Concise Scots Dictionary

The *Concise Scots Dictionary* is brought to you by Scottish Language Dictionaries Ltd, a registered charity. The Scottish Government generously funds some of our activities, but we rely on our supporters for additional help to continue our work on preserving, recording, and analysing the Scots language from its earliest records to the present day. Visit us at www.dsl.ac.uk/support-dsl/ to find out how you can support us.

Concise Scots Dictionary

Second Edition

EDINBURGH
University Press

Edinburgh University Press is one of the leading university presses in the UK. We publish academic books and journals in our selected subject areas across the humanities and social sciences, combining cutting-edge scholarship with high editorial and production values to produce academic works of lasting importance. For more information visit our website: edinburghuniversitypress.com

© Scottish Language Dictionaries Ltd, 2017
First edition published 1985
www.scotsdictionaries.org.uk

Edinburgh University Press Ltd
The Tun – Holyrood Road, 12(2f) Jackson's Entry, Edinburgh EH8 8PJ

Designed and typeset by Sharon McTeir, Creative Publishing Services, and printed and bound in Poland by Hussar Books

All rights reserved. No part of this publication may be reproduced, stored in a retrieval system, or transmitted in any form or by any means, electronic, mechanical, photocopying, recording or otherwise, without the prior permission of the publisher.

A CIP record for this book is available from the British Library

ISBN 978 1 4744 3231 3 (hardback)

CONTENTS

Acknowledgements		vii
Contributors		viii
Introduction: A History of Scots		ix
I	A general outline	ix
II	The position today	xiv
III	The principal chronological periods in the history of Scots and English	xvi
IV	Internal history: some important changes in the language itself	xvi
How to Use CSD2		**xxiii**
1	What does CSD2 contain and what are its sources?	xxiii
2	How to find a word in CSD2	xxiv
3	Variants	xxv
4	Headwords	xxviii
5	Pronunciation	xxix
6	Grammar and word-formation	xxxiv
7	Definitions	xxxiv
8	Dating	xxxv
9	Geographical distribution	xxxvii
10	Derivatives, compounds, phrases	xli
11	Etymologies	xlii
12	Cross-references	xliii
13	Typefaces	xliii
14	Abbreviations, labels and symbols	xliv
Scottish Money, Weights and Measures		xlvii
The A-Z Dictionary		1-852

*In memory of
Christian Kay*

ACKNOWLEDGEMENTS

Very many people have helped to make the second edition of the *Concise Scots Dictionary* (CSD2) possible. It builds on its predecessor, the first edition edited by Mairi Robinson and her team (CSD1). Like CSD1, CSD2 rests on the foundation of the great historical dictionaries: the *Scottish National Dictionary*, *A Dictionary of the Older Scottish Tongue* and the *Oxford English Dictionary*. First and foremost, the editors of CSD2 acknowledge the great debt they owe to these illustrious forebears.

CSD2 was initiated at the suggestion of Gavin Wallace of the Scottish Arts Council, who funded a pilot study carried out by Lorna Pike under the supervision of Marace Dareau. The Council continued to fund CSD2 until 2009, when the Scottish Government became the main source of income for Scottish Language Dictionaries Ltd, the overarching body for authoritative dictionaries of Scots. We are extremely grateful not only for the Scottish Government's financial support but also for their encouragement. We also gratefully acknowledge the generous financial support from the Strathmartine Trust. Finally, we would also like to thank our members and many donors for their contributions, large and small, and all those who took part – and continue to take part – in the 'Sponsor-a-Word' scheme.

Scottish Language Dictionaries Ltd (SLD) has been fortunate in having a very knowledgeable and active Board of Trustees. Chaired by Christian Kay (2002–10) and Jeremy Smith (2010–), and presided over by Margaret Mackay, members of the Board have given generously of their time and expertise. Much day-to-day leadership towards the end of the project, in addition to ongoing support throughout, was also exercised by the Treasurer, Jean Anderson, now succeeded by Rhona Alcorn. This dictionary also draws gratefully on the collective knowledge of SLD's Advisory Board, a body of experts in diverse fields from heraldry to curling and from church history to cookery. Thanks are also due to all the tradespeople, scholars, museum curators and others whom editors consulted; to the volunteer readers who added to the Word Collection; to those who took the trouble to contact us about words they had heard or read; and, not least, to the writers and speakers of Scots without whose spoken and written words this dictionary would not exist.

CONTRIBUTORS

The revision of the *Concise Scots Dictionary* was primarily undertaken by Pauline Cairns Speitel, Marace Dareau, Alison Grant and Chris Robinson. In the latter stages of the project, crucial input was given by Ann Ferguson, Eileen Finlayson and Ruth Martin of SLD, and Ian Brookes, Leonie Dunlop, Michael Munro, Thomas Widmann and Keith Williamson. Checking of etymologies was undertaken in particular by Keith Williamson, and by Gunhild Aamodt (Norwegian), Philip Bennett and Sabine Citron (French), Ian Brookes (Latin), Ian Felce (Old English), Heinz Giegerich (German), William Gillies (Gaelic), Bettelou Los (Dutch) and Katherine Miller (Old Norse). Former staff members who made a significant contribution to the project include Maggie Scott, who worked on the revision of CSD2 in the early stages, Lorna Pike, who, as flagged above, assisted with the preliminary planning of CSD2, and Henry Gratwick. Final delivery of this complex project to the publisher was managed by Alison Macaulay, Ruth O'Donovan and Anna Stevenson.

INTRODUCTION: A HISTORY OF SCOTS

The introduction to CSD1 was written by the Scots scholar and lexicographer Jack Aitken, and much of what he said remains true today; thus Aitken's discussion remains the basis of the Introduction to CSD2, with some necessary updatings and rephrasings. However, recent work in the study of language varieties means that our notions of dialect boundaries have changed, and there are also new insights available into the spread of Scots, notably in the Highlands and Islands. The revised Introduction below takes account of such changes.

Since Aitken wrote the original Introduction, steps have been taken to restore the status of Scots. The UK Government signed the European Charter for Regional or Minority Languages in 2000 and ratified it in 2001 in respect of Scots and Gaelic in Scotland and Ulster Scots and Irish in Northern Ireland. In February 2009, Linda Fabiani, then Scottish Minister for Europe, External Affairs and Culture, held a conference at the University of Stirling where it was announced that Scottish Language Dictionaries and the Scots Language Centre were to receive funding from the Scottish Executive (later the Scottish Government). The conference also resulted in the setting up of the Scots Language Working Group in November 2009 by Michael Russell, who succeeded Linda Fabiani. This Working Group submitted its report in 2011 and made wide-ranging recommendations for the furtherance of Scots, particularly in education, in broadcasting, in literature and the arts, internationally, academically and in the awareness of the general public. Later in 2011, a question on the Scots language was included in the Census for the first time. The response suggested that there were 1.5 million speakers of Scots at that time.

A significant development in recent years has been the appointment of four Scots Coordinators in 2014 for a two-year period to support education authorities and schools in developing learning, teaching and assessment of the Scots language within the new Curriculum for Excellence. In the same year, the Scottish Qualifications Authority launched two new Scots Language Awards for secondary pupils.

These changes suggest that we can be rather more optimistic about the future of Scots than Aitken was in 1985.

A HISTORY OF SCOTS

I A general outline

CSD2 is concerned with Scots, a distinctive language variety which historically has been primarily associated with Lowland Scotland. However, the Scots language is also found in parts of the Highlands, particularly within the burghs, where Scots functioned as the language of burghal law and record. In these Highland towns, Scots co-existed with the Gaelic language, rather than predominating as it did further south, which is perhaps why the Highland region has traditionally been excluded from maps delineating the extent of the Scots language. An insular form of Scots is also found in the Northern Isles, and a variety of Scots is spoken in large enclaves in Northern Ireland, as a result of settlements there in the seventeenth century and later, especially from the west and south-west of Scotland.

The first speakers of the Old English (Anglo-Saxon) ancestor of Scots arrived in what is now southern Scotland in the sixth century. This variety of Old English was Old Northumbrian, a northern sub-dialect of Old Anglian, the Old English dialect spoken over a wide territory stretching from the English Midlands to the Scottish Lowlands. The area that these first Old English speakers occupied, in what was later to become Scotland, is characterised by place-names with early Old English elements. This area consists of a wide swathe of what is now south-eastern and southern Scotland, with less extensive settlements along the Solway and, perhaps rather later, in Kyle in mid-Ayrshire.

Before the twelfth century the English-speaking part of Scotland was limited to these south-eastern and southern areas (except perhaps for the royal court of King Malcolm III and his queen, Margaret, a princess of the ancient royal house of Wessex, whom he married about 1070). There is also chronicle and place-name evidence that by the tenth and eleventh centuries the Gaelic language was socially dominant throughout much of Scotland, including the English-speaking south-east. In origin Gaelic was the native language of the Scots of Alba or Scotland, the kingdom centred north of the Forth and Clyde, whose kings in the tenth and eleventh centuries also gained dominion of the more southerly parts of what was to become an expanded Scottish kingdom.

Until the late eleventh century the increasing linguistic dominance of Scotland by Gaelic continued, but this trend was reversed with the accession of the Normanized kings of Scotland, particularly King David I (1124–53) and his immediate successors. Thereafter place-names and other indications show a spread of the English-speaking area beyond the south-east, first to other parts of southern Scotland, then in the late twelfth and thirteenth centuries to eastern Scotland north of the Forth.

This expansion of English in Scotland was brought about by several important groups of immigrants who came to Scotland at the invitation of the king: English-speaking servants and retainers of the new Anglo-Norman and Flemish landowners, and of the monks from England and France; and English-speaking pioneer burgesses, chiefly from south-east Scotland and from northern England, who settled in the new royal and baronial burghs of Scotland. Though the language of the royal court and the baronage of Scotland was now Norman French, later to become Anglo-Norman, the native tongue of many of these immigrants of lesser rank was a variety of Northern English heavily influenced in pronunciation, vocabulary and grammar by the Scandinavian language brought to northern and midland England by Viking-era invaders and settlers. This Scandinavian-influenced Northern English was the principal, though probably not the only, language of the early Scottish burghs, and its contribution to the formation of the language later known as Scots is probably even greater than that of the original Old Northumbrian spoken in south-eastern and southern Scotland.

Gradually the variety of Northern English spoken in Scotland began to diverge from the Northern English spoken in England, and the Scots language emerged: *Older Scots*, subdivided into *Early Scots* (up to around 1450) and *Middle Scots* (from around 1450 to around 1700), and *Modern Scots* (from around 1700 to the present day). (For a timeline comparing the periods traditionally identified for Scots with those for English, see section III below.)

By the fourteenth century this emerging language had become the dominant speech of all ranks in Scottish society east and south of the Highland Line (except in Galloway, where a form of Gaelic appears to have survived down to the seventeenth century). In other areas the rural inhabitants had abandoned their former Gaelic for the Scots language of the burghs, the local centres of government, law and trade. And the barons had also abandoned their minority tongue, French, for the Scots of the majority of the population. From about this time, too, the same Scots tongue was beginning to be used in Caithness, Orkney and Shetland, so beginning the long process of the supplanting by Scots of the Old Norse ('Norn') formerly spoken under the Norse earls of these territories.

Until the latter decades of the fourteenth century, written records of Early Scots ('pre-literary Scots') consist of no more than a few vernacular words and phrases and some descriptive place-names and surnames which crop up sporadically in early Latin documents from the twelfth century onwards. From these fragmentary written records, and by extrapolation from later evidence, we are able to reconstruct the development of Older Scots.

Continuous written records of Older Scots begin in 1376 with John Barbour's great poem *Brus*, an account of the exploits of the heroes Robert Bruce and James Douglas in the War of Independence. Other verse and prose writings in Older Scots followed, including (from 1424) the statutes of the Scottish Parliament. Gradually an ever-wider range of genres was written in Scots, so that, by the second half of the fifteenth century, Older Scots became the principal language of literature and of record for the Scottish nation, having successfully competed in this latter function with Latin.

Hence by the later fifteenth and the sixteenth centuries there were two prestigious vernacular languages in use in Britain: metropolitan Tudor English in the kingdom of England, and metropolitan Older Scots in the kingdom of Scotland. Linguistically these languages were distinct but quite closely related varieties, as different as are (for instance) Norwegian and Danish today. Because of this close relationship, elements originally English could appear in Scots writings and, later, speech without appearing particularly incongruous.

This process, which is known as *anglicization*, developed for a number of reasons. Traditionally, the anglicization of Scots is attributed to influences resulting from the Reformation of 1560, in particular the adoption by the Scots Reformers of the English Geneva Bible and a mainly English Psalter instead of a Bible and a Psalter in Scots, and from the much closer political and social contacts between the two nations which followed the Reformation and, still more, after the Union of the Crowns in 1603. Printing in Scotland was slow to emerge in comparison with England, and thus printed books in the vernacular imported from south of the border provided a linguistic model that was widely imitated.

Another element in anglicization was literary influence of English writings on Scots writers, long predating the Reformation. The sixteenth-century poet and courtier Sir David Lyndsay alluded to *Inglis bukis* and to New Testaments in English, both printed in England; such texts were being read by Scots of Protestant leanings before the Reformation. English poetry and prose writings were circulated in Scotland from the fourteenth century or earlier, including in particular the writings of Chaucer and his successors, and were admired and emulated by Scottish poets. Indeed, the Scottish fifteenth- and sixteenth-century *makars* seem to have included in their grandest poetry occasional imitations and quasi-imitations of the English spellings of Chaucer and their other English mentors, as alternatives to the corresponding native Scots forms, such as *quho* (Scots *quha*), *moste* (Scots *maist*); English words, like *frome* (Scots *fra*), *tho* (Scots *than*) and *twane* (Scots *twa*); and English verbal inflexions, such as the ending *-n* in *seyn* (Scots *se*, to see) and the ending *-ith* (corresponding to English *-eth*, Scots *-is*). By 1540 similar spellings were appearing, though still quite rarely, in Scots prose, but after 1560 the phenomenon was much more pervasive. By the end of the sixteenth century, written Scots admitted both Scots- and English-derived forms, in which pairs of spellings and spelling-symbols like *aith* and *oath*, *ony* and *any*, *gude* and *good*, *quh-* and *wh-*, *sch-* and *sh-*, co-existed as options.

Initially, few Scottish people seem to have had any strong feeling for a distinctive Scots linguistic identity. Not until 1494 did Scottish writers begin to apply the name *Scots* to their own tongue. Before that the language was always called *Inglis* (i.e. English), as no doubt befitted a variety which shared with the English of England a common Anglo-Saxon origin. And even after 1494 and indeed until the end of the Older Scots period both names continued in use, with no obvious predominance of either.

However, from early in the sixteenth century there are occasional hints that, even though Scots was now the preferred vernacular of at least Lowland Scotland, it was felt to be somewhat less elegant than literary English. As early as 1513 the poet Gavin Douglas thought of his own vernacular as *braid and plane* alongside *sudron* (i.e. English). This feeling was stated quite explicitly in 1603 (see p.xiii below), and from time to time thereafter.

The progressive anglicization of writings in manuscript (records, diaries, manuscript histories, and others) proceeded through the seventeenth century and into the eighteenth. In print, partly or largely as a result of commercial considerations by publishers and printers, the demise of literary Older Scots is far earlier and more sudden. After 1610, except for a few legal texts and one or two comic or satiric *tours-de-force*, most public writing in prose by Scottish authors, whether printed in Scotland or, as often, in London, is undeniably anglicized in form although still exhibiting some Scots words and phrases.

There were however some exceptions to the general trend towards anglicization. Scots survived for some time in private writings such as letters, and in public the tradition of printing heroic and comic poems of the classical Early and Middle Scots periods continued through the seventeenth century (albeit in somewhat anglicized spelling), e.g. Hary's *Wallace*, which was originally composed at the end of the fifteenth century but which went through at least six editions in Glasgow alone from the middle of the seventeenth century to the beginning of the eighteenth. These printed texts served as a springboard for the eighteenth-century revival of Scots writing launched by Allan Ramsay and his contemporaries in lyric, comic and descriptive verse, in balladry and, a little later, in humorous tales and ghost stories in prose, and prose dialogue and monologue. Such writings, however, were written in a more colloquial Scots than the formal style of most Older Scots literature. Some of the new features of spelling and grammar of this Modern literary Scots are mentioned below.

While Scottish writing was becoming anglicized in these ways from the sixteenth century or earlier, the indications are that the *speech* of almost all Scots outside the monolingual Gaelic-speaking areas continued to be the Scots language. Following the Reformation in 1560, however, Scottish people of all classes were coming not only into regular visual but also into aural contact with English: aural in that at least once a week, and in the case of devout people several times a week, they heard readings from the English Bible, and sermons in a language at least partly modelled on Biblical English. In the course of the seventeenth century there was also a considerable increase in personal interaction between Scots-speakers and English-speakers.

A further element in all these anglicizing influences was the great increase after 1603 in contacts of all sorts between the upper classes of the two countries. Intermarriage between the Scottish and English aristocracies was becoming common, and after the Restoration in 1660 every Scotsman of the nobility was likely to spend part of his time in southern England, at court or residing in the Home Counties, and nearly all other eminent Scots visited London for longer or shorter periods. Under these circumstances it is not surprising that the Scottish upper classes gradually gave up their native Scots speech for what had long been regarded as the more *elegant and perfect* English of the south (as it was called by one Scottish writer in 1603). It is doubtless possible to exaggerate the degree of anglicization by the late seventeenth century, and individuals no doubt varied, as they do today. But the overall impression is that, in contrast with the sixteenth century, when all Scots simply spoke Older Scots, the formal or 'polite' speech of Scotland's social elite now became increasingly closer to southern English usage; forms of speech which mostly favoured traditional Scots usages were identified with conservatives, eccentrics and, especially, with the common people. Some upper- and middle-class Scots certainly still used occasional Scotticisms, and spoke their English with a noticeable Scottish accent. But this was also the time when the Augustan culture of eighteenth-century England began strongly influencing the Scottish cultural scene. Augustanism was a fashion which laid great emphasis on 'propriety' and prohibited in 'polite' usage anything 'unrefined', 'vulgar' or 'provincial'.

These prescriptions were accepted by nearly all educated eighteenth-century Scots, who developed a greatly increased self-consciousness about the provinciality of their English speech (with some dissenting voices like those of the poets Allan Ramsay and Alexander Ross). Residual Scots features were now regarded as sullying what might otherwise have been exemplary refined English, and it was all but universally accepted as desirable for all those with pretensions to being 'polite' that they should write and speak English with 'propriety'. Such practices are already in evidence in the records of the Fair Intellectual Club, founded in 1719 for educated young ladies of Edinburgh, in which the first president complimented her members on the propriety of their English 'considering how difficult it is for our country people to acquire it'. The well-known consequences of these notions include the publication, from 1752 onwards, of several alphabetical lists of Scots words and expressions, compiled expressly so that people could learn to avoid them in their writing and speech, and also the appearance in Edinburgh, from 1748 onwards, of a long line of lecturers on elocution. Scottish Standard English (SSE) emerged as part of this process, during the eighteenth century, as an 'educated' variety, consisting of largely Standard English vocabulary and grammar, spoken in a Scottish accent much modified in the direction of usages south of the Border.

Though some continued to hold that the total extinction of vernacular Scots was desirable, this attitude seems to have changed early in the nineteenth century. We may perhaps associate this change with the publication of John Jamieson's *Etymological Dictionary of the Scottish Language* in 1808, together with the new wave of Scottish Romantic writers, the burgeoning of nineteenth-century antiquarianism, and with the sturdy assertion of the value of the Scots language by people like Lord Cockburn (1779–1854), the celebrated Edinburgh judge and raconteur. It was now accepted that Scots was 'going out as a spoken tongue every year', as Cockburn put it in 1838, but for some, such as Cockburn himself, this was a matter for nostalgic regret at the incipient demise of a rich and expressive old tongue. And as the nineteenth century progressed, there arose a further distinction between traditional, usually equated with rural, dialects of Scots, which were widely approved by cultural commentators of the time, and 'slovenly perversions of dialect', usually equated with urban dialects, which were not.

II The position today

The language of contemporary Scotland can fairly be described as fluid. It is marked by a wide and highly variable range of speech-styles, ranging from the broad Scots of some fishing and farming communities, through various intermediate 'mixtures of Scots and English', to a variety of Standard English spoken in a Scottish accent (i.e. SSE). Even the last of these usages retains obvious affiliations with the more fully Scottish speech-styles – in the accent with which it is pronounced, in its speakers' frequent recourse to a repertory of Scotticisms like *dinna fash yoursel*, *to swither* and *to miss yourself* and in the peculiarly Scottish pronunciations of certain words such as *length* (as [lɛnθ] rather than [lɛŋθ]), of *Wednesday* (with three clear syllables), of *fifth* and *sixth* (as *fift* and *sixt*), and of *loch*, *patriarch* and *technical* (with [x] not [k]). The speech of an individual will vary according to region (some regions being strikingly more 'Scottish' than others), social class, age, sex, circumstance (e.g. the well-known contrast between classroom and playground speech), and the national and local loyalties of the speaker. However, although a distinctively Scots legal terminology persists, the sixteenth-century situation in which Scots was the universal language of Scotland outside the *Gàidhealtachd* (the Gaelic-speaking areas) has long disappeared. It may therefore reasonably be asked if there is any sense in which

Scots is entitled to the designation of a language any more than any of the regional dialects of English in England.

In reply one may point out that Scots possesses several attributes not shared by any regional English dialect. In its linguistic characteristics it is more strongly differentiated from Standard English than any English dialect. The dictionary which follows displays a far larger number of words, meanings of words and expressions not current in Standard English than any of the English dialects could muster, and many of its pronunciations are strikingly different from their Standard English equivalents. Moreover, the evidence of modern linguistic surveys is that the Scots vernacular is less open to attrition in favour of standard usages than are the English dialects. One illustration of this is the fact that a fair number of dialect words – such as *aye* always, *pooch* a pocket, *shune* shoes, *een* eyes, and *nicht* night – have very recently died out in northern England but remain in vigorous use in many parts of Scottish society.

It is of course true that Scots shares many words with dialects of northern England. Words such as *hame*, *stane*, *doon*, *lass*, *bairn*, *bonny*, *loon* and *glaur*, which many Scots think of as purely Scots words, are indeed very much northern English words as well. But it is also true that a large number of Scotticisms are now confined within the border, and many of them perhaps always were. A number of the features of Scots described in section IV below are of this class. Indeed, easily the most definite dialect-boundary in the English-speaking world is the Scottish-English border.

But what most of all distinguishes Scots is its literature. Nowhere in the English-speaking world is there a non-standard literature which remotely compares with literature in Scots for antiquity, for extent and variety, and for distinction. This embraces the poetry of the great medieval *makars* together with later works by Robert Burns, Walter Scott, James Hogg, Hugh MacDiarmid and Lewis Grassic Gibbon. Modern urban prose writers such as Irvine Welsh, James Kelman and James Robertson can rightly be included in this list. Beyond this, Scots-language drama and comedy performed on both stage and screen, together with regional comic strips and cartoons in Scottish newspapers, continue to reach a wide audience.

From at least the first half of the eighteenth century, Scots has always been thought to be 'dying out' as a spoken language. From time to time suggestions have been made for 'restoring' or 'reviving' it, from the solid base of literary Scots, where its permanence has been less often in doubt. Various schemes for the perpetuation of the language have been suggested over the years, with varying degrees of success or failure, and yet in the midst all of these initiatives, spoken Scots demonstrably persists, and even thrives.

The special characteristics of Scots which we have just surveyed – its linguistic distinctiveness, its occupation of its own 'dialect-island' bounded by the border, its individual history, its own dialect variation, its varied use in a remarkable literature, the ancient loyalty of the Scottish people to the notion of the Scots language, as well as the fact that since the sixteenth century Scots has adopted the nation's name – all of these are attributes of a language rather than a dialect. Manifestly Scots is to be seen as much more than simply another dialect of English. The present dictionary is intended not only as a record of the copiousness and variety of the Scots language, but also as a contribution to asserting its social validity.

III The principal chronological periods in the history of Scots and English

The main periods in the history of Scots

Old English:	to 1100
Older Scots:	to 1700
Pre-literary Scots:	to 1375
Early Scots:	to 1450
Middle Scots:	1450 to 1700
Early Middle Scots:	1450 to 1550
Late Middle Scots:	1550 to 1700
Modern Scots:	1700 onwards

A corresponding list of the periods for English

Old English:	to 1100
Middle English:	1100 to 1475
Early Middle English:	1100 to 1250
Late Middle English:	1400 to 1475
Early Modern English:	1475 to 1650
Modern English:	1650 onwards

IV Internal history: some important changes in the language itself

(a) Sound changes: vowels and diphthongs

In the Early and Middle Scots periods, some important sound-changes resulted in differences in the pronunciation of vowels and diphthongs between Scots and Standard English (including SSE). These include the following contrasts:

(1) Scots *stane, gae*   (Sc)StEng *stone, go*

This contrast results from the twelfth-century rounding of the Old English long *ā* sound (e.g. in *stān* and *gān*) in midland and southern England to a sound of *o*-like quality, whereas no such rounding occurred in the north. The different sounds which resulted had different subsequent developments, leading ultimately to the modern contrast.

(2) Scots *buit, muin, puir*   (Sc)StEng *boot, moon, poor*
    (with front vowel)   (with back vowel)

This contrast results from a fronting of an original long *ō* sound in these words in the thirteenth century in Northern Middle English and, especially, Early Scots, yielding a sound of *ü*-like quality [œ:] in the ancestor of Scots, but leaving *ō* [o:] (which later became [u:]) in the ancestor of (Sc)StEng. Further development brought about dialect variations within Scots (*ee* in the Northern Highlands, *ai* or *i* in the Central region, and *ü* remaining in Shetland, Orkney, Tayside and the Borders).

(3) Scots *aw, au* [a, ɔ], *ow* [ʌu], *ou, u* [u]   (Sc)StEng *al(l), ol(l), ul(l)*
in *baw, saut, sowder,*   in *ball, salt, solder,*
row, mouter, fou   *roll, multure, full*

This contrast results from an early fifteenth-century Scots replacement of *l* by *u* in this position – the so-called 'vocalization of *l*'.

(4) Scots (and Northern English)   (Sc)StEng
coo, hoose, doon   *cow, house, down*

This contrast results from an important difference in the direction taken by the fifteenth-century Great Vowel Shift in the north from that taken in the midlands and south of England. Scots and Northern English retain the original Old and Middle English and Early Scots monophthong *ū* [u:], which became a diphthong in the fifteenth century in more southerly accents of English. The Scottish system of vowel length described at 5.4.3 below first arose at this time, partly as a result of the Great Vowel Shift.

(b) Spellings

The spelling system of Older Scots allowed considerable variation. Some features which distinguished it from the spelling of midland and southern English of the time are:

(1) Among the spellings of consonants, Scots *quh-, qwh-* corresponded to *wh-* in midland and southern English usage, e.g. in Scots *quhat, quhite*; Scots *sch-* corresponded to *sh-*, e.g. in *schip*; Scots *-ch* corresponded to *-gh*, e.g. in *lauch, nicht, dochter*; Scots *ʒ* corresponded to *y*, e.g. in *ʒere* ('year'), *ʒing* ('young'). Common variations within Scots in spellings of consonants included: for *-ch* as in *lauch* or *laich* ('low'), also *-cht*; for *-th* as in *baith* ('both') or *mouth*, also *-tht*; *v* and *w* interchanged, and *-v-* interchanged with *-u-, -w-* or *-f(f)-*.

(2) Among the vowels, the device of adding *-i* or *-y* to distinguish certain Early Scots long vowels from similarly spelled short vowels, e.g. *hait* ('hot') from *hat* ('hat'), *meit* ('meet' or 'meat') from *met*, *coit* (coat) from *cot*, *buit* (boot) from *but*; and some writers even use *yi* as in *byit* ('bite') to distinguish this vowel from that in *bit* in the same way.

As a consequence of the sound change mentioned at IV(a) (3) above, the following sets of spellings became interchangeable:

al, aul with *au, aw* e.g. in *halk, haulk, hawk* ('hawk'), or *walter, wawter, water* ('water');
ol, oul, owl, with *ou, ow* e.g. in *nolt, noult, nowlt, nowt, nout* ('cattle');
ul, oul, owl with *ou, ow* e.g. in *pulder, poulder, powlder, pouder, powder* ('powder').

As well as introducing new alternative English (or quasi-English) word forms such as *oath* beside *aith*, *most* beside *maist*, *quhich* beside *quhilk*, *church* beside *kirk*, *any* beside *ony*, *if* beside *gif*, the anglicization process (see section I above) also resulted in massive changes in ways of spelling Scots words themselves. By the eighteenth century many characteristic Older Scots spellings had been discarded, e.g. *quh-*, *sch-*, the letter *ȝ* (though this form did survive as a realization of *z* – see the entry for *ȝ* in DSL), the alternative spelling of *o[-]e* (where [-] = a consonant) as *oi*, *oy*, e.g. in *cote*, *coit* ('coat'). New forms of mainly southern English origin were introduced, e.g. *wh*, *sh*, *gh*, *ee*, *oo*, *ea* and *oa*, and word-final *-ae* and *-oe*. Where a Scots word differed from a corresponding English word in the apparent omission of a letter, this 'omission' was acknowledged with an intruded apostrophe, as *ha'e* beside *have*, *fu'* beside *full*. Some Older Scots spellings did, however, survive, notably *ch* as in *lauch*, *nicht* and *ai*, *ei* and *ui*.

Though still much more variable than Standard English, the new hybrid spelling system deployed for Modern Scots was much less variable than that of Older Scots. This spelling system continues in use in Scottish literature to this day (alongside some recent, highly innovative systems to represent localized varieties of spoken Scots). Attempts to make it more consistent, notably the *Scots Style Sheet* produced by the Makars' Club in 1947 or the *Recommendations for Writers in Scots* published by the Scots Language Society in 1985, have had at best only limited success.

(c) Grammar

Modern Scots inherits from Early Scots a number of characteristic Northern English grammatical features, of which the following is a small sample:

(1) irregular plurals: *een* ('eyes'), *shune* ('shoes'), *kye* ('cows'), *hors* ('horses'), *caur* ('calves'), and *thir* (pl. of *this*) and *thae* (pl. of *that*).
(2) a distinction between present participles in *-an* (*He's aye gutteran aboot*) and verbal nouns in *-in* (*He's fond o gutterin aboot*). This distinction is still found in extreme Northern and Southern dialects.
(3) past tense and past participle forms: *greet* ('weep'), pt *grat*, ptp *grutten*; *lauch* ('laugh'), pt *leuch*, ptp *lauchen*; *gae* ('go'), pt *gaed* (Older Scots *ȝeid*), ptp *gane*; *hing* ('hang'), pt *hang*, ptp *hungin*.
(4) a distinction in present-tense verb forms according to whether a personal pronoun is or is not immediately adjacent to the verb (e.g. *they say he's owre auld* but *them that says he's owre auld* or *thir laddies says he's owre auld*).

Modern Scots also has a number of features that have arisen since the Early Middle Scots period:
(1) reduced forms of the negative adverb: Older Scots *nocht*, Modern Scots *no* or *nae* and *-na* or *-ny*;
(2) new rules for negative and interrogative constructions: Older Scots *He gais nocht*, *Gais he nocht?*, Modern Scots *He's no gaun*, *Is he no gaun?*;
(3) new usages of auxiliary verbs such as *may* (common in Older Scots, little used in Modern Scots, where *can* and constructions with *maybe* take its place); similarly *sall* (and its reduced form *'se*) is almost obsolete.

(d) Vocabulary

Early Scots shared much of its word stock with contemporary Northern Middle English. This included virtually all of the vocabulary items borrowed from Scandinavian, since these forms had originally reached Scotland as part of the Northern English speech of the Anglo-Danish immigrants referred to on p.x. Among the hundreds of characteristic Modern Scots words from this source are such well-known items as *bairn*, *brae*, *gate*, *graith*, *nieve*, *kirk*, *lass*, *big* ('build'), *flit*, *hing*, *dreich* and *lowse*, and several of the grammatical features mentioned in the preceding section. It should be noted, however, that the history of the still more numerous Scandinavian borrowings into the dialects of Shetland, Orkney and Caithness is quite different. These words derive directly from the former Norn, or Norwegian language of the inhabitants of these regions, following their colonization by Norwegian settlers after c. AD 800.

Other sources contributed many words and expressions exclusive to Early Scots vocabulary as well as others shared with the English of England. From French (both the Norman French of the original twelfth-century Norman settlers, and the Central French which later superseded it) came many words originally shared with English but which have survived only in Scots, such as *leal*, *ashet*, *aumry*, *douce*, *hoolet* and *tassie*, and others, perhaps resulting from direct Scots–French contact through the Franco-Scottish Alliance (1296–1560), such as *deval*, *disjune*, *fash*, *spairge*, *vennel*, *vivers*, *gardyloo* and *Hogmanay*.

Other borrowings originally restricted to Scots rather than English include many from Gaelic, beginning at least as early as the twelfth century, e.g. *cairn*, *capercailzie*, *cranreuch*, *crine*, *glen*, *ingle*, *loch*, *messan*, *oe*, *quaich*, *sonse*, *strath* and *tocher*, along with more recent borrowings such as *ceilidh*, *claymore*, *gillie*, *pibroch*, *spleuchan*, *sporran* and *whisky*. Some of these forms, of course, have since spread to English (e.g. *whisky*).

Between the twelfth and the eighteenth centuries contact between Scotland and the Low Countries was constant and close, with Flemish craftsmen settling in the Scottish burghs and Scottish traders settling at the Scottish staple ports in the Netherlands. One result was the many Scots words of Dutch or Flemish origin, such as *bucht*, *callan*, *croon*, *cuit*, *mutch*, *pinkie*, *golf* and *scone*, the past tense *coft* ('bought'), and the names of measures such as *mutchkin* and coins such as *doit* and *plack*.

Other important elements of the distinctive vocabulary of Scots come from Anglo-Saxon itself, whence, for example, *bannock*, *but and ben*, *eldritch*, *gloamin*, *haffet*, *haugh*, *heuch*, *lanimer*, *wee* and *weird*, all of which died out south of the Border but were retained in Scots; a few of these forms have been re-borrowed from Scots into Standard English (e.g. *wee*).

Borrowing from Latin was in Older Scots frequently carried out independently of English. Many words of Latin origin were borrowed into the two languages at widely different dates and often in strikingly different meanings, with examples including: *liquid*, *liquidate*, *local*, *locality* and *narrative*. Additionally, Scots law has a large and distinctive vocabulary of Latin origin, with forms such as *executor-dative*, *homologate*, *hypothec*, *nimious* and *sederunt*. Scots often prefers a different form of the same word (often a verb) from that preferred by English: *dispone* (beside *dispose*), *promove* (beside *promote*), and others; and Scots often prefers ending-less (and thus more 'etymological') forms of Latin past participles, like (*weel*) *educate*, *depute*, and *habit and repute*. School Latin, partly borrowed in the modern period, has yielded such characteristic Scotticisms as *dominie, dux, fugie, pandie, vaig, vaik* and *vacance*.

From the foregoing it is evident that by the sixteenth century, Scots differed strikingly in vocabulary as well as in many other ways from contemporary dialects of English, not excluding Northern English. Since the seventeenth century the process of direct borrowing of vocabulary from foreign sources has largely, though not entirely, ceased, but the processes of coinage and word formation appear to continue apace, and indeed down to the present day: expressions of the latter origin include *fantoosh, henner, high-heid-yin, scheme, to miss yersel, to put yer gas at a peep, to be up to high doh* and many others. Even so, the many apparently new words which first appear in Modern Scots are by no means all of recent origin: many, such as *boorach, golach, gumption, gyte, slaister* and *theevil*, are doubtless older words which have emerged into record only in the modern period as a result of the rather different preoccupations of most writers of Older Scots (primarily a prestigious language of record) and of Modern Scots (primarily an informal usage). Many words which (approximately) coincide in form with Standard English words have very different meanings in Scots: this is true of some of the words of Latin origin mentioned above; others of diverse sources include *divider, find, flit, hold, hurl, mind, outcast, outcome, policy, sober, sort, travel, want, weave, word* and the definite article *the*.

(e) The spoken dialects

Some characteristic dialect features are:

(1) A well-known feature of the North-East and parts of the Northern Highlands is *f-* where other dialects have *wh-*, as in *fa* ('who'), *fite* ('white').
(2) A well-known characteristic of Borders Scots is the occurrence at the ends of words of *-ow* [-ɑʊ] where other dialects have *-oo* [-u], and *-ey* [-ai] where other dialects have *-ee* [-i], making this accent the so-called 'yow and mey' accent, e.g. *Yow and mey'll gang oot and pow a pey* 'You and me will go out and pull a pea'.
(3) Grammatical variations include the distinction between singular *thou, thee* and plural *ye* in Shetland, Orkney and parts of the Northern Highlands (cf. *tu* and *vous* in French), and that between the present participle and the verbal noun (see IV (c) above).
(4) As a result of their special histories certain localities favour words of a particular etymological source: words of Norse origin in Shetland, Orkney and the county of Caithness; a special group of words of Dutch origin in Shetland; Gaelic in the Northern and Western Highlands, in the North-East and in parts of Tayside; Romany in parts of the Lothians and the Borders; and some words specific to particular occupations (notably fishing and coal-mining) are localized to particular places and regions.

Beyond such brief sketches it is as yet not possible to offer further generalizations on the regional distributions of different classes of word within Scotland, except to point to the numerous variations between dialects in their terms for common notions: for instance, for 'little finger' the expression *peerie finger* and variants appear in Shetland, Orkney and Caithness, in comparison with North-Eastern *crannie*, East-Central *curnie* and *pinkie* everywhere else. Similarly, 'to rinse' appears as East-Central *synd* and West-Central *syne*, as the North-Eastern *sweel* and as the more widespread *reenge* and its variants; and words for 'mud' including *dubs*, *gutter*, *glabber*, *clabber* and *glaur* are scattered around the country, with *dubs* favoured in the North-East and the Northern Highlands, *gutters* in the East-Central dialect, *glabber* and *clabber* in the West-Central dialect, and *glaur* more generally across the Central Belt and also in the Borders. One could multiply these examples many times. CSD2 provides copious information on the present regional distributions both of words and of individual meanings of words.

A. J. Aitken, revised by Chris Robinson, Jeremy Smith, Pauline Cairns Speitel, Alison Grant, Ann Ferguson and Margaret Mackay.

Further reading

Dictionary of the Scots Language/Dictionar o the Scots Leid (= DSL, available at www.dsl.ac.uk): this online resource brings together the two major historical dictionaries of the Scots language: *A Dictionary of the Older Scottish Tongue* (DOST) and *The Scottish National Dictionary* (SND). It also includes two authoritative discussions: 'The Scots Language' by William Grant (1931), and 'History of Scots to 1700' by Caroline Macafee, the latter incorporating material by A. J. Aitken (2002).

A. J. Aitken (ed.), *Lowland Scots*, Association for Scottish Literary Studies, Occasional Papers No. 2, Edinburgh, 1973.

A. J. Aitken, Tom McArthur (eds), *Languages of Scotland*, W. & R. Chambers, Edinburgh, 1979.

John Corbett, J. Derrick McClure and Jane Stuart-Smith (eds), *The Edinburgh Companion to Scots*, Edinburgh University Press, Edinburgh, 2003.

Charles Jones (ed.), *The Edinburgh History of the Scots Language*, Edinburgh University Press, Edinburgh, 1997.

Caroline Macafee, 'Scots and Scottish English', in Raymond Hickey (ed.), *Legacies of Colonial English: A Study in Transported Dialects*, Cambridge University Press, Cambridge, 2004, 59–81.

Caroline Macafee and Iseabail Macleod (eds), *The Nuttis Schell: Essays on the Scots Language presented to A. J. Aitken*, Aberdeen University Press, Aberdeen, 1987.

J. Derrick McClure, *Why Scots Matters*, Saltire Society, Edinburgh, 2008 (third edition).

Iseabail Macleod and J. Derrick McClure (eds), *Scotland in Definition*, John Donald, Edinburgh, 2012.

David Murison, *The Guid Scots Tongue*, Blackwood, Edinburgh, 1977.

Susan Rennie, *Jamieson's Dictionary of Scots*, Oxford University Press, Oxford, 2012.

Jeremy J. Smith, 'Scots', in Glanville Price (ed.), *Languages in Britain and Ireland*, Blackwell, Oxford, 2000, 159–70.

Jeremy J. Smith, *Older Scots: A Linguistic Reader*, Scottish Text Society/Boydell: Edinburgh/Woodbridge, 2012.

HOW TO USE CSD2

1 What does CSD2 contain and what are its sources?

1.1 Sources

CSD2 is based mainly on two major dictionaries: the *Scottish National Dictionary* (SND) and its Supplements (1976, 2005) for the modern period from 1700 to the present day, and *A Dictionary of the Older Scottish Tongue* (DOST) for the centuries up to 1700. The main difference between these two works is that whereas DOST covers the whole of the Scots language of the period, including what is shared with English, SND concentrates on what is different from Standard English in the modern language (but including items found also in English dialects, especially Northern English).

1.2 Inclusions

1.2.1   CSD2 aims to include what is (or was) wholly or mainly Scots, including the Scottish elements in SSE, and in addition words and usages which, according to the evidence available, were used earlier or later in Scots than in the English of England. Meanings shared with the English of Southern England are however frequently included, often as the first definition of an entry.

1.2.2   CSD2, like its predecessor CSD1, contains a considerable amount of encyclopaedic information, e.g. names of Scottish regiments, religious sects, legal and educational institutions. Inclusion of such material, much appreciated by users of CSD1, will add greatly to its usefulness as a general reference book.

1.2.3   Efforts have been made to include new words and usages where possible and to keep abreast of changes in local government and education.

1.2.4   Rare items from major authors are included. See 1.3.2 below.

1.3 Exclusions

1.3.1   The *quotations*, which provide such a rich source of information and pleasure in the parent dictionaries, cannot be included in a dictionary such as CSD2, which aims at compression of information. Rarely, illustrative phrases are given in order to help clarify a meaning or usage (see 7.6 below). In addition, the following categories of material have been omitted:

1.3.2   **Rarities**. Most items for which there are only one or two pieces of evidence altogether in the parent dictionaries are omitted. In other words, normally a total of three quotations and/or references is required to justify inclusion. There are certain exceptions to this rule:

(a) Many items from the following historical authors have been included, even if there is only one occurrence, especially if it is thought that inclusion would be helpful to a reader of their works. The authors are Barbour, Henryson, Dunbar, Douglas, Ramsay, Fergusson and Burns.

(b) Current Orkney and Shetland items are included even with fewer than three quotations.

(c) Sometimes a meaning with sparse evidence has been included in order to clarify another meaning for which the evidence is more plentiful.

1.3.3   *Letters of the alphabet, prefixes, suffixes.* SND in particular does include entries for these (e.g. **M, ma-**), but they are normally omitted from CSD2. A few prefixes and suffixes, such as **un-, -some**, have however been included and the letter 3 (yogh) has its own entry.

1.3.4   *Transparent derivatives.* Derivatives, compounds and phrases whose meaning and form can easily be worked out from that of the base word(s) are often omitted, e.g. adverbs ending in *-ly*, nouns in *-ness* (see also 10 below).

2 How to find a word in CSD2

2.1 Order of entries

Material is entered in alphabetical order of the first headword. Words which have the same spelling but different etymological sources are entered separately with consecutive superscript numbers attached to the first headword, e.g. **gab^1, gab^2, gab^3**. Words which have the same spelling and are etymologically related have two-part superscript numbers, e.g. **gab$^{1.1}$** (a noun) and **gab$^{1.2}$** (the verb from which the noun is derived). These related items are ordered according to part of speech as follows: noun, verb, adjective, adverb, pronoun, determiner, numeral, preposition, conjunction and interjection.

2.2 Spelling variants

Scots has always had so many spelling variants that it would be impossible for a one-volume dictionary to list them all. Most entries in CSD2 do however contain several variants, many of them representing other variants (see 3 and 4 below).

2.3 How to find a word

2.3.1   Look in the obvious alphabetical position. If the word is not found:

2.3.2   Glance above and below for a similar spelling. If the word is still not found, ask the following question: could it be a compound or derivative form (such as **honestshift** or **honesty** from **honest**), a past tense or past participle of a verb, or a plural of a noun? Look under a likely base form: in the case of compounds try the first element first; in the case of past tenses or plurals, what might a normal English spelling of the present tense or singular be? If the word is still not found:

2.3.3   Consult the lists of variants (see 3 below). Vowel variation is more likely than consonant variation; try vowel lists first. Look up words with double consonants under single consonants and vice versa, e.g. **hog** under **hogg**.

3 Variants

Certain variant spellings are regarded as predictable, that is they regularly interchange with one another and if a word is not found under one spelling it is likely to be found under one of the variants.

3.1 List of variants

In the following list the entries in bold type consist of sets of variants, as far as possible in descending order of the spellings most likely to be found as headwords in CSD2. For example, suppose you meet a word containing the sequence *-cht-*. On looking this form up in the list below you are referred to the sets under **ch**.

Therefore you should try the dictionary for an entry containing *-ch-*. If there is no entry that fits, try *-th-*, and so on down the list ([-] = any consonant).

a	*see*	ai *or* au *or* o
ae	*see*	ai
a[-]e	*see*	ai *or* ui
ai, ae, a[-]e, ay, a, ea, i, y, ii, yi, oi, oy, ei, ey, o, oa, o[-]e;		
ai, e;		
ai	*also see*	ei *or* ui
al	*see*	au
au, aw, al, aul, a		
aul	*see*	au
aw	*see*	au
ay	*see*	ai *or* ei
b, bb		
c, s, t;		
c	*also see*	ck
ch, th, cht, tht, chtht, tch;		
ch, gh, ght;		
ch	*also see*	sh
cht	*see*	ch
chtht	*see*	ch
ck, c, k, kk, ct		
cks, x, ks		
ct	*see*	ck
d, dd, ld, t, tt, th		
dd	*see*	d
dg	*see*	g
e	*see*	ei *or* ai *or* i[-]e
é	*see*	ei
ea	*see*	ei *or* ai
ee	*see*	ei *or* ui
e[-]e	*see*	ei
ei, ee, e[-]e, ey, e, é, ea, i, ie, y;		
ei, ai, ay;		

ei	*also see*	ai *or* ui
eu, ew, ou, u, ui, ue, ow, yow		
ew	*see*	eu
ey	*see*	ai *or* ei *or* ui
f, ff, ph, v;		
f, th;		
f	*also see*	wh
g, gg;		
g, dg, j		
gg	*see*	g
gh	*see*	ch
ght	*see*	ch
i	*see*	ai, ei, i[-]e *or* ui
ie	*see*	ei *or* i[-]e
i[-]e, i, e, ie, ii, iy, y, y[-]e, yi		
ii	*see*	ai *or* i[-]e
iy	*see*	i[-]e
j	*see*	g
k	*see*	ck
kk	*see*	ck
l, ll		
ld	*see*	d
ll	*see*	l
m, mm, mb;		
m, n		
n, nn, nd, nt, ng;		
n, m		
nd	*see*	n
ng, nzie, ngie, nʒ(i)e, ny(i)e;		
ng	*also see*	n
ngie	*see*	ng
ngth	*see*	nth
nn	*see*	n
nt	*see*	n
nth, ngth		
ny(ie), nʒ(i)e, nzie,	*see*	ng
o, a;		
o	*also see*	ai, o[-]e, ou *or* u
oa	*see*	ai *or* o[-]e
oe	*see*	o[-]e *or* ui
o[-]e, o, oe, oi, oy, oa;		
o[-]e	*also see*	ai *or* ei
oi	*see*	ai, o[-]e *or* ui
ol	*see*	ou
oo	*see*	ou *or* ui

ou, ow, ol, oul, oo, u, o, ue, u[-]e;

ou	*also see*	eu *or* ui
oul	*see*	ou
ow	*see*	eu, ou *or* ui
oy	*see*	ai, o[-]e *or* ui

p, pp, pt

ph	*see*	f
pp	*see*	p
pt	*see*	p

qu, qw, quh;

qu	*also see*	wh
quh	*see*	qu *or* wh
qw	*see*	qu *or* wh

r, rr, rh

s, sc, ss, z;

s	*also see*	c *or* sh
sc	*see*	s *or* sk
sch	*see*	sh *or* sk

scl, skl, sl

sh, sch, ch, sk, s

sk, sc, sch;

sk	*also see*	sh
skl	*see*	scl
sl	*see*	scl
ss	*see*	s
t	*see*	c *or* d
tch	*see*	ch

th, tht;
th, y;

th	*also see*	ch, d *or* f
tht	*see*	ch *or* th
tt	*see*	d

u, o, v, w;

u	*also see*	eu, ou *or* ui
ue	*see*	eu, ou *or* ui
u[-]e	*see*	ou *or* ui
uee	*see*	ui

ui, uy, ue, u[-]e, u, oo, oi, oy, oe, o[-]e, ou, ow, ee, ei, ey, wee, uee, i, ai, a[-]e;

ui	*also see*	eu
uy	*see*	ui
v	*see*	f *or* u
w	*see*	u
wee	*see*	ui

wh, quh, qu, qw;
wh, f

x	*see*	cks

y, yh, ꜟ, ꜟh, z;

y	*also see*	ai, ei, i[-]e *or* th
yh	*see*	y
yi	*see*	ai *or* i[-]e
yow	*see*	eu
ꜟ	*see*	y
ꜟh	*see*	y
z	*see*	s, y

3.2 *Word beginnings and endings*

Many word beginnings and endings in Scots vary considerably and the following lists give just a few examples of these.

3.2.1 *Word beginnings*
en-, an-, in-

in-, on-, un-, wn-

ower-, over-, our-, ouer-, ovir-, owir-, owyr-, ovyr-

per-, par-

re-, ra-

3.2.2 *Word endings.* It should be noted that many words may also have a final 'e'.

-er, -eir, -eyr, -eur, -ar, -air, -ayr, -ir, -yr, -or, -oir, -oyr, -our, -ur

-ie, -y, -ye, -e, -é, -ee, -ey, -ay, -ae

-ing, -yng, -and, -an, -ant

-in, -yn, -en, -ein, -eyn, -eng, eing, -eyng

-ed, it(t), -yt(t), -et(t)

-le, -il(l), -yl(l), -el(l), -al(l), ol(l)

-ion, -ioun, -tio(u)n, -cio(u)n, -sio(u)n, -shio(u)n, -shun, -zhun

4 Headwords

4.1 *Headwords in CSD2*

Sections 4–12 of this user guide explain the components of a typical CSD2 entry. All entries in CSD2 begin with a headword printed in bold type. Headwords (printed in bold type) are normally selected from the numerous variants for which there is evidence in the parent dictionaries or SLD's database. The headword is generally the most frequently evidenced form. Occasionally, where there is a Scots spelling and a spelling shared with English, a distinctively Scots spelling will be given as the headword, even although it may be less common (e.g. **colleckshun**, **doactor**). The headword is followed by variants, separated by commas and ordered on the basis of frequency, geographical distribution and currency. Words are regarded as current if they have been recorded after 1900. Obsolete headwords and variants are marked with a dagger †. Up to three obsolete variants may be included. These are chosen on the basis of frequency and their capacity to illustrate the range and nature of spelling variation.

4.2 Cross-references

Every CSD2 variant headword also appears in its own alphabetical place, with a cross-reference to the leading headword of the CSD2 article in which the variant appears, except where it is alphabetically adjacent to that article (see 12 below).

5 Pronunciation

5.1 Introduction

5.1.1 *How is pronunciation shown?* For all current headwords, a broad phonetic transcription is supplied using the symbols of the International Phonetic Alphabet (IPA). These symbols are explained in 5.2 below. No pronunciation is given for obsolete words. Regional variations are often included but these are necessarily restricted to representative samples from the main dialect areas.

5.1.2 *How should a native speaker of Scots use CSD2 as a guide to pronunciation?* Native speakers of Scots can be guided by the spellings and the phonetic symbols, but as the transcriptions are very broad and not all variations are included, speakers are of course free to adopt pronunciations as appropriate to their own regional accent (see also 5.4).

5.1.3 *Can anyone learn to pronounce Scots from CSD2?* Reading a dictionary is no substitute for listening to native speakers, but non-native speakers of Scots will achieve a plausible Scots pronunciation if they interpret the phonetic transcriptions by giving the symbols their usual IPA values, as given at 5.2 below.

5.1.4 *On what evidence do the phonetic transcriptions depend?* The pronunciations of current forms represented in the phonetic transcriptions are derived from the transcriptions in SND and other authorities on the pronunciation of Scots, from recordings, from indications of spellings and rhymes in SND and writings in Scots, from personal knowledge of members of the editorial staff, and by consultation with local speakers.

5.2 Phonetic transcriptions

5.2.1 *Consonant symbols* For the most part the IPA consonant symbols have the same values as in varieties of English, e.g. [b] as in *butter* or *club*, [h] as in *house* or *hand*. Symbols of this kind are: [b], [d], [f], [g], [h], [k], [l], [m], [n], [p], [r], [s], [t], [v], [w], [z]. There are also special symbols or symbol-combinations. In CSD2 we have made use of the following symbols:

Phonetic symbol	Typical spellings	As in Scots words	As in Standard English words spoken by Scottish speakers
j	y	*yaird, tailye, nyaff*	*yard, million, William, onion*
x	ch	*bricht, ocht, pech*	*loch, dreich, Auchtermuchty*
ʍ	wh	*wha, whustle*	*when, which, whistle*
ʃ	sh	*shilpit, snash, ashet*	*she, ash, bishop*
ʒ	si, shi, su	*fushion, pleasure,*	*evasion, treasure*
tʃ	ch, tch	*chiel, fleech, wratch*	*child, beech, catch*
dʒ	j, dg, g	*jeelie, fadge, fugie*	*jam, lodge, magic*
ŋ	ng	*hing, ingan, fank*	*sing, bank*
θ	th	*thole, thrawn, graith*	*thin, three, cloth*
ð	th	*thae, thir, kythe*	*these, bathe, gather*

5.2.2 *Vowel symbols*

(a) Monophthongs

Phonetic symbol	Typical spellings	As in Scots words	As in Standard English words spoken by Scottish speakers
a	a	*gab, plack*	*man, cat*
ɔ	au, aw, a'	*fause, saut, baw*	*cause, caught, saw*
e	ai, ay, a[-]e	*graith, gate, tae*	*faith, gate, pay*
ɛ	e	*ken, hecht*	*pen, get*
i	ee, ei, ea	*deif, dee*	*leaf, meet, sea*
ɪ	i	*lit, birl, niz*	*bit, whirl, fix*
o	o, oa, o[-]e	*thole, dove*	*close, coat, coal*
u	oo, ou, ow, ui, u[-]e	*hoose, croup, doo*	*loose, shoe*
ʌ	u	*buss, buckle*	*bus, bud*
ə	e, a, i, o, u	the unstressed syllable in *faither, bannock, anent*	the unstressed syllable in *father, hillock, about* (see below)
ø	ö, eu, oo	especially in Shetland and Orkney *snöd, shö, sneuk, mooratoog*	(see below)
ɑ	aa	especially in Shetland and Orkney *sneerim/snaarim, baackie*	(see below)

The [ə] symbol is regularly used to represent indeterminate vowels in unstressed syllables, but it should be noted that some speakers sporadically use [ɪ], [ɛ], [ʌ] or [a] in such contexts. The [ø] symbol is used here only in Shetland, Orkney and occasional Northern Highland words to indicate a more or less rounded front vowel, ranging in quality from the vowels in French *lune*, German *über* to those in French *peu*, German *schön*. Following the practice of the *Scottish National Dictionary*, the [ɑ] symbol is used for vowels in Shetland, Orkney and occasional Northern Highland words, although there appears to be considerable overlap between this vowel and the [a] and [ɔ] vowels. Particularly in Central Scotland, there is a tendency to merge the [ɔ] and the [o] vowels in words such as *doctor* (see **doactor**) and **docken**.

The final vowel in words such as *happy* is variable in Scots with some areas (such as the Borders) having predominantly [e] and others (such as the Northern Highlands) preferring [i]. For many areas, the choice is determined largely by the height of the preceding vowel; so, after a high vowel, [i] is used as in **stooshie** [ˈstuʃi] but after a low vowel [e] is used as in **collie** [ˈkɔle].

(b) Diphthongs:

Phonetic symbol	Typical spellings	As in Scots words	As in Standard English words spoken by Scottish speakers
ʌɪ	i[-]e, y[-]e, ey, ay	gyte, ile, jine	bite, mile, line (see 5.4.3)
ae	i[-]e, y[-]e	kye, ay (yes), guise, rive	eye, rise, hive, die (see 5.4.3)
ɔɪ	oi, oy	droicht, hoy	Boyd, noise, boy
ʌu	ou, ow	ower, knowe	house, hour, cow

5.2.3 **Stress.** The mark [ˈ] denotes that the following syllable is stressed, e.g. [ˈmanədʒər] **manager**, [rəˈmen] **remain**.

5.2.4 *Regional pronunciations.* General Scots pronunciations are given first, followed by regional pronunciations in the following order: Shetland (*Sh*), Orkney (*Ork*), Northern Highlands (*N*), North-East (*NE*), Tayside (*T*), Western Highlands and Islands (*H&I*), East Central (*EC*) and West Central (*WC*), which may be combined as Central (*C*), South-West (*SW*), Borders (*Bor*) and Ulster (*Uls*).

Using **ploo**[1.1] as an example, pronunciations are listed in the following manner: [plu; *Sh* plɔx; *NE T* plux; *C SW* plʌx; *EC* pjʌx; *WC* pju; *SW Bor* plju, pljux]. The General Scots form is [plu]. Where there is more than one General Scots pronunciation for a word these are separated by commas, whereas regional pronunciations are separated by semicolons.

Although regions are assigned particular pronunciations, this does not mean that the General Scots pronunciation is absent in those areas. There may be overlap between regions which is not shown in CSD2 and, in many cases, there will be local pronunciations that are not given at all. However, the regional transcriptions provide a good indication of the range of variation available.

5.3 *Which pronunciations are and are not included in the phonetic transcriptions?*

5.3.1 *Are all the current principal Scottish pronunciations included?* We have aimed to give the commonest or best-attested variations, although predictable or regular variations may sometimes be omitted.

5.3.2 *Predictable variations.* The following predictable or regular variations in certain districts are not always shown in CSD2's phonetic transcriptions:

(a) Word-initial consonant sequences, formerly general in both Scots and English, but now surviving only in a few dialects, that is [kn-] and [gn-], now widely [n-], in words such as **knee**[1.1], **knit, knip**[3.1]; the obsolete [wr-], in some dialects north of the Tay [vr-], elsewhere now [r-], e.g. in **wrang, writ;**
(b) The simplification of word-initial [tʃ] to [ʃ] in Shetland, Orkney, the Northern Highlands and the Borders, e.g. in **chance**[1.1] [tʃans, tʃɔns, tʃʌns; *Sh Ork N* ʃans];
(c) The change of word-initial [dʒ] to [tʃ] in Orkney and the Northern Highlands, e.g. in **jaud** [dʒɔd; *Ork* tʃad];
(d) The replacement of [θ] with [t], and [ð] with [d], in Shetland and Orkney, e.g. in **thrang**[1.3] [θraŋ, θrɔŋ]; *Sh Ork* [traŋ] and **thee** [ði; *Sh Ork* di];
(e) The omission of initial [ð] in the Northern Highlands and the North-East, e.g. in **the** [ɪ];
(f) The substitution of [f] for [ʍ], particularly in the Northern Highlands and the North-East, e.g. in **whalp**[1.1] *N NE* [fɔlp, fʌlp]. An intermediate pronunciation is not uncommon;
(g) The change of [-ək] (**-ock, -ack**) to [-əg] (**-ag**) in Northern. See **-ock**;
(h) Variation in weak past tense and past participle endings such as final devoicing whereby, in **bemangit**, the variant *bemang'd* [bəˈmaŋd] has the alternative voiceless final sound [bəˈmaŋt];
(i) For the ending of the present participle and verbal noun SSE uses **-ing** [-ɪŋ]. Scots favours **-in** [-ən] or [-ɪn]. For some Scots speakers (especially Shetland, Orkney and the Northern Highlands), a distinction is made between the present participle in [-ən] and the verbal noun in [-ɪn], although for most speakers the two endings have become indistinguishable. See 6.3. In many but not all cases, CSD2 preserves the distinction. In some cases, where our evidence is limited, transcriptions are given with only the velar nasal [-ŋ] or only the alveolar nasal [-n]. In most cases, it should be assumed that either may be used;
(j) The final unstressed vowel in words such as **cosie** [ˈkozi, ˈkoze] varies according to dialect area and, in some dialects, according to the vowel in the preceding syllable and the intervening consonant(s). Where only one pronunciation is given, the other should not be ruled out.

See also 5.2.2., 5.4.1, 5.4.4.

5.4 *How precise are the phonetic transcriptions?*

5.4.1 *CSD2's transcriptions are intentionally broad.* Many of CSD2's phonetic symbols cover a range of sound qualities, ignoring local variations. For example:

(a) [ɛ] as in *get*, *ken*, *hecht* ranges from a fairly close pronunciation in the North-East (verging on [e] as in *gate*) to a much more open pronunciation in the South (rather like the vowel [æ] in *cat* in RP). CSD2 [ɛ] represents both of these sounds as well as Central Scots [ɛ];
(b) [ɔ] as in *saut* (salt), *cause*, *saw* generally represents a vowel similar to that in *bought* in most varieties of British Standard English. As noted at 5.2.2, there is some variation between this [ɔ] and the [o] vowel;
(c) In words such as **theevil** [ˈθivəl] and **widden** [ˈwɪdən] an unstressed vowel is shown, although pronunciations with a syllabic [l] or [n] are possible. Epenthetic vowels are usually omitted, e.g. **airm**¹ [erm], not [ˈerəm].

5.4.2 *The glottal stop.* Many Scots speakers today substitute the glottal stop [ʔ], a sound made by momentarily closing the glottis, for the consonants [t], [p] or [k], but especially [t], in any position except the onset of a stressed syllable, as [ˈbʌʔər] *butter*. CSD2 does not record such variants, giving only the phonemic forms with [t] etc.

5.4.3 *How does CSD2 treat vowel length?* Scots and SSE have their own system of vowel length, which is different from that of all other parts of the English-speaking world:

(a) The vowels [ɪ] and [ʌ] are always pronounced short;
(b) [i], [u], [ʌɪ] and, for some dialects, [e], [a], [o], [ɔ], [ʌu] are normally longer
   - before the consonants [v], [ð], [z], [ʒ] and, for many dialects, [r]
   - when the vowel is final (in a word or in the first part of a compound word)
   - when the vowel is followed by an ending such as the past-tense ending.

In all other positions, in most dialects of Scots and in SSE, these vowels are short.

There is considerable variation in vowel length between the dialects and in these circumstances it is clearly impossible for a dictionary such as CSD2 to record the precise vowel length for each word in every dialect, and this has not been attempted. Consequently, vowels are not normally marked for length in the transcriptions, and it is left to the reader to pronounce the vowel in each case either with the length appropriate to his or her own dialect or according to the general indications set out above.

5.4.4 *Vowel + r.* In Scots and in SSE, *r* is always pronounced, unlike in some parts of England, where it is pronounced only before a vowel. The [ɛ] vowel before *r* does not usually alter in quality, as in **serve** [sɛrv]. However, increasingly [ɪr] is merging with [ʌr]; for example, **bird** [bɪrd] is becoming [bʌrd] (compare **hurl** [hʌrl]). Alternative pronunciations are usually given for these [ɪr], [ʌr] pairs. There is a growing tendency for [ɪr], [ʌr] and even [ɛr] to become [ɜr], as in General American. This tendency has not been reflected in CSD2.

6 Grammar and word-formation

6.1 *Parts of speech*

All headwords are given a part-of-speech label which follows the pronunciation information, if this is included; otherwise it immediately follows the headword and any variant spellings.

6.2 *Noun n*

Plural forms of nouns are not normally given if they are the same as the SSE plural or if they conform to one of the regular patterns of plurals in Older Scots (*-is*, *-ys*).

6.3 *Verb v*

6.3.1 **present participle** *presp* and **verbal noun** *(not abbreviated).* Regular Scots forms of the present participle (such as **-in²**, *-and*, *-an*) and the verbal noun (e.g. **-in¹**, *-ing*) are not normally given in CSD2 (see also 'A History of Scots' above). These are included only where a Scots meaning or usage is given, as a headword or in the derivatives section (see 10.1).

6.3.2 *past tense pt* and *past participle ptp*. These forms are not normally given when they follow the regular patterns of Scots and/or SSE. An exception is made where the standard British English form is attested earlier in Scots than in English, and these are included according to the rules set out in 1.2 above.

6.4 *Adjective adj* and **adverb** *adv*.
Comparatives and superlatives are given in the cases where these may differ from the South British English pattern, e.g. **dear**^{1,2}... *comparative also* **derrar**, †**darrer**, *superlative also* †**derrast**, **darrest**.

For a full list of abbreviations, see p.xlii.

7 Definitions

Definitions (in roman type) are largely based on those in the parent dictionaries. However every definition and every quotation in the parent dictionaries has been examined afresh, and often the DOST and SND definitions have been modified in the light of the more comprehensive information available to the editors of CSD2. Such changes will be incorporated eventually into the revised DSL.

The wording of definitions has been kept as simple as possible. Definitions from the parent dictionaries have therefore been simplified where necessary, although it is not always possible to avoid complicated or technical language. Sometimes a concept is complicated in itself.

7.1 *Synonyms*

Synonyms used in definitions are normally separated by commas; where a semicolon is used, this indicates a slight shift in meaning, e.g.:

> **tap**^{1,1}... **1** the highest, uppermost or most important place or position *la14-*. **2** a tuft of hair, wool or feathers; a forelock; a bird's crest *15-*.

7.2 Order

The ordering of meanings within an entry or sub-entry follows historical order with the most current coming first and those with wider geographical spread given precedence over those that are more dialectally restricted.

7.3 Dating and geographical distribution

All definitions are followed by a date indicating the period during which they were used, to the nearest half-century (see 8 below). Some are also followed by a label or labels indicating the regions in which they are found, especially when their use is restricted in the modern period (see 9 below).

7.4 Information on constructions

Such information is given in definitions in several ways. Usually, this is dealt with by treating the construction as a phrase, e.g.:

>**speir at** to put a question to, inquire of (a person) *la14-*.

Alternatively, a grammatical note is given, often with an illustrative phrase (7.6), e.g.:

>**see ... 3** *in imperative* hand or pass, give into a person's hand, let (a person) have: ◊*see me the teapot 19-*.

7.5 Field labels

Labels (such as *mining*, *law*) are occasionally used to indicate which field of knowledge the item belongs to. They are placed in italics before the definition, e.g.:

>**mandate**¹... **2** *law* a formal warrant authorizing one person to act on behalf of another (without payment); a commission of attorneyship or proxy *16-*.

7.6 Illustrative phrases

These are included occasionally to clarify a meaning or usage. They are given before the date, e.g.:

>**fine**¹·³ /fʌɪn/ *adv* very well, very much: ◊*I like it fine la18-*

8 Dating

8.1 General

Dates (in italic type) are given in half-centuries, as far as available evidence allows, for each sense. Thus:

e16	means that there is evidence of use between 1500 and 1550
la16	between 1550 and 1600
16	for the whole of the 16th century
la14-16	from the second half of the 14th century to the end of the 16th century
15-19	from the beginning of the 15th to the end of the 19th century
la16-e19	from the second half of the 16th to the first half of the 19th century

16-19, 20- *NE T*	in widespread use from the beginning of 16th century to the end of the 19th century, but only attested in specific regions from the 20th century onwards
16-20, 21- *historical*	in current use from the beginning of 16th century to the end of the 20th century, but now only referred to in a historical context
la14-	from the second half of the 14th century to the present day

Occasionally where there is a long gap in the evidence, two date ranges are given; for example *e16, 19-* means that there is early 16th-century evidence but nothing more until the early 19th century.

8.2 Place-names

Place-name evidence is often the earliest available for a Scots term, but these dates are generally not marked separately from those given for the lexical evidence. Where the usage of a word is particularly prevalent in place-names, or where the evidence is primarily from place-names, this is indicated with the phrase *frequently in place-names*.

9 Geographical distribution

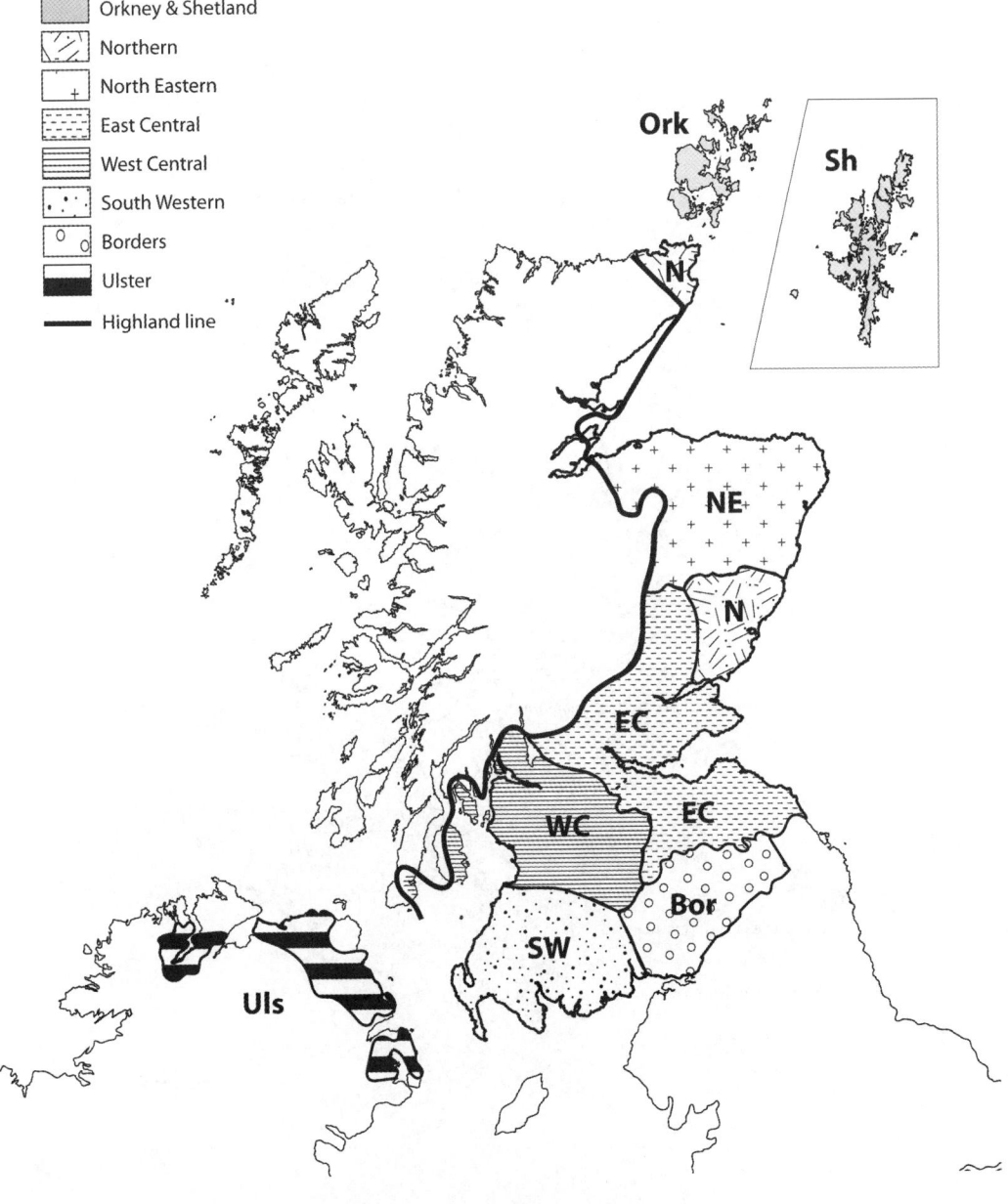

Dialect Areas of Scotland

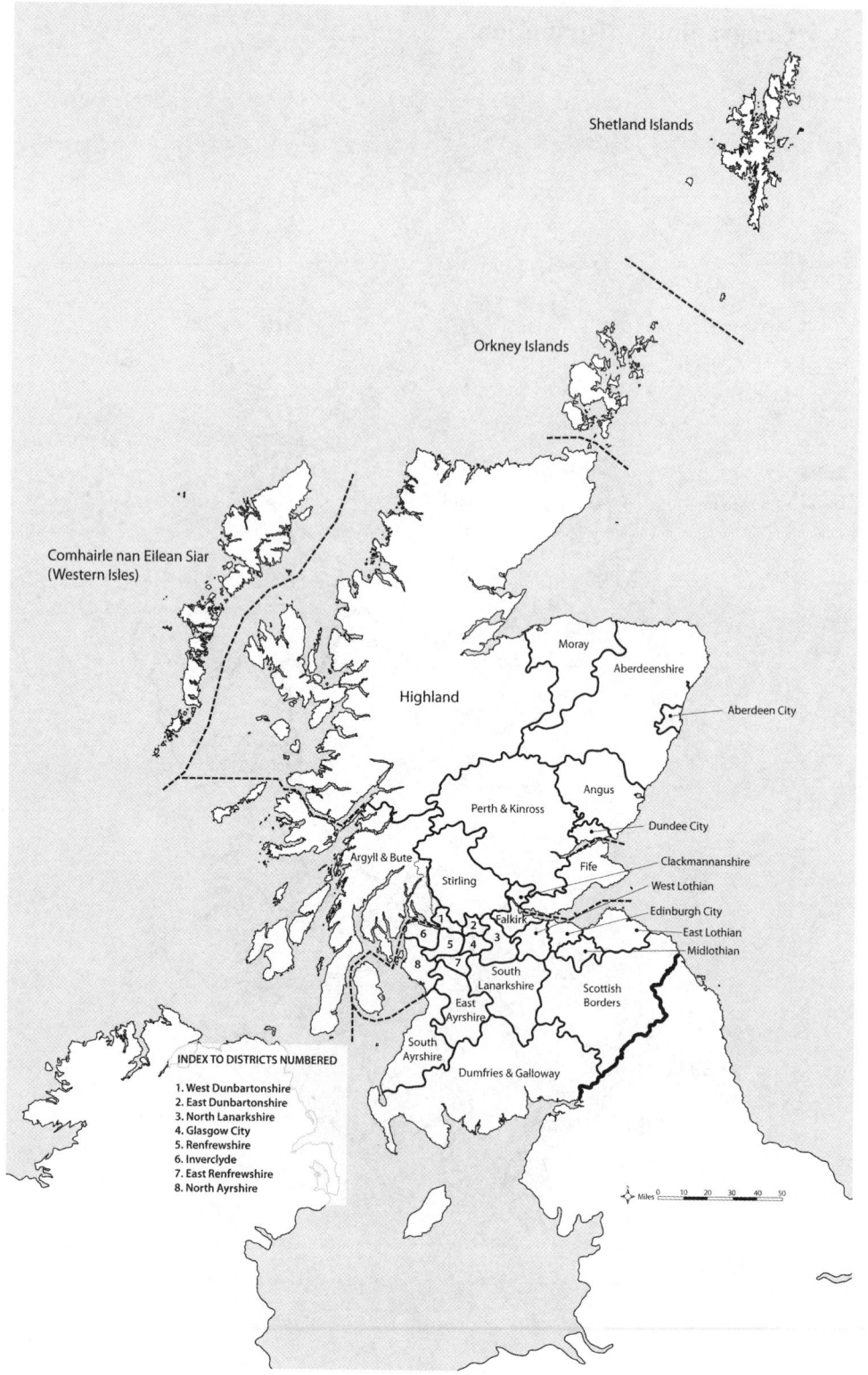

Administrative Areas of Scotland before 1975

xxxix HOW TO USE CSD2

Administrative Areas of Scotland after 1996

9.1 General

The geographic distribution of the regions used in CSD2 is illustrated on the map on p.xxxvii. The names of the regions have been altered from those used in both SND and in CSD1. The CSD2 regions are broadly based on the pre-1975 county boundaries, which have been divided into *east* and *west*, or *north* and *south* where necessary. The only exception to the pre-1975 system is that the Hebrides have been grouped together, rather than being listed under their respective separate counties.

It should be noted that, with increasing social mobility, words can move rapidly from one region to another. Hence, even where areas of distribution are specified in CSD2, this does not preclude the occurrence of the form, meaning or usage outwith the specified region. CSD2 reflects the current data held by SLD, which is being updated as new evidence becomes available with a view to being added to DSL.

Where evidence of a form, meaning, usage or pronunciation is limited to an area or areas, and especially where it is thus limited in the modern era, this is indicated by means of CSD2's system of abbreviations as set out below.

9.2 Dialect districts of Scots

The abbreviations (in italic type) normally precede the spellings and pronunciations to which they refer. When senses are distinguished, they follow the dates given.

CSD2 Region	*CSD2 Abbreviation*	*Pre-1975 Counties*
SHETLAND	*Sh*	Shetland
ORKNEY	*Ork*	Orkney
NORTHERN HIGHLANDS	*N*	Caithness
		Sutherland
		Ross & Cromarty (mainland)
		Inverness-shire (mainland)
		Nairnshire
NORTH-EAST	*NE*	Morayshire
		Banffshire
		Aberdeenshire
		Kincardineshire
TAYSIDE	*T*	Angus
		Perthshire
WESTERN HIGHLANDS AND ISLANDS	*H&I*	Inner and Outer Hebrides
		Argyllshire (mainland)
		Bute
EAST CENTRAL	*EC*	Fife
		Kinross-shire
		Clackmannanshire
		East Stirlingshire
		West Lothian

WEST CENTRAL	*WC*	Midlothian East Lothian West Stirlingshire Dunbartonshire Renfrewshire Lanarkshire North Ayrshire
SOUTH WEST	*SW*	South Ayrshire Wigtownshire Kirkcudbrightshire West Dumfriesshire
BORDERS	*Bor*	Berwickshire Peeblesshire Roxburghshire Selkirkshire East Dumfriesshire
ULSTER	*Uls*	Antrim Down Derry/Londonderry Donegal
CENTRAL	*C*	refers to *EC* and *WC* together

The order in which the regions are listed is *Sh, Ork, N, NE, T, H&I, C* (including *EC* and *WC*), *EC, WC, SW, Bor, Uls*. If an item is in general use throughout the country, this is indicated in entries by giving a current date (e.g. *1a14-*) with no restricting label.

Where two date ranges are given, any restriction refers only to the later date range, e.g. *1a14-16, 1a19- NE*. This means that the evidence from the late 19th century onwards is confined to the North-East, but that the restriction does not apply to the medieval period.

10 Derivatives, compounds, phrases

10.1 Derivatives

Derivatives, such as **flesher, fleshing, fleschlyk** from **flesh**, are presented immediately after the main article for each headword. They are in alphabetical order of the suffix, e.g. **flesh** *n* 1 ... 2 ... 3 ...**flesher** ... **fleshing** ... **fleschlyk.**

10.2 Compounds

Compounds which have the headword as first element follow the derivatives (where there are any). They are listed in alphabetical order of the second element, e.g. **maister**[1] ... **maisterman** ... **maistertree** ...

10.3 The possessive s

The presence or absence of the possessive s has been ignored in the alphabetization as its presence or absence is frequently inconsistent in Scots.

10.4 Phrases

These follow compounds in alphabetical order of the first significant element (whether or not this element is the headword). Function words such as pronouns, prepositions, and definite or indefinite articles are normally ignored. It is not, however, possible to make rigid rules about the order in which phrases appear.

10.5 Most compounds and phrases will be found under the first element. As there is not enough space in the dictionary to allow an item to be included more than once, users may not always find the item they are looking for at the first attempt. In such cases they should then try one of the other elements. In rare instances, a cross-reference is given from one element of a phrase or compound to another.

Derivatives, compounds and phrases may form self-contained entries if they are more common than their current main element, or where the main element has become obsolete and the derivative, compound or phrase is still in current use. They may also have other derivatives, compounds and phrases dependent on them.

11 Etymologies

See the list of abbreviations on pp.xliv–xlvi. Etymologies are included for all entries, within square brackets, at the end of each entry. They are necessarily brief and generally give the most likely source or sources of the headword, where known. Where no language of origin is given, it can be assumed that the source is Scottish English.

11.1 English in etymologies A very large number of words entered Scots from northern Middle English; the etymology for these words is given as their, usually, Old English or Old Norse precursor. Where a word appears first in Middle English and cannot be taken further back, or where a word has undergone a substantial change in form or meaning in Middle English, then the Middle English word is given as the etymon.

Datings for periods of English used in CSD2 are as follows:

Modern English	1650–
EModE	1475–1650
ME	1100–1475
OE	up to 1100

11.2 Latin in etymologies Vowel quantities (e.g. $\bar{a}$, $\bar{e}$) are given for all Latin words.

Nouns, adjectives and pronouns are normally given in the nominative case and verbs in the infinitive, where necessary with other parts in addition.

11.3 French in etymologies Datings for periods of French used in CSD2 are based on entries in the parent dictionaries and roughly correspond to the following:

OFr	up to 1350
MFr	1350–1600
Fr	1600–

11.4 Where the etymology of an item is uncertain it is given as [unknown].

11.5 The following annotations are used frequently:
(1) [onomatopoeic] where the meaning of the word is strongly suggested by its sound, e.g. **skrauch**;
(2) [imitative] where the sound of the word mimics the sound described, e.g. **cockieleerie**;

12 Cross-references

In all cross-references the first headword of the entry referred to is given in small capitals. This may be preceded by a subsidiary headword form or sub-entry in *italics*, e.g. *town guard* (TOUN).

Every variant form given in an entry also appears as a main-entry cross-reference in its own alphabetical place, e.g.

gabbart, †gabar, †gabert, †cabar ...

Therefore:
gabar *see* GABBART
gabert *see* GABBART
cabar *see* GABBART

The only exceptions to this are as follows:
(1) where the variant form would be alphabetically adjacent to the first headword, e.g. **gallant¹ galland** ...;
(2) a derivative or compound is not cross-referred unless it is difficult to recognize as coming from one of the headwords which have already been given.

13 Typefaces

CSD2 uses four typefaces:

(1) **bold** for
- all leading headwords and their variant headwords
- grammatical forms (such as plurals of nouns, past tenses and participles of verbs etc.)
- sub-entries (derivatives, compounds, phrases and their variants)
- numbers separating different senses

(2) roman for
- definitions (which thus stand out from surrounding information in bold and italic)
- etymologies except where a word form is given
- phonetic symbols

(3) *italic* for
- Latinate abbreviations
- labels (including those indicating semantic field or register)
- additional information on grammar or usage
- dates and geographical distribution

- illustrative phrases
- citation of words forms in etymologies
- sub-cross-references

(4) small capitals for
- cross-references

14 Abbreviations, labels and symbols

CSD2 contains a wide variety of different types of information and this has made it necessary to use a large number of abbreviations and other labels. Efforts have been made to keep these as simple and as easily understood as possible.

adj	adjective, adjectival
adv	adverb, adverbial
AF	Anglo-French
AN	Anglo-Norman
aux	auxiliary
Bor	Borders
c	*circa*, about
C	Central (= EC + WC)
conj	conjunction
CSD1	*Concise Scots Dictionary* (first edition)
CSD2	*Concise Scots Dictionary* (second edition)
Dan	Danish
def art	definite article
dial	dialect, dialectal
dim	diminutive
DOST	*A Dictionary of the Older Scottish Tongue*
DSL	*Dictionary of the Scots Language*
Du	Dutch
e	early (as in *e16* = early 16th century)
E	East: (1) in general; (2) = Sh Ork N + EC dialects (see 9 above)
EC	East Central
ed.	editor, edition
eds	editors, editions
e.g.	for example
EModDu	Early Modern Dutch
EModE	Early Modern English
Eng	English
etc	et cetera
Faer	Faeroese
Fr	French
fem	feminine
Flem	Flemish
Gael	Scottish Gaelic
Ger	German
H&I	(Western) Highlands and Islands
HibEng	Hiberno-English
Icel	Icelandic
i.e.	that is
indef art	indefinite article

infl	influence, influenced
interj	interjection
Ir	Irish
IrGael	Irish Gaelic
Ital	Italian
la	late (as in *la16* = late 16th century)
Lat	Latin
LG	LowGerman
M	Middle (of languages)
masc	masculine
MDu	Middle Dutch
ME	Middle English
MFr	Middle French
MHG	Middle High German
MLG	Middle Low German
ms(s)	manuscript(s)
n	noun; northern
N	Northern Highlands; North
NE	North-East
Norw	Norwegian
O	Old, Older (of languages)
OE	Old English
OED	*Oxford English Dictionary*
OFr	Old French
OFris	Old Frisian
OIr	Old Irish
ON	Old Norse
orig	original, originally, origin
Ork	Orkney
pers	person
pl	plural
Port	Portuguese
ppl	participle, participial
prep	preposition
pres	present, present tense
presp	present participle
pron	pronoun
pt	past, past tense
ptp	past participle
ref	reference
Rom	Romany
Sc	Scots
Gael	Scottish Gaelic
Sh	Shetland
sing	singular
SLD	Scottish Language Dictionaries
SND	*Scottish National Dictionary*
SSE	Scottish Standard English
SW	South-West
Swed	Swedish
T	Tayside
Uls	Ulster

US	United States
v	verb
W	West
WC	West Central

Symbols (see also Pronunciation Key in 5 above)

* in etymologies, indicates a hypothetical form

= used to cross-refer to an item with identical meaning (and the same dates and geographical distribution unless otherwise stated)

& and

SCOTTISH MONEY, WEIGHTS AND MEASURES

Money

The Scots currency was roughly equivalent in value to that of England till the later 14th century, when it began to depreciate by stages till at the time of the Act of Union in 1707, by the terms of which the Scots currency was abolished. The following values obtained:

SCOTS	STERLING	DECIMAL
1 penny	$1/12$ penny	-
2 pennies = 1 BODLE	$1/6$ penny	-
2 bodles = 1 PLACK	$1/3$ penny	-
3 bodles = 1 BAWBEE	1 half penny	-
2 bawbees = 1 SHILLING	1 penny	.42 penny
13 shillings 4 pence = 1 MERK	1s. $1^{1}/3$d.	5.5 pence
20 shillings = 1 pound	1s. 8d.	8 pence

> 1826 Galt *The Last of the Lairds* ii: 'For on that day [Union of 1707] the pound Stirling came in among our natural coin, and, like Moses' rod, swallow't up at ae gawpe, plack, bodle, mark, and bawbie.'

Weights and measures

There was much confusion and diversity in early Scottish weights and measures and a succession of enactments from the 15th century failed to improve matters till in 1661 a commission was set up by Parliament which recommended the setting up of national standards, the exemplars of which were to be kept in the custody of certain burghs, the *ell* for lineal measure to be kept by Edinburgh, the *jug* for liquid capacity by Stirling, the *firlot* for dry measure by Linlithgow, and the *troy stone* for weight by Lanark. These recommendations in the main prevailed throughout Scotland, though there was some irregularity between commodities in dry measure; a further recommendation that *tron* weight should be entirely abolished was ignored and this measure fluctuated within fairly wide limits as between 22 and 28 ounces per pound. By Act 5 Geo. IV. c.74, 1824 uniformity of weights and measures was statutorily established and gradually this was conformed to, although the names of the older measures like FIRLOT, FORPET, LIPPIE were transferred to fractions of the Imperial hundred-weight and are still sometimes heard.

(a) According to the standard of Lanark, for TROY weight:

SCOTS	AVOIRDUPOIS	METRIC WEIGHT
1 drop (see DRAP)	1.093 drams	1.921 grams
16 drops = 1 ounce	1 oz. 1.5 drams	31 grams
16 ounces = 1 pound	1 lb. 1 oz. 8 dr.	496 grams
16 pounds = 1 stone	17 lbs. 8 oz.	7.936 kilograms

(b) According to the standard of Edinburgh, for TRON weight:

SCOTS	AVOIRDUPOIS	METRIC WEIGHT
1 drop	1.378 drams	2.4404 grams
16 drops = 1 ounce	1 oz. 6 drams	39.04 grams
16 ounces = 1 pound	1 lb. 6 oz. 1 dram	624.74 grams
16 pounds = 1 stone	1 stone 8 lbs. 1 oz.	9.996 kilograms

Capacity

Liquid measure according to the standard of Stirling. See JOUG.

SCOTS	IMPERIAL	METRIC
1 gill	.749 gill	.053 litres
4 gills = 1 MUTCHKIN	2.996 gills	.212 litres
2 mutchkins = 1 CHOPIN	1 pint 1.992 gills	.848 litres
2 chopins = 1 PINT	2 pints 3.984 gills	1.696 litres
8 pints = 1 gallon	3 gallons .25 gills	13.638 litres
1 pint = 104.2034 Imp. cub. in. ((I)CI)	1 pint = 34.659 ICI	1 litre = 61.027 CI

 1731 *Two Students* (Dickinson 1952) lxvi: 'Each Bursar hath for breakfast the thrid part of a Scon & mutckine of ale.'

Dry measure according to the standard of Linlithgow.

For wheat, peas, beans, meal, etc.

SCOTS	IMPERIAL	METRIC
1 LIPPIE (or FORPET)	.499 gallons	2.268 litres
4 lippies = 1 PECK	1.996 gallons	9.072 litres
4 pecks = 1 FIRLOT	3 pecks 1.986 gallons	36.286 litres
4 firlots = 1 BOLL	3 bushels 3 pecks 1.944 galls	145.145 litres
16 bolls = 1 CHALDER	7 quarters 7 bushels 3 pecks, 1.07 galls	2322.324 litres
1 firlot = 2214.322 cub. in.	1 gallon = 277.274 cub. in.	1 litre = 61.027 cub. in.

 1887 P. McNeill *Blawearie* 161: 'It's no jist so easy now ... to run off wi' a sheep or a firlot o' tatties'.

For barley, oats, malt

SCOTS	IMPERIAL	METRIC
1 lippie (or forpet)	.728 gallons	3.037 litres
4 lippies = 1 peck	1 peck .912 gallons	13.229 litres
4 pecks = 1 firlot	1 bushel 1 peck 1.650 gallons	52.916 litres
4 firlots = 1 boll	5 bushels 3 pecks .600 gallons	211.664 litres
16 bolls = 1 chalder	11 quarters 5 bushels 1.615 gallons	3386.624 litres

1 firlot = 3230.305 cub. in.

> 1894 P. H. Hunter *James Inwick* 171: 'A faur-seein chiel, wha kent hoo mony lippies gae to the peck.'

Linear and square measures

According to the standard ell of Edinburgh.

Linear

SCOTS	IMPERIAL	METRIC
1 inch	1.0016 inches	2.54 cm
8.88 inches = 1 scots link	8.8942 inches	22.55 cm
12 inches = 1 foot	12.0192 inches	30.5287 cm
$3^{1}/_{12}$ feet = 1 ell	37.0598 inches	94.1318 cm
6 ells = 1 fall (fa)	6.1766 yards	5.6479 metres
4 falls = 1 chain	24.7064 yards	22.5916 metres
10 chains = 1 furlong	247.064 yards	225.916 metres
8 furlongs = 1 mile	1976.522 yards	1.8073 km

1 fall = 1.123 English poles; 1 chain = 1.123 English chains; 1 furlong = 1.123 English furlongs; 1 mile = 1.123 English miles

Square

SCOTS	IMPERIAL	METRIC
1 sq. inch	1.0256 sq. inch	6.4516 sq. cm
1 sq. ell	1.059 sq. yards	.8853 sq. m.
36 sq. ells = 1 sq. fall	38.125 sq. yards (1 pole 7.9 sq. yards)	31.87 sq. m.
40 falls = 1 sq. rood	1525 sq. yards (1 rood 10 poles 13 sq. yards)	12.7483 ares
4 roods = 1 sq. acre	6100 sq. yards (1.26 acres)	.5099 hectare

> 1845 *Second Statistical Account* I. 196: 'The extent of the glebe is 10 acres, 3 roods, 17 falls, 4 ells, Scotch measure.'

Yarn measure

1 CUT = 300 yards
1 HEERE = 2 cuts or 600 yards
1 HEID = 2 heeres or 1200 yards
1 HANK or HESP = 3 heids or 3600 yards
1 SPINLE = 4 hanks or 14400 yards

The above applies to linen and handspun woollen yarn in the early 19th century. Earlier the measure was considerably shorter and varied with the kind of yarn spun.

> 1748 *Aberdeen Journal* (6 Sept.): '54 Hesps of Thread were stole from the Bleaching at Marnoch Kirk, they consisted some of 3, some 6, some 7, and some of 8 Cuts in the Hesp.'

A

a[1], †**o** /a, ə/ *indef art* a, an *la14-*. [OE *ān* one; compare AN[1]]
a[2] /e, ə/ *prep frequently suffixed to the preceding word to:* ◊*I'm gaunna dance wi' him la19-*. [reduced form of TAE[3,4]]
a[3] /a, ə/ *prep* **1** on, at: ◊*a west* ◊*a horseback la15-*. **2** engaged in ◊*her dress is a-making la16-*. [OE *a*; reduced from *on*]
a *see* AE, HAE[1,2], O[2]
A *see* AH
a' *see* AW[1.1], AW[1.2], AW[1.3]
aa *see* AVE[3], AW[1.1], AW[1.2], AW[1.3]
aaber[1.1], **aber** /'abər, 'abər/ *v* to sharpen; to quicken or brighten *20- Sh*. [see the adj]
aaber[1.2], **aber**, †**auber** /'abər, 'abər/ *adj* eager, keen, sharp *la19- Sh*. **aaberness** eagerness *20- Sh*. [OE *apr* sharp, hard, bad]
aaber[2] /'abər/ *v* to half-thresh a sheaf of corn (for feeding horses) *la19- Ork*. **aaber-tait** a small quantity of feed given to horses at night *20- Ork*. [perhaps OE *berian* to beat, crush and hull (barley), ON *berja* to beat, thresh]
aabody *see* AWBODY
aal, aald *see* AULD[1,2]
aaler *see* AULDER
aalest *see* AULDEST
aal-farrant *see* AULD-FARRANT
aamal /'aməl/ *n* an equal *20- Ork*. [altered form of YAMAL]
aamos *see* AMOS[1.1], AMOS[1.2]
aan *see* AWE, YAWIN
aandoo, andoo, *Ork* **ando,** *N* **anno,** *N* **anoo** /'andu; *Ork* 'ando; *N* 'anu; *N* 'anu/ *v* to row a boat to maintain position; to move slowly *la19- Sh Ork N*. **annosman** the rower in a boat *20- N*. [ON *andóf*]
aapron *see* APRIN
aar *see* ARR
aaricht *see* AWRIGHT[1.1], AWRIGHT[1.2]
aat *see* AWTE
aathegither *see* AWTHEGITHER
aathing *see* AWTHING
ab /ab/ *n* an impediment, an objection *la19- Ork*. [unknown]
ab *see* ALB
aback, †**abak** /ə'bak/ *adv* **1** back, backwards; back again *15-*. **2** behind, in the rear, at a distance; in the past *16-*. **3** away; aloof *la19-*. †**abakwrittin** written on the back of a document *la16-e17*. **aback o** behind, to the rear of *19-*. [OE *onbæc*]
†**abade, abaid, abayd** *n* the action of waiting or delaying; a stay; a delay *la14-16*. [from the verb ABIDE, with vowel influenced by the pt, ptp]
abade *see* ABIDE
abaid *see* ABADE
†**abais** *v* **1** to discourage or dismay *la14-e17*. **2** to be taken aback, be surprised *16*. **abaisit** discouraged, dismayed; taken aback *la14-e17*. **abaysitnes** alarm; discouragement *la14-e16*. [ME *abaishen, abaissen*]
abaise *see* ABUISE[1,2]
abak *see* ABACK
abandon[1.1], †**abandoun** /ə'bandən/ *n* the action of relinquishing *20-*. †**abandonly** impetuously, recklessly *la14-15*. †**at abandoun** without restraint; furiously *la14-e15*. †**in abandoune** = *at abandoun la14*. [AN *abandun*]

abandon[1.2], †**abandoun** /ə'bandən/ *v* **1** to give up, relinquish; to desert *la16-*. **2** to subdue, conquer *la14-16*. **3** to risk oneself; to rush headlong; to venture *la14-15*. [AN *abanduner*]
abane *see* ABUNE[1.1]
abatement, †**abaytment** /ə'betmənt/ *n* **1** a reduction, a decrease; the amount by which something is reduced *la17-*. **2** relaxation, recreation, amusement *16*. [EModE *abatement*]
abay *see* ABYE
abayd *see* ABADE
abaysitnes *see* ABAIS
abaytment *see* ABATEMENT
abbacee *see* EBBASAY
abbacy, †**abbasy** /'abəsi/ *n* **1** the office or jurisdiction of an abbot or abbess *15-*. **2** an abbey *la15-*. [AN *abbacie*]
abbates *see* ABBOTESSE
abbay *see* ABBEY
abbeit *see* HABIT
abbey, †**abbay** /'abe/ *n* (the building or buildings housing) a community of monks or nuns *la14-*. †**abbay croun** a coin minted at Holyrood *la16*. **Abbey Laird** *humorous* a debtor taking sanctuary in the precincts of Holyrood Abbey *18-e19, la19- historical*; compare *laird in the Abbey* (LAIRD[1.1]). **the Abbey** the precincts of Holyrood Abbey in Edinburgh, which was used as a sanctuary for insolvent debtors until the late 19th century *la17-19, 20- historical*. [ME *abbeie*]
abble /'abəl/ *adj* weakly *la19- Ork*. [compare AB]
abbot /'abət/ *n* the head of an abbey *la12-*. **Abbot of Na Rent** = *Abbot of Unreason la15-16, 20- historical*. **Abbot of Unreason** a figure of misrule who acted as the leader of the revels in a burgh festival which burlesqued religious institutions (a practice which was suppressed at the Reformation) *la15-16, 19- historical*. **Abbot of Unrest** = *Abbot of Unreason la15, 20- historical*. [OE *abbot*]
†**abbotesse, abbates** *n* the female head of an abbey, an abbess *la16*. [OE *abbodesse*]
abbreviate[1.1], †**abbreviat** /ə'briviət/ *n* **1** an abstract, an abridgement, a summary *17-*. **2** *law* a brief notice registering a decree of adjudication or, in bankruptcy, of the petition of sequestration *18-*. †**abbreviature** abridgement *la16*. [Lat *abbreviātum*]
abbreviate[1.2], †**abbreviat** /ə'briviət/ *v* to shorten; to abridge; to summarize *16-*. †**abbreviatour** an abridger *e16*. [Lat *abbreviāre*]
abbryge *see* ABREGE
A B C *see* EBBASAY
abeen *see* ABUNE[1.1], ABUNE[1.2]
abeese *see* ABUISE[1.2]
abeet *see* ABUIT
abefore *see* OF-BEFORE
abeich, abeigh, †**abiegh** /ə'bix, ə'bex/ *adv* aloof, aside, away, at a distance *la16-*. [unknown]
aber *see* AABER[1.1], AABER[1.2]
Aberdeen, Aiberdeen, Eberdeen, †**Abirdene,** †**Aberdon,** †**Aberdein** /abər'din, ebər'din, ɛbər'din/ *n* a city in North-East Scotland *12-*. **Aberdeen Angus,** †**Aberdeen and Angus** a breed of black, hornless, beef cattle, originally from Aberdeenshire and Angus *la18-*. **Aberdeen sweetie** a sharp tap on the head with a flick

of the thumb *la19, 20- NE*. [a Celtic place-name meaning 'mouth of the River Don']

Aberdeen-awa[1.1], **Aiberdeen-awa** /abərdin ə'wa, ebərdin ə'wa/ *n* Aberdeen or its neighbourhood or dialect *19, 20- NE*. [ABERDEEN + AWA[1.1]]

†**Aberdeen-awa**[1.2] *adj* pertaining to Aberdeen or its neighbourhood or dialect *e19*. [see the noun]

Aberdein, Aberdon *see* ABERDEEN

Aberdonian[1.1], **Aiberdonian** /abər'donıən, abər'donjən, ebər'donıən, ebər'donjən/ *n* a native or citizen of Aberdeen *la17-*. [see the adj]

Aberdonian[1.2], **Aiberdonian** /abər'donıən, abər'donjən, ebər'donıən, ebər'donjən/ *adj* of or pertaining to the city of Aberdeen or its inhabitants *17-*. [Lat *Aberdōnia* Aberdeen]

†**abetwix, abetuix** *prep* between *16*. [A[3] + BETWIXT]

abid *see* ABIDE

abidden *see* ABIDE

abide, †**abyde,** †**abid,** †**abyd** /ə'bʌɪd/ *v pt* †**abade,** *ptp* †**abidden 1** to stay, remain *la14-*. **2** to endure, put up with *la15-*. **3** to stay behind; to wait for; to expect *la14-19*. **4** to remain faithful to; to adhere to *la15-18*. **5** to continue *la15-e18*. †**abide at** to stand by, adhere to *15-e17*. †**abide fra** to stay away from (a person or place) *la16-e17*. [OE *ābīdan*]

abiegh *see* ABEICH

abies /ə'biz/ *prep* in comparison with; in addition to; except *19-*. [unknown]

abiet *see* AW[1.2]

abil *see* ABLE[1.2]

abill *see* ABLE[1.1], ABLE[1.2]

†**abilʒeit, abulʒeit, habilyiet** *adj* arrayed, dressed; equipped *la15-e17*. [Fr *habiller*, compare Picard *habilliet*]

abilʒement *see* HABILIMENT

abin *see* ABUNE[1.2]

abine *see* ABUNE[1.1]

Abirdene *see* ABERDEEN

abit[1], **abut,** *Bor* **ebbit** /'abɪt, 'abʌt; *Bor* 'ɛbɪt/ *interj* a term expressing disagreement *la19-*. [Scots *ah* or AYE[1] + BUT[1.5]]

abit[2] *see* HABIT

ablach, ablich, aiblich, †**ablack** /'abləx, 'eblək/ *n* **1** a contemptible person; one lacking will or intellect *la18- N NE T H&I*. **2** a small or unimportant person; a dwarf *la18- NE*. **3** a mangled carcass *18-19*. [Gael, IrGael *ablach* carrion; a useless person or thing]

able[1.1], *Sh Ork* **eeble,** *Bor* **yable,** *Bor* **yibble,** †**abill,** †**ebill** /'ebəl; *Sh Ork* 'ibəl; *Bor* 'jebəl; *Bor* 'jıbəl/ *adj* **1** having ability or power, capable *la14-*. **2** suitable, fitting, sound, substantial *la14-*. **3** ready, prepared; on the point of *16-*. **4** physically fit, strong *20-*. **5** possible *la16-e17*. **6** liable, likely *16-e17*. **able for** having an appetite for *20-*. [ME *able*]

able[1.2], **abil,** †**abill** /'ebəl/ *adv* perhaps, possibly *la15-19, 20- Bor*. [see the adj]

ableeze[1.1] /ə'bliz/ *adj* on fire, ablaze; excited, emotionally charged *19-*. [A[3] + BLEEZE[1.1]]

ableeze[1.2] /ə'bliz/ *adv* on fire, ablaze *19-*. [see the adj]

ablens *see* AIBLINS

ables, *Bor* **yibbles,** †**aibles,** †**yeables** /'ebəlz; *Bor* 'jıbəlz/ *adv* maybe, perhaps, possibly *la18-19, 20- Bor*. [ABLE[1.1], with adv-forming suffix]

ablich *see* ABLACH

ablins *see* AIBLINS

ablow[1.1], **ablo** /ə'blo/ *adv* below, beneath, lower down *la19-*. [A[3] + BELOW[1.2], by analogy with *above*]

ablow[1.2], **ablo** /ə'blo/ *prep* under, below, further down from *la19-*. [see the adv]

aboard *see* ABOORD

abody *see* AWBODY

aboif *see* ABOVE[1.1]

aboil /ə'bɔɪl/ *adv* at or to boiling point *la18-*. [A[3] + *boil* (BILE[1.1])]

abön *see* ABUNE[1.2]

abone, aboon *see* ABUNE[1.1], ABUNE[1.2]

aboord, aboard, †**aburde** /ə'burd, ə'bord/ *adv* on board *16-*. [A[3] + BUIRD and ME *abord*, EModE *aborde*]

aboot[1.1], **about,** *N* **eboot,** †**abowt** /ə'but, ə'bʌut; *N* i'but/ *adv* **1** around, round or near *la14-*. **2** on all sides, in every direction *la14-*. **3** in turn *la15-*. **4** approximately *la19-*. **5** able to move about, going about (after an illness): ◊*Tam's aboot again 20-*. **6** with circular motion *15-16*. †**about spech** a circumlocution *e16*. †**be about wi** be even with, avenged on *18-19*. [OE *abūtan*]

aboot[1.2], **about,** *N* **eboot,** †**abowt** /ə'but, ə'bʌut; *N* i'but/ *prep* **1** around, on every side of; near *14-*. **2** concerning, regarding *15-*. **3** during *20- Sh*. **aboot it** about the same: ◊*hoo are ye? Muckle aboot it la19-*. [see the adv]

aboot-gaain /ə'butgaɪn/ *adj* whirling; veering; wandering *20- Sh Ork*. [ABOOT[1.1] + presp of GAE]

aboot-kast /ə'butkast/ *n* **1** a sudden veering of the wind *20- Ork*. **2** the equinox *20- Sh*. [ABOOT[1.1] + CAST[1.1]]

aboucht *see* ABYE

aboun *see* ABUNE[1.1], ABUNE[1.2]

about *see* ABOOT[1.1], ABOOT[1.2]

above[1.1], †**abufe,** †**abuf,** †**aboif** /ə'bʌv/ *adv* aloft, on or in a higher level or place; higher up *la14-*. **above written** earlier (in a text) *15-*. [OE *ābufan*]

above[1.2], †**abufe,** †**abuif,** †**abowe** /ə'bʌv/ *prep* **1** over, higher up than; superior to *la14-*. **2** beyond, more than, in addition to *la14-*. [see the adv]

†**abovin**[1.1], **abufin** *adv* above *la14-15*. **abovin writtin** earlier (in a text) *la14-16*. [OE *ābufan*]

†**abovin**[1.2] *prep* above, over *la14-15*. [see the adv]

abowe *see* ABOVE[1.2]

abowt *see* ABOOT[1.1], ABOOT[1.2]

†**abraid** *v* to start, move suddenly *la15-16*. [OE *ābregdan*]

abraird, abreard, †**abreird** /ə'brerd, ə'brird/ *adv of grain* sprouted *la15-19, 20- Uls*. [A[3] + BRAIRD[1.1]]

abree *see* AVREE

abreed, abreid, †**abrede** /ə'brid/ *adv* **1** wide, apart, open *16-*. **2** to or in pieces *20- WC SW*. **3** on or in breadth; widely, far and wide; abroad *16-19, 20- Bor*. [A[3] + BREED[1]]

†**abrege, abbryge** *v* to abridge *15-e17*. [ME *abbreggen*]

abreid *see* ABREED

abreird *see* ABRAIRD

abreist /ə'brist, ə'brɛst/ *adv* on the same level, side by side; abreast *la18-*. [A[3] + BREIST[1.1]]

†**abrico** *n* an apricot *la16-e17*. [MFr *abricot*]

absence, †**absens** /'absəns/ *n* the state of being absent *la14-*. [ME *absence*]

†**absent** *n pl* also **absence absens** an absentee (from a court of justice) *15-e18*. [ME *absent*]

absolvitor[1.1], †**absolvitour** /ab'zɔlvıtər/ *n law* a decision by a court in favour of the defender *16-*. [Lat *absolvitor* let him (her) be absolved]

†**absolvitor**[1.2], **absolvitour** *adj law* in favour of the defender *e17*. [see the noun]

†**absolʒe** *v* to absolve *la15-e16*. [conflation of ASSOILZIE with ME *absolve*]

absteen, abstain, †**abstene,** †**obstene** /əb'stin, əb'sten/ *v* to refrain (from); to resist *la15*. [ME *absteinen*]

abstract, †**abstrak** /əb'strakt/ *v* to take away, withdraw; to steal, purloin *la15-*. [Lat *abstract-*, ptp stem of *abstrahere* to drag away]

abthane, †**abthan** /'abθen/ *n* **1** the lands of an abbey, an abbacy *e14, la19- historical*. **2** a senior or chief thane

16- historical. [Gael *abth-aine*; sense 2 from mistaken division as *ab-thaine*]

abuf *see* ABOVE[1.1]

abufe *see* ABOVE[1.1], ABOVE[1.2]

abufin *see* ABOVIN[1.1]

abuif *see* ABOVE[1.2]

abuilyiement *see* HABILIMENT

abuin *see* ABUNE[1.1], ABUNE[1.2]

abuise[1.1], **abuse** /əˈbjis, əˈbjus/ *n* improper use or treatment; offensive language or behaviour *la16-*. [ME *abus*, Lat *abūsus*]

abuise[1.2], **abuse**, *NE* **abeese**, *SW Bor* **abaise** /əˈbjiz, əˈbjuz; *NE* əˈbiz; *SW Bor* əˈbez/ *v* **1** to misuse; to mistreat; to behave in an offensive manner; to take advantage of *15-*. **2** to disuse, discontinue the use of *la15-16*. [ME *abusen*, Lat *abūs-*, ptp stem of *abūtī*]

abuit, *NE* **abeet** /əˈbut; *NE* əˈbit/ *adv* into the bargain *19-*. [A[3] + BUIT[2.1]]

abulʒeit *see* ABILʒEIT

abune[1.1], **aboon**, **abuin**, *Ork N NE* **abeen**, *NE* **abane**, *EC* **abine**, †**abone**, †**aboun** /əˈbun; *Ork N NE* əˈbin; *NE* əˈben; *EC* əˈbʌɪn/ *adv* **1** above, higher, over *la14-*. **2** in good cheer, in or into better condition *la18-*. **3** *mining* on the surface, above ground *20- EC.* †**abone writtin**, **aboun writtin** above-written *la15-17.* **get abune** to recover from an illness, get over a disappointment *19, 20- NE T.* [by v-deletion from ABOVIN[1.1]]

abune[1.2], **aboon**, **abuin**, **abin**, *Sh* **abön**, *Ork N NE* **abeen**, †**abone**, †**aboun** /əˈbun, əˈbɪn; *Sh* əˈbøn; *Ork N NE* əˈbin/ *prep* above, over, higher than; louder than; more than *la14-.* **abune the breath** above the nostrils or the windpipe *19, 20- Ork N NE T.* [see the adv]

aburde *see* ABOORD

abuse *see* ABUISE[1.1], ABUISE[1.2]

†**abusioun**, **abusion** *n* **1** misuse; misconduct *la15-16.* **2** deceit *16.* [ME *abusioun*, Lat *abūsio* use of a wrong synonym, loose use of a term]

abut *see* ABIT

aby *see* ABYE

abyd, **abyde** *see* ABIDE

†**abye**, **aby**, **abay** *v ptp* **aboucht** to pay, suffer (for); to endure *15-19.* [OE *ābicgan* to redeem]

abyte *see* HABIT

academy, †**academie**, †**achademya** /əˈkadəme/ *n* **1** a place of learning *16-.* **2** a public or private secondary school, originally set up in a burgh to replace or improve a grammar school or provide a more modern curriculum *la18-.* [Lat *acadēmia*]

acamy *see* AKAMY[1.2]

acause /əˈkɔz/ *conj* because *la19-.* [CAUSE[1.1], with *a-* prefix by analogy with AFORE[1.3], AHINT[1.2]]

acavite *see* AQUAVITAE

accep, **accept**, †**except**, †**exsep** /əkˈsɛp, əkˈsɛpt/ *v ptp* also †**accept** †**except**, †**exceppit** to receive or take willingly; to agree (to) *la15-.* [ME *accepten*, Lat *acceptāre*]

accep *see* EXCEP[1.1]

accept *see* ACCEP, EXCEP[1.1]

acceptilation /ˌaksɛptəˈleʃən/ *n law* the extinction of a debt by an arrangement other than by full payment *la17-.* [Lat *acceptilātio* an accounting of a thing as received]

acces *see* AIXIES, EXCESS

accession /əkˈsɛʃən/ *n* **1** an addition, an increase *17-.* **2** *law* complicity, concurrence or assent in an action *17-.* **3** the attainment of a throne *18-.* [EModE *accession*, Fr *accession*, Lat *accessio*]

accessory, †**accessor**, †**accessour** /əkˈsɛsəre/ *n* **1** something additional; an ornament or accompaniment *la15-.* **2** *law* an accomplice to a criminal; an assistant or adjunct *la15-.* [AN *accessorie*, AN, MFr *accessoire*]

accident /ˈaksɪdənt/ *n* **1** a fortuitous occurrence, chance *la15-.* **2** a mishap, a disaster, an unavoidable casualty *la16-.* **3** a casual sum *la15-e17.* **4** an inessential attribute *la15-16.* [ME *accident*, Lat *accidēns*]

Accies /ˈakiz/ *npl* **1** a nickname for Hamilton Academicals Football Club *la19-.* **2** a nickname for pupils or former pupils of an academy, especially when organized as a team *20-.* [abbreviated from *academicals*]

†**acclame**[1.1] *n* a claim *16-17.* [see the verb]

†**acclame**[1.2] *v* to claim or lay claim to *16-e18.* [Lat *acclamāre* to shout]

accomie *see* ALCOMY

accompt *see* ACCOONT[1.1], ACCOONT[1.2]

accomptant *see* ACCOONTANT

accoont[1.1], **account**, †**accompt** /əˈkunt, əˈkʌunt/ *n* **1** a report, a (financial) statement, an explanation; a description, a narrative *15-.* **2** worth, value, importance; consideration, basis; behalf *la16-.* [ME *account*]

accoont[1.2], **account**, †**accompt** /əˈkunt, əˈkʌunt/ *v* to explain, offer a reckoning (for); to give consideration to *16-.* [ME *accounten*]

accoontant, **accountant**, †**accomptant** /əˈkuntənt, əˈkʌuntənt/ *n* **1** a person who maintains or prepares financial accounts *18-.* **2** the chief clerk in a bank branch, the deputy of the manager or assistant manager *20-.* **Accountant of Court** *law* an officer of court who supervises the conduct of judicial factors *19-.* [AN *acomptant*]

account *see* ACCOONT[1.1], ACCOONT[1.2]

accountant *see* ACCOONTANT

accoutre /əˈkutər/ *v* to dress, array or equip *la16-.* [MFr *accoustrer*]

accresce, †**accress**, †**accres** /əˈkrɛs/ *v* **1** to accrue or fall to *la16-.* **2** to increase *16-18.* **3** to be added or united *la16-e17.* [Lat *accrescere*]

accur *see* OCCUR

accusable, †**accusabil** /əˈkjuzəbəl/ *adj* liable to be accused *la15-.* [Lat *accūsābilis* reprehensible]

†**accusator**, **accusatour** *n* an accuser *15-19.* [Lat *accūsātor*]

accustom /əˈkʌstəm/ *v* to get or be used to, in the habit of *la15-.* †**accustomat**, †**accustomit** customary, usual *16-e17.* [ME *accustomen*]

ace, *Ork* **eace**, *NE T* **ess**, *Uls* **eyiss**, *Bor* **yiss**, †**ais** /es; *Ork* is; *NE T* ɛs; *Uls* ˈejɪs; *Bor* jɪs/ *n* **1** the smallest possible amount *16-.* **2** a playing card bearing a single symbol *la18-.* **3** something or someone superlative, the best *la18-.* **4** the side of a dice marked with a single spot *16.* [EModE *ace*, ME *as*]

ach, †**auch** /ax, əx/ *interj* an expression of impatience, disappointment, contempt or remonstrance *16-.* [probably onomatopoeic of a sigh]

-ach *see* -OCK

achademya *see* ACADEMY

achan *see* AUCHAN

achar *see* AJAR

acherspyre[1.1], *N* **aikerspir** /ˈaxərspaer; *N* ˈɛkərspir/ *n* **1** the sprouting of grain during malting; a sprout of such grain *19, 20- T.* **2** a shoot; the first growth (of a plant) *20- N.* [see the verb]

acherspyre[1.2], *N* **aikerspir**, *NE* **ackiespyre**, †**akyrspire** /ˈaxərspaer; *N* ˈɛkərspir; *NE* ˈakispaer/ *v of grain* to sprout during malting *15-19, 20- N NE T.* [perhaps OE *eher* an ear of corn + OE *spryttan* to sprout]

†**achesone**, **aitchesoun** *n* a silver-plated copper coin of low value *17*. [named after Thomas Achesoun, master of the mint 1581-1611]

achet *see* ESCHEAT[1.1], ESCHEAT[1.2]

acht *see* AUCHT[1], AUCHT[2], ECHT[1.1], ECHT[1.2], AWE

achteen *see* ECHTEEN

ack[1.1], **act**, †**ak** /ak, akt/ *n* **1** a formal agreement *la14*-. **2** (a written record of) a piece of legislation, an ordinance or statute *15*-. **3** an action, a deed; something done *la15*-. **act of adjournal 1** *pl* the records and regulations of the High Court of Justiciary *18*-. **2** a court decision requiring one person to give satisfaction to another within a specified time *la15-17*. †**act of litiscontestation** the judicial act admitting a case to proof *17*. **Act of Union** the Acts of the Scottish and English Parliaments uniting Scotland and England *18*-; compare TREATY OF UNION. [ME *act*, Lat *actus* motion, Lat *actum* a deed, a written record of events]

ack[1.2], **act**, †**ak** /ak, akt/ *v* **1** to do (an action), behave or conduct oneself *la16*-. **2** to enact or decree *15-e18*. **3** to enter (an agreement or obligation) in a record-book *la15-16*. **4** to pledge (oneself) to an undertaking or obligation *la16-17*. †**be actit** to be recorded as pledged to an undertaking or obligation *la15-17*. [Lat *act*-, ptp stem of *agere*]

-ack *see* -OCK.

ackadür *see* AKKADÖR

ackavity *see* AQUAVITAE

acker *see* ACRE[1.1], ACTOR

ackiespyre *see* ACHERSPYRE[1.2]

ackir *see* ACTOR

acknawledge, †**acknawlege** /əkˈnɔlədʒ/ *v* to acknowledge *la16*-. [ME *acknowleche*]

ackre *see* ACRE[1.2]

ackwa *see* AQUA

ackwal, **actual** /ˈakwəl, ˈaktuəl, ˈakʃəl/ *adj* real *la15*-. **2** sexual *la15-16*. **ackwally**, **actwally**, **actually** in reality, in fact *la15*-. [EModE *actual*]

ackwart[1.1], **awkward**, †**acquart**, †**awkwart** /ˈakwərt, ˈɔkwərd/ *adj* **1** difficult, cumbersome, inconvenient *la15*-. **2** *of people* perverse, ill-natured, hostile; obstinate *la15*-. **3** clumsy *18*-. **4** backhanded *la15-16*. [ME *aukward* backhanded; upside-down, awry]

ackwart[1.2], **awkward** /ˈakwərt, ˈɔkwərd/ *adv* **1** in a difficult position, uncomfortably *19*-. **2** with a backward stroke *la15*. [see the adj]

acquant[1.1], **acquent**, **acquaint** /əˈkwant, əˈkwɛnt, əˈkwent/ *v* **1** to make oneself known, become familiar (with) *15*-. **2** to make acquainted with a fact, inform *15*-. **acquantance**, **acquaintance**, †**acquyntance 1** the state of knowing or being familiar with; friendship *la14*-. **2** a person one knows, a friend *la14*-. [ME *aqueinten*]

acquant[1.2], **acquent**, **acquaint**, †**acquynt** /əˈkwant, əˈkwɛnt, əˈkwent/ *adj* acquainted, known, familiar (with) *la14*-. [ME *aquointe*, MFr *accointe*]

acquart *see* ACKWART[1.1]

acqueesh *see* ATWEESH

acquent *see* ACQUANT[1.1], ACQUANT[1.2]

acquynt *see* ACQUANT[1.2]

acquyntance *see* ACQUANT[1.1]

acre[1.1], **acker**, †**aiker**, †**akir**, †**aker** /ˈekər, ˈakər/ *n* **1** a land measure, originally approx 6000 square yards (0.5 hectares); *in place-names* fields, arable land *la12*-. **2** a piece of ground (of at least an acre) rented by a villager from a neighbouring proprietor *19*-. [OE *æcer* a field, a plot of land]

acre[1.2], **ackre** /ˈekər, ˈakər/ *v* to harvest crops (at a stated rate per acre) *la19*- NE T. [see the noun]

acroass[1.1], **across** /əˈkros, əˈkrɔs/ *adv* from one side to another, on the other side; crosswise *19*-. [ME *acros*]

acroass[1.2], **across** /əˈkros, əˈkrɔs/ *prep* from one side to the other of, on or at the other side of; beyond *18*-. [see the adv]

act *see* ACK[1.1], ACK[1.2]

actentik *see* AUTENTIK

action, †**actioun** /ˈakʃən/ *n* **1** *law* a legal process; a claim at law *15*-. **2** an act or deed; the process or state of being active *la15*-. **3** a matter concerning a person or their interests; a cause *15-e17*. **4** the celebration of the sacrament of the Lord's Supper or the Mass *la16-17*. **5** *law* a charge against a person; a civil or criminal offence *15-e16*. **action sermon** *Presbyterian Church* the sermon preceding the celebration of the sacrament of the Lord's Supper *18-19, 20- historical*. **action of declarator** *law* an action brought by an interested party to have some legal right or status declared, but without claim on any person called as defender to do anything *18*-. **action of division** *law* an action by which common property is divided *la18*-. **action of ejection** *law* an action either to eject a person or to recover property lost as in an ejection *17*-. **action of spuilzie** *law* a legal process or claim in a case of alleged spoliation *18*-. [ME *accioun*]

†**actitate** *adj* obligated (in an official document) *16*. [Lat *actitāt*-, ptp stem of *actitāre* to act]

actor, *NE* **ackir**, †**acker**, †**actour** /ˈaktər; *NE* ˈakər/ *n* **1** a person who performs or takes part in an action; a theatrical performer *la16*-. **2** *law* an agent; one who acts on behalf of another *la15-17*. **3** an author, originator *16*. **4** *law* the pursuer in a court case *15-e17*. [ME *actour*, Lat *actor*]

actornay, **actorney** *see* ATTORNEY

actoun *see* HOGTOUN

actour *see* ACTOR

actual *see* ACKWAL

adae[1.1], **ado**, *NE* **adee**, *Bor* **adow** /əˈde, əˈdu; *NE* əˈdi; *Bor* əˈdʌu/ *n* **1** fuss, commotion; trouble *la15*-. **2** business, occupation; *pl* concerns, affairs *la16-e19*. **hae yer ain adaes**, **hae yer ain ados** to have one's own difficulties or trouble *19*-. [A[3] + DAE[1.1]]

adae[1.2], **ado**, *NE* **adee**, *Bor* **adow** /əˈde, əˈdu; *NE* əˈdi; *Bor* əˈdʌu/ *adv* **1** to do, be done: ◊*quhat is the best ado?; I hae naething ado; I widna hae naething adee wi ye la14*-. **2** going on, being done: ◊*what's adee? 17*-. **3** the matter with: ◊*fat's adee wi ye? la19*-. [see the noun]

Adam-an-Eves /adəm ən ˈivz/ *npl* the tubers of the orchis *20*-. [from the Old Testament characters after a supposed resemblance to two inseparable human figures]

Adam's wine /adəmz ˈwʌɪn/ *n humorous* water *18*-. [from the Old Testament character + WINE]

add /ad/ *v* **1** to combine; to give in addition; to calculate the total (of) *la15*-. **2** *Presbyterian Church* to make an addition to the exposition or discussion of a passage of Scripture *la16-19*. †**adder** *Presbyterian Church* a person who makes the addition to the scriptural discussion *17*. [Lat *addere*]

†**addebted**, **addettit**, **adettyt** *adj* **1** in debt to, owing *16-e19*. **2** owed, due *la16-e19*. **3** obliged, bound to *la15-16*. [ME *andetted*]

adder, **adder bell** *see* ETHER

addettit *see* ADDEBTED

addiscence *see* AUDIENCE

addition, †**additioun** /əˈdɪʃən/ *n* **1** something (or someone) added; an increase; the action or fact of adding *16*-. **2** *Presbyterian Church* a discourse made after the exposition or discussion of a passage of Scripture *la16-19, 20- historical*. [ME *addicioun*, Lat *additio*]

addle, **aidle**, †**adill** /ˈadəl, ˈedəl/ *n* foul, putrid liquid, the run-off from dung; slime, ooze *16-19, 20- C SW Bor*. [OE *adela*]

address[1.1], †**addres** /əˈdrɛs/ *n* **1** a (formal) speech; originally an application or appeal *16-*. **2** a state of preparedness or resourcefulness *la18-*. **3** the name or location of a place where a person lives or an organization is based; a postal address *la18-*. **4** the stance of a golfer addressing the ball *la19-*. [see the verb]

address[1.2], †**addres** /əˈdrɛs/ *v* **1** to direct one's remarks to, speak formally to, apply in speech to (a person) *18-*. **2** to apply in writing to; to write a postal address (on a letter or parcel) *la18-*. **3** *golf* to position oneself relative to the ball (in order to strike it) *la18-*. **4** to direct one's attention to, deal with a matter *20-*. **5** to prepare oneself, make ready; to put in order, arrange *la14-e19*. **6** to proceed, set about; to remove oneself to or bring to (a place) *la15-e17*. **7** to dress oneself *15-e17*. [ME *adressen*]

adduce /əˈdʒus/ *v* **1** to cite as pertinent, quote as evidence *la16-*. **2** *law* to produce (an item of) evidence in proof; to bring forward a person as a witness *la17-*. [Lat *addūcere*]

adee *see* ADAE[1.1], ADAE[1.2]

adest *see* ATHIST

adettyt *see* ADDEBTED

†**adew**[1.1] *adv* away, gone, departed *la15-e16*. [see the interj]

†**adew**[1.2] *interj* farewell *la15-17*. [ME *adieu*]

adge *see* AGE

adheir *see* ADHERE

†**adherde** *v* to adhere to *e16*. [altered form of ANHERD, with influence from ADHERE]

adhere, †**adheir** /ədˈhir/ *v* **1** to continue to support, remain faithful to; to be a follower of (a person or idea) *16-*. **2** *law* to cohabit and be faithful (to the other spouse) *16-*. **3** *law* to confirm or sustain the judgement of a lower court *17-*. **4** *of a thing* to cling or stick to; to become attached *la18-*. [EModE *adhere*, Lat *adhaerere*]

adherence /ədˈhirəns/ *n* **1** allegiance, devotion; compliance *la16-*. **2** *law* the fulfilment of the legal obligation of residing with one's spouse *la16-*. [EModE *adherence*, Lat *adhaerent-*, prp stem of *adhaerere* to cling]

adherent /ədˈhirənt/ *n pl* also †**adherence 1** a follower, supporter; a devotee *la16-*. **2** *Presbyterian Church* a person who attends the services but is not in full communion *la19-*. [ME *adherent*]

adhibit /ədˈhɪbɪt/ *v* **1** to administer or apply a remedy; to make use of, allow *la16-*. **2** to add, append; to attach or affix; to put (one's signature or seal) to a document *la17-*. [Lat *adhibit-*, ptp stem of *adhibēre* to add to, employ]

adience *see* AUDIENCE

adill *see* ADDLE

adione *see* ADJOIN

adist *see* ATHIST

†**adiutorie, adiutory** *n* help; a helper *16*. [Lat *adjūtōrium*]

adjoin, †**adjune**, †**adione** /əˈdʒɔɪn/ *v* **1** to join or attach, add to *la15-*. **2** to be adjacent to *18-*. **3** to unite with other people *16*. [ME *ajoinen*]

adjourn /əˈdʒʌrn/ *v* **1** to put off or defer a matter; to postpone or suspend the sitting of parliament or court proceedings *la16-*. **2** to go to another place for rest or relaxation *19-*. **3** to summon for trial *la16*. [ME *ajournen*]

†**adjournal** *n law* the record of the proceedings of a justice aire *la15-16*. [ADJOURN, with *-al* suffix]

†**adjournay** *v* **1** to summon for trial *15-e17*. **2** to adjourn, put off *la15-17*. [Lat *adjurāre* to swear on oath]

adjudge, †**adjuge** /əˈdʒʌdʒ/ *v* **1** *law* to sentence judicially (to a certain fine); to condemn *la15-*. **2** *law* to make a judicial decision *16-*. **3** *law* to assign property by adjudication *la17-*. [ME *ajugen, ajuggen*]

adjudication, †**adjudicatioun** /ədʒudəˈkeʃən/ *n* **1** *law* the seizure of land or other heritable estate to pay a debt *17-*. **2** a judicial or official ruling; a formal judgement (of a competition) *la18-*. [MFr *adjudication*, Lat *adjūdicatio*]

adjuge *see* ADJUDGE

adjune *see* ADJOIN

admeeration *see* ADMIRATION

admeir *see* ADMIRE

adminicle /ədˈmɪnəkəl/ *n* **1** *law* supporting or corroborative evidence *la16-*. **2** an aid, an accessory *20-*. [EModE *adminicle*, Lat *adminiculum*]

†**adminiculate** *v law* to support with evidence *la17-19*. [Lat *adminiculāt-*, ptp stem of *adminiculāre* to prop up]

administrate /ədˈmɪnəstret/ *v ptp* also **administrat 1** to manage, direct; to run, govern *la16-*. **2** to administer a sacrament or oath *la16-*. [Lat *administrāt-*, ptp stem of *administrāre*]

admiral, †**amerale**, †**ammyral**, †**almeral** /ˈadmərəl/ *n* the (chief) commander of a fleet of naval vessels *15-*. †**admiralite** admiralship *la15*. [ME *amiral*]

admirald *see* EMERANT[1.1]

admiration, †**admeeration**, †**admiratioun** /adməˈreʃən/ *n* **1** appreciation *16-*. **2** a marvel, a wonder; astonishment *16-*. [ME *admiracion*, Lat *admīrātio*]

admire, †**admeir** /ədˈmaer/ *v* **1** to feel or express admiration; to regard with esteem or approval *la16-*. **2** to express wonder, marvel at; to be amazed or surprised (by something) *la17-*. [EModE *admire*]

†**admoneis, admonis, amonest** *v* to admonish *la14-e17*. [ME *admonesten, admonishen*]

†**admove** *v* to appoint *16-e17*. [Lat *admovēre*]

ado *see* ADAE[1.1], ADAE[1.2]

adoir *see* ADORE

adoon[1.1], †**adoun**, †**adown** /əˈdun/ *adv* down, downwards; to a lower position or condition *la15-19, 20- literary*. [O² + DOON[1.3]]

adoon[1.2], †**adoun**, †**adown** /əˈdun/ *prep* down *17-19, 20- literary*. [see the adv]

adore, †**adoir** /əˈdor/ *v* **1** to worship; to venerate *la15-*. **2** to love deeply; to admire greatly *la16-*. [EModE *adoure*, Lat *adōrāre*]

adorn, †**odorne** /əˈdɔrn/ *v* **1** to embellish or decorate *la15-*. **2** to adore or worship *15-16*. [ME *adournen*, Lat *adornāre*]

adoun *see* ADOON[1.1], ADOON[1.2]

adow *see* ADAE[1.1], ADAE[1.2]

adown *see* ADOON[1.1], ADOON[1.2]

†**adred**[1.1] *adj* afraid *la15-16*. [ME *adredde*]

†**adred**[1.2] *conj* for fear that, lest *15-e16*. [see the adj]

adreigh, adreich /əˈdrix/ *adv* afar, at a distance *16-*. [reduced form of *on dreich* (DREICH[1.1])]

aduertence, aduertens *see* ADVERTENCE

†**adune** *v* to unite *la15-16*. [MFr *adunir*]

advancear *see* ADVANCER

Advanced Higher *n* a secondary education qualification normally taken after the Higher examination *21-*. [Scots *advanced* + HIGHER[1.1]]

†**advancer, advancear, avancear** *n* a person who pays money in advance; a money lender *la16-e19*. [Older Scots *advance*, with agent suffix]

adveece *see* ADVICE

adventur /ədˈvɛntər/ *n* an adventure *la15-*. Compare AVENTURE[1.1]. [ME *aventure, adventure*]

†**adversar, adversarie** *adj* opposing; hostile *15-e17*. [AN, MFr *adversaire*, Lat *adversārius*]

adversary, †**adversar**, †**adversour** /ədˈvɛrsəre/ *n* **1** an opponent; an enemy *la14-*. **2** Satan, the Devil *la19-*. [AN, MFr *adversaire*, Lat *adversārius*]

†**advert** *v* to give heed; to observe; to inform, warn *16-17*. [ME *adverten*]

adverteese, **advertise**, †**adverteis**, †**advertish**, †**avertese** /ˈadvərtiz, advərˈtiz, ˈadvərtaez/ *v pt* also †**advertist** to publicize, promote; to notify, warn *la15-*. **adverteesement**, **advertisement**, †**avertissiment** (public) notification; warning *la15-*. [ME *advertisen*]

†**advertence**, **aduertence**, **aduertens** *n* heed, attention *la15-e16*. [ME *advertence*]

advertise, **advertish**, **advertist** *see* ADVERTEESE

advice, †**adveece**, †**advise** /ədˈvʌɪs/ *n* **1** consideration, opinion; guidance or recommendations; legal counsel; formal notice (of a sale) *la14-*. **2** a piece of advice *la18-19*. †**be myne avyse** in my opinion *la15-16*. [ME *avis*]

advise, *Bor* **aveese**, †**avise**, †**avis** /ədˈvaez/; *Bor* əˈviz/ *v* **1** to give advice or guidance, recommend *la14-*. **2** to consider; to deliberate upon; to bethink oneself *la14-e19*. **3** *law* to reserve for further consideration; to review or reconsider *17-*; compare AVIZANDUM. **4** to inform, tell *17-*. **5** to plan, devise or arrange *15-e17*. **avised** informed, aware (of) *19, 20- WC Bor*. **advisedly**, †**advisitly**, †**auysitlie** after due consideration *15-*. **advisement**, †**avisement** deliberation, consideration; counsel, advice *la14-*. †**be avisit**, **be advisit** to take counsel; to come to a decision after reflection; to attain a clear understanding *la14-17*. [ME *avisen*]

advise *see* ADVICE

advocat *see* ADVOCATE[1.1], ADVOCATE[1.2]

advocate[1.1], †**advocat** /ˈadvəkət/ *n* **1** *law* a professional pleader in a court of justice, a barrister *la14-*. **2** a person who intercedes for or speaks on behalf of another; a person who publicly supports a cause *15-*. **3** *law* a solicitor *18- NE*. **advocate depute** a salaried advocate appointed by the LORD ADVOCATE to prosecute under his directions *19-*. [ME *advocat*, Lat *advocātus*]

advocate[1.2], †**advocat** /ˈadvəket/ *v ptp* also †**advocat 1** *in criminal cases* to appeal from a lower court to a higher one *la19-*. **2** *of a higher court* to summon a case before its jurisdiction from a lower court; originally also to designate a matter as appropriate to its jurisdiction *16-*. [Lat *advocāt-*, ptp stem of *advocāre*]

advocation, †**advocatioun** /advəˈkeʃən/ *n* **1** guardianship or patronage of a church or benefice *la15-*. **2** *law* the calling of an action before a superior court *la16-19*. **3** the position, office or calling of an advocate *16-e17*. [ME *advocacion*]

ae, *Sh Ork* **ee**, *C Bor* **yae**, †**yee**, †**a**, †**ya** /e; *Sh Ork* i; *C Bor* je/ *numeral* **1** the number one *la14-*. **2** a certain or particular (person or thing) *la14-*. **3** one of two or more; one (and not another) *15-*. **4** very, really *15-*. **5** the same *16-*. **6** only: ◇*ma ae wean 16-*. **7** about, approximately *la19, 20- H&I*. **aesome** single, solitary *la19, 20- NE*. **ae coo's meat** enough land to support one cow *20-*. **ae ee** a favourite, a pet *19, 20- NE*. **ae-fur-land** land which can only be ploughed in one direction (because of its steepness) *19-*. **ae-pointitgairss** various single-pointed grasses, mainly couch-grass *19, 20- T*. **ae wey**, **ae wy** one way *19, 20- Ork NE T*. **the ae 1** one of two or more, one (and not another) *15-*. **2** the one, the only *la15-*. **this ae** this (particular) one, this very *16-*. [OE *ān* one]

ae *see* AY

aefauld, **aefaul**, †**afald**, †**afauld**, †**efauld** /eˈfɔld, eˈfɔl/ *adj* **1** single *la14-*. **2** simple, sincere; honest, faithful; single-minded *la15-*. **aefauldlie**, †**afaldly** sincerely, honestly, faithfully *la15-*. [OE *ānfeald*]

aeger /ˈegər/ *n* an auger *20- Sh NE C*. [Du *egger*]

ae noo *see* EENOO

aeque *see* EQUE[1.1]

aer *see* AIR[2], AIR[3]

aerrow *see* ARRA

aert *see* YIRD[1.1]

aertfast *see* YIRDFEST[1.2]

aes[1.1], *Ork* **aize**, *Ork* **uiz** /es; *Ork* ez; *Ork* øz/ *n* a blazing fire *la19- Sh Ork*. [ON *eisa* glowing embers]

aes[1.2], **aize** /es, ez/ *v of a fire* to blaze fiercely *20- Ork*. **aizer**, **uizer**, **eezer** a blazing fire *20- Ork*. **aesin**, **esin** *of a fire* blazing *20- Sh*. [ON *eisa* to shower down, dash]

aeshin *see* EASIN

aesin *see* AES[1.2]

aess *see* ASS

aessi-pattle *see* ASSIEPATTLE

aest[1.1], **est** /øst, ɛst, est/ *n* envy *20- Ork*. [see the verb]

aest[1.2], *Ork* **est**, *N* **ayest**, *N* **eyst** /øst; *Ork* ɛst; *N* ˈeəst; *N* est/ *v* to envy, desire eagerly *20- Ork N*. [ON *æsta* to ask for, demand, request]

aester *see* EASTER[1.2]

aesy *see* EASY[1.1]

aet, **et** /et, ɛt/ *n* agitation, eagerness *20- Sh*. [ON *etja* to incite]

aet *see* EAT[1.2]

aetion *see* AISHAN

af *see* AFF[1.3], AFF[1.4]

afald, **afauld** *see* AEFAULD

afeard, **afeart**, †**aferd**, †**afferyt**, †**efferd** /əˈfird, əˈfirt/ *adj* afraid *15-*. Compare FEART. [OE *āforht*; compare AFFEIR[1.2]]

afeild *see* AFIEL

aferd *see* AFEARD

aff[1.1], **off** /af, ɔf, of/ *v* to go off, depart; to take off, remove *19-* [see the prep]

aff[1.2], **off** /af, ɔf, of/ *adj* **1** lying away from, situated aside from (the main part) *19-*. **2** farther off; *of a horse or vehicle* designating or relating to the right side *la19-*. [see the prep]

aff[1.3], **off**, †**af**, †**of** /af, ɔf, of/ *adv* **1** away, so as to be removed or separated *la14-*. **2** *with ellipsis of verb* going away, departing: ◇*Ah'm aff 19-*. **3** *of the age of livestock* less than one year past the age specified: ◇*he's three aff la19-*. **4** *of a person* in a poor condition, feeling unwell *20-*. **5** *of food* stale or sour *20-*. **aff o**, **aff of** off, from, away from *17-*. **off or on** decided one way or the other, settled *la16-*. †**be aff wi** to have done with, disengage oneself from *18-e19*. [see the prep]

aff[1.4], **off**, †**af**, †**of** /af, ɔf, of/ *prep* **1** down from, removed from *la14-*. **2** away from, out of (a place) *la15-*. **3** opening out from *18-*. **affin** off (of) *19-*. **off the first end** first of all *18, 20- Sh*. **off the foot** ailing *19, 20- N NE*. [OE *of*]

aff- /af/ *prefix* expressing removal, separation or change of direction *la15-*. [AFF[1.2], AFF[1.3]]

affa *see* AWFY[1.1], AWFY[1.2]

affair *see* EFFEIR[1.1]

affaird *see* AFFOORD

affcast, **offcast** /ˈafkast, ˈɔfkast/ *n* a reject; a cast-off, an unwanted person; discarded clothing *la16-19, 20- NE T*. [AFF- + ptp of CAST[1.2]]

affcastin, **offcasting** /ˈafkastɪn, ˈɔfkastɪŋ/ *n* something which is shed or cast off, unwanted clothing; the action of casting off, rejection *la16-19, 20- Sh*. [AFF- + verbal noun from CAST[1.2]]

affcome, **offcome** /ˈafkʌm, ˈɔfkʌm/ *n* **1** an outcome, a result; a verdict or judgement (of someone) *la17-*. **2** a saying, a witty remark *20-*. **3** an excuse, a pretext; a subterfuge, an evasion *la17-e19*. [AFF- + COME[1.2]]

affeck, **affect** *see* EFFECK

†affeir[1.1], **effeir** *n* fear *16*. [see the verb]
†affeir[1.2], **effer, effeir** *v* to fear; to be afraid *16*. [OE *āfǣran* to frighten]
affeir, affere *see* EFFEIR[1.1], EFFEIR[1.2]
affen, aften, oaffen, oaften, often, †oftin /ˈafən, ˈaftən, ˈɔfən, ˈɔftən, ˈɔfən/ *adv* frequently; in many instances *la16-*.
aftentimes oftentimes *la16-19, 20- literary*. [AFT[1.2], with *-en* suffix]
afferme *see* AFFIRM
afferyt *see* AFEARD
affeurd *see* AFFOORD
aff faˈins, off fallings, †aff-fawings /ˈaf fɔɪnz, ˈɔf fɔlɪŋz/ *npl* **1** things fallen or discarded; scraps, remnants *17-*. **2** a decline or lapse in health or morals *17-e19*. [AFF- + verbal noun from FA[1.2]]
affgaun[1.1]**, affgaˈin, affgoin, offgoing** /ˈafgɔn, ˈafgɔɪn, ˈafgɔɪn, ˈɔfgɔɪŋ/ *n* **1** a start; a departure *17-*. **2** fading away; death *17-*. [AFF- + verbal noun from GAE]
affgaun[1.2]**, affgaˈin, †off-going** /ˈafgɔn, ˈafgɔɪn/ *adj* **1** departing, outgoing *20-*. **2** dilapidated, worse for wear *la19*. **3** *of a market* brisk *e19*. [AFF- + pr esp of GAE]
affgo, off-go /ˈafgo, ˈɔfgo/ *n* a start, a beginning, an outset *la19-*. [AFF- + GAE]
affgoin *see* AFFGAUN[1.1]
aff-hand[1.1]**, offhand** /ˈafhand, ˈɔfhand/ *adj* unpremeditated, casual; brusque *17-*. [AFF- + HAN[1.1]]
aff-hand[1.2]**, offhand** /ˈafhand, ˈɔfhand/ *adv* **1** without deliberation, casually; brusquely; at once *la17-*. **2** achieved, off one's hands *e19*. [see the adj]
affin /ˈafɪn/ *n* offing *19-*. [AFF[1.3], with *-ing* suffix]
affin *see* AFF[1.4]
affirm, †afferme, †efferme /əˈfɪrm/ *v* **1** to confirm, ratify; to assert strongly *la14-*. **2** to open a court by affirming (by oath) agreement to avoid disorderly interruption *la15-17*. [ME *affermen*]
affix, †effix /əˈfɪks/ *v* **1** to attach (a seal) to a document; to fix, fasten; to fix up *la15-*. **2** to assign or appoint *16-e17*. [Lat *affix-*, ptp stem of *affīgere*]
aff-lat, afflet, offlet /ˈaflat, ˈaflət, ˈɔflət/ *n* **1** a drainage outlet *18-*. **2** a holiday, a spell of leisure *20- NE*. [AFF- + LAT]
aff-leef *see* AFF-LOOF
afflick, afflict /əˈflɪk, əˈflɪkt/ *v* to cause suffering to; to distress *16-*. [Lat *afflict-*, ptp stem of *afflīgere* to strike, dash down, Lat *afflictāre* to damage, injure]
aff-loof, aff luiff, *Uls* **aff-leef, †off-loof** /afˈluf; *Uls* afˈlif/ *adv* without delay, at once; offhand *18-*. [AFF- + LUIF]
affoord, affeurd, affuird, affaird, afford /əˈfurd, əˈferd, əˈfɔrd/ *v* **1** to yield; to furnish or supply; to offer *la16-*. **2** to be able to meet the expense of; to have the resources for *18-*. [OE *forþian* to offer, contribute (something)]
†affordell *adv* in hand; in front *16-e17*. [unknown]
afforrow *see* AFFORROW
aff-pit, offpit, offput /ˈafpɪt, ˈɔfpɪt, ˈɔfput/ *n* **1** an excuse, an evasion, a reason for delay *18-*. **2** a delay, a waste of time *la19- NE T SW*. **3** a procrastinator *la19- NE T SW Bor*. **4** a makeshift or a hasty meal *la19- N EC Bor*. **off-put o time** a waste of time *la19, 20- Bor*. [AFF- + PIT[2]]
aff-pittin[1.1]**, aff-putting, offputting, †ofputting** /ˈafpɪtɪn, ˈafputɪŋ, ˈɔfputɪŋ/ *n* postponement, procrastination, evasion; an excuse, a delay *la15-*. [AFF- + verbal noun from PIT[2]]
aff-pittin[1.2]**, aff-putting, offputting** /ˈafpɪtɪn, ˈafputɪŋ, ˈɔfputɪŋ/ *adj* delaying, procrastinating; trifling, dilatory *19-*. [AFF- + pr esp of PIT[2]]
affraitlye *see* AFFRAY[1.2]
affray[1.1]**, effray** /əˈfre, ɛˈfre/ *n* **1** a cause, occasion or instance of alarm; a public fight or disturbance; *law* an assault on a person which constitutes a breach of the peace *15-*. **2** a state of alarm or fear; fright, terror *la14-e17*. [ME *affrai*]
†affray[1.2]**, effray** *v* to frighten or terrify; to feel fear *15-e17*. **affrayit, effrayt, effrait** afraid; alarmed *la14-17*. **affrayitly, effraytly, affraitlye** in alarm or fear *la14-16*. [ME *affraien*]
affront[1.1]**, †effront** /əˈfrʌnt/ *n* an act which causes offence; disgrace, humiliation *17-*. [see the verb]
affront[1.2] /əˈfrʌnt/ *v* to disgrace, humiliate *17-*. [OFr *afronter*]
affrontit, affronted, †effrontit /əˈfrʌntɪt, əˈfrʌntəd/ *adj* **1** ashamed, humiliated *la18-*. **2** impudent, shameless *e17*. **†affrontitly** impudently *17*. [ptp of AFFRONT[1.2]]
affset, offset, †af set /ˈafsɛt, ˈɔfsɛt/ *n* **1** an ornament, an embellishment *17-*. **2** a (cause of) delay; a setback; a hindrance, a stoppage; an excuse *la18-*. **3** an outset, a start *la19-*. **4** a diversion of water forming a mill-race *18-*. [AFF- + SET[1.2]]
afftak, *Sh Ork* **aftak** /ˈaftak; *Sh Ork* ˈaftak/ *n* **1** a mocking remark, a jeer *19-*. **2** a person who ridicules others, a mimic *la19-*. **3** a deduction of wages *la19- C*. **4** a lull in a storm *20- Sh Ork*. [AFF- + TAK[1.2]]
afftakin[1.1]**, †offtaking** /ˈaftakɪn/ *n* **1** mockery, imitation *19-*. **2** taking off, removal *la15-e18*. [AFF- + verbal noun from TAK[1.2]]
afftakin[1.2]**, aff-takkin, offtakin** /ˈaftakɪn, ˈɔftɛkɪn/ *adj* mocking, sarcastic *la19-*. [AFF- + pr esp of TAK[1.2]]
affuird *see* AFFOORD
†affy *v* to trust *la14-16*. **affyance** trust, confidence *e16*. [ME *affien*]
affy *see* AWFY[1.1], AWFY[1.2]
afiel, afield, †afeild /əˈfil, əˈfild/ *adv* **1** away (from home); abroad *16-*. **2** out in the fields *la19-*. [OE *on felda*]
afit[1.1]**, afoot** /əˈfɪt, əˈfut/ *adj* upright; up and about; on the move *la18-*. [EModE *a foote*]
afit[1.2]**, afoot** /əˈfɪt, əˈfut/ *adv* **1** on foot; on the move *18-*. **2** in preparation or progress *19-*. [see the adj]
†afleyd *adj* dismayed, afraid *la18-19*. [ptp of OE *āflȳgan* to drive away; compare FLEY[1.2]]
aflocht[1.1]**, †aflought** /əˈflɔxt/ *adj* agitated, in a flutter *16-*. [A[3] + FLOCHT[1.1]]
aflocht[1.2]**, †aflought** /əˈflɔxt/ *adv* in or into a state of agitation *la18-*. [see the adj]
afoot *see* AFIT[1.1], AFIT[1.2]
afor *see* AFORE[1.3]
afore[1.1]**, †effoir** /əˈfor/ *adv* **1** *of time* before, previously *la15-*. **2** at an earlier point in a piece of writing or document *la15-*. **3** *of place* before, in front; in advance *la16-*. **4** *of a clock* fast *20-*. **afoirhand, †efforhand** in advance, beforehand *16-*. **afoirtyme, †afortyme** formerly, before *16-*. [OE *onforon*]
afore[1.2]**, †effore** /əˈfor/ *prep* **1** before, earlier than, in front of, in advance of; in the presence of *16-*. **2** *of what is to come* confronting, in store for *19-*. **3** *of rank or consequence* above, before; in preference to *la19-*. [see the adv]
afore[1.3]**, †afor** /əˈfor/ *conj* **1** *of time* before *16-*. **2** rather than *la19-*. [see the adv]
†afornent, afornens *prep* beside, next to *15-19*. [AFORE[1.1] + ANENT]
†aforrow, afforrow *adv* before, previously *16*. [altered form of AFORE[1.1]]
afouth /əˈfuθ/ *adv* in abundance *la18-*. [AT[1.2] or ON[1.2] + FOUTH]
af set *see* AFFSET
†aft[1.1]**, oft** *adj* frequent *16-19*. [OE *oft*]
aft[1.2]**, oft** /aft, ɔft/ *adv* often *la14-*. **aft-times, oft-times** often, frequently *la14-*. [see the adj]
aftak *see* AFFTAK
aften *see* AFFEN
after *see* EFTER[1.2], EFTER[1.3], EFTER[1.4]

after- *see* EFTER-[1.5]
afterhend *see* EFTERHIN[1.2]
afternoon *see* EFTERNIN, EFTERNUN
aftir *see* EFTER[1.3]
ag[1.1] /ag, ɑg/ *n* the wash of the sea; foam or debris on the shore *20- Sh*. [Norw *aga* to float; to swell]
ag[1.2] /ag, ɑg/ *v* to drive towards the shore; to be driven shoreward *20- Sh*. [see the noun]
-ag *see* -OCK
again[1.1], **agen**, **agin**, *Sh* **ageen**, †**agane**, †**agayn** /əˈgen, əˈgɛn, əˈgɪn; *Sh* əˈgin/ *adv* **1** back; once more; additionally on a further occasion *la14-*. **2** in return *la15-*. **3** a request for a reminder: ◊*what was I at again? 19-*. †**agane bring** to bring back, restore *15-e16*. †**agane call**, **again call** to recall; to revoke *la14-e17*. †**agane cuming** a return, returning *la14-16*. [OE *ongēan*]
again[1.2], **agen**, **agin**, †**agane**, †**agayn** /əˈgen, əˈgɛn, əˈgɪn/ *prep* **1** in opposition to; in defiance of; to the hurt or disadvantage of; unfavourable to *la14-*. **2** in anticipation of, in preparation for; about, before, by (a time or occasion) *la15-*. **3** striking against, into collision with *la18-*. **4** leaning or resting against; close to or touching *la19-*. **5** facing; towards, so as to meet or greet *la14-16*. †**agaynstandand** standing in opposition or in the way *15*. [see the adv]
again[1.3], **agen**, **agin**, †**agane** /əˈgen, əˈgɛn, əˈgɪn/ *conj* in anticipation of, in preparation for (a time or occasion when); until *16-*. [see the adv]
against, **agenst**, **aginst**, †**againis**, †**aganis**, †**aganyst** /əˈgenst, əˈgɛnst, əˈgɪnst/ *prep* **1** in opposition to; hostile to *la14-*. **2** in preparation for; in anticipation of, about, before, by *la15-*. **3** facing, next to; in contact with; supported by *la14-*. **4** towards, near *la14-*. **5** with reference to *15-*. [ME *agaynes*]
agait, **agate** /əˈget/ *adv* **1** on the road; going about (after an illness) *19-*. **2** away *19-*. **3** in motion *la16-e17*. †**agaitward** on the road or way *la16-e17*. †**agaitwards** = agaitward *16-17*. [ON[1.2] + GATE]
a'gait *see* ALGATE
agane *see* AGAIN[1.1], AGAIN[1.2], AGAIN[1.3]
aganis, **aganyst** *see* AGAINST
agate *see* AGAIT
a'gates *see* ALGATES
agayn *see* AGAIN[1.1], AGAIN[1.2]
age, †**aige**, †**adge**, †**eage** /edʒ/ *n* **1** the length of a life or existence; a period or stage of a life or time *15-*. **2** the state or fact or being old, old age *la15-*. **be ages wi** to be of the same age as *la19-*. [ME *age*]
agee *see* AJEE[1.1], AJEE[1.2]
ageen *see* AGAIN[1.1]
agen *see* AGAIN[1.1], AGAIN[1.2], AGAIN[1.3]
agenst *see* AGAINST
agent[1.1], **awgent** /ˈedʒənt, ˈɔdʒənt/ *n* **1** a person who acts for another; *law* a solicitor or law agent *la16-*. **2** a part-time representative of a firm; a country bank manager or stationmaster *la18-20, 21- historical*. **agentry**, **agentrie** the office or function of agent *la16-*. [EModE *agent*, Lat *agēns*]
agent[1.2] /ˈedʒənt/ *v* to act as an agent or legal representative *17-*. [see the noun]
aggle[1.1] /ˈagəl/ *n* a mess *20- Sh Ork*. [see the verb]
aggle[1.2], **uggle** /ˈagəl, ˈʌgəl/ *v* to dirty, make a mess *la19- Sh Ork*. [Norw *alka*]
aggrage *see* AGGREGE
aggre *see* AGREE
aggreance *see* AGREEANCE
†**aggrege**, **aggrage** *v* **1** to exaggerate; to aggravate *la15-e18*. **2** to heap wrath on *e16*. [ME *aggreggen*]

agile, †**agill** /ˈadʒʌɪl/ *adj* able to move or act quickly, nimble *15-*. [MFr *agile*]
agility, †**agilitie**, †**agilite** /əˈdʒɪlətɪ/ *n* nimbleness, skill, mental dexterity *la15-*. [ME *agilite*, Lat *agilitās*]
agill *see* AGILE
agin *see* AGAIN[1.1], AGAIN[1.2], AGAIN[1.3]
aginst *see* AGAINST
agitate[1.1], †**agitat** /ˈadʒətet/ *v* **1** to perturb or disturb; to stir up *la16-*. **2** to discuss or debate *e19*. [Lat *agitāt-*, ptp stem of *agitāre*]
†**agitate**[1.2], **agitat** *adj* **1** tossed about; perturbed *la16-e17*. **2** debated, discussed *17-e18*. [ptp of AGITATE[1.1], Lat *agitātus*]
agley[1.1], **aglee** /əˈgle, əˈglɪ/ *adj* squint, not straight; awry, wrong *la19-*. [GLEY[1.2], with *a-* prefix]
agley[1.2], **aglee** /əˈgle, əˈglɪ/ *adv* off the straight, obliquely; wrong, awry, astray *la18-*. [see the adj]
agmentatioun *see* AUGMENTATION
agname /ˈagnem/ *n* a byname or nickname *la17-*. **agnamed** bynamed, nicknamed; styled *la17-*. [Lat *agnōmen*, with substitution of *name*]
agnate, †**agnat** /ˈagnet/ *n* a relative on the father's side *la15-*. Compare COGNATE[1.1]. [Lat *agnātus*]
†**agnosce** *v* **1** to acknowledge; to confess *la16*. **2** to investigate, establish by proof *la16*. [Lat *agnoscere*]
agree, †**agre**, †**aggre** /əˈgrɪ/ *v* to come to an agreement, be in accord with; to be the same as or similar to *la15-*. **agree with** to consent to *19-*. [ME *agreen*]
†**agreeance**, **agreance**, **aggreance** *n* agreement *16-e19*. [AGREE, with noun-forming suffix]
agrouf, **agroof**, **agrufe**, *SW* **agruff**, †**a growfe** /əˈgruf; *SW* əˈgrʌf/ *adv* face downwards, prone *16-*. [ME *a gruf*; compare GROOF]
†**agrys** *v* to terrify *e16*. [OE *agrīsan* to be afraid of]
Ah, **A**, **Aw**, **I**, *T* **E**, *T* **Eh**, †**ik**, †**ic** /a, ɔ, ae; *T* ɛ; *T* e/ *pron* I *la14-*. [OE *ic*]
ahaint *see* AHINT[1.2]
ahame /əˈhem/ *adv* at home *la18-*. [AT[1.2] + HAME[1.1]]
ahaud /əˈhɔd/ *adv* on fire *20- Bor*. [A[3] + HAUD[1.1] in the grip (of fire)]
ah-bay-say *see* EBBASAY
ahead *see* AHEID
aheat /əˈhit/ *adv* in or into a hot or warm condition *la19, 20- EC Bor*. [A[3] + HEAT[1.1]]
a heater *see* HECTURI
aheid, **ahead** /əˈhid, əˈhɛd/ *adv* in front, in a forward direction; in advance, in the future *19-*. **come ahead** an invitation to start a fight (with the speaker) *la20-*. [A[3] + HEID[1.1]]
ahin han *see* AHINT HAND
ahint[1.1], **ahin**, **ahent**, †**ahind** /əˈhɪnt, əˈhɪn, əˈhɛnt/ *adv* **1** at a later time, late, too late *la18-*. **2** behind; in the past *19-*. **3** *of a clock* slow *la19-*. [OE *æthindan*]
ahint[1.2], **ahin**, **ahent**, **ahaint**, **ahind** /əˈhɪnt, əˈhɪn, əˈhɛnt, əˈhʌɪnd/ *prep* **1** behind *la18-*. **2** later than, after, in view of *la19-*. **ahint the hand**, **ahin the hand** **1** in reserve *20- NE*. **2** late, after the event *la18-19*. **come in ahint** to take advantage of (a person) *19, 20- NE*. [see the adv]
ahint hand, **ahint han**, **ahin han** /əˈhɪnt hand, əˈhɪnt han, əˈhɪn han/ *adv* behind, late, in arrears *20-*. [AHINT[1.2] + HAN[1.1]]
ahpron *see* APRIN
Aiberdeen *see* ABERDEEN
Aiberdeen-awa *see* ABERDEEN-AWA[1.1]
Aiberdonian *see* ABERDONIAN[1.1], ABERDONIAN[1.2]
aibles *see* ABLES
aiblich *see* ABLACH
aiblins, *Bor* **yiblins**, †**ablins**, †**ablens** /ˈeblɪnz; *Bor* ˈjɪblɪnz/ *adv* perhaps, possibly *la16-*. [ABLE[1.1], with *-lins* suffix]

†**aich** *interj* an expression of surprise or sorrow [probably onomatopoeic of a sigh]

aich *see* AUCHT², EETCH

aichan /'exən, 'ɛxən/ *n* an ear of corn *20- Ork.* [compare AICHER]

aicher, *Sh* **akker**, *Sh Ork* **aiker**, *NE* **eacher**, †**icker**, †**echer**, †**eichyr** /'exər; *Sh* 'akər; *Sh Ork* 'ekər; *NE* 'ixər/ *n* **1** an ear of corn *la19- Sh NE*. **2** a fragment, a small quantity; a piece, a drop *la19- Sh NE*. [OE *eher*]

aicht *see* AUCHT², ECHT¹·²

aichteen *see* ECHTEEN

aickle *see* YACKLE¹·¹

aidder *see* ETHER

aider *see* EDDER¹·²

aidge *see* EDGE¹·¹

aidle *see* ADDLE

aifter *see* EFTER¹·², EFTER¹·³, EFTER¹·⁴

aifterneen, aifternoon *see* EFTERNIN

aigar /'egər/ *n* dried grain ready to be ground *19-*. **aigar brose** brose made of oatmeal *19-*. †**aigar meal** ground oats or barley mixed with peasemeal *19*. [altered form of AICHER]

aige *see* AGE

aigle *see* EAGLE

aik, **oak**, *Bor* **yik**, †**ake**, †**ayk**, †**ak** /ek, ok; *Bor* jɪk/ *n* **1** the oak, a tree of the genus *Quercus 13-*. **2** oak timber *la15-*. [OE *āc*]

aik *see* YAWK

aikaspire /'ekəspʌɪr/ *adj* mouldy *20- Ork*. [altered form of ACHERSPYRE¹·²]

aiken, †**akin**, †**akyn**, †**oken** /'ekən/ *adj of objects* made of oak wood; *of places* consisting of or characterized by oak trees *la13-19, 20- literary*. [AIK with adj-forming suffix]

aiker *see* ACRE¹·¹, AICHER

aikerspir *see* ACHERSPYRE¹·¹, ACHERSPYRE¹·²

†**aiky, aikie, aky** *adj in place-names* consisting of or characterized by oak trees *la16-19*. [AIK + -IE²]

ail¹·¹, †**aill** /el/ *n* an illness; an ailment *la15-*. **ail break** absence from work due to illness *20- EC*. [see the verb]

ail¹·² /el/ *v* **1** to trouble or afflict in mind or body *la14-*. **2** *of a person* to suffer from an illness; to be ill *15-*. **3** to hinder or prevent: ◊*what suld ail me to ken it? 19-*. **what ails ye** what is the matter *la14-*. **what ails ye at** what objection or grounds for complaint have you against *la15-*. [OE *eglan*]

ailay *see* ALLEY

aild *see* AULD¹·²

aile *see* AISLE

aile cruk *see* ELCRUKE

ailiss, aillis /'elɪs/ *n* a blaze, a roaring fire *20- N*. [unknown; compare AES¹·¹]

aill *see* AIL¹·¹, ALE¹·¹

aillis *see* AILISS

Ailsa cock /elsə 'kɔk/ *n* the puffin *Fratercula arctica 19-*. [shortened form of AILSA CRAIG + COCK¹·¹]

Ailsa Craig /elsə 'kreg/ *n* a curling stone made from the volcanic rocks of Ailsa Craig *la19-*. [from the name of the island off the Ayrshire coast]

Ailsa parrot /elsə 'parət/ *n* the puffin *Fratercula arctica la19-*. [shortened form of AILSA CRAIG + Scots *parrot*]

aim, *Sh EC Bor* **em** /em; *Sh EC Bor* ɛm/ *v* **1** to direct (a shot); to throw (a stone) *la17-*. **2** to seek to achieve *la17-*. [EModE *aim*]

aime *see* EEM²

aimers *see* EMMERS

ain¹·¹, **aine, own**, †**awin**, †**awn**, †**owin** /en, on/ *adj* **1** belonging to oneself or itself *la14-*. **2** proper or natural *la15-e17*. **ain think** a person's own private thoughts or opinion *19, 20- NE*. [OE *āgen*]

ain¹·², **own**, †**awne** /en, on/ *pron* the kinsfolk, friends or property belonging to a person; that which belongs to oneself *la14-*. **o my ains** belonging to me *la19, 20- H&I*. [see the adj]

ain *see* ANE¹·¹, ANE¹·²

aince¹·¹, **wance, ance, eence, once**, *Sh* **anes**, *C SW Bor* **yince**, *WC Uls* **yinst**, *H&I WC Uls* **wanst**, †**anis**, †**anys**, †**onis** /ens, wans, ans, ins, wʌns; *Sh* 'anəs; *C SW Bor* jɪns; *WC Uls* jɪnst; *H&I WC Uls* wanst/ *adv* **1** one time or on one occasion only *la14-*. **2** on one or the first of two or more occasions *15-*. **3** formerly *15-*. **4** one day, at some time in the future *la15-e17*. **5** of one mind, in harmony *la15-e16*. **the once** on one occasion only *la20-*. **ance a day** = *ance in a day 18-19, 20- EC*. **ance in a day** once upon a time *19, 20- NE Bor*. **at aince, at wance, at eence**, †**atanis**, †**attanis** **1** at one and the same time, together *la14-*. **2** immediately *16-*. [OE *ǣnes*]

aince¹·², **wance, eence, once**, *C SW Bor* **yince**, †**ance**, †**anes**, †**anys** /ens, wans, ins, wʌns; *C SW Bor* jɪns/ *conj* when once, if once; as soon as *la15-*. [see the adv]

aince errand¹·¹, **aince erran**, *H&I* **enseerin** /'ens ɛrənd, 'ens ɛran; *H&I* 'ɛnsirən/ *n* a (particular) purpose; a special design or errand *19-*. [see the adv]

aince errand¹·², *NE* **eence-eerin**, *EC* **anes-eerand**, *WC* **yince erran**, *Bor* **yins yirrint**, †**anis eirand** /'ens ɛrənd; *NE* 'ɪns ɪrən; *EC* 'anəs irənd; *WC* 'jɪns ɛrən; *Bor* 'jɪns jɪrənt/ *adv* for the express purpose, as a special errand *la16-*. [AINCE¹·¹ + EERAN; compare Norw *eins ærend*]

aind *see* END, YIND

aine *see* AIN¹·¹

ainlie, ainly *see* ANELY¹·¹, ANELY¹·²

ainsel, ainsell, †**awin self** /'ensɛl, en'sɛl/ *pron* own self *15-*. **ma ainsel** myself *19-*. [AIN¹·¹ + SEL¹·¹]

aint *see* ENT

aip *see* APE

aipple, apple, *NE* **epple**, †**appil**, †**apill**, †**aple** /'epəl, 'apəl; *NE* 'epəl/ *n* an apple, the fruit of a tree of the genus *Malus la14-*. †**appill garnet** a pomegranate *16-e17*. †**appill orange** an orange *la15-e16*. †**apille rubye** a variety of apple *e16*. **aipple tree, apple tree**, *NE* **epple tree**, †**apil trie** a tree which bears apples *14-*. [OE *æppel*]

aippleringie, appleringie, *T* **aipple reengie**, *WC* **aipplerhynie**, †**overeengie** /'epəlrɪŋi, 'apəlrɪŋi; *T* 'epəlrindʒi; *WC* 'epəlrʌɪni/ *n* southernwood *Artemisia abrotanum 19, 20- T C SW Bor*. [AN *averoine*, with first element altered by popular association with AIPPLE]

aiqual *see* EQUAL¹·¹, EQUAL¹·²

air¹, *WC Bor* **err**, †**are**, †**aire**, †**ayr** /er; *WC* ɛr/ *n* **1** (the space occupied by) the atmosphere, air *la14-*. **2** a light breeze *la16-*. **ar o wind**, †**are of wind** a gentle breeze, a breath of wind *la16-17, 20- Sh*. **tak the air 1** to experience the air or environment *la14-*. **2** *of frost* to rise, disperse *19, 20- Sh Ork N*. **tak the air aff** to take the chill off *la18-*. [ME *air*]

air², *Sh* **ar**, *Sh* **aer**, *Sh* **er**, *Ork* **ere** /er; *Sh* ɑr; *Sh* eər; *Sh Ork* ɛr/ *n* a small quantity, a particle, a morsel, a taste *la16, la19- Sh Ork N NE*. [unknown; compare HAIR¹·¹, Icel *ar* a speck of dust]

air³, **oar**, *Sh* **aer**, †**ar**, †**ayr**, †**ore** /er, or; *Sh* eər/ *n* an oar, the blade or pole used to propel a boat *la14-*. [OE *ār*, ON *ár*]

air⁴ /ɛr/ *v* to taste; to sniff or smell *19, 20- Ork*. [probably AIR¹]

air⁵·¹, †**ayr** /er/ *adj* early *16-19, 20- NE*. [OE *ǣr*, ON *ár*]

air⁵·², **ere, ear**, †**are**, †**ayr**, †**eyr** /er, ɛr, ir/ *adv* **1** early, soon *la14-*. **2** before, formerly *la14-16*. [see the adj]

air *see* AIRE, AYRE, HEIR¹·¹, HEIR¹·²

airand *see* EERAN

airch[1.1], **arch**, †**ark** /ertʃ, artʃ/ *n* 1 a curve, a curved structure (forming part of a bridge or doorway); compare ARK[2] *15-*. 2 an aim (in shooting or archery) *19- N NE T Bor*. [ME *arch*]

airch[1.2], **arch**, *N NE* **erch** /ertʃ, artʃ; *N NE* ɛrtʃ/ *v* 1 to bend or curve; to form an arch *la18-*. 2 to take aim *19- N NE Bor*. [AN *archer*]

†**aire**, **air** *n* a circuit court held by itinerant judges or officers *15-e19*. [AN *eire*]

aire *see* AIR[1]

†**airel** *n* in the Borders a flute *e19*. [unknown]

airgh *see* ERCH[1.2]

airgument, **argument** /ˈɛrgjəmənt, ˈargjumənt/ *n* a heated debate, an altercation; a set of reasons or process of reasoning *15-*. [ME *argument*, Lat *argūmentum*]

airie[1] /ˈere/ *n* a shieling *la18-*. [Gael *àirigh*]

airie[2] /ˈere/ *n* an aeroplane *la20-*. [shortened form of AIRYPLANE]

airieplane *see* AIRYPLANE

airish /ˈerɪʃ/ *adj of weather* cool, chilly *19-*. [AIR[1], with adj-forming suffix]

airk *see* ARK[1]

airle penny *see* ARLE PENNY

airles *see* ARLES

airm[1], **erm**, **arm**, †**arme** /erm, ɛrm, arm/ *n* 1 the upper limb of the human body *la14-*. 2 a bar or beam *la16-*. †**army** having arms or branches *la18*. **arm bane**, †**arme bane** a bone in the arm *la15-*. **airmchair**, **armchair**, †**arme-schair** a chair with arms *la16-*. †**armyt chair**, **armed chyre** an armchair *17*. **arm of the sea**, †**arme of the se** a long, narrow inlet of the sea *la14-*. [OE *earm*]

airm[2], **erm**, **arm** /erm, ɛrm, arm/ *v* 1 to equip with weapons or armour *la14-*. 2 to protect oneself, take up arms *la15-*. [OFr *armer*]

airmie *see* AIRMY

airmour, **ermour**, **armour** /ˈermər, ˈɛrmər, ˈarmər/ *n* 1 defensive armour *la14-*. 2 weapons *16-*. [ME *armüre*]

airmy, **ermy**, **army**, †**armie**, †**airmie**, †**armee** /ˈerme, ˈɛrme, ˈarme/ *n* 1 a body of troops, the military *16-*. 2 a multitude of people *20-*. **Tartan Army** *see* TARTAN[1.1]. [OFr *armee*]

airn[1.1], **ern**, **iron**, †**irne**, †**erne**, †**iren** /ern, ˈerən, ɛrn, ˈɛrən, aern, ˈaerən/ *n* 1 the metal, iron *la14-*. 2 a tool or implement made of iron *la14-*. 3 *pl* iron shackles *la15-*. 4 a flat implement for pressing clothes *17-*. 5 *golf* a type of club with a narrow head, originally made of iron *19-*. 6 *pl* surgical instruments *la15-19, 20- EC Bor*. 7 a tool for cutting peats; the number of peats cut with this tool in one day *la18- H&I*. 8 a girdle, a grill *17 20- Sh*. †**irnehous** a room in a prison where prisoners were kept in irons *la16-18*. **fresh aff the erns** brand new; fresh from one's studies *la18-19, 20- SW*. **new aff the airns** = *fresh aff the erns*. [OE *īren*]

airn[1.2], **ern**, **iron**, †**iren**, †**irne**, †**yrn** /ern, ˈerən, ɛrn, ˈɛrən, aern, ˈaerən/ *adj* made of iron *la14-*. **iron eer** ferric oxide; rust *la19- N NE*. **iron eerie** impregnated with iron; rusty *18- NE*. **iron fit** a shoemaker's last *19-*. †**iron graith** iron equipment, accessories or tackle *la15-e18*. **iron mail** a rust stain *19- C Bor*. **iron man** *fishing* a winch used on boats to haul in the nets *la19-*. [see the noun]

airn *see* EARN

airnest *see* EARNEST[1.1], EARNEST[1.2]

airra, **airrow** *see* ARRA

airschip *see* HEIRSKIP

airse *see* ERSE[1.1]

airt[1], **ert**, **art** /ert, ɛrt, art, ɛrt/ *n* (a branch of) learning; a skill; fine art *la14-*. †**art-magician** one skilled in sorcery *e16*. **airt and pairt**, **art and part** *law* (acting as) accessory or accomplice in a crime *15-*. †**airt and partaker** an accessory or accomplice = *airt and pairt 16-e17*. [ME *art*]

airt[2.1], *Sh Ork* **ert**, *EC* **airth**, *Uls* **art**, †**arth** /ert; *Sh Ork* ɛrt; *EC* erθ; *Uls* art/ *n* 1 a point of the compass, a quarter *15-*. 2 a direction, way or manner *la16-*. [perhaps Gael *àird*]

airt[2.2] /ert/ *v* 1 to direct or guide; to point a direction *la17-*. 2 to direct one's way; to make for (a direction or place) *la18-*. 3 to discover by search *20- Bor*. **airtan** direction; tendency *la19-*. **airt oot** to discover by search *19- Bor*. [see the noun]

airt[3], *EC* **airth**, †**art**, †**arct** /ert; *EC* erθ/ *v* to urge on; to incite, impel *15-19, 20- EC SW*. [ME *arten*]

airth *see* AIRT[2.1], AIRT[3]

airticle, **article**, †**artikil**, †**articule** /ˈertɪkəl, ˈartɪkəl/ *n* 1 a clause or paragraph in a (legal) document or ordinance *la14-*. 2 an object; an item; a commodity *17-*. 3 a written composition published in a newspaper or periodical *19-*. 4 a useless or insignificant person *20-*. 5 an iota, a small amount *la19- T*. **articles of roup** a formal statement of the conditions of sale at an auction *18-*. **Lords of the Articles** *see* LORD. [ME *article*]

airtist, **artist** /ˈertɪst, ˈartɪst/ *n* 1 one skilled in the learned arts; a scholar; a craftsman *16-*. 2 a creator of works of art *la18-*. [MFr *artiste*, Lat *artista* one who excels in a particular task]

air-yesterday *see* EREYESTERDAY

air yestreen *see* EREDASTREEN

airyplane, **airieplane** /ˈereplən, ˈerɪplən/ *n* an aeroplane *20-*. Compare AIRIE[2]. [altered form of Eng *aeroplane*]

ais *see* ACE

aise *see* ASS, EASE[1.1]

aish *see* ESH

aishan, **ation**, **aetion**, †**etion** /ˈeʃən/ *n* derogatory stock, kindred, breed *18- N NE EC*. [wrong division of A[1] + NATION]

aisiament *see* EASEMENT

aislar, **ashlar**, *WC Bor* **ezlar**, †**astler**, †**esler**, †**estlair** /ˈeslər, ˈaʃlər; *WC Bor* ˈɛzlər/ *n* square-hewn stone for building or paving *16-*. **ashlar stone**, †**estler stane** hewn stone *16-*. **ashlar work**, **aislar wark** masonry constructed of square-hewn stone *16-*. [AN *aiseler* from OFr *ais* a plank of wood]

aisle, †**ile**, †**aile**, †**yll** /ʌɪl/ *n* 1 a passageway in a church; a walkway between rows of seats in a public building *la14-*. 2 a passage between shelves in a shop or supermarket; a passageway between rows of seats on public transport *20-*. 3 an enclosed and covered (family) burial place, apparently adjoining a church *17-19*. [ME *ele*]

aisle *see* AIZLE[1.1], AIZLE[1.2]

aisle-tuith, **assle-tuith** /ˈezəl tuθ, ˈasəl tuθ/ *n* a molar tooth; a bicuspid tooth *la19- SW Bor*. [ON *jaxl* grinder + OE *tōþ*]

aisment *see* EASEMENT

aiss *see* ASS

aissy *see* ASSIE

aist *see* EAST[1.1], EAST[1.2], EAST[1.3]

aisy *see* EASY[1.1], EASY[1.2]

aisy-hole *see* ASSIE

ait, **ate**, **oat**, *EC Bor* **yit**, †**ote** /et, ot; *EC Bor* jɪt/ *npl* oat, oats, a cereal plant *la14-*. **aiten** relating to the oat plant; composed of the grain of oats; made with oatmeal *la18-*. **ait breed**, †**ate brede**, †**eat-breid** oat bread or oatcakes *16-*. **ait cake**, **oat cake**, †**ait caik** a thin, crisp, savoury biscuit made from oatmeal and other ingredients *la16-*. **ait laif** a loaf of oat bread *16-*. **ait meal**, **oat meal**, †**eit meill** flour made from the oat, oatmeal *la15-*. **ait seed**, **ate seed** 1 the seed of the oat *16-*. 2 (the season for) sowing oats *la16-19*. [OE *āte*, *ǣte*]

ait *see* EAT[1.1], EAT[1.2]

aitchesoun see ACHESONE

†**aiten, eaten** *n* juniper *la18-19*. Compare ETNACH[1.1]. [Gael *aitionn*]

aiten see AIT

aith, oath, †**othe,** †**athe,** †**hathe** /eθ, oθ/ *n* **1** a formal or legal declaration, a sworn pledge *la14-*. **2** a swear-word or expletive *16-*. **oath in litem** *law* an oath sworn by the pursuer in an action regarding the amount of loss suffered *la17-*. †**oath in supplement** an oath by which a litigant could give evidence in their own favour when impartial legal evidence was lacking *la17-19*. **oath of calumny** an oath taken at the outset of an action by which both parties swear that the facts pleaded are true *la16-20, 21- historical*. **oath of credulity** an oath as to the truth of the averment of debt required to be made by a creditor petitioning for or claiming in sequestration *19-*. †**aith of neibourhede** the oath sworn by a person on becoming a burgess *la16-e17*. †**oath of verity 1** an oath as to the truth of the case as stated *16-e19*. **2** an oath volunteered by the pursuer or defender which has the effect of concluding the case *17-e18*. **3** a pledge of loyalty or allegiance *16-17*. [OE *hāt*]

aithehen see HAITHEHEN

aither[1.1], *Sh NE* **edder,** †**ather,** †**athir,** †**eather** /ˈeðər; *Sh NE* ˈedər, ˈɛdər/ *adj* **1** each of two, one or other of two, either *la14-*. **2** *with plural noun* both *la15-17*. [OE *ǣgþer* each, both, OE *āwþer* one or other of two]

aither[1.2], *NE* **edder,** *NE* **eyther,** †**ather,** †**ether** /ˈeðər; *NE* ˈedər, ˈɛdər; *NE* ˈʌɪðər/ *adv* either; any more than another *la14-*. **edderin, eidderin, eitheran** either *19, 20- Sh NE H&I*. **aithers** either *19-*. [see the adj]

aither[1.3], **ayther,** *NE* **eyther,** †**athir,** †**ether** /ˈeðər; *NE* ˈʌɪðər/ *pron* also *pl* †**atheris,** †**ethers** one or other; each (of two people or things) *la14-*. †**athir uther** each other, one another *la14-16*. [see the adj]

aither[1.4], **ayther,** *Sh NE* **edder,** *NE* **eyther,** †**eather,** †**ether** /ˈeðər; *Sh* ˈedər, ˈɛðər; *NE* ˈʌɪðər/ *conj* either *16-*. [see the adj]

aithken /ˈeðkɛn/ *n* a mark of ownership (on a sheep) *la19- Ork*. Compare EITH-KENT[1.2]. [ON *auðkenni* a mark, distinction, with form influenced by EITH[1.2]]

aitnach see ETNACH[1.1]

aitrie see ETTERY

aive see AVE[2]

aiven see EVEN[2.2], EVEN[2.3]

aiver, †**aver** /ˈevər/ *n* a workhorse, a carthorse; an old or worthless horse *16-19, 20- NE*. †**averill** a worthless horse *e16*. [ME *aver* property, stock, a beast of burden]

aiver see YIVVER

aivis /ˈevɪs/ *n* a silly or useless occupation; a trick *20- NE*. [unknown]

aivrin see AVERIN, EFTERHIN[1.1]

aiwal see AVAL[1.2]

aix, axe, *NE* **yax,** *Bor* **yix,** †**ax,** †**ex** /eks, aks; *NE* jaks; *Bor* jɪks/ *n* an axe *la14-*. [OE *æx*]

aixies, axes, exies, †**acces** /ˈeksɪz, ˈaksɪz, ˈɛksɪz/ *n* an attack of ague; hysterics *15-*. [ME *acces*]

aixle, exle, †**axile** /ˈeksəl, ˈɛksəl/ *n* an axle *17-*. [ME *axle-*, in compounds such as *axle-tree*; compare OE *eax*]

aixtra[1.1], **aixtrae, extrae** /ˈekstrə, ˈekstre, ˈɛkstre/ *n* something or someone extra or additional *20-*. [altered form of Eng *extra*]

aixtra[1.2], **aixtrae, extrae,** †**yaxtra** /ˈekstrə, ˈekstre, ˈɛkstre/ *adj* extra, additional *la19-*. [see the noun]

aixtra[1.3], **aixtrae, extrae** /ˈekstrə, ˈekstre, ˈɛkstre/ *adv* extra, to a greater extent, in addition *20-*. [see the noun]

aixtree, extrie, †**axtre,** †**extre,** †**axtree** /ˈekstri, ˈekstri/ *n* an axle (of a wheel) *la15-19, 20- NE Bor*. Compare ASSLE-TREE. [OE *eax* + OE *trēow* tree, wood, timber, beam]

aize see AES[1.1], AES[1.2]

aizle[1.1], *NE* **eizel,** *NE* **eyzle,** *T* **izzle,** †**aisle** /ˈezəl; *NE* ˈʌɪzəl; *T* ˈɪzəl/ *n pl* also †**isillys 1** an ember; a spark; compare AES[1.1] *16-*. **2** a burnt-out cinder *19*. **eyzly** fiery, flashing *20- NE*. [OE *ysl* ashes]

†**aizle**[1.2], **aisle** *v of a fire* to glow *la19*; compare AES[1.2]. **aislin** *of a fire* glowing *la19*. [see the noun]

ajar, †**achar** /əˈdʒar/ *adv* slightly open *16-*. [ON[1.2] + CHAR[1.1]]

ajee[1.1], **agee** /əˈdʒi/ *adj* **1** *of a door, gate or window* slightly open, ajar *la18-*. **2** askew, awry, crooked *19-*. [see the adv]

ajee[1.2], **agee** /əˈdʒi/ *adv* **1** *of a door, gate or window* so as to be partly open, ajar *la17-*. **2** so as to be to one side; aside, off the straight; awry, askew *18-*. **3** *of the mind* so as to be in a disturbed or disordered state *18-*. [A[2] + JEE[1.1]; compare AJAR]

†**a-jour, ajower** *adj in needlework* having an openwork pattern *la16*. [MFr *a jour* openwork allowing light to pass through]

ak see ACK[1.1], ACK[1.2], AIK

akamy[1.1], **akami** /ˈakəmi/ *n* a weak or infirm person or animal *20- Sh Ork*. [unknown]

†**akamy**[1.2], **acamy** *adj in Orkney* diminutive, undersized, infirm *e19*. [unknown]

ake see AIK

aker, akir see ACRE[1.1]

akin see AIKEN

a'kin, awkin, †**alkin,** †**alkind,** †**alkynd** /ˈakɪn, ˈɔkɪn/ *adj* of every kind, every kind of *la14-*. **a' kin o, a' kind o',** †**all kynd of** every kind of, of every kind *15-*. **a'kin kind** *NE* **a' kin-kine,** †**alkyn kynd** every kind (of) *15-*. [AW[1.2] + KIND[1.1]]

akkadör, ackadür /akəˈdør, akəˈdør/ *v* to persevere, endeavour *la19- Sh*. [unknown]

akker see AICHER

†**aknawin** *adj* known to (a person) *la14-e16*. [ptp of OE *oncnāwan*]

aky see AIKY

akyn see AIKEN

akyrspire see ACHERSPYRE[1.2]

al see ALL, AW[1.1], AW[1.2], AW[1.3]

†**alabast** *n* alabaster *la14-e17*. [OFr *albastre*, Lat *alabaster*]

alacampine, †**allicompain** /alikəmˈpen, aləˈkampən/ *n* (candy flavoured with) the elecampane plant *Inula helenium la16-*. [Lat *enula campāna*]

alace, alas see ALESS

alack, †**alake,** †**allake,** †**allaik** /əˈlak/ *interj* an exclamation of sorrow *la15-*. †**alakanee, alackanie** = ALACK *18-e19*. [probably LACK[1.1]]

alacreische see ALICREESH

alaek see ALIKE[1.1], ALIKE[1.2]

alaft, aloft /əˈlaft, əˈlɔft, əˈloft/ *adv* above, up or upwards, in or into the air, on high *16-*. [reduced form of *on loft* (LAFT[1.1])]

alagrugous /aleˈgrugəs/ *adj* grim, ghastly; sour; woebegone *la18- NE T*. [unknown]

alagust /əleˈgʌst/ *n* disgust; suspicion *18- NE*. [unknown]

alainerly see ALLENARLY[1.1]

alairm[1.1], **alerm, alarm, alarum** /əˈlerm, əˈlɛrm, əˈlarm, əˈlarəm/ *n* **1** a warning, an alert *16-*. **2** a call to arms; an assault *16*. [ME *alarm*, EModE *alarum*]

alairm[1.2], **alerm, alarm, alarum** /əˈlerm, əˈlɛrm, əˈlarm, əˈlarəm/ *v* to frighten or disturb; to warn of danger *la17-*. [see the noun]

alaiven see ELEEVEN

alakanee, alake see ALACK

alamootie, **allamotti**, †**alamonti** /ˈalamuti, ˈalamɔti/ *n* the storm petrel *Hydrobates pelagicus la18- Sh Ork*. [unknown; second element perhaps Norn *muti* a small being, a storm petrel]

alan, **allen** /ˈalən, ˈɑlən/ *n* the Arctic skua *Stercorarius parasiticus 19- Sh Ork*. Compare SCOOTIE-ALAN. **allan-hawk 1** the great northern diver *Gavia immer 19- H&I Uls*. **2** the Arctic skua *Stercorarius parasiticus la19*. [unknown]

†**alandward**, **alandwart** *adv* in or into the countryside *la16-e19*. [A³ + LANDWARD¹·¹]

alane¹·¹, *NE T* **aleen**, †**allane**, †**allone** /əˈlen; *NE T* əˈlin/ *adj* solitary, unaccompanied; unaided; sole, exclusive *la14-*. [ME *all ane*]

alane¹·², *NE T* **aleen**, †**allane** /əˈlen; *NE T* əˈlin/ *adv* only, solely, exclusively; merely, no more than *16-*. [see the adj]

alanerly *see* ALLENARLY¹·¹, ALLENARLY¹·²

alang¹·¹ /əˈlaŋ/ *adv* along *18-*. [OE *andlang*]

alang¹·² /əˈlaŋ/ *prep* along *la16-*. **alangside** beside *19-*. [see the adv]

alangis *see* ALANGST¹·²

alangst¹·¹, *N* **alangse**, †**alongst**, †**alongis**, †**allongs** /əˈlaŋst; *N* əˈlaŋse/ *adv* along *la16-19*, *20- N NE*. †**alangst with**, **alongis with** along with, accompanying, as well as *17-e19*. [OE *andlanges*]

alangst¹·², **alongst**, *Ork* **alonks**, †**alangis**, †**alongis** /əˈlaŋst, əˈlɔŋst; *Ork* əˈlɔŋks/ *prep* along *16-*. [see the adv]

†**alar** *n* a garden walk *16-e18*. [AN *alure* a place to walk in]

alarm, **alarum** *see* ALAIRM¹·¹, ALAIRM¹·²

†**alasant** *n* an Egyptian striped silk *la17-e18*. [AN *alisandrin*, OFr *alexandrin* cloth from Alexandria]

†**alaw** *adv* down, low down *15-19*. Compare ALOW¹·¹. [A³ + LOW¹·²]

alb, †**ab** /alb/ *n* an ecclesiastical vestment with sleeves *15-*. [Lat *alba*]

Albany /ˈalbəne/ *n* one of the Scottish heralds *15-*. **Albany herald** = ALBANY. [Lat *Albānia* Scotland north of Forth and Clyde]

albuist, †**alpuist**, †**apiece** /alˈbuəst/ *conj* although, albeit *la18- NE*. [probably **all beis it* all be it]

†**alcomy**, **accomie** *n* a metal alloy, mainly used for making cutlery *16-e19*. [EModE *alchemy*]

ald *see* AULD¹·²

alderman, †**elderman** /ˈaldərmən, ˈɔldərmən/ *n* the head of a guild; a town provost or magistrate; a bailie *la14-17*, *18- historical*. [OE *alderman* a nobleman, a chief]

alders *see* AULDERS

ald man *see* AULD MAN

Ald Toon, **ald toun** *see* AULD TOON

ald wife *see* AULD WIFE

ale¹·¹, *Sh Ork* **eel**, *N* **ile**, *C Bor* **yill**, †**aill**, †**yeal**, †**yale** /el; *Sh Ork* il; *N* ʌil; *C Bor* jɪl/ *n* **1** an alcoholic drink; a type of beer *la14-*. **2** a non-alcoholic drink, such as lemonade or ginger beer *20- NE T*. **aleberry**, †**ailberrie** ale boiled with bread, sugar, and spice; oatmeal boiled in ale *17-*. †**aillcap**, **ailcop**, **yill-caup** a wooden ale-cup *16-e19*. †**aill cunnare** an official inspector of ale offered for sale *la15-16*. †**aile sellar** a cellar for storing ale *la15-16*. †**aill sellar** an ale-vendor *la16-17*. †**ail tastare** = *aill cunnare 15*. †**aill wand** an official wand or staff indicating that ale is for sale *15-16*. †**yill-wife** a woman who sold ale (of her own brewing) *la18-19*. [OE *ealu*]

†**ale**¹·², **yill** *v* to treat to ale; to drink ale *19*. [see the noun]

aleen *see* ALANE¹·¹, ALANE¹·²

alemosener *see* ELEMOSINAR

alenth /əˈlɛnθ/ *adv* onward, forward, to a more advanced stage in a process *19- Sh N NE T*. [A³ + LENTH¹·¹]

alerm *see* ALAIRM¹·¹, ALAIRM¹·²

ales *see* UNLESS¹·²

aless, **alas**, *Ork NE* **aliss**, †**alace**, †**allace** /əˈlɛs, əˈlas; *Ork NE* əˈlɪs/ *interj* an exclamation expressing grief, sorrow or pain *la14-*. [ME *alas*]

aless *see* UNLESS¹·¹

algate, **a'gait**, **augait** /ˈɔlget, ˈaget, ˈɔget/ *adv* **1** everywhere *19-*. **2** always *la14-16*. [AW¹·² + GATE]

algates, †**a'gates**, †**algatis** /ˈɔlgets/ *adv* always, in any case; in any way; nevertheless *15-*. [ALGATE, with adv-forming suffix]

Alhallow /ɔlˈhalo/ *n* **1** the first of November, All Saints Day *16-20*, *21- historical*. **2** all of the saints collectively *15-18*. **Allhallows day** All Saints Day *la14-*. **Alhallow e'en**, **All Hallows eve** Halloween *la15-*. **All Hallows fair** a fair held in early November in various Scottish towns *16-*. **All Hallowmass**, †**Alhallowmes** the feast of All Saints *15-*. †**All-Hallowtide** the period around All Saints Day *la15-18*. [OE *Alle Hālge*]

aliament *see* ALIMENT¹·¹

alicht¹·¹, **alight**, †**alyght** /əˈlɪxt, əˈlʌɪt/ *v* **1** to shed light on, light up, illuminate *16-*. **2** to set fire to, ignite *16-*. **alichtin** to light up *e16*. [OE *alīhtan*]

alicht¹·², **alight** /əˈlɪxt, əˈlʌɪt/ *adj* on fire; glowing with light *la19-*. [ptp of ALICHT¹·¹]

alicht¹·³, **alight** /əˈlɪxt, əˈlʌɪt/ *adv* on fire, in or into flames; provided with light *la19-*. [see the adj]

alicht², **alight** /əˈlɪxt, əˈlʌɪt/ *v* to dismount, get down; to land, descend *16-*. [OE *alīhtan*]

alicreesh, **allycreesh**, *Bor* **allacreesh**, †**alacreische** /aliˈkriʃ, aleˈkriʃ; *Bor* alaˈkriʃ/ *n* liquorice *la16*, *19- C SW Bor*. [shortened form of *sucker alacreische* (SUGAR); compare SUGARALLIE, LICKERY]

alien *see* AWLIEN

aligaster /əliˈgastər/ *n* disgust *20- NE*. [unknown]

alight *see* ALICHT¹·¹, ALICHT¹·², ALICHT¹·³, ALICHT²

alike¹·¹, *Sh* **alaek**, †**elike**, †**elyk**, †**ylyke** /əˈlʌɪk; *Sh* əˈleək/ *adj* identical; similar *la14-*. †**the elike** the same *la16-e17*. [OE *anlīc*, ON *álíkr*, OE *gelīc*]

alike¹·², *Sh* **alaek**, †**elik**, †**elyke**, †**ylyke** /əˈlʌɪk; *Sh* əˈleək/ *adv* equally, in a like manner *la14-*. [see the adj]

†**alikeways**, **elikeways**, **alykewayes** *adv* likewise *16*. [ALIKE¹·¹, with adv-forming suffix]

†**alikewise**, **elikewise**, **alykewys** *adv* likewise; also *la15-16*. [ALIKE¹·¹, with adv-forming suffix]

aliment¹·¹, †**aliament** /ˈalɪmənt/ *n law* maintenance or support, especially support claimed from another; alimony *la16-*. †**alimentar** connected with maintenance or support *e17*. [MFr *aliment*, Lat *alimentum* food]

aliment¹·² /ˈalɪmənt/ *v* **1** to maintain, support or sustain *la17-*. **2** *law* to make provision for the maintenance (of a person); to provide for *la17-*. [MFr *alimenter* to nourish, sustain]

alishunners *see* ALSHINDERS

alisone *see* ELSHIN

aliss *see* ALESS

alist /əˈlɪst/ *adv* revived (from a swoon) *la18-*. **come alist** to recover consciousness; to wake up *la18-*. [unknown]

alite *see* ALYTE

alkin, **alkind**, **alkynd** *see* A'KIN

†**all**, **al** *conj* even if, although *la14-15*. [perhaps reduced form of ME *albeit*]

all *see* AW¹·¹, AW¹·², AW¹·³

allacay *see* ALLEKAY

allace *see* ALESS

allacreesh *see* ALICREESH

allage *see* ALLEGE

allaik, allake see ALACK
allamotti see ALAMOOTIE
allane see ALANE¹·¹, ALANE¹·²
allanerly see ALLENARLY¹·¹, ALLENARLY¹·²
allan-hawk see ALAN
alla-volie see ALLEVOLIE
allay see ALLEY
†**alleadgeance, allegeance** *n* an allegation or assertion (made in a court of law) *la15-18*. [ME *allegeaunce, allegeance*]
allegance see ALLEGIANCE
allege, †**allage,** †**alleage** /əˈlɛdʒ/ *v* **1** to assert, affirm, claim *la14-*. **2** to appeal; to plead in support of *la15*. †**allege ane remissioun** to appeal or have recourse to a pardon *la16-e17*. [ME *alleggen*]
allegeance see ALLEADGEANCE, ALLEGIANCE
allegiance, †**allegeance,** †**allegance** /əˈlidʒəns/ *n* (sworn) loyalty, fealty *15-*. [ME *alligeaunce*]
†**allekay, allacay** *n* **1** in Angus the best man, the bridegroom's attendant *la18-e19*. **2** a footman, a lackey *16-e17*. [MFr *alacays* a foot-soldier]
allen see ALAN
allenarly¹·¹, *Bor* **alainerly,** †**allanerly,** †**alanerly** /əˈlɛnərle; *Bor* əˈlenərle/ *adj* **1** alone, lonely *20- Bor*. **2** sole, single, only *la15-16*. [**all** (AW¹·³) + ANERLIE¹·¹]
allenarly¹·², †**allanerly,** †**alanerly** /əˈlɛnərle/ *adv* **1** only, solely, exclusively *la14-*. **2** singly, solitarily *la14-e15*. [see the adj]
aller, †**ouler** /ˈalər/ *n* the alder tree *Alnus glutinosa 16-*. [OE *aler*]
allering see ALLOURING
†**alleris, allyris** *adj* of us all, of all of them *la14-e16*. [OE *ealra* genitive plural of *eall*, with genitive ending *-is*]
allevin see ELEEVEN
†**allevolie, alla-volie** *adv* at random *17-e19*. [Fr *à la volée*]
alley, †**aylay,** †**allay,** †**ailay** /ˈale/ *n* **1** a lane or passageway; a narrow street *18-*. **2** a garden walk or path *la15-e17*. †**alley bowlis, alla boulis** the game of bowls *la16-e17*. [ME *alei*]
allicompain see ALACAMPINE
alligrant /ˈaligrant/ *n* a fit of the sulks; a bad mood *20- NE*. [unknown; compare MOLLIGRANT¹·¹]
allocate, †**allocat** /ˈaləket/ *v ptp* also †**allocate** to assign *la16-*. [Lat *allocāt-*, ptp stem of *allocāre*]
allone see ALANE¹·¹
allongs see ALANGST¹·¹
alloo, allow /əˈlu, əˈlʌu/ *v* **1** to credit or grant (a sum of money); to put to one's account *la14-*. **2** to approve, sanction; to permit or let *la15-*. **3** to agree, admit, accept *la16-*. **4** *omitting verb of motion*: to be permitted to go ◊*he was allowed ashore 20-*. **5** to praise, commend *15-16*. [ME *allouen*]
allooance, allowance /əˈluəns, əˈlʌuəns/ *n* **1** a sum of money granted or allotted *la15-*. **2** approval, approbation, sanction; the act of allowing *la16-*. **at nae allooance, at ane allowance** without stint, with the utmost vigour *la18-19, 20- Ork NE T*. [ME *allouaunce, allouance*]
†**allouring, allering, alrinn** *n* the stone pavement placed behind the battlements of a building *16-17*. [ME *alour* a place to walk in, with noun suffix]
allow see ALLOO
allowance see ALLOOANCE
all quhair see A'WHERE
all samyn see ALSAMMYN
all thing see AWTHING
†**alluterly, aluterly, all wtirly** *adv* wholly, completely, entirely, absolutely *la14-19*. [*all* (AW¹·³) + *utterly* (UTTER)]
all wtirly see ALLUTERLY

†**allya¹·¹, allye** *n* **1** an ally or associate *la14-17*. **2** *pl* **allies** members of an alliance *15-17*. **3** alliance, kinship *15-17*. [ME *allie*]
†**allya¹·²** *v* to unite in or enter into alliance *16-17*. [ME *allien*]
†**allyat** *adj* allied *16*. [Latinized form of *allyit*, ptp of ME *ally* or ALLYA¹·²]
allycreesh see ALICREESH
allye see ALLYA¹·¹
allyris see ALLERIS
†**Almaine¹·¹, Almany** *n* Germany *la14-16*. [ME *Alemaine*]
†**Almaine¹·²** *adj* German *16*. **Almaine whistle** a small whistle (originally imported from Germany) *e19*. [see the noun]
almaist see AWMAIST
Almanie whistle see ALMAINE¹·²
Almany see ALMAINE¹·¹
almark /ˈalmark/ *n* a sheep that jumps over or breaks through fences *la19- Sh*. **eil-mark sheep** = ALMARK *19- Sh*. [reduced form of Shetland dial *almark sheep*; compare Norw *ålmark* a common]
almaser see AMOS¹·¹
almast see AWMAIST
alme see AUM¹·¹, AUM¹·²
almeral see ADMIRAL
almery see AUMRY
†**almicht** *adj* only in rhymes almighty *15-e16*. [reduced form of ALMICHTY]
almichty, a'michty, almighty /alˈmɪxte, ɔlˈmɪxte, aˈmɪxte, ɔlˈmʌɪte/ *adj* all powerful, omnipotent; extreme, terrible *15-*. †**almichtine** almighty, powerful *16*. **the Almichty** God *la16-*. [OE *eallmihtig*]
almorie see AUMRY
almosar, almoseir see AMOS¹·¹
almost see AWMAIST
almous, alms see AMOS¹·¹
aloft see ALAFT
alom see AUM¹·¹
alongis, alongst see ALANGST¹·¹, ALANGST¹·²
alonks see ALANGST¹·²
aloor, ill oor /əˈlur, ɪˈlur/ *interj* an expression of anguish or despair *la19- Ork*. [probably ILL¹·³ + OOR¹]
alow¹·¹ /əˈlo/ *adv* below *19-*. Compare ALAW. [A³ + LOW²·² or altered form of BELOW¹·² by analogy with AFORE¹·¹]
alow¹·² /əˈlo/ *prep* below, under *la19-*. [see the adv]
alow² /əˈlʌu/ *adv* on fire, ablaze *19-*. Compare LOWE¹·¹ [A³ + LOW¹·¹]
†**Alpha** *n* God *e16*. [Lat *alpha* first letter of the Greek alphabet]
alpuist see ALBUIST
alquhare see A'WHERE
alrady, already, alreddy see A'READY
alricht see AWRIGHT¹·¹, AWRIGHT¹·²
alrinn see ALLOURING
alrische see ELDRITCH
alrone see ARN
als see AS²·¹, AS²·²
alsa, alsae see ALSO
†**alsammyn, all samyn** *adv* all together *la14-e16*. [*all* (AW¹·³) + *samin* (SAME²·³)]
alse see ALSO
†**alset** *conj* although *la14-15*. [*all* (AW¹·³) + SET¹·⁴]
alshin see ELSHIN
alshinders, alishunners, †**elshinders** /ˈalʃɪndərz, ˈalɪʃʌnərz/ *n* horse-parsley; bishopweed *19, 20- SW*. [altered form of Eng *Alexanders*; AN *alisaundre* wild parsley]

also, alsae, †alse, †alsa, †alswa /ˈɔlso, ˈɔlse/ *adv* in addition, as well, likewise, in the same way; further *la14-*. [OE *alswā*]

alssone *see* AS[2.1]

alsswith as *see* AS[2.2]

alsswyth *see* AS[2.1]

alsswyth as *see* AS[2.2]

alswyith *see* AS[2.1]

alter /ˈɔltər/ *v ptp* also †**alterat** †**alterait** **1** to change *la15-*. **2** *law* to reverse the judgement of a lower court *la18-*. [ME *alteren*]

althing *see* AWTHING

altho, althoch, althocht *see* ALTHOUGH[1.2]

although[1.1] /əlˈθo, ɔlˈðo/ *adv* though, all the same, however: ◊*I wisna invitet but I'm gaun although* 20- *NE H&I EC*. [see the conj]

although[1.2], **altho**, *Sh* **alto**, †**althoch**, †**althocht** /əlˈθo, ɔlˈðo; *Sh* əlˈto/ *conj* **1** even if, despite the fact that; however *la14-*. **2** although it be so, nevertheless: ◊*even although?* *la19, 20- EC*. [*all* (AW[1.3]) + THO[2]]

†**altyme** *adv* at all times, always *la14-e16*. [*all* (AW[1.3]) + TIME]

†**aluff** *adv nautical* close or closer to the wind *e16*. [A[3] + OFr *lof*]

alum *see* AUM[1.1]

alunt /əˈlʌnt/ *adv* alight, on fire *19- SW Bor*. [A[3] + LUNT[1.1]]

†**alurryt** *adj* furnished with ALLOURING, provided with a stone walkway *la14*. [AN, OFr *alure* a place to walk in + -IT[2]]

aluterly *see* ALLUTERLY

alway /ˈɔlwe/ *adv* always *la14-*. [OE *ealneg*]

always, †**alwayis**, †**awayis** /ˈɔlwez/ *adv* **1** at every time; at all times, on all occasions; continually *la14-*. **2** still *la14-*. **3** in any event; nevertheless *la15-*. [ALWAY, with adv-forming suffix]

alwhair *see* A'WHERE

†**alwise** *adv* in every way; always; nevertheless *la16-18*. [*all* (AW[1.2]) + WISE[1]]

alyght *see* ALICHT[1.1]

alykewayes *see* ALIKEWAYS

alykewys *see* ALIKEWISE

†**alyte**, **alyt**, **alite** *adv* a little *la15-16*. [*a* (AW[1]) + ME *lite* little]

am *see* BE

amae *see* AMANG

amagger /əˈmagər/ *adv* in spite of *19, 20- N NE*. [ME *amaugrey*]

amains *see* AMENDS

amaist *see* AWMAIST

†**amal**, **amel** *v* to enamel *16*. [ME *amal* enamel]

amand /əˈmand/ *n* a fine *la16-e19, la19- historical*. [OFr *amende* amends]

amang, **among**, *NE T* **amon**, *NE* **amo**, *T* **amae**, †**imang**, †**emang** /əˈmaŋ, əˈmʌŋ; *NE T* əˈmɔn; *NE* əˈmo; *T* əˈme/ *prep* **1** surrounded by, in the midst of; between, in relation to *la14-*. **2** *with non-count noun* amid, in: ◊*I stuck amang the snaw* 16-. **amang my feet** at or beside my feet *19-*. **amang oor hands** *of work* engaged on, in hand *19-*. **amang you be it** settle it among yourselves *19-*. [OE *āmang*]

amangst, **amongst**, †**amangis** /əˈmaŋst, əˈmʌŋst/ *prep* **1** among, surrounded by, in the midst of *15-*. **2** divided between *15-*. [AMANG, with genitive suffix]

amast *see* AWMAIST

†**ambaxiatour** *n* an ambassador *la15-e16*. [Lat *ambaxiātor*]

†**ambland**, **amland** *adj* ambling *15-e17*. [presp of ME *aumble*]

ambrie *see* AUMRY

ame *see* BE, EEM[1]

†**amedon** *n* a preparation of wheat flour; starch *la16*. [OFr *amidon* starch]

amel *see* AMAL

amend /əˈmend/ *v* **1** to correct; to alter; to improve *la14-*. **2** to make amends *la14-16*. [ME *amenden*]

amends, *NE* **amens**, *NE* **amains**, †**amendis** /əˈmendz; *NE* əˈmenz; *NE* əˈmenz/ *n* compensation, satisfaction, reparation *la14-*. **amends o** revenge, retaliation on, the upper hand of *la18-19, 20- NE*. [ME *amende*]

†**amene** *adj* agreeable, pleasing, pleasant *la15-16*. [Lat *amoenus*]

amens *see* AMENDS

amerale *see* ADMIRAL

amerant *see* EMERANT[1.1], EMERANT[1.2]

amerciate /əˈmersiet/ *v ptp* **amerciat** *law* to fine; to impose a discretionary penalty *la15-*. [Lat *amerciāt-*, ptp stem of *amerciāre*]

amers *see* EMMERS

amerswakk *see* AMMERSWAK

†**amervail**, **amervel** *v* to strike with wonder or surprise *la15-16*. [ME *amervelen* to be astonished]

amery *see* AUMRY

†**ames**, **ameys** *v* to appease, placate; to mitigate, assuage *la14-e16*. [AN *ameiser*, OFr *amaisier*]

amest *see* AWMAIST

a'michty *see* ALMICHTY

†**amid**[1.1], †**amyd** *adv* in the middle *e16*. [OE *onmiddan*]

amid[1.2], †**amyd** /əˈmɪd/ *prep* in the middle (of), among *la14-*. [see the adv]

†**amids**[1.1], **amyds**, **amyddis** *adv* in the midst (of) *la14-19*. [AMID[1.1], with genitive suffix]

†**amids**[1.2], **amyddis**, **ymyddis** *prep* in the midst of *la14-e16*. [see the adv]

†**amidwart**[1.1] *adv* in the middle *e16*. [AMID[1.1], with OE *-weard* suffix]

†**amidwart**[1.2] *prep* in the middle of *e16*. [see the adv]

amind /əˈmʌɪnd/ *adv* in mind (of), disposed (to do) *la18-19, 20- Sh*. [A[3] + MIND[1.1]]

amis *see* AMOS[1.1], AMOS[1.2]

amissing, **amissin** /əˈmɪsɪŋ, əˈmɪsɪn/ *adj* missing; lacking *la16-*. [A[3] + presp of MISS[1.2]]

†**amissioun** *n law* loss *16-e17*. [MFr *amission*, Lat *āmissio*]

amitan /ˈamɪtən/ *n* a foolish person *19- N SW*. [Gael *amadan*]

amiter /ˈamətər/ *n* an infirm or foolish person *20- Ork*. [ON *úmáttugr* weak, infirm]

amland *see* AMBLAND

ammel /ˈaməl/ *n* the swingle-tree of a plough *20- Sh Ork N*. [Norw *humul*]

ammers *see* EMMERS

ammerswak, **amerswakk** /ˈamərswək/ *n* a state of unrest or agitation *20- Sh*. [unknown]

ammunition, †**amonitioune** /amjuˈnɪʃən/ *n* (a supply of) powder, shot or shells; military supplies *la16-*. [MFr *amonition, amunition*]

ammyral *see* ADMIRAL

amna, amnae *see* BE

amo, amon *see* AMANG

amonest *see* ADMONEIS

among *see* AMANG

amongst *see* AMANGST

amonitioune *see* AMMUNITION

amos[1.1], **alms**, *Sh* **aamos**, *Ork* **amis**, *SW Bor* **awmous**, †**almous** /ˈamos, amz; *Sh* ˈaməs; *Ork* ˈamɪs; *SW Bor* ˈɔməs/ *n* **1** food or money given to the poor, a charitable gift or act *la14-*. **2** *ironic* a well-deserved punishment, one's just deserts *la15-19, 20- NE*. **3** a gift offered in a vow or given in fulfilment of a vow; a gift promised in the hope that a wish will be granted to the donor *19- Sh*. **4** payment for a small service; a child's pocket-money *20- NE*. **†almosar, almoseir, almaser** an almoner, an official distributor of alms *la15-e17*; compare ELEMOSINAR. [ON *almusa*, OE *ælmesse*]

amos[1,2], **aamos, amis** /'amos, 'aməs, 'amɪs/ *adj* **1** deserving of charity; pitiable, poor, wretched *la19- Sh Ork*. **2** well-deserved *20- Ork*. [see the noun]

†amour *n* **1** *pl* lovemaking; love affairs *la14-e19*. **2** affection *la15-16*. [ME *amour*]

†amove[1], **amuff** *v* **1** to affect with strong emotion, excite or anger *la14-e16*. **2** to move to action, influence *la14-e16*. **3** to bring about, cause *15*. **4** to be excited *la15*. [eME; OF *amover*, Lat *admovēre*]

†amove[2] *v* to remove; to put or take away *la15-e16*. [Lat *āmovēre*]

amp /amp, ɑmp/ *n* anxiety, watchfulness, restlessness *la19- Sh*. [Norw *ampe* trouble]

ampersyand /'ampərsʌiand/ *n* an ampersand *20-*. Compare EPPERSHAND. [corruption of Eng *and per se and*; compare A PER SE]

†ample, ampill *v* to amplify *16*. [OFr *amplier*]

†amplefeyst, wumplefeyst *n* a sulky humour, the sulks *e19*. [unknown]

amry see AUMRY

amshach, †hamshoch /'amʃəx/ *n* an accident, a misfortune; an injury *la18- NE*. [probably Gael *aimsith* mischance + *-ach* (-OCK)]

amuff see AMOVE[1]

amyd see AMID[1,1], AMID[1,2]

amyddis see AMIDS[1,1], AMIDS[1,2]

amyds see AMIDS[1,1]

an[1], **†ane** /an, ən/ *indef art* **1** before vowels or *h* an *la14-*. **2** before consonants a *la14-e18*. [OE *ān* one; compare A[1]]

an[2], **in, and** /an, ən, ɪn, and, ənd/ *conj* **1** as well as, in addition to, also; along or together with *14-*. **2** if *la14-*. **3** expressing a contrast or objection to the preceding besides, moreover: ◇*an me wi a bad leg tae; and I sae weary, fu o care! la15-*. **4** even if, although *la16-19*. **and some** and more so *la18-*. **and thing** and so on, et cetera *20- Bor*. [OE *and*]

an see ANE[1,1], ANE[1,2], THAN[1,2]

-an see -IN[2]

ana see AN AW, ANNA[2]

an a, an aa see AN AW

anaith see ANEATH[1,1], ANEATH[1,2]

analy see ANNALZIE

anamal see ENAMEL

anarmit see ENARM

an aw, an a, an aa, ana /ə'nɔ, ə'na/ *adv* **1** and everything else: ◇*tae see the kye bedded an a 19-*. **2** besides, also: ◇*I want a piece ana la19-*. **3** giving emphasis as well: ◇*big an strong an aw as she is la19-*. [AN[2] + AW[1,1]]

anawin, †inawing /ə'nɔən/ *adj* **1** of people owing, indebted *la16-19, 20- SW Uls*. **2** of a sum owed *la16-e17*. [AWE, with *in-* verbal prefix]

ance see AINCE[1,1], AINCE[1,2]

anchor-stock see ANKERSTOCK

ancien, ancient see AUNCIENT

†anciente, anciente, ancienitie *n* antiquity *la14-17*. [AN *ancienté*]

and see AN[2]

-and see -IN[2]

Andermas, Andermes, Andersmes see ANDREWSMASS

ando, andoo see AANDOO

Andrea Ferrara, †Andrew Ferrary, †Andro Ferrara /andreə fə'rara/ *n* a Scottish broadsword *19, 20- historical*. [from the name of the 16th century swordsmith *Andrea dei Ferrari*]

Andrewsmass, Andermas, †Andersmes, †Androsmes, †Andermes /'andrusmas, 'andərmas/ *n* St Andrew's Day, 30th November *la15-19, 20- historical*. **Andrewsmass Fair, †Andersmas Fair** a fair held in late November or early December in the towns of Aberdeen, Braemar and Perth *la18-19, 20- historical*. [from the saint's name *Andrew* + MASS[2]]

Andro Ferrara see ANDREA FERRARA

Androsmes see ANDREWSMASS

ane[1,1], **ain, one, wan**, *Sh Ork NE T* **een**, *N* **ein**, *C Bor* **yin**, **†an, †yane, †on** /en, wʌn, wan; *Sh Ork NE T* in; *N* ʌin; *C Bor* jɪn/ *pron* **1** a single person or thing *la14-*. **2** *pl* these or those ones (in particular): ◇*I'll tak them yins* ◇*youse yins'll hae tae hurry* ◇*wherr youse wans gaun? la19-*. **3** a woman: ◇*a braa een 20- Sh N T*. **4** a certain person, someone in particular: ◇*ane telt me to gae up by la14-19*. **eenerie, onerie, †anerie** in children's counting rhymes one *19-*. **eenickie, eenie, †anie** an infant, a baby animal *20- NE*. **ane or twa**, *NE* **een or twa** one or two, a very small number *la14-*. **†in ane 1** unanimously; together *la15-16*. **2** continuously *la14-16*. **†of ane** of all, beyond all: ◇*the best of ane la14-16*. **there's no ane o them tae mend anither** they're all equally bad *19- C Bor*. [OE *ān* one]

ane[1,2], **ain, one, wan**, *Sh Ork NE T* **een**, *N* **ein**, *C Bor* **yin**, **†an, †on, †ȝane** /en, wʌn, wan; *Sh Ork NE T* in; *N* ʌin; *C Bor* jɪn/ *numeral* one, designating a single individual or unit *la14-*. [see the pron]

ane see AN[1]

aneath[1,1], **anaith, aneth** /ə'niθ, ə'neθ, ə'nɛθ/ *adv* beneath, below, under *19-*. [altered from BENEATH[1,1], with prefix *a-* replacing *be-* by analogy with AFORE[1,2] and ATWEEN[1,1]]

aneath[1,2], **anaith, aneth** /ə'niθ, ə'neθ, ə'nɛθ/ *prep* **1** under, below, beneath *16-*. **2** under the authority, control or influence of *19-*. **aneth the breath** in a whisper *la19-*. [see the adv]

anee /ə'ni/ *interj* a cry of lamentation *19, 20- SW Uls*; compare *alakanee* (ALACK), *ochanee* (OCHONE). [perhaps reduced form of *ochanee* (OCHONE)]

aneest[1,1], **†aneist, †aneixt** /ə'nist/ *adv* next *la15-19, 20- NE*. [A[3] + NEIST[1,2]]

aneest[1,2], **†aneist, †anist, †anext** /ə'nist/ *prep* **1** nearest or next to, adjoining, adjacent to *la15-19, 20- Bor*. **2** on this side of, not as far as; short of (an outcome) *18-19, 20- NE*. [see the adv]

†anefald, anefauld *adj* sincere, honest *la15-e17*; compare AEFAULD (sense 2). **anefaldly** honestly, sincerely *16*. [ANE[1,2] + FAULD[1,1]]

aneist see ANEEST[1,1], ANEEST[1,2]

aneival /ə'nivəl/ *adv* upside down, tumbled over *20- N*. [wrong division of *on aival* (AVAL[1,3])]

aneixt see ANEEST[1,1]

†ane levin *numeral* eleven *16-e17*. Compare ELEEVEN. [misinterpretation of the first vowel as numeral and expansion to ANE[1,2]]

anely[1,1], **ainly, ainlie, only, †onlie** /'enle, 'onle/ *adj* sole, single *la14-*. [OE *ǣnlīc*]

anely[1,2], **ainly, ainlie, only, †anly, †onely** /'enle, 'onle/ *adv* solely, exclusively; merely *la14-*. [see the adj]

anenst, †anens, †anentis /ə'nɛnst/ *prep* **1** over against; opposite *la14-*. **2** in respect of, concerning *la14-*. [ANENT, with genitive suffix]

anent /ə'nɛnt/ *prep* **1** opposite, in front of, before *la14-*. **2** concerning, about; in view of *la14-*. **3** in a line with; on a

level with, alongside of *19-*. **4** in the presence of *la14-15, 20- NE*. [OE *on efen* on even ground, near]
anentis *see* ANENST
anerie *see* ANE[1.1]
anerlie[1.1], **anerly** /'anərle/ *adj* only, lone, single; alone *la14-*. [altered form of ANELY[1.1]; compare ALLENARLY[1.1]]
anerlie[1.2], **anerly** /'anərle/ *adv* only, solely *la14-*. [see the adj]
anes *see* AINCE[1.1], AINCE[1.2]
anes-eerand *see* AINCE ERRAND[1.2]
aneth *see* ANEATH[1.1], ANEATH[1.2]
anet seed *see* ENNET SEID
aneuch *see* ENEUCH[1.1], ENEUCH[1.2], ENEUCH[1.3]
anew *see* ENEW[1.1], ENEW[1.2]
anext *see* ANEEST[1.2]
angeller *see* ANGULAR
anger[1.1], †**angir** /'aŋgər, 'aŋər/ *n* **1** a feeling of displeasure or hostility; rage, wrath *la14-*. **2** a cause of vexation; distress, grief *la14-19, 20- NE*. **3** a fit or spell of rage *la16-e19*. **angersome** causing anger, provocative, vexatious *19-*. [ON *angr* trouble, affliction]
anger[1.2] /'aŋgər, 'aŋər/ *v pt* also †**angrit 1** to make angry *la14-*. **2** to become angry *la15-e19*. **3** to distress or trouble *la14-e15*. [ON *angra* to vex]
angilberre *see* ANGLEBERRY
angir *see* ANGER[1.1]
anglar *see* ANGULAR
angleberry, *EC SW* **ingleberry**, †**angilberre** /'aŋgəlbɛri; *EC SW* 'ɪŋgəlbɛri/ *n* a fleshy growth or sarcoid on horses, cattle or sheep *la16-*. [unknown]
angrit *see* ANGER[1.2]
†**angular, angeller, anglar** *n* a brace-piece or tie in the interior angle of a wooden frame *16-e17*. [Lat *angulāris* angular]
Angus /'aŋgəs/ *n* **1** a former county in eastern Scotland *12-*. **2** the name of a breed of cattle, the *Aberdeen Angus* (ABERDEEN) *19-*. **Angus doddies** a breed of hornless cattle *19-*. †**Angus herald** *heraldry* a Scottish herald *la15*. [perhaps from Gael *Oengus*, a personal and tribal name]
†**anherd, enherde, inherd** *v* **1** to adhere to, join with (a person or party) *la14-16*. **2** to hold firmly to; to consent to *15-e16*. **anherdance, inherdance** adherents, supporters *15-e16*. **anherdandis** adherents *la15-e16*. [OFr *enherdre*]
anidder *see* ANITHER[1.1], ANITHER[1.2]
an'int *see* ANOINT
anis *see* AINCE[1.1], AWN[1]
anis eirand *see* AINCE ERRAND[1.2]
anist *see* ANEEST[1.2]
anither[1.1], **another**, *Sh Ork NE* **anidder**, †**anothir** /ə'nɪðər, ə'nʌðər; *Sh Ork NE* ə'nɪdər/ *adj* a second, further or different person or thing *la14-*. †**anither sang** a different attitude *la18-e19*. [AN[1] + ITHER[1.1]]
anither[1.2], **another**, *Sh Ork NE* **anidder**, †**anothir** /ə'nɪðər, ə'nʌðər; *Sh Ork NE* ə'nɪdər/ *pron* a second, further or different person or thing *15-*. [see the adj]
anker /'aŋkər/ *n* a liquid or dry measure, 8⅓ gallons (approx 38 litres) *18- Sh Ork N*. [Du *anker*]
†**ankersaidell, hankersaidil** *n* an anchorite, a hermit *16-e17*. [OE *ancorsetl* a hermit's cell]
ankerstock, †**anchor-stock** /'aŋkərstɔk/ *n* a large, long loaf (of rye-bread) *19, 20- historical*. **ankerstock gingerbread** a large, long loaf of gingerbread (made with rye flour and seasoned with spices and currants) *20-*. [from supposed resemblance to an *anchor-stock*]
†**anklet, ankleth, hanckleth** *n* the ankle *15-19*. [OE *ancleōw* ankle + OE *lið* a limb]

anly *see* ANELY[1.2]
anmark, onmark /'anmark, 'ɔnmark/ *n* a troublesome animal or person *20- Ork N*. Compare ALMARK. [ON *annmarki* a defect, a flaw]
†**ann** *n* an ANNAT *17-18*. [shortened form of ANNAT or ANNA[1]]
ann *see* YAWIN
†**anna**[1], **annay** *n* an ANNAT *la15-e16*. [MFr *annate*]
anna[2], †**ana**, †**annay** /'anə/ *n* a river island, a holm *17- EC Bor*. †**annay land** alluvial land, land exposed to inundation *la18-e19*. [unknown]
Annacker's midden, Annicker's midden /anəkərz 'mɪdən/ *n* a mess, a dreadful muddle *la20-*. [from the surname of a Glasgow pork butcher + MIDDEN[1.1]]
†**annalzie, annailʒe, analy** *v law* to transfer (property) to the ownership of another, alienate *15-e19*. [unexplained variant of Older Scots *alien*]
†**annat** *n* **1** *law* the stipend or income of a charge or benefice for the (half) year after the death paid to the estate of a deceased incumbent *16-18*. **2** *Roman Catholic Church* the first year's revenue of a see or benefice paid to the Pope *la16-17*. [MFr *annate*]
annay *see* ANNA[1], ANNA[2]
annet seid *see* ENNET SEID
annex, annexe /'anɛks/ *n* **1** an addition (to a building or property); an appendix to a document *la19-*. **2** *law* an appurtenance of property *16-e19*; compare CONNEX. [MFr *annexe*, Lat *annexus*]
Annicker's midden *see* ANNACKER'S MIDDEN
anniuersar *see* ANNIVERSAR[1.2]
anniversar[1.1] /anɪ'vɛrsər, 'anɪvɛrsər/ *n* **1** (a celebration marking) the yearly recurrence of the date of a past event *la15-*. **2** (a payment for) a mass said annually on the anniversary of a person's death *15-16*. [see the adj]
anniversar[1.2], †**anniuersar** /anɪ'vɛrsər, 'anɪvɛrsər/ *adj* recurring annually, annual *15-*. [Lat *anniversārius*]
anno *see* AANDOO
annorn *see* ENOURN
annoy *see* ENNOY
annoynt *see* ANOINT
anns /anz, anz/ *npl* the chaff or husks of oats or other grain *la19- Sh T*. [ON *agnar* husks, plural of *ögn*]
annual[1.1], †**onwal**, †**annuel** /'anjuəl/ *n* **1** yearly interest on money *la16-19, 20- N*. **2** an annual payment of rent, quit-rent or duty *la14-19*. †**annuallar, annuellar** one who receives an annual rent *la16*. [see the adj]
annual[1.2], *NE* **annwal**, *NE* **onwal**, †**anwall** /'anjuəl; *NE* 'anwəl; *NE* 'ɔnwəl/ *adj* occurring yearly *18-*. [ME, OFr *anuel*]
annualrent, †**annuel rent**, †**anwall rent** /'anjuəlrɛnt/ *n* **1** rent paid yearly *15-*. **2** interest on borrowed money *17-*. [ANNUAL[1.2] + RENT[2]]
annuel *see* ANNUAL[1.1]
annwal *see* ANNUAL[1.2]
anoint, *NE* **an'int**, †**enoynt**, †**annoynt**, †**anoynt** /ə'nɔɪnt, ə'nʌɪnt; *NE* ə'nint/ *v ptp* also †**envnte 1** to smear (with ointment) *la14-*. **2** to beat, thrash *20- NE*. [ME *enointen*]
anonder *see* ANUNDER
anone *see* ON-ANE
anoo *see* AANDOO
anorn *see* ENOURN
another, anothir *see* ANITHER[1.1], ANITHER[1.2]
anouch *see* ENEUCH[1.1], ENEUCH[1.2], ENEUCH[1.3]
anournement *see* ENORNAMENT
anower *see* INOWER[1.2]
anoy *see* ENNOY
anoynt *see* ANOINT
anoyous *see* ENNOYUS

anse *see* ENSE
ansenȝe *see* ENSENYIE
anshent *see* AUNCIENT
anslacht *see* ONSLAUCHT
answer[1.1], †**answar**, †**ansuer**, †**ansowr** /'ansər/ *n* a reply, a response; a solution *la14-*. [OE *andswaru*]
answer[1.2], †**ansuere**, †**ansueir** /'ansər/ *v* **1** to reply or respond; to account for *la14-*. **2** *law* (to appear before an authority) to reply to a charge *15-*. **3** to respond to a command, obey *la14-19, 20- Sh Ork NE*. **4** to look good in, suit: ◊*I always answered pink 20- C*. **5** to requite, compensate (a person) *16*. [OE *andswarian*]
ant *see* AUNT, ENT
†**antecessour** *n* a predecessor (in office); an ancestor or forefather *15-e17*. [MFr *antecesseur*, Lat *antecessor* predecessor in office]
†**antecestor** *n* = ANTECESSOUR *16-17*. [ANTECESSOUR, with influence from *ancestor*]
†**antefit, antefute** *n* a part of a hood or other headgear *e17*. Compare TIPPET (sense 1). [unknown]
†**antepend** *n Christian Church* a covering for the front of an altar *16*. [Lat *antependulus* hanging before]
†**anter**[1.1], **aunter** *n* **1** an adventure, an enterprise *15-e16*. **2** chance, risk; fortune *la15-16*. **anterous, aunterus** adventurous *la15-16*. **antercast** a misfortune, a mischance *la18-e19*. [ME *aunter*]
†**anter**[1.2], **awntyr** *v* **1** to venture; to risk *la14-18*. **2** to chance upon, find by chance *la18-e19*. [ME *auntren*]
Antiburgher /'antibʌrgər/ *n Presbyterian Church* a member of that section of the Secession Church which seceded over the burgess oath *la18-19, 20- historical*. Compare BURGHER. [Lat *anti-* against + BURGHER]
antisyzygy, antisizigy /anti'sızıdʒi/ *n* a union of opposites; the presence of duelling polarities within one entity *20-*. Compare *Caledonian antisyzygy* (CALEDONIAN[1.2]) and *Scottish antisyzygy* (SCOTS[1.2]). [Greek *anti* opposite + Greek *syzygia* union]
antle /'antəl/ *v* to complain repetitively, grumble; to nag, insist on *20- N SW*. [compare ON *annt* eager, anxious; pressing]
antran *see* ANTRIN[1.2]
antrin[1.1] /'antrın/ *n* an occasional one *la19- NE T*. [verbal noun from ANTER[1.2]]
antrin[1.2], *NE* **antran**; *Bor* **hantrin** /'antrın; *NE* 'antrən; *Bor* 'hantrın/ *adj* **1** occasional, single; rare *la18-*. **2** odd, peculiar, strange *20- literary*. [presp of ANTER[1.2]]
†**antrum** *n* in the South-West, (the meal taken in) the afternoon or early evening *19*. [OE *undern* morning]
anunder, †**anonder** /ə'nʌndər/ *prep* under, beneath *la16-19, 20- Sh Ork NE Bor Uls*. [ME *anunder*]
anwall *see* ANNUAL[1.2]
anwall rent *see* ANNUALRENT
anxeeity, anxiety /aŋ'ziəte, aŋ'zaeəte/ *n* anxiousness, concern, worry *18-*. [Lat *anxietās*]
anyoch *see* ENEUCH[1.2], ENEUCH[1.3]
anyow *see* ENEW[1.1]
anys *see* AINCE[1.1], AINCE[1.2]
apae *see* UPON
apairt, apert, apart /ə'pert, ə'pɛrt, ə'part/ *adv* separate, aside, in or to pieces *16-*. [MFr *à part*]
apane *see* APAYN
†**apardoun, aperdon, appardone** *v* to pardon, forgive; to make allowances for, excuse *16-e17*. [ME *pardoune*, with *a-* prefix]
apart *see* APAIRT

apartment /ə'partmɛnt/ *n* a room in a house or flat (excluding the kitchen and bathroom): ◊*a three-apartment waterfront flat la20- C*. [Fr *appartement*]
†**apayn, apane** *adv* by chance, possibly; with difficulty *la14-e16*. **apayn of** on pain of, under the penalty of *15*. [OFr *a peine* in or with difficulty]
ape, †**aip**, †**yape** /ep/ *n* **1** an ape or monkey *la15-*. **2** a foolish person *16-*. [OE *apa*]
apen *see* OPEN[1.2], OPEN[1.3]
aper *see* APPER
aperdon *see* APARDOUN
Aperell *see* APRILE
†**a per se, e per sie** *n* someone or something unique or pre-eminent, a paragon *la15-16*. [ME *A* the letter + Lat *per sē* by itself, a formula used of a symbol which itself forms a word; compare AMPERSYAND]
†**apert** *adj* open; bold *la14-16*. **in apert** in an open or overt manner; in public *la14-15*. [ME *apert*, Lat *apertus*]
apert *see* APAIRT
apeynt *see* APPOINT
apiece *see* ALBUIST
apill *see* AIPPLE
apil trie *see* AIPPLE
apin *see* OPEN[1.2]
†**apirsmert, apirsmart** *adj* sharp, severe *e16*. [probably OFr *aspre* harsh + SMERT[1.3]]
aple *see* AIPPLE
apo, apon *see* UPON
aponlande *see* UPONLAND
apont *see* APPOINT
†**aporte, apport** *n* bearing, demeanour *la14-e16*. [OFr *port* demeanour]
†**apostata** *n* an apostate *15-16*. [Lat *apostata*]
†**aposteme** *n* a large abscess *16-17*. [ME *apostem*, EModE *aposteme*, Lat *apostēma*]
†**apostol, apostil, apostill** *n* an apostle *la14-e17*. [OE *apostol*, originally from Greek]
†**apothecarie, ypothecary, hipoticary** *n* a person who prepared and sold medicines *16-18*. Compare APOTHICAR, POTHECAR, POTICARY, POTTINGAR and IPOTINGAR. [ME *apothecarie*, EModE *apothecarie*, Lat *apothēcārius* a warehouseman]
apotheck *see* HYPOTHEC
†**apothicar, ipotecar, ypothegar** *n* an apothecary *16-18*. Compare APOTHECARIE, POTHECAR, POTICARY, POTTINGAR and IPOTINGAR. [OFr *apotecaire*, Lat *apothēcārius* a warehouseman]
†**appair, appare** *v* to injure or damage; to impair *la15-16*. [ME *apeiren*, EModE *appayre*, to worsen]
appale *see* APPEAL[1.1], APPEAL[1.2]
apparand *see* APPEARAND[1.2]
appardone *see* APARDOUN
appare *see* APPAIR
apparelling, appareling, †**apparaling,** †**apperrelling** /ə'parəlıŋ/ *n* **1** equipment, rigging; dress, attire *la14-*. **2** the action of making ready or fitting out *la15-e17*. [verbal noun from ME *aparail*]
†**apparitour** *n* a court officer or sergeant *la15-e16*. [Lat *apparātor* one who prepares]
appatite *see* APPETEET
appeal[1.1], *NE* **appale**, †**appell**, †**appele** /ə'pil; *NE* ə'pel/ *n* **1** an earnest request or entreaty *15-*. **2** *law* an application to a higher court (for the reversal of a decision of a lower court) *15-*. **3** a challenge *la15-e19*. [ME *apel*]
appeal[1.2], *NE* **appale**, †**appel**, †**appelle** /ə'pil; *NE* ə'pel/ *v* **1** to make an earnest request or entreaty *la14-*. **2** *law* to apply to a higher court (for the reversal of a decision of a lower

appearance

court) *la14-*. **3** to charge or accuse *15-16*. **4** to challenge *la15-16*. [ME *apelen*]

appearance, †**apperance**, †**apperans** /əˈpɪrəns/ *n* the action or fact of appearing; an outward impression or condition *15-*. †**be apperance** seemingly, apparently *la15-16*. [ME *aparaunce*, Lat *appārentia*]

†**appearand**[1.1], **appeirand** *n* an heir apparent *la15-17*. [see the adj]

†**appearand**[1.2], **apparand**, **apperand** *adj* apparent; likely, intended *la14-18*. **appearand air**, **apperand air** heir apparent *la14-e18*. [presp of ME *appere*]

appearandly, †**appeirandlie** /əˈpɪrəndli/ *adv* apparently, evidently, obviously *la15-19*, *20-* NE. [APPEARAND[1.2], with adv-forming suffix]

appearingly, **appearinly**, †**apperinglie**, †**appeiringlie** /əˈpɪrɪŋli, əˈpɪrɪnli/ *adv* apparently, seemingly *la16-*. [presp of ME *appere*, with adv-forming suffix]

appeirand *see* APPEARAND[1.1]
appeirandlie *see* APPEARANDLY
appeiringlie *see* APPEARINGLY
appel *see* APPEAL[1.2]
appele, **appell** *see* APPEAL[1.1]
appelle *see* APPEAL[1.2]

append /əˈpɛnd/ *v* **1** to add (an appendix or supplement) to the end of a document *18-*. **2** to hang or attach (a seal to a document) *la15-e18*. [Lat *appendere*]

†**appense** *v* to append (a seal) to a document *la15-16*. [MFr *appenser*]

apper, **aper** /ˈapər/ *v* to detain, recall; to hinder *la19-* Sh. [ON *aptra* to take back, hinder, withdraw]

apperance *see* APPEARANCE
apperand *see* APPEARAND[1.2]
apperans *see* APPEARANCE
apperinglie *see* APPEARINGLY
apperrelling *see* APPARELLING
appeteesement *see* APPETIZE

appeteet, **appetite**, †**eppiteet**, †**appetyte**, †**appatite** /ˈapətit, ˈapətʌɪt/ *n* hunger, a desire for food; physical desire or inclination *la14-*. [ME *apetit*, Lat *appetītus*]

†**appetize** *v* to cause to feel hungry *la18-e19*. **appetized**, **appetezed** having an appetite, hungry *la18-e19*. **appeteesement** appetite, hunger *e19*. [Fr *appétissant* appetizing]

appety /ˈapəti/ *n* appetite *19-*. [Fr *appétit*]
appetyte *see* APPETEET
appil *see* AIPPLE
appin *see* OPEN[1.3]
appint *see* APPOINT
apple *see* AIPPLE
appleis *see* APPLESE
appleringie *see* AIPPLERINGIE

†**applese**, **appleis** *v* to please; to gratify or satisfy *la15-e17*. [A[3] + PLEASE[1.2]]

apply /əˈplae/ *v* **1** to utilize, employ, put to use; to be applicable or appropriate *la15-*. **2** to put something onto the skin or other surface *la15-*. **3** to make an application *la17-*. **4** to attach oneself to, give support to (a person or party) *15-16*. **5** to incline, be inclined *la15-16*. [ME *applien*, *aplīen*]

appoint, *NE* **appint**, *SW* **apeynt**, †**appoinct**, †**apont**, †**appunct** /əˈpɔɪnt/; *NE* əˈpɪnt; *SW* əˈpent/ *v ptp* also †**appunctuat** to determine or decree; to assign (a role or job) *15-*. **appointment**, †**appunctment 1** an arrangement to meet *17-*. **2** a placement in or appointment to an office or position *18-*. **3** a settlement or agreement *15-18*. [Lat *appunctuāre*]

appone *see* OPPONE
apport *see* APORTE

appreciate, †**appretiate** /əˈpriʃɪet/ *v ptp* also †**appreciate 1** to be grateful for, regard highly; to recognize, comprehend *la18-*. **2** *law* to appraise, estimate the value of *16-18*. [Lat *appretiāt-*, ptp stem of *appretiāre*]

appreciation, **appretiation** /əpriʃɪˈeʃən/ *n* **1** *law* the valuing of property or (poinded) goods *la17-*. **2** critical appraisal, recognition of value; gratitude *19-*. [AN, MFr *appreciation*]

apprehend /aprəˈhɛnd/ *v* **1** to catch, arrest, take into custody *16-*. **2** to understand *la16-*. **3** to find and seize goods *la15-17*. **4** to come upon, find (a person) *la15-e17*. [MFr *apprehender*, Lat *apprehendere*]

appreif *see* APPRUVE
appretiate *see* APPRECIATE
appretiation *see* APPRECIATION
appreve *see* APPRUVE

apprise /əˈpraez/ *v* **1** to appraise, estimate the value of (goods or property); *law* to value and sell a debtor's property to pay off the debt *16-*. **2** to appreciate, prize *16*. [ME *aprisen*]

apprisement /əˈpraezmənt/ *n* an appraisement, an estimation of value (of goods or property prior to sale) *la18-*. [OFr *aprisement*]

†**appriser**, **appryser** *n* a valuer or appraiser; *law* a creditor who appraises a debtor's land *la16-e19*. [APPRISE, with agent suffix]

approbate[1.1] /ˈaprəbet/ *v law* to approve as valid *la18-*. **approbate and reprobate** to assent to part of a deed and object to the rest (a course disallowed by law) *la18-e19*. [see the adj]

†**approbate**[1.2], **approbat** *adj* approved, sanctioned *16*. [Lat *approbātus*]

†**appropry**, **appropir**, **approper** *v* to assign possession of property; to appropriate, take possession of *15-16*. [ME *appropren*]

appruve, **approve**, **appruv**, †**appreve**, †**appreif** /əˈpruv, əˈprʌv/ *v ptp* **approved** †**approvit 1** to affirm, sanction; to commend *la14-*. **2** to prove, demonstrate *la15-16*. [ME *apreven*]

appryser *see* APPRISER
appunct *see* APPOINT

Aprile, **April**, *NE* **Awprile**, *NE* **Awpril**, †**Aprill**, †**Aperell**, †**Apreill** /əˈprʌɪl, ˈeprɪl; *NE* ˈɔprʌɪl; *NE* ˈɔprɪl/ *n* the fourth month of the year *la14-*. **Aprile eeran**, **April erran** an errand on which an April fool is sent *18-*. **April gowk** an April fool *19-*. [Lat *Aprīlis*]

aprin, **apron**, *NE* **aapron**, *NE* **ahpron**, *NE* **awpron**, †**aproun**, †**naperon**, †**naiproun** /ˈeprən; *NE* ˈaprən; *NE* ˈɔprən/ *n* **1** a protective garment worn over the clothes, an apron *14-*. **2** *in plumbing* a strip of lead folded over the edge of a gutter to conduct rain-water into it *19-*. **3** the abdomen of a crab *la19-*. **apron washing** an initiation rite of apprentices *la19-* NE. [ME *napron*]

apud acta /apud ˈakta/ *adv of notices given in open court during the proceedings la15-*. [Lat *apud acta*]

aqua, †**ackwa** /ˈakwə/ *n* whisky *19*, *20-* Sh H&I. [reduced form of AQUAVITAE]

aqual *see* EQUAL[1.1], EQUAL[1.2]

aquavitae, **aquavita**, †**acavite**, †**ackavity**, †**awka veety** /akwəˈvite, akwəˈvita/ *n* spirits; whisky *la15-*. [Lat *aqua vītae* water of life]

ar[1.1] /ar/ *n* a slight movement *20-* Sh. [see the verb]

ar[1.2] /ar/ *v* to move feebly *20-* Sh. [compare Norw dial *arra* to walk with difficulty]

ar *see* AIR[2], AIR[3], ER

-ar *see* -ER

Arab /'arəb/ *n* **1** a nickname for a Dundee United Football Club supporter *20-.* **2** *pl* a nickname for Dundee United Football Club *20-.* [perhaps because of the use of a lot of sand on their pitch after adverse weather in 1963]

arage, arriage, †arrage, †harrage, †average /'arədʒ/ *n* feudal service including the carriage of goods, or payment in lieu, due by a tenant to his landlord *la15-19, 20- historical.* **arriage and carriage, †harrage and carrage** = ARAGE. [AN *average*, perhaps from OFr *averail* possessions, livestock]

araise *see* ARISE

arang *see* HARANGUE

arange *see* ARREENGE

arasees, arrasees /'arasiz/ *npl* tricks, capers *20- Ork.* [Norn *arasees*]

arays *see* ARISE

arbiter[1], **†arbitour** /'arbɪtər/ *n law* a person appointed to decide in a dispute between parties, an arbitrator *la15-.* [Lat *arbiter*]

†arbiter[2] *n* will, pleasure; arbitration *la15-16.* [ME *arbitre*, Lat *arbitrium* free will]

arbitral, †arbitrale, †arbitrall /'arbɪtrəl/ *adj law* relating to or resulting from the use of an arbitrator *la15-.* [Lat *arbitrālis*]

†arbitrar *adj law* relating to or resulting from the use of an arbitrator *la16-17.* [MFr *arbitraire*, Lat *arbitrārius*]

arbitrator, †arbitratour /'arbɪtretər/ *n* a person appointed to decide in a dispute between parties *la14-.* [MFr *arbitrateur*, OFr *arbitreor*, Lat *arbitrātor*]

Arbroath Smokie /ar'broθ 'smoki/ *n* a haddock smoked whole in Arbroath *la19-.* [from the place-name *Arbroath* + SMOKIE]

arch *see* AIRCH[1.1], AIRCH[1.2], ERCH[1.1], ERCH[1.3]

archebischop *see* ARCHIBISCHOP

archedekyne *see* ARCHIDIACONE

†archedene, archidene, ersdene *n* an archdeacon *la14-e17.* [Lat *archidiāconus*]

†archibischop, archebischop, arsbischop *n* an archbishop *15-e17.* [Lat *archiepiscopum*, OE *arcebiscop*]

archidene *see* ARCHEDENE

†archidiacone, archedekyne *n* an archdeacon *15-16.* [Lat *archidiāconus*]

archilowe, archilagh *n* a drink offered in return for one received *e19.* [unknown]

archly *see* ERCH[1.3]

†archpriestrie *n* the office of head priest (at Dunbar) *la16-e17.* [EModE *archprest*, with noun-forming suffix]

arct *see* AIRT[3]

are *see* AIR[1], AIR[5.2], BE, EAR[2]

a'ready, awreddie, already, †alreddy, †alrady /a'redi, ɔ'redi, əl'redi/ *adv* at or prior to this time *16-.* [ME *al redie* all ready]

†arear, areir *adv* **1** behind, in the rear or background *la15-19.* **2** backwards *la15-16.* [A[3] + REAR; compare ME *arrēre*]

†areke, areik *v* to reach *e16.* [OE *aræcan*]

arel *see* ARL

arena, arenae *see* BE

arer *see* HEIR[1.2]

arest *see* ARREIST[1.1], ARREIST[1.2]

arestment *see* ARREISTMENT

†arettit *adj* accused *la14-15.* [ME *aretten* to accuse]

†arff, eerif *n in Shetland and Orkney* inheritance; (a court held for) the division of property among heirs *16-19.* [ON *arfr*]

†argentar, argenter *n* the officer having charge of royal finances *16.* [MFr *argentier*, Lat *argentārius* a money-changer]

†argentie *n* a type of fabric *la16-e17.* [probably Fr *argenté* silvered]

argew *see* ARGIE[1.2]

argh *see* ERCH[1.3]

argie[1.1] /'argi/ *n* an assertion *19-.* [see the verb]

argie[1.2], **argyie, argue, †argu, †argew** /'argi, 'argjə, 'argju/ *v* **1** to dispute, call in to question; to reason for or against, quarrel *la14-.* **2** to accuse *la14-e16.* [ME *arguen*]

argie-bargie[1.1], **argy-bargy** /'ardʒi'bardʒi/ *n* a quarrel, a disturbance *la19-.* [rhyming compound from ARGIE[1.2]]

argie-bargie[1.2], **argy-bargy** /'ardʒi'bardʒi/ *v* to quarrel, cause a disturbance *la19-.* [see the noun]

argify, argufy, arguify, argufee, †argifee /'argɪfae, 'argjufae, 'argjufi/ *n* to argue *la18-.* [ARGIE[1.2], with verb suffix]

†argle-bargain, aurgle-bargain *v* to dispute *18-e19.* Compare HAGGLE-BARGAIN[1.2]. [conflation of ARGLE-BARGLE[1.2] with BARGAIN[1.2]]

argle-bargle[1.1] /'argəl'bargəl/ *n* contention, dispute; a quarrel *la19-.* **argle-barglous** quarrelsome *19-.* [perhaps a rhyming compound based on ARGIE[1.2]]

argle-bargle[1.2], **†argol-bargol, †hargle-bargle** /'argəl-'bargəl/ *v* to dispute; to quarrel *19-.* [see the noun]

argown *see* ARGUN

argu, argue *see* ARGIE[1.2]

argufee, argufy, arguify *see* ARGIFY

argument *see* AIRGUMENT

†argun, argown *v* to argue, hold an argument *la15-e17.* [ARGIE[1.2]]

argy-bargy *see* ARGIE-BARGIE[1.1], ARGIE-BARGIE[1.2]

argyie *see* ARGIE[1.2]

Argyll, Argyle, †Ergyll, †Ergile, †Ergyle /ar'gʌɪl/ *n* **1** a former county in western Scotland *la15-.* **2** a pattern of fabric based on the tartan of the Argyll branch of the Campbell clan *19-.* **Argyllshire Highlanders** a Scottish regiment raised in 1794; linked in 1881 with the Sutherland Highlanders to form the *Argyll and Sutherland Highlanders* (Princess Louise's) *la18-19, 20- historical.* **Argyll and Sutherland Highlanders** a Scottish regiment formed in 1881 from the *Argyllshire Highlanders* and the *Sutherland Highlanders* (SUTHERLAND) *la19-20, 21- historical.* [Gael *Oirer Gháidheal*, IrGael *Airer Gáidel*]

ari /'ari/ *n* the first slight movement of the water after the turn of the tide *20- Sh.* [compare AR[1.1]]

aricht /ə'rɪxt/ *adv* correctly, properly *16-.* [OE *arīht*]

arise, †arays /ə'raez/ *v pt* **araise, arose, †arays** to rise, get up or start up *16-.* [A[3] + RISE[1.2]]

ark[1], **airk** /ark, erk/ *n* **1** Noah's Ark *15-.* **2** a large chest (for storing grain or fruit) *15-.* **3** something large or unwieldy *20- Sh Ork.* **4** an enclosure for confining or catching fish *18-19*; compare *eel ark* (EEL). **5** the Ark of the Covenant *la15-17.* [OE *arc*]

ark[2] /ark/ *n* the curved structure which carries the water off from a breast-shot mill-wheel; the waterway under a mill-wheel *la18-.* Compare AIRCH[1.1]. [probably Lat *arcus* a bow]

ark *see* AIRCH[1.1]

arl, arel /arl, 'arəl/ *v* to crawl or move feebly *20- Sh.* [unknown; compare AR[1.2]]

arle, erl /arl, ɛrl/ *v* **1** to engage for service by payment of earnest money; to hire or rent *la14-.* **2** to become engaged to be married; to marry *19, 20- C.* **3** to secure a right or an outcome *19.* [from the noun ARLES]

†arle penny, airle penny *n* earnest money *18-e19.* Compare *arlis penny* (ARLES). [ARLES + PENNY]

arles, erles, *Bor* **airles, †arlis, †erlis** /arlz, ɛrlz; *Bor* erlz/ *npl* **1** money given to seal a bargain (in confirmation of engagement of services), earnest money *la15-.* **2** a foretaste (of

arm | 20 | **aschame**

something more to come) *15-19.* †**arlis penny, erlispennie** earnest money *la16-17*; compare ARLE PENNY. [probably ME *erles*]
arm *see* AIRM¹, AIRM²
arme *see* AIRM¹
armee, armie *see* AIRMY
†**armipotent, armypotent** *adj* mighty in arms *16.* [Lat *armipotens*]
armony *see* HARMONY
armour *see* AIRMOUR
army *see* AIRM¹, AIRMY
armypotent *see* ARMIPOTENT
arn, ern, †**alrone** /arn, ɛrn/ *n* the alder tree *Alnus glutinosa la15-19, 20- NE T*. Compare ALLER. [OE *aler*]
arna *see* BE
arnit, arnut, ernit /ˈarnɪt, ˈarnʌt, ˈɛrnɪt/ *n* an edible plant root, earthnut *Bunium bulbocastanum* or *Conopodium majus 16-*. Compare HORNECK. [OE *eorð hnutu*]
aroon¹·¹, **aroond, around,** †**arown** /əˈrun, əˈrund, əˈrʌund/ *adv* (round) about; on every side; in a circle *la16-*. [ME *aroun*]
aroon¹·², **aroond, around** /əˈrun, əˈrund, əˈrʌund/ *prep* (in a circle) around; on all sides of; encompassing; throughout *17-*. [ME *around*]
arose *see* ARISE
arow *see* ARRA
arown *see* AROON¹·¹
arr, aar, †**aur** /ar/ *n* a scar, the mark left by a wound *19, 20- Sh C Uls*. **arred, ard** scarred or scratched; pockmarked *19, 20- Sh*. [ON *ørr*]
arra, arrie, airra, airrow, arrow, *Sh* **aerrow,** †**arow,** †**harow** /ˈarə, ˈare, ˈɛrə, ˈero, ˈaro; *Sh* ˈeərə/ *n* a slender bolt fired from a bow, an arrow *la14-*. †**arrow-bag** a quiver *16-17*. †**arrow cace** a quiver *e16*. **arra heid, arrow head** the tip or pointed part of an arrow *la15-*. **arrow shot,** †**arow schot** a shot with an arrow; *as a measure of distance* a bowshot *16-*. [OE *arwe*]
†**arrace, arrais, arras** *v* to pull out, snatch away or tear down *15-16*. [ME *aracen*]
arrage *see* ARAGE
arrais *see* ARRACE
arrange *see* ARREENGE
arras /ˈarəs/ *n* the sharp edge at the angle between two surfaces *19-*. [perhaps Fr *arase* building blocks used to level a wall; compare ARRIDGE]
arras *see* ARRACE
arrasees *see* ARASEES
arreenge, arrange, †**arange** /əˈrindʒ, əˈrendʒ/ *v* to put in order; to make plans; to come to an agreement *la14-*. [OFr *arengier*]
arreist¹·¹, **arrest,** †**arest** /əˈrist, əˈrɛst/ *n* **1** the action of apprehending, legal restraint (of a person) *15-*. **2** *law* seizure of goods; the seizure of a person's wages in payment of a debt *17-*. **3** the act of stopping or staying; a halt, a delay *la14-e16*. [OFr *areste*]
arreist¹·², **arrest,** †**arest** /əˈrist, əˈrɛst/ *v* **1** *law* to apprehend, take into custody; to seize property *la14-*. **2** to cause to stop; to halt; to catch the attention of *la14-*. **arrestee** *law* the third party currently in possession of the moveable property arrested by a creditor *18-*. †**arrester, arrestar** *law* a person who makes an arrest or seizes goods (in payment of debt) *la15-e18*. [ME *aresten*]
arreistment, arrestment, †**arestment** /əˈristmənt, əˈrɛstmənt/ *n law* **1** the action of arresting, apprehending or seizing by legal authority *la15-*. **2** the seizing of money or goods currently in the hands of a third party in payment of a debt *la16-*. [OFr *arestement*]
arrest *see* ARREIST¹·¹, ARREIST¹·²
arrestment *see* ARREISTMENT
arriage *see* ARAGE
arridge, †**awrige** /ˈarɪdʒ/ *n* the sharp angle of the ridge made by ploughing *19- Ork SW*. [OFr *areste* an edge, a ridge; the backbone of a fish, Lat *arista* the bones of a fish; compare ARRAS]
arrie *see* ARRA
arro, arrow /ˈaro, ˈaro/ *n* a young hen commencing to lay *20- Ork*. [Gael *eireag*, compare EAROCK]
arrour *see* ERROR
arrow *see* ARRA, ARRO
arr-tree *see* AR-TREE
ars *see* ERSE¹·¹
arsbischop *see* ARCHIBISCHOP
arscap, arschip *see* HEIRSKIP
arse *see* ERSE¹·¹, ERSE¹·²
art *see* AIRT¹, AIRT²·¹, AIRT³
artailliarie *see* ARTILƷERIE
†**artailƷeit** *adj* provided with artillery *16*. [OFr *arteille*, ptp of *artiller* to provide with war-engines]
artailƷerie *see* ARTILƷERIE
artation, †**artatioun** /arˈteʃən/ *n* compulsion, constraint; instigation, incitement *la15-e16, 20- literary*. [Lat *artātio* compression]
arth *see* AIRT²·¹
†**Arthuris hufe, Arthuris Hove** *n* = ARTHUR'S OON *15-e17*. [a misreading of ARTHUR'S OON]
Arthur's Oon, Arthur's Oven /arθərz ˈun, arθərz ˈɔvən/ *n* an ancient monument near the Roman Wall at Falkirk, demolished 1743, traditionally associated with King Arthur, so called because of its oven-like shape *17-19, 20- historical*. [from the personal name *Arthur* + OAVEN]
article, articule, artikil *see* AIRTICLE
†**artilƷerie, artailƷerie, artailliarie** *n* artillery *la15-e17*. [ME *artelrie*]
artist *see* AIRTIST
ar-tree, arr-tree /ˈartri/ *n in Shetland and Orkney* (a piece of wood nailed to) a plough beam *19-20, 21- historical*. [Norw *ard* plough + TREE¹·¹]
arvi, *Ork* **arvo** /ˈarvi; *Ork* ˈarvo/ *n* chickweed *Stellaria media 20- Sh Ork*. [ON *arfi*]
†**as**¹ *n* a donkey, an ass; a foolish person *15-16*. Compare ASINE. [OE *assa*]
as²·¹**, is,** *H&I WC* **ass,** †**als** /az, ɪz; *H&I WC* as/ *adv* **1** in the same way, to the same extent, like *la14-*. **2** than *la16-*. †**alssone, as sune, as sone** immediately, at once *la14-17*. †**alsswyth, alswyith** at once, immediately *la14-16*. **as monie, as mony,** †**alsmony** as many *15-*. **as muckle,** †**as mekill,** †**alsmekill** as much *15-*. †**as of** as regards, in respect or consideration of *la14-15*. **as weill,** †**alswele** also, in the same way, equally *la15-*. [reduced form of OE *alswā*; compare ALSO]
as²·²**, is,** *H&I WC* **ass,** †**has,** †**als** /az, ɪz; *H&I WC* as/ *conj* **1** in the same way, to the same extent, like *la14-*. **2** when, while; during *15-*. **3** that, who, which: ◊*this is the yin as telt me la19-*. **4** as if *la14-19, 20- Sh*. **5** than *16-*. **6** how *la16-e19*. **7** that *17-18*. **8** such as *16*. †**alsswyth as, alsswith as** as soon as *e16*. **as weill,** †**alswele,** †**alsweill** as well *la14-*. [see the adv]
as *see* ASS, AX
†**aschame, ashame, eschame** *v* **1** to put to shame *16-e19*. **2** to feel shame *15-e17*. [OE *āsceamian*]

†**aschamit**, †**eschamit** *adj* **1** affected with shame *la14-17*. **2** disgraced *16*. [ptp of ASCHAME]
aschape *see* ESCHAPE¹·²
asche *see* ESH
Asch Wedinisday *see* ASK-WEDINSDAY
†**ascrive** *v* to ascribe to, reckon or consider; to assign *la15-17*. [ME *ascriven*]
ase *see* ASS, AX
aseth *see* ASSYTH¹·²
ash *see* ESH
ashair, **assure**, *NE* **asseer**, *NE* **asheer**, †**asseure**, †**assover** /əˈʃer, əˈʃur; *NE* əˈsir; *NE* əˈʃir/ *v* to assert, convince; to make sure, secure or confirm *la14-*. [ME *assuren*]
ashairance, **assurance**, †**assoverance** /əˈʃerəns, əˈʃurəns/ *n* **1** confidence *la14-*. **2** a pledge, a promise; a guarantee (of safety or immunity) *la14-*. **3** certification; security; insurance *16-*. [OFr *aseurance, asegurance*]
ashame *see* ASCHAME
asheer *see* ASHAIR
ashet /ˈaʃət/ *n* **1** a (large) oval serving plate *la17-*. **2** a metal pie-dish *20- WC*. **ashet pie** a pie made in a plate or shallow dish *20-*. [Fr *assiette*]
ashlar *see* AISLAR
ashy *see* ESHY
ashypet *see* ASSIEPET
aside¹·¹ /əˈsaɪd/ *adv* **1** to one side, out of the way *16-*. **2** close by *la18-*. [ME *asyde*]
aside¹·² /əˈsaɪd/ *prep* beside; close to, alongside; in comparison with *la18-*. [see the adv]
asides¹·¹ /əˈsaɪdz/ *adv* besides *20-*. [ASIDE¹·¹, with adv-forming suffix]
asides¹·² /əˈsaɪdz/ *prep* beside *20-*. [see the adv]
†**asine** *n* an ass *16-e17*. Compare AS¹. [OFr *asne*, Lat *asina*]
ask¹, **esk**, †**awsk** /ask, ɛsk/ *n* a newt, an eft, a lizard *15-*. [OE *āþexe*]
ask²·¹, **eesk**, **yask**, **hask** /ask, isk, jask, hask/ *n* a haze, mist or fog; drizzle *la19- Sh Ork*. [unknown]
ask²·² **eesk** /ask, isk/ *v* to rain slightly, drizzle; to sleet *19- Sh Ork*. [unknown]
ask *see* AX
askis *see* ASS
asklent, **aslent** /əˈsklɛnt/ *adv* on the slant, askew, to the side; astray *la16-*. [ME *on slent*; compare SKLENT¹·¹]
†**Ask-Wedinsday**, **As Wodinsday**, **Asch Wedinsday** *n* Ash Wednesday *16-e17*. [*ash* the powdery residue + WEDNESDAY]
asleep, †**asleip** /əˈslip/ *adv* **1** in or into a state of sleep, sleeping *la16-*. **2** *of a civil action* where no further step in procedure has been taken within a year and a day after it was first lodged *18-*. [OE *on slæpe*]
aslent *see* ASKLENT
asoond, †**asound** /əˈsund/ *adv* in a faint; unconscious *17-19, 20- Sh Ork*. [altered form of ME *aswoon* after SOUND¹·¹]
†**aspar**, **a spar** *adv* (with legs or feet) apart *17-e19*. [A³ + SPAR¹·¹]
asperans *see* ESPERANCE
†**asposit** *adj* disposed *la15-16*. [altered from ptp of DISPOSE]
aspy *see* ESPY¹·¹, ESPY¹·²
†**aspyne**, **hespyne**, **espyne** *n* a ship's boat *la14*. [ON *espingr*]
ass, **ase**, *Sh* **ess**, *N NE* **aise**, *N* **aiss**, *NE* **aess**, *Bor* **auss**, †**as** /as; *Sh* ɛs; *N NE* es; *Bor* ɔs/ *n pl* also †**assis** †**askis 1** ash, ashes *la14-*. **2** wood ash, potash *15-e17*. **ass-hole**, *EC Bor* **assole** a place below or in front of the grate, or a hole outside the house, for ashes *19-*. **ass-midden** a refuse heap for ashes *19- NE Bor*. **ass-pit** a pit for dumping ashes *19-*. [ON *aska*]
ass *see* AS²·¹, AS²·²
†**assail**¹·¹, **assaill**, **assale** *n* an attack *la14-e19*. [OFr *assaille*]
assail¹·², †**assailze**, †**assailʒe**, †**assalʒe** /əˈsel/ *v* **1** to attack, assault; to impinge upon, beset *la14-*. **2** to attempt, make trial of *15-16*. †**assailʒeour** an assailant, an attacker; a prosecutor *la14-e16*. [OFr *assaillir*]
†**assassinate** *n* an assassin *la17-e19*. [Fr *assassinat*]
assassor *see* ASSESSOUR
assay /əˈse/ *n* **1** a quality test; the testing of the composition of metal or oil *la15-*. **2** a demonstration of ability or capacity *la16-e17*. **3** a trial of courage or endurance *la14-16*. **4** an attack or assault *la14-16*. †**assayour** a tester of metal or coins *16*. [ME *assai*]
†**assedat**, **assidat** *v law* to let or lease *16-e18*. [Lat *assedāre*]
assedation, †**assedatioun** /asəˈdeʃən/ *n law* a lease; originally also the act of letting *15-*. [ASSEDAT, with noun-forming suffix]
asseer *see* ASHAIR
assembly, †**assemble** /əˈsɛmble/ *n* **1** (a formal or social) gathering *la14-*. **2** the GENERAL ASSEMBLY *la16-*. **3** a hostile encounter *la14-15*. **4** a muster of armed men *la15-16*. **5** *Presbyterian Church* a meeting of a congregation or kirk session *la16*. **Assembly School** a school set up by the General Assembly in a parish where the heritors' provision for education was inadequate *19, 20- historical*. [ME *asemble*]
†**assessour**, **assassor** *n* an adviser to a judge or magistrate *la15-17*. [ME *assessour*, EModE *assessor*]
asseth *see* ASSYTH¹·¹
asseure *see* ASHAIR
assidat *see* ASSEDAT
assie, *Sh* **essi**, *Sh* **essie**, *NE* **aissy** /ˈasi; *Sh* ˈɛsi; *NE* ˈesi/ *adj* covered with ashes; ash-coloured; dirty *19-*. **essibacket** an ash-bucket *20- Sh*. **aisy-hole** a hole for ashes beneath an open-hearth fire *20- N*. **essikert**, **essie-kaert**, *Ork* **assiecart** a refuse vehicle *20- Sh Ork*. **essimidden** a dunghill where ashes are deposited *20- Sh*. [ASS + -IE²]
assiepattle, †**aessi-pattle** /ˈɑsipatəl/ *n* a neglected or dirty child; a lazy person *19- Sh Ork*. [perhaps ASS + ON *patla* to poke; compare Ger *Aschenputtel*]
assiepet, **ashypet** /ˈasipɛt, ˈaʃipɛt/ *n* a scullery-maid, a drudge *19- SW Bor*. [probably reduced form of ASSIEPATTLE; compare Dan *askepot* a Cinderella]
†**assigna**, **assignay**, **assigne** *n pl* also †**assignis** *law* an assignee, the person to whom a property or right is formally assigned *15-17*. [MFr *assigné*]
assignation, †**assignatioun**, †**assignacioune** /asɪɡˈneʃən/ *n* **1** *law* an assignment of a right; the formal record of assignment *la15-*. **2** an appointment *la18-*. **3** the act of assigning something *15-e19*. [MFr *assignation*; compare AN *assignacion*, Lat *assignātio*]
assignay, **assigne** *see* ASSIGNA
assilag /ˈasilaɡ/ *n* the storm petrel *Hydrobates pelagicus la17-19, 20- N*. [Gael *asaileag*]
assiltre *see* ASSLE-TREE
assis *see* ASS
assise *see* ASSIZE
assisour *see* ASSIZER
assist /əˈsɪst/ *v* **1** to support; to help, aid *15-*. **2** to assent or agree to an opinion *16*. **3** to take sides with, agree with *16-e17*. [MFr *assister*, Lat *assistere*]
assith *see* ASSYTH¹·¹, ASSYTH¹·²
assithment *see* ASSYTHMENT

assize, †**assise**, †**assyse**, †**assyis** /əˈsaez/ *n* **1** *law* a trial by jury; a jury or panel; a judicial inquiry *la14-*. **2** a regulation governing the quality, quantity or price of commodities *15-18*. **3** size, dimension *e16*. †**assyse ale** *in the North-East* a duty on ale *17*. †**assise fish** = *assise herring 17-e18*. †**assise herring** a duty of herring paid to the crown *16-e18*. †**assise of errour** *law* a panel appointed to reduce an erroneous service of heirship *la15-18*. [ME *assise*]

†**assizer**, **assisour**, **assysar** *n law* a member of an assize, a juryman *15-19*. [ME *assisour*]

assle-tree, *Ork* **ossiltree**, †**assiltre** /ˈasəltri; *Ork* ˈɔsəltri/ *n* an axle *16-19, 20- Ork SW*. [ME *axiltre*; compare AIXTREE]

assle-tuith *see* AISLE-TUITH

associate, †**associat** /əˈsoʃɪət/ *adj* associated, joined; allied *la15-*. **Associate Presbytery** the Secession Church *18, 19- historical*. **Associate Synod 1** the section of the Secession Church which upheld the lawfulness of swearing the burgess oath *18-e19, 20- historical*; compare GENERAL ASSOCIATE SYNOD. **2** the section of the Secession Church which seceded over the swearing of the burgess oath *18, 20- historical*. [Lat *associātus*]

assoilzie, †**assoilʒe**, **assolʒe**, †**assoly** /əˈsɔɪlji/ *v* **1** *law* to acquit of a charge; to find in favour of the defender in an action *la15-*. **2** *Roman Catholic Church* to absolve from sin, grant absolution *la14-e19*. **3** *law* to clear (oneself) of a charge *16-19*. **4** to free from an obligation *la15*. **5** to resolve (a question or issue) *15-e16*. [OFr *assoille*, pres subjunctive of *assoldre*]

assole *see* ASS

assoly, assolʒe *see* ASSOILZIE

assonʒe *see* ESSONʒE[1.1], ESSONʒE[1.2]

assover *see* ASHAIR

assoverance *see* ASHAIRANCE

†**assucurit** *adj* assured, certain *e16*. [Lat *assecūrāre*]

assume /əˈsjum/ *v* **1** to take upon oneself, undertake; to take on, adopt *la15-*. **2** to suppose, believe *17-*. **3** to levy, collect as a due (from ecclesiastical property) *la16*. [Lat *adsūmere*]

assumption, †**assumptioun** /əˈsʌmʃən/ *n* **1** *Roman Catholic Church* (the feast of) the ascent into heaven of the Virgin Mary *la14-*. **2** the action of assuming responsibility or control *la15-*. **3** a supposition *la16-*. **4** the collecting of the ecclesiastical revenues used to provide for the clergy *la16-e17*. [Lat *assumptio*]

assurance *see* ASHAIRANCE

assure *see* ASHAIR

assyis, assyse *see* ASSIZE

assysar *see* ASSIZER

†**assyth**[1.1], **assith, asseth** *n* satisfaction, reparation, compensation *la14-15*. [ME *asseth*]

†**assyth**[1.2], **assith, aseth** *v* **1** to compensate (for an injury or offence), pay a sum in compensation *la14-e18*. **2** to satisfy *la14-e17*. [see the noun]

assythment, assythement, †**assithment** /əˈsʌɪðmənt/ *n* satisfaction, compensation for loss or injury; reparation, indemnification *la15-19, 20- historical*. [ASSYTH[1.2], with noun-forming suffix]

ast *see* AX

astabill *see* ESTABILL

astablis *see* ESTAIBLISH

astarn, astern /əˈstarn, əˈstɛrn/ *adv* **1** behind; in the rear *la16-*. **2** in debt, insolvent *20-*. [A^3 + STARN[2]]

†**astart, estert** *v* to avoid, shun; to escape, depart from *15-16*. [ME *asteorte*]

astate *see* ESTATE

asteep /əˈstip/ *adv* steeping, soaking *la19-*. **lay yer brains asteep** to make a mental effort, think hard *la19-*. **set yer brains asteep** = *lay yer brains asteep*. [A^3 + STEEP[1.1]]

asteer, astir, †**asteir** /əˈstir, əˈstɪr/ *adv* up and about, stirring; in a commotion *16-*. Compare *on steer* (STEER[1.1]). [A^3 + STEER[1.1]]

astent *see* EXTENT[1.1]

astern *see* ASTARN, AUSTERN

†**asthmatics** *n* asthma *e19*. [Lat *asthmaticus*]

astir *see* ASTEER

astler *see* AISLAR

†**astonait, estonyt** *adj* astounded, astonished *15-e16*. [ME *astoned*]

†**astonist**, †**estonist**, †**astonysit** *adj* astounded, astonished *16*. [altered form of ASTONAIT]

astragal /ˈastrəgəl/ *n* a glazing bar in a window *19-*. [Lat *astragalus* a moulding on a column]

†**astrenʒe** *v* to bind or constrain *la15-e16*. [ME *astreinen*]

astrict, †**astrick** /əˈstrɪkt/ *v ptp* also †**astrict 1** to restrict, limit *la16-*. **2** *law* to bind tenants or servants by a legal obligation *16-19, 20- historical*. **3** to bind to a belief or moral obligation *la16-e17*. **astricted multures, astrictit multures** multures to which a mill is entitled from the tenants of lands thirled to it *la16-19, 20- historical*. †**astrict multures** = *astricted multures la16-e17*. [Lat *astrict-*, ptp stem of *astringere* to bind]

astriction /əˈstrɪkʃən/ *n* a bond; a moral or legal obligation *16-*. [Lat *astrictio*]

†**astrolog, astrologue** *n* an astronomer or astrologer *la14-e17*. [MFr *astrologue*, Lat *astrologus*]

†**astuce** *adj* astute *e16*. [OFr *astuce*]

As Wodinsday *see* ASK-WEDINSDAY

at[1.1] /at, ət/ *adv* **1** expressing energetic action away: ◊*he was layan at for a he was worth 20- Sh Ork*. **2** expressing continuance of action on: ◊*hei blethert an blethert at 20- Bor*. [see the prep]

at[1.2] /at, ət/ *prep* **1** in, on; near to, beside; in the direction of, towards *la14-*. **2** from, of (a person) *la14-*; compare AX. **3** to, towards: ◊*few can keep anger at a bairn la18-*. **4** within reach of (so as to thrash); meddling with, hurting: ◊*whae was at ye? 19-*. **5** in repeated contact with: ◊*so a' the lads are wooing at her! 19-*. **at yersel 1** in one's right mind; in a calm state *la17-*. **2** healthy, flourishing *19-*. **be at someone** to talk continuously; to urge; to solicit; to nag *20-*. **what are ye at?** what do you mean? *19-*. [OE *æt*]

at[2], **it** /ət/ *pron* that *la14-*. [reduced form of THAT[1.2], perhaps with influence from ON *at* relative pronoun]

ata, at a, at all /əˈta, əˈtɔl/ *adv* in all respects or any respect, altogether *15-*. Compare AVA. [AT[1.2] + AW[1.2]]

a'taist *see* ATHIST

atanis *see* AINCE[1.1]

atap, atoap /əˈtap, əˈtop/ *adv* atop, above *la19-*. [A^3 + TAP[1.1]]

atdraw /ˈatdrɔ/ *n* a quarrel, a dispute *la19- Sh*. [A^3 + DRAW[1.1]]

ate *see* AIT, EAT[1.2]

aten *see* EAT[1.2]

atfirt, atferd, atvird, *Ork* **atfare** /ˈatfɪrt, ˈatfɛrd, ˈatvɪrd; *Ork* ˈatfer/ *n* odd or clumsy behaviour; antics *la19- Sh Ork*. [ON *atferð* exertion, activity]

atgauns /ˈatgɑnz/ *npl* behaviour, goings-on *20- Ork*. [A^3 + pl of verbal noun from GAE]

athe *see* AITH

atheen, athin /əˈθin, əˈθɪn/ *prep* above *20- NE*. [perhaps altered form of *abeen* (ABUNE[1.2])]

athegidder, a'thegither *see* AWTHEGITHER

ather *see* AITHER[1.1], AITHER[1.2]

ather-bill *see* ETHER

atheris *see* AITHER[1.3]
athin[1.1] /əˈθɪn/ *adv* within *20-*. [altered form of WITHIN[1.1]]
athin[1.2], *Sh* **ithin** /əˈθɪn; *Sh* ɪˈθɪn/ *prep* within *la19-*. [see the adv]
athin *see* ATHEEN
athing *see* AWTHING
athir *see* AITHER[1.1], AITHER[1.3]
athist, a'taist, †adist, †adest /əˈðɪst, əˈtɛst/ *prep* on this side of *17-19, 20- WC SW*. Compare AYONT[1.2]. [perhaps AT[1.2] + THIS[1.3], at this side]
Atholl brose, Athole Brose /aθəl ˈbroz/ *n* a blend of honey, oatmeal and whisky *la18-*. [from the Earl of *Atholl* + BROSE]
athoot[1.1] /əˈθut/ *adv* outside; on the outside *20-*. [altered form of WITHOOT[1.1]]
athoot[1.2], **ithoot** /əˈθut, ɪˈθut/ *prep* without *la19-*. [see the adv]
athoot[1.3] /əˈθut/ *conj* unless, except (that) *20-*. [see the adv]
athort[1.1] /əˈθɔrt/ *adv* across in various directions, all over, about *16-*. [AT[1.2] + THORT[1.1]]
athort[1.2] /əˈθɔrt/ *prep* across, from one side to the other of, and fro over; all over; through, among *la15-*. [see the adv]
athraw /əˈθrɔ/ *adv* awry *la18-*. [AT[1.2] + THRAW[1.1]]
atifer, atifore /ˈatifər, ˈatifor/ *n* shame *20- Ork*. [unknown]
atil /əˈtɪl/ *prep* in, into *20- Sh*. [altered form of INTIL[1.2]]
ation *see* AISHAN
atoap *see* ATAP
atour[1.1], **attour** /əˈtʌur, əˈtur/ *adv* 1 besides, over and above, moreover; in addition *15-*. 2 farther off or out; back; away; across; over; out; apart *la16-*. 3 all over, everywhere *15-e16*. [see the prep]
atour[1.2], **attour, atower, †attouir** /əˈtʌur, əˈtur/ *prep* 1 across; (down) over; out of; above; beyond *la14-*. 2 more than; besides, in addition to; beyond, after *la14-e19*. 3 outside, in violation of (a law) *la14-e17*. **by and attour** *see* BY. [AT[1.2] + OWER[1.3] or altered form of OOT OWER[1.1]]
attach, †atteche, †atteich /əˈtatʃ/ *v* 1 *law* to seize (goods or earnings); to arrest, summon a debtor to appear in court *15-*. 2 to join or fasten *16-*. [OFr *atachier*]
†attachiament *n* = ATTACHMENT *15-e17*. [Lat *attachiamentum*]
attachment, †attechement /əˈtatʃmənt/ *n* 1 *law* arrest, the summons of an offender; seizure of goods or earnings *15-*. 2 the act or state of being attached; something attached *18-*. [AN *atachement*, Fr *attachement*]
attain, *Sh* **atteen, †attene, †atteyn, †attane** /əˈten; *Sh* əˈtɪn/ *v* to reach, gain; to obtain or achieve *la14-*. [ME *atteinen*]
attanis *see* AINCE[1.1]
†atteal, atteil *n* a species of wild duck *la16-19*. [unknown]
atteche *see* ATTACH
attechement *see* ATTACHMENT
atteen *see* ATTAIN
atteich *see* ATTACH
atteil *see* ATTEAL
attemp[1.1], **attempt** /əˈtɛmp, əˈtɛmpt/ *n* a try, an effort, an endeavour *la16-*. [see the verb]
attemp[1.2], **attempt** /əˈtɛmp, əˈtɛmpt/ *v* to make an effort, try *la15-*. [AN *attempter*, OFr *atenter*]
†attemptat *n* an action involving violence or wrong; an outrage *la14-e17*. [AN, MFr *attemptat*]
attene *see* ATTAIN
†attent[1.1] *n* attention *la15*. **attentfully** attentively *e16* [OFr *atente*]
†attent[1.2] *adj* attentive *16*. **attentlie** attentively *la15-16*. [Lat *attentus*]
attentik *see* AUTENTIK

†attenuat *adj* thin or weak *16*. [Lat *attenuāt-*, ptp stem of *attenuāre* to make thin]
atter *see* ETTER[1.1]
attercap, attercep *see* ETTERCAP
attery *see* ETTERY
atteyn *see* ATTAIN
†attingent *adj* touching; near or close (in age or relationship) *la16-e17*. [Lat *attingent-*, presp stem of *attingere* to touch]
attir *see* ETTER[1.1]
attircop *see* ETTERCAP
†attolerance *n* permission or licence granted by authority; the right to grant such permission *la16-19*. [altered from TOLERANCE]
attorney, †actorney, †actornay, †attournay /əˈtʌrne/ *n* one appointed to act for another in matters of law or business; an authorized agent *la14-*. [ME *attourne*]
attouir *see* ATOUR[1.2]
attour *see* ATOUR[1.1], ATOUR[1.2]
attournay *see* ATTORNEY
attrack, attract /əˈtrak, əˈtrakt/ *v* to draw (the attention of), pull in *19-*. [Lat *attract-*, ptp stem of *attrahere*]
attry *see* ETTERY
atvird *see* ATFIRT
atwae, †atwa /əˈtwe/ *adv* in two *19- SW Bor*. [altered form of OE *ātwā*]
atweel /əˈtwil/ *adv* assuredly, certainly, indeed *la18-*. [probably shortened form of the Scots phrase *I wat weel*]
atween[1.1] /əˈtwin/ *adv* between *la18-*. **atween and** between this place or time and that indicated: ◊*you'll be back this wey atween and three months 18-19, 20- C SW*. [altered form of BETWEEN[1.1], by analogy with AFORE[1.1], ANEATH[1.1]]
atween[1.2] /əˈtwin/ *prep* between *la18-*. **atween the een** before one's eyes; with one's own eyes; in the face *la18-*. **atween hands** in the intervals of regular occupation; at intervals; in the meantime *19-*. **atween whiles** between times *la19-*. [see the adv]
atweesh, atwixt, atweest, acqueesh /əˈtwiʃ, əˈtwɪkst, əˈtwɪst, əˈkwiʃ/ *prep* between *la18-*. [perhaps altered form of BETWIXT]
auaill *see* AVAIL[1.1]
auber *see* AABER[1.2]
aubirchoun *see* HABERSCHOUN
auch *see* ACH, ECHT[1.2]
†auchan, achan *n* a variety of pear *la17-19*. [named after Auchans House in Ayrshire]
auchful *see* AWFY[1.1]
auchlet, auchlot *see* ECHT[1.1]
aucht[1], **acht** /ɔxt, axt/ *n* 1 possession, ownership *15-*. 2 property; land, premises *la14-e18, 20- N*. 3 applied to a wife or child a possession of great value, a treasure *20- Sh*. 4 a person of little value, a troublemaker *la18-e19*. **†aucht and wont** according to use and custom *la15-16*. **best aucht** *see* BEST[1.2]. **in yer aucht, †in your aught** in your possession *16-*. [OE *ǣht*]
aucht[2], **acht**, *Ork NE* **aicht**, *NE* **yaucht**, *NE* **echt**, *T* **aich**, **†ought** /ɔxt, axt; *Ork NE* ext; *NE* jɔxt; *NE* ɛxt; *T* ɛx/ *v* to owe *16-*. **†auchtin, auchtand** 1 *of money* owing, due *16-19*. 2 *of a person* owing, indebted *la16-17*. **†auchtingis** debts *la16*. [pt of AWE used as pres; compare OCHT[2]]
aucht *see* AWE, ECHT[1.1], ECHT[1.2], OCHT[1.1], OCHT[2]
auchteen, †auchtand, †auchtane, †auchten /ˈɔxtin/ *adj* eighth *15-19, 20- historical*. **auchteen part** an eighth share (of land) *la15-19, 20- historical*. [ON **ahtande*; compare ECHT[1.1]]
auchteen *see* ECHTEEN

auchteent see ECHTEENT
auchten see AUCHTEEN
auchtene see ECHTEEN, ECHTEENT
auchtent see ECHTEENT
auchtin see AWE
auchtsome, auchtsum see ECHTSOME
†**auctenty** *adj* authentic *e16*. [probably altered form of AUTENTYFE]
auctour see OWTHOR
audience, *NE* **addiscence**, *NE* **owdience**, †**adience**, †**audiens**, †**awdience** /ˈɔdɪəns; *NE* ˈadɪsəns; *NE* ˈʌudɪəns/ *n* (the action, state or condition of) hearing or being heard; (a body of) listeners; a formal interview or reception *la14-*. [ME *audience*]
auditor, †**auditour** /ˈɔdɪtər/ *n* 1 a person who audits accounts *15-*. 2 a judicial hearer (of complaints or suits) *15*. 3 a listener, one of an audience *16-e17*. †**auditouris of chekker** those appointed by commission under the Quarter Seal to hold the audit and, constituting the court of exchequer, hear cases relating to the royal revenues *la15-e17*. **Auditor of the Court of Session** an examiner of the accounts of the Court of Session *19-*. **Auditor of the Sheriff Court** an examiner of the accounts of the Sheriff Court *19-*. [ME *auditour*]
†**auditour** *n* an audience *16*. [Lat *audītōrium*]
auedent see EVIDENT[1.1]
auentour see AVENTURE[1.1]
aufull see AWFY[1.1]
augait see ALGATE
aught see AWE
augmentation, †**augmentatioun**, †**agmentatioun** /ɔgmənˈteʃən/ *n* 1 the action or process of augmenting *15-*. 2 an increase in income or rent; *law* an increase of the stipend of a parish minister *16-*. [ME *augmentacioun*]
augsome see UGSOME
†**augurian**[1.1] *n* an interpreter of omens *e16*. [see the adj]
†**augurian**[1.2] *adj* pertaining to an augur or augury *e16*. [Lat *augurius*]
aul see AULD[1.2]
auld[1.1], **old** /ɔld, ald, old/ *n* 1 a person, animal or thing of the age indicated: ◊*a wheen o ten year aulds la16-*. 2 old people *17-*. **the auld 1** old people *la15-*. 2 an old person *la14-e16*. **in the auld** or **of old**, formerly *la16-19, 20- NE*. **of the auld** formerly *la15-19, 20- T*. [see the adj]
auld[1.2], **aald**, **ald**, **aul**, **aal**, **old**, *Sh Ork N H&I Uls* **owld**, *Sh Ork N H&I Uls* **ould**, †**aild** /ɔld, ald, ɔl, al, old; *Sh Ork N H&I Uls* ʌuld/ *adj* 1 having lived or existed for a long time, not young or new *la14-*. 2 belonging to ancient times; former, previous *la14-*. 3 long standing; long established, current *la14-*. 4 of a specified age: ◊*twae year auld 15-*. 5 the same, usual: ◊*Pate will still be the auld man 18-*. 6 *of siblings or children* oldest *18-*. 7 *of family relationships* at one generation's remove, great-, grand- *la18-*. 8 *of bread* stale *la18-*. **auld boy** the father of the speaker or person referred to *la20-*. **Auld Clootie** the Devil *la18-*. **Auld Cloots** the Devil *la18-*. **aald daa** the grandfather of the speaker or person referred to *20- Sh*. **auld day** the day after a celebration or market, when only essential work is done *la19- NE*. **old dear** the mother of the speaker or person referred to *la20-*. **auld doll** an old woman; a grandmother *la20-*. *NE* **Aul Eel** Christmas Day, according to the old Julian calendar, variously dated the 5th, 6th or 7th of January *la19- Sh NE*. †**auld extent** the Scottish land valuation made in the reign of Alexander III (c. 1380) *la15-e19, 20- historical*; compare *new extent* (NEW[1.2]). **aul' fernyears** stories of long ago *la18- NE*. †**auld-gabbit** speaking an ancient tongue; ancient looking *e18*. **Auld Hangie** the Devil *la18-19, 20- N*. **Auld Hornie** the Devil *la18-*. **Auld Kirk** the established CHURCH OF SCOTLAND (as distinguished from the FREE KIRK) *19-*. **auld laird** the current laird where there is a male heir *16-*. **auld mither 1** the mother or grandmother of the speaker or person referred to *la18-*. 2 Scotland *20-*. **auld mossie** the ace of spades *20- WC*. †**auld-mou'd** *in the North-East* wise, wily, crafty *18-e19*. **Auld Nick** the Devil *la18-*; compare NICK. †**Auld Sanny, Auld Saunders** the Devil *19*; compare SANDY (sense 3). **auld shune** an old sweetheart, a jilted lover *la18-*. **Auld Smith** the Devil *la19- NE*. **auld style, old style** *of dates* according to the Julian calendar *17-*. **Auld Suitie** the Devil *la18-*. **auld-tasted** musty *19-*. **auld-warld** belonging to past time, old, antique; old-fashioned *18-*. **auld young** middle-aged, mature *19- Sh SW*. **auld yule, the Auld Alliance**, †**the old Alliance** the traditional friendship between Scotland and France *la17-*. **auld claes an parritch** a person's usual daily routine; the daily grind *la19-*. **the Auld Enemy 1** the English or England *16-*. 2 the Devil *16-e19*. †**our auld enemies, our ald ennemyis** the English *la15-e19*. **the auld hech how**, †**auld heigh-ho** the same old thing, the old routine *la18-19, 20- EC Bor*. **auld in the horn** wise because of age or experience *19-*. **the Auld Hundert, the Auld Hunder, the Old Hundredth** (the tune of) the 100th Psalm, in the Scottish psalter *la19-*. **auld maid's bairn** a hypothetical well-behaved child which a spinster has in mind when criticizing the children of others *la19-*. **auld maid's wean** = *auld maid's bairn 20-*. **the auld mune in the airms o the new** the disc of the full moon faintly illuminated within the crescent moon, believed to be a sign of an approaching storm *la18-*. **Auld New Year's Day** New Year's Day according to the old Julian calendar *19- Sh Ork N H&I*. **da Aald Rock, the Old Rock** Shetland *la19- Sh*. **the Auld Thief** the Devil *19-*. †**auld used hand** a person accustomed to a situation, an experienced person *la18-e19*. [OE *ald*]
auld ane see AULD YIN
aulder, auler, *NE* **aaler**, †**oulder**, †**oldar** /ˈɔldər, ˈɔlər; ˈalər/ *adj* older, elder *la16-*. [AULD[1.2], with comparative suffix]
aulders, †**alders** /ˈɔldərz/ *npl* 1 day-old bread or cakes sold at a reduced price *20- T EC*. 2 older people, seniors *la19*. 3 ancestors, forefathers *la19*. [plural noun from the adj AULDER]
auldest, aullest, aulest, *NE* **aalest**, †**ouldest** /ˈɔldəst, ˈɔləst; *NE* ˈaləst/ *adj* oldest *17-*. [AULD[1.2], with superlative suffix]
auld-farrant, auldfarran, *NE* **aal-farrant**, †**old farrant** /ɔldˈfarənt, ɔldˈfarən; *NE* alˈfarənt/ *adj* 1 old-fashioned; quaint *la18-*. 2 *of children or young people* having the ways or shrewdness of older people; precocious *18-*. 3 *of people* sagacious, prudent, witty, ingenious *18-*. 4 *of proverbs* old and wise *la18-*. [AULD[1.2] + FARRANT, presp of FARE[1.2]]
auld lang syne, †**old long syne** /ˈɔld laŋ ˈsʌɪn/ *n* 1 bygone times, old friendship, memories of the past *la17-*; compare LANG SYNE[1.1]. 2 the song by Robert Burns sung at the close of social gatherings and at midnight on Hogmanay *18-*. [AULD[1.2] + LANG SYNE[1.1]]
Auld Lichts /ɔld ˈlɪxts/ *npl* 1 the stricter, conservative and evangelical section of the Church of Scotland *18-e19, 20- historical*. 2 one of the two corresponding groups which split both branches of the Secession Church, the Burghers in 1799 and the Antiburghers in 1806, the Auld Lichts from both combining in 1842 to form the Synod of Original Seceders *la18-e19, 20- historical*. Compare NEW LICHTS. [AULD[1.2] + LICHT[1.1]]

auld man, old man, ald man, *Ork H&I Uls* **owld man** /ɔld 'man, old 'man, ald 'man; *Ork H&I Uls* ʌuld 'man/ *n* **1** an old man; a man of the older generation *la14-*. **2** a person's father *la20-*. **3** southernwood *Artemisia abrotanum* 20- *EC Bor*. **4** a grey lichen *Parmelia saxatilis* providing a yellowish or reddish brown dye *la19- Sh*. **auld man's girse** a grey lichen *20- Sh*. **auld man's milk** eggnog *18-*. **auld gray man on the stane** a grey lichen (growing on stones) *20-*. **auld mairriet man** a married man (from the day after his marriage) *20-*. **the Auld Man 1** the Devil *18-*. **2** a person unchanged in character *18-e19*. [AULD^{1,2} + MAN]

Auld Reekie, †**Auld Reikie** /ɔld 'riki/ *n* a nickname for Edinburgh *18-*. [AULD^{1,2} + *reekie* (REEK^{1,1})]

Auld Toun, Old Town, *Ork* **Ald Toun**, †**Auld Town**, †**ald toun** /'ɔld tun, 'old tʌun; *Ork* 'ald tun/ *n* **1** a name for the oldest part of Aberdeen *16-*. **2** the part of Edinburgh along the Castle ridge, so called since the building of the NEW TOWN in the late 18th century *19-*. **3** the oldest part of any Scottish town *19-*. [AULD^{1,2} + TOUN]

auld wife, *Ork* **ald wife** /ɔld 'wʌif; *Ork* ald 'wʌif/ *n* **1** an old woman *la17-*. **2** a rotating chimney cowl *19-*. **3** a fussy, gossipy man *20-*. **4** the mother of the speaker or person referred to *la20-*. **auld wifie, old wifie 1** an old woman *20-*. **2** the mother of the speaker or person referred to *la20- WC*. **auld wives' mutches 1** a plant with a bonnet-like flower, the columbine *Aquilegia vulgaris* or monkshood *Aconitum napellus la19-*. **2** a rotating chimney cowl *20-*. **auld wifie's sooker** a mint imperial *20- NE T EC Bor*. [AULD^{1,2} + WIFE]

Auld Year /ɔld 'jir/ *n* the year that is about to end *19-*. Compare NEW-YEAR. **Auld Year's Day** the last day of the year *la19-*. **Auld Year's Nicht** the last night of the year, New Year's Eve *20-*. [AULD^{1,2} + YEAR]

auld yin, auld ane /'ɔld jɪn, 'ɔld en/ *n* **1** an old person *la19-*. **2** something old *la19-*. **the auld yin** a person's father or mother *la19-*. **the Auld Yin** the Devil *19-*. [AULD^{1,2} + ANE^{1,1}]

auler *see* AULDER

aulest, aullest *see* AULDEST

aum^{1,1}, alum, †**alme,** †**alom** /ɔm, 'aləm/ *n* a mineral salt used in dyeing or tanning *15-*. [ME *alum*]

†**aum^{1,2},** †**alme** *v* to treat with alum; to cure leather in this way *17-19*. [see the noun]

aumeril /'ɔmərəl/ *n* a foolish or awkward person *19, 20- NE*. Compare GOMERIL^{1,1}. [unknown]

aumers *see* EMMERS

aumry, almery, amery, amry, †**almorie,** †**ambrie** /'ɔmri, 'alməri, 'aməri, 'amri/ *n* **1** a place for storing domestic utensils or food, a cupboard, a pantry, a wooden piece of furniture *la15-*. **2** a clumsy or foolish person *19*. [ME *almerie*]

auncient, ancient, anshent, †**ancien** /'ɔnʃənt, 'enʃənt, 'anʃənt/ *adj* **1** very old; belonging to times long past *la15-*. **2** *of children* precocious; having the ways or intelligence of an adult *la19-*. [ME *auncien*]

aunction *see* UNCTION^{2,1}

aunt, †**awnt,** †**ant,** †**aynt** /ant/ *n* the sister of a person's mother or father *15-*. [ME *aunte*]

aunter, aunterus *see* ANTER^{1,1}

auntie /'ante, 'anti/ *n* **1** a familiar term for an aunt *la18-*. **2** an unmarried woman who kept an inn; drink obtained in such an establishment *19*. **Auntie Beenie** a rather old-fashioned looking woman *la20- C*. **eat up, ye're at yer Auntie's** *humorous* an invitation to guests to help themselves *la20-*. **I wouldn't call the Queen my auntie** an assertion of satisfaction about one's family or circumstances *la20-*. [AUNT + -IE^{1}]

aur *see* ARR

aurea *see* AURRIE

aureate, †**aureat** /'ɔriət/ *adj* **1** *of poetry* brilliantly written, highly ornamental *16-*. **2** golden, gold-coloured *16-e19*. [Lat *aureātus* decorated with gold]

argle-bargain *see* ARGLE-BARGAIN

aurrie, orry, aurea /'ɔre, 'ɔri, 'ɔreə/ *n* an area, an open space; the space below ground level in front of a basement; a school playground *la18-*. [altered form of Scots *area*]

auss *see* ASS

austern, †**owsteran,** †**astern** /'ɔstərn/ *adj* austere *15-19, 20- SW Bor*. [ME *austere*]

†**autentik, attentik, actentik** *adj* authentic *15-e17*. [ME *autentik*]

†**autentyfe** *adj* authentic *la15-e16*. Compare AUCTENTY. [OFr *autentif*]

authir *see* OWTHER^{1,4}

author, authour, autour *see* OWTHOR

auysitlie *see* ADVISE

ava, avaa, awa /ə'va, ə'wa/ *adv* **1** at all *la18-*. **2** of all: ◊*warst ava la18-e19*. Compare ATA. [*of* (O^{2}) + A^{3}]

avail^{1,1}, †**auaill,** †**avale** /ə'vel/ *n* **1** advantage, use, worth, validity *15-*. **2** material or monetary value, price *la15-e19*. **avail of marriage** *law* the sum payable to the feudal superior by the heir of a deceased ward vassal on his becoming marriageable *e18, la18- historical*. †**to the maist availl** at the highest possible price or rate *16*. †**within the awaill** at or below the proper value *la16-17*. [see the verb]

avail^{1,2}, †**awail,** †**availʒe,** †**avalʒe** /ə'vel/ *v* to be of use or advantage; to help or benefit *la14-*. [ME *availen*, Lat *valēre*, perhaps with *ad-* prefix]

availlour *see* AVALOUR

availʒe *see* AVAIL^{1,2}

aval^{1,1}, awalt /'aval, 'awalt/ *v of a sheep* to become cast, fall onto its back *19, 20- Bor*. [unknown; compare ON *velta* to roll, WALT^{2}, WELTER^{2,2}]

aval^{1,2}, avil, aiwal, *NE* **yaval,** †**avald,** †**awald,** †**awalt** /'aval, 'ewal; *NE* 'javəl/ *adj* **1** *of a sheep* lying on its back and unable to rise *la18-*. **2** *of a person* prostrate, helpless; in a state of intoxication or insensibility *la18-*. [see the verb]

aval^{1,3}, †**awald,** †**awalt** /'aval/ *adv of a sheep* lying helplessly on its back *la18-*. [see the verb]

aval^{2,1}, yavil /'aval, 'javəl/ *n* **1** a crop sown for the second year on the same field *18- NE*. **2** land lying the second year without being ploughed *la16-e17*. [unknown]

aval^{2,2}, avel, *Ork* **yaavel,** *NE* **yaval,** *T* **awat,** †**avald,** †**awald,** †**awal** /'aval; *Ork* 'javəl; *NE* 'javəl; *T* 'awət/ *adj of a grain crop* grown for the second year on the same land *16-*. **yaval broth** soup eaten the day after it has been made *la19- NE*. [unknown]

avald *see* AVAL^{1,2}, AVAL^{2,2}

avale *see* AVAIL^{1,1}

†**avalour, availlour** *n* value; validity *16*. [altered form of VALOUR^{1,1}]

avalʒe *see* AVAIL^{1,2}

†**avance, avans** *v* **1** to raise in rank or status; to promote, make prosperous *la14-16*. **2** to provide beforehand, advance money *16-e17*. **3** to raise in spirit or repute; to praise *la15-16*. **4** to go forward, progress *16*. [ME *avauncen*]

avancear *see* ADVANCER

†**avant^{1,1}** *n* boasting; a boast *15-e16*. [see the verb]

†**avant^{1,2}** *v* to praise or commend; to boast, glorify oneself *la14-e17*. [ME *avaunten*]

†**avantage** *n* advantage *la14-17*. **at avantage** in a position of superiority; having the upper hand *la14-16*. [ME *avauntage*]

†**avareis** *n* a duty on goods; a charge additional to the freight *16-e17*. [OFr *avarie* damage caused to goods]

†**avay**[1.1] *n law* an argument or plea advanced in court *15*. [see the verb]

†**avay**[1.2] *v law* to plead or present evidence in court *15*. **avayment** a legal declaration *15*. [ME *avaien*]

ave[1] /av/ *n* a small net used mainly in herring fishing, an AVNET *20- N NE*. [unknown; compare HAAF-NET]

ave[2], **aive** /ev/ *n* the eve or brink (of something) *20- NE*. **in the ave o** on the point of *20- NE*. **in the ave o't** in the mood for *20- NE*. [ME *eve*]

ave[3], †**awe**, †**aw**, †**aa** /av/ *n* a float-board on an undershot water-wheel *la16-*. [unknown]

aveese *see* ADVISE

aveet *see* EVITE

avel *see* AVAL[2.2]

†**avenand, awendand** *adj* convenient, agreeable; handsome *la14-16*. [ME *avenaunt*]

†**aventure**[1.1], **eventure, auentour** *n* **1** an adventure; an unusual incident *la14-16*. **2** chance, fortune; accident *la14-16*. **3** commercial enterprise or risk *15-16*. Compare ADVENTUR. **the wild aventouris** customs duty levied on goods imported by foreigners or unfreemen (outwith the control of the authorities) *la15-16*. [ME *aventure*]

†**aventure**[1.2], **eventure** *v* to adventure; to venture; to risk; to dare *la15-e17*. [ME *aventuren*]

aver *see* AIVER, EEVER

average *see* ARAGE

Averil, †**Averill** /'evərəl/ *n* April *la14-19, 20- literary*. [ME *averil*]

averill *see* AIVER

averin, avern, *T* **aivrin,** †**everon** /'evərən, 'evərn; *T* 'evrən/ *n* the cloudberry *Rubus chamaemorus la18-19, 20- NE T*. [unknown]

avertese *see* ADVERTEESE

†**averty** *adj* well-advised, prudent *la14*. [ME *averti*]

avil *see* AVAL[1.2]

avis *see* ADVISE

avisandum *see* AVIZANDUM

†**avise** *n* manner, fashion, style *e16*. [probably altered form of WISE[1]]

avise *see* ADVISE

avizandum, avisandum /avɪ'zandəm/ *n law* further or private consideration (outside the court) *17-*. [gerund of Lat *avizāre* to consider]

avnet /'avnɛt/ *n* a small net used in herring fishing *20- Sh*. [perhaps AVE[1] + NET; compare HALVE-NET]

†**avow**[1.1] *n* a vow *la14-e19*. [see the verb]

avow[1.2], †**awow** /a'vʌu/ *v* to make a vow, swear; to undertake or promise with a vow *la14-*. [ME *avouen*]

avpone *see* UPON

avree, abree /a'vri, a'bri/ *adv* away: ◊*come, hurry avree! la20-*. [Travellers' language]

aw[1.1], **a', aa, all,** †**al** /ɔ, a, ɔl, al/ *n* everything, the whole thing *15-*. **aa ae oo** all one wool; all one, all the same; of one stock; on an equal footing *19, 20- Sh N EC*. [see the adj]

aw[1.2], **a', aa, all,** †**al** /ɔ, a, ɔl, al/ *adj* **1** the whole, the whole of *la14-*. **2** every, any *la14-*. †**alhale, alhail** complete, entire *la14-16*. †**all and ane** every one *16*. **all and haill** *law* the entire amount, the whole of (something) *15-19, 20- historical*. †**al and sum** all without exception, everyone, everything; the whole matter *la14-16*. †**all and summyn** = *al and sum e16*. †**all be it, abiet** although *15-e18*. †**all maist** almost all *e16*. †**all our ane** all together *e16*. **aa ither thing** everything else *la19- NE*. **a wey** everywhere *la19-*. **a weys** in every way or respect *20-*. **like aw that** with the utmost speed or energy *la19-*. [OE *eall*]

aw[1.3], **a', aa, all,** †**al** /ɔ, a, ɔl, al/ *adv* altogether, completely, entirely, quite *la14-*. †**al bedene** at once *la14-16*. †**alhale, alhail** completely, entirely *la14-16*. †**alhalely** = *alhale la14-16*. †**allout, all owt** completely, absolutely *la14-16*. **aw throu,** †**all thrwch** entirely, throughout *16-*. †**all thus** just like this, in this precise manner *la15*. [see the adj]

†**aw**[2] *v* **1** to have a claim or right, be entitled; to deserve or merit *la14-17*. **2** to be bound or under obligation *la14-17*. [compare OCHT[2]]

aw[3] /ɔ/ *interj* an expression of disappointment *20-*. [a natural utterance]

aw *see* AVE[3], AWE

Aw *see* AH

awa[1.1], **awaa, away** /ə'wa, ə'wɔ, ə'we/ *adv* **1** to or at a distance; apart; elsewhere, out of sight *la14-*. **2** dead *17-*. **3** *indicating motion, continuation or encouragement* on, along: ◊*come awa to your bed* ◊*ca awa, la19-*. †**away biding** staying away *16-e17*. †**away cuming** a departure *la16-17*. †**away had** removed: ◊*our gudis to be tane and away had 15*. †**away led** carried off; removed *la14-17*. †**away passing** a departure *la16-e17*. **away a place** dead *la20-*. **awa frae** incapable of: ◊*he wis awa frae speakin la19- Sh N*. †**awa frae himsel** out of his wits *e19*. **awa tae skin and bane** wasted, reduced in flesh *la19-*. **awa wi 't, away wi 't** done for; broken in health; ruined; out of one's senses; lost; dead *19-*. [OE *āweg*]

awa[1.2], **away** /ə'wa, ə'wɔ, ə'we/ *interj* an expression of incredulity, contempt or dismissal: ◊*awa wi ye! 19-*. [see the adv]

awa *see* AVA

awaar *see* AWAUR

†**awach** *v* to keep watch *e16*. [A[3] + *wach* (WATCH[1.2])]

awaik *see* AWAUK[1.1]

awail *see* AVAIL[1.2]

†**await** *n* a lying in wait, an ambush *la15-e17*. [ME *await*]

await *see* AWYTE[1], AWYTE[2]

awake *see* AWAUK[1.1], AWAUK[1.2]

awal *see* AVAL[2.2]

awald *see* AVAL[1.2], AVAL[1.3], AVAL[2.2]

awalk, awalknyt *see* AWAUK[1.1]

awalt *see* AVAL[1.1], AVAL[1.2], AVAL[1.3]

awand *see* AWE

awant /ə'wɒnt/ *adv* wanting *la19- NE T C*. **awant o** for want of, lacking *la19- NE T C*. [A[3] + WANT[1.1]]

awanting, †**awantand** /ə'wɒntɪŋ/ *adj* lacking, missing *la16-*. [A[3] + WANT[1.1]]

awapwt *see* AWAY PUT

awar, aware *see* AWAUR

†**a-wastle, awestill** *prep* to the west of *la15-e19*. [A[3] + *wastle* (WAST[1.4])]

awat *see* AVAL[2.2], AWYTE[2]

awauk[1.1], **awake,** †**awalk,** †**awaik** /ə'wɔk, ə'wek/ *v pt* **awoke,** †**awoik,** †**awoilk,** †**awalkeit,** *ptp* **awauken,** †**awalknyt 1** to wake up *la15-*. **2** to keep watch (over) *16*. [OE *āwæcnan* to wake up, OE *āwacian* to keep watch]

awauk[1.2], **awake** /ə'wɔk, ə'wek/ *adj* not asleep, roused from sleep *18-*. [altered from the ptp of AWAUK[1.1]]

awaur, awaar, awar, aware /ə'wɔr, ə'war, ə'wer/ *adj* informed, alert; conscious, cognizant *17-*. [OE *gewær*]

away *see* AWA[1.1], AWA[1.2]

awayis *see* ALWAYS

†**away put, awapwt** *v* to set aside, exclude; to sell *15-17*. **away putting** removal, suppression, destruction *la15-17*. [*away* (AWA[1.1]) + *put* (PIT[2])]

†**away take, awaytak** *v* to steal; to carry off *la15-19*. [*away* (AWA[1.1]) + *take* (TAK[1.2])]

†**awaywart** *adv* away; turned away *la14-e16*. [away (AWA¹·¹) + -WART]
awband *see* AWEBAUND
†**awblaster** *n* **1** an arbalest, a cross-bow *15-e16*. **2** an arbalester, a cross-bow man *la14*. [ME *arblaster*]
awbody, abody, aabody /ˈɔbəde, ˈɔbde, ˈabədi, ˈabəde/ *pron* everybody *19-*. **abody's body** a general favourite; a sycophant *19-*; compare *ilka body's body* (ILKA¹). [AW¹·² + BODY]
awdience *see* AUDIENCE
awe, owe, *NE* **yaw, †aw, †ow** /ɔ, o; *NE* jɔ/ *v pt* **awed, aucht, acht, ocht, awe, owe, †aught,** *ptp* also †**auchtin 1** to be indebted or obliged (to someone), owe *la14-*. **2** to own, possess *la14-*. **awin, awn, owe, yaw,** *H&I* **aan,** *Bor* **awnd, †awand, owand, †owne 1** owing, indebted (to someone) for: ◊*A'm awnd'im naething* ◊*I'm owe 'im a shilling 15-*. **2** *of money* owed, due *15-*. †**aucht and wont** due and customary *la15-e16*. **wha's aucht?, wha's awe?** who owns?, to whom does this belong? *la16-*. [OE *āgan* possess; compare AUCHT²]
awe *see* AVE³
awebaund, †aweband, †awband /ˈɔbʌund/ *n* a check, a curb, a restraint, a deterrent *16-19, 20- Sh*. [ON *agi* discipline + BAND¹·¹]
awee /əˈwi/ *adv* **1** to a small extent or degree, somewhat *18-*. **2** a little while, a short distance *la18-*. [A¹ + WEE¹·¹]
aweel /əˈwil/ *adv* well: ◊*aweel, Jamie, what think ye? 19-*. †**aweel a wat** assuredly *la18-19*. [Scots *ah* + WEEL¹·³]
aweers /əˈwirz/ *adv* on the point (of) *19- NE*. [IN¹·⁴ + WEER]
awendand *see* AVENAND
awestill *see* A-WASTLE
awfy¹·¹, awfie, affy, affa, awfu, awful, *NE* **yafu, †awfull, †aufull, †auchful** /ˈɔfe, ˈafe, ˈafa, ˈafə, ˈɔfu, ˈɔfəl; *NE* ˈjafu/ *adj* **1** inspiring awe or dread; terrifying *la14-*. **2** shocking, terrible, dreadful *la18-*. **3** remarkable, very great *la18-*. **an awfu** a great many: ◊*thir wiz an affy wasps this year 20-*. **in an awfy wey** in a state of great distress *20-*. [OE *egefull*]
awfy¹·², awfie, affy, affa, awfu, awful /ˈɔfe, ˈafe, ˈafa, ˈafə, ˈɔfu, ˈɔfəl/ *adv* very, extremely; very much *19-*. [see the adj]
awgent *see* AGENT¹·¹
a'where, †alquhare, †all quhair, †alwhair /ˈɔmer/ *adv* everywhere *la14-*. †**our alquhare, our alquhair** everywhere; throughout *la14-16*. [AW¹·² + WHAUR¹·¹]
awhing *see* AWTHING
awid /əˈwɪd/ *adj* eager, longing *la19- T*. [A³ + WUD¹·¹]
awill /əˈwɪl/ *adv* astray *20- Ork*. [AT³ + WILL³·¹]
†**a will** *adv* of one's own accord, of itself *e18*. [AT³ + WILL³·²]
awin *see* AIN¹·¹, AWE
awite *see* AWYTE²
awka veety *see* AQUAVITAE
awkin *see* A'KIN
awkward *see* ACKWART¹·¹, ACKWART¹·²
awkwart *see* ACKWART¹·¹
awlien, alien /ˈɔliən, ˈeliən/ *n* a stranger, an outsider; a foreigner *la14-*. †**alienar** a foreigner or stranger *la15-e16*. [ME *alien*]
awmaist, amaist, almost, *Sh* **amest, †almaist, †almast, †amast** /ˈɔmest, aˈmest, ɔlˈmost; *Sh* aˈmɛst/ *adv* very nearly, all but; approximately *la15-*. **almost never** seldom or never *la18-*. [OE *eallmǽst*]
awmous *see* AMOS¹·¹
†**awn¹** *n pl* also **anis** an ass; a fool *la15-16*. [OFr *asne* an ass]
awn², own, †owen /ɔn, on/ *v* **1** to possess *la17-*. **2** to acknowledge as a relation or acquaintance, give recognition to; to have to do with; to come into contact with; to lay claim to *la17-*. **owner, †ownar 1** a proprietor, possessor *la15-*. **2** a shipowner *la16-17*. [OE *āgnian*; compare AWE]

awn *see* AIN¹·¹, AWE
awnd *see* AWE
awne *see* AIN¹·², YAWIN
awner *see* AWN²
awnie *see* YAWIN
awnt *see* AUNT
awntyr *see* ANTER¹·²
awny *see* YAWIN
awoik, awoilk, awoke *see* AWAUK¹·¹
†**awonder** *v* to astonish, surprise *e16*. [probably OE *ofwundrian*]
awow *see* AVOW¹·²
†**awppis** *npl* curlews or bullfinches *e16*. [perhaps erron for *quhawppis* (WHAUP¹·¹)]
Awpril, Awprile *see* APRILE
awpron *see* APRIN
awreddie *see* A'READY
awrige *see* ARRIDGE
awright¹·¹, awricht, alricht, aaricht /ɔˈrʌɪt, ɔˈrɪxt, alˈrɪxt, aˈrɪxt/ *adj* satisfactory, fine, acceptable *20-*. [AW¹·³ + RICHT¹·³]
awright¹·², awricht, alricht, aaricht /ɔˈrʌɪt, ɔˈrɪxt, alˈrɪxt, aˈrɪxt/ *adv* satisfactorily, well; certainly, indeed *20-*. [see the adj]
awsk *see* ASK¹
awte, aat /ɔt, at/ *n* the grain of wood or rock; a flaw; a crack in the skin *19- NE*. [perhaps Gael *alt* joint]
awthegither, a'thegither, aathegither, athegidder /ɔðəˈgɪðər, aðəˈgɪðər, ɔðəˈgɪdər/ *adv* altogether *19-*. [AW¹·³ + THEGITHER]
awthing, athing, aathing, awhing, †all thing, †althing /ˈɔθɪŋ, ˈaθɪŋ, ˈɔhɪŋ/ *pron* everything *la14-*. [AW¹·² + THING¹]
awyte¹, await /əˈwʌɪt, əˈwet/ *v* **1** to wait for *la16-*. **2** to wait upon, attend on *la15-16*. **3** to lie in wait for, waylay *16*. Compare AWAIT. [ME *awaiten*]
awyte², awite, awat, †await /əˈwʌɪt, əˈwat/ *adv* assuredly, indeed *19, 20- NE*. [AH + *wat* (WIT¹·²); compare ATWEEL]
ax, ask, †as, †ase /aks, ask/ *v pt* also **ast** to inquire, question; to request; to require or demand *la14-*. **ask at** to ask (a person) *15-*. [OE *ascian*]
ax, axe *see* AIX
axes *see* AIXIES
axile *see* AIXLE
axtre, axtree *see* AIXTREE
ay, ae /e/ *interj* an expression of surprise or wonder *19-*. [ME *ei*]
ay *see* AYE¹, AYE², O²
aye¹, ay /ae, e/ *adv* **1** yes *19-*. **2** hello: ◊*aye aye Souter! 19-*. **3** an ironic expression of disbelief *20-*. **aye right** an ironic expression of disbelief *la20-*. [unknown]
aye², ay, ey /ae, e/ *adv* **1** always, continually; at all times *la14-*. **2** still; all the same *19-*. †**ay lestand** everlasting *la14-15*. †**aye and while, ay and quhill** *law* until, during the time that *la15-19*. [ON *ei*]
ayen *see* EEAN
ayest *see* AEST¹·²
ayewis, eywis /ˈaewɪz/ *adv* always *la20-*. [probably conflation of ALWAYS and AYE²]
†**aying, eyne** *n in Orkney* inherited property *16-e17*. [ON *eign*]
ayk *see* AIK
aylay *see* ALLEY
ayler *see* ELDER¹·¹
ayme *see* EEM²
aynd *see* END, YIND
aynt *see* AUNT

ayont[1.1], *NE* **ayon** /əˈjɔnt; *NE* əˈjɔn/ *adv* further on, on the other side, beyond *la18-*. [see the prep]

ayont[1.2], *NE* **ayon** /əˈjɔnt; *NE* əˈjɔn/ *prep* beyond; later than *la18-*. [A³ + YONT[1.1]]

ayr *see* AIR¹, AIR³, AIR[5.1], AIR[5.2], AYRE, HEIR[1.1]

ayre, **air**, *Ork* **ire**, *Ork* **oire**, †**ayr**, †**ere** /er; *Ork* aer; *Ork* ɔɪr/ *n* **1** a gravelly beach; a gravel bed; a sandy or gravelly spit or bank of land *16- Sh Ork*. **2** hard earth around a house; hard, gravelly clay; muddy puddles which collect on hard ground *20- Ork*. [ON *eyrr* a gravel bank]

Ayrshire /ˈerʃaer, ˈerʃər/ *n* **1** a county in the South-West of Scotland *18-*. **2** (one of) a breed of dairy cattle *19-*. **Ayrshire blanket** a cream-coloured woollen blanket with coloured stripes woven into both ends *la19-*. †**Ayrshire Lassie** a set opening in the game of draughts *la19*. **Ayrshire needlework** fine needlework on muslin *19-*. **Ayrshire rose** (one of the) varieties of cultivated roses developed from the species rose *Rosa arvensis 19-*. [from the name of the town of *Ayr* + SHIRE¹]

ayther *see* AITHER[1.3], AITHER[1.4]

B

ba[1], **baa**, **baw**, **ball** /ba, bɔ, bɔl/ *n* **1** a ball (used in playing games) *15-*. **2** a sphere, a spherical object *la15-*. **3** a testicle *16-*. **4** a game played with a ball *la18-*. †**ba cod**, **ball cod** the scrotum *la15-e17*. **ba-day** the day of an annual football or HAND-BA game *la19-*. **ball-green**, †**balgrene** a piece of grass on which ball games are played *17-19, 20- historical*. **ba-money** coins thrown for children at a wedding *20-*. **ba-siller** coins thrown for children at a wedding *la19-*. **ba' stane**, **bawstane** a testicle *16-*. **the ba 1** the annual game of football played in some areas on Shrove Tuesday *la19-*. **2** a game of HAND-BA played on certain annual holidays *20-*. †**the ba'in** a game of football *la18-19*. **the baw's burst**, **the ba's up on the slates** it's a hopeless situation, the game is over *la20-*. **it's ma ba'** a (childish) assertion uttered during a disagreement by a participant who insists on having his or her own way *la20-*. [probably ME *bale*]

ba[2], **baw** /ba, bɔ/ *v* to lull, hush (a child) to sleep *la16-*. **baw baw**, **baw baws**, **ba bas** a child's word for a bed or for going to sleep *la19-*. Compare *beddie ba* (BED[1.1]). [nonsense word]

ba see BAA[2], BALL[1]

baa[1.1], †**bae** /ba/ *n* the cry or bleat of a sheep or goat *16-*. **baa lamb** a lamb *17-*. [onomatopoeic]

baa[1.2], †**bae** /ba/ *v* **1** *of a sheep or goat* to bleat *la18-*. **2** *of a person* to speak in a bellowing or bleating tone *la19-*. [see the noun]

baa[2], **ba** /bɑ, ba/ *n* **1** the surf created by sunken rocks *19- Sh*. **2** a sunken rock in the sea *20- Sh*. **bafall** the rush of a wave; a splash *20- Sh*. Compare BO[3]. [Norn *ba*, ON *boði* submerged rock, breaker]

baa see BA[1]

baak see BAUK[1.1], BAUK[2]

baakie, **baagie**, **baggie**, †**bawgie**, †**baukie** /'bɑki, 'bagi/ *n* **1** the great blackbacked gull *Larus marinus* *la19- Sh Ork NE H&I*. **2** the razorbill *Alca torda la19- Sh Ork*. [ON *bak* the back]

baal, **bal**, **ball** /bɑl, bal/ *v* to throw or fling; to strike noisily *20- Sh Ork*. [ON *bella* to hit]

baal see BAULD[1.3]

baalie see BALLIE

baand see BAND[1.1], BAND[1.2]

baat see BITE[1.2]

baathe see BATH[1.2]

bab /bab/ *n* a baby *16-*. [variant of ME *babe*]

bab see BOB[1], BOB[2.2]

bab-at-the-bowster, **bob-at-the-bowster**, **babbity bowster**, **bobbity bowster** /'babətɔɪ'bʌustər, 'bɔbətɔɪ'bʌustər, 'babəte'bʌustər, 'bɔbəte'bʌustər/ *n* **1** a country dance; the dance which closed a ball *19-*. **2** a children's game (of hopping or leaping) *la19-*. [BOB[2.2] + BOWSTER]

babben see BABBIN

babbie, **babby** /'babi, 'babe/ *n* a baby, an infant *16-*. [BAB with diminutive suffix *-ie*]

babbin, †**babben** /'babɪn/ *n* a bobbin, a reel of thread *la17-19, 20- WC*. [unknown]

babbinqua see BOBBINQUAW

babbity bowster see BAB-AT-THE-BOWSTER

babby see BABBIE

babie see BAWBEE

babord, †**baburd**, †**bawburd** /'babərd/ *n* larboard, the port side of a ship *16-19, 20- historical*. [Fr *bâbord*; compare OE *bæcbord*, Du *bakboord*, ON *bakborði*]

baby's piece /bebez 'pis/ *n* a bag containing a slice of cake, some cheese and a coin offered to the first person to see a baby after its christening *la19- NE T C*. [possessive of Older Scots *babie* + PIECE]

bachelor, **bacheleer**, †**bachelere**, †**bachiller**, †**bachleir** /'batʃələr, batʃə'lir/ *n* **1** a university student who has completed a first degree *15-*. **2** an unmarried man *18-*. **3** *Scottish Universities* a third-year student *18-19, 20- historical*. **4** a young knight *la14-17*. **bachelor's buttons** a mint-flavoured hard sweet, a mint imperial *20-*. **bachelor coal** a type of dead coal which turns white in the fire *la19-*. [ME *bachelor*]

bachle see BAUCHLE[1.1], BAUCHLE[1.2]

back[1.1], **bak**, †**bake** /bak/ *n* **1** the back (of a person, animal or object) *la14-*. **2** the reverse (of a thing), the side opposite the front *16-*. **3** the outermost boards from a sawn tree *la17-19, 20- NE T*. **4** the turf placed at the back of the fire *20- NE*. **5** a backer, backing; support *la15-19*. **6** *mining* a fault in a seam; a main (almost) vertical joint by which strata are intersected *e19*. **at a back** at a loss *20- NE*. **at the back o'** not long after: ◊*at the back o' six 19-*. **at the back o' the mune** at a very great distance *la19-*. **at yer back** behind you *la20-*. †**bak and bed** possession or provision of clothing and bedding *la14-16*. **the back o' beyond**, **the back o' beyont** a remote, inaccessible place *19-*. **the back o' ma hand tae** a gesture or expression of farewell or dismissal *la18-*. **come up yer back** come into one's mind, fit in with one's own inclination (to do something) *la19-*. **go up yer back** be beyond one's power *la19- NE T*. **on the back o'** = *at the back o'*. **wi yer back tae the wa'** hard-pressed, facing desperate odds *la16-*. **ye'll get the back o ma hand** a threat to strike a (young) person *20-*. [OE *bæc*]

back[1.2] /bak/ *v* **1** to support, assist; to back up *16-*. **2** to furnish with a back; to cover the back of *la16-*. **3** to carry on the back *la16-*. **4** to address (a letter); to endorse a (folded document) *18-*. **5** *mining* to throw coal along the face to the roadhead *la19-*. **6** to bank up a fire (for the night) *20-*. **7** to drive back; to repress or harm *la15-16*. **backing turf**, **backing truff** a turf laid on a low fire to keep it burning through the night *19, 20- NE*. [see the noun]

back[1.3] /bak/ *adj* **1** situated to the rear *15-*. **2** late, falling behindhand; *of payments* overdue, in arrears *19-*. **hae aw yer back teeth** to be wise or astute *la20-*. [see the noun]

back[1.4] /bak/ *adv* in a direction to the rear or already travelled; rearwards, in a reverse direction *15-*. **back and fore**, †**bak and foir 1** backwards and forwards *la17-*. **2** *of land and property* including both the front and rear *la16-19*. **back oot owre** backwards; away (from) *la19, 20- NE*. **back owre**, †**bak owir** behind; backwards *17-*. [see the noun]

back[2], **bauk** /bak, bɔk/ *n* an instrument for toasting; a girdle *19, 20- NE T*. [unknown]

back[3] /bɑk/ *n* in Orkney a partition wall dividing the animals' part of a building from the house *20- historical*. [ON *bálkr* a partition, a low wall in a house]

back see BAUK[1.1], BAUK[2]

back-aboot /ˈbakabut/ *adj* **1** *of a place* remote, lonely *la19- Sh.* **2** *of a person* old-fashioned, out-of-date *20- Sh.* [BACK[1.3] + ABOOT[1.1]]

backagruf *see* BAKKAGROF

backart[1.1], **backwart**, †**bakwart** /ˈbakərt, ˈbakwərt/ *adj* backward; late, slow; perverse; hesitant *la16-.* [BACK[1.3], with *-ward* suffix]

backart[1.2], **backwart**, †**bakwart**, †**bakward** /ˈbakərt, ˈbakwərt/ *adv* backwards, towards the rear *la14-.* [see the adj]

backarts, **backwarts**, †**bakwarts** /ˈbakərts, ˈbakwərts/ *adv* backwards *16-.* **backarties** backwards *20- NE T EC.* [BACK[1.4], with adv-forming suffix denoting direction]

backband, **backbond** /ˈbakband, ˈbakbɔnd/ *n law* a deed attaching a qualification or condition to the terms of a conveyance or other instrument *la16-.* Compare BACK-LETTER. [BACK[1.3] + BAND[1.1]]

backbane, *NE T* **backbeen** /ˈbakben; *NE T* ˈbakbin/ *n* a backbone *la18-.* [BACK[1.1] + BANE]

back-bid /ˈbakbɪd/ *v* to bid at an auction merely to raise the prices *la19- NE.* Compare BACK-ROUP. [BACK[1.3] + BID[1]]

back-birn /ˈbakbɪrn/ *n* a burden carried on the back *la18-19, 20- NE.* [BACK[1.1] + BIRN]

backbond *see* BACKBAND

back-brack /ˈbakbrak/ *n* excessive fatigue *20- Sh.* [BACK[1.1] + BRAK[1.1]]

†**back-breed** *n* a fall or throw on the back *la19.* [BACK[1.1] + BREED[1]]

back-calver /ˈbakkavər/ *n* a cow which calves towards the end of the year *la19-.* [BACK[1.3] + Eng *calver*]

backcast /ˈbakkast/ *n* **1** a setback in luck or health *18-19, 20- Bor.* **2** an unexpected blow *19- literary.* [BACK[1.3] + CAST[1.1]]

back chap /ˈbak tʃap/ *n* **1** an answering blow made by a helper with a smaller hammer (when a blacksmith makes a blow with a large hammer) *19-.* **2** a retort, a response *la19- NE T.* **3** a helping hand *la19- NE T.* [BACK[1.3] + CHAP[3.1]]

back close /bak ˈklos/ *n* **1** an enclosure or passageway to the rear of a building; a narrow lane (lined with houses) giving access to a larger building *19-.* **2** the part of a tenement close beyond the stairway giving access to the rear garden or courtyard *20-.* [BACK[1.3] + CLOSE[1]]

backcome /ˈbakkʌm/ *n* **1** a return *19-.* **2** recrimination; an expression of regret or disappointment *la19-.* **backcoming**, †**bak cuming** a return *la16-.* [BACK[1.4] + COME[1.2]]

back court, **back coort** /bak ˈkort, bak ˈkurt/ *n* the (enclosed) communal courtyard or garden at the rear of a tenement *la17-.* [BACK[1.3] + COORT[1.1]]

backdoor, †**bak dure** /bakˈdor/ *n* a rear entrance *la16-.* **back-door trot** diarrhoea *la18-.* [BACK[1.3] + DOOR]

backdraa *see* BACK-DRAW

backdraucht /ˈbakdrɔxt/ *n* a drawing in of the breath; the gasp in whooping cough *19- NE T EC.* [BACK[1.3] + DRAUCHT[1.1]]

back-draw, *Sh* **backdraa** /ˈbakdrɔ; *Sh* ˈbakdrɑ/ *n* **1** a drawback, a disadvantage *20-.* **2** a drawing back from an agreement *20- NE Bor.* **3** a sharp inhalation of breath (as with whooping cough) *20- Sh.* [BACK[1.3] + DRAW[1.1]]

backdyke, †**bak-dyke** /bakˈdʌɪk/ *n* a rear wall (of a yard or garden) *16-.* [BACK[1.3] + DYKE[1]]

backen, **back end** /bakˈɛn, bak ˈɛnd/ *n* the end of harvest, late autumn *19-.* [BACK[1.3] + EN[1.1]]

backet, †**bakkat** /ˈbakət/ *n* **1** a shallow wooden receptacle (used for carrying mortar, flour, fuel or ashes) *15-.* **2** a dustbin *20- N NE EC*; compare BUCKET. **backetfu'** as much as a backet would hold *la19- NE T Bor.* [MFr *bacquet*]

backfa /ˈbakfɔ/ *n* the outlet of a mill lade *la19, 20- Bor.* [BACK[1.3] + FA[1.1]]

back-feast, **backfaeste** /ˈbakfist, ˈbakfast/ *n* an entertainment given by the best man in response to the wedding feast *19- Sh Ork.* [BACK[1.3] + Older Scots *fest*, Scots *feast*]

backfet /bakˈfɛt/ *adj* bent backwards *20- Ork.* [BACK[1.4] + ON *fattir* bent backwards]

†**back-friend** *n* a supporter; one who does his best for another *18-e19.* [BACK[1.1] + FREEND[1.1]]

backfu /ˈbakfu/ *n* as much as can be carried on one's back *19-.* [BACK[1.1] + -FU]

back-gane, **back-gaen**, **back-gaun** /ˈbakgen, ˈbakgɔn/ *adj of people and animals* not thriving *la18-19, 20- SW.* [from the verb *gae back* (GAE)]

back gangin /ˈbakgaŋɪn/ *n* a relapse *19-.* [from the verb *gae back* (GAE)]

backgate /ˈbakget/ *n* a back road *19, 20- NE.* **go the backgate** to act cunningly or deceitfully *20- NE T.* [BACK[1.3] + GATE[1]]

backgates, †**backgate** /ˈbakgets/ *adv* backwards *la18-.* [BACK[1.3] + GAIT[3]]

back-gaun *see* BACK-GANE

back green /bak ˈgrin/ *n* a back garden, a communal (grassed) area behind a tenement *la18-.* [BACK[1.3] + GREEN[1.1]]

back-hand rent /bakhand ˈrɛnt/ *n law* rent payable by agreement later than at the legal term *la19-.* [Scots *back-hand* overdue + RENT[2]]

backhash, **baghash** /ˈbakhaʃ, ˈbaghaʃ/ *v* to abuse, scold vigorously *19- NE T.* [probably BACK[1.4] + HASH[1.2]]

backie[1] /ˈbaki, ˈbake/ *n* **1** a hoist on the back; a piggy-back *la19-.* **2** a ride on the back of a bicycle *la20-.* **3** a back green or back garden *la20-.* **4** a defensive position in football *la20-.* **buckie up** a hoist on the back *la20-.* [BACK[1.1], with *-ie* suffix]

backie[2], **bawkie**, **baukie** /ˈbaki, ˈbɔki/ *n* a name for various species of bat, especially *Pipistrellus pipistrellus la19-.* **backie-bird**, **bawkie-bird**, †**bauckie-bird** a bat *la18-.* [BAK, with *-ie* diminutive suffix]

backie *see* BAIKIE[2]

backing, **backin** /ˈbakɪŋ, ˈbakɪn/ *n* **1** provision of a back; material for this *la16-.* **2** the address (on a letter) *la19-.* **3** *pl* refuse of wool or tow *la18-19.* **backing rock** a distaff used in spinning *la19, 20- historical.* [verbal noun from BACK[1.2]]

back-jar /bak dʒar/ *n* a setback in health or circumstances *la19- NE.* [BACK[1.3]; second element perhaps related to Older Scots *jar* discord]

back-jaw /ˈbakdʒɔ/ *n* impudence, abusive language *la19- NE WC.* [BACK[1.3] + Eng *jaw* impudent talk]

backland /ˈbakland/ *n* the rear section of a piece of ground; a building erected on the rear section of a plot of land; a tenement or house built behind another *la15-.* [BACK[1.3] + LAND[1.1]]

back-letter /ˈbaklɛtər/ *n law* a deed attaching a qualification or condition to the terms of a conveyance or other instrument *la18-.* Compare BACKBAND. [BACK[1.3] + LETTER]

backlick /ˈbaklɪk/ *n* **1** a back-handed or low blow; a final or decisive blow *19, 20- NE.* **2** a return stroke in a ball game *20- NE T.* [BACK[1.1] + LICK[1.1]]

backlins, †**backlingis** /ˈbaklɪnz/ *adv* backwards *15-.* [BACK[1.4], with adv-forming suffix denoting direction; compare OE *bæclinge*, Dan *baklengis*]

back-lyin', **back-lying** /ˈbaklaɪən, ˈbaklaeən/ *adj* **1** *of land* having a northern, bleak exposure; remote *19-.* **2** *of money* overdue, in arrears; payable at a later date *la19-.* [BACK[1.3] + LIE[1.2]]

backman /ˈbakman/ *n* **1** a porter, a person who carries loads on his back *17-19, 20- historical.* **2** a retainer, a follower *la16-e19.* [BACK[1.3] + MAN[1.1]]

back-peat, **backpaet** /ˈbakpit, ˈbakpɛt/ *n* the peat against which a domestic fire is built *20- Sh Ork*. [BACK[1.3] + PEAT[1.1]]

back-rape, †**bak-raip** /ˈbakrep/ *n* the rope which keeps the traces in place over a horse's back *17-19, 20- WC*. [BACK[1.1] + RAIP[1.1]]

back-rope /ˈbakrop/ *n fishing* a rope from which nets are hung; the messenger or warp-rope in a fleet of herring nets *19- Sh Ork H&I*. [BAUK[2] + rope (RAIP[1.1])]

†**back-roup** *v* to bid at an auction merely to raise the prices *la18-19*; compare BACK-BID. [BACK[1.3] + ROUP[1.1]]

backset[1] /ˈbakset/ *n* something which hinders or causes a relapse *18-*. [BACK[1.4] + SET[1.1]]

backset[2] /bakˈsɛt/ *v* to weary or fatigue; to worry; to disgust or upset *la19- NE*. [BACK[1.4] + SET[1.1]]

backsey /ˈbakse/ *n* a name for various parts of the loin of beef (or other meat) *la17-19, 20- NE SW*. [BACK[1.1] with variant of *-sie* familiar suffix]

backside /bakˈsʌɪd, ˈbaksʌɪd/ *n* 1 the back part of a house or tenement; the space, yard or fields at the rear of a building *la15-*. 2 the rear or reverse *16-*. 3 the posterior *19-*. 4 *pl* the parts of a town off the main streets *19, 20- Bor*. **backside foremaist, backside foremost** back to front, inside out, the wrong way round *19-*. **on the backside** on the side facing the back, behind *la15-*. [BACK[1.3] + SIDE[1]]

backspang /ˈbakspaŋ/ *n* 1 (the taking of) an underhand advantage *19-*. 2 a legal flaw or loophole *19*. [BACK[1.3] + SPANG[2.1]]

backspeir /bakˈspir/ *v* to question closely, cross-examine *la16-*. [BACK[1.4] + SPEIR]

†**back-sprent** *n* 1 the back bone *19*. 2 a spring or catch used as a hold or check *la16-e19*. [BACK[1.3] + SPRENT[1.1]]

backstair, †**bakstair** /bakˈster/ *n* stairs at the back of a building; a secondary staircase *16-*. [BACK[1.3] + STAIR[1]]

backstane /ˈbaksten/ *n* a stone forming the back of a hearth or fireplace *19- Sh T SW Uls*. [BACK[1.3] + STANE[1.1]]

†**back tack**, **bak tak** *n* a deed whereby the actual possession of land was continued, or returned to the proprietor, on payment of a rent corresponding to the interest of the loan *17-19*. [BACK[1.3] + TACK[2]]

back-water, †**bak water** /ˈbakwɔtər/ *n* the excess water in a mill lade *la16-20, 21- historical*. †**gar someone's een stan in back-water** to reduce someone to a state of helplessness *la17-19*. [BACK[1.3] + WATTER[1.1]]

†**back widdie** *n* the band over a cart saddle (supporting the shafts) *19*. [BACK[1.1] + WIDDIE]

back yett, †**bak ȝet** /bak ˈjɛt/ *n* a back gate or door *15-*. [BACK[1.1] + YETT]

bacon *see* BAWCON

bad[1.1] /bad/ *adj* 1 not good; of poor quality *la15-*. 2 unwell, ill; in pain *la19-*. **bad minded** having evil thoughts or intentions *la19-*. **bad yin** a wicked, dissolute person *20-*. **the bad fire** hell *20-*. **the bad man** the devil *la19-*. **the bad place** hell *la19-*. **nae bad, no bad** not bad, quite good *19-*. [unknown]

bad[1.2] /bad/ *adv* badly *20-*. **bad use** to ill-treat; to misuse; to abuse *la19- Sh NE T*. [unknown]

bad *see* BATH[1.2], BAUD, BID[1]

badd, bad, †**baud** /bɑd, bad/ *n* an article of clothing *la19- Sh*. [Norn *bad*]

badder *see* BATHER[1.1], BATHER[1.2]

badderlock, batherlock /ˈbadərlɔk, ˈbaðərlɔk/ *n* an edible variety of seaweed *Alaria esculenta la18-*. [unknown]

baddock /ˈbadək/ *n* (the young of) the coalfish *Pollachius virens la18- NE Bor*. [perhaps Gael *bodach ruadh* a codfish, from *bodach* an old man]

†**bade, baid** *n* waiting; delay, pause *la14-16*. **but bade** without (further) delay *la14-16*. **withoutin baid** = *but bade*. [from the past tense of BIDE[1.2]]

bade *see* BID[1], BIDE[1.2]

badkin *see* BAUDKIN

badly /ˈbadli, ˈbadle/ *adj* ill, ailing *la18-*. [BAD, with -*ly* adj-forming suffix]

bad-money, †**bald-money** /ˈbadmʌne/ *n* the herb gentian *Gentiana lutea* or the spignel *Meum athamanticum*, used medicinally *19, 20- Bor*. [unknown]

badness /ˈbadnəs/ *n* 1 wickedness *la16-*. 2 inferior quality, poor condition *18-*. 3 illness *18-*. 4 spite, malice *la20-*. **for badness** out of mischief, for spite *la20-*. [BAD, with -*ness* noun forming suffix]

badock, †**badoch** /ˈbadək/ *n* 1 the great skua *Catharacta skua la19-*. 2 the arctic skua *Stercorarius parasiticus e19*. [perhaps Gael *beadach* forward, impertinent]

badrans *see* BAUDRONS

bae *see* BAA[1.1], BAA[1.2]

baelt *see* BELD[1.3]

baeshin /ˈbeʃən/ *n* a bowl or open container; a basin *19- SW*. [altered form of BASIN]

baess *see* BEAST[1.1]

baet /bet/ *n* a bundle of grass stalks or straw *la19- Sh Ork*. [altered form of BEET[1]]

baet *see* BATE[1.1], BATE[1.2]

baff[1.1] /baf/ *n* a (soft) blow *la16-*. [OFr *baffe*]

baff[1.2] /baf/ *v* to beat or strike; to struggle *la19, 20- Sh NE*. [see the noun; compare BEFF[1.2]]

baff[2] /baf/ *n* a slipper, a shoe for indoor use *20-*. [probably BAFF[1.1]]

baff[3] /baf/ *n* a poultice *la19- Sh*. [Norn *baf* to warm, poultice; probably from ON *baða* to warm up, but the form influenced by BAFF[1.1]]

baffie[1], **baffy** /ˈbafi, ˈbafe/ *n* a type of golf club equivalent to the modern no. 4 wood *la19- historical*. [shortened form of BAFFING SPOON]

baffie[2], **baffy** /ˈbafi, ˈbafe/ *n* a slipper, a shoe for indoor use *20-*. [probably BAFF[1.1]]

baffing, baffin /ˈbafɪŋ, ˈbafɪn/ *n of waves or weather* the action of beating or dashing; a drenching *e16, 20- Ork*. [probably derivative of BAFF[1.2]]

baffing spoon /ˈbafɪŋ spun/ *n* a type of golf club equivalent to the modern no. 4 wood *la19, 20- historical*. [BAFFING + SPUIN]

baffy *see* BAFFIE[2]

bafuff, ballfuff /baˈfʌf, balˈfʌf/ *n* a (remote and unspecified) fictitious place *la19- NE T*. **the back o bafuff, the back o balfuff** the back of beyond *la19- NE T*. [nonsense word]

bag[1.1], *NE* **bug** /bag; *NE* bʌg/ *n* 1 a money-bag, a pouch; a purse *15-*. 2 a small sack; a piece of luggage *16-*. 3 the stomach; the paunch *18-*. 4 *pl* the bagpipes *19-*. **bagrel** a small fish, a minnow; a child or small person *19, 20- T Bor*. **Baggie Aggie** a woman wearing large ill-fitting clothes *la20- C*. **bag-a-rintle** sacking *20- Sh*. **bag irnis** the metal mountings of a bag *la15*. **bag raip** the double rope fastened round the eaves to secure thatching *19- NE T*. [probably ON *baggi*]

bag[1.2] /bag/ *v* 1 to put in a bag *19-*. 2 to stuff or cram; to cause to swell like a bag *la20-*. [see the noun]

†**bagcheik** *n* the Henry VIII groat *e16*. [so called from the appearance of the king's face on the coin]

†**bage, baige** *n* a heraldic badge *16-17*; compare BAGIE. [ME *bage*, Lat *bagea, bagia*]

bagening /ˈbɛdʒənɪŋ/ *n* rough horseplay; a thrashing, rough treatment *la19, 20- Bor*. [unknown]

baggage /ˈbagədʒ/ *n* **1** luggage *la16-*. **2** rubbish *la19- NE T*. [ME *bagage*]
bagget *see* BAGGIT¹·¹
baggie¹, baggy /ˈbagi, ˈbagɛ/ *n* **1** a minnow *19-*. **2** a small bag *la20-*. **3** the stomach, the belly *la18-e19*. **baggie minnie, baggie minnow, baggie minnen** a minnow *19-*. [BAG¹·¹, with *-ie* diminutive suffix]
baggie², *Bor* **baigie** /ˈbagi; *Bor* ˈbegɛ/ *n* the swede *Brassica napobrassica la19- EC Bor*. [compare Swed dial *rotabagge*]
baggie *see* BAAKIE
baggit¹·¹, baggot, †bagget /ˈbagət/ *n* **1** the coalfish *Pollachius virens la19- NE*. **2** an unspawned salmon *19-, 20- C*. [see the adj]
baggit¹·² /ˈbagət/ *adj* **1** big with young, pregnant *15-19, 20- literary*. **2** *of a fish* full of spawn *la16-19, 20- Bor*. **3** bulging, swollen; baggy *19-*. **4** corpulent, big-bellied *19-, 20- Sh Bor*. [probably ptp of BAG¹·²]
†baggit² *adj of a stallion* having testicles, entire *e16*. [BAG¹·¹, with *-it* adj forming suffix]
baggonet, baigonet, †baignet, †bagnet, †bagonet /ˈbagənɛt, ˈbegənɛt/ *n* a bayonet *la17-*. [altered form of Eng *bayonet*]
baggot *see* BAGGIT¹·¹
baghash *see* BACKHASH
†bagie *n* a heraldic badge *16*; compare BAGE. [ME *bagy*]
bagle *see* BAIGLE
baglin /ˈbaglɪn/ *n* a puny or wayward child *20- N*. [BAG¹·¹ with *-ling* suffix]
bag off¹·¹ /ˈbag ɔf/ *n* a prospective sexual partner; a casual pick-up *la20- NE EC*. [unknown]
bag off¹·², bag oaf /bag ˈɔf, bag ˈof/ *v* to have casual sex or a casual sexual relationship *la20- NE C*. [unknown]
bagpipe, †bagpype, †bagpyp /ˈbagpʌɪp/ *n* a musical instrument consisting of an airtight wind-bag and reed-pipes into which the air is pressed by the performer *la15-*. **bagpipes** = BAGPIPE. [BAG¹·¹ + PIPE]
ba heid *see* BAW HEID
bahookie, behooky, behouchie, bahoochie /bəˈhuki, bəˈhuxi/ *n* the buttocks, the backside *20-*. [conflation of Eng *behind* with *houch* (HOCH¹·¹)]
†bahuif, bahuv, balhuif *n* a chest, a coffer; a trunk (for storing clothes) *16-e17*. [OFr *bahu* a large trunk with an arched lid]
baible /ˈbebəl/ *v* to spill whilst drinking *19, 20- SW*. [perhaps related to Eng *beb* drink, with *-le* frequentative suffix]
baid *see* BADE, BED¹·¹, BED¹·²
baif *see* BEFF¹·¹
baige *see* BAGE
baigle, bagle, beegle /ˈbegəl, ˈbagəl, ˈbigəl/ *n* **1** a beagle, a small hound *19-*. **2** a disagreeable, dirty person *19-*. **3** a constable or sheriff officer *19*. [Eng *beagle*]
baik *see* BAKE¹·¹, BAKE¹·², BAUK¹·¹, BECK¹·¹, BECK¹·²
baikie¹, †bakie /ˈbeki, ˈbekɛ/ *n* **1** a square wooden container (for ashes, coal or rubbish) *17- C*; compare BACKET. **2** a (wooden) trough used for animal feed *20- WC SW*. [perhaps reduced form of BACKET]
baikie², *N* **backie, †baikine** /ˈbeki, ˈbekɛ; *N* ˈbaki/ *n* a stake or peg to which an animal's tether is fastened *la16-*. [unknown]
baikin *see* BAUDKIN
bailie, baillie, beylie, bylie, biley, †bailʒe, †ballie, †belʒe /ˈbeli, ˈbelɛ, ˈbʌɪli/ *n* **1** a town magistrate next in rank to the provost *la14-20, 21- historical*. **2** an administrative officer of a barony or regality *la14-19, 20- historical*. **3** a steward; a landlord's agent; a water-bailiff *la15-*. **4** a cattle-man on a farm *la19- NE*. **5** a title given to senior councillors in certain local authorities *la20-*. **bailiary, †baillerie, †bailliary** the jurisdiction of a bailie; the district administered by a bailie *la15-19, 20- historical*. **bailie court** a local court held by a bailie *16-20, 21- historical*. **†bailie work** work to be done by tenants as prescribed by the landlord's steward *la16-18*. [ME *bailli*]
bailiff, †bailive /ˈbelɪf/ *n* **1** a town magistrate *la16-18, 19- historical*. **2** a sheriff's officer *la17-*. **3** a landlord's agent; an overseer *19-*. [ME *bailiff*]
baill *see* BALE¹, BALE²
†baillie, bailʒe *n* a bailey, the (upper or lower) court of a castle *la15-e17*. [ME *bailly*]
baillie *see* BAILIE
bailyament /ˈbeljəmənt/ *n* prosperity *20- Ork*. [unknown]
bailʒe *see* BAILIE, BAILLIE
baim-flooer /bemˈfluər/ *n* a flower with radiating petals; a daisy *20- Ork*. [OE *bēam* a beam, a ray of light + FLOOER¹·¹]
bainish, *SW* **benish, †banis, †bannis, †bennisch** /ˈbenɪʃ; *SW* ˈbɛnɪʃ/ *v* to banish *la14-*. **bainishment, bannisment** banishment, exile *la16-*. [OFr *baniss-*, stem of *banir* to make a formal proclamation]
bair, †bare, †bore, †boir /ber/ *n* a boar *la14-19, 20- Sh*. [OE *bār*]
bair *see* BAR¹, BARE, BEAR²
baird *see* BARD¹, BEARD
bairdal, berdel /ˈberdəl/ *n* steatite, soapstone *la19- Sh*. [unknown]
bairdie *see* BEARDIE¹·¹, BEARDIE¹·²
bairge¹, barge /berdʒ, bardʒ/ *n* a small vessel, a barge *la14-*. [ME *barge*]
bairge² /berdʒ/ *v* to strut; to walk jerkily *19, 20- SW Bor*. [unknown]
bairge³·¹, berge /berdʒ, bɛrdʒ/ *n* (a person with) a loud, strong voice *la19- NE*. [unknown]
bairge³·², berge /berdʒ, bɛrdʒ/ *v* **1** to speak loudly and angrily; to scold or taunt loudly *19, 20- NE SW Bor*; compare ARGIE-BARGIE¹·². **2** *of a dog* to bark loudly *la19- NE*. [unknown]
bairge⁴ /berdʒ/ *v* to collide violently; to threaten with violence; to move clumsily and noisily *19, 20- NE*. [unknown]
bairge⁵, †barge, †bardge /berdʒ/ *n* **1** a slatted shutter similar to a venetian blind (used in drying-sheds) *la19-*. **2** a slat of wood to protect windows or doors from rain or floodwater *18-19*. [unknown]
bairn¹·¹, bern, †barne /bern, bɛrn/ *n* **1** a child; a baby, an infant; a young person; a son or daughter *la14-*. **2** a native of Falkirk (from the town's motto 'Better meddle wi' the Deil than the bairns o' Falkirk') *19-*. **3** a nickname for a player for, or supporter of, Falkirk Football Club *19-*; compare FALKIRK BAIRNS. **bairndom** childhood *20- Sh*. **bairnheid, bairnhood, †barnehede** childhood, infancy *la14-*. **bairnless, †bernles** childless, deprived of children *la14-*. **bairnlike, †barnelike** childlike *la16-*. **†barnage** childhood; youth *15-17*. **†bairnbed, †barnebed** the womb; a condition affecting the womb *16-19*. **bairn's bargain** a bargain that can be easily broken *19, 20- NE T EC*. **bairn's part, †barnis part** *law* a child's portion of heritable property; a legitim *la15-20, 21- historical*. **bairn's piece** a bag containing a slice of cake, some cheese and a coin offered to the first person to see a baby after its christening *la19- NE T EC*; compare BABY'S PIECE. [OE *bearn*, ON *barn*]
bairn¹·² /bern/ *v* to make pregnant *19-*. [see the noun]
bairne *see* BARN, BERN
bairnie /ˈberni, ˈbernɛ/ *n* a baby or small child *la17-*. [BAIRN¹·¹, with *-ie* diminutive suffix]

bairnly, **bairnlie**, †**barnelie** /ˈbernli, ˈbernle/ *adj* childish; childlike *16-*. **bairnliness** childishness *la16-*. [BAIRN[1.1], with *-lie* adj-forming suffix]

bairnrhyme /ˈbernrʌim/ *n* a poem for children *20-*. [BAIRN[1.1] + RHYME[1.1]]

†**bairntime**[1], **barneteme**, **barnetyme** *n* a brood of children; offspring (of people or animals) *15-19*. [OE *bearntēam*].

bairntime[2] /ˈberntʌim/ *n* childhood *19-* literary. [BAIRN[1.1] + TIME]

bais *see* BAISS[1], BAISS[2]

baise, **bease** /bez, biz/ *n* confusion, bewilderment *19-* T. [reduced form of ABUISE[1.1]]

baised, †**baisit**, †**basit**, †**bazed** /bezd/ *adj* dismayed, confused, bewildered *15-19, 20- SW*. [reduced form of ABUISE[1.2]]

baisies /ˈbesiz/ *n* the game of rounders *la19- NE* T. [Eng *base*, with *-ie* diminutive suffix]

baisit *see* BAISED

baiss[1], *Sh* **bess**, †**bais** /bes; *Sh* bɛs/ *v* to baste, sew loosely with long stitches *16-*. [ME *basten*]

†**baiss**[2], **bais**, **base** *v* to beat soundly *16-19*. [unknown]

baissin /ˈbesən/ *n* a beating *19- NE T C Bor*. [derivative of BAISS[2]]

baissin *see* BASIN

baist *see* BUIST[1]

bait[1.1] /bet/ *n* **1** food used to entice fish, fishing bait *la15-*. **2** food, refreshment; a feed for horses; a halt in a journey (for food or rest); pasturage for animals *la15-*. **3** a seed potato *la19- Sh*. [ON *beit* grazing, something to eat]

bait[1.2] /bet/ *v* **1** to stop (on a journey) for food or rest; to feed or pasture a horse (during a break in a journey) *14-*. **2** to attack or assail with dogs *16-*. **3** to bait a fishing line; to entice with bait *la16-*. [ON *beita* to graze]

bait *see* BAT[2], BITE[1.2], BOAT[1.1]

baitchel, **betchell** /ˈbetʃəl, ˈbetʃəl/ *v* to beat soundly, thrash *19- Bor*. [related to BATE[1.2]]

baith[1.1], **both**, †**bathe**, †**beith** /beθ, boθ/ *adj* one and the other; two together, both *la14-*. †**baith tway** both *e16*. †**play with baith the handis** to act dishonestly or with duplicity *16*. [ON *báðar*]

baith[1.2], **both**, †**bathe**, †**beith** /beθ, boθ/ *adv* both; jointly *la14-*. †**bathe as ane and ane as bathe** *law* jointly and equally *15-16*. [see the adj]

baith[1.3], **both**, †**bathe**, †**beith** /beθ, boθ/ *pron* the one as well as the other, both *la14-*. [see the adj]

baith[1.4], **both** /beθ, boθ/ *conj* not only, both *19-*. [see the adj]

baith *see* BATH[1.1]

baittle, †**battill** /ˈbetəl/ *adj* of grass or pasture rich, luxuriant *16-19, 20- Bor*. [unknown]

baiver *see* BEVER[1], BEVER[2.2]

baiverage *see* BEVERAGE

baivis, **beevis** /ˈbevɪs, ˈbivɪs/ *n* a large fire, a great blaze *19, 20- NE EC*. [unknown]

bajan, **bajon** *see* BEJAN

†**bak** *n* a bat, a nocturnal animal capable of flight *la15-16*. [ME *bakke*]

bak *see* BACK[1.1], BAUK[1.1]

bak dure *see* BACKDOOR

bak-dyke *see* BACKDYKE

bake[1.1], †**baik** /bek/ *n* **1** a (usually thick or soft) biscuit *16-*. **2** a share of something *19- SW*. **3** a peat kneaded from wet peat dust *la18*. **bakie** a peat kneaded from wet peat dust *19- SW*. [see the verb]

bake[1.2], *NE* **byaak**, †**baik** /bek/ *NE* bjak/ *v pt also* **beuk**, †**buke**, *ptp* **baken**, †**ybaik** **1** to cook by dry heat (in an oven); to harden by exposure to heat *15-*. **2** to knead dough *19*. **baker**, †**bakar** a person who bakes *14-*. **bake-board**, **bake-brod**, **bakebreid**, †**baikbuird**, †**bakbred**, †**baikbraid** a board for kneading and rolling dough *la15-*. †**baikstule**, **bakstule** a stool used in bread-making *la14-16*. [OE *bacan*]

bake *see* BACK[1.1]

baken *see* BAKE[1.2]

bakflakki /bakˈflaki/ *n* a protective mat *20- Sh*. [ON *bakflaki* a raft of wicker or boards nailed together]

bakflan /bakˈflan/ *n* a sudden, backwards gust of wind *20- Sh*. [BACK[1.3] + FLAN[1.1]]

bakie *see* BAIKIE[1]

bakister *see* BAXTER

bakkagrof, †**backagruf** /bakəˈgrɔf/ *n* the face of peat at the bottom of a peat-bank *la19- Sh*. [ON *bakki* bank + *gróf* pit]

bakkat *see* BACKET

bakon *see* BAWCON

bak-raip *see* BACK-RAPE

bakstair *see* BACKSTAIR

bakstar *see* BAXTER

bak tak *see* BACK TACK

bakwarts *see* BACKARTS

bak water *see* BACK-WATER

bak ȝet *see* BACK YETT

bal *see* BAAL

Balaam /ˈbaləm/ *n* **1** the name of a prophet from *The Book of Numbers la16-*. **2** *in printing and publishing* second-rate copy kept in reserve to fill a gap in a newspaper or magazine *19-*. [from the name of the prophet]

balance *see* BALLANCE

balbe *see* BAWBEE

bald *see* BAULD[1.1], BAULD[1.2], BAULD[1.3], BELD[1.3]

baldairie *see* BALDERRY

baldeen, **baldin** /ˈbaldin, ˈbaldɪn/ *n* the halibut *Hippoglossus hippoglossus la19- Sh*. [compare ON *baldinn* untractable, unruly]

balderonis *see* BAUDRONS

balderry, **baldairie**, **beldairy**, **bulldairy**, *Ork* **puldary** /ˈbɔldɛri, ˈbalderi, ˈbɛlderi, ˈbʌlderi; *Ork* ˈpʌlderi/ *n* any of several types of wild orchids including *Dactylorhiza maculata* (sometimes thought to have aphrodisiac powers) *la18-19, 20- Sh Ork SW Bor*. [unknown]

baldie *see* BAULDIE

baldin *see* BALDEEN

bald-money *see* BAD-MONEY

baldy *see* BAULDY[1.1], BAULDY[1.2]

bale[1], †**baill**, †**bele** /bel/ *n* a large fire; a bonfire or beacon-fire *la15-19, 20- historical*. **bale-fire**, †**bailfyre** a beacon fire *la14-*. [ON *bál*, OE *bǣl*]

bale[2], †**baill** /bel/ *n* misery, sorrow, pain *la14-19, 20- literary*. [OE *balu*]

bale *see* BEAL

baleen, †**ballane**, †**balling**, †**bellan** /baˈlin/ *n* whalebone *16-*. †**ballant boddice**, **balling bodys** a whaleboned bodice *17-e19*. [ME *baleine*]

balhuif *see* BAHUIF

balk *see* BAUK[1.1]

ball[1], **baw**, **ba** /bɔl, bɔ, ba/ *n* **1** a (formal) gathering for dancing; a social gathering *la18-*. **2** a bustle, disturbance; a period of noisy entertainment *19, 20- Sh NE*. **balling** dancing; the holding or frequenting of balls *la16-19, 20- NE*. **on the ball** constantly drinking *la19-*. [Fr *bal* dance]

†**ball**[2] *n* boot-blacking *18-19*. [shortened form of Eng *blacking ball*]

ball *see* BA[1], BAAL

ballage /ˈbaledʒ/ *n* ballast *20- Sh*. [unknown; compare BALLISTEN]

ballaloo *see* BALLOO¹·¹, BALLOO¹·²

ballance, balance /ˈbaləns/ *n* **1** scales (for weighing) *la15-*. **2** a comparative reckoning; the remainder or rest *17-*. **3** equilibrium; stability *18-*. **4** a plate, a flat dish *e16*. †**ballandis** (a pair of) scales *15-16*. [MFr *balance*]

ballane *see* BALEEN

ballant, ballat, †**ballett** /ˈbalənt, ˈbalət/ *n* a ballad *la15-*. **a hole in the ballant** a blank or omission (a reference to the excuse made by ballad-singers that their broadside was torn) *la19-*. [EModE *balate*]

ballfuff *see* BAFUFF

ballie, baalie /ˈbɑli/ *n* a thick (oatmeal) cake *la19- Sh*. [ON *bǫllr*, Norw dial *ball*, Swed *ball*]

ballie *see* BAILIE

balling *see* BALEEN

ballisten /ˈbɑlistən/ *n* a round sea-worn stone or pebble *la19- Sh*. [ON *bǫllr* + STANE]

balloch, bealach /ˈbaləx, ˈbjaləx/ *n* a narrow pass (on a hill or mountain); frequently in place-names *la16-*. [Gael, IrGael *bealach*]

ballock, †**ballok,** †**bollok** /ˈbɔlək/ *npl* †**bellox** a testicle *la15-*. [BA¹, with diminutive suffix -*ock*]

balloo¹·¹**, ballaloo,** †**baloue,** †**balulalow** /baˈlu, baləˈlu/ *n* a lullaby *la16-*. [nonsense word]

balloo¹·²**, ballaloo,** †**balow** /baˈlu, baləˈlu/ *interj* a word used to hush a child to sleep *18-*. [see the noun]

balloon /baˈlun, blun/ *n* a boastful or foolish person *la20-*. [figurative from Eng *balloon*]

ballop /ˈbaləp/ *n* a trouser-flap; trouser-flies *la16- NE C SW Bor*. [probably BAG¹·¹ + LAP¹·¹]

bally *see* BELLY¹·¹

bally-cog /ˈbalikɔg/ *n* a milk pail *19- NE*. [compare Dan *balje* a tub]

Balmoral /balˈmɔrəl/ *n* a broad, flat woollen bonnet with a pom-pom on the crown, worn to one side *19-*; compare KILMARNOCK. **Balmorality** enthusiasm for the superficial elements of Scottish culture *19-*. **Balmoral Bonnet** = BALMORAL. [from the name of the royal estate in Deeside]

baloue *see* BALLOO¹·¹

balow *see* BALLOO¹·²

baltic /ˈbɔltɪk/ *adj* extremely cold *la20-*. [from the name of the region in Northern Europe]

balulalow *see* BALLOO¹·¹

bam /bam/ *n* **1** a joke, a trick; the butt of a joke *19-*. **2** an idiotic or contemptible person *la20-*. **bammer** a rowdy or aggressive person *la20-*. [probably reduced form of Eng *bamboozle*]

bambaize *see* BUMBAZE

bambirr /ˈbɑmbɪr/ *n* a state of haste or excitement *20- Sh*. [ON *bang* hammering + BIRR¹·¹ or BIRL¹·¹]

bambor *see* BAOMBE

Bamff *see* BANFF

bamfouleerie /bamfuˈliri/ *numeral* a meaningless word used in children's counting-out rhymes *20- EC*. [nonsense word derived from a system of counting of sheep]

bampot /ˈbampɔt/ *n* a term of contempt for a person *la20-*. [probably from Eng *barmpot*]

bamstick /ˈbamstɪk/ *n* a term of contempt for a person *la20-*. [probably from Eng *barmstick*]

ban /ban/ *v* to curse; to scold, utter curses, swear profusely *la14-*. [ON *banna* to prohibit, interdict, curse]

ban *see* BAND¹·¹, BAND²

bancat *see* BANKET¹·¹, BANKET¹·²

†**bancour, bankure, banquhoir** *n* a covering for a seat or bench *la15-16*. [compare BUNKER]

band¹·¹**, ban,** *Sh* **baand** /band, ban; *Sh* bɑnd/ *n* **1** something which binds; a strip for fastening or reinforcing *la14-*. **2** the marriage bond *la14-*. **3** a promise, an agreement, a contract; a mortgage *la14-*. **4** *pl* the two short, white, linen strips hanging from the collar, worn as part of the officiating dress of an ordained minister *18-*. **5** a long stone laid cross-wise through a wall *20-*. **6** a hinge or fastening for a door or gate *la14-19, 20- NE T EC*. **7** a rope or straw-twist used to bind corn *la15-19, 20- Sh NE Uls*. **8** a timber or rib of a boat *20- Sh*. **9** a range of hills; a ridge (of a hill) *16-19*. **bander** a person who signed the Covenant, a covenanter *17-e19, la19- historical*. **bandsman,** †**bandisman** = *bandster la16-19, 20- NE*. **bandster, banster** the member of a party of harvesters who binds the sheaves *17-*. **band-stane** a stone going through the width of a wall *la15-*. **bandwin** the band of three to eight reapers who work together and are served by one *bandster 17-19, 20- NE Bor*. †**band of manrent** a contract agreed between a free man and his feudal superior *la15-17*. [ON *band* that which binds, MFr *bande* a flat strip, a strap]

band¹·²**,** *Sh* **baand** /band; *Sh* bɑnd/ *v* **1** to secure with bands; to bind; to string together or tether *la15-*. **2** to furnish with a band or edging *la16-*. **3** to join together as a company, unite, confederate *la16-*. **bandit, banded 1** secured or strengthened with (metal) bands *15-*. **2** *of a wall* made secure with bond-stones *19, 20- Ork*. [see the noun]

band²**, ban** /band, ban/ *n* **1** a company, a group *16-*. **2** a group of musicians, originally a company of musicians attached to an army regiment *la18-*. **3** a (church) choir *19-*. **an what did the band play?** a sarcastic expression of disbelief: ◊*Ye won the lottery? Aye, an what did the band play? la20-*. **tae a band playin** to do something with enthusiasm and relish: ◊*I could drink tea tae a band playin la20-*. [MFr *bande* a group]

band *see* BIND¹·²

bandie /ˈbandi/ *n* a minnow or stickleback *la19- NE T*. [probably contracted from BANSTICKLE]

†**bandis** *npl* banns of marriage *la16-17*. [altered form of Older Scots *bannis*]

banditch /ˈbandɪtʃ/ *n* a bandage *la19- NE T EC*. [altered form of Eng *bandage*]

bandoune¹·¹**,** †**bandoun,** †**bandown** /ˈbandun/ *n* **1** control, authority *15-19, 20- literary*. **2** subjection, a state of servitude *la15-19, 20- literary*. [ME *bandoun*]

†**bandoune**¹·²**,** †**bandoun,** †**bandown** *v* **1** to give up *15-16*. **2** to control, dominate *la15-16*. [see the noun]

†**bandrell, bendrole** *n* a bandoleer *la16-17*. [altered form of Fr *banderole*]

bandwin *see* BAND¹·¹

bane, bone, *Sh* **bonn,** *Ork NE T* **been,** †**bayn,** †**bean** /ben, bon; *Sh* bɔn; *Ork NE T* bin/ *n* **1** part of a skeleton, a bone *la14-*. **2** pith, marrow, life *la19-*. **baney, bainie,** *NE* **beeny** bony *la18-*. **bane kaim, bane kame** a comb made of bone; a small, fine-toothed comb *la16-*. †**beanshaw** sciatica; hip gout *la16-e19*. **benwark, bonwark,** †**bone wrak** muscular pain; rheumatic pain in the bones *la19- Sh*. †**bane and lire** bone and flesh *la14-e19*; compare *lyre and bane* (LIRE¹). †**keep the banes green** preserve good health and youthfulness; be in comfortable circumstances in later life *la15-19*. [OE *bān*]

bane *see* DAYNE¹·¹, DEAN

banefire, †**benfire,** †**bonefire** /ˈbɛnfɑre/ *n* a bonfire *la16-*. [BANE + FIRE¹·¹]

baner *see* BANNER

banesoun *see* BENISON

banestikill *see* BANSTICKLE

Banff, Bamff, †Banf /banf, bamf/ *n* a coastal town in Aberdeenshire *la14-*. **Banff bailies** large white snowy clouds rising along the horizon, regarded as a sign of bad weather *la19- N NE*. **go to Banff!** a term of dismissal *19, 20- NE*. [unknown]

banffie /'banfi/ *n* a kind of kite *20- Ork*. [unknown]

bang[1.1] /baŋ/ *n* **1** a resounding blow or thump; a loud noise *la16-*. **2** an attack, an onslaught *la18-*. **3** a throbbing pain *la18-*. **in a bang** in haste *18-*. [see the verb]

bang[1.2] /baŋ/ *v* **1** to beat, thrash, strike *la16-*. **2** to overcome, surpass *la16-*. **3** to hurry, dash *la16-*. **†bangie** impetuous; quarrelsome *19*. **bangster 1** a violent or lawless person; a bully *la16-*. **2** a victor, a winner *la18-e19*. **bangstrie** violence; bullying behaviour *la16-*. **bankstership** compulsion, force *la19- Sh*. **bang out** to rush out, fall out violently *18-*. **bang up 1** to jump; to rise hastily *18-*. **2** to strike up a tune *la18-*. [ON *banga* to hammer, knock]

bang[1.3] /baŋ/ *adj* **1** fierce, violent, strong *la18-19, 20- Bor*. **2** agile and powerful *19- Bor*. [see the verb]

bang[2] /baŋ/ *n* a crowd *18-19, 20- NE*. **†the bang-dollop** the whole lot *la19*. **the bang-jing** the whole lot *la19- T EC*; compare JING-BANG. [unknown]

bang[3] /baŋ/ *n* a logging chain *20- T*. **bang chain** a chain for fastening a load (of wood) to a cart *la19-*. [unknown]

bangie /'baŋi/ *n* a man appointed to watch the Solway and the River Annan for salmon poachers *la19- SW Bor*. [reduced form of BANG-THE-BEGGAR]

bangster *see* BANG[1.2]

bang-the-beggar /'baŋðəbɛgər/ *n* **1** a police constable *19- SW Bor Uls*. **2** a strong staff, a police truncheon *19, 20- Bor*. [metonymic form based on BANG[1.2] and Older Scots *beggar*]

bangyal *see* BANYEL

bani /'bɑni/ *n* a serious injury, a deadly wound *20- Sh*. [ON *bani* death]

†banis, benis *n* a kind of fur *la15-e16*. [unknown]

banis *see* BAINISH

banjo /'bandʒo/ *v* to hit, thrash *la20-*. [unknown]

bank[1] /baŋk/ *n* **1** the (sloping) ground bordering a river or loch *la14-*. **2** a hillside; a slope *la15-*. **3** the boundary-line of a farm *19-*. **4** the place in a peat moss where peats are cut *la19-*. **5** a raised footpath; a raised ridge of ground *20-*. **6** *pl* sea cliffs, a steep cliff; steep rocks; the seashore *la19- Sh*. **banks-broo** a cliff edge *la20- Sh*. **banksflooer** sea-pink, thrift *Armeria maritima 20- Sh*. **banks-gaet** a cliff-top path; the way up or down a cliff; a difficult undertaking *la20- Sh*. **banks-girse** common scurvy grass *Cochlearia officinalis* (growing on a cliff) *la19- Sh*. **bank sparrow** the rock pipit *Anthus petrosus la19- Sh*. [ME *banke*]

bank[2] /baŋk/ *n in weaving* the basket of bobbins of yarn used in making up the warp in a loom; a section of the warping frame in which the bobbins are set up *19, 20- WC*. [OFr *banc* a bench]

bank[3] /baŋk/ *n* the beating of a drum (as used in making a public proclamation) *17-18, 19- historical*. **†beat a bank** proclaim (to the beat of a drum) *17-18*. [ON *banga* to hammer, knock]

†banket[1.1], **bancat** *n* a banquet *la15-e17*. [EModE *bankett*]

†banket[1.2], **bancat** *v* to hold or attend a banquet *16-e17* [see the noun]

Bankies /'baŋkiz/ *npl* a nickname for Clydebank Football Club *20-*. **the Bankies** = BANKIES. [shortened form of *Clydebank* with plural suffix]

bankit siller /ˈbaŋkɪt ˈsɪlər/ *n* money saved (and put in the bank) *la19-*. [Older Scots *bank*, with adj-forming suffix *-it* + SILLER[1.1]]

bankstership *see* BANG[1.2]

bankure *see* BANCOUR
bannage *see* BONDAGE
banner, †baner, †benner /'banər/ *n* a flag, a sign *la14-*. **†bannerer, banerer** a banner-bearer *16-19*. **†bannerman, banerman** a banner-bearer *la14-e19*. [ME *baner*]
bannet *see* BUNNET[1.1]
bannie *see* BANNOCK
bannis *see* BAINISH
bannock, bannok, *Ork* **banno,** *Ork* **binnack,** *Bor* **bannie, †bonnock** /'banək; *Ork* 'bano; *Ork* 'bɪnək; *Bor* 'banɛ/ *n* **1** a pancake; a round flat cake (originally of oat-, barley- or pease-meal) usually baked on a girdle *la16-*. **2** a quantity of meal sufficient to make a bannock, due to the servant of a mill from each of those using it *la16-18*. **3** a flat cake (of tallow or wax) *la16-e19*. **Bannock Day** Shrove Tuesday *la19-*. **bannock fluke** the turbot *Scophthalmus maximus 19-*. **bannock hive,** *Ork* **bannoo-hive** *humorous* a gastric upset caused by overeating *la16-*. **†bonnock iron** an iron utensil for baking bannocks *la17*. **Bannock Night** Shrove Tuesday *19-*. **bannock stane** a heated stone on which bannocks were baked *la18-19, 20- historical*. **bannock stick** a wooden rolling pin for bannocks *19-*. [OE *bannuc*; compare Gael *bonnach, bannach*]

banno-corn /'banokorn/ *n* a small corn-stack *20- Ork*. [extended use of ON *barn* a child + CORN[1.1]]

banno-disty /'banodɪsti/ *adj* ill-humoured *20- Ork*. [ON *barn* a child + second element perhaps derived from ON *dust* a fight, a tilting]

bannok *see* BANNOCK
banquhoir *see* BANCOUR
†banrent *n* a banneret, a knight entitled to bring a company of vassals into the field under his own banner *la14-e17*. [ME *baneret*]

banshee, benshie /'banʃi, 'bɛnʃi/ *n* a female supernatural being, whose wail was believed to forecast death or disaster for the family who heard her *la18-*. [Gael *ban-sìth*, IrGael *bean-sídhe* a fairy-woman]

banstickle, banstikkel, †banestikill /'banstɪkəl/ *n* a stickleback, a fish of the family *Gasterosteidae la15-* [probably BANE + OE *sticel* a prick, sting]

banter[1.1] /'bantər/ *n* **1** nonsense, ridicule; a jest; an exchange of teasing remarks *18-*. **2** amusing, light-hearted discussion; chatter *20-*. [unknown]

banter[1.2] /'bantər/ *v* **1** to make fun of a person; to ridicule; to tease in fun *18-*. **2** to speak loquaciously, engage in conversation *la20-*. **3** to cheat, trick, bamboozle *18-19*. **4** to scold, drive away by scolding *18-e19*. [unknown]

bantie /'banti/ *n* a bantam *19-*. **bantie cock** a male bantam; a (small) self-important person *la19-*. [reduced form of BANTIM with *-ie* suffix]

bantim, †bantin, †banting /'bantəm/ *n* a bantam, a small domestic fowl *19-*. [named from *Bantam* (now *Banten*), a trading-port in Java]

†banwart *n* the daisy *16-e17*. [OE *bānwyrt*]

banyan day, *Ork* **banyar day** /'banjən de; *Ork* 'banjər de/ *n* a day on which little food is available; a day with no meat; hard times *18-*. [Arabic *banyan* an ascetic Hindu merchant + DAY]

banyel, bangyal, bengle, bengyal /'banjəl, 'baŋjəl, 'bɛŋəl, 'bɛŋjəl/ *n* a bundle; a heap; a crowd *19, 20- NE SW Bor*. [unknown]

baombe, bambor /'bʌumbe, 'bambər/ *numeral in children's counting rhymes* the numeral five *la19, 20- SW*. [nonsense word derived from a system of counting of sheep]

bap[1.1] /bap/ *n* **1** a bread roll *la16-*. **2** a stupid person *20-*. **bap-faced** soft and stupid-looking *20-*. **bap-fit** a flat foot *la19- NE.* **bapp-nose** a person with a large flat nose *la19- NE T EC.* **they couldna knock the stew aff a bap** *of a person* ineffectual *la20- NE T.* [unknown]

bap[1.2] /bap/ *v* to walk in a plodding, flat-footed way *20- NE.* **bappin' on** getting on with something, not wasting time *20- NE.* [unknown]

bapteese, bapteeze, baptise, †baptese /bap'tiz, bap'taez/ *v* to christen; to name or designate, baptize *la14-.* [OFr *baptisier*, Lat *baptīzāre*]

†baptime, bapteme *n* baptism *la14-e17.* [ME *bapteme*]

bar[1.1]**, baur** /bar, bɔr/ *n* **1** a rod of solid material; a broad line or band *15-.* **2** *law* the place in a court where business is transacted, the court itself *15-.* **3** a barrier *la15-.* **4** a bank of sand or silt across the mouth of a river or harbour; frequently in place-names *la15-.* **5** a public house *19-.* **like the bars o' Ayr** *of movement* fast and noisy; energetic (after the sea bar formerly at the mouth of the River Ayr) *19-.* [ME *barre*]

bar[1.2]**, baur** /bar, bɔr/ *v* **1** to secure (with a bar); to create a barrier *la14-.* **2** to exclude, shut out *la15-.* [ME *barren*]

bar[2]**, barr, bawr, baur** /bar, bɔr/ *n* a joke, a humorous situation; a practical joke *la19-.* [unknown]

bar[3]**, barr** /bar/ *n* the outside cut of a fish such as halibut, the fin *20- Sh.* **barr cut** a slice of halibut *la19- Sh.* [ON *barð* brim, edge]

bar[4] /bar/ *n* the bearded end of an ear of corn *20- Sh Ork.* [perhaps ON *barð* a beard]

bar *see* BARE
barat *see* BARRAT

†barbar[1.1] *n* a barbarian *16-17.* [ME *barbar*]

†barbar[1.2]**, barbour, barbir** *adj* barbarous, barbarian *16-17.* [OFr *barbare* barbarous]

barbar *see* BARBER[1]

†barbe *n* a beard *la14.* [ME *barbe*, Lat *barba*]

barber[1]**, †barbour, †barbar** /'barbər/ *n* a men's hairdresser (originally also a minor surgeon) *la13-.* **†barbarize** to act as a barber; to shave *17-e18.* [AN *barber*]

barber[2]**, berber** /'barbər, 'bɛrbər/ *n* a freezing, coastal mist in calm frosty weather *20- Sh NE.* [unknown]

barbir *see* BARBAR[1.2]
barbour *see* BARBAR[1.2], BARBER[1]

†barbulyie, barbulʒe *v* to disorder or confuse; to besmear *la16-e19.* [Fr *barbouiller* to smear]

barcatt *see* BARKET

Barchan's Day /'barkənz de/ *n* a horse fair usually held in December *19-e20, la20- historical.* [from the name of St Berchan + DAY]

bar-claw /'barklɔ/ *n* a dew-claw *20- Sh.* [perhaps ON *barð* brim, edge + CLAW[1.1]]

bard[1]**, †baird** /bard/ *n* **1** a poet; a strolling singer or player *14-.* **2** a scold, a noisy woman *16-19, 20- Sh N.* **3** a scurrilous person; a buffoon *16-18.* **†bardrie** scurrility; scurrilous language *16.* [Gael *bard*, Lat *bardus*]

bard[2] /bard/ *n* a (steep) headland whose top projects beyond its base; frequently in place-names *la19- Sh.* [ON *barð* brim, edge]

bard *see* BARRIT

bardach /'bardəx/ *adj* fearless, arrogant, difficult *la18-19, 20- T.* [derivative of BARD[1]]

bardasoga /bardə'soga/ *n* an unreasonably long time, an eternity *20- Sh.* [ON *Bardolsvaka* St Bartholomew's Day]

bardge *see* BAIRGE[5]

bardie[1.1] /'bardi/ *n* a minor poet, a humble bard *18-.* [BARD[1] + -IE[1]]

bardie[1.2]**, baurdy** /'bardi, 'bɔrdi/ *adj* bold, impudent, quarrelsome *18-.* [see the noun]

†barding *n* horse armour *16.* [MFr *barde*, with *-ing* suffix]

†bardis *npl* horse armour *la15-16.* **bardit, bairdit** *of a horse* armoured *16-e19.* [MFr *bardis*; possibly from OFr *barde* pack-saddle]

bare, †bar, †bair, †beare /ber/ *adj* **1** naked, uncovered *la14-.* **2** *of places* barren, infertile; desolate *la14-.* **3** *of weapons* unsheathed *la14-.* **4** destitute, needy *la15-.* **5** scant, minimal; simple, plain *la15-.* **barelies** scarcely, barely *la18- NE T.* **baries** bare feet *la20-.* **†bair-leg** bare-legged *la16-e17.* **†bairman, bareman** a destitute person; a debtor, a bankrupt *15-17.* **bare scud** naked skin, a state of nudity *20-.* **baretail** naked, left with nothing *20- N.* **as bare as birkie** completely bare *la19- WC SW Bor Uls.* **as bare as da birk o' Yule een** completely bare *20- Sh.* [OE *bær*]

bare *see* BAIR, BEAR[1], BEAR[2]

barefit, barfit, †barefute, †barfwte /'bɛrfɪt, 'barfɪt/ *adj* barefoot *la14-.* **barefittit, barefitted, †bare-futit** barefooted *16-.* **barefit broth, barfit broth** broth made without meat *la19- NE T.* **bare-feeted broth** = *barefit broth 20- N.* **†barefit kail** = *barefit broth la18-19.* [BARE + FIT[1.1]]

Bar-Ell *see* BAR-L

barfit *see* BAREFIT

barfljug /'bar'flug/ *v* to separate corn from the stalks after thrashing *20- Sh.* [probably BAR[4] + ON *fleygja* to throw]

barflog /'bar'flɔg/ *v* to beat one's hands crosswise around the shoulders to keep warm *20- Sh.* [probably ON *berja* to beat + ON *flóki* something tangled]

barfwte *see* BAREFIT

bargain[1.1]**, bergin, †bargane, †bergane** /'bargən, 'bɛrgən/ *n* **1** a business transaction; an advantageous deal *la16-.* **2** contention, conflict, struggle *la14-19.* [ME *bargain*]

bargain[1.2]**, bergin, †bargane** /'bargən, 'bɛrgən/ *v* **1** to negotiate a deal or agreement; to haggle *la17-.* **2** to contend or fight with *la14-18.* [OFr *bargaignier*, MFr *barguiner*]

†barganour *n* a quarreller, a wrangler, a fighter *15-e16.* [BARGAIN[1.2], with agent suffix]

barge *see* BAIRGE[1], BAIRGE[5]

bargle /'bargəl/ *v* to wrangle, argue *la19-.* [shortened form of ARGLE-BARGLE[1.2]]

barisdale, †barisdall /'barɪsdel/ *n* an instrument of torture invented and used only by MacDonald of Barisdale *e18, 20- historical.* [from the name of the inventor]

bark[1.1]**, berk** /bark, bɛrk/ *n* a loud noise made by a dog; a hard cough *19-.* [see the verb]

bark[1.2]**, berk** /bark, bɛrk/ *v* **1** to utter a barking sound *la14-.* **2** to cough *la19-.* [OE *beorcan*]

bark[2.1] /bark/ *n* **1** the rind of the trunk and branches of trees; tree rind used in tanning *15-.* **2** the skin *18-19, 20- Sh.* **3** the scab formed over a wound or sore *20- NE Bor.* **4** the root of the tormentil *Potentilla erecta* (used in tanning) *20- Sh.* **†barkhole** a tanner's bark-pit *la16-e19.* **bark-kettle** a kettle for boiling bark *la19- Sh NE.* **bark loft** a loft in which tanner's bark is stored *la16-19.* **†bark pot** a pot or pit for tanner's bark *la16-19.* [ON *börkr*]

bark[2.2] /bark/ *v* to tan leather *15-.* **†barker, barkar** a tanner *la13-17.* [see the noun]

barken /'barkən/ *v* to encrust; to plaster over; to blacken *la18-.* **barkened, †barknit 1** dried into a crust, encrusted *16-.* **2** *of leather* tanned *la18-.* [BARK[2.1], with verb-forming suffix *-en*]

†barket, barcatt *n* a wooden trestle or support; the wooden timbers of a pier *la16-e19.* [unknown]

barking and fleeing /'barkɪŋ ənd 'fliɪŋ/ *n* spending wastefully and over-extravagantly; being on the verge of ruin *19, 20- EC.* [perhaps Swed *barka* to fly + FLEE[2]]

barkit, †**berkit** /ˈbarkət/ *adj* **1** dried into a crust, encrusted (with dirt); filthy *16-*. **2** *of leather* tanned *15-17*. [ptp of BARK[2,2]]

Bar-L, **Bar-Ell** /barˈɛl/ *n* a nickname for Barlinnie Prison in Glasgow *la20-*. [shortened form of the name of the prison]

barlaw *see* BIRLEY

barley[1], **baurley**, †**barlie**, †**berlik** /ˈbarle, ˈbɔrle/ *n* a hardy cereal of the genus *Hordeum 15-*. †**barleyhood**, **barlickhood** violent ill-temper; obstinacy resulting from drunkenness *18-19*. **barley fever**, **barrel-fever** intoxication, drunkenness *la18-19, 20- NE T EC*. **barley pickle 1** a grain of barley *19- C*. **2** a kind of linen weave with a lumpy texture *19*. †**barley-sick**, **barrel-sick** drunk *la18-e19*. [OE *bærlic*]

barley[2], **baurley** /ˈbarle, ˈbɔrle/ *n* in *children's games* a truce or pause *la18-*; compare PARLEY[1,1]. **barley brack**, *Ork* **barley brock 1** a chasing and catching game *19- NE T*. **2** in *children's games* (a call for) a truce or pause *20- Ork*. †**barley-bracks**, **barla-breikis**, **barlabreikis** a chasing and catching game *la16-19*. †**barley fummel**, **barlafummil** (a call for) a truce or pause in a game or fight *16-19*. **barley-play** in *children's games* (a call for) a truce or pause *la19- Sh Ork Uls*. **cry barley** call for a truce *la18-19, 20- T*. [perhaps Fr *parler*]

barleybree, †**barley-broo** /barleˈbri/ *n* malt liquor, whisky *18-*. [BARLEY[1] + BREE[1,1]]

barley-door *see* BAR-THE-DOOR

barlie *see* BARLEY[1]

barm[1,1], †**berme** /barm/ *n* **1** the froth that forms on the top of fermenting malt liquors, yeast *15-*. **2** an insult; blame *20- NE*. **barm biscuit** a round biscuit made of fermented dough, with added sugar and lard *20- H&I*. [OE *beorma*]

barm[1,2] /barm/ *v* **1** to mix with yeast; to ferment *19-*. **2** to become enraged; to rant or rave noisily *19-*. **barmin**, **barman 1** fermenting *la19- Sh Ork*. **2** frothing; seething *la20- Sh Ork N*. [see the noun]

†**barme horse** *n* a horse without a saddle; a pack-horse *15-e19*. [unknown first element + HORSE[1,1]]

barminskin *see* BARMSKIN

barmkin, †**barnekin**, †**barmkyn** /ˈbarmkɪn/ *n* a battlement; a defensive wall; a turret or watchtower on an outer wall *la15-19, 20- historical*. [perhaps altered form of ME *barbican*]

barmskin, **barminskin** /ˈbarmskɪn, ˈbarmɪnskɪn/ *n* a tanned sheepskin used by fishermen as a covering for the breast or knees *19- Sh*. [OE *barm* bosom + SKIN[1,1]; compare BRAMSKIN]

barmy /ˈbarme/ *adj* **1** yeasty; frothy *la15-*. **2** flighty, foolish; excitedly active *la16-*. **3** passionate *e19*. [BARM[1,1] + -IE[2]]

barn, **bern**, †**bairne**, †**born** /barn, bɛrn/ *n* a building for the storage of grain or hay, or housing livestock *14-*. **barnman**, †**bernman** a worker in a barn, a thresher *la16-*. **barnyard**, †**bairnyaird**,†**bernʒarde** the area around a barn (where unthreshed grain is stored) *15-*. [OE *bereern* barley place]

†**barnage**[1] *n* the collective body of barons, the baronage *la14-16*. [ME *barnage*]

†**barnage**[2] *n* childhood, youth *15-e17*. [BAIRN[1,1], with *-age* suffix]

†**barne**, **barny** *n* the nobility, the baronage *la14-e15*. [OFr *barné*]

barne *see* BAIRN[1,1]

barnekin *see* BARMKIN

barnelie *see* BAIRNLY

barneteme, **barnetyme** *see* BAIRNTIME[1]

†**barns-breaking** *n* an idle frolic; a mischievous action *19*. [BARN + verbal noun from BRAK[1,2]]

barny *see* BARNE

baron, †**baroun**, †**barroun**, †**barron** /ˈbarən/ *n* one who holds land directly of the Crown; the owner of a freehold estate (including commoners and lesser landowners); a member of the lowest rank of the nobility *la14-*. [ME *baroun*]

baron bailie /ˈbarən bele/ *n* a baron's deputy with both civil and criminal jurisdiction in the BARON COURT *la16-19, 20- historical*. [BARON + BAILIE]

Baron court, †**barroun court** /ˈbarən kort/ *n* a court held by a baron or his deputy in his barony *la16-19, 20- historical*. [BARON + court (COORT[1,1])]

baronial /bəˈronɪəl/ *adj* **1** pertaining to a baron or his rank *la18-*. **2** = *Scottish Baronial 19-*. **Scottish Baronial** an ornate style of architecture characterized by turrets and crow-stepped gables (found especially in 19th-century countryhouses and Edinburgh Old Town tenements) *19-*. [BARONY, with adj-forming suffix *-ial*]

baron officer, †**barroun officer** /ˈbarən ɔfɪsər/ *n* an estate official *la17-19, 20- historical*. [BARON + OFFICER]

baronry, †**barounry** /ˈbarənre/ *n* the lands or domain held by a baron *15-19, 20- historical*. [BARON, with *-ry* suffix]

Barons of Exchequer /ˈbarənz əv ɛksˈtʃɛkər/ *npl* the judges of the Scottish Court of Exchequer *18-19, 20- historical*. [plural of BARON + EXCHEQUER]

barony, †**barrownie** /ˈbarəne/ *n* the lands or domain held by a baron *la14-*. †**in barony** by baronial tenure *15-e16*. [ME *baronie*]

baroun *see* BARON

barounry *see* BARONRY

barp /barp/ *n* a chambered cairn *19- N H&I*. [Gael *barpa*]

barr /bar/ *n* a ridge, a hill *19-*. [Gael *bàrr*]

barr *see* BAR[2], BAR[3]

barra, **barrae**, **barry**, **borra**, **borry**, **barrow**, **borrow** /ˈbarə, ˈbare, ˈbɔrə, ˈbɔre, ˈbaro, ˈbɔro/ *n* a wheelbarrow; a handcart or hand-barrow *la14-*. **barraman**, **barrowman**, †**borrowman** a person who carries building materials in a barrow; a person who helps to carry or push a hand-barrow *la14-*. **barrowsteel** the shaft of a wheelbarrow *16-19, 20- NE Bor*. **barrowtram** = *barrowsteel 16-19, 20- EC Bor*. **the Barras**, **the Barrows** a street market in the East End of Glasgow *20-*. **set doon the barra** to go bankrupt *la19-*. [ME *barewe*]

barrace, **barras**, †**barres** /ˈbarəs/ *n* **1** a barrier (in front of a castle); a barricade *la14-19, 20- historical*. **2** an enclosure used for tournaments, duelling or judicial combats *la15-e19*. †**barras dore** a (reinforced) door in or beside a barrier *la17-e19*. **barrasgate**, †**barras ʒet** a gate in or beside a barrier *16-19, 20- historical*. [ME *barre*]

barrack *see* BERRICK

barrae *see* BARRA

barrall *see* BARREL[1,2]

†**barrane**, **barrand**, **barrant** *adj* barren *la14-e17*. [ME *barain*]

barras *see* BARRA, BARRACE

†**barrat**, **barret**, **barat** *n* **1** fraud; contention *15-16*. **2** distress, trouble, vexation *la15-e17*. **barratour** a person who obtained benefices by underhand means *15-16*. [ME *barat*]

barratry, †**barratrie** /ˈbarətre/ *n* **1** law the corrupt purchase of benefices by an ecclesiastic *15-19, 20- historical*. **2** law the crime committed by a judge, of pronouncing a particular judgement in return for a bribe *18-19, 20- historical*. **3** law fraud or negligence committed by the crew of a ship, especially desertion, sinking or embezzling cargo *la18-*. [OFr *baraterie*]

barr cut *see* BAR[3]

barred *see* BARRIT

†barrekin, barriquin, berrykan *n* a small cask or barrel *la16-e17.* [Fr *barrique*]

barrel[1.1], **†barrell, †berrell** /'barəl/ *n* 1 a cylindrical (wooden) container *15-.* 2 the quantity or measure which a barrel can hold; a dry measure of varying amounts *la15-.* **†barrell-ferrar** a vessel in which water or liquor was carried on a journey *la14-e15.* [ME *barel*]

barrel[1.2], **†barrall, †berrell** /'barəl/ *v* to pack in a barrel *la15-.* [see the noun]

barrel-fever see BARLEY[1]

barrell see BARREL[1.1]

barrer see BARRIER

barres see BARRACE

barrie[1] /'bare, 'bari/ *n* 1 a baby's flannel coat; a binder, a wrapper *18-.* 2 a lady's undergarment *18-e19.* [perhaps related to OE *beorgan* to protect]

barrie[2], **barry** /'bare, 'bari/ *adj* fine; big; smart in appearance *20-.* [Travellers' language]

barrie-masherie /'barimaʃəri/ *n* a preparation of sour milk *20- N.* [Gael *bainne maistridh* whipped cream]

barrier, †barrer /'barıər/ *n* a barricade, an impediment *la15-.* **Barrier Act** an act passed by the General Assembly of the Church of Scotland in 1697, which provided that acts involving an important change in church law must be approved by the presbyteries as well as by the General Assembly *la17-.* [ME *barrer*]

barriquin see BARREKIN

barrit, barred, †bard /'barıt, bard/ *adj* furnished with bars *16-.* **†barrit grote, bard grote** a kind of coin *la16.* [BAR[1.1] + -IT[2]]

barritchfu /'barıtʃfu/ *adj* harsh *19- NE.* [perhaps related to BARRAT, with -*ful* suffix]

barron, barroun see BARON

barroun court see BARON COURT

barroun officer see BARON OFFICER

barrow see BARRA, BORROW[1.2]

barrownie see BARONY

barry see BARRA, BARRIE[2]

barse see BERS

Bartane see BERTANE

Bartanʒe see BRETANʒE

bartesein, barteshing see BARTIZAN

bar-the-door, barley-door /'barðədor, 'barledor/ *n* a children's game of capture and release *20-.* [BAR[1.2] + DOOR]

Barthol, Bartill see BARTLE

bartizan, *EC* **baterson, †barteshing, †bartesein, †bartissing** /bartə'zan; *EC* 'batərsən/ *n* 1 a battlement, a parapet *la16-.* 2 a barrier *19- NE.* [metathesis of ME *bretasynge*]

Bartle, †Bartill, †Barthol /'bartəl/ *n* St Bartholemew *la15-.* **Bartle Day, †Bartholl day** St Bartholomew's Day, 24 August *la17-e20, la20- historical.* **Bartle Fair, †Bartill fair** a fair held on St Bartholomew's Day (at Kincardine O'Neil) *la16-e20, la20- historical.* **†Bartlemas** the festival of St Bartholomew *la15-17.* [reduced form of the personal name Bartholomew]

bas see BASE, BERS

†basan skin *n* sheepskin tanned with bark *la15-16.* [MFr *basane*]

†basar *n* an executioner *la14-15.* [IrGael *básaire*]

base, †basse, †bas /bes/ *adj* 1 *of the voice or a musical instrument* low-toned *la15-.* 2 low in position, forming a base *16-.* 3 of low rank or status; illegitimate *la16-.* 4 dishonourable, immoral; inferior, worthless *la16-.* **base fee, †bas fee** a type of conditional tenure (originally based on service to a feudal lord) *la15-19, 20- historical.* **base holding** a FEU granted by a VASSAL to a SUBVASSAL *la16-.* [ME *baas*]

base see BAISS[2]

basel see BASSEL[1.1], BASSEL[1.2]

bash[1.1] /baʃ/ *n* a heavy blow, a smashing motion *19-.* **on the bash** having a drinking bout *20-.* [see the verb]

bash[1.2] /baʃ/ *v* to beat, thump or smash *la18-.* [unknown; compare Dan *baske* to beat, Swed *basa* to flog]

†bash[2] *v* to be abashed or confused *la18.* [aphetic form of Older Scots *abaise* to abash]

basin, bassin, basson, †bassing, †baissin, †bassyne /'besın, 'basən/ *n* a wide dish; a hollow containing water; a bay or harbour *la14-.* Compare BAESHIN. **†baising siluir, basin silvir** a gratuity to certain royal servants at special seasons *la15-e16.* [ME *bacin*]

basit see BAISED

bask /bask/ *adj* 1 *of weather* dry, withering *19-.* 2 unpleasant, distasteful *la16.* [ON *beiskr* acrid, bitter]

†baslar *n* a dagger or short sword worn at the girdle *la15-e16.* [MFr *badelaire, baselare*]

bass /bas/ *n* 1 a mat of bark fibre, coarse straw or rushes; a doormat *18-.* 2 a workman's tool-basket or bag *20- NE T EC.* 3 a fish-basket *20- NE T EC.* **†basten, bassyn, bastin** made of bark fibre *15-17.* **bass-bottomed** *of chairs* with a seat of woven rushes or bark *la19, 20- NE.* **bass mat** a bark or rush mat *18-.* [variant of EModE *bast*]

basse see BASE

bassel[1.1], **basel** /'basəl/ *n* a struggle; a commotion *20- Sh.* [see the verb]

bassel[1.2], **basel** /'basəl/ *v* to struggle, toil; to splash around *la19- Sh.* [compare Swed *basa*]

bassened see BAWSONT

bassie[1.1], **bawsey** /'basi, 'bɔze/ *n* an old horse; a name for a horse with a blaze on the face *la18-19, 20- SW.* [OFr *baucent*, Fr *balzan* piebald; compare BAWSONT]

†bassie[1.2] *adj* having a white mark or blaze on the face *la17-e18.* [see the noun]

bassie[2], **bossie** /'basi, 'bɔsi/ *n* a wooden basin or bowl (for carrying meal to the baking board or in which meal is mixed and kneaded) *18-19, 20- NE.* [perhaps reduced form of BASIN]

bassin, bassing, basson, bassyne see BASIN

bastailʒe see BASTLE

†bastant *adj* sufficient, sufficiently strong *la16-17.* [MFr *bastant*]

†bastardry, bastardrie *n* illegitimacy of birth *la15-e17.* [AN *bastardrie*, OFr *basterderie*]

bastart[1.1], **bastard, †bystart** /'bastərt, 'bastərd/ *n* 1 a person of illegitimate birth *15-.* 2 a despicable or unpleasant person *20-.* [ME *bastard*]

bastart[1.2], **bastard, †byster** /'bastərt, 'bastərd/ *adj* 1 of illegitimate birth *15-.* 2 not proper or genuine; unauthorized *la15-.* 3 oddly sized, irregular; inferior *16-.* 4 difficult, unpleasant *la20-.* **bastard fallow** *agriculture* the giving of three or four furrows to a piece of ground to prepare it for another crop *la18-.* **bastard verdict** an informal name for the 'not proven' verdict in Scots law *19-.* [OFr *bastard*]

bastartin, bastarding, bastardn, bastarn /'bastərtən, 'bastərdıŋ, 'bastərdən, 'bastərn/ *adj* difficult, unpleasant, annoying *la20-.* [derivative of BASTART[1.1]]

baste see BEAST[1.1]

bastion see BASTON

bastle, †bastile, †bastell, †bastailʒe /'bastəl, 'basəl/ *n* a fortified tower; a siege-tower *la15-19, 20- historical.* **bastel-house, bastle house** a fortified house *16-19, 20- historical.* [OFr *bastille* a building]

†baston, bastoun, bastion *n* a cudgel, a truncheon; a staff of office *la15-e19.* [ME *bastoun*]

bat[1.1], †**batt** /bat/ *n* **1** a blow *la15-*. **2** a stick, a club; an implement for hitting a ball *18-*. **3** a lead wedge for securing lead flashings in masonry joints *19-*. **4** a gust of wind *20- Sh Ork N*. **5** an iron bar, a staple or loop of iron *17-19*. **aboot a bat** equal in ability *19- SW Bor*. [ME *botte* a stout piece of wood]
bat[1.2], †**batt**, †**bot** /bat/ *v* **1** to fasten or secure with an iron bar or a lead wedge *la16-*. **2** to beat, strike *la17-*. [MFr *battre*]
†**bat**[2], **bait** *n* a small extra amount given free to a buyer *la15-e16*. [MDu *baet*]
bat[3] /bat/ *n* a drove of sheep *20- Bor*. [Gael *bad* a cluster; a flock]
†**bataill**, **batayle**, **battell** *n* **1** a battle, a fight *la14-e17*. **2** a battalion *la14-16*. [ME *batail*]
batalrus *see* BATTALOUS
batayle *see* BAWTIE
batchie[1] /'batʃe/ *n* a baker; a baker's man *19, 20- C Bor*. [derivative of Scots *batch*]
batchie[2], **batchy** /'batʃi/ *n* **1** a bachelor *la19- NE T*. **2** (the loser in) a card game *la19- NE*. [shortened form of BACHELOR]
bate[1.1], **baet**, **beyt**, **beat** /bet, bit/ *n* **1** musical rhythm; a drum beat; (the sound of) a stroke or blow *la17-*. **2** something greater, better or in excess of another; that which surpasses something else *la19-*. [see the verb]
bate[1.2], **baet**, **beat**, †**beit**, †**bet**, †**batt** /bet, bit/ *v* **1** to hit, strike; to inflict blows upon *la14-*. **2** to hammer down, crush; to press hard, fix firmly *15-*. **3** to throb or pulsate *16-*. **4** to overcome, defeat; to surpass *17-*. **5** *of butter* to soften (by beating); to melt *19-*. [OE *bēatan*]
bate *see* BOAT[1.1]
baterson *see* BARTIZAN
bath[1.1], †**baith** /baθ/ *n* a tub for washing; the act of washing in a bath-tub *la14-*. †**bath fat**, **baith fatt** a bath-tub *la15-16*. [OE *bæþ*]
bath[1.2], **bathe**, **baathe**, **bawthe**, *Sh* **bad**, †**baith** /baθ, beð, bɔð; *Sh* bɑd/ *v* to wash or immerse in water *15-*. [OE *baþian*]
bathe *see* BAITH[1.1], BAITH[1.2], BATH[1.2]
bather[1.1], **boather**, *Sh Ork N NE* **badder**, *Sh NE* **budder**, *NE* **bither** /'baðər, 'boðər; *Sh Ork N NE* 'badər; *Sh NE* 'bʌdər; *NE* 'bɪðər/ *n* (an) annoyance, trouble; bother *19-*. [unknown]
bather[1.2], **boather**, *Sh Ork N NE* **badder**, *Sh NE* **budder**, *NE* **bither**, †**bauther**, †**bodder** /'baðər, 'boðər; *Sh Ork N NE* 'badər; *Sh NE* 'bʌdər; *NE* 'bɪðər/ *v* to trouble or annoy; to bother *la18-*. **batheration**, *Sh NE* **badderation** vexation, annoyance *la19-*. [unknown]
batherlock *see* BADDERLOCK
†**batie**, **bawtie** *adj* round, plump *19*. **batie bum**, **baty bummill** a feckless person *16-e19*. [unknown]
batie *see* BAWTIE
baton[1.1], †**battoun**, †**batton** /'batən/ *n* **1** a cudgel, a truncheon *16-*. **2** a rod or staff of office *16-*. †**batonman**, **battonman 1** a constable *la18-19*. **2** a hired mourner at a funeral *18-19*. [MFr *baston*]
baton[1.2], †**battoun**, †**batton** /'batən/ *v* to strike with a baton *la16-*. [see the noun]
bats *see* BATTS
batt *see* BAT[1.1], BAT[1.2], BATE[1.2]
battalation /batə'leʃən/ *n* a struggle *la19, 20- literary*. [compare Fr *bataille*]
†**battalous**, **batalrus**, **battailous** *adj* bellicose, warlike *la15-18*. [ME *bataillous*]
†**battard**, **battart** *n* a small cannon *16-e17*. [MFr *bastard* Fr *bâtard*]
battell *see* BATAILL
batter[1.1] /'batər/ *n* **1** an assault, (an act of) beating *la16-*. **2** *cookery* flour beaten with egg, water or milk *la18-*. **3** a paste or glue *la18-*. **4** a medicinal plaster *la19-*. **5** the cover of a book *la19-*. **batter-horn** a horn for holding shoemakers' paste *la18-19, 20- NE*. **on the batter** having a night of revelry *19-*. [see the verb]
batter[1.2] /'batər/ *v* **1** to beat; to mix by beating *la15-*. **2** to paste, stick or fasten; to stiffen with paste or glue *la16-*. †**battering** stiffening, lining *e16*. [OFr *batre*, with frequentative suffix *-er*]
battes *see* BATTS
battill *see* BAITTLE
battle *see* BOTTLE[2.1], BOTTLE[2.2]
batton, **battoun** *see* BATON[1.1], BATON[1.2]
batts, †**bats**, †**battes** /bats/ *npl* **1** bots, a disease caused by the parasitical larvae of flies of the genus *Oestrus*, especially in horses *la17-19, 20- NE SW*. **2** colic in humans *la16-19, 20- Bor*. [unknown]
bauch, †**baugh**, †**bawch** /bɔx/ *adj* **1** poor, pathetic; ineffective, indifferent *16-*. **2** timid, sheepish, foolish *18-*. **3** weak, exhausted, feeble *18-19, 20- T*. **4** *of a cutting implement* blunt, dull, turned on edge *19, 20- NE*. **5** *of blows* inflicted with a blunt instrument *16-e17*. **6** unpleasant, unsavoury *16*. †**bauchly** sorrily, indifferently *17-19*. **bauch ice**, †**baugh ice** *curling* soft, unslippery ice affected by thaw *19-*. [perhaps ON *bagr* awkward, clumsy or ON *bágr* uneasy; poor]
bauchill *see* BAUCHLE[1.2]
bauchle[1.1], **bachle** /'bɔxəl, 'baxəl/ *n* **1** an old, worn-out shoe; a loose or ill-fitting slipper or shoe *la18-*. **2** an old, useless, worn-out person *19-*. **3** *derogatory* an untidy or clumsy person, a figure of fun *20-*. **bauchlie**, **bauchly** worn or bent out of shape *20-*. **mak a bauchle o** make a laughing-stock or botch of *17-*. [unknown; compare BAUCH]
bauchle[1.2], **bachle**, *NE* **beochle**, †**bauchill** /'bɔxəl, 'baxəl; *NE* 'bjɔxəl/ *v* **1** to wear shoes out of shape; to distort or spoil *la19-*. **2** to shuffle; to walk awkwardly *20-*. **3** to treat contemptuously, cause trouble or harm to; to bother or be bothered by *19, 20- NE*. **4** to denounce openly; to disgrace, discredit (publicly) *la15-16*. **bauchled**, **bauchlt** *of footwear* out of shape; worn-out, battered *19-*. [see the noun]
baucon, **baucun** *see* BAWCON
baud, **bawd**, †**bad** /bɔd/ *n* **1** a clump of thick worms strung together on twine (used for fishing for eels) *20- WC*. **2** a thicket, a clump of bushes or plants *la18-e19*. [Gael *bad* a tuft]
baud *see* BADD
†**baudkin**, **badkin**, **baikin** *n* a richly embroidered cloth; a baldachin, a canopy *la14-16*. [ME *baudekin*]
baudrons, **bawdrons**, **baudrins**, **bauldrins**, †**badrans**, †**balderonis** /'bɔdrənz, 'bɔldrənz/ *n* **1** (a pet name for) a cat *la15-*. **2** a hare *20- NE*. Compare BAWD. [unknown]
baugh *see* BAUCH
bauk[1.1], **balk**, **back**, **bak**, **baak**, †**baik** /bɔk, bak/ *n* **1** an unploughed ridge (in a cultivated field), a strip of unploughed land used to mark a boundary (between farms); frequently in place-names *14-*. **2** a wooden beam *la14-*. **3** the beam of a balance or pair of scales *15-*. **4** a hen roost *la15-*. **5** a crossbeam, a rafter *16-*. **6** a ridge still apparent in a field after tilling *18-*. **7** *pl* a church gallery *la19-*. **8** a narrow track, a garden path *20-*. **9** a seat in a (fishing) boat *20-*. **bauk hicht**, †**bawk-hight** as high as the rafters *18-19, 20- literary*. **bauk tree**, **back tree** a joist *20- Bor*. **bauk and brade** a beam with scales for weighing large articles *15-19, 20- Bor*. **balk and burrel** *of the pattern on a ploughed field* corrugated, ribbed *la18-19, 20- Bor*. [OE *balca*]
bauk[1.2], **baulk** /bɔk/ *v* **1** to leave small strips of land inadvertently unploughed *19, 20- NE H&I*. **2** to fail to use or hold

onto; to let slip *e18*. **3** to pass over; to overlook, miss *la16*. [see the noun]

bauk², baak, back /bɔk, bak/ *n* the head rope in fishing lines and nets *19- Sh Ork N NE*. Compare BACK-ROPE. [unknown; compare ON *bakka-kólfr* a thick arrow without a point]

bauk *see* BACK²

baukie *see* BAAKIE, BACKIE²

baul *see* BELD¹·³, BAULD¹·²

bauld¹·¹, †bald /bɔld/ *v* to embolden; to kindle or blow up a fire *15-19, 20- Bor*. [see the adj]

bauld¹·², baul, bawl, †bald /bɔld, bɔl/ *adj* **1** *of people* courageous, daring; confident, presumptuous *la14-*. **2** *of animals* fierce; courageous *la15-*. **3** *of things* strong, powerful *la15-* **4** *of fire* burning fiercely *la15-e19*. [OE *bald*]

†bauld¹·³, bald, baal *adv* boldly, strongly, fiercely *la14-e19*. [OE *balde*]

bauld *see* BELD¹·³

bauldie, baldie /'bɔldi, 'baldi/ *n* a carvel-built fishing boat *la19-*. [perhaps shortened form of the name *Garibaldi*; the boat was earlier termed a 'Garibaldi boat']

bauldrins *see* BAUDRONS

bauldy¹·¹, baldy /'bɔlde/ *n* a very short haircut *la20-*. [see the adj]

bauldy¹·², baldy /'bɔlde/ *adj* bald, hairless *20-*; compare BELD¹·³. **Baldy Bain, Baldy Bayne** a nickname for a bald man *la20-*. **bauldy-heidit, bauldy-heided** bald-headed *20-*. [BELD¹·³ + -IE²]

baulk *see* BAUK¹·²

baur *see* BAR¹·¹, BAR¹·², BAR²

baurdy *see* BARDIE¹·²

baurley *see* BARLEY¹, BARLEY²

bausined *see* BAWSONT

bausy, bawsy /'bɔze, 'bɔzi/ *adj* large, fat, coarse *la15-*. **Bawsy Broon, †Bausie Broun** a name for a demon *16- literary*. [compare Norw dial *basse* a big, well-fed animal; a big, strong man]

bauther *see* BATHER¹·²

bavary, bavarra /'bavəre, bə'vara/ *n* a greatcoat or cloak *la18-19, 20- NE*. [probably Fr *bavarois* Bavarian]

baver *see* BEVER¹

bavin *see* BOWIN

baw *see* BA¹, BA², BALL¹

bawaw /bɔ'wɔ/ *n* a sideways glance (of scorn or contempt) *la18-19, 20- literary*. [unknown]

bawbag /'bɔbag/ *n* **1** the scrotum *la20-*. **2** *derogatory* a person *la20-*. [*baw* (BA¹) + BAG¹·¹]

bawbee, †bawbe, †balbe, †babie /bɔ'bi/ *n* **1** a halfpenny *18-20, 21- historical*. **2** *pl* money *la19-*. **3** a copper or base silver coin valued at six pennies Scots *16-18*. **ken the richt side o a bawbee** to be shrewd with money *la20-*. [probably from *Sillebawbe* the land and territorial designation of Alexander Orrock, a 16th-century master of the mint]

bawbrek /bɔ'brɛk/ *n* a kneading trough or board *19, 20- Bor*. [probably altered form of *bake-board* (BAKE¹·²)]

bawburd *see* BABORD

bawcan, bawkin, bockan /'bɔkən/ *n* a spectre, a ghost *20- H&I WC*. [probably Gael *bòcan* a hobgoblin; a ghost]

bawch *see* BAUCH

bawcon, baucon, baucun, bacon, †bakon /'bɔkən, 'bɛkən/ *n* **1** cured pig's meat, bacon *la15-*. **2** an animal (possibly a pig) *la15*. [ME *bacoun*]

bawd /bɔd/ *n* a hare *la18-*. Compare BAUDRONS. [unknown]

bawd *see* BID¹, BAUD

bawdrons *see* BAUDRONS

baw face /'bɔ fes/ *n derogatory* a person with a round face *20- C*. [*baw* (BA¹) + FACE¹·¹]

baw faced /bɔ 'fest/ *adj derogatory* having a round face *20- C*. [BAW FACE, with adj-forming suffix]

bawgie *see* BAAKIE

baw-hair /'bɔher/ *n* a hair's breadth, a tiny distance *la20-*. [*baw* (BA¹) + HAIR¹·¹]

baw heid, ba heid /'bɔ hid, 'ba hid/ *n* **1** *derogatory* a person with a (large) round head *la20- C*. **2** *derogatory* a foolish person *la20- C*. [*baw* (BA¹) + HEID¹·¹]

bawkie *see* BACKIE²

bawkin *see* BAWCAN

bawl *see* BAULD¹·²

bawr *see* BAR²

baws /bɔz/ *interj* an expression of disbelief or dismissal *la20-*. [plural of *baw* (BA¹)]

bawsey *see* BASSIE¹·¹

bawsont, bawsant, bawsened, bassened, †bausined, †bawsand, †basownit /'bɔsənt, 'bɔsənd, 'basənd/ *adj of a horse or other animal* having a white marking or stripe on the face *15-*. [ME *bausand*]

bawsy *see* BAUSY

bawthe *see* BATH¹·²

bawtie, †bawte, †batie /'bɔti/ *n* **1** (a name for) a dog *16-19, 20- literary*. **2** a hare, a rabbit *19- Bor*. Compare BAWD. [unknown]

bawtie *see* BATIE

baxter, †baxtar, †bakstar, †bakister /'bakstər/ *n* a baker *14-*. **†baxtarie, baxtrey** (the craft of) baking *16-e18*. [OE *bæcestre*, feminine of *bæcere*]

†bay *n* the singing of birds *e16*. [perhaps transferred sense of Eng *bay* baying of hounds]

bayin *see* BOWIN

bayn *see* BANE

†bayne¹·¹, bane *adj* ready, willing *la15-16*. [perhaps ON *beinn* straight; hospitable]

†bayne¹·² *adv* readily, willingly *la15-e16*. [see the adj]

bayt *see* BOAT¹·¹

bazed *see* BAISED

be, *Bor* **bey** /be; *Bor* beɪ/ *v* *present singular* **is, am, †ame**, *present singular and plural* **are, er, ir, irr, ur**, also *Sh* **bees**, **†beis, †bene, †be**, *imperative* **be, †beis**, *ptp* **been, bin, †bein, †ybe** **1** to exist, live *la14-*. **2** to take place, happen *la14-*. **3** to occupy a place or position *la14-*. **4** to continue or remain *la14-*. **5** *with ellipsis of* HAE¹·² have been: ◊ *I been consulting with a lawyer la14-*. **6** to have as followers (in battle) *la14-16*. **amna, amnae, immen, umnae** am not *20-*. Compare WIRNIE and WISNAE. **arna, arena, arenae, urnae** are not *19-*. Compare WIRNIE and WISNAE. **†beid** be it *la15-16*. **sae beins, sae bein as** that being so *18- NE*. **'twar** it were *19-*. [OE *bēon*]

be *see* BEE¹, BY¹·², BY¹·³

bead, bede, †beid /bid/ *n* **1** a rosary; a bead *la15-*. **2** a glass or quantity of spirits *19-*. **3** (a measure of) the strength of spirits *19- WC SW*. **4** *weaving* the eyelet through which the warp thread passes in a harness or jacquard loom *la20- WC SW*. **5** a prayer *la14-16*. **beadhouse, bedehouse, †bedhous** an almshouse; a hospital *la16-19, 20- historical*. **†bead lams** short heddles fitted with glass beads through which the warp threads passed in a silk-loom *19*. **bedeman 1** a pauper receiving alms, a person receiving alms from the monarch to pray for him; a dependant *15-19, 20- historical*. **2** an inmate of an almshouse or hospital *la15-19, 20- historical*. **†bedewoman** a female inmate of a hospital or almshouse *16*. [ME *bede* prayer; compare OE *biddan* to pray]

beadle, beddal, †bedral, †betheral, †pedell /'bidəl, 'bɛdəl/ *n* **1** a church officer *16-*. **2** a gravedigger *19*. **3** a

town bellman *e19*. **4** an officer in the service of a university *la16-17*. **5** a herald or officer of justice *la14-e17*. [OE *bydel*]
beak, †**beke**, †**beik** /bik/ *n* **1** a bird's bill *15-*. **2** a rocky projection or point; a headland *la16-*. **3** the nose, the face *19-*. **4** impudence *19- Bor*. **5** *pl* the projecting hip-bones of an old horse *e16*. [ME *bek*]
beal, **beel**, **bale**, †**bele**, †**beil** /bil, bel/ *v* **1** to fester, suppurate *la15-*. **2** to swell with rage; to fill with rancour *15-*. **3** to be filled with pain or remorse; to suffer intense pain *18-*. **bealin**, **beelin** *n* a suppuration; a festering sore, boil or pimple *17-*. **bealin**, **beelin**, **beeling** *adj* **1** festering, suppurating *la19-*. **2** enraged; highly agitated *la20-*. **3** disgusting, foul *la20-*. [probably related to OE *bȳl* a boil]
bealach *see* BALLOCH
†**beall** *n* bail *la17*. [EModE *bail*]
beam[1], †**beme** /bim/ *n* **1** a ray of light *la14-*. **2** a long thick piece of wood (used in construction) *16-*. [OE *bēam*]
beam[2] /bim/ *v* to propel a swing (by standing on it and bending the knees) *20- EC Bor*. [perhaps related to Eng *crossbeam* the highest part of a swing]
beam *see* BEEM
beamer /'bimər/ *n* a blushing face (as a sign of embarrassment) *la20-*. [perhaps a derivative of BEAM[1] in the sense of a bright, shining light]
beamfill, †**beymfill** /'bimfɪl/ *v* **1** *in building* to fill in the space between the wall-plate and the roof *16-*. **2** to fill completely, cram, stuff *la19-*. **beamfill't** filled to overflowing; indulged; intoxicated *19- NE*. **beamfoo** = *beamfill't*. [ME *bemefelle*]
bean, †**bene** /bin/ *n* a legume, a bean *15-*. **King of Bane**, **King of Bene** the man in whose portion of Twelfth-Night cake the bean was found *la15-16*, *19- historical*. **Queen of Bane** the woman in whose portion of Twelfth-Night cake the bean was found *e16*, *19- historical*. [OE *bēan*]
bean *see* BANE
bear[1], **bere**, **beer**, **bare**, †**beir** /bir, ber/ *n* a hardy, coarse variety of barley *Hordeum hexasticon* or *Hordeum tetrasticon* (having four or six rows of grain in the ear) *la14-*. **bere bannock** a cake made of barley meal *la16-*. †**bearland**, **beirland** land on which barley is grown *16-19*. **bear-meal**, **bare-meal**, †**beire mele** barley meal *15-*. †**bear-pundlar**, **beir pondler** *in Orkney* an instrument for weighing barley *la16-19*. †**bear-root crop**, **bar-reet crop** the first crop after a barley crop *18-19*. †**bear seed**, **beirseid 1** (the time for) sowing of barley *16-e19*. **2** the seed of the barley; barley for sowing *16*. **bear-sowing**, †**beir sawing** the sowing of barley; seed barley *16-*. [OE *bere*]
bear[2], **beir**, †**bere**, †**bare**, †**bair** /ber, bir/ *v pt* **bore**, †**bair**, †**bure**, *ptp* **borne**, †**yborn 1** to support or hold up; to carry or convey *la14-*. **2** to give birth to; to produce *la14-*. **3** to carry oneself; to act, behave *la14-*. **4** to endure, withstand; to tolerate *15-*. **5** to signify, mean or imply; *of writing* to state *la15-*. **bearer** *mining* a (female) worker who carried coal in baskets from the workings to the shaft *la19*, *20- historical*. †**bore breiff** a birth certificate *la16-e18*. **bear the gree** to win; to carry off the prize *15-*. †**borne man of** a native (of a place) *16-e17*. †**bere on hand** to maintain; to continue in; to assert *la14-e17*. [OE *geberan*]
bear[3], †**bere**, †**beir** /ber/ *n* **1** a large heavy mammal with a shaggy coat *la14-*. **2** a rough working man; an oilrig worker *la20-*. **bearpit** a rough pub *la20-*. [OE *bera*]
beard, **baird**, †**berde**, †**beird** /bird, berd/ *n* the hair that grows on the chin of an adult man, a beard *la14-*. [OE *beard*]
beardie[1.1], **bairdie** /'birdi, 'berdi/ *n* **1** the three-spined stickleback *Gasterosteus aculeatus 19-*. **2** the greater whitethroat *Sylvia communis la19-*. **3** the rubbing of a man's rough chin against another person's chin or cheek, the squeezing of someone's chin with the hand *la19-*. **4** a person with a beard *20-*. **5** a large jar (with the figure of a bearded man on it) *19*. **6** the loach *Barbatula barbatula e19*. **beardie lotchie** the loach *Barbatula barbatula 19*, *20- Bor*. [BEARD + -IE[2]]
beardie[1.2], **bairdie** /'birdi, 'berdi/ *adj of cheese* mouldy, hair moulded *la20- EC SW*. [see the noun]
beare *see* BARE
beas *see* BEAST[1.1]
bease, †**behss** /bes/ *n* bustle, hurry *la19- NE T*. [unknown]
bease *see* BAISE, BEAST[1.1], BOOSE[1.1]
beasing *see* BOOSE[1.2]
beast[1.1], **baste**, †**beste**, †**beist** /bist, best/ *n pl also* **beas**, **bease**, **baess**, **beise**, †**bes 1** a (wild) animal *la14-*. **2** a cow, a bovine, a farm animal; *pl* livestock *15-*. **3** an ignorant, brutal person *16-*. **4** a bird, a fish, an insect *la18-*. **5** a loser at cards *19- NE*. **6** the skin of a fur-bearing animal *la15-e16*. **beastie 1** an animal, a beast *la18-*. **2** *fisherman's taboo* a pig *20- T Bor*. [ME *best*]
beast[1.2], **beest** /bist/ *v* to beat (at cards); to overcome, vanquish *19*, *20- NE*. **get beasted in** to approach something enthusiastically; to eat heartily *la20-*. [see the noun]
beat, *N H&I* **beyt** /bit; *N H&I* bʌit; *N H&I* bet/ *v* to bet, wager *18-19*, *20- N NE T H&I*. [EModE *bet*]
beat *see* BATE[1.1], BATE[1.2]
beatac *see* BEETYACH
beauty *see* BYOUTY
becam *see* BECOME
beck[1.1], **baik**, †**bek** /bɛk, bek/ *n* a bow; a curtsy; a gesture of respect *la15-*. [see the verb]
beck[1.2], **bek**, **baik** /bɛk, bek/ *v* to bow; to curtsy; to make a gesture of respect *la15-*. [shortened form of BEKIN[2]]
become, †**becum** /bə'kʌm/ *v pt* **became**, †**become**, †**becam**, *ptp* †**becummin**, †**becum**, †**becummit 1** to come to be *la14-*. **2** to befit, be suitable *16-*. **3** to acquire *15-17*. [OE *becuman*]
bed[1.1], †**bede**, †**beid**, †**baid** /bɛd/ *n* **1** an article of furniture for sleeping on *la14-*. **2** a flat base or foundation; a level structure *16-*. **3** a garden plot *16-*. **4** a bank in the sea *la16-*. **beddie ba**, **beddie baa** a child's word for a bed or for going to sleep *la19-*. **bed buirds**, **bed bewards** boards used to form a bed *19*, *20- NE WC*. †**bed-evil** an illness confining one to bed *15-e17*. **bedfast** bedridden, confined to bed *la16-*. **bedmat** a thick, woollen bedcover *19-*. **bed-pand**, **bed-pan** the valance of a bed *la17-*. **bed plaid** a plaid used as a bed-covering; a top-cover for a bed *la16-19*, *20- NE C*. **bed recess** an alcove in a room (designed to hold a bed), commonly found in tenement flats *19-*. **bed stock** the beam of wood that runs along the front of a bed *la17-19*, *20- NE*. [OE *bedd*]
bed[1.2], †**bede**, †**baid** /bɛd/ *v* **1** to go to bed; to lie in bed (with someone) *la14-*. **2** to put to bed *la18-*. **beddit up** confined to bed through illness *20- NE*. [OE *beddian*]
bed *see* BIDE[1.2]
beddal, **beddel** /'bɛdəl/ *n* a bedridden person *19*, *20- NE*. [probably variant form of BEDLAR[1.1]]
beddal *see* BEADLE
beddie ba *see* BED[1.1]
bedding /'bɛdɪŋ/ *n* **1** bedclothes *la15-*. **2** straw for bedding an animal *17-*. **3** the ceremony of putting a bride to bed *19*, *20- historical*. **4** sleeping accommodation *15-17*. †**ane bedding of clathis** a supply of bedclothes for one bed *la16-17*. [derivative of BED[1.1]]
beddral[1.1], **bedril**, **bedral** /'bɛdrəl/ *n* **1** a bedridden person *16-19*, *20- Sh NE*. **2** an inmate of a hospital or almshouse *16-e17*. [probably a metathesized form of BEDLAR[1.1]]

beddral[1.2], †**bedrall** /'bɛdrəl/ *adj* confined to bed, bedridden *la15-19, 20- NE*. [see the noun]

bede see BEAD, BED[1.1], BED[1.2]

bedeen, †**bedene**, †**bedeyn** /bə'din/ *adv* **1** immediately, at once; quickly, soon *15-19, 20- literary*. **2** altogether, entirely *la14-16*. [unknown]

bedellus /bə'dɛləs, 'bidələs/ *n* the chief porter and macebearer in a Scottish University *18-*. [Lat *bedellus*]

bedene see BEDEEN

†**bedettit** *adj* indebted *e16*. [*be-* prefix + derivative form of DEBT]

bedeyn see BEDEEN

bedhous see BEAD

bedink /bə'dɪŋk/ *v* to bedeck *19, 20- literary*. [DINK[1.2], with verb-forming prefix]

bedirten see BEDRITE

†**bedlar**[1.1], **bedlare**, **beiddellar** *n* a bedridden person *la16-19* [perhaps BED + ON *lag* lying, with agent suffix]

†**bedlar**[1.2], **bedlare** *adj* bedridden *la15*. [see the noun]

†**bedovin**, **bedowyn** *adj* immersed, plunged *15-e16*. [OE *bedofen*, ptp of *bedūfan* to submerge]

bedraigle /bə'dregəl/ *v* to soil, bedraggle *la19-*. **bedraigled** soiled, wet, muddied *la19-*. [*be-* prefix + DRAIGLE[1.2]]

bedrait see BEDRITE

bedral see BEADLE, BEDDRAL[1.1]

bedrall see BEDDRAL[1.2]

bedrate see BEDRITE

bedril see BEDDRAL[1.1]

bedrite /bə'draɪt/ *v pt* **bedrate**, †**bedrait** †**bedret** *ptp* **bedritten**, †**bedirten** to foul with excrement or dirt *16-19, 20- Bor*. [*be-* prefix + DRITE[1.2]]

bedrucken /bə'drʌkən/ *adj* drunken *la19- Sh T EC*. [*be-* prefix + DRUCKEN]

beds /bɛdz/ *npl* the spaces chalked on the street for playing hopscotch; the game itself *la19-*. **beddies** = BEDS. [plural of BED[1.1]]

bee[1], †**be** /bi/ *n* **1** a honey bee, an insect of the family *Hymenoptera la14-*. **2** a whim, a fanciful idea *16-*. **3** a crustacean *Aega tridens la19- Sh*. **bee-ale** a type of mead *19- N NE T*. **bee-bole** a recess in a wall for holding a beehive *20- T*. **bee-heidit**, **bee-heided** harebrained, scatty *19-*. **bee-skep** a beehive *la16-*. [OE *bēo*]

bee[2], *Bor* **bei** /bi; *Bor* bae/ *n* a metal ring or ferrule *19- SW Bor*. [OE *bēah* a ring]

†**be-east**[1.1], **be-est** *adv* to or towards the east; on the east side *la15-17*. [OE *be ēastan*]

be-east[1.2], **be'st**, **beest**, *Sh* **be-aest**, †**be-est** /bi'ist, bist; *Sh* bi'est/ *prep* to the east of, eastwards from *15-*. [see the adv]

bee-baw-babbety /bibɔ'babəte/ *n* a kissing game; a dance *20-*. [variant of BAB-AT-THE-BOWSTER]

beef, **beif** /bif/ *n* **1** the flesh of cattle *la14-*. **2** any butcher's meat *20- NE*. **3** an ox or cow intended for slaughter *17-19*. **4** human flesh; the body *la16-18*. **beef brose** brose made with the liquid in which beef has been boiled *19- NE T EC*. **beef cheese** a mixture of hard-boiled eggs and gravy set in a mould *20- NE T*. †**beefie coal** a type of coal *19*. †**beef stand** a tub for holding salted beef *la17-e18*. **beef and greens** beef and cabbage (the traditional meal at a curling club dinner) *19-*. **put on the beef** to gain weight *la20-*. [ME *bef*]

beefle see BIFFLE

†**be-eft** *prep* after, behind *15-17*. [OE *beæftan*]

beegle see BAIGLE

beein /'biən/ *n* a dwelling *la19- Sh*. [perhaps an altered form of BIGGIN[1]]

beek[1.1] /bik/ *n* an act or period of warming oneself *18-19, 20- NE*. [unknown]

beek[1.2], †**beik**, †**beke** /bik/ *v* **1** to warm oneself; to bask in heat *la14-*. **2** *of the sun* to shine brightly *18-*. **3** to add fuel to a fire *la19-*. **4** to overheat, warm to the point of discomfort *la20-*. [unknown]

beek[2] /bik/ *v* **1** to bathe, wash *la19- Sh Bor*. **2** to pat, stroke; to comfort or cuddle *la19- Sh*. [perhaps from BEEK[1.2] with influence from BEET[2.1]]

beel see BEAL

beell see BILL[1]

beem, **been**, *Sh* **bem**, †**beam** /bim, bin; *Sh* bɛm/ *v* to steep a barrel or tub to make it watertight *19- Sh N NE*. [unknown]

been see BANE, BE, BOON[1]

beenge, †**binge**, †**beynge** /binʒ/ *v* to bow; to cringe or fawn *la15-19, 20- Bor*. [unknown]

been-hook /'binhʊk/ *n in Orkney* harvest-work required of a tenant as part of their rent; the cottar under this obligation *19, 20- historical*. [probably OE *bēn* prayer, supplication + HEUK]

beenkie /'binki/ *n* a ledge or rock *20- Sh Ork*. [compare BINK[1]]

beenmost see BOONMOST

beer see BEAR[1]

beerach, **burrach**, †**bourach** /'birəx, 'bʌrəx/ *n* a rope used to keep a cow from kicking during milking *19, 20- N H&I*. [Gael *buarach* a cow fetter]

beeran, **bioran** /'birən, 'bjɔrən/ *n* a small trout *la19- N H&I*. [Gael *bioran* a little stick]

beerial, **burial**, **bural**, *Sh* **bürol**, *N* **bewrial**, **buriall**, †**beryall** /'birɪəl, 'birɪəl, 'bʌrɪəl, 'berɪəl, 'bʌrəl; *Sh* 'børəl; *N* 'bjurɪəl/ *n* **1** the interment of a body; a funeral *16-*. **2** a burial ground; a grave, a tomb *la16-17*. **burial bread** cakes eaten by mourners after a funeral service *la18-19, 20- historical*. **burial letter** an intimation of or invitation to a funeral *la17-19, 20- Ork N SW*. †**buriall silver** payment for a funeral *e17*. **burial yaird**, **burial yard** a burial ground *la16-*. [ME *biriel*]

beerie, **bury**, *Ork* **booray**, *N* **bewry**, †**bery** /'bire, 'bɪre, 'bʌre, 'bere; *Ork* 'bure; *N* 'bjuri/ *v ptp* †**yberyit** to inter, bury *la14-*. **buryin** a funeral *19-*. [OE *byrgan*]

bees see BE

beest, **beist** /bist/ *n* the first milk of a cow after calving *la16-*. **beesnin** = BEEST *19- SW Bor Uls*. **beestie** = BEEST *20-*. **beestin**, **beistyn** = BEEST *19-*. [OE *bēost*]

beest see BEAST[1.2], BE-EAST[1.2]

be-est see BE-EAST[1.1], BE-EAST[1.2]

beester /'bistər/ *v* to outdo; to beat in a game *20- NE T*. [unknown]

beesweel, **beswell** /bi'swil, bə'swɛl/ *adv* however *la19- Ork*. [shortened form of Eng *be as it will*]

†**beet**[1], **beit** *n* a sheaf or bundle of flax *la15-19*. [perhaps OE *bēatan* beat]

†**beet**[2.1] *n* **1** a needful thing *e19*. **2** a repair; material for mending a garment *e16*. [see the verb]

beet[2.2], †**bete**, †**bet** /bit/ *v pt* **bet**, *ptp* **bet**, †**ybet 1** to repair, mend *la15-*. **2** to furnish a want or supply something needed; to replace something missing or worn out *18-*. **3** to plant trees to replace others *la18-*. **4** to relieve or lessen distress or need; to assist, help or comfort *la14-e19*. **5** to kindle or add fuel to a fire *la14-e19*. **6** to amend or correct *la14-16*. **7** to make, constitute *e16*. †**beitment** repairing, mending *16-e17*. †**beet a mister** to fulfil a need, make good a deficiency *la14-19*. **beet the wants** to replace lost hooks on a fishing line *19-*. [OE *bētan*]

beet see BEHOVE, BUIT[1.1], BUIT[1.2], BUIT[2.1], BUIT[2.2]

beetle see BITTLE[1.1], BITTLE[1.2]

beetleheid /ˈbitəlhid/ *n* a tadpole *20- H&I*. [Older Scots *bettill* a beetle + HEID[1.1]]

beetyach, beatac, †bittock /ˈbitjəx, ˈbitək/ *n* a sword, a dagger, a small knife *19-*. [Gael *biodag* a dagger]

beevis see BAIVIS

beezer /ˈbizər/ *n* **1** something bigger or better than usual; something extreme of its kind *la19-*. **2** a smart fellow *20-*. [unknown]

beezim see BESOM

befa, befaw, befall /bəˈfa, bəˈfɔ, bəˈfɔl/ *v* **1** to occur, happen *la14-*. **2** to receive as one's lot or share *la15-16*. [OE *befeallan*]

beff[1.1], **baif** /bɛf, bef/ *n* a blow; a swelling (as a result of a blow) *la18- NE*. [probably a variant of BAFF[1.1]]

†beff[1.2] *v pt, ptp* **beft** to strike, beat *la14-19*. [see the noun]

beff[2] /bɛf/ *n* a foolish or overweight person *la19- NE*. [unknown]

beffan /ˈbɛfən/ *n* a foolish or overweight person *la19- NE*. [unknown]

†beforn[1.1] *adv* before *la14-e17*. **of beforne** before in time; formerly *15-e17*. [OE *beforan*]

†beforn[1.2] *prep* before *la14-e19*. [see the adv]

†beforrow *adv* before *la16*. [*be-* prefix + FOROW]

befram /bəˈfram/ *adv* to seaward *la19- Sh*. [*be-* prefix + FRAM[1.2]]

befreen /bəˈfrin/ *v* to befriend *la19- NE*. [*be-* prefix + FREEND[1.2]]

beft see BEFF[1.2]

befundered /bəˈfʌndərd/ *adj* amazed *20- Ork*. [*be-* prefix + foonert (FOONDER[1.2]) foundered, dismayed]

befyle /bəˈfʌil/ *v* to soil, defile *16-19, 20- literary*. [OE *befȳlan*]

beg see BIG[1]

begaik see BEGECK[1.1], BEGECK[1.2]

began see BEGIN

begar see BEGGAR

begare see BEGARY[1.2]

†begary[1.1] *n* a trimming, facing, or stripe of different material on a garment *la16-e17*. [see the verb]

†begary[1.2], **begare** *v* **1** to ornament a garment with stripes or trimmings of another material or colour *la15-e17*. **2** to variegate with streaks of colour *16-17*. [MFr *bigarrer*]

begeck[1.1], **begeik, begaik, begick** /bəˈgɛk, bəˈgek, bəˈgɪk/ *n* a trick, a disappointment *la18- N NE T*. [see the verb]

begeck[1.2], **†begaik** /bəˈgɛk/ *v* to deceive, disappoint *la16-19, 20- NE*. [probably derivative of GECK[1.1]; compare MDu, MLG *begecken* deride]

begeik see BEGECK[1.1]

be ges see BEGUESS

beggar, †begar /ˈbɛgər/ *n* a mendicant, someone who begs *la14-*. **†beggartie** beggary *16*. **†beggar's bed** *in a farm or country house* a bed made up for beggars, usually in the barn *la18-19*. **†beggar's broon** light brown snuff made from tobacco stems *19*. **beggar man** a fish, usually a flounder *20- NE*. **†beggar-plaits** creased garments *19*. [ME *beggare*]

begick see BEGECK[1.1]

begin /bəˈgɪn/ *v pt* **began, begouth, beguid, begood**, *ptp* **begun, begunnyn** to commence, start *la14-*. **begin to** to start on: ◊*he began to his dinner la16-*. [OE *beginnan*]

beglamour, †beglaumer /bəˈglamər/ *v* to bewitch *19-*. [*be-* prefix + GLAMOUR[1.1]]

begood see BEGIN

begotted, bigotit /bəˈgɔtəd, bəˈgɔtɪt/ *adj* **1** intolerant, obstinate *la18-*. **2** infatuated *19-*. [Fr *bigot*]

begouth see BEGIN

begowk /bəˈgʌuk/ *v* to trick, fool *19-*. [*be-* prefix + GOWK[1]]

begoyt see BEGYTE

begrutten, †begrouttin /bəˈgrʌtən/ *adj* tear-stained, sorrowful *17-*. [*be-* prefix + ptp of GREET[1.2]]

beguess, †be ges /bəˈgɛs/ *adv* by guessing; at random *15-19, 20- NE*. [BY[1.2] + GUESS[1.1]]

beguid, begun see BEGIN

begunk[1.1] /bəˈgʌŋk/ *n* **1** a trick, a cheat *18-*. **2** a disappointment, a misfortune *la18-*. [derivative of GUNK[1.1]]

begunk[1.2] /bəˈgʌŋk/ *v* **1** to cheat, deceive; to jilt *19-*. **2** to befool, play a trick on *la19- T C Bor*. [see the noun]

begunnyn see BEGIN

begyte, †begoyt /bəˈgʌit/ *adj* foolish, mad *la18- NE Bor*. [*be-* prefix + GYTE[1.2]]

beh see BUY

behad, behald see BEHAUD

behalf, †behalve, †behaw /bəˈhaf/ *n* on the part of (someone or something) *15-*. [ME *bihelue*]

behand, behan /bəˈhand, bəˈhan/ *adv* finished, over and done with *la19- NE*. **come weel behand** to manage well *19- NE Bor*. [*be-* prefix + HAN[1.1]]

behangt /bəˈhaŋt/ *interj* an expression of impatience *la19-*. [BE + ptp of HING[1.1]]

behaud, behad, †behald /bəˈhɔd, bəˈhad/ *v ptp* also **behudden 1** to look at, regard, contemplate *la14-*. **2** to suspend action, hold back, wait *17-*. **3** to scrutinize, spy on or monitor *19-*. [OE *behealdan*]

behaw see BEHALF

behear /bəˈhir/ *interj* an expression of surprise *20-*. [perhaps shortened form of *losh be here* (LOSH)]

beheave see BEHEEF

†behecht[1.1] *n* a promise *e16*. [see the verb]

behecht[1.2], **behight** /bəˈhext, bəˈhʌit/ *v* to vow, promise *la15-19, 20- Bor*. [ME *behiȝt*]

beheef, *N* **beheave, †behufe, †behove, †behuve** /bəˈhif; *N* bəˈhiv/ *n* behoof, advantage, benefit *la14-19, 20- N NE*. [OE *bēhof*; compare BEHOVE]

beheeve see BEHOVE

behight see BEHECHT[1.2]

behint[1.1], **behin, behind,** *H&I* **behunt** /bəˈhɪnt, bəˈhɪn, bəˈhʌind; *H&I* bəˈhʌnt/ *adv* in the rear *la14-*. Compare AHINT[1.1]. [OE *behindan*]

behint[1.2], **behin, behind,** *H&I* **behunt** /bəˈhɪnt, bəˈhɪn, bəˈhʌind; *H&I* bəˈhʌnt/ *prep* at the back of, to the rear of *la14-*. Compare AHINT[1.2]. [see the adv]

behooky, behouchie see BAHOOKIE

behove, behoove, †beheeve, †behufe, †behuve /bəˈhov, bəˈhuv/ *v pres* **†behus**, *pt* **bude, bit, bud, bode,** *NE* **beet, †bute, †behud †bewyt 1** to be necessary or incumbent on *la14-*. **2** *of a person* to be under an obligation or necessity *la14-*. **beet-tae-be, bude-be** something which one was obliged to do *19-*. [OE *behōfian*; compare BEHOOF]

behove see BEHEEF

behss see BEASE

behud see BEHOVE

behudden see BEHAUD

behufe see BEHEEF, BEHOVE

†behuffull, behufull *adj* behoveful, necessary; advantageous *15-e16*. [Eng *behoof*, with adj-forming suffix *-ful*]

behunt see BEHINT[1.2]

behus see BEHOVE

behuve see BEHEEF, BEHOVE

bei see BEE[2]

beid see BEAD, BED[1.1]

beiddellar see BEDLAR[1.1]

beif see BEEF

beig see BIG[2]

beik see BEAK
beil see BEAL
beild see BIELD¹·¹, BIELD¹·², BUILD
beilybucht see BELLIBUCHT
bein see BE, BIEN¹·²
†**beir**¹·¹, **bere** *n* an outcry, clamour; noise, a din *la14-19*. [OE *gebǣre* behaviour]
†**beir**¹·², **bere** *v* to cry, roar *la14-19*. [OE *gebǣran* to behave]
beir see BEAR¹, BEAR², BEAR³
beird see BEARD
beirdly see BUIRDLY
beis see BE
beise see BEAST¹·¹
beist see BEAST¹·¹, BEEST
beit see BEET¹
beith see BAITH¹·¹, BAITH¹·²
beitment see BEET²·²
bejan, bejant, *WC* **bajan,** †**bajon** /ˈbedʒən, ˈbidʒən, ˈbidʒənt; *WC* ˈbadʒən/ *n* a first-year student at a Scottish university (especially St Andrews) *17-*. **bejanella** a female first-year student at the University of Aberdeen *la19-*. **bejantine** a female first-year student at the University of St Andrews *la19-*. [Fr *béjaune* inexperienced youth]
bek see BECK¹·¹, BECK¹·²
beke see BEAK
†**beken** *v* **1** *law* to admit as possessor *la14-e16*. **2** *law* to acquaint, instruct *e16*. [*be-* prefix + KEN¹·²]
†**bekin**¹ *n* **1** a beacon; a signal-fire *16-17*. **2** a sign, a signal; a gesture *la15-e16*. [OE *bēacen*]
†**bekin**² *v* to beckon; to give a sign *la14-e17*. [OE *bīcnan*]
bekkle /ˈbɛkəl/ *v* to twist, distort *la19- Sh*. [compare Faer *bekla* to walk crookedly, Norw *begla* to bungle, botch]
belaggeret, belaggirt /bəˈlagərət, bəˈlagərt/ *adj* clogged with wet mud *la19- NE EC*. [*be-* prefix + Eng *lag*, with *-irt* suffix]
belang /bəˈlaŋ/ *v* **1** to be the property of *la15-*. **2** to concern or relate to, appertain to; to be appropriate to *la15-*. **3** to own, possess *la19-*. **4** to be born in or live in (a place), be a native of: ◊*he belangs Glesca* ◊*where dae ye belang tae? la19-*. †**as belangand** as concerning *la15-e16*. [ME *bilong*]
belanter /bəˈlantər/ *v* to delay; to hinder or thwart *20- Ork*. [*be-* prefix + Orkney dial *lanter* to foil, hinder]
belaubir, belauber /bəˈlɔbər/ *v* to belabour, thrash *la19- Sh NE T Bor*. [altered form of Eng *belabour*]
belaw see BELOW¹·², BELOW¹·³
belch¹, **bilch, bilge,** †**bilsh** /bɛltʃ, bɪltʃ, bɪldʒ/ *n* **1** *derogatory* a (short, fat or thickset) person or child *la18-*. **2** the belly *15*. **bilchy, bilshy,** †**belshie** short, plump and thriving *18-19, 20- SW Bor*. [ON *belgr* a bag; bellows]
†**belch**² *n* a deep pool or abyss *e16*. [unknown]
†**beld**¹·¹, **bell** *n* a white mark on a horse's face *la16-19*. [see the adj]
beld¹·², **bell** /bɛld, bɛl/ *v* to go bald; to make bald *la19- NE*. [see the adj]
beld¹·³, **bell't, bauld, bald, baelt, bell,** †**bellit,** †**baul** /bɛld, bɛlt, bɔld, balt, bɛl/ *adj* **1** hairless, bald *15-*. **2** *of horses or cattle* having a white spot or mark on the forehead *16-19, 20- historical*. **beld-heided, beld-headed** bald-headed *19-*; compare *bauldy-heidit* (BAULDY¹·²). **bell-kite** the bald coot *Fulica atra la19- EC Bor*. **bel-poot** = *bell-kite*. [ME *ballid*]
†**beld**² *adj* bold *la15-e19*. [compare BAULD¹·²]
beld see BIELD¹·¹
beldairy see BALDERRY
belde see BIELD¹·²
bele see BALE¹, BEAL

†**belechere** *n* good cheer; entertainment *e16*. [ME *bel cher*]
beleif, beleve see BELIEF, BELIEVE
belget see BELLIGET
†**belgh** *n* an outburst *e17*. [variant of ME *belche*; compare BILSH]
Belgian Biscuit /ˈbɛldʒən ˈbɪskət/ *n* an iced shortcake biscuit with a jam filling *20-*. Compare *empire biscuit* (EMPIRE¹·¹). [Eng *Belgian* + Older Scots *bisquet*, Scots *biscuit*]
belief, †**beleve,** †**beleif** /bəˈlif/ *n* **1** the act or state of believing, faith *la14-*. **2** *Presbyterian Church* the Apostle's Creed *la16-18*. **3** expectation, anticipation *e16*. [ME *byleve*]
believe, †**beleve,** †**beleif** /bəˈliv/ *v* **1** to put trust in, accept as true *la14-*. **2** to expect: ◊*he belevis to lerne 16*. [ME *beleve*]
†**beligger** *v* to beleaguer *e17*. [ME *belegar*]
belike, †**belyke** /bəˈlʌɪk/ *adv* to all appearances, surely; presumably, probably *la16-19, 20- literary*. [probably ME *belyke*]
belive see BELYVE
belky /ˈbɛlki/ *v* to drink in great quantities *20- Ork*. [ON *belg* possibly with diminutive suffix *-ie*]
bell¹·¹ /bɛl/ *n* a (cast metal) instrument designed to ring when struck *la14-*. **bell-cast** *building* a decrease in the pitch of a roof near the eaves; a taper, a slant *la19-*. †**bell custom** a custom-due (for the upkeep of a bell) *la16-19*. **bell heather** the fine-leaved heath *Erica cinerea* or the cross-leaved heath *Erica tetralix 19-*; compare *heather bell* (HEATHER). †**belheidit** *of nails* having a bell-shaped head *e17*. **bellhouse 1** a belfry *15-*. **2** *fisherman's taboo* a church *20-*. **bell-penny** money set aside to pay for one's funeral *19- NE T*. †**bell string** a bell rope *la16-19*. **bell tow** a bell rope *la16-*. **bell tree** a tree near a church from which the bell was hung (in the absence of a proper belfry) *19, 20- historical*. **bellware, bellwar, belliwar** a coarse seaweed, bladderwrack *Fucus vesiculosus la18-19, 20- N NE*. **the bell of the brae** the highest part of the slope of a hill *18-*. **the Bells** the striking of midnight on Hogmanay *la20-*. **on the bell** a person's turn to buy a round of drinks *la20-*. [OE *bell*]
bell¹·² /bɛl/ *v* **1** to furnish with a bell *la16-*, to ring a bell; to alert or wake people with a bell *la19, 20- historical*. **3** to swell out, bulge *e19*. **bell the cat** *v* **1** to undertake a hazardous action; to grapple or contend with a dangerous opponent *la16-19, 20- historical*. **Bell the Cat** *n* a nickname given to Archibald Douglas, fifth Earl of Angus, who daringly offered to remove James III's favourite in 1482 *la18- historical*. [see the noun]
bell²·¹ /bɛl/ *n* a bubble *16-19, 20- Bor*. [Flem *belle*; compare Du *bel*]
†**bell**²·² *v* to bubble up *e19*. [Du *bellen*]
bell see BELD¹·¹, BELD¹·², BELD¹·³
†**bellamy** *n* a man; an unpleasant or rough person *la15-16*. [ME *belami*, OFr *bel ami* fair friend]
bellan see BALEEN
belleis see BELLIES
bellibucht, beilybucht /ˈbɛlɪbʌxt, ˈbilɪbʌxt/ *n* a hollow in a hill, running across the slope *19- SW*. [probably BIELD¹·¹ + BUCHT¹·¹]
bellies, †**bellis,** †**belleis** /ˈbɛliz, ˈbɛlez/ *npl* (a pair of) bellows *la14-*. **bellises, bellowses,** †**bellesis** (a pair of) bellows *16-*. [plural of OE *belg*; compare BELLY]
belliget, belget /ˈbɛlɪgət, ˈbɛlgət/ *adj* gluttonous *20- Sh*. [ON *belgr*, OE *belg* a bag]
belli-hooin¹·¹ /bɛliˈhuɪn/ *n* riotousness *la19- EC*. [unknown]
belli-hooin¹·² /bɛliˈhuɪn/ *adj* riotous, rough *la19- EC*. [see the noun]

†**bellis, bellish** *v* to embellish *15-e17*. **bellisant** serving to embellish; beautiful *la15-e17*. [aphetic form of OFr *embelissant*, presp of *embelir* to make beautiful]
bellis see BELLIES
bellit, bell't see BELD[1.3]
belliwar see BELL[1.1]
belloch /'bɛlɔx/ *v* **1** *of cattle* to bellow *la19, 20- literary*. **2** *of children* to cry loudly *la19, 20- NE*. [unknown]
bellox see BALLOCK
bellum /'bɛləm/ *n* **1** noise, a din; a blow; force *18-*. **2** a person who talks nonsense *19-*. [perhaps Lat *bellum* war]
bellwaver, *Sh* **bulwaaver** /bɛl'wevər; *Sh* bʌl'wavər/ *v* to straggle, go astray; to move about aimlessly, stroll *la18-*. [perhaps related to Eng *bellwether*]
belly[1.1], †**bally** /'bɛli, 'bɛle/ *n* the abdomen, the stomach *la14-*. **belly blind** blind man's buff; a blindfolded person (in the game) *la15-19, 20- Bor*. **belly brace 1** *building* a cross-brace *la17-*. **2** a girth for a horse *la15-e17*. **belly-flaucht**, †**belly-flaught 1** flat on one's face or stomach *18-*. **2** (flayed) with the skin pulled off over the head *la14-e19*. **3** in full flight, headlong *18-e19*. **bellygut** *n* a glutton *20-*. †**bellygut, belly-god** *adj* gluttonous *la16-19*. **belly-huddroun** a large-bellied person or a sluggard *e16*. **belly rive** a great feast; eating to repletion *20- NE*. **bellythraw** colic, bellyache *16-19, 20- literary*. **belly timber** food, provisions *la18-*. †**over the belly of** in spite of *18*. [OE *belg* a bag]
belly[1.2] /'bɛli/ *v* to eat or drink voraciously *19- NE*. [see the noun]
belly see BULLY[2.2]
belovit, beloved, †**beluffit** /bə'lʌvɪt, bə'lʌvəd/ *adj* much loved *la15-*. [ME *biluuede*]
†**belovits, belovittis** *npl* beloved subjects *la15-e17*. [plural formed for substantive use of BELOVIT]
below[1.1] /bə'lo/ *v* to lower (oneself) *19-*. [*be-* prefix + LOW[1.1]]
below[1.2], **belaw** /bə'lo, bə'lɔ/ *adv* in a lower position *la16-*. [see the verb]
below[1.3], **belaw** /bə'lo, bə'lɔ/ *prep* under, lower *17-*. **in below** underneath *la19-*. [see the verb]
bel-poot see BELD[1.3]
belshach /'bɛlʃəx/ *n* rapid, incoherent speech *20- N*. [perhaps related to Gael *beulachas*]
belt[1.1] /bɛlt/ *n* **1** a strip of leather or fabric encircling the waist *la14-*. **2** a blow (with a belt) *19-*. **3** a narrow strip of trees *la19-*. **4** a tawse, a leather strap formerly used to punish children *20, 21- historical*. **beltie** a breed of cattle with a broad white band round a black body *20-*; compare *belted Galloway* (BELTED). **beltin** a clump or line of trees *20-*. [OE *belt*]
belt[1.2] /bɛlt/ *v* **1** to put a belt on (a person); to invest (an earl) with a belt *15-*. **2** to beat or thrash (with a belt) *la15-*. **3** to secure with a belt; to fasten on (a sword) with a belt *16-*. **4** to move rapidly, hurry, rush *20-*. **5** to surround, encircle *15-16*. †**belting silk** silk cord (for making belts) *la16*. [see the noun]
Beltane, †**Beltyme**, †**Beltan** /'bɛlten/ *n* **1** the first of May; an old Scottish term-day or quarter-day *15-*. **2** a pagan fire festival (marking the beginning of summer) held either in early May or late June *la18-*. **3** *Roman Catholic Church* the feast of the Invention of the Cross (on the third of May) *la15-16*. †**Beltane buke** an account book in which the reckoning was made annually at the beginning of May *la16-e17*. **Beltane Cake** a cake (with an uneven surface) baked to celebrate Beltane *la18-19, 20- historical*. **Beltane Day 1** the day of the Beltane festival or fair *16-19, 20- historical*. **2** a local festival held in Peebles *la19- Bor*. **Beltane Eve** the last day of April *la19- historical*. **Beltane Fair** a local fair held in Peebles *17- Bor*. **Beltane Fire** a ceremonial bonfire lit on the first of May *19, 20- EC*. **Beltane Queen** the girl who is crowned Queen at the annual Beltane celebrations in Peebles *la19- Bor*. **Beltane Ree** a period of stormy weather at the beginning of May *la19- Sh*. [Gael *bealltainn*, IrGael *bealtaine*]
belted, beltit /'bɛltəd, 'bɛltɪt/ *adj* **1** fastened with a belt *16-*. **2** *of cattle* having a band of a different colour round the body *la16-*. **belted earl** an aristocrat *la16-*. **belted Galloway** a breed of cattle with a broad white band round a black body *20-*. **belted knight** an aristocrat *la18-*. **belted plaid** a long plaid fastened round the body with a belt *18-*. **belted plaidie** = *belted plaid 18- literary*. [derivative of OE *belt*]
Belter /'bɛltər/ *n* **1** a nickname for a native or inhabitant of Tranent *la20-*. **2** a member of Tranent Football Club or Rugby Club *la20-*. [perhaps with reference to the former tannery in the town]
beltit see BELTED
Beltyme see BELTANE
beluffit see BELOVIT
belyf see BELYVE
belyke see BELIKE
belyore[1.1], **bilyore** /bɛl'jor, bɪl'jor/ *n* a loud noise; a noisy person *20- Uls*. [unknown]
belyore[1.2], †**bilyore** /bɛl'jor/ *v* to make a loud noise; to shout incessantly *la19- Uls*. [unknown]
belyve, belive, †**belyf**, †**belif** /bə'laev/ *adv* quickly, at once; soon *la14-19, 20- literary*. [ME *bilife*]
belȝe see BAILIE
bem see BEEM
bemang'd, bemangit /bə'maŋd, bə'maŋɪt/ *adj* hurt, injured *19- literary*. [unknown]
†**beme**[1.1] *n* a trumpet *la15*. [OE *bȳme*]
†**beme**[1.2] *v* to sound loudly; to ring or resound; to echo *e16*. [OE *bȳmian* to blow a trumpet]
beme see BEAM[1]
bemean /bə'min/ *v* to disparage, humiliate *19, 20- NE Bor*. [EModE *bemean*]
bemilded /bɪ'mɪldəd/ *adj* fatigued, lacking energy *20- Ork*. [unknown]
ben[1.1] /bɛn/ *n* **1** the inner room, the best room (in a house) *la18-*. **2** *mining* a miner's right to enter the pit *la19, 20- EC*. **3** one's place in a queue *la19- C*. [see the prep]
ben[1.2] /bɛn/ *adj* inner, interior *19-*. [see the prep]
ben[1.3] /bɛn/ *adv* **1** in or towards the inner part of a house; in or to the best room; inside, indoors *15-*. **2** *mining* inwards, towards the workings *19-*. **benmist, benmaist, benmost** furthest in; in the second or inner room *la18-*. **benner** inner *la16-*. **benward, benwart** inward *la15-*. [see the prep]
ben[1.4] /bɛn/ *prep* through (a house) towards the inner part; in or to the best room *la16-*. **ben the hoose** through the house, towards the inner part of the house *17-*. [OE *binnan* within]
ben[2], **binn, bin** /bɛn, bɪn/ *n* a mountain, usually applied to the higher Scottish mountains; frequently in place-names *la18-*. [Gael *beann, beinn* peak]
ben see BEND[1]
bencape, benkep /bɛn'kep, bɛn'kɛp/ *adj* first-rate, excellent *20- NE*. [unknown]
bench /bɛnʃ/ *n* a rack in a kitchen where dishes are kept *19- NE*. Compare BINK. [OE *benc* bench]
bend[1], †**benn**, †**ben** /bɛnd/ *n* **1** *heraldry* a diagonal band running across the shield *la15-*. **2** = *bend leather 18-*. **3** a sash or ribbon (worn on clothing or in the hair) *16-19*. **bend**

leather toughened ox leather used for boot soles *18-*. [OE *bend*, OFr *bende*]

bend[2.1] /bɛnd/ *n* **1** a curve *15-*. **2** readiness; a start *20- Sh SW*. **3** the complete harness of a peat pony *la20- Sh*. **4** a spring, a leap *16-18*. **5** a pull of liquor *e18*. [see the verb]

bend[2.2] /bɛnd/ *v ptp* **bent**, †**bendit**, †**ybent** **1** to (cause to) curve *la14-*. **2** to pull tight, stretch, put under tension; to draw a bow *la15-*. **3** to harness a horse; to equip a pack-horse *e16, la19- Sh*. **4** to spring, leap *la16-e19*. **5** to drink hard *18-e19*. †**bended**, **bendit** *of a gun or other weapon* cocked, made ready for firing *la16-e19*. **bender** a hard drinker *18-19, 20- T*. †**bentnes** inclination, intentness *la16-17*. **bend the bicker** to drink hard (by turning up the tankard) *la18- literary*. [OE *bendan*]

bendrole see BANDRELL

bene see BE, BEAN, BIEN[1.1], BIEN[1.2], BIEN[1.3]

beneath[1.1], †**beneth** /bəˈniθ/ *adv* below *la14-*. [see the prep]

beneath[1.2], †**beneth** /bəˈniθ/ *prep* under *la14-*. [OE *beneoþan*]

benefit, †**benefite** /ˈbɛnəfɪt/ *n* **1** an advantage; a kindness, a favour *la15-*. **2** payment in kind as part of a farmworker's wages *la18- SW*. **benefit-man** a farmworker who receives part of his wages in kind *la18- SW*. [ME *benefet*]

beneth see BENEATH[1.1], BENEATH[1.2]

benevolence, †**benevolens** /bəˈnɛvələns/ *n* **1** goodwill, kindness *15-*. **2** free will, voluntary action *16*. [ME *benevolence*, Lat *benevolentia*]

benfire see BANEFIRE

benge see BINGE

bengle, **bengle** see BANYEL

benibiter /bɛnɪˈbʌɪtər/ *n fisherman's taboo* a dog *20- Sh*. [BANE + Scots *biter*]

benichtit, **benichted**, **benighted** /bəˈnɪxtɪt, bəˈnɪxtəd, bəˈnʌɪtəd/ *adj* **1** unenlightened *la17-*. **2** overtaken by darkness *18-*. [ptp of NICHT[1.1]]

†**bening** *adj* benign *15-16*. [ME *benigne*, Lat *benignus*]

benis see BANIS

benish see BAINISH

benison, **bennison**, †**benisoun**, †**banesoun** /ˈbɛnəsən/ *n* a blessing *la14-19, 20- literary*. [ME *benisoun*]

benk see BINK[1]

benkep see BENCAPE

benkle /ˈbɛŋkəl/ *v* to dent, dimple or bend *20- Sh*. [compare BINK[1]]

benlin, *N* **benleen**, *N* **benlane** /ˈbɛnlɪn; *N* ˈbɛnlin; *N* ˈbɛnlɛn/ *n* a (stone) weight attached to a rope (used to secure a thatch) *20- Ork N*. **benlin steen** = BENLIN *la19- Ork*. [ON *bendill* a small cord, string]

benmost see BEN[1.3]

benn see BEND[1]

Benna Sunday, †**Bonny Sunday** /bɛnə ˈsʌnde/ *n* the Sunday before Christmas *la18- Sh*. [ON *bón* a request, prayer + SUNDAY]

bennel[1.1] /ˈbɛnəl/ *n* **1** long, reedy grass *19 WC SW Bor*. **2** a reed or rush mat (used to line ceiling rafters) *19- Bor*. [unknown]

bennel[1.2] /ˈbɛnəl/ *v* to tie together; to plait together *20- Sh Ork*. [unknown]

benner see BANNER, BEN[1.3]

bennisch see BAINISH

bennison see BENISON

benny /ˈbɛne/ *n* a fit of rage *la20- C*. [unknown]

†**benok** *n* a type of skin or hide *la16-e17*. [probably diminutive form of Gael *bian*]

benon[1.1] /bɪˈnɔn/ *adv* as well, over and above, additionally *20- Sh*. [perhaps a corruption of Eng *anon*, OE *on ān(e)*]

benon[1.2] /bɪˈnɔn/ *prep* on the top of *la19- Sh*. [see the adv]

benorth[1.1] /bəˈnɔrθ/ *adv* to or in the north *la16-*. [OE *benorðan*]

benorth[1.2], *Sh* **benort** /bəˈnɔrθ; *Sh* bəˈnɔrt/ *prep* to the north of *la14-*. [see the adv]

bense /bɛns/ *v* to walk or move energetically; to bounce *19-*. **bensin** bouncing, vigorous *la19- NE*. [probably back-formation from BENSELL[1.1]]

bensell[1.1] /ˈbɛnsəl, ˈbɛnzəl/ *n* **1** vigorous action; force; violent movement (of a storm or fire) *la17-*. **2** a place exposed to storm *19- T EC*. **3** a severe scolding or rebuke *la18-19*. **4** a state of eagerness or excitement; a strong inclination *17*. **5** bending, straining *e16*. [ON *benzl* bent state of a bow]

bensell[1.2] /ˈbɛnsəl, ˈbɛnzəl/ *v* **1** to beat or thrash *19, 20- NE Bor*. **2** to crash around; to press forward *19, 20- NE Bor*. [see the noun]

benshie see BANSHEE

bensin see BENSE

bent /bɛnt/ *n* **1** coarse, rush-like grass; reed-grass *15-*. **2** a stretch of open ground (covered with coarse grass); moorland, hill-ground *la15-*. **3** *pl* a sandy hillock or sand-dune covered with bent-grass *la15-*. **4** the slope or ridge of a hill *e19*. **benty** covered with bent-grass; frequently in place-names *la16-*. **bent bands** woven bent-grass (used to make ropes) *la19- Ork*. **bent day** a holiday given to schoolchildren for the purpose of gathering bent *la16-19, 20- historical*. **bent links** sand-dunes covered with bent-grass *la18- Sh Ork T*. **bent silver** money paid by schoolchildren to provide bent to cover the schoolroom floor *la15-19, 20- historical*. †**go to the bent** to flee (from danger or from one's creditors) *18-e19*. †**take to the bent** = *go to the bent* *e18*. [OE *beonet-*]

bent see BEND[2.2]

benweed, **bunweed**, †**bunwede**, †**benwod** /ˈbɛnwɪd, ˈbʌnwɪd/ *n* (a stalk of) ragwort *Jacobaea vulgaris la15-19, 20- WC SW Uls*. **bennie-weed** = BENWEED *20- H&I WC*. [OE *bune* reed + OE *weōd* herb, grass]

beoch see BOICH

beochle see BAUCHLE[1.2]

beouty see BYOUTY

beowl'd see BOWLT

bequeyst /bɪˈkwʌɪst/ *n* a bequest *20- NE*. [ME *biquyste*]

berber see BARBER[2]

berde see BEARD

berdel see BAIRDAL

bere see BEAR[1], BEAR[2], BEAR[3], BEIR[1.1], BEIR[1.2]

Bereans /ˈbɛrɪənz, bəˈrɪənz/ *npl* a Protestant sect *la18-19, 20- historical*. [from the name of the biblical people of *Berea*]

bereis see BERIS[1.2]

berg /bɛrg/ *n* a prominent rock; a small rocky hill *20- Sh*. Compare BERRY[4]. **bergseat**, †**bersit** a rock on the seashore (used by anglers) *la19- Sh*. [ON *berg*]

bergane see BARGAIN[1.1]

berge see BAIRGE[3.1], BAIRGE[3.2]

bergel, **bergal**, **bergylt**, †**bergell** /ˈbɛrgəl, ˈbɛrgɪlt/ *n* a wrasse, a fish of the family *Labridae la18- Sh Ork NE*. [Norw *berggylte* wrasse, literally rock-pig]

bergin see BARGAIN[1.1], BARGAIN[1.2]

†**beriall**, **buriall** *n* beryl (the precious stone); fine crystal *la14-e17*. [altered form of ME *beril*, Lat *bēryllus*]

†**beris**[1.1] *n* a burying place; a burial *la15-e16*. [perhaps OE *byrgels*]

†**beris**[1.2], **bereis** *v* to bury *la15-16*. [see the noun]

berk see BARK[1.1], BARK[1.2]

berkimal /ˈbɛrkɪməl/ *n* a large tangle *20- Ork*. [perhaps related to ON *börkr* bark]

berkiny /'bɛrkjəni/ *adj of a person* short and stout *20- Ork*. [compare Norn *bjarki*]

berkit *see* BARKIT

berlik *see* BARLEY[1]

berme *see* BARM[1.1]

†**bern, beyrne, bairne** *n* a (fighting) man, a warrior *15-e17*. [OE *beorn*]

bern *see* BAIRN[1.1], BARN

Berr /bɛr/ *n* a player for or supporter of Rangers Football Club *la20-*. [rhyming slang based on GERS, a shortened form of 'Rangers'; compare TEDDY BERRS]

berrell *see* BARREL[1.1], BARREL[1.2]

berrick, barrack /'bɛrɪk, 'barək/ *n* **1** sleeping accommodation for male farmworkers *19-*. **2** a hut used as temporary sleeping accommodation *20- Sh NE*. [Fr *baraque*]

berry[1], †**bery** /'bɛre/ *n* **1** a small, juicy, stoneless fruit *la15-*. **2** *pl* jam made from berries *20- NE*. **berry-bug** the harvest mite *20-*. **berry hedder** the crowberry *Empetrum nigrum la19- Sh*. **the berries 1** berry-picking; the berry-picking season *20-*. **2** something very good *la20-*. **nae the berry** not the thing; not to be trusted *la19- NE*. [OE *berie*]

berry[2] /'bɛre/ *v* to thresh corn; to thrash a child *19- Sh SW Bor*. [ON *berja*]

berry[3], †**burry** /'bɛri/ *n* a name for a dog *la15, 20- Sh*. [unknown]

berry[4] /'bɛri/ *n* a rock *20- Ork*. Compare BERG. [ON *berg*]

berrykan *see* BARREKIN

†**bers, bas, barse** *n* a small cannon *16-e17*. [MFr *berce*]

bersit *see* BERG

bert, burth, †**birt,** †**birth** /bɛrt, bʌrθ/ *n* an ebb-tide or backtide *la18- Ork N*. [ON *burðr* a bearing]

†**Bertane, Bartane** *n* **1** Britain *la14-16*. **2** Brittany *la15-e16*. **Bartane canves** canvas from Brittany *16*. **Bartane claith** cloth from Brittany *la15-16*. [metathesized form of BRETANȜE]

Bertanȝe *see* BRETANȜE

berthy *see* BIRTH[1]

Bertie Auld /'bɛrti 'ɔld/ *adj rhyming slang* cold *la20-*. [from the name of a former player for Celtic Football Club]

†**bertisse** *n* a brattice, a breastwork or parapet *15-17*. [metathesis of ME *bretise*]

†**Bertonar** *n* a man or ship of Brittany *e16*. [metathesized form of BRETANȜE]

bertyn *see* BRITTYN

bervie /'bɛrvi/ *n* a split, dried haddock *la19-*. **Bervie Haddock** a smoked Haddock (from Inverbervie) *18-*. [from the Aberdeenshire place-name *Inverbervie*]

Berwick cockle /bɛrɪk 'kɔkəl/ *n* a kind of toffee made in the Borders (shaped like a cockle) *20- Bor*. [from the place-name + Older Scots *cokkill*, Scots *cockle*]

bery *see* BEERIE, BERRY[1]

bes *see* BEAST[1.1]

beschop *see* BISHOP[1.1]

beseek, beseik, †**beseke** /bə'sik/ *v pt* **besocht** to beseech, beg, entreat *la14-*. [*be-* prefix + SEEK[1]]

beskae /bə'ske/ *v* to befall *la19- Sh*. [*be-* prefix + SKAE]

beslabber /bə'slabər/ *v* to eat or drink messily; to slobber; to spit whilst speaking *19, 20- NE T*. [*be-* prefix + SLABBER[1.1]]

besocht *see* BESEEK

besom, bizzum, bissum, bissom, *Sh* **bussom,** *NE* **beezim,** †**boosome** /'bɪzəm, 'bɪsəm; *Sh* 'bʌsəm; *NE* 'bizəm/ *n* **1** a sweeping-brush, a broom *16-*. **2** a derogatory term (for a woman or girl) *19-*. **3** a comet; the tail of a comet *la16-17*. **4** a bunch of twigs used as a scourge *16*. [OE *besma*]

besooth, besouth /bə'suθ, bə'sʌuθ/ *prep* to the south of *15-*. [*be-* prefix + SOOTH[1.3]]

bess /bɛs/ *v* to sing in a bass voice *la19- NE*. [ME *bas* deep-sounding]

bess *see* BAISS[1]

bessie[1] /'bɛsi/ *n* an ill-mannered, boisterous, or sharp-tempered female *la19, 20- NE*. [from the personal name *Bess* + -IE[1]]

bessie[2] /'bɛsi/ *n* the loach *Barbatula barbatula 19- Bor*. **bessie beardie, bessie bairdie** the loach *20- Bor*. **bessie lotchie** = *bessie beardie*. [unknown]

best[1.1] /bɛst/ *n* that which is best; the most outstanding person or thing *la14-*. **the Best** Providence, God *19- Ork N T*. **Best kens** God knows *19- Ork N T*. [see the adj]

best[1.2] /bɛst/ *adj* most excellent *la14-*. **best aucht** the most valuable article or animal owned by a person; originally claimed by a superior on the death of a tenant *16-19, 20- NE*. †**best cheip** cheapest *16*. †**best lyk** of best appearance *16*. **best maid** a (chief) bridesmaid at a wedding *la18-*. **best man** the chief attendant on a bridegroom *la18-*. [OE *betst*]

beste *see* BEAST[1.1]

bestial, †**bestiall,** †**bestiale** /'bɛstɪəl/ *n* **1** domestic animals, livestock *la14-19, 20- literary*. **2** wild animals *la15-e17*. [ME *bestaile*, Lat *bestiālis* like a beast]

†**beswakkit** *adj* drenched *e16*. [*be-* prefix + SWACK[1.2]]

beswell *see* BEESWEEL

besy *see* BUSY

bet *see* BATE[1.2], BEET[2.2]

be tae /'bi te/ *v* to be under an obligation or necessity *20-*. [*bude* (BEHOVE) + TAE[3.4]]

betak /bi'tak/ *v* **1** to hand over, deliver; to inflict *la14-19, 20- NE*. **2** to recover *la19- NE*. **3** to overtake *la16-19*. [ME *bitaken*]

betaken, betoken /bi'tekən, bi'tokən/ *v* to signify, indicate *la14-19, 20- literary*. [ME *betacnien*]

betchell *see* BAITCHEL

bete *see* BEET[2.2]

†**beteach, beteche** *v* **1** to commit, commend (to God or the Devil) *la14-19*. **2** to hand over; to give up, entrust *la14-e17*. **3** to teach *e16*. [OE *betǣcan*]

bethankit[1.1] /bɪ'θaŋkɪt/ *n* a grace or prayer, a blessing *la18-*. [see the interj]

bethankit[1.2] /bɪ'θaŋkɪt/ *interj* an expression of joy or relief *la18-19, 20- literary*. [shortened form of Scots *God be thankit*]

betheral *see* BEADLE

betide *see* BETYDE

betill *see* BITTLE[1.1]

betimes, †**bytimes** /bɪ'tʌɪmz/ *adv* **1** occasionally, sometimes *la15-*. **2** early, in good time *la16-*. [ME *betimes*]

betoken *see* BETAKEN

†**betraise, betrase, betrese** *v* to betray, deceive *la14-e17*. [ME *bitraishen*, lengthened stem of *trahir*]

†**betrump** *v* to deceive, elude *e16*. [*be-* prefix + TRUMP[3]]

†**betteis** *npl* remedies *e16*. [unknown; compare BEET[2.1]]

better[1.1] /'bɛtər/ *n* something superior; an advantage or superior position *15-*. [OE *betera*]

better[1.2], †**bettir,** †**bettyre** /'bɛtər/ *adj* **1** of greater excellence, of a superior quality; preferable *la14-*. **2** completely recovered from an illness *18-*. **betterlike** more promising, better-looking *la19-*. **bettermaist** better-class, superior *19-*. **betterness** improvement; recovery *19-*. **on the better side of** older or younger than *20- NE*. [see the noun]

better[1.3], †**bettir,** †**bettyr** /'bɛtər/ *adv* **1** in a better way *la14-*. **2** to a greater degree or extent; more; further; more completely or fully *16-*. **3** with renewed effort: ◇*ran and better ran 17-*. †**bettir chepe** more cheaply *la15-e17*. **better-faured** better-looking *19-*. **the better of** the better for *la18-*. **I am better to** I had better *la18-*. [see the noun]

betuxe see BETWIXT
between[1.1], †**betwene**, †**betwine** /bəˈtwin/ *adv* amidst, among *la15-*. **between the lights** twilight *20-*. [OE *betwēon*]
between[1.2], †**betwene**, †**betwine** /bəˈtwin/ *prep* amidst, among *la14-*. [see the adv]
betwees, †**betweesh**, †**betwis** /bəˈtwis/ *prep* between *15-19, 20- NE*. [compare BETWIXT]
betwene see BETWEEN[1.1], BETWEEN[1.2]
betwex see BETWIXT
betwine see BETWEEN[1.1]
betwis see BETWEES
betwixt, †**betwix**, †**betwex**, †**betuxe** /bəˈtwɪkst/ *prep* between *la14-*. [OE *betwēoh, betweox*]
betyde, betide /bəˈtʌɪd/ *v* **1** to happen, befall *la14-*. **2** to succeed, fare well *la16-19, 20- NE*. [ME *bitiden*]
beuch, bouch /bjux, bux/ *n pl* also †**bewis 1** a branch of a tree, a bough *la15-*. **2** the bow of a ship *17-18, la19- N NE*. **3** the shoulder of an animal or person *la16-19*. [OE *bōh*]
beufsae /ˈbjufse/ *adj* ungainly, clumsy *la19- Ork*. [ON *bufsa*]
beuk see BAKE[1.2], BUIK[1.1], BUIK[1.2]
beukin see BUIKIN
beul see BØL[1.1], BØL[1.2]
beuld[1.1], **buil** /bøld, bøl/ *n* a shelter for livestock, a stall *19- Ork*. Compare BØL[1.1]. [ON *ból* a lair, a bed, a farm]
beuld[1.2], †**bool** /bøld/ *v* to drive livestock to a stall, shelter or pasture *la18- Sh Ork*. Compare BØL[1.2]. [see the noun]
beuld see BØL[1.1], BØL[1.2], BOOLD
†**beune**[1.1] *adv* above *la14*. [OE *beufan*]
†**beune**[1.2] *prep* above *la15-16*. [see the adv]
beuse up see BOOSE[1.2]
beuss /bøs/ *n* a bad job, a botch *20- Ork*. [perhaps variant of BUSS[4.1]]
beust /bist/ *n* withered grass (from the previous year) *19- SW*. [unknown]
beut see BUIT[1.1]
beute see BYOUTY
†**bevel, bevell** *n* a staggering blow *17-e19*. [unknown]
†**bever**[1], **baiver, baver** *n* a beaver *15-e19*. [OE *befor*]
†**bever**[2.1] *n* shaking; a trembling fever *la17*. **bevir hair, bevar hoir** a trembling old man *la15*. [see the verb]
bever[2.2], *Ork* **baiver** /ˈbɛvər; *Ork* ˈbevər/ *v* **1** to shake, tremble; to shiver with cold or fear *la18- Bor*. **2** to struggle against the wind *20- Ork*. [frequentative form of OE *beofian*]
beverage, *Uls* **baiverage** /ˈbɛvərɪdʒ; *Uls* ˈbevərɪdʒ/ *n* **1** a drink *la18-*. **2** a fine in the form of money, alcohol, or a kiss demanded from a person wearing something new *19, 20- SW Uls*. [OFr *bevrage*]
bew see BLUE[1.1], BLUE[1.2]
bewaar, bewar see BEWAUR
beward see BOORD[1.1]
beware see BEWAUR
bewast, bewest /biˈwast, biˈwɛst/ *prep* to the west of; on the west side of *15-*. [OE *bewestan*]
bewaur, bewaar, beware, †**bewar** /bɪˈwɔr, bɪˈwar, bɪˈwer/ *v* to be cautious or wary *la14-*. [OE *bewarnian*]
†**bewave** *v ptp* to toss about; to blow or sweep away *16-e19*. [*be-* prefix + *wave* (WAFF[1.2])]
†**bewchit** *adj* branched *e16*. [BEUCH + -IT[2]]
bewest see BEWAST
bewis see BEUCH
bewry see BEERIE
bewte see BYOUTY
bewyt see BEHOVE
bey see BE
beyld see BIELD[1.1]

beylie see BAILIE
beymfill see BEAMFILL
beynge see BEENGE
beyo /ˈbʌɪu/ *n* a kind of scythe *20- Ork*. [unknown]
beyont[1.1], **beyond,** †**beʒond,** †**beyon,** †**beʒound** /biˈjɔnt, biˈjɔnd/ *adv* at a greater distance, farther away *la14-*. [see the prep]
beyont[1.2], **beyond,** †**beʒond,** †**beyon,** †**beʒound** /biˈjɔnt, biˈjɔnd/ *prep* **1** on the farther side of *la14-*. **2** *of time or numbers* above, more than *la15-*. [OE *begeondan*]
beyrne see BERN
beyt see BATE[1.1], BEAT
beʒond, beʒound see BEYONT[1.1], BEYONT[1.2]
bi see BY[1.2]
biach, byauch /bjax, bjɔx/ *n* a familiar form of address *20- N*. [perhaps Gael *beathach* beast]
bibble see BUBBLE[1.1], BUBBLE[1.2]
bibbly see BUBBLY
†**bibliothecar** *n* a librarian *la16-19*. [Lat *bibliothecārius*, compare Fr *bibliothécaire*]
bibliotheck, †**bibliothick,** †**bibliothek** /ˈbɪblɪoθɛk/ *n* **1** a library *la16-e18, la19- historical*. **2** a librarian *la19, 20- historical*. [Lat *bibliothēca*]
biche see BITCH
bicht /bɪxt/ *n* a loop in a length of rope *la19-*. [OE *byht* bend]
bichter, †**bighter** /ˈbɪxtər/ *n* a stone used as an anchor to long lines *19- Sh*. [perhaps from the noun BICHT]
bick, bik /bɪk/ *n* a bitch, a female dog *16-*. [ON *bikkja*]
bick birr /ˈbɪk bɪr/ *n* an imitation of the call of the grouse *19- NE Bor*. [onomatopoeic]
bicker[1.1], †**bikkir,** †**bikker** /ˈbɪkər/ *n* **1** a skirmish, an attack with missiles; a quarrel, an altercation *la15-*. **2** a street-fight or school-fight (where stones are thrown) *la18-19*. **3** a rapid, noisy movement, a short run *la18-19, 20- NE*. **at the bicker of liquid** boiling briskly, starting to bubble *la20- NE*. [ME *biker*]
bicker[1.2], †**bikker** /ˈbɪkər/ *v* **1** to quarrel, squabble; originally to attack or fight with missiles *la14-*. **2** *of a watercourse* to move quickly and noisily; *of rain* to pelt, patter *la18-19, 20- NE*. **3** *of living creatures* to move quickly and noisily, rush *19, 20- N EC*. **4** *of boiling water* to bubble quickly *20- NE*. **5** to laugh heartily *20- NE*. **6** *of children* to engage in (stone-throwing) street fights or school fights *la18-19*. **7** *of light or fire* to gleam, flicker, sparkle *e19*. [see the noun]
bicker[2], †**bikker** /ˈbɪkər/ *n* a beaker, a (wooden) drinking vessel; a (wooden) porridge bowl *16-*. **bickerfu'** a cupful; a bowlful *19, 20- Bor*. [ON *bikarr*]
bid[1], †**byd** /bɪd/ *v pt* **bad, bade,** †**bawd 1** to offer a price (for goods) *la14-*. **2** to request or command (someone to do something) *la14-*. **3** to desire or seek (to do something) *15-*. **4** to invite to a social gathering *16-*. **5** to offer a greeting *16-*. **biddable** obedient, amenable to discipline *la18-*. **bidding 1** a command *la14-*. **2** the offering of a price for an article *18-*. **3** an invitation *19-*. [OE *bēodan*]
bid[2] /bɪd/ *n* a small length of line (used to fasten a hook to another line) *la19- Sh*. [ON *bit* a bite, also ON *biti* a bit, a mouthful]
bidden see BIDE[1.2]
biddie /ˈbɪdi/ *n* a (thick) cake of oatmeal or barley-meal *19- Sh*. [ON *biti* a bit, a mouthful]
bide[1.1] /bʌɪd/ *n* **1** something endured, pain *19, 20- NE*. **2** a prolonged visit *20- NE*. [see the verb]
bide[1.2], †**byde,** †**byd** /bʌɪd/ *v pt* **bade, bed, bided, bode,** *ptp* **bade, bed, bidden 1** to remain; to stay temporarily (in a place) *la14-*. **2** to wait; to await, stay for *la14-*. **3** to tolerate, endure; to withstand *15-*. **4** to dwell, reside, live (in

a place) *16-*. **bide-in** = BIDIE-IN *20- NE*. **bide by** to stand by, adhere to, submit to *17-*. †**lawful time bidden** at the time appointed by law *la15-16*. [OE *bīdan*]

bidie-in, bidey-in /bʌɪdi ˈɪn/ *n* a live-in lover or partner *20-*. [BIDE¹·² + -IE³ + IN¹·²]

bieenter *see* BJINTER

bield¹·¹, **beild**, *NE* **biel**, †**beld**, †**beyld** /bild; *NE* bil/ *n* **1** a place giving refuge or shelter; a byre or cattle fold *la15-*. **2** protection; relief, succour; refuge, shelter *15-19, 20- literary*. **3** a person acting as a protector or comforter *la14-18*. **bieldless** without shelter *19- literary*. **bieldy** sheltered, cosy *la18- literary*. [OE *beald* boldness, courage]

bield¹·², **beild**, †**belde** /bild/ *v pt* **bieldit, beild 1** to shelter; to cover over *la15-*. **2** to assist, aid; to protect or strengthen *la15-19, 20- literary*. [OE **bealdian* embolden]

bield¹·³ /bild/ *adj* sheltered, cosy *la18-19, 20- literary*. [see the verb]

bieldit *see* BIELD¹·²

†**bien**¹·¹, **bene** *v* **1** to make comfortable *e19*. **2** to fill abundantly *la15*. [unknown]

bien¹·², **bein**, †**bene** /bin/ *adj* **1** in good condition *la14-*. **2** pleasant, agreeable; cosy, comfortable *la15-*. **3** well-off, wealthy *17-*. **4** *of a larder or store* well-stocked *18-*. **bienly** pleasantly; comfortably; cosily *15-19, 20- literary*. †**bienness** prosperity *19, 20- Bor*. [unknown]

bien¹·³, †**bein**, †**bene** /bin/ *adv* handsomely; liberally; comfortably *la15-19, 20- literary*. [unknown]

biffle, beefle /ˈbɪfəl, ˈbifəl/ *v* to strike or beat repeatedly *20- Ork*. [perhaps ON *bifast* to shake, tremble, be moved, with frequentative suffix *-le*]

big¹, **bigg**, †**bige**, †**beg** /bɪg/ *v pt* **biggit**, *C Bor* **bug 1** to build, construct, erect *14-*. **2** *of birds* to build nests *15-*. **3** to build or make a fire *16-*. **4** to stack hay or corn *la19-*. **5** to occupy land (by building on it); to build on or develop (land or ground) *15-17*. **6** to dwell or remain, make one's home *la14-17*. **biggit 1** built, constructed *la14-*. **2** *of land* occupied, inhabited; cultivated; built on, built up *la14-*. **3** *of a person* well built, sturdy *17-*. **bigly** habitable, pleasant, commodious, well-made *la15-19 20- literary*. †**big sanny mills wi** to be intimate with, be a friend or playmate of *la18-19*. †**big up 1** to build or rebuild; to repair *la14-*. **2** to close or block up by building *16-*. [ON *byggja* to inhabit, settle]

big², *N NE EC Bor* **beig**, †**byg** /bɪg; *N NE EC Bor* beg/ *adj* **1** large, mighty, grand; physically stout or strong *la15-*. **2** conceited; elated; of some consequence *18-*. **3** main, principal *19-*. **4** friendly, intimate *la19-*. †**biggen** to swell, grow larger; to be pregnant *18-19*. **bigsie, bigsy** proud, conceited *la19- Ork NE*. **Big Aggie's man** an imaginary character (onto whom blame can be shifted); an unspecified person *20-*. **big-coat** a greatcoat, an overcoat *18-*. **big end** the larger room of a small school (where the senior pupils are taught) *la20-*. **big hoose** the principal dwelling house (of the laird) on an estate *la18-*. **big man** a respectful form of address *la20-*. **big miss** a great loss (by death, or departure) *20-*. **big school** secondary school *la19-*. **big sma' faimily** a large family of young children *la19-*. †**big spell** a spelling book written in capital letters *19*. **Big Wednesday** the main (cattle) market of the winter (held at Martinmas, in November) *19-*. **Big Yin** a tall person; a person in authority; a big man *la19-*. **big yins** older children *la19-*. [unknown]

bige *see* BIG¹

bigg /bɪg/ *n* a variety of barley *la18-*. [ON *bygg* barley]

bigg *see* BIG¹

biggin¹, **bigging**, †**byggyng** /ˈbɪgɪn, ˈbɪgɪŋ/ *n* **1** a building, a house; frequently in place-names *la12-*. **2** the act of building; building work *15-*. **3** *pl* subsidiary buildings on an estate, outbuildings; farmworkers' cottages *16-*. **4** a cluster of houses, a hamlet *19-*. [verbal noun from BIG¹]

†**biggin**² *n* a linen cap *e19*. **bigonet, biginet** a woman's cap *17-e19*. [Fr *béguin* a cap]

biggit *see* BIG¹

bighter *see* BICHTER

bightsom /ˈbʌɪtsəm/ *adj* easy, relaxed; ample *la18-19, 20- literary*. [OE *byht* bend, with *-som* suffix]

bigotit *see* BEGOTTED

bik *see* BICK

bike *see* BYKE¹·¹, BYKE³

bikker *see* BICKER¹·¹, BICKER¹·², BICKER², BUCCAR

bikkir *see* BICKER¹·¹

bilbie /ˈbɪlbi/ *n* shelter, lodging; protection, freedom or scope *19- T*. [probably ON *ból* a lair, a bed, a farm]

bilch *see* BELCH¹

bile¹·¹, **boil**, *N* **bweil** /bʌɪl, bɔɪl; *N* bwʌɪl/ *n* a state of boiling; boiling point *18-*. **in a boil** in a state of perspiration *20-*. **through the boil** completely boiled *20-*. [see the verb]

bile¹·², **boil**, †**builʒe** /bʌɪl, bɔɪl/ *v* to heat to boiling point; to cook by boiling; to become excessively hot *15-*. **biler, boiler** a kettle *la18-*. **bilin, boiling 1** a boiled sweet *la19-*. **2** a quantity of food large enough for one serving *la20-*. **bile hoose, boil house** a building containing a boiler (for washing or bleaching, rendering fish-oil or cooking food for animals) *19-*. **bile yer heid** an expression of contempt or dismissal *20-*. [ME *boillen*]

bile², **byle**, †**byll** /bʌɪl/ *n* a swelling, a suppuration, a tumour *la14-*. [OE *bȳl*; compare BEAL]

biley *see* BAILIE

†**bilf**¹, **bulf** *n* a blow *19*. [probably onomatopoeic]

bilf², **bulf** /bɪlf, bʌlf/ *n* **1** a sturdy, growing young man *20- NE T*. **2** something large and clumsy *e19*. **bilfert, belfert** a larger than usual person or object *20- NE*. [unknown; compare BELCH¹]

bilge, †**billage**, †**bylge** /bɪldʒ/ *n* the lower part of a ship's hull *16-*. †**bilgeit** large-hulled *e16*. [probably OFr *bouge* a bag or trunk]

bilge *see* BELCH¹

bilge-kod /ˈbɪlʒkɔd/ *n* a piece of wood nailed to the bilge of a boat in order to make it make it seaworthy *20- Sh Ork*. [BILGE + ON *koddi* a pillow]

bilget¹, **billgate**, †**billiet** /ˈbɪlgət, ˈbɪlgɛt/ *n* a billet, a document (containing a military order); a billeting order *17-20, 21- historical*. [Fr *billet (de logement)* a written order (with instruction to lodge]

bilget², †**bilʒett** /ˈbɪldʒət/ *n* joinery a piece of wood; a support or bevel for shelves or doors *la16-19, 20- Sh Ork Bor*. [Fr *billette*]

bilkie /ˈbɪlki/ *n* the breast *20- Sh*. [compare ON *búlki* cargo or freight of a ship, Norw *bulk* a bump]

bill¹, **bull**, *N NE* **beell** /bɪl, bʌl; *N NE* bil/ *n* **1** a letter; a formal document, a contract *la14-*. **2** *law* a petition, claim, charge or complaint used to initiate proceedings in a court (or with another authority) *la15-*. **3** a (printed sheet) or poster containing public information or an advertisement *la15-*. **4** an account of money owed (for goods or services) *la15-*. **5** a bill of exchange *18-*. **Bill Chamber** a court separate from, but staffed by judges of, the Court of Session *la17-e20, la20- historical*. †**burn one's bill** to perform an act of recantation *16*. †**in bill** in a written document, in writing *15-e17*. [ME *bille*, Lat *bulla*]

bill² /bɪl/ *n* an eddy or streak of foam from an oar *20- Sh*. [compare ON *bulla* to bubble up]

bill *see* BULL¹

billage *see* BILGE
billaix *see* BULLAX
billet *see* BULLET
billgate *see* BILGET¹
billie *see* BILLY
billiet *see* BILGET¹
billy¹, **billie** /ˈbɪle, ˈbɪli/ *n* **1** a lover *16-*. **2** a (close) friend, a comrade *la16-*. **3** a fellow, a lad *la18-*. **4** a brother; a brother member of a craft or guild *19-*. **5** a person particularly suited to, good at or characterized by something *la19-*. **bill blin folklore** a brownie, a benevolent spirit *19, 20- historical*. [unknown]
Billy² /ˈbɪle, ˈbɪli/ *n* a nickname for a Protestant or Orangeman *20- WC*. **Billy Boy 1** a member of a Glasgow gang named the Billy Boys *20-*. **2** a supporter of Rangers Football Club *la20-*. [shortened form of the name of the Scottish king William II]
billy *see* BULLY²·²
billy-nut /ˈbɪlenʌt/ *n* a horse-chestnut, a conker *la20- WC*. [BULLY²·¹ + NIT¹]
bilsh /bɪlʃ/ *v* to boast; to speak loudly or angrily *19- Bor*. [altered form of Eng *belch*]
bilsh *see* BELCH¹
bilyore *see* BELYORE¹·¹, BELYORE¹·²
†**bilʒard**, **bulʒard**, **bullyeart** *n* the game of billiards *la16-17*. [Fr *billard*]
bilʒett *see* BILGET²
bin /bɪn/ *n* humour, mood *19- NE*. Compare BON. [unknown]
bin *see* BE, BEN², BIND¹·²
†**binage** *n* in the *North-East* service due from a tenant to his superior or from a farmworker to a farmer *18-e19*. Compare BONAGE. [altered form of EModE *boonage*, with additional confusion with BONDAGE]
bind¹·¹, **binnd** /bʌɪnd, bɪnd/ *n* **1** a person's capacity for drinking alcohol *19-*. **2** measurement, size; capacity *16-e19*. **3** a standard measure for the barrels in which fish were packed *15-e18*. **4** a standard measure for wine and tar *la16-e17*. **5** a bundle of hides *15-e16*. [see the verb]
bind¹·², **bin**, **binn**, *Sh* **binnd** /bʌɪnd, bʌɪn, bɪn; *Sh* bɪnd/ *v pt* **bound**, **band**, *ptp* **bund**, †**bundin**, †**ybondyn**, †**ybond 1** to tie, tether; to fasten, make fast *la14-*. **2** to unite; to come or bring together *la14-*. **3** to agree or pledge oneself, make a bond; to place under obligation, constrain or restrict someone *15-*. **4** to fasten together the pages of a book *17-*. **binnen**, *Sh* **bennen 1** a tether for cattle *la19- NE WC Uls*. **2** *fishing* a cord used to attach the end of a line to the one previously shot *20- NE*. **bindle**, **binnle** a tether for cattle *19, 20- NE T*. **bindwood**, **bindwud** a term used of various plants including ivy *Hedera helix*, woodbine or honeysuckle *Lonicera* and bindweed *Convolvulus 19-*. [OE *bindan*]
bine, **boyne**, †**bowen**, †**bowine** /bʌɪn, bɔɪn/ *n* **1** a shallow tub (used for steeping), a wash-tub *16-*. **2** a broad shallow container used for skimming milk *19-*. [unknown]
bing¹·¹ /bɪŋ/ *n* **1** a heap or pile *16-*. **2** a pile of stored coal; a slag-heap, a mound of coal, shale or ore waste *18-*. **3** a temporary, makeshift storage receptacle (for grain or animal feed) *19-*. **4** a crowd, a large number *la19-*. **5** a funeral pile *e16*. **in the bing** *of a horse* having lost a race *la20-*. **on the bing** = *in the bing*. [ON *bingr* a bed, a bolster, a heap]
bing¹·², †**bink** /bɪŋ/ *v* to heap or pile up; to store in a pile *16-*. [see the noun]
bing² /bɪŋ/ *v* to go; to come; to walk or run *19-*. [Travellers' language]
†**binge**, **benge** *n* a bow of obeisance *la15-e16*. [BEENGE to bow]
binge *see* BEENGE

binger /ˈbɪŋər/ *n in racing* a losing horse or dog *la20-*. [BING¹·¹ with agent suffix]
bink¹, *Sh Ork* **benk** /bɪŋk; *Sh Ork* bɛŋk/ *n* **1** a bench, a long seat *la14-*. **2** a peat bank, a bank of earth *16-*. **3** a wall rack or shelf for dishes; a kitchen dresser *16-*. **4** a hob or grate on a fireplace; a shelf or ledge at the side of a fireplace (used for warming) *la18-*. **5** a beehive or wasps' nest *19- EC Bor*. **6** a ledge of rock *20- N*. [ME *bynk*]
†**bink**²·¹ *n* a bending movement, a crease, a fold *e19*. [unknown]
†**bink**²·² *v* to bend, bow *19*. [unknown]
bink *see* BING¹·²
binn *see* BEN², BIND¹·²
binna¹·¹ /ˈbɪnə/ *v* **1** is not *la18-19, 20- literary*. **2** *imperative* don't be *la18-19, 20- NE*. [Scots BE + Scots -NA]
binna¹·² /ˈbɪnə/ *prep* except for *19- literary*. [see the verb]
binna¹·³ /ˈbɪnə/ *conj* unless, except *la19, 20- C*. [see the verb]
binnack *see* BANNOCK
binnd *see* BIND¹·¹, BIND¹·²
binnen *see* BIND¹·²
binner¹·¹ /ˈbɪnər/ *n* **1** a noise, a blow *20- NE*. **2** speed, a rush; a flurry *20- NE*. [unknown]
binner¹·² /ˈbɪnər/ *v* **1** to knock, crash, move noisily *19-*. **2** to run, gallop, scamper *la18- NE*. [unknown]
binner² /ˈbɪnər/ *n* temper, humour; style *20- NE*. [perhaps a derivative of BIN]
bioran *see* BEERAN
biorlinn *see* BIRLINN
bir *see* BIRR¹·¹
bird¹, **burd**, †**bred** /bɪrd, bʌrd/ *n* **1** a feathered creature, a fowl, a bird *15-*. **2** a nestling, a young bird; an unhatched bird *15-19, 20- Sh*. **3** the young or offspring of an animal *16-19, 20- N*. **4** a term of endearment (to children) *19- Sh Ork*. **5** a child, the offspring of a person *16-e19*. **bird-mouthed** unwilling to speak out *18-19, 20- WC*. [OE *brid* a young bird]
bird², **burd** /bɪrd, bʌrd/ *n* a girl, a woman; originally a maiden or lady *la15-*. [probably OE *brȳd* a woman, a woman about to be married]
bird-alane¹·¹, **burdalane** /ˈbɪrdəˈlen, ˈbʌrdəˈlen/ *n* an only child, the only child left in a family *la16-*. [BIRD¹ + ALANE¹·¹]
bird-alane¹·², **burdalane**, *NE* **bird aleen** /ˈbɪrdəˈlen, ˈbʌrdəˈlen; *NE* ˈbɪrdəˈlin/ *adj* quite alone; single, solitary *la16-*. [see the noun]
birdie, **birdy**, **burdie** /ˈbɪrdi, ˈbʌrdi/ *n* **1** a bird *la18-*. **2** a term of endearment (for a child) *19-*. **3** a young halibut *Hippoglossus hippoglossus la19- NE*. **birdie's een 1** the speedwell plant *Veronica chamaedrys 20- NE*. **2** boiled tapioca or sago *la20- NE*. **birdie's eenies** boiled tapioca or sago *la20- NE*. [BIRD¹ + -IE¹]
birdik, **birdek** /ˈbɪrdək/ *n* a heavy burden *20- Sh*. [derivative of ON *byrðr* a burden]
birding *see* BURDEN¹·¹
birdy *see* BIRDIE
birge, **birges** *see* BURGES
birk¹ /bɪrk/ *n* **1** a birch tree *Betula pendula 14-*. **2** *pl* birch woodland *la18-*. **3** a (birch) roof-timber *18- Ork N*. **4** *pl* birch twigs (used for decoration) *la15-17*. **birk wine** birch-sap *19-*. [OE *birc*, ON *bjǫrk*]
birk² /bɪrk/ *v* to move energetically or restlessly *la18- WC SW*. [unknown]
birk³ /bɪrk/ *n* a well-built lad *20- NE*. [perhaps back-formation from BIRKIE¹·¹]
birk⁴ /bɪrk/ *n* the bark of a tree; the outer skin on seaweed tangles *20- Sh Ork*. [perhaps altered form of BARK¹·¹]
birk *see* BUIRK
birken¹·¹ /ˈbɪrkən/ *n* a birch tree *19- literary*. [see the adj]

birken[1,2] /ˈbɪrkən/ *adj* consisting of birch-wood; frequently in place-names *la12*-. [BIRK[1], with adj-forming suffix]

birkie[1.1] /ˈbɪrke, ˈbɪrkɪ/ *n* **1** a smart or active (young) man *la18*-. **2** a conceited fellow *la18-19, 20- EC*. **3** a sharp-tongued, quick-tempered woman or child *20- EC Uls*. †**auld birkie** an old chap, an old codger *18-19*. [unknown]

birkie[1.2] /ˈbɪrke, ˈbɪrkɪ/ *adj* **1** lively, spirited; nimble *19*-. **2** sharp-tongued, tart in speech *19*-. **3** easily offended, huffy *20- T*. [unknown]

†**birkie**[2] *n* the card game beggar-my-neighbour *19*. [unknown]

birl[1.1], **burl** /bɪrl, bʌrl/ *n* **1** a spin, a twist, a revolving movement *la19*-. **2** a brisk dance; a circular dancing motion *la19*-. **3** a turn, a try, a shot *la19*-. **4** a whistle; the sound made by a whistle *20*-. **5** *piping* a grace-note introducing the note A, produced by two rapid touches on G, the lowest note on the chanter *20*-. **6** a drive or ride *20*-. **7** a rattling or ringing noise *19*. †**byrl quheil** a spinning wheel *e17*. **gie it a birl** to have a go, make an attempt *la20*-. [see the verb]

birl[1.2], **burl** /bɪrl, bʌrl/ *v* **1** to revolve rapidly, spin, whirl round; to dance; to move with a rattling or whirring sound *la18*-. **2** to move rapidly, hurry *la18*-. **3** to toss a coin; to pool funds; to spend money *19*-. **4** to whistle *la19- WC*. [probably onomatopoeic]

birl[2] /bɪrl/ *v* **1** to pour out, serve alcohol; to ply with drink *la15*-. **2** to drink, carouse *la16-e19*. [OE *byrelian*, from *byrele* a cup bearer]

birley, **burley**, **burlaw**, **birlaw**, †**boorlaw**, †**bourlaw**, †**barlaw** /ˈbɪrle, ˈbʌrle, ˈbʌrlə, ˈbɪrlə/ *n* local customary law *15-19, 20- historical*. **burlaw bailie** an officer employed to enforce the laws of the BIRLEY court *18-19, 20- historical*. **burlaw court**, **birlaw court** a neighbourhood court for the settlement of local disputes or complaints *la16-18, 19- historical*. **burley man**, **birlaw man**, **burlaw man 1** a judge or arbiter in local disputes *la15-19, 20- historical*. **2** a man who estimates the value of a crop *18-19, 20- NE*. **crying of the burley** the proclamation of a town's charter at the annual Riding of the Marches *20- Bor*. [ME *byerlar*, ON **byjar-lǫg* town-law]

birlie /ˈbɪrle, ˈbɪrlɪ/ *adj* swirly, revolving *la20*-. [BIRL[1.1] + -IE[2]]

birlinn, **biorlinn**, †**birlin**, †**birling** /ˈbɪrlɪn, ˈbɪərlɪn/ *n* a large rowing boat or galley used in the West Highlands *la16-19, 20- historical*. [Gael *birlinn*]

birn, †**byrne** /bɪrn, bʌrn/ *n* **1** a burden, a load, a heap *la14*-. **2** a group; a crowd of people or animals, a tribe *la18*-. [altered form of BURDEN[1.1]]

birn *see* BURN[2.1], BURN[2.2]

†**birnis**, **burnys** *v ptp* also **yburnyst** to burnish, polish *la14-16*. [ME *burnishen*]

†**birny**, **byrne** *n* a mail-coat; a cuirass or breastplate *la14-16*. [altered form of OFr *broigne*, ON *brynja*]

birr[1.1], †**bir**, †**byr** /bɪr/ *n* **1** force, energy, an onrush; bustling activity *15*-. **2** enthusiasm, verve *18*-. **3** a whirring sound *la19*-. **4** passion; rage *20- Sh*. **5** a breeze *20- Sh*. [ON *byrr* a breeze]

birr[1.2] /bɪr/ *v* **1** to (cause to) whirr or vibrate; to make a whirring noise *16*-. **2** to move rapidly and energetically *16*-. [see the noun]

birr[2] /bɪr/ *n of hair* a tousle; stiffness, a bristle *20*-. [compare BURR[1] and BIRSE[1.1]]

birrat *see* BURRAT

birrel *see* BURREL

birs *see* BIRSE[1.1]

birsall *see* BRISSELL

birse[1.1], †**birs**, †**byrs** /bɪrs/ *n* **1** a bristle, bristles *16*-. **2** a beard; hair *la16*-. **3** anger, temper *17*-. **4** the bristle fixed on a shoemaker's thread *la18*-. **5** a sheaf or plume of bristles *la19*-. **6** a brush *la16-e17*. **birsie 1** bristly; hairy *16-19, 20- Sh*. **2** hot-tempered, passionate *la19, 20- Ork SW Bor*. †**birsit** bristly *e16*. **get yer birse up** to get angry *la19*-. **set yer birse up** to get angry *19*-. [OE *byrst*]

birse[1.2] /bɪrs/ *v* **1** to bristle up; to become angry or defensive *19*-. **2** *of shoemakers* to attach a bristle to a thread *la19, 20- EC Bor*. †**birsit**, **birset** *of thread* supplied with a bristle *la16-19*. [see the noun]

birse *see* BRIZZ[1.2]

birse-cup /ˈbɪrskʌp/ *n* = BIRSE TEA *la19- NE*. [perhaps from the name of Aberdeenshire parish + CUP]

†**birsell foul**, **brissell fowl** *n* a game bird *la16-e17*. Compare BRISSEL-COCK. [perhaps ME *brustle* + FOOL]

birse tea /bɪrs ti/ *n* a (final) cup of tea with whisky (or other spirit) instead of milk *la19- NE T EC Bor*. [perhaps from the name of Aberdeenshire parish + TEA]

birsi /ˈbɪrsi/ *n* a sea-taboo term for a pig *20- Sh*. [derivative of BIRSE[1.1]]

birsil *see* BIRSLE

†**birsket**, **briscat**, **brescat** *n* baked dough, biscuit *la15-17*. **birsket breid** = BIRSKET. [BISKET, with intrusive *r*]

birsket *see* BRISKET

birsle, **brissle**, **bristle**, †**birsil**, †**brissill** /ˈbɪrsəl, ˈbrɪsəl/ *v* **1** to scorch or burn *16*-. **2** to warm thoroughly; to toast or broil (on the fire) *19*-. **birsled** warmed, toasted; well-cooked *20*-. **birsling 1** completely dry *la19*-. **2** scorching *20*-. [EModE *burstle*]

birst[1.1], **burst** /bɪrst, bʌrst/ *n* **1** a rent, a tear; a sudden eruption; an instance of bursting *19*-. **2** an injury caused by over-exertion *la19*-. **3** a big feed *la19*-. **4** a bout of drunkenness *20*-. **a hunger or a burst** *see* HUNGER[1.1]. [OE *byrst*]

birst[1.2], **burst**, **brust**, **brast**, †**brist**, †**brest** /bɪrst, bʌrst, brʌst, brast/ *v pt* **bristit**, **brast** †**brist**, †**brest 1** to break open or out, issue suddenly *la14*-. **2** to cause to burst, rupture *15*-. **bursen**, †**bursten**, †**brusten 1** burst, ruptured; broken, spoilt *la15*-. **2** filled to bursting; fat *18*-. **3** winded, breathless, exhausted *la18*-. **burster** *mining* a blast into a seam without previous cutting or boring *la19, 20- EC*. **burstit**, **bursted** broken, spoilt *19*-. **bursen grease** lubricating grease which has become thin (through friction) *20- NE*. **bursen oil** = *bursen grease 20*-. [OE *berstan*]

birstle /ˈbɪrsəl/ *n* a bristle, the stubble on an unshaved chin *la20- Sh Ork N*. [probably altered form of Eng *bristle*; compare BIRSE[1.1]]

birt *see* BERT

birth[1] /bɪrθ/ *n* **1** childbirth, the fact of being born; offspring *la14*-. **2** ancestry, rank *15*-. **3** produce of the soil, a crop *15-16*. †**birthful** = *birthy la16*. †**birthy**, **berthy** prolific, fertile *la15-19*. [probably ON *burðr*]

†**birth**[2] *n* the carrying capacity (of a ship) *la15-e17*. [ON *byrðr*]

birth *see* BERT

birthing, **birthinsake** *see* BURDEN[1.1]

birze *see* BRIZZ[1.1], BRIZZ[1.2]

biscat, **biscuit** *see* BISKET

bishop[1.1], †**bischop**, †**byschape**, †**beschop** /ˈbɪʃəp/ *n* **1** a high-ranking member of the clergy *la14*-. **2** an instrument for ramming down stones and earth *19, 20- NE Bor*. **bishopric**, †**bischoprik** the office or diocese of a bishop *la14*-. †**bischoprie** = *bishopric 16-e17*. †**bishop-sattin** a kind of satin *17-18*. **bishop weed** ground elder *Aegopodium podagraria 19*-. †**the bishop's foot has been in the broth** the broth is burnt *18-e19*. [OE *biscop*]

bishop[1.2] /ˈbɪʃəp/ *v* to beat or ram down stones and earth with a machine *la19- NE*. [see the noun]

bisket, biscuit, †**bisquet,** †**biscat** /ˈbɪskət/ *n* a small baked piece of dough, a biscuit *16-*. [ME *bisquit*, EModE *bisket*]

bisket *see* BRISKET

†**bismair, bysmer** *n* a disreputable woman *16*. [OE *bismer* abomination, disgrace]

bismar, bismer, †**pismire** /ˈbɪsmər/ *n* **1** a beam used for weighing goods, a steelyard *la16- Sh Ork NE T*. **2** a species of stickleback *Spinachia spinachia 19- Sh Ork*. [ON *bismari*]

bisquet *see* BISKET

biss *see* BOOSE[1.1]

bissart *see* BUZZARD

†**bisset** *n* a narrow trimming or lace (for cloth) *la16*. [MFr *bisette* a narrow strip of lace often embellished with gold or silver]

bissing *see* BOOSE[1.2]

bissum *see* BESOM

bissy *see* BUSY

bist *see* BUIST[2.1], BUIST[2.2]

bit[1.1], †**byt** /bɪt/ *n* **1** a small piece or portion (of something) *la15-*. **2** a small piece of food; a bite, a mouthful *16-*. **3** a small piece of ground; a spot, a place *la16-*. **4** one's place of residence or employment; one's situation or job; one's local area *la19-*. **5** a distance *la19-*. **aff the bit** off the mark, wrong *la19- T SW Bor*. †**at the bit** at the critical point or moment *la16-19*. †**bit and brat** food and board *19*. **bit and the buffet** food and blows, the good with the bad *la16-*. **bits o things** meagre possessions *19-*. **come to the bit** to come to the point of decision *19-*. **nae a bit** an expression of surprise or incredulity *20- NE*. [OE *bita*]

bit[1.2] /bɪt/ *adj* small; trivial, insignificant *18-*. [see the noun]

bit[1.3] /bɪt/ *adv* in a small way, to a small degree *la20-*. [see the noun]

bit[2], †**byt** /bɪt/ *n* the mouth-piece of a horse's bridle; a curb, a restraint *la15-*. **cannae get oot o the bit** to be unable to make any progress *20-*. **never aff the bit** always on duty *la20-*. [OE *bite* a pain, a bite]

bit *see* BEHOVE, BITE[1.1], BITE[1.2], BUIT[1.1]

bitch, †**biche** /bɪtʃ/ *n* **1** a female dog *16-*. **2** a term of contempt for a woman *la16-*. **3** a term of contempt for a man *la18-19, 20- literary*. †**bitchify'd** intoxicated *la18*. **bitch fou,** †**bitch fu** drunk (and beastlike) *la18- literary*. [OE *bicce*; compare BICK]

bite[1.1], †**byit,** †**byt,** †**bit** /bʌɪt/ *n* **1** the action of biting *la15-*. **2** a morsel of food *16-*. **bite and sup** something to eat and drink *la16-*. [see the verb]

bite[1.2], †**byt** /bʌɪt/ *v pt* **bit, bait,** *Sh* **baat** to use the teeth to pierce or injure; to take a bite (of something) *la14-*. **no be able tae bite yer thoum** to be very drunk *la18-*. [OE *bītan*]

bither *see* BATHER[1.1]

bittag *see* BITTOCK

bittel /ˈbɪtəl/ *n* **1** an abnormal or prominent tooth *20- Sh*. **2** an animal's tusk or fang *20- Sh*. **bitlek** a small or broken tooth; a growing tooth *la19- Sh*. [Norw dial *bitel, bitle* a small solitary tooth]

bitterie /ˈbɪtəri/ *n* the sand martin *Riparia riparia la19- Bor*. [shortened form of Scots *bitterbank, biter bank*, from its habit of excavating a nest in sandy banks with its bill]

bittie[1.1] /ˈbɪte, ˈbɪti/ *n* **1** a small piece, a little bit *la19-*. **2** a short time or distance *la19-*. [BIT[1.1] + -IE[1]]

bittie[1.3] /ˈbɪte, ˈbɪti/ *adj* a small amount *20-*. [see the noun]

bittie[1.3] /ˈbɪte, ˈbɪti/ *adv* a bit, somewhat *19-*. [see the noun]

bittle[1.1], **beetle,** †**betill** /ˈbɪtəl, ˈbɪtəl/ *n* **1** a (wooden) mallet *la15-*. **2** a kitchen implement for bruising barley or mashing potatoes *18-19, 20- SW Bor*. [OE *bȳtel*]

bittle[1.2], **beetle** /ˈbɪtəl, ˈbɪtəl/ *v* **1** to beat (linen or clothes) *19, 20- Bor*. **2** to thrash *la19- EC Bor*. **3** to pound barley or corn *19*. [see the noun]

bittock, *N* **bittag** /ˈbɪtək; *N* ˈbɪtəg/ *n* a small piece or portion *la18-*. **bittickie, bittockie** an especially small piece or portion *la19- NE*. [BIT[1.1], with diminutive suffix]

bittock *see* BEETYACH

bizz[1.1] /bɪz/ *n* **1** a buzzing, humming or hissing sound *la18-*. **2** a state of commotion or excitement, a bustle *la18-*. **3** a rumour *la19-*. [see the verb]

bizz[1.2], †**bys** /bɪz/ *v* **1** to make a buzzing or humming sound *16-*. **2** *of liquids* to hiss or fizz *16-*. **3** to bustle about; to become excited *la19-*. [onomatopoeic]

bizz[2] /bɪz/ *interj* an expression of disapproval *20- NE*. [unknown]

bizzard *see* BUZZARD

bizzie[1] /ˈbɪzi/ *n* bedding for cattle *la19- Sh Ork*. Compare BUSS[4.1]. [Norw dial *bys* litter, straw]

bizzie[2] /ˈbɪzi/ *n* a stall or stance in a byre *20- Sh Ork N*. [probably ON *bás*, with influence from BIZZIE[1]]

bizzum *see* BESOM

bjakk, †**byack,** †**byauch** /bjak/ *n* **1** a small or puny person or animal *19- Sh Ork N*. **2** a useless or insignificant person *la19*. [compare Norw *pjakk* a young salmon, *pjokk* a little boy]

bjelset *see* BYELSIT

bjinter, bieenter, bjanter /ˈbjɪntər, ˈbjantər/ *n* a spell of cloudy, cold and windy weather *la19- Sh*. [compare Shetland dial *binder* a cold, dry wind]

bjog *see* BYOAG

bla *see* BLAE[1.1], BLAE[1.2]

blaa *see* BLAW[1.1], BLAW[1.2]

blaand *see* BLAND[1.1]

blab[1.1], †**bleb** /blab/ *n* a large quantity of spirits *la19- NE*. Compare BLIB, BLYBE[1.1]. [see the verb]

blab[1.2], **bleb** /blab, bleb/ *v* to drink noisily or excessively *19- NE T*. [probably onomatopoeic]

blab *see* BLOB[1.1], BLOB[1.2]

blabber, †**blaber** /ˈblabər/ *v* to speak inarticulately; to babble *15-*. [ME *blaberen*; compare ON *blabbra*]

black[1.1], †**blak** /blak/ *n* **1** the colour black *la15-*. **2** *pl* mourning clothes *la19-*. **3** *pl* coal shale *la19- C*. **4** a scoundrel, a blackguard *19, 20- T* **5** black cloth *la15-e17*. Compare BLECK[2.1]. [OE *blæc, blac*]

black[1.2], †**blak,** †**blake** /blak/ *adj* **1** black-coloured *la12-*. **2** *of landscape* indicating the presence of coal; *of a hill* covered in heather; frequently in place-names *13-*. **3** *of complexion or hair* dark; frequently attached to a personal name: ◊*Black Douglas 14-*. **4** dismal, unfortunate, shameful, sad *16-*. **5** utter, downright, out-and-out *la19-*. **blackie 1** a blackbird *la19-*. **2** a black-faced sheep *20-*. **black back** a nickname for a miner *la20- C*. †**black baised** depressed *e19*. **blackberry** the blackcurrant *Ribes nigrum*; the crowberry *Empetrum nigrum 16-*. **blackbide, black byde,** †**black boyd** the berry of the bramble *Rubus fruticosus 19-*. **black bitch 1** a native of Linlithgow *la19-*. **2** a bag for fraudulently catching meal from the mill spout *19- SW Bor*. **black broun** dark brown *la16-*. **black bun** a rich spiced fruit cake, baked in a pastry crust and eaten at Hogmanay *la19-*. **black coal** coal which has been slightly burned by igneous rock *18-*. **black coat** a clergyman, a minister *la18-*. †**black crap, black crop** a crop of peas or beans *la17-e19*. **black dooker** the cormorant *Phalacrocorax carbo la19- SW*. **black fish** a recently-spawned salmon *la16-*. **black fisher** a night poacher of fish *17-*. **black fishing** night salmon-fishing with torches *la18-*. **black fit, black foot** a lovers' go-between *19-*.

black gate the road to ruin *19- NE T Bor.* **black gray** dark grey (colour or cloth) *la15-.* **black house** a Hebridean or West Highland dwelling, with dry-stone and turf walls, a thatched roof and a central fireplace on an earthen floor, traditionally accommodating both livestock and people *la19-.* **black hut** = *black house la18-e20, la20- historical.* **black jack** the saithe or coalfish *Merlangius merlangus 20- Sh.* **blackmail**, †**blak meill** a payment extorted by threats, originally in return for protection from plunder *16-.* **black malvoisie** a white grape from which malvoisie wine is made *19-.* **blackman 1** a kind of toffee; liquorice; a dark-coloured sweet *19-.* **2** an ice-cream with a plain wafer on one side and a marshmallow-filled wafer with chocolate edges on the other *la20-.* **3** a piece of black, hard mucus in the nose *20- C.* **black money 1** counterfeit coins; originally low value copper or mixed metal coins *la15-.* **2** an extra payment made to workers undertaking especially dirty work *la19-.* **black neb 1** a person with democratic or anti-government sympathies *19-.* **2** a strike-breaker *19-.* **3** a carrion crow *Corvus corone la19- SW Bor.* **4** an immature sea-trout *20- SW.* **black ox** a metaphorical black ox associated with bereavement or calamity *18-.* **Black Parliament** a name given to various parliaments considered to be unfortunate or shameful *16, la19- historical.* †**black rizzar** the blackcurrant *Ribes nigrum e18.* **Black Saturday**, †**Blak Sattirday** the day of the Battle of Pinkie, 10 Sept 1547 *la16- historical.* **black sight** a curse *20- Ork.* **blacksmith 1** a smith who works iron; a farrier *la15-.* **2** the halibut *Hippoglossus hippoglossus la19- NE.* †**black sole** a lovers' go-between *18-e19.* **black spauld** a disease in cattle *la18-19, 20- Ork WC.* **black spit** a lung disease formerly common among miners *19-.* **blackstone**, †**blackstane** *in Scottish Universities* a dark-coloured stone, later part of a chair, on which students sat during an annual public examination *la16-19, 20- historical.* **black strap** molasses *20- NE T.* **black-strippit ba** a hard boiled sweet, a bullseye *20-.* **black sugar** liquorice or liquorice juice *la18-.* **black tang** bladderwrack seaweed *Fucus vesiculosus la18-19, 20- Sh Ork.* **black traicle** molasses *la19-.* **black victual** peas and beans *la18-19, 20- EC.* †**black ward** *law* the holding in ward by a subvassal of another vassal who also held ward of his superior *la17-e19.* **Black Watch** a Scottish regiment, raised from the Independent Companies in 1739, so called from their dark green and black tartan; now part of the Royal Regiment of Scotland *18-.* **black weet** rain (as opposed to snow) *19-.* **as black as the pot** very black or dirty *la19-.* **black as the Earl o' Hell's waistcoat 1** pitch black *20-.* **2** very dirty *20-.* **black burning shame** utter shame *18-.* **the black man 1** the bogy-man *la19-.* **2** the Devil *la19-.* †**the blak spyce** pepper *la15.* **say black is the white o yer ee** to speak ill of a person *19, 20- NE T.* [see the noun]

black[1,3] /blak/ *adv* completely, utterly; intensely, extremely *la16-.* **black-avised**, **black-aviced** dark-complexioned *18-.* **black affrontit**, **black affronted** mortified; utterly embarrassed or humiliated *la19-.* **black oot** *of a fire* completely out *la19-.* [see the noun]

black cock, †**blak cok** /'blak kɔk/ *n* the (male of the) black grouse *Tetrao tetrix 15-.* †**mak a black cock o** to shoot (a person) *la18-e19.* [BLACK[1,2] + COCK[1,1]]

blacken, †**blakin** /'blakən/ *v* **1** to make or become black *15-.* **2** to polish shoes *20-.* **blacken someone's door** to appear at a door, make an unwanted visit *la19- Ork T EC.* [BLACK[1,2], with verb-forming suffix]

blackening /'blakənɪŋ/ *n* **1** shoe polish *19-.* **2** the traditional smearing of a bride or bridegroom with substances such as boot polish or treacle the night before their wedding *la20- Ork N NE.* [verbal noun from BLACKEN]

blackgaird, **blackguard**, *NE* **blaegart**, *EC* **blackyirt**, *WC* **blagyird** /'blakgerd, 'blagard; *NE* 'blegərt; *EC* 'blakjɪrt; *WC* 'blagjɪrd/ *n* a villain, a scoundrel *18-.* [BLACK[1,2] + GAIRD[1,1]]

blackin girse, **blacking grass** /'blakɪn gɪrs, 'blakɪŋ gras/ *n* the meadowsweet plant *Filipendula ulmaria* (from which a black dye is extracted) *la19- Sh.* [Scots *blacking* + GIRSE[1,1]]

black puddin, **black pudding** /blak 'pʌdən, blak 'pʊdɪŋ/ *n* a sausage made of pig's blood, suet and oatmeal (or flour) *18-.* [BLACK[1,2] + PUDDIN]

blackyirt *see* BLACKGAIRD

blad[1] /blad/ *n* a portfolio; a writing pad or blotting-pad *19, 20- EC Bor.* Compare BLAUD[2]. [ON *blað* the leaf of a plant or book]

blad[2] /blad/ *n* a deceptively weak or feeble person *19- Sh.* [probably OE *blæd* a blade, a leaf]

blad *see* BLAUD[1,1], BLAUD[1,2], BLAUD[2]

bladarie *see* BLADRY

bladder *see* BLETHER[1,2], BLETHER[2]

bladderskate *see* BLETHERSKITE

bladdoch, **bleddoch**, *Sh* **bleddick**, *Ork* **blathoo**, †**bladdo**, †**bledoch** /'bladəx, 'blɛdəx; *Sh* 'blɛdɪk; *Ork* 'blaðu/ *n* buttermilk *la16-.* [Gael *blàthach*]

bladdy *see* BLAUD[1,1]

blade[1,1], *Sh* **bled**, †**blaid**, †**blead** /bled; *Sh* blɛd/ *n* **1** the cutting part of a knife, weapon or tool *la14-.* **2** a broad flattened bone; the scapula *la15-.* **3** a leaf of grass; a vegetable leaf *la16-.* **4** a man *la18- literary.* **5** a tea-leaf *19, 20- Ork NE T.* [OE *blæd*]

blade[1,2], *Sh NE* **bled** /bled; *Sh NE* blɛd/ *v* to strip the leaves from (a plant) *19-.* [see the noun]

blad haet /'blad 'het/ *n* absolutely nothing *19- SW Bor.* [perhaps intensive use of BLAD[2] + *haet* (HAE[1,2]) used as a strong negative]

bladry, **blaudry**, †**blaidry**, †**bladarie** /'bladre, 'blɔdre/ *n* **1** filth, filthiness; waste *la16-19, 20- NE.* **2** harm, abuse, rough usage *18-19, 20- NE.* **3** foolishness, ostentation *18-e19.* [unknown]

†**bladʒean** *n* term of abuse for a person *e16.* [unknown]

blae[1,1], †**bla** /ble/ *n* **1** the colour blue; an expanse of blue *19- literary.* **2** a bruise; a scar *la16-e19.* [ON *blár*]

blae[1,2], †**bla**, †**blay**, †**blea** /ble/ *adj* **1** *of flesh* bruised; cold, bloodless, livid *13-.* **2** blue in colour; bluish or grey *la14-.* **3** *of weather* bleak, dreary, sunless *16-.* **4** *of skin colour* black *la15.* Compare BLUE[1,2]. **blaeness** lividness *la19-.* **blaeberry**, †**blaberry** the bilberry *Vaccinium myrtillus la15-.* **blae wing** *angling* an artificial fly tied with a bluish-grey wing *la19-.* [see the noun]

blae[2], †**blea** /ble/ *n* a bluish-grey hardened clay or soft slate *17-.* **blae beds**, †**blea beds** layers of clay or slate *la18-19, 20- EC.* [a specialized use of BLAE[1,2]]

blae *see* BLEA

blaeflum *see* BLAFLUM[1,1]

blaegart *see* BLACKGAIRD

blaeget, **blaget** /'blegət, 'blagət/ *adj of animals* spotted, speckled *20- Sh.* [compare Swed *blaga*]

blaes, **blaze**, **blaize** /blez/ *n pl* **1** a bluish-grey hardened clay, soft slate or shale *18-.* **2** *pl* (red-coloured) spent shale, used in road building, tennis courts and hard football pitches *20-.* **blaes and balls** shale with ironstone nodules embedded *la19, 20- EC.* [derivative of BLAE[1,2]]

blaewort, **blaewart** *see* BLAWORT

blaff[1,1] /blaf/ *n* a blast, a gust; a bang, a crash *la19-.* [perhaps imitative]

blaff[1,2] /blaf/ *v* to blast or bang *la19- literary.* [see the noun]

blaffart see BLUFFERT

blaflum[1.1], †**blafum**, †**bleflume**, †**blaeflum** /ˈblafləm/ *n* a deception, a hoax, an illusion; nonsense, idle talk *la16-19, 20- literary*. [unknown]

blaflum[1.2] /bləˈflʌm/ *v* to cajole, deceive *18-19, 20- literary*. [unknown]

blaget see BLAEGET

blagyird see BLACKGAIRD

blaid see BLADE[1.1], BLAUD[1.2], BLAUD[2]

blaidry see BLADRY

blaik see BLECK[2.3]

blaiken, †**blakyn** /ˈblekən/ *v* to make pallid; to become pale *la15-19, 20- NE*. [ON *bleikja*]

blaiken see BLECKIN

blaikent, †**blaiknit**, †**blaknit** /ˈblekənt/ *adj* made pale, pallid; bleached *la15-*. [ON *bleikr*]

blaiker see BLECK[1]

blain[1], †**blane** /blen/ *n* a scar, a sore; a wound or weal *16-19, 20- NE*. **blainag** a pimple *20- N*. [OE *blegen*]

blain[2] /blen/ *n* a bare patch (in a field of crops) *19, 20- NE*. **blainy** *of crops* bare in patches *19, 20- NE*. [metaphorical derivative of BLAIN[1]]

blairdie /ˈblerdi/ *n* the bilberry *Vaccinium myrtillus la19- NE*. [diminutive derived from BLAE[1.2] with diminutive suffix *-die*]

blaised, **bleezed** /blezd, blizd/ *adj of milk* slightly soured *19- NE T SW*. [participial adj from BLEEZE[1.2]]

blait, †**blate**, †**blete** /blet/ *v* to bleat *15-*. [OE *blǣtan*]

blaith see BLITHE[1.2]

blaize see BLAES

blak see BLACK[1.1], BLACK[1.2]

blak cok see BLACK COCK

blake see BLACK[1.2]

blakin see BLACKEN

blaknit see BLAIKENT

blakyn see BLAIKEN

blame[1.1] /blem/ *n* 1 reproof, censure; responsibility, culpability *la14-*. 2 *with a possessive pronoun* fault: ◊*it's not my blame 19-*. [OFr *blasme*]

blame[1.2], *Ork* **bleem** /blem; *Ork* blim/ *v* to hold responsible; to find fault with, reprove *la14-*. [OFr *blasmer*]

blan see BLIN[1]

blancat see BLANKET[1.1]

blanche see BLENCH[1.1], BLENCH[1.2], BLENCH[1.3]

blancheferme see BLENCH FARM[1.1]

blanchferme see BLENCH FARM[1.2], BLENCH FARM[1.3]

bland[1.1], **blaand** /bland, bland/ *n* a beverage of buttermilk and water; sour whey *17- Sh Ork*. [ON *blanda*]

bland[1.2] /bland/ *v* to mix, mingle *la15-19, 20- Ork*. †**blanded bear** bear mixed with barley *la18-e19*. [see the noun]

†**bland**[2] *adj* flattering, pleasant *la15-16*. [Lat *blandus*]

†**blander** *v* to diffuse or disperse too scantily or thinly *la17-19*. [unknown]

blane see BLAIN[1]

blanket[1.1], **blunket**, †**blancat**, †**bloncat**, †**blankid** /ˈblaŋkət, ˈblʌŋkət/ *n* 1 a large woollen cloth or bed-covering *14-*. 2 grey or blue undyed wool (woven into cloth) *16-e17*. †**blanket blue** blue woollen cloth *16-e17*. **blanket preaching** an open-air religious service commemorating the field-preaching of the Covenanters *la19-*. **blue blanket** the banner of the craftsmen of Edinburgh *la16-*. **wet blanket** a person who puts a damper on events *19-*. [ME *blanket*, OFr *blanquette*]

†**blanket**[1.2], **blunket**, **bloncat** *adj of cloth* greyish blue *15-e17*. [see the noun]

blankid see BLANKET[1.1]

blansht, **blenched** /blanʃt, blɛnʃt/ *adj of milk* slightly sour *19- NE*. [shortened form of Scots *blenched milk*]

†**blanter** *n* bread or porridge made from oats *la18-19*. [perhaps related to BLANDER]

blare[1.1], †**blere** /bler/ *n* the bleat of a sheep *19- Bor*. [see the verb]

blare[1.2], †**blere** /bler/ *v* 1 to emit a loud noise; to roar or bellow *la16-*. 2 to weep; *of an animal* to bleat *la16-19, 20- Bor*. [ME *bleren*]

blase see BLEEZE[1.1], BLEEZE[2]

blash[1.1] /blaʃ/ *n* 1 a splash of liquid *la18-*. 2 a heavy or drenching shower of rain or sleet *19-*. 3 a weak drink, a thin soup *la19-*. 4 a semi-liquid or soft slimy mass, a dirty mess *19- NE EC*. 5 a large draught of liquor *19, 20- NE T*. 6 a torrent of words *la19, 20- NE T*. Compare PLASH[1.1]. **blashy** 1 rainy, wet, gusty *18-*. 2 *of food or drink* weak, thin; mushy, wet *19, 20- NE Bor*. [onomatopoeic]

blash[1.2] /blaʃ/ *v* 1 *of rain, sleet or snow* to batter or lash (against a person or thing) *19-*. 2 to pour or drip with a splashing noise *20- NE T EC*. Compare PLASH[1.2]. [see the noun]

blason see BLAZON[1.1], BLAZON[1.1]

blasphemation, †**blasphematioun** /blasfəˈmeʃən/ *n* 1 insult, calumniation *la15-16, la20- literary*. 2 blaspheming; blasphemy *16, la20- literary*. [Lat *blasphēmātio*]

blast[1.1], †**blist** /blast/ *n* 1 a violent gust of wind *la14-*. 2 a loud noise, an explosion; a loud musical note *15-*. 3 a smoke or puff of a pipe *19-*. 4 a sudden attack of illness; a stroke *18-19, 20- NE*. [OE *blǣst*]

blast[1.2] /blast/ *v* 1 to strike, crash, destroy *la16-*. 2 to shout loudly, boast, declaim *la16-*. 3 to pant, breathe hard *la18-*. 4 to blow on the pipes *la19-*. 5 to smoke tobacco *19, 20- Bor*. **blastit** paralysed; having suffered a stroke *la18- NE*. [see the noun]

blaster see BLEESTER[1.2]

blastie[1.1] /ˈblasti, ˈblaste/ *n* 1 an undersized person; a bad-tempered, unmanageable child or animal *la18-*. 2 a nickname for a native of Kilbirnie, Ayrshire *la19-*. 3 **the Blasties** a nickname for Kilbirnie Football Club *la20-*. [perhaps a development from BLAST[1.1]]

blastie[1.2], **blasty** /ˈblasti, ˈblaste/ *adj* 1 boisterous, noisy; *of weather* gusty *19, 20- NE T C Bor*. 2 puffing, panting *la18*. [see the noun]

blate, †**bleat** /blet/ *adj* 1 bashful, sheepish, timid, awkward, modest *la15-*. 2 dull, stupid, easily deceived *la15-*. 3 *of crops* backward in growth *20- NE T*. **blately** bashfully, stupidly *16-18, 19- literary*. [unknown]

blate see BLAIT

blather see BLETHER[1.1], BLETHER[1.2], BLETHER[2]

blatherskite see BLETHERSKITE

blathoo see BLADDOCH

blatter[1.1] /ˈblatər/ *n* 1 a loud rattling or rustling noise *18-*. 2 a blow; a heavy fall; a gunshot *la18-*. 3 a storm of rain or hail *19-*. 4 an incoherent flow of words *19-*. [see the verb]

blatter[1.2] /ˈblatər/ *v* 1 to speak noisily and fast; to babble *16-*. 2 to beat noisily or violently; *of rain or hail* to rattle or crash *17-*. 3 to run noisily with short steps *19-*. 4 to flicker, flutter or flap *19-*. [perhaps from Lat *blaterāre*]

blaud[1.1], **blad**, †**blawd** /blɔd, blad/ *n* 1 a blast of wind, a downpour of rain *19, 20- literary*. 2 a large raindrop *20- Sh*. 3 a blow; an injury; a disease like smallpox *la16-19*. **bladdy** *of weather* unsettled *19- N NE*. [see the verb]

blaud[1.2], **blad**, †**blaid** /blɔd, blad/ *v* 1 to damage or spoil; to harm or injure *16-*. 2 to beat or pound; to slap, strike; to thrust or drive violently *16-*. 3 to defame or deface *la16-*. 4

blaud / **bleem**

of rain or wind to buffet, beat *la17-19, 20- NE T*. **5** to spoil a child *20- NE*. [probably onomatopoeic]

blaud², **blad**, †**blaid** /blɔd, blad/ *n* **1** a sample of written text; a snippet of verse; a specimen or promotional page *16-*. **2** a lump; a piece of dirt; a dirty mark *la16-19, 20- T*. **3** a newsletter, an information page *la20- Uls*. **4** a piece or portion of something, a fragment *16-e19*. **5** a strip of cloth *la16-e19*. [unknown]

blaudry *see* BLADRY

blaugh *see* BLEACH²·²

blaver /'blɛvər/ *n* a name for various flowers including the cornflower *Centaurea cyanus 19- NE Bor*. Compare BLAWORT. [unknown]

blaw¹·¹, **blaa**, **blow**, *NE* **blyave** /blɔ, bla, blo; *NE* 'bljav/ *n* **1** a blast of noise; the blowing of a musical instrument *la15-*. **2** a gust of wind *19-*. **3** a puff of a pipe *20-*. **4** boasting, a boast; a boaster *19-*. **5** a pull of liquor *la18-e19*. **at full blow** at full blast *20-*. [see the verb]

blaw¹·², **blaa**, **blow**, *NE* **blyave**, *NE* **byauve** /blɔ, bla, blo; *NE* 'bljav; *NE* 'bjav/ *v* **1** *of air or wind* to move around, cause (something) to move *la14-*. **2** to breathe out; to breathe heavily *la14-*. **3** to sound or blow an instrument *la14-*. **4** to boast or brag; to exaggerate *la14-*. **5** *draughts* to take a piece from one's opponent *19-*. **6** to smoke a pipe *la18- C*. **7** to inflate; to cause meat to swell to improve its appearance *la15-19*. **8** to make known, advertise *16-19*. **blawy**, **blowy** windy *la18-*. **blaw doon** a back-draught in a chimney or fireplace *20-*. **blaw grass** a hill-grass, a variety of bent *la18- T WC SW*. †**blaw a cauld coal** to suffer failure, engage in a hopeless task *18-e19*. **blaw in yer lug** to flatter someone *19-*. **blaw lown** to make little or no noise; to avoid boasting *19- NE Bor*. †**blaw out on** to denounce formally (after blowing a horn to attract public attention) *15-16*. **blaw up 1** to blow up, explode *17-*. **2** to flatter, coax or deceive *19-*. [OE *blāwan*]

blaw² /blɔ/ *n* a hard stroke or knock *la15-*. [ME *blaw*]

blaw³ /blɔ/ *v* to blossom *19-, 20- NE SW*. [OE *blōwan*]

blaw⁴ /blɔ/ *n* oatmeal *19-, 20- NE T H&I SW*. [compare Scots *blawkie* a porridge pot]

blawd *see* BLAUD¹·¹

blawn, **blown**, †**blowen**, †**blawin** /blɔn, blon/ *adj* **1** driven or tossed by the wind; windswept *16-*. **2** inflated, swollen, bloated *la16-*. **3** *of meat or fish* dried in the open air without salt *19- Sh Ork NE*. **4** *of land* over-manured by seaweed *20- N*. †**blawin flesh** meat inflated to improve its appearance *la16-e17*. †**blawn land**, **blawin land** (light, sandy) land liable to be damaged by the wind *16-19*. **blown milk** a preparation of sour milk *20- N*. **blawn up** blocked *la18- NE*. [participial adj from BLAW¹·²]

blawort, **blaewort**, **blaewart**, †**blewart** /'blawərt, 'blewərt/ *n* **1** the cornflower *Centaurea cyanus la18-*. **2** the harebell *Campanula rotundifolia 19-*. **3** the germander speedwell *Veronica chamaedrys 19*. Compare BLAVER. [BLAE¹·² + OE *wyrt*]

blay *see* BLAE¹·²

blaze *see* BLAES, BLEEZE¹·¹, BLEEZE¹·², BLEEZE²

blazon¹·¹, †**blason** /'blezən/ *n* **1** a shield; a heraldic shield, a coat of arms *15-*. **2** *law* the badge of office displayed by a King's or Queen's messenger; latterly the badge of a sheriff officer *la16-*. [ME *blasoun*]

blazon¹·², *T* **blezzin**, †**blason** /'blezən; *T* 'blɛzɪn/ *v* **1** to describe in heraldic terms *15-*. **2** to proclaim, make public, publish; to propagate or glorify *la15-*. **3** to proclaim with reproach *la16-e17*. [see the noun]

blea, **blae** /bli, ble/ *v of a lamb or kid* to bleat or cry *19- Bor*. [probably onomatopoeic]

blea *see* BLAE¹·², BLAE²

†**bleach**¹·¹, **bleech** *n* a blow, a stroke *18-19*. [ME *bleche*]

bleach¹·², **bleech** /blitʃ/ *v* to strike, beat *19, 20- NE*. [ME *blechen*, OFr *blecier*, *blecher* to injure]

bleach²·¹ /blitʃ/ *n* the bleaching process; a bleaching substance *18-*. **bleachfield** a bleaching works and adjacent drying-ground; frequently in place-names *18-*. **bleachgreen** = *bleachfield 18-*. [see the verb]

bleach²·², †**bleche** /blitʃ/ *v* to whiten (cloth or clothes) *16-*. **bleached**, †**blechit**, †**blacht**, †**blaugh 1** treated with a bleaching substance, whitened by bleaching *16-*. **2** pale, livid *19*. **bleaching-green**, †**bleachin grien** a bleaching works and adjacent drying-ground *la17-*. [OE *blǣcan*]

blead *see* BLADE¹·¹

blear¹·¹ /blir/ *n* something which obscures the sight; matter in the eye *17-*. **blearach** short-sighted *20- N NE*. **draw the blear ower yer ee** to deceive *la18- NE*. [see the verb]

blear¹·², †**blere** /blir/ *v* **1** to beguile, deceive *15-*. **2** to weep; to look blearily *la16-*. **3** to shine dimly; to dim (a light) *la18-*. †**blear yer ee** to deceive someone *15-19*. [ME *blere*]

blearie¹·¹ /'bliri/ *n* liquid food, gruel *19-*. [see the adj]

blearie¹·² /'bliri/ *adj* **1** watery-eyed *19-*. **2** dim, gloomy *20-*. **3** *of food or drink* thin, watery, insipid *19*. **bleary e'et** watery-eyed *20- NE*. [BLEAR¹·¹ + -IE²]

blearit, **bleart**, **bleared**, †**blerit**, †**blerde** /'blirɪt, blirt, blird/ *adj* **1** *of the eyes* dimmed, bleary *16-*. **2** *of food or drink* thin, watery, insipid *19-*. **3** debauched-looking *20-*. **4** *of writing* blotted *20-*. [ptp of BLEAR¹·²]

bleart *see* BLEARIT

bleat *see* BLATE

bleater, **blitter** /'blitər, 'blɪtər/ *n* the (cock) snipe *Gallinago gallinago la18- SW Bor*. [so called from the bleating note of both male and female during breeding season]

bleatery *see* BLEETER

bleb *see* BLAB¹·¹, BLAB¹·²

bleche *see* BLEACH²·²

bleck¹ /blɛk/ *v* **1** to baffle; to puzzle *19- NE T*. **2** to surpass, beat or excel *19, 20- NE T*. **blaiker** a puzzle, a challenge *20- NE*. [unknown]

bleck²·¹, **blaik**, †**blek** /blɛk, blek/ *n* **1** blacking (for leather) *16-*. **2** a black mark; a spot or stain *16-*. **3** (a particle of) soot or smut *la19-*. **4** mildew on plants *la19-*. **5** a blackguard, scoundrel *la19-*. [ON *blek* ink]

bleck²·², **blaik**, †**blek** /blɛk, blek/ *v* **1** to blacken; to dirty or stain *15-*. **2** to defile or defame, blacken a person's character *15-*. **3** to blacken with ink; to write on paper *16-*. **4** to apply polish or blacking *la19-*. †**bleckit quheitt** mildewed wheat *la17*. [see the noun]

bleck²·³, **blek**, **blaik** /blɛk, blek/ *adj* black-coloured, dark *la19-*. **bleckie** a blackbird *la20-*. [see the noun]

bleckin, **blaiken**, †**blekin** /'blɛkən, 'blekən/ *v* **1** to blacken *la16-*. **2** to polish shoes *la20-*. **blecknin** blacking (for leather) *la19-*. [BLECK²·², with *-en* suffix]

bled *see* BLADE¹·¹, BLADE¹·²

bledder *see* BLETHER¹·¹, BLETHER¹·², BLETHER²

bleddick, **bleddoch** *see* BLADDOCH

blede *see* BLEED¹

bledoch *see* BLADDOCH

bleech *see* BLEACH¹·¹, BLEACH¹·²

bleed¹, †**blede**, †**bleid** /blid/ *v* to draw or discharge blood; to cause to bleed; *of blood* to flow *la14-*. Compare BLUID¹·². [OE *blēdan*]

bleed² /blid/ *v of grain* to yield (well) *19-*. [probably related to OE *blōwan* to blow, bloom]

bleed *see* BLUID¹·¹, BLUID¹·²

bleedie *see* BLUIDY

bleem *see* BLAME¹·², BLUME¹·¹, BLUME¹·²

bleester[1.1] /'blistər/ *n* a blast of wind; a passing storm *20- NE H&I.* [ON *blástr*]

bleester[1.2], †**blaster** /'blistər/ *v* to blast, make an explosive noise; *of wind* to blow in blasts *la15-19, 20- Ork NE H&I.* [see the noun]

bleeter /'blitər/ *n* a passing storm *19-*. **bleatery** cold, raw, showery *20- NE.* [unknown; compare BLOOTER[1.1], BLATTER[1.1]]

bleeter *see* BLOOTER[1.1], BLOOTER[1.2]

bleeze[1.1], **blaze**, †**blese**, †**blase**, †**bles** /bliz, blez/ *n* 1 a bright, fiercely-burning fire *la14-*. 2 a blazing brand or a torch (used whilst spearing fish) *15-*. 3 a beacon or signal fire, a bonfire *16-19, 20- T.* **bleeze money** a gratuity given by pupils to their schoolmasters at Candlemas *la19, 20- historical.* †**bleis silver** = *bleeze money la16.* **in a bleeze** *of a crop* suddenly ripe; ready to be thinned *20- NE T.* [ME *blese*]

bleeze[1.2], **blaze**, †**blese** /bliz, blez/ *v* 1 to burn brightly and fiercely *16-*. 2 to light up water to attract fish *18-*. **bleezed** very drunk *19-*. **bleezin** very drunk *19-*. †**bleezy** *of the eyes* showing signs of intoxication *19.* [see the noun]

bleeze[2], †**blase**, †**blaze** /bliz/ *v* 1 to proclaim (loudly) *la16-*. 2 to boast, brag *19, 20- NE EC.* **bleeze awa** to brag, exaggerate *19-, 20- NE.* [ON *blása* to blow]

bleezed *see* BLAISED

bleffart *see* BLUFFERT

bleflume *see* BLAFLUM[1.1]

bleg *see* BLIG

bleib *see* BLOB[1.2], BLOB[1.2]

bleid *see* BLEED[1]

blek *see* BLECK[2.1], BLECK[2.2], BLECK[2.3]

blekin *see* BLECKIN

blellum /'blɛləm/ *n* an idle, ignorant, talkative man *la18-19, 20- literary.* [perhaps conflation of BLABBER with SKELLUM]

blemish /'blɛmɪʃ/ *v* 1 to stain, spoil or mar *17-*. 2 to damage *la19-.* [OFr *blesmiss-*, stem of *blesmir* to render livid or pale]

blen /blɛn/ *n* a light wind, a breath of wind *20- Sh.* [cognate with ON *blása*, OE *blāwan*]

blench[1.1], †**blanche** /blɛnʃ/ *n law* a small or nominal quitrent *16-20, 21- historical.* [shortened form of BLENCH FARM[1.1]]

blench[1.2], †**blanche** /blɛnʃ/ *adj of land* held for a small or nominal rent *16-20, 21- historical.* **blench duty** a nominal rent or fee *17-20, 21- historical.* **blench holding** the holding of land for a nominal rent *17-20, 21- historical.* [see the noun]

blench[1.3], †**blanche** /blɛnʃ/ *adv* by the payment or on the tenure of a nominal rent *la15-20, 21- historical.* [see the noun]

blenched *see* BLANSHT

blench farm[1.1], †**blancheferme**, †**blencheferme** /'blɛnʃfarm/ *n law* a small or nominal quit-rent *la14-19, 20- historical.* [OFr *blanche ferme* white rent, rent paid in silver]

blench farm[1.2], †**blancheferme**, †**blencheferme** /'blɛnʃfarm/ *adj of land* held for a small or nominal rent *la15-18, 20- historical.* [see the noun]

blench farm[1.3], †**blancheferme**, †**blencheferme** /'blɛnʃfarm/ *adv* by the payment or on the tenure of a nominal rent *la15-19, 20- historical.* [see the noun]

blenk *see* BLINK[1.1], BLINK[1.2]

blenshaw /'blɛnʃɔ/ *n* a drink made of oatmeal, sugar, milk, water, and nutmeg *19-.* [Fr *blanche eau* white water]

†**blent**[1.1] *n* a glance *e16.* [pt of BLINK[1.2]]

blent[1.2], **blint** /blɛnt, blɪnt/ *v* 1 to shine; to shed a gleam of light; to flash *19-*. 2 to glance (at) *la15-e16.* [see the noun]

blent *see* BLINK[1.2]

blenter *see* BLINTER[2.1], BLINTER[2.2]

blerde *see* BLEARIT

blere *see* BLARE[1.1], BLARE[1.2], BLEAR[1.2]

blerit *see* BLEARIT

blese *see* BLEEZE[1.1], BLEEZE[1.2]

blessit *see* BLISSIT[1.1], BLISSIT[1.2]

blete *see* BLAIT

blether[1.1], *Sh NE* **bledder**, †**blather** /'blɛðər; *Sh NE* 'blɛdər/ *n* 1 foolish or trivial talk; long-winded (boasting) talk *18-*. 2 a person who talks foolishly; a chatterbox *19-*. 3 a chat, a conversation *la19-.* **blethers** a piece of nonsense, a foolish whim or notion *la19-.* [see the verb]

blether[1.2], *Sh NE* **bledder**, †**blather**, †**bladder** /'blɛðər; *Sh NE* 'blɛdər/ *v* 1 to talk foolishly or in a trivial way; to prattle, speak boastfully *15-*. 2 to stammer, speak indistinctly *la16-e19.* **bletheration** foolish talk *la19-.* **bletherer** a person who talks foolishly or too much *la18-.* **bletherie** foolish talk *la19- NE.* **blethering fou** drunk enough to speak loquaciously or foolishly *20-.* **blethering Tam** the whitethroat *Sylvia communis 19- C SW.* [ON *blaðra* to utter inarticulately, move (the tongue) to and fro]

blether[1.3] /'blɛðər/ *interj pl* an expression of dismissal or contempt *19-.* [see the verb]

blether[2], **bledder**, **blather**, **bladder** /'blɛðər, 'blɛdər, 'blaðər, 'bladər/ *n* 1 the organ which collects urine, a bladder *la14-.* 2 a bagpipe; the windbag of a bagpipe *16-.* 3 a (leather) football *la20-.* **blether an' leather** a football *20-.* [OE *blēdre*]

bletherskite, **blatherskite**, **bletherskate**, *WC* **bletheranskite**, *Uls* **bletherkumskite**, †**bladderskate** /'blɛðərskʌɪt, 'blaðərskʌɪt, 'blɛðərsket; *WC* 'blɛðərənskʌɪt; *Uls* 'blɛðərkəmskʌɪt/ *n* 1 a silly foolish person; a babbler, a prattler *la17-.* 2 a boaster, a bragger *la19- N NE T EC.* [BLETHER[1.2] + SKATE or SKITE[1.2]]

blett /blɛt/ *n* a spot, a blotch; a piece of ground of a distinct colour *la19- Sh Ork.* [Icel *blettr*]

bleud *see* BLUID[1.1]

bleupsy /'blupsi/ *adj of the face* flabby, heavy-looking and expressionless *la20- Ork.* [unknown]

blew *see* BLUE[1.1], BLUE[1.2]

blewart *see* BLAWORT

blezzin *see* BLAZON[1.2]

blib /blɪb/ *n* weak tea; watery soup *20- NE.* [compare BLAB, BLYBE[1.1]]

blibbans /'blɪbənz/ *npl* strips of soft, slimy seaweed *19- NE SW.* [perhaps conflation of BLIB with RIBBON]

blibber *see* BLUBBER

blibe /blʌɪb/ *n* a bubble *la19- Sh.* [compare BLIB, BLYBE[1.1]]

blichan /'blɪxən/ *n* 1 a term of contempt for a person *19- T EC SW.* 2 a worn-out, worthless animal *19- SW.* [unknown; compare Gael *blianach* a lean animal, an inactive person]

blicht[1.1] /blɪxt/ *a* disease in plants; blight, ruin *19-.* [unknown]

blicht[1.2] /blɪxt/ to blight, destroy *la19-.* [unknown]

blicker /'blɪkər/ *n* 1 a boaster, a talkative person; a foolish person *20- NE.* 2 prattle, nonsense *20- NE.* [unknown]

blid *see* BLUID[1.1], BLUID[1.2]

bliddy *see* BLUIDY

blide *see* BLITHE[1.2]

bliffert *see* BLUFFERT

blig, **bleg** /blɪg, blɛg/ *n* a wooden wedge used to keep a hoe securely fixed to a handle *la19- Sh.* [compare Norw *blegg*, Swed *bligd*, Dan *blejr*]

blin[1], †**blyn**, †**blyne** /blɪn/ *v pt* **blindit**, **blan** to cease, stop; to come to an end *la14-19, 20- literary.* [OE *blinnan*]

blin[2.1], **blind**, *Sh* **blinnd** /blɪn, blʌɪnd; *Sh* blɪnd/ *n* 1 something which obstructs vision; a pretence, a deception *la16-.* 2 a wink of sleep *20- Sh.* 3 a small degree of light, a gleam *20- Sh.* [see the adj]

blin[2.2], **blinn**, **blind**, *Sh* **blinnd** /blɪn, blʌɪnd; *Sh* blɪnd/ *v* **1** to make blind; to deprive of sight *la14*-. **2** to close the eyes, go to sleep *19*-. **3** to pack the large stones forming the bed of a road with smaller stones to give strength and firmness *19*-. **blinner** to move the eyelids like a person with defective sight *20*- *N NE*. **blinners** blinkers *20*-. [see the adj]
blin[2.3], **blinn**, **blind**, *Sh* **blinnd** /blɪn, blʌɪnd; *Sh* blɪnd/ *adj* **1** *of places or landscape features* hidden, covered, closed up; *of land* infertile, unproductive, barren *13*-. **2** *of people or animals* unable to see, devoid of sight *la14*-. **3** *of people or animals* lacking discernment; *of actions* reckless, foolish *la14*-. **4** excluding light, dark, dense *16*-. **5** secret, misleading; *of a transaction* executed without full knowledge *17*-. **6** *of a cow's teat* having no opening *20*-. **blinder** to blind *20- Ork*. **blindlins**, †**blyndlyngis** blindly; heedlessly; with eyes shut *16-19, 20- WC*. **blin bargain** a bargain made without care or full knowledge *la18-19, 20- NE SW*. **blind coal** a kind of anthracite *la18-*. **blin drift** drifting snow *19-*. **blin' ee**, **blind eye** the dogfish *Scyliorhinus canicula 19-*. **blind-een** with the eyes shut, without needing to look *19, 20- NE*. **blind fair** extremely fair; albino *19-*. **blin fou** very drunk *19-*. **blind Harrie** blindman's buff *la18-19, 20- EC Bor*. **blin hooie** an (unfavourable) exchange *20-*. **blin lump**, **blind lump** a boil which does not come to a head *20-*. †**blinmen's baw** = *blindman's buff la18-19*. **blindman's buff** the common puffball *Bovista plumbea 20-*. **blind nail**, †**blynd naill** a headless nail *16-*. **blin' oors** the late hours of the night *la19-*. **blind parables**, **blin parables** a form of communication using signs and whispers to conceal the information from someone present *la19- NE*. **blin Seturday**, **blind Saturday** the Saturday of the week in which no pay is given to those paid fortnightly *la19-*. **blind sieve** a basket or tray for carrying grain *19- Sh Ork NE*. **blin swap** the exchange of articles by schoolboys with their eyes shut or with the articles in closed hands *20-*. [OE *blind*]
†**blind** *n* a spritsail *16-e17*. [Du *blind*]
blind *see* BLIN[2.1], BLIN[2.2], BLIN[2.3]
blindit *see* BLIN[1]
blink[1.1], †**blenk** /blɪŋk/ *n* **1** a glance, a glimpse *la15-*. **2** a gleam, a glimmer (of light); a short period of sunshine (between clouds) *16-*. **3** a short time, a moment *19-*. **4** the action of blinking the eyes *20-*. **5** a wink of sleep *20-*. **6** a momentary use of borrowed light: ◊*gie me the blink o a candle 19- Sh NE*. [see the verb]
blink[1.2], †**blenk** /blɪŋk/ *v pt* †**blent 1** to close the eyelids briefly *la16-*. **2** *folklore* to give the evil eye; to bewitch; to turn milk sour *18-*. **3** to glance kindly, look fondly at; to ogle *18-19, 20- NE T*. **4** to make a spark; to light a lamp *la19- Sh EC*. **5** to be drunk, be under the influence of drink *19, 20- WC SW*. **6** to deceive or cheat *19, 20- NE*. **7** to miscarry *20- Sh*. **8** to give a glance or a sudden look *la14-16*. **9** to gleam or glitter *e16*. **blinker 1** the eye *19-*. **2** the sun *19, 20- Sh*. **3** *pl* the eyelashes *la19- NE EC*. **4** a blow to the eye *la19- NE*. **5** a person who is nearly blind or is blind in one eye *19, 20- NE*. **6** a lively, attractive girl *la18-19, 20- Bor*. **7** a cheat, a spy *la18-e19*. **blinkin eed** weak-eyed *la19- NE EC*. [ME *blenk*]
blinkie /'blɪŋki/ *n* an electric torch *la20- Sh*. [BLINK[1.2] + -IE[3]]
blinkie *see* PLINKIE
blinn, **blinnd** *see* BLIN[2.2], BLIN[2.3]
blinochs *see* BLUNOCHS
blint *see* BLENT[1.2]
blinter[1] /'blɪntər/ *v* **1** to glimmer, flicker *19- NE T EC*. **2** to squint; to blink *19, 20- NE*. **blinterer** a short-sighted person *20- NE*. **blintrin**, **blinterin 1** short-sighted; blinking *19- N NE*. **2** glimmering, flickering *la20- T C*. [probably frequentative form of BLENT[1.1]]
blinter[2.1], **blenter** /'blɪntər, 'blɛntər/ *n* **1** a boisterous gusty wind *19- NE T EC*. **2** a flat stroke, a strong sharp blow *19- NE T EC*. [unknown]
blinter[2.2], **blenter** /'blɪntər, 'blɛntər/ *v* **1** to rush, make haste *19- NE T*. **2** to strike *la19- NE EC*. [unknown]
blirt[1.1] /blɪrt, blʌrt/ *n* **1** an outburst (of weeping) *la18-19, 20- NE*. **2** a gust of wind with rain *19, 20- NE Bor*. **3** an ineffectual, crying person *20- Uls*. **blirtie** *of weather* changeable, showery *19, 20- NE Bor*. [probably onomatopoeic]
blirt[1.2] /blɪrt, blʌrt/ *v* to weep; to burst into tears *18-19, 20- NE T*. [see the noun]
blirt[2] /blɪrt, blʌrt/ *n* the female genitals *19-*. [unknown]
bliss, †**blis** /blɪs/ *v* to bless *la14-*. [OE *bletsian*]
blissit[1.1], **blessit** /'blɪsət, 'blɛsət/ *n* an animal with a white face *la19- Sh Ork*. [compare ON *blesòttr*]
blissit[1.2], **blessit** /'blɪsət, 'blɛsət/ *adj of an animal* having a white head or a white streak down the forehead *19- Sh Ork*. [see the noun]
blist *see* BLAST[1.1]
blith *see* BLITHE[1.2]
†**blithe**[1.1], **blyth** *v* to gladden *la15*. [see the adj]
blithe[1.2], **blythe**, **blaith**, *Sh Ork* **blide**, †**blith**, †**blyth** /blæð, bleð; *Sh Ork* blʌɪd/ *adj* **1** happy, joyous; cheerful, in good spirits *la14-*. **2** kind, friendly *la14-19, 20- Sh Ork*. †**blithfull**, **blythfull** joyful, glad; pleasant *la14-16*. **blitheness**, *Sh* **blydeness**, †**blytheness**, †**blithnes**, †**blythnes** happiness, cheerfulness, gladness *la14-*. **blithesome** cheerful, merry *la17-*. **blithemeat**, *Sh Ork* **blyde-maet 1** a thanksgiving feast after the birth of a child *la17-19, 20- Sh Ork Uls*. **2** food distributed amongst family and neighbours at the time of a birth *19, 20- Sh Ork C Bor*. **blithe o**, **blithe of** happy because of, glad of *la14-*. [OE *blīðe*]
blithe[1.3] /blʌɪð/ *adv* happily, cheerfully, kindly *la18-*. [see the adj]
blitter[1.1] /'blɪtər/ *n* a thin watery mess *20-*. [ON *blautr* soft, wet]
blitter[1.2] /'blɪtər/ *v* to work in water; to splash about *20-*. [see the noun]
blitter *see* BLEATER, BLOOTER[1.2]
blivert /'blɪvərt/ *n* the bilberry *Vaccinium myrtillus 20- NE*. [altered form of BLAWORT]
blob[1.1], **blab**, **bleib** /blɔb, blab, blʌɪb/ *n* **1** a drop of moisture, a bubble; a blotch, a globule *15-*. **2** a pimple or pustule; a blister *16-*. **3** *pl* a rash, chickenpox *18-*. **4** the bag of a honey bee *19, 20- NE*. **5** a gooseberry *18-19*. [unknown]
blob[1.2], **blab**, **bleib** /blɔb, blab, blʌɪb/ *v* **1** to besmear (with dirt or moisture) *19, 20- NE*. **2** to mark or stain with ink, blot *15-19*. [unknown]
blocher[1.1], *Uls* **bloigher** /'blɔxər; *Uls* 'blɔɪxər/ *n* a loose, catarrhal cough *20- T Uls*. [see the verb]
blocher[1.2] /'blɔxər/ *v* to make a gurgling noise in coughing *19- NE T Uls*. [probably onomatopoeic]
block[1.1], †**blok** /blɔk/ *n* **1** a quantity of goods (sold together) *la15-*. **2** a large lump or chunk of wood or stone; a tree-stump *16-*. **3** a foolish or clumsy person *la16-*. **4** the base in hide-and-seek *la20-*. **5** a pulley or sheaf of pulleys *16-e17*. **block, hammer and nail** a children's game *la19, 20- NE*. [MFr *bloc*]
block[1.2], †**blok** /blɔk/ *v* **1** to hinder, impede (from progress) *15-*. **2** to sketch out, draft *la16-*. **3** to obstruct, block off; to blockade *17-*. **block the ice** *curling* to obstruct the run of the stones with guards *19-*. [MFr *bloquer*]
block[2.1], †**blok** /blɔk/ *n* **1** a bargain or agreement in buying and selling; a commercial or business transaction;

something bought or sold *16-19, 20- literary*. **2** a scheme, a plot *16*. [see the verb]

block²·², †**blok** /blɔk/ *v* **1** to bargain; to trade; to exchange (money for goods) *16-19, 20- NE*. **2** to acquire by bargaining *la16-e17*. †**blocker** a trader, a broker *e17*. **blockin ale** a drink taken (by all parties concerned) to seal a bargain *19- NE*. [extended sense of BLOCK¹·²]

block³ /blɔk/ *n* the cod *Gadus morhua 20- NE*. **blockie** a small cod *20- N NE*. [unknown]

blockan, bluchan /'blɔkən, 'blʌxən/ *n* the (young) coalfish *Pollachius virens la17- WC SW Uls*. [unknown]

blod, blöd *see* BLUID¹·¹

bloigher *see* BLOCHER¹·¹

bloit *see* BLOUT²

blok *see* BLOCK¹·¹, BLOCK¹·², BLOCK²·¹, BLOCK²·²

blome *see* BLUME¹·¹, BLUME¹·²

bloncat *see* BLANKET¹·¹, BLANKET¹·²

blondin /'blɔndən/ *n* a cableway between two towers with a skip which can carry stone in a quarry backwards and forwards or up and down *20-*. [from the name of the French tightrope walker Charles *Blondin*]

†**blonk** *n* a steed *la15-16*. [OE *blanca*]

blood *see* BLUID¹·¹, BLUID¹·²

bloody *see* BLUIDY

bloom *see* BLUME¹·¹, BLUME¹·²

blooro /'bluro/ *n* a slight quarrel, a disagreement *20- Ork*. [unknown]

blooter¹·¹, bluiter, *NE* **bleeter** /'blutər; *NE* 'blɪtər/ *n* **1** a big, clumsy or slovenly person *la16-*. **2** a foolish person; a senseless talker *la16-*. **3** a rumbling noise *19-*. **4** a wild kick or a hard thump *la19-*. **5** a badly executed or unskilful job *la20-*. [unknown]

blooter¹·², bluiter, blitter, *NE* **bleeter** /'blutər, 'blɪtər; *NE* 'blɪtər/ *v* **1** to make a rumbling noise *la18-*. **2** to work in an inefficient or messy manner *la19-*. **3** to talk foolishly, prattle *la19-*. **4** to strike hard or kick wildly *la20-*. **5** *of an animal* to defecate *la20- NE*. **blootered, blootert** extremely drunk *20-*. **blitter blatter** a rattling irregular noise *la18-*. [unknown]

blost *see* BLOUST¹·¹, BLOUST¹·²

bloster *see* BLOUSTER¹·¹, BLUSTER

blot¹ /blɔt/ *n* **1** water prepared for washing clothes or vegetables *la19- Sh Ork*. **2** *pl* dirty soapsuds *la19- Sh Ork*. [ON *blautr* soft, wet]

blot²·¹ /blɔt/ *n* a spot or stain, an ink blotch; a blemish *la16-*. †**blot-book** a blotting-block *la19*. **blot-sheet** blotting-paper *la19-*. [ME *blot*]

blot²·² /blɔt/ *v* **1** to mark or spot with ink; to stain; to stigmatize, accuse *la16-*. **2** to efface, make illegible *la17-*. [see the noun]

blotch /blɔtʃ/ *v* **1** to blot out, delete *la19- NE SW Bor*. **2** to stain or blot with ink *20- NE SW*. [EModE *blotch*]

bloust¹·¹, *N* **blost**, *SW Bor* **bluist** /blʌust; *N* blɔst; *SW Bor* blust/ *n* **1** a boast; boasting *19-*. **2** an explosion *20- N*. **3** the blast of trumpet *20- N*. [back-formation from BLOUSTER¹·¹]

bloust¹·², *N* **blost**, *SW Bor* **bluist**, †**blowst** /blʌust; *N* blɔst; *SW Bor* blust/ *v* to boast, brag *19-*. [see the noun]

blouster¹·¹, bloster, bluister /'blʌustər, 'blɔstər, 'blostər, 'blustər/ *n* **1** a boaster, a braggart *19-*. **2** a violent squally wind *la19-*. [unknown]

blouster¹·², bluister /'blʌustər, 'blustər/ *v* **1** to brag, boast *19-*. **2** *of the wind* to blow gustily and with violence *20-*. [unknown]

†**blout¹, blowt** *adj* barren, bare *e16*. [compare Du *bloot* bare and ON *blautr* soft, wet]

blout², bloit /blʌut, blɔɪt/ *n* **1** a sudden burst of wind or rain *la18-19, 20- WC SW*. **2** a sudden noisy eruption of gas or liquid; diarrhoea *19, 20- WC SW*. **3** a mess, a wet mass; dirty water *la19- Ork T EC*. **4** *derogatory* a person *la19- Ork T*. **blouter, bloiter** a blast of wind *19- NE Bor*. [perhaps ON *blautr* soft, wet or OE *blāwan* blow]

blow *see* BLAW¹·¹, BLAW¹·²

blowder /'blʌudər/ *n* a sudden gust of wind *la19- NE*. [compare BLOUT²]

blowen, blown *see* BLAWN

blowst *see* BLOUST¹·²

blowt *see* BLOUT¹

bluachie /'bluəxi/ *adj* bluish *20- NE T*. [BLUE¹·¹ + *-ach* (-OCK) + -IE¹]

blubber, blibber, †**blubbir** /'blʌbər, 'blɪbər/ *v* **1** to sob, sniffle; to make a bubbling sound *15-*. **2** to besmear, spatter *la16-19, 20- NE*. **blibberin** slobbering; making a noise when drinking soup *20- NE*. **blubber-totum** weak tea or thin gruel; a drink of oatmeal and buttermilk *20- NE*. [probably onomatopoeic]

bluchan *see* BLOCKAN

bluchtan /'bluxtən/ *n* a piece of hollow stem used as a peashooter *19- SW*. [unknown]

blud *see* BLUID¹·¹

bludder *see* BLUTHER

blude *see* BLUID¹·¹, BLUID¹·²

bluder *see* BLUTHER

bludie, bludy *see* BLUIDY

blue¹·¹, *NE* **byoo**, *C* **bew**, †**blew** /blu; *NE C* bju/ *n* **1** the colour blue; blue cloth *la15-*. **2** whisky or other spirits *la18-19*. [see the adj]

blue¹·², blew, *Sh* **blyue**, *NE* **blyew**, *NE* **byoo**, *C* **bew** /blu; *Sh NE* blju; *NE C* bju/ *adj* blue-coloured *15-*. Compare BLAE¹·². **bluebell 1** the harebell *Campanula rotundifolia la18-*. **2** the English bluebell *20-*. **blue blanket** *see* BLANKET¹·¹. **blue bonnet 1** a man's flat-topped round cap without a peak *la16-*. **2** the wearer of a blue bonnet; a Scottish soldier or Border raider *17-19, 20- historical*. **3** the cornflower *Centaurea cyanus* or knapweed *Centaurea scabiosa la18-*. **4** the bluetit *Cyanistes caeruleus 19-*. **Blue Brazil** Cowdenbeath Football Club *la20-*. **blue cap 1** *mining* the blue haze over the flame of a safety-lamp when firedamp is present in the air *la19, 20- EC*. **2** a man's broad, flat bonnet *la16-e19*. **3** a wearer of a broad, flat bonnet, a Scotsman *e19*. **blue clue, blue clew** a ball of blue wool or yarn used in divining at Halloween *la18-19, 20- NE*. **blue day 1** a very cold or frosty day *19-*. **2** a day when one is very anxious or depressed *la19-*. **3** a day on which an uproar or disturbance takes place *19- NE Bor*. **blue do** a poor performance, a failure, a black outlook *la20-*. **blue ee** a black eye *19-*. **blue gown** a (licensed) beggar, beadsman (so called because they wore blue cloaks) *la17-19, 20- historical*. **blue grass** a sedge grass, a plant of the genus *Carex 19-*. **blue grey** *of cattle* a crossbreed of a Galloway cow and a shorthorn bull *la19-*. **blue keeker** a black eye *la19-*. **blue merle** *of a collie-dog* having a marbled or blotchy coat *la19-*. **blue mogganer** a nickname for native of Peterhead (originally a Peterhead fisherman) *la19- NE*; compare MOGGAN. **blue nose 1** *derogatory* a supporter of Rangers Football Club *la20-*. **2** *derogatory* a Protestant *la20-*. **blue snaw, blue snaa** something impossible or highly unlikely *la19-*. †**blue spur hawk** the sparrowhawk *Accipiter nisus e19*; compare *spur hawk* (SPUR²). **blue threid** an indecent or smutty touch (in a story) *19-*. **Blue Toon, Blue Toun 1** a nickname for the town of Peterhead *20-*. **2** a nickname for Peterhead

Football Club *la20-*. **I've seen as licht a blue** I've seen as much *20- NE*. [ME *bleu*]

bluemelt[1.1] /ˈblumǝlt, bluˈmɛlt/ *n* a bruise *20- Sh*. [Faer *blóðmelta*, Norw *blodmelte*]

bluemelt[1.2] /ˈblumǝlt/ *v* to bruise, to strike so that coagulated blood appears under the skin *20- Sh*. **blue-meltet** bruised *20- Sh*. [Faer *blóðmelta*, Norw *blodmelta*]

blueniled, **bluenild** /bluˈnʌɪld/ *adj* musty, mildewed *20- Sh Ork*. [BLUE[1.2] + unknown second element]

bluester *see* BLUSTER

bluff[1] /blʌf/ *n* a credulous person *la18-19, 20- NE*. [unknown]

bluff[2] /blʌf/ *v* to blow (small objects) through a tube *la19, 20- NE*. [onomatopoeic]

bluffert, **bleffart**, **bliffert**, **blaffart** /ˈblʌfǝrt, ˈblɛfǝrt, ˈblɪfǝrt, ˈblafǝrt/ *n* **1** a squall (of wind and rain) *19-*. **2** a blow, slap *19- NE T*. [probably derivative of BLUFF[2]]

blugga /ˈblʌga/ *n* the marsh marigold *Caltha palustris 20- Sh*. [unknown]

bluid[1.1], **blude**, **blid**, **blood**, *Sh* **blud**, *Sh* **blöd**, *Ork* **bleud**, *N NE* **bleed**, †**blod** /blud, blɪd, blʌd; *Sh Ork* blød; *N NE* blid/ *n* **1** the red fluid that circulates in the body, blood *la14-*. **2** kinship, family, race; a blood relation *la14-*. **3** bloodshed; an assault causing bleeding *16-e18*. **4** a fine for bloodshed *e17*. †**bluid drawing** the crime of wounding (by the drawing of blood) *15-e17*. **blud fastin**, **blöd-fastin** having eaten nothing all day *la19- Sh*. **blud friend**, **blöd-freend** a blood relation *17-19, 20- Sh*. **blud kercake** a CARCAKE mixed with hog's blood, eaten on Easter Sunday *19-20, 21- historical*. **blood puddin** black pudding *18-*. †**blude roll** a roll of people accused of bloodshed *16*. **blood-run** bloodshot *18-19, 20- NE*. **bloodshed** bloodshot *la19-*. **bluidspring** in great haste; with great speed *20- Sh*. **bloodwite**, **blood-wit**, †**bloudweck 1** a fine for bloodshed; the right of imposing or collecting such a fine *15-18, 19- historical*. **2** guilt or liability for a penalty for bloodshed; an action against a person for bloodshed *la13-18*. **blude abune the breath** *folklore* to scratch or wound on the forehead (to bring bad luck) *20- Ork*. **no a blud** *fishing* not a bite *la19- Sh T EC*. [OE *blōd*]

bluid[1.2], **blude**, **blid**, **blood**, *NE* **bleed** /blud, blɪd, blʌd; *NE* blid/ *v* **1** to draw blood, cause to bleed *16-*. **2** to be bleeding; to have blood flowing *17-*. [see the noun]

bluidy, **bludie**, **bliddy**, **bloody**, *Sh Ork NE* **bleedie**, †**bludy** /ˈblude, ˈblɪde, ˈblʌde; *Sh Ork NE* ˈblidi/ *adj* **1** stained or covered with blood; bleeding *la12-*. **2** made of or containing blood *16-*. **3** bloodthirsty, brutal *la16-*. **bludie bells** the foxglove *Digitalis purpurea 19, 20- N*. **bluidy fingers** = *bludie bells la18-19, 20- WC*. **bluidy puddin**, **bloody puddin 1** black pudding *la18-*. **2** a nickname for an inhabitant of Stromness in Orkney *20- Ork N*. [OE *blōdig*]

bluist *see* BLOUST[1.1], BLOUST[1.2]

bluister *see* BLOUSTER[1.1], BLOUSTER[1.2]

bluiter /ˈblutǝr/ *n* the bittern *Botaurus stellaris 19- SW*. [probably onomatopoeic]

bluiter *see* BLOOTER[1.1], BLOOTER[1.2]

blume[1.1], **bloom**, *N NE* **bleem**, †**blome** /blum; *N NE* blim/ *n* **1** a flower, a blossom *la14-*. **2** *pl* potato tops *20- N T*. [ON *blóm*]

blume[1.2], **bloom**, *N NE* **bleem**, †**blome** /blum; *N NE* blim/ *v* to flourish or thrive; to yield blossom *la15-*. [see the noun]

blumf /blʌmf/ *n* a dull, stupid person *19-*. [unknown; compare SUMPH[1.1]]

blunderbush /ˈblʌndǝrbʌʃ/ *n* a blunderbuss *18-19, 20- NE T*. [altered form of Du *donderbus*]

blunk[1] /blʌŋk/ *n* **1** a small block (of wood or stone) *la19- NE*. **2** a dull, lifeless person *19- NE*. [unknown]

†**blunk**[2] *n* a cloth woven to be printed on *la18-19*. [perhaps shortened form of BLANKET[1.1]]

blunk[3] /blʌŋk/ *v* to spoil or mismanage *19- SW*. [unknown]

blunkart, **blunkert** /ˈblʌŋkǝrt/ *n* **1** a small block (of stone or wood) *la19- NE*. **2** a thickset or stupid person *la19- NE*. [unknown]

blunket *see* BLANKET[1.1], BLANKET[1.2]

blunochs, **blinochs** /ˈblʌnǝxs, ˈblɪnǝxs/ *npl* clothes *20- NE*. [unknown]

blunt[1.1] /blʌnt/ *n* a foolish person *19-*. [see the adj]

blunt[1.2] /blʌnt/ *adj* dull; stupid; lacking in force; not sharp *la15-*. [ME *blunt*]

bluntie[1] /ˈblʌnti/ *n* a sniveller; a foolish person *la18-19, 20- literary*. **look like bluntie** to look stupid *la18-19, 20- NE*. [BLUNT[1.1], with diminutive suffix *-ie*]

bluntie[2] /ˈblʌnti/ *n* a disappointment; a scolding *20- Sh*. [unknown]

blush, †**blusch** /blʌʃ/ *v* **1** to go red in the face *la16-*. **2** to (raise a) blister *19- Bor*. **blushing** a blister, a pustule *19- SW Uls*. [ME *blussche*]

bluster, **bloster**, **bluester** /ˈblʌstǝr, ˈblɔstǝr, ˈblustǝr/ *n* rough, mossy peat; peaty soil of a bluish colour *la19- Sh*. [unknown]

bluther, †**bludder**, †**bluder** /ˈblʌðǝr/ *v* to soil or disfigure (with tears); to be stained or disfigured (with something wet) *16-19, 20- T*. [onomatopoeic]

blyave *see* BLAW[1.1], BLAW[1.2]

blybe[1.1] /blʌɪb/ *n* a large quantity of liquid, especially of spirits *la19- NE*. [compare BLIB, BLAB[1.1]]

blybe[1.2] /blʌɪb/ *v* to drink heavily *la19- NE*. [see the noun]

blyew *see* BLUE[1.2]

blyn, **blyne** *see* BLIN[1]

†**blype** *n* a layer of skin as it peels or is rubbed off *la18-19*. [compare FLYPE[1.1]]

blyter /ˈblʌɪtǝr/ *v* to talk unceasingly and incoherently *20- NE*. [compare BLOOTER[1.2]]

blyth *see* BLITHE[1.1], BLITHE[1.2]

blythe *see* BLITHE[1.2]

blyue *see* BLUE[1.2]

bo[1], **boo**, **bu** /bo, bu/ *n* a hobgoblin *19, 20- Sh N*. **boo-man**, †**bu-man** a bogyman *19, 20- Sh NE C*. [Norw dial *bó*]

†**bo**[2] *v* to make a face *e16*. [from the interj *bo* (BOO[4])]

bo[3] /bo/ *n* a submerged rock *la19- Sh H&I*. Compare BAA[2]. [ON *boði* a wave breaking on a rock]

bo *see* BOO[2], BOO[4]

boach *see* BOCH

boadie, **boady** *see* BODY

boag *se* BOG[1.1], BOG[2]

boak[1.1], **boke**, **bock**, **bowk**, *NE* **byock**, †**bok** /bok, bɔk, bʌuk; *NE* bjɔk/ *n* **1** a belch, a retch; vomit *15-*. **2** nausea; a feeling of disgust or revulsion *20- NE*. **bochan** to vomit *20- N*. **boky** feeling sick *la20-*. **boak up**, **boke up** to vomit *20-*. **get the dry boak**, **get the dry boke** to feel disgust; to retch on an empty stomach *20-*. **gie ye the boak**, **gie ye the boke** to cause to feel sick or disgusted *20-*. [probably onomatopoeic]

boak[1.2], **boke**, **bock**, **bowk**, *NE* **byock**, *Uls* **book**, †**bok**, †**bolk** /bok, bɔk, bʌuk; *NE* bjɔk; *Uls* buk/ *v* **1** to vomit; to retch; to belch *la15-*. **2** *of fluids* to gush, spurt; *of smoke* to emit, reek *la18-19, 20- Bor*. **byochy-byochy** to retch, vomit *la19- T*. [see the noun]

boakie, **bockie** /ˈboki, ˈbɔki/ *n* a piece of hard matter in the nose *20- NE*. [altered form of Eng *bogey*]

boal *see* BOWAL[1.1]

boam, †**bolm**, †**bome** /bom/ *n* **1** a wooden framework on which yarn is hung to be shaken and dried *la19- T EC*. **2** a heavy beam or bar; a boom used to close a river or harbour *16-17*. **3** a boat- or punt-pole *e16*. [Du *boom* tree, punt-pole, boom; compare OE *bēam* tree, beam]

boannie *see* BONNY[1.1]

boar *see* BORE[2]

board *see* BOORD[1.1], BOORD[1.2]

boarder *see* BORDER

boardly *see* BUIRDLY

boar stone *see* BORE[1.1]

boart *see* BOORD[2]

boast[1.1], **bost** /bost, bɔst/ *n* **1** bragging; proud or arrogant speech *la14-*. **2** a threat, a scolding *la15-*. [ME *boost* outcry, clamour]

boast[1.2], **bost** /bost, bɔst/ *v* **1** to brag, speak arrogantly *16-*. **2** to utter threats, threaten; to scold or reprove *la15-19, 20- Sh N NE*. **boaster**, †**bostour 1** a braggart *16-*. **2** an engine of war *14-e15*. [see the noun]

boat[1.1], *N NE* **bait**, *N NE* **bate**, †**bayt**, †**bote**, †**boit** /bot; *N NE* bet/ *n* **1** a vessel for travelling on water *la14-*. **2** a ferry *la16-*. **boatic**, **bottick**, *N* **buttag** a boat-hook *20- Sh N NE*. **boatie** a ferryman *20- NE*. **boatman**, †**bateman 1** a ferryman *la14-*. **2** a coastguard *20- NE EC Bor*. **boatshiel**, †**batschele** a boatshed (for a ferry-boat) *la15-19, 20- Bor*. **boatwricht**, †**baitwrycht** a boatbuilder *16-*. [OE *bāt*]

boat[1.2] /bot/ *v* **1** to travel by boat, sail *16-*. **2** to transport by boat *16-*. †**boated men** men hired for occasional work in boats *la18*. [see the noun]

boat[2], †**bote**, †**bott** /bot/ *n* **1** a barrel or tub (used for pickling meat) *15-19, 20- T*. **2** a flat vessel for skimming the cream off milk *19, 20- NE*. **3** a cask or butt (for wine) *15-e17*. [MFr, Ital *botte*, Spanish, Port *bota*; compare *butt*]

boather *see* BATHER[1.1], BATHER[1.2]

boat hoose *see* BUY

boatil, **boattle** *see* BOTTLE[1]

boattom *see* BODDAM[1.1]

boax *see* BOX[1.1], BOX[2]

boay *see* BOY

bob[1], **bab** /bɔb, bab/ *n* **1** a cluster, a bunch; a posy or bunch of flowers, a knot of ribbons *la15-*. **2** a small luxuriant patch of grass or corn *la19- NE SW*. [unknown]

bob[2.1] /bɔb/ *n* **1** a dance *la16-*. **2** *in angling* any fly on a cast other than a tail-fly *19-*. [see the verb]

bob[2.2], **bab** /bɔb, bab/ *v* to move up and down; to dance *la16-*. †**bobber** *in angling* any fly on a cast other than a tail-fly *e19*. **bab an ee** to shut one's eyes *19-*. [perhaps onomatopoeic]

bob[3] /bɔb/ *n* **1** a target *19, 20- H&I Uls*. **2** a taunt, scoff *la18-19, 20- Sh*. [perhaps OFr *bobe* deception, mocking]

bob *see* BUB

bob-at-the-bowster *see* BAB-AT-THE-BOWSTER

bobbantilter /bɔbən'tıltər/ *n* something dangling; an icicle *20- N*. [probably BOB[2.2] + TILT to tip up]

bobbie, *N* **bubba** /'bɔbi; *N* 'bʌbə/ *n* **1** a grandfather *la18- N NE*. **2** the Devil *20- N*. **auld Bobbie** the Devil *la18-19, 20- NE*. [compare PAWPIE, Ger *Bub* boy]

bobbin john, **bobbing john** /'bɔbın dʒɔn, 'bɔbıŋ dʒɔn/ *n* **1** a hand-sower used for turnip-seed, consisting of a metal box with holes attached to a long wooden handle *la18- NE*. **2** a nickname for John Erskine, the Earl of Mar (1675-1732), who frequently changed sides politically *e18, la19- historical*. [BOB[2.2] with *-ing* + the personal name *John*]

bobbinquaw, **babbinqua** /'bɔbınkwɔ, 'babınkwa/ *n* a quaking bog, a quagmire *19, 20- NE Bor*. [BOB[2.2] with *-ing* + QUAW]

bobbity bowster *see* BAB-AT-THE-BOWSTER

boch, **boach** /box/ *n* **1** a child's toy, a knick-knack *20- N*. **2** an untidy or disagreeable person *20- N*. [unknown]

bocht *see* BUY

bock *see* BOAK[1.1], BOAK[1.2]

bockan *see* BAWCAN

bockie *see* BOAKIE, BOKY

bod[1] /bɔd/ *n* a (small) person *la18-*. [perhaps shortened form of Gael *bodach*]

bod[2], *N* **bowd** /bɔd; *N* bʌud/ *n* a wave, a breaker; ground-swell on a sunken rock *la19- Sh Ork N*. [ON *boði*]

bod *see* BODE[1.1], BODE[1.2]

böd, **büid** /bød, bud/ *n* a booth or shed, a fisherman's hut *la19- Sh*. [perhaps altered form of BUITH or ON *búð*]

bodach, **boddach**, †**boddoch** /'bɔdəx/ *n* **1** an old man *la19-*. **2** a small or insignificant person *la19-*. **3** a spectre, a malevolent spirit *19, 20- literary*. **4** a cormorant *Phalacrocorax carbo 20- N NE*. **5** a mutchkin *e17*. **bodach-back** a wedge-shaped peat which has to be removed from a fresh peat-bank to make room for a peat-cutting implement *20- N*. [Gael *bodach* an old man; a bad-tempered old man; a MUTCHKIN]

†**boday** *n* bow-dye, a scarlet dye *la17*. [from the Essex place-name *Bow* + Scots *dye*]

bodda *see* BUDDO

boddach *see* BODACH

boddam[1.1], **boddom**, **boattom**, **bottom**, *Sh Ork NE* **botham**, *SW* **buddom** /'bɔdəm, 'bodəm, 'botəm, 'bɔtəm; *Sh Ork NE* 'bɔθəm; *SW* 'bʌdəm/ *n* **1** the lowest part or underside of anything *15-*. **2** the bottom of a slope; low-lying ground, a valley; frequently in place-names *16-*. **3** the fundament, the buttocks *la17-*. **4** a thorough cleaning *la20-*. **5** the hold or hull of a ship *16-17*. **bottomer** *mining* the person who loads and unloads the cages at the bottom or intermediate landings in a shaft *19, 20- T C*. **boddom breadth** = *bottom room la19- NE T*. **bottom room** the amount of space necessary for a person to sit, especially in a church pew *19-*. [OE *botm*]

boddam[1.2], **boddom**, **bottom**, *NE* **bothom** /'bɔdəm, 'bodəm, 'bɔtəm; *NE* 'bɔθəm/ *v* **1** to provide with a (new) bottom *la16-*. **2** to touch the bottom of the sea *20- Sh*. **3** to comprehend, understand *20- NE*. [see the noun]

bodder *see* BATHER[1.2]

böddie *see* BUDDIE

boddin *see* BODEN

boddle *see* BOTTLE[1], BODLE

boddoch *see* BODACH

boddom *see* BODDAM[1.1], BODDAM[1.2]

boddy *see* BODY

bode[1.1], **bod** /bod, bɔd/ *n* **1** an offer, a bid (at auction) *la15-*. **2** the price asked by a seller; the offer of goods at a certain rate *19, 20- NE T EC*. **3** an invitation (to a wedding) *19, 20- Sh*. **bod penny** the sum fixed (in advance) to be the regular increase between bids at an auction *18-19, 20- NE*. **bodword**, †**boydword**, †**bodwart** an invitation; a message, an announcement, a report *la14-19, 20- NE*. [OE *bod*, from ptp stem of *bēodan* to offer]

bode[1.2], **bod** /bod, bɔd/ *v* **1** to bid for; to aim at *la16-*. **2** to expect; to desire *18-*. **3** to offer with insistence, press on someone *19-*. [see the noun]

bode *see* BEHOVE, BIDE[1.2]

bodefu, **bodeful** /'bodfu, 'bodful/ *adj* ominous *19- literary*. [BODE[1.1], with noun-forming suffix *-ful*]

bodely *see* BODILY[1.1], BODILY[1.2]

bodement /'bodmənt/ *n* foreboding *19, 20- NE Bor*. [perhaps OE *bodian*, with noun-forming suffix *-ment*]

boden, †**bodin**, †**boddin**, †**bowden** /'bodən, 'bɔdən/ *adj* **1** provided, prepared; fitted out, dressed *15-19, 20- Ork NE*. **2** furnished with arms; equipped for fighting *la14-e19*. **weel**

boden well equipped or provided *15-19*, *20- Sh*. **weel-boddened** = *weel boden la18-19*, *20- Ork*. [OE *boden*, ptp of *bēodan* announce and ON *boðinn* prepared for service]

bodie see BODY

bodilik see BODYLIKE

bodily[1.1], †**bodely**, †**bodyly** /ˈbɔdəli/ *adj* **1** of the body, physical, corporeal *la14-*. **2** as a whole, entirely *19-*. †**bodily athe**, **bodely aith** a corporal oath, ratified by touching a sacred object *la14-e17*. [BODY, with adj-forming suffix]

bodily[1.2], †**bodely**, †**bodyly** /ˈbɔdəli/ *adv* **1** in person, in the flesh *la14-*. **2** by an oath ratified by touching a sacred object *la14-16*. [see the adj]

bodle, **boddle** /ˈbɔdəl/ *n* **1** a small copper coin worth two pence Scots, a TURNER *la17-19*, *20- historical*. **2** something of little value *la18-*. **bodle preen**, †**boddle prin** a large safety-pin (originally costing a bodle) *19*, *20- NE Bor*. **no care a boddle** see CARE[1.2]. [unknown]

bodsy, **bodsie** /ˈbɔdzi/ *n* a little, dapper, or neat person *la18- NE*. [derivative of BOD]

bodword, †**bodwart** /ˈbɔdwərd/ *n* **1** a message, an announcement, a report; an invitation *la14-19*, *20- NE*. **2** a warning, a forewarning *19*. [ME *bodeworde*]

body, **bodie**, **boddy**, **boady**, **boadie**, **buddy**, **buddie**, *Ork* **bothy**, †**bothie** /ˈbɔdi*,* ˈbɑde, ˈbɔdi, ˈbode, ˈbʌdi, ˈbʌde; *Ork* ˈbɔθi/ *n* **1** the physical form of a person or animal *la14-*. **2** a carcass, a corpse *la14-*. **3** a person, a human being; oneself *la14-*. **4** the main portion of something; the substance of something *15-*. **5** a number of people, a crowd *16-*. **6** a small, sickly or pathetic person *la18-*. **7** a great quantity of something, a mass; a great number of fish *la18-*. **a'body's body** everybody's favourite; a person who tries to be all things to all people *19-*. **a bodie's sel** oneself *19-* **the Buddies 1** the inhabitants of Paisley *la19-*. **2** the supporters of St Mirren Football Club *la19-*. Compare PAISLEY BUDDY. **nae ither body** no one else *la18-*. [OE *bodig*]

†**bodylike**, **bodylyke**, **bodilik** *adv* alive, in the flesh *la14-18*. [BODY, with adv-forming suffix -*like*]

bodyly see BODILY[1.1], BODILY[1.2]

bog[1.1], **boag**, †**boig** /bɔg, bog/ *n* a piece of wet, spongy ground, a morass, a mire *13-*. **bog-bleater** the bittern *Botaurus stellaris 19-*. **bog-cotton** cotton-grass *19-*. **bog-hay** hay gathered from uncultivated or marshy ground *la18-*. **bog hyacinth** the wild orchid *Orchis mascula la19-*. **bog-stalker**, †**bog-staker** an idle, bashful man *18-*. **bog-thistle** the thistle *Cirsium palustre la19-*. [Gael, IrGael *bogach*]

bog[1.2] /bɔg/ *v* **1** to sink into a bog, become sunk and entangled *19-*. **2** to work in wet, dirty surroundings; to work slowly *19- N NE Uls*. **3** *of liquid* to flow or spurt out *20- Sh NE*. **4** *of wet shoes* to make a squelching sound *20- Sh NE*. **5** *of shoemakers* to work in a customer's house at a daily rate *la19*. [see the noun]

bog[2], **boag** /bɔg, bog/ *n* an insect; a bed bug *Cimex lectularius*; a louse *Phthiraptera la19-* [altered form of Eng *bug*]

bogan see BUGGIN

bogel see BUGGLE

bogentully /ˈbogəntʌli/ *n* a heavy boot *20- NE*. [unknown]

boggar see BOUGAR

boggin, **bogging** /ˈbɔgɪn, ˈbɔgɪŋ/ *adj* dirty, disgusting, smelly *la20-*. [unknown]

boggle /ˈbɔgəl/ *v of the eyes* to protrude, bulge (with fear or pain) *20-*. [probably related to BOGLE[1.2]]

boggle see BOGLE[1.1]

bogie, **bogey** /ˈbogi/ *n* a hobgoblin, a bugbear *la19-*. **the game's a bogie** a call to cancel a game (and start again) when there has been a fault *20-*. [unknown]

bogie see BUGGIE

bogie roll, **bogie rowe** /ˈbogi rol, ˈbogi rʌu/ *n* a coarse black tobacco of a medium twist *19-*. [named from the river Bogie, near which it was first manufactured + ROW[1.1]]

bogle[1.1], †**boggle**, †**bogill** /ˈbogəl/ *n* **1** a ghost or spectre, a hobgoblin; a terrifying sight *16-*. **2** a scarecrow; an untidy person *la19-*. **bogly**, †**bogilly** haunted (by bogles) *19*, *20- NE*. **bogle-bo** a hobgoblin, spectre *17-19*, *20- literary*. **bogle about the stacks** a kind of hide-and-seek *19*, *20- Bor*. [unknown]

bogle[1.2] /ˈbogəl/ *v* **1** to start with fright; to take alarm; to terrify or bewitch *17-*. **2** to hesitate, demur; to quibble or equivocate *17-*. **3** to wander about aimlessly; to waste time; *of an animal* to sniff around *20-*. [unknown]

bogle[2] /ˈbogəl/ *v* to shout, bellow *la19- Ork*. [perhaps development from BOGLE[1.1] or perhaps altered from Eng *bugle*]

boglo /ˈboglo/ *n* the outside peat on a peat-bank *20- Ork*. [compare Norw dial *boke* something that is dug up]

bogshaivelt, **buckshaivelt**, **bogshammelt**, **bumshayvelt** /bɔgˈʃevəlt, bʌkˈʃevəlt, bɔgˈʃaməlt, bʌmˈʃevəlt/ *adj* knocked out of shape, distorted *20- NE*. [OE *būgan* to bend + ptp of SHEVEL[1.2]]

bogwar see BOUGWAAR

bogy see BUGGIE

boich, **byoch**, **beoch** /bɔɪx, bjɔx/ *v* to cough with difficulty; to cough up phlegm *19*, *20- NE*. [onomatopoeic]

boick see BYKE[1.1]

boig see BOG[1.1]

†**boikin**, **boitkin** *n* a bodkin, a dagger *16-19*. [ME *bodkin*]

boil see BILE[1.1], BILE[1.2]

boilyiemint see BULIMENT

boir see BAIR

boist see BUIST[1]

boit see BOAT[1.1]

boitkin see BOIKIN

bok, **boke** see BOAK[1.1], BOAK[1.2]

boky, **bokie**, *Ork* **bockie** /ˈboki; *Ork* ˈbɔki/ *n* **1** a hobgoblin; a supernatural being *19- Sh Ork N NE*. **2** a scarecrow; a badly-dressed person *19- Sh Ork N NE*. [probably ON *bokki* a he-goat; a fellow, with influence from *bogey*]

böl[1.1], **beul**, **beuld**, †**bull**, †**buill** /bøl, bøld/ *n* a sheepfold, a byre; a resting-place for animals, a stall in a stable; a person's bed *la18- Sh Ork*. [ON *ból* a lair, a bed, a farm]

böl[1.2], **bøl**, **beul**, **beuld**, †**bool**, †**bule** /bøl, bøld/ *v* **1** to drive livestock to a resting place *la18- Sh Ork*. **2** *of animals* to rest in a fold or shelter; *of people* to shelter or hide *20- Sh Ork*. [see the noun]

boldin see BOWDEN[1.1], BOWDEN[1.2]

bole see BOWAL[1.1], BULL[1]

bolk see BOAK[1.1]

boll, **bow** /bɔl, bʌu/ *n* **1** a dry measure of weight or capacity varying according to commodity and locality, but frequently equivalent to 6 imperial bushels *la14-*. **2** payment in food to a farmworker *la18-*. **3** a valuation of land according to the quantity of bolls it produced *18-e19*. †**bollman** in Orkney a cottager *la18-19*. [OE *bolla* or ON *bolli* a bowl, a small vessel]

boll see BOW[2], BOW[3], BULL[3]

bölliment see BULIMENT

bollok see BALLOCK

bolm see BOAM

bolne see BOWDEN[1.1]

bolster see BOWSTER

bolt see BOWT[1.1], BOWT[1.2]

boltastane, **boltisten** /ˈbɔltəsten, ˈbɔltɪsten/ *n fishing* a heavy stone attached to buoy-ropes for sinking long lines *la19- Sh*. [compare BALLISTEN]

bomb, *Sh NE* **boomb** /bɔm; *Sh NE* bum/ *n* **1** an explosive projectile *18-*. **2** a puff or belch of smoke; a blow-down in a chimney *la20- N T H&I*. [Fr *bombe*]

bombaise *see* BUMBAZE

†**bombasie, bumbasy** *n* bombasine cloth *16-17*. [MFr *bombasin*]

bome *see* BOAM

bomer *see* BUMMER

bommi *see* BUMMIE[2]

bon, bone /bɔn, bon/ *n* humour, mood *20- NE T*. [compare Norw dial *bunsa* to burst out, rush violently on]

Bonaccord /bɔnə'kɔrd/ *n* **1** the motto of the city of Aberdeen *19-*. **2** a nickname for the city of Aberdeen *19-*. **3** concord; friendly agreement; good fellowship *17-19, 20- historical*. **4** an Aberdeen toast *17*. **Abbot of Bonaccord** a citizen elected annually by the town council of Aberdeen to organize public sports and entertainments and act as master of the revels *15-16, 19- historical*. **Lords of Bonaccord** a name for the *Abbot of Bonaccord* and the *Prior of Bonaccord 16, 19- historical*. **Prior of Bonaccord** a citizen elected annually by the town council of Aberdeen to assist the *Abbot of Bonaccord* in the organization of public entertainments *15-16, la19- historical*. [OFr *bone acorde* good accord, harmony]

bonage *see* BONDAGE

bonailie, bonalie, †**bonallay** /bɔn'eli, bɔn'ale/ *n* a drink with or toast to a departing friend; a farewell gathering *la15-19, 20- literary*. [MFr *bon* good + MFr *aller* going]

bonat *see* BUNNET[1.1]

bonce *see* BOONCE[1.1], BOONCE[1.2]

bond[1], **bund, bund**/ *n* **1** a peasant farmer *18- Sh*. **2** a peasant or serf, a bondman *15-16*. [OE *bōnda*, ON *bóndi*]

bond[2] /bɔnd/ *n* **1** an agreement, a covenant *la15-*. **2** a binding or fastening *la17-*. **3** *law* a mortgage *la17-*. **bond and disposition in security** a form of heritable security consisting of obligation to pay debt and security as well as DISPOSITION of the property *19-*. **bond of manrent** a firm contract between two people; originally a contract agreed between a free man and his feudal superior *16-*. [compare BAND[1.1]]

bond *see* BOUN[2.1]

bondage, bonnage, bunnage, †**bundage,** †**bannage,** †**bonage** /'bɔndədʒ, 'bɔnədʒ, 'bʌnədʒ/ *n* **1** servitude, serfdom *15-*. **2** service due from a farmworker to a farmer, or from a farm-tenant to the proprietor *la15-e20, la20- historical*. **bondager** a female field-worker supplied by a farm-tenant in accordance with the conditions of his tenancy (in addition to his wife) *19-e20, la20- historical*. [ME *bondage*]

bonday wark *see* BONE[2]

†**bondelesoure, bonelesew** *n* pasturage connected with service rendered as a tenant; bond-service or boon-service *la15*. [BOND + LIZOUR[1.1]]

bone[1] /bon/ *v* to pester someone for money owed *la19- NE T WC*. [probably an extension of Eng *bone* to remove bones from]

†**bone**[2], **boyn** *n* a boon, a prayer; the thing prayed for *la14-16*. **bonday wark** work done without payment as part of tenant service *la16-e17*. **bon ploughs, bondpluys, bone plews** the ploughs used in unpaid tenant service; the ploughing service itself *la15-e18*. **boneservice** = *bonday wark la16*. **boyne silver** money paid in lieu of service *e16*. [ON *bón*]

bone *see* BANE, BON

bonefire *see* BANEFIRE

bonegrace *see* BONGRACE

bonelesew *see* BONDELESOURE

bonespell *see* BONSPIEL

bonet *see* BUNNET[1.1]

†**bonevale** *n* a farewell toast or gathering *e17*. [conflation of BONAILIE with Lat *valē* farewell]

boney, bonnie /'boni, 'bɔni/ *n* a bonfire *la20- T C*. [shortened form of BANEFIRE, with diminuitive suffix *-ie*]

bonfrost /bɔn'frɔst/ *n* a very severe frost *20- Sh*. [perhaps ON *botn* bottom + *frjósa* frost; compare Norw *botnfrjosa* to freeze to the bottom]

†**bongall** *n* silk material imported from Bengal (used as a neck-covering) *e18*. [from the Indian place-name]

bongrace, †**bonegrace** /bɔn'gres/ *n* **1** a coarse straw hat (worn by country-women) *la18-19, 20- Bor*. **2** a shade attached to a woman's bonnet *16-18*. [Fr *bonne-grâce* coarse cloth used for covering clothes]

bonhoga, bonnhoga /bɔn'hoga/ *n* a place of one's childhood; a former haunt *la19- Sh*. [Shetland dial *bonn* a child + HOGA]

bonhus, bønhus /bɔn'hus, bøn'hus/ *n fisherman's taboo* a church *la19- Sh Ork*. [ON *bón* request, petition + *hús* house]

bonie-words, bonnie wirds /boni 'wʌrdz, bɔni 'wɪrdz/ *npl* bedtime prayers *20- Ork*. [BONNY[1.1] + WORD, with plural suffix *-s*]

bonkard, bonker *see* BUNKER

bonn *see* BANE

bonnage *see* BONDAGE

bonnet *see* BUNNET[1.1], BUNNET[1.2]

bonnhoga *see* BONHOGA

bonnie *see* BONNY[1.1], BONNY[1.2]

bonnie wirds *see* BONIE-WORDS

bonnilie *see* BONNY[1.1]

bonnock *see* BANNOCK

bonny[1.1], **bonnie, boannie,** †**bony** /'boni, 'bɔne, 'bone/ *adj* **1** beautiful, pretty *la15-*. **2** good, excellent, fine *la15-*. **3** beloved, dear: ⋄*my bonnie bairn 16-*. **4** *of boys or men* handsome, attractive *la16-*. **5** great, considerable, substantial *la16-*. **6** *of a space of time* short *la15-e17*. **bonnily, bonnilie 1** beautifully, finely *la16-*. **2** well, satisfactorily *la16-*. **bonnieness, bonniness** beauty, handsomeness *la18-*. **bonnie die, bonny die** a trinket, a toy *19, 20- literary*. †**bonnie wallie, bonny wallie** = *bonnie die 18-e19*. **a bonny fechter** an intrepid person; a zealot *la19-*. **a bonny penny, a bonnie penny** a considerable sum *la19-*. **nae bonnie, no bonnie** unattractive *la20-*. [unknown]

bonny[1.2], **bonnie** /'boni, 'bone/ *adv* **1** in an attractive or fine way, well *19-*. **2** very, extremely, exceedingly *la19-*. **bonny and** extremely: ⋄*he was bonny and angry about it la19-*. [unknown]

Bonny Sunday *see* BENNA SUNDAY

bonspiel, bonspeil, †**bonspell,** †**bonespell,** †**bonspale** /'bɔnspil/ *n* **1** a grand or significant curling match played between two distinct clubs or districts (played outdoors on a frozen body of water) *la18-*. **2** a match or contest *la16-*. [perhaps Du **bond spel*]

bontath, bonteth *see* BOUNTITH

bontie *see* BOUNTY

bonxie /'bɔŋksi/ *n* the great skua *Catharacta skua la18- Sh Ork NE H&I SW*. [ON *bunki* a heap, pile; compare Norw *bunke* a heap, a corpulent woman, hence any dumpy body]

bony *see* BONNY[1.1]

boo[1.1], **bow** /bu, bʌu/ *n* an inclination of the body (in greeting) *19-*. [see the verb]

boo[1.2], **bow** /bu, bʌu/ *v* **1** to incline the body (in respect to another); to submit or defer to (someone) *la14-*. **2** to bend, curve; to become bent or crooked; to bend over or curl up *la14-*. **booed, bowit** bent, curved; crooked *16-*. **bowed rig** a strip of land on a hillside ploughed in winding curves to prevent erosion *la19- WC*. **no boo an ee** to not close one's eyes, fail to sleep *19-*. [OE *būgan*]

boo², **bo** /bu, bo/ *n* a louse *la19- N*. [Fr *pou*]

boo³ /bu/ *v* to speak loudly, monotonously and to little purpose *la19- NE T EC*. [onomatopoeic]

boo⁴, †**bo** /bu/ *interj* a noise indicating disapproval *17-*. **boo to yer blanket** a term of reproach or condemnation *17-*. [imitative]

boo⁵, **bu** /bu/ *n* a spell of (good or bad) weather *la19- Sh*. [unknown]

boo⁶, **bu**, †**bow** /bu/ *n* a homestead, a farmhouse; a large undivided farm; a hamlet *16-19, 20- Ork*. Compare BULL³. [ON *bú*]

boo *see* BO¹, BOW¹, BOW³

booce *see* BOOSE²·²

booch *see* BOUCH¹·²

boodie /'budi/ *n* 1 a ghost, a hobgoblin *19- NE*. 2 a scarecrow *19- NE*. **tattie boodie** *see* TATTIE. [probably Gael *bodach*, as in *bodach ròcais* a scarecrow, with influence from BO¹]

boof *see* BUFF²·¹, BUFF²·², BOUFF¹·¹

boofel, **buffle** /'bufəl/ *v* to pummel; to beat with repeated blows *20- Sh*. [frequentative form of BUFF²·²]

booil /'buəl/ *v of an animal* to gore; to push with the head or horns *20- Sh*. [variant of *bowel*]

book *see* BOAK¹·², BOUK¹, BOUK², BUIK¹·¹, BUIK¹·²

booking *see* BUIKIN

bookit *see* BOOKIT

booklag, **boucklag**, **bucklag** /'buklag, 'bʌklag/ *n* 1 a big stone *20- N*. 2 a field border *20- N*. [unknown]

bool¹, †**boull**, †**boule** /bul/ *n* 1 the ball used in the game of bowls *la15-*. 2 a ball or rounded object; a stone ball (used in games); a cannon ball *16-*. 3 a marble *19-*. 4 a round sweet *20-*. 5 a small potato *la20-*. **booler** a bowler *la19-*. **bools 1** the game of bowls *la15-*. 2 the game of marbles *19-*. †**boull maill** rent or hire of a bowling green *la17-e18*. **the boolie rows fine** things are going well *20- NE*. **the bools row smooth** things are going well *la19-*. **hae a bool in yer mou** to speak in an affected way; to have an over-refined accent *la20-*. [ME *boule*]

bool², **boul**, †**boull** /bul/ *n* 1 the handle of a pot or bucket; a curved or semi-circular band *la15-*. 2 the ring of a key *la16-19*. 3 the ring joining the blades of a pair of shears; the finger and thumb holes in scissors *la16-19*. **bool back-it** hump-backed; round-shouldered *19, 20- NE*. **bool fit** a club foot *la19- NE T EC*. **boul horned 1** perverse, obstinate *la18-19, 20- literary*. 2 having curved or twisted horns *18*. [MDu *boghel*]

bool³ /bul/ *n* a term of contempt for a man *la18-19, 20- NE*. [unknown]

†**bool⁴** *v in the Borders* to weep or sing with a long-drawn-out mournful sound *e19*. [compare OE *bellan* to roar, ON *baula* to low like a cow]

bool⁵ /bul/ *v of fish* to play on the surface of the water *la19- Sh Ork*. [compare Icel *bulla* to bubble, boil]

bool *see* BEULD¹·², BÖL¹·²

boold, **beuld** /buld, bøld/ *n* the festivities held by people at night during the big markets (when there was no proper accommodation available) *20- Ork*. [compare BEULD¹·¹]

boolder /'buldər/ *n* a boulder *la19-*. Compare BOWDER². [EModE *boulder*]

bool-hive *see* BOWEL HIVE

boolik, **bulek** /'bulək/ *n* a pimple, a blister *la19- Sh*. [ON *bóla* a blain, with diminutive suffix *-ock*]

boolsie /'bulzi/ *n* a three-legged pot (supported by iron grips from a fire-crane) *20- N*. [BOOL², with diminuitive suffix *-ie*]

boomb *see* BOMB

boon¹, **bune**, *NE* **been** /bun; *NE* bin/ *prep* above *la18-*. [aphetic form of ABUNE¹·²]

boon² /bun/ *n* a band of reapers, shearers or turf-cutters *la18-19, 20- Uls*. [ON *bón* a request, a petition]

boon *see* BOUN¹·², BOUN²·¹

boonce¹·¹, **bunce**, **bounce**, *Bor* **bonce** /buns, bʌns, bʌuns; *Bor* bɒns/ *n* a rebound, a bounce; a knock *18-*. **bounce game** *in sports* a friendly or non-competition game *20-*. [see the verb]

boonce¹·², **bunce**, **bounce**, *Bor* **bonce** /buns, bʌns, bʌuns; *Bor* bɒns/ *v* 1 to rebound; to bounce *18-*. 2 *in sport* to challenge to a friendly game *la20-*. [ME *bunsen*, *bounse*]

boonie¹·¹, **boona** /'buni, 'bunə/ *n* 1 a harness; a piece of equipment or clothing *19- Ork*. 2 a state of readiness or preparation; good order, good spirits *19- Ork*. [ON *búningr*]

boonie¹·² /'buni/ *v* 1 to prepare or equip (oneself); to dress and tidy oneself *la19- Ork*. 2 to castrate a farm animal *20- Ork*. [see the noun]

boonmost, **beenmost** /'bunmost, 'binmost/ *adj* uppermost *la18-19, 20- NE*. [contracted form of OE *bufan* + superlative suffix *-most*]

boonspal, **bonspell** /'bunspal, 'bɒnspɛl/ *n* a rush, a leap, a bound *la19- Sh Ork*. [perhaps Orkney dial or Shetland dial *boon* a bound + Shetland dial *spjal* to sprawl]

boonta *see* BOUNTY

boonyach /'bunjəx/ *n* diarrhoea *la20- H&I*. [Gael *buinneach*]

boor, **bower**, †**bour**, †**bowr** /bur, bʌur/ *n* 1 an inner or private chamber; a lady's private apartment *la14-*. 2 a shady spot (arched with foliage) *la15-*. 3 a lodging-place, an inn; a rustic cottage, a rural abode *18-19, 20- Sh*. [OE *būr*]

boorach¹·¹, **bourach**, **bourock** /'burəx, 'burək/ *n* 1 a crowd, a group, a cluster *18-*. 2 a (disorderly) heap or mass *la19-*. 3 a muddle, a mess, a state of confusion; a fuss *20-*. 4 a small, humble house *la18-19, 20- T*. 5 a mound, a knoll *19, 20- T*. [probably Gael *bùrach* a mess, a shambles]

boorach¹·², **bourach**, *EC* **boorock** /'burəx; *EC* 'burək/ *v* 1 to burrow in the soil (in search of something); to poke around, hunt about *20-*. 2 to heap up; to mass profusely *20-*. 3 to crowd together; to cluster *la18-19, 20- NE*. [see the noun]

boorag /'burəg/ *n* a rough piece of turf used as a peat, or for thatching houses *la19- N*. **Boorag-town** a nickname for a part of Thurso *20- N*. [compare Gael *bùrach* digging]

booray *see* BEERIE

boord¹·¹, **buird**, **board**, *NE* **beward**, †**burd** /burd, bord; *NE* 'buərd/ *n* 1 a plank, a panel; a notice-board *la14-*. 2 a table (spread for a meal) *la14-*. 3 food and accommodation supplied in a person's house *la15-*. 4 a council, a committee *18-*. 5 a board for laying out a corpse; a bier *la19- Sh NE*. 6 *fishing* the net closest to the side of the boat *20- N*. 7 *nautical* a course or tack *16-e17*. †**buird bed** boards used as a bed *la16*. **buird-claith**, †**burdclath** a tablecloth *la15-*. †**board-heid**, **buird-heid** the head of a table *la16-19*. **bed buirds**, **bed boards** boards forming the bottom layer of a bed *19-*. [OE *bord*; compare BROD²·¹, BRED¹·¹]

boord¹·², **buird**, **board**, †**burd** /burd, bord/ *v* 1 to fit or cover with boards *la16-*. 2 to go on board (a vessel) *la16-*. 3 to furnish with board and lodging *la16-*. [see the noun]

boord², **boart**, **bort**, †**burd** /burd, bort, bɔrt/ *v* 1 to split stratified stone *19, 20- N*. 2 *of a bed of rock or stone* to split; to separate into layers or strata *20- Ork*. [probably extended sense of ME *bord* plank]

boorik /'burək/ *n fisherman's taboo* a cow *19- Sh*. [Norw *bure* to bellow]

boorlaw *see* BIRLEY

boorly *see* BUIRDLY

boorock *see* BOORACH[1.2]

boos *see* BOOSE[2.1]

†**boosach** *adj in Argyllshire* sulky, blubber-lipped *19*. [Gael *busach*]

boosam *see* BOWSOME

boose[1.1], **bease**, **biss** /buz, biz, bɪs/ *n* a stall for a horse or cow *la18- H&I C SW Uls*. [OE **bōs*; compare ON *báss*]

boose[1.2], **buiss** /buz, bus/ *v* to enclose cattle in a stall *19-*. **beasing**, **bissing** a partition between cattle in a byre *20- H&I*. **buisin stane** the wall between stalls *18- H&I WC SW*. **buiss up**, **beuse up** a command to a cow to take its place in a stall *19- WC SW*. [see the noun]

boose[2.1], **boos** /bus/ *n* excessive haste, a rush; turmoil *la19- Sh*. [see the verb]

boose[2.2], **booce** /bus/ *v* to bustle, rush about; to work energetically *la19- Sh Ork NE*. **boocin**, **busen** energetic, bustling *la19- Sh*. [compare Norw *buse*, Swed *busa* to dash, bound]

boose[3.1], *N NE* **buss**, *H&I* **bush** /bus; *N NE* bʌs; *H&I* buʃ/ *n* 1 a mouth; an animal's snout *la19- N H&I*. 2 a pout, a sulky, bad-tempered expression *20- N NE H&I WC*; compare PUS. **have a bus on** to pout, look sulky *20- N H&I*. [Gael *bus* a mouth, especially that of an animal or one with protruding lips]

boose[3.2] /bus/ *v* to pout, sulk *la19- H&I WC*. [see the noun]

boosome *see* BESOM

boost /bust/ *v* to drive off or away; to cause to move *la19- WC SW Bor*. [compare BOAST[1.2]]

booster *see* BOWSTER

boot *see* BOUT[2], BOWT[1.1], BUIT[1.1], BUIT[1.2]

bootch[1.1], *T* **boutch** /butʃ; *T* bʌutʃ/ *n* a botch, a bungle, a muddle *la19-*. [see the verb]

bootch[1.2], *T EC* **boutch** /butʃ; *T EC* bʌutʃ/ *v* to botch, bungle or muddle *la19-*. [perhaps MDu *butsen* strike, patch up]

booth *see* BUITH

bootie /ˈbuti/ *n* a piece of cloth used (by women) as a headwrap *19- Ork N*. [ON *bót* a remedy, a patch]

†**bootyer** *n* a glutton *e19*. [unknown]

booyangs /ˈbujaŋz/ *npl* straps buckled over the trousers below the knees; compare NICKIE-TAMS *20-*. [unknown]

boozy *see* BOWSIE[3]

borag /ˈborəg/ *n* a bradawl *20- N*. [probably BORE[1.1], with diminuitive suffix *-ag*]

boral *see* BORE[1.2]

borch, **borcht** *see* BORROW[1.1]

bord /bɔrd, bord/ *n* 1 an edging or border on a garment or hat; a hem, a frill *la16-19, 20- NE SW*. 2 a ridge or rim of a hill *15-e17*. [OE *borda*, OFr *bord*]

†**bordel**, **bordale** *n* a brothel *la14-e19*. **bordeller** a keeper or frequenter of brothels *la14-e19*. [ME *bordel*]

bordel house, †**bordale hous** /ˈbɔrdəl hʌus/ *n* a brothel *15-19, 20- NE Bor*. [BORDEL + HOOSE[1.1]]

border, **boarder**, †**bordour**, †**bordwr** /ˈbɔrdər, ˈbordər/ *n* 1 a frontier, a boundary *15-*. 2 an edge; an edging *la15-*. 3 one's furthermost limit *la18-19, 20- NE T*. **Borderer**, †**Bordourar** a dweller in *the Borders* or on the border between Scotland and England *15-*. **Border man** a man dwelling in *the Borders* or on the border between Scotland and England *la16-*. **Border Marriage** an irregular marriage performed at Gretna (usually for runaway couples from England) *la19, 20- historical*. **the Borders** the area of southern Scotland adjacent to the border with England *la15-*. **Borders Region** a region formed from the former counties of Peebles, Berwick, Roxburgh and Selkirk and part of the former county of Midlothian *la20-*. [ME *bordure*]

bördly *see* BUIRDLY

bore[1.1] /bor/ *n* 1 a hole (made by boring); a natural hole (in a stone); a crevice (used as a shelter or hiding-place) *la15-*. 2 *curling* a passage between two guards *la18-*. 3 an opening in the clouds showing blue sky *17-19, 20- NE*. 4 a hole in a sequence, the space between holes (on a belt or the yarn beam of a loom) *la18-19, 20- NE*. 5 the opening in a cow's teat *20- Sh*. **borie** 1 a clear opening in the sky during wet weather *la19- NE*. 2 a clearing, a passage *20- NE*. **blue bore** an opening in the clouds showing blue sky *17-19, 20- NE*. **borestaff** the part of a loom which maintains tension on the warp *19, 20- historical*. **bore stone**, **boar stone**, **boar stane** 1 a stone bored to hold a flagstaff *la18- historical*. 2 a boundary stone; frequently in place-names *la19-*. **neist bore tae butter** the next best thing *20- NE*. **tak in a bore** to turn over a new leaf *19- NE*. [see the verb; compare also ON *bora* a hole]

bore[1.2] /bor/ *v* 1 to drill, make a hole; to pierce (by boring) *la15-*. 2 to press against, crash into *la19-*. **boral**, †**borell** a boring tool, an auger *la15-19, 20- Sh Bor*. **bore at** to study deeply or intently *20-*. **bore in** = *bore at la19-*. [OE *borian*]

bore[2], **boar** /bor/ *n* a large wave breaking on the beach (amid smaller ones); a tidal race *20- Ork N*. **borek** a short breaking wave *la19- Sh*. [perhaps ON *bára*]

bore *see* BAIR, BEAR[2]

bore breiff *see* BEAR[2]

borek *see* BORE[2]

borell *see* BORE[1.2]

born *see* BARN

borne *see* BEAR[2]

borough *see* BURGH

borow *see* BORROW[1.2]

borra *see* BARRA, BORROW[1.1], BORROW[1.2]

†**borrel**, **burell** *adj* rough, rude *la15-19*. [ME *borel*]

borrow[1.1], **borra**, **borry**, †**borch**, †**borcht** /ˈbɔro, ˈbɔrə, ˈbore/ *n* 1 a surety, a pledge *la14-19, 20- historical*. 2 a loan *la19-*. †**borrowgang**, **borowgang** suretyship *la14-e17*. †**brogh and hammell**, **brough and hamehald**, **borch and hamehald** *law* proof or a pledge that something offered for sale is not stolen *15-e19*. †**draw in borch** to put in pledge *la14-15*. †**lat to borch** to allow security or a pledge to be given for (a person or thing) *la14-e17*. †**to borch** as a pledge or security *la14-e16*. [OE *borg, borh*]

borrow[1.2], **borra**, **borry**, †**borow**, †**barrow** /ˈbɔro, ˈbɔrə, ˈbore/ *v* 1 to obtain on loan *la14-*. 2 *law* to stand surety for; to bail a person *15-*. 3 to ransom, redeem or release (a person's life or soul) *la15-*. **borrowed reek** smoke from a chimney blown down a neighbouring one by the wind *20- NE*. **borrowing days** the last three days of March (from the fable that March borrowed three days from April) *16-*. [OE *borgian*]

borrow[2] /ˈbɔro/ *n* in *curling* and *golf* the allowance made in directing the stone or ball for unevenness or irregularity in the playing surface *19-*. [probably extended sense of BORROW[1.1]]

borrow *see* BARRA, BURGH

borry *see* BARRA, BORROW[1.1], BORROW[1.2]

bort *see* BOORD[2]

†**bos** *n* 1 a leather bottle (for wine) *la14-16*. 2 *derogatory* a person *16*. [unknown]

bos *see* BOSS[2.2], BUSK[1.1], BUSS[4.2]

bosie[1.1] /ˈbozi/ *n* 1 a bosom *la18-*. 2 a cuddle *20- NE*. [reduced form of BOSOM]

bosie[1.2] /ˈbozi/ *v* to clasp to one's bosom; to cuddle *20- NE*. [see the noun]

boskill *see* BOSS[3]

bosom, buzzum, bowsom, †bosum /ˈbuzəm, ˈbʌzəm, ˈbʌuzəm/ *n* **1** the breast *la14-*. **2** the womb *la15-16*. **†bosom chimney** a fireplace with a built-out chimney *la18-e19*. [OE *bōsum*]

boss[1.1] /bɔs/ *n mining* the waste or exhausted workings of a mineral *la19- C*. [unknown]

boss[1.2] /bɔs/ *v mining* to undercut a thick seam *la19- C*. [unknown]

boss[2.1] /bɔs/ *n* **1** the fore-part of the body (from the chest to the loins) *la18- literary*. **2** a cupboard in a wall recess *20- Ork*. **the boss of the body** the fore-part of the body *19- literary*. [unknown]

boss[2.2], **†bos**, **†bosse** /bɔs/ *adj* **1** hollow; concave *16-*. **2** foolish; helpless, destitute *la16-*. **3** empty *la18-*. **bossing** the woodwork on the recessed part on the inside of a wall below a window *20-*. **bossness** hollowness *la17-*. **boss-heid, boss-head** the piece of metal on a door frame into which the bolt of a lock fits *19-*. **†bois lok** a type of lock *16-e17*. **†bos windo** a bow or bay window *16-17*. [unknown]

boss[3] /bɔs/ *n* the wooden frame on which a cornstack is built *19-*. **bossin** a ventilation hole in a cornstack *19- H&I C*. **boskill** a ventilation funnel in a cornstack *19, 20- NE Bor*. [unknown]

boss *see* BUSS[1], BUSS[2], BUSS[4.1]
bosse *see* BOSS[2.2]

bossie /ˈbɔsi/ *n* a metal button used in the game of *buttony* (BUTTON) *20- NE*. [perhaps *boss* (BUSS[2]) + -IE[1]]

bossie *see* BASSIE[2]
bost *see* BOAST[1.1], BOAST[1.2]
böst *see* BUIST[1]
boster *see* BOWSTER
bosum *see* BOSOM
†bot, bott *n* a bolt *la15-e17*. [unknown]
bot *see* BAT[1.2], BUT[1.4], BUT[1.5]
böt *see* BUIT[1.1]
†botano *n* a kind of bombazine or fustian *17*. [Ital *bottana*]
bote *see* BOAT[1.1], BOAT[2], BUIT[1]
both *see* BAITH[1.1], BAITH[1.2], BAITH[1.3], BAITH[1.4]
botham *see* BODDAM[1.1]

bothan /ˈbɔθən/ *n* an unlicensed drinking house or hut, a kind of shebeen *la19- N H&I WC*. [Gael *bothan* a hut, a bothy]

bothe *see* BOTHY[1.1], BUITH

botherer /ˈbɔðərər/ *n* an annoyance *19- NE EC Bor Uls*. [*bother* (BATHER[1.2]), with agent suffix]

bothie *see* BODY
bothom *see* BODDAM[1.2]

bothy[1.1], **†bothe** /ˈbɔθe, ˈbɔθi/ *n* **1** a primitive dwelling; a rough hut used as temporary accommodation (by shepherds, fishermen or mountaineers) *la14-*. **2** a hut or cottage on a farm used as permanent living quarters for (unmarried, male) workers *la16-*. **3** a workman's hut *la20-*. **bothy ballad** a traditional song (originally sung in bothies) *la19-*. **bothy laft** an attic in a bothy *la19- NE T*. **bothy man, bothie man** a farmworker living in a bothy *19-*. **bothy nicht, bothy night 1** a night of entertainment and singing held by shepherds and farmworkers *20, 21- historical*. **2** a (public) event featuring traditional songs from farm bothies *20-*. **bothy wife** the woman who takes charge of a bothy *la19-*. [altered form of Gael *bothan* a hut; perhaps borrowed into Gael from BUITH]

bothy[1.2] /ˈbɔθe, ˈbɔθi/ *v* **1** to stay (temporarily) in a bothy *la19-*. **2** to live in a bothy on a farm *la19-*. **bothier 1** a (farm) worker living in a bothy *la19-*. **2** a regular user of mountaineering huts *la20-*. **bothyism** the system of lodging male workers (on a farm) *la19-*. [see the noun]

bothy *see* BODY
†bothyn *n* a sheriffdom or lordship *e15*. [unknown]
†boting, botyn *n* a boot *16*. [MFr *botine* a light boot]
bott *see* BOAT[2], BOT
bottall *see* BOTTLE[1]
bottel *see* BOTTLE[2.1]
bottell *see* BOTTLE[1]
bottick *see* BOAT[1.1]

bottle[1], **boattle, boatil, boddle, †bottell, †bottall** /ˈbɔtəl, ˈbɔtəl, ˈbɔdəl/ *n* a hollow narrow-necked vessel for holding liquids *la15-*. **bottlin', bottling 1** a festive gathering of friends at a wedding or a hen-party *la19-*. **2** the act of stuffing the neck of a bottle down a person's throat to induce vomiting *20- NE*. [ME *botel*, OFr *bouteille*]

bottle[2.1], **battle, buttle, †bottel** /ˈbɔtəl, ˈbatəl, ˈbʌtəl/ *n* a bundle of hay or straw; a sheaf *16-*. [ME *botel*, EModE *bottell*]

bottle[2.2], **battle, buttle** /ˈbɔtəl, ˈbatəl, ˈbʌtəl/ *v* to bundle up hay or straw for fodder *la17-*. **gang to Banff and bottle skate** get lost! *20-*. **go to Birse and bottle skate** get lost! *20-*. [see the noun]

bottle[3] /ˈbɔtəl/ *n* a rounded piece of timber running along the ridge of a roof, over which a covering of lead or zinc is fixed *20-*. [EModE *boltel* a rounded moulding]

bottom *see* BODDAM[1.1], BODDAM[1.2]
†botwand *n* a wand or staff of some kind *e16*. [unknown]
botyn *see* BOTING

bouch[1.1], **bowch** /bʌux/ *n* the bark of a dog *19- SW*. [probably onomatopoeic]

bouch[1.2], **booch** /bʌux, bux/ *v* **1** to cough *la19-*. **2** *of a dog* to bark *20- SW*. [see the noun]

bouch *see* BEUCH
boucheour, boucher *see* BUTCHER
boucht *see* BUCHT[1.1], BUCHT[1.2], BUCHT[2.1], BUCHT[2.2], BUCHT[3], BUY
boucklag *see* BOOKLAG
bouet *see* BOWET

bouff[1.1], **bowff, Sh boof** /bʌuf; Sh buf/ *n* **1** a dog's bark; a loud, hard cough *la19-*. **2** a dull sound; *mining* the thud heard when a roof is cracking *la19-*. **3** a dog *20- NE*. **bowffie, bouffie** a dog *20- NE*. [onomatopoeic]

bouff[1.2], **bowff** /bʌuf/ *v* **1** to cough loudly; *of a dog* to bark *19-*. **2** to make a loud dull sound *19-*. **bowfer** a dog *la19- NE*. [see the noun]

bouff[2] /bʌuf/ *n* a large or stupid person *la19- NE*. [unknown]
bouff *see* BUFF[2.1]

boug, bowg /bʌug/ *n* the stomach, the belly (of a child) *20- N*. [Gael *balg, bolg* a bag; the belly]

bougar, bugger, boggar /ˈbugər, ˈbʌgər, ˈbɔgər/ *n* a cross-beam in a roof; a rafter *16-19, 20- NE T Bor*. **bougar-stake** the lower part of the cross-beam that reached to the ground in old houses *la17-19, 20- Bor*. [unknown]

bought *see* BUCHT[2.1], BUCHT[2.2], BUCHT[3]

bougwaar, bogwar /ˈbʌugwar, ˈbɔgwar/ *n* a kind of seaweed *Fucus vesiculosus 20- N*. [probably BOUG + WARE[1.1]]

bouk[1], **bowk, NE book** /bʌuk/ *NE* buk/ *v* to steep (dirty linen) in lye before bleaching *18-*. **bookin' graith, boukin' graith** liquid prepared for soaking clothes *la19- NE*. **†boukin' washing** the annual washing of the family linen *19*. [ME *bouken*]

bouk[2], **book, †bowk, †buke, †boulk** /bʌuk, buk/ *n* **1** the carcass of a slaughtered animal *15-*. **2** the body of a person (living or dead) *16-*. [ON *búkr* the body, OE *būc* the belly, trunk of the body]

bouk[3.1], **buik, †boulk, †bowk** /bʌuk, buk/ *n* **1** a quantity or load of merchandise; a cargo, a big load *la15-*. **2** bulk, size, quantity, volume *16-*. **bookie** obese, bulky; imposing *la18-*.

bouksome, booksome large, bulky *18- NE T.* **brek bouk** see BRAK[1.2] [conflation of BOUK[1] with ON *búlki* cargo]

bouk[3.2] /bʌuk, buk/ *v* **1** to increase in size, swell out; to have weight or importance *la17-.* **2** *of a rope* to increase by the accumulation of its coils on a capstan *la19, 20- NE T EC.* **3** to store grain or pack goods *19.* **bookin** pregnant *20- NE.* **bouking** *mining* segments of wood used to increase the diameter of a drum *la19-, 20- T EC.* [see the noun]

†**bouk**[4] *v* to stop up the touch-hole of a cannon *la16.* [MFr *boucher*, influenced by *bouk*buck or bulk]

boukit, bookit, †**bowkit** /'bukɪt/ *adj* **1** bulky, swollen *16-.* **2** pregnant *18-.* **sma boukit** see SMA[1.2]. **weel boukit** see WEEL[1.3]. [BOUK[3.1] + -IT[2]]

boul see BOOL[2], BOWEL

bould see BUILD

boule see BOOL[1]

boulk see BOUK[2], BOUK[3.1]

boull see BOOL[1], BOOL[2]

boult /bult/ *n* a grassy border (between crofts); the edge of a field *20- N.* [unknown]

boult see BOWT[1.1]

boulyiement see BULIMENT

bouman see BOW[1]

boun[1.1], †**bound** /bʌun, bun/ *v ptp* **bound, bun, bounit 1** to get ready to go; to set out *la14-.* **2** to make ready, prepare *15-.* **3** to make oneself ready, betake oneself *la14-e19.* [ON *búinn*, ptp of *búa* to make ready]

boun[1.2], **bun', boon,** †**bowne** /bʌun, bʌn, bun/ *adj* **1** prepared, organized; equipped, dressed *la14-.* **2** ready to start (a journey), heading for (a place) *15-.* **3** *of things* made ready, put in order *la14-16.* [see the verb]

boun[2.1], **boon, bound,** †**bond,** †**bund** /bʌun, bun, bʌund/ *n* **1** a boundary or limit (of land or a territory) *la14-.* **2** a district or area of land (within specific boundaries) *la14-.* **3** extent, width *la19-.* **bounding,** †**boundand** *of a charter* specifying the bounds of property *16-19, 20- historical.* †**bound court** a district court *la15.* **bound road 1** a boundary road or track; a boundary *la16-19, 20- historical.* **2** the border between Scotland and England (near Berwick) *la16-e18.* †**biggit bouns** a cluster of buildings with their grounds *18.* [ME *bound*]

boun[2.2], **bound** /bʌun, bun, bʌund/ *v* **1** to fix or mark (land) boundaries *la15-.* **2** to have a common land boundary (with) *16-.* [see the noun]

boun' see BUND

bounce see BOONCE[1.1], BOONCE[1.2]

†**bound**[1] *n* a bundle (of flax) *16-18.* [Flem *bond*]

†**bound**[2] *adj* pregnant *e16.* [ptp of BIND[1.2]]

bound see BIND[1.2], BOUN[1.1], BOUN[2.1], BOUN[2.2], BUND

†**boundance** *n* abundance *la15.* [aphetic form of Older Scots *aboundance*]

†**boundand** *adj* abundant *la15.* [aphetic form of Older Scots *aboundant*]

bounit see BOUN[1.1]

bountay, bounte see BOUNTY

bountith, †**bonteth,** †**bounteth,** †**bontath** /'buntɪθ/ *n* a gratuity; a gift (stipulated in a contract of employment) in addition to wage-money *16-19, 20- literary.* [ME *bountith*]

bountree see BOURTREE

bounty, Ork boonta, †**bounte,** †**bontie,** †**bountay** /'bunti, 'bʌunti; *Ork* 'bunta/ *n* **1** generosity, kindness *la14-.* **2** a gift, a reward; a gratuity *la16-.* **3** a bonus paid to fishermen for the season's fishing in addition to the price for the fish caught *20- N NE.* **4** valour, courage *la14-e17.* [ME *bounte*]

bour see BOOR

bourach see BEERACH, BOORACH[1.1], BOORACH[1.2]

bourd[1.1] /burd/ *n* **1** a jest, a joke; a cause of amusement, a funny or mocking story *la15-19, 20- NE.* **2** sport or play, fun *15-16.* †**na bourd** no joke, no trivial matter *la15-e18.* [ME *bourde*]

bourd[1.2] /burd/ *v* to speak merrily or in jest, joke, have fun or sport *la14-19, 20- literary.* [ME *bourden*]

bourie /'buri/ *n* a rabbit's burrow, an animal's lair *19, 20- literary.* [perhaps altered form of Scots *burrow* or diminutive form of BOOR, with extended meaning]

Bourignonism /bə'rinjonɪzm/ *n* the religious doctrines of Antoinette Bourignon, a 17th-century French mystic who was popular among the Episcopalians and Jacobites of the North-East in the early 18th century *18, 19- historical.* [from the surname *Bourgignon*]

bourlaw see BIRLEY

bourock see BOORACH[1.1]

bourtree, bourtrie, bountree, †**bourtre** /'burtri, 'buntri/ *n* the elder tree *Sambucus nigra 14-.* **bourtree gun, bountry-gun** a popgun, a peashooter *19-.* [unknown]

boushty, bushtie /'buʃti, 'bʌʃte/ *n* a bed *la18-19, 20- NE.* **bushtie ba** a bed *la19- NE.* [OFr *boiste* a box, a receptacle made of wood]

bouster see BOWSTER

bousterous, bowsterous, †**boustrous** /'bʌustərəs/ *adj* boisterous, fierce; rowdy *la19-.* [ME *boistrous* rough, coarse]

bout[1] /bʌut/ *n* a hank or skein of thread or worsted *19, 20- Ork NE EC.* [OE *byht* bend]

bout[2], *NE* **boot** /bʌut; *NE* but/ *n* **1** a prolonged session of drinking *18-.* **2** a spell of work or exercise *19-.* **3** a contest, a match; a round of fighting *19-.* **4** the extent of ground covered as the mower, driller or ploughman moves across a field (and back again) *19-.* **5** the sweep of a scythe; the amount of corn cut in a single sweep *20- Ork NE.* **6** a row in knitting *20- NE.* **lying in the bout** *of corn or hay* lying in rows after being cut *19- NE T.* [OE *byht* a bending]

bout[3], † **bult** /bʌut/ *v* to sift (flour) through a sieve or fine cloth *15-19, 20- WC.* †**boutclaith, boutcloath** cloth of a thin or open texture used for sieving *14-e19.* †**boutclaithing** = *boutclaith la16-e17.* †**bouthous** a building in which flour is sifted *la16-17.* [ME *bulten*]

bout see BOWT[1.1], BOWT[1.2]

boutch see BOOTCH[1.1], BOOTCH[1.2]

boutgate, boutgait /'bʌutget/ *n* **1** a roundabout way, a circumvention; an evasion; underhand means *la16-19, 20- literary.* **2** *mining* a secondary access road to a mine from the surface, independent of the shaft (in a shallow pit) *19- T C.* **3** a round of work; the ploughing of two furrows, outwards and back *la19, 20- NE SW.* [aphetic form of ABOOT[1.1] + GAIT[3]]

bouth see BUITH

bouzy see BUSS[1]

bow[1], **boo, bu** /bʌu, bu/ *n* **1** a stock or herd of cattle (on a farm) *15-19, 20- Sh.* **2** a field for cows, a leased cow pasture; a fold for cows *19, 20- historical.* **bower,** †**booer** a tenant who hires dairy cattle and grazing rights *18- C SW Bor.* **bowin, bowing** the holding or lease of stock and grazing land *19- WC SW.* **bowhouse,** †**bowhous** a cattle shed *16-19, 20- NE T EC.* **bowman, booman,** †**bouman** a man having charge of cattle on a farm; a tenant who leases a herd of cows and grazing land (from a farmer) *la15-19, 20- N WC.* **bow teind** a tithe on cows *17- Sh Ork.* [ON *bú* household, farm, livestock]

bow[2], †**boll** /bʌu/ *n* the seed-pod of flax *la15-19, 20- NE.* [OE *bolla* bowl, small vessel]

bow[3], *NE* **boo,** †**boll** /bo; *NE* bu/ *n* **1** an archer's bow *la14-.* **2** an archway; an arched gateway; the arch of a bridge; frequently in street-names: ◇*Netherbow la15-.* **3** the curve of

a street; the curve of a furrow; a bend in a river *la16-*. **4** a fiddler's bow *la18-*. **5** (the bow of) an ox-yoke *16-19, 20- NE*. **6** the semi-circular handle of a pail or pot *19- NE T*. †**bower, bowar** a maker of bows, a bowyer *15-e18*. †**bowit 1** provided with a curved handle *16*. **2** provided with an archery bow *e15*. **bow-backit, bow-backed, boobackit** humpbacked *19-*. **bowbrig** an arched bridge *16-*. **bowbutts** ground used for archery practice; frequently in place-names *la16-19, 20- historical*. **bow-cheer** an armchair *la19- NE*. †**bow draucht** the distance of a bow-shot *la14-e18*. **bow hand, bow haun** a style of fiddling; skill in fiddle-playing *19-*. **bow houghed, bow houcht** bandy-legged *la18-19, 20- NE T EC*. **bow-maker** a maker of bows, a bowyer *14-*. **bow-marks,** †**bowmerkis** ground used for archery practice *15-17, 19- historical*. **bowsaw** a narrow-bladed saw on an arched frame *la16-*. †**bowsting** a bowstaff, a stick suitable for making into a bow *la15-e17*. **gae owre the bows** to go beyond all bounds *la19- NE T*. **gae through the bows** to go too far; to over-imbibe *la19- NE*. **take a person throw the bows** to take a person severely to task *19- NE*. [OE *boga*; compare BOO[1.1]]
bow[4]**, bowe,** †**buy,** †**boy** /bʌu/ *n* a buoy *17-19, 20- Sh NE*. **bowrope,** *Sh* **bürep,** *Sh* **börep,** †**boy rap,** †**buyrope,** †**burop** a buoy rope *16-19, 20- Sh NE*. [EModE *buoy*]
bow see BOLL, BOO[1.1], BOO[1.2], BOO[6], BULL[2]
bowal[1.1]**, bole, boal,** †**bowall** /'bʌuəl, bol/ *n* **1** a recess in a wall (used as a cupboard) *16-*. **2** an aperture, an opening in a wall to admit light or air (fitted with a shutter rather than glazed) *la16-*. **3** a pay-desk window *20- T C*. **boley hole** a small storage space (for odds and ends) *20-*. **boley window** a pay-desk window *20- T C*. [unknown]
†**bowal**[1.2] *v* to build a recess into a wall *e16*. [unknown]
bowall see BOWAL[1.1]
bowat see BOWET
†**bowbart, bowbard** *n* a dull or sluggish person *e16*. [OFr *bobert* a fool, lout]
bowcaill see BOW-KAIL
bowch see BOUCH[1.1]
bowcht see BUCHT[1.1]
bowd see BOD[2]
bowden[1.1]**,** †**boldin,** †**bowdin,** †**bolne** /'bʌudən/ *v* to swell (up), rise in flood; to bloat (with heat) *la14-19, 20- NE*. **bowdent, bowdened 1** *of people or animals* swollen from overeating *19- NE*. **2** *of people* swollen with pride or grief *la16-19*. [ON *bólgna*]
†**bowden**[1.2]**, bowdyn, boldin** *adj* **1** physically swollen or distended *la14-18*. **2** affected by extreme grief or pride *16-18*. [see the verb]
bowden see BODEN
bowder[1]**,** *NE* **byowder** /'bʌudər; *NE* 'bjʌudər/ *n* a heavy squall, a storm of wind and rain *20- NE SW*. [unknown]
bowder[2] /'bʌudər/ *n* a boulder *la19- SW*. Compare BOOLDER. [compare Swed *bullersten*]
bowdin see BOWDEN[1.1]
bowdy /'bʌudi/ *adj* bandy-legged *20-*. [derivative of BOW[3]]
bowdyn see BOWDEN[1.2]
bowe see BOW[4]
bowel, boul, bowl /'bʌuəl, bul, bol/ *n* a basin, a bowl *la17-*. †**bowlman** a hawker of crockery *19*. [OE *bolla*]
bowel hive, bool-hive, †**bowellhywe** /'bʌuəl haev, 'bul haev/ *n* enteritis, inflammation of the bowels in children *la17-*. **bowel-hive grass** the plant *Alchemilla arvensis* (believed to be a remedy for enteritis) *la19-*. [OFr *boële* + EModE *hives*]
bowen see BINE
bower see BOOR

bowet, bowat, bouet, buat /'bʌuət, 'buət/ *n* a small (hand) lantern *la15-*. **bowater** a night poacher of salmon (who uses a lantern) *20- Bor*. **MacFarlane's Bowat, M'Farlane's buat** the moon *19- literary*. [MFr *boiste*, Lat *boeta* a box]
bowf[1.1]**, bowff** /bʌuf/ *n* an offensive smell *la20-*. [unknown]
bowf[1.2]**, bowff** /bʌuf/ *adj* smelly, foul, unpleasant *la20-*. [unknown]
bowfarts /'bʌufarts/ *n* a difficult situation *la19- NE*. **in the bowfarts** in difficulty; unable to get up or free oneself *la19- NE*. [unknown]
bowfer /'bʌufər/ *n* an unattractive person *la20-*. Compare *bowfer* (BOUFF[1.2]). [unknown]
bowff see BOUFF[1.1], BOUFF[1.2], BOWF[1.1], BOWF[1.2]
bowfin, bowffin, bowfing /'bʌufɪn, 'bʌufɪŋ/ *adj* stinking, foul, unpleasant *la20-*. [unknown]
bowfit steel see BUFFET STOOL
bowg see BOUG
bowglag waar /'bʌuglag war/ *n* a type of seaweed characterized by bladder-like vesicles *20- N*. [compare BOUGWAAR]
bowie, †**bowy** /'bʌui/ *n* **1** a broad, shallow dish or bowl *16-*. **2** a barrel (for water or ale) *la16-*. **3** a small tub *19-*. **4** a bucket *18-19, 20- SW Bor*. [probably diminutive form of OE *bolla* or ON *bolli*]
bowin, †**bayin,** †**bavin** /'bʌuɪn, 'boən/ *n* a species of wrasse *Labrus bergylta 18-19, 20- SW*. [probably IrGael *ballán*]
bowine see BINE
bowk see BOAK[1.1], BOAK[1.2], BOUK[1], BOUK[2], BOUK[3.1]
bow-kail, †**bowcaill** /'bʌukel, 'bokel/ *n* cabbage *16-*. [unknown; compare BOWSTOCK, KAIL]
bowkit see BOUKIT
bowl see BOWEL
bowlie[1] /'bʌuli, 'boli/ *n* a bowl *la19- NE EC*. [derivative of BOWEL]
bowlie[2.1] /'bʌuli, 'boli/ *n* a bow-legged person *19- T EC SW Bor*. [probably BOW[3], with adj-forming suffix; compare MDu *boghel* a bow, a hoop]
bowlie[2.2]**, bowly** /'bʌuli, 'boli/ *adj* crooked, bent; *of legs* bandy *18-*. **bowly legged, bowly-leggit** bow-legged *20- WC*. [see the noun]
†**bowllin, bowland** *adj* bending, curving, twisting *16*. [perhaps MDu *boghelen* to curve]
bowl-money /'bolmʌne/ *n* money thrown to children at a wedding *la19- NE T C SW*. [BOWL + MONEY]
bowlocks /'bʌuləks, 'boloks/ *n* ragweed *Jacobaea vulgaris 19- SW*. [compare Gael *buaghallan*]
bowlt, beowl'd /bʌult, bjʌuld/ *adj* crooked, distorted *19- T EC SW Bor*. [perhaps MDu *boghelen* to curve]
bowne see BOUN[1.2]
bow-net see POW-NET
bowr see BOOR
bowse /bʌus/ *v* **1** to swing out (of a boat); to haul with tackle *la18-19, 20- NE T*. **2** to bounce *la19- NE T*. [compare BOOSE[2.2]]
bowsh /bʌuʃ/ *n in Inverness* an errand *20- N H&I*. **bowsher** *in Inverness* an errand-boy *20- N H&I*. [unknown]
bowsie[1] /'bʌuzi/ *adj* crooked; bandy-legged *19, 20- Ork T*. [perhaps Fr *bosse* a hump, or derivative of BOW[3]]
bowsie[2]**, boosie** /'bʌuzi, 'buzi/ *n* a bogeyman (invoked to frighten children) *la19- C SW*. **bowzie-man, boosie-man** a bogeyman *la19- WC SW*. [compare BO[1]]
bowsie[3]**,** †**boozy** /'bʌuzi/ *adj* big, fat, corpulent, puffed up *19, 20- NE T*. [compare MHG *Bûs* inflation]
bowsom see BOSOM
bowsome, *Sh Ork* **boosam,** †**bowsum** /'bʌusəm, 'bosəm; *Sh Ork* 'busəm/ *adj* **1** obedient, willing, compliant *la14-*. **2** *of a woman* buxom, handsome, pleasant, agreeable *la16-*. [ME *buhsum* obedient]

bowsplit, †**bowspleit** /ˈbʌusplɪt/ *n* a spar running out from the stem of a boat *16-19, 20- NE SW*. [altered form of EModE *bowsprit*]

bowster, bouster, bolster, *Sh* **booster,** †**boster** /ˈbʌustər, ˈbolstər; *Sh* ˈbustər/ *n* **1** a long pillow, a bolster *la15-*. **2** a piece of timber or metal used to prevent chafing; a bearing for a wheelshaft in a watermill *16-19, 20- Sh NE*. [OE *bolster*]

bowsterous *see* BOUSTEROUS

bowstock /ˈbʌustɔk, ˈbostɔk/ *n* a cabbage with a properly-developed heart *18-19, 20- NE*. [unknown; compare BOW-KAIL, STOCK¹·¹]

bowsum *see* BOWSOME

bowt¹·¹, **bout, bolt,** *Sh* **boot,** †**boult** /bʌut, bolt; *Sh* but/ *n* **1** a roll of cloth *14-*. **2** a short, heavy arrow *15-*. **3** a stout metal pin, a bolt for fastening *16-*. **4** a spring, a leap; a sudden movement *la16-*. **5** a club foot *20- T*. †**bout fitted** having a club-foot *e19*. †**boltfoot** a club-footed person *e19*. [OE *bolt* a bolt, an arrow]

bowt¹·², **bout, bolt** /bʌut, bolt/ *v* to start, spring; to take flight; to break or rush away; *of liquid* to well up *15-*. †**bowt fou, bowt fow** welling up, full to the brim *e18*. [see the noun]

bowy *see* BOWIE

box¹·¹, **boax** /bɔks, boks/ *n* **1** a (rectangular) case or receptacle (with a lid) *la15-*. **2** a strong-box (for the funds of a guild or corporation); a guild treasury *16-19, 20- historical*. **3** *mining* a hutch *la18-19, 20- EC*. **4** *law* a box in the corridor of Parliament House, Edinburgh, containing an advocate's professional papers *20-*. **5** a melodeon or accordion *20-*. **box-day** *law* the day in the schedule of the Court of Session on which papers for the coming session were to be lodged *18-e20, la20- historical*. **box-ladder** a narrow staircase (enclosed in wooden casing) *la19- C*. **box-master, box-maister** a treasurer (of a guild or corporation) *17-*. †**box pennie** a market duty levied for the benefit of a craft or burgh funds *17*. **box-seat** an enclosed pew in a church *20-*. **on the box** in receipt of National Health Insurance benefit, originally in receipt of weekly assistance from a poor fund or a friendly society *18-*. **oot yer box** drunk, drugged; not responsible for one's actions *la20-*. **out the box** = *oot yer box*. **the whole box and dice** the whole lot, everything or everybody *19-*. [OE *box* a receptacle for medicines]

box¹·² /bɔks/ *v* **1** to put into a box *18-*. **2** to add wainscoting; to panel *18-19, 20- historical*. **3** *law* to lodge papers (required in a lawsuit by the Court of Session) with the clerk *19-20, 21- historical*. [see the noun]

box², **boax,** *Ork* **bucks** /bɔks, boks; *Ork* bʌks/ *v* **1** to fight with the fists; to engage in a boxing match *18-*. **2** *of rams* to attack with the horns, butt *la19-*. [EModE *box* to beat, thrash]

box-bed /ˈbɔksbed/ *n* a bed enclosed in wooden panelling, the front having either sliding panels, hinged doors, or curtains *la17-*. [BOX¹·¹ + BED¹·¹]

boxie /ˈbɔksi/ *n* **1** a (small) box *19-*. **2** a melodeon or an accordion *20- N NE*. [BOX¹·¹ + -IE¹]

boxin /ˈbɔksɪn/ *n* wainscotting *18-19, 20- WC SW Bor*. [verbal noun from BOX¹·²]

boy, boay /bɔɪ, boe/ *n* **1** a male child; a lad; a (young) servant *15-*. **2** a familiar form of address to a man *la18-*. **3** a bachelor (of any age) still living with his parents *la19-*. **4** an apprentice *20-*. **5** a man (of any age) *20-*. **boyackie** a little boy *la19- N NE*. **boyses** belonging to the boys: ◊*the boyses brose 20- WC SW*. **boyag** a boy *20-*. **the boy** a term of commendation and praise *20-*. **the Bhoys** a nickname for Celtic Football Club *la19-*. **boys a day** an exclamation or a greeting to a child *20- H&I C*. [ME *boy*]

boy *see* BOW⁴

†**boyart** *n* a small one-masted vessel *16*. [MDu, MLG *bojert*]

†**boyis, boyes** *npl* leg-irons, fetters *la14-e17*. [OFr *boie, buie*]

boyn *see* BONE²

boyne *see* BINE

bra *see* BRAE, BRAW¹·¹, BRAW¹·²

braa *see* BRAW¹·¹

braad /brad/ *n* a brooding goose *20- N*. [compare BROD³]

braad *see* BRAD¹·¹

braaly *see* BRAWLY¹·²

braand, *N* **bron** /brand; *N* brɔn/ *n* a burning peat or glowing cinder *la19- Sh N*. [OE *brand*, ON *brandr* a fire, a piece of burning wood]

brabanar *see* BRABONER

brabble /ˈbrabəl/ *n* something small or worthless *20- T*. **brabblach** refuse, dross *19- H&I EC*. [probably Gael *prabar* rabble]

braboner, †**brabanar,** †**brebnar** /ˈbrabənər/ *n* a weaver *15-e18, 20- historical*. [Du *Brabander* a native of Brabant, surviving in the Scottish surnames *Brebner* and *Bremner*]

brace, †**brase,** †**bras** /bres/ *n* **1** *building* a band of stonework or wood used to strengthen a structure *15-*. **2** a fireplace; the breast or arch of a chimney *16-*. **3** a mantelpiece *18-*. **4** a chimney made of straw and clay *19*. **5** a (supporting) strap, thong or belt *15-19*. **6** *archery* a wrist guard *15-e17*. **brace-piece** a mantelpiece *19, 20- T*. **brace steen** a stone behind the fire in old houses *la19- Ork N*. [ME *brace*]

brace *see* BRESS

bracelet, †**braslat,** †**breslet** /ˈbreslət/ *n* a decorative band for the wrist *la15-*. [ME *bracelet*]

brachan *see* BRECKEN, BROCHAN

brachtan /ˈbraxtən/ *n* a young chaffinch *20- N*. [unknown; compare BRICHTIE]

brachton /ˈbraxtən/ *n* a large, heavy, clumsy man; something weighty or unwieldy *la18- SW*. [unknown]

†**brack**¹·¹ *n* brine *e19*. [see the adj]

†**brack**¹·², **brak** *adj* briny, salty *e16*. **brackit** salty, bitter *e19*. [probably Du *brak*]

brack *see* BRAK¹·¹, BRAK¹·²

bracken *see* BRAK¹·², BRECHAN, BROKEN

brack-fur¹·¹ /ˈbrakfʌr/ *n* a kind of light ploughing *la19- NE*. [BRAK¹·¹ + FURR¹·¹]

brack-fur¹·² /ˈbrakfʌr/ *v* to plough (land) lightly *la19- NE*. [see the noun]

brad¹·¹, **braad** /brad, brɑd/ *n* a sharp tug on a fishing line *20- N*. [ON *bregða* to move swiftly]

brad¹·², **brawd** /brad, brɑd/ *v* to jerk a fishing line (so as to hook a fish) *20- Ork N*. [see the noun]

†**brad**² *n in the South-West* a term of abuse for a thing or a person; an old man *18-e19*. [unknown]

brade *see* BRAID¹·¹, BRAID¹·², BRAID²·¹

brae, †**bra,** †**bray,** †**brea** /bre/ *n* **1** the (steep or sloping) bank of a river, lake or seashore *13-*. **2** a bank or stretch of ground rising fairly steeply; a hillside *la14-*. **3** an upland mountainous district: ◊*the Braes o Balquhidder la15-*. **4** a road with a steep gradient; frequently in street names *19-*. **5** the brow of a hill *la19-*. **6** (the site of) a salmon trap consisting of an artificial gravel-and-stone bank across a river *18- NE*. **brae face** a slope, a hillside *la18-*. **brae foot** the bottom of a hill or slope *la18-*. **braeheid, braehead** the top of a hill or slope *16-*. **brae man,** †**bray man** a hill-man; an inhabitant of a hilly region, such as the southern slopes of the Grampians *18-19, 20- historical*. **brae-set** situated on a slope; steep *19-*. **gae doon the brae** to go to ruin, cease to prosper; *of an old person* to fail physically *17-*. [ON *brá* eyelash, compare OE *brū* eyelash, eyebrow, brow, brow of a hill; Gael *bràighe* the upper part (of places); also BROO², BREE³]

braeth *see* BRAITH

brag¹·¹ /brag/ *n* **1** a boast; bragging *15-*. **2** a challenge *18-*. **3** a defiant note (on a trumpet) *la15-e16*. **braggle, braggal** boastful, smug *20- N*. **braggie** ostentatious, boastful *19- T*. [ME *brag*]

brag¹·² *NE* **braig** /brag; *NE* breg/ *v* **1** to boast *la15-*. **2** to challenge or defy *18-e19*. **3** to reproach, scold *18-e19*. **4** to threaten, taunt *la16*. [see the noun]

bragglement /ˈbragəlmənt/ *n* a dispute, a disturbance, a quarrel *20-*. [*braggle* (BRAG¹·¹), with noun-forming suffix *-ment*]

bragwort, bregwort, †brogat /ˈbragwɔrt, ˈbrɛgwɔrt/ *n* a drink made of ale and honey *la16-19, 20- SW Bor*. [Welsh *bragod*]

braicham *see* BRECHAM

†braid¹·¹, **brade** *n* a sudden movement, a jerk; a blow, an attack *la14-e19*. [OE *gebregd*]

†braid¹·², **brade** *v* **1** to make a sudden movement; to start, spring or stride *la15-19*. **2** to catch, lift or throw (suddenly) *la14-16*. [OE *bregdan*]

braid²·¹, **broad, †brade, †bread, †bred** /bred, brɔd/ *adj* **1** wide, broad *13-*. **2** plain, clear *16-e19*. **†braidlingis 1** broadwise *e17*. **2** flat (on the ground); with the limbs extended *la16*. **†braid band** *of corn* lying unbound or unstooked on the harvest field *la18-19*. **†braid benisoun** full blessing *la15-e16*. **braid bonnet** a wide, flat, woollen bonnet *19-*. **†braid malesone** full blessing *la15-e16*. **braid Scotland, broad Scotland** the whole (breadth) of Scotland *la17-*. **braid Scots, broad Scots** the Scots language *la17-*. **braid sword, broad sword** a cutting sword with a broad blade *la16-*. [OE *brād*]

braid²·² /bred/ *adv* **1** widely, broadly; in an extended manner; laid or squeezed flat *la14-*. **2** unrestrainedly; indiscreetly; fully, frankly *16-*. **look braid in the face** to look straight or squarely in a person's face *19-*. [OE *brāde*]

braid *see* BRED¹·¹, BREED¹, BREED², BREID

braidside /ˈbredsʌɪd/ *n* **1** the broad side of something *16-*. **2** a strong attack *19-*. **at the braidside** in a hurry; suddenly, unexpectedly *19-*. [BRAID²·¹ + SIDE¹]

braig /breg/ *n* a large knife *16-e17, 20- T*. **†braig knyfe** = BRAIG *la16-e17*. [unknown]

braig *see* BRAG¹·²

braiggle /ˈbregəl/ *n* a useless, worn-out or unsafe tool *19- SW*. [unknown]

braik *see* BRAK¹·¹, BRAK¹·², BRAKE

braikfast *see* BRAKFAST

braikshaw *see* BREAKSHUGH

brail, *N* **brile** /brel; *N* brʌɪl/ *n* a strong or intense outburst *20- Ork N*. [Icel *bræla* thick smoke and fire]

brain¹·¹ /bren/ *n* a loud noise or voice *19- NE*. [unknown]

brain¹·² /bren/ *v* to roar, bellow *la18- NE WC*. [unknown]

brain²·¹, *T* **brehn, †brayn** /bren; *T* brɛn/ *n* the organ of thinking *la15-*. **brainish** confused, wandering in the mind *la19- NE T C*. **brainy 1** clever *20-*. **2** high-spirited, lively *19- EC*. **†brain wud, brayne wode** mad *la14-e19*. [OE *brægen*]

brain²·², **†brane** /bren/ *v* **1** to smash the skull; to dash out the brains *16-*. **2** to hurt with a blow to the head; to wound or beat severely *18-*. [see the noun]

brain²·³ /bren/ *adj* mad, enraged, furious *15-19, 20- literary*. [perhaps shortened form of *brain wud* (BRAIN²·¹)].

brainch, branch, brench /brenʃ, branʃ, brɛnʃ/ *n* **1** a bough or branch of a tree *la14-*. **2** a subdivision *15-*. **3** a tributary of a river *17-*. **4** *heraldry* an addition or attachment to an escutcheon *la17*. [ME *braunch*]

brainge *see* BREENGE¹·¹, BREENGE¹·²

braingel *see* BRANGLE¹·¹

†brainyell¹·¹ *n* an uproar; an outburst *e19*. [compare Norw dial *brengja* to wriggle, twist]

brainyell¹·², **†brainzell** /ˈbrenjəl/ *v* to break out; to rush violently *19- SW Bor*. [see the noun]

braird¹·¹, **beird, breer, †breard, †brerd** /brɛrd, bird, brir/ *n* **1** the first shoots of a crop (above the ground); germination *la15-*. **2** the surface; the brim *la15-e19*. **3** *spinning* the short flax obtained from a second hackling of the first tow *18-19*. [OE *brerd* a brim, a margin]

braird¹·², **beird, breer, †brierd, †brerd** /brɛrd, bird, brir/ *v* to sprout (above the ground); to germinate *la15-*. [see the noun]

braisant *see* BRESS

braise *see* BRAZE, BRIZZ¹·²

braiss *see* BRESS

braissle *see* BRASTLE

braith, breith, breeth, breath, *Sh* **braeth, †breth** /brɛθ, briθ, brɛθ; *Sh* ˈbrɛəθ/ *n* **1** (an act of) respiration; a movement of air *la15-*. **2** an opinion, a line of thought *la18-*. [OE *bræþ* smell, stench]

braith *see* BRATH¹, BRATH²

braithe, breath, bred /breθ, briθ, brɛd/ *v* to melt, liquefy *la19- Sh Ork*. [ON *bræða*]

braize *see* BROOSE

brak¹·¹, **brack, brek, break, †braik** /brak, brɛk, brek/ *n* **1** a rupture, a breach; a separation *16-*. **2** ground broken up for cultivation; a strip of uncultivated land (between two plots of land); a division of land (in crop rotation) *la18-*. Compare BRECK. **3** a hollow in a hill *la18-*. **4** the breaking up of a storm or a hard freeze *19- NE T EC Bor*. **5** the breaking of waves on the shore *19- Sh*. **6** a fall of snow or rain; a layer or deposit of snow *19- Bor*. **7** failure, bankruptcy *la19- NE T EC*. **8** the breaking up of a market *la19- NE T*. **9** a breach of a promise; a breach of friendly relations *la15-17*. [see the verb]

brak¹·², **brack, brek, break, †braik, †brik** /brak, brɛk, brek/ *v pt* **brak**, *Sh Ork Uls* **bruk**, *ptp* **bracken, braken, brok, broken, †ybrokkyn 1** to destroy; to fracture; to force open; to burst forth *la14-*. **2** to transgress, fail to keep or observe (a law or a promise) *la14-*. **3** to divide into portions or pieces; to separate; to disband (a company) *15-*. **4** *of milk* to curdle; to coagulate *20-*. **5** to cause a change in (the weather) *19, 20- N NE*. **6** to apportion a tax on (a person) *la16-e17*. **7** to throw into disorder; to scatter *la14-e16*. **8** to overcome (by persuasion or force) *16*. **breaker, †brekar, †bracker, †braiker 1** a violator (of laws or peace) *la14-*. **2** a person who breaks something *la18-*. **brakins** the remains of a meal *19- NE T*. **break a bottle** to open a new bottle *19-*. **brak bouk** to open up and unload a cargo; to unpack merchandise *15-*. **brack doon** to carve, cut up *la19- Sh*. **brak an egg** *curling* a command to strike a stone with another with a force such as would break an egg *19-*. **brack in, break in** to prepare a field for seed by harrowing *19- NE EC*. **†brak lowse 1** to become lawless; to rise in arms *15-e18*. **2** to leave one's job; to take to vagrancy *17*. **brack on, brack o 1** to begin to use stored food or drink *la19-*. **2** to change a banknote or coin for smaller money *la19-*. **3** to break up sod by delving *20- Sh*. **†brek the price** to fail to observe the officially prescribed prices *15*. **†brek the theats** to break free of restraints *18*. **brack up** to start a conversation *la19- Sh*. **brak the wand** *of an official* to break the insignia of office, indicate obstruction in the course of duty *la15-e18, 19- historical*. **break wi a fu han** to make a fraudulent bankruptcy *la19-*. **brak the wind** *of a medicine* to relieve flatulence *20- Sh N NE*. †**brak Yule gird** to disturb the peace of Christmas and so incur bad luck for the following year *16-19*; compare *Yule girth* (YULE). **ye've pu'd a stick tae brak yer ain back** you will suffer from the consequences of your own actions *20- NE T EC*. [OE *brecan*]

brak *see* BRACK[1,2]

brakan *see* BRECKEN

brakane *see* BRECHAN

brake, †**braik** /brek/ *n* **1** a heavy harrow (drawn by horses) *17-19*, *20- NE T*. **2** a flax-harrow *la16-17*. [MLG *brake*, ODu *braeke* a flax harrow]

braken *see* BRAK[1,2]

brakfast, brakfist, brekfast, breakfast, braikfast, *Sh* **brakwist,** *N* **brekwus** /ˈbrakfəst, ˈbrakfɪst, ˈbrɛkfəst, ˈbrɛkfəst; *Sh* ˈbrakwɪst; *N* ˈbrɛkwʌs/ *n* the first meal of the day, breakfast *16-*. [BRAK[1,2] + ON *fasta* a fast]

bralans *see* BRAWLINS

†**brall** *v* to soar, fly *la16*. [perhaps MFr *bransler* shake]

bram /bram/ *n* a mixture of oatmeal and water, eaten cold *la19- Ork*. [perhaps altered form of BARM[1,1]]

bramble *see* BRAMMLE

brammel, bramlin /ˈbraməl, ˈbramlɪn/ *n* a striped worm found in old dunghills and leaf-heaps (used as bait for freshwater fish) *19-*. **brammel worm** = BRAMMEL. [compare Eng *brandling*]

brammer /ˈbramər/ *n* a term of approbation; an excellent specimen of its type *la20- H&I WC*. **brammed up** dressed up *la20- WC*. [from the name *Brahma*, the first god in the Hindi triumvirate]

brammle, brummle, bramble, †**brimmle,** †**brymmyll** /ˈbraməl, ˈbrʌməl, ˈbrambəl/ *n* the blackberry *Rubus fruticosus*; a blackberry bush *16-*. [OE *brēmel*]

†**bramskin** *n* a leather apron worn by tanners and curriers *16-19*. [metathesized form of OE *bearm* bosom + SKIN[1,1]; compare BARMSKIN]

bran, brawn, †**brand,** †**brawyne** /bran, brɔn/ *n* **1** the flesh or muscle of an animal (as food) *la14-*. **2** the calf of the leg; a rounded muscle of the arm; a fleshy part of the body *15-19*, *20- Sh H&I*. **3** (the flesh of) a boar *la14-19*, *20- SW Bor*. **upo da bran** upon the point of doing something *20- Sh*. [ME *braun*]

branch *see* BRAINCH

brand *see* BRAN

Brandane, †**Brandan** /ˈbrandən/ *n* **1** a native of the island of Bute *la19-*. **2** *pl* the followers of Stewart of Bute *15-e17*, *la18- historical*. [probably from the name of St Brandan or Brendan of Clonfert, who had a foundation in Bute]

brandeis *see* BRANISH

brander[1,1]**, branner,** †**brandreth,** †**brandrie,** †**brandraucht** /ˈbrandər, ˈbranər/ *n* **1** a gridiron *la14-*. **2** a supporting framework; a trestle; scaffolding used in the construction of buildings, bridges or the foundations of structures *la15-*. **3** the iron grating over a drain *19-*. **brander bannock** a thick oatcake baked on a gridiron *19- NE T*. [ON *brandreið*; compare OE *brandrād*]

brander[1,2] /ˈbrandər/ *v* **1** to grill or broil on a gridiron *la18-*. **2** *joinery* to fix cross-strips of wood to ceiling joists to support a ceiling *la19- T WC SW*. **3** to support with a framework or scaffolding *16-18*. †**brandering** the material or structure forming a scaffolding or retaining framework *la16-19*. [see the noun]

brandered /ˈbrandərd/ *adj* brindled, dun-striped *19- N H&I*. [compare BRANDIT]

brandie, †**branie** /ˈbrandɪ/ *n* a name for a brindled cow *19- NE SW Bor*. [altered form of BRANDIT]

brandie *see* BRANDY

brand iron /ˈbrand aerən/ *n* a gridiron *20- Sh Ork*. [ON *brandr* + AIRN[1,1]]

brandis, brandish *see* BRANISH

brandit, brannet, †**brawnit** /ˈbrandɪt, ˈbranɪt/ *adj* of a reddish-brown colour with darker stripes or markings, brindled *la14-19*, *20- Sh Ork NE T*. [compare Norw *brandut*]

brandreth *see* BRANDER[1,1]

brandy, †**branny,** †**brandie** /ˈbrandɪ/ *n* spirits distilled from wine or grapes *la17-*. [shortened form of Du *brandewijn* burnt (distilled) wine]

brane *see* BRAIN[2,2]

brang *see* BRING

brangle[1,1]**,** †**braingel,** †**brangil** /ˈbraŋɡəl/ *n* **1** a state of confusion, a tangle; a disturbance *la16-19*, *20- literary*. **2** a confused crowd *19*, *20- N*. **3** a lively dance *16-19*. **4** a movement; an impulse *17*. [MFr *bransle* movement]

brangle[1,2]**,** †**brangil** /ˈbraŋɡəl/ *v* **1** to shake, sway; to confuse or tangle *16-19*, *20- Ork NE*. **2** to brandish a weapon; to batter down; to brawl or squabble *16-19*. [MFr *bransler*]

branie *see* BRANDIE

branish, brandish, †**brandis,** †**brandeis** /ˈbranɪʃ, ˈbrandɪʃ/ *v* **1** to wave (a weapon) in threat or display *la14-*. **2** to act showily, swagger *15-e16*. [MFr *brandiss-*, lengthened stem of *brandir*]

brank[1] /braŋk/ *v* **1** to prance or strut; to bear oneself proudly *16-19*, *20- NE EC*. **2** to dress up in finery *16-19*, *20- NE EC*. **3** to behave violently or without restraint *e15*. †**brankie** finely or showily dressed *la18-e19*. [unknown]

brank[2] /braŋk/ *v* **1** to bridle, halter; to restrain *17-*. **2** to punish with an iron bridle, put the branks on a person *la16-e17*. [back-formation from BRANKS[1]]

branks[1]**,** †**brankis** /braŋks/ *npl* **1** a bridle or halter (with wooden side-pieces) *16-*. **2** an instrument of public punishment, an iron bridle and gag used to punish breaches of the peace or abusive language *la16-18*, *19- historical*. **put the branks on** to restrain, curb, cut down to size; *in chess* to checkmate *20-*. [unknown]

branks[2]**, branx** /braŋks/ *npl* the mumps *la18-*. [perhaps extended sense of BRANKS[1]]

branner *see* BRANDER[1,1]

brannet *see* BRANDIT

branny *see* BRANDY

branx *see* BRANKS[2]

brar *see* BRITHER[1,1]

bras *see* BRACE, BRESS

brase *see* BRACE

brash[1,1]**,** †**brasche** /braʃ/ *n* **1** an onset; a bout; an extra effort *17-*. **2** a short bout of illness *17-*. **3** a sudden gust of wind or burst of rain *19-*. **4** a short spell of churning *19*, *20- H&I Uls*. **5** a noisy throng of people *19*, *20- Ork*. **6** an attack, an assault in battle *la16*. **brashy 1** delicate in constitution, subject to illness *19- N NE EC SW*. **2** stormy, wet and windy *19*, *20- EC Bor*. [compare MLG *brasch* a crash]

brash[1,2]**,** †**brasche** /braʃ/ *v* **1** to break through or down; to bash or batter *la16-19*, *20- literary*. **2** to bring up liquid into the mouth (by belching) *19- NE SW*. **3** to rush *19- SW*. [see the noun]

†**brashloch** *n in the South-West* a mixed crop of rye with oats or barley *17-e19*. [unknown]

braslat *see* BRACELET

brass *see* BRESS

brasser /ˈbrasər/ *n* a blushing face (from embarrassment) *la20- C*. [perhaps from BRESS]

brast *see* BIRST[1,2]

brastle, braissle /'brasəl, 'bresəl/ *v* to struggle, exert oneself or toil *19- Bor.* †**brastling** noisy and menacing *la17.* [compare BREESHLE[1,2]]

brat /brat/ *n* **1** a (poor or ragged) garment; a rag *la15-.* **2** a bib, a pinafore *19-.* **3** a coarse (hessian) apron (worn by workers) *19-.* **4** scum on the surface of liquid; a skin on porridge; curdled cream on milk *la17-19, 20- Ork Bor.* **5** a cloth put on a tup-hog to prevent mating *19- C.* **6** a shepherd's plaid *19-20, 21- historical.* **7** the crust that forms on harrowed land *20- WC SW.* [OE *bratt* a cloak; compare Gael *brat* a mantle]

†**brath**[1], **braith** *adj* fierce, violent, strong *la14-e16.* [ON *bráðr*]

brath[2], **braith** /braθ, breθ/ *v* to weave straw-ropes round a stack *la18-19, 20- Ork.* [ON *bregða* to bind, pass a rope round, OE *bregdan* to weave]

brattach /'bratəx/ *n* a banner, a flag, an ensign *19, 20- literary.* [Gael *bratach* a banner; compare BRAT]

brattle[1.1], †**brattill** /'bratəl/ *n* **1** a loud clatter or rattle *16-.* **2** a peal of thunder *la19-.* **3** a short rush; a sudden bound; a race *18-19, 20- NE.* **4** a sudden blast of wind and rain, a spell of bad weather *la19- Sh NE.* **5** a noisy assault; a fight, a struggle *17-e19.* [onomatopoeic]

brattle[1.2], †**brattill** /'bratəl/ *v* **1** to make a clattering or clashing noise; to crash or rattle *16-.* **2** to rush noisily; to scamper *18-e19.* [see the noun]

brave /brev/ *adj* **1** courageous, daring; stout-hearted *16-.* **2** splendid, excellent, fine *16-.* **bravely 1** splendidly, very well *16-.* **2** courageously *17-.* **bravity, bravetie** splendour, elegance; ornament, finery *la16-19, 20- NE T C.* **brave and** very, extremely: ◊*brave and early la19-.* [MFr *brave*; compare BRAW[1.1]]

braw[1.1], **bra**, *Sh* **braa**, *NE* **brow** /brɔ, bra; *Sh* brɑ; *NE* brʌu/ *adj* **1** fine, splendid; excellent; worthy *17-.* **2** elegant, well-dressed, showy *17-.* **3** handsome, beautiful; strong, able-bodied *17-.* **4** *of a sum of money* considerable *18-.* **5** *of weather* pleasant *19-.* **braws**, *Ork* **braas 1** finery; good clothes, one's best clothes: ◊*Sunday braws 18-.* **2** beautiful or good things *19-.* **brawlike** fine, splendid, nice *20-.* **Braw Lad** the young man chosen annually by the people of Galashiels to represent the Burgh at the Braw Lads' Gathering on 29 June *20- Bor.* **Braw Lads and Braw Lasses** the young people of Galashiels *20- Bor.* **Braw Lass** the girl chosen to accompany the *Braw Lad* at the Braw Lads' Gathering in Galashiels *20- Bor.* **braw an', braw and** very, extremely: ◊*braw and weel 19-.* **a braw penny** a considerable sum of money *la19-.* **in braw time** in very good time *la19-.* [variant of BRAVE, from which it is not clearly separable in early examples with -*w*- for -*v*-]

braw[1.2], **bra** /brɔ, bra/ *adv* **1** well, finely *la19-.* **2** very, extremely *la19-.* [see the adj]

brawd *see* BRAD[1.2]

brawlins, †**bralans** /'brɔlɪnz/ *npl* the berries of the cowberry *Vaccinium vitis-idaea* or cranberry *Vaccinium oxycoccus la18- N NE T.* [Gael *braoileagan*, pl of *braoileag* a whortleberry, with additional plural -*s* suffix]

brawly[1.1], **brawlie** /'brɔli/ *adj* well, in good health: ◊*the bairns is brawly 19-.* [BRAW[1.1], with redundant adj-forming suffix -*ly*]

brawly[1.2], **brawlie**, *Sh* **braaly**, *NE* **browlie** /'brɔli; *Sh* 'brɑli; *NE* 'brʌuli/ *adv* **1** very well, excellently; thoroughly *la18-.* **2** fairly, reasonably *20- Sh EC.* **3** finely, elegantly *17.* [see the adj]

brawn *see* BRAN

brawnit *see* BRANDIT

brawyne *see* BRAN

braxy /'braxi/ *n* **1** an infection of the fourth stomach in sheep (caused by *Clostridium septicum*) *la18-.* **2** the salted flesh of a sheep that has died of braxy *la18-.* **braxy bree** soup made from a sheep that has died of braxy *20-.* **braxy ham** the ham of a braxy sheep *19-.* [unknown]

bray /bre/ *v* to push or shove *20- NE.* [perhaps ON *bregða* to cause to move quickly or OE *bregdan* to drag, pull]

bray *see* BRAE

brayn *see* BRAIN[2.1]

braze, braise /brez/ *n* the seabream *Pagellus centrodontus* or roach *Rutilus rutilus la18-.* [OE *bærs* a fish of the perch family, a bass or Norw dial *brasen* a bream]

†**bre** *v* to frighten *15-e16.* [OE *brēgan*]

bre *see* BREE[3]

brea *see* BRAE

breach *see* BRETSH

bread *see* BRAID[2.1], BREED[2], BREED[3], BREID

breadth *see* BREEDTH

break *see* BRAK[1.1], BRAK[1.2]

breakfast *see* BRAKFAST

†**breakshugh, braikshaw** *n* an intestinal disease in sheep, dysentery *la18-e19.* [Compare BRAXY]

breard *see* BRAIRD[1.1]

breast *see* BREIST[1.1], BREIST[1.2]

breath *see* BRAITH, BRAITHE

brebnar *see* BRABONER

brecan *see* BRECKEN

brecham, *NE* **braicham**, †**brechan** /'brɛxəm; *NE* 'brɛxəm/ *n* **1** a collar for a draught-horse (or ox) *16-.* **2** a bulky scarf *20-.* [OE *beorg*-, stem of *beorgan* to protect + HAIM]

brechan, †**brochan**, †**bracken**, †**brakane** /'brɛxən/ *n* a (highland) plaid; a tartan *16-19, 20- literary.* [Gael *breacan*]

brechan *see* BRECHAM

breck, brek /brɛk/ *n* poor, thin soil; a tract of barren or uncultivated land *la19- Sh Ork N.* [ON *brekka* a slope]

brecken, brecan, brachan, †**brakan** /'brɛkən, 'braxən/ *n* bracken; ferns of the genus *Pteridium*; frequently in place-names *la13-.* [ME *braken* or perhaps ON **brakni*]

bred[1.1], †**braid** /brɛd/ *n* **1** a church offertory or collection plate; the offering itself *la15-19, 20- SW.* **2** a board, a plank *16-19, 20- SW.* **3** a (wooden) pot lid *19, 20- Bor.* **4** one of the boards of a book *la19, 20- Bor.* **5** a shutter *19.* Compare BROD[2.1]. [OE *bred* a plank, a table]

†**bred**[1.2] *v* to furnish with boards *15-e16.* [see the noun]

†**bred**[2] *n* a quantity of lambskin *la15-e16.* [perhaps BREED[1]]

bred *see* BIRD[1], BRAID[2.1], BRAITHE, BREID

brede *see* BREED[1], BREED[4], BREID

breder *see* BRITHER[1.1]

bredth *see* BREEDTH

bree[1.1], **brie** /bri/ *n* **1** cooking liquid; soup, stock, gravy *la18-.* **2** whisky *la18-*; compare BARLEYBREE. **3** liquid or moisture of any kind *la19-.* **4** fruit juice *20-.* **through the bree** boiling; over-boiled *la20-.* [unknown; compare BROO[1]]

bree[1.2] /bri/ *v* to drain the cooking water (from boiled potatoes or vegetables) *la19- NE.* [see the noun]

bree[2] /bri/ *n* the consequences, the brunt *la19- NE EC.* [perhaps figurative use of BREE[1.1]]

bree[3], †**bre** /bri/ *n* **1** the brow, the forehead *18-19, 20- EC.* **2** the rim or edge; the top *la18-19, 20- N H&I.* **3** the eyebrow *la15-e19.* Compare BROO[1]. †**move neither ee nor bree** to remain absolutely motionless *la18-e19.* [OE *brū*; compare BROO[2]]

bree[4] /bri/ *n* a favourable opinion *la19, 20- Bor.* [unknown; compare BROO[3]]

breechin *see* BRITCHIN

breed¹, *NE* **breeth**, †**brede**, †**breid**, †**braid** /brid; *NE* briθ/ *n* **1** breadth, width *la14-*. **2** *with specification of measurement* distance across: ◊ *of fourty fute brede 15-16*. **i the breed o yer face** to one's face, in the face *19, 20- NE*. †**on brede** in extent; in an open manner, in the open *la14-16*. **on the breeth o yer back** flat on your back *la19, 20- NE*. [BRAID¹·²]

breed², †**bread**, †**braid** /brid/ *v* to resemble, take after; to have the nature or quality of *15-19, 20- NE EC*. [OE *bregdan on* to turn into; compare ON *bregða til* to resemble]

breed³, **breid**, **bread** /brid, brɛd/ *n* **1** favour, regard *la18-*. **2** circumstances, livelihood *la18-*. **in bad bread 1** in disfavour, on bad terms with *la19-*. **2** in difficulty or out of work *19*. [unknown]

breed⁴, †**brede** /brid/ *n* **1** *pl* the innards of an animal, the pancreas (of a sheep), sweetbreads *16-19, 20- Sh Ork NE*. **2** a piece of meat (for roasting) *e16*. [OE *brǣde* roasted meat]

breed⁵ /brid/ *n* **1** a brood, a litter of young *20- NE*. **2** a tribe, an (extended) family *la20- NE T C*. Compare BROD³. **breedy** prolific (in breeding) *19- N EC SW*. [OE *brōd*]

breeder *see* BRITHER¹·¹

breedth, **breidth**, **breadth**, †**bredth** /bridθ, brɛdθ/ *n* width; extent *la16-*. **breadth an lenth** one's full length, prone *19- EC SW*. [BRAID¹·², with noun-forming suffix *-th*]

breeg *see* BRIG

breek¹·¹, †**breke**, †**breik** /brik/ *n* **1** a cloth put on a ewe to prevent mating *20- NE Bor*. **2** (a pair of) breeches or trousers *la14-19*. **3** the crotch *la15*. **breekless** without trousers; wearing a kilt *16-*. **breeklums** an affectionate term for a small child *la19- NE T*. **breekums 1** short trousers; knee-breeches *la19- NE T EC*. **2** a small person; an affectionate term for a little boy *la19- NE T*. **breekband** a trouser waistband *20- Sh Ork NE SW*. **breekbridder**, **breek-brother** a rival in love *la16-19, 20- Sh*. †**breekumstoich** a small stout child in breeches *19*. [OE *brōc* (a pair of) breeches, trousers; buttocks]

breek¹·² /brik/ *v* **1** to tuck up (a dress) to the knees (for farm work) *19-*. **2** to put into trousers *la19-*. **3** to set to work *20- NE*. [see the noun]

breeks, *NE* **briks**, †**brekis** /briks; *NE* brɪks/ *n* **1** trousers; breeches *la15-*. **2** underpants, knickers *20-*. **3** *in draughts* the position when a king lies between two opposite men and is able to take either of them *20-*. **4** a forked stick used for a catapult; a fork in a tree *20- T EC*. **it's no in yer breeks** you won't succeed *18-19, 20- NE EC*. **pull up yer breeks** to pull oneself together, make an effort *la19-*. **wear the breeks** to be the dominant partner in a relationship *la19-*. [plural of BREEK¹·¹]

breel /bril/ *v* to move quickly and noisily; to hurtle *19- T SW Bor*. [perhaps metathesis of BIRL¹·²]

breem¹, **brim** /brim, brɪm/ *v of a sow or other animal* to be in heat *la16-19, 20- Ork EC SW*. [ME *bryme*]

†**breem**², **breme**, **brim** *adj* **1** furious, fierce, violent *la15-e19*. **2** bright, clear *e15*. [OE *brēme* famous, ME *breme* fierce, rough]

breem *see* BROOM

breenge¹·¹, **brainge** /brindʒ, brɛndʒ/ *n* a violent or clumsy rush, a dash, a plunge *la18-*. [unknown]

breenge¹·², **brainge** /brindʒ, brɛndʒ/ *v* **1** to rush violently; to barge forward recklessly or carelessly *la18-*. **2** to drive with a rush, impel vigorously; to batter, bang or slam *la19-*. **breengin 1** wilful, pushing, sharp-tongued *19-*. **2** bustling, surging *19-*. **let breenge** to aim a blow *20-*. [unknown]

breenger /ˈbrindʒər/ *n* **1** a rash, impetuous person *20-*. **2** a formidable or wilful person *la19- T C*. **3** *in football* a rash or forceful shot *la19- T*. [BREENGE¹·², with agent suffix]

breenth *see* BRENTH

breer, †**brere** /brir/ *n* a briar; a bramble or rose bush *15-*. [OE *brēr*]

breer *see* BRAIRD¹·¹, BRAIRD¹·²

†**breerie**¹·¹, **brierie** *n* a place covered with briers *19*. [see the adj]

breerie¹·², **brierie**, **briary**, †**brery** /ˈbriri, ˈbriəri, ˈbraeəri/ *adj* **1** covered with briars; frequently in place-names *la14-*. **2** sharp, clever; troublesome *la19*. [BREER + -IE²]

breers /brirz, ˈbriərz/ *npl* **1** the eyelashes *la19- NE T*. **2** the eyebrows *20- Sh NE*. **hing by the breers o yer een** to be in a very precarious position; to be on the verge of bankruptcy *la19- NE T*. [probably double plural form of ON *brár* eyelids or OE *brǣw* eyelid]

breese /briz/ *n* crushed sandstone or limestone *20-*. [probably BRIZZ¹·²]

breese *see* BREWIS

breeshle¹·¹ /ˈbriʃəl/ *n* the act of rushing; a rush *19- N NE T C*. [compare BRASTLE]

breeshle¹·² /ˈbriʃəl/ *v* to hurry, rush *19- N NE T C*. [see the noun]

breest *see* BREIST¹·¹

breet *see* BRUIT

breeth *see* BRAITH, BREED¹

breether *see* BRITHER¹·¹, BRITHER¹·²

breeze *see* BRIZZ¹·¹, BROOSE

bregwort *see* BRAGWORT

brehn *see* BRAIN²·¹

breid, **bread**, † **brede**, †**braid**, †**bred** /brid, brɛd/ *n* **1** baked dough, bread *la14-*. **2** an oatcake; oatcakes *20- N NE*. **3** a loaf; a bread-roll *15-e19*. **bread-berry** small pieces of bread with hot milk poured over the top, originally bread-and-water *18-*. **bread-house**, †**breid-hous** a store-room for bread; a pantry *la15-*. **breidsnapper** a (hungry) child; a mouth to feed *20- C*. **bread-and-cheese 1** the inside of a thistle head *20-*. **2** the first green shoots on a hedge in early spring *20- C SW*; compare *cheese-an-breid* (CHEESE¹). **he disna aet the breid o idleseat** he works hard for his living *20-*. [OE *brēad* a fragment, bread]

breid *see* BREED¹, BREED³

breidth *see* BREEDTH

breif *see* BRIEF¹·¹, BRIEF¹·², BRIEF²

breik *see* BREEK¹·¹

breird *see* BRAIRD¹·¹, BRAIRD¹·²

breist¹·¹, **breest**, **briest**, **breast**, †**brest**, †**brist** /brist, brɛst/ *n* **1** the chest; the bosom *la14-*. **2** the front or a projecting part (of something) *15-*. **3** a perpendicular cut in peat *19-*. **4** a (cobbled) slipway forming the front of a harbour *19-*. **5** the desk board of a pew *19- NE T*. **6** the gable end of a house *la18- Ork*. **7** a panelled partition (enclosing a box-bed and cupboard) *la18- NE*. **breist bane**, *NE* **breist been** the breast-bone *la15-*. **breast-bore** an instrument for boring *19- C*. †**brest curch** a kerchief for covering the breast *la15-e16*. **breast-seat** the front seat in the gallery of a church *la18- NE*. **breist-spade** a type of peat-spade *20- NE*. **breist o the laft** the front of the gallery in a church *20-*. **breist tae breist** face to face *20-*. **in a breist** abreast *20-*. [OE *brēost*]

breist¹·², **breast** /brist, brɛst/ *v* to spring up; to press forward; to climb *la16-*. [see the noun]

breith *see* BRAITH

brek *see* BRAK¹·¹, BRAK¹·², BRECK

brekanetyne *see* BRIGANTINE

breke *see* BREEK¹·¹

brekfast, **brekwus** *see* BRAKFAST

brekis *see* BREEKS

breme see BREEM²
brench see BRAINCH
brenn see BURN²·²
brennastyooch, brennastjuch /ˈbrɛnəstjux/ *n* fine spray rising from the sea breaking on a rocky shore *20- Sh.* [ON *brenna* to burn + STEW¹·¹]
brennik /ˈbrɛnək/ *n* a parhelion, a mock sun; the end of a rainbow *la19- Sh.* [Faer *brenning*]
brent¹·¹ /brɛnt/ *v* to spring forward *la19, 20- NE.* [compare ON *bruna* to advance quickly]
brent¹·² /brɛnt/ *adv* with a sudden bound or spring; directly, squarely *19- NE EC Bor.* [see the verb]
brent² /brɛnt/ *adj* **1** smooth, unwrinkled *la14-*. **2** steep, precipitous *19-*. **3** lofty, upright *16*. [OE *brant* steep]
brent see BRUNT²
brenth, breenth /brɛnθ, brinθ/ *n* breadth *la19- H&I WC SW Uls.* [altered form of BREEDTH, with influence from LENTH¹·¹, STRENTH¹·¹]
brerd see BRAIRD¹·¹, BRAIRD¹·²
brere see BREER
brery see BREERIE¹·²
bres see BRESS
brescat see BIRSKET
brese see BRIZZ¹·²
breslet see BRACELET
bress, braiss, brass, †**bras,** †**brace,** †**bres** /brɛs, brɛs, bras/ *n* brass, an alloy of copper and tin or zinc *la14-*. **braisant** brazen-faced, shameless *la18- NE T C Bor.* **brassy coal** *mining* coal with veins of iron pyrites *la19- C*. [OE *bræs*]
bressell see BRISSELL
bressie /ˈbrɛsi/ *n* a fish, the bib or pout *Trisopterus luscus 18-19, 20- EC.* [perhaps altered form of Eng *wrasse*]
brest see BIRST¹·², BREIST¹·¹
Bret see BRETT
Bretane see BRITANE¹·¹
†**Bretanʒe, Bertanʒe, Bartanʒe** *n* Brittany *la14-e17.* [OFr *Bretaigne*]
breth see BRAITH
brethering, brethir see BRITHER¹·¹
bretsh, †**breach** /brɛtʃ/ *n* the breaking of waves on a rocky shore (by which sailors navigate at night) *18-19, 20- Sh.* [OE *bryce*, Fr *brèche* a breach]
brett /brɛt/ *v* **1** to tuck up, roll *20- Ork.* **2** to strut; to square up *20- Ork.* [ON *bretta* to turn upwards]
Brett, †**Brit,** †**Bret** /brɛt/ *n* a (Strathclyde) Briton; a Brittonic-speaker *15- historical.* [OE *brit*]
Brettoner see BRITONER
†**Brettowne, Brettone, Brettane** *n* a Briton, a Brittonic-speaker *15.* [ME *Britoun*]
breu see BROO¹
breuk see BROOK¹·¹
breukie see BROOKIE¹·¹
breve see BRIEF¹·¹, BRIEF¹·², BRIEF²
brew /bru/ *v ptp* **brewed,** †**browin,** †**brewin 1** to make beer; to ferment malt *15-*. **2** to boil or steep; to concoct *la16-*. **brewer,** †**brewar** one who brews (beer) *la16-*. **browst, brewst 1** a brewing (of alcohol) *la16-*. **2** a brew (of tea) *19, 20- Sh.* †**brew caldroun** a brewing vessel *la15-e17.* †**brewcreesh** = *brew tallow 17-e19.* **brewcroft** a croft ranking as *brewland 17-19, 20- historical.* **brewhouse,** †**brew hous** a place where beer is brewed, a brewery *la14-*. †**brewing lume** a brewing vessel *16-18.* **bewland, browland** land connected with brewing on an estate *la13-19, 20- historical.* **brewseat** a brewery *la18-19, 20- historical.* †**brewstead** a place for brewing, a brewery *17-e19.* †**brew-tak** a tack of *brewland la16-17.* †**brew tallow, brew talloun** tallow paid as a tax for the privilege of brewing *17-e19.* [OE *brēowan*]
brewis, brooze, †**breese,** †**bruise,** †**browis** /bruz/ *n* broth, stock made from meat and vegetables *16-19, 20- T SW.* [ME *broues*, EModE *brues*]
brewster, *NE T* **browster,** †**brostar,** †**broustar** /ˈbrustər/; *NE T* ˈbrʌustər/ *n* a brewer or seller of ale *la14-19, 20- historical.* †**browster hous** a brewhouse, a brewery *la16-e17.* **brewsterland, browsterland** land connected with brewing on an estate *la14-19, 20- historical.* **brewster wife, browster wife** a woman who brews or sells ale; a landlady *18-19, 20- NE T EC.* [BREW, with (originally) feminine agent suffix *-ster*]
†**bricht**¹·¹ *n* a beautiful woman *la15-16.* [see the adj]
bricht¹·², **bright** /brɪxt, brʌɪt/ *adj* **1** shining, glowing, reflecting light; pure, clear *la14-*. **2** lively, cheerful, clever; *of colour* vivid *la14-*. **brichtsome** bright-looking *la19-*. [OE *briht, beorht*]
bricht¹·³ /brɪxt/ *adv* brightly *la14-*. [OE *brihte, beorhte*]
brichten, brichtin /ˈbrɪxtən/ *v* to brighten *la15-*. [OE *beorhtian*, or from the adj BRICHT¹·²]
brichtie /ˈbrɪxti/ *n* the chaffinch *Fringilla coelebs la19- SW.* Compare BRISKIE. [BRICHT¹·² + -IE³]
brick /brɪk/ *n* a loaf (of bread): ◊*penny brick la18-19, 20- EC Bor.* [figurative use of Eng *brick*]
bridder see BRITHER¹·¹
bride, †**bryd** /brʌɪd/ *n* a woman about to be married or newly married *la14-*. **bridal,** †**brithal,** †**brithell,** †**brydale** a wedding or wedding-feast *la14-*. **bride's bun** = *bride's cake 19, 20- Sh.* **bride's cake** a wedding cake, originally an oatcake or shortbread which was broken over the head of the bride *la18-*. **bride's cog** a three-handled wooden bowl containing a hot alcoholic drink, handed round the wedding party *19- Ork N.* †**bride's pie** a pie made by the bride's friends and distributed among the company at a wedding *la18-19.* †**bride's scone** = *bride's cake la18.* [OE *brȳd*]
bridie /ˈbrʌɪdi/ *n* a pasty made of a circle of pastry folded over and filled with meat and onions, originally made in Forfar *19-*. [probably shortened form of *bride's pie* (BRIDE)]
bridle¹·¹, †**bridill,** †**brydill** /ˈbrʌɪdəl/ *n* **1** a harness for a horse; a check, a restraint *la14-*. **2** a retaining band or beam; a crossbeam supporting the ends of joists *la16-*. †**bridil silver** a gratuity given to a servant for leading a horse *la15-e16.* **keep a bridle hand** to keep in control *18-19, 20- T EC.* [OE *brīdel*]
bridle¹·², †**bridill** /ˈbrʌɪdəl/ *v* **1** to put a bridle on (a horse); to check, restrain *15-*. **2** to rope a stack *19- Ork NE SW.* **3** to punish or ill-treat a person by the application of a bridle or branks *la16-e17.* [see the noun]
brie, brye /bri, brʌe/ *n* sandstone pounded down to use for rubbing on doorsteps *20- H&I WC.* **brie-stane** sandstone *20- C.* [ME *brayen* to pound, grind small, or back-formation from BREESE]
brie see BREE¹·¹
brief¹·¹, **brieve,** †**breve,** †**breif** /brif, briv/ *n law* an official document; a summons; a legal writ; a warrant (from chancery) authorizing an inquest or inquiry by a jury *la14-*. **brieve of division** *law* a brief of chancery providing for the dividing of lands between heirs-portioners *la15-*. **brieve of inquest** *law* a retourable brief directing the sheriff or bailies to try the validity of a claimant's title *la15-19, 20- historical.* †**brieve of lining** *law* a non-retourable brief of chancery directed to the provost and bailies of a burgh for settling the boundaries of holdings by measuring out the holdings *la15-17.* †**breff of mortancestor** = *brieve of mortancestry 14-15.* **brieve of mortancestry** *law* a brief of

chancery directing an inquest into a claim that the raiser is heir to certain property formerly possessed by an ancestor and now wrongfully held by another *15-18, 19- historical.*
†**brieve of right, brieve of richt** a brief setting up an inquest to determine the title to land *15-18.* [ME *bref,* Lat *breve* a letter, a note]
brief[1.2]**,** †**breve,** †**breif** /brif/ *v* **1** to instruct, inform *19-* **2** to express in writing *15-e17.* **3** to compose or narrate (a letter or book) *e16.* [see the noun]
brief[2]**,** †**breve,** †**breif** /brif/ *adj* **1** of a short duration; concise *la15-.* **2** energetic, forcible *la19- Sh Ork.* **3** curt, abrupt *e19.* †**the brief and the lang o it** the long and the short of it *e19.* [ME *bref,* Lat *brevis*]
brierd *see* BRAIRD[1.2]
brierie *see* BREERIE[1.1], BREERIE[1.2]
briest *see* BREIST[1.1]
brieve *see* BRIEF[1.1]
brig, brigg, *N* **breeg,** †**bryg** /brɪg; *N* brig/ *n* **1** a bridge; frequently in place-names *la12-.* **2** the division between flues in a chimney *la19-.* **3** a reef, a long low ridge of sea-rocks; frequently in place-names *la19- NE T EC.* **4** a large flat stone, a flagstone *e18.* **5** a gangway for a boat *la14-e17.* **6** a connecting part of a mechanism or implement *16-17.* **7** a drawbridge *la14-15.* **brig penny** a tax or toll for the upkeep of a bridge *17-19, 20- NE.* **brig stane,** *Sh* **briggsten,** *Ork* **brig steen 1** *pl* a footpath of flagstones laid in front of a house *20- Sh Ork.* **2** a stepping stone; a stone forming part of a bridge *la15-19.* †**brig work, bryg wark** the work of building or maintaining a bridge *la15-19.* [ON *bryggja* a pier, a landing-stage, a gangway, a bridge]
brigand, †**brigant,** †**brigane** /ˈbrɪgənd/ *n* a robber, a bandit *la15-.* †**brigancy** robbery with violence *la16-e17.* **briganer,** †**briganner** a thief, a ruffian *17-19, 20- NE.* [ME *brigaunt*]
†**brigantine, brekanetyne** *n* a kind of body armour *la15-e16.* [ME *brigantines,* variant of *briganders*]
brigdi, *Ork* **brigde** /ˈbrɪgdi; *Ork* ˈbrɪgdə/ *n* a basking shark *19-, Sh Ork N.* [ON *bregða,* OE *bregdan* to move quickly]
brigg *see* BRIG
bright *see* BRICHT[1.2]
†**brigue** *v* to intrigue; to solicit by underhand means; to canvass *la16-e19.* [MFr *briguer* to try to get]
brik *see* BRAK[1.2]
briks *see* BREEKS
brile *see* BRAIL
brim *see* BREEM[1], BREEM[2], BRIME[1.1], BRIME[1.2]
brime[1.1]**,** *Sh Ork* **brim,** †**bryme** /brʌɪm; *Sh Ork* brɪm/ *n* **1** salt water; brine (used for pickling) *17-19, 20- N NE T.* **2** (the sound of) surf breaking on the shore; sea-spray *19- Sh Ork.* **3** a stretch of water; a river or stream *la14-15.* **brimtud** the sound of breaking waves *la19- Sh.* [OE, ON *brim* the sea]
brime[1.2]**, brim** /brʌɪm, brɪm/ *v* **1** to fill a boat with salt water to swell and close the timbers (after it has been lying ashore) *20- N NE T.* **2** to draw a boat up out of reach of the surf *20- Ork N.* [see the noun; compare also ON *brýna upp skipi* to drag a boat or ship half ashore]
brimmle *see* BRAMMLE
brimstane *see* BRUMSTANE
brin *see* BURN[2.1], BURN[2.2]
brind /brɪnd/ *v of animals* to be in heat; to copulate *20- Sh.* [compare ON *brundtíð* the time when ewes are in heat]
brindle, brintle /ˈbrɪndəl, ˈbrɪntəl/ *n slang* money, cash *19- NE Bor.* [reduced form of *brint silver* (BRUNT[2])]
bring, †**bryng** /brɪŋ/ *v pt* **brocht, brang,** *ptp* **brocht, broucht, brung** to fetch, convey; to lead or accompany; to (cause to) come *la14-.* [OE *bringan*]

brinkie-brow /ˈbrɪŋkɪbrʌu/ *n* a child's word for the forehead *la19- NE T.* [unknown]
brint *see* BRUNT[2], BURN[2.2]
brintle *see* BRINDLE
bris *see* BRIZZ[1.1], BRIZZ[1.2]
briscat *see* BRISKET, BRISKET
brisk *see* BRÜSKI
brisken up /ˈbrɪskən ˈʌp/ *v* to freshen up, stimulate; to smarten up *la19-.* [EModE *brisk,* with verb-forming suffix]
brisket, *NE* **bisket,** †**briscat,** †**birsket** /ˈbrɪskət; *NE* ˈbɪskət/ *n* **1** the breast of an animal *la16-.* **2** the breast of a person *16-19, 20- NE T EC.* [compare OFr *brichet*]
briskie /ˈbrɪski/ *n* the chaffinch *Fringilla coelebs la19- SW.* [perhaps Scots *brisk* + -IE[3]; compare BRICHTIE]
brismic, brismac /ˈbrɪsmək/ *n* a young cusk fish *Brosme brosme 19- Sh N.* [ON *brosma* a type of cod fish]
briss /brɪs/ *n* a crack, a fissure; a defect *la19- Sh.* [ON *brestr*]
briss *see* BRIZZ[1.1]
†**brissel-cock, brissill cok** *n* a (game) bird *la16-e19.* Compare BIRSELL FOUL. [perhaps ME *brustle* + COCK[1.1]]
†**brissell, birsall, bressell** *n* brazil wood or the dye-stuff obtained from it *16-e19.* [ME *brasile,* Spanish *brasil* the wood of the sappan tree]
brissell fowl *see* BIRSELL FOUL
brissill cok *see* BRISSEL-COCK
brissle *see* BIRSLE
brist *see* BIRST[1.2], BREIST[1.1], BIRST[1.2]
bristit *see* BIRST[1.2]
bristle *see* BIRSLE
Brit *see* BRETT[1.2]
†**Britane**[1.1]**, Bretane** *n* Britain *la14-e17.* Compare BERTANE. [Lat *Britannus*]
†**Britane**[1.2] *adj* relating to Britain; British *16-e17.* [see the noun]
britch *see* BROOTSH
britchin, breechin /ˈbrɪtʃən, ˈbrɪtʃən/ *n* a breeching, a strap round the hindquarters of a shaft horse to let it push backwards *19-.* **hing in the breechin** to hang back, hesitate *la19-.* **sit in the breechins** to refuse to move; to fail to do one's fair share of work *19-.* [OE *brōc* (a pair of) breeches, trousers; buttocks]
brithal, brithell *see* BRIDE
brither[1.1]**, brother, bruther, brar, brur,** *NE* **bridder,** *NE* **breeder,** *NE* **breether,** *WC* **brurra,** †**broder,** †**bredir** /ˈbrɪðər, ˈbrʌðər, braər, brʌər; *NE* ˈbrɪdər; *NE* ˈbridər; *NE* ˈbriðər; *WC* ˈbrʌrə/ *n pl* †**brethir,** †**brethering,** †**breder 1** a male sibling, a brother *la14-.* **2** a dear friend, a colleague; a fellow man *la14-.* **3** a member of a religious order, or of a gild or corporation *15-.* **4** an equal, one of a pair *la19-.* **brither bairn,** †**brother barn,** a brother's child; a cousin *la16-19, 20- N.* †**brother bairns, brethir barnis** the children of brothers; cousins, kinsmen *15-19.* **brither dochter, brother dochter** a niece on one's brother's side *la16-.* **brither son, brother son** a nephew on one's brother's side *15-.* [OE *brōþor*]
brither[1.2]**, brother,** *NE* **breether** /ˈbrɪðər, ˈbrʌðər; *NE* ˈbriðər/ *v* **1** to admit or initiate into a trade, corporation or society *la17-19, 20- T WC SW.* **2** to match, equal; to accompany *la18-19, 20- NE T.* **3** to accustom; to inure *la19- NE.* **4** to receive as a brother, make a brother of *15-e19.* [see the noun]
british /ˈbrɪtɪʃ/ *n mining* a wall or a block of minerals which supports the roof of a working *la19, 20- EC.* [altered form of Scots *brattice*]
†**Britoner, Brettoner** *n* a Breton *15-16.* [ME *brutiner*]
brittle /ˈbrɪtəl/ *adj* **1** easily broken, fragile *la17-.* **2** difficult *19-.* [ME *bretil*]

brittyn, **bertyn** *v* to hack or hew to pieces; to slaughter *la15-16*. [OE *brytnian* to divide, distribute]

brizz[1.1], **bris**, **bruise**, *NE T* **birze**, *WC SW* **breeze**, †**briss** /brɪz, brɪs, bruz; *NE T* bɪrz; *WC SW* briz/ *n* **1** a contusion, a bruise *la18-*. **2** pressure; a push or struggle *19-*. [see the verb]

brizz[1.2], **bruise**, **braise**, **birse**, **birze**, †**brese**, †**bris**, †**birze** /brɪz, bruz, brez, bɪrs, bɪrz/ *v* **1** to crush; to break; to injure (by pressure); to inflict a bruise *la14-*. **2** to squeeze or strain; to push, shove or press forward *la18-*. [ME *brisen*]

bro, **brö** *see* BROO[1]

broach[1.1], †**brutch**, †**broche**, †**bruche** /brotʃ/ *n* **1** a brooch, a buckle *la14-*. **2** the spindle on which newly-spun yarn is wound *16-19, 20- NE*. **3** a pointed rod; a spit *la15-e19*. [ME *broche*]

broach[1.2], †**brotch**, †**broche** /brotʃ/ *v* **1** to prick or pierce; to open by piercing *la15-*. **2** to open a discussion; to tackle a person on a matter *17-*. [see the noun]

broad *see* BRAID[2.1], BROD[2.1]

broag *see* BROG[1.1]

broakie-faced *see* BROCKY

broath *see* BROTH[1]

brob[1.1] /brɔb, brob/ *n* a prick, a jab *la20- NE*. [perhaps onomatopoeic; compare BROD[1.1], BROGUE[1]]

brob[1.2] /brɔb, brob/ *v* to jab, prick *la20- NE*. [see the noun]

broch, **brough**, **bruch**, †**brouch**, †**brugh** /brɔx, brʌx/ *n* **1** a borough, a town *la15-*; compare BURGH. **2** an Iron Age structure consisting of a large round tower with hollow stone-built walls (especially common in Caithness and the Northern and Western Isles) *la17-*. **3** a halo round the moon (indicating bad weather) *la18-*. **4** *curling* a circle round the tee *19, 20- NE*. **5** a ring or halo *17-19*. **the Broch** a name for the nearest town, used particularly of Fraserburgh and Burghhead *19-*. [metathesis of BURGH, or ON *borg* a castle]

brochan, **brochen**, †**brachan** /ˈbrɔxən, ˈbroxən/ *n* **1** gruel, porridge; a hot drink containing oatmeal, butter and honey (used as a cure for a cold) *18-*. **2** a cereal mixture for feeding young calves *19, 20- NE*. [Gael *brochan*, IrGael *brochán* gruel; porridge]

brochan *see* BRECHAN

broche *see* BROACH[1.1], BROACH[1.2], BROTH[2.2]

brochen *see* BROCHAN

brochle /ˈbrɔxəl/ *n* a lazy person *19- N SW*. [unknown; compare BROCK[1]]

brocht *see* BRING

brock[1], **brok**, †**broke** /brɔk/ *n* **1** the badger *Meles meles 15-*. **2** *derogatory* a person *19-*. [OE *brocc*, Gael *broc*]

brock[2.1], *Sh Ork NE* **bruck**, *SW* **broke**, †**brok** /brɔk; *Sh Ork NE* brʌk; *SW* brok/ *n* **1** broken or small pieces; fragments, rubbish *16-*. **2** scraps of food, leftovers; kitchen refuse used for feeding pigs *18-*. **3** the rakings of straw from a harvested field *20- N NE T Bor*. **4** small potatoes *20- NE WC SW*. **da brucks o Yöl**, **the brucks o Yule** **1** the last days of the Christmas festive season *20- Sh*. **2** the last drop left in a bottle after Christmas celebrations *la20- Sh*. [OE *broc* a fragment, a piece; compare BRAK[1.1]]

brock[2.2], *Sh Ork* **bruck**, †**brok** /brɔk; *Sh Ork* brʌk/ *v* **1** to crush or bruise *la19- Sh Ork*. **2** to handle carelessly or unskilfully; to spoil *la17-19, 20- NE*. [see the noun]

brock *see* BROK

brocked *see* BROCKIT

brock-faced, †**brook-faced** /ˈbrɔkfest/ *adj of an animal* having a streaked or striped face *la18-*. [BROCK[1] + derivative of FACE[1.1]]

brockit, **brocked**, **bruckit**, †**brokit** /ˈbrɔkɪt, ˈbrɔkəd, ˈbrʌkɪt/ *adj* **1** *of an animal* having black and white stripes or spots *la16-*. **2** *of an animal* having a white streak down its face *la16-*. **3** *of people* streaked with dirt; filthy; disfigured *la19-*. **4** *of oats* black and white growing together *la16-19, 20- NE*. **5** *of things* marked with soot or mud, streaky, lined *la19, 20- literary*. Compare BROOKIT. **brockit grun** a mixture of clay and boggy ground *la19- Uls*. [compare Norw dial *brokut*, Dan *broget* flecked, streaked]

brocklie *see* BRUCKLE[1.2]

brocky /ˈbrɔki/ *n* a name for a cow with a black and white face *la18-19, 20- NE*. **brockie-faced**, *N* **broakie-faced** having a streaked or striped face *20-*. [back-formation from BROCKIT]

brod[1.1] /brɔd/ *n* **1** a goad, spur, pointed implement *la14-19, 20- NE EC*. **2** a prod or stroke (from a goad) *15-19, 20- NE EC*. **3** a stimulus, strong influence *la14-e16*. [ON *broddr*]

brod[1.2] /brɔd/ *v* **1** to goad, prick or pierce; to jab *la15-19, 20- NE EC*. **2** to appear, emerge *20- Sh*. [see the noun]

brod[2.1], **broad** /brɔd, brod/ *n* **1** (one of) the covers of a book *16-*. **2** a flat piece of wood, a panel; a notice-board *la16-*. **3** a games board (for chess or draughts) *la16-*. **4** a table spread for a meal *la16-*. **5** a church offertory or collection plate *16-19, 20- NE T EC*. **6** a (window) shutter *17-19, 20- T*. **7** a committee or council *la19- Sh NE T EC*. **8** a pot-lid *la19- NE T*. **9** *pl* the platform or scales of a weighing-machine *15-e18*. **10** the dial of a clock *la16-e17*. [metathesis of OE *bord*; compare BOORD[1.1]]

brod[2.2] /brɔd/ *v* **1** to cover with a lid *la19- Sh*. **2** to fit with a board or boards, especially shutters *la16-e17*. [see the noun]

brod[3], **brood**, †**brude** /brɔd, brud/ *n* **1** offspring, a family, a tribe *la15-*. **2** a goose that has hatched goslings *19- Sh Ork N*. **3** a young child, the youngest of a family *19*. **broody**, **brodie**, †**brudy** prolific; able or apt to breed *16-*. **brood goose**, †**brodguse** a breeding goose *16-19, 20- NE*. **brodmal**, †**brodmell** a brood *16-19, 20- NE*. [OE *brōd*]

bröd[4] /brød/ *n* a (cattle) track, a path *la19- Sh*. [ON *braut* a road]

broder *see* BRITHER[1.1], BROWDER

brodikyn *see* BROTEKIN

brodinster *see* BROWDINSTAR

brodstar *see* BROWDSTARE

brog[1.1], *Sh* **broag**, *N* **browg** /brɔg; *Sh* brog; *N* brʌug/ *n* **1** a bradawl; a goad *19-*. **2** a spike *la15-e16*. **brogit staff**, **broggit staff** a staff with an iron point, a pike *15-19, 20- historical*. [unknown]

brog[1.2] /brɔg/ *v* to prick; to pierce (a hole) *19-*. **broggle** to prick or pierce; to patch or mend; to work shoddily, botch or bungle *19, 20- Bor*. [unknown]

brog *see* BROGUE[1], BROGUE[2]

brogat *see* BRAGWORT

brogh and hammell *see* BORROW[1.1]

brogue[1], †**brog** /brog/ *n* a heavy shoe (decorated with a distinctive pierced pattern along the seams); originally a Highlander's shoe of untanned hide stitched with leather thongs *18-*. **broguer**, **brogger** a maker of brogues or clogs *19, 20- NE*. [Gael *bròg*, IrGael *bróg* a shoe]

brogue[2], *Sh* **brog** /brog; *Sh* brɔg/ *n* a trick, a hoax *la18, 20- Sh*. [EModE *brogge*]

broider *see* BROWDER

broigh *see* BROTH[2.1], BROTH[2.2]

broik *see* BROOK[1.2]

†**brok**, **brock** *n* the profit or interest on capital; usufruct *la15-e17*. [OE *broc* use, advantage; compare BROOK[2]]

brok *see* BRAK[1.2], BROCK[1], BROCK[2.1], BROCK[2.2]

broke *see* BROCK[1] BROCK[2.1], BROCK[2]

broken, **brokken**, **bracken**, †**brokin**, †**brokkyn** /ˈbrɔkən, ˈbrɔkən, ˈbrakən/ *adj* **1** damaged, fragmented; not

broken   76   **brot**

functioning *la14-*. **2** *of people* outlawed (for a crime); having no feudal superior or chief and living lawlessly *16-18, 19- historical.* **3** ruined, bankrupt; impoverished *la19-*. **4** *of milk* curdled, coagulated (as butter) *19- Sh NE SW.* **broken men** outlawed men (who had no feudal superior or chief) *16-18, 19- historical.* **broken milk** curds; whisked cream *la19- N NE T.* [ptp of BRAK[1.2]]
broken *see* BRAK[1.2]
brokill *see* BRUCKLE[1.2]
brokin *see* BROKEN
brokit *see* BROCKIT
brokken, brokkyn *see* BROKEN
bröl[1.1] /brøl/ *n* a bellow; the lowing of a cow *20- Sh.* **brolik** a taboo-name for a cow *20- Sh.* [see the verb]
bröl[1.2], **brüil** /brøl, brul/ *v* to bellow *la19- Sh.* [compare Norw dial *braula* to scream]
brolach /ˈbrolǝx, ˈbrɔlǝx/ *n* **1** a mess; rubbish; confusion; ruin *19- N NE.* **2** an old or feeble person *la19- NE T.* [Gael *brollach* a mess; compare IrGael *brothlach* the cooking pit of the Fiann]
broltie /ˈbrolti/ *n* the corn bunting *Emberiza calandra 20- Ork.* [unknown]
brome *see* BROOM
bron *see* BRAAND
†**brone** *n* a twig *e16.* [unknown]
brongie /ˈbrɔŋgi/ *n* the great cormorant *Phalacrocorax carbo 19- Sh.* [ON *bringa* chest]
brönnie *see* BRUNIE
bront *see* BRUNT[1], BRUNT[2]
broo[1], **brue**, *Sh* **brö**, *Ork* **breu**, †**bro** /bru; *Sh Ork* brø/ *n* **1** broth, soup; gravy, water in which food has been boiled *16-*. **2** moisture, liquid; slushy snow *la19, 20- T WC.* [ME *bro*; compare BREE[1.1]]
broo[2], **brow, brou** /bru, brʌu/ *n* **1** the eyebrow *la14-*. **2** the crest or slope of a hill *15-*. **3** the forehead *la15-*. **4** a (moss) bank; the top or surface level of a peat bank *la18-19, 20- Sh.* **5** the overhanging bank of a river *20- WC Bor Uls.* †**browband** a band for the front of a hat *la16-e17.* **broo o' brinkie** a child's word for the forehead *20- Ork*; compare BRINKIEBROW. **lat doon a broo** to frown, show displeasure *20- Ork NE.* [OE *brū* eyebrow]
broo[3], **brow** /bru, brʌu/ *n* a favourable opinion: ◊*I've nae broo o him 18- NE C SW Bor.* [unknown]
broo *see* BUROO
brood *see* BROD[3]
brook[1.1], **bruik, breuk** /bruk/ *n* soot (on pots or kettles) *la19- N NE T EC.* [compare BROCKIT]
brook[1.2], †**broik**, †**bruik** /bruk/ *v* to make black or dirty, streak or smear with soot *la15-19, 20- NE T.* [see the noun]
brook[2], †**bruik**, †**bruke**, †**broke** /bruk/ *v* **1** to have the use or possession of (lands, property or office) *la14-*. **2** to put up with, endure *18-*. **3** to wear or bear appropriately: ◊*weel may he brook it 18-19.* †**brookable** bearable *19.* [OE *brūcan*]
brook[3] /bruk/ *n* a deep layer of seaweed cast ashore (by stormy weather) *la19- Sh Ork N.* **brook o waar**, †**brook of ware** a heap of seaweed on a beach *la18- Sh Ork N.* [ON *brúk* a heap, especially of seaweed]
brook[4] /bruk/ *n* (a circle drawn in) a game of marbles *20- H&I WC.* [probably variant of BROCH]
brook[5], †**bruke** /bruk/ *n* a boil, ulcer or sore *15-19, 20- EC Uls.* [compare Icel *brúk* a swelling, rising (of yeast), ON *brúk* a heap, and BROOK[3]]
brook-faced *see* BROCK-FACED
brookie[1.1], †**breukie** /ˈbruki/ *n* **1** a nickname for a blacksmith *18-19, 20- NE T.* **2** a nickname for the Devil *19- NE.* [BROOK[1.2] + -IE[3]]

brookie[1.2] /ˈbruki/ *adj* grimy, dirty; covered with soot *19- NE Bor.* [see the noun]
brookit, broukit, †**bruiked,** †**brukit** /ˈbrukɪt/ *adj* **1** *of animals* marked or streaked with black *15-*. **2** streaked with dirt, grimy, sooty *16-*. Compare BROCKIT. [ptp of BROOK[1.2]]
broolie *see* BRULYIE
brooly *see* BRULZIE
broom, brume, *NE* **breem,** †**broum,** †**brome,** †**broume** /brum; *NE* brim/ *n* the plant broom *Cytisus scoparius*; bushes, a stretch or an expanse of broom; frequently in place-names *14-*. **broom cow,** †**broom kow** a branch of broom *la17-*. **broom park, brume park** a park or enclosure grown with broom *la15-*. **sing the brooom, sing the breem** to cry out because of punishment inflicted *20- NE.* [OE *brōm*]
broon[1.1], **broun, brown** /brun, brʌun/ *n* **1** the colour brown; brown-coloured cloth *la15-*. **2** a horse of a brown colour *15-19, 20- NE T EC.* **3** porter, ale *19, 20- NE.* [see the adj]
broon[1.2], **broun, brown,** †**brun** /brun, brʌun/ *adj* brown-coloured *13-*. **brown lintie** the linnet *Linaria cannabina la19, 20- N SW.* **broon pig** an earthenware whisky jar *19- NE T.* **broon robin, brown robin** home-brewed ale *la19- NE T C Bor.* **broon troot** the brown trout *Salmo trutta 20-.* [OE *brūn*]
brooncaidis *see* BROONKATIES
broonie, brownie, †**brunie** /ˈbruni, ˈbrʌuni/ *n* **1** *folklore* a benevolent sprite (supposed to perform household tasks in the night) *16-*. **2** *folklore* a malevolent goblin or evil spirit *18-*. [BROON[1.2] + -IE[3]]
broonie *see* BRUNIE
broonkaties, brooncaidis /brunˈketiz, brunˈkedɪs/ *n* bronchitis *20- Sh NE T C Bor.* [altered form of Eng *bronchitis*]
broose, braize, *NE* **breeze,** †**brouze** /bruz, brez; *NE* briz/ *n* a race at a country wedding from the church or the bride's home to the bridegroom's home *la18-*. **ride the broose** to participate in the BROOSE on horseback *la18-*. **run the broose** to participate in the BROOSE on foot *la18-*. **win the broose;** *NE* **win the breeze** to finish first in the BROOSE *20-.* [pl of BROO[1], a bowl of specially seasoned soup being originally the prize]
broostle *see* BRUSSLE[1.1], BRUSSLE[1.2]
brootsh, britch /brutʃ, brɪtʃ/ *v* to crush; to break or cut into small pieces *la19- Sh.* [ON *brytja* to chop]
brooze *see* BREWIS
broozle /ˈbruzǝl/ *v* to bruise, crush or smash *19, 20- NE EC.* [probably frequentative of *bruise* (BRIZZ[1.1])]
brose /broz/ *n* **1** a dish of oat- or pease-meal mixed with boiling water or milk (seasoned with salt and butter) *la17-*. **2** food; a meal (of which brose was the chief ingredient); one's living or livelihood *la19- NE T.* **brose-bicker** a wooden dish for brose *19- NE T EC.* **brose-caup, brose-cap** a wooden bowl in which brose was made *19- NE T EC Bor.* **brosemeal** parched pease-meal for making brose *19, 20- NE T EC.* **brose-time** meal-time *19, 20- NE.* **brosing-time,** †**browsing time** *mining* a meal-time *19-, 20- EC.* [unknown]
brosie, brosy /ˈbrozi/ *adj* **1** fed with brose; healthy, substantial *19-*. **2** stout, bloated (with food); soft, inactive *19-*. **3** covered or bedaubed with brose *la18-19, 20- NE T C.* **4** coarse, clumsy *20- NE C.* **brosy-faced** having a fat, flaccid face; looking well-fed *19-*. **brosie-headit** foolish or clumsy *la19-.* [BROSE + -IE[2]]
bröski *see* BRÜSKI
brostar *see* BREWSTER
brosy *see* BROSIE
brot[1] /brɔt/ *n* **1** a rag *la19- N T.* **2** an apron *19- NE T.* [Gael *brot* a veil; an upper garment; compare BRAT]

brot[2] /brɔt/ *n* a tangle, a muddle *la19- NE T*. [unknown]

brotch see BROACH[1,2]

†**brotekin, brodikyn** *n* a high boot *16-17*. [MFr *brodequin*]

broth[1], **broath** /brɔθ, broθ/ *n* soup usually made from mutton, barley and vegetables, Scotch broth; *frequently treated as pl*: ◊*they are guid broth 16-*. [OE *broþ*]

broth[2,1], †**broigh** /brɔθ/ *n* excessive perspiration *19- Bor*. **broth o sweat** a heavy sweat *19- EC Bor*. [see the verb]

broth[2,2], †**broche**, †**broigh** /brɔθ/ *v* to sweat profusely *la16-19, 20- SW Bor*. [compare Gael *bruich, bruith* to boil, cook, and BROTH[1]]

brother see BRITHER[1,1], BRITHER[1,2]

brottlet, †**brotlet** /ˈbrɔtlət/ *n* **1** a small coverlet *la18- T*. **2** a tablecloth *e17*. [compare BROT[1], BRAT]

brou see BROO[2]

brouch see BROCH

broucht see BRING

broud see BROWD

brough see BROCH

brough and hamehald see BORROW[1,1]

broukit see BROOKIT

†**broulery** *n* a struggle, a disturbance *la17-e19*. [Fr *brouillerie*; compare BRULZIE]

broume, broume see BROOM

broun see BROON[1,1], BROON[1,2]

brount see BRUNT[1]

broustar see BREWSTER

brouze see BROOSE

brow see BRAW[1,1], BROO[2], BROO[3]

†**browd, broud** *v* to embroider *la15-e16*. **browdin, brodin** **1** embroidered, decorated *la14-e19*. **2** stained (with blood) *16*. **browdry, broderie** embroidery *15-16*. [ME *brouden*, with influence from BROWDER]

browden, †**browdin** /ˈbrʌudən/ *adj* **1** enamoured, extremely fond of; intent on, eager for *la16-19, 20- NE*. **2** bold, impudent *la19- Sh Ork*. [extended sense of OE *brogden* ptp of *bregden* to weave]

browdened, brodent, †**broudned** /ˈbrʌudənd, ˈbrɔdənt/ *adj* **1** enamoured, extremely fond of *la17-*. **2** brazen, forward *20- Sh*. [derivative of BROWDEN]

†**browder, broder, broider** *v* to embroider *la15-e19*. **browderer** an embroiderer *e16*. [OFr *broder*]

†**browdinstar, brodinster, browdister** *n* an embroiderer *15-e17*. [irregular variant of BROWDSTARE]

†**browdstare, brodstar, browstare** *n* an embroiderer *la15-e17*. [BROWD, with agent suffix]

browg see BROG[1,1]

browin see BREW

browis see BREWIS

browl /brʌul/ *n* a dry piece of firewood *20- NE EC*. [unknown]

browlie see BRAWLY[1,2]

brown see BROON[1,1], BROON[1,2]

brownie see BROONIE

browst see BREW

browstar see BROWDSTARE

browster see BREWSTER

broynd see BRUND[1,1]

bruch see BROCH

bruche see BROACH[1,1]

bruck see BROCK[2,1], BROCK[2,2]

bruckit see BROCKIT

bruckle[1,1] /ˈbrʌkəl/ *v* to crumble; to crush or crumple *la19- Sh*. [see the noun]

bruckle[1,2], †**brukill**, †**brukle**, †**brokill** /ˈbrʌkəl/ *adj* **1** easily broken, brittle; crumbling *la14-*. **2** unstable, uncertain; hazardous *la15-19*. **3** morally weak; readily yielding to temptation *la14-16*. **brucklie, brocklie 1** crumbly, breakable *la18- Sh NE T EC*. **2** *of people* in a weak state of health; *of weather* unsettled *la19- Sh NE*. **bruckleness**, †**brukilnes** brittleness, fragility; uncertainty *la14-*. [OE **brucol*, from *bruc-*, variant of *brecan*; compare BRAK[1,2]]

bruckles /ˈbrʌkəlz/ *npl* the prickly-headed carex, a sedge *Carex echinata la19- NE*. [perhaps Gael *brù-chorc* stool-bent, dirk grass]

brude see BROD[3]

brudge /brʌdʒ/ *v* to bruise; to crush, chop finely *20- Ork*. [ON *brytja* to chop]

brue see BROO[1]

brug /brʌg/ *n* a hillock, a flat-topped mound *la19- Sh*. [unknown]

brugh see BROCH

bruik see BROOK[1,1], BROOK[1,2], BROOK[2]

bruiked see BROOKIT

bruilzie see BRULZIE

brüil see BRÖL[1,2]

bruind see BRUND[1,2]

bruise see BREWIS, BRIZZ[1,1], BRIZZ[1,2]

bruit, brute, *NE* **breet**, *C SW* **brit** /brut; *NE* brɪt; *C SW* brɪt/ *n* **1** an animal; a brutal person *17-*. **2** a poor fellow or creature *la18- NE*. [Fr *brute*]

bruk see BRAK[1,2]

bruke see BROOK[2], BROOK[5]

brukit see BROOKIT

brukle see BRUCKLE[1,2]

brulie see BRULZIE

†**brulyie, broolie, brulʒe** *v* to broil, burn *la14-e19*. [ME *broilen*]

brulzie, brulie, brooly, †**brulʒe**, †**bruilzie** /ˈbrulji, ˈbruli/ *n* a turmoil, a commotion; a quarrel, an affray *16-19, 20- N NE T WC*. **brulziement** = BRULZIE *18-*. [MFr *brouiller* to confuse]

†**brumaill** *adj* wintry *e16*. [Lat *brūmālis*]

brume see BROOM

brummle see BRAMMLE

brumple, brumplo /ˈbrʌmpəl, ˈbrʌmplo/ *n* a small fish of various different varieties *20- Sh Ork N*. **brumplick** = BRUMPLE *la19- Sh*. [unknown]

brumstane, brimstane, brunstane, †**bruntstane**, †**brynstane** /ˈbrʌmsten, ˈbrɪmsten, ˈbrʌnsten/ *n* brimstone, sulphur *la14-*. [ME *brynstane*; compare ON *brennisteinn*]

brund[1,1], †**broynd** /brʌnd/ *n* **1** a fragment, a vestige *19- T*. **2** a brand, a burning or burnt piece of wood *la14-17*. Compare BRAAND. [OE *brand*]

†**brund**[1,2], **bruind** *v* to emit sparks, blaze *e19*. [see the noun]

brung see BRING

brunie, broonie, brönnie /ˈbruni, ˈbrøni/ *n* a round, thick scone or bannock made with beremeal or oatmeal *19- Sh Ork*. [compare Norw dial *bryne* a slice of cake]

brunie see BROONIE

brunstane see BRUMSTANE

brunt[1], †**bront**, †**brount** /brʌnt/ *n* **1** (the chief impact of) an attack *la15-*. **2** the front ranks of an army *16*. [ME *brunt* a sharp blow]

brunt[2], **brent, burnt**, †**brint**, †**bront** /brʌnt, brɛnt, bʌrnt/ *adj* **1** burned; injured, damaged or destroyed by fire *15-*. **2** hardened by fire; prepared or refined by heating *16-*. **3** branded, marked by burning *la16-*. **4** harmed, suffering; cheated *19-*. **bruntie** a blacksmith *la19- Ork NE T*. **brunt ale, burned yill 1** the refuse of a whisky still *la18- Ork NE C*. **2** warmed ale *20- NE C*. †**Brunt Candlemes, Brint Candilmes** the Candlemas of 1355 when Edward III burnt much of southern Scotland *la15-17*. **burnt coal** *mining* coal which has been altered and carbonized by the intrusion of igneous rock *la19, 20- T C*. **burnt end** *carpet bowls* the replaying of an end (when the jack goes out of play) *20-*. **bruntland, brintlin** rough ground or moorland, periodically burned *17-19, 20- Sh NE T WC*. **burnt-nebbit** *of tawse* having ends hardened by fire *la19- NE EC*. **brent new** brand new *la18-*. †**brint silver** refined silver *la15-16*. [ptp of BURN[2.2]]

brunt *see* BURN[2.2]
bruntstane *see* BRUMSTANE
brur, brurra *see* BRITHER[1.1]
brus *see* BRUSH[1.1]
brusche *see* BRUSH[1.1], BRUSH[1.2]
†**brusery** *n* embroidery *e16*. [compare BRUSIT]
†**brush**[1.1], **brusche, brus** *n* a violent rush or onset *15-e19*. [ME *brusche*]
†**brush**[1.2], **brusche** *v* 1 to force or drive violently; to cause to rush or gush *15-e19*. 2 to burst or spring out *15-e16*. [see the noun]
brush[2] /brʌʃ/ *v mining* to remove part of the roof or pavement of a working (by blasting) to heighten the roadway *la19- C*. **brushing** *mining* the part of the roof or pavement of a working removed to heighten the roadway *la19, 20- EC*. **brusher** *mining* a person employed in heightening the roadway *la19- NE T C Bor*. [unknown]
†**brusit** *adj* embroidered *la15-e16*. [Lat *brusdus*; compare BRUSERY]
brüski, bröski, *Ork* **brisk** /ˈbrøski; *Ork* brɪsk/ *n* gristle, cartilage *la19- Sh Ork*. [ON *brjósk*]
†**brusour** *n* an embroiderer *la15-e16*. [Lat *brusdus*; compare BRUSERY, BRUSIT]
brussle[1.1], †**broostle** /ˈbrʌsəl/ *n* a rush, a bustling state; hard exertion *19- WC SW Bor*. [probably onomatopoeic]
brussle[1.2], **bruzzle,** †**broostle** /ˈbrʌsəl, ˈbrʌzəl/ *v* to rush, hurry or bustle about *19- Bor*. [see the noun]
brust *see* BIRST[1.2]
brutal /ˈbrutəl/ *adj* 1 brutish, stupid; cruel; violent *16-*. 2 of or like an animal *la15-16*. [Lat *brūtus* dull, stupid, unreasonable, with adj-forming suffix]
brutch *see* BROACH[1.1]
brute[1.1], †**bruyt** /brut/ *n* 1 noise, a din *16-e19, 20- literary*. 2 (a) rumour, a report; fame, ill repute *la15-19, 20- WC SW*. [MFr *bruit*]
†**brute**[1.2] *v* 1 to spread a rumour, make a noise *la16-e19*. 2 to accuse or credit (a person) by rumour *la16-e17*. [see the noun]
brute *see* BRUIT
bruther *see* BRITHER[1.1]
bruyt *see* BRUTE[1.1]
bruzzle *see* BRUSSLE[1.2]
bryd *see* BRIDE
brydill *see* BRIDLE[1.1]
brye *see* BRIE
bryg *see* BRIG
bryme *see* BRIME[1.1]
brymmyll *see* BRAMMLE
bryng *see* BRING
brynstane *see* BRUMSTANE
bu *see* BO[1], BOO[6], BOW[1]
buat *see* BOWET
†**bub, bob** *n* a blast of wind, a sudden squall *16-e19*. [perhaps onomatopoeic]
bubba *see* BOBBIE
bubble[1.1], **bibble,** †**bubbil** /ˈbʌbəl, ˈbɪbəl/ *n* 1 a hollow globule of liquid *16-*. 2 *pl* mucus from the nose *19-*. 3 a bout of weeping *la20-*. [see the verb]

bubble[1.2], **bibble** /ˈbʌbəl, ˈbɪbəl/ *v* to weep, blubber *18-*. [ME *bubble* to form bubbles]
bubbly, bibbly, †**bubly** /ˈbʌble, ˈbɪble/ *adj* 1 emitting bubbles *la16-*. 2 snotty, dirty with nasal mucus *la18-*. 3 tearful, blubbering, snivelling *la19-*. **Bubbly Babies** *derogatory* a nickname for the Boys Brigade *la20-*. **Bubbly Bairns** = *Bubbly Babies*. [BUBBLE[1.1] + -IE[2]]
bubbly-jock /ˈbʌble dʒɔk/ *n* a turkey (cock) *la18-*. **sair hauden doun by the bubbly jock** overwhelmed with too much to do *la19, 20- NE SW*. [BUBBLY + JOCK]
bubby /ˈbʌbe/ *n* a breast *18-*. [probably imitative from baby language]
bubly *see* BUBBLY
buccar, †**bucker,** †**bikker** /ˈbʌkər/ *n* a fast-sailing boat used in smuggling *la18-19, 20- SW*. [perhaps altered form of Eng *buccaneer*]
buccassy *see* BUCKASIE
Buchan cheese /ˈbʌxən ˈtʃiz/ *n* cheese made with skimmed milk *19- NE*. [from the name of the Scottish district + CHEESE[1]]
Buchan humlie, Buchan hummlie /ˈbʌxən ˈhʌmle/ *n* a breed of black, hornless beef cattle; an Aberdeen Angus *la19- NE T*. [from the name of the Scottish district + derivative form of HUMMEL[1.1]]
Buchanite /ˈbʌxənʌɪt/ *n* a member of a fanatical religious sect, founded by Mrs Elspeth Buchan, in the South-West of Scotland *la18-e19, la19- historical*. [from the surname of the founder]
bucher, byoocher /ˈbʌxər, ˈbjuxər/ *n* a fit of uncontrollable coughing; a cough which causes this *la19- NE*. [onomatopoeic]
bucht[1.1], **bught, boucht,** †**bowcht** /bʌxt, bʌuxt/ *n* 1 a sheepfold; a small pen (within a fold) for milking ewes *15-*. 2 the pulpit in which the precentor sat *20- T*. 3 a square pew in a church *19*. [Flem *bocht, bucht* an enclosure for swine or sheep]
†**bucht**[1.2], **boucht** *v* to bring together; to enclose ewes (for milking) in a fold *18-19*. [see the noun]
bucht[2.1], †**boucht,** †**bought** /bʌxt/ *n* 1 a length of fishing line (of 40-50 fathoms) *17- Sh Ork*. 2 a bend, a fold; a knot; a coil of rope *19, 20- NE WC*. [Norw *bukt*]
†**bucht**[2.2], **boucht, bought** *v* to bend, fold (over) *18-e19*. [see the noun]
bucht[3], †**bought,** †**boucht** /bʌxt/ *n* 1 the bend of the arm or leg *la18- NE EC*. 2 a branch, twig; a fork of a tree *la18- T Uls*. [perhaps Norw *bukt* or BEUCH, with infl from BUCHT[1.1]]
buck[1] /bʌk/ *v of water* to pour or gush out; to make a gurgling noise *19, 20- Sh NE*. [probably onomatopoeic]
buck[2] /bʌk/ *v* 1 to push, butt; to strike, fight *la16-19, 20- NE*. 2 to walk to and fro *la19-, NE SW*. **buckie** *n* a smart blow (to the face) *19- NE T*. **buckie** *v* to strike or push roughly *la19- NE*. [perhaps related to BUCK[3]]
buck[3], †**buk** /bʌk/ *n* the male of the goat *Capra aegagrus* or fallow deer *Dama dama 15-*. †**bukhed, bukhud** the game of blindman's buff; peep-bo *la15-16*. **buck tooth,** †**buktuth** a large projecting tooth *la15-*. [OE *bucca*]
buckartie-boo /ˈbʌkərtiˈbu/ *v* to coo like a pigeon *la19- NE*. [onomatopoeic]
†**buckasie, buckesie, buccassy** *n* bocasin, a kind of fine buckram *la15-e17*. [Spanish *bocaci*]
buckdealling *see* BUGDALIN
bucker[1.1] /ˈbʌkər/ *n* 1 a mess, a bungle *20- NE*. 2 vexation, annoyance; a nuisance *20- NE*. [see the verb]
bucker[1.2] /ˈbʌkər/ *v* 1 to move or work aimlessly or awkwardly; to fuss, detain with trivialities *la19- NE*. 2 to make

a mess of, bungle *20- NE*. [probably frequentative form of BUCK²]

bucker² /'bʌkər/ *n* the killer whale *Orcinus orca* or porpoise *Phocoena phocoena la18- H&I WC*. [perhaps from its bucking movements]

bucker³ /'bʌkər/ *n* a boat used in herring fishing *19, 20- N*. [perhaps derived from the place-name *Buckie*]

bucker⁴ /'bʌkər/ *n* **1** a nickname for a native of Buckie *19-*. **2** a nickname for a native of Buckhaven *20-*. [derived from the name of the towns]

bucker *see* BUCCAR

buckesie *see* BUCKASIE

bucket, †**bukket**, †**bukkit**, †**buket** /'bʌkət/ *n* **1** a pail; a (square-sided) wooden vessel for transporting goods and waste *la13-*. **2** *mining* the metal tub used for transporting workers and ore within a pit *la18-20, 21- historical*. **3** a glass of spirits; a quantity of drink: ◇*he taks a fair bucket la19-*. **4** a dustbin; a wastepaper basket *20-*. †**bucket money, buckit monye** *in Glasgow* a sum paid by entrant burgesses, originally used by the Merchants' and Trades' Houses in the provision of (leather) buckets for public services including fire-fighting *la17-19*. †**bucket pot, buckitt pat** a pit dug to receive sea water for evaporation in a salt-works, a salt-pan *17-19*. **the buckets** rubbish collection *la20-*. [MFr *bacquet*]

buckie¹, †**bukky** /'bʌke, 'bʌki/ *n* **1** (the shell of) the common whelk *Buccinum undatum*; a mollusc of the family *Buccinidae 16-*. **2** something of little value: ◇*no worth a buckie la19- NE EC*. **3** a snail-shell *20- EC*. **4** a small hut or shed *la20-*. **5** a protuberance on the cheek *16-e17*. **come oot o yer buckie** to lose your shyness *20- NE T*. [perhaps Lat *buccinum* a shellfish used in purple dyeing]

buckie² /'bʌke, 'bʌki/ *n* a hip, the fruit of the wild rose *Rosa canina 19, 20- NE H&I Uls*. **buckie breer** a wild-rose bush *la19- SW Uls*. [unknown; compare BUCKIE-FAULIE]

buckie³ /'bʌki/ *n* a child's rattle made of plaited rushes and dried peas *la18- NE*. [unknown]

buckie⁴ /'bʌke, 'bʌki/ *n* a perverse, obstinate person *18-*. [perhaps derived from BUCK³]

buckie-faulie, buckie-faalie /bʌki'fɔli, bʌki'fali/ *n* the fruit or flower of the briar *Rosa canina* or *Rubus fruticosus*; the primrose *Primula vulgaris 20- N*. [Gael *bocaidh-fhàileag* the hip, the fruit of the wild rose; compare BUCKIE²]

bucklag *see* BOOKLAG

buckle¹·¹, †**bukkill**, †**bukle** /'bʌkəl/ *n* **1** a clasp or fastening (on a belt or strap) *15-*. **2** a tussle, a tangle *la19- Sh NE*. **3** the clamp which holds the coulter of a plough to the beam *20- NE EC*. **up in the buckle 1** elated *19- T C Bor*. **2** conceited *la19- EC SW*. [MFr *boucle*]

buckle¹·², †**bukkill**, †**bukle** /'bʌkəl/ *v* **1** to fasten with a buckle; to secure firmly *16-*. **2** to join or be joined in marriage *18-*. **3** to partner (in a dance) *19-*. **4** to wrap up; to fasten up *la18-19, 20- Sh Ork*. **5** to dress *la19- NE*. **6** to entangle *20- Sh*. **bucklins** clothes, trappings (of marriage) *20- NE*. †**buckle-beggar** a hedge parson *18-19*. **buckle-the-beggars 1** a person who performs irregular marriage ceremonies *19, 20- Uls*. **2** a registry-office marriage *la20- Uls*. [see the noun]

bucks, bux /bʌks/ *v* to tramp down, walk clumsily; to splash through water *la19- Sh Ork*. [compare ON *byxa sér* to jump]

bucks *see* BOX²

buckshaivelt *see* BOGSHAIVELT

bucksturdie /bʌk'stʌrde, 'bʌkstʌrde/ *adj* obstinate *19- T*. [perhaps BUCK³ + STURDY¹·²]

†**bud¹·¹, budd** *n* a bribe; a private reward for services rendered *15-e18*. [unknown; compare OE *bēodan* bribe, offer]

†**bud¹·²** *v* to bribe *la16-e19*. [see the noun]

bud *see* BEHOVE

budd *see* BUD¹·¹

budder *see* BATHER¹·¹, BATHER¹·²

buddie *see* BODY

buddie, böddie /'bʌdi, 'bødi/ *n* a (straw) basket (carried on the shoulders) *19- Sh*. [compare Icel *biða* a little tub]

buddo, *Sh* **bodda** /'bʌdo; *Sh* 'boda/ *n* a term of endearment (for a child) *20- Sh Ork*. [unknown]

buddom *see* BODDAM¹·¹

buddy *see* BODY

bude *see* BEHOVE

†**budgell, budyel, budʒell** *n* **1** a bottle; an earthenware jar (for holding alcohol) *la16-19*. **2** a bag, a pack; a bundle *19*. [Gael *buideal*]

buff¹·¹ /bʌf/ *n pl* the lungs *la19- C SW*. [see the verb]

buff¹·² /bʌf/ *v* **1** to toast (herring) on a grid-iron *18-19, 20- EC*. **2** to laugh aloud *19, 20- Bor*. **3** to puff out (clothing or the cheeks) *la16-e19*. **4** to stuff furniture *e18*. **buffie, baffy** fat, chubby *19-*. †**buffing** a puffed part of a pair of breeches *la16-e17*. [perhaps OFr *bofer* to snort, breathe heavily, MFr *bouffer* to puff out, snort]

buff²·¹, *NE* **bouff**, *NE* **boof** /bʌf; *NE* bʌuf; *NE* buf/ *n* a blow; a dull sound *19-*. **not play buff** to make no impression *la19, 20- NE*. **play buff** to strike (on something) making a dull sound *la19-*. [probably onomatopoeic; compare OFr *buffe*, LG *buff* a blow, and BAFF¹·¹]

buff²·², *NE H&I* **boof** /bʌf; *NE H&I* buf/ *v* **1** to strike, beat or buffet *la18-*. **2** to thresh grain without untying the sheaf *19-*. **3** *of a storm* to beat down or flatten (grain) *19- NE*. **4** to emit a dull sound *20- N*. **5** to make a soft or puffing sound *e16*. †**the best o him is buffed** he is in decline, his strength is going *19*. [see the noun]

buff³ /bʌf/ *n* silly or irrelevant talk *la18- Sh NE T EC*. **neither buff nor stye** neither one thing nor the other; nothing at all *19-*. [probably onomatopoeic]

buff⁴ /bʌf/ *adj* buff-coloured, a light brownish yellow *18-*. **AB buff** the alphabet, so called from the colour of the school primer; hence something very simple or elementary *la19- NE T WC SW*. Compare *penny buff* (PENNY). [shortened form of Fr *buffle* buffalo]

buffate stule *see* BUFFET STOOL

buffets /'bʌfəts/ *npl* a swelling in the glands of the throat; mumps *19- T C*. [compare BUFF¹·²]

buffet stool, *NE* **bowfit steel**, *T C* **buffy stool**, †**buffate stule** /'bʌfət stul; *NE* 'bʌufət stil; *T C* 'bʌfe stul/ *n* a kind of square stool *la15-19, 20- NE T C Bor*. [unknown first element + STUIL]

buffle *see* BOOFEL

buftie /'bʌfte/ *n offensive* a homosexual *la20-*. [unknown]

bug *see* BAG¹·¹, BIG¹

bugdalin, †**buckdealling**, †**buk denning** /'bʌgdələn/ *n* **1** packing material or bedding-straw (used in the hold or bottom of a boat) *18- Sh Ork N H&I*. **2** the inner planking of a ship *16-e18*. [Du *buikdenning, buikdelling*]

†**buge¹** *n* lambskin *15-16*. [ME *buge*]

†**buge²** *n* a kind of (hooked) weapon *e16*. **buge staff** = BUGE² *la15-e16*. [MFr *bouge*]

bugger *see* BOUGAR

buggerize /'bʌgəraez/ *v* to mess around (whilst pretending to work hard) *20- Sh EC*. [compare Eng *bugger about*]

buggerlugs /'bʌgərlʌgz/ *n* a term of abuse for a person *la20-*. [nonsense formation from Eng *bugger* + LUG¹, with pl suffix]

buggie, bogy, bogie /'bʌgi, 'bogi/ *n* a sheepskin leather bag *17- Sh Ork*. **buggiflay, buggie-flay** to skin a sheep whilst keeping the skin in one piece *la19- Sh*. **buggiflooer** sea

buggin | 80 | **buliment**

campion 20- *Sh*. [ON *belgr* the skin of an animal taken off whole; a bag, bellows]
buggin, †**bogan** /'bʌgən/ *n* a boil, a pimple *la18-19, 20- Uls*. [IrGael *bócán* a blister caused by a burn]
buggle, bogel /'bʌgəl, 'bogəl/ *n* a large BANNOCK (made of oatmeal or barley meal) *la19- Sh*. **buggle day** a historic feast day on which a BANNOCK was baked for each member of a family *la19- historical*. [probably related to Faer *bøkul*]
bught *see* BUCHT[1.1]
†**bugrist** *n* a person who practised buggery *e16*. [MFr *bougre*, with agent suffix]
büid *see* BÖD
buik[1.1], **buke, book, beuk**, *NE* **byeuk** /buk; *NE* bjuk/ *n* 1 a (bound) printed or written work; a section or division of a text *la14-*. 2 the bible *15-*. 3 a record book or register *la15-*. 4 the reading of the bible; family worship *19, 20- NE T EC SW*. 5 a packet of gold leaf (resembling a book) *la15-17*. **buikie**, †**byuckie** a book *19-*. **buik board**, †**buik buird** a bookshelf in a pew or pulpit *la18-*. **buik lare, beuk lear** learning, education *19- NE T C*. **at the buiks** reading, studying *la19- N NE C*. **be i the gudeman's buiks** to be in favour, in a person's good books *19- NE T*. **book of adjournal 1** the records and regulations of the High Court of Justiciary *18-*. 2 a register containing the records of criminal trials *16-17*; compare ADJOURNAL. †**buke of responde** a record book in which decrees and acts were entered by the Clerk of the Session for the charging of fees *16-17*; compare *responde book*, RESPONDE. **Buik of Sederunt** *see* SEDERUNT. **far i the buik** well-read, learned, clever *la19, 20- Ork NE*. **tak the Buik** to hold family worship *19, 20- NE C Bor*. [OE *bōc*]
buik[1.2], **buke, book, beuk** /buk/ *v* 1 to record, register; to enter into a (record) book *la16-*. 2 to record the names of a betrothed couple in the register of the session clerk before marriage *la19- NE T WC*. [OE *bōcian* to give (a grant of land) by charter]
buik *see* BOUK[3.1]
buikin, beukin, booking, †**buiking** /'bukɪn, 'bjukɪn, 'bukɪŋ/ *n* 1 the act of entering (a name) in a book or register *la16-*. 2 the giving in of the names (to the session clerk) for the proclamation of the banns; the festivities held in celebration of such a betrothal *la18- NE T C*. **beukin nicht, booking night** a celebration held on the evening of a formal betrothal *20- Ork NE*. **tenure of booking** *law* a system of land tenure in the burgh of Paisley requiring registration in the burgh register *19, 20- historical*. [presp of BUIK[1.2]]
buil *see* BEULD[1.1]
build, †**beild**, †**buld**, †**bould** /bɪld/ *v ptp* also †**ybeldyt** to construct or erect; to increase *la15-*. Compare BIG[1]. †**beildar, beilder** a builder *16*. **building stance** a building site for a house *la18-*. **built up on** devoted to (someone) *la19- NE C*. [ME *bylden*]
buill *see* BÖL[1.1]
buily, builo /'bøli, 'bølo/ *n* a feast; a titbit, something nice to eat *19- Ork*. [compare Dan *bolsje*, Swed *bulle*]
builʒe *see* BILE[1.2]
buin *see* BUNE
buird /burd/ *adj* strong, sturdy *la19- EC SW*. [reduced form of BUIRDLY]
buird *see* BOORD[1.1], BOORD[1.2]
buirdly, buirlie, boorly, burly, *Sh* **bördly**, †**boardly**, †**beirdly**, †**burelie** /'burdli, 'burli, 'bʌrli; *Sh* 'børdli/ *adj* 1 sturdy, well-built; strong, powerful, robust; stout *15-*. 2 rough *19- NE*. [ME *borelich*]
buirk, *EC* **birk** /børk; *EC* bɪrk/ *v* to belch *20- Ork EC*. [unknown; compare BOAK[1.2]]
buirlie *see* BUIRDLY

buiss *see* BOOSE[1.2]
buist[1], *Sh* **böst**, *EC* **baist**, †**boist**, †**bust** /bust; *Sh* bøst; *EC* best/ *n* 1 a small box for storing documents, valuables, sweets or medicines *la14-19, 20- Sh Ork NE T*. 2 a casket or chest *15-19, 20- NE EC*. 3 a pad placed under a garment *la16-e17*. [ME *boist*]
buist[2.1], *SW* **bist** /bust; *SW* bɪst/ *n* 1 an identification mark branded or painted on sheep *la18-19, 20- N NE SW*. 2 an iron stamp for marking sheep *20- WC SW Bor*. [perhaps extended sense of BUIST[1]]
buist[2.2], *SW* **bist** /bust; *SW* bɪst/ *v* to brand or mark cattle or sheep with their owner's mark *19, 20- N WC SW Bor*.
buister 1 a person who brands or marks sheep *19, 20- N WC Bor*. 2 the instrument used for marking sheep *20- SW Bor*. **buisting iron** an instrument used for marking sheep *19, 20- H&I SW*. [see the noun]
buit[1.1], **bute, boot**, *Sh* **böt**, *Ork* **beut**, *N NE* **beet**, *C* **bit**, †**bote**, †**butt** /but; *Sh Ork* bøt; *N NE* bit; *C* bɪt/ *n* 1 footwear covering the ankle (and lower leg), a boot *la14-*. 2 an instrument of torture *la16-18, 19- historical*. 3 a term of abuse for a woman *la20-*. †**butcatcher** a servant who removes and cleans boots *la17*. [ME *bote*]
buit[1.2], **boot**, *NE* **beet**, †**bute** /but; *NE* bit/ *v* 1 to wear or be provided with boots *18-*. 2 to kick *18-*. 3 to place a person in an instrument of torture *la16-17, 19- historical*. [see the noun]
buit[2.1], *N NE* **beet**, †**bute** /but; *N NE* bit/ *n* 1 an amount added to one side of a bargain to make up a deficiency of value, something thrown in *la16-*. 2 help, remedy, relief *la14-e17*. †**na bute** no alternative or choice *la14-e19*. **to the bute** in addition, in to the bargain, boot *la18- NE T C*. **to the beet of the bargain** in addition *20- N NE*. [OE *bōt*]
buit[2.2], *N NE* **beet**, †**bute** /but; *N NE* bit/ *v* 1 to complete a bargain; to make up the balance *20- NE*. 2 to help, benefit *la15-17*. Compare BEET[2.2]. [see the noun]
buith, booth, †**buth**, †**bothe**, †**bouth** /buθ, buð/ *n* a covered (market) stall; a shop *14-*. **booth-holder**, †**buith haldar** the occupant of a booth, a shopkeeper *la15-*. †**buthman** a shopkeeper *15-e16*. †**booth-meal, buith maill** the rent of a booth; shop-rent *la15-18*. **buith raw, booth row** a row of shops or stalls (especially in Edinburgh) *15-17, la18- historical*. [ON *búð* a booth, a shop]
buk *see* BUCK[3]
buk denning *see* BUGDALIN
buke *see* BAKE[1.2], BOUK[2], BUIK[1.1], BUIK[1.2]
buket, bukket *see* BUCKET
bukkill, bukle *see* BUCKLE[1.1], BUCKLE[1.2]
bukkit *see* BUCKET
bukky *see* BUCKIE[1]
bul *see* BULL[3]
buld *see* BUILD
bulder *see* BULLER[1.1], BULLER[1.2]
bule *see* BÖL[1.2], BULL[1]
bulek *see* BOOLIK
bulf *see* BILF[1], BILF[2]
bulfie[1.1] /'bʌlfi/ *n* a stout or fat person *20- T*. [see the adj]
bulfie[1.2] /'bʌlfi/ *adj* 1 fat, stout *20- NE T*. 2 stupid, foolish *19- NE*. [derivative of BILF[2]]
Bulgan's Day, Bullion's Day /'bʌlgənz de, 'bulɪənz de/ *n* = MARTIN BULLION'S DAY *la19, 20- N*. [perhaps reduced form of MARTIN BULLION'S DAY]
bulger /'bʌldʒər/ *n golf* a (wooden) driver with a convex face *la19- T C*. [probably derivative of Eng *bulge*]
bulget *see* BULLGIT
buliment, bullament, *Sh* **bölliment**, *NE* **boulyiement**, *Uls* **boilyiemint**, †**buljament**, †**bulziement** /'bulɪmənt,

'bulǝmǝnt; *Sh* 'bølimǝnt; *NE* 'buljǝmǝnt; *Uls* 'bɔɪljǝmɪnt/ *n* **1** an outer garment of a ragged or ridiculous type *20- NE Uls*. **2** *pl* odds and ends; belongings *la19- Sh*. **3** *pl* equipment, arms *e19*. **4** a garment; clothing *la16-e18*. Compare HABILIMENT. [OFr *habillement*]

bulister *see* BULLISTER

buljament *see* BULIMENT

bulkie /'bʌlki/ *n* a policeman; a sheriff's officer *19- NE T EC Uls*. [probably Eng *bulky* of large bulk]

bull[1], **bill**, †**bule**, †**bole** /bul, bʌl, bɪl/ *n* **1** the male of a bovine *Bos taurus la14-*. **2** a variety of trout *Salmo trutta la19- SW Bor*. **bullsbags** the green-veined or purple orchid *19- NE T*. **bull-grass** brome grass *Bromus la19- NE Bor*. **bull's head** *folklore* a symbol of condemnation to death, warning of immediate execution; a bad omen *la16-19, 20- historical*. **bull-o-the-bog** the bittern *Botaurus stellaris 19- Bor*. **bull-reel** a reel danced by men only *19- NE EC Bor*. **bull-segg** a bull which has been castrated when fully grown *19- NE SW Bor*. **bullock-yellow** a kind of turnip *19- N NE T H&I*. **bullyhorn** a kind of hide-and-seek *la19- T*. **as prood as bull beef** very proud or conceited *la19- NE T*. [apparently ON *boli*]

bull[2], †**bow** /bul/ *n* (the seal attached to) a papal letter *15-*. [Lat *bulla*]

bull[3], **bul**, †**boll** /bul, bʌl/ *n* a homestead; the chief house or principal farmhouse on an estate *16- Ork*. Compare BOO[5] [perhaps ON *ból* a lair, a bed, a farm]

bull *see* BILL[1], BÖL[1.1]

bullament *see* BULIMENT

bullax, †**billaix** /'bʌlaks/ *n* an axe, a hatchet *16-19, 20- NE*. [ON *bol-öx*]

bulldairy *see* BALDERRY

buller[1.1], *Sh Ork N* **bulder** /'bʌlǝr, 'bulǝr; *Sh Ork N* 'bʌldǝr/ *n* **1** a bubble; a bubbling or boiling up of water; a whirlpool or eddy; frequently in place-names *la15-19, 20- NE Bor*. **2** a roar, a loud gurling noise *19- N NE T*. **3** blustering talk, nonsense *la19- Sh Ork N*. **4** a (spasmodic) cry *20- N*. [see the verb]

buller[1.2], *Sh Ork* **bulder** /'bʌlǝr, 'bulǝr; *Sh Ork* 'bʌldǝr/ *v* **1** *of water* to boil or bubble up; to rush noisily; to make a loud gurgling sound *la15-*. **2** to roar, bellow (like a bull) *16-*. **3** to bluster, blurt out; to speak unintelligibly *20- Sh Ork*. **4** to blunder clumsily *20- Sh*. †**bullerand in his blude** with blood issuing from the body, bleeding profusely *15-e17*. [compare OFr *bolir*, Icel *bulla* to boil; Swed *bullra*, Dan *buldre* to rumble]

bullet, †**billet** /'bulǝt/ *n* **1** a ball or shot used as ammunition *16-*. **2** a large round stone *19-*. **3** a game in which iron balls were hurled (using a leather sling) *18-19, 20- historical*. **bullet gun**, †**billet gun** a pop-gun made from a branch of elder *19- SW Bor*. **bulletstane 1** a hailstone *20- NE*. **2** a round stone *17-e19*. [MFr *boulette*]

bullgit, †**bulget** /'bʌldʒɪt/ *n* **1** a large, shapeless, untidy bundle *20- NE T*. **2** a (leather) pouch, bag or sack *la15-e17*. [ME *bouget*]

bullie /'buli/ *n* the bullfinch *Pyrrhula pyrrhula la19- NE T EC Bor*. [abbreviated form of Eng *bullfinch*]

bullie *see* BULLY[2.1]

bullin, **bullon** /'bʌlǝn/ *n* a heap, a pile (of peats or seaweed) *la19- Sh Ork N*. [ON *bulungr* a pile of logs, firewood]

Bullion's Day *see* BULGAN'S DAY

bullister, †**bulister** /'bulɪstǝr/ *n* a wild plum or sloe (tree or bush) *Prunus spinosa 16-19, 20- WC*. [ME *bullester*]

bulliwan *see* BULWAND

bullon *see* BULLIN

bullox[1.1] /'bʌlǝks, 'bulǝks/ *n* a mess *20-*. [related to BULLAX]

bullox[1.2] /'bʌlǝks, 'bulǝks/ *v* to spoil, make a mess of *20-*. [see the noun]

bully[1] /'buli/ *n* the game of conkers *20-*. [compare BARBULYIE to disorder, Gael *buille* a blow]

bully[2.1], **bullie** /'buli/ *n* a bellow, a howl *la19- NE*. [related to Eng *bellow*]

bully[2.2], **belly**, †**billy** /'buli, 'bɛli/ *v* to bellow, howl or roar; to weep loudly *la18- N NE SW*. [see the noun]

bullyeart *see* BILƷARD

Bully Wee /buli 'wi/ *n* a nickname for Clyde Football Club *la19-*. [Eng *bully* first-rate + WEE[1.2] because they are a minor team]

bult /bʌlt/ *v* to butt (with the head or horns) *la19- Sh*. [Swed *bulta*]

bult *see* BOUT[3]

bulwaaver *see* BELLWAVER

bulwand, *Sh* **bulwaand**, *Ork* **bulwint**, *N* **bulliwan** /'bʌlwǝnd; *Sh* 'bʌlwand; *Ork* 'bʌlwɪnt; *N* 'bʌliwǝn/ *n* **1** mugwort *Artemisia vulgaris 19- Sh Ork N*. **2** the bulrush *Typha latifolia 19- Sh SW*. **3** the common dock plant *Rumex la19- Ork N*. [Eng *bull* big + WAND[1.1]; compare BUNEWAND]

bulʒard *see* BILƷARD

bulziement *see* BULIMENT

bum[1.1] /bʌm/ *n* **1** a humming or droning sound; a buzz of voices *la19-*. **2** a musical note *la19- NE T*. **3** a person who reads, sings or plays badly *la19- NE*. **4** a boasting person *la20- WC*. **bum clock** a humming beetle *la18-*. [see the verb]

bum[1.2] /bʌm/ *v* **1** to make a humming or buzzing noise *la16-*. **2** *of bagpipes* to make a droning sound; *of a person* to sing or intone in a droning manner *18-*. **3** to weep or sob *la19-*. **4** to brag, boast *19-*. **5** to proceed vigorously, prosper *20- NE T*. **bummin** very good, worth boasting about *20- NE T*. **bum bummin** a continuous humming sound *la19- NE EC*. **bum yer chat** to try to put something over on someone *la20-*. **bum yer load** = *bum yer chat*. [onomatopoeic]

bum[2] /bʌm/ *v* **1** to strike or knock *19- C SW Bor*. **2** to throw away carelessly or noisily; to dismiss without ceremony *20- C SW Bor*. [perhaps onomatopoeic]

bum[3] /bʌm/ *n* a kind of Dutch fishing boat *20- Sh NE*. [Du *bom*, *bomschuit*, LG *boomschip*, *bumboot*]

bumbar, †**bumbard**, †**bumbart** /'bʌmbar/ *n* **1** a big clumsy person *20- N*. **2** a bumblebee *la16-e17*. **3** a lazy or stupid person *e16*. [probably a derivative of BUM[1.2]]

bumbase *see* BUMBAZE

bumbasy *see* BOMBASIE

bumbaze, **bumbase**, **bombaise**, †**bambaize** /bʌm'bez, bǝm'bez/ *v* to perplex, confuse or stupefy *la17-*. **bumbazement**, **bombaisement**, **bambaizment** confusion *20-*. [unknown]

bumbee /'bʌmbi, bʌm'bi/ *n* a bumblebee *la17-*. **bumbee tartan** a mock tartan, a ludicrous checked pattern *20-*. [BUM[1.2] + BEE[1]]

bumble *see* BUMMEL[1.2]

bumfle[1.1], **bumphle** /'bʌmfǝl/ *n* an untidy bundle; a pucker, a ruffle, an untidy fold *20-*. **bumfly**, **bamphly** bundled up, rumpled; untidily put on *la19-*. [probably BUMPH, with frequentative suffix *-le*]

bumfle[1.2], **bumphle** /'bʌmfǝl/ *v* **1** to puff out, bulge *la19-*. **2** to roll up untidily; to rumple up *20-*. [see the noun]

bumfy /'bʌmfi/ *adj* clumsy or lumpy *20-*. [BUMPH + -IE[2]]

bumlick, **bumlack** /'bʌmlɪk, 'bʌmlǝk/ *n* **1** a stone on which one might trip; a stumbling-block; a pebble *19- NE*. **2** a large clumsy person or thing *20- NE*. [perhaps BUMMLE[1.1], with diminutive suffix]

bumlie /'bʌmli/ *n* something which is larger than usual *20- NE*. **bumlers** heavy masses of clouds *20- NE*. [perhaps reduced form of BUMLICK]

bummack *see* BUMMOCK

bummasal, bymasal /bʌmə'sal, bʌImə'sal/ *interj* an expression of astonishment *20- NE T*. [shortened form of Scots *by my soul*]

bummel[1.1] /'bʌməl/ *n* a splash; a floundering (in water) *19- Sh*. [Icel *bumbla*]

bummel[1.2], **bumble** /'bʌməl, 'bʌmbəl/ *v* to boil up, bubble; to splash or flounder in water *19- Sh EC Bor*. [see the noun]

bummer, Ork bomer /'bʌmər; Ork 'bomər/ *n* 1 an insect that hums or buzzes; a bumblebee; a bluebottle *19-*. 2 a humming toy; a humming top *19, 20- NE T C*. 3 a blunderer, an ineffective singer or player *19- NE T C SW*. 4 a mill or factory siren *20-*. 5 a thing or person or animal which is very large or wonderful of its kind; a bulky person or thing *20-*. 6 a manager, a prominent or officious person *20-*. [BUM[1.2], with agent suffix]

bummie[1] /'bʌmi/ *n* 1 a bumblebee *la19-*. 2 a foolish person *la18- Sh NE T EC*. **bummie bee** a bumblebee *la20-*. [BUM[1.2] + -IE[3]]

bummie[2], **bommi** /'bʌmi, 'bomi/ *n* a wooden vessel for water or milk, a shallow churn *la18- Sh Ork*. [probably ON *bumba* a drum, the belly of a large vessel]

bummle[1.1], †**bummill** /'bʌməl/ *n* 1 a wild bee *la18-*. 2 a person who reads, sings or plays badly *la18-*. 3 indistinct, blundering reading *la19-*. 4 a bungle, a mess *la19-*. 5 an idle or clumsy person *la18-e19*. †**bummillbaty** a feckless person *e16*; compare *batie bum* (BATIE). [frequentative form of BUM[1.1]]

bummle[1.2] /'bʌməl/ *v* 1 to read, play or sing badly *18-*. 2 to work ineffectively; to blunder about *19-*. 3 *of a bee* to hum *20-*. 4 to stammer; to speak carelessly *20-*. 5 to weep *la19- NE*. **bummler, N boomalar, †bumlar** a blundering or awkward person, a bungler *la16-*. **bummlin**, *Sh* **bemlin, †bamling** clumsy, careless *19-*. [see the noun]

†**bummock, bummack** *n* 1 *in Orkney and Caithness* the brewing of a large quantity of malt; the liquor that is brewed *la17-e19*. 2 *in Orkney* an entertainment given at Christmas by tenants to their landlords *la18-e19*. [unknown]

bump /bʌmp/ *n* 1 *pl* fast turns of a skipping rope *la20-*. 2 a thump on the back or on the bottom (for each year of life) as a birthday ritual *la20-*; compare DUMP[1.1]. [onomatopoeic]

bumph /bʌmf/ *n* 1 a lump, a bundle *20- SW*. 2 a stupid person *20- SW*. [variant of Eng *bump*]

bumphle *see* BUMFLE[1.1], BUMFLE[1.2]

bumpy /'bʌmpi/ *n* the buttocks *la19, 20- NE*. [Eng *bump* + -IE[1]]

bumshayvelt *see* BOGSHAIVELT

bun[1] /bʌn/ *n* 1 a small cake; a bread roll *la16-*. 2 a very rich spiced fruit cake, baked in a pastry crust and eaten at Hogmanay, compare *black bun* (BLACK[1.2]) *18-*. [ME *bun*]

bun[2], †**bune** /bʌn/ *n* 1 the tail of a hare or rabbit *18-19, 20- Bor Uls*. 2 the buttocks *16-e19*. [compare Gael *bun* base, bottom]

†**bun**[3] *n* a cask (for water or beer) *la16-e19*. [unknown]

bun *see* BOUN[1.1], BUND

bun' *see* BOUN[1.2]

bunce[1.1] /bʌns/ *n* a share *19- EC*. [unknown, compare Eng *bunce*]

bunce[1.2] /bʌns/ *v* to club together; to share equally *19- T EC*. [see the noun]

bunce *see* BOONCE[1.1], BOONCE[1.2]

bunch /bʌnʃ/ *n* a small, stout girl or young woman *19- WC SW Uls*. [unknown]

bund, bun, boun', bound /bʌnd, bʌn, bʌun, bʌund/ *adj* 1 tied, secured with bonds *15-*. 2 joined or fitted together; secured with mortise-and-tenon joints or beading *16-*. 3 under obligation; compelled *la16-*. **bun bed** a box-bed *la17-19, 20- NE T*. **bun breest** a box-bed which incorporates a cupboard with panelled doors *la19- NE*. **bun shafe** someone engaged to be married *20- NE*. †**bund wark** a piece of work fitted together with joints or beading *16-17*. [ptp of BIND[1.2]]

bund *see* BIND[1.2], BOND[1], BOUN[2.1]

bundage *see* BONDAGE

bundin *see* BIND[1.2]

bundling /'bʌndlɪŋ/ *n* a form of courtship which was common in the Highlands and Isles, in which the partners laid in bed together with their clothes on *19-20, 21- historical*. [derivative of ME *bundel*]

bune, buin /bun/ *adj* upper *20- SW Bor*. [aphetic form of ABUNE[1.1]]

bune *see* BOON[1], BUN[2]

†**bunewand, bunwand** *n* a hollow plant stem of the dock plant *Rumex* or cow parsnip *Heracleum sphondylium*; the plant itself *la16-e19*. [OE *bune* reed + WAND[1.1]; compare BULWAND]

bung[1.1] /bʌŋ/ *n* 1 the act of throwing forcibly *19- NE T EC*. 2 a blow, a slap *20- Sh EC SW*. 3 a violent rush *la19- NE*. **bungy** huffy, sulky *19- NE*. **in a bung** in a temper or sulking *la19- NE*. **tak the bung** to go into a huff *19- NE*. [perhaps related to BANG[1.1]]

bung[1.2] /bʌŋ/ *v* 1 to throw violently, hurl *19-*. 2 to offend; to take offence *la19- NE*. [see the noun]

bung[1.3] /bʌŋ/ *adv* with sudden impetus or impact *la19- NE T H&I EC*. [see the noun]

bung[2] /bʌŋ/ *v* to make a booming or twanging sound *19, 20- NE EC*. [onomatopoeic]

bung[3] /bʌŋ/ *n* 1 an old worn-out horse *19- EC Bor*. 2 a worthless or worn-out person *20- NE T Bor*. [unknown]

bung[4.1] /bʌŋ/ *n* a stopper (for a cask or barrel) *16-*. **bung fu** 1 very drunk *la18-*. 2 completely full up *19-*. [ME *bung*]

†**bung**[4.2] *adj* tipsy *e18*. [perhaps shortened form of *bung fu* (BUNG[4.1])]

bungle[1.1] /'bʌŋgəl/ *n* a big clod of earth *20- Sh*. [Norw *bungl*, Faer *bungla*]

bungle[1.2] /'bʌŋgəl/ *v* to throw a big clod of sod or turf *la19- Sh*. [see the noun]

bungs *see* BUNKS

bunk[1.1] /bʌŋk/ *n* 1 a chest used as a seat *20- NE T EC*. 2 the lodgings of a St Andrews University student *la19- EC*. **bunk wife** a landlady of a student lodging-house *20- EC*. [unknown]

bunk[1.2] /bʌŋk/ *v* to occupy a bunk or lodging; to share a lodging with *la19-*. [unknown]

bunker, NE bunkart, †bonker, †bonkard /'bʌŋkər; 'bʌŋkərt/ *n* 1 a chest or box (used also as a seat); a bench or pew *16-*. 2 a receptacle for coal on a ship; a press or storage bin for household coal *18-*. 3 a small sandpit; a sandtrap on a golf-course *19-*. 4 a rough outdoor seat; a bank of earth at the roadside *19- NE T Uls*. 5 a large heap (of stones or clay) *la19- NE*. 6 a kitchen work surface *la20-*. **bunker iron** *golf* a club used to dislodge a ball from a sand bunker *19-*. [unknown]

bunks, bungs /'bʌŋks, 'bʌŋz/ *v* to wrap up well; to overdress *20- Sh Ork*. [ON *bunki* a heap, a pile]

bunnage *see* BONDAGE

bunnel /'bʌnəl/ *n* the cow parsnip *Heracleum sphondylium 19- WC*. [compare BUNEWAND]

bunnet[1.1], **bannet, bonnet, †bonet, †bonat** /'bʌnət, 'banət, 'bɔnət/ *n* 1 a soft flat brimless hat or peaked cloth cap

la14-. **2** a woman's (brimmed) head-dress *la15-*. **3** *mining* a portion of a seam left as a roof *la19- C*. **4** an additional piece laced to a sail *la15-e17*. **5** a metal helmet *16-e17*.
bonnety, bonnetie a boys' game played with their caps *la19-*. **bonnet fir** the Scots pine *Pinus sylvestris la19- T*. **bonnet fleuk** the brill *Scophthalmus rhombus la17- C*. **bonnet hill** a (wooded) hill overlooking the land or town below *18-*. **bonnet laird** a small landowner who farmed his own land; a self-important person *19-*. †**Bonnet Monday** *in Glasgow* the day following the Spring Sacrament, on which women traditionally strolled along the main streets to show off their new spring bonnets *la19*. †**bonnet mutch** a woman's bonnet-like cap *e17*. **bonnet piece** a gold coin from the reign of James V, depicting the king wearing a bonnet *la16-e17, la17- historical*. **Bonnet Toon, Bonnet Town** a nickname for Stewarton in Ayrshire, a town noted for the manufacture of bonnets *20-*. **bonnets on the green** a quarrel *20-*. **do yer bunnet** to fly into a rage *la20- C*. [OFr *bonet* cloth for making headgear]
bunnet[1.2], **bonnet** /ˈbʌnət, ˈbɔnət/ *v* to cover the top of something; to put one's cap on the top of (a mast or a tree) as a feat of daring *e16, la19- NE T*. [see the noun]
bunnle /ˈbʌnəl/ *n* a bundle *la19-*. [ME *bundel*]
bunsucken /bʌnˈsʌkən/ *adj* **1** *of a farm* obliged (under the terms of their lease) to take their grain to a certain mill *la19- NE*. **2** under an obligation, beholden *20- NE*. [OE *bōnda* a peasant proprietor + OE *sōcn* jurisdiction]
bunt[1] /bʌnt/ *n* (the end of) an animal's tail *19- Bor*. [variant of BUN[2]; compare RUNT[1]]
bunt[2] /bʌnt/ *n* **1** a short plump person *20-*. **2** a hen without a rump *18-e19*. **bunty** a nickname for a plump little girl *la19-*. [unknown]
buntin[1] /ˈbʌntɪn/ *adj* plump, short and stout *19, 20- Bor*. [unknown]
buntin[2] /ˈbʌntɪn/ *n* a bantam *20- NE EC*. [probably variant of BANTIM]
†**buntlin**[1] *adj* short and thick *19*. [perhaps a variant of BUNTIN[1]]
†**buntlin**[2] *n* the corn bunting *Emberiza calandra la18-19*. [unknown]
bunwand *see* BUNEWAND
bunwede, bunweed *see* BENWEED
bur /bʌr/ *n* the tongue or top edge of the upper of a shoe *la18, 19- Sh NE*. [ON *borð* a board, a plank]
bural *see* BEERIAL
burble[1.1] /ˈbʌrbəl/ *n* a tangle, a mess *19- WC SW*. [see the verb]
burble[1.2] /ˈbʌrbəl/ *v* to tangle or muddle *19- WC SW*. [Fr *barbouiller*]
burch *see* BURGH
burd *see* BIRD[1], BIRD[2], BOORD[1.1], BOORD[1.2], BOORD[2]
burdalane *see* BIRD-ALANE[1.1], BIRD-ALANE[1.2]
Burdeaulx *see* BURDEOUS
burden[1.1], **burthen**, †**burding**, †**birding**, †**birthing** /ˈbʌrdən, ˈbʌrðən/ *n* **1** a (heavy) load; an amount (serving as a measure of quantity) *15-*. **2** a responsibility or obligation; a difficulty or hardship *la16-*. **3** *law* a restriction or encumbrance on property *la17-*. †**burdinabill, burthinabill** burdensome *la16-17*. †**burdiner** = *burdin-taker 17*. †**birthinsake, burdingseck** a theft of as much as could be carried on the back *13-17*. †**burdin-taker** one who undertakes (especially financial) responsibility for another, a guarantor *17*. †**takand the burding on you** assuming responsibility *la16-e17*. [OE *byrþen*]

burden[1.2], **burthen**, †**burding**, †**burthing** /ˈbʌrdən, ˈbʌrðən/ *v* to load heavily, weigh down; to encumber or oppress *la16-*. [see the noun]
burden[2] /ˈbʌrdən/ *n piping* a drone *la18-*. [OFr *bourdon*]
†**Burdeous, Burdeaulx** *n* Bordeaux *16*. [from the name of the French city]
burdie *see* BIRDIE
†**burdin** *adj* made of boards *15-16*. [ME *borden*]
burding *see* BURDEN[1.1], BURDEN[1.2]
†**burdoun** *n* a stout staff, a cudgel *15-e19*. [ME *burdoun*]
†**bure** *n* a coarse woollen cloth *la16*. Compare BURR[2]. [OFr *bure*; compare BURRAT]
bure *see* BEAR[2]
burelie *see* BUIRDLY
burell *see* BORREL
burgage /ˈbʌrgədʒ/ *n* **1** the tenure by which land within a royal burgh is held of the king *16-19, 20- historical*. **2** land held in burgage tenure *la16-e17*. **burgage land** land held in burgage tenure *la17-19, 20- historical*. [EModE *burgage*]
burgar *see* BURGHER
burge *see* BURGES
burgeis *see* BURGESS[1.1]
†**burgen** *n* a BURGESS[1.1] *15*. [Lat *burgensis*]
burger *see* BURGHER
burges, burgess, †**birges**, †**birge**, †**burge** /ˈbʌrdʒəs/ *n* the city of Bruges in Flanders *la15-19, 20- Sh Ork N*. **birge satyne** satin from Bruges *16*. **Burgess treed**, †**Birgis threid** thread from Bruges *la15-16, 20- Sh Ork N*. [metathesized form of the place-name]
burgess[1.1], †**burges**, †**burgeis** /ˈbʌrdʒəs/ *n* a citizen or freeman of a BURGH *la14-*. †**burgesry** the status or privileges of a burgess *la15-16*. **burgess oath** the oath sworn by a person on becoming a burgess *17-*. **burgess ticket** a certificate of *burgesry 17-*. **burgess of guild** a burgess elected by virtue of his membership of the GUILD *18-*. [ME *burgeis*]
†**burgess**[1.2], **burges** *v* to make a person a burgess *la17-e19*. [see the noun]
burgh, borough, †**burch**, †**burrow**, †**borrow** /ˈbʌrə/ *n pl* also †**burrowis**, †**burrois** **1** a town with special privileges conferred by charter and having a municipal corporation *la11-*; compare *royal burgh* (ROYAL). **2** town (as opposed to country) *15-e19*. **3** *pl* towns or burgesses collectively *la14-17*. †**burrowage, borowage** = BURGAGE *15-e17*. **burghal**, †**burgall** of a burgh *la16-*. **burgh acres, borough acres** the land belonging to a burgh *17-20, 21- historical*. **burgh clerk**, †**borrow clerk** a town clerk *la15-20, 21- historical*. **burgh court**, †**burrow court** a court held within a burgh, equivalent to the sheriff court *15-20, 21- historical*. †**burrow dalis** = *burgh acres 16-18*. †**borow greff** a magistrate of a burgh *e15*. **burgh land**, †**burrow land**, †**borrowland** land belonging to or situated within a burgh *la15-20, 21- historical*. **burgh laws**, †**burrow lawes**, †**borrow lawis** the code of law governing the burghs, translated in the early 15th century from *Leges Quatuor Burgorum la15-18, 19- historical*. †**burrow maill, borrow meall** the annual duty payable by a burgh to the Crown in return for its rights *15-e18*. †**borowman** a burgess, a burgage tenent *15*. **burgh muir**, †**borough muir**, †**burrowmure**, †**borrowmure** the moorland belonging to a burgh *15-*. **burgh roods**, †**burrow rudis** cultivated land belonging to a burgh *16-20, 21- historical*. **burgh school** a school maintained by a burgh *19-e20, la20- historical*. **burrowstoun, borrowstoun** a burgh *15-19, 20- literary*. †**burgh in barony** = *burgh of barony la15-16*. **burgh of barony**, †**burgh of barronie** a burgh under the jurisdiction of a BARON *17-*. **burgh of**

regality a burgh under the jurisdiction of a Lord of Regality *la16-19, 20- historical*. [OE *burh*, a fortified place]

Burgher, burgher, †burger, †burgar, †burcher /'bʌrgər/ *n* **1** a burgess or citizen of a town *15-*. **2** *Presbyterian Church* a member of that section of the Secession Church which upheld the lawfulness of swearing the burgess oath *la18-19, 20- historical*. Compare ANTIBURGHER. [Du *burger*]

burial *see* BEERIAL

buriall *see* BEERIAL, BERIALL

buriawe *see* BURRIO

burker /'bʌrkər/ *n* a murderer *19-*. [derived from the surname of William *Burke*, who sold his murder victims for anatomical dissection]

burking house /'bʌrkɪŋ hʌus/ *n* a house used for dissections *la19-*. [derived from the surname of William *Burke* + HOOSE[1.1]]

burl *see* BIRL[1.1], BIRL[1.2]

†burlat *n* a pad; a padded addition to a garment or a saddle *la15-16*. [MFr *bourlet*; compare BURR[2]]

burlaw, burley *see* BIRLEY

burly, Ork **burlo** /'bʌrle; Ork 'bʌrlo/ *n* a crowd, cluster *19-*. [reduced form of Eng *hurly-burly*]

burly *see* BUIRDLY

burn[1] /bʌrn/ *n* **1** a brook, a stream; frequently in place-names *la12-*. **2** well-water; water for use in brewing or washing *16-*. **3** urine *18-* WC SW. **burnbaker, burnbecker** the dipper *Cinclus cinclus 19-* SW. **†burn-bearer** a water-carrier *la16-e18*. **burn-drawer** = *burnman la18-19, 20- historical*. **†burneledar, burnlader** a water-carrier *16*. **†burnman, burneman** a water-carrier *la16-e17*. **burnside** land beside a stream, a valley containing a watercourse *16-*. **†burnstand, burnestand** a large tub or barrel for holding water *la16-19*. [OE *burna*]

burn[2.1], **birn, †brin, †birne, †byrne** /bʌrn, bɪrn/ *n* **1** an injury or mark caused by burning *16-*. **2** a brand of ownership (on an animal or barrel) *16-*. **3** the scorched stem of heather remaining after the small twigs are burnt *18-*. **4** a pasture on dry, heathy land *la18-e19*. **5** a flash, a gleam *la18-19*. **birny, birnie 1** *of land* on which heather has been burned, scorched, blackened *la16-*. **2** rough, hard; dried-up *la18-19, 20-* Ork. [see the verb]

burn[2.2], **birn, brenn, †brin, †byrn** /bʌrn, bɪrn, brɛn/ *v ptp* also **brunt, †brint, †ybrynt 1** to be or set on fire; to be destroyed by fire *la14-*. **2** to injure by burning; to brand with a burning iron *la14-*. **3** to glow, give off light or heat *15-*. **4** to experience extreme emotion *15-*. **5** *in curling or bowling* to spoil a game by improper interference with a stone or bowl *19-*. Compare BRUNT. **†birnar, burnear** a brander *15-16*. **†birning** branding as a punishment *la15-16*. **burny** (extremely) hot; burning *la20-*. **†burne-coill** charcoal *la16-e17*. **burn iron, †burn irne, birn irne 1** a brand of ownership on an animal *la18-19*. **2** a branding iron *16-e19*. **burn-the-wind** a blacksmith *la18-19, 20-* NE T C. **burnwood** wood for burning *16-19, 20-* NE T EC. **the burning fire** a euphemism for hell *la20-*. **burn nits** to burn nuts at Halloween to predict the outcome of courtship *la18-*. **burn tobacco** to smoke *la19-* NE. **burn the water** to spear salmon by torchlight *la18-19, 20-* NE C. [OE *byrnan* and OE *bærnan*]

burnock /'bʌrnək/ *n* a type of curling stone *la19-* T WC SW. [named after Burnock Water in Ayrshire, where the stones originate]

Burns Night, Burns Nicht /'bʌrnz nʌɪt, 'bʌrnz nɪxt/ *n* an annual celebration of the birthday of Robert Burns on the 25th of January, usually featuring a BURNS SUPPER, toasts and speech-making, and the reciting and singing of Burns' poems and songs *la19-*. [from the surname of the poet + NICHT[1.1]]

Burns Supper /bʌrnz 'sʌpər/ *n* a meal served to celebrate the birthday of Robert Burns on the 25th of January, usually consisting of haggis, neeps and tatties, often as part of a BURNS NIGHT *la19-*. [from the surname of the poet + SUPPER[1.1]]

burnt *see* BRUNT[2]

burnys *see* BIRNIS

buroo, burroo, broo /bə'ru, bru/ *n* **1** the Jobcentre, formerly the Labour Exchange *20-*. **2** unemployment benefit *20-*. **broo money** unemployment benefit *la20-*. **on the burroo, on the broo** unemployed, claiming benefits *20-*. [altered form of Eng *bureau*]

burop *see* BOW[4]

burr[1] /bʌr/ *n* **1** a rough or prickly seed case or flower-head of a plant *18-*. **2** a fir-cone *19-* NE T. **3** a sea-urchin *la19-* NE. [Fris *burre*]

†burr[2] *n* a pad; a padded addition to a garment or a saddle *16-e17*. **burrit, burred** padded *16-e17*. [MFr *bourre*]

burra /'bʌra/ *n* the heath rush *Juncus squarrosus 19-* Sh Ork. [compare Norw *borda* a long narrow leaf]

burrach *see* BEERACH

†burrat, birrat *n* a coarse woollen cloth *la16-e17*. [MFr *burat*; compare BURE]

burreau *see* BURRIO

burrel, birrel /'bʌrəl, 'bɪrəl/ *n* a ridge or strip in balk and burrel ploughing *la18-19, 20-* NE Bor. [unknown; compare BORREL]

burrie[1] /'bʌri/ *n* a children's catching game *19-* NE. [BAR[1.2] + -IE[1]]

burrie[2] /'bʌri/ *v* to push roughly, jostle *19-* NE. [perhaps variant of BERRY[2]]

†burrio, burreau, buriawe *n* an executioner *16-e19*. **burreour** = BURRIO *16-17*. [MFr *bourreau*]

burrois *see* BURGH

burroo *see* BUROO

burrow, burrowis *see* BURGH

burrow duck, †burrough duck /'bʌro dʌk/ *n* the shelduck *Tadorna tadorna 19-*. [from its habit of nesting in rabbits' burrows]

burr-thistle, burr-thrystle /bʌr'θɪsəl, bʌr'θrɪsəl/ *n* the spear thistle *Cirsium vulgare la18-*. [BURR[1] + THRISSEL]

burry *see* BERRY[3]

burry man /'bʌre man/ *n* **1** *in South Queensferry* a man covered with burrs who parades through the town in an annual ceremony to bring good luck *la19-*. **2** *in the North-East* a public scapegoat on whom was symbolically laid all the bad luck of the fishing season (who was then chased out of the village) *la19, 20- historical*. [BURR[1] + -IE[1] + MAN; historically ghosts and evil spirits were thought of as sticking like burrs to the skin of the living]

bursar, †bursour, †busser /'bʌrsər/ *n* **1** a treasurer (of a school or university) *la15-*. **2** a holder of a BURSARY *la16-*. [Lat *bursārius*, from *bursa* a purse]

bursary, †bussary /'bʌrsəre/ *n* a school or university scholarship *la17-*. **bursary competition** a competitive examination for university bursaries *19-20, 21- historical*. [from the noun BURSAR]

†burse *n* **1** a bursary *la16-19*. **2** a purse *16-17*. **3** a financial exchange *la16-e17*. [MFr *bourse*, Lat *bursa*]

bursen *see* BIRST[1.2]

bursour *see* BURSAR

burst *see* BIRST[1.1], BIRST[1.2]

bursten, burstin /'bʌrstən/ *n* meal made from corn dried in a kettle over a fire *19-* Sh Ork N. **bursten brönnie, †bursten broonie 1** a nickname for a native of Sandness

20- Sh. **2** a scone made from dried corn *19.* [probably from presp or strong ptp of BIRST[1,2], because of the ears of corn bursting when being roasted]
burth /'bʌrθ/ *n* the distance between fishing boats when setting lines *20- N NE T.* [perhaps altered form of Eng *berth*]
burth *see* BERT
burthen *see* BURDEN[1.1], BURDEN[1.2]
burthing *see* BURDEN[1.2]
bury *see* BEERIE
bus *see* BUSS[1]
busch *see* BUSH[2]
†**buschbome, buschboun** *n* boxwood *Buxus sempervirens e16.* [EModDu *busboom*; compare MLG *busbōm*]
†**busche** *n* an allowance of food (in a household) *15-16.*
  busche of court = BUSCHE. [OFr *bouche*]
busche *see* BUSS[1], BUSS[3]
bush[1] /bʌʃ/ *v* to move about or work nimbly; to clean or tidy up *la19- C SW.* [compare BUSK[1.2], BUSS[4.2]]
†**bush**[2], **busch** *v* to rush or gush (out) *15-e19.* [unknown]
†**bush**[3] *n* a warehouse or timberyard *17-19.* Compare *Timber Bush* (TIMMER[1.1]). [perhaps Fr *bourse* an exchange]
bush *see* BOOSE[3.1], BUSS[1], BUSS[3]
bushle-breeks /'buʃəlbriks/ *npl* wide, baggy trousers *la19- WC SW.* [Older Scots *buschel* + BREEKS]
bushock *see* BUSS[1]
bushtie *see* BOUSHTY
busk[1.1], *Sh* **bos**, †**buss** /bʌsk; *Sh* bɔs/ *n* **1** a trimming, an adornment; the decoration on a woman's cap or bonnet *la17-19, 20- Sh.* **2** a woman's head-dress *16-e17.* [see the noun]
busk[1.2], **buss** /bʌsk, bʌs/ *v* **1** to prepare, get ready; to make ready, equip *la14-.* **2** to dress (oneself); to adorn or deck; to dress up *la15-.* **3** to dress hooks or a fly for fly-fishing *la17-.* **4** to decorate (a flag) with ribbons (on the eve of the Common Riding in the Borders) *18-.* **5** to set out, go with haste *la14-15.* **6** to disguise oneself, put on a disguise *16.* †**buskie** well-dressed *e19.* †**buskin, bussin, busking 1** a cap or hood worn by women *17-e19.* **2** decoration, adornment *17-18.* [ME *busken*, ON *búask* to make preparations, prepare oneself, get ready]
busk *see* BUSS[1]
buss[1], **busk, bush,** †**boss,** †**bus,** †**busche** /bʌs, bʌsk, buʃ, bʌʃ/ *n* **1** a thicket; a clump or stand of trees; a wood *13-.* **2** a shrub or bush, a clump of bushes *15-.* **3** a clump of ferns, grass or heather *16-.* **4** a mass of seaweed *19.* **5** a bunch, a tuft *16-e17.* **bushock** the hedge-sparrow *Prunella modularis la19- EC.* **bussy, bussie,** *SW Bor* **bouzy,** †**buskie,** †**busky** bushy; covered with bushes *17-.* †**bush sparrow** = *bushock 19.* †**wag as the bus wags** to agree sycophantically with someone *la16-e17.* [perhaps ME *bush*]
buss[2], **boss** /bʌs, bɔs/ *n* **1** a rounded prominence; a projection, a round mass *16-.* **2** a ledge of rock (covered with seaweed) projecting into the sea; a small sea rock exposed at low tide; a mass of rock *19-.* [ME *boce*; perhaps with later confusion with BUSS[1]]
buss[3], **bush,** †**busche,** †**busk** /bʌs, bʌʃ/ *n* a type of cargo boat or fishing boat *15-.* **bush rope** *fishing* the rope to which drift nets are attached *la19- N NE T.* [ME *bus* and MDu *buysse* a fishing vessel]
buss[4.1], **byss, boss** /bʌs, bɪs, bɔs/ *n* chaff, straw, bedding for animals; (the lining of) a bird's nest *la19- Sh Ork N.* [Norw *bos, boss* or Norw dial *bus, bys*]
buss[4.2], **bos** /bʌs, bɔs/ *v* to sift oats, rummage through chaff *20- Sh Ork.* [see the noun]
buss *see* BOOSE[3.1], BUSK[1.1], BUSK[1.2]

bussack /'bʌsək/ *n* a smack or thump *20- N.* [compare Gael *bosag* a slap]
bussart *see* BUZZARD
busser *see* BURSAR
bussie *see* BUSY
bussom *see* BESOM
bust *see* BUIST[1]
†**busteous, bustuous** *adj* boisterous, rough *15-19.* [unknown]
buster /'bʌstər/ *n* chips and hot peas (sold from a stall or takeaway) *20-.* [probably intensive form of *burst* (BIRST[1.1])]
†**bustine, bustiane** *n* bustian, a cotton fabric *la14-18.* [unknown]
bustuous *see* BUSTEOUS
busy, †**bissy,** †**bussie,** †**besy** /'bɪzi/ *adj* occupied with tasks, active, engaged *la14-.* **busy bee,** †**besy be** a very busy person *la14-.* [OE *bysig*]
but[1.1] /bʌt/ *n* the kitchen or outer room, usually of a *but and ben 19-.* **but and ben** a two-roomed cottage *la18-.* [see the adv]
but[1.2] /bʌt/ *adj* **1** outer, outside; relating to the kitchen *la19- Sh Ork N NE EC.* **2** relating to the parlour or best room *la19- NE.* **but-end 1** the best room in a house; the living room *la19- Sh N NE.* **2** the outer room of a house, the kitchen *20- Sh N.* [see the adv]
but[1.3] /bʌt/ *adv* **1** in or towards the outer part of a house; into the kitchen or outer room; out *15-.* **2** *as a tag at the end of a phrase or sentence* however, by the way: ◇*he skint his knee but la20-.* **but and ben 1** in (or to) both the outer and inner parts; backwards and forwards, to and fro; everywhere *la14-19, 20- Ork.* **2** at opposite ends of the same house, passage or landing *la18-19, 20- NE.* [OE *būtan*]
but[1.4], †**bot** /bʌt/ *prep* **1** out or away from the speaker or spectator; over; across; through a house towards the outer part *la16-.* **2** without, lacking; free from *la14-e19.* **3** excluding, not counting; in addition to *la14-15.* **but the hoose 1** in or into the kitchen or outer end of a house *19, 20- N NE T.* **2** in or into the best room *20- NE.* †**but mair 1** without more delay, at once *la14-16.* **2** without anything or anyone else, in all *la14-15.* [see the adv]
but[1.5], †**bot** /bʌt/ *conj* nevertheless, yet; unless, except that *la14-.* †**but and** besides, and also *la14-e18.* [see the adv]
but *see* BUTT[1], BUTT[2]
butch /butʃ, bʌtʃ/ *v* to slaughter an animal for meat *la18-19, 20- NE.* **butching gullie** a knife used by butchers *20- Ork.* **butch-hoose** a slaughterhouse *20- NE EC.* [back-formation from BUTCHER]
butcher, †**boucheour,** †**boucher** /'butʃər/ *n* **1** a slaughterer; an executioner *la15-.* **2** a dealer in meat *la17-.* †**bucherie** a butcher's shop or stall *e16.* **butcher meat** butcher's meat *18-.* [ME *bocher*]
bute *see* BEHOVE, BUIT[1.1], BUIT[1.2], BUIT[2.1], BUIT[2.2]
Bute pursuivant, †**Bute pursevant** /bjut 'pʌrswɪvənt/ *n* one of the Scottish pursuivants *la16-.* [from the name of the island in the Firth of Clyde + PURSUIVANT]
buterflee *see* BUTTERFLEE
buth *see* BUITH
butt[1], †**but** /bʌt/ *n* a small piece of ground disjointed from the adjacent lands, a small freehold; a ridge or strip of ploughed land; frequently in place-names *13-.* [Lat *butta*]
butt[2], †**but** /bʌt/ *n* **1** *archery* a target, (a pair of) targets *la15-.* **2** ground used for archery practice *19-.* **3** *games* a line drawn on the ground to indicate the starting point *19- C SW Uls.* **4** *grouse-shooting* a wall or bank of earth erected to hide the guns *20-.* **5** a measure of distance (between a pair of

targets) *la16-e19*. †**butlenth** the length of a pair of targets *16*. [MFr *but*]
butt *see* BUIT¹·¹
buttag *see* BUTTOCK
butter /'bʌtər/ *n* the solidified, fatty substance made by churning cream *14-*. **butter bannock** a bannock spread with butter *20-*. **butter bap** a scone made with butter *20- NE T C*. **butter blob** the globeflower *Trollius europaeus la19- NE WC SW Bor*. **butter brods** a pair of wooden paddles for working butter *la19- NE T WC*. **butter clappers** = *butter brods 20- WC SW*. **butter day** the day on which a tenant presented a certain quantity of butter to their landlord *20- Sh*. **butter kit** a container for butter *la19-*. **butter man** a dealer in butter; a butter-maker *la16-*. **buttermilk-anmeal** a bowl of buttermilk with oatmeal on top *la19- NE T*. **butter poki** a small thin bag used for straining water from freshly-churned butter *20- Sh*. **butter tron** in Edinburgh a public weighing-machine used for butter *la15-e19, la19- historical*. **butter well** a well whose water is considered good for washing the buttermilk out of butter *la18- EC*. **butterylippit** smooth-tongued, flattering *20- T SW*. **butter an breid** bread and butter *la18-*. [OE *butere*]
butterage, buttereis *see* BUTTRAGE
butterflee, †**buterflee** /'bʌtərfli/ *n* a butterfly *la15-*. [OE *buttorflēoge*]
butterie /'bʌtəri, 'bʌtəre/ *n* a butterfly *la19- NE T*. [shortened form of BUTTERFLEE]
buttery, butterie /'bʌtəri, 'bʌtəre/ *n* a morning roll made of a high-fat dough, originating in the North-East; a butter biscuit *la19-*. **butterie rowie** a morning roll *20-*. [from the noun BUTTER + -IE²]
buttery willie collie /'bʌtəri wɪli 'kɔli/ *n* a red-gowned undergraduate student at Aberdeen University; the gown itself *la19- NE*. [unknown]
buttie *see* BUTTY
buttle *see* BOTTLE²·¹, BOTTLE²·²
buttock, *N* **buttag,** †**buttok** /'bʌtək; *N* 'bʌtəg/ *n* one of the buttocks; a rump *15-*. †**buttock hire** a fine for sexual immorality *la18-e19*. **buttock mail 1** a spanking *20- NE*. **2** a fine for sexual immorality *16-e19*. [ME *buttok*]
button, †**buttoun** /'bʌtən/ *n* **1** a disc or knob used for fastening clothes *15-*. **2** *pl* a game played with buttons with distinctive names and values *la19- NE*. **3** *in Orkney* a sheepmark made by pinching the skin on the nose and tying it with thread *18-e19*. **buttony** a game played with buttons *20- NE SW*. **buttonhole** a slit through which a button may pass *16-*. [ME *botoun*]
†**buttrage, butterage, buttereis** *n* a buttress *la14-e18*. [ME *boteras*]
butts /bʌts/ *npl* a fire-engine; the fire-brigade *la19- C SW*. **the butts** = *butts*. [probably Older Scots *butt* a cask]
butty, buttie /'bʌte/ *n* **1** an intimate companion; a friend, a workmate *la19-*. **2** an escort *20-*. **gie someone a butty** to accompany someone on their journey *20-*. [unknown; compare Eng *buddy*]
bux *see* BUCKS
buy, *T* **beh,** †**by** /bae; *T* bɛ/ *v pt* **bocht, boucht,** *ptp* **bocht, boucht,** †**ybocht 1** to purchase; to pay for *la14-*. **2** to buy over, bribe *la15-*. **3** to gain, procure; to redeem or ransom *16-*. †**buy a broom** to take out a warrant *e19*. **bought house, boat hoose** a house which is owned rather than rented *la20-*. [OE *bycgan*]
buy *see* BOW⁴
buzzard, †**bizzard,** †**bussart,** †**bissart** /'bʌzərd/ *n* a large bird of prey *Buteo buteo la15-*. [ME *busard*]

buzzle /'bʌzəl/ *v* **1** to (cause to) buzz *la20-*. **2** *of grain crops* to rustle (indicating ripeness) *20- NE*. **ma heid's buzzled** my head is buzzing *la20-*. [onomatopoeic, with frequentative suffix]
buzzum *see* BOSOM
bweil *see* BILE¹·¹
by¹·¹, bye /bae/ *adv* **1** near, nearby; present *la14-*. **2** *of place* past, so as to pass *15-*. **3** aside *la15-*. **4** *of time* past, over *la16-*. †**by board, by burd** a side-table *la16-e18*. †**bycumming** the act of coming past a place *la16-e17*. †**bygate** an indirect way, a side-path *16-*. †**bygottin** illegitimate *la15-16*. **by-hand, by-han** finished, over and done with *17-19, 20- NE*. **by-hours** unassigned time at work; overtime *19, 20- NE*. **bye-job 1** an additional job on the side *la18-*. **2** fornication *la18*; compare JOB¹·². †**byknife, byknyff** a knife carried beside a dagger *la15-17*. **bypast,** †**bypassit 1** *of time or a specific date* past, elapsed: ◊*August last by past la14-*. **2** *of events or actions* passed or in or belonging to past time *la15-*. **by-place** an out-of-the-way place *la18-19, 20- NE*. **by-put, by-pit** *n* **1** a temporary substitute, a pretence *la19- NE*. **2** a procrastinator *la19- NE*. †**by put** *v* to set aside *15-e16*. †**bysleeve, bysleve** an additional or over-sleeve; a hanger-on, nonentity *la16-e18*. †**bystand** to stand beside or near; to witness *15-16*. †**by-table** a side-table *18-e19*. †**bywent** bygone, past *la15-e16*. **bye and aboon** over and above *la19- NE EC*. **by and attour** *law* in addition to, besides *la16-19, 20- T*. †**by and besyde** in addition to, besides *la16-e17*. **by and gane** completely over, finished *20-*. **by and out owre** in addition to, besides *la17-19, 20- NE EC*. **by the way 1** incidentally *la16-*. **2** *as an intensifier* in fact, in truth: ◊*Ah dinnae ken, by the way la20-*. **by wi** over and done with, finished *la19-*. **b'wye** as it were, by the way *20- NE T EC*. [OE *be, big*]
by¹·², **bye, be, bi** /bae, bɪ, bi/ *prep* **1** beside; near, at *la14-*. **2** as a result of, by means of *la14-*. **3** *of time* not later than *la14-*. **4** in comparison with, as distinct from *la14-*. **5** past, further than *la14-*. **6** in the name of: ◊*by Jupiter 15-*. **7** above, beyond; more than *16-*. **8** except *la16-*. **9** *of age or quality* past: ◊*by their best 20-*. **10** concerning, about *la18-19, 20- N NE SW*. **11** apart from, away from, laid aside from *16-e19*. **12** contrary to, at variance with, against *15-e17*. **13** in addition to, besides *la15-e17*. **by common** out of the ordinary, unusual *19-*. **by-south, besooth** *prep* on or to the south of; below, beyond *15-19, 20- Sh NE*. **by-south, besooth** *adv* in the south; on the side *16-*. **by-usual** unusual *la19- NE T EC*. **by the common** = *by common 19-*. **by himsel, by himself** out of his mind, beside himself *16-*. †**by his mind** out of his mind, insane *16*. **by the ordinar** unusual *la19-*. **by yer ordinar** out of one's usual health *20- NE T SW*. [see the adv]
by¹·³, be /bae, bɪ, bi/ *conj* **1** by the time that, as soon as *la14-*. **2** than *la18-*. [see the adv]
by *see* BUY
byaak *see* BAKE¹·²
byack *see* BJAKK
†**byas bowl** *n* a bowl (used in bowling) *17*. [compare Eng *biassed bowl* a bowl with a weight or bias]
byauch *see* BIACH, BJAKK
byauve *see* BLAW¹·²
by-bite, bye-bit /'baebʌɪt, 'baebɪt/ *n* a snack between meals *19, 20- NE WC SW*. [BY¹·¹ + BITE¹·¹]
byd *see* BID¹, BIDE¹·²
byde *see* BIDE¹·²
bye *see* BY¹·¹, BY¹·²
bye-bit *see* BY-BITE

byelsit, bjelset /ˈbjɛlsət/ *adj of a sheep* having a white ring around the neck *20- Sh.* [perhaps ON *helsi* a collar]

bye's, by's, beis /baez, biz/ *prep* **1** compared with *19-*. **2** except; instead of *20-*. **3** than: ◊*ye're an aulder man beis A thocht ye wis 20-*. [BY¹·³, with adv-forming suffix]

byeuk *see* BUIK¹·¹

byg *see* BIG²

bygane, †begane /ˈbaegən/ *adj* **1** *of a period of time* past; gone by *15-*. **2** *of actions or events* earlier, former; done in the past *la15-*. **3** *of payments* made or due for past periods of time *la15-e18*. **in the bygane** in the past, of old *19-*. [BY¹·¹ + *gane* (GAE)]

byganes, †byganis /ˈbaegənz/ *npl* **1** things occurring or done in the past, past offences or injuries *la16-*. **2** payments for past periods; arrears *la16-18*. [from the adj BYGANE]

by-gaun, by-going, by-ganging /ˈbaegɔn, ˈbaegɔən, ˈbaegɔɪŋ, ˈbaegəŋɪŋ/ *n* the act of passing by *17-*. **in the by-going, in the by-gaun** in the passing, incidentally *17-*. [BY¹·¹ + *gaein* (GAE)]

byggyng *see* BIGGIN¹

by-going *see* BY-GAUN

byit *see* BITE¹·¹

byke¹·¹, bike, *NE* **boick** /bʌɪk; *NE* bɔɪk/ *n* **1** a bees', wasps' or ants' nest; a beehive *15-*. **2** a swarm, a crowd (of people) *16-*. **3** a dwelling, a habitation *la15-19, 20- NE C*. **4** a beehive-shaped cornstack *la18- N NE*. **5** a collection, a hoard, something acquired *19, 20- N NE*. [unknown]

byke¹·² /bʌɪk/ *v* **1** *of bees* to swarm *la18-19, 20- NE T*. **2** to dwell *20- EC*. **†byked in** closed in *e17*. [unknown]

byke² /bʌɪk/ *n* the nose *la19, 20- T*. [unknown; compare BECK¹·¹]

byke³, bike /bʌɪk/ *n* the bend of a hook; the hook attached to the chain holding a pot over a fire *la19, 20- NE*. [unknown; compare BYKE²]

byke⁴ /bʌɪk/ *v* to weep, whine or sob *19- WC SW Bor*. [unknown]

byle *see* BILE²

bylge *see* BILGE

bylie *see* BAILIE

byll *see* BILE²

bymasal *see* BUMMASAL

byoag, bjog /bjog/ *n* **1** a plaited-straw horse collar *la19- Sh*. **2** a circular stripe (of a different colour) on a stocking or sock *la19- Sh*. **3** a triangular wooden collar placed around the neck of a sheep to prevent it from going through fences *20- Sh*. **bjoget, bioget 1** *of stockings and wool* having circular stripes of a contrasting colour; a mark on a garment caused by badly-mixed wool *20- Sh*. **2** *of an animal* having a circular stripe (around the belly or neck) *20- Sh*. [ON *baugr* a ring]

byoch *see* BOICH

byochy-byochy *see* BOAK¹·²

byock *see* BOAK¹·¹, BOAK¹·²

byoo *see* BLUE¹·¹, BLUE¹·²

byoocher *see* BUCHER

by-ordinar¹·¹, byordnar, byornar /baeˈɔrdənər, baeˈɔrdnər, baeˈɔrnər/ *adj* extraordinary, unusual *19-*. [BY¹·² + ORDINAR¹·²]

by-ordinar¹·², byordnar, byornar /baeˈɔrdənər, baeˈɔrdnər, baeˈɔrnər/ *adv* extraordinarily, unusually *la19-*. [see the adj]

byous¹·¹ /ˈbaeəs/ *adj* wonderful, extraordinary, exceptional *19-*. [BY¹·², with adj-forming suffix]

byous¹·² /ˈbaeəs/ *adv* exceedingly, very *19-*. [see the adj]

byouty, byowty, beouty, beauty, †bewte, †beute /ˈbjʌuti, ˈbjuti/ *n* attractive or pleasing appearance, beauty *la14-*. **byowtifu, byoutifu** beautiful *la19- NE*. **ya beauty** an exclamation of approbation or triumph *la20-*. [ME *beaute*]

byowder *see* BOWDER¹

byr *see* BIRR¹·¹, BYRE

†byrd *v* **1** should, ought (to) *la14-16*. **2** it behoves (one) *la14-e15*. [OE *byrian*]

byre, †byr /baer/ *n* **1** a cow-house, a cattle-shed *13-*. **2** a dwelling, an abode *la16*. **byre-claut** a scraper for cleaning out a byre *la19- T SW*. **byreman** a cattleman *la16-*. **byrewoman** a woman who looks after cows *la17-*. [OE *bȳre*]

by-rins, †byrinnis, †byrunnis /ˈbaerɪnz/ *npl* arrears *la16-17, 20- NE*. **by-rinnins** = BY-RINS *20- NE*. [BY¹·¹ + RIN¹·¹, RIN¹·²]

byrl quheil *see* BIRL¹·¹

byrne *see* BIRN, BIRNY, BURN²·¹

†byrun *adj* **1** *of time* past; expired *la15-16*. **2** *of payments* due for a period in the past *16-17*. **byrunnyn, byrinnin** = BYRUN *la15-16*. [BY¹·¹ + *run* (RIN¹·²)]

byrunnis *see* BY-RINS

†by-ryne *v* to pass *e16*. [BY¹·¹ + RIN¹·²]

bys *see* BIZZ¹·²

by's *see* BYE'S

byschape *see* BISHOP¹·¹

bysen, †bysyn /ˈbaezən/ *n* **1** a person presenting a ludicrous or disgusting spectacle *20- Bor*. **2** a prostitute, a loose woman *e19*. **3** a monster *la14-e17*. [ON *býsn* a marvel, a portent]

bysmer *see* BISMAIR

†bysnyng¹·¹, bysning *n* a monster *la14-e16*. [ON *býsn* a wonder, an omen]

†bysnyng¹·², bysning *adj* monstrous *la14-e16*. [see the noun]

byspel, byspale /ˈbaespɛl, ˈbaespəl/ *n* **1** an extraordinary person or thing *19- T Bor*. **2** an illegitimate child *e19*. [OE *bigspell*]

byss *see* BUSS⁴·¹

bystart *see* BASTART¹·¹

byster *see* BASTART¹·²

†bystour *n* a boastful or bullying person *16*. [unknown]

byt *see* BIT¹·¹, BIT², BITE¹·¹, BITE¹·²

by-time /ˈbaetʌɪm/ *n* spare moments, free time *la19- NE EC Bor*. **at a by-time** occasionally *19, 20- NE*; compare BETIMES (sense 1). [BY¹·¹ + TIME]

bytimes *see* BETIMES

C

ca[1.1], **caa, cau, caw, call** /ka, kɔ, kɔl/ *n* **1** a cry, a shout; a request; a summons *16-*. **2** a turn of a skipping rope or handle *20-*. **3** the motion of the waves *19- Sh N NE T*. **4** a drove of sheep *20- Sh NE SW*. **5** a search *la19- NE T EC*. **6** a knock, a blow *20- NE T EC*. **7** a hurry, a rush *20- NE*. **8** a school of whales *la19- Sh*. **ca' knowe** a knoll where cattle are rounded up *19- Bor*. **have the ca'** to have the right to call upon the next performer *la19- NE EC*. [see the verb]

ca[1.2], **caa, caw, call,** †**cal** /ka, kɔ, kɔl/ *v pt* **ca'd, cald, callit 1** to shout, cry; to summon by calling *la14-*. **2** to name *la14-*. **3** to drive a vehicle or plough *la14-*. **4** *law* to summon before or to attend a court *15-*. **5** to urge on or drive (animals) *la15-*. **6** to drive in nails; to fix (on or in) by hammering *16-*. **7** to transport goods or produce; to bring home a harvest from the fields *la16-*. **8** to order a drink *18-*. **9** to knock, push *la18-*. **10** to be driven on; to proceed; to keep going, plod on *la18-*. **11** to set or keep in motion; to circulate *la18-*. **12** to ransack, search *la18-*. **13** to sell or hawk goods *la19-*. **14** to swing a skipping rope *20-*. **15** to drive whales into shallow water in order to beach them *la19- Sh Ork NE*. **16** to abuse, miscall *la19- T EC SW*. **cawin rope** a skipping rope *la20-*. **ca-the-shuttle** a weaver *19- NE Bor*. **be called to a church** to be invited formally by a congregation to be its minister *la16-*. **ca' aboot a story** to spread gossip *20- NE T*. **ca' again, call again 1** to oppose or contradict *19- NE T*. **2** to recall, revoke or retract *14-16*; compare *again-call* (AGAIN[1.1]). **ca' awa, caw awa** to proceed; to work away; to carry on *19-*. **ca canny, caw cannie** to proceed warily; to be moderate *19-*. **ca' the cat frae the cows** = *ca' the cows out o the kail-yaird 19, 20- T*. **ca' the clash** to spread gossip *19- NE T*. **ca' the cows out o the kail-yaird** to perform a very simple or reasonable act *19, 20 N NE T*. **ca' the crack** to converse, talk *la19-*. **ca' doon, caa doun** to knock down, demolish *la20-*. **ca for 1** to call on, visit *la18-*. **2** to name after someone *19-*. **3** to abuse someone *20-*. **ca' a nail to the heid** to go to extremes, exaggerate *la19-*. **ca' for awthing** to heap abuse on someone *la19-*. **ca' on, call on 1** to ask, request *15-*. **2** to be in demand *la19-*. **3** to attach or nail on *17*. **ca' oot** to dislocate *20-*. **ca tae, caw tae** to shut a door *la19-*. **ca' yer gird, caa yer gird** to proceed, carry on *la19-*. **no worth ca'in oot o a kail-yaird** valueless *la19- N T EC*. [ON *kalla*]

ca[2.1], **caa** /kɔ, ka/ *n* a calf *19-*. [probably back-formation from CAUR calves]

ca[2.2] /kɔ, ka/ *v* to calve *la18- WC SW*. [from the noun]

caa see CA[1.1], CA[1.2], CA[2.1], KAE[1.1]

caaf see CAFF

caain' whale, caa'in whale /ˈkaən ʍel, ˈkɔən ʍel/ *n* the pilot whale *Globicephala melas* or *Globicephala macrorhynchus la19- Sh Ork NE T*. [presp of CA[1.2] + WHAAL]

caak[1.1] /kak/ *n* a hen's cackle *20- N*. [onomatopoeic]

caak[1.2] /kak/ *v of a hen* to cackle *20- N*. [see the noun]

caak see CAUK[1.2]

caal see CAUL, CAULD[1.1], CAULD[1.3]

caams see CALMES

caav see CAUF[1.1], CAUF[1.2]

caavie see KAAVIE[1.1]

cab, kab /kab/ *v* to pilfer, filch, snatch *19- Ork N NE EC Bor*. [shortened form of Eng *cabbage* to pilfer]

cabal see CABBLE[1.1], CABBLE[1.2]
cabane see CAIBIN
cabar see GABBART
cabbage, cabbitch /ˈkabɪdʒ, ˈkabɪtʃ/ *n* **1** a plant of the family *Brassica oleracea*, cabbage *la17-*. **2** a nickname for Hibernian Football Club *la20-*. **cabbage kail** cabbage *la17- NE T*. **cabbage-runt** a cabbage stalk *la18-*. **cabbage stock** = *cabbage-runt 19-*; compare CASTOCK. **cabbage and ribs** a rhyming slang nickname for Hibernian Football Club *la20-*. [EModE *cabbage*]

†**cabbiclaw** *n* a dish of salt cod *18-19*. [unknown; compare CABELEW]

cabbie, kabby /ˈkabɪ/ *n* a small cod caught near the shore *20- Sh Ork*. [probably Norw *kabbe* a stump, a block, a log]

cabbitch see CABBAGE

cabble[1.1], **cabal** /ˈkabəl, kəˈbal/ *n* **1** a secret group of plotters; intrigue, plotting *17-*. **2** a group of people gathered together for gossip or drinking *18-19, 20- NE*. **3** a violent dispute *19, 20- NE*. [Fr *cabale*]

cabble[1.2], **cabal,** †**gabal** /ˈkabəl, kəˈbal/ *v* **1** to quarrel, dispute *18- NE T H&I*. **2** to find fault *la19- NE*. [see the noun]

cabbrach[1.1] /ˈkabrəx/ *n* **1** a big, disagreeable or uncouth person *la18- NE SW*. **2** carrion *19, 20- Bor*. [see the adj]

†**cabbrach**[1.2], **cabroche** *adj* **1** lean, scraggy *16-e19*. **2** rapacious, greedy *la18-e19*. [perhaps Gael *cabrach* having antlers or rafters]

cabby-labby[1.1], *Sh* **cabbi-labbi,** *WC* **kebbie-lebbie** /ˈkabɪlabe; *Sh* ˈkabɪlabɪ; *WC* ˈkɛbɪ lɛbe/ *n* a quarrel, an altercation; a hubbub *la18-*. [reduplicative compound; compare MDu *kebbelen*]

†**cabby-labby**[1.2] *v* to quarrel, wrangle *19*. [see the noun]

cabe see KABE

cabelew, kabbilow /ˈkabəlʌu/ *n* a young cod; salt cod; pike; a dish of this *18-19, 20- Sh*. Compare CABBICLAW and KABBELOW. [compare Ger *Kabeljau*]

caber, †**kaber,** †**kebar,** †**kebber** /ˈkebər/ *n* **1** a heavy pole, a long slender tree-trunk; the pole tossed in competition in the Highland Games *16-*. **2** a rafter, a beam *la16-*. **3** a large stick or staff *19- N NE*. **4** an old useless horse *20- N NE*. **5** a large coarse or clumsy man *19- NE*. **6** wood laid across the main rafters to support the thatch *18-19*. **caber tree** the pole used in the Highland Games *la19- NE T*. **tossing the caber** an event in the Highland Games which involves throwing a heavy pole *19-*. [Gael *cabar* a pole, a rafter]

cabil see CABLE
cabin see CAIBIE[1], CAIBIN
cabinet see CAIBNET
cable, †**cabil,** †**capill,** †**kabill** /ˈkebəl/ *n* a strong thick rope *la15-*. †**cabill stok** a capstan *e16*. **cable tow,** †**kabill tow** a cable-rope *la16-*. †**cabilȝarne** yarn for making cables *la16*. [ME *cable*]

cabok see KEBBOCK

†**caboschoun** *n* a precious stone polished but not cut or faceted *la16*. [MFr *cabochon*]

cabroche see CABBRACH[1.2]
cace see CASE[1], CASE[2]
cach see CATCH[1.2]
cache[1], †**caitch,** †**caich,** †**catche** /katʃ, kaʃ/ *n* the game of hand-tennis *15-e17, 20- historical*. [MDu *caetse*]

†**cache²**, **caich**, **catch** v **1** to chase, drive *la15-e17*. **2** to make one's way; to go *la15-e17*. [ME *cacchen*]

cachepell see CATCHEPOOLE

cachet¹·¹, †**caschet** /ˈkaʃe/ n a seal or stamp for impressing documents *la16-18, la19-* historical. [MFr *cachet* a seal]

†**cachet¹·²**, **caschet** v to authorize with a seal *17*. [see the noun]

cack¹·¹, *Sh* **kukk** /kak; *Sh* kuk/ n **1** excrement *la18-*. **2** the act of voiding excrement *20-*. **cackie 1** excrement *19-*. **2** the act of voiding excrement *20-*. **caukie stammackit** having imperfect digestion; squeamish *20- NE*. [see the verb; compare KEECH¹·¹]

cack¹·², **kach**, †**cawk** /kak, kax/ v to void excrement *16-*. **cackie** to void excrement *18-*. [Lat *cacāre*; compare KEECH¹·²]

cacker see CAUKER¹

ca'd see CA¹·²

†**cadda**, **caddow** n a rough woollen covering or rug; a saddle cloth *la16-19*. [EModE *caddow*]

caddal nal see CADDLE¹

caddas see CADDIS

caddel¹·¹, **caudle**, †**cathel**, †**caudil** /ˈkadəl, ˈkɔdəl/ n **1** a warm reviving drink (of gruel mixed with spices or alcohol) *la15-20, 21-* historical. **2** beaten or scrambled eggs; a sloppy mixture *20- Sh NE*. **3** a kind of eggnog *18-19*. [ME *caudel*]

caddel¹·², †**cathel** /ˈkadəl/ v **1** to stir or mix into a mess *20- NE SW*. **2** to be violent or disordered; to beat severely *la18-19*. [see the noun]

caddel²·¹, **kadel** /ˈkadəl, ˈkɑdəl/ n a sheep-mark of coloured thread (through the ear or round the neck) *20- Sh*. [ON *kaðall* a rope]

caddel²·², **kadel** /ˈkadəl, ˈkɑdəl/ v to attach an identifying thread to a sheep *20- Sh*. [see the noun]

cadden nail, †**caddone nail** /ˈkadən nel/ n a large nail or iron pin (holding the body of a cart to the axle) *16-19, 20- NE*. Compare CANNON NAIL and CARRON-NAIL, CADDLE¹, CADDY NAIL. [unknown first element + NAIL¹·¹]

caddes see CADDIS

caddie¹·¹, †**cadie** /ˈkadi, ˈkade/ n **1** *golf* an attendant who carries a player's clubs *la18-*. **2** a ragamuffin, a rough lad or fellow *la18-19, 20- NE EC Uls*; compare KADDIE. **3** a messenger or errand-boy; a member of an organized corps of porters in Edinburgh and Glasgow *18-19, 20-* historical. **4** a military cadet *17-e19*. [Fr *cadet*]

caddie¹·² /ˈkadi, ˈkade/ v *golf* to carry a player's clubs *la19-*. [see the noun]

caddie², †**keddie** /ˈkadi/ n an orphan lamb; a pet lamb *la16- Sh Ork*. [unknown]

caddis, †**caddas**, †**caddes** /ˈkadɪs/ n **1** fluff, dust *la19- NE T EC SW*. **2** rags, shreds of material; ends of thread *la19, 20- NE T EC*. **3** surgical lint *18-19*. **4** cotton wool, flock; padding material *la16-e17*. [EModE *caddow*]

caddle¹, **cathel** /ˈkadəl, ˈkaθəl/ n a large nail or iron pin *20- NE*. Compare CADDEN NAIL. **cathel nail**, †**caddal nal** a large nail or iron pin *16, 19- T C SW*. [unknown]

caddle², **caudle** /ˈkadəl, ˈkɔdəl/ n a set of cherry stones used in a game of PAIP *20- EC*. [unknown]

caddone nail see CADDEN NAIL

caddow see CADDA

caddroun see CAUDRON

caddy bolt /ˈkadi bolt/ n a bolt used in fixing the body of a cart to its axle *19, 20- T*. [unknown first element + BOWT¹·¹]

caddy nail /ˈkadi nel/ n an iron pin used in fixing the body of a cart to its axle *la19, 20- T*. [unknown first element + NAIL¹·¹]

†**cadent** n a cadet, a younger son *17*. [altered form of Fr *cadet*]

cadge¹·¹ /kadʒ/ n a round or district used by beggars; the action of begging *la17-*. [see the verb]

cadge¹·² /kadʒ/ v **1** to peddle wares or produce *18-*. **2** to carry loads or parcels *19-*. **3** to beg; to sponge *la19-*. [ME *caggen* to bind or fasten]

cadge²·¹ /kadʒ/ n a shake, a jolt; a nudge, a hint *la18- NE*. [unknown]

cadge²·² /kadʒ/ v to shake up; to knock about; to jostle *la18- NE*. [unknown; compare KEYTCH¹·²]

cadger, †**cadgear**, †**cadgyar**, †**cagger** /ˈkadʒər/ n **1** an itinerant dealer, a hawker (of fish); a carrier of goods, a carter *la15-*. **2** an ill-tempered person *la19- NE*. **Cadger's brose** a dish made by stirring oatmeal into boiling water *la19-*. **Cadger's dizzen**, **Cadger's dozen** thirteen *19-*. **Cadgers' Fair** an annual fair held by the Carters Society in Stewarton, Ayrshire *19, 20- WC SW*. **bolt the cadger** to vomit *la19- T*. **Cadger's news** stale news *la19- NE T EC*. **Cadger's whips** a child's term for the letter *r*, believed to have a curve resembling a cadger's whip *la19- T*. **cowp the cadger** to vomit *la19- T*. **the king will come in the cadger's road** a great man may need the services of a humble one *la19-*. [CADGE¹·², with agent suffix]

cadget, †**cageat** /ˈkadʒət/ n a small box, a casket; *in Elgin* a chest for official documents *la14-19, 20-* historical. [unknown]

cadgy, **caidgie**, **caigy**, †**kidgie** /ˈkadʒi, ˈkedʒi/ adj cheerful, in good spirits; friendly, hospitable *la18-*. **caigily**, †**cadgily** cheerfully, in a friendly manner; wantonly, lustfully *18-19, 20- SW*. [unknown]

cadgyar see CADGER

cadie /ˈkedi/ n a man's or boy's cap *la19- C*. [unknown]

cadie see CADDIE¹·¹

†**caduac**, **cadouk** n an accidental gain, a windfall *17-19*. [CADUC, Lat *cadūca* transitory things]

†**caduc** adj transitory *16*. [MFr *caduc* old, lapsed, Lat *cadūcus*]

†**caduciar** adj = CADUCIARY *la17*. [Lat *cadūcārius*]

caduciary /kəˈdjuʃəre/ adj *law* caducary, subject to or by way of escheat *la17-20, 21-* historical. [Lat *cadūcārius*]

ca'er, **cawer**, **caller** /ˈkaər, ˈkɔər, ˈkɔlər/ n **1** a driver, a carter; a person who guides plough horses *la15-*. **2** a visitor *19-*. **3** a person who swings (one end of) a skipping rope *la20-*. [CA¹·², with agent suffix]

caerd see CAIRD²·¹, CAIRD²·²

caff, **kaff**, **caaf**, **cauf**, †**calf**, †**caf**, †**caffe** /kaf, kɔf/ n chaff, winnowed grain (used for stuffing mattresses) *la15-*. **caff bed** a bed-tick filled with chaff *la16-*. †**calf bouster** a chaff-filled bolster *la16-e17*. **caff hoose**, **cauf hoose** the compartment connected with a corn-threshing machine where the chaff collects after threshing *20-*. **caff-seck** = *caff bed la20- N NE*. [OE *ceaf*]

caff see CAUF¹·¹

†**caffunʒe** n a type of footwear *la15-e16*. [unknown]

cag, **keg**, *Sh* **kig**, †**kaig**, †**caig**, †**quag** /kag, kɛg; *Sh* kɪg/ n **1** a small cask, a keg *la15-*. **2** the stomach, the belly *20- N NE EC*. [ON *kaggi*]

cageat see CADGET

cagger see CADGER

cahoo, **cahow** /kəˈhu, kəˈhʌu/ interj the call beginning of the search in the game of hide-and-seek *19- NE*. [compare KEEHOY]

cahoochy, **cahootchy** /kəˈhutʃi/ n rubber *la19-*. **cahootchy ba** a rubber ball *la19-*. **cahoochy padlock** humorous a condom *la20- EC*. [Fr *caoutchouc*]

cahow see CAHOO

†**cahute**, **kahute** *n* a ship's cabin; a separate room or space *e16*. [MFr *cahute*]
caib *see* CAIP²
caibe /keb/ *n* a cabinet-maker *20-*. [unknown]
caibie¹, **cabin** /'kebi, 'kabın/ *n* a hen's crop or gizzard *20- N NE*. [Gael *geuban*]
caibie² /'kebi/ *n* a hen coop *20- N*. [altered form of CAVIE¹·¹]
caibin, **cabin**, *Sh Ork* **kjaebin**, †**cabane** /'kebın, 'kabın; *Sh Ork* 'kjebın/ *n* **1** a hut, a shelter; an apartment (in a ship) *17-*. **2** a flat-topped bread roll *la20- EC*. [Fr *cabane*]
caibnet, **caibinet**, **cabinet** /'kebnət, 'kebənət, 'kabənət/ *n* **1** a piece of furniture used for storage or display; a repository for valuables *17-*. **2** a committee of senior government ministers *18-*. **3** a small chamber, a private apartment *16-e19*. [MFr *cabinet*]
caich *see* CACHE¹, CACHE²
caidgie *see* CADGY
caif /kef/ *adj of birds or animals* tame, unafraid; *of people* familiar, intimate *19- Bor*. [OE *cāf* swift, eager]
caif *see* CAVE¹
caig *see* CAG
caigy *see* CADGY
caik *see* CAKE
caikal /'kekəl/ *n* a worm, a tape-worm *20- N*. [compare Gael *ceigean* a small lump]
caikie *see* CAKEY
caikle *see* KECKLE¹·²
cailleach, **caillach**, *NE* **culloch**, †**cailliach** /'kaljəx, 'keljəx, 'kaləx, 'keləx; *NE* 'kʌləx/ *n* **1** an old woman *la18-*. **2** the festival of harvest-home *20- NE H&I Uls*. **3** the last sheaf of corn cut at harvest *20- NE Uls*. Compare CLYACK. [Gael *cailleach* an old woman, a nun]
cailʒard *see* KAILYARD
cain *see* KAIN
caip¹·¹, **cape**, †**kaip**, †**kape** /kep/ *n* **1** a coping; the highest part of a wall *la17-19, 20- NE*. **2** a coping-stone *16-17*. **3** an ecclesiastical cloak *15-16*. **cap-house**, †**cape house** a small erection on top of another building *la16-*. **caipstane**, *NE* **capesteen** a coping stone *la16-*. †**a cape of leid** a lead coffin *la15-16*. [ME *kape*, ON *kápa* a cloak]
caip¹·², †**kaip** /kep/ *v* to furnish with a coping; to cover with a roof *la16-19, 20- Bor*. **caipin' stone** a coping stone *17-*. [see the noun]
caip², †**caib** /kep/ *n* a spade for cutting divots; the iron or cutting part of a spade *la18- N*. [Gael *ceaba*]
caip *see* KEP¹·¹, KEP¹·²
cair, *N* **keir** /ker; *N* kir/ *v* **1** to scrape or rake up *19-*. **2** to stir *19- NE T*. **3** to prepare threshed corn for winnowing by separating out the broken pieces of straw *la19- N NE*. **4** to mix together *la19- Sh NE*. [Norw *kara* to rake, scrape]
cair *see* CARE¹·¹, CAUR
cairban /'kerbən/ *n* the basking shark *Cetorhinus maximus la18-*. [Gael *cearban*]
caird¹·¹, *NE* **kyaard**, †**kaird**, †**kard** /kerd; *NE* kjard/ *n* **1** a tinker; a craftsman who mends pots and kettles *la16-*. **2** a vagrant or rough person *18-*. **3** a person who scolds *19- N NE*. **kyaard tung't** given to loose talk *20- NE*. [Gael *ceàrd* a craftsman, a tinker]
caird¹·², *NE* **kyaard** /kerd; *NE* kjard/ *v* to abuse, scold *19- NE T*. [see the noun]
caird²·¹, **card**, *Sh* **caerd**, *NE* **cyard**, †**kard** /kerd, kard; *Sh* 'keərd; *NE* kjard/ *n* an instrument for carding wool (or hemp), or dressing cloth to raise the nap *la15-*. [MFr *carde* a teasel]
caird²·², **card**, *Sh* **caerd**, *NE* **cyard** /kerd; *NE* kjard; *Sh* 'keərd; *NE* kjard/ *v* to prepare wool for spinning; to dress cloth with cards *16-*. **caerdin** a party of women gathered by invitation at a neighbour's house in order to card wool *20- Sh*. [MFr *carder*]
caird³, **cerd**, **card**, **cairt**, †**cart**, †**kert** /kerd, kɛrd, kard, kert/ *n* **1** a playing card; a piece of cardboard *la15-*. **2** a photograph *la19- Sh NE T EC*. **3** a chart, a map *la15-19, 20- WC*. †**cairder**, **carder** a card-player *16-e18*. **cairtin**, †**carding**, †**carting** card-playing *16-19, 20- NE*. **the cards** a game of cards *la15-*. **up by cairts** up in the world, in an exalted position *18- NE T*. [MFr *carte*]
caird⁴, **kairt** /kerd, kert/ *v* to mix *18-*. **caird through ither**, **kaird through ither** to mix together *18-*. [CAIRD³, perhaps with influence from CAIR]
cairie¹·¹ /'keri/ *n* a breed of sheep local to Caithness with wool of mixed colours *20 N*. Compare KEERIE¹·¹. [Gael *caora* a sheep]
cairie¹·², **kairy** /'keri/ *adj of fleece* streaked, striped *20- N*. [see the noun]
cairl *see* CARLE¹·¹
cairlin *see* CARLINE
cairn¹·¹, *NE* **cyarn**, *NE* **cyaarn**, †**carne**, †**kairn**, †**kearn** /kern; *NE* kjarn/ *n* **1** a pile of stones used as a boundary-marker; a mound of stones placed as a way-marker (on a mountain) *la14-*. **2** heaped stones marking a grave; a memorial *16-*. **3** a loose heap of stones; rubble *la16-*. **4** a heap or quantity of anything *la18- N NE T*. **5** a particular type of small West Highland terrier *20-*. **Cairn Master** the official in a mountaineering club who marks the route up a hill with heaps of stones *la19- T*. **cairn net** a small net for catching fish lying behind stone-piles in a river *19-*. **Cairn terrier** a particular type of small West Highland terrier *la19-*. [Gael *càrn*]
cairn¹·², **cyarn** /kern, kjarn/ *v* to heap or pile (up); to mark with a pile of stones *la18- NE T*. **cairnit**, **cairned**, †**carnit** piled up; furnished with heaped stones (as boundary marks) *16-*. [see the noun]
cairngorm /kern'gɔrm/ *n* a yellowish semi-precious stone *la18-*. [from the name of the mountain range]
cairpet, **cerpet**, **carpet** /'kerpət, 'kɛrpət, 'karpət/ *n* a floor-covering, originally a thick table-cloth or coverlet *la14-*. **carpets** carpet slippers *20- NE T*. **carpet bowling** indoor bowls, played on a carpet *la19-*. **carpet bowls** = *carpet bowling 19-*. [ME *carpet*]
cairrage, **kerridge**, **carriage**, †**cariage**, †**careage** /'kerədʒ, 'kɛrədʒ, 'karədʒ/ *n* **1** the action of carrying; the conveyance of goods or baggage *la15-*. **2** a wheeled (horse-drawn) vehicle; a railway coach *17-*. **3** behaviour, demeanour *17-*. **4** (those responsible for) the baggage of an army *la14-e16*. †**careage hors** a pack-horse *16-e17*. †**careage man**, **carrage man** a man engaged in transporting goods *la14-e17*. [ME *cariage*]
cairrier, **carrier**, †**caryar**, †**cariour** /'keriər, 'kariər/ *n* a person who carries; a transporter of goods *la15-*. **come wi the blin cairrier** to return after a very long time or not return at all *19- T C*. [CAIRRY¹·², with agent suffix]
cairry¹·¹, **cerry**, **carry** /'kere, 'kɛre, 'kare/ *n* **1** a (heavy) weight, a burden *19-*. **2** a means of transport; a lift (in a vehicle) *19-*. **3** the motion of the clouds; the sky *19-*. **4** the action of carrying *la19-*. **5** the distance travelled and trajectory of a golf-ball *la19-*. **6** employment as a golf caddie *20-*. [see the verb]
cairry¹·², **cerry**, **carry**, †**cary**, †**care**, †**carie** /'kere, 'kɛre, 'kare/ *v* **1** to transport, convey; to lift or bear *la14-*. **2** to conduct, escort, lead *16-19*. **3** to act, behave *17-e18*. **4** to make one's way, proceed *la15-e16*. **5** to drive *e16*. **carried**, **cairriet 1** carried away; transported; elated *18-*. **2** conceited *19-*. **3** delirious, not rational *19-*. **4** *of food* packed to be

consumed elsewhere *la20-*. **carrying** being carried: ◊*she came past with some tins carrying la19-*. **cairry oan, cairryon** unseemly behaviour; a fuss, a row *20-*. **cairry oot, carryout** (hot) food or alcohol bought to be consumed off the premises *20-*. [AN *carier*]

Cair Sonday *see* CARE SUNDAY

cairt[1.1], **cart, cert,** †**kart** /kert, kart, kɛrt/ *n* **1** a wagon, a cart *la14-*. **2** a chariot *16, la20- literary*. **cairtie, cartie** a small cart, a child's home-made cart *la19-*. **cairtle,** †**cartill** a cart-load *16-19, 20- NE T*. **cairt-door** the tail-board of a cart *20-*. **cairt draucht, cart draught** a cart-load *17-19, 20- NE EC*. †**cartgate, kairt gait** a road suitable for carts *16-17*. **cairt gird** a rope used to secure a load *20- NE*. **cairtraik** the time taken to transport and unload a cart-load *20- NE SW Bor*. **cairt-wheel** the ox-eye daisy *Leucanthemum vulgare 20-*. [ON *kartr*]

cairt[1.2], **cart, cert,** †**kart** /kert, kart, kɛrt/ *v* **1** to convey by cart *la15-*. **2** to break in a horse for cart work *20- H&I*. [see the noun]

cairt *see* CAIRD[3]

cairter, carter, †**cartar,** †**kerter** /'kertər, 'kartər/ *n* **1** a transporter of goods, a carter *la13-*. **2** a charioteer *e16*. **Carters' Play** a yearly procession held by Carters' Societies *19- EC*. **kill the cairter** a name for a very strong variety of whisky *la19- NE T EC*. [CAIRT[1.1], with agent suffix]

cais *see* CASE[1], CASE[2]

caishen *see* CAITION[1.2]

caishin *see* KAISHIN

caisie *see* CASSIE

caitach *see* KETACH

caitch *see* CACHE[1], KEYTCH[1.1], KEYTCH[1.2]

caitch-pule *see* CATCHEPOOLE

caition[1.1], **caution,** †**catioun,** †**cautioun,** †**casioune** /'keʃən, 'kɔʃən/ *n* **1** *law* bail; security or surety (for an obligation) *la15-*. **2** one who stands surety *16-*. **3** a warning *la17-*. **4** prudence, wariness *18-*. **caishoner, cautioner** one who stands surety (for another) *16-*. **caishionry, cautionary,** †**cawtionarie** surety; the obligation entered into by a *caishoner la16-*. [MFr *caution*, Lat *cautio*]

caition[1.2], **caishen, caution,** *NE T* **cowshin,** †**cooshin,** †**cawshion,** †**catioun** /'keʃən, 'kɔʃən; *NE T* 'kʌuʃən/ *v* **1** to warn, advise or admonish *17-*. **2** to guarantee; to wager *la19-*. **3** to pacify, quieten *la19- NE T*. [see the noun]

caivel *see* CAVEL[1.1]

cake, *NE* **cyaak,** †**caik,** †**kake,** †**kaik** /kek; *NE* kjak/ *n* **1** an oatcake, a bannock *15-*. **2** a sweet cake *18-*. **3** a fruit loaf given to children or callers at New Year *la19- EC Bor*. **4** a sheet or slab of metal, especially lead *16-17*. **caking** the children's custom of visiting people on Old New Year's Day to ask for cakes *la19-20, 21- historical*. †**caik baxter, kaik bakstar** a baker of (oat)cakes *16-e17*. **Cake day** Hogmanay *19- T EC Bor*. †**caik fidler** a parasite, a hanger-on *e16*. **cake of breid** an oatcake *la17-19, 20- NE*. †**nocht worth ane cake** worthless *15-16*. [ON *kaka*]

caked *see* CAKIT

caker *see* CAUKER[3]

cakey, caikie /'keke, 'keki/ *adj* silly, foolish *la20- C*. [unknown]

cakit, caked /'kekɪt, kekt/ *adj* covered or smeared with mud or dirt *19-*. [ptp of Scots *cake* to smear, plaster]

cal *see* CA[1.2]

calamy /'kaləme/ *n* calomel *19, 20- NE C*. [Fr *calomel*]

calchen *see* KILCHAN

†**calcul**[1.1], **calcule** *n* a reckoning, a calculation *la16-18*. [MFr *calcul*]

†**calcul**[1.2], **calkil** *v* to calculate *16*. [ME *calculen*]

calculat /'kalkjulət/ *adj* calculated *la16-19, 20- NE*. [Lat *calculāt-*, ptp stem of *calculāre*]

calcule *see* CALCUL[1.1]

cald *see* CA[1.2], CAULD[1.1], CAULD[1.3]

caldron *see* CAUDRON

cale *see* KAIL

Caledon /'kalədən/ *n* a reduced form of CALEDONIA *17- literary*. [reduced form]

Caledonia /kalə'donɪə/ *n* **1** a (romantic or literary) term for modern Scotland *17-*. **2** the Roman name for northern Britain *la18-*. [Lat *Calēdonia*]

Caledonian[1.1] /kalə'donɪən/ *n* **1** a native of Scotland *18-*. **2** a native of the ancient province of Caledonia *la18- historical*. [see the adj]

Caledonian[1.2] /kalə'donɪən/ *adj* **1** of or pertaining to Scotland *la18-*. **2** of or pertaining to the ancient province of Caledonia *la18- historical*. **Caledonian antisyzygy** the presence of duelling polarities within one entity, considered to be characteristic of the Scottish temperament *20-*. **Caledonian cream** a dessert of whipped cream with marmalade, sugar, brandy and lemon juice *19-*. [derivative form of CALEDONIA]

caleeried /kə'lirid/ *adj* scatter-brained, giddy; full of mischief; conceited *la19- Uls*. [IrGael *caleer* to caper]

caleery /kə'liri/ *n* a silly, light-hearted person; a vain, conceited person *20- Uls*. [IrGael *caleer* to caper]

calendis *see* KALENDS

calf *see* CAFF, CAUF[1.1], CAUF[1.2], COLF

†**calfat** *v* to make watertight; to caulk *la16-17*. **calfatar, calfettour** a ship-caulker *16-e17*. **calfating** the action of caulking *16-e17*. [MFr *calfater*, Du *kalfaten*, and COLF]

calfie *see* CAUFIE

calfing *see* COLF

calk *see* CAUK[1.1], CAUK[1.2]

calkil *see* CALCUL[1.2]

call *see* CA[1.1], CA[1.2]

†**callan** *n* in Galloway a girl *la18-19*. [compare Gael *caile* a girl, diminutive *cailin*]

callant, callan, *N* **calland,** *H&I WC SW* **cullan** /'kalənt, 'kalən; *N* 'kalənd; *H&I WC SW* 'kʌlən/ *n* **1** a youth, a lad; a friend or associate *la16-*. **2** an affectionate or familiar term for an older man *20-*. **3** a customer *16-e17*. [MDu *caland*]

caller[1.1] /'kalər, 'kɔlər/ *v* to freshen; to cool *19, 20- NE*. [see the adj]

caller[1.2], **cauler,** †**callour** /'kalər, 'kɔlər/ *adj* **1** *of fish or vegetables* fresh, just caught or gathered *la14-*. **2** *of air or water* cool, refreshing *16-*. **3** healthy, vigorous *la18-*. **as caller as a kail-blade** very cool and fresh *19, 20- NE*. **caller ou,** †**caller oo** *in Edinburgh* a street cry used by vendors of fresh oysters *19, 20- historical*. [unknown]

†**callet**[1] *n* a disparaging term for a girl *la18-19*. [unknown]

†**callet**[2] *n* a mutch or cap *19*. [Fr *calotte*]

callivan *see* KEELYVINE

calloo /ka'lu/ *n* the long-tailed duck *Clangula hyemalis la18- Sh Ork*. [probably onomatopoeic]

callour *see* CALLER[1.2]

callow, kallow /'kalo/ *v of a cow* to calve *17- Sh Ork SW Bor*. [altered form of Older Scots *calf* to calve]

calm *see* CAM[1.1], CAUM[1.1], CAUM[1.2]

calmes, caums, †**cams,** †**caams** /kamz, kɔmz/ *npl* weaving heddles *18-19, 20- T*. [unknown]

calms, cams, caums, †**calmis** /kamz, kɔmz/ *npl* matrices; (bullet) moulds *16-19, 20- Sh N NE SW*. [unknown]

calmstone *see* CAM[1.1]

calp, †**caulp,** †**cawp** /kalp/ *n* **1** the most valuable article or animal owned by a person, claimed by a superior on the death of a tenant *16-17, la19- historical.* **2** *in Galloway and Carrick* a gift required of a tenant by his superior or chief (in return for his support and protection) *la15-16.* [Gael, IrGael *colpa* a full-grown cow or horse, taken as the unit for grazing animals; compare Gael *colpach* duty payable by tenants to landlords, and COLPINDACH]

calsay *see* CAUSEY¹·¹, CAUSEY¹·²

calshes, *T* **kilches** /'kalʃəz; *T* 'kɪlʃəz/ *npl* boys' trousers with a jacket or vest attached *19, 20- T H&I WC SW Bor.* [altered form of CALSOWMIS]

calshie, †**kelshie** /'kalʃi/ *adj* ill-tempered, surly *la18- NE T.* [unknown]

†**calsowmis** *npl* hose, trousers *la16-17.* [MFr *caleçons*; compare CALSHES]

Calton Entry Boys /kaltən 'ɛntre bɔɪz/ *n* the name of a gang who operated in the east of Glasgow *20, 21- historical.* [from the name of a district of Glasgow + ENTRY + plural form of BOY]

Calton Tongs /kaltən 'tɔŋz/ *n* the name of a Glasgow gang *20-.* [from the name of a district of Glasgow + a gang name of obscure origin]

†**calumpne**, **calumpny** *n* calumny *la15-17.* [Lat *calumnia*]

†**calumpniat** *v* to accuse falsely and maliciously *la16-17.* [Lat *calumniāt-*, ptp stem of *calumniāri*]

calumpny *see* CALUMPNE

calve *see* CAUF¹·²

†**calȝe** *n* a scale *la16.* **calȝeit** *of a horse's trappings* embroidered with scales *la16.* [MFr *escaille*]

cam¹·¹, **caum**, †**calm** /kam, kɔm/ *n* **1** pipeclay *la19-.* **2** a slate pencil *la19- WC SW.* **3** limestone *la15-19.* **camstane**, **caumstane**, †**calmstone 1** pipeclay (used for whitening) *19-.* **2** limestone *16-19.* [unknown]

cam¹·², **caum** /kam, kɔm/ *v* to whiten with pipeclay *la19- T C SW.* [unknown]

cam² /kam/ *n ploughing* the tilt or angle given to a furrow as it falls over from the ploughshare, adjusted by the setting of the coulter *la20- NE EC.* [probably reduced form of Eng *camber*]

cam *see* COME¹·²

camack, **cammock**, *Sh* **kammik**, *N* **cammag**, †**cummock**, †**cammok** /'kamək; *Sh* 'kamɪk; *N* 'kaməg/ *n* **1** a walking stick; a crooked staff or stick *16-19, 20- N NE SW.* **2** the game of shinty *19- N H&I.* **3** an obstruction *19- Sh.* [ME *kambok*, Lat *cambuca*]

caman, †**cammon** /'kamən/ *n* **1** a shinty stick *la19-.* **2** the game of shinty *e19.* **3** a crooked stick *e18.* [Gael *caman*; compare CAMACK]

cambreche, **cambrige** *see* CAMRICK

camceil /'kamsil/ *n* a sloping ceiling or roof *20- NE H&I C.* **camceiled**, **camsiled** having a sloping roof *la19- NE C.* **camiceiling**, †**camesillane** a sloping ceiling (in an attic room) *18, 20- WC.* [CIEL, with unknown first element; compare *coomceil* (COOM²)]

came *see* COME¹·², KAME¹·¹, KAME¹·²

cameill, **camel** *see* CAUMEL

camerage *see* CAMRICK

cameral, **kemerel**, **gamrel** /'kamərəl, 'kɛmərəl, 'gamrəl/ *n* a haddock after spawning *19- NE.* [compare IrGael *camramhail* dirty]

Cameron Highlander /kamərən 'hʌɪləndər/ *n* **1** a soldier in The Queen's Own Cameron Highlanders (QUEEN) *19-20, 21- historical.* **2** *pl* an informal name for The Queen's Own Cameron Highlanders (QUEEN) *la19-20, 21- historical.* [from the name of the Clan *Cameron* + plural form of HIELANDER]

Cameronian /kaməˈroniən/ *n* **1** a soldier in the Cameronian Regiment (Scottish Rifles) raised in 1689 in the west of Scotland in support of William of Orange *la17-20, 21- historical.* **2** a follower of Richard Cameron, the Covenanter; a member of the Reformed Presbyterian Church *la17-19, 20- historical.* [derived from the name of the Clan *Cameron*]

cammag *see* CAMACK

cammas *see* CANNAS

cammavyne *see* CAMOVINE

cammock, **cammok** *see* CAMACK

cammon *see* CAMAN

camovine, †**cammavyne** /'kamovʌɪn/ *n* camomile *16-19, 20- Ork NE T.* [probably irregular variant form of OFr *camomille*]

camp *see* KEMP¹·²

campie *see* KEMPIE¹·¹

†**campioun**, **campion** *n* a champion *la14-17.* [ME *champioun*]

campsho *see* CAMSHEUGH

campstarie *see* CAMSTAIRY¹·²

campy *see* KEMPIE¹·²

camrick, †**camerage**, †**cambreche**, †**cambrige** /'kamrɪk/ *n* cambric *la15-19, 20- NE EC.* [from the name of the French town of *Cambrai*]

cams *see* CALMES, CALMS

camschach *see* CAMSHEUGH

camshauchle¹·¹, **camshachle** /kamˈʃɔxəl, kamˈʃaxəl/ *v* to distort; to bend or twist; to disorder *19- NE EC Bor.* [probably Gael *cam* crooked + SHAUCHLE¹·²]

camshauchle¹·², **camshachle** /ˈkamʃɔxəl, ˈkamʃaxəl, kamˈʃɔxəl, kamˈʃaxəl/ *adj* twisted, distorted; quarrelsome *19- C Bor.* [see the verb]

camshell *see* KAMSHELL

camsheugh, *Ork* **camsho**, *NE* **camschach**, †**campsho** /kamˈʃux; *Ork* ˈkamʃo; *NE* ˈkamʃəx/ *adj* **1** surly, ill-tempered, perverse *17-19 20- Ork NE.* **2** crooked, distorted, deformed *16-e19.* [probably Gael *cam* crooked + SHAUCH]

camsiled *see* CAMCEIL

camstairy¹·¹, **camsteery** /kamˈstere, kamˈstiri/ *n* an uproar *la19, 20- T EC.* [unknown]

camstairy¹·², **camsteery**, *H&I* **camsterrie**, †**campstarie**, †**gamsterrie** /kamˈstere, kamˈstiri; *H&I* kamˈsteri/ *adj* perverse, unruly, quarrelsome *17-.* **camsterious** *of a horse* frisky *20- N.* [unknown]

can¹, **kan** /kan/ *n* **1** a (metal) container, a drinking-vessel, an earthenware jug *la14-.* **2** a chimney-pot *19-.* **3** a liquid measure (of approximately one gallon) *17- Sh.* [OE *canne* jug]

can²·¹, **kan** /kan/ *n* **1** skill, knowledge, ability *17-19, 20- Sh Ork N NE WC.* **2** supernatural power, witchcraft *la18-19, 20- Ork.* [see the verb]

can²·² /kan, kən/ *v pt* **cuid**, **coud**, **cud**, *NE* **quid**, †**culd**, †**couth**, †**cuth 1** *as an auxiliary verb* to be able to *la14-.* **2** *with ellipsis of the main verb* can do *la15-.* **3** to know, have knowledge of or skill in *15-16.* **canna**, **cannae**, **canny** cannot *la16-.* **cannin** can't: ◊*cannin ye be serious?* *20- NE.* **cudna**, **cudnae 1** could not *la18-.* **2** couldn't have: ◊*it coudna been better 19- NE T EC.* **cudnin** couldn't: ◊*cudnin ye hae telt me la19- NE.* †**can skeill** to have knowledge (of) *la15.* [OE *cunnan*]

†**can³** *v pt* did: ◊*to Parys can he ga la14-18.* Compare CULD. [substitution for ME *gan*, pt of *gin*, used as an auxiliary verb]

can, **canage** *see* KAIN

canally, *NE* **kinallie**, †**cannaille**, †**canailly**, †**canalzie** /kəˈnale; *NE* kɪnˈali/ *n* a rabble, a mob; an unruly crowd *la16-19, 20- NE T C.* [MFr *canaille*]

cance, †**canse** /kans/ *v* to speak impertinently or self-importantly *19- SW Bor.* [unknown]

†cancellar, cancellair *n* a chancellor *16-17*. [Lat *cancellārius*]

†cancellat *v* to cancel *16*. [Lat *cancellāt-*, ptp stem of *cancellāre*]

†candavaig *n* a variety of salmon *la18-e19*. [unknown]

candill *see* CAUNLE

Candillismes, Candilmes *see* CANDLEMAS

candle *see* CAUNLE

candle coal, cannel coal, †kennel-coal /ˈkandəl kol, ˈkanəl kol/ *n* a bituminous type of coal *la17-*. Compare PARROT COAL. [EModE *canel* + COAL]

Candlemas, Can'lemas, †Candilmes, †Kandelmes, †Candillismes /ˈkandəlməs, ˈkanəlməs/ *n* a religious feast-day falling on February 2nd; a Scottish quarter-day *15-*. **Candlemas ba'** a football match played (at Jedburgh) on the second of February *la19-*. **Candlemas bleeze** *in the Borders and South-West* a gift made by pupils to a teacher at Candlemas *19, 20- historical*. **Candlemas crown** a crown bestowed upon the Candlemas king or queen *la18-19, 20- historical*. **Candlemas day, †Candilmes day** = CANDLEMAS *la14-*. **Candlemas king** the title given to the boy who gave the largest gift of money to the schoolmaster at Candlemas *la18-19, 20- historical*. **Candlemas queen** the title given to the girl who gave the largest gift of money to the schoolmaster at Candlemas *la19, 20- historical*. **Candlemas term** the second or spring term in the Universities of St Andrews and Glasgow *20-*. [OE *candelmæsse*]

candy[1.1] /ˈkandi/ *n* crystallized sugar; hard sweets *17-*. Compare *succar candy* (SUGAR). **candybob** (the candy given by) a hawker or ragman *la19- NE T*. **candibrod, †candy-broad 1** sugar-candy *20- NE T EC Bor*. **2** loaf or lump sugar *18-e19*. **candy-glue** candy made from treacle *la19- NE T*. **candyman** a hawker or ragman (who gave candy in exchange for rags) *la19-20, 21- historical*. **candy-rock** candy in blocks or sticks *19-*. [Fr *sucre candi*]

candy[1.2] /ˈkandi/ *v ptp* **candied, †candeit** to preserve by boiling with sugar *17-*. [see the noun]

cane, caner *see* KAIN

cangle[1.1], **†cungle** /ˈkaŋəl/ *n* noise, disturbance; a quarrel *la19- T C Bor*. [perhaps onomatopoeic]

cangle[1.2] /ˈkaŋəl/ *v* to wrangle, dispute *17-*. [see the noun]

canker[1.1], **†kanker, †chanker, †schanker** /ˈkaŋkər/ *n* **1** an ulcerous sore *la14-*. **2** ill-temper *la18- NE T C*. **cankersome** ill-natured *la19- T SW*. **cankry** = cankersome *la18- WC SW*. [Lat *cancer*, ME *canker*]

canker[1.2] /ˈkaŋkər/ *v* **1** to infect or corrupt; to fester; to corrode *la18-*. **2** *of plants* to become infected with blight *la18-19, 20- NE SW*. **3** to fret; to become ill-tempered *19- NE T EC*. **4** to put into a bad temper *19- NE WC*. [see the noun]

cankert, cankered, †cankerit, †kankyrryt /ˈkaŋkərt, ˈkaŋkərd/ *adj* **1** affected with canker, infected, poisoned, gangrenous *la14-*. **2** ill-natured; malignant, corrupt *la15-*. **3** *of weather* gusty, stormy *la18-19, 20- NE EC*. **4** bent, twisted *19, 20- NE*. [ptp of CANKER[1.2]]

canlie /ˈkanli/ *n* a variety of the game of tig; the player who is 'it' *19- NE*. [perhaps altered form of KING]

canna *see* CAN[2.2], CANNACH

†cannabie, cannobie *n* a canopy (for a bed) *16-17*. [MFr *canopé* or *conopee* a bed curtain]

cannach, †canna /ˈkanəx/ *n* cotton-grass *Eriophorum vaginatum 19, 20- H&I*. **canna down** = CANNACH *20- NE T H&I EC*. [Gael *canach*]

cannae *see* CAN[2.2]

cannaille *see* CANALLY

cannas, canvas, †canves, †cammas, †cannowse /ˈkanəs, ˈkanvəs/ *n* **1** a heavy-duty fabric, canvas *la15-*. **2** a canvas sheet for catching grain or seeds *19- NE*. **3** linoleum *20- NE*. **cannas braid** a canvas-breadth; a small patch (of land) *la18- NE C*. [ME *canevas*, OFr *canevas*]

cannel[1.1] /ˈkanəl/ *n* the sloping edge of an axe, chisel or plane after sharpening *19, 20- NE T SW*. [Fr *canneler* to groove, Lat *canālis* a groove]

cannel[1.2] /ˈkanəl/ *v* **1** to give the wrong bevel to the edge of a tool being sharpened *20- NE*. **2** to chamfer, bevel *19, 20- NE*. [see the noun]

†cannel[2], **cannell** *n* cinnamon *la15-18*. **cannell water** a drink flavoured with cinnamon *17*. [ME *canel*]

cannel coal *see* CANDLE COAL

cannellie *see* TANNY[1.1]

cannie *see* CANNY[1.1]

cannin, canny *see* CAN[2.2]

cannle *see* CAUNLE

cannobie *see* CANNABIE

Cannogait breikis *see* CANONGATE BREEKS

†cannonar, cannoner, cannoneir *n* a gunner, a cannoneer *16-17*. [Older Scots *cannoun*, with agent suffix]

cannon nail /ˈkanən nel/ *n* the nail or pin which attaches a cart to its axle *19- EC Bor*. Compare CARRON-NAIL. [unknown first element + NAIL[1.1]]

cannon pin /ˈkanən pɪn/ *n* the nail or pin which attaches the cart to its axle *20- NE WC SW*. [unknown first element + PEEN[1]]

cannowse *see* CANNAS

canntaireachd /ˈkɔntarəxk/ *n piping* the chanting of pipe music in syllables (generally the vowels representing melody notes, the consonants grace-notes); also a written representation of this *la19-*. [Gael *canntaireachd* chanting]

canny[1.1], **cannie, †kanny** /ˈkane, ˈkani/ *adj* **1** cautious, careful, prudent, astute *la16-*. **2** pleasant; good, kind *la17-*. **3** favourable, lucky, of good omen *18-*. **4** gentle, quiet, steady *la18-*. **5** skilful, dexterous *19-*. **6** frugal, sparing: ◇ *be canny wi the butter 19-*. **7** comfortable, easy *19-*. **8** safe, free from risk *la16-19*. **cannily** carefully, cautiously, skilfully *la16-*. **canniness** cautiousness, prudence *17-*. **canny-weys, cannywise** cautiously, gently *19-*. **canny ca** woodworm *19- EC*. **canny man** a man who deals in the supernatural *la19- NE EC*. **canny moment, cannie moment** the moment of childbirth *18-19, 20- NE EC*. **canny-nanny** a species of yellow stingless bumblebee *20- C Bor*. **canny wife 1** a midwife *18-19, 20- NE EC*. **2** a woman who deals in the supernatural *19*. **no canny, nae cannie 1** uncanny, unnatural, supernatural *19-*. **2** risky, unwise *19-*. [probably CAN[2.2] + -IE[2]; compare ON *kunnigr* versed in magic]

canny[1.2] /ˈkane, ˈkani/ *adv* cautiously, carefully *la18-*. **ca canny** *see* CA[1.2]. [see the adj]

canny *see* KANNIE

†Canongate breeks, Cannogait breikis *n* venereal disease *la16-e18*. [from the name of the Edinburgh district + BREEKS]

†canous, canos *adj* hoary; grey-haired *15-e16*. [Lat *cānus*]

canse *see* CANCE

cant[1.1] /kant/ *n* **1** insincere pious or moral talk *17-*. **2** slang or jargon; dialectal speech, the language of Travellers *18-*. **3** a poem, a story, a merry tale *la16-e19*. **4** a song, music *e16*. [Lat *cantus* singing, *cantāre* to sing]

cant[1.2] /kant/ *v* **1** to talk in an affected or insincere manner; to use jargon or slang *18-*. **2** to speak monotonously or piously *18-*. **3** to chatter; to tell stories *18-e19*. **4** to sing, chant *la17-e19*. [see the noun]

cant[2] /kant/ *n* a trick; a habit, a custom *19- NE*. [perhaps connected with CANT[1.1]; compare CANTRIP]

†**cant**³ *adj* brisk, lively, smart *la14-e16*. [compare LG *kant* lively, Du *kant* neat, clever]
cant⁴, †**kant** /kant/ *n* **1** a rise of rocky ground *19- SW*. **2** an edge, the brink (of a hill or the sea) *la14-e17*. [perhaps Ger *Kante*, MDu *cant*, MLG *kant* a border, a side]
cant *see* KANT
†**cantailʒe, cantrailʒe** *n* a tuft, a tassel; trimming (for garments) *la16*. [MFr *canetille* braided gold or silver thread]
cantation /kanˈteʃən/ *n* talk, conversation *la18- T*. [Lat *cantātio* singing, incantation, or CANT¹,² with noun-forming suffix *-ation*]
canteelim *see* KANTEELAM
cantell *see* CANTLE¹
canter /ˈkantər/ *v* to chant music orally (when an instrument is unavailable) *20- T H&I*. [frequentative form of CANT¹,²]
cantie *see* CANTY
cantily, †**cantilly** /ˈkantəli/ *adv* cheerfully, joyfully *18-*. [CANTY, with adv-forming suffix *-ly*]
cantle¹, †**cantell** /ˈkantəl/ *n* **1** a corner, a nook; a projection, a ledge, a hill-summit *15-*. **2** (the crown of) the head *19, 20- NE Bor*. **3** the crown of the road *la18-e19*. [ME *cantel*]
cantle² /ˈkantəl/ *v* **1** to stand or set on high *la19, 20- T*. **2** to stimulate; to strengthen *20- NE*. **cantle up 1** to brighten up; to recover one's health or spirits *la19- NE*. **2** to bristle with anger *la19- NE*. [compare CANTLE¹ and *cant* tilt]
cantrag /ˈkantrag/ *n* a festivity to celebrate a marriage *20- N*. [altered form of CONTRACK¹,¹]
cantrailʒe *see* CANTAILʒE
cantrip, †**cantraip**, †**cantrep** /ˈkantrɪp/ *n* **1** a spell, a charm; magic *la16-*. **2** antics, a piece of mischief; a trick *19-*. [unknown]
canty, cantie /ˈkanti/ *adj* **1** lively, cheerful; pleasant *18-*. **2** small and neat *19-*. **3** comfortable *20-*. [derivative of CANT³]
canvas, canves *see* CANNAS
caochan, keechan /ˈkuxən, ˈkixən/ *n* **1** a stream, a rivulet *la19- N NE*. **2** *in distilling* fermented liquor before it goes through the still *19, 20- T H&I*. [Gael *caochan*]
cap¹, **caup**, †**cop** /kap, kɔp/ *n* **1** a (wooden) bowl or dish *la14-*. **2** a bowl used as a measure for liquor, grain or potatoes *16-*. **3** a snail's shell *e19*. **4** a leper's alms-bowl *15-16*. Compare CUP. **capper, cauper**, †**cappar 1** a maker of wooden bowls or other articles *16-19, 20- NE T*. **2** a nickname for a late riser *20- NE*. **3** a cupbearer; a keeper of cups *16-17*. **capfu, capfull**, †**copfull 1** a dishful *la16-*. **2** a quarter of a peck *18-19, 20- NE EC*. **cappie** hollow, bowl-shaped *20- WC SW*. †**cap-ale** a kind of beer *19*. †**copalmery, capalmrie** a cupboard *la15-e17*. †**cappy hole** *marbles* a game involving hollows made in the ground *18-e19*. †**cophous** a store-room for cups or plates *e16*. †**cap out** = *clean caup oot 16*. **clean caup oot** to completely drain (a vessel) *19-*. **drink oot o a toom cappie** to be in want *20- NE*. **he's as fou's cap or staup'll mak him** he is completely drunk *la19- NE*. **kiss a cap** to drink together (from the same vessel); to share a refreshment *la18-*. †**play cop out** to empty the cup; to carouse *16*. [OE *copp*, ON *koppr* cup]
†**cap**² *v* **1** to sail; to keep a course *16*. **2** to drift *16*. [unknown]
cap³, **caup** /kap, kɔp/ *v* to bend, twist or warp *19, 20- WC*. [unknown]
cap⁴ /kap/ *v* **1** to grab, seize; *of a child* to take another child's toy *19- EC*. **2** to stop; to prevent; to hold back *la19- Bor Uls*. [OFr *caper* to seize]
cap *see* KEP¹,¹, KEP¹,²
†**cape** *v* to seize vessels unlawfully *la17-18*. **caper** a privateer *la17-e19*. **capering** privateering *la17*. [Du, Flem *kapen* to plunder, *kaper* a privateer]
cape *see* CAIP¹,¹

†**capellane** *n* a chaplain *16*. [Lat *capellānus*]
†**caper, kaeper** *n* a piece of bread or oatcake with butter and cheese *la18-19*. [Gael *ceapaire*]
caper *see* CAPE
capercaillie, capercailzie, †**capercailʒe**, †**caper keily** /kapərˈkeli, kapərˈkelji/ *n* the wood-grouse *Tetrao urogallus 16-*. [Gael *capull coille*]
capernicious /kapərˈnɪʃəs/ *adj* short-tempered, fretful, fault-finding *la19- NE*. [conflation of Eng *capricious* with CAPERNOITIE]
capernoited, *Sh* **kappernoitit** /kapərˈnɔɪtəd; *Sh* kapərˈnɔɪtɪt/ *adj* **1** irritable, peevish *la18-19, 20- Sh NE T EC*. **2** capricious, nonsensical *18-19, 20- NE WC*. **3** intoxicated, giddy *19, 20- NE EC*. [unknown]
capernoitie, capernoity /kapərˈnɔɪti/ *adj* **1** intoxicated, dizzy *la18-19, 20- NE*. **2** irritable *19, 20- NE*. [unknown]
†**capes** *npl* grain retaining some part of the chaff or husk *la18-e19*. [unknown]
capesteen *see* CAIP¹,¹
capey-dykey, cappie-dykey /kepeˈdʌɪke, kapiˈdʌɪki/ *n* a game played with marbles or a ball (thrown against a wall) *la19- T*. [diminutive form of DYKE¹,¹, with unknown first element]
cap-house *see* CAIP¹,¹
†**capidose, cappiedosie, capie-dossie** *n* a (velvet) cap *16-e19*. [ME *capados*]
capill *see* CABLE, CAPPEL
†**capilowe** *v* to outdistance *e19*. [unknown]
†**capitanry, captanery** *n* the office of captain *15-e17*. [MFr *capitainerie*]
†**capitbirne** *n* a hood for a cloak *la15*. [unknown]
capoosh, †**capusche** /kəˈpuʃ/ *n* a hood *la16-e17, 20- NE*. [MFr *capoosh* a monk's cowl, from OFr *capusse* a head]
cappar *see* CAP¹, CAPPER
†**cappel, cappill, capill** *n* a horse, a cart-horse or workhorse *15-19*. [Gael *capull* a horse; a mare]
†**capper**, †**cappar** *n* copper *la17-e19*. [OE *copor*]
capper *see* CAP¹
cappie¹ /ˈkɑpi/ *n* a sinker for a fishing-line *19- Sh*. [ON *köppu-steinn* boulder]
cappie² /ˈkapi/ *n* an ice-cream cone or cornet *20- NE*. [diminutive form of Scots *cap*; compare POKEY-HAT]
cappiedosie *see* CAPIDOSE
cappie-dykey *see* CAPEY-DYKEY
cappill *see* CAPPEL
cappit /ˈkapɪt/ *adj* peevish, ill-humoured *la16-19, 20- Bor*. [unknown]
†**capprois** *n* copperas *la16-17*. [MFr *couperose*]
†**capricht** *n* part of the dress or armour of a horse *e16*. [unknown]
†**caprowsy** *n* an article of clothing *e16*. [unknown]
capshin *see* CAPTION
capstride /kapˈstrʌɪd/ *v* to anticipate, pre-empt; to perform a task sooner or better *la18-19, 20- Bor*. [unknown]
captanery *see* CAPITANRY
caption, capshin /ˈkapʃən/ *n* **1** *law* arrest; a warrant for an arrest (of a debtor) *la15-20, 21- historical*. **2** a lucky or valuable acquisition; a windfall, a prize *19- NE*. **3** seizure, capture *e15*. [Lat *captio* apprehension]
captire, captyre /ˈkaptɪr, ˈkaptaer/ *n* suspense *20- N NE*. **keep in captire** to keep a person in suspense *20- N NE*. [Fr *capture* arrest]
†**captour** *n* a person appointed to catch or detect offenders *la16-17*. [Lat *captor*]
captyre *see* CAPTIRE
capusche *see* CAPOOSH

car¹, kerr, caur, †kar /kar, kɛr, kɔr/ *n* **1** a wheeled vehicle; a cart, wagon *la15-*. **2** a sledge (for transporting peats or hay) *la15-19, 20- SW*. **3** a tram car *20-*. **†kerfull** a cart-load *la15-e16*. [ME *carre*]

car², caur, ker /kar, kɔr, kɛr/ *adj* **1** left (hand or side), left-handed *14-*. **2** awkward; wrong *18-*. Compare CORRIE². **car-handit, kaur-handit, ker-handit, †carhanded** left-handed *la16-*. [Gael *cearr* wrong, awkward; left(-handed)]

carb¹·¹ /karb/ *n* wrangling, an argument *la19- NE*. [probably altered form of Scots *carp*]

carb¹·² /karb/ *v* to wrangle, quarrel *19- NE EC*. **carble** = CARB¹·². [see the noun]

carcage, carkidge, *Sh* **karkish, †carkace, †karkage, †kerkage** /ˈkarkədʒ; *Sh* ˈkarkɪʃ/ *n* **1** a carcass, a dead animal *la15-*. **2** a corpse, a dead body *la16-e19*. [Lat *carcagium*, variant of Lat *carcosium*]

carcake, kercake, †caur-cake /ˈkarkek, ˈkɛrkek/ *n* a kind of small cake eaten on Shrove Tuesday or at YULE *19, 20- historical*. [CARE¹·¹ + Scots *cake*]

†carcan *n* an ornamental collar or necklace *16*. [MFr *carcan* a decorative necklace from OFr *carcan* an iron restraining collar]

†carcansoun *n* a kind of cloth *e16*. [perhaps from the French place-name *Carcassonne*]

†card *n* a kind of fabric *e14*. [unknown]

card *see* CAIRD²·¹, CAIRD²·², CAIRD³

†cardique, kerdikew, kairdique *n* a French silver coin *17-e19*. [Fr *quart d'écu*]

cardower, curdooer, †cardooer /karˈdʌuər, kʌrˈduər/ *n* **1** a person who undertook casual tailoring (without being a freeman of the burgh) *la18-19, 20- historical*. **2** an itinerant seamstress or tailor *19, 20- NE Bor*. [perhaps CAR² + DAE¹·¹, with agent suffix]

care¹·¹, C kerr, †cair /kɛr/ *C* kɛr/ *n* **1** worry, anxiety; misery, grief, sorrow; trouble *la14-*. **2** benevolent attention; protection; caution *la16-*. **careful, †carefull 1** attentive; painstaking; cautious *la16-*. **2** mournful, grieving; unhappy, anxious *la15-e18*. **care bed** a sick-bed *la14-19, 20- literary*. **†cair weid** mourning attire *e16*. **care's my case** woeful is my plight *19- NE T*. **hae a care o** to watch over, protect; to be cautious over *19- NE T EC Bor*. **tak care o** to be a match for *la19- NE T*. [OE *caru*]

care¹·², C kerr /kɛr/ *C* kɛr/ *v* **1** to look after, tend *16-*. **2** to be concerned for; to have regard for; to like or enjoy *la16-*. **3** to be cautious or reluctant *la16-*. **care na by** to be indifferent *la18-19, 20- T*. **care tae** to have objections to; to scruple *la16-19, 20- NE T*. **no care a boddle** to not care at all *la18-*. **no care the crack o a thoum** to be completely indifferent *19, 20- NE*. [OE *carian*]

care *see* CAIRRY¹·²

careage *see* CAIRRAGE

Care Sunday, †Cair Sonday /kɛr ˈsʌnde/ *n* the fifth Sunday in Lent, Passion Sunday *16-19, 20- historical*. [CARE¹·¹ + SUNDAY; compare ON *Kærslusunna*]

carfuffle¹·¹, curfuffle /karˈfʌfəl, kʌrˈfʌfəl/ *n* **1** a disorder, a mess *19-*. **2** a state of excitement or agitation; a fuss *19-*. **3** a disagreement, a quarrel *20-*. [see the verb]

carfuffle¹·², curfuffle /karˈfʌfəl, kʌrˈfʌfəl/ *v* to disorder, throw into confusion *la16-*. [intensifying prefix *car-* + FUFFLE¹·²]

cariage *see* CAIRRAGE

†caribald, carrybald *n* a term of abuse for a person *16*. [unknown]

carie *see* CAIRRY¹·²

cariour *see* CAIRRIER

cark¹·¹, †kark /kark/ *n* **1** care, anxiety *la18-19, 20- NE T WC SW*. **2** a certain weight, a load *15-e16*. **cark an' care** trouble and strife; financial difficulties *la18-*. [ME *cark*]

cark¹·², SW kerk /kark; *SW* kɛrk/ *v* **1** to complain or grumble; to nag *la19- N NE T SW*. **2** to load a ship *15*. **carking care** penury; distress; trouble *18-*. [ME *carken*]

carkidge *see* CARCAGE

carl-doddie /ˈkarlˈdɔdi/ *n* the ribwort plantain *Plantago lanceolata* and greater plantain *Plantago major* *19- NE T C*. [conflation of CURL-DODDY with CARLE¹·²]

carle¹·¹, carl, cairl, SW kerl, †karle /karl, kɛrl; *SW* kɛrl/ *n* **1** a man, a fellow; an old or miserable man, a miser *la14-*. **2** a man of the common people, a labourer *la14-19, 20- NE T C*. **3** a tall candlestick *19- SW*. **†carlish, carlich** rustic *15-e19*. **the auld carle** the Devil *la19- NE T EC*. **†play carle again** to give as good as one gets *18-e19*. [ON *karl* a man]

carle¹·², carl /karl/ *adj* **1** male, masculine *la16-*. **2** strong, large *18-19, 20- NE*. **carl-cat** a tom-cat *la16- literary*. **stalk of carl hemp** tough fibre, a firm or stubborn element *17-*. [see the noun]

carle² /karl/ *npl* small cakes given to carol-singers *la19- T*. **carl-scones** scones given to carol-singers *20- T*. [Scots *carol*]

carlie /ˈkarli/ *n* a small or elderly man *la17-19, 20- NE T EC*. **Carlie market** a market held annually for the engagement of married male farm-servants *la19- NE T*. **Carlie's Fair** = *Carlie market* *20- NE T*. [CARLE¹·¹ + -IE¹]

carline, carlin, carling, kerlin, *N* **cairlin, †karling, †kerlyng** /ˈkarlɪn, ˈkarlɪŋ, ˈkɛrlɪn; *N* ˈkɛrlɪn/ *n* **1** a woman; an old woman, a crone *la14-*. **2** a witch *la14-19, 20- NE EC*. **3** (the corn-dolly made with) the last sheaf of corn in the harvest field *20- NE*. **carlin heather** bell-heather *Erica cinerea* *19- T*. **carline spurs** needle furze *Genista anglica* *19- NE*. [ON *kerling*]

carlings /ˈkarlɪŋz/ *npl* cooked peas (eaten on Passion Sunday) *17-19, 20- historical*. [CARE¹·¹, with *-ling* suffix]

carmagnole /ˈkarmanjɔl/ *n* **1** a lively song and dance (popularized by French Revolutionaries) *la18-*. **2** a soldier in the French Revolutionary army *la18-e19*. **3** the Devil; an upstart; a rogue, a rascal *la18*. [Fr *carmagnole*]

carmele /ˈkarmɛle/ *n* the heath-pea *Lathyrus linifolius* *18, 20- historical*. [Gael *carra-meille*]

carmudgelt /ˈkarmʌdʒəlt/ *adj* bashed, crushed, damaged *19, 20- NE*. [intensifying, depreciatory prefix *car-* + ptp of MUDGE¹·²]

†carmusche¹·¹ *n* a skirmish *16-e17*. [MFr *escarmuche*]

†carmusche¹·² *v* to skirmish *la16*. [see the noun]

Carmyllie clover /karmʌɪle ˈklɔvər/ *n* the plant *Prunella vulgaris* *la19- T*. [from the place-name + CLAVER²]

carnaptious, carnapshus, curnaptious /karˈnapʃəs, kʌrˈnapʃəs/ *adj* irritable, quarrelsome, bad-tempered *la19-*. [intensifying prefix *car-* + derivative form of KNAP²·²]

carne *see* CAIRN¹·¹

carneed, curneed /karˈnid, kʌrˈnid/ *n* the runt of a litter (of pigs) *20- NE*. [unknown; compare DORNEEDY]

†Carnwath-like *adj* awkward; odd-looking *19*. [from the place-name + -LIKE³]

†carolus *n* a French coin of Charles VIII, worth 10 silver pence *16*. [a Latinized form of the personal name *Charles*]

carp, *Sh* **kjirp, †karp** /karp; *Sh* kjɪrp/ *v* **1** to dispute, find fault; to talk censoriously *16-*. **2** to speak or converse *la14-19*. **3** to sing or recite; to produce musical sounds *la15-19*. [probably ON *karpa* to brag]

carpet *see* CAIRPET

†carpoll *n* a pole or spar *la16*. [unknown]

carr *see* CAUR

carrant, carrunt, coorant /kaˈrant, kaˈrʌnt, kuˈrant/ n **1** an expedition; a sudden journey la19, 20- N SW. **2** a social gathering; an escapade; an uproar 20- NE T C. [Fr courante a dance]

carriage see CAIRRAGE

carrick /ˈkarɪk/ n **1** the game of shinty 19- EC. **2** a shinty stick 19- EC. [perhaps Gael carraig a knot of wood, wooden ball]

Carrick pursuivant, †**Carrik pursewant** /karɪk ˈpʌrswɪvant/ n heraldry a Scottish PURSUIVANT la15-. [from the district-name + ME pursevaunt]

carrie see CORRIE[2]

carried see CAIRRY[1,2]

carrier see CAIRRIER

Carrik pursewant see CARRICK PURSUIVANT

carritch /ˈkarɪtʃ/ n Presbyterian Church the catechism la18-. **mither's caridge**, †**mother's carritch** a simplified form of the Shorter Catechism la18-. [carritches as a variant of CATECHIS, thought of as plural and new singular formed]

carron-nail /ˈkarənnel/ n the nail fixing a cart to its axle la19- NE Bor. Compare CANNON NAIL. [perhaps from the name of the Carron Iron Works, or variant of garron nail (GARRON[2]); compare CADDEN NAIL, CANNON NAIL]

carrunt see CARRANT

†**carry** n a weir la18-19. [Gael caraidh]

carry see CAIRRY[1,1], CAIRRY[1,2]

carrybald see CARIBALD

carryvan /ˈkarevan/ n a caravan 20-. [altered form of Eng caravan]

carsackie, cursackie, kerseckie /karˈsaki, kʌrˈsaki, kɛrˈsɛki/ n an overall; a labourer's smock or jacket 19-. [perhaps MDu kasacke a cloak, a linen garment]

†**car saddle, cursaddle, carsadil** n a small saddle put on the back of a horse for supporting the shafts of a cart or carriage la15-19. [CAR[1] + SAIDLE[1,1]]

†**carse**[1], †**kerse**, †**cars**, †**kers** /kars/ n (an extensive stretch of) low alluvial land along the banks of a river; frequently in place-names la13-. [unknown]

†**carse**[2], **kerse**, **kers** n cress 15-19. [metathesis of OE cærse]

carsey coal, †**carsy coal** /ˈkarse kol/ n a kind of coal found near Bo'ness 19- EC. [unknown]

cart /kart/ n the crab-louse Pthirus pubis 20- NE. **kartie** = CART 19, 20- Sh. **carts** the skin-disease caused by the crab louse 20- NE. [specific sense of CAIRT[1,1]]

cart see CAIRD[3], CAIRT[1,1], CAIRT[1,2]

†**cartar** n a charter e17. [Lat carta]

†**cartar, carter** see CAIRTER

cartoush /karˈtuʃ/ n a woman's short jacket or gown la18-19, 20- Bor. [probably Fr courte short + housse a cloth covering for people, animals and objects]

cartow /ˈkartʌu/ n a quarter-cannon, throwing a ball of a quarter of a hundredweight (12.7 kilos) 17, la19- historical. [OFlem kartouwe]

†**cartyke** adj a type of taffeta la16. [unknown]

carvey, carvie /ˈkarve, ˈkarvi/ n **1** the caraway seed or plant Carum carvi 16-. **2** a sweet containing caraway seed 19- EC SW. **carvied** flavoured with caraway 19, 20- NE. **carvey sweetie** a sugar-coated caraway seed la19- NE H&I WC. [MFr carvi]

cary see CAIRRY[1,2]

caryar see CAIRRIER

†**casar** n a board or box for displaying bread for sale la16-e17. [unknown]

casay see CAUSEY[1,1]

caschelawis see CASHIELAWS

caschet see CACHET[1,1], CACHET[1,2]

caschie see CASSIE

caschielawis see CASHIELAWS

caschrom, cas crom /ˈkasxrom, ˈkaʃkrom, ˈkaskrom/ n a crook-handled spade or foot-plough traditionally used in the Highlands and Islands 19-. [Gael cas chrom crooked foot]

case[1], **kess**, †**cais**, †**cace** /kes, kɛs/ n **1** a situation, an occurrence, a state of affairs la14-. **2** a matter for consideration or investigation; a law-suit la14-. **3** a state or condition 15-. **caseable** natural or appropriate to a particular case la16-19, 20- Sh. **case-alaek** all the same 20- Sh. **case be, case by** in case, lest; perhaps 19, 20- NE WC. **in a case** in a state of excitement 20- NE. [ME cas, Lat cāsus]

case[2], **cace**, †**cays**, †**kace**, †**cais** /kes/ n **1** a receptacle or container; a suitcase la14-. **2** a window frame; a casing 16-. **cased**, †**casit** fitted with a frame or casing 16-. †**cais camb** a comb kept in a case la16-17. **case window**, †**cais windo, cais windok** a casement window 16-. [ME case]

†**caser, caysere** n an emperor 15-16. [OE cāser]

cash[1] /kaʃ/ n a sum of money, a fund; ready money (in the form of coins or notes) la17-. **cash account** in banking a loan-system allowing credit on the surety of two guarantors la18-20, 21- historical. **cash credit** = cash account 19-20, 21- historical. **cash keeper**, †**cash-keiper** a treasurer, a cashier la17-. [Fr caisse, Ital cassa a box]

cash[2] /kaʃ/ n mining soft, coaly blaes la19, 20- EC. **cashy blaes** = CASH[2]. [unknown; compare CASHIE]

cash[3] /kaʃ/ n a tobacco pouch la19- Sh. [Dan kasse a case, purse, Fr casse a box]

cashie /ˈkaʃi/ adj **1** delicate, soft, perishable 19- SW Bor. **2** of vegetation luxuriant, succulent 19. [unknown]

cashielaws, †**caschelawis**, †**caschielawis** /ˈkaʃilɔz/ n an instrument of torture la16-e17, la18- historical. [unknown]

cashti, casti /ˈkaʃti, ˈkasti/ n a stick 20- SW Bor. [Travellers' language; compare Sanskrit káshtha]

†**cashub, cassup** n a kind of wood ash used in bleaching 18. [Polish kaszub, from Kaszubja the name of a village in Poland]

cashy blaes see CASH[2]

casie see CAUSEY[1,2]

casioune see CAITION[1,1]

†**casnat, casnett** n unrefined cane-sugar la16-17. [reduced form of MFr cassonade]

†**cassacioun** n cancellation 15. [Lat cassātio]

cassay see CAUSEY[1,1], CAUSEY[1,2]

cassie, Sh **kishie**, Ork N NE **caisie**, N **keizie**, NE **cazzie**, †**caschie** /ˈkasi; Sh ˈkiʃi; Sh ˈkɪʒi; Ork N NE ˈkesi; N ˈkezi; NE ˈkazi/ n a straw-basket or creel la16- Sh Ork N NE. **kishiefoo**, †**kessieful**, †**cassiefull** the load or quantity carried in a straw basket or creel 17- Sh Ork. **kishielepp** (the remains of) a worn-out or broken basket la19- Sh. [ON kass a case, a creel]

cassie see CAUSEY[1,1], CAUSEY[1,2]

cassin see CAST[1,2]

cassup see CASHUB

cast[1,1], **kast**, Ork **kest**, NE T **kiest** /kast; Ork kɛst; NE T kʌɪst, kɪst/ n **1** a throw; the act of throwing; the distance covered by a throw la14-. **2** one's lot, fortune, fate la14-. **3** a turn or twist; a trick, a contrivance la15-. **4** aspect, demeanour, appearance la15-. **5** a ditch; a cutting or excavation; a sunken road la16-. **6** a particular quantity or amount 17-. **7** help, assistance; a friendly turn 18-. **8** a casting of lots, a share apportioned by casting lots 18-. **9** an opportunity, a chance of getting something 19-. **10** a course, a route 19- literary. **11** a (short-term) loan 19, 20- Sh. **12** a taint, a bad taste 20- Sh. **13** skill 19, 20- Sh. **14** a tumble, a fall 20- T. **15** an assessment or rating *la17*. **cast of yer hand** a helping hand *19- Sh EC*. **hae a cast upo de** to put on airs *20- Sh*. [see the verb]

cast[1,2], **kast** /kast/ *v pt* **cast, coost, cuist, kiest,** *Sh* **cöst,** †**kist,** †**kest,** *ptp* **cast, cuist, casten, cuisten,** *Sh* **cassen,** †**cassin 1** to throw or hurl; to send forth *la14-*. **2** to shed or discard; to remove clothing *la14-*. **3** to direct the gaze; to glance *la14-*. **4** to dig or excavate; to clear out a drain or ditch; to cut peats or turf; to cut a trench *15-*. **5** to estimate; to reckon an amount; to assess quality; to devise or plan *15-*. **6** to set in a mould *la15-*. **7** to emit light; to throw a shadow *16-*. **8** *of bees* to swarm *la16-*. **9** *of a horse* to throw its rider *18-*. **10** to toss the head *la18-*. **11** to sow seed *la19-*. **12** to vomit *la14-19, 20- EC*. **13** *of animals* to give birth *15-19, 20- NE T EC*. **14** to thresh grain; to dismantle a stack of grain for airing or threshing *16-19, 20- T Bor*. **15** to make fast; to knot a rope or thread *la16-19, 20- N NE SW*. **16** to spread dung (in a stable or on a field) *20- Ork N*. **17** to cover with lime or rough-cast *17-e19*. **18** to reject or oppose as illegal or improper; to annul *la16-e17*. **cassen, casten;** *Sh Ork* **kassen 1** *of colours* faded *20-*. **2** rejected, defeated (in an election) *la19- NE*. **3** *of food* tainted, sour; decaying *la19- Sh*. **castings** cast-off clothing *16-*. **cast awa** a waste *la19- NE T EC*. **castback** a setback, a relapse *la19- NE EC SW*. †**cast-bye** an outcast *e19*. **cast line** the thin casting-line attached to the reel-line of a fishing-rod *19-*. †**be castin lowse** to lose one's job *e17*. **cast aboot** to manage, arrange, look after *19-*. **cast aff** to recover from (an illness) *20-*. **cast aff wi** to cut oneself off from *19- NE*. **cast at** to spurn, condemn *18-*. **cast that at** to reproach someone (with something) *la19-*. **cast by** to discard *16-19, 20- Sh*. **cast a clod at** to reproach *20- N NE*. **cast the colours** to perform the flag-waving ceremony at Selkirk Common Riding *la19-*. **cast the cup** to tap a cup prior to reading the tea-leaves *la19- Sh NE*. **cast a dash** to make a great show; to cut a dash *18-19, 20- NE*. **cast eggs 1** to drop eggs into water for the purpose of divination *19, 20- NE*. **2** *in cooking* to beat eggs *18-e19*. †**cast in** to take in, store or stack (a crop) *la15-16*. †**cast a laggen-gird** to have an illegitimate child *18-e19*. **cast the mell** to assign the stations in half-net fishing *20- SW Bor*. **cast oot** *v* to disagree, quarrel *18-*. **cast oot** *n* a quarrel *20-*. **cast owre** to consider, think over *la19-*. **cast a shae** to have an illegitimate child *20-*. **cast up 1** to reproach; to taunt someone *17-*. **2** to appear, turn up; to befall *18-*. **3** *of storm-clouds* to gather *19- NE EC Bor*. **4** *of the weather* to clear up *19, 20- T*. **5** to throw open *15-17*. [ON *kasta*]

castell *see* CASTLE

†**castellane, castilean** *n* one of the garrison of a castle *15-17*. [OFr *chastelain*]

†**castellaw** *n* in Argyllshire a measure of flour or cheese *14-16*. [unknown]

†**castelward** *n* **1** a payment in commutation of the feudal service of guarding a castle *15-e17*. **2** ground pertaining to a castle *la15*. **3** a castle-guard *e15*. [CASTLE + OE *weard* keeper, warden or WARD[1,1]]

casti *see* CASHTI

castilean *see* CASTELLANE

castle, †**castell** /'kasəl/ *n* **1** a fortified building, a stronghold *14-*. **2** an isolated pillar of rock in the sea *20- Ork*. **castle toun** a collection of houses lying near or under a castle *la16-*. [ME, AN *castel*]

castock, custock, *Sh* **kastik** /'kastɔk, 'kastək, 'kʌstək; *Sh* 'kastɪk/ *n* a stalk of kale or cabbage *17-*. [KAIL + STOCK[1,1], ME *caulstok*]

casual /'kaʒəl/ *adj* accidental, irregular; arising from a mistake *la15-19, 20- NE*. [MFr *casuel*, Lat *cāsuālis* depending on chance]

casualty, †**casualte,** †**casualite** /'kaʒəltɛ/ *n* **1** *law* an incidental item of income or revenue due from a tenant or vassal on the transmission of land *16-20, 21- historical*. **2** the aggregate of incidental items of the royal revenue *e16*. [MFr *casualité* uncertainty]

cat[1], *Sh Ork* **katt** /kat; *Sh Ork* kɑt/ *n* **1** a small domesticated animal, cat *Felis domesticus la14-*. **2** a stick used in the game of tip-cat *19-20, 21- historical*. **cat's carriage** a seat formed by two people's crossed hands *19- NE EC*. †**catcluke** the bird's-foot trefoil *Lotus corniculatus 16*. **cat's een** the germander speedwell *Veronica chamaedrys la19- C SW Bor*. **cataface** an owl *Asio accipitrinus la- Ork*. **cat's face** a round of six scones or buns *20-*. **cat's fur** an expression of dismissiveness: *What fir? Cat's fur!* *la20-*. **cat's hair** cirrus or cirrostratus cloud *la19- NE*. **cat heather** a species of heath *Erica tetralix, Erica cinerea* or *Calluna vulgaris 19- NE T EC*. **cat-kindness** false affection (for personal profit) *19-*. **cat's lick** a hasty, superficial wash *la19-*. **catloup** a short distance or time *19-*. **cat-steps** crow-steps on a gable *19- Bor*. **cat's tails** cotton-grass *Eriophorum vaginatum la18-*. **cat wa', kat waa** a partition between two rooms; an internal wall not built up as far as the roof *la19- Sh Ork*. **cat-wittit, cat-witted 1** hare-brained, scatty *19-*. **2** spiteful; savage; short-tempered *la18-19, 20- H&I Bor*. **atween you an me an the cat** between ourselves, confidentially *la19- NE*. **cat and bat** the game of tip-cat *la19-* compare CATTIE. **cat and dog** = *cat and bat la19-*. **meet the cat in the mornin** to suffer a setback, have bad luck *la19- NE*. [OE *cat*]

cat[2,1] /kat/ *n* **1** straw mixed with soft clay used in building or repairing walls *la16-19, 20- Bor Uls*. **2** a handful of straw or reaped grain laid on the ground without being put into a sheaf *19- Bor*. [unknown]

cat[2,2] /kat/ *v* to build or repair a structure with straw and clay *la17- Bor*. [unknown]

catakeese *see* CATECHEEZE

catale *see* CATTLE

catalogue, †**cataloge,** †**catholog** /'katələɡ/ *n* **1** a descriptive list of items (for sale) *la16-*. **2** a register of those present; a list or roll of names *la16-e20, la20- historical*. [MFr *catalogue*]

cat and clay /kat ənd 'kle/ *n* straw mixed with soft clay used in building or repairing walls *la16-19, 20- Bor Uls*. [compare CLAT AND CLAY and CAT[2,1]]

†**catband** *n* an iron strap or bar for securing a door or gate *16-19*. [BAND[1,1]; first element unknown]

catch[1,1] /katʃ/ *n* **1** a haul of fish *la18-*. **2** a hold, a grasp *la19-*. **3** a sharp pain, a stitch *la19- NE EC*. **4** a knack *la19- NE EC*. [see the verb]

catch[1,2]**, ketch,** †**cach,** †**cawch** /katʃ, kɛtʃ/ *v pt* **catchit, caucht, cotch 1** to take hold of; to seize; to obtain *15-*. **2** to chase, drive; to proceed *la15-e17*. **catchers** a game played with a ball, or a bat and ball *20- EC SW*. **catchy** disposed to take advantage of another *19- NE EC SW*. **catchy-clappy** games bouncing a ball against a wall *la20- NE EC*. **catchie-hammer** one of the smallest of a stonemason's hammers *19-*. †**cachkow** a cow-catcher *e16*. †**catch-match** an advantageous marriage *e19*. **catch grup o** to take hold of *la19-*. **catch the salmon** a catching game played with a piece of rope *la19- NE*. **catch-the-ten** a card game *19-*. **catch yerself on** to pull yourself together *la20-*. [ME *cacchen*]

catch *see* CACHE[2]

catche *see* CACHE[1]

catchepoole, kaitchpull, caitch-pule, †cachepell, †kachepele, †kechepule /ˈkatʃpul, ˈketʃpʌl/ *n* **1** the game of hand-tennis *la16-e17, 19- historical*. **2** a ground or court for playing hand-tennis *16-17, 19- historical*. **†caitchpeller, kaichpellar** a keeper of or attendant at a tennis-court *la16-e17*. [MDu, Flem *caets-spel*; compare CACHE¹]

catecheeze, catakeese, catechize /katəˈtʃiz, katəˈkiz, ˈkatəkaez/ *v* to teach scripture or doctrine *la16-*. [MFr *catechiser*]

catechis, cattiches, cattages /ˈkatətʃɪs, ˈkatədʒɪz/ *n* **1** the catechism *la16-*. **2** a catechizing; a cross-questioning *la16-19, 20- NE*. [MFr *catechese*]

catechize *see* CATECHEEZE

cater *see* CATTER²

cateran, catheran, †catherein, †katherane, †ketterine /ˈkatəran, ˈkaθəran/ *n* (one of) a band of a Highland marauders *16-19, 20- historical*. [Gael *ceatharn* a troop]

†caterve *n* catarrh *la16*. [irregular variant of Older Scots *catar*]

caterwoul, cater-wail /ˈkatərwʌul, ˈkatərwel/ *v* to whine, cry *la17-19, 20- NE T*. [ME *caterwawe*, EModE *caterwawl*]

cat-harrow /ˈkat haro/ *n* **1** a type of harrow (for turnips) *la19- T EC*. **2** a time of strain *20- Ork*. **3** a nursery game, played by pulling crossing loops of thread *16-e19*. **†draw the cat-harrow** to pull in different directions; to thwart one another *16-e19*. [perhaps related to CAT¹]

cathead /ˈkathɛd/ *n* an inferior kind of ironstone *la18-19, 20- historical*. [unknown]

cathel *see* CADDEL¹·¹, CADDEL¹·², CADDLE¹

cathel nail *see* CADDLE¹

catheran, catherein *see* CATERAN

Catholic creditor /kaθlɪk ˈkrɛdɪtər/ *n law* a person who holds security for his debt over more than one piece of property belonging to his debtor *la19-*. [Older Scots *catholik* in the older sense of 'universal' + Older Scots *creditour*]

catholog *see* CATALOGUE

ca through¹·¹, ca thro, ca throw /ˈkɔ θru, ˈka θru, ˈkɔ θro/ *n* **1** a disturbance *19- NE T EC Bor*. **2** drive, energy *la19- NE T EC*. **3** a slight or preliminary wash of clothing *20- NE T EC SW Bor*. **4** a search *20- NE T EC*. [see the verb]

ca through¹·², †ca thro /ˈkɔ θru, ˈka θru/ *v* **1** to display great drive or energy; to work steadily *la18-*. **2** to pull through an illness *la19- NE T EC*. [CA¹·² + THROU¹·²]

cat-hud /ˈkathʌd/ *n* the large stone used as a back to the fire on the hearth of cottage *19- SW Bor*. [perhaps CAT¹ + HUD]

catioun *see* CAITION¹·¹, CAITION¹·²

catlill /ˈkatlɪl/ *v* to punish by pressing the finger into the hollow under a child's ear *19- SW*. [perhaps CAT¹ + Du *lel* the ear-lobe]

cat loup *see* CAT¹

catma, catmaw /ˈkatma, ˈkatmɔ/ *n* a somersault *19- T*. **tumble a catmaw** to perform a somersault *19- T*. [CAT¹ + MAW⁵·¹]

catmoagit *see* KATMOGIT

catour *see* CATTER²

catrail /ˈkatrel/ *n* the name of an early earthwork in southern Scotland *18- SW Bor*. [unknown]

cattages *see* CATECHIS

cattell *see* CATTLE

†catter¹ *n* a type of cloth *la16-e17*. [unknown]

catter², cowder, †catour, †cater /ˈkatər, ˈkʌudər/ *n* **1** money, cash *la18-19, 20- NE*. **2** a household officer, a furnisher of provisions, a purveyor *la15-17*. [ME *catour* a buyer of provisions]

catterbatter¹·¹ /ˈkatərbatər/ *n* a quarrel, a disagreement *19, 20- Bor*. [see the verb]

catterbatter¹·² /ˈkatərbatər/ *v* to wrangle, quarrel *19- Bor*. [perhaps Du *kater* a tom-cat + BATTER¹·²]

cattercavie /katərˈkevi/ *n* a species of crab *20- EC*. Compare KEAVIE. [unknown]

catter-wurr /katərˈwʌr/ *n* an ill-tempered person *20- NE*. [unknown]

cattiches *see* CATECHIS

catticloo, kattaklu /katiˈklu, katəˈklu/ *n* a disorderly crowd; a noisy quarrel *la19- Sh*. [Norw *katteklo* cat's claw]

cattie /ˈkate, ˈkati/ *n* **1** a cat *la19-*. **2** a catapult *20-*. **3** the game of tip-cat *19- NE EC*. **4** a woman's fur necklet *20- NE T*. **5** the core of an apple or pear *20- T*. **cattie buckie** the whelk *Nucella lapillus 20- Ork*. **cattie and battie** the game of tip-cat *la20-*. **lat the cattie dee** to allow a swing to come gradually to rest *20-*. [CAT¹ + -IE¹]

cattiewurrie¹·¹ /ˈkateˈwʌre/ *n* a violent dispute *la19- NE*. [compare Du *kater* a tom-cat, and WIRR¹·¹]

cattiewurrie¹·² /ˈkateˈwʌre/ *v* to wrangle violently *la19- NE*. [see the noun]

†cattill *n* a kettle or pot *16-e17*. Compare KETTLE. [ON *katl-*, dative and plural stem of *ketill*]

cattle, †catale, †cattell, †kettell /ˈkatəl/ *n* **1** livestock, cattle *la14-*. **2** vermin, lice *la18-19, 20- NE WC*. **3** birds and beasts *la19, 20- NE*. **4** *derogatory* people *19, 20- C*. **5** property *e15*. **cattler** a cattleman on a farm *20- NE*. **cattlie** a cattleman on a farm *20- NE*. **cattle beasts** livestock *19-*. **cattle bucht** a cattle yard *la19- NE T EC*. **cattle court** a cattle yard *19-*. **cattle creep** a low arch or gangway for cattle under or over a railway *19-*. **cattle raik** a cattle pasture; a road along which cattle are driven to fairs *19- NE T EC*. **cattle reed** a cattle yard *19- NE T C*. [ME *catel*]

catton *see* CUTTEN

cau *see* CA¹·¹

caucht *see* CATCH¹·²

caudil *see* CADDEL¹·¹

caudle *see* CADDEL¹·¹, CADDLE²

caudron, caldron, †caddroun /ˈkɔdrən, ˈkɔldrən/ *n* a large pot, a cauldron *la14-*. [ME *caudroun*]

cauf¹·¹, calf, caff, caav, †cawf /kɔf, kaf, kav/ *n* **1** the young of a cow, a calf *la12-*; compare CAUR. **2** a smaller island lying off the shore of a larger one *la18- Sh Ork*. **calf grund, cauf ground** the place of one's birth and early life *la19- T EC Bor*. **calf kintra** = *cauf grund 19-*. **calf's lick** an unruly tuft of hair *20-*. **calf ward** an enclosure for calves *la18-*. [OE *cealf*]

cauf¹·², calf, calve, caav /kɔf, kaf, kav/ *v* to give birth to a calf *la15-*. [OE *cealfian*]

cauf² /kɔf/ *n* the calf of the leg *19-*. [ON *kálfi*]

cauf *see* CAFF

caufie, calfie /ˈkɔfe, ˈkafi/ *n* a calf *la19- Ork N NE T*. **calfie's cheese** a soft cheese or curd made with the milk of a newly-calved cow *la20- NE T*. **calfie's lick** an unruly tuft of hair *20- NE*. **calfie's mooie** a small cowrie shell *20- NE*. [CAUF¹·¹ + -IE¹]

cauk¹·¹, *Sh* **kaak,** *T* **kalk, †calk, cawk** /kɔk; *Sh* kak; *T* kalk/ *n* chalk, lime *la15-*. **caukie, cauky** chalky, covered with chalk *20-*. **†cauk and keel** chalk and ruddle, as used by fortune-tellers *18-e19*. **†calke is na sheares, cawk's nae sheers** *proverb* marking the pattern on the cloth with chalk is not the same as cutting it *la16-18*. [OE *calc*]

cauk¹·², cawk, caak, *NE T* **kalk, †calk** /kɔk, kak; *NE T* kalk/ *v* **1** to mark, treat or wash with chalk *la15-*. **2** to mark up with chalk something to be remembered or paid; to chalk up *20- NE T EC*. **3** to make someone pay dearly *20- NE*. [see the noun]

cauk² /kɔk/ *v* to fix a guard on or turn down and sharpen the ends of a horseshoe to prevent slipping *19-*. [compare OE *calc* a sandal, Lat *calx* a heel]

cauker¹, cacker /ˈkɔkər, ˈkakər/ *n* **1** a calkin, (the turned-down ends of) a horseshoe *la18-*. **2** an iron rim fixed on a clog or shoe to minimize wear *20- NE EC SW Bor*. **3** *pl* a pair of boots (studded with large tacks) *20- N NE*. [derivative of CAUK²]

cauker², caulker /ˈkɔkər/ *n* a dram of liquor, a bumper *la18-19, 20- NE T C*. [nautical slang]

cauker³, caker /ˈkɔkər, ˈkakər/ *n* a stroke on the palm of the hand from a strap *la19- NE T EC*. [unknown]

caul, caal, †cauld /kɔl, kal/ *n* a weir or dam (to divert water into a mill lade) *la16- NE EC SW Bor*. [unknown]

cauld¹·¹, cald, cowld, cold, caul, caal /kɔld, kald, kʌuld, kold, kɔl, kal/ *n* **1** coldness; a spell of cold weather *la14-*. **2** the common cold *16-*. **cauldrife, cauldrif 1** cold, causing or susceptible to cold *18-*. **2** cold in manner; lacking in cheerfulness; cold-hearted *la17-19, 20- NE T EC*. **3** lacking in religious zeal *la17-19, 20- literary*. **cauldit, calded, colded** suffering from a cold *19-*. [see the adj]

cauld¹·² /kɔld/ *v* to grow cold; to make cold *la16-*. [see the adj]

cauld¹·³, cald, cowld, cold, caul, caal /kɔld, kald, kʌuld, kold, kɔl, kal/ *adj* **1** lacking warmth, cold; *la12-*. **2** *of land* stiff, clayey *la19-*. **cauld comfort** inhospitality *19-*. **cauld gab, caul gab** a period of stormy weather at the beginning of May *20- NE EC*. **cauld iron 1** *fisherman's taboo* a phrase intended to ward off possible bad luck when a prohibited word has been uttered *19-*. **2** a solemn pledge by schoolchildren *20- NE T EC SW*. **cauld kail het again** reheated broth; a stale or repetitive story *19-*. **cauld morality** a sermon lacking Evangelical fervour *la19-*. **cauld seed, cold seed** late oats or peas *la18-19, 20- Bor*. **cauld steer, caul steer** sour milk or water and oatmeal stirred together; cold brose *19- N NE T H&I EC*. **cauld steerie** = **cauld steer cauld straik** neat whisky (as opposed to toddy) *19- Bor*. **cauld wamed** cold in manner, cold-blooded *la19- EC SW*. **cauld water** apathetic, indifferent *la19- NE T EC*. **cauld wind pipes** the Lowland or Border bellows bagpipe *la20-*. [OE *cald*]

cauler *see* CALLER¹·²

caulker *see* CAUKER²

caulp *see* CALP

caum¹·¹, cawm, calm /kɔm, kam/ *v* to make or become calm *16-*. [see the adj]

caum¹·², cawm, calm /kɔm, kam/ *adj* still, tranquil, calm *16-*. [MFr *calme*]

caum *see* CAM¹·¹, CAM¹·²

caumel, camel, †cameill, †kemel /ˈkɔməl, ˈkaməl/ *n* a large ruminant quadruped, a camel *la14-*. [OE *camel*]

caums *see* CALMES, CALMS

caunle, cannle, candle, †candill /ˈkɔnəl, ˈkanəl, ˈkandəl/ *n* **1** a source of artificial light, made of tallow or wax, a candle *la14-*. **2** *in singular form as a collective noun* candles; tallow, wax *la15-19, 20- NE*. **3** a corpse candle *la19- NE*. **4** the sun *e16*. **candle doup, caunle dowp** a candle-end *19-*. **candle fir** split fir-wood used instead of candles *la18-19, 20- NE*. **candle maker, †candilmakir** a chandler *16-*. **candle shears, †candill scheris** candle snuffers *16-e17, la19- historical*. **neither dance nor haud the cannle, neither dance nor hold the candle** to take no part, refuse to participate *18-19, 20- T WC*. [OE *candel*]

caup *see* CAP¹, CAP³

caupable *see* CAWPABLE

cauper *see* CAP¹

caur, carr, †cair /kɔr, kar/ *npl* calves *16-19, 20- NE T*. [altered form of OE *calfur*, plural of *cealf*; compare CAUF¹·¹]

caur *see* CAR¹, CAR²

caur-cake *see* CARCAKE

caurie *see* CORRIE²

causay *see* CAUSEY¹·¹

cause¹·¹, †caus /kɔz/ *n* a reason, an origin, a source; a matter or a concern; a case (at law), *la14-*. **†for caus** because *la14-16*. **†in the hour of cause** at the time appointed for a trial *la15-e19*. [Fr *cause*, Lat *causa*]

cause¹·² /kɔz/ *v* **1** to be the cause of *la14-*. **2** to bring about, order or make happen: ◇*cause build a loft la16-19*. [Lat *causāre*]

cause², kis /kɔz, kəz, kɪz/ *conj* because *la16-*. [aphetic form of Older Scots *becaus*]

causey¹·¹, causay, cassie, †calsay, †cassay, †casey /ˈkɔze, ˈkasi/ *n* **1** a paved road, a street or pavement laid with cobbles; a causeway *la14-*. **2** the paved or hard-beaten area around or in front of a farmhouse *la19-*. **3** a cobblestone, a paving stone *20-*. **4** the cobbled part of a byre or stable *20- NE*. **causey bool** a round boulder used in paving, a cobblestone *20- T*. **causey clash** street-talk; gossip *19- NE T C*. **causey croon** = *crown of the causey la19-*. **causey maker, †calsay makar** a layer of paving blocks or cobbles *16-*. **causey paiker, †calsay paiker** a street-walker *16-19, 20- T*. **†causey raker** a street-sweeper, a scavenger, a wanderer *e18*. **causey saint** a person who is well-behaved and pleasant when away from home *19-*. **causey stane, †calsay stane** a paving stone or cobblestone *la16-*. **crown of the causey** the middle of the road; a conspicuous, public place; a respectable or dominant position *17-*. **kiss the causey** to meet defeat *la18-19, 20- EC*. [ME *cauce*]

causey¹·², cassie, †cassay, †calsay, †casie /ˈkɔze, ˈkase/ *v* to pave (with small stones); to lay cobbles *16-*. **causeyer, †calsier** a road-maker, a paver *17-*. [see the noun]

caution *see* CAITION¹·¹, CAITION¹·²

cautioun *see* CAITION¹·¹

cautious *see* COWSHUS

cavack /ˈkavək/ *n* a flock of seabirds calling and diving over a shoal of herring *20- H&I*. [perhaps Gael *cabag* blether]

cave¹, †caif /kev/ *n* **1** a natural cavern, a hollow in the earth *la14-*. **2** a case for holding bottles of wine or spirits *17-19, 20- Sh*. **3** a square-shaped bottle (for spirits) *18- Sh Ork*. **4** a cellar, a wine-cellar *16-17*. **5** a dungeon *la15*. [OFr *cave*]

cave², SW Bor keave /kev; SW Bor kiv/ *v* **1** to topple, fall (over); to faint or swoon *16-19, 20- Sh*. **2** to toss the head; to butt with horns *la17-19 20- NE SW Bor*. **3** to pitch or throw; to knock or push *19, 20- EC*. **cavie 1** to swoon; to fall asleep *20- Ork*. **2** to walk affectedly *18-e19*. **3** to rear, prance *e19*. [unknown]

cave³ /kev/ *v* to separate the grain from broken straw (after threshing) *19, 20- NE*. **cavings** broken straw *19, 20- NE*. [altered form of CAFF]

cavel¹·¹, caivel, kevil, cavil, †cavill, †kavill /ˈkevəl, ˈkavəl/ *n* **1** a lot cast *16-19, 20- N NE*. **2** a division or share of property (assigned by lot) *la15-e19*. **3** one's fate; chance *la16-18*. **4** a piece of wood used in casting lots *15-16*. **5** division or assignment by lot *la12-e16*. **†be cavillis** by lot *16-17*. **cast cavels** to draw lots *la15-19, 20- N NE T EC*. [MDu *cavele*, MLG *kavele*; compare ON *kafli*]

cavel¹·², †cavill /ˈkevəl, ˈkavəl/ *v* to draw lots; to divide or assign by lot *la14-19, 20- T*. [see the noun]

cavel², kivel, †kevel /ˈkevəl, ˈkɪvəl/ *n* a rough or uncouth man *16-19, 20- NE*. [unknown]

cavell *see* KEVEL³, KEVEL⁴·¹

caver *see* QUAVER

cavey see KEAVIE
cavie[1.1], **†kavie** /ˈkevi/ n a hen-coop 16-19, 20- T C SW Bor. [Flem kavie]
†cavie[1.2], **kavie** v to coop up (poultry); to confine la17-e19. [see the noun]
cavie[2] /ˈkevi/ n (a den used in) the game of Prisoners' Base la19- T EC Bor. [CAVIE[1.1] or CAVE[1]]
cavie see CAVE[2]
cavil see CAVEL[1.1], KAVVEL[1.1], KAVVEL[1.2]
cavill see CAVEL[1.1], CAVEL[1.2], KEVEL[2], KEVEL[4.2]
caw see CA[1.1], CA[1.2]
ca way see COME[1.2]
cawch see CATCH[1.2]
cawer see CA'ER
cawf see CAUF[1.1]
cawk see CACK[1.2], CAUK[1.1], CAUK[1.2]
cawm see CAUM[1.1], CAUM[1.2]
cawp see CALP
cawpable, caupable /ˈkɔpəbəl/ adj capable 19- NE T EC. [altered form of Older Scots capable]
cawshion see CAITION[1.2]
cayne see KAIN
cays see CASE[2]
caysere see CASER
cazzie see CASSIE
†cedar, ceder n cider la15-e18. [ME sider]
cedent /ˈsidənt/ n law a person who assigns property to another la16-19, 20- historical. [Lat cēdent-, presp stem of cēdere to grant, concede]
cedull see SCHEDULE
ceecle /ˈsikəl/ n a bicycle 20- NE. [altered form of Eng cycle]
ceeliehoo see SEELY
ceepher, seefer, cipher, †sipher, †syphir, †chiffer /ˈsifər, ˈsaefər/ n 1 an unimportant or worthless person, a nonentity 16-. 2 (a symbol used in) a secret method of writing la16-. 3 a monogram, a letter design la16-. 4 zero, a numerical figure 16-e17. [ME cifre, EModE cipher]
ceetie, city, †cite, †cete /ˈsiti, ˈsɪte/ n 1 a large town la14-. 2 in Scotland a name for some of the (especially larger) burghs, originally those which were episcopal seats 15-. **City Chambers** the municipal offices of Edinburgh, Glasgow, Dundee and Perth 19-. **City Guard** an armed corps (of ex-soldiers) enrolled for police duties la17-e19, la19- historical. **city officer** an officer charged with keeping public order la19-20, 21- historical. **The Four Cities** a collective name for Glasgow, Edinburgh, Dundee and Aberdeen 20-. [ME cite]
ceevil, civil /ˈsivəl, ˈsɪvɪl/ adj 1 relating to ordinary citizens 15-. 2 proper, polite, civilized 16-. **†civil rebellion** law the state of being a debtor who has been put to the horn e19. [ME civil, Lat civīlis]
ceil see CIEL
ceilidh[1.1], Uls **kailyee, †kailie** /ˈkeli, ˈkele; Uls ˈkelji/ n 1 an informal social gathering among neighbours (with singing, music and story-telling); a visit, a chat, a gossip 19- N NE H&I Uls. 2 an organized evening entertainment of Scottish music and dancing (in a hall or hotel) 20-. **ceilidh hoose, ceilidh house** a house which is frequently visited (where ceilidhs are held) la19- N NE T H&I. [Gael céilidh]
ceilidh[1.2], **kailie** /ˈkeli, ˈkele/ v to hold a dance or social evening; to visit; to chat, gossip 19-. **kailier** a person who outstays his welcome 20- N Uls. [see the noun]
ceiling see SYLING
celdre see CHALDER
cellar[1.1], **†sellar** /ˈsɛlər/ n an (underground) storeroom; a pantry la15-. [ME celer, Lat cellārium]

cellar[1.2], **†sellar** /ˈsɛlər/ v to store in a cellar la16-. [see the noun]
cellar[2], **seller**, Sh **saller** /ˈsɛlər; Sh ˈsalər/ n 1 the best or main room in the house; a room in the inner part of a house la16- Sh Ork N. 2 the apartment leading off the living-room and used as a bedroom la19- Sh Ork N. [ON salr a room]
celsitude, †celsitud /ˈsɛlsɪtjud/ n lofty position, high rank or majesty, sometimes used as a form of address or title la15-19, 20- literary. [Lat celsitūdo]
Celts /kɛlts, sɛlts/ npl a nickname for Celtic Football Club la19-. [shortened form of Celtic]
cense see SENS
censement see SENSEMENT
censor, †censour /ˈsɛnsər/ n 1 a person who supervises or corrects (morals or conduct) 16-. 2 a supervisor in a university or school; the person who kept the attendance register la16-20, 21- historical. [Lat censor]
†centiner, sentiner n a hundredweight 16-17. [Ger Zentner]
Central Belt /ˈsɛntrəl bɛlt/ n an area of Scotland comprising Glasgow, Edinburgh and the surrounding area la20-. [Scots central + BELT[1.1]]
Central Region /ˈsɛntrəl rɪdʒən/ n a REGION formed from the former county of Clackmannan and parts of the former counties of Perth, Stirling and West Lothian la20, 21- historical. [Scots central + REGION]
centreis see SENTRICE
†centrell, sentrell n a hundredweight e17. [altered form of CENTINER]
centries see SENTRICE
ceptna /ˈsɛptnə/ prep except, save for 20- NE C. [reduced form of Scots except na]
cerd see CAIRD[3]
cerpet see CAIRPET
cerry see CAIRRY[1.1], CAIRRY[1.2]
cerse see SEARCH[1.2]
cert see CAIRT[1.1], CAIRT[1.2]
certain[1.1], **†certane, †sertane** /ˈsɛrtən/ n 1 certainty, truth; knowledge la14-. 2 a definite (but unspecified) number of people or things: ◊a certane of landis 15-e17. [see the adj]
certain[1.2], **†certane, †sertan** /ˈsɛrtən/ adj 1 sure, inevitable, fixed; confident la14-. 2 definite (but not named or specified): a certain sum of money la14-. [ME certain]
certain[1.3], **†certane** /ˈsɛrtən/ adv certainly, assuredly la15-. **certain sure** absolutely certain 19-. [see the adj]
certaint /ˈsɛrtənt/ adj certain 17-. [altered form of CERTAIN[1.2]; compare SUDDENT[1.1]]
certane see CERTAIN[1.1], CERTAIN[1.2], CERTAIN[1.3]
certie, serty, certes, †sartie, †certis /ˈsɛrti, ˈsɛrte, ˈsɛrtəs/ adv certainly, assuredly la14-. **my certie 1** most certainly 19-. **2** astonishingly 19-. [ME certes]
certificate, †certificat /sərˈtɪfɪkət/ n a document attesting or certifying something 16-. **Certificate of Sixth Year Studies** the certificate awarded in a state secondary school examination at a more advanced level than the Higher Grade examinations la20, 21- historical. **Intermediate Certificate** a certificate awarded to pupils completing the three-year INTERMEDIATE course of education e20, la20- historical. **Leaving Certificate** a certificate awarded for proficiency in certain subjects or groups of subjects on the results of examinations conducted annually by the Scottish Education Department from 1888 to 1961 in secondary schools la19-20, 21- historical. **Scottish Certificate of Education** the certificate which was awarded for Highers, Ordinary Grades and the Certificate of Sixth Year Studies la20, 21- historical. [MFr certificat]

certification, †**certificatioun** /sɛrtɪfə'keʃən/ *n* **1** assurance; attestation; notification *la15-*. **2** *law* a warning of the penalty to be inflicted for non-compliance with an order *la15-*. **with certification** *law* a phrase used to introduce the penalty clause *la15-*. [MFr *certification*]

certify /'sɛrtɪfae/ *v* **1** to assure, confirm; to set down in writing *la14-*. **2** to warn *16-e17*. [OFr *certefier*, MFr *certifier*]

certiorate, †**certiorat** /'sɛrʃəret/ *v ptp* **certiorat** to certify, make certain; to inform authoritatively *la16-*. [Lat *certiōrāt-*, ptp stem of *certiōrāre*]

certis *see* CERTIE

cess[1.1], †**sess** /sɛs/ *n* **1** a tax based on land values *la17-19, 20- historical*. **2** a local tax, taxation in general *la18-19, 20- NE T EC Bor*. **3** an exaction; a tribute *18-19, 20- NE*. **4** a person who is a burden (to another) *19, 20- NE*. [see the verb]

cess[1.2], †**sess** /sɛs/ *v* to tax, burden *la17-19, 20- NE*. [EModE *cess* to assess]

cessio bonorum /'sɛsɪo bɔ'norəm/ *n law* a process whereby a debtor could escape imprisonment if he surrendered all his means and was innocent of fraud *la18-e20, la20- historical*. [Lat *cessio bonōrum* the surrender of one's goods]

†**cessioner, cessionar** *n* a person to whom a cession of property was made *la15-e18*. [MFr *cessionaire*, Lat *cessionarius*]

cessioun *see* SESSION[1.1]

cete *see* CEETIE

ceteȝenere *see* CITISINAR

ceul, kul /køl/ *n* a slight breeze, a movement of clouds *la19- Sh Ork*. [ON *kul*]

ceuler, kuiller /'kølər/ *n* a small tub without handles *20- Ork*. [compare Norw *kolle*]

ceur *see* CURE[1.1]

chaa *see* CHAW[1.1], CHAW[1.2], JAA

chaamer *see* CHAUMER

chabbard *see* JABBART

chabble *see* JABBLE[1.1]

chace *see* CHASE[1.1], CHASE[1.2]

chack[1.1], **check**, †**chak**, †**chek** /tʃak, tʃɛk/ *n* **1** a restraint, a curb; a sudden stop *15-*. **2** a mechanical device to limit movement *la15-*. **3** a groove or notch cut to receive an edge or serving as a check, a rabbet *la16-*. **4** a test of correctness or accuracy; supervision *17-*. **5** a door-key *la19- C*. [ME *chek* a check in chess]

chack[1.2], **chak, check** /tʃak, tʃɛk/ *v* **1** to examine, investigate or verify *la15-*. **2** to arrest, halt; to restrain or diminish *la16-*. **3** to rebuke or reprove *la16-*. **4** to cut a groove or notch to receive an edge or serving as a check *17-*. **check reel, check reel** a reel with a check or catch to control the amount of yarn *17-19, 20- historical*. †**chakwache** a patrol *la14-e17*. [ME *chekken*]

chack[2.1], **chak** /tʃak/ *n* **1** a bite of food, a snack; a slight or hurried meal *19-*. **2** a cut or hack; a bruise, a nip *la19-*. **3** a clicking noise, a snapping sound *19- Sh SW Bor*. [onomatopoeic]

chack[2.2], **chak** /tʃak/ *v* **1** to bite or snap; to close with a snap *16-19, 20- WC SW Bor*. **2** to make a clicking noise; *of the teeth* to chatter *la17-19, 20- NE WC*. **3** to hack or chop; to catch (fingers in a door) *19- T EC Bor*. [see the noun]

chack[3] /tʃak/ *n* a checked pattern; checked fabric *la19- NE T C*. **chackit, chacket** checked, tartan *19- NE T C*. [ME *chek*]

chack[4] /tʃak/ *n* the wheatear *Oenanthe oenanthe la18-19, 20- Ork*. [onomatopoeic]

chack *see* CHUCK[2]

chackart, chackert /'tʃakərt/ *n* **1** a name for various birds, including the stonechat *Saxicola torquata*; the whinchat *Saxicola rubetra*; and the ring ouzel *Turdus torquatus 19- NE WC*. **2** a term of endearment or affectionate reproof *la19- NE*. [onomatopoeic, with agent suffix *-art*]

chackert, †**chakkerit** /'tʃakərt/ *adj* chequered *la16-e17, 20- NE*. [ME *chekkerit*]

chackie /'tʃaki/ *n* a striped cotton bag used by farmworkers for carrying their clothes *20- NE*. [probably CHACK[3] + -IE[1]]

chackie mill, chackie mull /'tʃaki mɪl, 'tʃaki mʌl/ *n* the death-watch beetle *Xestobium rufovillosum 19- NE*. [CHACK[2.2]; second element unknown]

chack-purse /'tʃak pʌrs/ *n* a sporran *la19- NE T*. [unknown first element + Scots *purse*]

chad /tʃad/ *n* gravel *18- NE T*. [unknown]

chad *see* JAUD

chadders *see* CHATTERS

chafer *see* CHAFFER[1]

chaff[1.1] /tʃaf/ *n* **1** a worn part *19- NE*. **2** a temper; passion *17-e19*. [see the verb]

chaff[1.2], †**chauf** /tʃaf/ *v* **1** to rub, wear or chafe *18-*. **2** to knead or mould (individual loaves) *la19-*. **3** to warm, heat *la15-e16*. [ME *chaufen*]

chaffer[1], **choffer, chauffer,** †**chafer,** †**chowfer** /'tʃafər, 'tʃɔfər/ *n* **1** a portable stove (used as a heater) *18-*. **2** a moveable grate (in a corn-kiln or a baker's oven) *20-*. **3** a vessel for heating water or warming food, a chafing-dish *la15-19*. [ME *chaufour*]

chaffer[2] /'tʃafər/ *n* the round-lipped whale *Delphinus orca la18- Sh*. [unknown]

†**chafferon, schaffron** *n* an ornament on a woman's hood *16*. [probably EModE *chaffron* part of the armour for a horse's head]

†**chaffery** *n* merchandise *la15-e19*. [Older Scots *chaffer* to bargain, with noun-forming suffix *-ery*]

chaffie /'tʃafi/ *n* a chaffinch *Fringilla coelebs la19-*. [reduced form]

chaft[1], *Sh* **shaft,** †**schaft** /tʃaft; *Sh* ʃaft/ *n* **1** the jaw *15-*. **2** the cheek *18-19, 20- NE C SW*. **big-chafted** big-jawed *la19, 20- NE*. **chaft-blade,** †**shaft-blade 1** the jaw-bone *16-*. **2** the cheek-bone *19, 20- NE EC*. **chaft tooth** a molar *19, 20- EC*. [ON *kjöptr*]

†**chaft**[2] *n* a shaft, a long handle *16*. [OE *sceaft*]

chaickad *see* JAIKET

chainge *see* CHYNGE[1.2]

chainȝe *see* CHENȜE[1.2]

chainzie *see* CHENȜE[1.1]

†**chaip, chape** *v* to escape *la14-e19*. [aphetic form of ESCHAPE[1.2]]

chaip *see* CHAPE[1.2]

chaipel, chapel, †**cheppell,** †**schapell** /'tʃɛpəl, 'tʃapəl/ *n* **1** a place of worship, a chapel *la14-*. **2** a Roman Catholic or Scottish Episcopal church *18-*. **3** a royal or an ecclesiastical chancellery *15-16*. †**chapell bed** a canopied bed *17*. [ME *chapele*]

chaipter, chapter, *NE* **chipter,** †**cheptour,** †**chapiter,** †**scheptour** /'tʃɛptər, 'tʃaptər; *NE* 'tʃɪptər/ *n* **1** a division of a book *la14-*. **2** the members of an organization (meeting) as a body; originally the body of canons of a cathedral or church *la14-*. [ME *chapitre*]

chair *see* CHARE

chairakter, chairacter /'kɛrəktər/ *n* character *la20-*. [Fr *caractère*]

chairge[1.1], **cherge, charge,** †**scharge** /tʃɛrdʒ, tʃɛrdʒ, tʃardʒ/ *n* **1** a task or duty; a burden, a load *la14-*. **2** an expense, a price; a payment *la14-*. **3** a command, an order; a legal summons *15-*. **4** an accusation *15-*. **5** an impetuous attack, an onset, a rush *la16-*. **6** *law* an injunction issued under warrant of the signet to compel an heir to a debt-encumbered estate or other debtor to act in relation to the debt or to obey the decree of a court, originally a command or summons *18-*. †**under all payne and charge** a legal formula used to emphasize a command *la15-e16*. [ME *charge*]

chairge[1,2], **cherge**, **charge**, †**scharge** /tʃɛrdʒ, tʃɛrdʒ, tʃardʒ/ *v* **1** to make an impetuous attack (in battle) *la14-*. **2** to make a (formal) accusation *la14-*. **3** to impose a fee or cost; to demand payment *la14-*. **4** to make responsible for (a commission or errand) *la14-*. **5** to burden; to load or fill *la14-*. **6** to chaff, tease (a person) *20- SW Bor*. **7** to order or commit to prison *la15-16*. †**chargeand** burdensome, oppressive *la14-16*. **charger**, †**chargeour**, †**chargear 1** a warhorse *la18-*. **2** a creditor trying to recover his money (by use of a legal summons) *18-19*. **3** one who makes a charge; an accuser, a plaintiff *la16-18*. **4** an appliance for charging a gun *la15-e16*. [ME *chargen*]

chairity *see* CHARITY

chairk *see* CHIRK

chairm[1.1], **cherm**, **charm** /tʃɛrm, tʃɛrm, tʃarm/ *n* an attractive quality; a trinket; a spell *16-*. [MFr *charme*]

chairm[1.2], **cherm**, **charm** /tʃɛrm, tʃɛrm, tʃarm/ *v* to delight or influence; to enchant, put a spell on *16-*. [MFr *charmer*]

chairt, **chert**, **chart** /tʃɛrt, tʃɛrt, tʃart/ *n* a map; a table; a feu charter *18-*. [OFr *charte*]

chairter *see* CHARTER[1.1]

chais *see* CHASE[1.2]

chaise *see* CHASE[1.1]

chaistain, †**cheston**, †**chestane** /'tʃɛstən/ *n* a chestnut *17- 18, 20- literary*. [ME *chesteine*, EModE *chasten*]

chaistifie *see* CHASTIFY

chaisty *see* CHASTY

chaitry *see* CHEATRY

chak *see* CHACK[1.1], CHACK[1.2], CHACK[2.1], CHACK[2.2]

chakker *see* CHEKKER

chakkerit *see* CHACKERT

chalange *see* CHALLENGE[1.1], CHALLENGE[1.2]

chalder, †**chawder**, †**chelder**, †**celdre** /'tʃaldər/ *n* **1** a measure of grain equalling 16 bolls, frequently as part of a minister's stipend; the stipend itself *la14-*. **2** a variable quantity of salt, lime or coal (usually several tons) *15-19*. [OFr *chaldre* a measure of quantity of coal]

chalder, **chaldroo** *see* SHALDER

†**chalf** *n* chaff *la17*. [erroneous form of CAFF]

chalking the door /'tʃɔkɪŋ ðə 'dor/ *n law* a warning to (burghal) tenants to remove *la16-19, 20- historical*. [from the practice of marking the principal door of the tenement with chalk forty days before Whitsunday]

challance *see* CHALLENGE[1.1], CHALLENGE[1.2]

†**challender** *n* a maker of coverlets *la16-e17*. [derivative of ME *chaloun* a kind of tapestry, a bedspread or hanging made from this material]

challenge[1.1], †**chalange**, †**challance** /'tʃaləndʒ/ *n* **1** a calling to account; an accusation; a claim (against another) *la14-*. **2** an invitation to a trial or contest *17-*. **3** a call or summons *la18- NE*. [ME *chalenge*]

challenge[1.2], †**chalange**, †**challance** /'tʃaləndʒ/ *v* **1** to call in question; to dispute; to accuse *15-*. **2** to summon or invite to a trial or contest *15-*. **3** to lay claim to; to demand as one's right; to make a claim *15-*. **4** to reprove, find fault with *17-*. [ME *chalengen*]

challop *see* SHALLOP

chalmer *see* CHAUMER

chalmerlane *see* CHAMBERLAIN

chalmirleir *see* CHAUMER

chalowse *see* JALOUSE

cham /tʃam/ *v* to bite or chew *19- SW Bor*. [compare CHAMP[1.2]]

chamber *see* CHAUMER

chamberlain, †**chalmerlane**, †**chammerlane**, †**chawmerlane** /'tʃɛmbərlɪn/ *n* **1** one of the chief officers of the royal household *la14-18, 19- historical*. **2** a steward; a factor (of a nobleman's estate) *15-19, 20- H&I*. **3** a city official dealing with revenue, a treasurer *18-*. **chamberlainry**, †**chalmerlanrie**, †**chaumerlanry** the office of chamberlain *15-19, 20- historical*. **chamberlain ayre**, †**chaumerlane aire** the circuit court held by the Chamberlain of Scotland *15-19, 20- historical*. **chamberlain court**, †**chalmerlane court** = *chamberlain ayre 16-17, 19- historical*. **Chamberlain of Scotland**, †**Chaumerlan of Scotland** one of the chief officers of the royal household *la14-18, 19- historical*. [ME *chaumberlein*]

chamer *see* CHAUMER

chammerlane *see* CHAMBERLAIN

chammoy *see* SHAMBO

champ[1.1] /tʃamp/ *n* **1** a stretch of muddy trodden ground; a quagmire *19- Bor*. **2** mashed potatoes *la19- Uls*. **champers** mashed potatoes *la19- C SW*. **champies** mashed potatoes *19- NE EC SW Bor*. [see the verb]

champ[1.2] /tʃamp/ *v* to crush, pound or mash; to trample *la18-*. **champit tatties** mashed potatoes *19-*. [probably EModE *champe* munch]

†**champ**[2] *n* **1** a raised or overlaid pattern on a (rich) cloth *16*. **2** *heraldry* the field in a heraldic shield *la15*. **champit of cloth** having a raised or overlain pattern; stamped or embossed *la15-19*. [ME *chaump*]

†**champart** *n law* assistance given to a party in a suit in return for a share in the gains *14-17*. [OFr *champart* produce received by a feudal lord from land leased]

chance[1.1], **chaunce**, **chunce**, *Sh Ork N* **shance**, †**chans** /tʃans, tʃɔns, tʃʌns; *Sh Ork N* ʃans/ *n* **1** a fortuitous event or circumstance; accident, fortune, fate *la14-*. **2** an opportunity *18-*. **3** possibility; probability *la18-*. **4** a tip, a perquisite; a share (of a profit) *la18-*. [ME *chaunce*]

chance[1.2], **chaunce**, *Sh Ork N* **shance**, †**chans** /tʃans, tʃɔns; *Sh Ork N* ʃans/ *v* **1** to happen (fortuitously); to come about by chance *16-*. **2** to risk *la19-*. [see the noun]

†**chancellar**, **chanslar** *adj* pertaining to the chancel of a church *15-16*. [Lat *cancellārius*]

†**chancellary**, **chancellerie** *n* the office or department of chancellor; the office which authenticated documents (by the addition of a seal) and issued documents so authenticated *15-19*. Compare CHANCERY. [ME *chancelrie*]

chancellor, †**chancellar**, †**chancellour**, †**chanslar** /'tʃansələr/ *n* **1** a court, ecclesiastical or university dignitary *la14-*. **2** the foreman of a jury (especially in a fiars court) *la15-*. **3** the highest officer of the Crown and chief legal authority *la14-e18, 19- historical*. **Chancellor of Scotland** the highest officer of the Crown and chief legal authority *15-e18, la18- historical*. [Lat *cancellārius*]

chancellour *see* CHANCELLOR

chancery /'tʃansəri/ *n* the office of government dealing with the service of heirs, originally issuing brieves directing an inferior judge to try a specified issue with a jury *la17-*. [reduced form of CHANCELLARY]

chancy, **chancie** /'tʃanse, 'tʃansi/ *adj* fortunate, lucky; bringing good fortune *16-*. **no chancy**, **nae chancy** not to be relied on, dangerous *19-*. [CHANCE[1.1] + -IE[2]]

chandler, †**chandelare**, †**schandellar**, †**chanler** /'tʃandlər/ *n* **1** a dealer in provisions and hardware; the keeper of a general store; originally a person who made or sold candles *18-*. **2** a candlestick, a chandelier; a lantern *la15-e18*.

chandler chafted, chandler chaftit lantern-jawed *18-*.
†**chandler chafts** lantern-jaws *18*. [ME *chaundeler*]
chang /tʃaŋ/ *n* a ringing sound *la18-19, 20- historical*. [onomatopoeic]
change *see* CHYNGE[1.1], CHYNGE[1.2]
chanker *see* CANKER[1.1]
chanler *see* CHANDLER
channel[1.1], *Sh* **shannel**, †**chinnell** /'tʃanəl; *Sh* 'ʃanəl/ *n* **1** a watercourse; the main course of running water in a river or estuary *la15-*. **2** shingle, gravel *la16-*. **3** a gutter *16-19, 20- T*. [ME, OFr *chanel*]
channel[1.2] /'tʃanəl/ *v* to play at curling *la19- SW*. **channel stane**, *NE* **channel steen** a curling-stone *la18-*. [see the noun]
channer[1] /'tʃanər/ *n* shingle, gravel *19- NE WC SW*. **channery** gravelly *20- WC Uls*. [altered form of CHANNEL[1.1]]
channer[2], **chawner, chunner** /'tʃanər, 'tʃɔnər, 'tʃʌnər/ *v* to grumble, mutter *la14-*. [perhaps onomatopoeic]
chanonry, chanry, †**channery,** †**chanounrie,** †**channorie** /'tʃanənri, 'ʃanənri, 'tʃanri/ *n* a canonry, an establishment of canons; the office or benefice of a canon *la15-19, 20- historical*. [MFr *chanoinerie*]
chans *see* CHANCE[1.1], CHANCE[1.2]
chanslar *see* CHANCELLAR, CHANCELLOR
†**chansoune** *n* a song *la15-e17*. [OFr *chanson*]
chant[1.1], **chaunt** /tʃant, tʃɔnt/ *n* **1** a song, a melody; a monotonous drone or dirge *19-*. **2** pert language *la19- NE*. [see the verb]
chant[1.2], **chaunt** /tʃant, tʃɔnt/ *v* **1** to sing; to intone; to recite musically *la15-*. **2** to chatter; to speak pertly *19-*. **3** to speak with a English accent *la19- Ork*. [OFr *chanter*]
chanter, †**chantour** /'tʃantər/ *n* **1** a singer; originally a chanter in a church service or the precentor in a church choir *15-*. **2** the double-reeded pipe on which a bagpipe melody is played *la17-*. **3** an English accent *20- Ork*. [ME *chauntour*]
chanty, chunty, *Sh* **shantie** /'tʃanti, 'tʃʌnte; *Sh* 'ʃanti/ *n* **1** a chamber-pot *la18-*. **2** a toilet (pedestal) *la20- C*. **chantie wrassler** a waster, an unreliable or unscrupulous person *la20-*. **knee-high tae a chanty** very young *la20- NE WC*. [probably from the place-name *Chantilly*; the French town famous for the manufacture of soft-paste porcelain in the early eighteenth century]
chanʒe *see* CHENʒE[1.1], CHENʒE[1.2]
chap[1] /tʃap/ *n* **1** a fellow, a lad *18-*. **2** a lover *20-*. **3** a customer, a buyer *18-e19*. **chappie 1** a fellow, a man *18-*. **2** a little boy *la19-*. [shortened form of CHAPMAN]
chap[2] /tʃap/ *n* the threshing-floor *20- NE*. [perhaps CHAP[3.1], CHAP[3.2]]
chap[3.1], *Sh Ork N* **shap** /tʃap; *Sh Ork N* ʃap/ *n* **1** a knock, a blow *16-*. **2** a stroke of a clock or bell *la16-*. **3** a spell or turn of work *la19- NE T*. **4** a swell, choppiness of the sea *la19- Sh T EC*. [see the verb]
chap[3.2], *Sh Ork N* **shap** /tʃap; *Sh Ork N* ʃap/ *v* **1** to strike, hit *la16-*. **2** to knock or rap (at a door or window) *la16-*. **3** *of a clock* to strike *la16-*. **4** to mash (vegetables) *18-*. **5** to chop, cut into pieces *la18-*. **6** to strike with a hammer (in a smithy) *la19-*. **7** *curling* to strike away a stone *la19-*. **8** *in dominoes or card games* to rap on the table as an indication that one cannot play at one's turn *20-*. **9** to finely grind sand *la19- WC SW Bor*. **10** *mining* to signal by means of a striking apparatus *la19, 20- EC*. **chapping-stick**; *Sh Ork N* **shappin-stick 1** a stick used for striking *18-*. **2** a potato masher *la19- Sh Ork N T*. **chappin tree, shappin tree** a potato masher *la19- Sh Ork*. **chappit tatties** mashed potatoes *19-*. **chap and lie** *curling* to strike away a stone *la19-*. **chap hands** to shake hands *17-*. **chap in aboot** to take a person down a peg; to snub *la19- NE*. **chap in taes** = *chap in aboot 20- NE*. [ME *chappen* to crack open fruit, chap skin]
chap[4] /tʃap/ *v* **1** to choose, select; to pick sides *la18-19, 20- NE T EC*. **2** to strike a bargain with; to agree to or ratify *la19, 20- NE T EC*. **chap and chuse** to make a choice *18-19, 20- NE*. [OE *cēapian* to buy and sell, make a bargain, trade]
chap *see* CHEEP[1.2]
†**chape**[1.1], **cheip, schaip** *n* a sale price *15-17*. [OE *cēap*]
chape[1.2], **chaip, cheap,** *Sh Ork N* **shape,** †**cheip,** †**schap** /tʃep, tʃip; *Sh Ork N* ʃep/ *adj* inexpensive, cheap *17-*. **be cheap o** to get off lightly; to serve (someone) right: ◊*ye've got your fairin, an I maun say I think ye're cheap o't 19-*. [see the noun]
chape *see* CHAIP
chapeau, †**schapio,** †**schappeo** /'ʃapo/ *n* a smart or formal hat *16-*. †**chapeau bras** a small three-cornered, flat, silk hat *e19*. [MFr *chapeau*]
chapel *see* CHAIPEL
chapellane, chapellanry *see* CHAPLAIN
chapin *see* CHOPIN
chapiter *see* CHAIPTER
chaplain, †**cheplane,** †**chapellane,** †**schaplane** /'tʃaplən/ *n* a clergyman *14-*. **chaplainry,** †**chapellanry,** †**chaplanry** the office of chaplain, a chaplaincy *15-19, 20- historical*. [ME *chapelein*, OFr *chapelain*]
chapman, †**chepman,** †**schapman** /'tʃapmən/ *n* an itinerant merchant or dealer, a pedlar *14-*. Compare CHOPMAN. [OE *chēapmann* a trader]
chapper, *Sh Ork N* **shapper** /'tʃapər; *Sh Ork N* 'ʃapər/ *n* **1** a beetle for pounding or mashing *20-*. **2** a door knocker *20-*. **3** a person who misses a turn in dominoes *20-*. **4** a *chapper-up la19- T C*. **chapper-up** a person whose job is to wake people up in time for work by banging on their doors *la19- T C*. [CHAP[3.2], with agent suffix]
chappie *see* CHAP[1]
chappin *see* CHOPIN
chapple *see* JAPPLE[1.2]
chaps, *NE* **chips** /tʃaps; *NE* tʃips/ *v* **1** to pick out, select *19-*. **2** to choose sides for a game *la19-*. **chaps me,** *NE* **chips me** I claim, I prefer *la19-*. [probably derivative of CHAP[4]]
†**chaptane** *n* a captain *e16*. [ME *chaptein*]
chapter *see* CHAIPTER
†**chapterlie, chaptourlie** *adj* having or belonging to an ecclesiastical chapter *17*. [*chapter* (CHAIPTER), with adj-forming suffix *-lie*]
chapterly, †**cheptourly** /'tʃaptərle/ *adv* as a chapter, in full chapter *16-e19, la19- historical*. †**cheptourly gadderit, chaptourlie gaiderrit** assembled in a chapter *16*. [*chapter* (CHAIPTER), with adv-forming suffix *-ly*]
chaptourlie *see* CHAPTERLIE
†**char**[1.1] *n* a turn *la16*. **on char** ajar *16*. [OE *cierr*]
†**char**[1.2] *v* to cause to turn aside or back *la15-e16*. [OE *cierran*]
†**charbukyll** *n* a fabric used for church vestments or cloths *e15*. [unknown]
†**chare, chair, schare** *n* a wheeled conveyance; a chariot *la14-e16*. [ME *char*]
charet *see* CHARRIT
charge *see* CHAIRGE[1.1], CHAIRGE[1.2]
charity, chairity, cherity, *NE* **chirity,** †**charite,** †**cherite,** †**cheretie** /'tʃarəti, 'tʃerəte, 'tʃerəte; *NE* 'tʃɪrəti/ *n* **1** a donation to the poor or needy; alms *la14-*. **2** a small additional amount given to the purchaser (in a grain transaction) *la15-18*. †**chereteit, chirretit** with a small amount added or given in addition *la16-18*. [ME *charite*]
chark *see* CHIRK

charlie /'tʃarli/ *n* a chamber-pot *la20- NE SW*. [from the personal name]

†Charl Wayn *n* the constellation Ursa Major, the Great Bear or Plough *e16*. [OE *Carles wægn*]

charm *see* CHAIRM[1.1], CHAIRM[1.2]

†charnel *n* a hinge *la15-e18*. **charnle-pins** the pins on which the hinges of machinery turn *e19*. Compare SHARLPIN. [ME *channel*]

†charrit, charet, cherret *n* a carriage *la16-19*. [ME *charret*, EModE *charet*]

chart *see* CHAIRT

charter[1.1], **chairter, †chartour** /'tʃartər, 'tʃertər/ *n* a document granting a right, privilege or possession *14-*. **charter chest, †charter chist, †chartour kist** a chest for the keeping of charters *16-19, 20- historical*. **†charterhous** a room for the keeping of charters *la16*. [ME, OFr *chartre*]

†charter[1.2] *v* to put in possession (of lands) by a charter *15-e16*. [see the noun]

†Charterour *n* a Carthusian monk *la15-e16*. [MFr *chartreur*]

chartour *see* CHARTER[1.1]

chasbow *see* CHESBOW

chase[1.1], **†chace, †chays, †chaise** /tʃes/ *n* **1** pursuit; a hunt *la14-*. **2** haste, hurry *la19- NE T EC*. [ME *chace*]

chase[1.2], *Sh* **shaste**, *Ork* **chiss**, *N* **cheis, †chace, †chais, †chece** /tʃes; *Sh* ʃest; *Ork* tʃis; *N* tʃʌis/ *v* **1** to pursue; to hunt; to drive out *la14-*. **2** to hurry, run at speed *20- NE T EC*. **chaser, †chasar** a ram with imperfectly-developed genitals *la16-19, 20- N SW*. **chasie 1** a game of marbles *20- NE T C*. **2** the game of tig *la20- C*. [ME *chacen*]

chassal, chisell, †cheswell, †chesell /'tʃasəl, 'tʃɪzəl/ *n* a cheese-press *la17-19, 20- NE WC*. **†the cheswell ye were staned in** your original social class *18-19*; compare *the chisset ye were staint in* (CHESSART). [CHEESE[1] + WALL[1]]

chasteeze /tʃa'stiz/ *v* to chastise *la19- T EC*. [ME *chastisen*]

chastify, †chaistifie /'tʃastəfae/ *v* to chastise, castigate *16-19, 20- EC*. [OFr *chastifier*]

†chasty, chaisty, chestee *v* to reprove; to chastise *la14-e16*. [ME *chastien*]

chat[1] /tʃat/ *n* **1** light conversation *19-*. **2** impudence, impertinent talk *la19-*. [reduced form of CHATTER[2]]

chat[2.1] /tʃat/ *n* a snack; a morsel *19- NE T EC*. [perhaps aphetic form of Fr *achat* a purchase; compare AN *chat* in the same sense]

chat[2.2] /tʃat/ *v* to bite or chew *19- NE*. [see the noun]

chat[3] /tʃat/ *n* a pig; a call to a pig *19- NE*. **chattie** a pig, a boar *la19- NE*. [perhaps onomatopoeic or extended sense of CHAT[2.1]]

chat[4] /tʃat/ *n* **1** a small haddock *20-*. **2** a small potato *20-*. [probably ME *chit* the young of an animal]

chat[5] /tʃat/ *v* to chafe; to fray *19, 20- NE*. [compare CHACK[2.2]]

chate *see* CHEAT[1.1], CHEAT[1.2]

chathers *see* CHATTERS

chatter[1] /'tʃatər/ *v* to shatter *la17-19, 20- NE Uls*. [ME *schater*]

chatter[2] /'tʃatər/ *v of the teeth* to rattle together with cold or fear *la15-*. **chatterin-bite** a snack eaten after bathing *20-*; compare *chittering bit* (CHITTER). **chatterin piece** = *chatterin-bite la19- NE*. [onomatopoeic]

chatters, *N* **shatters,** *NE T* **chadders,** *NE T EC* **chathers** /'tʃatərz; *N* 'ʃatərz; *NE T* 'tʃadərz; *NE T EC* 'tʃaðərz/ *npl* the iron staples in a rudder-post of a boat into which the rudder is fixed *20- N NE T EC*. [unknown]

chattert, chattered /'tʃatərt, 'tʃatərd/ *adj* chewed; frayed, tattered *la18- NE SW Bor*. [compare CHAT[2.2]]

chattery /'tʃatəri/ *adj* gravelly, stony; hard *19, 20- NE T*. [perhaps CHATTER[2] + -IE[2]]

chattie *see* CHAT[3]

chattle, *T* **chowtle** /'tʃatəl; *T* 'tʃʌutəl/ *v* to nibble, chew feebly *19- NE T Bor*. Compare CHITTLE. [frequentative form of CHAT[2.2]]

†chatton *n* the collet of a ring *la16-e17*. [MFr *chaton*]

chatty-puss /'tʃatipus/ *n* **1** a call to a cat *19- Ork NE EC Bor*. **2** a cat *20- Ork NE*. Compare CHEET. [perhaps CHAT[4] + -IE[1] + EModE *puss* a name for a cat; compare CHAT[3] and CHEET]

chaud melle, †chaudmellay /'tʃɔd mɛle/ *n of a murder* committed in the heat of the moment *la14-*. [OFr *chaude meslee* heated affray]

chaudpis *see* JAWPISH

chauf *see* CHAFF[1.2]

chauffer *see* CHAFFER[1]

chaumer, chalmer, chamer, chamber, *NE* **chaamer, †chawmer, †schalmer** /'tʃɔmər, 'tʃalmər, 'tʃemər, 'tʃembər; *NE* 'tʃamər/ *n* **1** a (private) room, a bedroom *la14-*. **2** a parlour, the best room in a house *19-*. **3** a sleeping place (in a stable or outbuilding) for farmworkers *19- Ork NE SW*. **4** a one-roomed cottage *20- Ork N*. **†chalmerer, chaumerer** a chamberlain or chambermaid *la14-e17*. **†chaumerit, chamber'd** lodged (in a chamber); closeted, shut up *16-19*. **†chalmirleir** a chambermaid *e16*. **†chaumer chiel, chalmer cheild** a young attendant; a valet *16-e19*. **chalmer glew** sexual activity *la15-16, la20- literary*. **chamber of dais, †chamber of deas** a best bedroom or sitting-room, originally a private room (at the dais end of a hall) *16-e19, la19- historical*. [ME *chaumbre*]

chaunce *see* CHANCE[1.1], CHANCE[1.2]

chaunge *see* CHYNGE[1.2]

chaunt *see* CHANT[1.1], CHANT[1.2]

chauve *see* TYAUVE[1.1], TYAUVE[1.2]

chavie, chavvie /'tʃavi/ *n* **1** (a term of address for) a boy or young man *la19-*. **2** a boyfriend *20- T SW*. [Travellers' language *chabó* a boy, Sanskrit *śāva* the young of any animal]

chaw[1.1], **chaa, chow,** *Sh* **show,** *Ork* **jow** /tʃɔ, tʃa, tʃʌu; *Sh* ʃʌu; *Ork* dʒʌu/ *n* **1** the act of chewing; something chewed *19-*. **2** a small lump of chewing tobacco *20-*. **3** a disappointment, a snub; a cutting retort *20- NE T C*. **chaw throu** a toilsome attempt *20- NE*. [see the verb]

chaw[1.2], **chaa, chow,** *Sh* **show,** *Ork* **jow** /tʃɔ, tʃa, tʃʌu; *Sh* ʃʌu; *Ork* dʒʌu/ *v* **1** to chew *16-*. **2** to provoke, vex; to make jealous *19-*. **chawl** to eat noisily or listlessly *19- SW*. **chawsome** causing envious disappointment; galling *la19- C SW*. **chaw yer words** to mumble *20- NE*. **like a chowed moose** having a debauched or worn-out appearance *la19- EC SW Bor*. [OE *cēowan*]

chaw[2] /tʃɔ/ *n* a lecture, a reprimand *20- N NE*. [altered form of JAW[1.2]]

chaw *see* HAW[1], CHOW

chawder *see* CHALDER

chawl *see* CHAW[1.2]

chawmer *see* CHAUMER

chawmerlane *see* CHAMBERLAIN

chawner *see* CHANNER[2]

chay /tʃe/ *interj* a call to cows to calm them *la19- Uls*. [unknown]

chays *see* CHASE[1.1]

chealous *see* JEELOUS

chean *see* CHEEN[1.1]

cheap *see* CHAPE[1.2]

chear *see* CHEER[1]

cheat[1.1], **chate, †chete** /tʃit, tʃet/ *n* **1** a deception, a fraud; a person who acts dishonestly, a swindler *17-*. **2** an escheat; forfeiture of goods *15-16*. [ME *chete*]

cheat[1.2], **chate, che't,** *N* **cheit,** †**chete,** †**scheit** /tʃit, tʃet; *N* tʃʌɪt/ *v* **1** to deceive; to act dishonestly *18-*. **2** to escheat, confiscate *16-e17*. **cheater,** †**cheiter** a deceiver, a cheat *la17-*. **chate-the-belly** an insubstantial cake or pastry *20- NE EC*. **chate-my-guts** = *chate-the-belly NE T*. **cheat-the-wuddy** one who has cheated the gallows, a scoundrel *19-*. **it cheats me** (unless) I am very much mistaken *19-*. [see the noun]

cheatry, cheatery, *Sh* **shaetry,** *NE* **chaitry,** †**chetry** /'tʃitri, 'tʃitəri; *Sh* 'ʃetri; *NE* 'tʃetri/ *n* **1** the practice of cheating; deceit, fraud *la17-*. **2** an escheat; forfeiture of goods *la15-16*. [CHEAT[1.2], with noun-forming suffix *-ry*]

†**cheats** *npl* sweetbreads *la17-e19*. [unknown]

chece *see* CHASE[1.2]

check *see* CHACK[1.1], CHACK[1.2]

cheek[1.1], *Sh* **sheek,** *N* **shick,** †**cheke,** †**scheik** /tʃik; *Sh* ʃik; *N* ʃik/ *n* **1** the side of the face below the eye *la14-*. **2** the side posts of a door or gate; the sides of a window-frame or fireplace *la14-*. **cheek stane, cheek stone** one of two upright stones which support a grate *19, 20- NE*. **cheek warmer** a short-stemmed tobacco pipe *20-*. **cheek for chow,** *Sh* **sheek for showe,** *N* **chick for chowl,** †**cheek for chew** cheek by jowl, close together, very friendly *18-*. [OE *cēace*]

cheek[1.2], *N* **shick,** †**cheik** /tʃik; *N* ʃik/ *v* **1** to flatter *la18, 20 NE*. **2** to turn the face; to set the head *20- N*. **3** to join, fit *la17*. **cheek in wi** to court the favour of *la19- NE*. **cheek up** to use insolent language to *20- NE T EC*. **cheek up till** to make up to; to make amorous approaches to *la19-*. [see the noun]

cheekaside /'tʃikəsʌɪd/ *adj* askew *18-19, 20- Ork Bor*. [compare EModE *chekasyde* a profile on a coin]

cheelder, sheelder /'ʃildər, 'tʃildər/ *n* a child, a fellow *20- Sh Ork*. [compare *childer* (CHILD)]

cheen[1.1], *NE* **chine,** *NE* **cheyne,** †**chene,** †**chean** /tʃin; *NE* tʃʌɪn/ *n* a chain *la14-*. Compare CHEN3E[1.1]. [ME *chaine*]

cheen[1.2], *NE* **chine** /tʃin; *NE* tʃʌɪn/ *v* to fasten with a chain *20-*. Compare CHEN3E[1.2]. [see the verb]

cheena *see* CHEENY

cheenge *see* CHYNGE[1.1], CHYNGE[1.2]

cheeny, cheenie, cheena, china /'tʃini, 'tʃinə, 'tʃʌɪnə/ *n* **1** porcelain; crockery, tableware *la18-*. **2** a china marble *20- NE T EC SW*. [from the name of the country *China*]

cheep[1.1], †**chepe** /tʃip/ *n* **1** a whisper, a hint, a word *19-*. **2** a light kiss *la19-*. **cheeper** a kiss (on the cheek) *la19-*. **keep a quiet cheep** to be silent *la19, 20- NE*. **play cheep** to make a sound; to say a word *la18-19, 20- EC*. **say cheep** = *play cheep 20- N*. [see the verb]

cheep[1.2], *N* **chap,** †**chepe** /tʃip; *N* tʃap/ *v* **1** *of a bird* to chirp; *of a mouse* to squeak *16-*. **2** to speak softly, whisper; to murmur *la16-*. **3** *of inanimate objects* to squeak; to creak *19- N NE T EC*. [onomatopoeic]

cheepin shoppie /'tʃipɪn ʃɔpi/ *n* a shebeen *la19- T EC*. [probably altered form of Eng *shebeen* + SHOP]

cheer[1], **cheir, chyre, chire, cherr,** *Sh* **shair,** †**chear,** †**chyar,** †**shire** /tʃir, tʃaer, tʃer; *Sh* ʃer/ *n* a chair *la14-*. **draw in yer chair an sit doon** to acquire affluence without any effort of your own *la19- N NE T*. [ME *chaier, cheier*]

cheer[2.1], †**chere,** †**cheir** /tʃir/ *n* **1** joy, rejoicing *la14-*. **2** feasting, entertainment *la14-*. **3** a shout of encouragement or approval *la18-*. **4** the face; facial expression *la14-e17*. [ME *chere*]

cheer[2.2], †**cheir** /tʃir/ *v* **1** to entertain; to raise the spirits *la16-*. **2** to shout in approval or encouragement *19-*. †**cheerer** a glass of spirits; a toddy *la18-e19*. [see the noun]

cheerie-bye, cheery-bye /'tʃiri 'bae/ *interj* a farewell greeting *20-*. [conflation of Eng *cheerio* with Eng *goodbye*]

cheery, †**chery** /'tʃiri/ *adj* cheerful *16-*. **cheerisome** cheerful, merry *la19- Sh C SW*. **cheerie pyke** a tasty morsel, a treat *20- NE*. [CHEER[2.1] + -IE[2]]

cheese[1], †**cheis,** †**scheis** /tʃiz/ *n* **1** food made from milk curd, cheese *la15-*. **2** the receptacle of the thistle *Cirsium vulgare 20-*. **3** *spinning* a cylindrical yarn-bobbin without flanges *la20- Ork C*. **cheese-an-breid** the first green shoots on (hawthorn) hedges *20- EC SW Bor*; compare *bread-and-cheese* (BREID). **cheese bandages** wrappings for cheese while it is being cured *20- H&I SW*. **cheese bauk** a board or rafter on which cheeses mature *19- NE WC*. **cheese cloots** wrappings for cheese while it is in the cheese-press *20-*. **cheese stane** a stone worked with a screw for pressing cheese *20- NE SW*. **hung cheese** cheese made by suspending the curds in a cloth *la18-19, 20- NE*. [OE *cēse*]

cheese[2] /tʃiz/ *n* something good; someone important *20-*. **never say cheese** do not mention something, keep quiet *20- N NE T EC*. [perhaps Urdu *chīz* thing, as in the phrase *the (real) cheese* applied to anything good, which originated among Anglo-Indians]

cheese *see* CHUSE

cheesie /'tʃizi/ *adj* a nonsense word in a children's rhyme: ◊*cheesie bat, come into my hat la19- T*. [unknown]

cheet /tʃit/ *n* **1** a call to a cat *19-*. **2** a cat *19-*. **cheetie-pussy** = CHEET *20-*. [compare CHATTY-PUSS]

cheetle, †**chittle** /'tʃitəl/ *v* to chirp, warble *19, 20- WC*. [onomatopoeic]

cheeve /tʃiv, ʃiv/ *n* a sheave, a pulley-wheel *20- N NE T*. [ME *shive*]

chef *see* CHIEF[1.1]

chefe *see* CHIEF[1.1], CHIEF[1.2]

cheggie /'tʃege/ *n* a chestnut *la20- C SW Bor*. [unknown]

cheif *see* CHIEF[1.1], CHIEF[1.2]

cheiftane *see* CHIEFTAIN

cheik *see* CHEEK[1.2]

cheil, cheild *see* CHIEL

cheinge *see* CHYNGE[1.1], CHYNGE[1.2]

cheip *see* CHAPE[1.1], CHAPE[1.2], SHEEP

cheir *see* CHEER[1], CHEER[2.1], CHEER[2.2], SHEAR[1]

cheis *see* CHASE[1.2], CHEESE[1], CHICE

cheit *see* CHEAT[1.2]

chek *see* CHACK[1.1]

cheke *see* CHEEK[1.1]

chekin *see* CHUCKEN

†**chekker, chakker, scheker** *n* **1** a chess board *15-e19*. **2** the annual audit of royal revenues; the royal exchequer or court of account *la14-17*. **chekker compt** an account laid before the audit or exchequer *16-e17*. †**chekker hous** the house occupied by the exchequer *16-e17*. [ME *cheker*]

chel *see* CHILL

cheld *see* CHIEL

cheldbed lare *see* CHILDBEDLAIR

chelder *see* CHALDER

†**chelleis, chelise** *n* a chalice *la14-e17*. [OE *calic*]

†**chemer, chymmer** *n* a loose, upper robe *la14-e17*. [MFr *chamarre*]

chemlay *see* CHIMLEY

chemois, chemis, †**chymmis,** †**schimmeis** /'ʃemwa, 'ʃemɪs, 'tʃemɪs/ *n* **1** the principal mansion or manor house of an estate *la14-e17, 19- historical*. **2** a chief town or city *15-e16*. **3** a dwelling, a house *e16*. [MFr *chiefmes*]

chene *see* CHEEN[1.1]

chenge *see* CHYNGE[1.1], CHYNGE[1.2]

†**chen3e**[1.1], **chan3e, chainzie** *n* a chain *la14-e19*. Compare CHEEN[1.1]. [ME *chenye*, variant of *chaine*]

†**chenʒe**[1,2], **chanʒe**, †**chainʒe** v to fasten with a chain *la15-16*. Compare CHEEN[1,2]. [see the noun]
chepe see CHEEP[1,1], CHEEP[1,2]
cheplane see CHAPLAIN
chepman see CHAPMAN
cheppell see CHAIPEL
cheptour see CHAIPTER
cheptourly see CHAPTERLY
†**cherarchy**, **jerarche** n an angelic hierarchy *la15-e16*. [ME *jerarchi*]
chere see CHEER[2,1]
cheretie see CHARITY
cherge see CHAIRGE[1,1], CHAIRGE[1,2]
cheriot /ˈtʃɛrɪət/ n a chariot *16-e17, la20- literary*. [ME *chariot*]
cherite, **cherity** see CHARITY
cherk see CHIRK, JIRK
cherm see CHAIRM[1,1], CHAIRM[1,2]
cherr see CHEER[1]
cherret see CHARRIT
cherry-coal /ˈtʃɛre ˈkol/ n a type of shiny, freely-burning coal *la18- NE T C*. [perhaps Older Scots *chery* cherry, from the bright lustre when burning + COAL]
chert see CHAIRT
chery see CHEERY
†**chesabill**, **chesapill** n an ecclesiastical vestment, a chasuble *15-16*. [ME *chesible*]
†**chesbow**, **chasbow**, **chesboll** n a poppy *16-e17*. [unknown]
chese see CHUSE
†**cheseb** n = CHESABILL *e16*. [shortened form of CHESABILL]
chesell see CHASSAL
†**cheson**[1,1], **chessoun** n 1 an occasion, a cause, a reason *la14-15*. 2 an objection, an exception; a cause or grounds for complaint *15-16*. [aphetic form of ENCHESONE[1,1]]
†**cheson**[1,2], **chessoun** v to find fault with; to blame or accuse *15-16*. Compare ENCHESONE[1,2]. [see the noun]
chess, *Sh* **shess**, †**chesse**, †**shass** /tʃɛs; *Sh* ʃɛs/ n a window-sash, a window frame *18-*. **chass window**, †**chess window** a framed window *18, 20- N*. [MFr *chasse*]
chessart, **chesser**, **chesset**, **chisat**, **chisset** /ˈtʃɛsərt, ˈtʃɛsər, ˈtʃɛsət, ˈtʃɪsət/ n a cheese-press; a cheese-vat *18-*. †**the chisset ye were staint in** your original social class *e19*. [derivative of CHEESE[1]; compare KAISART, Flem *kaeshorde*]
chesse see CHESS
chesʒer, **chesset** see CHESSART
chessoun see CHESON[1,1], CHESON[1,2]
chest see KIST[1,1]
chestane see CHAISTAIN
chestee see CHASTY
†**chester**, **chestre** n a circular fortification; a farm or hamlet near a Roman earthwork; frequently in place-names *la11-e19*. [OE *ceaster*]
chester barley /ˈtʃɛstər ˈbarle/ n = CHESTER BEAR *la18- T*. [unknown first element + BARLEY[1]]
chester bear /tʃɛstər ˈber/ n a variety of barley *la18- NE T EC*. [unknown first element + BEAR[1]]
chesting see KIST[1,2]
cheston see CHAISTAIN
chestre see CHESTER
cheswell see CHASSAL
che't see CHEAT[1,2]
chete see CHEAT[1,1], CHEAT[1,2]
chetry see CHEATRY
cheuch see TEUCH[1,1]
cheuchter see TEUCHTER

cheuer see SHIVER[1]
†**cheveron**, **scheverone**, **schiveron** n 1 a kid glove *17-e19*. 2 kid-skin *la16-17*. [altered form of ME *cheverel* kid-leather; compare OFr *chevrele* a kid, a young goat]
Cheviot /ˈtʃiviət/ n a breed of sheep *la18-*. [from the name of the range of hills on the Scottish-English border]
chew /tʃu/ interj a reprimand to a dog *19, 20- SW Uls*. [instinctive utterance]
cheyne see CHEEN[1,1]
chib[1,1] /tʃɪb/ n a knife or razor used as a weapon *la20-*. **chib mark** a scar from a knife or razor wound *la20-*. [variant of Travellers' language *chiv*]
chib[1,2] /tʃɪb/ v to stab or slash with a knife or razor *la20-*. [see the noun]
chice, **cheis**, **choice**, †**chois**, †**chose** /tʃʌɪs, tʃɔɪs/ n the act of choosing; choice *la14-*. [ME, OFr *chois*]
chick[1,1] /tʃɪk/ n 1 a clicking noise (made to encourage horses) *20-*. 2 the tick of a watch or clock; a moment of time *la18-19, 20- EC*. [onomatopoeic]
chick[1,2] /tʃɪk/ v 1 to make a clicking noise (to encourage horses) *19, 20- NE EC*. 2 *of a watch or clock* to tick *e19*. [see the noun]
chicken see CHUCKEN
chickie-mellie, **chickymelly** /ˈtʃɪkiˈmɛli/ n a game or trick involving knocking on a door or window *la19- NE T C*. [probably CHICK[1,1] + MELL[1,2]]
chief[1,1], †**chefe**, †**cheif**, †**chef** /tʃif/ n 1 a leader *la14-*. 2 the head of a clan or feudal community *15-*. 3 a principal town, a city, a capital *la14-e16*. †**in chefe** in the feudal system as an immediate vassal *la14-17*. [ME *chef*]
chief[1,2], †**chefe**, †**cheif** /tʃif/ adj 1 highest in rank, most important *la14-*. 2 intimate, friendly *la19-*. [see the noun]
chieftain, †**chiftane**, †**cheiftane**, †**scheiftane** /ˈtʃiftən/ n 1 a clan chief *la16-*. 2 a military leader or commander *la14-e17*. [altered form of ME *chevetain*]
chiel, **cheil**, **chield**, *Sh N* **sheeld**, †**cheld**, †**schyld**, †**cheild** /tʃil, tʃild; *Sh N* ʃild/ n 1 a young man, a fellow; a lad; originally a young servant or apprentice *la14-*. 2 a child *la14-*. 3 a young woman *la16-19, 20- EC*. **the Auld Chiel** the Devil *20- Sh NE EC*. [OE *cild*; compare CHILD]
chiffer see CEEPHER
chiffin /ˈtʃɪfən/ n a particle, a crumb, a fragment *20- NE*. [unknown]
chifmakir see SHEATH
chikkin see CHUCKEN
child, *NE* **tsill**, *Uls* **chile** /tʃʌɪld; *NE* tʃɪl; *Uls* tʃʌɪl/ n 1 a child, a young boy or girl; (a person's) offspring *la14-*. 2 *pl* the crew of a ship *15-16*. 3 *pl* fellows, people *la16*. **childer** children *la15-*. **chillie**, **chullie** a child *20- NE*. †**child ill** the pains of childbirth *la14-e16*. **children's panel** a tribunal of lay people who conduct hearings intended to combine justice and welfare for children and young people *la20-*. [OE *cild*; compare CHIEL]
†**childbedlair**, **cheldbed lare** n childbirth; the confinement of a woman *la15-e17*. [Older Scots *childbed* + LAIR[1,1]]
childer see CHILD
chile see CHILD
chilfie see SHILFA
chill, *Ork SW* **shill**, †**schill**, †**chel**, †**chyll** /tʃɪl; *Ork SW* ʃɪl/ adj cold *la14-*. [OE *cele*]
chillie see CHILD
chilp[1,1] /tʃɪlp/ n a chirp *20- NE*. [onomatopoeic]
chilp[1,2] /tʃɪlp/ v to chirp, squeak; to cry; to make a shrill sound *e17, 20- NE*. [see the noun]
chilpy /ˈtʃɪlpi/ adj chilly *la19- NE*. [altered form of CHILL + -IE[2]]

chim /tʃɪm/ *v* to make up to a person; to ingratiate oneself *20- NE*. **chim in wi** to agree with fawningly *la19- NE*. [variant of CHUM]

chimley, chimlay, chimla, chimbley, chumla, *Sh Ork N* **shimley,** *N* **chumley,** *Bor* **chumlay,** †**chemlay,** †**schimlay** /ˈtʃɪmle, ˈtʃɪmlə, ˈtʃɪmble, ˈtʃʌmlə; *Sh Ork N* ˈʃɪmle; *N Bor* ˈtʃʌmle/ *n* **1** a funnel used to vent smoke, a chimney *16-*. **2** a grate, a hearth, a fireplace *la16-19, 20- NE*. **chimley brace** a mantelpiece *17-*. **chimley cheek, chimla cheek** the side of the fireplace or grate *19, 20- NE T EC*. **chimley heid, chimla heid 1** a chimneytop *16-19, 20- NE T C SW*. **2** a mantelpiece *la19- NE T EC*. **chimley lug** the fireside *la18-19, 20- NE EC*. **chimley neuk,** *N* **chumley neuk** the chimney corner *la16-*. **chimley rib** a bar of a grate *19- NE T EC*. [altered form of ME *chimene*]

chin see CHUN[1.1]

china see CHEENY

chincough, *N H&I* **chincoch** /ˈtʃɪŋkɔf; *N H&I* ˈtʃɪŋkɔx/ *n* whooping cough *18-20, 21- historical*. Compare *kink cough* (KINK[2.2]). [ME *chinke* asthma or whooping cough + Older Scots *coche* a cough]

chine see CHEEN[1.1], CHEEN[1.2]

chiner see JINER

chinge see CHYNGE[1.1], CHYNGE[1.2]

chingle, *Ork* **gingle,** *SW Uls* **jingle,** †**chingill,** †**chyngill** /ˈtʃɪŋəl; *Ork SW Uls* ˈdʒɪŋəl/ *n* coarse gravel, shingle; a shingly or pebbly beach *15-*. **chingly, jingly** gravelly, pebbly *la18-*. [unknown]

chinnell see CHANNEL[1.1]

chip[1.1] /tʃɪp/ **1** a small piece of something; a thin strip of wood; a thin slice of fruit *18-*. **2** a piece of deep-fried potato *la19-*. **chippy sauce** a combination of brown sauce and vinegar, served in chip shops *la20- EC*. [ME *chippe*]

chip[1.2] /tʃɪp/ *v* **1** to cut, gouge; to break off fragments; to break a surface *19-*. **2** *curling* to knock or strike a stone *20-*. **3** to throw small objects *la20-*. **4** *of buds or seeds* to break open; to germinate *la15-e19*. **chippit 1** *of fruit or eggs* damaged *20-*. **2** tipsy *20- NE*. **chippy** a large marble; a game of marbles *20-*. **chip the winner** *in curling* to avoid the guard stones and strike what can be seen of the winning stone *la19-*. [perhaps OE **chippian*; compare Fris *kippen* to cut, MDu, MLG *kippen* to chip eggs, hatch]

chips see CHAPS

chipter see CHAIPTER

chirawk[1.1] /tʃəˈrɔk/ *n* a squawk *20- NE*. [onomatopoeic]

chirawk[1.2] /tʃəˈrɔk/ *v* to squawk *20- NE*. [see the noun]

chirche see CHURCH

chire see CHEER[1]

chirity see CHARITY

chirk, *WC SW* **chark,** *Bor* **chairk,** †**cherk** /tʃɪrk; *WC SW* tʃɑrk; *Bor* tʃɛrk/ *v* **1** to make a harsh strident noise; to creak or croak *17-*. **2** to gnash or grind the teeth *19-*. **3** to chirp, chirrup *19-*. Compare CHORK. **chirker** the house-cricket *Acheta domesticus la19- SW Bor*. [OE *cearcian*; compare CHORK]

chirl[1.1], **churl** /tʃɪrl, tʃʌrl/ *n* a chirp, a trill, a warble *17-19, 20- SW Bor*. [onomatopoeic]

chirl[1.2], **churl** /tʃɪrl, tʃʌrl/ *v* to chirp, warble *17- T C SW Bor*. [see the noun]

chirle /tʃɪrl/ *n* a roll of fat beneath the chin, a flap of skin on the neck of a bird *la18-19, 20- Ork*. [perhaps metathesis of *chuller* (CHOLLER)]

chirls, churls /tʃɪrlz, tʃʌrlz/ *npl* **1** small coal *19- NE T EC*. **2** kindling wood *la19- N NE T H&I*. [unknown]

chirm[1.1] /tʃɪrm/ *n* a bird's call, a chirp *16-19, 20- literary*. [see the verb]

chirm[1.2] /tʃɪrm/ *v* **1** to warble, chirp *la15-19, 20- literary*. **2** to fret, complain *17-19, 20- Uls*. [OE *cirman*]

chirnel see KERNEL

†**chirple** *v of a swallow* to twitter *19*. [frequentative form of Eng *chirp*]

chirry /ˈtʃɪre/ *n* a cherry, the fruit of the *Prunus cerasus* or *Prunus avium 16-19, 20- NE WC*. [OE *ciris*, OFr *cerise*]

chirt[1.1] /tʃɪrt/ *n* **1** a squeeze, a hug *19, 20- SW Bor*. **2** a small quantity (of liquid) *19, 20- N Bor*. **3** a chirping or squirting sound *e17*. [onomatopoeic]

chirt[1.2] /tʃɪrt/ *v* to squeeze or press; to spurt or squirt *16-*. [see the noun]

†**chirurgian, cirugiane** *n* a surgeon *16-e18*. **chirurgenair** = CHIRURGIAN *la16*. **chirurgianrie** surgery *la16-17*. [ME *cirurgien*]

chisat see CHESSART

chisell see CHASSAL

chisouris see CHIZORS

chiss see CHASE[1.2]

chisset see CHESSART

chist see JIST[1.2], KIST[1.1]

chit /tʃɪt/ *n* a packed lunch; a piece of bread *19, 20- H&I SW*. [unknown; compare CHAT[2.1]]

chitter /ˈtʃɪtər/ *v* **1** to shiver (with cold or fear); *of teeth* to chatter *la19-*. **2** *of birds* to twitter *la18-*. **3** to flicker or flutter *20- literary*. **chittering bit** a snack eaten after bathing *19-*. †**chittering piece** = *chittering bit 19*. **chitter chatter** to chatter, shiver *la19- NE T*. [onomatopoeic]

chitties /ˈtʃɪtiz/ *npl* tripod irons with a chain and cleek to hold a cooking pot over a fire *20-*. [unknown]

chittle /ˈtʃɪtəl/ *v* to nibble, gnaw *19- SW*. [variant of CHATTLE]

chittle see CHEETLE

chitty wran /tʃɪti ˈran/ *n* the common wren *Troglodytes troglodytes la19- H&I WC Uls*. [compare *kittie wren* (KITTIE[1])]

chiver see SHIVER[1]

chizors, †**shissors,** †**chisouris** /ˈtʃɪzərz/ *npl* scissors *la16-*. [EModE *cizars*]

chob see JOB[1.1]

chock[1], **choke,** *SW Bor* **chowk** /tʃɔk, tʃok; *SW Bor* tʃʌuk/ *v* to throttle, strangle; to clog or choke *la16-*. **chockit** suffering from quinsy *la19, 20- NE C*. **chock roap, choak roap** a flexible appliance for clearing an obstruction in an animal's throat *20- N NE*. [ME *choken*]

†**chock**[2] *n* a set of sixty pieces *17-e18*. [Du, LG *schok*]

choffer see CHAFFER[1]

choice see CHICE

choir see QUEIR

chois see CHICE

choise see CHUSE

chok see SHOCK

choke see CHOCK[1], CHOWK

†**chokis, chowkkis** *npl* **1** quinsy *e16*. **2** the JOUGS *la16*. [*choke* (CHOCK[1])]

choll see CHOWL[1]

choller, †**chollare,** †**chuller** /ˈtʃɔlər/ *n* **1** the jowls, a double chin *16-18, 19- NE SW Uls*. **2** *pl* the gills of a fish *la18- WC SW Bor*. **3** *pl* the wattles of a cock *19- SW Bor*. [OE *ceolor* throat]

choochter see TEUCHTER

chook see CHOWK, CHUCK[1]

chookie[1], **chuckie** /ˈtʃuki, ˈtʃʌke/ *n* **1** a chicken; a bird *18-*. **2** a fool *la20- H&I WC*. **chookie burdie** a bird *la20-*. [CHUCK[1] + -IE[1]]

chookie[2] /ˈtʃuke/ *n humorous* the Duke of: *Chookie Wellington la20-*. [devoicing and analogy with CHOOKIE[1]]

choop, jupe /tʃup, dʒup/ *n* the hip of the wild rose *Rosa canina 19- SW Bor.* [ON *hjúpa, júpr* a doublet, compare OE *hēope*]

choop *see* JUPE¹

chop¹·¹ /tʃɔp/ *n* a stroke, a blow; a knock *17-*. Compare CHAP³·¹. [see the verb]

chop¹·² †**schop** /tʃɔp/ *v* 1 to cut, hack or slice *la15-*. 2 to strike, knock *16-*. †**chop handis** to shake hands *17*. [variant of CHAP³·²]

chop² †**chowp** /tʃɔp/ *n* a jaw *16-*. [unknown]

chop *see* SHOP

chopin, chappin, *Sh* **shapin,** †**choppin,** †**schoppin,** †**chapin** /'tʃɔpən, 'tʃapən; *Sh* 'ʃapən/ *n* 1 *weights and measures* a Scots half-pint *15-*. 2 a container of this capacity *la15-16*. †**choppin stoup, choppyne stowp** a drinking vessel holding a Scots half-pint *16-e19*. [ME *chopin*]

†**chopman, shopman** *n* a chapman; a shopkeeper *la16-e18*. [variant of CHAPMAN]

choppie *see* SHOP

choppin *see* CHOPIN

chore¹·¹ /tʃɔr/ *n* stolen goods *la20-* C. **on the chore** engaging in theft *la20- EC*. [see the verb]

chore¹·² /tʃɔr/ *v* to steal *la19-*. **chorie, chory** to steal *la20- EC*. [Travellers' language *chor, choar*]

chork /tʃɔrk/ *v* to make a squelching noise *18-19, 20- Bor.* [variant of CHIRK]

chorus /'kɔrəs/ *n* the backside *la20-*. [rhyming slang reduced from *chorus and verse* ERSE¹·¹]

chose *see* CHICE

chottill *see* SHOTTLE

chou *see* CHOWL¹

chouk, choulk *see* CHOWK

choup /tʃup/ *n* a single word, a cheep *20- NE.* [onomatopoeic; compare CHEEP¹·¹]

chow, †**chaw** /tʃʌu/ *n* 1 the game of shinty *la16- NE.* 2 a shinty ball *19- NE.* [OFr *choule* a stick and ball game similar to golf or croquet]

chow *see* CHAW¹·¹, CHAW¹·², CHOWL¹

chowfer *see* CHAFFER¹

chowk, chouk, choke, *NE* **chook,** *H&I* **juke,** †**choulk** /tʃʌuk, tʃok; *NE* tʃuk; *H&I* dʒuk/ *n* the cheek, the jaw *la15-*. **choke band,** †**cholkband** the jaw-strap of a bridle *16-19, 20- NE SW.* [compare ON *kjálki* a jaw-bone, Norw *kjake* a cheek]

chowk *see* CHOCK¹

chowkkis *see* CHOKIS

chowl¹**, chow,** †**chou,** †**choll** /tʃʌul, tʃʌu/ *n* the jowl *la15-19, 20- Bor.* [ME *cholle*]

chowl² /tʃʌul/ *v* 1 to grimace, distort the face *19- T.* 2 to howl or cry mournfully *19.* **chowl yer chanler-chafts** to make a face *19- T.* [see the noun]

†**chowp** *v* to mumble *e16.* [see the noun CHOP²]

chowp *see* CHOP²

chows, †**shows** /tʃʌuz/ *npl* small coal *la17-*. [unknown]

chowtle *see* CHATTLE

chree *see* THREE

Chrissenmas *see* CHRISTENMAS

christen *see* KIRSEN¹·¹

Christendie, †**Christintie** /'krɪsəndi/ *n* the Christian world, Christendom *la16- literary.* [ME *Cristianite, Cristante*]

christening *see* KIRSENIN

Christenmas, Chrissenmas, †**Christinmes,** †**Christinmesse** /'krɪsənməs/ *n* Christmas *16-19, 20- NE T EC.* [ME *Cristes mæsse*]

christin *see* KIRSEN¹·²

Christinmes, Christinmesse *see* CHRISTENMAS

Christintie *see* CHRISTENDIE

Christmas, †**Crystmaesse** /'krɪsməs/ *n* 1 the feast of the nativity, celebrated on December 25th *16-*. 2 a Christmas present; a seasonal gratuity *la19-*. [OE *cristes-mæsse*]

chuck¹**, chook** /tʃʌk, tʃuk/ *n* a chick, a chicken *19-*. Compare CHOOKIE¹. [onomatopoeic]

chuck² *T C* **juck,** *EC SW* **chack** /tʃʌk; *T C* dʒʌk; *EC SW* tʃak/ *n* 1 a pebble; a marble *19-*. 2 *pl* a game involving throwing and catching pebbles *19-*. [perhaps Eng *chuck* to throw]

chuck³ /tʃʌk/ *n* food *20-*. [perhaps Eng *chuck* a block of wood]

chucken, chicken, *Sh* **shicken,** †**chekin,** †**chikkin** /'tʃʌkən, 'tʃɪkən; *Sh* 'ʃɪkən/ *n* a domestic fowl; its flesh as food *15-*. **chickenweed** chickweed *Stellaria media 19-*. **chickenwort,** *Sh* **shickenwirt** = *chickenweed 19-*. [OE *cicen* a young chicken, a chick]

chuckie /'tʃʌke, 'tʃʌki/ *n* 1 a pebble, a marble *20-*. 2 *pl* a game involving throwing and catching pebbles *20- NE WC.* 3 *pl* testicles *la20-*. [CHUCK² + -IE¹]

chuckie *see* CHOOKIE¹

chuckie-stane, chucky-stane /tʃʌke'sten, tʃʌki'sten/ 1 a pebble; a flat stone used for skimming across water *la18-*. 2 a game involving throwing and catching pebbles *19, 20- NE H&I SW.* [CHUCKIE + STANE¹·¹]

chucks mei /tʃʌks 'mae/ *v* I claim *20- T Bor.* [compare *chaps me* (CHAPS)]

chucky-stane *see* CHUCKIE-STANE

chuddy /'tʃʌde, 'tʃʌdi/ *n* chewing gum *20-*. [unknown]

chudge *see* JUDGE¹·¹, JUDGE¹·²

chuff /tʃʌf/ *n* a fool; a rustic or coarse person *la15-19, 20- Uls.* [unknown]

chuffell *see* SHUIL¹·¹

chuffie, chuffy /'tʃʌfe, 'tʃʌfi/ *adj* chubby, fat-faced *la18-*. **chuffy-cheeked** chubby-cheeked *18-*. [probably CHUFF + -IE²]

chug *see* TUG¹·¹, TUG¹·²

chuggle *see* TUGGLE¹·²

chugle *see* TUGGLE¹·¹

chukery-packery *see* JOUKERIE-PAWKERIE

chuller *see* CHOLLER

chullie *see* CHILD

chum /tʃʌm/ *v* to accompany (as a friend) *20-*. [Eng *chum* a friend]

chumla, chumlay, chumley *see* CHIMLEY

chummle *see* JUMMLE

chump /tʃʌmp/ *n* a thickset (young) person *la19- NE.* [compare Eng *chump* a thick lump (of wood)]

chump *see* JUMP

chun¹·¹ *SW* **chin** /tʃʌn; *SW* tʃɪn/ *n* a sprout, a shoot (of a potato) *19- SW Bor.* [OE *cinu* a fissure]

chun¹·² /tʃʌn/ *v* 1 to remove the sprouts from potatoes *19- SW Bor.* 2 *of potatoes* to sprout *la19- SW.* [OE *cīnan* to crack open]

chun *see* SHON

chunce *see* CHANCE¹·¹

chund *see* JUND

chunner *see* CHANNER²

chunty *see* CHANTY

church, †**chirche** /tʃʌrtʃ/ *n* a building used for public worship *12-*. **church officer** an official charged with keeping order in the church and parish, attending the *kirk-session* and carrying out its edicts *la18-*. Compare KIRK¹·¹. [OE *cyrice*]

Church of Scotland /'tʃʌrtʃ əv 'skɔtlənd/ *n* the reformed church in Scotland, which became Presbyterian in 1690 *la16-*. [CHURCH + SCOTLAND]

churl *see* CHIRL¹·¹, CHIRL¹·²

churls see CHIRLS
churn see KIRN²
churr muffet, *EC* **shirmuffet** /ˈtʃʌrmʌfət; *EC* ˈʃɪrmʌfət/ *n* the whitethroat *Sylvia communis la19-*. [onomatopoeic, the second element refers to its light-coloured head and neck feathers]
chuse, chyse, cheese, †choise, †chese, †scheis /tʃuz, tʃʌɪz, tʃiz/ *v* to select, to decide; to make a preference *la14-*. [OE *cēosan*]
chust see JIST¹,²
chyar, chyre see CHEER¹
chye /tʃae/ *n* the chaffinch *Fringilla coelebs* 20- *NE*. [onomatopoeic]
chyll see CHILL
chymmer see CHEMER
chymmis see CHEMOIS
chynge¹·¹, **cheenge, cheinge, chinge, change, †chenge** /tʃʌɪndʒ, tʃindʒ, tʃɪndʒ, tʃendʒ/ *n* **1** an alteration, a substitution; variety or novelty *la14-*. **2** exchange, trade; custom, business, patronage *la15-19, 20- NE*. **3** an inn, an alehouse *17-19*. **changefu'** changing; changeable *19, 20- NE T.* **change ale** home-brewed ale (shared with the neighbours) *20- Ork*. **change hoose, change house, cheenge hoose** an inn, an alehouse *17-*. **change keeper** an innkeeper *18-19, 20- historical*. **†change wife** a female innkeeper *la18-e19*. **†change yearn** a different yarn from the remainder of the piece *la17*. [ME *chaunge*]
chynge¹·², **cheenge, cheinge, chinge, change, †chenge, †chaunge, †chainge** /tʃʌɪndʒ, tʃindʒ, tʃɪndʒ, tʃendʒ/ *v* **1** to alter, transform *la14-*. **2** to exchange or substitute *la14-*. **3** *of food* to deteriorate, go off *20- N NE*. **chyngin, cheengin, chingin, †cheinging 1** undergoing or causing change *la15-*. **2** *of fabric* showing different colours in different aspects or lights *la16-*. **chyngin ba, chingin ball** a sweet that changes colour as it is sucked *20- NE T*. **change words wi** to converse, talk to *20-*. **change yer breath** to have a drink *20-*. **change yer feet** to put on dry shoes and stockings *la19-*. **change yersel** to change your clothes *18-*. **change yer tune** to change your opinion or way of behaving *la16-*. [ME *chaungen*]
chyngill see CHINGLE
chyre see CHEER¹
chyse see CHUSE
chyvir see SHIVER¹
ciel, †ceil, †syle /sil/ *n* a ceiling *e16, 19- literary*. Compare SYLE. [SYLE]
†ciete *n* a city *la15-e17*. [ME *cite*]
cietenar see CITINER
cieteȝan see CITEȜAN
cieteȝour see CITEȜOUR
cile see SYLE
cinner, *NE* **shinner**, *NE C SW* **shunner**, *Bor Uls* **shunder, †schinder** /ˈsɪnər; *NE* ˈʃɪnər; *NE C SW* ˈʃʌnər; *Bor Uls* ˈʃʌndər/ *n* a cinder *la16-*. **†cinner-coal** coal deprived of its bitumen *la17*. [OE *sinder*]
cipher see CEEPHER
cipir see SYPER
†circuat *adj* encircled, surrounded *la16-e17*. [Lat *circuāt-*, ptp stem of *circuāre*]
†circue *v* to encircle, surround *la15-e17*. [MFr *circuir*]
†circuilie *adv* in turn *e16*. **circuilie inquerit** asked in turn *e16*. [Lat *circu-* round, with adv-forming suffix *-lie*]
†circule *v* **1** to encircle, surround (with) *15-16*. **2** to place round in a circle *16*. [MFr *circuler*, Lat *circulāre*]
†circumcide *v* to circumcise *la14-e17*. [Lat *circumcīdere* to cut round]

circumduce /sɪrkəmˈdjus/ *v* **1** *law* to declare or claim the time allowed for leading a proof to have elapsed *la16-*. **2** to carry round *e16*. [Lat *circumdūcere* to lead round, annul]
†circumferat *adj* surrounded, encircled *16*. [Lat *circumferre* to bear round]
circumscription, †circumscriptioun /sɪrkəmˈskrɪpʃən/ *n* an encircling inscription *15-19, 20- historical*. [Lat *circumscriptio* an encircling, an outline]
circumstance /ˈsɪrkəmstans/ *n* **1** a condition, a detail, an attendant fact *la15-*. **2** elaborateness of detail, a formal display or ceremony *15-16*. [ME *circumstance*, Lat *circumstantia*]
†circumstantiate, circumstantiat *adj* affected by particular circumstances; detailed *la17-19*. [EModE *circumstantiate*]
†circumvene *v* **1** to circumvent *la15-18*. **2** to encircle, surround *16-18*. [MFr *circonvenir*, Lat *circumvenīre*]
cirugiane see CHIRURGIAN
cister see SISTER¹
†Cisteus, Systeus *n* Cistercian *15-e16*. [AN *Cisteus*, the site of an abbey near Dijon, the mother-house of the order]
†citat *adj* cited, summoned *la16-e17*. [Lat *citāt-*, ptp stem of *citāre*]
cite see CEETIE
†citeȝan, cieteȝan, citesane *n* a citizen *la14-16*. [ME *citisein*]
†citeȝour, cieteȝour *n* a citizen *15-e16*. [irregular variant of *ceteȝener* (CITISINAR)]
†citiner, citionar, cietenar *n* a citizen *la15-e17*. [ME *citener*]
†citisinar, ceteȝenere *n* a citizen *la15-e17*. [ME *citisain*]
cituat see SEETUATE
city see CEETIE
civil see CEEVIL
claa see CLAW¹·¹, CLAW¹·²
claag¹·¹, **†claug** /klag/ *n* noisy speech; the sound of chattering birds *la19- Sh*. [ON *klak* the chirping of birds]
claag¹·², **klag, †claug** /klag/ *v of hens* to cackle; *of people* to prattle *la19- Sh*. [ON *klaka* to twitter]
clabber, glabber, *SW* **clobber** /ˈklabər, ˈglabər; *SW* ˈklɔbər/ *n* soft mud, clay, mire *19-*. **clabbery, glabbery, glaubery** muddy, dirty *la19-*. **clabbered** covered with mud or dirt *20-*. [Gael *clàbar*]
clabbydhu, clappy doo /klabiˈdu, klapi ˈdu/ *n* a large variety of mussel of the family *Mytilidae 19- H&I C*. [probably Gael *clab* an enormous mouth + Gael *dubh* black]
claber see KLEEBER
clachan, †clauchan, †clauching, †clachane /ˈklaxən/ *n* **1** a hamlet, a small village; frequently in place-names *la15-*. **2** a village inn *la19*. [Gael *clachan*]
clack¹·¹, **cleck, †clak** /klak, klɛk/ *n* **1** a sharp impact, a sharp sound *la16-*. **2** gossip, chatter, insolence *19-*. **3** the clapper of a mill *19, 20- T*. [see the verb]
clack¹·², **cleck, †clak** /klak, klɛk/ *v* **1** to make a sharp noise *la16-*. **2** to gossip; to talk loudly and idly *18-*. [compare Fr *claquer*, Du *klakken*]
clack² /klak/ *n* a kind of treacle toffee *la19-*. [unknown; compare *claggum* (CLAG¹·¹)]
clack see CLAIK³, CLAIK⁴
clackan, †cleckin, †clekane /ˈklakən/ *n* **1** a wooden bat or racquet *la19, 20- historical*. **2** a shuttlecock *la16-19*. **†cleckinbrod** a wooden board used in handball *18-e19*. [unknown]
clack mill see KLICK-MILL
clad /klad/ *v* to cover or line with wood; to reinforce *18-*. **cladding** flooring or lining with wood; boarding, lagging *la19-*. Compare *cleedin* 3 (CLEED). [OE *gecladed*]

claddach, **cloddach** /'kladəx, 'klɔdəx/ *n* the gravelly bed or edge of a river; a shingly beach or ridge *19- NE SW*. [Gael *cladach* a shore, a beach]

claes, **clathes**, **claithes**, **clothes**, †**claise**, †**cleis**, †**clathis** /klez, kleðz, kloðz/ *npl* clothing, apparel; bed-coverings *la14-*. **claes beetle** a mallet for beating clothes when washing them *la19- NE T C SW*. **claes line** a clothes-line *20-*. **claes pole** a clothes-prop; a fixed pole to which the clothes-line is attached *la19-*. **claes rope** a clothes-line *19-*. **claes screen** a clothes-horse *19-*. [OE *claðas*]

claff, **claft** /klaf, klaft/ *n curling* a piece of iron studded into the ice to act as a foot-grip *la19- WC*. **tak the claft** *curling* to come between the two guards *20- WC*. [compare ON *klof* the fork of the legs]

claff *see* CLOFF[1]

clag[1.1], *Sh Uls* **cleg** /klag; *Sh Uls* klɛg/ *n* 1 a lump or mass of clay, mud or snow; a sticky or dirty mess *19-*. 2 a quantity of soft (sticky) food *19, 20- NE SW*. 3 a hindrance, something surplus to requirements *19- C*. 4 *law* an encumbrance on or claim against property *la16-e19*. 5 a fault, a cause for reproach *la16-e19*. **claggum** treacle toffee *la19- Ork NE EC Bor*. **claggy**, *Sh* **glaggy**, *Sh Uls* **cleggy** sticky, adhesive; soft, wet *19-*. [see the verb]

clag[1.2], *Sh Uls* **cleg** /klag; *Sh Uls* klɛg/ *v* 1 to besmear (with mud or dirt) *la15-*. 2 to clog, clot or stick together; to stop up *la15-*. **clagger**, *N* **clyager** to besmear or daub (with muck); to make sticky *20- N NE EC*. [unknown; compare Dan *klag* sticky mud, clay]

clag *see* CLEG

claich *see* CLAIK[2]

claif *see* CLEAVE[1.2]

claik[1.1] /klek/ *n* 1 a shrill, raucous cry of a goose or other bird *la15-*. 2 gossip, chatter, insolence *19- NE T EC*. 3 a gossip, a tattler *19- NE T EC*. [compare ON *klak*]

claik[1.2], †**clake** /klek/ *v* 1 to gossip, chatter *la18-*. 2 *of birds* to cry or squawk *16-19, 20- NE*. 3 to cry incessantly and impatiently; to clamour for *19- NE T*. [compare ON *klaka*]

claik[2], **claich** /klek; klex/ *v* to besmear, dirty (with something sticky) *19- NE T*. [compare CLAG]

claik[3], †**clack** /klek/ *n* the barnacle *Lepas anatifera la17- Sh Ork NE*. [unknown; compare CLAIK[1.1], CLAIK[4]]

†**claik**[4], **clack** *n* the barnacle-goose *Branta leucopsis la15-19*. **caik goose** = CLAIK[4] *16-e19*. [unknown; compare CLAIK[3]]

clainging *see* CLENGE

clair[1.1] /kler/ *v* 1 to prepare *20- Sh*. 2 to settle; to free from obstruction; to clear up *15-e17*. [see the adj]

clair[1.2] /kler/ *adj* 1 evident, certain; visible, bright; unobstructed *la15-*. 2 prepared, ready *16-18, 19- Sh Ork N*. [ME *cler*; compare CLEAR[1.3]]

clair[1.3] /kler/ *adv* completely; unequivocally; precisely *la15-19, 20- NE*. **clair tae Goad** an expression denoting exasperation *la20-*. [see the adj]

†**clair**[2] *v* to harm, injure *la16*. [unknown]

clairschow, **clairshocher** *see* CLARSACH

clairt *see* CLART[1.1], CLART[1.2]

clairty *see* CLARTY

clairy *see* CLARY[1.1]

claische *see* CLASH[2]

claise *see* CLAES

claisp *see* CLESP[1.1], CLESP[1.2]

claister *see* CLEESTER[1.1], CLEESTER[1.2]

clait *see* CLEIT

claith, **clathe**, **cloath**, **cloth**, †**cleth**, †**cloith** /kleθ, kloθ, klɔθ/ *n* a piece of woven material; cloth or fabric; a tablecloth *la14-*. **cloth-brush** a clothes-brush *la18-*. †**clath of lede** a sheet of lead *la14-16*. [OE *clāþ*]

claith *see* CLEED

claithes *see* CLAES

†**claitt** *n* a cleat *17-e18*. [ME *clet*]

claitter *see* CLATTER[1.1], CLATTER[1.2]

clak *see* CLACK[1.1], CLACK[1.2]

clake *see* CLAIK[1.2]

clam[1] /klam/ *n* a scallop or mussel; a scallop shell *la16-*. **clam shell** a scallop shell *16-*. [OE *clam* a fetter, a constriction, anything that holds tight]

clam[2], †**claum** /klam/ *v* to grope, grasp *19- NE WC SW*. [Norw *klemme* to grip hard; to squeeze]

clam[3], †**clamm** /klam/ *adj* sticky, damp, clammy *la16- NE Bor*. [ME *clammi*; compare Ger *klamm*]

clam *see* CLEM[1], CLEM[2], CLIM

clamant /'klamənt/ *adj* crying out, clamorous; urgent, calling for redress *18-*. [Lat *clāmant-*, prp stem of *clāmāre*]

clamb *see* CLIM

clame *see* CLEME[1.1], CLEME[1.2], CLIM

clamel *see* KLEMMEL

clamersum, **clammersome** /'klamərsʌm/ *adj* noisily discontented, contentious *la19- NE T*. [OFr *clameur*, with adj-forming suffix *-sum*]

clamihewit /klami'hjuit/ *n* 1 a blow, a drubbing; an accident or misfortune *la18-19, 20- NE*. 2 a hubbub, an uproar, a commotion *la19- NE T C*. [unknown]

clamjamfry[1.1], **clamjamphrey**, **clamjamfrey**, **clamjamfray**, **clamjamphrie**, †**clanjamfry** /klam'dʒamfre, klam'dʒamfri/ *n* 1 a company, a crowd of people; a rabble, riff-raff *19-*. 2 rubbish, junk *19-*. 3 a row, a commotion *20-*. [unknown]

clamjamfry[1.2], **clamjamphrie** /klam'dʒamfre, klam'dʒamfri/ *v* 1 to crowd, clutter up *la19-*. 2 to chatter or gossip *e19*. [unknown]

clamm *see* CLAM[3]

clammer, *NE* **claumer** /'klamər; *NE* 'klɔmər/ *v* to clamber *19-*. [ME *clambren*]

clammersome *see* CLAMERSUM

clammys *see* CLAMS

clamp[1.1] /klamp/ *n* a patch *la19- Sh Ork NE*. [perhaps an extended sense of Scots *clamp* a brace]

clamp[1.2] /klamp/ *v* to patch; to make or mend clumsily *la15-19, 20- Sh NE*. †**clamper**, **clampar** *n* 1 a metal plate or patch *17-e19*. 2 a patched-up argument or charge *la17-e18*. †**clamper** to patch up, put together *la17-e19*. [see the noun]

clamp[2.1] /klamp/ *n* a heavy footstep or tread *la18-*. [onomatopoeic; compare Eng *clump*]

clamp[2.2] /klamp/ *v* 1 to walk noisily or heavily *19-*. 2 to move something noisily *19-*. **clamper**, **clumper** *v* 1 to walk noisily or clumsily *19-*. 2 to crowd, clutter or litter *19- C SW Bor*. **clamper**, **clumper** *n* a stout heavy shoe, a clog *19- NE EC*. [see the noun]

clamp[3] /klamp/ *n* 1 *in curling* a piece of spiked iron worn on the shoe to prevent slipping *la19-*. 2 a spiked iron protector for the toe or heel of a boot *la19- T*. [Scots *clamp* something that grasps]

clamp[4] /klamp/ *n* a small stack of peats or turf; an uncovered heap of potatoes *la19- NE T EC SW Uls*. [perhaps variant of Eng *clump*]

†**clamper** *v* to quarrel; to struggle *17-18*. [perhaps CLAMP[2.2]]

clampet /'klampət/ *n* an iron spike fixed to the shoe; a crampon for walking on ice *17-19, 20- Bor*. [compare CRAMPET]

clams, *N* **glaums**, †**clammys** /klamz; *N* glʌumz/ *npl* a clamp; pincers, a vice *la14-*. [OE *clammas* bonds, fetters]

clan /klan/ *n* 1 a local or family group bearing a common name (from a supposed joint ancestor) and united under a chief (especially in the Highlands or Borders) *15-*. 2 a class or group of people *16-*. **3** a tribe or race *16*. †**clannit** belonging to a clan *16-e17*. †**clanman** = *clansman e17*. **clansman** a man belonging to a clan *19-*. **clan system** (government based on) the organization of local or family groups into clans *19-*. **clanswoman** a woman belonging to a clan *19-*. [Gael *clann* children; especially in kin-names, descendants]

clane *see* CLEAN¹·³

clang /klaŋ/ *v pt* clung *19, 20- NE T EC*. [probably by analogy with Scots *rang*, pt of *ring*]

clange *see* CLENGE

clanjamfry *see* CLAMJAMFRY¹·¹

clank¹·¹ /klaŋk/ *n* **1** a loud noise *18-*. **2** a resounding blow *18-19*. [MDu *klank* a clinking sound, and CLINK¹·¹]

clank¹·² /klaŋk/ *v* **1** to throw or slam down *17-*. **2** to sit or flop down *la18-*. **3** to strike, beat *la18-e19*. **4** to snatch or clutch; to seize violently *e19*. [see the noun]

clap¹·¹ /klap/ *n* **1** a sharp noise, the sound of two surfaces striking together *la14-*. **2** a heavy blow or stroke *16-*. **3** an affectionate pat *la19-*. **4** (a clapper used by) a town-crier *la17-19, 20- historical*. **5** the clapper of a mill *la16-e19*. **clap and happer** the symbols used in the sasine of a mill *la16-19, 20- historical*. **clap o the hass** the uvula *20- Ork T EC*. †**clap o the throat** = *clap o the hass 17*. **in a clap** all of a sudden; immediately *17-*. [ME *clappe*; compare MDu *clap*]

clap¹·², *Ork* **klepp** /klap; *Ork* klεp/ *v* **1** to pat affectionately; to fondle *15-*. **2** to make a clapping noise; to strike (the palms) together *la15-*. **3** to place or move (abruptly) *la15-*. **4** to adhere or cling (together) *17-*. **5** to press down, flatten; to compress (soil) *la18-*. **6** to flop down; to crouch; to sit down abruptly *19-*. **7** to bury a person *19, 20- Sh*. **8** to shrink or shrivel *19, 20- Sh*. **clappers** small wooden tools used for making butter *20-*. **clappit** having the flesh clinging to the bones; shrunken *19-*. **clap dyke** a wall of turf or compressed earth *la18-*. **clapped in** *of the face* sunken *20-*. **clap a piece** to make a sandwich *la20-*. **clap yer thoum on** to keep secret, keep silent about *19-*. [ME *clappen*; compare MDu *klappen*]

clap² /klap/ *n* a rabbit burrow or hare's form *20- WC SW Bor*. [OFr *clapier* a rabbit warren]

†**clappard** *n* a rabbit burrow or hole *la16*. [ME *claper*, EModE *clapper*]

clapperdin /klapər'dɪn/ *n* a gossip *20- NE*. [Eng *clapper* the tongue + DIN¹·¹]

clappy doo *see* CLABBYDHU

clapshot /'klapʃɔt/ *n* a dish originating in Orkney, consisting of boiled potatoes and turnips mashed together *20-*. [unknown]

clare constat *see* PRECEPT

clargy /'klardʒi/ *n* **1** a Protestant clergyman *19- Uls*. **2** the Protestant clergy *19- Uls*. [altered form of Older Scots *clergy*]

clark¹·¹, **clerk**, †**cleirk** /klark, klɛrk/ *n* **1** a keeper of records or accounts; a scribe; a secretary, a junior office worker *la14-*. **2** a cleric; a scholar *la14-e19*. †**clerk-play** a play composed or acted by clerics or scholars *la15-16*. †**Clerk of the Register** the official responsible for the state registers and records *la15-17*; compare LORD CLERK REGISTER. **Clerk of the roup** an auctioneer's clerk *la19, 20- N NE T*. **Clerk of Session** a clerk of court in the Court of Session *la18-*. **Clerk of the Signet** a clerk in attendance on the royal secretary, in charge of the privy signet *la15-19, 20- historical*. **Clerk of Teinds** the clerk of the Court of Teinds, the person in charge of the Teind Office *19-20, 21- historical*. [ME *clerk*, Lat *clēricus*]

clark¹·², **clerk** /klark, klɛrk/ *v* **1** to record in writing *la18-*. **2** to work as an office clerk *la19-*. **3** to write, compose *19, 20- NE*. [see the noun]

clarsach, †**clarschach**, †**clairschow**, †**clersha** /'klarsax/ *n* **1** a Highland or Irish harp *la15-*. **2** a Highland harper *15-e16*. †**clairshocher** a harper; a harp *16-e17*. [Gael *clàrsach*, IrGael *cláirseach*]

†**clarschar** *n* a Highland harper *16-e17*. [Gael *clàrsair*]

clart¹·¹, **clairt**, *Sh Ork* **klurt**, *NE* **clort**, *WC SW* **clert** /klart, klɛrt; *Sh Ork* klʌrt; *NE* klɔrt; *WC SW* klɛrt/ *n* **1** a lump or clot of something unpleasant or sticky *19-*. **2** mire, mud *la19-*. **3** a dirty or untidy person *la19-*. [see the verb]

clart¹·², **clairt**, *Sh Ork* **klurt**, *NE* **clort**, *WC SW* **clert** /klart, klɛrt; *Sh Ork* klʌrt; *NE* klɔrt; *WC SW* klɛrt/ *v* **1** to besmear, dirty; to spread thickly *19-*. **2** to act in a slovenly, dirty way; to work with dirty or sticky substances *20-*. [ME *biclarten* to soil, defile]

clart² /klart/ *v* to clear or scrape with a muck-rake *19- C SW*. [probably conflation of CLAUT¹·² with CLART¹·²]

clarty, **clairty**, *Sh* **clurty**, *NE T* **clorty**, *WC SW Bor* **clerty** /'klarte, 'klɛrte; *Sh* 'klʌrte; *NE* 'klɔrte; *WC SW Bor* 'klɛrte/ *adj* **1** dirty, muddy; sticky *la16-*. **2** *of a painting* daubed, smudgy *20- Sh NE*. Compare CLATTY. [CLART¹·¹ + -IE²]

clary¹·¹, **clairy** /'klare, 'klere/ *n* a mess; a thick daub or liberal smear (of something) *la19- H&I WC SW Uls*. [perhaps related to *glaurie* (GLAUR¹·¹) muddy]

clary¹·², **clairy** /'klare, 'klere/ *v* to besmear *20- H&I WC SW Uls*. [see the noun]

clash¹·¹, †**clasche** /klaʃ/ *n* **1** a resounding impact, a blow; a conflict, a skirmish *16-*. **2** chatter, talk, gossip *la17-*. **3** a mass of something soft or moist *la19-*. **4** a large number or amount *la19-*. **5** a tale, a story *19, 20- NE T EC*. **6** a downpour of rain *19, 20- EC SW*. **7** a gossiping person *20- C SW Bor*. **clashy** given to gossip *20-*. **clash bag** a tell-tale, a gossip *la18-*. **clash pyet** = *clash bag la19-*. [onomatopoeic]

clash¹·², †**clasch** /klaʃ/ *v* **1** to strike or slap; to make a loud noise *16-*. **2** to tell tales; to gossip or chatter *la17-*. **3** to repair by throwing wet mortar into joints and crevices *18-*. **4** to collide with; to fight, conflict with *la18-*. **5** to throw forcefully or noisily (especially anything wet or liquid) *19-*. **6** to slam a door *la19-*. **7** *of rain* to fall with a crash or splash *la19-*. **clasher** a tell-tale, a gossip *la18-*. **clashing** soaking, dripping *la18-*. [see the noun]

clash¹·³ /klaʃ/ *adv* with a crash or bump *la19-*. [see the noun]

clash², †**claische** /klaʃ/ *n* a hollow in a hill or between hills; a cavity, a natural ditch; frequently in place-names *la15-*. [Gael *clais* a furrow, a ditch]

clash-ma-clavers /klaʃmə'klevərz/ *npl* gossip, idle tales *la19-*. [CLASH¹·¹, by analogy with CLISHMACLAVER¹·¹]

clasp *see* CLESP¹·¹, CLESP¹·²

class, **cless**, †**classe** /klas, klɛs/ *n* **1** a social division of people *16-*. **2** (a meeting held for the tuition of) a group of pupils or students *la16-*. **3** a set or category (of things) *18-*. **4** *Presbyterian Church* a presbytery meeting for religious exercises and study *18-e19*. [MFr *classe*, Lat *classis*]

clat¹·¹, *Sh* **klett** /klat; *Sh* klɛt/ *n* **1** a lump, a clot, a (soft) clod of muck or dung *la16-*. **2** a mess, a muddle *la19-*. **3** a messy or dirty person *la20-*. [compare OE *clott*]

clat¹·², *Sh* **klett** /klat; *Sh* klɛt/ *v* **1** to besmear, dirty *19-*. **2** to form (tough) lumps *20- Sh*. [see the noun]

clat *see* CLAUT¹·¹, CLAUT¹·²

clat and clay, †**claut and clay** /klat ənd 'kle/ *n* straw mixed with mud and clay and plastered onto a wooden frame to build a wall *la18-19, 20- Bor*; compare CAT AND CLAY. [perhaps CLAT¹·¹ + CLAY; but compare EModE *clate* a hurdle]

clatch¹·¹, *NE* **clotch** /klatʃ; *NE* klɔtʃ/ *n* **1** a splashing sound *19-*. **2** a wet mass, a clot *19-*. **3** a dirty or untidy person; a large or clumsy person *19-*. **4** a badly built, clumsy structure, one unfit for use *19-*. **clatchy**, †**klaitchie** muddy, sticky *19-*. [onomatopoeic]

clatch¹·², *NE* **clotch** /klatʃ; *NE* klɔtʃ/ *v* **1** to besmear; to spread thickly *19-*. **2** to move with a splashing or squelching sound *20-*. **clatch up 1** to build carelessly or clumsily *19, 20- T WC SW*. **2** to fill or stop up with mud or clay *19, 20- SW* [see the noun]

clatch², †**clotch** /klatʃ/ *v* to sit lazily, lounge *19- SW*. [perhaps back-formation from CLATCHIN]

clatch see CLAUTCH

clatchin /'klatʃin/ *n* a brood of chickens; a clutch of eggs *la19- WC SW Uls*. [palatalized variant of *cleckin* (CLECK¹·²)]

clathe see CLAITH

clathes, clathis see CLAES

clatter¹·¹, **claitter, cletter,** †**kletter** /'klatər, 'kletər, 'klɛtər/ *n* **1** noisy idle chatter; gossip, scandal; rumour *la16-*. **2** a loud noise *la18-*. **3** a chatterer, a gossip *20- NE*. [see the verb]

clatter¹·², **claitter, cletter,** †**clattir** /'klatər, 'kletər, 'klɛtər/ *v* **1** to make a loud noise *16-*. **2** *of birds* to chatter or call *16-*. **3** to gossip, talk scandal *17-*. **clatterer,** †**clatterar** a chatterer; a tale-bearer *la15-19, 20- NE Bor*. **clatter bag, clatter bags** a tell-tale *19, 20- NE EC*. **clatter banes 1** bones which rattle together *18-*. **2** pieces of bone used like castanets *19, 20- Bor*. **clatter traps** odds and ends *19, 20- NE Bor*. [ME *clateren*]

clatty /'klate/ *adj* **1** dirty, muddy *17-*. **2** disagreeable, unscrupulous *la19-*. Compare CLARTY. [CLAT¹·¹ + -IE²]

clauchan see CLACHAN

claucher /'klɔxər/ *v* to move with difficulty; to struggle *19, 20- EC*. [perhaps back-formation from CLAUGHT¹·²]

clauching see CLACHAN

claucht see CLEEK¹·²

claug see CLAAG¹·¹, CLAAG¹·²

claught¹·¹ /klɔxt/ *n* **1** a clutch, a grasp, a grab *la18-19, 20- NE T H&I*. **2** *pl* clutches *19- NE SW*. **3** a handful *19- NE WC*. **4** a blow *la19- N T EC*. [see the verb]

claught¹·² /klɔxt/ *v* to grasp, seize or clutch *18-19, 20- NE T*. [pt or ptp of CLEEK¹·²]

claught see CLEEK¹·²

claum see CLAM²

claumer see CLAMMER

clause /klɔz/ *n* a (part of a) sentence; a stipulation or proviso in a legal document *la14-*. **clause of return** *law* a provision whereby the granter of a right provides that in certain circumstances it may return to themselves or their heirs *18-*. [ME *clause*]

claut¹·¹, **clat** /klɔt, klat/ *n* **1** a claw; a grasping hand *la17-*. **2** a hoe; an implement for scraping dung or dirt *la17-*. **3** a handful; a lump, a scraping *19-*. **4** a clutch, a grasp or hold *la18-19, 20- NE T*. [perhaps related to CLAUGHT]

claut¹·², **clat** /klɔt, klat/ *v* **1** to claw, scratch or tear *la16-*. **2** to rake or scrape; to clean by scraping *la17-*. †**clautings, clattings** street refuse, sweepings *la18-19*. **claut oot** to snatch *19, 20- SW Uls*. [see the noun]

claut and clay see CLAT AND CLAY

clautch, clatch /klɔtʃ, klatʃ/ *n* a sudden grasp, a clutch *la19, 20- EC*. [variant of Eng *clutch*, perhaps influenced by CLAUGHT¹·¹]

clautie-scone /klʌuti'skɔn/ *n* a kind of oat bread or scone *19, 20- NE*. [probably CLAUT¹·¹]

claver¹·¹, *EC* **glaver** /'klevər; *EC* 'glevər/ *n* **1** gossip; foolish talk, nonsense *18-*. **2** a fuss; a murmur or muttering *19- EC Bor*. **3** a foolish, idle talker *20- C SW Bor*. [unknown]

claver¹·², *EC* **glaver** /'klevər; *EC* 'glevər/ *v* to talk idly or foolishly; to gossip *la16-*. **claverer** a prattler, a chatterbox *17-19, 20- Bor*. [unknown]

claver², *NE* **clivver,** †**clever** /'klevər; *NE* 'klıvər/ *n* clover *16-*. [OE *clæfre*]

clavey see KLIVVY

clavie /'klevi/ *n* **1** a tar-barrel burned in the village of Burghead on January 11th (the old New Year's Eve) for good luck *la19-*. **2** a torch carried round the fishing boats on New Year's Eve in Morayshire to ensure a successful season *la17-e18, 20- historical*. [compare Gael *cliabh* a basket, a creel]

claw¹·¹, *Sh* **claa,** †**clow** /klɔ; *Sh* kla/ *n* **1** a claw, the sharp, hooked nail of an animal or bird *16-*. **2** a scratching (of the head) *la18-*. **3** injury or illness; a setback *20- Sh*. **4** a blow *18-19*. [OE *clawu*]

claw¹·², *Sh* **claa,** *WC SW* **clow** /klɔ; *Sh* kla; *WC SW* klʌu/ *v* **1** to scratch or tear with claws *la15-*. **2** to scratch an itch; to scratch the head in astonishment or uncertainty *la15-*. **3** to scrape; to clean out; to empty *la18-*. **4** to beat or strike *17-19, 20- N NE T*. **claw aff** to do something with speed or eagerness *la18- NE*. **claw awa** = *claw aff*. **clawin post** a rubbing post for cattle *la19-*. **claw someone's back** to flatter someone; to ingratiate oneself *16-*. **claw someone's hide** to punish; to beat *la18- NE EC*. **claw someone's skin** = *claw someone's hide*. **claw up someone's mittens** to kill someone *19- EC Bor*. **gar claw whaur it's no yeuky** to give someone a drubbing *19-*. †**gar claw without a youk** = *gar claw whaur it's no yeuky e18*. **never claw an auld man's heid** to fail to live to a ripe old age *19-*. [OE *clāwian*]

claw² /klɔ/ *n* an excited state (of anger or anxiety) *20- NE*. [perhaps extended meaning of Older Scots *claw* to scratch, scrape]

clay, cley, kley /kle, klae/ *n* a fine-grained soil *la14-*. **clayey** a clay marble *20-*. **clay cat** a clump of straw mixed with clay used in the building of a wall *19- T*. **clay davie** an agricultural labourer or navvy *20- NE SW*. [OE *clǣg*]

clayme see CLEME¹·¹

claymore /'klemor/ *n* the Highlanders' large two-edged sword; a basket-hilted single-edged broadsword *18-*. [Gael *claidheamh* a sword + Gael *mór* great]

clean¹·¹ /klin/ *n* the afterbirth of an animal, especially of a cow *19- N NE T Bor*. [see the adj]

clean¹·², †**clene,** †**clenʒe** /klin/ *v* **1** to make clean *16-*. **2** to clear, remove *19, 20- NE T*. **cleanin** the afterbirth of an animal, especially of a cow *19- N NE T Bor*. [see the adj]

clean¹·³, †**clene,** †**cleyn,** †**clane** /klin/ *adj* **1** free from dirt, unsoiled; fresh, innocent *la14-*. **2** uncontaminated, absolute, complete *15-*. **clean lan** land after a root crop has been grown on it *20- Sh Ork NE*. **Clean Pease Strae** a Scottish country dance *19-*. **clean as a leek** cleanly, wholly, completely, thoroughly *18-19, 20- EC*. **the clean tattie** the right person, one who can be trusted or relied on *la19-*; compare *the tattie* (TATTIE). **mak a clean breast wi** to speak one's mind to, have it out with *19, 20- NE T WC*. **mak a clean house** *of servants or farmworkers* to quit or be dismissed all at one time *18-19, 20- NE*. **mak a clean toun o** = *mak a clean house*. [OE *clǣne*]

cleanger see CLENGE

†**clear**¹·¹, **clere** *n* a fair lady *16-e17*. [see the adj]

clear¹·², †**clere,** †**cleir** /klir/ *v* to make clear; to clear away or remove *la15-*. [see the adj]

clear¹·³, †**clere** /klir/ *adj* **1** unclouded, bright *la14-*. **2** transparent, obvious, plain *15-*. **3** unobstructed *la15-*. **the clear stuff** whisky *19-*. **luik wi clear een** to look long and earnestly *19, 20- NE WC*. [ME *cler*]

clear[1,4], †**clere** /klir/ *adv* **1** brightly; with visual clarity *la14*-. **2** distinctly, plainly *15*-. **3** fully, completely *15-16*. [see the adj]

clearance /ˈklirəns/ *n* **1** approval, authorization; the clearing of a ship at Customs *18*-. **2** removal of an obstacle or encumbrance *la19*-. **3** proof; revelation, clarification *la19*, *20- NE*. **4** *pl* a call in a game of marbles requiring removal of an obstacle *20- NE EC*. **5** = *the Clearances 19, 20- historical*. **the Clearances** *pl* a series of mass evictions of tenants by Highland landlords in order to enclose the land and introduce sheep *20- historical*. [CLEAR[1,3], with noun-forming suffix *-ance*]

†**clearin** *n* a scolding, a beating *19*. [perhaps verbal noun from CLEAR[1,2]]

cleathin /ˈkliðən/ *n* the mould-board of a plough *19- N NE EC*. [perhaps CLEED]

cleave[1,1] /kliv/ *n mining* a division of a seam of ironstone *la19- EC*. [see the verb]

cleave[1,2], †**cleve**, †**cleif** /kliv/ *v pt* also †**claif**, *ptp* **cloven**, *NE* **clowen 1** to split; to sever *la14*-. **2** *in ploughing* to split a ridge *la18- NE T EC*. **cleavins**, *Sh* **kleevins**, *Ork* **klivvens**, †**cleavings** the crotch *16*-. **cleave cannles** to make candles of fir roots *la19- NE*. [OE *clēofan*]

cleck[1,1] /klɛk/ *n* idle talk, gossip; insolence *19*-. [see the verb]

cleck[1,2], †**clek** /klɛk/ *v* **1** to hatch *la15*-. **2** to bring forth; to give birth to *16*-. **3** to invent; to conceive *la16*-. **4** to gossip; to chat idly *19, 20- EC*. **cleckin**, **clecking 1** the act of hatching or giving birth *la16*-. **2** a brood, a litter *19*-. [ON *klekja*]

cleck *see* CLACK[1,1], CLACK[1,2], COLLECK

cleckin, **cleckinbrod** *see* CLACKAN

cleed, **claith**, *NE* **cleethe**, †**clethe**, †**cleid**, †**cleith** /klid, kleð; *NE* kliðd/ *v pt, ptp* **clad cled**, **cleed**, †**cleedet**, †**clethit 1** to clothe, dress; to provide with clothes *la14*-. **2** to cover; to fill; to throng *la15*-. **3** *of a tailor* to make (a suit of) clothes for *la19*-. **cled 1** clothed, clad *la14*-. **2** *of a measure or weight* heaped, full *19- SW Bor*. **3** *law* provided with a husband or wife; invested with a right or authority *la15-17*. **cleedin**, **claiding**, **cleathing 1** clothing; a garment, a suit of clothes *la14*-. **2** *mining* a lining of timber, the wood of the box of a hutch *la19, 20- EC*. **3** a covering or facing applied to a surface or framework *16-e17*; compare *cladding* (CLAD). **cledscore**, **cladscore** twenty-one sheep *la18- SW*. [OE *clāþian*, ON *klæða*; compare CLAD]

cleek[1,1], **click**, †**cleke**, †**cleik** /klik, klɪk/ *n* **1** a substantial metal hook for holding, pulling or suspending *15*-. **2** a latch, a catch *18*-. **3** *mining* a hook attaching the hutches to the pulley; the process of raising the coal *19*-. **4** a golf club corresponding to the no. 4 iron *19*-. **5** a crochet-hook *19*-. **6** a salmon gaff *la19*-. **7** a muck-rake *20*-. **8** *pl* leg cramps in horses *la16-19, 20- NE*. **9** an inclination to trickery; a trick *18-19, 20- NE*. **10** the hooked piece of iron used by children for guiding a hoop *20, 21- historical*. **cleekie** *adj* cunning, astute *18-19, 20- NE*. †**cleekie** *n* a walking stick with a crook *19*. **cleekit 1** crocheted *20*-. **2** *of horses* having stringhalt *20- NE T*. **cleek anchor** a small anchor *la19- N SW*. †**cleeksman** *mining* the man who unhooked the baskets of coal at the pithead *la18-19*. [see the verb]

cleek[1,2], **click**, †**cleke**, †**cleik** /klik, klɪk/ *v pt, ptp* **cleekit**, **claucht**, **claught 1** to seize, snatch or steal; to get hold of *la15*-. **2** to link arms; to walk arm in arm with *la18*-. **3** *in dancing* to link arms and whirl round *la18*-. **4** to hook, catch or fasten with a hook *19*-. **5** to ensnare a husband *19- NE T EC*. **cleek in wi** to associate or be intimate with *19, 20- NE WC*. †**cleke on** to put on clothes *16*. **cleek up wi** = *cleek in wi*. [OE *clyccan* to bend, incurve (the fingers)]

cleek *see* CLICK[1,2]

cleem *see* CLEME[1,2]

cleepie *see* KLEEPIE

cleerich *see* CLORACH[1,2]

cleesh[1,1] /kliʃ/ *n* room to manoeuvre, elbow-room *20- T EC*. [unknown]

cleesh[1,2] /kliʃ/ *interj in marbles and bowls* a call made by a player to clear a path for a shot *20- T*. [unknown]

cleesh[2,1] /kliʃ/ *n* a lash with a whip; a blow *20- SW Bor*. **cleisher** a lash, a crack with a whip *20- literary*. [compare CREESH[1,1]]

cleesh[2,2] /kliʃ/ *v* to lash with a whip; to crack a whip *19- Bor*. [see the noun]

cleester[1,1], *Sh* **clester**, *Bor* **claister** /ˈklɪstər; *Sh* ˈklɛstər; *Bor* ˈklɛstər/ *n* a glutinous mass; a mess *la19*-. [see the verb]

cleester[1,2], *Sh* **clester**, *Ork* **klyster**, *N* **claister** /ˈklɪstər; *Sh* ˈklɛstər; *Ork* ˈklʌɪstər; *N* ˈklɛstər/ *v* to smear, bedaub or plaster *19*-. [compare Dan *klistre* to paste]

cleester[2], †**cleister** /ˈklɪstər/ *n* an enema, a clyster *la16-19, 20- Bor*. [MFr *clistere*, Lat *clystēr*, originally Greek]

cleet *see* CLOOT[3]

cleethe *see* CLEED

cleg, *N* **clag**, *NE* **gleg**, *Bor* **gled** /klɛg; *N* klag; *NE* glɛg; *Bor* glɛd/ *n* **1** a gadfly or horsefly, a biting insect of the family Tabanidae *15*-. **2** a missile used by rioters against troops or police, especially during the Radical movement *e19*. [ON *kleggi*]

cleg *see* CLAG[1,1], CLAG[1,2]

cleid *see* CLEED

cleif *see* CLEAVE[1,2]

cleik *see* CLEEK[1,1], CLEEK[1,2]

cleinge *see* CLENGE

cleip *see* CLEPE[1,2]

cleir *see* CLEAR[1,2]

cleirk *see* CLARK[1,1]

cleis *see* CLAES

cleish-clash *see* CLISH-CLASH

cleisher *see* CLEESH[2,1]

cleister *see* CLEESTER[2]

cleit, **clait** /klit, klɛt/ *n* a small dry-stone structure used for drying peat and storing food on St Kilda *19-e20, la20- historical*. [Gael *cleit*]

cleith *see* CLEED

clek *see* CLECK[1,2]

clekane *see* CLACKAN

cleke *see* CLEEK[1,1], CLEEK[1,2]

†**cleket** *n* a catch, bolt or trigger *la14*. [ME *cliket*]

clem[1], **clam** /klɛm, klam/ *v* to stop up a hole; to stick in place *19- Sh N NE EC*. [OE *clǣman* to plaster]

clem[2], †**clam** /klɛm/ *adj* mean, unprincipled *19, 20- Bor*. [unknown]

†**cleme**[1,1], **clame**, **clayme** *n* a claim *la14-e17*. [ME *claim*]

†**cleme**[1,2], **cleem**, **clame** *v* to claim *la14-19*. [ME *claimen*]

clemel *see* KLEMMEL

clench *see* CLINCH[1,1], CLINCH[1,2]

clene *see* CLEAN[1,2], CLEAN[1,3]

†**clenge**, **clange**, **cleinge** *v* **1** to cleanse, make clean *la14-17*. **2** *law* to clear oneself; to declare or prove oneself not guilty *15-17*. **3** *law* to clear by a judicial verdict; to find not guilty *la16-17*. **clengear**, **cleanger**, **clangear** a cleanser of infected people or places; a cleaner *la15-e17*. **clenging**, **clainging 1** cleansing, disinfecting *15-e17*. **2** *law* clearing from a charge *15-e17*. [altered form of OE *clǣnsian*]

clenkett *see* CLINK[2,2]

clenny /ˈklɛne/ *n* the cleansing department *la20- C*. [shortened form of *cleansing department*]

clenȝe see CLEAN¹·²
clep¹·¹, clip /klɛp, klɪp/ *n* **1** a device for seizing or grasping *la15-*. **2** *fishing* a gaff *18-*. **3** *pl* an adjustable iron handle for suspending a pot over the fire *17-19, 20- Bor*. **4** *pl* a wooden instrument for pulling thistles out of standing corn *la18-19, 20- H&I Uls*. [see the verb]
†**clep¹·²**, **clip** *v* to catch hold of; to grapple *la15-19*. [OE *clyppan* embrace]
clep², **klepp** /klɛp/ *n* a lump of something soft; a thick bannock *20- Ork*. [ON *kleppr* a lump]
†**clepe¹·¹** *n* a call, a cry *14-16*. **clepe and call** a legal summons *14-16*. [see the verb]
†**clepe¹·²**, **cleip** *v ptp also* †**yclepit 1** to call, name *15-16*. **2** to cry out to *e16*. Compare CLIP³. [OE *clipian*]
clepped /klɛpt/ *adj of fingers or toes* webbed *la19- WC SW*. [unknown]
clere see CLEAR¹·², CLEAR¹·³, CLEAR¹·⁴
clerk see CLARK¹·¹, CLARK¹·²
clersha see CLARSACH
clert see CLART¹·¹, CLART¹·²
clerty see CLARTY
†**clesch** *v* to verbally abuse *la16*. [compare CLASH¹·², CLISH-CLASH, CLISH]
clesp¹·¹, **claisp**, **clasp**, *T* **glasp** /klɛsp, klesp, klasp; *T* glasp/ *n* something which serves to fasten or secure, a hook or pin *la15-*. [ME *claspe*]
clesp¹·², **claisp**, **clasp**, †**glasp** /klɛsp, klesp, klasp/ *v* **1** to fasten or fit with a hook or pin *la15-*. **2** to join (the hands) together; to embrace *la16-*. [see the noun]
cless see CLASS
clester see CLEESTER¹·¹, CLEESTER¹·²
cleth see CLAITH
clethe see CLEED
clett, klett, †**clet** /klɛt/ *n* a detached rock (in the sea), a low-lying coastal rock; frequently in place-names *18- Sh Ork N*. [ON *klettr* a rock]
cletter see CLATTER¹·¹, CLATTER¹·²
cleuch, cleugh, †**clewch** /klux/ *n pl* †**clewis 1** a gorge, a ravine; frequently in place-names *la12-*. **2** a cliff, a crag; frequently in place-names *15-19*. [ME *clough*]
cleuk¹·¹, **clook,** †**cluke,** †**cluik** /kluk/ *n* **1** a claw *la14-*. **2** a hand *la18-*. **3** *pl* clutches *la19-*. **4** a pulled thread (in a garment) *la20- NE*. [unknown]
cleuk¹·² /kluk/ *v* to claw, scratch; to seize (with the claws) *18- NE*. [unknown]
†**cleuk²**, **cluik** *n* a cloak *la15-19*. [irregular variant of CLOCK³·¹]
cleush see CLOOSE
clev, cliv /klɛv, klɪv/ *v* to make up a fishing line after use *20- N NE WC*. **cliv the line** to protect the tippin and hooks before treating a deep-sea fishing line with a preservative after use *20- N NE*. [unknown]
cleve see CLEAVE¹·²
†**clever** *v* to clamber or scramble; to cling or grip *15-18*. [altered form of ME *claveren*; compare Du *kleveren* to climb, OE *clifer* a claw]
clever see CLAVER², CLIVER¹
†**cleverus** *adj* quick or adroit at grasping *e16*. [compare CLIVER¹]
†**clew** *n* a claw *16-19*. [perhaps related to CLAW¹·¹]
clew see CLOO
clewch, clewis see CLEUCH
cley see CLAY
cleyn see CLEAN¹·³
cliack see CLYACK
clib see CLIP¹

clibber, klibber /ˈklɪbər/ *n* a wooden pack saddle *18- Sh Ork N*. [ON *klyf-beri*, from *klyfa* pack, and *bera* to carry]
click¹·¹ /klɪk/ *n* a boyfriend or girlfriend *la20-*. [CLEEK¹·²]
click¹·², **cleek** /klɪk, klik/ *v* to start a romantic relationship with someone *la20-*. [see the noun]
click see CLEEK¹·¹, CLEEK¹·²
click-clack /ˈklɪk klak/ *n* loquacity *19- NE*. [onomatopoeic]
clicksie, kliksi /ˈklɪksi/ *n* an eagle *la19- Sh*. [perhaps Norw *klikka* to screech (of eagles)]
Clide see CLYDE
clier see CLYRE
clift¹ /klɪft/ *n* a cliff *15-19, 20- H&I WC*. [ME *clift*]
clift² /klɪft/ *n* **1** a cleft, a fissure; a cave *16-*. **2** a plank, a board *la15-19, 20- Sh*. **3** the crotch *16-19, 20- NE*. [ME *clift*, compare OE *geclyft*]
clifty, †**cliftie** /ˈklɪfte, ˈklɪfti/ *adj* clever, active, nimble *la17-19, 20- NE T EC*. [compare MLG *kluftich* clever, MDu *cluchtich* capable]
clim, †**clym** /klɪm/ *v pt* **clam, clamb, climmed,** †**clame,** †**clum,** *ptp also* †**clummyn,** †**clum** to climb *la14-*. [OE *climban*]
climp¹ /klɪmp/ *v* to snatch; to grab hold of *19- T EC*. [compare Eng *clamp* fasten together, clasp]
climp² /klɪmp/ *v* to limp *19- SW Bor Uls*. [perhaps conflation of Eng *limp* with CLINCH¹·²]
clinch¹·¹, **clench** /klɪnʃ, klɛnʃ/ *n* a limp *la18-19, 20- NE*. [unknown]
clinch¹·², **clench,** †**clinsch** /klɪnʃ, klɛnʃ/ *v* to limp; to falter *la15-19, 20- NE*. [unknown]
cline see KLINE
†**cling¹·¹** *n* diarrhoea in sheep *e19*. [see the verb]
cling¹·² /klɪŋ/ *v* **1** to dry up; to shrink *la15-*. **2** to adhere, stick; to hold onto firmly *la16-*. [OE *clingan*]
clink¹·¹ /klɪŋk/ *n* **1** a clinking sound *16-*. **2** money, cash; coins *18-*. **3** a blow *la19-*. **4** a sudden fall *19- N NE*. **the clean clink** the genuine article *la20- Ork*. **in a clink** in a flash, in a moment *la19, 20- NE T*. [see the verb]
clink¹·² /klɪŋk/ *v* **1** to make a clinking sound *15-*. **2** to strike, slap or beat *19-*. **3** to move quickly; to hurry *19-*. **4** to gossip; *of news* to spread *19- NE T C*. **5** to seize or snatch (up) *19, 20- EC*. **6** to compose verses *18-19*. **7** to dump, deposit *e18*.
clinker 1 a coin; money *19-*. **2** a broken piece of rock *19-*. **clink doun 1** to flop, sit or fall suddenly *19-*. **2** to dump, deposit; to set down *19, 20- NE*. [ME *clinken*; compare Norw *klinka*, MDu *klincken*]
clink²·¹ /klɪŋk/ *n* a rivet *19- NE SW*. [see the verb]
clink²·² /klɪŋk/ *v* to rivet, join; to mend *la18-*. **clinker** something astonishing *19-*. **clinkit,** †**clenkett** riveted; joined *la16-*. [OE *beclencan*; compare LG, Du *klinken*, Norw *klinka*]
clink³ /klɪŋk/ *v* to lose weight; to diminish in size *la19- Ork SW*. [probably LG *klinken* contract, wither; compare CLING¹·²]
†**clinkand** *adj* spangled, tinselled *la16*. [MFr *clinquant* showy]
†**clinkard¹·¹**, **clinker** *n* a spangle *la16-e17*. [altered form of CLINKAND, with influence from CLINK¹·²]
†**clinkard¹·²**, **clinker** *adj* spangled, tinselled *e17*. [see the noun]
clinkit /ˈklɪŋkɪt/ *adj* thin, emaciated *la19-*. [ptp of CLINK³]
†**clinkum** *n* a bellman, town-crier; a gravedigger *la18-19*. [CLINK¹·²]
clinkum-clank /ˈklɪŋkəmˈklaŋk/ *n* the ringing sound of a bell *19- literary*. [CLINK¹·²]
clinoo see KLINE
clinsch see CLINCH¹·²
clint¹·¹ /klɪnt/ *n* **1** a cliff, a crag, a precipice *16-19, 20- NE SW Bor*. **2** a rock, a stone *19- SW Bor Uls*. **3** a cleft or crevice (in

rocks) *la18-19, 20- SW.* **4** *curling* a rough stone thrown first as being likely to keep its place on the ice *la18-19, 20- WC.*
clinty stony, rocky *16-.* [ME *clint*; compare Dan, Swed *klint* a steep cliff]
clint[1.2] /klɪnt/ *v of a sheep* to become stranded on a ledge of rock *20- SW Bor.* [see the noun]
clip[1], *SW Uls* **clib** /klɪp; *SW Uls* klɪb/ *n* **1** a colt; a young mare *la19- NE Uls.* **2** a cheeky girl *la19- NE SW.* **3** a mischievous child *la19- Uls.* [Gael *cliobag* a filly, IrGael *cliobóg* a filly, a colt]
clip[2] /klɪp/ *v* **1** to snip, cut *la15-.* **2** to trim hair; to shear sheep *16-.* **3** to destroy false coin by cutting it in pieces *la15-16.* †**clip hous** a place where false coin was destroyed *la16.* †**clipping-hous** = *clip hous.* **in clipping time** at the right moment, in the nick of time *19, 20- NE.* [ON *klippa*]
†**clip**[3] *v* to call, name *la15-16.* Compare CLEPE[1.2]. [OE *clipian*]
clip *see* CLEP[1.1], CLEP[1.2]
clipe *see* CLYPE[1.1], CLYPE[1.2]
clippie[1.1] /ˈklɪpi/ *n* a cheeky, sharp-tongued girl *19-.* [probably CLIP[1], with influence from CLIP[2]; compare *a tongue that wad clip cloots* (CLOOT[1.1])]
clippie[1.2] /ˈklɪpi/ *adj* cheeky, cutting *la19-.* [see the noun]
clipshear, **clipsher** /ˈklɪpʃɪr, ˈklɪpʃər/ *n* an earwig *la19- C.* [from the pincer-like appendages]
clis-clas *see* CLISH-CLASH
clish /klɪʃ/ *v* to repeat gossip *19- NE EC.* [compare CLASH[1.2], CLISH-CLASH, CLESCH]
clish-clash, **cleish-clash**, †**clis-clas** /ˈklɪʃklaʃ, ˈkliʃklaʃ/ *n* idle talk, gossip; chatter *la17- NE H&I C SW.* [compare CLASH[1.1], CLISH, CLESCH]
clishmaclash /ˈklɪʃməklaʃ/ *n* **1** idle talk, gossip *la19- C.* **2** a chatterbox *la19- EC.* [altered form of CLISH-CLASH]
clishmaclaver[1.1] /ˈklɪʃməklevər/ *n* **1** idle talk, gossip; prattle *18-.* **2** a gossip; a talkative busybody *19-.* [CLISH + CLAVER[1.1]]
clishmaclaver[1.2] /ˈklɪʃməklevər/ *v* to gossip, chatter *19-.* [see the noun]
clit *see* CLOOT[3]
clitter *see* CLOITER[1.1], CLOITER[1.2]
clitter-clatter[1.1] /ˈklɪtərklatər/ *n* **1** a rattling, clattering noise; a continuous sharp crackle *16-.* **2** noisy animated talk, senseless chatter *16-.* [reduplicative compound from CLATTER[1.1]]
clitter-clatter[1.2] /ˈklɪtərklatər/ *v* **1** to clatter, rattle *19-.* **2** to talk endlessly, chatter *19-.* [see the noun]
cliv, *Sh Ork* **klov**, *N* **clive**, †**cluif**, †**clufe** /klɪv; *Sh Ork* klov; *N* klaev/ *n* **1** a (cloven) hoof; a paw *16-19, 20- Sh Ork N.* **2** *humorous* a human hand or foot *la19- Sh Ork N.* [ON *klauf*, Dan *klov*]
cliv *see* CLEV
cliver[1], **clivver**, **kliver**, **clever**, *H&I* **cluvver** /ˈklɪvər, ˈklevər; *H&I* ˈklʌvər/ *adj* **1** intelligent; skilful *la17-.* **2** swift, speedy, nimble *la18-.* **3** handsome, well-made *19-.* **4** good, nice *la19-.* **5** generous, liberal, ample *20- Uls.* **cleverality** cleverness *19- C Bor.* [unknown; compare OE *clifer* a claw]
cliver[2] /ˈklɪvər/ *n* a tether for a cow *18-19, 20- NE.* [perhaps related to ON *klofi* a cleft implement; compare CLIVVIE]
clivgeng *see* CLOWGANG
clivoo *see* KLIVVY
clivver *see* CLAVER[2], CLIVER[1]
clivvie /ˈklɪvi/ *n* a cleft *19- Ork NE.* [perhaps ON *klyfja* to cleave, or Eng *cleave*]
cloak, †**cloke** /klok/ *n* a clock *16-.* [variant of Eng *clock*]
cloak *see* CLOCK[1.1], CLOCK[1.2]
cloath *see* CLAITH
clobber *see* CLABBER
cloch /klɔx/ *v* to cough *19, 20- N.* [onomatopoeic]

†**clocharet** *n* the wheatear *Oenanthe oenanthe* or the stonechat *Saxicola torquata la18-19.* [compare Gael *clacharan*]
clocher[1.1] /ˈklɔxər/ *n* **1** bronchial mucus; phlegm *19-.* **2** a rough or wheezing cough *19-.* [onomatopoeic]
clocher[1.2] /ˈklɔxər/ *v* to cough, expectorate *19-.* [see the noun]
clock[1.1], **cloak** /klɔk, klok/ *n* the clucking sound made by a broody hen *19-.* [see the verb]
clock[1.2], **cloak**, *N* **clook**, †**clok** /klɔk, klok; *N* kluk/ *v* **1** to cluck *16-.* **2** *of a bird* to sit on or hatch eggs *18-.* **3** to sit idly for a long time *19- N NE SW Bor.* **4** to cower; to hunch the shoulders *20- N.* **clocker** a broody hen *19-.* **clockin 1** the noise made by a hen *19-.* **2** the desire to brood; *of people* the desire to marry *19-.* **3** freedom from disturbance, quiet *20- NE.* **clocking hen 1** a broody hen *la18-.* **2** a woman past the age of childbearing *19, 20- EC SW.* **3** a woman during the time of bearing and rearing a family *20- NE EC SW.* **4** a sum of money earning interest *20- NE EC SW.* **clockin-time** *of women* a time of fertility; *of birds* hatching time *la18-19, 20- NE.* **clocks-midder**, **clocksmither** a hen with chickens *20- Sh Ork.* [OE *cloccian*]
clock[2], **clok**, *NE* **cloke** /klɔk; *NE* klok/ *n* a beetle *16-.* **clocker** a large beetle; a cockroach *Blatta orientalis la19- EC Bor.* **clock bee** a flying beetle *19, 20- NE WC.* **clok leddy** the ladybird *Coccinella septempunctata 19, 20- EC Bor.* [unknown; compare Swed *klocka* a beetle]
clock[3.1], †**clok** /klɔk/ *n* a cloak *la14-19, 20 NE T EC.* †**clock bag**, **clokbag** a portmanteau *17-19.* [ME *cloke*]
†**clock**[3.2] *v* to cloak, cover up *la16-17.* [see the noun]
clod[1.1] /klɔd/ *n* **1** a lump (of earth); a sod *16-.* **2** a small (hard) peat *20- Sh N NE.* **3** a type of flat (wheaten) loaf *la18-19, 20- EC.* **4** a cast or throw *la17.* †**clod coal** strong homogeneous coal *la18-19.* [variant of ME *clot*]
clod[1.2] /klɔd/ *v* **1** to pelt with missiles *16-.* **2** to throw (forcibly) *la18-.* **3** to free land from clods or stones *18-19, 20- H&I.* **4** to pile up (peats or turnips) *la19- SW.* [see the noun]
cloddach *see* CLADDACH
clof *see* CLOIF
cloff[1], **cloft**, †**claff** /klɔf, klɔft/ *n* **1** a cleft between hills *19- EC Bor.* **2** a cleft of branches in a tree *la18-19, 20- Bor.* **3** the cleft of the crotch *16.* [ON *klof* the cleft between the legs, compare ON *klofi* a cleft or rift in a hill]
†**cloff**[2], **clove** *n* the apparatus which separates the bridgeheads in a mill *la16-e19.* [unknown; compare ON *klyfja* to cleave]
clog, *Sh* **klug** /klɔg; *Sh* klʌg/ *n* **1** a log or block of wood *16-.* **2** a clog, a wooden shoe *la17-.* **cloggie** a log for the fire *19- NE T.* [unknown]
clogang *see* CLOWGANG
†**clogbag**, **clogbog** *n* a saddle-bag *16-e19.* [perhaps a variant form of *clock bag* (CLOCK[3.1])]
†**cloif**, **clof** *n* a certain weight of iron *15-e17.* [unknown]
cloit[1.1], **clyte** /klɔɪt, klʌɪt/ *n* a sudden heavy fall *19-.* [unknown]
cloit[1.2], **clyte** /klɔɪt, klʌɪt/ *v* **1** to fall heavily or suddenly *18-.* **2** to sit down suddenly *19-.* **clyter** to fall, tumble *la19- NE.* [unknown]
cloit[1.3], **clyte** /klɔɪt, klʌɪt/ *adv* heavily, suddenly *la19-.* [unknown]
cloit[2.1], **clyte**, †**gloit** /klɔɪt, klʌɪt/ *n* a dull, heavy, inactive person *19-.* [compare Flem *kluite*]
cloit[2.2], **gloit** /klɔɪt, glɔɪt/ *adj* soft, delicate *20- SW.* [see the noun]
cloiter[1.1], **clowter**, **clitter** /ˈklɔɪtər, ˈklʌutər, ˈklɪtər/ *n* **1** a disgusting, wet or sticky mass *la19-.* **2** a badly built heap, a precarious pile *20- Ork Uls.* **cloitery**, **clytrie** wet,

disagreeable, dirty *la18-*. [compare MDu *clāteren* to dirty, MLG *kladeren*]

cloiter¹·², **clowter, clyter, clitter** /ˈklɔɪtər, ˈklʌutər, ˈklʌɪtər, ˈklɪtər/ *v* **1** to be engaged in dirty or wet work *19-*. **2** to work in a dirty, disgusting way; to splash about *19- N NE T EC*. **3** to walk in a slovenly way, especially in wet or muddy conditions *la19- N NE T Bor*. **4** to snuffle or sneeze; to cough or wheeze *la20- EC*. [see the noun]

cloith *see* CLAITH

clok *see* CLOCK¹·², CLOCK², CLOCK³·¹

cloke *see* CLOAK, CLOCK²

clomph, clumph /klɔmf, klʌmf/ *v* to walk heavily *19- C SW Bor*. [probably altered form of Eng *clump*]

cloo, clue, clew, †**clow** /klu/ *n* **1** a ball of wool, yarn or thread *la16-19, 20- Sh NE*. **2** a ball of straw-rope used in thatching stacks *la18- Ork NE*. [OE *cliwen*]

clood¹·¹, **clud, cloud,** †**clude** /klud, klʌd, klʌud/ *n* water vapour in the sky, a cloud; a mass of smoke or dust *la14-*. †**clud of nicht** darkness of night *16-17*. †**under cloud of night, under clud of nicht** under cover of darkness *16-e19*. [OE *clūd* a hill, a rock]

clood¹·², **clud, cloud** /klud, klʌd, klʌud/ *v* to become cloudy; to obscure *19-*. [see the noun]

clood² /klud/ *v* to cart in small loads *20- NE*. [unknown]

clooder *see* CLUTHER

clook *see* CLEUK¹·¹, CLOCK¹·²

cloor¹·¹, **kloor** /klur, ˈkluər/ *n* a cat's claws; a scratch (made by claws) *la19- Sh Ork*. [ON *klóra* to scratch like a cat]

cloor¹·², **kluir** /klur, ˈkluər/ *v* to scratch (with claws); to tear by scratching *la19- Sh Ork*. [see the noun]

cloor *see* CLOUR¹·¹, CLOUR¹·²

cloose, cluse, †**clous,** †**cleush** /klus/ *n* a sluice *la15-*. [OE *clūse* a confine, an enclosure, a cell]

clooster, clooshter /ˈklustər, ˈkluʃtər/ *n* a mass of something wet or sticky; mud or muck *19- NE SW* [compare CLEESTER¹·¹]

cloot¹·¹, **clout,** †**clowt** /klut, klʌut/ *n* **1** a piece of cloth, a rag; a dishcloth, a duster *la14-*. **2** a cloth patch on clothes or fabric *16-*. **3** a patch of metal on pans or tools *18-*. **4** *pl* derogatory clothes *la18-*. **5** a baby's nappy *19-*. **6** *archery* a (white cloth) target; a successful hit on the target *19-*. **7** *pl* bedclothes *la20- NE T*. **8** the sail of a boat *20- Ork*. **9** a piece of cloth used as a pin-cushion *16-17*. **10** a small piece of land *la15-17*. **a tongue that wad clip cloots** a person with a sharp tongue *la19-*. [OE *clūt*]

cloot¹·², **clout,** †**clowt** /klut, klʌut/ *v* **1** to patch; to mend fabric or clothes *la15-*. **2** to repair pots and pans; to mend or reinforce footwear *la16-*. †**clouter** a patcher, a cobbler *16-19*. [ME *clouten*]

cloot²·¹, **clout** /klut, klʌut/ *n* a blow, a slap *16-*. [see the verb]

cloot²·², **clout** /klut, klʌut/ *v* to strike, slap *la18-*. [extended sense of CLOOT¹·²]

cloot³, **cluit,** *H&I* **cleet,** *WC SW* **clit** /klut; *H&I* klit; *WC SW* klɪt/ *n* **1** one of the divisions in the hoof of cloven-footed animals; the whole hoof *la18-*. **2** a person's foot *la19- EC Bor*. **3** a cloven-footed animal *18, 20- Uls*. [compare CLAUT¹·¹]

clootie¹, †**clouty** /ˈkluti/ *adj* **1** made of strips of cloth or rags *la19-*. **2** *of food* cooked in a cloth *la19-*. **Clootie City** a nickname for Dundee *la20-*. **clootie dumpling, cloutie dumpling** a rich (fruit) pudding, wrapped in a cloth and boiled *la19-*. **clootie rug** a rug made from rags *20- NE*. **clootie well** a wishing well where strips of cloth are tied to the surrounding trees in the belief that this will cure illness *20-*. [CLOOT¹·¹ + -IE²]

clootie²·¹ /ˈkluti/ *n* a left-handed person *la19- NE Uls*. [unknown]

clootie²·² /ˈkluti/ *adj* left-handed; clumsy *20- SW Uls*. [unknown]

clootie³·¹ /ˈkluti/ *n* a name for the devil *la18-*. **Auld Clootie** *see* AULD¹·² [see the adj]

clootie³·² /ˈkluti/ *adj* cloven, split; cloven-hoofed *19-*. [CLOOT³ + -IE²]

Cloots /kluts/ *n* a name for the devil *19-*. **Auld Cloots** *see* AULD¹·² [CLOOT³]

clorach¹·¹ /ˈklɔrəx/ *n* a disgusting mass; a dirty or sticky mess *20- NE T EC SW*. [unknown]

clorach¹·², *NE* **cleerich** /ˈklɔrəx; *NE* ˈklirəx/ *v* **1** to work in a slovenly way *la19- NE T*. **2** to clear the throat noisily; to hawk or spit *20- NE T*. **3** to sit lazily by the fire as if unwell *la19- NE*. [unknown]

clort *see* CLART¹·¹, CLART¹·²

clorty *see* CLARTY

close¹, †**clos,** †**cloys** /kloz/ *v* *ptp* †**yclos 1** to shut; to enclose or cover; to conclude *la14-*. **2** to suffer from congestion of the respiratory system *la19- NE T EC*. **closer** an argument which silences a person; a person who has the last word *19, 20- NE*. **closing** respiratory congestion; croup *la18-19, 20- NE*. **closed-in bed** an enclosed bed, a box-bed *19- NE T*. [OE *clýsan*]

close²·¹, *Sh Ork N NE* **closs,** †**closse,** †**clos** /klos; *Sh Ork N NE* klɔs/ *n* **1** an enclosure (adjacent to a building); a courtyard *la15-*. **2** a passageway between buildings, an alley; a narrow lane with houses on each side *16-*. **3** a farmyard, the yard round which the farm buildings are arranged *18-*. **4** the passageway giving access to a common stair; the communal area in a block of flats *la19-*. **5** a tenement building *la20-*. **close mouth, close mooth** the entrance to a tenement *19-*. **in the wrang close** in an irretrievable predicament, in grievous error *18-19, 20- NE WC*. **it's a' up a closie** it is a hopeless position, it is a poor outlook *20- NE T C*. [see the adj]

close²·², †**clos,** †**cloys,** †**closse** /klos/ *adj* **1** shut up, shut away; sealed, closed, secret *la15-*. **2** near, intimate; close-fitting *16-*. **3** *of weather* sultry, muggy *17-*. **4** *of work* constant, unremitting *la18-*. **close bed** an enclosed bed, a box-bed *la16-*. **close cairt 1** a farm cart with fixed shafts *la18-19, 20- EC Bor*. **2** an enclosed cart *la15-16*. **close cap** an older or married woman's head-dress *19-*. **close eared** *of a cap* fitting snugly round the ears *19, 20- NE T EC*. **close fish** a (smoked) fish that has been gutted but not fully split open *la19-*. **close fit** with feet close together *20- NE T Bor*. **close luggit** *of a cap* fitting snugly round the ears *19, 20- NE T EC*. **close weather** a heavy snowfall *la18-19, 20- NE*. [MFr *clos*, Lat *clausum*]

close²·³, †**clos** /klos/ *adv* **1** closely; close by *15-*. **2** completely; constantly *la16-*. [see the adj]

close coort /klos ˈkurt/ *n* the square yard round which a farm steading is built *20- NE T*. [CLOSE²·² + COORT¹·¹]

closhach, clossach /ˈklɔʃəx, ˈklɔsəx/ *n* **1** a corpse; a carcass (of a fowl) *19- NE*. **2** a mass of something (semi-liquid) *la19- NE*. **3** a hoard of money *la19- NE*. **the haill clossach** the whole quantity or number *la19- NE*. [Gael *closach* a carcase]

closs *see* CLOSE²·¹

closse *see* CLOSE²·¹, CLOSE²·²

clotch *see* CLATCH¹·¹, CLATCH¹·², CLATCH²

cloth *see* CLAITH

clothes *see* CLAES

clottert, †**clotter'd** /ˈklɔtərt/ *adj* clotted, congealed, caked *19-*. [ptp of frequentative of Eng *clot*]

cloud *see* CLOOD¹·¹, CLOOD¹·²

cloupie /ˈklupi/ *n* a walking stick with a curved handle *19- SW*. [LG *kluppel*, MDu *cluppel* a club]

clour[1.1], **cloor** /klur/ *n* **1** a lump or swelling caused by a blow *16*-. **2** a blow, a knock *la18*-. **3** a dent or hollow (in metal) *19*-. [unknown; compare CLOOR[1.1]]

clour[1.2], **cloor**, †**clowr** /klur/ *v* **1** to deal a blow to; to batter or thump; to dent, damage or disfigure *la16*-. **2** to dress or chisel stone *la19*-. **clourer**, **cloorer**, **clurer 1** a stone-dressing chisel *la19*-. **2** a mason's hammer *la19*- *N T*. [unknown; compare CLOOR[1.2]]

clous *see* CLOOSE

cloush, **klush** /klʌʃ, klʌʃ/ *n* a lump; an ungainly, clumsy person *la19*- *Sh N*. **clushit** very clumsy *la20*- *Sh*. **klushy** clumsy *20*- *Sh*. [compare Norw *kluns* a lump, a clod]

clout *see* CLOOT[1.1], CLOOT[1.2], CLOOT[2.1], CLOOT[2.2]

clouty *see* CLOOTIE[1]

clove[1.1] /klov/ *n* an instrument used in the preparation of flax *la19*- *Uls*. [see the verb]

†**clove**[1.2] *v* to break or split (flax) fibres before heckling *la18-19*. [altered form of Scots *cleave*, with influence from ptp *cloven*]

clove *see* CLOFF[2]

clow[1], **clowe** /klʌu/ *n* a clove, the dried flower-bud of *Syzygium aromaticum la15*- *Sh NE T EC*. **clow gillie flower** the carnation or clove pink *Dianthus caryophyllus 18-e19*. [MFr *clou (de girofle)*]

clow[2] /klʌu/ *n* a (young) sea-gull *la20*- *EC*. [unknown]

clow[3], **klow** /klʌu/ *n* a cloven hoof, a foot *la19*- *Ork*. [altered form of *cluif* (CLIV)]

clow *see* CLAW[1.1], CLAW[1.2], CLOO

clowder *see* CLUTHER

clowen *see* CLEAVE[1.2]

clowgang, **clogang**, **clivgeng**, **klovgeng** /ˈklʌugaŋ, ˈklogaŋ, ˈklɪvgɛŋ, ˈklɒvgɛŋ/ *n* **1** pasture land; a portion of pasture to which sheep or cattle have become attached; home-ground or native environment *17*- *Sh Ork*. **2** (the sound of) a crowd of moving people or animals, a procession *la19*- *Sh*. **3** a herd of (driven) cows or sheep *20*- *Ork*. [ON *klaufagangr* the tramp of cattle]

clowr *see* CLOUR[1.2]

clowt *see* CLOOT[1.1], CLOOT[1.2]

clowter *see* CLOITER[1.1], CLOITER[1.2]

cloys *see* CLOSE[2.2]

†**club** *n* a member of a trade, especially shoemaking, who has not gone through a full or formal apprenticeship *18-e19*. [compare the Eng phrase *prentices and clubs*, the rallying cry of London apprentices]

clud *see* CLOOD[1.1], CLOOD[1.2]

clude *see* CLOOD[1.1]

cludgie /ˈklʌdʒi/ *n* a lavatory *la20*- *T C*. [unknown]

clue *see* CLOO

clufe *see* CLIV

cluff[1.1] /klʌf/ *n* a cuff or slap *la19*- *EC SW Bor*. [probably onomatopoeic]

cluff[1.2] /klʌf/ *v* to cuff; to thrash *19*- *SW Bor*. [see the noun]

cluif *see* CLIV

cluik *see* CLEUK[1.1], CLEUK[2]

cluit *see* CLOOT[3]

cluke *see* CLEUK[1.1]

clum, **clummyn** *see* CLIM

clump /klʌmp/ *n* **1** a compact mass or heap *la18*-. **2** a cluster of trees, a piece of woodland *la18*-. **3** a heavy, inactive person *19, 20*- *NE*. [compare Ger *Klumpen*, MLG *klumpe*, MDu *clompe*, OE *clympre* a lump, a metal of metal]

clumper *see* CLAMP[2.2], KLUMPER

clumph *see* CLOMPH

clumpse, *Ork* **klimse** /klʌmps; *Ork* klɪms/ *v* **1** to be parched with thirst *19*- *Sh Ork*. **2** to silence, render speechless *la19*- *Sh*. [OE *clumian* to remain silent, Norw *klumse* to root to the spot by means of witchcraft; to render speechless]

clung /klʌŋ/ *adj* **1** dried up, contracted, shrivelled; adhering *16*-. **2** shrunken with hunger, hungry *la18-19, 20*- *NE EC*. [ptp of CLING[1.2]]

clunk[1.1], *Ork N* **glunk** /klʌŋk; *Ork N* glʌŋk/ *n* **1** a hollow, gurgling sound made by liquid in motion *19*-. **2** a dull, thudding sound; a plopping or popping sound *19*-. **3** a gulp of liquid *19, 20*- *Sh*. [onomatopoeic; compare Norw *klunk*]

clunk[1.2], **klunk**, *Ork N* **glunk** /klʌŋk; *Ork N* glʌŋk/ *v* **1** *of pouring liquid* to make a hollow gurgling sound *la18*-. **2** to make a dull, thudding sound *19*-. **3** to gulp liquid quickly *20*- *Sh Ork N NE T*. [onomatopoeic; compare Swed *klunka*]

clunk[2] /klʌŋk/ *v* to walk heavily *20*-. [perhaps onomatopoeic]

clunk[3] /klʌŋk/ *n* a blow, a thump *20*- *NE*. [extended sense of CLUNK[1.1] from the sound to the action producing it]

clunkart /ˈklʌŋkərt/ *n* a very large piece or lump; a dumpy person *la19*- *NE T*. [altered form of CLUNKER[1]]

clunker[1] /ˈklʌŋkər/ *n* a lump, a bump *la18*- *T*. [probably LG *klunker* a lump of dirt]

clunker[2] /ˈklʌŋkər/ *n* a draught, a drink *20*- *Sh*. [CLUNK[1.1], with intensive suffix]

clunkertonie /ˈklʌŋkərˌtoni/ *n* a jellyfish *la19*- *Ork N*. [compare Dan *klynger-torn* a bramble]

clurer *see* CLOUR[1.2]

clurty *see* CLARTY

cluse *see* CLOOSE

clushit *see* CLOUSH

cluther, **clowder**, †**clooder** /ˈklʌθər, ˈklʌðər, ˈklʌudər/ *n* a heap, a close group, a (disordered) crowd *la18*- *WC SW*. [perhaps altered form of Eng *clutter*]

clyack, **cliack**, **gliack** /ˈklaɛək, ˈglaɛək/ *n* **1** the last sheaf of corn of the harvest dressed to represent a girl or decorated with ribbons *la18*- *NE*. **2** the end of harvest *la18*- *NE*. **3** the harvest-home supper *19*- *NE*. [Gael *caileag* a girl; compare MAIDEN]

clyager *see* CLAG[1.2]

Clyde, †**Clyd**, †**Clide** /klʌɪd/ *n* the name of a river which flows though Glasgow *14*-. **Clydebuilt** built in the Clydeside shipyards; solid, well-constructed *19*-. **Clydesdale** a heavy draught horse (originally bred near the River Clyde) *19*-. **Clydesider 1** a person who lives near the River Clyde *20*-. **2** a (hardline) Labour politician (representing Glasgow in Westminster) *20*-. **he could fall into the Clyde and come up wi a salmon** he is a very lucky person *la20*-. **I didn't come up the Clyde in a banana boat** I'm not stupid *la20*-. [Old Welsh *Clūt*, *Clūd*]

clym *see* CLIM

clype[1.1], **clipe**, †**klype** /klʌɪp/ *n* **1** a gossip; an idle tale; a lie *la18*-. **2** a tell-tale *la19*-. **3** *in rick-building* the person who passes hay or sheaves from the forker to the builder *20*- *SW*. **clypach** a gossip *la19*- *NE*. **clypie** talkative, tale-telling *19*- *NE C*. [see the verb]

clype[1.2], **clipe** /klʌɪp/ *v* **1** to tell tales; to inform on someone *20*-. **2** to report or relate information *19, 20*- *NE H&I SW Bor*. **3** to be talkative; to gossip *19, 20*- *NE SW*. **clypach** to gossip *la19*- *NE*. **clype clash** a tale-bearer *la19, 20*- *SW Uls*. [OE *clipian* to call, name]

clype[2.1] /klʌɪp/ *n* **1** a big, uncouth, awkward or ugly person *la15-19, 20*- *NE T SW*. **2** a mass of something wet *la19*- *NE T*. **3** a large piece (of something) *la19*- *Uls*. **clypach** a mess, a wet mass *la19*- *NE*. [unknown]

clype[2.2] /klʌɪp/ *v* to work or walk in a slovenly way *la19*- *NE*. [unknown]

clype[3.1] /klʌɪp/ *n* a heavy, noisy fall *19*- *NE*. **clypach** a heavy fall *19*- *NE SW*. [unknown]

clype³·² /klʌɪp/ *v* to fall *19- NE*. **clypach** to fall flat (with a crash) *la19- NE*. [unknown]
clype⁴ /klʌɪp/ *n* a blow *la19-*. [unknown; compare Eng *clip* a slap]
clype⁵·¹ /klʌɪp/ *n* a scratch *20- N*. [compare Norw *klype* a pinch]
clype⁵·² /klʌɪp/ *v* to scratch, claw or scrape *20- N*. [compare Icel *klypa* to pinch]
clyre, clier /klaer/ *n* **1** a gland in meat; a glandular swelling or sore *19-*. **2** a source of grievance *19-*. **3** *pl* a disease in cattle similar to glanders *19-*. **clier't**, †**clyred** affected with tumours or sores *la17-19, 20- Bor*. [MDu *cliere* a gland]
clytach¹·¹ /'klʌɪtəx/ *n* talk, chatter *la18- literary*. [unknown]
clytach¹·² /'klʌɪtəx/ *v* to talk, chatter *19- NE T*. [unknown]
clyte¹·¹ /klʌɪt/ *n* a sharp blow *20- NE Bor*. [unknown; compare CLOIT¹·¹, CLOOT²·¹]
clyte¹·² /klʌɪt/ *v* to strike; to rap the knuckles against a hard object *20- NE WC*. [unknown]
clyte *see* CLOIT¹·¹, CLOIT¹·², CLOIT¹·³, CLOIT²·¹
clyter *see* CLOITER¹·²
co¹ /ko/ *n* a sea cave *19- WC SW*. [reduced form of COVE¹·¹]
co *see* QUO
Co² /ko/ *n* a Co-operative store *la20-*. [reduced form of CO-OPERATIVE]
coach, †**coche**, †**cotch** /kotʃ/ *n* **1** a carriage; a bus *la16-*. **2** a baby's pram *la19- NE T*. [MFr *coche*, from Magyar *kocsi* from Kocs]
coachbell, *WC Bor* **scodgebell** /'kotʃbəl; *WC Bor* 'skɔdʒbəl/ *n* the earwig *Forficula auricularia 19-*. [altered form of Eng *twitch-ballock, twitch-bell*]
coad *see* COD¹
coaf¹·¹, **coaff**, *N* **coch**, †**coche**, †**cogh** /kof; *N* kɔx, kox/ *n* a cough *la16-*. †**coghle** to cough weakly; to gasp *19*. [see the verb]
coaf¹·², **coaff** /kof/ *v* to cough *la20-*. [ME *coughen*]
coaffee *see* COFFEE
coag, koog /kog, kug/ *v* to peer (cautiously) *la19- Sh*. [ON *kaga* to pry]
coag *see* COG¹·¹, COG²·¹
coal, *Sh* **coll**, *NE* **quile**, *NE* **cwyle**, †**cole**, †**coil** /kol; *Sh* kɔl; *NE* kwʌɪl/ *n* **1** a combustible black rock; an ember, a cinder; charcoal *la14-*. **2** a coal mine *16-17*. †**coal bearer** the woman who carried the coal on her back from the workings to the surface *17-e19*. **coal and candle-light** the long-tailed duck *Clangula hyemalis la19- Ork EC*. **col-cannel-week** = *coal and candle-light 20- EC*. **coal coom** coal dust *la19-*. †**collever** a horse used for carrying coal *e16*. **coal fauld** a coal yard; a recess or cellar for keeping coal *18-19, 20- EC*. **coal grieve**, †**coall greive** the manager of a coal mine *17-19, 20- historical*. **coal gum** coal dust *la19, 20- EC*. **coal heuch, coal heugh**, †**cole heuch**, †**coil heuch** a coal-working or pit *15-19, 20- historical*. **coal hewer**, †**coilhewar** a coal miner *la16-*. **coal hill** ground occupied at a pit-head for colliery purposes *la17-*. †**coal hood, colehood** any of several species of black-headed birds *18-19*. **coal mosie**, †**coal mozey** in the Clackmannanshire coalfield a coal of inferior quality found in narrow, seams of variable thickness, frequently not worth working *la18- EC*. **coal neuk** a recess for keeping coal; a coal-cellar *la17-19, 20- NE*. **coal peat** a peat which has almost acquired the consistency of coal *20- Ork*. **coal pit**, †**coil pit** a coal-working or pit *16-*. †**colpot, coillpot** = *coal pit 16-17*. **coal press** a cupboard for storing coal *19-*. **coal ree** a store from which coal is sold *18-*. **coal wheecher** a coal-carter, coalman *la19- EC*. **bring oot ower the coals** to haul over the coals *18-*. **tak ower the coals** = *bring oot ower the coals*. [OE *col*]

coalie buckie, colly buckie /'kole 'bʌki, 'kɔle 'bʌki/ *n* a piggy-back ride *la20- NE H&I EC*. [altered form of Eng *coalback* to carry coals on one's back]
coallege *see* COLLEGE
coamic¹·¹, **comic** /'komɪk, 'kɔmɪk/ *n* **1** a comedian *la19-*. **2** a children's periodical featuring picture stories *20-*. [see the adj]
coamic¹·², **comic**, †**comick** /'komɪk, 'kɔmɪk/ *adj* amusing, funny; comical *18-*. [Lat *cōmicus*]
coammon *see* COMMON¹·³
coarn *see* CORN¹·¹, CURN¹
coarner, corner /'kornər, 'kɔrnər/ *n* a corner, an edge; a corner stone; a street-corner *la15-*. [ME *corner*]
coarse *see* COORSE¹
coarum *see* QUORUM
coast¹, †**cost** /kost/ *n* **1** (the land along) the sea coast; the shoreline *la14-*. **2** the trunk, the bodily girth or frame *la15-19, 20- Bor*. **coast side** the sea coast *15-*. **coast-wester** a nickname for a person from the Western Isles *la20- N H&I*. [ME *coste*, Lat *costa* a rib, a flank]
coast²·¹, **cost**, †**coist** /kost, kɔst/ *n* expense, cost; outlay, expenditure *la14-*. [ME *cost*]
coast²·², **cost**, †**coist** /kost, kɔst/ *v* to be priced at; to cause the loss of *la15-*. [ME *costen*]
coat, cot, *NE* **cwite**, *NE* **quite**, †**coit**, †**cote**, †**cott** /kot, kɔt; *NE* kwʌɪt/ *n* **1** an outer garment, a coat *la15-*. **2** a woman's or child's petticoat; a skirt *19-*. **gae coats kilted** = *hae yer coat kilted*. **hae yer coat kilted** to be pregnant *19-, 20- C*. **on yer ain coat-tail, on yer ain quite-tail** forced to make or pay your own way *19, 20- NE*. [OFr *cote*]
cob¹·¹, †**keb** /kɔb/ *n* **1** a blow *19, 20- T*. **2** the game of tip-cat; the bat or stick used in the game *20- SW Bor*. [see the verb]
†**cob**¹·², **keb** *v* to beat or strike (on the buttocks) *19*. [ME *cob* to fight, give blows]
cob² /kɔb/ *n* a pea-pod *19- N SW Bor*. [unknown]
cobill *see* COBLE²
coble¹ /'kɔbəl, 'kobəl/ *v* to rock, bob out *19-*. [perhaps related to Eng *cobble* a rounded stone or COBLE²]
coble², †**cowbill**, †**cobill** /'kɔbəl/ *n* **1** a short flat-bottomed rowing-boat, used especially in salmon-fishing (in a lake or river) *la13-*. **2** a ferry-boat *15-*. †**coble and net** *law* the symbols used in the transference of the ownership of fishing rights *la16*. **net and coble** a method of fishing in tidal rivers (also used symbolically to refer to fishing rights) *la18-*. [Lat *cobellus, cobella*; compare OE *cuopel* a boat, Welsh *ceubal* a ferry-boat]
coble³ /'kɔbəl, 'kobəl/ *n* **1** a water-hole for steeping flax; a pond, a watering place (for cattle) *la19- NE*. **2** brewing a vat for steeping malt *16-e19*. **3** a drainage cistern, a cesspool *16-e17*. [perhaps COBLE²]
cob-worm /'kɔbwʌrm/ *n* the larva of the cockchafer *Melolontha melolontha la18- EC*. [unknown first element + WORM]
coch, coche *see* COAF¹·¹
coche *see* COACH
cock¹·¹, †**cok**, †**coik**, †**kok** /kɔk/ *n* **1** a male bird, especially of the domestic fowl *Gallus gallus domesticus la14-*. **2** a weather-cock *la16-*. **3** curling the target circle at the end of the rink *la18-*. **4** a tap or spigot *la16-19, 20- Ork*. †**cocked of eggs** fertile *la18-19*. **cockie-bendie** **1** a small, bumptious or effeminate man; a small boy *la19-*. **2** a dance tune *la19-*. **cocky-breeky, cock-a-breeky** a small boy *la19-*. **cock's eggs** the small yolkless eggs laid by a hen about to stop laying *19, 20- NE EC*. **cock's eye** a halo round the moon, thought to be a sign of stormy weather *la19- N NE*. **cock fight** a playground game in which the players hop on

one foot and fold their arms and try to knock their opponents off balance *la18-20, 21- historical*. **cock laft** the gallery in a church *20-*. **cock laird** a small landowner who farmed his own land; a self-important person, compare *bonnet laird* (BUNNET[1.1]) *18-19, 20- NE T*. **cock paddle** the lumpfish *Cyclopterus lumpus 18-19, 20- NE*. **cock-a-bendy boat** a boat made by folding a sheet of paper *la19- NE*. **cocks and hens** the leaf-buds of the plane-tree *Acer pseudoplantanus la19- Bor*. **2** the flowers of the bird's-foot trefoil *Lotus corniculatus 20- H&I SW*. **cock and pail** a mechanism for drawing off liquid from a pipe *17-19, 20- Ork*. **cock of the north 1** a nickname for the Marquis of Huntly *la17-*. **2** a nickname for someone in authority or who is very successful *la20-*. [OE *coc*]

cock[1.2] /kɔk/ *v* **1** to stick or set up assertively or defiantly; to turn up jauntily *la18-*. **2** to raise a fist in a threatening manner *la18-*. **3** to bend a limb or joint at an angle *19-*. **4** to revive; to pick up (after an illness) *20- NE EC*. **5** to drink, tipple *18-19, 20- T*. **cockit bonnet, cocked bonnet** a boat-shaped cap of thick cloth, with the points at the front and back *la19-*. **cock its fud** *of an animal* to cock its tail *la18-*. **cockit hat, cocked hat** a three-cornered curling stone *18, 19- historical*. **cock yer neb** to look haughtily *la19-*. **cock yer wee finger** to drink, tipple *la19-*. [see the noun]

cock[2] /kɔk/ *v* to indulge or pamper *la19-*. [EModE *cock*]

cock-a-law, †**cockie-law** /kɔkəˈlɔ/ *n Presbyterian Church* the Thursday preceding the spring Communion, kept as a fast day *la19- C SW*. [perhaps Gael *cóigeamh là* fifth day]

cock-a-leekie, †**cockie leekie** /kɔkəˈliki/ *n* chicken and leek soup *18-*. [COCK[1.1] + LEEK, with diminutive suffix]

cockaleerie see COCKIELEERIE

cock-a-lorie /kɔkəˈlore/ *n* in a counting-out rhyme a nonsense word: ◊*Eetum, peetum, penny pie, Cock-a-lorie, jinky jye la19- NE*. [compare Sussex shepherds' numeral *cocktherum*]

cockapentie /kɔkəˈpɛnti/ *n* a snob, a pretentious person *19-*. [unknown]

cocker /ˈkɔkər/ *v* to rock; to totter, walk unsteadily *19- NE C Bor*. **cockerie** unsteady, shaky *la19- NE C Bor*. [EModE *cocker*; compare COCKLE]

cockerdecosie, cockertie-coozie /kɔkərdiˈkozi, kɔkərtiˈkuzi/ *adv* (riding) on someone's shoulders *19- NE C*. [unknown]

cockerdehoy see COCKERTIE-HOOIE

cockernony, †**cockernonny** /kɔkərˈnɔne/ *n* **1** a women's hairstyle in which the hair is gathered up on top of the head *18-19, 20- historical*. **2** a woman's cap with starched crown *19, 20- historical*. [unknown]

cockertie-coozie see COCKERDECOSIE
cockertie-hooie, cockerdehoy /kɔkərtiˈhui, kɔkərdiˈhɔɪ/ *adv* = COCKERDECOSIE *19- NE T*. [unknown]
cockie-bendie see COCK[1.1]
cockie-law see COCK-A-LAW
cockie leekie see COCK-A-LEEKIE
cockieleerie, cockaleerie /kɔkiˈliri, kɔkəˈliri/ *n* **1** the crowing of a cock *19- NE C SW*. **2** the cock itself *la19- NE T H&I C*. **cockieleerie-law** = COCKIELEERIE. [onomatopoeic]
cockle /ˈkɔkəl/ *v* to totter, walk unsteadily *la19-*. †**cockle brained** frivolous *e19*. †**cockle headed** whimsical *e19*. [compare COCKER, COGGLE]
cockmaleerie /kɔkməˈliri/ *n* a name for the barnyard cock *19- NE WC SW*. [variant form of COCKIELEERIE]
cock-up /ˈkɔkʌp/ *n* (a pad of false hair used to heighten) a coiffure *18-19, 20- historical*. [derived from COCK[1.2], compare COCKERNONY]

cocky-rosie, cocky-roosie /kɔkiˈrozi, kɔkiˈrusi/ *n* a children's game of riding on each other's shoulders *19-*.
cockie-ridie-roosie = COCKY-ROSIE. [perhaps variant of COCKERDECOSIE]
coclink see COWCLINK
cod[1], **coad** /kɔd, kod/ *n* **1** a cushion, a pillow *15-*. **2** an axle-bearing *la18-*. **3** a support or bearing for a bell *la16-17*. **codding 1** stones acting as supports for various constructions *la19-*. **2** the last course of short slates below the roof ridge *la20-*. †**codbere** a pillowcase *la15-e17*. †**codware** = *codbere la15-19*. [ON *koddi*]
cod[2] /kɔd/ *n* a pod or husk (of peas or beans) *18- N NE C*. [OE *codd* a pod, a shell, ON *koddi* a pillow]
codgie /ˈkɔdʒi/ *adj* comfortable, content *la19- NE*. [probably variant of CADGY]
cod-needle /ˈkɔdnidəl/ *n* a curved needle with the eye in the point for binding besoms *20- NE*. [probably from COD[1]]
†**codroch**[1.1], **codrach, codracht**, *n* an idle low-class person *la15-17*. [unknown]
†**codroch**[1.2] *adj* **1** rustic; rough-mannered *18-e19*. **2** low-class *17*. [unknown]
coer see COVER[1.2]
†**cofe** *n* an exchange *la15*. **coffing** = COFE *la15-e16*. [related to COFF]
coff /kɔf/ *v* to buy, purchase *la18-19, 20- literary*. [back-formation from COFT]
coff see COOF
coffee, coaffee /ˈkɔfi, ˈkofe/ *n* a hot drink made from coffee-beans *17-*. **gie someone his coffee** to scold, chastise *la19-*. [Arabic *qahwah*]
coft /kɔft/ *v pt, ptp* bought, purchased *15-*. [MDu *cofte*, pt, ptp of *copen* to buy]
cog[1.1], **coag, cogue**, *Sh* **cug**, *N* **coug**, †**coig** /kɔg, kog; *Sh* kʌg; *N* kʌug/ *n* **1** a wooden container made of staves; a pail or bowl *16-*. **2** a dry measure *19*. **cog wame** a pot-belly *la18-19, 20- EC*. **coup the cog** to drink *19- NE*. [compare Eng *keg* and ON *kaggi*]
cog[1.2], **cogue** /kɔg, kog/ *v* **1** to feed (calves) from a wooden container *20- NE*. **2** to empty into a wooden container *18-19*. [see the noun]
cog[2.1], **coag** /kɔg, kog/ *n* **1** a cog (in machinery) *16-*. **2** a small iron wedge fixed in a horse's shoe to prevent it slipping on ice *20-*. **3** a wedge or support *la19- SW Uls*. [ME *cogge*]
cog[2.2] /kɔg/ *v* to steady by means of a wedge; to wedge, scotch (a wheel) *17-19, 20- NE SW*. [see the noun]
coggle, *Sh* **kugl**, *Sh* **cuggle** /ˈkɔgəl; *Sh* ˈkogəl/ *v* **1** to rock, totter or shake *la18-*. **2** to cause to rock, so as to seem ready to overturn *19, 20- Sh NE*. **coggly**, *Sh SW* **cuggly** unsteady, easily overturned *la19-*. [compare COCKLE]
cogh see COAF[1.1]
coghle see COAF[1.1]
cognate[1.1] /ˈkɔgnet/ *n law* a relative on the mother's side *la18-*. Compare AGNATE. [see the adj]
cognate[1.2], †**cognat** /ˈkɔgnet/ *adj* belonging by kinship; descended from a common ancestor *17-*. [Lat *cognātus*]
cogneezance, cognizance, †**cognossance** /kɔgˈnizəns, kɔgˈnezəns/ *n* **1** knowledge *16-*. **2** heraldic cognizance *16-e17*. [OFr *conoissance*, Lat *cognōscentia*]
cognition, †**cognitioun** /kɔgˈnɪʃən/ *n* **1** knowledge, perception *la15-*. **2** *law* an inquiry as to the facts of a matter; (the acquisition by inquiry or investigation of) authoritative or judicial knowledge *la15-*. **tak cognition** to acquire authoritative or judicial knowledge *16-*. [Lat *cognitio*]
cognizance see COGNEEZANCE
cognosce, †**cognos**, †**cognosche** /kɔgˈnos/ *v* **1** *law* to investigate, examine; to inquire into *la16-*. **2** *law* to declare or

cognossance | **collogue**

assign judicially; to adjudicate *la16*-. **3** *law* to make judicial inquiry; to take cognizance or jurisdiction (upon) *16-e18*. [Lat *cognōscere*]

cognossance *see* COGNEEZANCE

cogster /'kɔgstər/ *n* a person involved in the dressing of flax, a scutcher *19- Bor.* [compare Eng *cog* to beat]

cogue *see* COG¹·¹, COG¹·²

coif *see* COVE¹·¹

coig *see* COG¹·¹

coik *see* COCK¹·¹

coil *see* COAL, COLE¹·¹, COLE¹·²

coin *see* QUINE

†**coine-house** *n* the mint *17*. [altered form of *cunyie house* (CUNYIE¹·¹)]

coinzie *see* CUNYIE¹·¹

coist *see* COAST²·¹, COAST²·²

coit *see* KITE¹·²

coitter *see* COTTAR¹·¹

cok *see* COCK¹·¹

†**cokalane, cuckolane** *n* a lampoon or satire *la16-17*. [MFr (*saillir du*) *coq a l'asne* to change subject illogically, the title of a satirical poem by C. Marot]

cöl *see* CUIL

col-cannel-week *see* COAL

cold *see* CAULD¹·¹, CAULD¹·³

coldoch *see* CUDDOCH

cole¹·¹, quile, *Sh* **col,** *H&I* **quoil,** *C SW Bor* **kyle,** †**coil** /kol, kwʌɪl; *Sh* kɔl; *H&I* kwɔɪl, kʌɪl; *C SW Bor* kʌɪl/ *n* a raked heap of hay, a haycock *18*-. [perhaps related to ON *kollr* a top, a summit, a head, a shaven crown]

cole¹·², quile, kyle, †**coil** /kol, kwʌɪl, kʌɪl/ *v* to rake up hay into haycocks *la17-*. †**collar** a maker of haycocks *la16*. [see the noun]

cole *see* COAL, COLL

colf, culf, †**calf** /kɔlf, kʌlf/ *v* to fill in or stop up (a hole); to caulk *la17, 19- NE.* **colfing,** †**calfing,** †**cuffing** *n* **1** gunwadding *17-19, 20- NE.* **2** material for caulking or stopping *16-17*. [reduced form of CALFAT]

coll, cole /kɔl, kol/ *v* **1** to cut (obliquely); to taper; to shape *la16-19, 20- Sh NE SW Bor.* **2** to clip or trim hair; to remove the horns of cattle *la16-19, 20- Sh T.* Compare COW²·² and KOILLET. [unknown; compare ON *kollr* a top, a summit, a head, a shaven crown]

coll *see* COAL

collady-stane *see* COW-LADY-STANE

collap *see* COLLOP

collar *see* COLE¹·²

collate /kə'let/ *v* **1** to arrange in sequence; to examine; to compare *la17-*. **2** *law* to pool inheritances *la17-*. [Lat *collāt-*, ptp stem of *conferre* to bring together]

collation¹·¹, †**collatioun** /kə'leʃən/ *n* **1** *Christian Church* formal admission to a benefice *15-*. **2** a meal or repast; a refreshment *la15-*. **3** the action of bringing together (for the sake of comparison) *la15-*. **4** *law* the pooling of inheritances with a view to their equitable distribution amongst the heirs *la17-*. **5** conversation, discourse *15-e16*. †**collatioun ordinar** regular induction to a benefice *la15-16*. [ME *collacioun*, Lat *collātio* the act of bringing together]

†**collation¹·²** *v* to compare, collate *17*. [see the noun]

†**collationate, collationat** *adj* **1** collated, compared *16-e17*. **2** put in possession of or appointed to a benefice *16*. [Lat *collātionāt-*, ptp stem of *collātionāre*]

collatioun *see* COLLATION¹·¹

collcoom, kolkoom /kɔl'kum/ *v* to char, burn (food) *20- Sh*. [*col coal, charcoal + COOM¹·²]

†**colleague¹·¹** *n* partnership, alliance; collusion *16-19*; compare COLLOGUE¹·¹. [see the verb]

colleague¹·², *NE* **collig,** †**colleg** /kə'lig; *NE* kə'lɪg/ *v* **1** to associate with for crime or mischief; to plot or conspire *la18-*. **2** to associate or be friendly with *la19, 20- NE.* **3** to join, ally (with) *16*. [OFr *colliguer* to join in alliance]

colleck, collect, *Bor* **cleck,** †**collec** /kə'lɛk, kə'lɛkt; *Bor* klɛk/ *v* to gather, assemble, accumulate or collect *16-*. [MFr *collecter* or Lat *collecta* a gathering (of taxes)]

colleckshun, collection /kə'lɛkʃən/ *n* **1** the act of collecting; an accumulation or gathering of things *la15-*. **2** *Presbyterian Church* the offering *17-*. [ME *colleccioun*, Lat *collectio*]

collect *see* COLLECK

collection *see* COLLECKSHUN

†**collectorie** *n* **1** the office of (tax) collector *la15-17*. **2** that part of the royal revenue derived from the collection of the *thirds of benefices* (THIRD¹·¹) *la16*. [perhaps OFr *collecterie* the office of tax collector]

colleg *see* COLLEAGUE¹·²

college, coallege /'kɔlədʒ, 'kolədʒ/ *n* **1** a university; an institute of further or higher education; an association of scholars *15-*. **2** (the place of residence of) a society or incorporation of ecclesiastics *15-*. **3** a course of lectures *18*. **College of Justice** the body of judges, Lords of Council and Session and others composing the supreme civil court *16-*; compare *Court of Session* (COORT¹·¹). [Lat *collēgium*]

college *see* COLLIG

collegeaner *see* COLLEGIANER

colleged /'kɔlədʒd/ *adj* educated at a university *19, 20- C.* [derivative of COLLEGE]

collegianer, †**collegeaner,** †**colleginer** /kə'lidʒənər/ *n* a student at a college or university *la17-19, 20- NE C Uls.* [EModE *colligener*]

†**collep** *n* a drinking vessel *e16*. [unknown]

coll-ever *see* COAL

collie¹, †**colley,** †**coly** /'kole, 'kɔli/ *n* a sheepdog *17-*. **collie dug 1** a sheepdog *la18-*. **2** *rhyming slang* a gullible person, a mug *la20-*. **he never asked, Collie, wull ye lick** he did not even invite me to have something to eat *19-*. [unknown]

collie², colly, *Ork* **koly** /'kɔli; *Ork* 'koli/ *n* a small iron lamp; a paraffin lamp *la19- Sh Ork.* [ON *kola* a small open lamp]

†**collie³** *n* *curling* a stone that fails to score by falling short of a line drawn across the rink; the scoring line itself *19*. [unknown]

colliebuction /kɔli'bʌkʃən/ *n* a noisy squabble *19- N NE T EC.* [compare COLLIESHANGIE; perhaps with influence from *ruction*]

collie-fox /'kɔlefɔks/ *v* to tease *la19- Uls.* [unknown]

collieshangie, killieshangie, cullieshangie /kɔli'ʃaŋi, kɪli'ʃaŋi, kʌli'ʃaŋi/ *n* **1** a noisy dispute, an uproar *18-*. **2** a dog-fight *la19- NE SW Bor.* **3** a talk; animated conversation *la19- NE T.* [unknown]

†**collig, colligue, college** *n* a colleague *16-17*. [altered form of Lat *colligāre* assemble]

collig *see* COLLEAGUE¹·²

collik, kullyak, †**cullock** /'kulək, 'kʌljək/ *n* a clam or other shellfish *la18- Sh.* [diminutive form of ON *kollr* a top, a summit, a head, a shaven crown or ON *kúla* a ball, a knob]

†**collitigant** *n* an opponent in a lawsuit *16-e17*. [Lat *cum* with + Older Scots *liticant, litigant*]

collogue¹·¹ /kə'log/ *n* **1** a (whispered) conversation, a private interview *la19-*. **2** a meeting, a conference *la20-*. [unknown]

collogue¹·², *Uls* **colloug** /kə'log; *Uls* kə'lʌug/ *v* **1** to converse together, chat *la19-*. **2** to be in league, have an understanding (with); to plot or scheme *19, 20- NE EC Uls.* [unknown]

collop, †**collap** /'kɔləp/ *n* a slice of meat *16-*. [ME *collop* a dish of fried or roasted meat, a morsel (for a king); compare Swed *kalops*]

colloug see COLLOGUE[1,2]

colly see COLLIE[2]

colly buckie see COALIE BUCKIE

colmie /'kolmi/ *n* the mature coalfish *Pollachius virens 19, 20- NE.* **coalman**, †**colman** = COLMIE *18-19, 20- NE.* [COAL, with unknown second element or perhaps shortened form of COLMOUTH]

†**colmouth**, **colemoth** *n* the mature coalfish *Pollachius virens 15-17.* [COAL, with unknown second element]

colour, †**coullour**, †**cullour**, †**culler** /'kʌlər/ *n* 1 hue, colour *la14-.* 2 appearance, aspect *15-.* 3 paint, pigment, dye *la15-.* 4 *pl* a flag or standard *17-.* 5 a small quantity *20- Uls.* 6 rhythm, metre *16-e17.* †**colour-de-roy** a purple or tawny dress material *16-e17.* [ME *colour*]

colpindach, †**cowpendoch**, †**copindo**, †**cupnow** /'kɔlpɪndax/ *n* a young cow or ox; a heifer *11-18, 19- historical.* [related to Gael *colpach* a female calf, a heifer; compare CALP, CUDDOCH]

colrach see CULREACH

colt see COWT

†**columbie** *adj of cloth* dove-coloured *la16-e17.* [OFr *colombe*, Lat *columba* a dove]

†**columby** *n* the columbine *Aquilegia la15-e16.* [ME *columbine*, perhaps from MFr *fleur colombine* the dove flower, alternative name of the *ancolie*]

†**colvin** *n* a sea-going vessel *e16.* [unknown]

coly see COLLIE[1]

†**colȝear**, **colȝar** *n* a coal miner; a charcoal-burner *la15-17.* [ME *colier*]

com see COME[1,1]

comatee, **commatee**, **committee** /kɔməˈti, kɔməˈti, kəˈmɪte/ *n* a group of people appointed to perform a service or function *17-.* [AN *committé*, ptp of *committer* to empower]

comb see KAME[1,1], KAME[1,2]

combster see KAMESTER

comburges see CONBURGES

come[1,1], †**com** /kʌm/ *n* 1 a thaw; moisture in the air *20- WC SW Bor.* 2 the angle between a tool and its user *20- NE.* 3 coming, arrival *la14-e16.* [OE *cyme* coming]

come[1,2], **cum** /kʌm/ *v pt* **cam**, **came**, **come**, **cum**, †**coyme**, *ptp* also **cummyn**, **cumyn**, **cum**, **cumit**, **cummed** 1 to approach, move towards; to arrive *14-.* 2 to occur, arise; to become; to attain *la14-.* 3 to stretch, expand *la19, 20- NE EC.* 4 to equal, match *20- NE WC.* 5 *of a time of the day* to draw near ◊*it came four o'clock 20- NE T.* **come again** a scolding; a beating *la19- NE.* **come-o-will** an illegitimate child *19, 20- NE Bor.* **come aifter** to court, seek to marry *la19- NE.* **come at** *of a misfortune* to befall; to affect; to distress *20- Sh NE T.* **come ather** a call to a horse to turn to the left *19- NE T.* **come away 1** to come along *19-.* **2** *of seeds or plants* to germinate; to grow rapidly *la19-.* **3** *imperative* stop talking nonsense *la20-.* **come back an fore** to visit regularly *20-.* **come back on** *of food* to repeat *20-.* **come back ta der auld haglet** to return to their old haunts *20- Sh.* **come doon** *of a river* to be in flood *la18-19, 20- NE EC.* **come doon with yer spirit** to humble yourself *19, 20- NE WC.* **come forrit** to make progress; to grow *20-.* **come and gang a wee** to compromise *19, 20- NE C.* **come guid for** to be surety for; to back up *19, 20- EC.* **come hame** to be born *la19- NE T EC.* **come in** to collapse *20- EC.* **come in aboot** to come into a place; to arrive *la20-.* **come in by**, **come in bye** to come in, draw near *la18-.* **come in to the fire** to draw near to the fire *la18-.* **come o** to become of or happen to someone *20-.* **come on 1** to come along *la19-.* **2** to be about to do something *la19-.* **3** *imperative* stop talking nonsense *la20-.* **come oot** to study or qualify for a particular profession *20-.* **come oot ower** to strike *19- NE T EC.* **come ower 1** to happen to, befall *19-.* **2** to repeat; to make mention of *la19-.* **come paddy owre** to get round a person *la19- T C.* **come speed** to make progress, get on quickly; to succeed *16-.* **come tae**, **come to 1** to regain one's composure after a time of mental stress *19-.* **2** to become reconciled; to comply *la18- NE T EC.* **3** to come near *la18- NE.* **4** to grow up *la17-19, 20- NE.* **come tae the door** *of a knock* to sound on the door *la18-19, 20- NE.* **come tae yer thoum** to dawn on one, reach one's consciousness *20- NE.* **come tee te** to overtake *la19- NE.* **come through** to recover from an illness *19-.* **come the time** on someone's next birthday, on the next anniversary of an event ◊*I'm just now five and threty come the time 19, 20- N NE T.* **ca way**, **c'way**, **quay 1** to come along *19-.* **2** *imperative* stop talking nonsense *la19-.* **come yer ways** to come along *19-.* [OE *cuman*]

comic see COAMIC[1,1], COAMIC[1,2]

comick see COAMIC[1,2]

comman[1,1], **command** /kəˈman, kəˈmand/ *n* 1 an order, a command *la15-.* 2 *pl* the ten commandments *16-.* [see the verb]

comman[1,2], **command** /kəˈman, kəˈmand/ *v* to order, give a command *la14-.* **commanding** *of pain* severe, disabling *la19-.* [ME *commaunden*]

†**commandiment**, **commandement** *n* a commandment *la14-19.* [ME *commaundement*]

commatee see COMATEE

†**commend**[1] *n* 1 commendation, praise *la15-e17.* 2 trust, recommendation *15-16.* **in commend** *of a benefice* to be held by a bishop (in addition to his own preferment) or by a layman *la15-16.* [Fr *commend*]

†**commend**[2] *n* a comment, a commentary *la15-16.* [variant of Older Scots *comment*]

commendator, †**commendatour**, †**commendatare** /'kɔməndetər/ *n* a holder of a benefice made over to them in trust *16-18, 19- historical.* [Lat *commendātor*]

†**commentar** *n* an exposition, a commentary *la16-e17.* [MFr *commentaire*, Lat *commentārium*]

commere see KIMMER[1,1]

commie /'kɔmi/ *n* an ordinary marble *20- WC.* Compare COMMONIE. [shortened form of COMMON[1,3]]

†**commissar** *n* 1 *law* a civil official taking the place of the former ecclesiastical diocesan commissary *la16-e18.* 2 a commissary; a delegate or representative *la14-17.* 3 a representative of a burgh at the annual convention of burghs *15-e17.* [MFr *commissaire*]

commissariat /kɔmɪˈserɪət/ *n law* a commissary court; the office or jurisdiction of a commissary; the district included in such jurisdiction *la16-20, 21- historical.* [Fr *commissariat*]

commissary /'kɔmɪsəre/ *n law* a civil official appointed to act in matters of marriage or divorce, which previously came under ecclesiastical law *16-19, 20- historical.* [Lat *commissārius*]

commissary clerk /'kɔmɪsəre 'klark/ *n* the sheriff clerk when acting in relation to confirmation of executors *la18-.* [COMMISSARY + *clerk* (CLARK[1,1])]

Commissary Court /'kɔmɪsəre 'kort/ *n law* the court which appointed and confirmed executors of deceased people leaving personal property in Scotland *la18-19, 20- historical.* Compare *commissariat.* [COMMISSARY + *court* (COORT[1,1])]

commission, †**commissioun** /kəˈmɪʃən/ n 1 (a document conveying) authority granted for a particular action or function 15-. 2 the body which carries out a particular action or function la15-. 3 the action of committing a sin or a crime la15-. **Commission of Justiciary** a court for trying criminal cases, later absorbed into the Court of Justiciary 16-e17, 19- historical. †**Commission of Plat** Presbyterian Church the body which implemented and administered the organization of the Presbyterian system 17-18. [MFr commission, Lat commissio]

commissioner, †**commissionar** /kəˈmɪʃənər/ n 1 a person charged with an official task la15-. 2 a member of the General Assembly of any of the Scottish Presbyterian Churches 18-. 3 a factor, an agent, a steward la19, 20- NE. 4 a member of the Scottish Parliament la16-e18, 20- historical. 5 a representative of a burgh at the annual convention of burghs la15-e18. †**Commissioner of Police** a member of a popularly elected body in a burgh which supervised the watching, lighting and cleansing of the town 19. **Commissioners of Supply** the group of landowners in each county which exercised various administrative functions la17-20, 21- historical. †**Commissioners of Teinds** the parliamentary body administering the tithes as part of the *Court of Session* (COORT[1.1]) since the Union of the Parliaments la17-20, 21- historical. [AN commissioner]

commissioun see COMMISSION
committee see COMATEE
commixtion, †**commixtioun** /kəˈmɪkstʃən/ n 1 law a mixture of property belonging to different people 18-. 2 mingling la15-16. [Lat commixtio]

commodate /ˈkɔmədət/ n a COMMODATUM la18-. [ptp of Lat commodāre to lend]

commodatum /kɔməˈdetəm/ n law a free loan of an article which must be returned exactly as lent la17-. [ptp of Lat commodāre to lend]

†**commodite** n 1 pl advantages or benefits deriving from the possession or use of property la14-e17. 2 advantage, convenience 15-16. [Lat commoditās]

common[1.1], †**commoun** /ˈkɔmən/ n 1 communal pasture la15-. 2 a debt, an obligation la16-. 3 the common people la14-e18. 4 pl the foot-soldiers in an army 15-16. †**the commounis, the commonis** the common people la14-e17. †**in someone's common** in debt or under an obligation to someone la16-e18. †**quit a common** to repay a debt or injury la16-e17. [see the adj]

†**common**[1.2], **commoun** v to have dealings with; to discourse or discuss; to negotiate about la15-e18. [ME communen]

common[1.3], **coammon**, NE **cowmon**, †**commoun** /ˈkɔmən, ˈkoːmən; NE ˈkʌumən/ adj 1 shared (by the community); public la14-. 2 ordinary, usual; regular, general 15-. 3 base, low; lacking in manners or taste la15-. **common debtor** when a person owes money to a second person which the second person recovers by taking from a third person a sum owed by the third person to the first person, the first person is known as the common debtor 18-. **common good** the property and revenues of the corporation of a royal burgh which are not held under special acts of parliament nor raised by taxation 15-. †**common head** a religious exercise or discourse on a general point 17. †**common hird** a shepherd employed by the community 15-e18. **common law** the usual civil law 15-. †**common menstrall** a musician in the service of a burgh 16-e17. †**common mett** a public standard system or unit of measurement; a standard instrument for measuring la15-e18. †**common piper** the official bagpiper of a municipality la15-17. †**the common popular** the common people la16. †**the common profit** the benefit of the whole community la14-16. **common seal** the seal of a religious community or burgh used in community business or by a person who did not have his own seal la14-20, 21- historical. **common stair** the communal staircase giving access to the flats in a tenement 18-. **for common** commonly, generally 15-19, 20- NE T. **than common** than usual 18-19, 20- Sh T. **common five-auchts** an average or ordinary person or thing la19-. [ME commun, Lat commūnis]

commonate see COMMONITE
commonie /ˈkɔməni/ n an ordinary marble 20- EC Bor. Compare COMMIE. [derivative of COMMON[1.3] + -IE[3]]

†**commonite**, **commonate** n 1 a community of people 15-e17. 2 a common pasture 17. [variant of Older Scots communité]

Common Riding /ˈkɔmən ˈrʌɪdɪŋ/ n the name for the Riding of the Marches in certain Borders towns, including Selkirk and Hawick la18-. [COMMON[1.3] + RIDING]

commoun see COMMON[1.1], COMMON[1.2], COMMON[1.3]

†**commove** v 1 to move to anger; to excite to passion la15-19. 2 to set in motion or agitation 16. [OFr commovoir, AN commoveir]

communing /kəˈmjunɪŋ/ n debate, discussion la16-19, 20- NE EC. [verbal noun from COMMON[1.2]]

communio bonorum /kəmjunɪo bəˈnorəm/ n law the stock of moveable property owned jointly by a husband and wife 19, 20- historical. [Lat commūnio bonōrum mutual participation in goods]

compaingen /kəmˈpeŋən/ n a companion 20- N NE. [altered form of Scots companion]

†**companionrie** n companionship la16-17. [Older Scots companȝeon, with abstract noun suffix]

compare[1] /kəmˈper/ n comparison, resemblance 16-19, 20- NE EC. †**in compare of** in comparison with 16. [COMPARE[2.2]]

†**compare**[2.1], **compere** n an equal, a rival la14-e17. [MFr compere a godfather, a companion]

compare[2.2], †**compere** /kəmˈper/ v to make comparison la14-. [OFr comparer, Lat comparāre to pair together, match]

†**compare**[2.3] adj comparable, equal e16. [Lat compar]

†**comparisoun** n a covering spread over the saddle or harness of a horse e16. [altered form of MFr caparaçon]

†**compartiner** n a co-partner la16-17. [OFr comparçonnier]

compear, compeir, †**compere** /kəmˈpir/ v 1 law to appear or be represented before a court 15-. 2 to appear before a congregation, minister or kirk session, especially for rebuke la16-. 3 to present oneself, appear la15-18. **compearance** law the formal act of appearing in court la15-. [ME comperen, Lat compārēre]

†**compeditour** n a competitor 16-e17. [altered form of Older Scots competitour]

compel, †**compell** /kəmˈpɛl/ v 1 to force, constrain 15-. 2 to distrain goods or property la15-16. [ME compellen, Lat compellere]

compend /ˈkɔmpənd/ n a compendium, a summary la16-. [Lat compendium]

†**compendize** v to abridge, summarize la17-e18. [COMPEND, with verb-forming suffix]

compensatio injuriarum /kɔmpənˈsɛʃɪo ɪnjuriˈarəm/ n law a plea that a defender should not be compelled to pay damages to a pursuer on the grounds that the pursuer is liable for as great or greater damages to the defender 19-. [Lat compensātio injūriārum]

compensation /kɔmpənˈseʃən/ n 1 recompense, redress la16-. 2 law = COMPENSATIO INJURIARUM 18-. [Lat compensātio]

compere see COMPARE[2.1], COMPARE[2.2], COMPEAR

†**compesce** *v* to restrain or repress *17-19*. [Lat *compescere*]
†**competable** *adj* competent, suitable *la15-e16*. [OFr *competable*]
competeetion /kɔmpə'tiʃən/ *n* a competition *la19-*. [Lat *competītio*]
complain *see* COMPLEEN
complainer, †**complenar**, †**complenʒear** /kəm'plenər/ *n law* a victim of a crime who has reported it to the authorities; a plaintiff *16-*. [*complain* (COMPLEEN), with agent suffix]
compleen, **complain**, †**complene**, †**complenʒe** /kəm'plin, kəm'plen/ *v* **1** to make a complaint; to express dissatisfaction *la14-*. **2** to be ailing or unwell *19-*. [ME *compleinen*]
complenar *see* COMPLAINER
complent /kəm'plent/ *n* a complaint *16-*. [ME *compleint*]
complenʒe *see* COMPLEEN
complenʒear *see* COMPLAINER
†**complese**, **compleis** *v* to please, satisfy *la14-16*. [OFr *complaisir*]
compliment /'kɔmpləmənt/ *n* **1** an expression of praise; a (formal) act of civility or greeting *la17-*. **2** a gift, a present *la19, 20- NE T EC*. [Fr *compliment*]
complouter *see* COMPLUTHER[1,2]
complowsible /kəm'plʌuzɪbəl/ *adj* reasonable *la19- EC*. [altered form of PLOSIBLE]
compluther[1.1] /kəm'pluθər/ *n* a mix-up; confusion *19, 20- Bor*. [unknown; compare OFr *complote* a crowd, a mêlée]
compluther[1.2], †**complouter**, †**comploiter** /kəm'pluθər/ *v* **1** to mix or associate with *la19- T Bor*. **2** to agree, coincide or fit in with *19, 20- Bor*. [see the noun]
†**compone** *v* **1** to come to an agreement; to settle a dispute with payment *la15-18*. **2** to compound or combine *la15-17*. **3** to compose in speech or writing *la15-16*. **4** to compound a payment for a certain sum *16-e17*. **5** to compose or calm oneself *16*. [Lat *compōnere*]
†**componitour**[1] *n* a person who settled disputes or arranged agreements *la15-16*. [erroneous expansion of scribal *compōitour*; compare COMPOSITOR]
†**componitour**[2] *n* an agreement (which settled a dispute) *15-16*. [Lat *compōnitur* it is settled]
composition, †**compositioun** /kɔmpə'zɪʃən/ *n* **1** *law* a sum paid in settlement of a claim, dispute or obligation; the amount fixed by mutual agreement *la15-*. **2** a piece of writing; a work of literature, music or art *la16-*. **3** a combination of elements, a mixture *la16-*. **4** an agreement for the settlement of a dispute *la14-e17*. [ME *composicioun*, Lat *compositio*]
†**compositor**, **compositour** *n* a person who settled disputes; an arbitrator *la14-e18*. [AN *compositour*, Lat *compositor*]
comprise /kəm'praez/ *v* **1** to include or contain; to consist of *la14-*. **2** to appraise, value *la16-19, 20- N*. **3** *law* to attach or distrain property *16-17*. **4** to understand or comprehend *la14-16*. [MFr *compris*, ptp of *comprendre*]
†**compromis** *n* an agreement, a settlement *la15-e16*. [MFr *compromis* ptp of *compromettre*, Lat *comprōmissum*]
†**compromit**[1.1] *n* a settlement, an agreement *la15-e17*. [see the verb]
†**compromit**[1.2] *v* to agree; to settle; to pledge (oneself) *la15-16*. [Lat *comprōmittere*]
compt[1.1], †**coumpt** /kɔmpt/ *n* **1** a monetary account *15-17, 20- literary*. **2** a list, a register, an inventory *la15-17*. **3** counting, addition *la16-e17*. †**to gude compt** to the full amount *la15-16*. [ME *counte, compte*]
†**compt**[1.2] *v* to make a count or reckoning; to add up *15-19*. [ME *counten, compten*]

†**comptar**, **compter** a person who kept or rendered accounts; a treasurer *la15-e18*. **comptar wardane** a counter in the Scottish Mint *16-17*. [COMPT[1.2], with agent suffix]
†**comptes** *n* a countess *16-e17*. [MFr *comtesse*]
compulsitor[1.1], †**compulsatour** /kəm'pʌlsɪtər/ *n law* a writ ordering the performance of a particular act; something which compels an action *16-*. [see the adj]
†**compulsitor**[1.2], **compulsatour** *adj law* compelling performance *e16*. [Lat *compulsātōrius*]
con /kɔn/ *n* a squirrel *la15-19, 20- literary*. [unknown]
con *see* CUN
†**conand**, **connand**, **cunnand** *n* a covenant, an agreement *la14-16*. Compare COVENANT. [ME *covenaunt, conaunt*]
†**conburges**, **comburges** *n* a fellow burgess *la15-17*. [Lat *cum* with + BURGESS[1.1]]
concait, conceat *see* CONCEIT
conceit, consait, concait, *Sh* **consaet**, †**conceat** /kən'sit, kən'set; *Sh* kən'seat/ *n* **1** a fancy article, a quaint or dainty object or person *la16-*. **2** vanity, arrogance; a good opinion of oneself *la18-*. **3** an idea, a thought *15-19, 20- NE T*. **4** interest, lively attention, concern *18-19, 20- NE EC*. **5** a good opinion of another; esteem, high regard *16-e19*. **6** a scheme, stratagem *15-16*. **conceity, conceaty 1** conceited, vain, proud *la17-*. **2** neat, tidy, dainty *la18-*. **3** witty, apt; clever *la19- WC SW*. **4** fanciful, flighty *la16-17*. **tak a conceit in** to take an interest in, take a pride in *la19, 20- NE EC*. [ME *conceit*]
conclusion /kən'kluʒən/ *n* **1** an end or close; a result or settlement *la14-*. **2** *law* the clause in a court of session summons which states the precise relief sought *19-*. [ME *conclusioun*]
concord[1.1] /'kɔnkɔrd, 'kɔŋkɔrd/ *n* agreement, harmony *15-*. [ME *concord*, Lat *concordia*]
concord[1.2] /kən'kɔrd/ *v* to concur, agree; to come to an agreement *la14-*. [OFr *concorder*, Lat *concordāre*]
concordedly /kən'kɔrdədle/ *adv* calmly, contentedly *la19- Ork*. [ptp of CONCORD[1.2], with adv-forming suffix]
concourse, †**concurse** /'kɔnkors, 'kɔŋkors/ *n* **1** conjunction, coming together; a gathering (of people) *la16-*. **2** *law* concurrence, especially of an authority whose consent is necessary to a legal process, particularly of the public prosecutor in a private prosecution *17-*. **3** *law* the simultaneous existence of two actions based on the same grounds *19-*. [MFr *concours*, Lat *concursum* a running together]
†**concredit** *adj* entrusted *la16-17*. [Lat *concrēditus*]
†**concreour** *n* a conqueror *16*. [metathesis of Older Scots *conqueror*]
concurrent /kən'kʌrənt/ *n law* one who accompanies a sheriff's officer as a witness or as an assistant *18-*. [from the adj Older Scots *concurrant*]
concurse *see* CONCOURSE
condame, condamp *see* CONDAMPNE
†**condampnatioun** *n* condemnation *15-16*. [MFr *condampnation*]
†**condampnatour**[1.1] *n* a condemnatory sentence or decree *la16-e17*. [see the adj]
†**condampnatour**[1.2] *adj* condemnatory *16-e17*. [MFr *condamnatoire*; compare CONDAMPNATIOUN]
†**condampne, condamp, condame** *v* **1** to condemn *la14-e17*. **2** to cause damage (with artillery fire) *la16-e17*. **3** to block off or fill up (a door) *la16-e17*. [MFr *condampner*]
condeetion, condition, †**conditioun**, †**condiscioune** /kən'diʃən, kən'dɪʃən/ *n* **1** a stipulation or requirement *la14-*. **2** the nature or state of something *15-*. [ME *condicioun*]
†**condempnatour** *n* a condemnatory sentence or decree *la16-17*. [CONDAMPNATOUR[1.1], with influence from EModE *condemnatorie*]

condescend /kɔndəˈsɛnd/ v 1 to descend, deign *16-*. 2 to specify, give details *16-*. 3 to acquiesce, agree *15-e18*. **condescendence** 1 agreement, acquiescence; condescension *17-*. 2 *law* a statement of the facts in a case; a specification or statement of particulars *17-*. †**condescendency** = *condescendence la17-e19*. [ME *condescenden*, Lat *condēscendere*]
condie see CUNDY
condign, †**conding**, **condigne** /kənˈdʌɪn/ *adj* 1 appropriate, suitable *15-*. 2 worthy, valuable *la15-e17*. [ME *condigne*, Lat *condignus*]
condingly, **condignly** /kənˈdɪŋle, kənˈdʌɪnle/ *adv* 1 fittingly, deservedly *16-*. 2 agreeably, lovingly *19- NE*. [CONDIGN, with adv-forming suffix]
condiscioune, **condition**, **conditioun** see CONDEETION
†**conditionate** *adj* agreed in a bargain, stipulated *16-e17*. [Lat *conditionātus*]
conduce /kənˈdjus/ v 1 to lead, contribute *la15-*. 2 to engage the services of, hire *la15-17*. 3 to bargain, deal with *la16-e18*. [Lat *condūcere*]
conduck[1.1], **conduct** /ˈkɔndʌk, ˈkɔndʌkt/ *n* 1 (good) behaviour; guidance or leadership *la16-*. 2 a safe-conduct; an assurance of safe passage or immunity *la15-19, 20- NE EC*. 3 a conduit, a channel for water *16-e17*. [Lat *conductus*]
conduck[1.2], **conduct** /kənˈdʌk, kənˈdʌkt/ v 1 to behave (well); to lead, guide or direct *la16-*. 2 to engage or hire; to make a bargain *16*. [Lat *conduct-*, ptp stem of *condūcere*]
confabble[1.1] /ˈkɔnfabəl, kənˈfabəl/ *n* a confabulation, a discussion *19- NE C*. [Lat *confabūlātio*]
confabble[1.2] /kənˈfabəl/ v to confabulate, discuss *19- NE C*. [Lat *confabūlāri*]
confaise see CONFEESE
confaision see CONFEESHIN
confeerence, **confeerance**, **conference** /ˈkɔnfirəns, kənˈfirəns, ˈkɔnfərəns/ *n* 1 a meeting for consultation or discussion *la16-*. 2 comparison, congruence *la16-19, 20- NE*. [MFr *conference*]
confeerin[1.1] /kənˈfirən/ *adj* suitable, corresponding *la19- NE*. **confeerin to** in accordance with, according to *la18- NE T*. **confeerin wi** = *confeerin to*. [participial adj from CONFER]
confeerin[1.2] /kənˈfirən/ *adv* considering; taking everything into consideration *la18- NE*. [see the adj]
confeese, **confuse**, †**confaise** /kənˈfiz, kənˈfjuz/ v to bewilder, perplex; to mix up, disorder, jumble *la15-*. [back-formation from ptp *confusit* from Fr *confus* or Lat *confūsus* with redundant *-it* suffix, originally the ptp of *confound*]
confeeshin, **confaision**, **confusion**, †**confusioun** /kənˈfiʃən, kənˈfeʒən, kənˈfjuʒən/ *n* 1 disorder, chaos; lack of clarity *la14-*. 2 a mixture of liquids *la17-*. 3 *law* a mode of extinguishing a debt, a right or a claim where either party acquires the title of the other by inheritance or otherwise *la17-*. [ME *confusioun*, Lat *confūsio*]
confer /kənˈfer/ v 1 to talk together, hold conference *15-*. 2 to grant or bestow *la16-*. 3 to compare, collate *16-e17*. [Lat *conferre*]
conference see CONFEERENCE
confidder see CONFIDER
confide, †**confyd** /kənˈfʌɪd/ v to trust, entrust; to impart, disclose *la15-*. [Lat *confidere*]
†**confider**, **confidder** v to form a league; to ally (with) *la15-16*. [MFr *confederer*]
†**confiderat** *n* a confederate, an ally *16-e17*. [Lat *confoederātus*]
†**confideratioun** *n* confederation *la15-e17*. [Lat *confoederātio*]
confirmation, †**confirmatioun** /kɔnfərˈmeʃən/ *n* 1 the action of confirming; verification, corroboration *la14-*. 2 *law* a process whereby executors are judicially recognized or confirmed in their office and receive a title to the property of a deceased person *17-*. [ME *confirmacioun*, Lat *confirmātio*]
conflummix[1.1] /kənˈflʌməks/ *n* a shock *20- NE*. [see the verb]
conflummix[1.2] /kənˈflʌməks/ v to confuse, bewilder *20- NE*. [Lat *cum* with + Eng *flummox*]
confoond, **confoon**, **confound**, †**confund** /kənˈfund, kənˈfun, kənˈfʌund/ v to astonish, confuse; to contradict; to overthrow, thwart *la14-*. [ME *confounden*]
confooter /kənˈfutər/ v to confound *20- NE*. **confooter ye** a mild oath *20- NE*. [conflation of CONFOOND with FOUTER[1.2]]
conform /kənˈfɔrm/ *adj* 1 conformable; corresponding to *la15-*. 2 *of furnishings* matching, in keeping with the rest *la17*. **conform to** in accordance with *16-*. [Lat *conformis*]
†**confortable** *adj* comfortable *15-19*. [ME *comfortable*]
confound, **confund** see CONFOOND
confuse see CONFEESE
confusion, **confusioun** see CONFEESHIN
congregation, †**congregatioun** /kɔŋgrəˈgeʃən/ *n* 1 an assembly of people (in a church) *la14-*. 2 the body of those forming the Protestant party during and after the Reformation *la16*. [ME *congregacioun*, Lat *congregātio*]
conjoin, †**conjone**, †**conjune** /kənˈdʒɔɪn/ v 1 to unite, join together *la15-*. 2 *law* to order a joint trial of two processes involving the same subject and the same parties *19-*. [MFr *conjoindre*]
conjunct /kənˈdʒʌŋkt/ *adj* 1 *law* possessed or shared in jointly *15-*. 2 combined, united; associated *16-*. 3 connected by blood *la15-19*. †**conjunct fiar**, **conjunct fear** *law* a person who holds property jointly with another *16-18*. **conjunct probation** *law* the process of disproving by evidence an opponent's allegations, carried on as part of the process of proving a party's own case *la18-*. **conjunct and confident persons** *law* people related by blood and connected by interest (such as in a bankruptcy case where recent transfer of property is challengeable) *17-*. [Lat *conjunctus*]
conjune see CONJOIN
connach[1.1] /ˈkɔnəx/ *n* a botch; an unskilled worker *la19-*. [unknown]
connach[1.2] /ˈkɔnəx/ v 1 to waste, be wasteful *la18-*. 2 to spoil or destroy; to devour *la18-*. 3 to fuss over, pet *la19-*. [unknown]
connached /ˈkɔnəxt/ *adj* 1 ruined, spoilt, exhausted *la19-*. 2 indulged, petted, fussed over *20-*. [ptp of CONNACH[1.2]]
connand see CONAND
†**conneck**[1.1] *n* a connection, a link *la19*. [see the verb]
conneck[1.2] /kəˈnɛk/ v to connect *19-*. [Lat *cōnectere*]
conneeve /kəˈniv/ v to connive *19, 20- NE*. [Lat *cōnīvēre* to shut the eyes]
†**connex** *n* an item of property connected with another, an appurtenance *16-e19*. Compare ANNEX. [MFr *connexe* related]
†**connoch** *n* an illness; a cattle plague, murrain *15-e19*. **connochworm** the caterpillar larva of the hawk-moth *Sphingidae 19*. [Gael *conach*]
†**connotar** *n* a notary acting conjointly with another *la16-e19*. [MFr *conotaire*; compare NOTAR]
conqueis see CONQUIS, CONQUESS
conqueist see CONQUEST[1.1], CONQUEST[1.2]
conques see CONQUIS
conquess, †**conques**, †**conqueis** /ˈkɔnkwɛs/ v ptp also †**yconquest** 1 to conquer, overcome by force *15-*. 2 to gain; to acquire land or property otherwise than by inheritance *la15-19*. [back-formation from *conquest*, pt, ptp of CONQUEST[1.2]]

conquest[1.1], †**conqueist** /'kɔŋkwɛst/ *n* 1 the act of conquering *15-*. 2 something gained by conquest *15-*. 3 *law* acquisition of land; property acquired rather than inherited *la15-19*. [ME *conquest, conqueste*]

†**conquest**[1.2], †**conqueist** *v* to conquer *15-17*. [ME *conquesten*]

†**conquis, conqueis, conques** *n* 1 the act of conquering *16-e17*. 2 something gained by conquest *la16-e18*. [OFr *conquis, conquise,* ptp of *conquerre*]

†**conray, cunray,** *v* to overwhelm; to deal with severely *e15*. Compare CUMRAY. [OFr *conrëer* equip, supply with]

consaet, consait *see* CONCEIT

consanguinean /kɔnsaŋ'gwiniən/ *adj law* descended from the same father but not the same mother *18-*. [Lat *consanguineus* of the same blood]

conseeder, consider, consither /kən'sidər, kən'sɪdər, kən'sɪðər/ *v* to think about, reflect upon; to take into account *la14-*. [OFr *considerer,* Lat *consīderāre*]

†**conserjary, consergerie** *n* the house used as an inn by the Scottish merchants at Campvere, Holland *17-e18*. [Fr *conciergerie* lodge]

conservator, †**conservatour** /kən'sɛrvətər/ *n* 1 a keeper, a custodian; a curator *la15-*. 2 an officer of the staple at Campvere, Holland, appointed to protect the rights of the Scottish merchants and settle their disputes *16-e19, la19- historical*. 3 an official defender of the privileges of an institution or corporate body *16*. [ME *conservatour,* Lat *conservātor*]

consider *see* CONSEEDER

considerin /kən'sɪdərɪn/ *adj* considerate, thoughtful *20- NE EC*. [presp of CONSEEDER]

consign, †**consing** /kən'sʌɪn/ *v* 1 to commit, deliver, entrust *la16-*. 2 *law* to deposit money as a pledge or pending judicial action *la16-*. 3 to lodge money as a pledge of good conduct at a wedding *17-19* **consignation,** †**consignatioun** *law* 1 the depositing of a sum of money pending a judicial outcome *la16-*. 2 the depositing of money (with a church) as a pledge for good conduct at a wedding *18, la19- historical*. [EModE *consign,* Lat *consignāre*]

consistore *see* CONSISTORY

consistorial /kɔnsɪ'stɔrɪəl/ *adj law* pertaining to actions between spouses involving status (for divorce or separation); originally pertaining to a bishop's consistory or a commissary court *la15-*. [CONSISTORIE, with adj-forming suffix]

consistory, †**consistorie,** †**consistore** /kən'sɪstəre/ *n* an ecclesiastical court, originally a bishop's court or the commissary court *la15-*. [ME *consistorie,* Lat *consistōrium*]

consither *see* CONSEEDER

consolidate, †**consolidat** /kən'sɔlədet/ *v law* to combine the superiority and ownership of property in one person *la16-*. **consolidation** *law* the joining of the superiority and ownership of property in one person *17*. [Lat *consolidāt-,* ptp stem of *consolidāre*]

constabilry *see* CONSTABULARY

constable, †**constabill,** †**counstable** /'kʌnstəbəl, 'kɔnstəbəl/ *n* 1 an officer of the peace; a police officer *la15-*. 2 the commander of an army under the king; the warden of a royal castle *la14-e18*. **Constable of Scotland** one of the chief officers of the royal household *15-19, 20- historical*. [ME *constable*]

constabulary, †**constabilry** /kən'stabjulərə/ *n* 1 a police force *19-*. 2 the district under the jurisdiction of a constable *la15-18, 19- historical*. 3 the rank or office of constable *16-e18*. [Lat *constabulāria*]

constancy /'kɔnstənsɛ/ *n* steadfastness; regularity *la16-*. **for a constancy** incessantly, always *19, 20- WC*. [Lat *constantia*]

constant[1.1] /'kɔnstənt/ *adj* 1 faithful, firm, steadfast *15-*. 2 unchanging, invariable; continual, persistent *16-*. 3 evident, proved *17*. [MFr *constant,* Lat *constans*]

constant[1.2] /'kɔnstənt/ *adv* constantly, always *19- Ork NE T EC*. [see the adj]

†**consterie, constrie** *n* an ecclesiastical court *la15-e18*. [reduced form of CONSISTORY]

constitute[1.1] /'kɔnstɪtjut/ *v* 1 to appoint; to place, situate *la15-*. 2 to make up, form *16-*. 3 to open formally; to give legal or official form to an assembly or church *17-*. [Lat *constitūt-,* ptp stem of *constituere*]

†**constitute**[1.2] *adj* constituted, appointed *16-e19*. [Lat *constitūtus,* ptp of *constituere*]

†**constrene, constryne** *v* to constrain *la15-16*. [OFr *constreindre*]

†**constrenʒe** *v* to constrain *la15-16*. [ME *constreinen, constrenen*]

constrie *see* CONSTERIE

construct /kən'strʌkt/ *v* 1 to build, make or assemble *16-*. 2 to construe, interpret *17-e19*. [Lat *construct-,* ptp stem of *construere*]

constryne *see* CONSTRENE

consuetude /'kɔnswɪtjud, kən'suɪtjud/ *n* custom, habit; a convention, an unwritten law *la15-*. [ME *consüetude,* Lat *consuētūdo*]

consumpt /kən'sʌmt/ *n* consumption, the amount consumed *18-*. [Lat *consumpt-,* ptp stem of *consumere* consume]

†**consuming dyke** *n* = CONSUMPTION DYKE *19*. [Scots *consuming* + DYKE[1.1]]

consumption dyke /kən'sʌmʃən dʌɪk/ *n* a wall built to use up the stones cleared from a field *la19- NE*. [Older Scots *consumptioun* + DYKE[1.1]]

cont *see* COONT[1.1], COONT[1.2]

contain *see* CONTEEN

containow *see* CONTEENA

conteen, contain, †**contene,** †**conteyn** /kən'tin, kən'ten/ *v* 1 to have or hold within *la14-*. 2 to hold back; to restrain *la14-*. †**contenyng** behaviour, demeanour *la14-e15*. [ME *conteinen*]

conteena, conteenie, continue, †**continow,** †**containow** /kən'tinə, kən'tini, kən'tɪnju/ *v* 1 to keep going; to maintain; to remain *la14-*. 2 *law* to adjourn, prorogue, put off (a judicial case or parliamentary session) for an interval of time *15-*. 3 to grant (a person) a delay or respite *16*. [OFr *continuer*]

†**contempn** *v* to despise, show contempt *la15-e17*. **contempnandlie** contemptuously, scornfully *la15-e17*. [ME *contempnen*]

†**contemporane** *adj* contemporaneous *15-16*. [Lat *contemporāneus*]

†**contemptioun** *n* 1 contempt; insolent disregard of authority *la15-e17*. 2 the state of being scorned *16*. [Lat *contemptio*]

contenance *see* COONTENANCE

†**contene, contine, conteyne** *v* to continue *la14-16*. [irregular variant of *continue* (CONTEENA)]

contene *see* CONTEEN

content[1.1] /kən'tɛnt/ *n* 1 satisfaction, pleasure *la15-*. 2 a drink of hot water, milk and sugar *19-*. [OFr *contente*]

content[1.2] /kən'tɛnt/ *adj* 1 satisfied *15-*. 2 happy, pleased *19-*. [MFr *content*]

conter[1.1] /'kɔntər/ *n* 1 a reverse, a misfortune *la18- NE T*. 2 the contrary *20- NE T*. [see the prep]

conter¹,² /ˈkɔntər/ *v* to oppose, contradict, thwart *la18-*. [see the prep]

conter¹,³ /ˈkɔntər/ *adj* opposite *20- NE T.* **contirgates** contrariwise *20- NE.* **contermint, conterminit** contrary, perverse *la19- NE.* †**conter-tree** a crossbar preventing a door being opened from the inside *e19*. [see the prep]

conter¹,⁴ /ˈkɔntər/ *adv* against *19- NE C.* **gae conter tae** to go against *19-*. [see the prep]

conter¹,⁵ /ˈkɔntər/ *prep* against *la18-19, 20- EC.* [Fr *contre*, Lat *contra*]

conterdick /ˈkɔntərˌdɪk/ *v* to contradict *la19- NE T.* [Lat *contrādict-*, ptp stem of *contrādicere* speak against]

conterfait *see* COUNTERFUTE²,², COUNTERFUTE²,³

contermacious, contramashious /ˌkɔntərˈmeʃəs, ˌkɔntrəˈmeʃəs/ *adj* perverse, self-willed, obstinate *19-*. [altered form of Eng *contumacious*, with influence from CONTER¹,³]

†**contermaister, countermaister** *n* the mate of a ship *la16-e17*. [MFr *contremaistre*]

contermit, contermt /kənˈtɛrmɪt, kənˈtɛrmt/ *adj* determined, stubborn *la15-*. [unknown]

conteyn *see* CONTEEN

conteyne *see* CONTENE

†**contigue** *adj* contiguous, adjacent *la15-19*. [MFr *contigu*, Lat *contiguus*]

contine *see* CONTENE

continow, continue *see* CONTEENA

continuation /kənˌtɪnjuˈeʃən/ *n* 1 the act of continuing *15-*. 2 *law* adjournment, postponement; an extension *la15-*. **with continuation of days** *law* with provision or allowance for a case or other legal matter to be continued or adjourned to a later date *la14-*. [ME *continuacioun*, Lat *continuātiō*]

Continuing United Free Church /kənˈtɪnjuɪŋ juˈnʌɪtəd fri ˈtʃʌrtʃ/ *n* the minority group of members of the UNITED FREE CHURCH who did not rejoin the Church of Scotland in 1929 *e20, la20- historical*. [compare UNITED FREE CHURCH]

contra, †**contray** /ˈkɔntrə/ *prep* against *la15-*. †**in contra of** in violation of *la15-e16.* **pro and contra** for and against *la15-*. [Lat *contra*; compare CONTER¹,⁵]

contrack¹,¹, **contract,** †**contrak** /ˈkɔntrak, ˈkɔntrakt/ *n* a (written) agreement *la14-*. [ME *contract*]

contrack¹,², **contract** /kənˈtrak, kənˈtrakt/ *v* 1 to bring upon oneself; to incur; to become infected with *16-.* 2 to enter into a contract; to agree *16-.* 3 to bring together, collect *e16*. [Lat *contract-*, ptp stem of *contrahere*]

contrair¹,¹, †**contrar,** †**contrer** /ˈkɔntrer, kənˈtrer/ *n* the contrary or the opposite *la14-*. [see the adj]

contrair¹,², **contrar** /kənˈtrer, kənˈtrar/ *v* to oppose, contradict; to go contrary to *la14-*. [see the adj]

contrair¹,³, †**contrare,** †**contrar,** †**contrer** /kənˈtrer, ˈkɔntrer/ *adj* contrary, opposite; unfavourable, adverse *la14-*. [OFr *contraire*]

contrair¹,⁴ /kənˈtrer/ *adv* in a contrary way *la15-*. [see the adj]

†**contrair**¹,⁵, **contrar** *prep* 1 in opposition to, against *15-e19*. 2 contrary to, at variance with *la15-e17*. [see the adj]

contrak *see* CONTRACK¹,¹

†**contramand** *v* to countermand *16*. [ME *countremaunden*, with influence from CONTRA]

contramashious *see* CONTERMACIOUS

†**contrapart** *n* the opposing party or side *16*. [Lat *contra* against + *part* (PAIRT¹,¹)]

contrar *see* CONTRAIR¹,¹, CONTRAIR¹,², CONTRAIR¹,³, CONTRAIR¹,⁵

contrare *see* CONTRAIR¹,³

†**contrary** *v* 1 to act or speak against; to oppose *la14-e16.* 2 *of the wind* to be contrary *15-e17*. [ME *contrarien*]

†**contravaill** *v* to equal in value, counterbalance or reciprocate *la16*. [EModE *countervail*, with influence from CONTRA]

contravene /ˌkɔntrəˈvin/ *v* to act contrary to; to violate, infringe or transgress *16-*. [MFr *contrevenir*, Lat *contrāvenīre*]

contray *see* CONTRA

contre *see* KINTRA

†**contremandment** *n* a counter-order *la14-e15*. [MFr *contremandement*]

contrer *see* CONTRAIR¹,¹, CONTRAIR¹,³

†**contryne** *v* to constrain *la16*. [variant of CONSTRENE after OFr *constreindre*]

†**contumax** *adj* contumacious, insolent, wilfully disobedient, showing contempt of court *la15-17*. **contumaxit, contumaxed** declared guilty of contumacy *la16-17*. [Lat *contumāx*]

contynance *see* COONTENANCE

convalesce, †**convales,** †**convoles** /ˌkɔnvəˈlɛs/ *v* 1 to recover from illness, regain health *16-*. 2 to become strong, acquire or regain strength *16-e17*. [Lat *convalēscere*]

conveen *see* CONVENE¹,²

conveevial, convivial /kənˈvivɪəl, kənˈvɪvɪəl/ *adj* festive, jovial *19-*. [Lat *convīviālis* pertaining to a feast]

convenar *see* CONVENER

†**convene**¹,¹ *n* 1 a gathering *e19.* 2 an agreement, a compact *16*. [MFr *convine*]

convene¹,², †**conveen,** †**convine** /kənˈvin/ *v* 1 to meet, gather or assemble *15-.* 2 to convoke a meeting *16-.* 3 to suit, be fitting; to pertain naturally to *la15-19.* 4 to summon before a tribunal *15-17.* 5 to come to an accord, agree *16-e17*. [MFr *convenir*, Lat *convenīre*]

convener, †**convenar** /kənˈvinər/ *n* 1 the president of the Incorporated Trades in a burgh, the deacon convener *la16-.* 2 the chair of a committee *la17-.* 3 a person who assembles along with others *la16.* **convenery** 1 the court of the conveners of the Trade Incorporations *la18-.* 2 a body met for official purposes, a convention *la18-e19*. [CONVENE¹,², with agent suffix]

convention, †**conventioun** /kənˈvɛnʃən/ *n* 1 an agreement; a rule or custom *15-.* 2 an assembly, a gathering; a conference *16-.* 3 the (annual) meeting of the representatives of Scottish Local Authorities (originally the commissioners of burghs) *16-.* 4 an extraordinary meeting of the Estates of Scotland to deal with emergencies *16-18, 19- historical.* **Convention of Burghs** a meeting of the commissioners of burghs *la16-20, 21- historical.* **Convention of Royal Burghs** = *Convention of Burghs la18-20, 21- historical.* **Convention of Scottish Local Authorities** the national association of Scottish councils *la20-.* **COSLA** = *Convention of Scottish Local Authorities*. [ME *convencioun*, Lat *conventio*]

conversation /ˌkɔnvərˈseʃən/ *n* 1 discourse, discussion; association, intercourse *la14-.* 2 a flat sweet inscribed with a motto *la19-.* **conversation lozenge** a flat sweet inscribed with a motto *la19-.* **conversation sweetie** = *conversation lozenge 20-.* [ME *conversacioun*]

conveth /ˈkɔnvəθ, kənˈvɛθ/ *n* hospitality due by a vassal to a superior *12-16, la19- historical*. [IrGael *coinmeadh*]

convey /kənˈve/ *v* 1 to transport, carry *16-.* 2 *law* to transfer (property) *la18-.* 3 to communicate an idea *19-.* 4 to escort, conduct *la16-19, 20- NE*. [ME *conveien*; compare CONVOY¹,²]

†**convict**¹,¹ *n* a conviction, a guilty verdict *la16*. [see the verb]

†**convict**¹,², **convick** *adj* proved or found guilty, convicted *15-e18*. [Lat *convict-*, ptp stem of *convincere*]

convine *see* CONVENE¹,²

convivial *see* CONVEEVIAL

convoles see CONVALESCE

convoy[1.1], †**conwoy** /ˈkɔnvɔi/ n 1 escorting, guiding; the accompanying of a guest (all or part of the way) on their journey home *la16-*. 2 an escort, a guide *la16-e17*. 3 the management of affairs *la16*. 4 deportment, bearing *e16*. **a Hielan convoy** accompanying a person some or all the way on their journey home (sometimes being accompanied in return some of the way back) *la19- Ork T Bor*. **a Scots convoy** accompanying a person some or all the way on their journey home (sometimes being accompanied in return some of the way back) *19-*. [OFr *convoi*]

convoy[1.2], †**conwoy** /kənˈvɔi, ˈkɔnvɔi/ v 1 to escort or accompany; to lead or conduct *la14-*. 2 to carry, transport goods *16-*. 3 to manage, accomplish *16-e17*. 4 to pursue *la14-e15*.

convoyance 1 escort, escorting *16, 20- N NE T*. 2 conveyance, carrying; a carriage *17-19*. 3 management, contrivance *16-17*. [ME *convoien*, OFr *convoier*; compare CONVEY]

†**convyne, convyine** n 1 an agreement *la15-e16*. 2 a company *e16*. [OFr *covine*; compare COVIN]

conyng see KINNEN

conyngare see CUNINGAR

conȝe see CUNYIE[1.1], CUNYIE[1.2]

conȝeour see CUNȜEAR

coo, cow, †**kow,** †**quow** /ku, kʌu/ n 1 a large bovine animal, a cow *Bos taurus la14-*; compare KYE. 2 a cow given as a payment to the clergy on the death and burial of a householder *16*. **cooie, cowie** a (baby's) teat *20- EC Bor*. **coo's arse, coo's erse** a botched job, a mess *la20-*. **coo bailie, cow bailie** a cow-man *la19-*. **cow cakes** the cow parsnip *Anthriscus sylvestris la19- EC Bor*. †**cow cracker** the bladder campion *la19*. **coo's drink** hot treacle (given to sick cows); a hot drink *la19- T EC*. **coo feeder, cowfeeder** a dairy farmer *18- N NE T C Bor*. **coo gang, cowgang** a cow pasture; enough pasturage for one cow *19- Bor*. **coo's gress,** †**kyis girs** enough pasturage for one cow *la19-, 20- SW Bor*. **coo-haughed** knock-kneed; bow-legged *20- T WC SW*. **cowkeep** enough pasturage for one cow *19- Ork EC*. **cow plat** a cow-pat *19-*. **coo quake, cow quake** a short spell of bad weather in May *17-19, 20- Ork NE T EC*. [OE *cū*]

cooard, coord, coward, †**cowart** /ˈkuərd, kurd, ˈkʌuərd/ n a person lacking courage *la14-*. **cooardiness, cowardiness** cowardliness *la19-*. **cooardly, cooartly,** †**cowartly** cowardly *la14-*. [ME *couard*]

cooardy, coordie /ˈkuərdɪ, ˈkurdi,/ adj cowardly *la19-*. **cooardy lick, coordie lick** a blow given as a challenge to fight *la19-*. [COOARD + -IE[2]]

cooch[1.1]**, couch,** †**cuche** /kutʃ, kʌutʃ/ n 1 a bed, a sofa *16-*. 2 a dog's kennel *la19- NE*. 3 a cradle-cloth *la14-e16*. **cooch bed, couch bed** a couch used as a bed; a divan *la15-*. [ME *couche*]

cooch[1.2]**, couch,** †**cuche** /kutʃ, kʌutʃ/ v 1 to lie down; to settle, fix in place *la15-*. 2 to command (a dog) to lie down; to kennel a dog *20 NE*. **coocher, coucher** 1 a coward, a base person *15-19, 20- SW Bor*. 2 a blow or tap on the shoulder as a challenge to fight *19- C Bor*. **cooch up** to go to bed *20 NE T EC*. [ME *couchen*]

cood[1], N **keed,** NE **quid,** NE **cweed,** †**cude** /kud/ N kid/ N kwid/ n the cud of a ruminant *la16-*. [OE *cudu*]

cood[2], NE **quid,** NE **cweed,** †**cuyd** /kud/ NE kwid/ n 1 a shallow tub, a wooden dish or basin *la16-*. 2 a large tub for washing, storage or transportation *17-*. [unknown]

coodie see CUDDIE[1]

coo'er see COOR

coof, cuif, †**coff** /kuf/ n 1 a foolish or incompetent person *18-*. 2 a coward *19- NE T EC*. 3 an ill-mannered or rough person *19, 20- EC*. 4 a rogue *la16*. [unknown]

coo-heel /kuˈhil/ v to command a dog to come away or come to heel *la19- T*. [probably corruption of Scots *come to heel*]

cook[1.1] /kuk/ n 1 the game of hide-and-seek *la19, 20- EC*. 2 a look, a peep *19- H&I WC*. **cookerty, cookerty, I, I, I** a warning call in the game of hide-and-seek *la20- Bor*. [see the verb]

cook[1.2] /kuk/ v 1 to disappear suddenly from view; to dart in and out of sight *la18-*. 2 to peep at, glance slyly *19- H&I WC* [perhaps related to KEEK[1.2]; compare Ger *gucken*, LG *kucken* to peep]

cook see CUIK[1.1], CUIK[1.2]

cookie, †**cukie** /ˈkuki, ˈkuke/ n 1 a plain bun *18-*. 2 a prostitute *20- C*. **cookie shine** a tea party *19-*. **cream cookie** a yeast-baked bun split sideways and filled with cream *20-*. **currant cookie** a bun with currants in it *la19-*. **kiss my cookie** kiss my arse *la20-*. [perhaps Du *koekje* a small cake]

cool, cowl, †**coule,** †**cule** /kul, kʌul/ n 1 a hooded garment (worn by monks) *la14-*. 2 a (woollen) close-fitting cap, a night-cap *18-*. [OE *cugele*]

cool see CUIL

coolye see CULYIE

coom[1.1]**, koom, culm,** C **gum,** †**cowm** /kum, kʌlm; C gʌm/ n 1 soot; coal-dust; dross *16-*. 2 peat dust; fine turf mould *la19- SW Uls*. 3 dust, powder; small particles *20- Sh Ork Uls*. **coomy** n a miner *la19- C*. **coomy** adj sooty, covered in coal-dust *19- C*. [ME *colme*]

coom[1.2]**,** †**cowm** /kum/ v to dirty, blacken, stain *la16-*. [see the noun]

coom[2]**,** †**cowm** /kum/ n 1 the wooden frame supporting the building of the arch of a bridge *16-19, 20- historical*. 2 the sloping part of an attic ceiling *20-*. 3 a (curved) coffin-lid *19*. 4 an arch or vault *la16-18*. **coomed** vaulted, arched; *of a ceiling* sloping *18-*. **coomceil, cumseil, cumsyle** v 1 to lath and plaster a ceiling *la18-*. 2 to furnish with an arched ceiling *la16-17*. **coomceil, cumseil,** †**coomesyle** n the timbering of an arched ceiling; a sloping roof *17-19, 20- WC*; compare CAMCEIL. **coomceiled** having a sloping ceiling *la17-*. [unknown]

coomle see CUMMEL

cooncil, council, †**counsale,** †**councell,** †**counsell** /ˈkunsəl, ˈkʌunsəl/ n 1 an assembly; a body of advisors *la14-*. 2 a local authority, the administrative body of a town or district *la15-*. **cooncil hoose, council house** 1 a house rented from the local authority *20-*. 2 a house where town-council meetings were held; a town hall *la15-19, 20- historical*. **cooncil juice, council juice** water *la20-*. **cooncil telly** 1 satellite television *21-*. 2 free terrestrial television *21-*. [ME *counseil*, Lat *concilium*]

coont[1.1]**, count,** †**cont,** †**cunt** /kunt, kʌunt/ n 1 an account or reckoning (of money); the act of counting; the total sum as reckoned *la14-*. 2 an account or description (of matters); a point of consideration *16-*. 3 pl arithmetic, sums *20-*. [ME *counte*]

coont[1.2]**, count,** NE **cwint,** †**cont** /kunt, kʌunt; NE kwɪnt/ v 1 to count, reckon; to take into account *la14-*. 2 to do arithmetic *19-*. 3 to settle an account; to pay *18-19, 20- NE*. **count kin wi** to compare one's pedigree with that of another; to claim relationship with *19-*. **count a pye** to point to or itemize the players in a game to identify the MANNIE *la20- NE*. [ME *counten*]

coontenance, countenance, †**contenance,** †**contynance** /ˈkuntɪnəns, ˈkʌuntɪnəns/ n appearance, manner; the face; a facial expression *la14-*. [ME *contenaunce*]

coonter¹, counter, †countour /ˈkuntər, ˈkʌuntər/ *n* **1** a (display) counter in a shop, originally a counting table *la15-*. **2** a disc used in playing games, originally for counting with *la15-*. **coonter louper, counter lowper** *derogatory* a person who serves behind a counter, a shop-assistant *la19-*. [ME *countour*]

coonter², counter /ˈkuntər, ˈkʌuntər/ *n* a person who keeps or renders accounts; a treasurer or accountant; a mathematician *la15-*. [ME *countour*]

coontra *see* KINTRA

coonty, county /ˈkunti, ˈkunte, ˈkʌunte/ *n* a shire, a county *17-*. [AN *counté*]

coonyie *see* CUNYIE¹·¹

coop¹ /kup/ *n* a small heap of manure or hay *19-*. [unknown; compare Gael *coip* a heap of foam]

†coop² *v* to make or repair casks *la18-e19*. [back-formation from COOPER]

coop *see* COWP¹·², CUP

co-op /ˈkoɔp, kɔp/ *n* a Co-operative store *20-*. Compare *the Store* (STORE¹·¹). [reduced form of CO-OPERATIVE]

cooper *see* COUPER²

Co-operative /koˈɔprətɪv, koˈɔpərətɪv, kɔpəˈretɪv/ *n* **1** an organization operated by its members for their mutual benefit *19-*. **2** a store run by a co-operative society *la20-*. **co-operative society** a society in which goods are distributed and the profits are shared by all the contributing members *19-*. **co-operative store** a shop belonging to a *co-operative society* providing goods at cost price and distributing any profits among the members *19-*. [Lat *cooperāt-*, ptp stem of *cooperāri*, with adj-forming suffix]

coopie, co-opie /ˈkope, ˈkopi/ *n* a Co-operative store *la20- NE T*. [CO-OP + -IE¹]

coopin *see* COUPON¹

coor, cour, coo'er, curr, †cowr /kur, ˈkuər, kʌr/ *v* **1** *v* to cower, cringe; to crouch down *la15-*. **2** to bend, lower or fold *la18-*. [unknown; compare Dan *kure* to squat, Ger *kauern* to cower]

coor *see* COVER¹·²

coorag¹ /ˈkurəɡ/ *n* a woollen cap; a nightcap *20- N*. [Gael *currachd*, apparently from CURCH]

coorag², currag /ˈkurəɡ, ˈkʌrəɡ/ *n* the index finger *20- N*. Compare COORIE³. [Gael *corrag*]

coorant *see* CARRANT

coord *see* COOARD

coordie /ˈkurdi/ *v* to be cowed, shrink *20- NE EC*. [COOARD + -IE¹]

coordie *see* COOARDY

coorgy /ˈkurdʒi/ *n* a blow or push given as a challenge to fight; a dare *20- C*. [unknown]

coorie¹·¹, †curry /ˈkuri, ˈkure/ *v* **1** to stoop, bend or crouch down; to cringe *18-*. **2** to snuggle, nestle *20-*. **coorie-hunker, curry-hunker** to squat, crouch *20-*. **coorie doon, †curry down 1** to crouch down *18-*. **2** to snuggle down (in bed) *20-*. [COOR + -IE¹]

coorie¹·² /ˈkuri, ˈkure/ *adj* timid, cringing *19- EC Bor*. [see the verb]

†coorie² *n* the stables of the royal household *e17*. [aphetic form of Fr *écurie*]

coorie³, curry /ˈkuri, ˈkʌri/ *n* the index finger *20- N*. Compare COORAG². [Gael *corrag*]

coorly, kooerly /ˈkuərli/ *adj* cowardly, timid; miserly *20- Ork*. [perhaps altered form of *cooardly* (COOARD)]

coorse¹, coarse, †cours /kurs, kors/ *adj* **1** rough, harsh, vulgar; not fine *16-*. **2** *of weather* foul, stormy *la18-*. **3** *of people* wicked, bad; mischievous *la19-*. **4** hard, trying;

disagreeable *la19-*. **5** *of people* rough, vulgar, awkward; over-direct in manner *20-*. [ME *cours*]

coorse², course, †cours, †cowrs, †curs /kurs, kors/ *n* **1** a route, a direction; the path or channel taken; a track *la14-*. **2** a part of a meal *15-*. **3** a diet of instruction or study *la16-*. **4** a charge (on horseback) *la14-16*. **5** currency, circulation *la15-16*. **†coursable** *law* according with usual legal procedure *la15-e16*. **an' coorse** of course *la19- NE*. **†cours of commoun law** usual legal procedure *15-16*. **in coorse 1** of course *la19- NE*. **2** in due course *la19- NE*. [ME *cours*]

coort¹·¹, court, †curt /kurt, kort/ *n* **1** a formal assembly; the royal court; a court of justice or administration *la14-*. **2** a quadrangular area used for ball games, a tennis court *17-*. **3** a lane or narrow courtyard enclosed by houses; a courtyard behind a tenement *18-*. **4** a (covered) enclosure for cattle *la19-*. **†court plaint** the privilege of dealing with complaints made to a court of justice *la15-e17*. **Court of Admiralty** the court in which the High Admiral of Scotland exercised extensive jurisdiction (civil and criminal) *la18-19, 20- historical*. **Court of Exchequer** a court having jurisdiction in revenue cases (merged since 1856 in the Court of Session) *18-19, 20- historical*. **†Court of Justice 1** *law* the supreme criminal court of Scotland *la17-e19*. **2** *law* a court presided over by a Justice *la15-17*. **Court of Justiciary** *law* the supreme criminal court of Scotland, originally a court presided over by a JUSTICIAR *16-*; compare HIGH COURT. **court of regality** a court held by a lord of regality *la16-18, 19- historical*. **Court of Session** the supreme civil judicature in Scotland *la16-*. **Court of Teinds** the Commissioners of Teinds, the body administering the tithes after the Union of the Scottish and English Parliaments *18-20, 21- historical*. [ME *court*]

coort¹·², **court** /kurt, kort/ *v* to make advances towards; to seek favour from *17-*. [see the noun]

coorteen /ˈkurtin/ *n* a curtain *20- Sh N*. [altered form of Eng *curtain*]

coosar *see* COOSER

coose¹·¹, koos, *Ork* **kest** /kus; *Ork* kɛst/ *n* a heap or pile (of refuse); a dunghill *la19- Sh Ork*. [Norw dial *kos* a heap]

coose¹·², kus, †kest, †kase /kus/ *v* to heap or pile up peat or seaweed for drying *la18- Sh Ork*. [ON *kasa* to heap earth on]

cooser, coosar, †cuisser, †cusser, †cursour /ˈkusər/ *n* **1** a stallion *16-19, 20- NE EC*. **2** a war-horse, a charger *la14-e17*. [altered form of ME *courser*]

cooshin *see* CAITION¹·²

cooshious *see* COWSHUS

coosie /ˈkuzi/ *n* a challenge to a feat of dexterity or daring *la19- T*. [unknown]

coost *see* CAST¹·²

coot *see* CUIT, QUEET

cooter, Uls coother, †culter, †couter /ˈkutər; *Uls* ˈkuθər/ *n* **1** the coulter of a plough *la14-*. **2** *humorous* a name for the nose *la19-*. [OE *culter*]

coothie *see* COUTHIE

coothin, kuithin /ˈkuθɪn, ˈkøðɪn/ *n* a young coalfish *19- Ork*. Compare *cuddin* (CUDDIE²). [Norw dial *kot*, the *-in* is probably the def art]

cootie /ˈkuti/ *adj of fowls* having feathered legs *la18- SW*. [probably CUIT + -IE²]

cootie *see* CUDDIE¹

cop /kɔp, kʌp/ *interj* a call to a horse to approach *20-*. **cop cop** = COP. [altered form of Scots *come up*]

cop *see* CAP¹

copar *see* COUPER²

copburd *see* CUBBART

cope *see* COUP¹·², COWP¹·²

copeburd see CUBBART
cope-carlie see COWP[1,2]
coper see COUPER[2]
copindo see COLPINDACH
†**coping-boit** a herring-buyer's boat *la16*. [ON *kaupa*, MDu *copen* + BOAT[1,1]]
copy[1,1], †**coppe** /ˈkɔpi, ˈkope/ *n* **1** a duplicate; an imitation *la15-*. **2** a copy-book *20-*. **3** plenty, abundance *la14-e15*. [ME *copie*]
copy[1,2], †**coppe** /ˈkɔpi, ˈkope/ *v* **1** to make a copy; to imitate *la15-*. **2** to note, observe *la15-e16*. **copy wattie** to copy without acknowledgement; to take note of *20- NE*. [ME *copien*, Lat *copiāre* to transcribe]
coral, †**curale**, †**currell**, †**curle** /ˈkɔrəl, ˈkorəl/ *n* **1** coral, the substance and the colour *la15-*. **2** a lightweight fabric; coral-coloured cloth *17*. [ME *coral*]
coram see QUORUM
†**corbell**, **corball** *n* a corbel *15-17*. **corbel sailʒe** a series of corbels *e16*. [ME *corbel*]
Corbett /ˈkɔrbət/ *n* a name for a Scottish mountain of between 2500 and 3000 feet in height *la20-*. Compare MUNRO, DONALD[2]. [from the surname of J R Corbett, who first listed them]
corbie, **corby** /ˈkɔrbi, ˈkorbe/ *n* **1** the raven *Corvus corax 15-*. **2** the carrion crow *Corvus corone* or hooded crow *Corvus cornix la19-*. **3** the rook *Corvus frugilegus 20-*. **corbie messenger** a slow or unreliable messenger, originally the raven sent out by Noah *la15-19, 20- NE C*. **corbie stanes** step-like projections on the sloping part of a gable *20-*; compare *crawsteps* (CRAW[1]). **be a gone corbie** be done for *19-*. [OFr *corp*, *corbe*]
corcag /ˈkɔrkəg/ *n* a small knife *20- N*. [Gael *corcag*]
†**corchat** *n* a crotchet (in music) *e16*. [metathesis of CRUCHET]
cord[1] /kɔrd/ *v* to accord, agree *la14-19, 20- SW*. [aphetic form of Older Scots *accord*]
cord[2] /kɔrd/ *n* **1** a string or thin rope *la14-*. **2** one of the ropes held by relatives and friends of the deceased by which a coffin is lowered into the grave *20-*. **3** *pl* an intestinal inflammation in calves *19- WC Bor*. **4** a bundle of skins *la16-17*. [ME *corde*]
cordecedron see CORDISIDRON
†**cordell** *n* a rope (as part of a ship's tackle) *16-e17*. [OFr *cordele*]
cordiner, †**cordenar**, †**cordonar**, †**cordinare** /ˈkɔrdənər/ *n* a shoemaker, a cordwainer *15-*. [ME *cordewaner*, OFr *cordoanier*, originally a maker of or dealer in Cordovan leather]
†**cordisidron**, **cordecedron** *n* lemon peel *17-e18*. [Fr *écorce de citron*]
cordonar see CORDINER
cordovan Cordovan leather *la15-e17*. [irregular variant of Older Scots *cordwane*]
core /kor/ *n* **1** a (convivial) party or company *la18-*. **2** *curling* a team of players *la18-19, 20- NE T*. [EModE *chore* a choir, a company]
†**corf** *n* a basket *16-e17*. [MDu *corf*]
corfhouse /ˈkɔrfhʌus/ *n* a salmon-curing shed; a storage shed for salmon nets *la16-*. [perhaps CORF + HOOSE[1,1]]
cork /kɔrk/ *n* **1** an overseer; a master tradesman; a small employer; a manufacturer's agent *19-*. **2** a person in authority *19-*. [unknown]
corkir /ˈkɔrkər/ *n* **1** a lichen *Lecanora tartarea* used as a red dye *18-19, 20- Sh*. **2** a red or purple colour *la19- Sh*. [Gael *corcur* crimson]
corklit, *Sh* **korkalit** /ˈkɔrklɪt; *Sh* ˈkɔrkəlɪt/ *n* **1** a lichen *Lecanora tartarea* used for dyeing red *la17-19, 20- SW*. **2** a red dye *19- Sh*. [CORKIR + LIT[1,1]]

corky[1,1] /ˈkɔrki/ *n* a foolish, giddy or frivolous person *18-*. [see the adj]
corky[1,2] /ˈkɔrki/ *adj* light, springy; frivolous, foolish *18-*. †**corky heidit**, **corky headed** silly, foolish *la18-19*. †**corky noddle** a giddy person *19*. [Older Scots *cork* the light substance made from oak bark + -IE[2]]
†**cormundum** *n* a clean heart *16-19*. **cry cormundum** to confess one's fault *16-19*. [Lat *cor mundum*]
corn[1,1], **coarn** /kɔrn, korn/ *n* **1** cereal, grain *la14-*. **2** *pl* crops of grain *la14-*. **3** oats *la18-*. **4** a single grain, a seed *la15-19 20- Ork SW*. **corn crake**, †**corn craik 1** the landrail *Crex crex la15-*. **2** a toy rattle *19-*. **corn harp** an instrument for separating grain and weed seeds *18- NE*. **corn kist** a storage-bin for grain *17-*. **corn kister** a type of song sung at farmworkers' gatherings *20- NE T EC*. **corn pipe** a music-pipe made from an oat stem *16-19, 20- Bor*. **corn rig** a ridge or strip of growing corn; the strip between two furrows in a cornfield *la18-*. **corn willie** the yellow wagtail *Motacilla flava la20- WC*. **corn yaird**, †**corn ʒard** a yard where corn is stacked *la15-*. [OE *corn*]
corn[1,2] /kɔrn/ *v* **1** to feed with oats or grain; to provide with grain *la15-*. **2** *of people* to take food *18-*. **corned** exhilarated with drink, tiddly *19, 20- NE*. **cornin time** a meal-time *la19- T EC*. **waur to water than to corn** addicted to alcohol *19-*. [see the noun]
corn beef, **corned beef** /kɔrn ˈbif, kɔrnd ˈbif/ *adj* deaf *la20-*. [rhyming slang; compare DEEF]
†**corneill** *n* a cornelian *16-e17*. [OFr *corneole*]
†**cornel**, **kornal** *n* a colonel *la17-19*. [reduced form of CORONELL]
corner see COARNER
cornet, †**quarnat** /ˈkɔrnət/ *n* **1** the chief rider and standard-bearer of the burgh in ceremonies of riding of the marches *18-*. **2** a cavalry officer who carried the colours *la16*. **3** a ladies' head-dress; an appendage to a head-dress *16*. [MFr *cornette*]
†**cornicle**, **cornikill** *n* a chronicle *la14-e17*. [metathesis of Older Scots *cronicle*]
coronach, †**correnoch** /ˈkɔrənəx/ *n* **1** a funeral lament, a dirge *16-*. **2** an outcry, a shout from a crowd *16-17*. Compare CRONACH[1,1]. [Gael *corranach*, IrGael *coránach*]
†**coronell** *n* a coroner *la16-e17*. [confusion of Older Scots *coronare* with Older Scots *coronell* a colonel]
corp /kɔrp/ *n* a corpse *la15-*. **corp-candle** a will-o'-the-wisp *la19- H&I WC SW*. **corp-lifter** a body-snatcher *la19-*. **the corp** the deceased *la19-*. [probably erroneous singular from ME *corps*]
corps-present see CROCE-PRESENT
corpus /ˈkɔrpəs/ *n* the live body of a person or animal *19- NE T EC*. [Lat *corpus*]
correck[1,1], **correct** /kəˈrek, kəˈrekt/ *v* to put right, rectify, amend; to reprove *la15-*. [Lat *correct-*, ptp stem of *corrigere*]
correck[1,2], **correct** /kəˈrek, kəˈrekt/ *adj* free from error; true, accurate *16-*. [see the verb]
correll see QUARREL[1]
correnoch see CORONACH
corrie[1] /ˈkɔri, ˈkore/ *n* a (circular) hollow on the side of a mountain or between mountains *16-*. [Gael *coire* a cauldron or place resembling one; a kettle]
corrie[2], **caurie**, **carrie** /ˈkɔri, ˈkore, ˈkare/ *adj* left; left-handed *19-*. **corry-fisted** left-handed *20-*. **corrie-fister** a left-handed person *20-*. **caurry-handit** left-handed; awkward *la19-*. **carrie-pawed** left-handed; awkward *la19- T EC*. [derivative of CAR[2]]
corrieneuchin[1,1] /kɔriˈnjuxən/ *n* an intimate conversation *la19- NE T EC Bor*. [see the verb]

corrieneuchin[1,2] /kɔriˈnjuxən/ v to be conversing intimately 19- *NE T EC*. Compare CURNEUCH. [perhaps altered from presp of CRONACH[1,2]]

corruption, †**corruptioun** /kəˈrʌpʃən/ n **1** dishonesty, depravity *la15-*. **2** ill temper, anger *19-*. [MFr *corruption*, Lat *corruptio*]

corrydander /kɔriˈdandər/ n coriander *19- NE WC*. Compare CURLY-ANDRA. [altered form of Older Scots *coriander*]

cors *see* CROSS[1,1], CROSS[1,2]

†**corse**, **cors** v to search for or seek out; to visit *16*. [unknown]

corse *see* CROSS[1,1]

†**cors-gard**, **crose-gaird** n a small body of soldiers on guard-duty; a guard-room *la16-e17*. [OFr *cors*, Lat *corpus* body + GAIRD[1,1]]

†**corshous** n a house standing crossways to others *16-e17*. [probably aphetic form of ACROASS[1,2] + HOOSE[1,1]; compare CROSS[1,2]]

cors-presand *see* CROCE-PRESENT

Corstorphine cream /kərstɔrfɪn ˈkrim/ n a dessert made of thickened milk and sugar *18-*. [from the name of a district in Edinburgh + CREAM]

corsy-belly /ˈkɔrsibɛli/ n a child's pleated shirt *la18- NE WC*. [unknown]

corter *see* QUARTER[1,1]

†**cortrik** n cloth from Courtray *la14-15*. [from the Dutch place-name]

cosche *see* QUOSCHE

†**cose**[1,1], **cosse**, **coys** n an exchange (of lands) *la15-e17*. [unknown; compare Lat *cociātor* a broker]

cose[1,2], **kos**, †**coss**, †**quoss** /koz, kɔs/ v to exchange; to barter *15-19, 20- Sh Ork*. [see the noun]

cosey /ˈkozi/ n a woollen scarf *la19-*. [COSIE]

cosh /kɔʃ/ adj **1** snug, comfortable, cosy *la18-*. **2** friendly, intimate *la18-*. [unknown]

cosie, **cosy**, †**cozie** /ˈkozi, ˈkoze/ adj **1** *of people* warm and comfortable, well wrapped-up *la17-*. **2** *of places* sheltered, providing comfort and protection *la18-*. [unknown]

cosing *see* KIZZEN

COSLA *see* CONVENTION

cosnant *see* COSTANENT[1,1]

cosnent *see* COSTANENT[1,1], COSTANENT[1,2]

coss *see* COSE[1,2]

cosse *see* COSE[1,1]

cost /kɔst/ n payment in kind for rent, dues or wages *16- Sh Ork N*. [ON *kostr* food]

cost *see* COAST[1], COAST[2,1], COAST[2,2]

cöst *see* CAST[1,2]

costanent[1,1], †**cosnent**, †**cosnant** /ˈkɔstənɛnt/ n wages without board *la17-19, 20- Uls*. †**cosnent work** work unpaid either in money or board *e19*. [unknown]

costanent[1,2], †**cosnent** /ˈkɔstənɛnt/ adv (working) for wages without board *19, 20- Uls*. [unknown]

cosy *see* COSIE

cot[1,1], †**cote** /kɔt/ n **1** a (farm) cottage, a house occupied by a cottar; frequently in place-names *14-*. **2** a sheep-house *16-*. **cot-folk** people who live in farm cottages *la18-*. **cot-house**, †**coathous**, †**cote hous** a (farmworker's) cottage *16-*. †**cotland** (arable) land attached to a cottage *la14-18*. **cotman** a cottage-dweller, a tenant with a cottage *la16-19, 20- WC SW*. [OE *cott*]

cot[1,2] /kɔt/ v to cohabit; to live in a (farm) cottage *19- NE T*. [see the noun]

cot *see* COAT, KET[2,1]

cotar *see* COTTAR[1,1]

cotch *see* CATCH[1,2], COACH

cote *see* COAT, COT[1,1], QUOT

cotinoy *see* CUTTANOY

†**cotonar** n a piece of small fur, used for lining *e16*. [OFr *cotoners*]

cott *see* COAT

cottar[1,1], †**cotar**, †**coitter** /ˈkɔtər/ n a married farmworker who has a cottage as part of his contract; a tenant occupying a cottage with or without land attached to it *15-*. †**cottary**, **cottery** a cottar's holding *la15-19*. †**cottar beer** barley grown as part of a cottar's remuneration *18-e19*. **cottar house** a farmworker's cottage, a tied cottage *la16-*. †**cottar land** land attached to a cottage *la16-19*. **cottar toun** a hamlet (of farm cottages) *17-19, 20 NE T*. [COT[1,1], with agent suffix]

cottar[1,2], **cotter** /ˈkɔtər/ v to live in a cottage (as a cottar) *20- NE*. [see the noun]

cotter /ˈkɔtər/ v to scramble eggs *la19- T EC*. [EModE *cotter* to clot, coagulate]

cotter *see* COTTAR[1,2]

cottery *see* COTTAR[1,1]

cotting, **cottoun** *see* CUTTEN

cottown, **cotton**, †**cottoun** /ˈkɔttʌun, ˈkɔtən/ n a hamlet (occupied by cottars); farm cottages *15-19, 20 NE T EC*. [COT[1,1] + TOUN]

†**cottrall** n a tenant occupying a cottage *la15-16*. [OFr *coterel* a marauder]

couch *see* COOCH[1,1], COOCH[1,2]

coud *see* CAN[2,2]

coug *see* COG[1,1]

cougher /ˈkɔxər/ v to cough continuously *19, 20- NE*. [frequentative form of Scots *cough*]

couk *see* COWK[1,2]

coukuddy *see* CURCUDDIE

coule *see* COOL

coulichin *see* KILCHAN

coulie *see* COWLIE

†**coulter**, **coutter** n a cautery *la17-e18*. [Fr *cautère*]

coumpt *see* COMPT[1,1]

councell, **council** *see* COONCIL

counger /ˈkunʒər, ˈkʌnʒər/ v **1** to keep in order, put down; to scold; to beat *19- NE WC Bor* **2** to overawe or intimidate *19- NE Bor*. [OFr *coignier* to beat, coin, wedge]

counsale, **counsell** *see* COONCIL

counstable *see* CONSTABLE

count *see* COONT[1,1], COONT[1,2]

countenance *see* COONTENANCE

†**counter** n the part of a horse's breast immediately under the neck *16*. [unknown; perhaps related to *counter* in the opposite direction]

counter *see* COONTER[1], COONTER[2]

countercheck /ˈkʌuntərtʃɛk/ n a tool for cutting the groove which unites the two sashes of a window *19, 20- NE SW*. [unknown]

counterfait *see* COUNTERFUTE[2,2], COUNTERFUTE[2,3]

†**counterfute**[1] n a kind of plate or dish *16*. [unknown]

†**counterfute**[2,1], **conterfete** n a counterfeit, a copy, a model *la15-e17*. [see the adj]

†**counterfute**[2,2], **counterfait**, **conterfait** v to counterfeit *la15-17*. [see the adj]

†**counterfute**[2,3], **counterfait**, **conterfait** adj counterfeited *la15-e17*. [ME *countrefet*]

countermaister *see* CONTERMAISTER

countour *see* COONTER[1]

countra, **countre**, **country** *see* KINTRA

county *see* COONTY

county of the city /ˈkʌunte əv ðə ˈsɪte/ *n pl* **counties of cities** any of the county burghs of Edinburgh, Glasgow, Dundee and Aberdeen, now all altered into districts with extended boundaries and more limited responsibilities *la18-20, 21- historical*. [AN *counté* + of the CITY]

coup¹·¹, cowp /kʌup/ *n* a deal, a trade; a bargain *la16-19, 20- NE EC*. [see the verb]

coup¹·², cowp, *Sh* **kop,** †**cope** /kʌup; *Sh* kop/ *v* to buy or trade (goods or livestock); to barter or exchange *16-19, 20- Sh NE EC Bor*. [ON *kaup* a bargain]

†**coup², cowp** *n* **1** a basket for catching salmon; a pannier *la15-19*. **2** a closed cart for carrying manure or earth *la15-e19*. [ME *coupe* a basket]

coup *see* COWP¹·², CUP

Coupar justice *see* CUPAR JUSTICE

coup-cart *see* COWP-CAIRT

†**couper¹, coupar, cupar** *n* a maker or mender of barrels and casks *la13-e18*. [MLG *kuper*, MDu *cuper*]

couper², cowper, cooper, †**copar,** †**coper** /ˈkʌupər, ˈkupər/ *n* **1** a trader, a merchant *16-*. **2** a horse-dealer *la16-*. **3** a buyer of herring *16-e19*. †**couper boit** a herring-buyer's boat *la16-e17*. [COUP¹·², with agent suffix]

couple¹·¹, cupple, kipple, †**coupill,** †**cuppill,** †**kipill** /ˈkʌpəl, ˈkɪpəl/ *n* **1** (one of) a pair of rafters, forming a V-shaped roof support; a principal rafter *15-*. **2** a pair, a set of two *la15-*. **3** a measure of butter and cheese sold together *la17-e18*. **4** a standard of length of 12 feet in (the roofspace of) a building *la15-17*. **5** a leash for two dogs *16-17*. **couple bauk** the crossbeam connecting the ends of a rafter *la18-*. **couple-leg** one of a pair of rafters *19- Ork N NE EC*. **in a couple of hurries** without delay *19-*. [ME *couple*]

couple¹·², cupple, kipple, †**coupill** /ˈkʌpəl, ˈkɪpəl/ *v* **1** to join, unite *la14-*. **2** to marry *la14-*. **3** to frame a roof with a pair of rafters *la15-16*. **coupling, cupplin 1** joining, uniting; marrying *la14-*. **2** a rafter *19-*. **3** the bottom of the spine where it joins the sacrum *19- NE EC*. **4** the framing of a roof with a pair of rafters *la15-e16*. [ME *couplen*]

coupon¹, coopin, †**coupoun,** †**cowpon** /ˈkʌupən, ˈkupən/ *n* a small piece (cut off), a fragment *16-*. [ME *culpoun*, OFr *copon*]

coupon² /ˈkupən/ *n* a face *la20-*. [probably specific use of COUPON¹]

cour *see* COOR, COWER

courchay *see* KURCHIE

courche *see* CURCH

cours *see* COORSE¹, COORSE²

course *see* COORSE²

court *see* COORT¹·¹, COORT¹·²

courtesy, †**curtassy,** †**courtasy** /ˈkʌrtəse/ *n* **1** courteous behaviour; a courteous act *la14-*. **2** = the courtesy of Scotland *la15-20, 21- historical*. **3** a reward; an entertainment *la15-e17*. **the courtesy of Scotland** *law* a life-rent conferred on a widower of the estate of his deceased wife *la15-20, 21- historical*. [ME *courteisie*]

†**courtician, curtician** *n* a courtier *la15-16*. [MFr *courtisien*]

cousie *see* COWSY

cousin, cousing *see* KIZZEN

cousinace, cousingnes *see* CUSINES

cout *see* COWT

couter *see* COOTER

couth, †**cowth,** †**kowth** /kuθ/ *adj* **1** comfortable, snug, neat *18-19, 20- C Bor*. **2** soft, flabby *19- Bor*. **3** *of people* agreeable, friendly *18-e19*. **4** known *la14-16*. [OE *cūþ*, ptp of CAN³]

couth *see* CAN²·², CULD

couther *see* CUITER

couthie, coothie /ˈkuθi, ˈkuθe/ *adj* **1** *of people* agreeable, sociable, friendly, sympathetic *18-*. **2** *of places or things* comfortable, snug, neat; pleasant *la18-*. **3** affected, overly sentimental, twee *la20-*. [COUTH + -IE¹]

coutter *see* COULTER

covatis *see* COVETICE

cove¹·¹, †**coif** /kov/ *n* a cave, a cavern; a recess *la14-*. **cove ceiling** a vaulted or sloping ceiling *la19-*. [OE *cofa* a cave]

cove¹·² /kov/ *v* to hollow or scoop out (earth) *18-19, 20- Sh*. [see the noun]

coven *see* COVIN

covenant, †**covenand** /ˈkʌvənənt/ *n* a contract, a pledge; an agreement or pact *la14-*. Compare CONAND. **the Covenant** the National Covenant of 1638 or the Solemn League and Covenant of 1643 *17, 18- historical*. [ME *covenaunt*]

Covenanter /kʌvəˈnantər, ˈkʌvənəntər/ *n* a supporter of the National Covenant of 1638 or the Solemn League and Covenant of 1643 *17, 18- historical*. [COVENANT, with agent suffix]

Covenanting /kʌvəˈnantɪŋ/ *adj* (belonging to a community) actively supporting the National Covenant or the Solemn League and Covenant *17, 18- historical*. [COVENANT, with -ing suffix]

cover¹·¹, kivver /ˈkʌvər, ˈkɪvər/ *n* **1** a cover or covering; a tablecloth or bedcover *la15-*. **2** the maximum livestock a farm will carry *la18-*. **3** *mining* the strata between the workings and the sea-bed *la19, 20- EC*. [see the verb]

cover¹·², kivver, *NE T EC* **coor,** †**cuver,** †**coer** /ˈkʌvər, ˈkɪvər; *NE T EC* ˈkuər/ *v* **1** to place a covering on or over; to extend across or over *la14-*. **2** to protect, conceal or cover up *15-*. **cover the table** to lay a cloth on a table *la18-19, 20- NE*. [ME *coveren*]

cover *see* COWER

†**covetice, covatis, cuvetice** *n* covetousness, greed *la14-19*. [ME *coveitise*]

covetta /kəˈvɛtə/ *n* a plane for moulding framed work, a quarter-round *19-*. [Eng *cavetto* a hollow moulding whose profile is a quadrant, originally Ital diminutive of *cavo* hollow]

covin, coven, †**covine,** †**covyne** /ˈkovən, ˈkʌvən/ *n* **1** a company, a band; a rabble *16-*. **2** a group of witches *la17-*. **3** a compact, an agreement; a plot *la14-16*. **covin tree** a tree in front of a Scottish mansion at which guests were met and from which they were sent off *19, 20- historical*. [ME *covine*]

cow¹ /kʌu, ku/ *n* **1** a twig or branch (of heather, whin or broom) *la15-*. **2** *curling* a besom or broom *19-*. **3** a birch used for whipping *19- NE*. [OFr *coue* tail, hair-like extremity of many objects]

cow²·¹ /kʌu/ *n* a haircut *la19-*. [see the verb]

cow²·² /kʌu/ *v* **1** to poll or crop; to cut (hair) *16-*. **2** to cut down, cut short *16-*. **3** to eat up, consume *18-*. **4** to surpass, outdo *la19-*. **cowit 1** *of cattle* polled *la16-*. **2** *of hair* cropped *16-17*. **cow a'** to surpass or beat everything *20-*. **cow a' green thing** = *cow a'* *20- NE*. **cow a'thing** = *cow a'* *la19-*. **cow the cadger** = *cow a'* *la19- NE T*. **cow the cuddy** = *cow a'* *la19-, NE T C*. **cow the gowan** = *cow a'* *19-*. [unknown; compare COLL]

cow³, †**kow** /kʌu/ *n* a hobgoblin; an object of terror *16-19, 20- N*. [unknown]

†**cow⁴** *v* to scold or rebuke *la18-e19*. [perhaps ON *kúga* to force, tyrannize]

cow *see* COO

cowan¹ /ˈkʌuən/ *n* **1** a builder of dry-stane dykes *la16-*. **2** *freemasonry* one outside the brotherhood; a curious interloper *la18-*. **3** *derogatory* one who works as a mason without having served an apprenticeship *19-*. **4** an unskilled or uninitiated person; an amateur *19-*. [unknown]

†**cowan**² *n* a fishing boat *17-e19*. [perhaps Gael *cobhan* a box, an ark]

coward, cowart *see* COOARD

cowbill *see* COBLE²

†**cowbrig** *n* the orlop-deck of a vessel *16-e17*. **cowbryging** material for an orlop-deck *e16*. [Du *koe-brugg* a cowbridge]

†**cowclink, coclink** *n* a prostitute *16*. [unknown]

†**cowd** /kʌud/ *v* to float slowly, rock or bob gently (on water) *19-*. **cowdle** = COWD. [unknown]

cowda, cowdach *see* CUDDOCH

cowdeich *see* CUDEIGH

cowder *see* CATTER²

cowdrum, cowdram /'kʌudrəm/ *n* a scolding, a beating *19- NE*. **get cowdrum** to get one's deserts; to be punished *19- NE*. [Gael *co(mh)throm* justice]

cower, cour, †**cover,** †**cuver** /'kʌuər, 'kuər/ *v* **1** to recover, get well *la14-*. **2** to get over or recover from (something) *la18-19, 20- NE*. **3** to restore or revive *la14-e17*. [ME *coveren*]

†**cowffyne** *n* a term of endearment *16*. [unknown]

†**cowgrane** *n* a kind of fabric *la16*. [perhaps altered form of GROWGRANE]

†**cowhuby, kouhuby** *n* a weakling or foolish person *16*. [unknown]

cowk¹·¹ /kʌuk/ *n* a retch *20- NE*. [see the verb]

cowk¹·², **couk** /kʌuk/ *v* to retch; to vomit *la18- NE T C*. [compare Dan *kulka* to gulp, Du *kolken* to belch]

cowl *see* COOL

cow-lady-stane, collady-stane /'kʌulede'sten, 'kɔləde'sten/ *n* a variety of quartz *19- Bor*. [perhaps EModE *cow-lady* a ladybird + STANE¹·² from the colouring of the quartz]

cowld *see* CAULD¹·¹, CAULD¹·³

cowlie, †**coulie** /'kʌuli/ *n* **1** *derogatory* a man *la17-*. **2** *derogatory* a boy *19- EC*. [unknown; compare EModE *cully*]

cowm *see* COOM¹·¹, COOM¹·², COOM²

cowmon *see* COMMON¹·³

cown /kʌun/ *v* to weep; to lament *la19- Ork N EC*. [Gael *caoin*]

cowp¹·¹, **coup** /kʌup/ *n* **1** an upset, an overturning; a fall *16-*. **2** a rubbish tip; a recycling centre *la19-*. **3** *mining* a sudden break in a stratum of coal *la18-19, 20- EC*. **4** *derogatory* a company, a group *18-19*. **free coup** a place where rubbish may be dumped free of charge *la19-*. **the haill coup** the whole lot *19-*. [see the verb]

cowp¹·², **coup,** *Sh Ork* **coop,** *H&I Uls* **cope** /kʌup; *Sh Ork* kup; *H&I Uls* kop/ *v* **1** to overturn, upset; to ruin *la16-*. **2** to overbalance, fall over or capsize; to go bankrupt *17-*. **3** to tilt up or over; to empty by upturning *la17-*. **4** to bend, incline or heel over *la19-*. **5** to have sexual intercourse with *la20-*. **6** to set a church-bell *17*. **cowpy** a sheep that has turned over on its back and is unable to get up *20- SW Bor*. **cope-carlie** to turn head over heels *19- SW Uls*. **coup fauch** to plough up the green strip between furrows after ploughing lightly *20- NE*. **coup fauchin, coup facken** ploughing lightly to let the frost into the ground *20- NE*. **coup by the heels** to prostrate someone; to lay a person low *20-*. **coup the crans** to turn head over heals; to be ruined *la18-*. **coup the creels 1** to turn a somersault; to fall head over heels *18- EC*. **2** *of a woman* to have an illegitimate child *19, 20- EC Bor*. **3** to die *19- WC Bor*. **4** to foil the plans of or get the better of *la19- NE*. **cowp the kirn** to finish the harvesting (and avoid being last in the field) *la19-*. **cowp the laidle** to play a game of see-saw *19- NE EC*. [OFr *couper* to strike]

cowp *see* COUP¹·¹, COUP¹·², COUP²

cowp-cairt, coup-cart /'kʌup kert, 'kʌup kart/ *n* **1** a tipping cart *18-*. **2** a closed cart for carrying manure or earth *la18-*. [COWP¹·¹, COWP¹·² + CAIRT¹·¹]

cowpendoch *see* COLPINDACH

cowper *see* COUPER²

cowpon *see* COUPON¹

cowr *see* COOR

cowrs *see* COORSE²

cowschet *see* CUSHAT

cowshin *see* CAITION¹·²

cowshus, cooshious, cautious /'kʌuʃəs, 'kuʃəs, 'kɔʃəs/ *adj* **1** careful, prudent, wary *la17-*. **2** unassuming, kindly, considerate *la19- NE T*. [adj from Older Scots *catioun*]

cowslem /'kʌusləm/ *n* the evening star *19- Bor*. [perhaps from COO + LEAM¹·¹, the gleam of the star when the cattle are being driven home]

cowstick¹·¹ /'kʌustɪk/ *n* caustic soda *la19- NE T C SW*. [see the adj]

cowstick¹·² /'kʌustɪk/ *adj* caustic, corrosive; biting *la19- NE C SW*. [altered form of Eng *caustic*]

cowsworth *see* KOWISWORTH

cowsy, cousie /'kʌuzi, 'kʌusi/ *n mining* a self-acting incline on which full descending hutches pull up a corresponding number of empties *la19- C*. **cowsy wheel, cousie wheel** the drum or pulley on a COWSY *la19, 20- EC*. [perhaps extension of CAUSEY¹·¹]

cowt, cout, colt, *N* **cyowt** /kʌut, kolt; *N* kjʌut/ *n* **1** a young horse, a colt *15-*. **2** a rough, awkward person; an adolescent child *19-*. **cowt foal** a young horse when suckling *17, la18- SW Bor*. **cowt helter, cowt halter** a halter made of rope or straw *17-*. [OE *colt*]

cowth *see* COUTH

†**coy, koy, cwe** *n* a bed or bunk (in a cabin); a berth (in a ship) *16-19*. [Du *kooi*]

coyd *see* CUDE³

coygerach *see* QUIGRICH

coyme *see* COME¹·²

coys *see* COSE¹·¹

coyst *see* CUST

cozie *see* COSIE

cra *see* CRAW²·¹

craa *see* CRAW¹, CRAW²·²

craal¹·¹, **crawl,** *NE* **crowl** /kral, krɔl; *NE* krʌul/ *n* **1** the act of crawling; a slow movement or journey *la19-*. **2** a swarm, a large number *20- Bor*. †**tak my crawl** to creep away *la19*. [see the verb]

craal¹·², **crawl,** *NE T EC* **crowl,** †**creull,** †**crale** /kral, krɔl; *NE T EC* krʌul/ *v* to crawl *la16-*. [unknown; compare Norw, Dan *kravle*]

crab, †**craib** /krab/ *v* **1** to become angry *la15-19, 20- SW*. **2** to annoy, make angry *la15-19*. [perhaps back-formation from CRABBIT]

crab-apple /'krabapəl/ *n* the wild apple *Malus sylvestris 18-*. Compare SCRAB¹. [unknown first element + APPLE]

crabbit, crabbed, †**crabit,** †**craibit** /'krabɪt/ *adj* **1** ill-natured; bad-tempered, angry *la14-*. **2** *of land or weather* rough, difficult *19-*. [Older Scots *crab* + -IT², from the gait and supposed disposition of the crustacean]

crack¹·¹, †**crak,** †**craik** /krak/ *n* **1** a loud or sharp noise *la14-*. **2** a split, a gap, a fissure *la15-*. **3** a loud boast or brag *la15-*. **4** a chat, a gossip, a conversation *la16-*. **5** a moment, a short space of time *18-*. **6** a story, a tale *18-*. **7** an entertaining talker, a gossip *19-*. **8** a try or turn in a game; an attempt *la19-*. **9** a sudden onset of stormy weather *20- Sh*. **cracky** talkative, affable, amusing *19-*. **the crack o a thoum** a snap of the fingers *19-*. **get on the crack** to start a conversation *20-*.

gie's yer crack give us your news *18-*. [see the verb; borrowed into IrGael as *craic*]

crack[1,2], †**crak**, †**craik** /krak/ *v* **1** to snap, splinter; to break (with a sharp noise) *15-*. **2** to talk, converse, gossip *la16-*. **3** to boast or brag *la15-19, 20- NE*. **4** to strike sharply *la19- N NE*. **cracker**, †**crakkar 1** a boaster, a braggart *16-*. **2** a talker, a gossip *la19-*. **3** *pl* pieces of bone or wood used like castanets *la19-*. **4** the lash of a whip *19-*. **crack net** a hazelnut, the fruit of the hazel *Corylus avellana la19- T SW*. †**crakraip** a gallows-bird *la15*. **crack crouse 1** to talk in a lively, cheerful way *la18-*. **2** to boast *la17-18*. **crack like a pen-gun** to talk in a lively way, chatter loudly *la18-19, 20- NE EC*. †**crack looves** to shake hands; to seal a bargain *la18-e19*. **crack a match** to strike a match *20- N NE SW*. **crack on** to carry on, hurry on *20-*. †**crack yer credit** to become bankrupt; to lose one's reputation or trust *19*. **crack yer thoums** to snap one's thumbs *19, 20- Sh NE*. [OE *cracian* to make a harsh noise]

crack[2] /krak/ *adj* foolish or stupid *19- NE*. **crack wittet** scatter-brained, foolish *20- NE*. [probably reduced form of Older Scots *crakkit* cracked]

cracken *see* KREKIN

crackie, †**crocky** /'krake, 'kraki/ *n* a low three-legged stool *19- T Bor*. **crackie stool** = CRACKIE. [compare Norw dial *krakk*]

crackins, **crakkings** /'krakınz, 'krakıŋz/ *npl* **1** the residue of tallow melting *la16-19, 20- NE*. **2** the residue from any rendered fat or oil *20- WC SW Uls*. **3** a dish of fried oatmeal *20- N NE*. **craklins**, **cracklings 1** the residue of tallow melting *la16-19, 20- NE*. **2** the residue from any rendered fat or oil *20- NE*. **3** a dish of fried oatmeal *20- SW*. †**crackling house** a building in which tallow for candles was boiled down *17-18*. [verbal noun from CRACK[1,2]]

crackit, †**crakkyt** /'krakıt/ *adj* cracked *16-*. [ptp of CRACK[1,2]]

cracklings *see* CRACKINS

cradill *see* CRAIDLE[1,1]

cradle *see* CRAIDLE[1,1], CRAIDLE[1,2]

cradoun *see* CRAWDOUN

craeme *see* CRAME

craft /kraft/ *n* **1** skill, art; a handicraft; a profession or occupation *la14-*. **2** a craftsman; (an association of) those following a particular trade or occupation *15-*. **3** cunning, trickery *15-e17*. **crafty 1** skilful, ingenious, clever *la14-*. **2** cunning *la16-*. **the craft** the freemasons *19-*. [OE *cræft* strength]

craft *see* CROFT

crafter *see* CROFTER

craftin *see* CROFTING

crag *see* CRAIG[1], CRAIG[2,1]

craggit *see* CRAIGIT

cragy *see* CRAIGIE

craib *see* CRAB

craibit *see* CRABBIT

craichle *see* CRAIGHLE[1,1], CRAIGHLE[1,2]

craidle[1,1], **cradle**, **creddle**, †**cradill**, †**credill** /'kredəl, 'krɛdəl/ *n* **1** a baby's crib *la14-*. **2** a supporting framework *la15-*. **3** a frame for carrying glass; the quantity of glass held in such a frame *16-e17*. [OE *cradol*, **crædel*]

craidle[1,2], **cradle**, **credle** /'kredəl, 'krɛdəl/ *v* **1** to fit with a cradle; to line a shaft (of a mine or well) with stone *17-19, 20- C SW*. **2** to rear a child *20- WC*. **3** to reduce to a childish state *la18*. [see the noun]

craif *see* CRAVE[1,2]

craig[1], **crag** /kreg, krag/ *n* **1** a steep rock, a cliff; frequently in place-names *la13-*. **2** a projecting spur of rock *la18-*. **3** *pl* rocky ground *18-19, 20- NE EC*. **4** *pl* rock-fishing *la19- Sh*. **5** rock as a material *16-e19*. **craig-and-tail**, **crag-and-tail** a geological formation consisting of a hill with a steep rockface at one end sloping towards the other in a mass of drift or moraine, caused by the obstruction and splitting of a glacier by hard rock *19-*. †**craig leif** permission to dig coal from a HEUCH *16-18*. †**craig mail** rent or other charges for quarrying *17-18*. †**craig stane** a detached rock; a large stone *15-19, 20- Sh*. [Gael *creag*]

craig[2,1], **crag** /kreg, krag/ *n* **1** the neck of a person or animal *15-*. **2** the throat, the gullet *la18-*. **3** the neck of a garment *la16-e17*. †**craig claith** a cravat *la17-e19*. **craig's close** *humorous* the gullet *19-*. †**craig piece** armour for the neck *17*. **pit ower yer craig** to swallow *la19- NE EC*. [Ger *Kragen*, MDu *craghe*, MLG *krage*]

†**craig**[2,2] *v* to drink, swallow *la19*. [see the noun]

craighle[1,1], **craichle**, **creachle**, **crechle**, **crickle** /'krexəl, 'krıxəl, 'krɛxəl, 'krıkəl/ *n* a dry, husky cough; wheezing or hoarseness in the throat *la19-*. Compare CROICHLE[1,1]. [probably onomatopoeic]

craighle[1,2], **craichle**, **creichle**, **crechle** /'krexəl, 'krıxəl, 'krɛxəl/ *v* to cough drily or huskily; to wheeze *19-*. Compare CROICHLE[1,2]. [see the noun]

craigie, **craigy**, †**cragy** /'krege, 'kregi/ *n* **1** the neck *18-*. **2** the throat *la18-*. **craigy heron** the heron *Ardea cinerea 19- N NE C SW*. [CRAIG[2,1] + -IE[1]]

craigit, **craggit**, †**craiggit**, †**craiged** /'kregıt, 'kragıt/ *adj* having a neck of a particular sort *la16-*. **craggit heron** the heron *Ardea cinerea la19- NE*. [CRAIG[2,1] + -IT[2]]

craigy *see* CRAIGIE

craik[1,1] /krek/ *n* **1** the harsh cry of a bird; a croak *16-*. **2** the landrail or corncrake *Crex crex la18-19, 20- NE EC*. **3** ill-natured gossip; grumbling *la19- Bor*. [onomatopoeic]

craik[1,2], †**crak** /krek/ *v* **1** *of birds* to utter a harsh cry; to croak *la15-*. **2** to ask persistently, clamour (for) *19-*. **3** to grumble, complain *19-*. **4** *of objects* to creak *19-*. †**craikar** a clamorous person *e16*. [see the noun]

craik *see* CRACK[1,1], CRACK[1,2]

Crail capon /'krel kepən/ *n* a dried or smoked haddock *la18-20, 21- historical*. [from the Fife place-name + Older Scots *capon*]

crainroch *see* CRANREUCH

craip *see* CRAPE

craishan /'kreʃən/ *n* a withered, shrunken person *la19- N*. [unknown]

craiter, **craitur** *see* CRATUR

craive *see* CRUIVE[1,1]

crak *see* CRACK[1,1], CRACK[1,2], CRAIK[1,2]

crakkings, **craklins** *see* CRACKINS

crakkyt *see* CRACKIT

crale *see* CRAAL[1,2]

cram /kram/ *v* **1** to stuff full; to pack tightly *la17-*. **2** *of people* to push or crowd (into) *la18-*. [OE *crammian*]

cram *see* KRAM

cramasie *see* CRAMMASIE[1,1], CRAMMASIE[1,2]

crambo /'krambo/ *n* **1** doggerel verse, poetry *18-*. **2** a rhyming game *la18-20, 21- historical*. **crambo clink** doggerel verse *la18-*. †**crambo jingle** = *crambo clink la18*. †**crambo jink** = *crambo clink 19*. [Lat *crambē* a kind of cabbage]

crame, †**craeme**, †**creame**, †**creme** /krem/ *n* **1** a merchant's booth, a market stall *la15-*. **2** a portable case of goods, a chapman's pack *la16-e18*. [MDu *kraem* a stall]

crame *see* CREAM

†**cramer**, **creamer**, **cremare** *n* a merchant who sells goods from a stall; a chapman or pedlar *la15-18*. **cramerie**, **creamery**, **cremary** a stall-holder's or pedlar's goods *16-e18*. [Ger *Krämer*, MDu, MLG *kraemer*]

cramish *see* CRAMSH

crammasie[1.1], **cramasie**, **crammasy**, *NE* **crammosie** /ˈkraməse, kraməˈsi; *NE* ˈkramosi; *NE* krəˈmozi/ *n* crimson cloth *la15-*. [see the adj]
crammasie[1.2], **cramasie**, **crammasy**, *NE* **crammosie** /ˈkraməse, kraməˈsi; *NE* ˈkramosi; *NE* krəˈmozi/ *adj of cloth* crimson *15-*. [OFr *cramoisi*]
cramp[1] /kramp/ *n* **1** curling an iron spike fastened to the shoe to prevent slipping on the ice *19-*. **2** curling an iron sheet laid at the end of the rink to keep a player from slipping when throwing the stone *19-*. [probably MDu *krampe* a cramp-iron]
cramp[2] /kramp/ *v* to munch *20- N*. [probably onomatopoeic; compare CRUMP]
†**cramp**[3] *v* to strut or swagger; to prance *la15-e17*. [unknown]
†**cramp**[4] *n in Orkney* vitrified glass and stone found in tumuli *19*. [probably Norw dial *krampa* to press, squeeze]
crampet, **crampit** /ˈkrampɪt/ *n* **1** curling a spike fixed to the shoe; a crampon for walking on ice *17-*. **2** curling the iron footboard from which a player throws the stone *la19-*. **3** a roof-gutter bracket, a support *19- NE*. **4** a cramp-iron, a grappling iron *16-e19*. **5** the iron guard at the end of a staff *18-e19*. **6** the guard of the handle of a sword *16-e18*. [CRAMP[1], with diminutive suffix]
cramsh, **cramish** /kramʃ, ˈkramɪʃ/ *v* to grit one's teeth; to crunch *20- NE*. [onomatopoeic]
cran[1.1], **crane**, †**cren** /kran, kren/ *n* **1** the crane *Grus grus la12-*. **2** the heron *Ardea cinerea la18-*. **3** the swift *Apus apus la19-*. [OE *cran*; compare MDu *crane*]
cran[1.2] /kran/ *v* to (strain the neck to) eavesdrop *20- NE*. [see the noun]
cran[2], **crane** /kran, kren/ *n* **1** a crane, a machine for lifting and moving heavy weights *la14-*. **2** an iron frame or tripod placed across the fire (to support a pot or kettle); a trivet *la18-*. [MDu *crane*, from the similarity to the bird; compare OE *cran*]
cran[3], †**crane** /kran/ *n* a measure of fresh uncleaned herrings, relating to one barrel (37.5 gallons) *18-*. [Gael *crann*]
cran[4], **crane** /kran, kren/ *n* a tap *19-*. [Du *kraan*]
cranachan, **crannachan** /ˈkranəxən/ *n* a dessert made with whipped cream, toasted oats, whisky, honey and raspberries *20-*. [Gael *crannachan*]
†**crance** *n* **1** a (circular) brass fitting *la16-e17*. **2** a wreath *la16*. [Du *krans* a chaplet, a wreath]
crane /kren/ *n* the cranberry *Vaccinium oxycoccos la18- Bor*. [probably CRAN[1.1]]
crane *see* CRAN[1.1], CRAN[2], CRAN[3], CRAN[4]
crang, **kraang** /kraŋ/ *n* a carcass; a corpse *20- Sh WC*. [Du *kreng* carrion]
†**crank**[1.1] *n* a snare; a wile; a twist; a difficulty; a whim *la18-19*. [EModE *crank* a bend, a crooked path]
crank[1.2] /kraŋk/ *adj* difficult; odd; stubborn *la18-*. **crankous** fretful, captious *la18-*. **crankum** something odd or difficult to understand; a complicated piece of machinery *19- Bor*. [see the noun]
†**crank**[2.1] *n* a harsh noise *la18*. [probably onomatopoeic]
†**crank**[2.2] *v* to make a harsh noise *la19*. [see the noun]
crankie /ˈkraŋki/ *adj* **1** bad-tempered; eccentric *19-*. **2** unsteady, insecure, unreliable *la19-*. [CRANK[1.1] + -IE[2]]
crannachan *see* CRANACHAN
crannak *see* CRANNOG
cranner /ˈkranər/ *n fishing* a person employed to count the baskets of herring and verify their contents as they are unloaded *la19- Sh NE*. [CRAN[3], with agent suffix]
crannie[1] /ˈkrani, ˈkrane/ *n* **1** a crevice, a crack, a gap *la18-*. **2** a square or oblong recess in a wall *19, 20- NE*. [ME *crani*]

crannie[2] /ˈkrani, ˈkrane/ *n* the little finger *20- N NE T*. **crannie doodlie** the little finger *20- NE*. **crannie wannie** the little finger *la18- NE*. [probably CRAN[4]]
crannog, †**crannak** /ˈkranəg/ *n* an ancient fortified (circular) dwelling constructed on a loch or estuary *17- historical*. [Gael *crannag*, IrGael *crannóg*]
cranreuch, †**crainroch**, †**cranra** /ˈkranrux/ *n* hoar-frost *16-*. [Gael *crann* to shrink, shrivel + Gael *reothadh* frost]
cranzie *see* KRANSI
crap *see* CREEP[1.2], CROP[1.1], CROP[1.2]
crape, †**craip**, †**creap** /krep/ *n* **1** crêpe fabric *la16-*. **2** a band of crêpe on a garment *16-e18*. [MFr *crespe*]
crape *see* CREEP[1.2]
crappened *see* CROPPENED
crappin[1], †**crapine** /ˈkrapɪn/ *n* the crop of a fowl; the throat, breast, or stomach of a man *18-19, 20- SW Bor*. [CROP[1.1], with *-ing* suffix]
crappin[2], **krappen** /ˈkrapɪn/ *n* a dish of oatmeal and fish-livers cooked in a fish-head *la19- Sh*. Compare CRAPPIT HEID. [probably verbal noun from CROP[1.2]]
crappit heid /krapɪt ˈhid/ *n* a haddock head stuffed with roe, oatmeal and spices *19-*. [ptp of CROP[1.2] + HEID[1.1]]
crase *see* CRAZE[1.2]
crasie, **crazy** /ˈkrezi, ˈkreze/ *n* a sunbonnet *19-20, 21- historical*. [altered form of CRUISIE, from its shape]
cratur, **craitur**, **craiter**, **crater**, **creature**, *H&I* **crettir** /ˈkretər, ˈkritʃər; *H&I* ˈkretər/ *n* **1** a person or animal, a creature *la14-*. **2** a nickname for whisky *la20-*. **the craitur**, **the cratur**, **the creature** a nickname for whisky *19-*. [ME *creature*]
†**crauch** *interj* an expression of submission *e16*. [unknown; compare CRAIK[1.1]]
crave[1.1] /krev/ *n* **1** *law* a formal request or petition (to a court) *18-*. **2** a desire, a hankering after (something) *19, 20- NE T*. [see the verb]
crave[1.2], †**craif** /krev/ *v* **1** to beg or entreat; to ask for humbly *la14-*. **2** *law* to ask for as of right; to demand or claim as properly or legally due *15-*. **3** to press or pester for payment of a debt *la15-*. **4** to long for something; to strongly desire food or drink *la16-*. [OE *crafian*]
craw[1], **craa**, **crow** /krɔ, kra, kro/ *n* **1** a crow, in Scotland usually applied to the rook *Corvus frugilegus 15-*. **2** *pl* an inferior type of coal *la19- EC*. **craw aipple** the crab-apple *Malus sylvestris la19- EC*. **craw berry** the crowberry *Empetrum nigrum* or cranberry *Vaccinium oxycoccos 16-*. **craw bogle** a scarecrow *20- NE EC SW*. **craw coal** *mining* an inferior sort of coal *la18-*. **craws court**, **craas court** a parliament of rooks; a flocking of crows *19- Sh T EC*. **craw crooks 1** the crowberry *19-*. **2** the cranberry *Vaccinium oxycoccos la19- NE T EC*. †**craw iron**, **craw irne** a crowbar (with a claw for drawing nails) *la16-19*. **craw mill 1** a child's rattle *19- T*. **2** a rattle used to frighten crows *20- Ork*. **craw nancy** a scarecrow *20- WC Bor*. **craw pea** the meadow vetchling *Lathyrus pratensis la19- NE Bor*. **craw picker** *mining* a person who picks stones from coal or shale at the pit-head *la19- C*. **crawstep** a step-like projection up the sloping edge of a gable *19-*. **craw taes 1** the creeping crowfoot *Ranunculus repens 18-*. **2** crow's feet, wrinkles at the corner of the eye *19-*. **3** the bird's-foot trefoil *Lotus corniculatus la19-*. **4** the wild hyacinth *Hyacinthoides non-scripta la19, 20- SW*. **5** caltrops (for impeding cavalry) *18-e19*. **craw's weddan** a large assembly of crows *19- N NE T EC*. **craw widdie** a rookery *20-*. **be shot amo the craws** to be involved in trouble through bad associates *la20-*. **craw in someone's crap** to irritate, annoy or henpeck someone; to give cause for regret *la18- NE T EC*. **the craw road**, **the**

crow road the road to death; the way to a hopeless situation *la20-*. **sit like craws in the mist** to sit in the dark *19- NE T EC*. [OE *crāwe*]

craw[2.1], †**cra** /krɔ/ *n* 1 the crowing of a cock *la15-*. 2 a similar sound made by other birds, especially the rook *la18- NE*. [see the verb]

craw[2.2], **craa** /krɔ, krɑ/ *v pt* also **crew**, *ptp* also **crawn** to make a crowing noise; to boast *la14-*. **craw crouse** to boast *la16-*. **craw on yer ain midden** to be boastful in one's own environment *19-*. [OE *crāwan*]

craw[3] /krɔ/ *n* a pigsty; a goat-pen *la19- N C Uls*. [compare CRUE; but the vowel is anomalous]

craw *see* CRUE

†**crawdoun, cradoun** *n* a coward *16-e17*. [unknown]

Crawfordjohn /krɔfərd'dʒɔn/ *n* dark granite, used to make curling stones *la19-*. [from the name of the Lanarkshire village where the stone is quarried]

crawl *see* CRAAL[1.1], CRAAL[1.2]

crawn *see* CRAW[2.2]

crax *see* CREX[1.2]

cray *see* CRUE, CRY[1.2]

†**crayer, crear** *n* a small trading vessel *15-19*. [MFr *crayer*; compare MDu *kraajer*]

†**craze**[1.1] *n* a crack, a blow *18-e19*. [see the verb]

craze[1.2], **crase** /krez/ *v* to render infirm (through age or injury) *16-19, 20- SW Bor*. [ME *crasen* to be diseased or deformed]

crazy *see* CRASIE

†**cre** *v* to create *la15-e16*. [Lat *creāre*]

creachle *see* CRAIGHLE[1.1]

creagh, †**creach** /krex/ *n* 1 a Highland foray, a cattle raid *la18- historical*. 2 booty or plunder; stolen cattle *19*. [Gael *creach* plunder]

cream, *NE SW* **crame** /krim; *NE SW* krem/ *n* the fatty part of the milk, cream *16-*. **cream of the water** the first water from a well on New Year's morning *18-*. **cream of the well** = *cream of the water*. [OFr *cresme*]

creame *see* CRAME

creamer *see* CRAMER

creap *see* CRAPE

crear *see* CRAYER

creash *see* CRESS[1.2]

creature *see* CRATUR

crechle *see* CRAIGHLE[1.1], CRAIGHLE[1.2]

creddle *see* CRAIDLE[1.1]

crede *see* CREED

credill *see* CRAIDLE[1.1]

credit, *Sh NE T* **creedit**, *NE* **crydit** /'krɛdɪt; *Sh NE T* 'kridɪt; *NE* 'krɑedɪt/ *n* 1 trustworthiness; (good) reputation or qualities; (public) commendation *16-*. 2 lending on trust; a loan *la16-*. **earn yer credit** to gain approval or esteem *la19- NE T*. [EModE *credite*]

credle *see* CRAIDLE[1.2]

cree *see* CRUE

creed, †**crede** /krid/ *n* 1 doctrine; belief *la14-*. 2 a severe rebuke *19, 20- EC*. [OE *crēda*, from Lat *crēdō* I believe]

creedit *see* CREDIT

creek[1], †**creik**, †**cryke** /krik/ *n* 1 a cleft in a rock-face *la14-*. 2 a narrow inlet of the sea *17-*. **creeks and corners** nooks and crannies *19- NE*. [MDu *krēke*]

creek[2] /krik/ *n* the break of day, dawn *18, 20- NE T*. Compare GREEK, SKREEK. [MDu *krieke*, MLG *krik*]

creel[1.1], †**crele**, †**creill**, †**kreill** /kril/ *n* 1 a deep basket for carrying peats, fish or eggs, either on the back or loaded onto a horse; a crate *15-*. 2 a fish-trap, a lobster-pot *la15-*. 3 the stomach; the womb *18- NE T*. 4 a basketful (of peats) *la15-e18*. **creelman**, †**creillman** 1 a fisherman who uses creels to catch lobster (and other shellfish) *la20-*. 2 a porter, one who carries or transports goods (to market) in a creel *16-19*. **in a creel** in confusion or perplexity; mad *la18-*. [unknown]

creel[1.2], †**crele** /kril/ *v* 1 to put into a creel (for carrying) *16-*. 2 *fishing* to land a fish with a rod (and place it in a creel) *la19-*. 3 *fishing* to fish for shellfish using baited creels *la20-*.

creeling 1 a custom involving a creel to which a newly-married man is subjected *18-*. 2 the practice of fishing for shellfish using baited creels *la20-*. [unknown]

creeminal *see* CRIMINAL

creenge, cringe /krinʒ, krɪnʒ/ *v* to crouch or shrink in fear *la15-*. [apparently OE **crengan* to cause to cringe]

creep[1.1], †**crepe** /krip/ *n* 1 a low archway in a railway embankment, allowing livestock to pass safely *la19-*. 2 a contemptible fellow, a sneak *la20-*. **cattle creep** a passage for livestock (over or under a railway) *19-*. **cauld creeps** gooseflesh, the creeps *19-*. [see the verb]

creep[1.2], †**crepe**, †**creip** /krip/ *v pt* **creepit**, **crept**, *NE T* **crap**, †**crape**, *ptp* **creepit**, **crept**, **cruppin**, †**croppin** 1 to sneak, move stealthily *la14-*. 2 to crawl, move slowly or gradually *15-*. 3 *of a curling stone* to move slowly or gently *19-*. **creeper**, †**crepar** a grappling iron, a grapnel *16-*. †**creiping craip** a variety of crape or grogram *la16-e17*. **creep afore ye gang** *proverb* walk before you run *19-*. **creep-at-even** someone out late courting *la19- NE*. **creep in** 1 to grow smaller, shrink *19-*. 2 *of daylight hours* to shorten *la19-*. **creep in 's ye crap oot** to go to an unmade bed *20- NE T SW*. **creep oot** *of the hours of darkness* to lengthen *20- NE EC*. **creep ower** to swarm, be infested (with vermin) *la19- NE C*. **creep thegither** to shrink or huddle up with cold or age *19-*. [OE *crēopan*]

creepie, †**crepie** /'kripi/ *n* 1 a low three-legged stool *17-*. 2 a footstool *19-*. 3 the stool of repentance *18-e19*. †**creepie chair** 1 a small chair *19*. 2 the stool of repentance *la18*. **creepie stool** 1 a low stool *la17-*. 2 a footstool *la19-*. [CREEP[1.2] + -IE[3]]

creepin eevie /kripən 'ivi/ *n* bindweed *la19- NE*. [presp of CREEP[1.2] + variant of Older Scots *ivy*]

creepit *see* CREEP[1.2]

creesh[1.1], *Sh* **greesh**, †**cresche**, †**cres**, †**creisch** /kriʃ; *Sh* griʃ/ *n* 1 fat, grease, tallow *15-*. 2 a knock, a blow *la18-19*. [AN *gresse*]

creesh[1.2], †**cresch** /kriʃ/ *v* 1 to grease; to oil; to lubricate *la15-*. 2 to beat or thrash *19, 20- NE SW*. **creesh someone's loof** to pay; to tip; to bribe *la18-*. [see the noun]

creeshie, †**creischie** /'kriʃi/ *adj* greasy; fat; dirty *16-*. **creeshie-mealie** oatmeal fried in fat *20- T*; compare *mealie creeshie* (MEALIE). [CREESH[1.1] + -IE[2]]

creest[1.1], **creist**, †**creste**, †**crist**, †**cryst** /krist/ *n* 1 a crest *16-*. 2 a self-important or officious person *19- EC SW Bor*. 3 conceit, self-importance *la19- SW*. [ME *creste*]

creest[1.2] /krist/ *v* to brag; to put on airs *la18- WC SW Bor*. [see the noun]

creichle *see* CRAIGHLE[1.2]

creik *see* CREEK[1]

creill *see* CREEL[1.1]

creip *see* CREEP[1.2]

creis *see* CREYS

creisch *see* CREESH[1.1]

creischie *see* CREESHIE

creist *see* CREEST[1.1]

crele *see* CREEL[1.1], CREEL[1.2]

cremare *see* CRAMER

creme *see* CRAME

cren see CRAN[1.1]
crepe see CREEP[1.1], CREEP[1.2]
crepie see CREEPIE
crepill see CRIPPLE[1.1], CRIPPLE[1.2], CRIPPLE[1.3]
crept see CREEP[1.2]
cres, cresche see CREESH[1.1]
cresch see CREESH[1.2]
cress[1.1] /krɛs/ *n* a crease, a fold *19- NE SW*. [EModE *crease*]
cress[1.2], **creash** /krɛs, kriʃ/ *v* to crease, fold *la18- NE C SW*. [EModE *cress, crease*]
†**cressent, cressen** *n* a crescent-shaped decoration on a harness or armour *e16*. [ME *cressaunt*, OFr *creissant*]
creste see CREEST[1.1]
†**cretar** *n* a writing-case *la16-e17*. [aphetic form of MFr *escritoire*]
crettir see CRATUR
creull see CRAAL[1.2]
crew see CRAW[2.2]
crewels see CROOELS
crewk see CRUIK[1.1], CRUIK[1.2]
crex[1.1] /krɛks/ *n* (the sound of) clearing the throat *la19- Sh*. [Norw dial *krække* to cough up]
crex[1.2], **krekks, crax** /krɛks, kraks/ *v* to clear the throat, cough up phlegm *la19- Sh*. [see the noun]
†**creys,** †**creis** *adj of hair* waved *e16*. [perhaps related to CRESS[1.2]]
crib[1] /krɪb/ *n* 1 a manger, a fodder-box *15-*. 2 a hen-coop *la18- N NE T EC*. Compare CRUB[2]. [OE *crib*]
†**crib**[2] *n in the Borders* a reel for yarn *e19*. **cribbie** a measure of yarn *e19*. [unknown]
crib[3], †**krib** /krɪb/ *n* 1 a kerb *18- T EC SW*. 2 a coping, a raised rim (on a brewing vessel) *18-19, 20- NE*. Compare CRUB[1.1]. **cribbie** a kerb *20- T*. **cribstane** a kerb stone *la19- NE T*. [metathesis of Eng *curb*]
cricket /ˈkrɪkət/ *n* 1 a grasshopper, an insect of the suborder *Caelifera 19-*. 2 a cricket, an insect of the family *Gryllidae la19-*. [AN *criket*]
crickle see CRAIGHLE[1.1]
cricklet /ˈkrɪklət/ *n* the smallest of a litter, the weakest of a brood *19- WC SW*. [compare LG *kriik* small]
criffins see CRIVVENS
crile, †**cryll,** †**croyll** /krʌɪl/ *n* a stunted person; a misshapen creature *la16-*. [unknown; compare Du *kriel* a small person]
crimch see CRUMCH
†**criminabill** *adj* 1 capable of being regarded or indicted as a crime *la15-16*. 2 capable of being accused of a crime *16-17*. [Lat *criminābilis*]
criminal, *NE* **creeminal,** †**criminall** /ˈkrɪmɪnəl; *NE* ˈkrimɪnəl/ *adj* relating to crime; forbidden by law *15-*. **criminal letters** *law* a form of criminal charge in which the sovereign summoned the accused to answer the charge *la16-*. †**criminal Lord** a LORD OF SESSION who became a judge of the Court of Justiciary by the Act of 1672 *la17*. [ME *criminal*]
crimpet /ˈkrɪmpət/ *n* 1 a large thin drop scone *la20-*. 2 a muffin, a crumpet *20- NE*. [altered form of Eng *crumpet*]
crimple /ˈkrɪmpəl/ *v* to crumple *19- NE T EC*. [altered form of Eng *crumple*]
†**crimpson** *adj* crimson *17*. [altered form of ME *cramesyn*]
crinch[1.1], **crunch** /krɪnʃ, krʌnʃ/ *n* a very small piece *19- NE EC*. **crinchie, crunchie** a tiny piece *20- N NE EC*. [see the verb]
crinch[1.2], **crunch** /krɪnʃ, krʌnʃ/ *v of the teeth* to grind; to crunch *19-*. [altered form of Eng *crunch*]
crine, †**cryne** /krʌɪn/ *v* 1 to shrink, shrivel *16-*. 2 to reduce in size, cause to grow smaller *16-*. [Gael *crìon* little, withered]

cring[1.1], **kring** /krɪŋ/ *n* a halter; two animals roped together *la19- Sh*. Compare KRINGLE. [compare Norw dial *kring* a circle]
cring[1.2] /krɪŋ/ *v* to fasten two animals together with a halter *20- Sh*. [compare Norw dial *kringa* to encircle]
cringe see CREENGE
cripple[1.1], †**crippill,** †**crepill** /ˈkrɪpəl/ *n* a disabled person *la14-*. [OE *crypel*]
cripple[1.2], †**crepill** /ˈkrɪpəl/ *v* to walk lamely, hobble *la15-*. [see the noun]
cripple[1.3], †**crippill,** †**crepill** /ˈkrɪpəl/ *adj* lame; unable to walk *la14-*. **cripple Dick** a lame person *19-*. [see the noun]
crisdim /ˈkrɪsdəm/ *n* an obvious statement of fact *la20- N H&I*. [unknown]
crisp /krɪsp/ *v* to fold cloth lengthwise after weaving *la19- T Uls*. [Eng *crisp* curled, crimped, folded]
crist see CREEST[1.1]
†**cristalline** *n* crystal *16*. [ME *cristalline*, Lat *crystallinus* resembling crystal]
cristin see KIRSEN[1.1]
cristyn see KIRSEN[1.2]
crit see CRUIT
criticeese, criticeeze /ˈkrɪtəsiz/ *v* to criticize *la19-*. [altered form of Eng *criticize*]
crittle see CROTTLE[1.1]
crive see CRUIVE[1.1], CRUIVE[1.2]
crivvens, crivens, criffins /ˈkrɪvənz, ˈkrɪfənz/ *interj* an expression of astonishment *19-*. [perhaps reduced form of Scots *Christ fend us*]
†**cro**[1] *n* compensation or satisfaction for a killing *15-19*. [IrGael *cró*]
cro[2], **kro** /kro/ *n* a corner or nook; a corner-space used for storage *20- Sh*. [ON *krá* a nook]
cro, crö see CRUE
croak see CROG
croam, krom /krom/ *adj* hoarse (from a cold) *20- Ork*. [unknown]
croap see CROUP[1]
croass see CROSS[1.1], CROSS[1.2]
croce see CROSS[1.1], CROSS[1.3]
†**croce-present, cors-presand, corps-present** *n* a gift due to the clergy from the goods of a householder on his death and burial *la15-16*. [OFr *cors*, Lat *corpus* body + PRESENT[2]]
crochle[1.1] /ˈkrɔxəl, ˈkroxəl/ *n* a disease of cattle causing lameness *19- NE*. **crochlie** lame *la20- NE*. **crochle-girs** the plant self-heal *Prunella vulgaris*, believed to cause a disease in cattle *la19- NE*. [unknown; compare CROICHIT]
crochle[1.2] /ˈkrɔxəl, ˈkroxəl/ *v* to limp *la19- NE*. [see the noun]
crock[1], †**crok** /krɔk/ *n* an old ewe *la15-*. [unknown; compare Norw *krake* a sickly beast]
crock[2] /krɔk/ *n* 1 an earthenware vessel or container *la19-*. **crocker** an earthenware marble *19, 20- NE SW*. [OE *crocca*]
crock[3] /krɔk/ *v* to die *20- Ork NE EC*. [altered form of Eng *croak*]
crockanition, crockanation, crockaneetion /krɔkəˈnɪʃən, krɔkəˈneʃən, krɔkəˈnɪʃən/ *n* complete destruction, smithereens *19-*. [Eng *crock* a broken piece of earthenware, with suffix by analogy with *ruination* and *perdition*]
crocky see CRACKIE
croft, *NE T* **craft** /krɔft; *NE T* kraft/ *n* 1 a small land-holding (leased by a tenant); frequently in place-names *16-*. 2 a piece of enclosed land (adjoining a house), a small field (used for tillage or pasture); frequently in place-names *13-19*. [OE *croft* an enclosed field]

crofter, *NE T* **crafter** /ˈkrɔftər; *NE T* ˈkraftər/ *n* a person who occupies a CROFT or smallholding *17-*. **Crofters Commission** a commission set up to administer the Crofting Acts *la19-*. [CROFT, with agent suffix]

crofting, *NE T* **craftin** /ˈkrɔftɪŋ; *NE T* ˈkraftɪn/ *n* the practice of croft-holding; the holding itself *la16-*. **crofting counties** those Scottish counties where crofting is important and which receive special treatment by government; since 1975 used loosely of the former counties *20-*. [CROFT, with *-ing* suffix]

crog, *N* **croak** /krɔg; *N* krok/ *n* a big hand, a paw *19- N NE T*. [Gael *cròg*]

†**croichit** *adj of animals* lame *e17*. Compare CROITTOCH. [unknown; compare CROCHLE[1.1], CROCHLE[1.2]]

croichle[1.1], **cruchle** /ˈkrɔɪxəl, ˈkrʌxəl/ *n* a dry, husky cough *19-*. Compare CRAIGHLE[1.1]. [probably onomatopoeic]

croichle[1.2], †**cruichle** /ˈkrɔɪxəl/ *v* to cough huskily *19-*. Compare CRAIGHLE[1.2]. [see the noun]

croip *see* CROP[1.1]

croishtarich *see* CROSTARIE

croittoch /ˈkrɔɪtəx/ *n* lameness in cattle *19, 20- SW*. [probably related to Gael *crotach* humpbacked]

krok *see* CROCK[1]

croke *see* CRUIK[1.1]

cröl, krul /krøl, krʌl/ *n* 1 a confused heap, a tangle *la19- Sh Ork*. 2 a hump; a humpback *20- Sh*. [Norw dial *kryl* a hump]

crom[1.1] /krɔm/ *v* to bend *la19- NE*. [see the adj]

crom[1.2], **crum** /krɔm, krʌm/ *adj* bent, crooked *16-*. [Ger *krumm*, OE *crumb*, MLG *krum*, MDu *cromp*, Gael *crom* crooked, bent]

cromack, crommack *see* CRUMMOCK[2]

cromag *see* KRUMMICK

crommie *see* CRUMMIE[1]

crommt *see* CRUMMET

†**cronach**[1.1] *n* a funeral lament *la18-e19*. Compare CORONACH. [reduced form of CORONACH]

cronach[1.2] /ˈkrɔnəx/ *v* 1 to wail or lament; to grumble *19-*. 2 to gossip, tattle *19*. [see the noun]

crone *see* CROON[1.1], CROON[2.1]

croo /kru/ *v of doves* to coo *la19-*. [onomatopoeic]

croo *see* CRUE

crooban *see* CRUBAN[1]

crooch /krutʃ/ *v* to crouch *20-*. [ME *crouchen*]

†**crood**[1], **croude, crowd** *v of doves* to coo *16-19*. [onomatopoeic]

crood[2.1] /krud/ *n* a crowd, a throng of people *18-*. [see the verb]

crood[2.2], †**croud** /krud/ *v* to press together, throng; to gather into a crowd *17-*. [OE *crūdan* to push, shove]

crood *see* CRUD

croodie *see* CROWDIE[2]

croodle[1] /ˈkrudəl/ *v* 1 to hum or sing quietly *19- N NE WC*. 2 *of doves* to coo *la19- NE T C*. **croodlin doo** 1 a term of endearment *19- NE EC*. 2 a wood-pigeon *Columba palumbus 20- NE T*. [onomatopoeic]

croodle[2] /ˈkrudəl/ *v* to cower; to nestle *19-*. [probably frequentative form of CROOD[2.2], perhaps with influence from CROODLE[1]]

crooels, cruels, †**crewels,** †**crowells** /ˈkruəlz/ *npl* scrofula *la16-*. [aphetic form of MFr *escroeles, escrouelles*]

croog, crug, krug /krug, krøg/ *v* to crouch, huddle, to shelter from bad weather *la19- Sh*. [Norw dial *krukka*]

crook *see* CRUIK[1.1], CRUIK[1.2]

crooked *see* CRUIKIT

Crookston Dollar /ˈkrukstən ˈdɔlər/ *n* a large silver coin struck in the reign of Mary Queen of Scots *19- historical*. [from the name of the estate and DOLLOUR or DALLAR]

crool *see* CRULL

croolge *see* CRULGE

croon[1.1], **croun, crown,** †**crone** /krun, krʌun/ *n* 1 a (monarch's) crown; the monarch *la14-*. 2 the top of the head; the highest part of a hill *15-*. 3 a (gold or silver) coin *la15-20, 21- historical*. 4 the first furrow in ploughing *20- N SW*. **Crown Agent** *law* the chief Crown solicitor in criminal matters *la18-*. †**croun as** a superior kind of potash *la16*. †**croun matrimonial** *in the reign of Mary* a regal crown claimed or obtained through marriage with the sovereign *la16*. †**croun of wecht** a coin of full weight *16*. [ME *coroune, croun*]

croon[1.2], **crown** /krun, krʌun/ *v* to crown a monarch *la14-*. [ME *corounen, crounen*]

croon[2.1], †**crone** /krun/ *n* 1 a wail, a lament, a mournful song *la18-*. 2 a low murmuring tune *18-*. 3 a bellow *16-19*. [see the verb]

croon[2.2], **cruin,** †**crune,** †**croyn** /krun/ *v* 1 to sing in a low tone; to mutter, hum *la16-*. 2 to lament, mourn, sing a dirge; to wail *17-19, 20- N NE*. 3 to bellow, roar *16-19, 20- SW*. **croon ower** to sing or hum a tune *la18-*. [MDu *kronen* to groan]

crooner[1], †**crunner** /ˈkrunər/ *n* the gurnard *Eutrigla gurnardus 18-*. [CROON[2.2], with agent suffix; from the sound it makes when taken from the water]

crooner[2] /ˈkrunər/ *n* that which beats all, the best or worst *la19- N T EC SW*. [CROON[1.2], with agent suffix]

croonge /krunʒ/ *v* to crouch *la19- NE T*. [probably conflation of CREENGE with CROOCH]

croonick /ˈkrunɪk/ *n* the gurnard *Eutrigla gurnardus la19- NE*. [CROON[2.2], with diminutive suffix; from the sound it makes when taken from the water]

croopan /ˈkrupən/ *n* 1 the body, the torso *la19- Sh Ork*. 2 an odd or poor individual *la19- Sh Ork*. [Norw *kroppen*]

croose *see* CROUSE

croot *see* CROUT, CRUIT

croove *see* CRUIVE[1.1]

crop[1.1], **crap,** †**crope,** †**croip,** †**cropt** /krɔp, krap/ *n* 1 the top, the head, the highest part *15-*. 2 the top of a tree or plant; a head of corn *15-*. 3 the produce of arable land *15-*. 4 the stomach; the throat; the crop of a bird *15-*. 5 the substance which rises to the top of boiled whey *19- SW*. **crappin** a bird's crop; *humorous* the stomach *19- C SW Bor*. **clear yer crap** to get a piece of news off your chest *la19- NE T*. **crap and root, crap and reet** completely, root and branch *17-19, 20- NE EC*. †**crop and rute** the complete embodiment, everything *16-18*. †**crop and year** a whole or entire year: ◊*for and after crop and year 1724 la16-18*. **crap o the wa** the space between the top of a wall and the roof of a building *19- Sh NE T SW*. **get the crap on** to grow afraid *20- NE WC*. **have a crap for all corn** to be greedy; to have a capacity for absolutely anything *18-*. **shake yer crap** to give vent to grievances *la18- NE*. **stick in your crap** to cause resentment, stick in your throat *19- NE C*. [OE *crop* a sprout, a shoot, a stalk, a head]

crop[1.2], **crap** /krɔp, krap/ *v* to cut short, cut the head off; to reap, gather as a crop *la15-*. **crop the causey** to take or hold the crown of the road *la17-*. [see the noun]

croppen, cruppen /ˈkrɔpən, ˈkrapən/ *adj* bent, twisted; shrunk *la19- Sh Ork EC*. **cruppen down** shrunk, shrivelled or bent with age *la18-*. [ON *kroppinn*]

croppened, *Ork* **crappened** /ˈkrɔpənd; *Ork* ˈkrapənd/ *adj* shrunken, contracted, narrowed *20- Sh Ork*. [CROPPEN, with redundant suffix]

croppin see CREEP[1.2]
cropt see CROP[1.1]
cros see CROSS[1.2]
†**crosat ducat** *n* a variety of ducat *16*. [unknown first element + Fr *ducat*]
crose /kroz/ *v* to fawn or flatter; to wheedle or whine *la19- NE*. [unknown]
crose see CROSS[1.1], CROSS[1.2]
crose-gaird see CORS-GARD
cross[1.1], **croass**, *NE* **corse**, †**cors**, †**croce**, †**crose** /krɔs, kros; *NE* kɔrs/ *n* **1** a crossing, a cross-roads; a market cross, a market-place; frequently in place-names *13-*. **2** the symbol of a cross; a crucifix *la14-*. **3** a coin with a cross on one side *la15-19, 20- WC*. **4** part of a sail; a cross-sail *16-19, 20- NE*. **5** a cross as a boundary marker; a cairn, a pile of stones on a hill-top *15-18*. **corsie crown** a game like noughts and crosses *19- SW*. †**cros-dollar, croce dolour** a Spanish dollar with a cross on one side *la16-17*. **cross-fit** the starfish *Asterias rubens la18- NE T*. **cross kirk**, †**croce kirk**, †**cors kyrk 1** a church founded because of a cross *la15-*. **2** a transept *15-16*. †**crostailit band, corstallitt band** a tie or connecting piece with a crossed end *la16-e17*. **cross-tig** a variant of the game of tig *la19- T SW*. [OE *cros*, ON *kross*]
cross[1.2], **croass**, †**cors**, †**cros**, **crose** /krɔs, kros/ *v* **1** to make the sign of the cross *la14-*. **2** to go across; to move or place cross-wise *15-*. **3** to thwart, impede *17-*. **4** to harrow (a field) across the ploughing *20- NE*. **5** to mark or incise with a cross *la15-e19*. [see the noun]
cross[1.3], †**croce** /krɔs/ *prep* across *17-*. [probably aphetic form of ACROASS[1.2]]
cross-speir /ˈkrɔsspir/ *v* to cross-question *la19- NE EC*. [probably aphetic form of ACROASS[1.1] + SPEIR[1.2]]
crostarie, †**croishtarich**, †**crosstarrie** /krɔˈstari/ *n* a burnt or burning wooden cross used as signal for the gathering of the clans *18- historical*. Compare *fiery cross* (FIRE[1.1]). [Gael *crois-tàraidh* a signal of defiance before a battle]
crotal see CROTTLE[2]
†**crote** *n* a particle, a crumb *e15*. [ME *crot*]
crottle[1.1], **crittle** /ˈkrɔtəl, ˈkrɪtəl/ *n* a fragment, a crumb; a lump of coal or stone *19- WC SW Bor*. **crotly**, *NE* **grottly** fragmentary, crumbly *19- NE T SW*. [diminutive form of CROTE]
crottle[1.2] /ˈkrɔtəl/ *v* to crumble *20- Bor*. [see the noun]
crottle[2], **crotal** /ˈkrɔtəl, ˈkrotəl/ *n* a dye-producing lichen *la18-*. [Gael *crotal*]
croud see CROOD[2.2]
croude see CROOD[1]
croun see CROON[1.1]
croup[1], **crowp**, †**croap** /krup, krʌup/ *v* **1** *of a bird* to croak, caw *16-*. **2** to speak hoarsely *19- N NE EC Bor*. **3** to grumble, complain, fret *20- NE*. **croupie, crowpie 1** the common street pigeon *la20- EC*. **2** the raven *19*. **croopit** croaking, hoarse *la19- N EC Bor*. [onomatopoeic]
croup[2] /krup/ *n* an inflammatory disease of the larynx and trachea in children *18-*. [probably onomatopoeic]
croupan see CRUBAN[2]
croupert, **crowpert** /ˈkropərt, ˈkrʌupərt/ *n* the crowberry *Empetrum nigrum la19- NE*. [unknown; compare KNOWPERT]
crouse, **croose**, †**crous**, †**crowse** /krus/ *adj* **1** satisfied; cheerful, merry *la15-*. **2** bold, courageous, spirited *la15-19, 20- Sh NE*. **3** conceited, arrogant, proud *la15-19, 20- NE T*. **4** cosy, comfortable *19- NE EC*. **5** ill-tempered, touchy *la19- Ork NE Uls*. **crouseness 1** boldness, valour *la18- NE T*. **2** self-satisfaction, cheerfulness *la19- T EC*. **crouse i the craw** full of self-confident talk *20-*; compare *craw crouse* (CRAW[2.2]). [ME *crous*]

†**crout, croot** *v* to croak *la17-19*. [onomatopoeic]
crove see CRUIVE[1.1]
crow /kro/ *n* a wasting disease of cattle *20- N*. [unknown; compare CROCHLE[1.1]]
crow see CRAW[1]
crowat see CRUET
crowd see CROOD[1]
crowdie[1], †**crowdy** /ˈkrʌudi/ *n* oatmeal and water mixed and eaten raw; porridge, brose *la17-*. †**crowdy-mowdy 1** a mixture similar to crowdie *18*. **2** a nonsensical term of endearment *e16*; compare *towdy mowdy* (TOWDY). **crowdie time, crowdy time** mealtime, breakfast time *la18- literary*. [unknown]
crowdie[2], **crowdy**, *N* **croodie** /ˈkrʌudi; *N* ˈkrudi/ *n* a kind of soft cheese *19-*. [CRUD + -IE[1], with influence from CROWDIE[1]]
crowells see CROOELS
crowl /krʌul/ *n* **1** a (tiny) child *19- H&I WC Uls*. **2** *derogatory* a diminutive person *la19- SW*. **3** the smallest pig of a litter *20- Uls*. [unknown]
crowl see CRAAL[1.1], CRAAL[1.2]
crown see CROON[1.1], CROON[1.2]
crownar see CROWNER
†**crownell**[1] *n* a circlet, a coronet *la15-e17*. [ME *coronal*]
†**crownell**[2] *n* a colonel *la16-e17*. [altered form of Older Scots *coronell* with influence from Older Scots *croune* a crown]
†**crowner, crownar** *n* a colonel *la16-19*. [altered form of Older Scots *coronell* with influence from Older Scots *crowner* a coroner]
crowp see CROUP[1]
crowpert see CROUPERT
crowse see CROUSE
croy[1] /krɔi/ *n* a tiny crustacean on which herring feed *la19- H&I WC*. [perhaps Gael *cruimh* a worm, a maggot]
croy[2] /krɔi/ *n* a (projecting) mound or quay built to break the force of the stream and protect the riverbank *16- T*. [Gael *cró* a fold, a hut, Icel *kró* a sheepfold]
croy see CRUE
croyll see CRILE
croyn see CROON[2.2]
crub[1.1] /krʌb/ *n* **1** the curb on a horse's bridle *19- NE T EC*. **2** the rim (on a brewing vessel) *17-18*. Compare CRIB[3]. **crub stane** a kerb stone *20- T*. [metathesis of Eng *curb*]
crub[1.2], †**crubb**, †**crube** /krʌb/ *v* to curb or restrain *17- NE T EC Bor*. **crub in aboot** to keep under strict discipline *20- NE*. [see the noun]
crub[2] /krʌb/ *n* **1** a manger (for cattle-fodder), a trough *e17, la19- Sh NE*. **2** a small enclosure for growing cabbages *la19- Sh*. **crubbit** narrow, confined *la19- Sh NE*. [Norw *krubbe* a feeding trough]
cruban[1], **crooban** /ˈkrubən/ *n* a crab *Cancer pagurus 19- H&I WC SW Uls*. [Gael *crùbag*]
cruban[2], **croupan** /ˈkrubən, ˈkrupən/ *n* a disease of the legs and feet of animals *19- N H&I WC*. [Gael *crùban* crouching; probably related to CRUBAN[1]]
cruban[3], **crubban** /ˈkrubən, ˈkrʌbən/ *n* a (wooden) pannier (carried by a horse) *e16, la18- N*. [Gael *crùbag*]
crubb, crube see CRUB[1.2]
†**cruchet** *n* a little hook *la14*. [OFr *crochet*]
cruchle see CROICHLE[1.1]
crucifee, crucify /ˈkrusəfi, ˈkrusəfae/ *v* to put to death, crucify *la14-*. [ME *crucifien*]
cruckle see KRUGGLE
crud, crood /krʌd, krud/ *n* **1** coagulated or curdled milk, curds *la15-*. **2** soft cheese, crowdie *20-*. **3** frog-spawn *20- NE EC*. Compare CURD. [ME *crud*]

cruddy /ˈkrʌdi/ *adj* curdled, full of curds *la18-*. **cruddy butter** soft cheese, crowdie *20- NE*. [CRUD + -IE²]

crudle /ˈkrʌdəl/ *v* to curdle *18-19, 20- NE WC SW*. [frequentative of verb from CRUD]

crue, cray, craw, *Sh Ork* **crö,** *N* **cree,** †**cro,** †**croo,** †**croy** /kru, kre, krɔ; *Sh Ork* krø; *N* kri/ *n* 1 an animal pen or fold; a pigsty, a hen-coop *16-*. 2 a wooden or wickerwork fish trap used in a river *la13-e19*. 3 a hovel, a hut *la16-19*. Compare CRUIVE¹·¹. [Gael *cró* a fold, a hut, Icel *kró* a sheepfold]

cruels *see* CROOELS

cruet, †**crowat** /ˈkruət/ *n* 1 a small vessel for liquids; a cruet *la14-*. 2 a carafe; a decanter *la19, 20- NE*. [ME *cruet*]

crufe *see* CRUIVE¹·¹

crug *see* CROOG

crugset, kruggset /ˈkrʌgsɛt/ *v* to drive an animal into a corner (to catch it) *la19- Sh*. [probably ON *krókr* a hook, a bend, a corner + ON *setja* to place]

cruichle *see* CROICHLE¹·²

cruik¹·¹, crook, †**cruke,** †**crewk,** †**croke** /kruk/ *n* 1 a curved or crooked piece of land, a nook or corner; frequently in place-names *13-*. 2 a curve, a bend; a river-bend *la13-*. 3 a metal hook; a pot-hook *la14-*. 4 a hooked shepherd's staff *la16-*. 5 (a disease causing) curvature or lameness; a limp *16-18, 20- Bor*. 6 a hook on which a door or gate is hung *la15-19*. 7 a misfortune, a difficulty *la18-e19*. †**cruikie, crucky** a sixpence *e19*. **crook baak** a beam above the fire from which pot-hooks are hung *la19- Sh*. **crook saddle,** †**cruik saddell** a saddle with hooks for supporting panniers *la16-*. †**cruik studie** a beaked anvil *la16-e17*. **crook tree** = *crook baak 19-*. **as black as the crook** very black, very dirty *la18-*. †**a crook in yer lot** a misfortune, a difficulty *18-e19*. **like the links o the crook** very poor; very thin, meagre *20- NE*. [ON *krókr* a hook, a bend, a corner]

cruik¹·², crook, †**cruke,** †**crewk** /kruk/ *v* 1 to bend; to become curved or crooked *la15-*. 2 to (cause to) become lame; to limp *la16-e19*. **crook yer elbow** to drink alcohol freely *19-*. **crook yer mou 1** to speak or whistle *la18- NE T EC*. 2 to grimace, scowl *18-19*. **not to crook a finger** not to make the least exertion *19-*. [see the noun]

cruikit, crooked, †**crukit** /ˈkrukɪt, ˈkrukəd/ *adj* 1 bent, crooked; curved *14-*. 2 *of a person or animal* lame; *of a limb* twisted or misformed *15-19, 20- N*. **tak up wi the crookit stick** to accept an inferior suitor *la19- T EC*. [CRUIK¹·¹ + -IT²]

cruin *see* CROON²·²

cruise, †**cruse** /kruz/ *n* = CRUISIE *la16-*. [shortened form of CRUISIE]

cruisie, crusie /ˈkruzi/ *n* an open, boat-shaped lamp with a rush wick; a candleholder *16-*. [OFr *creuset* a crucible]

cruit, crit, †**croot** /krut, krɪt/ *n* 1 a small person, a puny child *19- C SW Bor*. 2 the youngest of a brood; the smallest of a litter *19- C SW Bor*. [compare Welsh *crwt* a boy]

cruive¹·¹, croove, *NE* **crive,** *EC* **craive,** †**cruve,** †**crove,** †**crufe** /kruv; *NE* kraev; *EC* krev/ *n* 1 a wooden or wickerwork fish trap used in a river *14-*. 2 a pen, a fold; a pigsty; a hen-coop *16-*. 3 a hovel, a hut *16-*. Compare CRUE. **cruive-dyke** a rubble dyke extending across a river to hold fish traps *19-*. [CRUE, with excrescent *-v-*]

cruive¹·², crive /kruv, kraɪv/ *v* to shut up in a pen or stall *e17, 20- NE*. [see the noun]

cruke *see* CRUIK¹·¹, CRUIK¹·²

crukit *see* CRUIKIT

crül *see* KRÖL

crulge, croolge /krʌldʒ, kruldʒ/ *v* to cower, crouch *la18-*. [conflation of CRULL with Older Scots *crenge* to cringe]

crull, crool /krʌl, krul/ *v* to huddle, cower *19-*. [compare ME *crul* curly]

crum, crumb /krʌm/ *n* 1 the soft part of a loaf *la14-*. 2 a small particle, a crumb *la15-*. **crumlick** a small piece, a crumb *la19-*. [OE *cruma*]

crum *see* CROM¹·²

crumch, crimch /krʌmʃ, krɪmʃ/ *n* a small particle of something *la19- NE*. **crumshie, krimchie** a morsel, a small piece *la19- NE*. **crumchick** = *crumshie*. [diminutive form of CRUM]

†**crummet, crumet, crommt** *adj* crooked; having crooked horns *17-e19*. [*crum* (CROM¹·²) + -IT²]

crummie¹, crommie /ˈkrʌmi, ˈkrɔmi/ *n* a cow with crooked horns; a name for a pet cow *18-*. [*crum* (CROM¹·²) + -IE³]

†**crummie²** *n* a staff with a crook as a handle *19*. [*crum* (CROM¹·²) + -IE³]

crumle¹·¹ /ˈkrʌməl/ *n* 1 a crumb; a particle, a scrap *la19-*. 2 a fruit crumble *la20-*. [diminutive form of CRUM]

crumle¹·² /ˈkrʌməl/ *v* to crumble or break into pieces *20-*. [see the noun]

†**crummock¹** *n* a cow with crooked horns; a pet name for a cow *18-e19*. [*crum* (CROM¹·²) + -OCK]

crummock², crommack, cromack /ˈkrʌmək, ˈkrɒmək, ˈkromək/ *n* a stick with a crooked head, a shepherd's crook *la18-*. [Gael *cromag* a hook, a crook]

†**crummock³** *n* the skirret plant *Sium sisarum la17-e18*. [Gael *cromag*, *crumag*]

crump /krʌmp/ *v* 1 to crunch or munch *la18-*. Compare CRAMP². 2 *of snow or ice* to crackle (underfoot) *la18-19, 20- Sh NE*. [onomatopoeic; compare CRAMP²]

crumpie /ˈkrʌmpi/ *adj* crisp, brittle *19-*. [onomatopoeic; compare CRAMP²]

crumshy /ˈkrʌmʃi/ *adj* brittle; crusty *20- NE*. [CRUMP, with adj-forming suffix]

crunch *see* CRINCH¹·¹, CRINCH¹·²

crune *see* CROON²·²

crunkle, *NE T* **grunkle** /ˈkrʌŋkəl; *NE T* ˈgrʌŋkəl/ *v* to crinkle; to wrinkle; to crackle *19-*. [perhaps back-formation from ME *crunkeld*, possibly derived by analogy from *crimple*, *rumple*, and *wrinkle*]

crunluath /ˈkrunluə/ *n piping* a movement consisting of a combination of grace-notes (at the climax of a tune) *19-*. [Gael *crunluath*]

crunner *see* CROONER¹

crunt¹·¹ /krʌnt/ *n* a heavy blow *la18- WC SW*. [probably onomatopoeic]

crunt¹·² /krʌnt/ *v* to hit; to strike a blow (on the head) *la19- NE C SW*. [see the noun]

cruppen *see* CROPPEN

cruppin *see* CREEP¹·²

crupple *see* CURPLE

cruse *see* CRUISE

crusie *see* CRUISIE

crutchie *see* CURCHIE¹·²

cruttle¹·¹, kruttle /ˈkrʌtəl/ *n* a rattling noise; a gurgling or bubbling sound; a ripple *la19- Sh Ork*. [probably onomatopoeic]

cruttle¹·², kruttle /ˈkrʌtəl/ *v* to gurgle; to rattle; to ripple *20- Sh Ork*. [see the noun]

cruve *see* CRUIVE¹·¹

cry¹·¹ /kraɪ/ *n* 1 a loud call, a shout; a cry of grief or pain, a call for help *la14-*. 2 a proclamation, an official summons *15-*. 3 the distance a call can carry *la17-*. 4 *pl* proclamation of banns *la19-*. 5 a short visit (in passing) *la19-*. [ME *cri*]

cry¹·², †cray /kraɪ/ *v* 1 to call, shout; to call (on a person) for help *la14-*. 2 to proclaim publicly *la14-*. 3 to summon *la15-*. 4 to denominate, give a name to *18-*. 5 to proclaim

crya

marriage banns *18*-. **6** to be in labour *la17-19, 20- NE EC*. **crying 1** calling, proclaiming *la15*-. **2** labour; a confinement *19*-. **crying cheese** a cheese specially made at a birth *la19- NE*. **cry at the cross** to make public *la19*-. **cry back** to call back *19*-. **cry by** to call in, visit *20*-. †**cry down 1** to forbid, suppress; to disown by proclamation *la15-17*. **2** to reduce (money) in value by proclamation *la16-17*. †**a cryit fair** a fair or market proclaimed in advance *16-e17*. **cry in** to call in, visit *la19*-. **cry names** to call (someone) names *20*-. **cry a roup** to proclaim publicly that an auction sale is to take place *19*-. **cry tae** to call upon, visit *la20- NE*. †**cry up** to raise (money) in value by proclamation *17*. **cry upon** to call upon, visit *20*-. **cry up to** to call upon, visit *la19- NE T*. **a far cry** a very long distance, a long way (from) *la18*-. **like a cried fair** in a state of bustle *19*-. [ME *crien*]

†**crya**, **crye** *n* a proclamation; a hue and cry *la14-e16*. [OFr *crié* ptp of *crier* shout]

crydit see CREDIT

crye see CRYA

cryke see CREEK[1]

cryll see CRILE

†**cryne** *v* to fear *e16*. [compare MFr *craign*-, stem of *craindre*]

cryne see CRINE

cryreck /krae'rɛk/ *n* calling distance *la19- Sh*. [CRY[1.1] + RECK[1.2]]

cryst see CREEST[1.1]

Crystmaesse see CHRISTMAS

crystynnyng see KIRSENIN

cubbart, **cubbirt**, **cupboard**, †**copeburd**, †**copburd** /'kʌbərt, 'kʌbərd/ *n* **1** a storage closet or cabinet *la16*-. **2** a table for displaying cups and other plate *la15-e17*. **3** the vessels displayed on or kept in a cupboard *la15-16*. †**copbuird claith** a cloth placed upon a display table *16-e17*. [ME *cuppeborde*]

cubbie, **kubby**, *Sh* **kubi** /'kʌbi; *Sh* 'kubi/ *n* a small cup-shaped basket with a carrying-band *19- Sh Ork N*. [MDu *cubbe*]

cubbirt see CUBBART

†**cubical coal** *n* mining a type of coal located close to the surface *e19*. [unknown first element + COAL]

cuche see COOCH[1.1], COOCH[1.2]

cuckolane see COKALANE

cuckoo's-spittens /kukuz'spɪtənz/ *npl* cuckoo-spit, a frothy insect secretion *la19- NE T EC*. [from the appearance]

†**cud** *n* a cudgel *la18-e19*. [MDu *codde*]

cud see CAN[2.2]

cudbear /'kʌdber/ *n* a purple dyestuff (prepared from lichens); the lichen *Lecanora tartarea la18*-. [perhaps from the name of the patentee *Cuthbert Gordon*]

cuddane see CUDDIE[2]

cuddeich see CUDEIGH

cuddie[1], **cootie**, *NE* **cweedie**, *EC* **keddie**, †**coodie**, †**cudde** /'kʌde, 'kuti; *NE* 'kwidi; *EC* 'kede/ *n* a (wooden) dish or tub *17*-. [perhaps Gael *cùdainn* a large tub; compare ON *kútr* a cask]

cuddie[2] /'kʌdi/ *n* a young coalfish *Pollachius virens la18*-. Compare CUITHE. **cuddin**, **cudding**, **cuddane** = CUDDIE[2] *19- Ork N H&I*. Compare COOTHIN. [compare Gael *cudaig*]

cuddie[3], **koddi** /'kʌdi, 'kɔdi/ *n* a small storage basket *19- Sh*. [unknown]

cuddie see CUDDY

cuddle /'kʌdəl/ *v* **1** to hug, embrace *la18*-. **2** to squat, sit close *19*-. **3** *in the game of marbles* to throw or place a marble close to the target *la19- NE*. **cuddle up tae** to coax, wheedle or flatter *20- NE T EC*. [perhaps derivative of COUTH]

cuit

cuddoch, †**coldoch**, †**cowdach**, †**quoddoch** /'kʌdəx/ *n* a young cow or ox *16-19, 20- SW*. Compare COLPINDACH. **cowda**, †**kowda** = CUDDOCH *la16-19, 20- Bor*. [perhaps reduced form of COLPINDACH]

cuddum /'kʌdəm/ *v* to train, accustom *la18*-. [unknown]

cuddy, **cuddie** /'kʌde, 'kʌdi/ *n* **1** a donkey *19*-. **2** a stupid person *19*-. **3** a horse *20*-. **4** a joiner's trestle *20*-. **5** a gymnasium horse *20*-. **6** *mining* a loaded bogie used to counterbalance the hutch on a *cuddie-brae la19, 20- EC*. **cuddy-ass**, **cuddie-ass** a donkey *19*-. **cuddieback** a piggyback *la20- T EC*. **cuddie brae** *mining* an inclined roadway with a bogie on it *la19, 20- EC*. **cuddie-heel** an iron heel on a boot or shoe *19- C*. **cuddie loup** the game of leapfrog *la19- C Bor*. **cuddy-loup-the-dyke** = *cuddie loup 20- Bor*; compare *loup the cuddy* (LOWP[1.2]). **never said cuddy wid ye lick** failed to offer someone (a share of) food *la20*-. [unknown]

cuddy see CUTTY[1.1]

†**cude**[1] *n* a chrisom-cloth *la14-e17*. [unknown]

cude[2] /kud/ *n* the butler or storekeeper at George Heriot's Hospital in Edinburgh *19, 20- historical*. [perhaps related to COOD[2]]

cude[3], †**coyd** /kud/ *adj* foolish or hare-brained *la16- Bor*. [unknown]

cude see COOD[1]

†**cudeigh**, **cuddeich**, **cowdeich** *n* **1** a gift, a bribe; a premium for the use of money *18-e19*. **2** a night's entertainment due from a tenant to a superior, or its equivalent in value *16-e17*. [Gael *cuid* a share + Gael *oidhche* a night]

cudna, **cudnae**, **cudnin** see CAN[2.2]

cuff[1] /kʌf/ *n* the nape or scruff of the neck *18*-. [altered form of Eng *scuff* the nape of the neck]

cuff[2] /kʌf/ *v* **1** to remove a layer of soil with a rake before sowing *la18*-. **2** to winnow (corn or barley) for the first time *la18- NE*. [perhaps altered form of SCUFF[1.2]]

cuffing see COLF

cuffock /'kʌfək/ *n* a coil in a ball of wool, made with the strands wound in one direction *20- NE*. [probably Older Scots *cuff* the bottom part of a sleeve, with diminutive suffix]

cug see COG[1.1]

cuggle see COGGLE

cuid see CAN[2.2]

cuif see COOF

cuik[1.1], **cook**, *NE* **kyeuk**, †**cuke**, †**kuke** /kuk; *NE* kjuk/ *n* a person who cooks, a chef *14*-. †**maister cuke** the head cook of the royal or other large household *la15-e17*. [OE *cōc*]

cuik[1.2], **cook**, *NE* **kyeuk**, †**cuke** /kuk; *NE* kjuk/ *v* **1** to prepare food *la16*-. **2** to coax, cajole *19*-. [see the noun]

cuil, **cool**, **cule**, *Sh* **cöl**, *NE* **queel**, *NE* **cweel** /kul; *Sh* køl; *NE* kwil/ *v* **1** to mitigate, lessen; to become less fervent *la14*-. **2** to become or make cold or cool *la15*-. **cool-the-loom** a lazy worker *19- Bor*. **queelin stane**, †**cooling stone** a stone at or near a school, on which boys who had been whipped were made to sit *19, 20- historical*. **cuil-an-sup** to live from hand to mouth *19, 20- Bor*. [OE *cōlian*]

cuintrie see KINTRA

cuir see CURE[1.1], CURE[1.2]

cuisser see COOSER

cuist see CAST[1.2], CUST

cuisten see CAST[1.2]

†**cuists** *npl* pieces of stone used in building an oven *16-e17*. [unknown]

cuit, *NE* **queet**, †**cute**, †**coot** /kut; *NE* kwit/ *n* **1** an ankle *16*-. **2** a fetlock *17, 20- WC SW*. †**not a cute** not a jot *la16-e17*. [MDu *cote* a (finger) joint, MLG *kote*]

cuit see KITE[1.1]

cuiter, couther /ˈkutər, ˈkuθər/ v **1** to nurse; to pamper, fuss over *la18-*. **2** to coax, wheedle *19-*. **3** to mend, patch up, put to rights *19*. [unknown]

cuithe, *Ork* **kuithe**, *NE* **queeth**, †**kuythe** /kuð; *Ork* køð; *NE* kwið/ n the young coalfish *Pollachius virens la17- Sh Ork NE*. [compare Norw dial *kot* and CUDDIE²]

cuitikins, *NE* **queetikins**, *NE* **cweetikins** /ˈkutɪkɪnz; *NE* ˈkwitɪkɪnz/ *npl* **1** cloth gaiters *19-*. **2** knitted socks which cover the ankles *la19- Sh Ork*. [CUIT, with diminutive suffix]

cuittle, cuttle, †**kuitle,** †**cutle** /ˈkutəl, ˈkʌtəl/ v **1** to coax, flatter *18- SW Bor*. **2** to cuddle or caress *la18-19*. **3** to smile ingratiatingly *la18-e19*. **4** to whisper *la15-17*. [unknown]

cuittle see CUTTLE¹·², KITTLE¹·²

cuitty-boyne /ˈkute bɔɪn/ n a small tub used for foot-washing *19- WC SW*. [CUIT + *boyne* (BINE)]

cuke see CUIK¹·¹, CUIK¹·²

cukie see COOKIE

†**culd, couth, cuth** v did: *to Parys culd he ga la14-e17*. Compare CAN³. [OE *cunnan* to know, understand]

culd see CAN²·²

Culdee, †**Kilde** /ˈkʌldi/ n a member of an ascetic religious movement (from the eighth to the early fourteenth century) in the Celtic Church *15- historical*. [IrGael *céle Dé* a companion or servant of God]

cule see COOL, CUIL, QUEEL

culf see COLF

†**cullage** n shape, form, appearance *e16*. [unknown]

cullan see CALLANT

Cullen skink /kʌlən ˈskɪŋk/ n soup made with smoked fish *20-*. [from the name of the village + SKINK¹]

culler see COLOUR

cullie see CULYIE

cullieshangie see COLLIESHANGIE

cullion, †**culyeon** /ˈkʌljən/ n a base or disagreeable person *la17-19, 20- NE*. [Fr *couillon* a testicle]

culloch see CAILLEACH

cullock see COLLIK

cullour see COLOUR

culm see COOM¹·¹

†**culmas** n a curved sword; a sabre *e16*. [unknown]

culome see CULUM

culpable, †**culpabill** /ˈkʌlpəbəl/ *adj* guilty, deserving of blame *la14-*. **culpable homicide** *law* a killing caused by fault which falls short of the evil intention required to constitute murder; manslaughter *la18-*. [ME *coupable*, Lat *culpābilis*]

culpe see CUP

culreach, †**culrach,** †**colrach** /ˈkʌlreəx/ n *law* the surety given on removing a case from one court to another; the person acting as surety *15-18, 19- historical*. [probably Gael *cùl* back + Gael *rath* surety]

†**culroun**¹·¹ n a base person; a rascal *la15-16*. [unknown]

†**culroun**¹·² *adj* base, low *16-e19*. [unknown]

culsh /kʌlʃ/ n a big, disagreeable person *la19- NE*. [unknown]

†**cultellar** n a cutler *16-17*. [Lat *cultellārius*]

culter see COOTER

†**culum, culome** n the buttocks; the anus *la15-16*. [Lat *cūlum*, accusative of *cūlus*]

culverin, †**culvering** /ˈkʌlvərɪn/ n **1** a hand-gun *la15-19, 20- historical*. **2** a large cannon *16-19, 20- historical*. [OFr *coluevrine*]

culyeon see CULLION

culyie, *N* **coolye,** *NE* **cullie,** †**culʒe** /ˈkʌlji; *N* ˈkulji; *NE* ˈkʌli/ v **1** to fondle or caress *la15-*. **2** to cherish *16-*. **3** to coax or entice *17-*. **4** to receive or entertain kindly *la16-e17*. [AN *coilli* ptp of *coillir* to gather, take]

cum see COME¹·²

cumar see KIMMER¹·¹

cumber see CUMMER¹·¹, CUMMER¹·²

cumbir see CUMMER¹·¹

cumble see CUMMEL

cumit, cummed see COME¹·²

cummel, cummle, coomle, cumble /ˈkʌməl, ˈkuməl, ˈkʌmbəl/ v to turn upside down *la19- Sh*. **gae in coomle** to capsize *la20- Sh*. [variant of WHUMMLE¹·²]

cummen see KIMMIN

cummer¹·¹, **cumber,** †**cumbir** /ˈkʌmər, ˈkʌmbər/ n **1** a hindrance or encumbrance *16-*. **2** trouble, distress; a difficulty, a disturbance; a nuisance *15-e17*. †**cummerance, cumbrans** trouble; annoyance *15-16*. **cummersome, cumbersome,** †**cummersum 1** troublesome, causing trouble or difficulty *16-*. **2** *of places* difficult to pass through, full of obstructions *la14-16*. †**cummerwarld** a useless encumbrance *e16*. †**be quit of someone's cumber** to be free of trouble (caused by the person mentioned) *16-e19*. [see the verb]

cummer¹·², **cumber,** †**cummyr** /ˈkʌmər, ˈkʌmbər/ v to hamper or impede; to disturb or harass *la14-19, 20- literary*. **cumbered, cumert** benumbed (with cold) *19-*. [ME *combren*]

cummer see KIMMER¹·¹, KIMMER¹·²

cummering see KIMMERIN

cumming see KIMMIN

cummins /ˈkʌmɪnz/ n the rootlets of malt *la19, 20- NE Bor*. [plural verbal noun from COME¹·²]

cummle see CUMMEL

cummock see CAMACK

cummyn see COME¹·²

cummyr see CUMMER¹·²

cumper /ˈkʌmpər/ n a type of fish, the father-lasher or short-spined sea scorpion *Myoxocephalus scorpius 19- Ork NE T*. [unknown]

†**cumray** v to overpower, throw into disorder *la14-e16*. [perhaps conflation of CONRAY with CUMMER¹·²]

cumseil see COOM²

cumyn see COME¹·²

cun, con /kʌn, kɔn/ v **1** to get to know; to learn *la14-*. **2** to taste ale; to evaluate by tasting *la15-e19*. **3** to taste food; to eat *16-e19*. †**cunnar, kuner** a person appointed to test the quality of ale and fix its price; a taster *15-19*. †**cunstar, quenster** = *cunnar 16-17*. **cun someone thanks** to feel or express gratitude *la15-*. [OE *cunnian* to try, OE *cunnan* to know]

cundy, cundie, condie /ˈkʌndi, ˈkɔndi/ n **1** a covered drain, the entrance to a sewer or drain; a culvert for water *19-*. **2** a hole in a wall (for the passage of animals) *19-*. **3** a tunnel, a passage *20-*. [ME *conduit*, *cundit*]

cungle, kungle /ˈkʌŋəl/ n a large, water-worn stone; a pebble *la19- Ork*. [unknown]

cungle see CANGLE¹·¹

cunigar see CUNINGAR

cuning see KINNEN

cuningar, *Ork* **cunningair,** †**cunigar,** †**conyngare** /ˈkʌnɪŋər, ˈkunɪŋər; *Ork* ˈkʌnɪŋer/ n a rabbit-warren; frequently in place-names *15-e19, la19- historical*. [OFr *conniniere*]

cunnand see CONAND

cunningair see CUNINGAR

cunray see CONRAY

cunstar see CUN

cunt see COONT¹·¹

†**cuntbittin** *adj* suffering from a venereal disease *e16*. [ME *cunte* + ptp of BITE¹·²]

cuntre see KINTRA

cunyie[1.1], **cunzie**, *N* **coonyie**, *N* **quinie**, †**conӡe**, †**cunӡe**, †**coinzie** /ˈkʌnji, ˈkʌnzi; *N* ˈkunji; *N* ˈkwɪni/ *n* **1** a corner of a wall or building; a corner-stone; a quoin, a keystone *la14-19, 20- Ork N EC Bor*. **2** coined money, a coin; coinage *la14-19, 20- NE EC Bor*. **3** a corner piece of ground *la15-17*. **4** a coining-house, the mint *la15-e17*. **cunyie house, cunzie house,** †**cunӡehous,** †**counӡehous,** †**coinӡiehous** the mint *la15-17, 18- historical*. Compare COINE-HOUSE. †**quinestane, cunӡie stane** a corner-stone *17-18*. [OFr *coigne*, AN *cuigne* a wedge, a corner, a die for stamping money]

†**cunyie**[1.2], **cunӡe, conӡe** *v* to coin money *15-18*. [see the noun]

†**cunӡear, cunӡeour, conӡeour** *n* a coiner, someone who makes coins; a counterfeiter of coins *la15-17*. [CUNYIE[1.2], with agent suffix]

cunzie see CUNYIE[1.1]

cup, *Ork* **coop,** †**coup,** †**cupe,** †**culpe** /kʌp; *Ork* kup/ *n* **1** a cup, a drinking-vessel; a chalice *la14-*. **2** a cup as a prize in a competition *17-*. Compare CAP[1]. **cuppie** a cup *la19- NE T*. [OE *cuppe*]

cupar see COUPER[1]

Cupar justice, Coupar justice /ˈkupər dʒʌstɪs/ *n* summary punishment (prior to a trial) *la17-19, 20- historical*. Compare *Jeddart justice* (JETHART). [from the name of the town in Fife + JUSTICE]

cupboard see CUBBART

cupe see CUP

cupnow see COLPINDACH

cuppill see COUPLE[1.1]

cupple see COUPLE[1.1], COUPLE[1.2]

cur- /kʌr/ *prefix* **1** wrongly, awry; confusedly *la16-*. **2** very, exceedingly *la16-*. **currie-** closely, intimately *18-*. [unknown]

curale see CORAL

curate, †**curat,** †**keerate** /ˈkjurət/ *n* **1** *Roman Catholic Church* a pastor *la15-*. **2** a parish priest of the Scottish Episcopal Church *18- historical*. **3** a curator *la15*. †**curatry** *law* the office of a curator; curatorship *la15*. [Lat *cūrātus*]

curator, †**curatour** /kjuˈretər/ *n* **1** *law* a person either entitled by law or appointed by the Court or an individual to manage the affairs of a legally incapable person (such as a minor) *15-*. **2** a manager or overseer; a (museum) curator *17-*. **3** *pl* the seven people appointed by Edinburgh District Council and the University Court, who have the power of appointing to the office of Principal and some professorships in the University of Edinburgh *la19-*. **curator bonis** the person appointed to manage the estate of a minor or of a person suffering from mental or physical infirmity *la18-*. [ME *curatour*, Lat *cūrātor*]

curatory /ˈkjurətəre/ *n law* the office of a curator; curatorship *la15-*. [Lat *cūrātōria*]

curatrix /kjuˈretrɪks/ *n* **1** *law* a female legal guardian (to a minor) *la16-*. **2** a female curator or manager *la19*. [Lat *cūrātrix*]

curch, †**courche,** †**querche** /kʌrtʃ/ *n* a kerchief, a woman's head covering *la14-*. [reduced form of CURCHEFFE]

curchay see KURCHIE

†**curcheffe, curchif** *n* a kerchief *16-17*. [ME *coverchef, courchef*]

curchie[1.1], **curtchie** /ˈkʌrtʃi/ *n* a curtsy *la18-*. [altered form of Eng *curtsy*]

curchie[1.2], **curtchie,** *Bor Uls* **crutchie** /ˈkʌrtʃi; *Bor Uls* ˈkrʌtʃe/ *v* to curtsy *19, 20- Bor Uls*. [see the noun]

curchif see CURCHEFFE

curcuddie, †**coukuddy** /kʌrˈkʌdi/ *n* a crouching, rustic dance *la18-19, 20- T*. [CUR- + CUDDY]

curcuddoch /kʌrˈkʌdəx/ *adj* **1** sitting close together or side by side *la18-19, 20- Uls*. **2** cordial, kindly *18-e19*. [probably altered form of CURCUDDIE]

curd /kʌrd/ *n* **1** coagulated or curdled milk *16-*. **2** *pl* frogspawn *la19*. Compare CRUD. **Curd Fair** a holiday in Kilmarnock around the time of the old hiring fair in May *la19- WC*. **Curd Saturday** = *Curd Fair*. [metathesis of CRUD]

curdie see CURDY

curdoo /kʌrˈdu/ *v* to coo (like a pigeon); to make love *19- C*. [onomatopoeic]

curdooer see CARDOWER

curdy, curdie /ˈkʌrdi/ *n* a very small coin; a farthing *la19-*. [Travellers' language *curdy* a halfpenny, perhaps from Spanish *cuarto* a small coin, or Romany *xurdo* little]

cure[1.1], *Ork* **ceur,** *NE* **keer,** †**cuir,** †**kuir** /kjur; *Ork* kjør; *NE* kir/ *n* **1** a remedy, a treatment for illness *la15-*. **2** care, charge; attention, diligence *la14-17*. **3** an ecclesiastical living or parish; the office of a pastor *16-17*. †**cure of** concern for or interest in *la15-16*. [ME *cure*]

cure[1.2], **cuir,** *NE* **keer,** †**kuir,** †**kure** /kjur; *NE* kir/ *v* **1** to heal; to restore *la14-*. **2** to dress or preserve meat or fish *16-*. **3** to care for, value; to attend to *16-19*. [ME *curen* to take care of]

curfuffle see CARFUFFLE[1.1], CARFUFFLE[1.2]

†**curie** *n* the royal stables *la16-e17*. [aphetic form of MFr *escurie*]

curious see KEERIOUS

curiousitie, curiousity see KEERIOSITY

curius see KEERIOUS

curl[1.1] /kʌrl/ *n* **1** a lock of hair; a curved or spiral shape *17-*. **2** *curling* the curving motion given to the stone *19*. [see the verb]

curl[1.2] /kʌrl/ *v* **1** to (cause to) bend, twist or coil; *of hair* to form curls or be curled *16-*. **2** to play the game of curling *18-*. [ME *crullen* to curl (the hair), bend, twist]

curl-doddy, †**curl-dodie** /ˈkʌrldɔdi/ *n* **1** the ribwort plantain *Plantago lanceolata* or greater plantain *Plantago major 16-*; compare CARL-DODDIE. **2** the devil's-bit scabious *Succisa pratensis* or field scabious *Knautia arvensis 19- Bor Uls*. **3** clover *Trifolium pratense* or *Trifolium repens 19- Ork EC*. [probably CURL[1.1] + DODDIE[1.1]]

curle see CORAL

curler /ˈkʌrlər/ *n* a person who plays at curling *17-*. **curler's grip** a secret handshake used by curlers *la18-19, 20- historical*. **curler's word** a word or formula used as a password in curling societies *la18-19, 20- historical*. [CURL[1.2], with agent suffix]

curlie, curly /ˈkʌrli, ˈkʌrle/ *adj* twisting, forming curls *la17-*. **curly-doddy** a kind of confectionery *19- C Bor*. **curlygreens** = *curly kail 19-*. **curly kail** curly colewort, a cultivar of *Brassica oleracea la18-*. **curly Kate** the rounded top crust of a loaf of bread *20- T*. **curlie murlie** a kind of confectionery *la19- T*. **curlie-willie** = *curlie murlie la19- EC*. †**curlie-wurlie** an elaboration, an ornamentation *la18-19*. [CURL[1.1] + -IE[2]]

curlies /ˈkʌrliz/ *npl* curly colewort, a cultivar of *Brassica oleracea 19-*. [substantive use of CURLIE, with plural suffix]

curling /ˈkʌrlɪŋ/ *n* a game played by sliding heavy stones on ice at a target *17-*. **curling court** a mock court of curlers held after a curling-club supper *18-*. **curling house** a hut near the pond for storing curling stones *la19-*. **curling stane, curling stone,** *NE* **curling steen** the smooth rounded stone, frequently of polished granite, used in curling *17-*. **curling word** = *curler's word* (CURLER) *la18-19 20- historical*. [verbal noun from CURL[1.2]]

curly see CURLIE

curly-andra /kʌrli'andrə/ *n* a sugared coriander or caraway seed *la19- EC*. Compare CORRYDANDER. [altered form of Older Scots *coriander*]

curmud /kʌr'mʌd/ *adj* close, near, intimate; snug *19- Bor*. [CUR-, with unknown second element]

curmur /kʌr'mʌr/ *n* flatulence, stomach rumbling *20- NE*. [CUR- + MURR[1,1]]

curmurring, curmurrin /kʌr'mʌrɪŋ, kʌr'mʌrɪn/ *n* **1** a stomach rumble; flatulence *la18-*. **2** (a source of) grumbling or complaining *la19-*. **3** a murmur of talk *20- NE EC*. [verbal noun from CUR- + MURR[1,2]]

curn[1], *Sh* **coarn**, *NE* **quern**, *NE* **curran**, †**kurn** /kʌrn; *Sh* korn; *NE* kwern; *NE* 'kʌrən/ *n* **1** a seed; a single grain (of corn), a particle, a granule *la15-*. **2** a small number or quantity; a few *17-*. **3** a lump or piece (of molten metal or wax) *15-16*. **curny** grainy, coarse *la18-*. [related to OE *corn*; compare CORN[1,1], KIRN[2]]

curn[2] /kʌrn/ *n* a currant *la19- Sh EC Bor*; compare CURRAN. **curny** containing currants or dried fruit *20- Sh Bor*. **curn bap** a fruit loaf *20- Sh EC*. **curn-loff** = *curn bap 20- Sh*. [reduced form of CURRAN, perhaps with influence from CURN[1]]

curn *see* KIRN[1,1], QUERN

curnaptious *see* CARNAPTIOUS

curnawin /kʌr'nɔən/ *n* a gnawing sensation of hunger *19- NE T*. [CUR- + Older Scots *gnawin*]

curneed *see* CARNEED

curneuch /kʌr'njux/ *v* to converse intimately *20- NE*. Compare CORRIENEUCHIN[1,2]. [perhaps altered form of CRONACH[1,2]]

curnie /'kʌrne/ *n* a child's word for the little finger *19- EC*. **curnie wurnie** = CURNIE. [perhaps metathesis of CRANNIE[2]]

curpall *see* CURPLE

curpin, †**curpon**, †**curpan** /'kʌrpən/ *n* **1** a saddle strap (passing under the horse's tail) *la16, 19- NE T*. **2** the hindquarters, the rump *18-19, 20- NE*. [metathesis of ME *croupoun*]

curple, *Bor* **crupple**, †**curpall** /'kʌrpəl; *Bor* 'krʌpəl/ *n* **1** a saddle strap (passing under the horse's tail), a crupper *la15-19, 20- SW Bor*. **2** the buttocks *la18- WC SW*. [variant of CURPIN]

curpon *see* CURPIN

curr *see* COOR

currach[1], *NE* **currick**, †**currok** /'kurəx; *NE* 'kʌrək/ *n* a coracle; a small boat or skiff *la15-*. [Gael *curach*]

†**currach**[2], **curreck** *n* a wickerwork pannier carried by horses *la17-19*. [Gael *curach*]

currack /'kʌrək/ *n* tangle seaweed *Laminaria digitata la19- NE*. [perhaps Gael *currac* headdress, or *corrag* a finger]

currag *see* COORAG[2]

curran /'kʌrən/ *n* a currant, a raisin or dried fruit *18-*; compare CURN[2]. **curran bun 1** a festive cake, a black bun *la18-*. **2** a bump on the behind when one sits down forcibly *la19- WC*. [from the place-name *Corinth*, originally AN *raisin de courance*; compare Fr *raisin de Corinthe*]

curran *see* CURN[1]

curreck *see* CURRACH[2]

currell *see* CORAL

currick *see* CURRACH[1]

currie[1] /'kʌri/ *n* a small stool *19, 20- WC*. **curry-stool** = CURRIE[1] *19- WC Bor*. [probably COORIE[1,1]]

currie[2], **kurrie** /'kʌri/ *adj* loveable, pretty, neat *la19- Sh*. [unknown]

currieboram /kʌri'borəm/ *n* a confused, noisy or frightened crowd *la19- NE*. [*currie-* (CUR-), with obscure second element]

curriebuction /kʌri'bʌkʃən/ *n* = CURRIEBORAM *la19- NE T*. [*currie-* (CUR-) + BUCK[2], with noun-forming suffix]

currieshang /kʌri'ʃaŋ/ *n* a dispute, a quarrel *20- N*. [*currie-* (CUR-) + back-formation from SHANGIE[2]]

curriewumple, curriewimple /kʌri'wʌmpəl, kʌri'wɪmpəl/ *n* a disturbance, a quarrel *20- N*. [*currie-* (CUR-) + WIMPLE[1,1]]

currie-wurrie[1,1] /kʌri'wʌri/ *n* a violent dispute *19- NE T C*. [perhaps reduplicative compound based on *currie-* (CUR-); compare *gurry-wurry* **2** (GURR[1,1])]

currie-wurrie[1,2] /kʌri'wʌri/ *v* to dispute violently *la19- NE*. [see the noun]

currok *see* CURRACH[1]

curroo, kirroo /kʌ'ru, kɪ'ru/ *v of a bird* to coo *19- T C*. [onomatopoeic]

†**currour, curriour** *n* **1** a forest ranger *la13-e16*. **2** a messenger, a courier *la15-16*. [OFr *coreor*]

curry *see* COORIE[1,1], COORIE[3]

curs *see* COORSE[2]

cursackie *see* CARSACKIE

cursaddle *see* CAR SADDLE

cursen *see* KIRSEN[1,1]

Curse of Scotland /'kʌrs əv 'skɔtlənd/ *n in cards* the nine of diamonds *18-*. [Older Scots *curse* + SCOTLAND]

cursit *see* CURST

cursnin *see* KIRSENIN

†**curson** *n* a fruit-bearing shoot *la18*. [Fr *courson*]

cursour *see* COOSER

curst, cursit /kʌrst, 'kʌrsɪt/ *adj* **1** cursed, accursed *la14-*. **2** very cross; fierce *la18- NE T*. [ptp of Older Scots *curs*]

curt *see* COORT[1,1]

curtassy *see* COURTESY

curtchie *see* CURCHIE[1,1], CURCHIE[1,2]

†**cury** *n* a cooked dish; a concoction *16-e17*. [ME *curie*]

curyus *see* KEERIOUS

cuschen *see* CUSHIN

cuschet *see* CUSHAT

cusching *see* CUSHIN

cush /kuʃ, kʌʃ/ *n* a soft, useless person; a coward *la19- Bor*. [perhaps back-formation from Eng *cushy* easy, comfortable]

cushat, cushet, †**cuschet**, †**cowschet** /'kuʃət, 'kʌʃət/ *n* the ring-dove or wood-pigeon *Columba palumbus la15-*. [OE *cusceote*]

cushie, cushy /'kuʃi, 'kʌʃi/ *n* the ring-dove or wood-pigeon *la19-*. **cushie doo 1** the ring-dove or wood-pigeon *19-*. **2** a term of endearment *la19-*. [OE *cusceote*]

cushie-dreel /'kuʃidril/ *n* a trouser opening *20- T*. [GUSHET + DREEL[2,1]]

cushin, †**cuschen**, †**cusching**, †**quissan** /'kʌʃən, 'kuʃən/ *n* a cushion *la15-*. [ME *cusshen*]

cushle-mushle /'kʌʃəl'mʌʃəl/ *n* whispering, muttering (of gossip) *18- NE EC*. [reduplicative compound based on a frequentative form of MUSH[2]]

cushy *see* CUSHIE

cusine *see* KIZZEN

†**cusines, cousinace, cousingnes** *n* a female cousin; a kinswoman *15-16*. [ME *cosin*; compare KIZZEN]

cusser *see* COOSER

cussie, kussie /'kusi, 'kʌsi/ *n* **1** a pet- or call-name for a cow *la19- Sh*. **2** a call-name for a pig *20- Ork N*. **3** a fool *20- Sh*. [Norw dial *kusse* a calf]

†**cust, cuist, coyst** *n derogatory* a person *la15-16*. [compare CUSTRIL, CUSTRIN]

custock *see* CASTOCK

custodier /kʌ'stodɪər/ *n* a custodian *19-*. [Lat *custōdia* custody, with agent suffix]

custom¹·¹, †custume /ˈkʌstəm/ n 1 a habitual or usual practice, a convention la14-. 2 a duty or levy 15-. 3 a customary right or privilege e15. **custom free, †custome frie** free of customs duty la15-19, 20- historical. [ME custum]

†custom¹·², custume v to impose or collect customs duty 16-e17. [OFr costumer to collect a customary tax]

†customary, custumarie n the office of collector of customs la15-e17. [CUSTOMER, with noun suffix]

customary weaver /ˈkʌstəmərə ˈwivər/ n a weaver who works for private customers 19-20, 21- historical. [CUSTOMER (sense 1), with adj-forming suffix + WEAVER]

customer, †custumar /ˈkʌstəmər/ n 1 a buyer, a purchaser (of goods or services) 17-. 2 a customs officer la14-18. **†customer wark** weaving orders carried out for a private customer (as opposed to factory) 19. **customer weaver** = CUSTOMARY WEAVER 19-. [AN custumer]

custril /ˈkʌstrəl/ n a fool 19- Bor. [EModE custrell a groom, an esquire]

†custrin, custrone n a rogue, a knave 16-19. [ME quistroun, EModE coystrowne]

custumar see CUSTOMER

custumarie see CUSTOMARY

custume see CUSTOM¹·¹, CUSTOM¹·²

cut¹·¹ /kʌt/ n 1 a piece cut off; a joint of meat or fish; a length of timber or cloth 16-. 2 a quantity of linen or woollen yarn (120 rounds of a 93-inch reel) 17-. 3 a skein of wool (weighing four ounces) 20-. 4 a group of sheep divided from the rest 20-. 5 temper, (bad) humour: ◊he's in bad cut 20-. 6 a substantial amount of time 20- Sh. 7 a score in handball 20- Bor. 8 pl the clevis of a plough 19- SW. **a cut of a man** a sturdy, middle-sized man 20- N NE. [see the verb]

cut¹·², †cute, †kut /kʌt/ v pt **cuttit**, ptp **cuttit** to chop, trim; to sever by cutting la14-. **cutter, †cuttar** 1 a reaper, a harvester la19- NE. 2 a crack or crevice in a stratum of rock la18-19. 3 a person who cuts (wood) without permission la16-17. **cutting** 1 the action of cutting la15-. 2 piping (the playing of) a single very brief grace-note, prefixed to a lower melody note la18-. 3 a cut piece (of wood or cloth) la16-17. **cuttit** curt, abrupt, snappish 19-. **†cuttitly** abruptly, curtly 17-e19. **cuttin breid** bread old enough to be easily cut 21-. **cut coal** mining coal cut on two sides where two working-spaces meet la19, 20- EC. **†cut luggit** crop-eared 17-e19. **cut note** piping an accented short note preceding an unaccented long one; occasionally an unaccented short note following an accented long one 20-. **cutting loaf** bread old enough to be easily cut 20-. **cut-throat** 1 a murderer 16-. 2 a dark lantern la17-e19. 3 a piece of light artillery; a firearm 16-e17. **†cut widdie, cut wuddie** the linkage attaching a plough or harrow to the traces la16-e19. **cut and dry** cut-and-dried tobacco 17-. **cut before the point** to anticipate 19, 20- SW. **cut harrows** to sever relations; to stop being on speaking terms 20- Bor. **cut out** to cut off la18-19, 20- EC. [ME cutten]

cut² /kʌt/ n an appetite la19- NE. **cut pock** the stomach la18- NE. [altered form of GUT]

cutchack, gushoch /ˈkutʃək, ˈkʌtʃək, ˈguʃəx/ n a small, blazing coal or peat fire; the fireside 18- NE. [perhaps Gael cùilteag a small corner]

cute see CUIT, CUT¹·², KITE¹·²

cuth see CAN²·², CULD

†cuthill, cuthyll n a grove, small wood 15-e17. [unknown]

cutlack, cutlich /ˈkʌtlək, ˈkʌtləx/ n impertinence, impudence 20- NE. [unknown]

cutle see CUITTLE

cutler, Bor cuittler, †cutelere /ˈkʌtlər; Bor ˈkutlər/ n a maker of or dealer in knives la14-. [OFr coutelier]

cutlich see CUTLACK

cuttack, kuttack /ˈkʌtək/ n a field mouse or vole 20- Ork. [CUTTY¹·³, with -ack diminutive suffix]

cuttag /ˈkʌtəg/ n a sturdy, middle-sized woman 20- N. [Gael cutag a little dumpy woman]

cuttance, cuttans see QUITTANCE

cuttanoy, kuttanoy, cotinoy /ˌkʌtəˈnɔɪ, ˌkutəˈnɔɪ, ˌkɔtəˈnɔɪ/ n a disturbance; turmoil, annoyance la19- Sh Ork. [unknown]

cutten, †catton, †cotting, †cottoun /ˈkʌtən/ n cotton 15-19, 20- Sh N. [MFr coton]

cutter /ˈkʌtər/ n a hip-flask; a small whisky bottle la19- N NE T EC. **rin the cutter** 1 to carry out alcohol from a public house or brewery unobserved 20-. 2 to act as a bookie's runner la20- WC. [perhaps extended sense of Eng cutter a boat used for smuggling]

cutter see CUT¹·²

†cuttie, cutty n a hare la18-19. [compare Gael cutach bob-tailed]

cuttie see CUTTY¹·¹, CUTTY¹·², CUTTY¹·³

cuttit see CUT¹·²

cuttle¹·¹, Sh køtel /ˈkʌtəl; Sh ˈkøtəl/ n 1 (the act of) sharpening la19- NE. 2 a (blunt) knife 20- Sh. [see the verb]

cuttle¹·², Bor cuittle /ˈkʌtəl; Bor ˈkutəl/ v to sharpen or whet 19-. [back-formation from CUTLER]

cuttle see CUITTLE

cutty¹·¹, cuttie, kutty, WC cuddy /ˈkʌte, ˈkʌti; WC ˈkʌde/ n 1 a short pipe 18-. 2 a short, dumpy girl 19-. 3 an affectionate name for a child, or for a mischievous or disobedient girl 19-. 4 derogatory a woman 19-. 5 the black guillemot Cepphus grylle; the common gull 19-. 6 an oat bannock 20- Ork N. 7 a short-handled spoon la17-19. [see the adj]

cutty¹·², cuttie /ˈkʌte, ˈkʌti/ v to sup greedily la18-. [shortened form of cutty spoon (CUTTY¹·³)]

cutty¹·³, cuttie /ˈkʌte, ˈkʌti/ adj short, stumpy 18-. **cutty-clay** = cutty pipe la19-. **cutty-gun** a short tobacco pipe 18-19, 20- historical. **†cutty-mun** the name of a dance 18-e19. **cutty pipe, cuttie pipe** a short, stumpy (clay) pipe 19-. **cutty quine, †cutty quean** derogatory a woman la18-19, 20- NE. **cutty-rung** a crupper for use with a pack-saddle 19- N NE. **cutty sark, cuttie sark** a short chemise or undergarment la18-19, 20- historical. **cutty spoon** a short-handled spoon (made of horn) la17-. **cutty-stool** 1 a low (three-legged) stool 19-. 2 the stool of repentance, the place in a church where wrongdoers were obliged to sit la18-19, la19- historical. **†cutty stoup** a pewter vessel holding 1/8 of a chopin 18-e19. **cutty-wran** the wren Troglodytes troglodytes 19-. [CUT¹·² + -IE²]

cutty see CUTTIE

cuver see COVER¹·², COWER

cuvetice see COVETICE

cuvy see KUIVY

cuyd see COOD²

cwe see COY

cweed see COOD¹, COOD²

cweedie see CUDDIE¹

cweel see CUIL

cweetikins see CUITIKINS

cwint see COONT¹·²

cwintry see KINTRA

cwite see COAT

cwyle see COAL

cyaak see CAKE

cyaarn see CAIRN¹·¹

cyard see CAIRD²·¹, CAIRD²·²

cyarn see CAIRN¹·¹, CAIRN¹·²

cyowt see COWT

D

'd *see* IT

da[1] /da/ *n* an informal word for father *la19-*. [shortened form of DADDY]

†**da**[2], **day**, **dea** *n* a canopy over a throne or chair of state *la16-e17*. [MFr *days*, AN *deis*; compare DEAS]

da *see* DAE[2], DAW[2], DAY, THE[1,2]

daable *see* DAUBLE

daak[1.1] /dak/ *n* 1 a lull in bad weather; an easing of pain *20- N NE*. 2 a short nap *20- N*. [see the verb]

daak[1.2] /dak/ *v* 1 *of bad weather* to lull, abate *la19- Sh N*. 2 to doze, have a brief sleep *20- N*. **daachen, dachen** *of bad weather* to lull, abate *la19- Sh*. [Norw *daka* to go slowly]

daaken, dawken /'dakən, 'dɔkən/ *v* to dawn, grow light *20- N*. [compare Norw dial *dagna*]

daal /dɑl/ *n* a valley, a dale *la19- Sh*. **daalamist** mist which gathers in valleys or on low-lying water at night *20- Sh*. [ON *dalr*]

daander *see* DAUNER[1.1], DAUNER[1.2]

daar *see* DAUR[1]

dab[1.1], †**daub** /dab/ *n* 1 a peck, a poke, a tap *18-*. 2 a blow, a slap *18-19, 20- NE T*. 3 melted fat or gravy in which potatoes are dipped; compare *tatties and dab* (TATTIE) *la19-*. 4 a throw in a children's game *la19, 20- T*; compare DOB[1.1]. **dabach** a stroke, a blow *19- NE*. **dabbie,** *NE* **dibbie,** *Ork* **dobie** a game played with marbles or tops *20-*. **the very dab** the very thing *la19-*. [see the verb]

dab[1.2], †**dawb** /dab/ *v* 1 to poke or prod; to peck (at) *la16-*. 2 to pierce slightly, stab *19-*. 3 to aim at or hit a marble *20- T EC Bor*. 4 to push, shove smartly *la19- NE T*; compare DOB[1.2]. **dabber, dauber** a large kind of marble *20- Bor*. **let dab** to disclose information *20-*. [ME *dabben* hit]

dab[2] /dab/ *n* a plain, ordinary or unpretentious person or thing *20- NE T*. [Eng *daub* clay]

dabbity /'dabəti/ *n* 1 an ornament, a knick-knack *la19-*. 2 a sticker, a transfer *20-*. 3 a game of chance played with small cut-out pictures *la19- WC*. [diminutive form of DAB[1.1]]

daberlack /'dabərlək/ *n* 1 an edible seaweed BADDERLOCK *19- NE*. 2 wet, dirty scraps of cloth or leather *19- NE*. 3 hair in lank, tangled, separate locks *19- NE*. 4 a tall ungainly person *la19- NE*. [metathesis of BADDERLOCK]

dablet *see* DEBLAT

dacent, daicent, decent, *Sh NE* **dassint** /'desənt, 'disənt; *Sh NE* 'dasənt/ *adj* appropriate, respectable; adequate, satisfactory; kind, generous *16-*. [MFr *decent*]

dachle *see* DACKLE[1.1], DACKLE[1.2]

dacker[1]**, daiker, dicker,** *Sh* **dekkir,** †**daker** /'dakər, 'dekər, 'dɪkər; *Sh* 'dɛkər/ *v* 1 to bargain *la17-*. 2 to walk slowly, aimlessly or weakly; to saunter; to loiter *19-*. 3 to be engaged in undemanding work; to fiddle around with *19, 20- Sh EC SW*. 4 to grapple with; to interfere *18- N NE*. **daiker on,** *Sh* **dekkir on** to continue, carry on; to get along (with) *la18-*. [MDu *daeckeren* to flutter, move about, shake]

dacker[2], †**daker** /'dakər/ *v* to search a house or person for stolen goods (by official warrant) *la16- NE*. [perhaps related to DACKER[1]]

dackle[1.1], **dachle** /'dakəl, 'daxəl/ *n* 1 a hesitating step *20- NE*. 2 a lull, a state of uncertainty *19*. [see the verb]

dackle[1.2], **dachle, dauchle** /'dakəl, 'daxəl, 'dɔxəl/ *v* 1 to hesitate, dawdle, slacken *19- NE T*. 2 to cause to hesitate; to impede or hold back *20- NE*. [altered form of DACKER[1]]

dad[1.1], **dod, daud,** †**dade** /dad, dɔd/ *n* 1 a heavy blow, a thud, a thump *la16-*. 2 a large piece, a lump, a quantity (knocked off); compare DOD[4] *18-*. **come dad** to fall with a heavy thud *20-*. **play dad, play dod** = *come dad 18-*. [probably onomatopoeic]

dad[1.2], **daud** /dad, dɔd/ *v* 1 to strike heavily, beat violently *la16-*. 2 to bump about; to dash or thud *19-*. 3 *of wind or rain* to blow in gusts, drive *la18-*. 4 to bang; to slam (a door) *la18-*. 5 to pelt; to spatter *19, 20- Sh NE WC*. [see the noun]

dad[2] /dad/ *v* to plod, trudge *20- Sh*. **daddery, dadery** drudgery *la19- Sh*. **daddit, daddet** weary, worn out by overwork *20- Sh*. [extension of DAD[1.2]]

daddy, *N* **deddy,** *Bor* **daidie,** †**dady,** †**dadie** /'dadi; *N* 'dɛdi; *Bor* 'dede/ *n* an informal word for father *16-*. **be a' their daddies** to excel, be the best, be an extreme example *20-*. [unknown]

†**dade** *n* dad, father *16-e19*. [unknown]

dade *see* DAD[1.1]

†**dadgeon, dajon** *n* an outcast *19*. **dajon wabster** a weaver of linen or woollen material for country neighbours *19*. **dadgeon weaver** = *dajon wabster*. [unknown]

dadie, dady *see* DADDY

dae[1.1], **dee, do,** *Ork* **deu,** †**dow** /de, di, du; *Ork* dø/ *v pres also* **dis** †**dois,** *also* **div,** *pt* **did** †**dyde,** *presp* **daein,** †**deand** †**dowand,** *ptp* **dune, deen, din, done,** †**downe,** †**doun,** †**doin** 1 to do, perform an act *la14-*. 2 *as an auxiliary* to do *la14-*. 3 to cause (to do something) *la14-19*. 4 to consign, dispatch; to proceed, betake oneself *la14-e19*. 5 to put, place *la14-e16*. **daeinless** unprosperous, feckless; clumsy, awkward *19, 20- EC*; compare DAELESS. **dain't** don't *20-*; compare DINNAE. **deester** *derogatory* a person in a position of authority *la19- NE*. **disnin** don't *20- NE*. **diven, divna** don't *la19-*. **dae-nae-better** a poor substitute *19, 20- EC SW*. **dae-na-gude** a disreputable person *19, 20- NE EC Bor*. **be daein** to be content, be satisfied; to put up with *18-*. **be deen wi' it** to be dying *20- NE T EC*. **dae awa** 1 to get along, continue (to work or live) *20-*. 2 to desist or refrain from something *la14-16*. **dae ill wantin** to spare with difficulty *19-*. **dune oot** exhausted *la19-*. **do the turn** to serve a purpose, suffice *la16-*. [OE *dōn*]

dae[1.2] /de/ *v* do not ◊*Ah dae ken* I don't know *20- C Bor*. [reduced form of DINNAE]

†**dae**[2]**, da, de, day** *n* doe, the female of the fallow deer *la14-18*. [OE *dā*]

daein, doin, doing /'deən, 'duən, 'duɪŋ/ *n* 1 a beating; a scolding *20-*. 2 an action, a deed, an event *la16-19*. [verbal noun from DAE[1.1]]

daek *see* DYKE[1.1]

dael *see* DALE[1.1], DALE[2]

daeless, doless, dowless, *Sh* **döless,** *H&I* **deelus** /'deləs, 'duləs, 'dʌuləs; *Sh* 'døləs; *H&I* 'diləs/ *adj* 1 lazy, improvident, useless *18-*. 2 helpless, feeble, lacking strength or energy *la18-*. [DAE[1.1], with adj-forming suffix]

daer, doer, †**doar** /'deər, 'duər/ *n* 1 a person who performs an act or deed *la14-*. 2 an agent, a factor; a person who acts for another *la15-*. **3** an animal which thrives *20-*. [DAE[1.1], with agent suffix]

daeth *see* DAITH

daev *see* DEAVE[1.2]

daff /daf/ *v* to act playfully or foolishly *16-*. **daffery**, †**dafrie** **1** fun, merriment *la18- NE EC*. **2** folly, foolishness *la16-18*. [unknown]

daffik, daffick, *Ork* **daffo**, †**daffok** /'dafək; *Ork* 'dafo/ *n* a small wooden tub or bucket for carrying water *17- Sh Ork*. [Gael *dabhach*]

daffin, daffing /'dafın, 'dafıŋ/ *n* **1** fun, merriment; foolish behaviour *16-*. **2** immoral behaviour; indecent, obscene language *18-e19*. **on the daffin** out for fun, on holiday *la19- NE EC*. [unknown]

daffins /'dafınz, 'dafınz/ *npl* the cords used to fasten driftnets to the rope from which they are hung *20- Ork N NE*. [unknown]

daffo, daffok *see* DAFFIK

daft /daft/ *adj* **1** stupid, lacking intelligence *15-*. **2** crazy, insane; of unsound mind *la15-*. **3** frivolous, thoughtless *la16-*. **daftie** a foolish person; a person with learning difficulties *la19-*. **daftish** slightly foolish, somewhat daft *19, 20- NE EC*. **daftness** foolishness; lasciviousness *la16-*. **daft days** **1** the period of festivity around Christmas and New Year *la18-*. **2** a time of frivolity and fun; one's youth *19, 20- NE EC*. **act the daft laddie** *of a male* to pretend naivety, ignorance or stupidity *20-*. **act the daft lassie** *of a female* to pretend naivety, ignorance or stupidity *20-*. **as daft as a maik watch** completely silly *20-*. **daft aboot** extremely fond of, mad for *la18-*. **daft for** crazy for or in desperate need of *19-*. **daft on** = *daft aboot 20-*. [OE *gedæfte* gentle, meek]

dag[1.1] /dag/ *n* **1** a thin drizzling rain *19, 20- Sh Ork Bor*. **2** a heavy shower of rain *19, 20- N NE H&I*. **daggy** drizzling, moist, misty *19, 20- NE C Bor*. [ON *dögg* dew]

dag[1.2] /dag/ *v* to rain gently, drizzle *19, 20- Bor*. [ON **dagg-*, stem of *döggva* to bedew]

dag[2], *NE* **dyaug** /dag; *NE* djɔg/ *n fisherman's taboo* woollen mittens or pieces of cloth used to protect the hands *la19- Sh NE*. [unknown]

dag[3], **dog, deg** /dag, dɔg, dɛg/ *interj as a mild oath* confound it *la19, 20- N NE*. **dag it** confound it *la19-*. **dag on it** = *dag it 19-*. [perhaps euphemistic form of Scots *God damn*]

daggen, daghan, daggon /'dagən/ *n* a large piece, a thick slice; a lump *19- Sh Ork*. [unknown]

daggle, daigle /'dagəl, 'degəl/ *v* to move, act or work slowly or idly *19- EC Bor*. [EModE *daggle* to clog with wet mud, wet or soil; compare DAG[1.2]]

daggon, daghan *see* DAGGEN

†**Dagone** *n* a Philistine deity *e16*. [Lat *Dagon*]

dai *see* DY

daible /'debəl/ *v* to dabble; to wash perfunctorily; to move around feebly or sloppily *19- Bor*. [Du *dabbelen*]

daice *see* DEAS[1.1]

daicent *see* DACENT

daich, daigh, *Bor* **deuch**, †**dauch**, †**dewche** /dex; *Bor* djux/ *n* **1** dough *16-*. **2** a mixture of meal and hot water for chicken food *19-*. **daichie, daighie, daikie, duchy** **1** doughy, half-baked *19-*. **2** *of a person* inactive, lacking in spirit *19-*. [OE *dāg* dough]

daichie *see* DAIKIE

daid *see* DEID[1.2]

daidie *see* DADDY

daidle[1] /'dedəl/ *n* **1** a (child's) pinafore or bib *19-*. **2** an apron *19-*. **3** the scoop-net which removes herring from the ringnet into the boat *20- NE Bor*. **4** a napkin *la20- T*. **daidlie,** **dedley** **1** a (child's) pinafore or bib *19-*. **2** an apron *la19-*. a doily *20- WC*. [unknown]

daidle[2] /'dedəl/ *v* **1** to idle, waste time; to potter about *la18-*. **2** to waddle; to stagger *19, 20- EC*. **daidler** an idler, a timewaster *19, 20- EC*. **daidle and drink** to wander from place to place drinking; to tipple *19, 20- T*. Compare DODDLE[2.2] [unknown]

daidle[3] /'dedəl/ *v* to dirty or wet one's clothes *19, 20- NE*. **daidlet, daudl't** battered, soiled; buffeted by the wind *20- NE*. [perhaps frequentative form of DAD[1.2]]

daidle[4] /'dedəl/ *v* to dandle or cuddle a child; *of a child* to be dandled or cuddled *la19, 20- NE WC*. [unknown]

daiffy *see* DEEFIE[1.3]

daig *see* DEG[1.1]

daigh *see* DAICH

daigie, deggie /'degi, 'dɛgi/ *n* a variety of the game of marbles *la19-*. [perhaps diminutive form of DEG[1.1]]

daigle *see* DAGGLE

daik[1.1] /dek/ *n* a smoothing down *la18-19, 20- NE*. [see the verb]

daik[1.2], †**dek** /dek/ *v* **1** to deck, adorn; to cover (with something rich or ornamental) *16-*. **2** to smooth down the hair *19, 20- NE T*. [MDu *deken* to cover]

daiker /'dekər/ *v* to decorate, deck out; to lay out a corpse *19-*. [perhaps Fr *décorer*, or frequentative form of DAIK[1.2]]

daiker *see* DACKER[1], DAKER

daikie, †daichie /'deke/ *n* the bivalve smooth-shelled mollusc *Arctica islandica 19- C*. [unknown]

dail *see* DALE[1.1], DALE[2], DALE[3]

daill *see* DALE[1.1], DALE[1.2]

daily[1.1], †**dayly**, †**daly** /'dele/ *adj* of each day, occurring every day *la15-*. **daily day** every day, constantly *la17-*. [OE *dægic*]

daily[1.2], †**dayly**, †**daly** /'dele/ *adv* on every day, day by day *la15-*. [DAY, with adv-forming suffix]

daim *see* DEM

daimen, †**demmin** /'demən/ *adj* rare, occasional *la18-*. [unknown]

daimish *see* DAMISH[1.2]

daimishel *see* DAMISHELL

daimish't *see* DAMMISHED

daine *see* DANE

dainner *see* DENNER[1.1]

dainshach, danshach, denshag /'denʃəx, 'danʃəx, 'dɛnʃəg/ *adj* fastidious; fussy about food *19, 20- N*. [unknown; compare DAINTY[1.2]]

dainte *see* DAINTY[1.1]

daintess, daintis, dentice /'dentəs, 'dɛntəs/ *n* a delicacy, a rarity *19-*. [plural of DAINTY[1.1]]

†**daintith, danteth** *n* a choice piece of food, a delicacy *la15-19*. [ME *deinteth*]

dainty[1.1], †**daynte**, †**dante**, †**dainte** /'denti, 'dente/ *n* **1** a delicacy, a choice piece of food *la14-*. **2** a large toffee sweet *20-*; compare *penny dainty*. **3** esteem, affection *la14-16*. **4** joy *la14-e16*. [ME *deinte*]

dainty[1.2], †**deintie, dentie**, †**dennty**, †**danty**, †**dayntie** /'denti, 'dente, 'dɛnte/ *adj* **1** small and neat; delicate, refined *la15-*. **2** pleasant, agreeable *la17-19, 20- NE T EC*. **3** large, fair-sized; *of time* considerable *la19, 20- Ork C*. [see the noun]

dainty-lion *see* DENTYLION

dair *see* DEAR[1.1], DEER[2]

dairk *see* DERK[1.1], DERK[1.3]

dairt *see* DART, DERT[1.1], DERT[1.2]

dais *see* DEAS[1.1]

daise *see* DAIZE

daiss see DASS

daith, daeth, deeth, deith, death, †**dethe** /deθ, diθ, dɛθ/ *n* the end of life, death *15-*. **death candle** *folklore* a will-o'-the-wisp thought to foretell death *19-, 20- NE EC*. **death-chap** a knocking thought to foretell death *19- N NE EC*. **death dwam** a death-like faint *la19, 20- NE*. †**the head of deathbed** = *law of deathbed 18-19*. †**law of deathbed** the law by which an heir could annul deeds made to his disadvantage by a terminally ill predecessor within 60 days before death, *la17-19*. **tak yer death** to die *la19-*. [OE *dēaþ*]

daiver *see* DAVER

daize, daze, *Bor* **dease,** †**daise** /dez; *Bor* diz/ *v* **1** to dazzle, bewilder or stupefy; to benumb with cold *15-*. **2** to become rotten or spoiled by age or damp *19, 20- SW Bor*. [ME *dasen*; compare ON *dasaðr* weary and exhausted]

daizzle /'dezəl/ *v* to dazzle *19-*. [frequentative form of DAIZE]

dajon *see* DADGEON

†**daker, daiker** *n* a set of ten (hides) *15-18*. [AN *daker*]

daker *see* DACKER[1], DACKER[2]

dale[1.1], **dail, deal,** *Sh* **dael,** †**dele,** †**deill,** †**daill** /del, dil; *Sh* deəl/ *n* **1** a part, a portion, a share *la14-*. **2** a quantity, an amount, a number *15-*. **3** a share, portion or division of land; a piece of land, a field *la15-*. **4** a share in a herring-fishermen's profit-sharing scheme *18-*. **5** a quantity or measure of coal *la17-19*. **6** a dealing out, division or distribution *15-e18*. **7** sexual intercourse *15-16*. **8** dealings with others, association *la15-16*. **dealsman, dailsman** a sharer or partner in a ship or fishing boat *la16-*. †**dail silver, daill silver** money given as dole or alms *la16-17*. [OE *dǣl* a part, a division]

dale[1.2], **deal,** †**daill** /del, dil/ *v* **1** to have dealings with, trade with *la14-*. **2** to divide, separate; to distribute *la14-*. [OE *dǣlan* to divide]

dale[2], **dail,** *Sh* **dael,** *N* **deyl,** †**dell** /del; *Sh* 'deəl; *N* dʌɪl/ *n* **1** a plank of wood *la15-*. **2** a shelf *19-*. **3** a container for holding milk *18, 20- N Bor*. **4** a diving-board at a swimming pool *20- WC*. **5** a plank bridge; loose planks *20- Sh*. [MLG *dele*]

dale[3], **dail, dell** /del, dɛl/ *n games* a goal; a stopping place, a base *19-*. [probably altered form of DOOL[2]]

dalk *see* DAUGH

dall *see* DOLL[2]

†**dallar** *n* a dollar *17*. Compare DOLLOUR. [Ger *Taler*, LG, Du *daler*]

†**dalldrums, dauldrums** *npl* foolish imaginings *19*. [altered form of Eng *doldrums*]

dallop *see* DOLLOP

†**dalphin, dolphin, daulphin** *n* the dauphin of France *la15-e17*. [ME *dauphin, dolphin*]

daly *see* DAILY[1.1], DAILY[1.2]

dam[1.1], †**dame** /dam/ *n* **1** (a body of water confined by) a retaining wall; a mill-dam *la13-*. **2** the amount of urine discharged at a time *19, 20- NE*. **damdike** the retaining wall of a dam *la13-19, 20- SW*. **damheid** (the body of water confined by) a weir *16-*. [Ger *Damm*, MDu *dam(m)*]

dam[1.2], †**dame** /dam/ *v* **1** to build a dam; to obstruct by means of a dam *la16-*; compare DEM. **2** to pass urine *e16*. †**damming and laving, damming and leving** a method of removing water, used in mining and poaching *18-19*; compare *dem and lave* (DEM). [see the noun]

dam[2] /dam/ *n* **1** *pl* the game of draughts *la17-*. **2** a piece in the game of draughts *19*. **dam heed** the top or bottom of a draughtboard *20- NE*. [Fr *dame* a piece in the *jeu de dames*]

dam *see* DAME

†**damacella** *n* a type of cloth *e17*. [unknown]

damage *see* DAMISH[1.1], DAMISH[1.2]

damas *see* DAMIS

dambrod[1.1] /'dambrɔd/ *n* a draught board *18-*. **the dambrod** the game of draughts *19, 20- NE EC Bor*. [DAM[2] + BROD[2.1]]

dambrod[1.2] /'dambrɔd/ *adj* chequered, having a chequered pattern *la18-*. [see the noun]

dame, deem, †**dam,** †**deme** /dem, dim/ *n* **1** a lady, a matron (used as a form of address or title) *la14-*. **2** a mother *la14-*. **3** a young (unmarried) woman *la18-19, 20- N NE T C*. **4** a (farmer's) wife, a housewife *la18-19, 20- NE EC*. **5** an elderly woman *la19- Ork NE*. **6** a kitchenmaid on a farm *20- NE*. **damie, deemie 1** a young woman *la18-*. **2** a sweetheart *20- NE*. [ME *dame*]

dame *see* DAM[1.1], DAM[1.2]

dameack, deimack /'demək, 'dimək/ *n* **1** a young woman *20- N NE*. **2** a sweetheart *20- NE*. **dameackie, deemachie** a little girl, a young woman *20- N NE*. [DAME + -OCK]

dames *see* DAMIS

damesel *see* DAMISHELL

†**damis, damas, dames** *n* damask *la15-e18*. [altered form of OFr *Damasc* the city of Damascus]

damish[1.1], **damage,** †**demmish,** †**damnage,** †**dampnage** /'damɪʃ, 'daməʤ/ *n* (loss caused by) injury, harm *la15-*. †**dampnis** reparation for injury sustained, damages *la15-e16*. [ME *damage*]

damish[1.2], **damage,** *Bor* **daimish,** †**dampnage,** †**damnis** /'damɪʃ, 'daməʤ; *Bor* 'demɪʃ/ *v* to injure or harm; to break, ruin *la15-*. [see the noun]

damishell, daimishel, demishel, †**damesel,** †**damycele,** †**damoysell** /'damɪʃəl, 'demɪʃəl, 'dɛmɪʃəl/ *n* a young woman, a damsel; the daughter of the house *la14-17, 18- NE*. [ME *damisele*]

dammer *see* DAUMER

dammished, *Bor* **daimish't,** †**demmished,** †**dammest,** †**dammischit** /'damɪʃd; *Bor* 'demɪʃt/ *adj* **1** spoilt, broken; injured *18-*. **2** stunned, stupefied, bewildered *la16-19, 20- Sh NE*. [ptp of DAMISH[1.2]]

dammle *see* DEMMEL[1.1]

damnage *see* DAMISH[1.1]

damnifeit *see* DAMPNIFEIT

damnis *see* DAMISH[1.2]

damnum fatale /'damnʌm fə'tale/ *n law* a loss due to an unavoidable accident or 'act of God' *18-*. [Lat *damnum fatāle* a loss ordained by fate]

damoysell *see* DAMISHELL

damp /damp/ *n fisherman's taboo* the end of a line or rope *19- Sh Ork*. [compare Norw, LG *tamp*]

dampnage *see* DAMISH[1.1], DAMISH[1.2]

†**dampnifeit, damnifeit** *adj* damaged or injured; sustaining material loss *la16-e17*. [OFr *dampnifier*, Lat *damnificāre* to damage]

dampnis *see* DAMISH[1.1]

damster *see* DEMPSTER

damycele *see* DAMISHELL

Dan /dan/ *n* a nickname for a Roman Catholic *20- WC*. **Dannie boy** = DAN *la20-*. [from familiar form of the personal name *Daniel*, which is popular among Irish Roman Catholics]

dance[1.1], **daunce,** †**dans** /dans, dɔns/ *n* (an occasion of) dancing, a dance *la15-*. **dancie** a dancing master *la19- NE T EC*. [ME *daunce*]

dance[1.2], **daunce,** †**dans,** †**daunse** /dans, dɔns/ *v* to move in time to music, perform or take part in a dance *15-*. **dancers** the aurora borealis *18-*; compare *merry dancers* (MERRY) and *pretty dancers* (PRETTY). **dance-in-my-loof** a very small person *19- T Bor*. **dancin mad** in an intense rage *la19-*. **dance the miller's reel** = *dance the reel o Bogie*. **dance the reel o Bogie** to have sexual intercourse

18-. **dance the reel o Stumpie** = *dance the reel o Bogie.* **dance yer lane** to be filled with joy or rage *18-19, 20- NE.* **ya dancer!** an exclamation of delight or approval *la20-.* [ME *dauncen*]

dandelion see DENTYLION

dander[1] /'dandər/ *n* the refuse of a smith's fire; clinker *la18-.* [unknown]

dander[2] /'dandər/ *n* a kind of sweet bun or biscuit, a rock-cake *20- C.* [perhaps humorous extension of DANDER[1]]

dander see DAUNER[1.1], DAUNER[1.2]

dandie[1.1] /'dandi/ *n* a DANDY LINE *la19- NE.* [reduced form of DANDY LINE]

dandie[1.2] /'dandi/ *v fishing* to keep moving a line up and down in the water *20- Sh NE.* **dandie handline** a DANDY LINE *19- Sh NE.* [compare Faer *danda* to dandle]

†**dandiefechan** *n* a slap; a blow *e19.* [unknown]

†**dandillie** *adv* in a petted manner *e16.* [perhaps Older Scots *dandill* to dandle, with adv-forming *-ly* suffix; compare DANDILLY[1.2]]

dandilly[1.1], †**dandillie** /'dandəli/ *n* a spoilt pet *la17-19, 20- Uls.* [perhaps Older Scots *dandill* + -IE[2]]

†**dandilly**[1.2] *adj* petted, pampered; fancy, over-ornamented *la18-19.* [see the noun]

dandrum /'dandrəm/ *n* a whim, a curiosity *la19- NE.* [altered form of TANTRUM]

dandy[1] /'dandi, 'dande/ *n* a man who is vain about his appearance *la18-.* [unknown]

dandy[2] /'dandi, 'dande/ *n* a stiff brush for cleaning horses *20- N NE SW.* [probably DANDY[1]]

dandy line /'dandi lʌɪn/ *n in herring fishing* a type of fishing line, a series of lines and hooks fastened together and dropped into the shoal *19-.* [DANDIE[1.2] + LINE[1.1]]

†**dane**, **daine** *adj* haughty, reserved, dignified *16.* [ME *digne, deine*; compare DIGNE]

dane see DEAN

dang[1] /daŋ/ *v* to strike, knock *la19, 20- EC SW.* [pt of DING[1.2]]

dang[2] /daŋ/ *v* to damn *19-.* [euphemistic form of Older Scots *damn*]

dang see DING[1.2]

danger, †**daunger**, †**denger** /'dendʒər/ *n* 1 risk or harm, peril *15-.* 2 power to control, affect or harm *la14-19, 20- WC.* 3 the state of being in debt *la15-19.* 4 disdain; displeasure, enmity *16.* 5 reluctance *16.* [ME *daunger*]

dank see DUNK[1.1], DUNK[1.2]

dans see DANCE[1.1], DANCE[1.1]

danshach see DAINSHACH

†**Danskin**[1.1], **Danskene**, **Danskyn** *n* the town of Danzig (now Gdansk) *la15-e17.* [see the adj]

†**Danskin**[1.2], **Danskene** *adj* connected with, made in, or imported from Danzig (now Gdansk) *la15-e17.* [from the former place-name *Danzig*, with adj-forming suffix]

dant see DAUNT, DUNT[2.2]

dante see DAINTY[1.1]

danteth see DAINTITH

danton, **dantoun** see DAUNTON

danty see DAINTY[1.2]

daover, **dover** /'dovər/ *numeral in counting rhymes* nine *la19- NE EC SW.* [nonsense word derived from a system of counting sheep]

dar, **dare** see DAUR[1], DAUR[2.2]

dareen see DOREEN

darett see DIRECK[1.1]

darf see DERF

darg[1.1], **daurg**, †**dargue**, †**daurk**, †**dawerk** /darg, dɔrg/ *n* 1 a day's work (in the fields) *15-.* 2 work, a task *19-.* 3 the result or product of a day's work (a quantity of hay, peat or coal) *la15-.* 4 the area of meadow which can be mowed in a day *la16-17.* **darger**, †**darker** a casual labourer *18- NE C.* [reduced form of DAY + WARK[1.1]]

darg[1.2] /darg/ *v* to work, toil *la19-.* [see the noun]

darg[2] /darg/ *n* a young whiting *Merlangius merlangus la19- NE.* **dargie** the (fry of the) coalfish *Pollachius virens la19- T.* [unknown]

dargue see DARG[1.1]

dark see DERK[1.1], DERK[1.2], DERK[1.3]

Dark Blues /dark 'bluz/ *npl* a nickname for Dundee Football Club *20-.* [from the colour of their jerseys]

darken see DERKEN

darkness see DERKNESS

darle see DORLE

darloch see DORLACH

darn[1], †**dern** /darn/ *n* 1 a disease of cattle associated with constipation or diarrhoea *19- NE.* 2 excrement *la19- NE.* **dry darn** constipation *la17- NE.* [unknown]

darn[2], **dern** /darn, dɛrn/ *v* 1 to mend by darning *18-.* 2 to thread one's way in and out (of) *19.* [unknown]

darn see DERN[1.2], DERN[1.3], DERN[1.4]

darr see DAUR[1]

darra see DORRO

darrer, **darrest** see DEAR[1.1]

†**dart**, **dairt** *adj of oxen and horses* no longer capable of work, worthless *la15-16.* [unknown]

dart see DERT[1.1], DERT[1.2]

darth see DEARTH[1.1], DEARTH[1.2]

dasche see DASH[1.1], DASH[1.2]

†**daseyne** *n* a daisy *e16.* [Eng *daisy* altered for rhyme]

dash[1.1], †**dasche** /daʃ/ *n* 1 a (violent) impact, a blow *16-.* 2 a splash; a small quantity *la17-.* 3 a fast, short run *20-.* **dashy** ostentatious *19, 20- NE.* **cast a dash** see CAST[1.2]. **a dash of rain** a sudden fall of rain *la18-19, 20- NE WC.* [see the verb]

dash[1.2], †**dasche** /daʃ/ *v* 1 to beat or throw sharply or violently; to smash; to splash *la16-.* 2 to go at great speed, rush *19-.* [ME *dashen*]

dash see DASS

dashle /'daʃəl/ *v* to soil, batter, wear out *19- H&I WC SW.* [perhaps frequentative form of DASH[1.2]]

dask, **desk** /dask, dɛsk/ *n* 1 a piece of (school or office) furniture, a desk *16-.* 2 a seat or pew in a church (with a shelf to put a book on) *la17-.* [ME *deske*]

dass, *Sh Ork* **dess**, *Ork* **dash**, †**daiss**, †**deas** /das; *Sh Ork* dɛs; *Ork* daʃ/ *n* 1 a shelf or ledge on a hillside or cliff; a stratum of stones *la18-.* 2 (a section or layer in) a stack of hay, peats or heather; a small stack of sheaves set up in a field *la18-.* 3 a cut of hay, corn or coal *19- C.* [perhaps ME *deis*, ON *des* a hay rick]

dassint see DACENT

da streen see THE STREEN[1.1], THE STREEN[1.2]

dat see DAUT[1.2], THAT[1.1], THAT[1.2], THAT[1.3], THAT[2]

date see DAUT[1.2]

dather see DOCHTER

†**dative**[1.1] *n law* (a person appointed to) the post of *tutor dative* (TUTOR) or *executor dative* (EXECUTOR) *la16-17.* [see the adj]

dative[1.2] /'detɪv/ *adj of an executor or tutor* appointed by a court *la15-*; compare *tutor dative* (TUTOR). [EModE *dative*, Lat *datīvus*]

daub see DAB[1.1]

dauble, **daable** /'dɔbəl, 'dabəl/ *v* to work ineffectively, waste time *18-19, 20- NE.* [altered form of Eng *dabble*]

dauch see DAICH, DAUGH, DAVACH

dauchie see DAUGHY

dauchle see DACKLE[1.2]

dauchter see DOCHTER
daud see DAD[1.1], DAD[1.2]
daugh, dauch, †dalk /dɔx/ *n* soft coaly fire clay, found in a coal seam *la18-*. **daugher** a long thin pick for use in a DAUGH seam *20- C.* [unknown]
daugh see DAWK[1.1]
daughter see DOCHTER
daughy, †dauchie /'dɔxe/ *adj of the ice in curling* dull and sticky *19-*. [perhaps DAUGH + -IE[2]]
dauk /dɔk/ *adj* stupid; sluggish *la19- NE.* [unknown; compare DAAK[1.1], DACKER[1]]
dauldrums see DALLDRUMS
daulphin see DALPHIN
daumer, dammer /'dɔmər, 'damər/ *v* to stun, confuse *19, 20- NE.* [unknown]
daunce see DANCE[1.2]
dauner[1.1]**, donner, daunder, dander,** *Sh* **daander** /'dɔnər, 'dɔndər, 'dandər; *Sh* 'dɑndər/ *n* a stroll, a leisurely walk *19-*. [unknown]
dauner[1.2]**, donner, daunder, dander,** *Sh* **daander** /'dɔnər, 'dɔndər, 'dandər; *Sh* 'dɑndər/ *v* to stroll, saunter *la16-*. [unknown]
daunger see DANGER
daunse see DANCE[1.2]
daunt, †dant /dɔnt/ *v* **1** to overcome, subdue; to intimidate *la14-*. **2** to correct, chastise *16*. **3** to tame *e16*. **†dantar 1** a subduer, a controller *16*. **2** a horse-tamer *16*. [ME *daunten*]
daunt see DUNT[2.1], DUNT[2.2]
daunton, daunten, †dantoun, †danton /'dɔntən/ *v* **1** to subdue; to intimidate or frighten; to discourage *16-19, 20- C.* **2** to bring under control; to suppress; to tame *la16-17*. [altered form of DAUNT]
daunts /dɔnts/ *npl* discouraging words *19, 20- C.* [from the verb DAUNT]
daupit see DAWPIT
daur[1]**, dare,** *Sh* **daar, †dar, †darr** /dɔr, der; *Sh* dɑr/ *v pres* also **durst,** *pt* **daured †dard, †durst 1** to venture, have courage (to) *la14-*. **2** to challenge *la19-*. **3** *imperative* don't you dare! *la19- NE EC.* **4** to forbid *la18, 20- SW.* **daurna, darena** dare not *la18-*. [OE *durran*]
daur[2.1] /dɔr/ *n* a feeling of awe or fear *19- Sh T EC Bor.* [see the verb]
daur[2.2]**, †dare, †dar** /dɔr/ *v* **1** to terrify, intimidate *19-, 20- NE WC.* **2** to be afraid *19.* **3** to lurk, crouch *15.* **†dare at** to be afraid of *19.* [OE *darian* to lie still or hidden]
daurg see DARG[1.1]
daurk see DARG[1.1], DERK[1.3]
daurkness see DERKNESS
daut[1.1]**, dawt** /dɔt, dot/ *n* **1** a caress *la18-*. **2** a darling *20- N NE Uls.* **dautie, dawtie** a pet, a darling *la17-*. [unknown]
daut[1.2]**, †dawt, †dat, †date** /dɔt, dot/ *v* to pet, fondle; to make much of *16-*. [unknown]
davach, davoch, †dauch, †dawach /'davəx/ *n* a measurement of land of variable area (possessing the necessary resources for a group of people to survive throughout the year); a unit of land assessed for taxation and military service *la12-19, 20- historical*. [Gael *dabhach*]
dave /dɛv, dev/ *v* to dive *18-19, 20- T.* [altered form of Eng *dive*]
dave see DEAVE[1.2]
davel see DEVEL[1.1], DEVEL[1.2]
daver, daiver, *Bor* **dever** /'devər; *Bor* 'dɛvər/ *v* **1** to wander aimlessly or dazedly; to stagger *la16-*. **2** to stun, stupefy or daze *la18-*. **3** to be stupid or senile *19- Sh Ork NE Bor.* **4** *in imprecations* damn, confound *19- WC SW Bor.* **5** to dawdle *19- NE SW.* **6** to make numb, chill *la18- NE.* [perhaps Du *daveren* to shake, quake]
daviely /'devəle/ *adv* listlessly, languidly *la18- WC SW.* [unknown]
davoch see DAVACH
daw[1.1] /dɔ/ *n* dawn *la19, 20- Bor.* [see the verb]
daw[1.2] /dɔ/ *v pt* also **†dew,** *ptp* also **†dawin, dawyn** to dawn *la14-*. **†dawin, dawyng** dawn, dawning *la14-e19.* [OE *dagian*]
daw[2]**, da** /dɔ, da/ *n* **1** a lazy person *16-19, 20- N.* **2** a slattern *la16-19, 20- Uls.* [extension of ME *dawe* a jackdaw]
†daw[3] *n* an atom, a jot *e19.* [unknown]
daw see DAY
dawach see DAVACH
dawb see DAB[1.2]
daweling see DEVELLING
dawerk see DARG[1.1]
dawin see DAW[1.2]
dawk[1.1]**, daugh** /dɔk, dɔx/ *n* fog, drizzle *19- C.* **dawkie, daughie** drizzly, damp *la17-19, 20- EC SW.* [unknown]
†dawk[1.2] *v* to drizzle *19.* [unknown]
dawlie /'dɔli/ *adj* physically or mentally slow *la18-*. [probably DAW[2], with adj-forming suffix]
dawpit, †daupit /'dɔpət/ *adj* stupid, slow to learn *la18-19, 20- NE.* [unknown]
dawrin see DOREEN
dawt see DAUT[1.1], DAUT[1.2]
dawyn see DAW[1.2]
day, *T* **dey, †da, †daw** /de; *T* dae/ *n* a period of 24 hours; the working day; daytime; daylight, dawn *la14-*. **day daw** dawn *la18- NE EC SW.* **day set** sunset; nightfall *17, 18- Sh Ork N.* **†day sky** daylight *16-e19*; compare SKY[1.1] (sense 2). **†daysman** an arbitrator, umpire *la16-19.* **day tale** (the daily wage of) a day labourer *la19- Bor.* **aw the days o yer life** the whole of one's life *la14-.* **day and daily** constantly, every day *la19-.* **day and day about** on alternate days *19-.* **†day of march** (a day appointed for) a court held by the Wardens of the Marches of England and Scotland, under truce, to settle disputes *15-16.* **†day of trew** = *day of march la15-16.* **get day aboot wi** to get one's own back on *la19- EC.* **here the day and awa the morn** said of someone unreliable or changeable *20-.* **see day aboot wi** = *get day aboot wi 20- H&I Bor.* [OE *dæg*]
day see DA[2], DAE[2]
dayell see DIAL
†dayis licht *n* daylight *15-e16.* [possessive of DAY + LICHT[1.1]]
daylicht, *T* **deylicht, †day lycht** /'delɪxt; *T* 'daelɪxt/ *n* daylight *la15-*. **not be able to see daylicht til** to be blind to the faults of *la19- NE EC.* **not be able to see daylicht for** = *not be able to see daylicht til.* [DAY + LICHT[1.1]]
dayligaun /'deləgɔn/ *n* twilight *19-.* [reduced form of DAYLICHT + *gaun* (GAE)]
dayly see DAILY[1.1], DAILY[1.2]
day lycht see DAYLICHT
day-nettle /'de nɛtəl/ *n* **1** either of two types of hemp-nettle *Galeopsis tetrahit* or *Galeopsis speciosa 19-.* **2** the dead-nettle, a plant of the genus *Lamium 19-.* [perhaps altered form of Eng *dead-nettle*]
daynte see DAINTY[1.1]
dayntie see DAINTY[1.2]
dayster see DYESTER
daze see DAIZE
dazent /'dezənt/ *adj* **1** dazed, stupefied *20- T*; compare DOZEN. **2** damned *20 N NE.* [unknown; compare DAIZE, DOZENT]
dazzle /'dazəl/ *n* a fizzy drink *20- NE.* [compare DAIZZLE]
de see DAE[2], DEE[1], THE[1.2]

dea *see* DA².

deacon, *NE T* **dykon**, †**dekin**, †**deakin**, †**decane** /ˈdikən; *NE T* ˈdʌikən/ *n* **1** *Christian Church* a member of the clergy below the level of a priest *la14-*. **2** the chief official of a craft or trade; the president of one of the Incorporated Trades *15-*. **3** *Presbyterian Church* a member of the clergy below the level of a minister appointed to manage the temporal affairs of a congregation *la16-*. **4** a master of a craft or skill; an expert *19, 20- NE EC SW*. †**deikenheid** the right of a trade to have a deacon; the control exercised by a deacon *17*. †**deaconrie 1** the right of a trade to have a deacon; the control exercised by a deacon *17-e18*. **2** (the holding of) the office of deacon of a trade *la16*. **deaconship 1** *Presbyterian Church* the office of deacon *la16-*. **2** the right of a trade to have a deacon; the control exercised by a deacon *la16-e17*. **deacon convener** the deacon who convenes and presides over meetings of the Incorporated Trades of a town *la16-*. **Deacons' Court** *Presbyterian Church* a committee which runs a congregation's temporal affairs, consisting of the ministers, elders and deacons *20-*. [Lat *decānus* one in charge of ten]

dead *see* DEID¹·¹, DEID¹·².

deadlike, †**dedlik**, †**dedelike** /ˈdɛdlʌik/ *adj* **1** deathlike, suggestive of death *la15-*. **2** mortal, liable to death *la14-e15*. †**al dedlyke, al dedelike** mortals *la14-e15*. [OE *dēadlic*]

deadly *see* DEIDLY

deaf *see* DEEF

deafen /ˈdɛfən/ *v* to make soundproof by pugging *19-*. [*deaf* (DEEF), with verb-forming suffix]

deafie *see* DEEFIE¹·¹

deafy *see* DEEFIE¹·³

deakin *see* DEACON

deal *see* DALE¹·¹, DALE¹·²

†**deambulatour** *n* a place to walk in; a walk *16*. [Lat *dēambulatōrium*]

dean, †**dene**, †**dane** /din/ *n* **1** a title prefixed to the names of ecclesiastics *la14-*. **2** *Scottish Universities* the head of a faculty *16-*. **3** the elected leader of the Bar, whether of the Faculty of Advocates or of a local Bar of solicitors *18-*. †**denry** deanery *15-17*. **Dean of Guild** a member of the town council, who presided over the *Dean of Guild Court*, originally the head of the craft guild or merchant company of a royal burgh *15-*. †**Dean of the guild** = *Dean of Guild 15*. **dean o guil, dean o guild, dinnygill** to test and stamp (weights) officially; to investigate thoroughly *20- NE*. **Dean of Guild Court** a court with jurisdiction over the buildings of a burgh (some of them earlier having jurisdiction also over weights and measures) *18-20, 21- historical*. [ME *den*, Lat *decānus* one in charge of ten; compare DEACON]

dean *see* DEN¹

deand *see* DAE¹·¹

dear¹·¹, †**dere**, †**dair**, †**deir** /dir/ *adj* **1** beloved, highly valued, precious *la14-*. **2** expensive *15-*. **dearer**, †**derrar**, †**darrer** more costly or precious *15-*. **dearest**, †**derrast**, †**darrest** most costly or precious *la14-*. **dear meal** a time of famine or high price of meal *la18-19, 20- historical*. **dear be here** good gracious! *19- N NE EC*. **dear keep us** Lord save us! *19- NE EC*. **dear kens** God knows! *la19-*. [OE *dēore*]

dear¹·² /dir/ *adv* **1** at a high cost *la14-*. **2** dearly, fondly *la14-*. [see the adj]

dearch *see* DWERCH

dearth¹·¹, *NE* **darth**, †**derth** /dɛrθ; *NE* darθ/ *n* **1** a scarcity, a shortage *15-*. **2** dearness, high price *15-19, 20- NE WC*. †**dearthfu** expensive *18*. [DEAR¹·¹, with noun-forming *-th* suffix]

†**dearth¹·²**, **darth** *v* to make dear in price (to cause a scarcity) *la15-19*. [see the noun]

deas¹·¹, **deese**, **dais**, †**dese**, †**deys**, †**daice** /ˈdiəs, dis, ˈdeəs/ *n* **1** a dais, a raised platform *15-*. **2** a desk or pew in a church *la16-*. **3** a stone or turf seat outside a cottage *19-*. **4** a wooden seat or settle, which could also be used as a table, or as a bed *19- NE WC*. [ME *deis*]

†**deas¹·²** *v* to provide with a dais, seats or benches *17-e18*. [see the noun]

deas *see* DASS

dease *see* DAIZE

deasil¹·¹, **dessil** /ˈdjeʃəl, ˈdɛsəl/ *n* (the custom of) walking left to right round a person or thing (for good luck) *la18-*. Compare WIDDERSHINS. [Gael *deiseil* southward, sunward]

deasil¹·², **diesel** /ˈdjeʃəl, ˈdɛsəl, ˈdizəl/ *adv* sunwise, southward *la18-*. [see the noun]

death *see* DAITH

deave¹·¹, **deeve** /div/ *n* an interminable talker *20- NE*. [see the verb]

deave¹·², **deeve**, *Sh* **daev**, *Ork* **dave**, †**deve**, †**deif** /div; *Sh Ork* dev/ *v* **1** to deafen *15-*. **2** to annoy with noise or talk; to bore *15-*. **deavance** annoyance, nuisance *19- NE Bor*. **deavesome** deafening, noisy *la19-*. [OE *dēafian*; Sh Ork forms perhaps from ON *deyfa* to make blunt]

debar /dəˈbar/ *v* **1** to exclude, prohibit; to shut out *la16-*. **2** *Presbyterian Church* to exclude formally from Communion (those guilty of certain sins) *la16-19*. [ME *debarren* compare MFr *desbarrer* to smash open, rout an army]

debatabill land *see* DEBATEABLE LAND

debatable /dəˈbetəbəl/ *adj* **1** admitting of debate or dispute *15-*. **2** *of land or boundaries* subject to dispute *15-e17*. [OFr *debatable*]

debate¹·¹ /dəˈbet/ *n* **1** conflict, fighting; a fight, dissension, strife *la14-*. **2** disputation, discussion, consideration *la15-*. **3** *in court procedure* the legal argument submitted by the parties on the closed record *la19-*. **4** a struggle *la19*. **5** a dispute as to legal rights or claims *la14-17*. †**but debate** without resistance; without effort; peacefully *la14-e17*. †**mak debate** to begin or maintain a fight, in attack or defence *la14-16*. [ME *debat*]

debate¹·² /dəˈbet/ *v* **1** to discuss, argue about *la16-*. **2** to fight for; to defend *la14-e17*. **3** to maintain or support by action or argument *16-e17*. **4** to fight against; to stop by force; to overcome *16-e17*. [ME *debaten*]

Debateable land, †**debatabill land** /dəˈbetəbəl land/ *n* the land on the Scottish-English border between the Esk and the Sark, ownership of which was disputed, and which in consequence was effectively lawless *la15-16, 17- historical*. [DEBATABLE + LAND¹·¹]

†**deblat**, **dablet** *n* a little devil, imp *la15-16*. [ME *deblet*]

debosh¹·¹ /dəˈbɒʃ/ *n* (a bout of) excessive eating or drinking *la17-*. [Fr *débauche*]

debosh¹·², **debush** /dəˈbɒʃ, dəˈbuʃ/ *v* **1** to corrupt or deprave *17-19, 20- NE EC*. **2** to behave immorally *17*. **3** to squander *17*. [Fr *débaucher*]

†**debowaill**, **debowal** *v* to disembowel *la14-e16*. [OFr *boële*, with verb-forming prefix denoting removal]

debt, †**det**, †**dett** /dɛt/ *n* something owed, an outstanding sum of money; an obligation *la14-*. †**detful**, **debtfull 1** proper, due *15-17*. **2** *of a person* indebted *la16-e17*. **3** *of money* owing, owed *e17*. †**detfully 1** duly, properly *la15-16*. **2** dutifully *15*. †**dettit 1** indebted *15-e17*. **2** due, owing *la14-16*. †**detbund 1** bound by an obligation *la15-e17*. **2** obligatory, due *la16-e17*. [OFr *dete*, Lat *debita*]

†**debuish** *v in skittles* to oust (from a winning position), get rid of *e19*. [perhaps a specific sense of DEBOSH¹·²]

†**deburse, deburs** *v* to pay out, disburse *16-18*. [MFr *desbourser*]
debush *see* DEBOSH[1.2]
decane *see* DEACON
decanter /dəˈkantər/ *n* **1** a vessel for decanting wine or liquor *18-*. **2** a table jug *la19- NE*. [Fr *décanteur* a decanting or clarifying glass]
†**decart** *v* to set aside; to discard *la16-e17*. [OFr *descarter* to disperse]
decay, †**dekey** /dəˈke/ *n* **1** decomposition, degeneration; a declining state *la16-*. **2** a decline in health caused by tuberculosis *la17-e19*. **3** downfall, death *e15*. [OFr *decaīr*, compare AN *en decay* in ruins]
decease[1.1], †**deces**, †**decesse**, †**disses** /dəˈsis/ *n* death *la14-*. [ME *deces*, Lat *dēcessus* departure, death]
decease[1.2], †**deces**, †**deceis**, †**disces** /dəˈsis/ *v* to die *la14-*. [see the noun]
deceis *see* DECEASE[1.2]
deceive, *T* **desave**, †**dissave**, †**desaif**, †**dissaif** /dəˈsiv; *T* dəˈsev/ *v* to mislead, cheat *la14-*. [ME *deceiven*]
deceivery, deceiverie /dəˈsivəre, dəˈsivəri/ *n* deceit, trickery *19-*. [DECEIVE with noun-forming suffix]
December, †**Discembre** /dəˈsɛmbər/ *n* the last month of the year, December *la14-*. [Lat *December*]
decent *see* DACENT
decern, †**discerne** /dəˈsɛrn/ *v* **1** *law* to pronounce judicially; to decide judicially or formally; to decree *15-*. **2** to determine or settle *15-17*. **decerniture**, †**decernitour** a decree or sentence of a court *17-*. [Lat *dēcernere* to decide]
decerne *see* DISCERN
deces *see* DECEASE[1.1], DECEASE[1.2]
decesse *see* DECEASE[1.1]
decht *see* DICHT[1.2]
declaration, †**declaratioun** /deklaˈreʃən/ *n* **1** an announcement or proclamation *15-*. **2** *law* the statement made before a committal and in the presence of the sheriff by a person whom it is intended to try on indictment *18-*. [ME *declaracioun*, Lat *dēclārātio*]
declarator /dəˈklarətər/ *n law* **1** a judicial declaration *16-*. **2** an action brought by an interested party to have some legal right or status declared, but without claim on any person called as defender to do anything *la16-*. [MFr *declaratoire* declaratory]
declare, †**declere**, †**disclar** /dəˈkler/ *v* **1** to state openly; to announce, proclaim *la14-*. **2** to make clear, settle *15*. [ME *declaren*, Lat *dēclārāre*]
declinature, †**declinator**, †**declinatour** /dəˈklɪnətʃər/ *n* **1** *law* the refusal by a judge to exercise jurisdiction, appropriate in a case in which by reason of relationship to a party or pecuniary or other interest his decision might be thought affected *la16-*; compare *exceptioun declinatour* (EXCEPTION). **2** refusal to accept some office, appointment or benefit, *18-*. [Lat *dēclīnātōria*]
decline, †**declyne** /dəˈklʌɪn/ *v* **1** to turn away from; to deviate; to avoid; to turn down, refuse *la14-*. **2** to descend or sink; to fail in strength or value; to deteriorate *15-*. **3** *law* to reject the jurisdiction of a judge or court *la15-*. **4** to consent (to) *16*. [OFr *decliner*]
†**decore**[1.1] *n* adornment *16*. [Lat *decor*]
decore[1.2] /dəˈkor/ *v* **1** to decorate, adorn or embellish *16-*. **2** to invest with an honour or distinction *16-17*. **decorement**, †**decoirment 1** a decoration, an ornament *la16-*. **2** the act of decoration; embellishment *la16-e19*. [ME *decoren* to beautify]
†**decore**[1.3] *adj* beautiful, comely *16*. [Lat *decōrus*]

†**decourt** *v* to force out of or dismiss from Court *la16-17*. [*court* (COORT[1.1]), with prefix denoting separation, departure]
decree, †**decre** /dəˈkri/ *n* **1** an edict, a civil or ecclesiastical order *la15-*. **2** *law* a final judgement *la18-*. **decree arbitral** a judgement or order made by an arbiter *la17-*. **degree conform** *law* a judgement by one court to render effective the decree of another *19-*. **decree dative** *law* the judgement appointing a person executor *la18-*. **decree of lining** permission to proceed with building after due inspection of the boundaries *la18-*. [ME *dēcre*]
decreet[1.1], †**decrete** /dəˈkrit/ *n* **1** *law* the judgement or decree of a court or judge *la14-*. **2** a decision; a civil or ecclesiastical decree *15-16*. **decreet arbitral** a judgement or order made by an arbiter *la15-*. †**decreet of plat** an official ruling or authorized scheme of the *Commission of Plat* (COMMISSION) *17-18*. [OFr *decret*, Lat *dēcrētum*]
†**decreet**[1.2], **decrete**, **decreit** *v* **1** to order, ordain; to decree judicially *la14-e19*. **2** to decide, determine to do *la15-16*. [OFr *decreter*]
decrippit, decrepit, decript, †**decripped** /dəˈkrɪpɪt, dəˈkrɛpɪt, dəˈkrɪpt/ *adj* wasted, worn out or enfeebled with age or infirmity *la15-*. [Lat *dēcrepitus*]
ded *see* DEID[1.1]
deddy *see* DADDY
dede *see* DEED[1], DEID[1.1], DEID[1.2]
dedeigne *see* DEDEN3E[1]
dedelike *see* DEADLIKE
dedely *see* DEIDLY
†**deden3e**[1], **dedeigne, dedeyn** *v* to deign, condescend *la14-16*. [*den3e* (DENZIE) with prefix meaning 'down']
†**deden3e**[2.1], **dedigne** *n* disdain *la14-15*. [see the verb]
†**deden3e**[2.2] *v* to disdain *e16*. [altered form of DISDENE[1.2]]
dedlik *see* DEADLIKE
deduce /dəˈdʒus/ *v* **1** to surmise or infer *la16-*. **2** to deduct, subtract *16-18*. **3** to conduct, prosecute (a process or cause) *la15-17*. [Lat *dēdūcere* to lead down, derive]
dee[1], **die**, †**de**, †**dey** /di, dae/ *v* to suffer death, cease to live *la14-*. **die in the harras** to die while still working, die in harness *19- N NE T Bor*. **die wi** to die of *19-*. [ON *deyja*]
Dee[2] /di/ *n* a nickname for Dundee Football Club *la20-*. [shortened form of *Dundee*]
dee *see* DAE[1.1], DEY[1], THEE[3], THY
deed[1], †**dede**, †**deid** /did/ *n* **1** an act, an action; an exploit, an achievement *la14-*. **2** a legal document *17-*. **3** a criminal act or act of violence *la14-e17*. **4** an act of legal import or consequence *16-e17*. †**deid-doar** the doer of a deed of violence; a murderer *15-17*. †**by my deed** upon my word *la18-19 Ork NE*. **deed of accession** a deed executed by the creditors of an insolvent, approving and accepting an arrangement by him for settling his affairs *19-*. †**dede of armis** an act of charity *la15-16*. †**into deid** in fact, indeed *15-e16*. †**upon my deed** = *by my deed*. [OE *dǣd*]
deed[2] /did/ *adv* indeed *la18-*. **deed aye** yes indeed *20-*. **deed no** no indeed *la18-*. [aphetic form of Older Scots *indede*]
deed *see* DEID[1.1], DEID[1.2]
deedle *see* DIDDLE[1.2], DIDDLE[2.1], DIDDLE[2.2]
deef, deaf, †**defe,** †**deif** /dif, dɛf/ *adj* **1** unable to hear; having impaired hearing *la14-*. **2** *of soil* poor, unproductive, barren; springy, spongy *la18-*. **deaf nit** a nut without a kernel *19-*. †**nae deaf nit** no inconsiderable thing or person *18-e19*. **not fed on deaf nits** plump, well-fed, well-developed *18-*. [OE *dēaf*]
deefie[1.1], **deafie** /ˈdifi, ˈdɛfi/ *n* **1** *derogatory* a deaf person *la20-*. **2** a pretence of deafness; an act of ignoring or avoiding *la20-*. [DEEF + -IE[3]]
deefie[1.2] /ˈdifi/ *v* to ignore *la20-*. [see the noun]

deefie[1,3], **deafy**, *C* **daiffy**, *WC* **diffy** /'difi, 'dɛfi; *C* 'defe; *WC* 'dɪfe/ *adj* **1** *of a ball* without bounce *20- H&I C Bor.* **2** *of sound* dull *20- C.* [see the noun]

deek[1.1] /dik/ *n* a peep; a look *19-.* [see the verb]

deek[1.2] /dik/ *v* to look, catch sight of, see *la18-.* [Travellers' language]

deelus *see* DAELESS

deem, †**deme** /dim/ *v* to judge, pass sentence; to consider, decide *la14-.* **deemster**, †**demestar** a judge *la15-.* [OE dēman]

deem *see* DAME

deemachie *see* DAMEACK

deemis, deemous, †**deemas** /'diməs/ *adv* extremely, very *19, 20- NE SW.* Compare DOOMS. [aphetic form of UNDEEMOUS]

deem's day /'dimz de/ *n* doomsday *la19- NE.* [possessive of DOOM[1.1] + DAY]

deen /din/ *v* to suit, befit *20- Sh Ork.* **deenin, deenan 1** a sufficiency of food *la19- Sh Ork WC.* **2** that which is requisite *la19- Ork.* [Du *dienen* to serve]

deen *see* DAE[1.1], DUNE

deep, †**depe**, †**deip** /dip/ *adj* **1** extending or situated far down; broad, wide *la14-.* **2** profound, intense, serious *15-.* **deepth** depth *la19- N NE T C Bor.* **deep plate** a soup plate or similarly-shaped smaller dish *la18-.* [OE *dēop*]

deepdrauchtit /dip'drɔxtɪt/ *adj* crafty, cunning *19-.* [DEEP + DRAUCHT[1.1] + -IT[2]]

deepin, †**depin**, †**dipin** /'dipən/ *n* a section or part of a fishing net *16-19, 20- H&I WC.* [EModE *deeping*]

deer[1], †**dere**, †**deir**, †**deyr** /dir/ *n* a quadruped of the genus *Cervidae*, a deer *la14-.* **deer forest** a large stretch of open land used for deer-stalking *la19-.* **deer-hair 1** the scaly-stalked club rush *Scirpus cespitosus la18-19, 20- Bor.* **2** the scaly-stalked spike rush *Eleocharis 19.* [OE *dēor* a wild animal]

deer[2], †**dair** /dir/ *v* to affect, make an impression on; to make progress *19- Sh Ork.* [perhaps an extended sense of DERE[1,2]]

deese *see* DEAS[1.1]

deest *see* JIST[1.2]

deeth *see* DAITH

deeve *see* DEAVE[1.1], DEAVE[1.2]

deevil *see* DEIL

deface, †**defase**, †**defas** /də'fes/ *v* **1** to spoil, mar *16-.* **2** to disgrace or discredit *la15-e17.* [ME *defacen*]

defaik *see* DEFALK

defaisance *see* DEFEASANCE

defait *see* DEFEAT

†**defalk, defaik, defalc** *v* to deduct, subtract; to diminish or lessen *la15-17.* [MFr *defalquer*]

defalt *see* DEFAULT[1.1], DEFAULT[1.2]

defamation, †**defamatioun** /dɛfə'meʃən/ *n* **1** discredit, disgrace, dishonour *15-.* **2** *law* libel, slander *la17-.* [ME *defāmacioun*, Lat *diffāmātio*]

†**defamatoir** *adj* defamatory *la15-17.* [MFr *diffamatoire*]

†**defame, diffame** *n* **1** defamation *15-16.* **2** infamy; disgrace, discredit *la14-e17.* [ME *defame*]

defas, defase *see* DEFACE

defase *see* DEFACE, DEFESE

default[1.1], **defaut**, †**defalt** /də'fɔlt, də'fɑt/ *n* lack or absence (of something); neglect, negligence; the failure to pay (a debt) *la14-.* †**in his defalt** through his fault, failure, or negligence *la15-17.* [ME *defaut*]

default[1.2], †**defawt**, †**defalt** /də'fɔlt/ *v* to fail to fulfil an obligation or pay a debt *la14-.* [OFr *defaillir*]

defe *see* DEEF

defeasance, †**defesance**, †**defaisance** /də'fizəns/ *n* **1** *law* a condition by which a document is rendered null and void; the document expressing this condition *la18-.* **2** acquittance, discharge *la14-16.* [AN *defeasaunce*, OFr *defesance* undoing]

defease *see* DEFESE

defeat, †**defait**, †**defett** /də'fit/ *adj* **1** defeated *16-19, 20- NE T EC.* **2** exhausted, worn out *18-19, 20- NE.* [OFr *desfait* ptp of *desfaire* to undo or put an end to]

defeck, defect /'difɛk, 'difɛkt/ *n* a shortcoming; an imperfection, a flaw *la16-.* [Lat *dēfectus*]

defection, †**defectioun** /də'fɛkʃən/ *n* **1** desertion; failure in duty *16-.* **2** a defect, flaw; a failure *la16-19, 20- T.* [Lat *dēfectio*]

defeeckwalt *see* DIFFEECULT

defeeckwalty *see* DIFFEECULTY

defence, †**defens** /də'fɛns/ *n* **1** the action of defending; protection, resistance; a protector *la14-.* **2** *law* the denial of a charge; a defendant's case in a court of law *la15-.* **3** *pl law* the pleading of a defender in a civil action *la18-.* **4** *pl* arguments (in favour of something) *la16-18.* [ME *defens, defense*]

defend, †**diffend** /də'fɛnd/ *v* **1** to guard or protect against attack or injury *la14-.* **2** *law* to contest or deny a charge; to protect property; to maintain a legal right *la14-.* **3** to maintain an argument; to vindicate one's reputation against attack *15-.* **4** to ward off, avert; to resist against *la15-e19.* **5** to prohibit or exclude *15-e17.* **defender**, †**defendar**, †**defendour 1** a protector or supporter *la14-.* **2** *law* a defendant (in a civil case) *15-.* [ME *defenden*, Lat *dēfendere*]

defens *see* DEFENCE

defer, †**deffer**, †**differ** /də'fɛr/ *v* **1** to give way, yield (to someone) *la15-.* **2** to allot, assign, consign; to refer for consideration *la15-16.* **3** to refer (something) to someone's oath *la15.* **4** to agree or assent (to a legal exception) *la15.* [Lat *dēferre*]

defesance *see* DEFEASANCE

†**defese, defase, defease** *v* **1** to allow as a deduction, deduct *la15-17.* **2** to acquit or discharge from an obligation or penalty *la15-16.* **3** to expunge or cancel *e16.* [OFr *desfes-*, stem of *desfaire* to undo; compare DEFEASANCE]

defett *see* DEFEAT

deffeckwalt *see* DIFFEECULT

†**deficient** *n* a person who fails to comply with a requisition or demand; a defaulter of payment *17-19.* [Lat *dēficere* to desert, fail]

deficill *see* DIFFICIL

deficultat *see* DIFFICULTED

deficulte *see* DIFFEECULTY

de fideli /de fɪ'dɛli/ *n law* an oath taken by people appointed to perform certain public or other duties that they will faithfully carry them out (a breach of which does not amount to perjury) *17-.* [shortened form of Lat *dē fidēlī administrātiōne officii* on the faithful performance of a duty]

define /də'fʌɪn/ *v* **1** to explain, describe, determine *16-.* **2** to decide, settle or arrange *16.* [ME *diffinen*, Lat *dēfinīre*]

defluction, †**defluxion** /də'flʌkʃən/ *n* a discharge (from the nose or eyes); expectoration, phlegm *16-19, 20- H&I C.* [MFr *defluxion*, Lat *dēfluxio*]

†**deforce**[1.1] *n* the crime of preventing an officer of the law from carrying out his duty *la14-17.* [see the verb]

deforce[1.2], †**defors** /də'fors/ *v* **1** to impede, prevent by force (an officer of the law or a body of officials) from the discharge of duty *la15-.* **2** to rape, violate (a woman) *la14-e17.* **3** to take or retain by force *15-e17.* **deforcement**, †**deforsment** the crime of preventing an officer of the law from carrying out his duty *la15-.* †**deforcer, deforcear** the committer of a *deforcement 15-19.* [AN *deforcer*]

†**deforciament** *n* = *deforcement* (DEFORCE[1.2]) *e16.* [Lat *dēforciāmātum*]

†**deformate** *adj* deformed, transformed *15-16*. [Lat *dēformātus*]
defors see DEFORCE[1.2]
†**defoul**[1.1] *n* cruel treatment, outrage *la14-15*. [see the verb]
†**defoul**[1.2], **defoylȝe, defowll** *v* **1** to trample underfoot *la14-16*. **2** to make foul, defile *la14-16*. **3** to treat with scorn; to disparage; to disgrace, bring shame on *la14-e16*. [ME *defoulen*]
†**defound, defund** *v* to pour down; to diffuse *16*. [Lat *dēfundere*]
defowll, defoylȝe see DEFOUL[1.2]
defund see DEFOUND
deg[1.1], †**daig** /dɛg/ *n* a sharp stroke; a dig or poke *19, 20- NE*. [unknown]
deg[1.2] /dɛg/ *v* to strike a sharp-pointed object quickly into something; to stab or pierce *19, 20- NE*. [unknown]
deg see DAG[3]
degest see DIGEST[1.1], DIGEST[1.2]
deggie see DAIGIE
†**degraduat, degraduit** *adj* deposed, degraded *e17*. [ptp of EModE *graduate*, with prefix signifying reversal]
degree, †**degre,** †**degrie** /dəˈgriː/ *n* **1** a stage in a scale of intensity or amount *la14-*. **2** a stage in a scale of rank or kinship *la14-*. **3** an academic qualification *16-*. **4** a stage in elevation, a step *16-*. **5** *freemasonry* one of the steps of proficiency within the order *19-*. †**in al degre** in all respects, in every way *la14-e16*. †**in na degre** to no extent *15-16*. [ME *dēgre*]
deid[1.1], **deed, dead,** †**dede,** †**ded** /did, dɛd/ *n* **1** death; a fatality *la14-*. **2** the cause of (someone's) death *la17-*. **3** a corpse, a dead person *la16-17*. **4** a pestilence, a plague *15-e16*. †**deadal** connected with death *19*. †**dead bed, deid bed, ded bed** a deathbed *la15-e17*. **dead bell, deid bell 1** a passing bell *la16-*. **2** a sudden sensation of deafness and a ringing in the ears, thought to foretell death *19, 20 Sh Ork*. **deid box, dead box** a coffin *20-*. **dead candle** a strange light believed to foretell death *la19- NE*. **deid chack, dead chack 1** the ticking of the deathwatch beetle, believed to foretell death *la17-19, 20- Ork*. **2** a dinner prepared for magistrates after a public execution *e19*. †**dead chist** a coffin *la17-e19*. **deid claes, dead clothes** a (linen) shroud *18-19, 20- NE T EC*. **dead-deal** the board on which a corpse is laid *la18-19, 20- EC*. **deid drap, dead drap** a drop of water dripping on the floor, believed to foretell death *19, 20- NE*. **dead house 1** a mortuary *19, 20- NE T C Bor*. **2** a grave *e19*. **dead ill** a mortal illness *15-*. **deid kist, dead kist** a coffin *17-*. **deid licht, dead light** a strange light believed to foretell death *la18-*. †**dead lift** a state in which one can exert oneself no more, a crisis *18-19*. **deid-rap** an unexplained knocking, believed to foretell death *la19- Bor*. **deid ruckle** the death rattle *19- EC Bor*. **deid sark** a shroud *la19- Sh Ork*. **deid spale** a shroud-like shape of candlegrease on a guttered candle, thought to foretell the death of the person in whose direction it forms *19- Bor*. †**dead-straik** a death blow *17*. **dead thraw, deid thraw,** *Sh* **deadtraa,** †**dedthraw** a death throe *15-19, 20 Sh NE SW*. **dead watch** the deathwatch beetle; its ticking sound *la18-*. **the deed o** the cause of (something bad); the culprit *20- NE Bor*. **dead's part,** †**dedis pairt** *law* that part of a person's moveable estate which a testator can freely dispose of by will *la16-*. †**deidis thrid** = *deid's part la16-17*. **in the deadthraw 1** between hot and cold *19, 20- NE T*. **2** between one state and another; undecided *19, 20- N NE*. †**tak the dede** to die *la14-15*. [variant of *dethe* (DAITH), with influence from the adj]

deid[1.2], **deed, dead,** *Sh Ork T Bor* **daid,** *N* **deyd,** †**dede** /did, dɛd; *Sh Ork N T Bor* ded/ *adj* **1** no longer alive, dead *la14-*. **2** inanimate; unconscious; lacking vigour *15-*. **3** *of a golf ball* so near the hole that it is certain of being holed at the next stroke *19-*. **4** *of opponents' bowls* equidistant from the tee *la19, 20- NE EC*. **5** *of ground* barren, infertile; away from the sun, facing northwards; *of water* stagnant; frequently in place-names *la16-19, 20- NE*. **dead man's bellows** the bugle *Ajuga reptans la19- WC SW Bor*. **deid man's bells, dead man's bells** the foxglove *Digitalis purpurea 19, 20- NE Bor*. **dead man's mittens** gentian *Gentiana 20- Sh*. †**the deid dreich** (a piece of) completely level ground *16*. **like a deid dog** out of sorts *20 NE*. [OE *dēad*]
deid see DEED[1]
deidly, deadly, †**dedely,** †**dedly** /ˈdidle, ˈdɛdle/ *adj* **1** causing death, fatal *la14-*. **2** liable to death, mortal *15-e18*. **3** hostile, implacable *la15-e17*. **4** deathlike, dismal *la15-17*. †**against all deadly, aganis all dedelie** *law* against all people *15-19*. [OE *dēadlic*]
deif see DEEF, DEAVE[1.2]
†**deificate, deificait, deificat** *adj* deified *la15-16*. [Lat *deificātus*]
deigh see DEY[1]
deik, dick /dik, dʌɪk, dɪk/ *v* to hide, duck down *20- Ork T EC*. [unknown]
deil, deevil, deivil, devil, *NE* **divil,** *N NE H&I* **duvvle,** †**deill,** †**deuill** /dil, ˈdiəl, ˈdivəl, ˈdɛvəl; *NE* ˈdɪvəl; *N NE H&I* ˈdʌvəl/ *n* **1** Satan; a demon or an evil spirit *la14-*. **2** an evil or fiendish person *la15-*. **3** a shoemaker's last *la19- NE*. **deevilock,** *NE* **divilick** a little devil, an imp *19- NE T EC*. **deviltry, deeviltry** devilry *la19-*. **deil's bairn,** †**deels bairn** a mischievous person, a rascal *18-*. **devil's bird** the magpie *Pica pica la19, 20- NE*. **deil's darning needle** the dragonfly *19- WC SW Bor*. **deil's dizzen, devil's dozen** thirteen *la18-*. **deil's fit** a shoemaker's last *20- NE WC Bor*. **devil's limb** a wicked or mischievous person or animal *la14-*. **deil's luck** bad luck *20- H&I C*. **deil's mark, devil's mark 1** *folklore* an insensitive spot on the body of a witch believed to indicate adherence to the Devil *17-18, 19- historical*. **2** a crescent-shaped mark on the foreleg of a pig *la19- NE EC*. **deil's milk** the white milky sap of many plants *19- WC SW*. **deevil's mutches** the plant monkshood *Aconitum napellus 20- Sh*. **deil's pictur buiks** playing cards *la20- NE SW*. **devil's snuffbox** the common puffball *Lycoperdon perlatum 19, 20- T WC SW*. **deil's testament** a pack of playing cards *20- Sh*. **deil a** no; not a; never a *19-*. **deil a', deil all** nothing at all *20- NE SW*. **deil a fear, devil a fears** not likely, no fear *la19- Sh N NE EC Bor*. **deil a haet** not a bit, damn all *la16-*. **deil ane** not one; no one at all *la18-19, 20- T EC*. **deil ava** nothing at all *19- NE EC Bor*. **deil be-licket** devil a bit, absolutely nothing *18-19, 20- SW*. **devil in a bush** the herb Paris *Paris quadrifolia la19- NE T*. **deil kens** goodness knows *19-*. **deil ma care, deil may care** no matter; for all that *la18-*. †**deil-mak-matter** all the same, for all that *19*. **Deil mane ye, Deil moan ye** Devil take you *18-*. **deil speed the liars** a quarrel, dispute *18-19, 20- NE*. [OE *dēofol*]
deill see DALE[1.1], DEIL
deimack see DAMEACK
deintie see DAINTY[1.2]
deinȝe see DENZIE
deip see DEEP
†**deir** *v* to make dear or expensive *15*. [from DEAR[1.1]]
deir see DEAR[1.1], DEER[1]
deith see DAITH

deivil *see* DEIL

†deject, dejeck *v* to throw or cast down *16*. [Lat *dēject-*, ptp stem of *dēicere*]

dek, dick, dock /dɛk, dɪk, dɔk/ *numeral in sheep-counting and children's rhymes* ten *la19- NE WC SW Bor.* [nonsense word derived from a system of counting sheep]

dek *see* DAIK[1.2]

dekey *see* DECAY

dekin *see* DEACON

dekkir *see* DACKER[1]

del *see* DELL

delait *see* DELETE[1.1]

Delap *see* DUNLOP

delapidat *see* DILAPIDAT

†delasch, delash *v* to discharge, let fly *la16-e17*. [OFr *deslachier*]

delate[1], **†dilate** /dəˈlet/ *v* **1** to accuse, inform against or denounce (to a kirk session or presbytery) *la15-*. **2** to allege *16-17*. **delation, †dilatioun** a denouncement, an accusation *16-19, 20- literary*. **delator, †delater, †dilatour** an accuser, an informer *16-19, 20- historical*. [Lat *dēlāt-*, ptp stem of *dēferre*]

†delate[2] *v* to dilate, extend; to enlarge upon a report *16-e17*. [MFr *dilater*, Lat *dīlātāre*]

delatour *see* DILATOR[1.1], DILATOR[1.2]

dele *see* DALE[1.1]

delectus personae /dɪˈlɛktəs pɜrˈsoneɪ/ *n law* the right of selection of a particular person to occupy a position (as a tenant in a lease or as partner in a firm) *la18-*. [Lat *dēlectus persōnae* choice of the person]

deleerit, †deleeret /dəˈlirɪt/ *adj* delirious, mad; temporarily out of one's senses *la18-*. [MFr *delirer*, Lat *dēlīrāre* to be mad]

†delegat, deligat *adj* delegated *la15-e17*. [Lat *dēlēgāt-*, ptp stem of *dēlēgāre*]

deleit *see* DELETE[1.2]

delete[1.1], **†delait** /dəˈlit/ *v* to strike out; to erase or expunge *15-*. [Lat *dēlēt-*, ptp stem of *dēlēre*]

†delete[1.2], **deleit** *adj* deleted; destroyed *15-19*. [see the verb]

delf, †delph /dɛlf/ *n* **1** an excavation in a peat-bank, a place dug out; a quarry, a pit, a grave *14-19, 20- N NE SW*. **2** that which is removed by digging; a sod, a mass of vegetation *19- Sh NE*. **3** an act of digging *la16*. [OE *delf* a trench, a ditch, a water-channel]

delf *see* DELVE

†deliberat[1.1] *v* to consider, decide *la16-e17*. [Lat *dēlīberāre*]

†deliberat[1.2] *adj* carefully considered or deliberated, resolved *la16-e18*. [ptp of DELIBERAT[1.1]]

†delicate[1.1], **diligat** *n* a delicacy, a dainty *16-e17*. [see the adj]

delicate[1.2], **†deligat, †dilicat, †diligat** /ˈdɛlɪkət/ *adj* delicate, dainty *la14-*. [Lat *dēlicātus*]

delicht[1.1], **delyte, †delyt, †delite** /dəˈlɪxt, dəˈlʌɪt/ *n* delight, pleasure *la14-*. **delichtsum, †delytsum** delightful *16, 20- literary*. **†delytable, delytabill** delectable, delightful *la14-16*. **†delytably** delightfully, daintily *la14-15*. [ME *delit*, modern velar fricative by analogy with LICHT[1.1]]

delicht[1.2], **†delyte, †delyt** /dəˈlɪxt/ *v* to delight or take pleasure in, enjoy oneself *la14-*. [ME *deliten*, modern velar fricative by analogy with LICHT[1.1]]

delict /dəˈlɪkt/ *n law* a (civil) offence *la17-*. [Lat *dēlictum* an offence, a crime]

deligat *see* DELEGAT, DELICATE[1.2]

delite *see* DELICHT[1.1]

deliver[1.1] /dəˈlɪvər/ *v* **1** to hand over *la14-*. **2** to set free, rescue; to assist in a birth *la14-*. **3** to allow or enable to leave on completion of business *15-16*. **4** to give a decision or judgement; to settle (an action) *15-16*. **5** to declare, state or utter *15-e17*. **†deliverit** deliberate, determined, resolved *la15-16*. [ME *deliveren*]

†deliver[1.2], **delyver** *adj* **1** delivered (of a child) *la14-e17*. **2** active, agile *la14-16*. **deliverly 1** actively, nimbly *la14-e16*. **2** continuously, incessantly *e19*. [ME *deliver*]

deliverance /dəˈlɪvərəns/ *n* **1** *law* a formal decision or judgement; the orders of the court in sequestrations, including any order, warrant, judgement, decision, interlocutor or decree *la14-*. **2** liberation, release *15-*. **3** *Presbyterian Church* the findings or decision of the General Assembly or other Church court on a report from a committee or special commission *19-*. **4** the act of handing over, delivery *la15-e17*. **5** the freedom or permission to leave; the completion of an errand entitling one to this *15-16*. **6** the act of surrendering (a stronghold, hostage or prisoner) *15-16*. **7** activity, agility *e16*. [ME *deliveraunce*]

dell, del /dɛl/ *v* to delve, dig *18- Sh Ork N NE*. [altered form of DELVE]

dell *see* DALE[2], DALE[3]

dellow /ˈdɛlo/ *n* a small patch of cultivated ground *19- Ork*. [from DELL]

delph *see* DELF

†delphyn fysch *n* a dolphin *e16*. [Lat *delphīnus* dolphin + FISH[1.1]]

deltit, diltit /ˈdɛltɪt, ˈdɪltɪt/ *adj* petted, spoilt *la18- N NE*. [perhaps related to Gael *dalta* a foster child]

delve, †delf /dɛlv/ *v ptp* **†dollin 1** to dig; to turn over the soil *la14-*. **2** to bury *la14-e16*. Compare DELL. [OE *delfan*]

delyt, delyte *see* DELICHT[1.1], DELICHT[1.2]

delyver *see* DELIVER[1.2]

dem, daim /dɛm, dem/ *v* to dam; to build a dam *15-19, 20- NE Bor*; compare DAM[1.2]. **dem and lave** an extravagant profusion *la19- NE*. [OE *fordemman* to shut up, stop up (ears)]

dem *see* THAIM[1.1], THAIM[1.2]

†demaim *v* to injure, maim *17-e18*. [conflation of DEMAIN with Older Scots *maim*]

demain, †demean, †demayne, †demane /dəˈmen/ *v* **1** to maltreat; to injure; to treat as a traitor or enemy *la14-19, 20- NE*. **2** to control, govern; to treat or deal with *la14-e18*. **3** to behave oneself *la14-17*. [ME *demeinen*]

demand /dəˈmand/ *n* **1** an urgent requirement; a peremptory claim *la14-*. **2** a question *la14-e16*. **†without ony demand** without question or delay *e16*. [ME *demaunde*]

demane, demayne *see* DEMAIN

demble *see* DEMMEL[1.2]

deme *see* DAME, DEEM

demean *see* DEMAIN

†demember *v* to dismember, mutilate *15-e18*. **demembration** *law* dismembering, mutilation *la16-19*. [OFr *desmembrer*]

dementit, demented, *NE* **dimintit** /dəˈmɛntɪt, dəˈmɛntəd; *NE* dɪˈmɪntɪt/ *adj* **1** mentally unbalanced or ill *la17-*. **2** highly excited; extremely worried or annoyed *18-*. [ptp of EModE *dement* to drive mad]

†demi-bever *n* an inferior beaver or mixed fur; a hat made of this *17*. [OFr *demi* half + AN *bevere*]

demishel *see* DAMISHELL

demissioun *see* DIMISSIOUN

demit, †dimit /dɪˈmɪt, dɪˈmɪt/ *v* **1** to resign, give over (an office or possession) *16-*. **2** to dismiss; to allow to go, release *la16-*. [Lat *dīmittere*]

demmel[1.1], **demmle** /ˈdɛməl/ *n* a commotion in the sea, a splash *la19- Sh Ork*. [see the verb]

demmel[1.2], **demble,** *Ork* **dammle** /ˈdɛməl, ˈdɛmbəl; *Ork* ˈdaməl/ *v* to dip or plunge into water; to draw water in a vessel; to splash *la19- Sh Ork*. [Norw dial *demla* to splash, fill a vessel by emersing it water]

demmin *see* DAIMEN

demmish *see* DAMISH¹·¹

demmished *see* DAMMISHED

demmle *see* DEMMEL¹·¹

†demoleis, dimolische *v* to demolish, pull down, destroy *la16-e17*. [MFr *demoliss-*, stem of *demolir*]

dempster, †dempstar, †demstar, †damster /'dɛmpstər, 'dɛmstər/ *n* **1** *law* the officer of a court who pronounced sentence as directed by the clerk or judge *la14-18, 19- historical*. **2** a public executioner *la18-20, 21- historical*. [short vowel variant of *deemster* (DEEM)]

demuired /də'mjurd/ *adj* **1** sad, downcast *20- N Bor*. **2** disconcerted, abashed *20- T EC*. [ptp of EModE *demure* to look or make demure]

†demy, dimy *n* a gold coin *15-e19*. [elliptical for MFr *demi-couronne* a half-crown of gold]

†demygrane, dimmegrane, dummygrane *n* a type of woven fabric *16*. [perhaps MFr *demigraine* a pomegranate, with influence from MFr *gros grain* a coarse fabric]

†demyostage *n* a woven fabric (of mixed wool and flax) *16-19*. [OFr *demie ostade* half worsted]

den¹, dean, †dene /dɛn, din/ *n* a narrow (wooded) valley; a ravine (with a watercourse); frequently in place-names *12-*. [OE *denu* a valley]

den²·¹ /dɛn/ *n* **1** the lair of a wild beast *15-*. **2** *games* a base, a place of safety *20-*. **3** the forecastle of a fishing boat *20-*. [OE *denn*]

†den²·² *v* to hide *19*. [see the noun]

den³ /dɛn/ *n* a groove (to hold a blade or a mill-stone) *19, 20- NE*. [perhaps an extension of DEN¹]

†den⁴ *v* to dam *la14*. [perhaps altered form of DEM]

Dence *see* DENS¹·¹, DENS¹·²

†Dene *n* a Dane *16-e17*. Compare DENS¹·². [OE *Dene* the Danes]

dene *see* DEN¹, DEAN

†denere, dinneir *n* a silver penny; a French coin worth one twelfth of a sou *15-17*. [OFr *dener*, Lat *dēnārius*]

denger *see* DANGER

denk *see* DINK¹·¹, DINK¹·²

denkie /'dɛŋki/ *n* a shallow depression in the ground *la19- Sh*. [ON *dökk* a pit, a pool]

denner¹·¹, dinner, *NE* **dainner, †dennar, †dyner, †dinnar** /'dɛnər, 'dɪnər/ *NE* 'denər/ *n* dinner, the main meal of the day; lunch *la14-*. **dinner-school** a place where school dinners are served *20- T C SW*. [ME *diner*]

denner¹·², dinner /'dɛnər, 'dɪnər/ *v* **1** to dine, have dinner *la18-19, 20- NE WC Bor*. **2** to entertain, supply with dinner *19, 20- NE EC*. [see the noun]

dennty *see* DAINTY¹·²

dennounce, †denunce /də'nʌuns/ *v* **1** to condemn, proclaim as wrong *la15-*. **2** to formally proclaim as rebel or traitor; to sentence or condemn *16-19*. **3** to announce, notify *la15-e19*. **4** *Roman Catholic Church* to proclaim as condemned, curse *15-e16*. **†denounce to the horn** to proclaim publicly as a rebel *16-19*. [ME *denouncen*, Lat *dēnuntiāre*]

denry *see* DEAN

†Dens¹·¹, Dence *n* the Danish language; a Dane *16-e17*. [see the adj]

†Dens¹·², Dence *adj* Danish *la15-17*. **Danesaxe, dense axe** a long-bladed axe *16-e19*. **Densman** a Dane *la15-e17*. [OE *denisc*]

†denschyre *n* the English county of Devonshire *la16-e17*. **densyre cairsay** a type of coarse cloth, Devonshire kersey *la16-e17*. [reduced form of the place-name *Devonshire*]

denshag *see* DAINSHACH

dent *see* DINT¹, DUNT²·¹

dent-de-lyon *see* DENTYLION

dentice *see* DAINTESS

dentie *see* DAINTY¹·²

dentylion, dainty-lion, dandelion, †dent-de-lyon, †dentilioun /'dɛntelaeən, 'dɛntelaeən, 'dandilaeən/ *n* the dandelion *Taraxacum officinale 16-*. [MFr *dent de lion*, *dandelyon*]

denude¹ /də'njud/ *v* **1** to strip (off); to make naked *16-*. **2** *of a trustee* to hand over the trust estate on giving up the office of trustee *18-*. **3** to deprive (of a possession or right); to exclude *la15-17*. **4** to divest oneself of a right, resign *la17*. **5** to make empty; to clear (of inhabitants) *e16*. [Lat *dēnūdāre*]

†denude² *adj* made bare or destitute, denuded *la15-e17*. [shortened form of *denudit* (DENUDE¹)]

denum, †denumb /də'nʌm/ *v* to confound, perplex *19, 20- NE*. [Scots *numb*, with intensifying prefix]

denumpt, denummt /də'nʌmpt, də'nʌmt/ *adj* stupid, confounded *la19- NE*. [ptp of DENUM]

denunce *see* DENOUNCE

denunciation, †denunciatioun /dənʌnsɪ'eʃən/ *n* **1** condemnation *19-*. **2** *law* the act by which a person was proclaimed a rebel *la16-19, 20- historical*. **3** an announcement, a proclamation *la16-e18*. [EModE *denunciation*, Lat *dēnunciātiō*]

deny /də'nae/ *v* **1** to declare to be untrue, refuse to admit *la14-*. **2** to refuse to give or allow, forbid *la14-*. **3** to refuse to move or do something *la14-16, la18- NE*. **it winna deny** it cannot be denied *19, 20- NE*. [ME *denien*]

†denzie, denʒe, deinʒe *v* to condescend, deign *la14-18*. [ME *deinen*]

deochandorus, dochan doris /'djɔxəndorəs, 'dɔxəndorəs/ *n* a stirrup cup, a parting drink *la17-*. [Gael *deoch an doruis* a drink at the door]

deochray, dyochree /'djɔxre, 'djɔxri/ *n* a kind of gruel or SOWANS *la19- N Uls*. [Gael *deoch-rèith*]

deow *see* DEW¹·¹

†depairt¹·¹, depart *n* a departure *la16-e18*. [MFr *depart*]

depairt¹·², depart, †depert /də'pert, də'part/ *v* **1** to leave, go away *la14-*. **2** to die *la14-*. **3** to part, divide or separate; to distribute *la14-e17*. **4** to give birth *16*. **departel, †departal** departure, death *19- WC SW*. [ME *departen*]

depairtment, depertment, department /də'pertmənt, də'pertmənt, də'partmənt/ *n* **1** a division, a self-contained section within a business or organization *18-*. **2** a departure *la16*. [MFr *departement*]

depart *see* DEPAIRT¹·¹

†departising *n* division *la15*. [perhaps from OFr *departision*]

department *see* DEPAIRTMENT

depasche *see* DEPESCHE¹·²

†depauper *v* to impoverish, reduce to poverty *la16-17*. [OFr *depauperer*, Lat *dēpauperāre*]

depauperat, depauperate *see* DEPOOPERIT

depe *see* DEEP

depend /də'pɛnd/ *v* to rely on; to be contingent upon *la15-*. **†dependand** being still in process or undecided; awaiting settlement or payment *la15-e17*. **†dependar** a dependant, an adherent *la16-e17*. **†dependentis** amounts still owing *16-e17*. [ME *dependen*]

depert *see* DEPAIRT¹·²

depertment *see* DEPAIRTMENT

†depesche¹·¹ *n* **1** a sending off *16*. **2** a message, a messenger *16*. [EModE *depech*]

†depesche¹·², depasche *v* to dispatch, send away *16*. [EModE *despesche*]

depin see DEEPIN

depone /dəˈpon/ v 1 law to make a sworn statement, swear; to testify, give evidence on oath la15-. 2 to remove from office; to resign 16-e17. 3 to deposit la16-17. †**deponer, deponar** law a witness; one who gives testimony under oath la16-19. [Lat dēpōnere to deposit]

depooperit, depauperate, †**depauperat** /dəˈpupərɪt, dəˈpɔpəret/ adj impoverished; bankrupt la16-18, la19- Sh. [Lat dēpauperātus]

†**depose** n a deposit; something entrusted to one; an accumulated amount; a store la14-16. **in depose** on deposit, in trust la14-16. [from the verb OFr deposer to set aside]

deposit /dəˈpɔzɪt/ n law = DEPOSITATION la18-. [Lat dēpositum that which is deposited]

†**depositate** adj deposited la17-18. [ptp of Lat dēpositāre]

depositation /dəpɔzɪˈteʃən/ n a contract under which a moveable property is entrusted by a depositor to another to be kept either for payment or without reward la18-. [Lat dēpositāre to deposit]

depredation, †**depredatioun** /dɛprəˈdeʃən/ n 1 ravaging, plundering 16-. 2 law the offence of driving away livestock with armed force la18-19, 20- historical. [AN depredation, depredatioun, Lat dēpraedātiō]

†**deprise** v to depreciate, despise la15-16. [OFr depriser]

†**deprivat** adj deprived, excluded la16. [Lat dēprīvātus]

†**depulȝe** v to despoil e16. [MFr despouiller]

†**depurse** v to disburse la16-18. [conflation of DEBURSE with PURSE[1.1]]

depute[1.1] /ˈdɛpjut/ n a deputy la14-. [see the adj]

depute[1.2], †**deput** /dəˈpjut/ v 1 to appoint as one's deputy, substitute a representative (to act in some official capacity) la14-. 2 to appoint, assign or ordain la14-16. †**deputrie** the office of deputy la15-16. [OFr deputer]

depute[1.3], †**deput,** †**deputt** /ˈdɛpjut/ adj 1 law appointed or acting as deputy 15-. 2 appointed, assigned la14. [OFr deputé deputed]

Deputy Clerk Register /ˈdɛpjute ˈklark ˈrɛdʒɪstər/ n the official appointed to carry out the duties of the LORD CLERK REGISTER 19-e20, la20- historical. [Scots deputy + reduced form of LORD CLERK REGISTER]

der see THERE

deray /dəˈre/ n 1 noise; revelry or mirth 15-. 2 disturbance, trouble, disorder, confusion la14-e19. †**at deray** impetuously e15. [ME derai]

derb, dirb, durb /dɛrb, dɪrb, dʌrb/ n in children's games an ordinary marble 20- N. **derbs, dirbs** a game of marbles la20- N. [unknown]

derdel /ˈdɛrdəl/ n the tail-root (of pigs and sheep) la19- Sh Ork. [Icel dirðill a short tail, the tail of a sheep; compare DIRL[1.1]]

†**dere**[1.1] n hurt, harm, injury la15-e19. [see the verb]

†**dere**[1.2] v to harm, hurt, injure la14-16. [OE derian]

dere see DEAR[1.1], DEER[1]

dereck see DIRECK[1.3]

derect see DIRECK[1.1], DIRECK[1.2]

dereeshion, dereeshin, derision, †**derisioun** /dəˈriʒən, dəˈriʃən, dəˈrɪʒən/ n 1 scorn, mockery la15-. 2 an object of ridicule, a foolish person 20- Sh. [ME derisioun, Lat dērīsiō]

dereliction /dɛrəˈlɪkʃən/ n law abandonment of something owned la19-. [Lat dērelictiō]

†**derenȝe**[1.1], **dereyn, derene** n a conflict, a contest, an encounter la14-16. [ME dereine]

†**derenȝe**[1.2], **dereyn, derene** v 1 to vindicate, claim la14-15. 2 to challenge, attack 15-16. [ME dereinen]

derf, †**darf** /dɛrf/ adj 1 of people bold, daring, hardy la14-. 2 unbending, sullenly taciturn 19-. 3 of things hard, rough, violent 16-e19. 4 of land difficult to traverse la15-16. †**derfly** boldly, courageously; roughly, violently 15-e19. [ON djarfr bold, daring]

derige see DIRGIE

derision, derisioun see DEREESHION

derk[1.1], **dairk, dark, dork,** †**dirk,** †**dyrk** /dɛrk, derk, dark, dɔrk/ n darkness, absence of light la15-. [see the adj]

derk[1.2], **dark,** †**dirk** /dɛrk, derk, dark/ v 1 to slink, lurk la18-19, 20- T. 2 to darken 16-19. [see the adj]

derk[1.3], **dairk, daurk, dork, dark, dirk,** †**dyrk** /dɛrk, derk, dɔrk, dark, dɪrk/ adj having no or little light, unilluminated; dark-hued; sinister la15-. **dark-avised** having dark hair and eyes; dark-complexioned 20- Sh Ork NE H&I; compare black-avised (BLACK[1.3]). **Dark Blues** see DARK BLUES. [OE deorc]

derken, darken /ˈdɛrkən, ˈdarkən/ v 1 to make or become dark, darken 16-. 2 to lurk, lie hidden e16. **darkenin, derkenin** twilight, dusk; nightfall 19-. †**darkening broad** a shutter e18. [DERK[1.3], with verb-forming suffix]

derkness, daurkness, darkness, †**dirknes** /ˈdɛrknəs, ˈdɔrknəs, ˈdarknəs/ n a lack of light la15-. [OE deorcnes]

dern[1.1] /dɛrn/ n secrecy; a secret place; darkness la14-. [see the adj]

dern[1.2], **darn** /dɛrn, darn/ v 1 to hide, conceal; to go into hiding la16-. 2 to loiter; to eavesdrop 19- EC. [OE dyrnan]

dern[1.3], **darn,** †**derne** /dɛrn, darn/ adj 1 secret, hidden; serving to conceal, secluded 12-. 2 dark, dreary, desolate, remote 16-. [OE dyrne]

†**dern**[1.4], **darn** adv secretly; in secret or concealment 16-e17. [see the adj]

derne see DERN[1.3]

†**deroub, derob** v to rob, despoil la15-16. [OFr desrober]

†**deroy** adj purple; tawny 17. [shortened form of colour-deroy (COLOUR)]

derrar, derrast see DEAR[1.1]

derril /ˈdɛrəl/ n a broken piece of bread or cake 19, 20- T. [variant of DORLE]

derry see DYRIE

dert[1.1], **dairt, dart** /dɛrt, dert, dart/ n a pointed weapon, a dart la14-. [ME dart]

dert[1.2], **dairt, dart** /dɛrt, dert, dart/ v to pierce with a weapon; to thrust or move quickly or suddenly 17-. [see the noun]

derth see DEARTH[1.1]

dery dan see DIRRYDAN

desaif, desave see DECEIVE

†**descense, discens, discence** n 1 descent by lineage 15-16. 2 a downward course or movement, a downward slope 15-16. [ME descense, Lat dēscensus]

desch see DISH[1.1]

descrive, †**descryve,** †**discrive,** †**discryve** /dəˈskraev/ v to describe la14-. [ME descriven]

dese see DEAS[1.1]

desert[1.1] /dəˈzɛrt/ v 1 to abandon, give up; to abscond la15-. 2 law to discontinue (a summons, action or diet) la15-. 3 to (cause to) come to an end, adjourn a parliament la16-e17. [OFr deserter]

†**desert**[1.2] adj 1 given up; annulled; null and void la15-e17. 2 of parliament adjourned 16-e17. 3 deserted, abandoned 16. [ME desert]

design[1.1], †**desing,** †**desseing,** †**desine** /dəˈzʌɪn/ n 1 a plan; a plot la16-. 2 a pattern 18-. 3 a small amount 20- Uls. [MFr desseing]

design[1.2], †**desing** /dəˈzʌɪn/ v 1 to plan, conceive; to intend 16-. 2 law to assign to a person; to bestow (manses and glebes) to the clergy la16-19. 3 to name, entitle, identify a person la17. [EModE desyne]

designation /dɛzɪgˈneʃən/ *n* **1** a name, a title; a descriptive identification *la17-*. **2** *law* a title or description used as a means of identifying witnesses (written on the back of a document) *la17-*. **3** *Presbyterian Church* (the document recording) the assigning of a manse and glebe to a parish minister *la16-19, 20- historical*. [Lat *dēsignātio*]

desine *see* DESIGN[1.1]

desing *see* DESIGN[1.1], DESIGN[1.2]

desk *see* DASK

desolate, †**dissolate** /ˈdɛsələt/ *adj* alone; empty, abandoned *la14-*. [Lat *dēsōlātus*]

desperate, **despert**, **desprit** *see* DISPERT[1.1], DISPERT[1.2]

desperation, †**disperatioun** /dɛspəˈreʃən/ *n* **1** a state of being desperate or despairing *la15-*. **2** a great rage *la19, 20- NE*. [ME *desperacioun*, Lat *dēspērātio*]

†**despite**[1.1] *n* contempt; animosity *la14-e17*. **dispytfullie**, **dispitfully** **1** spitefully, cruelly *la14-16*. **2** scornfully, contemptuously *la14-e17*. [ME *despit*]

despite[1.2], †**dispite** /dɪsˈpʌɪt/ *v* to regard with dislike or contempt; to despise *la14-19, 20- literary*. [OFr *despiter*]

despone *see* DISPONE

dess *see* DASS

desseing *see* DESIGN[1.1]

dessil *see* DEASIL[1.1]

destany, **destenie** *see* DESTINE

†**destinat** *v ptp* **destinat** to ordain, appoint *16-e18*. [Lat *dēstināt-*, ptp stem of *dēstināre*]

destination /dɛstəˈneʃən/ *n* **1** *law* a direction as to the people who are to succeed to property, mainly in a will affecting heritable property *la17-*. **2** the end-point of a journey *18-*. **destination over** a legal direction to one person on failure of a precedent gift, usually by will, another *20-*. [Lat *dēstinātio*]

†**destine**, **destany**, **destenie** *n* destiny *la14-e16*. [ME *destine*]

destrick *see* DISTRICK

desuetude /dəsˈjuətjud/ *n law* disuse, discontinuance *la16-*. [Fr *désuétude*, Lat *dēsuētūdo*]

†**desy**[1.1] *v* to make dizzy *e16*. [OE *dysigan* to be foolish]

†**desy**[1.2], **dissy** *adj* dizzy, giddy *la14-e17*. [OE *dysig* foolish]

det *see* DEBT

detain, *NE EC* **deteen**, †**detene** /dəˈten/; *NE EC* dəˈtin/ *v* to delay, hamper; to keep in custody; to retain, withhold *16-*. †**detenar** detainer *la16-e17*. [OFr *detenir*]

†**deteriorat** *adj* deteriorated, impaired *la16-17*. [Lat *dēteriorāt-*, ptp stem of *dēteriorāre*]

†**determ** *v* to determine, decide *la14-e17*. [Lat *dētermināre*]

dethe *see* DAITH

dett *see* DEBT

deu *see* DAE[1.1]

deuch, **teuch**, †**dyoch** /djux, tjux/ *n* an (alcoholic) drink *19, 20- NE*. [Gael *deoch* a drink]

deuch *see* DAICH

deugend, **deugan** /ˈdjugənd, ˈdjugən/ *adj* wilful, obstinate; litigious *19- N*. [unknown]

deugle *see* JOUGAL

deugs, †**dewgs**, †**duigis** /ˈdjugz/ *npl* small pieces, shreds; fragments *la16-19, 20- N*. **juggins** tatters, smithereens *19, 20- H&I Uls*. [unknown]

deuill *see* DEIL

deuk, **jeuk**, **jook**, **duck**, *C* **juck**, †**duke** /djuk, dʒuk, dʌk; *C* dʒʌk/ *n* a duck, a bird of the genus *Anas la15-*. **deuk dub**, †**duke dub** a duck pond *18-19, 20- EC SW Bor*. **deuk-fittit** splay-footed *20-*. [OE *dūce*]

deuk *see* JOUK[2]

deulder *see* DILDER[1.1]

deuoreis *see* DEVORYIS

†**devanter**, **dewanter** *n* a dress-front; an apron *la16*. [MFr *devantier* apron]

devat *see* DIVOT[1.1]

devaul[1.1], **deval**, **devall**, †**devald** /dəˈvɔl, dəˈval/ *n* **1** a sloping surface, a slope; the amount of downward slope required by a ditch or drain *la17-19, 20- Sh NE*. **2** a cessation, a stop *19, 20- NE*. [see the verb]

devaul[1.2], **deval**, **devall**, **divall**, †**devald**, †**devale**, †**devail** /dəˈvɔl, dəˈval/ *v* **1** to stop, cease, leave off *la16-*. **2** to move downwards; to sink, fall or bend down *la15-e17*. [OFr *devaler*]

†**devay** *v* to go astray, wander *16*. [AN *desveier*]

deve *see* DEAVE[1.2]

devel[1.1], **davel** /ˈdɛvəl, ˈdevəl/ *n* a severe and stunning blow *la18-19, 20- SW Bor*. [unknown; compare DAVER]

devel[1.2], **davel** /ˈdɛvəl, ˈdevəl/ *v* to strike with violence; to beat; to dash *19, 20- Bor*. [see the noun]

†**develling**, **daweling** *n* a covering of centres or COOM[2] used in building arches *16-e17*. [unknown]

dever *see* DAVER

device, †**devise** /dəˈvʌɪs/ *n* **1** a purpose, a design, a plan *la14-*. **2** a (mechanical) contrivance *la16-*. **3** disposition (of property); one's will *15-e17*. †**at all devys**, **at all dewys** in all respects, completely *la14-16*. [ME *devis*]

devide *see* DIVIDE

devil *see* DEIL

devise, †**devis**, †**devyse**, †**devyis** /dəˈvaez/ *v* **1** to design, plan or contrive *la14-*. **2** to describe, tell or explain; to consider *la14-16*. **3** to appoint; to assign *15-16*. [ME *devisen*]

devise *see* DEVICE, DIVISE[1.1], DIVISE[1.2]

†**devoid** *v* **1** to remove, clear; to free *la14-e17*. **2** to depart, withdraw *15-16*. **3** to vacate land *15-e16*. [ME *devoiden*]

devoir *see* DEVOOR

devoit *see* DEVOTE

devolution, †**devolucioun** /divəˈluʃən/ *n* **1** transference (of a right) *la15-*. **2** *law* the referring of a decision to an oversman by arbiters who differ in opinion *la19-*. **3** the transference of certain powers from Westminster to a new Scottish Assembly based in HOLYROOD *la20-*. **clause of devolution** a clause devolving some office, obligation or duty on a person (to act as an arbiter) *la19-*. [Lat *dēvolvere* to roll down]

devolve /dəˈvɔlv/ *v* **1** to transfer (rights or power) *la15-*. **2** *law* to pass a decision over from arbiters to an oversman *20-*. [Lat *dēvolvere* to roll down]

devolved /dəˈvɔlvd/ *adj* relating to the Scottish Parliament at HOLYROOD (rather than Westminster) *la20-*. [ptp of DEVOLVE; compare DEVOLUTION]

devoor, **devour**, †**devore**, †**devoir** /dəˈvur, dəˈvʌur/ *v* to swallow, consume, absorb; to destroy *la15-*. [ME *devouren*, OFr *devorer*, Lat *dēvorāre*]

†**devoryis**, **deuoreis** *npl* dues or duties payable *la15-16*. [OFr *devoir* that which is owing]

†**devote**, **devoit** *adj* **1** devout, pious *la14-17*. **2** devoted (to) *la14-16*. [Lat *dēvōtus*]

devour *see* DEVOOR

devyde *see* DIVIDE

devyis, **devyse** *see* DEVISE

dew[1.1], *NE* **deow**, *NE* **dyow** /dʒu, dju; *NE* djʌu/ *n* **1** moisture, dew *la14-*. **2** whisky *la19-*; compare *mountain dew* (MOUNTAIN). **3** light rain *la19- NE*. [OE *dēaw*]

dew[1.2] /dʒu, dju/ *v* to rain gently, drizzle *19- N NE*. [ME *deuen*]

dew *see* DAW[1.2], DUE

dewanter *see* DEVANTER

Dewar /'djuər/ *n* the hereditary keeper of a relic of a (Celtic) saint, especially a bell or staff *19- historical*. [Gael *deòradh* an alien, a stranger; a pilgrim]

dewche *see* DAICH

†**dewgard** *interj* God preserve you; a greeting in these words *la15-e17*. [ME *dugarde*, OFr *Dieu (vous) garde*]

dewgs *see* DEUGS

dewite *see* DUTY

†**dewlie** *adj* due, proper *la15-e16*. [Older Scots *dew* due, with adv-forming suffix]

dewty *see* DUTY

dey[1], *Ork* **deigh**, †**dee** /dae; *Ork* de/ *n* a dairymaid *18-19, 20- Ork N*. †**deywyff** a dairywoman *la16*. [OE *dǣge* a female servant, a baker, ON *deigja* a dairymaid, a baker-woman]

dey[2], *EC Bor* **tae** /de; *EC Bor* te/ *n* **1** a child's word for a father *19- NE C Bor*. **2** a grandfather; a respectful term of address for an old man *la19- Sh NE EC Bor*. **3** a grandmother *20- NE*. [shortened form of *daidie* (DADDY)]

dey *see* DAY, DEE[1]

deyd /ded, daed/ *n* a grandfather; a grandmother *20- NE*. [shortened form of *daidie* (DADDY)]

deyd *see* DEID[1,2]

deydie /'dedi, 'daedi/ *n* a grandfather *20- NE*. [probably altered form of DADDY]

deyl *see* DALE[2]

deylicht *see* DAYLICHT

deyr *see* DEER[1]

deys *see* DEAS[1,1]

dhuine wassel *see* DUNIWASSAL

diacle, **diakel** *see* DYCAL

dial, †**dyall**, †**dayell** /'daeəl/ *n* the face of a clock or watch; a sundial *16-*. **dial stane** a sundial *la19- NE T EC*. [ME *dial*]

dialectician /daeəlɛk'tɪʃən/ *n* a person skilled in argument *la16-*. [MFr *dialecticien*]

diamond, †**dyamont**, †**diamant**, †**diamaunt** /'daemənd/ *n* **1** a precious stone, a diamond *15-*. **2** a diamond-shaped piece of iron, especially a spearhead *la15-e16*. **diamond coal** a high-grade coal from the diamond seam *19- NE T EC*. **the Diamonds** a nickname for the Airdrie United and Airdrieonians football teams (from the red diamond design on their jerseys) *la20-*. [ME *diamaunt*]

†**diapason** *n music* the concord based on intervals of an octave; harmonious music or speech *16-19*. **dyapason symple** the interval of an octave *la15*. [Lat *diapāsōn*]

dib *see* DUB[1,1]

dibber-dabber[1,1] /'dɪbərdabər/ *n* wrangling, argument *18- NE*. [reduplicative compound]

dibber-dabber[1,2] /'dɪbərdabər/ *v* to wrangle, argue *la19- NE*. [see the noun]

dibe /dʌɪb/ *v* **1** to dip in water *la19- Sh*. **2** to plod, trudge; to work laboriously *la19- Sh*. [ON *dýpka* to become deeper, deepen]

dice[1,1], †**dyce**, †**dys** /dʌɪs/ *n* **1** *pl* small cubes with numbered faces *15-*. **2** a game of chance played with dice *15-*. **3** a pellet of iron used as shot *la15-16*. [ME *des*, pl of *de*]

dice[1,2], †**dyce**, †**dys** /dʌɪs/ *v* **1** to play at dice *16-*. **2** to cut into cubes *la16-*. **3** to ornament or mark with a chequered pattern *17-*. **4** to make trim and neat *la18-*. †**dysour**, **dysar**, **dysser** a dice-player *16-e17*. **dice-board** a draught- or chess-board *la19- N WC*. [see the noun]

dich *see* DUTCH

†**dichels**, **dichells** *npl* corporal punishment, a beating *17-19*. [unknown]

dichens /'dɪxənz/ *npl* a reproof, a beating *19- SW Bor*. [unknown]

dicht[1,1] /dɪxt/ *n* **1** a wipe, a cursory wash; a rub *la19-*. **2** a blow, a smack, a swipe; a trouncing, a heavy defeat *la19, 20- NE EC Bor*. [OE *diht* a setting on order]

dicht[1,2], †**dight**, †**decht** /dɪxt/ *v* **1** to clean, sweep; to dust or polish; to make tidy *15-*. **2** to sift or winnow grain; to sift meal *la15-*. **3** to wipe or rub clean or dry *16-*. **4** to scold or reproach; to thrash, strike *18-19, 20- NE WC Bor*. **5** to prepare meat or fish for cooking, cook a meal *la14-18, 19- Sh Ork*. **6** to equip or dress oneself; to make (oneself) ready; to prepare *la14-e19*. **7** to finish cloth; to dress or plane wood *15-17*. **8** to deal with, treat *la14-e17*. **9** to dress a wound *la14-e16*. †**dicht with** to finish off, decorate with *la14-e16*. **dicht yer ain door steen** be sure that you are beyond reproach before criticizing others *20- NE*. **he may dight his neb and flee up** his opinions are of no importance *18-*. [OE *dihtan* to compose, command, prescribe]

dichty water /dɪxte 'wɔtər/ *n* the affected speech of a Scot trying to sound English *la19- T WC*. [perhaps a reference to *Dichty Water* near Dundee]

dick /dɪk/ *n* a schoolmaster *20- NE T*. [unknown]

dick *see* DEK, DEIK, DYKE[1,1], DYKE[1,2]

dicker *see* DACKER[1]

dictay *see* DITTAY

dictionar, †**dictioner** /'dɪkʃənər/ *n* a dictionary *la16-*. [MFr *dictionnaire*]

dictum /'dɪktəm/ *n* a saying; an authoritative pronouncement *la16-*. [Lat *dictum*]

did *see* DAE[1,1]

didder, †**diddir** /'dɪdər/ *v* to tremble, shiver; to move jerkily *la14, la19- Sh NE T WC*. [onomatopoeic]

didderums, **dodrums** /'dɪdərʌmz, 'dɔdrʌmz/ *npl* foolish notions, intractable behaviour *19- T H&I WC*. [DIDDER, with *-ums* suffix]

diddle[1,1] /'dɪdəl/ *n* a short, jerky, lively tune *19-*. [see the verb]

diddle[1,2], *N Bor* **deedle** /'dɪdəl; *N Bor* 'didəl/ *v* **1** to dance with a jigging movement *18-*. **2** to move (the elbow) to and fro in fiddling; to fiddle *la18-*. **3** to dandle a child *19-*. [onomatopoeic]

diddle[2,1], **deedle** /'dɪdəl, 'didəl/ *n* wordless singing (as an accompaniment for dancers) *la19-*. [see the verb]

diddle[2,2], **deedle**, *WC* **teedle** /'dɪdəl, 'didəl; *WC* 'tidəl/ *v* to sing without words, usually in imitation of instrumental dance music *19-*. **diddler**, **daidler** a person who sings to accompany dancing *20-*. Compare DOODLE[1,2]. [onomatopoeic]

diddle[3,1] /'dɪdəl/ *n* a slow, inefficient worker *la19- NE*. [see the verb]

diddle[3,2] /'dɪdəl/ *v* to busy oneself without getting much done; to waste time; to potter or dawdle *19-*. [perhaps an extension of DIDDLE[1,2]; compare Eng *fiddle*]

diddle-daddle[1,1] /'dɪdəldadəl/ *n* great activity with little result; trifling activity *la19- NE*. [reduplicative compound based on DIDDLE[3,2]]

diddle-daddle[1,2] /'dɪdəldadəl/ *v* to loiter, dawdle *la19- NE*. [see the noun]

diddle-doddle /'dɪdəldɔdəl/ *n* a model boarding house *la20-*. [rhyming slang from *model*]

didgy /'dɪdʒe/ *n* a dustbin *la20- WC*. [probably altered form of MIDGIE]

didnae, **didny**, **didna** /'dɪdne, 'dɪdni, 'dɪdnə/ *v* didn't *19-*. [*did* (DAE[1,1]) + -NAE]

†**die** *n* a toy, a trinket *19*. [perhaps related to DICE[1,1]]

die *see* DEE[1], DY

diesel *see* DEASIL[1,2]

diet[1], †**dyet** /'daeət/ *n* **1** food, what is eaten *la15-*. **2** a meal *18-*. †**diet cake** a kind of sponge cake *19*. **diet hour**, **diet**

oor meal time *19, 20- N NE T EC*. **diet loaf** = *diet cake la18-19, 20- N*. [ME *diete*]

diet[2], **†dyet**, **†dyat** /ˈdaeət/ *n* **1** a meeting, a sitting (of a council) *la15-*. **2** *law* a session of a court; the hearing of a case *la15-*. **3** a day or date fixed for a meeting or for a market *la16-*. **4** a church service or meeting *17-*. **5** a particular day or date *la16-17*. **6** a journey or its date; the movements of a person travelling *la16-17*. **7** the list of summonses set down to come before the Court of Session from each quarter of the country *16-e17*. **†dyet buke, diat buke** a day-book; a journal; the book containing the deliberations of a meeting *la16-e17*. **†by dyet** beyond the proper time or measure *la16-e17*. **†diet of examination** a meeting held by a minister to examine the religious knowledge of the residents of a district *la18-19*. **diet of examinations** a group of (university degree) examinations at a particular time *la19-*. **diet of worship** a church service *la19-*. **†keep dyet** to appear (at a court or meeting) on the day appointed *la15-e18*. [Lat *diēta* a day's journey, a day's work]

diffame *see* DEFAME

diffat *see* DIVOT[1.1]

diffeecult, defeeckwalt, *SW* **deffeckwalt** /ˈdɪfɪkəlt, ˈdɪfɪkwəlt/; *SW* /ˈdɪfɛkwəlt/ *adj* difficult *19-*. [EModE *difficult*]

diffeeculty, diffeekwalty, defeeckwalty, difficulty, †difficulte, †deficulte /ˈdɪfɪkəlti, ˈdɪfɪkwəlti, ˈdɪfɪkəltɛ/ *n* the fact of being difficult *la14-*. [ME *difficulte*, Lat *difficultās*]

diffend *see* DEFEND

differ[1.1] /ˈdɪfər/ *n* **1** a difference of opinion; a disagreement or dispute *la16-*. **2** a difference, a dissimilarity *17-*. **†in differ** in dispute *la16-e17*. [see the verb]

differ[1.2] /ˈdɪfər/ *v* **1** to be dissimilar or distinct *la15-*. **2** to quarrel; to disagree *16-*. [MFr *differer*]

differ *see* DEFER

†difficil, difficle, deficill *adj* difficult *15-17*. [OFr *difficile*, Lat *difficilis*]

difficulte *see* DIFFEECULTY

†difficulted, deficultat *adj* placed in a difficulty *la17-19*. [MFr *difficulter*]

difficulty *see* DIFFEECULTY

diffy *see* DEEFIE[1.3]

digeedoo *see* DIGGIE-DOO

digest[1.1], *NE C* **digeest, †degest** /dɪˈdʒɛst, daeˈdʒɛst; *NE C* dɪˈdʒɪst, dʌɪˈdʒɪst/ *v* **1** to absorb food in the stomach *15-*. **2** to consider, process information *15-*. [Lat *dīgest-*, ptp stem of *dīgerere* to separate, dissolve, digest]

†digest[1.2], **degest** *adj* composed, settled; mature, serious *la15-16*. **digestlie, degestlie** maturely, with careful deliberation *la15-e17*. [Lat *dīgestus*]

diggie-doo, digeedoo /ˈdɪɡɪdu/ *n* the game of hide-and-seek *20- Ork*. [unknown; compare ON **dika* to run]

dight *see* DICHT[1.2]

dighter *see* DOITER

†digne, ding, dyng *adj* worthy, deserving; of great or exceptional merit *la14-19*. Compare DANE. [MFr *digne*]

dike *see* DYKE[1.1]

†dilapidat, delapidat *adj* dissipated, squandered *16-17*. [Lat *dīlapidātus*]

dilate *see* DELATE[1]

†dilator[1.1], **dilatour, delatour** *n* **1** a delay (in giving a legal decision); a dilatory plea *la15-e19*. **2** = DILATORY DEFENCE *la15-e18*. [see the adj]

†dilator[1.2], **dilatour, delatour** *adj* dilatory, causing delay (in a legal action) *la15-e18*. [MFr *dilatoire*, Lat *dīlātōrius*]

dilatory defence /ˈdɪlətəre dəˈfɛns/ *n law* a defence which is purely technical, not touching the merits of the case *la19-*. [Lat *dīlātōrius* dilatory + DEFENCE]

dilce *see* DILSE

dilder[1.1], **deulder** /ˈdɪldər, ˈduldər/ *n* a shake, a jolt; a trembling frightened state *la19- Ork*. [see the verb]

dilder[1.2] /ˈdɪldər/ *v* **1** to shake, tremble; to jolt or rattle *la19- Ork*. **2** to dangle behind; to dawdle or loiter *la19- Ork*. Compare DIDDER. [Norw dial *dildra*]

diled *see* DOILT

dilgit, dulget /ˈdɪldʒət, ˈdʌldʒət/ *n* a lump; an untidy heap or bundle *19, 20- NE*. [unknown]

dilicat *see* DELICATE[1.2]

diligat *see* DELICATE[1.1], DELICATE[1.2]

diligence, †diligens /ˈdɪlədʒəns/ *n* **1** assiduity, industry *15-*. **2** *law* the application of legal means against a person, especially for the enforcing of a payment or recovery of a debt; a warrant issued by a court to enforce the attendance of witnesses, or the production of writings *la16-*. [MFr *diligence*, Lat *dīligentia*]

dill /dɪl/ *v* **1** to soothe, quieten down, die away *la15-*. **2** *of a rumour* to fade, be forgotten *17-19, 20- Sh NE*. [ON *dilla* to trill, lull]

dills *see* DILSE

dilly daw /ˈdɪle dɔ/ *n* a slow, slovenly, untidy person *19-*. [reduced form of Eng *dilly-dally* + DAW[2]]

dilmont *see* DINMONT

dilp[1.1] /dɪlp/ *n* **1** a limp *20- T*. **2** a lazy or thriftless woman *la18-19*. [unknown]

dilp[1.2] /dɪlp/ *v* to hobble or limp *la19- T*. [unknown]

dilse, dills, dulse, †dilce /dɪls, dʌls/ *n* the edible seaweed *Palmaria palmata*, dulse *17-*. [Gael *duileasg*]

diltit *see* DELTIT

†diminew, dymynew *v* to diminish *la15-16*. [ME *diminuen*, Lat *dēminuere*]

dimintit *see* DEMENTIT

†dimissioun, demissioun *n* the action of giving up (an office or possession), a resignation *16-e18*. [Lat *dīmissio*]

dimit *see* DEMIT

dimmegrane *see* DEMYGRANE

dimolische *see* DEMOLEIS

dimple[1.1] /ˈdɪmpəl/ *n* a dibble; a tool for making holes in the ground *18-19, 20- Sh NE*. [perhaps altered form of DEMMEL[1.2]]

dimple[1.2] /ˈdɪmpəl/ *v* to plant by means of a dibble *la19- Ork NE*. [see the noun]

dimy *see* DEMY

din[1.1], **†dyn, †dyne** /dɪn/ *n* **1** a loud, continuous confused noise *15-*. **2** loud talk or discussion; a fuss, a disturbance *15-*. **3** a report, a rumour; a scandal *la19- NE T SW*. **4** a slight noise; the sound of running water *18-19*. **dinsome** noisy, riotous, brawling *18-*. **din-raisin** quarrelsome; trouble-making; gossip-spreading *la19- NE*. [OE *dyne*]

†din[1.2], **dyn** *v* **1** to ring with sound or noise; to resound or re-echo *16-e19*. **2** to make a loud noise or outcry *la14-16*. [OE *dynian*]

din[2] /dɪn/ *adj* **1** of a dull or dingy colour, dun-coloured *16-*. **2** *of people* dark-complexioned, sallow *la16-*. **dinness** sallowness, darkness *19, 20- N NE*. **nae dinbonnets** not to be despised, first-rate *la19- NE*. [OE *dun*]

din *see* DAE[1.1]

dindee, dundee /ˈdɪndi, ˈdʌndi/ *n* a noise, an uproar; a fuss, a disturbance *la19- NE*. **dinniedeer** = DINDEE. [DIN[1.1] + *adee* (ADAE[1.1])]

dine[1.1], **†dyne** /dʌɪn/ *n* **1** (a) dinner; dinnertime *la15-*. **2** *pl* (the location of) communal university dinners (at St Andrews University) *20-*. [see the verb]

dine[1.2], **†dyne** /dʌɪn/ *v* to eat a meal, take dinner *la14-*. [ME *dinen*]

dine *see* THINE

ding¹·¹ /dɪŋ/ *n* a knock or blow, a shove *19-*. [see the verb]

ding¹·² /dɪŋ/ *v pt* **dang, dung,** *ptp* **dung, †dungin, †doung, †dang 1** to beat or strike with heavy blows; to thrash *la14-*. **2** to drive or dash with violence; to push suddenly and forcibly; to pierce with a weapon *la14-*. **3** to force out or drive off; to beat back *15-*. **4** to overcome, defeat, get the better of *16-*. **5** *of rain or snow* to fall heavily and continuously; *of wind* to blow with great force *16-*. **6** to drive, cause to become *18- NE EC SW*. **7** to drive into the mind, force someone to remember something *la16-19, 20- SW Uls*. **8** to smash to pieces; to reduce to fragments *la16-19, 20- NE*. **9** to curse, invoke evil; ◊*ding it! 19, 20- N NE*. **dingie** to snub, reject; to fail to keep a (romantic) appointment *la20-*. **ding dust** very fast *20- Uls*. **ding doun Tantallon** to perform the impossible *18-*. **ding on puir men and pike staves** to rain heavily *18- NE*. **†ding to dede** to kill by blows *la14-16*. [ON *dengja*]

ding *see* DIGNE

ding dang /ˈdɪŋ daŋ/ *adv* speedily, in rapid succession; in confusion *18-19, 20- NE EC*. [reduplicative compound based on DING¹·²; compare Eng *ding-dong*]

dinge¹·¹ /dɪndʒ/ *n* a blow; a dent *19- H&I WC SW Uls*. [unknown]

dinge¹·² /dɪndʒ/ *v* to dent or bruise *la19- Sh WC SW Uls*. [unknown]

dinger /ˈdɪŋər/ *n* **1** a smashing blow; a vigorous course of action *20-*. **2** a masterful or vigorous person *la19- C Bor*. **3** a beater *e17*. **go yer dinger** to do something with extreme vigour *20-*. [DING¹·², with agent suffix]

dingle /ˈdɪŋəl, ˈdɪŋgəl/ *v* **1** to tingle (with cold or pain) *19-*. **2** to vibrate, resound, jingle *la18-19, 20- NE*. [conflation of DINNLE¹·² with TINGLE¹·²]

dingle-doozie, dingle-dousie /ˈdɪŋəlduzi, ˈdɪŋgəlduzi/ *n* **1** a lighted stick or peat waved rapidly to form an arc of light *19- C SW Bor Uls*. **2** an active bustling person *la19- SW Bor*. [altered form of Eng *dangle* + DOOZIE]

Dingwall pursuivant /ˈdɪŋwəl ˈpʌrswɪvənt/ *n heraldry* one of the Scottish pursuivants *la16-19, 20- historical*. [after the town in Ross]

dink¹·¹, **denk** /dɪŋk, dɛŋk/ *v* to dress neatly or finely, adorn *19- Sh NE EC Bor*. [unknown]

dink¹·², **†denk** /dɪŋk/ *adj* **1** neat, trim, finely dressed, dainty *16-19, 20- NE EC*. **2** fastidious, precise; haughty *16-19, 20- EC*. **dinkie** neat, trim *la18-*. **dinkly** neatly, sprucely, trimly *la18-19, 20- Bor*. [unknown]

dinmont, †dunmont, †dilmont, †dynmonth /ˈdɪnmənt/ *n* a (Cheviot) wether sheep between the first and second shearing *14-*. [unknown]

dinnae, dinny, dinna, *Sh* **dunna** /ˈdɪne, ˈdɪni, ˈdɪnə; *Sh* ˈdʌnə/ *v* don't *19-*. [DAE¹·¹ + -NAE]

dinnar *see* DENNER¹·¹

dinneir *see* DENERE

dinnen skate /ˈdɪnən sket/ *n* a kind of skate (the fish) *Dipturus batis 18-19, 20- NE*. [unknown first element + SKATE]

dinner *see* DENNER¹·¹, DENNER¹·²

dinnle¹·¹ /ˈdɪnəl/ *n* **1** a vibrating or tingling sensation (caused by a knock); a thrill (of emotion) *19- NE T C SW Bor*. **2** a vibration, a tremor *19- NE T*. [unknown]

dinnle¹·², **dinnil, †dynnill, †dyndill, †dyndle** /ˈdɪnəl/ *v* **1** to (cause to) shake or tremble; to vibrate or ring *16-*. **2** to (cause to) tingle or twinge with cold or pain *18-*. **3** *of bells or thunder* to peal, roll or drone *la18-*. [unknown]

dinny *see* DINNAE

dint¹, **†dent** /dɪnt/ *n* affection, liking, regard *la18-19, 20- NE T*. **dint of** fondness for *la18-19, 20- NE T*. [reduced form of DAINTY¹·¹]

dint² /dɪnt/ *n* **1** a dint, a blow *la14-*. **2** a chance, occasion or opportunity *18-e19*. **3** a shock, an assault; a deep impression, an impact *la14-19*. [OE *dynt*]

dint³ /dɪnt/ *n* a rumour, a report *20- Ork*. [unknown]

dint *see* DUNT¹·¹, DUNT¹·²

dintle /ˈdɪntəl/ *n* thin leather (used for soling shoes) *la19, 20- Sh Ork*. [unknown; compare Norw *tynn* thin]

†diocesie *n* a diocese *15-17*. [Lat *diocesis*]

†diocie, diocy *n* **1** a diocese *la14-19*. **2** a jurisdiction, a district *la16*. [shortened form of DIOCESIE]

dip¹·¹ /dɪp/ *n* **1** a descent; a decline *la18-*. **2** a (brief) immersion *19-*. **3** melted fat in which potatoes are dipped *la19-*. [see the verb]

dip¹·² /dɪp/ *v* **1** to descend, go downwards *15-*. **2** to immerse (briefly) in liquid *15-*. **3** to investigate, question; to touch upon *la16-19, 20- NE*. **4** to sit down *la19- Sh*. **dippin** a place by a river with steps leading down, where pails or clothes are dipped *la18-*. **dippins** melted fat *20- Ork*. [OE *dyppan*]

dipin *see* DEEPIN

dippit /ˈdɪpɪt/ *adj* silly, confused *la20-*. [unknown; perhaps from DIP¹·²]

dirb *see* DERB

dird¹·¹ /dɪrd, dʌrd/ *n* **1** a hard blow, a knock *18- N NE T EC*. **2** a bump; a bounce; a fall *la18- N NE*. **3** a fuss *20- Sh N*. **4** a mighty deed, an achievement *la18-e19*. [probably onomatopoeic]

dird¹·² /dɪrd, dʌrd/ *v* **1** to push or thrust violently, shove *la19- Ork N NE*. **2** to bump, bounce or jolt *19- N NE*. **3** to act or walk conceitedly; to fuss or flit about *20- N*. **dog-dirder** a dog-handler, a kennel attendant *la19- NE SW*. [see the noun]

dird¹·³ /dɪrd, dʌrd/ *adv* with a bang or bump *la19- NE*. [see the noun]

dirdum, durdum /ˈdɪrdəm, ˈdʌrdəm/ *n* **1** tumultuous noise, uproar; an altercation *la15-*. **2** blame; punishment; a scolding; retribution *la17-*. **3** bad temper, ill humour; violent excitement *19- T WC SW Bor*. **4** a quandary, a problem *19- T Bor*. **5** a heavy stroke or blow *19- NE EC*. **6** an achievement, a great deed *la18-19, 20- NE*. **dree the dirdum** to bear the punishment, take the consequences *19- T EC Bor*. [probably onomatopoeic]

dirdy-lochrag, dirdy-wachlag, dirdy-waflag /ˈdɪrdə-lɔxrag, ˈdɪrdewɔxləg, ˈdɪrdewɔfləg/ *n* a lizard *20- N*. [Gael *dearc luachrach*]

direck¹·¹, **direct, †direk, †derect, †darett** /dɪˈrɛk, daeˈrɛk, dɪˈrɛkt, daeˈrɛkt/ *v ptp* **direckit, directit, †direck, †direct, †derect** to guide, instruct, to point; to send, address *la15-*. [Lat *direct-*, ptp stem of *dirigere* to straighten, guide, direct]

direck¹·², **direct, †derect** /dɪˈrɛk, daeˈrɛk, dɪˈrɛkt, daeˈrɛkt/ *adj* straightforward, straight; direct *la16-*. [ME *direct*, Lat *directus*]

direck¹·³, **direct, †dereck** /dɪˈrɛk, daeˈrɛk, dɪˈrɛkt, daeˈrɛkt/ *adv* directly; in a direct course or manner *la15-*. [MFr *direct*, Lat *directus*]

†direckar, directair, directour *n* a director (of the chancellery) *la15-e17*. [EModE *directour*]

†dirgie, dirige, derige *n* **1** a funeral service, the office for the dead *15-19*. **2** a song of mourning, a lament *16-19*. **3** a funeral feast (consisting mainly of drink) *17-19*. Compare DREDGIE. [Lat *dirige* direct, the first word of the antiphon at Matins in the Office of the Dead]

dirk¹·¹, **†durk** /dɪrk/ *n* **1** a Highlander's short dagger worn in the belt *la16-*. **2** a stab, a prod *la19, 20- Sh Ork*. [unknown]

dirk¹·², **†durk** /dɪrk/ *v* to stab with a dagger *la16-*. [unknown]

dirk *see* DERK[1.2], DERK[1.3]

dirken /ˈdɪrkən/ *n* a fir-cone (used in smoking fish) *20- N NE.* [Gael *duircean*]

dirkin *see* DERKEN

dirknes *see* DERKNESS

dirl[1.1], †**dirle** /dɪrl/ *n* **1** the pain caused by a blow; a tingling sensation *18-.* **2** a knock or blow (causing a vibration or a sting); a shock, a jar, a clatter *19-.* **3** a sharp noise, a clatter or rattle; a vibration *19-.* **4** a gust of wind *20- Sh NE.* **5** a hurry, a bustle; a rattling pace, an energetic movement *20- Sh NE.* [see the verb]

dirl[1.2], †**dirle** /dɪrl/ *v* **1** to pierce, sting; to thrill, quiver or tingle *la16-.* **2** to vibrate, rattle or reverberate; to ring, whirl *la18-.* **3** to cause to vibrate or shake; to throw noisily *20-.* **dirler** a chamber-pot *20- N NE.* **dirlie-bane** the funny-bone *la19-.* **dirl aff 1** to reel off poetry or songs *la18-.* **2** *of an alarm clock* to go off with a whirring noise *20- NE EC.* **dirl tee, dirl to** to shut with a bang *20- NE EC.* **dirl up 1** to strike up a tune (on the bagpipes), play vigorously *la18-19, 20- NE.* **2** to push over backwards *20- Sh.* [unknown; compare THIRL[1.2]]

dirl[1.3] /dɪrl/ *adv* with a crash or clatter *la18-19, 20- Sh NE EC.* [see the verb]

dirl[2.1] /dɪrl/ *n* a dangling object; a swaying motion *la19- Sh.* [Norw dial *dirla* to hang loosely; compare DERDEL]

dirl[2.2], **dirrel** /dɪrl, ˈdɪrəl/ *v* to dangle loosely; to lag behind *20- Sh.* [see the noun]

dirle *see* DIRL[1.2]

dirr[1.1] /dɪr, dʌr/ *n* a humming, a buzzing sound *19- Sh Ork SW Bor.* [onomatopoeic]

dirr[1.2] /dɪr, dʌr/ *v* to vibrate, quiver *19- Sh Ork Bor.* [see the noun]

dirrel *see* DIRL[2.2]

dirry[1] /ˈdɪri/ *n* the ashes on top of a pipe *20- NE.* [unknown]

dirry[2] /ˈdɪri/ *n* haste; a hastening *20- NE.* **haud on the dirry** to whip up (horses) *20- NE.* [unknown]

dirrydan, †**dery dan** /ˈdɪrɪdan/ *n* sexual intercourse; riotous behaviour *e16, 20- EC.* [unknown]

†**dirrye dantoun** *n* the name of a dance *e16.* [unknown]

dirt[1.1], **durt** /dɪrt, dʌrt/ *n* **1** excrement, filth; muck, mud *16-.* **2** *derogatory* a person; a troublesome child *19-.* **3** *in mining* material produced other than coal, ore or minerals *20- EC.* **4** nonsense *20- Sh.* Compare DRITE[1.1]. **dirtie, dirtry** worthless people or things *19- EC SW Bor.* **dirt-bee** the common dung beetle *Geotrupes stercorarius la19- NE T.* **dirt deen** extremely tired *20- NE.* †**dirt fear** extreme terror *e18.* **dirt-flee** = *dirt-bee 19- N NE T.* [metathesis of ON *drit* excrement]

dirt[1.2], **durt** /dɪrt, dʌrt/ *v* to defecate, befoul; to soil *18-.* Compare DRITE[1.2]. [see the noun]

dirten, †**dirtin** /ˈdɪrtən/ *adj* **1** filthy, soiled with excrement *16-19, 20- NE T.* **2** mean, contemptible; conceited, disdainful *18- N NE.* **dirtnist** utmost *20- NE.* **dirten allen** the skua, a seabird of the genus *Stercorarius la18-19, 20- N NE.* [from the noun DIRT[1.1], with adj-forming suffix]

dirty[1.1], **durty**, †**dirtie** /ˈdɪrti, ˈdʌrte/ *adj* **1** soiled, filthy; covered in dirt *la16-.* **2** *of land or crops* weed-infested *la19-.* **dirty allen** the skua, a seabird of the genus *Stercorarius la18-19, 20- NE.* **dirty coal** a coal seam with a lot of blaes or fireclay; a very ashy coal *la19- EC.* **dirty thow** a thaw brought on by rain *20-.* [from the noun DIRT[1.1] + -IE[2]]

dirty[1.2] /ˈdɪrti/ *adv* very, completely, ignominiously *20-.* [see the adj]

dirvin /ˈdɪrvɪn/ *n* a thick clumsy-looking object; a large untidy woman *20- Ork.* [unknown]

†**dis, dys** *n* a double interval in music *la15.* [Lat *dis-* two-]

dis *see* DAE[1.1], THIS[1.1], THIS[1.2], THIS[1.3]

disabuse[1.1] /dɪsəˈbjus/ *n* damage, bad usage; disturbance *19- NE.* [see the verb]

disabuse[1.2], *NE* **disabeeze** /dɪsəˈbjuz; *NE* dɪsəˈbiz/ *v* **1** to disabuse, undeceive *19-.* **2** to misuse, damage; to spoil *17-18, 19- NE.* [an intensive form of ABUISE[1.2]]

disagreeance, †**disagrieance** /dɪsəˈgriəns/ *n* disagreement *la16-.* [EModE *desagreeance*]

†**disagyse** *v* to disguise *15-17.* [altered form of Older Scots *disgyse*]

disannul /dɪsəˈnʌl/ *v* to make null and void, cancel, do away with; to obliterate, demolish (material objects) *17-.* [an intensive form of Older Scots *annul*]

†**disassent** *v* to refuse or withhold assent; to disagree *16-17.* [an intensive form of Older Scots *assent*]

disays *see* DISEASE[1.1]

Discembre *see* DECEMBER

discence, discens *see* DESCENSE

discern, †**decerne** /dəˈsɛrn/ *v* to perceive, distinguish *la15-.* [Lat *discernere* to separate, distinguish, determine]

discerne *see* DECERN

disces *see* DECEASE[1.2]

disch *see* DISH[1.1]

dischairge[1.1], **discharge** /ˈdɪstʃɛrdʒ, ˈdɪstʃardʒ/ *n* **1** the act or fact of discharging; an unloading; an outflow *16-.* **2** an acquittance or receipt; a dismissal *16-.* **3** the fulfilment of an obligation *la16-.* **4** a prohibition *la16-e17.* [ME *discharge*]

dischairge[1.2], **discharge** /dɪsˈtʃɛrdʒ, dɪsˈtʃardʒ/ *v* **1** to relieve of a burden or obligation, set free; to acquit (of a debt) *15-.* **2** to remove from office, dismiss; to resign *15-.* **3** to deliver; to fulfil an obligation; to unload a cargo; to resign a claim *la15-.* **4** *law* to forbid, prohibit *16-.* **5** to fire a weapon *la16-.* **6** to abolish, cancel *la15-17.* [ME *deschargen*]

dischort *see* DISHORT

discipline, †**disciplene** /ˈdɪsəplɪn/ *n* **1** training; correction, punishment *la14-.* **2** a branch of learning *16-.* **Book of Discipline** either of two books adopted in 1560 and 1581 respectively, laying down the constitution of the Reformed Church and also dealing with education *la16-17, 18- historical.* [ME *discipline*, Lat *disciplīna*]

disclamation, †**disclamatioun** /dɪskləˈmeʃən/ *n* **1** a repudiation; a disclaimer *la18-.* **2** *law* a disclaiming of connection with an action in court (where one's name has been used) *la18-.* **3** *law* the renunciation by a tenant or vassal of obligation to his superior *16-19.* [Lat *disclāmātio* a disclaimer]

disclar *see* DECLARE

discomfish, †**discomfis**, †**discumfys**, †**disconfeis** /dɪsˈkʌmfɪʃ/ *v* to discomfit, overcome, defeat *la15-19, 20- literary.* [OFr *desconfis-*, pres stem of *desconfire*; compare SCOMFISH[1.2], DISCOMFIT]

discomfit /dɪsˈkʌmfɪt/ *v* **1** to frustrate, put to inconvenience or discomfort *la19-.* **2** to overcome, defeat *la14-e19.* [OFr *desconfit*, ptp of *desconfire*; compare DISCOMFISH]

disconfeis *see* DISCOMFISH

disconform /dɪskənˈfɔrm/ *adj law* not conforming (to), different (from), disagreeing (with) *la16-19, 20- historical.* [negative prefix *dis-* + CONFORM]

†**disconformable** *adj* not conforming (to), disagreeing (with) *la16-19.* [negative prefix *dis-* + Older Scots *conformable*]

†**discontigue** *adj of areas of land* not adjacent, disconnected *16-19.* [negative prefix *dis-* + CONTIGUE]

discontiguous /dɪskənˈtɪgjuəs/ *adj* not contiguous, disconnected *17-.* [negative prefix *dis-* + Lat *contiguus*]

disconvainient *see* DISCONVENIENT

disconvenience[1.1] /dɪskən'vinjəns/ *n* an inconvenience *19-*. [MFr *disconvenience*]

disconvenience[1.2] /dɪskən'vinjəns/ *v* to inconvenience *19-*. [see the noun]

disconvenient, *NE* **disconvainient** /dɪskən'vinjənt; *NE* dɪskən'venɪənt/ *adj* inconvenient *la15-*. [Lat *disconveniēns*]

discoorse[1.1], **discourse**, †**discurs** /'dɪskurs, 'dɪskors/ *n* a (formal) discussion; a conversation *la16-*. [Lat *discursus*]

discoorse[1.2], **discourse**, †**discurse** /dɪs'kurs, dɪs'kors/ *v* to speak authoritatively; to discuss; to converse with *la16-*. [see the noun]

discover, †**discure** /dɪs'kʌvər/ *v* **1** to find; to find out, realize *16-*. **2** to reveal, make known; to uncover *la14-e19*. **3** to reconnoitre *la14-15*. †**discoverour, discurriour, discurrour** a reconnoiterer, a scout *la14-16*. [ME *discoveren*]

discreet, discrete, †**discreit** /dɪs'krit/ *adj* **1** discerning, judicious, prudent *la14-*. **2** civil, polite, well-behaved *la16-*. [ME *discret*]

†**discrepance, discrepans** *n* disagreement, dissension; difference, variance *15-e19*. [OFr *discrepance*]

discrete see DISCREET

discrive, discryve see DESCRIVE

discumfys see DISCOMFISH

discure, discurriour, discurrour see DISCOVER

discurs see DISCOORSE[1.1]

discurse see DISCOORSE[1.2]

discuss, †**discus** /dɪ'skʌs/ *v* **1** to debate, consider; to settle *15-*. **2** *law* to proceed against one of two possible debtors such as a principal debtor and a cautioner, before proceeding against the other *la16-*. [ME *discussen*, Lat *discuss-*, ptp stem of *discutere* to examine]

†**disdaine** *v* to deign *16*. [altered form of *dedeigne* (DEDENƷE[1]), with influence from *disdain*]

†**disdene**[1.1], **disdenƷe** *n* (a feeling of) disdain *la14-e16*. [ME *disdein*; compare DEDENƷE[2.1]]

†**disdene**[1.2], **disdenƷe** *v* to disdain *16*. [OFr *disdeinen*; compare DEDENƷE[2.2]]

disease[1.1], *EC* **disays,** †**disese,** †**dises,** †**diseis** /də'ziz; *EC* də'ses/ *n* **1** (an) illness; sickness, a malady *la14-*. **2** discomfort, distress, hardship *la14-16*. [ME *disese*]

†**disease**[1.2], **diese** *v* to deprive of ease, trouble or molest *la14-e17*. [AN *deseaser*]

diseis, dises see DISEASE[1.1]

disese see DISEASE[1.1], DISEASE[1.2]

†**disfigurate** *adj* disfigured, deformed *la15-16*. [Lat *disfigūrāre*]

disgeest, disjeest, *Sh* **digest** /dɪs'dʒist; *Sh* dɪs'dʒest/ *v* to digest *la16-*. **disgeester** digestion *la19- NE EC SW.* **disgeestion, disjastion** digestion *la19, 20- NE T.* [variant of DIGEST[1.1]; compare EModE *disgest*]

dish[1.1], †**disch,** †**desch** /dɪʃ/ *n* **1** a plate or bowl (for food); a shallow vessel *la14-*. **2** a dishful of food; food served at a meal *la16-*. **dish cloot, dish clout** a dish-cloth *18-*. **dish man** a hawker of crockery *19-*. **dish washins,** †**dische weschingis** dishwater *la15-19, 20- Sh Ork.* **a dish o want** no food at all *la19- N NE.* [OE *disc*]

dish[1.2] /dɪʃ/ *v* to rain heavily, pour with rain *19, 20- NE T SW.* [see the noun]

†**dishabilitate** *v law* to subject to legal disqualification *17-19*. [MFr *deshabiliter*, with Latinate suffix *-ate*]

dishairten, disherten /dɪs'hertən, dɪs'hertən/ *v* to dishearten *la19-*. [negative prefix *dis-* + HERTEN]

dishaunt, †**dishant** /dɪs'hɔnt/ *v* **1** to cease to attend, stay away from (church services) *la16-19, 20- historical.* **2** to give up, discontinue (a practice) *la16-17*. **dishaunter** a person who neglects to attend church *la16-19, 20- historical.* [OFr *deshanter*]

dishealth /dɪs'helθ/ *n* ill-health, illness *la18- N NE T C.* [negative prefix *dis-* + HALTH]

†**disherish, disheris** *v* to disinherit *la14-19*. [probably back-formation from Older Scots *disherisoun* disinheritance]

disherten see DISHAIRTEN

dishilago see TUSHILAGO[1]

dishle see DISSLE[2]

dishort, †**dischort** /dɪ'ʃɔrt/ *n* an injury, a mischief, hurt; a loss *16-19, 20- literary.* [unknown]

disjacket see DISJECKIT

disjaskit /dɪs'dʒaskɪt/ *adj* **1** dilapidated, neglected, untidy *18-*. **2** dejected, downcast, depressed *19-*. **3** exhausted, worn out; weary-looking *19-*. [unknown; compare DISJECKIT]

disjeckit, disjacket /dɪs'dʒɛkɪt, dɪs'dʒakɪt/ *adj* **1** dejected *la19-*. **2** worn-out, dilapidated *la19-*. [perhaps altered form of Eng *dejected*, or perhaps derived from Lat *disject-*, from *disicere* to throw asunder]

disjeest see DISGEEST

disjoin /dɪs'dʒɔɪn/ *v* **1** to detach, sever, disunite *la16-*. **2** *law* to detach or separate (one church or parish from another) *17-*. [ME *disjoinen*]

disjone see DISJUNE[1.1], DISJUNE[1.2]

disjoyne see DISJUNE[1.1]

disjunction /dɪs'dʒʌŋkʃən/ *n* **1** separation, disconnection *15-*. **2** *law* the disjoining or dividing up (of parishes) *19-*. [ME *disjunccioun*]

disjune[1.1], †**disjone,** †**disjoyne** /dɪs'dʒun/ *n* breakfast; forenoon refreshment *la15-19, 20- literary.* [OFr *desjëun*]

†**disjune**[1.2], **disjone** *v* to eat breakfast *16-e17*. [OFr *desjëuner*]

disloaden /dɪs'lodən/ *v* to unload (a ship) *17-19, 20- N.* [negative prefix *dis-* + Older Scots *lodin, loaden*]

†**dislock** *v* to dislocate a joint *19.* [Fr *disloquer*]

†**disluge** *v* to remove or depart from a lodging *la15-16*. [ME *disloggen*]

dismall, dysmall, dysemale *n* an evil or unlucky time, being or circumstance *15-16*. [ME *dismal*, Lat *diēs malī* evil days]

disnae, disna, doesnae, doesny /'dɪzne, 'dɪznə, 'dʌzne, 'dʌzni/ *v* doesn't *18-*. [*dis* (DAE[1.1]) + -NAE]

disnin see DAE[1.1]

disobeyance /dɪso'beəns/ *n* disobedience *16, 20- NE.* [compare DISOBEYSANCE]

†**disobeysance** *n* disobedience *15-16*. [ME *disobeissaunce*]

†**disparissing** *n* unequal matching (in marriage) *la15-e16*. [perhaps altered form of Lat *dispar, disparis* unequal, with noun-forming suffix]

†**dispasche** *v* to dispatch *16-e17*. [EModE *dispatch*, with influence from DISPESCHE; compare Ital *dispacciare*, Spanish *despachar*]

dispeace /dɪs'pis/ *n* dissension, enmity, disquiet *19-*. [negative prefix *dis-* + PEACE[1.1]]

†**disperne** *v* to disperse, drive away; to despise *16.* [Lat *dispernere*]

†**disperson** *v* to treat with indignity; to insult or abuse *15-e17*. [Lat *dispersōnāre*]

dispert[1.1], **desprit, desperate,** *Uls* **despert,** †**disperat,** †**disparit** /'dɪspərt, 'dɛsprət, 'dɛspərət; *Uls* 'dɛspərt/ *adj* **1** despairing, hopeless *la14-*. **2** terrible, awful; reckless, violent *la17-*. [Lat *dēspērātus*]

dispert[1.2], **desprit, desperate,** *Uls* **despert** /'dɪspərt, 'dɛsprət, 'dɛspərət; *Uls* 'dɛspərt/ *adv* extremely, excessively *la18-*. [see the adj]

†**dispesche** *v* to dispatch *16-e17*. [OFr *despechier*; compare DEPESCHE[1.2], DISPASCHE]

dispite see DESPITE[1,2]

displeesure, displeasure, †**displesour,** †**displeisour,** †**displeaser** /dɪsˈpliʒər, dɪsˈplɛʒər/ *n* (a cause or source of) dissatisfaction or annoyance; vexation, grief *la15-*. [ME *displesir*]

displenish[1.1] /dɪsˈplɛnɪʃ/ *n* **1** a sale held to dispose of farm equipment and stock *19- Sh NE T.* **2** a disposal of goods; the dispersal of farm equipment or stock (at the expiry of the lease) *19*. **displenish sale** a sale held to dispose of farm equipment and stock *19-*. [negative prefix *dis-* + PLENISH[1.1]]

displenish[1.2] /dɪsˈplɛnɪʃ/ *v* to strip or deprive of property; to sell off furnishings, equipment or stock (from a farm) *la16-*. **displenishing sale** a sale of the furnishings, equipment or stock on a farm *la19-*. [see the noun]

displesour see DISPLEESURE

†**dispoilʒe, dispulʒe, dispolʒe** *v* to despoil *la14-e16*. [ME *despoilen*]

dispone, †**dispoune,** †**despone** /dɪsˈpon/ *v* **1** *law* to assign, grant or convey (property or land) *la15-*. **2** to exercise disposition, authority or control (over something) *15-e19*. **3** to set in order, arrange *la14-e18*. **4** to deal with, dispose of, hand over *la14-e18*. **5** to make oneself ready, prepare oneself *la14-16*. **6** to put (a person) in a suitable frame of mind *la15-16*. **disponer,** †**disponar 1** *law* the person who conveys property *la16-*. **2** a giver, a donor, a distributor *la15-16*.

disponee *law* the person to whom property is conveyed *18-*. [Lat *dispōnere*]

dispose /dɪˈspoz/ *v* **1** to arrange, settle; to incline towards *la15-*. **2** to get rid of *17-*. †**dispose on** to exercise disposition, authority or control upon *17-e19*. [ME *disposen*]

disposition, †**dispositioun** /dɪspəˈzɪʃən/ *n* **1** arrangement, position *la14-*. **2** outlook, nature *15-*. **3** the power or right to dispose of something *la15-*. **4** *law* a deed of conveyance, an assignation of property *la15-*. [MFr *disposition*]

dispositive clause /dɪˈspozɪtɪv klɔz/ *n law* the operative clause of a deed by which property is conveyed *18-*. [Fr *dispositive* + CLAUSE]

dispoune see DISPONE

†**disprise**[1.1]**, disprys** *n* blame, disparagement *la16*. [see the verb]

†**disprise**[1.2]**, disprese, disprys** *v* to depreciate, undervalue *15-16*. [ME *dispreisen*]

dispulʒe see DISPOILʒE

disremember /dɪsrəˈmɛmbər/ *v* to fail to remember, forget *la17-*. [negative prefix *dis-* + REMEMBER]

†**disrentell** *v* to remove from a rent-roll *la16*. [negative prefix *dis-* + RENTAL[1.2]]

disrespeck, †**disrespek** /dɪsrəˈspɛk/ *v* to treat without respect; to insult *la18-*. [negative prefix *dis-* + RESPECK[1.2]]

†**disrig** *v* to unrig (a ship or mill) *17-18*. [negative prefix *dis-* + RIG[1.1]]

disruption /dɪsˈrʌpʃən/ *n* disturbance, separation *19-*. **the Disruption** the split which took place in the Established Church of Scotland in 1843 when 450 of its 1200 ministers formed themselves into the Free Church *19, 20- historical*. [Lat *disruptio*]

dissaif see DECEIVE

†**dissasine** *n* withdrawal of seisin, dispossession *16-17*. [ME *disseisin*, OFr *dessaisine*]

dissave see DECEIVE

disseck /dɪˈsɛk, daeˈsɛk/ *v* to dissect *19-*. [Lat *dissect-*, ptp stem of *dissecāre*]

disses see DECEASE[1.1]

dissie see DISSY[1.1], DISSY[1.2]

†**dissimil, dissymyll, dissimule** *v* to dissemble; to conceal, feign *la14-16*. [ME *dissimulen*, Lat *dissimulāre*]

†**dissimilance, dissymilance, dissimulans** *n* dissimulation, deception *la15-16*. [Lat *dissimulantia*]

†**dissimulate, dissimulait, dissimilit** *adj* feigned, disguised; deceitful *la15-e17*. [Lat *dissimulātus*]

dissimule see DISSIMIL

†**dissle**[1] *n* a slight shower, a drizzle *18-19*. [compare Norw *dysja* to drizzle]

dissle[2]**, dishle** /ˈdɪsəl, ˈdɪʃəl/ *v* to struggle forward, push on; to jolt around *19, 20- T*. [unknown]

dissolate see DESOLATE

dissone see DIZZEN

dissy[1.1]**, dissie, dizzy** /ˈdɪse, ˈdɪze/ *n* a rejection; failure to keep a (romantic) appointment *la20- C*. **dissy corner** a nickname for the corner of Union Street and Argyle Street in Glasgow (a popular meeting place) *la20- WC*. [see the verb]

dissy[1.2]**, dissie, dizzy** /ˈdɪse, ˈdɪze/ *v* to jilt, stand up; to fail to turn up (for a rendezvous) *la20- C*. [probably a reduced form of Eng *disappointment*]

dissy see DESY[1.2]

dissymilance see DISSIMILANCE

dissymyll see DISSIMIL

dist, dust /dɪst, dʌst/ *n* **1** earth or dirt in fine particles, dust *15-*. **2** particles of meal and husk produced in grinding corn *la16-19, 20- N NE*. **disty, dusty** a name for a miller *19, 20- NE WC*. [OE *dūst*]

†**distene, disteyn, disteynʒe** *v* to stain, discolour; to cause to lose brightness *la15-16*. [ME *disteinen*]

dister, duster /ˈdɪstər, ˈdʌstər/ *n* a drizzle *20- Sh Ork N*. [compare Norw *dustra* to drizzle]

disteyn, disteynʒe see DISTENE

distil, †**distell** /dɪˈstɪl/ *v* to purify (liquid) by heating, distil; to (let) fall in drops *16-*. [Lat *dēstillāre*]

†**distingue, disting** *v* to distinguish *la15-16*. [ME *distinguen*, Lat *distinguere*]

distrack, distrak, distract /dɪˈstrak, dɪˈstrakt/ *v* **1** to divert the attention *la16-*. **2** to become troubled in mind or mentally ill *la17-18*. **distrackit, distractit** troubled in mind, mentally ill *17-*. [Lat *distract-*, ptp stem of *distrahere*]

†**distrenzie, distrenʒe, distreinʒie** *v* to distrain; to subject to constraint; to seize (land or goods) by way of enforcing fulfilment of an obligation *la14-e19*. **distrenʒeabill** liable or subject to distraint *15-e16*. [ME *distreinen* to restrict, be severe with]

distress[1.1]**,** †**distres** /dɪˈstrɛs/ *n* **1** affliction or misfortune; sorrow or anxiety *la14-*. **2** illness *la19, 20- T EC*. **3** severe weather, a storm *20- Sh*. **4** *law* seizure of goods *15-19*. **5** *law* goods seized against a debt by legal officials *15-e17*. [ME *distresse*]

distress[1.2]**,** †**distres** /dɪˈstrɛs/ *v* **1** to afflict, harass *18-*. **2** *law* to subject to distraint; to seize goods (from) *15-19*. [ME *distressen*]

distribulance see DISTROUBLE

distribut, distribute /dɪˈstrɪbət, dɪˈstrɪbjut/ *adj* distributed *15-19, 20- NE*. [Lat *distribūtus*]

districk, destrick, district /ˈdɪstrɪk, ˈdɛstrɪk, ˈdɪstrɪkt/ *n* **1** a region or division of territory; an area (within a place) *la17-*. **2** one of nine local government areas into which mainland Scotland was formerly divided *la20, 21- historical*. [Fr *district*]

†**distrouble, distruble, distroble** *v* to disturb, harass, trouble greatly *la14-e19*. **distroublance, distribulance, distrublans** disturbance, trouble, harassment *la14-16*. [ME *distroublen*]

†**distroy** *v* to destroy, commit destruction *la14-e17*. [ME *destroien*]

distruble see DISTROUBLE

disturs *v* to rob or plunder; to deprive *la15-e17*. [metathesis of ME *distrussen*]

disty, dusty /'dɪste, 'dʌsti/ *adj* covered with dust *16-*. **dustyfoot, †dustifute** a travelling merchant, a pedlar; a vagabond *15-19, 20- literary*. **dusty-melder 1** the last milling of a season's crop *la18-*. **2** the last born child in a large family *20-*. **dusty miller 1** a species of primula *Primula auricula la19-*. **2** a kind of bumble-bee *20-*. [DIST + -IE²]

†disuse *v* to discontinue *la15-17*. **disusit** out of practice, unaccustomed *la14-e16*. [negative prefix *dis-* + USE¹·²]

dit, †dytt /dɪt/ *v* **1** to shut up, close (the mouth) *la14-19, 20- NE Bor*. **2** to obstruct, block (water or light) *la17-19, 20- NE*. **3** to darken, dim *19, 20- NE SW Bor*. [OE *dyttan* to close, shut]

ditch *see* DUTCH

†dite¹·¹, **dyte, dyt** *n* **1** a composition, writing or written work *15-16*. **2** style of composition, diction *15-16*. **dyter** an inditer, a writer *la16*. **dytment, ditement 1** a written composition *la16-e17*. **2** dictation, direction, instruction *la16-e17*. [ME *dit*]

†dite¹·², **dyte, dyt** *v* **1** to compose, put in writing *15-e19*. **2** to dictate *16-e19*. **3** to direct or instruct *15-e17*. **4** to indict, summons *la15-e16*. [ME *diten*]

dite *see* DOIT¹

†diton *n* a phrase or sentence; a motto *la16-17*. [MFr *dicton*]

dittay, †ditty, †ditta, †dictay /'dɪte/ *n* **1** *law* a statement of the charge(s) against an accused person; an indictment *15-*. **2** *law* formal accusation, information forming a basis of indictment *la15-19*. **3** *law* a body or list of indictments coming before a court for trial *15-16*. **point of dittay** a statement of the charge(s) against an accused person; an indictment *la16-19, 20- historical*. **†take dittay** to obtain information and proof with a view to prosecution *la15-19*. [MFr *dicté*]

ditter *see* DOITER

ditty *see* DITTAY

div *see* DAE¹·¹

divall *see* DEVAUL¹·²

dive /daev/ *v* to argue *la19- Ork*. [unknown]

divert /dɪ'vert, dae'vert/ *n* an entertainment or amusement; an amusing person or thing *19-*. [substantive use of the verb from OFr *divertir* to turn aside]

divide, †devide, †devyde /də'vʌɪd/ *v* **1** to share out, assign (possession of land), distribute (goods) *la14-*. **2** to split, part, separate *15-*. **divider, †devyder 1** a ladle, a serving spoon *la18-*. **2** a person appointed to divide land *la16*. **dividing spoon** = *divider* (sense 1) *la18-*. [Lat *dīvidere*]

†dividual *adj* particular, distinct *19*. [Lat *dīviduus* separated, with *-al* suffix]

divil *see* DEIL

†divise¹·¹, **devise** *n* a boundary between lands *la14-e17*. [OFr *devise*]

†divise¹·², **devise** *v* to divide *la14-16*. [ME *devisen*]

division, †divisioun /də'vɪʒən/ *n* **1** the action of dividing *15-*. **2** *law* formal partition (of land or property) *15-*. **3** (splitting into) factions, dissension *15-*. [ME *divisioun*, Lat *dīvīsio*]

†divortioun *n* (a) divorce *16*. [Lat *divortio*]

divot¹·¹, **divvit, †devat, †duvat, †diffat** /'dɪvət/ *n* **1** a piece of turf, a sod; a peat *15-*. **2** a lump or chunk; a thick clumsy piece of bread or meat *la19-*. **†divot-seat** a turf bench at a cottage door *18-19*. [unknown]

divot¹·² /'dɪvət/ *v* **1** to cut sods or peat *la18-19, 20- N*. **2** to thatch with turf *la17-19*. [unknown]

divso /'dɪvso/ *n derogatory* an untidily-dressed woman *20- Ork*. [unknown]

divvish /'dɪvɪʃ/ *v* to set in order, tidy, to arrange; to finish off, prepare food (for the table) *la19- Sh Ork*. [unknown]

divvit *see* DIVOT¹·¹

dixie /'dɪksi/ *n* a sharp scolding *19, 20- Ork NE*. **get yer dixies** to be given a scolding *20- Ork NE*. [probably Lat *dixī* I have said]

dizzen, dizen, dozen, †dosane, †dissone, †dussoun /'dɪzən, 'dʌzən/ *n* a set of twelve, a dozen *15-*. **†the dusane** the body of ordinary councillors in a burgh (regardless of the actual number) *15*. [ME *dosein*]

dizzy *see* DISSY¹·¹, DISSY¹·²

djoll *see* JOLE

djur *see* JURE²

do *see* DAE¹·¹

doach, †doagh /dɔx/ *n* a salmon-trap or weir *la18- SW*. **the Doachs** a name for a rocky stretch of the River Dee at Tongland (where salmon is trapped) *19- SW*. [Gael *dabhach* a vat, a tub]

doactor¹·¹, **doctor, †doctour** /'dɔktər, 'dɔktər/ *n* **1** a scholar (with a doctorate); a university lecturer *la14-*. **2** a doctor of medicine *la15-*. **3** a large minnow; the red-breasted minnow *la19- C*. **4** an assistant-master in a school *la16-18*. [ME *doctour*, Lat *doctor* a teacher]

doactor¹·², **doctor** /'dɔktər, 'dɔktər/ *v* **1** to give medical treatment to *19-*. **2** to defeat (in a fight): ◇ *he fairly doctored Jock this time 19- Sh C*. [see the noun]

doadles *see* DODDLES

doag *see* DUG

doagh *see* DOACH

doaken *see* DOCKEN

doakie, dokey /'doki/ *n* a feat, a somersault *20- WC*. [perhaps DOCK¹·¹ + -IE¹]

doar *see* DAER

dob¹·¹ /dɔb/ *n* a prick; a peck; a thorn *19- N NE*. **dobbie** having spikes, prickly *la19- NE T*. [variant of DAB¹·¹]

dob¹·² /dɔb/ *v* to prick; to peck *la16-*. Compare DAB¹·². **dobbing** pricking *17- NE*. [see the noun]

dobber /'dɔbər/ *n* **1** a penis *la20-*. **2** *derogatory* a person *la20-*. [DOB¹·², with agent suffix]

dobbie, doobie, †doby /'dɔbi, 'dubi/ *n* **1** a stupid or clumsy person; the dunce of a class *19- T C SW Bor*. **2** a sprite *e19*. [unknown]

dochan doris *see* DEOCHANDORUS

docher, docker /'dɔxər, 'dɔxər, 'dɔkər/ *n* **1** injury; rough handling, wear and tear *la18- Sh Ork NE*. **2** strength, stamina; durability (of a material) *la19- Sh NE*. [Gael *dochair* hurt, damage]

dochle /'dɔxəl/ *n* a dull, stupid person; a fool *19, 20- NE*. [compare DACKLE¹·², DACKER¹]

†docht, doucht *n* power, strength *la18-19*. [back-formation from DOCHTY]

docht *see* DOW¹

dochter, dauchter, douchter, daughter, *Ork* **dowter,** *NE T* **dother, †douchtir, †dowthir, †dather** /'dɔxtər, 'dɔxtər, 'dʌuxtər, 'dɔtər;* Ork* 'dʌutər; *NE T* 'dɔθər; *NE T* 'doθər/ *n* a female child, a daughter *la14-*. **†dochter dochter** a granddaughter *15-16*. **†dochter sone** a grandson *15-16*. **daughter of the manse** a daughter of a Presbyterian minister *la19-*. [OE *dohtor*]

dochtless /'dɔxtləs/ *adj* powerless, worthless *19, 20- EC*. [DOCHT, with adj-forming suffix]

dochty, douchty, †dowchty, †duchtie, †dughty /'dɔxte/ *adj* doughty, bold, valiant *la14-*. [OE *dyhtig*, later OE *dohtig*]

dock¹·¹, *EC Bor* **dook, †dok** /dɔk/; *EC Bor* duk/ *n* **1** the buttocks *16-*. **2** the rear or butt of something; the stern of a ship *la16-19, 20- NE*. **3** a haircut *la19- NE T EC*. **docky** neat, tidy *19- SW*. **docknail 1** the nail used to fix a blade or handle on a scythe or plough *20- NE*. **2** a ploughman *20- NE*.

3 any person or part indispensable to the efficiency of a job or a tool *20- NE*. **docky-doon** help in descending from a vehicle *20- Bor*. **dookie-up** a hoist (up) *20- EC Bor*. [ME *dok* trimmed hair (of tail and forelock)]

dock[1.2], *EC Bor* **dook** /dɔk; *EC Bor* duk/ *v* **1** to cut short, crop; to shorten clothes; to put an infant into short clothes *la19-*. **2** to push someone upwards by placing one's head or shoulder to their buttocks and hoisting them up *20- Bor*. **3** to beat (on the buttocks) *la18*. **docketie** short, round and jolly *19- Bor*. **dockit** *of speech or temper* clipped, short *19, 20- NE EC*. [see the noun]

dock[2], †**dok** /dɔk/ *n* a dock, a berth for a vessel *la15-*. †**dockmaill** dock dues, the charges made for the use of a dock *17-e18*. **dok silver** = dock maill *16-e17*. [Du *dok*]

dock see DEK

docken, doaken, †**dokane** /'dɔkən, 'dɔkən/ *n* **1** the dock plant *Rumex obtusifolius* or *Rumex crispus 15-*. **2** something of no value or significance: ◊ *it disna maitter a doaken la19-*. **docken sporrow** the corn bunting *Emberiza calandra 20- Sh*. **no care a docken** not to care at all *la20-*. [OE *docce*]

docker see DOCHER
docket see DOCQUET[1.1], DOCQUET[1.2]
dockie see DUCK

docquet[1.1], **docket** /'dɔkət/ *n* an abstract, a minute *la16-*. **2** *law* a statement appended to an instrument of sasine declaring its authenticity *17-*. [perhaps ME *doket* rag]

docquet[1.2], **docket** /'dɔkət/ *v* to furnish with a minute or abstract; to endorse a letter or document with a short note of contents *17-*. [see the noun]

doctor see DOACTOR[1.1], DOACTOR[1.2]
doctour see DOACTOR[1.1]

doctrine, †**doctryne,** †**doctring,** †**doctreine** /'dɔktrɪn/ *n* instruction (in religion), preaching; teaching; dogma *la15-*. [ME *doctrine*, Lat *doctrīna* teaching]

†**doctrix** *n* **1** an assistant school-mistress *18*. **2** a female doctor *la18*. [Lat *doctrix* a female teacher]

doctryne see DOCTRINE

document /'dɔkjumənt/ *n* **1** a written statement or record; written evidence *la15-*. **2** teaching, a lesson *la15-17*. **3** proof, evidence, testimony *la15-e16*. [OFr *document*, Lat *documentum* a lesson, proof, written evidence]

docus /'dɔkəs/ *n* a stupid person *la18- C*. [unknown]

dod[1] /dɔd/ *v* to move slowly and unsteadily; to totter, tododder *19-*. [perhaps onomatopoeic]

dod[2], *NE* **dyod** /dɔd; *NE* djɔd/ *interj* God *la19-*. [euphemistic form of GOD]

dod[3] /dɔd/ *n* a sulk *la18-*. **doddy** sulky, bad-tempered *19-*. **tak the dods** to take a fit of bad temper, sulk *19-*. [Gael *dod* a huff, a tantrum]

dod[4], **dodd** /dɔd/ *n* a bare hill with a rounded top; a (rounded) lump or shoulder on a larger hill *la12-*. [unknown; compare DODDIE[1.1]]

dod[5], **dodd** /dɔd/ *n* **1** a tuft, a matted lump (of wool of hair) *20- Sh Ork*. **2** a simple or foolish person *20- N*. [Norw dial *dodd* a tuft]

dod see DAD[1.1]

doddie[1.1] /'dɔdi/ *n* **1** a hornless bull or cow *la18-19, 20- N NE T EC Bor*. **2** a hornless sheep *19- Bor*. **3** *derogatory* a person *la19, 20- NE*. [ME *dodden* to shear or shave + -IE[3]]

doddie[1.2] /'dɔdi/ *adj of cattle* hornless *19, 20- NE T EC Bor*. **doddie mitten** a mitten; a worsted glove with a separate division for the thumb only *la18- NE T EC*. [see the noun]

doddit /'dɔdət/ *adj of cattle or sheep* hornless *17-*. [ptp of ME *dodden* to shear or shave (a person's head), poll (cattle)]

doddle[1] /'dɔdəl/ *n* a small lump of home-made toffee which was sold in corner-shops *20, 21- historical*. [probably DAD[1.1]]

doddle[2.1] /'dɔdəl/ *n* something attractive or easy to do *20-*. [see the verb]

doddle[2.2], †**dodle** /'dɔdəl/ *v* to toddle, saunter, dawdle; to walk feebly or slowly *la16, 19- NE T EC*. Compare DAIDLE[2] [unknown]

doddles, doadles /'dɔdəlz, 'dɔdəlz/ *npl* the male genitals *18, 20- N NE T*. [unknown]

dodge /dɔdʒ/ *v* to jog, trudge along *19-*. [perhaps altered form of DOD[1]]

dodgel /'dɔdʒəl/ *n* something large of its kind, a lump; a clumsy person *19- Ork NE Bor*. [perhaps DODGE, with *-le* suffix]

†**Dodgill Reepan** *n* the marsh orchid *Dactylorhiza majalis 19*. [unknown]

dodle see DODDLE[2.2]
dodrums see DIDDERUMS
doer see DAER
doesnae, doesny see DISNAE

dog, dug, †**doug** /dɔg, dʌg/ *v* **1** to play truant from school *20-*. **2** to draw coal-tubs up the shaft of a mine *la19- WC*. [from the noun DUG]

dog see DAG[3], DUG

doggar /'dɔgər/ *n* (a concretion of) coarse ironstone *la18- C*. [unknown]

doggar see DUG

dogger /'dɔgər/ *n* a truant (from school) *la20- C*. **dogger man** a truant officer *21- C*. [DOG, with agent suffix]

dogon see DUGON
doif see DOWF[1.3]
doig see DUG

doilt, *NE* **diled,** *NE* **dylt,** †**doillit,** †**doild,** †**doylt** /dɔɪlt; *NE* dʌɪld; *NE* dʌɪlt/ *adj* **1** dazed, confused *16-19, 20- Sh NE SW*. **2** wearied, fatigued; grief-stricken *la18-19, 20- NE*. [unknown; compare DOOL[1.3]]

doin see DAE[1.1], DAEIN
doing see DAEIN
dois see DAE[1.1]

doist[1.1], **dyst, doisht,** †**doish,** †**dois** /dɔɪst, dʌɪst, dɔɪʃt/ *n* a heavy blow; a thud, a bump, a crash *16-19, 20- NE T*. **doister, dyster** a stormy wind blowing from the sea *19, 20- NE WC SW*. [perhaps onomatopoeic]

doist[1.2], **dyst** /dɔɪst, dʌɪst/ *v* **1** to fall, sit or throw (down) with a thud or bump *19- NE T WC*. **2** to move energetically *la20- NE*. [see the noun]

doit[1], †**dite** /dɔɪt/ *n* **1** something of little value; a small amount *18-*. **2** a small Dutch copper coin; a coin of low value *la16-19, 20- historical*. [Du *duit*]

doit[2.1] /dɔɪt/ *n* a confused or foolish person *19-*. [see the verb]

doit[2.2], †**dyte** /dɔɪt/ *v* **1** to act foolishly; to be confused in mind *16-*. **2** to walk with a stumbling or short step *la18-*. **doitit, doited, dowtit,** †**dotit** not of sound mind, confused, foolish *la15-*. [perhaps irregular variant of DOTE[2]]

doiter, ditter, dighter /'dɔɪtər, 'dɪtər, 'dʌɪtər/ *v* to walk or move unsteadily; to potter about *19-*. **doitered, doitert** confused; senile *19-*. **doitrified** stupefied, dazed, senseless *19, 20- NE T EC*. [frequentative form of DOIT[2.2]]

dok see DOCK[1.1]
dokane see DOCKEN
dokey see DOAKIE
döl see DOOL[1.1], DOOL[1.4]
dolder, doldie see DOLL[1]

dole /dol/ *n law* the corrupt, malicious, or evil intention which is an essential constituent of a criminal act *la17-*. [Lat *dolus* deceit, cunning]

doless, döless see DAELESS
dolf see DOWF[1.3]

doll¹ /dɔl, dol/ *n* **1** a portion, a large piece *18-19, 20- NE*. **2** a lump (of dung) *20- NE*. **dolder** something large of its kind *la19- NE*. **doldie, toldie 1** a lump *19- NE T*. **2** a large marble *la19- T EC SW*. **3** animal excrement *20- NE*. **doller** a large marble *la19- NE T*. **dollicker** a very large marble about six to eight times the normal size *la19- EC*. **dollie** = *dollicker la20-*. [probably related to ME *dol* a portion; compare Norw dial *dall* a hard lump]

doll², **dall** /dɔl, dal/ *n* a girl, a woman, often used as a term of (affectionate) address *la18-*. **dolly, dally** a term of (affectionate) address *19-*. [a shortened form of the female personal name *Dorothy*]

dollin *see* DELVE

dollop, †dallop /'dɔləp/ *n* **1** a tuft, a clump (of weeds); a lump, a portion (of food) *19-*. **2** an untidy or slovenly woman *20- NE*. [unknown; compare Norw dial *dolp* a lump]

†dollour, dolour *n* a dollar, a coin *la16-17*. [variant of DALLAR]

dolly /'dɔli/ *n* an old-fashioned oil-lamp, a CRUISIE *19- NE*. [reduced form of *eelie dolly* (ILE¹·¹)]

dolly *see* DOWIE¹
dolour *see* DOLLOUR
dolp *see* DOWP¹·¹
dolphin *see* DALPHIN
doly *see* DOOL¹·¹

dom /dɔm/ *n* a schoolmaster *20- NE*. **domsie** = DOM *la19- NE EC*. [reduced form of DOMINIE]

domaless /'dɔmələs/ *adj* weak, impotent; stupid *19- Ork*. [Norw dial *dåm* taste, flavour, appearance, with *-less* suffix]

dome *see* DOOM¹·¹
domicile *see* DOMINSELL

dominant tenement /'dɔmənənt 'tɛnəmənt/ *n law* a piece of land whose ownership includes a servitude right over adjoining land *la17-*. [Fr *dominant* + TENEMENT]

domineer /dɔmə'nir/ *v* **1** to govern or act despotically *la18-*. **2** to deafen, stupefy with loud noise or too much talk *la19- NE*. [EModDu *domineren* to rule, EModE *domineer* to revel, roister]

dominie /'dɔməni/ *n* **1** a (male or female) school teacher *la17-*. **2** a clergyman *e18*. [Lat *domine*, vocative of *dominus* a master]

dominium directum /də'mɪnɪəm dae'rɛktəm/ *n law* the right in land enjoyed by the superior; legal right of dominion *18-*. [Lat *dominium dīrectum* simple right of ownership]

dominium utile /də'mɪnɪəm 'jutʌɪl, də'mɪnɪəm 'utɪle/ *n law* the substantial right in land enjoyed by the vassal; actual possession of property *18-*. [Lat *dominium ūtile* advantageous right of ownership]

†dominsell, domicile *n* household effects; a household article *la15-e18*. [Lat *domicilii*, genitive sing of *domicilium* a household]

dominus litis /'dɔmɪnəs 'laetəs/ *n law* the person technically though not nominally behind legal proceedings, liable to be ordered to pay expenses *la19-*. [Lat *dominus lītis* the master of the lawsuit]

domra /'dɔmrə/ *n* fog or haze *20- Sh*. [unknown]
domsie *see* DOM
domster *see* DOOMSTER

Donald¹, **Donal** /'dɔnəld, 'dɔnəl/ *n* **1** a Highlander *19-*. **2** a measure of whisky (about half a gill) *19-*. [from the personal name]

Donald² /'dɔnəld/ *n* a hill in the Scottish Lowlands of 2000 feet (610m) or over *la20-*. [named after Percy Donald, who first listed them; compare CORBETT, MUNRO]

donatar *see* DONATOR
donatary *see* DONATORY

†donator, donatour, donatar *n law* the receiver of a donation (in cases of a forfeiture or failure of succession) *16-19*. [ME *donatour*]

donatory, donatary /'dɔnətəri, 'dɔnətəri/ *n law* the receiver of a gift of forfeited property (latterly only from the Crown) *18-*. [Lat *dōnātārius*]

donatour *see* DONATOR

†donatrix *n* a female DONATOR *la16*. [altered sense of Lat *dōnātrix* she who gives]

doncie *see* DONSIE
done *see* DAE¹·¹, DOON¹·³, DOON¹·⁴
dongeoun *see* DUNGEON

dongerees /dɔŋgə'riz/ *npl* dungarees *20-*. [Hindi *dungri* a kind of course calico]

dongle *see* DUNGEL¹·¹

donie /'dɔni/ *n* a hare *19- T SW*. [unknown]

†donk, dounk *v* to make damp or wet *16*. [from the adj DUNK¹·²]

donk *see* DUNK¹·¹, DUNK¹·²
donnard *see* DONNERT

donner, †donnar /'dɔnər/ *v* to daze, stun or stupefy *19-*. [unknown]

donner *see* DAUNER¹·¹, DAUNER¹·²

donnert, dunnert, †donnard /'dɔnərt, 'dʌnərt/ *adj* dull, stupid *18-*. [unknown]

Dons /'dɔnz/ *npl* a nickname for Aberdeen Football Club *20-*. [shortened form of *Aberdonians*]

donsie, †doncie /'dɔnsi/ *adj* **1** unfortunate, unlucky *la18-*. **2** sickly, feeble, delicate *la18-*. **3** dull, stupid *19- Bor*. **4** neat, tidy, prim *18-19*. **5** glum, dejected *18-19*. **6** badly behaved, ill-tempered *la18-e19*. [Gael *donas* bad luck, mischief + -IE²]

dont *see* DUNT¹·¹, DUNT¹·²
dontybour *see* DUNTIBOUR

doo, *Bor* dow /du; *Bor* dʌu/ *n* **1** a dove or pigeon, usually *Columba livia la14-*. **2** a familiar term of endearment (for a sweetheart or child) *la15-*. **3** a kindly loving person *20-*. **4** *pl* female breasts *la20-*. **doo's cleckin** a family of two, usually a boy and a girl *la19-*. **doo-docken** coltsfoot *Tussilago farfara 19- N*. **doo-lander** a tweed cap with a large peak *20-*. **doo-lichter** = *doo-lander*. **doo's sittin** = *doo's cleckin*. **†dow talit** *of a joint* dove-tailed *16-e17*. **no care a doo's ee** not to care a jot *20- C SW*. [by v-deletion from ME *duve*]

doobie *see* DOBBIE

dooble¹·¹, **double**, **†duble**, **†dowbill** /'dubəl, 'dʌbəl/ *n* **1** a double sum or amount *la14-*. **2** a duplicate or copy (of a document) *16-*. [see the adj]

dooble¹·², **double** /'dubəl, 'dʌbəl/ *v* **1** to multiply by two, increase twofold *la14-*. **2** to make a duplicate or copy of *17-e18*. **doubling 1** making double *la15-*. **2** *piping* in pibroch, the form in which a variation may be repeated, usually with more complete or perfect development *la18-*. **3** an ornament prefacing a note *20-*. [see the adj]

dooble¹·³, **double**, **†duble**, **†dowbill**, **†doubill** /'dubəl, 'dʌbəl/ *adj* **1** twofold; composed of two parts or pieces *la14-*. **2** of twice the usual thickness, size or value *la15-*. **3** deceitful, false *la15-16*. **dooble cairt** a cart pulled by two horses, one in the shafts and one in the traces *20- NE EC*. **double distress** *law* two or more claims on a single fund, an essential of a MULTIPLEPOINDING *la18-*. **double letter** a capital letter *19- N NE*. **†double pild** *of velvet* a particular length of nap *la16*. **†double-poinding** = MULTIPLEPOINDING *la16-17*. **double raip** a straw rope twisted double *la15, 20- NE*. **†double solit** having a double sole *la15-17*. [ME *double*]

dooble¹·⁴, **double**, **†duble** /'dubəl, 'dʌbəl/ *adv* doubly, to twice the amount or extent *la14-*. [see the adj]

doobrack, dubreck /'dubrak, 'dubrɛk/ *n* the smelt or sparling *Osmerus eperlanus la18- NE*. [Gael *dubh bhreac*]

doocot, †doocat, †dowcot, †ducat /'dukət/ *n* **1** a dovecote *15-*. **2** a pigeonhole, a recess *la20-*. **3** a room which is too small *la20-*. **doocot hole** a pigeon-hole *19-*. [DOO + COT[1.1]]

doodle[1.1] /'dudəl/ *n* a musical instrument made from a reed *20- Bor*. [see the verb]

doodle[1.2], **†doudle** /'dudəl/ *v* **1** to sing or hum over a tune to accompany dancers *20- NE H&I C*; compare DIDDLE[2.2]. **2** to play a wind instrument or the bagpipes *19, 20- Bor*. [Ger *dudeln*]

doodle[2], *Bor* **dowdle**, **†doudle** /'dudəl; *Bor* 'dʌudəl/ *v* to dandle, lull (a child) to sleep *la18-19, 20- SW Bor*. [onomatopoeic]

doof *see* DOWF[1.3]

dook[1.1], **douk** /duk/ *n* **1** the act of ducking or diving *la15-*. **2** a drenching, a soaking *la18-*. **3** liquid into which something is dipped *19-*. **4** a bathe, a swim *la19-*. **5** *mining* an inclined roadway *la19- C*. **dook workings** *mining* workings below the level of the pit bottom *la19, 20- EC*. [see the verb]

dook[1.2], **douk**, **†dulk** /duk/ *v* **1** to duck, dive; to dip or immerse (in water) *la15-*. **2** to bathe, swim *19-*. **3** *Christian Church* to baptize as a Baptist *20- T EC*. **4** *of the day* to draw to a close; *of the sun* to go down *19*. **dookit folk** members of the Baptist Church *20- NE*. **dook for apples** to seize an apple floating in a tub with one's teeth (in a game played on Halloween) *la19-*. **†the dooking** (sea) bathing *e19*. [Ger *ducken*, MDu, MLG *duken*]

dook[2.1] /duk/ *n* **1** a wooden peg driven into a wall to hold a nail *18-*. **2** a plug, a bung of a cask or a boat *19- NE*. **dook hole 1** a hole cut in a wall for a wooden peg *20- NE T SW*. **2** the plug hole of a cask or boat *20- N NE SW*. [unknown]

dook[2.2] /duk/ *v* **1** to insert a wooden peg into a wall *20-*. **2** to bung up a cask *la19- NE*. [unknown]

dook *see* DOCK[1.1], DOCK[1.2]

dooker, †ducker, †doukar, †dowcare /'dukər/ *n* **1** a diver, a swimmer *16-*. **2** a diving bird, a sea bird *la18-*. **3** a piece of bread dipped in gravy or soup *la20-*. **4** *pl* a swimming costume *la20-*. [DOOK[1.2], with agent suffix]

dool[1.1], **dule**, *Sh* **döl**, **†duill**, **†duyl** /dul; *Sh* døl/ *n* **1** grief, distress, sorrow; mourning, lamentation *la14-*. **2** mourning clothes *16-17*. **†dullie, doly, duly** gloomy, dismal *la15-e17*. **†doolfu, duleful** = *doolsome la14-19*. **doolsome, †dulesum** causing or expressing grief, sorrowful *16-*. **†dule habit** = *dule weed e16*. **†dool-string** a piece of black crepe worn round the hat as a sign of mourning *la18-19*. **dule tree** a gallows tree *la18-19, 20- literary*. **†dule weed, dooleweid** mourning attire *16-e19*. [ME *dol*]

†dool[1.2], **dule** *v* to be sorrowful; to lament, mourn *16-19*. [EModE *dool*]

dool[1.3] /dul/ *adj* sad, sorrowful, gloomy *18-*. [see the noun]

dool[1.4], *Sh* **döl** /dul; *Sh* døl/ *interj* an expression of dismay *18-19, 20- Sh*. [see the noun]

dool[2], **dull**, *WC* **dult**, **†dule** /dul, dʌl; *WC* dʌlt/ *n* **1** *games* the goal or place of safety *16-*. **2** a boundary mark *la16-19, 20- Ork*. Compare DALE[3]. **dully** *games* a prisoners' base; the game of rounders *la17*. **the dools** = *dully*. [Du *doel*]

dool[3.1], **†doule, †dowl** /dul/ *n* a dowel, a headless peg, pin or bolt *16-*. [perhaps related to ME *doule* a wooden rim of a wheel]

dool[3.2] /dul/ *v* to pin or fasten with dowels *la17-19, 20- Uls*. **†dovelling** the pinning together of the cooms used in building arches and the pends of windows with dowels *16-e17*. [see the noun]

doolie /'duli, 'dule/ *n* **1** a hobgoblin, a spectre *19- N NE T*. **2** a foolish, dithering, nervous person *20- T C*. [unknown]

doom[1.1], **†dome, †dume, †doym** /dum/ *n* **1** fate, destiny *la14-*. **2** destruction, ruin *la14-*. **3** *law* a formally pronounced judgement, a judicial sentence *la14-20, 21- historical*. **†but dome** without proper (trial and) sentence *la15-e17*. **†day of dome** the last judgement *la14-e16*. **†give for dome** to give as judgment *la14-e17*. **pronounce for doom** to judge, condemn to death *17-20, 21 historical*. [OE *dōm*]

doom[1.2], **†dume** /dum/ *v law* to pronounce sentence on, condemn *16-*. [see the noun]

dooms /dumz/ *adv* extremely, very *19-*. Compare DEEMIS. [perhaps altered form of DOONS]

doomster, †domster /'dumstər/ *n law* the official who reads out a sentence in court; a hangman *16-19, 20- historical*. [variant of DEMPSTER]

doon[1.1], **down** /dun, dʌun/ *v* **1** to knock down; to overthrow, get the better of *20-* **2** to drink down *la20-*. [see the adv]

doon[1.2], **doun, down** /dun, dʌun/ *adj* **1** in a low position *15-*. **2** *of a river* in flood *la19-*. **3** *of a school* closed for the holidays *20- EC SW*. **doon o mooth** in low spirits *20-*. [see the adv]

doon[1.3], **doun, down, †done** /dun, dʌun/ *adv* **1** in a descending direction; to a lower or inferior position; to or on the ground *la14-*. **2** *of prices or reckonings* by way of reduction *la15-*. **3** *of seed sown la19- N NE EC*. **4** *of a coal stratum* requiring support from below *20- EC*. **dooner, douner, downer** lower *la17-*. **doonlins** downwards *19- N NE*. **doonmaist, downmost** lowest *18-*. **dooncome, downcome 1** a fall in status, humiliation *19-*. **2** a heavy fall of snow or rain *la19-*. **3** a fall, a collapse, a descent *15-19*. **doun-ding** *n* a heavy fall of rain or snow *19- NE T EC*. **†doun-ding** *v* to beat down, todefeat *la19*. **doondrag, downdrag** an impediment, a disadvantage *19- NE T*. **doondraught, downdraught** a depressing influence, a heavy load, an impediment *19, 20- T EC Bor*. **doon-draw** = *doondraught 19- T C Bor*. **doonefter** following downwards or behind *la19- Sh*. **doonfa** a downward slope *19-*. **†doun falling** the act of falling; nightfall *15-16*. **†doun gangin** nightfall *15*. **doongaun, †doun-going** sunset, the end of the day *17-*. **†doun getting** the obtaining of a reduction or remission (of custom dues) *16-17*. **doonhame** at home (applied to Dumfries by the locals) *20-*. **Doonhamers 1** a nickname for the inhabitants of Dumfries *20-*. **2** a nickname for Queen of the South Football Club *20-*. **doonhaud** a disadvantage, something that prevents one rising in the world *19-*. **doon-hauden** kept in subjection *la19-*. **doonleuk, downlook 1** a hangdog expression *la19- NE*. **2** disapproval *17-18*. **doon lookin, downlooking** sullen, guilty looking *18-*. **doon-lyin** confinement, lying in *la16-*. **doon-moued** depressed *la19-*. **doon mouth** a sad expression *19-*. **†downe passing** the setting of the sun *la15-e17*. **doonpish** a downpour *la20-*. **downpouring** the pouring down (of rain) *la19, 20- Sh T*. **†dounraxter** a knocking down *e17*. **doontak** a humiliation, a taunt *la19-*. **†doun thring** to press or thrust down; to suppress *la14-16*. **doon through** in(to) the lower-lying part of the country or the coastal areas *19- N NE*. **downthrow** *mining* a fault which has displaced the strata downwards relative to the workings ahead *19, 20- EC*. **doonwith** downwards, downhill *la15-19, 20- N NE*. **be on the doon-hand** *of prices* to fall *20- NE*. **doon by, doon bye, down by** down there, in the neighbourhood *19-*. **doon o, down of** *of prices or reckonings* below *la18-*. [OE *dūne*]

doon[1.4], **doun, †done** /dun, dʌun/ *prep* **1** in a downward or descending direction *16-*. **2** along *16-*. **doon the gate** down the road, yonder *16-*. **doon the hoose** in the best room *19- SW Uls*. **doon the watter** down the river Clyde (on a pleasure trip or holiday) *la16-*. **gae doon the brae** to go downhill, deteriorate in health or fortune *la18-*. [see the adv]

doon², †**doun** /dun/ *n* down, (soft) feathers or plumage *16-*. [ON *dúnn*]

†**doon**³ *n* in Dumfries and Galloway the goal or home in a game *la18-19*. [perhaps DUN, with infl from DOOL²]

doon see DUN

doonie /'dune,'duni/ *n* a member of the HAND-BA team playing towards the downward goal, usually coming from the lower part of the town *20- Ork Bor*. Compare UPPIE. [DOON¹,³ + -IE³]

†**doons** *adv* very, extremely *18-19*. [ptp of DAE¹,¹, with adv-forming suffix; compare DOOMS]

doonset /'dunsɛt/ *n* **1** a (marriage) settlement *19-*. **2** a scolding *19-*. **3** a heavy blow, a misfortune *19, 20- NE EC*. **4** a good spread of food, a feast *20- Ork NE SW*. [DOON¹,³ + SET¹,¹]

doonsit /'dunsɪt/ *n* a settlement (obtained by marriage or inheritance) *la19-*. [DOON¹,³ + SIT¹,¹]

doonsittin, down-sittin, downsitting /'dunsɪtən, 'dʌunsɪtən, 'dʌunsɪtɪŋ/ *n* **1** a settlement (obtained by marriage or inheritance) *19-*. **2** the action of settling in a place *la16, la19- NE*. **3** the opening session of a deliberative body *la16-e18*. **at a doonsittin, at ae down-sitting** at a single sitting *la18-19, 20- NE T EC*. [verbal noun from DOON¹,³ + SIT¹,²]

doop see DOWP¹,¹

door, *T* **duir**, *H&I* **dorr**, †**dure** /dor; *T* dur; *H&I* dɔr/ *n* a hinged barrier at an entrance, a door; a doorway or entrance; *in place-names* a pass or gap between hills *la12-*. **doorie** a game of marbles played against a door *20- NE*. **doorcheek**, †**dur cheik** a door-post; a door, doorway *la16-*. **doorheid, doorhead** the upper part of a door-case *la16-19, 20- NE Bor*. **door-neighbour** a next-door neighbour *17-19, 20- NE*. **door sole** the threshold *19- Ork N NE*. **door stane** a flagstone at the threshold of a door; the threshold itself *19-*. **door-staple, door-steeple** an iron hook on a door-post to secure the bar or bolt on the inside of a door *la19- NE T*. **door-thrashel** the threshold *20- NE*. **the door's nivver aff the turn** I am inconvenienced by frequent visitors *la19- T WC SW*. **gie somebody the door in their face** to show someone the door, slam the door in someone's face *la19-*. †**make open doors** *law* to force open a locked door (under legal authority) *18-e19*. **put someone to the door** to ruin someone *18, 20- NE*. **tak the door after you** to close the door behind you *19-*. †**tak the door on your back** to go away, clear out *19*. **tak the door tae ye** = *tak the door after you 20-*. **tak the door wi ye** to go away; to shut the door as you go out *la18-19, 20- NE*. [OE *duru*]

doorie, *H&I* **durrie** /'duri; *H&I* 'dʌri/ *n* a pig; the smallest pig of a litter *la19- H&I WC SW Uls*. **doorkie** = DOORIE *la20- H&I*. [Gael *durra(i)dh* a pig, a sow, Gael *durrag* a little pig]

doose¹,¹, †**dous** /dus/ *n* a heavy blow; a butt, a push; a thud *16-19, 20- Sh Ork NE T*. [unknown]

doose¹,², **douce** /dus/ *v* to strike, knock, thrash *18-*. [unknown]

doosht¹,¹ /duʃt/ *n* a dull, heavy blow; a push; a thud *la18- Sh N NE*. [onomatopoeic]

doosht¹,² /duʃt/ *v* **1** to strike with a dull, heavy blow; to thump *la19- Sh NE*. **2** to throw (down) in a violent, careless way *la19- NE*. [see the noun]

doosie see DOOZIE

doost see JIST¹,²

doot¹,¹, **doubt**, †**dout** /dut, dʌut/ *n* **1** (a feeling of) uncertainty; perplexity; an unresolved difficulty *la14-*. **2** (a cause of) alarm or fear; dread *la14-16*. **dootsome, doubtsome, doutsum 1** doubtful, undecided; ambiguous, uncertain *16-19, 20- EC*. **2** involving risk or danger, formidable *16*. †**doutwise, dowtwisse** doubtful *la14-e16*. **I hae my doots** an expression of doubt *la19-*. [ME *dout*]

doot¹,², **doubt**, †**dout**, †**dowt** /dut, dʌut/ *v* **1** to distrust or disbelieve; to be uncertain *la14-*. **2** to fear, be afraid, suspect *la14-*. **3** to believe, expect, anticipate *la18-*. [ME *douten*]

doozie, dousie, doosie /'duzi/ *n* **1** a light; a flame (of a candle or lamp); a miner's lamp *la19- C SW*. **2** a lighted stick or peat waved rapidly to form an arc of light, a DINGLE-DOOZIE *19- SW*. [unknown]

dorb¹,¹ /dɔrb/ *n* a peck; a prod *20- NE*. [altered form of DOB¹,¹]

dorb¹,² /dɔrb/ *v of birds* to peck, grub *20- NE*. [see the noun]

dorbie¹ /'dɔrbi/ *n* **1** a stonemason *19, 20- N NE T Bor*. **2** the dunlin *19- NE*. [unknown; compare DORB¹,¹, DORB¹,²]

dorbie² /'dɔrbi/ *adj* delicate, weak *la19- NE*. [unknown]

dorche see DWERCH

†**dorder-meat** *n* a snack between meals (given to farmworkers between dinner and supper) *la18-19*. [development of OE *undernmete* food eaten in the morning]

dore /dor/ *v* **1** to deafen, bewilder with noise *19- Sh Ork*. **2** to repeat loudly and emphatically; to impress upon *20- Sh Ork*. [unknown]

doreen, dareen, doren, dawrin /'dorin, 'darin, 'dorən, 'dɔrən/ *n* damnation, the Devil *19- Sh Ork*. **doren apae thee** the devil take you *20- Ork*. **ill doren** to the devil *20- Sh*. [verbal noun from DORE]

Doric¹,¹ /'dɔrɪk/ *n* **1** a (rural or working-class) dialect of the Scots Language *la19-*. **2** the dialect of Scots spoken in the North-East *20-*. [see the adj]

Doric¹,² /'dɔrɪk/ *adj* **1** of or relating to the Scots language *la18-*. **2** of or relating to the dialect of Scots spoken in the North-East *20-*. [Lat *Dōricus* pertaining to the Dorians or their dialect]

dork see DERK¹,¹, DERK¹,³

dorlach, †**dorloch**, †**darloch** /'dɔrləx/ *n* **1** a large piece of something solid; a lump *la19- NE*. **2** a quiver (for arrows) *la16-e19*. **3** a bundle, a pack; a Highland soldier's knapsack; a portmanteau *e19*. [Gael *dorlach* a handful, a bundle; a quiver]

dorle, †**darle** /dɔrl/ *n* a small quantity; a piece of food *la17-19, 20- NE*. [perhaps back-formation from DORLACH]

dorloch see DORLACH

dormie /'dɔrme, 'dɔrmi/ *adj golf* as many holes up on an opponent as still remain to be played *19-*. [unknown]

dorneedy, dorneed /dor'nidi, dor'nid/ *n* the runt of a litter *la19- NE*. Compare DOORIE. [unknown]

†**dornell** *n* darnel, the weed *16*. [ME *darnel*]

†**dorne werk** *n* a kind of linen used for tablecloths *16*. [conflation of DORNICK with *werk* (WARK¹,¹)]

dornick, †**dornock**, †**dornik** /'dɔrnɪk/ *n* Tournai linen used for tablecloths, wall-hangings, napkins and towels *la15-*. [from *Doornik* (Tournai) in Flanders where the cloth was originally made]

dorr see DOOR

dorro, darra /'dɔro, 'dara/ *n* **1** a trailing cord with hooked lines attached, used in catching fish *la19- Sh Ork NE*. **2** the wooden frame on which the fishing-lines are wound *la19- Sh Ork*. **dorro-bullet** a lead sinker at the end of a mackerel line *20- T*. [ON *dorg*]

dort¹,¹ /dɔrt/ *n* **1** *pl* the sulks *17-*. **2** ill-humour, a huff *la18-*. **dorty 1** haughty, supercilious; impudent *16-*. **2** bad-tempered, sulky *la16-*. **3** feeble, delicate, sickly; *of plants or animals* difficult to rear *19- NE T*. **4** fastidious, difficult to please *la18- SW*. †**Meg Dorts** a sulky, bad-tempered woman *18-19*. [unknown]

dort[1,2] /dɔrt/ *v* **1** to sulk, take offence *17-*. **2** *of a bird* to forsake a nest or eggs *20- Ork*. [unknown]

dos *see* DOSS[1.1]

dosan *see* DOSSAN

dosane *see* DIZZEN

Do-School *see* DOUGH SCHOOL

dose /doz, dɔs/ *n* **1** a quantity of medicine (taken at one time) *la17-*. **2** a large quantity or number *19-*. **a dose of the cold** a bout of cold *la19-*. [Fr *dose*]

dose *see* DOZE

do service *see* DUE

dosh /dɔʃ/ *n* a term of endearment for a girl *la19- Sh NE*. [unknown]

dosinnit *see* DOZENT

doss[1.1], †**dos** /dɔs/ *v* to dress (up); to tidy, make neat *15-*. [Du *dossen*]

doss[1.2] /dɔs/ *adj* spruce, neat, tidy *19-*. [see the verb]

doss[2] /dɔs/ *n* a knot or bow (of ribbon or flowers) *19- N NE*. **dossie** a small knob or heap *la19- NE*. [Gael *dos* a tuft; a bow; a bunch of hair]

doss[3] /dɔs/ *n* a box or pouch for tobacco or snuff *la18-19, 20- T*. [Du *doos* a box]

doss[4] /dɔs/ *v* to pay; to make a payment *18-19, 20- NE*. **dossie down, dossie doon** to toss down payment; to pay money down *18-19, 20- NE*. [unknown]

doss[5] /dɔs/ *adj* stupid *la20- EC*. [unknown]

dossach /'dɔsəx, 'dɔsəx/ *v* to fondle, coddle, fuss over *19- NE*. [unknown]

dossan, dosan /'dɔsən, 'dosən/ *n* a forelock *la19- N NE H&I*. [Gael *dosan*, diminutive of *dos*; compare DOSS[2]]

dossie doon, dossie down *see* DOSS[4]

dot[1] /dɔt/ *n* a nap, a short sleep *19- N*. [compare Icel *dotta* to nod from sleep]

dot[2.1] /dɔt/ *n* **1** a speck, a spot; a small (round) mark *la18-*. **2** a person of small stature *la19- NE EC*. [EModE *dot* a small lump]

dot[2.2] /dɔt/ *v* **1** to mark with a dot or dots *19-*. **2** to scatter around *19-*. **3** to walk (about) with short quick steps *la19-*. [see the noun]

†**dotate** *adj* **1** endowed *16*. **2** given as an endowment *la16*. [Lat *dōtāt-*, ptp stem of *dōtāre* to give as a dowry]

dote[1.1] /dot/ *n* a dowry *16-19, 20- NE*. [EModE *dote*, Lat *dōt-*, oblique stem of *dōs*]

†**dote**[1.2] *v* **1** to endow; to give as an endowment *16-19*. **2** to provide (a woman) with a dowry *la16*. [OFr *doter*, Lat *dōtāre*]

dote[2] /dot/ *v* to think or act foolishly; to show excessive devotion (for) *la14-*. **dottered** stupid or confused; senile *la19- N NE EC*. **dotterel**, †**dotrell 1** a plover *16-*. **2** a confused or foolish person *la19-*. †**dottet, dotit** = dottered *la15-19*. [ME, MDu *doten*]

dote *see* DOUT

dother *see* DOCHTER

dotter /'dɔtər/ *v* to walk unsteadily, stagger *18-*. **dottery** unsteady, stumbling; drunk; senile *20-*. [perhaps related to DOD[1], or TOTTER]

dottered, dotterel *see* DOTE[2]

dottle[1.1] /'dɔtəl/ *n* **1** the plug of tobacco left at the bottom of a pipe after smoking *19-*. **2** the core of a boil *la19-*. **3** a cigarette end *20-*. **4** a particle, a jot; something small *19- C SW Uls*. **5** a person of small stature *19- NE*. **6** a stopper or plug *18, 20- Sh*. [diminutive form of DOT[2.1]]

dottle[1.2] /'dɔtəl/ *v* to stop up, plug *20- Sh*. [see the noun]

dottle[2.1] /'dɔtəl/ *v* **1** to be in or fall into a state of senility, become confused *19- N NE T*. **2** to cause confusion or make confused *19- NE*. [frequentative form of DOTE[2] or DOIT[2.2]]

dottle[2.2] /'dɔtəl/ *adj* in a state of senility *19-*. [see the verb]

dottled /'dɔtəld/ *adj* mentally impaired, confused; stupid *19-*. [ptp of DOTTLE[2.1]]

doub *see* DUB[1.1]

doubill *see* DOOBLE[1.3]

double *see* DOOBLE[1.1], DOOBLE[1.2], DOOBLE[1.3], DOOBLE[1.4]

doublet, †**doublat**, †**dublit**, †**dowlet** /'dʌblət/ *n* **1** a close-fitting body garment *15-18, 19- historical*. **2** *pl* clothes, garments *19, 20- NE*. [ME *doublet*]

doubt *see* DOOT[1.1], DOOT[1.2]

douce, *Sh* **dowse**, †**douse** /dus; *Sh* dʌus/ *adj* **1** sweet, pleasant, lovable *la16-*. **2** sedate, sober, respectable *18-*. **3** neat, tidy, comfortable *19- EC SW Bor Uls*. **doucely**, †**dousely** soberly, sedately *18-*. [ME *douce*]

douce *see* DOOSE[1.2]

doucht *see* DOW[1]

douchter, douchtir *see* DOCHTER

douchty *see* DOCHTY

doudle *see* DOODLE[1.2], DOODLE[2]

douff *see* DOWF[1.3]

doug *see* DOG, DUG

dougal /'dugəl/ *n* a penis *20- H&I*. [unknown]

douget *see* DUGGED

Dough School, Do-School /'do skul/ *n* a familiar name for any of the Colleges of Domestic Science *20, 21- historical*. [perhaps Scots *dough* or shortened form of *Domestic Science*]

†**Douglas grot** *n* a groat coined during the domination of Archibald Douglas, Earl of Angus, early in the reign of James V *16*. [from the surname + GROAT]

douk *see* DOOK[1.1], DOOK[1.2]

doukar *see* DOOKER

doule *see* DOOL[3.1]

†**doun** *n* a hill *15-16*. [OE *dūn*]

doun *see* DAE[1.1], DOON[1.2], DOON[1.3], DOON[1.4], DOON[2]

doung *see* DING[1.2]

dounk *see* DONK

doup[1.1] /dup/ *n* the end, the close *18-19, 20- literary*. **doup o' day** the end of the day, the approach of darkness *18- literary*. †**doup o e'en** = *doup o' day 18*. †**in a doup** in a trice *e18*. [see the verb]

doup[1.2] /dup/ *v* **1** to stoop, bend, duck *la17-19, 20- NE EC*. **2** *of the day* to draw to a close; *of darkness* to fall *la18-e19*. [compare Norw dial *duppa* to nod]

†**doup**[2] *v* to stab (a person); to thrust a weapon (into) *la16-17*. [unknown]

doup *see* DOWP[1.1], DOWP[1.2]

dour[1.1], †**dowr**, †**dure** /dur/ *adj* **1** stern, severe, harsh *la14-*. **2** obstinate, stubborn, unyielding; dogged *la14-*. **3** sullen, humourless, dull *la15-*. **4** *of stone or wood* hard *16-*. **5** slow, sluggish, reluctant *18-*. **6** *of weather* bleak, gloomy *la18-*. **7** *of land* hard, barren *la18-*. **8** *of work or a task* troublesome, difficult *la18-*. **9** *of a curling stone or ice* dull, sticky, dragging *19- WC SW*. **dourly** stubbornly; sullenly; sternly *15-*. †**dour seed** late-ripening oats *la18-e19*. [probably Lat *dūrus* hard]

†**dour**[1.2] *adv* severely, relentlessly, obstinately; extremely *15-e19*. [see the adj]

dourles /'durəlz/ *n* a stubborn fit, the sulks *19-*. [DOUR[1.1], with noun-forming suffix]

dous *see* DOOSE[1.1]

douse *see* DOUCE

dousie *see* DOOZIE

dout, dowt, *H&I* **dote** /dʌut; *H&I* dot/ *n* a cigarette-end; a half-smoked cigarette *20- H&I C*. Compare DOWP[1.1] (sense 4), DOTTLE[1.1] (sense 3). [probably altered form of DOWP[1.1], with possible influence from DOTTLE[1.1]]

dout *see* DOOT[1.1], DOOT[1.2]

douth, *Bor* **dowth** /duθ; *Bor* dʌuθ/ *adj* **1** dispirited, depressed *19- C Bor.* **2** *of places* gloomy, dreary, dark *19- SW Bor.* [probably altered form of DOWF¹·³]

dove /dov/ *v* to become drowsy, doze *19- Sh N NE T EC.* **dovie** *n* a stupid-looking person *19- T EC.* **dovie** *adj* stupid; sleepy *19- EC.* [compare Norw *dova* to weaken, become drowsy, ON *dofinn* drowsy, OE *dofung* nonsense, stupidity, dullness, and DOVER]

dovekie /'dʌvəki, 'dʌvki/ *n* the black guillemot *Cepphus grylle 19-.* Compare *sea doo* (SEA). [Eng *dove* + -OCK + -IE¹]

dover¹·¹ /'dovər/ *n* a doze, a nap *19-.* [see the verb]

dover¹·², †**dovyr** /'dovər/ *v* **1** to doze (off), drop into a light sleep *19-.* **2** to wander hesitatingly, walk unsteadily *19-.* †**doverit** sunk in sleep *16.* [probably frequentative form of DOVE]

dover *see* DAOVER

dovyr *see* DOVER¹·²

dow¹, †**dowe** /dʌu/ *v pt* **docht** †**doucht 1** to be able, have the ability to do something *la14-.* **2** to be willing, have the courage to do something; to dare (to) *18-.* **3** to be of value or use, be worthwhile *la14-18.* **4** to thrive, prosper *18-e19.* **dowless** feeble, lacking in strength or energy *la18-*; compare DAELESS. [OE *dugan*]

dow² /dʌu/ *v* to fade away, wither, wilt; to become musty or stale *18-.* **dowit**, **dowed 1** *of food* no longer fresh; dried out *17-19, 20- Sh N NE Bor.* **2** dull, faded, withered *18-19.* [unknown, compare DOWIE¹, DULL¹·¹]

dow³ /dʌu/ *adj* dismal, sad *19-.* [probably shortened form of DOWIE¹]

dow *see* DAE¹·¹, DOO

dowand, **downe** *see* DAE¹·¹

†**dowarer**, **dowariar**, **dowriar** *n* a dowager *16-17.* [MFr *doariere*]

dowbart *see* DULBERT

dowbill *see* DOOBLE¹·¹, DOOBLE¹·³

dowcare *see* DOOKER

dowchty *see* DOCHTY

dowcot *see* DOOCOT

dowdle *see* DOODLE²

dowe *see* DOW¹

dowf¹·¹, *Ork* **duff**, *Bor* **duiff** /dʌuf; *Ork* dʌf; *Bor* duf/ *n* **1** a stupid or gloomy person *18-19, 20- Ork NE EC.* **2** a dull blow with something soft *19, 20- N NE Bor.* [see the adj]

dowf¹·² /dʌuf/ *v pt* also *Bor* **duifft 1** to strike with something soft, thump *19, 20- NE T Bor.* **2** to bounce (a ball) *19, 20- EC.* **3** to be dull, slow or cautious *19, 20- NE.* [see the adj]

dowf¹·³, *Sh Ork* **duff**, *WC SW* **doof**, †**douff**, †**dolf**, †**doif** /dʌuf; *Sh Ork* dʌf; *WC SW* duf/ *adj* **1** dull, spiritless; stupid; weary *la15-.* **2** sad, melancholy *18-.* **3** *of a sound* dull, hollow *la18- NE T EC Bor.* **4** *of a part of the body* numb, insensitive *19- Sh Ork WC SW.* **5** *of excuses* feeble, failing to carry conviction *la18-19.* **6** *of ground* poor, infertile *19.* **dowfart** *adj* dull, spiritless; stupid *la18-19, 20- literary.* †**dowfart**, **doofart** *n* a dull stupid person *18-19.* †**dowffie** *adj* dull, slow, stupid *19.* **dowffie**, *H&I* **diffie** *n* a stupid person *19-.* [perhaps ON *daufr* deaf; compare Du *doof* deaf, benumbed]

dowg *see* DUG

dowie¹, †**dolly** /'dʌui/ *adj* **1** sad, dismal; dull, dispirited *la15-.* **2** ailing, weak, delicate *la19-.* **dowiely** sadly, mournfully *19-.* [probably OE *dol* foolish, stupid, unwise; compare DULLY]

dowie² /'dʌui/ *n in Eskdale* large granite stones deposited in the ice-age *20- SW Bor.* **dowie-stane** a large granite stone *20- SW Bor.* [unknown]

dowite *see* DUTY

dowl *see* DOOL³·¹

dowless *see* DAELESS

dowlet *see* DOUBLET

dowll *see* DWALL¹

dowly /'dʌule/ *adj* sad, doleful *la18-19, 20- Bor.* [perhaps ON *daufligr* or DOWIE¹]

down *see* DOON¹·¹, DOON¹·², DOON¹·³

downe *see* DAE¹·¹

down-sittin, **downsitting** *see* DOONSITTIN

dowp¹·¹, **doup**, *Ork* **doop**, †**dolp** /dʌup; *Ork* dup/ *n* **1** the buttocks *la17-.* **2** the end of a used candle *18-.* **3** the lower part or furthest edge (of something) *la18-.* **4** the stub of a cigarette or cigar *20-.* **5** the bottom of an eggshell *la16-19, 20- Ork N NE EC.* **6** the seat of a pair of trousers *19, 20- NE T EC.* **7** a loop or the set of loops of the short HEDDLE used in weaving gauze *19.* **doup-end** the bottom end *20-.* **doup-scour** a thump on the buttocks *19- NE.* †**e dolp** *see* EE¹. [compare Du *dop* a shell, a knob; MDu *dop* an eggshell; LG *dop* an eggshell, a nutshell, a fingertip]

dowp¹·², **doup** /dʌup/ *v* to dump a person down smartly on the buttocks (in the initiation ceremony of burgesses) *la18- NE EC.* **doup doon** to sit down, squat *19- NE.* [see the noun]

dowr *see* DOUR¹·¹

dowriar *see* DOWARER

dowse *see* DOUCE

dowt *see* DOOT¹·², DOUT

dowter, **dowthir** *see* DOCHTER

dowth *see* DOUTH

dowtit *see* DOIT²·²

†**doxie** *n* a sweetheart *19.* [EModE *doxy* a beggar's mistress, a prostitute]

doxy, **duxy** /'dɔksi, 'dʌksi/ *adj* lazy, slow, lethargic *19- NE T.* [unknown]

doylt *see* DOILT

doym *see* DOOM¹·¹

doze, **dose** /doz/ *v* **1** to sleep (lightly), fall in to a light sleep, drowse *la18-.* **2** to spin a top so fast that it appears not to move; to spin like a top *19- EC Bor.* **3** to stupefy, stun *la18-19, 20- Ork EC.* **dosed** *of wood, cloth or rope* rotten *19- N Uls.* [compare rare ON *dúsa* to doze]

†**dozen** *v* to be or become cold or numb *18-19.* [back-formation from DOZENT]

dozen *see* DIZZEN

dozent, **dozened**, †**dosinnit** /'dozənt, 'dozənd/ *adj* **1** stupefied, dazed, stupid *la14-.* **2** physically weakened (through age or drink) *la14-.* **3** *of wood or fruit* rotten *18, 20- T EC.* **4** damned *la19- NE.* **5** numb, stiff with cold *la18-19.* [unknown; compare DAIZE, DAZENT]

dozie¹·¹ /'dozi/ *n* a stupid person *20- EC SW Bor.* [see the adj]

dozie¹·², **dozy** /'dozi/ *adj* stupid *20-.* [reduced form of DOZENT]

drabble¹·¹, **draible** /'drabəl, 'drebəl/ *n* **1** a spot of dirt; a dribble of food spilt while eating *19- NE T H&I SW.* **2** a small quantity of liquid food *la19- NE EC.* **3** refuse, rubbish; anything too small for use *19- T.* **drablich 1** a muddy or dirty person *20- NE.* **2** a small quantity; left-overs, refuse *20- NE.* [see the verb]

drabble¹·², **draible** /'drabəl, 'drebəl/ *v* **1** to dirty or wet (clothing or boots) *19-.* **2** to spill *19-.* **3** to drizzle with rain *20- NE T.* **drabbly** *of weather* showery, drizzly *20- NE.* **drabblichy** = *drabbly.* [LG *drabbeln*]

dracht *see* DRAUCHT¹·¹

drack *see* DRAIK

draem *see* DREAM¹·¹, DREAM¹·²

draff, †**draf** /draf/ *n* dregs; the refuse of malted grain after brewing *la15-.* **draffie** out of condition, unable to walk or run easily *20- N NE T Bor.* **†draff-pock, draff-poke** a sack for carrying dregs or refuse; an imperfection, a blemish *17-e19.* [ME *draf*]

draft *see* DRAUCHT[1.1]

drag *see* DREG[3.1], DREG[3.2]

draggle *see* DRAIGLE[1.1], DRAIGLE[1.2]

dragle *see* DRAIGLE[1.2]

dragon, dragoun *see* DRAIGON

†dragy, dregy *n* a piece of confectionery, a sweetmeat *14-16*; compare DROG[1.1] (sense 2). **dragie muskie** sweetmeats flavoured with musk *la16-e17.* [ME *dragge, dragie*]

draible *see* DRABBLE[1.1], DRABBLE[1.2]

draidgy *see* DREDGIE

draidle *see* DRIDDLE[1.2]

draif *see* DRAVE, DRIVE[1.2]

draig *see* DREG[1], DREG[3.1], DREG[3.2]

draigle[1.1], **draggle** /ˈdregəl, ˈdragəl/ *n* a dirty, untidy person *19-.* [see the verb]

draigle[1.2], **draggle, †dragle** /ˈdregəl, ˈdragəl/ *v* **1** to make (a garment) wet and dirty *16-.* **2** to move slowly or wearily, plod through rain or mud *la16-.* **3** to mix flour or meal with water *la19- NE.* **draigelt** soaked through, drenched *20-.* **†draggly** straggly, untidily dressed *e19.* [frequentative form of ME *dragge* to drag]

draigon, dragon, *SW* **dreggen, †dragoun** /ˈdregən, ˈdragən; *SW* ˈdregən/ *n* **1** a dragon *la14-.* **2** a paper kite *la18-.* **†rais dragoun** to cause devastation *la14.* [ME *dragoun*]

draik, drawk, drack, †drak /drek, drɔk, drak/ *v* to drench, soak *15-.* **drackie, drachy** *of weather* damp, wet, misty *19, 20- WC SW Uls.* [unknown]

dram[1.1] /dram/ *n* a (small) drink of whisky (or other alcohol); originally a weight or measure *la16-.* **be yer dram** to pay your share of the drinks *19- T EC.* [ME *dragme, dram*, Lat, Greek *drachma*]

dram[1.2] /dram/ *v* to drink alcohol, tipple *19-.* [see the noun]

dram[2] /dram/ *n* a piece of wool or cloth threaded through the ear of a sheep to identify it *la19- Sh.* [compare Norw *dram* show]

dram *see* DRUM[1]

drame *see* DREAM[1.1]

drammach *see* DRAMMOCK

drammlick /ˈdramlɪk/ *n* a small piece of oatmeal dough; a fragment of oatcake *la19- NE.* [unknown]

drammock, drummock, *SW* **drammach** /ˈdramək, ˈdrʌmək; *SW* ˈdraməx/ *n* a mixture of raw oatmeal and cold water; crowdie *la16-.* [Gael *dramag*]

drang, dreng, dring /draŋ, dreŋ, drɪŋ/ *v* to draw together, tie tightly *la19- Sh.* [ON *drengja*]

drangle *see* DRING[2.2]

drant *see* DRAUNT[1.1], DRAUNT[1.2]

drap[1.1], **droap, drop** /drap, drop, drɔp/ *n* **1** a drop (of liquid); a small quantity *la15-.* **2** the dripping of water or the line down which it drops from the eaves of a house *16-.* **3** *with omission of 'of'* a drop of, a small quantity of: ◊ *a wee drap whisky 19-.* **4** a fall; the action of dropping *la19-.* **5** a disappointment *20-.* **6** *pl* small shot, pellets *17-19, 20- NE T EC.* **7** 1/16th of an ounce Scots *17-e19.* **drappie, droppie 1** a small quantity *18-.* **2** an alcoholic drink *19-.* **†drap wecht, drop wecht** 1/16th of an ounce Scots *la16-18.* **†a drappie in yer ee** just enough drink to make you mildly intoxicated *la18-19.* **have a drap at yer nose** to have an outstanding obligation of a sensitive or private nature, such as the paying of a debt *20- NE T.* **no a drap's bluid** not a blood-relation *19-.* [OE *dropa*]

drap[1.2], **droap, drop** /drap, drop, drɔp/ *v* **1** to fall in drops; to drip *la15-.* **2** to fall vertically; to let go of (accidentally) *la16-.* **3** to cease, lapse; to stop working *la16-.* **4** to rain slightly, drizzle *la19- NE SW.* **dropping** *of weather* showery *la18-.* **drappy, droppy** *of weather* showery, drizzly *19- NE.* **drappin drouth** a showery day during a dry spell *20- NE T EC.* **†drapping pan, dropping pan** a pan used to catch the dripping from roast meat *la16-e18.* **drap-ripe, drop-ripe** *of fruit* ready to drop from ripeness *18-19, 20- T.* **drop scone** a small, round, flat cake, made by allowing thick batter to drop onto a girdle or frying pan; a pancake *20-.* **drap glasses** to drop part of an egg-white into a glass of water in order to foretell the future *la19, 20- Sh NE.* [OE *dropian*]

drappit, droppit, drapped, dropped /ˈdrapɪt, ˈdrɔpɪt, drapt, drɔpt/ *adj* **1** lowered, fallen; spilt, discarded *la17-.* **2** rare, occasional *la19- NE.* **3** *of material* spotted, speckled *16-17.* **drappit egg** a poached egg (originally poached in gravy made from the liver of a fowl) *la18-19, 20- NE.* **dropped honey** honey drained from the comb *19- SW.* **dropped scone** a pancake *20-*; compare *drop scone* (DRAP[1.2]). [ptp of DRAP[1.2]]

dratch, †drich /dratʃ/ *v* to delay, dawdle; to move slowly and heavily *la14-19, 20- Sh N T.* [unknown]

drate *see* DRITE[1.2]

draucht[1.1], **draught, draft,** *N EC* **dracht** /drɔxt, draft; *NE EC* draxt/ *n* **1** the act of pulling or hauling; haulage *15-.* **2** a load *15-.* **3** a drink; the act of drinking *15-.* **4** a drawing, a plan, an outline; a preliminary version of a document *16-.* **5** the entrails of an animal *la16-19, 20- NE T SW Bor.* **6** a sheep or cow withdrawn from the flock or herd (as unfit for breeding) *la15-19, 20- NE SW Bor.* **7** breathing; a convulsive gasping or choking *la19- NE EC.* **8** two or more cartloads brought at one time *la19- N NE.* **9** the process of drawing off water from a stream or well; a water channel or ditch *la15-19, 20- N.* **10** a scheme, a plot, a plan *la15-e19.* **11** fishing rights; a place where fish are caught *la15-e17.* **12** a cesspit *la15-16.* **13** a quantity of sawing or sawn goods; planks *16.* **†draughty** cunning, scheming *la18-19.* **draught ewe, draft ewe** a ewe withdrawn from the flock as no longer fit for breeding *la18- SW Bor.* **†draucht net** a net drawn to catch fish *15-16.* **†draucht trumpet** a war trumpet or trumpeter *16.* [ME *draucht*]

draucht[1.2], **draught** /drɔxt, draft/ *v* **1** to draw or map out, plan *la17-.* **2** to line off land with the plough by means of straight furrows *20- N NE T.* **3** to train, break in (a horse); to harness for work *20- NE.* [see the noun]

draunt[1.1], **drant, †drawnt** /drɔnt, drant/ *n* a slow, drawling way of speaking, a whine *18-.* [onomatopoeic]

draunt[1.2], **drant** /drɔnt, drant/ *v* to drawl, whine or drone *18-.* [see the noun]

drave, *Ork N* **dreef, †dreave, †draif** /drev; *Ork N* drif/ *n* **1** the annual herring fishing; compare *herrin drave* (HERRIN) *la16-19, 20- EC Bor.* **2** a shoal of fish; a catch *la16-19, 20- Ork N.* **3** a herd, a flock *16-19, 20- NE.* **4** a crowd *20- Ork N.* **†drave-boat, dreave boat, draif boit** a herring boat *la16-e19.* [OE *drāf* a drove, a herd, a crowd; compare DROVE[1.1]]

drave *see* DRIVE[1.2]

draw[1.1] /drɔ, dra/ *n* **1** a tug, a pull, a wrench *la18-.* **2** a puff at a pipe, a smoke *la19-.* **3** *in curling and bowls* a shot played so that it comes to rest on a particular spot *la19-.* [see the verb]

draw[1.2] /drɔ, dra/ *v pt* **drew, †dreuch, †drewch,** *ptp* **drawn, †drawin, †draw, †ydraw 1** to pull, drag; to cause to move *la14-.* **2** to cause to flow; to lead water in channels; to make ditches *la14-.* **3** to aim a blow; to raise one's hand or foot in attack *la15-.* **4** *in curling and bowls* to aim a shot so as to land on a particular spot at the tee *la18-.* **5** to supply, produce *la18-*. **6** *of tea* to infuse or become infused *la18-*. **7** *of a teapot* to make good tea *19-*. **8** to cart a load *19- SW Uls*. **9** *of people* to get on together *19- C SW*. **10** to milk a cow *la19- Sh NE*. **11** to pull straw or hay from a stack *18, 20- Sh N*. **12** to close shutters *20- NE T*. **13** to ornament a garment with a different material *16*. **drawin 1** *pl* earnings *la20-*. **2** a collection for charitable purposes *la20- EC*. **draars, draavers, drawers** undergarments *19-*. †**draw bed** a truckle bed, a low bed on wheels *la16-e18*. †**draw boord** an extending table *e17*. †**draw dyk** a drainage ditch *la15-16*. **draw-kiln** a lime-kiln in which the burned lime is drawn at the bottom *la18- C*. **draw-moss** the harestail cotton-grass *Eriophorum vaginatum la19-*. **draw a body's leg** to pull someone's leg *la19-*. **draw the door on yer back** to shut the door behind you *19-*. †**draw in borrowgang** to offer (land) as security *la14-15*. **drawn length** curling the force needed to bring a stone to the tee or level with another stone *la19- C SW*. **drawn sheaf** a sheaf of drawn straw *18-19, 20- Sh Ork*. **draw strae** *in thatching* to pull straw through the hands so that pieces short of the required length fall to the ground *la18-19, 20- Sh NE SW*. **draw straes** to draw lots with straws *20-*. **draw a strae afore** to tease, make fun of someone; to deceive someone *la15-19, 20- Sh N*. **draw thegither** *of the eyes* to close in sleep *19, 20- NE EC*. **draw tae 1** to come to like (someone) gradually *la19-*. **2** to head for *19, 20- NE EC*. **draw tae rain** to be likely to rain *19-*. **drawn teind** every tenth sheaf taken as tithe *18-19, 20- historical*; compare *teind sheaf* (TEIND[1.1]). **draw the tether** *in witchcraft* to wrap a tether round a cow or over a container, obtain some desired end *la16-19, 20- historical*. **draw up** to become friendly (with), get to know *18-19, 20- T EC*. [OE *dragan*]

drawk *see* DRAIK

†**drawlie** *adj* slow and slovenly *e19*. [Du *dralen* to linger]

drawn *see* DRAW[1.2]

drawnt *see* DRAUNT[1.1]

dray *see* DRY[1.2], DRY[1.3]

dre *see* DREE[1.2]

dread *see* DREID[1.1], DREID[1.2]

dreaddour *see* DRITHER[1.1]

dream[1.1], *Sh* **draem**, *Ork T* **drame**, †**dreme**, †**dreym** /drim; *Sh* ˈdrɛəm; *Ork T* drem/ *n* a vision or fantasy (during sleep); a whim, a wish, an ideal *15-*. **my dream is redd** my wish has come true; my fate is sealed *18-19, 20- NE*. [ME *drem*; compare ON *draumr*, OFris *drām*]

dream[1.2], *Sh* **draem**, †**dreme** /drim; *Sh* ˈdrɛəm/ *v* to have a dream *15-*. **dreaming bread** wedding or christening cake (placed by the recipients under their pillows) *la18-19, 20- T*. [ME *dremen*; compare ON *dreyma*, MDu *dromen*]

dreary, †**drery**, †**drerie** /ˈdriri/ *adj* dismal, gloomy, dull *la14-*. **drearifu** dismal, sad *19- NE T EC*. **drearysome** = *drearifu la18- NE T EC*. [OE *drēorig* grief-stricken, sorrowful, doleful]

dreave *see* DRAVE

drede *see* DREID[1.1], DREID[1.2]

†**dredge box** *n* a flour-dredger *la18-19*. [ME *dreg* + BOX[1.1]]

dredgie, †**draidgy**, †**dregy** /ˈdrɛdʒi/ *n* **1** a funeral feast *18-*. **2** a song of mourning, a lament *la16-19*. Compare DIRGIE. [metathesis of DIRGIE]

dree[1.1] /dri/ *n* trouble, misfortune *la18-*. [see the verb]

dree[1.2], †**dre**, †**drey**, †**drie** /dri/ *v* **1** to endure; to suffer pain or misfortune *la14-*. **2** to last or hold out; to continue *la14-*. **3** to pass or spend time miserably; to drag out an existence *18-19*. **dree yer weird** to endure your fate; to suffer the consequences of something *19-*. [OE *drēogan* to suffer, endure]

dree[2] /dri/ *v* to suspect; to fear *19, 20- NE T*. †**dreesome** dreadful, fearsome *19*. [reduced form of DREID[1.2]]

dree *see* DREICH[1.2]

dreeble *see* DRIBBLE[1.1], DRIBBLE[1.2]

dreedle *see* DRIDDLE[1.2]

dreef *see* DRAVE

dreefle *see* DRIFFLE[1.2]

dreel[1.1], **drill** /dril, drɪl/ *n* **1** formal training or exercise (for soldiers) *17-*. **2** an instrument for drilling or boring *la19-*. **3** a scolding, a dressing-down *19- N NE T*. **4** energy, forcefulness *la18-19, 20- T*. **a dreel o wind** a gale *la18-*. [probably Du *dril*]

dreel[1.2], **drill**, †**dreill** /dril, drɪl/ *v* **1** to exercise or train (soldiers) *17-*. **2** to bore, make a hole (by drilling) *la18-*. **3** to scold or rebuke *19-*. **4** *of things* to move rapidly *la18- N NE T EC*. **5** to drive with force; to hustle *la18-19, 20- Sh Ork NE*. **6** *of people* to work quickly and smoothly *20- N NE*. [MDu *drillen*]

dreel[2.1], **drill** /dril, drɪl/ *n* a shallow furrow in which seeds or potatoes are sown *18-*. **oot o ma dreel** out of one's routine *la20- NE*. **up the wrang dreel** mistaken; having taken the wrong route *la20-*. [unknown]

dreel[2.2], **drill** /dril, drɪl/ *v* to make furrows; to plant seed in furrows *18-*. [unknown]

dreep[1.1], **drip** /drip, drɪp/ *n* **1** a drop (of fluid); a very small quantity *19-*. **2** an ineffectual person *20-*. **3** (the line of) water dripping from the eaves *la19- NE T EC*. **4** a steady fall of light rain *20- NE EC Bor*. **5** a wet, dripping condition *19, 20 NE EC*. **6** a disappointment *20- N EC*. **7** a drainage channel; a ditch *la19- C*. **dreeple** a drip, a trickle *20- Sh NE T*. **Sammy dreep** an ineffectual person *20-*. [see the verb]

dreep[1.2], **drip**, †**drepe**, †**dreip** /drip, drɪp/ *v* **1** to (let) fall in drops; to shed drops *15-*. **2** to drain or strain (potatoes after boiling) *19-*. **3** to descend (from a wall) by letting oneself down to the full stretch of the arms and dropping *la19-*. **dreeper**, †**dreiper** a strainer; a draining board or frame *17-*. **dreepin 1** *pl* the last drops *la20- NE T EC*. **2** an alcoholic drink *19*. **dreeple**, **dripple** to drip, trickle *19, 20- Sh N NE*. **dreepin drought** a showery day during a spell of dry weather *20- NE T*. **dreeping roast** a constant source of income *19-*. [OE *drēopan*]

dreetle *see* DRIDDLE[1.1], DRIDDLE[1.2]

dreev *see* DRIVE[1.2]

drefle *see* DRIVEL

dreg[1], **draig**, *NE* **drig** /drɛg, dreg; *NE* drɪg/ *n pl also* †**dreggis 1** *pl* sediment *15-*. **2** *distilling* the refuse of malt from the still *18-*. **3** a small quantity, a drop (of spirits) *19, 20- EC*. **4** fine powdery lime after slaking *19*. **5** inferior wine made from the refuse of grapes *17*. **draigle, dreggle** a small quantity, a paltry sum *19-, 20- C SW*. **dreglin, draiglin** a small quantity *19-*. †**dreg wine** inferior wine made from the refuse of grapes *la16-17*. [probably ON *dreggjar* dregs]

dreg[2.1] /drɛg/ *n* a dredge used by fishermen to collect shellfish *la19- Sh*. [see the verb]

dreg[2.2] /drɛg/ *v* to dredge (for shellfish) *16-19, 20- Sh*. †**dregar** a man who dredges oysters or mussels *16*. †**dreg-boat** a dredging boat *18-19*. [perhaps specific use of DREG[3.2]]

dreg[3.1], **drag**, **draig** /drɛg, drag, dreg/ *n* **1** a sledge, a large heavy harrow *17-*. **2** the motion of the tide *la19- Sh Ork N EC*. **3** a half-load *20- Uls*. **4** haulage *la16*. **never out o the drag** never finished *la19- NE EC*. [see the verb]

dreg[3.2], **drag**, **draig** /drɛg, drag, dreg/ *v* **1** to pull along; to haul or drag *18-*. †**dreg boit, drag boit** a fishing-boat (which used a drag-net) *la15-e17*. [Du *dreggen*]

dreggen *see* DRAIGON

dregy *see* DRAGY, DREDGIE

dreich[1.1], **driech** /drix/ *n* dreariness, gloom *20-*. **the deid dreich** *see* DEID[1.2]. †**on dreich** at or to a distance *15-16*. [see the adj]

dreich[1.2], **dreigh**, *SW* **dree** /drix; *SW* dri/ *adj* **1** extensive, persistent; tiresome; hard to bear *15-*. **2** inaccessible, difficult to reach *la16-*. **3** *of people* depressed, doleful; dull, boring *17-*. **4** *of sermons or speeches* long-winded; uninteresting *17-*. **5** *of time or journeys* long, wearisome *18-*. **6** *of people* slow; backward; tardy; slow to pay debts *18-*. **7** *of the weather or scenery* dreary, bleak *la18-*. **8** *of tasks* difficult, requiring close attention *19, 20- Sh Ork NE*. **dreich drawin** slow to move, slow in deciding *la18-19, 20- NE WC SW*. [ON *drjúgr* enduring, ample]

dreid[1.1], **dread**, †**drede**, †**dred** /drid, drɛd/ *n* **1** fear, apprehension *la14-*. **2** doubt *la14-e16*. †**dreidles**, **dredles** without doubt *la14-e16*. **in a dreedfu wey** in a state of great distress *la19-*. [see the verb]

dreid[1.2], **dread**, †**drede** /drid, drɛd/ *v pt also* †**dred**, †**dredd** **1** to fear; to be afraid or in apprehension of *la14-*. **2** to suspect, surmise *la18-*. **3** to be in doubt *la15-e16*. †**ydred** awe-inspiring *e16*. [ME *dreden*, probably aphetic from OE *ondrǣdan*]

dreifle *see* DRIVEL
dreigh *see* DREICH[1.2]
dreill *see* DREEL[1.2]
†**drekters** *n* a drake's penis *la15*. [Older Scots *drake* + TERS]
dreme *see* DREAM[1.1], DREAM[1.2]
dreng *see* DRANG
drenk *see* DRINK[1.1], DRINK[1.2]
drepe *see* DREEP[1.2]
drerie, **drery** *see* DREARY

dress[1.1], †**dres** /drɛs/ *n* **1** clothing, attire *16-*. **2** a woman's gown *la18-*. **3** the action of settling affairs; a settlement *la16-e17*. [see the verb]

dress[1.2], †**dres**, †**drese** /drɛs/ *v* **1** to clothe (oneself) *la14-*. **2** to arrange, prepare; to decorate; to attend to, bandage (a wound) *la14-*. **3** to cut and smooth stone, prepare for building *16-*. **4** *weaving* to prepare a web for the loom (with starch) *18-*. **5** to iron linen *19-*. **6** to neuter an animal *20-*. **7** to put in order; to bring affairs to a satisfactory conclusion *la15-e17*. **dressed** wearing clean clothes *la20-*. †**dressory** a room in which food is dressed *e16*. **dressing iron** a smoothing iron *la17-19, 20- N*. [ME *dressen*]

dreuch *see* DRAW[1.2]
drevel *see* DRIVEL
drevin *see* DRIVE[1.2]
drew, **drewch** *see* DRAW[1.2]
†**drewellis** *npl* drudges or menials *e16*. [MDu *drevel* a scullion, a turnspit]
drey *see* DREE[1.2], DRY[1.2]
dreym *see* DREAM[1.1]

drib[1.1] /drɪb/ *n* **1** a drop, a small quantity (of liquid) *18-19, 20- NE EC Bor*. **2** *pl* dregs *18-19*. [perhaps reduced form of DRIBBLE[1.1]]

drib[1.2] /drɪb/ *v* to extract the last drops of milk from a cow *la19- NE*. [see the noun]

drib[2] /drɪb/ *v* **1** to beat, thrash *la19- Sh N NE*. **2** to scold *la19- N NE*. [probably variant of DRUB; compare Norw dial *dribba* to thump, strike against something]

dribble[1.1], **dreeble** /'drɪbəl, 'drɪbəl/ *n* **1** a trickle; a drop (of alcohol) *la17-*. **2** *weather* a light drizzle *la18-19, 20- NE C SW*. **dribblach** a slight trickle *la19- NE*. **dribbly beards** curly kail boiled in fat broth *18-19, 20- Uls*. [see the verb]

dribble[1.2], **dreeble** /'drɪbəl, 'drɪbəl/ *v* **1** to drizzle *19-*. **2** to trickle or fall in drops; to spill or slobber *la19-*. **3** to tipple, drink alcohol *la18-19, 20- T*. [EModE *drible*]

drich *see* DRATCH
dridder *see* DRITHER[1.1], DRITHER[1.2]
driddle[1.1], *Sh* **druttil**, *NE* **dreetle** /'drɪdəl; *Sh* 'drɒtəl; *NE* 'drɪtəl/ *n* **1** a slow, awkward or helpless person *19- Sh NE SW*. **2** a small quantity of something *la19- Sh NE T*. [see the verb]

driddle[1.2], **draidle**, **dreedle**, *Sh* **drittle**, *NE* **dreetle** /'drɪdəl, 'drɛdəl, 'drɪdəl; *Sh* 'drɪtəl; *NE* 'drɪtəl/ *v* **1** to walk slowly or uncertainly; to dawdle, saunter *la18-*. **2** to potter, idle, waste time *19-*. **3** to spill, dribble; to let fall through carelessness *19-*. **4** to urinate in small quantities *19- T EC*. **5** to play the fiddle, strum an instrument *19- WC SW*. †**dridland** dribbling excrement *la16*. [onomatopoeic with infl from DRIBBLE[1.2], DIDDLE[3.2]]

drie *see* DREE[1.2]
driech *see* DREICH[1.1]
dri'en *see* DRIVE[1.2]

drieshach /'drɪʃəx/ *n* the glowing embers of a peat fire *19- N NE*. [Gael *grìosach* burning embers]

drife *see* DRIVE[1.2]

driffle[1.1] /'drɪfəl/ *n* **1** a flurry of rain or snow *19- SW Bor*. **2** a scolding *la19- NE T*. **3** a gale, a strong wind *la19- NE*. [see the verb]

driffle[1.2], *NE T* **dreefle** /'drɪfəl; *NE T* 'drifəl/ *v* **1** to drizzle; to rain or snow lightly *17-18, 19- SW Bor*. **2** to scold *la19- NE T*. **3** to delay, put off *la16*. [compare Norw dial *drivla* to drizzle]

drift[1.1] /drɪft/ *n* **1** (slow) movement, impetus *la15-*. **2** driving snow; an accumulation of snow (driven by the wind) *la16-*. **3** a set of fishing-nets suspended from a cable and allowed to drift with the tide *19, 20- NE*. **4** a drove, a flock, a herd *la15-e19*. **5** delay, procrastination *la16-e17*. **drifty** snowy *18-*. **drift net** a fishing net with weights attached to the bottom and floats attached to the top (allowed to drift with the tide) *19-*. [ME *drift*, related to OE *drīfan* to drive; compare ON *drift* a snow-drift]

drift[1.2] /drɪft/ *v* **1** to move with a current or the wind; to wander aimlessly *la18-*. **2** to delay *la16-e17*. †**drift time** to make delays *la16-17*. [see the noun]

drifter /'drɪftər/ *n* a fishing vessel which uses drift nets *la19-*. [DRIFT[1.2], with agent suffix]

drig *see* DREG[1]
drill /drɪl/ *v* to move slowly, loiter *20- Sh Ork*. [Norw dial *drila*]
drill *see* DREEL[1.1], DREEL[1.2], DREEL[2.1], DREEL[2.2]

drilt[1.1], **drult** /drɪlt, drʌlt/ *n* **1** a person who loiters or drags behind; a clumsy person *la19- Sh Ork*. **2** a heavy trudge, laborious effort in carrying *20- Sh Ork*. [see the verb]

drilt[1.2], **drult** /drɪlt, drʌlt/ *v* **1** to walk clumsily or heavily *la19- Sh Ork*. **2** to carry something heavy *20- Sh Ork*. [Norw dial *drilta*]

†**dring**[1] *v* to sing in a slow, droning way *18-19*. [probably onomatopoeic]

dring[2.1] /drɪŋ/ *n* a lazy person *la18- WC Uls*. [unknown]

dring[2.2] /drɪŋ/ *v* to loiter, delay *19, 20- literary*. **dringle**, †**drangle** to saunter, dawdle *la18-19, 20- Ork Bor*. [unknown]

†**dring**[3] *n* a poor or miserly person *16*. [probably OE *dreng* a lad, a warrior]

dring *see* DRANG

drink[1.1], †**drynk**, †**drenk** /drɪŋk/ *n* **1** drinkable liquid; a beverage *la14-*. **2** alcohol; an alcoholic beverage *la15-*. **drink siller** a gratuity (to be spent on drink) *la15-19, 20- NE EC*. **nae sma drink** of considerable importance *la18-*. [OE *drenc*]

drink[1.2], *Bor* **drenk**, †**drynk** /drɪŋk; *Bor* drɛŋk/ *v ptp* **drunken**, †**drucken**, †**drukken** **1** to swallow liquid *la14-*. **2** to

consume alcohol (to excess); to squander by drinking alcohol *la14-*. **drinkin** *of the day* to draw in *20- N NE*. †**ydrunkin** drowsy, as if intoxicated *e16*. **drinking sowans** the liquor left after straining sowans *19, 20- NE*. [OE *drincan*]
†**drint, drynt** *adj* drowned *e16*. [ME *dreinte*]
drip see DREEP¹·¹, DREEP¹·²
dripple see DREEP¹·²
drite¹·¹, *Sh Ork* **drit**, †**dryt** /drʌɪt; *Sh Ork* drɪt/ *n* **1** dirt, excrement *la14, la19- Sh Ork NE EC*. **2** *derogatory* a person *20- Ork*. [see the verb]
drite¹·², *NE* **drate**, †**dryte** /drʌɪt; *NE* dret/ *v pt* **drate**, *ptp* **dritten**, †**drate** to defecate *16-*. [OE *gedrītan*]
drither¹·¹, †**dridder**, †**dreaddour**, †**dredour** /'drɪðər/ *n* fear, dread; apprehension, distrust *15-19, 20- EC*. [DREID¹·¹, with suffix by analogy with words such as TERROR]
†**drither**¹·², **dridder** *v* to fear or dread; to hesitate *la18-19*. [see the noun]
drittle see DRIDDLE¹·²
driv /drɪv/ *n* drizzle, a passing shower *20- Sh Ork*. [Faer, Swed *driv* fine rain]
driv see DRIVE¹·²
drive¹·¹ /drʌɪv/ *n* **1** the act of driving; a trip in a vehicle *la18-*. **2** a forceful blow or swipe *19-*. **3** a private road *19-*. [see the verb]
drive¹·², †**drife**, †**dryf** /draev/ *v pt* **drave**, **driv**, *NE* **dreev**, †**draif**, *ptp* **driven**, *SW Uls* **druv**, *Bor* **dri'en**, †**drevin** †**dryve 1** to cause to go (with force or speed), direct a course; to chase *la14-*. **2** to convey (in a vehicle) *la14-*. **3** *golf* to strike the ball for a distance shot (in playing off the tee) *la15-*. **4** *of a ship or wreckage* to wash or drift ashore *15-18, la19- Sh*. **5** to throw with force or speed *19, 20- NE*. **6** to smash or burst open *la15-19*. **7** to pass time idly, live out *la14-e17*. **driver**, †**dryffar 1** a person who drives livestock or vehicles *15-*. **2** *in curling and bowls* the team leader *19*. **driving putter** *golf* the club used for pitching shots onto the green *19-*. †**drive aff** to pass time *e18*. †**drive on** *of time* to pass *la18*. **drive ower** to spend one's life; to pass or waste time; to delay *15-e19*. **drive pigs** to snore loudly *20-*. †**drive the pigs through somebody's game** to interfere with; to upset plans *e19*. **drive swine** = drive pigs. [OE *drīfan*]
drivel, †**drevel**, †**drefle**, †**dreifle** /'drɪvəl/ *v* to talk or think incoherently *16-*. †**dreflyng, dravillyng** confused thinking in sleep *e16*. [ME *drevelen* to dribble; to talk childishly]
driven see DRIVE¹·²
drizzen /'drɪzən/ *v* to make a low, plaintive sound; to moan *la18-19, 20- NE SW Uls*. [MDu *druysschen* to emit a hollow, roaring sound]
droap see DRAP¹·¹, DRAP¹·²
drob /drɔb/ *v* to prick with a sharp instrument *19- T*. [onomatopoeic]
droch see DROICH
drochle¹·¹ /'drɔxəl, 'drɔxəl/ *n* **1** a short, dumpy person; a puny, insignificant person *19-*. **2** a fat, dumpy animal, small of its kind *la19- NE EC*. [perhaps diminutive form of DROICH]
drochle¹·² /'drɔxəl, 'drɔxəl/ *v* to walk slowly and feebly; to dawdle *la19- NE*. **drochlin**, †**droghling 1** puny, dwarfish *la18-19, 20- NE*. **2** lazy *19, 20- NE*. [see the noun]
drocht see DROUTH
drod /drɔd/ *n* a short, thickset person *19- Bor*. [unknown]
droddum /'drɔdəm/ *n* the buttocks *la18-19, 20- NE T*. **dress yer droddum** to give someone a thrashing *la18-*. [unknown]
drog¹·¹, *EC* **drogue**, †**droig** /drɔg; *EC* drog/ *n* **1** a medicinal preparation; a drug *la15-19, 20- N NE EC SW Uls*. **2** a kind of confectionery (made of spices) *16-e17*; compare DRAGY.

†**drogester** a pharmacist *17*. **droggie** a nickname for a pharmacist *la19- NE EC*. **droggist**, †**drogest** a pharmacist *la17-19, 20- N NE*. [ME *drogge*]
drog¹·² /drɔg, drog/ *v* to administer a drug *20- NE*. [see the verb]
†**drogarie** *n* medicine; a drug *16-17*. [MFr *droguerie*]
drogat see DRUGGET
drogester see DROG¹·¹
droggat, drogget, droggit see DRUGGET
drogue see DROG¹·¹
droich, droch /drɔɪx, drɔx, drox/ *n* a dwarf, a person of restricted growth *16-*. [perhaps altered form of DWERCH; compare Gael *troich*]
droig see DROG¹·¹
droin see DRUNE¹·²
droity /'drɔɪti/ *n* an old clay pipe *20- Sh*. [Norn *droiti*]
drokin see DRUCKEN
drøn see DRUNE¹·¹
drone¹·¹ /dron/ *n* **1** the bass pipe of a bagpipe *16-*. **2** a monotonous (buzzing) sound *17-*. **3** a bagpipe *16-e19*. [unknown]
drone¹·² /dron/ *v* to talk monotonously; to make a low, continuous, buzzing sound *16-*. **droner** a bumble-bee *la19- NE T*. [unknown]
drone² /dron/ *n* the buttocks, the backside *la18-19, 20- NE T*. [Gael *dronn*]
dronk see DRUNK
dronkart see DRUNKART
dronkin see DRUNKEN
droog see DRUG¹·¹, DRUG¹·²
drooglan /'druglən/ *adj* messy, dirty; heavy *20- N*. [voiced frequentative variant of presp of DROOK¹·²]
droogled /'drugəld/ *adj* drenched, soaked *20- NE*. [voiced frequentative variant of ptp of DROOK¹·²]
drook¹·¹, **drouk** /druk/ *n* a drenching, a soaking state *19, 20- T EC*. [see the verb]
drook¹·², **drouk**, †**drowk** /druk/ *v* to drench, soak; to steep *16-*. **droukin** dripping with moisture *la19-*. **drookle** to drench, soak *20- Sh NE EC*. [unknown; compare ON *drukna* to be drowned]
drookit, droukit, drooked /'drukət, 'drukəd/ *adj* drenched, soaked *17-*. **drookit stour** mud *20-*. [ptp of DROOK¹·²]
drool¹ /drul/ *v* to utter or cry sadly; to sound mournfully *19- Bor*. [unknown]
drool² /drul/ *n* a lazy person *19, 20- Bor*. [unknown]
droon, droun /drun/ *v ptp* also **droondit 1** to (cause to) suffer death by drowning *la14-*. **2** to flood, inundate; to submerge, sink *la14-*. **3** to spoil a drink by over-dilution *la19-*. **droon the miller 1** to dilute alcohol with too much water; to add too much milk to tea *19-*. **2** to go too far, go to excess *19-*. **3** to (cause to) go bankrupt *19- WC Bor*. [ME *drounen*]
droosy, †**drousy** /'druzi/ *adj* sleepy, drowsy *la16-19, 20- NE*. [EModE *drowsy*]
drooth see DROUTH
droothy see DROUTHY
drop see DRAP¹·¹, DRAP¹·²
dropped, droppit see DRAPPIT
droppie see DRAP¹·¹
drop scone see DRAP¹·²
dross, †**dros**, †**drosse** /drɔs/ *n* **1** impurities, slag (from melted metal) *la16-*. **2** small coal, coal-dust *la18-*. **3** rubbish, something worthless *la18-*. **4** small change *20-*. **5** small particles; fragmented plant material *16-e19*. [OE *drōs*]
droucht see DROUTH
drouchty see DROUTHY
droud /drʌud/ *n* a (poor quality) codfish *19- WC*. [unknown]
drouk see DROOK¹·¹, DROOK¹·²

droukit see DROOKIT
droun see DROON
drousy see DROOSY
drouth, drooth, drocht, droucht, †drowth /druθ, drɔxt, druxt/ *n* **1** drought, very dry weather; drying breezy weather *la15-*. **2** thirst *16-*. **3** a drunkard, a habitual drinker *la19-*.
drouchtit thirsty, parched *20- NE*. [OE *drūgað*]
drouthy, droothy, drouchty, druchty /ˈdruθi, ˈdruθe, ˈdrʌxte/ *adj* **1** dry *la16-*. **2** thirsty; addicted to drinking alcohol *la18-*. [DROUTH + -IE²]
drove¹·¹ /drov/ *n* **1** a flock, a crowd; compare DRAVE *18-*. **2** a stonemason's broad-faced chisel *19- N NE*. [OE *drāf*]
drove¹·² /drov/ *v* **1** to prepare stone for building using a broad-faced chisel *la18-19, 20- N NE T*. **2** to drive cattle or sheep, work as a drover *la17-19*. [see the noun]
drove road /ˈdrov rod/ *n* a road or track originally used for driving cattle or sheep to markets *18-*. [DROVE¹·¹ + ROAD¹·¹]
drow¹·¹ /drʌu/ *n* **1** a cold, wet mist, a sea-fog; a drizzle *17-*. **2** a squall *e17*. **drowy** misty, drizzling, damp *19-*. [unknown]
drow¹·² /drʌu/ *v* to drizzle *19, 20- Bor*. [unknown]
drow² /drʌu/ *n* an attack of illness, a fainting fit; a spasm of anxiety *la16-19, 20- NE T EC*. [unknown]
drowarier, drowiar see DROWRIAR
drowk see DROOK¹·²
drowlack /ˈdrʌulək/ *n* a seat with a rope attached for lowering a person over a precipice *19- N NE*. [Gael *drolag* a swing]
drowre see DRURIE
†drowriar, drowiar, drowarier *n* a dowager *16*. [MFr *doariere*; compare DOWARER]
†drowry *n* love, a love token; a sweetheart *la14-16*. [ME *druerie*]
drowry see DRURIE
drowth see DROUTH
drub /drʌb/ *v* **1** to beat, thrash *la18-*. **2** to scold, verbally abuse *19, 20- NE T EC*. [EModE *drub*]
druchty see DROUTHY
drucken, drukken, †drukkin, †drokin /ˈdrʌkən/ *adj* inebriated, drunken *16-*. **druckenness, †drukkennes** drunkenness *16-19, 20- Ork*. **†druckensome, drukkinsum** inclined to drink too much *la16-19*. [ON *drukkinn*, ptp of *drekka* to drink]
drucken see DRINK¹·²
drug¹·¹, **N droog** /drʌg; N drug/ *n* a rough pull, a tug *la18-19, 20- N*. [see the verb]
drug¹·², **N droog** /drʌg; N drug/ *v* to pull forcibly, drag *15-19, 20- N NE SW*. [ME *druggen* to do menial tasks, labour, drudge]
drug¹·³ /drʌg/ *adj of slightly thawed ice used for curling* dragging, slow, sticky *19, 20- C SW*. [see the verb]
drugget, druggit, *H&I* **droggat, †drogget, †drogat, †droggit** /ˈdrʌgət; *H&I* ˈdrogət/ *n* a coarse wool or wool-blend cloth *la16-*. **druggit scone** an oatmeal and potato scone *20- WC SW Bor*. [Fr *droguet*]
drukken see DRUCKEN, DRINK¹·²
drukkin see DRUCKEN
drult see DRILT¹·¹, DRILT¹·²
drum¹, **†dram** /drʌm/ *adj* sad, dejected; sulky *16-19, 20- NE*. [unknown]
drum² /drʌm/ *n* **1** a percussion instrument *la16-*. **2** the cylindrical part of a threshing machine *19-20, 21- historical*. **drum fu, drum fou** as tight as a drum, full (of food) *la19- NE T EC*. **drum-major** *n* a domineering woman *19-*. **drum-major** *v* to domineer, order around *20-*. [ME *drom*]
drum³ /drʌm/ *n* **1** a long narrow ridge or knoll; frequently in place-names *18-*. **2** *pl* an area of ridged land intersected by marshy hollows *19- SW*. **†drumeheid** the head of a ridge *e17*. **drumlin** a ridge, especially a long whaleback mound of glacial deposit (occurring in groups in low-lying areas) *la19-*. [Gael, IrGael *druim* back, the ridge of a hill]
Drum⁴ /drʌm/ *n* an informal name for the Drumchapel district of Glasgow *la20- WC*. **The Drum** Drumchapel *la20- WC*. [shortened form of *Drumchapel*]
drumble see DRUMLE¹·²
drumblie see DRUMLIE
drumle¹·¹ /ˈdrʌməl/ *n* **1** a confusion, a jumble *la19- NE T*. **2** mud raised when water is disturbed *19- Bor*. [see the verb]
drumle¹·², **†drumble** /ˈdrʌməl/ *v* to make muddy, confuse, disturb *17-19, 20- Bor*. [probably back-formation from DRUMLIE]
drumlie, drumly, †drumblie /ˈdrʌmli/ *adj* **1** *of water* clouded, muddy, unsettled *16-*. **2** *of weather* cloudy, gloomy, dark *16-*. **3** *of people and things* troubled, disturbed, muddled, confused *17-*. **4** *of alcohol* full of sediment *la18-19*. [perhaps altered form of ME *drubli* turbid]
drummock see DRAMMOCK
drummoid /drʌˈmɔɪd/ *adj* dull, dejected *20- N*. [altered form of DRUMMURE, DEMUIRED]
drummure /drʌˈmjur/ *adj of people* serious, sad-looking, dejected *19- N NE SW Bor*. [altered form of Older Scots or EModE *demure*; compare DEMUIRED]
drumshorlin /drʌmˈʃɔrlɪn/ *adj* miserable, dejected; sulky *19- WC*. [unknown; compare *Drumshoreland* in West Lothian]
drunckart see DRUNKART
drune¹·¹, **drøn** /drun, drøn/ *n* a low, plaintive sound; a wail, a cry *19, 20- Sh N*. [Norw dial *dryn* a weak bellowing]
drune¹·², **droin** /drun, drɔɪn/ *v* to moan, complain; *of cows* to low plaintively *19, 20- Sh Ork*. [Norw dial *drynja* to utter a weak, drawn-out sound]
drunk, †dronk /drʌŋk/ *adj* intoxicated *la16-*. **as drunk as muck** very drunk *la19, 20- Sh T*. [ptp of DRINK¹·²]
drunkart, drunkard, †drunckart, †dronkart, †drunkat /ˈdrʌŋkərt, ˈdrʌŋkərd/ *n* a person who is habitually drunk, an inebriate *la15-*. [from the adj DRUNK, with noun-forming suffix]
drunken, †drunkin, †drunkyn, †dronkin /ˈdrʌŋkən/ *adj* inebriated; addicted to alcohol *la14-*. **drunkensome, drunkensum** inclined to drink too much *la15-19, 20- NE*. [ptp of DRINK¹·²]
drunken see DRINK¹·²
drunt¹·¹ /drʌnt/ *n* the sulks, a fit of ill humour *19- EC SW Bor*. **take the drunt** to take offence *la18-19, 20- SW*. [unknown]
drunt¹·² /drʌnt/ *v* to sulk *19, 20- NE SW*. [unknown]
Druntin /ˈdrʌntən/ *n* Trondheim, Norway *18-19, 20- Ork*. [altered form of the place-name *Trondheim*]
†drurie, drowry, drowre *n* **1** a dowry *la15-19*. **2** a gift *e16*. [altered form of Older Scots *dowry*, with infl from DROWRY affection, a love-gift]
drush¹ /drʌʃ/ *n* powdery waste, small fragments (of peat) *18-19, 20- Sh NE*. [compare DROSS]
drush² /drʌʃ/ *n* a great multitude (of people or fish) *20- Ork*. [Norw dial *drose* a troop, a flock, a large shoal]
druttil see DRIDDLE¹·¹
druv see DRIVE¹·²
dry¹·¹ /drae/ *n* a flaw or crack in a stone *19, 20- NE EC*. [see the adj]
dry¹·², **†dray, †drey** /drae/ *v* to make or become dry; to rid of moisture *15-*. **dryster, †drystar** the person in charge of the drying of grain in a kiln *la15-19, 20- N NE T EC*. **dry yer greetin een** to stop complaining *21-*. [OE *drȳgan*]
dry¹·³, **†dray** /drae/ *adj* **1** *of land* not under water; not subject to flooding; not marked by a watercourse *la12-*. **2** lacking

water; not exposed to wetting; free from moisture; dried out *15-*. **3** cold, unfriendly, impassive *15-*. **4** thirsty *16-*. **dryward** dull, prosy *la19- Sh*. **dry blows** blows not drawing blood *la16-19, 20- Ork*. †**dry burgh, dry burrow** a burgh not situated on the coast *la16-17*. **dry darn** see DARN[1]. **dry drift** powdery snow *la19- NE T C*. **dry-dyke** a DRYSTANE wall *19-*. **dry-dyker** a builder of DRYSTANE walls *19-*. **dry-field** land above flood level, especially in the Forth and Tay valleys *la18-*. **drying green** a grassy patch (with clothes poles) for the drying of laundry *20-*. **dry-haired** *of cattle* not sleek-coated, having a rough coat *19, 20- NE*. **dry-keep** *farming* cattle feed consisting of turnips and straw *20- N NE*. †**dry lodging** lodging without board *la18-e19*. †**dry march** a land boundary not marked by the sea or a river *15-17*. **dry-mou'd** not drinking, not having a glass of alcohol *19- NE EC*. **dry multure** *law* an annual duty of money or grain paid to a mill, whether the grain was ground there or not *la15-19, 20- historical*. †**dry seat** a commode *17-e19*. **dry shave** the rubbing of another's cheek with an unshaven chin or with the fingers *20-*. **dry siller** money, hard cash *la19- NE EC*. †**dry stool, dry stule** a commode *la16-e18*. †**dry tapstar** a retailer of ale who does not brew it *la15-e17*. **dry thow** a thaw after a high wind *20-*. **dry time** a spell of dry weather *20- NE*. †**dry ware, dry wair 1** goods packed in barrels for transport by sea *16-17*. **2** the casks used for transporting goods *16-e17*. **as dry as a horn** thoroughly dry *19-*. [OE *drȳge*]

dryachty /ˈdraeəxti/ *adj of the weather* inclined to be dry *20- NE*. [DRY[1.3], with *-achty* suffix]

dryf, dryffar see DRIVE[1.2]

drynk see DRINK[1.1], DRINK[1.2]

drynt see DRINT

drystane, drystone, *NE* **drysteen** /ˈdraestən, ˈdraeston; *NE* ˈdraestin/ *adj of a stone wall* constructed without mortar *la16-*. **drystane dyke** a stone wall built without mortar *18-*. **drystane dyker** a person who builds *drystane dykes la19-*. [DRY[1.3] + STANE[1.1]]

dryt see DRITE[1.1]

dryte see DRITE[1.2]

dryve see DRIVE[1.2]

du see THOU

dub[1.1], *WC SW* **dib,** †**doub** /dʌb; *WC SW* dɪb/ *n* **1** a muddy or stagnant pool, a pond; a water-hole in a moss *la15-*. **2** a puddle, a pool of rain water *la15-*. **3** *humorous* the ocean, the sea *la18-*. **4** a sea pool (only visible at low tide) *19- EC Bor*. **5** *pl* mud *16-19, 20- NE*. **6** a bog *20- Sh*. **dub-skelper** a person who travels rapidly regardless of the state of the roads; a rambling fellow *18-19, 20- NE EC*. **dub water** dirty water *18-19, 20- EC*. [MLG *dobbe*]

dub[1.2] /dʌb/ *v* to cover with mud *19- NE*. [see the noun]

†**dub**[2] *v* to consign, condemn *e16*. [unknown]

dubby, dubbie /ˈdʌbe, ˈdʌbi/ *adj* **1** muddy, miry *19-*. **2** abounding in puddles or small pools; wet, rainy *19-*. [DUB[1.1] + -IE[2]]

duble see DOOBLE[1.1], DOOBLE[1.3], DOOBLE[1.4]

dublit see DOUBLET

dubreck see DOOBRACK

ducat see DOOCOT

†**duchall quhite** *adj of hose* made from light-coloured material *e16*. [unknown]

duchas /ˈduxəs/ *n* the (right to) possession of land on which one's ancestors have lived *18-19, 20- historical*. [Gael *dù(th)-chas* the place of one's birth; a hereditary right]

†**Ducheland, Dutchland** *n* Germany *15-17*. [MDu *Dutsch* + LAND[1.1]]

†**duchery** *n* a dukedom, a duchy *la15-16*; compare *dukerie* (DUKE). [Older Scots *duché*, with *-ery* suffix]

duchtie see DOCHTY

duck /dʌk/ *n* a small stone used in a children's game; the game itself *19-*. **duckie, dockie 1** a rounded stone used in roadmaking *20- T EC*. **2** a small stone used in a children's game *20- T*. [unknown]

duck see DEUK

ducker see DOOKER

dud /dʌd/ *n* **1** a (ragged) article of clothing; a cloth or a rag; *pl* rags, ragged clothes *16-*. **2** a coarse linen or cotton cloth used for domestic purposes, a duster, a dishcloth *la18-*; compare *hand dud* (HAN[1.1]). **3** a dull, spiritless person *19*. **duddie** ragged, tattered *18-*. **duddies** (ragged) clothing *la18-*. **Dudsday** one of various Ayrshire hiring markets *19-20, 21- historical*. [unknown]

†**dudderon, duddroun** *n* a lazy, slovenly or ragged person *16-e19*. [unknown]

†**dude** *v* do it *la15-e19*. [reduced form of 'do it']

dudgit /ˈdʌdʒət/ *n* a clumsy parcel or pack *20- NE*. [variant of DILGIT or DULSHET, probably conflated with Eng *budget*]

Dudsday see DUD

due, †**dew** /dʒu/ *adj* **1** rightful, fitting, proper *la15-*. **2** *of a payment or obligation* owing *17-*. †**dew service, do service, deservice** feudal service to a SUPERIOR *la15-e17*. **be due** *of people* to be indebted, owe *la17-*. [ME *du*]

duell see DWALL[1]

due sober /dʒu sobər/ *adj* quite sober *la19- WC SW Uls*. [Older Scots *dew* exactly + SOBER[1.2]]

duff[1] /dʌf/ *v* to pull out of an undertaking *20- Bor*. [unknown]

duff[2] /dʌf/ *n* **1** the soft or spongy part of something *19-*. **2** peat moss or fallen leaves *19-*. **3** soft peat (unsuitable for burning) *20- Sh*. **duffie 1** soft, spongy; dry *19- Sh C Bor*. **2** *of coal* soft, inferior *19- EC*. **dufftin** a soft, crumbly, inferior peat *la19- NE*. **duff mould** peat moss or fallen leaves *19-, 20- Sh*. [variant of Scots *dough* or onomatopoeic]

duff see DOWF[1.1], DOWF[1.3]

duffie /ˈdʌfe, ˈdʌfi/ *n* a lavatory *la19- Ork EC Bor*. [unknown; compare YUFFIE]

dug, doag, dog, doug, dowg, †**doig** /dʌg, dog, dɔg, dʌug/ *n* **1** a dog, a hound *15-*. **2** a lever used by blacksmiths in hooping cart-wheels *18-19, 20- NE*. **3** a kind of cannon *16-17*. **4** a grapple for hoisting weights *16*. †**doggar** a dog-keeper *e16*. **dog daisy** the ox-eye daisy *Leucanthemum vulgare la19- SW*. †**dog dollour** the Dutch lion dollar *e17*. †**dog drave** ruin, utter confusion *18-19*. **dog's flourish** one of various umbelliferous plants *20-*. **dog flower** the dandelion *Taraxacum officinale 20- Ork*. **dog-heather** ling heather *Calluna vulgaris 19- NE T*. **dog-hillock** a small mound or hillock covered with long grass *la16- N NE T*. **dog-hip** the fruit of the dog rose *Rosa canina*, the rosehip *18-*. **dog-hole** a hole left in the wall of a building as an entrance for a dog *la19- NE T*. **dog's paise** the meadow vetchling *Lathyrus pratensis 20- Ork NE*. **dog-thistle** the sowthistle *Sonchus oleraceus 20- Ork NE*. **dog too** = *dog hillock 20- Sh Ork*. **dog's wages** food given as the only wages for service *la18-19, 20- NE*. **dog afore his maister** the swell of the sea that often precedes a storm *la19- N NE*. **the dug's baws** something very good of its kind *20-*. [ME *dogge*, rare and probably stylistically marked in OE]

dug see DOG

†**dugged, douget, doggit** *adj* **1** obstinate; determined *la19*. **2** ill-tempered, cruel *15-17*. [DUG + -IT[2]]

†**duggeoun** *n* dudgeon, a kind of hard wood *16-e17*. [ME *dogeon*, EModE *dudgeon*]

dughty see DOCHTY

†**dugon, dogon** *n* a term of abuse for a man *16-e19*. [probably altered form of DAGONE]
duiff *see* DOWF[1.1]
duifft *see* DOWF[1.2]
duigis *see* DEUGS
duik *see* DUKE
duill *see* DOOL[1.1]
duir *see* DOOR
duist *see* JIST[1.2]
duke, †**duk**, †**duik** /dʒuk/ *n* **1** a hereditary title of nobility ranking below prince, a duke *la14-*. **2** a ruler, a leader, a commander of an army *15-16*. †**dukerie** a dukedom *la16-19*; compare DUCHERY. [ME *duk*]
duke *see* DEUK
Duke of Argylls /dʒuk əv ar'gʌɪlz/ *n* haemorrhoids, piles *21-*. [rhyming slang]
dukes /dʒuks/ *npl* haemorrhoids, piles *21-*. [shortened form of DUKE OF ARGYLLS]
Dulap *see* DUNLOP
†**dulapse** *n* Presbyterian Church a second offence against church discipline *la18*; compare TRILAPSE. [Lat *du-* two- + Lat *lapsus* a fall; compare TRILAPSE, QUADRULAPSE, RELAPSE[1.1]]
dulbert, †**dowbart** /'dʌlbərt/ *n* a person considered to be stupid or foolish *16-17, 19- SW Bor*. [perhaps DULL[1.2] + BARD[1]; compare Ger *Dummbart*]
†**dulcorate, dulcorait** *adj of the voice* endowed with sweetness *16*. [Lat *dulcōrātus*]
dule *see* DOOL[1.1], DOOL[1.2], DOOL[2]
dulget *see* DILGIT
dulk *see* DOOK[1.2]
dull[1.1] /dʌl/ *v* **1** to make dull *15-*. **2** to become dull or inert *la15-e16*. [see the adj]
dull[1.2], †**dul** /dʌl/ *adj* **1** slow to understand or learn *la15-*. **2** deaf, hard of hearing *16-*. **3** lacking interest or excitement, not lively or bright; listless *la16-*. **dull o hearing** hard of hearing *18-*. [OE *dol* foolish, stupid, unwise]
dull *see* DOOL[2]
†**dully** *adj* doleful, gloomy, dismal *la15-16*. Compare DOWIE[1]. [unknown]
dulse *see* DILSE
dulshet, dulshoch /'dʌlʃət, 'dʌlʃəx/ *n* a small or untidy bundle *19- NE*. [unknown; compare DILGIT, DUDGIT]
dult /dʌlt/ *n* **1** a dolt, a person considered to be stupid *la18-19, 20- Sh N WC SW*. **2** the pupil at the bottom of the class, the dunce *19, 20- WC SW*. [variant of EModE *dolt*]
dult *see* DOOL[2]
dumb, †**dum** /dʌm/ *adj* **1** unable to speak; refraining from speech, silent, taciturn *la14-*. **2** lacking intelligence *19-*. **dummie 1** a mute person *la16-*. **2** a foolish person *19-*. **dumb window** a blocked-up window *la19- T EC*. **the dumb deid** the dead of night *20-*. [OE *dumb*]
dumba /'dʌmba/ *n* fine particles of corn removed by winnowing *la19- Sh*. [ON *dumba* dust, a cloud of dust]
†**Dumbarton youth** *n* a person (usually a woman) over thirty-five years old *e19*. [from the place-name + YOUTH]
dume *see* DOOM[1.1], DOOM[1.2]
dumfooner, dumfouner /dʌm'funər/ *v* to bamboozle, astonish *la19-*. [emphatic form of Eng *dumbfound*]
dumfoonert, dumfounert /dʌm'funərt/ *adj* dumbfounded *19-*. [ptp of DUMFOONER]
dumfoutter /dʌm'futər/ *v* to bewilder; to startle or irritate *19- N NE T*. [conflation of DUMFOONER with FOUTER[1.2]]
dummie *see* DUMB
dummygrane *see* DEMYGRANE
dump[1.1] /dʌmp/ *n* a blow, a thump, a thud *19, 20- Sh NE*. **the dumps** a children's birthday ritual in which the recipient is lifted or struck a number of times, corresponding with the age reached *20-*. [unknown]
dump[1.2] /dʌmp/ *v* **1** to beat, thump or kick *la16-*. **2** to walk with short, heavy steps; to stump about *19- N EC SW*. **dumper 1** *mining* a tool for keeping a borehole circular *la19-*. **2** a tool used in paving roads, a rammer *la19- C*. [unknown]
dump[1.3] /dʌmp/ *adv* with a thump or thud *19- NE EC SW*. [unknown]
dump[2] /dʌmp/ *n* a hole scooped in the ground for playing marbles *19- T Bor*. **dumps** a game of marbles played in a hole *19- T Bor*. [compare Norw *dump* a depression in the ground]
dumpik /'dʌmpɪk/ *n* a lump; a divot *la19- Sh*. [perhaps Eng *dump* an object of dumpy shape, with diminutive suffix]
dumplin, dumpling /'dʌmplɪn, 'dʌmplɪŋ/ *n* **1** a rich, boiled or steamed fruit pudding *18-*; compare *clootie dumpling* (CLOOTIE[1]). **2** a stupid person *la20-*. [perhaps Eng *dump* an object of dumpy shape, with *-ling* suffix]
dumpy[1.1] /'dʌmpe, 'dʌmpi/ *n* **1** a breed of short-legged fowl *la19-*. **2** a short, thickset person *e19*. [unknown]
dumpy[1.2] /'dʌmpe, 'dʌmpi/ *adj* short and stout *19-*. [unknown]
dun, †**doon** /dun/ *n archaeology* an iron-age stone-walled defensive homestead; a fortified eminence *la17-*. [Gael *dùn*, IrGael *dún* a fort, a fortification]
Dunbar wether, Dunbar wedder, †**Dunbar weather** /dʌn'bar weðər, dʌn'bar wɛdər/ *n* a salted herring *la18, 19- Bor*. [from the East Lothian coastal town + WEDDER]
dunch[1.1], **dunsh** /dʌnʃ/ *n* **1** a blow; a bump, a nudge *19-*. **2** a butt from an animal *la19- WC SW Uls*. **dunchach**, *T* **dunsheugh 1** a heavy blow, a thud; a nudge *la19- NE T*. **2** a large, untidy bundle (of rags) *la19- NE*. [unknown]
dunch[1.2], **dunsh**, †**dunsche** /dʌnʃ/ *v* **1** to punch, thump; to bump or nudge *la17-*. **2** *of an animal* to butt with the head or horns *la18- C SW Uls*. [unknown]
dundee *see* DINDEE
Dundee, †**Dundie**, †**Dunde** /dʌn'di/ *n* a city on the Firth of Tay *15-*. **Dundee cake** a rich fruit cake usually decorated with almonds *19-*. †**Dunde gray, Dundie gray** a type of cloth produced in Dundee *16*. **Dundee steak** processed meat, Spam *la20- EC*. [Gael *Dùn Dèagh* Fort of Daig(h)]
dunder[1.1], **dunner**, *NE* **dinner** /'dʌndər, 'dʌnər/ *NE* 'dɪnər/ *n* **1** a loud rumbling noise; a commotion; *la18-*. **2** a violent, noisy blow *la18-*. [see the verb]
dunder[1.2], **dunner** /'dʌndər, 'dʌnər/ *v* **1** to make a noise like thunder; to rumble, thump or bang *la18-*. **2** to move quickly and noisily *la18-19, 20- Bor*. [perhaps frequentative form of DIN[1.2]; compare Norw *dundre* to thunder, rattle, bang]
dunderheid, †**dunnerheid** /'dʌndərhid/ *n* a person considered to be stupid or foolish *la19-*. [altered form of EModE *dunderhead*]
Dundie *see* DUNDEE
dune, *NE* **deen** /dun/ *NE* din/ *adv* very, extremely *19, 20- NE EC Bor*. [ptp of DAE[1.1]]
dune *see* DAE[1.1]
dung *see* DING[1.2]
dungel[1.1], **dongle** /'dongəl, 'dɒŋgəl/ *n* a lump, a clod; a lump of unbaked dough *la19- Sh*. [Norw *dunge* a heap, a mass, with diminutive suffix]
dungel[1.2] /'dɒŋgəl/ *v* to pelt with clods of earth *la19- Sh*. [see the noun]
dungeon, †**dungeoun**, †**dongeoun** /'dʌnʒən/ *n* **1** the great tower or keep of a castle; a dark subterranean place of confinement *la14-*. **2** a person of great knowledge *18-*. **a dungeon of learning** a deep repository of knowledge or a very knowledgeable person *20-*. [ME *dongoun*]
dungin *see* DING[1.2]

dungstead /'dʌŋstɛd/ *n* a midden, a dunghill *19, 20- NE T EC SW Bor*. [Older Scots *dung* + *stead* (STEID¹·¹)]

duniwassal, dhuine wassel /duni'wasəl/ *n* a clansman of rank below the chief; a gentleman of secondary rank *la16-18, 19- historical*. [Gael *duin(e)-uasal*]

dunk¹·¹, †**dank**, †**donk** /dʌŋk/ *n* moisture, a mouldy dampness; a damp building or place *16-*. **dunky** somewhat damp or moist *16-19, 20- Sh Ork*. [unknown]

dunk¹·², **dank**, †**donk** /dʌŋk, daŋk/ *adj* damp, moist *15-*. [unknown]

dunk²·¹ /dʌŋk, døŋk/ *n* a bang or thump *20- Ork*. [Norw *dunk*]

dunk²·² /dʌŋk, døŋk/ *v of a boat* to bump around on the waves *20- Ork*. [see the noun]

dunkle¹·¹ /'dʌŋkəl/ *n* a dent or depression *19- WC SW*. [see the verb]

dunkle¹·² /'dʌŋkəl/ *v* to dent or make a slight depression in *19, 20- SW*. [diminutive and frequentative of DUNT¹·²]

Dunlop, †**Dunlap**, †**Dulap**, †**Delap** /dʌn'lɔp/ *n* **1** a village and parish in Ayrshire *16-*. **2** = Dunlop Cheese *19-*. **Dunlop cheese** a kind of sweet milk cheese originally made in West-Central Scotland *la18-*. [Gael *dùn* fort + unknown second element]

dunmont *see* DINMONT

dunna *see* DINNAE

dunner *see* DUNDER¹·¹, DUNDER¹·²

dunnerheid *see* DUNDERHEID

dunnert *see* DONNERT

dunny /'dʌni/ *n*, a basement, a cellar; an underground passage in a tenement building *19- C*. [reduced form of DUNGEON]

dunsche *see* DUNCH¹·²

dunsh *see* DUNCH¹·¹, DUNCH¹·²

dunt¹·¹, †**dint**, †**dynt**, †**dont** /dʌnt/ *n* **1** a heavy or dull-sounding blow or stroke, a knock *la14-*. **2** a shock; a deep impression, an impact; a blow to the fortunes, a disappointment *la14-*. **3** a throb or quickened beat of the heart *la18-*. **4** (the sound of) a heavy fall, thud, or bump *19-*. **5** a dig, an insult; a slanderous lie *19-*. **6** a lump, a large piece (of food) *19-*. **7** the wound caused by a heavy blow *la19-*. **8** a dent *20-*. **9** a chance, occasion or opportunity *16-19, 20- Sh*; compare *steal a dint* (STEAL¹·²). **the verra dunt** the very thing *20- NE SW*. [OE *dynt*]

dunt¹·², †**dint**, †**dont** /dʌnt/ *v* **1** to beat, strike or stamp heavily; to thump, bump or knock (so as to produce a dull sound) *la15-*. **2** *of the heart* to thump, beat violently; to palpitate *la16-*. **3** to crush or dent (by striking) *la19-*. **4** to shake together the contents of a container or a sack by knocking on the ground *la19- NE T SW*. **5** *of an injury* to throb *20- N NE T*. **dinted** *folklore* struck by an elf-arrow or Cupid's arrow *la18-19, 20- SW*. **dunt-aboot** a servant who is roughly shifted from one piece of work to another *20- T SW Bor*. **duntle doon** to pay a forfeit in a game played with a teetotum *19- T*. **dunt oot** to settle (a quarrel or misunderstanding) by discussion, thrash out *la18- NE T*. [see the noun]

dunt²·¹, †**daunt**, †**dent** /dʌnt/ *n* a wooden disc (made of two barrel-heads nailed together) used to press down salted herrings into barrels; the action of pressing down with such a disc *la18-19, 20- NE*. [see the verb]

dunt²·², †**daunt**, †**dant** /dʌnt/ *v* to press salted herrings into a barrel with a wooden disk *17-19, 20- NE*. [probably a specialized sense of DUNT¹·²]

dunter /'dʌntər/ *n* **1** the porpoise *Phocoena phocoena*; the dolphin *Grampus griseus 19- Sh Ork N NE Bor*. **2** = *dunter duck 18- Sh EC SW Bor*. **dunter duck** the eider duck *Somateria mollissima la18- Sh Ork N SW Bor*. †**dunter goose** = *dunter duck la17-e19*. [probably DUNT¹·², with agent suffix]

†**duntibour, dounteboir, dontybour** *n derogatory* a woman, an attendant at court *16*. [unknown]

†**dunty** *n* a mistress *18-e19*. [shortened form of DUNTIBOUR]

duoy /'duɔɪ/ *n* a great-grandchild *la19- Sh Ork*. [Gael *dubhogha* a great-grandson's grandson]

†**duplar** *adj* = DUPLATE *la15*. [Lat *duplāris* containing double]

†**duplate** *adj music* having two beats in the bar *la15-e16*. [Lat *duplātus* doubled]

duplicand /duplɪ'kand, 'duplɪkand/ *n law* a doubling or doubled amount of feu-duty for one year at certain specified intervals or occasions *la18-*. [Lat *duplicandō* with or by doubling]

duply¹·¹ /du'plae/ *n law* a second answer, the defender's rejoinder to the pursuer's reply *la16-19, 20- historical*. [MFr *duplique*]

duply¹·² /du'plae/ *v law* to answer, make a rejoinder or second reply *16-*. [OFr *dupliquer*]

†**durand** *prep* throughout, during *la14-16*. [perhaps ME *duraunt*]

†**durato** *n* duretto, a coarse durable cloth *e17*. [Ital *duretto*]

durb *see* DERB

durdum *see* DIRDUM

dure *see* DOOR, DOUR¹·¹

durk¹·¹, *SW* **durg** /dʌrk; *SW* dʌrg/ *n* something big and clumsy; a lump; a large clumsily-built person *la19- Sh Ork NE SW*. **durky 1** thickset, squat *19- T*. **2** clumsy *20- Ork*. [Norw dial *dorg* a heap; a heavy, slovenly woman; compare Gael *dorc, durc* a lump, a shapeless piece]

durk¹·² /dʌrk/ *v* to bungle, ruin (a job) *19- NE EC*. [see the noun]

durk *see* DIRK¹·¹, DIRK¹·²

durkin /'dʌrkən/ *n* a short, thickset person; a short thick weapon *la19- NE Uls*. [Gael *durcan*, diminutive of *durc* (see DURK¹·¹)]

durrie *see* DOORIE

durst *see* DAUR¹

durt *see* DIRT¹·¹, DIRT¹·²

durty *see* DIRTY¹·¹

dush¹·¹, †**dusch** /dʌʃ, duʃ/ *n* a heavy blow, a violent jolt *la14-19, 20- NE T*. [perhaps onomatopoeic; compare DOOSE¹·¹, DOOSHT¹·¹, DOIST¹·¹]

dush¹·² †**dusch** /dʌʃ, duʃ/ *v* **1** to push, beat or strike with force; to butt with horns *la14-*. **2** to fall heavily *la14-16*. **3** to rush or dash (violently) *15-e16*. [see the noun]

dussoun *see* DIZZEN

dust *see* DIST

duster *see* DISTER

dusty *see* DISTY

dutch, ditch, †**dich**, †**dych** /dʌtʃ, dɪtʃ/ *n* a trench, a ditch *16-*. [OE *dīc*]

Dutchland *see* DUCHELAND

duty, †**dewty**, †**dewite**, †**dowite** /'djuti, 'dʒute/ *n* **1** a payment required by an authority, a tax *la15-*. **2** an obligation *la15-*. **3** a service or payment owed to a feudal superior; feu duty *15-20, 21- historical*. [ME *duete*]

duvat *see* DIVOT¹·¹

duvvle *see* DEIL

dux /dʌks/ *n* the best pupil in a school, class or subject *la18-*. [Lat *dux* a leader]

duxy *see* DOXY

duyl *see* DOOL¹·¹

dwaam *see* DWAM¹·¹, DWAM¹·²

dwabble *see* DWAIBLE¹·¹, DWAIBLE¹·², DWAIBLE¹·³

dwadle /'dwadəl, 'dwɔdəl/ *v* to loiter, tarry *la19- N EC SW*. [perhaps altered form of DODDLE²·² or Eng *dawdle*]

dwaffle /ˈdwafəl, ˈdwɔfəl/ *adj* limp, soft; weak, feeble *19, 20- NE*. [unknown]

dwaible[1.1], *SW* **dwabble** /ˈdwebəl; *SW* ˈdwabəl/ *n* a weak, helpless person *la19, 20- SW*. [unknown]

†**dwaible**[1.2], **dwabble** *v* to totter, walk feebly *la19*. [unknown]

dwaible[1.3], *NE* **dweeble**, †**dwabble** /ˈdwebəl; *NE* ˈdwibəl/ *adj* **1** weak, feeble; shaky *la18- NE T EC*. **2** flexible; flabby *la19- NE T EC*. **dwaiblie**, *WC* **dwobbly** shaky, wobbly, weak *la19-*. [unknown]

dwall[1], **dwell**, †**duell**, †**dowll** /dwal, dwɛl/ *v* **1** to reside, stay, live permanently *la14-*. **2** to remain or continue (in a state or situation); to linger over, think habitually about *la14-*. **3** to delay *la14-15*. **dwallin**, **dwalling**, **dwelling 1** a place of residence, an abode *la14-*. **2** a person's household or retinue *la14-e15*. [OE *dwellan* to lead into error, mislead, deceive]

dwall[2.1] /dwɑl/ *n* a snooze; a lull *la19- Sh*. [Norw *dvale* sleep, hibernation]

dwall[2.2] /dwɑl/ *v* to fall into a light slumber *la19- Sh*. [see the noun]

dwam[1.1], **dwalm**, **dwaam**, **dwaum**, †**dwawm** /dwam, dwɔm/ *n* **1** a swoon, a fainting fit; a sudden attack of illness *16-*. **2** a stupor; a daydream *19-*. **3** a doze *la19- Sh*. **dwamie** sick, faintish, dreamy *la19-*. **dwaamish** = *dwamie la19- Sh NE EC*. **dwamle** a sick or faint turn *19-*. [compare OE *dwolma* confusion, MDu *dwelm* stupefaction]

dwam[1.2], **dwalm**, **dwaam**, **dwaum** /dwam, dwɔm/ *v* **1** to faint or swoon *la16-*. **2** to sicken or ail; to decline in health *19, 20- EC*. **3** to fall asleep, take a nap *20- Sh*. **4** to grow faint, fade *la18-19*. **dwamle** to faint; to appear faint *la19, 20- NE*. **dwaam ower** to fall asleep *20- Sh*. [see the noun]

dwamfle /ˈdwamfəl/ *adj* flexible, loose, sagging *20- NE*. [variant of DWAFFLE]

dwamle *see* DWAM[1.1], DWAM[1.2]

dwang[1.1] /dwaŋ/ *n* **1** a transverse piece of wood inserted between joists or posts to strengthen them *la15-*. **2** an iron lever or wrench *la18-*. **3** toil, labour; rough handling *la18- NE T*. **4** a bar of wood used for tightening ropes *la19, 20- NE*. [compare Du *dwang* compulsion, restraint]

dwang[1.2] /dwaŋ/ *v* **1** to compel; to oppress, harass or worry *la16-19, 20- NE T*. **2** to toil, work hard *la18- T*. [compare Du *dwingen* to force]

dwaum *see* DWAM[1.1], DWAM[1.2]
dwawm *see* DWAM[1.1]
dweeble *see* DWAIBLE[1.3]
dwell *see* DWALL[1]

†**dwerch**, **dorche**, **dearch** *n* a dwarf *la15-e16*; compare DROICH. [OE *dweorh*]

dwimish *see* WINNISH

dwine[1.1], **dwyne** /dwʌɪn/ *n* a decline, a waning *19-*. [see the verb]

dwine[1.2], **dwyne** /dwʌɪn/ *v* **1** *of people or animals* to pine, waste away, fail in health *la15-*. **2** *of things* to (cause to) fade or wither *16-*. **dwiney** sickly, pining *20- N NE EC*. [OE *dwīnan*, ON *dvína* to dwindle, pine away]

dwinnle /ˈdwɪnəl/ *v* to dwindle *19-*. [diminutive form of DWINE[1.2]]

dwyne *see* DWINE[1.1], DWINE[1.2]

dy, **dai**, †**die** /dae/ *n* a wave; a swell in the sea *la19- Sh Ork*. [unknown]

dy *see* THY
dyakill *see* DYCAL
dyall *see* DIAL
dyamont *see* DIAMOND
dyang *see* GANG[1.2]
dyat *see* DIET[2]
dyaug *see* DAG[2]
dyaun *see* GAE

dycal, **diakel**, †**diacle**, †**dyakill** /ˈdʌɪkəl, ˈdʌɪəkəl/ *n* a small compass or dial (used in a fishing boat) *la15-18, 19- Sh Ork*. [probably diminutive form of DIAL]

dyce *see* DICE[1.1], DICE[1.2]
dych *see* DUTCH
dyde *see* DAE[1.1]

dyester, †**dyster**, †**dayster** /ˈdaestər/ *n* a dyer *la17-19, 20- N NE Bor*. [ME *deister(e)*]

dyet *see* DIET[1], DIET[2]

dyke[1.1], **dike**, *Sh* **daek**, *N* **dick** /dʌɪk; *Sh* dɛk; *N* dɪk/ *n* **1** a wall (of stones or turf), a mound (of earth); frequently in place-names *14-*. **2** *in geology and mining* a vein of igneous rock in a vertical fissure in the earth's strata *la18-*. **3** a hedge *20- WC SW*. **4** new-cut peats built like a wall to dry *20- Sh*. **5** a ditch, a trench; frequently in place-names *13-16*. **dykie** the hedge-sparrow *Prunella modularis 19- WC SW Bor*. **dykeback** the back of a wall *la18-*. **dyke-end 1** the end of a dyke *la19-*. **2** a dyke built on the ebb-shore, running seaward (to prevent animals from trespassing) *la19- Sh*. **dike louper**, **dyke louper 1** an animal which leaps the dyke surrounding its pasture *la18-19, 20- NE EC Bor*. **2** a person of immoral habits *19- EC Bor*. **dykeside** the ground alongside a dyke *la16-*. [OE *dīc* a ditch]

dyke[1.2], *N* **dick** /dʌɪk; *N* dɪk/ *v* **1** to surround, enclose, shut (in or out) with a wall *la14-*. **2** to build or repair a stone or turf dyke *la15-*. **dyker**, †**dikar** a builder of dykes *la13-*. **dykit 1** *of land* enclosed with a dyke *16-*. **2** *of a road in a mine* cut off by a fault *20- EC*. [see the noun]

Dyker /ˈdʌɪkər/ *n* a nickname for a native of Cellardyke in Fife *19- T EC*. [shortened form of the place-name *Cellardyke*]

dykon *see* DEACON
dylt *see* DOILT
dymynew *see* DIMINEW
dyn *see* DIN[1.1], DIN[1.2]
dyndill *see* DINNLE[1.2]
dyne *see* DIN[1.1], DINE[1.1], DINE[1.2]
dyner *see* DENNER[1.1]
dyng *see* DIGNE
dynmonth *see* DINMONT
dynnill *see* DINNLE[1.2]
dynt *see* DUNT[1.1]
dyoch *see* DEUCH
dyochree *see* DEOCHRAY
dyod *see* DOD[2]
dyour *see* DYVOUR
dyow *see* DEW[1.1]
dyowr *see* DYVOUR

dyper /ˈdʌɪpər/ *v* to adorn, deck out *la19- NE Uls*. [OFr *diasprer*]

dyrie, †**derry** /ˈdaeri/ *n* a dairy *19, 20- NE*. [variant of Eng *dairy*]

dyrk *see* DERK[1.1], DERK[1.3]
dyrkyn *see* DERKEN
dys *see* DICE[1.1], DICE[1.2], DIS
dysemale, **dysmall** *see* DISMALL
dyst *see* DOIST[1.1], DOIST[1.2]
dyster *see* DYESTER
dyt *see* DITE[1.1], DITE[1.2]
dyte *see* DITE[1.1], DITE[1.2], DOIT[2.2]
dytt *see* DIT

dyvour, †**dyour**, †**dyowr**, †**dyver** /ˈdaevər/ *n* **1** a debtor, a bankrupt *15-*. **2** a rogue, a good-for-nothing person *19-*. †**dyvourie**, **dyvorie** debtorship, bankruptcy *la16-17*. [unknown]

E

e see EE[1], HE[1.2]
E see AH
eace see ACE
eacher see AICHER
eachy peachy[1.1] /ˈitʃi ˈpitʃi/ *n* a word used in children's counting-out rhymes *la20-*. [see the adj]
eachy peachy[1.2] /ˈitʃi ˈpitʃi/ *adj* much alike, even, six and half-a-dozen *la20- WC*. [probably altered form of EEKSIE-PEEKSIE]
eadwul see EEDOL
eage see AGE
eaggle-baggle see HAGGLE-BAGGLE
eaggle-bargin see HAGGLE-BARGAIN[1.2]
eagle, †aigle, †egill, †egle /ˈigəl/ *n* a bird of prey, an eagle *15-*. [ME *egle*]
eame see EEM[2]
ear[1], **†ere, †er, †eyr** /ir/ *n* the organ of hearing; hearing, attention *la14-*. **†ear whoop, ear woup** an earring *la17*. [OE *ēare*]
†ear[2], **ere, are** *v* to plough *15-19*. [OE *erian*]
ear see AIR[5.2]
'ear see YEAR
-ear see -ER
eard see YIRD[1.1], YIRD[1.2]
eardfast see YIRDFEST[1.2]
eariwig[1.1] /ˈiriwɪg/ *n* an earwig *20- T H&I C SW Uls*. [altered form of Eng *earwig*]
eariwig[1.2] /ˈiriwɪg/ *v* to eavesdrop *la20-*. [see the noun]
earl, *Sh* jarl, *NE SW Bor* yirl, *Bor* yerl, †erle, †eryll, †ʒerl /ɛrl/; *Sh* jarl; *NE SW Bor* jɪrl; *Bor* jɛrl/ *n* **1** a nobleman; a count *la14-*. **2** in Shetland the principal guiser in the Up-Helly-Aa celebrations *20-*, compare *guizer jarl* (GUISER). **Earl Marischal** a title conferred on Sir William Keith and his heirs *la15-*. **Earl o Hell 1** the Devil *19-*. **2** a wild lawless character *19*. [OE *eorl*, ON *earl, jarl* nobleman]
ear leather, †ere ledder /ˈir ˈlɛðər/ *n* a strap in a horse's harness *la15-19, 20- SW*. [altered form of *near leather* (NEER); initial *n-* lost by wrong division after *a*]
earn, erne, *Ork* yirn, †yearn, †eirn, †airn /ɛrn; *Ork* jɪrn/ *n* **1** an eagle *la14-*. **2** the white-tailed or sea eagle *Haliaeetus albicilla la18- Sh Ork NE*. **3** the golden eagle *Aquila chrysaetos la18-19, 20- Sh Ork N*. [OE *earn*]
earn see YIRN[1]
earn-bleater /ˈɛrn ˈblitər/ *n* the common snipe *Gallinago gallinago la18-19, 20- NE*. [unknown; compare *heather bleater* (HEATHER)]
earnest[1.1], **airnest, eernest, †ernist, †eirnist, †ernest** /ˈɛrnəst, ˈɛrnɛst, ˈɪrnəst/ *n* seriousness *la14-*. **†ernystfull, ernistfull** serious *la15-16*. [OE *eornost*]
earnest[1.2], **airnest, eernest** /ˈɛrnəst, ˈɛrnəst, ˈɪrnəst/ *adj* sincere, serious; intense *la16-*. [OE *eornoste*]
earock, *Uls* errick /ˈirək; *Uls* ˈɛrɪk/ *n* a young hen, a pullet *la18-19, 20- Sh NE H&I WC Uls*. Compare ARRO. [Gael *eireag*]
Earse see ERSE[2.1], ERSE[2.2]
eart, earth see YIRD[1.1]
earthfast see YIRDFEST[1.2]
ease[1.1], **†ese, †eys, †aise** /iz/ *n* **1** comfort, freedom from hardship or difficulty; advantage, convenience *la14-*. **2** a reduction or remission of an amount or service due *la17-18*. **3** (the act of) relieving the bowels *15-e17*. **4** (a source of) pleasure, satisfaction *la14-16*. **easedom** comfort, leisure, relief from anxiety *19- Sh NE*. **easefu** giving ease or comfort *la14-*. **†do your ese** to relieve the bowels *15-16*. **†put to ane ese** to bring to a settlement, arrange satisfactorily *e17*. [ME *ese*]
ease[1.2], **†ese, †eys** /iz/ *v* **1** to relieve (hardship or pain); to give comfort to *la14-*. **2** to take one's ease, enjoy ease *la14-e15*. **3** to supply (with); to provide; to advance (money) *la16-e18*. [see the noun]
ease[2] /iz/ *n* a children's ball-game *la19- NE*. [unknown]
†easedrop, esedrop *n* (the space receiving) the dripping of water from the eaves of a house *la15-16*. [OE *efes* eaves + *drop* (DRAP[1.1])]
easel see EASTLE[1.1], EASTLE[1.2]
easement, *T* aisment, †esement, †aisiament, †esiament /ˈizmənt; *T* ˈɛzmənt/ *n* **1** personal comfort or convenience; relief from physical discomfort or inconvenience *la15-*. **2** the act of relieving the bowels *20-*. **3** comfortable accommodation or lodgings *la18-e19*. **4** a material advantage in connection with the occupation of a property *la14-e17*. [ME *esement*]
easin, eezin, easing, *Sh* esin, *Sh* aeshin, †eising /ˈizɪn, ˈizɪŋ; *Sh* ˈesɪn, ˈeʒɪn/ *n* **1** *pl* the eaves of a building *la16-*. **2** the part of a haystack where the thatch begins *la18-*. **3** *pl* the angular space between the top of the side wall and the roof inside a house *la17-19, 20- Sh Ork NE H&I*. **4** the edge of the sky, the horizon *20- NE*. **†easing drop** = EASEDROP *la16-19*. **easin-gang** the course of sheaves which makes a projecting edge to the thatch to keep rain off a stack *19-*. [OE *efesung* haircut, tonsure]
easlins see EAST[1.3]
east[1.1], **aist, †est, †eist** /ist, est/ *n* the direction of the rising sun *la14-*. [OE *ēast*]
east[1.2], **aist, †est, †eist** /ist, est/ *adj* situated in or towards the east, eastern *13-*. **†eastlin** eastern, easterly *18-19, 20- Bor*. **eastmaist, eastmost, †estmast** most easterly *15-*. **†eastlan, eistlan** belonging to or of the east *17-19*. [OE *ēastan* from the east]
east[1.3], **aist, †est, †eist** /ist, est/ *adv* **1** towards the east *la14-*. **2** in the east; on the east side *la15-*. **3** in a particular direction: ◊*move that ashet a bittie east 18-*. **eastlins, *NE* easlins** eastwards *la18-19, 20- Sh NE*. [see the adj]
east[1.4], **†eist** /ist/ *prep* in an easterly direction (along a road), eastwards *la16-*. **east the toun** towards the east of the town *19- N T EC Bor*. [see the adj]
eastart[1.1], **eastard** /ˈistərt, ˈistərd/ *n* the east *la18-*. [see the adj]
eastart[1.2], **eastard** /ˈistərt, ˈistərd/ *adj* easterly *la19-*. [OE *ēast-weard*]
eastart[1.3], **eastard, †estwart** /ˈistərt, ˈistərd/ *adv* eastwards *la15-*. [see the adj]
easten[1.1], **esten** /ˈistən, ˈɛstən/ *n* the eastern part of a district *la19- Sh*. [see the adj]
easten[1.2], **†estin** /ˈistən/ *adj* east, eastern *16-19, 20- Sh T Bor*. [EAST[1.3], with *-en* suffix]
easter[1.1] /ˈistər/ *n* the east wind *la19, 20- NE*. [see the adj]

easter[1,2], *Sh* **aester** /ˈistər; *Sh* ˈestər/ *v of wind* to shift towards the east *20- Sh NE T*. [see the adj]

easter[1,3], †**ester**, †**eister** /ˈistər/ *adj* eastern, lying towards the east, the more easterly of two places (contrasted with wester); frequently in place-names *13-*. †**the eister seas** the Baltic *la16-e17*. [OE *ēastra*]

eastick, **istek** /ˈistək/ *adj of weather* cold, showery *la19- Sh*. [unknown]

Eastie /ˈisti/ *n* the occupant of a farm which includes 'east' or 'easter' in its name *la19- NE T*. Compare WASTIE. [EAST[1,2] + -IE[1]]

eastle[1,1], **easel** /ˈistəl, ˈisəl/ *adv* towards the east, eastwards *19, 20- Bor*. [EAST[1,3], with -*le* suffix]

eastle[1,2], **easel**, †**eistell**, †**estald** /ˈistəl, ˈisəl/ *prep* to the east of *la18- Bor*. †**an eistell** to the east of *la15-e17*. [see the adv]

easwas, **eizewas**, **eisewaas** /ˈizwaz, ˈeɪzwaz/ *npl* the top of the walls of a house on which the rafters rest; the inner angle between the level top of a wall and the sloping edge of roof, often serving as a shelf *20- N*. [OE *efes* eaves + WA[1,1]]

easy[1,1], **aisy**, *Sh* **aesy**, †**esy** /ˈizi, ˈeze; *Sh* ˈɛzi/ *adj* **1** free from trouble or difficulty, requiring little effort *15-*. **2** accommodating; unconstrained; moderate; gentle *la15-* **3** simple, straightforward: ◊*it's easy speakin 19-*. **be easy said til** to be yielding or amenable *la19- NE T*. [ME *esi*]

easy[1,2], **aisy**, †**esy** /ˈizi, ˈeze/ *adv* easily *la16-*. [see the adj]

easy-osy[1,1] /ˈizi ˈoze/ *n* an easy-going or lazy person *la19, 20- Bor*. [see the adj]

easy-osy[1,2], **easy-ozy** /ˈizi ˈoze/ *adj of people* easy-going, inclined to be lazy; *of things* involving the minimum of effort *19-*. [reduplicative compound based on EASY[1,2]]

eat[1,1], *Sh* **et**, *NE* **ett**, *NE* **ait** /it; *Sh NE* ɛt; *NE* et/ *n* **1** the action of eating *19- NE*. **2** what is eaten, a meal or feast *20- NE*. [OE *ǣt*]

eat[1,2], *Sh Uls* **aet**, *N* **eyt**, *NE* **ait**, *NE Bor* **ett**, †**ete** /it; *Sh N NE Uls* et; *NE Bor* ɛt/ *v pt* **ate**, *NE Bor Uls* **eet**, *C Bor* **ett**, *T EC* **eated**, †**eit**, *ptp* **etten**, *N* **eytin**, *SW* **aten**, †**eattin 1** to consume food *la14-*. **2** to cause or allow grass to be eaten by grazing animals: ◊*he eats the herbage with his sheep la14-19, 20- Sh NE T H&I SW*. **eaten corn** growing oats eaten by trespassing animals *la17-20, 21- historical*. **ate meat**, **eat meat** an idler, a parasite *la19- NE*. **eaten an spued pale**, unhealthy-looking *la18-*. **eat the cow and wirry on the tail** to fail or lack success because of one small thing; to be a stickler for trivialities *18-*. †**eat in your words** to eat your words, retract *18-e19*. **aten oot o ply** *of an animal* lean despite being well-fed *19- SW*. **eat yersel** to be extremely annoyed or vexed *la19- Sh NE T*. **eat yer thoom** = *eat yersel la18-*. [OE *etan*]

eat-breid *see* AIT

eatch *see* EETCH

eated *see* EAT[1,2]

eaten *see* AITEN

eather *see* AITHER[1,1], AITHER[1,4]

eattin *see* EAT[1,2]

eavesdrop /ˈivzdrɔp/ *n law* the SERVITUDE permitting the shedding of rainwater from a roof on to an adjoining property *la18-*. [OE *efes* eaves + *drop* (DRAP[1,1]); compare EASEDROP]

eb *see* EBB[1,1], EBB[1,2], EBB[1,3]

ebb[1,1], †**eb** /ɛb/ *n* **1** the going out of the tide *16-*. **2** the foreshore *la15-19, 20- Sh Ork N NE H&I*. **ebb sleeper** the dunlin *Calidris alpina 19- Sh*. [OE *ebba*]

ebb[1,2], †**eb** /ɛb/ *v* **1** *of the sea or tide* to recede *la14-*. **2** *of a boat* to be grounded at low tide *la14-17*. [OE *ebbian*]

ebb[1,3], †**eb** /ɛb/ *adj* **1** *of the sea or the tide* low, at the ebb *15-*. **2** *of the mind* lacking depth or capacity, frivolous *17-*. **3** *of furrows or ditches* shallow; *of mining excavations* near the surface *18-*. **4** *of liquid in a container* shallow *17-19, 20- NE EC Bor*. **5** *of cloth* narrow *la17-19, 20- Bor*. †**ebness** shallowness, scarcity *17*. [see the verb]

ebbasay, **abbacee**, **ah-bay-say**, **A B C** /ˈɛbase, ˈabasi, ˈa be se, ˈe bi si/ *n* **1** the alphabet *15-*. **2** an alphabetical list or table *la16-17*. [from the first three letters of the alphabet]

ebbit *see* ABIT

ebdomadare, **ebdomidrye** *see* HEBDOMADAR

Eberdeen *see* ABERDEEN

ebersiand *see* EPPERSHAND

ebill *see* ABLE[1,1]

eboot *see* ABOOT[1,1], ABOOT[1,2]

ebor *see* EBURE

ebraik *see* EEBREK

†**ebure**, **ebor** *n* ivory *15-16*. [Lat *ebur*]

eccle /ˈɛkəl/ *n* a lump on the neck or in the fat of an animal *20- Ork*. [Norw dial *økel* an excrescence]

eccle-grass, *Sh* **ekelgirs** /ˈɛkəl gras; *Sh* ˈɛkəlgɪrs/ *n* butterwort *Pinguicula vulgaris 19- Sh Ork*. [unknown first element + GIRSE[1,1]]

ech /ɛx/ *interj* an expression of pity, surprise or disgust *19-*. [variant of ACH]

eche *see* EETCH

echer *see* AICHER

echt[1,1], **aucht**, **acht**, **eight**, **eighth** /ɛxt, ɔxt, axt, ext, et, etθ/ *adj* the ordinal number after seventh *15-*. **auchlet**, †**auchlot** a measure of grain; one eighth of a BOLL, half a FIRLOT *la16-19, 20- SW*. **echt-pairt** the eighth part of an inch *20-*. [OE *eahtoþa*]

echt[1,2], **aucht**, **acht**, **eicht**, **aicht**, **eight**, †**eght**, †**auch** /ɛxt, ɔxt, axt, ext, et/ *numeral* the cardinal number after seven *la14-*. **echt day** *adj* ordinary, everyday, typical; of its kind *20-*. **echt day** *n* a common daily occurrence *20- NE*. **aucht days**, **echt days** a week *15-*. **was echt days a week ago**: ◊*he cam on Setterday was eicht days 18-*. [OE *eahta*]

echt *see* AUCHT[2]

echteen, **auchteen**, **eichteen**, **aichteen**, **achteen**, †**auchtene**, †**eightein** /ˈɛxtin, ˈɔxtin, ˈextin, ˈaxtin/ *numeral* the cardinal number after seventeen *la14-*. [OE *eahtatȳne*]

echteent, **auchteent**, **echteenth**, **eichteenth**, †**auchtent**, †**auchtene** /ˈɛxtint, ˈɔxtint, ˈɛxtinθ, ˈextinθ/ *adj* eighteenth *la15-*. [ECHTEEN with ordinal suffix]

echteenth *see* ECHTEENT

echtsome, **auchtsome**, **eightsome**, †**auchtsum** /ˈɛxtsʌm, ˈɔxtsʌm, ˈetsʌm/ *n* **1** a group of eight (people) *16-*. **2** a dance involving eight people *20-*. **eightsome reel** a reel danced by a group of eight *19-*. [ECHT[1,2], with -*some* suffix]

Eck /ɛk/ *n* an affectionate, familiar form of Alexander *20-*. **Eckie** a diminutive of ECK *la20-*. [diminutive form of the personal name *Alec*, itself a shortened form of *Alexander*]

economist *see* OECONOMUS

edder[1,1], **ether** /ˈɛdər, ˈɛðər/ *n* a straw rope used in thatching a hay- or corn-stack *20- NE* [unknown]

edder[1,2], **ether**, **aider** /ˈɛdər, ˈɛðər, ˈedər/ *v* to rope a stack to secure the thatch *18- NE*. **edderin**, **eddrin**, †**etherin** the straw-rope fastened at right angles to the other ropes on stacks or loads, a cross-rope *la18- Ork NE T*. [unknown]

edder *see* AITHER[1,1], AITHER[1,2], AITHER[1,4], ETHER, UDDER

eddicate, **eddycate**, **educate** /ˈɛdɪket, ˈɛdjuket, ˈɛdʒəket/ *v ptp* **educate** †**educat** to instruct, inform or train; to provide with an education *la16-*. [Lat *ēducāre*]

eddication, **eddycation**, **education**, †**educatioun** /ɛdɪˈkeʃən, ɛdəˈkeʃən, ɛdjuˈkeʃən, ɛdʒəˈkeʃən/ *n* formal instruction or training; upbringing *la16-*. [EModE *education*, Lat *ēducātiō*]

eddir *see* ETHER

eddycate *see* EDDICATE

eddycation *see* EDDICATION

edge[1.1], **aidge**, †**ege**, †**egge**, †**eyge** /ɛdʒ, edʒ/ *n* **1** the sharpened side of a tool or weapon, the cutting edge *15-*. **2** the crest of a ridge *la15-*. **3** the boundary of a surface, a border, a verge; an end or extremity; edging *16-*. **edge coals** *mining* coal seams lying at a very steep angle *la19- EC*. †**egge lume**, **edgelome** an edged tool or weapon *16-17*. **edge seams** = *edge coals 19-*. **at the aidge o a time** from time to time, occasionally *19- Sh NE*. **the edge o** the verge of; almost *la19-*. **in the edge o a time** = *at the aidge o a time*. [OE *ecg*]

edge[1.2], †**ege** /ɛdʒ/ *v* **1** to furnish with an edging or border *16-*. **2** to provide with a cutting edge *la16-*. **3** to creep *la19-*. **edge hame** to proceed slowly homewards *la19-*. [see the noun]

edgie, **edgy** /'ɛdʒi/ *adj* quick, active; sharp, smart *la19- EC Bor*. [EDGE[1.1] + -IE[2]]

edict, †**edick** /'idɪkt/ *n* **1** a command, a decree *16-*. **2** *Christian Church* a legally authoritative public announcement made from the pulpit or originally also at (the door of) a parish church *16-*. **3** *law* a proclamation or decree made in a public place and having the force of law *16-e18*. **edictally** by means of an EDICT or *edictal citation la17-*. **edictal citation 1** a citation made by by sending copies of the summons to the Keeper of Edictal Citations *20-*. **2** a citation made by EDICT *la17-19*. [Lat *ēdictum*]

edify /'ɛdəfae/ *v* **1** to instruct, enlighten *la16-*. **2** to build *la15-16*. [MFr *edifier*, Lat *aedificāre*]

Edinburgh rock /'ɛdɪnbʌrə 'rɔk/ *n* a stick-shaped confection with a soft, crumbly texture (originally made in Edinburgh) *la19-*. [from the name of the city + ROCK[1]]

Edinburry, **Edinburrae** /'ɛdɪnbʌre/ *n* Edinburgh *19-*. Compare EMBRA [spelling reflecting local pronunciation of *Edinburgh*]

educat, **educate** *see* EDDICATE

education, **educatioun** *see* EDDICATION

edyan *see* EIDENT

ee[1], **eye**, †**e**, †**ey**, †**eie** /i, ae/ *n pl* **een**, **eyes**, **ees**, †**ene**, †**eyne** **1** the eye, the organ of sight or means of seeing *la14-*. **2** *mining* an entrance into a shaft *16-*. **3** regard, liking, craving, covetousness: ◊*you wi a lang ee till anither lad la19-*. **4** the hole in the head of a pick or hammer into which the shaft is fitted *20- H&I WC SW*. **5** an opening through which water passes *la16-19, 20- Sh Ork*. **6** the hole in the centre of a millstone *la16-, 20- Sh NE*. **7** the loop in a snare *19, 20- Sh NE*. **8** a globule of fat in liquid *19- NE Bor*. **9** one of the loops of a straw creel or basket *20- Sh*. **10** the opening of a running sore *19, 20- Sh*. **11** an eyelet or a loop of metal to receive a hook *16-e17*. **eesome** handsome, pleasing to the eye *19, 20- NE EC*. **ee-bree** = *ee-broo 16-19, 20- EC SW Bor*. **ee breer** an eyelash *20- Sh NE*. **ee-broo** an eyebrow *la19-*. †**e dolp** = *ee hole e16*. **ee hole** an eyesocket *18-*. **ee string** the eyelid, an eye muscle *19, 20- Sh*. **ee wharm** = *ee breer 19- Sh*. **ee winker 1** an eyelash *19- C Bor*. **2** an eyelid *19- C Bor*. †**ee o the day** midday *e19*. **hae yer ee in**, **hae yer een in** to covet *la19-*. †**have ee to** to have regard or consideration for, pay heed to *la14-16*. **pit oot a person's ee** to obtain an advantage over, supplant *la19-*. **yer ee is yer merchant** the buyer has responsibility for (the quality of) a purchase, *caveat emptor la17-*. [OE *ēage*]

ee[2] /i/ *interj* an expression of dismay or foreboding *20- NE*. [probably a natural alarm call]

ee *see* AE, THE[1.2]

eean, **ion**, **ayen** /'iən, 'aeən, 'eən/ *n* a one-year-old horse or cow *19- NE*. [unknown]

eeble *see* ABLE[1.1]

†**eebrek**, **ebraik** *adj of land* ploughed the third year after being left fallow *la16-e19*. [unknown]

eechie nor ochie, **eechie nor ochie** /'ixi ɔr 'ɔxi, 'ixi nɔr 'ɔxi/ *n* neither one thing nor another; nothing *la18-*. [perhaps derivative forms of ECH + OCH]

eediocy, **eediot**, **eedit** *see* EEJIT

eedle-doddle[1.1], **eedle-oddle** /'idəl 'dɔdəl, 'idəl 'ɔdəl/ *n* a person who shows no initiative *20- N NE*. [see the adj]

eedle-doddle[1.2], **eedle-oddle** /'idəl 'dɔdəl, 'idəl 'ɔdəl/ *adj* easy-going, lacking initiative, muddle-headed *la19- N NE*. [reduplicative compound perhaps with influence from *idle* and DODDLE[2.1]]

eedol, **idol**, †**eadwul**, †**ydoll**, †**idole** /'idəl, 'ʌɪdəl/ *n* **1** an object of worship *la14-*. **2** an image, a representation *la15*. **idoleeze** to idolize *19-*. [ME *idol*]

eejit, **eedyit**, **eediot**, **eedit**, **idiwut**, **idiot** /'idʒɪt, 'idɪət, 'idɪt, 'idiwʌt, 'idiət/ *n* **1** a fool, a stupid person; a person with learning difficulties *la14-*. **2** a person without knowledge or expertise; a layperson *16-e17*. **eediocy**, **idiocy** insanity; stupidity *19-*. [ME *idiot*]

eekfow *see* EQUAL[1.2]

eeksie-peeksie, **icksy-picksy** /'iksi 'piksi, 'ikse 'pɪkse/ *adj* much alike, six and half-a-dozen *19-*. [perhaps reduplicative compound based on EQUAL[1.2]]

eel, †**ele**, †**eill** /il/ *n* a snake-like fish of the genus *Anguilla la14-*. **eel ark**, †**ele ark** an eel trap *16-*. **eel backit**, †**eill bakit** *of a horse or other animal* having a dark stripe along its spine *la16-*. **eel drooner** a person who can do the impossible, an exceedingly clever person *19, 20- Bor*. [OE *æl*]

eel *see* ALE[1.1], YELD[1.2], YULE

eela, **ile** /'ila, 'ilə/ *n* inshore rod-fishing from a small boat *19- Sh N*. [Norw dial *ile* a stone used as an anchor]

eelat /'ilət/ *n* the hagfish *Myxine glutinosa la19- NE*. [unknown]

eeldins *see* EILD[1.1]

eelic passun *see* ELIC PASSION

eelie *see* ILE[1.1], ELY

eelins *see* EILD[1.1]

†**eelist**, **ilest**, **eyelist** *n* **1** a fault, flaw or defect *16-e19*. **2** a cause of dissension, a grudge, a grievance, a quarrel *la16-e17* [perhaps EE[1] + ME *les(e)* a falsehood, a lie].

eelshard *see* YULE

eelstab, **eel stob** /'il stab, 'il stɔb/ *n* a V-shaped incision in the ear of an animal as a mark of ownership *19, 20- T H&I SW*. †**eelstabbed**, **eelstobbed** marked with an EELSTAB *la17-19*. [EEL + STAB[1.1]]

†**eem**[1], **eme**, **ame** *n* **1** an uncle *la14-18*. **2** a close male relative, kinsman or friend *15-19*. [OE *ēam*]

eem[2], **ime**, **eame**, **aime**, **ayme** /im, em/ *n* **1** a blast of hot air, steam; (a smell from) a warm stuffy atmosphere *20- Ork N*. **2** condensation or vapour (from the ground or seashore) *20- N*. Compare YOAM[1.1] and IME. [ON *eimr* reek, vapour]

eemach *see* EEMOCK

eemage, **image**, †**ymage** /'iməḏʒ, 'ɪməḏʒ/ *n* **1** a representation; a mental picture, an impression; a likeness *la14-*. **2** a person in a poor state of health, a pitiful figure; a spectacle *19, 20- Sh Ork NE Bor*. [ME *image*]

eemir *see* HUMOUR

eemis *see* IMMIS

eemock, **emmock**, **immick**, *NE* **eemach**, †**imock**, †**emot** /'imək, 'ɛmək, 'ɪmɪk; *NE* 'iməx/ *n* **1** an ant, an insect of the family *Formicidae la14-*. **2** a tiny person; a fairy *20- NE T*. [OE *æmette*]

eemost *see* UMEST[1.2]

een *see* ANE[1.1], ANE[1.2], EE[1]

e'en *see* EVEN[1], EVEN[2.2], EVEN[2.3]

eenach /ˈinəx/ *n* the natural grease in sheep's wool *la19- NE*. [perhaps Gael *igheach* greasy]

een-cake *see* OAVEN

eence *see* AINCE[1.1], AINCE[1.2]

eence-eerin *see* AINCE ERRAND[1.2]

eend *see* EVEN[2.1]

eend on *see* EVEN[2.3]

eendy *see* EENTY

eenerie *see* ANE[1.1]

eengan *see* INGAN

eenickie *see* ANE[1.1]

eenie[1.1] /ˈini/ *n* an eye *la19- NE*. [*een*, plural of EE[1] + -IE[1]]

eenie[1.2], **eeny** /ˈini/ *adj of liquid* containing globules of fat *19-*. [*een*, plural of EE[1] + -IE[2]]

eenie *see* INGY

eenigar /ˈinɪgər, ˈinɪgər/ *adj* unwell, not thriving *20- Ork*. [unknown]

eenil *see* EINDLE

eenin *see* EVENIN

eenoo, evenoo, ae noo, *NE* **ivnoo,** †**enow,** †**evin now** /iˈnu, ivəˈnu, eˈnu; *NE* ɪvˈnu/ *adv* **1** just now, at the present time, a moment ago *16-*. **2** in a short time, soon, at once *la17-*. [EVEN[2.3] + NOO]

eent *see* EVEN[2.3]

eenty, eendy /ˈinti, ˈindi/ *numeral in children's rhymes* one *la19-*. [nonsense word derived from a system of counting sheep]

eeny *see* EENIE[1.2]

eer[1.1] /ir/ *n* a scream *la19- Sh*. [onomatopoeic]

eer[1.2] /ir/ *v* to scream; to squeal *19- Sh*. [see the noun]

eer *see* URE[3], YER

eeran, eerant, erran, errand, *Bor* **yirran,** †**erand,** †**herand,** †**airand** /ˈirən, ˈirənt, ˈɛrən, ˈɛrənd; *Bor* ˈjɪrən/ *n* **1** business one is sent to accomplish; the purpose of a journey, an errand *la14-*. **2** *pl* purchases, parcels, shopping *la19-*. [OE *ǣrende*]

eer farnyher *see* EREFERNYEAR

eerie, †**ery** /iri/ *adj* **1** affected by fear or dread (of the supernatural); apprehensive *la14-*. **2** weird, uncanny; strange, spooky *la18-*. **3** gloomy, dismal, melancholy *18-19*. **eerily** weirdly; drearily *la19-*. **eeriness,** †**eiryness,** †**erynes** fear, dread *la14-*. **eeriesome, eerisome** uncanny, gloomy *19, 20- Sh NE EC*. [unknown]

eerif *see* ARFF

eeriorums /iriˈorəmz/ *npl* details; fancy work, ornamentation *la19- Sh Ork NE*. [probably altered form of VARIORUM]

Eerish *see* IRISH[1.1], IRISH[1.2]

Eerishman *see* IRISHMAN

eerison *see* ORISON

eernest *see* EARNEST[1.1], EARNEST[1.2]

eeroy, ereoy, †**ieroe,** †**eroy** /irˈɔɪ, ˈirɔɪ/ *n* a great-grandchild *17-19, 20- Sh Ork N*. [Gael *iar-ogha*; compare OE]

eerȝisterday *see* EREYESTERDAY

ees *see* EE[1]

eesage *see* USAGE

eese *see* USE[1.1], USE[1.2]

eeseless *see* USELESS[1.2]

eeseral /ˈisərəl/ *adj* worthless *20- Ork*. [unknown]

eeshan, ieshan /ˈiʃən, ˈaeʃən/ *n* a small child; a small and puny person *la19- N NE T*. [Gael *isean* a chicken; a small person]

eeshogel, †**iceshoggle,** †**ice schockle,** †**ise schokkyll** /ˈiʃɔgəl/ *n* an icicle *la15-19, 20- T SW Bor*. [MLG *isjokel*]

eesk *see* ASK[2.1], ASK[2.2]

eesless *see* USELESS[1.1]

eest wi *see* USE[1.2]

eeswal *see* USUAL

eet *see* EAT[1]

eetch, eatch, †**eitche,** †**eche,** †**aich** /itʃ/ *n* **1** an adze *16-*. **2** a mattock or hoe *20- Ork*. [OE *adesa*]

eetim, item /ˈitəm, ˈaetəm/ *n* **1** an individual article, object or instance *19-*. **2** a task *la19- Sh NE T EC*. **eetimtation** a very small amount, an iota *20- Sh*. [Lat *item* in like manner, moreover]

eetle ottle[1.1] /ˈitəl ˈɔtəl/ *n in counting-out rhymes* this one, that one: *eetle ottle black bottle, eetle ottle out la19-*. [nonsense word]

eetle ottle[1.2] /ˈitəl ˈɔtəl/ *v* to choose by counting out *20- WC*. [see the noun]

eettie-ottie /ˈiteˈɔte/ *n in counting-out rhymes* this one, that one *la19- NE SW*. [nonsense word]

eever, ever, aver /ˈivər, ˈevər/ *n* something or someone of unusually great size *20- Sh*. [unknown]

eezer *see* AES[1.2]

eezin *see* EASIN

efauld *see* AEFAULD

efeir *see* YFERE

effair *see* EFFEIR[1.1]

effeck, effect, †**effek,** †**affect,** †**affeck** /əˈfɛk, əˈfɛkt/ *n* **1** the state of being functional; that which has force, efficacy, or validity *la14-*. **2** a result, a (desired) outcome; a change or consequence *15-*. **3** the essential part or substance of anything *15-16*. **in effect** in fact, in reality *la15-*. †**of effect** of worth or importance *la15-16*. [ME *effect*]

effeckwal, effectwal, effectual, †**effectuale** /əˈfɛkwal, əˈfɛktwal, əˈfɛktʃuəl/ *adj* effective, valid *la15-*. **Effectual Calling** the name for and opening phrase in the answer to Question 31 in the Shorter Catechism *17-*. [ME *effectual*]

effect *see* EFFECK

†**effectionat** *adj* affectionate, well-disposed; loving *la16-e17*. [EModE *affectionat*]

†**effectioun** *n* affection *15-e17*. [ME *affeccioun*]

effectual, effectuale, effectwal *see* EFFECKWAL

effeir[1.1], **affeir, affair,** †**affere,** †**effair** /əˈfer, əˈfir/ *n* **1** a business matter; a matter of concern, a situation; an event *15-*. **2** an array or display of armed force; equipment *la14-e19*. **3** bearing, demeanour; appearance, aspect; manners *la14-16*. **4** state, condition *la14-15*. [ME *aferes*]

effeir[1.2], **affeir,** †**affere,** †**effere** /əˈfir/ *v* **1** to belong to, pertain to; to be appropriate to, be fitting or proper *la14-*. **2** to concern a person; to be of concern to *15-16*. **as effeirs** *law* in the proper way, in due form *la14-*. **effeiring to, effeiring till, affeirin ti,** †**efferand to** *law* pertaining or belonging to; in relation or proportion to, corresponding to *la15-*. [AN, OFr *aferir*]

effeir *see* AFFEIR[1.1], AFFEIR[1.2]

effek *see* EFFECK

effer *see* AFFEIR[1.2]

efferd *see* AFEARD

effere *see* EFFEIR[1.2]

efferme *see* AFFIRM

effix *see* AFFIX

effoir *see* AFORE[1.1]

effore *see* AFORE[1.2]

efforhand *see* AFORE[1.1]

effrait *see* AFFRAY[1.2]

effray *see* AFFRAY[1.1], AFFRAY[1.2]

effront see AFFRONT¹·¹
effrontit see AFFRONTIT
effusion, †**effusioun** /ɛˈfjuʒən/ n a shedding (of blood or tears); a pouring forth *15-*. **to the effusion of blood** *law* applied to a case of assault in which blood has been shed *16-*. [MFr *effusion*, Lat *effūsio*]
eft¹·¹ /ɛft/ *adj* aft, belonging to the after part; back, rear *19-*. †**eft castell** the poop of a vessel *e16*. †**eft schip** the stern of a vessel *e16*. [OE *æftan*]
eft¹·² /ɛft/ *adv* 1 *nautical* aft *17-*. 2 towards the rear of anything *20-*. [see the adj]
efter¹·¹ /ˈɛftər/ *v* to strip a cow; to obtain all of her milk *20- H&I EC Bor*. [see the prep]
efter¹·², **aifter**, **after**, †**eftir** /ˈɛftər, ˈɛftər, ˈaftər/ *adv* 1 afterwards, subsequently *la14-*. 2 behind, in the rear *la14-*. 3 as a remainder *la19- Sh*. **efterins**, †**afterings** 1 the last drops of milk taken in milking *la18-*. 2 final results, consequences *19-*. **efterlins** afterwards *20- Sh*. **efterward**, **efterwart** subsequently *la14-*. **efterwards**, †**efterwairds**, †**efterwartis** subsequently *la14-*. **eftir specifeit** specified below *la16-17*. †**efter writtin** = *eftir specifeit la15-16*. †**as efter followis** *in a document* below *la14-16*. †**efter as** according as *la14-e17*. [see the prep]
efter¹·³, **aifter**, **after**, †**eftir**, †**aftir** /ˈɛftər, ˈɛftər, ˈaftər/ *prep* 1 following upon, behind *la14-*. 2 according to, in accordance with; in the style of *la14-*. 3 in pursuit of; in search of, desirous of *la14-*. 4 by derivation from (a name) *15-*. 5 *in telling the time past: half an oor efter ten la18-*. 6 as heir to *20- Sh*. **efterklap**, **afterclap** a result, a consequence *la16-19, 20- Sh*. **be after** to have done; *◊I am after telling him 19- H&I Uls*. **efter the back** back foremost, backwards, on the back *la19- N NE*. **efter een**, †**after ane** alike, uniform, unchangeable, all the same: *◊it's aa efter een tae me 16-19, 20- NE*. **aifter the heid** headfirst *20- Ork N NE T*. [OE *æfter*]
efter¹·⁴, **aifter**, **after** /ˈɛftər, ˈɛftər, ˈaftər/ *conj* later than, at a later time than *la20-*. [see the prep]
efter-¹·⁵, **after-**, †**eftir-** /ˈɛftər, ˈaftər/ *prefix* later, following; behind, secondary *la14-*. **after-burn** the last wort drawn off malt *20- Ork*. **eftercast**, **aftercast** an effect, a consequence, a result *19, 20- Sh Bor*. **aftercome**, †**eftercum** a result, a consequence *la16-19, 20- Sh Ork*. **after dayset**, **efter dayset** the evening; a social gathering held in the evening *20- Sh N*. †**eftremes** a second course, a dessert *la14*. **aftershot**, †**efter schot** 1 the last alcohol from a distillation *la19, 20- Ork*. 2 a supplementary or additional action, race or event *17-e18*. [EFTER¹·², EFTER¹·³]
efterhaand, **efterhan**, **efterhend** see EFTERHIN¹·²
efterhin¹·¹, **efterin**, **aivrin** /ˈɛftərhɪn, ˈɛftərɪn, ˈɛvrɪn/ *adj* the port side (of a boat) *20- N NE T*. [see the adv]
efterhin¹·², **efterhend**, **efterhan**, *Sh* **efterhaand**, †**eftirhend**, †**afterhend** /ˈɛftərhɪn, ˈɛftərhɛnd, ˈɛftərhan; *Sh* ˈɛftərhɑnd/ *adv* afterwards *la14-*. [EFTER¹·³ + HAN¹·¹]
efterhin¹·³, **efterin**, †**eftyrehend** /ˈɛftərhɪn, ˈɛftərɪn/ *prep* after, subsequent to, in addition to *la14-19, 20- N NE EC*. [see the adv]
efterin see EFTERHIN¹·¹, EFTERHIN¹·³
efternin, **efternuin**, **efternune**, **aifternoon**, **afternoon**, *N NE* **aifterneen**, *N NE* **efterneen**, †**eftirnone** /ˌɛftərˈnɪn, ˌɛftərˈnun, ˌɛftərˈnun, ˌaftərˈnun; *N NE* ˌɛftərˈnɪn; *N NE* ˌɛftərˈnin/ *n* 1 the part of the day after midday, afternoon *la16-*. 2 a meal taken during the afternoon *la16-19, 20- Sh*. [EFTER¹·³ + NUNE]
†**efternun**, **afternoon**, **efternone** *adv* after midday; in the afternoon *15-e19*. **at efter none** in the afternoon *la16-e17*. [EFTER¹·³ + NUNE]
efternune see EFTERNIN

eftir see EFTER¹·², EFTER¹·³
eftir- see EFTER-
eftirhend see EFTERHIN¹·²
eftirnone see EFTERNIN
eftyrehend see EFTERHIN¹·³
eg see EGG¹, EGG²
†**egal** *adj* equal *16-e19*. [ME *egal*]
ege see EDGE¹·¹, EDGE¹·²
egg¹, †**eg** /ɛg/ *n* 1 a bird's egg *15-*. 2 an egg-shaped jewel *la15*. **eggalourie**, **eggaloorie** a dish of eggs and milk *19- Sh Ork*. **eggler**, **egglar** a hawker who collected eggs from outlying farms and villages for sale at local markets *la18-19, 20- historical*. **egg-bed** an ovary *19-*. **egg-siller** money from selling eggs *20- NE T EC*. **aff yer eggs** 1 mistaken *la18-*. 2 nervous *19-*. [OE *æg*]
egg², **eig**, *Sh* **igg**, †**eg** /ɛg, eg; *Sh* ɪg/ *v* to incite, urge on *la14-*. Compare EIK³. **eggle** to incite, stir up; to quarrel *la19-, Ork NE*. **egg up** to incite, urge on *la19-*. [ON *eggja*]
egge see EDGE¹·¹
eght see ECHT¹·²
egill see EAGLE
Egiptian see EGYPTIAN
egither see THEGITHER
egle see EAGLE
†**Egypt** *n* an Egyptian *15*. [Lat *Aegyptius*]
Egyptian, †**Egiptian** /əˈdʒɪpʃən/ *n* 1 an (ancient) Egyptian *la15-*. 2 a gipsy *16-19, 20- historical*. †**Egyptian herring** a type of fish found in the River Forth; a GOWDANOOK *la18-19*. [EYGPT, with adj-forming suffix]
eh /ɛ, e/ *interj* an expression of affirmation, surprise or dismay *19-*. **eh aye** = EH *la19-*. **eh man** = EH *20- NE T C*. **eh no** a tag question inviting confirmation *la20-*. **eh sirs** = EH *19, 20- NE T C*. [an involuntary utterance]
Eh see AH
ei see HE¹·²
eicen see EISEN
eicht see ECHT¹·²
eichteen see ECHTEEN
eichteenth see ECHTEENT
eichyr see AICHER
eicid see ISET
eickel see EIK³
eidderin see AITHER¹·²
eident, **eydent**, *Ork* **ydant**, *Ork* **edyan**, †**ithand**, †**idand**, †**ythand** /ˈaedənt; *Ork* ˈaedənt; *Ork* ˈɛdjən/ *adj* 1 assiduous, diligent, busy *la14-*. 2 *of wind or rain* continuous, persistent *15-*. 3 conscientious, careful, attentive *19-*. [ON *iðinn*]
eidistreen see EREDASTREEN
eie see EE¹
eig see EGG²
eight see ECHT¹·¹, ECHT¹·²
eightein see ECHTEEN
eighth see ECHT¹·¹
eightsome see ECHTSOME
eik¹ /ik/ *n* 1 the natural grease in sheep's wool *la15-19, 20- Bor*. 2 human perspiration *19- Bor*. [MDu *iecke*]
eik²·¹, †**eke** /ik/ *n* 1 an addition, extension or increase; an additional part or piece *16-*. 2 *law* an addition or supplement to a document; an addition made by an executor to cover property not included in a will *la16-*. 3 an addition or extension to a garment; a patch, a gusset *17-*. 4 an extension to a beehive *18-*. 5 an additional drink; a little drop more *la19-*. **eik-name** a nickname *20- Sh Ork NE*. [OE *ēaca*]
eik²·², †**eke** /ik/ *v* 1 to increase, add, supplement *la14-*. 2 to repair, enlarge, patch *la15-*. 3 *law* to make an addition to a

document *la15-19*. **4** to join or unite *la18-e19*. **eik up** to fill up (a container) *la19- EC*. [OE *ēcian*]

eik³ /ik/ *v* to stir up, urge on, incite *19- NE*; compare EGG². **eickel** to incite or urge on *20- NE*. [EIK².², with semantic influence from EGG²]

eild¹·¹, yeild, †elde, †eyld, †heild /ild, jild/ *n* **1** old age *la14-*. **2** antiquity, long ago *la15-*. **3** a person's age *la14-19*. **4** mature or legal age, full age *15-16*. **5** an age of the world *15-e16*. **eildins**, *SW* **eelins**, *Uls* **yealins, †yealings, †eeldins, †yellings** contemporaries, people born in the same year *18-*. **eildit** aged *16-*. **†within elde** under age *15*. [OE *eald*]

†eild¹·², elde *v* to grow old *la15-e16*. [OE *eldan* to tarry, OE *ealdian* to grow old]

eild see YELD¹·²

eilding see ELDING

eill see EEL

eil-mark sheep see ALMARK

ein see ANE¹·¹, ANE¹·², EVEN²·², YIND

eindle, †eenil, †eindill /ˈɪndəl, ˈʌɪndəl/ *v* to be or become jealous *la16-19, 20- Sh*. [unknown]

eining see EVENIN

einins see EVEN²·¹

einyaree /ˈʌɪnjari/ *n* diarrhoea (in sheep) *la19- Sh*. [unknown; compare Faer *innrið*]

eird see YIRD¹·¹

eirn see EARN

eirnist see EARNEST¹·¹

Eirse see ERSE²·¹

eisen, †eicen, †yssen /ˈizən, ˈaezən/ *v of a cow* to desire the male *la17-19, 20- Bor*. [perhaps OE **œxnian*]

eisewaas see EASWAS

eising see EASIN

eist see EAST¹·¹, EAST¹·², EAST¹·³, EAST¹·⁴

†eistack *n* something rare, surprising or eyecatching *la18-e19*. [perhaps EE¹ + STICK¹·²]

eistell see EASTLE¹·²

eister see EASTER¹·³

Eistland see ESTLAND

eit see EAT¹·²

eitche see EETCH

†eith¹·¹, eth *adj* easy *la14-19*. [OE *ēaþe*]

†eith¹·² *adv* easily *la14-e19*. [see the adj]

either /ˈaeðər, ˈɛðər/ *v* to drizzle *20- Ork*. [unknown]

eitheran see AITHER¹·²

eith-kent¹·¹, ethkent /ˈeθkɛnt, ˈɛθkɛnt/ *n* a distinctively dressed or easily recognizable person *20- Sh*. Compare AITHKEN. [see the adj]

eith-kent¹·², ethkent /ˈeθkɛnt, ˈɛθkɛnt/ *adj* well-known, easily recognizable *la19- Sh*. Compare AITHKEN. [EITH¹·² + ptp of KEN¹·²; compare ON *auð-kendr*]

eithly, eithlie /ˈiθli, ˈeθli/ *adv* easily *la16-*. [OE *ēaðelice*]

eit meill see AIT

eivendoon see EVENDOON¹·¹

eizel see AIZLE¹·¹

eizewas see EASWAS

ejection, †ejectioun /əˈdʒɛkʃən/ *n* **1** expulsion *16-*. **2** *law* unlawful and violent expulsion of a person from their property, ejectment *16-*. **3** eviction *18-*. [Lat *ējectio*]

ek /ɛk, ek/ *n* a whiff of a bad smell *20- Ork*. [unknown]

eke see EIK²·¹, EIK²·²

ekelgirs see ECCLE-GRASS

eken /ˈɛkən/ *adj* thin, meagre *20- Sh*. [unknown]

eksis girse /ˈɛksɪs gɪrs/ *n* **1** hawkweed, a plant of the genus *Hieracium 20- Sh*. **2** a dandelion *Taraxacum officinale 20- Sh*. [AIXIES + GIRSE¹·¹]

elaskit /əˈlaskɪt/ *n* elastic *20-*. [metathesis of Eng *elastic*]

elba, elby, elbie, elbow, †elbo /ˈɛlba, ˈɛlbe, ˈɛlbi, ˈɛlbo/ *n* the exterior of the joint between the upper arm and forearm *la14-*. **elbow grass** foxtail grass *Alopecurus geniculatus 19- WC Uls*. [OE *elnboga*]

elbuck, elbock, elbick, †elbok /ˈɛlbʌk, ˈɛlbɔk, ˈɛlbɪk/ *n* an elbow *16-*. [OE *elnboga*, with phonologically irregular *-k*]

elby see ELBA

†elcruke, aile cruk, eulcruik *n* a hook for lifting meat out of a pot *la15-e17*. [OE *āwel* awl + CRUIK¹·¹]

El D, Eldee, Eldo /ɛlˈdi, ɛlˈdo/ *n* a type of strong (cheap) fortified South African wine *20, 21- historical*. [from the name *El Dorado*, a type of proprietary fortified wine]

eldar see ELDER¹·¹, ELDER¹·²

eldast see ELDEST

elde see EILD¹·¹, EILD¹·²

Eldee see EL D

elder¹·¹, *NE* **elyer,** *NE* **ayler, †eldar** /ˈɛldər; *NE* ˈeljər; *NE* ˈelər/ *n pl* also **†eldris 1** *pl* forefathers, ancestors *la14-*. **2** *Presbyterian Church* a person elected and ordained to take part in church government as a member of the ecclesiastical courts (such as the kirk session) *la16-*. **eldership 1** the office of a church elder *la16-*. **2** the body of elders or kirk session of a church *la16-*. **3** an assembly composed of ministers and elders of a number of parishes *la16*. **elders' hours** respectable hours, usually considered to be before about 10 pm *la19-*. [ME *eldre* a parent, an elderly person]

elder¹·², †eldar /ˈɛldər/ *adj* older *15-*. [OE *ealdra*]

eldering see ELDERN

elderman see ALDERMAN

eldern, †eldrin, †eldering /ˈɛldərn/ *adj* **1** *of people* old, elderly *16-19, 20- Sh Bor*. **2** *of things* old *la16-e17*. [ELDER¹·², with *-en* suffix]

eldest, †eldast /ˈɛldəst/ *adj* oldest *la14-*. [OE *ealdest*]

†eldfader *n* **1** a grandfather *la14-15*. **2** a father-in-law *e16*. [OE *ealdfæder*]

elding, eldin, †eilding /ˈɛldɪŋ, ˈɛldɪn/ *n* fuel *la15-19, 20- EC Bor*. [ON *elding*]

†eldmodir *n* a mother-in-law; a female relative, a stepmother *e16*. [OE *ealdmōdor*]

†eldnyng, endling, indilling *n* jealousy *e16*. [EINDLE, with *-ing* suffix]

Eldo see EL D

eldricht see ELDRITCH

eldrin see ELDERN

eldris see ELDER¹·¹

eldritch, eldricht, †elrich, †erlish, †alrische /ˈɛldrɪtʃ, ˈɛldrɪxt/ *adj* **1** weird, ghostly; strange, uncanny *16-*. **2** belonging to or resembling elves or similar beings *16-e17*. [perhaps OE **aelfrīce* fairy kingdom]

ele see EEL

eleck¹·¹, elect /əˈlɛk, əˈlɛkt/ *n* **1** a person elected or chosen *16-*. **2** a bishop elect *15-e16*. [Lat *ēlectus*]

eleck¹·², elect /əˈlɛk, əˈlɛkt/ *v* to elect, choose *16-*. [Lat *ēlect-*, ptp stem of *ēligere*]

electric soup /əˈlɛktrɪk sup/ *n* strong fortified wine (providing maximum intoxication in the shortest possible time) *la20- C*. [Eng *electric* + SOUP]

†electuare, electuary *n* a medicinal syrup *15-16*. [Lat *ēlectuārium*]

eleeven, eleiven, eleven, *Sh* **ileeven,** *NE* **alaiven, †ellevin, †allevin, †lewyne** /əˈlivən, əˈlɛvən; *Sh* iˈlivən; *NE* əˈlevən/ *numeral* the number after ten, eleven *la14-*. Compare ANE LEVIN. **eleevent, eleveenth, †elevint, †allevint** eleventh *la14-*. [OE *endleofan*]

eleid see ELIDE

eleiven see ELEEVEN

†elementar *adj* basic, elemental *16*. [MFr *elementaire*, Lat *elementārius*]

element money /ˈɛlɪmənt ˈmʌne/ *n* money paid for the bread and wine used in the sacrament of communion *18-*. [Older Scots *element* bread or wine used in the sacrament + MONEY]

†elemosinar, alemosener *n* an almoner *la14-17*. Compare *almosar* (AMOS[1.1]). [MFr *elemosinaire*, Lat *elimosinārius*]

eleven *see* ELEEVEN

elf, †elph /ɛlf/ *n pl* also **†elvys** *folklore* a supernatural or magical creature *la15-*. **elf arrow** a flint arrowhead, thought to be used by elves *la16-*. **†elf candle** a spark or flash of light, thought to be of supernatural origin *la18-e19*. **elf cup** a perforated stone *19- Bor*. **elf mill** the death-watch beetle *Xestobium rufovillosum 19- N NE*. **elf ring** a fairy ring *19- NE SW Uls*. **elf stone** = *elf arrow la17-*. [OE *ælf*]

Elfin[1.1], **†Elphyne**, **†Elfame** /ˈɛlfɪn/ *n* 1 *folklore* fairyland, the land of the elves *la16- literary*. 2 Hell *19-*. [unknown; compare ON *álfheimar*]

Elfin[1.2] /ˈɛlfɪn/ *adj folklore* pertaining to elves, elvish *19-*. [probably EModE *elfin*]

elf-shot[1.1], **†elf schot** /ˈɛlfʃɔt/ *n* 1 a flint arrowhead, compare *elf arrow* (ELF) *la18-19, 20- historical*. 2 a sickness (usually of cattle) thought to be caused by fairies *16-19*. [ELF + SHOT[1.1]]

elf-shot[1.2] /ˈɛlfʃɔt/ *adj* 1 *folklore* shot by a fairy arrow, bewitched *17-19, 20- Uls*. 2 *of cattle* suffering from a sickness thought to be caused by fairies *17-19, 20- historical*. [see the noun]

elic passion, eelic passun /ˈɛlɪk ˈpaʃən, ˈilɪk ˈpasən/ *n* 1 colic *19- NE EC*. 2 appendicitis *19*. [altered form of Eng *iliac passion*]

elide, †eleid /əˈlʌɪd/ *v* 1 *law* to annul, quash, exclude *la16-*. 2 to omit a vowel or syllable in pronunciation *la18-*. 3 to join together, merge *la20-*. [Lat *ēlīdere* to crush out]

elik *see* ALIKE[1.2]

elike *see* ALIKE[1.1]

elikeways *see* ALIKEWAYS

elikewise *see* ALIKEWISE

ell, †elne, †ellin /ɛl/ *n* a measure of length, approximately 0.93m (37.2 inches) *15-19, 20- historical*. **†elne braid** ell wide *16-e17*. **ell coal** *mining* a type of coal (usually found in seams about an ELL thick) *la18- C*. [OE *eln*]

ellach *see* YELLOCH[1.2]

eller, elder /ˈɛlər, ˈɛldər/ *n* the elder tree *Sambucus nigra 19-*. [ME *eller(n)*]

ellevin *see* ELEEVEN

ellin *see* ELL

ellis *see* ELSE

ellishon *see* ELSHIN

ellwand[1.1], **ellwan**, *T* **elvin**, **†elnwand**, **†elvand**, **†elvan** /ˈɛlwɔnd, ˈɛlwən, ˈɛlwən; *T* ˈɛlvɪn/ *n* 1 a rod one ELL long; a yardstick *15-*. 2 *astronomy* Orion's Belt *16-19, 20- Ork NE*. [ELL + WAND[1.1]]

†ellwand[1.2] *adj of limbs* like a rod or yardstick; long and thin *e19*. [see the noun]

elne *see* ELL

elnwand *see* ELLWAND[1.1]

elph *see* ELF

Elphyne *see* ELFIN

elrich *see* ELDRITCH

else, †ellis /ɛls/ *adv* 1 other, different; in addition, besides *la14-*. 2 already, previously *16-*. 3 otherwise *la14-19, 20- WC SW Uls*. **elsewhere**, **†ellis quhar** in another place *la14-*. **or else no** maybe not, hardly *19, 20- T Bor*. [OE *elles*]

elshin, *Sh* **ellishon**, *Bor* **alshin**, *Uls* **elsin**, **†elsing**, **†elson**, **†alisone** /ˈɛlʃɪn; *Sh* ˈɛlɪʃən; *Bor* ˈalʃɪn; *Uls* ˈɛlsɪn/ *n* a shoemaker's awl *16-*. [MDu *elssene*]

elshinders *see* ALSHINDERS

elsin, elsing, elson *see* ELSHIN

elsket *see* ILSKET

elt[1.1] /ɛlt/ *n* 1 dough *20- Sh N*. 2 a heavy, laborious job *20- Sh*. 3 a stout or slovenly woman *20- N*. **mak an elt o** make a mess of *20- Sh*. [see the verb]

elt[1.2] /ɛlt/ *v* 1 to mix (so as to form a thick mass); to knead (dough) *20- Sh Ork N*. 2 to handle roughly, damage by rough or too much handling *la19- Sh Ork*. 3 to dirty or begrime; to smear *la19- Sh N*. 4 to work hard; to dig or rake in the dirt *la19- Sh Ork*. [ON *elta* to knead]

elvan, elvand, elvin *see* ELLWAND[1.1]

elvys *see* ELF

elwin-skud /ˈɛlwɪn skʌd/ *adv* head-over-heels *20- Ork*. [unknown]

ely, yillee, yealie, †eelie /ˈili, ˈjuli, ˈjɪli/ *v* to disappear, vanish; to disperse gradually *19- Bor*. **ely awa** to vanish away *19- Bor*. [unknown]

elyer *see* ELDER[1.1]

elyk *see* ALIKE[1.1]

elyke *see* ALIKE[1.2]

em *see* AIM

emang *see* AMANG

embassel *see* IMBAZEL

ember-goose *see* IMMER-GOOSE

Embra, Embro, Enbra, †Enbrough, †Embrough /ˈɛmbra, ˈɛmbrə, ˈɛmbro, ˈɛnbrə/ *n* Edinburgh *la18-*. Compare EDINBURRY. [contracted form of *Edinburgh*]

embrace[1], **†enbrace**, **†imbrace**, **†inbrace** /əmˈbres/ *v* 1 to clasp, put the arms round *la14-*. 2 to accept (eagerly); to get *15-*. [ME *embracen*]

†embrace[2], **enbrace, imbrace** *v* to put a shield on the arm; to put on or enclose in armour *la14-16*. [ME *embracen*]

Embro, Embrough *see* EMBRA

emby *see* INBY[1.2]

emdie, emdy *see* ONIEBODIE

eme *see* EEM[1]

emerald *see* EMERANT[1.1], EMERANT[1.2]

emerant[1.1], **emerald**, **†emeraud**, **†amerant**, **†admirald** /ˈɛmərənt, ˈɛmərəld/ *n* a bright green precious stone *la14-*. [ME *emeraude*]

emerant[1.2], **emerald**, **†amerant** /ˈɛmərənt, ˈɛmərəld/ *adj* bright green in colour *16-*. [see the noun]

emeraud *see* EMERANT[1.1]

†emergent *n* an accidental or unforeseen event; an emergency *17-18*. [Lat *emergent-em*]

emmer-goose *see* IMMER-GOOSE

emmers, amers, ammers, aumers, aimers /ˈɛmərz, ˈamərz, ˈɔmərz, ˈɛmərz/ *npl* embers *16-*. [OE *æmerge*, ON *eimyrja*]

emmerteen /ˈɛmərtin/ *n* an ant, an insect of the family *Formicidae la19- NE*. [probably altered form of OE *æmette*]

emmledeug /ˈɛmaldjug/ *n* butcher's offal, scraps *19, 20- SW*. [unknown; compare EMMLINS]

emmlins /ˈɛmlɪnz/ *npl* scraps; entrails, giblets *20- NE*. [Norw dial *emmel* a strip; with diminutive plural suffix]

emmock *see* EEMOCK

†emoliment *n* emolument; revenue *la15-17*. [Lat *ēmolimentum*]

emot *see* EEMOCK

emperiall *see* IMPERIAL

emperice *see* EMPRICE

emperor, †**emperour**, †**imperiour**, †**empreour** /'ɛmpərər/ n **1** the ruler of an empire la14-. **2** a military commander 15-16. [ME *emperour*, Lat *imperātor*]

empesche see IMPESCHE

empire[1.1], †**impire** /'ɛmpaer/ n **1** territory ruled by a sovereign ruler 16-. **2** supreme power; domination, rule 16-. **empire biscuit** an iced shortcake biscuit with a jam filling la20-. †**the empire, the impire** the Roman or Holy Roman Empire la14-17. [MFr *empire*]

†**empire**[1.2], **impire** v **1** to rule as emperor 16-e17. **2** to wield (tyrannical) authority la16-e17. **3** *of desires* to hold sway, prevail la16-e17. [see the noun]

†**emplese, implese, enplese** v to please or give pleasure to; to satisfy or suit la14-e16. **emplesance** pleasure, satisfaction 15. **empleseir** = *emplesance* la15-e16. **emplesour** = *emplesance* la15-16. [OFr *emplais-*, stem of *emplaire*]

emprent see IMPRENT

empreour see EMPEROR

†**emprice, emperice** n an empress la14-e17. [ME *emperesse*]

emprisoun see IMPRESON

†**emprunt, enprunt** n a loan la16. [MFr *emprunt*]

†**emptive, emptyve** adj empty la15-16. [empty (EMPY[1.2]), with adj-forming suffix]

empy[1.1], **impty, empty** /'ɛmpe, 'ɪmpte, 'ɛmpte/ v to make or become empty 17-. [see the adj]

empy[1.2], **impty, empty** /'ɛmpe, 'ɪmpte, 'ɛmpte/ adj containing nothing; vacant 16-. [OE *æmtig*]

en[1.1], **end**, *NE* **ine**, *NE* **eyn**, †**hend** /ɛn, ɛnd; *NE* ʌɪn, en/ n **1** an extremity, an edge la14-. **2** *in place-names* a quarter or division of a settlement or district; the outlying part of a settlement or district; a corner, a spot la14-. **3** a conclusion, a result; a cessation; the final part (of something) la14-. **4** *shoemaking* the thread used in sewing leather 18-. **5** a room; originally one room of a two-roomed cottage 19-. **6** *curling, bowling* the portion of play played from one end of the rink or green; a unit of play la19-. **7** *weaving* a warp thread la18- NE C Bor. **8** a part or instalment (of money) 16-19. **endless**, †**endles 1** without end la14-. **2** persistent; long-winded 19-. **endmaist, endmost** nearest to the end, furthest, most distant la19-. †**end day** the last day of a person's life la14-e17. **end gird** the end-hoop of a barrel 20- Sh NE Bor. †**end hooping** = *end gird* la18-e19. **end pickle** the grain of corn at the top of a stalk la19- NE T WC. **en rig, end rig** the land at the end of the furrow on which the plough is turned 17-. **en ways, end ways** forward, straight ahead; successfully 19- EC Bor. **endwye** progress la19- Sh EC. **the end o an auld sang** the last of an old custom or institution, the end of an era (from the remark by the Earl of Seafield after signing the Act of Union in 1707, 'Now there's ane end of ane old song') 18-. **the end o yer tedder** the limit of your resources la19- Sh Ork N. **frae end tae wynd** from end to end, completely 19- WC Uls. [OE *ende*]

en[1.2], **end** /ɛn, ɛnd/ v **1** to come or bring to an end; to finish, complete or conclude la14-. **2** to die 15-. **3** to stand on end la19-. **4** to kill, despatch la19-. **5** to settle, come to an agreement la15-e17. †**end out** to bring to completion la16-e17. [OE *endian*]

†**enache** n amends or satisfaction (for a fault) 15-16. [Gael *eineach* honour]

enact, †**inact** /əˈnakt/ v **1** to enter a statute in a register; to ordain or decree; to adjudge 17-. **2** to pledge oneself, be pledged (to an undertaking or obligation) 17-e19. [ME *enact*]

enamel, †**anamal**, †**inamal**, †**innemel** /əˈnaməl/ v **1** to cover or decorate with enamel la14-. **2** to colour with brilliant colours as if enamelled; to make brilliant 16. [ME *enamelen*]

†**enarm, inarme** v ptp also **enermit, anarmit** to equip with weapons 15-e19. [ME *enarmen*]

†**enbandown** v **1** to overcome or subdue e15. **2** to abandon, give up la14. [OFr *en bandon*]

Enbra see EMBRA

enbrace see EMBRACE[1], EMBRACE[2]

Enbrough see EMBRA

†**enbusch, inbusch** v **1** to ambush la14-e16. **2** to place under cover; to take shelter e15. [ME *embushen*, Lat **imboscāre*]

†**encheif, encheve** v to achieve, win la14-e16. Compare ESCHEVE. [ME *encheven*]

†**enchesone**[1.1], **enchessoun** n **1** reason la14-e17. **2** objection la15-e16. [ME *enchesoun*]

†**enchesone**[1.2], **enschesoun** v to challenge, accuse or blame 15-e16. [see the noun]

enchessoun see ENCHESONE[1.1]

encheve see ENCHEIF

enchew see ENSCHEW

enclose see INCLOSE

enclyne see INCLINE

encoonter[1.1], **encounter**, †**enconter** /ənˈkʌntər, ənˈkʌuntər/ n a casual or unexpected meeting; a conflict, a skirmish la15-. [ME *encountre*]

encoonter[1.2], **encounter**, †**enconter**, †**incountar** /ənˈkʌntər, ənˈkʌuntər/ v to confront (in combat); to come across; to experience 15-. [ME *encountren*]

encourage, †**incurage** /ənˈkʌrədʒ/ v to stimulate, incite; to make confident, embolden la16-. **encouragement**, †**encurragment**, †**incurragment 1** the action or fact of encouraging; support la16-. **2** payment, salary la17-18. [EModE *encorage*, ME *encouragen*]

encres see INCRES[1.1], INCRES[1.2]

end, †**aynd**, †**aind** /ɛnd/ n breath la14-19, 20- Sh. Compare YIND. **ayndles** out of breath la14-e16. [ON *andi*]

end see EN[1.1], EN[1.2]

endaivour[1.1], **endeavour**, *NE* **endeevour**, †**endevoir**, †**indevoir** /ənˈdevər, ənˈdɛvər; *NE* ənˈdivər/ n an attempt or effort la16-. **dae yer endeavour** to do one's utmost la16-. [see the verb]

endaivour[1.2], **endeavour**, *NE* **endeevour**, †**endevore**, †**indevoir** /ənˈdevər, ənˈdɛvər; *NE* ənˈdivər/ v to try, attempt 16-. [ME *endevoyre*]

endew see ENDUE[1], ENDUE[2]

endill scheit see ENEL-SHEET

endite see INDYTE[1.1], INDYTE[1.2]

endland see ENDLANG[1.4]

endlang[1.1], **enlang** /ˈɛndlaŋ, ˈɛnlaŋ/ v to harrow a ploughed field along the furrows 19- NE WC SW. [see the adv]

endlang[1.2], †**enlang** /ˈɛndlaŋ/ adj at full length la18-19, 20- Sh. [see the adv]

endlang[1.3], **enlang** /ˈɛndlaŋ, ˈɛnlaŋ/ adv **1** lengthwise, at full length 19, 20- NE EC Bor. **2** right along, straight on; in quick succession, continuously la14-19. [OE *andlang*, ON *endilangr*]

endlang[1.4], †**enlang**, †**endland**, †**inlang** /ˈɛndlaŋ/ prep along, by the side of; from end to end of la14-19, 20- literary. †**endlangis, inlangis** along, by the side of 16-e17. [see the adv]

endling see ELDNYNG

endoo, endow, †**indow** /ənˈdu, ənˈdʌu/ v to invest; to provide with funding la14-. [ME *endouen*]

†**endue**[1], **endew, indew** v to invest; to endow la16-e17. [ME *endeuen*]

†**endue**[2], **endew, indew** adj **1** *of people* owing, indebted la17-19. **2** *of debt* due to be paid, owing la17. [DUE, with *en-* prefix]

endurand

†**endurand, indurand, induring** *prep* during, while *15-e17*. [presp of Older Scots *endure*]
ene *see* EE¹
†**enel-sheet, endill scheit** *n* a winding sheet, a shroud *la16-19*. [unknown first element + SHEET¹]
enemy, †**inemy,** †**inimy,** †**ennymy** /ˈɛnəme, ˈɛnəmi/ *n* **1** an adversary, an antagonist, a foe *la14-*. **2** the Devil *la15-*. **the Auld Enemy** *see* AULD¹·². [ME *enemi*]
enermit *see* ENARM
eneuch¹·¹, **aneuch, enouch, anouch,** †**enewch,** †**ennuche,** †**yneuch** /əˈnjux, əˈnjʌx/ *n* a sufficiency, enough *la14-*. [see the adj]
eneuch¹·², **aneuch, enouch, anouch,** *Sh N* **anyoch,** *Sh* **enyoch,** †**ineuch,** †**enewch,** †**inuch** /əˈnjux, əˈnjʌx; *Sh N* əˈnjɔx/ *adj* sufficient, enough *la14-*. [OE *genōh*]
eneuch¹·³, **aneuch, enouch, anouch,** *Sh N* **anyoch,** *Sh* **enyoch,** †**enuch,** †**inewch,** †**yneuch** /əˈnjux, əˈnjʌx; *Sh N* əˈnjɔx/ *adv* sufficiently, adequately, enough *la14-*. [see the adj]
enew¹·¹, *NE* **anyow,** †**anew,** †**inew,** †**enow** /əˈnju; *NE* əˈnjʌu/ *n* a sufficient number or quantity *la14-19, 20- NE Bor.* [variant of ENEUCH¹·¹]
enew¹·², †**anew,** †**inew,** †**enow** /əˈnju/ *adj* sufficient in number or quantity *la14-19, 20- NE.* [see the noun]
enewch *see* ENEUCH¹·¹, ENEUCH¹·²
enfeff *see* INFEFF
enfeftment *see* INFEFTMENT
enflambe *see* INFLAME
engage, †**engadge,** †**ingadge,** †**ingage** /ənˈgedʒ/ *v* **1** to agree to, undertake (a commitment) *16-*. **2** to offer or accept employment, enlist; to hire or rent out, secure the use of (a vehicle or property) *la17-*. **3** to enter into combat with *la17-*. **4** to pray, launch into prayer *la19- NE T.* **5** to pawn, pledge or mortgage (property) *la16-e17*. †**engadger** one who took part in the military engagement of 1647-48, *17-18*. **engagement 1** a formal agreement or commitment; a betrothal; an appointment; a period or state of employment *17-*. **2** a military encounter, a battle *la17-*. **3** the undertaking of 1647-48 to send an army to England in support of Charles I *17*. [MFr *enguagier*]
†**engaigne** *n* resentment *la14*. [OFr *engaigne*]
engender, †**ingener,** †**engener,** †**ingender** /ənˈdʒɛndər/ *v* to beget, produce, give rise to *la14-*. [ME *engendren*]
engill *see* INGILL
engine *see* INGINE
engineer *see* INGINEER
England *see* INGLAND
Englify /ˈɪŋgləfae/ *v* to Anglicize (in speech or manner) *la18-*. [*Engli-* stem with *-fy* verb-forming suffix]
Englis, English *see* INGLIS¹·¹, INGLIS¹·²
engral /ˈɛŋrəl, ˈɪŋrəl/ *adj* greedy, ravenous *20- Ork.* [unknown]
†**engranyt, ingranit** *adj* dyed scarlet with a fast dye, dyed in grain *16-17*. [EModE *ingrain'd*]
engrave *see* INGRAVE
†**engreve, engreif, ingreve** *v* **1** to do harm to; to injure, hurt *la14-e17*. **2** to annoy *la15-e16*. [OFr *engrever*]
engyne *see* INGINE
engynour *see* INGINEER
engyre *see* INJEER
enhaunse *see* INHANCE
enherde *see* ANHERD
e'ning *see* EVENIN
eniose *see* ENJOYS
enjape *see* ENNAPI

†**enjoys, eniose, inioyse** *v* to enjoy, possess *16-e17*. [ME *enjoicen*]
enk¹·¹, **yink** /ɛŋk, jɪŋk/ *n* **1** a person engaged to be married; a sweetheart *la19- Sh.* **2** ownership of a young animal (invested in a child or friend) *20- Sh.* **3** a possession, something of one's own *20- Sh.* [ON *eign* property]
enk¹·², **yink** /ɛŋk, jɪŋk/ *v* to give or acquire nominal ownership of an animal *la19- Sh.* [see the noun]
enkrely *see* INKIRLY
enlairge, enlarge, †**inlarge,** †**inlairge** /ənˈlerdʒ, ənˈlardʒ/ *v* **1** to extend, make bigger *la16-*. **2** to release, set free *la16-*. [ME *enlargen*]
enlang *see* ENDLANG¹·¹, ENDLANG¹·², ENDLANG¹·³, ENDLANG¹·⁴
enlarge *see* ENLAIRGE
enlichten, †**inlichten** /ənˈlɪxtən/ *v* to enlighten *17-*. [ME *inliʒten*]
enlichtment, enlightenment /ənˈlɪxtmənt, ənˈlʌɪtənmənt/ *n* **1** the act of enlightening; the state of being enlightened *19-*. **2** a period in the eighteenth-century characterized by intellectual and scientific accomplishment *la20-*. [EModE *enlightenment*]
†**enlumyne** *v* to light up, illuminate *la14-e16*. [ME *enluminen*]
ennapi, enjape, †**jennapie** /ˈɛnapi, ˈɛnjapi/ *n* a frail, tiny creature *la19- Sh.* [unknown]
enner *see* INNER
†**ennet seid, annet seid, anet seed** *n* dill seed *16-18*. [MFr *anet* + SEED¹·¹]
ennis, innis /ˈɛnɪs, ˈɪnɪs/ *n* a very poor or ruined house *20- Ork.* [shortened form of Scots *innhouse*]
ennowe *see* INWITH¹·¹, INWITH¹·²
†**ennoy, annoy, anoy** *n* annoyance, vexation, trouble *la14-19*. [ME *anoi*]
†**ennoyus, anoyous** *adj* troublesome, vexatious *la14-e16*. [ENNOY, with adj-forming suffix]
ennuche *see* ENEUCH¹·¹
ennymy *see* ENEMY
ennyrmar *see* INNER
enorm, †**enorme,** †**inorme** /əˈnɔrm/ *adj* **1** *of harm or injury* considerable, severe *16-*. **2** enormous; unusual *16-19, 20- historical.* **3** *of crimes, offences or vices* heinous, outrageous *16-e18*. **4** *of people* acting irregularly or without regard for law *la16-e17*. **enorm lesion** *law* severe damage or injury, great detriment *la16-*. [MFr *enorme*, Lat *ēnormis*]
enormity, †**innormite** /əˈnɔrməte/ *n* **1** extreme wickedness *la14-*. **2** an outrageous or criminal act *15-*. [MFr *enormité*, Lat *ēnormis* unusual]
†**enornament, anournement** *n* adornment, ornament *la14-e16*. [ENOURN, with noun-forming suffix]
enouch *see* ENEUCH¹·¹, ENEUCH¹·², ENEUCH¹·³
†**enourn, anorn, annorn** *v* to adorn; to add lustre to *la14-e16*. [ME *enournen*]
enouth *see* INWITH¹·¹, INWITH¹·²
enow *see* EENOO, ENEW¹·¹, ENEW¹·²
enoynt *see* ANOINT
enplese *see* EMPLESE
enprent *see* IMPRENT
enprunt *see* EMPRUNT
enquere, enquire *see* INQUIRE
enquest *see* INQUEST
enschesoun *see* ENCHESONE¹·²
†**enschew, enchew** *v* to avoid, eschew *15*. [variant of ESCHEW]
ense, anse /ɛns, ans/ *adv* else, otherwise *la18-19, 20- NE T EC Bor.* **or ense no** maybe not, hardly *19, 20- T EC.* [an (THAN¹·²) + *-se*, reduced from ELSE]

enseerin *see* AINCE ERRAND[1.1]

†**ensence** *v* to perfume with incense *e16*. [from the noun ENSENS]

†**ensens** *n* incense *e16*. [ME *encens*]

ensens *see* INSENSE

†**ensenyie, ansenʒe, handsenʒe** *n* 1 a war cry, a rallying cry or signal; a slogan, a motto *la14-19*. 2 a distinguishing emblem or symbol; insignia *la15-e17*. 3 a banner, a small military flag *la15-e19*. 4 the standard-bearer of a company *16-17*. 5 a company of soldiers under one banner *la16*. [OFr *enseigne*]

ensolence *see* INSOLENCE

ent, ant, aint /ɛnt, ɑnt, ant, ent/ *v* to obey, heed; to care for *19- Sh Ork*. [Norw dial *enta*]

†**entechment** *n* instruction *e16*. [*techement* (TEACH), with *en-* prefix]

enteece, entice, †**entyse,** †**intyse** /ənˈtis, ənˈtʌɪs/ *v* to tempt or allure; to persuade *la14-*. [ME *enticen*]

enteetle, entitle, †**entitil,** †**entetil** /ənˈtitəl, ənˈtʌɪtəl/ *v* 1 to provide with a title *la15-*. 2 to qualify or give a right to *la18-*. 3 to dedicate to *e16*. [ME *entitelen, entītlen*]

entent *see* INTENT[1.1]

†**ententely, entintily** *adv* attentively *la14-e15*. [perhaps MFr *entente*, with adv-forming suffix *-ly*]

enter, *NE T* **inter,** †**entir,** †**entyr** /ˈɛntər; *NE T* ˈɪntər/ *v* 1 to go or come into (a place) *la14-*. 2 to put a person formally in possession or occupation of property; to obtain or assume possession of property *la14-*. 3 to record in an official register *15-*. 4 to take up the duties of an office; to become a member of a religious order or trade association *15-*. 5 to record or register as a member of a body, note by name *la15-*. 6 to enrol or admit to a school *la18-*. 7 to (cause to) engage in a task, begin work *15-19, 20- NE T EC Uls*. 8 to appear or present (oneself or another) in a court of justice to undergo trial *15-17*. **enter appearance** *law* to signify one's intention of defending an action *20-*. **entered prentice** *see* PRENTICE[1.1]. **enterin mornin** a morning with weather suitable for work *la19- NE*. **enter prentice** *see* PRENTICE[1.1]. [OFr *entrer*, Lat *intrāre*]

enterchangeably *see* INTERCHANGE

entercomoun *see* INTERCOMMUNE

enterdick *see* INTERDICT[1.1]

enteres *see* INTERES[1.1]

enteres silver *see* ENTRESS

enterest *see* INTEREST

entermell *see* INTERMELL

enterprise, enterpreeze, †**interprys** /ˈɛntərpraez, ˈɛntərpriz/ *n* 1 an undertaking, an attempt *la15-*. 2 the willingness or capacity to undertake (something) *la16-*. 3 a project; a commercial or industrial venture *la19-*. [ME *enterprise*]

enterprit *see* INTERPRET

†**enterpryse, interpryse** *v* to undertake *la15-e17*. **interprysar** a person who undertakes work or action *la16*. [from ENTERPRISE and MFr *entrepris*, ptp of *entreprendre*]

enterteen, entertain, †**entertene,** †**intertene,** †**intertain** /ɛntərˈtin, ɛntərˈten/ *v* 1 to amuse; to show hospitality to *16-*. 2 to treat or deal with; to accommodate *16-*. 3 to maintain (an idea), keep up, support *16-*. [MFr *entretenir*]

†**entertenyr** *v* to entertain *e16*. [MFr *entretenir*]

entetil *see* ENTEETLE

entice *see* ENTEECE

entir *see* ENTER

entitil, entitle *see* ENTEETLE

entone *see* INTONE

entra, entre *see* ENTRY

entremas *see* INTERMEIS

entres *see* ENTRESS

†**entress, entres, intres** *n* 1 the right or opportunity to enter; entrance (to a place) *la15-17*. 2 a point or place of entry, an access point *la15-e17*. 3 (a payment due for) entry into possession or occupation of land or property *la15-e18*. 4 (a payment fee for) entry into a trade, office or occupation *la15-17*. 5 entry of imported goods *16-17*. 6 *law* appearance or presentation in court *la15-16*. **entres silver, enteres silver, interes silver** 1 money paid on entering into the occupation of land *16-e17*. 2 money paid on being admitted as an apprentice *la16*. 3 money paid on goods brought into a port *e17*. **non entres** 1 *law* failure to enter into possession of property *la15-17*. 2 *law* failure to appear or present in court *la15-e16*. [ENTER, with noun-forming suffix]

entrest *see* INTEREST

entromet *see* INTROMIT

entromettour *see* INTROMITTER

entry, †**entre,** †**entra,** †**intre** /ˈɛntre/ *n* 1 the act, right or opportunity of entering *la14-*. 2 a place of entry *la14-*. 3 an alley or covered (public) passageway *18-*. 4 the front doorway of a house; an entrance-lobby or porch, especially in a block of flats *la18-*. 5 the entrance to an avenue leading to a house; the avenue itself *18-19, 20- EC Bor*. 6 (the recording of) the coming of goods into a port *15-e16*. 7 the appearance of an accused person in a court of justice to undergo trial *15-e17*. 8 *law* the taking on of occupation or ownership of property; the establishment of ownership by an heir's being created vassal of the superior of inherited property *15-19*; compare NON-ENTRY. 9 entry into employment or office *la15-e16*. †**entre silver** money paid on entering into the occupation of land, on being admitted as an apprentice, or on bringing goods into port *16*; compare *entres silver* (ENTRESS). [OFr *entree*]

entyr *see* ENTER

entyrdyt *see* INTERDICT[1.2]

entyre *see* INTER

†**entyrmyddill, intermiddill** *v* to intermingle *16*. [ME *entermedlen*]

entyse *see* ENTEECE

enuch *see* ENEUCH[1.3]

enunctment *see* INUNCT

envenfer *see* INVENTAR[1.2]

†**enveron, inviroun, inveroun** *v* to encircle, surround *la14-e17*. [ME *environen*]

envious *see* INVY[1.1]

envnte *see* ANOINT

envy *see* INVY[1.1], INVY[1.2]

enyoch *see* ENEUCH[1.2], ENEUCH[1.3]

e per sie *see* A PER SE

ephesian /əˈfiʒən/ *n* a pheasant *19- EC SW*. Compare FEESANT. [perhaps a humorous development from Scots *a pheesant*]

Episcopawlian[1.1]**, Episcopalian,** †**Episcopaulian** /əpɪskəˈpɔliən, əpɪskəˈpeliən/ *n* a member of the Scottish Episcopal Church *la18-*. [see the adj]

Episcopawlian[1.2]**, Episcopalian** /əpɪskəˈpɔliən, əpɪskəˈpeliən/ *adj* having an Episcopal character or belonging to an Episcopal church *la18-*. [Lat *epīscopālis*, with *-an* suffix]

eppershand, eppersheeand, *Sh* **ebersiand,** †**eppersyand** /ˈɛpərʃand, ˈɛpərʃand; *Sh* ˈɛbərsjand/ *n* an ampersand *la19- Sh NE*. [corruption of Eng *and per se and*]

eppiteet *see* APPETEET

epple *see* AIPPLE

equaill *see* EQUAL[1.2]

equal[1.1], **aiqual**, †**aqual** /'ikwəl, 'ekwəl/ *n* a person or thing equal to another *la16-*. [see the adj]

equal[1.2], **aqual**, **aiqual**, †**equaill**, †**eekfow** /'ikwəl, 'akwəl, 'ekwəl/ *adj* 1 the same as *la15-*. 2 just, fair; impartial *16-*. 3 in line or on a level with *la16-*. [Lat *aequālis*]

†**equal**[1.3] *adv* equally, on a level *16*. [see the adj]

equalaqual[1.1] /'ikwəl'akwəl/ *adj* equally balanced, alike, similar *19, 20- N NE T EC Bor.* [rhyming compound]

equalaqual[1.2] /'ikwəl'akwəl/ *adv* equally, alike *19, 20-* literary. **equalaquals**, †**equalsaquals** = EQUAL-AQUAL[1.2] *19- EC Bor.* [see the adj]

†**eque**[1.1], **equie**, **aeque** *n* 1 the contribution paid annually by each constituent burgh to the Convention of Royal Burghs *la17-e19*. 2 an acquittance or receipt for a properly balanced account, or for money paid *la16-17*. [shortened form of Lat *et sīc aequē*, written at the foot of a settled account]

†**eque**[1.2] *adj of accounts* duly balanced *16*. [see the noun]

equie *see* EQUE[1.1]

equipage, †**equippage** /ɛ'kwɪpɪdʒ, 'ɛkwɪpɪdʒ/ *n* 1 the harness and trappings of a horse; a competition in which these are displayed *la16-*. 2 a retinue, a following, an entourage *la16-*. 3 style or manner of living; the appurtenances of rank or office *la16-*. 4 small articles of domestic furniture; china, a tea-service *18-*. 5 a carriage and horses; a train of vehicles *19-*. 6 (the style or equipment of) a military retinue; military uniform *la16-e19*. 7 a ship's crew *la16-e17*. †**equippagit**, **equippaged** *of a ship* manned *la16-e17*. [MFr *esquipage*]

equivalent[1.1] /ə'kwɪvələnt/ *n* something of equal value *17-*. **The Equivalent** the sum of money which the English government guaranteed to pay to Scotland as compensation for Scotland's prospective share in the English public debt as part of the new United Kingdom *e18, la19- historical*. [see the adj]

equivalent[1.2] /ə'kwɪvələnt/ *adj* equal in value *la15-*. [Lat *aequivalent-*, presp stem of *aequivalēre*]

er, †**ar** /ɛr/ *conj* before, until *la14, 20- Sh NE T*. [OE ǣr]

er *see* AIR[2], BE, EAR[1], ERR

-er, -ar, †**-our,** †**-ear** /ər/ *suffix* indicating a person associated with the attached verb: ◊*fermer* ◊*beggar* ◊*arbitour 13-*. [OE *-ere, -are*]

erand *see* EERAN

†**erar** *adv* sooner, rather *la14-16*. [comparative of OE ǣr]

erast *see* EREST[1.2]

erbe *see* YERB

erch[1.1], **arch,** †**ergh,** †**erf** /ɛrtʃ, ɛrx, artʃ, arx/ *n* doubt, fear, timidity *19, 20- Sh NE*. [see the adj]

†**erch**[1.2], **ergh, airgh** *v* to be timid, feel reluctant, hesitate *la16-e19*. [see the adj]

erch[1.3], **arch, argh, erf,** †**ergh** /ɛrtʃ, ɛrx, artʃ, arx, ɛrf/ *adj* 1 timorous *15-19, 20- NE*. 2 hesitant, reluctant *16-19, 20- Sh NE EC*. 3 scanty, insufficient; miserly *19, 20- EC Bor.* †**archly** timidly; scarcely *la14-15*. **archness,** †**arghnes** doubt, fear, timidity *15-19, 20- NE*. [OE *earg* cowardly, craven, timid, ON *argr* emasculate, effeminate]

erch *see* AIRCH[1.2]

erchin *see* HURCHEON

erd *see* YIRD[1.1], YIRD[1.2]

erdfast *see* YIRDFEST[1.2]

ere *see* AIR[2], AIR[5.2], AYRE, EAR[1], EAR[2]

ereck, erect, †**erek** /ə'rɛk, ə'rɛkt/ *v* 1 to raise or set up; to construct or build; to establish or create *la15-*. 2 to raise or lift up *la15-e19*. [Lat *ērect-*, ptp stem of *ērigere*]

erection, †**erectioun** /ə'rɛkʃən/ *n* 1 the setting up of an institution; originally the raising of a town to a particular status *la15-*. 2 the action of building *18-*. 3 something built *18-*. 4 an erect state of the penis *la20-*. 5 *law* the post-Reformation creation of temporal lordships from former spiritual benefices; a lordship so created *la16-18*; compare LORD OF ERECTION. [Lat *ērectio*]

eredastreen, *N* **eidistreen,** *N SW* **erethestreen,** *SW* **air yestreen,** †**heer-yestreen** /ɛrdə'strin; *N* aedi'strin; *N SW* ɛrðə'strin; *N SW* 'ɛrðəstrin; *SW* ɛr'jɛstrin/ *n* the night before last *18-*. [ER + THE STREEN[1.1]]

erefernyear, †**eer farnyher** /'ɛrfɛrnjir, ɛrfɛrn'jir/ *n* the year before last *la15-19, 20- Sh SW*. [ER + FERNYEAR]

erek *see* ERECK

ere ledder *see* EAR LEATHER

ereoy *see* EEROY

†**erest**[1.1] *adj* first, earliest *15-16*. [superlative of OE ǣr]

†**erest**[1.2], **erast** *adv* 1 in the first place, by choice or preference *la15-16*. 2 earliest, first *la14-e16*. [see the adj]

erethestreen *see* EREDASTREEN

ereyesterday, *SW* **ever yesterday,** †**air-yesterday,** †**eerʒisterday** /ɛr'jɛstərde; *SW* ɛvər'jɛstərde/ *n* the day before yesterday *la16-19, 20- N SW Uls*. [ER + Older Scots ʒisterday]

erf *see* ERCH[1.1], ERCH[1.3]

ergh *see* ERCH[1.1], ERCH[1.2], ERCH[1.3]

Ergile, Ergyle, Ergyll *see* ARGYLL

Erische *see* IRISH[1.1], IRISH[1.2]

Erischman *see* IRISHMAN

eritabill *see* HERITABLE

eritage *see* HERITAGE

erl *see* ARLE

erle *see* EARL, HERLE

erles, erlis *see* ARLES

erlish *see* ELDRITCH

erm *see* AIRM[1], AIRM[2]

ermony *see* HARMONY

ermour *see* AIRMOUR

ermy *see* AIRMY

†**ern, urn** *v* to hurt or cause pain; to irritate *la15-e19*. [unknown]

ern *see* AIRN[1.1], AIRN[1.2], ARN

erne *see* AIRN[1.1], EARN

ernest *see* EARNEST[1.1]

†**ernfern, hernfern** *n* a variety of fern *Polypodium vulgare* or bracken *Pteridium aquilinum 19*. [EARN + FERN]

ernist *see* EARNEST[1.1]

ernit *see* ARNIT

eroy *see* EEROY

erp *see* ORP

err, †**er** /ɛr/ *v* to go astray; to wander, stray *la14-*. †**errand** wandering; straying *16*. **errant** wandering; straying *16-*. [OFr *errer*, Lat *errāre*]

err *see* AIR[1]

erran, errand *see* EERAN

†**errasy** *n* heresy *15-e17*. [ME *heresi*]

errick *see* EAROCK

error, †**errour,** †**arrour** /'ɛrər/ *n* 1 a mistaken belief or principle *la14-*. 2 a mistake *la14-*. 3 *law* a mistaken or wrongful decision on a brief of inquest or other legal matter *15-17*. 4 wandering, straying *e16*. [ME *errour*]

erruction *see* ERUCTION

ers *see* ERSE[1.1]

Ersche *see* ERSE[1.1], ERSE[1.2]

ersdene *see* ARCHEDENE

erse[1.1], **arse, airse,** †**ers,** †**ars** /ɛrs, ars, ɛrs/ *n* 1 the fundament, the buttocks *15-*. 2 the bottom of an object *16-*. 3 the hinterland, the interior away from the coast *la19- Ork N NE*. **ersie** 1 situated at the back *20- Sh Ork*. 2 stubborn, perverse *20- SW*. **ersit, essart** stubborn, perverse *la19- EC SW Bor*. **erselins, arselins** backwards *18-*. **aa erse an**

pooches used to describe a stout dumpy man (seen from behind) *la19- NE*. [OE *ears*]

erse[1,2], **arse** /ɛrs, ars/ *v* **1** to move or propel across the ground in the sitting position *20- Ork EC*. **2** to move backwards, push back; to back out *la19- NE*. **3** to consume food or (alcoholic) drink *la20- C*. **4** to destroy something by breakage *la20- C*. [see the noun]

Erse[2,1], †**Earse**, †**Eirse**, †**Ersche** /ɛrs/ *n* **1** Scottish Gaelic *16-*. **2** Irish Gaelic *20-*. Compare IRISH[1,1]. [see the adj]

Erse[2,2], †**Earse**, †**Ersche**, †**Irsche** /ɛrs/ *adj* **1** Irish *la14-*. **2** belonging or pertaining to the Scottish Highlands; Gaelic *la15-e19*. Compare IRISH[1,2]. †**Erschry**, **Irschery** **1** the Irish people or nation *15*. **2** the Gaelic language or the area where it was spoken *e16*. †**Irscheman** a person of Irish or Scottish Highland origins *la14-e16*. [OE *Yrisc* Irish, IrGael *Ériu* Ireland]

ersel *see* YERSEL

ersie, ersit *see* ERSE[1,1]

ert /ɛrt/ *v* **1** to threaten; to argue with *20- Sh*. **2** to strive for, attempt *20- Sh*. **ert up** to strive *19- Sh*. [ON *erta* to taunt; also compare AIRT[3]]

ert *see* AIRT[1], AIRT[2,1]

ertfast *see* YIRDFEST[1,2]

erth *see* YIRD[1,1], YIRD[1,2]

eruction, †**erruction** /əˈrʌkʃən/ *n* a violent outburst *19-*. [compare RUCTION]

erumption /əˈrʌmpʃən/ *n* an outburst, an uproar *20- EC SW Bor*. [altered form of Eng *eruption*]

ery *see* EERIE

eryll *see* EARL

eschaet *see* ESCHEAT[1,1]

eschame *see* ASCHAME

eschamit *see* ASCHAMIT

†**eschape**[1,1] *n* an escape *la14-e17*. [see the verb]

†**eschape**[1,2], **aschape**, **escheap** *v* to escape *la14-e17*. [ME *escapen, eschapen*]

esche *see* ESH, ISH[1,1]

escheap *see* ESCHAPE[1,2]

escheat[1,1], †**eschete**, †**achet**, †**eschaet** /ɛsˈtʃit/ *n law* **1** the forfeiture of a person's property on conviction for certain crimes, and until 1748 for non-payment of debts *15-*. **2** forfeited or confiscated property, possessions or goods, especially that falling to the Crown *la14-17*. [ME *eschete*]

escheat[1,2], †**eschete**, †**achet** /ɛsˈtʃit/ *v ptp also* **escheat**, **eschete** to confiscate; to forfeit *15-*. [see the noun]

escheif *see* ESCHEVE

eschete *see* ESCHEAT[1,1], ESCHEAT[1,2]

†**escheve**, **escheif** *v* **1** to accomplish or achieve; to overcome or vanquish; to succeed *la14-16*. **2** to succeed in escaping (from) *la15-16*. Compare ENCHEIF. [OFr *eschever*]

eschew /ɛsˈtʃu/ *v* **1** to avoid, shun *la14-*. **2** to escape *la14-e17*. **3** to draw back or withdraw (from); to draw aside *15-e17*. [ME *escheuen* to avoid]

eschie *see* ESHY

escok *see* ESSCOCK

ese *see* EASE[1,1], EASE[1,2]

esedrop *see* EASEDROP

esement *see* EASEMENT

esh, ash, aish, †**esche**, †**asche** /ɛʃ, aʃ, eʃ/ *n* (the wood of) the ash tree *Fraxinus excelsior* *12-*. [OE *æsc*]

†**eshy, ashy, eschie** *adj in place-names* covered with ash trees *la15-19*. [ESH + -IE[2]]

esiament *see* EASEMENT

esikis gray *see* ESSEX GRAY

esin *see* AES[1,2], EASIN

esk *see* ASK[1], YESK[1,1], YESK[1,2]

esler *see* AISLAR

esp /ɛsp/ *n* the aspen tree *Populus tremula* *16-19, 20- Bor*. [OE *æsp*]

†**esperance, esperaunce, asperans** *n* hope *la15-17*. [MFr *esperance*]

†**espy**[1,1], **aspy** *n* the action of spying; a spy *16-e17*. [ME *aspie*]

espy[1,2], †**aspy** /əˈspae/ *v* **1** to catch sight of; to perceive *la14-*. **2** to spy out, find out by spying; to spy on *la15-e19*. **3** to look, be observant *la15-e16*. [ME *aspien*]

espyne *see* ASPYNE

ess[1] /ɛs/ *n* a waterfall; frequently in place-names *19- Ork NE H&I SW*. **esscock** the dipper *Cinclus cinclus la19- NE*. [Gael *eas* + COCK[1,1]]

ess[2] /ɛs/ *n* an S-shaped hook *19-*. [from the letter shape]

ess *see* ACE, ASS

essart *see* ERSE[1,1]

essay /ˈɛse/ *n* **1** a piece of writing, a composition *la16-*. **2** a demonstration of ability, capacity or acquired skill, especially an object made to demonstrate skill *la16-19, 20- historical*. †**essayar** a tester of metal or coins *la16-17*; compare *assayour* (ASSAY). [MFr *essai*]

esscock, †**escok**, †**nescok** /ˈɛskɔk/ *n* an inflamed pimple *17-19, 20- NE*. [altered form of Scots *arse-cockle* a pimple on the buttock]

esscock *see* ESS[1]

†**Essex gray, esikis gray** *n* a grey cloth made in Essex *e17*. [from the English place-name + GRAY[1,1]]

essi, essie *see* ASSIE

†**essonʒe**[1,1], **assonʒe** *n* an excuse, a pretext; legal defence *la14-17*. [ME *essoine*, Lat *essonia*]

†**essonʒe**[1,2], **assonʒe** *v* to excuse *la14-16*. [ME *essoinen*]

est /ɛst/ *n* a nest *19- Bor*. [wrong division of Scots *a nest*]

est *see* AEST[1,1], AEST[1,2], EAST[1,1], EAST[1,3]

†**estabill, astabill** *v* to settle, establish *e16*. [OFr *establir*]

estaiblish, establish, †**establis**, †**establisch**, †**astablis** /əˈstɛbliʃ, əˈstabliʃ/ *v* to put in place; to create or set up; to prove or show to be valid *16-*. **estaiblishment, establishment** **1** the action or fact of establishing *la17-*. **2** the CHURCH OF SCOTLAND *la17-19*. **Established Kirk** the CHURCH OF SCOTLAND *20-*. [OFr *establiss-*, stem of *establir*]

estait *see* ESTATE

estald *see* EASTLE[1,2]

estate, †**estait**, †**astate** /əˈstet/ *n* **1** personal position, status or rank *15-*. **2** state, condition or situation *la15-*. **3** a landed property *17-*. **4** (heritable) possessions *17-*. **5** a housing development or scheme *20-*. **6** an industrial park *20-*. **7** class, order or rank in a community or country *15-e17*. **8** the body politic, the realm *la16-17*. Compare STATE[1,1]. **The Estates** the three classes of the community of Scotland (prelates, nobility and burgesses) which, with the king, made up the Scottish Parliament; the Scottish Parliament itself, compare *The Three Estates* (THREE) *la16-17, 18- historical*. [ME *estat*]

esten *see* EASTEN[1,1]

estent *see* EXTENT[1,1]

ester *see* EASTER[1,3]

estert *see* ASTART

†**estimy** *v* to esteem; to estimate *la15-16*. [ME *estemen*]

estin *see* EASTEN[1,2]

estlair *see* AISLAR

†**Estland, Eistland** *n* Estonia, or another eastern Baltic country *14-16*. **Estland burdis** boards or timber from the Eastern Baltic *15-16*. [EAST[1,2] + LAND[1,1]]

estonist *see* ASTONIST

estonyt *see* ASTONAIT

estreen *see* YESTREEN[1,2]

estwart see EASTART[1.3]
esy see EASY[1.1], EASY[1.2]
et see AET, EAT[1.1]
ete see EAT[1.2]
†**eterne, etern** *adj* eternal *la15-16*. **in eterne** to eternity *e16*. [ME *eterne*]
eth see EITH[1.1]
ether, edder, adder, *NE* **aidder,** †**eddir** /'ɛðər, 'ɛdər, 'adər; *NE* 'edər/ *n* an adder, a venomous snake of the family *Viperidae*; originally any snake or serpent *la14-*. **heather bill,** †**ether bell,** †**ather-bill,** †**adder bell** a dragonfly, an insect of the order *Odonata 19, 20- N NE*. †**ether stane, adderstone** a small perforated prehistoric stone or bead, used as an amulet *la18-19*. [wrong division of *a* NETHER[1]]
ether see AITHER[1.2], AITHER[1.3], AITHER[1.4], EDDER[1.1], EDDER[1.2], UDDER
ether-cap see ETTERCAP
ethers see AITHER[1.3]
ethkent see EITH-KENT[1.1], EITH-KENT[1.2]
†**ethnik**[1.1] *n* a heathen, a pagan *la14-16*. [see the adj]
†**ethnik**[1.2], **heathnick, hethnike** *adj* heathen, pagan *la16-17*. [Lat *ethnicus*]
etin, †**yetin,** †**etyne** /'ɛtɪn/ *n* a giant *la15-19, 20- literary*. [OE *eoten*]
etion see AISHAN
etle, etlyng see ETTLE[1.2]
etnach[1.1], **aitnach** /'ɛtnəx, 'ɛtnəx/ *n* the juniper *Juniperus communis*, the juniper berry *la18- N NE*. [see the adj]
etnach[1.2] /'ɛtnəx/ *adj* made of or pertaining to the juniper *la18- N NE*. [Gael *aitionnach*; compare AITEN]
ett see EAT[1.1], EAT[1.2]
etten see EAT[1.2]
etter[1.1], *N* **atter,** †**attir** /'ɛtər; *N* 'atər/ *n* **1** pus, poisonous matter *16-19, 20- Sh Bor*. **2** quarrelsomeness *20- N*. **ettersome 1** contentious, disagreeable *20- Sh NE T*. **2** *of weather* bitterly cold *20- Sh*. [OE *attor* poison]
etter[1.2], *SW* **yitter** /'ɛtər; *SW* 'jɪtər/ *v* to exude pus; to fester *19, 20- NE SW Bor*. [OE *ættrian* to poison]
ettercap, *Ork* **uiter-kap,** *N* **attercep,** *EC Uls* **attercap,** †**ether-cap,** †**ettercope,** †**attircop** /'ɛtərkap; *Ork* 'ətərkap; *N* 'atərkɛp; *EC Uls* 'atərkap/ *n* **1** a spider *15-*. **2** a spiteful or venomous person *16-*. Compare NETTERCAP. [OE *attorcoppa*]
etterlin, †**etterling** /'ɛtərlɪn/ *n* a two-year old cow or heifer in calf *19, 20- H&I*. †**etterlyne kow, otterline cow** = ETTERLIN *la16-17*. [perhaps Gael *atharla* a heifer]
etterskab, etterscab /'ɛtərskab/ *n* an ill-natured, troublesome person *20- Sh*. [perhaps altered form of ATTERCAP]
ettery, attery, *Ork* **aitrie,** *Ork* **attry,** †**attrie** /'ɛtəri, 'atəri; *Ork* 'etri; *Ork* 'atri/ *adj* **1** containing or exuding pus *la16-19, 20- NE Bor*. **2** grim, angry, forbidding; quarrelsome, spiteful *18-19, 20- Ork N NE Bor*. **3** *of weather* bleak, bitterly cold *19, 20- Sh Ork NE Bor*. **4** venomous, malignant *16*. [ETTER[1.1] + -IE[2]]
ettill see ETTLE[1.2]
ettle[1.1] /'ɛtəl/ *n* **1** one's aim or purpose, one's design or object *la18- literary*. **2** an effort, an attempt *19-*. **3** an ambition, a desire *20-*. **in ettle earnest** in deadly earnest *la19- Bor*. [see the verb]
ettle[1.2], †**tetle,** †**ettill** /'ɛtəl/ *v* **1** to intend, plan or propose *la14-*. **2** to aim or direct a blow or missile; to take aim at *la15-*. **3** to direct one's course or efforts towards; to attempt or venture *la15-*. **4** to desire very much *la19- Sh NE T H&I*. **5** to be about to or be on the verge of *la19- NE T EC*. **6** to expect, anticipate, guess *19- C SW Bor*. **ettling,** †**etlyng** purpose, intention; effort, endeavour; eagerness, ambition *la14-*. **ettle at** to try to express, get at *19-*. [ON *ætla*]

ettlement /'ɛtəlmənt/ *n* earnings, recompense; a fair share *20- EC Bor*. [ON *ætla*, with addition of *-ment* suffix]
Ettrick Shepherd /'ɛtrɪk 'ʃɛpərd/ *n* the assumed name of James Hogg *la18-*. [from the name of the village in the Scottish Borders + SHEPHERD]
etyne see ETIN
eucharist, †**ewcrist,** †**ocarist** /'jukərɪst/ *n* **1** *Christian Church* the sacrament of the Lord's Supper *15-*. **2** the vessel containing the consecrated bread, the pyx *15-16*. [ME *eukarist*, Lat *eucharistia*]
euer see IVER
euident see EVIDENT[1.1], EVIDENT[1.2]
euir see EVOR
euirlastande see IVERLAISTIN[1.2]
eulcruik see ELCRUKE
euse see USE[1.1]
euseless see USELESS[1.1]
eusteen see OST
euswal see USUAL
euther see YOWDER
evade, †**evaid** /ə'ved/ *v* to avoid or shun; to escape (from), elude; to get away *la15-*. [MFr *evader*]
†**evangel** *n* **1** *Christian Church* one of the four gospels; a gospel book (used in swearing an oath) *la14-e19*. **2** a political doctrine viewed as capable of redeeming society *e19*. [ME *evauegel*, Lat *ēvangelium*]
evanish, †**evanisch,** †**evanis** /ə'vanɪʃ/ *v* to disappear, vanish *la15-19, 20- T*. **evanishment** the act or fact of having disappeared *la19- NE T WC*. [ME *evanishen*]
eve /ev/ *n* doubt; irresolution *20- Sh*. [ON *ef*]
eveet, eveit see EVITE
even[1], **e'en,** †**evin,** †**evyn,** †**ewyn** /'ivən, in/ *n* evening; the eve of a particular day, especially a saint's day *la14-*. **at een** in the evening *15-*. [OE *ǣfen*]
even[2.1], *NE* **eyven** /'ivən; *NE* 'evən/ *v* **1** to estimate, appraise, compare with *15-*. **2** to divide equally or fairly; to make equal or even; to resolve or settle *la15-*. **3** to make level, smooth or straight *16-*. **4** to bring to the same level or condition; to lower, demean *19, 20- T SW*. **5** to malign or impugn, denigrate (someone or something) *la18-19, 20- NE H&I*. **6** to think oneself entitled to; to presume *19, 20- NE*. †**evinar** a person appointed to apportion lands *e16*. **eend** straight, level, exact *19- Bor*. **evener** weaving an instrument for spreading out the yarn on the beam *19- EC*. **einins** marbles (the right to change to) a more favourable position at an equal distance from the ring *20- SW Bor*. **even tae** to consider as a marriage partner *la18-19, 20- T*. **even yer wit tae** to condescend to argue with *la19- WC Uls*. [OE *efnan*]
even[2.2], **e'en,** *NE T EC* **aiven,** *SW* **ein,** †**evin** /'ivən, in; *NE T EC* 'evən; *SW* ain/ *adj* **1** straight; level *la14-*. **2** *of numbers* not odd, exactly divisible by two *la14-*. **3** equal, regular; impartial, just *la14-*. **be evens wi** to be even or quits with *la18-19, 20- EC SW*. **even hands wi** on an equal footing with *19- Bor*. **even heads** = *even hands wi la19- SW Bor*. [OE *efen*]
even[2.3], **e'en,** *NE T EC* **aiven,** †**evin,** †**evyn,** †**ewin** /'ivən, in; *NE T EC* 'evən/ *adv* **1** quite, fully, actually *la14-*. **2** just, simply: ◊*I may een gae hang la18-*. **3** directly, in a straight line, straight *la14-19*. **4** exactly, precisely *la14-e19*. **5** in a direct line of descent *la14-e15*. **6** in a level position *la14-16*. **7** no less or no other than; just *la14-17*. **8** in a regular, proper or normal manner *la14-e16*. **9** equally, evenly *la14-16*. **eent** indeed: ◊*I am not. Ye are eent 19- T H&I C*. **eend on** = *even on 20- EC Bor*. **even on** continuously, without ceasing, straight on *19-*. **even out** forthrightly, without restraint

19- *T EC Bor.* †**even up** *adj* straight, erect *la16-19.* **even up** *adv* straight up *la18, 20- Sh T.* [OE *efne*]

evendoon[1.1], *N* **eivendoon** /ˈivəndun; *N* ˈɛvəndun/ *adj* **1** *of heavy rain* straight, perpendicular *la18-.* **2** honest, frank, sincere *18-19, 20- NE H&I EC Bor.* **3** sheer, absolute, downright *la18-19, 20- N T SW.* [EVEN[2.3] + DOON[1.1]]

evendoon[1.2] /ˈivəndun/ *adv* absolutely, completely, downright *19, 20- NE.* [see the adj]

†**even doun** *n* candour, frankness *la17.* [from the adj EVENDOON[1.1]]

evenforrit /ˈivənfɔrɪt/ *adj* straightforward *18-19, 20- NE T EC Bor.* [EVEN[2.3] + FORRIT[1.2]]

evenin, eenin, evening, †**e'ning,** †**eining,** †**evining** /ˈivnɪn, ˈinɪn, ˈivənɪŋ/ *n* the last part of the day *la14-.* †**on e'enin's edge** on the verge of evening *la18*; compare *the edge o* (EDGE[1.1]). [OE *ǣfnung*]

evenly[1.1], †**evinly,** †**evynly** /ˈivənle/ *adj* **1** smooth, even, level *la16-19, 20- T H&I.* **2** equal; equitable *la14-e17.* **3** impartial *la15-16.* †**evenliness, evinlynes** equality; equanimity *15-19.* [OE *efenlic*]

evenly[1.2], †**evinly,** †**evinlie,** †**evynly** /ˈivənle/ *adv* **1** equally *la14-.* **2** uniformly, without variation *la14-.* **3** in an even or level position *la15-16.* **4** exactly, precisely *la14-16.* **5** equitably, impartially *15-e16.* [OE *efenlice*]

evenoo *see* EENOO

eventure *see* AVENTURE[1.1], AVENTURE[1.2]

ever *see* EEVER, IVER, OWER[1.2]

evere *see* IVERY[1.1]

everilk, evirilk /ˈɛvərɪlk/ *adj* every, each *la14-e19, la20- literary.* †**everilkane, everilkone** every one *la14-e19* †**euerilkdeill** every whit, altogether *la14-16.* [ME *ever ilk*]

everlastin *see* IVERLAISTIN[1.1], IVERLAISTIN[1.2]

everlesteen *see* IVERLAISTIN[1.1]

everlestin *see* IVERLAISTIN[1.1], IVERLAISTIN[1.2]

everly *see* IVER

evermair, evermar, evermoir, evermore *see* IVERMAIR

everon *see* AVERIN

†**evert** *v* **1** to refute (an argument or tenet of faith) *la16-19.* **2** to overturn, overthrow or destroy *16-e17.* [Lat *ēvertere*]

every *see* IVERY[1.1], IVERY[1.2]

ever yesterday *see* EREYESTERDAY

evidence, †**evidens** /ˈɛvɪdəns/ *n* **1** proof *15-.* **2** a document establishing a legal right or title to something *la14-e16.* [MFr *evidence* what is clearly visible or comprehensible, Lat *ēvidentia*]

evident[1.1], †**euident,** †**auedent** /ˈɛvɪdənt/ *n* **1** *law* a document establishing a legal right or title to something *la14-.* **2** *law* a piece of evidence, a proof *15.* [see the adj]

evident[1.2], †**euident** /ˈɛvɪdənt/ *adj* clear, plain, obvious *la15-.* [Lat *ēvidens*]

evil[1.1], **evill,** †**iwill** /ˈivəl/ *n* wrongdoing; harm; wickedness *la14-.* †**euil avisit** disposed to wrong-doing *la15-16.* †**evill gevin** inclined to do evil or cause trouble *16-e17.* †**evill won, evill win** ill-gotten *la15-16.* †**tak in evil** to resent *la15.* Compare ILL[1.1]. [see the adj]

evil[1.2], †**evill,** †**ivill,** †**iwill** /ˈivəl/ *adj* **1** wicked, vicious, immoral, depraved *la14-.* **2** inferior, of poor quality; badly made or maintained *la14-.* **3** harmful, unpleasant, offensive, difficult; unfortunate, miserable *15-.* †**evill dedy** evildoing *16.* †**euill myndit** having a wicked nature *la15-16.* †**evil willy** malevolent *16.* †**evil at eis** indisposed, unwell *la16.* Compare ILL[1.2]. [OE *yfel*]

evil[1.3], †**evill,** †**ivill** /ˈivəl/ *adv* **1** wickedly, with bad intent; wrongly, unjustly *la14-.* **2** severely, harshly, violently *la15-17.* **3** improperly, poorly; unhappily; in bad health *15-17.* †**evill disposit 1** inclined to evil, of an obnoxious nature *la15-e17.* **2** not in good health or condition *16.* †**evill facit** ugly *e16.* †**evill farit** ugly *e16.* †**evill farrand** ugly *e16.* **evil vickid** ill-disposed, malignant *20- Sh.* Compare ILL[1.3]. [OE *yfle*]

†**evin** *n* (subject) matter; substance *la15.* [ON *efni*]

evin *see* EVEN[1], EVEN[2.2], EVEN[2.3]

evining *see* EVENIN

evinlie *see* EVENLY[1.2]

†**evinlik**[1.1], **ewynlyk** *adj* equal; just, equitable *15.* **ewynlykly** exactly; directly *e15.* [OE *efenlic*]

†**evinlik**[1.2], **ewynlyk** *adv* equally, evenly *la14-e15.* [OE *efenlice*]

evinly *see* EVENLY[1.1], EVENLY[1.2]

evin now *see* EENOO

evir *see* IVER

evirilk *see* EVERILK

evirlestand *see* IVERLAISTIN[1.2]

evirmair *see* IVERMAIR

evite, eveet, †**aveet,** †**eveit** /əˈvʌɪt, əˈvit/ *v* to avoid, escape *17-19, 20- NE C.* [Fr *éviter*, Lat *ēvītāre*]

†**evor, yvor, euir** *n* ivory *15-16.* **evor bane, iver bane** ivory *16.* [ME *īvori*]

evyn *see* EVEN[1], EVEN[2.3]

†**evyneild** *n* a person of the same age *e16.* [OE *efeneald*]

evynly *see* EVENLY[1.1], EVENLY[1.2]

ewcrist *see* EUCHARIST

ewder *see* YOWDER

ewe *see* YOWE

ewest[1.1], †**ewis,** †**ewous** /ˈjuəst/ *adj* near, next to *la15-19, 20- SW.* [wrong division of ME *anewest*, OE *on nēaweste* in the neighbourhood]

†**ewest**[1.2], **ewis, ewous** *prep* near; beside *la15-e17.* [see the adj]

ewin *see* EVEN[2.3]

ewindrift *see* YOWDENDRIFT

ewiry *see* IVERY[1.1]

ewis, ewous *see* EWEST[1.1], EWEST[1.2]

ewyn *see* EVEN[1]

ewynlyk *see* EVINLIK[1.1], EVINLIK[1.2]

ex *see* AIX

exack[1.1], **exact** /ɛgˈzak, ɛgˈzakt/ *adj* precise *la16-.* **exackly, exactly 1** precisely *la16-.* **2** without more ado *la19-.* **3** in every respect *la19-.* [Lat *exactus*]

exack[1.2], **exact** /ɛgˈzak, ɛgˈzakt/ *adv* precisely *la16-.* [see the adj]

exaemin *see* EXAMINE[1.1]

exaimen *see* EXAMINE[1.2]

exaimple, example, exemple, †**exampill,** †**exempil** /ɛgˈzɛmpəl, ɛgˈzampəl, ɛgˈzɛmpəl/ *n* a typical or signal instance; a sample; a guide to conduct *15-.* [Lat *exemplum*]

exame *see* EXEM

†**examinat** *v pt* **examinate, examinat, exemenat** to examine, investigate *la15-e19.* **examinator, examinatour** an examiner, an interrogator *la16-19.* [Lat *exāmināre*]

examination, *NE* **exemination,** †**exeminatioun** /ɛgzaməˈneʃən; *NE* ɛgzɛməˈneʃən/ *n* testing, a test; investigation; interrogation *15-.* [Lat *exāminātio*]

examine[1.1], **examin,** *NE* **exaemin** /ɛgˈzamən; *NE* ɛgˈzemən/ *n* **1** examination *la15-19, 20- NE.* **2** *Presbyterian Church* an examination by a minister of the theological knowledge of his parishioners, in preparation for Communion *18-20, 21- historical.* [Lat *exāmen*]

examine[1.2], *NE* **exemin,** *NE T* **exaimen,** †**examin,** †**exemyn** /ɛgˈzamən; *NE* ɛgˈzɛmən; *NE T* ɛgˈzemən/ *v* to inspect; to question; to investigate *15-.* †**examinable persons** those eligible for theological examination by a minister prior to Communion *la17-e19*. [MFr *examiner*, Lat *exāmināre*]

exampill, example *see* EXAIMPLE

†**exauctorate** *v ptp* **exauctorate** to depose from office, relieve of authority *18-19*. [Lat *exauctōrāre*]

excaise[1.1], **excuse**, *NE* **exkeese**, †**excus**, †**excuis** /εk'skes, εk'skjus; *NE* εk'skis/ *n* a plea or explanation offered in extenuation or defence; an excuse *la15-*. [ME *excuse*]

excaise[1.2], **excuse**, *NE* **exkeese**, †**excus**, †**excuis** /εk'skez, εk'skjuz; *NE* εk'skiz/ *v* **1** to offer an excuse or defence; to defend or seek to clear oneself *la14-*. **2** to pardon, forgive; to exempt from blame or obligation; to furnish with an excuse *15-*. [ME *excusen*]

excamb[1.1] /'εkskam, 'εkskamb/ *n* an exchange; a piece of land given in exchange for another *19-*. [see the verb]

excamb[1.2] /εk'skam, εk'skamb/ *v law* to exchange (land) *la15-*. [Lat *excambiāre*]

excambion /εk'skambɪən/ *n law* an exchange of land or property *la15-*. [altered form of EXCAMBIUM]

†**excambium** *n* EXCAMBION *la15-e16*. [Lat *excambium*]

ex capite lecti /εks 'kapɪte 'lεktae/ *adv of a change to a person's last wishes* made on their deathbed, so open to judicial annulment *19, 20- historical*. [Lat *ex capite lectī* from the head of the bed]

exceed, †**excede**, †**exceid** /εk'sid/ *v* **1** to be greater or more than; to go past a limit *la14-*. **2** to surpass, outdo, be superior to *la14-*. **3** to be in excess *la15-16*. [MFr *exceder*, Lat *excēdere*]

excellence /'εksələns/ *n* **1** superior quality or worth *la15-*. **2** a title of honour, excellency *la14-16*. [MFr *excellence*, Lat *excellentia*]

excep[1.1], **except**, †**accept**, †**accep** /εk'sεp, εk'sεpt/ *v ptp* also †**excep**, †**except 1** to exempt; to exclude *15-*. **2** *law* to make an objection, protest; to plead as an objection *la15-e17*.

exceptin, excepting, *Sh T EC* **exceppin**, †**excepand** with the exception of, not including, other than *15-*. [MFr *excepter*, Lat *except-*, ptp stem of *excipere*]

excep[1.2], **except** /εk'sεp, εk'sεpt/ *prep* **1** with the exception of, not including, other than *la15-*. **2** in addition to, besides *la15-16*. [Lat *exceptus*]

excep[1.3], **except** /εk'sεp, εk'sεpt/ *conj* unless *la15-*. [see the prep]

exceppit *see* ACCEP

except *see* ACCEP, EXCEP[1.1], EXCEP[1.2], EXCEP[1.3]

exception, †**exceptioun** /εk'sεpʃən/ *n* **1** the action or state of excluding or exempting, or being excluded; exclusion *la14-*. **2** *law* a plea against a charge, a defence *15-*. **3** *law* an objection to a judge's charge to the jury in a civil case *19-*.

†**exceptioun declinatour** a DECLINATURE *la15-e17*. [AN *exception*]

excers *see* EXERCE[1.2]

excerse *see* EXERCE[1.1]

excess, †**exces**, †**acces** /εk'sεs/ *n* **1** intemperance, immoderate behaviour *15-*. **2** a superabundance, too much *la15-*. [MFr *exces*, Lat *excessus*]

exchequer, †**exchaker**, †**exchecker**, †**exchekker** /εks'tʃεkər/ *n* the government department concerned with revenue; the royal exchequer *17-*. Compare CHEKKER. [ME *escheker*, EModE *exchequer*]

†**excipient** *n law* a person who raises an EXCEPTION in law *la16-17*. [Lat *excipient-*, presp stem of *excipere* to except]

excise[1.1], †**excys**, †**exsis** /'εksaez/ *n* a tax on (imported) goods *16-*. [MDu *excijs*]

†**excise**[1.2] *v* to force to pay tax; to overcharge *e19*. [see the noun]

exclaim /εk'sklem/ *n* a shout, an exclamation *19, 20- Bor*. [from the Scots verb *exclaim*]

†**excres** *v* to increase, exceed *la16-e17*. [Lat *excrēscere*]

†**excresce, excres** *n* an increase; a surplus *16-e19*. [from the verb EXCRES]

excrescence /εks'krεsəns/ *n* **1** a growth, a protuberance *la17-*. **2** an excess amount, an increase, a surplus, a profit *la15-18*. [Lat *excrēscentia*]

excuis, excus, excuse *see* EXCAISE[1.1], EXCAISE[1.2]

excys *see* EXCISE[1.1]

execkiter, exectour *see* EXECUTOR

execute /'εksəkjut/ *v ptp* **executed**, †**execute 1** to perform a task *la15-*. **2** to put into effect as required by law, make legally effective *15-*. **3** to put to death *la16-*. [Lat *execūt-*, ptp stem of *exequi* to follow out]

execution, †**executioun** /εksə'kjuʃən/ *n* **1** the action of settling a matter or executing a task *la14-*. **2** *law* the formal putting into effect of a warrant, brief or decree *15-*. **3** *law* the writing in which an officer of the law narrates his fulfilment of duty *18-*. **4** the infliction of capital punishment *18-*. †**put to executioun** to execute, perform, put into effect *la15-16*. [ME *execucioun*, Lat *executio*]

executor, †**execkiter**, †**executour**, †**exectour** /εg'zεkjutər, εk'sεkjutər/ *n law* **1** the legal administrator of the estate of a deceased person *15-*; compare EXECUTRIX. **2** a person who serves a writ or executes a warrant; originally also a person who carried out a task or performed an action *15-*. †**executory, executry** the office of a legal executor *16-18*. **executry** the whole moveable property of a deceased person *la17-*.

executor dative the legal executor nominated by a sheriff when the deceased has failed to nominate an *executor testamentar 16-*. **executor nominate** = *executor testamentar la18-*. **executor testamentar** the legal executor nominated in a will *16-*. [ME *executour*, Lat *executōr*]

†**executorials, executoriallis, executoriellis** *npl* instructions or legal authority for executing a decree or sentence *16-e18*. †**letters executorialis** = EXECUTORIALS *la15-16*. [Lat *executōriālis*]

executour *see* EXECUTOR

executrix, †**executrice** /εg'zεkjutrɪks, εk'sεkjutrɪks/ *n* a female EXECUTOR (sense 1) *la15-*. †**executrix testamentar** the EXECUTRIX nominated in a will *16*. [Lat *executrīx*]

executry *see* EXECUTOR

exeem, exeme, †**exime** /εg'zim/ *v* **1** to free; to exempt *16-19, 20- Bor*. **2** to remove, exclude *e17*. [Lat *eximere* to take out]

exem, †**exame**, †**exeme** /εg'zεm/ *v* to examine *la14-19, 20- NE*. [reduced form of EXAMINE[1.2]]

exeme *see* EXEEM

exemenat *see* EXAMINAT

exemin *see* EXAMINE[1.2]

exemination, exeminatioun *see* EXAMINATION

exemp, exempt /εg'zεmp, εg'zεmpt/ *v* to free from; to except or exclude *la15-*. [MFr *exempter*]

exempil, exemple *see* EXAIMPLE

exempt *see* EXEMP

exemyn *see* EXAMINE[1.2]

exequies, †**exequeys** /'εksəkwiz/ *npl* funeral rites *la14-*. [OFr *exeques*, Lat *exequias*, accusative of *exsequiae* a train of followers]

†**exerce**[1.1], **excerse** *n* exercise, function *16-e18*. [see the verb]

†**exerce**[1.2], **exers, excers** *v* **1** to discharge the duties of an office *la15-18*. **2** to perform an act *la15-18*. **3** to use *la15-e18*. **4** to carry on a trade or calling *la15-17*. **5** to exert, apply strength *la15-17*. **6** to act in a certain capacity *16-e18*. **7** to

hold a fair or market *16-e17*. **8** to practise a virtue or vice *15-16*. **9** to occupy oneself in practice or exercise *16*. **exercit** exercised, made expert, experienced *16*. [ME *exercen*, Lat *exercēre*]

exerceese[1.1], **exercise** /'ɛksərsiz, 'ɛksərsaez/ *n* **1** physical exertion or training *la16-*. **2** practice or occupation in an activity; the activity performed *la16-*. **3** *Presbyterian Church* the exposition or discussion of a passage of Scripture, as part of a church service or by the members of a presbytery; an exegetical sermon or discourse delivered to a presbytery, especially prior to ordination *la16-*. **4** the using of a faculty *18-*. **5** work or written composition required by an educational establishment of its pupils or students *19-*. **6** family worship, prayers *18-19, 20- NE EC*. **7** a presbytery *la16-17*. †**make exercise** to hold family worship *19*. †**mak the exercise** to perform the exposition of Scripture *e17*. [ME *exercise*, Lat *exercitium*]

exerceese[1.2], **exercise** /'ɛksərsiz, 'ɛksərsaez/ *v* **1** to perform an activity; to act; to discharge the duties of an office *16-*. **2** to exert oneself physically, take exercise *la16-*. **3** to use an ability or power *17-*. **4** to engage in prayer or expound scripture as part of public or private worship *la16-19, 20- NE*. **5** to train by practice *la16-e17*. **6** to use a weapon *la15-16*. †**exerciser** the minister performing an exposition of Scripture *17*. [see the noun]

†**exercitioun, exercisioun** *n* **1** the exercise of a pursuit or office *la15-e17*. **2** an occupation *la15-16*. **3** physical exercise; practice or training in a skill *16*. [Lat *exercitio*]

exers see EXERCE[1.2]

exhaust see EXOWST

exhibition, †**exhibitioun** /ɛksə'bɪʃən/ *n* **1** *law* the production or delivery of documents at the instance of a court *la16-*. **2** the action of exhibiting; a show, display or manifestation *la16-*. **3** the presentation of a person in a court of law *la16*. [ME *exhibicioun*, OFr *exhibicion*, Lat *exhibitio*]

exhoner see EXONER

exhorbitant see EXORBITANT

exhort, †**exort** /ɛɡ'zɔrt/ *v* to urge, admonish *la15-*. †**exortar, exhortar** *Presbyterian Church* a person appointed to give religious exhortation under a minister *la16-e17*. [Lat *exhortāri*]

exhoust see EXOWST

exies see AIXIES

exime see EXEEM

exkeese see EXCAISE[1.1], EXCAISE[1.2]

exle see AIXLE

exoner, †**exhoner** /ɛɡ'zɔnər/ *v law* **1** to discharge from or relieve of an obligation or responsibility; to pay or acknowledge payment of a debt *16-*. **2** to resign from an office *16-19*. **3** to free from blame *17*. **4** to free from a burden; to unload *e16*. [MFr *exonerer*, Lat *exonerāre*]

exoneration, †**exoneratioun** /ɛɡzɔnə'reʃən/ *n* **1** an act of relieving or discharging *la16-*. **2** *law* the act of being legally disburdened of, or liberated from, the performance of a duty or obligation *la16-*. [Lat *exonerātio*]

exorbitant, †**exhorbitant** /ɛɡ'zɔrbɪtənt/ *adj* **1** *of prices* excessively high *16-*. **2** grossly excessive or unfair; transgressing *la15-e17*. [Lat *exorbitant-*, presp stem of *exorbitāre* to go out of the track]

exort see EXHORT

exowst, exhaust, *Bor* **exhoust** /ɛɡ'zʌust, ɛɡ'zɔst; *Bor* ɛks'hʌust/ *v ptp* also †**exhaust** to use up, empty *16-*. **exhausted teinds** the tithes already used in their entirety for payment of a minister's stipend leaving no surplus for increments *19-*; compare *valued teinds* (VALUE[1.2]). [Lat *exhaust-*, ptp stem of *exhaurīre*]

expairience see EXPERIENCE

expairt /ɛk'spɛrt/ *n* an expert *la20- NE T EC SW*. [Fr *expert*]

expawtiate /ɛk'spɔʃɪet/ *v* to expatiate *19, 20- NE T EC*. [Lat *exspatiāt-*, ptp stem of *exspatiāri*]

expeck, expect /ɛk'spɛk, ɛk'spɛkt/ *v* **1** to wait for, await *la16-*. **2** to anticipate, look forward to *17-*. **3** to think reasonable or appropriate *la18-*. †**expectant** the prospective occupier of a post; especially a prospective or probationary minister *17-e19*. [Lat *expectāre*]

expede, †**exped,** †**expeid** /ɛk'spid/ *v pt, ptp* **expede,** †**exped 1** *law* to complete and issue a document *la16-*. **2** to accomplish or complete; to deal with promptly and effectively *16-18*. **3** to send, expedite *la16-18*. [MFr *expedier*, Lat *expediāre* to make ready]

expense, †**expens,** †**expence** /ɛk'spɛns/ *n* **1** money or means for spending, financial support *15-*. **2** expenditure, money spent *la15-*. **3** *law* costs *18-*. †**for thair expence** for their pains *la15*. [ME *expense*, Lat *expēnsa*]

expensive /ɛk'spɛnsɪv/ *adj* **1** costly *17-*. **2** extravagant *19, 20- Sh NE EC Bor*. [Lat *expendere* to weigh out, and by suffixation of EXPENSE]

experience, *NE T* **expairience,** †**experiens** /ɛk'spɪrɪəns; *NE T* ɛk'spɛrɪəns/ *n* knowledge resulting from what has been experienced; an event which leaves a lasting impression *la15-*. [MFr *experience*, Lat *experientia*]

expire, †**expyre** /ɛk'spaer/ *v* **1** to render void; to cease to be valid *15-*. **2** to die *la15-*. **3** to come to an end *16-*. **expiry** the termination of a contract; the close of a period of time *18-*. [MFr *expirer*, Lat *exspīrāre*]

expiscate /ɛk'spɪsket/ *v* to examine; to discover by investigation *la17-*. **expiscation** investigation *la17-*. [Lat *expiscāri* to fish out]

†**exploratour** *n* a scout, a spy *16-e17*. [Lat *explōrātor*]

†**expone** *v* **1** to expose, lay open *15-e17*. **2** to expound, explain *la14-17*. **3** to state, declare, make known *la15-e17*. [Lat *expōnere*]

expoond, expund, expound /ɛk'spund, ɛk'spʌund/ *v* to explain; to interpret (scripture) *la14-*. [ME *expounen*, OFr *espundre*, Lat *expōnere*]

export[1.1] /'ɛksport/ *n* **1** the selling of goods abroad; a commodity sold to a foreign country *la17-*. **2** a superior-quality, stronger beer, slightly darker in colour than HEAVY[1.1] *20-*. [see the verb]

export[1.2] /ɛk'sport/ *v* to sell goods to a foreign country *16-*. [MFr *exporter*, Lat *exportāre*]

exposeetion, exposition, †**expositioun** /ɛkspo'zɪʃən, ɛkspo'zɪʃən/ *n* a detailed explanation (of a passage of Scripture) *15-*. [MFr *exposition*, Lat *expositio*]

†**expositour** *n* someone who explains or expounds texts *la15-16*. [ME *expositour*, Lat *expositor*]

expound see EXPOOND

†**expreme, exprime, expreym** *v* to express in words; to state or name *15-17*. [MFr *exprimer*, Lat *exprimere*]

†**expugnate** *adj* taken by storm *16*. [Lat *expugnātus*]

†**expuls** *n* expulsion *la15*. [Lat *expulsāre* to drive out]

expund see EXPOOND

expyre see EXPIRE

exsep see ACCEP

exsis see EXCISE[1.1]

extend /ɛk'stɛnd/ *v* **1** to stretch in length; to continue; to stretch out; to prolong; to enlarge *15-*. **2** *law* to make a final copy of a legal document for signature *19-*. **3** *of a law or effort* to apply or exert *la15-17*. †**extand to, extend till** to amount or come to a specified sum or quantity *la15-e18*. [Lat *extendere*]

extension, †**extensioun** /ɛkˈstɛnʃən/ *n* **1** a prolongation; an enlargement; something which has been extended *18-*. **2** a holding out of the hand *la15-16*. [Lat *extentio*]

extent[1.1], †**estent**, †**astent** /ɛkˈstɛnt/ *n* **1** the valuation of land or property; the assessed value *15-19, 20- historical*. **2** a levy or tax based on the valuation of land or property *la15-e17*. [ME *extente*]

†**extent**[1.2] *v* **1** to assess the value of land and property; to be assessed *15-16*. **2** to tax according to the assessed value of land or property *16-e17*; compare STENT[2.2]. **extentour** an assessor *15-e17*. [see the noun]

†**exterminioun** *n* extermination, destruction; expulsion *16-17*. [Lat *exterminium*]

extirpit, **extirpite** /ˈɛkstɪrpət, ɛkˈstɪrpət/ *adj* extirpated *18-19, 20- NE*. [Lat *extirpātus* + -IT[1]]

†**extors** *v* to subject to extorsion or oppression *la16-e18*. [Lat *extors-*, rare ptp stem of *extorquēre*]

extract[1.1], **extrack**, †**extrect**, †**extrek** /ˈɛkstrakt, ˈɛkstrak/ *n* **1** an excerpt *la15-*. **2** *law* an official, certified copy of a judgement of a court or of any other publicly-recorded document *16-*; compare EXTRETE. **3** extraction *la17*. [Lat *extractum*]

extract[1.2], **extrack** /ɛkˈstrakt, ɛkˈstrak/ *v ptp* also **extract 1** to take or draw out; to excerpt; to elicit, derive or obtain (from) *16-*. **2** *law* to make an official, properly authenticated copy of a publicly-recorded document *la15-*. [Lat *extract-*, ptp stem of *extrahere*]

extrae *see* AIXTRA[1.1], AIXTRA[1.2], AIXTRA[1.3]

extranean[1.1] /ɛkˈstrɛnɪən/ *n* an outsider, a stranger; a pupil from outside Aberdeen attending Aberdeen Grammar School to study for the university bursary competition *19- NE*. [Lat *extrāneus* a stranger]

extranean[1.2] /ɛkˈstrɛnɪən/ *adj* of external origin, added from without; foreign (to the burgh) *la16-19, 20- NE*. [Lat *extrāneus* foreign]

†**extraneare**[1.1], **extranier** *n* an outsider; one not belonging to the burgh or district; a stranger *16-17*. [Lat *extrāneus* a stranger]

†**extraneare**[1.2], **extranier** *adj* foreign; coming from outside; not belonging to the burgh *16-17*. [Lat *extrāneus* foreign]

†**extraordinar**[1.1] *n* an unusual or additional event, item or person *16-e19*. [see the adj]

extraordinar[1.2], †**extrornar** /ɛkˈstrɔrdɪnər, ɛkˈstrɔrdnər, ɛkstrəˈɔrdɪnər/ *adj* **1** out of the ordinary, exceptional *la15-*. **2** additional, extra *la16-17*. **3** excessive, extreme *la16-e19*. [Lat *extraordinārius*]

†**Extraordinar Lord of Session**, **extraordinary Lord of session** *n* a person nominated by the sovereign to join the fifteen regular Lords of Session as an additional or supernumerary member of the Court *la16-17*. [EXTRAORDINAR[1.2] + LORD OF SESSION]

extravage /ɛkˈstravədʒ, ɛkstrəˈveg/ *v* to wander about; to digress or ramble in talking *la17-*. [Lat *extravagārī* to wander, stray beyond limits; compare STRAVAIG[1.2]]

extre *see* AIXTREE

extrect *see* EXTRACT[1.1]

extreit *see* EXTRETE

extrek *see* EXTRACT[1.1]

†**extrete**, **extreit** *n law* (a certified copy of) the fines imposed by a court *la15-16*. [AN *estrete*, Lat *extracta*; compare EXTRACT[1.1]]

extrie *see* AIXTREE

extrinsic /ɛkˈstrɪnzɪk/ *adj of a fact or circumstance given under oath* not essentially qualifying the matter attested, not inherent to the point immediately at issue *18-*. Compare INTRINSIC. [Fr *extrinsèque*, Lat *extrinsecus*]

extrornar *see* EXTRAORDINAR[1.2]

ey *see* AYE[2], EE[1], THAE[1.1]

eydent *see* EIDENT

eye *see* EE[1]

eyelist *see* EELIST

eyes *see* EE[1]

eyge *see* EDGE[1.1]

eyiss *see* ACE

eyld *see* EILD[1.1]

eyll *see* ISLE

eyllan *see* ISLAND

eyn *see* EN[1.1]

eyne *see* AYING, EE[1]

eyntment, **intment**, **ointment**, †**oyntment**, †**oynment** /ˈʌɪntmənt, ˈɛntmənt, ˈɪntmənt, ˈɔɪntmənt/ *n* a medical preparation, an unguent or salve, originally also a cosmetic *la14-*. [ME *ointement, ointment, oinement*]

eyr *see* AIR[5.2], EAR[1]

eyrisland *see* URISLAND

eys *see* EASE[1.1], EASE[1.2]

eyst *see* AEST[1.2]

eyt, **eytin** *see* EAT[1.2]

eyther *see* AITHER[1.2], AITHER[1.3], AITHER[1.4]

eyven *see* EVEN[2.1]

eywis *see* AYEWIS

eyzle *see* AIZLE[1.1]

ezlar *see* AISLAR

F

fa[1.1], **faw**, **fall**, *Sh* **faa** /fa, fɔ, fɔl; *Sh* fɑ/ *n* **1** a drop, a tumble, a (sudden) descent *la14-*. **2** the distance over which a measuring rod falls; a lineal measure of land equal to 6 ells; the corresponding square measure *la14-*. **3** a dip or hollow in the ground; a small ravine *19- NE*. **4** a waterfall in a tide-race between two points of land *20- Ork*. **5** a share, a portion; a subdivision of land *la18-19*. **6** that which befalls one; a person's fate or fortune *la18-19*. [see the verb]

fa[1.2], **faw**, **fall**, **faa**, †**fal** /fa, fɔ, fɔl, fɑ/ *v pt* **fell**, *ptp Sh NE* **faaen**, **faen**, **fawn**, **fallen**, **fa'n**, *Sh WC* **faan**, †**fawin 1** to descend, drop; to collapse downwards, tumble *la14-*. **2** *of night* to come on *la14-*. **3** to happen, occur, befall *la14-*. **4** to get involved (in a state or activity); to become *la14-*. **5** *of possessions* to come into a person's ownership *la14-*. **6** to be under obligation or necessity; to have (to) *18-*. **7** to diminish in bulk; to crumble, fall to pieces *la18-*. **8** to aspire to, lay claim to; to be able to afford *la18-19, 20- Ork NE*. **9** to fall (to someone) as a duty or turn; to be appropriate, suit *15-19, 20- Sh*. **10** to obtain, win or come by *la15-19*. †**fall-brig** a boarding-bridge on the side of a ship *la14*. **fa-tae 1** a lean-to building *20-*. **2** a set-to, a quarrel *la19, 20- Sh Ork*. **fa about**, **fall about** to set about, fall to (a task) *17-*. **fa aff ane's feet** to tumble, fall down *la19-*. **fa afore** to occur to, come to one's mind *19- Sh*. **fa awa**, **fall away 1** to waste away; to decline in health *la19-*. **2** to faint *20- Sh NE T*. **fa by**, **fall by 1** to faint or collapse *20- Sh Ork*. **2** to take to one's bed through illness or childbirth *19- NE*. **3** to go missing, be mislaid *18-e19*. **fa in**, **fall in 1** *of the body* to shrink or shrivel *la19-*. **2** *of a river* to subside *19 20- SW*. **fa in fancy wi** to take a fancy to *la19- Sh Ork T WC*. †**fall in scatfall** *of land in Orkney* to be subject to confiscation due to failure to pay skatt tax *la16-e17*. **fa on** to start courting (with) *la19-, 20- NE*. **fa oot on**, **fall out on** to lose one's temper with, speak angrily to *la19- NE T*. **fa ower**, **fall ower** to fall asleep *la18-*. **fa ower the brim** to go to one's death or destruction *20- literary*. **fa through** to botch, mismanage *la18-19, 20- NE*. **fall through wi** to abandon a task from negligence or laziness *19, 20- T*. **fa wi bairn** to become pregnant *18-19, 20- NE EC*. †**fall with child** to become pregnant *18*. [OE *feallan*]

fa[2], **faw**, †**fall** /fa, fɔ/ *n* a falling mouse-trap or rat-trap *la15-19, 20- EC*. [OE (mūs) *fealle*]

fa *see* FAE[1], WHA

faa /fɑ, fɑ/ *n* the entrails of a slaughtered animal *la18- Sh Ork N NE*. [ON *fall* a slaughtered animal carcass]

faa *see* FA[1.1], FA[1.2]

faad *see* FAD

faader *see* FAITHER[1.1]

faaen *see* FA[1.2]

faal *see* FAULD[2.1], WHAAL

faan *see* FA[1.2]

faap *see* WHAUP[1.1]

faar[1] /far/ *n* an epidemic disease *la19- Sh*. [ON *fár* a dangerous disease]

faar[2], **far** /fɑr, far/ *n fisherman's taboo* a boat, a vessel *la19- Sh*. [ON *far* a ship]

faar *see* WHAUR[1.1]

faase /faz/ *v* to flatter insincerely; to fawn upon *la19- Sh*. [altered form of FALS]

faase *see* FAUSE

faat *see* FAUT[1.1]

faaver *see* FAVOUR[1.1]

†**fab**[1] *n* a small pocket, a pouch *la18-19*. [EModE *fob*]

fab[2] /fab/ *n* a truant *20- EC*. [unknown]

fab *see* FOB

fabala /'fabəla/ *n* a flounce; trimming on a garment *19, 20- NE*. [compare Eng *furbelow*]

fabric /'fabrɪk/ *n* an ungainly or ugly object, animal or person *la19- Sh NE T EC*. [extended sense of Eng *fabric*]

Fabruar *see* FEBRUAR

face[1.1], *N* **feice**, *N NE* **feece**, *T* **fess**, *T* **fiss** /fes; *N* fʌɪs; *N NE* fis; *T* fes; *T* fɪs/ *n* **1** the front of the head, the countenance; a facial expression *la14-*. **2** appearance, semblance, form *la15-*. **3** the surface or side of an object; the surface of the ground; a slope or vertical edge *16-*. †**Facers** an Edinburgh drinking club *e18*. **facie** bold, ready to face danger; cheeky *19- EC Bor*. **face cairt**, **face caird** *in playing cards* a court card *19-*. **face claith** a cloth for wiping the face *17-*. **face clout** a face-cloth *20-*. **face-dyke** a wall consisting of stones on one side and earth and turf on the other *la18-*. **the face of clay** any person, anyone at all *19, 20- NE H&I*. **oot o face** without a break, in orderly sequence *20- H&I SW Uls*. **oot o the face o't** bewildered; in a muddle *20- T*. **put in a face** to put in an appearance *20-*. [ME *face*]

face[1.2] /fes/ *v* **1** to look in the direction of; to confront or deal with *la16-*. **2** to cover (a surface) with another material *17-*. [see the noun]

facheon *see* FACHOUN

facherie *see* FASHERIE

†**fachoun**, **fachioun**, **facheon** *n* a curved broad sword with the edge on the convex side *la14-e16*. [ME *fauchoun*]

facile, †**facil** /'fasʌɪl/ *adj* **1** easy, straightforward *16-*. **2** *law* easily influenced, gullible *16-*. **facility 1** easiness *la16-*. **2** *law* the state of being easily influenced or gullible *la16-*. [EModE *facile*]

facin, **facing**, †**fasing** /'fesɪn, 'fesɪŋ/ *n* the action of applying an outside layer or surface *16-*. **facing iron** a smoothing iron with a polished surface *20- NE*. †**facing-tools** drinking vessels *e18*. **facing the monument** *in Glasgow* being hanged in the place of public execution (which faced the Nelson Monument) *19, 20- historical*. [derivative of FACE[1.1]]

fack[1.1], **fact** /fak, fakt/ *n* **1** something known to be true, a fact *18-*. **2** an act, deed *la15-17*. [Lat *factum* a deed]

fack[1.2], **fact** /fak, fakt/ *adj* true *la19, 20- NE Uls*. **as fack as** as sure as *la19, 20- N NE T SW Uls*. [see the noun]

†**fack**[1.3] *interj* an expression of affirmation *19*. [see the noun]

fact *see* FACK[1.1], FACK[1.2]

faction, †**factioun** /'fakʃən/ *n* **1** a small dissenting group within a larger group *16-*. **2** *in Aberdeen Grammar School* a section of a class; the bench on which each section sat *18-19*. [EModE *faction*, Lat *factio*]

factor[1.1], †**factour** /'faktər/ *n* **1** an agent or steward who manages property for its owner *15-*. **2** a business agent *16-*. **3** *law* a person appointed by a court to manage forfeited property *18-e19*. **factorship** the office of agent or steward *19-*. **factory 1** the office or jurisdiction of factor *17-*. **2** *law* a deed granting authority to a person to act on behalf of another *la16-19*. **factrix** a female agent or factor *la16-19, 20- historical*. [ME *factour*]

factor¹·² /'faktər/ *v* to act as an agent or steward *la19-*. [see the noun]

†**factour** *see* FACTOR¹·¹

faculty, †**faculte**, †**facultie** /'fakəlti/ *n* **1** a branch of learning; a department of study in a university *15-*. **2** privilege or permission to do something *15-*. **3** (the members of) a profession or trade *la15-*. **4** ability, skill *la15-*. **5** *law* the power to do something at will *18-*. **6** character, disposition *la15-e17*. **7** (the value of) personal possessions *la14-e16*. **8** social position *15-16*. **the Faculty of Advocates** the members of the Scottish bar *18-*. [ME *faculte*, Lat *facultās*]

fad, **fade**, *Sh* **faad**, †**faid**, †**feid** /fad, fed; *Sh* fɑd/ *v* to disappear gradually; (to cause) to lose colour or strength *la14-*. [ME *faden*]

faddom¹·¹, **fathom**, **foddom**, †**fadam**, †**fawdom**, †**faldom** /'fadəm, 'faðəm, 'fɔdəm/ *n* **1** a linear measure of about 6 feet, a fathom *la14-*. **2** a quantity of peat or wood *16-18*. [OE *fæþm* an embrace; a measurement of length]

faddom¹·², **fathom**, †**falddome** /'fadəm, 'faðəm/ *v* **1** to measure (by the fathom); to ascertain the depth of water *la18-*. **2** to understand, get to the bottom of *la18-*. **3** to encircle with the arms; *folklore* to encircle a corn-stack in this way at Halloween to conjure up an apparition of one's future spouse *17-19, 20- historical*. [OE *fæþman* to embrace, enfold, contain]

fade *see* FAD, FAID

fader *see* FAITHER¹·¹

faderils *see* FALDERALS

fadge, †**fage**, †**faige** /fadʒ/ *n* **1** a round, thick loaf or bannock, originally one made of barley meal *15-19, 20- N SW Bor*. **2** a kind of potato scone *la19- Uls*. [unknown]

fadge *see* FODGE

fadmal, **fedmel**, †**fedmill** /'fadməl, 'fɛdməl/ *n* a very overweight person, especially a woman *20- Sh*. [probably related to ON *feitr* fat]

fadmel *see* FOTMELL

fae¹, **foe**, †**fa**, †**fay**, †**fo** /fe, fo/ *n pl* †**fois**, †**foyn** an enemy; a foe *la14-*. †**faeman**, **famen** an enemy *la14-19*. [OE *gefā*]

fae²·¹, **frae**, **fro**, *Bor* **thrae**, †**fra**, †**fray**, †**fre** /fe, fre, fro; *Bor* θre/ *prep* **1** away from; free from *la14-*. **2** having come from; altered from *la15-*. †**fra that** from the time that *la14-e16*. †**fra this furth** from this time forward *la16-*. [ON *frá*]

fae²·², **frae**, *Bor* **thrae**, †**fra** /fe, fre; *Bor* θre/ *conj* **1** from the time that, as soon as *la14-*. **2** since, because, seeing that *16-e19*. [see the prep]

fael *see* FAIL¹

faem¹·¹, **foam**, *Ork* **feem**, †**fame**, †**fome** /fem, fom; *Ork* fim/ *n* froth, foam; the sea *la14-*. **faemy**, **faimie**, †**famy**, †**fomy** frothy, foamy *16-*. [OE *fām*]

faem¹·², **foam**, *Ork* **feem** /fem, fom; *Ork* fim/ *v* **1** to froth or foam *la15-*. **2** to gush *la19, 20- Ork WC*. [OE *fǣman*]

faen *see* FA¹·²

faerachin, †**ferekin**, †**firikin**, †**ferdekyn** /'fɛrəxɪn/ *n* a firkin, a small cask *la15-19, 20- N H&I*. [MDu *vierdekijn diminutive of fourth, fourth part]

faerdie-maet, **ferdimet**, **fardy maet**, **faraday maet** /'fɛrdimɛt, 'fɛrdimɛt, 'fɑrdi mɛt, 'farədə mɛt/ *n* food for a journey *19- Sh*. [ON *ferð* travel, journey + *matr* food, meat]

faered *see* FEART

fag¹ /fag/ *n* a sheep-tick *la18-19, 20- WC*. [unknown]

fag² /fag/ *v* to fail from weariness; to flag or falter *18-19, 20- literary*. [unknown]

fag³ /fag/ *v of a boat* to drift to the lee *20- Ork*. [unknown]

fage *see* FADGE

faggald, **faggot**, **faggal**, †**flaggat**, †**faggat** /'fagəld, 'fagət, 'fagəl/ *n* **1** a bundle of twigs, sticks or small branches (used for fuel) *la14-*. **2** an (untidy) bundle, a large amount *19, 20- N*. **3** an exasperating child; a clumsy or slovenly woman *19-20, 21- historical*. [ME *fagot*]

†**faid**, **fade** *n* **1** the leader of the hunt; a leader in a game or sport *16-19*. **2** a company of hunters *16*. [Gael *faghaid*]

faid *see* FAD

faider *see* FAITHER¹·¹

faige *see* FADGE

faik¹·¹, *NE* **fyaak**, *NE* **fyawk** /fek; *NE* fjak; *NE* fjɔk/ *n* **1** a strand of rope *20-*. **2** a fold of a garment *18-19, 20- NE*. **3** a plaid, a wrap, a shawl *18-19, 20- NE*. **4** *in mining and quarrying* a layer of shaly sandstone or limestone *19, 20- SW*. [unknown]

faik¹·², **fake**, *NE* **fyaak**, *NE* **fyawk** /fek; *NE* fjak; *NE* fjɔk/ *v* **1** to coil a rope or line *la19-*. **2** to fold or tuck (cloth or a garment) around *18-19, 20- Sh NE T*. **3** to fold down the mouth of a sack *20- NE T*. **4** to search through clothing; to rummage *20- T*. [unknown]

†**faik**² *v* to grasp or grip; to get hold of *16*. [unknown]

faik³, †**falk** /fek/ *v* **1** to spare or excuse; to let someone off *la18-19, 20- SW*. **2** to lower, abate or remit a price or a sum of money *15-19*. [aphetic form of *defaik* (DEFALK)]

†**faikin** *adj* deceitful *15*. [OE *fācne*]

fail¹, **fael**, **feal**, **fell**, †**faill**, †**fale**, †**feill** /fel, fil, fel/ *n* **1** turf as a material for building or roofing *15-*. **2** a piece of turf, a sod *16-*. **fail dyke**, **feal dyke**, **fell dyke** a field wall built or covered with sods *16-*. **fealy dyke**, **faelly-daek** = *fail dyke la19- Sh Ork*. **fail and divot** *law* an obligation attached to a piece of land giving the right to cut turf *18-*. [unknown]

†**fail**²·¹, **faill**, **fale** *n* a failure, a fault; a decline in strength *la14-19*. **but fale**, **but fyle** without fail, assuredly *la14-16*. **foroutin faill** = *but fale la14-16*. [ME *faile*; compare FAILZIE¹·¹]

fail²·², †**fell**, †**fayle**, †**feal** /fel/ *v* **1** to be unsuccessful, lose; to fail to achieve *la14-*. **2** to be insufficient or lacking; to fall short or default *la14-*. **3** to lose strength or vigour; to give way under strain; to collapse from exhaustion *la14-*. **failed**, **failit 1** *of people* impaired in health, infirm *la14-*. **2** *of things* broken down, worn out by age or use *16-*. †**fail of** fall short of *la14-e16*. [ME *failen*; compare FAILZIE¹·²]

faill *see* FAIL¹, FAIL²·¹

failzie¹·¹, **failie**, †**failȝe**, †**faillie** /'fɛlji, 'fɛli/ *n* **1** failure, default, non-performance of an obligation *la15-*. **2** a (state of) deficiency, a lack *la14-e18*. **3** a sum payable in case of failure, a penalty *17-18*. †**but failȝe** without fail *15*. †**in case of failȝe** in the event of failing to comply with a condition or fulfil an obligation *la16-17*. †**under the failȝe of** under the penalty of (a certain sum) *17-e18*. [OFr *faille*]

failzie¹·², †**failȝe**, †**falȝe**, **falye** /'fɛlji/ *v* **1** to fail, cease; to dwindle or fade *la14-19, 20- literary*. **2** to be absent or wanting; to default or fall short *la14-19*. †**failȝeand**, **failȝeing 1** failing; transitory *la14-17*. **2** in the absence or lack of (a designated heir) *la14-e17*. †**failȝeit 1** *of people* impaired in health, infirm *la14-e17*. **2** in bad condition, dilapidated *16*. faded in colour *16*. †**failȝeand of** in the event of something not happening or not being obtainable *15-e17*. †**failȝeand that** = *failȝeand of la15-16*. †**gif it failȝes** if it so befalls *la15*. [OFr *faillir*]

faimily, **faimly**, **family**, †**familie**, †**famyllye** /'fɛməle, 'fɛmle, 'fɑmli, 'fɑməli/ *n* a group of related people, kindred; a household *16-*. **family exerceese**, **family exercise** family worship or prayers *17-19, 20- NE EC*. [EModE *familie*, Lat *familia*]

faimish, famish, †**famis** /ˈfemɪʃ, ˈfamɪʃ/ v to starve, famish *la15-*. [ME *famishen*]

faimly see FAIMILY

fain[1.1] /fen/ v to express affection or pleasure; to fawn *la14-19, 20- Sh Ork*. [OE *fægnian* to be glad, ON *fagna* to welcome]

fain[1.2], †**fane**, †**fayne** /fen/ adj **1** pleased, glad *la14-*. **2** loving, affectionate, amorous *la18-*. **fainly** adj attractive; showing or inspiring fondness *19- Sh*. **fainly** adv gladly, fondly *19, 20- Sh C*. **fainness 1** gladness, joy *16-*. **2** liking, love *la18-19, 20- Sh*. **fain o** fond of *18-19, 20- Sh Ork NE*. [OE *fægn*]

fain[1.3], †**fane**, †**fayne** /fen/ adv gladly, fondly; longingly *la14-19, 20- literary*. †**fainest** most gladly *15-16*. [see the adj]

faint[1.1], †**fent** /fent/ n a fainting fit, a swoon *la18-*. [see the adj]

faint[1.2], *Sh NE* **fant**, *WC SW* **fent**, †**faynt**, †**faunt** /fent; *Sh NE* fant; *WC SW* fɛnt/ v **1** to become weak or feeble; to lose consciousness temporarily *la15-*. **2** to starve *19- Sh*. [see the adj]

faint[1.3], *Sh NE T* **fant**, †**fent**, †**faynt** /fent; *Sh NE T* fant/ adj **1** weak, feeble, timid; feeling dizzy *15-*. **2** lacking brightness or clarity *15-*. **3** *of weather* close, oppressive *20- T*. †**fantise**, **fantice** faintheartedness, weakness *la14-15*. [ME *feint*]

faiple, *SW Bor* **firple** /ˈfepəl; *SW Bor* ˈfɪrpəl/ n a loose, drooping underlip (on a human or an animal) *19- EC SW Bor*. [unknown; compare FIPPILL, Icel *flipi* the lip of a horse]

fair[1.1] /fer/ v *of weather* to clear up, become fine *19-*. [OE *fægrian*]

fair[1.2] /fer/ adj **1** beautiful, good-looking; attractive, fine *la14-*. **2** *of hair or complexion* light in colour *la14-*. **3** honest, just, unbiased *la14-*. **4** *of behaviour* commendable; desirable *la14-*. **5** *of weather* calm, dry, bright *la14-*. **6** *of wind* favourable *16-*. **7** absolute, utter: ◊*ye're a fair disgrace la19-*. †**fairheid**, **farhed** beauty, fairness *la14-16*. **fairleens**, **fairlins** completely, absolutely *la19- Sh*. **fairly 1** in a pleasing manner *la14-*. **2** absolutely, certainly *20- NE*. **fair avised** fair-complexioned *20-*. **fair ca'in** smooth-tongued, flattering *19, 20- T EC*. **fair daylight** broad daylight *16-19, 20- NE T SW*. **fair-faced** superficially polite, deceitful *la19-*. **fair- farrant**, **fair-farrand 1** plausible, flattering *la15-*. **2** handsome *la15-e17*. **fair furth-the-gate** candid, straightforward *la19- NE*. **fair gyaun** *of crops* quite good *20- NE*. **fair hornie** fair play *19-*. **fair play** honest dealing *la15-*. **fair-spoken** frank, friendly *20-*. **the Fair City** a nickname for Perth *19-*. **fair fa** may good fortune befall *18-*. **fair fa masel** an expression of self-satisfaction *20- N NE*. **fair oot** candid, blunt *la19- NE T SW*. **a fair-strae death** a death from natural causes *la18- literary*. [OE *fæger*]

fair[1.3] /fer/ adv **1** impartially, justly; in a pleasing or acceptable manner *la14-*. **2** completely, absolutely, simply *la18-*. **3** directly, without deviating *la18-*. **4** frankly, openly *la18*. **fair away wi**, **fair away with** very pleased with *20-*. **fair furth the gate** in a straight line; candidly, straightforwardly *la19- NE*. **fair oot** candidly, bluntly *la19- NE EC SW*. [OE *fægere*]

fair[2], †**fayr**, †**fare** /fer/ n **1** a gathering of people at which goods and livestock are bought and sold and workers are hired, and refreshments and entertainment are often available *15-*. **2** a gift bought at a fair *la18-19*. **fairin**, **fairing** a present of food from a fair or at a festive season; a souvenir gift from a holiday *18-*. **fair day** the day on which a fair is held *la15-*. **Fair Fortnight** the last fortnight in July taken as the annual summer holiday in Glasgow; compare GLESCA FAIR *20-*. **be taken to the fair** *of an over-confident person* to be taken aback or discomfited *la19-*. **the Fair** an established annual summer holiday (in a specific town or city) *20-*. **get yer fairins** to be punished, get one's deserts *18-*. **gie him his fairins** to punish a person *19-*. **tak yer fairins** = *get yer fairins*. [ME *feire*]

†**fair**[3] n *fisherman's taboo* a boat *19*. [ON *far* a ship]

fair see FARE[1.1], FARE[1.2]

†**fairce**, **fers** adj fierce *la14-19*. [ME *fers*]

faird, **fard** /ferd, fard/ n **1** a hasty or impetuous movement; a rush or onset *16-19, 20- Sh*. **2** fuss, bustle *e18*. [unknown; compare FARE[1.2]]

faird see FARD[1.1], FARD[1.2], FEART

fairleens see FAIR[1.2]

fairlie see FERLIE[1.1], FERLIE[1.2]

fairlins see FAIR[1.2]

fairly see FAIR[1.2]

fairm see FERM[1.1], FERM[1.2]

fairmer see FERMER

fairn see FERN

fairnietickle see FERNTICKLE

fairnᴈer see FERNYEAR

fairrie /ˈferi/ v to collapse from exhaustion or sudden illness *19- NE*. [unknown]

fairs see FARCE[1]

fairse see FARCE[2]

fairsie see FIERCIE

fairt[1.1], **fert**, **fart** /fert, fɛrt, fart/ n a breaking of wind *la15-*. [OE *feorting*]

fairt[1.2], **fert**, **fart** /fert, fɛrt, fart/ v to break wind *16-*. [ME *ferten*]

fairway /ˈferwe/ n a stretch of mown grass on a golf course between the tee and the green *la19-*. [OE *færweg* a thoroughfare, or FAIR[1.2] + *way* (WEY[1])]

fairy, **ferry**, †**fary**, †**phary**, †**pharie** /ˈferi, ˈfɛri/ n **1** *folklore* a mythical being *la16-*. **2** *folklore* fairyland; the fairy-folk *la15-17*. **3** a vision; a dazed or excited state of mind *la15-e16*. **fairy's caird**, **ferry's kaird** the fern *Pteridium aquilinum*, a type of bracken *19- Sh*. †**fairy raid** *folklore* the ride of the fairies to their celebrations at Beltane *e19*. [ME *fairie*]

faise see FAIZE[1], FAIZE[2]

faisible, **feasible** /ˈfezəbəl, ˈfizəbəl/ adj **1** practicable; easily done *19-*. **2** *of things* neat, satisfactory *la18-19, 20- C Bor*. **3** *of people* decent, respectable; presentable *19, 20- T EC Bor*. [OFr *faisible*]

faist see FEST[1.1], FEST[1.2]

faisten see FESTEN

faith see FETH[1.1]

faither[1.1], **feyther**, **fether**, **father**, *Sh* **faider**, *Sh* **faader**, *Sh NE* **fader** /ˈfeðər, ˈfɛðər, ˈfaðər; *Sh* ˈfedər; *Sh* ˈfɑdər; *Sh NE* ˈfadər/ n **1** a male parent, a father *la14-*. **2** God *la15-*. †**father better** (a person) better than one's father *17-e19*. †**father brother**, **fader broder** a paternal uncle *16-e17*. †**fader brother son**, **fader broder son** a paternal cousin *16-e17*. †**father-side** the paternal side of a family *17-e18*. †**father sister**, **fader sister** a paternal aunt *16-19*. †**fader-war**, **fatherwar** (a person) worse than one's father *la15-16*. **fathers and brethren** the members of the General Assembly or of the Synods or Presbyteries *19-*. **Father o' mercy** an exclamation of surprise or disbelief *19-*. [OE *fæder*]

faither[1.2], **father** /ˈfeðər, ˈfaðər/ v **1** to beget; to be the father of *la18-*. **2** to indicate one's own paternity through physical resemblance *19, 20- Ork N NE SW*. [see the noun]

faithfu, **faithful**, *Ork* **fatifu** /ˈfeθfu, ˈfeθfəl; *Ork* ˈfatɪfu/ adj **1** loyal, reliable; accurate *la15-*. **2** possessed of religious faith *la15-*. **3** affectionate *19- Ork*. [ME *feithful*]

faizart, †**fazart** /ˈfezərt/ n **1** a hermaphrodite fowl la16-19, 20- Sh. **2** a puny or effeminate man; a weakling; a coward 16-19, 20- Sh. [unknown]

faize[1], **faise**, †**feaze** /fez, fes/ v **1** of something woven or spun to unravel, fray 19, 20- Sh N NE EC Bor. **2** of metal or wood to make rough, splintered or jagged la16-19, 20- NE. [EModE feaze; compare FAS[1.1] a fringe]

faize[2], **faze**, **faise** /fez, fes/ v **1** to annoy, inconvenience or disturb la19-. **2** to make an impression (on) 19, 20- H&I WC Uls. [OE fēsian to drive away]

fake see FAIK[1.2]

faks see FAX[1.2]

fal see FA[1.2]

†**fala** n a kind of kerchief or small shawl worn by Dutch women e18. [Du falie]

falcon, †**falcoun**, †**fawcown** /ˈfɔlkən/ n **1** a bird of prey of the family Falconidae 15-. **2** a kind of light cannon la15-17, 19- historical. **falconer**, †**falconar**, †**fauconer** a falconer la12-. [ME faucoun, falcon]

fald see FAULD[1.1], FAULD[1.2], FAULD[2.1], FAULD[2.2]

falddome see FADDOM[1.2]

falderals, †**faderils**, †**fatt'rels** /faldəˈralz/ npl **1** trifles, idle fancies; a fuss about trivial things 19-. **2** ribbon ends, loose pieces of trimming la18-19, 20- T. [probably from a meaningless refrain in songs]

faldom see FADDOM[1.1]

fale see FAIL[1], FAIL[2.1]

falk see FAIK[3]

Falkirk Bairns, Fawkirk Bairns /ˈfɔlkɪrk bernz, ˈfɔkɪrk bernz/ npl **1** the natives of Falkirk 18-. **2** Falkirk Football Club and their supporters 20-. Compare BAIRN[1.1] (sense 2). [from the place-name + plural of BAIRN[1.1]]

Falkirk Tryst /ˈfɔlkɪrk traɪst/ n the cattle market held near Falkirk, the largest of its kind in Scotland la18-19, 20- historical. [from the place-name + TRYST[1.1]]

Falkland bred /ˈfɔlkland bred/ n well-mannered (as if bred at court) 18-19, 20- historical. [from the name of a village in Fife with a royal palace + Eng bred]

fall see FA[1.1], FA[1.2], FA[2]

falla see FELLAE

fallachan /ˈfaləxan/ n a hoard, a concealed store la19- N H&I WC. [Gael falachan hidden treasure]

fallae see FOLLAE

fallauge see VOLAGE

fallen see FA[1.2]

fallie see FELLAE

falloch /ˈfaləx/ n a lump or bundle; a large chunk of food; a big bulky object la19- NE Uls. [perhaps Gael eallach a burden]

fallow see FELLAE, FOLLAE

falou see FELLAE

†**falow, falu** adj withered; of grass pale, yellowish 13-14. Compare FAUGH. [OE falu]

falow see FELLAE

falowar see FOLLAE

†**fals** v **1** to maintain or prove to be false 15-e17. **2** to break an oath or promise la15-e17. **3** to forge (a document) la15-e17. **falser, falsar 1** a forger la15-e17. **2** a person who challenges a legal judgement 16-e17. **falsing** the act of questioning a legal judgement la15-e17. **fals a dome** to deny the equity of a sentence and appeal to a superior court 15-e17. [see FAUSE]

fals, false see FAUSE

falset, falsehood, †**falshede,** †**falshad,** †**falsed** /ˈfalsət, ˈfalshud/ n **1** deceit, lack of truth la14-. **2** law a crime of fraud or forgery la17-. [ME falshede]

falsify, †**falsife** /ˈfalsəfae/ v **1** to make (something) false; to counterfeit la16-. **2** to challenge a legal judgement la16-e17. [ME falsifien]

falt see FAUT[1.1], FAUT[1.2], VAT

falteis see FAUTISE

†**faltive, fautif** adj **1** of people having committed a fault, guilty of wrongdoing, delinquent la14-16. **2** of things faulty, defective la15-16. [MFr fautif]

falu see FALOW

falye, falʒe see FAILZIE[1.2]

fama /ˈfama/ n a scandal 20- N NE T C. [reduced form of FAMA CLAMOSA]

fama clamosa /fama klaˈmoza/ n in church law a widely-circulating rumour of scandalous behaviour (usually against a minister or probationer in Presbyterian Churches) la17-. [Lat fāma clāmōsa a noisy rumour]

fame see FAEM[1.1]

fameeliar, familiar, NE **fameeler,** †**famyliar,** †**famylyere,** †**familier** /faˈmɪljər, faˈmɪljər/; NE faˈmilər/ adj **1** intimate, personal; friendly, closely associated (with); originally pertaining to one's household 15-. **2** well-known, thoroughly conversant with; usual, normal, habitual 16-. †**familiar servant** a servant in a position of intimacy or trust; a member of one's household la15-16. [ME familier]

†**famell**[1.1] n females; a female 15-16. [Lat famella]

†**famell**[1.2] adj female la15-e17. [see the noun]

famell see FAMYLE

†**famh** n folklore a small animal somewhat like a mole, supposed to emit a glutinous substance reputedly fatal to horses la18-e19. [Gael famh a mole]

familiar see FAMEELIAR

familie see FAIMILY

familier see FAMEELIAR

family see FAIMILY

famis, famish see FAIMISH

famos, famous, famows, famus see FAWMOUS

†**famyle, famell** n related people, kindred; a household la14-16. Compare FAIMILY. [OFr famille]

famyliar see FAMEELIAR

famyllye see FAIMILY

famylyere see FAMEELIAR

fan see FANN[1.1], FIND[1.2], WHAN[1.1], WHAN[1.2]

fa'n see FA[1.2]

fanatic[1.1], †**phanatik** /fəˈnatɪk/ n a religious zealot, an unreasoning enthusiast 17-. [see the adj]

fanatic[1.2], †**phanatik** /fəˈnatɪk/ adj **1** over-zealous in religious matters, excessively enthusiastic; extreme la16-. **2** mad, frenzied e16. [Lat fānāticus pertaining to a temple]

fancy, NE **funcy** /ˈfansi; NE ˈfʌnsi/ adj elaborate; highly decorated la18-. **fancy piece, funcy piece** an individual, decorated cake la20- NE. [contracted form of Older Scots fantasie]

†**fand, faynd** v **1** to put to the test, make trial of la14-15. **2** to test by exercise; to exert la14-15. **3** to try, endeavour la14-16. [OE fandian]

fand see FIND[1.2]

fan dabby dozie /fan dabi ˈdozi/ adj extremely good la20-. [catchphrase of the Scottish comedy duo The Krankies]

†**fane, phane, fen** n a weathercock; a flag, pennant 16-18. [OE fana a banner, a standard]

fane see FAIN[1.2], FAIN[1.3]

fang[1.1] /faŋ/ n **1** the capacity for suction of a pump 19-. **2** a capture; something seized; booty, plunder, stolen goods la14-19, 20- Sh Ork NE. **3** a find, a bargain 20- Ork N Bor. **aff the fang 1** of a pump having lost its suction 19-. **2** of a person not in a good state; without one's usual spirit or skill *la19-.* †**in a fang** in a predicament *la18-19.* †**in the fang** in the act of stealing *la17-e18.* **lose the fang 1** *of a pump* to lose the power of retaining water *19- NE C.* **2** to fail; to lose the knack or skill (of something) *la18-19.* **oot o fang** *of a pump* having lost its suction *la19-.* †**with the fang** law in possession of stolen goods *18-19.* [OE *fang* booty, plunder, spoils]

fang[1,2] /faŋ/ *v* **1** to prime a pump (in a well) *19, 20- NE T EC SW.* **2** to acquire; to catch, seize or capture *la14-19, 20- Sh.* **3** to pull or draw in *e16.* [OE *fōn*]

fang[2] /faŋ/ *n* a heavy bundle *20- N NE.* [ON *fōng* baggage]

fang[3] /faŋ/ *n* a coil or bend of a rope, a hitch; a tether *e16, 19- Sh Ork EC Bor.* Compare FANK[1.1]. [ON *fang* grasp]

fang *see* WHANG[1.1], WHANG[1.2]

fangle *see* FANKLE[1.1], FANKLE[1.2]

fank[1.1] /faŋk/ *n* a coil of rope, a noose; a tangle *la18-.* **fank o tows** a coil of rope *19-.* [altered form of FANG[3]]

fank[1.2] /faŋk/ *v* **1** to tangle or twist *19-.* **2** to catch in a noose; to snare *18-19.* **fankit, fanked** entangled, mixed up *17-.* [altered form of ON *fanga* to grip, capture]

fank[2.1] /faŋk/ *n* a sheepfold *19-.* [Gael, IrGael *fang*]

fank[2.2] /faŋk/ *v* to drive into a sheepfold *19-.* [see the noun]

fankle[1.1], *NE T* **fangle** /ˈfaŋkəl; *NE T* ˈfaŋɡəl/ *n* a tangle, a muddle *19-.* [frequentative form of FANK[1.1] and FANG[3]]

fankle[1.2], *NE T* **fangle** /ˈfaŋkəl; *NE T* ˈfaŋɡəl/ *v* **1** to tangle or mix up *19-.* **2** to become tangled *la19, 20- C SW.* **3** to trap, ensnare *18-19, 20- C SW.* **4** to stumble or fumble *la19, 20- WC SW.* [see the noun]

fann[1.1], **fan** /fan/ *n* a drift or wreath of snow *la19- Sh Ork N.* [Norw dial *fann*]

fann[1.2] /fan/ *v of snow* to drift *20- Sh Ork.* [see the noun]

fanner /ˈfanər/ *n* **1** a winnowing machine, a grain-sifter *la18-.* **2** a blowing fan *la16.* **fanners** a winnowing machine *19-.* [OE *fann*]

fanny /ˈfani, ˈfane/ *n* **1** the female genitalia *20-.* **2** a term of contempt for a (male) person *la20- C.* **fanny baws** a term of contempt for a (male) person *21-.* [unknown]

fant *see* FAINT[1.2], FAINT[1.3]

fantation, fantashen /fanˈteʃən, fanˈtaʃən/ *n* (a state of) ravenous hunger; exhaustion from want of food *la19- Sh.* [FAINT[1.2], with noun-forming suffix]

fantice *see* FAINT[1.3]

†**fantise** *n* fantasy, illusion, deceit *la14-16.* [altered form of ME *fantasie*]

fantise *see* FAINT[1.3]

fanton[1.1], †**fantone** /ˈfantən/ *n* an unreal thing or state, a phantom *e16, 20- literary.* [ME *fantom, fanton*]

fanton[1.2], **fantoun**, †**fantown** /ˈfantən/ *adj* illusory, imaginary *e15, 20- literary.* [see the noun]

fantone *see* FANTON[1.1]

fantoosh /fanˈtuʃ/ *adj* overdressed; flashy, fancy; ultra fashionable *20-.* [probably coined during the 1914–18 War under the influence of *fanty-sheeny* a marionette, showy, fanciful, from Ital *fantoccino* a puppet]

fantoun, fantown *see* FANTON[1.2]

far[1.1], **faur, ferr, fer** /far, fɔr, fɛr/ *adj* distant, a long way away *la14-.* **farrer, ferrer, faurer** more distant *la14-.* **farrest**, †**ferrest** most distant *la14-.* **farmost** furthest *la19-.* **farness**, †**farnes** the amount of distance; remoteness *la16-.* †**farland** foreign, connected with distant countries *la16-e17.* †**at farrest, at the farrest** at the latest, at most *la16-17.* **far back 1** in debt *la19- T EC Bor.* **2** backward in terms of progress or education; ignorant or uncouth *20- N NE T.* †**far to seik** to be looked for far away; hard to find *15-16.* [OE *feorr*]

far[1.2], **faur, ferr, fer** /far, fɔr, fɛr/ *adv* distantly; to a great extent *la14-.* **farrer, ferrer, faurer** further *la14-.* **farrest**, †**ferrest** furthest *la14-.* **far-aff** distant in relationship *19, 20- Sh NE T EC.* **far and about** from far and near *20- NE T Uls.* **far awa wi't** feeble; frail, seriously ill *la19- Sh Ork NE T Bor.* **far back** long ago *20-.* **far ben 1** intimate, friendly, in great favour *16-.* **2** in favour with God *17-20, 21- historical.* **3** *of the eyes* dreamy, abstracted *20-.* **4** deeply versed, having deep or specialized knowledge *19, 20- Ork NE.* **far frae aa yonner** having learning difficulties *la19- NE.* **far in** intimate, friendly, in great favour *19-.* **far in wi yer feet stickin oot** in great favour *20-.* **far kent** known far and wide, famous *la18-.* **far north** astute, wide-awake *la19- NE WC Bor.* **far oot 1** distant in relationship *la19-.* **2** on bad terms, not friendly *20- NE T EC.* **far oot aboot** remote, out-of-the-way *20- Ork NE T.* **far seen** far-sighted; deeply-skilled *la18-19, 20- T Uls.* **far thochted** shrewd, perceptive *20- Sh Ork N.* **far throu, far through 1** nearly finished, worn out *19-.* **2** very ill, at death's door *la19-.* †**nae farrar gane** recently *la18-19.* **nae farrar gane than** as recently as *la19-.* [see the adj]

far *see* FAAR[2], FARE[1.1], WHAUR[1.1], WHAUR[1.2]

faraday maet *see* FAERDIE-MAET

faran, farran, forin /ˈfarən, ˈfɔrən/ *adj* belonging to or situated on the starboard side of a boat *la19- N NE T.* [reduced form of FOREHAND]

farand *see* FARRANT

farandman *see* FARE[1.2]

farawa, far awa /ˈfarəwa/ *adj* remote, distant *18-.* **farawa skreed** a letter or news from abroad *19-.* [FAR[1.2] + AWA[1.1]]

farce[1], †**fars**, †**fairs**, †**ferse** /fars/ *n* **1** a stage farce, a play *16-.* **2** a funny story, a joke *20- N NE T EC.* [MFr *farce*]

†**farce**[2], **fars, fairse** *v* to stuff or cram (with food); to stuff in preparation for cooking *la14-17.* [ME *farsen*]

†**farcost, fercost, farkost** *n* a small cargo-vessel *la14-e17.* [ON *farkostr*]

farcy *see* FIERCIE

†**fard**[1.1], **faird** *n* face paint *la16-18.* [MFr *fard*]

†**fard**[1.2], **faird** *v* to paint (the face); to embellish; to gloss over *16-e19.* [MFr *farder*]

fard *see* FAIRD

fardel[1], †**fardell**, †**farthel** /ˈfardəl/ *n* **1** a quarter of a flat loaf; a three-cornered cake, especially an oatcake, usually the fourth part of a round *17-19, 20- NE EC.* **2** a large slice or piece (of food) *19- NE.* **3** a fourth part, a quarter *la15-e17.* [OE *fēorþa dǣl* fourth part]

fardel[2], †**fardell**, †**ferdell**, †**farthell** /ˈfardəl/ *n* **1** the third stomach of a ruminant *19, 20- historical.* **2** a bundle, a parcel, a pack *la14-e19.* †**fardel-bound** a disease of cattle in which the contents of the third stomach become impacted *19.* [ME *fardel*]

farden *see* FAURDIN

farder *see* FORDER[1.3], FORDER[1.4]

fardest[1.1], **furthest** /ˈfardəst, ˈfʌrðəst/ *adj* most advanced, most distant, at the greatest interval *la16-.* Compare *farrest* (FAR[1.1]). †**at fardest, at the fardest** at the furthest, at the latest *la16-17.* [ME *ferthest*]

fardest[1.2], **furthest** /ˈfardəst, ˈfʌrðəst/ *adv* to or at the greatest distance, furthest *la17-.* [see the adj]

farding *see* FAURDIN

fardy maet *see* FAERDIE-MAET

fare[1.1], †**fair**, †**far** /fer/ *n* **1** a course of action; an activity, an event *la14-.* **2** (the provision of) food and drink, or entertainment *la14-.* **3** a passage for which a price is paid, the cost of conveyance *15-.* **4** a person's fortune or experience *la14-18.* **5** a journey, a voyage *la14-e16.* **6** conduct, demeanour;

bearing, appearance *la14-e16*. **7** ceremony, pomp; commotion, fuss *la14-15*. †**sae fares o** = *sic fares o la19*. †**sae fares wi** = *sic fares o e19*. **sic fares o** that's just typical of: ◊*he's fallen again, sic fares o' Sawtie 18-19, 20- NE*. [OE *fær*, ON *far*]

fare[1,2], †**fair** /fer/ *v pt also* †**fure**, *ptp also* **forn 1** to travel, go, proceed *la14-*. **2** to progress (well or badly); to get on, prosper; to advance through life *la14-*. **3** to be provided with food and drink or entertainment *la14-16*. **4** to act, behave, conduct oneself *la14-16*. **farin** food, fare *19- NE T EC*. †**farandman** an itinerant pedlar, a travelling person *15-e17*. [OE *faran*]

fare *see* FAIR[2]
fargis *see* FARKISH
farhed *see* FAIR[1,2]
farin *see* FARE[1,2]
farkish, *Ork* **fargis**, †**farkage** /ˈfarkɪʃ; *Ork* ˈfargɪs/ *n* an untidy heap or bundle; odds and ends *19, 20- Ork T Bor*. [unknown]
farkost *see* FARCOST
farl, **farle**, **farrel** /farl, ˈfarəl/ *n* **1** a three-cornered oatcake, a quarter of a loaf; a fardel *la17-*. **2** a section of scone, roll or shortbread baked in a round *la17-*. [reduced form of FARDEL[1]]
farlan *see* FARLIN
farley *see* FERLIE[1,2]
farlie *see* FERLIE[1,1]
farlin, **farlan** /ˈfarlən/ *n* a box in fish-curing yards into which herrings are emptied for gutting *la19- Sh N NE EC Bor*. [Shetland variant of FORELAND the foreshore, on which curing originally took place]
farly *see* FERLIE[1,2], FERLIE[1,3], FERLIE[1,4]
farm *see* FERM[1,1], FERM[1,2]
farmor *see* FERMER
farmourar *see* FERMORAR
farne *see* FERN
farntickle *see* FERNTICKLE
farnʒer *see* FERNYEAR
farra *see* FARROW
farrach /ˈfarəx/ *n* **1** a bustle; a mix-up; a state of agitation *la19- NE T*. **2** strength, energy *18-19, 20- NE*. [Gael *farrach* force]
farran *see* FARAN
farrant, †**farand** /ˈfarənt/ *adj* **1** having a specified disposition: ◊*auld-farrant* ◊*fair farrand la14-*. **2** comely; well-favoured *la14-e16*. [participial adj from FARE[1,2]]
farrel *see* FARL
farrer, **farrest** *see* FAR[1,1], FAR[1,2]
farrow, *Sh* **forro**, *NE* **farra**, *NE* **ferro**, †**ferow**, †**ferrow**, †**forrow** /ˈfaro; *Sh* ˈfɔro; *NE* ˈfara; *NE* ˈfero/ *adj of a cow* not in calf; barren, no longer capable of bearing young *la15-*. [MDu *verre-koe* a cow past bearing young]
fars *see* FARCE[1], FARCE[2]
farskal *see* FORSKAL
fart *see* FAIRT[1,1], FAIRT[1,2]
farthel *see* FARDEL[1]
farthell *see* FARDEL[2]
farthing *see* FAURDIN
†**fartingaill**, **fartigard**, **verdingale** *n* a hooped petticoat *16-17*. [MFr *vertugale* from Spanish *verdugado*, so called from *verdugo* a rod, a stick]
fary *see* FAIRY
†**far yaud**, **far yaw** *interj in the Borders* a call to a sheep-dog to drive sheep at a distance *e19*. [perhaps FAR[1,2] + YONT[1,1]]
†**fas**[1,1] *n* **1** a tassel, a fringe, a border *la15-17*. **2** something of little value *la15-16*. [OE *fæs* a fringe; compare FAIZE[1]]
†**fas**[1,2] *v* to provide with tassels *16-e17*. [see the noun]

fasand *see* FEESANT
fasch *see* FASH[1,2]
fascheonat *see* FASHION[1,2]
fascherie *see* FASHERIE
faschioun *see* FASHION[1,1]
faser *see* FOSSER
fasgird *see* FESGAR
fash[1,1] /faʃ/ *n* **1** trouble, bother; annoyance *18-*. **2** a troublesome person *19, 20- NE C*. **fashious 1** troublesome, annoying; difficult *16-*. **2** fractious, peevish *18-*. [see the verb]
fash[1,2], †**fasch** /faʃ/ *v* **1** to irritate or annoy; to anger; to inconvenience *16-*. **2** to take trouble over; to take pains with *la16-*. **3** to vex or bother oneself *17-*. **4** to afflict (with a disease) *18-19, 20- WC*. **5** to make trouble *la16-17*. **fash at** to be impatient with *18-*. **fash o** to grow weary of *18-19, 20- H&I*. **fash yer heid** to worry over, be put out by; to be concerned with *18-*. **fash yer thumb** = *fash yer heid la18-19, 20- NE T SW*. [MFr *faschier*]
fasherie, †**fascherie**, †**facherie**, †**fasscherye** /ˈfaʃəri/ *n* trouble, annoyance; fuss *la16-*. [MFr *fascherie*]
fashion[1,1], †**faschioun**, †**fassoun**, †**fassioun** /ˈfaʃən/ *n* **1** mode, form, custom; appearance, style *la14-*. **2** workmanship, the art or process of making *la15-*. **fashions** social intercourse or relations; manners, demeanour, behaviour *la16-19, 20- Sh NE T EC Uls*. **mak a fashion**, †**mak ane fassone** to pretend, make a show *17-19 20- NE*. [ME *facioun*]
fashion[1,2], †**fawson**, †**fassoun**, †**fasson** /ˈfaʃən/ *v* to form, mould, make; to give shape to *la14-*. **fashiont**, **fashioned**, †**fascheonat 1** of a specified appearance, manner or design *la15-*. **2** well-mannered, respectable *la18-19, 20- C*. [see the noun]
fashious *see* FASH[1,1]
fasiane *see* FEESANT
fasing *see* FACIN
fasscherye *see* FASHERIE
fassin *see* FESTEN
fassioun *see* FASHION[1,1]
fasson *see* FASHION[1,2]
fassoun *see* FASHION[1,1], FASHION[1,2]
fast, **fasti** /fast, ˈfasti/ *n* a rope attached to a (submerged) stone used as an anchor; a mooring-rope; a weighted rope used to secure hay *la19- Sh*. **fastibaand**, †**fasta band 1** a crossbeam running under the thwarts of a boat to secure the ribs *19- Sh*. **2** a rope attached to a stone *la19- Sh*. [ON *festr*]
fast *see* FEST[1,1], FEST[1,2]
fastern's een, **fasten een**, †**fasternisevin**, †**fasterisevin**, †**fastingisevin** /ˈfastərnz ˈin, ˈfastən ˈin/ *n* Shrove Tuesday *la14-*. [OE *fæsten* + EVEN[1]]
fasti *see* FAST
fastingisevin *see* FASTERN'S EEN
fat[1] /fat/ *adj* plump, corpulent, obese; rich in fat *15-*. †**fat brose** brose made with hot stock or fat instead of boiling water *la18-19*. **fattie cuttie** an individual semi-sweet cake *20- Ork*. [OE *fætt*]
fat[2] /fat/ *adj of marbles* disqualified if they come to rest inside the ring *20-*. **fattie** *of a marble* disqualified *20- T*. **fatum** = *fattie*. [unknown]
fat *see* VAT, WHIT[1,1], WHIT[1,2], WHIT[1,3]
fatal, *NE Bor* **fattal**, †**fatale**, †**fatell**, †**fatall** /ˈfetəl; *NE Bor* ˈfatəl/ *adj* **1** deadly, doomed, resulting in death; ruinous, disastrous, final *la15-*. **2** assigned or decreed by fate or destiny *la15-16*. [Lat *fātālis*]
father *see* FAITHER[1,1], FAITHER[1,2]
fa'ther *see* FORDER[1,4]
fathom *see* FADDOM[1,1], FADDOM[1,2]

fatifu *see* FAITHFU

†fatigacioune *n* a state of fatigue; the action of fatiguing *la15*. [MFr *fatigation*, Lat *fātigātiō*]

fat like *see* WHIT[1.1]

fatt *see* VAT

fattal *see* FATAL

fatten *see* WHATTEN

fattie *see* FAT[2]

fatt'rels *see* FALDERALS

fatuity, **†fatuitie** /fəˈtjuəti/ *n* **1** stupidity, folly; fatuousness *la19-*. **2** *law* imbecility *la16-19*. [MFr *fatuité*, Lat *fatuitās*]

fatum *see* FAT[2]

fatuous /ˈfatʃuəs/ *adj* **1** vacantly silly *17-*. **2** *law* in a state of imbecility and therefore incapable of managing one's own affairs *18-*. [Lat *fatuus*]

fauch[1.1], **faugh**, **†faulch** /fɔx/ *n* **1** a fallow field; a part of the outfield ground that is tilled and left fallow alternately for several years at a time; unploughed ley ground *14-19, 20- Sh N NE Bor*. **2** the breaking up of fallow land by light ploughing, harrowing or both *la18-19, 20- NE*. [unknown; compare OE *fealh* a harrow]

fauch[1.2], **faugh**, *NE* **fyauch** /fɔx; *NE* fjɔx/ *v* **1** to plough or harrow (fallow ground); to plough and leave fallow *16-19, 20- Sh N NE*. **2** to prepare ground for spring sowing *20- EC Bor*. **3** to work with speed; to toil away *la19- NE*. **4** to scratch or claw; to rub or scrub hard *20- NE*. **fauchinless** weak, without strength or energy *la19- NE*. [see the noun]

†fauch[1.3], **faugh** *adj of land* fallow, not sowed, untilled; growing only natural grass; frequently in place-names *la16-19*. [see the noun]

fauch *see* FAUGH

fauchat /ˈfɔxət/ *v* to throw or give up; to scatter coins at a wedding *la19- H&I WC*. [unknown; compare Gael *fadhadh* a little handful, a sprinkling]

fauchie, *NE* **fyauchie** /ˈfɔxi; *NE* ˈfjɔxi/ *adj* **1** *of colour* pale yellowish grey, faded or washed-out *20- N NE T*; compare FAUGH. **2** *of people* pasty-faced, sickly looking *20- N NE T*. [FAUGH + -IE[2]]

fauchle[1.1] /ˈfɔxəl/ *n* a slow, inept worker, a bungler *la19, 20- WC SW*. [unknown]

fauchle[1.2], *N* **fouchle**, *NE* **fyachle** /ˈfɔxəl; *N* ˈfʌuxəl; *NE* ˈfjaxəl/ *v* **1** to work lazily, listlessly or ineffectually *19, 20- N NE*. **2** to walk with difficulty due to lack of strength; to trudge or plod *la19- N NE*. **fauchled**, **faughlit** tired, worn-out, harassed *20-*. [unknown]

faucht *see* FECHT[1.1], FECHT[1.2]

faucon /ˈfɔkən/ *n* a mock sun, a parhelion *20- N NE*. [unknown]

fauconer *see* FALCON

faud *see* FAULD[1.2]

fauderie *see* FOUD

†faugh, **fauch**, **fawch** *adj* pale; pale brown, yellowish *16-19*. [conflation of FALOW with FAUCH[1.1]]

faugh *see* FAUCH[1.1], FAUCH[1.2], FAUCH[1.3]

faughlit *see* FAUCHLE[1.2]

faul *see* FAULD[1.1], FAULD[1.2], FAULD[2.1], FAULD[2.2]

faulch *see* FAUCH[1.1]

fauld[1.1], **fald**, **faul** /fɔld, fald, fɔl/ *n* **1** something folded; a pleat, a bend; a fold of cloth *15-*. **2** a strand of rope *20- Sh Ork NE T*. **3** a layer *20- N*. [see the verb]

fauld[1.2], **fald**, **faul**, **faud** /fɔld, fald, fɔl, fɔd/ *v* **1** to fold; to bend or fold over *la14-*. **2** to give in, yield; to give way; to lose courage *la14-*. **3** to shut or close *la18-19, 20- NE*. **4** *of the limbs* to double up or bend under one *la18-19, 20- Sh T*. **5** to embrace *la15*. **†faldit**, **falded** *of the fists* clenched *la16-e17*. **fauld yer fit**, **†fald yer feit 1** to sit down *18-19, 20- NE*. **2** to kneel; to bend the knees *16*. **fauld yer houch** to sit down *19- T*. [OE *fealdan*]

fauld[2.1], **fold**, **faul**, *NE* **faal**, **†fald** /fɔld, fold, fɔl; *NE* fal/ *n* **1** a pen, an enclosure for animals *13-*. **2** an enclosed piece of ground used for cultivation; a small field *15-*. **3** a halo round the moon, an indicator of possible stormy weather *19, 20- NE WC SW*. **4** a herd of (twelve) Highland cows used for breeding *la18-19, 20- H&I*. **5** the part of the outfield which was manured by folding cattle on it *18-19*. **6** the penning of cattle for milking; the milking of cattle *19*. **fauld dyke** a wall enclosing a fold *15-19, 20- NE T*. [OE *fald*]

fauld[2.2], **fold**, **faul**, **†fald** /fɔld, fold, fɔl/ *v* to shut animals in a pen or on a piece of land *la16-*. **†fauldin** a cattle-fold or sheepfold *la18-19*. [see the noun]

fault *see* FAUT[1.1], FAUT[1.2]

faunt *see* FAINT[1.2]

fauour *see* FAVOUR[1.1]

faup *see* WHAUP[1.1], WHAUP[2]

faur *see* FAR[1.1], FAR[1.2], FAVOUR[1.1], FAVOUR[1.2]

faurder *see* FORDER[1.4]

faurdin, **farden**, **farthing**, **†farding**, **†ferding** /ˈfɔrdən, ˈfardən, ˈfarðɪŋ/ *n* **1** a coin of low value, a farthing *15-20, 21- historical*. **2** a fourth part of a noble or rider *la15*. **farthing-land**, **†farden-land** a quarter of a PENNYLAND *la16-19, 20- historical*. [OE *fēorþing*]

faurer *see* FAR[1.1], FAR[1.2]

fause, **false**, *Sh* **faase**, **†fals** /fɔs, fɔls; *Sh* fas/ *adj* **1** untrue, incorrect *la14-*. **2** counterfeit, not genuine *14-*. **3** deceitful, treacherous *la14-*. **fause face** a mask *19-*. **2** facial cosmetics, make-up *la20-*. **fause hoose** a conical structure of wooden props built inside a corn stack to facilitate drying *la18-*. [OE *fals*, Lat *falsus*]

faut[1.1], **fault**, *Sh* **faat**, **†falt** /fɔt, fɔlt; *Sh* fɑt/ *n* **1** an error, a mistake; an offence or misdemeanour *15-*. **2** blame or responsibility for failure or error *la15-*. **3** a flaw or defect *la15-*. **4** a want, a lack (of food) *la14-19, 20- NE EC Uls*. **5** harm, injury *la19- Sh NE*. **hae a faut tae** to have a fault to find with *la18-*. **hae nae faut tae** to have no fault to find with *la18-*. **in a faut** in the wrong, at fault *15-*. [ME *faute*]

faut[1.2], **fault**, **†falt** /fɔt, fɔlt/ *v* **1** to find fault with, blame *15-*. **2** to commit a fault *15-*. **3** to penalize *e16*. **fauter**, **fautour**, **†faltour** a wrongdoer, an offender; a person who offends against Church discipline *la15-19, 20- literary*. [see the noun]

fautif *see* FALTIVE

†fautise, **falteis** *adj* **1** faulty, defective *la16-e17*. **2** at fault *15*. [MFr *fautise*]

favillo /ˈfavəlo/ *n* a lazy, clumsy person *la19- Sh Ork*. [unknown; compare Norn *vavlet* having a weak grasp, fumbling, handless, Norw *vavla* to waver, vacillate]

favour[1.1], **faur**, *NE* **faaver**, **†fauour** /ˈfevər, fɔr; *NE* ˈfavər/ *n* **1** (an act of) goodwill; approval *la14-*. **2** appearance, looks *la15-19*. **for ony favour** for any sake, for goodness' sake *la19-*. **in favours of** in favour of *la15-19, 20- NE EC*. [ME *favour*]

favour[1.2], **faur** /ˈfevər, fɔr/ *v* **1** to be well disposed to; to support, accept or prefer *15-*. **2** to resemble *la19-*. [ME *favouren*]

†faw *adj* variegated; frequently in place-names *13-e16*. [OE *fāh*]

faw *see* FA[1.1], FA[1.2], FA[2]

fawch *see* FAUGH

fawcht *see* FECHT[1.2]

fawcown *see* FALCON

fawdom *see* FADDOM[1.1]

fawin *see* FA[1.2]

Fawkirk Bairns *see* FALKIRK BAIRNS

fawl see WHAAL

fawmous, famous, †**famus,** †**famows,** †**famos** /'fɔməs, 'fɛməs/ *adj* **1** renowned, celebrated *15-*. **2** *of people* reputable, reliable; *of things* fit, proper *la15-19, 20- EC*. **3** *of trial witnesses* of good repute, respectable *16-e19*. [ME *famous*]

fawn see FA[1.2]

fawson see FASHION[1.2]

fax[1.1] /faks/ *n* **1** a foam topped wave, a heavy swell *20- Sh*. **2** the hair of the head *la14-16*. [ON *fax* a mane]

fax[1.2], **faks** /faks/ *v of the sea* to form foam-crested waves; to swell up *20- Sh*. [see the noun]

†**fay** *n* faith; faithfulness *la14-16*. **Inglis fay** allegiance to England *la14-15*. **Scottis fay** allegiance to Scotland *15*. [ME *feith, fei*]

fay see FAE[1], FEY[3]

fayle see FAIL[2.2]

faynd see FAND

fayne see FAIN[1.2], FAIN[1.3]

faynt see FAINT[1.2], FAINT[1.3]

fayr see FAIR[2]

fayth see FETH[1.1]

fazart see FAIZART

faze see FAIZE[2]

†**fe, fee** *n* **1** live-stock; cattle or sheep *la14-19*. **2** property, wealth *la14-e16*. **fee master** a master herdsman *e16*. [OE *feoh*, ON *fé*]

fe see FEE[1.1], FEE[1.2]

fead see FEID

†**feal** *adj* loyal, faithful *la16-e19*. [OFr *feal*]

feal see FAIL[1], FAIL[2.2]

feale, feall see FIALL

fear[1.1], †**fere,** †**feir** /fir/ *n* **1** dread, horror; anxiety, worry *15-*. **2** a fright, a scare *19-*. **fearsome** frightening, terrifying *la18-*. **nae fears** not likely *la19-*. [OE *fær* a sudden calamity, danger]

fear[1.2], †**feir,** †**fere** /fir/ *v* **1** to be afraid (of) *la15-*. **2** to frighten, scare *la16-*. [OE *fǣran* to terrify, frighten]

fear see FIAR[1], FIAR[2]

feardie see FEARTIE

fearie see FERE[3]

feart, feared, *Sh Ork* **faered,** *Sh Ork* **faird,** †**ferd,** †**ferit,** †**feirt** /firt, fird; *Sh Ork* ferd/ *adj* afraid *la14-*. **feartit** afraid *20-*. **dinna be feart o** *humorous* don't be so sparing with *20- NE T H&l EC*. **feart at** frightened or afraid of *16-*. **feart fae** scared of *20-*. **feart for 1** afraid of *19-*. **2** concerned about *20-*. **ye're nae feart** *ironic* you are very daring *20-*. [ptp of FEAR[1.2]]

feartie, fearty, feardie /'firti, 'firdi/ *n* a coward, a timorous person *20-*. **feardie gowk** a coward *20- EC*. [FEART + -IE[3]]

feasible see FAISIBLE

feat, †**feit** /fit/ *adj* **1** neat, trim; fitting, suitable *la16-19, 20- NE T EC SW*. **2** clever, adroit *18-19*. [ME *fet*, EModE *feat*]

feather[1.1], **fedder,** †**fether** /'fɛðər, 'fɛdər/ *n* **1** a barbed shaft forming plumage on a bird, a feather *15-*. **2** the projecting wing on the sock of a plough, which cuts out the furrow *la18-*. **3** the cutting edge of a peat spade *19-*. **4** the lines and graining in polished wood *la19, 20- H&I WC*. **5** one of the paddles on a horizontal water mill *la19- Sh*. **6** a sheep's ear mark *20- Sh*. **feddery craw** a toy made by sticking feathers in a potato so that the wind propels it along *20, 21- historical*. **shak yer feathers** to get out of bed; to stir oneself *19, 20- NE*. [OE *feþer*]

feather[1.2], **fedder** /'fɛðər, 'fɛdər/ *v* **1** to fit or provide with feathers *la15-*. **2** *of a bird* to get its feathers, fledge *la18-19, 20- NE C Bor*. **3** to smooth the top and sides of a rick *20- T WC SW Uls*. **4** to cut in the shape of a feather; to notch; to clip an animal's ear in this way *la19- Sh*. **5** to beat or chastise *20- NE*. [see the noun]

featherfooly, feather-foullie, †**feverfoylie** /'fɛðərfuli/ *n* featherfew, feverfew *Tanacetum parthenium 17-19, 20- NE T*. [altered form of ME *feverfew*, with infl from FEATHER[1.1] and FULZIE[2] from the appearance of the foliage]

feathery /'fɛðəri/ *n* a golf ball cased in leather and stuffed with feathers *la19, 20- historical*. [FEATHER[1.1] + -IE[2]]

feaze see FAIZE[1]

Februar, Feberwar, February, †**Feverʒere,** †**Fabruar,** †**Feberwerrie** /'fɛbruar, 'fɛbərwar, 'fɛbruəre/ *n* the month of February *la14-*. [Lat *Februārius*]

fech see FESH

fecht[1.1], *Ork* **feight,** *NE* **fyaacht,** *C SW* **faucht,** †**ficht,** †**feicht** /fɛxt; *Ork* fɛxt; *NE* fjaxt; *C SW* fɔxt/ *n* a fight, a struggle; exertion; aggression *15-*. **fechtie, fechty** courageous, ready to fight *la19- NE T EC*. [OE *feohte*]

fecht[1.2], †**ficht,** †**fycht** /fɛxt/ *v pt* **focht** †**faucht,** †**fawcht,** †**feught,** *ptp* **focht 1** to fight, do battle; to quarrel *la14-*. **2** to struggle against misfortune or poverty *la18-*. **3** to wrestle, kick or fling the limbs about *la19- NE T*. **fechter,** †**fichter,** †**fechtar** a fighter *la14-*. **fochten,** †**foughten** harassed, worn out *la18-19, 20- NE*. [OE *feohtan*]

feck, †**fect,** †**fek** /fɛk/ *n* **1** the majority, the greater part *la15-*. **2** a (large) quantity, number or amount *17-*. **3** value, worth; effect, force *la15-19, 20- Ork*. **feckfu, feckful,** †**fectfull 1** effective, capable, efficient *16-*. **2** sturdy, forceful, powerful *16-19, 20- NE EC Uls*. **feckless** ineffective, weak, incompetent *la16-*. **fecklessness** weakness, incompetence *17-*. **feckly,** †**fectlie 1** mostly, almost *la18-19, 20- NE T*. **2** effectively *la17*. [aphetic form of EFFECK]

fecket /'fɛkət/ *n* a woollen or heavy cotton garment with sleeves and buttoned front, worn under or over a shirt *la18-*. [unknown]

fect see FECK

fed see FEID

fedder see FEATHER[1.1], FEATHER[1.2]

feddrame see FETHERAME

fede see FEED, FEID

fedill see FEEDLE

fedmel, fedmill see FADMAL

fee[1.1], †**fe,** †**fey** /fi/ *n* **1** a payment or remuneration, a price *la14-*. **2** a servant's wages, especially those paid half-yearly or for specific services *la14-*. **3** an engagement as a servant *la19-*. **4** *law* a feudal holding, the right of holding land as a fief *la14-20, 21- historical*. **in fee and heritage** in feudal possession with heritable rights *la14-19, 20- historical*. [ME *fe*]

fee[1.2], †**fe,** †**fey,** †**fie** /fi/ *v* **1** to engage as a servant; to employ *15-*. **2** to accept an engagement as a servant *la17-*. **3** to take something on hire *la15-e17*. **feein fair, feeing fair** a fair usually held at Whitsun and Martinmas, where farmers engaged servants for the coming term *19-20, 21- historical*. **feein market, feeing market** a market held for the purpose of engaging farm workers *19-20, 21- historical*. [see the noun]

fee see FE

feece see FACE[1.1]

feech[1] /fix/ *n* the knob under the bowl of a clay pipe, to hold it by when the bowl becomes hot *la19- NE*. [unknown]

feech[2], **feuch,** †**figh** /fix, fjux/ *interj* an expression of disgust, pain or impatience *18-*. **feechie, fichie 1** foul, dirty, disgusting *20- NE T*. **2** *of the weather* rainy, puddly, unpleasant *20- NE T*. [compare Gael *f(u)ich*]

feed, †**fede,** †**feid** /fid/ *v* **1** to provide with food, feed *la14-*. **2** to eat; *of animals* to graze *la16-*. **3** to fatten livestock *19-*.

4 to pasture animals *la17-18*. **feeder 1** a cow or bullock being fattened for market *la19-*. **2** a lodger *20- Ork*. **feeding of livestock** fattened for market *19-*. **feedin storm** a storm which adds more snow to that already lying *17-*. [OE *fēdan*]

feedie /ˈfidi/ *n* an oath, a curse *la19- Ork*. [unknown]

feedle, fiedle, †fedill /ˈfidəl/ *n* a field, an enclosure *16-19, 20- NE*. [metathesis of FIELD¹·¹]

feefle¹ /ˈfifəl/ *v* **1** to work clumsily or foolishly; to act foolishly *la19- Sh Ork*. **feefly** feeble, clumsy *20- Ork*. [ON *fífl* a fool]

feefle² /ˈfifəl/ *v of snow* to swirl *la20- Sh Ork*. Compare FEEVIL. [probably onomatopoeic]

feegarie *see* FIGMAGAREY

feegie /ˈfigi/ *n* a nickname for the Ferguslie Park area in Paisley *la20-*. [shortened form of the place-name, with influence from WEEGIE]

feegur¹·¹, figger, figure, †figour, †fegour /ˈfigər, ˈfɪgər/ *n* **1** form, shape; appearance or representation *la14-*. **2** a symbol; a figure of speech *la15-*. **3** a number, a numeral *17-*. **in yer figure** without a coat or jacket *la20- C*. [MFr *figure*]

feegur¹·², figure /ˈfigər, ˈfɪgər/ *v* **1** to represent by a figure *la15-*. **2** to calculate, consider *18-*. **3** to be represented *19-*. **feegured, figured, †figorit, †figurit 1** patterned *la15-*. **2** figurative, metaphorical *16-e17*. [see the noun]

feel¹·¹, †feill, †fele /fil/ *n* **1** mental perception, knowledge *la15-*. **2** an idea; a shrewd suspicion *la15-16*. **†feelless** insensible; numb *la17-e19*. [see the verb]

feel¹·², †fele, †feill /fil/ *v* **1** to perceive by touch *la14-*. **2** to perceive mentally *la14-*. **3** to perceive by smell or taste *la14-*. **4** to seek to know *16*. [OE *fēlan*]

feel² /fil/ *adj* **1** cosy, neat; comfortable *19- SW Bor*. **2** soft, smooth *la18-19, 20- SW Bor*. [OE *fǣle* faithful, good, pleasant]

feel *see* FUIL¹·¹, FUIL¹·³

feelimageery *see* WHIGMALEERIE

feelish *see* FUILISH

feem¹·¹ /fim/ *n* **1** a state of sudden heat; a sweat *19- NE*. **2** a state of agitation or rage *19- NE*. [OE *fām* foam]

feem¹·² /fim/ *v* to be very hot; to sweat profusely; to be in a fit of rage *19- NE*. [OE *fǣman* to emit foam]

feem *see* FAEM¹·¹, FAEM¹·²

feenal, †finale, †fynale /ˈfinəl/ *adj* final *15-*. [MFr *final*, Lat *finālis*]

feenich /ˈfinəx/ *n* knot grass *Polygonum aviculare*, especially its flowerhead and seed *18- NE*. [perhaps Gael *fianach* moor-grass]

feenish¹·¹, finish /ˈfinɪʃ, ˈfɪnɪʃ/ *n* **1** the end or conclusion of something; the last stage or final part *19-*. **2** a (smooth or fine) surface or coating; polish, refinement *19-*. **3** ploughing the final furrow (which separates one rig from another) *la19-*. **4** a mixture of alcohol and shellac used in varnishing, and as an intoxicant by meths-drinkers *la19- C SW*. [see the verb]

feenish¹·², finish, †fynys /ˈfinɪʃ, ˈfɪnɪʃ/ *v* **1** to bring or come to an end *15-*. **2** *ploughing* to plough the final furrow in a rig *20-*. **†finished within itself** *of a house* self-contained *e19*. [ME *finishen*, stem of *fenir*]

feenk /fiŋk/ *n* a bad smell *20- Sh Ork*. [variant of Eng *funk* a stink]

feer /fir/ *v ploughing* to make the first guiding furrow *18-*. **feerin** the act of making the first furrow; the first furrow made *18-*. **feering pole, feerin pole** a pole set up as a guide when making the first furrow *19-*. [OE *fȳrian* to cut a furrow]

feerd *see* FUIRD¹·¹, FUIRD¹·²

feerdy *see* FERDY

feerich /ˈfirəx/ *n* **1** ability, activity, energy *19, 20- N NE*. **2** a state of agitation or excitement; a fit of rage or panic *19, 20- N NE*. **3** an impulse *la20- NE*. **feerichin** bustling, fumbling because of excitement *19, 20- N NE*. [unknown; compare FEERY-FARRY]

feerie /ˈfiri/ *n* **1** an epidemic disease; distemper in dogs *19- Sh*. **2** a stomach bug; diarrhoea *20- Sh*. [unknown]

feerie *see* FERE³

feerious *see* FURIOUS¹·¹, FURIOUS¹·²

feery-farry, †fery fary /ˈfirifari/ *n* a bustle, a state of excitement or confusion *16-19, 20- NE Bor*. [reduplicative compound from FAIRY]

feesant, pheasant, †fasiane, †phesand, †fasand /ˈfizənt, ˈfɛzənt/ *n* a pheasant *Phasianus colchicus la15-*. [ME *fesaunt*]

feesh *see* FESH

feesick *see* PHYSIC

feesp, fiesp /fisp/ *v* to move smartly or nimbly about (despite being feeble) *la19- Sh*. [perhaps altered form of Norn *fip* to trip about]

feess *see* FESH

feet *see* FIT¹·¹

†feeth, feith *n* a salmon net fixed on stakes and planted into the bed of a river *la15-19*. [unknown]

feetie, feeties *see* FITTIE¹·¹

feetle *see* FITTLE

feetock *see* FITTOCK

feetspur *see* FIT¹·¹

feevil, feevl /ˈfivəl/ *n* a light fall or thin covering of snow *la19- Sh*. Compare FEEFLE². [ON *fǫl*]

feeze¹·¹, †fize /fiz/ *n* a screw; a screwing or twisting motion *17-19, 20- historical*. **†feeze-nail** a screw *la17-19*. **feeze pin, veeze-pin, †veese pin** a threaded wooden pin *18- Sh Ork*. [Flem *vize, vijze*, MDu *vise*; compare VICE²]

feeze¹·² /fiz/ *v* **1** to turn, twist or screw; to cause to revolve *la18-19, 20- Sh Ork N*. **2** to wriggle; to wiggle the body *19- NE T EC*. **3** to fawn, ingratiate oneself *19, 20- Sh NE*. **4** to work hard at *la19-, NE*. **†feeze up** to flatter; to work up a passion *19*. [see the noun]

feff /fɛf/ *n* a bad smell *20- N*. [probably ON *þefr* a smell]

feftie *see* FIFTY

feg, fig /fɛg, fɪg/ *n* the fruit of the fig-tree *Ficus carica la14-*. [ME *fige*]

fegour *see* FEEGUR¹·¹

fegs /fɛgz/ *interj* an expression of emphatic assertion or surprise *la18-*. **†by my fegs** by my soul *19*. **guid fegs** good gracious *la18- Sh NE*. [reduced form of Scots *(by my) faikins*]

feice *see* FACE¹·¹

feicht *see* FECHT¹·¹

feid, †fede, †fed, †fead /fid/ *n* (a state of) enmity or hostility; a feud *la14-19, 20- WC*. **†at feid, at fede** in a state of enmity or feud (with) *15-18*. [ME *fed*]

feid *see* FAD, FEED

feidom *see* FEY³

feifteen¹·¹, fifteen, †fiftene, †fyften /fʌɪfˈtin, fɪfˈtin/ *adj* fifteenth *la14-19, 20- NE EC*. [see the numeral]

feifteen¹·², fifteen, †fiftene, †fyftene /fʌɪfˈtin, fɪfˈtin/ *numeral* the cardinal number after fourteen *la14-*. **†fifteint, fyftend** fifteenth *15-17*. **the Fifteen 1** a name for the Jacobite rising of 1715 *la18- historical*. **2** the Court of Session (consisting of fifteen judges), when acting as a court of appeal *la18-e19, la19- historical*. [OE *fíftīne*]

feight *see* FECHT¹·¹

feik *see* FYKE¹·²

†**feilamort, philamort, feildamort** *n* the colour of a dead leaf; yellow or brown *la16-17*. [AN *feile* + *morte*]
feild *see* FIELD[1.1], FIELD[1.2]
feill *see* FAIL[1], FEEL[1.1], FEEL[1.2]
feind *see* FIENT[1.2]
feingie, †**fenʒe**, †**fenzie**, †**fenye** /ˈfɛŋi, ˈfɛŋji/ *v* **1** to feign or pretend; to imagine *la14-19, 20- NE*. **2** to counterfeit, forge; to act deceitfully or falsely *la14-19, 20- NE*. †**fenʒear, fenʒeour** a person who feigns *la15-e16*. **fenged, fenyeit**, †**fenʒeit 1** feigned, pretended; imaginary, fictitious *la14-19, 20- literary*. **2** deceitful *la15-e17*. **3** forged, spurious *la15-e17*. [ME *feinen, feinyhen*]
†**feir** *n* a band, a host, a following *15-19* **in feir** in company, together *15-e16*. [OE *gefēre* a community, a company (of people)]
feir *see* FEAR[1.1], FEAR[1.2], FERE[1], FERE[3], FIAR[1], FIER
feird *see* FOURT
feirrie *see* FERE[3]
feirt *see* FEART
feisik *see* PHYSIC
feit *see* FEAT, FIT[1.1]
feith *see* FEETH
†**feitho, fethok** *n* (the skin of) a polecat *15*. [ME *ficheux*]
fek *see* FECK
felba *see* FILBOW
felde *see* FIELD[1.1]
feldefer, feldifare *see* FELTIEFLIER
fele *see* FEEL[1.1], FEEL[1.2]
fell[1] /fɛl/ *n* **1** a skin or hide *la15-*. **2** the pile or nap of cloth, the direction of an animal's coat *20- SW*. [OE *fell*]
fell[2] /fɛl/ *n* a steep, rocky hill; a tract of hill-moor; frequently in place-names *15-*. [ON *fjall*]
fell[3.1] /fɛl/ *n* a knock-down or stunning blow *20- NE SW Bor*. [see the verb]
fell[3.2] /fɛl/ *v* **1** to strike down; to slaughter, kill *la14-*. **2** to injure; to thrash *la18-*. **3** *in salmon fishing* to cast a net from a boat into a river *la18-19*. **felled** prostrate, especially with illness *la19-*. **felled sick** too ill to move *19- WC*. **fell twa dugs wi ae bane** to kill two birds with one stone *la18-19, 20- Sh Ork NE T*. **fell twa dugs wi ae stane** = *fell twa dugs wi ae bane 18- EC SW*. [OE *fellan*]
†**fell**[4.1] *n* fate, destiny *la18-e19*. [see the verb]
†**fell**[4.2] *v* to befall; to be the fate of *la18-19*. [probably back-formation from *fell*, pt of FA[1.2]]
fell[5.1] /fɛl/ *adj* **1** fierce, cruel, harsh *la14-*. **2** remarkable, considerable; extremely strong, big or loud *la14-*. **3** *of weather* violent, inclement *la14-*. **4** energetic and capable, sturdy *18-19, 20- C SW Bor*. **5** clever, shrewd *18-19, 20- C SW Bor*. **6** *of food or drink* pungent, strong *la18-19*. [ME *fel*]
fell[5.2] /fɛl/ *adv* **1** extremely, very, severely *la14-*. **2** vigorously, energetically *la19, 20- EC*. [see the adj]
fell *see* FA[1.2], FAIL[1], FAIL[2.2]
fellae, felly, fella, fulla, filla, fallie, fallow, fellow, *Sh N NE Uls* **follow,** *SW* **falla,** †**folow,** †**falow,** †**falou** /ˈfɛle, ˈfɛlə, ˈfʌlə, ˈfɪlə, ˈfale, ˈfalo, ˈfɛlo;* Sh N NE Uls* ˈfɔlo; *SW* ˈfalə/ *n* **1** an associate, a comrade, a companion *la14-*. **2** an equal, a match; an equivalent, a counterpart *15-*. **3** a male person *15-*. **4** a member of a society or incorporation *la15-*. **5** a boyfriend, a partner, a husband *20-*. **fellow-craft** *freemasonry* a person who has taken the second degree, originally one who has passed his apprenticeship and is a full member of his craft *18-*. [OE *fēolaga*, ON *félagi*]
†**felloun**[1.1], **fellon** *adj* **1** fierce, cruel *la14-e17*. **2** great, huge *la14-16*. **3** loud, strong *la14-16*. [ME *feloun*]
felloun[1.2], **fellan** /ˈfɛlən/ *adv* extremely, greatly *la15-19, 20- literary*. [see the adj]

fellow, fellow-craft *see* FELLAE
†**fellow deir** *n* fallow deer *la16-17*. [altered form of OE *fealu* + DEER[1]]
felly *see* FELLAE
†**felny** *n* wickedness, felony *la14-15*. [OFr *felonie*]
felt[1] /fɛlt/ *n* **1** a soft matted fabric; a matted fibrous substance *la16-*. **2** worn-out arable pasture consisting mainly of fine bent-grass *19, 20- T*. **3** couch grass or creeping wheat grass *la18-19*. [OE *felt*]
†**felt**[2] *n* a condition involving a build-up of urinary crystals *16*. **felt gravel** = FELT[2] *17-18*. [unknown]
felter[1.1] /ˈfɛltər/ *n* *weaving* a defect or a mistake *19- EC*. [see the verb]
†**felter**[1.2] *v ptp* **feltrat 1** to tangle (hair); to weave faultily or work ineffectively *la15-e19*. **2** to entangle or encumber *la16-e19*. [ME *filteren*]
feltie /ˈfɛlti/ *n* **1** the mistle thrush *Turdus viscivorus la19-*. **2** the fieldfare *Turdus pilaris 20-*. [shortened form of FELTIEFLIER]
feltieflier, feltifer, felty fare, †**feldefer,** †**feldifare** /ˈfɛltifliər, ˈfɛltifər, ˈfɛlti fer/ *n* **1** the fieldfare *Turdus pilaris la15-*. **2** the mistle thrush *Turdus viscivorus la19-*. [OE *feldefare*]
feltrat *see* FELTER[1.2]
felty fare *see* FELTIEFLIER
fely *see* FILLIE
fen /fɛn/ *n* **1** a marsh *la15-*. **2** filth, mud, excrement *la15-16*. [OE *fen*]
fen *see* FANE, FEND[1.1], FEND[1.2]
fence[1.1], †**fens** /fɛns/ *n* **1** an enclosing barrier or a railing, a fence *16-*. **2** defence *la14-17*. **3** an enclosure or enclosed area *16-17*. **4** *law* an arrest of goods or lands *16*. **fence-fed** *of animals* fed with titbits at the fence; pampered *19- NE T*. [aphetic form of DEFENCE]
fence[1.2], †**fens** /fɛns/ *v* **1** to enclose with a fence; to secure or fortify *15-*. **2** *law* to open the proceedings of a court or parliament by uttering a formula forbidding interruption *15-*. **3** *law* to arrest or seize goods *16-18*. †**fensment, fencement 1** legal arrest or attachment *la15-e16*. **2** the formal opening of a court or of parliament *la16*. **fence the tables** *Presbyterian Church* to admonish intending communicants to examine their consciences *18-19, 20- T H&I EC Bor*. [see the noun]
fencible[1.1] /ˈfɛnsɪbəl/ *n* a soldier called up for home defence *la18-19, 20- historical*. [see the adj]
fencible[1.2], †**fensabill,** †**fensible** /ˈfɛnsɪbəl/ *adj* **1** *of men* capable of and liable for (defensive) military service *16-19, 20- historical*. **2** *of buildings or settlements* suitable for defensive purposes *la15-e19*. **3** *of dykes or hedges* suitable for use as a fence or stock-proof enclosure *la17-e19*. **4** *of arms or amour* suitable for defensive use *la15-16*. [aphetic form of ME *defensable*]
fend[1.1], **fen** /fɛnd, fɛn/ *n* **1** defence, resistance *17-19, 20- historical*. **2** an effort or an attempt to maintain oneself *18-19, 20- T C SW*. **3** sustenance, provisions *19- NE*. **fendfu, fenfa** resourceful, energetic *19, 20- T WC SW*. **fendless, fenless 1** lacking resource or energy *la19- Sh Ork N NE SW*. **2** without flavour *la19- NE*. **3** *of cereal crops* short, thin, without substance *la19- NE*. **fenny, fendy 1** self-sufficient, resourceful, thrifty *la18-19, 20- SW*. **2** active, lively, healthy *18-19, 20- WC SW*. **3** *of a boat* buoyant, riding the waves *la19- Sh*. **mak a fend, mak a fen** to make an attempt *18-19, 20- T C SW*. [see the verb]
fend[1.2], **fen** /fɛnd, fɛn/ *v* **1** to maintain or support oneself; to scrape an existence *la16-*. **2** to defend, protect or shelter *la14-19, 20- N NE*. **3** to provide with sustenance; to maintain

or support another *la15-19, 20- NE T*. **4** to defend oneself, resist attack *15-19*. †**how do ye fend?** how are you doing? *la18-e19*. [aphetic form of DEFEND]

fend, fende *see* FIENT¹·¹

fenged *see* FEINGIE

fens *see* FENCE¹·¹, FENCE¹·²

fensabill, fensible *see* FENCIBLE¹·²

fent /fɛnt/ *n* a slit or opening in a garment *la15-19, 20- Ork NE T EC*. [ME *fente*]

fent *see* FAINT¹·¹, FAINT¹·², FAINT¹·³

fenye, fenʒe, fenzie *see* FEINGIE

feppill *see* FIPPILL

fer *see* FAR¹·¹, FAR¹·², FOR¹·¹

fercost *see* FARCOST

ferd *see* FEART, FOURT

ferdekyn *see* FAERACHIN

ferdell *see* FARDEL²

ferdimet *see* FAERDIE-MAET

ferding *see* FAURDIN

ferdy, feerdy /ˈfɛrdi, ˈfirdi/ *adj* strong, active, fit, quick *la16-19, 20- Sh Ork EC*. [obscurely related to FARE¹·¹]

fere¹, fiere, †feir, †pheare /fir/ *n* **1** a companion, a comrade; a mate or spouse *la14-19, 20- literary*. **2** a match or equal; an opponent *16*. †**feer for feer** equal in every respect *la18-e19*. [OE *ᵹefēra* a companion, a comrade, a friend]

†**fere²** *v* to belong or pertain to; to be appropriate to *la14-16*. [aphetic form of EFFEIR¹·²]

fere³, fier, †feir /fir/ *adj* **1** healthy, sturdy *la14-19, 20- NE T EC*. **2** sound, undamaged *la14-16*. **fearie, †feerie, †feirrie, †fery** active, nimble, strong *15-19, 20- literary*. [OE *fēre*, from pt stem of *faran* to go]

fere *see* FEAR¹·¹, FEAR¹·², FIER

ferekin *see* FAERACHIN

ferfochen *see* FORFOCHEN

ferge /fɛrdʒ/ *v* to work hard (with little result) *la19- NE*. [variant of FIRK]

†**feriale** *adj* pertaining to an ordinary weekday *15-16*. **feriale time** *law* a period in which no legal proceedings can be taken *la15-e18*. [ME *ferial*, Lat *feriālis*]

†**feriat, feriot** *adj* **1** *law* pertaining to a time in which no legal proceedings can be taken *la15-e19*. **2** pertaining to a holiday period *16-e19*. **feriat time** *law* a period in which no legal proceedings can be taken *la15-e19*. [Lat *feriāt-*, ptp stem of *feriāri* to keep holiday]

Ferintosh /ˈfɛrɪntɔʃ/ *n* a whisky distilled at Ferintosh, on the Cromarty Firth *18-19, 20- historical*. [from the place-name]

feriot *see* FERIAT

ferit *see* FEART

ferk *see* FIRK

ferkishin /ˈfɛrkəʃɪn/ *n* **1** a large (untidy) amount *19- Bor*. **2** a crowd, a seething mob *20- Bor*. [verbal noun from FARKISH]

ferle *see* FERLIE¹·²

ferlie¹·¹, ferly, fairlie, farlie /ˈfɛrli, ˈfɛrle, ˈfɛrli, ˈfɑrli/ *n* **1** a strange sight; a marvel, a wonder; a curiosity *la14-*. **2** a piece of surprising news; (a piece of) gossip *19-*. **3** a monstrous or unpleasant creature *la18-19, 20- NE*. **4** a whim, a fanciful notion *19, 20- Ork*. **fairlyfu**, *NE* **ferlifee**, †**ferliful 1** filled with wonder *19- NE*. **2** wonderful, marvellous *la14-16*. †**have ferly** to marvel, wonder *la14-16*. **nae ferly** no wonder *18-*. **spy ferlies, spy farlies** to interfere in someone else's business; to be inquisitive *la18-*. [see the adj]

ferlie¹·², **ferly, fairlie, farly, farley, †ferle** /ˈfɛrli, ˈfɛrle, ˈfɛrli, ˈfɑrli/ *v* **1** to wonder, marvel, be surprised *la14-*. **2** to cause to wonder; to be the cause of surprise: ◊ *it fairlies me la14-e15, 20- Sh*. [see the adj]

ferlie¹·³, ferly, †farly /ˈfɛrli, ˈfɛrle/ *adj* strange, wonderful *la14-*. [ON *ferligr* monstrous, dreadful]

†**ferlie¹·⁴, ferly, farly** *adv* strangely, wonderfully *la14-18*. [see the adj]

ferlot *see* FIRLOT

ferly *see* FERLIE¹·¹, FERLIE¹·², FERLIE¹·³, FERLIE¹·⁴

ferm¹·¹, fairm, farm /fɛrm, fɛrm, fɑrm/ *n* **1** land cultivated as a unit, originally land leased at a fixed rent *la14-*. **2** a fixed yearly amount paid as rent for land *la14-19*. **3** grain paid as rent in lieu of money *la16-19*. †**farm bear, ferme beir** barley paid as rent *16-e19*. **ferm-corn** grain paid as rent *16-19, 20- NE*. **farm meal, †ferme meill** meal paid as rent *16-19, 20- NE Bor*. **farm onstead** farm buildings, the homestead *19-*. **farm stead** farm buildings, the homestead *la18-*. **farm steading, †ferme stedyng** the farm buildings with or without the farmhouse *la16-*. **farm stocking** the livestock of a farm *19-*. **farm toun, fairm toon, †farm town** the homestead of a farm *17-*. †**farm victual** meal paid as rent *la15-18*. †**set for ferme** to let land for a fixed amount *la14-e16*. [MFr *ferme* a legal agreement for payment in return for a benefit]

ferm¹·², **fairm, farm** /fɛrm, fɛrm, fɑrm/ *v* **1** to cultivate a farm or estate *la17-*. **2** to let out or rent *la17*. [see the noun]

ferm *see* FIRM

fermance, fermans *see* FIRMANCE

fermer, fairmer, †fermour, †farmor /ˈfɛrmər, ˈfɛrmər/ *n* **1** a person who cultivates a farm, a (tenant) farmer *15-*. **2** a collector of dues or imposts *la16-17*. [ME *fermour*]

†**fermorar, firmorar, farmourar** *n* **1** a rent-paying tenant of land, a farmer *la15-17*. **2** a lessee of a mill *la15-e17*. **3** a collector of duties, revenues or tithes *la15-17*. **4** a tenant or lessee of church lands *la15-16*. [Lat *fermarius*]

fermour *see* FERMER

fern, †fairn, †farne /fɛrn/ *n* bracken; a fern or ferns; frequently in place-names *la15-*. **fern-owl** the nightjar *la18-19, 20- NE*. [OE *fearn*]

fernacket *see* FORNACKET

ferntickle, *Uls* **farntickle** /ˈfɛrntɪkəl; *Uls* ˈfɑrntɪkəl/ *n* a freckle *18-*. **fernytickle, fairnietickle** a freckle *19-*. [ME *ferntikel*]

fernyear, †fernʒere, †farnʒer, †fairnʒer /ˈfɛrnjir/ *n* last year; the preceding year *la15-*. [OE *fyrngēar*]

ferow *see* FARROW

ferr *see* FAR¹·¹, FAR¹·²

ferre *see* FERRY¹·¹, FERRY¹·²

ferrer, ferrest *see* FAR¹·¹, FAR¹·²

ferriar *see* FERRY¹·²

ferrick /ˈfɛrɪk/ *n* a mock sun, a parhelion *la19- NE SW*. [unknown]

ferrier /ˈfɛriər/ *n* **1** a farrier *18-*. **2** a veterinary surgeon *la19- NE EC*. [OFr *ferrier*]

ferriour *see* FERRY¹·²

ferro, ferrow *see* FARROW

ferry¹·¹, †fery, †ferre /ˈfɛri, ˈfɛre/ *n* a boat for conveying (passengers and goods) across a body of water; frequently in place-names *la13-*. **ferry louper** an incomer to the Northern Isles; a stranger to a district *la17-*. [ON *ferja*]

ferry¹·², †fery, †ferre /ˈfɛri, ˈfɛre/ *v* to convey by ferryboat *la14-*. †**ferriar, ferriour** a ferryman *15-e17*. [OE *ferian*, ON *ferja*]

ferry² /ˈfɛri, ˈfɛre/ *v of a sow* to give birth, have a litter *la14-19, 20- Sh Ork NE T EC*. [derivative of OE *fearh* a young pig]

ferry *see* FAIRY

fers *see* FAIRCE

ferse *see* FARCE¹

fersell /ˈfɛrsəl/ *adj* energetic, active *la19- NE*. [unknown]

ferst see FIRST¹·¹
fert see FAIRT¹·¹, FAIRT¹·²
†**ferter, fertor** *n* 1 a bier, a litter *16-e19*. 2 a shrine, a reliquary *la14-e16*. [ME *fertre*, Lat *feretrum*]
ferther, ferthyrmor see FORDER¹·⁴
fertigue see FIRTIG¹·¹
fertor see FERTER
fery see FERE³, FERRY¹·¹, FERRY¹·²
fery fary see FEERY-FARRY
fesch see FISH¹·¹
fesgar, fasgird /ˈfɛzɡər, ˈfasɡɪrd/ *n* a ring of twisted straw, sewn or laced round the rim of a basket *20- Sh Ork*. [Norw dial *fastgard* a facing of straw or heather]
fesh, fetch, fess, *NE* **feesh,** †**fech** /fɛʃ, fɛtʃ, fɛs; *NE* fiʃ/ *v pt* **fuish,** *NE* **feess,** *T C SW* **fotch,** *ptp* **fessen,** *NE T* **feshen,** *EC Bor* **fuishen** 1 to bring or fetch *la14-*. 2 to breathe with difficulty; to pant or gasp *la18-19, 20- Sh*. 3 *of a horse* to pull by jerking *la18*. **fesh on** to bring forward; to advance; to bring to maturity *la19, 20- NE T*. **fesh up** to bring up, rear or nurture *la18- NE T*. [OE *feccean*]
fess see FACE¹·¹, FESH
fessin see FESTEN
fest¹·¹, fast, *NE* **faist** /fɛst, fast; *NE* fɛst/ *adj* 1 fixed, firm *15-*. 2 quick, hasty *18-*. 3 busy, occupied *la19- NE*. **fast place in mining** a working place in advance of the others *la19, 20- EC*. **fast in the foot** *of a mining pump* choked *la19, 20- EC*. [OE *fæst*]
fest¹·², fast, *NE* **faist** /fɛst, fast; *NE* fɛst/ *adv* 1 firmly, securely *la14-*. 2 quickly, rapidly *la14-*. 3 diligently, earnestly, vigorously *la14-16*. [OE *fæste*]
festen, fessin, *NE* **faisten,** †**fassin,** †**festin** /ˈfɛsən; *NE* ˈfɛsən/ *v pt, ptp* †**festnyt** 1 to make fast, fasten; to fix or close *la14-*. 2 to puzzle or perplex *20- Bor*. **fessener** a puzzle, a baffling problem *20- EC Bor*. [OE *fæstnian*]
†**festinance** *n* custody, confinement *15-16*. [FESTEN, with noun-forming suffix]
fetch see FESH
fete see FIT¹·¹
feth¹·¹, faith, †**fayth** /fɛθ, feθ/ *n* confidence, trust; religious belief *la14-*. [ME *feith*]
feth¹·² /fɛθ/ *interj* an expression of emphasis or affirmation *19, 20- Sh Ork*. [see the noun]
fether see FAITHER¹·¹, FEATHER¹·¹, FORDER¹·⁴
†**fetherame, feddrame** *n* a coat of feathers, plumage *15-e17*. [OE *feðerhama*]
fethok see FEITHO
fetonas see PYTHONESS
fetter¹·¹ /ˈfɛtər/ *n* a shackle; a restraint *la14-*. †**fetters** *law* the restrictions imposed by a deed of entail *la18-19*. [OE *feter*]
fetter¹·², †**fettir** /ˈfɛtər/ *v ptp* †**yfetterit** 1 to secure with chains; to restrain or control *la14-*. 2 *law* to impose restrictions by a deed of entail *20-*. [see the noun]
fettill see FETTLE¹·²
fettle¹·¹ /ˈfɛtəl/ *n* strength, vigour, condition *la18-*. **what fettle?** how are you? *la19-*. [see the verb]
fettle¹·², †**fettill** /ˈfɛtəl/ *v* 1 to put to rights; to repair; to settle or arrange *19-*. 2 to fall upon; to tackle *la19, 20- Sh Bor*. 3 to attend to the needs of; to feed or clothe *la19, 20- WC*. 4 to make oneself ready *e15*. [ME *fetlen* to shape, fix or prepare; to bestow]
fettle¹·³ /ˈfɛtəl/ *adj* neat, trim; exactly suited *19, 20- T SW Uls*. [see the verb]
fettle² /ˈfɛtəl/ *n* a rope of twisted straw or heather (used as a handle for a creel or basket) *19- Sh Ork N*. [ON *fetill* a band, a strap]

feu¹·¹, †**few** /fju/ *n* 1 *law* a perpetual lease of land or other property at a fixed yearly rent; originally a feudal tenure of land where a vassal made a return in grain or money to their superior in place of military service *la15-20, 21- historical*. 2 a piece of land held by feu tenure *18-20, 21- historical*. 3 the fixed annual payment for a feu lease *16-20, 21- historical*. **feuar,** †**feuer,** †**fewar** a person who held land in perpetual lease; the tenant of a feu *16-20, 21- historical*. **feu charter,** †**few chartoure** the document granting a new feu lease *la16-20, 21- historical*. **feu duty,** †**few dewtie** the fixed annual payment for a feu lease *la16-20, 21- historical*. **feu-farm,** †**feuferme,** †**fewferme** 1 the tenure of land (or other property) in feu *15-20, 21- historical*. 2 the payment made by a tenant of a feu *la15-17*. †**fewfermar** the holder of a feu lease *15-16*. †**fewfermorar** = *fewfermar 15-17*. **feu holding** the tenure of land in feu *18-20, 21- historical*. †**feu-mail, few maill** the fixed annual payment for a feu lease *16-18*. **feu right** the right established by feu charter *18-20, 21- historical*. **hold feu** *of lands* to be held in feu tenure *17-20, 21- historical*. [AN *feu*, cognate with FEE¹·¹]
feu¹·², †**few** /fju/ *v* to grant or let land in feu *la16-20, 21- historical*. [see the noun]
feu see FEW¹, FEW²
feuach /ˈfjuax/ *n* a sparse crop of grain or grass *la19- NE*. [perhaps Gael *feochadh* withering]
feuch¹·¹ /fjux/ *n* a draw or a puff at a pipe *20- NE T*. [onomatopoeic]
feuch¹·² /fjux/ *v* to puff at a pipe; to smoke *la18-19, 20- NE*. [see the noun]
feuch² /fjux/ *n* a resounding blow *18- NE T*. [unknown]
feuch³ /fjux/ *n* a state of excitement or rage; a commotion *la18-19, 20- T EC*. [unknown]
feuch see FEECH²
feuchter /ˈfjuxtər/ *n* a slight fall of snow *la19- NE T*. [perhaps altered form of FLOCHTER¹·¹]
feught see FECHT¹·²
feul see FUIL¹·¹, FUIL¹·³
feurce /førs/ *adj* violent, uncontrolled, unmanageable *19- Ork N*. [Norw dial *fors*]
feverfoylie see FEATHERFOOLY
Feverȝere see FEBRUAR
fevvar see FIVVER
few¹, fyow, †**feu** /fju, fjʌu/ *adj* small in number, not many *la14-*. **a few broth** a small amount of broth *la18-19, 20- C*. †**few menyie, few menȝe** few companions, a small party *la14-e17*. †**a few nowmer** a small number *16*. **a few porridge** a small amount of porridge *la18-19, 20- C*. **a guid few** a good many, a considerable number *19-*. [OE *fēawe*]
few², feu /fju/ *v* to show promise or aptitude *la19- SW Bor*. [unknown]
few see FEU¹·¹, FEU¹·²
†**fewale,** †**fwaill,** †**fooll** *n* fuel *la14-e18*. [ME *feuel*]
fewl see FOOL
†**fewtyr** *v* to close in combat; to fight at close quarters *e16*. [unknown]
fey¹ /fae/ *n* the infield or the arable land nearest the farm buildings *la17- SW*. [perhaps related to FEY²]
fey² /fae/ *v* to clean out a ditch or a drain *la19- NE T*. [ON *fægja* to cleanse]
fey³, †**fay** /fae, fe/ *adj* 1 fated to die, doomed; at the point of death *la14-*. 2 behaving in an irresponsible or excited way (as if bewitched) *19-*. 3 leading to death; fatal *la15-e16*. 4 feeble, timid *e16*. **feydom,** †**feidom** the state of being doomed; a portent of death; destiny *18-19, 20- EC*. †**fey token** a sign of approaching death *la18-e19*. [OE *fǣge*, ON *feigr*]

fey see FEE¹·¹, FEE¹·²
feyr see FIAR¹
feyt see FIT¹·¹
feyther see FAITHER¹·¹
†fiall, feale, feall *n* **1** payment for services, wages *la15-18*. **2** a feudal tenant; a paid servant or workman *16-e18*. **3** feudal tenure *la15-e17*. [perhaps FEAL, with infl from FEE¹·¹]
fiar¹, fear, †feir, †feyr /'fiər/ *n* the price of (each variety of) grain fixed for the year by the local sheriff in the Fiars Court (used to determine ministers' stipends) *16-20, 21- historical*. [ME *feor*]
fiar², †fear /'fiər/ *n* the owner of a property in fee-simple or absolute possession *la15-*. [FEE¹·¹, with agent suffix]
fiarter /'fjartər/ *n* an insignificant or undersized person or animal *19- N*. [FAIRT¹·² with agent suffix]
ficher¹·¹, fucher /'fɪxər, 'fʌxər/ *n* a fiddling, inept way of working *19- NE*. [unknown]
ficher¹·², fucher /'fɪxər, 'fʌxər/ *v* **1** to fumble; to fiddle awkwardly or nervously with the fingers *19- Sh NE T*. **2** to work in an inept way *19, 20- NE*. **ficher wi** to handle (a woman) indelicately; to grope *19- Sh NE T*. [unknown]
fichie see FEECH²
ficht see FECHT¹·¹, FECHT¹·²
fickill see FICKLE¹·³
fickle¹·¹ /'fɪkəl/ *n* a puzzle, a riddle *la19- EC Bor*. **ficklie** puzzling, difficult, tricky *19- T EC*. [see the adj]
fickle¹·² /'fɪkəl/ *v* to puzzle or perplex *19-*. **fickler** a puzzle, a baffling problem *20- EC Bor*. [see the adj]
fickle¹·³, †fickill, †fikkill /'fɪkəl/ *adj* **1** changeable, inconstant *15-*. **2** difficult, tricky; dangerous *19-*. [OE *ficol*]
ficks facks see FYKE-FACK
fidder /'fɪdər/ *v* to flutter; to be in a state of excitement; *of a bird* to hover *19- SW*. [frequentative form of FUD¹·²]
fidder see FUTHER
fiddick /'fɪdək/ *n* a wooden bucket, a keg *la19- Sh*. Compare VATICK. [diminutive form of ON *fat* a pail, a vat]
fiddle, †fidill /'fɪdəl/ *n* **1** a violin, a fiddle *la15-*. **2** a hand-machine for sowing grain (worked by drawing a rod over an opening in the seed-container with a similar motion to bowing a violin) *18-*. **fiddler, †fithelar 1** a fiddle-player, a violinist; frequently in place-names *13-*. **2** the sandpiper *Actitis hypoleucos 19-*. **fiddlie** a nickname for a fiddler *20- NE T*. **fiddler's biddin** a last-minute invitation *la19- NE T C*. **fiddler's news** old news *la19-*. **fiddltie-fa** a fuss; a feeble excuse *la19- NE*. **fiddle diddle** an imitation of the sound of a fiddle *19-*. **fiddle face** a long face; a sad face *la19-*. **find a fiddle** to come upon something rare or precious; to get a pleasant surprise *la18-19, 20- NE*. **look like the far end of a French fiddle** to have a long face; to look sour or disdainful *18-*. [OE **fiðele*]
fidge¹·¹ /fɪdʒ/ *n* a shrug, a twitch, a jerk *18-19, 20- Sh NE T EC*. [unknown]
fidge¹·² /fɪdʒ/ *v* to fidget; to twitch, itch *la16-*. **fidgin fain** restlessly or excitedly eager *la17-19, 20- NE T EC*. [EModE *fidge*]
fidill see FIDDLE
fie see FEE¹·²
fiedle see FEEDLE
field¹·¹, fiel, †felde, †feild /fild, fil/ *n* **1** (a piece of) open or cleared ground; a piece of land used for pasture or tillage; frequently in place-names *13-*. **2** a battlefield *la14-*. **fieldy** the dunnock or hedge-sparrow *Prunella modularis 20- H&I C Bor*. **field conventicle** a meeting of Covenanters in the open air *la17-18, 19- historical*. **†field land, feild land** unenclosed land (suitable for pasture or cultivation); land comprised of fields *15-19*. **†feildland aittis** oats growing on land divided into fields *la16-e17*. **field meeting** a religious service held in the open air *17-19, 20- historical*. **field-preaching** a religious service held in the open air *19, 20- historical*. **field sparrow** the dunnock or hedge-sparrow *Prunella modularis 19-*. [OE *feld*]
field¹·², †feild /fild/ *v* **1** to fight, confront; to deal with; to handle or deflect *16-*. **2** to sink a margin around a wooden panel *19-*. [see the noun]
fie na see FY
fient¹·¹, fiend, †fende, †fend /fint, find/ *n* a demon; the Devil *la14-*. [OE *fēond* an enemy]
fient¹·², fiend, †feind /fint, find/ *interj* an invocation of the Devil; an expression of strong negation *la17-*. **fient a** not one, never one *16-*. **fient aw** nothing at all, not a thing *20-*. **fient haet, feint a haet** not a bit, not a jot *la18-*. **fient may care** the Devil may care *la18-19, 20- N*. **†fient nor** would to the Devil (that) *la18*. **†feint o me** certainly not *19*. **†fient that** = *fient nor e18*. [see the noun]
fier, †feir, †fere /fir/ *n* bearing, demeanour *15-19, 20- literary*. Compare EFFEIR¹·¹. **†feris** bearing, manners *15-e16*. **in fier of war, †in fere of were** in warlike array *la14-19, 20- literary*. [aphetic form of EFFEIR¹·¹]
fier see FERE³
fiercelins /'fɪrslɪnz/ *adv* hurriedly, impetuously, violently *la18-19, 20- Sh*. [Older Scots *fers* fierce, with *-lins* adv-forming suffix]
†fiercie, farcy, fairsie *n* farcy, a disease of animals (especially horses) *16-19*. [MFr *farcin*]
fiere see FERE¹
Fiersday see THURSDAY
fiesp see FEESP
Fife /fʌɪf/ *n* an area of eastern Scotland between the Forth and the Tay *la14-*. **Fifan** belonging to Fife *la17-19, 20- historical*. **Fifer 1** a native of Fife *la19-*. **2** a kind of soft, dull brown marble *20- NE*. **Fifie 1** a type of herring fishing boat (first built and used on the Fife coast) *20-*. **2** the nickname of the ferry-boat that formerly crossed from Dundee to Newport before the building of the Tay Road Bridge *20- T*. **Fifish** eccentric; outlandish or unbalanced *19, 20- T EC*. **Fife Region** a local government region formed from the former county of Fife *la20, 21- historical*. **ye need a lang spoon tae sup wi a Fifer** be wary of a person from Fife *20-*. [Gael *Fìb*]
fiffe see FIVE
fift, fifth, †fyft, †fyift /fɪft, fɪfθ/ *adj* the ordinal number after fourth *la14-*. [OE *fífta*]
fifteen, fiftene see FEIFTEEN¹·¹, FEIFTEEN¹·²
fifth see FIFT
fifty, fufty, †feftie /fɪfti, fʌfte/ *numeral* the cardinal number after forty-nine *la14-*. [OE *fíftig*]
fig see FEG
figger see FEEGUR¹·¹
figh see FEECH²
figmagarey, †feegarie /fɪgmə'gere/ *n* a frippery, a bauble *19, 20- Uls*. Compare WHIGMALEERIE. [altered and extended form of Scots *vaigrie* vagary; compare FLAGARIE]
figmaleerie, figmalirie see WHIGMALEERIE
†figorata *n* a kind of figured fabric *e17*. [Ital *figurata* or Spanish *figurada*]
figorit see FEEGUR¹·²
figour see FEEGUR¹·¹
†figurate, figurait *adj* **1** expressed or compared metaphorically *la15-16*. **2** patterned, figured *16*. [Lat *figūrātus*]
figure see FEEGUR¹·¹, FEEGUR¹·²
fik see FYKE¹·²
fike see FYKE¹·¹, FYKE¹·²

fikey see FYKIE
fikkill see FICKLE¹·³
fil see FILL¹·²
filbow, felba /'fɪlbo, 'fɛlbə/ *n* a blow, a thump *19- NE*. [unknown]
file see WHILE¹·¹, WHILE¹·²
fileock see WHILEOCK
files see WHILES¹·¹
filget, filjit /'fɪldʒət/ *n* an untidy, disreputable looking person *20- NE*. [unknown]
filiate /'fɪlɪet/ *v law* to determine the paternity of a child *19-*. **filiation,** †**filiacioune** 1 the act of, or legal action for, determining paternity *19-*. 2 adoption as a son *la15*. [Lat *fīliāt-*, ptp stem of *fīliāre* to have a child]
filie see WHILIE
filit see FYLE
filjit see FILGET
filk see WHILK³·¹
fill¹·¹ /fɪl/ *n* 1 a full supply, enough to satisfy *la14-*. 2 the action of filling, the amount necessary to fill (a container) *19-*. [OE *fyll*]
fill¹·², †**fil** /fɪl/ *v* 1 to make full; to fill something up or in *la14-*. 2 to pour out (into) *16-*. 3 to load peats *la18- Sh NE*. 4 *weaving* to fill bobbins with yarn *la19- T EC*. 5 *of the sea* to flow landward *15-19*. 6 to comply with; to complete *la14-16*. **filler,** †**fillar** 1 a person who fills something up or in *16-*. 2 a funnel for liquids *17-*. **fill an fesh ben** extravagant living *19- NE*. **fill an fesh mair** = *fill an fesh ben 19 20- NE T SW*. **fill drunk, fill fou** to make drunk *19-*. **fill up** to increase in bulk or girth *la19- NE T H&I SW*. [OE *fyllan*]
fill¹·³ /fɪl/ *adj* full *18-19*, *20- Ork NE*. Compare FOU²·³. [see the verb]
fill see WHILE¹·²
filla see FELLAE
fillad see FILLET
fillebeg, philabeg /'fɪləbɛg/ *n* a kilt *18-19*, *20- literary*. [Gael *féileadh-beag* little kilt, *féileadh* being originally the whole PLAID¹·¹ which, when belted, was a significant development towards the modern KILT¹·¹]
fillet, *N* **fillad,** *NE* **fullet** /'fɪlət; *N* 'fɪləd; *NE* 'fʌlət/ *n* 1 a joint or strip of meat or fish *16-*. 2 a strip of wood or cloth (used for decoration) *16-*. 3 the loin or thigh (of a person or animal) *la15-19*, *20- N NE*. [ME *filet*]
fillie, †**filly,** †**fely** /'fɪli/ *n* the exterior of a wheel rim, the felloe *la14-19*, *20- literary*. [OE *felg*]
†**fillock, fillok** *n* a giddy or silly girl *15-19*. [unknown]
fillum /'fɪləm/ *n* a film *20-*. [altered form of Eng *film*]
filly see FILLIE
filsh¹ /fɪlʃ/ *n* a big, disagreeable person; a lout *19- NE EC*. **filschach** a dishonest or greedy person *20- NE*. [unknown]
filsh² /fɪlʃ/ *adj* weak, faint *19- C*. [unknown]
filska /'fɪlska/ *n* high-spirited fun, flighty behaviour *la19- Sh*. [ON *fólska* foolishness]
filsket, filskit /'fɪlskət/ *adj* high-spirited, frisky *la19- Sh*. [from the noun FILSKA]
filth see FULTH
filthie, filthy, filty see FULTHY
fimis¹·¹, **fimmish** /'fɪmɪs, 'fɪmɪʃ/ *n* a flurry, a state of excitement or perplexity *la19- Sh Ork*. [compare ON *fimr* agile]
fimis¹·², **virmish** /'fɪmɪs, 'vɪrmɪʃ/ *v* to be excited or worked up; to long anxiously for *20- Sh Ork*. [ON *fimask* to hasten]
fimmish see FIMIS¹·¹
fin see FIND¹·¹, FIND¹·², WHAN¹·¹, WHAN¹·²
finale see FEENAL
finance, †**fynans** /'fʌɪnans, fɪ'nans/ *n* 1 the management of money; money lent, advanced or spent *15-*. 2 fineness, metallic content (of gold or silver) *la15-16*. 3 ransom money *15*. †**mak finance** to collect, lend or spend money *la15-e16*. [ME *finaunce*]
find¹·¹, **fin** /fɪnd, fʌɪnd, fɪn, fʌɪn/ *n* 1 something found *19-*. 2 the feel of something, the impression produced by touch *19-*. 3 the indecent handling of a woman *20-*. [see the verb]
find¹·², **fin,** †**fynd** /fɪnd, fʌɪnd, fɪn, fʌɪn/ *v pt* **fund,** *H&I WC* **fan, fand,** *ptp* **fund,** *Sh* **fun,** †**foundin,** †**fundin** 1 to come across, discover; to locate *la14-*. 2 to encounter, experience; to sense or become aware of *la14-*. 3 *law* to decide and declare after consideration or judicial proceedings *la14-*. 4 to feel or search with the fingers; to grope *la18-*. 5 to procure; to provide for *la14-17*. **finding,** †**fyndyn** 1 the act of finding *la14-*. 2 provision, maintenance *15-e17*. **finster** a discovery, a (worthwhile) find *19- Sh*. **fin yer mooth** to put food in your mouth *20- Sh Ork NE SW*. [OE *findan*]
Findon haddock see FINNAN HADDOCK
†**fine**¹·¹, **fyne** *v* 1 to sort out wool by separating the fine from the coarse parts *18-19*. 2 to refine metal *la14-e17*. †**fyning quhele** a spinning wheel for making a fine woollen yarn *17*. [see the adj]
fine¹·², †**fyne** /fʌɪn/ *adj* 1 of superior quality *la14-*. 2 delicate; slender; minute *la14-*. 3 comfortable, contented; in good health *la18-*. 4 pleasant-mannered, likeable *la18-*. **fineries** delicacies, luxury foods *19, 20- Sh*. **fine ham** an exclamation of incredulity or dismissal *20- NE C*; compare HAM-A-HADDIE. **fine and, fine an** very, properly, really: ◊*fine an ripe, thae aipples la18-*. **fine day** an exclamation of incredulity or dismissal *20-*. **a fine time o day** an inappropriate or inconvenient time *20-*. [ME *fin*]
fine¹·³ /fʌɪn/ *adv* very well, very much: ◊*I like it fine la18-*. **fine that** very well indeed; certainly *la19-*. [see the adj]
fine²·¹ /fʌɪn/ *n* 1 a sum of money imposed as a penalty for an offence *17-*. 2 a final result or settlement *15-e17*. 3 aim, purpose *la15-e17*. 4 an end or termination *la14-16*. **come tae fine** to come to a decision *20- Ork*. [ME *fin*]
fine²·² /fʌɪn/ *v* to impose a monetary penalty for an offence *17-*. †**fine with** *of a magistrate* to accept a payment from an accused person as the price of connivance *16-e17*. [see the noun]
†**fine**²·³ *v* to cease, desist; to come to an end *la14-16*. [ME *finen*]
fineer /fɪ'nir/ *v* 1 to veneer *19-*. 2 to ornament fancifully *la19- NE T EC Bor*. [Ger *furnieren*]
fineries see FINE¹·²
finger, †**fyngar** /'fɪŋər, 'fɪŋgər/ *n* one of the digits on a hand *la14-*. **fingerfu, fingeful** a pinch, a small quantity *la19-*. **finger-fed** pampered *la15-19, 20- NE T*. **finger-neb** a fingertip *la18- C*. **finger-steel, finger-stuil** a finger-stall *19-*. [OE *finger*]
fingering, †**fingram,** †**finʒering** /'fɪŋgərɪŋ/ *n* 1 a kind of worsted, originally spun from combed wool on the small wheel *17-*. 2 a kind of coarse, woollen cloth *17-e18*. [unknown]
finish see FEENISH¹·¹, FEENISH¹·²
†**finkle, finkil** *n* fennel, the plant *16-e19*. [Lat *faeniculum*]
finn /fɪn/ *n folklore* a mythical being associated with the sea *la19- Sh Ork*. [ON *Finnar* the Finns]
Finnan haddock, Finnan haddie, †**Findon haddock** /fɪnən 'hadək, fɪnən 'hadi/ *n* a haddock cured with the smoke of green wood, peat or turf *18-*. [from the place-name *Findon* and HADDOCK or HADDIE]
finner /'fɪnər/ *n* a whale of the genus *Balaenoptera la18- Sh Ork*. [from its prominent dorsal fin]
†**finnie** *adj of grain* full of substance *18-e19*. [perhaps ME *findi* suitable or proper for a certain purpose]

finnis /ˈfɪnɪs/ v to fidget with eagerness or anxiety *20- T.*
finnissin fidgeting, anxious *20- T.* [unknown]
finnock, finnoch,†phinoc, †fynnak /ˈfɪnək, ˈfɪnəx/ n a young sea-trout *Salmo trutta*, originally also a young salmon *17-19, 20- N NE H&I C.* [Gael *fionnag* a sea-trout; a young salmon]
†finour n a refiner of metal *15-16.* [ME *finour*]
†finster n a trade of some kind *la17.* [compare FINOUR]
finster see FIND[1.2]
finȝering see FINGERING
†fippill, feppill v to pout; to whimper *la15-e16.* [unknown; compare FAIPLE, Icel *flipi*]
fir, †fyr /fɪr, fʌr/ n an evergreen coniferous tree or its timber *15-.* **†firrin, fyrryn, fyrne** made of fir-wood *la15-e17.* **fir candle** a thin length of fir-wood used as a candle; see *candle fir* (CAUNLE) *19- NE.* **†fir-fecket** a coffin *19.* **fir gullie** a knife used for splitting candle fir *la19- NE.* **fir peerie** a fir cone *20- Uls.* **fir-tap** a fir cone *18-19, 20- C SW Bor.* **fir yowe** a fir cone *19, 20- NE T.* [ME *firre*, ON *fýri*]
fir see FOR[1.1]
firdoun see FRIDDON
fire[1.1], **†fyre, †fyir** /faer, ˈfaeər/ n 1 burning matter; a bonfire *la14-.* 2 fuel *la16-.* 3 a foreign (metallic) body in the eye *la19-.* 4 the phosphorescence of the sea *la19, 20- NE.* 5 a kindling of tobacco; a lit pipe *la19- Sh.* **firies** very fast turns of a skipping rope *20- T.* **†fyre bitt** a crate containing combustible material which could be set on fire as a beacon *17.* **fire burn** sea phosphorescence *la19- NE EC SW.* **fire coal 1** soft, bright-burning coal *la18-19, 20- NE T EC.* **2** coal supplied to workmen connected with a colliery *la19, 20- EC.* **†fire cros, fyre cors** = *fiery cross 16-17.* **fiery cross** a wooden cross burnt at one end and dipped in blood at the other, carried from place to place to summon men to arms *18, 19- historical*; compare CROSTARIE. **fire-edge 1** the sharp edge of a new tool *20- NE H&I EC.* **2** an initial wave of enthusiasm *19- NE SW.* **fire-en, fire-en** (the location of) the fireside in a room *la18-.* **firefangit** scorched; spoilt by excessive fermentation *16-19, 20- Ork Bor.* **fire-flaucht 1** lightning, lightning-flashes; a thunderbolt *15-.* **2** a shooting star; a will-o'-the-wisp *19- NE C SW.* **fire-glud** the glow of the fire *20- Sh.* **fire-hoose, fire-house, †fyre hous 1** a house with a fireplace, a dwelling-house *15-19, 20- N NE.* **2** a kitchen *20- Ork.* **fire kettle** a three-legged pot for containing fire in an open fishing-boat *la19- Sh.* **fire-kinlin** a house-warming party *19- NE.* **fire master 1** the chief officer of a fire-brigade *la19-.* **2** one of a group of citizens appointed to take charge of fire-fighting *e18.* **fire new** brand new, as new as metal from the fire *la18- NE EC.* **fire raising, †fyir rasing** *law* arson *la16-.* **fire room** a room with a fireplace *la16-19, 20- H&I.* **fireside tartan** mottled skin on the legs caused by sitting too close to a fire *20- NE T C*; compare *grannie's tartan* (GRANNIE[1.1]), *tinker's tartan* (TINKER). **†fire-slaucht, fire-slacht** lightning *la14-e19.* **†fyre spere** a flaming spear *16-17.* **fire stane** a hearth stone *20- Ork NE.* **fire stife** *mining* the smell of coal burning spontaneously *la19, 20- EC.* **†fyre vessell, fyre veschell** cooking utensils *la16-17.* **fire wark, †fyre werk 1** a firework *17-.* **2** *pl* fittings for guns *la16-e17.* **3** a firearm *la16-17.* **fire and tow** rash, impetuous *la19, 20- NE T.* **like fire and tow** rashly, impetuously *19, 20- NE T.* [OE *fȳr*]
fire[1.2], **†fyre, †fyir** /fʌɪr, ˈfʌɪər/ v 1 to set fire to *15-.* 2 to discharge a gun *16-.* 3 to bake bread or cakes in an oven or on a girdle *18-.* 4 to inflame a part of the body by chafing *la18-.* 5 to heat a house *20-.* **fired** *of perishable food* spoiled by hot weather conditions *19, 20- EC SW.* [see the noun]
firikin see FAERACHIN

firk, ferk /fɪrk, fɛrk/ v to jerk; to poke about or rummage *la19- Ork NE.* [OE *fercian* to bring]
firlot, †ferlot, †furlot, †forlot /ˈfɪrlɔt, ˈfɪrlət/ n 1 a dry measure, the fourth part of a BOLL *la13-.* 2 a vessel used to measure this amount *15-19.* [ON *fjórði* fourth + ON *hlutr* a lot, a portion]
firm, †ferm /fɪrm, fʌrm/ *adj* 1 fixed, settled, constant *la14-.* 2 strong, solid; secure, safe *la14-.* **†ferme and stabill** *in legal agreements* without alteration, revocation or retraction *la14-e17.* [OFr *ferm*, Lat *firmus*]
firm see FURM
†firmance, fermance, fermans n 1 confinement, custody *la15-18.* 2 secure safekeeping *la15-e16.* 3 an enclosure *e16.* [OFr *fermance* an enclosure, a guarantee]
firmorar see FERMORAR
firnenst see FORENENT
firple see FAIPLE
firr /fɪr/ n a state of agitation or excitement *20- NE.* [unknown]
firris /ˈfɪrɪs/ n 1 excitement or rage *la19- NE.* 2 a predicament *la19- NE.* [unknown]
firsle see FISSLE[1.2]
first[1.1], **furst, †fyrst, †ferst** /fɪrst, fʌrst/ *adj* 1 the ordinal number corresponding to one *la14-.* 2 earliest, foremost; preceding all others *la14-.* **firsten, †firstin** first *la18- literary.* **†first end** the first instalment of a payment *la16-18.* **first flat** the ground floor of a building *la18-.* **first floor** = *first flat la19-.* **First Minister** the head of the Scottish Government and chair of the Scottish cabinet *la20-.* **†first Maryday** the Annunciation (25 March) or the Assumption (15 Aug) *la15-16.* **†in the first** in the first place *la14-e17.* **Monday first** next Monday *la18-.* [OE *fyrst*]
first[1.2], **furst, †fyrst** /fɪrst, fʌrst/ *adv* initially; before all others *la14-.* [see the adj]
first see FRIST[1.1]
first fit[1.1], **first foot** /fɪrst ˈfɪt, fʌrst ˈfut/ n 1 the first person to enter a house on New Year's morning, traditionally considered to bring good (or bad) luck for coming the year *la18-.* 2 the first person or animal met on a journey, especially by a wedding or christening party on the way to church *18-19, 20- N NE T EC.* [FIRST[1.1] + FIT[1.1]]
first fit[1.2], **first foot** /fɪrst ˈfɪt, fʌrst ˈfut/ v to be the first to visit (a household) in the New Year; to go on a round of such visits *19-.* **first fitter, first footer** a person who goes first-footing *19-.* [see the noun]
firth[1], **frith** /fɪrθ, fʌrθ, frɪθ/ n a wide inlet of the sea; an estuary *14-.* [ON *fjörðr*]
†firth[2], **fyrth** n a wood; wooded country, land overgrown with brushwood; frequently in place-names *la14-19.* [OE *fyrhþ*]
firtig[1.1], **†fertigue** /ˈfɪrtɪg/ n fatigue, tiredness *la19- Sh NE.* [altered form of Scots *fatigue*]
firtig[1.2], **fortig** /ˈfɪrtɪg, fərˈtɪg/ v to tire or fatigue *la19- Sh NE T.* [see the noun]
fiscal, †fischall, †phiscall /ˈfɪskəl/ n the Procurator Fiscal *la16-.* [shortened form of PROCURATOR FISCAL]
fischer see FISHER
fish[1.1], **fush, †fisch, †fesch** /fɪʃ, fʌʃ/ n 1 an aquatic creature, a fish *la11-.* 2 a salmon *19-*; compare *reid fish* (REID[1.2]). 3 white fish (as opposed to herring) *20- N T EC.* **fish-boat, †fische boit** a fishing boat *16-.* **fish cadger** an itinerant fish seller *19-20, 21- historical.* **fishy-flee** a bluebottle fly *Calliphora vomitaria 20- Sh.* **fish side** the flesh side of a split fish (as opposed to the skin side) *la19- Sh.* **fish supper** a meal of fish and chips *la19-.* **fish tea** a meal of fish and chips with bread and butter and tea *la19-.* **fish toun** a fishing village *la18- NE.* [OE *fisc*]

fish¹,², **fush**, †**fisch**, †**fysche** /fɪʃ, fʌʃ/ *v* **1** to catch or attempt to catch fish; to work in the fishing industry *15-*. **2** to endeavour; to contrive *19- H&I WC*. **fishing-wand** a fishing rod *17-*. [OE *fiscian*]

fisher, **fusher**, †**fyschare**, †**fischer** /ˈfɪʃər, ˈfʌʃər/ *n* **1** a fisherman *14-*. **2** a member of a fishing community *19-*. **fisher folk**, **fisher fowk** the people of a fishing community *19-*. **fisher's hen** a seagull *la20- NE T*. **fisher land** land along the shore used by fishermen to dry fish or spread nets *la18-*. **fisher toun**, **fisher toon** a fishing village *la16-*. **fisher wife**, †**fischar wyf** a woman employed in the fishing industry or living in a fishing community *la16-*. [OE *fiscere*]

†**fisk**¹ *n* the public treasury; the revenue of the Crown or that which fell to the Crown by forfeiture or escheat *17-18*. [Fr *fisc*, Lat *fiscus*]

fisk² /fɪsk/ *n fisherman's taboo* a fish *19- Sh*. **fiskafeal** the boards dividing a boat into compartments *la19- Sh*. [ON *fiskr*]

fiskalie /ˈfɪskali/ *adj* suitable or lucky for fishing *la19- Sh*. [ON *fiskiligt*]

fismal /ˈfɪsməl/ *n* a small quantity, a particle *20- Sh*. [derivative of Norw dial *fisma* anything too thin or flimsy]

fiss¹ /fɪs/ *n* fine rain, drizzle *20- Ork*. [perhaps onomatopoeic]

fiss² /fɪs/ *v* to make a hissing noise *la19- NE*. [onomatopoeic]

fiss *see* FACE¹,¹

fissle¹,¹, †**fistle** /ˈfɪsəl/ *n* **1** a rustling sound *19, 20- SW Bor Uls*. **2** a bustle, a commotion, a fuss *18-19*. [onomatopoeic]

fissle¹,², **fistle**, *SW Uls* **firsle** /ˈfɪsəl; *SW Uls* ˈfɪrsəl/ *v* **1** to make a rustling or scuffling noise *18-19, 20- EC SW Bor Uls*. **2** to fidget; to bustle *la18-19, 20- literary*. [see the noun]

fit¹,¹, **foot**, **fuit**, **fut**, †**fute**, †**fwt** /fɪt, fut, fʌt/ *n pl* **feet**, **fits**, †**fete**, †**feit**, †**feyt** **1** the lowest part of the leg below the ankle, the foot *la14-*. **2** a measure of distance, 12 inches; the length of a foot *la14-*. **3** the bottom of a hill; the lower or far end of a street or a piece of ground; the lower reaches or mouth of a watercourse; frequently in place-names *la14-*. **4** the lower part or base of an object *la15-*. **5** a foothold; one's footing *18-*. **6** a bringer of (good or bad) fortune: ◇*be an ill fit 18-19, 20- NE*. **fits** the foot of the class, the dunce *20- T Bor Uls*. **fit ale**, †**foot yill** a celebratory drink *19, 20- N EC*. **fit breed**, **fit breedth**, †**futbreid** the breadth of a foot; a very small distance *la14-19, 20- N NE T Bor*. **fit brod**, **foot broad** a footboard, a treadle, a foot-rest *la16-19, 20- NE*. **fit eitch**, †**fute-eache** an adze; a ship's carpenter's long-handled adze held in place by the foot *17-19, 20- Sh Ork N NE*. **fit fang**, *Sh NE* **fit wang** a strap used by cobblers looped round knee and foot and over the work to keep it in position *la18- Sh NE*. **fit feal**, †**futefell** the skin of a young lamb *15-e18, 20- Bor*. **fit folk** people who attend an event on foot, pedestrians *la18-19, 20- NE T SW Bor*. †**fitgang**, **footgang 1** a plank or planks to walk on *16-19*. **2** a long footstool or chest beside a bed, used as a step *la16-e18*. †**fute hate**, **fut het**, **fute hoyt** in haste; with all speed; immediately *la14-e16*. **fitick** the chain and hook connecting the muzzle of the plough with the fit-tree *20- H&I WC SW Uls*. **fitman**, **footman**, †**futeman 1** an attendant, a servant *16-*. **2** a foot soldier *la14-17*. **fit market**, **foot market** the part of a fair or market with stalls and stands as opposed to livestock for sale, frequented by those seeking work *la18- NE T*. **fit pad** a footpath *la19- WC SW*. **fit pan** a bed valance *la19- NE SW*. **fit rig** an end-rig; the piece of land at the end of a field on which the plough is turned *19- Sh NE*. **fit road** a footpath *16-*. †**fit side**, **fut syde 1** even with; in line or step with *17-e18*. **2** *of a garment* reaching to the feet *e16*. †**fit sides** even with; in line or step with *la18-19*. †**fute sok** a short sock *la15-e17*. †**fute spade** an ordinary digging spade *la15-17*.

fitspar, **feetspur** a wooden bar across the floor of a boat for pressing the feet against when rowing *la19-*. †**fit-stead** a footprint *16-19*. **fitstep**, **futstep**, †**futestep** a footstep *la15-*. **fit-stramp** a footstep *20- Sh*. **fit stuil**, †**futstule 1** a footstool *la16-*. **2** the earth *la19- Sh SW*. **fit tree 1** the wooden spar to which the traces are attached in ploughing *20-*. **2** the treadle of a spinning-wheel or loom *la19- Sh Ork*. **feetwashin** the ceremony of washing the feet of a bridegroom or bride, performed by friends on the eve of the wedding *18-*. **a yer feet** at full speed *la19- NE*. **aff yer feet 1** unfit for work *19- N NE*. **2** having loose morals *la19- NE EC Bor*. †**at hir fute** *of a calf or stirk* still going with the cow *16*. **fit an a half**, **foot and a half** (a call in) a game of leapfrog *la19-*. **fit fair** *curling* to take up position for delivering a shot at the proper distance from the far tee *19-*. **fit for fit** step by step, side by side, closely *16-*. **fit for leg** immediately, as quickly as possible *la19- NE Uls*. †**fute of the compt** (the total shown at) the bottom line of an account *la15-17*. **Fit o the Toon** the harbour area of Arbroath *la19- T*. **Fit o the Walk**, **Foot of the Walk** the bottom of Leith Walk in Edinburgh *la20-*. **get up yer fit** to be scolded *la19- NE T SW*. **gie him up his fit** to scold, rebuke *19-*. †**ilka fit and fur** every detail *19*. **mak yer feet yer freen** to go off at a great pace, take to one's heels *la19- NE T*. **on fit 1** standing, walking *la14-*. **2** well, in good health *19- Sh Ork NE T*. **3** alive *20- EC Bor*. †**on the fete** alive *e16*. **pit in a fit** to walk more quickly *19-*. **tak yer fit in yer hand**, **tak yer foot in your hand** to depart *la18-19, 20- Sh Ork NE T*. **till yer fit** recovered from illness, up and about *la19-*. **upon the fit** *of a crop* standing, uncut; unthreshed *la18-19, 20- NE*. [OE *fōt*]

fit¹,², **foot**, **fut**, †**fute** /fɪt, fut, fʌt/ *v* **1** to provide with a foot or base *la15-*. **2** to add up (an account) and insert the total *la15-*. **3** to move the feet; to tread; to travel on foot *16-*. **4** to set peats up on end to dry *la16-*. **5** to attach a foot to a stocking; to knit a new foot for a sock *la18-19, 20- Sh*. **6** *of a horse* to kick *19, 20- SW*. **fitted account** *law* an account rendered by one party and accepted as correct by the other *la17-*. †**futit compt** an account which has been added or reckoned up *16-17*. †**fute the field** to go out to fight *la16*. **fit the fluir**, **foot the floor** to dance *la18-19, 20- Sh NE WC SW*. [see the noun]

†**fit**² *n* a strain of music *la15-18*. [OE *fitt* a section of a poem or song]

fit³ /fɪt/ *v* **1** to suit, meet the requirements of *17-*. **2** to be the correct shape or size; to fill a space exactly *la18-*. **fittit**, **fitted 1** appropriate, suited *la17-*. **2** made to fit closely *la17-*. **3** pleased, satisfied *la18-*. [EModE *fit*]

fit *see* WHIT¹,¹, WHIT¹,², WHIT¹,³

fitakaleerie /fɪtəkəˈliri/ *n* a dance performed in a sitting position with an ale-cog in hand *20- Ork*. [FIT¹,¹, FIT¹,², with a fanciful ending]

fitba, **fitbaw**, **football**, †**fut bal**, †**futeball**, †**fut baw** /ˈfɪtba, ˈfɪtbɔ, ˈfutbɔl/ *n* **1** a game involving two opposing teams in which a ball is kicked with the aim of scoring goals *15-*. **2** the ball used in a game of football *la15-*. [FIT¹,¹ + BA¹]

fitch¹ /fɪtʃ/ *n* vetch, the plant *Vicia sativa la15-*. [ME *fecche*, *ficche*]

fitch² /fɪtʃ/ *v* to move slightly or restlessly; to edge along; to move from one place to another *la15-19, 20- Sh Ork N*. [unknown; compare FIDGE¹,², FOTCH]

fite *see* WHITE¹,¹, WHITE¹,², WHITE²

fiteichtie *see* WHITE¹,²

fithelar *see* FIDDLE

fither *see* WHITHER¹,²

fitin *see* WHITIN

fitless, †**futles** /ˈfɪtləs/ *adj* **1** lacking a foot or feet *la15-*. **2** unsteady on the feet; accident prone *la19-*. **fitless cock** a kind of oatmeal dumpling *19-*. [FIT¹·¹, with adj-forming suffix]

fit like *see* WHIT¹·¹

fits *see* FIT¹·¹

fitter¹ /ˈfɪtər/ *n* **1** a person who is a harbinger of (good or bad) fortune *la19- NE Uls*. **2** *fisherman's taboo* a cat *20- Sh*. [Norn *fitter* a mouse or cat]

fitter² /ˈfɪtər/ *v* **1** to move restlessly; *of feet* to tap or patter *19-*. **2** to totter, walk unsteadily; to stumble *19, 20- N*. [perhaps frequentative form of FIT¹·²]

fittie¹·¹, **fitty** /ˈfɪte, ˈfɪti/ *n* **1** a foot *la18-*. **2** a stocking foot or short sock worn as a shoe or as an extra sock, or put on over a boot *la19- Sh Ork NE*; compare FITTOCK. **3** the least able pupil in a school class *20- T SW Bor*. **4** a nickname for an agile, nimble dog *18-e19*. †**feetie** feet *18-19*. **feeties** feet *la19- NE*. [FIT¹·¹ + -IE¹]

fittie¹·² /ˈfɪte, ˈfɪti/ *adj* nimble, surefooted *18-19, 20- WC SW*. [see the noun]

fittiefie /ˈfɪtefae/ *n* a whim, a fancy; a quibble or complaint *19- NE*. [altered form of WHEETY-WHATTIE¹·¹]

fittin, **fitting** /ˈfɪtɪn, ˈfɪtɪŋ/ *n fisherman's taboo* a cat *la19- Sh Ork*. [FIT¹·¹ the footed-one, with ending by analogy with FOODIN]

fittininment /fɪtənˈɪnmənt/ *n* concern, interference; a footing in something *la18- NE*. [presp of FIT¹·² + IN¹·³, with noun-forming suffix]

fittle, **feetle** /ˈfɪtəl, ˈfitəl/ *v* to take short steps *la19- Sh Ork N*. **fittlan** bungling *20- Ork*. **fittlie** shaky on the feet *20- Ork*. [perhaps frequentative or diminutive form of FIT¹·²]

fittock, *Ork* **feetock** /ˈfɪtək; *Ork* ˈfitək/ *n* **1** a stocking foot or short sock worn as a shoe or as an extra sock, or put on over a boot *la19- Ork N NE*. **2** a peat cut from the bottom of a peat-bank *20- NE*. [FIT¹·¹ with diminutive suffix *-ock*]

fittret *see* FUTRET

fitty *see* FITTIE¹·¹

five, †**fiffe**, †**fyve**, †**fywe** /faev/ *numeral* **1** the cardinal number after four *la14-*. **fives** = *five stanes 20- NE T SW*. **fivesome**, †**fivesum**, †**fyvesum** five in all; a set or group of five *la14-*. **five stanes** the game of chucks played with five stones or pebbles *la19- N NE T EC*. **like five ell o wind** at great speed; like lightning *la19- T C Bor*. [OE *fīf*]

fivver, *N* **fevvar**, †**fiver** /ˈfɪvər/ *N* ˈfevər/ *n* fever; scarlet fever *la16-*. [OE *fēfer*]

fize *see* FEEZE¹·¹, FIZZ¹·¹, VICE²

fizz¹·¹, †**fize** /fɪz/ *n* **1** effervescence; a hissing sound *17-*. **2** a bustle, a commotion; a state of excitement or rage *19-*. [onomatopoeic]

fizz¹·² /fɪz/ *v* **1** to effervesce; to make a hissing sound *la18-*. **2** to make a fuss; to bustle; to be in a great rage *la18-*. **fizzin' deevil** a pellet of wet gunpowder set alight as a kind of firework *la19-20, 21- historical*. [see the noun]

fizzy *see* FUZZIE

fla *see* FLAE¹, FLAE²

flaa *see* FLAW¹·¹, FLAW¹·²

flaacht *see* FLAUCHT¹·¹

flaachter *see* FLOCHTER¹·²

flaachter-spade *see* FLAUCHTER-SPADE

flaag *see* FLAG⁶

flacat *see* FLAKKET

flaccon *see* FLAGON

flacht *see* FLAUCHT¹·¹, FLAUCHT¹·²

flack *see* FLAG²·¹

flackie, **flakki** /ˈflaki/ *n* **1** a straw mat to protect a horse's back *18- Sh Ork*. **2** a mat over which corn is winnowed or meal is sifted *la19- Sh Ork*. **3** a draught-screen for a doorway *20- Ork N*. [ON *flaki* a wickerwork hurdle]

flacon *see* FLAGON

†**flad**, **flaud** *n* a large, flat piece; a slab *19*. [compare FLAG²·¹, FLAT¹·¹, BLAUD²]

flae¹, †**fla** /fle/ *n* **1** a fly *la14-*. **2** a flea *16-*. †**flae luggit**, **flea lugged** scatterbrained *18-e19*. [OE *flēah* a flea, the vowel is irregular; compare FLECH¹·¹]

flae², **flay**, †**fla**, †**fle** /fle/ *v pt also* †**flew**, *ptp* **flain** †**flane**, †**flead 1** to skin, flay *la14-*. **2** to strip ground of turf, especially before cutting peat *la16-*; compare FLAW¹·². [OE *flēan*, ON *flá*]

flaesick /ˈflezək/ *n* **1** a wood shaving *19- NE*. **2** a small particle (of ash, soot or fluff) *20- NE*. [perhaps ON *flís* a splinter, with diminutive suffix]

flaff¹·¹ /flaf/ *n* **1** a fluttering or flapping movement *19-*. **2** a flick, a slap, a light blow *19-*. **3** a gust or puff of wind *19-*. **4** something light or insubstantial; a vain empty-headed person *19-*. **5** a brief moment, an instant; a flash (of lightning) *19*. [see the verb]

flaff¹·² /flaf/ *v* **1** to flap, flutter; to make unsteady; to fan a flame *la15-*. **2** *of the wind* to blow in gusts *19, 20- Sh T EC*. **3** *of light* to flicker or gleam *19, 20- SW*. [onomatopoeic]

flaff¹·³ /flaf/ *adv* with a sudden fluttering movement *la19, 20- NE*. [see the verb]

flaffer¹·¹ /ˈflafər/ *n* **1** a pound note *la19-*. **2** a fluttering, flapping movement *19, 20- Sh NE T EC*. [FLAFF¹·², with agent suffix]

flaffer¹·² /ˈflafər/ *v* to flutter or flap; to throb or palpitate *la18-19 20- NE T EC Bor*. [frequentative form of FLAFF¹·²]

flag¹ /flag/ *n* a large, clumsy, slovenly woman *e16, 19- Sh NE*. [unknown]

flag²·¹, †**flack**, †**flaik** /flag/ *n* **1** a flat stone, a flagstone *16-*. **2** a piece of turf cut from the surface of the ground, a sod *18-19, 20- Bor*. Compare FLAW¹·¹ (sense 5). [compare Icel *flag* a place where turf has been cut]

flag²·² /flag/ *v* to pave with flagstones *16-*. [see the noun]

†**flag**³ *n* a blast or gust; a flash (of lightning) *16*. [compare FLAW²]

flag⁴·¹ /flag/ *n* a large snowflake *19- N NE T*. [compare Dan *flage*, Norw *flak*, ON *flaki*]

flag⁴·² /flag/ *v of snow* to fall in large flakes *19- NE*. [see the noun]

flag⁵ /flag/ *v* to flog, whip *19- literary*. [altered form of Eng *flog*]

flag⁶, **flaag** /flag, flɑg/ *v* to hang loosely, flap *20- Sh*. [perhaps related to OFr *flac* feeble, drooping]

flag⁷, †**flaig** /flag/ *n* a cloth banner; an emblem *la16-*. [EModE *flagg*]

flagarie /fləˈgeri/ *n* **1** a whim; a piece of frivolity *19, 20- NE Bor*. **2** an ornament, something excessively fancy *18-19*. **3** an overdressed or frivolous person *19*. [altered form of *feegarie* (FIGMAGAREY)]

flaggat *see* FAGGALD

flaggert /ˈflagərt/ *n* a loose flapping garment *20- NE*. [derivative of FLAG⁶]

flagon, **flaggon**, †**flagoun**, †**flaccon**, †**flacon** /ˈflagən/ *n* **1** a bottle or jug (for holding alcohol) *la15-*. **2** a small metal can (for carrying milk) *19- NE T EC*. [ME *flagon*]

flaich *see* FLECH¹·¹

flaig *see* FLAG⁷

flaik *see* FLAG²·¹, FLAKE¹·¹

flail, †**flaill** /flel/ *n* **1** an instrument for threshing grain *la14-*. **2** a tall, gangling person *la19- N NE*. **flail soople** the part of a flail which beats out the grain *la19- Sh Ork NE*. [OE *fligel*, OFr *flaiel*]

flain see FLAE²
flainen see FLANNEN
flaip /flep/ *n* (the sound of) a dull heavy fall; a thud *19- Bor.* [variant of FLAP¹·¹; compare FLYPE²·¹]
flair¹·¹, **fluir**, *Sh* **flör**, *NE* **fleer**, *WC* **fler**, †**flure**, †**flour** /fler, flur; *Sh* flør; *NE* flir; *WC* fler/ *n* a floor *la14-*. [OE *flōr*]
flair¹·², **fluir**, *NE* **fleer**, †**flure** /fler, flur; *NE* flir/ *v* to provide with a floor; to lay flooring *la15-*. **flairing**, †**fluiring**, †**flouring 1** flooring *la15-*. **2** a flooring nail *e17*. †**fluring nail** a flooring nail *la16-e17*. [see the noun]
flair² /fler/ *v* to flatter; to boast *la18-19, 20- SW.* [unknown]
flairdie¹·¹ /'flɛrde/ *n* **1** flattery; insincerity *20- SW.* **2** a wheedling child or person; a two-faced person *20- SW.* [derivative of FLAIR²]
flairdie¹·² /'flɛrde/ *v* to flatter, cajole *la19- SW.* [see the noun]
flait see FLET³
flake¹·¹, **fleck**, †**flaik** /flek, flɛk/ *n* **1** a (portable) hurdle or framework of crossed slats used as a fence or gate *la15-*. **2** *distilling* a wooden box containing water through which a spiral tube or worm passes, to condense the liquid inside it *18-*. **3** *pl* (a number of hurdles used as) a temporary pen for sheep or cattle *18-19, 20- NE SW.* **4** a weir or lattice fence across a river *18-19, 20- SW.* **5** a rack used for displaying goods for sale or feeding hay to animals *la16-19*. **flake stand 1** *distilling* a wooden box containing water through which a spiral tube or worm passes, to condense the liquid inside it *18-19, 20- T.* **2** a rack used for displaying goods for sale or feeding hay to animals, or a stand to support one *la16-17*. [ON *flaki* a wicker hurdle]
flake¹·² /flek/ *v* **1** to pen sheep with hurdles *la18-19, 20- NE Bor.* **2** to screen with a frame or rack *e16*. [see the noun]
flake² /flek/ *n* a side of bacon *20- EC SW Bor.* [ON *flikki*, with influence from FLAKE¹·¹]
†**flakket**, **flacat**, **fleckit** *n* a flask, a flagon *la15-e19*. [ME *flaket*]
flakki see FLACKIE
†**flam** *n* a kind of tart or flan *la16-e19*. [variant of ME *flaun*]
flam see FLAME¹·¹, FLAN¹·¹, FLAN¹·²
flamagaster /flamə'gastər/ *n* a stunning shock of surprise or disappointment *20- NE.* [variant of STAMMYGASTER ¹·¹, based on *flabbergast*]
flamb see FLAME¹·²
flame¹·¹, *Bor* **flam**, †**flambe**, †**flawm** /flem; *Bor* flam/ *n* **1** ignited gas; fire, a blaze *15-*. **2** a flare; a glare of light *20- Bor.* [ME *flaume, flaumbe*]
flame¹·², †**flamb**, †**flawme** /flem/ *v* **1** to burn with flame; to emit flames *la14-*. **2** to baste meat *16-e19*. †**flammer**, **flamer** a basting ladle *17-e18*. †**flamming spoon**, **flaming spoon** a basting spoon *la17-19*. [ME *flaumen, flaumben*]
flan¹·¹, **flann**, **flam** /flan, flam/ *n* **1** a blast or sudden gust of wind *18-*. **2** a surge of smoke blown down a chimney by a gust of wind, a back-draught *18-19, 20- Sh N NE T.* **3** a storm *la15.* **flannie** squally *19- Sh T EC.* [compare Icel *flan* a rush]
flan¹·², *N* **flam** /flan; *N* flam/ *v of wind or smoke* to blow in sudden gusts; to blow down a chimney *19-*. [compare Icel, Norw dial *flana* to rush blindly]
flanan see FLANNEN
Flanders baby /'flandərz 'bebe/ *n* a Dutch doll, a jointed doll *19-20, 21- historical.* [from the place-name + Eng *baby*]
flane, †**flayn** /flen/ *n* an arrow *la15-19, 20- literary.* [OE *flān*]
flane see FLAE²
flang see FLING¹·²
flann see FLAN¹·¹
flannen, †**flanan**, †**flannin**, †**flainen** /'flanən/ *n* flannel *16-*. **flannenette** flannelette *la19-*. **flannan broth** sweetened milk-sops *20- NE T.* [variant of Scots *flannel*]

flap¹·¹ /flap/ *n* **1** a blow, a slap *15-*. **2** a flapping motion; something hanging loosely *18-*. **3** the form or lair of a hare or other animal *20- NE T SW.* **4** a rest, a lie-down *20- NE.* [onomatopoeic]
flap¹·² /flap/ *v* **1** to strike a blow *16-*. **2** to sway, swing or flutter *17-*. **3** to fall down flat suddenly (in order to hide); to flop down *la19-*. **4** to rest *20- NE.* **flapper** to move in a loose, unsteady, flapping way; to flutter noisily *19, 20- N EC.* [see the noun]
flary /'flere/ *adj* gaudy, showy *la19- SW Bor.* [derivative of Eng *flare* to display, flaunt]
†**flas¹**, **flass** *n* a flask *16-e18*. [perhaps Flem *flasch*]
†**flas²** *adj* flat *la15-e17*. [unknown]
flash /flaʃ/ *n* **1** a burst of light, a glimpse or glimmer *la17-*. **2** the tab of cloth worn on the garter of a kilt stocking and visible below the turndown *20-*. [from the Eng verb *to flash*]
flash see FLUSH
flass see FLAS¹
flat¹·¹, **flet** /flat, flɛt/ *n* **1** a piece of level ground; a flat place; frequently in place-names *13-*. **2** a saucer; a flat plate for placing under a dish *18-*. **3** a skate or other flat fish *20- Ork EC Bor.* **4** a level part of a structure; a landing on a staircase *17-18*. **flattie** a saucer, a teapot stand *20- NE T.* [see the adj]
flat¹·², **flet** /flat, flɛt/ *adj* level, horizontal; smooth; shallow *15-*. †**flatling** flat *la15-16*. **flatlins**, **flatlings**, †**flatlingis** prostrate, horizontally *la14-19, 20- Sh NE.* **flat sausage** sausage-meat cut into slices and grilled or fried *la20-*. [ON *flatr*]
flat², **flet** /flat, flɛt/ *n* **1** a floor or storey of a house *18-*. **2** a set of rooms on a single floor comprising an individual dwelling within a larger building *la18-*. [OE *flett* the floor, ground; a dwelling, ON *flet* a house; compare FLET¹]
†**flat³** *v* to flatter *e16*. [MFr *flater*]
flatch¹·¹ /flatʃ/ *n* something large and flat *la19, 20- Sh.* [variant of FLAT¹·², with influence from ON *fletja*]
flatch¹·² /flatʃ/ *v* **1** to flatten, press flat *19- Sh EC Bor.* **2** to walk clumsily *la19- Sh.* [see the noun]
flatchie, **flatshie** /'flatʃi/ *n* a shakedown bed, a straw bed *20- Sh.* [perhaps altered form of Norw *flatseng*]
flate see FLYTE¹·²
flauchin see FLAUCHT¹·²
flaucht¹·¹, **flaught**, *Sh* **flaacht**, †**flacht** /flɔxt; *Sh* flaxt/ *n* **1** a burst of flame; a flash of lightning *la15-19, 20- Sh NE T.* **2** a flake; a snowflake *la18-19, 20- Sh T EC.* **3** a lock or tuft of hair or wool *la18-19, 20- N.* [ME *flaught*]
flaucht¹·², †**flacht** /flɔxt/ *v* **1** to flicker, flash *20-*. **2** *of snow* to fall in flakes *19, 20- T.* **3** to card wool into thin flakes *la16-19, 20- Sh.* **flauchin**, *SW* **fleuchin** a fleck or flake *19, 20- NE EC SW.* [see the noun]
†**flaucht²** *v* to weave, intertwine or put together *19.* [perhaps related to OE *fleohta* wickerwork]
flaucht see FLOCHT¹·¹, FLOCHT¹·²
flauchter, **flaughter** /'flɔxtər/ *v* to cut turf *18-19, 20- H&I C SW Bor.* [perhaps frequentative form of FLAUCHT¹·¹]
flauchter see FLOCHTER¹·¹, FLOCHTER¹·²
flauchter fail, **flauchter feal**, †**flawchtir fail** /'flɔxtər fel, 'flɔxtər fil/ *n* a piece of turf cut with a FLAUCHTER-SPADE *la16-19, 20- historical*. [FLAUCHTER + FAIL¹]
flauchter-spade, **flaughter-spade**, *Sh* **flaachter-spade** /'flɔxtər sped; *Sh* 'flaxtər sped/ *n* a two-handed spade with a broad heart-shaped blade used for cutting turf *la15-*. [FLAUCHTER + SPADE]
flaud see FLAD
flaught see FLAUCHT¹·¹
flaughter see FLAUCHTER
flaughter-spade see FLAUCHTER-SPADE

flaunce see FLUNCE

flaunter /ˈflɔntər/ v 1 to quiver; to tremble with excitement or agitation *la18-19, 20- literary*. 2 to waver or falter in speech; to prevaricate *18-e19*. [unknown]

flauntie, flaunty /ˈflɔnti/ adj 1 capricious, flighty *la18-19, 20- NE Uls*. 2 showy, gaudy *19, 20- T EC SW*. [Scots *flaunt* + -IE²]

†**flaur, fleur, flevour** n flavour, smell *la14-19*. [AN *flaur*; compare OFr *fleur, flavor*]

flaw¹·¹, *Sh* **flaa** /flɔ/; *Sh* fla/ n 1 a fault, a defect *15-*. 2 a flake or particle *la18-*. 3 the broken-off point of a horseshoe nail *16-19, 20- Bor*. 4 a thin layer of turf pared off the surface of a peat bank (used for thatching) *18-19, 20- Sh*. 5 a falsehood, a lie *18-19, 20- Ork*. 6 a flash or spark (of fire) *15-e16*. [perhaps ON *flaga* a slab of stone]

flaw¹·², *Sh* **flaa** /flɔ/; *Sh* fla/ v 1 to remove turf from a peat bank before cutting peat *19, 20- Sh*. 2 to boast, exaggerate; to tell lies *la16-19*. [see the noun]

flaw² /flɔ/ n a gust or squall of wind (bringing rain) *16-19, 20- NE*. [perhaps OE *flagu*; compare MDu, MLG *vlage*]

flaw³ /flɔ/ n a stretch of grassland, a broad ridge *la16- Sh Ork*. [ON *flá*]

flaw see FLEE²

flawchtir fail see FLAUCHTER FAIL

flawm see FLAME¹·¹

flawme see FLAME¹·²

flay see FLAE²

flayn see FLANE

fle see FLAE², FLEE¹, FLEE², FLEE³, FLEY¹·²

flead see FLAE²

fleam see FLEEM²

Fleams see FLEMIS

flech¹·¹, *Sh* **flaich** /flɛx; *Sh* flex/ n 1 a flea *17-*. 2 a restless, active person *19- NE T*. 3 a small, unprepossessing person *20- Sh*. **flechy** adj covered or infested with fleas *19- Sh NE EC*. **flechy** n a flea-infested person or place *20- NE*. [OE *fléah*]

flech¹·² /flɛx/ v 1 to rid (oneself or another) of fleas *19- N EC*. 2 to be restless, fidget *20- NE T*. [see the noun]

flech see FLESH

fleche, flechour see FLEECH

fleck see FLAKE¹·¹

Fleckie¹·¹ /ˈflɛki/ n a pet name for a spotted cow *19- Sh*. [from the adj]

fleckie¹·² /ˈflɛki/ adj flecked, spotted *17-*. [EModE *fleck* + -IE²]

fleckit, †**flekkit** /ˈflɛkɪt/ adj flecked, spotted *la15-*. [EModE *fleck* + -IT²]

fleckit see FLAKKET

fled see FLEE², FLEE³

flee¹, **flie, fly**, †**fle** /fli, flae/ n 1 an insect of the order *Diptera*, a fly *la15-*. 2 a small amount; a thing of little value *15-*. **fleeock** a fly *19- Ork*. **let that flee stick tae the wa**, †**let that flie stick i the wa** to drop a particular subject, say no more about a topic *la18-*. [OE *fléoge*]

flee², **fly, †fle, †fley, †flie** /fli, flae/ v pt †**flaw**, *Sh Ork* **fled** ptp **flown, floon, flewn, †flowin, †fleyn** 1 to take wing, fly; to move with speed *la14-*. 2 to be violently excited or intoxicated *la19-*. **fleein** very drunk *la19-*. **flee about** a flighty or fickle person *la19, 20- Sh Ork N NE T*. **fleein bent** mountain melick *Melica nutans 19-*. **fleein draigon** a paper kite *19-*. **fleein ether** a dragonfly *19- Bor*; compare *heather bill* (ETHER). **fleein merchant** a travelling salesman, a hawker *19- NE*. **fleein tailor** a travelling tailor *19, 20- T*. **flee up** a frivolous or pretentious person *la19, 20- NE T EC SW*. **flee the blue doo** to send out a messenger surreptitiously for whisky *20- NE*. **flee intae** to berate, scold *20- NE EC Bor*. **flee laich** to act prudently and cautiously; to be modest and unambitious *20-*. **flee out** *of a rash* to appear *20- Bor*. [OE *fléogan*]

flee³, †**fle, †fley, †flie** /fli/ v pt, ptp **fled** †**fleid** to run away (from danger); to avoid *la14-*. †**flear** a fugitive, a person who flees *la14-e17*. [OE *fléon*]

flee see FLEY¹·²

fleece see FLEESH

fleech, †**fleche** /flitʃ/ v to coax or flatter; to entreat or cajole *la14-19, 20- C SW Bor*. †**fleecher, flechour** a flatterer, a wheedler *15-19*. [unknown]

fleed /flid/ n the piece of land at the end of a field, on which the plough is turned *18- NE*. [unknown]

fleed see FLUDE¹·¹

fleegarie see FLAGARIE

fleein see FLEE²

fleem¹, *Sh Ork* **fleum**, †**fleume**, †**flewme** /flim; *Sh Ork* fløm/ n phlegm *la15-19, 20- Sh Ork T SW Bor*. [ME *fleum*]

fleem², †**fleam** /flim/ v to flow or gush *la19- Sh*. [Eng *fleam*]

fleeock see FLEE¹

fleep /flip/ n a lazy, stupid man or boy, a lout *la18- Ork N NE*. [unknown]

fleep see FLUP

fleepie /ˈflipi/ n a somersault; a state of agitation *la19- T*. [unknown]

fleepsy, fleepy see FLUP

fleer see FLAIR¹·¹, FLAIR¹·²

fleerish /ˈflirɪʃ/ n a piece of steel for striking fire with a flint *18- NE T EC*. [shortened form of FLEERISHIN]

†**fleerishin, furisine** n = FLEERISH *16-18*. [MLG *vúrisern* a fire-iron; compare FRIZZLE]

fleesh, fleece, †**fleis,** †**fleische** /fliʃ, flis/ n 1 a sheep's fleece *la15-*. 2 a large number; a flock or herd *19, 20- NE Bor*. 3 a sheep *18-19*. [OE *fléos*]

fleesome see FLEY¹·¹

fleet¹·¹, †**fleit** /flit/ n 1 a number of vessels sailing together or jointly owned *17-*. 2 *fishing* a set of nets or lines carried by a single boat *la17-*. [see the verb]

fleet¹·², †**flete, †fleit** /flit/ v 1 to flow with moisture; to be very wet or flooded *16-*. 2 to float; to rise to the surface of a liquid *la14-19, 20- Sh Ork*. 3 *of water* to flow or overflow *15-19, 20- Bor*. †**fleting** floating *la14*. **fleetings** the thick curds formed on top of boiling whey *20- NE T*. **fleet-dyke** a wall built to prevent flooding; a breakwater *19- WC SW Bor*. **fleet water** water which overflows on to ground *19- C SW Bor*. [OE *fléotan*]

fleet² /flit/ adj 1 swift, nimble; active, smart *la16-*. 2 easy to deal with, manageable *20- NE*. [perhaps ON *fljótr*]

fleeter¹, **fleetir** /ˈflitər/ n a wooden utensil for skimming a pot of liquid *19- Sh*. [FLEET¹·², with agent suffix]

fleeter² /ˈflitər/ v to flutter or flit about *20- Sh Ork*. [altered form of Eng *flitter*]

fleg¹·¹ /flɛg/ n a fright, a scare *18-*. **get a fleg** 1 to get a fright *la18-*. 2 to diminish appreciably; to disappear *la19, 20- Ork NE T*. [unknown]

fleg¹·² /flɛg/ v 1 to frighten, scare *17-*. 2 to dispel, drive away *la18-19, 20- NE T Bor*. 3 to take fright, be scared *la18-19, 20- NE*. [unknown]

fleg²·¹ /flɛg/ n a severe blow, a kick *18-19, 20- EC Bor*. [unknown]

fleg²·² /flɛg/ v 1 to fly or rush from place to place; to dash about *la18- SW*. 2 to work hard; to press on *20- SW*. [unknown]

†**flegear** n a fletcher, an arrowmaker *la15-e17*. [OFr *flecher*]

†**fleggar** n a liar, a braggart *16-19*. [unknown]

fleid see FLEE³

fleidnes *see* FLEY¹·²
fleis, fleische *see* FLEESH
fleit *see* FLEET¹·¹, FLEET¹·², FLEY¹·²
flekkit *see* FLECKIT
†**fleme** *v* **1** to banish; to drive into exile; to put to flight *15-e19*. **2** to refrain from; to put away from oneself *la15*. [OE *flīeman*]
†**Flemis, Fleymes, Fleams** *adj* Flemish *la15-17*. [MDu *Vlaemisch*]
flench¹, **flinch** /flɛnʃ, flɪnʃ/ *v* **1** to draw back from, shrink from *19-*. **2** *of weather* to be unreliable; to give a false impression of improvement *la19- NE*. **flinchin Friday** a fine Friday followed by deteriorating weather *la19- NE*. [OFr *flenchir*]
flench² /flɛnʃ/ *v in coopering* to bevel the stave ends of a barrel *la19- NE*. [unknown]
flenderis, flenders, flendris *see* FLINDERS
flenk *see* FLINK¹·¹, FLINK¹·², FLINK¹·³
fler *see* FLAIR¹·¹
flesh, †**flesch**, †**flech** /flɛʃ/ *n* **1** soft tissue, muscle *la14-*. **2** butcher's-meat *la14-*. **3** *pl* carcasses *18-19*. **flesher**, †**fleschar**, †**fleschour** a butcher *15-*. †**fleschowar** a butcher *la14-e15*. **fleshing** the trade of a butcher *19-*. **fleshly**, †**fleschly** of the flesh, carnal; fleshy, plump *la14-*. †**fleschlyk** fleshy, corporeal *la14-15*. †**flesh-crook**, **flesch cruik** a meat hook *la16-e18*. †**flesch fatt** a beef-barrel *16-e17*. **flesh market**, **flesh mercat** a meat market *la16-19, 20- historical*. **flesh meat** butcher's-meat *19-*. **flesh-mens** physical retribution *20- Ork*. †**fles pryssar** a fixer of meat prices *la15-e16*. **fleshstock** a butcher's block *16-19, 20- T*. [OE *flǣsc*]
†**flet**¹ *n* the inner part of a house *15-e19*. [OE *flett* the floor, ground; a dwelling, ON *flet* a house; compare FLAT²]
flet² /flɛt/ *v* to pour tea into one's saucer *20- C*. [from the noun FLAT²]
flet³, **flait** /flɛt, flet/ *n* **1** a straw mat *la18- Ork N*. [ON *flétta* a braid, a string]
flet *see* FLAT¹·¹, FLAT¹·², FLAT², FLYTE¹·²
flete *see* FLEET¹·²
†**flether**¹·¹ *n* flattery *19*. [see the verb]
flether¹·² /ˈflɛðər/ *v* to flatter, cajole *la18-19, 20- literary*. [perhaps conflation of Older Scots *flatter* + BLETHER¹·²; compare ON *flaðra* to fawn upon]
fleuchin *see* FLAUCHT¹·²
fleuk, fluke /fluk/ *n* the flounder *Platichthys flesus la15-*. [OE *flōc*]
fleum, fleume *see* FLEEM¹
fleur, flevour *see* FLAUR
flew *see* FLAE²
†**flewit** *n* a blow, a slap *18-19*. [unknown]
flewme *see* FLEEM¹
flewn *see* FLEE²
fley¹·¹ /fle/ *n* **1** a fright, a scare *la18-*. **2** a source of fear; a fearsome-looking person *20- NE WC SW*. **fleysome, fleesome** terrifying, terrible *la18-19, 20- NE SW Bor*. [see the verb]
fley¹·², †**flee**, †**fle**, †**flie** /fle/ *v* **1** to frighten, scare *la14-*. **2** to put to flight; to scare away *15-*. **fleyd**, †**fleit**, †**fleyit** frightened, scared *la14-*. †**fleyitnes, fleidnes** fear, alarm *la15-16*. **fley awa** to frighten off *la18-*. **fleyed for** frightened of *19, 20- C SW*. [OE *flecgan*, ON *fleygja* to put to flight]
fley *see* FLEE², FLEE³
Fleymes *see* FLEMIS
fleyn *see* FLEE²
flichan *see* FLICHT³

flicher /ˈflɪxər/ *v* to giggle or give a silly laugh *19- NE*. [extended sense of Older Scots *flikker* to flutter, quiver]
flicher *see* FLICHTER¹·²
flicht¹·¹, **flight**, †**flycht** /flɪxt, flʌɪt/ *n* **1** the act of flying *15-*. **2** a number of birds flying together; a number of arrows shot at once *la15-*. **3** one of a set of hooks or prongs on the fly of a spinning-wheel, to guide the thread to the spool *19- Sh NE T*. **flichtrife** unsteady, fickle, changeable *19- NE*. **flichty, flichtie** flighty, capricious *19-*. †**flicht speid** full speed *la16*. †**at the flicht** about to set out; in all haste *16*. [OE *flyht*]
flicht¹·² /flɪxt/ *v* to take wing; to fly *la18-*. [see the noun]
flicht²·¹, **flight**, †**flycht** /flɪxt, flʌɪt/ *n* the act of fleeing *la14-*. [ME *fliht*]
flicht²·² /flɪxt/ *v* to flee, run away *la18- N NE T*. [see the noun]
flicht³ /flɪxt/ *n* a flake, a speck *19- WC Bor*. **flichan** a flake of snow, a small particle or speck of something *19, 20- EC SW Bor*. [compare FLAUCHT¹·¹]
flichter¹·¹ /ˈflɪxtər/ *n* **1** a flutter, a fluttering *19- NE EC SW*. **2** a small particle of soot or a flake of snow *la19- N EC*. **3** a state of excitement *19- NE*. **4** a flicker, a glimmer of light *19, 20- EC*. **flichterie** changeable; excitable, flighty *20- NE T*. **flichtersome** changeable, whimsical *la19- NE*. **flichter-lichtie** a scatterbrained or flighty person *la19- NE*. [see the verb]
flichter¹·², †**flighter**, †**flicher** /ˈflɪxtər/ *v* **1** *of birds* to flutter; to fly (awkwardly); *of people* to rush about (excitedly) *la14-*. **2** to flicker or gleam *19- EC SW*. **3** *of the heart* to flutter, quiver or palpitate *la17-19, 20- NE EC*. **4** to run with outspread arms to greet someone *la18-19, 20- literary*. **5** to startle, frighten *18-19, 20- T*. **6** to make fluttering movements or efforts *16-17*. [perhaps onomatopoeic]
†**flichter**², **flighter** /ˈflɪxtər/ *v* to bind the limbs with cords; to pinion *la16-18*. [unknown]
flick /flɪk/ *n* a glimmering, a streak of light *la19, 20- EC*. [variant of EModE *fleck*]
flickament /ˈflɪkəmənt/ *n* a state of excitement *la20- Sh*. [unknown]
flie *see* FLEE¹, FLEE³, FLEY¹·²
flight *see* FLICHT¹·¹, FLICHT²·¹
flighter *see* FLICHTER¹·², FLICHTER²
flim /flɪm/ *n* **1** a haze or mist rising from the ground *19-*. **2** something unsubstantial or illusory *19-*. [metathesis of Eng *film*]
flinch *see* FLENCH¹
flinders, *Bor* **flenders**, †**flenderis**, †**flendris** /ˈflɪndərz; *Bor* ˈflɛndərz/ *npl* fragments, splinters, pieces *15-*. [compare Norw dial *flindre* a splinter, a flake]
flindrikin¹·¹, **flinrikin** /ˈflɪndrɪkən, ˈflɪnrɪkən/ *n* **1** something light, flimsy and insubstantial *la19- Sh NE SW*. **2** a light snow-shower *20- Ork*. **3** a term of contempt for a person *la16-19*. [unknown]
flindrikin¹·², **flinrikin** /ˈflɪndrɪkən, ˈflɪnrɪkən/ *adj* light, flimsy *la19, 20- Ork NE Bor Uls*. [unknown]
fling¹·¹ /flɪŋ/ *n* **1** a fit or spasm; a fit of extravagance *la16-*. **2** a throw, a toss *18-*. **3** (a name for) a dance *18-*; compare **Highland fling** (HIELAND¹·²). **4** the act of kicking; a kick from a horse *19-*. **get the fling** to be jilted *19, 20- NE EC*. **gie somebody the fling** to jilt someone *19, 20- NE EC*. **tak the flings** to sulk *18-19, 20- Sh EC*. [see the verb]
fling¹·² /flɪŋ/ *v pt* **flung, flang**, *ptp* **flung, flang 1** to cast, throw *la14-*. **2** *of animals* to kick *la14-*. **3** to dance (a Scottish dance); to move with vigour *16-*. **4** to jerk the head or body sideways as a gesture of displeasure, flounce *la18-*. **5** to jilt *la18-19, 20- NE EC*. **flinger**, †**flingar 1** a cow that kicks

20- *NE.* **2** a dancer *16-e19.* †**flingin tree** the part of a flail which strikes the grain *la18-19.* [related to ON *flengja* to whip]

flink[1.1], **flenk** /flɪŋk, flɛŋk/ *n* **1** a conceited or jaunty air *20- Sh Ork.* **2** a frolic or flirtation *20- Sh.* [see the verb]

flink[1.2], **flenk** /flɪŋk, flɛŋk/ *v* **1** to move nimbly or jauntily *la19- Sh Ork.* **2** to flirt or frolic *20- Sh Ork.* [perhaps conflation of FLING[1.2] with Norw dial *flingsa* to gad about]

flink[1.3], **flenk** /flɪŋk, flɛŋk/ *adj* nimble, agile *la19- Sh.* [see the verb]

flinrikin see FLINDRIKIN[1.1], FLINDRIKIN[1.2]

flint, †**flynt** /flɪnt/ *n* an exceptionally hard stone *la14-.* **flinty 1** having flint-like qualities; hard, unsympathetic *la18-.* **2** keen, sharp, lively *19, 20- SW.* [OE *flint*]

flipe see FLYPE[1.1], FLYPE[1.2]

flird[1.1] /flɪrd/ *n* **1** something thin, flimsy or tawdry *la18-19, 20- NE SW Bor.* **2** a vain, dressy or fickle person *la18-19.* **flirdie** fickle, giddy, skittish *19, 20- NE Bor.* [unknown]

flird[1.2] /flɪrd/ *v* **1** to flutter; to flounce; to move restlessly or frivolously *19, 20- WC Bor.* **2** to talk idly; to flirt; to mock or scoff *16, 20- Bor.* [unknown]

flirr /flɪr/ *v* to stir; to ruffle *20- NE.* [onomatopoeic]

flisk[1.1] /flɪsk/ *n* a sudden sweeping movement, a flick or whisk *19-.* **fliskie, flisky 1** restless, flighty, skittish *la18-19, 20- NE WC SW.* **2** *of a horse* restive, apt to kick *19, 20- NE WC SW.* [onomatopoeic]

flisk[1.2] /flɪsk/ *v* **1** to dart from place to place; to frolic about; to caper *la17-.* **2** to make an abrupt sweeping motion; to whisk or swipe *19-.* [see the noun]

fliskmahaigo, fliskmahoy /flɪskməˈhego, flɪskməˈhɔɪ/ *n* a flighty or frivolous woman *19, 20- NE SW Bor.* [unknown]

fliss[1.1] /flɪs/ *n* a flake, a splinter, a chip *la19- Sh.* [ON *flís*]

fliss[1.2] /flɪs/ *v* to peel in flakes; to peel off *la19- Sh.* [see the noun]

flist[1.1] /flɪst/ *n* **1** an explosion, a sudden puff or flash *la16-19, 20- N NE.* **2** a sudden outburst of rage, a fit of temper *19- NE T.* **3** a lie; a boast *la19- N NE.* **4** a boaster; a liar *la19- N NE.* **flisty** irascible, irritable *19- NE T.* [unknown]

flist[1.2] /flɪst/ *v* **1** to puff or whizz; to explode with a sharp hiss or bang *la17-19, 20- N NE T.* **2** to boast or brag; to exaggerate *la16-19, 20- N NE.* **3** to fly into a rage *19, 20- NE.* **let flist** to let fly with a blow, lash out *20- N NE.* [unknown]

flit[1.1] /flɪt/ *n* a removal *19-.* **flit boat** a small boat used for transferring passengers or goods from ship to shore or for other short journeys *la19- Sh N NE H&I.* **Flit Friday** the Whitsunday or Martinmas removal day for farm workers *19- T.* **flitman** a ferryman *la19- Sh.* [see the verb]

flit[1.2], †**flyt** /flɪt/ **1** to remove or convey (a person or object) from one place to another *la14-.* **2** to leave a place, go elsewhere *la14-.* **3** to move house; to remove (one's household) to another house *la15-.* **4** to move quickly or lightly; to change or alter suddenly *16-.* **5** to move tethered animals to fresh grazing *la18-.* **6** to die *la16-19, 20- literary.* **flitter 1** a person who moves house frequently *19-.* **2** *pl* removal men *20-.* †**flit and remove** to remove (one's household) to another house *16-17.* [ON *flytja* to carry, deliver]

flit see FLYTE[1.2]

flither see FLUTHER[1.1]

flitten see FLYTE[1.2]

flitter /ˈflɪtər/ *n* a shred, a splinter *19, 20- Uls.* [unknown]

flitting, flittin /ˈflɪtɪŋ, ˈflɪtɪn/ *n* **1** household goods being moved (during a house-removal) *15-.* **2** the act of moving from one house to another *17-.* **3** the removal of a thing or person from one place to another *16-e17.* †**Flitting Friday** the Whitsunday removal day *16.* [verbal noun from FLIT[1.2]]

flix /flɪks/ *n* a fright, a state of excitement *20- Ork.* [variant of FLEG[1.1]]

flixed /flɪkst/ *adj* frightened; flurried *la19- Ork.* [FLIX + -IT[2]]

floamie /ˈflomi/ *n* something flat and spread out, an expanse *19- Sh.* [Norw dial *flaum* a flood]

floan, flon /flon, flɔn/ *v* **1** to show affection (in an overly sentimental way) *la18- NE.* **2** to lounge or loaf *la19- NE.* [compare Norw dial *flana*, Dan *flane* to gad about, be flighty or frivolous]

float[1], †**flott** /flot/ *n* fat, grease or scum (on a boiling pot of soup or jam) *la16-19, 20- WC SW.* **float-whey, †flot quhaye** a dish made by boiling whey, often with meal and milk, to form a soft floating curd *16-19, 20- Bor.* [ON *flot* floating fat]

float[2.1], †**flot**, †**floit** /flot/ *n* **1** the act of floating; an object designed to float *la14-.* **2** a flat spring cart without sides; a lorry for carrying livestock *20-.* **3** *mining* a sheet of intrusive rock lying roughly in the same plane as the surrounding strata *la19, 20- WC SW.* **4** (a state of) flooding, a flood *la15-16.* [OE *flota* a seagoing vessel, *on flote* afloat]

float[2.2], †**floitt** /flot/ *v pt, ptp* †**floatit** to be buoyant; to rest on the surface of a liquid *la16-.* [OE *flēotan*]

flocht[1.1], **flaucht**, *NE* **flucht**, †**flought** /flɔxt; *NE* flʌxt/ *n* **1** a flutter, a state of excitement or uncertainty *la15-19, 20- Sh NE.* **2** the act of fleeing, flight *16-19, 20- Sh NE.* **3** a flight or flock of birds *19, 20- Sh.* **4** a sudden gust of wind *19, 20- NE Bor.* **5** a bustle, a flurry, a great hurry *19, 20- literary.* **6** excitement, stress *19, 20- NE.* **at the flaucht** at full speed *19- NE.* [perhaps OE *flyht* flight]

flocht[1.2], **flaucht**, **flucht** /flɔxt, flʌxt/ *v* **1** to bustle; to go off in a flurry *19- NE T.* **2** to shake, tremble or vibrate; to flutter or palpitate *19- Sh Bor.* **3** to excite; to startle or frighten *la19- N NE.* [see the noun]

flochter[1.1], **flauchter** /ˈflɔxtər/ *n* **1** a fluttering or flapping *la18-.* **2** a state of excitement or stress *la19, 20- NE T.* †**flochtrous, floughtrous** hurried and confused, fluttering *la18-e19.* [frequentative form of FLOCHT[1.1]]

flochter[1.2], **flauchter**, *Sh* **flaachter** /ˈflɔxtər; *Sh* ˈflaxtər/ *v* **1** to flutter, flap *la18-.* **2** to spread open, sprawl *19-.* **3** to fluster; to rush about *la19-.* **4** to knock down; to knock out *19, 20- NE EC Bor.* [see the noun]

†**flodder, floddyr** *v* to flood, overflow *e16.* [derivative of FLUDE[1.1]]

flodge[1.1] /flɔdʒ/ *n* a fat, slovenly or lazy person *19, 20 NE SW Bor.* [onomatopoeic]

flodge[1.2] /flɔdʒ/ *v* to walk clumsily; to waddle *19, 20- Ork NE Bor.* [see the noun]

†**flog**[1.1] *n* a flapping or trailing mass *la19.* [see the verb]

flog[1.2] /flɔg/ *v* to hang loose, flap or flutter *20- Sh.* [variant of FLAG[6]]

flog[2] /flɔg/ *n* a patch used to mend a split board in the hull of a boat *la19- Sh.* [compare Norw *flak* a strip]

flog[3] /flɔg/ *v* to pilfer *la20- N H&I.* [unknown]

floit see FLOAT[2.1]

floitt see FLOAT[2.2]

flokrit see FLUKRA

flon see FLOAN

floo /flu/ *n* the core of an animal's horn *20- Ork.* [compare SLO]

flood see FLUDE[1.1], FLUDE[1.2]

flooer[1.1], **flouer**, **flower**, **floor**, **flour**, †**flowr** /ˈfluər, ˈflʌuər, flur, flʌur/ *n* **1** the blossom of a plant, a flower *la14-.* **2** the finest part, the best specimen *la14-.* **3** a bunch of flowers, a bouquet *la18-.* **4** the first water drawn from the well in the New Year *19-20, 21- historical.* **flowers of Edinburgh** (the

flooer   218   **flunkie**

smells arising from) garbage and night soil thrown into the streets of Edinburgh *18, 19- historical.* [ME *flour*]

flooer[1.2], **flouer, flower,** †**flour** /'fluər, 'flʌuər/ *v* **1** to embroider (flowers or similar designs) *19-.* **2** to adorn with flowers *15-17.* **flooerin-soorik** spotted persicaria *Persicaria maculosa 20- Sh.* [see the noun]

flooer[2], **floor, flour** /'fluər, flur, flʌur/ *n* finely ground wheat, flour *la14-.* [ME *flour*]

floon *see* FLEE[2]

floop *see* FLUP

floor *see* FLOOER[1.1], FLOOER[2]

floorish *see* FLOURISH[1.1]

flooster *see* FLUISTER

flootchie /'flutʃi/ *n* a flat-bottomed boat (with a square stern); a skiff *20- Sh.* [perhaps Du *vlotje* a raft]

flör *see* FLAIR[1.1]

Florence /'flɔrəns/ *adj* made in or imported from Florence *la15-.* [from the name of the Italian city]

florie[1.1] /'flori/ *v* to swagger, strut about conceitedly *19- N SW.* [unknown]

†**florie**[1.2], **flory** *adj* vain, showy *la18-e19.* [unknown]

floris *see* FLOURISH[1.2]

florisch *see* FLOURISH[1.1]

†**flory** *n* = *flory boat la19.* **flory boat, florry boat** a boat carrying passengers to and from steamers which could not get alongside the pier *19.* [unknown]

flory *see* FLORIE[1.2]

flosche, flosh *see* FLUSH

floss /flɔs/ *n* the rush *Juncus effusus* (used for thatch, ropes and wicks) *17- Sh Ork N.* [unknown]

flot[1], **flott** /flɔt/ *n* an area of land ploughed at one turn; the portion allotted to a competitor in a ploughing-match *20- N.* [Norw dial *flot* level ground]

†**flot**[2], **flote, floyt** *n* **1** a fleet *la14-17.* **2** a float or raft *16.* [OE *flota,* ON *floti*]

†**flot**[3], **floyt** *n* a troop or company *la14-e16.* [ME *flote*, OFr *flote* a fleet]

flot *see* FLOAT[2.1]

†**flote** *v* to line or back a garment *la15.* **floting** lining or backing for a garment or saddle *la15-e17.* [unknown]

flote *see* FLOT[2]

flot quhaye *see* FLOAT[1]

flott *see* FLOAT[1], FLOT[1]

†**flotter**[1] *v* to float awkwardly; to flounder *la15-e19.* [OE *floterian*]

†**flotter**[2], **flottyr** *v* to splash or soak; *of liquid* to overflow *16-e19.* [unknown]

flouer *see* FLOOER[1.1], FLOOER[1.2]

flought *see* FLOCHT[1.1]

floughtrous *see* FLOCHTER[1.1]

flour *see* FLAIR[1.1], FLOOER[1.1], FLOOER[1.2]

†**flour dammes** *n* the auricula, the flower *Primula auricula e16.* [FLOOER[1.1] + OFr *damas*]

†**floure jonet** *n* a variety of yellow flower *e15.* [FLOOER[1.1] + OFr *jaunet* the yellow water lily]

flouring *see* FLAIR[1.2]

flouris *see* FLOURISH[1.2]

flourish[1.1], **floorish,** †**florisch,** †**fluris** /'flʌrɪʃ, 'flurɪʃ/ *n* **1** blossom (on fruit or hawthorn trees) *la15-.* **2** an embellishment, a decoration *19-.* †**florist, flurist** flourishing, flowery *15-16.* [see the verb]

flourish[1.2], †**floris,** †**flouris,** †**flureis,** †**fluris** /'flʌrɪʃ/ *v* **1** to thrive or prosper *la14-.* **2** to blossom, be in flower; to grow luxuriantly *la14-.* **3** to add ornament or embellishment; to gesticulate or move dramatically *la14-.* **4** to embroider *la19- Ork NE T SW.* [ME *florishen*]

flouw *see* FLOW[2]

flow[1] /flo/ *n* **1** a wet peat bog, a morass; a low-lying piece of watery, uncleared land *17-.* **2** an arm of the sea; a deep-water channel with strong tides *la19- Sh Ork N.* **3** quicksand *19.* **flow land** marshland *20- N.* **flow-moss** mossy, boggy ground; the spongy moss which grows on boggy ground *18-.* [perhaps ON *flói*]

flow[2], **flouw** /flo, flʌu/ *v of liquid* to move or issue forth; to surge; *of the tide* to come in *la15-.* **flowin, flowing,** †**flowand 1** moving in a fluid state *15-.* **2** unstable, changeable, fickle *la15-16.* [OE *flōwan*]

flow[3] /flo/ *n* a small quantity of something; a small amount of flour, meal or dust *19, 20- NE T.* **flowin, flowan** small particles or a small quantity of something *19-.* [unknown]

flowder *see* FLUTHER[1.1]

flower *see* FLOOER[1.1], FLOOER[1.2]

flowin *see* FLEE[2], FLOW[2], FLOW[3]

flown *see* FLEE[2]

flowr *see* FLOOER[1.1]

floyt *see* FLOT[2], FLOT[3]

flozent /'flozənt/ *adj* swollen, flabby, puffed up *19- NE.* [unknown]

flucht *see* FLOCHT[1.1], FLOCHT[1.2]

fludda *see* FLUTHER[1.1]

fludder *see* FLUTHER[2]

flude[1.1], **flood,** *N NE* **fleed** /flɪd, flʌd; *N NE* flid/ *n* **1** a deluge or overflow of water *la14-.* **2** high tide *15-.* **3** a body of water, a river or sea *la14-e19.* **flood mark,** †**flude mark** the high-water mark *15-.* [OE *flōd*]

flude[1.2], **flood** /flɪd, flʌd/ *v* to inundate with water; to become submerged *18-.* [see the noun]

fluff[1.1] /flʌf/ *n* **1** a puff of wind or smoke *19, 20- Ork N NE.* **2** a small amount, an insubstantial quantity *19, 20- NE.* **fluffy** puffy, chubby *20- NE EC SW.* [onomatopoeic; compare FLAFF[1.1], FUFF[1.1]]

fluff[1.2] /flʌf/ *v* **1** to puff, blow *la18-.* **2** to flutter; to move lightly in a breeze *19, 20- Sh.* **3** *of a bird* to take a dust-bath *19, 20- NE.* [see the noun]

fluffer[1.1] /'flʌfər/ *n* **1** a flapping, fluttering motion *la19, 20- NE.* **2** something which flaps or flutters *20- NE.* [frequentative form of FLUFF[1.1]]

fluffer[1.2] /'flʌfər/ *v* **1** to flutter, flap *la19-.* **2** to excite, agitate *la19- literary.* [see the noun]

fluir *see* FLAIR[1.1], FLAIR[1.2]

fluise /fluz/ *v* to roughen; to blunt *19, 20- SW.* [unknown]

fluister, flooster /'flustər/ *v* **1** to hustle or bustle; to be flustered *la19- Sh Ork T EC Bor Uls.* **2** to coax, flatter; to make a fuss over *20- Uls.* [perhaps onomatopoeic; compare Icel *flaustra* to bustle]

†**fluke** *n* diarrhoea *18-e19.* [altered form of Older Scots *flux*]

fluke *see* FLEUK

flukner /'flʌknər/ *n fisherman's taboo* a hen *la19- Sh.* [ON *-flognir* *-flier*]

flukra /'flʌkra/ *n* snow falling in large flakes *19- Sh.* **flukret, flokrit** speckled with white *20- Sh.* [compare Faer *flykra* a snowflake]

flumgummery /flʌm'gʌməri/ *n* foolishness, frivolity; fanciful ornamentation or trimmings *19- NE.* [reduplicative formation based on Eng *flummery* nonsense]

flunce, †**flaunce** /flʌns/ *v* to flounce *18-19, 20- Sh NE.* [perhaps Norw dial *flunsa* to hurry]

flung *see* FLING[1.2]

flungs /flʌŋs/ *v* to swing, shake; to turn with a jerk *la19- Sh.* [Norw dial *flunsa* to hurry]

flunkie /'flʌŋki/ *n* a manservant (in livery), a footman; a lackey *la18-.* [unknown]

flunner /ˈflʌnər/ *n* **1** the flounder *Platichthys flesus 18-19, 20- N H&I*. **2** the halibut *Hippoglossus hippoglossus 20- Sh*. [AN *floundre*]

flup, *Ork N NE* **fleep**, †**floop** /flʌp/; *Ork N NE* **flip**/ *n* a stupid, clumsy person *la17-*. **fleepsy**, **fleepy** lacking in pluck or stamina *20- Ork N*. [probably onomatopoeic]

flure *see* FLAIR[1.1], FLAIR[1.2]

flureis *see* FLOURISH[1.2]

fluris *see* FLOURISH[1.1], FLOURISH[1.2]

flush, flosh, †**flus,** †**flosche,** †**flash** /flʌʃ, flɔʃ/ *n* a piece of boggy ground (where water lies on the surface); a pool of water; frequently in place-names *la14-19, 20- H&I WC SW Bor*. **floshen** a large shallow puddle *19- SW*. [unknown]

fluther[1.1], *Sh* **fludda**, *NE* **flowder**, *EC* **flither** /ˈflʌðər; *Sh* ˈflʌda; *NE* ˈflʌudər; *EC* ˈflɪðər/ *n* a flutter, a flurry; confusion, bustle *19-*. [see the verb]

fluther[1.2] /ˈflʌðər/ *v* to flutter, flap about; to rush about or bustle *la18-19, 20- NE T*. [probably variant of FLOTTER[1]]

fluther[2], **fludder** /ˈflʌðər, ˈflʌdər/ *n* **1** a boggy piece of ground, a marsh *16-*. **2** a slight rise or turbidity in a river *la18- NE T*. [unknown]

fly *see* FLEE[1], FLEE[2]

flycht *see* FLICHT[1.1], FLICHT[2.1]

fly cup /ˈflae kʌp/ *n* a quick or surreptitious cup of tea *la19- NE T*. **fly cuppie** = FLY CUP *20- NE T EC SW*. [Scots *fly* shrewd + CUP]

flynt *see* FLINT

flype[1.1], **flipe** /flʌɪp/ *n* **1** a fold or flap; a hat-brim; a turn-up on a garment *la17-e19, la19- Sh*. **2** the cutting of a strip of skin; a loose piece of skin *18-19, 20- Ork N EC*. **3** a shred, a fragment *la20- N*. [unknown]

flype[1.2], **flipe** /flʌɪp/ *v* **1** to fold back; to turn a garment wholly or partially inside out *16-*. **2** to tear off the skin in strips; to peel *18-*. **3** to pluck wool from a sheepskin *20- Bor*. **4** *of the lip* to curl; *of torn skin* to hang down in shreds *19*. [unknown]

flype[2.1] /flʌɪp/ *n* a slap *la19- NE*. [onomatopoeic; compare FLAIP]

flype[2.2] /flʌɪp/ *v* to fall heavily; to flop down for a short rest *la18- NE T*. [see the noun]

†**flyre** *v* to grimace; to mock *la15-19*. **flyrdome** mockery; an object of scorn *la15-e17*. [ME *flerien*]

†**flyrok** *n* a deformed person *e16*. [unknown]

flyt *see* FLIT[1.2]

flyte[1.1] /flʌɪt/ *n* **1** a scolding, a reproof *la18-19, 20- Sh H&I WC SW*. **2** a scolding match *19, 20- Sh EC Bor*. **flyte pock** a double chin *19, 20- T*. [OE *flit*]

flyte[1.2] /flʌɪt/ *v pt* **flytit, flet, flit,** †**flate,** *ptp* **flitten 1** to scold; to wrangle violently; to employ abusive language towards; to quarrel with someone *la14-*. **2** *of poets* to engage in an exchange of abuse *19-*. **flyter,** †**flytar** a scold; a person who engages in FLYTING *la15-*. **flyte at** to scold; to use abusive language towards; to contend in abuse with, rail at *19-*. **flyte on** = *flyte at la19-*. [OE *flītan*]

flyting, flytin /ˈflʌɪtɪŋ, ˈflʌɪtɪn/ *n* **1** scolding, quarrelling; employing abusive language *la15-*. **2** a contest between poets in mutual abuse *16-*. †**flyting free** blameless *17-e19*. [verbal noun from FLYTE[1.2]]

fo *see* FAE[1]

foal[1.1], †**fole,** †**foill,** †**foll** /fol/ *n* the young of a horse or other equine *15-*. [OE *fola*]

foal[1.2], †**fole** /fol/ *v* **1** *of a mare* to give birth *15-*. **2** *of a horse* to throw its rider *19- NE T*. [see the noun]

foally *see* FOLLY

foam *see* FAEM[1.1], FAEM[1.2]

foat *see* FOT

fob, fab /fɔb, fab/ *v* to pant with heat or exertion *18- NE*. [onomatopoeic]

†**foche** *v* to move away, depart *la16*. [perhaps variant of Older Scots *fetch*]

focht *see* FECHT[1.2]

fock *see* FOWK

foddom *see* FADDOM[1.1]

fodge, fudge, †**fadge** /fɔdʒ, fʌdʒ/ *n* **1** a bundle (of sticks) *19, 20- historical*. **2** a fat, clumsy person *la18-19, 20- EC Bor*. [unknown]

fodgel[1.1] /ˈfɔdʒəl/ *n* a plump, good-humoured person *19, 20- NE Uls*. [probably derivative of FODGE]

fodgel[1.2] /ˈfɔdʒəl/ *adj* plump, buxom *18-19, 20- NE*. [see the noun]

fodmell *see* FOTMELL

foe *see* FAE[1]

fog[1.1] /fɔg/ *n* **1** moss or lichen (originally used as thatching material or for packing walls) *la15-*. **2** grass left standing in the field in winter *la15-e16*. **foggage,** †**fogage 1** (the hire of land for) winter grazing; the right to pasture cattle on standing hay *15-*. **2** the second crop of grass after hay *18-*. **fog house** a small, garden summer-house built or lined with mossy turf *19, 20- NE*. [ME *fogge* rank tall grass]

fog[1.2] /fɔg/ *v* **1** to gather moss; to become moss-grown *18-*. **2** to thatch a roof or pack a wall with moss *18-19, 20- NE*. **3** to save money; to make money at another's expense *la19-, NE T WC SW*. **foggin** savings, a large sum of money *20- NE T*. [see the noun]

foggie[1.1], **foggy** /ˈfɔgi/ *n* the wild or moss carder bee *Bombus muscorum 19-*. **foggie bee** a bee *19-*. **foggie bummer** a bee *19, 20- NE*. **foggy toddler** a bee *la19- NE T EC*. [see the adj]

foggie[1.2], **foggy** /ˈfɔgi/ *adj* **1** mossy *18-*. **2** *of a turnip* soft, spongy *20- NE*. **Foggie** a nickname for Aberchirder in Banffshire *20- NE*. **Foggie Loan** a nickname for Aberchirder in Banffshire *19- NE*. **foggie peat, foggy peat** a rough, spongy peat *20- Ork N NE Uls*. [FOG[1.1] + -IE[2]]

foggie[2], †**fogie** /ˈfɔgi/ *n* **1** an old, infirm person *la18-*. **2** a veteran soldier, an army pensioner *19, 20- EC*. [perhaps FOGGIE[1.2], compare Eng *fogey*]

foggy *see* FOGGIE[1.1], FOGGIE[1.2]

fogie *see* FOGGIE[2]

†**foichal** *n* a girl in her late teens *la18-e19*. [unknown]

foill *see* FOAL[1.1]

foir *see* FORE[1.1], FORE[1.2], FOWER

foirbuith *see* FOREBOOTH

foircoipe *see* FORCOP

foirend *see* FORE-END

foir entres *see* FORE ENTRES

foirfute *see* FOREFIT

foirgrantschir *see* FOREGRANTSIRE

foirhous *see* FOREHOUSE

foiriugeit *see* FORJUGIT

†**foirlappis** *npl* the overlapping front flaps of a garment *la16-e17*. [OE *fore* + OE *lappa*, with plural suffix]

foirnemmit *see* FORENEMMIT

foirsate *see* FORESEAT

†**foirschete** *n* part of a mill *la16*. [unknown]

foir stair *see* FORESTAIR

foir streit *see* FORESTREET

foirsyde *see* FORESIDE

foirwall *see* FOREWA

foir ȝet *see* FOREȜETT

fois *see* FAE[1]

foisted *see* FOOST[1.2]

fold *see* FAULD[2.1], FAULD[2.2], FOUD

fole /fol/ *n* a small, soft, thick oatcake *18- Ork NE.* [unknown]
fole *see* FOAL¹·¹, FOAL¹·², FUIL¹·¹
foley *see* FOLLAE
folk *see* FOWK
foll *see* FOAL¹·¹
follae, folly, folla, follow, *EC* **fallae,** *WC* **foley, †fallow, †folow** /ˈfɔle, ˈfɔlə, ˈfɔlo; *EC* ˈfale; *WC* ˈfole/ *v* **1** to go or come after; to occur subsequently *la14-*. **2** to imitate, copy; to conform or comply with *la14-*. **3** to accompany, escort on a journey *la19- Sh Ork Uls*. **4** to pamper, indulge *20- NE*. **5** *law* to pursue, prosecute *15-e17*. **follower, followar, †falowar 1** the young of a domestic animal still dependent on or in the company of its mother *15-*. **2** someone or something which follows; a supporter or adherent *16-*. **3** a pursuer or claimant at law *la14-e17*. **following 1** a body of supporters or adherents *18-*. **2** *mining* an overlying, soft stratum which came down as the coal was extracted from under it *la18-19*. **3** a plaintiff at law, the prosecution of a suit or claim *la14-e16*. **†as efter followis** as follows *la14-e16*. **†follow furth** to follow up; to go on with; to prosecute *la15-e17*. **†follow out** to follow up *18*. [OE *folgian*]
follow *see* FELLAE, FOLLAE
folly, *Sh* **foally, †foly** /ˈfɔli; *Sh* ˈfoli/ *n* **1** foolishness *la14-*. **2** a prank, a piece of fun *la19- Sh Ork N*. **follyfou** mischievous, fond of pranks *la19- Sh*. **†folyhat** a hat resembling a fool's cap *e16*. [ME *folie*]
folly *see* FOLLAE
folm¹·¹, †whelm /fɔlm/ *n* something which rolls (over); a wave, a surge of water; a billow (of mist or cloud) *19, 20- NE*. [see the verb]
folm¹·², †whalm, †wholme, †quhelm /fɔlm/ *v* **1** to overturn; *of a boat* to capsize *16-19, 20- NE*. **2** *of a wheel* to turn downwards; to roll over (someone) *la15-e17*. [perhaps OE *hwelman*]
folow *see* FELLAE, FOLLAE
folp *see* WHALP¹·¹, WHALP¹·²
foly *see* FOLLY
fome *see* FAEM¹·¹
fommle *see* WHUMMLE¹·²
†fon¹·¹ *n* folly, foolishness *la15*. [unknown]
†fon¹·² *v* to be foolish; to play the fool *la15-16*. [unknown]
fond /fɔnd/ *adj* **1** foolish, silly *la15-*. **2** overly keen; infatuated, doting *17-*. **3** affectionate, caring *18-*. **4** eager (to), glad (to) *20- H&I WC SW Bor*. **fond of** attracted by, keen on *17-*. **I'd be very fond tae dae** I would certainly not do; I would be foolish to attempt *la19-*. [ptp of FON¹·²]
fond *see* FOOND¹·¹
†fontale *adj* coming from a fountain *la15*. [Lat *fons* fountain, with adj-forming suffix]
fontane, fontayne *see* FUNTAIN
fonȝeis *see* FUNȜE¹
foo, fu, fow /fu, fʌu/ *adv* **1** how, in what way *16-19, 20- Sh Ork N NE T*. **2** why, for what reason *19, 20- NE T EC*. **†foo ca ye im** what-do-you-call-him *19*. **foo ca y'it** what-do-you-call-it *19, 20- NE Bor*. **fooever** however *la19- Sh NE*. **†funabeis** nevertheless, however *la18-e19*. **fusomever** however *la19- Sh Ork N*. **fousticait, fousticat** what-do-you-call-it *18-19, 20- Sh Bor*. **foo that, fou that** how, in such a way that *19, 20- NE*. **fu's a?** how are you? *la18- N NE T*. [*quhow* (HOO¹), with the *f-* by analogy with other interrogatives; compare *fa* (WHA)]
foo *see* FOU²·²
food *see* FUDE
foodin /ˈfudən/ *n fisherman's taboo* a cat *la19- Sh Ork*. [probably derivative of ON *fótr* a foot, with noun-forming suffix *-ing* the footed one]

foof /fuf/ *interj* an expression of impatience or disgust *la19- Sh NE EC*. [onomatopoeic]
fooit *see* FOU¹
fool, foul, †fowle, †fewl /ful, fʌul/ *n* a (game or wild) bird or domestic fowl *la14-*. **foolie bree** chicken broth *19- NE*. [OE *fugel*]
fool *see* FOUL, FUIL¹·¹, FUIL¹·², FUIL¹·³
foolish *see* FUILISH
fooll *see* FEWALE
foon¹·¹ /fun/ *n* a small amount; a few *la19- Sh*. [unknown]
foon¹·² /fun/ *adj* few *la19- Sh*. [unknown]
foon *see* FOOND¹·²
foond¹·¹, found, *NE* **fond** /fund, fʌund; *NE* fɔnd/ *n* **1** the foundation of a building or wall *17-*. **2** a fund of money *la17-19, 20- Sh NE T EC*. **3** a ring of stones and brushwood on which a haystack is built *20- NE*. [see the verb]
foond¹·², foon, found, †fund /fund, fun, fʌund/ *v* **1** to lay the foundations of, begin the building of *la14-*. **2** to establish or bring into being *la14-*. **†foundit, foundat** provided for by the foundation of a college *la16-17*. **foonin pint, founding pint** a drink given to workmen after laying the foundations of a building as an omen of good luck *19-*. [OFr *fonder*]
foonder¹·¹, fooner, founder /ˈfundər, ˈfunər, ˈfʌundər/ *n* **1** a collapse, a breakdown in health *19-*. **2** a severe chill *20- WC Uls*. [see the verb]
foonder¹·², fooner, founder, †fundir /ˈfundər, ˈfunər, ˈfʌundər/ *v* **1** to stumble, fall *la15-*. **2** to exhaust, prostrate or cause to collapse *18-*. **3** to fell, strike down *la18-*. **4** to collapse, break down *la19-*. **foonert, foundert** in a state of collapse; exhausted; overcome by cold *la19-*. [ME *foundren*]
foondit *see* FOUNDIT
fooneral *see* FUNERAL¹·¹
foonge /fundʒ/ *v* to fawn over or flatter; to show affection in an overly sentimental way *la18- NE EC*. [unknown]
foongil /ˈfundʒəl/ *n* a lazy, slovenly or careless person *la19- NE T*. [unknown]
foorach /ˈfurəx/ *n* buttermilk, whipped cream or whey mixed with oatmeal *20- NE*. [Gael *fuarag* a mixture of meal and water, from *fuar* cold; compare *cauld steer* (CAULD¹·³)]
foord *see* FUIRD¹·¹, FUIRD¹·²
foording *see* FURE
foorich¹·¹ /ˈfurəx/ *n* bustle, confusion *la18-19, 20- NE*. [probably extended sense of FOORACH]
foorich¹·² /ˈfurəx/ *v* to bustle about; to get excited *20- NE*. [see the noun]
foort *see* FOURT
foorth *see* FURTH¹·²
foos, foose *see* FOU¹
foosh /fuʃ/ *n* dust or soot *la19- NE T*. [onomatopoeic]
fooshion *see* FUSHION
foosht *see* FOOST¹·¹, FOOST¹·²
fooshtie, fooshty *see* FOOSTY
foosome *see* FOUSOME
foost¹·¹, *NE* **foosht** /fust; *NE* fuʃt/ *n* **1** a mouldy condition or smell *19-*. **2** a suppressed breaking of wind *la19- NE*. **3** a dirty person, someone with disagreeable habits *la19- NE*. [see the verb]
foost¹·², fuist, *NE* **foosht** /fust; *NE* fuʃt/ *v* **1** to become or smell mouldy *19, 20- NE EC SW Bor*. **2** to break wind in a suppressed way *la19- NE*. **foostit, fuisted,** *NE* **fooshtit, †foisted** stale, mouldy, mildewed *la16-*. [OFr *fust*]
foosty, foustie, *NE* **fooshtie,** *NE* **fooshty** /ˈfuste, ˈfusti; *NE* ˈfuʃti/ *adj* stale, musty, mouldy *19-*. [FOOST¹·¹ + -IE²]
foot *see* FIT¹·¹, FIT¹·²
football *see* FITBA

footer[1.1], **fouter** /ˈfutər/ n **1** an exasperating person; an objectionable person *18-*. **2** a troublesome, fiddly job *19-*. **3** a slacker, a muddling, aimless person *19-*. **4** a chap, a fellow: ◊ *a tough auld fouter la18-19, 20- literary*. **footery, footerie, fouterie 1** *of a task* trivial; fiddly, time-consuming *20-*. **2** *of a person* fussy, inept *20-*. [see the verb]

footer[1.2], **fouter** /ˈfutər/ v **1** to potter, fiddle around; to work in a tinkering, unskilled way *la19-*. **2** to thwart; to inconvenience *19, 20- Sh Ork N T*. **footering, footrin** clumsy, awkward *la19-*. [perhaps OFr *foutre*, Lat *futuere* (of a man) to have sexual intercourse]

footie, foutie, †**futie** /ˈfuti/ adj **1** mean-spirited, base, despicable, underhand *la17-19, 20- NE T SW Bor*. **2** miserly *20- NE SW Uls*. **3** obscene, indecent *19, 20- literary*. [unknown]

Foot of the Walk see FIT[1.1]

foozie see FOZIE[1.2]

for[1.1], **fur, fir, fer,** †**fore** /fɔr, fʌr, fɪr, fɛr/ prep **1** in consideration of, to the advantage of *la14-*. **2** because of, as a result of, through *la14-*. **3** with the object or purpose of; for the sake of; on behalf of *la14-*. **4** in place of *la14-*. **5** in spite of *la14-*. **6** in return for, in payment of *15-*. **7** during, for the period of *15-*. **8** in honour of, named after (a person) *la18-*. **9** for fear of, to prevent: ◊ *I canna luik doon for fawin la18-*. **10** for want of *19-*. **11** inclined towards, desirous of: ◊ *are ye for pudding?* ◊ *are ye for bidin? 19-*. **12** of, on account of: ◊ *the creature was terrified for him 19-*. **13** concerned for, interested in (the health of): ◊ *folk were spearing for the laird la19-*. **14** *in exclamations* as being: ◊ *see til her noo! for a braw sonsey lass la19, 20- Sh NE*. **a that's for somebody** what there is of someone *19-*. **for a, for aa 1** for all that, all the same, notwithstanding *la19-*. **2** all the time, forever *20- NE*. **for ordinar** usually *18-*. **for tae, fur tae, for to, for till** in order to (do) *la14-*. †**for that** because, since *la14-e15*. **for that o't** for that matter, as far as I am concerned *20-*. [OE *for*]

for[1.2] /fɔr/ conj **1** because, since *14-*. **2** until *la19- Sh*. [see the prep]

for- /fɔr, fər/ prefix utterly, completely; intensely *la14-*. Compare FORDOVERIT, FORDWEBLIT. [OE *for-*]

for- see FORE-

foraneen see FORENUIN

foranent see FORENENT

forasmuckle, †**forasmickle,** †**forasmekle** /fɔrəzˈmʌkəl/ conj forsasmuch as *la17-19, 20- literary*. [compare *as muckle* (AS[2.1]), FORSAMEKLE]

foraye, †**for ay** /fəˈrae/ adv forever *15-*. [FOR[1.1] + AYE[2]]

forayer, †**forrayour,** †**furriour** /ˈfɔreər/ n **1** a person engaged in foraging or making a raid *la14-19, 20- literary*. **2** a person sent in advance to secure quarters or supplies *la16-e17*. [ME *forreour*]

forbare see FOREBEAR

†**forbatie, forbate** adj *of taffeta* imitation, counterfeit *la16*. [unknown]

forbear, †**forbere,** †**forbeir** /fərˈber/ v pt **forbear** †**forbare,** †**forbure 1** to refrain or abstain from; to keep away from *la14-*. **2** to endure; to have patience with; to tolerate *la14-19, 20- EC*. [OE *forberan*]

forbear, forbeer see FOREBEAR

forbeir, forbere see FOREBEAR

forbidden, †**forbiddin,** †**forbodin,** †**forbodyn** /fərˈbɪdən/ adj **1** prohibited *la14-*. **2** ill-fated, unlucky *18*. **forbidden time 1** *law* the close season for fishing *15-19, 20- historical*. **2** Lent *la16-e17*. [ptp of Older Scots *forbid*]

forbure see FOREBEAR

forby[1.1], **forbye** /fərˈbae/ adj extraordinary, strange; unusually good *19, 20- NE SW Uls*. [see the adv]

forby[1.2], **forbye** /fərˈbae/ adv **1** beyond, past *la14*. **2** besides, in addition, as well *la16-*. **3** near, beside; to one side *la18-19, 20- Uls*. **4** unusually, extraordinarily: ◊ *he was forby kind 19, 20- Uls*. **forbyes** whereas *20- NE*. [FOR[1.1] + BY[1.1]]

forby[1.3], **forbye** /fərˈbae/ prep **1** besides, in addition to *16-*. **2** except *19-*. **3** beside, beyond *19-*. **4** let alone, not to mention, far from, much less *la19- NE*. **5** compared with, relative to *la19, 20- Sh NE*. **forbyes,** †**forbyse** besides, in addition to *la19- NE*. **be forby yersel** to be beside yourself, be out of your wits *20- Sh T EC SW*. **forby that** besides the fact that *20- NE*. [see the adv]

force[1.1], †**fors** /fɔrs/ n **1** strength, power *la14-*. **2** violence, compulsion *la14-*. **3** *law* validity *la14-*. **4** a body, troop or company *la16-*. **5** the greater part, the majority *la19- NE Uls*. **6** (a matter of) necessity *la15-16*. **force and fear** *law* illegal pressure to make a person do something, duress (translating *vis et metus*) *18-*. †**the maist fors** the greatest part; for the most part *la14-15*. [ME *force*]

force[1.2], †**fors** /fɔrs/ v **1** to compel, oblige; to bring about by force *la15-*. **2** to exert oneself, strive *la14-e16*. **3** to matter, be of consequence *la15-e16*. **4** to strengthen, reinforce *16*. **forced grun** banked-up ground, ground made up in levelling *la19, 20- H&I WC SW Uls*. [ME *forcen*]

†**forcely, forsely** adv forcibly, strongly *la14-e16*. [FORCE[1.1], with adv-forming suffix]

forcie, forcey, †**forsy,** †**forcye** /ˈforsi, ˈforse/ adj **1** vigorous, active; forceful, strong *la14-19, 20- Sh NE T*. **2** *of weather* warm and dry, favourable for crops *la19- NE*. [FORCE[1.1] + -IE[2]]

forcop, †**foircoipe** /ˈfɔrkɔp/ n a kind of tax formerly collected in Orkney *16-e17, 20- historical*. [perhaps Norw *forkaup* or ON *fararkaup*]

forcye see FORCIE

†**ford** prep for it *la15-16*. **I stand ford** I guarantee *la15-e16*. [compare 'd (IT)]

ford see FUIRD[1.1], FUIRD[1.2]

fordards see FORDERTS

fordel[1.1], †**fordell** /ˈfɔrdəl/ n **1** advantage, profit; advancement *16-19, 20- literary*. **2** a store, a reserve supply *19- NE*. [FOR- + DALE[1.1]]

fordel[1.2], †**fordell** /ˈfɔrdəl/ adj **1** in reserve, laid by *la16- N NE T*. **2** done ahead of time; paid in advance *19- N NE T*. **3** extra, spare; odd; wasteful, dilatory *19- Ork*. [see the noun]

fordel[1.3] /ˈfɔrdəl/ v pt, ptp **fordled** to store, keep in reserve or hoard *19- NE*. [see the noun]

fordell see FORDEL[1.1], FORDEL[1.2]

forder[1.1], **further,** †**forthyr,** †**furder** /ˈfɔrdər, ˈfʌrðər/ n furtherance, assistance; progress *la15-19, 20- Uls*. **fordersome, furthersome 1** active, rapid *18-19, 20- N NE*. **2** *of weather* fine, favourable for work *la19- NE Uls*. **3** rash, impetuous *la18-19*. **4** advantageous, helpful *17-e19*. **guid forder** good luck *la18-19, 20- Uls*. [see the verb]

forder[1.2], **further,** †**forthir,** †**furthir** /ˈfɔrdər, ˈfʌrðər/ v **1** to promote, help forward, further *la14-*. **2** to make progress, thrive, succeed *la16-*. [OE *fyrþran*]

forder[1.3], **further,** †**forthir,** †**furthir** /ˈfɔrdər, ˈfʌrðər/ adj **1** additional *15-*. **2** more forward, at the front *15-19*. †**forthirly, furtherlie** forward; in addition *15-16*. [OE *furþra*]

forder[1.4], **faurder, further, furder,** *EC* **fa'ther,** *EC Bor* **fether,** *Bor* **ferther,** †**forthir,** †**farder** /ˈfɔrdər, ˈfʌrðər, ˈfʌrdər; *EC* ˈfaðər; *EC Bor* ˈfɛðər; *Bor* ˈfɛrðər/ adv **1** in addition, moreover *la14-*. **2** at or to a greater distance or extent *16-*. **3** more forward, in front *la14-19*. **furthermair,** †**forthirmare,** †**ferthyrmor** furthermore *la14-*. †**na forder** no more; no longer *la16-e17*. [OE *furþor*]

forderts, †**fordards**, †**fordwartis**, †**forthwartis** /'fɔrdərts/ *adv* forwards, ahead *15-19, 20- NE*. [FORDER¹·³, with adv-forming suffix]

†**fordin** *v* to (cause to) resound *e16*. [FOR- + DIN¹·²]

fordled *see* FORDEL¹·³

†**fordo** *v* to destroy, spoil; to do away with *la14-15*. [FOR- + DAE¹·¹]

fordone /fər'dʌn/ *adj* exhausted, worn out *19, 20- literary*. [FOR- + DONE]

†**fordoverit** *adj* overcome with sleep *la15-16*. [FOR- + pt p of DOVER¹·²]

†**fordullit** *adj* made dull or stupid *16-e17*. [FOR- + pt p of DULL¹·¹]

†**fordward¹** *n* a covenant, a promise *la15-e16*. [altered form of ME *foreward* a promise, OE *foreweard* a precaution]

†**fordward²·¹**, **fordwart** *adj* inclined to action, enterprising; well advanced *15-17*. Compare FORRIT¹·². [altered form of OE *foreweard* the front part]

†**fordward²·²**, **fordwart** *adv* forward, onward *16-e17*. Compare FORRIT¹·³. [see the adj]

fordwartis *see* FORDERTS

fordweblit /fər'dweblɪt/ *adj* very weak, enfeebled *19, 20- NE*. [FOR- + pt p of DWAIBLE¹·²]

fore¹·¹, †**foir** /for/ *n* **1** the front part *la16-*. **2** advantage, profit *19, 20- SW*. †**fore-bar** *law* the bar in the Court of Session at which advocates pleaded causes of first instance *18-e19*. **to the fore 1** on hand, in reserve *la16-*. **2** alive, still in existence *17-*. **3** in advance, ahead *17-19*. [aphetic form of AFORE¹·¹ or Older Scots *before*]

fore¹·², †**foir** /for/ *adj* situated in front; facing the front *16-*. [see the adv]

fore¹·³ /for/ *adv* at or to the front; forwards, foremost *la16-*. [OE *fore*]

fore¹·⁴ /for/ *interj golf* a call used to warn anyone in the path of the ball *la19-*. [see the adverb]

fore *see* FOR¹·¹

fore-, for- /for, fɔr/ *prefix* earlier, in front *la14-*. [OE *fore*]

forebear, forbear, *NE* **forbeer** /'forber, 'fɔrber; *NE* 'fɔrbir/ *n* an ancestor, a forefather *15-*. [FORE- + agent noun formed from BE]

forebearer, †**forebearar** /'forberər/ *n* an ancestor, a forefather *la16-*. [erroneous variant of FOREBEAR]

forebooth, †**forebuthe**, †**foirbuith** /'forbuθ/ *n* a front booth or shop *la15-e17, 19- historical*. [FORE- + BUITH]

forebreed /'forbrid/ *n* the front of a skirt or dress *20- Sh NE*. [FORE- + BREED¹]

forebreist, forebreast /'forbrist, 'forbrɛst/ *n* **1** the forefront or front part of something *la15-*. **2** the front seat of the gallery in a church *la17-*. **3** the front seat of a cart *la19- Ork NE T*. **4** the breast of a garment *16-e17*. **forebreist o the loft** the front seat of the gallery in a church *la17-19, 20- EC*. [FORE- + BREIST¹·¹]

†**forebroads** *npl* the first milk from a cow after calving *e19*. [FORE-; for second element compare Icel *broddur, brodd mjólk* the first milk]

†**forebront, forebrunt** *n* the vanguard of an army or a charge *16-e17*. [FORE- + BRUNT]

forebuthe *see* FOREBOOTH

†**fore-cadie** *n golf* a caddie who went on ahead of the player to watch where the ball fell *la18-19*. [FORE- + CADDIE¹·¹]

†**forechalmer** *n* a front room *la15-e17*. [FORE- + CHAUMER]

†**foredask** *n* a desk or pew in a front position in a church *17-e18*. [FORE- + DASK]

foredoor /'fordor/ *n* **1** the front door of a building *la16-19, 20- NE T C SW*. **2** the front part of a box cart, with a seat on top for the driver *20- NE H&I SW*. [FORE- + DOOR]

fore-elder, †**fore-eldar** /'forɛldər/ *n* an ancestor *15-20, 21- historical*. [ON *forellrar*]

fore-end, †**foirend** /'forɛnd/ *n* **1** the first or front part or portion of something *17-*. **2** the beginning or earlier part of a period of time *la17-*. [FORE- + EN¹·¹]

†**fore entres, foir entres** *n* a front entrance, a vestibule *16-17*. [FORE- + ENTRESS]

fore entry, †**fore entre** /'forɛntre/ *n* a front entrance, a vestibule *16-19, 20- NE*. [FORE- + ENTRY]

fore-face /'forfɛs/ *n* **1** the front of a fireplace (consisting of an iron framework) *la19- EC*. **2** the front or forward-facing part of something *la16-17*. [FORE- + FACE¹·¹]

forefit, †**foirfute** /'forfɪt/ *n* **1** a front foot (of an animal) *15-*. **2** the front part of the foot *la16-19, 20- Sh NE EC SW*. [FORE- + FIT¹·¹]

forefolk /'forfok/ *npl* ancestors, forefathers *la19-*. [FORE- + folk (FOWK)]

forefought *see* FORFOUCHT

fore-front /'forfrʌnt/ *n* the fore part or front of something *15-*. [FORE- + FRONT]

foregain, †**forgane** /for'gen/ *prep* opposite to, in front of, over against *la14-19, 20- Ork NE*. [FORE- + AGAIN¹·²]

†**foregainst, forganest, forganis** *prep* opposite to, over against *la15-19*. [FORE- + AGAINST]

fore gait *see* FOREGATE

foregang, *Sh* **foregeng** /'forgaŋ *Sh* 'forgɛŋ/ *n folklore* a wraith or other supernatural sign (thought to foretell a death); a premonition of misfortune *la19- Sh N NE*. [FORE- + GANG¹·²]

†**foregate, fore gait, forgait** *n* the street in front of a building *16-e18*. [FORE- + GAIT³]

foregeng *see* FOREGANG

†**foregere** *n* armour for the front of the body *la15-16*. [FORE- + GEAR¹·¹]

foregill /'forgɪl/ *n* the curved part of the beam of the old Orkney plough which would slide along the surface while the plough was in the ground *20- historical*. [FORE- + perhaps KEEL²·¹]

forego /'forgo/ *n folklore* a wraith, a premonition *la19, 20- literary*. [anglicized variant of FOREGANG]

†**foregranddame** *n* a great-grandmother or a great-great-grandmother *16-17*. [FORE- + *grandam* (GRAND)]

†**foregrandfather** *n* a great-grandfather *la16-17*. [FORE- + *grandfaither* (GRAND)]

†**foregrantsire, fore grandschir, foirgrantschir** *n* a great-grandfather or a great-great-grandfather *la15-17*. [FORE- + *grandsher* (GRAND)]

forehaimmer, forehammer /'forhemər, 'forhamər/ *n* a sledgehammer *la16-*. [FORE- + HAIMMER¹·¹]

forehand¹·¹ /'forhand/ *n* **1** a position at the front; a head start, an advantage *19-*. **2** *in curling* the first stone to be played; the player to make the first shot on either side *19-*. **3** *in curling and bowling* a shot coming in from the right of the tee or jack *20-*. **4** a leading horse in a team *e19*. **forehandit, forehanded 1** paid in advance *la19-*. **2** prudent, far-seeing; having thought for the future *la19-*. **to the forehand of** straight ahead, in front of *19, 20- Sh*. [FORE- + *hand* (HAN¹·¹)]

forehand¹·² /'forhand/ *adj* **1** *of payments* made in advance; *of rent* paid in advance of the usual time *la17-*. **2** first, foremost, leading *19-*. **3** *of bowls or curling stones* approaching the tee or jack from the right and curving in anticlockwise *20-*. [see the noun]

foreheid, forehead, †**forehede**, †**foret**, †**forret** /'forhid, 'forhɛd/ *n* **1** the part of the face above the eyes; the brow *la14-*. **2** the front compartment of an open boat *la19- Sh Ork*

forehorn /'fɔrhɔrn/ *n* the top of the stem-post in a boat *la19- Sh*. [FORE- + HORN]

N. **3** the line up to which a peat moss has been dug *la15-16*. [FORE- + HEID¹·¹]

forehouse, †**foirhous** /'fɔrhʌus/ *n* a house facing the street; an outer apartment by which a house may be entered *15-20, 21- historical*. [FORE- + *house* (HOOSE¹·¹)]

foreland /'fɔrlənd/ *n* **1** a foreshore or beach *18-*. **2** a building or piece of land facing onto a street *la15-18*. **3** a headland, a cape *16*. [FORE- + LAND¹·¹]

†**foremail¹·¹, foremale** *n* prepaid rent *la15-e18*. [FORE- + MAIL¹]

†**foremail¹·², foremale** *v* to let property for a prepaid rent; to require rent to be paid in advance *la15-e18*. [see the noun]

foremaist¹·¹, foremost, †formast, †formest /'fɔrmɛst, 'fɔrmost/ *adj* at the front; in first place *la14-*. [FORE- + MAIST¹·¹]

foremaist¹·², foremost, †formast, †formest /'fɔrmɛst, 'fɔrmost/ *adv* at the front; in first place *la15-*. [see the adj]

foremale *see* FOREMAIL¹·¹, FOREMAIL¹·²

foremost *see* FOREMAIST¹·¹, FOREMAIST¹·²

forenail, †fornale /fɔr'nel/ *v* to let or sell property in advance; to pledge money before it is earned or designate how it will be spent in advance *la15-19, 20- NE*. Compare FOREMAIL¹·². [perhaps FORE- + NAIL¹·²]

foreneen *see* FORENUIN

†**forenemmit, foirnemmit, fornamyt** *adj* previously mentioned by name *la14-17*. [FORE- + pt p of NEM¹·²]

forenent, fornent, fornenst, *Sh* **firnenst, †foranent, †fornentis, †fornens** /fɔr'nɛnt, fɔr'nɛnst; *Sh* fɪr'nɛnst/ *prep* **1** opposite to, in front of *15-*. **2** in return for, in exchange or payment for *la18-*. **3** in opposition to, against *la19- Sh*. **4** concerning, with regard to *la15-19*. [FORE- + ANENT, ANENST]

forenicht, forenight /'fɔrnɪxt, 'fɔrnʌɪt/ *n* the early part of the night, the evening; the winter evening (as a time of relaxation and entertainment) *16-*. [FORE- + NICHT¹·¹]

forenun, forenoon, *NE* **foreneen**, *NE* **foraneen** /fɔr'nun; *NE* fɔr'nin; *NE* fɔrə'nin/ *n* the morning (prior to noon) *17-*. **forenoon bite** a mid-morning snack or drink; elevenses *19- NE EC Bor*. [FORE- + NUNE]

†**forepartie** *n* a vanguard *la17*. [FORE- + *partie* (PAIRTY¹·¹)]

†**foreplace** *n* a building or piece of land facing onto a street *16-e17*. [FORE- + PLACE¹·¹]

forerin, for-rin /fɔr'rɪn/ *v* **1** to outrun; to outstrip in running *16-*. **2** to play truant from school *20- SW*. **forerinner, †forrinner** a precursor, a harbinger *la14-*. †**for-ron, forrvn, forrown** exhausted by running *la15-e16*. [FORE- + RIN¹·²]

foreroom /'fɔrrum/ *n* the front part of a boat; the compartment in front of the mast *la16-19, 20- Sh EC*. [ON *fyrirrúm*]

foresaid /'fɔrsɛd/ *adj* aforesaid, above-mentioned *la14-*. [FORE- + pt p of SAY¹·²]

foresaids¹·¹, †foresaidis /'fɔrsɛdz/ *npl law* the people or matters previously mentioned *16-*. [see the adj]

†**foresaids¹·², foresaidis** *adj* **1** *of people or things* aforesaid, above-mentioned *la14-e18*. [FORESAID, with plural suffix]

foreschot *see* FORESHOT

foreseat, †foirsate /'fɔrsɪt/ *n* **1** the (moveable) seat in the front of a carriage or car *19-20, 21- historical*. **2** a bench forming the front part of an enclosed pew *la16-e19*. [FORE- + SEAT]

foresee /fɔr'si/ *v* **1** to anticipate in advance *15-*. **2** to consider something beforehand; to see someone previously *la16-e17*. **3** to catch sight of beforehand *la15*. [FORE- + SEE]

†**foreshop** *n* a shop fronting the street *18-19*. [FORE- + SHOP]

foreshot, †foreschot /'fɔrʃɔt/ *n* **1** *distilling* the whisky that comes over first *la18-*. **2** a projecting part of a building overhanging the street *la17-18, 19- historical*. [FORE- + SHOT¹·¹]

foresicht, †forsicht /'fɔrsɪxt/ *n* **1** anticipation, foresight *la14-*. **2** divine providence *la14-16*. **forsichty** foresighted, provident *19, 20- N*. [FORE- + SICHT¹·¹]

foreside, †forside, †foirsyde /'fɔrsʌɪd/ *n* the front or front part of something *la15-*. **on da foreside o'** *of time* a little before *20- Sh*. [FORE- + SIDE¹]

foresman /'fɔrzmən/ *n* a foreman, the head workman *la18-*. [altered form of Scots *foreman*]

forespeaker *see* FORSPEAKER

forespeik, forespoken *see* FORSPEAK

forest, †forrest /'fɔrəst/ *n* **1** a large area of woodland (sometimes including cultivated land); frequently in place-names *la12-*. **2** *law* a large area of (wooded) ground, originally reserved for deer-hunting and belonging to the Crown *18-19, 20- historical*. †**forestary** the office of forester *la15-e17*. **forester, †forestar, †forstar, †forster, 1** the keeper of a forest *12-*. **2** a forest-dweller *e16*. **forestry, †forstry 1** the cultivation of forests *19-*. **2** *law* the district of a forester; a hunting forest; the rights of hunting in such a forest *la15-19, 20- historical*. †**forestar stede** the land and dwelling of a forest-keeper *15*. **The Flowers of the Forest** the name of a tune traditionally said to be a lament for the young men of Ettrick killed at Flodden *la18-*. †**the Forest** Ettrick Forest in Selkirk *18-19*. **the muckle forester** the wind *20- NE*. [OFr *forest*]

fore-sta /'fɔrsta/ *n* a feeding trough in a byre *la19- NE T*. [FORE- + STA¹·¹]

forestair, †foir stair, †forstair /'fɔrster/ *n* an outside staircase leading to the first floor of a building *16-*. [FORE- + STAIR¹]

forestall, †foresta, †forstaw /fɔr'stɔl/ *v* **1** to hinder or thwart; to prevent by advance action *la16-*. **2** to buy merchandise before it is brought to the burgh market (to increase the price on resale) *15-19, 20- historical*. [OE *foresteall* an ambush, a plot]

fore-stem, †forestam, †forstam /'fɔrstɛm/ *n* **1** the prow of a boat *la15-19, 20- NE*. **2** the forehead *e18*. [FORE- + OE *stefn* a prow]

†**forestreet, foir streit** *n* the street directly in front of a building *la17-19*. [FORE- + STREET¹]

foresupper /'fɔrsʌpər/ *n* the period between the end of work and supper-time *la18-19, 20- EC Bor Uls*. [FORE- + SUPPER¹·¹]

foresye /'fɔrsae/ *n* a cut of beef from the shoulder *18-*. [FORE- + SEY³]

foret *see* FOREHEID

foretaft *see* FORETHAFT

†**foretaiking, foretaking** *n* a foretoken, an omen *la16*. [altered form of OE *foretācn*]

†**foretenement** *n* a tenement fronting a street *la16-19*. [FORE- + TENEMENT]

forethaft, *Sh* **foretaft** /'fɔrθaft; *Sh* 'fɔrtaft/ *n* the seat next to the bow in a rowing boat *la19- Sh Ork NE EC*. [FORE- + THAFT]

forethocht¹·¹ /'fɔrθɔxt/ *n* forethought *la19-*. **forethochty** cautious, having foresight *19- EC Bor*. [FORE- + THOCHT]

forethocht¹·², forethought /'fɔrθɔxt, 'fɔrθɔt/ *adj* premeditated *la14-*. **forethought felony** *law* malice aforethought *la14-*. [FORE- + pt p of THINK¹·²]

forewa, forewall, †foirwall /'fɔrwɔ, 'fɔrwɔl/ *n* the front wall of a building *16-*. [FORE- + WA¹·¹]

†**forewerk** *n* a front portion of a building *la15-17*. [FORE- + WARK¹·¹]

forewey /'fɔrwʌɪ/ *adv* forward *la19- Ork*. **i mae forewey** in front of me *la19- Ork*. [FORE- + WEY¹]

forewin, forewind /ˈforwɪn, ˈforwɪnd/ *n* **1** *in hand-reaping* the first strip to be cut, done by the most experienced worker *la19- T H&I WC*. **2** the worker who leads or sets the pace in any farming task *20- H&I WC*. [FORE- + WIN²; compare *bandwin* (BAND¹·¹)]

†**fore-writin, forwretyne** *adj* already set down in writing *la14-e16*. [FORE- + ptp of WRITE¹·²]

†**foreʒett, foir ʒet** *n* a front gate *15-e17*. [FORE- + YETT]

†**forfaictour, forfactour** *n* forfeiture *15-16*. [Latinate variant of *forfature* (FORFAULT¹·²)]

†**forfair, forfare** *v* **1** to go amiss; to perish or decay *la14-16*. **2** to bring to ruin; to destroy *la14-e17*. [OE *forfaran*]

forfairn, †**forfarn** /fərˈfern/ *adj* **1** ruined, destitute *la15- literary*. **2** exhausted; worn out (with age) *la18- literary*. [ptp of FORFAIR]

forfalt *see* FORFAULT¹·¹, FORFAULT¹·²

Forfar bridie /ˌforfər ˈbrʌɪdi/ *n* a BRIDIE made in Forfar *19-*. [from the place-name + BRIDIE]

forfare *see* FORFAIR

forfarn *see* FORFAIRN

forfat *see* FORFAULT¹·²

forfauchlet /fərˈfɔxəlt/ *adj* worn out, exhausted *19, 20- T C Bor*. [FOR- + *fauchled* (FAUCHLE¹·²)]

†**forfault¹·¹, forfalt** *n* **1** a fault, an offence *15-e17*. **2** a fine; a forfeiture *15-17*. [ME *forfet*, with influence from fault (FAUT¹·¹)]

forfault¹·², †**forfalt,** †**forfat,** † **forfaut** /fərˈfɔlt/ *v ptp* **forfaultit, forfault 1** to confiscate; to take as forfeited *la14-19, 20- historical*. **2** to commit a fault *la15-18*. **3** to subject a person to confiscation of rights or property *la15-18*. **4** to condemn *la15*. †**forfaulter, forfaltour** a forfeiter, a wrongdoer *la15-16*. †**forfaulter, foirfaltour, forforture** forfeiture, deprivation of property as a penalty *la15-19*. †**forfaultry** forfeiture; the property forfeited *16-18*. [see the verb]

forfecht /fərˈfext/ *v* to exhaust; to tire oneself out *la19- NE*. [back-formation from FORFOCHEN]

forfeit, †**forfett** /ˈfɔrfət/ *v* **1** to lose the right to or be deprived of (something) *15-*. **2** *law* to subject a person to forfeiture; to confiscate a person's estates and heritable property as a penalty for treason *17-19*. Compare FORFAULT¹·². [ME *forfeten*]

forfeuchen *see* FORFOCHEN

forflitten *see* FORFLUTTEN

forfluther /fərˈflʌðər/ *v* to fluster, agitate *19, 20- literary*. [FOR- + FLUTHER¹·²]

forflutten, †**forflitten** /fərˈflʌtən/ *adj* severely scolded, excessively abused *16-e17, 20- NE*. [FOR- + ptp of FLYTE¹·²]

forfochen, ferfochen, forfoughen, forfochten, forfoughten, *EC Bor* **forfeuchen,** †**forfochtin** /fərˈfɔxən, fərˈfɔxtən/; *EC Bor* fərˈfjuxən/ *adj* **1** exhausted with fighting *15-*. **2** exhausted with effort or exertion *17-*. [FOR- + ptp of FECHT¹·²]

forfoucht, †**forefought,** †**forfocht** /fərˈfɔxt/ *adj* exhausted (from fighting or effort) *la16-19, 20- literary*. [FOR- + ptp of FECHT¹·²]

forfoughen, forfoughten *see* FORFOCHEN

forgadder, forgaddir *see* FORGAITHER

forgae, †**forga** /fərˈge/ *v* to do without, give up or forgo *la14-19, 20- literary*. [OE *forgān*]

forgae, forgaff *see* FORGIE

forgait *see* FOREGATE

forgaither, forgather, *Sh* **forgadder,** †**forgaddir** /fərˈgeðər, fərˈgaðər; *Sh* fərˈgadər/ *v* **1** to assemble, gather together *la15-*. **2** to meet, encounter *16-*. **3** to associate or keep company with *19, 20- NE EC*. **4** to come together in marriage; to get married *la18- NE*. **forgaitherin, forgathering** a meeting, an assembly *19-*. **forgaither wi, forgather with 1** to meet with *16-*. **2** to keep company with *la18- NE EC*. **3** *of ships* to encounter another vessel in battle; to run into a storm *la16-17*. [FOR- + GAITHER]

†**forgane** *adj* exhausted *la14-16*. [ME *forgon* exhausted]

forgane *see* FOREGAIN

forganest, forganis *see* FOREGAINST

forgat *see* FORGET¹·²

forgather *see* FORGAITHER

forgeif *see* FORGIE

forget¹·¹ /fərˈgɛt/ *n* (an instance of) forgetfulness, absent-mindedness *19-*. [see the verb]

forget¹·², *Sh NE* **foryet,** †**forʒet** /fərˈgɛt; *Sh NE* fərˈjɛt/ *v pt Sh* **foryat,** *Sh T* **forgat** to lose recollection of; to fail to remember *la14-*. **forgetfu, forgetful,** †**forgetfull,** †**forʒetfull** liable to forget, having a bad memory *la16-*. [OE *forgietan*]

forgettle, *NE* **foryettle,** †**forʒetil** /fərˈgɛtəl; *NE* fərˈjɛtəl/ *adj* forgetful *la14, 19- NE T SW Bor*. [OE *forgitel*]

forgie, forgive, †**forgeve,** †**forgif,** †**forgeif** /fərˈgi, fərˈgɪv/ *v pt* **forgied, forgae,** †**forgaff,** *ptp* **forgien** †**forgevine** to pardon, excuse; to stop being angry (at someone) *la14-*.

†**forgevance** forgiveness *la15-16*. [OE *forgiefan*]

forhoo, forhooie, *NE* **forvoo,** †**forhow** /fərˈhu, fərˈhui; *NE* fərˈvu/ *v* to forsake or desert; *of a bird* to abandon a nest *16-19, 20- NE EC Bor*. [OE *forhogian* to despise; compare PERVOO]

forin *see* FARAN

forisfamiliate /ˌforɪsfəˈmɪliet/ *v law* to provide separately for a son or daughter *la16-*. [Lat *forisfamiliāre*]

forisfamiliated, †forisfamiliate, †forisfamiliat /ˌforɪsfəˈmɪlietəd/ *adj of a minor* living independently of his or her parents because of being married or having a separate estate *la16-*. [ptp of FORISFAMILIATE]

forisfamiliation, †forisfamiliatioun /ˌforɪsfɪmɪliˈeʃən/ *n of sons or daughters* the state of living independently with independent means *17-*. [FORISFAMILIATE, with noun-forming suffix]

forjeskit, forjaskit /fərˈdʒɛskɪt, fərˈdʒaskɪt/ *adj* exhausted, worn out *la18-*. [FOR- + JASKIT]

†**forjidget** *adj* extremely tired, exhausted *la18-e19*. [probably extended sense of FORJUGIT condemned, as good as dead]

†**forjugit, foiriugeit** *adj* sentenced; condemned *la15-e16*. [ptp of OFr *forjugier*]

fork¹·¹ /fɔrk/ *n* **1** a pronged agricultural implement *la14-*. **2** a branch or branching of a stream *la16-*. **3** a piece of cutlery *17-*. **4** a forkful *19-*. **5** a thorough search *la19- Sh NE EC*. [OE *forc*]

fork¹·² /fɔrk/ *v* **1** to dig or move with a fork *17-*. **2** to divide into branches *19-*. **3** to search about, hunt for *19- Sh NE T EC*. **4** to fend for oneself *la19- Sh NE T EC*. **forker** an earwig *20- EC Bor*. **forkin, forking 1** the point where a river divides into two or more streams; frequently in place-names *19-*. **2** the branching of a tree or road *19- WC SW Bor*. **3** the crotch *19, 20- Bor*. **forkit** forked; branching *16-*. [see the noun]

forkie /ˈfɔrki/ *n* an earwig, an insect of the order *Dermaptera 20-*. **forky golach** an earwig *20- NE*. **forkie tail 1** an earwig *19-*. **2** a tail coat *20- Ork NE T*. [FORK¹·¹ + -IE¹]

†**forky** *adj* forceful, powerful *e16*. [compare FORCIE]

forl *see* WHURL²

forlaithie¹·¹, forlethie /fərˈleθi, fərˈlɛθi/ *n* **1** a surfeit, an excess *la18- N NE T*. **2** a feeling of disgust or revulsion *la19- NE*. [FOR- + LAITH¹·¹ + -IE²]

forlaithie¹·² /fərˈleθi/ *v* to sicken; to disgust through excess *la19- NE*. [see the noun]

†**forlane** *adj* **1** set aside, disregarded *la15-16*. **2** despicable, worthless *e16*. [ptp of ME *forlien* to lie with, commit adultery; to rape]

forleet, †**forleit**, †**forlete** /fər'lit/ *v* **1** to neglect, forsake or leave behind *la15-19, 20- literary*. **2** to forget *la18-e19*. [OE *forlǣtan*]

forlegen /fər'legən/ *adj* exhausted, worn out *la19- Sh Ork*. [compare FORLANE and Norw, Dan *forlegen* embarrassed, perplexed]

forleit, forlete *see* FORLEET
forlethie *see* FORLAITHIE[1.1]
†**forloff** *n* a furlough, a leave of absence *17-e18*. [Du *verlof*]
forloir *see* FORLORE
†**forloppin** *adj of an ecclesiastic* runaway, renegade *16-17*. [FOR- + *loppin* (LEAP)]
†**forlore, forlor, forloir** *adj* lost, forlorn, destroyed *la15-16*. [ptp of OE *forlēosan*]
forlot *see* FIRLOT
form *see* FURM
formast *see* FOREMAIST[1.1], FOREMAIST[1.2]
formest *see* FOREMAIST[1.2]
forn *see* FARE[1.2]
fornacket, †**fernacket** /fər'nakət/ *n* a hard slap or thump *19- NE*. [FOR- + derivative of KNACK[1.1] or KNACK[1.2]]
fornale *see* FORENAIL
fornamyt *see* FORENEMMIT
fornens, fornenst, fornent, fornentis *see* FORENENT
fornes *see* FURNISH
forniaw *see* FORNYAW
fornicatrix /'fɔrnɪketrɪks/ *n* a woman guilty of fornication *la16-18, 19- historical*. [Lat *fornicātrix*]
†**fornie, forny** *n* fornication *la18-e19*. [shortened form of Older Scots *fornicatioun*]
fornyaw, forniaw /fər'njɔ/ *v* to fatigue, tire, wear out *la18-19, 20- EC SW*. [FOR- + Older Scots *gnaw*; compare GNYAUVE]
†**forout** *prep* without *la14-e17*. [OE *forūtan*; compare FOROUTEN]
forouten, †**foroutin**, †**forowtyn** /fər'ʌutən/ *prep* **1** without, lacking *la14-e17, 20- literary*. **2** besides, not taking into account *la14-16*. †**foroutin mair** only, without more *la14-15*. [OE *forūtan*; compare FOROUT]
†**forouth**[1.1], **forrouth** *adv* **1** forward *la14-e15*. **2** before, previously *la14-e15*. [ME *forwith*]
†**forouth**[1.2], **forrowth** *prep* **1** before, in front of *la14-e16*. **2** prior to, previous to *la14-e15*. [see the adv]
†**forow**[1.1], **forrow** *adv* beforehand, previously *la14-16*. [reduced form of FOROUTH[1.1]]
†**forow**[1.2], **forrow** *prep* **1** previous to *la14-e17*. **2** in front of *la14-15*. [see the adv]
forowtyn *see* FOROUTEN
forpit, forpet, †**forpett** /'fɔrpɪt, 'fɔrpət/ *n* a measure of weight used mainly for the sale of root vegetables *17-*. [reduced form of FOURT + PAIRT[1.1]]
†**forquhy** *conj* **1** for which reason, why *la14-16*. **2** because, since *la14-16*. [OE *forhwȳ*]
forrad *see* FORRIT[1.3]
†**forray**[1.1], **furrow, forra** *n* an armed, hostile raid, a foray *la14-17*. **ride a forray** to make an attack *16*. **rin a forra** = ride a forray. [see the verb]
†**forray**[1.2], **furrow, forrow** *v* to raid, pillage *la14-e17*. [probably back-formation from FORAYER]
forrayour *see* FORAYER
forrest *see* FOREST
forret *see* FOREHEID
for-rin *see* FORERIN
forrit[1.1], *WC* **furrit** /'fɔrɪt; *WC* 'fʌrɪt/ *v* to put forward in time; to promote or assist *19-*. [see the adv]

forrit[1.2], **forward**, *WC* **furrit**, †**forwart** /'fɔrɪt, 'fɔrwərd; *WC* 'fʌrɪt/ *adj* **1** towards the front *la16-*. **2** bold, audacious; pushy, keen, precocious *la16-*. **3** well advanced; near completion *la18-*. **4** *of a clock or watch* fast *la19-*. **5** *of goods or livestock* appearing in public for sale; *of a person or a team* entered into a contest *20-*. **6** present, at hand *la19, 20- C Bor*. Compare FORDWARD[2.1]. **forritsome** forward, impudent, bold *19-*. **forrit owre** bent forward, stooped *20- Sh Bor*. [see the adv]

forrit[1.3], **forward**, *Sh N* **forrad**, *WC* **furrit**, †**forwart** /'fɔrɪt, 'fɔrwərd; *Sh N* 'fɔrəd; *WC* 'fʌrɪt/ *adv* **1** towards the front, forwards *16-*. **2** available for sale, on public display *20-*. Compare FORDWARD[2.2]. [OE *forweard*]

forro *see* FARROW
for-ron *see* FORERIN
forrouth *see* FOROUTH[1.1]
forrow /'fɔro/ *adv* in reserve, in hand, in readiness for use *la19- Ork*. [compare ON *fyrir höndum*]
forrow *see* FARROW, FOROW[1.1], FOROW[1.2], FORRAY[1.2]
forrown *see* FORERIN
forrowth *see* FOROUTH[1.2]
forrvn *see* FORERIN
†**fors**[1.1] *n in Shetland* the coarse outer wool on a sheep's fleece *la18*. [see the verb]
fors[1.2] /fɔrs/ *v* to pluck out the coarse outer wool on a sheep's fleece *la18- Sh*. [MFr *forcer* to clip with shears]
fors *see* FORCE[1.1], FORCE[1.2]
forsake, *NE* **forsak**, †**forsaik**, †**forsaek** /fər'sek; *NE* fər'sak/ *v* to abandon; to refuse or decline *la14-*. [OE *forsacan*]
†**forsamekle, forsameikle** *conj* forasmuch (as) *la15-17*. [FOR[1.1] + SAE[2.1] + *meikle* (MUCKLE[1.1])]
Forsday *see* THURSDAY
†**forseeth, forsuth, forsuyth** *adv* truly, forsooth *la14-e19*. [OE *forsōð*]
forsel[1.1] /'fɔrsəl/ *n in Orkney* a protection of straw and bands for a horse's back when loaded *19, 20- historical*. [unknown; compare ON *seli* harness]
forsel[1.2] /'fɔrsəl/ *v* **1** to harness a horse *19- Ork*. **2** to spread with butter *20- Ork*. **3** to cover with dung *20- Ork*. [see the noun]
†**forsellet, forslat** *n* a fortress *15*. [ME *forcelet*]
forsely *see* FORCELY
forsicht *see* FORESICHT
forside *see* FORESIDE
forskal, farskal /'fɔrskəl, 'farskəl/ *n* a porch; a shelter at the front of a house *20- Ork N*. [ON *forskáli* an antechamber, an entrance hall]
forslat *see* FORSELLET
forsmo /fər'smo/ *n* an insult, an affront, a snub *20- Sh*. [ON *fyrirsmá* to despise]
†**forsocht** *adj* premeditated, planned *15-16*. [altered form of FORETHOCHT[1.2]]
forspeak, †**forespeik** /fər'spik/ *v* **1** *folklore* to put under a spell, bewitch; to charm with excessive praise *17-19, 20- Sh Ork N NE*. **2** to foretell, predict *la16-e17*. **3** to mention; to agree beforehand *la14-16*. **forspoken, forespoken 1** *folklore* bewitched *la16-19, 20- Sh Ork N NE*. **2** agreed, settled or mentioned beforehand *la14-19, 20- Uls*. **forspoken water** *folklore* water used to undo a spell *18-19, 20- Ork N*. [ME *forspeken*]
forspeaker, forespeaker, †**forspekar** /fər'spikər/ *n* a person who speaks on behalf of another, an advocate *15-19, 20- historical*. [OE *forspeca*]
forspoken *see* FORSPEAK
forsta /fər'sta/ *v* to understand, comprehend *19- Sh Ork NE*. [probably Du *verstaan*]

forstair see FORESTAIR
forstam see FORE-STEM
†**forstand** v to understand *18-19*. [OE *forstandan* to defend, understand]
forstar, forster see FOREST
forstaw see FORESTALL
forstry see FOREST
†**forsume** v to neglect, misuse *la15-e16*. [compare Du *verzuimen*]
forsuth, forsuyth see FORSEETH
forswifted, †**forswiftit** /fərˈswɪftəd/ adj hurried along or swept away *e16, 20- Ork*. [FOR- + pt p of ON *svipta* to pull quickly, sweep off]
forsy see FORCIE
fort[1.1], †**forth** /fɔrt, fort/ n a fortified building or place *16-*. [MFr *fort*]
fort[1.2], †**forth** /fɔrt, fort/ v to fortify *la16-*. [see the noun]
fort see FOURT
fortak /fərˈtak/ v to hit; to aim a blow at *la19- NE*. [FOR- + TAK[1.2]; compare Norw dial *fortaka* to assail; to put a strain on]
fortalice, †**fortalise,** †**fortales** /ˈfɔrtəlɪs/ n a fortress, a fortification *15-*. [OFr *fortelesce*]
fortefie see FORTIFEE
forteres see FORTRESS
forth see FORT[1.1], FORT[1.2], FURTH[1.2]
forthink /fərˈθɪŋk/ v pt **forthocht** 1 to regret, repent *la14-19, 20- NE*. 2 to have second thoughts; to reconsider *18-19, 20- NE*. [FOR- + OE *þyncan* to seem]
forthir see FORDER[1.2], FORDER[1.3], FORDER[1.4]
forthirly see FORDER[1.3]
forthirmare see FORDER[1.4]
†**forthirward, forthirwart** adv further, forward *la14-15*. **forthirwartis** forward *16*. [OE *furþorweard*]
forthocht see FORTHINK
†**forthwart**[1.1], **furthwart** adj forward; promising *la15-e16*. [see the adv]
†**forthwart**[1.2], **furthwart** adv forward, onward, outward *la14-16*. [OE *forðweard*]
forthwartis see FORDERTS
†**forthy**[1.1] adv for that reason, therefore *15-16*. **forthy that** for the reason that, to the end that *la14-15*. [OE *forþī*]
†**forthy**[1.2] conj for this reason, therefore *la14-e16*. [OE *forþȳ*]
forthy see FURTHIE
forthyr see FORDER[1.1]
fortifee, fortify, †**fortefie** /ˈfɔrtəfi, ˈfɔrtəfae/ v 1 to strengthen (against attack); to support *la15-*. 2 to pet, pamper or spoil (a child or a pet) *la19- NE*. †**fortifiar, fortifear** an upholder, a supporter *la16-17*. [MFr *fortifier*]
fortig see FIRTIG[1.2]
fortin see FORTUNE[1.1]
fortnicht, fortnight /ˈfɔrtnɪxt, ˈfɔrtnʌɪt/ n a period of two weeks *17-*. [shortened form of OE *fēowertȳnenihte*]
forton see FORTUNE[1.1]
fortoun see FORTUNE[1.1], FORTUNE[1.2]
fortress, †**forteres,** †**fortres,** †**fortrace** /ˈfɔrtrəs, ˈfɔrtrəs/ n a fortified stronghold *la14-*. [ME *forteress*]
fortunate, †**fortunat,** †**fortunait** /ˈfɔrtʃənət/ adj 1 favoured by fortune, lucky *la15-*. 2 destined by fortune *la15*. [Lat *fortūnātus*]
fortune[1.1], **fortin,** †**fortoun,** †**forton** /ˈfɔrtʃun, ˈfɔrtən/ n 1 chance, luck; fate, destiny *la14-*. 2 wealth, a large sum *la16-*. [ME *fortune*, Lat *fortūna*]
†**fortune**[1.2], **fortoun** v pt, ptp **fortunit, fortunat** 1 to be endowed with a fortune *e19*. 2 to happen to; to befall *16-e17*. 3 of God to assign a particular fate *15-16*. **fortunit** favoured, fortunate *la15*. [ME *fortunen*, Lat *fortūnāre*]
forty[1.1], **fowertie,** †**fourty** /ˈfɔrti, ˈfɔrte, ˈfʌuərte/ numeral the cardinal number after thirty-nine *la14-*. **the Forty-five 1** the Jacobite rising of 1745 *e18, la18- historical*. **2** the forty-five members representing Scotland in the British parliament (1707-1832) *18*. **the Forty Thieves** a group of ministers in the Synod of Glasgow who withdrew their support from the Disruption as it became imminent and tried to find a compromise *e19, la19- historical*. **the Forty-twa** the Black Watch, originally the 42nd Highland Regiment of Foot *19-20, 21- historical*. [OE *fēowertig*]
†**forty**[1.2], **fourty** adj fortieth *la15-e16*. [see the numeral]
†**forvey, forvay, forway** v to go astray; to err *la15-16*. [ME *forveien*]
forvoo see FORHOO
†**forwakit, forwakyd, forwalkit** adj tired out from staying awake *15-e19*. [FOR- + pt p of WAUK[1.2]]
forwandert, forwandered /fərˈwɔndərt, fərˈwɔndərd/ adj weary with wandering; bewildered, lost *la19- literary*. [ME *forwandren* to exhaust oneself with wandering]
forward, forwart see FORRIT[1.2], FORRIT[1.3]
forway see FORVEY
†**forwonderit** adj amazed, astounded *la14-15*. [FOR- + pt p of *wonder* (WUNNER[1.2])]
†**forworthin** adj malformed, useless *la14-e16*. [OE *forworden*, ptp of *forweorþan*]
forwretyne see FORE-WRITIN
†**forwrocht** adj overcome with toil, exhausted *la15-16*. [OE *forworhton* ruined, lost, ptp of *forwyrcan*]
foryat see FORGET[1.2]
†**foryeild, forȝelde, forȝeild** v to repay, recompense *la14-19*. [OE *forgyldan*]
foryet see FORGET[1.2]
foryettle see FORGETTLE
forȝet see FORGET[1.2]
forȝetil see FORGETTLE
föshin see FUSHION
föshinless see FUSHIONLESS
fosser, †**faser** /ˈfɔsər/ n a rush mat laid on a horse to prevent chafing from a wickerwork pannier *la16, 19- NE*. [unknown]
foster[1.1] /ˈfɔstər/ n 1 an adopted child *18-19, 20- N*. 2 a foster-child *16-17*. 3 a home-bred animal *e17*. [OE *fōstorcild*]
foster[1.2] /ˈfɔstər/ v 1 to bring up a child, nurture *la14-*. 2 to promote, encourage *la14-*. 3 *of a mother* to feed, nourish; to suckle *la14, la19- Sh Ork N NE*. **fosterer,** †**fostar** a foster-parent, a nurturer *la15-*. [OE *fōstran*]
†**foster**[2] n a foster-parent, a nurse *16-17*. [OE *cildfēstre* a children's nurse]
†**fosterschip** n the office of forester *16-e17*. [Older Scots *foster* a forester, with abstract noun-forming suffix]
†**fostery** n = FOSTERSCHIP *la15*. [Older Scots *foster* a forester, with abstract noun-forming suffix]
fosy see FOZIE[1.2]
fot, foat /fɔt, fot/ n a footless stocking used as a gaiter *19- SW Bor*. **fottie** a baby's bootee *la19- Bor*. [unknown]
fotch /fɔtʃ/ v to shift position; to turn *17-19, 20- literary*. [variant of FITCH[2]]
fotch see FESH
fother[1.1] /ˈfɔðər/ n 1 hay or straw for feeding livestock, fodder *la15-*. 2 food *la16-*. [OE *fōdor*]
fother[1.2] /ˈfɔðər/ v 1 to feed livestock with hay or straw *18-*. 2 to feed a person or animal *19-*. [see the noun]
†**fotmell, fodmell, fadmel** n a weight or quantity of lead *15-16*. [OE *fōtmǣl* a foot-measure]
fottie see FOT

fou¹, †**fow** /fu/ *n pl* also **foos**, **foose** the houseleek *Sempervivum tectorum 17-19*, *20- NE*. **fooit**, †**fuet**, †**fouat** the houseleek *19- C Bor*. [unknown]

fou²·¹, **fu**, **full**, †**fow** /fu, ful, fʌl/ *n* **1** the fill of a container; a full load *la16-*. **2** one's fill, enough to satisfy one *la19-*. **3** a herring full of milt or roe *la19- Sh Ork N NE EC*. **4** a firlot, a bushel *la17-e19*. **5** a quantity of pans or small boxes *16-e17*. [see the adj]

fou²·², **foo**, **full** /fu, ful, fʌl/ *v pt, ptp* **fullt**, **fult**, **fulled**, †**fu'd 1** to fulfil *la15-*. **2** to fill; to load *la16-*. **fuller** a filler, a funnel *la19- NE T*. [see the adj]

fou²·³, **fu**, **full**, †**fow**, †**ful** /fu, ful, fʌl/ *adj* **1** filled to capacity, full *la14-*. **2** complete, perfect, absolute *la14-*. **3** full of food, well-fed *la15-*. **4** drunk, intoxicated *16-*. **5** proud, pompous, conceited *la19-*. **6** *of a herring* full of milt or roe, sexually mature *la19- Sh Ork N EC*. **7** comfortably well-off, well-provided for *19, 20- SW Bor Uls*. **full bench** a sitting of the High Court of Justiciary or of the Inner House of the Court of Session consisting of more than the quorum required for the hearing of criminal appeals generally *la19-*. **full handit** having the hands full; having enough *16-19, 20- NE*. **fou as a puggie** extremely drunk *20-*. **fou as a wulk** very drunk or full of food *la19-*. **a fou man's leavins** a very small portion of food left by someone who can eat no more *19, 20- Ork N T*. **full slap** at full speed *20-*. **ower fou hauden** too well provided for; too well off *la18- Bor*. [OE *full*]

fou²·⁴, **fu**, **full**, †**fow** /fu, ful, fʌl/ *adv* very, exceedingly; completely, perfectly *la14-*. [see the adj]

†**fouat**, **fowat** *n* a cake baked with butter and raisins, similar to black bun *16-e19*. [OFr *fouace* a cake baked in the ashes]

fouchle *see* FAUCHLE¹·²

foud, †**fold**, †**fowde** /fʌud/ *n* **1** an official in Shetland and Orkney acting as a sheriff, steward or bailiff *la15-19, 20- historical*. †**foudrie**, **fauderie**, **fowdrie** the district or office of a FOUD *la16-e19*. [Norw *foged*, ON *foguti*]

foud *see* FOWD

foughten *see* FECHT¹·²

fouk *see* FOWK

foul, **fule**, **fool**, †**fowle** /fʌul, ful/ *adj* **1** loathsome, vile *la14-*. **2** dirty, unwashed *15-*. **3** infected with plague *la16-17*. **4** guilty of an offence *15-16*. **foulness**, †**fulnes 1** a foul condition, filth *la14-*. **2** *mining* an impurity or irregularity in a seam *la19, 20- EC*. **foul-farren** dirty, untidy; nasty, unpleasant *18- literary*. †**foul fa**, **foull fall** may evil befall *15-e19*. **the Foul Thief** a nickname for the Devil *la18-*. [OE *fūl*]

foul *see* FOOL

foule *see* FUIL¹·¹

foulsome *see* FOUSOME

foumart, **fumart**, *WC SW* **thoumart**, †**fowmart**, †**fulmart**, †**thummart** /'fumərt; *WC SW* 'θumərt/ *n* **1** the ferret *Mustela putorius furo* or weasel *Mustela nivalis*, or the polecat *Mustela putorius 15-*. **2** a term of abuse for a person *16-*. [OE **fūl meard* foul marten]

†**found** *v* to travel, make one's way *la14-16*. [OE *fundian*]

found *see* FOOND¹·¹, FOOND¹·²

†**foundatour**, **fundatour** *n* a founder *la15-17*. [Lat *fundātor*]

founder *see* FOONDER¹·¹, FOONDER¹·²

foundin *see* FIND¹·²

foundit, **foondit** /'fʌundɪt, 'fundɪt/ *n* the slightest thing *19, 20- N SW*. **not a foundit** not a thing *19, 20- N SW*. [shortened form of Scots *not a confounded*]

fountain *see* FUNTAIN

four *see* FOWER

fourme *see* FURM

fourt, **foort**, **fort**, †**fowrt**, †**feird**, †**ferd** /fʌurt, furt, fort/ *adj* fourth *la14-*. **fourtie** a quarter of the regulation barrel, a firkin (of salt herring) *20- NE*. †**the ferd corne** a measure of grain *la15-16*. †**the ferd penny** one penny in every four *16*. [OE *fēorþa*]

†**fourteen**¹·¹ *n* a fourteen-shilling piece *la17-e18*. [see the numeral]

†**fourteen**¹·², **fourtene** *adj* fourteenth *la15-17*. [see the numeral]

fourteen¹·³, **fowerteen**, †**fourtene** /'fortin, for'tin, 'fʌutin, fʌuər'tin/ *numeral* the cardinal number after thirteen *la14-*. **fourteent**, †**fourteint** fourteenth *16-*. [OE *fēowertýne*]

fourtht *see* FURTH¹·²

fourty *see* FORTY¹·¹, FORTY¹·²

†**fous**¹·¹, **fows**, *n* a (defensive) ditch *la15-e17*. [compare FOUSSIE¹·¹]

†**fous**¹·², **fowse** *v* to furnish with a ditch *la15-16*. [compare FOUSSIE¹·²]

fousome, **foosome**, **fusome**, *WC SW* **foulsome**, †**fowsum**, †**fulsum** /'fusəm; *WC SW* 'fʌulsəm/ *adj* **1** dirty, filthy; loathsome *la14-*. **2** *of food* cloying, nauseating; filling, over-rich *17-19, 20- Sh NE T WC*. [conflation of ME *fulsom* full, abundant with FOUL]

foussie¹·¹, **fowsie** /'fusi, 'fʌuzi/ *n* a (defensive) ditch, a moat *16-19, 20- historical*. [OFr *fossé*; compare FOUS¹·¹]

†**foussie**¹·², **fowsie** *v* to provide or surround with a moat or ditch *la16-e17*. [OFr *fossé* a ditch; compare FOUS¹·²]

fousticait, **fousticat** *see* FOO

foustie /'fusti/ *n* a kind of large, thick floury bread roll *20- T*. [shortened form of *fustean skon* (FUSTIAN)].

foustie *see* FOOSTY

fouter *see* FOOTER¹·¹, FOOTER¹·²

fouth, **fowth**, †**fulth** /fuθ, fʌuθ/ *n* abundance, plenty; an ample supply *la14-*. **fouthie**, **fouthy** abundant, prosperous *19-*. **at fouth** in abundance, fully, copiously *16-e17*. [FOU²·³, with noun-forming suffix]

foutie *see* FOOTIE

fow¹·¹ /fʌu/ *n* **1** a pitchfork *la15-19, 20- NE SW Bor*. **2** a kick or kicking movement *la19- NE*. [unknown]

fow¹·² /fʌu/ *v* **1** to lift or toss straw or hay with a pitchfork *19- NE SW Bor*. **2** to kick in a restless manner *la19- NE*. [unknown]

fow *see* FOO, FOU¹, FOU²·¹, FOU²·³, FOU²·⁴

fowat *see* FOUAT

fowd, **foud** /fʌud/ *n* withered vegetation; worn-out thatch; broken down sods previously used for building or roofing *la18- NE*. [Gael *fòd* a turf]

fowde, **fowdrie** *see* FOUD

fower, **fowre**, **four**, †**foir** /'fʌuər, fʌur, for/ *numeral* the cardinal number after three *la14-*. **fowersie**, **foursy** a group of four stones or marbles which have to be picked up while another is thrown in the air in a game of chuckies *la19-*. **fowersome**, **foursome 1** a group of four people or things *la15-*. **2** *golf* a match consisting of four players, with two on each side *la19-*. **3** = *foursome reel 20-*. **fourtie** a quarter of the regulation barrel, a firkin (of salt herring) *20- NE*. **fourareen**, **fowereen**, †**four airing** a four-oared boat *la16- Sh Ork*. **fower fittit**, †**four futtit** having four feet *16-*. **four hours 1** a snack eaten in the late afternoon *17-*. **2** four o'clock in the afternoon *16-e17*. **four neukit**, **four nooked**, †**four nukit** four-cornered *la15-*. **four quarters**, **fower quarters 1** personal influence *la18-19, 20- literary*. **2** the body, the person *la18*. **foursome reel** a reel danced by four people *la18-*. **the four posts o misery** the four-posted hand-loom (from the poor living it provided in competition with industrial looms) *19, 20- historical*. †**on four half about**, **on the four halfis about** in the surrounding neighbourhood *15-e17*. **upon yer fowers** on all fours *la19-*. [OE *fēower*]

fowerteen *see* FOURTEEN[1.3]

fowertie *see* FORTY[1.1]

fowk, folk, *Sh Ork* **fock,** †**fouk** /fʌuk, fok; *Sh Ork* fɔk/ *n* **1** people, the human race *la14-*. **2** family members, relatives; a community or group of people *la14-*. **3** the inhabitants of a place *15-*. **4** servants, employees *18-*. **5** two or more individual people: ◊*here's twae folks come frae Glasgow18-*. **6** human beings as opposed to animals or supernatural beings *19, 20- Ork NE SW*. **ferm fowk** the workers on a farm *20- NE EC SW*. [OE *folc*]

fowle *see* FOOL, FOUL

fowmart *see* FOUMART

fownk *see* FUNK[2]

fowre *see* FOWER

fowrt *see* FOURT

fows *see* FOUS[1.1]

fowse *see* FOUS[1.2]

fowsie *see* FOUSSIE[1.1], FOUSSIE[1.2]

fowsum *see* FOUSOME

fowth *see* FOUTH

fox /fɔks/ *n* a red bushy-tailed animal *Vulpes vulpes la14-*. **fox-fit 1** the creeping buttercup *Ranunculus repens 20- EC Bor*. **2** the fir clubmoss *Huperzia selago* or *Lycopodium clavatum 19- Bor*. †**foxter-leaves, foxtrie leaves, fochsterrie leavis** the leaves of the foxglove *Digitalis purpurea 17-e19*. [OE *fox*]

foy[1] /fɔi/ *n* a farewell drink or feast; a party to celebrate a special occasion *la15-*. †**drink yer foy** to toast someone's farewell *18-e19*. [MDu *foye*, *voye* a celebration of a departure, MFr *voie* a journey]

foy[2] /fɔi/ *interj* an expression of dismissal or reproof *19, 20- NE*. [variant of Eng *fie*]

foylȝe *see* FULZIE[1.1]

foyn *see* FAE[1], FUNȜE[2]

foysoune *see* FUSHION

foze *see* WHEEZE[1.1], WHEEZE[1.2]

fozie[1.1] /ˈfozi/ *n* a person with learning difficulties *20- T EC*. [see the adj]

fozie[1.2], **fosy, fozzie,** *H&I* **foozie,** †**fozzy** /ˈfozi, ˈfɔzi; *H&I* ˈfuzi/ *adj* **1** *of people* unintelligent, stupid *18-*. **2** *of fruit or vegetables* soft, spongy *la18-*. **3** *of people and animals* fat, out of condition *la18-*. **4** *of rope* ragged, frayed *18- NE*. **foziness 1** sponginess *19-*. **2** flabbiness *19-*. **3** stupidity *19-*. [Du *voos* spongy, porous + -IE[2]]

fozle *see* WHEEZE[1.1], WHEEZE[1.2]

fozzie, fozzy *see* FOZIE[1.2]

F.P. *see* FREE PRESBYTERIAN

†**fra, frae** *adv* away *la14-17*. **to and fra** back and forth *la14-17*. [ON *frá*]

fra *see* FAE[2.1], FAE[2.2]

fraacht *see* FRAUCHT[1.1]

fra'at, †**frithat** /frat, frəˈat/ *adv* for all that, nevertheless *la18-19, 20- NE*. [shortened form of Scots *for all that*]

fraca, fracaw /ˈfraka, frəˈka, frəˈkɔ/ *n* **1** a fuss, a bother *19-*. **2** an intimate friendship; a warm affection *la19- NE EC*. [Fr *fracas*]

fracht *see* FRAUCHT[1.1], FRAUCHT[1.2]

frack *see* FRECK

fraction /ˈfrakʃən/ *n* **1** a fragment or small part; a share; a section *18-*. **2** a proportional payment for horses used for military service; a certain number of people required to provide and pay a leader of horse *la17*. [EModE *fraction*]

frae *see* FAE[2.1], FAE[2.2], FRA, FROE[1.1]

frael *see* FRAIL[1]

†**fraer, frear, frayar** *n* a basket (of figs, dates or almonds) *14-17*. [altered form of *frael* (FRAIL[1])]

fraesta *see* FRESTA

fraik[1.1], **frake** /frek/ *n* **1** flattery; affectionate fussing *19-*. **2** a flatterer, a wheedler *la19- T EC SW*. **3** a weak, delicate person; a spoilt over-protected child *la19- Sh Ork*. **4** a slight or imaginary ailment *20- Ork T*. **5** a whim, a capricious change; an odd notion *la16-e19*. **fraikie, fraiky** coaxing, wheedling *19- Ork N NE T*. **frixie** a fuss *20- N*. **mak a fraik** to make a fuss *19-*. [see the verb]

fraik[1.2], **freck** /frek, frɛk/ *v* **1** to flatter, wheedle, cajole *19- Ork T EC*. **2** to make a fuss of; to pet or pamper *19- Ork T EC*. **3** to pretend to be ill; to make a fuss about a minor ailment *20- Ork T*. **freksit, frekkid** spoilt, peevish *la19- Sh Ork*. [perhaps from Eng *freak*]

frail[1], †**frael** /frel/ *n* **1** a container with a circular wooden frame and a sheepskin bottom, used for winnowing corn *20- EC SW Bor*. **2** a rush-basket *e15*. [ME *fraiel*; compare FRAER]

frail[2] /frel/ *n* a flail *19- EC Bor*. [altered form of FLAIL]

Frainch *see* FRENCH

†**fraine, frane, frayn** *v* to ask for; to enquire about *la14-16*. [OE *fregnan*, ON *fregna*]

frainesy *see* FRENZY

fraise *see* PHRASE[1.1], PHRASE[1.2]

frait *see* FREIT

fraith *see* FREITH[1.2]

fraized /frezd/ *adj* astonished, startled *19- Bor*. [conflation of FAIZE[2] with RAISE[1.2]]

†**frak** *v* to move swiftly *e16*. Compare FRECK. [OE *frec*, *fræc*]

frak *see* FRECK

frake *see* FRAIK[1.1]

fram[1.1] /fram/ *adj* seaward, far out at sea; far off *la19- Sh*. [ON *fram* forward, outward]

fram[1.2] /fram/ *adv* out to sea, seawards *19- Sh*. [see the adj]

frame[1.1] /frem/ *n* **1** a supporting structure, a framework *la16-*. **2** an emaciated person or animal *la19-*. **3** a square or hoop of wood hung from the shoulders on which to carry pails *la19- Ork N NE*. **4** an instrument of torture, the rack *la14-e15*. [see the verb]

frame[1.2] /frem/ *v* to construct, devise, contrive; to shape or form *la16-*. [OE *framian* to do good, bring about benefit, ON *frama* to further]

frame *see* FREMIT[1.2]

franazy *see* FRENZY

France, Franche *see* FRENCH

frandie /ˈfrandi/ *n* a small hay-rick or corn-rick *19- T EC*. [unknown]

frane *see* FRAINE

frank /fraŋk/ *adj* **1** open, sincere, straightforward *la15-*. **2** willing, eager, ready *la18-19, 20- N T*. [ME *frank*]

†**Frankis** *adj* Gaulish *e15*. [Lat *Francus*]

†**franktenement** *n* freehold *la14-e17*. **frank tenementar** a freeholder *la15-16*. [AN, OFr *franc tenement*; compare FRANK, TENEMENT]

fratch /fratʃ/ *v* to quarrel, argue, dispute *19- SW Bor*. [ME *fracchen* to make a harsh or strident noise; to creak]

fraucht[1.1], **fracht, fraacht** /frɔxt, fraxt/ *n* **1** the commercial transport of goods, a ship's cargo *la15-*. **2** as much as can be transported by one person, a load or burden *18-*. **3** the hire of a boat; the fare or freight charge for transport by water *la14-19, 20- N H&I WC*. **4** a large amount, a plentiful supply *la18- NE*. **5** a number or quantity *la15-17*. †**frauchtisman** a person who loads a ship *15-16*. [Ger *Fracht*, MDu, MLG *vracht*]

fraucht[1.2], **fracht** /frɔxt, fraxt/ *v* **1** to load a ship with cargo *15-19, 20- NE*. **2** to hire a boat *la16-18*. **3** to transport by water *15-16*. †**frauchtar** a person who loads a ship *la16-17*. **fraughted**, †**fraughtit** loaded, burdened, weighed down *16-19, 20- NE*. [see the noun]

fraud, †**frawd** /frɔd/ *n* (criminal) deception; deceitfulness; insincerity; trickery *15-*. **fraudful**, †**fraudfull** fraudulent; given to practising fraud *15-19, 20- Uls*. †**fraudfully** fraudulently *la14-e19*. [ME *fraude*]

Fraunce *see* FRENCH

frawart[1.1], †**fraward**, †**frawerd** /ˈfrawərt/ *adj* contrary, perverse; adverse, unfavourable *la14-19, 20- literary*. [FRA, with adj-forming suffix with the sense of having a specified direction]

†**frawart**[1.2] *prep* away from *15-e16*. [see the adj]

frawd *see* FRAUD

fray[1.1] /fre/ *n* **1** fighting; an attack, a brawl *15-*. **2** a noise, a fuss, a stir *la16-*. **3** (a state of) fear or alarm; a fright *la14-e19*. **4** a noise made to raise an alarm *16-17*. [aphetic form of AFFRAY[1.1]]

†**fray**[1.2] *v* **1** to alarm, frighten; to scare away *la14-e19*. **2** to be afraid *16-e17*. **frayed, frayit** afraid, frightened *la15-19*. [see the noun]

fray *see* FAE[2.1]

frayar *see* FRAER

Frayday *see* FRIDAY

frayn *see* FRAINE

fre *see* FAE[2.1], FREE[1.2], FREE[1.3]

frear *see* FRAER

freat *see* FREET[2]

freath *see* FREITH[1.1], FREITH[1.2]

freche *see* FRESH[1.3]

†**freck, frack, frak** *adj* **1** bold, eager, impetuous *la15-e19*. **2** able-bodied, vigorous, active *la18-19*. Compare FREKE. **frakly** boldly, eagerly *la14-e17*. [OE *frec* bold, greedy]

freck *see* FRAIK[1.2]

Freday, Fredday *see* FRIDAY

fredome *see* FREEDOM

free[1.1] /fri/ *v* **1** to set at liberty; to rescue; to relieve of a burden or restriction; to exempt *15-*. **2** to place beyond suspicion: ◊*I widna free her tae play a trick on him 19- Sh NE*. **3** *in hide-and-seek* to put out of the game by reaching 'home' first *20-*. [OE *frēogan*]

free[1.2], *Bor* **frei**, †**fre** /fri; *Bor* fre/ *adj* **1** not in subjection, at liberty; unrestricted, unobstructed *la14-*. **2** liberal, generous *15-*. **3** not requiring to be paid for; without financial cost *la15-*. **4** *of days between a summons and a trial* clear, noninclusive *17-*. **5** ready or willing (to do something) *la18-*. **6** *of baked goods* brittle, crumbly *la18-*. **7** single, unmarried *18-19, 20- NE T EC*. **8** guiltless, not subject to any charge or accusation *la16, la19- Sh*. **9** *of a person* enjoying the privileges and rights of a burgess *la15-19, 20- historical*. **10** *of good or noble character or birth la14-e19*. **11** *of stone* easily cut or hewn *16-e19*. **freelins** somewhat, rather, quite *20- NE*. **free coal** coal which breaks or burns easily *19-*. **free forest** a forest in which the hunting rights were granted to the proprietor by the Crown under charter *15-19, 20- historical*. **free forester** a person who was granted or claimed the rights of *free forest*; latterly a person who poached in deer forests *la19- historical*. **freeholder, †frehaldar 1** a person who possesses a freehold estate *15-*. **2** *law* a person who could elect or be elected a member of Parliament by virtue of holding lands direct of the Crown assessed at or over forty shillings (prior to the 1832 Reform Act) *18-e19*. **freeliving** self-indulgent *19, 20- Sh NE EC Uls*. †**fre money** surplus or ready money *la15-16*. **free port** a port open to all traders for loading and unloading their vessels *la16-*. †**frie prisoun** imprisonment without fetters or with the privilege of going out temporarily *la15-17*. †**fre tailʒe** stone which can be cut easily *la14-e16*. **free teinds** that part of the tithe of a parish not yet allocated to a minister's stipend *18-19, 20- historical*; compare UNEXHAUSTED TEINDS. **free tenant** a lessee who enjoyed all the rights and privileges of a feudal vassal or tenant-in-chief *la14-17, 18- historical*. **free trade 1** unrestricted trade *la17-*. **2** smuggling *19-*. †**frie ischew and entrie** = *free ish and entry 16-17*. **free ish and entry** *law* the right or means of access to or from property; egress *15-*. †**that fre** that woman *la14-16*. [OE *frēo*]

free[1.3], †**fre** /fri/ *adv* freely *la14-*. [see the adj]

Free[1.4] /fri/ *n* **1** the Free Church of Scotland; the United Free Church of Scotland *la19-*. **2** a member of one of the free churches *la19-*. Compare WEE FREE. [see the adj]

Free Church of Scotland /fri tʃʌrtʃ əv ˈskɔtlənd/ *n* **1** a name adopted by the body which broke away from the Established Church at the Disruption of 1843 *19-*. **2** a name applied to the minority which refused to enter the union with the UNITED PRESBYTERIAN CHURCH in 1900 *20-*. Compare FREE KIRK. [FREE[1.3] + CHURCH + SCOTLAND]

freedom, †**fredome** /ˈfridəm/ *n* **1** liberty; the state of being free *la14-*. **2** an exemption or immunity attached or pertaining to lands, corporations or burghs *la14-*. **3** permission *19-*. **4** a piece of common land allotted by certain communities to their members *la18-e19, la19- historical*. **5** the area over which the immunities of a burgh extended *la15-17*. **6** full membership of a merchant guild or trade incorporation; liberty to engage in business or trade as a member of an incorporation *15-17*. [OE *frēodōm*]

Free Kirk /ˈfri kɪrk/ *n* **1** a name adopted by the body which broke away from the Established Church at the Disruption of 1843 *19-*. **2** a name applied to the minority which refused to enter the union with the UNITED PRESBYTERIAN CHURCH in 1900 *20-*. Compare FREE CHURCH OF SCOTLAND, WEE FREE. **Free-kirker** a member of the Free Kirk *la19-*. [FREE[1.3] + KIRK[1.1]]

†**freely**[1.1], **frely** *adj* noble, handsome *la14-18*. [OE *frēolic*]

freely[1.2], †**frely**, †**frelie** /ˈfrili/ *adv* **1** in a free manner, without constraint *la14-*. **2** entirely, completely, fully *la15-*. [OE *frēolice*]

freend[1.1], **freen, friend**, †**frende**, †**freynd**, †**freyind** /frind, frin, frɛnd/ *n* **1** a person with whom one has a close relationship, a friend *la14-*. **2** a relative, a kinsman *15-*. †**frendful, freindfull** friendly *la14-16*. **friendlyk** *adj* friendly *15-16*. **friendlyk** *adv* in a friendly way *e16*. **freendship, friendship**, †**frendschip**, †**frenschip 1** the relationship between friends; friendly relations *la14-*. **2** kinship; kindred, a group of friends *la15-e17*. **be friends to** to be related to *la19, 20- NE Uls*. **be friends with** = *be friends to*. [OE *frēond*]

†**freend**[1.2], **friend, frend** *v* **1** to befriend *e19*. **2** to join in friendship; to reconcile *15-e17*. [see the noun]

freenge, fringe, †**freinge**, †**frenʒe**, †**frenʒie** /frɪndʒ, frɪndʒ/ *n* a decorative border (with tassels), a fringe *la15-*. [ME *frenge*]

Free Presbyterian /fri prɛzbəˈtiriən/ *n* a member of the body which seceded from the FREE CHURCH OF SCOTLAND in 1892 *la19-*. **F.P.** = FREE PRESBYTERIAN. [FREE[1.2] + PRESBYTERIAN[1.1]]

freer *see* FRIAR

freest, freist, friest /frist/ *n* frost *la19-*. [altered form of FROST[1.1]]

freestane, freestone, †**fre stane** /ˈfristen, ˈfriston/ *n* (a block of) an easily worked sandstone *16-*. [FREE[1.2] + STANE[1.1]]

freet[1] /frit/ *n* milk products; butter or cheese *19- N*. [extended sense of FRUIT]

freet², †**frete**, †**freat**, †**freit** /frit/ v **1** to fret; to be vexed *la16-*. **2** to rub or chafe; to injure or damage *la14-19, 20- EC*. [OE *fretan* to devour, eat voraciously]
freet *see* FREIT
†**freeth, frethe, freith** v **1** to free or release from a claim or obligation *la14-e18*. **2** to set free, liberate *15-e17*. **3** to free or absolve oneself *la16-e17*. [OE *friþian* to free, keep in peace]
freeth *see* FREITH¹·¹
freevolous /ˈfrivələs/ adj frivolous *19-*. [Lat *frīvolus*; compare FRIVOLE]
freff /frɛf/ adj shy; cold, distant *la19- EC Bor*. [probably altered form of THARF]
frei *see* FREE¹·²
freid *see* THREID¹·¹
freik *see* FREKE
freinge *see* FREENGE
freist *see* FREEST
freit, freet, frait, †**frete** /frit, frɛt/ n **1** a superstitious belief, observance or act *15-*. **2** an omen *18-*. **3** a whimsical notion, a fad *la18-*. **4** a superstitious saying, an adage *19-*. **freitie, freety** strongly believing in superstition *18-19, 20- EC*. **stand on fraits** to be fussy or difficult *la18-19, 20- N*. [unknown]
freit *see* FREET²
freith¹·¹, freeth, †**freath** /friθ, frið/ n **1** froth, foam, lather *la18-19, 20- SW Bor*. **2** a hasty wash given to clothes *19, 20- H&I WC SW*. [see the verb]
freith¹·², **freath**, †**fraith** /friθ, frið/ v **1** to foam, froth *la18-19, 20- T C SW*. **2** to work up into a froth; to make a lather *18-19, 20- literary*. **3** to swill clothes quickly through soapsuds *19- SW*. [OE *āfrēoþan*, ON *freyða*]
freith *see* FREETH
†**freke, freik, frek** n **1** a man *la15-e17*. **2** a warrior; a champion *la14-e16*. Compare FRECK. [OE *freca*]
frelie *see* FREELY¹·²
frely *see* FREELY¹·¹, FREELY¹·²
fremd /frɛmd/ n *fisherman's taboo* a human head *19- Sh*. [Norn *fremd* a fish-head, a projection]
fremit¹·¹, fremmit, fremd, fremt, frem /ˈfrɛmɪt, frɛmd, frɛmt, frɛm/ n a stranger, a foreigner; a person who is not kin *la14-*. **the fremit, the fremmit,** *Sh* **da fremd 1** strangers, foreigners *la16-*. **2** the wider world *20-*. [see the adj]
fremit¹·², fremmit, fremd, fremt, frem, †**fremmyt,** †**frame** /ˈfrɛmɪt, frɛmd, frɛmt, frɛm/ adj **1** strange, unfamiliar, foreign; unrelated *la14-*. **2** estranged; distant, aloof *16-e19*. **3** unusual, uncommon *la15-e17*. †**fremmitlie, fremmytly** strangely, in a strange or unfriendly way *la15-16*. **fremitnes, fremmitnes** strangeness, unfamiliarity; unfriendliness *la15-*. [OE *fremede*]
French, Frainch, †**Franche,** †**France,** †**Fraunce** /frɛntʃ, frɛntʃ/ adj **1** of or relating to France *15-*. **2** Gaulish *e16*. †**franchly** after the French fashion *e16*. **French cake** a small iced and decorated sponge cake *20-*. **French loaf 1** a long, thin loaf *20-*. **2** a loaf made from dough containing a small quantity of fat and sugar and shaped so as to give a heart-shaped slice *20-*. **Frenchman,** †**Franche man 1** a man from France *15-*. **2** a man from Gaul *15-e17*. **French peerie** a humming top *19, 20- C*. **French and English** a boys' game *la19- Ork N EC*. [OE *frencisc*]
frend *see* FREEND¹·²
frende *see* FREEND¹·¹
frenesy *see* FRENZY
frenʒe, frenʒie *see* FREENGE
frenzy, *Bor* **frainesy,** †**frenesy,** †**franazy** /ˈfrɛnzɪ; *Bor* ˈfrɛnəze/ n **1** rage, madness; wild excitement; furious activity *la14-*. **2** a sudden illness; feverishness *20- Ork Bor*. [OFr *frenesie*]
frequent¹·¹, †**frequant** /friˈkwɛnt/ v **1** to visit often or habitually *la15-*. **2** to associate or keep company with; to meet up with *17-*. **3** to exercise or practise regularly *la15-16*. **4** to be accustomed to *la16-e17*. [Lat *frequentāre*]
frequent¹·² /ˈfrikwənt/ adj **1** often repeated, recurring, habitual *16-*. **2** abundant, numerous *16-*. **3** *of an assembly* crowded, full; well-attended *la16-17*. **frequently,** †**frequentlie 1** often, repeatedly *la16-*. **2** in large numbers *17*. [Lat *frequens*]
frere *see* FRIAR
fres, fresche *see* FRESH¹·³
frese *see* FRIZZ
fresh¹·¹ /frɛʃ/ n **1** (the setting in of) a thaw, a period of open weather *18-*. **2** the upper part of an estuary (containing fresh water); an influx or stream of fresh water *18-*. [see the adj]
fresh¹·² /frɛʃ/ v **1** to thaw *19, 20- NE T*. **2** to pack herring in ice ungutted (for consumption as fresh) *20-*. **fresher** a herring-buyer who packs fish in ice ungutted, for consumption as fresh *20-*. [see the adj]
fresh¹·³, †**fresche,** †**fres,** †**freche** /frɛʃ/ adj **1** new, novel, not previously known *la14-*. **2** *of food* not stale or preserved; *of water* not salty *15-*. **3** *of a person* sober, recovered from a drinking bout *18-*. **4** *of weather* not frosty; thawing *la18-*. **5** *of animals* thriving, fattening *20- EC SW Bor*. **freshly,** †**freschlie** afresh *la14-*. [ME *fresh*]
fresh¹·⁴ /frɛʃ/ adv freshly, afresh *15-*. [see the adj]
frest *see* FRIST¹·¹
fresta, †**fraesta** /ˈfrɛsta/ interj a polite request *19- SW Bor*. [unknown]
fre stane *see* FREESTANE
frete *see* FREET², FREIT
frethe *see* FREETH
freuch, *Sh* **froch** /frux; *Sh* frɔx/ adj dry and brittle, liable to break *la15-19, 20- Sh NE*. [unknown]
freuchan /ˈfruxən/ n the toecap of a boot *19- N NE H&I*. [Gael *fraochan*]
Freuchie /ˈfruxi, ˈfrui/ n a village in Fife *18-*. **gae tae Freuchie** to get lost; to go away; to lose oneself *19- T C*. **gae tae Freuchie and fry mice** = *gae tae Freuchie*. [Gael *fraoch* + *-in* suffix, place of heather]
frevoll *see* FRIVOLE
freyind, freynd *see* FREEND¹·¹
friar, freer, †**frere** /fraeər, frir/ n **1** *Roman Catholic Church* a brother in or member of a religious order *la14-*. **2** pl a friary *la14-16*. †**friar's chicken** a soup made with veal, chicken and beaten eggs *la18-e19*. [ME *frer*]
fricht¹·¹, fright /frɪxt, frʌɪt/ n fear, a sudden terror or alarm *17-*. **frichtsome, frightsome** fearful, terrifying *la18-*. **nae frichts** no fear *la19, 20- EC*. [OE *fyrhtu*]
fricht¹·² /frɪxt, frʌɪt/ v to frighten, terrify *18-*. **frichtit for** afraid of *18-*. [OE *fyrhtan*]
frichten /ˈfrɪxtən/ v to frighten *la19-*. **frichtened for** frightened of *la19-*. [FRICHT¹·¹, with verb-forming suffix]
Friday, *NE* **Freday,** †**Fryday,** †**Frayday,** †**Fredday** /ˈfrʌɪde; *NE* ˈfrede/ n **1** the day of the week before Saturday and after Thursday *la14-*. **2** *in the North-East* a hiring market held on a Friday *la19*. **Friday penny, Friday's penny** children's pocket-money *la19- NE*. [OE *frīgdæg*]
†**friddon, firdoun** v to warble *16-e17*. [MFr *fredonner* to ornament a phrase of music by modulation]
friend *see* FREEND¹·¹, FREEND¹·²
frie prisoun *see* FREE¹·³
friest *see* FREEST
fright *see* FRICHT¹·¹
frill *see* FRULL

frimse /frɪms/ *n* a display of disdain or peevishness *la19- Sh*. [unknown]

fringe *see* FREENGE

frisel *see* FRIZZLE

†**frist**[1.1], **first**, **frest** *n* **1** delay, respite *la14-e18*. **2** the allowing of time for payment; credit *la15-16*. [OE *first* a space of time]

†**frist**[1.2] *v* **1** to sell goods on credit *15-e19*. **2** to give a person extra time to pay a debt; to extend credit *la15-e19*. **3** to delay or allow to be delayed; to suspend or postpone *la15-17*. [see the noun]

frith *see* FIRTH[1]

frithat *see* FRA'AT

†**frivole**, **frevoll**, **fruell** *adj* **1** frivolous, of little account or worth *la15-e17*. **2** fickle, unreliable *la15-16*. **3** frail, brittle *la15*. [MFr *frivole*, Lat *frīvolus*]

frixie *see* FRAIK[1.1]

frizz, †**frese** /frɪz/ *v* **1** *of cloth* to fray or wear out *20- NE EC Bor*. **2** to put a nap on cloth *e16*. [MFr *friser*]

frizzle, **frisel**, †**frizzel** /ˈfrɪzəl/ *n* **1** the steel used for striking fire from a flint *17-19, 20- EC SW Bor*. **2** the hammer of a flintlock pistol or gun *18-19*. [perhaps MDu *vierijzer*; compare FLEERISH]

fro *see* FAE[2.1], FROE[1.1]

froad *see* FROTH[1.1], FROTH[1.2]

froak *see* FROCK

froath *see* FROTH[1.1], FROTH[1.2]

froch *see* FREUCH

frock, **froak**, †**frog** /frɔk, frok/ *n* **1** a woman's dress *la16-*. **2** a sailor's or fisherman's knitted jersey or guernsey *19- Sh Ork NE*. **3** a short oilskin coat or cape *20- Sh N EC*. **4** a coat, a cloak; a tunic or smock *la14-19*. [ME *frok*]

frock *see* THROCK

froe[1.1], **fro**, **froh**, *SW Bor* **froo**, *Bor* **frae** /fro; *SW Bor* fru; *Bor* fre/ *n* froth, foam *la18-*. **froh milk** a mixture of cream and whey beaten up and sprinkled with oatmeal *20- NE T*. **frostick** a whisk made of wood and cows' hair *la19, 20- NE*. [probably altered form of FROTH[1.1]]

froe[1.2] /fro/ *v* to froth, foam; to bubble *la18-19, 20- NE T EC Bor*. [see the noun]

frog[1] /frɔg/ *n* a colt, a male horse from one to three years old *19- NE*. [unknown]

frog[2] /frɔg/ *n* an amphibian *Rana temporaria 16-*. **frogs mooth 1** the monkey flower or mimulus, a plant of the family *Phrymaceae la19- EC SW Bor*. **2** the wild snapdragon *Antirrhinum majus la18-19, 20- Sh*. [OE *frogga*]

frog *see* FROCK

froh *see* FROE[1.1]

froist *see* FROST[1.1]

froith *see* FROTH[1.1]

†**fronsit**, **frosnit** *adj* wrinkled *la15*. [ME *frouncen* to wrinkle + -IT[2]]

front, †**frunt** /frʌnt/ *n* **1** the anterior or foremost part *la14-*. **2** the front line of an army *la14-*. **3** the forehead *la14-19*. **frontyways**, **frontieweys** with the front end first *la20-*. **front-breist** the front seat in the gallery of a church *20-*. **front-door flat** a ground-floor flat with direct access to the street *20-*. **the front** the front garden *la19-*. **in front of 1** *of place* positioned before *19-*. **2** *of time* before, prior to *20- Sh NE EC*. [ME *frount*, Lat *frons* the forehead]

†**frontale** *n* **1** a covering for the front of an altar *la15-16*. **2** a curtain for a bed *16*. [ME *frountel*]

frontier, †**fronter**, †**fronteir** /ˈfrʌntɪr/ *n* the border of a country *16-*. [ME *frounter*]

froo *see* FROE[1.1]

froon[1.1], **froun**, **frown** /frun, frʌun/ *n* a furrowing of the brow *19-*. [see the verb]

froon[1.2], **froun**, **frown** /frun, frʌun/ *v* to wrinkle the brow; to frown *la16-*. [ME *frounen*]

frosin *see* FROZEN

frosnit *see* FRONSIT

frost[1.1], †**froist** /frɔst/ *n* **1** frozen dew or vapour; extreme cold *la14-*. **2** ice *la16-19, 20- Sh Ork NE T EC*. **frosty** covered in frost; affected by frost; frozen; extremely cold *la15-*. **frost nail** a special nail used in a horse's shoe to give grip on ice or frozen ground *16-*. **find frost** to run into self-created difficulties *18-19, 20- Ork*. **it is frost** it is freezing, there is frost *la18-*. [OE *forst*]

frost[1.2] /frɔst/ *v* **1** to protect a horse from slipping on ice by using frost nails in its shoes *16-*. **2** to cover with frost; to become frosty; to freeze *la18-*. [see the noun]

†**frostar** *n* a forester *la14-e17*. [variant of *forester* (FOREST)]

froth[1.1], **froath**, *Sh* **froad**, †**frothe**, †**froith** /frɔθ, froθ; *Sh* frod/ *n* foam, froth; bubbles *la15-*. †**froath stick** a whisk made of wood and cows' hair *e18*. [ON *froða*]

froth[1.2], **froath**, *Sh* **froad** /frɔθ, froθ; *Sh* frod/ *v* **1** to foam, froth *20-*. **2** to whisk into a foam *20-*. **3** to wash in soapsuds *la19*. [see the noun]

frothe *see* FROTH[1.1]

frothy *see* FURTHIE

froun *see* FROON[1.1], FROON[1.2]

frow /frʌu/ *n* a big buxom woman *la18-19, 20- NE T*. [Du *vrouw* a woman]

frowdie /ˈfrʌudi/ *n* an old woman's cap, with a seam at the back *19, 20- literary*. **frowdie mutch** = FROWDIE *la19- NE T EC*. [FROW + -IE[1]]

frown *see* FROON[1.1], FROON[1.2]

froyt *see* FRUIT

frozen, †**frosin** /ˈfrozən/ *adj* freezing cold; turned to ice *la15-*. **frozened** frozen *la19- Ork T C SW*. [ptp of ME *fresen*]

fruct *see* FRUIT

fructuous, †**frutuus** /ˈfrʌktjuəs/ *adj* abounding in fruit, fruitful; profitable, beneficial *la15-*. [ME *fructuous*, Lat *fructuōsus*]

fruell *see* FRIVOLE

frugal, *WC* **througal** /ˈfrugəl; *WC* ˈθrugəl/ *adj* **1** sparing, meagre; thrifty, economical *la18-*. **2** kindly, hospitable, generous *la18-19, 20- Sh N NE*. [Lat *frūgālis*]

fruit, †**frut**, †**fruct**, †**froyt** /frut/ *n* **1** the edible product of a plant or the land; a crop *la14-*. **2** revenue accrued from the produce of the land *15-*. **3** result, benefit, profit *la15-*. **4** offspring *16-*. [ME *fruit*, Lat *frūctus*]

fruitman /ˈfrutmən/ *n* a dealer in fruit *17-*. [FRUIT + MAN]

frull, **frill** /frʌl, frɪl/ *n* an ornamental edging, a frill *19-*. [unknown]

frump[1.1] /frʌmp/ *n* a sulk, a bad mood *18-*. [unknown]

frump[1.2] /frʌmp/ *v* **1** to be fretful or peevish *20- Sh*. **2** to rumple *20- Sh*. [unknown]

frumple /ˈfrʌmpəl/ *v* to crease, crumple *19, 20- NE T EC Bor*. [perhaps MDu *verrompelen*, compare ME *frumpel* a wrinkle, a fold]

frunt *see* FRONT

†**frusch**[1.1] *n* **1** fragments, splinters *e19*. **2** a crashing noise; the crash of breaking weapons *la14-15*. **3** a violent rush, a charge *la14*. [ME *frush*]

†**frusch**[1.2], **frush** *v* **1** to shatter; to smash to pieces *la14-e19*. **2** to drive back an army *la14-e16*. [ME *frushen*]

frush[1.1] /frʌʃ/ *n* **1** a frothy jet, a squirt; a hiss; a splutter *20- Sh*. **2** a sudden outburst of anger *la20- Sh*. [see the verb]

frush[1.2] /frʌʃ/ *v* **1** to splutter, spurt or froth *la19- Sh*. **2** *of an angry cat* to hiss or spit *20- Sh*. [Norw dial *frusa*]

frush² /frʌʃ/ *adj* **1** *of pastry* crisp, short, crumbly *18-*. **2** *of soil* crumbly, loose *18-*. **3** *of wood or vegetable matter* brittle, decayed, rotten *la18-*. **4** *of cloth* frayed, apt to disintegrate *la18-*. **5** frank, bold, rash *la18-19, 20- NE*. **6** tender, frail; easily hurt or destroyed *19- literary*. [probably FRUSCH¹·¹]
frush see FRUSCH¹·²
†**fruster**¹·¹ *v* to frustrate; to come to nothing; to render useless *16*. [MFr *frustrer*, Lat *frustrāri* to deceive]
†**fruster**¹·² *adj* ineffective, useless *la15-e16*. [see the verb]
frut see FRUIT
frutuus see FRUCTUOUS
fry¹·¹ /frae/ *n* **1** a state of worry or distraction, a disturbance *la18-*. **2** a number of fish for frying, sufficient for a meal (presented as a gift) *la19-*. **3** a quantity of food for frying; a meal of fried food *la20-*. [see the verb]
fry¹·² /frae/ *v* **1** to cook in fat in a shallow pan *16-*. **2** to be painfully hot or inflamed *16-*. **frying pan** a shallow pan for frying *la14-*. [OFr *frire*]
Fryday see FRIDAY
fryne /frʌɪn/ *v* to grumble, whine *la18-19, 20- SW*. [compare Norw dial *fryna* to wrinkle up one's nose, make a wry face]
†**frythe** *v* to fry; to burn with rage *la18-19*. **frything pan** a frying pan *17-e18*. [FRY¹·²]
fu see FOO, FOU²·¹, FOU²·³, FOU²·⁴
-fu, -ful, †-full /fu, fə, ful, fəl/ *suffix* **1** indicating fullness, or having a capacity for (something) *la14-*. **2** indicating the quantity contained when full *la14-*. [*fu* (FOU²·³)]
fucher see FICHER¹·¹, FICHER¹·²
fuck, †fukk /fʌk/ *v offensive* to have sexual intercourse *16-*. [perhaps related to Du *focken* to mock]
fud¹·¹ /fʌd/ *n* **1** the tail of an animal, especially of a hare or rabbit *18-*. **2** the female genitals or pubic hair *19-*. **3** the buttocks *18-19, 20- N WC SW Bor*. **4** *offensive* a term of abuse for a person *la20-*. **fuddie** *n* **1** *fisherman's taboo* a rabbit *20- EC*. **2** a hare *19*. **fuddie** *adj* **1** *of an animal* short-tailed *la19-*. **2** *of a person* short, stumpy *la19, 20- Ork*. **3** *of an object* thick, squat *la19, 20- Ork*. [compare Icel *fuð* the genitals of a female animal, Norw *fud* the buttocks]
fud¹·² /fʌd/ *v* **1** to frisk about; to walk briskly *la18-19, 20- NE*. **2** *of an animal* to whisk the tail *19*. [see the noun]
fu'd see FOU²·²
fudder see FUTHER, WHITHER¹·² WHIDDER¹·¹, WHIDDER¹·²
fuddle /'fʌdəl/ *v* **1** to get drunk *la18-*. **2** to drink the proceeds of; to spend time drinking *19, 20- literary*. [unknown]
fude, fuid, food /fud/ *n* nourishment, sustenance, food *la14-*. **2** a person, a child *la14-e16*. [OE *fōda*]
fudge see FODGE
fuet see FOU¹
fuff¹·¹ /fʌf/ *n* **1** a puff or gentle gust of wind; a whiff *16-*. **2** the hiss or spit of a cat *19-*. **3** a sudden outburst of temper, a huff *19-*. **fuffy** short-tempered, impatient *la19, 20- Bor*. [onomatopoeic]
fuff¹·² /fʌf/ *v* **1** to emit smoke or vapour (in puffs) *16-*. **2** to puff, blow; to breathe hard *la16-*. **3** *of a cat* to spit, hiss *la17-*. **4** to fly into a temper; to go off in a huff *la18-*. **5** to smoke a pipe; to blow smoke (from a pipe or up a chimney) *la18-*. **6** *of a hen* to puff its feathers out or up *20- Sh Ork NE*. **7** to sniffle as if about to cry *19, 20- EC*. [see the noun]
fuff¹·³ /fʌf/ *interj* an expression of annoyance or contempt *19-*. [see the noun]
fuffle¹·¹ /'fʌfəl/ *n* fuss, commotion; violent exertion *19- SW Bor*. [frequentative form of FUFF¹·¹]
fuffle¹·² /'fʌfəl/ *v* **1** to dishevel, ruffle; to disarrange clothing *19, 20- N NE EC Bor*. **2** to walk awkwardly, shuffle; to fumble or be clumsy *20- Sh N WC SW*. †**fuffiling** rough moving about *e16*. [see the noun]

fufty see FIFTY
fuggle /'fʌɡəl/ *n* **1** a small bundle of hay or grass; a bundle of rags (used to stop up a hole) *la19- NE T*. **2** an unburnt plug of tobacco in a pipe, the dottle *20- NE*. [compare Norw dial *fugge* a small bundle]
fugie¹·¹ /'fjudʒi, 'fudʒi/ *n* **1** a runaway, a fugitive; a coward *la18-*. **2** a truant; an absentee *la19- N NE*. **3** a challenge to fight *la19, 20- historical*. **4** a runaway cock (from a cockfight) *la18-19*. **fugie-warrant** *law* a warrant issued by a sheriff to a creditor to apprehend a debtor on sworn information that he intends to leave the country *19, 20- H&I*. [perhaps FUGITIVE¹·¹, FUGITOUR or Lat *fugiō* I flee]
fugie¹·² /'fjudʒi, 'fudʒi/ *v* **1** to play truant *la19- N NE SW*. **2** to take flight, back away *19, 20- NE*. [see the noun]
fugie¹·³ /'fjudʒi, 'fudʒi/ *adj* cowardly *19- EC Bor*. [see the noun]
fugitate /'fjudʒətet/ *v ptp* **fugitate, fugitated** *law* to declare a fugitive from justice; to outlaw, banish *la17-19, 20- historical*. **fugitation 1** *law* a judicial sentence declaring a person a fugitive from justice, with confiscation of moveable property for failing to appear in court on a criminal charge *18-e20, la20- historical*. **2** flight, the act of fleeing *19*. [Lat *fugitāt-*, ptp stem of *fugitāre* to flee]
fugitive¹·¹ /'fjudʒətɪv/ *n* a person fleeing from the law; a runaway *la14-*. [see the adj]
fugitive¹·² /'fjudʒətɪv/ *adj* **1** fleeing from justice *la14-*. **2** exiled *la15-18*. †**decern and adjudge fugitive** *law* to outlaw; to pronounce a sentence of fugitation on *la17-e19*. [ME *fugitif*, Lat *fugitīvus*]
†**fugitour** *n* a fugitive *15-16*. [Lat *fugitor*]
fuid see FUDE
fuil¹·¹, **fule, fool**, *Ork* **feul**, *N NE* **feel**, †**fole**, †**foule**, †**full** /ful/; *Ork* føl; *N NE* fil/ *n* **1** a person lacking in wisdom, a foolish person *la14-*. **2** a person with learning difficulties *15-*. **3** a jester *la15-*. **fools and bairns shouldnae see things half done** judgements should not be made on anything until it has been completed *la20-*. [ME *fol*]
fuil¹·², **fool**, †**fule** /ful/ *v* **1** to dupe, trick *la18-*. **2** to mess around; to behave in a flippant manner *19-*. **3** to act foolishly *la14*. [see the noun]
fuil¹·³, **fule, fool**, *Ork* **feul**, *N NE* **feel** /ful/; *Ork* føl; *N NE* fil/ *adj* foolish, silly *la14-*. **fule-like**, *NE* **feel-like** foolish *19- NE C SW*. **feuly, feulie** foolish *20- Ork*. **as feel as a maik watch** completely silly *20- NE*. [see the noun]
fuilish, foolish, fuilitch, *NE* **feelish**, †**fulische** /'fulɪʃ, 'fulɪtʃ; *NE* 'filɪʃ/ *adj* lacking wisdom, foolish *15-*. [FUIL¹·¹, with adj-forming suffix]
fuiltachs, fuilteachs see FUTTICK
fuilzie see FULZIE¹·¹
fuird¹·¹, **foord, ford**, *NE* **feerd**, *NE* **fyoord**, †**furd** /furd, fɔrd; *NE* fird; *NE* fjurd/ *n* a shallow crossing-place in a river or stream; frequently in place-names *la11-*. [OE *ford*]
fuird¹·², **foord, ford**, *NE* **feerd** /furd, fɔrd; *NE* fird/ *v* to wade across a river or stream at a ford *18-*. [see the noun]
fuirday /'furde/ *n* **1** the earlier part of the day, the morning, the forenoon *19, 20- SW Bor*. **2** the later part of the day *16-e19*. **3** broad daylight *18-e19*. [unknown; compare ME *forth daies* late in the day, and FORE¹·²]
Fuirsday see THURSDAY
fuish, fuishen see FESH
fuist, fuisted see FOOST¹·²
fuit see FIT¹·¹
fukk see FUCK
ful see FOU²·³
-ful see -FU
fule see FOUL, FUIL¹·¹, FUIL¹·², FUIL¹·³

fulische *see* FUILISH
full *see* FOU²·¹, FOU²·², FOU²·³, FOU²·⁴, FUIL¹·¹
-full *see* -FU
fulla *see* FELLAE
fullalie *see* FULLELY
fulled *see* FOU²·²
†**fullely, fullily, fullalie** *adv* fully *la14-16*. [**full** (FOU²·³), with adv-forming suffix]
fuller *see* FOU²·²
fullet *see* FILLET
fullie *see* FULLY
fullily *see* FULLELY
fullt *see* FOU²·²
fully, fullie /ˈfule/ *adv* **1** completely, entirely *la14-*. **2** somewhat, slightly *19-*. [OE *fullīce*]
fullyery, †**fulȝery** /ˈfuljere/ *n* foliage *16, 20- literary*. [OFr *fueillier*]
fulmar /ˈfulmər/ *n* a seabird *Fulmarus glacialis* of the petrel species, originally recorded as breeding in St Kilda but now more widespread *la17-*. [Gael *fulmar*, ON *fúll* foul + *már* gull, because of its offensive smell]
fulmart *see* FOUMART
fulp *see* WHALP¹·¹, WHALP¹·²
fulsum *see* FOUSOME
fult *see* FOU²·²
fulth, filth, †**fylth** /fʌlθ, fɪlθ/ *n* **1** obscenity *la14-*. **2** foul matter, repulsive dirt *15-*. [OE *fȳlþ*]
fulth *see* FOUTH
fulthy, filthy, *Sh Ork N* **filty,** †**filthie** /ˈfʌlθe, ˈfɪlθe; *Sh Ork N* ˈfɪlti/ *adj* dirty, foul; disgraceful, vile, disgusting *16-*. **as filthy as the Earl o Hell's waistcoat** very dirty *la20-*; compare *black as the Earl o' Hell's waistcoat* (BLACK¹·²). [FULTH + -IE²]
fulye *see* FULZIE²
fulyie *see* FULZIE¹·¹
fulȝe *see* FULZIE¹·¹, FULZIE¹·², FULZIE²
fulȝery *see* FULLYERY
fulzie¹·¹, fuilzie, †**fulyie,** †**fulȝe,** †**foylȝe** /ˈfulji, ˈfulzi/ *n* filth, dirt, garbage; dung, excrement *la14-19, 20- Bor*. [unknown]
fulzie¹·², †**fulȝe** /ˈfulji/ *v* **1** to defile, pollute *16-17, 18- literary*. **2** to trample underfoot; to beat down; to overcome *la15-16*. †**fulȝeit** worn out, exhausted *16*. [ME *foilen*]
†**fulzie², fulȝe, fulye** *n* **1** a leaf of a plant or tree *la15-e19*. **2** gold leaf *la15-e19*. [OFr *fueille*]
fum¹ /fʌm/ *n* **1** a wet or spongy peat or turf *la19- WC SW Uls*. **2** *derogatory* a useless person; a large or dirty person *la19- WC SW Uls*. [unknown]
fum² /fʌm/ *n* a disagreeable smell *la19- EC SW Bor*. [unknown]
fumart *see* FOUMART
fumble *see* FUMMLE¹·²
fummle¹·¹ /ˈfʌməl/ *n* the act of fumbling; a botched job *la18-*. [see the verb]
fummle¹·², fumble, †**fummyll** /ˈfʌməl, ˈfʌmbəl/ *v* to handle clumsily or ineffectually; to grope about *16-*. **fummler,** †**fumler** a fumbler *16*. [Ger *fummeln*]
fummle *see* WHUMMLE¹·²
fummyll *see* FUMMLE¹·²
fumper *see* WHIMPER¹·¹
fun *see* FIND¹·², WHIN¹, WHIN²
funabeis *see* FOO
funceless *see* FUNSELESS
funcy *see* FANCY
fund *see* FIND¹·², FOOND¹·²
fundatour *see* FOUNDATOUR

fundeit *see* FUNDY
fundin *see* FIND¹·²
fundir *see* FOONDER¹·²
fundit *see* FUNDY
†**fundlin, fundling, funlin** *n* a foundling *la14-19*. [ptp of FIND¹·², with noun-forming suffix]
†**fundy, funnie** *v* to suffer a chill; to become stiff with cold *la14-18*. **fundyit, fundeit, fundit** chilled; sensitive to cold *la16-e19*. [OFr *enfondre*]
funeral¹·¹, *Bor* **fooneral** /ˈfjunrəl; *Bor* ˈfunərəl/ *n* the ceremony associated with the burial or cremation of the dead *la16-*. **funeral cairn** a cairn to mark resting places for the pallbearers on the way to the graveyard *19- H&I*. **funeral letter** an invitation by letter to a funeral *la19-*. [EModE *funeral*]
funeral¹·², †**funerale** /ˈfjunərəl/ *adj* associated with a funeral *la15-*. [ME *funeral*]
fung /fʌŋ/ *adv* forcibly, violently; with a whizzing movement *la18- NE*. Compare FUNK¹·². [onomatopoeic]
fung *see* FUNK¹·¹, FUNK¹·²
fungible /ˈfʌndʒɪbəl/ *n law* consumable goods; a perishable commodity which may be estimated by weight, number or measure *la17-*. [Lat *rēs fungibilēs*]
funk¹·¹, fung /fʌŋk, fʌŋ/ *n* **1** a blow from a hand or foot; a cuff, a kick *la18-19, 20- NE EC SW*. **2** a throw, a toss *19, 20- NE*. **3** a bad temper; a huff, a tantrum *19- Sh SW*. **4** a whizzing or whooshing noise *la19- NE H&I*. **5** a state of excitement or enthusiasm; a commotion *la19*. †**funkie** apt to take offence, petulant *la19- WC*. **like fung** violently, vehemently *la19- WC*. [onomatopoeic]
funk¹·², fung /fʌŋk, fʌŋ/ *v* **1** *of a restive horse* to kick; to throw up the legs *18-19, 20- NE T EC Bor*. **2** to strike with the hands or feet *19, 20- NE T*. **3** to throw violently and abruptly; to toss or fling *19, 20- NE T*. **4** to fly at high speed (with a buzzing noise); to whizz along *19, 20- NE T*. **5** to fly into a temper or rage; to sulk *la19- NE*. **funker** an animal that kicks *19, 20- NE Bor*. **lat fung, let fung** to throw violently *20- NE*. [see the noun]
funk², N fownk /fʌŋk; *N* fʌuŋk/ *n* thick smoke; a strong smell *la19- Sh Ork N*. [OFr *fungier, funkier* to raise smoke]
funlin *see* FUNDLIN
funnie *see* FUNDY
funny /ˈfʌne, ˈfʌni/ *n* a game of marbles, played for fun, where no score is kept and all winnings are restored to the loser *la19-*. [from the Scots adj *funny*]
funseless, funceless /ˈfʌnsləs/ *adj* dry and sapless; without flavour or substance *20- N*. [unknown]
funtain, fountain, †**funtane,** †**fontane,** †**fontayne** /ˈfʌntən, ˈfʌuntən/ *n* a natural spring; a source; a fountain *la15-*. [ME *fountain*]
†**funȝe¹, fonȝeis** *n* (the fur of) the beech marten *Martes foina la14-e16*. [OFr *foine*]
†**funȝe², fuyn, foyn** *v* to fence; to make thrusts with a pointed weapon *la14-e16*. [unknown]
fup *see* WHUP¹·¹, WHUP¹·²
fupperty jig /ˈfʌpərte dʒɪg/ *n* a trick, a dodge *19- NE*. [nonsense formation]
fur *see* FOR¹·¹, FURR¹·¹
†**furch** *n* the hindquarters of a deer *16-17*. [MFr *forche* anything that is forked]
furd *see* FUIRD¹·¹
furder *see* FORDER¹·¹, FORDER¹·⁴
†**fure** *v* **1** to carry, convey (by sea) *la14-e17*. **2** to bear, endure *la15-16*. **furing, foording 1** transporting by sea *la15-e18*. **2** the cargo of a vessel *16-e17*. **3** the amount of

cargo allowed to a mariner for his own business use *e17*. [compare Du *voeren*]

fure *see* FARE¹⁻², FURR¹⁻¹

furght *see* FURTH¹⁻²

furious¹⁻¹, *NE* **feerious**, †**furyus** /ˈfjurɪəs; *NE* ˈfiːrɪəs/ *adj* **1** raging, full of fury *la15-*. **2** extraordinarily good, excellent *la19- NE*. **3** *law* insane; given to violent outbursts *la15-19*.
†**furiosity, furiosite** *law* insanity *la15-19*. [ME *furious*]

furious¹⁻², *NE* **feerious** /ˈfjurɪəs; *NE* ˈfiːrɪəs/ *adv* exceedingly, very *19- NE*. [see the adj]

Furisday *see* THURSDAY

furisine *see* FLEERISHIN

furl *see* WHURL¹⁻¹, WHURL¹⁻²

furlie-fa *see* WHIRLIWHA¹

furlie-majigger, furly-giggy /fʌrliməˈdʒɪgər, fʌrliˈgɪgi/ *n* a whirligig; a cheap ornament; a piece of machinery or equipment (that revolves or has wheels) *la19- NE*. [compare WHIRLIGIG, Eng *thingamajig*]

furligig *see* WHIRLIGIG

furlot *see* FIRLOT

furly-giggy *see* FURLIE-MAJIGGER

furm, form, *Sh Ork T* **firm**, †**furme**, †**fourme** /fʌrm, fɔrm; *Sh Ork T* fɪrm/ *n* **1** shape, appearance; pattern, style *la14-*. **2** a long bench *15-*. [ME *forme*, Lat *forma*]

furn /fʌrn/ *v* to coagulate and form a mouldy deposit *20- Ork*. [probably ON *fyrnast* to grow old, decay]

furnish, †**furnis**, †**fornes**, †**furneis** /ˈfʌrnɪʃ/ *v* to provide; to supply; to equip *la15-*. **furnisher**, †**furnessar** a provider, a supplier *16-*. **furnishing**, †**furnessing 1** materials, supplies *la15-*. **2** the action of supplying *16-*. †**furnisment** provisioning *la16-e17*. [ME *furnishen*]

†**furour, furon** *n* fury *la15-16*. [AN *furour*, Lat *furor*]

furr¹⁻¹, fur, *N* **fure** /fʌr; *N* fur/ *n* **1** a furrow; a strip of earth turned over by a plough *15-*. **2** a small piece of ground *15-*. **3** a land-drainage trench *18-19, 20- Sh Ork H&I*. **4** a single ploughing; a turning over of the earth with a spade *18-19, 20- Ork NE Bor*. **5** a deep furrow or trench separating one rig or one garden bed from another *la18-19, 20- Sh Ork NE*. **furr ahin**, †**fur-ahin** the horse in a team immediately in front of the plough on the right-hand side *la18- WC*. **fur-beast** = *furr ahin 19-*. **fur-horse** = *furr ahin 19-*. **one fur ley** grassland after its first ploughing *18-19, 20- WC*. [OE *furh*]

furr¹⁻² /fʌr/ *v* **1** to make drills for sowing seeds; to earth up potatoes *18- Sh EC SW*. **2** to plough; to furrow *la18-19, 20- NE SW*. [see the noun]

furrier, †**furriour**, †**furrour** /ˈfʌrɪər/ *n* a dealer in or dresser of furs *la15-*. [MFr *fourreur*, OFr *forreor*]

furriour *see* FORAYER, FURRIER

furrit *see* FORRIT¹⁻¹, FORRIT¹⁻², FORRIT¹⁻³

furrour *see* FURRIER

furrow /ˈfʌro/ *n* **1** a trench separating ridges in ploughing *la17-*. **2** the earth turned over by a plough *la18-*. [OE *furh*]

furrow *see* FORRAY¹⁻¹, FORRAY¹⁻³

Furry Boots City /ˈfʌri buts sɪti/ *n* a nickname for the city of Aberdeen *la20-*. [jocular formation based on local pronunciation of WHAUR¹⁻¹ + ABOOT¹⁻¹ + city]

furst *see* FIRST¹⁻¹, FIRST¹⁻²

furt *see* FURTH¹⁻²

furth¹⁻¹ /fʌrθ/ *n* the outdoors, the open air *la19, 20- NE T*. **the furth** out of doors, in the open; away from home *19, 20- NE*. [see the adv]

furth¹⁻², **forth**, *Sh* **furt**, †**furght**, †**fourtht**, †**foorth** /fʌrθ, forθ; *Sh* fʌrt/ *adv* **1** forwards; onwards; outwards *la14-*. **2** outside, out of doors, in(to) the open air *18-19, 20- Sh NE T*. **3** out *la14-17*. †**furth-bering 1** personal bearing, conduct *la15-e16*. **2** carrying out, discharging *e16*. †**furthbok** to vomit *e16*. †**furthborn** carried forth *e16*. †**furth bring** to bring forth, produce *la14-16*. †**furth bringing** the act of carrying forth (a corpse for burial) *la15-16*. **furthcoming** *n law* an action which the arrester of property must bring against the arrestee in order to obtain possession of property to be seized for debt *la17-*. **furthcoming, †furthcummand** *adj* ready to be produced when required *15-*. †**furthfill** to fulfil *la16-17*. **furthga'in** the feast given at a bride's departure from her parents' home; a wedding entertainment *19- NE T*. †**furthganging** going out *e16*. †**furthgif** to give out; to pronounce (a decision) *la15-16*. †**furthgo** to go out *la15-e17*. †**furthpas** to go out, depart *la14-16*. †**furthputting 1** the exercising of authority *la15-e16*. **2** eviction *la15-16*. †**furthrin** to run out, elapse or expire *16*. †**furthschaw** to display or exhibit *la14-16*. †**furthschet** shut out, excluded *e16*. †**furthseik** to seek or search out *la16*. †**furthset** to put forward or promote *la16*. †**furthsprede** to spread out *e16*. †**furth sprent** outstretched; spread out *e16*. †**furthstreke** to stretch forth *e16*. †**furthʒet, furtheyet** to pour forth *e16*. †**do furth** to carry out, perform *la14-15*. **furth of 1** out of, away from; beyond the confines or limits of *la15-*. **2** out of the revenues of, at the expense of *la16-e19*. [OE *forþ*]

furth¹⁻³ /fʌrθ/ *prep* out of, from; outside *18-*. **furth the gait** *adj* candid, honest, straightforward *la19- NE*. **furth the gait** *adv* candidly, honestly, straightforwardly *la19- NE*. [see the adv]

Furth /fʌrθ/ *n* a mountain in England or Wales of Munro height (above 3000 feet) *la20-*. [FURTH of Scotland]

further *see* FORDER¹⁻¹, FORDER¹⁻², FORDER¹⁻³, FORDER¹⁻⁴

furtherlie *see* FORDER¹⁻³

furthermair *see* FORDER¹⁻⁴

furthest *see* FARDEST¹⁻¹, FARDEST¹⁻²

furthie, *NE* **frothy**, †**forthy** /ˈfʌrθi; *NE* ˈfroθi/ *adj* **1** bold; energetic; impulsive *15-*. **2** generous, hospitable, liberal *18-19, 20- C*. **3** producing or reproducing plentifully *la19, 20- Ork*. **4** frank, friendly, affable *18-19*. [FURTH¹⁻² + -IE²]

furthir *see* FORDER¹⁻²

furthwart *see* FORTHWART¹⁻¹, FORTHWART¹⁻²

fury /ˈfjuri/ *n* **1** rage; frenzy *16-*. **2** *law* violent insanity *17*. [MFr *furie*, Lat *furia*]

furyus *see* FURIOUS¹⁻¹

fush *see* FISH¹⁻¹, FISH¹⁻²

fushach *see* FUSSOCH

fusher *see* FISHER

fushion, fusion, fooshion, *Sh* **föshin**, †**fusioun**, †**foysoune**, †**fusoun** /ˈfuʃən, ˈfuʒən; *Sh* ˈføʃən/ *n* **1** the nourishing or sustaining element in food or drink *17-*. **2** physical strength or energy; bodily sensation *18-*. **3** mental or spiritual force or energy; strength of character, power *18-*. **4** abundance, plenty *la14-e16*. [ME *foisoun*]

fushionless, fusionless, *Sh* **föshinless** /ˈfuʃənləs, ˈfuʒənləs; *Sh* ˈføʃənləs/ *adj* **1** *of people* physically weak, without energy or stamina *18-*. **2** *of people* faint-hearted; lacking initiative or ability *19-*. **3** *of plants* without sap or pith; dried, withered *19-*. **4** *of food* lacking in nourishment; tasteless, insipid *19-*. **5** *of actions, writing or speech* without substance; dull, uninspired *19-*. **6** *of objects* without strength or durability; weak from decay *19-*. [FUSHION, with adj-forming suffix]

fushloch, fushnach *see* FUSSOCH

fusht *see* WHEESHT¹⁻⁴

fusion *see* FUSHION

fusionless *see* FUSHIONLESS

fusioun *see* FUSHION

fusker /ˈfʌskər/ *n* facial hair, a whisker; a moustache *la18- NE T EC.* [altered form of Eng *whisker*]

fuskie *see* WHISKY

fusome *see* FOUSOME

fusoun *see* FUSHION

fusper[1.1] /ˈfʌspər/ *n* a whisper *20- NE.* [altered form of WHUSPER[1.1]]

fusper[1.2] /ˈfʌspər/ *v* to whisper *20- NE.* [see the noun]

fussle *see* WHUSTLE[1.1], WHUSTLE[1.2]

fusslebare *see* WHUSTLE[1.2]

fussler *see* WHUSTLER

fussoch, *NE* **fushach**, *SW* **fushnach**, *SW* **fushloch** /ˈfʌsəx; *NE* ˈfʌʃəx; *SW* ˈfʌʃnəx; *SW* ˈfʌʃləx/ *n* **1** the grass that grows in stubble; waste fragments of straw or grass *19, 20- NE SW*. **2** a loose, untidy bundle of something *la19- NE.* [diminutive form of Eng *fuss, fuzz* loose fluffy matter].

fussy /ˈfʌsi/ *adj* **1** overly fastidious *19-*. **2** affected in dress or manner, overly dressy *20- NE T EC Bor.* [Eng *fuss* + -IE[2]]

fustian, †**fustean** /ˈfʌstiən, ˈfʌstʃən/ *n* a kind of thick cloth *la14-*. †**fustian scone**, **fustean skon** a kind of large, thick, white and floury bread roll originally containing oatmeal (probably so called from its coarse texture) *16-e19*. Compare FOUSTIE. [ME *fustian*]

fut *see* FIT[1.1], FIT[1.2]

fut bal, **fut baw** *see* FITBA

fute *see* FIT[1.1], FIT[1.2]

futeball *see* FITBA

†**futher**, **fudder**, **fidder** *n* **1** a large number of people, a company *16-e19*. **2** a cartload *15-17*. **3** a quantity of lead *la15-16*. **peat-futherer** a person who carried peat for door-to-door sale *19*. [OE *fōþer* a load, a cartload]

futher *see* WHIDDER[1.2]

futie *see* FOOTIE

futles *see* FITLESS

futley bealin *see* WHITTLE[2]

futret, **futrat**, **whitret**, *Sh* **whitrit**, *NE* **futteret**, *Uls* **whiteret**, †**quhitret**, †**fittret**, †**quhitred** /ˈfʌtrət, ˈmɪtrət; *Sh* ˈmɪtrɪt; *NE* ˈfʌtərət; *Uls* ˈmɪtərət/ *n* **1** an animal of the genus *Mustela*, mainly the weasel, stoat or ferret *15-*. **2** a small, thin, sharp-featured person *19-*. **whitterick** a restless or furtive person; a small child *la19-*. **whittrock**, **whitrick** a weasel, stoat or ferret *20-*. [ME *whitrat* a white rat]

futtick /ˈfʌtɪk/ *n pl* **fuiltachs**, †**fuilteachs** a period of time falling at least partly in February (often stormy and sometimes seen as predicting the weather later in the year) *19, 20- NE*. [Gael *faoilteach* the last fortnight of January and the first of February, usually a period of stormy weather]

futtle *see* WHITTLE[1.1], WHITTLE[1.2]

fuyn *see* FUNƷE[2]

fuzzie, **fizzy** /ˈfʌzi, ˈfɪzi/ *adj* effervescent, hissing, fizzing *19-*. [onomatopoeic]

fwaill *see* FEWALE

fwt *see* FIT[1.1]

fy, †**fye** /fae/ *interj* **1** an expression of disgust, indignation or reproach *15-19, 20- historical*. **2** an emphatic exclamation of agreement or disagreement *la19- NE T*. **3** an exclamation inciting a person to hurry *la17-19*. **fy ay** indeed yes *20- NE T.* **fie na** indeed not *la19- NE T.* [ME *fi*]

fy *see* WHEY

fyaacht *see* FECHT[1.1]

fyaak *see* FAIK[1.1], FAIK[1.2]

fyachle *see* FAUCHLE[1.2]

†**fyall**, **fyell** *n* a finial *16-e17*. [OFr *fiole*]

fyauch *see* FAUCH[1.2]

fyauchie *see* FAUCHIE

fyawk *see* FAIK[1.1], FAIK[1.2]

fycht *see* FECHT[1.2]

fycket *see* FYKE[1.2]

fye *see* FY, WHEY

fyell *see* FYALL

fyft *see* FIFT

fyften *see* FEIFTEEN[1.1]

fyftene *see* FEIFTEEN[1.2]

fyift *see* FIFT

fyir *see* FIRE[1.1], FIRE[1.2]

fyk *see* FYKE[1.2]

fyke[1.1], **fike** /fʌɪk/ *n* **1** a fuss or bustle; commotion or excitement *18-*. **2** a whim, a fad *18-*. **3** (an act or state of) restlessness, fidgeting *la18-*. **4** trouble, worry; a petty care *la18-*. **5** an amorous dalliance, a flirtation *la18-*. **6** a trivial piece of work *19-*. **7** a fussy, fastidious person *20- C SW Bor.* **fykerie** fuss, over-fastidiousness *19- Sh T WC.* **the fykes 1** a mood of restlessness; a state of fidgeting *19, 20- N T*. **2** itchiness (of the anus) *la16-e18*. **mak a fyke** to make a fuss *la18-*. [see the verb]

fyke[1.2], **fike**, *Sh* **fik**, †**fyk**, †**feik** /fʌɪk; *Sh* fɪk/ *v pt* †**fycket 1** to move about restlessly; to fidget *16-*. **2** to exert oneself; to work laboriously; to take trouble over *18-*. **3** to bustle about or fiddle around; to make a fuss about nothing *la18-*. **4** to be anxious or troubled *19, 20- C.* **5** to trouble or vex; to cause pain *la16-19*. [ON *fíkjast* to be eager or restless]

fyke-fack /ˈfʌɪkfak/ *n pl* **fyke-facks**, †**ficks facks 1** an inconsequential or fiddly piece of work; a small domestic job *la16-*. **2** a trivial fuss *la18- NE*. **3** a whim, a contrary mood *e19*. [reduplicative compound from FYKE[1.1]; compare Du *fik-fak* unnecessary fuss]

fykie, **fikey** /ˈfʌɪki/ *adj* **1** fussy, finicky, overly fastidious *19-*. **2** restless, fidgety *19-*. **3** *of a task* tricky, troublesome; difficult to manage *19-*. [FYKE[1.1] + -IE[2]]

fyle /fʌɪl/ *v pt, ptp* †**filit** †**fyllit**, †**fyld 1** to make dirty; to soil or defile; to infect *la14-*. **2** to debauch; to defame or dishonour *la14-*. **3** to defecate; to soil with excrement *16-*. **4** to find guilty; to convict or blame *la15-18*. **5** to allow land to become overgrown with weeds *15-e16*. †**fyle a bill** to find the charge made in a bill justified and the accused guilty *la16*. **fyle the fingers** to soil the hands *la18-19, 20- NE T H&I C.* †**file my thumb** = *fyle the fingers la18*. **fyle the stamach**, **fyle the stomach** to upset the stomach *19, 20- NE H&I C Bor.* [OE *fȳlan*]

fyles *see* WHILES[1.1]

fylth *see* FULTH

fynale *see* FEENAL

fynans *see* FINANCE

fynd *see* FIND[1.2]

fyne *see* FINE[1.1], FINE[1.2]

fyngar *see* FINGER

fynnak *see* FINNOCK

fynys *see* FEENISH[1.2]

fyoord *see* FUIRD[1.1]

fyow *see* FEW[1]

fyr *see* FIR

fyre *see* FIRE[1.1], FIRE[1.2]

fyrne, **fyrryn** *see* FIR

fyrst *see* FIRST[1.1], FIRST[1.2]

fyrth *see* FIRTH[2]

fyschare *see* FISHER

fysche *see* FISH[1.2]

fyve, **fywe** *see* FIVE

G

g' *see* GAE

ga, gaa, gaw, gall /ga, gɔ, gɔl/ *n* **1** bile; the gall-bladder *la14-*. **2** a disease of cattle *la19- Sh*. **gaa bursen** breathless *la19- Sh NE*. **ga girse, gaa girse** stonewort *Chara vulgaris*, at one time boiled and given to cattle as a cure for disease *la19- Sh*. **gaa sickness** a disease of cattle *la19- Sh*. [OE *gealla* gall, bile]

ga *see* GAE

gaa *see* GA, GAW[1.1]

†**gaady, gaude** *n* one of the larger beads on a rosary; a bead *16-e18*. [Lat *gaudium* joy]

gaain *see* GAE

gaa-knot, gal-knot /'ga nɔt, 'gal nɔt/ *n* a knot tied in such a manner as to make it difficult to unloosen *la19- Sh Ork*. [Norw dial *gald* hard ground + KNOT[1.1]]

gaan, gan /gɑn, gan/ *v* to stare, gaze, gawp *la19- Sh Ork*. [ON *gana*]

gaan *see* GAE

gaapus *see* GAWPUS

gaar *see* GAR[2]

gaase, †**garse** /gaz/ *v* to compel, force *la19- Sh*. [probably voiced variant of CAUSE[1.2]]

gaat *see* GAUT

gaave /gav/ *n Scottish Travellers* a large village; a town *20- SW Bor*. [Romany *gav* a village]

gaavlo *see* GOLACH

gab[1.1] /gab/ *n* **1** speech, conversation; manner of speaking *la18-*. **2** light entertaining talk, chat; cheek *la18-*. **3** a talkative person, a chatterbox, a gossip *19-*. **gabbie** *n* a chatterbox, a gossip *18-*. **gabbie** *adj* garrulous, chatty; fluent *18-*. **gabbit** talkative, gossipy *18-19, 20- Sh SW Bor*. [see the verb]

gab[1.2] /gab/ *v* to talk (idly or volubly) *18-*. Compare GAB[4]. [perhaps onomatopoeic; compare GAB[2]]

gab[2] /gab/ *n* **1** the mouth *18-*. **2** the palate, taste *18-19*. **gabbit** mouthed: ◊*he's foul gabbit la18-*. **gab gash** petulant or voluble chatter *la19, 20- N Bor*. **gab stick** a (wooden) spoon *19, 20- T Bor*. †**dight yer gab** = *haud yer gab 18-e19*. **haud yer gab** to hold your tongue, be quiet *la18-*. **set up yer gab** to speak out boldly or impertinently *19-*. **steek yer gab** = *haud yer gab la18-*. **thraw yer gab** to grimace *18-19, 20- NE*. Compare GUB[1.1]. [variant of GUB[1.1]]

gab[3] /gab/ *n* commencement *la19-*. **the gab o' May**, *Ork N* **the gob o' May** stormy weather at the beginning of May *la19-*. [probably an extension of GAB[2]]

†**gab**[4] *v* to deceive, lie *la14-e16*. [OFr *gaber* to mock, ON *gabb* mockery]

gabal *see* CABBLE[1.2]

gabar *see* GABBART

†**gabart, gabert, galbert** *n* a gaberdine, a loose upper garment *la15-16*. [shortened form of MFr *galvardine*]

gabbart, †**gabar,** †**gabert,** †**cabar** /'gabərt/ *n* a sailing vessel used for inland navigation *la16-*. [MFr *gabarre*]

gabber /'gabər/ *v* to jabber, gibber *19-*. [onomatopoeic or frequentative form of GAB[1.2]]

gabbit *see* GAB[1.1], GAB[2]

gaberlunzie, †**gaberlungy** /gabər'lʌnzi/ *n* a beggar; a tramp, a travelling tinker *16-*. **gaberlunzie man** a beggar; an itinerant musician *18-*. [perhaps GABART + LUNYIE]

gabert *see* GABBART

gaberts /'gabərts/ *npl* scaffolding *la19-*. [probably altered form of CABER]

gable-ender /gebəl'ɛndər/ *n* **1** a nickname for an inhabitant of Montrose *la19-*. **2** *pl* a nickname for Montrose Football Club *la19-*. [because small plots of land leased in the town necessitated building houses with gable-ends facing the street]

gable-endie /gebəl'ɛndi/ *n* **1** *pl* a nickname for Montrose Football Club *la19-*. **2** a nickname for an inhabitant of Montrose *20-*. [see GABLE-ENDER]

gad, *N NE H&I* **gyad** /gad; *N NE H&I* gjad/ *interj* an expression of disgust *la19-*. [altered form of GOD]

gad *see* GAUD[1]

gadder *see* GAITHER

gaddering *see* GAITHERIN

gade *see* GAUD[1], GAUD[2]

gader *see* GAITHER

gadering *see* GAITHERIN

†**gadge** *v* to talk haughtily without justification *e18*. [unknown]

gadge *see* GAUGE[1.1], GAUGE[1.2]

gadger /'gadʒər/ *n* a sponger *la19, 20- NE*. [altered form of CADGER]

gadgie /'gadʒi, 'gadʒe/ *n* a boy or man *20-*. **gadge** = GADGIE *la20-*. [Romany *gadgi* a man, especially a non-gipsy]

†**gadloup, gateloupe, goad-loup** *n* a punishment in which the culprit had to run between two rows of men who struck him with a stick or a knotted cord *la17-e18*. [Swed *gatlopp*]

gadman *see* GAUDSMAN

gadther *see* GAITHER

gadwand *see* GAUD[1]

gae, ga, go /ge, ga, go/ *v unstressed also* **g'**, *pt* **gaed, geed**, *N NE T C* **gied,** †**ʒeid,** †**ʒude**, *presp* **gaein, gaun, gaan, gan**, *Sh* **gyaain**, *Sh Ork N NE* **gyaan**, *Sh NE* **gaain**, *Ork NE* **gyaun**, *NE* **gyan**, *NE* **dyaun**, *ptp* **gane, gein**, *Sh N* **geen 1** to walk; to move; to make one's way, proceed *la14-*. **2** to go away, depart; to pass, end *la14-*. **3** to become; to enter a state or condition *la15-*. **4** to cover on foot; to travel as a pedlar *19-*. **5** to want, desire, like: ◊*I could go a cup o tea. 20-*. **6** *of machinery* to use or operate: ◊*I cannae go a bike. 20-*. **7** to act, take action: ◊*I maun gae ride la14-20*. **go-between** a maid who assists the cook and housemaid *la19, 20- NE T*. **gaun gear 1** the machinery of a mill *la18-*. **2** money or property that is being wasted *la19- NE T SW*. **3** a person in declining health; one about to die *19- NE SW*. **gae aboot 1** *of a disease* to be prevalent *20-*. **2** *of animals* to graze, search for food *19- Sh NE SW*. **go about the bush** to approach in a roundabout or tactful way *19, 20- T NE Uls*. **gae afore** to fall off a cliff, bank or quay into the sea and perish; to drown *la19- Sh Ork*. **gae awa 1** to express impatience, incredulity or derision *19-*. **2** to die *19- Ork NE T Bor*. **3** to faint, swoon *la19- T EC SW*. **gae back, go back** to deteriorate *18-*. **gae by the door, gae by their door** to pass someone's house without calling in *la18-*. †**ga chat** an expression of contempt *16*. **gae done, go done** to be used up or worn out, come to an end *la19-*. **gae doon the wrang hause** *of food* to go down the wrong way *19-*. **gae fae** to stop, abstain from; to lose the taste for *20-*. **gae fae**

the hauch tae the heather to go from a better to a worse situation *20- NE EC*. **gae in, go in 1** *of a congregation or school* to assemble *19-*. **2** to shrink, contract *19-*. **3** *of time* to approach (a period or point): ◊*it's gaein in twa years noo 18-e19*. **gae intae, go into** to open and search (a bag or drawer) *la19-*. **gae in twa** to break in two, snap *19, 20- NE*. **gae in wi** to agree with *la19-*. **gae lie** to retire to bed *18-19, 20- WC SW Bor*. **gae on** to make a fuss, scold continuously *la19-*. **gae ower** to be out of control; to get the better of *19-*. **gae tae** to shut, close *la19-*. **gae thegither 1** to come together, unite; to close *la19-*. **2** *of lovers* to court *la19-*. **3** to get married *la18-19*. **gae through, go through 1** to waste, squander; to become bankrupt or penniless *19-*. **2** to bungle, muddle (speech or a discourse) *19-*. **gae through the flair** to be overcome with shame, embarrassment or astonishment *19-*. **gae through ither** to make a mess of things *la19- NE T EC*. **gae through the yirth** = *gae through the flair*. **gae wi 1** to keep company with; to court a lover *19-*. **2** to go pleasantly or smoothly for *la18-19, 20- NE T EC*. **gaun yersel, go on yersel** an exclamation of encouragement *la20-*. Compare GANG[1.2], WEND. [OE *gān*]

gae *see* GIE
gaebie *see* GEBBIE
gaed *see* GAE
gaein *see* GAE
Gael, †**Gathel** /gel/ *n* a Gaelic speaker, a Highlander *la16-*. **Gaeldom** the Gaelic-speaking regions of Scotland *la19-*. [Gael *Gàidheal*]
Gaelic[1.1], †**Galeig**, †**Gathelik**, †**Gallic** /'galık/ *n* **1** a Celtic language spoken in Scotland *16-*. **2** Irish Gaelic or Manx Gaelic *la18-*. **the Gaelic** Scottish Gaelic *la18-*. [Gael *Gàidhlig*, Lat *Gathelicus*]
Gaelic[1.2] /'galık/ *adj* of the Gaels *la16-*. [see the noun]
gaenfore *see* GANFER
gaesintie, gizintie /gə'zınte, gə'zınti/ *n* a children's term for sums in division *la20-*. [altered form of Scots *gaes intae* goes into]
gaet *see* GAIT[3]
gaevalos, gaivalis /'gevələs/ *adj* **1** awkward, clumsy; feeble *la19- Sh Ork*. **2** mumbling, lisping, indistinct in speech *20- Sh Ork*. [Norw dial *geivla* to mumble; to throw to and fro]
gaff[1.1], †**gawfe**, †**gawf** /gaf/ *n* a boisterous laugh *16-*. [unknown, perhaps onomatopoeic]
gaff[1.2], †**gawff**, †**gauf** /gaf/ *v* **1** to laugh boisterously *18-*. **2** to babble, chatter *e19*. [see the noun]
gaff *see* GIE
gaffaw *see* GUFFAW[1.1], GUFFAW[1.2]
gafs /gafs/ *v* to eat ravenously *20- Ork*. [Norw dial *gafsa*]
gag[1.1] /gag/ *n* a filthy mass of liquid or semi-liquid *la19- Sh NE*. Compare GAGGLE[2.1]. [unknown]
gag[1.2] /gag/ *v* to stir a porridge-like mass; to work in the wrong way *20- Sh*. Compare GAGGLE[2.2]. [unknown]
gage[1.1] /gedʒ/ *n* **1** a pledge, security *15-*. **2** *pl* wages *la16-e17*. [ME *gage*]
†**gage**[1.2] *v* to pledge; to give or take in pledge *la15-e17*. [OFr *gagier*]
gage *see* GAUGE[1.1], GAUGE[1.2]
gaggit *see* GAIG[1.2]
gaggle[1] /'gagəl/ *v* to laugh, giggle, cackle *la19- EC*. [ME *gagelen* to cackle]
gaggle[2.1] /'gagəl/ *n* a moist, soft mass; a mess *20- Sh Ork*. Compare GAG[1.1]. [perhaps ON *gogli* mire]
gaggle[2.2] /'gagəl/ *v* to make a mess of; to work with something messy *20- Sh Ork*. Compare GAG[1.2]. [see the noun]
gaibie /'gebe/ *n* a stupid person *19- Bor*. **gaibie lippit** having a projecting under-lip *20- Bor*. [unknown]

gaiblick /'geblık/ *n* an unfledged bird *19- EC Bor*. [GAB[2], with diminutive suffix]
Gaidhealtachd /'geltəxt/ *n* the Gaelic-speaking regions in Scotland *20-*. [Gael *Gàidhealtachd*]
gaif *see* GIE
gaiflock *see* GAVELOCK
gaig[1.1], **geg** /geg, gɛg/ *n* **1** a crack, a chink *19- N T SW*. **2** a chap in the skin *19- NE WC SW*. **3** a deep cut, a festering sore *la19- NE*. [Gael *gàg*, IrGael *gág* a cleft, a chink; a chap, a hack]
gaig[1.2], †**geg** /geg/ *v ptp* †**gaggit 1** to cut, wound *la19- NE*. **2** *of skin* to chap *20- N SW*. **3** to split or crack from heat or dryness *la16-e19*. [see the noun]
gaikit *see* GECK[1.2]
gaill *see* GELL[3]
gaillie, gellie, galley, †**galay,** †**gallay,** †**gale** /'gele, 'gɛle, 'gale/ *n* **1** a type of ship, a galley *la14-*. **2** *Scottish Travellers* a type of tent *20-*. **3** a garret, a bothy, a workshop *la19- NE T*. **4** a dirty or untidy house *20- T*. †**gallay brekis** wide trousers *la16*. [ME *galei*]
†**gain, gane** *v* **1** to suffice, serve, last *18-e19*. **2** to be fitting or suitable *la14-17*. **ganand, gaynand, gainand** suitable, appropriate, convenient *14-e17*. [ON *gegna* to meet, suit (a person)]
gain *see* GIN[3.1]
gain-, †**gayne-,** †**gaine-,** †**gane-** /gen/ *prefix* **1** back again *la14-*. **2** against, in opposition to *15-*. [OE *gegn-*]
†**gaincall, gayn call, ganecall** *v* **1** to revoke, withdraw *15-16*. **2** to call to mind, recollect *la16*. [aphetic form of *agane call* (AGAIN[1.1])]
gainder *see* GANNER[1.1]
gaine- *see* GAIN-
†**gaine-cuming, gayne cummyng** *n* a return *la14-16*. [aphetic form of *agane cuming* (AGAIN[1.1])]
gainer *see* GANNER[1.1]
†**gainest, ganest, gaynest** *adj* **1** *of a route or way* most direct *la15-18*. **2** most suitable, most fit *e16*. [superlative from ON *gegna*]
gaing *see* GANG[1.1], GANG[1.2]
†**gainhekling, gamhekling** *n* a kind of yarn; the cloth made with it *la16-e17*. [unknown]
gainin /'genın/ *adj* winning, winsome *18-*. [presp of Eng *gain* to obtain, persuade]
gainsay, †**gaynsay,** †**ganesay** /'gense/ *v* to contradict, deny; to speak against *15-*. **gainsaying** contradiction, opposition *la14-*. [GAIN- + SAY[1.2]]
†**gainshot, ginshot** *n* a cover over the inlet to a millwheel *la18-e19*. [GIN[1] + SHOT[2]]
gainstand, †**gaynstand** /gen'stand/ *v* to withstand, resist, be opposed *15-19, 20- literary*. †**gainstander** an opponent, enemy *la15-19*. [GAIN- + STAND[1.2]]
gainʒe *see* GANʒE
gair[1] /ger/ *n* **1** a gore, a triangular piece of cloth in a garment *la15-*. **2** a (dirty or worn) stripe or streak on clothes *19-*. **3** a strip of green grass (on a hillside); a patch of marshy ground in heather *la18-19, 20- Ork EC SW Bor*. **4** a triangular opening in a garment *la18-e19*. **gairit** striped *la16-*. [OE *gāra*, ON *geiri*]
gair[2] /ger/ *adj* **1** greedy, covetous *18-19, 20- Bor*. **2** parsimonious; thrifty *la18-19, 20- Bor*. **3** eager, keen *16-e18*. [ON *gjarn* eager, willing]
gair *see* GEAR[1.1]
†**gaircule, gairguill, gardecule** *n* a jupon, a short outer skirt *la16-17*. [MFr *gardecul*]
gaird[1.1], **guaird, guard,** †**gard,** †**gward** /gerd, gard/ *n* **1** a guard or sentinel; a body of armed men (engaged to watch

gaird and protect) *15-*. **2** a state of vigilance; care, protection *la15-*. **3** a protective device or safety mechanism *16-*. **4** curling a stone played so as to lie in front of and guard the tee or another stone *19-*. **gairdhoose, †gairdhous** a guardhouse *la16-*. **brak aff the gaird** curling to strike away a guard stone *19- SW*. **flee the gairds** curling to fail to strike the guard stone *19-*. **†the gaird 1** the Edinburgh town guard *la17-e19*; compare *toun guard* (TOUN). **2** the headquarters of the guard, the lock-up *18*. [ME *gard*]

gaird¹,², **guaird, guard, †gard** /gerd, gard/ *v* **1** to maintain a state of vigilance, protect *la16-*. **2** curling to protect a stone lying on or near the tee by placing another in front of it *la18-*. **3** to trim or ornament (a garment) *la15-e19*. **gaird ma sowl** an exclamation of surprise *20- Sh Ork*. [OFr *garder*]

gairden, garden, †gardin /ˈgerdən, ˈgardən/ *n* a plot of ground attached to a house; an area given over to horticulture; a public recreation area *la15-*. [ME *gardin*]

gairdener see GAIRDNER

gairding see GARDIN

gairdner, gairdener, gardener, †gairner /ˈgerdnər, ˈgerdənər, ˈgardnər, ˈgardənər/ *n* a person who tends a garden *14-*. **gairdener's gairtens, gairner's gartens, gardener's garters** reed canary grass, ribbon-grass *Phalaris arundinacea 19-*. [AN *gardiner*]

gairdy see GARDY

†gair-fowl *n* the great auk *Pinguinus impennis la17-19*. [ON *geirfugl*]

gairguill see GAIRCULE

gairner see GAIRDNER

gairnish, †garnis /ˈgernɪʃ/ *v* **1** to ornament, embellish, garnish *la15-*. **2** to furnish with means of defence or attack *la15-16*. [ME *garnishen*]

gairsty see GORSTIE

gairten, garten, *Sh Ork* **gerten, †gartane** /ˈgertən, ˈgartən; *Sh Ork* ˈgertən/ *n* **1** a garter *la15-*. **2** a leaf of ribbon-grass *Phalaris arundinacea 20- T Bor*; compare *gairdener's gairtens* (GAIRDNER). **†gairtanit** gartered *la16-19*. **get the green gairten** an expression used of an older sister or brother when a younger sibling marries first *la18-*. **wear the green gairten** = *get the green gairten*. [altered form of ME *garter*]

gairy¹ /ˈgere/ *n* a vertical outcrop of rock, a crag *19- SW*. [probably Gael *gàradh* a wall, a dyke]

†gairy²·¹ *n* a name for a striped cow *la18-e19*. [see the adj]

gairy²·² /ˈgere/ *adj* striped *19-*. **gairy bee** the black-and-yellow-striped wild bee *19, 20- NE T Bor*. [GAIR¹ + -IE²]

gais see GAUZE

gaishon /ˈgeʃən/ *n* a thin, emaciated person *19, 20- SW Bor Uls*. [unknown]

gaislin, †gaisling /ˈgezlɪn/ *n* a gosling *16-*. [ON *gæslingr*]

gaist see GHAIST

gait¹, **goat, †gate, †gote** /get, got/ *n* a goat, an animal of the genus *Capra la13-*. **gait hair, goat's hair** cirrus cloud *la19-*. **†gate whey** the whey of goat's milk; a restorative diet or lifestyle *18-e19*. [OE *gāt*]

gait²·¹, *NE* **gyte** /get; *NE* gʌɪt/ *n* a single sheaf of grain tied near the top and set up to dry *17-*. [unknown]

gait²·², **gyte, gaut** /get, gʌɪt, gʌut/ *v* to tie a sheaf of grain near the top and set it up to dry *la18-19, 20- NE*. [unknown]

gait³, **gate, gaet,** *N* **gett, †gat, †get, †ʒat** /get; *N* get/ *n* **1** a way, a path; a road; a street (in a town); frequently in place-names *13-*. **2** a course or direction; a means or manner of doing something *la14-*. **3** the length of a way, a distance *16-*. **4** a way of behaving; conduct, manner; habit *18-*. **5** a journey, a trip *la18-19, 20- C*. **†gating** a drift or passage in a mine *e17*. **†gaitlins, gatelins** directly, straight; towards *la18-19*. **gateward, †gatewards** straight on, straight to *17-18, la20- Bor*. **gate en, gate end** a neighbourhood, a locality *19-*. **gate farrin** presentable, comely *la19- NE*. **†gatesman, gaitisman** a person who made drifts or passages in a coalmine *17-19*. **†gate penny** a tax on merchants and dealers selling goods in a market *16-e18*. **at the gate again** recovered from an illness *la19- NE Uls*. **come the gate o** to come (to), reach *la19- NE SW*. **gae your gate, go your gait 1** to go on one's way *la14-*. **2** to follow one's own opinions *18-*. **†gang to gait 1** to set out *la17-e19*. **2** to go to wrack and ruin, be destroyed *la18-19*. **gang your ain gait** to follow one's own opinions *19-*. **gang your gait 1** to go on one's way *la14-*. **2** to follow one's own opinions *18-*. **†gie someone his gate** to give someone his way, allow someone free rein *19-*. **haud the gate, †hald his gate 1** to keep to the road or route, stick to the proper way *la14-*. **2** to hold one's own (when ill); to be in a good state of health or prosperity *la19, 20- NE*. **in the gait, in the gate 1** in someone's way, causing an obstruction to someone *15-*. **2** on the way, along the road *16-*. **oot the gait 1** on one's way, along the road, up the road *16-*. **2** out of the way *20-*. **oot o the gait, out of the gate** out of the way *la18-*. **tae the gate again** recovered from an illness *la19-*. **tak the gait, tak the gate 1** to set off on a journey *la18-*. **2** to run away *19-*. **that gate** that way *la18-*. **weel ti the gate** at an advanced stage, well on *20- Bor*. **your gait, your gate** the way one (habitually or regularly) takes; one's course of action *la14-*. [ON *gata*]

gait see GATE, GET¹·²

gaither, gether, gather, *Sh NE* **gadder,** *NE* **gedder, †gader, †gadther** /ˈɡeðər, ˈɡeðər, ˈɡaðər; *Sh NE* ˈɡadər; *NE* ˈɡedər/ *v* **1** to bring or come together; to collect or compile *la14-*. **2** to accumulate wealth, save *16-*. **3** *in ploughing* to throw the soil into a central ridge *18-*. **4** to pull oneself together; to rally *la18-*. **5** to prepare a fire for the night or a long period without attention; to place a large piece of coal or peat on the raked embers *la18-*. **6** to collect money, contributions or subscriptions *la19-*. **7** *of butter* to form, collect in the churn *la19-*. **8** *in harvesting* to bring together enough corn to form a sheaf *la19- NE EC Bor*. **gaithered** rich, well-to-do *la19- NE T Bor*. **gatherer** a person whose job is to collect corn into sheaves *la18-*. **gaddery, geddery 1** an accumulation, a miscellaneous collection *19, 20- Sh NE*. **2** a gathering *20- Sh*. **gaither dam** a dam which collects water from drainage and rainfall only *18- NE*. **gether up** a motley collection *20-*. **gather the feet** to recover from a fall, regain one's footing *la17-19, 20- NE EC Bor*. **gather yer feet** = *gather the feet*. [OE *gaderian*]

gaitherin, gaithering, gathering, †gaddering, †gadering /ˈɡeðərɪn, ˈɡeðərɪn, ˈɡaðərɪn/ *n* **1** an assembly or meeting; an assembled group, a company of followers *la14-*. **2** a signal on drum or bagpipe to (fighting) men to assemble; a tune used for this purpose; one of the types of pibroch *la17-*. **3** a gathering; a type of festival featuring piping, dancing and athletics contests *19-*. **gathering coal** fuel laid on the embers to keep a fire alive over a long period without attention *19-*. **gathering note** a lengthened note sung at the beginning of the first and sometimes certain subsequent lines of a hymn or psalm *20-*. **gathering peat** = *gathering coal*. **gathering psalm** the psalm sung at the beginning of a church service *la19-*. [verbal noun from GAITHER]

gaivalis see GAEVALOS

gaive /gev/ *v* to move clumsily, aimlessly or restlessly *19- SW Bor*. [unknown; compare CAVE²]

gaivle see GAVEL¹

Gala /ˈgala/ *n* **1** a nickname for the town of Galashiels *la19-*. **2** = GALASHIELS GREY *la19*. [shortened form of the place-name *Galashiels*]

galash, †**gallash** /gəˈlaʃ/ *n* a waterproof overshoe *17-*. [Fr *galoche*]

Galashiels grey /galəʃilz ˈgre/ *n* a coarse grey woollen cloth manufactured at Galashiels *18-19, 20- historical*. [from the place-name *Galashiels* + GRAY¹·¹]

galat /ˈgalət/ *n* term of endearment used to address a girl *19- N NE H&I*. [Gael *galad*]

Galatian *see* GALOSHAN

galay *see* GAILLIE

galbert *see* GABART

†**galcoit** *n* a coat or jacket *e16*. [unknown]

gald *see* GAUD¹

galder¹·¹ /ˈgaldər/ *n* **1** a noisy, vulgar laugh; a loud yell *19- Sh Ork*. **2** noisy, foolish chatter *19- Sh Ork*. Compare GULLER¹·¹, GULLER¹·². [Norw dial *galder* a roar]

galder¹·² /ˈgaldər/ *v* **1** to laugh in a coarse manner *la19- Sh Ork*. **2** to talk or sing boisterously *la19- Sh Ork*. Compare GULLER¹·¹, GULLER¹·². [Norw dial *galdra* to bawl]

galderie /ˈgaldəri/ *n* a large, barn-like building or room *la19- Sh Ork*. [probably altered form of Scots *gallery*]

gale, **gell** /gel, gɛl/ *n* **1** a very strong wind *17-*. **2** a spiritual uplift *18-*. **3** a state of excitement *19-*. **4** a brawl, a row, a squabble *19- WC*. **5** a breeze *17-19*. **6** a time of noisy enjoyment; a drinking bout *19*. **gell o wind** a very strong wind *19- Sh H&I EC*. [EModE *gale*]

gale *see* GAILLIE, GAVEL¹, GEIL, GELL³

Galeig *see* GAELIC¹·¹

galenʒe *see* GILLENʒE

gal-knot *see* GAA-KNOT

gall /gɔl/ *n* bog myrtle *Myrica gale 18-*. [OE *gagel*]

gall *see* GA, GAW¹·¹

gallafer /ˈgaləfər/ *n* loud mirth *la19- Sh*. [perhaps onomatopoeic; compare GOLLIE]

gallant¹·¹, †**galland** /ˈgalənt/ *n* a handsome, well-dressed young man *la15-*. †**gallantish** *of women* flirtatious, ostentatious *la18-e19*. [see the adj]

gallant¹·² /ˈgalənt, gəˈlant/ *v* to gad about; to pursue pleasure; to flirt *19-*. [see the adj]

gallant¹·³, †**galland** /ˈgalənt/ *adj* **1** noble, courteous, brave *16-*. **2** large, ample *19-*. [ME *galaunt*, EModE *gallant*]

†**gallant**² *n* galloon, a kind of ornamental ribbon *la16-e17*. [MFr *galon* possibly influenced by MFr *galant* elegant]

gallash *see* GALASH

gallay, galley *see* GAILLIE

gallayniel *see* GILEYNOUR

galliard *see* GALʒEART

Gallic *see* GAELIC¹·¹

†**gallivaster** *n* an idle, boastful person, a gadabout *e19*. [Scots *gallivant*, with agent suffix]

gallo *see* GALLOW

gallon, †**galloun** /ˈgalən/ *n* **1** a gallon; a measure of capacity equal to 277.25 cubic inches *19-*. **2** = *gallon Scots 15-e19*. †**gallon Scots** a measure of capacity equal to approximately 3 times the Imperial gallon *18*. [ME *galoun*]

galloper /ˈgaləpər/ *n* a five-shilling piece with a design of St George on horseback *la19-20, 21- historical*. [after the design]

gallopin Tam /ˈgaləpɪn ˈtam/ *n Presbyterian Church* a much used sermon, especially one preached in several places by a candidate for a church *19-*. [probably from the fact it was being used in different places]

galloun *see* GALLON

gallous *see* GALLOWS, GALLUS²

Gallovidian¹·¹ /galəˈvɪdɪən/ *n* **1** a native of Galloway *19-*. **2** the language of Galloway *19-*. [Lat *Gallovidia*]

Gallovidian¹·², †**Gallowedian** /galəˈvɪdɪən/ *adj* of or relating to Galloway *17-*. [see the noun]

†**gallow, gallo, galu** *n* a GALLOWS; frequently in place-names *13-e19*. **gallow-breid** a hanged man; a person who deserved to be hanged *16-e17*. **gallow-tre, gallow treis** a gallows *la14-16*. [OE *galga*]

Galloway, Gallowa, †**Gauway** /ˈgalǝwe, ˈgalǝwa/ *n* **1** a small, sturdy type of horse *18-*. **2** a breed of hardy black (or red) hornless cattle *la18-*; compare *belted Galloway* (BELTED). †**Gallowais** men of Galloway *la14*. †**Galloway dyke** a whinstone wall (usually about five feet high), the lower part of a drystane construction topped by a thin course of projecting flat stones, and the upper part a tapering construction of round stones *la18-e19*. **Galloway hedge** a combination of hedge and dyke *20-*. †**Galloway white** a type of woollen cloth *17-e18*. [from the name of the district in South-West Scotland]

Gallowedian *see* GALLOVIDIAN¹·²

gallows, †**gallowis**, †**gallous** /ˈgaləz, ˈgaloz/ *n* **1** an apparatus used to execute people by hanging *15-*. **2** a device for suspending a pot over a fire *16-17, 20- Uls*. †**gallousis** a gallows *e17*. Compare GALLUSES. [OE *galga*, with plural -*s* suffix]

gallows *see* GALLUS¹, GALLUS²

gallowses *see* GALLUSES

gallus¹, **gallows** /ˈgaləs, ˈgaloz/ *n* a single brace or suspender; braces *19-*. Compare GALLUSES. [GALLOWS]

gallus², **gallous, gallows** /ˈgaləs, ˈgaloz/ *adj* **1** villainous, rascally *la18-*. **2** wild, unmanageable, bold; impish, mischievous, cheeky *20-*. [an attributive use of GALLOWS, in the sense of deserving to be hanged]

galluses, gallowses /ˈgaləsəz, ˈgalozəz/ *npl* **1** trouser braces; stocking suspenders *19-*. **2** a yoke for carrying pails *20-*. [GALLOWS, with additional plural suffix]

gallyie, gellie /ˈgalje, ˈgɛle/ *n* a roar, cry *19-*. [perhaps onomatopoeic; compare GOLLIE¹·¹]

gallytrough *see* GELLYTROCH

†**galopin** *n* an underservant; a roving youth *la16-e19*. [MFr *galopin* an errand boy]

galore¹·¹, †**gillore** /gəˈlor/ *n* plenty, superabundance *la18-*. [see the adj]

galore¹·² /gəˈlor/ *adj* in abundance *la18-*. [Gael *gu leòir, gu leòr*, IrGael *go leor* sufficiently]

Galoshan, Galoshin, Galatian /gəˈlɔʃən, gəˈleʃən/ *n* **1** the name of the hero in a mumming play; a mummer, a harlequin *19- H&I C SW Bor*. **2** a play performed by mummers or guisers at Hogmanay or Halloween *19- C SW Bor*. **3** *pl* guising; a performance by guisers *la19- C SW Bor*. [from the name of the ancient province of *Galatia*]

galravich *see* GILRAVAGE¹·¹

galshachs /ˈgalʃaxs/ *npl* **1** sweets, titbits *la19- NE*. **2** luxuries, treats *20- NE*. [perhaps altered form of GULSOCH]

galt *see* GAUT

galtags /ˈgaltagz/ *npl* inflammation of the skin between the toes *20- N*. [perhaps derivative of *gall* (GAW¹·¹), with diminutive suffix]

galu *see* GALLOW

†**galya** *n* a safe-conduct *e16*. [LG, Du *geleide* a conveyance, an escort]

†**galʒeart, galliard** *adj* **1** gallant; lively *la15-e17*. **2** *of dress* spruce, bright, gaudy *16-e17*. [ME *gaillard*]

gam /gam/ *n* **1** a large tooth *19- Ork N NE T Bor*; compare GAMS¹. **2** the gum, the jaw *19, 20- Ork NE*. **gam teeth** large teeth *la19- NE*. [GAMS influenced by *gum*]

gam see GAME¹·¹
gamaleerie¹·¹ /'gaməliri/ *n* a foolish, clumsy person *19, 20- T EC*. [perhaps altered form of GOMERIL¹·¹]
†gamaleerie¹·² *adj* of clumsy build, gawky *19*. [see the noun]
†gambade, gambat, gamound *n* a leap; a caper *16-e19*. [MFr *gambade*]
game¹·¹, gemme, gemm, gem, †gam /gem, gɛm/ *n* **1** amusement, fun, sport; a competitive pastime, a sporting contest *la14-*. **2** that which is hunted; the quarry in the sport of hunting *la14-*. **Games** a meeting for the purpose of holding contests in athletics, piping and dancing, held originally in the Highland area *19-*; compare *Highland Games* (HIELAND¹·²). **†gamin** sport, play; hunting *la14-e16*. **gaming, gamming** sport, sporting *15-*. **gamster, †gemster, †gamester 1** a frivolous woman *20- SW*. **2** a player in a game *18-e19*. **3** a gambler *17-18*. **4** an actor *la16*. **game watcher** a gamekeeper *la19-*. **make game** to joke *19-*. **oot the game** unable to continue because of exhaustion *20-*. [OE *gamen*]
game¹·² /gem/ *v* to play games, make sport, joke *15-*. **†gam-in** to sport; to disport oneself *15*. [see the noun]
gamf¹·¹, gomf /gamf, gɔmf/ *n* a buffoon *la19-*. **gamphrell, †gamphrel** a buffoon *la18- WC SW Bor Uls*. [perhaps onomatopoeic]
gamf¹·², gamp /gamf, gamp/ *v* to be merry *19- WC SW*. [see the noun]
gamfer see GANFER
gamfle /'gamfəl/ *v* to idle, dally *19, 20- T SW*. [GAMF¹·²]
gamhekling see GAINHEKLING
gamie, gemmie /'gemi, 'gɛmi/ *n* a nickname for a gamekeeper *la19-*. [shortened form of Eng *gamekeeper*]
gamin see GAME¹·¹, GAME¹·²
gamming see GAME¹·¹
gammis see GAMS¹
†gammon, gamon *n* a person's leg or thigh *18-19*. [AN *gamboun* ham]
gamound see GAMBADE
gamp /gamp/ *v* **1** to gape *18- SW Bor*. **2** to eat or drink greedily, devour *19- Bor*. **gampy** gaping *20- Bor*. [perhaps onomatopoeic]
gamp see GAMF¹·²
gampherd /'gamfərd/ *adj of embroidery* bespangled, adorned *19, 20- SW Bor*. [unknown]
gamphrel, gamphrell see GAMF¹·¹
gamrel /'gamrəl/ *n* a piece of wood used to separate the legs of a carcass to facilitate butchering *19- SW Bor*. [MFr *gamberel* a piece of forked wood for capturing animals]
gamrel see CAMERAL
gams¹, †gammis /gamz/ *npl* teeth, jaws *la15-19, 20- Ork N NE T Bor*. Compare GAM. [unknown]
gams² /gams/ *v* to behave in a rude, reckless manner; to make rough movements *20- Sh*. [Norw dial *gamsa* to play, romp]
gamse¹·¹ /gams/ *n* a playful snap (by a dog) *20- Sh Ork*. [see the verb]
gamse¹·² /gams/ *v of a dog* to bite playfully *20- Sh Ork*. [Dan *gamse* to snatch, bite]
gamster see GAME¹·¹
gamsterrie see CAMSTAIRY¹·²
gan, †gane /gan/ *v* to go *la14- C SW Bor*. **gane on aboot** to make a fuss about *20- EC SW*. [ME *gan, gane* infinitive of GAE; latterly with infl from GANG¹·¹ or presp forms of GAE]
gan see GAAN, GAE
ganand see GAIN
gandaguster /'gandə'gʌstər/ *n* a strong gust of wind, a squall *20- Sh*. [Norn *gander* a high wind + GOWSTER¹·¹]
gandiegow /gandi'gʌu/ *n* **1** a squall, a heavy shower *20- Sh T Bor*. **2** a quarrel; a prank; an uproar *20- Sh N*. [Norn *gander* noisy chatter, a high wind, with alliterating second element]
gandy, gannie /'gandi, 'gani/ *v* to talk in a blustering, boastful or pert way *19- NE*. [Norn *gander* noisy chatter]
gane¹·¹ /gen/ *adj* mad, crazy *20-*. [ptp of GAE]
gane¹·² /gen/ *adv* **1** past, ago: ◊*a week gane 18-*. **2** over, more than (a certain age): ◊*he's but eighteen gane* ◊*she's gane forty-twa la19-*. [see the adj]
†gane² *n* an ugly face *16*. [perhaps related to OE *gānian* to yawn]
gane see GAE, GAIN, GAN
gane- see GAIN-
ganecall see GAINCALL
†gane-come, gaynecome *n* a return *15*. [GAIN- + COME¹·²]
ganer see GANNER¹·¹
ganesay see GAINSAY
ganest see GAINEST
ganfer, gamfer, †gaenfore /'ganfər, 'gamfər/ *n* **1** a ghost; an apparition of a living person (regarded as a portent of the person's death) *la18- Sh Ork*. **2** an atmospheric sign or phenomenon; drizzle or mist foretelling a snowstorm *20- Ork*. [Norw *gjenferd*]
gang¹·¹, ging, *Sh* **geng,** *Sh* **gaing,** *Sh* **gjang,** *Ork* **geong** /gaŋ, gɪŋ; *Sh* gɛŋ; *Sh* geŋ; *Sh* gjaŋ; *Ork* gjɔŋ/ *n* **1** a range or stretch of pasturage, a pasture *16-*. **2** gait, a way of walking *16-*. **3** a journey, a trip (especially one made when carrying or transporting goods) *la16-*. **4** a single load; the quantity (of water or liquor) that can be carried at one time *la16-*. **5** a layer of corn-sheaves in a cart or stack *la18-*. **6** a passage, a thoroughfare *20-*. **7** a set or usual number of articles; a related group of objects *la16-18, 20- Sh*. **8** *in knitting or weaving* a row *la18-19, 20- Sh Ork N*. **9** the course or channel of a stream *la15-e19*. **10** a row of decoration on a garment *17-e18*. **11** a family or Border clan *la16*. **gang aboot** a hawker *20- Ork WC*; compare GAUN-ABOOT. **gang water 1** the water supplied by the normal flow of a stream to a mill, without a dam *20- NE*. **2** (enough money for) the bare necessities *la19- NE*. [OE *gang*, ON *gangr*]
gang¹·², *Sh* **gaing,** *Sh H&I* **geng,** *NE* **ging,** *NE* **gyang,** *NE* **dyang** /gaŋ; *Sh* geŋ; *Sh H&I* gɛŋ; *NE* gɪŋ; *NE* gjaŋ; *NE* djaŋ/ *v* **1** to go, proceed, take a course *la14-*. **2** to go on foot, walk *la14-*. **3** to happen; to continue *la14-*. **4** to become; to pass or change (out of or into) *la14-*. **5** to be carried, taken or used *15-*. **6** to go away, depart *la15-*. **7** *of a road* to stretch, extend *la15-*. **8** to be current, have currency *la15-e17*. **ganger 1** a person who goes on foot *15-*. **2** a person who is going away for some purpose *la16-*. **gang awa** to faint, swoon *la18-*. **gang by oneself** to go mad *la19, 20- NE*. **gang done** to be used up, come to an end *19, 20- NE*. **gang doon the hoose** to go to the parlour of a farmhouse, where it is down a step *la19- SW Uls*. **gang hail-heid erran, gang heildeeran** to go for one express purpose *20- N*. **gang hailheidit** to devote one's entire energy to *la19- Sh NE T*. **gang lie** to go to bed *la19- SW*. **gang oot amang folk** to work as a cleaner in private houses *la19-*. **gang ower** to overcome, beat *la19, 20- Ork NE*. **gang ower the march** *of a couple from England* to elope to Scotland (to be married according to the speedier and less formal procedure of Scots law) *18- Bor*. **gang skerp** to be torn or ripped *20- Ork*. **†gang tae, gang to** *of the sun* to set *15-e17*. **gang throw** to squander *19-*. **gang throu it** to dissipate one's resources, go bankrupt *la19- NE T*. **gang together,** *NE* **ging thegither** to get married *la18- Sh NE*. **gang one's ways** to depart, take oneself off, go away *19-*. [OE *gangan*]
gangand see GANGIN

gange /gandʒ/ v **1** to chatter, gossip; to talk insolently *19- NE*. **2** to brag; to exaggerate *la19- NE*. [variant of GANSH¹·²]

gangin, ganging, †**gangand** /'gaŋɪn, 'gaŋɪŋ/ adj **1** going (on foot), walking *la14-*. **2** moving or functioning *la15-*. **gangin aboot body** a Traveller, a tramp *la19-*. **gangin body, gengin body** = gangin aboot body. †**ganging gear, gangand geir** the working parts of a machine or implement *la16-17*. †**ganging graith** moving parts (of a mill) *la15-19*; compare *standing graith* (STANDING¹·²). [presp of GANG¹·²]

ganglin, gangling /'gaŋlɪn, 'gaŋglɪŋ/ adj lanky, loosely built *19-*. [GANG¹·², with *-le* and *-ing* suffixes]

gangrel, †**gangrell** /'gaŋrəl, 'gaŋgrəl/ n **1** a tramp, a vagrant, a vagabond *16-*. **2** a child just able to walk, a toddler *la18- N NE T*. **3** a toad *la15-16*. [probably GANG¹·², with *-rel* suffix]

gangs /gaŋz/ npl spring shears, sheep-shears *20- N*. [perhaps GANG¹·¹]

ganner¹·¹, **gainer, gainder**, *Sh* **genner**, †**ganer** /'ganər, 'genər, 'gendər/ *Sh* 'gɛnər/ n a male goose, a gander *15-*. [OE *gandra*]

ganner¹·² /'ganər/ v to wander aimlessly or foolishly about *19- NE Bor*. [see the noun]

gannie see GANDY

gansel¹·¹ /'gansəl/ n **1** a disagreeable comment, an insolent remark; a scolding *18-*. **2** garlic sauce served with goose *la15-e18*. [OFr *ganse aillie* garlic sauce]

gansel¹·², *SW* **gaunsel** /'gansəl; *SW* 'gɔnsəl/ v to scold *la19-*. [see the noun]

gansey, genzie /'ganzi, 'gɛnzi/ n a guernsey, a jersey, especially one worn by fishermen *19-*. [from the island-name *Guernsey*, in a non-rhotic dialect]

gansh¹·¹ /ganʃ/ n **1** a stupid, clumsy or stammering person *la19- Uls*. **2** a stammer *20- T H&I*. [see the verb]

gansh¹·², **gaunch** /ganʃ, gɔnʃ/ v **1** to snatch (at), snap; *of a dog* to snarl *18-*. **2** to stammer *19-*. [unknown; compare GAMSE¹·²]

ganska /'ganska/ adv *fisherman's taboo* quite well *la19- Sh*. [Norw *ganske* quite]

gant¹·¹, **gaunt** /gant, gɔnt/ n a yawn, a gape, a gasp *la15-*. [see the verb]

gant¹·², **gaunt** /gant, gɔnt/ v **1** to yawn; to gasp *la15-*. **2** to stammer or stutter *20- N*. [perhaps a frequentative form of OE *gānian* to yawn]

gant² /gant/ n the gannet *Morus bassanus la19- NE C*. [perhaps OFr *jante, gante* a wild goose]

gant see GENT

gantree, gantry /'gantri, 'gantre/ n **1** the shelves behind the bar in a pub *la20- C*. **2** a wooden stand for barrels *18*. [perhaps back-formation from GANTREES]

gantrees, *T WC* **gantrice**, †**gantreis** /'gantriz; *T WC* 'gantris/ npl a four-legged wooden stand for barrels *16-*. [unknown]

gantry see GANTREE

†**ganʒe, gainʒe, genʒie** n an arrow or a bolt for a crossbow *15-16*. [Gael *gàinne*, IrGael *gáinne*]

†**gapeshot** adj *in Shetland* open-mouthed *19*. [Scots *gape*, with unknown second element]

gapus see GAWPUS

gar¹·¹, †**gare** /gar/ n **1** filth, slime *15, 19- Sh Ork N NE T EC*. **2** a soft, doughy mixture; a poultice *la19- Sh*. **garrie** sticky, clammy, slimy *20- Sh Ork*. [OE *gor* slime, excrement]

gar¹·² /gar/ v to mix; to mess up *la19- Sh*. [see the noun]

gar², **gaar, ger, gare**, †**gere** /gar, gɛr, ger/ v pt **gart, gert** **1** to cause something to be done *la14-*. **2** to make a person or thing do something *la14-*. **3** to give instructions; to take steps to do or make something *la14-e19*. **gar-me-true** a hypocrite; a philanderer *la19- NE*. †**gar someone as gude** to pay someone back, retaliate *la17-e19*. **gar someone grue** to cause someone to have a feeling of horror or dread *19-*. [ON *gera*]

garb /garb/ n **1** fashion, dress *17-*. **2** (clothing made of) poor, thin cloth *20- NE*. **3** a thin coating of frost *20- SW*. [Ital *garbo* grace, elegance]

gard see GAIRD¹·¹, GAIRD¹·²

gardecule see GAIRCULE

garden see GAIRDEN

†**gardenap, gardenat** n a plate or mat for putting under dishes at a table *la15-16*. Compare GARDIN. [OFr *gardenape*]

gardener see GAIRDNER

†**gardeviant, gardevyance, gardevyat** n a chest for holding or transporting valuables *la15-16*. [AN *gardevyand*, ME *gardeviaunt*]

gardevine /'gardevʌɪn/ n **1** a (large) bottle of wine or spirits *la18-*. **2** a case or chest for holding wine bottles or decanters *la19*. [altered form of GARDEVIANT, the second element being from Fr *vin* wine]

gardevyance, gardevyat see GARDEVIANT

†**gardin, gairding, guarden** n a protective (brass) mat or plate placed under dishes at a table *16-e18*. [reduced form of GARDENAP]

gardin see GAIRDEN

gardy, gairdy /'gardi, 'gerdi/ n **1** pl the hands or fists *la18-*. **2** the arm, the forearm *16-19, 20- NE*. †**gardy chair** an armchair *la18-e19*. [unknown; compare Gael *gàirdean*]

gardyloo /garde'lu/ interj *in Edinburgh* a warning call that rubbish or sewage was about to be poured into the street from an upper storey *la17-19, 20- historical*. [altered form of Fr *gare à l'eau!* or *gardez(-vous de) l'eau!* beware of the water!]

gare see GAR¹·¹, GAR²

garfa see GILFA

garibaldi /garə'bɔldi/ n a kind of bun or scone *la19, 20- NE EC*. [from the name of the Italian general]

†**garitour** n a watchman *15-e17*. [OFr *garite* a watch tower, with agent suffix]

garment, †**garmound** /'garmənt/ n an article of clothing *15-*. †**garmond of clais** a suit of clothes *la16-e17*. [ME *garnement, garment*]

†**garnach** n a wine from the eastern Pyrenees *la14-e15*. [OFr *garnache*]

garnale, garnel see GIRNEL¹·¹

garnis see GAIRNISH

garron¹, †**garrein** /'garən/ n **1** a small sturdy horse *17-*. **2** an old, worn-out horse *19-*. **3** a strong, thickset man or sturdy boy *19- NE*. [Gael, IrGael *gearran* a gelding, a hack]

garron², †**garroun** /'garən/ n **1** a wooden beam *16- Ork N NE*. **2** = *garron-nail la17-*. **garron nail** a large nail or spike, especially as used in fixing the body of a cart to its axle *16-*; compare CANNON NAIL and CARRON-NAIL. [AN *garoun*, OFr *jarron* a branch of a tree, a beam for building]

garse see GAASE

gart see GAR²

gartane, garten see GAIRTEN

garth /garθ/ n **1** an enclosure, a yard, a garden; frequently in place-names *la15-*. **2** a shallow part of a river or stretch of shingle used as a ford; frequently in place-names *la18- NE*. [ON *garðr* a yard, a fence]

gartlins see GREAT¹·²

garvie /'garvi/ n a sprat *Sprattus sprattus la17-*. **garvuck** †**garvock** a sprat *la18-19, 20- N*. [unknown]

gascon, gaskin, †**gascoigne** /'gaskən/ n **1** a native of Gascony *la14-*. **2** a variety of gooseberry *la18-20*,

21- *historical*. **3** a wine of Gascony *e16*. **gascon wine** a wine of Gascony *la15-*. [from the name of the region in France]

†**gash**¹·¹ *n* a protruding chin *e19*. [unknown]

†**gash**¹·² *v* to gnash, bare the teeth, snap *19*. [unknown]

gash²·¹ /gaʃ/ *n* prattle, talk; impudent language *la18-*. [unknown]

gash²·² /gaʃ/ *v* to talk volubly, gossip or prattle *la18-19, 20- N EC*. [unknown]

gash²·³ /gaʃ/ *adj* talkative, loquacious *la17-19, 20- EC*. [unknown]

gash³ /gaʃ/ *adj* pale or ghastly in appearance; grim, dismal *la18-*. [EModE *gash*; compare GASHLY]

gash⁴ /gaʃ/ *adj* **1** sagacious, shrewd *18-*. **2** well-dressed, respectable, smart *la18-*. [unknown]

gash⁵·¹ /gaʃ/ *n* refuse, rubbish; something useless or awful *20-*. [unknown]

gash⁵·² /gaʃ/ *adj* terrible, awful *la20-*. [unknown]

gash-gabbit¹ /'gaʃ gabɪt/ *adj* **1** having a protruding lower jaw *18-*. **2** having a sagging, misshapen mouth *19, 20- T*. [GASH¹·¹ + *gabbit* (GAB²)]

gash-gabbit² /'gaʃ gabɪt/ *adj* loquacious, glib *e18, 19- EC*. [GASH²·³ + *gabbit* (GAB²)]

gashle¹ /'gaʃəl/ *v* to distort *19- NE*. [frequentative form of GASH¹·²]

gashle² /'gaʃəl/ *v* **1** to argue bitterly *19, 20- WC*. **2** to gossip *20- NE*. [frequentative form of GASH²·²]

gashly /'gaʃle/ *adj* ghastly *20- T SW*. [altered form of Older Scots *gastly*]

gash-mou'd /'gaʃ mud/ *adj* having a sagging, misshapen mouth *19- NE EC*. [GASH¹·¹ + *mou'd* (MOOTH¹·¹)]

gaskin *see* GASCON

gasoliery /gasə'liri/ *n* a gas chandelier *la19-20, 21- historical*. [Eng *gasolier* + -IE¹]

gast¹·¹ /gast/ *n* a fright *la17-*. **in a gast** in a fright *la17-*. [ME *gastan* to frighten, terrify; compare OE *gǣsten*]

†**gast**¹·², **gaste** *adj* frightened *la14-e16*. [ME *gast*]

gast *see* GHAIST, GUEST

gastrous /'gastrəs/ *adj* horrifying, unearthly *19-*. [EModE *gaster* to frighten, with adj-forming suffix]

†**gat** *n* a navigable channel *16-19*. [ON *gat* a hole]

gat *see* GAIT³, GET¹·²

gate, **gait**, †**gaitt** /get/ *n* an opening in a wall for access *la16-*. **gate slap** an opening, a gateway *la19- NE T SW*. [OE *geat*]

gate *see* GAIT¹, GAIT³, GET¹·²

gateloupe *see* GADLOUP

Gathel *see* GAEL

Gathelik *see* GAELIC¹·¹

gather *see* GAITHER

gathering *see* GAITHERIN

gattin *see* GET¹·²

gatting *see* GYTE²

gaud¹, **gad**, **goad**, †**gade**, †**gald** /gɔd, gad, god/ *n* **1** a goad for driving cattle *la17-*. **2** a fishing-rod *la18- C Bor*. **3** a wooden slat used to direct standing grain into the teeth of the binder or to the scythe of the reaper *20, 21- NE*. **4** a bar of iron to which prisoners could be shackled *17-19, 20- historical*. **5** a rod or bar of iron or steel *15-19*. **6** a spear *e19*. †**gadwand** a goad *la14-e16*. [OE *gād*, ON *gaddr* a goad, a spike]

†**gaud**², **gade** *n* a trick; a prank *15-e19*. [ME *gaud*]

gaude *see* GAADY

gaudeamus /gʌudi'aməs/ *n* **1** the title of a student song, named from its opening word *la19-*. **2** a student feast or merry-making; celebration *18-19*. [Lat *gaudeāmus* let us rejoice]

gaudsman, **goadsman**, †**gadman**, †**goadman** /'gɔdsmən, 'godsmən/ *n* **1** the man who holds a goad before the reaper *20- NE*. **2** one who directed a team of oxen or horses with a goad *la15-19*. [derivative of GAUD¹ + MAN]

gaudy /'gɔde, 'gɔdi/ *adj* **1** excessively ornate; tastelessly showy *la17-*. **2** lively, dashing *e19*. [EModE *gaudy*]

gauf *see* GAFF¹·²

gauge¹·¹, †**gage**, †**gadge** /gedʒ/ *n* **1** a standard measure *la16-*. **2** a template to regulate mesh size in net-making *20- Sh N SW*. [ME *gauge*, EModE *gauge*; compare JEDGE¹·¹]

gauge¹·², †**gage**, †**gadge** /gedʒ/ *v* **1** to measure (against a standard), inspect *la16-*. **2** to ascertain the contents of a cask; to perform the duties of an exciseman *18-e19*. **gauger**, **gadger** **1** person who collects the duty payable on alcohol and other goods *18-*. **2** an assessor, an inspector *15-e17*. [ME *gaugen*; compare JEDGE¹·²]

†**gaun**¹ *n* the butterbur *Petasites hybridus 19*. [altered form of GOWAN]

gaun² /gɔn/ *adj* **1** *of a child* at the walking stage *18- Sh Ork EC*. **2** brisk, active, busy *18-19*. **gaun bodie** a tramp, a Traveller, a tinker *la19-*. Compare **gang aboot** (GANG¹·¹). [presp of GAE]

gaun *see* GAE

gaun-aboot /gɔnə'but/ *adj* on the move, wandering; vagrant, itinerant *20-*. **gaun-aboot bodie** a tramp, a Traveller, a tinker *la19-*. [presp of GAE + ABOOT¹·¹]

gaunch *see* GANSH¹·²

gaunna, **gaunnae** *see* GONNAE

gaunsel *see* GANSEL¹·²

gaunt *see* GANT¹·¹, GANT¹·²

gaup¹·¹, **gawp**, **gowp** /gɔp, gʌup/ *n* **1** a stupid person; a person who gapes *19-*. **2** a stare *la19-*. **gaupit** stupid, silly *la19-*. [see the verb]

gaup¹·², **gawp**, **gowp** /gɔp, gʌup/ *v* **1** to stare open-mouthed *19-*. **2** to devour *19-19, 20- NE*. **gowp-the-lift** a nickname for a person who carries his head high, or has a cast in the eye *19- NE*. [ME *galpen* to gape, yawn]

gaup *see* GOWP²·¹, GOWP²·²

gaut, **galt**, **golt**, *Sh N* **gaat** /gɔt, gɔlt, golt; *Sh N* gat/ *n* **1** a pig; a (castrated) boar *la15-19, 20- Sh Ork N NE*. **2** a rocky point, a large rounded rock *20- Sh Ork*. **3** a fisherman's taboo name or pet name for a pig *20- Sh*. [ON *galti*, *göltr* a hog]

gaut *see* GAIT²·²

gauten *see* GYTE²

Gauway *see* GALLOWAY

gauze, †**gais**, †**gawis**, †**gaze** /gɔz/ *n* a thin, semitransparent fabric *la16-*. [MFr *gaze*]

†**gaval** *v* to revel, carouse *19*. [altered form of CABAL]

gave *see* GIE

gavel¹, *Sh* **gaevil**, *NE* **gaivle**, *NE* **gale**, †**gavill**, †**gayl**, †**gevill** /'gavəl; *Sh NE* 'gevəl; *NE* gel/ *n* **1** the gable of a building *la14-*. **2** one of the side ropes of a herring-net *20- Ork NE EC*. **3** the buttocks or female genitals *la18-19, 20- NE*. **4** the end of a box *16-17*. **gavel end** a gable-end *la18-*. **like the gale o a hoose**, **like the gavel en o a hoose** *of people* extremely overweight *20- NE SW*. [ON *gafl*]

gavel² /'gavəl/ *v of a door* to stand wide open *20- NE*. [probably an extended sense of GAVEL¹]

gavelag *see* GOLACH

gavelock, *SW* **gellock**, †**gavillok**, †**gaiflock** /'gevlək; *SW* 'gɛlək/ *n* a crowbar, a lever *la15-*. [OE *gafeluc* javelin]

gavill *see* GAVEL¹

gavillok *see* GAVELOCK

gaw¹·¹, **gaa**, †**gall** /gɔ, ga/ *n* **1** a gall, a pustule or sore *la16-*. **2** a drainage furrow or channel; a boggy patch of land (with a spring) *la16-*. **3** a defect, a blemish; a mark or flaw *la18-*.

4 *mining* a narrow vein of igneous rock intersecting the coal strata *la18-*. 5 *weaving* a gap in cloth where weft threads are missing (between the end of one piece and the beginning of the next) *20-*. **gaw fur** a furrow at an end-rig used for drainage *19-*. **a gaw in yer back** 1 a bad habit, a weak spot *18-*. 2 a grievance *19-*. [OE *gealla* gall, bile]

†**gaw**[1.2] *v* 1 to make sore (by rubbing) *la16-e19*. 2 to vex, irritate *18-19*. [see the noun]

gaw see GA

gawdnie see GOWDIE

gawf, gawfe see GAFF[1.1]

gawff see GAFF[1.2]

gawis see GAUZE

gawk[1.1] /gɔk/ *n* an awkward, clumsy person; a foolish person *la18-*. **gawkit** stupid, clumsy *19-*. [unknown]

gawk[1.2] /gɔk/ *v* 1 to behave foolishly or giddily; to flirt *19, 20- T WC Uls*. 2 to wander around aimlessly *la19- NE T SW*. [unknown]

gawk[2] /gɔk/ *v* to stare idly or vacantly *la19-*. [unknown]

gawkus /'gɔkəs/ *n* a foolish person *la19- Ork T EC*. [altered form of GAWK[1.1]]

gawky[1.1] /'gɔke/ *n* an awkward, clumsy person; a foolish person *18-19, 20- SW*. [see the verb]

gawky[1.2] /'gɔke/ *v* to behave foolishly or giddily; to flirt *la19- N T Bor Uls*. [altered form of GAWK[1.2]]

gawp see GAUP[1.1], GAUP[1.2]

gawpus, gaapus, gapus /'gɔpəs, 'gapəs, 'gepəs/ *n* a foolish person; a clumsy, awkward person *19-*. [altered form of GAUP[1.1]]

gawsie /'gɔzi, 'gɑsi/ *adj* 1 *of people* plump, fresh-complexioned; jovial-looking; handsome *18-*. 2 *of things* large, ample; imposing, showy *la18-*. 3 *of animals* in good condition *19-*. [unknown]

gay see GEY[1.1], GEY[1.2]

gayl see GAVEL[1]

gaynand see GAIN

gayn call see GAINCALL

gayne- see GAIN-

gaynecome see GANE-COME

gayne cummyng see GAINE-CUMING

†**gayne gevyng** *n* restoring, giving back *la14-e15*. [GAIN- + verbal noun from GIE]

gaynest see GAINEST

gaynsay see GAINSAY

gaynstand see GAINSTAND

†**gayn-ȝeld** *n* a return; recompense *16*. [GAIN- + YIELD[1.1]; compare Dan *gengæld*]

gaze see GAUZE

gazen see GIZZEN[1.1]

geal see JEEL[1.1], JEEL[1.2]

gean, †**gein** /gin/ *n* the wild cherry tree and its fruit *17-*. [Fr *guigne*]

geand see GEEANT

geanis see GENE[2]

Geanis see JANIS

gear[1.1], †**gere,** †**geir,** †**gair** /gir/ *n* 1 equipment *la14-*. 2 property; goods, money or livestock *la14-*. 3 personal possessions, household effects; odds and ends *la18-*. 4 food or drink *la18-*. 5 rubbish, detritus *19-*. 6 arms and armour; weapons *la14-17*. **gerit** provided with arms and armour *la15-16*. **gear gatherer** a person who acquires or amasses wealth, a hoarder *19-*. **guid gear gangs in sma buik** good things come in small bulk (applied to a small but capable person) *la19-*. †**nae gear** not an iota, not a jot *19*. **naither gear nor guid** not a thing *la19- NE*. [ON *gervi*]

†**gear**[1.2] *v* to equip *19*. [see the noun]

gearcairlin see GYRE[1.1]

geat see GET[1.1]

gebbie, *EC* **gaebie** /'gɛbi; *EC* 'gebi/ *n* 1 a person's stomach *la18-*. 2 the crop of a bird *19-*. 3 a person's mouth; a bird's beak *19-*. 4 a horn spoon *la19- Sh Ork NE*. [probably diminutive form of GAB[2]; compare Gael *geuban* a crop, a gizzard]

geck[1.1], †**gek** /gɛk/ *n* 1 a gesture of derision, a gibe *16-*. 2 a fool *la18-*. 3 a scornful or disdainful manner *19*. **geck neckit** having a twisted neck *19- N NE*. †**get a geck** to be made to look foolish *la16-e19*. [Du, LG *gek* a fool]

geck[1.2], †**gek** /gɛk/ *v* 1 to mock, deride *la16-*. 2 to toss the head in scorn; to raise the head proudly or disdainfully *18-*. 3 to sport, play the fool *19-*. 4 to stare rudely *la19- N NE SW*. 5 to turn the head in a vain or vacant manner *19, 20- NE T WC*. 6 to go off the straight, go awry *20- N NE*. 7 to trick, cheat *la16-19*. **geckin** lively, playful *la19- NE SW*. **gaikit** silly *20- Sh NE T*. [Du, LG *gekken* to make a fool of]

ged /gɛd/ *n* the pike *Esox lucius la14-*. [ON *gedda*]

gedder see GAITHER

geddick /'gɛdɪk/ *n* the lesser sand eel *Ammodytes tobianus 19- Sh*. [GED, with diminutive suffix]

Gedward see JETHART

gee /gi/ *n* 1 a fit of sulkiness or temper *17-*. 2 a notion, a fancy *18-*. **tak the gee** to take offence, sulk *la18-*. **tak gees** to have a notion or fancy *20- NE*. [unknown]

gee see JEE[1.1], JEE[1.2]

geeant, gian, †**giand,** †**gyand,** †**geand** /'dʒiənt, 'dʒiən/ *n* a giant *15-19, 20- Sh NE*. [ME *geant, gyant*]

geebald, jeebauld /'dʒibɔld/ *n* a type of long-handled sickle *20- Bor*. [probably altered form of Eng *G-bill* a G-shaped hedgebill]

geed see GAE, GUID[1.1], GUID[1.3]

geedin see GUIDIN

geegaw /'gigɔ, 'dʒidʒɔ/ *n* a bauble, a gaudy trifle *la19-*. [EModE *gewgaw*]

geel, †**guild** /gil/ *n* wort in the process of fermentation *18- Sh Ork*. [Du *gijl*]

geel fat, †**gyle fat,** †**guill fat,** †**geilfat** /'gil fat/ *n* the brewing vessel in which wort is left to ferment *la13-19, 20- Ork*. [GEEL + OE *fæt* a vessel]

†**geel house, geil house** *n* the place where the wort was set to cool *16-e18*. [GEEL + HOOSE[1.1]]

geelum /'giləm/ *n* a rabbet-plane *la19-*. [Fr *guillaume*]

geems see GOOMS

geen see GAE

geenie, †**guinie** /'gini/ *n* a guinea *la17-*. [EModE *guinny*]

geenyoch /'ginjəx/ *adj* ravenous, voracious; greedy *19, 20- literary*. [Gael *gionach*]

geese see GUSE[1.1]

geeskin see JOSKIN

geet see GET[1.1]

geetle see JUITLE[1.1]

gef see GIE, GIF

gefe see GIF

geffin see GIE

geg[1] /gɛg/ *n* a poacher's hook for catching fish *20- Bor*. [compare Eng *gig* a kind of fish spear]

geg[2], **gegg** /gɛg/ *n* a joke, a trick *19, 20- NE Bor*. **geggery** trickery, a practical joke *19, 20- SW*. [compare Eng *gag*]

geg[3], **gig** /gɛg, gɪg/ *n* an article such as a penknife or a piece of wood, used in the game *smuggle-the-gig* (SMUGGLE[1.2]) *19-*. [perhaps altered form of keg (CAG)]

geg see GAIG[1.1], GAIG[1.2]

gegg see GEG[2]

†**gegger** *n* a (protruding) under-lip *e19*. [compare Norw dial *gag, gagar* bent back, and EModE *gag-tooth* a projecting tooth]
geggie /ˈgɛgi/ *n* a travelling theatrical show *19-*. [probably from GEG²]
geiffin *see* GIE
geig *see* JEEG²
geigget *see* GIGOT
geil, *Bor* **gale**, †**gell** /gil; *Bor* gel/ *v* to tingle, smart, ache *16-19, 20- Sh N Bor*. [unknown]
geilfat *see* GEEL FAT
geil house *see* GEEL HOUSE
geill *see* JEEL¹·²
gein *see* GAE, GEAN
geing, **ging** /gɛŋ, giŋ/ *n* human excrement; filth, mud *19-*. **gingie** filthy *19, 20- C Bor*. [OE *genge* a drain, a latrine]
geir *see* GEAR¹·¹
geisen *see* GIZZEN¹·¹
geist *see* JEEST¹·¹, JEEST¹·²
geisting *see* JEESTING
†**geit**¹·¹ *n* a border on a garment *e16*. [perhaps OFr *giez* jesses for a bird of prey]
†**geit**¹·², **jeit** *v* to put a border on a garment *16*. [see the noun]
geit *see* GET¹·¹, JEET
geizan *see* GIZZEN¹·¹
gek *see* GECK¹·¹, GECK¹·²
gell¹·¹ /gɛl/ *n* a crack in wood *19, 20- Sh SW Bor*. [unknown]
gell¹·² /gɛl/ *v of unseasoned wood* to split or crack in drying *19, 20- Sh Ork SW Bor*. [unknown]
gell² /gɛl/ *n* a leech *18-*. **gellie** a leech *19-*. [IrGael *geal*]
†**gell**³, **gale**, **gaill** *v* **1** to yell; to sing raucously *16-19*. **2** to scold *la19*. [OE *galan* to sing, call]
gell⁴ /gɛl/ *adj* brisk, keen *la18-*. [compare GEIL]
gell *see* GALE, GEIL
gellie *see* GAILLIE, GALLYIE, GELL²
gellock *see* GAVELOCK, GOLACH
gelly *see* JEELY, JELLIE
†**gellytroch**, **gallytrough** *n* the Arctic char *Salvelinus alpinus la18-e19*. [unknown]
gem, **gemm** *see* GAME¹·¹
†**gemel**, **gemmel**, **jammall** *adj* twin, double *la15-16*. Compare YAMAL. [AN *gemel*, OFr *jumel*, Lat *gemellus*]
†**gemma band**, **gemmay band**, **jammay band** *n* a hinge *16-e17*. [ME *gemeu* hinge + BAND¹·¹]
gemme *see* GAME¹·¹
gemmel *see* GEMEL
†**gemmell** *n* a two-part harmony *e16*. Compare YAMAL. **gemilling**, **gemynyng** *music* an extra treble line *la15*. [particular sense of GEMEL]
gemmie *see* GAMIE
gemster *see* GAME¹·¹
†**gend** *adj* foolish, simple *la15-e19*. [unknown]
gender *see* GENER¹·²
†**gene**¹, **jayne** *n* an instrument of torture *la16-e17*. [OFr *gehine* a confession extracted by torture, MFr *jaine* a door-jamb]
†**gene**², **genes**, **geanis** *adj of cloth* from Genoa *la16-17*. [from the name of the Italian city]
gener¹·¹ /ˈdʒɛnər/ *n* **1** gender *16-*. **2** progeny *19-*. [AN, OFr *gendre*]
†**gener**¹·², **gender** *v* to engender, beget, cause *la14-e17*. [AN, OFr *gendrer*]
†**general**¹·¹ *n* the master of the mint *la16-17*. [see the adj]
general¹·² /ˈdʒɛnərəl/ *adj* **1** common, relating to a whole class, not specific *la14-*. **2** *in Scottish Universities* designating a first-year, non-specialized course *18-*; compare ORDINAR¹·² (sense 3). **general merchant 1** a shopkeeper of a grocery or general store *20-*. **2** a grocery or general store *20-*. **general service** *see* SERVICE. [ME *general*]
General Assembly /ˈdʒɛnərəl əˈsɛmbli/ *n Presbyterian Church* the highest church court as represented by delegate ministers and elders, assembled annually and presided over by a moderator *la16-*. [GENERAL¹·² + ASSEMBLY]
General Associate Synod /ˈdʒɛnərəl əˈsosɪət sɪnəd/ *n* that section of the Secession Church which refused to take the burgess oath, the ANTIBURGHERS *18-19, 20- historical*. [GENERAL¹·² + ASSOCIATE + SYNOD]
General Council /ˈdʒɛnərəl ˈkʌunsəl/ *n* **1** the deliberative body in the four oldest Scottish Universities, the main functions of which are to elect the Chancellor and four Assessors of the Court and to represent the graduate body *19-*. **2** a council of the realm; a convention of the Estates, taking the place of a parliament *15-16*. [GENERAL¹·² + council (COONCIL)]
general disposition /ˈdʒɛnərəl dɪspəˈzɪʃən/ *n law* a deed meant as a conveyance but lacking the prerequisites of INFEFTMENT, such as a proper description of the land *la19-*. [GENERAL¹·² + DISPOSITION]
†**generat** *adj* generated *16*. [Lat *generātus*, ptp of *generāre*]
genes *see* GENE²
†**genetrice** *n* a female parent *16*. [OFr *genitrice*]
geng *see* GANG¹·¹, GANG¹·²
†**genie** *n* an inherent ability, a natural bent *19*. [Fr *génie*, Lat *genius* a tutelary spirit]
genner *see* GANNER¹·¹
gennick *see* JONICK¹·²
gent, *Sh* **gant** /gɛnt; *Sh* gant/ *n* a tall, thin person *19- Sh SW Bor*. [Norw dial *gand* a pointed stick; a tall thin fellow]
genteelity, **gentility**, †**gentilite** /dʒɛnˈtiləti, dʒɛnˈtɪləti/ *n* **1** good breeding, refinement *19-*. **2** gentry, people born into a high social rank *20- Sh H&I WC Uls*. **3** paganism *16*. [EModE *gentilitie*, Lat *gentīlitās*]
gentie /ˈdʒɛnti/ *adj* **1** neat, dainty, graceful *18- NE EC SW*. **2** genteel; courteous, well-bred *18- NE EC*. **3** *of dress* tasteful *19*. [Fr *gentil*]
gentilite, **gentility** *see* GENTEELITY
gentilman *see* GENTLEMAN
gentle¹·¹, †**gentill** /ˈdʒɛntəl/ *n* a person of high social rank *15-19, 20- historical*. **gentle and semple** gentry and commoners alike *16-*. [see the adj]
gentle¹·², *Sh* **jantle**, †**gentill**, †**gentil** /ˈdʒɛntəl; *Sh* ˈdʒantəl/ *adj* **1** (characteristic of one) of high social birth; gentlemanly, genteel *la14-*. **2** courteous, mild, tender *la15-*. **the gentle persuasion** *Christian Church* the Episcopalian denomination, adhered to by many of the upper classes *la18- NE*. [ME *gentil*]
gentleman, *Sh* **jantleman**, †**gentilman**, †**gentyllman** /ˈdʒɛntəlmən; *Sh* ˈdʒantəlmən/ *n* a man of high birth or rank *la14-*. [ME *gentilman*]
gentlemanny, †**gentlemanie** /ˈdʒɛntəlmani/ *adj* gentlemanly *la16-19, 20- Sh NE T*. [GENTLEMAN + -IE²]
gentre *see* GENTRY
gentrice, †**gentris** /ˈdʒɛntrɪs/ *n* **1** good birth or breeding, gentility *18-*. **2** people of good birth or breeding, gentry *la19-*. **3** the character or behaviour natural to a person of high social status or rank *la14-16*. [ME *gentris*]
gentry, *Sh* **jantry**, †**gentre** /ˈdʒɛntre; *Sh* ˈdʒantri/ *n* **1** a wealthy, land-owning class of people *la19-*. **2** the character or behaviour natural to a person of high social status or rank *16-18, 20- NE T*. **3** a person of high social status; the rank of a gentleman *18-19, 20- T*. [ME *gentri*]
gentyllman *see* GENTLEMAN
genȝie *see* GANȜE
genzie *see* GANSEY

geo /gjo, gjʌu/ *n* an inlet of the sea with steep, rocky sides; a cleft with deep water among rocks, frequently in place-names *17- Sh Ork N*. [ON *gjá*]

geong *see* GANG[1.1]

Geordie /'dʒɔrdi/ *n* **1** a diminutive form of the name George *la16-*. **2** a rustic, a yokel; a miner *la19-*. **3** a guinea coin *la18-e20, la20- historical*. [altered from the personal name *George*]

gep-shot, gjep-shot /'gɛpʃɔt, 'gjɛpʃɔt/ *adj* having the lower jaw projecting beyond the upper *la19- Sh*. [Norw *geip* a grimace, a mouth + participial adj from SHUIT]

ger *see* GAR[2]

†**geraflour, gerofle, jereflour** *n* the gillyflower *15-16*. [MFr *giroflee*]

gere *see* GAR[2], GEAR[1.1]

gerofle *see* GERAFLOUR

gerrock /'gɛrək/ *n* a coalfish *Pollachius virens* in its first year *19- NE*. [probably Gael *geàrr* short, squat + diminutive suffix]

Gers /dʒɛrz/ *n* a nickname for Glasgow Rangers Football Club *la20-*. [shortened form of *Rangers*]

gers, gerse *see* GIRSE[1.1]

†**gersone** *n* a fellow *e16*. [ME *garsoun*]

gersting *see* GIRTH[2.2]

gersty *see* GORSTIE

gersum *see* GRASSUM

gert /gɛrt/ *n* a piece of unenclosed ground for grazing cattle; waste ground; frequently in place-names *la19- Sh*. [ON *gerði* a fenced field]

gert *see* GAR[2]

gerten *see* GAIRTEN

ges *see* GUESS[1.1], GUESS[1.2]

geskafoo /'gɛskəfu/ *adj* affable *20- Ork*. [ON *gæðska* goodness, kindness + *fullr* full]

†**gess** *n* a wooden container of standard measure for fruit; the amount thus measured *la17-e18*. [unknown]

gest *see* GHAIST, GUEST, JEEST[1.1], JEEST[2.1], JEEST[2.2]

gester, jester /'dʒɛstər/ *v* **1** to gesture *20- Sh Ork EC Bor*. **2** to strut, swagger *la18- EC Bor*. [from the Older Scots noun *gesture*]

gesting *see* JEESTING

gesyne *see* JIZZEN

get[1.1], **geet, geat, geit, gyte** /gɛt, git, gʌit/ *n* **1** offspring, progeny; a child *15-*. **2** *derogatory* a brat; a bastard *16-*. **3** a coalfish in its second stage *20- NE EC*. **4** begetting, birth *la14-16*. **getling** a young child, infant; a bastard *18-19, 20- EC SW*. [see the verb]

get[1.2], **git, gete, gait** /gɛt, gɪt, get/ *v pt* **got, goat,** †**gat,** †**gate,** *ptp* also **gottin** †**gattin,** †**getten,** †**get 1** to beget, engender *14-*. **2** to obtain *la14-*. **3** to find, locate by looking: ◊*ye'll get it in ma pooch 18-*. **4** to manage or accomplish; to find an opportunity: ◊*I couldnae get sleeping*; ◊*I got wachled hame some wey or anither 18-*. **5** to marry, take as a spouse *la18-*. **6** to be called, be addressed as: ◊*Mackenzie's ma name but I aye get Jock frae her la18-*. **7** to be able or allowed to go somewhere: ◊*can I get downstairs? la19-*. **8** to accompany: ◊*I'll get ye as far as the bus stop la20-*. **9** to be struck, receive a blow: ◊*I gat in the lug wi a steen 19- NE T*. **gettin, getting** becoming: ◊*she's gey auld getting la20-*. **get a mens o** to get satisfaction from, to get the better of; to get even with *17-19, 20- Sh Ork NE*. **get a moyen o** to get news or a forewarning of something *la19- NE*. **get away** to die *la19-*. **get by 1** to get past, succeed in passing *20-*. **2** to avoid or dispense with *19, 20- Sh NE*. **get forth** to succeed in going onwards, make progress (on a journey) *19, 20- SW Bor*. **get one's hands on** to catch someone (for the purposes of punishment) *la18-*. **get intae 1** to succeed in opening something *la19-*. **2** to become familiar with or practised in (a subject or technique) *la20-*. **get it ower the fingers** to be reprimanded *20-*. **get on for** to get a job as; to be promoted to *19-*. **get on tae** to attack verbally, scold *la20-*. **get on tae be** = *get on for*. **get oot** to give full vent to, finish off *la18-19, 20- Sh NE EC*. **get oot wi** to speak suddenly or forcibly *la18-*. **get ower 1** to get the upper hand of *la19-*. **2** to last out; to subsist *19- NE*. **get roon** to accomplish, master *la19-*. **get through** to escape; to recover from *18-*. **get tore in** to tackle vigorously *20-*. **get up in years** to grow old *19-*. **get weel up** to rise in position, succeed *19-*. [ON *geta*]

get *see* GAIT[3]

gete *see* GET[1.2]

gether *see* GAITHER

gett *see* GAIT[3]

getten *see* GET[1.2]

geud *see* GUID[1.1], GUID[1.3]

geup[1.1] /gep, gøp/ *n* a foolish person *20- Ork*. [Norw dial *gap*]

geup[1.2] /gep, gøp/ *v* to make a fool of *20- Ork*. [see the noun]

geve *see* GIE, GIF

gevill *see* GAVEL[1]

†**gevilling, geweling** *n* a javelin *16*. Compare JAVELING. [MFr *javeline*]

gevin *see* GIE

gey[1.1], **gie, gay** /gae, ge/ *adj* **1** excellent, splendid *la15-*. **2** *of a quantity or amount* considerable, good-sized, great *19-*. **3** disreputable, wild *la19-*. **4** bright, showy, handsome *15-e19*. **geylies 1** *of health* well enough, tolerably well *18-*. **2** quite, rather; very *la18-*. **3** fairly well, pretty nearly *la18-*. **geylike** excellent, splendid *la19-*. **gaily, gayly 1** in a joyous, showy or pleasing fashion *15-*. **2** quite, rather; very *la17-19, 20- Bor*. **a gey penny** a considerable sum of money *19-*. [OFr *gai*]

gey[1.2], **gay** /gae, ge/ *adv* **1** considerably, very; rather *la17-*. **2** brightly, showily *la15-e16*. **gey and, gey an'** rather, very *18-*. **gey kind o, gey kinna** rather badly *20-*. [see the adj]

geyler *see* JILE[1.1]

geyze /gaez/ *v* to become leaky; to warp *la18-19, 20- H&I EC*. [back-formation from *geisen* (GIZZEN[1.1])]

gezy *see* JEEZY

ghaist, †**gast,** †**gaist,** †**gest** /gest/ *n* **1** an apparition, a ghost *la14-*. **2** a term of contempt for an emaciated, sickly or undersized person *16-*. **3** (a piece of) shaly coal burnt to its ashy state, a white slaty cinder *19-*; compare GUEST (sense 3). [OE *gāst* breath, the soul, a spirit]

gheeho /gi'ho/ *n* an uncouth, blustering man *20- H&I*. [unknown]

ghillie *see* GILLIE[1.1], GILLIE[1.2]

gian, giand *see* GEEANT

Giant's Grave /'dʒaeənts grev/ *n* a popular name for the ruins of prehistoric remains *la19-*. [GEEANT + GRAVE[1.1]]

†**gib**[1], **jib** *n* a kind of sweet made with treacle and spices *19*. [perhaps shortened form of *Gibraltar rock*]

gib[2] /gɪb/ *n* **1** a name for a cat; a cat *la15-*. **2** a (castrated) tom-cat *19-*. **gibbie** a cat *la18-*. **gib cat** a tom-cat *19-*. [shortened from the name *Gilbert*]

gib[3] /gɪb/ *n mining* a wooden prop *la19-*. [probably Eng *gib* a piece of metal used for keeping parts of a machine tight]

gibbery[1], **jibbery** /'dʒɪbəri/ *n* gingerbread *la18-*. [aphetic form of GINGEBREID[1.1]]

gibbery[2] /'dʒɪbəri/ *n* a game of marbles *la19- NE*. [unknown]

gibbi-gaa /'gɪbi 'ga/ *n* the name applied to the person counted out in children's games *20- Sh*. [from the last line of a counting rhyme]

gibble /'gɪbəl/ *n pl* tools, articles, wares *la18- NE T EC.*
  gibblet an implement, a tool, a utensil *19, 20- NE EC SW.* [unknown]
gibble-gabble[1.1] /'gɪbəl gabəl/ *n* chatter, tittle-tattle *la18-.* [reduplicative compound from Eng *gabble*]
gibble-gabble[1.2] /'gɪbəl gabəl/ *v* to prattle, chatter *18-.* [see the noun]
gibblet *see* GIBBLE
giblet-check /'dʒɪblət tʃɛk/ *n* a rabbet cut in masonry to allow a door to fit flush with the wall *19, 20- NE T.* [unknown]
gid *see* GIE
gide *see* GUIDE[1.1]
gid gad, gid gow /'gɪd gad, 'gɪd gʌu/ *interj* an expression of disgust *la19- Ork T EC Bor.* [altered form of Eng *Good God*; compare GAD, GUID[1.3]]
gie, gae, give, †**gif,** †**gef,** †**geve** /gi, ge, gɪv/ *v pt* **gied, gae, gid, gave, gien,** *NE* **gya,** †**geve,** †**gaif,** †**gaff,** †**gef,** *ptp* **gien, gied, given,** †**giffin,** †**gevin,** †**geffin, geiffin 1** to grant, bestow, give *la14-.* **2** to strike: ◊*give him across the head with the butt of your rod 16-.* **3** to feed *20- Sh Ork NE.* **gies** give us, give me *20-.* **gimme, gimma** give me *la18-.* **given** damned, accursed: ◊*A had tae sit twa given hoors 20-.* **given name** a first name, a forename *la19-.* †**give down 1** to admit, acknowledge (legally) *18-19.* **2** to reduce or remit an amount *la16-e18.* **gie a stane feet** *in curling* to speed the progress of a stone by sweeping the ice in front of it *19-.* **gie someone a hat** to salute someone in passing by raising one's hat *18-19, 20- T EC Bor.* **gie him heels** = *gie a stane feet 19- WC SW.* **gie a ploo mair land** to adjust the width of the cut to be made by a plough *20-.* †**gif obedience** to render obedience or dutiful service; to submit *17.* **gie ower** to give up, abandon *18-.* **gie's-a-piece** a hanger-on, a parasite *19, 20- T Bor.* **gie up** to hold up a child for baptism *20-.* **no give a tinker's curse** to not care at all *19-.* [OE *giefan*]
gie *see* GEY[1.1]
gied *see* GAE, GIE
gielainger *see* GILEYNOUR
gien, gies *see* GIE
gif, *SW* **give,** †**gef,** †**gefe,** †**geve** /gɪf; *SW* gɪv/ *conj* if *la14-.* [variant of Scots *if*, with initial consonant assimilated to gif (GIE)]
gif *see* GIE
giff-gaff[1.1] /'gɪf gaf/ *n* **1** mutual help, give and take, fair exchange *18-.* **2** interchange of talk, repartee *19-.* [reduplicative compound from *gif* (GIE)]
giff-gaff[1.2] /'gɪf gaf/ *v* **1** to exchange or barter *la18-.* **2** to bandy words, exchange banter *la18-.* [see the noun]
giffin *see* GIE
gift /gɪft/ *n* **1** that which is given; a present, a donation *la14-.* **2** a natural talent or quality *la15-.* **3** *law* a royal gift, a royal grant of property which has reverted to the Crown *la19-.* **giftie** a sense of power, an ability *la18.* [OE *gift*]
gig /gɪg/ *n mining* a winding engine *19-.* **gigman, gigsman** the man in charge of a winding engine *19-.* [unknown; compare Eng *gig, whirliegig* something that whirls]
gig *see* GEG[3], JEEG[1.2]
gigot, †**geigget** /'dʒɪgət/ *n* **1** a leg of mutton or lamb (sometimes also used of pork or beef) *la16-.* **2** a lump or hunk *20- Ork.* [MFr *gigot*]
†**gild**[1] *n* clamour, din *16-e19.* [unknown]
gild[2] /gɪld/ *adj* **1** *of cattle or fish* of full value *16-19, 20- Sh Ork.* **2** great; clever *18-19, 20- Sh.* [ON *gildr*]
gild *see* GILT[3], GUILD
gildee /gɪ'di/ *n* the whiting, pout or bib *Trisopterus luscus la18- H&I.* [unknown]

gilder[1.1] /'gɪldər/ *n* a giggle *20- Ork.* [perhaps altered form of GALDER[1.1]]
gilder[1.2] /'gɪldər/ *v* to giggle, snigger *20- Ork.* [see the noun]
gildro /'gɪldro/ *n* a game in which two people are tied together and cannot untangle themselves *20- Ork.* [Norw *gildre* a trap, a snare]
gileynour, †**golenʒeour,** †**gielainger,** †**gallayniel** /gə'lɛnjur/ *n* a cheat, a swindler *la16-19, 20- literary.* [compare OFr *Gilain* a quasi-proper name designating a swindler, with allusion to *guiler* to deceive]
gilfa, garfa /'gɪlfə, 'garfə/ *n* **1** the failure of the wort to ferment in the brewing process *20- Sh Ork.* **2** a fit of idleness *20- SW.* [GEEL + FA[1.1]]
gilgal, gill-gall /'gɪlgal, 'gɪlgɔl/ *n* a commotion, an uproar *la18- Sh N NE.* [onomatopoeic]
gill[1] /dʒɪl/ *n* one fourth of a MUTCHKIN, about three quarters of the imperial gill; a vessel holding this measure *la18-19, 20- historical.* **gillie** = GILL[1] *la18-e19.* †**gill bells** the bells of St Giles church in Edinburgh which were rung at 11.30 am (the time when many paid a visit to a tavern) *18-19.* [OFr *gille*]
gill[2], **gyll,** *Sh* **gyill** /gɪl; *Sh* gjɪl/ *n* a ravine, a gully; frequently in place-names *13-.* [ON *gil*]
†**gillenʒe, golenʒe, galenʒe** *n* a deceitful or evasive statement or argument *16-17.* [unknown]
†**gillet, gillat** *n* a mare *la14-e17.* [perhaps diminutive form of *Gill* the female name]
gillet *see* JILLET
gill-gall *see* GILGAL
gillie[1.1], **ghillie** /'gɪli, 'gɪle/ *n* **1** a lad, a youth *17-.* **2** a sportsman's attendant (in deerstalking or angling in the Highlands) *19-.* **3** a male servant, an attendant on a Highland chief; a Highlander *15-.* **gillie callum, killumkallum** the sword-dance; the name of the tune to which it is danced *la18-.* †**gilliecasflue** the attendant who carried the Highland chief over wet places *18-e19.* †**gilliewetfoot** an attendant; a scoundrel *la18-e19.* [Gael *gille* a lad, a servant]
gillie[1.2], **ghillie** /'gɪli, 'gɪle/ *v* to act as a sportsman's attendant *20-.* [see the noun]
†**gillie**[2], **jilly** *n* a high-spirited girl *la17-e19.* [diminutive form of *Gill* the female name]
gillieperous /gə'lipərəs/ *n* a fool; a rough ungainly person *20- NE.* [unknown]
gillore *see* GALORE[1.1]
gillravager *see* GILRAVAGE[1.2]
gilly *see* GULLY[1.1]
†**gillygacus** *n* a foolish person *18-e19.* [perhaps alliterating compound of GAWKUS]
†**gillygawkie** *n* a silly young person, a foolish girl *la18-e19.* [perhaps variant of GILLYGACUS]
gilly-gawpus /gɪle'gɔpəs/ *n* a foolish person; a tall awkward person *la18-19, 20- T.* [perhaps variant of GILLYGACUS]
†**gilly-gawpy** *n* a foolish person *18-19.* [perhaps variant of GILLYGACUS]
gilp *see* JILP[1.2]
gilpie /'gɪlpi/ *n* **1** a lively young girl; a tomboy *18-.* **2** a lively, mischievous youth *18-19.* Compare KELPIE[2]. [perhaps variant of GILPIN]
gilpin, gulpin /'gɪlpən, 'gʌlpən/ *n* **1** a big, stout or well-grown young person *19, 20- N NE SW.* **2** a loutish person *19, 20- NE Uls.* [variant of GALOPIN]
gilravage[1.1], **gulravage,** *SW* **galravich,** †**gilravitch** /gɪl'ravədʒ, gʌl'ravədʒ; *SW* gal'ravɪtʃ/ *n* **1** merrymaking, horseplay; a lively commotion, an uproar *la18-19, 20- SW Bor Uls.* **2** a state of confusion, a disturbance *19- EC Bor.* **3** a noisy disorderly crowd, a mob *19- SW Uls.* [see the verb]

gilravage[1,2], **gulravage**, *SW* **galravitch** /gɪlˈravədʒ, gʌlˈravədʒ; *SW* galˈravɪtʃ/ *v* **1** to eat and drink immoderately; to indulge in high living *18-19, 20- Sh C SW*. **2** to make merry, enjoy oneself noisily, create a noisy disturbance *la18-19, 20- C SW Bor*. **3** to rove about, plunder *19, 20- Bor*. **4** to devour *19, 20- literary*. **gillravager** a wild or lawless person *19, 20- Uls*. [unknown; compare Eng *ravage*, RAVISH]

gilse *see* GRILSE

gilt[1] /gɪlt/ *n* a young sow, especially before her first farrowing *la15-*. [ON *gyltr*]

gilt[2] /gɪlt/ *n* a rectangular stack of hay or heather *la19- Sh Ork N*. [extended sense of GILT[1]; compare SOO[1]]

gilt[3], **gild** /gɪlt, gɪld/ *v* **1** to cover with gold, gild *la14-*. **2** *of decaying fish* to become yellow *18-19, 20- Bor*. [ptp of Older Scots *gild*]

†giltin *adj* gilded, gilt, golden *la15-16*. [ptp of Older Scots *gild*]

†gilty *adj* gilted, gilt, golden *e16*. [Older Scots *gilt* gilding + -IE[2]]

gim, **†gym** /dʒɪm/ *adj* neat, spruce *16-19, 20- NE T*. **jimmy 1** neat, spruce *19, 20- Uls*. **2** ingeniously made *la20- Sh*. [perhaps JIMP[2,2]]

gimme *see* GIE

gimmer, *Sh* **gjimmer** /ˈgɪmər; *Sh* ˈgjɪmər/ *n* a year-old ewe; a ewe between its first and second shearing *15-*. [ON *gymbr* a ewe-lamb]

gimmer *see* KIMMER[1,1]

gimp *see* JIMP[2,2]

gimse /gɪms/ *v* to toss the head *20- Ork*. [Norw dial *gimsa*]

gin[1], **†gyn** /dʒɪn/ *n* **1** a (mechanical) device, a trap *la14-*. **2** a bolt, a lock, a latch *la15-19*. **3** a contrivance, a stratagem *la14-e16*. **4** a military engine *la14-e16*. [ME *gin*]

gin[2] /gɪn/ *conj* **1** if, whether *la16-*. **2** if only *la18-*. [perhaps reduced form of *given* (GIE), compare GIF]

gin[3,1], **†gain** /gɪn/ *prep* **1** *of time* by, before *la18-*. **2** in anticipation of, in readiness for *19- NE T*. **3** against *19, 20- Uls*. [aphetic form of AGAIN[1,2]; compare GAIN-]

gin[3,2] /gɪn/ *conj* **1** by the time that; before *la18-*. **2** until *la18-*. [see the prep]

gin[4] /gɪn/ *conj* than *la19- NE T*. [extended use of GIN[3,2]]

ging *see* GANG[1,1], GANG[1,2], GEING

ginge /dʒɪndʒ/ *n* ginger *18-19, 20- NE*. [back-formation from GINGEBREID[1,1]]

gingebreid[1,1], **gingebreed** /ˈdʒɪndʒbrid/ *n* gingerbread *la16-19, 20- NE*. [ME *gingebred*, OFr *gingembras* preserved ginger]

†gingebreid[1,2] *adj* gaudy, extravagant; insubstantial *la18-19*. [see the noun]

ginger /ˈdʒɪndʒər/ *n* a sparkling soft drink (of any flavour) *la19-*. [reduced form of Eng *ginger beer*]

gingle *see* CHINGLE

†gink *n* a trick, a prank *la19*. [voiced variant of KINK[1,1]]

ginkum /ˈgɪŋkəm/ *n* **1** a trick, a dodge *la19- NE*. **2** a habit, a trait *la19- NE*. [GINK, with diminutive suffix]

ginnle /ˈgɪnəl/ *v* to catch a fish by the gills *19- WC SW Bor Uls*. [from the noun GINNLES]

ginnles /ˈgɪnəlz/ *npl* **1** the gills of a fish *19- NE WC*. **2** the cheeks *19- NE WC*. [unknown]

ginshot *see* GAINSHOT

giola *see* GYOLA

gip[1] /gɪp/ *n* the jaw of a fish *20- N NE EC*. [compare Norw dial *gip* a gap, a jaw]

gip[2,1] /gɪp, gjɪp/ *n* a cut in the belly of a fish for gutting; herring guts *20- Sh*. [compare Norw dial *gipe* a cut, a large wound]

gip[2,2] /gɪp, gjɪp/ *v* to gut fish *20- Sh*. [compare Norw dial *gipa* to make gape]

gipe *see* JUPE[1]

gird[1,1], **girr**, **†gir** /gɪrd, gɪr/ *n* **1** a saddle-girth *16-*. **2** a band or hoop for a barrel *la16-*. **3** a child's hoop *la18-e20, la20- historical*. **4** a hoop-shaped frame hung from the shoulders for carrying two pails *19, 20- literary*. **5** a hoop for a skirt or petticoat *la19-e20, la20- historical*. **6** a band or strap used to support a bed *16*. **†gordie** *mining* a rope and chain for pulling hutches *e19*. **gurdy** *mining* the pulley on a self-acting incline *la19- C*. **girdsting** a length of wood for making hoops *16-e17*; compare *girthsting* (GIRTH[2,2]). [see the verb]

gird[1,2], **girr** /gɪrd, gɪr/ *v* **1** to provide a barrel with hoops *16-*. **2** to encircle, fasten with a band; to put a saddle-girth on a horse *la14-19, 20- Sh*. **girdin 1** the act of furnishing with bands or hoops *la15-*. **2** a saddle-girth *la15-19, 20- Sh*. **3** a rope *la19- NE*. **4** material for girths or hoops *17*. [OE *gyrdan*; compare GIRTH[2,2]]

gird[2,1] /gɪrd/ *n* **1** a knock, a blow *la14-19, 20- NE T Bor*. **2** a gust, a blast *19*. **3** a moment, a quick spasm *la18-19*. [unknown]

gird[2,2] /gɪrd/ *v* **1** to rush (at); to perform vigorously or with force *la14-19, 20- Sh*. **2** to push or drive forward *la19*. **3** to strike, deliver a blow *la15-e19*. **4** to pierce *15-e16*. **†let gird**, **leit gird** to strike, deliver a blow *la15-e19*. [unknown]

girdle, **†girdill** /ˈgɪrdəl/ *n* an iron plate used for baking, traditionally circular with a hooped handle for hanging over a fire *15-*. **girdle scone** a type of scone baked on a GIRDLE, or on a frying-pan or a hot-plate *la19-*. [metathesis of ME *grydel*]

girg *see* JIRG[2,2]

girke *see* JIRK

girkienet, **girkin** *see* JERKIN[2]

girl, **grill**, **†grile** /gɪrl, gɪrl/ *v* to shiver, shudder *e16, 19- Bor*. [ME *grillen* to offend, grieve, shudder]

girls *see* GRILSE

girn[1,1], **gurn** /gɪrn, gʌrn/ *n* **1** a snarl *18-*. **2** a whine, a whimper; grumbling or fault-finding *la18-*. **3** a grin, a grimace *la19-*. **4** a gaping furrow *20-*. **5** a bad-tempered or fault-finding person *20-*. **girnie**, **girny** *adj* peevish, ill-tempered *19-*. **girnie**, **girny** *n* a fretful, bad-tempered person *la19-*. **girnigo** a peevish person *19-*. **girnigo gabbie**, **girnigo gibbie** term of address to a petulant child *la18-19, 20- Ork EC Uls*. **girny gib** a fretful person, a peevish child *la19, 20- Bor Uls*. [see the verb]

girn[1,2], **gurn** /gɪrn, gʌrn/ *v* **1** to snarl, grimace *la14-*. **2** to complain peevishly, moan or grumble *18-*. **3** to grin, sneer *la18-*. **4** *of soil* to crack *la19-*. **5** *of clothes* to gape *19, 20- EC*. **girner** a moaning, peevish person *la20-*. [metathesis of Older Scots *grin*]

girn[2,1] /gɪrn/ *n* a noose, a snare *la14-*. [metathesis of OE *grin*]

girn[2,2] /gɪrn/ *v* to ensnare *15-*. [see the noun]

girnel[1,1], **girnal**, *SW* **garnel**, **†garnale**, **†grinnale**, **†granale** /ˈgɪrnəl; *SW* ˈgarnəl/ *n* **1** a storage chest for meal or cereals *la15-*. **2** a granary, a storehouse *15-19, 20- NE*. [compare GIRNER]

†girnel[1,2], **girnal** *v* to store (food); to hold in storage *16-e18*. [see the noun]

†girner *n* a storage chest for meal or cereals *la16-e17*. [AN *gerner* a storehouse]

girnigo *see* GIRN[1,1]

girr *see* GIRD[1,1], GIRD[1,2]

girran /ˈgɪrən/ *n* a small boil or pustule *19, 20- N H&I SW*. [Gael *guirean*]

girse[1,1], **gress**, **gerse**, **grass**, **†gres**, **†gers**, **†gyrs** /gɪrs, grɛs, gɛrs, gras/ *n* **1** grass, grassland, pasture *la14-*. **2** a stalk or blade of grass *la19- NE*. **girsie, gressy 1** grassy *16-*. **2** *of cereal crops* interspersed with grass *la19-*. **grass beef** beef from grass-fed cattle *la18-*. **girse-gawed** having cuts or cracks between the toes *19- NE SW*. **girse-guide** = *girse-heuk 20- Sh*. **girse-heuk** the hooked metal cross-stay between shaft and blade of a scythe *20- Ork NE T*. **grass-ill 1** a disease of young lambs *19-*. **2** a disease of horses *20- T*. †**gres maill, grassmaill** rent for pasturage *la15-18*. †**girseman, gersman, gresman** a landless tenant with only rights of pasturage *la12-19*. **grass-nail** = *girse-heuk 19-*. **grass sickness 1** a disease of lambs, apparently a form of BRAXY *20-*. **2** a disease of horses *20-*. **get girsie stibble** to enjoy the best of fare *20- NE*. [OE *græs, gærs*]

girse[1,2], **gress, grass** /gɪrs, grɛs, gras/ *v* **1** to pasture animals *16-*. **2** to remove from office *la18-19, 20- historical*.

girsin pasturage, grazing land *la16-17, 18- Ork N NE*. [see the noun]

girsell *see* GIRSLE

girsill *see* GRILSE

girsin *see* GIRSE[1,2]

girsle, grissle, †**girsell** /'gɪrsəl, 'grɪsəl/ *n* **1** cartilage in meat, gristle *la16-*. **2** a fragment of crisp or caked porridge from the inside of the pan; something charred *19-*. **3** (the shaft or stump of) a quill pen *la18-e19*. [OE *gristle*]

girst, grist /gɪrst, grɪst/ *n* corn for grinding *15-*. [OE *grīst*]

girt *see* GREAT[1,2]

†**girth**[1], **gyrth** *n* **1** (a place of) sanctuary *la14-e19*. **2** security; immunity *la14-16*. [metathesis of OE *griþ*, ON *grið*]

girth[2,1] /gɪrθ/ *n* **1** a saddle-girth *la15-*. **2** a child's hoop *la18-19, 20- Bor*. **3** a band or hoop for a barrel *la15-19*. **gurthie,** †**gurdy 1** corpulent, fat *19, 20- EC*. **2** heavy, oppressive *19, 20- EC*. [ON *gjörð*; compare GIRD[1,1]]

†**girth**[2,2] *v* to provide a barrel with hoops; to surround *16-e17*. **girthing, girthin 1** providing with hoops *16-e17*. **2** material for girths *e17*. **girthsting, gersting** a length of wood suitable for use as a barrel-hoop *15-e17*. [see the noun; compare GIRD[1,2]]

girth cross, †**girth cors** /gɪrθ 'krɔs/ *n* a cross marking the limits of a place of sanctuary; frequently in place-names *16-19, 20- historical*. [GIRTH[1] + CROSS[1,1]]

girtling *see* GREAT[1,2]

girzie /'gɪrzi/ *n* a maidservant, a young woman *19, 20- T EC*. [metathesized diminutive of the female name *Grizel*]

gising, gissan *see* JIZZEN

gissie *see* GUSSIE[1,1], GUSSIE[1,2]

git *see* GET[1,2]

gitter *see* GUTTER[1,1], GUTTER[1,2]

gitteral /'gɪtərəl/ *adj* low, mean, vulgar *la19- Ork*. [compare GUTTER[1,1], KITERAL]

give *see* GIE, GIF

given *see* GIE

gizen *see* GIZZERN

gizintie *see* GAESINTIE

gizz, †**jiz** /dʒɪz/ *n* **1** the face *19, 20- literary*. **2** a wig *la18*. †**jeezy, gezy** a wig *la18-e19*. [shortened form of Eng *jasey*]

gizzen[1,1], *Ork Uls* **gazen**, *Bor* **geizan,** †**geisen,** †**gyzen** /'gɪzən; *Ork Uls* 'gezən; *Bor* 'gʌɪzən/ *v* **1** to shrink; to warp, leak *18-*. **2** to dry up, wither or shrivel *la18-*; compare KIZEN. **3** *of the throat* to be or become parched *la18-*. [compare Icel *gisna* to become leaky]

gizzen[1,2] /'gɪzən/ *adj* **1** dry, parched, shrivelled *la18-*. **2** *of containers* cracked, leaky *la18-*. [ON *gisinn* leaky]

gizzent /'gɪzənt/ *adj* sated, surfeited; saturated *20- NE T Bor*. [unknown]

gizzern, guzzern, gizen, *Sh* **gjuseren,** †**guisserne** /'gɪzərn, 'gʌzərn, 'gɪzən; *Sh* 'gjøzərn/ *n* the throat *la16-*. [ME *giserne*]

gjaevel, gyevel /'gjavəl, 'gjevəl/ *v* to nibble *la19- Sh*. [Norw dial *geivla* to chew slowly]

gjang *see* GANG[1,1]

gjep-shot *see* GEP-SHOT

gjimmer *see* GIMMER

gjoger, gyoger /'gjogər/ *n* a sprain *la19- Sh*. [Norw dial *gjøgr*]

gjonger /'gjɔŋgər/ *n fisherman's taboo* a horse *20- Sh*. [ON *gangari* an ambling nag, a palfrey]

gjoppen *see* GOWPEN[1,2]

gjot *see* GYTE[2]

gjuseren *see* GIZZERN

glaab /glab/ *n* **1** an opening between hills or between islands through which a distant object may be seen *la19- Sh*. **2** a dale, a hollow *20- Sh*. [Norw dial *glap*]

glaan[1,1] /glɑn/ *n* a whetstone *la19- Sh*. [compare Icel *glan* burnished gloss]

glaan[1,2] /glɑn/ *v* to whet, sharpen *20- Sh*. [Norw dial *glana* to gleam]

glabber *see* CLABBER

glack, †**glak** /glak/ *n* **1** a hollow between hills, a defile, a ravine *16-*. **2** an open area in woodland *19- NE T*. **3** the angle between thumb and forefinger *19, 20- N*. **4** the fork of a tree or road *19, 20- NE*. **5** a handful, a morsel *la18-19*. **glackefu** a small handful, a pinch *20- NE*. **glack someone's mitten** to put money in someone's hand, tip someone *18-*. [Gael, IrGael *glac*]

glad *see* GLED[2,1], GLED[2,2]

glade *see* GLED[2,2]

glaep[1,1] /glep/ *n* a gulp, a bite; the act of swallowing greedily *20- Sh Ork*. [see the verb]

glaep[1,2], **glep** /glep, glɛp/ *v* to gulp, swallow greedily *20- Sh Ork N*. **glaeit and spued** unhealthy looking *20- Ork*. [ON *gleypa*]

glaerl *see* GLAUR[2]

glaff *see* GLIFF[1,1]

glafter /'glɑftər/ *n* loud, foolish laughter *20- Sh Ork*. **glafter-it** boisterously jolly; excitable *20- Sh Ork*. [perhaps onomatopoeic with infl from *laughter*]

glag *see* GLUG[1,1], GLUG[1,2]

glagger /'glagər/ *v* to desire eagerly, long for *la19- NE*. [probably extended sense of GLAG]

glaiber /'glebər/ *v* to talk incessantly or idly, babble *19, 20- N Bor Uls*. [probably onomatopoeic]

glaid *see* GLED[1], GLED[2,1], GLED[2,2], GLID

glaik[1,1] /glek/ *n* **1** a foolish, thoughtless person *16-*. **2** a flash or gleam of reflected light *la18-19, 20- WC*. **glaikery,** †**glaikrie** foolish behaviour *la16-19, 20- Sh*. **glaikie** thoughtless, foolish *la19-*. [unknown]

glaik[1,2] /glek/ *v* **1** to trifle or flirt with; to play around *la16-*. **2** to look foolishly or idly *la16-19*. [unknown]

glaikit, *NE* **gleekit** /'glekɪt; *NE* 'glikɪt/ *adj* **1** foolish, stupid; thoughtless, irresponsible *la15-*. **2** *of a child* over-fond, clinging *19- NE EC*. **3** playful, full of pranks; flirtatious *la18-e19*. [unknown]

glaiks[1], †**glaikis,** †**glaykis** /gleks/ *npl* **1** trickery, deception; practical jokes or tricks *16-*. **2** a puzzle; a game or toy *la16-19*. **3** sexual desire, wantonness *16*. †**cast the glaiks in a person's een** to deceive *19*. †**fling the glaiks in a person's een** to deceive *19*. †**get the glaiks** to be deceived *la16-18*. **gie somebody the glaiks** to deceive someone *18-*. [unknown]

glaiks² /gleks/ *npl* **1** a lever or shaft attached to a churn-staff to facilitate churning *19- SW Uls*. **2** an implement for twisting straw into ropes *20- SW Uls*. [IrGael *glac* a grip, a handle; compare GLACK]

glaim, gleam, †gleme /glem, glim/ *n* **1** a shaft of light; a flash of lightning *la15-*. **2** a flame *la18- NE T*. [OE *glǣm*]

glairy /ˈglere/ *adj* gaudy, showy *19- Sh NE EC*. [Eng *glare* + -IE²]

glaise /glez/ *n* a heat from a fire; a burn from a fire *la16-19, 20- Sh N T*. [unknown]

glaiss *see* GLESS¹·¹, GLESS¹·², GLESS¹·³, GLAIZE¹

glaister¹ /ˈglestər/ *n* a thin covering of snow or ice *19, 20- SW Bor*. [variant of GLISTER¹·¹]

†glaister², glaster *v* **1** to brag, prattle *16-e19*. **2** to shout, bawl *18-e19*. [unknown]

glaive *see* GLAVE

glaize¹, glaze, *NE* **glaiss** /glez/; *NE* gles/ *v* **1** to furnish with glass *20-*; compare GLESS¹·². **2** to make shiny *20-*. **3** to smooth over, make smooth *20- Sh NE*. [ME *glasen*]

glaize² /gles, glez/ *adj of knitting or weaving* open or coarse in texture *20- Sh Ork*. [Norw dial *glesen* sparse]

glaizie, glazey /ˈglezi, ˈgleze/ *adj* **1** glittering, shiny *18-*. **2** *of sunshine* bright but watery (indicating more rain) *20- H&I WC SW Uls*. [GLAIZE¹ + -IE²]

glak *see* GLACK

glam *see* GLAUM¹·²

†glamer, glawmir *n* noise, tumult; outcry; scandal *15-16*. [compare Older Scots *clamour*, ON *glamm* noise]

glammach¹·¹ /ˈglaməx/ *n* a snatch, a grab; a grope *19, 20- NE*. [GLAUM¹·¹, with diminutive suffix]

glammach¹·², glammoch, glaumach /ˈglaməx, ˈglɔməx/ *v* **1** to grasp eagerly, grab *la19, 20- NE*. **2** to grope blindly *19, 20- NE*. [see the noun]

glamour¹·¹ /ˈglamər/ *n* **1** magic, enchantment, witchcraft *18-*. **2** charm; attractiveness, allure, beauty *20-*. [altered form of GREMMAR; compare GRAMARIE]

glamour¹·² /ˈglamər/ *v* **1** to bewitch; to dazzle *18-*. **2** to deceive, bamboozle *la19-*. [see the noun]

glamourie /ˈglaməri/ *n* enchantment *18-*. [GLAMOUR¹·¹ + -IE³; compare GRAMARIE]

glamp¹·¹ /glamp/ *n* **1** a grab, a grope *la18- Ork N NE*. **2** a large mouthful *la19, 20- N*. [GLAUM¹·¹, with excrescent *p*]

glamp¹·² /glamp/ *v* **1** to clutch at, grope *19, 20- NE*. **2** to snap up greedily; to gobble *20- N*. [see the noun]

glamse¹·¹, *N* **glamsh** /glams; *N* glamʃ/ *n* a snap, a quick attempt to bite *20- Sh Ork N*. [see the verb]

glamse¹·², *N* **glamsh** /glams; *N* glamʃ/ *v* **1** to snap at *20- Sh Ork T*. **2** to make a snapping or smacking noise; to eat greedily *20- Ork N NE*. [Dan *glamse*]

glamshach /ˈglamʃəx/ *adj* greedy, grasping *19, 20- NE*. [GLAUM¹·¹, with adj-forming suffix]

glance¹·¹, glaunce, glence, †glans /glans, glɔns, glɛns/ *n* a flash of light; a glimpse; a deflected movement *16-*. **glancy** shiny, shining, bright *18-19, 20- NE*. **glansin** sparkling *20- Sh*. [unknown]

glance¹·², glaunce, glence, †glans /glans, glɔns, glɛns/ *v* to strike obliquely; to shine or gleam; to glimpse *la16-*. **glance on** to occur to *20- EC*. **†glance upon** = *glance on 19*. [unknown]

glant /glant/ *n* jollification *20- Sh*. [unknown]

glar *see* GLAUR¹·¹, GLAUR¹·²

glare *see* GLAUR¹·¹

glas *see* GLESS¹·¹, GLESS¹·², GLESS¹·³

glase *see* GLESS¹·¹, GLESS¹·³

Glasgow bailie /ˈglazgo bele/ *n* a salt herring of fine quality; a red herring *20- C SW*. [from the place-name + BAILIE]

Glasgowegian *see* GLASWEGIAN¹·¹

Glasgow Fair, Glesca Fair /glazgo ˈfer, glɛska ˈfer/ *n* the last fortnight in July taken as the annual summer holiday in Glasgow, the Glasgow Trades holiday fortnight *20-*. [from the place-name + FAIR²]

Glasgow Highlanders /ˈglazgo hʌiləndərz/ *n* a battalion of part-time volunteers, latterly the 9th (Territorial) Battalion of the Highland Light Infantry *la19-20, 21 historical*. [from the place-name + HIELANDER]

Glasgow keelie *see* GLESCA KEELIE

Glasgow kiss *see* GLESCA KISS

Glasgow magistrate /ˈglazgo madʒɪstret/ *n* a salt herring of fine quality; a red herring, compare GLASGOW BAILIE *la18- C*. [from the place-name + MAGISTRATE]

Glasgow punch /glazgo ˈpʌnʃ/ *n* a punch made with rum, cold water, sugar, lemons and limes *19-*. [from the place-name + Eng *punch*]

Glasgow roll /glazgo ˈrol/ *n* a type of bread roll *20-*. [from the place-name + ROW¹·¹]

Glasgow screwdriver /glazgo ˈskrudraevər/ *n* a hammer *20-*. Compare *Paisley screwdriver* (PAISLEY SCREW). [from the place-name + Eng *screwdriver*]

Glasgow smile, Glesca smile /glazgo ˈsmʌɪl, glɛska ˈsmʌɪl/ *n* a scar caused by cutting the face from ear to ear *la20-*. [from the place-name + SMILE¹·¹]

glashan, gleshan /ˈglaʃən, ˈglɛʃən/ *n* the coalfish *Pollachius virens* in its second or third year *la19- H&I SW Uls*. [Gael *glaisean*]

glasin *see* GLESSIN

glasinwricht *see* GLASSINWRICHT

Glasite /ˈglasʌɪt/ *n* a member of the religious sect founded by the Reverend John Glas (1693-1773) *la18-20, 21- historical*. Compare SANDEMANIAN. [from the surname]

glasp *see* CLESP¹·¹, CLESP¹·²

glass *see* GLESS¹·¹, GLESS¹·², GLESS¹·³

glassin *see* GLESSIN

†glassinwerk *n* glass fitted in windows, glazing *la15-e17*. [GLESSIN + *werk* (WARK¹·¹)]

†glassinwricht, glasinwricht, glessinwrycht *n* a glazier *15-17*. Compare *glaswricht* (GLESS¹·¹). [GLESSIN + WRICHT]

glaster *see* GLAISTER²

Glaswegian¹·¹, Glasgowegian /glazˈwidʒən, glasˈwidʒən, glazgoˈwidʒən/ *n* **1** a native or inhabitant of Glasgow *19-*. **2** the dialect of Scots spoken in Glasgow *20-*. [derivative of the place-name, by analogy with *Galwegian* a native or inhabitant of Galloway]

Glaswegian¹·² /glazˈwidʒən, glasˈwidʒən/ *adj* native to or living in Glasgow *20-*. [see the noun]

glaubery *see* CLABBER

glauf *see* GLIFF¹·¹

glaum¹·¹ /glɔm/ *n* a clutch or grab *19-*. [see the verb]

glaum¹·², glam /glɔm, glam/ *v* **1** to snatch, grab at *la18-*. **2** to seize or snatch at with the jaws; to devour *19, 20- EC Bor*. **3** to grope *la18-19, 20- SW*. **glammer** to grope *la19- N NE*. [Gael *glàm* to snatch, grab; to devour]

glaumach *see* GLAMMACH¹·²

glaums *see* CLAMS

glaun, glaund /glɔn, glɔnd/ *n* a clamp *19, 20- SW*. [probably altered form of GLAUM¹·¹; compare CLAMS]

glaunce *see* GLANCE¹·¹, GLANCE¹·²

glaur¹·¹, glar, †glare /glɔr, glar/ *n* **1** soft, sticky mud; ooze, slime; dirt *16-*. **2** term of contempt or abuse for a person or thing *19, 20- EC*. **glaurie** muddy, dirty *la18-*. **glaursel** completely covered with mud *la20- SW Bor*. [unknown]

glaur¹·², †glar /glɔr/ *v* to make muddy; to dirty or soil; to make slimy *la15-*. [unknown]

glaur[2] /glɔr/ *n* slippery ice; slipperiness *la19- NE*. **glaerl**, **glerel** slippery ice or frost *20- Sh*. [Eng *glare* a sheet of ice]
†**glave, glaive** *n* a sword *la15-16*. [ME *glaive* a lance]
glaver *see* CLAVER[1.1], CLAVER[1.2]
glawmir *see* GLAMER
glayd *see* GLED[2.2]
glaykis *see* GLAIKS[1]
glaze *see* GLAIZE[1]
glazey *see* GLAIZIE
gle *see* GLEE[1]
gleam *see* GLAIM
glebe[1.1], *Bor* **glibe,** †**gleib** /glib; *Bor* glʌɪb/ *n* **1** the portion of land assigned to a parish minister in addition to his stipend *la15-*. **2** a lump, a piece; a small quantity *16-19, 20- Sh*. **3** a plot of cultivated land *18-19, 20- Sh Bor*. **gleebrie** a large piece of (waste) ground *20- NE*. [Lat *glēba* a clod, soil]
†**glebe**[1.2] *v* to divide land into lots *la18*. [see the noun]
gled[1], †**glaid** /glɛd/ *n* **1** the kite *Milvus milvus*; frequently in place-names *12-*. **2** a rapacious or greedy person *la16-*. **3** the buzzard *Buteo buteo la18-*. **as gleg as a gled** as keen or eager as a hawk; very hungry *19, 20- WC*. **as if they had fa'en frae the gled's feet** in disorder, dishevelled, confused *19, 20- EC Bor*. †**in the gled's grups** in mortal danger or dire trouble *19*. [ON *gleða*]
†**gled**[2.1], **glad, glaid** /glɛd, glad, gled/ *v* to make glad, gladden *15-19, 20- literary*. **gladar** a person who made people glad *e16*. [see the adj]
gled[2.2], **glad, glaid,** †**glayd,** †**glade** /glɛd, glad, gled/ *adj* pleased, happy, cheerful *la14-*. [OE *glæd* shining, cheerful]
gled *see* CLEG
glede *see* GLEED[1]
gledge[1.1] /glɛdʒ/ *n* a glimpse, a sidelong glance *19, 20- Bor*. [unknown; compare GLEY[1.1]]
gledge[1.2] /glɛdʒ/ *v* to squint, look sidelong *19, 20- Bor*. [see the noun]
glee[1], †**gle,** †**glew,** †**glie** /gli/ *n* **1** mirth; entertainment, sport *la14-*. **2** music, melody *la15-e18*. [OE *glīw*]
glee[2.1] /gli/ *n* an oily or fatty film on water *20- Sh Ork*. [Norw dial *glya* slime; compare ON *gljá* to glisten]
glee[2.2] /gli/ *v* to glisten (especially of an oily or fatty film on liquid) *20- Sh Ork*. [ON *gljá*]
glee *see* GLEY[1.2], GLEY[1.3], GLEY[1.4]
gleebrie *see* GLEBE[1.1]
gleed[1], **gleid,** †**glede,** †**gleyd** /glid/ *n* **1** a live coal or peat, an ember; a glowing fire *la14-*. **2** a spark, a glimmer of fire or light *19-*. **3** a tiny amount *19-*. †**in a glede** burnt to an ember, completely burnt *la14-16*. [OE *glēd*]
gleed[2] /glid/ *adj* set far apart, scattered *20- Sh Ork*. [Norw dial *gleid* spread out]
gleed *see* GLEYD
gleek /glik/ *v* **1** to look, peep *20- NE Uls*. **2** to jeer, gibe *la18-19*. [unknown; compare GLAIK[1.2], GLEY[1.2]]
gleekit *see* GLAIKIT
gleem-glam *see* GLIM-GLAM
gleer /glir/ *v* to blink, peer *20- Sh Ork WC*. [Norw *glire*; compare GLEY[1.2]]
gleesh /gliʃ/ *n* a large bright fire or flame *19- NE*. **gleeshach** = GLEESH. [altered form of GREESH, GREESHACH[1]]
gleet[1.1] /glit/ *n* a sheen, a shine; glitter *19- Bor*. [see the verb]
gleet[1.2], †**glete,** †**gleit** /glit/ *v* to gleam, shine, glitter *la14-16, 19- Bor*. [ON *glita*]
gleet *see* GLIT
gleg[1.1] /glɛg/ *adj* **1** quick, nimble; smart, alert *15-*. **2** *of cutting implements* sharp, keen *la18-*. **3** *of a mechanism* working smoothly, quick-acting *la18-*. **4** lively, sprightly; merry *19-*. **glegly 1** briskly, quickly *la18-*. **2** keenly, quickly, attentively *la18-19*. **3** smartly, skilfully, adroitly *la18-e19*. **4** brightly *17-e19*. **glegness** sharpness, keenness, cleverness *19- Sh NE Bor*. **gleg eared** with ears cocked *20- WC*. **gleg eed** sharp-eyed; perceptive *18-*. **gleg gabbit** smooth-tongued, glib; voluble *la19-*. **gleg lug'd** sharp of hearing *19-*. **gleg sighted** sharp-eyed; perceptive *19-*. **gleg tongued** smooth-tongued, glib *19-*. **gleg witted** smart, quick, alert *la19-*. **gleg in at the uptak** quick-witted, perceptive *19-*. [ON *glöggr* clear-sighted, clever, distinct]
gleg[1.2] /glɛg/ *adv* keenly, sharply *18-*. [see the adj]
gleg *see* CLEG
gleib *see* GLEBE[1.1]
gleid *see* GLEED[1], GLEYD
gleit *see* GLEET[1.2]
gleme *see* GLAIM, GLIME[1.2]
glen[1] /glɛn/ *n* a (narrow, steep-sided) mountain valley traversed by a river or stream *la12-*. [Gael *gleann*]
glen[2] /glɛn/ *n* a daffodil *19- WC*. [back-formation from GLEN SATURDAY]
†**glen**[3] *v* to glean *la16-e17*. [ME *glenen*, EModE *gleane*]
glence *see* GLANCE[1.1], GLANCE[1.2]
Glengarry /glɛn'gare/ *n* a man's flat-sided cap, pointed at the front and back, with an ornamental tuft on top and frequently two ribbons hanging behind *19-*. Compare *cockit bonnet* (COCK[1.2]). [named after Macdonnell of Glengarry who popularized it].
†**glengore, glengoir** *n* venereal disease, syphilis *16-e19*; compare GRANDGORE. **glengorie** syphilitic *la16-17*. [MFr *grand gorre*]
glennie /'glɛni/ *n mining* a flame safety-lamp for testing for the presence of gas *20-*. **glennie blink** miner's nystagmus (oscillation of the eyeballs) *20-*. [from the name of the inventor Dr W R Clanny]
Glen Saturday /'glɛn satərde/ *n in Ayrshire* the first or third Saturday in April when the children of Kilmarnock went to the glen of Crawfurdland Castle to pick daffodils *la19-20, 21- historical*. [GLEN[1] + *Saturday* (SETERDAY)]
glent[1.1], **glint** /glɛnt, glɪnt/ *n* **1** a gleam, a flash of light; a faint or momentary glitter *18-*. **2** a look, a glance *la18-*. **3** a glimpse *19-*. **4** a scrap, a vestige *la19-*. **5** a flash of intuition, a slight suspicion *la19-*. **6** a glancing blow, a slap *19- SW*. **in a glent** in a flash, in a moment *la18-*. [see the verb]
glent[1.2], **glint** /glɛnt, glɪnt/ *v* **1** to (cause to) gleam or glint; to shine, sparkle *18-*. **2** to move quickly; to dart or flash past *la18-*. **3** to glance, peep, squint *la18-*. **glintin** dawn, daybreak *la19, 20- NE*. **glent aff** to glance off *20- Bor*. [ME *glenten*]
glep *see* GLAEP[1.2]
glerel *see* GLAUR[2]
gles *see* GLESS[1.1], GLESS[1.2]
Glesca, Glesgie, Glesco, Glesky /'glɛska, 'glɛzge, 'glɛsko, 'gleske/ *n* Glasgow *la19-*. [altered form of *Glasgow*]
Glesca Fair *see* GLASGOW FAIR
Glesca hoosie /glɛska 'husi/ *n* a variety of the game of rounders *la19-*. [GLESCA + *hoosie* (HOOSE[1.1])]
Glesca Jock /glɛska 'dʒɔk/ *n* coir rope used in binding haystacks *20- NE*. [GLESCA + JOCK]
Glesca keelie, Glasgow keelie /glɛska 'kili, glazgo 'kili/ *n* **1** an uncouth (male) Glaswegian; a street urchin or ruffian *la19-*. **2** *pl* a nickname for the Highland Light Infantry *20, 21- historical*. [GLESCA + KEELIE[2]]
Glesca kiss, Glasgow kiss /glɛska 'kɪs, glazgo 'kɪs/ *n* a headbutt *20-*. [GLESCA + KISS]
Glesca smile *see* GLASGOW SMILE
Glesco *see* GLESCA

glesgend, glesgin /ˈglɛzgənd, ˈglɛzgɪn/ *adj* greedy *20- Ork*. [unknown]

Glesgie *see* GLESCA

gleshan *see* GLASHAN

Glesky *see* GLESCA

gless[1.1]**, glaiss, glass, †glas, †gles, †glase** /glɛs, gles, glas/ *n* **1** a hard transparent substance, glass *la14-*. **2** an article made of glass; a drinking vessel *la15-*. **3** a measure of spirits, half a gill (approximately 71 ml) *20-*. **glessack** a small glass marble *20- N*. **glesser, glasser** a glass marble *20-*. **glesses** spectacles *19-*. **glessie 1** toffee *la19-*. **2** a glass marble *20-*. **†glas band** a strip of metal or wood for securing the panes of glass in a window *la16-17*. **†glas window, glase windock** a glazed window *16-e18*. **†glaswricht** a glazier *la14-17*; compare GLASSINWRICHT. **casting the glass, casting the glasses** a method of fortune-telling involving mixing egg-white in a glass of water *19- Sh Ork N*. **talk gless haunles** to speak very politely, use an over-refined accent *20- C SW Bor*. [OE *glæs*]

gless[1.2]**, glaiss, glass, †glas, †gles** /glɛs, gles, glas/ *v* **1** to fit (windows) with glass *la16-*; compare GLAIZE[1] (sense 1). **2** to assault or injure with a glass *la20-*. **3** to find or identify with a telescope or binoculars *la20- T*. **†glasser** a glazier *17*. [see the noun]

gless[1.3]**, glaiss, glass, †glas, †glase** /glɛs, gles, glas/ *adj* made of glass; glazed *16-*. [see the noun]

glessack *see* GLESS[1.1]

†glessin, glassin, glasin *adj* made of glass; fitted with glass *la14-17*. [ptp of GLESS[1.2]]

glessinwrycht *see* GLASSINWRICHT

glet, glett /glɛt/ *n* a break in rain; a temporary clearing of the sky *la19- Ork*. [Norw *glette*]

glet *see* GLIT

glete *see* GLEET[1.2]

†glevyn, gleuin *v* to glow *e16*. [unknown]

glew *see* GLEE[1]

gley[1.1] /gle/ *n* **1** a sidelong or sly look, a glance; a squint in the eye *19- Sh N NE T EC*. **2** squintness, irregularity; error *19- NE T*. **3** aim; the act of aiming *la19- NE T*. **†be aff the gley** to fail to reach an objective, be wrong *la19- NE EC*. [unknown]

gley[1.2]**, *Sh* gly, †glee** /gle; *Sh* glae/ *v* **1** to squint; to cast a sidelong glance; to look askance *la16-*. **2** to swerve, go astray; to miscarry *19-*. **3** to look with one eye; to take aim *19, 20- NE T*. **4** to avert the eyes, look away *18-19*. [unknown]

gley[1.3]**, *H&I* glee** /gle; *H&I* gli/ *adj* squint-eyed *20-*. **gley-eyed** squint-eyed *la19-*. [unknown]

gley[1.4]**, glee** /gle, gli/ *adv* off the straight, awry *19-*; compare AGLEY[1.2]. **gae glee, gang glee** to go awry *la18-*. [unknown]

gleyd, gleyed, gleed, *Sh* glyed, †gleyit, †gleid /gled, glid; *Sh* glaed/ *adj* **1** having a squint in the eye *la15-*. **2** not straight, slanting; crooked, awry *la16-*. **3** mistaken, misguided *19- T EC Bor*. **4** one-eyed, blind in one eye *19- N NE T*. **gleytness, †gleidnes 1** the condition of having a squint *17-*. **2** obliqueness *19, 20- NE*. **gleed eed** squint-eyed *la19- Sh Ork T EC Bor*. **gleed necked** having a twisted neck *19- N EC Bor*. **glyed shield** *fisherman's taboo* the halibut *Hippoglossus hippoglossus la19- Sh*. **gae gleyd, gang gleyd** to go (morally) astray *la18-19, 20- T EC*. [ptp of GLEY[1.2]]

gleyd *see* GLEED[1]

gliack *see* CLYACK

†glib[1.1] *v* to talk volubly or smoothly *18-19*. [see the adj]

glib[1.2]**, †glibe** /glɪb/ *adj* **1** talkative, fluent *19-*. **2** voluble but insincere or superficial *la19-*. **3** smooth, slippery, moving without friction *18-19, 20- SW Bor Uls*. **4** sharp in one's dealings; smart, cunning *19, 20- Sh T*. **†glibby** talkative, fluent *la19*. **glib gabbit** gossipy; smooth-tongued *la18-*. **glib moued** = *glib gabbit la19-*. [EModE *glib*; compare Du *glibberig* slippery]

†glib[1.3] *adv* smoothly, easily, readily *18-19*. [see the adj]

glibe *see* GLEBE[1.1]

glid, †glaid /glɪd/ *adj* **1** moving smoothly; free from friction *16-19, 20- literary*. **2** slippery *19*. **glidder** *pl* small stones, scree *la18- Bor*. [related to GLED[1], MDu *glad*, OFris *gled*]

glie *see* GLEE[1]

gliff[1.1]**, gluff, gloff, glaff, glowff, glauf, †glufe** /glɪf, glʌf, glɔf, glaf, glʌuf/ *n* **1** a (startled) glance; a glimpse *16-*. **2** a sudden fright, a shock; a surprise, a thrill *18-*. **3** a moment, a short while; a short snatch of sleep *la18-*. **4** a momentary resemblance *la19-*. **5** a flash, a glint *19-*. **6** a slight attack, a touch (of an illness) *la19-*. **7** a whiff, a slight smell; a gust of air *19-*. **8** a rumour *20-*. **a gliff o the cauld** a slight cold *la19-*. **in a gliff** in a moment *la18-*. [see the verb; compare Norw dial *glufs* a gust of wind]

gliff[1.2]**, gluff, †gloff** /glɪf, glʌf/ *v* **1** to frighten, startle; to be frightened *la18-*. **2** to glance at *la19-*. **3** to gasp (with surprise or cold) *19- Ork NE*. [ME *gliff*]

gliffin[1]**, †gliffing** /ˈglɪfɪn/ *n* a moment, an instant *19- literary*. [GLIFF[1.1], with *-ing* suffix]

†gliffin[2]**, gluffin, glowffin** *v* to look, glance *la14-16*. [GLIFF[1.2], with *-in* suffix]

glig, gligg /glɪg/ *n* an opening in the wall or roof of a barn or byre *la19- Sh*. [ON *gluggr*]

glim /glɪm/ *n* **1** a gleam, a glimmer *19, 20- Sh Ork N Uls*. **2** a glimpse, a glance *17, 20- Sh Ork*. [unknown; compare Norw dial *glim*]

glime[1.1] /glʌɪm/ *n* a sidelong look, a sly glance *la18-19, 20- Bor*. [see the verb]

glime[1.2]**, †gleme** /glʌɪm/ *v* to take a sidelong glance, squint *16-19, 20- Bor*. [unknown; compare Norw dial *glyma* to look sly or roguish]

glim-glam, gleem-glam /ˈglɪm glam, ˈglim glam/ *n* the game of blind-man's buff *la18-19, 20- NE*. [reduplicated compound from GLAUM[1.2]; compare also GLIM]

glimmer, †glymmer /ˈglɪmər/ *v* **1** to glitter, emit a faint or wavering light *16-*. **2** *of the eyes* to be dazzled; to blink or wink; to look unsteadily *16-*. **glimmerin** *of the eyes* half-closed, peering *19, 20- NE*. [OE **glimorian*]

glimp /glɪmp/ *n* a glimpse *la19-*. [probably back-formation, but compare MDu *glimpen* to burn, glow, shine, Du *glimp* a glimpse, a show]

glinder /ˈglɪndər/ *v* to peep or peer; to blink *la19- Sh*. [Norw dial *glindra*]

glink[1.1] /glɪŋk/ *n* **1** a sidelong look, a peep, a squint *19-*. **2** a gleam, a flash *la19- Sh*. [variant of *glint* (GLENT[1.1])]

glink[1.2] /glɪŋk/ *v* **1** to glance, look sidelong (at) *19-*. **2** to shine, gleam *la19- Sh*. [see the noun]

glint *see* GLENT[1.1], GLENT[1.2]

glinted /ˈglɪntəd/ *adj* flighty, rather foolish *la19- Sh Ork*. [probably Norw dial *glenta* to dally, be foolish]

glintin *see* GLENT[1.2]

glipe /glʌɪp/ *n* **1** a thoughtless or foolish person *19- Bor Uls*. **2** an uncouth, clumsy person *19- Bor Uls*. [unknown]

glipek, glippik /ˈglɪpək/ *n* an opening; a fissure, a rent *20- Sh*. [derivative of Norw dial *glip*]

glisk[1.1] /glɪsk/ *n* **1** a glance, a glimpse *la17-*. **2** a moment, an instant *la18-*. **3** a gleam, a sparkle, a flash *19-*. **4** a momentary sensation or reaction; a short spell; a whiff, a trace *19-*. **5** a resemblance, a slight similarity *la19-*. **a glisk o cauld** a touch of cold, a slight cold *19-*. [unknown]

glisk¹,² /glɪsk/ *v* **1** to glance, glimpse *18-*. **2** to glimmer *la19- Sh*. [unknown]

†glist *adj* shiny, glistening *18-e19*. [perhaps reduced form of Eng *glisten*]

glister¹,¹ /ˈglɪstər/ *n* glitter, brilliance *la16-*. [see the verb]

glister¹,² /ˈglɪstər/ *v* to glisten, glitter *la16-*. [MLG *glistern*, MDu *glisteren*]

glit, glut, glet, gleet, *Ork* **gloot**, **†glute** /glɪt, glʌt, glɛt, glit; *Ork* glut/ *n* **1** filth; slimy, greasy or sticky matter *15-*. **2** phlegm, mucus; the liquid discharging from a wound; pus *16-*. **3** the slimy vegetation found in ponds *19-*. **4** slime on fish or decomposing meat *19-*. **5** pulp *20- Ork*. **glittie, gluttie 1** slimy, greasy, oily *la18-*. **2** covered with or producing mucus *19-*. **3** smooth, slippery *19- SW Bor*. **†glittous** filthy, base, vile *16*. [ME *glet*]

gliv see GLOVE

gloam¹,¹ /glom/ *n* twilight; a faint light *18-*. [back-formation from GLOAMIN]

gloam¹,² /glom/ *v* to become dusk, grow dark *18-*. [see the noun]

gloamin, gloaming, †gloming, †glowming /ˈglomɪn, ˈglomɪŋ/ *n* **1** evening twilight, dusk *15-*. **2** morning twilight, dawn *19- Sh SW Uls*. **gloamin fa** dusk *19-*. **gloamin grey** dusk *19*. **gloamin hour** dusk *19-*. **†gloamin shot** a twilight interval before the lighting of lights, a short time of relaxation in the evening *la18-e19*. **gloamin tide** dusk *18-*. [OE *glōmung*]

gloan, glone /glon/ *n* energy, excitement *19- NE*. **in a gloan** in a state of excitement *20- NE*. [unknown]

glock see GLUG¹,¹, GLUG¹,²

glocken /ˈglɔkən/ *v* to start with fright *19- SW*. [ON *glúpna* to be downcast]

glöd see GLUDE¹,¹

gloe see GLOVE

gloff see GLIFF¹,¹, GLIFF¹,²

glog /glɔg/ *adj* black, dark *19, 20- literary*. [unknown]

glog see GLUG¹,¹, GLUG¹,²

gloggo see GLUGG

gloid /glɔɪd/ *v* to do something in a slovenly, messy or awkward way *la19- T*. [perhaps voiced variant of CLOITER¹,²]

gloir see GLORY¹,¹, GLORY¹,²

gloit see CLOIT²,¹, CLOIT²,²

gloming see GLOAMIN

glondouris see GLUNNERS

glone see GLOAN

gloom¹,¹, **†glowme** /glum/ *n* **1** a frown, a scowl *la16-*. **2** darkness; despondency *19-*. **3** *pl* the sulks, a state of depression *19, 20- NE*. [see the verb]

gloom¹,², **glum, glowme** /glum, glʌm, glʌum/ *v* **1** to look sullen, frown, scowl *16-19, 20- C*. **2** *of a horse* to show signs of ill-temper or viciousness *20- N H&I*. **3** to suspect; to doubt *20- Sh Ork*. **4** to grow dark *18-19, 20- NE*. [OE **glūmian*]

gloondie /ˈglundi/ *adj* gluttonous *19- Ork*. [unknown]

gloop see GLOUP

gloor¹,¹ /glur/ *n* sunshine through a haze; a glimmer or light *20- Sh*. [see the verb]

gloor¹,² /glur/ *v* to shine through a haze; to emit a faint or phosphorescent light *20- Sh*. [Norw dial *glora* to glisten]

gloot see GLIT

glorg, glurg /glɔrg, glʌrg/ *v* to engage in dirty work *19, 20- Sh*. [probably onomatopoeic]

glorgie /ˈglɔrgi/ *adj of weather* sultry, close *19- WC SW*. [probably GLORG + -IE²]

glorifee /ˈglɔrəfi/ *v* to glorify *la19-*. [Fr *glorifier*]

†gloriositie *n* self-importance, boastful bearing *la16-17*. [MFr *glorieuseté*]

glorious, †glorius, †gloryus /ˈglorɪəs/ *adj* **1** magnificent, of great fame or splendour, marvellous *15-*. **2** in a state of elation from drinking alcohol *la18-*. **3** vainglorious, boastful *la15-16, 20- T*. [ME *glorious*, Lat *glōriōsus*]

glory¹,¹, **glore, †gloir, †glor** /ˈglore, glor/ *n* **1** (a cause of) praise, honour or renown *la14-*. [ME *glorie*, Lat *glōria*]

glory¹,², **†glore, †gloir, †gloyr** /ˈglore/ *v* **1** to take pride in, boast of *16-*. **2** to give glory to *e16*. [Lat *glōriāri*]

glose /gloz/ *v* to strike with violence *la19- Ork*. [unknown]

gloss¹ /glɔs/ *n* **1** shine, lustre *la18-*. **2** a bright glow, a fire without smoke or flame *la18-19, 20- Bor*. **glossy 1** lustrous *la18-*. **2** *of a fire* glowing, clear *20- EC Bor*. [EModE *glosse*]

gloss²,¹ /glɔs/ *n* a doze, a light sleep *20- Ork NE*. **a gloss o sleep** a wink of sleep *20- NE*. [extended sense of GLOSS¹]

gloss²,² /glɔs/ *v* to doze, be half asleep *20- Ork NE*. **gloss ower** to read cursorily *20- NE T*. [see the noun]

glotten /ˈglɔtən/ *v* to thaw partially *19, 20- Bor*. [unknown]

†glottenit, glotnyt *adj* **1** *of a river* slightly swollen and discoloured *19*. **2** clotted or wet with blood; bloodshot *e16*. [unknown]

gloup, gloop /glup/ *n* a sea cave or chasm *la18- Sh Ork N*. [Norw dial *glup*]

glour see GLOWER¹,²

glourik, †glowrik /ˈglurɪk/ *n fisherman's taboo* an eye *19- Sh*. [unknown; compare GLOWER¹,¹]

glouster /ˈglʌustər/ *v* to bluster; to be loud-mouthed *20- N*. [conflation of BLOUSTER¹,² with GOWSTER¹,²]

glousterin, glowsterin, *Bor* **glysterin** /ˈglʌustərɪn; *Bor* ˈglʌɪstərɪn/ *adj* **1** *of weather* squally *19-*. **2** *of people* blustering; loud-mouthed *20- N*. [presp of GLOUSTER]

glove, gliv, gluive, †gloe, †gluve, †gluf /glʌv, glɪv, gluv/ *n* a garment for the hand, a glove *la14-*. **†gluff of plate** a gauntlet *15-e16*. [OE *glōf*]

glowe, glow /glʌu, glo/ *n* bright heat or light; a blaze *19-*. [OE *glōwan* to glow, radiate heat and light]

glower¹,¹, **†glowr** /ˈglʌuər/ *n* **1** a wide-eyed stare, an intent look *17-*. **2** a scowl, a fierce look *17-*. [unknown]

glower¹,², **†glowr, †glowir, †glour** /ˈglʌuər/ *v* **1** to stare fixedly; to gaze intently *la15-*. **2** to be drunk and glassy-eyed *18-*. **3** to scowl; to look angry *18-*. **4** *of the sun and moon* to gleam, shine brightly *la18-19*. **glower frae** to have a fixed or vacant look, stare stupidly *19, 20- Bor*. [unknown]

glowff see GLIFF¹,¹

glowffin see GLIFFIN²

glowme see GLOOM¹,¹, GLOOM¹,²

glowming see GLOAMIN

glowr see GLOWER¹,¹, GLOWER¹,²

glowrik see GLOURIK

glowsterin see GLOUSTERIN

gloy¹,¹ /glɔɪ/ *n* unbroken straw (used for thatching) *la15-19, 20- Sh Ork N*. [Du *glui*; compare ME *gloi*]

gloy¹,² /glɔɪ/ *v* to thresh corn partially or hastily *la18-19, 20- SW*. [see the noun]

gloyd see GLYDE

gloyr see GLORY¹,²

gloze¹,¹ /gloz/ *n* a blaze *la19- T*. [see the verb]

gloze¹,² /gloz/ *v* to blaze, shine brightly *19- T*. [variant of GLOSS¹; compare MLG *glosen* to gleam, glitter]

gluck see GLUG¹,¹, GLUG¹,²

gludder /ˈglʌdər/ *n* a glow of heat (from the sun) *la19- Sh*. **gluddery** *of the sky* having an unsettled appearance *la19- Sh*. [intensive form of GLUDE¹,¹]

gludder see GLUTHER¹,¹, GLUTHER¹,²

glude¹,¹, **glöd** /glød/ *n* a glow of heat or light *19- Sh*. [ON *glóð* red hot embers]

glude¹,² /glød/ *v of a fire* to glow *la19- Sh*. [ON *glæða*]

gludyr see GLUTHER[2]
gluf see GLOVE
glufe see GLIFF[1.1]
gluff see GLIFF[1.1], GLIFF[1.2]
gluffin see GLIFFIN[2]
gluffus /ˈglʌfəs/ *n* a rough, uncouth or unattractive person *la19- Sh Ork N.* [unknown]
glug[1.1], **gluck**, **glock**, **glog**, **glag** /glʌg, glʌk, glɔk, glɔg, glag/ *n* a noisy gulp; a gurgling noise *la19-.* [onomatopoeic]
glug[1.2], **gluck**, **glock**, **glog**, **glag** /glʌg, glʌk, glɔk, glɔg, glag/ *v* to gulp; to gurgle; to make a gurgling noise in swallowing *la18-.* **glugger** to make a gurgling noise *la19-.* [see the noun]
glugg /glʌg/ *n* slime on fish skins *20- Sh Ork.* **gluks**, †**glugs** a thick mixture (of oatmeal and milk); thick lumps *la19- Sh.* **gloggo** a thick mixture (of oatmeal and milk) *19- Ork.* [onomatopoeic]
gluive see GLOVE
gluks see GLUGG
glum see GLOOM[1.2]
glumch see GLUMSH[1.2]
glumph[1.1] /glʌmf/ *n* a sulky or morose person *19-.* **glumpy**, †**glumfie** sulky, sullen, morose *19- T Uls.* [onomatopoeic]
glumph[1.2], **glump** /glʌmf, glʌmp/ *v* to be glum or look gloomy; to sulk; to look sourly at *19-.* [see the noun]
glumse[1.1], *N* **glumsh** /glʌms; *N* glʌmʃ/ *n* 1 a curt, rude reply *la19- Sh.* 2 the snap of a dog; a greedy bite *20- Sh N.* [variant of GLAMSE[1.2]]
glumse[1.2], *N* **glumsh** /glʌms; *N* glʌmʃ/ *v* to reply curtly; to snap at; to eat greedily *20- Sh N.* **glumsit** surly, sulky *20- Sh.* [see the noun]
glumsh[1.1] /glʌmʃ/ *n* a sulky, sullen mood; a surly look or reaction; a pout *la19, 20- T EC.* **glumshie** sulky, sullen *la19-.* [see the verb]
glumsh[1.2], **glumch** /glʌmʃ/ *v* to look sulky; to be morose; to grumble or whine *19-.* [perhaps related to ME *gloumen* to look sullen]
glumsh[1.3] /glʌmʃ/ *adj* 1 sulky, sour-looking *la19-,* 2 melancholy *la19-, 20- T.* [see the verb]
glumsh see GLUMSE[1.1], GLUMSE[1.2]
glunch see GLUNSH[1.1]
glundie /ˈglʌndi/ *n* a fool *la18-19, 20- WC SW.* [unknown]
†**Glunimie** *n derogatory* a Highlander *18-e19.* [perhaps derivative of Gael *glùn* a knee, or *glùineanach* gartered, (one) wearing garters; compare GLUNTOCH]
glunk see CLUNK[1.1], CLUNK[1.2]
†**glunners**, **glondouris** *npl* sulks *16-19.* **in the glunners**, **in the glondouris** in the sulks *16-19.* [unknown]
glunsh[1.1], **glunch** /glʌnʃ/ *n* a sour look, a scowl; a sulky, sullen mood *la18-19, 20- C SW Bor.* **glunshy** sulky, sour, bad-tempered *19, 20- Bor.* [variant of GLUMSH[1.1]]
glunsh[1.2] /glʌnʃ/ *v* to look sour or sullen, scowl; to grumble *18-.* [see the noun]
glunsh[1.3] /glʌnʃ/ *adj* sulky, sour, bad-tempered *19-.* [see the noun]
glunsh[2.1] /glʌnʃ/ *n* 1 a greedy bite, a large mouthful; a snap *20- Sh N.* 2 a glutton *20- Ork.* [compare GLUMSE[1.1]]
glunsh[2.2] /glʌnʃ/ *v* to gobble; to gulp food *20- N SW.* [see the noun]
gluntie /ˈglʌnti/ *adj* tall, lean, haggard *19- Bor.* [unknown]
†**gluntoch** *n* 1 a stupid or sullen person *19.* 2 a contemptuous term of address to a Highlander *e16.* [probably Gael *glùineach* having large knees; compare GLUNIMIE]
glurg see GLORG
glush /glʌʃ/ *n* slush or snow; soft mud *19-.* **glushie** *of snow* soft, slushy *19- NE T EC.* [onomatopoeic]

glut[1.1] /glʌt/ *n* a gulp, a draught (of liquid) *19- C SW Bor.* [OFr *glout*]
glut[1.2] /glʌt/ *v* to swallow; to gulp down *la18- C SW Bor.* [OFr *gloutir*]
†**glut**[2] *n* a wooden wedge for adjusting a plough *18-e19.* [perhaps related to *cleat*]
glut, **glute** see GLIT
gluther[1.1], **gludder** /ˈglʌðər, ˈglʌdər/ *n* a gurgling noise *19- C Bor.* **gluthery** muddy, greasy *19, 20- T C.* [see the verb]
gluther[1.2], **gludder**, †**glutter** /ˈglʌðər, ˈglʌdər/ *v* 1 to gurgle, splutter *19- C Bor.* 2 to swallow greedily or noisily *19- C Bor.* [frequentative form of GLUT[1.2]; compare Swed dial *gluddra* to gargle, gurgle]
†**gluther**[2], **gludyr** *v* to flatter *la14-16.* [unknown]
glutter see GLUTHER[1.2]
†**gluttery** *n* gluttony *la15-e16.* [ME *gloteri*]
gluve see GLOVE
gly see GLEY[1.2]
glyde, †**gloyd** /glʌɪd/ *n* 1 an old, worn-out horse *la16-19, 20- H&I.* 2 an old, feeble or disagreeable person *la18-19.* [unknown]
glyed see GLEYD
glymmer see GLIMMER
glysterin see GLOUSTERIN
gnaff see NYAFF[1.1]
gnap see KNAP[4.1], KNAP[4.2]
gnappar see KNAP[4.2]
gnapperts see KNAPPARTS
gnash see NASH[1]
gnashack, *N* **nashag** /ˈgnaʃək; *N* ˈnaʃəg/ *n* the red bearberry, a plant of the genus *Arctostaphylos* *19- N NE.* [Gael *cnàimhseag*]
gnauve see GNYAUVE
gneck[1.1] /gnɛk/ *n* a notch *19- NE.* [probably variant of NICK[1.1]]
gneck[1.2] /gnɛk/ *v* to cut notches *la19- NE.* [see the noun]
gnepin see KNYPE[2]
gniaf see NYAFF[1.1]
gnib, *Sh* **knib** /gnɪb; *Sh* knɪb/ *adj* quick, nimble, eager *18- Sh NE.* [imitative of a snapping action]
gnick see KNICK[1.2]
gnidge see NIDGE[1.1], NIDGE[1.2]
gnip see KNIP[3.1], KNIP[3.2]
gnyauve, **gnauve**, *Sh Ork* **nyauve** /gnjɔv, gnɔv; *Sh Ork* njav/ *v* to gnaw *la18- Sh Ork N NE.* [perhaps Norw dial *gnava* to gnaw quietly]
gnyp see KNIP[3.2]
go[1] /go/ *n* 1 going, movement *19-.* 2 a state of anxiety or excitement *la19-.* †**go o' the year** the latter part of the year *19*; compare GOESUMMER, GO-HARVEST. **in a go** in a fuss, in a state of anxiety *la19-.* **upon go** restlessly active; much in use *19- Sh NE T.* [from the verb *go* (GAE)]
go[2] /go/ *interj* an expression of surprise or admiration *la19- NE T EC Bor.* [euphemistic form of GOD]
go see GAE
goad see GAUD[1], GOD
goad-loup see GADLOUP
goadman, **goadsman** see GAUDSMAN
goam /gom/ *v* to heed, notice; to recognize, greet *la18- C SW Bor.* [ON *gaumr*]
goamless /ˈgomləs/ *adj* stupid *20- T C SW Bor.* [*gome* understanding, judgement; compare GOAM]
†**goan** *n* a wooden bowl or dish *18-19.* [altered form of GALLON]
goat see GAIT[1], GET[1.2], GYTE[2]
goave see GOVE[1.2]

gob[1.1] /gɔb/ *n* a mass or lump (of something soft); a lump of spit *19-*. [ME *gobbe*]

gob[1.2] /gɔb/ *v* to spit *20-*. [see the noun]

gob *see* GUB[1.1]

†**gobble**[1.1] *n golf* a rapid, straight putt at the hole *la19*. [see the verb]

gobble[1.2] /ˈgɔbəl/ *v golf* to make a rapid putt towards the hole *20-*. [probably Eng *gobble* to swallow hurriedly]

goblet /ˈgɔblət/ *n* **1** a bowl-shaped drinking vessel *la15-*. **2** an iron pot or pan with a straight handle (and convex sides) *18-*. [ME *gobelet*]

gob o' May *see* GAB[3]

†**gock** *n* a deep wooden dish *la18-19*. **gockie** = GOCK. [compare COG[1.1]]

gock *see* GOWK[1]

god, goad, gode /gɔd, god/ *n* a deity *la14-*. †**god's penny, goddis penny** a small sum given as earnest-money *15-19*. †**god-bairne gift** a baptismal gift to one's godchild *16-e18*. †**god's gorbie** a clergyman *e19*. [OE *god*]

godderlitch, gutherlidge /ˈgɔdərlɪtʃ, ˈgʌðərlɪdʒ/ *adj* slovenly, dirty, sloppy *19- NE*. [unknown]

gode *see* GOD

Godsend, God's send /ˈgɔdsɛnd, ˈgɔds sɛnd/ *n* a shipwreck or other profitable flotsam *18- Sh Ork SW*. [possessive of GOD + SEND[1.1]]

godspel *see* GOSPEL

†**goesummer, goesomer, goe o simmer** *n* a spell of mild weather in late autumn, an Indian summer *17-18*. [probably Eng *gossamer*; compare Ger *altweibersommer* (old woman's summer), gossamer, Indian summer]

goff *see* GOWF[1]

goffer, *NE T* **guffer,** †**gouffer** /ˈgofər; *NE T* ˈgʌfər/ *v* to pleat, crimp; originally to decorate (cloth) with an impressed design *la16-*. †**goffring** pleating, crimping *la16-e17*. [MFr *gaufrer*]

gog *see* GUGS

goggie /ˈgɔgi/ *n* **1** a child's word for an egg *20- H&I WC*. **2** an unfledged bird, a nestling *20- T SW*. [Gael *gogaidh* a child's word for an egg]

goggles, †**gogillis** /ˈgɔgəlz/ *npl* **1** protective spectacles *la16-*. **2** blinkers *17-*. [ME *gogeler* someone who squints]

goglet /ˈgɔglət/ *n* an iron pot or pan with a long handle *18- NE T*. [altered form of GOBLET]

†**go-harvest** *n* the late autumn, between harvest time and winter *18-19*. Compare GOESUMMER. [by analogy with GOESUMMER]

goich /gɔɪx/ *n* a haughty carriage of the head *20- H&I*. [Gael *goic* a tossing of the head]

†**goif** *n pl* **goifis, govis, golfis** the pillory *la15-e17*. [unknown]

goif *see* GOVE[1.2]

goiff *see* GOWF[1]

goik *see* GOWK[2]

goillya *see* GOLLA

goind /gɔɪnd/ *adj of an animal* emaciated *20- Ork*. [unknown]

gointek, gointack /ˈgɔɪntək/ *n* the rope by which a girth is fastened to a pack-saddle *la19- Sh*. [ON *gagn-tak*]

goiry *see* GOORIE[1.2]

goishalk *see* GOSHAWK

goit /gɔɪt/ *n* an unfledged nestling *19- SW Bor*. [variant of GET[1.1]]

goit *see* GYTE[2]

gok *see* GOWK[1]

†**gokstule** *n* a cuckstool, a chair in which an offender was fastened and exposed to public shame *la16*. [variant of ME *cukstol*]

golach, golack, *Ork* **gaavlo,** *N* **gavelag,** *SW* **gellock,** †**goulock** /ˈgolax, ˈgɔlək; *Ork* ˈgavlo; *N* ˈgavələg; *SW* ˈgɛlək/ *n* **1** an earwig *19-*. **2** an insect; a carnivorous ground beetle *19-*. **3** a term of abuse; a nickname for people from Caithness used by people from Sutherland *20- N NE H&I*. [Gael *gobhlag* an earwig; a fork-shaped stick]

golaich /ˈgoˈlex/ *n* a breed of short-legged hen *19, 20- NE T*. [go (GAE) + LAICH[1.4]]

gold *see* GOWD

†**goldeine** *n* the golden-eye duck *Bucephala clangula la16*. Compare GOWDY DUCK. [*gold* (GOWD) + *een* (EE[1]) or *gold* (GOWD) + EE[1], with adj-forming suffix]

golden crest /ˈgoldən krɛst/ *n* the goldcrest *Regulus regulus la19-*. **golden crestie** = GOLDEN CREST. [*gowden* (GOWD) + *creste* (CREEST[1.1])]

†**golden knap, gowdnap** *n* an early variety of pear grown around Stirling *e19*. [*gowden* (GOWD) + KNAP[1]]

golder *see* GULLER[1.1], GULLER[1.2]

goldie[1], **gooldie** /ˈgoldi, ˈguldi/ *n* the goldfinch *Carduelis carduelis 19-*. Compare GOWDSPINK. [shortened form of Eng *goldfinch*]

goldie[2] /ˈgoldi/ *n* a glass of whisky *la20-*. **wee goldie** a small measure of whisky *la20-*. [*gold* (GOWD) + -IE[1]]

goldilocks /ˈgoldilɔks/ *n* the wood crowfoot *Ranunculus auricomus la19, 20- Bor*. [from the name of the fairy-tale character]

goldspink *see* GOWDSPINK

gole *see* GOWL[1.1]

golenȝe *see* GILLENȜE

golenȝeour *see* GILEYNOUR

golf *see* GOWF[1]

golfis *see* GOIF

gölgriv, guilgruff, †**golgrav** /ˈgølgrɪv, ˈgulgrʌf/ *n* **1** an open drain from a byre or midden *19- Sh*. **2** liquid manure (in a drain or midden) *19- Sh*. [ON *gröf* a pit, a hole, with unknown first element; compare OLGER]

golk *see* GOWK[1], GOWK[2]

golla, gulya, goillya /ˈgola, ˈgulja, ˈgɔɪlja/ *n* a young woman who assists at the christening of a child; a godmother *la19- Sh*. [ON *kolla* a hind, a cow, a ewe]

gollach /ˈgɔlax/ *v* to yell, bawl *19, 20- H&I*. [onomatopoeic; compare GULLER[1.2], GOLLIE[1.2]]

gollan, gullan /ˈgɔlən, ˈgʌlən/ *n* **1** name for various wild flowers, including the daisy, the corn marigold and ragwort *la19, 20- Ork N*. **2** a bright spot in the sky on either side of the sun, a parhelion *20- N NE*. **3** a frumpy woman *20- N*. [ME *gollan*; compare GOWAN]

gollar *see* GULLER[1.2]

goller *see* GULLER[1.1]

gollie[1.1], **gullie** /ˈgɔli, ˈgʌli/ *n* a shout, a roar, a yell *la18-19, 20- NE SW*. [see the verb]

gollie[1.2] /ˈgɔli/ *v* **1** to roar, shout, scold *la18-*. **2** to weep noisily *la18- NE*. [onomatopoeic; compare GULLER[1.2], GOLLACH]

gollop[1.1] /ˈgɔləp/ *n* a gulp *20-*. [probably variant of Eng *gulp*]

gollop[1.2] /ˈgɔləp/ *v* to gulp *20-*. [see the noun]

golt *see* GAUT

gomach /ˈgomax/ *n* a foolish person *19, 20- Uls*. [IrGael *gamach*]

gomeril[1.1], **gomeral** /ˈgɔmərəl/ *n* **1** a foolish or stupid person *19-*. **2** a person whose lower teeth project beyond the upper teeth *la19- Ork*. [GOAM, with -*ril* suffix; compare *gamphrell* (GAMF[1.1])]

†**gomeril**[1.2], **gomral** *adj* foolish, stupid *e19*. [see the noun]

gomf *see* GAMF[1.1]

gomphion *see* GUMPHION

gomral *see* GOMERIL[1.2]

gon see GOUN

goniel /'gɔniəl/ *n* **1** a foolish person *la19- Bor.* **2** (the meat of) a sheep found dead, usually after suffering from braxy *19- Bor.* [unknown; compare Eng *gawney, gony*]

gonnae, gaunnae, gonny, gaunna /'gone, 'gɔne, 'gɔnə/ *v* **1** to be about to; to have the intention of: ◊*Ah'm gonnae ask hur the noo 19-*. **2** *as an imperative* will you (do something): *gonnae answer the door 20-. EC.* **gaun-a-du** a resolution *19, 20- EC.* **gonnae no** *as an imperative* do not (do something): ◊*gonnae no ask stupit questions la20-.* [derivative of GAE]

gonterns /'gɔntərnz/ *interj* an expression of surprise or delight *la18-19, 20- Bor.* [perhaps altered form of Eng *conscience*]

goo¹, gou /gu/ *n* **1** a strong, persistent (disagreeable) taste *18-.* **2** a liking or relish for something *18-.* **3** an offensive smell *19-.* **gooey** tasty, having a distinctive flavour *20-.* [Fr *goût*]

goo²·¹ /gu/ *n* a bout of retching *20- SW.* **get the goo** to retch, suffer nausea or disgust *20- SW.* [perhaps extended sense of GOO¹]

†**goo²·²** *v* to retch *la19.* [see the noun]

goo³ /gu/ *v of a baby* to coo *la19-.* [onomatopoeic]

goo see GOW⁶·¹

good see GUID¹·¹, GUID¹·³

goodfather see GUID-FAITHER

goodin see GUIDIN

goodman see GUIDMAN

gooey see GOO¹

goog /gug/ *n* something soft, moist or messy *19- N NE T.* **googar** = GOOG *20- NE.* [perhaps imitative; compare GAGGLE²·¹]

gool, guil, †**gowl,** †**guld,** †**guild** /gul/ *n* the corn marigold *Glebionis segetum 15-.* [OE *gold*; compare GOWD, GULE]

goold see GOWD

gooldie see GOLDIE¹

gooldspink see GOWDSPINK

gooms, gums, *NE* **geems,** *NE* **gweems,** †**gumes** /gumz, gʌmz; *NE* gimz; *NE* gwimz/ *npl* the firm flesh at the base of the teeth *15-.* [OE *gōma* the inside of the mouth or throat]

goon see GOUN

goor¹·¹, gore, *Sh* **gurr,** †**gor** /gur, gor; *Sh* gʌr/ *n* **1** mucus; muck in the eye *16-19, 20- Sh Ork N NE T.* **2** mud, dirt; muddy, stagnant water; slush *la19- Sh NE.* **3** fish slime, fish refuse *20- Sh Ork NE.* **4** wax in the ear *20- Ork.* **5** bodily matter, faeces *e15.* [OE *gor* dung, dirt, ON *gor* slimy matter]

goor¹·² /gur/ *v of a stream* to become choked with thawing snow and ice *la19- NE.* [see the noun]

goorie¹·¹, †**gowrie** /'guri/ *n pl* †**gouries** fish refuse *la16-17, 20- NE.* [GOOR¹·¹ + -IE¹]

goorie¹·², †**gorry,** †**goiry** /'guri/ *adj* muddy, slimy *la15-, 20- NE.* [see the noun]

goose see GUSE¹·¹, GUSE¹·²

goose hawk, gooshauk see GOSHAWK

gooshet see GUSHET

goosy see GUSSIE¹·²

gopin see GOWPEN¹·¹

gor /gɔr/ *interj* an expression of surprise or incredulity; a mild oath *19-.* [euphemistic form of GOD]

gor see GOOR¹·¹, GORE¹·²

gorb¹·¹ /gɔrb/ *n* **1** an unfledged bird *la18-.* **2** an infant, a young child *19-.* **3** a glutton *la19-.* **gorbel 1** an unfledged bird *19-.* **2** an infant, a young child *19, 20- WC.* **gorbellit** *of an egg* containing a developing chick *20- NE T Bor.* **gorbet 1** an unfledged bird *16-.* **2** an infant, a young child *19- T.*

†**gorbie** an unfledged bird *la19.* **gorblin,** *NE* **gordlin** an unfledged bird *18-.* [unknown]

gorb¹·² /gɔrb/ *v* to eat greedily *20- SW Uls.* [unknown]

gorble /'gɔrbəl/ *v* to eat ravenously *18-19, 20- SW Bor.* [perhaps a variant of Eng *gobble*]

gor-cock /'gɔrkɔk/ *n* the male of the red grouse *Lagopus lagopus la18-19, 20- NE T.* [obscure first element + COCK; compare GORMAW]

gordie see GIRD¹·¹

gordlin see GORB¹·¹

Gordon /'gɔrdən/ *n* a soldier in the *Gordon Highlanders la18-20, 21- historical.* **Gordon Highlanders** the name of an infantry regiment originally raised by the fourth Duke of Gordon in 1794 *la18-20, 21- historical.* [named after the Duke of Gordon]

gore¹·¹, gurr /gor, gʌr/ *n* a deep furrow *la18-19, 20- NE.* [unknown]

gore¹·², †**gor** /gor/ *v pt, ptp* also †**gorrit 1** to stab, pierce; to maul *la15-.* **2** to plough deeply *la18-19.* [unknown]

gore see GOOR¹·¹

gorfy /'gɔrfe/ *adj* coarse *19- T.* [probably metathesis of of GROFF]

gorge, gurge, grudge /gɔrdʒ, gʌrdʒ, grʌdʒ/ *v* **1** to choke up a channel with mud or snow *16-19, 20- Sh Bor.* **2** to swell, surge *16-19, 20- Bor.* [ME *gorgen*]

gorget, †**gorgeat** /'gɔrdʒət/ *n* **1** a piece of armour to protect the throat; a covering for the throat *15-e17, 19- historical.* **2** an iron collar used as a form of pillory *e19.* **3** a woman's neck covering *la16-e19.* †**the gorgets** a form of pillory *17-e19.* [ME *gorget*]

gorlin /'gɔrlɪn/ *n* **1** an unfledged bird *la18-.* **2** a young child; an urchin *18-19, 20- SW.* [compare *gorblin*]

†**gormaw** *n* the cormorant *Phalacrocorax carbo 16-e19.* [perhaps GOOR¹·¹ + MAW⁴]

gornal /'gɔrnəl/ *n* a button *20- N.* [altered form of KIRNEL]

gorroch¹·¹ /'gɔrəx/ *n* **1** a trampled, muddy spot *la19- SW.* **2** a mess *20- EC.* [derivative of GOOR¹·¹]

gorroch¹·² /'gɔrəx/ *v* **1** to mix or stir something soft and messy *19- SW.* **2** to make a mess of, spoil *20- EC SW.* [see the noun]

gorry see GOORIE¹·²

gorsk see GOSK

gorstie, gersty, gairsty /'gɔrsti, 'gɛrsti, 'gersti/ *n* a ridge of rough ground left uncultivated as a boundary between two plots of arable land *la18- Sh Ork.* **gorstie girse** the grass growing on a uncultivated ridge *la19- Sh.* [ON *garðstaðr* the site of a fence or boundary]

†**gos** *n* the goshawk *la18.* [shortened form of GOSHAWK]

gosh /gɔʃ/ *interj* an expression of surprise *19-.* **gosh be here** an expression of surprise *la19- Sh NE.* **gosh bliss me** Gold bless me *la19- Sh N NE T.* **gosh me** goodness me *la19-.* [euphemistic form of GOD]

goshawk, goose hawk, †**goshalk,** †**goishalk,** †**gooshauk** /'gɔʃɔk, 'guʃɔk/ *n* the hen harrier *Circus cyaneus*; the goshawk *Accipiter gentilis*, or another species of hawk *la15-.* [OE *gōshafoc* goose-hawk]

gosk, gorsk /gɔsk, gɔrsk/ *n* coarse, rank grass *18- NE T.* **goskie, gorskie** overgrown; luxuriant *19, 20- NE T SW.* [perhaps GOOR¹·¹ + REESK]

gospel, †**gospell,** †**godspel** /'gɔspəl/ *n* **1** religious teaching (especially from the four books of the Evangelists) *la14-.* **2** something believed to be true *la15-.* **gospel greedy** regularly attending church, fond of churchgoing *la19-.* [OE *godspel* good tidings]

†**goss, gosse** *n* a familiar form of address to a friend *17-19.* [reduced form of Older Scots *gossop* a godparent; a friend]

got *see* GET¹,²
gote *see* GAIT¹, GYTE²
goth /gɔθ/ *interj* a mild oath *19, 20- Ork N SW.* [euphemistic form of GOD]
gott *see* GYTE²
gottin *see* GET¹,²
gou *see* GOO¹
goudie, †**gowdie** /ˈgʌudi/ *n* Gouda cheese *la19-.* [from the name of the Dutch city]
goudie *see* GOWD
gouf /gʌuf/ *v* to underpin or underbuild a wall or building to secure its foundations or put in a damp-course *18- C.* [perhaps variant of COLF]
gouff *see* GUFF¹, GUFF²,¹, GUFF³,¹
gouffer *see* GOFFER
goug *see* GUGA
goukmey /ˈgʌukme/ *n* the grey gurnard *Eutrigla gurnardus 19, 20- literary.* [unknown]
goul *see* GOWL¹,²
gould *see* GOWD
goule *see* GOW⁶·¹, GOWL²
goulf *see* GOWF¹
goul-mau *see* GOW⁶·¹
goulock *see* GOLACH
goum *see* GUM¹
goun, goon, gown, †**gon** /gun, gʌun/ *n* **1** a loose upper garment, a dress; a formal robe of office *la14-.* **2** a nightgown or nightshirt *la19-.* **goonie, gounie** a nightgown or nightshirt *la19-.* †**gown class** a course at Glasgow University leading to an Arts degree *la18-e19.* †**gown curriculum** = *gown class.* †**gown student** a matriculated student attending a *gown class* and intending to take the full course for a degree *18.* [ME *goune*]
goun *see* GUN¹,¹
gourd¹,¹ /gurd/ *v of water* to become pent up *18-19, 20- NE Bor.* [see the adj]
†**gourd**¹,² *adj* stiff *15-19.* [MFr *gourd* numb, stiff]
gouries *see* GOORIE¹,¹
†**Gourlay** *n* a superior brand of golfball *la18-e19.* [from the name of the manufacturer]
gourlins /ˈgurlɪnz/ *npl* the edible roots or tubers of the earthnut *Bunium bulbocastanum* or *Conopodium majus 19- SW.* [Gael *cutharlan* the earthnut]
Gourock /ˈgurək/ a town on the Clyde *la17-.* **it's all to one side like Gourock** it is lop-sided *20- C.* [Gael **guireóc, *guireág* small protuberance]
gouster *see* GOWSTER¹,¹, GOWSTER¹,²
goustrous *see* GOWSTER¹,¹
gousty *see* GOWSTIE
govanenty /ˈgɔvənenti, gɔvəˈnenti/ *interj* an expression of surprise *la19- N SW.* [perhaps altered form of Scots *God defend ye* or similar phrase; compare GOVIE]
gove¹,¹ /gov/ *n* a vacant stare *19- T SW Bor.* [unknown]
gove¹,², **goave**, †**goif** /gov/ *v* **1** to gaze, look at; to stare stupidly or vacantly *la14-.* **2** to wander aimlessly about *20- SW Bor.* **3** *of animals* to start with fright; to toss the head *19, 20- NE.* [unknown]
Gove² /gɔv/ *n* a nickname for a headmaster or school governor *20- EC.* **Govie** = GOVE *la19- NE EC.* [shortened form of Older Scots *governour*]
†**gove**³ *v* to put in a pillory *la15-e17.* [from GOIF]
govie /ˈgovi/ *interj* an expression of surprise *19-.* **govey dick** = GOVIE *la19-.* **govey ding** = GOVIE *20-.* [euphemistic form of GOD]
Govie *see* GOVE²
govis *see* GOIF

gow¹ /gʌu/ *n* a foolish person *19- SW.* [probably Eng *gull* a fool]
gow² /gʌu/ *n* a blacksmith *la15-19, 20- literary.* [Gael *gobha*]
gow³ /gʌu/ *n* a halo around the sun or moon (supposed to be a sign of storms) *19-.* [unknown]
gow⁴ /gʌu/ *v* to wheedle, persuade *la19- NE.* **goo ower** to win over *la19- NE.* [Eng *gull* to cheat]
gow⁵ /gʌu/ *v* to bawl, howl, squeal *20- Ork.* [probably shortened form of GOWL¹,²]
gow⁶·¹, **goo**, †**goule** /gʌu, gu/ *n* a gull, a bird of the family *Laridae la15-.* †**goul-mau** a gull *e16.* [ME *gulle*]
gow⁶·² /gʌu/ *v* to eat greedily *la20- N NE.* [see the noun]
gowan /ˈgʌuən/ *n* **1** the daisy *Bellis perennis 16-.* **2** the ox-eye daisy *Leucanthemum vulgare 20-.* **3** the corn marigold *Glebionis segetum la18- NE.* **4** marsh ragwort *Jacobaea aquatica 20- Sh.* †**gowan'd** covered with daisies *19.* **gowany 1** covered with daisies *18-.* **2** *of weather* (deceptively) bright or fine *19- NE EC.* **ewe gowan** the daisy *19- T Bor.* **gowan gabbit** covered with daisies *19- EC Bor.* **horse gowan 1** the ox-eye daisy *19-.* **2** the dandelion *Taraxacum officinale 19- NE.* **3** the sowthistle *Sonchus arvensis 20- N.* **lapper gowan** the globeflower *Trollius europaeus 19- Bor.* **lucken gowan,** †**luikin gowane** the globeflower *Trollius europaeus la16-19, 20- Bor.* **May gowan** the daisy *19- T Bor.* **white gowan** the ox-eye daisy *19-.* **yellow gowan** a name for various yellow wild flowers including the buttercup or marigold *18-.* **not care a gowan** to not care in the least *19-.* [variant of GOLLAN]
gowd, gould, goold, gold /gʌud, guld, gold/ *n* a precious yellow metal, gold *la14-.* **gowden, gooldin** made of gold; golden *la14-.* **goudie,** †**gowdie** the treasurer of a trade corporation *la19-, 20- WC.* **gowds** a pet name for a child or a married woman *20- N.* †**gold foilzie, gowden foolyie** gold leaf *e19;* compare FULZIE². †**goldin myne** a gold mine *e16.* †**golden penny, gold penny** a shipping due *la16-17.* †**gae gowdie lane** *of a child* to walk unaided *19.* [OE *gold*]
gowdanook, gowdnook, †**gowfnack** /ˈgʌudənuk, ˈgʌudnuk/ *n* the skipper or saury *Scomberesox saurus la18-19, 20- NE.* [*gowden* (GOWD), with *-ock* diminutive suffix]
gowdie, †**gowdnie,** †**gawdnie** /ˈgʌudi/ *n* **1** the gurnard, a fish of the family *Triglidae 18- NE T EC.* **2** the father lasher *Taurulus bubalis 18- Ork NE T.* **3** the common dragonet *Callionymus lyra 18-19.* [GOWD + -IE³]
gowdie *see* GOUDIE
gowdnap *see* GOLDEN KNAP
gowdnook *see* GOWDANOOK
gowdspink, Uls **gooldspink,** †**goldspink** /ˈgʌudspɪŋk; Uls ˈguldspɪŋk/ *n* the goldfinch *Carduelis carduelis 16-.* [GOWD + SPINK²,¹]
gowdy duck /ˈgʌudi dʌk/ *n* the golden-eye duck *Bucephala clangula la18-19, 20- Sh.* [GOWD + -IE² + *duck* (DEUK)]
gowf¹, **golf,** †**goulf,** †**goiff,** †**goff** /gʌuf, gɔlf/ *n* the game of golf *la15-.* **gowfin** golf *18-.* **gowf ba, golf ball** the ball used in playing golf *16-.* **golf club,** †**goff club** the club used to strike the ball in golf *16-.* **golf house,** †**goff house** a golf club house *la18-.* **golf links, gowf links** a golf course by the seashore *la18-.* **gowf stick** a golf club *20- NE EC.* [probably MDu *kolf* a club used in a game similar to golf]
gowf²,¹, **gowff** /gʌuf/ *n* a blow, a slap *18-.* †**tae the gowf** to wrack and ruin *19.* [GOWF¹ or onomatopoeic]
gowf²,² /gʌuf/ *v* to hit, strike, slap *18-.* [see the noun]
gowfnack *see* GOWDANOOK
gowk¹, *Sh Ork* **gok**, *NE* **gock,** †**golk** /gʌuk; *Sh Ork NE* gɔk/ *n* **1** the cuckoo *Cuculus canorus la15-.* **2** a foolish person *la16-.* **3** a joke or trick; an April Fools' Day joke *20-.*

gowkie foolish *la19-*. **gowkoo** the cuckoo *la19- NE T EC*. **gowk aits** oats sown in May, after the arrival of the cuckoo *la19- NE Bor*. **gowk's day** April Fools' Day *la19-*. **gowk's days** the first two or three days of April *la19- Ork Bor*. **gowk's errand** a fool's errand *19-*. **gowk's hose** a bell-shaped flower, especially the Canterbury bell *Campanula medium 19, 20- NE*. **gowk's meat** the wood sorrel *Oxalis acetosella la18- Bor*. **gowk spit 1** the frothy secretion of the froghopper *19-*. **2** *derogatory* a weak person *19- Bor*. **gowk spittle, gowks' spittle** the frothy secretion of the froghopper *19-*. **gowk's storm, gowk storm 1** a brief spring storm coinciding with the arrival of the cuckoo *19-*. **2** a minor dispute *la16-e19*. **gowk's-thimles** the harebell *la19- NE*. **gowk and titlin, the gowk and the titling 1** the cuckoo and the meadow pipit (frequently seen together) *19-*. **2** a name for two inseparable or incongruous companions *19-*. [ON *gaukr*]

gowk[2], †**goik**, †**golk** /gʌuk/ *v* to stare *la15-*. [unknown; compare GAWK[2]]

gowk[3] /gʌuk/ *v* **1** to fool or deceive; to play an April Fools' Day joke *18-*. **2** to wander aimlessly; to loiter *la19-*. [GOWK[1] or GOWK[3]]

gowkit, †**gukit**, †**guckit**, †**gukkit** /'gʌukɪt/ *adj* foolish *la16-*. [GOWK[1] + -IT[2]]

gowl[1.1], †**gule**, †**gole** /gʌul/ *n* **1** a yell, a howl; a loud cry *la15-*. **2** a noisy gust of wind *19, 20- Sh Bor*. **gowlie 1** *of people* sulky, scowling *19, 20- Sh*. **2** *of weather* windy *20- Bor*. [see the verb]

gowl[1.2], †**goul** /gʌul/ *v* **1** to howl, yell; to weep noisily *la14-*. **2** to scold angrily *19-*. **3** to scowl *19-*. **4** *of a seal* to bark *20- Sh*. **5** *of the wind* to gust noisily *la17-19*. [ON *gaula* to low, bellow]

gowl[2], †**goule** /gʌul/ *n* **1** the throat, the jaws *16-*. **2** a narrow pass or hollow between hills; frequently in place-names *la16-*. [probably OFr *goule* a throat, a neck, a cleft]

gowl[3] /gʌul/ *n* the crotch, the perineal region *20- Sh N NE*. [probably Gael *gobhal* bifurcation]

gowl *see* GOOL
gown *see* GOUN

gowp[1.1] /gʌup/ *n* a throb of pain *19-*. [unknown]

gowp[1.2] /gʌup/ *v* **1** *of the heart or pulse* to beat strongly or wildly, palpitate *la18-*. **2** *of sores or pains* to throb, ache violently *19-*. [unknown]

gowp[2.1], **gulp**, †**gaup** /gʌup, gʌlp/ *n* a large mouthful, a gulp *17-*. [see the verb]

gowp[2.2], **gulp**, †**gaup** /gʌup, gʌlp/ *v* to swallow greedily, gulp *18-*. [ME *gulpen*; compare Du *gulpen*]

gowp[3] /gʌup/ *v* to scoop up with the hands; to hollow out *la19-*. [back-formation from GOWPEN[1.2]]

gowp *see* GAUP[1.1], GAUP[1.2]

gowpen[1.1], *Uls* **gopin**, †**gowpin** /'gʌupən/; *Uls* 'gopən/ *n* **1** two hands held together to form a bowl *la15-*. **2** the receptacle formed by the hands held together *la18-*. **gowpenfu** a handful *la18-*. [ON *gaupn*]

gowpen[1.2], *Sh* **gjoppen** /'gʌupən/; *Sh* 'gjɔpən/ *v* to scoop up or ladle out with both hands *19-*. [see the noun; compare Norw dial *gaupna*]

gowrie *see* GOORIE[1.1]
gowsel *see* GUSEL

gowst[1.1] /gʌust/ *n* **1** a gust, a blast *la19-*. **2** an angry shout *20- Sh SW*. [perhaps back-formation from GOWSTER[1.1]]

gowst[1.2] /gʌust/ *v* to boast, bluster *19-*. [see the noun]

gowster[1.1], **gouster** /'gʌustər/ *n* **1** a wild, violent, blustering or swaggering person *18-19, 20- Ork SW*. **2** a strong wind *la19- Sh Ork*. **3** a violent outburst *20- Sh Ork SW*. **goustrous 1** hearty, vigorous *19- C SW Bor*. **2** *of weather* dark and stormy *19- C SW Bor*. **goustery** wet and windy, blustery *20- Sh SW*. [see the verb]

gowster[1.2], **gouster** /'gʌustər/ *v* **1** to boast, bluster *la19- Sh Ork SW*. **2** to be stormy; to lash with wind and rain *la19- Sh Ork*. [perhaps Eng *gauster, goster* to behave in a noisy, blustering manner]

gowstie, gousty /'gʌusti/ *adj* **1** vast, dreary, desolate; eerie *16-*. **2** ghastly, emaciated, pale *16-19, 20- NE*. **3** wild, stormy *19, 20- NE Bor*. **4** short of breath; fat and flabby *20- NE*. [unknown]

gra *see* GRAY[1.1], GRAY[1.3]
graav *see* GRAVE[1.1]
graavut *see* GRAVAT

grab /grab/ *n* **1** something which has been grabbed; plunder, booty *la18-*. **2** a miserly or avaricious person *19-*. **3** a clutch, a snatch, a sudden grip *la19-*. **4** an advantageous bargain (with the implication of greed or dishonesty) *la19- N NE T*. **grabbie** greedy, avaricious *19-*. [from the Eng verb *to grab*]

grabble[1.1] /'grabəl/ *n* a grab, a grasping motion *la19- T EC*. [see the verb]

grabble[1.2] /'grabəl/ *v* to grab; to grope *la19- Sh T EC Uls*. [frequentative form of Eng *grab*; compare Du *grabbelen*]

grace /gres/ *n* **1** spiritual virtue; divine favour *la14-*. **2** favourable disposition; benevolence *15-*. **3** a prayer said before or after a meal *la15-*. **4** a courtesy title or form of address *16-*. **gracie** full of spiritual grace, devout, virtuous *18-*. **gracious 1** full of grace, goodness or kindness *15-*. **2** friendly, on good terms *la18-*. **3** happy, prosperous *18-19*. **4**; *of soil* fertile *la18*. †**grace-drink** the drink taken at the end of a meal after grace had been said *18*. **grace note** *in bagpipe music* an extremely short note, theoretically not counted in the time of the music *19-*. **act of grace** *law* the act of 1696 providing for the maintenance of an indigent debtor in prison by the creditor responsible for his imprisonment *la17-19, 20- historical*. **du ony grace** to make any progress; to be worthwhile *20- Sh*. [ME *grace*]

graddan[1.1], †**gradʒan** /'gradən/ *n* **1** coarse oatmeal made from parched grain ground by hand *la16-19, 20- NE*. **2** home-made snuff *19, 20- NE*. **3** powdery refuse, sweepings of peat *19, 20- NE*. [Gael *gradan*]

†**graddan**[1.2] *v* to parch grain in the ear *la18-e19*. [see the noun]

graduand /'gradʒuənd/ *n* a person about to receive a university degree *la19-*. [Lat *graduāndus*, gerundive of *graduāri* to take a degree]

gradʒan *see* GRADDAN[1.1]
graefster *see* GREFSTER
graf, grafe, graff *see* GRAVE[1.1]

graft /graft/ *n* a grave *19, 20- SW Bor*. [MDu *graft* a ditch, ON *gröftr* the action of digging]

Grahame's Dike *see* GRIMES DYKE

graif *see* GRAVE[1.1], GRAVE[1.2]

graig /greg/ *v* to make a noise in the throat *17- NE*. [onomatopoeic; compare CRAIK[1.1]]

grain[1], †**grane** /gren/ *n* **1** the seed of cereals *la15-*. **2** the smallest unit of measurement, 1/576 ounce SCOTS[1.2] *16-*. **3** a small quantity; a little bit *la18-*. **4** a seed, berry *la15-e17*. **5** a scarlet dye *15-e16*. †**grainit, grainyt** dyed with a scarlet dye *la15-e17*. [ME *grain*]

grain[2], †**grane** /gren/ *n* **1** a branch of a tree or family *15-*. **2** a branch of a river, an arm of a valley or loch; frequently in place-names *la15-*. **3** a prong (of a fork or salmon spear) *16-*. †**grainit** pronged *16-e19*. [ON *grein*]

grain[3.1], **grane, groan,** †**grone** /gren, gron/ *n* a low sound of grief or pain, a groan *la14-*. **groaning malt** ale brewed to celebrate a birth *19, 20- historical*. [see the verb]

grain³,², **grane**, **groan**, †**grone** /gren, grɔn/ v **1** to utter a low sound of grief or pain; to groan *la14-*. **2** to complain, grumble; to be ailing *18-*. [OE *grānian*]

grainery /ˈgrenəre/ n a place where grain is stored *19-*. [Lat *grānārium*, with influence from GRAIN¹]

graip¹·¹, **grape**, *Sh* **grep**, †**grap** /grep; *Sh* grɛp/ n an iron-pronged fork used in farming and gardening *la15-*. [ON *greip* the space between the thumb and fingers; compare Norw dial *greip* a dung-fork]

graip¹·² /grep/ v to fork up land *20-*. [see the noun]

graip², **grape**, **growp**, **grope** /grep, grʌup, grop/ v **1** to search with the hands; to probe *la14-*. **2** to handle or touch indecently; to grope *la15-*. **3** to examine the conscience or an argument *la15-18*. [OE *grāpian*]

graisle, †**graizle**, †**grassil**, †**grasle** /ˈgresəl/ v to fizzle, crackle; to make a grating, grinding or creaking noise *16-19, 20- SW*. [probably onomatopoeic; compare Fr *grésiller* to crackle]

grait *see* GREAT¹·²

graith¹·¹, *Sh* **greth**, †**grayth**, †**grathe**, †**greath** /greθ; *Sh* greθ/ n **1** equipment; tools, implements, machinery *la14-*. **2** clothes, articles of dress *15-*. **3** mechanical accessories for a mill or plough; the heddles for a loom *la15-*. **4** the rigging or tackle of a ship *la15-*. **5** furnishings, effects *la15-*. **6** merchandise; supplies; cargo *la15-*. **7** archery equipment *la15-*. **8** trappings or harness for a horse *la15-*. **9** possessions, wealth, money *16-*. **10** a soapy lather; dirty soapsuds *18-*. **11** stale urine used in washing and dyeing *19, 20- historical*. **12** *fishing* the attachment, consisting of the snood and tippin, by which the hook is suspended from the line *20- N NE*. **13** the penis *18-19*. **14** liquor, medicine *la18-19*. **15** a contemptuous term for a mob of people *19*. **16** the accessory apparatus of a gun or cannon; ammunition powder and shot *la15-e18*. **graithin** equipment, trappings; dress *la18-19, 20- EC*. †**graithly** well; carefully; clearly *la14-16*. [ON *greði* arrangement, order; compare Norw dial *greide* implements, tackle]

graith¹·², †**grath** /greθ/ v **1** to prepare, make ready *la14-*. **2** to harness or tack up a horse *la16-*. **3** to equip, dress *la15-19*. **4** to deal with (a person) *la14-16*. **5** to ornament, decorate *la15-17*. †**graith your gate** to make a way for oneself *15*. [ON *greiða* to arrange, make ready]

†**graith**¹·³ adj ready, clear, direct *la14-15*. [see the noun]

graitifee /ˈgretəfi/ v to gratify *la19- Sh NE*. [Fr *gratifier*]

graititeed *see* GRATITUDE

graivel, **gravel**, †**gravell** /ˈgrevəl, ˈgravəl/ n **1** small stones, pebbles; coarse sand *15-*. **2** urinary crystals, renal calculus *la15-18*. [ME *gravel*]

graizle *see* GRAISLE

gralloch¹·¹ /ˈgraləx/ n **1** a deer's entrails *19-*. **2** the disembowelling of a deer *la19-*. [Gael *greallach* entrails, intestines]

gralloch¹·² /ˈgraləx/ v to disembowel a deer *19-*. [see the noun]

gram¹·¹, **grame** /gram, grem/ n **1** sorrow, grief *la15-19, 20- literary*. **2** anger, malice *16-19, 20- literary*. [OE *grama*]

gram¹·² /gram/ adj **1** eager, keen; delighted *la19- Sh*. **2** fierce *la15*. [OE *gram*]

gramarie /ˈgraməri/ n magic, enchantment, witchcraft *19, 20- Ork*. Compare GLAMOUR¹·¹. [ME *gramari*]

gramashes *see* GROMMASHENS

grame *see* GRAM¹·¹

gramer, grammar *see* GREMMAR

gramse /grams/ n a grab or snatch *20- Sh Ork*. [Norw *gramse*]

gran *see* GRAND, GRIND²

†**grana crescentia** n *law* the corn grown on a THIRLAGE *18-e19*. [Lat *grāna crescentia* growing grains]

granale *see* GIRNEL¹·¹

grand, gran, graund, graun /grand, gran, grɔnd, grɔn/ adj **1** great, of high rank or importance *16-*. **2** fine, splendid *la19-*. **grandbairn** a grandchild *la19-*. **grandchilder** grandchildren *19, 20- Uls*. **granda** a grandfather *la19-*. **grandam**, †**grannam**, †**grandame 1** a grandmother *15-*. **2** a great-grandmother *15-17*. **grandey** a grandfather *19- T EC*. **grand-dochter** a grand-daughter *la19-*. **grandfaither, granfader** a grandfather *la16-*. **grandminnie** a grandmother *20-*. **grandmither** a grandmother *la19-*. **grandsher**, †**grandschir**, †**grantschir 1** a great-grandfather *16-19, 20- Sh*. **2** a grandfather *15-e16*. **grandwean** a grandchild *la19-*. [MFr *grand*]

grand *see* GRIND²

†**grandgore**, **grangour** n venereal disease, syphilis *la15-e17*. [MFr *grand gorre*; compare GLENGORE]

grane *see* GRAIN¹, GRAIN², GRAIN³·¹, GRAIN³·²

grangour *see* GRANDGORE

granich /ˈgranəx/ v to sicken, disgust *la19- NE*. [Gael *gràinich*]

†**granitar, grintar** n the official in charge of a granary *la15-16*. [MFr *grenetier*, Lat *granitārius*]

Granite City /ˌgranɪt ˈsɪte/ n a nickname for the city of Aberdeen *19-*. [a reference to the granite from which much of the city was historically built + city]

†**grank**¹·¹ n a groan *16*. [frequentative form of GRAIN³·¹]

†**grank**¹·² v to groan *16-e19*. [see the noun]

grannam *see* GRAND

grannie¹·¹, **granny** /ˈgrane, ˈgrani/ n **1** a familiar name for a grandmother *la18-*. **2** a hairy caterpillar *la19-*. **3** the last sheaf cut at harvest-time *la19- Uls*. **4** a chimney cowl *20-*. **grannie's bairn** a grandchild, especially one brought up by its grandmother and spoilt *20-*. **grannie mutch, granny mutchie 1** a nickname for an old woman *20-*. **2** a nickname for a solemn little girl *la20-*. **granny's mutches, granny's mutch 1** the columbine *Aquilegia vulgaris la19-*. **2** the snapdragon *Antirrhinum majus 20-*. **grannie preen** a large pin for fastening a shawl *20-*. **grannie's sooker, granny sooker** a mint imperial or other hard sweet which can be sucked for a long time *20- NE T EC Bor*. **grannie's tartan** mottled skin on the legs *la20- C SW*. **grannie's tuith, grannie's teeth** *carpentry* a router plane *20- NE T*. **grannie's hieland hame** a sentimental view of the rural Highlands (from the song title) *20-*. **yer grannie** a phrase expressing derision; a sarcastic retort *la19-*. [shortened form of *grandam* (GRAND)]

grannie¹·², **granny** /ˈgrane, ˈgrani/ v to defeat heavily in a game (without the loser scoring) *la20-*. **grannie at** to address a person as 'granny' *20-*. [see the noun]

grant /grant/ v ptp †**ygrant 1** to bestow a favour or possession; to transfer property by formal grant *la14-*. **2** to permit; to consent to *la14-*. **3** to admit, acknowledge, confess *la14-*. [ME *graunten*]

grantschir *see* GRAND

granzie /ˈgranzi/ n *Travellers' language* a barn *19-*. [probably altered form of Older Scots *grange*]

grap *see* GRAIP¹·¹

†**grape** n a vulture *16*. [perhaps altered form of ME *grip(e)* a griffon]

grape *see* GRAIP¹·¹, GRAIP²

grapple /ˈgrapəl/ v **1** to fight at close quarters, wrestle with *la18-*. **2** to drag water when searching for a corpse *20-*. **3** to grope *la19- NE T*. **grappling** a method of catching salmon by means of an arrangement of hooks *la18-*. [OFr *grapeler* to seize violently, with influence from OFr *grape* a hook]

grapus /'grapəs/ *n* a name for the Devil or for a hobgoblin *19, 20- T.* [unknown]

†**grashloch** *adj* stormy, blustering *19.* [unknown]

grasle *see* GRAISLE

grass *see* GIRSE[1.1], GIRSE[1.2]

grassil *see* GRAISLE

grassum, †**gressum**, †**grissum**, †**gersum** /'grasəm/ *n law* a sum over and above the rent paid by a tenant at the granting or renewal of a lease *la13-*. [OE *gærsum* a treasure, something costly]

grat *see* GREET[1.2]

grate /gret/ *n* a grating *18-19, 20- N H&I.* [ME *grate*]

grath *see* GRAITH[1.2]

grathe *see* GRAITH[1.1]

gratification /gratəfɪ'keʃən/ *n* 1 satisfaction *la19-*. 2 a reward, a gratuity *la16-e19.* [Lat *grātificātio*]

†**gratinȝied** *adj of cloth* pinked *la16-17.* [aphetic form of MFr *esgratigner*]

gratis /'gratɪs/ *adv* free, without payment *16-*. †**gratis burgess** a burgess exempted from paying the regular entry fee for burgess-ship *la17-e19.* [Lat *grātis* out of kindness]

gratitude, *NE* **graititeed**, †**gratitud** /'gratɪtʃud; *NE* 'gretɪtid/ *n* 1 gratefulness *la16-*. 2 a gratuity *la16-*. 3 a service performed, a favour conferred *16-e17.* 4 a grant or contribution to the sovereign or a ranking clergyman *la15-16.* 5 a goodwill payment to a landlord in addition to the rent and GRASSUM *16.* [MFr *gratitude*]

grauin *see* GRAVE[1.2]

graun *see* GRAND

graund *see* GRAND

gravat, gravit, *N* **gravad**, *T* **graavut** /'gravət; *N* 'gravəd; *T* 'grɔvət/ *n* a scarf or muffler; a cravat *la17-*. [Fr *cravate*]

†**gravatour** *n* a letter of censure from an ecclesiastical court *la15-16.* [Lat *gravātōrium* aggravation of sentence]

grave[1.1], **graff, greff**, *Sh* **graav**, †**graif**, †**grafe**, †**graf** /grev, graf, grɛf; *Sh* grɑv/ *n* 1 a place of burial, a grave *la14-*. 2 the bottom of a peat-bank *la19- Sh.* 3 *fisherman's taboo* (ooze on) the sea bottom *la19- Sh.* **graveyaird deserter** a sickly looking person; a person who looks terminally ill *la19-*. **graveyaird hoast** a cough which appears to indicate a deadly disease *la19-*. [OE *græf*]

grave[1.2], †**graif** /grev/ *v ptp also* †**grauin** †**ygraven** 1 to bury, inter a corpse *la14-19, 20- Sh.* 2 to dig *la14-16, 20 Sh.* 3 to incise, engrave *la15-e17.* [OE *grafan* to dig, engrave]

†**grave**[2] *n* a grove *15-16.* [OE *grāf*]

grave *see* GRAVY

gravel, gravell *see* GRAIVEL

gravit *see* GRAVAT

gravy, †**grave** /'greve/ *n* 1 thickened meat juices *19-*. 2 a hot sauce *la18-19, 20- T EC.* [ME *grave*]

grawl /grɔl/ *n* a young salmon on its first return to fresh water *19- SW.* [altered form of GRILSE]

gray[1.1], **grey**, †**gra** /gre/ *n* 1 dawn; twilight *19-*. 2 grey cloth, compare *hodden gray* (HODDEN[1.2]) *la15-e19.* [see the adj]

gray[1.2], **grey** /gre/ *v* 1 to dawn *la19-*. 2 to cover with a thin sprinkling of snow *20- SW.* [see the adj]

gray[1.3], **grey**, †**gra** /gre/ *adj* having a colour between black and white *la14-*. **grayback** 1 the immature herring gull or lesser black-backed gull *20-*. 2 the hooded crow *Corvus cornix 20- Ork N T.* 3 the flounder *Platichythys flesus 20- NE EC.* 4 a salmon or salmon trout in the autumn run *20- SW Bor.* **graybeard, greybeard** a large jug or pitcher *la18-*. †**gray breid** bread made of rye or oats *15-e19.* **gray cheeper** the meadow pipit *Anthus pratensis la19- T Bor.* †**gray corn** a kind of light, inferior grain; the refuse of oats *la16-19.* **gray dark** dusk *la19-*. **gray day, grey day** dawn *19- Sh N NE Bor.* **grayface, greyface** a crossbred sheep, a Blackface crossed with a Leicester *19-*. **gray fish, grey fish** the coalfish *Pollachius virens*, especially in its second or third year *18-19, 20- Sh Ork N.* †**gray groat, grey groat** a silver fourpenny piece; something of little value *la18-e19.* **gray hen, grey hen** the female black grouse *Tetrao tetrix 15-*. **gray horse** a louse *20- T EC.* **gray lintie, grey lintie** 1 the male linnet (which has bright red plumage during the breeding season) *Linaria cannabina 19-*. 2 the lesser redpoll *Acanthis cabaret la19, 20- H&I.* **gray lord** the fully-grown coalfish *Pollachius virens la17-*. **gray meal, grey meal** the refuse of oats *17-*. †**gray oats, grey oats, gray aittis** an inferior kind of oats *la16-e19.* **gray paper** brown paper *19- Sh Ork N NE T.* **gray plover, grey plover** the golden plover *Pluvialis apricaria* in its summer plumage; the knot *Calidris canutus la18-*. **grey schule** an inferior variety of salmon *19- Bor.* †**gray sisteris** nuns of the third order of St Francis *16.* **gray skate** the skate *Dipturus batis 19, 20- NE EC.* **gray slate, grey slate** laminated sandstone, a kind of flagstone used in roofing *la18- Ork NE T EC.* **gray stane, grey stane** a grey volcanic rock; a grey boulder or monolith used as a landmark or boundary stone *la15-*. **gray thrums, grey thrums** the purring of a cat *19-*. **gray willie** the herring gull *Larus argentatus 20- N NE.* **a gray gate, a grey gate** a disastrous course or path *18-*. [OE *græg*]

gray[2] /gre/ *n* a light wind, a gentle breeze *la19- Ork N NE EC.* [Norw dial *gråe* a wind that just ripples the surface of water]

Gray[3] /gre/ *n* an arithmetic textbook *la19-e20, la20- historical.* [from the author of the book, James Gray of Peebles]

grayth *see* GRAITH[1.1]

gre *see* GREE[1.1], GREE[1.2], GREE[2]

greance *see* GREEANCE

grease /gris/ *v* to serve the ball in the game of rounders *20- H&I.* [perhaps extended sense of Scots *grease*, in the sense of making something run smoothly]

great[1.1], **gryte**, †**gret**, †**grete** /gret, grʌɪt/ *n* noble people *la14-*. **the grytes o the legs** the thighs *la19- NE.* †**in gret** in large quantities, in bulk *15-17.* [see the adj]

great[1.2], **grete, gret, grit, gryte**, †**girt**, †**greit**, †**grait** /gret, grɛt, grɪt, grʌɪt/ *adj* 1 large (in size, quantity, extent or importance) *la12-*. 2 coarse (in grain or texture) *la15-*. 3 intimate, friendly *17-*. 4 boastful, proud, elated *19-*. 5 thick, bulky; roomy, substantial *16-19, 20- Sh Bor.* 6 *of people* big, stout *la19- Sh NE.* 7 *of a river* in flood, high *la16-e19, 20- Ork.* 8 *of people or animals* pregnant and about to give birth *la14-19, 20- NE WC.* 9 *of the heart* filled with grief *18-19.* 10 *of an official* chief, principal *16.* †**Great Admiral** the commander-in-chief of the navy *la15-17*, compare LORD HIGH ADMIRAL. †**great assise** an assize consisting of 25 nobles or gentlemen appointed to try charges against an ordinary assize *15-16.* **great avizandum** *law* an AVIZANDUM from a judge in the Outer House to the judges in the Inner House; a report by the Lord Ordinary to the Inner House in certain actions *la19-*. †**grete effere** pomp, ceremony, display *la14-15.* **great ewe** a pregnant ewe *la18-*. **great fish** white fish *18- NE.* **great folk** people of rank or position *18-19, 20- NE T.* **great hearted** filled with emotion; ready to cry, sorrowful *19, 20- NE T EC.* †**Gret Justice** *law* one of the officers of state charged with the holding of justice aires and justice courts as presiding judge in the name of the sovereign *la15-e16.* **great-line**, *Bor* **gartlins**, †**girtling** the line used in deep-water fishing *la16-*. **great pipes** the Scottish bagpipes *16-*. **Great Seal**, †**grete sele** 1 the seal of the monarch or head of state used to authenticate royal charters and other documents of importance *la14-*. 2 the government department dealing with authentications under

the Great Seal *16-17*. **great teinds** the tithe of grain originally paid to the minister of a benefice or parish *17-20, 21- historical*. †**the great shot** the main aim or purpose of an activity *la16-17*. **a great warrior** a humorous term for a lively, spirited person or a bold child *18-*. [OE *grēat*]
greath *see* GRAITH¹·¹
Great Steward of Scotland /gret stjuərd əv ˈskɔtlənd/ *n* **1** a subsidiary title of the Duke of Rothesay; a title of the Prince of Wales *la14-*. **2** the chief officer of the Royal Household *17-e18*. [GREAT¹·² + *Stewart of Scotland* (STEWART)]
†**grece**¹ *n* a grey fur *la14-16*. [ME *gris*]
†**grece**² *n pl* **greissis** a flight of stairs; steps *la15-17*. Compare GREE². [ME *gres*]
gree¹·¹, †**gre** /gri/ *n* goodwill *la14-16, la19- literary*. [ME *gre*]
gree¹·², †**gre** /gri/ *v* **1** to come or bring to terms; to reconcile; to make an agreement or settlement *la16-*. **2** to be in harmony; to correspond or fit *16-*. **greeable 1** harmonious *la19, 20- NE H&I SW*. **2** agreeable, suitable, fitting *15-e16*. **greement**, †**griment** agreement, harmony *la16-19, 20- Ork NE T H&I*. [aphetic form of AGREE]
gree², †**gre** /gri/ *n* **1** first place, victory in a contest; the prize for coming first *15-19, 20- literary*. **2** rank, social position *la14-19*. **3** a step, a tier, a shelf *la14-17*. **4** a degree of relationship *15-16*. **5** a level of intensity or quality *15-16*. **6** a degree in measurement in geometry or astronomy *16*. **7** a university degree *15-e16*. [ME *gre*]
gree³ /gri/ *n* fish oil or fish-liver oil *la19- Sh*. **greed** *of fish* cooked with fish-liver oil *la19- Sh*. [back-formation from Older Scots *grese* grease]
greeance, †**greance** /ˈgriəns/ *n* concord, agreement *la16-19, 20- NE*. [aphetic form of AGREEANCE]
greed, †**greid** /grid/ *n* avarice *la16-*. [back-formation from OE *grǣdig*]
greed *see* GREE³
greek /grik/ *n* dawn *18-19, 20- Sh Ork N*. Compare CREEK², SKREEK. [back-formation from GREIKIN]
greek *see* GREET²
greemik *see* GRIMEK
greemit *see* GRIMET
green¹·¹, †**grene**, †**greyn** /grin/ *n* **1** land grown with grass; a grassy place; frequently in place-names *14-*. **2** a piece of communal grassy ground within a town or village *14-*. **3** green colour, greenness *15-*. **4** the grassy area forming part of the grounds of a house or tenement *la15-*. **5** *golf* the piece of finely-turfed grass used as the putting ground; originally also the fairway or the whole course *18-*. **greens** green vegetables, especially kail *la18-*. [see the adj]
green¹·², †**grene**, †**gren** /grin/ *adj* **1** covered with grass, grassy; frequently in place-names *12-*. **2** green-coloured *la14-*. **3** young, youthful; full of vitality *la14-*. **4** *of timber* unseasoned *15-*. **5** *of hides* untanned *la16-*. **6** *of milk* new, fresh *18-*. **7** *of manure* fresh, unrotted *la18-*. **8** *of cloth or yarn* unbleached, untreated *la18-*. **9** *of a fire* newly kindled and smouldering *la19-*. **10** *of herring or other fish* fresh, unsalted *la16-19, 20- Sh N SW*. **11** *of a cow* recently calved *19- EC Bor*. **12** *of a woman* having just given birth *18*. **green- ichtie** greenish *20- NE*. **greenichy** greenish *la19- NE T*. **green bane** the garfish or sea needle *Belone belone 18-19, 20- Sh Ork*. **green berry** the green gooseberry *20-*. **green brees** seepage from a dunghill or cesspool *19- NE*. **green gaw** green slimy seaweed; green algae *20- N NE*. **green grass** a children's rhyme; the game in which it occurs *19, 20- NE T*. **green kail** (soup made from) a non-curly variety of kail *17-*. **green kailworm** the caterpillar of the cabbage butterfly *Pieris rapae 19-*. **green lady 1** a spectre *19-*. **2** a local authority health visitor (from the colour of the uniform)

la20- WC. **green lintie** the greenfinch *Carduelis chloris 19-*. **green paek** the first grass in Spring *20- Sh*. †**Green Ribbon** the ribbon of the Order of the Thistle *18-19*. **Green Rod** the baton of the Order of the Thistle *18-*. **green wood 1** growing trees or branches, living wood *15-*. **2** a wood or forest in leaf *la15-16*. **aa green thing** everything *la19- NE T*. **the Green Tables** an informal name for the Court of Session (apparently from the green cloth with which the Court was originally furnished) *20-*. [OE *grēne*]
green², **grien**, †**grene**, †**grein** /grin/ *v* **1** to long or yearn for *16-*. **2** *of pregnant women* to crave particular foods *18-*. [perhaps ON *girna* to desire]
green grape /ˈgrin grep/ *n derogatory* a Roman Catholic *la20-*. [rhyming slang from PAPE]
greenhorn /ˈgrinhɔrn/ *n* **1** a raw inexperienced person; a person with learning difficulties *la17-*. **2** a spoon made of a green-coloured horn *18-*. [GREEN¹·² + HORN]
greenichtie, **greenichy** *see* GREEN¹·²
greenwife /ˈgrinwʌif/ *n* a female greengrocer *19-*. [GREEN¹·¹ + WIFE]
greesh /griʃ/ *n* a stone abutment built against the gable wall inside a building, forming the back of the fireplace *la18-19, 20- N NE*. [Gael *grì(o)s* fire, heat]
greesh *see* CREESH¹·¹
greeshach¹, **greisoch**, †**greeshoch**, †**greishoch** /ˈgriʃəx, ˈgrisəx/ *n* red-hot embers (in a glowing fire) *19-*. [Gael *grìosach*]
greeshach², **greesoch** /ˈgriʃəx, ˈgrisəx/ *adj* shivery, shuddery, chilly *20- N NE*. [Gael *grìs* horror, shuddering]
greet¹·¹, †**grete**, †**greit** /grit/ *n* (a fit of) weeping; tears *la14-*. **get your greet out** to relieve one's feelings by weeping *la19-*. **the greet in your craig** the sob in your throat *19- Ork NE*. **the greet in your throat** = *the greet in your craig*. [see the verb]
greet¹·², †**grete**, †**gret** /grit/ *v pt* **grat**, **gret**, *ptp* also **grutten 1** to weep, cry *la14-*. **2** to lament; to complain; to grumble or whine *16-*. **greetin ee** a watering eye *la19-*. **greetin face 1** a person who continually looks tearful or sad *19-*. **2** a bad-tempered, complaining person *19-*. **greetin faced 1** looking tearful *19-*. **2** bad-tempered, complaining *la20-*. **greetin fou** at the tearful stage of drunkenness *19-*. **greetin meetin** a farewell meeting; the last meeting of a town council before an election *la19-*. **greetin Teenie** a crybaby; a person who is always complaining *20-*. [OE *grētan*]
greet², *T EC* **greek**, †**greit** /grit; *T EC* grik/ *n* **1** the grain or texture of a stone *18-*. **2** sand, gravel *e16*. [OE *grēot*]
greetie¹·¹ /ˈgriti/ *n* a child's whimper *la18-19, 20- NE*. [GREET¹·¹ + -IE¹]
greetie¹·² /ˈgriti/ *adj* **1** weepy, given to tears *20-*. **2** inclined to rain, showery *20- NE T*. [see the noun]
greeve *see* GRIEF¹·²
greff *see* GRAVE¹·¹
grefster, †**graefster** /ˈgrɛfstər/ *n* an unusually low ebb tide; the stretch of foreshore exposed by a low ebb tide *la19- Sh*. [compare Faer *grefstur* a digging, deep waves whipped up by a gale]
†**Gregioun** *n* a Greek *15-e16*. [compare OFr *Gregeois*, Lat *grājugenus*]
greid *see* GREED
greif *see* GRIEF¹·², GRIEVE¹·¹, GRIEVE¹·²
greiff *see* GRIEF¹·¹
greikin, †**greking** /ˈgrikɪn/ *n* daybreak *16-19, 20- literary*. [MDu *griekinge*]
grein *see* GREEN²
greind *see* GRIND²
greip *see* GRIP²

†**greis**[1] *npl* greaves, pieces of armour for the shins *15*. [ME *greves*]
†**greis**[2] *npl* twigs, branches *e16*. [OE *græfe* a thicket, a copse]
greishoch, greisoch *see* GREESHACH[1]
greissis *see* GRECE[2]
greit *see* GREAT[1,2], GREET[1,1], GREET[2]
greive *see* GRIEVE[2]
gremmar, grammar, †**gramer** /ˈgrɛmər, ˈgramər/ *n* the rules of language, grammar *15-*. [ME *gramere*]
gremster *see* GRIMSTER
gren *see* GREEN[1,2]
grene *see* GREEN[1,1], GREEN[1,2], GREEN[2]
grep *see* GRAIP[1,1]
gres *see* GIRSE[1,1]
greschip *see* GRIEVE[1,1]
gress *see* GIRSE[1,1], GIRSE[1,2]
gressum *see* GRASSUM
†**gret**[1], **grete** *adv* greatly, much, very *la14-16*. [from the adj GREAT[1,2]]
†**gret**[2], **grete** *n* a Flemish groat *15-e16*. [Du *groot*]
gret *see* GREAT[1,1], GREAT[1,2], GREET[1,2]
grete *see* GREAT[1,1], GREAT[1,2], GREET[1,1], GREET[1,2], GRET[1], GRET[2]
greth *see* GRAITH[1,1]
†**gretumly, grettumly, grittumlie** *adv* greatly *la14-17*. [OE *grēatum*, dative of *grēat*]
greve *see* GRIEF[1,1], GRIEVE[1,1], GRIEVE[2]
grew[1] /gru/ *n* a greyhound *16-*. **groo-men** greyhound owners *la20-*. †**grew whelp** a greyhound puppy *16-17*. **the grews** greyhound racing *20-*. [shortened form of *grewhund* (GREW-HOUN)]
grew *see* GROWE[1,2], GRUE[1,1], GRUE[1,2]
†**Grew**[2], **Grewe** *n* Greece *15-16*. [ME *Greu*]
grew-houn, grewhund, †**grwhund** /ˈgruhən, ˈgruhənd/ *n* a greyhound *15-*. [OE *grīghund*]
grey *see* GRAY[1,1], GRAY[1,2], GRAY[1,3]
greyn *see* GREEN[1,1]
grice, Ork **grize,** N **griss,** †**gryse** /grʌɪs; Ork grʌɪz; N grɪs/ *n* a young pig or piglet; a sucking pig *la14-*. **grice ingans** the vernal squill *Scilla verna 20- Sh*. **grice mites 1** small potatoes fed to pigs *20- Sh*. **2** the wild hyacinth *Hyacinthoides non-scripta 20- Sh*. **grice murr** small potatoes fed to pigs *20- Sh*. [ON *gríss*]
grief[1,1], †**greve,** †**greiff** /grif/ *n* **1** sorrow, distress; suffering, hardship *15-*. **2** an injury *la14-e17*. **3** *law* a documentary statement of a grievance; a formal complaint *15-e17*. [ME *gref*]
grief[1,2], **greeve,** †**greif** /grif, griv/ *adj* **1** heavy, arduous *la15, 20- N*. **2** *of weather* stormy, adverse *20- NE*. [see the noun]
grien *see* GREEN[2]
grieve[1,1], †**greve,** †**greif** /griv/ *n* **1** the overseer on a farm; a farm bailiff *la15-*. **2** the overseer of a mine or gang of workmen *16-19*. **3** the chief magistrate or provost of a burgh *e15*. †**greveschip, greschip** the district under the jurisdiction of the chief magistrate or provost of the burghs of Cullen, Elgin and Inverness *la14-e17*. [ME *greive* a steward, the headman of a town or village]
grieve[1,2] /griv/ *v* to oversee *18-19, 20- NE T*. [see the noun]
grieve[2], †**greve,** †**greive,** †**greif** /griv/ *v* **1** to distress; to annoy *la14-*. **2** to be distressed *16-*. **3** to injure, hurt; to wrong or oppress *la14-e17*. †**grevand** grievous, painful, hurtful *la14-15*. [ME *greven*]
grile, grill *see* GIRL
grilse, Bor **gilse,** †**grissill,** †**girsill, girls** /grɪls; Bor gɪls/ *n* a young salmon on its first return to fresh water *la14-*. [unknown]

grim /grɪm/ *adj* **1** grey or mottled black and white *19-*. **2** grimy, dirty-looking *la19-*. **da grims o de morning** early dawn *20- Sh*; compare GRIMLINS. [unknown; compare GRIMA, GRIME, GRIMLINS]
grima /ˈgrɪmə, ˈgrɪmə/ *n* a name given to an animal with spots or stripes *la19- Sh*. [Norw dial *grime* a streak of dirt on the face; compare GRIME]
grime, gryme /grʌɪm/ *v* to sprinkle or cover thinly with snow *19- SW Bor*. **a griming of snow** a light covering of snow *19- SW Bor*. [Norw dial *grim* a fine shower of snow or rain; compare GRIMA]
grimek, grimik, greemik /ˈgrɪmək, ˈgrɪmək/ *n* a rope halter with a loop which allows it to be used as a bridle *la19- Sh*. [Norw *grime* a halter, with *-ek* suffix]
griment *see* GREE[1,2]
Grimes Dyke, Grahame's Dike /ˈgrɪmz dʌɪk, ˈgreəmz dʌɪk/ *n* a name for the Antonine Wall *la14-19, 20- historical*. [probably ON *Grímr* nickname for Odin + DYKE[1,1]]
grimet, greemit /ˈgrɪmət, ˈgrɪmət/ *adj* **1** *of a face* streaked with dirt *la19- Sh Ork*. **2** *of cattle* having a white face with spots or stripes *la19- Sh Ork*. **3** *of the ground* having a patchy covering of snow *20- Sh*. [ptp of GRIME]
grimik *see* GRIMEK
grimlins /ˈgrɪmlɪnz/ *npl* twilight *20- Ork N*. [derivative of Norw dial *grimla* to glimmer]
grimster, gremster, grinster /ˈgrɪmstər, ˈgrɛmstər, ˈgrɪnstər/ *n* a very low ebb-tide *la19- Sh*. [perhaps nasalized form of GREFSTER]
grind[1] /grɪnd/ *n* **1** a gate; a passage through a wall; frequently in place-names *18- Sh Ork*. **2** a rectangular wooden frame around which fishing-line is wound for catching mackerel and coalfish *la19- Sh*. [ON *grind* a barred gate]
grind[2], **grun, grund,** †**greind** /grʌɪnd, grʌn, grʌnd/ *v pt also* **grun, grund, gran, grand,** *ptp also* **grun, grund,** †**grundin,** †**grind 1** to reduce to small particles by crushing; to mill *14-*. **2** *of a cat* to purr *20- Sh*. †**grindable** *of grain* suitable or intended for grinding *17-e18*. **grunstane,** NE **grinsteen** a grindstone *la18-*. [OE *grindan*]
grinnale *see* GIRNEL[1,1]
grinsteen *see* GRIND[2]
grinster *see* GRIMSTER
grintar *see* GRANITAR
grip[1,1], **grup,** †**gryp** /grɪp, grʌp/ *n* **1** a tight hold or grasp *15-*. **2** control, mastery, power *la15-*. **3** *pl* a sharp pain *la16-*. **4** *pl* an embrace; clutches *18-*. **5** a hand-clasp; a particular handclasp as used between Freemasons *la18-*. **6** *piping* a throw in which all the finger holes are closed, so sounding the lowest note G *20-*. **grippie** avaricious, mean; inclined to sharp practice *la18-*. †**grip grass** goose-grass, cleavers *Galium aparine 19*. **come tae grips** to engage in a struggle at close quarters (with) *17-*. **the grip** the system of sub-contracting work to casual labour in the building industry *la20-*. **hae a guid grip o Scotland** to have large feet *20-*. **hae a guid grip o yer gear 1** to be well off *la19-*. **2** to be miserly *20-*. **haud the grip** to keep a firm hold; to endure *19, 20- H&I WC SW*. †**in grips, in grippis 1** in custody *e19*. **2** in an embrace or a wrestling hold *16-e17*. [OE *gripe* a grasp, and OE *gripa* a handful, a sheaf]
grip[1,2], **grup,** †**gryp** /grɪp, grʌp/ *v ptp also* **gruppen 1** to grasp, clutch, grab tightly *la14-*. **2** to arrest a person; to seize or take possession of lands or belongings *15-*. **3** *of pain or disease* to attack *la16-*. **4** to get the better of, outsmart *la19- NE*. **5** *of a boat* to overtake *20- Sh*. **gripper** the person who catches and holds a sheep to be sheared *19, 20- SW*. **gripping** *n* a paralytic disease of sheep *la18-*. †**gripping** *adj* grasping, avaricious *la16-19*. **grippit 1** seized with pain

grip *la16-*. **2** sprained *19-*. **3** short of money *la19, 20- NE T.* **grip in** to pinch, constrict *20- Sh NE T.* **grip tae** to hold on to; to stick close to *la15-*. [OE *grīpan*]

grip², *NE* **greip**, †**grup**, †**gruip** /grɪp; *NE* grip, grʌip/ *n* **1** the gutter in a byre *la17-*. **2** a field drainage ditch; frequently in place-names *19, 20- Ork NE T.* [OE *grēp* a furrow, a ditch]

gripe /grʌip/ *v* **1** to vex, cause pain or envy *la16-19, 20- Sh.* **2** to grasp, seize *la14-e19.* **3** to search or grope for *la16-19.* [OE *grīpan* to grasp]

grisk /grɪsk/ *adj* greedy, avaricious *19- EC Bor.* [Norw, Dan *grisk*]

griss *see* GRICE
grissill *see* GRILSE
grissle *see* GIRSLE
grissum *see* GRASSUM

grist /grɪst/ *n* **1** the size or thickness of yarn *18-*. **2** volume, capacity, girth *la18-19, 20- Sh Ork Uls.* **3** strength, force *20- Sh Ork.* [unknown]

grist *see* GIRST

grit /grɪt/ *n* an oat kernel; a grain *19-*. [OE *grytta* groats, meal]
grit *see* GREAT¹·²
grittumlie *see* GRETUMLY
grize *see* GRICE

gro¹·¹, **groo** /gro, gru/ *n* a breeze or light wind *20- Sh Ork.* [see the verb]

gro¹·², **groo** /gro, gru/ *v of the wind* to freshen *la19- Sh Ork.* [Norw dial *grå* to become grey, cloud over, blow gently]

gro¹·³ /gro/ *adj* grey; frequently in place-names *la19- Sh.* [ON *grá*]

groan *see* GRAIN³·¹, GRAIN³·²

groat, †**grote** /grot/ *n* **1** a Scots fourpenny piece *la15-19, 20- historical.* **2** a coin of small denomination; a very small sum of money *16-19, 20- historical.* †**grote wecht** the weight of a groat (1/8 ounce) *16.* †**not a grote** nothing at all *16-17.* [MDu *groot* thick, big]

groatie-buckie, *Sh* **grottie-buckie** /'groti bʌki; *Sh* 'groti bʌki/ *n* a cowrie shell *Trivia monacha 20- Sh Ork N NE.* [from the place-name *John o' Groats* + BUCKIE¹]

groats, grotts, †**grotis**, †**grottis** /grots, grɔts/ *npl* hulled grain *la15-.* **ken your groats in among ither folk's kail** to recognize one's own property, handiwork or interests *la16-19, 20- NE.* [ME *grotes*]

groff, grof, grouff /grɔf, grʌuf/ *adj* **1** coarse in grain or texture, inferior *16-19, 20- Sh N NE.* **2** *of language* vulgar, coarse; smutty, obscene *la17-19, 20- SW Bor.* **3** *of people* coarse, rough *18-19, 20- Sh NE.* **4** *of the voice* harsh *20- Sh NE.* **groff guess** a rough guess, a pretty good idea *19, 20- Sh.* **groff print** large type *la19- N NE.* [MDu, MLG *grof*]

grograne *see* GROWGRANE
groitik *see* GRUDACK

grokoll /'grokɔl/ *n fisherman's taboo* a mouse *20- Sh.* [ON *grá* grey + ON *kollr* a top, a summit, a head, a shaven crown]

gromack *see* KRUMMICK
gromel *see* GRUMMLE¹·²

gromish /'gromɪʃ/ *v* to crush, bruise; to squeeze, grip *20- Sh N NE.* [compare Swed dial *gramsa* to grasp]

grommashens, †**gramashes** /grə'maʃənz/ *npl* leggings, gaiters *la17-19, 20- WC.* [altered form of EModE *gamash*]

gronach /'gronəx/ *v* to grumble, complain *20 NE.* [variant of CRONACH¹·²]

grond *see* GRUND¹·¹
grone *see* GRAIN³·¹, GRAIN³·²
gronʒe *see* GRUNYIE
groo *see* GRO¹·¹, GRO¹·², GRUE¹·², GRUE¹·³

groof, grufe, †**growf** /gruf/ *n* the face *la19- literary.* **grooflins**, *Sh* **gruflens**, †**gruflingis** prostrate, flat on one's face *15-19, 20- Sh NE SW.* **on your groof** face downwards, prone *18-.* Compare AGROUF. [ON *á grúfu* face down]

grool, grule /grul/ *n* **1** friable moss made into peats by mixing with water and drying *19- WC SW.* **2** gritty material, gravel; dusty refuse, coal dust *19.* **grooloch** gravel, stones; coal dust *20- SW.* [probably Scots *gruel*]

grool *see* GROWL
groo-men *see* GREW¹
groond *see* GROUND¹

groose, grouse /grus, grʌus/ *n* a game bird *18-.* [unknown]

grooshin, grushin, grushion /'gruʃən, 'gruʒən/ *n* a glutinous mess; soft, putrid food *la19- NE.* [GRUE¹·², with ending by analogy with PUSHION¹·¹]

†**groosie** *adj* dirty, greasy; unsavoury *19.* [probably conflation of GRUE¹·² with Scots *greasy*]

groosie *see* GRUSE¹·¹
groot *see* GRUTE¹·²
grootie *see* GRUTE¹·¹
grootin *see* GRUTE¹·²

groozle¹·¹ /'gruzəl/ *n* a grunting or gurgling noise *19, 20- SW.* [onomatopoeic]

groozle¹·², **gruzzle** /'gruzəl, 'grʌzəl/ *v* **1** to breathe heavily; to make a grunting noise *la18-19, 20- SW Bor.* **2** *of a child* to gurgle *19, 20- Bor.* [see the noun]

grop¹·¹ /grɔp/ *n* **1** coarsely ground corn *20- Sh Ork N.* **2** breadcrumbs; small potatoes; refuse *20- Sh N NE.* **3** drizzle *la19- Sh.* [Norw dial *grop* bruised grain, course meal]

grop¹·² /grɔp/ *v* **1** to rain in heavy drops *20- Sh.* **2** to crush coarsely *20- Sh.* [Norw dial *gropa* to grind coarsely]

grope *see* GRAIP²

gropsie /'grɔpsi/ *v* to eat gluttonously *la19- H&I WC.* [unknown]

†**gros** *n* a Flemish or German coin *la16-e17.* [Du, Flem *gros*]
grosar *see* GROSER
grosart *see* GROZET

groser, grozer, †**grosar** /'grozər/ *n* a gooseberry *16-.* [altered form of OFr *groseille*]

groset *see* GROZET

grossel, †**grozel** /'grozəl/ *n* a gooseberry *19- WC SW Bor.* [OFr *groseille*]

grote *see* GROAT, GROTT
grotis *see* GROATS

†**grotkin** *n* twelve dozen, a gross *la15-e17.* [Du, Flem *grootge*]
†**grott, grote** *n* a particle; a speck *15-18.* [OE *grot* a particle]

grotti /'grɔti/ *n* the nave of the under millstone through which the spindle passes to the sile in the upper millstone *la19- Sh.* [ON *Grotti* the name of a mythical hand-mill in the Edda]

grottie-buckie *see* GROATIE-BUCKIE
grottis, grotts *see* GROATS
grou *see* GRUE¹·¹

grouff¹·¹ /grʌuf/ *n* a snooze *19- EC.* [onomatopoeic]
†**grouff¹·²** *v* to sleep heavily but restlessly; to snore *la18-19.* [see the noun]

grouff *see* GROFF
ground *see* GRUND¹·¹, GRUND¹·²
grounds *see* GRUNDS
grounge *see* GRUNCH¹·²
grouse *see* GROOSE
grousome *see* GRUE¹·²
grouth *see* GROWTHE
grow *see* GROWE¹·¹, GROWE¹·², GRUE¹·²

growe¹·¹, grow /grʌu, gro/ *n* **1** growth *la18- NE.* **2** a sudden rise in a river; a flood *la19- NE.* [see the verb]

growe¹·², grow /grʌu, gro/ *v pt* **grew, growed**, *ptp* **growen, growin, grown, growed 1** to increase, develop, become bigger *la14-.* **2** *of vegetation* to thrive, flourish *la14-.* **3** *of* *a person* to advance or make progress *la14*-. **4** *of land* to be covered with vegetation *15*-. **5** *of a person* to cultivate a crop *18*-. **6** *of a river or sea* to rise *16*. **grow grey** made of natural, undyed wool *la19- NE T*. **grown-up** overgrown; choked with vegetation *20*-. [OE *grōwan*]

growen see GROWE¹,²
growf see GROOF
†**growgrane**, **grograne** *n* grogram fabric *la16-e17*. Compare COWGRANE. [MFr *gros grain* coarse cloth]
growin see GROWE¹,²
growk /grʌuk/ *v* to look intently or longingly *19*, *20- N NE T Uls.* [unknown]
growl, *NE* **grool** /grʌul/ *NE* grul/ *v* to utter a low sound expressing anger, growl *la18*-. [probably onomatopoeic]
growl see GRUEL
grown see GROWE¹,²
growp /grʌup/ *v* to grumble, complain *la19- NE*. [onomatopoeic; compare CROUP¹]
growp see GRAIP²
growthe, **grouth**, **growth** /grʌuθ, groθ/ *n* **1** the action or process of growing *la15*-. **2** growing plants; a yield or crop *la15*-. **3** rank vegetation, weeds *la19*-. **4** the deposit found on the bottom of a boat *20- Sh NE C SW*. **5** the rate of inflow of water in a mineworking *20- EC*. **growthie 1** *of weather* warm and moist, promoting growth *la18*-. **2** *of vegetation* growing fast, weedy *la19*-. **3** *of people or animals* well-grown, thriving *19*-. [GROWE¹,², with noun-forming suffix]
growze see GRUSE¹,¹, GRUSE¹,²
groze /groz/ *v* to crush or compress *19- EC*. [probably Du *gruizen*]
grozel see GROSSEL
grozer see GROSER
grozet, **groset**, **grosart** /ˈgrozət, ˈgrosət, ˈgrosərt/ *n* a gooseberry *la18*-. **grozet fair** an agricultural fair (held in Kilmarnock at the beginning of August) *la19- WC*. [GROSER + with excrescent -*t*]
†**gru** *n* a particle, an atom *18-19*. [ME *gru(e)* a bit]
grub /grʌb/ *v* **1** to dig around; to dig up *16*-. **2** to grasp at (money) *19*-. **grubber 1** an iron harrow for weeding in drills; a scarifier *19*-. **2** a scrounger *20*-. **in the grubber** short of money, in poverty *la20*-. [ME *grubben*]
gruch see GRUDGE¹,¹, GRUDGE¹,²
grudack, **groitik** /ˈgrʌdək,ˈgrɒtɪk/ *n* a large kettle for cooking fish and potatoes *la19- Sh*. [ON *grýta* a pot, with diminutive suffix]
grudge¹,¹, †**gruch** /grʌdʒ/ *n* **1** ill-will, resentment; a grievance *16*-. **2** discontent, dissatisfaction *la16-19*. [see the verb]
grudge¹,², †**gruch**, †**grutch** /grʌdʒ/ *v* **1** to complain; to be discontented or uncooperative *la14*-. **2** to give unwillingly or reluctantly *16*-. [ME *grucchen*]
grudge see GORGE
grudget /ˈgrʌdʒət/ *n* a gooseberry *19- SW*. [altered form of GROZET]
grue¹,¹, **grew**, **grou** /gru/ *n* a shudder, a shiver; a feeling of horror or repulsion *19*-. **tak the grue at** to become disgusted or fed up with *la19*-. [see the verb]
grue¹,², **grew**, **groo**, †**grow** /gru/ *v* **1** to feel horror or terror; to shudder in horror or fear *la14*-. **2** to make a wry face *la18*-. **3** to shiver with cold *18-19*, *20- C SW Bor*. **gruesome**, **grousome** horrible; arousing dread or loathing *la18*-. **it gars me grue** it disgusts me *19*-. [unknown; compare Du *gruwen*, Dan *grue*]
grue¹,³, **groo** /gru/ *adj* **1** ugly, horrible *19*-. **2** afraid; discontented *19*, *20- Ork N*. [see the verb]

grue² /gru/ *n* slush floating on water; the melting snow and ice found on rivers in early spring *la18*-. [probably Gael *gruth* curds]
gruel, **growl** /grul, ˈgruəl, grʌul/ *n* **1** boiled oatmeal; thin porridge *la15*-. **2** food *la19- NE T*. [ME *gruel*]
grufe, **gruflens** see GROOF
gruggle¹,¹ /ˈgrʌgəl/ *n* a fold, a crease, a wrinkle *20- NE T*. [see the verb]
gruggle¹,² /ˈgrʌgəl/ *v* to disorder, rumple, crease *19- NE T*. [Du *kreukelen* to crease, crumple, crimp]
grugous, **grugeous** /ˈgrugəs, ˈgrudʒəs/ *adj* grim, ugly, surly *la18-19*, *20- literary*. [Gael *grùgach* surly, sulky, scowling]
gruip, †**grup** /grøp/ *v carpentry* to cut a groove in a board for fitting into a corresponding tongue *17-19*, *20- Sh*. [compare GRIP²]
gruip see GRIP²
gruitly see GRUTE¹,¹
grule see GROOL
grulik /ˈgrølək/ *n in Shetland* a guiser, a member of a band of young men dressed in costumes of plaited straw who go masquerading on certain days of the year such as Halloween or Shrove Tuesday *la19*, *20- historical*. [ON *grýla* an ogre, a giantess]
grulsh /grʌlʃ/ *n* a fat, squat person or animal *19*, *20- SW Uls*.
†**grulshie** sturdy, fat; clumsy-looking *19*. [altered form of GRILSE]
grum¹ /grum/ *n* dregs *20- Sh N*. [Norw *grums* sediment]
grum² /grʌm/ *adj* **1** ugly, unattractive *la19- Sh*. **2** fierce, surly *20- Sh*. **3** *of weather* threatening *20- Sh*. [compare Norw *grum* cruel, Dan *grumme* ugly, harsh]
grumble see GRUMMLE¹,¹, GRUMMLE¹,²
grumlie /ˈgrʌmli/ *adj* **1** grumbling, irritable; sullen, surly *19*-. **2** *of weather* unsettled, blustery *la19*, *20- NE*. **3** *of the sea* ugly, threatening *19*, *20- NE*. [GRUM² + -IE²; compare *grumlie* (GRUMMEL¹,¹)]
grumlie see GRUMMEL¹,¹
grumlins see GRUMMEL¹,²
grummel¹,¹, †**grunmale** /ˈgrʌməl/ *n* **1** mud, dregs, sediment; loose earth and stones *16-19*, *20- Ork N SW Uls*. **2** crumbs, fragments *19- Sh Ork*. **grumlie**, *C* **gumlie** muddy, turbid, full of dregs or gravel *18*-. [compare Swed *grummel* sediment, OFlem *grommeling* rubble, GRUM¹]
grummel¹,², *C* **gumlie** /ˈgrʌməl/ *v* to make muddy or turbid; to confuse *19*, *20- Sh NE T C*. **grumlins** dregs *20- Ork SW*. [see the noun]
grummle¹,¹, **grumble** /ˈgrʌməl, ˈgrʌmbəl/ *n* **1** a complaint; the act of complaining *18*-. **2** a grudge or grievance, a quarrel *la19*-. [see the verb]
grummle¹,², **grumble**, †**gromel** /ˈgrʌməl, ˈgrʌmbəl/ *v* to complain *17*-. [unknown; compare Fr *grommeler* to mutter, Du *grommelen* to rumble, growl]
grumph¹,¹ /grʌmf/ *n* **1** a grunt *18*-. **2** a name for a pig *la19- NE T SW*. **3** a grumbler *20*-. **grumphie** *n* a name for a pig *la18*-. **grumphie** *adj* ill-natured, grumpy *20*-. [onomatopoeic]
grumph¹,² /grʌmf/ *v* to grunt; to grumble *19*-. **grumphie** to grunt *20- NE T*. [see the noun]
grun see GRIND², GRUND¹,¹
grunch¹,¹ /grʌnʃ/ *n* **1** a grumble, a moan *19*, *20- SW Bor*. **2** a grunt, a growl *19*, *20- Bor*. [see the verb]
grunch¹,², *Bor* **grounge**, †**grunsch** /grʌnʃ; *Bor* grʌunʒ/ *v* **1** to growl, grunt *18-19*, *20- Ork Bor*. **2** to grumble; to object, refuse *la15-19*, *20- Bor*. [perhaps nasalized from GRUDGE]
grund¹,¹, **grun**, **groond**, **ground**, †**grond** /grʌnd, grʌn, grund, grʌund/ *n* **1** the surface of the earth, the ground *la14*-. **2** the bottom or lowest part of something *la14*-. **3** farmland; a farm, an estate *la14*-. **4** earth, soil *15*-. **5** the bottom of the

sea *15*-. **6** the root of a matter; the basis of a discourse, the text of a sermon *la15*-. **7** the pit of the stomach *la15*-. **8** a piece of ground used for a particular purpose; a sports ground *16*-. **9** the foundation of a structure or building *16*-. **10** the theme in pibroch piping from which all the variations are derived *la18*-. **11** a burial ground or burial plot *19*-. **12** the people belonging to a farm or estate *la15-18*. **grunds** mining the seam next to the floor *19- C*. **ground annual, †grund annuell** *law* an annual rent on land, ground-rent *la15-*. **grund avy, groundavy** ground-ivy *Glechoma hederacea 19*-. **ground baulk** the weighted rope at the bottom edge of a fishing net *19- Sh Ork N*. **grund blackie** the blackbird *Turdus merula* that nests on the ground *20*-. **ground coal** mining the seam next to the floor *19- C*. **grun ebb 1** the ebb-tide at its lowest, low water *20- Sh N NE*. **2** the lower part of the foreshore *20- Sh N NE*. **grund heid** mining the stratum above the *grunds 20- C*. **†grund leif, ground leif** (payment for) leave given to vessels, especially in port, make use of ground on shore *la16-e17*. **grun officer, ground officer** the manager of an estate *18-*. **†ground-riche** extremely rich *la15-e17*. **†grund richt, ground richt** *law* heritable right; right of possession *la15-16*. **grund-shot, grunsher** mining one of a series of shots placed along the bottom of a seam where the coal is too hard to undercut *20- C*. **grund stane** a foundation stone *la16-19, 20- Sh*. **grounds and warrants** *law* the reasons and documentary evidence on which a decree was based and which might be called for in an action of restriction *19-*. [OE *grund*]

grund[1.2], **ground** /grʌnd, grʌund/ v to lay a foundation or base; to establish *15*-. [see the noun]

grund, grundin see GRIND[2]

grundiswallow /ˈgrʌndiswɔlo/ n groundsel *Senecio vulgaris 19, 20- NE T*. [OE *grundeswylige*]

grunds, gruns, grounds /grʌndz, grʌnz, grʌundz/ *npl* **1** dregs, lees *la19*-. **2** a kind of sowans *20- N*. **3** the refuse of flax after dressing *18-19*. [ptp of GRUND[1.2], with plural suffffix]

grunk[1.1] /grʌŋk/ n **1** a grunt *20- Ork*. **2** a glutton *19*. [onomatopoeic]

grunk[1.2] /grʌŋk/ v to grunt *20- Ork*. [see the noun]

grunkle see CRUNKLE

grunmale see GRUMMEL[1.1]

gruns see GRUNDS

grunsch see GRUNCH[1.2]

grunsher see GRUND[1.1]

grunstane see GRIND[2]

gruntie /ˈgrʌnti/ n a pig *la18*-. [Scots *grunt* + -IE[3]]

gruntle[1.1], **†gruntill** /ˈgrʌntəl/ n **1** a pig's snout; *derogatory* a person's face *16-19, 20- C SW Bor*. **2** a grunt *la18-19, 20- NE*. [see the verb]

gruntle[1.2], **†gruntill** /ˈgrʌntəl/ v to grunt *la16-19, 20- Bor*. [ME *gruntelen*]

grunyie, grunzie, †grunʒe, †gronʒe /ˈgrʌnji, ˈgrʌnzi/ n **1** the snout of an animal; *derogatory* a person's face *la14-19, 20- literary*. **2** a grudge *la18-19*. **grunyasie** of the face ugly, disagreeable *20- Ork*. [ME *groin*]

grup see GRIP[1.1], GRIP[1.2], GRIP[2], GRUIP

gruppen see GRIP[1.2]

gruse[1.1], **growze** /gruz, grʌuz/ n a shiver, a shudder *19, 20- C SW Bor*. **groosie** shivery *20- EC Bor*. [derivative of GRUE[1.2]]

gruse[1.2], **growze** /gruz, grʌuz/ v to shiver, shudder *19, 20- Bor*. [see the noun]

grush[1.1] /grʌʃ/ n grit, fine gravel *20- WC SW Bor*. [see the verb]

†grush[1.2] v to crush, grind *19*. [altered form of Eng *crush*]

grushie /ˈgrʌʃi/ *adj* abundant, lush *la18-19, 20- SW*. [Older Scots *gros* large, thick + -IE[2]]

grushin, grushion see GROOSHIN

grutch see GRUDGE[1.2]

grute[1.1] /grut, grøt/ n oil or oily sediment; liquid mess *20- Sh Ork N*. **grootie** dirty, messy; *of oil* full of sediment *20- Sh Ork*. **gruitly** messy *20- Ork*. [Norw *grut* sediment, grounds]

grute[1.2], **groot** /grut, grøt/ v to poke about in mess *20- Ork N*. **grootin** messy *20- Ork*. [see the noun]

grutten see GREET[1.2]

gruzzle see GROOZLE[1.2]

grwhund see GREW-HOUN

gry /grae/ n a horse *20*-. [Travellers' language]

gryme see GRIME

gryp see GRIP[1.1], GRIP[1.2]

gryse see GRICE

gryte see GREAT[1.1], GREAT[1.2]

guaird, guard see GAIRD[1.1], GAIRD[1.2]

guarden see GARDIN

gub[1.1], **gob** /gʌb, gɔb/ n the mouth; a bird's beak *la16-*. [Gael, IrGael *gob* a beak; a mouth; compare GAB[2]]

gub[1.2] /gʌb/ v to smack in the mouth; to defeat *la20-*. [see the noun]

gub[2.1] /gʌb/ n **1** foam, froth, lather *la19- Sh Ork*. **2** swampy ground, a puddle *la19- Sh Ork*. **gubless** latherless *20- Sh*. [probably Norw dial *gop* a pit]

gub[2.2] /gʌb/ v to lather *20- Sh*. [see the noun]

†gubernakil n a helm, a rudder *e16*. [Lat *gubernāculum*]

†guberne v to govern *la15-16*. [Lat *gubernāre* to steer, govern]

guchar see GUTCHER

guckit see GOWKIT

gud see GUID[1.1], GUID[1.3]

gud brother see GUID-BRITHER

guddame see GUID-DAME

guddaughter see GUID-DOCHTER

guddick /ˈgødək, ˈgʌdək/ n a riddle *19- Sh*. **lay up guddicks** to ask riddles *20- Sh*. [ON *gáta* a riddle, with diminutive suffix]

guddle[1.1] /ˈgʌdəl/ n **1** a mess, a muddle; a state of confusion *la19-*. **2** a person works in a messy, slovenly way *20-*. **3** hard, dirty or messy work *19- T C*. **4** a crowbar *20- T EC*. **5** a pointed iron bar for making holes for fence-posts *20- NE T*. [unknown]

guddle[1.2] /ˈgʌdəl/ v **1** to catch fish by groping with the hands under the stones or banks of a stream *19-*. **2** to do dirty work; to work in a careless, slovenly way *19-*. **3** to make a mess or mess about; *of children* to play messily *19-*. **4** to prod or poke; to stab or hack *19*. **guddled** disordered, in a muddle *20-*. [unknown]

gude see GUID[1.1], GUID[1.3], GUID[1.4]

gude brither see GUID-BRITHER

gude dochter, gude douchtyr see GUID-DOCHTER

gude een see GUID EEN

gudefather see GUID-FAITHER

gude-gaun see GUID-GAUN

gudein see GUID EEN

gudeless see GUIDLESS

gudely see GUIDLY

gudeman see GUIDMAN

gude-mither, gudmoder see GUID-MITHER

gudeschir, gudesire see GUTCHER

gude-sister see GUID-SISTER

gudeson, gudesone, gude son in law see GUID-SON

gudewife see GUIDWIFE

gude will see GUIDWILL

gudfadyr see GUID-FAITHER

gudge[1.1], †**guge** /gʌdʒ/ *n* **1** something short and thick; a short, strong, thickset person *la19-*. **2** a chisel with a concave blade, a gouge *17-19, 20- Sh Ork NE*. **3** a gudgeon, a pivot or axle-end *18-19, 20- historical*. **gudgie** short and thickset, squat *19-*. [Fr *gouge*]

gudge[1.2] /gʌdʒ/ *v* to gouge out *19- Sh Ork NE T EC*. **gudge up** to raise or separate by driving in wedges *la19- NE T*. [see the noun]

†**gudget** *n* a camp-follower; a servant, a drudge *la16-17*. [MFr *goujat* a soldier's servant]

gudgie see GUDGE[1.1]

†**gudling** *n* a Dutch silver coin, a guilder *la15-17*. [altered form of Du *gulden*]

gudman see GUIDMAN
gud systyr see GUID-SISTER
gud wif see GUIDWIFE
gud will see GUIDWILL

guess[1.1], *N NE T* **guiss**, †**ges** /gɛs; *N NE T* gɪs/ *n* **1** a conjecture, an estimate *15-*. **2** a riddle, a conundrum *19-*. [see the verb]

guess[1.2], *N NE T* **guiss**, †**ges** /gɛs; *N NE T* gɪs/ *v* to conjecture, estimate *la14-*. [MLG, MDu *gissen*]

guest, **gest**, †**gast** /gɛst/ *n* **1** a visitor *la14-*. **2** *folklore* an object believed to foretell the arrival of a stranger *19, 20- Sh Ork*. **3** shaly coal burnt to ash *19, 20- SW Bor*; compare GHAIST (sense 3). [OE *giest, gæst*]

guff[1], **gouff** /gʌf, gʌuf/ *n* a foolish person *19, 20- EC SW Bor*. [EModE *goffe*]

guff[2.1], **gouff** /gʌf, gʌuf/ *n* **1** a (bad) smell *19-*. **2** a puff or current of air, a gust *19-*. **3** a flavour or taste; an after-taste *18-19, 20- EC Bor*. [see the verb]

guff[2.2] /gʌf/ *v* to give off a smell; to emit steam, smoke or vapour *20-*. [onomatopoeic of a puff of wind; compare Norw *gufs* air, a puff of wind, *guva* to smoke]

guff[3.1], **gouff** /gʌf, gʌuf/ *n* **1** an animal noise, a grunt or a bark *16, la19- Sh Ork N*. **2** a giggle; a snort of laughter *20- N NE*. **guffie** a name for a pig *20-*. †**neither guff nor sty** nothing at all *19*. [see the verb]

guff[3.2] /gʌf/ *v* **1** to belch *20-*. **2** to snort, snuffle *18-19, 20- Sh Ork*. **3** to cackle with laughter; to babble or talk foolishly *la18-19, 20- WC Bor*. [onomatopoeic; compare Norw dial *goffa* to grunt, *guffa* to yelp]

guffaw[1.1], **guffa**, *Uls* **gaffaw** /gʌˈfɔ, gʌˈfa; *Uls* gaˈfɔ/ *n* a loud, hearty laugh *18-*. [onomatopoeic]

guffaw[1.2], *NE Uls* **gaffaw** /gʌˈfɔ; *NE Uls* gaˈfɔ/ *v* to laugh loudly and heartily *18-*. [see the noun]

†**guffer** *n* the eelpout *Zoarces viviparus la17-19*. [unknown]
guffer see GOFFER

guffie[1.1] /ˈgʌfi/ *n* a bully, an unpleasant person *la20-*. [see the adj]

guffie[1.2] /ˈgʌfi/ *adj* stupid *19, 20- SW Bor*. [GUFF[1] + -IE[2]]

guffie[2] /ˈgʌfi/ *adj* fat or flabby about the cheeks *19- Bor*. [unknown]

guga, **goug** /ˈguga, gʌug/ *n* the young of the gannet *Morus bassanus la19- H&I*. [Gael *guga*]

guge see GUDGE[1.1]

guggle[1.1] /ˈgʌgəl, ˈgugəl/ *n* dirt; a mess *20- Sh*. [ON *gogli* ooze, mud]

guggle[1.2] /ˈgʌgəl, ˈgugəl/ *v* **1** to dirty or defile; to get dirty *la19- Sh*. **2** to work with the hands in something soft and dirty *la19- Sh*. **3** to work in an incompetent way *20- Sh*. [see the noun]

gugs, †**gog** /gʌgz/ *n* the tee or mark in certain games *la18-19, 20- SW*. [unknown]

guid[1.1], **gude**, **good**, *Ork* **geud**, *N* **geed**, *NE* **gweed**, †**gud** /gɪd, gud; *Ork* gød; *N* gid; *NE* gwid/ *n* **1** something of benefit or value *la14-*. **2** virtue, morality *la14-*. **3** God *la18-*. **4** property; livestock, cattle *la14-16*. **guids**, **gudes**, †**gudis** **1** (moveable) property; commodities *la14-*. **2** cattle, livestock *la15-18*. †**guid reule** social order, the rule of law *la15-e17*. **dae guid** to get good results; to thrive or prosper *la19-*. **get the guid o** to get what advantage or benefit is to be had from (something) *20-*. **the Gude** God *la18-*. **guids and gear**, **gudes and gear** personal possessions *la16-*. †**goods in communion** *law* the moveable property of a husband and wife, regarded as jointly owned *la18-19*. †**gudis of airschip** (moveable) goods to which an heir in heritage was entitled *la15-e16*. **Guid save us** an exclamation of surprise or protest *19-*. **haena gude daein** to find something difficult to do *19, 20- Sh Ork N NE T*. **hae ye guid in yer mind?** = **hae ye guid on ye?** *20- H&I C*. **hae ye guid on ye?** are you feeling generous? *20- C*. **ken the guid o** to know what advantage or benefit is to be had from (something) *20-*. †**men of gude** men of property, rank or standing *la15-16*. **tak the guid o 1** to get what advantage or benefit is to be had from (something) *la20-*. **2** to damage or spoil *la20-*. [see the adj]

†**guid**[1.2] *v* to manure land *16-e19*. [OE *gōdian* to prosper, improve, enrich]

guid[1.3], **gude**, **good**, *Ork* **geud**, *N* **geed**, *NE* **gweed**, †**gud** /gɪd, gud; *Ork* gød; *N* gid; *NE* gwid/ *adj* **1** fine, proper, pleasing; of good quality *la14-*. **2** kind, pleasant; virtuous, morally excellent *la14-*. **3** *of people* distinguished in rank or social standing, worthy, respectable *la14-*. **4** *of extent, duration or degree* considerable, substantial *la14-*. **5** *of clothing* kept as best, formal; *of a room* used on formal occasions *19-*. **guidness**, **gudeness**, *NE* **gweedness 1** personal excellence; goodness *la14-*. **2** the benevolence of God *la15-*. **3** quality, excellence in things *la15-*. **4** God *19-*. **goody-good** sentimentally pious *la19-*. **gude breed**, bread baked for weddings, baptisms or funerals; the bread used at Communion *19- Bor*. †**gude deed** a benefit, a bribe *17-e18*. **gude gosh** an expression of surprise *19-*. †**gude speid** quickly *la14-16*. †**Gude Wednisday** the Wednesday before Easter *la15*. **gude words**, *NE* **gweed words** (children's) prayers *la19-*. †**gude zeill** good intent, kindly disposition *16*. **a guid bit** a long time or distance *20-*. **a good meat hoose** a house where there is always plenty of good food *18-*. **a guid mids** a compromise *18-19, 20- NE Bor*. **become guid for** to be surety for *19-*. **be guid mens upo** to serve someone right *20- Ork*. **guid and weel** well and good *la19-*. **the Gude Book** the Bible *la19-*. **guid day wi ye** good day to you *19-*. **the guid folk 1** the ordinary, respectable citizens *18-*. **2** *folklore* fairies or other mythical beings *19, 20- Sh NE T SW*. **guid in ye** kind of you *la18-e19*. **the Gude Man** a child's word for God *19-*. †**the gude neebors** fairy folk *la16-19*. **guid nicht wi ye**, **gude nicht wi ye** good night to you *19-*. **the gude place** Heaven *19-*. **the guid Scots tongue 1** the Scots language *20-*. **2** a Scots accent *20-*. **the guid toun** a complimentary title for a town; a nickname for Edinburgh *16-*. **hae a guid Scots tongue in yer heid** to be outspoken; to not be shy in sharing one's opinions *20-*. †**in gude effect** in fact, in reality *16*. **in gweed reel** in step; in good order, tidy *20- NE*. **in good tune** in a good mood *20-*. †**of gude memory** of happy or blessed memory *la14-16*. **some guid mair** a good many more *la18-19, 20- NE T*. [OE *gōd*]

guid[1.4], **gude** /gɪd, gud/ *adv* very, fairly: ◊*I'm very gude sure 19- EC*. [see the adj]

guid-brither, gude brither, *NE* **gweedbreeder**, †**gud brother** /ˈgɪd brɪðər, ˈgud brɪðər; *NE* ˈgwidbridər/ *n* a brother-in-law *la14-*. [GUID¹·³ + BRITHER¹·¹]

†**guid-dame**, **guddame** *n* a grandmother *15-19*. [GUID¹·³ + DAME]

guid-dochter, gude dochter, *NE* **gweed dothor**, †**gud-daughter**, †**gude douchtyr** /ˈgɪd dɔxtər, ˈgud dɔxtər; *NE* ˈgwid dəθər/ *n* a daughter-in-law *la15-*. [GUID¹·³ + DOCHTER]

guide¹·¹, †**gyde**, †**gyd**, †**gide** /gʌɪd/ *n* 1 a person who shows the way; someone who directs or influences *15-*. 2 a manager or controller of money or property *la18-19, 20- Sh N NE T*. **guideship** 1 treatment of one person by another *la18-19, 20- Sh NE T*. 2 guidance, leadership *16-19*. [MFr *guide*]

guide¹·², †**gyde**, †**gyd** /gʌɪd/ *v* 1 to show the way to; to steer *15-*. 2 to manage, control or govern *la15-*. 3 to handle or care for children or animals *17-*. 4 to manage money well; to use resources sparingly *18-*. 5 to conduct oneself, behave *la15-19, 20- Sh NE EC*. **guider**, †**gydar** 1 a person who guides *16-*. 2 a manager, an administrator *16-19, 20- Sh NE*. 3 a person put in charge of the guidance and upbringing of a child or young person *16*. †**guide us** an expression of surprise or consternation *19*. [MFr *guider*]

guid een, gude een, †**gudein** /gɪd ˈin, gud ˈin/ *n as a greeting* good evening *la16-*. [GUID¹·³ + EVEN¹]

guider /ˈgʌɪdər/ *n* a home-made children's cart steered by a rope *20- T EC*. [GUIDE¹·², with agent suffix]

guider *see* GUIDE¹·²

guid-faither, guid-feyther, gudefather, *NE* **gweed father**, †**gudfadyr**, †**goodfather** /ˈgɪd feðər, ˈgɪd feðər, ˈgud faðər; *NE* ˈgwid faðər/ *n* a father-in-law *la15-*. [GUID¹·³ + FAITHER¹·¹]

guid-gaun, gude-gaun /gɪdˈgɔn, gudˈgɔn/ *adj* going well, in good working order; active, flourishing *18-*. [GUID¹·³ + *gaun* (GAE)]

guidin, goodin, geedin /ˈgɪdɪn, ˈgudɪn, ˈgidɪn/ *n* the manuring of land; manure *la15-19, 20- Sh Ork N T*. [OE *godian*]

guidless, gudeless, *NE* **gweedless** /ˈgɪdləs, ˈgudləs; *NE* ˈgwidləs/ *adj* without good *19-*. **guidless ill-less** doing neither good nor harm; insipid or characterless *19- NE*. [GUID¹·¹, with *-less* suffix]

guidly, gudely, *NE* **gweedlie** /ˈgɪdle, ˈgudle; *NE* ˈgwidli/ *adj* 1 attractive, excellent *la14-*. 2 godly, pious *19, 20- NE T*. 3 appropriate, convenient, possible *la14-e17*. †**guidlyheid**, **gudlyheid** goodliness, sanctity *15-19*. [OE *godlic* godlike, *gōdlic* good, beautiful]

guidman, gudeman, goodman, *NE* **gweedman**, †**gudman** /ˈgɪdman, ˈgudman; *NE* ˈgwidman/ *n* 1 a term of address used between equals who are not on terms of familiarity *la14-*. 2 the head of a household; a woman's husband *la15-*. 3 the owner or tenant of a small estate or farm, ranking below a laird *la16-*. 4 the Devil *17-*. 5 the head of an establishment, a manager *la17-19*. **the gudeman's craft** a plot of land left uncultivated to propitiate the Devil *la18-*. [GUID¹·³ + MAN]

guid-mither, gude-mither, *NE* **gweedmither**, †**gud-moder** /ˈgɪdmɪðər, ˈgudmɪðər; *NE* ˈgwidmɪðər/ *n* a mother-in-law *la15-*. [GUID¹·³ + MITHER]

guid-sister, gude-sister, †**gud systyr** /ˈgɪdsɪstər, ˈgudsɪstər/ *n* 1 a sister-in-law *16-19, 20- literary*. 2 a term of courtesy to a sister *16*. [GUID¹·³ + SISTER¹]

guid-son, gudeson, *NE* **gweedsin**, †**gudesone** /ˈgɪdsʌn, ˈgudsʌn; *NE* ˈgwidsɪn/ *n* a son-in-law *15-19, 20- literary*. †**gude son in law** = GUID-SON *e16*. [GUID¹·³ + *son* (SIN¹)]

guidwife, gudewife, *NE* **gweedwife**, †**gud wif** /ˈgɪdwʌɪf, ˈgudwʌɪf; *NE* ˈgwidwʌɪf/ *n* 1 a term of address for the mistress of a house *la14-*. 2 a wife *18-*. 3 the landlady of an inn *la18-*. 4 the mistress of a particular place (especially a farm) *16-19, 20- NE T C SW*. [GUID¹·³ + WIFE]

guidwill, gude will, *NE* **gweedwull**, †**gud will** /gɪdˈwɪl, gudˈwɪl; *NE* gwidˈwʌl/ *n* 1 willingness to be helpful, ready consent, friendly disposition *la14-*. 2 readiness, eagerness *la14-16*. **guid-willed** zealous *19, 20- Sh*. **guidwillie**, *NE* **gweedwullie** willing, ready; kind, generous*16-*. †**give his gude will** to give his consent *15-e17*. [GUID¹·³ + WILL¹·²]

guil *see* GOOL

guild, †**gild** /gɪld/ *n* 1 an association of merchants in a burgh; an organization or club *15-*. 2 a member of a guild *15-17*. **guildry**, †**gildrie** 1 a merchant guild; the guilds collectively as a municipal corporation *16-*. 2 membership in a merchant guild *16*. †**gildschippe** membership in a merchant guild *la16-e17*. **guild box** (a vessel containing) the treasury or funds of the guild *17-*. **guild brother**, †**gilbroder** a male member of a guild *la15-*. [OE *gyld*]

guild *see* GEEL, GOOL

guildry *see* GUILD

guilgruff *see* GŌLGRIV

guill fat *see* GEEL FAT

guilt /gɪlt/ *n* culpability, remorse *la14-*. **tak guilt til anesel** to feel or show guilt, be conscience-stricken *la19-*. [OE *gylt*]

guinie *see* GEENIE

guise¹·¹, **guize**, *Ork NE* **gy**, †**gyse**, †**gys**, †**gyis** /gaez; *Ork NE* gae/ *n* 1 semblance, appearance *la15-*. 2 a masque or masquerade; merrymaking, a piece of fun *la15-*. 3 manner, fashion; habit or custom *16-*. **hae a guise** to have a bit of fun *19- Sh NE*. **hae the gy o** to have the knack of *20- Ork*. **haud a guise** = *hae a guise*. †**turn the guise** to reverse roles *18-19*. [ME *gise*]

guise¹·², †**gys** /gaez/ *v* 1 to disguise *16-19, 20- Ork T Bor*. 2 to go out dressed as a GUISER at Halloween *la19-*. [see the noun]

guiser, **guizer**, **guizard**, †**guyser**, †**gysar** /ˈgaezər, ˈgʌɪzərd/ *n* 1 a person in disguise taking part in a festival at Halloween, Christmas, Hogmanay or Up-Helly-Aa, originally a mummer or masquerader *la15-*. 2 an unprepossessing or odd-looking person *18-*. **guizer jarl**, **guiser jarl** the chief or leading guiser in the Up-Helly-Aa celebrations *20- Sh*. [GUISE¹·¹, GUISE¹·², with agent suffix]

guising, †**gysing** /ˈgaezɪŋ/ *n* masquerading; calling on houses dressed as a GUISER at Halloween *la16-*. [verbal noun from GUISE¹·²]

guiss *see* GUESS¹·¹, GUESS¹·²

guisserne *see* GIZZERN

guissie *see* GUSSIE¹·¹

guizard *see* GUISER

guize *see* GUISE¹·¹

guizer *see* GUISER

†**guk**¹·¹ *n* a mocking sound *la15-16*. **gukkis** a jocular title *16-e17*. [perhaps onomatopoeic; compare GOWK¹]

†**guk**¹·² *v* to talk or behave foolishly *la16-e17*. [see the noun]

gukit, **gukkit** *see* GOWKIT

gulbröl¹·¹ /gəlˈbrøl/ *n* a loud bellow *la19- Sh*. [Norw *gaul* a bellow + BRÖL¹·¹]

gulbröl¹·² /gəlˈbrøl/ *v* to bellow, roar *la19- Sh*. [see the noun]

gulch¹·¹ /gʌltʃ/ *n* a glutton *la19, 20- N*. [onomatopoeic]

gulch¹·² /gʌltʃ/ *v* to eat rapidly or greedily *la19, 20- NE*. [see the noun]

guld *see* GOOL

gulder *see* GULLER¹·¹, GULLER¹·²

†**gule** *adj* yellow *la15-e16*. **guletree** the barberry *Berberis vulgaris e19*. [ON *gulr*; compare GOOL]

gule *see* GOWL¹·¹

gull /gʌl/ *n* a thin cold mist accompanied by a chilly breeze *19- NE*. [Norw dial *gul* a (sea) breeze, which tends to bring mist]

gullan *see* GOLLAN

guller[1.1], **gulder, golder, goller** /'gʌlər, 'gʌldər, 'gɔldər, 'gɔlər/ *n* **1** a shout, a roar, a yell *19-*. **2** a gurgling noise *19-*. **3** an outburst of angry speech *la19-*. **4** a loud laugh *20- Ork SW Uls*. Compare GALDER[1.1], GALDER[1.2]. [onomatopoeic]

guller[1.2], **gulder, golder, gollar** /'gʌlər, 'gʌldər, 'gɔldər, 'gɔlər/ *v* **1** to roar, shout, bawl *18-*. **2** to make a gurgling sound *19-*. Compare GALDER[1.1], GALDER[1.2]. [see the noun]

gullet /'gʌlət/ *n* **1** the oesophagus *18-*. **2** a narrow, deep channel or rocky inlet of the sea *la18-*. **3** a gully, a ravine *la18-*. **4** a narrow channel made or used for catching fish *la16-e19*. [EModE *gullet*]

gullie[1.1], **gully** /'gʌle, 'gʌli/ *n* a large (blunt) knife *la16-*. †**gulliegaw** to wound; to cut or hack with a knife *19- N EC*. **gully knife, gullie knife** a large (blunt) knife *16-*. **guide the gully** to manage or control events *18-19, 20- Bor*. **haud the gullie ower the dyke** to stand up for oneself *la19- T*. [unknown]

†**gullie**[1.2], **gully** *v* to slash or cut with a knife *19*. [unknown]

gullie *see* GOLLIE[1.1]

gullion /'gʌljən/ *n* **1** a quagmire, a marsh *19- EC SW*. **2** a pool of mud or of semi-liquid manure and decayed vegetable matter *19- Uls*. [IrGael *goilín* a pit, a pool]

gully[1.1], **gilly, gullo** /'gʌli, 'gɪli, 'gʌlo/ *n* a familiar term of address *19- Ork*. [see the adj]

gully[1.2] /'gʌli/ *adj* pleasant, agreeable *20- Ork*. [compare Norw dial *gjøle* excellent]

gully *see* GULLIE[1.1], GULLIE[1.2]

gulmoget /gʌl'mɔgət/ *adj of an animal* having a dark-coloured body with a light underside *20- Sh*. [compare Faer *gulmøgutur*, Icel *golmögóttur*]

gulp *see* GOWP[2.1], GOWP[2.2]

gulpin *see* GILPIN

gulravage *see* GILRAVAGE[1.1], GILRAVAGE[1.2]

gulsa, gulset *see* GULSOCH

gulsh /gʌlʃ/ *n* a fat, thickset person *19, 20- Bor*. [perhaps variant of GRILSE]

gulsoch, *Sh* **gulsa**, †**gulset** /'gʌlʃəx; *Sh* 'gʌlsa/ *n* **1** jaundice *16-19, 20- Sh Ork NE*. **2** excessive eating; nausea caused by overeating *19, 20- NE*. [GULE yellow + OE *suht* illness; compare Norw dial *gulsott*, ON *gulu-sótt*]

gulya *see* GOLLA

gum[1], †**goum** /gʌm/ *n* adhesive, gum *16-*. **gum flower** an artificial flower *18-*. [ME *gomme*]

gum[2.1] /gʌm/ *n* **1** a disagreement, a dispute; ill-will, rancour *18-*. **2** a mist, a haze; condensation, a film on glass *16-19, 20- N NE T*. [unknown]

gum[2.2] /gʌm/ *v* to become misted over *la19- NE T*. [unknown]

gum *see* COOM[1.1]

gumes *see* GOOMS

gumlie *see* GRUMMEL[1.1]

gummle *see* GRUMMEL[1.2]

gump[1], **gumph** /gʌmp, gʌmf/ *v* to catch fish by groping with the hands under the stones or banks of a stream *19, 20- EC Bor*. [unknown]

gump[2] /gʌmp/ *n* **1** a large part or portion; a piece cut off *19- SW*. **2** *in lead mining* a pocket of lead *19- SW*. **gumping** the part of a crop left standing between two reapers *19- SW*. [unknown]

gump[3] /gʌmp/ *n* the rump of a horse (or other animal) *la19- Ork*. [ON *gumpr*]

gumph /gʌmf/ *n* **1** a fool *19-*. **2** a moan, a complaint *la20-*. **gumpus** a foolish person *19-*. **the gumphs** the sulks *19- EC*. [onomatopoeic]

gumph *see* GUMP[1]

†**gumphion, gunfioun, gomphion** *n* a standard; a funeral banner *15-e19*. [altered form of MFr *gonfalon*]

gumping *see* GUMP[2]

gumple-faced /'gʌmpəlfest/ *adj* in a bad mood *19, 20- NE*. [frequentative form of GUMPH + Older Scots *faceit* having a particular kind of face]

†**gumple-foisted** *adj* = GUMPLE-FACED *e19*. [frequentative form of GUMPH; second element unknown]

gumption /'gʌmʃən/ *n* **1** common sense, native wit *18-*. **2** pluck, self-confidence *la19-*. [unknown; compare RUMMLEGUMPTION]

gumptious /'gʌmʃəs/ *adj* self-important, bumptious *la19-*. [GUMPTION, with adj-forming suffix]

gumpus *see* GUMPH

gums *see* GOOMS

gumsh /gʌmʃ/ *v* to munch *la19- NE T*. [onomatopoeic; compare GANSH[1.2]]

gum-stick /'gʌmstɪk/ *n* a stick used by a teething child *18-19, 20- C*. [*gum* (GAM) + STICK[2.1]]

gun[1.1], †**goun**, †**gune** /gʌn/ *n* **1** a firearm, a cannon *la14-*. **2** a tobacco-pipe, a brier-pipe *19-*. **gun end** the best room, the parlour *20- NE*. **be great guns wi** to be close friends with *20- Sh N T*. [unknown]

gun[1.2] /gʌn/ *v* **1** to gossip; to talk rapidly or animatedly *19- NE*. **2** *of a mining or quarrying charge* to go off without splitting the mineral; to blow back out of the charge-hole *la19- NE T*. **gunner** a person who shoots game for sport *la18-19, 20- Ork T*. [unknown]

gunch /gʌnʃ/ *n* **1** a thick piece, a hunk *la18- N WC SW*. **2** a short, thickset person *20- N*. [unknown; compare LUNCH a thick piece]

gundie /'gʌndi/ *adj* greedy *18, 19- Bor*. [unknown]

gundy /'gʌndi/ *n* toffee *19-*. [perhaps altered form of CANDY[1.1]]

gune *see* GUN[1.1]

gunfioun *see* GUMPHION

gunk[1.1] /gʌnk/ *n* a bitter disappointment *la18-19, 20- WC SW Uls*. **gie the gunk** to upset or disappoint; to jilt *la18-19, 20- WC SW Uls*. [unknown]

gunk[1.2] /gʌnk/ *v* to disappoint, humiliate; to jilt *19- Sh H&I SW Uls*. [unknown]

gunnie /'gʌni/ *n* a kind of sea fish, the father-lasher or short-spined sea scorpion *la19- NE T*. [unknown; perhaps shortened form of GUNPLUCKER]

gunplucker /'gʌnplʌkər/ *n* a kind of sea fish, the father-lasher or short-spined cottus; or the long-spined sea scorpion *la19- NE*. [Norn *plukker* an angler fish, a sea scorpion, with unknown first element]

gupp /gʌp/ *v* to retch, vomit *la19- Sh*. [Norw *gurpa*]

gurblot[1.1] /gʌr'blɔt/ *n* a hasty wash *20- Sh*. [unknown]

gurblot[1.2] /gʌr'blɔt/ *v* to wash (clothes) inefficiently *la19- Sh*. [unknown]

gurdy *see* GIRD[1.1]

gurg *see* JORG

gurge *see* GORGE

gurgis /'gʌrgɪs/ *n* a nasty, sticky mess *20- Ork*. [unknown]

gurk /gʌrk/ *n* a stout, heavily-built person *18- N NE*. [unknown]

gurl[1.1] /gʌrl/ *n* **1** a growl, a snarl *la18- C SW Bor*. **2** a gale, a squall *19, 20- Sh Ork*. **3** a gurgling sound *la19- SW*. [onomatopoeic]

gurl[1.2] /gʌrl/ *v* **1** to gurgle *la19-*. **2** *of the wind* to roar, howl *la18- C SW Bor*. **3** to growl *19- C SW Bor*. [see the noun]

gurl[1,3] /gʌrl/ *adj* **1** *of weather* cold, stormy, wild *16-19, 20- C SW*. **2** *of a person* surly, grumbling *19- C SW*. [see the noun]

gurlie, gurly /'gʌrle, 'gʌrli/ *adj* **1** *of weather* stormy, threatening; bitter, bleak *18-*. **2** *of a person* surly, bad-tempered; *of an animal* growling, snarling *18-*. **3** *of water* gurgling *19-*. **4** *of a tree* gnarled; *of undergrowth* tangled, overgrown *19-*. [onomatopoeic]

gurm /gʌrm/ *v* to make dirty; to engage in dirty work *la19- Sh*. [Norw dial *gurm* mud, dregs]

gurn *see* GIRN[1,1], GIRN[1,2]

gurr[1,1] /gʌr/ *n* a growl, a snarl *19-*. **gurry 1** a dogfight, a brawl *19-*. **2** a bustle, a state of confusion *la19-*. **gurry-wurry 1** a growl, a snarl *19, 20- NE T*. **2** a dogfight, a brawl *la19, 20- C SW*. [onomatopoeic]

gurr[1,2] /gʌr/ *v* to growl, snarl *19-*. [see the noun]

gurr[2] /gʌr/ *n* a strong, thickset, ungainly person *19, 20- NE*. [perhaps Gael *geàrr* short, squat; compare GARRON[1]]

gurr[3] /gʌr/ *n* drive, spirit *20- NE*. [perhaps GORE[1,1] or GURR[1,1]]

gurr *see* GOOR[1,1], GORE[1,1]

gurth /gʌrθ/ *n* crushed curd for cheese-making *19- WC*. [voiced variant of CURD; compare Gael *gruth* curds]

gurthie *see* GIRTH[2,1]

gusch *see* GUSH

guschet *see* GUSHET

guse[1,1], **goose**, *Sh N NE* **geese** /gus; *Sh N NE* gis/ *n* **1** a large web-footed bird, a goose *la14-*. **2** a tailor's iron *17-*. **3** a bagpipe with a chanter but no drones *la19-*. **gusedub** a goose pond; frequently in place-names *la16-*. **guse grass** brome-grass, grasses of the genus *Bromus 19-*. **goose nest** a recess in an interior wall of a house *la19- Ork*. †**guse pan** a large cooking-pot *la15-17*. [OE *gōs*]

guse[1,2], **goose** /gus/ *v* to press with a tailor's iron *17-*. **gusing iron** a tailor's iron *17-19, 20- T Bor*. [see the noun]

gusel, gowsel /'gusəl, 'gʌusəl/ *n* a gusty wind *la19- Sh Ork*. [frequentative form of Norw dial *gus* a puff of wind]

gush, †**gusch** /gʌʃ/ *v* **1** to flow swiftly, rush forth *la16-*. **2** to salivate *19*. [ME *gushen*]

gushel[1,1] /'gʌʃəl/ *n* **1** a bungled job *20- Ork N*. **2** a bungler *20- Ork N*. **gushlie** inept *20- Ork*. [unknown]

gushel[1,2] /'gʌʃəl/ *v* to bungle, botch *20- N*. [unknown]

gushet, gusset, †**gooshet,** †**guschet** /'gʌʃət, 'gʌsət/ *n* **1** a triangle of material let into a garment; a gusset *la15-*. **2** a triangular piece of land, especially between adjacent properties; an odd corner of land; a nook *la16-*. **3** the breast pocket of a jacket or coat *la19-*. **4** a triangular patch left in ploughing or reaping *20-*. **5** the corner of a building; a corner in a building *20-*. **6** a clock or ornamental pattern on the side of a stocking *16-e19*. **gushet house** a house standing at a corner or forming the angle between two roads *la19-*. **gushet neuk** an odd corner of land *la19- NE T*. [ME *gusset*]

gushoch *see* CUTCHACK

gussie[1,1], **gissie, guissie** /'gʌsi, 'gɪsi, 'gusi/ *n* **1** a pig; a young pig or sow *19-*. **2** a nickname for a fat person *la19, 20- T*. **3** a segment of an orange (from the supposed resemblance to piglets huddled together) *20- T*. [see the interj]

gussie[1,2], **gissie, goosy** /'gʌsi, 'gɪsi, 'gusi/ *interj* a call to pigs *19, 20- T C SW Bor*. **guss-guss** a call to pigs *19, 20- C SW Bor*. [compare Norw dial *giss* a call to pigs]

gust[1,1] /gʌst/ *n* a taste or flavour *la15-*. **gustie** tasty *18-*. **gustily** with relish, heartily *19-*. †**gustit** flavoured *la15-18*. **gustless 1** tasteless, insipid *la16-19, 20- EC*. **2** having no sense of taste *la18-19, 20- EC*. [ME *gust*, Lat *gustus*]

gust[1,2] /gʌst/ *v* **1** to delight the palate, please with a delicious taste *la15-*. **2** to smell (strongly or badly) *16-e18, 20- T*. **3** to test by tasting *la15-e17*. **gust the gab** to delight the palate, whet the appetite *18-*. †**gust of** to take a taste (of) *la15-e16*. [ME *gusten*, Lat *gustāre*]

†**gustard** *n* a bustard *16-17*. [probably altered form of OFr *bistarde*]

gut[1,1] /gʌt/ *n* the intestine, the stomach, the belly *la18-*. **guts**, †**guttis** the intestines *la14-*. **gutser 1** a belly-flop *20-*. **2** a glutton *la20- NE T*. **gutsie 1** greedy, gluttonous *19-*. **2** *of a building* roomy, commodious *la19-*. **gut pock** the stomach of a fish *la19- N NE*. **gut pock herring** herring which feed mainly on small crustaceans *la19- N H&I*. **gut scraper** a fiddle player *la18-19, 20- NE*. **aw gutts an gangyls** all stomach and legs *la19- NE*. †**gut and ga, guts and ga** the stomach and contents *la18-19*. [OE *guttas* guts, entrails]

gut[1,2] /gʌt/ *v* to disembowel, eviscerate *la16-*. **guts** to eat greedily or gluttonously *20-*. **gutter** a woman employed in gutting fish *la19-*. †**gut fish afore you catch them** to count your chickens before they are hatched *19*. [see the noun]

gut *see* GYTE[2]

gutcher, gudesire, †**gudeschir,** †**gutsher,** †**guchar** /'gʌtʃər, 'gudsaer/ *n* a grandfather *15-*. [GUID[1,3] + Older Scots *sire*]

gutherlidge *see* GODDERLITCH

guts, gutser *see* GUT[1,1]

gutsher *see* GUTCHER

gutta *see* GUTTIE[2]

guttag /'gʌtəg/ *n* a fish-gutting knife *20- N WC SW*. [conflation of Gael *cutag* with GUT[1,2]]

guttam /'gʌtəm/ *n* a drop (of ink or spirits) *20- N NE*. [Lat *guttam*, accusative of *gutta* a drop]

gutter[1,1], **gitter,** †**guttar** /'gʌtər, 'gɪtər/ *n* **1** a drainage channel, a gutter *15-*. **2** mud, mire; muddy puddles *18-*. **3** an awkward, untidy or messy worker *la19-*. **4** a muddle, a mess *la20-*. **5** an unskilful or dirty way of working *la19- NE EC*. **gutterie** muddy, messy *la18-*. **gutters** mud, mire; muddy puddles *18-*. **gutter bluid 1** a lowly-born or ill-bred person *19, 20- SW Bor*. **2** a native of a particular town; a person whose ancestors have been born in the same town for generations, especially a native of Peebles *19, 20- Bor*. **gutter gaw** a sore on the foot *19- NE T EC*. **gutter hole** a drain or drainage hole for kitchen refuse *la16-19, 20- N NE*. [ME *goter*]

gutter[1,2], **gitter** /'gʌtər, 'gɪtər/ *v* **1** to furnish with a gutter *la14-*. **2** to do something in a dirty, slovenly or unskilful way *19-*. **3** to potter or tinker; to fritter away time *20-*. **4** to talk nonsense, gabble *20-*. [see the noun]

guttie[1,1] /'gʌti/ *n* **1** a corpulent, pot-bellied person; a glutton *19- WC SW Bor*. **2** a minnow *19- C*. [GUT[1,1] + -IE[1]]

guttie[1,2] /'gʌti/ *adj* **1** thick; gross; corpulent, pot-bellied *la18-*. **2** greedy, gluttonous *19- NE SW Bor*. [see the noun]

guttie[2], **gutta** /'gʌti, 'gʌtə/ *n* **1** something made wholly or partly of rubber *19-*. **2** a catapult *la20- T C*. **gutties** gymshoes *20- T C*. **guttie ba** a golf ball *19-*. **gutty-perky** gutta-percha sap *20-*. [Malay *getah* gum, exudation]

guttis *see* GUT[1,1]

gutty-perky *see* GUTTIE[2]

guy[1,1], †**gy** /gae/ *n* a guide *15-19, 20- NE*. **guys** the handlebars of a bicycle *20- NE T*. [ME *gi*]

guy[1,2], †**gy** /gae/ *v* to guide, steer *la14-16, 20- NE*. [ME *gien*]

guyser *see* GUISER

guzzern *see* GIZZERN

guzzle[1,1] /'gʌzəl/ *n* a bout of excessive eating and drinking *19-*. [see the verb]

guzzle[1,2] /'gʌzəl/ *v* **1** to eat greedily *18-*. **2** to take by the throat; to throttle *la19, 20- NE T EC*. [EModE *gussel*]

gward *see* GAIRD[1,1]

gweed see GUID[1.1], GUID[1.3]
gweedbreeder see GUID-BRITHER
gweed dothor see GUID-DOCHTER
gweed father see GUID-FAITHER
gweedless see GUIDLESS
gweedlie see GUIDLY
gweedman see GUIDMAN
gweedmither see GUID-MITHER
gweedsin see GUID-SON
gweedwife see GUIDWIFE
gweedwull see GUIDWILL
gweems see GOOMS
gweeshtens, gweeshtie /ˈgwiʃtənz, ˈgwiʃti/ *interj* an expression of surprise *la19- NE*. [derivative of *gweed* (GUID[1.1]); compare GOSH]
gwite see GYTE[2]
gy see GUISE[1.1], GUY[1.1], GUY[1.2]
gya see GIE
gyaain, gyaan see GAE
gyad see GAD
gyan see GAE
gyand see GEEANT
gyang see GANG[1.2]
gyaun see GAE
gyd, gyde see GUIDE[1.1], GUIDE[1.2]
gyel see JILE[1.1]
gyevel see GJAEVEL
gyill see GILL[2]
gyir carlyng see GYRE[1.1]
gyis see GUISE[1.1]
gyle fat see GEEL FAT
gyll see GILL[2]
gym see GIM
gymp see JIMP[1], JIMP[2.2]
gyn see GIN[1]
†gyne *v* to elect to an office; to get oneself elected *17*. [perhaps reduced form of ADJOIN]
gyoger see GJOGER
gyola, giola /ˈgjola/ *n* thin buttermilk; whey *la19- Sh*. [Norw dial *kjore* curdled milk]
gype[1.1] /gʌip/ *n* a foolish or awkward person *19- Sh NE T*. [perhaps ON *geip* nonsense]

gype[1.2] /gʌip/ *v* 1 to stare foolishly or open-mouthed *la19- N NE T*. 2 to play the fool; to make a fool of *la19- Sh NE T*.
gypit silly, foolish *19- Sh N T*. [perhaps ON *geipa* to talk nonsense; compare Norw dial *gipa* to let the mouth hang open]
gyper[1.1] /ˈgʌipər/ *n* nonsense; fun, joking *la19- NE*. [frequentative form of GYPE[1.2]]
gyper[1.2] /ˈgʌipər/ *v* to talk nonsense *20 NE*. **gyperie** nonsense, foolishness *19- NE*. [see the noun]
gyre[1.1] /gaer/ *n* 1 *folklore* an ogress, a giantess; a witch *19- Sh Ork*. 2 *in Orkney* a boy dressed as a hobgoblin who chased children in the street (on the evening of Shrove Tuesday) *20- historical*. **gyre-carling, gearcairlin, †gyir carlyng** *folklore* an ogress, a giantess; a witch *16-19, 20- Sh Ork N*. [ON *gýgr* an ogress, a witch]
gyre[1.2] /gaer/ *adj* 1 unpleasant, unnatural, repulsive *la19- NE*. 2 *of garments or colours* odd, gaudy *la19- NE*. [see the noun]
gyrs see GIRSE[1.1]
gyrth see GIRTH[1]
gys see GUISE[1.1], GUISE[1.2]
gysar see GUISER
gyse see GUISE[1.1]
gysing see GUISING
gyte[1.1] /gʌit/ *n* a mad person, a foolish person *19-*. **gyter** *n* 1 nonsense, foolish talk *la19- NE*. 2 a foolish, talkative person *19- NE WC*. **gyter** *v* to prattle in a foolish way *20- NE*. **gytit** foolish, mad *la19, 20- NE T*. [unknown]
gyte[1.2] /gʌit/ *adj* 1 *of a person* insane; mad with rage or pain *18-*. 2 *of things* nonsensical, awry *la18-*. 3 *of a person* lovesick, eager *19-*. [unknown]
gyte[2], **gote, gott, gut,** *Sh N* **gjot,** *NE* **gwite, †goit, †goat** /gʌit, got, gɔt, gʌt; *Sh N* gjɔt; *NE* gwʌit/ *n* 1 a ditch, a drain, a watercourse *la16-*. 2 a narrow rocky inlet of the sea, a creek; a navigable channel *18-*. 3 a bog *19- WC Bor*. **goting, †gatting, †gauten** *mining* a drainage gutter *la18- EC*. [MLG, MDu *gote* a ditch, a trench, a watercourse]
gyte see GAIT[2.1], GAIT[2.2], GET[1.1]
gyurd /gjørd/ *n* a gift *la19- Sh*. [probably ON *görð* an act, a deed]
gyzen see GIZZEN[1.1]

H

ha¹, haw, hall, *Sh* **haa**, *Sh NE T* **haal** /ha, hɔ, hɔl; *Sh* hɑ; *Sh NE T* hal/ *n* **1** a large, spacious building, the residence of a landowner *14-*. **2** the principal room of a palace, castle, or monastery *15-*. **3** a large public meeting room; a village or community hall, a market-hall; a school hall; a church hall *la16-*. **4** a farmhouse, the main dwelling of a farm or estate *18-*. **5** an entrance hall, a passageway in a house or other building *la19-*. **6** a (community) hall used as a port of call during the Up-Helly-Aa procession *la20- Sh*. **7** a parlour; the principal room of a farmhouse *18-19*. †**ha' bible** a large, family bible *la18-19*. †**ha' board, hall buird** a large table; the dining-table in a farmhouse *17-e19*. †**hall chamber** a small room or bedroom off a hall *15-e18*. **ha' hoose** the main house on a farm; a laird's residence *17-19, 20- Sh NE*. †**hall huntaris** scroungers *e16*. **the Hall** a Presbyterian theological college *la18-*. †**hall binks are sliddery** great men are not reliable in their support *la15-e18*. [OE *heall*]

ha², **haa** /ha/ *v* to eat *la19-*. [Travellers' language, Romany]

ha *see* HAE¹·²

haa *see* HA¹, HA²

haad *see* HAUD¹·¹, HAUD¹·²

haaf /haf, haf/ *n* **1** the deep or open sea *la18- Sh Ork*. **2** deep-sea fishing *19- Sh Ork*. **haf-fish**, †**haaf fish** a seal larger than the common seal, the grey seal *Halichoerus grypus la18- Sh*. **haaf fishing** deep-sea fishing *la18-*. **haaf-man** a deep-sea fisherman *la19- Sh*. [ON *haf*]

haaf-net, †**haf-net**, †**halve-net**, †**halfe-net** /'haf nɛt/ *n* a net on a frame set across the current to catch fish as the tide flows or ebbs *17- SW Bor*. [compare Norw *håv*, ON *háfr* a net for herring fishing + NET]

haag¹·¹ /hag, hag/ *n* order, good management; thrift *la19- Sh*. **haagless** careless; wasteful; remorseless *20- Sh*. [ON *hag*]

haag¹·², **hag** /hag, hag/ *v* to manage well, be economical, save *la19- Sh*. [ON *haga*]

haain, hain /'hain, hen/ *n* economy, restraint, moderation *20- Sh Ork N*. [perhaps ON *haga*; compare HAIN]

haal *see* HA¹, HAUL¹·²

haand *see* HAN¹·¹

haar¹, haur /har, hɔr/ *n* **1** a cold mist or fog, especially an east-coast sea fog *18-*. **2** a cold easterly wind *la18- Sh N NE EC Bor*. **haary 1** misty, foggy *19, 20- Sh EC Bor*. **2** *of wind* cold, piercing *19- Sh EC*. [MLG, MDu *hare* a biting cold wind]

†**haar²·¹** *n* a burr in a person's speech; 'r' pronounced as a uvular trill *la18-e19*. [onomatopoeic]

haar²·² /har/ *v* to speak with a burr *19- T WC*. [see the noun]

haar *see* HAIR²·²

haaver *see* HALVER¹·¹, HALVER¹·²

haavers *see* HAUFERS

haavie /'havi/ *n* **1** a knee-shaped piece of wood fixed to the end of the keel of a boat to secure it to the stern *20- Ork*. **2** a piece of wood built into the wall of a stable or byre to which animals are tethered *20- Ork*. [Norw dial *hav* a handle, the bent-up part of a sledge runner]

haavin /'havɪn/ *n* the practice of fishing with a HAAF-NET *la18- SW Bor*. [from HAAF-NET]

habbell *see* HOBBILL¹·¹

habben *see* HABEN

habber¹·¹ /'habər/ *n* **1** a stammer *20- Sh NE T*. **2** a snarl, a growl; the gobble of a turkey *19- NE*. [onomatopoeic; compare HABBLE¹·¹]

habber¹·², **hubber** /'habər, 'hʌbər/ *v* **1** to prattle, chatter *20-*. **2** to stammer, stutter *19, 20- Sh NE T*. **3** to snarl, growl; to make a gobbling noise *19- NE*. **habbergaw** to stumble; to mutter; to make objections *19, 20- SW*. [see the noun]

habbie /'habi, 'habe/ *n* **1** a form of poetic stanza used by Habbie Simpson and favoured by Robert Burns *18- literary*. **2** an inhabitant of Kilbarchan, Renfrewshire *20- WC*. [named from *Habbie Simpson*, a piper of Kilbarchan]

habbie-horse /'habi hɔrs/ *n* a hobby-horse, a child's play horse *la19-*. [altered form of Eng *hobby-horse*]

habbi-gabbi /'habi gabi/ *n* a child's game in which stones or other small objects are thrown into the air and then caught *la19- Sh*. [unknown]

†**habbitrot** *n* in the Borders a household fairy or brownie *19*. [unknown]

habble¹·¹ /'habəl/ *n* **1** a difficulty, a predicament; a state of perplexity *la18-*. **2** an uproar, a disturbance, a tumult; a quarrel, a fight *la18-*. **3** a coarse or slovenly person *19- Bor Uls*. Compare HOBBLE¹·¹, HUBBLE¹·¹. **habble jock** a turkey cock *la19- T*. [see the verb]

habble¹·² /'habəl/ *v* **1** to walk unsteadily, limp, hobble *la18-*. **2** to perplex, confuse, trouble; to hamper or foil *19- EC SW Bor*. **3** to tangle thread *20- EC SW Bor*. **4** to quarrel, wrangle *19*. **5** to stutter; to babble *e19*. [onomatopoeic; compare HABBER¹·², HOBBLE¹·², HUBBLE¹·²]

haben, habben /'habən/ *n* **1** bread *la19-*. **2** food in general *la19-*. [Travellers' language, Romany]

†**haberschoun, haubersione, aubirchoun** *n* a habergeon, a sleeveless coat of mail *la14-e17*. [AN *aubershun, haubergeon*]

habile¹·¹, †**habill**, †**hable** /'habəl/ *adj* **1** qualified, suitable, fit; able, powerful *la14-*. **2** *law* admissible, valid; apt, competent *la17-*. **3** liable, likely *la15-e17*. †**habilitie 1** ability; deftness, readiness *la15-19*. **2** *law* the legal competence of a witness *la17-e18*. [OFr *habile*, Lat *habilis*; compare ABLE¹·¹]

†**habile¹·²**, **habill** *adv* perhaps, possibly *16*. [see the adj]

habiliment, †**abuilyiement**, †**abilʒement**, †**habilʒement** /həˈbɪlɪmənt/ *n* **1** a garment; attire *la15-*. **2** equipment, arms *la15-e19*. Compare BULIMENT. [OFr *habillement*]

habill *see* HABILE¹·¹, HABILE¹·²

habilyiet *see* ABILʒEIT

habilʒement *see* HABILIMENT

habit, †**abit**, †**abbeit**, †**abyte** /'habɪt/ *n* **1** attire; the dress of a religious order *la14-*. **2** customary behaviour *la16-*. **3** mental or physical constitution *la15-e16*. †**in habits** on good terms *la18-e19*. †**on good habits** = *in habits*. [ME *habit*]

habit and repute¹·¹ /'habɪt and rə'pjut/ *n law* the fact of being held and reputed, the reputation of being a thief; the reputation of being married *18-*. [see the adj]

habit and repute¹·² /'habɪt and rə'pjut/ *adj law* held or reputed (to be a thief, witch, or a married person) *18-*. [Lat *habitus et reputatus* held and reputed (to be)]

habjaickle *see* HAPSHACKLE¹·¹

hable *see* HABILE¹·¹

hace *see* HAIRSE

hach *see* HAUCH¹·¹, HAUCH¹·²

†**hache** *n* a pain, a pang *e16*. [OE *aece*]

hack[1.1], **hak**, **hawk**, *Sh* **hakk** /hak, hɔk; *Sh* hɑk/ *n* **1** a pronged tool for breaking up or raking soil or dung *la18-*. **2** a crack or chap in the skin caused by cold or frost *19-*. **3** *curling* a metal footplate to steady the player's foot; originally a cut in the ice *19-*. **4** a joiner's adze; a miner's pick-ended hammer *19, 20- EC Bor*. **5** a choppy sea *20- Sh N*. **6** a notch on a graded scale; a certain amount (of time or distance) *20- NE*. **7** an indentation on a toothed wheel *17*. **8** a cut or gash *la15*. **hackmuck** a muck-rake *la18-*. **a hack abeen the common** a cut above (ordinary people) *la19- Sh NE*. **ca a hack i the crook** to mark, celebrate (an event) *la19-*. **ca a hack i the post** = *ca a hack i the crook*. **drive a hack i the crook** = *ca a hack i the crook*. **haul doon a hackie** = *tak doon a hackie*. **tak doon a hackie** to puncture a person's self-conceit, take down a peg *20- Sh NE*. [see the verb; compare Du *hak* a hoe and HAG[1.1]]

hack[1.2] /hak/ *v* **1** to cut, chop *la15-*. **2** *of skin* to crack, chap or roughen *la18-*. **3** to drag dung from a cart with a pronged rake *19- H&I EC*. **hackie** a robber of eggs from birds' nests *la19- WC Bor*. †**hak-hammer** a sharp-edged hammer for cutting *la16-e17*. †**hack-heid** the head of a cutting tool *la17*. **hacking stock** a chopping block *16-19, 20- N NE*. **hackstock** = *hacking stock 17-19, 20- N NE*. [OE *tohaccian*]

hack[2] /hak/ *n* the foot-rest on a peat-spade *20- Ork*. [Norw dial *hake* a hook, a spade]

hack *see* HECK[1.1]

hackberry *see* HAGBERRY

hackit, **hacket**, **hakkit**, **hakket** /'hakɪt/ *adj* **1** *of skin* chapped, roughened; scarred *la16-*. **2** ugly *la20-*. **hackit faced** ugly-faced, unattractive *la20-*. †**hacket kail** chopped kail or cabbage boiled in water or milk *18-19*. [ptp of HACK[1.2]]

hackit *see* HAWKIT

hackle *see* HECKLE[1.1], HECKLE[2]

hacksey-looked /'haksi lukəd/ *adj of a face* scarred, pitted, scratched *19- Sh Ork*. [compare Norw *haksa* to hack carelessly and HACK[1.2]]

hackum-plackum[1.1] /'hakəm plakəm/ *adj* equal in every way; in close accord *19- Bor*. [rhyming compound; perhaps based on HACK[1.2] and influenced by Lat *placēre* to be agreeable or PLACK]

hackum-plackum[1.2] /'hakəm plakəm/ *adv of payment or reward* distributed equally, in equal shares *19- Bor*. [see the adj]

hacky *see* HAWKIE

hacky duck, **hucky-duck** /'hake dʌk, 'hʌke dʌk/ *n* a children's game in which two teams take it in turn to leap on the lined-up backs of their opponents *20- T*. [unknown]

hacquebute *see* HAGBUTE

had *see* HAE[1.2], HAUD[1.1], HAUD[1.2]

hadd *see* HAUD[1.1], HAUD[1.2]

hadden *see* HAUD[1.2], HAUDIN

hadder *see* HEATHER

haddibaand /'hadibɑnd/ *n* a crossbeam under the thwart which fastens the frames of a boat *la19- Sh*. [HAUD[1.2] + BAND[1.1]]

haddie, **haddy**, **huddie**, †**haddo**, †**hady** /'hadi, 'hade, 'hʌde/ *n* **1** a haddock *la17-*. **2** a nickname for an Aberdonian *20-*. **3** a mild term of contempt for a person *20-*. **Aberdeen haddie** a nickname for an Aberdonian *20- WC*. [altered form of HADDOCK]

haddish, †**haddisch**, †**half-disch** /'hadɪʃ/ *n* a measure of grain equal to a third or a quarter of a peck *16- NE T*. **haddish cog** a container holding a measure of grain *la18- NE T*. [*half* (HAUF[1.3]) + DISH[1.1]]

haddit *see* HAUD[1.2]

haddo *see* HADDIE

haddock, *NE* **hathock**, *NE* **hoddock**, †**haddok**, †**hadok** /'hadək; *NE* 'haθək; *NE* 'hɔdək/ *n* **1** an edible North Atlantic fish *15-*. **2** a term of contempt for a person *e19*. Compare HADDIE. [unknown]

haddy *see* HADDIE

†**hade**, **haid** *n* rank, estate; quality, kind *la14-15*. [OE *hād*]

hade *see* HIDE[1]

hadok *see* HADDOCK

hadry *see* HEATHERY

hady *see* HADDIE

hae[1.1], *NE* **hiv** /he; *NE* hɪv/ *n pl* †**haves** **1** possession of material things or mental powers: ◊*a continual state of a hae an a want 20-*. **2** property, possessions *19*. †**hae and heal** health and wealth *19*. [see the verb]

hae[1.2], **hiv**, **huv**, **hev**, **have**, **ha**, **a**, †**haf**, †**haif**, †**hef** /he, hɪv, hʌv, hev, hav, ha, a/ *v present singular* **has**, **hes**, **his**, **hez**, **hais**, **haes**, *pt* **haed**, **hed**, **hid**, **hed**, †**haid**, *ptp* **haed**, **haid**, **hed**, **hid**, **hed**, *Ork NE* **heen**, *N NE T* **haen**, *N NE T* **hedden**, *NE* **hin** **1** to possess, hold, keep *la14-*. **2** to experience, undergo, endure *la14-*. **3** to put, bring, to take, send: ◊*he was had to bed la14-*. **4** to command, order: ◊*hae tak that, an' be aff wi you 18-*. **5** to credit, believe, think *la19-*. **6** was to, were to: ◊*if she had tae recover she wad hae bin a help tae him 20- T H&I SW*. **7** to behave, conduct oneself *15-16*. **husnae**, **hasnae**, **hisnae** has not *19-*. **huvnae**, **havnae**, **hivnae**, **hinna**, **hinnae**, *WC Bor* **henna** have not *la18-*. **hudnae**, **hidnae**, **hidny**, **hadnae**, *Ork* **hidno** had not *19-*. **be weel had** to be well off *la18- WC Uls*. **haet**, †**haid** **1** *in imprecations* have it *la16-*; compare *deil a haet* (DEIL). **2** a small amount, an iota; a whit *19-*. †**have at ill-will** to dislike *18-e19*. **hae a tune tae yersel** to play a tune by oneself *20-*. **hae easy daein** to be able to do easily, without difficulty *la18-19, 20- Sh NE T*. **hae eftir** to go after, follow *la19- T EC*. **hae guid daein** = *hae easy daein*. **hae had that tae dae** to have been compelled or predetermined by fate to take a course of action *19- NE T EC*. **had haen that tae dae** = *hae had that tae dae 20-*. **hae ill daein** to have difficulty doing *la19- Sh NE T*. †**have in thocht** to contemplate, consider *la14-16*. **hae't and haud it** to hide one's feelings *20- NE*. **hae wi** to go with, accompany *la18, 20- T*. †**hae yer meat and yer mense baith** said when one's hospitality has been refused, so that one has the credit of hospitality without any expenditure *17-19*. **what wad ye hae o't**, **what hae ye o't** would you believe it! *la19-*. [OE *habban*]

haegri *see* HEGRI

hael *see* HAIL[1.2], HEAL[1.2]

haen *see* HAE[1.2]

haet *see* HAE[1.2], HET[1.1]

haethin *see* HAITHEN[1.1], HAITHEN[1.2]

haf *see* HAE[1.2], HAUF[1.1]

haff *see* HAUF[1.1], HAUF[1.3]

haffet, †**halffet**, †**halfheid** /'hafət/ *n* **1** the temple, the cheek *la15-*. **2** a side-lock of hair *18-*. **3** *pl* locks of hair growing on the temples *18-*. **4** the wooden side of a box-bed, chair or pew; the vertical side of a dormer window *la18-*. [OE *healfhēafod* the forepart of the head]

haf-fish *see* HAAF

hafflins *see* HALFLINS[1.2]

hafles *see* HAIVELESS

haf-net *see* HAAF-NET

haft *see* HEFT[1.1], HEFT[3.1], HEFT[3.2]

hag[1.1], †**hagg** /hag/ *n* **1** a water-filled hole or marshy place in a moor (where channels have been made or peats cut) *16-*. **2** a tussock or hillock of firmer ground in a bog *19-*. **3** a notch, a hack *16-19, 20- WC SW Uls*. **4** brushwood; felled wood used for fuel *19, 20- NE T Bor*. **5** a ledge of turf overhanging a stream *19- SW Bor*. **6** a section of woodland marked for felling *17-e19*. **hagger** a deep jagged cut *la19- NE*. **hagger-snash** *of language* a conglomeration of scraps; spiteful or cutting remarks *19-*. †**hag-house** a woodshed *17-e18*. **hag pile** = *hag stack*. **hag stack** a stack or pile of firewood *la19- NE T SW*. **strike a hag in the post** to mark or celebrate (an event) *16-18, 19- WC SW Uls*. Compare HACK[1.1]. [ON *högg* a stroke, a blow]

hag[1.2] /hag/ *v* **1** to hack, cut; to chop wood *la15-*. **2** to cut down trees, prepare timber *19- C*. **hagger** to cut clumsily, hack *la19- NE*. †**hag-airn**, **hag-iron** a blacksmith's cutting tool *17-19*. **hag-block** a chopping block *la19- SW Uls*. **hag-clog** a chopping block *19- SW*. †**hagman** a woodcutter *18-e19*. **hag stock**, †**hag-stoke** a chopping block *e16, 20- SW*. Compare HACK[1.2]. [ON *hǫggva*]

hag *see* HAAG[1.2]

hagabag /'hagəbag/ *n* coarse linen, huckaback *la17-19, 20- SW*. [unknown]

hagard *see* HAGGARD

hagberry, **hackberry** /'hagbɛri, 'hakbɛri/ *n* the bird cherry *Prunus padus 18-*. [ON *heggr* + BERRY[1]]

†**hagbute**, **hakbut**, **hacquebute** *n* an early portable firearm, a harquebus *16-e19*. **hagbutter**, **hagbutar** a soldier armed with a hagbute *16-19*. **hagbut of crochat** = *hagbut of crok e16*. **hagbut of crok** a harquebus supported on a rest by an iron hook attached to the barrel *16-e17*. [MFr *hakebute*, altered form of *haquebuse* with influence from *buter* to strike with a thrusting motion]

hage *see* HEDGE

†**hagg**, **haig** *v of cattle* to butt with the head, fight *19*. [unknown]

haggard, †**hagard** /'hagərd/ *n* a stackyard *la16- EC SW Uls*. [ON *heygarðr*]

haggeis *see* HAGGIS

hagger *see* HAG[1.1], HAG[1.2]

†**haggirbald** *n* a term of abuse for a person *16*. Compare LUSCHBALD. [unknown]

haggis, *Ork* **heggis**, †**haggeis** /'hagɪs; *Ork* 'hɛgɪs/ *n* **1** the heart, lungs and liver of a sheep minced with suet, oatmeal, onions and seasoning (boiled in a sheep's stomach) *16-*. **2** a botched job, a mess *20- Ork*. **3** the stomach of a person or animal *la18-19*. **haggis bag** the sheep's stomach in which haggis is cooked *la18-19, 20- Bor*. [unknown]

haggit /'hagɪt/ *adj* weary, exhausted *19- NE EC*. [unknown]

haggle[1.1], *Bor* **haigle** /'hagəl; *Bor* 'hɛgəl/ *n* **1** an uneven cut, a hack; a bungle; a tangle *20-*. **2** a struggle, a laborious effort *la19- Bor*. [frequentative form of HAG[1.1]]

haggle[1.2], *Bor* **haigle** /'hagəl; *Bor* 'hɛgəl/ *v* **1** to stumble forward, struggle or plod on *18-*. **2** to cut unevenly, hack *19-*. **3** to carry (something cumbersome) with difficulty *19- EC Bor*. [see the noun]

haggle-baggle, †**eaggle-baggle** /'hagəl bagəl/ *v* to argue, wrangle over a price *la19-*. [rhyming compound from Eng *haggle*]

haggle-bargain[1.1] /'hagəl bargən/ *n* a haggler, someone who wrangles over a price *19- Bor*. Compare ARGLE-BARGAIN. [Eng *haggle* + BARGAIN[1.1]]

haggle-bargain[1.2], †**eaggle-bargin** /'hagəl bargən/ *v* to argue, wrangle over a price *la19-*. Compare ARGLE-BARGAIN. [see the noun]

haglet /'haglət/ *n* an enclosed piece of hill pasture *20- Sh*. [ON *hagi* pasture + Norw dial *leite* a particular place]

hagman /'hagmən/ *n* a farmhand considered only to be fit for tending stall-fed cattle *la19- EC*. [perhaps HAG[1.2]]

hagmark /'hagmark/ *n* a boundary marker between hill pastures *19- Sh*. [ON *hagi* pasture + MARK[1.1]]

hagmet /'hagmɛt/ *n* = HAGMARK *20- Sh*. [ON *hagi* pasture + MET[1.1]]

hagmonay *see* HOGMANAY

hagrie, †**hagra** /'hagri/ *n* a ride on the hill *la18- Sh*. **ride da hagri** to ride the marches, take part in the traditional ceremony of riding round the boundaries of common land to inspect boundary marks *la18- Sh*. [ON *hagi* pasture + ON *reið* a ride]

haiches, **yachis** /'hexəs, 'jaxəs/ *n* a heavy fall; a thud *la18- NE T*. [probably onomatopoeic]

haid *see* HADE, HAE[1.2]

haif *see* HAE[1.2]

haifar *see* HAVER[2]

haig *see* HAGG

haigle *see* HAGGLE[1.1], HAGGLE[1.2]

haigs *see* HEGS

haik[1.1] /hek/ *n* **1** a person or animal given to roaming about *19-*. **2** a trek, a journey *la20-*. **be on the haik for** to be on the lookout for *20-*. [unknown]

haik[1.2] /hek/ *v* **1** to trek, rove or roam; to wander aimlessly; to go laboriously, trudge *la15-*. **2** to carry or drag with difficulty *la18-*. **3** to treat roughly, drive hard *19, 20- NE*. [unknown]

†**haik**[2] *n* a hack, a hackney horse or vehicle *la18-e19*. [shortened form of Older Scots *Haknay* a Hackney]

†**haik**[3] *n* a (woman's) cloak or mantle *la14-16*. [Du *huik*]

haik *see* HECK[1.1]

haikit *see* HAWKIT

hail[1.1], **whole**, †**hale**, †**quhole** /hel, hol/ *n* the entirety, the full number or amount *15-*. [see the adj]

hail[1.2], **hale**, **haill**, **whole**, *Sh* **hael**, †**heal**, †**hele**, †**quhole** /hel, hol; *Sh* 'heal/ *adj* **1** sound, healthy; uninjured; wholesome; robust, vigorous *la14-*. **2** *of things* complete; undamaged *la14-*. **3** all, entire, whole; the full number of: ◊*the whole Heritors or their agents la14-*. **4** sole, only *la14-e18*. **hailly** completely *la14-*. †**hailumly** completely, undoubtedly *la18-e19*. **hale-heartit** undaunted, stalwart *19-*. **hale-heidit** completely, entirely *19- N NE*. **hail oot drink** a drink drunk in a single swallow *e18, 20- T*. **hale sale** wholesale *la17-*. **hailscart**, **hale-scart**, †**hailskarth** unscathed *16-19, 20- Bor Uls*. **hail-skinnt** having an unblemished skin *la19-*. **hale-tear** at full speed *20-*. **haleware** the whole number or amount *la16-19, 20- SW*. **hale-watter** *n* a downpour *la19-*. **hale-watter** *adv* torrentially *la19-*. **hail wheel** full tilt *la19- NE T*. **hale and fere** in full health and vigour; unharmed, undamaged *la14-*. **hael an hadden** entire; simple, ordinary *la19- Sh*. **whole at the heart**, **hale at the heart 1** in good spirits *20- NE T EC*. **2** having a hearty appetite *20- NE*. †**the hale heid** the whole amount, the total *la16-17*. **the hale rickmatick** the whole lot *la19-*. **the hail tot** the total *19- C SW*. †**in hail** in total *15-19*. [OE *hāl*]

hail[1.3], **whole**, †**hale**, †**thaill** /hel, hol/ *adv* completely; fully *la14-*. [see the adj]

hail[2], †**thaill**, †**hayle** /hel/ *n* **1** pellets of ice, hailstones *la14-*. **2** small shot *la17-*; compare *sparra hail* (SPARRA). **3** a small quantity of liquid *20- N*. †**hailshot**, **hailschot** shot which scatters like hail *16-19*. **hailstane**, *NE* **hailsteen** a pellet of hail *15-*. **haily-puckle**, **haily-pickle**, **haily-buckie** a hailstone *19- Sh Ork*. [OE *hagol*]

hail[3.1] /hel/ *n* **1** *games* a shout when a goal is scored *la18-*. **2** *games* the goal area *la18-*. **3** the scoring of a goal *17-19, 20- H&I Bor*. **4** *pl* a game similar to shinty played with clackans at Edinburgh Academy *la19- EC*. **hail-ba** a variety of handball *19- Ork SW*. **hail-post** a goalpost *20- Ork N*. [see the verb]

hail[3.2], †**hale** /hel/ *v games* to drive a ball through the goal or boundary; to score a goal *18-19, 20- Bor*. **hail the dools** to score a goal; to be the winner; to celebrate a win *16-19, 20- NE*. [specific use of HAIL⁴]

hail⁴, †**haill**, †**hale** /hel/ *interj* an exclamation of greeting or salutation *15-*. [specific use of HAIL¹·²]

hail *see* HALE¹·¹

haill *see* HAIL¹·², HAIL¹·³, HAIL², HAIL⁴, HALE¹·², HALE¹·³, HEAL¹·¹

hailly *see* HAIL¹·²

hailse *see* HELSE

hailsing *see* HELSIN

hailsome, halesome, †**hailsum,** †**helsum,** †**hoilsum** /ˈhelsəm/ *adj* **1** health-giving; beneficial *15-*. **2** curative, medicinal *la14-16*. **3** healthy, vigorous *16*. **4** able to protect from harm *e16*. [OE *healdsum* taking care of, protective]

hailumly *see* HAIL¹·²

hailykit *see* HELLICAT¹·²

hailzin *see* HELSIN

haim, hame, hem /hem, hɛm/ *n pl* the two curved pieces of wood or metal forming or covering the collar of a draught horse *la14-*. **hae the hems on** to curb, keep in order *20-*. **pit the hems on** to prevent, restrain *20-*. [MDu *hame*]

haim *see* HAME¹·¹

haimelt *see* HAMELT¹·¹

haimmer¹·¹, hemmer, hammer, *NE* **hawmer,** †**hamer,** †**halmer** /ˈhemər, ˈhɛmər, ˈhamər; *NE* ˈhɔmər/ *n* **1** a tool with a (metal) head for beating, breaking or driving nails *la14-*. **2** the heavy metal ball attached to a chain thrown in an athletic contest *la18-*. **3** clumsy or noisy working or walking; a clumsy noisy person *la18-19*. **hammerman 1** a craftsman using a hammer for metalwork *15-*. **2** *pl* the collective name for members of the Incorporation of Hammermen, traditionally craftsmen and now a charitable organization *la15-*. **hammer and block** a rough game in which a boy is swung by others against another boy who crouches on hands and knees *19, 20- NE*. **hammer, block and bible** = *hammer and block*. [OE *hamer*]

haimmer¹·², hammer, *NE* **haumer,** †**hamber** /ˈhemər, ˈhamər; *NE* ˈhɔmər/ *v* **1** to strike with a hammer (or other implement) *la16-*. **2** to work or walk in a clumsy, noisy way *la18-19, 20- N NE T*. **3** to thrash, beat up; to defeat heavily *la20-*. [see the noun]

hain, †**hane** /hen/ *v* **1** to enclose or protect (woodland or grassland) with a hedge or fence; to keep (ground) unused, preserve from grazing or cutting *15-*. **2** to keep back from use, spare, to save up; to be thrifty, hoard *16-*. **3** to protect from harm *18-*. **4** *of rain* to cease *la19- Sh*. [ON *hegna* to hedge, protect]

hain *see* HAAIN, HINE²

hainch¹·¹, hench, hinch, †**hanch** /ˈhenʃ, ˈhɛnʃ, ˈhɪnʃ/ *n* **1** the haunch *la15-*. **2** an underhand throw made by jerking the throwing arm against the thigh *19-*. **3** a limp, lameness *la19-*. **4** a boost or help up *20-*. **hench-bane** the hip-bone *16-*. **henchle-bane** = *hench-bane EC*. [ME *haunche*]

hainch¹·², hench, hinch /ˈhenʃ, ˈhɛnʃ, ˈhɪnʃ/ *v* **1** to throw (something) by jerking the arm against the thigh *la18-*. **2** to walk jerkily or with a limp *19-*. [see the noun]

haingle¹·¹, hingle, hangil /ˈheŋəl, ˈhɪŋəl, ˈhaŋəl/ *n* **1** an idle or slovenly person *la18-*. **2** *pl* influenza *19-*. **in the hangles** in a lazy mood *19- NE T*. [frequentative form of HING¹·¹]

haingle¹·², hingle /ˈheŋəl, ˈhɪŋəl/ *v* to move about feebly; to loiter, hang about *19-*. [see the noun]

haingle¹·³, hangel /ˈheŋəl, ˈhaŋəl/ *adj* lazy *19- NE*. [see the noun]

haining, hainin, †**haning** /ˈhenɪŋ, ˈhenɪn/ *n* **1** a piece of ground enclosed by a fence, hedge or wall (originally to protect a hay crop from cattle), frequently in place-names *la13-*. **2** a fence, hedge or wall forming the boundary of an enclosure *la15-*. **3** thrift, economy *la19- Ork NE*. **4** *pl* savings *19*. [verbal noun from HAIN]

haip *see* HEAP¹·¹, HEAP¹·²

hair¹·¹, *WC* **herr,** †**hare,** †**hayr,** †**heir** /her; *WC* hɛr/ *n* **1** the hairs growing on a person's scalp or skin; an animal's coat *la14-*. **2** something made of hair *la14-*. **3** a single hair *15-*. **4** the smallest amount, a whit or trace *15-*. **5** *of cattle* having a mixture of white and red or white and black hair, roan *16*. **haired, hairt,** †**harit 1** having hair (of a specified sort): ◊*lang-haired la15-*. **2** *of cattle* having a mixture of white and red or white and black hair, roan *16-e19*. **3** edged with fur or hair *16*. **hairen, hairin** made of hair *la16-19, 20- Sh Ork N NE T*. **hairclaith** cloth made of hair *la15-*. †**hairsay** a kind of serge or sey (partly made with hair) *17*. **hair-tether,** †**hairen tether,** †**herin teddir,** †**harin tedder** *witchcraft* a tether made of hair *la16-19, 20- Sh N NE*. **again the hair** contrary to the lie of hair or disposition; contrary to the meaning *17-19, 20- Sh H&I*. **a hair in the neck** a hold or means of influence or control over a person; a fault such as might give another such a hold *la15-19, 20- T WC*. **a hair to make a tether** a fuss about nothing, a trifle used as an excuse *18-*. **hae a hair on yer heid** to be clever, cautious or wise *19- H&I C*. **hair and hoof** every particle; the slightest particle *17-19, 20- Sh T*. †**of hair and of hyde** in its entirety, entirely *la15*. [OE *hǣr*]

hair¹·² /her/ *v* to free from hair *19-*. **hair the butter** to free farm butter from impurities such as hairs by passing a knife through it in all directions *19, 20- Ork*. [see the noun]

hair²·¹ /her/ *v of ploughed ground* to dry up *20- NE*. [OE *hārian* to grow grey]

hair²·², hare, har, haar, †**hayr** /her, har/ *adj* **1** grey or white with age *15-*. **2** *of weather* frosty, cold *la15-19, 20- literary*. **3** *of ground, rocks or stones* grey, greyish *14-e16*. **4** *of woods* bare, leafless or grey with lichen *13-16*. **hair-frost, haar-frost** hoarfrost *17-*. **hair-mould** mould on foods such as cheese, bread or jam exposed to damp *19-*. **hair-mouldit** mouldy, covered with mould *18-19, 20- NE T EC*; compare *hairy-mouldit* (HAIRY¹·²). **harestane, hairstane** a large, grey, moss-covered stone; a conspicuous stone used as a boundary mark, frequently in place-names *14-*. [OE *hār* grey, old]

hair *see* HARE, HEIR¹·¹

hairb *see* YERB

hairbour *see* HERBOUR¹·¹, HERBOUR¹·²

haird *see* HARD¹·²

hairie *see* HAIRY¹·²

hairm¹·¹, herm, harm, †**harme** /herm, hɛrm, harm/ *n* **1** injury, damage; hurt, wrong *la14-*. **2** *pl* sorrow, grief, distress *la15-16, 20- Sh*. **3** *pl* injuries, wounds *15-e16*. [OE *hearm*]

hairm¹·², herm, harm /herm, hɛrm, harm/ *v* to hurt, injure; to wrong *la15-*. [OE *hearmian*]

hairns *see* HARNS

hairp *see* HARP¹·¹, HARP¹·²

hairrial *see* HEREZELD

hairry *see* HERRY

hairse, *N* **hais,** *Bor* **hersh,** †**hers,** †**hace** /hers; *N* hes; *Bor* herʃ/ *adj* hoarse, rough-sounding, raucous *la15-*. [OE *hās*]

hairshach *see* HARESHARD

hairst¹·¹, hairvest, hervest, harvest, †**harst** /herst, ˈhervəst, ˈhɛrvəst, ˈharvəst/ *n* **1** (the time of) reaping and gathering in of crops or produce *15-*. **2** a job as a harvest labourer *19-*. **3** the autumn *la15-19, 20- Sh NE T*. **hairst blinks** summer lightning *20- Sh Ork*. **har'st fee** the wages paid to a harvest worker *la16, la19- Ork NE*. **hairst folk** workers hired for the harvest *la18-*. †**hervest hog** a young sheep once it has been smeared with liniment after the harvest *16-e19*.

hairst knot, harvest knot a loop of twisted straw worn in a buttonhole, or as a decoration by the horses at harvest time *20- Ork EC*. **harvest plait** = *hairst knot 20-*. **hairst play** school holidays taken during the harvest *19- N NE*. **hairst rig** a harvest field *18-*. †**hairst vacance** = *hairst play 17-19*. **awe a day in hairst** to owe a favour *19-*. **hae a day in hairst** to have a score to settle *19-*. [OE *hærfest*]

hairst[1,2], **hairvest, hervest, harvest** /hɛrst, 'hɛrvəst, 'hɛrvəst, 'harvəst/ *v* to gather in crops or other produce; to work in the harvest field *la19-*. [see the noun]

hairt *see* HAIRTH, HART, HERT[1.1]

hairth, herth, hearth, *Sh* **hert,** †**harth,** †**hairt** /hɛrθ, hɛrθ, harθ; *Sh* hɛrt/ *n* the base of a fireplace, a hearth *16-*. [OE *heorþ*]

hairt-scaud *see* HERTSCAD
hairtsome *see* HERTSOME
hairty *see* HERTY
hairvest *see* HAIRST[1.1], HAIRST[1.2]

hairy[1.1], *WC* **herry** /'hɛri, 'hɛre; *WC* 'hɛre/ *n* a woman from the slums thought to be promiscuous; a prostitute *20-*. [see the adj]

hairy[1.2], †**hairie,** †**hary** /'hɛri, 'hɛre/ *adj* **1** having or consisting of thick or coarse hair; covered with hair *la16-*. **2** *of work* untidy, rough, slovenly *20- SW*. **3** made of hair *la16-e17*. **hairy grannie** a large hairy caterpillar *20-*. **hairy heid** the red-breasted merganser *Mergus serrator 20- Ork*. **hairy hurcheon** a sea-urchin of the family *Echinidae 19- NE EC*. **hairy moggans** footless stockings *19- N NE EC*. **hairy-mouldit** mouldy; covered in mould filaments *20-*; compare *hair-mouldit* (HAIR[2.2]). **hairy-oobit** the woolly-bear caterpillar *19-*. **hairy tatties** mashed potatoes mixed with flaked, dried salt fish *20- NE*. **hairy-worm** the woolly-bear caterpillar *20- NE T EC*. [HAIR[1.1] + -IE[2]]

hais *see* HAE[1.2], HAIRSE
haisk *see* HASK[1.1]
haist *see* HEEST
haister *see* HASTER[1.1], HASTER[1.2]
haistine *see* HEEST
hait *see* HATE, HET[1.1], HET[1.2]

haith, heth /heθ, hɛθ/ *interj* a mild oath *17-*. [perhaps altered form of FETH[1.2]]

†**haithehen, aithehen, heath-hen** *n* the female of the black grouse, a heath hen *la16-e18*. [unknown]

haithen[1.1], **heathen,** *Sh* **haethin,** †**hethin** /'heðən, 'hiðən; *Sh* 'heθɪn/ *n* **1** someone who does not believe in an established religion; a person perceived to be uncultured or uncivilized *la14-*. **2** an intractable or difficult person or thing *20- Sh Ork EC Uls*. [see the adj]

haithen[1.2], **heathen,** *Sh* **haethin,** †**thethin,** †**theithin** /'heðən, 'hiðən; *Sh* 'heθɪn/ *adj* lacking religion; outlandish, incomprehensible *15-*. [OE *hæþen* heathen]

haithen[2], **heathen** /'heðən, 'hiðən/ *n* a lump of gneiss or similar stone, a glacial boulder *19- NE*. [perhaps reduced form of Eng *heath-stone*]

haither *see* HEATHER
haitrent *see* HATRED
haitsum *see* HATESUM
haive *see* HEAVE[1.2]

haiveless, haveless, haweless, †**hafles** /'hevləs, 'havləs, 'hɔləs/ *adj* **1** shiftless, incapable, careless, extravagant *19- NE*. **2** senseless, meaningless *19- NE*. **3** destitute *la15*. [OE *hafenlēas* poor]

haiven *see* HIVVEN

haiver[1.1] /'hevər/ *n* **1** *pl* nonsense, foolish talk, gossip, chatter *la18-*. **2** a piece of nonsense, a foolish whim or notion *19-*. **3** a chat, a gossip *19-*. **4** a person who talks nonsense *20-*. [unknown]

haiver[1.2], **haver** /'hevər/ *v* **1** to talk in a foolish or trivial way, speak nonsense *la18-*. **2** to dawdle, potter about; to lounge *la19-*. **3** to make a fuss about nothing, make a pretence of being busy *la19- NE WC Uls*. [unknown]

haiverel[1.1], **havrel,** *Sh* **hyveral,** †**haveril** /'hevərəl, 'hevrəl; *Sh* 'haevərəl/ *n* **1** a foolishly chattering or garrulous person, a silly person *la18-*. **2** a lazy person *e18, la19- Sh*. [unknown]

haiverel[1.2], †**haveril** /'hevərəl/ *adj* **1** garrulous, speaking foolishly *la18-19, 20- SW*. **2** foolish, stupid, nonsensical *la18-19, 20- Uls*. [unknown]

haiverin *see* HAIVERING[1.1], HAIVERING[1.2]

haivering[1.1], **havering, haverin, haiverin** /'hevərɪŋ, 'hevərɪn/ *n* chatter, gossip, nonsense *19-*. [verbal noun from HAIVER[1.2]]

haivering[1.2], **havering, haverin, haiverin,** †**havren** /'hevərɪŋ, 'hevərɪn/ *adj* babbling, gossiping, garrulous; nonsensical *18-*. [participial adj from HAIVER[1.2]]

haivins, havins, †**havings,** †**hauingis** /'hevɪnz, 'havɪnz/ *npl* behaviour, manners *la15-*. [verbal noun from *have* (HAE[1.2])]

haizer, hazer /'hezər/ *v of clothes* to dry partially, air in the open, bleach in the sun *19-*. [compare Norw *hesja* to dry hay or corn on a wooden frame]

hak *see* HACK[1.1], HAWK[1.1]
hakbut *see* HAGBUTE
†**hake, hak, heck** *n* a hook *15-17*. [ON *haki*, MDu *hake*]
hakk *see* HACK[1.1]
hakket, hakkit *see* HACKIT
halch *see* HAUGH
†**halcrek, halcrik** *n* a half-suit of light armour, worn by footmen and horsemen *16*. [MFr *halecret*]
halcrik *see* HALCREK
hald *see* HAUD[1.1], HAUD[1.2]

Haldaneite, †**Haldanite** /'haldənʌɪt/ *n* a follower of Robert and James Haldane, leaders of an early-nineteenth-century Scottish evangelical movement *19, 20- historical*. [from the surname *Haldane*]

haldin *see* HAUD[1.2]
halding *see* HAUDIN

hale[1.1], **hail** /hel/ *n* a haul of fish; the hauling in of nets *la18-19, 20- Sh*. Compare HAUL[1.1]. [see the verb]

hale[1.2], **haill** /hel/ *v* **1** *of rain or tears* to flow copiously, run down, pour *16-*. **2** *in nautical use* to haul, drag, pull (up) *15-19, 20- Sh NE*. **3** to move quickly *la15-e17*. Compare HAUL[1.2]. [ME *halen*]

†**hale**[1.3], **haill** *interj in nautical use* an exclamation used when hauling *16*. [see the verb]

hale *see* HAIL[1.1], HAIL[1.2], HAIL[1.3], HAIL[3.2], HAIL[4], HEAL[1.1], HEAL[1.2]
halesome *see* HAILSOME
†**half, haave** *n* = HAAF-NET *17-19*. [shortened form of HAAF-NET]
half *see* HAUF[1.1], HAUF[1.2], HAUF[1.3], HAUF[1.4]
half-disch *see* HADDISH
halfe-net *see* HAAF-NET
halfers *see* HAUFERS
halff *see* HAUF[1.1]
halffet *see* HAFFET
halfheid *see* HAFFET
halfins *see* HALFLINS[1.2]

halflin[1.1] /'haflɪn/ *n* **1** a half-grown boy, an adolescent youth *la17-*. **2** a person with learning difficulties *19- N Bor Uls*. **3** a half-mature herring *20- EC*. [HAUF[1.3], with -*ling* suffix]

halflin[1.2] /'haflɪn/ *adj* **1** half-grown *18-*. **2** of an intermediate or half-size *la18-*. **haflin-plane** a large plane used by carpenters *19-*. [see the noun]

†**halfling** *adv* halfway *15-16*. [HALFLIN[1.2]]

halflings see HALFLINS[1,2]

†**halflins**[1.1] *adj* half, partial; half-grown, young *19*. [HALFLIN[1.1], with -*s*]

halflins[1.2], **hafflins**, †**halflings**, †**halfins** /ˈhaflɪnz/ *adv* **1** halfway, midway *la18-*. **2** half, partly, almost *16-19, 20- NE*. [see the adj]

halgh see HAUGH

haliday see HOALIDAY

halie see HALY

halison see HELSIN

halk see HAWK[1.1], HAWK[1.2]

Halkerton's Cow /ˈhakərtənz kʌu/ *interj* an expression of disbelief *la17-*. **like Halkerton's Cow** a situation different from or the opposite of what was expected *la19-*. [from the name of a farm near Laurencekirk]

halkit see HAWKIT

hall see HA[1]

halla see HALLOW[1.1], HALLOW[1.3]

hallaby /ˈhaləbe/ *n* a word in children's counting rhymes *la19-*. [nonsense word]

hallach see HALLICH[1.2], HALLICH[1.3]

Hallaleen see HALLOWEEN

Hallamass see HALLOWMASS

hallan, †**halland**, †**hallen**, †**hallon** /ˈhalən/ *n* **1** an inner wall, partition or door-screen *16-19, 20- N NE*. **2** a cottage, a house *19, 20- EC*. **3** a hen-roost *20- Ork*. **4** an inside porch or passage formed by an inner wall or partition *19*. **hallan-end** the area between the outer wall of the house and the inner wall *la18-19, 20- SW*. **hallanshaker**, †**halland schekker** a beggar or tramp *16- literary*. **hallanstane** a stone dividing cattle stalls in a byre *20- N*. †**hallan-wa** an inner wall or partition *19*. [unknown]

hallet /ˈhalət/ *n* a wild, frivolous girl *20- Ork*. [altered form of HALLICH[1.1]]

hallicat see HELLICAT[1.2]

hallich[1.1], *SW* **hellock**, †**halok** /ˈhaləx; *SW* ˈhɛlək/ *n* a thoughtless, foolish young person *16-19, 20- NE SW Bor*. [unknown]

hallich[1.2], **hallach** /ˈhaləx/ *v* to behave in a crazy, wild or irresponsible way *la19, 20- T EC*. [unknown]

hallich[1.3], **hallach** /ˈhaləx/ *adj* **1** crazy, foolish *19- NE*. **2** uncouth, noisy *20- NE*. [unknown]

Halliday see HALLOWDAY

halligalant /halɪɡəˈlant/ *n* a boisterous celebration *20- Sh*. [unknown; compare HEELIEGOLEERIE[1.1]]

halligate see HELLICAT[1.1]

halliget see HELLICAT[1.2]

halligolum /halɪɡoˈlʌm/ *n* a word in children's counting rhymes *la19-*. [nonsense word]

halliket see HELLICAT[1.2]

hallion, *Sh SW* **hullion** /ˈhaljən; *Sh SW* ˈhʌljən/ *n* a slovenly-looking or clumsy person; a rogue; a fool *la18-*. [unknown]

hallirackit /ˈhalɪrakət, halɪˈrakət/ *adj* frivolous, crazy, boisterous *19-*. Compare HELLICAT[1.2]. [unknown]

†**hallirakus** *n* a foolish, hare-brained person *19*. [altered form of HALLIRACKIT]

hallo see HALLOW[3]

hallockit see HELLICAT[1.2]

hallok see HALLOW[3]

hallon see HALLAN

hallow[1.1], **halla** /ˈhalo, ˈhalə/ *n* a hollow, dip or valley *18-*. [OE *holh*]

hallow[1.2] /ˈhalo/ *v* to make hollow *19-*. [see the adj]

hallow[1.3], **halla** /ˈhalo, ˈhalə/ *adj* hollow, concave *la16-*. [ME *holwe*]

†**hallow**[2] *n* a saint *la14-15*. [OE *hālga*]

hallow[3], **hallo**, †**hallok** /ˈhalo/ *n* a bundle of straw *la16- Sh Ork N*. [compare Norw dial *halge*]

†**Hallow Court** *n* a meeting of a craft or trades court held on All Saints' Day, 1 November *17-18*. [shortened form of ALHALLOW + *court* (COORT[1.1])]

Hallowday, *Uls* **Halliday** /ˈhalode; *Uls* ˈhalɪde/ *n* All Saints' Day *la16-*. [shortened form of ALHALLOW + DAY]

Halloween, *C SW* **Hallaleen**, *Uls* **Halloweve**, †**Hallowen**, †**Hallow evin** /haloˈin; *C SW* haləˈlin; *Uls* haloˈiv/ *n* 31 October, the eve of All Saints' Day, a children's festival where guisers receive money or sweets in exchange for the performance of a joke or song; originally the last day of the year in the old Celtic calendar *la16-*. [shortened form of ALHALLOW + EVEN[1]]

Hallowfair /ˈhalofer/ *n* a market held on 1 November, especially a cattle market in Edinburgh *18-20, 21- historical*. [shortened form of ALHALLOW + FAIR[2]]

hallow-fire /ˈhalofaer/ *n* a Halloween bonfire *17-19, 20- historical*. [shortened form of ALHALLOW + FIRE[1.1]]

Hallowmass, *Sh* **Halomas**, *EC* **Hallamass**, †**Hallowmes** /ˈhalomas; *Sh* ˈhɑlomas; *EC* ˈhaləmas/ *n* All Saints' Day *16-19, 20- Sh NE T EC*. [shortened form of ALHALLOW + MASS[2]]

†**Hallowtide** *n* the first week (or day) in November *la17-e18*. [shortened form of ALHALLOW + TIDE[1.1]]

hally see HALY

halmer see HAIMMER[1.1]

halok see HALLICH[1.1]

Halomas see HALLOWMASS

halpeny see HAUF[1.3]

hals see HAUSE[1.1]

halse see HAUSE[1.2], HELSE

halsing see HELSIN

halslok see HAUSE[1.1]

halt see HAUT[1.1], HAUT[1.2]

halta dance /ˈhalta dans/ *n* **1** a frantic struggle, a mad rushing about *20- Sh*. **2** gossamer, a shimmering motion; a heat-haze *20- Sh*. [ON *haltr* halt, lame, limping + *danz* dance, the fairies, in Shetland tradition, limping when they dance]

haltagongi, **haltugonga** /ˈhaltaɡɔŋɡi, ˈhaltuɡɔŋɡa/ *interj fisherman's taboo* an invocation intended to check the running of a big fish after it is hooked *la19- Sh*. [ON *haltú göngu* stop your going]

haltand, **haltane** see HAUTANE

halth, **health**, †**helth** /halθ, hɛlθ/ *n* physical condition, well-being, health *16-*. [OE *hǽlþ*]

haltugonga see HALTAGONGI

halucket see HELLICAT[1.2]

halve see HAUF[1.1]

halve-net see HAAF-NET

halver[1.1], **haaver**, †**hawfar** /ˈhavər/ *n* a half-share *16-*. [HAUF[1.1], with -*er* suffix]

halver[1.2], **haaver** /ˈhavər/ *v* to halve, divide equally; to hold in partnership with someone *19- Sh Ork N NE*. [iterative form of HAUF[1.2]]

halvers[1.1], **havers** /ˈhavərz/ *adj* held in partnership, jointly owned *la19- Sh*. [see the adv]

halvers[1.2], **havers** /ˈhavərz/ *adv* jointly, as equal partners *la19- Sh*. [probably HALVER[1.1], with adv-forming suffix]

halvers see HAUFERS

haly, **halie**, **holy**, †**helly**, †**hally** /ˈheli, ˈhele, ˈholi, ˈhole/ *adj* sacred; pertaining or dedicated to God, venerated as such *13-*. †**haly band** the kirk session *18*. †**halyblude**, **halie bluid 1** the blood of Christ or a saint venerated as a relic *la15-17*. **2** the blood of Christ, adopted as the patron of the merchant guilds of pre-Reformation burghs *16*. †**halyblude mes** a mass in honour of the holy blood *la15-e16*. **holy**

dabbies a kind of shortbread used in place of bread at Holy Communion *19, 20-* historical. †**Holy Fair** the celebration of Communion in the Presbyterian Church *la18-e19*. **Haly Ghaist**, †**haligast**, †**holie gaist** *Christian Church* the third person of the Trinity *la14-*. **hallie hoo**, *C* **hully-hoo**, †**haly-how** the caul sometimes on the head of a newborn child, regarded as a good omen *18-*. **haly hoose** a church *la19-*. †**haly kirk** (the institution of) the Roman Catholic Church *la14-17*. **halyman's rig**, †**helliman rig** a strip of land left uncultivated to propitiate the Devil *17, 20-* historical. **Holy Rood**, †**halie rude** *Christian Church* the cross on which Jesus Christ was crucified *la15-*; compare HOLYROOD. †**Haly spreit, hellie spereit** = *Haly Ghaist la14-e17*. [OE *hālig*]

haly day see HOALIDAY

halyert, hal3ar see HAUF[1.3]

ham see HUM[1.1], HUM[1.2]

ham-a-haddie, **ham'n'haddie**, **hammy-haddie** /ˈhaməhadi, ˈhamənhadi, ˈhamihadi/ *n* **1** a breakfast dish of bacon and smoked haddock sometimes topped with a poached egg *20-*. **2** a confused situation or unlikely story; a mix-up; a fuss *20- T C Bor*. [Scots *ham* + HADDIE]

hamald see HAMELT[1.2]

hamart see HAMEART

hamber see HAIMMER[1.2]

†**Hamburgh barrel** *n* a large barrel, originally 14 gallons, commonly used for salmon *15-16*. [from the name of the German port + BARREL[1.1]]

hame[1.1], **haim**, **home**, *Sh* **hem**, *Ork* **heem**, †**haym** /hem, hom; *Sh* hɛm; *Ork* him/ *n* a person's house or native area, the place where a person was born or brought up *la14-*. **hame aboot 1** at home *20- Ork.* **2** homely *20- Sh.* **hamebider** a local resident; especially a native of Bo'ness, West Lothian or Anstruther, Fife *20-*. **hame-drauchtit 1** keen to further the interests of oneself or one's home; selfish *la19- NE.* **2** homesick; fond of, or drawn to home *20- NE.* **hame draw-in** selfish *la19- NE H&I SW Bor.* **hame folk** family, relatives *20- Sh NE.* **hame made 1** (something) made at home *19-.* **2** homely, rustic, unrefined *20-.* **hame trowe**, †**hame through**, †**hame throw** (straight) homewards *la16-19, 20- Sh.* [OE *hām*]

hame[1.2], **home**, *Sh* **hem**, *Ork* **heem** /hem, hom; *Sh* hɛm; *Ork* him/ *adv* **1** (back) to one's home *la14-.* **2** at home *la15-.* †**hame bring** to fetch from a distance; to import *la16-17*. †**hame bringar** an importer *la16-17*. †**hame bringing** the action of bringing home, or escorting or importing from a distance *la15-17*. **hame come 1** arrival *19, 20- Sh N NE.* **2** a coming or return home *la14-16.* **hame comin**, **hame coming**, †**hame cumming 1** a coming or return home *la14-*. **2** festivities on the arrival of a bride at her new home *la19-.* **3** a birth *20-*. **hame farin** staying at home *la19, 20- Sh WC.* **hame fir, hame fare** a coming or return home *19-.* †**hamefrie** in *Shetland* the security of one's home *e17.* **hame-gaun 1** a return (journey), the act of going home *la18-.* **2** death; the burial of the dead *la19-.* **3** homeward bound, returning home *la19-.* **bring hame 1** to fetch from a distance; to import *la14-.* **2** of *a mother or midwife* to cause to be born, bring to birth *la18-.* **come hame 1** of *a baby* to be born *la18-.* **2** to find or enter into employment *19-.* **3** to arrive at one's destination *20- Sh T H&I.* **enter hame** to find or enter into employment *17-.* **gae hame, gang hame** to die *19-.* **get hame** to import *17-18, 20- Ork H&I.* **pay hame** to pay back, avenge, punish *la16-19, 20- Sh.* [see the noun]

hame none see HAIM

hameart, *T EC SW* **hamer**, †**hamart** /ˈhemərt; *T EC SW* ˈhemər/ *adj* **1** home-made, home-grown *la15-*. **2** unsophisticated *la18-19, 20- T.* **3** of *speech* vernacular, Scots *la18-19*. Compare HAMELT[1.2]. **hamert-made** home-made *la19, 20- T.* [altered form of HAMELT[1.2], perhaps with infl from HAMEWART[1.1]]

†**hamehald, haymhald** *v law* to claim an animal as one's own property *15-e17*. [from the noun HAMELT[1.1]]

hamehald see HAMELT[1.1], HAMELT[1.2]

hameil see HAMELT[1.2]

hameint see HAMIT

hamel see HAMELT[1.2]

hamelott see HAMLOTT

hamelt[1.1], **haimelt, hemmald**, †**hamehald**, †**haymald** /ˈhemǝlt, ˈhɛmǝld/ *n* **1** pasture near a farm *20- Sh.* **2** fisherman's taboo a housewife; a wife *20- Sh.* **3** legal possession *14-e19*; compare *brogh and hammell* (BORROW[1.1]). [ON *heimild* title to or right of possession]

hamelt[1.2], **hammel, hamel, hamald**, †**hameil**, †**hamehald** /ˈhemǝlt, ˈhemǝl, ˈhemǝld/ *adj* **1** belonging to home, domestic, internal; home-made, home-bred, home-grown *16-.* **2** of *language* vernacular, Scots *18-.* **3** homely, familiar, plain *19- N NE T WC Bor.* [ON *heimoll* domestic]

hamely[1.1], †**hamly**, †**haymly** /ˈhemle/ *adj* **1** friendly, familiar, intimate; kind, courteous *la14-*. **2** simple, plain, unaffected *la15-.* **3** blunt, outspoken *16-e17*. **hameliness**, †**hamlynes 1** familiarity, lack of ceremony, intimacy; kindness *la14-.* **2** bluntness in speech *la15-e17*. [HAME[1.1], with adj-forming suffix]

hamely[1.2] /ˈhemle/ *adv* **1** in a friendly fashion, kindly, courteously *la14-*. **2** familiarly, as if at home *15-.* **3** candidly, bluntly *16.* [see the adj]

hameower[1.1], †**hame-o'er** /ˈhemʌur/ *adj* **1** of *speech* simple, plain, unaffected; in the Scots vernacular *18-.* **2** familiar, intimate *la19- T.* [HAME[1.1] + OWER[1.2]]

hameower[1.2], †**hame over**, †**hame-o'er** /ˈhemʌur/ *adv* homewards *la16-19, 20- Sh T.* [see the adj]

hamer see HAIMMER[1.1], HAMEART

hamesucken[1.1], †**hamesukkin**, †**hemsuckenn**, †**hamesokyn** /ˈhemsʌkən/ *n law* an assault upon a person in their dwelling-place *la13-*. [OE *hāmsōcn*, ON *heimsókn*]

†**hamesucken**[1.2] *adj* greatly attached to one's home; selfish *19.* [HAME[1.1] + SUCKEN[1.3]]

hamet see HAMIT

hamewart[1.1], **hameward, homeward**, *NE* **hamewith** /ˈhemwǝrt, ˈhemwǝrd, ˈhomwǝrd; *NE* ˈhemwɪθ/ *adj* towards home *la17-.* [see the adv]

hamewart[1.2], **hameward, homeward**, *NE T* **hamewith**, *T* **hamewath**, †**haymwart**, †**hamwart** /ˈhemwǝrt, ˈhemwǝrd, ˈhomwǝrd; *NE T* ˈhemwɪθ; *T* ˈhemwaθ/ *adv* to or towards home *la14-.* **hamewards**, †**hamewartis** homewards *la14-.* [OE *hāmweard*]

hamfish, hemfish, humfish, †**hamphise** /ˈhamfɪʃ, ˈhɛmfɪʃ, ˈhʌmfɪʃ/ *v* to surround, hem in, confine; to curb *la18- NE.* [altered form of Scots *handfast* to tie the hands of, manacle]

hamit, hamet, *EC Bor* **hameint**, †**hemmit** /ˈhemɪt; *EC Bor* ˈhemɪnt/ *adj* **1** home-produced, home-grown *la16-19, 20- T EC.* **2** home-loving, homely, familiar *20-.* **3** vernacular; rude, uncouth, untidy *20- EC.* [altered form of HAMELT[1.2] or HAMEART]

hamlock see HUMLOCK

†**hamlott, hamelott** *n* a quarter of the holding of a forest-keeper *la15-e16*. [unknown]

hamly see HAMELY[1.1]

hammel see HAMELT[1.2], HEMMEL

hammeler see HUMMEL[1.2]

hammer see HAIMMER[1.1], HAIMMER[1.2]

†hammer-stand *n* = HAMBURGH BARREL *la15-e16*. [from the place-name *Hamburgh* + STAND¹·¹]
hammle /'haməl/ *v* to walk with a limp, hobble *19- Bor.* [probably nasalized form from HABBLE¹·²]
hammy-haddie, ham'n'haddie *see* HAM-A-HADDIE
hamp /hamp/ *v* to stutter, stammer; to read with difficulty or hesitation *la18- C SW Bor.* [unknown]
Hampden Roar /hamdən 'rɔr/ *n* **1** the cheer of the crowd at Hampden Park in Glasgow *20-*. **2** *rhyming slang* score *la20-*. [from the name of the stadium + RAIR¹·¹]
hamper /'hampər/ *v* to confine or restrict; to hinder, cramp *15-*. [unknown; compare HAIM]
hamphise *see* HAMFISH
hamrel /'hamrəl/ *n* a person who often stumbles; an awkward person *19, 20- NE*. [unknown]
hamsh *see* HANCH¹·²
hamshoch *see* AMSHACH
hamsy /'hɑmsi/ *adj of a thing* coarse; *of a person* wild, erratic *20- Ork.* [unknown]
hamwart *see* HAMEWART¹·²
han¹·¹, haun, hon, hand, haund, *Sh* **haand** /han, hɔn, hand, hɔnd; *Sh* hand/ *n* **1** the palm, fingers and thumb; the hand *la14-*. **2** direction, quarter, neighbourhood: ◊*near han; frae aboot Auchneel han 15-*. **3** a horse that walks on the unploughed land at the left-hand side of a plough-team *la19-*. **4** a person who has a particular liking for something: ◊*I'm no much o a cake-hand la20-*. **5** a handle *la15-19, 20- Sh NE EC*. **6** a handful *20- Sh Ork*. **7** *pl* bearings, landmarks *20- Sh*. **8** a cuff *16-17*. **hanfu, †handfull** a quantity that fills the hand *la15-16*. **handit, handed** fitted with a handle or handles *la16-*. **handless, †handles** *of people* awkward, clumsy, incompetent, slow *la16-*. **hands** a pair of bats for shaping butter *la19-*. **far hand** *of applicants for membership of the Incorporated Trades* unrelated or unconnected to an existing or former member *la18-*. **hand band, haun band 1** the wristband or cuff of a shirt *la18-*. **2** *in Orkney* a handshake to seal a bargain *la15-16*. **hand barrow** a wooden frame with shafts, carried by two people *la18-*. **hand breed** the width of a hand *la15-*. **hand chair** a chair easily lifted by hand *20- NE T EC*. **hand clap, han clap** a clap of the hands; the time taken to clap the hands, an instant *la18-*. **hand cloot** a towel *la19-*. **†hand cuff** a wrist-piece or cuff *17*. **†han' daurk** labour *la18*. **hand dud** a coarse hand towel *20- NE EC*. **hand fast 1** to betroth; to become engaged (especially implying a probationary period of cohabitation before marriage) *la14-*. **2** fully occupied, busy *20- Sh NE*. **†hand habble** quickly, without premeditation *19*. **haund haill** healthy, fit for work *la19- Sh NE*. **†hand havand** *of a thief* with the stolen article in the hand *16-e17*. **hand idle** having nothing to occupy one's hands, with idle hands *19-*. **hanlawhile** a short space of time *19- Bor*. **hand lin, †hand ling, †hand lyne** a fishing-line worked by hand *16- Sh Ork N NE T*. **hand makin** the making of an article by hand *la19- Sh T*. **hand plane** a carpenter's smoothing-plane *19-*. **hand shaking** a handshake marking the conclusion of a bargain *20- Sh EC Bor*. **hand sho, hand skuve** a mitten, a fingerless glove *19- Ork N*. **haandspik, †handspaik, †handspake 1** one of a number of bars of wood used to carry a coffin *18-19, 20- Sh*. **2** a wooden bar used as a lever *16-18*. **hand staff** the handle of a flail *17-19, 20- Ork N*. **hand-trist 1** to separate threshed corn from the straw by hand-sifting; make straw into bundles by twisting *la19- Sh*. **2** to rummage, ransack *20- Sh*. **hand wale** to select or sort by hand *la19- NE EC SW*. **hand waled** hand-picked, choice *la17-*. **hand write, †hand writ** handwriting; penmanship; a person's signature *la15-19, 20- NE EC*. **nearhand** *of applicants for membership of the Incorporated Trades* related or connected to an existing or former member *la18-*. **aboot hans, about hand** at hand, in the vicinity *19-*. **†above yer hand** beyond one's authority or comprehension *19*. **aff yer hand** on one's authority, on one's initiative *la17-19, 20- C*. **amang hands** at spare moments, at intervals *18-19, 20- NE SW*. **amang one's hands 1** on hand, current *18-*. **2** in one's possession *17-18*. **at the far hand** *of applicants for membership of the Incorporated Trades* unrelated or unconnected to a member or former member *la18-*. **at the near hand** *of applicants for membership of the Incorporated Trades* related or apprenticed to a member or former member *la18-*. **†at your ain hand** by oneself, on one's own account or initiative *la15-19*. **†before the hand, befoir the hand** beforehand *la15-e17*. **behind the hand** in arrears, late, after the event *la15-19, 20- T WC Uls*. **between hands** in the interval *18-*. **by the hand** in reserve, at one's disposal, available *19, 20- Ork NE*. **by one's hand** *in oaths* used to signify assent or given as a pledge *la15, 20- Sh*. **for your own hand** for one's own part, in one's own interest *18-*. **†fra hand** at once *16-e17*. **hae through hands** to deal with, investigate *la18-*. **han' for nieve** hand in hand, abreast; hand in glove *la18-19, 20- N NE*. **hand in hand** side by side, together *15-*. **hand of write, hand o writ** handwriting, style of writing *18-*. **hand ower heid** indiscriminately *17-*. **†han' to nieve, hand to nive** hand to hand *18-e19*. **in hand** *of a sum of money* in cash *la15-16*. **†in hands 1** in captivity, under arrest *la14-e19*. **2** in close combat *la15-17*. **in hands with** occupied with, engaged in *17-*. **keep in hand** to keep in suspense; to delay *19, 20- H&I EC*. **†off a person's hand** on a person's authority *la17*. **tak through hands** = *hae through hands*. **there's my hand** an expression of assurance *la18- EC SW Bor Uls*. [OE *hand*]
han¹·², haun, hand /han, hɔn, hand/ *v* **1** to pass or deliver from one hand to another *la18-*. **2** to advise or assist a competitor at a ploughing match *20- H&I SW Uls*. **hander** an adviser, a helper *20- H&I SW Uls*. [see the noun]
hanch¹·¹ /hanʃ/ *n* a voracious snap or snatch *19- SW Uls*. [see the verb]
hanch¹·², hansh, *NE T* **hamsh,** *Uls* **hantch** /hanʃ; *NE T* hamʃ; *Uls* hantʃ/ *v* **1** to snap at, show the teeth; to snatch, bite, eat voraciously *17-*. **2** to take for one's own use *la19- NE T*. [ME *hanchen*, EModE *hansch*]
hanch *see* HAINCH¹·¹
hanchman, †haunchman /'hanʃmən/ *n* the personal attendant of a Highland chief, a trusted follower or bodyguard *18-19, 20- T*. [altered form of Eng *henchman*]
hanckleth *see* ANKLET
hand *see* HAN¹·¹, HAN¹·²
hand-ba, hand-ball /'hanbɔ, 'hanbɔl/ *n* **1** a game involving throwing or catching a ball with the hands *16-*. **2** an outdoor team game played between two goals, and in which a small ball is thrown and caught with the hands; particularly as played on certain annual holidays in the Borders *la19-*. [HAN¹·¹ + BA¹]
handie, handy, hannie /'handi, 'hande, 'hani/ *n* **1** a hand *18-*. **2** a small wooden tub or pail for carrying liquids, especially a milk-pail with one of the staves projecting to form a handle *la17-19, 20- T C SW Bor*. **hanifu** a handful *20- NE*. **handigrip** a handhold on a boat *20- Sh Ork*. [HAN¹·¹ + -IE¹]
handill *see* HANLE¹·²
handle *see* HANLE¹·¹, HANLE¹·²
handlin, handling *see* HANLIN
handsel *see* HANSEL¹·¹
handsenʒe *see* ENSENYIE
handy¹·¹ /'handi/ *adj* **1** done with the hands; dexterous, skilful *la15-*. **2** to hand, close by; available, accessible; convenient,

useful *16-*. **3** easy to accomplish or put up with *19-*. **4** *of an animal* quiet to handle, amenable, adaptable *la18- NE*. †**handie labourar** one who works with his hands, a manual worker *la16-e17*. **handy-wife** an unqualified midwife *la19-*. **nae handy** not easy to accomplish or put up with *19-*. [HAN[1.1] + -IE[2]]

handy[1.2] /'handi/ *adv* easily; skilfully; moderately *la19-*. [see the adj]

handy *see* HANDIE
hane *see* HAIN
hanet *see* HAUF[1.3]
hang *see* HING[1.1], HING[1.2]
hangar *see* HINGER
hangel *see* HAINGLE[1.3]
hanger *see* HINGER
hangie[1] /'haŋe/ *n* a hang-net *19-, 20- T SW Bor*. [shortened form of HANG-NET]
†**hangie**[2] *n* a hangman *18-19*. [shortened form of HANGMAN]
hangil *see* HAINGLE[1.1]
hanging *see* HINGIN
hangit *see* HING[1.2], HINGIT
hangman, †**thingman** /'haŋmən/ *n* **1** the person employed to execute people by hanging, an executioner *la15-*. **2** = *hangman cheese 20- NE*. **hangman cheese** a kind of cheese made by hanging the curds outdoors in a cloth *20- NE*. [ME *hangman*]
hang-net /'haŋnɛt/ *n* a vertical stake-net *19-*. [*hang* (HING[1.2]) + NET]
hangrell /'haŋrɛl/ *n* **1** a stick or arm on which something is hung; the pole supporting carcasses in a butcher's shop *19- SW Bor*. **2** a knotty tree-branch for holding bridles in a stable *19- Bor*. **3** a curved bar to which a sack can be attached and held open for filling *20- EC*. **4** the gallows *la16*. [perhaps altered form of Eng *hang rail*]
haning *see* HAINING
hank[1.1] /haŋk/ *n* **1** a loop, a coil *15-*. **2** a skein of yarn of a certain length or weight *la16-*. **3** a hesitancy in speech; hesitation *la18-*. **4** influence, control *18-19, 20- SW Bor*. **5** a skein or coil of (gold or silver) wire or thread *16-17*. †**hae the hank in yer ain han** to have control of a situation *19*. †**hald ane hank** = *hae the hank in yer ain han la16-17*. †**haud the hank in yer ain han** = *hae the hank in yer ain han 19*. [ON *hönk*]
hank[1.2] /haŋk/ *v* **1** to entangle, ensnare, catch *la14-*. **2** to gather into coils or hanks, loop *18-*. **3** to fasten, attach or secure *15-19, 20- C*. **4** to tie tightly or constrict *la18-19, 20- NE Bor*. **hankle 1** to entangle *18-19, 20- SW*. **2** to coil up *la19- Sh*. **hankle aff** to unwind *la19- Sh*. [ON *hankask* to be coiled up]
hank[2] /haŋk/ *n* **1** the (stem or) stern compartment of a boat *20- Sh N NE*. **2** the place on each side of a boat where the side-board turns towards the stem or stern *la16, la19- Sh*. **hanksman** a rower seated in the stern of an open boat *la19- NE*. [ON *hanki* an eye or ring on the edge of a sail or on the side of a boat, sense transferred in Scots to that part of a boat to which such a ring was fitted]
hanker[1.1] /'haŋkər/ *n* a hesitation, a pause *19-*. [see the verb]
hanker[1.2] /'haŋkər/ *v* to loiter, linger expectantly; to hesitate, stammer *la18-*. [Du *hankeren* to linger expectantly, crave]
hankersaidil *see* ANKERSAIDELL
hankle *see* HANTLE[1.1]
hanlawhile *see* HAN[1.1]
hanle[1.1], **haunle**, **handle** /'hanəl, 'hɔnəl, 'handəl/ *n* **1** (a part of) a thing by which an object is meant to be grasped or held, a handle *19-*. **2** the shaft of a golf club *la19*. [OE *handle*]
hanle[1.2], **haunle**, **handle**, †**handill** /'hanəl, 'hɔnəl, 'handəl/ *v* **1** to deal with, treat or manage; to prepare *la14-*. **2** to lay hands on (a person) in a hostile way; to seize or capture *la15-*. **3** *curling* to drag off a stone that has failed to reach the hog-score by the handle *la19, 20- SW*. †**handallit** afflicted; harassed *la16-e17*. [OE *handlian*]

hanlin, **handlin**, **handling** /'hanlɪn, 'handlɪn, 'handlɪŋ/ *n* **1** manipulation, use, treatment; management, governance *16-*. **2** commercial dealing, trade; a business transaction *la16-*. **3** a job in hand, a difficult task *18-*. **4** a share or hand in something *19-*. **5** a person who is difficult to manage *la19-*. **6** the rounding up and penning of sheep for dipping or shearing *la19-*. **7** an entertainment, a meeting, a social gathering *19- WC SW Uls*. **8** an unpleasant experience, an ordeal *la19, 20- Ork T*. **9** the preparation of food *la15-e17*. **10** seizure, capture *la15-e17*. [verbal noun from HANLE[1.2]]

hannie *see* HANDIE
hansel[1.1], **handsel**, †**hansell** /'hansəl, 'handsəl/ *n* **1** a good-luck gift for something new or a new beginning (such as the New Year, a new house or new undertaking) *la14-*. **2** the money received by a trader for his first sale of the day or of a new business, to bring good luck *18-*. **3** a light snack given to farmworkers before beginning work *19- SW Uls*. **4** the first taste or experience of something *18-19*. **5** a first instalment of payment *17-19*. **Hansel Monday** the first Monday of the New Year, on which the New Year's gift was given (regarded as a holiday) *17-20, 21- historical*. [OE *handselen* giving into the hands of another; mancipation, ON *handsal* a pledge, a bargain]

hansel[1.2] /'hansəl/ *v* **1** to give or offer a good-luck gift *la15-*. **2** to inaugurate with a ceremony or a gift to bring good luck *18-*. **3** to use for the first time; to be the first to try, test or taste *18-*. **4** *in Orkney* to make over formally by shaking hands *e14*. [see the noun]

hansell *see* HANSEL[1.1]
hansh *see* HANCH[1.2]
hansper /'hanspər/ *n* muscular pains or stiffness in the legs *20- Sh*. [compare Faer *andsperri*]
hant *see* HAUNT[1.1], HAUNT[1.2]
hantch *see* HANCH[1.2]
hantle[1.1], **hankle**, †**hantill** /'hantəl, 'haŋkəl/ *n* **1** an unspecified quantity (of things or people); a great deal *16-*. **2** *in Travellers' language* the settled population *la20-*. †**hantla** a great deal of *18-e19*. **a hantle sicht** a great deal, much *19-*. [unknown]

hantle[1.2] /'hantəl/ *adv* much, to a great extent *19-*. [unknown]
hantrin *see* ANTRIN[1.2]
hanty, **haunty** /'hanti, 'hɔnti/ *adj* convenient, handy *18-19, 20- literary*. [perhaps altered form of HANDY[1.1]]
hanvaeg, **hanvag** /han'veg, han'vag/ *v* to put off time, hesitate; to remain sleepless *20- Sh*. [ON *andvaka* sleeplessness]
hap[1.1] /hap/ *n* **1** a wrap, a shawl or plaid; a warm outer garment; a bed-quilt or blanket *la16-*. **2** a covering (for protection against the weather); a tarpaulin *la18-19, 20- C Bor*. **hapwarm** a warm wrap or thick outer garment *la18-19, 20- NE T*. [unknown]

hap[1.2] /hap/ *v* **1** to wrap up so as to shelter; to protect or keep warm *la14-*. **2** to cover so as to conceal *la16-*. **3** to cover with earth or straw as a protection against cold or wet; to thatch *la18-*. **4** to bury, inter *la18-*. **5** to clothe, dress *la18-*. **6** to cover a fire with ash or turf to keep it burning for a long time *19, 20- T*. **happer** the last hour of a mason's working day when work is covered up against frost *20- NE T H&I*. †**happin** clothing, a garment *la18-e19*. **hap in** to cover up dung or potatoes in drills with the plough *20- NE*. [unknown]

hap[2.1], **hop** /hap, hɔp/ *n* a small jump or bound *16-*. **hap, stap and lowp** the game of hop, step and jump, also used to describe the movement *la18-*. [see the verb]

hap²·², **hop** /hap, hɔp/ *v* **1** to spring, bound, jump *la15-*. **2** to walk with a limp *19, 20- T Uls*. **3** *of tears* to trickle, splash down *18-19*. **4** to rebound, bounce *16-e19*. **hap-the-beds** hopscotch *19- WC SW*; compare BEDS. **hoppin beds** = *hap-the-beds 20- NE EC*. [OE *hoppian*]

hap³, **haup**, **hip**, †**hep** /hap, hɔp, hɪp/ *n* a rosehip, the fruit of the wild rose *16-*. [OE *hēōpe*]

†**hap**⁴ *n in Dumfriesshire* an implement used to scrape up ooze from the seabed to make salt *18-e19*. [unknown]

hap *see* HUP¹·¹, HUP¹·²

hapenny *see* HAUF¹·³

†**hapning** *n* chance *la14-15*. [verbal noun from HAPPEN]

hapning *see* HAPPENIN

happen, hauppen, †**happin,** †**happyn** /ˈhapən, ˈhɔpən/ *v* **1** to occur by chance; to chance to be or to come *la14-*. **2** to befall: ◊*the fate that soon will happen Kirk or state la18- C Bor*. [ON *happ* chance, good luck, with verb-forming suffix]

happenin, †**happining,** †**hapning** /ˈhapənɪn/ *adj* casual, occasional, chance *la16-*. [presp of HAPPEN]

happer, hopper /ˈhapər, ˈhɔpər/ *n* **1** a receptacle, originally for feeding grain into a mill *15-*. **2** a basket or container, especially one for carrying seed to be sown *la16-19, 20- Ork NE T Bor*. **happrick** a pannier or basket *la19- Sh*. †**happer-arsed** = *happer-hippit la17-18*. †**happergaw** *n* a gap in growing corn caused by uneven sowing *17-e19*. †**happer-gaw** *v* to sow grain unevenly so that the resulting crop was patchy *e19*. **happer-hippit** with bony, protruding hips *19- Bor*. [HAP²·², with agent suffix]

happin¹·¹ /ˈhapɪn/ *n* a chance event *20- Sh*. [from HAPPEN]

†**happin**¹·² *adv* perhaps *la15-e17*. [subjunctive of HAPPEN]

happin *see* HAPPEN

happining *see* HAPPENIN

happity /ˈhapəti/ *adj* lame *19, 20- T*. [a fanciful extension of HAP²·²]

happy /ˈhapi/ *adj* **1** content, joyful *la14-*. **2** lucky, fortunate, auspicious *15-*. [ON *happ* chance, good luck + -IE²]

happyn *see* HAPPEN

hapshackle¹·¹, *N* **habjaickle,** †**hopschakil** /ˈhapʃəkəl; *N* ˈhabdʒekəl/ *n* a hobble for tethering a horse, a fetter, a shackle *16-19, 20- N*. [perhaps HAP²·² or HAMPER + OE *sceacel* a fetter]

hapshackle¹·², †**hapschakkel,** †**hopschakel** /ˈhapʃəkəl/ *v* to hobble (a horse); to tie up, prevent from straying *16-*. [see the noun]

har *see* HAIR²·², HARR

harangue, †**harrang,** †**arang** /həˈraŋ/ *n* a formal speech, a tirade *la15-*. [MFr *harangue*]

harber *see* HERBOUR¹·¹, HERBOUR¹·²

harbery *see* HERBERY¹·¹

harbin /ˈharbɪn/ *n* the two- or three-year-old coalfish *Pollachius virens la18- Ork*. [unknown]

harbory *see* HERBERY¹·²

harbour *see* HERBOUR¹·¹, HERBOUR¹·²

harboury *see* HERBERY¹·¹

harbry *see* HERBERY¹·²

harchatt *see* HARESHARD

hard¹·¹ /hard/ *n* **1** difficulty, hardship *18-*. **2** spirits, especially whisky *la19-*. **3** firm ground *la19, 20- EC SW*. **4** the rocky bottom of the seabed *19- Sh*. **hardie** *fisherman's taboo* a rock *20- Sh*. **come through the hard** to experience hardship or misfortune *19, 20- NE T EC*. **if hard goes to hard** if the worst comes to the worst *20- Uls*. †**when hard comes to hard** = *if hard goes to hard 18-19*. [see the adj]

hard¹·², **haurd, haird, herd,** †**harde** /hard, hɔrd, herd, herd/ *adj* **1** firm, solid; forceful, powerful *la14-*. **2** difficult; unpleasant; unyielding *la14-*. **3** *of intoxicants* strong, undiluted, raw *19-*. **4** close-fisted, stingy *19-*. **5** *of joints in carpentry or masonry* pressing closely together at one place and not at another *20- N EC*. **6** *of wind* dry *la15, 20- NE SW*. **7** *of a door* locked *20- Ork*. **hardie 1** a white bread roll with a hard crust *20- T*. **2** a hard type of butter biscuit, particularly those baked in Cupar, Fife and popular as ship's biscuits *20- NE EC*. **hard birdit** *of an egg* almost ready to hatch *20- T Bor*. **hard breid 1** stale bread, especially dried in the oven, for making breadcrumbs *20-*. **2** a type of thin oatcake *la17-19, 20- NE Uls*. **hard fish** dried or salt fish *16-*. **hard handed** stingy, close-fisted *19, 20- Sh WC*. **hard heads** to oppose directly as if butting with the head *17-e19*. **hard heid 1** the sea scorpion or father-lasher *Myoxocephalus scorpius 18-*. **2** ribwort *Plantago lanceolata 20-*. **3** black knapweed *Centaurea nigra*; the head of this plant *20- SW Bor*. **4** sneezewort *Achillea ptarmica 19*. **hard neck** impudence, effrontery, a brass neck *la20-*. **hard-necked, hard-neckit** lacking in modesty, forward *20- H&I C*. **hard nickle doon** a game of marbles *20- NE T*. **hard-set** wilful, obstinate *19, 20- EC*. **hard-sutten** *of eggs* almost ready to hatch *20-*. **hard tartan** tartan cloth of a hard, dense texture *19-*. **as hard as a horn, as hard as the horn** very hard, as hard as nails; *of a person* hardy *19-*. **as hard as Hinnerson's erse** extremely hard *20- NE T*. **hard pit tae** in difficulties *19-*. **the hard stuff** whisky *la19-*. **the hard tackle** whisky *19- EC Bor*. **hard up 1** *of people* in poor health, unwell *la19- T C Bor*. **2** in bad condition, in a state of disrepair *20- SW Bor*. [OE *heard*]

hard¹·³ /hard/ *adv* **1** violently, strenuously; severely *la14-*. **2** tightly, firmly, securely *la14-*. **3** near *16-17*. [OE *hearde*]

hard *see* HEAR

harde *see* HARD¹·²

harden, †**hardin** /ˈhardən/ *v* to solidify; to (cause to) become hard *la14-*. **harden up** *of weather* to clear up, become settled after rain *la19-*. [HARD¹·², with verb-forming suffix]

harden *see* HARN¹·¹, HARN¹·²

†**hardheid, hard-head** *n* a copper coin from the reigns of Mary and James VI *la16-19*. [OFr *hardit* a copper coin named after Philippe III le Hardi, king of France, who issued it + HEID¹·¹]

hardiment *see* HARDY

hardin *see* HARDEN, HARN¹·¹, HARN¹·²

hardis *see* HARDS

hardlie, hardly *see* HAURDLY

hards, †**hardis,** †**herdis** /hardz/ *npl* **1** the coarser woody fibres of flax or hemp, separated from the finer ones *la14-19, 20- N*. **2** cloth or yarn made of coarse fibres *20- Sh*. †**hardis weik** wick for candles *16*. [OE *heorde*]

†**hard weik** *n* candlewick made of fibres *la16*. [altered form of *hardis weik* (HARDS)]

hardy /ˈhardi/ *adj* **1** bold, resolute *la14-*. **2** robust, in good health *la19-*. **3** frosty *la19- C SW Uls*. †**hardyment, hardiment 1** boldness *la14-e17*. **2** a deed of valour *la14-e15*. **keep up a hardy heart** to be courageous *19- T EC SW Bor*. [ME *hardi*]

hare, †**hair,** †**hear** /her/ *n* **1** a rabbit-like mammal *15-*. **2** the last sheaf or handful of grain cut in the harvest-field *la19- SW Uls*. **hare lug, hare's lug** an angling fly, the body of which is dubbed with fur from the hare's ear *19-*. [OE *hara*]

hare *see* HAIR¹·¹, HAIR²·²

harebell /ˈherbɛl/ *n* the round-leaved bellflower *Campanula rotundifolia*, the bluebell of Scotland *la18-*. [HARE + BELL¹·¹]

hareshard, hareshaw, *EC* **hairshach,** *Bor* **hareshal,** *Uls* **hareskart,** †**harchatt** /ˈherʃard, ˈherʃɔ; *EC* ˈherʃəx; *Bor* ˈherʃəl; *Uls* ˈherskart/ *n* a hare-lip *la15-*. [OE *hærsceard*]

hargle-bargle *see* ARGLE-BARGLE¹·²

harigalds, harigalls, harigals *see* HARRIGALS

haring *see* HERRIN

harit see HAIR¹·¹
hark¹·¹ /hark/ *n* a whisper *19-*. [see the verb]
hark¹·², **herk** /hark, herk/ *v* **1** to listen *la15-*. **2** to whisper *la16-*. [ME *herken*]
harken, harkin see HEARKEN
harky see HIRKIE
harl¹·¹ /harl/ *n* **1** a muck-rake or scraper *16-*. **2** an accumulation (of something), a scraping *la17-*. **3** a dirty, untidy or coarse person *19- WC SW Bor Uls*. **4** the act of dragging, a tug *19, 20- EC Bor*. **a harl o banes** a very thin person *20- T EC Bor Uls*. [unknown]
harl¹·², **harle, haurl, †harrel** /harl, hɔrl/ *v* **1** to drag; to take by force *la14-*. **2** to drag oneself, trail along; to wear trailing garments *16-*. **3** to fish from a boat by trailing a baited line in a zigzag motion *19-*. **4** to scrape or rake together *la17-19, 20- Bor*. **5** to amass money or goods *la18- EC*. **6** to peel or rub off skin *la18, 20- Uls*. **7** to draw or drag in a vehicle *la16-e18*. **harlt** worried, tired-looking *20- EC Bor*. **harl aboot** to creep about, walk slowly and feebly *19, 20- Sh*. [unknown]
harl²·¹ /harl/ *n* (the mixture of sand and lime used for) roughcasting *la19-*. [unknown]
harl²·² /harl/ *v* to roughcast with lime and small stones *la16-*. **harling 1** the action of roughcasting *la16-*. **2** the material used for roughcasting *18-*. [unknown]
†harl³ *n* the reed or brittle part of the stem of flax *18-e19*. [MLG *harle* fibre of flax or hemp]
harle /harl/ *n* the red-breasted merganser *Mergus serrator la17-19, 20- Sh Ork*. Compare HERALD DEUK. [MFr *harle* a kind of shelduck]
harle see HARL¹·²
harly see HAURDLY
harm see HAIRM¹·¹ HAIRM¹·²
harme see HAIRM¹·¹
†harmisay *interj* an expression grief or distress *la14-e17*. [unknown]
harmony, †hermony, †harmonie, †armony, †ermony /'harməni/ *n* **1** agreement, concord *la15-*. **2** musical harmony *la15-*. [MFr *harmonie*]
harn¹·¹, **harden, †harran, †hardin, †herdin** /harn, 'hardən/ *n* a coarse cloth, originally also yarn, made from the coarser woody fibres of flax or hemp *la15-*. [derivative of HARDS]
harn¹·², **harden, †hardin, †herdin** /harn, 'hardən/ *adj* **1** of cloth or yarn made from the coarser woody fibres of flax or hemp *16-*. **2** of rope hempen *la16-17*. **harden gown, harn gown** a coarse linen gown worn by penitents under church discipline *18, 19- historical*. [see the noun]
harn², **†haurn** /harn/ *v* to roast on embers; to toast or bake on a fire *19- Sh Ork SW Bor Uls*. [HARDEN to make hard]
harness, herness, harnish, †harnes, †hernes, †harna /'harnəs, 'hɛrnəs, 'harnɪʃ/ *n* **1** a set of straps (to secure a horse) *15-*. **2** *weaving* the apparatus in a loom for moving the warp-threads *la17-*. **3** an intricate form of weaving common in Paisley *la18- WC*. **4** defensive armour for horses or people *la14-e17*. **harnessin** the accoutrements or trappings of a horse *15-*. **harnish plaid** = harness shawl *la19- C*. **†harnes sadle** a pack-saddle *la15-e16*. **harness shawl** a (Paisley-made) plaid or shawl of fine quality or intricate pattern *19- WC*. **harnish tying** the process of mounting a harness-loom *19- WC*. [ME *harneis*]
harnis see HARNS
harnish see HARNESS
harnless /'harnləs/ *adj* stupid *la19- Sh N NE WC*. [HARNS, with suffix denoting absence]
harnpan /'harnpan/ *n* the skull *la14-*. [HARNS + PAN¹·¹]
harns, hairns, †haurns, †harnis /harnz, hɛrnz/ *npl* brains, the brain; the intelligence *la14-*. [ON *hjarni*]

haroosh see HURROO¹·¹
harow see ARRA
harp¹·¹, **hairp, herp** /harp, hɛrp, hɛrp/ *n* **1** a stringed musical instrument *la15-*. **2** a sieve or riddle *la17-*. **3** the part of a meal-mill which separates the dust from the husks *19-*. **4** the lower fine-meshed sieve in a winnowing machine which separates weed seeds from grain *20- Ork NE*. **5** a sparred shovel used for lifting potatoes or filling coal *19- C*. [OE *hearpe*]
harp¹·², **hairp, herp** /harp, hɛrp, hɛrp/ *v* **1** to play on a harp *16-*. **2** to riddle, sift *18-19*. [see the noun]
harpo, harpi /'harpo, 'harpi/ *n* a scallop of the family *Pectinidae 20- Sh Ork*. [HARP¹·¹, from its appearance; compare Icel *hǫrpu(-skel)*]
harr, Ork herr, †har, †herre /har; *Ork* hɛr/ *n* the hinge of a door or gate *la15-19, 20- Sh Ork*. [OE *heorr*, ON *hjarri*]
harra¹·¹, **harrow** /'harə, 'haro/ *n* a spiked implement for breaking up (ploughed) ground, a harrow *la14-*. **†harrowbill, harroubull** a crossbar or spar of a harrow *la17-19*. **†get yer leg ower the harrows** = *have your leg ower the harrows*. **†have your leg ower the harrows** to get out of hand, become unmanageable *e19*. [ME *harwe*, ON *herfi*]
harra¹·², **harrow, †tharro** /'harə, 'haro/ *v* to break up ground with a harrow *la15-*. **†harrower** a young horse unbroken to the plough but used for harrowing *la18*. [see the noun]
harrage see ARAGE
harrald see HERALD
harran see HARN¹·¹
harrang see HARANGUE
harrel see HARL¹·²
harrigals, harigals, *Bor* **harigalds, †harigalls** /'harɪgəlz; *Bor* 'harɪgəldz/ *npl* viscera, entrails *la17-*. [MFr *harigot* a mutton stew]
harro, hirro /'haro, 'hɪro/ *interj* a cry of distress or alarm or encouragement *15-19, 20- N*. [ME *harou*; compare HURROO¹·³]
harro see HARRA¹·²
harrow see HARRA¹·¹, HARRA¹·²
harrowster /'harostər/ *n* a spawned haddock *la19- NE*. [unknown]
harry see HERRY
harsel see HIRSEL²·¹
harsk /harsk/ *adj* **1** harsh, hard; rough to the touch or hearing *la14-16, 20- Sh*. **2** severe; offensive, rude; unpleasant *15-17, 20- Sh*. **herskin** harsh, rough; rude *20- Ork*. Compare HASK¹·². [ME *harsk*]
harst see HAIRST¹·¹
hart, †hert, †hairt, †heart /hart/ *n* a stag *14-*. **†herthorne, hart horne** the antler of a stag *16-17*. [OE *heort*]
hart see HERT¹·¹, HERT¹·²
harth see HAIRTH
hartie see HERTY
hartskaid see HERTSCAD
hartsum see HERTSOME
harvest see HAIRST¹·¹, HAIRST¹·²
hary see HAIRY¹·², HERRY
haryng see HERRIN
†hary nobill *n* an English gold coin of Henry VI *la15-e17*. [from a familiar form of the king's name + NOBLE¹·¹]
has see AS²·², HAE¹·²
†hasard¹·¹ *n* a grey-haired old man *e16*. [unknown]
†hasard¹·² *adj* grey, grey-haired *e16*. [unknown]
†hasartour, hasatour, hasardour *n* a player at dice, a gambler *la15-16*. [ME *hasardour*]
has-been, †hes-beene /'hazbin/ *n* **1** something or someone no longer existing or past their best *17-*. **2** a good old custom *e19*. [third person singular present perfect of BE]
hasch see HASH¹·²

haschie see HASHIE[1.1]

haseing see HASSON

hash[1.1] /haʃ/ *n* **1** a stupid, careless, clumsy, slovenly person 18-. **2** a heap, a large quantity; a crowd 19-. **3** a rush or excessive pressure of work; work done in a hasty, careless way la19-. **4** grain dried in a kiln and then chopped 20-. **5** a strong wind, especially with rain la19- *Sh N EC*. **6** a row, an uproar, a brawl 19- *NE T*. **7** ribald talk, nonsense 19- *Sh EC*. **8** the complement of workers on a large farm 20- *NE Bor*. **9** the inside of a cow 20- *Sh*. **hashter** (a person who does) badly organized or slovenly work 19- *WC Uls*. [see the verb]

hash[1.2], †**hasch** /haʃ/ *v* **1** to cut (meat) into small pieces la16-. **2** to slash or hack 17-. **3** to slice or cut up; to chop (turnips) for fodder; to munch or chew 18-. **4** to spoil, destroy or deface la18-. **5** to fatigue, overwork, harass 19-. **6** to move or work in a muddling, flurried way 19-. **7** to talk volubly, emptily or illogically 20- *Bor*. **hashed** harassed la19, 20- *NE*. **hasher 1** a careless, hustling person; a workman who does fast but rough and ready work la19-. **2** a turnip slicer la19- *Sh Ork NE T EC*. †**hashter** to work in a hurried, slovenly and wasteful way 19. [MFr *hachier*]

hashie[1.1], †**haschie** /'haʃi, 'haʃe/ *n* a mixture of chopped meat and other ingredients la16- *NE T EC*. [MFr *hachis*, *hagis*]

hashie[1.2], **hashy** /'haʃi, 'haʃe/ *adj* **1** slapdash, careless or slovenly in dress, work or habits 19-. **2** wet or windy, stormy 19-. **hashily**, †**hashly** in a careless or slovenly fashion 18-. **hashie-bashie** a game in which smaller marbles are knocked out of holes by striking them with a larger one 20- *T*. †**hashie-holie** = *hashie-bashie* la19. [HASH[1.1] + -IE[2]]

hashloch see HUSHLACH[1.1]

hashy see HASHIE[1.2]

hasil see HAZEL[1.1]

hask[1.1], **haisk** /hask, hesk/ *v* to give a short dry cough, clear the throat noisily, cough up phlegm 19- *T EC SW Bor*. [see the adj]

hask[1.2] /hask/ *adj* **1** *of touch or taste* hard, dry, rough 19- *Bor*. **2** severe, rigorous, rough la16-19. **hasky 1** rough, coarse; unpalatable, stale, dry 19-. **2** husky, hoarse la18-19. [altered form of HARSK]

hask see ASK[2.1]

hasp see HESP[1.1], HESP[1.2], HESP[2]

haspal /'haspəl/ *n* an untidy, carelessly-dressed person 19- *SW*. [AN *haspal*, *haspel* riff-raff, a ragamuffin or variant of HASPAN]

†**haspan** *n* a young lad e19. [shortened form of *half-span*]

haspie see HI-SPY

hass see HAUSE[1.1], HAUSE[1.2]

hassbiles /'hasbʌɪlz/ *npl* infantile eczema la19- *Ork*. [ON *hauss* skull + BILE[2]]

hassen /'hasən/ *n* one of the boards on a boat, next but one to the keel 19- *Sh*. [HAUSE[1.1] a neck, a narrow part; compare Norw dial *hals* the forepart of a boat]

hassock, *Ork* **hasso**, *NE* **hussock** /'hasək; *Ork* 'haso; *NE* 'hʌsək/ *n* **1** a large round tuft of peat used as a seat 19, 20- *Ork NE T*. **2** a shock of bushy hair la18-19, 20- *Sh NE*. [OE *hassuc* coarse grass]

hasson, †**haseing** /'hasən/ *n* mining a vertical gutter or drainpipe between water rings in a shaft la17-19, 20- *EC*. [HAUSE[1.1] a neck, a narrow part, with *-ing* suffix]

hast, haste see HEEST

†**haster**[1.1], **haister** *n* a confusion, a muddle, a rush 19. [see the verb]

haster[1.2], **haister**, *T* **hester** /'hestər; *T* 'hestər/ *v* **1** to pester, harass 19-. **2** to cook too quickly, scorch (food) 19- *Bor*. †**haistered**, **hasterit** flustered, harassed, rushed la15-19, 20- *Bor*. †**hasterns** early-ripening oats or peas la18-e19. [frequentative form of HEEST]

hastie, **hasty** /'hesti/ *v* to hasten, hurry e16, 20- *NE*. [from the Scots adj *hasty* or perhaps Scots *haste ye*]

hastie see HEISTY

hasting see HEEST

hasty see HASTIE, HEASTY, HEISTY

hat[1], **hatt**, †**hate** /hat/ *n* **1** a covering for the head; a hat la14-. **2** a layer of froth or scum forming on the surface of a liquid, especially beer or yeast in brewing la16-. **hatless**, †**hatles** not wearing a hat la14-. **hattock**, †**huttok** a little hat 16-*literary*. **hatty**, **hattie** one of various games involving a hat or cap 19, 20- *N T EC*. †**hattit kit** a preparation of milk with a top layer of cream, variously flavoured 17-19. **hat maker**, †**hatmakar** a hatter la15-. †**hat pece** a James VI coin representing him wearing a hat la16-e17. **horse and hattock** see HORSE[1.1]. [OE *hæt*]

hat[2] /hat/ *v* to abuse or ill-treat 20- *Ork*. [ON *hata* to hate]

hat see HATE, HAUT[1.1], HAUT[1.2], HEAT[1.2], HET[1.2], HIT[1.2]

hatch /hatʃ/ *n* a peat bank; a row of peats spread out to dry 19, 20- *NE*. [probably OE *hæc* grating; compare HECK[1.1]]

†**hate**, **hait**, **hat** *v* to name or call la14-e16. **hattyn**, **hatine** named, called la14-e16. [OE *hātan*]

hate see HAT[1], HEAT[1.1], HEAT[1.2], HET[1.1]

haterent see HATRED

hatesum, †**hatsome**, †**haitsum** /'hetsəm/ *adj* hateful la15-e16, 20- *N*. [ME *hatsum*]

hathe see AITH

hather see HEATHER

hathock see HADDOCK

hathorne see HAWTHORN

hatine see HATE

hatred, †**haterent**, †**hettret**, †**haitrent** /'hetrəd/ *n* extreme dislike, loathing 15-. [ME *hatred*]

hatsome see HATESUM

hatt see HAT[1]

hatter[1.1], †**hettir** /'hatər/ *n* **1** a miscellaneous collection of things, a confused heap; a state of disorder 17-. **2** a skin eruption, a rash la18-19, 20- *N NE Bor*. **3** difficulty; a struggle, commotion 20- *Bor*. [see the verb]

hatter[1.2] /'hatər/ *v* **1** to move laboriously; to work in a careless or haphazard way 19, 20- *WC Bor Uls*. **2** to bruise, treat roughly, bully la15-19, 20- *Sh NE*. **3** to harass or vex; to overtire 19, 20- *Sh Bor*. **4** to impede, hinder or obstruct la19- *Sh Ork*. **5** to collect in crowds, swarm or abound 19, 20- *Bor*. [perhaps onomatopoeic]

hatter[2] /'hatər/ *n* a hat-maker 18-. **like a hatter** with maximum energy or vigour, with all one's might la19-. [HAT[1], with agent suffix]

hatterel /'hatərəl/ *n* **1** a confused heap, a jumble; a large number 19, 20- *Ork NE EC*. **2** a mass of sores 19, 20- *Ork NE Uls*. [HATTER[1.1], with frequentative suffix]

hattock see HAT[1]

hattyn see HATE

haubersione see HABERSCHOUN

hauch[1.1], **hach**, †**haugh** /hɔx, hax/ *n* **1** (a soft, loose) cough; (the sound of) a clearing of the throat; originally also a catch in the voice la17-. **2** a forcible expulsion of breath; a gasp 20- *NE*. **3** a sound expressing exertion, a grunt e16. [onomatopoeic]

hauch[1.2], **hach** /hɔx, hax/ *v* to cough; to cough up mucus to clear the throat la18-. **hocher** to cough up mucus la20- *C*. [see the noun]

hauch see HAUGH

hauchames see HOUGHAMS

hauchle see HOCHLE[1.1], HOCHLE[1.2]

hauchty /ˈhɔxte/ *adj* haughty *la18-19, 20- literary*. [altered form of EModE *hawty*]

haud[1.1], **hud**, **had**, **hadd**, **hald**, **howld**, **haul**, *Sh* **haad** /hɔd, hʌd, had, hald, hʌuld, hɔl; *Sh* had/ *n* **1** the act of taking or keeping (in the hand); a grasp or grip *la14-*. **2** property held, a holding; a habitation, a dwelling-place *la14-*. **3** a refuge, shelter or place of retreat; a den or lair of an animal *15-*. **4** something to hold on to, a support or prop *18-*. **5** restraint, control: ◊*he had no haud on his hand wi the butter 19- NE WC SW*. **6** a stone or an overhanging bank of a stream beneath which fish lurk *19, 20- Sh Bor*. **7** the action of a sheepdog in keeping sheep at a particular spot *20- H&I Bor*. **8** a dispute, a quarrel *la19- C*. **9** a stutter, a stammer *20- Ork*. **10** a stronghold *la15-e17*. **haud again**, †**hald agayn** opposition, an obstacle, a delay *16 15-19, 20- NE T EC*. **haad-dog** *in Shetland* a sheepdog trained to catch and hold a sheep *19, 20- historical*. **haud-doon** a handicap, a burden *20- Sh NE H&I EC*. **haud-fast** a staple used for fixing *19-*. **haud in** a stinting, a lack *20-*. **by the hauls**, **by the haulds** to walk around by holding on to fixed objects for support *19- Sh N NE Uls*. **get a haud** to grasp, grip, catch *19-*. **in a haud** in difficulties, in trouble *la19- C SW*. **on haud** on fire *la20- EC Bor*. [see the verb]

haud[1.2], **hud**, **had**, **hadd**, **hauld**, **hald**, **howld**, **hold**, *Sh* **haad**, *Ork* **hild**, †**hawd** /hɔd, hʌd, had, hɔld, hald, hʌuld, hold; *Sh* had; *Ork* hɪld/ *v pt* **held**, *Sh* **huild**, *Sh* **haddit**, *Ork* **heud**, *N* **heed**, *NE* **heeld**, *ptp* **hauden**, **hadden**, *N H&I* **howlded**, †**haldin**, †**holden** **1** to have or keep (in the hand), hold onto; to retain, possess *la14-*. **2** to confine or detain; to hinder, restrain *la14-*. **3** to continue as before; to maintain oneself in a certain state *la14-*. **4** to arrange an event; to hold a market or celebrate a festival *la14-*. **5** to continue on or along, proceed, keep to a path or route *la14-*. **6** to observe, adhere to, maintain (an opinion or practice) *la14-*. **7** to contain; to keep within; to have capacity to hold *15-*. **8** to restrain oneself, prevent; to govern one's feelings *la15-*. **9** (to command to) stop or desist *la18-*. **10** to keep farm animals to re-stock a herd; to keep or maintain animals *la14-19, 20- EC Bor*. **11** to remain in good health: ◊*how are ye haudin yersel? 19- T C*. **12** to round up or pen sheep; to corner a person *19- EC Bor*. **13** *of fish* to hide or lurk under stones; to seek shelter *19- NE Bor*. **14** to wager, bet *la18-19, 20- NE*. **15** *of seeds or plants* to grow *18-19, 20- NE*. **16** to save one's life *la14-e16*. **17** to administer the law; to keep a house or shop *la14-e17*. **18** to keep an appointment *la14-e16*. **19** to keep or store provisions *la15*. **hauden** to be obliged or required (to do something) *la14-*. **hauder** a holder *la14-*. **hauder-on** a riveter's assistant in a shipyard *20- C*. **haud aff 1** to keep off or away *la16-*. **2** *in a command to a draught animal* turn to the right *19-*. **haud aff yersel** to look after oneself, defend oneself or one's own interests *19, 20- NE T*. **haud again** to hold back *15-19, 20- NE T*. **haud at 1** to persist in, keep at *la19-*. **2** to exhort, pester, nag *19, 20- N NE WC*. **haud awa**, †**had awa**, †**had away 1** to keep away, keep out or off *15-*. **2** to continue on one's way, go away *la18-*. **haud awa frae** with the exception of *la19- NE T EC*. **haud back** *in a command to a draught animal* turn left or away *19-*. **haud by 1** to pass by, keep away from, abstain from *16-19, 20- NE*. **2** to have little respect for *19, 20- NE*. **haud for** to aim at, make for *la19-*. **haud forrit** to continue to improve (in health) *20- T EC*. **haud hale eel** to make merry, celebrate (Christmas and the New Year) *20- NE*. †**hald hand to**, **hold hand to** to support, assist *la16-e18*. **haud haul**, **had haal** to offer resistance; to prop, support *20- N*. **haud in**, **hold in**, †**hald in 1** to confine, retain; to restrain, keep in order *15-*. **2** *of a container* to retain the contents; *of a dam or river* to not leak, spill or flood *16-*. **3** to save, economize, be miserly *19-*. **haud in aboot 1** to keep in order, restrain or control *la18- Sh Ork NE T EC*. **2** to bring or come closer *la19- Sh Ork NE T Bor*. †**hold in the hals** to have in one's power *la14-e17*. **had in the mooth o** to feed by hand, fatten up *20- Sh*. **haud in wi**, **hold in with** to keep in with, curry favour with *19-*. **haud on 1** to carry on, continue *15-*. **2** to keep supplying *la18- Ork NE T*. **haud oot**, †**hald out 1** to extend, proffer *la15-*. **2** to keep out *16-*. **3** to persist *la17-*. **4** to live, reside *19-*. **haud oot a langer** to amuse, entertain *la16-19, 20- Sh Ork NE*. **haud sae** to pause; to cease; to issue a command to stop *la18-19, 20- Sh WC SW Bor*. **haud tae 1** *of a door* to shut or keep shut *19-*. **2** to keep hard at work *la18- Sh Ork NE T*. **haud till** to persist in asserting *19-*. **haud a time** to make a fuss of *20- Sh N NE T*. **haud up**, **hud up**, †**hald up 1** to support; to keep raised; to sustain *la14-*. **2** to stand still *la19-*. **3** to present a child for baptism *18-19, 20- NE*. **4** *of good weather* to continue *20-*. **5** to maintain, keep in a good state of repair *15-17*. **haud up to** to court, make up to *la19-*. **haud up wi** to keep pace with *19-*. †**hold ward** *of a vassal* to have tenure of land by military service; *of land* to be held under tenure of military service *la16-18*. **hold water to** to match, be equated or compared with *la18, 20- Sh*. **haud a wee** to wait a minute *20-*. **haud wi** to admit, agree to, accept *la19-*. **haud wide o** to keep clear of, avoid *20- N T SW*. **hauds ye** I accept your wager *la18- NE*. **hold yer face to** to vouch for *18-19, 20- NE*. **haud yer feet** to keep (on) one's feet *la15-*. **haud yer mooth** to be silent *20- Sh C*. **haud yer tongue** (a command to) be quiet, to stop talking *la18-*. **haud yer wheesht**, **haud yer weesh** to be quiet *la18-*. **neither tae haud nor bind** to be ungovernable, be beyond control *18-*. [OE *healdan*]

hauden *see* HAUD[1.2]

hauden doon /ˈhɔdən ˈdun/ *adj* burdened, oppressed, afflicted *la18-*. [ptp of HAUD[1.2] + DOON[1.3]]

haudin, **hauding**, **holding**, **hadden**, †**halding** /ˈhɔdən, ˈhɔdɪn, ˈholdɪn, ˈhadən/ *n* **1** the action of holding *la14-*. **2** the tenure or occupation of land *la14-*. **3** a small farm or house held on lease *la18-*. **4** possessions, means of support, property *la18-19, 20- NE EC*. **5** the stock a farm can support *la18- Bor*. **6** furniture or equipment on a farm *la18-e19*. [verbal noun from HAUD[1.2]]

hauf[1.1], **half**, **haf**, **haff**, †**halff**, †**halve** /hɔf, haf/ *n* **1** one of two equal parts; a half *la14-*. **2** one of the (two) sides of anything *la14-*. **3** one of two unequal parts into which something has been divided *18-*. **4** a half-measure of a specified amount, especially of whisky; a half-gill *la19-*. **5** *of time* 30 minutes before the hour specified: ◊*half five* (indicating half past four) *17-*. **6** *of time* 30 minutes past the hour specified: ◊*half five* (indicating half past five) *20-*. **7** one of three or more divisions or portions *20- N NE H&I*. **8** a half-share (in a boat or net) *la15-18*. **haufie**, **halfie 1** a half-holiday *19-*. **2** a half-measure *la19-*. **3** a half-sized loaf *la19- T*. **half-nabbie** a member of the middle class *la19-*. **a hauf an a hauf** a half-pint of beer with a small whisky as a chaser *20-*. [OE *healf*]

hauf[1.2], **half** /hɔf, haf/ *v* **1** to divide into two equal parts, halve; to share equally *19-*. **2** *golf* to play a hole, round or match in the same number of strokes as one's opponent *19-*. **3** to divide into more than two equal shares *20- NE EC*. [see the noun]

hauf[1.3], **half**, **haff** /hɔf, haf/ *adj* forming one of two (more or less equal) parts *la14-*. **half cousin** the child of one's parent's cousin, a second cousin *19-*. **half deal man** a half-share fisherman *19- EC Bor*. †**half deill** half *la14-e16*. **half foot** *in the Highlands and Islands* a system of land use where the landlord supplied (usually half of) the seed and the tenant grew and harvested the crop, which was divided between them in the same proportion *19-e20, la20- historical* †**half fou** a measurement corresponding to half a bushel *18-e19*. †**hauf gable, half gavill** one side of a gable which is common to two houses; the right to build on to the gable of another's house *la17-19*. **half gaits, haf gaits** halfway *la16-19, 20- Sh T EC.* †**half hag** a smaller size of HAGBUTE *16-e17*. **half house** a semi-detached house *la19- NE T.* †**half hyre** half of a seaman's pay for a voyage *la16-e17*. †**half landis** the half-portion of a landed estate *la15-17*. **half lang** *n* 1 a half-grown lad (working on a farm) *la17-19, 20- Bor.* 2 *in tanning* a hide of half length *la16-17*. **half lang** *adj* 1 *of a farmworker* adolescent, half-grown *la17-19, 20- Bor.* 2 of half or short length *la15-18*. **hauf loaf, half loaf** a loaf of plain bread, originally half the size of a standard quartern (four pound) loaf *19-*. †**haff manor, half manure** in Galloway, a *half foot* lease *16-19*. †**half manurer** a person who farmed land under the terms of a *half foot* lease *la17*. **half marrow** a marriage-partner, a mate *la16-19, 20- T.* **half merk, haff mark** 1 a coin of the value of half a merk *16-19, 20- historical.* 2 (the fee or symbol for) a clandestine marriage *la17-19, 20- historical.* †**halfmess, half mes** a small plate; half a portion of food *la16-e18*. †**half net, hanet** *in the North-East* a (half) share of fish caught in one net in a season *16-19*; compare HAAF-NET. **half note** a ten-shilling note *20, 21- historical.* **half one** *golf* the allowance to one's opponent of a stroke at alternate holes *19, 20- EC.* **hauf oor, half hour** 1 half an hour *16-*. 2 the mechanism in a clock for striking the half hours *la16-*. **halfpenny, hapenny,** †**haupny,** †**halpeny** a coin worth half a penny *15-20, 21- historical.* **halfpenny-land** half a pennyland *la15-19, 20- historical.* **hauf-roads, half-roads** halfway *la19-*. †**half seill** the matrix of a seal *la16*. **half water** halfway between a boat and the bottom of the sea *la19- Sh.* **half-waxed** *of rabbits* half-grown *20- Bor.* **half-ways, half-wyes** halfway; partly *la19-*. †**half web** the grey or red-necked phalarope *19*. **half year,** †**halȝar,** †**halyert,** †**hellier** a half year, six months *la15-*. †**ha-year auld, hei-yearald, high-year-old** *of Borders cattle* a year and a half old *19*. **hauf yin,** *Uls* **half wan** a half glassful of spirits *la19- C Uls.* **half an atween, half and between** neither one nor the other *19-*. **haff an haff** half-drunk *18-*. [see the noun]

hauf[1.4], **half** /hɔf, haf/ *adv* to the extent or measure of half; in part, partly *la14-*. **half-bred** *of sheep* crossed from the Border Leicester ram and the Cheviot ewe *la19-*. **half-chackit** drunk *20- EC.* **hauf cock** half-drunk *19, 20- NE.* **half gane** around the middle period of a pregnancy *19-*. **half-hung-tee** 1 pretentious, affected *20- NE.* 2 irresponsible *20- NE.* **half jackit** half-witted *20-*. **half jeck** = *half jackit*. [see the noun]

haufers, halfers, halvers, haavers /'hɔfərz, 'hafərz, 'havərz/ *npl* 1 a half-portion, an equal share *16-*. 2 an exclamation used (by children) to claim a half-share *19-*. **go halfers, ging halfers** to share equally; to split the cost *19-*. **in halfers, in haavers** jointly, in partnership *16, 20- Sh N.* [derivative of HAUF[1.1]]

haugh, hauch, †**halch,** †**halgh,** †**hawch** /hɔx/ *n* a piece of level alluvial ground on a riverbank, river-meadow land; frequently in place-names *la12-*. **haugh ground,** †**haugh-grund** low-lying meadowland (by the banks of a stream or river) *la18-19*. †**haughing ground** = *haugh-grund 18-e19*. **haughland, haughlan** land by a river *17-*. [OE *healh* a corner, a nook]

haugh see HAUCH[1.1], HOCH[1.1]
hauingis see HAIVINS

haul[1.1] /hɔl/ *n* a very large quantity (of something) *la19-*. Compare HALE[1.1]. [see the verb]
haul[1.2], **haal** /hɔl, hal/ *v* to pull or drag; to transport *la18-*. [variant of HALE[1.2]]
haul see HAUD[1.1]
hauld see HAUD[1.2]
hault see HAUT[1.2]
haumer see HAIMMER[1.2]
haun see HAN[1.1], HAN[1.2]
haunchman see HANCHMAN
haund see HAN[1.1]
haunle see HANLE[1.1], HANLE[1.2]
haunt[1.1], **hant** /hɔnt, hant/ *n* 1 a place of frequent resort or usual abode *la15-*. 2 the act of frequenting *16-*. 3 a custom, a habit, a practice *16-19, 20- T SW.* [see the verb]
haunt[1.2], **hant** /hɔnt, hant/ *v* 1 to visit habitually, frequent the company of *15-*. 2 to attend church regularly *la16-e17*. **hantit** accustomed, habituated, familiar *la15-19, 20- T EC.* [ME *haunten*]
haunty see HANTY
haup see HAP[3]
haupny see HAUF[1.3]
hauppen see HAPPEN
haur see HAAR[1]
haurd see HARD[1.2], HEAR
haurdly, haurly, harly, hardly, *Sh Ork* **herdly,** †**hardlie** /'hɔrdle, 'hɔrle, 'harli, 'hardli; *Sh Ork* 'hɛrdli/ *adv* 1 scarcely, barely *17-*. 2 harshly, severely; with difficulty *15-e17*. 3 certainly, assuredly *la15-16*. 4 vigorously, violently; courageously *la14-16*. **hardlies, harlies** hardly, scarcely *19- EC.* **hardlins** hardly, scarcely *19- Sh NE EC Bor.* [OE *heardlice* harshly, stoutly]
haurl see HARL[1.2]
haurly see HAURDLY
haurn see HARN[2]
haurns see HARNS
hause[1.1], **hawse, hass,** †**thals** /hɔs, has/ *n* 1 the neck *la14-*. 2 the throat, the gullet *la14-*. 3 a narrow neck of land; a narrow passage between hills, a defile, the head of a pass; frequently in place-names *la15-19, 20- SW Bor.* 4 a narrow stretch of water, a narrow inlet *16-19, 20- Ork.* 5 a narrow neck-like part, a spindle or axle; the neck of a vessel *16-18, 20- NE.* **hassband** a neck-band for tying a cow *20- Sh.* **hause bane, hawse bane** the collarbone *15-*. **hass-furr** ploughing the second furrow *20- WC SW.* **haslock,** †**hawslock,** †**halslok,** †**haslok** the fine wool on a sheep's neck *la16-19, 20- Sh NE.* **hause pipe** the throat, the windpipe *la19- T WC.* **hass o the thrapple** the back of the throat *21-*. [OE, ON *hals*]
hause[1.2], †**thass,** †**thawse,** †**thalse** /hɔs/ *v* to hug or embrace *15-19, 20- literary.* [see the noun]
†**haut**[1.1], **hat, halt** *n* lameness, a limp; a hop *la15-e19*. [see the verb]
haut[1.2], **hat,** †**halt,** †**hault** /hɔt, hat/ *v* to limp; to hop *la14-19, 20- WC.* [OE *haltian*]
†**hautane, haltane, haltand** *adj* haughty *la14-16*. [ME *hautein*]
hauthorn see HAWTHORN
hauyn empire see HEVIN IMPYRE
havar see HAVER[2]
have see HAE[1.2], HEAVE[1.2]
havel, †**theevil,** †**theawe-eel,** †**thave-eel** /'hevəl/ *n* the conger-eel *Conger conger 18-19, 20- NE.* [ON *haf* the open sea + Scots *eel*]
haveless see HAIVELESS
haven see HINE[2]

haver[1] /ˈhevər/ *n* the oat *Avena sativa*; oats *la17-19, 20- Bor.* **haver-meal** oatmeal *la17-19, 20- SW.* **haver straw** straw from oats *19- SW Bor.* [probably ON *hafr*; compare MDu, MLG *haver*]

haver[2], †**havar**, †**haifar** /ˈhavər/ *n* **1** *law* the holder of documents required for production as evidence in a court *la16-.* **2** a person who has something, an owner, keeper, or occupier *la15-18.* [*have* (HAE[1.2]), with agent suffix]

haver *see* HAIVER[1.2]

haverel /ˈhevərəl/ *n* a castrated male goat *19, 20- Uls.* [OE *hæfer* a he-goat]

haveril *see* HAIVEREL[1.1], HAIVEREL[1.2]

haverin, havering *see* HAIVERING[1.1], HAIVERING[1.2]

havers *see* HALVERS[1.1], HALVERS[1.2]

haves *see* HAE[1.1]

havie *see* HEAVY[1.3]

havin *see* HINE[2]

having /ˈhavɪŋ/ *n* **1** possessing, keeping *la14-.* **2** bearing, behaviour, deportment *la14-16.* **3** taking, removing *la15-16.* Compare HAIVINS. [verbal noun from *have* (HAE[1.2])]

havings, havins *see* HAIVINS

havnae *see* HAE[1.2]

havrel *see* HAIVEREL[1.1]

havren *see* HAIVERING[1.2]

havy *see* HEAVY[1.2]

havyn *see* HINE[2]

haw[1], *NE* **chaw** /hɔ; *NE* tʃɔ/ *n* the hawthorn *Crataegus monogyna*; a hawthorn berry *16-.* **hawberry** a hawthorn berry *la19- T EC.* **haw-buss, haw-bush** the hawthorn tree *19- T H&I EC Bor.* **haw-spitter** a peashooter *20- WC SW.* **hawstone** the seed in a hawthorn berry *19- SW Uls.* **hawtree** the hawthorn tree *19-.* [OE *haga* a hawthorn berry]

haw[2], *NE* **hyaave** /hɔ; *NE* hjav/ *adj* **1** bluish, lead-coloured; dull, wan *la15-19, 20- Sh NE.* **2** *of people* pale, sallow-looking *18- NE.* **hawee** pale, tinged with blue *20- Sh.* **haw clay, ha' clay** a kind of clay for whitening doorsteps, usually a tough, clammy, pale-blue clay *18, 19- Bor.* [OE *hǣwe*]

haw[3] /hɔ/ *interj* an exclamation to attract someone's attention *20- WC.* [a natural utterance; compare ON *hó*]

haw *see* HA[1]

hawch *see* HAUGH

hawd *see* HAUD[1.2]

hawee *see* HAW[2]

haweless *see* HAIVELESS

hawfar *see* HALVER[1.1]

Hawick ba, Hawick ball /ˈhɔɪk bɔ, ˈhɔɪk bɔl/ *n* **1** a round, brown, mint-flavoured boiled sweet made in Hawick *20-.* **2** a game played at Shrovetide with a football in the River Teviot *la19- Bor.* [from the place-name + BA[1]]

†**Hawick gill** *n* a measure of ale or spirits equivalent to half an Imperial pint (0.28 litre) *18-e19.* [from the place-name + GILL[1]]

hawk[1.1], †**halk**, †**hak** /hɔk/ *n* a bird of prey of the family *Falconidae 14-.* †**halk dog** *in Orkney* an annual tax of a dog (for upkeep of the royal hawks) *la16-e17.* †**halk hen** *in Shetland, Orkney and Caithness* a feudal tax of poultry *16-e19.* [OE *hafoc*]

hawk[1.2], †**halk** /hɔk/ *v* to hunt with a trained bird of prey *la15-.* [see the noun]

hawk *see* HACK[1.1]

hawkie, †**hacky** /ˈhɔki/ *n* **1** (a name for) a cow with a white face *18-.* **2** a stupid person *la18-e19.* [altered form of HAWKIT]

hawkit, haikit, hackit, †**halkit** /ˈhɔkət, ˈhekət, ˈhakət/ *adj* **1** *of livestock* having white markings; white-faced *la15-19, 20- N NE.* **2** *of people* stupid, rash *la18- NE.* [unknown]

hawm /hɔm/ *v* to work in a slovenly way; to lounge or laze about *la19- NE.* [unknown]

hawmer *see* HAIMMER[1.1]

hawse *see* HAUSE[1.1], HAUSE[1.2]

hawthorn, †**hathorne**, †**hauthorn** /ˈhɔθɔrn/ *n* a prickly tree, the hawthorn *Crataegus monogyna*, frequently in place-names *la13-.* [OE *hagaþorn*]

hay *see* HEY[1], HEY[3.2]

ha-year auld *see* HAUF[1.3]

hayle *see* HAIL[2]

haylis *see* HELSE

haym *see* HAME[1.1]

haymald *see* HAMELT[1.1]

haymhald *see* HAMEHALD

haymly *see* HAMELY[1.1]

haymwart *see* HAMEWART[1.2]

hayr *see* HAIR[1.1], HAIR[2.2]

hazel[1.1], *NE* **hizzel**, *Bor* **heezel**, †**hissel**, †**hesill**, †**hasil** /ˈhezəl; *NE* ˈhɪzəl; *Bor* ˈhizəl/ *n* **1** a bush or small tree *Corylus avellana 15-.* **2** a hazel stick used as a cudgel *19, 20- N NE Bor.* **hazelly**, †**hazly** covered with or abounding in hazels *la18-.* **hazel oil** *humorous* a caning, a beating *19, 20- T SW.* **hazelraw** the lichen *Lobaria pulmonaria la18.* [OE *hæsel*, ON *heslt*]

hazel[1.2] /ˈhezəl/ *v* to beat or thrash *la19- N NE Bor.* [see the noun]

hazer *see* HAIZER

hazy /ˈhezi/ *adj* **1** *of weather* misty, not clear *19-.* **2** weak in intellect; mentally unbalanced *19- H&I EC Bor.* [unknown]

he[1.1] /hi/ *n* a man, a male *la18-19, 20- N NE.* [see the pronoun]

he[1.2], *NE* **e**, *Bor* **ei**, †**hie** /hi; *NE* i; *Bor* ʌɪ/ *pron* **1** the male in question or referred to *la14-.* **2** *of objects or natural phenomena* it *15-.* **3** a male animal *la15-.* **4** *referring to a husband or master* him, himself *19-.* **he-deem** a woman perceived to have masculine manners or appearance *20- NE.* [OE *hē*]

he *see* HEICH[1.2], HEICH[1.4]

head *see* HEID[1.1], HEID[1.2], HEID[1.3]

headapeer *see* HEIDIEPEER

headicraa[1.1], **heidiecra** /hɛdiˈkra, hidiˈkra/ *n* a somersault *la19- Sh.* [unknown]

headicraa[1.2], **heidiecra** /hɛdiˈkra, hidiˈkra/ *adv* head-over-heels *19- Sh.* [unknown]

headie *see* HEIDIE[1.3]

heal[1.1], †**hele**, †**hale**, †**haill** /hil/ *n* **1** health, physical well-being *la14-19, 20- NE.* **2** a source of health or well-being *15-16.* **3** spiritual well-being, salvation *la14-16.* †**heleful** healthy; health-giving, salutary *la14-15.* [OE *hǣlu*]

heal[1.2], **hael, hale**, †**hele**, †**heill** /hil, hel/ *v* to restore to health, cure; to get well *la14-.* [OE *hǣlan*]

heal[2], **hele, heild**, *N* **heyl**, †**theil**, †**theld** /hil; hild; *N* hel/ *v* **1** to conceal; to keep secret *la14-.* **2** to cover *la14-e16.* **heal and conceal** *in freemasonry* to keep secret *la17-.* †**theil counsell** *in the oath of homage* to conceal or keep secret *15-16.* [OE *helian*]

heal *see* HAIL[1.2]

healing blade /ˈhilɪŋ bled/ *n* the greater plantain *Plantago major la19- N NE T.* [presp of HEAL[1.2] + BLADE[1.1]]

†**healing leaf** *n* = HEALING BLADE *e19.* [presp of HEAL[1.2] + LEAF]

health *see* HALTH

heap[1.1], **haip**, *Ork* **hipp**, †**hepe** /hip, hep; *Ork* hɪp/ *n* **1** a pile, a stack *15-.* **2** a large number or quantity, a great deal *la16-.* **3** a slovenly woman *19-.* **4** a coarse, rough person *20- NE T EC.* **5** a heaped measure of capacity *16-e19.* [OE *hēap*]

heap[1.2], **haip**, †**hepe** /hip, hep/ *v* **1** to pile up; to accumulate *la14-.* **2** to be untidy or careless in one's dress *20- NE.* [OE *hēapian*]

hear, †**here**, †**heir** /hir/ *v pt, ptp* **heard, hard, haurd,** *N* **heered,** †**herd 1** to listen, perceive by the ear; to be told *la14*-. **2** *law* to try a person or a case, give a judicial hearing to *15*-. **3** to attend and listen to a religious service or a lecture *15-e18*. **4** to accede to or grant a request *la15-17*. **5** to audit an account *la15-e16*. **hearer,** †**herar 1** an auditor, a listener *15*-. **2** one who listens to the preaching of a certain minister; a churchgoer *la16*-. **hearin, hearing 1** the faculty or action of hearing *la14*-. **2** *law* a judicial process *17*-. **3** a scolding *19*-. **4** news; a long or scarcely believable story *19*- *Sh.* **hear apon** to listen to *la19*- *Sh.* †**herd, heird** hear it *la15*. **hear o** to receive information about *la14*-. †**here record of** to hear tell of *15-16*. **hear till, hear tae** to listen to, heed *la18*-. **hear till her** just listen to her *19*-. **hear till him** just listen to him *19*-. **hear yer ears** to hear oneself speak *la19*- *H&I C Uls.* **nae hear o** to refuse to accept or consent to *la15*-. **not hear day nor door** to be unable to distinguish sounds *la18*-. [OE *hēran*]

hear *see* HARE

hearken, harken, herken, †**herkin,** †**harkin** /'harkən, 'hɛrkən/ *v* **1** to listen, pay attention to; to heed *la14*-. **2** *of the wind* to blow gently *19*-. **3** to eavesdrop *la19*- *NE T C.* **4** to whisper *19, 20*- *Sh Ork N NE.* **hearkener,** †**herkenare,** †**harkner** a listener; an eavesdropper *la15*-. **hearkenin** *of wind or weather* gentle; calm *20*- *NE.* **hearken intae** to whisper to a person *la19*- *Sh NE.* **hearken someone their lessons** to hear someone repeat lessons *19*-. [OE *hercnian*]

heart *see* HART, HERT[1.1], HERT[1.2]

hearten *see* HERTEN

hearth *see* HAIRTH

Heart of Midlothian /hart əv mɪd'loðɪən/ *n* **1** an Edinburgh football club *la19*-. **2** a nickname for the now-demolished Tolbooth prison in Edinburgh, the site of which is marked by a heart-shaped arrangement of cobbles on the Royal Mile *18-e19, la19- historical.* [HERT[1.1] + the county name *Midlothian*]

Hearts /harts/ *n* a nickname for Heart of Midlothian Football Club *20*-. **the Hearts** = HEARTS *la19*-. [shortened form of HEART OF MIDLOTHIAN]

heart scald *see* HERTSCAD

heartsome *see* HERTSOME

hearty *see* HERTY

heary, †**heery,** †**herie** /'hiri/ *interj* an expression of endearment (used by married couples to each other) *la18-e19, 20- EC.* [unknown]

hease *see* HEEZE[1.2]

heasty, †**heastie,** †**hasty** /'histi/ *n in Caithness and Sutherland* a disease of cattle, murrain *la17-19, 20- historical.* [unknown]

heat[1.1], **hate, heyt,** †**hete,** †**theit,** †**het** /hit, het/ *n* **1** warmth, hotness *la14*-. **2** an act of heating, a state of feeling hot *16*-. **get a heat** to make (oneself) warm, warm up *la18*-. **gie a heat** to make (oneself or another) warm *16*-. [OE *hǣtu*; compare HET[1.1]]

heat[1.2], **het, hate,** †**hete** /hit, hɛt, het/ *v pt* **het, hat, heatit,** *ptp* **het, heatit,** *EC* **hetten** to make or become hot; to warm up *la14*-. **heater** a wedge-shaped, glazed, sugared bun *20- NE.* **heat a wummle** a game with a young child held on the knee *19*-. **heat the hoose** to hold a housewarming party *19, 20- EC.* [OE *hǣtan*; compare HET[1.1]]

heathen *see* HAITHEN[1.1], HAITHEN[1.2], HAITHEN[2]

heather, haither, *Sh Ork NE* **hedder,** †**hether,** †**hadder,** †**hather** /'hɛðər, 'hɛðər; *Sh Ork NE* 'hɛðər/ *n* **1** a plant of the genus *Erica la11*-. **2** a place of concealment (in the heather-clad hills) *18- literary*. **3** an expression of surprise, doubt or disgust *la19- Bor.* **heather ale** a drink brewed from heather, hops, barm, syrup, ginger and water *19*-. **heather ask** the common lizard *Zootoca vivipara 20- NE EC.* **heather bell** the flower of the heather *Erica tetralix* or *Erica cinerea 18*-; compare *bell heather* (BELL[1.1]). **hedder berry** the black crowberry *Empetrum nigrum 20- Sh N NE.* **heather besom** a broom made of heather *la16*-. **heather birns** the stalks and roots of burnt heather *la18*-. **heather blackie** the ring ouzel *Turdus torquatus la19*-. **heather bleat** the common snipe *Gallinago gallinago 18- N NE SW Uls.* **heather bleater, heather bluitter** the common snipe *Gallinago gallinago la16*-. **heather blindness** a contagious eye disease of sheep *20*-. **heather claw** a (hunting) dog's dew-claw (frequently removed as liable to catch in heather) *20*-. **heather cock** the black grouse *Tetrao tetrix* or the red grouse *Lagopus lagopus la19, 20- N NE T EC.* **heather cowe,** *Sh* **hedder kowe 1** a large, bushy heather plant; a tuft or twig of heather *17-19, 20- Sh Ork N NE.* **2** a broom made of heather-twigs *19, 20- Sh Ork N NE SW.* **heather lintie 1** the twite *Linaria flavirostris 19*-. **2** the common linnet *Linaria cannabina la19- NE T EC Bor.* **heather lowper** a hill-dweller, a country-dweller *20- NE.* **heather peeper 1** the meadow pipit *Anthus pratensis la19- NE.* **2** the sandpiper *Actitis hypoleucos la20*- *T.* **heather piker** *derogatory* a person living in a poverty-stricken or miserly way *20- NE.* **heather range, heather reenge** a pot-scourer made of heather stems tied together *18*-. **heather-an-dub** *n* clay mixed with cut heather, used instead of mortar in house-building *la19- NE.* **heather-an-dub** *adj* rough, poor, unrefined *la19- NE.* **not set the heather on fire** to not cause a great furore or sensation *19*-. [unknown]

heather bill *see* ETHER

heather-reenge, †**heatherange** /'hɛðər rinʒ/ *n* the hydrangea *Hydrangea macrophylla la19- NE T EC.* [altered form of *heather range* (HEATHER)]

heathery, *NE* **heddery,** †**hadry,** †**heathry** /'hɛðəri; *NE* 'hɛdəri/ *adj* **1** heather-covered; of or like heather *la15*-. **2** rough, dishevelled; mountain-bred *la18*-. **heatherie head** (a person with) a tousled or shaggy head of hair *19- NE T Bor.* †**hedry pow** = *heatherie head la18*. [HEATHER + -IE[2]]

heath-hen *see* HAITHEHEN

heathnick *see* ETHNIK[1.2]

heathry *see* HEATHERY

heave[1.1] /hiv/ *n* a push, a shove; a heaving movement *19*-. **get the heave 1** to be pushed or shoved *la19*-. **2** to be sacked from a job *la20*-. [see the verb]

heave[1.2], **have,** *Sh* **höv,** *NE* **haive,** †**heve,** †**heif** /hiv, hav; *Sh* høv; *NE* hev/ *v pt, ptp* **hovin 1** to throw or pitch; to toss or fling *la18*-. **2** to rise up above the surface; to become prominent; to come into view *19*-. **3** to lift or hold up; to elevate *la14-19*. **4** to lift a child from the font as sponsor; to baptize *la14-17*. [OE *hebban*]

heaven *see* HIVVEN

heavy[1.1] /'hɛvi/ *n* a type of (strength of) Scottish beer *20*-. [see the adj]

heavy[1.2], **hivvy,** †**hevy,** †**havy,** †**heuie** /'hɛvi, 'hɪve/ *adj* **1** weighty, hard to lift or carry *la14*-. **2** severe, extreme; serious, oppressive *la14*-. **3** of great quantity or force *la14*-. **4** pregnant; in an advanced state of pregnancy *la14*-. **5** *of a river* swollen *19*-. **6** *of an alcoholic drink* large *la19*-. **heavysome** dull, gloomy, doleful *e18, 20- SW.* **heavy beer** a type of (strength of) Scottish beer *20*-. **heavy fittit** in an advanced state of pregnancy *19*-. **heavy handfu** a heavy burden, an oppressive responsibility *19*-. **heavy-heartit** threatening rain *19- EC.* **be a heavy neighbour on** to consume a great deal of food or drink *19*-. **be heavy on** to be hard on clothes; to consume a great deal of food or drink *19*-. **heavy o fit** = *heavy fittit la19*-. [OE *hefig*]

heavy[1,3], †**hevy**, †**havie** /ˈhɛvi/ *adv* heavily *15-*. [OE *hefige*]

heawe-eel *see* HAVEL

hebdomadar, †**ebdomadare** /hɛbˈdɔmədər/ *n* **1** *in Scottish universities* the member of staff whose turn it is to supervise the conduct of the students (originally also in Grammar schools) *17-*. **2** a member of a college or chapter taking a weekly turn in performing the services in the church *la15-e16*. †**habdomodary, ebdomidrye** a weekly turn of performing church services *16*. [Lat *hebdomadārius* a member of a college or chapter taking a weekly turn in performing church services, originally Greek]

hech[1.1] /hɛx/ *n* **1** the act of exclaiming the word 'hech' *la18-19, 20-* WC. **2** a fixed routine or habit *la18-19, 20-* *literary*. [see the interj]

hech[1.2] /hɛx/ *v* **1** to pant, breathe hard or uneasily *19, 20-* Bor. **2** to make the sound 'hech' *19*. [see the interj]

hech[1.3], †**hegh** /hɛx/ *interj* an expression of sorrow, fatigue, pain, surprise or contempt *la17-*. **hech aye** an expression of affirmation *20-*. **hech hey** an expression of weariness or regret *la18-19, 20-* T. **hech how** an expression of weariness or regret *18-19, 20-* SW Bor. **hech how hum** an expression of weariness or regret *19, 20-* NE T EC. **hech me** an expression of sorrow, fatigue or pain *19-*. **hech sirs** an expression of sorrow, fatigue or pain *la18-*. **hech wow** an expression of distress or regret *18-19, 20-* Bor. [imitative of a sigh]

hech *see* HECK[1.1]

hech how *see* HECH[1.3]

hech-how /ˈhɛxhʌu/ *n* **1** hemlock water dropwort *Oenanthe crocata la19-* H&I SW. **2** hedge parsley *Torilis arvensis la19-* SW Uls. [probably Gael *ith-eodha* hemlock, perhaps with influence from *hech how* (HECH[1.3])]

hechle[1.1] /ˈhɛxəl/ *n* a struggle; a difficulty; a perplexing piece of work *20-* EC Bor. [see the verb]

hechle[1.2], WC **hychle** /ˈhɛxəl/ WC ˈhʌɪxəl/ *v* **1** to puff, pant *19-*. **2** to walk with difficulty; to struggle or exert oneself *19-* C Bor. [frequentative form of HECH[1.2]; compare also HOCHLE[1.2]]

hecht[1.1], †**hicht**, †**heicht** /hɛxt/ *n* a promise *la14-19, 20-* *literary*. †**if a' hechts haud** if all comes true *18-19*. [see the verb]

hecht[1.2], †**hicht**, †**heicht** /hɛxt/ *v* **1** to promise, pledge *la14-*. **2** to foretell, prophesy *la18-* C SW. †**I hecht** I undertake, I avow, I dare say *la14-16*. [OE *hēht*, pt of *hatan* to command, order]

†**hecht**[2], **hicht** *v* to be called, have as one's name *la14-19*. [OE *hēht*, pt of *hatan* to be called]

hecht *see* HEICH[1.3], HEICHT[1.1], HEICHT[1.2]

hechten *see* HEICHTEN

heck[1.1], N NE EC **haik**, †**hek**, †**hack**, †**hech** /hɛk; N NE EC hek/ *n* **1** a slatted (wooden or iron) framework *la15-*. **2** a grating placed in and across a stream to obstruct flotsam, fish or livestock *16-*. **3** the toothed part of a spinning-wheel or warping machine for guiding the spun thread onto the bobbin *16-19, 20-* *historical*. **4** a plate-rack or bottle-rack *18-* Sh N NE T EC Bor. **5** a rack for drying fish *17-19, 20-* Sh NE T EC. **6** the ability to eat heartily, appetite *20-* SW Bor. **7** a framework attached to a cart to enable it to take a higher load *la19, 20-* NE. **8** a rack for drying cheeses *la17-19, 20-* N. **9** a metal hook or loop on a scabbard through which the sword-belt passed *e18*. **10** a space between the bars of a grating across a stream *15-17*. **hecker** a person with a hearty appetite *20-* C Bor. †**heck door** a hatch-door, a door divided in two horizontally *la16-e19*. **Auld Haiks, Auld Haikes** a name for a fishing-ground off the coast of Fife *la18-*. **live at heck and manger** to live extravagantly *la18-*. [OE *fōdorhec* a rack for food; compare MLG *heck* a fence]

heck[1.2] /hɛk/ *v* **1** to eat greedily *19-* EC Bor. **2** *in weaving* to work a fringe on a small loom *la18*. [see the noun]

heck[2] /hɛk/ *interj* a command to a horse to turn left *la19-* T EC. [unknown]

heck[3.1] /hɛk/ *n* a crutch *la19-* Sh. [ON *haekja*]

heck[3.2] /hɛk/ *v* to walk with a limp or on crutches; to hop *la19-* Sh Ork. **heckle** to go as if on crutches; to travel laboriously *la19-* Sh. [see the noun]

heck[4] /hɛk/ *v* to grasp, grab *la19-* Sh Ork. **hecked** closely linked, hand-to-hand *20-* Ork. [unknown]

heck *see* HAKE

heckapolo /ˈhɛkəpolo/ *n* a poor creature *20-* Ork. [unknown]

heckapurdes /ˈhɛkəpʌrdɪs/ *n* a poor, frail creature *20-* Ork. [unknown]

heckham-peckham, †**heckum-peckum** /ˈhɛkəmˈpɛkəm/ *n* an artificial fly used in trout-fishing *la19-*. [unknown]

heckle[1.1], **hackle**, †**hekkill** /ˈhɛkəl, ˈhakəl/ *n* **1** a flax comb *la15-*. **2** the long neck-feathers found on certain birds *la15-*. **3** a cockade of dyed hackle-feathers worn in the bonnets of some Scottish regiments *la18-*. **4** (a person who gives) a severe beating or sharp criticism *la18-19, 20-* SW. **5** *angling* an artificial fly (made with a hackle-feather) *la19*. [MLG, MDu *hekele*]

heckle[1.2], †**hekkill** /ˈhɛkəl/ *v* **1** to dress flax with a comb *la15-*. **2** to scold severely; to argue *17-*. **3** to badger with questions, interrogate *19-*. †**heckled**, **hecklit** having a border or fringe like a cock's hackle *la15-e17*. **hecklie** a type of hard biscuit with a pinhole surface *la19-* T. **heckle biscuit** = *hecklie la19-* NE T. **heckle pin** a tooth of a flax-comb; something sharp *la18-*. **be on heckle pins** to be in suspense or on tenterhooks *la19-*. **come through the heckle pins** to suffer a harsh or taxing experience *la18-19, 20-* T EC. [see the noun]

heckle[2], **hackle** /ˈhɛkəl, ˈhakəl/ *n* a net of straw ropes covering a haystack or a thatched roof *la19-* NE. [OE *hacele* a cloak, a mantle]

heckle[3] /ˈhɛkəl/ *n* the part of a knife to which the handle is attached, the tang *20-* Sh. [compare Faer *hekil* the metal connecting the blade of a scythe to the sned]

Hecklebirnie /ˈhɛkəlbɪrni, ˈhɛkəlbʌrni/ *n* a euphemism for Hell *19, 20-* NE. [euphemistic form of Scots *Hell*]

heckoo, **hecko** /ˈhɛku, ˈhɛko/ *n* (the combatants of) a hand-to-hand fight *20-* Ork. [unknown]

heckum-peckum *see* HECKHAM-PECKHAM

hecturi, †**heeturi**, †**a heater** /ˈhɛkturi/ *numeral in counting rhymes* six *19-* WC SW Bor. [nonsense word derived from a system of counting sheep]

hed *see* HAE[1.2], HEID[1.2], HIDE[1]

-hed *see* -HEID

hedden *see* HAE[1.2]

hedder *see* HEATHER

hedderkindunk, **hederkandunk** /ˌhɛdərkənˈdʌŋk/ *n* **1** a (game of) see-saw *la19-* Sh. **2** a seabird *la19-* Sh. **3** a bump, a thump; a heavy fall *20-* Sh. [unknown]

heddery *see* HEATHERY

heddle, †**theddill**, †**hiddle** /ˈhɛdəl/ *n in a loom* one of the cords or wires which separates the warp threads to allow passage of the shuttle *16-*. [OE *hefeld* a weaver's beam]

hede *see* HEED[1.1], HEID[1.1], HEID[1.2]

-hede *see* -HEID

hederkandunk *see* HEDDERKINDUNK

hedge, †**thege**, †**hage**, †**hegge** /hɛdʒ/ *n* a row of closely-planted bushes; frequently in place-names *la12-*. **hedgie** the hedge sparrow or dunnock *Prunella modularis 20-*. **hedge ruit** the bottom of a hedge *la19-* T EC SW Bor. †**hege**

skraper an avaricious person *la16*. **hedge spurdie, hedge spurgie** the hedge sparrow *la19- NE T*. [OE *hecg*]

hedger /'hɛdʒər/ *n* a hedgehog *20- NE T*. [shortened form of Eng *hedgehog*]

hedie *see* HEIDIE[1.3]

heding *see* HETHING

hedy peir *see* HEIDIEPEER

hee *see* HEICH[1.3]

heech /hix/ *interj* an expression of exhilaration, shouted by dancers in a reel *la19-*. [compare HOOCH[1.3]]

heed[1.1], **†hede, †heid** /hid/ *n* care, attention *la14-*. **tak heed** to pay attention *la14-*. [ME *hed*]

heed[1.2] /hid/ *v* to take notice, pay attention *18-*. **never heed** never mind, don't bother *18-*. [OE *hēdan*]

heed *see* HAUD[1.2], HEID[1.1], HOOD[1.1]

heedabo /'hidəbo/ *adj* reckless *20- Ork*. [unknown]

heedie *see* HEIDIE[1.1], HOODIE

heedin *see* HOODIN

heefer *see* HEIFER

hee haw /hi 'hɔ/ *n* nothing; not a thing *la20-*. [unknown]

heek *see* HICK[2]

heel[1.1], **†hele, †heill** /hil/ *n* **1** the back part of a foot *la14-*. **2** the end part of a loaf of bread or a piece of cheese *la18-*. **3** the part of an adze or scythe into which the handle is fitted *19-*. **4** *golf* the part of the head of a club nearest to the shaft *la19-*. **5** the fulcrum of a lever, a block of wood put under a crowbar to give leverage *20- T C*. **heel-cap** to mend or reinforce the heels of shoes or socks *19-*. **heel-ring** a metal protection on the heel of a boot or shoe *la19- NE T EC*. **heelshod** a piece of iron used to protect the heel of a heavy boot or shoe *la19-*. **at the heel o the hunt** last *la19- EC Bor Uls*. **come tae yer heel-hap** to come to grief *20- NE*. **heels ower heid 1** in disorder *la18-*. **2** head over heels *19-*. **heels ower hurdie** head over heels *la19-*. **heelster heids** head over heels *19-*. **mak your heels your freends** to run away *la19- NE T EC*. **tak yer heels** to take to one's heels, run away *18-*. [OE *hēla*]

heel[1.2] /hil/ *v golf* to mis-hit by striking the ball with the heel of the club *la19-*. [see the noun]

heel *see* HEELD[1.2]

Heeland *see* HIELAND[1.2]

heeld[1.1], **†held, †heild** /hild/ *n* **1** the close of day when the sun is low in the sky; the end of the year *20- Sh*. **2** sloping ground *la16*. **†on heild** *of posture* leaning or stooping *e16*. [OE *hielde* a slope]

heeld[1.2], **†helde, †heild, †heel** /hild/ *v* **1** to lean or tilt; to overturn *la14-19, 20- Sh Ork*. **2** to incline to an attitude or opinion; to submit to a person *la14-16*. [OE *hieldan*]

heeld *see* HAUD[1.2]

heelie *see* HOOLY[1.2]

heeliegoleerie[1.1] /hiligə'liri/ *n* confusion, noise, bustle *19, 20- NE EC*. [see the adv]

heeliegoleerie[1.2], **†hilliegleerie** /hiligə'liri/ *adv* topsy-turvy, in a state of confusion *19, 20- T EC*. [a fanciful formation, perhaps from a children's action rhyme; compare HEELSTERGOWDIE]

heelik *see* HELLICK

heelstergowdie, heels ower gowdie, heels ower gowrie /hilstər'gʌudi, hils ʌuər 'gʌudi, hils ʌuər 'gʌuri/ *adv* head over heels, upside-down *18-19, 20- NE T EC*. [HEEL[1.1], second element perhaps *ower gowdie* with *gowdie* in the sense of golden hair; compare GOWD]

heely[1.1] /'hili/ *n* an affront *19- N NE H&I EC*. **heeliefu** haughty, arrogant *la19- NE T EC*. [see the adj]

heely[1.2] /'hili/ *v* **1** to offend; to take offence *la19- NE EC*. **2** to despise *la19- NE EC*. [see the adj]

heely[1.3], **†hely, †hiely** /'hili/ *adj* haughty, arrogant *15-19, 20- N*. [OE *hēalic*]

heely[1.4], **†hely, †heyly, †hiely** /'hili/ *adv* **1** highly, extremely; *la14-17, 20- literary*. **2** arrogantly; loudly *15-17*. [OE *hēalice*]

heely *see* HOOLY[1.3], HOOLY[1.4]

heem *see* HAME[1.1], HAME[1.2]

heen *see* HAE[1.2]

heepochondreoch /hipə'kɔndriəx/ *adj* listless, melancholy *20- NE EC*. [altered form of Eng *hypochondriac*]

heepocondry /hipə'kɔndri/ *n pl* **†hypochonderies** hypochondria *19, 20- T EC*. [altered form of Eng *hypochondria*]

heepocreet *see* HYPOCREET

†heepy *n* a melancholy or foolish person *18-e19*. [shortened form of Eng *hypochondriac*]

†heere, heir, here *n* a length of 600 yards (548 metres) of linen yarn, one sixth of a hank *15-19*. [specialized sense of HAIR[1.1]]

heered *see* HEAR

heeren *see* HERRIN

heery *see* HEARY

heer-yestreen *see* EREDASTREEN

hee scoill *see* HIGH SCHOOL

heesh, hish /hiʃ, hɪʃ/ *interj* **1** an exhortation to be quiet *20-*. **2** a soothing sound (for rocking a child to sleep) *20- NE T*. [onomatopoeic]

heesh *see* HISH[1.2]

heeshie-baw *see* HISHIE-BA[1.2]

heest, haste, *NE EC* **hist, †hast, †hest, †haist** /hist, hest; *NE EC* hɪst/ *v* **1** to (cause to) go or act quickly; to hurry, hasten *la14-*. **2** to send (equipment or news) quickly from one place to another; to instruct (a person) to go quickly *15-*. **3** to carry out an action quickly, dispatch with speed *15-16*. **†hasting, haistine** an early flowering variety of pea *la17-e19*. **haste ye back** *v* to visit again soon *la18-*. **haste ye back** *n* a bargain, an extra given by a shopkeeper to encourage customers to return *la20- NE SW*. [ME *hasten*]

heeturi *see* HECTURI

heeven *see* HIVVEN

heevie *see* HOOVIE

heevil *see* HAVEL

heeze[1.1], *NE* **hyse, †heez** /hiz; *NE* haez/ *n* **1** help, assistance; encouragement *18-*. **2** a heave or hoist up *19-*. **3** a piece of clowning; a practical joke; banter, teasing *la19- NE*. **4** the act of swinging; a child's swing *e19*. **5** hoisting tackle *e17*. **heezie**, *NE* **hyzie 1** a heave or hoist up; a raising of the spirits *18-*. **2** a drubbing, rough handling *18-19, 20- Sh*. **heezie hozie** a game in which two players stand back to back, interlink arms, and, stooping alternately, raise each other from the ground *19-*. [see the verb]

heeze[1.2], **hease, hize, hyse, †these, †theis, †heys** /hiz, haez/ *v* **1** to hoist, lift or raise up *16-*. **2** to exalt or extol *la16-*. **3** to travel quickly; to hurry *la19, 20- NE T EC*. **4** to convey quickly; to hurry a person (off or along) *19, 20- NE EC*. **5** to abound, swarm or teem *20- NE EC*. **6** to dance in a lively way; to romp; to make merry *19, 20- NE*. **7** *of costs* to rise *la18-19*. **heyser** a clothes-prop *20- NE T*. **heeze your hert** to lift up one's own or another's heart; to take or give courage to; to embolden; to cheer *la16-*. [LG *hissen*, Du *hijsen*]

heezel *see* HAZEL[1.1]

hef *see* HAE[1.2]

heff *see* HEFT[3.1], HEFT[3.2]

heffer[1.1] /'hɛfər/ *n* a loud laugh, a guffaw *20- EC Bor*. [probably onomatopoeic]

heffer[1.2] /'hɛfər/ *v* to laugh heartily, laugh in a coarse manner *20- EC Bor*. **hefferer** a person who laughs loudly *20- EC Bor*. [see the noun]

heft¹·¹, **haft** /hɛft, haft/ *n* **1** the shaft of a hand tool; a haft *la14-*. **2** a fisherman's gaff (for landing big fish) *20- Ork*. **baith heft an blade in yer hand** to have complete control *16-19, 20- Sh NE*. [OE *hæft*]

heft¹·² /hɛft/ *v* **1** to fit with a handle *17-19, 20- Sh*. **2** to fix firmly *la16-17*. **heftit** handled, fitted with a handle *17-*. [see the noun]

heft² /hɛft/ *v* **1** to lift up; to remove by lifting *la18-*. **2** to lift in order to estimate the weight *20-*. [probably verbal extension of Older Scots *heft* weight, heaviness]

heft³·¹, †**heff**, †**haft** /hɛft/ *n* **1** a pasture to which sheep or cattle have become familiar; the attachment of sheep to a pasture *la17-*. **2** the number of sheep that a particular pasture will support *20-*. **3** a dwelling-place, one's situation or environment *18-19, 20- SW*. [see the verb]

heft³·², **heff**, †**haft** /hɛft, hɛf/ *v* **1** to accustom livestock to a new pasture by constant herding to prevent them from straying *18-*. **2** *of livestock* to become used to a pasture; *of people* to become settled in a place or occupation *18-19, 20- WC SW Bor*. **heftit 1** accustomed to a pasture, place or situation *18-*. **2** well off, well supplied, in a good situation *la19- Sh*. [unknown; compare ON *hefða* to get possession by long occupation]

heft⁴ /hɛft/ *v* to leave a cow unmilked so that her udder is distended *la19-*. **heftit 1** *of a cow* having a large quantity of milk in the udder *18-*. **2** *of milk* accumulated in the udder *19-*. **3** *of a person* full (of liquid or food) to bursting point or repletion *19-*. **4** *of a cow's udder* hard and dry through not being milked *20-*. **5** swollen with wind, flatulent *20- EC SW Bor*. [Norw dial *hefta* to hold up, restrain, check]

hege, **hegge** *see* HEDGE

heggis *see* HAGGIS

hegh *see* HECH¹·³

hegri, **hegrie**, **haegri** /ˈhɛgri, ˈhegri/ *n* **1** the heron *Ardea cinerea 19- Sh*. **2** thin, loose-fibred worsted yarn *la19- Sh*. **3** a tall, thin person *20- Sh*. **hagery wirsit** thin, loose-fibred worsted yarn *la19- Sh*. [ON *hegri*]

hegs, **haigs** /hɛgz, hegz/ *interj* an expression of emphatic assertion or surprise *la18-*. [altered form of HAITH by analogy with FEGS]

heh *see* HEICH¹·³

heich¹·¹, **high**, †**hich** /hix, hae/ *n* **1** a hill, a height, upland; rising ground *la16-*. **2** height, the highest point *16*. **heich and howe** hill and dale *19-*. **heichs and howes**, †**highs and hows** hills and hollows; ups and downs *18-*. [see the adj]

†**heich¹·²**, **high**, **he** *v ptp* **height**, **hichit** to raise, heighten; to exalt *la14-18*. [see the adj]

heich¹·³, **heigh**, **hee**, **hie**, **high**, *T* **heh**, †**hich**, †**heicht**, †**hecht** /hix, hi, hae; *T* hɛ/ *adj* **1** extending upward, lofty, tall *la14-*. **2** of high rank, exalted, noble *15-*. **3** situated far up, in an elevated position *la15-*. **4** arrogant, haughty *16-*. **5** *of a road* chief, principal *la16-*. **6** lively, excitable *19-*. **7** situated in the upper part or on the upper floor of a building *la16-19, 20- H&I WC*. **8** out of one's mind, raving in delirium *la19, 20- NE*. **9** *of wind or geographical location* north *20- SW*. **10** *of edging-lace or braid* broad *17*. †**High Admiral** the commander-in-chief of the navy *18-e19* **high-bendit** dignified in appearance; haughty, ambitious *18-19, 20- EC*. †**hie burde** the high table, the principal table in a dining-hall *la16-e17*. **high-cutter** a type of plough used in ploughing competitions *20-*. **high door** *mining* an upper landing-place in a shaft *la19- EC*. **high English** the stilted, affected, pedantic or distorted form of English used by Scots trying to imitate 'correct' English *la18-19, 20- T C*. **high-flyer** a name for a member of the Evangelical Church party, the successors of the Covenanters, as opposed to a Moderate *18-e19, 20- historical*. **high gate**, †**hie gate 1** a main road, a highway *la14-19, 20- historical*. **2** the main route through a town, the High Street *la15-18, 19- historical*. **3** the best or most direct way *la16-19*. **heich heidit**, **high heided** arrogant, haughty *la16-19, 20- Sh N NE T EC*. **high heid yin** a leader, a person in authority; *pl* the people in charge; the authorities *20-*. **high jinks** *see* JINK¹·¹. **high kirk** the principal church in a town or region *17-*. †**hie scule** *see* HIGH SCHOOL. **be high in the bend** to be very condescending *20- EC SW Bor*. **be heich upon ae shouther** to have one shoulder higher than the other *20- Sh NE*. **cairry a heich heid** to behave haughtily *la19- NE T EC*. **High Court of Admiralty** the court in which the High Admiral of Scotland exercised extensive jurisdiction (civil and criminal) *la18-19, 20- historical*. **High Steward of Scotland** *see* GREAT STEWARD OF SCOTLAND. †**on hie 1** aloud, loudly *la14-16*. **2** aloft, on high *15-e17*. **up to high doh** in a state of extreme agitation or excitement *20-*. [OE *hēah*]

heich¹·⁴, **high**, †**he**, †**hey**, †**heicht** /hix, hae/ *adv* **1** on high, at or to a height, loftily *la14-*. **2** loudly, in a loud voice *la14-*. **3** proudly, haughtily *la18-*. **heech oot**, **heich oot** aloud, audibly *la19- NE T C*. [see the adj]

heichen *see* HEICHTEN

heicher *see* HIGHER¹·²

Heichlan', **Heichland** *see* HIELAND¹·¹

heich-skeich /ˈhix skix/ *adj* irresponsible *20- literary*. [reduplicated compound based on SKEICH¹·²]

heicht¹·¹, **hecht**, **hicht**, **height**, †**hycht** /hixt, hɛxt, hɪxt, hʌɪt/ *n* **1** altitude, elevation, tallness *la14-*. **2** the highest point, the top, the summit; a high place; *la14-*. **3** the midst or busiest time (of something) *la15-*. **4** a degree, state or condition at the bounds of moderation *18-*. **5** haughtiness, arrogance *la15-16*. **6** exalted rank or worth *la14-16*. †**hichty**, **heichty 1** proud, haughty, arrogant *15-16*. **2** high, elevated *e16*. **the hicht 1** the high point; high ground; the Highlands *la14-19, 20- literary*. **2** the sky, the heavens *15-16, 20- literary*. **heights and howes**, †**hights and hows 1** hills and hollows; ups and downs *la16-*. **2** tantrums, quirks of character *18-*. †**on hicht**, **on heicht 1** aloud, loudly *la14-16*. **2** on high, aloft *la16-e17*. [OE *hiēhþ*]

heicht¹·², **hecht**, **hicht**, **height** /hixt, hɛxt, hɪxt, hʌɪt/ *v* **1** to make higher, lift or heighten *16-19, 20- NE*. **2** to raise in price or value; to increase prices or rents *16-e19*. [see the noun]

heicht *see* HECHT¹·¹, HECHT¹·², HEICH¹·³, HEICH¹·⁴

heichten, **hechten**, **hichten**, †**heichen**, †**highen** /ˈhixtən, ˈhɛxtən, ˈhɪxtən/ *v* to make higher, raise, increase in height *la17-*. [HEICHT¹·¹ or HEICHT¹·², with *-en* suffix]

heid¹·¹, **heed**, **head**, †**hede** /hid, hɛd/ *n* **1** the head, the mind or brain *la14-*. **2** the top or upper part (of something) *la14-*. **3** the highest part or upper end of a river, valley, hill or parish *la14-*. **4** the upper end of a town, street or passage; the end next to the main street *15-*. **5** a headland *la15-*. **6** a single one; *in counting livestock* one beast *la15-*. **7** the flat top or upper surface (of a floor, wall or piece of furniture) *16-*. **8** a measure of yarn, a bundle of (eight) one-ounce skeins, originally four cuts *la16-*. **9** *in curling or bowls* that part of the game in which all the stones or bowls on both sides are played to one end of the rink; their position once thus played *19-*; compare EN¹·¹ (sense 6). **10** the chief or essential point; the purpose or intention of a matter or action *20- Ork NE*. **11** the front part of a ploughshare, originally the part of the Scots plough corresponding to the modern sole *la17-19, 20- H&I SW*. **12** a postage stamp *18-19, 20- WC*. **13** the piece of cloth draped from the canopy at the head of a bed *la15-17*. **14** a chief point or section of a discourse; an item; a subject under discussion *la16-17.* **15** an article of faith *la16-e17.* **headlins, †heidling-is** headlong *la16-19, 20- Sh Ork NE.* **heidmaist, headmost** topmost, highest up *20-.* **heids** the top pupil in a class *20- Bor.* **head band 1** a headband *16-.* **2** the waistband of a pair of trousers or other garment *17-.* **3** a halter *la18-19, 20- Sh T EC Bor.* **heidbanger** a very stupid or unstable person *la20-.* **heid bauk 1** the vertical edge of a fishing-net *la18- Sh EC Bor.* **2** the float-rope of a herring-net *la19- Sh NE.* **head coal** the stratum of a coal seam next to the roof; the top portion of a coal seam when left unworked, either permanently, or to be taken down later *19- EC.* **head dyke, heid dyke** the boundary wall of an agricultural holding; a wall separating arable from uncultivated land *15-.* **head gear, †heid geir, †hede gere** something worn on the head; a head-dress; head armour *15-.* **heid heich** with the head high, proudly *20-.* **†head hemp** a measure of yarn *la16-17.* **head ill, heid ill 1** jaundice in livestock *18- Ork N Bor.* **2** a brain disease of livestock *20- Ork N.* **head koil** a straw covering for the top of a haystack *20- Sh.* **†head lace, heid lace** a hair-ribbon, a headband *16-e19.* **headlicht** giddy, light-headed *la19- Sh Ork N.* **†head mark, heid mark** a distinguishing characteristic on a farm animal *18-19.* **heid nipper** a person who nags or scolds *la20-.* **head rig, heid rig, †hedrig** the grass land at the edge of a field; originally land left unploughed to allow for the turning of the plough *la15-.* **head room, heid room 1** the higher or outer part of an agricultural holding; marginal or boundary land *la15-.* **2** scope for action, authority *la19-.* **†heid scheit** a sheet for the head of a bed *la15-e17.* **head sheaf 1** the crowning point, the finishing touch *18- NE T C.* **2** the last sheaf of grain placed on the top of a stook or ruck *la19-.* **heid steel, †heid staill, †hede stele** a headstall, the headpiece of a bridle *la15-.* **head stoop** headlong *la19- Sh Ork.* **†head suit** a set of ribbons for trimming a head-dress *e18.* **†hed tow, heid toll** a part of a ship's rigging *la15-e17.* **head washing, †heid wasching** the washing of the head as a ceremony of initiation, especially when a new apprentice enters his trade *la16-19, 20- WC.* **†heid werk** pain in the head *la15-e17.* **†hedʒard, heidyard** the (farther or outer) end of a yard or garden *la15-16.* **aff at the head** mad, crazy *19-.* **awa i the heid** mentally unbalanced *la19- C Bor.* **be at heid an aix wi** to be involved in a meddlesome or contentious way with *la19- NE.* **gae oot o heid** to be forgotten *la19-.* **get your heid in your hands and your lugs tae play wi** to receive a severe scolding or punishment *la19-.* **get yer heid oot** to launch out on one's own; to get one's freedom of action *20-.* **gie you your heid in your hands** to give someone a severe scolding or punishment *la19-.* **heids an heels** completely, wholly *20-.* **heid and horn** the characteristic features of an animal *20- NE.* **heids an thraws 1** lying in opposite directions, with alternating head and feet or top and bottom *18-.* **2** higgledy-piggledy *19-.* **3** a game played with pins *19, 20- WC Uls.* **heidicks and pinticks** a game played with pins *la19- NE.* **†head in the bees** confused, light-headed *la18-19.* **the heid o hairst** the height of the harvest *la19- NE.* **heid o' the heap** in the forefront, first *20- NE EC.* **†hede o kyn** the chief of a family or clan *la15-e16.* **in the heid o** busied or occupied with, deeply involved in *19- Sh NE WC Uls.* **ken by heid and horn** to know intimately *20- N NE.* **†ken by heidmark** to know by sight; to recognize *19.* **†lay the heid o the soo to the tail o the grice** to arrange in an orderly fashion, balance losses with gains *18-19, 20- Ork.* **lay your heid till** to eat *la19- NE T.* **on the heid o 1** busied or occupied with, deeply involved in *19-.* **2** immediately after, on top of *la19-.* **on the heids o** in confirmation of; on the strength or security of; concerning *la19-.* **ower the heid o** because of, in consequence of, concerning *la19-.* **pit the heid on** to headbutt *la20-.* **stick the heid on** to headbutt *la20-.* **tak yer head** to go to one's head, intoxicate *la19-.* **wi yer heid under yer oxter** looking downcast or dejected *20-.* **yer heid's fu o mince** you are mistaken, you are talking nonsense *la20-.* [OE *hēafod*]

heid[1,2], **head, †hede, †hed** /hid, hɛd/ *v* **1** to behead a person; to prune or cut back a plant or tree *la14-.* **2** to lead, go in front; to control, be in charge of *15-.* **3** to fit or provide (an object) with a head or top *16-.* **4** to finish and secure the top of a haystack *17-.* **5** to reach the summit of a mountain; to accomplish a task *la19-.* **6** *football* to strike the ball with the head *20-.* **heider** *football* a shot in which the ball is struck with the head *20-.* **heiders** a game of heading a ball *la20-.* **heading sheaf 1** the last sheaf of grain placed on the top of a stook or ruck *19-.* **2** the final straw, the last irritation *la19- NE EC.* **heid-the-baw 1** a game of bouncing a ball against a wall using only the head *la20-.* **2** a term of address or a term of abuse for a person *la20-.* [OE *hēafdian*; or see also above]

heid[1.3], **head** /hid, hɛd/ *adj* **1** chief, principal; most important *15-.* **2** situated at the head or top *la15-.* **heid bull, head bu** the chief house of an estate, a manor-house *la16- Sh Ork.* **heid bummer** a manager, an overseer, a prominent or important person; an officious person *la19-.* **†heid burgh** the principal town of an area *16-18.* **†head court** a court without judicial function, held once a year at Michaelmas, when each freeholder of a county met to make up the voters' rolls and elect an MP; originally one of the three principal sessions of a burgh-court, Sheriff Court or Baron court which a freeholder was obliged to attend *15-19.* **head-man 1** a chief, a commander; a leader; a foreman *la16-.* **2** a stalk of rib-grass *Plantago lanceolata*, used by children in mock duels *18-19, 20- Uls.* **heidsman, †hedisman** a chief, a commander; a leader; a foreman *la15-19, 20- Uls.* **†hed stenn** *in Orkney* an annual court session *16.* **heid yin** a leader, a person in authority; *pl* the people in charge, the authorities *20-*; compare *high heid yin* (HEICH[1.3]). **in the heid hurry o** at the busiest time of, in the peak of *la19- NE EC.* [see the noun]

heid see HEED[1.1]

-heid, †-hede, †-hed /hid/ *suffix* describing a state of being: ◊*bairnheid* ◊*youtheid la14-.* [OE *-hēd*]

heidie[1.1], **heedie** /'hidi/ *n* **1** a headteacher in a school *20-.* **2** *in ball games* a header *la20-.* **heidies** a street football game where players try to strike the ball mainly using the head *la20-.* [HEID[1.1] + -IE[1]]

heidie[1.2] /'hidi/ *v football* to strike a ball with the head *la20-.* [see the noun]

heidie[1.3], **heidy, †hedie, †headie** /'hidi/ *adj* **1** headstrong, passionate; impetuous, violent *la16-.* **2** clever, intelligent *la19-.* **3** apt to make one dizzy *la19-.* **4** proud, haughty *la19, 20- NE T.* **heidy knite** a clever person *la19- NE.* [see the noun]

heidiecra see HEADICRAA[1.1], HEADICRAA[1.2]

heidiepeer, headapeer, †hedy peir /hidi'pir, hɛdə'pir/ *adj* of equal stature or age *16-19, 20- NE.* [probably HEID[1.1] + OFr *de per* on an equality]

heidiepeers /hidi'pirz/ *npl* people of equal age or height *18-19, 20- NE.* [HEIDIEPEER]

†heid steke, heidstik *n* a piece of large artillery, a kind of cannon *16.* [MDu *hootstucke*]

heidy see HEIDIE[1.3]

heif see HEAVE[1.2]

heifer, heefer, †hiffer /'hɛfər, 'hifər/ *n* **1** a young cow before she has calved *17-.* **2** a big, awkward, clumsy (female) person *20- NE T EC.* [OE *hēahfore*]

heigh see HEICH[1.3]

heigher see HIGHER[1.2]

Heighland see HIELAND[1.2]
height see HEICH[1.2], HEICHT[1.1], HEICHT[1.2]
heil see HEAL[2]
Heilandman see HIELANDMAN
heild see EILD[1.1], HEAL[2], HEELD[1.1], HEELD[1.2]
heill see HEAL[1.2], HEEL[1.1]
heir[1.1], †**air**, †**hair**, †**ayr** /er/ *n law* the person who succeeds to the property of a deceased, an inheritor *la14-*. **heir general** an *heir at law* who succeeds to both the heritable and moveable property of a deceased *la16-*. **heir portioner 1** one of several female heirs (or their successors) who succeed to equal portions of a heritable estate *la16-*. **2** *in Shetland and Orkney* a joint heir under UDAL law *17-*. **heir substitute** *law* an heir nominated to replace a predeceasing heir; an heir of entail *la17-*. **heir at law** a person who inherits by succession and according to the normal functioning of the law without any special provision *18-*. **heir of conquest** *law* one who succeeds to lands or heritable rights acquired (not succeeded to) by his immediate predecessor *17-*. **heir of line** one who inherits by descent the property of a deceased person *la15-*. **heir of provision** a person who receives goods or property by bequest rather than by right of birth *17-*. [ME *heir*]
heir[1.2], †**air** /er/ *v* to become an heir to; to inherit *15-*. †**arer** an heir *la15*. [see the noun]
heir see HAIR[1.1], HEAR, HEERE, HERE[1], HERE[3.1]
heiranent see HEREANENT
heird see HEAR, HIRD[1.1]
heirschip see HERSHIP
heirskip, **heirship**, **heirskap**, †**airschip**, †**arschip**, †**arscap** /'erskɪp, 'erʃɪp, 'erskap/ *n* **1** the state or position of an heir; succession by inheritance *15-*. **2** an inheritance, a legacy *la15-19, 20- NE Bor*. †**airschip gudis** = *heirship moveables 16-e17*. †**heirship moveables** moveable goods to which an heir was entitled besides the heritable estate *la17-19*. [HEIR[1.1], with *-ship* suffix]
heis see HEEZE[1.2]
heisk[1.1] /hʌɪsk/ *adj* nervous, agitated; excited *la19- Ork*. [unknown]
heisk[1.2] /hʌɪsk/ *adv* haughtily, proudly *20- Ork*. [unknown]
heist[1.1], **hyste** /hʌɪst/ *n* a hoist, a lift; a device for lifting *la19- NE T EC*. [see the verb]
heist[1.2], **hyste** /hʌɪst/ *v* to hoist, lift up *la17-*. **heist in** to understand, take in *20- Ork*. [related to HEEZE[1.2], HOISE[1.2] + Older Scots *hoist*]
heist see HEST
heisty, **hastie**, **hasty** /'histi, 'heste/ *adj* **1** hurried, done quickly; occurring in haste *la14-*. **2** speedy, quick to act *la15-19, 20- EC*. **hasty brose**, **hastie brose** a kind of quickly made BROSE *19- NE*. **hasty puddin** a quickly made dish of oatmeal, suet and seasoning *20- H&I SW*. [ME *hasti*]
heit see HEAT[1.1], HET[1.2]
heithin see HAITHEN[1.2]
heiven see HIVVEN
hei-yearald see HAUF[1.3]
hek see HECK[1.1]
hekkill see HECKLE[1.1], HECKLE[1.2]
Heland see HIELAND[1.1], HIELAND[1.2]
Helandman see HIELANDMAN
Helands see HIELANDS
held see HAUD[1.2], HEAL[2], HEELD[1.1]
helde see HEELD[1.2]
hele see HAIL[1.2], HEAL[1.1], HEAL[2], HEAL[2], HEEL[1.1]
helf, **helve** /hɛlf, hɛlv/ *n* the handle of a tool or weapon *16-19, 20- Sh Uls*. [OE *hielfe*, MDu, MLG *helf*]
heliday see HOALIDAY
helland see HIELAND[1.2]

hellicat[1.1], *N* **halligate** /'hɛlɪkət; *N* 'halɪgɛt/ *n* a noisy, restless person; a foolish or useless person *19-*. [see the adj]
hellicat[1.2], **hallockit**, **halliket**, **hallicat**, *Sh* **halliget**, *WC* **hailykit**, †**halucket** /'hɛlɪkət, 'halǝkǝt, 'halɪkǝt; *Sh* 'halɪgǝt; *WC* 'hɛlɪkǝt/ *adj* **1** wild; frivolous; crazy *la17-*. **2** clumsy, ungainly *18-*. [altered from ptp of HALLICH[1.2]]
hellick, **heelik** /'hɛlɪk, 'hilɪk/ *n* a large, flat rock on the seashore, suitable for use as a landing place; *pl* coastal rocks *la19- Sh*. [diminutive form of ON *hella* a flat rock]
hellier see HAUF[1.3], HELYER
hellim see HELM[2]
hellio /'hɛlɪo/ *n* a stone with a rim of clay, used for drying corn *19- Ork*. [ON *hella* a flat stone]
hellisom /'hɛlɪsǝm/ *adj* pleasant, amiable *20- Sh*. [probably HELLY, with adj-forming suffix]
hellock see HALLICH[1.1]
helly /'hɛli/ *n* the weekend *la19- Sh*. [ON *helgr* a holiday]
helly see HALY
hellyiefer /'hɛljɪfǝr/ *n* a heavy shower, a downpour *20- Ork*. [probably ON *hella* to pour out, with unknown second element]
helm[1] /hɛlm/ *n* **1** a helmet *la14- literary*. **2** a crowd, a noisy gathering *20- NE T EC*. [OE *helm* a helmet]
helm[2], **hellim** /hɛlm, 'hɛlǝm/ *n* a tiller on a boat *la17-*. [OE *helma*]
helmein see HEMLIN
†**helmstok** *n* a tiller on a boat *e16*. [MDu, Flem *helmstoc*]
help[1.1] /hɛlp/ *n* **1** aid or assistance; relief, remedy *la14-*. **2** a person or thing that helps *15-*. [OE *help*]
help[1.2] /hɛlp/ *v* **1** to aid or assist; to support (oneself) *la14-*. **2** to remedy or amend; to repair *la14-19, 20- SW*. **helpender**, **hilpender** an assistant, a helper *la19- NE*. **helper**, †**helpar 1** a person who helps *la14-*. **2** a minister's or teacher's assistant *la17-*. **helplie**, **helply** helpful; willing to help *16-19, 20- N*. †**helplike**, **helplyk** helpful *la14-e16*. **help ma Boab**, **help ma Bob** an exclamation expressing annoyance or annoyance *la19-*. [OE *helpan*]
helse, †**hailse**, †**halse**, †**haylis** /hɛls/ *v* to greet, welcome *la14-19, 20- Sh*. [ME *heilsen*, ON *heilsa*]
helsin, **hailzin**, †**halison**, †**hailsing**, †**halsing** /'hɛlsɪn, 'hɛlzɪn/ *n* a greeting, a salutation; a welcome *15-19, 20- Sh NE*. [verbal noun from HELSE]
helsum see HAILSOME
helt see HILT[1]
helter /'hɛltǝr/ *n* **1** a halter *la15-*. **2** challenged or disputed possession of animals or goods; such goods themselves *15*. **helter shank** a rope attached to a halter *la19-*. †**in helter** in a state of disputed possession *15*. †**tak the helter of** to formally claim possession of animals or goods whose ownership is in dispute *la15*. [OE *hælfter*]
helter skelter see HILTER-SKILTER
helth see HALTH
helty-skelty see HILTIE-SKILTIE[1.2]
helve see HELF
hely see HEELY[1.3], HEELY[1.4]
helyer, **hellier** /'hɛljǝr/ *n* a cave into which the tide flows *19- Sh Ork*. [ON *hellir* a cave]
hem /hɛm/ *n* **1** the border of a garment *la14-*. **2** the outer part of a millstone *la16-*. **3** the edge of a piece of armour *e16*. [OE *hem*]
hem see HAIM, HAME[1.1], HAME[1.2]
hemfish see HAMFISH
hemliband /'hɛmlɪband/ *n* a tether for two animals *20- Ork*. [ON *helmingar* half + *band* a band, a bond; compare HUMLIBAAND]

hemlin, †**helmein** /'hɛmlɪn/ *n* a sheepmark, made by removing a semi-circular piece from an ear *17- Ork.* [metathesis of ON *helmingr* a half part]

hemlins /'hɛmlɪnz/ *n* the ledge inside a grain kiln, supporting the crossbeams under the straw on which the grain dried *19- Ork.* [derivative of HEMMEL]

hemmald *see* HAMELT[1.1]

hemmel, hammel /'hɛməl, 'haməl/ *n* **1** a shed and an open court communicating with it used for housing cattle *19, 20- EC Bor.* **2** a square rack on posts to hold fodder *19- Bor.* [metathesis of HELM[1] a helmet, a covering; compare Norw dial *hjelm* the straw covering of a rick, a slatted roof]

hemmer *see* HAIMMER[1.1]

hemmit *see* HAMIT

hemp, †hempt /hɛmp/ *n* (the fibre of) the plant *Cannabis sativa*; a hemp rope *15-*. **hempie, hempy** *n* **1** a mischievous or unruly young person; a naughty girl *19-*. **2** the hedge sparrow or dunnock *Prunella modularis la19- EC SW Bor.* **3** a person deserving to be hanged, a rogue *18-19, 20- EC SW.* **hempie, hempy** *adj* wild, romping, roguish *18-19, 20- SW Bor.* **hemp gravat** a hangman's noose *la18- literary.* **hempen gravat** = *hemp gravat la19- literary.* **hemp rigg** land where hemp is grown; frequently in field-names *la17- SW.* [OE *henep*]

hemp *see* IMP[1.1]

hempt *see* HEMP

hemsuckenn *see* HAMESUCKEN[1.1]

hen[1.1] /hɛn/ *n* **1** a female domestic fowl, a chicken *la15-*. **2** a term of address for a girl or woman *la18-*. **3** a dare, a challenge *20- SW Bor.* **hennie** timid, cowardly *20-*. **hen aipple** the fruit of the wild service tree *Sorbus torminalis la19- N NE H&I.* **henbauk** a tie beam on the roof of a country cottage (so called because hens roosted there) *18-*. **hen-broth** a thick chicken soup *la19-*. **hen cavie** a hencoop *17-*. **hen crae** a hencoop *20-*. **hen croft, hen craft** a piece of enclosed land where hens are kept; a part of a cornfield damaged by fowl *15-19, 20- NE T.* **hen's flesh** goose-flesh *19- Sh EC Bor.* **hen's gerse, hen's gress** as much grass or land as would feed a hen; something of very little value *la19- Sh EC Bor.* **hen-hertit** chicken-hearted *18-*. **hen laft** a hen-roost; a loft used for keeping hens *la19-*. **hen-pen** the droppings of fowls, used as manure *19-*. **hen plooks** goose-flesh *20- Bor.* **hen-ree** a hen run *20-*. **hen-taed, hen-toed** pigeon-toed *20-*. **hen-taes** creeping buttercup *Ranunculus repens 20-*. **hen's taes** bad handwriting, a scrawl *19-*. **hen toomal** a chicken enclosure *20- Ork.* **hen-ware** an edible seaweed *Alaria esculenta 19, 20- NE T.* **henwife 1** a woman who has charge of, or deals in poultry *la15-*. **2** a man who concerns himself about matters usually left to women *20-*. †**henwile** a petty or contemptible trick or stratagem *la16-e18.* **a hen's eeran** a fool's errand *20- N NE T.* **like a hen on a het girdle** restless, anxious, impatient *la18-*. **see ye by the hen's meat** to escort someone part of the way home *20-*. **sell yer hens on a rainy day** to sell at a disadvantage, make a bad bargain *la17-*. **sleep in a hen's feet-mark** to sleep in a very cramped position *20- N.* [OE *henn*]

hen[1.2] /hɛn/ *v* **1** to withdraw from an undertaking or promise through cowardice, lose one's nerve *19- T C SW Bor.* **2** to challenge, dare *20- EC Bor.* [see the noun]

hench *see* HAINCH[1.1], HAINCH[1.2]

henchle-bane *see* HAINCH[1.1]

hend *see* EN[1.1], HINT[1.2]

†**hende, hend, heynd** *adj* skilful, clever; pleasant, courteous *la15-16.* [probably aphetic form of OE *gehende* near, at hand]

hender *see* HINNER[1], HINNER[2.1], HINNER[2.2]

henderend *see* HINNEREN

hendirmost *see* HINNERMAIST

hendmost *see* HINMAIST[1.2]

†**henk**[1.1]**, hink** *n* a hesitation, a falter or a stutter *la16-19.* [see the verb]

henk[1.2]**, †hink** /hɛŋk/ *v* to walk with a limp; to walk unsteadily; to hop on one leg *la15-19, 20- Sh.* [Ger, MLG, MDu *hinken*]

henks up /'hɛŋks ʌp/ *v* to hitch up *la19- Sh.* [unknown first element + UP[1.2]]

henmast *see* HINMAIST[1.2]

henna *see* HAE[1.2]

henner /'hɛnər/ *n* **1** a somersault, an acrobatic feat *20- N EC.* **2** an upset, a disappointment; a fit of rage *la20- EC.* **3** a dare, a challenge *la20- EC*; compare HEN[1.1] (sense 3). [derivative of HEN[1.1]]

henshelstane, henshin-stane, *NE* **hinchin-steen** /'hɛnʃəlsten, 'hɛnʃənsten; *NE* 'hɪnʃɪnstin/ *n* a stone shelf or slab in front of a baker's oven-door, used to make it easier to slide trays or pans into the oven, or on which to square up loaves before baking *20-*. [perhaps derivative of HAINCH[1.1] from the approximate height of the stone + STANE[1.1]]

†**hensure, hensour** *n* a swaggering young fellow *16-e19.* [unknown]

hent[1.1]**, hint** /hɛnt, hɪnt/ *n* a gathering together *20- Sh Ork.* [see the verb]

hent[1.2]**, hint** /hɛnt, hɪnt/ *v* **1** to gather, collect *19- Sh Ork.* **2** to spirit (oneself) away, steal away, disappear *la19- Sh Ork.* [ON *henda* to catch, pick up, pick out]

†**hent**[2]**, hint, hynt** *v* **1** to take hold of, grasp or seize; to hold or raise up *la14-e19.* **2** to take; to acquire *la14-e19.* **hint to** lay hold of (a person or thing) *15-e16.* [OE *hentan*]

hent *see* HINT[1.2]

hentilagets /hɛntɪ'lagəts/ *npl* **1** loose tufts of wool from sheep's backs (gathered from pasture) *20- Sh.* **2** odds and ends *20- Sh.* [HENT[1.2] + LAGET]

hep *see* HAP[3]

hepe *see* HEAP[1.1], HEAP[1.2]

her[1.1]**, hur, hir** /hɛr, hʌr, hɪr/ *pron* **1** the female person or animal in question *la14-*. **2** *of an inanimate object* it *la14-*. **3** *in Highland speech* me, myself *la15-19.* [OE *hire*]

her[1.2]**, hur, hir** /hɛr, hʌr, hɪr/ *adj* **1** belonging to the female person or animal in question *la14-*. **2** *of an inanimate object* belonging to it *la15-*. **3** *in Highland speech* belonging to me *la17-19.* †**hirris** belonging to her *15-e17.* [see the pronoun]

her *see* HERE[1], HERE[3.1]

herald, †herauld, †herrod, †harrald /'hɛrəld/ *n* an officer of the crown who makes proclamations, carries messages and regulates matters of genealogy; a member of the Lyon Court *la14-*. [ME *heraud, herald*]

herald deuk, herald duck /'hɛrəld dʒuk, 'hɛrəld dʌk/ *n* the red-breasted merganser *Mergus serrator la17-19, 20- Sh.* Compare HARLE. [MFr *harle* a kind of shelduck + DEUK]

herand *see* EERAN

herauld *see* HERALD

herb *see* YERB

herber *see* HERBOUR[1.2]

†**herbery**[1.1]**, harboury, harbery** *n* **1** (a place of) shelter; lodging, an encampment *la14-e19.* **2** a harbour, a shelter for ships *16-17.* **harbrieles, herbriles** without shelter, homeless *e16.* **herbriour, herbrear** one who provides lodgings or shelter, a host *la14-16.* [OE *herebeorg*, ON *herbergi* temporary lodgings, quarters, an inn]

†**herbery**[1.2]**, harbory, harbry** *v* **1** to provide with shelter or lodging; to take shelter, lodge, encamp *la14-17.* **2** to provide a

harbour for a ship *16*. [OE *herebeorgian* to lodge, ON *herbergja* to lodge, harbour a person]

herbour[1.1], **hairbour, harbour, †harber** /ˈhɛrbər, ˈhɛrbər, ˈharbər/ *n* a shelter for ships, a harbour *la16-*. [OE *herebeorg*, ON *herbergi* temporary lodgings, quarters, an inn]

herbour[1.2], **hairbour, harbour, †herber, †harber** /ˈhɛrbər, ˈhɛrbər, ˈharbər/ *v* to give refuge or shelter to; to lodge or take shelter *la14-*. **†harbourous, harberous** hospitable *la16*. [see the noun]

herd see HARD[1.2], HEAR, HIRD[1.1], HIRD[1.2]
herda see HIRDA
herdin see HARN[1.1], HARN[1.2]
herdis see HARDS
herdly see HAURDLY

†here[1], **heir, her** *n* a lord, a chief; a man of high rank *la14-16*. [OE *herra*]

†here[2] *n* an army *la15-e16*. [OE *here*]

here[3.1], **†heir, †her** /hir/ *adv* **1** in or to this place; at this point or time, in this case *la14-*. **2** *with omission of the verb 'to be'* here is: ◊*here a sweetie shop la14-19, 20- C*. **†heir cumming** an arrival; a visit *la14-e17*. **†heir doun, heire downe** here below, here in this world *14-16*. **†heirintill** into this place; in this matter or case *la15-e17*. **here's me** an expression of a person's situation or state of mind: *here's me pregnant la20- C*. [OE *hēr*]

here[3.2] /hir/ *interj* an expression of surprise *20-*. [see the adv]

here see HEAR, HEERE

hereanent, †heiranent /hirəˈnɛnt/ *adv law* concerning this matter *la16-*. [HERE[3.1] + ANENT]

†hereatour, hereatowre *adv* furthermore, besides *la14-15*. [HERE[3.1] + ATOUR[1.1]]

hereawa, hereaway /ˈhirəwa, ˈhirəwe/ *adv* **1** in this quarter or neighbourhood, hereabouts *la16-*. **2** to this quarter, hither *19-*. **hereawa thereawa** hither and thither *la18-*. [HERE[3.1] + AWA[1.1]]

†hereditar *adj* hereditary *la16-e17*. [MFr *hereditaire*, Lat *hērēditārius*]

Hereditary Usher see USHER
hereschip see HERSHIP
heretage see HERITAGE
heretar see HERITOR

†heretrice *n* = *heretrix 16-e17*. [feminine form of HERITOR, with feminine suffix *-trice*]

heretrix, †heiritrix /ˈhɛrɪtrɪks/ *n law* a female heir or heritor; an heiress *la16-*. [feminine form of HERITOR, after Lat feminines in *-trix*]

herezeld, *NE* **herrial,** *NE* **hairrial, †herial, †hereʒelde, †heriald** /ˈhɛrəjɛld; *NE* ˈhɛriəl; *NE* ˈhɛriəl/ *n* **1** the best living animal (or cash payment) due to a landlord by feudal custom on the death of a tenant; the animal or payment itself *la15-18, 19- historical*. **2** a cause of ruin; an unwarranted expense, a drain on one's resources *la19- NE*. [perhaps HERE[1] + YIELD[1.1]; compare Eng *heriot* and OE *heregeld* a feudal custom]

herie see HEARY
hering see HERRIN

heritable, †heritabill, †eritabill /ˈhɛrɪtəbəl/ *adj* **1** pertaining to or connected with heritable property *la14-*. **2** *of people* holding property, office, or privilege by hereditary right *15-*. **3** *law* capable of being inherited, subject to inheritance; applied to that form of property (houses, lands, and rights pertaining to these) to be inherited by an heir at law *la15-*. **heritable bond** a bond for a borrowed sum of money, secured by heritable property *18-*. **heritable jurisdictions** various ancient rights formerly enjoyed by feudal proprietors of land or by holders of certain offices, entitling them to administer justice in local courts *18, 19- historical*. **heritable security** a security over heritable property, a standard security *18-*. [MFr *heritable*]

Heritable Usher see USHER

heritage, †heretage, †eritage /ˈhɛrətɪdʒ/ *n* **1** property that may be inherited, an inheritance *la14-*. **2** *law* (landed) property descending by succession to the heir at law; property inherited by a person as rightful heir; land inherited rather than acquired by purchase *la14-*. **3** a person's or nation's native land *15-16*. **in heritage** describing the possession of lands by heritable right *la14-*. **of heritage** by heritable right *la14-*. [ME *heritage, heritage*]

heritor, †heritour, †heretar, heriter /ˈhɛrɪtər/ *n* **1** an heir or heiress *la15-*. **2** *law* a property-owner or a landowner formerly liable to payment of public burdens connected with the parish, including upkeep of church property and schools, and administration of the poor *la16-19, 20- historical*. **3** the proprietor of heritable property *la15-18*. [ME *heriter*]

heritrix see HERETRIX
herk see HARK[1.2]
herken, herkin see HEARKEN

herle, erle, yerl /hɛrl, ɛrl, jɛrl/ *n* the grey heron *Ardea cinerea 16-19, 20- NE T EC*. [unknown]

herling, herlin, †hirling /ˈhɛrlɪŋ, ˈhɛrlɪn/ *n* an immature sea-trout *Salmo trutta la17- SW Bor*. [unknown]

herm see HAIRM[1.1], HAIRM[1.2]
hermony see HARMONY

hern, heron, †heroun, †huron /hɛrn, ˈhɛrən/ *n* the grey heron *Ardea cinerea 15-*. [ME *heiroun*]

hernes, herness see HARNESS
hernfern see ERNFERN

hernshaw, *Bor* **heronseugh, †heron-shew, †heronis sew** /ˈhɛrnʃɔ; *Bor* ˈhɛrənʃux/ the grey heron *Ardea cinerea la15-19, 20- SW Bor*. [ME *heironseu* a young heron]

heron see HERN

heronious, †hyronius /həˈroniəs/ *adj* misguided in behaviour; unconventional, outrageous *la16-19, 20- WC*. [variant of Older Scots *erroneous*]

heronis sew, heronseugh, heron-shew see HERNSHAW
heroun see HERN
herp see HARP[1.1], HARP[1.2]
herr see HAIR[1.1], HARR
herre see HARR
herrial see HEREZELD
herrie see HERRY

herrin, herring, *N* **herreen,** *NE* **heeren, †hering, †haring, †haryng** /ˈhɛrɪn, ˈhɛrɪŋ; *N* ˈhɛrin; *NE* ˈhirɪn/ *n* the Atlantic herring *Clupea harengus 15-*. **herrin drave** the annual herring-fishing *16-*. **herring hake** the hake *Merluccius merluccius la19-*. **herring hog** a species of dolphin *Grampus griseus* or *Tursiops truncatus*; the fin-whale *18-19, 20- NE T Uls*. **herrinsile** young herring *la19-*. [OE *hēring*]

herrin band /ˈhɛrɪn band/ *n* a string dividing cuts or a HEERE of yarn into separate bundles *19, 20- NE*. [derivative of HEERE + BAND[1.1]]

herrod see HERALD

herry, herrie, harry, *NE* **hairry, †hery, †hary** /ˈhɛri, ˈhari; *NE* ˈhɛri/ *v* **1** to devastate; to rob with violence; to raid *la14-*. **2** to plunder a bird's nest or a beehive *16-*. **3** to exhaust the fertility of land (by removing the topsoil) *la19- Sh Ork NE SW*. **4** to ruin or impoverish by extortion or oppression *la15-19, 20- NE SW*. **5** to cut away coal from pillars left as supports; to remove all coal from a working *19- C*. **6** *in fishing* to denude a stretch of water of fish *17- EC*. **herriement, harriement 1** ruination *la18-19, 20- NE*. **2** (the cause of) plundering, devastation *18-19*. **herry-hawk** a plunderer, a robber *20- C*. **herry-watter 1** a very selfish person *20- N*.

2 a fishing net which took all the fish from the water *15-18*. **heery oot** to dispossess or drive out; to make destitute *la18-NE*. [OE *hergian*]

herry *see* HAIRY¹·¹

hers *see* HAIRSE

herschip *see* HERSHIP

hersel, herself, †**hirself,** †**hir selwyn** /hərˈsɛl, hərˈsɛlf/ *pron* **1** the female mentioned or in question *la14-*. **2** a term of reference for the female head of an institution, the mistress of the house or a female boss *la19-*. **3** a wife *la20-*. **4** *in Highland speech* myself, I *la18-19*. [OE *hire self*]

hersh *see* HAIRSE

hership, herschip, †**hereschip,** †**heirschip** /ˈhɛrʃɪp/ *n* **1** an armed incursion, a predatory raid *la14-19, 20- historical*. **2** the act or practice of plundering or pillaging by an army or armed force *15-19, 20- historical*. **3** harm or hardship inflicted by violence or robbery; destitution or impoverishment caused by harrying or violent treatment *la15-19, 20 literary*. **4** booty, plunder; stolen cattle *la16-e19*. [HERE² or HERRY, wth noun-forming suffix; compare ON *herja* to harry, *herskapr* harrying]

herskit *see* HERTSCAD

hersle *see* HIRSEL²·¹, HIRSEL²·²

hert¹·¹, **hairt, heart,** †**hart** /hɛrt, hert, hart/ *n* **1** the bodily organ which pumps blood *la14-*. **2** a term of affection (for a woman) *15-*. **3** the central core of sheaves in a corn-rick *la18-*. **4** the stomach *16-19, 20- Sh Ork N NE*. **hertfully** heartily, wholly, sincerely *la14-*. †**hertily, hartily** *adj* heartily *16-e17*. **hertily, hartily** *adv* in a heartfelt manner, sincerely *la15-*. **hertless,** †**hartles 1** cheerless, dismal, discouraging *la17-*. **2** disheartened, discouraged, dejected *16-19*. †**hartly, hertly** *adj* **1** heartfelt, sincere *la14-e17*. **2** dear to the heart, beloved; loving, devoted *16*. †**hartly, hertly** *adv* sincerely, earnestly *la14-17*. †**hartlynes** sincerity, heartiness *15-e17*. **hert alane** absolutely alone; lonely, desolate *la19-*. **heart's care** anxiety, deep worry *19, 20- Sh Ork*. **hert dry** thoroughly dry *la19- NE T*. †**heart fever** a feverish condition; an exhausting illness *17-19*. **hert-gled** very glad, delighted *20-*. **heart hale 1** *of the body* organically sound *19-*. **2** whole-hearted, unafraid *la19-*. †**heart heezin** uplifting, encouraging, heartwarming *19*. **hert holl** the very centre *20- Sh*. **heart hunger** a longing for affection *19- Sh NE T*. **heart hungry 1** ravenous *19- NE T Bor*. **2** filled with longing *la19- Sh NE T*. **hert kake,** †**hart cake** heart-disease *e17, 20- Sh*. **heart lazy** extremely lazy *la19-*. **heart likin** affection, love *la19, 20- Sh NE*. **hert maegins** the central part (of the night) *20- Sh*. **hert peety** deep compassion *20- Sh NE*. †**hart pipes** the area of the body in front of the heart *16-e17*. **heart roasted, hert roastit** exasperated, annoyed *la20- C*. **heart rug** a strain on the emotions *19- Sh Ork NE*. **heart sab, hairt sab** a sob from the heart *20- T WC*. **hert sair,** †**hertsare** *n* grief, emotional pain *la14-*. **hert sair** *adj* sore at heart, grief-stricken *17-*. **hert shot** a loud burst of laughter or a loud sneeze *19- Sh*. **heart sorry, hert sorry** deeply grieved, sorry for someone *la19-*. **heart stound, hairt stound** a pain or pang at the heart *19-*. **heart warm** deeply affectionate, sincerely warm, cordial *la18-19, 20- Sh*. **gae tae yer heart** to be appetizing or palatable *19-*. **gang against yer heart** to be unpalatable or distasteful *19-*. **gang roond yer hert** to be appetizing or palatable *la20-*. **gar your hert rise** to nauseate *20- T EC Bor*. **hae yer hert an your ee in** to be extremely interested in, be eager to possess *la19-*. **the heart o corn** one of the best, a generous or popular person *la19-*. **heart of the yearth** the plant self-heal *Prunella vulgaris la19- Bor*. **taste your heart** to be appetizing or palatable *20- N NE*. **turn yer hert ower** to nauseate *20- NE T*. [OE *heorte*]

hert¹·², **heart,** †**hart** /hɛrt, hart/ *v* **1** to build up the inner sheaves of a cartload or stack of corn *19-*. **2** to embolden, hearten *la14-19, 20- SW Bor*. **3** to strike in the region of the heart so as to wind or knock out *17-19, 20- WC Bor*. **hearting** the building up of the inner sheaves of a cartload or stack; these sheaves themselves *19-*. [OE *hyrtan* to cheer, encourage]

hert *see* HAIRTH, HART

herten, hearten /ˈhɛrtən, ˈhartən/ *v* **1** to strengthen with food *la19-*. **2** to encourage *la19-*. **hertenin 1** strengthening with food *la18-*. **2** encouragement *la18-*. [HERT¹·¹, with verb-forming suffix]

herth *see* HAIRTH

hertscad, hairt-scaud, heart scald, *Sh Ork* **herskit,** †**hartskaid** /ˈhɛrtskad, ˈhɛrtskɔd, ˈhartskɔld; *Sh Ork* ˈhɛrskət/ *n* **1** heartburn *la16-*. **2** a source of bitter, trouble or disappointment *17-*. **3** a feeling of disgust or repulsion *la18-*. **hert-scalded** vexed, sorely grieved *20- Uls*. [HERT¹·¹ + SCAUD¹·¹]

hertsome, hairtsome, heartsome, †**hartsum** /ˈhɛrtsəm, ˈhertsəm, ˈhartsəm/ *adj* **1** encouraging, cheering; attractive, pleasant *la16-*. **2** merry, cheerful, lively *18-*. **3** *of a meal* satisfying, hearty *la18-19, 20- SW*. **heartsomely** cheerfully, heartily *la17-19, 20- Sh*. **heartsomeness** cheerfulness *la17-19, 20- Sh*. [HERT¹·¹, with adj-forming suffix]

herty, hairty, hearty, †**hartie** /ˈhɛrti, ˈherti, ˈharti/ *adj* **1** sincere, heartfelt *la15-*. **2** cordial, sociable, jovial, cheerful, merry *la18-*. **3** *of things* cheering; merry-looking: ◇*a hearty fire 19-*. **4** suffering from a weak heart *20-*. **5** intoxicated, tipsy, exhilarated by alcohol *la17-19, 20- Sh N*. **6** liberal, generous *la18-19, 20- NE T*. **7** having a healthy appetite *19, 20- NE T*. **you're awfy hertie when you laugh** a term of approbation to a parsimonious person *la20-*. [HERT¹·¹ + -IE²]

hervest *see* HAIRST¹·¹, HAIRST¹·²

hery *see* HERRY

hes *see* HAE¹·²

hes-beene *see* HAS-BEEN

hese *see* HEEZE¹·²

hesill *see* HAZEL¹·¹

hesp¹·¹, **hasp** /hɛsp, hasp/ *n* a catch or clasp; a hasp *la15-*. †**hesp and staple** *law* the symbols used in giving possession of property *la15-19*. [OE *hæpse*]

hesp¹·², **hasp** /hɛsp, hasp/ *v* to fasten with a catch or clasp; to fix *18-*. [OE *hæpsian*]

hesp², †**hasp** /hɛsp/ *n* a length or skein of yarn; sometimes equating to two hanks *la16-*. [extended sense of HESP¹·¹ or MDu *haspe*, ON *hespa*]

hespyne *see* ASPYNE

hessy *see* HI-SPY

†**hest, heste, heist** *n* bidding, command *16*. [OE *hæs*]

hest *see* HEEST

hester *see* HASTER¹·²

het¹·¹, **hoat, hate, hot,** *Sh* **haet,** †**heit,** †**hett,** †**hait** /hɛt, hot, het, hɔt; *Sh* ˈheət/ *adj* **1** at a high temperature, hot *la14-*. **2** warm, comfortable *19-*. **3** *of grain or root crops* fermenting, spoiled through being diseased or stored damp *20-*. **4** *of peas or oats* quickly growing, maturing early *la18- Bor*. **hot furr** newly ploughed ground; the practice of sowing into such ground *17-19, 20- NE*. **het hert 1** a heart suffering from bitter disappointment *19-*. **2** a state of disappointment *19-*. **het pint** a celebratory drink of hot spiced ale, with sugar, eggs and spirits *18-19, 20- historical*. **het-skinned** fiery, irascible *la18- N NE T EC*. **hot-trod,** †**hot tred 1** (the signal for) the tracking down and pursuit of Border marauders *la18-19, 20- historical*. **2** a fresh track *la16*. **get a het skin** to receive a beating *19-*. **get it het an reekin** to be scolded or thrashed *la19-*. **gie someone a het skin** to give someone a severe beating *19, 20- EC*. **gie it het** to scold or beat someone *la18-*. **gie it het an reekin** to scold or beat someone *la19-*. **het at hame** *of a person* having left home for no good reason *19-*. **het beans and butter** a children's game resembling hunt-the-thimble *19-20, 21- historical*. [ptp of HEAT¹·²; variant of OE *hāt*]

het¹·², **hoat**, †**hat**, †**hait**, †**hoyt** /hɛt, hot/ *adv* with great heat; intensely *la14-*. [see the adj]

het *see* HEAT¹·¹, HEAT¹·², HOOT¹·², IT

hete *see* HEAT¹·¹, HEAT¹·²

heth *see* HAITH

hether *see* HEATHER

hethin *see* HAITHEN¹·¹, HAITHEN¹·²

†**hething**, **heding** *n* scorn, derision, mockery *la14-e17*. **hethingfull**, **hedinful** derisive, scornful *la15-16*. [ON *haeðing*]

hethnike *see* ETHNIK¹·²

hett *see* HET¹·¹

hettell *see* HETTLE

hetten *see* HEAT¹·²

hettir *see* HATTER¹·¹

hettle, †**hettell** /'hɛtəl/ *n* a fishermen's term for the offshore stony sea-bottom beyond the area covered with seaweed *la17-19, 20- N*. [perhaps altered form of HECKLE¹·¹]

hettret *see* HATRED

heuch¹·¹, **heugh**, *NE* **hyoch**, †**hewch**, †**huche** /hjux; *NE* hjɔx/ *n* **1** a crag or precipice, a cliff or a steep bank (overhanging a river or the sea); frequently in place-names *la11-*. **2** a ravine with steep, overhanging sides *la15-*. **3** the shaft of a pit or mine; the steep face of a quarry *15-19, 20- C*. †**heuch heid** the top of a cliff or precipice *16-19*. [OE *hōh* a heel; a ridge, a promontory]

heuch¹·² /hjux/ *v* to earth up plants in drills; to trench *20- NE T EC*. Compare SHEUCH¹·². [see the noun]

heuch *see* HOOCH¹·³

heuchy *see* YEUKIE

heud *see* HAUD¹·², HOOD¹·¹

heudin *see* HOODIN

heugh *see* HEUCH¹·¹, HOOCH¹·², HOWK²

heuickin *see* HOOICK

heuie *see* HEAVY¹·²

heuk, **huke**, **hook**, *Sh* **hyook** /hjuk, hjʌk, huk; *Sh* hjøk/ *n* **1** a hook; a reaping-hook or sickle; a fish-hook *la14-*. **2** a proportion or amount; the share of the proceeds from the sale of coal cut by a group of miners allotted to each one *19, 20- NE*. **3** *derogatory* an old woman *20- NE*. **4** a reaper *16-19*. **5** the barb of an arrow *15-16*. **hooky 1** hook-shaped, crooked *19, 20- EC Bor*. **2** crafty; grasping *19, 20- Bor*. **heuk butter** a special portion of butter given to reapers *20- Ork*. **heuk hand** a reaper *20- Ork*. **cast da heuks** to use the throwing of sickles to predict the future *20- Sh*. [OE *hōc*]

heuk *see* YEUK¹·¹, YEUK¹·²

heukbane, †**hukebane**, †**hook bone** /'hjukben/ *n* the hipbone *16-*. [ME *hokebon*, early confused with HEUK, and perhaps also with HOCH¹·¹]

heukie *see* YEUKIE

heul *see* HULE

heuld *see* HOOD¹·¹

heumble, **heumle** *see* HUMMLE¹·²

hev *see* HAE¹·²

heve *see* HEAVE¹·²

hevin *see* HINE², HIVVEN

†**hevin impyre**, **hauyn empire** *n* the highest heaven *16*. [HIVVEN + EMPIRE¹·¹]

hevy *see* HEAVY¹·², HEAVY¹·³

hevyn *see* HIVVEN

hew *see* HOW¹·¹, HUE

hewch *see* HEUCH¹·¹

hewie *see* HOOIE

hewin *see* HIVVEN

hewmet, **hewmond** *see* HOOMET

Hexham /'hɛksəm/ *n* a euphemism for Hell *la19- Bor*. **tae Haexham** to Hell *la19- Bor*. [from the name of the town in Northumberland]

hey¹, **hay** /hae, he/ *n* **1** dried grass used as fodder, hay *la14-*. **2** the hay harvest *la18-*. **hay-bog** marshy ground whose grass was cut for fodder *19-*. **hay bogie** a low trailer for transporting hay *la19-*. **hay broo**, **hay bree** an infusion of hay *19, 20- N NE*. **hay-fog** the second growth of grass in a hayfield *19- N NE T EC Bor*. **hay folk** haymakers *la19- EC SW*. **hay fow**, **hey fow** a hay-fork *la19- NE SW*. **hay neuk** a corner of a byre or stable where hay is kept for immediate use *19- Sh SW Bor*. **hey sned** (the shaft of) a scythe *20- EC SW Bor*. [OE *hēg*, ON *hey*]

hey² /hae/ *n* a halfpenny *la19- T*. [shortened form of *halfpenny* (HAUF¹·³)]

hey³·¹ /hʌɪ, he/ *v* to exclaim to attract attention or to express high spirits (when dancing) *la18-*. [see the interj]

hey³·², **hay** /hae, he/ *interj* an exclamation, a call to attract attention *15-*. **hay-ma-nanny** a scolding; punishment *20- NE T Bor*. **like hie-ma-nanny** vigorously, quickly *la19-*. [a natural utterance]

hey⁴, †**hy**, †**hie** /he/ *v* to hasten, go quickly *la14-19, 20- literary*. [OE *hīgian*]

hey *see* HEICH¹·⁴

heyl *see* HEAL²

heyly *see* HEELY¹·⁴

heym *see* HIME

heynd *see* HENDE

heys *see* HEEZE¹·²

heyser *see* HEEZE¹·²

heyt *see* HEAT¹·¹

heyter *see* HYTER¹·¹, HYTER¹·²

hez *see* HAE¹·²

hi¹·¹, **hie** /hae/ *v* to direct a horse to the left with a verbal command *la19, 20- N T Bor*. [see the interj]

hi¹·², **hie** /hae/ *interj* a command to a horse to turn left *19-*. **hi here** a command to a horse to turn left *19-*. **hey up** = *hi here*. [probably HEY³·² or imperative of HEY⁴]

Hibernian¹·¹, †**Ibernien** /hɪˈbɛrnɪən, haeˈbɛrnɪən/ *n* **1** an Irish person *16-*. **2** an Edinburgh football club *la19-*. [see the adj]

Hibernian¹·², †**Ybernian** /hɪˈbɛrnɪən, haeˈbɛrnɪən/ *adj* **1** Irish *16-*. **2** relating to Hibernian Football Club *la19-*. [Lat *Hibernia* Ireland, with adj-forming suffix]

Hibs, **Hibbies**, **Hibees**, **Hi-bees** /'hɪbz, 'hɪbiz, 'haebiz/ *npl* a nickname for Hibernian Football Club and their supporters *la19-*. [altered form of *Hibernian*]

hich *see* HEICH¹·¹, HEICH¹·³, HITCH¹·²

hichit *see* HEICH¹·²

hicht *see* HECHT¹·¹, HECHT¹·², HECHT², HEICHT¹·¹, HEICHT¹·²

hichten *see* HEICHTEN

hick¹·¹ /hɪk/ *n* **1** a hiccup, hiccups; hiccuping *19- NE T*. Compare HIX¹·¹. **hicker** a hiccup *20- EC*. [onomatopoeic]

hick¹·² /hɪk/ *v* **1** to hiccup *19- NE T EC Bor*. **2** to catch the breath and make a hiccuping sound before bursting into tears; to sob noisily *19- EC Bor*. Compare HIX¹·². [see the noun]

hick², *EC* **heek** /hɪk; *EC* hik/ *v* **1** to delay or procrastinate; *of a horse* to jib *19- Sh C SW Bor*. **2** to hesitate in speaking *19, 20- NE Bor*. **hick an hum** to hum and haw *20- EC*. [compare

Norw dial *hika* to delay; to grope for a word; same ultimate origin as HICK^{1,2}]

hick^3 /hɪk/ *interj* a command to a horse to turn to the right *19- SW Bor*. [perhaps imperative of HICK^2]

hickertie-pickertie /ˈhɪkərti pɪkərti/ *adv* higgledy-piggledy *19- NE EC*. [reduplicative compound; compare EModE *hickletee-pickletee*]

†**hickery-pickery** *n* a purgative of bitter aloes and cinnamon *19*. [altered form of Lat *hiera picra* bitter remedy, originally from Greek]

hid *see* HAE^{1,2}, HIDE^1, HIDE^2, IT

hidden *see* HIDE^1

hidder *see* HITHER

†**hiddie-giddie, hiddy-giddy** *adv* topsy-turvy; in a confused or giddy state *la15-e19*. [reduplicative compound]

hiddie kiddie /ˈhɪdi kɪdi/ *n* wits, sense, mental stability *20- NE*. [reduplicative compound]

hiddill *see* HIDDLE^{1,1}

†**hiddillis, hidlis, hyddyllis** *n* a hiding place; hiding places *la14-e16*. **in hiddillis** in hiding, in concealment *la14-e16*. [OE *hȳdels*, from *hȳdan* to hide]

hiddin *see* HOODIN

hiddle^{1,1}, †**hiddill** /ˈhɪdl/ *n* 1 a hiding place, a sheltered spot *la19- T*. 2 a (confused) cluster of buildings *20- NE*. 3 hiding, concealment; secrecy *15-e16*. **hiddlie** hidden, sheltered, remote *la19, 20- T*. †**in hiddil** in hiding, in concealment *la15-e16*. [back-formation from the noun HIDDILLIS, erroneously perceived as plural]

hiddle^{1,2} /ˈhɪdəl/ *v* 1 to hide, conceal *19, 20- Sh T Bor*. 2 to nestle closely, take shelter *la19- NE T*. [see the noun]

hiddle *see* HEDDLE

hiddlins *see* HIDLINS^{1,1}, HIDLINS^{1,2}, HIDLINS^{1,3}

hiddous *see* HIDOWIS

hiddy-giddy *see* HIDDIE-GIDDIE

hide^1, *Sh* **hoid**, *NE T* **hod**, *EC* **howd**, *WC* **hid**, †**hyde** /hʌɪd; *Sh* hɔɪd; *NE T* hod; *EC* hʌud; *WC* hɪd/ *v pt* **hid**, *NE T* **hode**, *NE T EC* **hed**, *NE T Bor* **hade**, *N NE* **hidit**, *NE T* **hoddit**, †**hyd**, *ptp* **hid, hidden, hodden**, *T* **hod**, *NE* **hidit**, *T* **hoddit**, †**hide**, †**hyd**, †**huden** to conceal; to keep secret *la14-*. **hidie**, *T* **hoddy** *adj* carefully concealed; suitable for concealment *20- NE T EC Bor*. **hidie** *n* the game of hide-and-seek; the call given by a player to indicate that he is ready to be sought for *19- T EC*. **hiding** concealment, a hiding place *15-*. **hidance** = *hiding la19- WC*. [OE *hȳdan*]

hide^2, †**hid**, †**hyd** /hʌɪd/ *n* 1 the skin of an animal *la14-*. 2 human skin *la14-*. **hide-bind** a condition of horses and cattle which causes the hide to cling to the bone *19- Ork C*. †**hide and hair** the whole of (a person or thing) *la15-18*. **hide or hair** the slightest sign or trace of a person or animal *la14-*. †**hyd and hew** = *hyd or hew 15-e17*. †**hyd or hew** colouring or complexion *e19*. [OE *hȳd*]

hidie-hole, *Sh* **hoidie-holl** /ˈhʌɪdi hol; *Sh* ˈhɔɪdi hɔl/ *n* a hiding place *19-*. [*hidie* (HIDE^1) + HOLE^{1,1}]

hidit *see* HIDE^1

hidlin, †**hidling** /ˈhɪdlən/ *adj* hidden, secret; secretive, furtive *19, 20- T EC Bor*. **hidlin wise**, †**hidling ways** secretly, by stealth *la18-19, 20- SW*. [presp of HIDDLE^{1,2}, or back-formation from HIDLINS^{1,2}]

hidlins^{1,1}, **hiddlins**, †**hidlingis** /ˈhɪdlənz/ *npl* 1 hiding places; places of refuge or shelter *la16-*. 2 concealment, secrecy *19, 20- SW Uls*. **in hiddlins**, †**in hidlings** in secret, clandestinely *la16-*. [*hid* (HIDE^1), with *-ings* suffix]

hidlins^{1,2}, **hiddlins** /ˈhɪdlənz/ *adj* secret, clandestine, underhand *19, 20- WC SW Bor*. [see the noun]

hidlins^{1,3}, †**hiddlins**, †**hidlingis** /ˈhɪdlənz/ *adv* secretly, stealthily *la15-*. [see the noun]

hidlis *see* HIDDILLIS

hidmost *see* HINMAIST^{1,2}

hidnae, hidno, hidny *see* HAE^{1,2}

†**hidowis, hidwis, hiddous** *adj* hideous *la14-16*. [ME *hidous*]

hie *see* HE^{1,2}, HEICH^{1,3}, HEY^4, HI^{1,1}, HI^{1,2}

Hieland^{1,1}, **Highland, Heichlan'**, †**Heland**, †**Heichland** /ˈhilənd, ˈhʌɪlənd, ˈhɪxlən/ *n* 1 the Scottish Highlands *16-*. 2 high ground, a hill; a high part of a country *la16-19, 20- literary*. [see the adj]

Hieland^{1,2}, **Heeland, Hielan, Highland**, †**Heland**, †**Heighland**, †**helland** /ˈhilənd, ˈhilən, ˈhʌɪlənd/ *adj* 1 belonging to or characteristic of the Highlands of Scotland *16-*. 2 *of breeds of animals* native to the Highlands *16-*. 3 *of language* Gaelic; *of people* Gaelic-speaking *la16-*. 4 *of character traits* considered to be typical of Highlanders *la18-*. †**Highland anger** a violent, short-lived burst of anger *e18*. **Highland cow, Hielan coo** (one of) a long-haired, long-horned breed of cattle native to the Highlands, typically red in colour *16-*. **hielan dancer** *rhyming slang* a chancer *la20-*. **Highland dancing** a form of dancing, based on traditional Highland figures, performed competitively or as a spectacle *19-*. **Highland Donald** a nickname for a Highlander *la18-19, 20- N NE T*. **Highland dress** a tartan outfit consisting of the kilt and a jacket with silver buttons (and sometimes a sporran, hose, a bonnet and a plaid) *la18-*. **Highland fling, Hielan fling** a solo example of *Highland dancing 19-*. **Highland Games** an event consisting of athletics, piping and dancing competitions, originally held in the Highlands *19-*. **Highland Gathering** = *Highland Games la19-*. **Highland honours** the ceremonial drinking of a toast, where people stand with one foot on their chairs and one on the table *19-*. **Highland Light Infantry** a former Scottish regiment, raised in 1777 and so called from 1807 *19-20, 21- historical*. **the Highland line** the notional boundary between the Highlands and the Lowlands, considered to extend from Dumbarton to Ballater approximately and then across to Nairn *19-*. **Highland pony** a native Scottish pony originating in the Highlands *la18-*. **Highland pride** (exaggerated) pride in one's lineage *la18-*. **Highland pyot, hieland pyot** the mistle thrush *Turdus viscivorus la19- NE*. **Hieland reel** a Highland dance performed by two couples, similar to a foursome reel *la18-*. **Highland regiment** one of various regiments of the British Army, originally recruited from the Highlands, whose members are entitled to wear Highland dress *18-*. **Highland Region** the region formed from the former counties of Caithness, Sutherland and Nairn, and parts of the former counties of Ross and Cromarty, Inverness, Moray and Argyll *la20, 21- historical*. **Highland schottische** a dance combining a schottische and a reel *la19-*. **Highland sheltie, hielan sheltie** = *Highland pony la18-19, 20- N NE T H&I*. **Highland Show** an agricultural show now held annually at its showground at Ingliston, Midlothian (but originally held in a different town each year) *19-*. †**heilan walloch** = *Highland fling la18-19*. †**give highland bail** to liberate by force *e19*. **The Highland and Agricultural Society of Scotland** a society formed to inquire into the state of the Highlands and Islands *18-20, 21- historical*. [HEICH^{1,3} + LAND^{1,1}]

Hielander, Highlander /ˈhiləndər, ˈhʌɪləndər/ *n* 1 a native or inhabitant of the Scottish Highlands *17-*. 2 a soldier in one of the Highland regiments of the British Army *18-*. 3 a Highland cow *la18-*. [HIELAND^{1,1}, with agent suffix]

Hielandman, Heilandman, Hielanman, Hielantman, Highlandman, †**Helandman** /ˈhiləndmən, ˈhilənmən, ˈhilntmən, ˈhʌɪləndmən/ *n* a Scottish Highlander *15-*.

Highlandman's garters ribbon grass *Phalaris arundinacea 'Picta'* 20- *Sh NE WC*. **Hielanman's Umbrella, Highlandman's Umbrella** the bridge in Glasgow carrying the Central Railway Station over Argyle Street (under which Highlanders used to gather) 20-. [HIELAND¹·² + MAN]

Hielands, Hielans, Highlands, †Helands /ˈhiləndz, ˈhilənz, ˈhʌɪləndz/ *n* the mountainous district of Scotland lying north and west of the Highland line; the area historically occupied by the Gaelic-speaking clans 16-; compare LAWLANDS. **the Highlands and Islands** the area consisting of the Highlands and the Northern and Western Isles of Scotland *la18-*. [HEICH¹·³ + plural of LAND¹·¹]

Hielans *see* HIELANDS
Hielantman *see* HIELANDMAN
hiely *see* HEELY¹·³, HEELY¹·⁴
Hie Scole, hie scule *see* HIGH SCHOOL
hiffer *see* HEIFER
high *see* HEICH¹·¹, HEICH¹·², HEICH¹·³, HEICH¹·⁴

High Constable /hae ˈkɒnstəbəl/ *n* **1** one of the chief officers of the royal household; a hereditary title held by the Hays of Errol *17-*. **2** a member of a society of special constables in Edinburgh *19- EC*. [*high* (HEICH¹·³) + CONSTABLE]

High Court /hae ˈkɔrt/ *n* the supreme criminal court of Scotland *la19-*. **High Court of Justiciary** = HIGH COURT *la17-*. [*high* (HEICH¹·³) + *court* (COORT¹·¹)]

highen *see* HEICHTEN

Higher¹·¹ /ˈhaeər/ *n* an advanced examination or certificate, taken at the end of a secondary school course in Scotland *20-*. [shortened form of *Higher Leaving Certificate*; compare *Leaving Certificate* (CERTIFICATE)]

Higher¹·² /ˈhaeər/ *adj in secondary education* relating to the advanced examination or certificate: ◊*Higher English la19-*. [see the noun]

Highland *see* HIELAND¹·¹, HIELAND¹·²
Highlander *see* HIELANDER
Highlandman *see* HIELANDMAN
Highlands *see* HIELANDS

high school, †hie scule, †Hie Scole, †hee scoill /ˈhaeskul/ *n* a secondary school, originally the principal school in a town or burgh *16-*. [*high* (HEICH¹·³) + *school* (SCHULE)]

High Steward of Scotland /hae stuərd əv ˈskɒtlənd/ *n* an alternative name for the GREAT STEWARD OF SCOTLAND *la14-*. [*high* (HEICH¹·³) + *steward* (STEWART) + *of* + SCOTLAND]

high tea /hae ˈti/ *n* a meal eaten in the late afternoon or early evening, usually consisting of one (cooked) course followed by bread, cakes and tea *la19-*. [Eng *high tea*]

high-year-old *see* HAUF¹·³

Hi Hi /ˈhae hae/ *n* **1** a nickname for Haddington Athletic Football Club *20-*. **2** a nickname for Third Lanark Football Club *la19-20, 21- historical*. [perhaps from a supporters' chant]

hilch¹·¹ /hɪltʃ/ *n* a limp, an uneven gait; the act of walking with a limp *19- N SW Uls*. [see the verb]

hilch¹·², **hilsh** /hɪltʃ, hɪlʃ/ *v* to limp, hobble; to move with a rolling, lurching gait *la18-*. **hilch up** to move with a jerk; to hitch up (a load on one's back) *20- N SW*. [palatalized variant of HILT³]

hild *see* HAUD¹·²

hill¹, hull, †hyll /hɪl, hʌl/ *n* **1** an elevation, a (low) mountain *la12-*. **2** a pile of earth; an artificial mound *16-*. **3** a common moor where grazing rights are shared by the community *16-*. **4** upland or moorland on a farm used as rough grazing *la19-*. **5** community moorland where peats are cut; a peat moss *la17-19, 20- Sh Ork N NE*. **6** a flock of sheep pastured on a hillside *20- H&I SW Bor*. **7** a peat-stack *20- N NE*. **8** *mining* the pithead, the surface; the dump of hewn coal at the pithead, a coal-hill *16-19, 20- EC*. **hillag** a little hill, a small mound *20- N*. **hillan** a mound, a heap, a hillock; a molehill *la18-19, 20- EC SW*. **hiller, huller** a hillock, a small heap *20- N*. **hillin'** (common) grazing *la19- Sh*. **hillock** *NE* **hullock 1** a little hill, heap or mound *la15-*. **2** an overweight, sluggish person *20- Sh N NE T SW*. **3** a large quantity; a crowd of people *20- N NE T*. **hill-bark** tormentil *Potentilla erecta 20- Sh Ork*. **hill-berry** the crowberry *Empetrum nigrum 19, 20- N*. **hill-cart** a small, low cart *20- C SW*. **hill-clap** a rumbling noise in the upper air over hills; thunder *20- Sh T*. **hill-clerk** *mining* the person who weighs the coal when it is dispatched from the pit or from the depot *la19, 20- EC*. **hill-dyke** the wall dividing hill pasture from the (lower) arable land *la17-*. **hill-fit, hill-foot** (the ground at) the bottom of a hill; a foothill; frequently in place-names *16-*. **hill-folk 1** people who live in the hills *la19-*. **2** the Reformed Presbyterian Church, originally the Covenanters who, because of persecution, worshipped secretly in the hills *19, 20- historical*. **3** *folklore* hill fairies *la19- Sh Ork*. **hill-gaen** peat-cutting *20- Sh*. **hill-gaet** a track through hills *la19- Sh*. **hill-girse** common grazing *20- Sh*. **hill-grind** a gateway between hill pasture and enclosed arable land *20- Sh*. **hillheid, hillhead** the summit or upper part of a hill; frequently in place-names *la15-*. **hill-kishie** a creel for carrying peat *20- Sh*. **hill-lintie** the twite *Linaria flavirostris la19- Ork N T EC*. **hillman 1** a person who lives or works in the hills; a shepherd or gillie *la17-*. **2** *pl* the Reformed Presbyterian Church, originally the Covenanters who, because of persecution, worshipped secretly in the hills *la17-19, 20- historical*. **3** a man who works at the pithead; a colliery official *la17-19*. **hill-run 1** hilly, upland *la19- N NE*. **2** uncultured, rough, boorish *20- NE T EC*. **hill-shither** *folklore* fairy folk *20- Ork*. **hillsman** *mining* a man who worked at the pithead; a colliery official *la18-19, 20- literary*. **hill-sporrow, hill-sparrow** the meadow pipit *Anthus pratensis la19- Sh Ork*. **hill-tings** *folklore* fairy folk *20- Sh*. **hill-trows** *folklore* fairy folk *20- Sh Ork*. **hill-wife** *folklore* a fairy woman *la19- Sh*. **hill-woman** *mining* a female pithead worker *la19, 20- EC*. **gather the hill** to gather together flocks pastured on a hillside *20-*. **hill abeen e cairnie** topsy-turvy *20- N*. **hillie cairnie** a game involving children piling into a heap *20- N NE*. **†oot o hill an heap** from whatever lies to hand, from odds and ends; by one's own resourcefulness or imagination *19*. **to the hill** in an upward direction *19- NE SW*. [OE *hyll*]

hill², hull /hɪl, hʌl/ *v* to hurry, move at speed *la19-*. **hill on** to hurry along *20- NE*. [unknown]

hilliegeleerie *see* HEELIEGOLEERIE¹·²

hilsh *see* HILCH¹·²

hilt¹, hult, †hylt, †helt /hɪlt, hʌlt/ *n* **1** the handle of a sword or dagger *la14-*. **2** a plough-handle *20- N NE SW Bor*. [OE *hilte*]

hilt², *H&I* **hult** /hɪlt; *H&I* hʌlt/ *n* a trace, a vestige *18-*. **hilt nor hair** nothing at all, not a vestige *19-*. **ilka hilt and hair** every particle *18-19, 20- SW*. [unknown]

†hilt³ *v* to walk with a limp *la18-19*. [altered form of Older Scots *halt*]

hilter-skilter, helter skelter /ˈhɪltər skɪltər, ˈhɛltər skɛltər/ *adv* in rapid succession, confusedly *18-*. **†drink helter-skelter** to drink heavily, while also mixing one's drinks *18-19*. [EModE *helter skelter*]

hiltie-skiltie¹·¹, hilty-skilty /ˈhɪlti skɪlti/ *adj* harum-scarum, heedless *19- EC Bor*. [see the adv]

hiltie-skiltie¹·², helty-skelty /ˈhɪlti skɪlti, ˈhɛlti skɛlti/ *adv* in rapid succession, confusedly *la18-*. [altered form of HILTER-SKILTER]

hilty-skilty *see* HILTIE-SKILTIE¹·¹

him, um /hɪm, ʌm/ *pron* **1** the male person or animal in question *la14-*. **2** *of a thing or phenomenon* it *la18-19, 20- Sh Ork N*. [OE *him*, dative]

himberry *see* HINDBERRY

hime, hymn, †heym, †hympne, †ympne, †ymn /hʌɪm, hɪm/ *n* a song of praise to a deity; a hymn *la14-*. [Lat *hymnus*]

himp *see* IMP[1.1]

himsel, himsell, himself /hɪm'sɛl, hɪm'sɛlf/ *pron* **1** the male mentioned or in question *la14-*. **2** a term of reference to a clan chief, the man in a household or a male boss *la19-*. Compare *hissel* (HIS). [OE *him self*]

himst[1.1] /hɪmst/ *adj* **1** touchy, huffy *la19- Sh*. **2** foolish or flighty *la19- Sh*. **3** restless, hurried, agitated *la19- Sh*. [unknown]

himst[1.2] /hɪmst/ *adv* abruptly *20- Sh*. [unknown]

hin *see* HAE[1.2], HINT[1.2]

hinch *see* HAINCH[1.1], HAINCH[1.2]

hinchin-steen *see* HENSHELSTANE

hinc inde /ˈhɪŋk ɪndɛ/ *adv of legal claims and contracts* working reciprocally *la16-*. [Lat *hinc inde* on this side, on that side]

hincumsneevie *see* HINKUMSNEEVLIE

hind[1], **hyne** /hʌɪnd, hʌɪn/ *n* **1** a farm-servant, a ploughman *la15-19, 20- C SW Bor*. **2** a married skilled farmworker who occupies a farm-cottage; a farm foreman *la17-19, 20- C SW Bor*. **3** a youth, a stripling *la14-e19*. **hinding, hindin** the work of a farm hand *la19- EC Bor*. **hinds' raw** a row of farmworkers' cottages *20- EC Bor*. [OE *hīwan* members of a family, household, or religious house]

hind[2.1] /hʌɪnd/ *n* a skin or film (on the surface of a liquid) *19- Sh*. [ON *hinna*]

hind[2.2] /hʌɪnd/ *v* to coat or form a film *20- Sh Ork*. [see the noun]

hind *see* HINE[1], HINT[1.2], HYNE

hindbacks *see* HINTBACKS

hindberry, WC himberry /ˈhʌɪndbɛri; WC ˈhɪmbɛri/ *n* the wild raspberry *Rubus idaeus 19- N H&I C SW Bor*. [OE *hindberge*, from *hind* the female deer + BERRY[1]]

hinder *see* HINNER[1], HINNER[2.1], HINNER[2.2]

hinderend *see* HINNEREN

hindermost *see* HINNERMAIST

hinders *see* HINTERS

hindie *see* HYNE

hindmaist *see* HINMAIST[1.2]

hindmest *see* HINMAIST[1.2], HINMAIST[1.3]

hindmost *see* HINMAIST[1.2]

hine[1], **†hind** /hʌɪn/ *n* a HINDBERRY *19- SW Bor*. [shortened form of HINDBERRY]

hine[2], **hain, haven, †havin, †havyn, †hevin** /hʌɪn, hen, ˈhɛvən/ *n* a (natural) harbour, a port; frequently in place-names *la14-*. **†heavening** harbouring; a haven *15-e17*. **†havin silver** a harbour due *la15-17*. [OE *haefen*]

hiney *see* HINNIE[1.1]

hing[1.1], **hang** /hɪŋ, haŋ/ *n* **1** the act of hanging; a downward droop or bend *19-*. **2** the act of leaning out of a tenement window for amusement *la19- T C SW*. **3** a period of idleness or leisure *la19- C*. **4** a rope or pulley (by which something is suspended) *18-19*. **hingie** the act of leaning out of a tenement window for amusement *la20- T C*. **on the hing** in the balance *20- T C SW*. [see the verb]

hing[1.2], **hang** /hɪŋ, haŋ/ *v pt* **hingit, hangit, hung**, *Sh NE* **hang**, *ptp* **hung, hangit, †hungin, †hingin, †hyngyt 1** to suspend or be suspended *la14-*. **2** to be hanged; to execute by hanging *la14-*. **3** to be imminent or pending *la15-*. **4** to cling or hold fast to *la15-*. **5** to furnish or decorate (with wallpaper, paintings or hangings) *16-*. **6** to lean out of a window to watch events in the street below *la19-*. **7** to delay, hover indecisively; to shirk *la19-*. **8** to be in a poor state of health *la19-*. **9** *farming* to lay sheaves in a sloping position *19, 20- Ork*. **hung** of the notice of an intention to marry displayed on a registrar's notice board *20- EC SW*. **†hang-choice** a choice between two evils *e19*. **hingim-tringim** worthless, disreputable; barely presentable *la19- NE*. **hang net** a vertical stake-net *19-*. **hing on** a source or period of delay, tedium or weariness; an encumbrance, a hindrance *20-*. **hing-oot** a promiscuous woman *la20-*. **hing-tee** a mistress, a girlfriend *20- N NE T*. **hing-the-gither** clannish *19-*. **hing by a tack** to hang by a thread *17-*. **hing by yer ain heid** to be independent, self-supporting or self-reliant *18-*. **hing the cat** to work slowly or to rule; to lounge about; to hold things up *20- T EC*. **hang a faiple, hing yer faiple** to look glum or sour *19-*. **hing in 1** to carry out a task with energy; to persevere; to hurry *la19-*. **2** to pay court assiduously; to curry favour *20- Ork NE*. **hing in like a coo in a harrow** to persevere *20- Ork*. **hing on 1** to wait, hold on *17-*. **2** to delay or hinder someone, keep someone waiting *20- NE T*. **hing on a lang face** to look miserable *la19, 20- Sh Ork T*. **hing the pettit lip** to sulk *20-*. **hing tae** to join in; to adhere or attach oneself to something; to fall in with another's plans *19- N NE EC*. **†hing to** to attach or append one's seal to a document *15-e16*. **hing up** *of weather* to remain dry *20- H&I WC*. **hing yer lugs** to look dejected or abashed *la17-*. [ME *hingen*, the strong forms of the pt and ptp replacing earlier forms of OE *hangian* and ON *hengja*]

hing *see* THING[1]

hingand *see* HINGIN

hinger, hanger, †thingar, †hangar /ˈhɪŋər, ˈhaŋər/ *n* **1** a device by which something is hung *16-*. **2** hanging drapery; a curtain or tapestry *16-19, 20- Sh NE Bor*. **3** the layer of rock above a coal-seam *17-19, 20- EC SW*. **4** a pendant ornament *la15-19, 20- EC*. **hinger-in** a person who perseveres; a conscientious, hardworking person *20-*. **†hingars-at-lugs, hingaris-at-lugis** earrings *la16-19*. [HING[1.2], with agent suffix]

hingie, hingy /ˈhɪŋi/ *adj* slightly unwell *la20-*. [HING[1.2], with *-ie* suffix]

hingin, hinging, hanging, †hingand /ˈhɪŋən, ˈhɪŋɪŋ, ˈhaŋɪŋ/ *adj* **1** suspended; drooping; overhanging *la15-*. **2** *of coal* lying at a steep angle; undercut and ready to fall *la17-*. **3** *of a golf ball* lying on a downward slope *la19-*. **4** *of the sky* overcast, threatening rain *20-*. **hanging burn** a sheep-mark, a vertical stroke branded on the lower part of the face *la19- SW Bor*. **hanging chimney, †hinging chimney** a wide, old-fashioned chimney descending from the roof above a fire *la18-19, 20- NE*. **hanging gate** a bar or grating hung across a stream *19- C Bor*. **hingen-heedit** abashed *la19- N NE*. **hingin-like** ill-looking *la20-*. **hinging lock, hanging lock** a padlock *la15-*. **hingin-luggit** dejected, crestfallen, abashed *20-*. **hingin lum** = *hanging chimney la17-*. **hingin' mince 1** a non-existent thing, an absurdity for which people are sent on fool's errands *la20- NE T EC*. **2** a humorous term for sausages *21- NE T EC*. **hingin' mou'd** dejected, sulky *la19- NE*. **hanging post** a post supporting a roof *18-19, 20- T*. **hanging scaffold** *mining* a moveable platform in a shaft *la19, 20- EC*. **hanging stair** stone steps built into the wall at one side *la17-*. **hanging steps** = *hanging stair la19-*. **hingan stitch** *shoemaking* a stitch for attaching the upper to the sole *20- Ork*. **hingin witter** a sheepmark, a slanting upward slit in the side of the ear *20- Sh*. **hingin fae** *of an emotion* made obvious: ◇*embarrassment was just hingin fae her la20-*. [presp of HING[1.2]]

hingin *see* HING[1.2]

hinging see HINGIN

hingit, hangit /ˈhɪŋɪt, ˈhaŋɪt/ *adj* **1** executed by hanging *16-20, 21- historical*. **2** suspended, draped; decorated with hangings *19, 20- literary*. **hangit-faced** looking villainous or likely to hang *19- T Bor*. †**hangit-like** shamefaced *19*. **hangit-lookin** shamefaced, having an air of constraint or reluctance *20- EC*. [ptp of HING¹·²]

hingit see HING¹·²

hingle see HAINGLE¹·¹, HAINGLE¹·²

hingman see HANGMAN

hingmy see THINGMY

hingy see HINGIE

hink see HENK¹·¹, HENK¹·², THINK¹·²

hinkie-pinkie see INKIE-PINKIE

hinklin see INKLIN

hinkumsneevlie, hincumsneevie /hɪŋkʌmˈsnivli, hɪŋkʌmˈsnivi/ *n* **1** a foolish person *19- NE*. **2** a deceitful person; a tell-tale *19- NE*. [unknown]

hinmaist¹·¹, †**hinmost** /ˈhɪnmest/ *n* **1** the last, the furthest back *19, 20- NE*. **2** the finish, the end of a period of time *19, 20- NE*. [see the adj]

hinmaist¹·², hindmaist, hindmost, *Sh* **hidmost,** *T* **hendmost,** †**hindmest,** †**hinmest,** †**henmast** /ˈhɪnmest, ˈhɪndmest, ˈhʌɪndmost; *Sh* ˈhɪdməst; *T* ˈhɛndmost/ *adj* **1** furthest behind; in the rear *la14-*. **2** last in order or time; final *la15-*. **the hinmaist day** the Day of Judgement *20-*. **the hindmost rook** a person's last penny *la18-19, 20- WC SW*. [perhaps HINT¹·² rear, back or OE *heonan* from here, with superlative suffix]

hinmaist¹·³, †**hindmest** /ˈhɪnmest/ *adv* finally, last *15-*. [see the adj]

hinmest see HINMAIST¹·²

hinmost see HINMAIST¹·¹

hinna, hinnae see HAE¹·²

hinner¹, hinder, †**hyndir,** †**hender** /ˈhɪnər; ˈhɪndər/ *adj* **1** situated in the rear, coming from behind *la15-*. **2** *of time* (recently) past, previous *la14-19, 20- WC*. **hinderlands** the buttocks *19- literary*. †**hinnerlets, hinderlets** the buttocks *la18-e19*. †**hinderlins** the buttocks *19*. †**hinner nicht, hindernight** last night; the previous night *16-e19*. [HINT¹·² rear, back, with comparative suffix]

hinner²·¹, hinder, †**hender** /ˈhɪnər; ˈhɪndər/ *n* **1** a hindrance; an obstruction or impediment; a cause of delay *16-*. **2** damage *la16*. [see the verb]

hinner²·², hinder, *T EC* **hender** /ˈhɪnər; ˈhɪndər; *T EC* ˈhɛndər/ *v* **1** to obstruct, delay or impede; to interrupt; to prevent *la14-*. **2** to linger or dawdle; to waste time *la19- Sh NE T*. **hinnerance, hindrance,** †**hinderance,** †**henderance** impediment, obstruction; disadvantage, delay *la16-*. **hinderment** hindrance, delay *19- Sh NE EC*. **hinnersome, hindersome,** †**hindersum,** †**handersum 1** obstructive, troublesome, detrimental *la16-*. **2** *of weather* causing delay (to farm work) *19-*. **it'll hinder me tae dae** it will save me the trouble *la19- Sh*. **you'll no hinder me to do** nothing can prevent me from doing *19-*. [OE *hindrian*]

hinneren, hinnerend, hinderend, *NE* **hinnereyn,** *T* **henderend** /ˈhɪnərɛn, ˈhɪnərɛnd, ˈhɪndərɛnd; *NE* ˈhɪnərʌɪn; *T* ˈhɛndərɛnd/ *n* **1** the later or final part; the end (of life or time) *la15-*. **2** the back or rear portion of something; the extremity *19-*. **3** the buttocks *19-*. **4** the remains of something; leavings, refuse *19- NE EC Bor*. **the hinner-end o a'** the culmination *la18- NE Bor*. **at the hinnerend, at the hinneren** ultimately, in the end *la15-*. **in the hinnerend** in the end, latterly *20-*. **lauch yer hinderend** to die laughing *19- NE T*. [HINNER¹ + EN¹·¹]

hinnermaist, hindermost, *NE* **hinnermist,** †**hendirmost** /ˈhɪnərmest, ˈhɪndərmost; *NE* ˈhɪnərmɪst/ *adj* last, final, hindmost *la16-*. [HINNER¹, with superlative suffix]

hinnie¹·¹, hinny, hinney, honey, †**hiney,** †**huny,** †**hwny** /ˈhɪni, ˈhɪne, ˈhʌni, ˈhʌne/ *n* **1** a sweet fluid made by bees, honey *la14-*. **2** a term of endearment *la15-*. **hinny blob, honey blob 1** a large, yellow variety of gooseberry *Ribes uva-crispa 18-19, 20- SW Uls*. **2** a drop of honey; a term of endearment *e19*. †**hwnygukkis** a term of endearment *e16*. **hinny pear, honey perr,** †**hony per** a sweet pear *16-19, 20- C SW Bor*. **hinnie pig** an earthenware container for liquid honey *19, 20- NE SW*. **hinnie pots, honey pots** a children's game *19, 20- Bor*. **hinniesickle** honeysuckle *Lonicera la18-19, 20- T WC*. **hinnywar, hinniwir** an edible seaweed *Alaria esculenta 19- Sh N*. **aw hinny and jo** *of behaviour* insincerely affable *19-*. **nothing but hinny and jo** = aw hinny and jo *la17-19, 20- T EC*. [OE *hunig*]

hinnie¹·², hinny, honey, †**huny,** †**hony** /ˈhɪni, ˈhɪne, ˈhʌni, ˈhʌne/ *adj* sweetened or flavoured with honey; as sweet as honey *la15-*. [see the noun]

hinnie-spot /ˈhɪni spɔt/ *n* **1** a mole, a birthmark *20- Sh*. **2** the breast-hook in a boat, the three-cornered piece of wood which connects the gunwales with the stem *20- Sh*. [unknown first element + SPOAT]

hinny see HINNIE¹·¹, HINNIE¹·²

hint¹·¹ /hɪnt/ *n* **1** the back, the rear *19-*. **2** the end of a period of time *19-*. **3** the furrow left between two strips of ploughing *la19- WC SW Uls*. **hintin** the mould furrow *la18-*. [see the adj]

hint¹·², hin, hent, hind, †**hynd,** †**hend** /hɪnt, hɪn, hɛnt, hʌɪnd/ *adj* **1** situated at the back or in the rear *la14-*. **2** later in time *16*. **hin-door** the removable back-board of a box-cart *la19-20, 21- historical*. **hin-en, hint-en, hind-end 1** an extremity or rear part; the hindquarters *18-*. **2** the latter portion of a period of time *18-*. **hin-hairst** the period of the year after harvest and before winter *18-*. **hint-hand, hindhand 1** *of a curling stone* last, hindmost *19-*. **2** *of a person* dilatory, careless, late *la19-*. **hinhaun** curling the player of the last stone played in a rink *19, 20- SW*. †**hindhead, hindheid** the back of the head *la16-17*. **hin-hoch, hin haugh** a hind leg *la20-*. **hin-side** the rear *20- NE*. **hin'side afore** back to front *la19- NE*. **hint-side foremaist** backwards, back to front *20-*. [ME *hint*; compare OE *hindan* from behind]

†**hint¹·³** *adv* behind, in the rear *e19*. [see the adj]

hint¹·⁴ /hɪnt/ *prep* behind *la18-19, 20- NE T Bor*. **hint the han** stored for future use *la19- NE*. [see the adj]

hint² /hɪnt/ *n* a moment, an instant *la18-19, 20- Sh N*. [EModE *hint* an occasion, an opportunity]

hint³ /hɪnt/ *n* a trace; a clue *18-*. **neither hint nor hair** nothing at all, not a vestige *la19- NE T EC*. [altered form of HILT², with infl from *hint* a slight indication]

hint⁴ /hɪnt/ *v* to slink or flit about quietly or furtively *19- Sh NE*. [unknown]

hint see HENT¹·¹, HENT¹·², HENT²

hintbacks, †**hindbacks** /ˈhɪntbaks/ *adj* surreptitious *la18-19, 20- Sh Ork*. [HINT¹·² + BACK¹·¹ + -s; an adverbial formation used as an adjective]

hinters, †**hinders** /ˈhɪntərz/ *n* the hindquarters of an animal; the buttocks *la19, 20- Sh*. [substantive use of HINNER¹]

hip¹ /hɪp/ *n* **1** the upper thigh, the haunch *16-*. **2** a projecting or outlying piece of land; a curving projection of the lower slopes of a hillside *la15-19, 20- SW*. **hippit 1** having hips of a specified kind *19-*. **2** having a feeling of stiffness or overstraining in the lower back, hips or thighs *19-*. †**hipsie-dipsie** a thrashing *19*. **hip-grippit** discomfort in the back and thighs through stooping *20- N NE SW*. **hiplocks** the coarse wool which grows on the hips of sheep *la17-19, 20- Ork N SW*. [OE *hype*]

hip[2.1] /hɪp/ *n* an act of hopping, a hop *20- WC Bor*. [see the verb]

hip[2.2] /hɪp/ *v* **1** to pass over, miss *la15-19, 20- Sh EC*. **2** to hop, skip *19, 20- NE Bor*. [ME *hippen* to leap, spring, hop, bounce]

hip *see* HAP[3]

hipoticary *see* APOTHECARIE

hipp *see* HEAP[1.1]

hippan *see* HIPPEN[2]

hippen[1], †**hipping** /ˈhɪpən/ *n* **1** a baby's nappy *18-*. **2** *humorous* the curtain in a makeshift theatre *20- WC*. [HIP[1], with *-ing* suffix]

hippen[2], **hippan** /ˈhɪpən/ *n* the fruit of the wild rose *Rosa canina 19- NE*. [OE *hēope*, with diminutive *-ing* suffix]

hippertie-skippertie /ˈhɪpərti skɪpərti/ *adj* frivolous, frisky *19, 20- NE Bor*. [reduplicative compound based on HIP[1] and SKIP[1.2]]

hipping *see* HIPPEN[1]

hippity /ˈhɪpɪti/ *adj* lame, limping *la19- T SW*. [derivative of *hippit* (HIP[1])]

hipple /ˈhɪpəl/ *v* to walk with a limp; to hobble; to go lame *19- NE WC Bor*. [frequentative or diminutive form of HIP[2.2]; compare HIRPLE[1.2]]

hipsie-dipsie *see* HIP[1]

hir *see* HER[1.1], HER[1.2]

hird[1.1], **herd**, *Uls* **hurd**, †**heird** /hɪrd, hɛrd/ *Uls* hʌrd/ *n* **1** a person who tends or watches over sheep or cattle; a shepherd *la14-*. **2** a spiritual guide, a pastor *la14-19, 20- T*. **3** *curling* a stone played so as to guard the winning shot from the stones of opponents *la18-e19*. [OE *heord*]

hird[1.2], **herd**, *Uls* **hurd** /hɪrd, hɛrd/ *Uls* hʌrd/ *v* **1** to tend or watch over livestock; to prevent animals from straying *la17-*. **2** to keep land clear of animals *18-*. **3** to keep someone away; to alienate or drive someone away *la19- NE EC*. **4** to look after or attend to (a person or object) *la16-19, 20- SW*. **5** to bring in crops at harvest *la19- Sh*. **herdin, herding 1** the tending of sheep or cattle *la16-19, 20- N H&I SW Bor*. **2** a grazing allotted to a particular herdsman *la17-19, 20- N SW Bor*. **3** the post of herdsman *la19, 20- N EC Bor*. **herd craws, hird crows** to prevent rooks from damaging crops *20- NE T EC Bor*. [see the noun]

hirda, herda /ˈhɪrdə, ˈhɛrdə/ *n* a crop trampled by animals; husks, stubble *la19- Sh*. **in herda** in confusion; in ruins *20- Sh*. [unknown]

hirdum-dirdum /ˈhɪrdəm dɪrdəm/ *n* uproar, noisy mirth or revelry *18- NE C Bor*. [reduplicative compound based on DIRDUM]

hirdy-girdy[1.1] /ˈhɪrdi gɪrdi/ *n* uproar, confusion, disorder *la15-19, 20- T EC*. [variant of HIDDIE-GIDDIE]

hirdy-girdy[1.2] /ˈhɪrdi gɪrdi/ *adv* in disorder or confusion *la16-19, 20- T Bor*. [see the noun]

hire[1.1], †**hyre** /haer/ *n* **1** the act of hiring; payment for temporary use of something; payment for hired service *15-*. **2** a titbit (given as an inducement); a reward *19, 20- EC Uls*. **3** a seaman's pay for a voyage *15-e17*. **hirie** a titbit, a reward *la19- NE*. †**half-hyre** one half of a seaman's pay for a voyage *la16-e17*. [OE *hȳr*]

hire[1.2], †**hyre** /haer/ *v* **1** to obtain the (temporary) use of something in exchange for payment; to engage an employee *15-*. **2** to let (something) out on hire *16-*. **3** to find employment; to accept a position *17-*. **4** to season food; to make food more palatable *19, 20- NE Bor*. **hirer,** †**hyrare 1** a person who hires something or engages an employee *17-*. **2** a person who rents something out on hire *17-*. **3** a farmworker (engaged by the day or for a short period) *la19- Ork N*. †**hyregang** the lease of farm animals, utensils or land *16-e17*. **hirehoose 1** a farm bothy *la19- N NE*. **2** farm labour *20- NE*. †**hireman, hyreman** a male farmworker or servant *la15-19*. †**hire woman, hyre woman** a female farmworker or servant *la16-19*. †**as they war hyrit** willingly, eagerly, speedily; as if being paid *16-e19*. [OE *hȳrian*]

hiree *see* HURROO[1.1]

hiring, hirin, †**thyring** /ˈhaerɪŋ, ˈhaerɪn/ *n* **1** giving or taking on a lease; renting *17-*. **2** the occasion of engaging farmworkers *la19-*. **3** a batch of baking done with rich ingredients *20- NE Bor*. **4** the payment due for the hire of something *15*. **hiring fair** a fair held for the purpose of engaging farmworkers *19, 20- historical*. **hiring market** a market held for the purpose of engaging farmworkers *19, 20- historical*. [verbal noun from HIRE[1.2]]

hirkie, †**harky** /ˈhɪrki/ *n fisherman's taboo* a pig *19- Sh N*. [probably imitative of a grunt; compare Norw dial *harka* to make a rattling sound in the throat]

hirling *see* HERLING

hirmal *see* ORMAL

hirne, hurn, †**hyrn** /hɪrn, hʌrn/ *n* **1** a nook or corner, a hiding place *15-19, 20- literary*. **2** the lair of a lobster *20- Ork*.

hirnik 1 a corner, a hiding-place *20- Sh*. **2** a fragment, a particle *20- Sh*. [OE *hyrne*]

hirpill *see* HIRPLE[1.2]

hirpile[1.1] /ˈhɪrpəl/ *n* a limp; the act of walking unsteadily or limping *la18-*. [see the verb]

hirple[1.2], †**hirpill** /ˈhɪrpəl/ *v* to limp or hobble, walk lamely; to move unevenly *la15-*. [unknown; compare HIPPLE]

hirr[1.1], **yirr** /hɪr, jɪr/ *n* **1** a call made to a dog to attack or pursue *19, 20- Sh N*. **2** the snarl or growl of a dog *19, 20- Sh T*. [see the verb]

hirr[1.2], **irr, yirr** /hɪr, ɪr, jɪr/ *v* **1** *of a dog* to snarl or growl *18-19, 20- Sh N*. **2** *of a person* to make an outcry; to continue to complain *19, 20- Sh EC*. **3** to urge a dog to attack or pursue *19, 20- N*. [onomatopoeic; compare OE *gyrran* to sound, chatter]

hirr[1.3], †**yirr** /hɪr/ *interj* a command to a dog to attack or pursue *19, 20- Sh N*. [see the verb]

†**hirrie-harrie, hiry-hary** *interj* an outcry after a thief; a call to charge *16-e19*. [compare HERRY, HARRO]

hirris *see* HER[1.2]

hirro *see* HARRO

hirsally *see* HIRST

hirsel[1.1], †**hirsell** /ˈhɪrsəl/ *n* **1** a flock of sheep, the number of sheep looked after by a shepherd *la14-19, 20- NE Bor*. **2** the spiritual charge of a pastor; a church *la14-19, 20- literary*. **3** a large number or quantity; a crowd or multitude *15-19, 20- T C Uls*. **4** the pasturage grazed by a flock of sheep *19, 20- C SW Bor*. **5** a drove of cattle *19, 20- NE*. [ON *hirzla, hirðsla* safe-keeping]

hirsel[1.2] /ˈhɪrsəl/ *v* **1** to separate sheep into flocks *16-19, 20- Bor*. **2** to arrange or classify (people or things) into groups *19*. [see the noun; compare ON *hirða* to tend sheep]

hirsel[2.1], **hirsle,** *Bor* **hersle,** †**harsel** /ˈhɪrsəl/ *Bor* ˈhɛrsəl/ *n* **1** the act of sliding along a bench or pew *19-*. **2** a wheeze or cough *la19-*. **3** an iron pin or auger used for boring holes when red-hot *19- SW Bor*. **4** a sliding, slithering or shuffling motion or noise; a confused fall *la19- NE*. [onomatopoeic]

hirsel[2.2], **hirsle, hirstle,** *NE* **hurschle,** †**hirsill,** †**hyrsyl,** †**hersle** /ˈhɪrsəl/ *NE* ˈhʌrʃəl/ *v* **1** to slide along a seat; to move sideways *18-*. **2** to make to haste, scramble; to bustle about *19-*. **3** to shrug *la19-*. **4** to slouch *19-*. **5** to wheeze *20-*. **6** to move with a rustling or grating noise *19- NE T*. **7** to graze against or grate on *16-17*. †**hirsel aff the stage** = *hirsle off la18*. †**hirsle off** to die peacefully *19*. **hirsle yont,** *NE*

hurschle yont to move along; to move over or away *19-*. [see the noun]
hirself see HERSEL
hirsell see HIRSEL[1.1]
hir selwyn see HERSEL
hirsill see HIRSEL[2.2]
hirsle see HIRSEL[2.1], HIRSEL[2.2]
hirst, *NE* **hist**, †**hyrst** /hɪrst; *NE* hɪst/ *n* **1** a piece of barren, unproductive ground; a hard or rocky mound or ridge, the summit of a rocky hill *15-19, 20- Ork C SW Bor*. **2** a bank of sand or gravel in a harbour or river; a ford or shallow in a river *la16-19, 20- C SW Bor*. **3** the frame of a pair of millstones, the part of the mill where the stones revolve in their framework *la16-19, 20- Ork NE*. **4** a great number of people; a quantity or accumulation of things *la18-19, 20- NE*. **5** a threshold, a door-sill *16-e19*. **hirsty, hirstie** stony, rocky; *of soil* dry or barren *la18-*. **hirsly**, *Ork* **hirsally** stony, rocky *la19- Ork NE T*. [OE *hyrst*]
hirstle see HIRSEL[2.2]
hirtch[1.1] /hɪrtʃ/ *n* a push, a jolt, a hitch; a shrug of the shoulders *la19- NE T*. [unknown]
hirtch[1.2] /hɪrtʃ/ *v* **1** to move jerkily, edge forward *la19- NE T*. **2** to approach in a sly ingratiating way, sidle *la19- NE T*. **3** to shudder with cold or fear *la18-19*. [unknown]
hiry-hary see HIRRIE-HARRIE
his /hɪz/ *adj* **1** belonging to him *la14-*. **2** belonging to it *la15-19, 20- Sh Ork*. **hissel, hisself** himself *la15-*. [OE *his*]
his see BE, HAE[1.2], US
hisened /ˈhɪzənd/ *adj* very cold, shivering with cold *20- Ork*. [Norw *isne* to chill, freeze]
hish[1.1], **hiss**, †**hys** /hɪʃ, hɪs/ *v* **1** to make a hissing sound *16-*. **2** to drive or scare away (by making a hissing sound) *la16-*. **3** to incite a dog to attack *20-*. [see the interj]
hish[1.2], **heesh, hiss** /hɪʃ, hiʃ, hɪs/ *interj* a sharp hissing call to drive off animals, or incite a dog to attack *19-*. **hiss cat, hish cat** a call to frighten away a cat *19, 20- NE*. [onomatopoeic]
hish see HEESH
hish-hash, *Sh* **hiss-hass** /ˈhɪʃhaʃ; *Sh* ˈhɪshas/ *n* a muddle, confusion; a mess *20- Sh EC SW*. [reduplicative form of HASH[1.1]]
hishie[1.1], **hushie** /ˈhɪʃi, ˈhʌʃi/ *n* a very quiet sound, a whisper *19, 20- T EC*. **neither hishie nor wishie** not the slightest sound *19, 20- EC*. [onomatopoeic]
hishie[1.2], **hushie** /ˈhɪʃi, ˈhʌʃi/ *v* to lull to sleep, sing a lullaby *19, 20- C*. [see the noun]
hishie-ba[1.1], **hushaby** /hɪʃi ˈba, hʌʃəˈbae/ *v* to lull a child to sleep *la19-*. [see the interj]
hishie-ba[1.2], **heeshie-baw, hushie-baa** /hɪʃi ˈba, hɪʃi ˈbɔ, hʌʃi ˈba/ *interj* an expression used to lull a child to sleep *19-*. [HISHIE[1.2] + BA[2]]
hisk /hɪsk/ *interj* **1** a call to a pig to come and be fed *20- EC*. **2** a call to drive off animals, or incite a dog to attack *la18-19*. [onomatopoeic; compare ISKY]
hi-spy, *EC* **hessy**, *WC* **haspie** /ˈhae spʌɪ; *EC* ˈhɛse; *WC* ˈhaspi/ *n* the call used in the children's game of hide-and-seek; the game itself *19-*. [Eng *Hi!* + Eng *spy*]
hiss see HISH[1.1], HISH[1.2]
hissel see HAZEL[1.1]
hiss-hass see HISH-HASH
hist see HEEST, HIRST
hit[1.1] /hɪt/ *n* a blow, a stroke *15-*. [see the verb]
hit[1.2], †**hyt** /hɪt/ *v pt* **hut, hat, hit**, *EC* **huttit**, *ptp* **hutten, hut, hit**, *Sh N NE* **hitten 1** to deliver a blow, strike *la14-*. **2** to throw or pitch *la19- Sh*. [ON *hitta* to hit upon, meet with]
hit see HOOT[1.2], IT

hitch[1.1] /hɪtʃ/ *n* **1** a temporary difficulty, a snag *17-*. **2** a small hop made in playing hopscotch *la19, 20- NE EC*. **3** *mining* a fault or dislocation in a coal-seam *17-19*. [unknown]
hitch[1.2], †**hich**, †**hych** /hɪtʃ/ *v* **1** to hobble, walk with a limp; to hop *16-*. **2** to lift with a jerk; to move jerkily *la16-*. [unknown]
hitchie-koo /hɪtʃiˈku/ *n* a ball game *20- NE*. [from the title of a music-hall song]
hither, *Sh* **hidder** /ˈhɪðər; *Sh* ˈhɪdər/ *adv* to or towards this place *la14-*. †**hithercuming**, **hyddir cummyn** arrival *16*. **hiddertil**, †**hithertill** until now, hitherto *15-19, 20- Sh*. †**hiddertillis** = *hiddertil 15-17*. **hither an yon, hither an yont 1** hither and thither, this way and that *18-*. **2** untidy, careless; muddled *19, 20- NE EC*. [OE *hider*]
hits see HOOTS
hitten see HIT[1.2]
hiv see HAE[1.1], HAE[1.2], HUIF
hive /haev/ *n* a haven, a harbour; frequently in place-names *17- NE*. Compare HYTHE. [OE *hȳþ*, perhaps influenced by *haven*]
hives, †**hyvis** /haevz/ *npl* **1** a skin eruption, a rash; an ailment *16-*. **2** inflammation of the bowels in children *20-*. [unknown]
hivnae see HAE[1.2]
hivven, haiven, heiven, heeven, heaven, †**hevin**, †**hevyn**, †**hewin** /ˈhɪvən, ˈhɛvən, ˈhivən, ˈhɛvən/ *n* **1** *Christian Church* a place believed to be the home of God, the after-life destination of the redeemed *la14-*. **2** *pl* the sky, the upper air *la14-*. **3** *pl* heavenly power, God *la16-*. [OE *heofon*]
hivvet /ˈhɪvət/ *n* **1** a mass or clod (of earth or roots) *la19- Sh Ork N*. **2** a swelling or boil *la19- Sh*. [ON *höfuð* head]
hivvy see HEAVY[1.2]
hix[1.1] /hɪks/ *n* **1** a hiccup *la19- Sh Ork N*. **2** a whimper or stifled sob *20- N*. Compare HICK[1.1]. **hicksi**, †**hixie** the hiccups *la19- Sh Ork*. [ON *hixti* a hiccup]
hix[1.2] /hɪks/ *v* to hiccup *20- Sh Ork*. Compare HICK[1.2]. [ON *hixta* to hiccup]
hixy-pixy /ˈhɪksi pɪksi/ *adv* in confusion, topsy-turvy *20- T WC*. [perhaps conflation of EEKSIE-PEEKSIE with Eng *higgledy-piggledy*]
hiz see US
hize see HEEZE[1.2]
hizzel see HAZEL[1.1]
hizzie, hussy /ˈhɪzi, ˈhɪze, ˈhʌse/ *n* **1** an old-fashioned term for a woman thought to be promiscuous *16-*. **2** a young or frivolous woman; a servant girl *16-*. **3** a pocket needle-case *19, 20- Ork N*. **4** a housewife *15-e17*. **5** the mistress of a household *16-e17*. **hizzieskip, hussyskep** housekeeping, household management *16-20, 21- historical*. †**hussy fellow, hizzy fallow** a man who interferes with or undertakes women's duties *e19*. [reduced form of ME *hoswif* a housewife]
†**hjaudins, hjodens** *npl in Shetland* the remains of a dead animal *la19*. [unknown]
hjonek see HONNEK
ho[1], **hoy** /ho, hɔɪ/ *n* hope *19- NE* **nae ho but** no choice, no hope but *19- NE*. **nae idder hoy but** no other hope but *20- NE*. [hobbut hope but, with later wrong division as *ho but*]
†**ho**[2.1], **hoo** *n* a pause, a halt *15-e17*. [see the interj]
†**ho**[2.2] *v* to stop or pause *la15-16*. [see the interj]
†**ho**[2.3] *interj* a call to stop *16-17*. [ME *ho*, EModE *ho*]
hoachin, hoatchin, hoaching, hotchin, hootchin /ˈhotʃɪn, ˈhotʃɪŋ, ˈhɔtʃɪn, ˈhutʃɪn/ *adj* **1** infested, seething; overrun with or abounding in *la18-*. **2** restless with impatience, eager *la19-*. Compare HOTCH[1.2]. [presp of HOTCH[1.2]]
hoakker see HUCKER
hoaliday, holiday, *Sh* **heliday**, †**haly day**, †**haliday** /ˈholəde, ˈhɔləde; *Sh* ˈhɛlide/ *n* a day or period of leisure or

recreation, a vacation; originally a consecrated day or a religious festival *la14-*. †**haly day claithis** Sunday or best clothes *la15-e17*. [OE *hāligdæg* holy day]

hoamed, hoomed, hoomt /homd, humd, humt/ *adj* musty, mouldy *19- N NE T*. [altered form of YOAM[1.1] + -IT[2]]

hoard *see* HUIRD[1.1], HUIRD[1.2].

hoarse *see* HORSE[1.1]

hoaspital, hospital, ospital, †**hospitall,** †**hospitale,** †**ospittall** /ˈhɒspɪtəl, ˈhɔspɪtəl, ˈɔspɪtəl/ *n* **1** an institution for the care of the sick *15-*. **2** an asylum for the needy or lepers *la14-e18*. **3** a hostel for travellers *la15-e16*. [ME *hospital*]

hoast[1.1]**, host,** *Bor* **whust,** †**whoast** /host; *Bor* ʍʌst/ *n* **1** a fit of coughing, a persistent cough *la15-*. **2** a single cough *16-*. **3** a cough made to attract attention or to stop someone *19-*. **it won't cost a host** it is not worth hesitating over *19-*. **without a host** without hesitation *19-*. [ON *hósti*]

hoast[1.2]**, host,** †**whost** /host/ *v* **1** to cough *la15-*. **2** to clear the throat to attract attention, or to cover confusion *18-*. **hoast oot** to cough or spit out or up; to get something off one's chest *16-*. **hoast up** = *hoast oot 18-*. [OE *hwōsan*, ON *hósta*]

hoat *see* HET[1.1], HET[1.2]

hoatch *see* HOTCH[1.1], HOTCH[1.2]

hoatchin *see* HOACHIN

hoax /hoks/ *v* to spoil a game *la19- NE*. [unknown]

hobbell *see* HOBBILL[1.1]

hobbil *see* HOBBLE[1.2]

†**hobbill**[1.1]**, hobbell, habbell** *n* a part of a shoe; a patch *16-e17*. [unknown]

†**hobbill**[1.2] *v* to cobble, repair shoes *la16*. [unknown]

hobble[1.1] /ˈhɒbəl/ *n* **1** a difficulty, predicament; an awkward situation *19-*. **2** a swarm of living creatures *la19- NE*. **3** a swaying, tossing or bouncing movement *19*. Compare HABBLE[1.1], HUBBLE[1.1]. **hobblie of the ground** quaking under the feet *la19- NE Bor*. **hobble-bog** a quagmire *la19- NE*. **hobble-quo 1** a dilemma *19- SW Bor*. **2** a quagmire *e19*. [see the verb]

hobble[1.2]**,** †**hobbil** /ˈhɒbəl/ *v presp* **hobland 1** to walk unsteadily, limp along *la14-*. **2** to rock from side to side, bob up and down, wobble *la14-*. **3** to swarm with living creatures *la19- NE T*. **4** to perplex, bother *20- N Uls*. **5** to shake with mirth *la18- NE*. Compare HABBLE[1.2], HUBBLE[1.2]. [ME *hobblen*; compare Du *hobbelen* to toss, rock]

hobbleshow *see* HUBBLESHOO

hobby *see* HUBBIE[2]

hobillschowe *see* HUBBLESHOO

hobland *see* HOBBLE[1.2]

hobleshew *see* HUBBLESHOO

†**hobyn** *n* a small horse or pony *la14*. [AN *hobyn*]

hoch[1.1]**, houch, hough, haugh,** †**hoich,** †**howch,** †**howgh** /hɔx/ *n pl* †**howis 1** the hind-leg joint of an animal, the hock *la15-*. **2** the hollow behind a human knee; (the back of) the thigh *la15-*. **3** a joint of meat from the hind leg of an animal, the shin *16-*. **houghed, hought, hocht** having thighs or legs of a specified sort *18-*. **hoch-band** a strap or cord by which the hind-leg movement of an animal is restricted, a hobble *la17-*. **hochbane** to tie the hind leg of an animal, hobble *la18-19, 20- Sh*. **cruik yer hoch, crook yer hough 1** to sit down; to kneel *19, 20- T Bor*. **2** to dance *18-e19*. †**cut the hochis** to hamstring *16-e17*. **faud yer hoch** to sit down *19- T*. **fling yer houghs** to dance *20- WC*. **shak yer houghs** to dance *19, 20- WC*. [ME *hough* a hock, OE *hōh* a heel; compare HEUCH[1.1]]

hoch[1.2]**, hough,** †**houch** /hɔx/ *v* **1** to lame or disable by cutting the hamstrings *16-19, 20- historical*. **2** to traverse with difficulty, trudge over *la19- NE T WC*. **3** to throw a stone from beneath one's upraised thigh *19, 20- NE T Bor*. **4** to throw a leg over an oar while rowing (in order to rest) *20- Sh*. **5** to deprive of support; to disable; to defeat *17-e19*. †**hocher** a person who maims or hamstrings livestock *la16-18*. [see the noun]

hoch[2] /hɔx/ *interj* an expression of weariness, regret or disapproval *19-*. **hoch aye** an expression of assent (suggesting impatience or resignation) *la19-*. **hoch-hey** an expression of weariness or sadness *la18-*. [onomatopoeic of a sigh]

hoch *see* HOTCH[1.2]

hochems *see* HOUGHAMS

hocher *see* HAUCH[1.2]

hocherty-cocherty *see* HOCKERTY-COCKERTY

hochie /ˈhɔxe, ˈhɔxi/ *n* a store or stash, a hoard *la19- EC*. [unknown]

hochle[1.1]**, hauchle,** †**houghel** /ˈhɔxəl, ˈhɔxəl/ *n* **1** a heaving movement of the body, an awkward shifting of position *20-*. **2** a person who is ungainly or slovenly in gait, dress or appearance *19- H&I WC SW Bor Uls*. [see the verb]

hochle[1.2]**, hauchle,** †**houghel,** †**huch-yall** /ˈhɔxəl, ˈhɔxəl/ *v* to hobble, totter *la18-*. [frequentative verb from HOCH[1.2]]

hochmagandie, houghmagandie /hɔxməˈgandi/ *n* sexual intercourse *la17-*. [a ludicrous formation based on HOCH[1.1]]

hock *see* HOWK[1.1], HOWK[1.2]

hocken *see* HOCKIN

hockerty-cockerty, hocherty-cocherty /ˈhɔkərti kɔkərti; ˈhɔxərti kɔxərti/ *adv* seated astride another's shoulders *19- NE T*. [rhyming compound from HOCH[1.1] and COCKER; compare COCKERDECOSIE]

hockin, hocken /ˈhɔkən/ *adj* very hungry *la19- Sh*. [Norw dial *hæken*]

hocus /ˈhokəs/ *n* a foolish or ill-mannered person *la18-19, 20- N*. [extension of obsolete Eng *hocus* a conjuror, a cheat]

†**hod** *v* to jog along on horseback; to bump in the saddle *la18-19*. [perhaps onomatopoeic; compare HOTCH[1.2], HOWD[1.2], HODDLE[1.2]]

hod *see* HIDE[1]

hodden[1.1]**,** †**hodding,** †**hoddin,** †**hodin** /ˈhɔdən/ *n* woollen cloth of a greyish colour (due to mixing black and white wool) *la16-*. [unknown]

hodden[1.2] /ˈhɔdən/ *adj* **1** made of hodden cloth; homespun, undyed *la16-*. **2** rustic, homely *19-*. **hodden gray, hoddin grey 1** homespun wool or woollen cloth of the natural undyed colour *la16-*. **2** a person dressed in a simple rustic fashion; a homely, unaffected individual *la19-*. **3** a soldier of the London Scottish regiment *20-*. [unknown]

hodden *see* HIDE[1]

hoddin, hodding *see* HODDEN[1.1]

hoddit *see* HIDE[1]

hoddle[1.1] /ˈhɔdəl/ *n* a waddling gait, a quick toddling step *20- WC SW Bor*. [see the verb]

hoddle[1.2] /ˈhɔdəl/ *v* to waddle or toddle unevenly; to hobble *18-19, 20- T EC SW Bor*. [frequentative form of HOD]

hoddock *see* HADDOCK

hoddy, hode *see* HIDE[1]

hodge[1.1] /hɔdʒ/ *n* **1** a shove, a push, a hitch up *la18- Sh NE T*. **2** a large, awkward person *la19- Sh NE*. [see the verb]

hodge[1.2] /hɔdʒ/ *v* **1** to move or walk awkwardly or jerkily; to hobble *18- Sh Ork NE*. **2** to hitch up, tug, heave *la18- Sh NE*. **3** to fidget *19- NE*. **4** to shake or quiver with laughter *19, 20- NE*. **5** to have sexual intercourse *20- Ork*. **hodge aboot** to carry around a heavy load *la19- Sh NE*. [perhaps onomatopoeic; compare HOD, HODDLE[1.2], HOTCH[1.2]]

hodgehead *see* HOGGET

hodge-podge /ˈhɔdʒpɔdʒ/ *n* **1** a hotch-potch, a state of confusion *la17-*. **2** a thick vegetable broth *18-19, 20- NE T*.

[altered form of AN *hogepot* the pooling of marriage portions for redistribution after parents' deaths]

hodgil /'hɔdʒəl/ *n* an oatmeal dumpling *19- Bor.* [probably reduced form of HODGE-PODGE]

†**hodiern** *adj* of the present day *e16.* [Lat *hodiernus*]

hodin *see* HODDEN[1.1]

hoe[1] /ho/ *n* the piked dogfish *Squalus acanthias 18- Sh Ork.* **hobrin** the blue shark *Prionace glauca 19- Sh.* **hodry** a kind of very large dogfish *20- Sh Ork.* **homer** the basking shark *Cetorhinus maximus la18- Sh Ork.* **hoe-midder** = *homer la19- Sh Ork.* **ho-moothed** having a protruding upper jaw *20- Sh.* **hoe tusk** a small shark, the smoothhound *Mustelus mustelus 19- Sh.* [ON *hár* a dogfish, a shark]

hoe[2], **ho** /ho/ *n* one of a pair of stockings or hose *18-19, 20- NE.* [back-formation from HOSE[1.1]]

hoe *see* HOW[1.1]

hog[1.1] /hɔg/ *n curling* a stone which does not pass over the hog score *la18-.* **hog score** the lines at each end of the rink over which a shot must pass to score *la18-.* [unknown; perhaps related to HOGG[1.1]]

hog[1.2] /hɔg/ *v curling* to play a stone which fails to cross the hog score *19- WC SW.* **hogged** stuck; at a standstill *19- WC SW.* [see the noun]

hog[2] /hɔg/ *n* a hill, high ground; a landmark; frequently in place-names *19- Sh Ork.* **hogboon** *folklore* a helpful fairy, a brownie *la19- Ork.* [ON *haugr* a mound, a barrow]

hog *see* HOGG[1.1]

hoga /'hɔga/ *n* 1 pasture (on a hill or outfield); frequently in place-names *la18- Sh.* 2 a familiar place or haunt *20- Sh.* **hogaleave**, †**hagalef** (payment for) permission to cut peats or to graze cattle or sheep *la18-19, 20- Sh historical.* [ON *hagi* pasture]

†**hogeart** *n* a tired-out old man *e16.* [unknown]

hogg[1.1], †**hog** /hɔg/ *n* a year-old sheep *14-.* **hogget** a year-old sheep *19-.* †**hograll**, **hogrell** the skin of a yearling sheep *15.* **hog-fence** a pasture reserved for the wintering of weaned lambs *la18-19, 20- Bor.* †**hog-shouther** to push or jostle with the shoulder *la18-e19.* †**hog-wedder** a young castrated male sheep; compare *wedder hogg* (WEDDER) *e18.* †**hog in harst** a young sheep once it has been smeared with liniment after the harvest *e19.* [OE *hogg* a hog, a castrated boar]

hogg[1.2] /hɔg/ *v* to keep a lamb on winter pasture during its first year *19-.* **hogging** a pasture reserved for the wintering of weaned lambs *19-.* [see the noun]

hoggar, hogger *see* HUGGER

hogget, †**hugget**, †**hoghed**, †**hodgehead** /'hɔgət/ *n* 1 a large cask, a hogshead *la15-19, 20- WC.* 2 a measure of meal, wine or fish *la15-19, 20- Uls.* [altered form of ME *hoggeshed*]

hoggie /'hɔgi/ *n* 1 the fireplace of a kiln *la19- Sh Ork.* 2 a fireplace in a house *20- Sh.* Compare KILLOGIE. [altered form of OGIE]

hoghed *see* HOGGET

Hogmanay, hugmanay, †hogmanae, †hagmonay /hɔgmə'ne, hʌgmə'ne/ *n* 1 the last day of the year, New Year's Eve *17-.* 2 a New Year's gift, originally a gift of oatcakes offered to or requested by children on New Year's Eve *la18-.* 3 the cry uttered in asking for the New Year's gift *17-e19.* 4 an oatcake or biscuit baked to give to children on 31 December *19.* **haud your Hogmanay** to celebrate the New Year *la18-.* **your Hogmanay** a drink or a gratuity given to tradesmen or employees at Hogmanay *20-.* [Fr *hoguinane*, OFr *aguillanneuf* a gift given on New Year's Eve, the word shouted in asking for this]

hog-reek /'hɔgrik/ *n* driving snow or freezing mist *20- N NE.* [unknown first element + REEK[1.1]]

†**hogtoun, hugtoun, actoun** *n* 1 a padded jerkin (worn under mail) *la15-e16.* 2 a short sleeveless jacket *16.* [ME *aketoun, haketon*]

hoich *see* HOCH[1.1]

hoid *see* HIDE[1]

hoidie-holl *see* HIDIE-HOLE

hoidin /'hɔidin/ *n fisherman's taboo* a clergyman *19- Sh Ork.* [unknown]

hoilkit /'hɔilkit/ *adj* hunch-backed *20- Sh.* [Norw dial *hulk* a protuberance]

hoilsum *see* HAILSOME

hoip *see* HOUP, HOWP[1.1]

hois *see* HOSE[1.1]

hoise[1.1], †**hoyse** /hɔiz/ *n* a lift, a heave up *la18-19, 20- H&I C SW Bor.* [see the verb]

hoise[1.2] /hɔiz/ *v* to hoist, raise; to lift up, elevate *17-19, 20- Ork H&I C SW Bor.* [variant of HEEZE[1.2]]

†**hoit, hoyte** *v* to move awkwardly or clumsily; to waddle along *la18-e19.* **hoitle** to waddle *la19.* [probably onomatopoeic; compare HOD, HOTTER[1.2], HYTER[1.2]]

hoiter *see* HYTER[1.2]

hoitina /'hɔitəna/ *n* completion; the finishing touch *la19- Sh.* [perhaps ON *hætandi*, presp of *hætta* to leave off, cease]

hoke *see* HOWK[1.2]

hoker *see* HUCKER

holane *see* HOLLAND

hold, holden *see* HAUD[1.2]

holding *see* HAUDIN

hole[1.1], *Sh* **holl,** †**how** /hol; *Sh* hɔl/ *n* 1 an opening; a cavity, a gap *la14-.* 2 an excavation, cave or pit; a lair or burrow *15-.* 3 the anus or vagina *16-.* 4 a small bay *17-.* 5 *golf* the small circular cavity in the green into which the ball is played *18-.* 6 *golf* the distance between each tee and its hole; the point scored by the player who takes the fewest strokes to reach the hole *18-.* 7 a shallow pool, a puddle *la19-.* 8 a dungeon or prison cell *16-17.* 9 a ship's hold *la15-e16.* **hole i the wa, hole in the wall** 1 a small building recessed between larger buildings, often used as a shop or public house *la18-.* 2 a box-bed, a recessed bed *20- NE C Bor.* 3 a cash dispenser (in the wall of a bank) *la20-.* **in the hole** 1 on the point of childbirth *18-19, 20- NE EC.* 2 the position of the bottom couple in the Whalsay reel *20- Sh.* [OE *hol*]

hole[1.2], †**holl,** †**how** /hol/ *v* 1 to make a hole or holes in; to wear into holes *16-.* 2 to dig up, excavate *16-.* 3 *golf* to play the ball into the hole; to play a particular hole *la17-.* 4 to harvest potatoes *la19- NE T.* 5 to loiter, linger *la19- NE.* 6 to cut turf *20- Uls.* **hole on** to loiter, linger *19- NE.* **hole out** 1 to dig out, bring to the surface *18-.* 2 *golf* to complete the playing of a hole by striking the ball into the hole *la19-.* [see the noun]

holey *see* HOLIE[1.2]

holf *see* HOWF[1.1]

holiday *see* HOALIDAY

holie[1.1] /'holi/ *n* a game of marbles in which a marble is aimed at another in a hole in the ground *la19-.* [HOLE[1.1] + -IE[3]]

holie[1.2], †**holey** /'holi/ *adj* having holes; full of holes *la16-.* **holiepied, hollipiet** 1 *of fabric* full of holes; *of embroidery* done as open-work *la19- NE T.* 2 *of the shore or sea-bottom* uneven, pitted; full of holes or troughs *20- Sh N NE.* †**holie work** open-work *la16-e17.* [see the noun]

hölie *see* HOOLY[1.3]

holk *see* HOWK[1.2], HULK[1.1]

holkis *see* HOWK[2]

holl *see* HOLE[1.1], HOLE[1.2], HOWE[1.1], HOWE[1.2], HOWE[2]

hollan, †**hollin**, †**holyn** /'hɔlən/ *n* holly *la15-19, 20- NE Bor*. **hollan bus**, †**holing busk** a holly bush *16-19, 20- NE*. [OE *holen*]

Holland, †**holane** /'hɔlənd/ *adj* from or relating to Holland *la15-*. **Holland hawk** the great northern diver *Gavia immer 19, 20- Uls*. [from the name of the country]

hollin *see* HOLLAN

holm *see* HOWM

holograph[1.1] /'hɔləgraf/ *n law* a document wholly in the handwriting of one person (in Scots law such documents are valid without witnesses) *18-*. [see the adj]

holograph[1.2] /'hɔləgraf/ *adj of a legal deed or letter* wholly in the handwriting of one person and, in the case of a will, signed by that person *la17-*. [Fr *holographe*, Lat *holographus*, originally from Greek]

holter *see* HULTER

holy *see* HALY

holyn *see* HOLLAN

Holyrood /'hɔlirud/ *n* **1** the area of Edinburgh where Holyrood Palace and Abbey are located *16-*. **2** the Scottish Parliament *la20-*. **Holyroodhouse**, †**Halyrudhous** the palace of Holyroodhouse in Edinburgh *la14-*. [*Holy Rood* (HALY)]

Holy Willie /'hɔli wɪli/ *n* a sanctimonious person *20-*. [from the name of the character in Burns' poem *Holy Willie's Prayer*]

home *see* HAME[1.1], HAME[1.2], WHUM

homeward *see* HAMEWART[1.1], HAMEWART[1.2]

homing ground *see* HOWM

hommill *see* HUMMEL[1.3]

homologate /hə'mɔləɡət/ *v ptp* also †**homologat** †**homologate** to ratify, confirm or approve; *law* to render valid; to ratify a deed or document which was informal or defective *la16-*. **homologation** *law* an act of ratification *la17-*. [Lat *homologāre*, originally from Greek]

hon *see* HAN[1.1]

hondiklokk /'hɔndiklɔk/ *n* a horned or winged beetle *19- Sh*. [ON *hyrndr* horned + CLOCK[2]]

hone *see* HUNE[1.1]

honest, †**honnest**, †**onest** /'ɔnəst/ *adj* **1** truthful, trustworthy *15-*. **2** of good character, worthy, estimable *15-*. **3** *of actions or conduct* commendable, creditable *15-*. **4** *of things* of a high quality or standard *15-e17*. **5** distinguished, well-dressed *15-16*. **honest-like 1** *of a person* decent, respectable *la16-*. **2** *of a thing* substantial *la18-*. **honestly** in an honest manner *la14-*. **honesty 1** decency, respectability; good repute *la14-*. **2** truthfulness *16-*. **honest folk** a married couple who act as the chief attendants at a wedding *20- Sh Ork*. **for an honesty** as a mark of respectability *la18-*. †**honest shift** a respectable livelihood *la16-18*. **the Honest Lad** one of the leading participants in the annual festival in Musselburgh *20-*. **the Honest Lass** one of the leading participants in the annual festival in Musselburgh *20-*. **the Honest Men** a nickname for Ayr United Football Club *20-*. **the Honest Toun** a nickname for Musselburgh *la18-*. [ME *honest*, Lat *honestus*]

honey *see* HINNIE[1.1], HINNIE[1.2]

honnek, **hjonek** /'hɔnək, 'hjɔnək/ *n derogatory* a small person *la19- Sh*. [unknown]

honnest *see* HONEST

honor *see* HONOUR

†**honorary** *n* an honorarium *18-e19*. [Lat *honōrārium*]

honour, †**honure**, †**honor** /'ɔnər/ *n* **1** honesty, integrity, respect *la14-*. **2** *pl* (signs of) high rank, eminence or distinction *la15-*. **the Honours of Scotland** the regalia (Crown, Sceptre, and Sword of State) of the Kingdom of Scotland *la16-*. [ME *honour*, Lat *honor*]

hony *see* HINNIE[1.2]

hoo[1], **hou**, **how**, †**quhow**, †**whow** /hu, hʌu/ *adv* **1** in what way, by what means *la14-*. **2** to what extent *15-*. **3** why *16-*. **4** in what state or condition *16-*. **howanabe** however, nevertheless *la18-19, 20- Bor*. **hooanever** however *la18-*. †**howgate**, **howgatis** in what way, how *la14-15*. **hooseever**, *NE* **hoosaeiver**, †**howsaeiver** in what way *la16-*. **hoosomever**, †**quhowswmevir**, †**howsomdever** in whatever way, however; notwithstanding, nevertheless, *la16-19, 20- Sh Bor*. †**howsoon**, **howsone** as soon as *16-18*. **how no** why not *20- C SW Bor*. **how that** in what way, how *la14-*. Compare FOO. [OE *hū* with the *quh-*, *wh-* forms by analogy with the other *wh-* interrogatives; compare WHA]

hoo[2.1], †**how** /hu/ *n* **1** a cry to attract attention or scare off birds; a shout of encouragement *16-*. **2** the hooting of an owl *16-*. [a natural utterance, onomatopoeic]

hoo[2.2] /hu/ *v* **1** to shout to attract attention *la18-*. **2** to hoot like an owl *19, 20- T*. **3** *of wind* to howl *la19, 20- T*. **hooie**, †**hoohi** to shout to scare off birds or straying animals *la18- NE*. [see the noun]

hoo[2.3], †**how** /hu/ *interj* a call to attract attention *la15-*. [see the noun]

†**hoo**[3], **how** *n* **1** a cap *la14-e19*. **2** a roof rafter *17-19*. [OE *hūfe*, ON *húfa*, a hood; compare Norw dial *huv* the ridge of a roof]

hoo *see* HO[2.1]

hoob *see* HOPE[2]

hooch[1.1] /hux/ *n* **1** a shout or loud cry (made by dancers during a Highland reel) *la19-*. **2** a dance *20-*. **3** a sudden expulsion of the breath *la19- NE T*. [onomatopoeic]

hooch[1.2], **heugh** /hux, hjux/ *v* **1** to make an excited cry; to shout; to whoop with delight *19-*. **2** to breathe hard on an object before polishing it *19, 20- NE T*. [see the noun]

hooch[1.3], †**heuch**, †**whoogh** /hux/ *interj* an expression of excitement or exhilaration (uttered by dancers during a reel) *19-*. [see the noun]

hood[1.1], **huid**, *Ork* **heud**, *Ork* **heuld**, *N NE* **heed**, †**hude**, †**hud** /hud; *Ork* hød; *Ork* høld; *N NE* hid/ *n* **1** a covering for the head (and shoulders); a hood *la14-*. **2** one of a pair of sheaves of corn placed on the top of a stook or corn stack as a protection against rain *la18- SW Bor*. **3** the dead of night *la19- Ork*. †**hoodock 1** the hooded crow *Corvus cornix la18-19*. **2** an avaricious person *la18-19*. †**hood sheaf** one of a pair of sheaves of corn placed on the top of a stook *la18-19*. †**hudpyk** a miser, a mean person *16*. [OE *hōd*]

hood[1.2], **huid** /hud/ *v* **1** to put on or cover with a hood *la17-*. **2** to top a stook with two protective sheaves *19, 20- T SW*. [see the noun]

hooded *see* HOODIT

hoodie, **huidie**, *Sh N* **heedie**, *T* **huddie** /'hudi; *Sh N* 'hidi; *T* 'hʌdi/ *n* **1** the hooded crow *Corvus cornix la18-*. **2** a farmworker's sunbonnet *20- Ork T Bor*. **hoodie craw**, *NE* **heedie craa 1** the hooded crow *Corvus cornix* or the carrion crow *Corvus corone la18-*. **2** the black-headed gull *Chroicocephalus ridibundus la19- Sh N*. **3** derogatory a person with a sinister manner or appearance *20- NE T Bor*. **huidie maa** the black-headed gull *20- Sh*. **put the huidie on** to cap, top *20- Ork T Bor*. [HOOD[1.1] + -IE[1]]

hoodin, *Sh* **huidin**, *Ork* **heudin**, *N* **heedin**, *NE* **hiddin** /'hudɪn; *Sh Ork* 'hødɪn; *N* 'hidɪn; *NE* 'hɪdɪn/ *n* **1** the hinge of a flail *19- Sh Ork N NE*. **2** a knot used to join two parts of a fishing line *la19- Sh Ork NE*. **3** *pl* the places where the sides of a boat meet the stem-posts and stern-posts *20- Sh Ork N*. **4** the place where the couples of a roof meet the ridge *20- Sh*. [HOOD[1.1], with *-in* noun suffix]

hoodit, **huidit**, **hooded**, †**hudit** /'hʊdɪt, 'hʊdəd/ *adj* wearing a hood *16-*. **hoodit craw 1** the hooded crow *Corvus cornix 16-*. **2** the black-headed gull *Larus ridibundus 19, 20- Ork.* [HOOD[1.1] + -IT[2]]

hoof *see* HUIF

hooick, **howek** /'hʊɪk, 'hʌuək/ *n* a small rick of corn or hay or stack of peats *la19- NE T.* **heuickin** the preserving of corn in small ricks during a rainy harvest *20- NE T.* [HOO[3] + -OCK]

hooie, *NE* **hewie** /'hui; *NE* 'hjui/ *v* to exchange or barter *19- NE T EC Bor.* [unknown]

hook *see* HEUK

hook bone *see* HEUKBANE

hooker[1] /'hukər/ *n* a glass of whisky, a dram *19, 20- NE.* [unknown]

hooker[2] /'hukər/ *n* a cloth cap *20- WC.* **hooker doon** a cloth cap with a peak *20- C.* [probably from the action of pulling down the peak as if hooking it on]

hookers *see* HUK

hookie /'huki/ *n* a mild oath *19-*. [unknown]

hooky *see* HEUK

hool[1.1], **hull**, †**huill** /hul, hʌl/ *n* **1** the husk, pod, skin or shell of a fruit or nut *16-*. **2** the pericardium, the membrane surrounding the heart *la16-*. **3** the skin *18-19, 20- Ork N.* **4** *pl* clothes, garments *18-19.* **5** an exterior, an external covering *la18-19.* **pit oot o the hool** *of the heart* to jump with excitement or fear *la16-*. [OE *hulu* husk]

hool[1.2], **hull** /hul, hʌl/ *v* **1** to shell peas, beans or nuts; to husk *la18-*. **2** to encase *e18.* [see the noun]

hool[2] /hul/ *n* a knoll *20- Sh.* [ON *hóll*]

hoolachan, **hullachan** /'huləxən/ *n* a Highland reel, the Reel of Tulloch *19-*. [Gael (*ruidhle*) *Thulachain*]

hoolet[1.1], **houlet**, **oolet**, **howlat**, **howlet** /'hulət, 'ulət, 'hʌulət/ *n* **1** an owl *la15-*. **2** a furtive person, a prowler *la16-*. **3** a peevish, dismal person *la17-*. **4** a stupid person *20- EC Bor.* [MFr *hulotte*]

hoolet[1.2] /'hulət/ *v* **1** to dominate; to find fault with *19- T Bor.* **2** to be solitary or unsociable; to lurk around at night *19- T Bor.* [see the noun]

hooly[1.1] /'huli/ *v* to pause, halt or hesitate *la19- Sh NE C.* [see the adj]

hooly[1.2], **huilie**, *NE* **heelie**, †**huly** /'huli; *NE* 'hili/ *adj* slow, cautious, careful *15-19, 20- Sh NE.* **ca your hogs til a huilie mercat** to make a bad bargain *20- NE T.* [ON *hófligr* moderate]

hooly[1.3], **huly**, *Sh* **hölie**, *NE* **heely** /'huli; *Sh* 'høli; *NE* 'hili/ *adv* moderately, slowly, gently *16-*. **come heely tae** = *come hooly on la19- NE.* **come hooly on** to have indifferent success, fare badly *la19- NE C.* **hooly and fairly**, †**hooly and fair** slowly and gently but steadily *18- literary.* [ON *hófliga* with moderation]

hooly[1.4], *NE* **heely**, †**huly** /'huli; *NE* 'hili/ *interj* an expression of warning or admonishment *la18-*. [see the adv]

hoomble *see* HUMMLE[1.2]

hoomed *see* HOAMED

hoomet, **hoomit**, †**hewmet** /'humət, 'humɪt/ *n* **1** a nightcap; a hat or hood *19- NE.* **2** a helmet *16.* **hoomach 1** a nightcap *20- NE.* **2** *pl* fingerless gloves *20- NE.* †**hewmond** a helmet *16.* [Fr *heaumet*]

hoomie *see* HUMMIE[1]

hoomit *see* HOOMET

hoomt *see* HOAMED

hoond[1.1], **hound**, **hund** /hund, hʌund, hʌnd/ *n* a (hunting) dog *la14-*. [OE *hund*]

hoond[1.2], **hound**, **hund** /hund, hʌund, hʌnd/ *v* **1** to pursue or harass; to drive (a person) from a place *la15-*. **2** to hunt animals with hounds *16-*. **3** *of a male dog* to pursue females *20- NE WC.* **hundge** to chase, drive away *la19- Sh.* **hound oot 1** to drive out, chase away *la15-*. **2** to incite (to commit a crime) *la16-17.* †**hounder out** an instigator, an inciter *la16-17.* †**hounding out** instigation; incitement to crime *la16-18.* [see the noun]

hoop, †**hupe** /hup/ *n* **1** a circular ring or band of metal or wood *15-*. **2** the circular wooden frame enclosing millstones to prevent meal from being scattered *15-e19.* [OE *hōp*]

hoop *see* HOWP[1.1]

hoops[1] /hups/ *interj* an encouragement to someone to raise themselves or lift something heavy *20-*. **hoopse up** = HOOPS *20-*. [altered form of UP[1.2]]

Hoops[2] /hups/ *npl* a nickname for Celtic Football Club *la20-*. [from their green and white hooped strip]

hoor, **hure**, **whure**, †**whoor** /hur/ *n* **1** a prostitute *la14-*. **2** a term of abuse for a woman (perceived to be promiscuous) *16-*. **3** a difficult or extreme example of something: ◊*it was a hure o' a job to fix it la20-.* **hoor-hoose** a brothel *la20-*. [OE *hōre*, ON *hóra* a prostitute]

hoor *see* OOR[1]

hoorkle *see* HURKLE[1.2]

hoosal *see* HOOSEHOLD

hoose[1.1], **house**, †**hous**, †**huse** /hus, hʌus/ *n* **1** a dwelling, a building used for habitation *14-*. **2** a family or lineage *15-*. **3** a building used for a purpose other than dwelling; a storehouse *la15-*. **4** a set of rooms in a building occupied by one tenant or family, having a separate door opening upon a common passage or stair; a flat *16-*. **5** *in curling and bowls* the circle round the tee within which the stones or bowls must lie to be counted in the score *la19-*. **6** a stronghold, a castle *15-e17.* **7** a monastery or convent *la14-15.* **hoosie**, †**housie** a house; a flat in a tenement building *18-*. **hoose-a-gate** gossiping; gossip *20- Ork.* **hoosamil** a road or space between houses *la19- Sh.* **hoosaminya** an upheaval or disturbance; a quarrel *20- Ork.* **hoosamylla** from house to house *la19- Sh.* **hoosavel 1** the field nearest the house *20- Ork.* **2** food brought to harvesters in the field *20- Ork.* **hoose-ba** the game of rounders *la19, 20- N SW Bor.* **hoose devil an causey saint** a person who behaves badly at home and well in public *19- NE T EC Bor.* **hoose end 1** the gable of a house *la14-*. **2** a fat or heavily-built person *20-*. **house-fast** housebound, confined to the house *la19-*. **husfolk** the occupants of a house *20- Sh.* **hoose gear**, **house gear** household furnishings or equipment *19-*. **house-heating** a house-warming party *19-*. **hoose-heid**, †**houshede** the roof of a house *16-19, 20- N NE Bor.* **hoose-hicht** the height of a house *la16-19, 20- C Bor.* †**house knock**, **house clock** a domestic clock *17.* †**house mail 1** house rent *16-19.* **2** storage charges *la15-e16.* **hoose place** a job as a domestic servant *20- EC Bor.* **house side 1** the side of a house *la15-*. **2** a large, clumsy person *19, 20- T C.* †**housestead** the land on which a house is to be built, the site of a house *la15-e19.* **hoose-tied** housebound *la19-*. **hoose weddin**, **house wedding** a marriage ceremony conducted and celebrated at home *la20-*. **hoosie Frazer** *rhyming slang* a razor *la20- WC*; compare MALKIE[1.1]. **house within itself** a self-contained house or flat *la18-19, 20- NE.* **out of house an ha** out of one's home and all one has, out of one's last refuge *19-*. **oot o house and hald** = *out of house an ha 18-*. **your hoose at hame** one's home *la18-19, 20- NE T WC.* [OE *hūs*]

hoose[1.2], **huse**, **house**, †**hows** /hus, huz, hʌuz/ *v* **1** to provide with a house *15-*. **2** to provide animals with housing or shelter *la15-*. **3** to store goods or crops *15-19, 20- Sh NE Bor.* [OE *hūsian*]

hoose² /huz/ *n* a disease in cattle which produces a dry, wheezy cough *la19-*. [related to OE *hwaēsan* to wheeze, breathe hard]

hoosehold, household, *Sh* **hushad,** *Ork* **hoosal, †houshald, †housald, †housit** /'hushold, 'hʌushold; *Sh* 'hushad; *Ork* 'husəl/ *n* **1** the people living together in a house *15-*. **2** the maintaining and managing of a house and its inmates; housekeeping *15-19, 20- Sh*. **3** the master of ceremonies at a wedding *20- Ork*. **hoosehaudder, householder, †houshaldar** the person who holds or occupies a house; the head of a household *16-*. **hoose haddin, †houshalding** the management of a house, housekeeping *16-*. **†in houshald** included in the household *la15-e17*. [HOOSE[1.1] + HAUD[1.1]; compare MDu *huushoud*]

hooshlach *see* HUSHLACH[1.2]

hooshlich *see* HUSHLACH[1.1]

hoosing, hoosin, housing /'husɪŋ, 'husɪn, 'hʌuzɪŋ/ *n* **1** accommodation, houses *15-*. **2** the sheltering of birds or animals or storing of commodities in a building *la15-*. **3** a shelter, a dwelling-place *la16-19, 20- NE*. **4** a canopied niche or recess in a wall *16-17*. **housing scheme** a public-authority housing estate *la19-*. [HOOSE[1.1], HOOSE[1.2], with *-ing* suffix]

hoosle *see* HOSE[1.1]

hoot[1.1], **†hute** /hut/ *v* to express contempt or dismissal; to scorn or revile *16-*. **hoot oot o** to pour scorn on *20- Ork SW*. [see the interj]

hoot[1.2], *Bor* **het, †hout, †howt, †hit** /hut; *Bor* hɛt/ *interj* **1** an expression of anger or remonstrance *16-19, 20- Bor*. **2** an expression of incredulity, impatience or dismissal *16-19, 20- Bor*. **hoot awa, †hout awa 1** an expression of dismissal *18-*. **2** an expression of pity or sympathy (to soothe children) *la19- NE*. **hoot aye** an expression of affirmation *la18-*. **hoot fie** an expression of dismissal or disbelief *la18-*. **hoot na, hoot no** a strongly-asserted negative *19-*. **hoot toot** an expression of incredulity or dismissal *19-*. [a natural utterance; compare Gael *ut*]

hootchin *see* HOACHIN

hooter, huter /'hutər/ *v* to silence with threats *20- Sh*. [compare Norw *huta*]

hoots, hits, uts /huts, hɪts, uts/ *interj* **1** an expression of anger or remonstrance *19-*. **2** an expression of incredulity, impatience or dismissal *la19-*. **hoots toots** an expression of incredulity or dismissal *la19-*. [HOOT[1.2], with adverbial *-s*]

hoove *see* HUIF

hoovie, *Sh* **hövi,** *Ork N* **heevie** /'huvi; *Sh* 'høvi; *Ork N* 'hivi/ *n* **1** a woven basket or creel *la17- Sh Ork N*. **2** a basket-work fish-trap *la19- Sh Ork*. [probably Norw *håv* a fish creel, a river net]

hooze *see* HUS

hoozlin *see* HUIZLIN

hop *see* HAP[2.1], HAP[2.2], HOWP[1.1]

hope¹, *SW* **whup, †howp, †whope** /hop; *SW* ʍʌp/ *n* **1** a small, enclosed, upland valley; frequently in place-names *la12-19, 20- WC Bor*. **2** a hill *18- SW Bor*. [OE *hop* a piece of enclosed land]

hope², *Sh* **hoob,** *NE EC* **howp** /hop; *Sh* hub; *NE EC* hʌup/ *n* a small bay or haven; frequently in place-names *15-*. [ON *hóp* a landlocked bay]

hope *see* HOUP, HOWP[1.1]

hopper *see* HAPPER

hopschakel *see* HAPSHACKLE[1.2]

hopschakil *see* HAPSHACKLE[1.1]

hork[1.1] /hɔrk/ *n* the act of lounging; a lounger (who occupies the most comfortable position by the fire) *20- SW Bor*. [see the verb]

hork[1.2], **†hurk** /hɔrk/ *v* **1** to sit over a fire; to lounge about *19, 20- SW Bor*. **2** to grub in the dirt like a pig; to poke about, rummage *19- SW Bor*. [MDu *hurcken*, LG *hurken*]

horkel /'hɔrkəl/ *n* a tide-race; a commotion in the sea *20- Sh*.

horkli, hurkly *of weather* rough, stormy *la19- Sh*. [Norw dial *hurkl* rough breathing, gurgling, unevenness]

horl /hɔrl/ *n* the tag of a bootlace *18-19, 20- WC*. [perhaps related to VIRL]

horl *see* WHURL²

horn, *Bor* **whurn, †horne** /hɔrn; *Bor* ʍʌrn/ *n* **1** a hard pointed growth on the heads of some animals *la14-*. **2** a wind instrument (originally made of hollow horn) *la14-*. **3** *law* the horn blown to proclaim an outlaw *la14-19, 20- historical*. **4** the metal tip on a lace or thong *la15-19, 20- Ork T*. **5** a stem-post or stern-post, the prow of a boat *la16-19, 20- Sh*. **6** a handle or spout *la18-19, 20- Sh Ork*. **7** a horn used for blood-letting; blood drawn by cupping *18-19, 20- Sh Ork*. **8** the horn-like projection at the side of an anvil *19, 20- Ork N SW*. **9** a horn spoon or cup *la18-19, 20- Ork*. **10** a drink of alcohol *la18-19, 20- N*. **11** a corn on the foot, hard skin, a callus *18-19, 20- EC*. **12** the constellation Ursa Minor *16*. **horner, †thornar 1** a craftsman who makes articles out of horn (especially horn spoons or combs) *la16-19, 20- Bor historical*. **2** an earwig *la19- NE T*. **3** a person who had been proclaimed as an outlaw or bankrupt *la16*. **horning 1** *law* the procedure of declaring a person to be an outlaw, rebel or bankrupt *16-20, 21- historical*; compare *put to the horn*. **2** the inlaying or covering of an object with horn *la15-e17*. **horn daft** quite mad *19, 20- N T*. **horn dry** *of clothes* thoroughly dry *19, 20- Sh N NE*. **horned golach** an earwig *la18-19, 20- T WC SW*. **horn eel** the sand-eel *Ammodytes 17, 19- NE EC*. **horn en** the best room in a but-and-ben *19- NE T*. **horn hard 1** as hard as horn, extremely hard *la18-19, 20- Sh*. **2** *of sleep* deep, sound *la18-e19*. **horn-idle** doing nothing, unemployed *la18-*. **horn tow** a cow's tether *20- Sh N*. **†at the horn** outlawed *la14-19*. **†bear the horn** to carry off the prize; to win or excel *18-e19*. **get out yer horns** to become assertive; to break free of conventions *la19-*. **hae yer horn in somebody's hip** to criticize severely, be antagonistic towards *19- Ork NE H&I*. **put to the horn** proclaimed as an outlaw or bankrupt *la14-19, 20- historical*. **†win the horn** to carry off the prize; to win or excel *18-e19*. [OE *horn*]

†horneck *n* the earthnut *Bunium bulbocastanum* or *Conopodium majus 19*. [altered form of ARNIT]

hornie[1.1], *Ork* **hornoo** /'hɔrni, 'hɔrne; *Ork* 'hɔrnu/ *n* **1** a nickname for the Devil *la18-*. **2** a horned animal; a cow *19-*. **3** a policeman *la18-19, 20- T EC Bor*. **4** the game of tig *19, 20- Ork T*. [HORN + -IE²]

hornie[1.2] /'hɔrni, 'hɔrne/ *adj* relating to or made of horn *16-*. **hornie golach** an earwig or other insect *la18-*. **hornie holes** a game for four people where each couple tries to throw a stick into the hole defended by their opponents *19, 20- Bor*. **horny hoolet** the long-eared owl *Asio otus la19- NE EC Bor*. **horny owl** = *horny hoolet*. [see the noun]

hornoo *see* HORNIE[1.1]

horologe *see* ORLOGE

horoyally /horo'jali/ *n* a ceilidh, a singsong, a noisy party *la19- H&I WC*. [Gael *ho ro gheallaidh* bethrothal dancing]

horra-goose /'hɔrəgus/ *n in Shetland and Orkney* the brent goose *Branta bernicla la18-19, 20- historical*. **†hurrok** = HORRA-GOOSE *la16*. [unknown first element + GUSE[1.1]]

horrid[1.1] /'hɔrɪd/ *adj of prices* very high *la19- Sh Ork*. [extended sense of Scots *horrid*]

horrid[1.2] /'hɔrɪd/ *adv* extremely, especially *la18-19, 20- Sh Ork SW*. [see the adj]

horse¹·¹, hoarse, †hors /hɔrs, hors/ *n* **1** a hooved animal, a horse *Equus ferus caballus la14-*. **2** a trestle, a support for scaffolding *19-*. **horse beast** a horse *19-*. **horse buckie** the large whelk *Buccinum undatum la19-*. **†hors carriage** conveyance by horse *la16-e17*. **†horse-cock** the dunlin *Calidris alpina 17-19*. **horse couper** a horse-dealer *17-*. **horse-coupin** horse-dealing *la18-*. **horseflour** the dandelion *Taraxacum officinale 20- Sh*. **horsegang 1** the track trodden by the horses in driving a threshing mill *19, 20- historical*. **2** a fourth part of a ploughgate; the land occupied by one of four people sharing a plough worked by their four horses *18-19*. **†horse gell** a horseleech *Haemopis sanguisuga 19*. **horse gock, horse gowk** the snipe *Gallinago gallinago la18- Sh Ork*. **horse-gowan, horse-gollan 1** the ox-eye daisy *Leucanthemum vulgare* or field camomile *Anthemis arvensis 19-*. **2** the dandelion *Taraxacum officinale 19- NE*. **3** the marsh ragwort *Jacobaea aquatica 20-*. **horse heid, †hors hed 1** a horse's head *15-*. **2** a large clod of earth *20- Ork NE T*. **horse hoof** the marsh marigold *Caltha palustris 20- Sh*. **horse-kirn** a butter churn worked by a horse *20- EC Bor*. **horse knot, horse knop** the black knapweed *Centaurea nigra la18- SW Bor*. **†hors marschall** a horsedoctor *la15-16*. **horse mussel** a large, freshwater mussel *Modiolus modiolus 17-*. **horsepease** vetch *Vicia sativa la18-19, 20- N*. **†hors rinning** horse-racing *16*. **†horse-setter** a person who hired out horses *18-19*. **horse-tree** the swingletree of a plough or harrow *la17-*. **†horsward, horswaird** an enclosure or paddock for horses *16-e17*. **horse and hattock** folklore a call to mount their horses made by witches or fairies *la17-19, 20- Sh NE*. **†on hors** on horseback *15-16*. **sic mannie, sic horsie** derogatory all of one kind, birds of a feather *20- NE*. [OE *hors*]

horse¹·² /hɔrs/ *v* **1** to mount a horse; to go on horseback *la14-*. **2** to convey or carry on a person's back; to move or convey something heavy or awkward *16-*. [see the noun]

horseman, †horsman /ˈhɔrsmən/ *n* **1** a person who rides a horse; a mounted soldier *13-*. **2** a man who tends horses; a farmworker who looks after and works (a pair of) horses *la17-*. **horseman's word** a secret word by which a farmworker was said to gain complete control over his horses *la19-20, 21- historical*. [HORSE¹·¹ + MAN]

hort *see* HURT¹·¹, HURT¹·²

hose¹·¹, †hos, †hois /hoz/ *n pl* **hose, hosen, †hoses 1** a stocking; stockings, socks *15-*. **2** a tube for the conveyance of water *la18-*. **3** the socket for the handle on a metal implement; the neck of a golf club where the head is fitted on to the shaft *la16-19, 20- Sh Ork N EC*. **4** mining an iron clasp at the end of a rope *la19, 20- EC*. **5** the sheath enclosing an ear of corn *17-19, 20- EC*. **6** a case or covering for a flag *16*. **hosack** the cuttlefish *Sepia officinalis 19- NE*. **†hosing** the providing or making of hose; cloth for making hose *16*. **hoosle, housel** the socket for the handle on a metal implement *20- EC Bor Uls*. **†hosing claith** cloth for making hose *16-e17*. **hosefish** the cuttlefish *Sepia officinalis la17-19, 20- Bor*. **†hosegrass** meadow soft grass *Holcus lanatus 19*. **†hosing gray** = *hosing claith*. **†hose-net 1** a trap or snare *la16-e19*. **2** a stocking-shaped net for fishing in streams; a fish-trap *18-e19*. **hose and sheen** exaggeration of a story (in the telling) *20- NE SW*. [OE *hosa* an article of clothing for the leg]

hose¹·² /hoz/ *v* to remove the bark from the base of a tree before felling *la19, 20- T H&I*. [see the noun]

hose² /hoz/ *v of fish* to swallow bait; *of people or animals* to swallow voraciously *20- Sh NE*. [probably from HOSE¹·¹ in that the food goes down the gullet like water through a hose]

hosen, hoses *see* HOSE¹·¹

hoshen /ˈhoʃən/ *n* **1** a footless stocking used to protect legs or arms in cold weather *la18-19, 20- N WC SW*. **2** a stocking used as a purse *la18- N WC SW*. [probably altered form of *hosen* (HOSE¹·¹)]

hospital, hospitale, hospitall *see* HOASPITAL

hossack /ˈhɔsək/ *n* a knot tied in a fishing-line to strengthen a weak spot *la19- Sh*. [unknown]

host¹·¹, †ost, †oist /host/ *n* **1** an army *la14-*. **2** a very large number; an abundance *15-*. **3** a confrontation in battle, a warlike gathering *la15-e19*. **4** (the assembling of) armed men summoned by the sovereign for military service; the campaign for which an armed force was raised *15-17*. [ME *host*]

†host¹·², †oist *v* to serve in an armed force; to take part in a campaign or raid *16-e18*. [see the noun]

host *see* HOAST¹·¹, HOAST¹·²

hostan /ˈhøstan/ *n fisherman's taboo* a wife or mistress of a house (in Foula) *20- Sh*. [ON *hústrúin*, variant of *húsfrú*]

hostee, †hostie /ˈhosti/ *n Roman Catholic Church* the host, consecrated bread *la16-19, 20- historical*. [Fr *hostie*]

hostel, †ostel /ˈhɔstəl/ *n* **1** a place offering low-cost accommodation *20-*. **2** an inn, hotel *la14-19, 20- historical*. [ME *hostel*]

hostelry, †hostilary, †hostlary, †ostillary /ˈhɔstəlri/ *n* **1** a public house; an inn *15-*. **2** the keeping of an inn; the right to keep an inn *la15-e17*. **3** lodging provided as a right to a church dignitary; a lodging belonging to a monastic community *15-e16*. [ME *hostelrie*]

hostilar *see* HOSTLER

†hosting *n* **1** active military service *la15-e19*. **2** the discharging of military service as a feudal obligation; the assembling for military service *la15-e18*. [verbal noun from HOST¹·²]

hostlary *see* HOSTELRY

hostler, †hostlar, †ostlaire, †ostler, †hostilar /ˈhɔstlər/ *n* **1** an innkeeper *la14-19, 20- literary*. **2** a stableman at an inn, an ostler *la15-e19*. **3** a host *15-e17*. **†oistlair hous** a hostelry, an inn *la15-17*. **hostler-wife** a woman who keeps an inn *17-19, 20- literary*. [ME *hostler*]

hot *see* HET¹·¹, HUT¹·¹, HUT¹·²

hotch¹·¹, hoatch /hɔtʃ, hotʃ/ *n* **1** a jerk, jolt or bounce *la18-19, 20- H&I C SW Bor*. **2** a hitch; a shrug or twitch *la18-19, 20- H&I C SW Bor*. **3** a large, ungainly or untidy woman *la19- C SW Bor*. [see the verb]

hotch¹·², hoatch, †hoch /hɔtʃ, hotʃ/ *v* **1** to move jerkily up and down; to bump or jog along *la15-*. **2** to fidget with impatience or discomfort *la18-*. **3** to heave with laughter *la18-*. **4** to slide along a bench or pew *19, 20- EC SW Bor*. **5** to shrug; to hitch up *19, 20- EC SW*. Compare HOACHIN. [ME *hotchen*]

hotchin *see* HOACHIN

hote *see* HUT¹·¹

hotter¹·¹ /ˈhɔtər/ *n* **1** a confused, jumbled heap *19-*. **2** a shaking or jolting; a rattling sound *19- Sh NE Bor*. **3** the bubbling or boiling of liquid *20- NE EC SW*. **4** a seething mass, a swarm *19, 20- NE SW*. **hotterel 1** a great number; a crowd, a swarm *20- NE*. **2** a mass of festering sores or chaps; an open sore *20- NE*. **a hotter o fat** the quivering of an obese person *19- NE*. [see the verb]

hotter¹·² /ˈhɔtər/ *v* **1** to crowd together; to mill around, swarm *19-*. **2** *of liquid* to seethe, bubble or boil *19-*. **3** to move in an uneven jerky way; to jolt or bump *19- Sh NE EC Bor*. **4** to shudder, shiver or shake *19- NE T SW*. **5** to walk unsteadily, totter *19- NE Bor*. [unknown; compare MDu *hotten* to shake, jolt]

hottle /ˈhɔtəl/ *n* a hotel *19, 20- N NE EC*. [altered form of Eng *hotel*]

†Hottopyis *n* a variety of wine *la16*. [perhaps Fr *haut pays* a higher or more inland district]

hou *see* HOO¹
houch *see* HOCH¹·¹, HOCH¹·²
houcks *see* HOWK²
houf *see* HOWF¹·¹, HOWF¹·²
hough *see* HOCH¹·¹, HOCH¹·², HOWE¹·²
†**houghams, hochems, hauchames** *npl* wooden supports for panniers on a horse *17-e19*. [perhaps HOCH¹·¹ + plural of HAIM]
houghel *see* HOCHLE¹·¹, HOCHLE¹·²
houghmagandie *see* HOCHMAGANDIE
houk *see* HULK¹·¹
houlet *see* HOOLET¹·¹
houlk *see* HULK¹·¹
hound *see* HOOND¹·¹, HOOND¹·²
hounder *see* HUNNER¹·¹
hount *see* HUNT¹·¹, HUNT¹·²
houp, †**hope,** †**hoip** /hʌup/ *n pl* **houps,** †**houppes** the fruit of the hop-plant (used in brewing) *la16-19, 20- Ork NE*. [MDu *hoppe*]
houp *see* HOWP¹·¹
†**houpe** *n* a heap or pile; a lot of goods for sale *la15-16*. [MDu, Flem *hoop*]
houppes *see* HOUP
hour *see* OOR¹
†**hous** *n* a covering, a housing *la15-17*. [OFr *houce*]
hous *see* HOOSE¹·¹
housald *see* HOOSEHOLD
house *see* HOOSE¹·¹, HOOSE¹·²
household *see* HOOSEHOLD
housel *see* HOSE¹·¹
houshald *see* HOOSEHOLD
housing *see* HOOSING
†**housour, howsour** *n* a covering, a housing *e16*. [OFr *houssure*; compare HOOSE¹·¹]
houster¹·¹ /ˈhʌustər/ *n* a badly-dressed, untidy person *19, 20- SW*. †**houstrie** trash, rubbish *19*. [unknown]
houster¹·² /ˈhʌustər/ *v* to gather together in a confused way *18-19, 20- NE EC*. [unknown]
hout *see* HOOT¹·²
houxie /ˈhʌuksi/ *interj* a call to a cow *20- N*. [perhaps diminutive form of OX or Norw *okse*]
höv *see* HEAVE¹·²
hove¹·¹, *Sh* **huiv** /hov; *Sh* høv/ *n* **1** the swelling or distending of cattle (due to unsuitable food) *la19- C Bor*. **2** the swell of the sea *20- Sh*. **hovie** swollen, distended; *of bread* puffy, well-risen *la19- Ork C Uls*. [see the verb]
hove¹·², *Sh* **huve** /hov; *Sh* høv/ *v* **1** to (cause to) swell or distend *la18-*. **2** to throw or cast away *18-19, 20- Sh T Bor*. **3** to rise above the ground; *of light or loose soil* to rise or swell up *la18-19, 20- N EC SW*. **4** to raise or hold up *la14-e16*. **hoved** swollen, bloated; *of cattle* swollen from overeating on rich grazing *la18-*. **hovin, hoving** the state of being swollen *19-*. [back-formation from *hovin* (HEAVE¹·²)]
hove² /hov/ *interj* a call to cows to come *19- Bor*. [unknown]
hoven /ˈhovən/ *adj* swollen, bloated; *of cattle* swollen (from overeating on rich grazing) *19-*. [ptp of HOVE¹·²]
hover¹·¹, †**hovir,** †**hovyr** /ˈhəvər/ *n* a state of hesitation or uncertainty *16-19, 20- Sh*. [unknown]
hover¹·², †**hovir,** †**hovyr** /ˈhəvər/ *v* **1** to remain suspended in the air *la15-*. **2** to pause or wait; to hesitate *la15-*. **hover a blink** to wait a short time *19-*. [unknown]
hovery *see* OVER
hövi *see* HOOVIE
hovie *see* HOVE¹·¹
hovin *see* HEAVE¹·², HOVE¹·²
hovir *see* HOVER¹·¹, HOVER¹·²

hovyr *see* HOVER¹·¹
how¹·¹, **hoe,** *N NE* **hyow,** *NE* **hyew,** †**hew** /hʌu, ho; *N NE* hjʌu; *NE* hju/ *n* a weeding tool, a hoe *la14-*. **come tae the hyow** to be ready for hoeing *20- N NE*. [OFr *houe*]
how¹·² /hʌu/ *v* to dig up or uproot plants; to thin out plants with a hoe *17-*. [see the noun]
how² /hʌu/ *interj* a call to attract attention or urge action *la15-19, 20- NE*. [perhaps altered form of HO²·³]
how *see* HOLE¹·¹, HOLE¹·², HOO¹, HOO²·¹, HOO²·³, HOO³, HOWE¹·¹, HOWE¹·², HOWE¹·³, HOWE², HOWE³
howch *see* HOCH¹·¹
howd¹·¹ /hʌud/ *n* **1** a lurching, rocking movement *la18- N NE Bor*. **2** a sudden gale, a squall *19*. [see the verb]
howd¹·² /hʌud/ *v* **1** to sway or rock from side to side; to jolt or wriggle about *la18- N NE Bor*. **2** *of a boat* to toss about; to bob up and down *la18- N NE Bor*. [altered form of HOD]
howd *see* HIDE¹
†**Howdenite** *n* a follower of John Halden, an extreme Covenanter *la17-e18*. [derived from the surname *Halden*]
howder¹·¹, **howther** /ˈhʌudər, ˈhʌuðər/ *n* **1** a rocking, jolting or bumping motion *la19-*. **2** a blast of wind, a gale *19- NE*. **3** horseplay, rough-and-tumble *e19*. [see the verb]
howder¹·², **howther** /ˈhʌudər, ˈhʌuðər/ *v* **1** to swarm, mill around, bustle about *la18-*. **2** *of wind* to gust, blow *20-*. **3** to move with a rocking, jolting or bumping motion *19- NE H&I*. [frequentative form of HOWD¹·²]
howder² /ˈhʌudər/ *v* to conceal *18- literary*. [frequentative form of *howd* (HIDE¹)]
howdie /ˈhʌudi/ *n* a midwife *la17-*. **howdyin, howdying 1** a confinement *19-*. **2** midwifery *19-*. **howdie-wife** a midwife *la19-*. [unknown]
howdle¹·¹ /ˈhʌudəl/ *n* a swarm or crowd; an untidy heap *19- EC*. [see the verb; compare HOWDER¹·²]
howdle¹·² /ˈhʌudəl/ *v* to move with a rocking or bumping motion; to stagger or limp *19- NE T*. [frequentative form of HOWD¹·²]
howdy towdy, †**howdy dowdy** /ˈhʌudi tʌudi/ *adj* tawdry; dowdy, unkempt *19, 20- EC*. [reduplicative compound; compare HUDDERIE and *dowdy*]
howe¹·¹, †**how,** †**holl** /hʌu/ *n* **1** a depression, a hollow; a low-lying piece of ground *la15-*. **2** a basin-shaped stretch of country, a wide plain bounded by hills; frequently in place-names: ◊*Howe o the Mearns 16-*. **3** a hollow space or cavity *16-*. **4** = *howe ice la19, 20- SW*. **howe ice** *curling* the smooth stretch of ice down the centre of the rink *la18-*. **be in the howes** to be depressed, be in the dumps *la17-19, 20- C*. †**cast in the howes** to cast out, suppress, reject completely *17*. **howe o the neck** the nape of the neck *la19- NE EC*. **howe o the nicht** midnight or the period between midnight and 3am *19-*. **howe o winter** midwinter, November to January *19- C Bor*. **howe o the year** midwinter *19, 20- T*. [OE *hol*]
howe¹·², **how,** †**holl,** †**though** /hʌu/ *adj* **1** hollow, deep-set, sunken; lying in a hollow *la14-*. **2** hungry, famished; devoid of food *18-*. **3** deep, intense; innermost *19-*. **4** *of sound or the voice* deep, echoing, guttural *16-19, 20- Ork*. **howe-backit 1** *of a person* round-shouldered; hollow-backed *20-*. **2** *of a horse* saddle-backed *la18-19*. †**how barrow** a barrow with sides *16*. †**how eneuch** indifferent *la17-19*. [see the noun]
howe¹·³, †**how** /hʌu/ *adv* hollowly, deeply *la15-*. [see the noun]
howe², †**how,** †**holl** /hʌu/ *n* **1** the hull of a boat *16-17, 20- NE*. **2** a boat with neither mast nor sails up *20- NE EC*. **3** the hold of a ship *la15-16*. [extended sense of HOWE¹·¹]
howe³, †**how** /hʌu/ *n* a (pre-historic) burial mound *la18- Sh Ork*. [extended sense of HOWE¹·¹]

howe-dumb-deid /ˈhʌudʌmdid/ *n* the depth of winter; the darkest point of the night *19- literary*. [HOWE[1.1] + *the dumb deid* (DUMB)]

howek *see* HOOICK

howf[1.1]**, howff, houf, †holf** /hʌuf/ *n* **1** a (private) burial ground *17-.* **2** a meeting-place; a favourite haunt; a local public house *18-.* **3** an enclosed space, a yard (for storing timber) *17-19, 20- NE T EC.* **4** a refuge or place of shelter *la18-19, 20- T C.* **5** a rough or improvised shelter used by mountaineers; a hut used by workmen *20-.* **†the Houff** a burial ground in Dundee, which was originally the courtyard of the Greyfriars Monastery *la16-18.* [Du, Flem *hof* an enclosed place, a courtyard]

howf[1.2]**, houf** /hʌuf/ *v* **1** to dwell or lodge; to frequent a place *18-.* **2** to take shelter or refuge *la19, 20- NE T.* [see the noun]

howff *see* HOWF[1.1]

howfin[1.1]**, †howffing** /ˈhʌufɪn/ *n* a clumsy, shy or stupid person *e16, la19- NE.* [unknown]

howfin[1.2]**, howffing** /ˈhʌufɪn, ˈhʌufɪŋ/ *adj* **1** shabby-looking; unattractive, ugly *la16-.* **2** smelly, disgusting *la20-.* [unknown]

howgh *see* HOCH[1.1]

howis *see* HOCH[1.1]

howit *see* HUT[1.1]

howk[1.1]**,** *Sh Ork* **hock** /hʌuk; *Sh Ork* hɔk/ *n* **1** the act of digging or burrowing; a hole *la18-19, 20- Sh Ork C.* **2** a gathering place for idle people; a spell of idleness in one place *la19- NE T.* [see the verb]

howk[1.2]**,** *Sh Ork* **hock, †holk, †hoke** /hʌuk; *Sh Ork* hɔk/ *v* **1** to dig; to dig out or uproot *16-.* **2** to hollow out; to scoop out or excavate *16-.* **3** to mine coal; to quarry stone *16-.* **4** *of pigs* to root around in the earth *18-.* **5** to investigate, search thoroughly *19-.* **howker** a person who digs *19-.* **howkit, †holkit** hollowed out, made hollow by digging *la15-.* **howk aboot** to loiter, stand around idly *la19- NE Bor.* [MLG *holken*]

howk[2]**, heugh** /hʌuk, hjux/ *n pl* **†houcks, †holkis 1** a disease affecting the eyes of cattle *19, 20- NE.* **2** a skin ailment affecting people *16.* [extended sense of HOWK[1.2]]

howk *see* HULK[1.1]

howlat *see* HOOLET[1.1]

howld /hʌuld/ *n* the hold of a ship *18-.* [variant of Eng *hold*]

howlded *see* HAUD[1.1], HAUD[1.2]

howlded *see* HAUD[1.2]

howle *see* OOL[1.1]

howlet *see* HOOLET[1.1]

howm, holm /hʌum, hom/ *n* **1** a stretch of low-lying land beside a river, a haugh; frequently in place-names *13-19, 20- C SW Bor.* **2** an islet *16- Sh Ork.* **†holmin** land along a river *18.* **†homing ground** = *holmin.* **†homing land** = *holmin.* [ON *hólmr* a small island]

howp[1.1]**, houp, hope,** *Sh Ork* **hoop, †hoip, †hop** /hʌup, hop; *Sh Ork* hup/ *n* expectation or prospect of something desired *la14-.* **howpfu, hopeful** full of hope; inspiring hope, promising *17-.* **be hopeful that** to hope that *la18-.* **in houps** in the hope or expectation of *la16-.* **na houp bit** no alternative but *20- Sh NE.* [OE *hopa*]

howp[1.2] /hʌup/ *v* **1** to desire, want; to expect or anticipate *la14-.* **2** to believe, suppose, conjecture *la14-17.* [OE *hopian*]

howp[2] /hʌup/ *n* a mouthful or gulp of liquid, a draught, a dram *la19- N NE.* [probably onomatopoeic]

howp *see* HOPE[1], HOPE[2]

howre *see* OOR[1]

hows *see* HOOSE[1.2]

howsour *see* HOUSOUR

howt *see* HOOT[1.2]

howther *see* HOWDER[1.1], HOWDER[1.2]

howtowdie /hʌuˈtʌudi/ *n* **1** a large (young) chicken for the pot; a young hen which has not begun to lay *18-19, 20- H&I WC.* **2** an unmarried woman *19.* [OFr *hetoudeau, estaudeau*]

hox *see* OX

hoy[1.1] /hɔɪ/ *n* a heave, the act of heaving *20- Sh N EC SW Bor.* [back-formation or reduced form of HOISE[1.1]]

hoy[1.2] /hɔɪ/ *v* to heave, throw or toss up; to throw away, dispose of *20- Sh EC Bor.* [see the noun]

hoy[2] /hɔɪ/ *v* to hurry; to walk briskly *19- C SW Bor.* [variant of HEY[4]]

hoy[3] /hɔɪ/ *v* **1** to hail or summon with a shout of 'hoy' *la16-.* **2** to urge on or incite with cries of 'hoy' *16-19, 20- NE C Bor.* [from the Older Scots interjection *hoy*]

hoy *see* HO[1]

hoyes[1.1]**, †oyes** /ˈhoːjez/ *n pl* **hoyes, †oyesis** the crying of 'oyez' *la15-19, 20- literary.* [see the interj]

†hoyes[1.2]**, oyes, oyas** *interj* a call to attract attention made by a public officer or town crier *la15-19.* [ME *oyes*]

hoyse *see* HOISE[1.1]

hoyt *see* HET[1.2]

hoyte *see* HOIT

hree *see* THREE

hub /hʌb/ *v* **1** to blame, accuse or suspect *la19- Sh.* **2** to drive away *la19- Sh.* [unknown]

hubbelskyu *see* HUBBLESHOO

hubber *see* HABBER[1.2]

hubbie[1] /ˈhʌbi/ *n* a woman's cotton jerkin or smock *la19- Ork.* [diminutive form of ON *hjúpr* a doublet]

hubbie[2]**, †hobby** /ˈhʌbe/ *n* a coarse, slovenly person *18-19, 20- Bor.* [diminutive form of *Hob*, itself a diminutive of *Robert*]

hubbilschow *see* HUBBLESHOO

hubble[1.1] /ˈhʌbəl/ *n* **1** bustle, confusion, disorder *19-.* **2** an uproar, a fight; an unruly crowd *19-.* **3** a difficulty, a problem; trouble *la19-.* **be in a hubble o work** to be overwhelmed with work *19- Sh SW.* [onomatopoeic; compare HABBLE[1.1], HOBBLE[1.1]]

hubble[1.2] /ˈhʌbəl/ *v* to trouble, perplex; to put in a quandary *la19- WC SW Bor.* [see the noun]

†hubble-bubble *n* an uproar, a tumult, a hubbub *17.* [rhyming compound from HUBBLE[1.1] + BUBBLE[1.1]]

hubbleshoo, hubbleshew, hobbleshow, *Sh* **hubbelskyu, †hobillschowe, †hubbilschow, †hobleshew** /ˈhʌbəlʃu, ˈhɔbəlʃo; *Sh* ˈhʌbəlskju/ *n* **1** an uproar, a tumult, a hubbub *16-.* **2** a mob, a rabble *la18-e19.* [unknown]

huche *see* HEUCH[1.1]

huch-yall *see* HOCHLE[1.2]

hucker, *Bor* **hoakker, †hoker** /ˈhʌkər; *Bor* ˈhokər/ *v* to crouch or bend down *19, 20- N Bor.* Compare HUNKER. [ON *hokra* to crouch, go bent, slink away]

huckle /ˈhʌkəl/ *v* **1** to arrest, take into custody forcibly *la20-.* **2** to be manhandled or hustled *la20-.* Compare HOCHLE[1.2]. [unknown]

hucky-duck *see* HACKY DUCK

hud /hʌd/ *n* **1** the back of an open fireplace, consisting of a stone or clay block resembling a seat *la18- SW Bor.* **2** a small shelf or recess at each side of an old-fashioned fireplace, used as a hob for pots *19- SW Bor.* **3** the seat by the fire on a blacksmith's hearth *19- SW Bor.* **†hudstane** a stone which forms a seat or shelf *19.* [unknown]

hud *see* HAUD[1.1], HAUD[1.2], HOOD[1.1]

hudd /hʌd/ *n* a hod, a receptacle for carrying mortar *19, 20- SW.* [variant of Eng *hod*]

hudder[1.1]**, huther** /ˈhʌdər, ˈhʌðər/ *n* **1** an untidy person or slovenly worker *la19, 20- WC SW Bor.* **2** a confused crowd or heap *19- SW Bor.* [see the verb]

hudder[1,2], **huther** /'hʌdər, 'hʌðər/ v **1** to heap together in disorder; to throw on clothes hastily or untidily *la19-*. **2** to act in a confused or hasty way; to work or walk clumsily or hastily *19, 20- SW Uls*. [variant of HOWDER[1,2] or back-formation from HUDDERON]

hudderie, huddery, *NE* **huddry**, †**hutherie** /'hʌdəri; *NE* 'hʌdri/ *adj* **1** slovenly, untidy, dirty *19-*. **2** *of hair* shaggy, unkempt, dishevelled *la19- NE EC*. [probably altered form of HUDDERIN]

hudderin, hutherin, †**huderon** /'hʌdərɪn, 'hʌðərɪn/ *adj* **1** slovenly, shabbily-dressed *18-19, 20- SW Uls*. **2** awkward, clumsy *18-19, 20- Uls*. [probably from the noun HUDDERON]

hudderon, huddroun, †**huddron** /'hʌdərən, 'hʌdrən/ *n* a slovenly person *16-19, 20- Ork N WC SW*. [unknown]

huddery *see* HUDDERIE

huddie *see* HADDIE, HOODIE

†**huddoun, huddon** *n* a species of whale *la15-16*. [unknown]

huddron *see* HUDDERON

huddroun *see* HUDDERON, HUTHERON

huddry *see* HUDDERIE

hude *see* HOOD[1.1]

huden *see* HIDE[1]

huderon *see* HUDDERIN

hudge[1.1] /hʌdʒ/ *n* a large quantity, a vast amount *19- Ork N NE*. [voiced variant of HUTCH[1.1] a chest, a coffer]

hudge[1.2] /hʌdʒ/ *v* to amass or heap up *la19- Ork NE*. [see the noun]

hudge-mudge /'hʌdʒ mʌdʒ/ *n* secrecy; furtive whispering *18- NE T*. **hudgmudgin** whispering behind someone's back *19- NE T*. [rhyming compound; compare HUGGERY-MUGGERY[1.1]]

hudit *see* HOODIT

hudnae *see* HAE[1.2]

hue, †**hew** /hju/ *n* **1** colour *la14-*. **2** appearance, aspect *15-*. **3** the complexion *15-19, 20- Sh*. **4** a very small quantity or portion *19, 20- WC*. **neither hue nor hair** in no way, not at all *19, 20- Sh N*. [OE *hīw*]

huey *see* HUGHIE

hufe *see* HUIF, HUIVE

huff /hʌf/ *v* to swell or puff up *la19- Sh T SW*. [onomatopoeic]

huge[1.1] /hjudʒ/ *adj* massive, immense *15-*. [ME *huge*]

†**huge**[1.2] *adv* hugely, immensely *la15-e16*. [see the adj]

hugger /'hʌgər/ *v* **1** to crowd or huddle together as a protection against cold *la19- NE T*. **2** to shudder, shiver; to hug oneself (to keep warm) *19- NE*. **huggert, huggered 1** huddled up or shrunk with cold, pinched-looking *20- NE T*. **2** *of clothes* hanging untidily *20- T EC*. **3** round-shouldered *20- NE*. **huggerin** huddled or shrunk with cold *20- NE T*. [unknown]

huggery-muggery[1.1] /'hʌgəre mʌgəre/ *adj* **1** furtive *19- T C SW Bor*. **2** disorderly, untidy *19- T C SW Bor*. **huggerie** untidy *19- WC Bor*. [altered form of Eng *hugger-mugger*; compare HUDGE-MUDGE]

huggery-muggery[1.2] /'hʌgəre mʌgəre/ *adv* **1** furtively *19- T EC SW Bor*. **2** in a confused or disorderly state *19- T EC SW Bor*. **huggerie** messily *19- WC Bor*. [see the adj]

hugget *see* HOGGET

huggistaff, †**huggie staff** /'hʌgɪstaf/ *n* a gaff, a hook for landing fish *19- Sh*. [Norw *hugg*, ON *högg* a stroke, a blow + STAFF]

hughie, huey /'hjui/ *v* to vomit *la20- C*. [onomatopoeic]

hugly *see* UGLY[1.2]

hugmahush /hʌgmə'hʌʃ/ *n* a slovenly person; a lout *19- NE*. [unknown]

hugmanay *see* HOGMANAY

hugtoun *see* HOGTOUN

huid *see* HOOD[1.1], HOOD[1.2]

huidie *see* HOODIE

huidin *see* HOODIN

huidit *see* HOODIT

huif, hoof, *N NE* hiv, †**hufe**, †**hoove** /huf; *N NE* hɪv/ *n* **1** the horny growth on the foot of an animal; a hoof *la15-*. **2** a particle, the least thing *17-e18*. **hoofit, hoofed**, †**huffit**, †**hovit** having hoofs *la15-*. [OE *hōf*]

†**huik** *v* to pay attention to; to take into account *la16*. [unknown; compare OE *hycgan* to think, ON *huga* to mind]

huiken *see* HUK

huild *see* HAUD[1.2]

huilie *see* HOOLY[1.2]

huilk /hʌɪlk/ *n* a container for oil *19- Sh*. [Norw dial *holk* a wooden vessel, a bucket]

huill *see* HOOL[1.1]

huin *see* HUN[2]

huird[1.1], **hoard**, †**hurd** /hurd, hord/ *n* a hidden store of treasure or food; a hoard *la14-*. [OE *hord*]

huird[1.2], **hoard**, †**hurd** /hurd, hord/ *v* **1** to store treasure or food *la14-*. **2** to secretly harbour criminals *la15-e17*. [OE *hordian*]

huit *see* HUT[1.1]

huiv *see* HOVE[1.1]

huive, †**huve**, †**hufe** /huv/ *v* to cease, desist; to wait *14-19, 20- Bor*. [ME *hoven* to wait in readiness or expectation; to remain, stay, linger]

huizle *see* WHEEZLE[1.2]

huizlin, hoozlin /'huzlɪn/ *n* a beating *19- Bor*. [unknown]

huk /huk/ *v* to squat or crouch *la19- Sh*. **hookers** the haunches, bended knees *19- Sh Ork N*. **huiken** to squat (on the haunches) *la19- Ork*. [ON *húka*]

huke *see* HEUK

hukebane *see* HEUKBANE

hulbert /'hʌlbərt/ *n* a big, clumsy person or animal *19- Sh*. [unknown]

huldery *see* HULTER

hule, heul /hjul/ *n* **1** a perverse or objectionable person or animal; a troublesome child *19- EC SW Bor*. **2** a name for the devil *la19- SW Bor*. [unknown]

hulk[1.1], **houk**, †**holk**, †**houlk**, †**howk** /hʌlk, hʌuk/ *n* **1** a ship *15-*. **2** a big unwieldy mass; a hump *la18-*. [OE *hulc*]

hulk[1.2] /hʌlk/ *v* to loiter, lurk *la19- Sh N NE T EC*. **hulk aboot** to move around furtively *la19- NE*. [see the noun]

hull *see* HILL[1], HILL[2], HOOL[1.1], HOOL[1.2]

hullachan *see* HOOLACHAN

hullie[1.1] /'hʌle/ *n* a basket or box anchored in a harbour for storing live crabs and lobsters; originally a hole in the rocks below the high-water mark *19- EC Bor*. [altered form of HALLOW[1.1]]

hullie[1.2] /'hʌle/ *adj* hollow *la19- EC*. [variant of Eng *hollow*]

hullion /'hʌlɪən/ *n* a heap or accumulation (of money or property) *la18- NE*. [unknown]

hullion *see* HALLION

†**hullok** *n* a Spanish red wine *la16-e17*. [EModE *hollocke, hallocke*, Spanish *haloque*]

hulster[1.1] /'hʌlstər/ *n* an upwards hoist, a push *la19- NE T*. [unknown]

hulster[1.2] /'hʌlstər/ *v* **1** to hoist a load onto one's back; to struggle along under a heavy burden *la19- NE T*. **2** to walk heavily, drag one's feet *la19- NE*. **3** to be overburdened with too many clothes *20- NE Bor*. [unknown]

†**hulster**[2] *n* a holster for a pistol *la17-e18*. [Du, EModE *holster*]

hult *see* HILT[1], HILT[2]

hulter, holter /'hʌltər, 'hɔltər/ *n* **1** a large boulder or lump of rock *19- Sh*. **2** a heap of boulders; a rockfall *la20- Sh*.

huldery awkward, clumsy *20- Sh.* [Norw dial *holt* a rough stony hill]

huly see HOOLY[1.2], HOOLY[1.3], HOOLY[1.4]

hum[1.1], *Ork Uls* **ham** /hʌm; *Ork Uls* ham/ *n* a piece of food softened by chewing and given to a child *19- Ork N SW Uls.* [unknown]

hum[1.2], *Ork NE Uls* **ham** /hʌm; *Ork NE Uls* ham/ *v* **1** to chew; to soften by chewing *19-*. **2** to eat greedily; to take large mouthfuls *20- NE*. **hummle** to chew *19, 20- Ork.* [unknown]

hum[2] /hʌm/ *v of the sky* to grow dark *la19- Sh Ork.* **humin, hoomin** dusk, twilight *19- Sh Ork.* [ON *húma*]

humanity, †**humanitie** /hju'manɪtɪ/ *n* **1** the human race; human nature or form *la15-*. **2** kindness, benevolence *15-*. **3** *Scottish Universities* the study of the classical languages and literature; the Latin class *la16-*. [ME *humanite*, Lat *hūmānitās*]

humast see UMEST[1.2]

humble, humbly see HUMMLE[1.2]

humbug[1.1] /'hʌmbʌg/ *n* **1** deception, fraud *19-*. **2** a nuisance, an imposition *20- NE.* [unknown]

humbug[1.2] /'hʌmbʌg/ *v* to fool or deceive *la19*. **be humbugged with** to be pestered or bothered with *la19- N NE SW.* [unknown]

humch /'hʌmʃ/ *v* to be sulky or bad-tempered *la19- NE.* [unknown; compare GLUNSH[1.2]]

hum-drum[1.1] /'hʌmdrʌm/ *n* an apathetic, lazy-minded person *19- WC SW.* [see the adj]

hum-drum[1.2] /'hʌmdrʌm/ *adj* dejected, in low spirits; sullen *18-*. [EModE *humdrum* lacking variety]

humf see HUMPH[2.1], HUMPH[2.2]

humff see HUMPH[2.3]

humfish see HAMFISH

humfy see HUMPHY[1.2]

humil see HUMMLE[1.1]

humility, †**humilite**, †**humylitie** /hju'mɪlɪtɪ/ *n* **1** meekness; humbleness *la14-*. **2** creeping saxifrage *Saxifraga stolonifera la19- NE T EC.* [MFr *humilité*, Lat *humilitās*]

humill, humily see HUMMLE[1.2]

humle see HUMMLE[1.1]

humler see HUMMEL[1.2]

humlibaand, humliband /'hʌmlɪband/ *n* a loop of rope which functions as a rowlock *19- Sh Ork.* [Norw *hamleband*]

humlin /'hɵmlɪn/ *adj* disagreeable, disorderly *20- Ork.* [unknown]

humlock, †**hamlock**, †**humlok** /'hʌmlɔk/ *n* **1** hemlock *Conium maculatum* or any of the umbelliferous plants such as the cow-parsnip *Heracleum sphondylium la16-*. **2** a dried hemlock stalk used as a peashooter *19- EC Bor.* [OE *hymlic*]

humly see HUMMLE[1.2]

hummel[1.1] /'hʌməl/ *n* an animal that has no horns or has been dehorned *la19- N NE T.* **hummlie 1** a hornless animal *19- N NE.* **2** a native of Buchan *la19- NE.* **3** a Highlander *18-e19.* [LG *hummel* a hornless animal]

hummel[1.2] /'hʌməl/ *v* **1** to remove the awns or 'beards' from barley or other grains *la18-*. **2** to break up and shape stones or large pieces of driftwood *20- Sh Bor.* **hummelled**, †**hummillit 1** *of cattle or sheep* deprived of horns *la16-*. **2** *of driftwood* worn *20- Sh.* **hummeller, humler, hammeler** a machine, or the part of a threshing-mill, that removes the awns from barley *la18-*. [see the noun]

hummel[1.3], †**thummill**, †**hommill**, †**umel** /'hʌməl/ *adj* **1** *of cattle* hornless *16-*. **2** *of a boat* without a mast or sail; with mast and sail lowered *20- N NE.* **3** *of deer* naturally hornless *20- NE T.* **4** *of grain* without awns *la15-19, 20- Bor.* **5** *of surfaces* flat, smooth, level *18-19, 20- NE.* †**hummel bonnet, humble bonnet** a military bonnet without a crest *19.*

hummle-doddie *adj* hornless *la19- NE.* **hummle-doddie** *n* a mitten *20- NE.* **hummle mitten** a mitten *la19- NE.* [see the noun]

†**hummell** *n* a lazy person *e16.* [Ger *Hummel*, MLG *hummel* a wild bee]

hummer /'hʌmər/ *v* to mumble or murmur; to grumble *18-*. [onomatopoeic with frequentative suffix]

hummie[1], **hoomie**, †**hummock** /'hʌmi, 'humi/ *n* **1** a small quantity of meal or salt; a pinch, a handful *19, 20- N NE.* **2** the closing of the hand so that the thumb and the four fingertips are placed together *17-e19.* [unknown]

hummie[2] /'hʌmi/ *interj in shinty* a warning call given to an opponent to keep to his own side *19- EC Bor.* **hummie your side** = HUMMIE[2]. **hummie yer stick** = HUMMIE[2]. [unknown]

hummill see HUMMEL[1.3]

hummle[1.1], †**thumle**, †**humil** /'hʌməl/ *v* to make humble *la15-.* [see the adj]

hummle[1.2], **humble**, *Ork* **heumle**, *NE* **heumble**, *NE* **hoomble**, †**thumill** /'hʌməl, 'hʌmbəl; *Ork* 'hjuməl; *NE* 'hjumbəl; *NE* 'humbəl/ *adj* modest, humble *la15-.* **hummlie, humbly**, †**humly**, †**humily**, †**umbelie** in a humble manner *la14-.* [ME *humble*]

hummle see HUM[1.2]

hummlie see HUMMEL[1.1]

hummock see HUMMIE[1]

humour, *NE* **eemir**, †**yumer** /'hjumər, 'jumər; *NE* 'imər/ *n* **1** mood *17-.* **2** one of the four bodily fluids *la15-19, 20- historical.* **3** (capacity for) amusement *19-.* **4** pus from a wound or sore *20-.* **5** a skin eruption *20- NE Bor.* **6** resentment or ill temper *18-19, 20- Ork.* **7** moisture, dampness *la15-e16.* **humoursome** humorous, witty *19-.* [ME *humour*, Lat *ūmor*]

humph[1.1], **hump** /hʌmf, hʌmp/ *n* **1** a hump-back *19-.* **2** the act of carrying a heavy load *20-.* **humphed** hunched *20-.* **humph-backit** hunchbacked *19-.* **away an cuddle my humph** an expression of dismissal *la20- C.* **come up your humph** to come into one's head, occur to one to do something *la19- C SW Bor.* **set up your humph** to become angry and antagonistic *la19- C Bor.* [unknown; compare LG *hump* a portion, a hunk, LG *humperl* the hump of a camel]

humph[1.2], **hump** /hʌmf, hʌmp/ *v* **1** to carry, drag; to hoist or lift up (something heavy) *la19-.* **2** to move around laboriously as if under the weight of a heavy burden *20-.* [see the noun]

humph[2.1], **humf** /hʌmf/ *n* an offensive smell of decaying matter *19-.* **humphy** smelly, tainted; decaying, putrid *20-.* [see the interj]

humph[2.2], †**thumf** /hʌmf/ *v* to have a smell or taste of decay *la19-.* **humphed** stinking, putrid *la18-.* [see the interj]

humph[2.3], †**thumff**, †**umff**, †**umph** /hʌmf/ *interj* an expression of disgust or dissatisfaction *la16-.* **humph an hae** to prevaricate, hesitate *19-.* [perhaps onomatopoeic of the action of blowing or breathing out in disgust]

humph coal /'hʌmf kol/ *n* poor quality coal *la18- N NE T C.* [unknown first element + COAL]

humphy[1.1] /'hʌmfi, 'hʌmfe/ *n* a hunchbacked person *la18-20, 21- historical.* [see the adj]

humphy[1.2], **humfy** /'hʌmfi, 'hʌmfe/ *adj* **1** having a hump, hunchbacked *la18-.* **humfy back** a hunchbacked person *20-.* **humphy backit** hump-backed *la19-.* [HUMPH[1.1] + -IE[2]]

humple[1] /'hʌmpəl/ *n* a heap or mound, a hillock *la18- C SW Bor Uls.* **humplock** a small heap or mound *la17- C Bor.* [*hump* (HUMPH[1.1]), with diminutive suffix]

humple[2] /'hʌmpəl/ *v* to hobble *19- EC Bor.* [Du *hompeten*, Ger *humpeln*, LG *humpeln*]

humplock see HUMPLE[1]

humylitie see HUMILITY

hun[1], *Ork* **huin** /hun; *Ork* høn/ *n* **1** *pl* the ridge of a roof *20- Sh Ork*. **2** a projection at the top of a ship's mast *16-e17, 20- Sh*. [ON *húnn* the knob at the masthead]

Hun[2] /hʌn/ *n* **1** *derogatory* a supporter of Glasgow Rangers Football Club *20-*. **2** *derogatory* a Protestant *la20-*. [OE *Hūna* one of an Asiatic race of warlike nomads who invaded Europe in the late fourth century]

hunch[1.1] /hʌnʃ/ *n* **1** a protuberance, a hump *19-*. **2** a shrug *20- NE EC*. [see the verb]

hunch[1.2] /hʌnʃ/ *v* to heave or shove with the shoulder *la19- Sh Ork EC*. **hunch-cuddy-hunch** a boys' team-game *20- C*. [EModE *hunch* to shove]

hunchie /ˈhʌnʃe, ˈhʌnʃi/ *n derogatory* a hunchback *19- N NE EC Bor*. [HUNCH[1.1] + -IE[3]]

hund *see* HOOND[1.1], HOOND[1.2]

hunder, hundir, hundred, hundreth *see* HUNNER[1.1], HUNNER[1.2]

†**hune**[1.1], **hone, hwn** *n* delay, tardiness *la14-e19*. **but hune, bot hown** without delay *la14-e19*. **foroutin hone** = *but hune 15-16*. **withoutin hone** = *but hune 15*. [unknown]

†**hune**[1.2] *v* to stop; to linger; to delay *19*. [unknown]

hunert *see* HUNNER[1.2]

hung *see* HING[1.2]

hunger[1.1], †**thungir**, †**hungyr**, †**hungar** /ˈhʌnər, ˈhʌŋɡər/ *n* **1** the sensation caused by lack of food; starvation *la14-*. **2** greedy or eager desire *16-*. **hungersome 1** hungry, having a keen appetite *19-*. **2** causing or stimulating hunger *la19-*. **a hunger or a burst** starvation (or scarcity) followed by plenty *la19-*. [OE *hungor*]

hunger[1.2] /ˈhʌnər, ˈhʌŋɡər/ *v* **1** to suffer hunger *la14-*. **2** to subject to hunger; to starve *15-*. **hungered, hungert**, †**hungrit** starved-looking, famished *16-*. [OE *hyngran*]

hungin *see* HING[1.2]

hungir *see* HUNGER[1.1]

hungry, †**thungre** /ˈhʌngri/ *adj* **1** lacking food; famished, starving *15-*. **2** *of soil* barren, unproductive *la16-*. **3** mean, miserly; greedy *la19-*. **hungrysome 1** hungry, having a keen appetite *la19-*. **2** causing or stimulating hunger *19, 20- N EC*. [OE *hungrig*]

hungyr *see* HUNGER[1.1]

hunker /ˈhʌŋkər/ *v* **1** to squat *18-*. **2** to huddle; to sit or settle oneself in a crouching or cramped position *la18-*. **3** to stoop, submit; to resign oneself (to circumstances) *19-*. **hunker doon** to squat down *la18-*. [unknown; MDu *hucken*, ON *húka* to squat]

hunker-bane /ˈhʌŋkər ben/ *n* the thigh-bone *20- N NE T*. [HUNKER + BANE]

hunkers /ˈhʌŋkərs/ *npl* the haunches *la18-*. **on yer hunkers 1** in or into a squatting position *la18-*. **2** in a quandary; in reduced circumstances *19- T C SW*. [probably from HUNKER]

hunker slide /ˈhʌŋkər slʌid/ *v* **1** to slide on ice in a crouched position *19-*. **2** to evade a duty or a promise; to act in a shifty manner; to prevaricate *20-*. **hunker slider** a deceitful or undependable person *20-*. **hunker slidin** dishonourable, shifty or evasive behaviour *la19-*. [HUNKER + SLIDE[1.2]]

hunkle /ˈhʌŋkəl/ *n* a shrug *la19- Sh N*. [HUNCH[1.1], with *-le* suffix]

hunkse, hunks /hʌŋks/ *v* to lift, heave upwards, hoist *la19- Sh*. [variant of HUNCH[1.2]]

hunner[1.1], **hunder, hundred**, †**thundir**, †**hounder**, †**hundreth** /ˈhʌnər, ˈhʌndər, ˈhʌndrəd/ *numeral* **1** a hundred *la14-*. **2** *pl* an indeterminately large amount *la20-*. **3** a number of livestock or goods greater than 100 (usually 120) *16-19, 20- Ork H&I Bor*. **4** *in Orkney* a vegetable plot, enough ground for 100 plants *la18-19*. **5** *in weaving* a unit of measurement denoting the fineness of a web *18-19*. **get a hunder pound** to have a piece of good fortune, frequently a birth in the family *20- NE EC*. [OE *hundred* 100, ON *hundraþ* 120]

hunner[1.2], **hunder, hunert, hundred**, †**thundir**, †**hundreth** /ˈhʌnər, ˈhʌndər, ˈhʌnərt, ˈhʌndrəd/ *adj* hundredth *15-19, 20- Sh NE EC Bor*. [reduced form of Older Scots *hundredth*]

†**hunscot** *n* a name for a type of cloth made in southern Holland and Flanders *la16-e17*. [Du *honskote*]

hunse /hʌns/ *v* to hunt for; to rummage *la19- Sh*. [Norw dial *handska*]

hunt[1.1], †**hount** /hʌnt/ *n* **1** the action of hunting (wild animals); an organization which hunts (with hounds and horses) *la14-*. **2** a search *la19-*. †**hunthall** a hunting lodge *la15-e16*. †**Huntis up, Hunts up** the tune song or dance: 'The Hunt is up' *la15-17*. **hunt nor hare** nothing at all, not a vestige *la19- T C*. **neither hunt nor hare** = *hunt nor hare*. [see the verb]

hunt[1.2], †**hount** /hʌnt/ *v* to pursue, chase; to seek out or search about for *la14-*. **hunting**, †**ontyne 1** the practice or act of hunting *la14-*. **2** *pl* hunting-grounds *la15-17*. †**hunting hall** a hunting lodge *e18*. **hunt the staigie** a children's game in which one player has to catch the others *la19- NE*. [OE *huntian*]

huntegowk[1.1], **hunt the gowk** /ˈhʌntigʌuk, ˈhʌnt ðə gʌuk/ *n* **1** the game of April fool; a fool's errand *19-*. **2** April Fools' Day *la19-*. **3** a person sent on a fool's errand, an April fool *la19-*. [see the verb]

huntegowk[1.2], **hunt the gowk** /ˈhʌntigʌuk, ˈhʌnt ðə gʌuk/ *v* to go on a fool's errand; to be made a fool of, especially an April fool *18-19, 20- EC Bor*. [HUNT[1.2] + THE[1.2] + GOWK[1]]

huny *see* HINNIE[1.1], HINNIE[1.2]

hup[1.1], **hap** /hʌp, hap/ *v* **1** *of a horse in harness* to go to the right *19-*. **2** *of a driver* to command a horse to go to the right or speed up *19-*. **neither hup or wynd** to refuse to turn; to prove unmanageable or obstinate *18-19, 20- WC SW Bor*. [see the interj]

hup[1.2], †**hap** /hʌp/ *interj* **1** a command to a horse to speed up *19-*. **2** a command to a horse to turn right *la19-*. **hup aff** a command to a horse to turn right *20-*. **hup back** to come back, bearing right *20-*. [perhaps reduced form of *ho up* or *haud up*]

hupe *see* HOOP

huphallowday *see* UPHALIEDAY

huphally-evin *see* UPHALY-EVIN

huppo /ˈhʌpo/ *n* a frog or toad *la19- Ork*. [Norw dial *hopp*]

hur *see* HER[1.1], HER[1.2]

hurb /hʌrb/ *n* a rough or objectionable person; a mischievous child *la19- NE*. [unknown]

hurcheon, hurchin, *EC* **erchin**, †**hurcheoun**, †**hyrcheoune** /ˈhʌrtʃən; *EC* ˈɛrtʃən/ *n* **1** a hedgehog *la14-19, 20- C SW Bor*. **2** a scruffy, uncouth person *la16-19*. [ME *irchoun*, *hirchoun* a hedgehog]

hurd /hʌrd/ *n* **1** a boulder (on the seashore) *la19- Sh*. **2** a heap of peats *la19- Sh*. [Norw dial *urd* a heap of stones]

hurd *see* HIRD[1.1], HIRD[1.2], HUIRD[1.1], HUIRD[1.2]

hurdeis *see* HURDIES

hurdiekeckle, hurdie-caikle /ˈhʌrdikɛkəl, ˈhʌrdikekəl/ *n* a pain in the back and thighs caused by prolonged stooping *la19- NE SW*. [HURDIES + KECKLE[1.1]]

hurdies, †**thurdeis** /ˈhʌrdiz/ *npl* the buttocks; the hips, the haunches *16-*. **ower the hurdies** in difficulties, deeply in debt *la19- T WC*. [unknown]

hure *see* HOOR

hurk *see* HORK[1.2]

hurkill *see* HURKLE[1.2]

hurkle[1.1] /ˈhʌrkəl/ *n* **1** the hip, upper thigh or haunch *20- NE*. **2** a shrug *20- N*. **3** a hunchback *20- Sh*. **hurkle backit**

hunchbacked, misshapen *19- SW Bor*. **hurkle bane** the hipbone *18-*. [see the verb]

hurkle[1,2], *Sh* **hoorkle**, †**thurkill** /ˈhʌrkəl; *Sh* ˈhurkəl/ *v* **1** to crouch, huddle *16-*. **2** to walk in a hunched manner; to stumble or stagger *19- NE Bor*. **3** to submit, yield *19- NE T Bor*. **hurkle doon 1** to crouch down *la19-*. **2** to back down *20- NE*. [MLG *hurken*, with frequentative suffix]

hurkle[2] /ˈhʌrkəl/ *n* a horse-hoe (for weeding turnips) *19- WC Bor*. [HORK[1,2], with frequentative suffix]

hurkle[3] /ˈhʌrkəl/ *v* to make a gurgling or choking noise; to clear the throat *la19- Sh Ork*. [Norw *hurkla* to gurgle]

hurkly *see* HORKEL

hurl[1,1] /hʌrl/ *n* **1** a rush forwards or downwards *16-*. **2** a fall of stones or snow; an onrush of wind or water *16-*. **3** a ride in or on a wheeled vehicle *la18-*. **4** a violent altercation; a scolding *17-e19*. **5** a wheelbarrow *16-17*. **hurl barra**, *Sh* **hurl borro**, †**hurl barrow** a wheelbarrow; a handcart *16-*. †**hurle bed** a low bed on wheels *17*. †**hurle behind** diarrhoea *16*. **hurlygush** a noisy rush of water *19, 20- literary*. [see the verb]

hurl[1,2] /hʌrl/ *v* **1** to throw with force *15-*. **2** to convey in a wheeled vehicle; to drive or move along on wheels *la16-*. **3** to dash, hurtle, tumble *la15-19, 20- Sh EC*. **4** *of a ball* to roll *19- EC*. [ME *hurlen*]

hurl[2,1] /hʌrl/ *n* **1** a rumbling or grating noise; thunder *la18- Sh Ork NE T*. **2** wheezing *20- Sh Ork N NE*. **3** the death rattle *20- Ork N NE*. **4** a gurgling sound in the throat *20- Sh*. **5** monotonous, meaningless talk *20- Sh*. **hurlie** congested with phlegm *20- N NE T*. [see the verb]

hurl[2,2] /hʌrl/ *v* **1** to wheeze *20- Sh Ork NE T*. **2** *of moving water* to crash or rumble *20- Sh N Uls*. [probably onomatopoeic; compare Faer *hurla* to rumble]

hurl[3] /hʌrl/ *n* a coarse Dutch tobacco or shag formerly smoked in Shetland *20, 21- historical*. [unknown]

hurle *see* HURLIE[1]

hurless /ˈhʌrləs/ *adj* exhausted *19- Sh*. [perhaps Norw *hør* to hear, with *-less* suffix]

hurlie[1], **hurly**, †**thurle** /ˈhʌrle, ˈhʌrli/ *n* **1** a wheelbarrow, a handcart *19-*. **2** a low bed on wheels *la19-*. **3** a child's home-made cart *20-*. **4** *mining* a wheeled box for carrying coal *19*. **hurlie barrow** a wheelbarrow *la18-*. **hurlie bed** a low bed on wheels *la19-20, 21- historical*. **hurly cart 1** a child's home-made cart *20-*. **2** a common cart *e16*. †**hurlie hacket**, **hurly hakcat 1** sledging, tobogganing *16-19*. **2** a sledge; a poor-quality carriage *e19*. [HURL[1,1], HURL[1,2]]

hurlie[2], **hurley** /ˈhʌrle, ˈhʌrli/ *interj* a call to cows to come to be milked *19- SW*. **hurlie hawkie** = HURLIE[2] *19- SW*. [unknown]

hurly hinmaist /ˈhʌrli hʌɪnmest/ *n* the last, the hindmost *la19- NE T*. [first element unknown; compare HINMAIST[1,1]]

hurn *see* HIRNE

huron *see* HERN

hurr[1,1] /hʌr/ *n* a whirring or wheezing sound; the purr of a cat *20- Sh*. [onomatopoeic]

hurr[1,2] /hʌr/ *v* to make a whirring sound; to purr *la19, 20- Ork N*. [see the noun]

hurr[1,3] /hʌr/ *interj* a purring or murmuring sound expressing pleasure or contentment *19, 20- Sh*. [see the noun]

hurrack, *Ork* **hurro** /ˈhʌrək; *Ork* ˈhʌro/ *n* a part of a boat between the after-thwart and the stern *la19- Sh Ork*. [unknown]

hurrie *see* HURRY[2]

hurro *see* HURRACK, HURROO[1,1], HURROO[1,2], HURROO[1,3]

hurrok *see* HORRA-GOOSE

hurroo[1,1], *Sh* **hurro**, *NE* **hiree**, *NE T C* **haroosh** /həˈru; *Sh* həˈro; *NE* həˈri; *NE T C* həˈruʃ/ *n* a high-spirited, disorderly gathering; a tumult, an uproar *19-*. [see the verb]

hurroo[1,2], *Sh* **hurro** /həˈru; *Sh* həˈro/ *v* to urge on with shouts *la19- Sh Uls*. [onomatopoeic; compare Norw dial *hurra* to buzz, rush about noisily]

hurroo[1,3], *Sh* **hurro** /həˈru; *Sh* həˈro/ *interj* a cry of excitement; a rallying cry *19, 20- Sh*. [see the verb]

hurry[1,1] /ˈhʌri/ *n* **1** haste *18-*. **2** a disturbance or riot, a quarrel; commotion *18-*. **3** a rush of work, an exceptionally busy time *19-*. **4** a scolding *19- NE C*. **hurry burry**, *C Bor* **hurry gurry** a tumult; confusion *18-*. **in a hurry** suddenly, unexpectedly *la19-*. **tak yer hurry** to take your time *la19-*. **tak yer hurry in yer han** to take your time *la19- NE C Uls*. [EModE *hurry*]

hurry[1,2] /ˈhʌri/ *v* to rush, move quickly; to hasten someone along *la17-*. **hurried** harassed, hard-pressed *la19-*. [see the noun]

hurry[2], **hurrie** /ˈhʌri/ *n* a toolbox *20- Sh*. [perhaps shortened form of HURRACK]

hurschle *see* HIRSEL[2,2]

hurt[1,1], *N T* **hort** /hʌrt; *N T* hɔrt/ *n* an injury; damage *la14-*. **hurtsome** hurtful, injurious *la16-*. [ME *hurt*]

hurt[1,2], *N T* **hort** /hʌrt; *N T* hɔrt/ *v pt* **hurtit**, **hurt** to injure, damage, harm *la14-*. [ME *hurten*]

†**hurt-majeste** *n* treason *la14-e16*. [HURT[1,2] + MAJESTY, after LESE-MAJESTY]

hus, **hooze** /hus, huz/ *v* to rock or swing (a child) *20- Sh Ork N*. [Norw dial *hussa*]

husband /ˈhʌzbənd/ *n* **1** a married man *la14-*. **2** a farmer; a manorial tenant who had a holding in land in addition to his homestead *la13-e17*. **husbandry 1** farming *16-*. **2** the holding or letting of land as or to a manorial tenant *15-e16*. **3** the land occupied by manorial tenants *la14-15*. **husband-land** a measure of arable land, originally the land-holding of a manorial tenant *la15-19, 20- historical*. **husbandman 1** a farmer *15-*. **2** a manorial tenant *15-e17*. †**husband town** (one of a number of) homesteads occupied by a *husbandman*; a hamlet, a farm-steading *la14-17*. [ON *húsbóndi*]

husche paidill *see* HUSH PADLE

huschou *see* HUSH[2,1]

huse *see* HOOSE[1,1], HOOSE[1,2]

hush[1,1] /hʌʃ/ *n* **1** the sound of swiftly moving water; splashing *la19-*. **2** an onrush of people *la18-19, 20- Sh EC Bor*. **3** a large quantity; an abundance *19, 20- Sh NE Bor*. **4** a whisper, a slight sound; a rumour *19, 20- NE T*. **5** an ungainly, slovenly person *la19- NE*. **6** the sound of a swell in the sea *la19- Sh*. [onomatopoeic]

hush[1,2] /hʌʃ/ *v* **1** *of water* to rush or gush *19, 20- Sh Uls*. **2** to throw together or bundle up carelessly *19, 20- Sh EC*. [see the noun]

hush[2,1] /hʌʃ/ *n* a cry to frighten off birds or animals *la19- Sh N T Uls*. **huschou** a cry to frighten off birds *la19- NE*. [a natural utterance; compare Eng *shoo*]

hush[2,2] /hʌʃ/ *v* to scare away; to drive off birds or animals *18-*. [see the noun]

hushaby *see* HISHIE-BA[1,1]

hushad *see* HOOSEHOLD

hushie *see* HISHIE[1,1], HISHIE[1,2]

hushie-baa *see* HISHIE-BA[1,2]

hushion *see* HOSHEN

hushlach[1,1], **hooshlich**, †**hashloch** /ˈhʌʃləx, ˈhuʃləx/ *n* a confused heap, a tangled mass; a loose quantity *19, 20- NE EC*. [HUSH[1,1] or HUSHLE[1,1], with diminutive suffix]

hushlach[1,2], **hooshlach** /ˈhʌʃləx, ˈhuʃləx/ *adj* hurried, careless, slovenly *la19, 20- NE*. [see the noun]

hushle[1,1] /ˈhʌʃəl/ *n* **1** an untidy, carelessly-dressed person *20- Sh N NE SW*. **2** a heap; an unruly crowd *la19- Sh N NE*. **3** a

rustling sound *la19- N*. **4** an idle or incapacitated person *19, 20- N*. [frequentative form of HUSH¹·¹]
hushle¹·², *Bor* **hussle** /ˈhʌʃəl; *Bor* ˈhʌsəl/ *v* **1** to fidget; to move about awkwardly or restlessly *la18- NE*. **2** to work or dress in a careless or slovenly way *la19- Sh NE WC*. **3** to shrug *19, 20- Bor*. [see the noun]
hushle²·¹ /ˈhʌʃəl/ *n* a strong, drying, gusty wind *20- Sh Ork SW*. [see the verb]
hushle²·² /ˈhʌʃəl/ *v of wind* to blow in gusts *20- Sh Ork N Uls*. [onomatopoeic; compare Norw dial *hosa* to whistle, rustle]
husho /ˈhʌʃo/ *n* a shellfish such as *Mya arenaria 20- Ork*. [unknown]
hush padle, †**husche paidill** /ˈhʌʃ padəl/ *n* the lump-fish *Cyclopterus lumpus la16-19, 20- NE*. [perhaps Du *haasje* the lump-fish + PAIDLE³]
husk /hʌsk/ *v* to cough violently *19, 20- WC Bor*. **huskit** hoarse *la19- EC*. [unknown]
husky /ˈhʌski/ *adj of weather* rough, stormy *20- Sh Ork*. [compare Norw dial *huska* to shudder with cold, Swed *huska* to be raw and cold (of weather)]
†**huslyng** *n* violent shaking, clashing *e16*. [unknown; compare MDu *hutselen* to shake violently]
husnae *see* HAE¹·²
hussle *see* HUSHLE¹·²
hussock *see* HASSOCK
hussy *see* HIZZIE
husta /ˈhʌstə/ *interj* an expression of surprise, remonstrance or alarm *la18- NE*. [unknown]
hustack /ˈhøstək/ *n* a large, fat woman *20- Sh*. [Norw *høystakk* haystack]
hut¹·¹, *SW Bor* **hote**, †**hot**, †**howit**, †**huit** /hʌt; *SW Bor* hot/ *n* **1** a basket or pannier for carrying manure or earth *la16-19, 20- SW*. **2** a small heap of manure distributed over a field in preparation for spreading *la17-19, 20- C SW Bor*. **3** a small, temporary stack of corn *17-19, 20- NE T C SW Uls*. **4** a lazy person *19*. [ME *hotte*]
hut¹·², *SW Bor* **hot** /hʌt; *SW Bor* hɔt/ *v* **1** to stack sheaves in a field *la18- T C SW Bor Uls*. **2** to heap up or heap together; to shovel out in heaps *19- EC SW Bor*. [see the noun]
hut² /hʌt/ *n* **1** a (wooden) structure for temporary or casual accommodation or storage *18-*. **2** *in Edinburgh* a smaller second house built in the grounds of a larger mansion and occupied as a town or suburban house by wealthy families *la18-19*. [Fr *hutte*]
hut *see* HIT¹·², IT
hutch¹·¹ /hʌtʃ/ *n* **1** a chest, a box; a pen or coop for small animals *15-*. **2** *mining* a wheeled box for carrying coal *la17-20, 21- historical*. **3** a small, temporary stack of corn *19- WC SW Bor*. **4** an embankment *19- Bor*. **5** a small heap or pile of dung *la18-e19*. [MFr *huche*]
hutch¹·² /hʌtʃ/ *v* to set sheaves of corn in small temporary stacks to dry *20- WC SW*. [see the noun]
hute *see* HOOT¹·¹
huter *see* HOOTER
huther *see* HUDDER¹·¹, HUDDER¹·²
hutherie *see* HUDDERIE
hutherin *see* HUDDERIN
†**hutheron, huddroun** *n* (the skin or meat of) a heifer *la16-e19*. [unknown]
hutten, huttit *see* HIT¹·²
huttok *see* HAT¹
huv *see* HAE¹·²
huve *see* HOVE¹·², HUIVE
huvnae *see* HAE¹·²
huz *see* US
hwn *see* HUNE¹·¹

hwny *see* HINNIE¹·¹
†**hy, hye** *n* haste, speed *la14-16*. **in hy** quickly, in haste *la14-16*. [from the ME verb *hie* to hasten]
hy *see* HEY⁴
hyaave *see* HAW²
hych *see* HITCH¹·²
hychle *see* HECHLE¹·²
hycht *see* HEICHT¹·¹
hyd *see* HIDE¹, HIDE²
hyddyllis *see* HIDDILLIS
hyde *see* HIDE¹
hye *see* HY
hyew *see* HOW¹·¹
hyke /hʌɪk/ *v* **1** to move with a jerk *19- T SW Uls*. **2** to sway or rock; to swing *la19, 20- T SW*. [unknown]
hyll *see* HILL¹
hylt *see* HILT¹
hymn, hympne *see* HIME
hyn *see* HYNE
hynd *see* HINT¹·²
hyndir *see* HINNER¹
hyne, †**hyn**, †**hind** /hʌɪn/ *adv* **1** *of a place* far off, at a distance *la14-*. **2** *of time* far on, late *20- NE*. **3** from this world or life *la14-16*. **4** *of time* henceforth, thenceforth *15-16*. **hindie** far away, distant *20- NE*. †**fra hyne** far away, distant *la14-16*. †**fra hyne furth** henceforth *la14-e17*. †**fra hyne furthwart** henceforth *e15*. **hyne awa** *adj* distant *la19-*. **hyne awa** *adv* far away, at a great distance *19-*. **merry hyne tae ye** good riddance to you *19- NE*. [perhaps altered form of ME *hethen* or OE *heonon* hence]
hyne *see* HIND¹
hyngyt *see* HING¹·²
hynt *see* HENT²
hyoch *see* HEUCH¹·¹
hyog /hjog/ *n* one of the loops of straw with which a basket is made *20- Sh*. [ON *auga* an eye]
hyook *see* HEUK
hyow *see* HOW¹·¹
hypal /ˈhʌɪpəl/ *n* a person or an animal in poor condition *la18-19, 20- NE T SW Bor*. [unknown]
hype /hʌɪp/ *n* a large, unattractive person *la19- N NE*. [variant of HEAP¹·¹]
hypocras *see* YPOCRAS
hypocreet, heepocreet, hypocrite, †**ypocrit,** †**ypocreit** /ˈhɪpəkrit, ˈhipəkrit, ˈhɪpəkrɪt/ *n* a charlatan, a hypocrite *la14-*. [ME *ipocrite*]
hypothec, hypotheck, apotheck, †**ypothec,** †**ipothek** /hɪˈpɔθək, haeˈpɔθək, əˈpɔθək/ *n law* the right of a creditor to hold the effects of a debtor as security for a claim without taking possession of them *la15-*. **the hale hypothec, the haill apotheck** the whole business or concern *19-*. [MFr *hypotheque* a deposit, a pledge]
hypothecate /hɪˈpɔθəket, haeˈpɔθəket/ *v law* to give, take or pledge as security; to mortgage *17-*. **hypothecation** pledging *la17-*. [derivative of HYPOTHEC]
hyrcheoune *see* HURCHEON
hyre *see* HIRE¹·¹, HIRE¹·²
hyring *see* HIRING
hyrn *see* HIRNE
hyronius *see* HERONIOUS
hyrst *see* HIRST
hyrsyl *see* HIRSEL²·²
hys *see* HISH¹·¹
hyse *see* HEEZE¹·¹, HEEZE¹·²
hyste *see* HEIST¹·¹, HEIST¹·²
hyt *see* HIT¹·²

hyte¹ /hʌɪt/ *adj* **1** mad, insane; highly excited, enraged *la18-19, 20- literary*. **2** excessively or passionately keen *la18- WC*. **gae hyte** to go mad with rage or passion; to fly into a hysterical state *18- N SW*. [unknown]

hyte² /hʌɪt/ *interj* a call to a horse *la19- EC*. [a natural utterance; compare ME *hait*]

hyter¹·¹, **heyter** /ˈhʌɪtər, ˈhetər/ *n* **1** a lurch, a stumble *la19- NE*. **2** a stupid person *19- NE*. [unknown]

hyter¹·², **heyter**, **hoiter** /ˈhʌɪtər, ˈhetər, ˈhɔɪtər/ *v* to stagger or lurch; to stumble or trip *la19- NE T C*. [unknown]

hyter¹·³ /ˈhʌɪtər/ *adv* **1** with a weak or uncertain stumbling step *19- NE T*. **2** in a state of ruin *19- NE T*. [unknown]

hythe /haeð/ *n* a harbour, a landing place, an inlet among rocks; compare HIVE *18- NE*. [OE *hȳþ*]

hyveral *see* HAIVEREL¹·¹

hyvis *see* HIVES

hyzie *see* HEEZE¹·¹

I

i /i/ *n* a spring, a source of water *20- Sh.* [variant of EE¹]

I *see* AH

i' *see* IN¹·⁴

ibane *see* IBONE

Ibernien *see* HIBERNIAN¹·¹

†**Iberyne** *adj* Spanish *e16*. [Lat *Ibēria*, with adj-forming suffix]

†**ibone, ibane** *n* ebony *la16-17*. [Lat *ebenus*]

ic *see* AH

ice, †**yce** /ʌɪs/ *n* frozen water, (a sheet of) ice *la15-*. **ice-lowsing** a thaw *20- Ork SW*. **ice-stane** a curling stone *19- T C*. **ice-tangle** an icicle *19- NE T EC*. [OE *īs*]

ice schockle, iceshoggle *see* EESHOGEL

†**ichone** *adj* each one *15-e16*. Compare ILKANE¹·¹. [YCH + *one* (ANE¹·¹)]

-ick *see* -OCK

icker *see* AICHER

icksy-picksy *see* EEKSIE-PEEKSIE

iconomus *see* OECONOMUS

idaia /aeˈdeə/ *n* an idea *la19- NE T SW*. [altered form of Eng *idea*]

idand *see* EIDENT

idder *see* ITHER¹·¹, ITHER¹·², ITHER¹·³

idi *see* ITHY

idill *see* IDLE

idilsett *see* IDLESET¹·¹

idilteth *see* IDLE

idiocy, idiot *see* EEJIT

idiotical /ɪdeˈɔtɪkəl/ *adj* stupid *la18-*. [Lat *idiōticus* uneducated]

†**idiotry, ydeotry** *n law* idiocy, the inability to conduct one's own affairs because of mental weakness *la15-19*. [idiot (EEJIT), with noun suffix]

idiwut *see* EEJIT

idle, †**idill,** †**ydil** /ˈʌɪdəl/ *adj* unemployed, not working, lazy; unused *la14-*. **idledom** idleness *20- Ork N*. **idlety,** †**ydilteth** idleness *16-19, 20- Ork NE*. [OE *īdel* empty]

idleset¹·¹, *Sh NE* **idlesee**, *NE* **idleseat,** †**idilsett** /ˈʌɪdəlsɛt; *Sh NE* ˈʌɪdəlsi; *NE* ˈʌɪdəlsɪt/ *n* **1** idleness, laziness *la16-*. **2** unemployment, lack of work *la19, 20- NE WC Bor*. [IDLE + SET¹·¹]

idleset¹·², *NE* **idleseet** /ˈʌɪdəlsɛt; *NE* ˈʌɪdəlsɪt/ *adj* idle, lazy *19, 20- NE*. [see the noun]

idlety *see* IDLE

idol, idole, idoleeze *see* EEDOL

†**idoneus** *adj* fit, competent, suitably qualified *16-e17*. [Lat *idōneus*]

-ie¹**, -y** /i, e/ *suffix with names* forming diminutives, with shades of familiarity or affection; *with common nouns* forming diminutives; as a meaningless informal suffix, especially in the North-East *15-*. [perhaps OFr *-i, -é* in personal names]

-ie²**, -y** /i, e/ *suffix forming adjectives* full of the quality expressed in the root noun: ◊*clartie* ◊*skeely 16-*. [OE *-ig*]

-ie³**, -y** /i, e/ *suffix forming nouns from adjectives* signifying a person or thing having the quality expressed by the adjective: ◊*daftie* ◊*saftie la19-*. [extension of -IE¹]

ieroe *see* EEROY

ieshan *see* EESHAN

ievell *see* JEVEL

igg *see* EGG²

ignorant¹·¹ /ˈɪɡnərənt/ *n* an ignorant person *la15-*. [see the adj]

ignorant¹·²**, iggerant** /ˈɪɡnərənt, ˈɪɡərənt/ *adj* **1** lacking knowledge, uninformed, uneducated *la15-*. **2** ill-mannered, presumptuous *la19-*. [ME *ignoraunt*, Lat *ignorans*]

I-I /ˈae ae/ *interj* an exclamation of denial or protest *20- Sh*. [unknown]

ik *see* AH

iland *see* ISLAND

ile¹·¹**, oil, ulyie,** *Sh* **uilie,** *NE* **eelie,** †**olʒe,** †**oyll,** †**ule** /ʌɪl, ɔɪl, ˈulji; *Sh* ˈuli; *NE* ˈili/ *n* **1** oil *la14-*. **2** an oil lamp *la18-*. **uilie bunkie** a tub for holding oil *la19- Sh*. **uilie collie** an oil lamp *la19- Sh*. **oil colour,** †**oyle cullour** oil paint *la15-*. **uilie cruisie** an oil lamp *19, 20- T*. †**oil dolive, oyle de olive, ule doly** olive oil *la15-17*. **eelie dolly 1** an oil lamp *la19- NE*. **2** oil of any kind *19*. **uilie kig** an oil barrel *19- Sh*. †**ulie petir** rock oil, petroleum *la16*. **uily pig** a container for oil *la17-19, 20- Sh*. **uilie pot** an oil barrel *la19, 20- Sh*. †**the oly well, the oylie well** a well, dedicated to St Catherine, near Edinburgh from which oil flowed *la15-e17*. [ME *oil*]

ile¹·²**, oil** /ʌɪl, ɔɪl/ *v* to apply oil to, lubricate with oil *la16-*. [see the noun]

ile *see* AISLE, ALE¹·¹, EELA, ISLE

ileeven *see* ELEEVEN

ilest *see* EELIST

ilk¹·¹ /ɪlk/ *n* a family, a race; a kind, a type *la18-*. **that ilk 1** the same person, place or thing (already mentioned) *la14-*. **2** the same place, estate or name (distinguishing the head of a landed family in designations of landed proprietors): ◊*James of Dundas of that ilk; Grant of that ilk 15-*. **the ilk** the (very) same person or thing mentioned *la14-*. **this ilk** = *that ilk*. [OE *ilca* the same]

ilk¹·² /ɪlk/ *adj* same *la14-*. [see the noun]

ilk²·¹ /ɪlk/ *adj* each, every (of two or more) *la14-*. †**ilk dayis** *of clothes* worn everyday, not kept for Sunday or holiday best *la15-17*. †**ilk dele, ilk deill** altogether, entirely *la14-e16*. **ilk ither** each other, one another *la18-*. [OE *ǣlc* each]

ilk²·² /ɪlk/ *pron* each one, every one *15-*. [see the adj]

ilka, *NE* **ilkie,** *NE* **ilky** /ˈɪlkə; *NE* ˈɪlki/ *adj* each, every (of two or more) *la14-*. **ilka ane,** *NE* **ilkie een** each one, everyone *18-*. †**ilka dale, ilka dele** every whit, altogether, wholly, entirely *la14-e19*. †**ilka where** everywhere *19*. **ilka wye** everywhere *la19- NE*. **ilka body's body 1** a popular person, a friendly obliging person *la18-*. **2** *derogatory* a disingenuous person *20- NE EC*. **ilka sae lang** every so often, now and again *la18- NE T EC*. [ILK²·¹ + A¹]

†**ilka**² *adj* the same *15*. [substituted for ILK¹·² by analogy with ILK² and ILKA¹]

ilka day¹·¹ /ˈɪlkə de/ *n* a weekday *19, 20- NE T*. [ILKA¹ + DAY]

ilka day¹·² /ˈɪlkə de/ *adj* ordinary, everyday (as opposed to Sunday or festive) *19-*. **ilkaday claes** ordinary, everyday or working clothes *19-*. [see the noun]

ilkane¹·¹**,** *NE* **ilkeen,** †**ilkone** /ɪlkˈen; *NE* ɪlkˈin/ *pron* each one of two or more (people or things); everyone *la14-*. [ILK²·¹ + ANE¹·¹]

†**ilkane**¹·²**, ilkone** *adj* every *la14-e19*. [see the pronoun]

ilkie, ilky *see* ILKA¹

ill¹·¹**,** *NE* **ull** /ɪl; *NE* ʌl/ *n* **1** evil *la14-*. **2** harm, injury, mischief *la14-*. **3** illness, disease *la14-*. **4** misfortune, calamity *la14-*. **5** malice, hostility *20-*. **ill-ca'er** a detractor, a reviler *20- Sh EC*. **ill-daein, ill doing** wrong-doing, bad behaviour

la15-19, 20- Sh N NE T EC. **ill-daer** an evil-doer *18-.* **ill santafied** not carrying a blessing, failing to bring about spiritual change *la19- Sh Ork.* **ill-spaeker** a slanderer *la19- Sh.* **ill-tryvin** bad luck; the Devil, mischief *la19- Sh Ork.* †**for na ill** with no bad intention *la15.* **hadd i' ill** scorn, deride *20- Ork.* **ill thram** woe betide, confound *20- N.* [see the adj]
†**ill**[1,2] *v* to speak ill of, malign *15-e16.* [see the adj]
ill[1,3], *NE* **ull**, †**yl** /ɪl; *NE* ʌl/ *adj* 1 evil, wicked, depraved *la14-.* 2 malevolent; unfriendly, hostile *la14-.* 3 harsh, severe, cruel *15-.* 4 *of weather* bad, stormy *la15-.* 5 unfortunate, unlucky; wretched *la15-.* 6 *of language* bad, profane; abusive *la16-.* 7 difficult, troublesome: ◊ *it's ill carrying gudes up the stairs la16-.* 8 awkward, inexpert, clumsy *19-.* 9 unwholesome, harmful, noxious *la14-19, 20- Sh NE EC Bor.* 10 unsatisfactory, ineffective *la15-19, 20- Sh Ork NE.* 11 of poor quality, defective, scanty *16-19, 20- Sh NE Bor.* 12 *of coinage* counterfeit *la17-19, 20- Sh NE T*; compare WAUR[1,1], WARSE[1,2]. **ill-laek**, †**ill-like** 1 ugly *20- Sh.* 2 having the appearance of evil, suspicious-looking *la15-e18.* 3 sick-looking *17.* **ill-air** 1 unwholesome air, a cause of infection or illness *20- Sh.* 2 *mining* noxious gas *la17-19.* **ill-bist** a tendency to anger or bad temper, a bad disposition *20- Sh.* **ill-bistet, ill-bisted** awkward, bad-tempered *la19- Sh Ork.* **ill-bit** a poor, infertile piece of ground *20- EC SW Bor.* **ill-brew** an unfavourable opinion *la18- C SW.* **ill-cauld** a bad cold, a chill *la19- NE T.* **ill-chat** impudence *20- NE T C.* **ill-coloured** having a bad or unhealthy colour *18-.* **ill-deedie** mischievous, unruly, wicked *18-*; compare *evill dedy* (EVIL[1,2]). **ill-deedit** = *ill-deedie la18- N NE T WC.* **ill-dreid** grave suspicion, apprehension *19-.* **ill-ee** 1 *folklore* the evil eye, a malicious look with the power to do harm *17-19, 20- NE T H&I SW.* 2 dislike, ill-will *la19- Sh.* 3 a longing, a yearning for *20- NE T.* **ill-end** a miserable death *la19, 20- Ork.* **ill-fittit** bringing bad luck *la19- Sh NE Bor.* **ill-gab** insolent, impudent language *la19-.* **ill-gabbit** in the habit of using abusive language, foul-mouthed *la19-.* **ill-gaitedness** perverseness *19, 20- N NE T.* **ill-gate** a bad habit *la19- T EC.* **ill-gates** dissolute behaviour, mischievousness *la19- T.* **ill-gettit**, *NE* **ull-gaitit**, *EC* **ill-gitted** badly behaved, impolite; perverse *19-.* **ill-hairt, ill-haired** ill-tempered, surly *18-19, 20- SW Bor.* **ill-helt** an expression of annoyance; the Devil *la19- Sh Ork.* **ill-hertit** 1 malevolent *la18-.* 2 *of a corn-rick* not packed tightly enough in the centre *20- Ork N NE SW.* 3 greedy, mean *la19- NE.* **ill-hung-tee** awkwardly put together, clumsily built; dressed without care or taste *la19- Sh N NE SW.* **ill-hung thegither** = *ill-hung-tee.* **ill-jaw** coarse, abusive language; insolence *19, 20- Sh N NE T SW.* **ill-lair** a bad habit *20- N.* **ill-laits** bad habits; tricks *la18-.* **ill-mou** vile language, a disposition to use such language, an abusive tongue *19- NE.* **ill-mou'd** impudent, insolent, abusive *19- Sh NE T EC.* **ill-naiter, ill-nature** bad temper, irritability *18-.* **ill-naitered** bad-tempered, irritable *18-.* **ill-name** a bad name, a bad reputation *19-.* **ill-scathe**, †**yl scath** harm *la14, 20- Ork.* **ill-sneukit** disagreeable, malicious *la19- Sh Ork.* **ill-sonse** *in curses* bad luck *20- Sh.* **ill-speakin** slanderous talk *la19- Sh C.* **ill-thochtit** having evil or suspicious thoughts, nasty-minded *19- Sh Ork NE EC.* **ill-tongue** a malevolent or abusive tongue; bad language, abuse; slander *18-.* **ill-tongued** slandering, abusive, vituperative *la18-.* **ill-trickit** prone to play tricks, mischievous *18-.* **ill-vickit, ill-veekit** perverse, troublesome; malicious *la19- Sh Ork.* **ill-vik** a bad disposition *20- Sh.* **ill-wan** little or slight hope *la19- Sh.* **ill-wind** 1 scandal, slander *la19- NE.* 2 abusive language *la19- NE.* **gae an ill gate** to live an immoral life *19-.* **ill aboot** 1 desiring greatly, fond of *la18- NE T.* 2 vexed, sorrowful, annoyed *19-.* **ill at** 1 vexed at, sorrowful about *la19-.* 2 inexpert, awkward at *la19-.* **the ill bit** Hell *la19- SW.* **ill for** inclined to (a bad habit or evil behaviour) *19-.* **the ill man** the Devil *la17-.* **the ill pairt** Hell *la18-19, 20- NE.* **the ill place** Hell *19-.* **ill sicht be seen apo** *used as a curse* may the Devil take *19- Sh.* **ill tae dae til** difficult to please *20- Sh NE T.* **ill tae dae wi** = *ill tae dae til la19-.* **ill tae see** ugly *la19, 20- Sh T EC.* **the ill thief** the Devil *la18-.* **in ill tune** in a bad mood; temperamental *la16-.* **pit yer meat in an ill skin** to look thin or half-starved *19-.* **run an ill gate** = *gae an ill gate.* [ON *illr*]
ill[1,4], *NE* **ull** /ɪl; *NE* ʌl/ *adv* 1 badly, poorly; not well *la14-.* 2 severely, harshly *la14-.* 3 wickedly; wrongfully; unjustly *la14-.* 4 unfortunately, unprofitably *la15-.* **ill-able** unable, unfit *la19- Sh Ork.* **ill-aff** 1 miserable, ill-used *18-.* 2 poor *19-.* 3 perplexed, at a loss *19-.* **ill-bearin** intolerant *20- Sh EC.* **ill-cleckit** misbegotten *19- NE T C.* **ill-come** 1 ill-gotten *20- N NE T EC.* 2 illegitimate *20- NE.* **ill-contrived** 1 tricky, mischievous, badly-behaved *la19- Sh N NE T SW.* 2 contradictory, intractable *la19- Sh N NE.* 3 awkward, clumsy *la19- Sh SW.* 4 unfriendly *20- Ork.* **ill-daein, ill-doing** badly behaved, dissolute; not thriving *la19-.* **ill-daer** an animal that is not thriving *20-.* **ill-designed** evilly disposed, mischievously-minded *19- Sh NE T C.* **ill-dune, ill-done** wrong, badly-behaved, perverse, mischievous *19-.* †**ill-farandly** in poor condition *la15.* **ill-farrant** ugly, unkempt, unpleasant *19- NE EC Bor.* **ill-fashiont** quarrelsome, rudely inquisitive *19, 20- Sh NE.* **ill-faured, ull-faurt**, †**ill-fard** 1 ill-favoured; ugly, unbecoming *16-.* 2 poor in quality, unattractive, scruffy *la18-19, 20- Sh Ork NE T.* 3 ill-mannered, bad-tempered, coarse *19, 20- Ork NE T.* 4 unpleasant, horrible *19, 20- N SW.* 5 shabby, faded *20- Ork NE WC.* 6 unlucky *la19, 20- Sh.* 7 clumsy *19.* **ill-gaein** clumsy or awkward at walking due to deformity of the feet *20- Ork NE T.* **ill-gaishon'd** mischievous, ill-disposed *19- EC.* **ill-gien, ill-given**, †**ill gevin** ill-disposed, malevolent, stubborn, mean *la16-.* **ill-gotten** illegitimate *la17- Sh NE T SW.* **ill-greein** quarrelsome *20- N NE T C.* **ill-guide** to ill-use, maltreat *18-.* **ill-guideship** maltreatment, abuse *la19-.* **ill-guidit** 1 mismanaged *20-.* 2 badly brought up *la19-.* **ill-hauden** 1 oppressed, in difficulties *20 T SW.* 2 saved to no purpose, falsely economized *la19- NE.* **ill-hyvered** 1 bad-tempered, abusive *20- Ork N.* 2 awkward, ungainly *la19- Sh.* 3 having a blotchy complexion *20- Sh.* **ill-intendit** ill-disposed, with evil intentions *19- NE T.* **ill-kinded** cruel; having a wicked disposition *20- EC.* **ill-laired** *of a child* spoiled, badly-behaved *20- N.* **ill-likeit, Sh ill-laekit** unpopular *la19-.* **ill-looked-upon** held in disfavour, unpopular *la18, 20- Sh Ork EC.* **ill-marrowed** *of marriage partners* ill-matched *20- Sh NE.* **ill-minted** with mischievous intent *la19, 20- Sh Ork.* †**ill-muggent** malicious *la18-19.* **ill-pairtit** badly divided, shared out unequally *la19-.* **ill-peyd** extremely sorry *19- NE.* **ill-pit** in difficulties, baffled, hard pressed *20-.* **ill-pit on** badly dressed *la19-.* **ill-pretted** mischievous, naughty *19, 20- N.* **ill-run** going or running badly; cantankerous, grumpy *la18, 19- Ork.* **ill-run dyke** a fiasco *la19- NE T.* **ill-saired** not having had enough food at a meal *19, 20- NE.* **ill-scrapit** *of the tongue* slanderous, rude, bitter *la18-19, 20- Ork N NE T.* **ill-seen** unpopular, unwelcome *la19, 20- Sh.* **ill-shaken thegither** ungainly, shambling *20- NE.* **ill-shaken-up** untidy, disordered; awkward, clumsy; loutish *18-19, 20- Sh Ork NE.* **ill-snirled** *of children* peevish *20- Ork.* **ill-snored** bad-tempered, grumpy *20- Ork.* †**ill-sorted** upset *e19.* **ill-speakin**, *Sh* **ill-spaekin** given to repeating slander *17-19, 20- Sh C.* **ill-taen** taken amiss, resented *la18-.* **ill-thrawn** ill-natured, cantankerous *20- Sh Ork N SW.* **ill-thriven** badly-nourished, lean, scraggy *19-.* **ill-tongue** to vilify, abuse *la19- N NE.* **ill-towdent** poorly clad, neglected-looking;

unkempt *20- NE*. **ill-twartened** cross-grained, refractory *20- Sh Ork*. **ill-vamd** unpleasant, disagreeable (in smell or taste); malignant; perverse *la19- Sh*. **ill-whinnered** perverse, mean, malevolent *20- Ork*. **ill-yokit** ill-matched in marriage *la18-19, 20- NE*. **ill deen til** badly treated *20- NE*. **ill pit tae** in difficulties *la18-*; compare *hard pit tae* (HARD¹·²). **ill spoken o** slandered *la19- Sh T*. **tak ill wi** to take badly, find difficulty in *20-*. **tak it ill oot** to be upset at or offended by something *e18, la19- Ork N C Bor*. **tink ill o** to be sorry for *20- Sh*. [see the adj]

ill-best¹·¹ /'ɪl bɛst/ *n* the best of a bad lot *la19- Sh Ork NE T*. [see the adj]

ill-best¹·² /'ɪl bɛst/ *adj* least bad *17-19, 20- Sh Ork*. [ILL¹·³ + BEST¹·²]

illes, illess see ILL-LESS

ill-fain¹·¹ /'ɪl fen/ *v* to be unkind to; to look unfriendly or unpleasant *20- Sh Ork*. [see the adj]

ill-fain¹·² /'ɪl fen, 'ɪl fen/ *adj* ill-disposed towards, having a dislike of *20- Ork*. [ILL¹·⁴ + FAIN¹·²]

ill-less, illess, *NE* **ulless,** †**illes** /'ɪllɛs, 'ɪləs; *NE* 'ʌlɛs/ *adj* harmless, innocent, docile *la16-19, 20- Sh NE*. **ill-less guidless, ulless-guidless** lacking character, colourless *19, 20- NE*. [ILL¹·¹, with adj-forming suffix]

ill oor see ALOOR

ill set¹·¹ /'ɪl sɛt/ *v* to be unsuitable or inappropriate *la19- NE T EC*. **ill-setten 1** clumsy *la18, 20- Sh Ork*. **2** *of clothes* badly fitting *20- Sh*. [ILL¹·⁴ + SET¹·²]

ill set¹·² /'ɪl sɛt/ *adj* **1** unpleasant, harsh, cruel *la17-*. **2** surly, churlish, ungenerous *la19-*. **3** ungainly *20- Sh*. [see the verb]

illumine /ɪ'lumɪn/ *v* **1** to shed light on, (to cause) to become bright *15-*. **2** to illuminate manuscripts *e16*. **3** to enlighten, offer spiritual or intellectual enlightenment *la14-e16*. [OFr *illuminer*]

illustration, †**illustratioun** /ɪlə'strɛʃən/ *n* **1** a picture, an example; elucidation *la16-*. **2** (spiritual) enlightenment *la14-16*. [MFr *illustration*, Lat *illustrātio*]

ill-will¹·¹ /'ɪl wɪl/ *n* dislike, enmity, malevolence *la14-*. **hae an ill-will at** to dislike, take a dislike to *19-*. †**hae ill-will tae** = *hae an ill-will at la16-e19*. **tak an ill-will at** = *hae an ill-will at la19-*. [ILL¹·³ + WILL¹·¹]

ill-will¹·² /'ɪl wɪl/ *v* to wish evil to, hate *17-19, 20- NE*. **ill-willer,** †**ill-willar** a person who wishes evil on another *16-19, 20- N NE*. **ill-willed** hostile, disliking *19, 20- Sh*. [see the noun]

ill-willie, ill-willy, *NE* **ull-wullie** /'ɪl wɪli; *NE* 'ʌl wʌli/ *adj* **1** bad-tempered *16-19, 20- Sh Bor*. **2** grudging, unobliging, mean *18-19, 20- NE*. **3** unfriendly, hostile *19, 20- NE*. **4** malevolent, malignant *la15-e16*. Compare *evil willy* (EVIL¹·²). [ILL-WILL¹·¹ + -IE²]

ilsket, elsket /'ɪlskət, 'ɛlskət/ *adj* malicious, rude, irritable *la19- Sh*. [ON *ilska* wickedness, cruelty]

ilta, ilty /'ɪltə, 'ɪlte/ *n* anger, resentment, ill-will, spite, malice *19- Sh Ork*. **iltafu** angry, malicious, spiteful *19- Sh Ork*. [unknown]

image see EEMAGE

imaigine, imagine, †**ymagin,** †**ymagyn** /ɪ'medʒɪn, ɪ'madʒɪn/ *v* **1** to picture to oneself; to conceive, conjecture *la15-*. **2** to scheme, plot *15-16*. [ME *imaginen*]

imang see AMANG

†**imbazel, imbasil, embassel** *v* to embezzle *la17-e18*. [ME *embesilen*]

imbrace see EMBRACE¹, EMBRACE²

†**imbreve** *v* to write out in the form of a brief; to put in writing *la16*. [Lat *imbreviāre*]

imbring see INBRING

imbuik see INBUIK

ime /ʌɪm, im/ *n* **1** soot (on a pot or kettle) *19- Sh Ork N*. **2** scum *20- N*; compare EEM². **imet** *of colour* nondescript; dark, black *20- Sh*. **imy 1** sooty *la19- Sh Ork*. **2** *of the sky* dark *20- Sh*. [ON *ím* dust, ashes]

ime see EEM²

†**immatriculat** *adj* matriculated, registered as a student *17*. [ptp of Lat *immātrīculāre*]

immedantly, immidintly /ɪ'mɛdəntle, ɪ'mɪdəntle/ *adv* immediately *19- NE T C*. [altered form of Eng *immediately*, with intrusive *-n-* by analogy with words like *presently*]

immediate¹·¹, †**immediat** /ɪ'mɪdjət, ɪ'mɪdɪət/ *adj* **1** without delay; close, contiguous *la15-*. **2** *of inheritance* succeeding directly *15-*. †**immediat tennent** a lessee holding his lease directly from the feudal superior, the tenant-in-chief *16-e17*. [Lat *immediātus*]

†**immediate**¹·², †**immediat** *adv* **1** preceding or following without interval, next *la15-e16*. **2** *of feudal tenure or ecclesiastical rank* directly, without intermediary *e15*. [see the adj]

immen see BE

immer-goose, emmer-goose, ember-goose /'ɪmər gus, 'ɛmər gus, 'ɛmbər gus/ *n* the great northern diver *Gavia immer la17-19, 20- Sh Ork N SW*. [ON *himbrin* great northern diver + GUSE¹·¹]

immick see EEMOCK

immidintly see IMMEDANTLY

immis, eemis /'ɪmɪs, 'ɪmɪs/ *adj* **1** *of the weather* uncertain, gloomy, likely to rain *19, 20- NE*. **2** *of an object* insecurely balanced, unsteady *20- literary*. [ON *ýmiss* alternate, in turn, various]

†**immixtion** *n* = INTROMISSION *la17*. [Lat *immixt-*, ptp stem of *immiscere* to mingle, meddle]

immortal /ɪ'mɔrtəl/ *adj* eternal, everlasting *la15-*. **The Immortal Memory** the honorific speech in praise of Robert Burns given at Burns Suppers *19-*. [Lat *immortālis*]

immost see UMEST¹·²

immunity, †**immunitie** /ɪ'mjunəte/ *n* protection or exemption (from an obligation or penalty) *la15-*. **the immunitie of the kirk** the right of sanctuary in a church *e17*. †**immunitie of Tayne** (the area of) the sanctuary of St Duthac of Tain *15-e17*. [ME *immunite*, Lat *immūnitās*]

imock see EEMOCK

imp¹·¹, *Sh* **himp,** *EC* **hemp** /ɪmp; *Sh* hɪmp; *EC* hɛmp/ *n* **1** an offspring, a descendant *la16-*. **2** a cord of twisted horsehair forming part of a fishing-line, to which the hook is attached *18- Sh Ork N EC Bor*. **3** a young shoot or cutting of a plant, a sucker, a sapling *la15-19, 20- Bor*. **4** a small candle or taper *e16*. [OE *impa*]

imp¹·² /ɪmp/ *v* **1** to tie a twisted cord to a fishing-line *20- Ork Bor*. **2** to engraft; to implant *la15-19*. [OE *impian*]

impashe see IMPESCHE

impediment /ɪm'pɛdɪmənt/ *n* a hindrance, an obstruction, an obstacle *la14-*. **but impediment** = *without impediment*. †**mak impediment** *law* to offer hindrance, opposition or objection *15-e17*. †**without impediment** in legal precautionary formulae without obstruction, opposition or objection *la14-16*. [Lat *impedīmentum*]

imper¹·¹ /'ɪmpər/ *n* a murmur, a remark *20- Sh*. [see the verb]

imper¹·² /'ɪmpər/ *v* to make a sound or cursory remark; to hint *20- Sh*. [Norw dial *impra* to hint at]

†**imperatrice** *n* an empress *e16*. [MFr *imperatrice*, Lat *imperātrix*]

imperial, †**emperiall** /ɪm'pɪriəl/ *adj* **1** pertaining to an empire or emperor, originally the Roman or Holy Roman Empire *15-*. **2** supreme, excellent *16-*. [ME *imperial*, Lat *imperiālis*]

imperiour see EMPEROR

†**impertinat** *adj* improper; insolent *la15-16*. [altered form of Older Scots *impertinent*]

†**impesche, empesche, impashe** *v* to hinder or obstruct; to delay or prevent *16-e17*. [ME *empechen*]

impetrate[1.1], †**impetrat** /ˈɪmpɪtret/ *v* to obtain by request or formal application; *law* to obtain by fraud *la15-*. [Lat *impetrāre*]

†**impetrate**[1.2], **impetrat** *adj* **1** *law* gained or contrived by fraud *e18*. **2** obtained by petition or formal application to an authority *la15-17*. **3** obtained by request or solicitation *la16-17*. [Lat *impetrātus*]

imphm /ˈɪmhɪm/ *interj* an expression of assent, sarcastic agreement or hesitation *19-*. [onomatopoeic]

impident, impiddent, impudent /ˈɪmpɪdənt, ˈɪmpjudənt/ *adj* impertinent, cheeky; immodest *la16-*. **impiddence, impidence** insolence *18-*. [Lat *impudēns*]

impignorate, †**impignorat** /ɪmˈpɪgnəret/ *v ptp* **impignorated,** †**impignorat** to pawn, pledge, mortgage *la16-*. [Lat *impignorāre*]

impignoration, †**impigneracioun** /ɪmpɪgnəˈreʃən/ *n law* giving in pledge; pledging; mortgaging *la15-*. [Lat *impignorātio*]

impire see EMPIRE[1.1], EMPIRE[1.2]

impit see IMPUTE

implement[1.1] /ˈɪmpləmənt/ *n law* the fulfilment or execution of a contractual obligation *17-*. [Lat *implēmentum* a filling up]

implement[1.2] /ˈɪmpləmənt/ *v* to complete or execute (a contract or agreement); to fulfil (a condition or promise) *18-*. [see the noun]

implese see EMPLESE

†**imploy** *v* **1** to employ, hire *la16-18*. **2** to apply money to a particular purpose; to bestow, expend money *la16-17*. [MFr *employer*]

import /ɪmˈport/ *v* **1** to bring (goods) into the country from abroad *17-*. **2** to bring about, occasion *la16-19*. **3** to obtain for oneself, have: ◊*ye will import our special thanks la16*. [Lat *importāre*]

†**importable** *adj* unbearable, insupportable *la15-17*. [MFr *importable*, Lat *importābilis*]

importance /ɪmˈportəns/ *n* **1** significance *16-*. **2** income, revenue *e16*. [MFr *importance*]

†**importurate** *adj* depicted; adorned with pictures or carvings *e16*. [ptp of PORTURE, with intensifying prefix]

impreif see IMPREVE

†**imprent, emprent, enprent** *v* to print; to imprint, stamp; to fix indelibly; to keep in mind *la15-e17*. [ME *emprenten*]

†**impreson, emprisoun** *v* to imprison *la15-16*. [ME *emprisonen*]

†**imprestable** *adj* impossible to perform or discharge; impracticable *la17-19*. [PRESTABLE, with negative prefix]

†**impreve, impreif** *v* **1** to disprove a legal document as being forged or spurious *la15-e17*. **2** to refute an argument; to confute a person *16-e17*. **3** to repudiate; to disapprove, condemn *la15-16*. [Lat *improbāre*; compare IMPROVE, PRUIVE]

imprive see IMPRUVE

improbation, †**improbatioun** /ɪmproˈbeʃən/ *n law* disproof of a legal deed as invalid or forged; an action to annul a deed on these grounds *la16-*. [Lat *improbātio*]

improbative /ɪmˈprobətɪv/ *adj* liable to IMPROBATION; not proved to be true *la17-*. [Lat *improbāt-*, ptp stem of *improbāre*, with adj-forming suffix]

improper /ɪmˈprɔpər/ *adj* **1** incorrect, wrong *la16-*. **2** unsuitable, unfit; inappropriate *la16-*. **improper liferent** a LIFERENT where a trust holds property on behalf of a beneficiary *20-*.

†**improper wadset** a mortgage which entitled the creditor to a fixed sum derived from the property *la17-e19*. [PROPER[1.2], with negative prefix]

†**improve** *v law* to disprove *la15-e18*. [ME *improven*, Lat *improbāre*; compare IMPREVE]

improve see IMPRUVE

†**improvin** *adj* **1** *of legal deeds* proved to be forged or invalid *la16-17*. **2** *of people* convicted of forging documents *la16-e17*. [ptp of IMPREVE, IMPROVE]

impruve, impruive, improve, †**imprive** /ɪmˈpruv/ *v ptp* **impruved,** †**improvin** to make better, make profitable; to utilize to advantage *la17-*. [EModE *improve*]

impty see EMPY[1.1], EMPY[1.2]

impudent see IMPIDENT

impugn, †**impung** /ɪmˈpjun/ *v* **1** *law* to challenge the validity of a document *15-*. **2** to dispute the truth of; to criticize, censure or oppose *16-*. [MFr *impugner*, Lat *impugnāre*]

†**imput** *v pt, ptp* **imput, impute 1** to impose, bestow *15-e17*. **2** to levy a tax or tribute on *16*. [altered form of INPIT[2]]

imput see INPIT[1.2], INPUT

impute, †**imput** /ɪmˈpjut/ *v ptp* also †**imput,** †**impit** to lay blame, ascribe or attribute a fault or crime *la14-*. [OFr *emputer*, Lat *imputāre*]

imsh see NIMSH

in[1.1] /ɪn/ *n* **1** *pl* (one of) the sides in a children's game in possession of the goal or home, or whose turn it is to play *19, 20- Ork T EC*. **2** an entrance; an invitation or permission to enter *la19- NE*. [see the adv]

in[1.2] /ɪn/ *v* to bring (the harvest) in from the fields *la15-*. [see the adv]

in[1.3] /ɪn/ *adv* **1** towards a central place, inwards *la14-*. **2** in a position inside, within *15-*. **3** *omitting a verb of motion* (to go) in: ◊*the dog wants in 18-*. **4** *of a gathering or meeting* assembled, in session *19-*. **5** *of a debtor* in debt (to someone) *19-*. **6** *in golf* over the last nine holes of an 18-hole course *la19-*. **7** alert, attentive *20-*. **8** *of land* under crop, ploughed and sown *la18-19, 20- N SW Uls*. **9** *in major disputes* remaining on the side of established authority *la19*. **10** *preceding the verb* in, within: ◊*the place that he is first in set 15-16*. **in ablow** under *20- C Bor*. **in aboot** to or close to a person or place *la19- NE T*. **in and out 1** inside and outside, the whole of something, throughout, altogether *15-*. **2** *of motion or a journey* inwards and outwards, there and back *la15-*. **in laich** = *in tae yersel la19-*. **in o** *of motion or rest* in, into, inside *la18-*. **in tae yersel** under one's breath, in a whisper; soundlessly *la18-*. **in wi 1** (a command to) get in; push in: ◊*in wi ye! la19-*. **2** in debt with a creditor *20-*. [OE *in*]

in[1.4], **i'** /ɪn, ɪ/ *prep* **1** in, within *la14-*. **2** *of motion* into *la14-*. **3** *of place or position* on, upon, along *la14-*. **4** *of time* during, on, at *la14-*. **5** resident in, or tenant of (the place or farm named thereafter) *16-*. **6** *law* to the amount or extent of: ◊*fined in forty shillings 17-*. **7** with: ◊*provided in a living 18-*. **8** of: ◊*good in ye la18-19, 20- Sh*. **9** occupied with *la18, la19- Sh*. **10** through, because of (a person's fault or failure) *la14-16*. **in a mistake** in error, by mistake *19-*. **in a present** as a gift: ◊*see what I hae brought ye in a present 18-*. †**in presand** = *in a present la14-16*. **in remark** remarkable *20- Sh*. **in the road** along the road, in a direction near the speaker *19- N NE T EC*. **in't, in it** there, present, available: ◊*there's nae butter in it the day 19- N H&I Uls*. [see the adv]

in see AN[2], INN

-in[1], **-ing** /ɪn, ɪŋ/ *suffix* forming verbal nouns derived from verbs *12-*. [OE *-ing*]

-in[2], **-an,** †**-and** /ɪn, ən/ *suffix* forming the present participle and adjectives thus derived *12-*. [OE *-ende*]

in-aboot-comer /ɪnəˈbutkʌmər/ *n* a visitor, an immigrant *20-*. [*in aboot* (IN[1.3]) + COME[1.2], with agent suffix]

inact see ENACT

inadvertence /ɪnədˈvɛrtəns/ *n* negligence, carelessness *16-*. [MFr *inadvertance*, Lat *inadvertentia*]

inamal see ENAMEL

inamite see INIMITE

inane /ɪˈnen/ *adj* of no account, pointless; foolish *16-*. **inanity** emptiness (of ideas); vacuity *16-*. [Lat *inānis* empty]

†**inanimitie** *n* enmity, strife *la16*. [probably altered form of INIMITE]

inarme see ENARM

inawing see ANAWIN

inband /ˈɪnband/ *n building* a header, a stone placed through the width of a wall, a quoin or jamb stone *la18-*. [IN[1.3] + BAND[1.1]; compare *band-stane* (BAND[1.1]), OUTBAND]

inbearing /ˈɪnberɪŋ/ *adj* **1** officious, ingratiating, obsequious *19- NE T EC*. **2** meddlesome, intrusive *19- NE T EC*. **3** impressive, persuasive *la17*. [IN[1.3] + presp of BEAR[2]]

in below /ɪn bəˈlo/ *prep* under *19-*. **in below the bedfu** a large assortment of things (such as are frequently stored under a bed) *20- Bor*. [IN[1.3] + BELOW[1.3]]

†**inbering** *n* (the action of) carrying in *la16-e17*. [IN[1.3] + verbal noun from BEAR[2]]

inbi see INBY[1.2]

inbiggit, inbigget /ɪnˈbɪgɪt/ *adj* obstinate; morose, uncommunicative *20- Sh*. [IN[1.3] + ptp of BIG[1]]

inbö, inbu /ˈɪnbø, ˈɪnbu/ *n* a welcome *19- Sh*. [*in-* prefix + ON *bjóða* to offer, invite]

inbrace see EMBRACE[1]

†**inbreak** *n* a breaking in; intrusion by force; violation *la17-19*. [IN[1.3] + *break* (BRAK[1.2])]

inbring, †imbring /ˈɪnbrɪŋ, ɪnˈbrɪŋ/ *v pt* **inbrocht 1** to bring into or to a place, convey; to import *15-19, 20- NE T EC*. **2** to fetch in as prisoners; to arrest *la15-e19*. **3** to fetch in taxes or fines to the appropriate recipient or office, collect (payments) *la15-e18*. **4** *law* to seize or confiscate goods *la15-e18*. **5** to introduce, bring into use *la14-17*. **6** to cause, bring about *la14-16*. [OE *inbrengan*]

†**inbuik, imbuik** *v* to enter in a book; to record, enrol *la16-e17*. [IN[1.3] + BUIK[1.2]]

inbund /ˈɪnbʌnd/ *adj of a farm* hemmed in, having no access to hill land *20- Ork*. [IN[1.3] + ptp of BIND[1.2]]

inbusch see ENBUSCH

inby[1.1] /ˈɪnbae/ *adj* low-lying; inshore; *of farmland* close to the farm buildings *19- EC SW Bor*. [see the adv]

inby[1.2], **in by, inbye**, *Sh* **inbi**, *Sh Ork* **emby** /ˈɪnbae, ɪnˈbae; *Sh* ˈɪnbi; *Sh Ork* ˈɛmbi/ *adv* **1** (from outside to) inside; further in (a house or room); inland (from the coast) *17-*. **2** indoors, in the inner part (of a house), at someone's house *19-*. **3** on the farmland close to the farm buildings *20- N EC SW Bor*. [IN[1.3] + BY[1.1]]

inby[1.3] /ˈɪnbae/ *prep* close to, beside; in the neighbourhood of *la19, 20- NE EC*. [see the adv]

†**incarcer** *v* = INCARCERATE *la16-17*. [MFr *incarcerer*]

incarcerate, †incarcerat /ɪnˈkarsərət/ *v ptp* †**incarcerat** to imprison *la16-*. [Lat *incarcerāt-*, ptp stem of *incarcerāre*]

incast /ˈɪnkast/ *n* **1** something thrown in, an extra amount given by a seller in addition to the quantity stipulated *la18- T EC Bor*. **2** the action of putting forward or bringing in *17*. [IN[1.3] + CAST[1.2]]

†**incasting** *n* the action of putting or throwing in *la15-e18*. [IN[1.3] + verbal noun from CAST[1.2]]

incertitude /ɪnˈsɛrtɪtjud/ *n* uncertainty, insecurity, unpredictability *la15-*. [MFr *incertitude*]

inch[1], †**insh**, †**insch** /ɪnʃ, ɪntʃ/ *n* **1** a small island; frequently in place-names *la12-*. **2** a stretch of low-lying land near a river or other water, sometimes cut off at high tide; frequently in place-names *la15-*. **3** a piece of rising ground in the middle of a plain *la18-*. [Gael *innis* an island]

inch[2], †**ynsche** /ɪnʃ, ɪntʃ/ *n* a measure of length, the twelfth part of a foot *15-*. [OE *ynce*]

†**inchant, inshant** *v* to enchant *la16-e17*. **inchantment 1** the act or process of enchanting *la14-17*. **2** a method of enchanting, a spell or charm *la16-e17*. [ME *enchaunten*]

†**incident diligence** *n law* a warrant issued by a court to require the production of evidence in the possession of a third party *17-19*. [Older Scots *incident* + DILIGENCE]

incline, †enclyne /ɪnˈklʌɪn/ *v* **1** to bend, curve; to bow (down) *la14-*. **2** to be (favourably) disposed towards *la14-*. **3** to lean or slope (towards) *15-*. **4** to influence, direct *la15-*. [Lat *inclīnāre*]

inclose, enclose, †inclois /ɪnˈkloz, ɛnˈkloz/ *v* **1** to shut in; to surround, encircle *la14-*. **2** *law* to shut a jury in a room for consideration of the verdict *la17-*. **3** to include in a letter, send as an inclusion *la18-*. **4** *of a jury* to retire to consider the verdict *la17-18*. [CLOSE[1], with *in-* prefix]

income[1.1], †**incum** /ˈɪnkəm/ *n* **1** an entrance, arrival *la15-*. **2** a swelling or abscess, a festering sore *18-*. **3** an illness or infirmity with no obvious external cause *19-*. **4** a sharp attack of pain, a stitch in the side *la19-*. **5** a newcomer, a new arrival, especially one who comes to settle in a place *19*. [IN[1.3] + COME[1.2]]

income[1.2], †**incum** /ɪnˈkʌm/ *v ptp* **income** to come in, enter; to arrive in a new district; to take up a tenancy or post *15-*. [see the noun]

incomer, †incummer, †incumer /ˈɪnkʌmər/ *n* a stranger; an immigrant; an intruder *16-*. [INCOME[1.2], with agent suffix]

†**incoming**[1.1], **incuming, incummyn** *n* **1** arrival, entry; coming in *15-17*. **2** an invasion *la16-17*. **3** the entry of vessels into port *la15-e17*. [verbal noun from INCOME[1.2]]

incoming[1.2], **incomin, †incummand** /ˈɪnkʌmɪŋ, ˈɪnkʌmɪn/ *adj* **1** *of a person* newly arrived, succeeding (in a tenancy or post) *la18-*. **2** *of a period of time* about to begin, ensuing *19-*. **3** *of a title* available to the succession of an heir *la16*. [presp of INCOME[1.2]]

†**inconsumptive** *adj* incapable of being consumed *e16*. [ME *consumptife*, with negative prefix]

†**incontrare**[1.1], **incontrair** *adv* against, in opposition to *la15-16*. [IN[1.4] + CONTRAIR[1.1]]

†**incontrare**[1.2], **incontrair, incontrar** *prep* contrary to, in opposition to, against *la15-16*. [see the adv]

†**inconvenient** *n* **1** a (state or cause of) difficulty or disturbance; trouble, danger *15-17*. **2** (a) personal inconvenience; a logical difficulty *la15-e17*. [from the Older Scots adj *inconvenient*]

incorporate[1.1] /ɪnˈkɔrpərət/ *v* **1** to include in, add to, combine *la16-*. **2** *law* to formally constitute as a legal entity *la16-*. [see the adj]

†**incorporate**[1.2], **incorporat** *adj* **1** formally constituted as a corporation *18*. **2** incorporated, embodied *16-e17*. [ptp of INCORPORATE[1.1] or Lat *incorporāt-*, ptp stem of *incorporāre*]

incorporated /ɪnˈkɔrpərətəd/ *adj* **1** united as one; combined, included *la16-*. **2** constituted as a legal or formal corporation *la18-*. **Incorporated Trades** the trade associations in a burgh *la18-*. [ptp of INCORPORATE[1.1]]

incorporation, †incorporatioun /ɪnkɔrpəˈreʃən/ *n* **1** the act of incorporating *la15-*. **2** an association of craftsmen or tradesmen (with burgess rights and duties, and holding a monopoly of their craft in their burgh until 1846) *17-*. [Lat *incorporātio*]

†**incounsolabyll** *adj* refusing counsel or advice *e16*. [Older Scots *counsalabill* with negative prefix]

incountar see ENCOONTER[1.2]

incountrie see INCUNTREY

†**incre, inkyre** *adj* earnest, ardent *la14*. [unknown; compare INKIRLY]

†**incredule** *adj* unbelieving *16*. [Lat *incrēdulus*]

increly see INKIRLY

†**incres**[1.1], †**encres** *n* increase; advancement *la15-e17*. [see the verb]

†**incres**[1.2], †**encres** *v* to make or become greater, increase *15-17*. [ME *encresen*, Lat *incrēscere*]

incum see INCOME[1.1], INCOME[1.2]

incumer see INCOMER

incuming see INCOMING[1.1]

incummand see INCOMING[1.2]

incummer see INCOMER

incummyn see INCOMING[1.1]

†**incuntrey, incuntre, incountrie** *n* the inner part of a country, an inland district; the Scottish Lowlands *16-17*. [IN[1.3] + *country* (KINTRA)]

incurage, incurragment see ENCOURAGE

Inde see INDIE

Independent Companies /ɪndəˈpɛndənt ˈkʌmpəniz/ *npl* companies of Highland troops first recruited to keep order in the Highlands (formed in 1739 into the Black Watch) *e18, la18- historical*. [Scots *independent* + Scots *company*]

indevoir see ENDAIVOUR[1.1], ENDAIVOUR[1.2]

indew see ENDUE[1], ENDUE[2]

indict, †indick, †indyte, †indite /ɪnˈdʌɪt/ *v law* to accuse, charge with an offence *15-*. [ME *enditen*]

indictment, †indytment, †inditement /ɪnˈdʌɪtmənt/ *n law* a formal (written) charge or accusation; the form of process by which the accused is brought to trial at the instance of the LORD ADVOCATE *15-*. [ME *enditement*]

indie, †Indy, †Inde, †Ynd /ˈɪndi/ *n* 1 India rubber, natural rubber *la19-*. 2 India *la14-e19*. **Indie rubber** India rubber *20-*. [from the name of the country]

†**indigent** *n* a pauper *la16-e17*. [Lat *indigens*]

indigne see INDING

†**indilaitlie** *adv* immediately; without delay *la16-e17*. [*in-* prefix + MFr *dilater* to delay, with adv-forming suffix *-lie*]

indilling see ELDNYNG

†**inding, indyng, indigne** *adj* unworthy, undeserving *16-e19*. [MFr *indigne*, Lat *indignus*]

indiscreet, †indiscreit /ɪndəˈskrit/ *adj* 1 lacking discretion *16-*. 2 impolite, rude, uncivil *la17-19, 20- N NE*. **indiscreetly** impolitely *17-19, 20- NE*. [Lat *indiscrētus*]

indisgestion /ɪndɪsˈdʒɛstjən/ *n* indigestion *18-*. [altered form of Eng *indigestion*]

indite see INDICT

inditement see INDICTMENT

†**indoce** *v ptp* **indost** to endorse *16*. [ME *endosen*]

†**indors** *v* to endorse *la15-e17*. †**indorsation, indorsatioun** endorsement *la15-19*. [altered form of OFr *endosser*]

†**indorsate, indorsat** *adj* endorsed *la15-e17*. [Lat *indorsātus*]

indost see INDOCE

indow see ENDOO

indraught, *Sh NE* **indraacht,** *Ork* **indright** /ˈɪndraft; *Sh NE* ˈɪndraxt; *Ork* ˈɪndrʌɪt/ *n* 1 an intake of breath *20- Sh NE*. 2 encouragement; a promise of help *20- Sh Ork*. 3 a toll or duty collected at a port *e17*. [IN[1.3] + DRAUCHT[1.1]]

indrink /ˈɪndrɪŋk/ *n* shrinkage, diminution; evaporation *la17-19, 20- NE T EC*. [IN[1.3] + DRINK[1.1]]

induciae /ɪnˈdjuʃie/ *npl law* the period of time between a citation to appear in court and the date fixed for the hearing *18-*. [Lat *indūtiae* truces, delays]

induct /ɪnˈdʌkt/ *v* 1 to admit formally *la18-*. 2 *Presbyterian Church* to install a minister in a parish *19-*. [Lat *induct-*, ptp stem of *indūcere*]

induction, †inductioun /ɪnˈdʌkʃən/ *n* 1 introduction, initiation *16-*. 2 *Presbyterian Church* the act and ceremony of installing a minister in a parish *19-*. 3 inducement *la15*. [MFr *induction*, Lat *inductio*]

induellar see INDWELLER

indulge /ɪnˈdʌldʒ/ *v* 1 to treat with favour; to gratify; to spoil; to yield to desire *17-*. 2 to grant Presbyterian ministers a licence to conduct services *18- historical*. **indulgence** 1 *Roman Catholic Church* remission of sins *15-*. 2 kindness, favour; extravagance *16-*. 3 a licence permitting Presbyterian ministers to conduct services on condition of their recognition of episcopal authority and royal supremacy in the Church *la17, 18- historical*. [Lat *indulgēre*]

†**indult** *n* a special privilege, licence or permission (granted by the Pope) *la15-16*. [Lat *indultum*]

indurand, induring see ENDURAND

industrial /ɪnˈdʌstrɪəl/ *adj* 1 *law* brought about by the industry of man *la18-*. 2 pertaining to industry *la19-*. [Fr *industriel*]

indwell, †indwel /ˈɪndwɛl/ *v* to reside, remain in; to inhabit a place *15-19, 20- NE*. [IN[1.3] + *dwell* (DWALL[1])]

indweller, indwaller, †induellar /ˈɪndwɛlər, ˈɪndwalər/ *n* a resident, inhabitant *15-*. [INDWELL, with agent suffix]

Indy see INDIE

indyng see INDING

†**indyte**[1.1], **endite** *n* composition; (style of) writing *16*. [see the verb]

†**indyte**[1.2], **endite** *v* to put into writing, compose (verse) *la15-e17*. [ME *enditen*]

indyte see INDICT

indytment see INDICTMENT

ine see EN[1.1], OAVEN

inemite see INIMITE

inemy see ENEMY

ineuch see ENEUCH[1.2]

inew see ENEW[1.1], ENEW[1.2]

inewch see ENEUCH[1.3]

infa, infall /ˈɪnfɔ, ˈɪnfa, ˈɪnfɔl/ *n* 1 the inflow of a river, a confluence *17, 20- NE*. 2 a junction of two roads *20- NE*. 3 a wedge *20- Sh*. 4 an incursion, a raid *17*. [IN[1.3] + FA[1.1]]

†**infame**[1.1] *n* an infamous person *15-16*. [see the adj]

†**infame**[1.2] *adj* infamous *16*. [MFr *infame*, Lat *infāmis* of ill repute]

†**infamite** *n* infamy *la15-16*. [MFr *infameté*]

†**infang** *n law* theft committed within the boundaries of a manor or estate *16-19*. Compare OUTFANG. [shortened form of INFANGTHIEF]

infangthief /ˈɪnfaŋθif/ *n law* the right of the lord of a manor to try and to punish a thief arrested on his property *la12-e18, la18- historical*. Compare OUTFANGTHIEF. [OE *infangeneþēof*]

infare /ˈɪnfɛr/ *n* 1 the feast given by the bridegroom to celebrate the coming of his bride to her new home; the day after the wedding *la16-19, 20- historical*. 2 entry into a new situation in life *e19*. 3 an entertainment on entering a new house *la14*. **infar-cake** a piece of oatcake or shortbread broken over the head of a bride as she enters her new home *la19, 20- historical*. [OE *infaer* an entrance]

infeck, infect, †infek /ɪnˈfɛk, ɪnˈfɛkt/ *v ptp* †**infect** to contaminate with a disease; to poison; to pollute; to affect, taint *la14-*. [Lat *infect-*, ptp stem of *inficere*]

†**infeff, enfeff** *v* = INFEFT *la14-e15*. [OFr *enfeffer*]

infeft /ɪnˈfɛft/ *v pt* **infeft** 1 *law* to invest a person with legal possession of heritable property *15-*. 2 *law* to assign property by INFEFTMENT *la15-17*. [ptp of INFEFF]

infeftment, †**enfeftment** /ɪnˈfɛftmənt/ **1** *law* the investing of a new owner with legal possession of land or heritage by registration of the deed of transfer (originally accomplished by a symbolic act) *15-*. **2** *law* the document which conveys this right *15-*. †**infeftment in security** *law* temporary infeftment of a creditor in heritable property as security against a loan or debt *18-e19*. [INFEFT, with noun-forming suffix]

infeild *see* INFIELD

infek *see* INFECK

†**infeodacione, infeodation** *n* = INFEFTMENT *la15-16*. [Lat *infeodātio*]

infer /ɪnˈfɛr/ *v* **1** to deduce *la15-*. **2** to imply *la16-*. **3** to impose, inflict (an outcome or penalty) *16-e19*. **4** to relate, mention *la16*. †**infer the pains of law** to lead to or impose a certain penalty *la17-e19*. **infer a punishment** = *infer the pains of law 18-e19*. [Lat *inferre* to carry in]

infermite *see* INFIRMITY

infield, †**infeild** /ˈɪnfild/ *n* the field or land lying nearest to the farm or homestead; originally one of the two main divisions of an arable farm before the practice of crop rotation, consisting of the best land nearest the farm buildings, kept continuously under crop and well manured *la15-*. Compare OUTFIELD[1,1]. [IN[1,3] + FIELD[1,1]]

infirmity, †**infirmitie**, †**infermite** /ɪnˈfɪrməti/ *n* bodily weakness, illness; a defect in character *la14-*. [Lat *infirmitās*]

infit /ˈɪnfɪt/ *n* a state of favour *la19 NE*. **hae an infit wi** to have influence on, be in the good favour of *la19- NE*. [IN[1,3] + FIT[3]]

inflame, †**enflambe**, †**inflam**, †**inflamb** /ɪnˈflɛm/ *v* to set on fire, fire with desire or passion *la14-*. [ME *enflaumen*]

inflick, inflict /ɪnˈflɪk, ɪnˈflɪkt/ *v* to impose (as a penalty or punishment); to cause to suffer from *la16-*. [Lat *inflict-*, ptp stem of *inflīgere*]

information, †**informatioun** /ɪnfərˈmeʃən/ *n* **1** (the imparting of) facts or knowledge *la14-*. **2** *law* a formal written accusation or statement of the charge in criminal cases *18-*. **3** *law* a written argument ordered by a Lord Ordinary in the Court of Session, or by the Court of Justiciary when difficult questions of law arose *18-e19*. [ME *informacioun*, Lat *informātio*]

-ing *see* -IN[1]

ingadder, ingaddir *see* INGAITHER

ingadge *see* ENGAGE

ingaen *see* INGAUN[1,1]

ingage *see* ENGAGE

ingait *see* INGATE

ingaither, ingather, *Sh NE* **ingadder**, †**ingaddir** /ɪnˈgeðər, ɪnˈgaðər/; *Sh NE* ɪnˈgadər/ *v* **1** to collect money or dues *16-*. **2** to gather in, harvest crops *la16-*. [IN[1,3] + GAITHER]

ingaitting *see* INGETTING

ingan, ingin, *NE* **eengan**, †**ingʒoun**, †**unʒeon**, †**onʒeon** /ˈɪŋən; *NE* ˈiŋən/ *n* an onion *Allium cepa 15-*. **ingan Johnnie** an itinerant onion-seller, usually from northern France *20, 21- historical*. [ME *oinyon*]

ingang /ˈɪŋəŋ/ *n* **1** a lack, deficiency or shortage *la16- N NE T Bor*. **2** an entrance, entry *20- Sh NE T C*. **3** a beginning, a fresh start *20- Sh NE T C*. Compare INGAUN[1,1]. [IN[1,3] + GANG[1,1]]

ingangin, †**inganging** /ˈɪŋəŋɪn/ *n* the act of entering, an entrance, entry *15-19, 20- Ork NE SW Bor*. [IN[1,3] + verbal noun from GANG[1,2]]

ingate, †**ingait** /ˈɪŋet/ *n* admission, entry; a way in *la16- Sh SW Bor*. [IN[1,3] + GATE]

ingather *see* INGAITHER

ingaun[1,1], **ingoing**, *T Bor* **ingaen** /ˈɪŋən, ˈɪŋoɪŋ; *T Bor* ˈɪŋeən/ *n* **1** an entrance, a way in; the act of entering *17-*. **2** the assembling of people in a building (for a church service) *19-*. **3** the reveal of a door- or window-case where the stonework turns inward at right angles to the wall *la19-*; compare INGO (sense 2). **4** *law* entry to a new tenancy *20- Ork T SW*. **5** *ploughing* the beginning of a furrow *20- T*. [IN[1,3] + verbal noun from GAE]

ingaun[1,2], **ingoing** /ˈɪŋən, ˈɪŋoɪŋ/ *adj* **1** entering, taking possession (of a tenancy) *19-*. **2** *of the feet* turned in *20- Sh*. **ingaun ee** (the entrance to) a drift mine or coal seam close to the surface outcrop, especially where the seam is not entered vertically *19- C SW*. **ingaun tenant** the person entering the tenancy of a property on the departure of the previous occupier *19-*; compare INCOMING[1,2] (sense 1). [IN[1,3] + presp of GAE]

ingender, ingener *see* ENGENDER

ingere *see* INJEER

†**ingetting, ingaitting** *n* getting in, collecting (rents or debts) *16-e17*. [IN[1,3] + verbal noun from GET[1,2]]

ingevar *see* INGIVER

ingeving *see* INGIVING

ingie /ˈɪŋɡi/ *v in weaving* to hand the threads in a loom to the weaver *20- T EC Bor*. **ingier** the person who hands the threads to the weaver *20- T EC Bor*. [IN[1,3] + GIE]

†**Ingies** *npl* the Indies *19*. [altered form of *Indies*]

†**ingill, engill** *n* a goldsmith's weight, 1/20 ounce *la15*. [Flem *inghelsche, engels*]

ingill *see* INGLE

ingin *see* INGAN

ingine, ingyne, ingin, engine, *NE* **injine**, †**engyne** /ˈɪndʒɪn, ˈɛndʒən; *NE* ˈɪndʒʌɪn/ *n* **1** a machine or motor, a mechanical contrivance; an artillery piece *la14-*. **2** natural cleverness, wit, genius, ingenuity *15-19, 20- N NE*. **3** a great intellect, a person of intellectual ability *16-e19*. **4** mental quality, disposition, temperament *15-e17*. **5** deception, guile *la15-16*. [ME *engin*, Lat *ingenium* an innate quality]

ingineer, engineer, †**engynour**, †**ingynour** /ɪndʒəˈnir, ɛndʒəˈnir/ *n* **1** a designer or operator of engines or machines *la14-*. **2** a contriver, a practitioner; a schemer *16-*. [ME *enginour*]

†**ingiver, ingevar, ingivar** *n* a person who hands in or formally lodges a document (for recording or registration) *la16-19*. [IN[1,3] + *give* (GIE), with agent suffix]

†**ingiving, ingeving** *n* the submission of a document (for consideration) *la16-19*. [IN[1,3] + verbal noun from *give* (GIE)]

Ingland, England, †**Yngland** /ˈɪŋlənd/ *n* the country immediately to the south of Scotland, England *la14-*. [OE *Englaland*]

ingle, †**ingill** /ˈɪŋəl, ˈɪŋəl/ *n* **1** a fire (on a hearth) *16-*. **2** an open fireplace or hearth; the fireside, a chimney corner *18-*. **3** a kiln- or furnace-fire *17-19, 20- Ork N SW Uls*. **4** fuel for a fire, burning coal or peat *17-19*. **ingle-cheek** the fireside, chimney corner *la18-*. †**ingle-en** the side of a house or room where the fire is located *la18-19*. **ingle lowe** the flame or gleam of the fire *la18-19, 20- N NE*. **ingle neuk** the fireside *la18-*. **ingle-stane** a hearthstone *la19-*. [Gael *aingeal* fire]

ingleberry *see* ANGLEBERRY

Inglis[1,1], **English**, †**Englis**, †**Inglisch**, †**Inglish** /ˈɪŋlɪs, ˈɪŋlɪʃ, ˈɪŋɡlɪʃ/ *n* **1** one of the languages deriving from Old English, originally applied to the vernacular of England and Lowland Scotland, but now specifically applied to the English Language as distinct from the Scots Language *15-*. **2** English people *15-*. **3** *pl* the English troops of the Commonwealth *la17*. †**English School, Inglis schole** a school where English was taught (as opposed to a grammar school where Latin was taught) *la16-19*. **the English** the people of England, the English nation *17-*. **English and Scotch** a children's game imitating the old Border Raids *la18-19, 20- EC Bor*. [see the adj]

Inglis[1,2], **Inglish, English**, †**Inglisch**, †**Englis** /ˈɪŋlɪs, ˈɪŋlɪʃ, ˈɪŋɡlɪʃ/ *adj* **1** of or belonging to England or its inhabitants *la14-*. **2** designating the language of the English or of England, originally including Lowland Scots *la14-*. **3** episcopal, Episcopalian *la17-*. **Englisher**, †**Inglisher** an Englishman *la17-*. **English blanket** a blanket with a thick nap *18-19, 20- NE T C Bor.* **English man**, †**Inglisman** a man who is English by descent or birth; *pl* English men, English troops *la14-*. **English pint** the Imperial pint, ⅓ Scots pint *la18-19, 20- historical.* **English woman**, †**Inglis woman** a woman who is English by descent or birth *la16-*. [OE *Englisc*]

ingo /ˈɪŋgo/ *n* **1** the entry into a tenancy of land *20-*. **2** the reveal of a door- or window-case where the stonework turns inward at right angles to the wall *20-*. Compare INGAUN[1.1]. [IN[1.3] + *go* (GAE)]

ingoing *see* INGAUN[1.1], INGAUN[1.2]

†**ingottin** *adj of taxes or debts* collected *la16-e17*. [IN[1.3] + ptp of GET[1.2]]

ingranit *see* ENGRANYT

†**ingrave**, **engrave** *v* to bury *16*. [IN[1.3] + GRAVE[1.2]]

†**ingres** *n* inlying pasture *16*. [IN[1.3] + *gress* (GIRSE[1.1])]

ingreve *see* ENGREVE

ingy, **eenie** /ˈɪŋi, ˈini/ *v of a ewe* to give birth *20- N*. Compare YEAN. [Norw dial *yngja*]

ingyne *see* INGINE

ingynour *see* INGINEER

ingyrar *see* INJEER

ingʒoun *see* INGAN

†**inhabile**, **inhable** *adj law* unfit, unqualified, inadmissible *16-19*. [MFr *inhabile*, Lat *inhabilis*]

†**inhability**, **inhibilitie** *n* **1** *law* loss of legal rights; legal disqualification or unfitness *15-19*. **2** inability, physical infirmity *16-17*. [MFr *inhabilité*, Lat *inhabilitās*]

inhad /ˈɪnhad/ *n* a bare sufficiency *20- Sh*. **a inhad o life** just enough to survive *20- Sh*. [IN[1.3] + HAUD[1.1]]

inhaddin *see* INHAUDIN[1.2]

inhalding *see* INHAUDIN[1.1]

†**inhance**, **inhaunce**, **enhaunse** *v* to create a monopoly in a trade; to keep for one's exclusive use, appropriate goods or advantages *la17*. [unknown]

inhaudin[1.1], †**inhalding**, †**inholding** /ˈɪnhɔdən/ *n* **1** frugality *la17- NE*. **2** damming of water *la15-e17*. **3** holding back, withholding, detaining *la15-e17*. [IN[1.3] + verbal noun from HAUD[1.1]]

inhaudin[1.2], †**inhaddin** /ˈɪnhɔdən/ *adj* **1** frugal, stingy *la18-19, 20- NE*. **2** obsequious *19- N NE T EC*. [IN[1.3] + presp of HAUD[1.1]]

inhaunce *see* INHANCE

inherd *see* ANHERD

inhibilitie *see* INHABILITY

inhibit /ɪnˈhɪbɪt/ *v ptp* †**inhibit 1** to prevent, check; to prohibit *16-*. **2** *law* to place under a writ prohibiting a debtor from disposing of heritable property *la16-*. [Lat *inhibit-*, ptp stem of *inhibēre*]

inhibition, †**inhibitioun** /ɪnhɪˈbɪʃən/ *n* **1** prohibition; restraint *la14-*. **2** *law* a writ prohibiting a debtor from parting with or committing his heritable property to the prejudice of a creditor *la16-*. **3** an order by which a husband may prevent credit being given to his wife *la18-20, 21- historical*. [OFr *inhibition, inibicion*]

inholding *see* INHAUDIN[1.1]

†**inhonestie**, **inhoneste** *n* disgraceful conduct; indecency; filthiness *16-e17*. [Lat *inhonestās*]

†**inimite**, **inemite**, **inamite** *n* enmity *la15-17*. [AN *enemité*]

inimy *see* ENEMY

inioyse *see* ENJOYS

iniquity, †**iniquite** /ɪˈnɪkwəti/ *n* **1** wickedness; wrongful or immoral conduct *la14-*. **2** *law* lack of equity, partiality *17-18*. [ME *iniquite*, Lat *inīquitās*]

†**injeer**, **ingere**, **engyre** *v* **1** to push oneself in, obtrude oneself; to insinuate oneself *16-e19*. **2** to take upon oneself, presume *la15-e17*. **3** to press (something) upon the attention *16*.

ingyrar one who obtrudes presumptuously into a position *la16*. [Lat *ingerere* to put into (a place)]

injine *see* INGINE

†**injune**, **injone** *v* to enjoin *15-e17*. [ME *enjoinen*, Lat *injungere*]

†**injure**[1.1] *n* **1** (an) injustice, wrong, mischief done to a person *la14-16*. **2** physical injury, maltreatment *15-16*. **3** abuse, insult *16*. [OFr *injure*, Lat *injūria*]

injure[1.2] /ˈɪndʒər/ *v* to do wrong to, hurt, to harm; to maltreat, abuse or offend *la15-*. [probably back-formation from Older Scots *injury*]

ink, †**ynk** /ɪŋk/ *n* coloured liquid used for writing, ink *la14-*. **inker** an ink-bottle *la19- T*. **inkies** a local name for the dark-coloured peat sods on Eday *19- Ork N*. **ink-fish** the squid or cuttlefish *Sepia officinalis la18-*. **ink-pud** an ink-bottle *19- EC Bor*. [ME *inke*]

inkie-pinkie, **inky-pinky**, *T* **hinkie-pinkie** /ˈɪŋki ˈpɪŋki; *T* ˈhɪŋki ˈpɪŋki/ *n* **1** a dish made from cold roast beef and vegetables *19-*. **2** a nonsense word in children's rhymes *19, 20- NE T C*. **3** weak beer *19, 20- EC*. [unknown]

†**inkirly**, **increly**, **enkrely** *adv* earnestly, eagerly *la14-e16*. [ME *enkerli*; compare ON *einkar* specially, very]

inklin, *N* **hinklin** /ˈɪŋklɪn; *N* ˈhɪŋklɪn/ *n* **1** a small amount, a trace; a hint, a rumour *la16-*. **2** an inclination, a slight desire *19, 20- Sh Ork N NE T*. [ME *yngkiling*]

in-kneed, †**in-kne'd** /ˈɪn nid/ *adj* knock-kneed *17-19, 20- Ork N NE T Bor*. [IN[1.3] + KNEE[1.1] + -IT[2]]

inks /ˈɪŋks/ *npl* low-lying land on the banks of a river estuary (subject to flooding) *la17- SW*. [ON *eng* a meadow]

inky-pinky *see* INKIE-PINKIE

inkyre *see* INCRE

inlack, **inlaik** *see* INLEAK[1.1], INLEAK[1.2]

†**inlair**, **inlayer** *n* (a small dam leading to) the channel or lade of a millrace *la16-e19*. [*in-* prefix + derivative of LAY[1.2]]

inlairge *see* ENLAIRGE

inlake *see* INLEAK[1.1]

inland /ˈɪnlənd, ˈɪnlənd/ *n* **1** the inlying or central area of a country (away from the sea) *la16-*. **2** *in Aberdeen* the inner section of a tenement block (forming one side of a courtyard) *16-19, 20- historical*. **3** INFIELD land on a farm or estate *la15-e17*. [OE *inland* demesne land]

inlang, **inlangis** *see* ENDLANG[1.4]

inlarge *see* ENLAIRGE

inlat, **inlet** /ˈɪnlat, ˈɪnlət/ *n* **1** a small arm of the sea; a bay *18-*. **2** encouragement, a concession, an opportunity, a welcome *18-*. **3** an entrance; an avenue, a lane *19- NE T EC SW*. [IN[1.3] + LAT]

†**inlay** *n* the diverting of water to a mill *la18*. [IN[1.3] + LAY[1.2]]

inlayer *see* INLAIR

†**inlaying** *n* the building of the INLAIR of a mill *la16*. [IN[1.3] + verbal noun from LAY[1.2]]

inleak[1.1], †**inlaik**, †**inlake**, †**inlack** /ˈɪnlik/ *n* **1** a deficit, a deficiency (of money or goods); a shortage, a lack; a reduction *la14-*. **2** death *16-19*. [LACK[1.1], with intensifying prefix]

†**inleak**[1.2], **inlaik**, **inlack** *v* **1** to be deficient, lack, suffer loss (in weight or volume) *16-19*. **2** to die *16-19*. **3** to fail; to weaken, decline *16-e17*. **4** *of people* to be absent or unavailable, default *la16*. [see the noun]

inlet *see* INLAT

inlichten *see* ENLICHTEN

†**in like, in lyk** *adv* equally; likewise *15-e16*. **inlyk maner** likewise, also *la16*. **inlykwayis** likewise *la16*. **inlikewis** in a like manner *la15-16*. [altered form of ALIKE[1.2]]

†**inlok** *n* a lock built into a door *15-e16*. Compare *hinging lock* (HINGIN). [IN[1.3] + LOCK[1.1]]

†**inlow** *v* to accredit (to one) in an account *15-17*. [altered form of ALLOO]

inlying[1.1] /ˈɪnlaeɪŋ/ *n* a confinement in bed for childbirth *18-*. [IN[1.3] + verbal noun from LIE[1.2]]

inlying[1.2] /ˈɪnlaeɪŋ/ *adj* confined to bed for childbirth *la19-*. [IN[1.3] + presp of LIE[1.2]]

in lyk *see* IN LIKE

inmeat, *Bor* **inmate** /ˈɪnmɪt; *Bor* ˈɪnmet/ *n* 1 the viscera or edible internal organs of an animal *la17-19, 20- H&I Bor*. 2 food given to animals when kept under cover during winter *la19- Sh N*. [IN[1.3] + MEAT[1.1]]

†**in myd**[1.1] *adv* in the midst *la15-e16*. [altered form of AMID[1.1]]

†**in myd**[1.2] *prep* in the middle (of) *la14-15*. [see the adv]

inn, †**in** /ɪn/ *n* 1 a lodging house, a hotel *la14-*. 2 a place of residence, a dwelling *la14-19, 20- Sh*. [OE *inn* a dwelling]

innar *see* INNER

†**innative** *adj* innate *16-e17*. [Lat *innātus* inborn]

innemel *see* ENAMEL

inner, †**enner**, †**innar** /ˈɪnər/ *adj* situated inside; near the centre; interior *la14-*. †**inner house** an inner apartment of a building *la15-17*. **Inner House** the first and second divisions of judges of the Court of Session *la16-*. †**innermare, ennyrmar** further in *la14-16*. [OE *innera*]

inner *see* INVER

innerlie[1.1] /ˈɪnərli, ˈɪnərle/ *adj* 1 *of people* friendly, kindly, sympathetic, affectionate *19- Sh Ork SW Bor*. 2 *of land* not exposed; in the interior of a district *19- SW Bor*. 3 *of a ship or fishing grounds* near the shore *20- Sh NE*. [INNER, with adj-forming suffix]

innerlie[1.2] /ˈɪnərli, ˈɪnərle/ *adv* near the shore *20- Sh NE*. [ON *innarliga* far inward or INNER, with adv-forming suffix]

innery /ˈɪnəre/ *n* a tenement to which access is gained by a common passage and stair *20- Bor*. [INN, with *-ery* suffix]

innin /ˈɪnən/ *n* an entrance, an introduction, a friendly reception *la19-*. [IN[1.1] or INN + -IN[1]]

innis *see* ENNIS, INNS

†**innomerable, innowmerabill** *adj* innumerable *15-16*. [Lat *innumerābilis*]

innormite *see* ENORMITY

innouth *see* INWITH[1.1], INWITH[1.2]

innovate /ˈɪnəvet/ *v ptp* †**innovat** †**innovate** to alter or revise (established practice or the status quo); to introduce something new *la16-*. [Lat *innovāt-*, ptp stem of *innovāre*]

innovation, †**innovatioun** /ɪnəˈveʃən/ *n* 1 the alteration of an established form, practice or institution *la15-*. 2 *law* the alteration or replacement of a legal obligation or provision *la17-*. 3 something newly introduced *18-*. [Lat *innovātio*]

innowmerabill *see* INNOMERABLE

inns, †**innis**, †**innys, †ynnys** /ɪnz/ *n* 1 lodgings, a lodging house; a tavern, a hotel *la14-19, 20- C SW Bor*. 2 a dwelling, a townhouse *la14-19, 20- historical*. [plural of INN]

†**inoportunitie** *n* an unsuitable occasion or application *16*. [Lat *inopportūnitās*]

inopportune, †**inoportune**, †**inopportoun**, †**inoportoyn** /ɪnɔpərˈtjun/ *adj* 1 untimely, unseasonable, inconvenient *la16-*. 2 importunate, persistent *16*. [Lat *inopportūnus*]

†**inorderly**[1.1] *adj* disorderly *la16-19*. [see the adv]

†**inorderly**[1.2], **inordourly** *adv* improperly, irregularly *la15-17*. [Older Scots *orderlie*, with negative prefix]

inorme *see* ENORM

in oure *see* INOWER[1.2]

inower[1.1], †**in over** /ɪnˈʌuər/ *adv* inside, over the top of, near, close or closer in *16-*. **in ower and out ower** thoroughly *19- Bor*. [IN[1.3] + OWER[1.3]]

inower[1.2], *T* **anower**, †**in oure** /ɪnˈʌuər; *T* əˈnʌuər/ *prep* 1 in, inside, within *16-19, 20- Ork N NE T EC*. 2 over (a fence or boundary) into the area within *16-19, 20- Ork N NE T C*. [see the adv]

†**inpassing** *n* passing in or inwards *16*. [IN[1.3] + verbal noun from PASS[1.2]]

†**inpasture** *n in Orkney and Shetland* an INFIELD *16*. [IN[1.3] + *pasture* (PASTER[2.1])]

inpit[1.1], **input** /ˈɪnpɪt, ˈɪnput/ *n* 1 a contribution; a share or quota (of money); a stake; a donation *la17-*. 2 supplementary goods or livestock put into an auction (by someone other than the principal seller) *la19- Ork Bor*. 3 an insertion *e16*. [IN[1.3] + PIT[2]]

inpit[1.2], **input**, †**imput** /ˈɪnpɪt, ˈɪnput/ *v* 1 to put (a thing) in place, insert; to contribute *15-*. 2 to sow crops *la18- SW*. 3 to grant a lease to, install a tenant *la15-18*. 4 to appoint a person to an office or position *la15-17*. 5 to put a person in prison *16*. [see the noun]

†**input, imput** *adj* that which has been put in, sown or loaded *18-19*. **imput master** the appointed skipper of a ship *la16-17*. [IN[1.3] + ptp of PIT[2]]

input *see* INPIT[1.1], INPIT[1.2]

inqueist *see* INQUEST

inquere *see* INQUIRE

inquest, †**inqueist**, †**inquist**, †**enquest** /ˈɪnkwɛst, ˈɪŋkwɛst/ *n* 1 a formal or legal inquiry *la14-*. 2 *law* a body appointed to inquire into the cognition of the insane and matters of inheritance *la15-19*. [ME *enqueste*]

inquire, enquire, †**inquere**, †**enquere**, †**inquyre** /ənˈkwaeɪr/ *v* to make an inquiry, investigate, ask about *la14-*. **inquire at** to inquire of, ask for information from (a person) *15-*. **inquire for** to ask about the health of (a person) *19-*. [ME *enqueren*]

inquiry /ənˈkwaeɪre/ *n* 1 investigation, questioning; a question, a request *la14-*. 2 *law* an inquest, especially an investigation into a fatal accident *la19-*. 3 a formal investigation into a matter of public concern *la20-*. **make inquiry at** to ask or inquire from (a source of information) *18-*. [INQUIRE, with noun-forming suffix]

inquist *see* INQUEST

inquyre *see* INQUIRE

in retentis /ɪn rɪˈtɛntɪs/ *adv of evidence taken in advance of a court case* laid aside until required *la17-*. [Lat *in retentīs* among things retained]

†**inrin** *v* to commit an offence, incur a loss, fall into difficulty *15-e17*. [IN[1.3] + RIN[1.2]]

inring /ˈɪnrɪŋ/ *n* 1 *curling* the innermost part of the surface of a stone, that nearest the tee *19, 20- SW*. 2 *curling* a shot in which the stone being played strikes the inside edge of another, glancing off it to hit and displace the opponent's stone nearest the tee *la18-19, 20- WC SW Bor*; compare INWICK[1.1]. [IN[1.3] + RING[1.1]]

†**inrow, inroll** *v* to enter on a list, enrol *16-18*. [ME *enrollen*]

†**inscales, inskells** *npl* the gratings or racks placed at the lower end of a salmon-trap *la17-e19*. [IN[1.3] + Older Scots *scales* a series of steps, specifically of a salmon-ladder]

insch *see* INCH[1]

inseam /ˈɪnsim/ *n* the seam attaching the welt to the insole and upper of a boot or shoe *la19-*. [IN[1.3] + SEAM[1.1]]

inseat *see* INSET

inseean /ˈɪnsiən/ *adj* prying, inquisitive *20- Ork*. [IN[1.3] + SEE, with presp suffix]

insense, †**ensens** /ɪnˈsɛns/ v to inform, instruct e15, 19- SW Uls. **insense into** to convince, impress a fact on, enlighten la19- SW Uls. [ME ensensen]

†**insere** v ptp **insert, inserit** to include in a book or writing; to enter in an official record 16. [MFr inserer, Lat inserere]

†**inserve** v to serve la16-e17. [Lat inservīre]

†**inset, insett, inseat** n **1** a living room in a farmhouse la17-19. **2** law (part of) the INFIELD of a farm 17-18. [IN³ + SET¹·²]

†**insetting** n setting in position, installing 16-e17. [IN³ + SET¹·², with verbal noun suffix]

insh see INCH¹

inshant see INCHANT

†**insicht**¹ n furniture, household goods la15-19. Compare INSPRAICH. [unknown; compare OUTSIGHT]

insicht² /ˈɪnsɪxt/ n perception, awareness; a capacity to understand 17-. [IN³ + SICHT¹·¹]

inside¹·¹ /ɪnˈsʌɪd, ɪnˈsʌɪd/ n the inner side or surface of something, the interior 16-. **gae tae the inside** mining to go from the pit-bottom to the coal face 20- C. [IN³ + SIDE¹]

inside¹·² /ɪnˈsʌɪd/ adj on, of, belonging to the inside 19-. **inside claes** underclothing la19-. **inside twist** curling a twist causing a stone to revolve to the right 19- C. [see the noun]

insink /ˈɪnsɪŋk/ n a soft bottom in a body of water; a miry puddle 20- Sh Ork. [IN³ + SINK¹·²]

†**insinuat** v **1** to imply, suggest; to communicate indirectly la16-e18. **2** to announce publicly, publish la16-17. [Lat insinuāre]

insist /ɪnˈsɪst/ v **1** to demand forcefully, persist, refuse to give way la16-. **2** law to proceed with a charge or action, continue with a case la16-. **3** to continue talking or preaching 18-e19. **insist for** to insist on la17-19, 20- N EC. **insist in** law to proceed with, pursue la16-. [Lat insistere]

inskells see INSCALES

†**inskift** n in Orkney a parcel of land belonging to a single owner 16-17. [probably ON *einskipt a single division of land]

insnorl /ɪnˈsnɔrl/ v to entangle la19- N NE SW. [IN³ + SNORL¹·²]

insolence, †**ensolence** /ˈɪnsələns/ n **1** rude, disrespectful behaviour, impertinence 16-. **2** wild behaviour, licentiousness la15-16. [Lat insolentia]

insook /ˈɪnsuk/ n **1** a swindle, a bad bargain 20- Sh N NE. **2** the inrush of the tide 20- Sh N. **3** a light frost 20- N. [IN³ + SOOK¹·¹]

inspector of the poor see PUIR'S INSPECTOR

†**inspraich, insprecht, inspreth** n furniture, household furnishings la15-19. Compare INSICHT¹. [unknown]

instance /ˈɪnstəns/ n **1** law the pleading and procedure followed during the hearing of a legal action; a pleading 17-. **2** an example, a particular case 18-. **3** urgency or persistence of entreaty; earnest pleading or appeal la14-e17. **at the instance of** at the instigation, request or suit of la14-. †**with instance** part of the wording used in recording the procuring of a seal 15-16. [OFr instance, Lat instantia]

instant /ˈɪnstənt/ adj **1** of the year or month present, current 15-. **2** of the present time, contemporary, now in existence la15-. **3** immediate, urgent 16-. **4** of people insistent la16-e17. **instantly 1** immediately, at once, forthwith 16-. **2** now, at this moment; at the time specified 16-e18. **3** urgently; insistently 16-e17. [ME instant, Lat instans present, insistent]

insteid, insteed, instid, instead, Bor **isteed**, †**instede**, †**ynsted** /ɪnˈstid, ɪnˈstɪd, ɪnˈstɛd/; Bor ɪˈstɪd/ adv in the place of, in substitution for la14-. [IN¹·⁴ + STEID¹·¹]

institor /ˈɪnstɪtər/ n law an agent or manager la17-19, 20- historical. [Lat institor]

institute /ˈɪnstɪtjut/ n law the person first named in a testament or destination of property la17-. Compare SUBSTITUTE¹·¹. [Lat institūtus one instituted (as heir)]

instruct, †**instruck**, †**instruk** /ɪnˈstrʌkt/ v **1** to direct, command 15-. **2** to teach, educate; to inform la15-. **3** law to supply evidence or documentary proof of; to prove clearly, vouch for (a fact) la16-. **instruction 1** teaching, education la15-. **2** pl directions, orders 16-. **3** law evidence, proof la16-e18. [Lat instruct-, ptp stem of instruere]

instrument¹·¹ /ˈɪnstrəmənt/ n **1** an implement or tool; a weapon; a musical instrument la14-. **2** a means of doing something; a person by means of whom something is done la15-. **3** law a formal authenticated, record of a transaction or court proceedings la14-19, 20- historical. †**instrumentary witness** one who witnesses the signing of a notary instrument la17-19. **instrument of premonition** a formal notification made by the debtor to the creditor in a wadset to appear at an agreed place and receive payment of the debt la16-18, 20-historical. **instrument of sasine** the deed or document recording the transfer of property la16-. **tak instruments** to obtain documentary proofs la15-20, 21- historical. [MFr instrument, Lat instrūmentum]

†**instrument**¹·² v to register a protest against a person by means of a notary instrument 18. [see the noun]

†**insucken, insuckin** n law the multure payable by people within the sucken of a mill 16-18. **insucken multure** = INSUCKEN la17-19. [IN¹·⁴ + SUCKEN¹·¹]

inta see INTAE

intack, intact /ɪnˈtak, ɪnˈtakt/ adj whole, unbroken; untouched, unblemished la15-. [Lat intactus]

intack see INTAK¹·¹

intacking see INTAK¹·²

intae, inty, inta, into /ˈɪnte, ˈɪntə, ˈɪntu/ prep **1** to the inside of, towards the interior; so as to become la14-. **2** in, within la14-19, 20- Ork N NE T C. **3** during la14-16. **be intae 1** to find fault with, scold (a person) 20-. **2** of a cutting remark to be telling, score a hit la19- Ork NE EC Bor. **be intae a fish** to hook (a salmon) 20-. **come into** to come closer (to the table or the fire) 18-. **out intae** out of, from 19, 20- T EC Bor. **sit into** = come into la19-. [OE intō]

intaed, †**intoed** /ˈɪnted/ adj having turned-in toes, pigeon-toed la18-. [IN³ + TAE¹ + -IT²]

intak¹·¹, **intack, intake** /ˈɪntak, ˈɪntek/ n **1** the place where water is diverted from a river or burn (to supply a mill); the channel along which the diverted water flows la15-. **2** a piece of moor or common land enclosed by an adjacent farm 16-. **3** building the offset on a wall, a ledge in a wall where its thickness is reduced la17-. **4** the act of taking in or gathering 19-. **5** a fraud, deception; a swindler 19-. **6** knitting a decrease in the number of stitches in order to shape a garment la19-. [see the verb]

intak¹·², **intake** /ɪnˈtak, ɪnˈtek/ v to take in la15-. **intakin, intaking**, †**intakking**, †**intacking 1** the act of taking in 16-. **2** the decrease of stitches in knitting socks la19-. **3** the breaking in and cropping of previously fallow ground 18- NE. **4** the capture of a place by assault la16-e19. [IN³ + TAK¹·²]

intelleck, intellect /ˈɪntɛlɛk, ˈɪntəlɛkt/ n **1** the mind, the power of thought or reasoning 17-. **2** pl wits, senses la19, 20- H&I Bor. [Lat intellectus]

intend, inten /ɪnˈtɛnd, ɪnˈtɛn/ v **1** to plan, design; to mean to do 16-. **2** law to raise or pursue legal proceedings la16-e18. **3** to attend 15-16. **intender**, †**intendar** freemasonry a member chosen by a novice to instruct him in the mysteries of the craft la16-18, 20- historical. [MFr intendre, Lat intendere]

intent¹·¹, †**entent** /ɪnˈtɛnt/ n **1** intention, purpose la14-. **2** law the pursuer's action in a suit la16-e17. **3** mind, spirit, disposition; opinion la14-e16. **4** heed, attention la15. [MFr entent, Lat intentus]

†**intent**¹·² *v law* to raise or institute a legal action *16-e19*. [Lat *intentāre*]

inter, †**entyre** /ɪnˈtɛr/ *v* to bury *la14-*. [ME *enteren*]

inter *see* ENTER

interaist *see* INTEREST

interant *see* INTRANT¹·¹

interchange, †**intercheinge** /ɪntərˈtʃendʒ/ *v* to exchange, alternate *la14-*. †**interchangeably, enterchangeably** *law* mutually, reciprocally *la14-e16*. [OFr *entrechangier*]

intercommune, †**intercomoun**, †**intercommon**, †**entercomoun** /ɪntərkəˈmjun/ *v* **1** to be in communication, have to do with (enemies, rebels, or outlaws) *15-19, 20- historical*. **2** to take counsel together, consult *16*. †**intercommuned** denounced in letters of intercommoning; proscribed, outlawed *la17-19*. †**intercommuning** the fact or practice of being in communication with rebels or denounced people *la15-18*. [ME *entercomunen*]

interdict¹·¹, **enterdick** /ˈɪntərdɪkt, ˈɛntərdɪk/ *n law* a court order prohibiting some action complained of as illegal or wrongful, until the question of right is tried in the proper court; an injunction *la18-*. [OFr *interdit*, Lat *interdictum*]

interdict¹·², †**interdite**, †**entyrdyt** /ɪntərˈdɪkt/ *v* **1** to place under ecclesiastical interdict, cut off from religious rites *15-*. **2** *law* to restrain or prohibit a spendthrift or facile person from disposing of heritable property *la15-*. **3** *law* to prohibit or restrain from an action by a court order *19-*. **4** to forbid; to prevent *la15-e17*. **5** to renounce *la16-e17*. **interdictor**, †**interdytter** a person whose consent is necessary before a facile person can grant any deed involving his estate *17-*. [ME *enterditen*, Lat *interdīcere*]

interdiction, †**interdictioun** /ɪntərˈdɪkʃən/ *n* **1** *law* the means whereby the actions of a facile person are restrained either voluntarily or by a court *la16-*. **2** the state of being under an ecclesiastical interdict *la15-e17*. [Lat *interdictio*]

interdite, interdytter *see* INTERDICT¹·²

†**interes**¹·¹, **intres, enteres** *n* **1** (compensation for) damage, injury or loss *15-17*. **2** a right or claim to the use or possession of something *la15-17*. **3** interest on money *la16-17*. **4** interest, concern *17*. Compare INTEREST. [ME *interesse*]

†**interes**¹·², **intres** *v ptp* **intrest, interessit 1** to be interested or concerned; to have an interest in *la16-17*. **2** to damage, harm *la16-17*. [see the noun]

interes silver *see* ENTRESS

interest, *NE* **interaist**, *NE* **enterest**, †**intrest**, †**entrest** /ˈɪntrəst, ˈɪntərəst; *NE* ˈɪntərəst, *NE* ˈɛntərəst/ *n* **1** (a feeling of) concern, care, curiosity; eagerness *la16-*. **2** a financial return on money lent *la16-*. **3** a (financial or other) claim or right *la16-*. **4** a landed property, an estate *la17-18*. [altered form of INTERES¹·¹]

interim interdict /ˈɪntərɪm ɪntərdɪkt/ *n* a provisional interdict (which can be granted without the participation of the defender) *la19-*. [Lat *interim* meanwhile + INTERDICT¹·¹]

interlocutor, †**interlocutour**, †**interloquitor** /ɪntərˈlɔkjutər, ɪntərˈlɔkətər/ *n law* an order or judgement given in the course of a suit by the Court of Session or a Lord Ordinary before final judgement is pronounced; any court order *16-*. †**interlocutory** provisional, not finally decisive *la15-e17*. [MFr *interlocutoire* a provisional court order, Lat *interloquitur* he pronounced an interim sentence]

intermediate, †**intermediat** /ɪntərˈmɪdɪət/ *adj* **1** in the middle, coming between *la16-*. **2** applied to a three-year course of education for 12- to 14-year-old children leading to the *Intermediate Certificate* (CERTIFICATE) *e20, la20- historical*. **intermediate diet** *law* a court investigation of the stance that would be taken by the parties in a future criminal trial *la20-*. [MFr *intermediat*, Lat *intermedius*]

†**intermeis, entremas** *n* a dish served or entertainment occurring between the courses of a meal at a banquet *la14-16*. [ME *entermes*]

†**intermell, entermell** *v* **1** to meddle, concern oneself, have to do with *la15-16*. **2** to mix, mingle *15*. [ME *entermedlen*, *entermellen*]

†**intermelle** *adv* mixed together, in a confused or intermingled group or crowd *la14-e15*. [OFr *entremeslé*]

intermiddill *see* ENTYRMYDDILL

†**interpell** *v* **1** *law* to prohibit, prevent *18-19*. **2** to interrupt; to appeal to, call upon; to cite *la16-17*. [Lat *interpellāre*]

interpone /ɪntərˈpon/ *v law* to interpose *16-*. **interpone authority to** to intervene (so as to prevent something) *16-*. [Lat *interpōnere*]

interpret, †**interpreit**, †**enterprit** /ɪnˈtɛrprət/ *v* to explain, elucidate; to construe, understand *la15-*. [ME *interpreten*, Lat *interpretāri*] DOST Enterprit v, Interpret(e v

interprys *see* ENTERPRISE

interprysar, interpryse *see* ENTERPRYSE

†**interrogators, interrogatouris** *npl law* interrogatories, questions (put to the accused or to a witness) *16-e18*. [agent noun from Lat *interrogāre* to interrogate]

interrup, interrupt /ɪntəˈrʌp, ɪntəˈrʌpt/ *v* to stop, cut short, break off *la15-*. [Lat *interrupt-*, ptp stem of *interrumpere*]

interruption, †**interruptioun** /ɪntəˈrʌpʃən/ *n* **1** an act or instance of interrupting, the state of being interrupted *15-*. **2** *law* the step legally required to stop the period of prescription *la15-*. [Lat *interruptio*]

intertain, intertene *see* ENTERTEEN

†**intertrike** *v* to entangle *15-e16*. [perhaps *inter-* + Lat *trīcāri* to make difficulties, play tricks]

interval, †**intervall**, †**intervale** /ˈɪntərvəl/ *n* **1** an intervening period of time *15-*. **2** a gap or space *la16-*. **3** *Presbyterian Church* the interlude between morning and afternoon church services *la19, 20- Ork*. [Lat *intervallum* the space between the ramparts, an interval of time]

inthrow¹·¹, **introw**, †**inthro** /ɪnˈθrʌu, ɪnˈtrʌu/ *adv* inwards; towards a central point *la17-19, 20- Sh*. [IN³ + THROU¹·²]

inthrow¹·², †**inthrou** /ɪnˈθrʌu/ *prep* **1** right through; in the interior of *16-19, 20- Ork NE T*. **2** by means of, through the agency of *19 N NE*. [see the adv]

intil¹·¹ /ˈɪntɪl/ *v* to enter *la20- N NE T EC*. [see the prep]

intil¹·², **intill, intul**, †**intyll** /ˈɪntɪl, ɪnˈtɪl, ˈɪntʌl, ɪnˈtʌl/ *prep* **1** towards, into, to the inside of *la14-*. **2** in, inside; forming a part or ingredient of *la14-*. **3** during *la14-16*. Compare INTAE. **be intil** *of a remark* to be a dig or thrust at (someone) *la19-*. **intil yersel** under your breath, silently *19-*. [IN³ + TILL²·²]

intimate, †**intimat**, †**intimeit** /ˈɪntɪmet/ *v ptp also* **intimate**, †**intimat**, †**intimeit** to make known *16-*. [Lat *intimāre*]

intimation, †**intimatioun** /ɪntɪˈmeʃən/ *n* **1** the act of making known; a formal notification or public announcement *15-*. **2** *Presbyterian Church* an announcement from the pulpit *la16-*. **3** *law* an official notice given to the people concerned, of something required of them and the penalty in case of default *16-19, 20- historical*. [MFr *intimation*, Lat *intimātio*]

intime *see* INTIMY

intimeit *see* INTIMATE

intimmer, †**intimber**, †**intymmyr** /ˈɪntɪmər, ɪnˈtɪmər/ *n* **1** the timber used in the interior of a ship or a building *la15-*. **2** *pl* a humorous term for the internal organs of the human body, especially stomach and bowels *19-*. **3** *pl* the mechanism or workings of a mechanical contrivance *20- Sh Ork NE SW*. [IN³ + TIMMER¹·¹]

†**intimy, intime** *v* to intimate, make known *16-e17*. [MFr *intimer*]

†**intitulat** *adj of books or writings* entitled, named *16-17*. [Lat *intitulat-*, ptp stem of *intitulare*]
intment *see* EYNTMENT
into *see* INTAE
†**intocum** *adv of a year* coming next, immediately ahead *16*. [IN³ + *to come* (COME¹·²)]
intoed *see* INTAED
†**in-toll** *n* a payment made to the BAILIE upon entering into possession of burghal property *la13-19*. [IN¹·¹ + TOLL]
intone, †**entone** /ɪnˈton/ *v* to sing or chant *16-*. [ME *entunen*]
intoun¹·¹, **intoon**, †**intown** /ˈɪntun/ *n* the land adjacent to the farmhouse (originally kept in continuous cultivation); the infield *16-19, 20- NE*. [IN³ + TOUN]
intoun¹·², **intoon** /ˈɪntun/ *adj* pertaining to the infield lands *18-19, 20- NE*. [see the noun]
intown *see* INTOUN¹·¹
†**intrait, intreit, intrat** *v* to entreat *la16-e17*. [ME *entreten*, EModE *entreate*]
intrant¹·¹, †**interant** /ˈɪntrənt/ *n* **1** a person who enters or becomes a member of a college, institution, order or association *16-*. **2** *in the Universities of St Andrews and Glasgow* the student chosen by each of the regional divisions of the student body to represent it in voting for the rector *18-19, 20- historical*. **3** a person entering into occupation of property *16-19*. **4** *Presbyterian Church* a person who becomes a minister (in a parish) *la16-18*. **5** a person entering a place *17*. [Lat *intrant-*, presp stem of *intrāre*]
intrant¹·² /ˈɪntrənt/ *adj* newly appointed, just beginning or entering on a profession, function or office *la16-*. [see the noun]
intrat *see* INTRAIT
intre *see* ENTRY
intreit *see* INTRAIT
intres *see* ENTRESS, INTERES¹·¹, INTERES¹·²
intrest *see* INTERES¹·², INTEREST
intrinsic /ɪnˈtrɪnsɪk/ *adj of an explanation* admitted under *oath* not separate from what is sworn and thus qualifying the oath *18-*. [Fr *intrinsèque*, Lat *intrinsecus*]
intromet *see* INTROMIT
†**intromissatrix, intromissatrice** *n* a female INTROMITTER *la16-19*. [altered form of INTROMIT, with female agent suffix]
intromission, †**intromissioun** /ɪntroˈmɪʃən/ *n* **1** *law* the assuming of the possession or management of another's property with or without authority *18-*. **2** *pl* the transactions of an agent or subordinate *18-*. **3** the conducting of any piece of business *19-*. **4** *pl* interference, goings-on *20- Ork T EC SW*. [Lat *intrōmittere* to send in, cause to enter, with noun-forming suffix]
intromit, †**intromet**, †**entromet** /ɪntroˈmɪt/ *v* **1** *law* to handle or deal with funds or property of another person (living or dead), with or without legal authority *15-*. **2** to have to do with, consort with, interfere with *la15-19, 20- NE T EC*. [Lat *intrōmittere* to interfere with (the property of) another]
intromitter, †**entromettour** /ɪntroˈmɪtər/ *n* a person who deals with, manages or interferes with another's property *la15-*. [INTROMIT, with agent suffix]
introw *see* INTHROW¹·¹
intrude /ɪnˈtrud/ *v* **1** to push in without permission or authority; to usurp power *la16-*. **2** *Presbyterian Church* to impose oneself or another into a church post against the wishes of the congregation *18-*. [Lat *intrūdere*]
intruse /ɪnˈtruz/ *v* **1** to impose (oneself or another) into an office to which one has no claim *15-19, 20- historical*. **2** to break into a house *la19*. **3** to bring in, introduce *la15-16*. [Lat *intrūs-*, ptp stem of *intrūdere*]
intrusion, †**intrusioun** /ɪnˈtruʒən/ *n* **1** unwelcome or forcible entrance; occupation of a property or territory *15-*. **2** *Presbyterian Church* the introduction of a minister to a charge against the wishes of the congregation *18-*. [ME *intrusioun*]
intul *see* INTIL¹·²
in-turn /ˈɪntʌrn/ *n curling* the playing of a stone with the handle inwards, to make it swing to the right *20- WC SW Bor*. [IN¹·³ + TURN¹·²]
inty *see* INTAE
intyll *see* INTIL¹·²
intymmyr *see* INTIMMER
intyse *see* ENTEECE
inuch *see* ENEUCH¹·²
†**inunct** *v* to anoint *16*. **inunctment, enunctment** ointment *e16*. [Lat *inunct-*, ptp stem of *inunguere*]
†**inund** *v* to inundate *17*. [MFr *inonder*, Lat *inundāre*]
invade, †**invaid** /ɪnˈved/ *v* **1** to attack, enter forcefully; to occupy by force *la15-*. **2** to attack or assault a person *la15-18*. [Lat *invādere*]
†**invalesce, invales** *v of disease* to grow worse; *of trouble* to increase *16*. [Lat *invalēscere* to grow stronger]
invecta et illata /ɪnvɛkta ɛt ɪˈlata/ *n* **1** *law* goods or effects brought onto premises, which may be held as security for rent *la18-*. **2** grain brought from outside the sucken to be ground at the superior's mill *18-e19*. [Lat *invecta et illāta* things imported and brought in]
inveet¹·¹, **invite** /ˈɪnvit, ˈɪnvʌɪt/ *n* an invitation *la19-*. [see the verb]
inveet¹·², **invite**, †**inveit**, †**inwit** /ɪnˈvit, ɪnˈvʌɪt/ *v* to request formally, give an invitation; to induce *la16-*. [MFr *inviter*]
†**invennomit** *adj* poisoned; charged with venom *la15-16*. [OFr *envenimé*, ptp of *envenimer* to poison, with altered suffix]
inventar¹·¹, *NE* **inveter**, †**inventour**, †**inventure**, †**invitour** /ˈɪnvəntər/; *NE* ˈɪnvɪtər/ *n* **1** an inventory of goods and chattels; a list or catalogue *la15-*. **2** *pl* the stock and crops listed in the inventory of a farm and taken over by a new tenant *20- NE T EC*. [ME *inventari, inventare*, Lat *inventārium*]
†**inventar**¹·², **inventour, enventer** *v* to make an inventory of; to catalogue or list *la16-e18*. [see the noun]
inver, †**inner** /ˈɪnvər/ *n* a confluence of streams; the mouth of a stream or river; frequently in place-names *la15-19, 20- NE*. [Gael *inbhear*]
Inverness /ɪnvərˈnɛs/ *n* a heavy tweed knee-length cloak with a shoulder cape *la19-*. **Inverness cape** = INVERNESS. [from the name of the Highland city]
inveroun *see* ENVERON
inversion /ɪnˈvɜrʃən/ *n law* the act of changing the use to which a leased property is to be put *19-*. Compare *invert possession* (INVERT). [Lat *inversio*]
invert, †**inwert** /ɪnˈvɜrt/ *v* to overturn, change *la16-*. **invert possession** *law* to exercise proprietary rights over the property of another, especially of a tenant using property for a purpose not provided for in the lease *la19-*. [Lat *invertere*]
inveter *see* INVENTAR¹·¹
invious *see* INVY¹·¹
inviroun *see* ENVERON
invite *see* INVEET¹·¹, INVEET¹·²
invitour *see* INVENTAR¹·¹
invy¹·¹, **envy** /ˈɪnve, ˈɛnve/ *n* a feeling of jealousy or covetousness, envy *la14-*. †**invyar, invyour** a person who envies *la16-e17*. **envyfu, invyfow**, †**invyfull** full of malice or envy, envious *16-*. **invious, envious** feeling or showing envy *15-*. [ME *envie*]
invy¹·², **envy** /ˈɪnve, ˈɛnve/ *v* to be envious of *la15-*. [ME *envien*]
inwan /ˈɪnwan/ *adv* inwards *la19- EC*. [IN³ + WAN²]
inward *see* INWART¹·¹, INWART¹·²

inwark, inwork /ˈɪnwark, ˈɪnwʌrk/ *n* domestic or indoor work *la18-19, 20- Ork T.* [IN³ + WARK¹·¹]

inwart¹·¹, **inward** /ˈɪnwərt, ˈɪnwərd/ *adj* **1** situated within, inner *la14-*. **2** on intimate terms, in favour *la15-16*. **3** heartfelt, earnest, fervent *la15-16*. [see the adv]

inwart¹·², **inward** /ˈɪnwərt, ˈɪnwərd/ *adv* (towards the) inside, within *la14-*. [ME *inward*, OE *inweard*]

inwert *see* INVERT

inweys /ˈɪnwez, ˈɪnwaez/ *adv* inwards *20-*. [IN³ + WEY¹, with adv-forming suffix]

inwick¹·¹ /ˈɪnwɪk/ *n* curling (the playing of) a shot which strikes the inside of another stone and glances off it towards the tee *19-*. [IN³ + WICK⁴·¹]

inwick¹·² /ˈɪnwɪk/ *v* curling to strike an opponent's stone and knock it out of play *19-*. [see the noun]

inwit *see* INVEET¹·²

inwith¹·¹, †**innouth**, †**enouth**, †**ennowe** /ˈɪnwɪθ/ *adv* **1** within, inside *la14-*. **2** inwards *19- NE*. [IN³ + *with* (WI))

inwith¹·², †**innouth**, †**enouth**, †**ennowe** /ˈɪnwɪθ/ *prep* **1** within, inside *la14-*. **2** at less than, under (a certain price or value) *la16*. [see the adv]

inwork *see* INWARK

†**inȝet** *adj* poured in *e16*. [IN³ + YAT]

iolyus *see* JEELOUS

ion *see* EEAN

iorram, †**jorram** /ˈɪrəm, ˈɪrəm/ *n* a Gaelic rowing-song *la18-*. [Gael *iorram*]

ioy *see* JOY¹·¹, JOY¹·²

Ipar *see* YPER

iper /ˈʌɪpər/ *n* sludge, mud, ooze; liquid manure *la19- Ork N NE*. [unknown]

ipo *see* UPON

ipocras *see* YPOCRAS

ipotecar *see* APOTHICAR

ipothek *see* HYPOTHEC

†**ipotingar**, **ypothingar**, **ypotingair** *n* an apothecary *16*. Compare APOTHICAR, APOTHECARIE, POTHECAR, POTICARY and POTTINGAR. [conflation of APOTHICAR with POTTINGAR]

ir *see* BE, OR¹·²

ire *see* AYRE

Ireland¹·¹, †**Irland**, †**Yrland** /ˈaerlənd/ *n* Ireland, a country South-West of Scotland *la13-*. [OE *Írland*, *Íraland*]

†**Ireland**¹·², **Irland**, **Yrland** *adj* **1** Irish, belonging or deriving from Ireland *la15-17*. **2** designating a heraldic officer *la15-e16*. **Irland man** an Irishman *la15-e17*. [see the noun]

iremonger /ˈaermʌŋgər/ *n* an ironmonger *20- NE*. [variant of Eng *ironmonger*]

iren *see* AIRN¹·¹, AIRN¹·²

Irichman *see* IRISHMAN

Irish¹·¹, *SW* **Eerish**, †**Irische**, †**Yrysch**, †**Erische** /ˈaerɪʃ; *SW* ˈɪrɪʃ/ *n* **1** the Irish people *la15-*. **2** the Irish Gaelic language *la15-*. **3** the Scottish Gaelic language *la15-18*. **4** the Scottish Highlanders *la16-17*. Compare ERSE²·¹. [see the adj]

Irish¹·², *SW* **Eerish**, †**Irische**, †**Iris**, †**Erische** /ˈaerɪʃ; *SW* ˈɪrɪʃ/ *adj* **1** of or belonging to Ireland *la14-*. **2** *of writing* composed in the Irish language; *of people* Irish Gaelic-speaking *la16-*. **3** of or belonging to the Scottish Highlands *la14-19*. **4** *of writing* composed in the Scottish Gaelic language; *of people* Scottish Gaelic-speaking *la16-e19*. Compare ERSE²·². **Irisher 1** an Irish person *19-*. **2** an Irish-bred cow *e19*.

†**Irischery**, **Erischry**, **Erschry 1** the Irish people or nation *la14-15*. **2** the Scottish Highlanders *la14-15*. [OE *Yrīsc* Irish, IrGael *Ériu* Ireland]

Irishman, †**Eerishman**, †**Erischman**, †**Irichman** /ˈaerɪʃmən/ *n* **1** a man of Irish birth or descent *la15-*. **2** a Scottish Highlander *la15-e17*. **Irishman's cutting** a cutting taken from a plant, with a portion of the root attached *20-*. [IRISH¹·² + MAN]

†**irkit** *adj* wearied, tired, exhausted *la15-16*. [Scots *irk* with -*it* suffix]

Irland *see* IRELAND¹·¹, IRELAND¹·²

irne, iron *see* AIRN¹·¹, AIRN¹·²

irp *see* ORP

irr *see* BE, HIRR¹·²

irredeemable, †**irredemable**, †**irredimable** /ɪrəˈdiməbəl/ *adj* not redeemable *17-*. [Older Scots REDEMABILL, with negative prefix]

†**irregular**¹·¹ *n* a disobedient or disqualified ecclesiastic *la15-17*. [see the adj]

irregular¹·² /ɪˈrɛgjulər/ *adj* **1** non-conforming (to Church rules), lawless *la15-*. **2** uneven, unequal *la18-*. **irregular marriage** a marriage contracted without a religious ceremony or formal civil procedure *18-*. [ME *irreguler*]

irrelevancy, †**irrelevancie** /ɪˈrɛləvənsɪ/ *n law* lack of pertinence *la16-*. [IRRELEVANT, with noun-forming suffix]

irrelevant /ɪˈrɛləvənt/ *adj of a legal claim or charge* not sufficient or pertinent, inadmissible *la16-*. [OFr *irrelevant*]

†**irresponsall** *adj* not able or willing to be answerable; unable to pay, insolvent *17*. [RESPONSALL¹·², with negative prefix]

irrevocable, †**irrevocabill** /ɪˈrɛvəkəbəl/ *adj* **1** irreversible *la16-*. **2** *of an agent* authorized irrevocably, whose appointment may not be revoked or rescinded *15-e18*. [Lat *irrevocābilis*]

irritancy /ˈɪrɪtənsɪ/ *n law* the nullification of a deed resulting from neglect or contravention of the law or of an agreement *la17-*. **irritancy of feu** nullification of a tenure because of failure to pay feu-duty for two consecutive years *la18-20, 21- historical*. [IRRITANT, with noun-forming suffix]

irritant /ˈɪrɪtənt/ *adj law* rendering null and void *16-*. **irritant clause** a clause rendering an agreement null and void by its contravention *la16-*. [Lat *irritant-*, presp stem of *irritāre* to make void]

irritate /ˈɪrɪtet/ *v law* to make void, nullify *la17-*. [Lat *irritāre*]

†**irrogate**, **irrogat** *v ptp* **irrogat** to impose a penalty *la16-17*. [Lat *irrogāre*]

Irsche, Irscheman *see* ERSE²·²

is *see* AS²·¹, AS²·², BE, THIS¹·², THIS¹·³

Is *see* SALL

-is *see* -S

ische *see* ISH¹·¹

ischear *see* USHER

†**ischew**¹·¹, **ischue** *n* **1** a pouring forth, an outflow; an exit *la14-17*. **2** a military sortie *la14-16*. **3** the expiry of a lease; the end of a legal term *la16-e17*. **4** (the right of) egress *la16-17*. **5** offspring, progeny *la16-17*. **6** an outcome, result *la16-17*. [ME *issue*]

†**ischew**¹·², **ischue** *v* to issue, go or send forth, promulgate *16-e18*. [see the noun]

Ise, I'se, Ise' *see* SALL

ise schokkyll *see* EESHOGEL

iset, eicid /ˈɪsət, ˈaesəd/ *adj* mottled, speckled *la19- Sh*. [Norw dial *hysjut*]

ish¹·¹, *N* **ush**, †**ische**, †**esche**, †**usche** /ɪʃ; *N* ʌʃ/ *n* **1** the conclusion of a period of time, the termination of a legal term or a term of office; the expiry (date) of a lease *la14-*. **2** *law* right or means of egress *15-*. **3** *pl* the entrails of a slaughtered animal *la16-19, 20- N*. **4** the action of going out; a way out, an exit *la14-16*. **5** *pl* proceeds or profits (in the form of fines) of a local court of justice *la14-16*. **6** a military sortie *la14*. **ish and entry** *law* the right or means of access to or from property, egress *15-*. [see the verb]

ish¹·², *N* **ush**, †**usche**, †**isse** /ɪʃ; *N* ʌʃ/ *v* **1** to go or come out, go forth *la14*-. **2** to flow out, pour out *16-19, 20- N*. **3** to clear a place of occupants *la15-e18*. **4** to move troops, make a sortie *la14-17*. [ME *ishen*]

isillys *see* AIZLE¹·¹

isitt, †**izzet** /ˈɪzɪt/ *n* (the name of) the letter Z *la19, 20- Ork*. [variant of Eng *zed*]

isk *see* YESK¹·²

iskie bae *see* USQUEBAE

isky, iskie, iskis /ˈɪskɪ, ˈɪskɪ, ˈɪskɪs/ *interj* a call to a dog *19, 20- NE T EC*. †**isk isk** = ISKY *e18*. Compare HISK. [unknown]

island, †**iland**, †**yland**, †**eyllan** /ˈʌɪlənd/ *n* a piece of land surrounded by water *la15*-. **the Islands 1** Shetland and Orkney *la18- N H&I*. **2** the Hebrides *la19- H&I*. **islander** a person from the Hebrides *16*-. **Islands Council** each of the local government councils set up in 1975 in Shetland, Orkney and the Hebrides *la20-*. [OE *īegland*]

isle, †**ile**, †**eyll** /ʌɪl/ *n* an island *la14*-. **the Isles** the Hebrides *la14*-. **ilesman** a Hebridean *15*-. [ME *ile*]

isse *see* ISH¹·²

isteed *see* INSTEID

istek *see* EASTICK

it, hit, hut, 't, *Ork N* **hid**, *EC* **het**, †**'d** /ɪt, hɪt, hʌt, t; *Ork N* hɪd; *EC* hɛt/ *pron* **1** the thing previously mentioned; the animal or child in question *la14*-. **2** its, belonging to 'it' *16*-. **3** *in children's games* the player who acts as catcher *19*-. **4** there: ◊*sic ane ferly neuer it was 15-19, 20- Ork*. **5** so: ◊*I don't think it 20*-. **itsel, hitsel, itself** the thing in question *la14*-. **about it** in one's usual state of health *la19*-. **awa wi't** ruined in health or fortune *20*-. **by wi't** = *awa wi't la19*-. **for that o't** for that matter *20*-. †**it that** that which, what *la14-16*. **that o't** that state of affairs *la19*-. **this o't** this state of affairs *19*-. **throw wi't** = *awa wi't 20*-. [OE *hīt*]

it *see* AT²

-it¹ /ət, ɪt/ *suffix forming the past tense and past participle of verbs, and adjectives thus derived* having the quality of the verb: ◊*convictit* ◊*skelpit 14*-. [OE -*ed*-]

-it² /ət, ɪt/ *suffix forming adjectives from nouns* having the quality of the noun: ◊*plookit* ◊*scabbit la15*-. [OE -*ed*-]

-it³ /ət, ɪt/ *suffix* denoting the loss or absence of the noun to which it is affixed *eg* POUSTIT *16*-. [a specific use of the past participle]

ita, itae /ˈɪtə, ˈɪte/ *prep* into, within *la19- Sh Ork*. [reduced form of INTAE]

†**Itale, Ital** *adj* Italian *e16*. [Lat *Ītalus*]

†**Italianis, Italieans** *n* **1** an edging lace or braiding made in Italy *e17*. **2** the Italian language *la16*. [Older Scots *Italiane* with final -*is* perhaps by analogy with other national designations, *eg Scottis*]

itchy-coo /ˈɪtʃiku/ *n* **1** something tickly *20- T C*. **2** the prickly seeds of the dog-rose, put by children down each others' backs *20- T C*. [perhaps Eng *itchy* + COO or HITCHIE-KOO]

item *see* EETIM

ithand *see* EIDENT

ither¹·¹, other, *Sh NE* **idder** /ˈɪðər, ˈʌðər; *Sh NE* ˈɪdər/ *adj* **1** second of two; the remaining one *la14*-. **2** further, additional, successive *la14*-. **3** different, distinct *la14*-. Compare TITHER¹·¹. **ithergates, othergates**, †**uthirgatis 1** otherwise *15*-. **2** elsewhere *20- T EC*. †**other half, uther half** one and a half, half as much again *15-16*. †**uther ma, othyr ma** others besides *la14-15*. †**other mony** many; various others in addition *la14-e16*. †**uther morne** the day after tomorrow *la16*. **ither roads** otherwise *20- C Uls*. †**ithersome, othersome** some others, others *la14-19*. †**utherway** otherwise *la14-17*. **itherways, otherways**, †**otherwayes**, †**oderwayis 1** in another way; in a different manner *la14*-. **2** similarly *la14-e18*. **3** in all other respects, for the rest *15-e17*. **itherwhere**, †**utherquahre** elsewhere, in or to another place *la14*-. **otherwhiles**, †**other quhilis**, †**uther quhyllis** at other times, at one time or another, occasionally *15-19, 20- NE T Uls*. **itherwise, otherwise**, †**utherwyse**, †**oderwise** in another way; in a different manner *la14*-. **ither than, other than** different from, apart from *15*-. [OE *ōþer*]

ither¹·², other, *Sh NE* **idder** /ˈɪðər, ˈʌðər; *Sh NE* ˈɪdər/ *adv* otherwise, else; differently *la18*-. **nae ither** no other, nothing else *la19, 20- NE*. **naething ither** nothing else *la18- NE*. **what ither** naturally, of course *la19- Sh NE WC*. [see the adj]

ither¹·³, other, *Sh NE* **idder**, †**uther**, †**oder**, †**uder** /ˈɪðər, ˈʌðər; *Sh NE* ˈɪdər/ *pron* **1** the remaining person or thing, a further one *la14*-. **2** each other, one another *la14*-. **3** *in uninflected form* other people or things: ◊*the lasses looked what ither had la14*-. Compare TITHER¹·². **eftir ither** in turn, in succession *la16*-. **in o ither** together; in or into one compacted whole *20- N NE T*. **oot o ither** apart, in or into pieces, in disorder or a state of disintegration *la19- N NE T*. [see the adj]

ithin *see* ATHIN¹·²

ithoot *see* ATHOOT¹·²

ithy, idi, †**ydy** /ˈɪði, ˈɪdi/ *n* an eddy, a small whirlpool; a current of water *la15- Sh Ork*. [ON *iða*]

iuge *see* JUDGE¹·¹

Iulius Hoif *see* JULIUS HOFF

iuperdy *see* JEOPARDIE¹·¹

iustice *see* JUSTICE

iustify *see* JUSTIFY

iver, ivver, ever, evir, *N* **oor**, †**euer** /ˈɪvər, ˈɛvər; *N* ur/ *adv* always, at all times; at any time *la14*-. **everly** constantly, perpetually *19, 20- EC SW Bor*. **ever now** just now *20- Ork N H&I*. Compare EENOO. **at the ever-leevin gallop** as fast as possible, very fast *la19- NE*. **ever and on** continually *20*-. [OE *ǣfre*]

iver *see* OWER¹·²

iverlaistin¹·¹, **everlestin, everlastin**, *Bor* **everlesteen** /ɪvərˈlɛstən, ɛvərˈlɛstən, ɛvərˈlastən; *Bor* ɛvərˈlɛstin/ *n* a long time *19, 20- NE T EC Bor*. [see the adj]

iverlaistin¹·², **ivverlaistin, everlestin, everlastin**, †**evirlestand**, †**euirlastande** /ɪvərˈlɛstən, ɛvərˈlɛstən, ɛvərˈlastən/ *adj* eternal, perpetual, endless *la14*-. [IVER + Older Scots *lasting*]

ivermair, ivvermair, evermair, evermore, †**evermar**, †**evirmair**, †**evermoir** /ɪvərˈmer, ɛvərˈmer, ɛvərˈmor/ *adv* **1** for all future time *la14*-. **2** at all times, always *la14*-. [IVER + MAIR¹·¹]

ivery¹·¹, **iviry, ivvery, every**, †**evere**, †**ewiry** /ˈɪvre, ˈɪvəre, ˈɛvre, ˈɛvəre/ *adj* **1** every one, each one *la14*-. **2** each of two, both *la18*-. **everyday** a weekday (as opposed to Sunday) *la19- T EC SW Bor*. [OE *ǣfre*]

ivery¹·², **every** /ˈɪvre, ˈɪvəre, ˈɛvre, ˈɛvəre/ *interj in a game of marbles* a call for liberty to play in any position *20- NE EC Bor Uls*. [see the adj]

ivigar *see* UIVIGAR

ivill *see* EVIL¹·², EVIL¹·³

iviry *see* IVERY¹·¹

ivnoo *see* EENOO

ivver *see* IVER

ivverlaistin *see* IVERLAISTIN¹·²

ivvermair *see* IVERMAIR

ivvery *see* IVERY¹·¹

iwill *see* EVIL¹·¹, EVIL¹·²

†**I wis** *adv* certainly, indeed, truly *la14-16*. [OE *gewiss*]

iymp *see* †JIMP¹

iz *see* US

izzet *see* ISITT

izzle *see* AIZLE¹·¹

J

ja *see* JAW[1.1], JAY

jaa, jaw, *N* **chaa**, †**jow** /dʒa, dʒɔ; *N* tʃa/ *n* the bony framework of the mouth *16-*. **jaw-lock** lock-jaw *la19-*. [ME *jou*]

jab[1.1], *EC* **jeb** /dʒab; *EC* dʒɛb/ *n* a prick, the act of pricking; a sharp blow; a cutting remark *19-*. **jabbie** a jab *la20-*. [see the verb]

jab[1.2] /dʒab/ *v* to prick sharply, poke roughly, stab *19-*. [probably onomatopoeic; compare JOB[2.2]]

jabart *see* JABBART

jabb, jaup, japp /dʒab, dʒɔp, dʒap/ *v* to tire out, exhaust *19-*. [unknown]

jabbart, jabbard, chabbard, †**jabart** /'dʒabərt, 'dʒabərd, 'tʃabərt/ *n* **1** an old, thin or weak animal *16, 19- N NE*. **2** a lean fish, caught out of season *20- N*. **3** a big, awkward man *20- N*. [JABB, with noun-forming suffix *-art*]

jabble[1.1], *Ork N* **chabble** /'dʒabəl; *Ork N* 'tʃabəl/ *n* **1** a shaking of liquid; liquid and its sediment stirred up together *la18-*. **2** a weak mixture, watery soup or weak tea *la18-*. **3** a choppy area of water or the sea; a ripple on the surface of water *19-*. **4** confusion, agitation; incoherent speech *la19-*. [frequentative form of JAUP[1.1]]

jabble[1.2], *WC SW* **jaible** /'dʒabəl; *WC SW* 'dʒebəl/ *v* **1** *of a liquid* to splash or be splashed *19-*. **2** *of the sea* to become choppy *19-*. [see the noun]

jacat *see* JAIKET

jachelt, jauchelt /'dʒaxəlt, 'dʒɔxəlt/ *adj* tossed, buffeted by the wind *la19- NE SW*. [altered form of DACKLE[1.2]]

†**jacinct, jassink** *n* the gemstone jacinth or hyacinth *16-e17*. [ME *jacinct*, EModE *iacynkt*]

jack[1], **jeck, jake**, †**jak** /dʒak, dʒɛk, dʒek/ *n* **1** a generic male personal name (frequently used as a reference to the common man) *16-*; compare JOCK. **2** a mechanism for screwing, turning or winding *la17-*. **3** bowls a smaller bowl placed as a marker for the player to aim at *la17-*. **4** *pl* small stones, bones or metal objects used in the game of *chuckies* (CHUCKIE); the game itself *la19-*. **5** the jackdaw *Corvus monedula* or magpie *Pica pica la19- C SW Bor*. **6** a country dweller, a farmworker *20- NE*. **7** the jack in a pack of playing-cards *la20-*. **jackie, jaikie** the jackdaw *20-*. **jackie downie** the bib or pout *Trisopterus luscus*, a fish of the cod family *la19- NE*. †**jakfallow lyk** *of a servant* presumptuous, behaving like his master's equal *la16-e17*; compare *jock-fellow-like* (JOCK). **Jeck-a-lum** a children's game *20- Sh*. **jeck-easy, jack-easy** indifferent, not caring one way or the other; easygoing, offhand *la19-*. **jecky forty-feet** a centipede *20- N*. **jeck wi the monie feet** a centipede *20- H&I WC SW*. [familiar form of *John*; compare JOCK]

†**jack**[2] *n* a privy *la17-18*. [unknown]

jack *see* JAK

jacket *see* JAIKET

jackman *see* JAKMAN

jackteleg *see* JOCKTELEG

Jacob's ladder /'dʒekəbz 'ladər/ *n* deadly nightshade *Atropa belladonna 19- WC Uls*. [in reference to Genesis 28.12]

Jacob's stone /'dʒekəbz 'ston/ *n* an alternative name for the Stone of Destiny (which was traditionally reputed to have been used as a pillow by the biblical figure Jacob and subsequently transported to Scotland) *17-*. [in reference to Genesis 28.11]

jad *see* JAUD

†**jadden** *n* the stomach of a sow (used to make a pudding), a haggis *19*. Compare JAUDIE. [ME *chaudon*]

jadge *see* JEDGE[1.1], JEDGE[1.2]

jadgear, jadgerie *see* JEDGE[1.2]

jaffled /'dʒafəld/ *adj* exhausted, worn out *19- SW*. [unknown; compare JAMPH[2]]

jafs[1.1] /tʃafs/ *n* a greedy snap with the mouth when eating *20- Sh*. [see the verb]

jafs[1.2], **shafs**, *Ork* **shavs** /tʃafs, ʃafs; *Ork* ʃavz/ *v* **1** to eat noisily or greedily *la19- Sh*. Compare GAFS. **2** to scowl, grimace *20- Ork*. [Norw dial *kjafsa* to eat voraciously like a dog]

jafs[2] /tʃafs/ *v* to walk in a laborious manner *20- Sh*. [Norw *dafsa* to splash, walk carelessly]

jag[1.1] /dʒag/ *n* **1** a prick with something sharp; a sharp blow or prod *la17-*. **2** a prickle, a thorn; something causing a sting *19-*. **3** an injection, an inoculation *la20-*. **the Jags 1** a nickname for Partick Thistle Football Club *20-*. **2** a nickname for Buckie Thistle Football Club *20-*. **3** a nickname for Inverness Caledonian Thistle Football Club, originally used of the former Highland League club Inverness Thistle *20-*. [perhaps onomatopoeic]

jag[1.2] /dʒag/ *v* **1** to prick, pierce *16-*. **2** to inject (with a needle) *la20-*. **3** to feel the pain of a prick from something sharp *la20-*. †**jag-the-flae** a contemptuous name for a tailor *la18*. [see the noun]

jag[2.1] /dʒag/ *n* a sharp violent shake or jolt; a rut in the road (causing a jolt) *la19-, 20- Sh N*. **jaggie, jaggy** *of motion or a vehicle* jerky, uncomfortable; *of a road* bumpy *19, 20- T*. [perhaps onomatopoeic; compare SHOG[1.1], *jog*]

jag[2.2] /dʒag/ *v* **1** to shake violently, jolt, jerk *19- NE*. **2** to move with a jerking motion, bump *la19-, N NE T*. [see the noun]

†**jag**[3], **jaug, jeg** *n* **1** a bag or wallet; a saddlebag *16-19*. **jag purse** a purse or wallet *la17*. [unknown]

jag[4] /dʒag/ *n* a nip, a shot of alcohol *la20- C*. [extended sense of JAG[1.1]]

jagger *see* YAGGER

jaggie, jaggy /'dʒagi, 'dʒage/ *adj* **1** prickly, sharp-pointed, piercing *la18-*. **2** *of nettles* stinging *20-*. **jaggie wire, jaggy wire** barbed wire *la20-*. [from the noun JAG[1.1] + -IE[2]]

jaible *see* JABBLE[1.2]

jaicket *see* JAIKET

jaik, jeck /dʒek, dʒɛk/ *n* a large tin mug, a drinking vessel *20- Ork*. [perhaps Eng *jack*]

jaiket, jaicket, jaykit, jecket, jacket, *N* **chaickad**, †**jakat**, †**jakket**, †**jacat** /'dʒekət, 'dʒɛkət, 'dʒakət; *N* 'tʃekəd/ *n* a short coat *la15-*. **yer jaiket's oan a shooglie nail** *see* SHOOGLY. [ME *jaket*]

jaikie *see* JACK[1]

jail *see* JILE[1.1]

jailous *see* JEELOUS

jairble *see* JIRBLE[1.1], JIRBLE[1.2]

jairdine *see* JORDAN

jairg *see* JIRG[2.2]

†**jak, jack** *n* a jerkin or defensive doublet; a surcoat *la15-e19*. **jakmakar** a jerkin-maker *16*. [ME *jakke*]

jak *see* JACK[1], JAUK

jakat see JAIKET
jake see JACK¹
jakey /'dʒeke/ n a (homeless) alcoholic; a street-drinker; a waster la20-. [perhaps from jaikie a jackdaw, see JACK¹]
jakket see JAIKET
jakmakar see JAK
†jakman, jackman n an attendant, a retainer la16-e19. [unknown]
jalk /tʃɑlk/ v to walk in a clumsy, laborious manner; to trudge through a mire 20- Sh. [altered form of Norn dalk]
jalling-stane see JAW¹·¹
jallisie, jollisie /'dʒaləsi, 'dʒɔləsi/ n an illness la19- NE. [altered form of jeelousy (JEELOUS)]
jalme see JAMB
jalous see JEELOUS
jalouse, jaloose, N **chalowse, †jelous, †jealouse** /dʒəˈluz/; N tʃəˈlʌuz/ v 1 to suspect, be suspicious of (a person or thing) la17-. 2 to be regarded with suspicion la17-. 3 to suppose, guess, surmise la17-. **jaloosins, †jealousings** suspicions 19- NE EC Bor. [Fr jalouser to regard with jealousy]
jam¹·¹ /dʒam/ n 1 a crush, a blockage la19-. 2 a patch (in a torn garment) 20- Sh. [see the verb]
jam¹·² /dʒam/ v 1 to cram or squeeze; to block 19-. 2 to put in a quandary, cause to be at a loss la19-. 3 to inconvenience la19-. 4 to mend, patch la18-19, 20- Sh Ork. **jam fu** crammed full 20-. **jammin fu** = jam fu. **jam yersel** to occupy your time to the exclusion of all else, preoccupy yourself exclusively 20- NE T EC. [perhaps onomatopoeic]
jamb, SW Uls **jum, †jam, †jalme** /dʒam; SW Uls dʒʌm/ n 1 a side-post or cheek of a doorway, window or chimney piece 16-. 2 a projecting wing or addition to a building la16-. 3 an overlarge, rambling house 19, 20- NE SW Uls. 4 something large and clumsy 19, 20- NE Uls. **jam-stane** the upright of a fireplace 19-. [MFr jambe a leg]
jambo /'dʒambo/ n 1 a player for Heart of Midlothian Football Club la20-. 2 a supporter of Heart of Midlothian Football Club la20-. [reduced form of JAM TART]
jamf see JAMPH¹·²
jamffe see JAMPH¹·¹
jammall see GEMEL
jammay band see GEMMA BAND
jamp see JUMP
jamph¹·¹, **†jamffe** /dʒamf/ n mockery, a jeer; a jest 17-19, 20- SW. Compare GAMF¹·¹. [unknown]
jamph¹·², **†jamf** /dʒamf/ v 1 to fool or trick; to mock or jeer 17-. 2 to waste time; to slack off, move slowly 19- NE. Compare GAMF¹·¹. [unknown]
†jamph² v to struggle; to be exhausted or in difficulties la18-e19. [variant of jaup (JABB)]
jampt see JUMP
jampy see JIMP⁴
Jam Tart /dʒam 'tart/ n 1 a player for Heart of Midlothian Football Club la20-. 2 a supporter of Heart of Midlothian Football Club la20-. [rhyming slang]
jander /'dʒandər/ v of a female animal to be in heat la20- Sh. [variant of Eng gender]
jandies /'dʒandiz/ n jaundice la17-. [Fr jaunice]
janet flour see JONET FLOUR
Janet Jo /'dʒanət dʒo/ n a children's singing game 19, 20- T. [after the name in the folksong Jenny Jones]
jangle, †jangill /'dʒaŋgəl/ v 1 to chatter, talk incessantly la15-19, 20- Uls. 2 to dispute; to grumble; to find fault la15-17. [ME janglen]
†Janis, Geanis n Genoa 16-e17. **Jenis taffatie, geanis taffatie** taffeta from Genoa 16-e17. [OFr Jannes, Gennes]

janitor, †jonator /'dʒanıtər/ n 1 a doorkeeper, a porter; a caretaker of a public building, especially a school la16-. 2 an usher or junior master in a school la16-18. Compare JANNIE. [Lat jānitor]
Janiveer, Janiwar see JANUAR
jank /dʒaŋk/ v to evade, elude; to fob off la17-19, 20- T. [perhaps altered form of JINK¹·²]
janker /'dʒaŋkər/ n 1 a log-cart; a long pole on wheels used to transport timber suspended underneath it 19-. 2 a heavy stone or iron frame laid on a new grave to thwart graverobbers (transported to the site by a log-cart) 20- historical. [unknown]
janner see JAUNNER¹·²
jannie /'dʒane, 'dʒani/ n a (school) janitor la20-. [shortened form of JANITOR]
jantle see GENTLE¹·²
jantleman see GENTLEMAN
jantry see GENTRY
Januar, Janwar, January, Janiwar, Janiveer, †Jenuar, †Jenvarie, †Januer /'dʒanjuər, 'dʒanwar, 'dʒanjuəre, 'dʒanıwar, 'dʒanıvir/ n the first month of the year, January la14-. [ME januari]
jap see JAUP¹·¹, JAUP¹·²
japp see JABB
japple¹·¹ /'dʒapəl/ n slush; liquid mud, a mire; a mess la19- Sh. [probably frequentative form of JAUP¹·¹; compare JABBLE¹·¹]
japple¹·², N **chapple** /'dʒapəl/ N 'tʃapəl/ v 1 to stamp with the feet in water, splash about 20- Sh N T. 2 to wash clothes by tramping them la19- Sh. [see the noun]
jappy, japsy see JAUP¹·¹
†jar v to push, thrust e16. [unknown]
jar see JAUR
†jarbe, jerb n a piece of jewellery in the form of a sheaf la16-17. [OFr jarbe a sheaf]
jarg, jargle see JIRG²·²
jarie see JAURIE
jark see JIRG²·²
jarl see EARL
jarmer see YARM
jarrie see JAURIE
jasch see JASS
jaskit /'dʒaskıt/ adj jaded, worn out la19- Sh NE T. [reduced form of DISJASKIT or FORJESKIT]
jasp see JESP²
jass, †jasch /dʒas/ n 1 a splash, the dash of a wave 16-19, 20- NE. 2 a violent throw, a heavy blow 19, 20- NE. [unknown]
jassink see JACINCT
jauchelt see JACHELT
jauchle /'dʒɔxəl/ v to shuffle; to struggle through, do something with difficulty 19- C. [probably onomatopoeic; compare JUFFLE]
jaud, Ork **chad, †jad** /dʒɔd; Ork tʃad/ n 1 a derogatory term for a woman 17-. 2 a derogatory term for an old, worn-out horse 17-19, 20- NE T Bor. 3 a wilful, perverse animal la19-. 4 an old or useless article 19- NE EC. [perhaps conflation of YAUD with Older Scots jad, jade]
jaudie /'dʒɔdi/ n 1 the stomach of a pig or sheep (used in making haggis) 19- T EC Bor. 2 an oatmeal pudding (made from the stomach of a pig or sheep); a haggis 19- T EC Bor. [diminutive form of JADDEN]
jaug see JAG³
jaugle see JOOGLE¹·²
jauk, †jak /dʒɔk/ v 1 to idle, dawdle, slack or laze about la15-19, 20- NE SW Uls. 2 of footwear to be slack or loose-fitting 19- NE. [unknown]

jaunner[1.1], **jauner** /'dʒɔnər/ n **1** idle, foolish talk *la18- SW Bor.* **2** a chatterbox *19- SW Bor.* [variant of CHANNER[2]]

jaunner[1.2], **jaunder**, *SW* **janner** /'dʒɔnər, 'dʒɔndər; *SW* 'dʒanər/ v to talk idly, foolishly or jokingly *19-*. [see the noun]

jaup[1.1], **jap** /dʒɔp, dʒap/ n **1** the splashing of the sea, a dashing or breaking wave; a choppy sea *16-*. **2** a splash of water or mud; a dirty splatter (of something) *la18-*. **3** a small quantity, a drop (of alcohol) *19-*. **4** a spark from a fire or flying fragment of red-hot metal *la19, 20- EC.* **jaupy**, **jappy** **1** splashy, muddy *la19, 20- Sh.* **2** *of the sea* rough, choppy *20- Uls.* **japsy** splashy, muddy *20- Sh.* **gae to jaup** to be wrecked or brought to ruin *la19- SW.* [onomatopoeic]

jaup[1.2], **jawp**, **jap** /dʒɔp, dʒap/ v **1** *of liquid* to splash, spill; *of waves* dash *16-*. **2** to cause (liquid) to splash or spill, make a splash *18-*. **3** to bespatter with water or mud *la18-*. **jaupin fu** brimming over *20-*. [see the noun]

jaup[1.3], **jawp** /dʒɔp/ adv with a splash or splashing sound *la18-19, 20- EC.* [see the noun]

jaup *see* JABB

jaur, **jar** /dʒɔr, dʒar/ n a (broad-mouthed) glass or earthenware vessel *la18-*. [Fr *jarre*]

jaurie, **jorrie**, **jarrie**, **jarie** /'dʒɔri, 'dʒari/ n an earthenware marble *la19-*. **have a jorrie in yer mouth** to speak in an affected way; to have an over-refined accent *la20-*. [JAUR + -IE[1]]

†**javeling**, **jeffeling** n a javelin; a spear *16-e17.* Compare GEVILLING. [MFr *javeline*]

†**javell**, **jevill** n a jail *17.* Compare JILE[1.1]. [OFr *javiole*]

javell *see* JEVEL

†**javelor**, **javellour**, **jevellour** n a jailer *la15-e18.* Compare *jiler* (JILE[1.1]). [OFr *jaiolëor*]

jaw[1.1], *NE* **ja** /dʒɔ; *NE* dʒa/ n **1** a wave, a breaker; the surge or swell of the sea *16-*. **2** a sudden outpouring of water, a cascade; a spurt or splash of liquid; liquid splashed or thrown *19-*. **3** a draught, a drink *la18-19, 20- NE SW.* †**jallingstane** = *jaw-hole e16.* †**jaurhole**, **jawer-hoill** = *jaw-hole la16-e19.* **jaw-box** a sink in a kitchen or on a common stair *19- C Uls.* **jaw-hole 1** a primitive drain; originally a hole in the wall of a house for pouring away dirty water or sewage *la17-*. **2** the mouth of a cesspool; a sewer; a foul place *19-*. **3** a (communal) sink, a water-trough *19-*. †**jawe stane** a stone sink in a scullery *e16.* [unknown]

jaw[1.2] /dʒɔ/ v **1** to pour or throw liquid abruptly; to splash, spill *16-*. **2** *of water* to gush, splash, overflow; *of waves* to surge *18-*. [unknown]

jaw *see* JAA

jawp *see* JAUP[1.2], JAUP[1.3]

†**jawpish**, **chaudpis** n urethritis *la16-18.* [MFr *chaude pisse* hot piss]

jay, †**ja** /dʒe/ n **1** the bird *Garrulus glandarius la15-*. **2** the mistle thrush *Turdus viscivorus la19- Uls.* **jay pyot** the bird *Garrulus glandarius 19-*. [ME *jai*]

jaykit *see* JAIKET

jayle *see* JILE[1.1]

jayne *see* GENE[1]

jealous *see* JEELOUS

jealouse *see* JALOUSE

jeanie /'dʒini/ n a spinning-jenny; a spinning factory *la18-19, 20- historical.* [altered form of Eng *spinning-jenny*]

jeast *see* JEEST[2.2]

jeb *see* JAB[1.1]

jebber *see* JIBBER

jeck[1] /dʒɛk/ v **1** to neglect work *la18-19, 20- NE.* **2** to throw (up), discard, abandon *20- WC Bor.* **3** to dislocate a joint *20- SW Bor.* [perhaps variant of JAUK]

jeck[2] /dʒɛk/ v to move correctly or smoothly; to fit in (with) *18- NE T.* [variant of CHACK[1.2]]

jeck *see* JACK[1], JAIK

jecket *see* JAIKET

Jedburgh, **Jeddart** *see* JETHART

†**jedge**[1.1], **jadge** n **1** a gauge; an instrument used to verify the dimensions of a standard measure or a vessel of a standard capacity; the standard to which such measures or vessels must conform *la16-e18.* **2** *law* an order from a Dean of Guild authorizing repairs or rebuilding of a property *17.* [MFr *jauge*; compare GAUGE[1.1]]

†**jedge**[1.2], **jadge** v to verify the capacity of a standard measure or vessel (by means of a gauge) *la16-e17.* **jadgear** a gauger (who verified that the fish barrels were of a standard size) *la16-e17.* **jadgerie** the action or office of gauging *la16-e17.* [MFr *jauger*; compare GAUGE[1.2]]

jedge and warrant, †**jedge and warrand** /'dʒɛdʒ ənd wɔrənt/ n *law* an order from a Dean of Guild authorizing repairs or rebuilding of a property *17-*. [JEDGE[1.1] + WARRANT[1.1]]

Jedwart *see* JETHART

jee[1.1], **gee** /dʒi/ n a move, a motion, a sideways turn *19-*. **jee e'ed** squint-eyed *la19- T C.* **gee-ways** squint, sideways *18-19,20- T EC.* **on the jee**, **on the gee** awry, off the straight *19-*. [unknown]

jee[1.2], **gee** /dʒi/ v **1** to move or budge; to move to one side or another, swerve; *18-*. **2** to cause or command to move, stir; to shift to one side; to raise *18-*. **3** *of horses* to turn to one side *19-*. **jeed** awry, squint *la19- N T C.* **jee yer ginger**, **gee yer ginger** to show concern, get upset; to become flustered *la18-*. [unknown]

jeebauld *see* GEEBALD

jeedge *see* JUDGE[1.1], JUDGE[1.2]

jeedgement *see* JUDGEMENT

jeeg[1.1], **jig**, †**jeig** /dʒig, dʒɪg/ n **1** a lively dance, a jig *la16-*. **2** a jerking movement, a sudden pull *la18-*. **3** *pl* high jinks, capers *la18-*. **4** an instrument for catching fish, a sinker or wire frame with fish hooks attached *la19-*. [unknown]

jeeg[1.2], **jig**, †**gig**, †**jeig** /dʒig, dʒɪg/ v **1** to dance *la18-*. **2** to move in a brisk or jerky fashion *la18-*. **3** to catch fish with a sinker or wire frame *la19-*. **the jigging, the jiggin** dancing; a dance *19-*. [unknown]

jeeg[2], †**geig** /dʒig/ v to creak, make a creaking noise *16-19, 20- NE Uls.* [onomatopoeic]

jeeger, **jigger** /'dʒigər, 'dʒɪgər/ n an odd or eccentric person *19-*. [JEEG[1.2], with agent suffix -*er*]

jeegle[1.1], **jiggle**, *Sh* **shiggle** /'dʒigəl, 'dʒɪgəl; *Sh* 'ʃɪgəl/ n a shake, a jog *19-*. [see the verb]

jeegle[1.2], **jiggle**, *Sh* **shiggle** /'dʒigəl, 'dʒɪgəl; *Sh* 'ʃɪgəl/ v to shake, wiggle *19-*. **jeegly**, **jiggly**, *Sh* **shiggly** unsteady, shaky *la19-*. [frequentative form of JEEG[1.2]]

jeel[1.1], **geal** /dʒil/ n **1** jelly *la15-*. **2** extreme coldness, frostiness *la19-*. **3** a severe chill, a chilling sensation *20- NE T.* **jeel cauld**, **geal cauld** cold as ice, stone-cold *la19- NE.* [OFr *gel*, *giel*]

jeel[1.2], **geal**, **geill** /dʒil/ v **1** *of jam or jelly* to set, congeal; *of stock* to thicken or solidify *18-*. **2** to freeze, become numb with cold *la18-*. [OFr *geler*]

jeelie[1.1], **jeely**, **jelly** /'dʒili, 'dʒɛli/ n **1** a set fruit dessert; originally a savoury preparation made with gelatin *18-*. **2** jam *19-*. **jeelie can**, **jeely can** a jam pot *20-*. **jeelie jaur**, **jeely jar** a jam pot *20-*. **jeelie-mug** a jam pot *20-*. **jeelie neb** a bloody nose *20-*. **jeely nose** a bloody nose *20-*. **jeelie pan**, **jeely pan** a (brass) pan for making jam or jelly *la19-*. **jeelie piece**, **jeely piece** a jam sandwich *19-*. **jeelie pig**, **jeely pig** a jam pot *la19- NE T.* [Fr *gelée*]

jeelie[1.2], **jeely, jelly** /'dʒili, 'dʒɛle/ v 1 to set like jelly 20-. 2 to cause the nose to bleed (by punching it) la19- T EC. [see the noun]

jeelous, jailous, jealous, Ork **chealous,** †**jelous,** †**jalous,** †**iolyus** /'dʒiləs, 'dʒɛləs, 'dʒɛləs; Ork 'tʃɛləs/ adj 1 envious, covetous (of) la15-. 2 suspicious, apprehensive 16-. **jeelousy, jailousy,** †**jolesy,** †**jelosy** 1 jealousy la14-. 2 suspicion 16- [ME jelous]

jeely see JEELIE[1.1], JEELIE[1.2], JELLIE

Jeen see JUNE

jeeng-bang see JING-BANG

jeep see JUPE[1]

jeest[1.1]**, jeist,** †**jest,** †**geist,** †**gest** /dʒist, dʒʌist/ n a large timber beam supporting a floor or bridge; a joist la14-. [ME giste]

†**jeest**[1.2]**, jeist, geist** v to furnish with joists la16-18. [see the noun]

jeest[2.1]**, jest,** †**gest** /dʒist, dʒɛst/ n 1 a joke, fun 16-. 2 a tale, a legend; deeds, exploits la14-e17. **nae jeesty** no laughing matter la19- NE. [ME gest, jeste]

jeest[2.2]**, jest,** †**jeast,** †**gest** /dʒist, dʒɛst/ v to joke, mock la16-. [see the noun]

jeest see JIST[1.2]

jeesting, †**jeisting,** †**geisting,** †**gesting** /'dʒistɪŋ/ n (the furnishing of) timber work; joisting 16-. [JEEST[1.1], with -ing suffix]

jeet, †**geit,** †**jeit** /dʒit/ n a hard black mineral, jet; a bead made of jet 16-19, 20 NE T. **jeety** 1 bright, sparkling la19- NE. 2 neat, fastidious 20- NE T. [ME get, AN geit]

jeet see JOOT

jeetle see JUITLE[1.1], JUITLE[1.2]

†**jeezy, gezy** n a wig la18-e19. [unknown; compare GIZZ]

jeezy see GIZZ

jeffeling see JAVELING

jeg see JAG[3]

jeho, jehoy /dʒə'ho, dʒə'hɔɪ/ v to give over, stop, cease la19- NE Uls. [JEE[1.2] + HO[2.2]]

jeig see JEEG[1.1], JEEG[1.2]

jeist see JEEST[1.1], JEEST[1.2]

jeisting see JEESTING

jeit see GEIT[1.2], JEET

jellie, jelly, jeely, †**gelly** /'dʒɛli, 'dʒili/ adj 1 light-hearted, merry, joyous la16-. 2 pleasant, attractive, agreeable; splendid, fine, grand la16-. 3 upright, honest, worthy, excellent 18-19, 20- literary. [ME joli]

jelly see JEELIE[1.1], JEELIE[1.2]

jelous see JALOUSE, JEELOUS

jenepere, jeniper /'dʒɛnɪpər/ n juniper 19-. [Lat jūniperus]

jenet see JONET

Jenkin's hen, Jinken's hen /'dʒɛŋkɪnz hɛn, 'dʒɪŋkɪnz hɛn/ n a hen which never knew the cock; an old maid, a spinster la18-. **die the death of Jenkin's hen** to die an old maid la18-19, 20- literary. [from the surname Jenkin + HEN[1.1]]

jennapie see ENNAPI

jennock see JONICK[1.1]

Jenny, Jinny /'dʒɛne, 'dʒɪne/ n 1 a generic term for a woman or girl, especially a country girl 17-. 2 pl hermaphrodite callipers with one leg with a short bend and the other with a point la19-. 3 derogatory a man who occupies himself with what others regard as female concerns; an effeminate man 20-; compare JESSIE. **Jennt a'thing, Jenny a'things** the female owner of a small general store; a shop with a variety of merchandise la19-; compare Johnnie a'thing (JOHN). **Jenny's blue een** the speedwell Veronica officinalis 20-. **Jenny Gray, Jenny Grey** the black guillemot Cepphus grylle in its first or winter plumage la19- N. **jennie heron** the grey heron Ardea cinerea la19-. **Jennie-hunder-feet, Jenny-hunnert-feet** a centipede of the family Chilopoda la19-. **Jennie-hunder-legs** a centipede 20-. **Jennie-lang-legs** the cranefly or 'daddy-long-legs' of the family Tipulidae 19-. **Jenny Lind** a fancy loaf named after the Swedish opera singer 20-. **Jenny meggie** = Jennie-lang-legs la19- C. **Jenny-mony-feet** a centipede 19, 20- NE T EC. **Jenny Muck, Jinny Muck** a working woman; a female farmworker la19- N NE. **Jenny-nettle, Jenny-nettles** 1 the cranefly or 'daddy-long-legs' of the family Tipulidae 19-. 2 the stinging nettle Urtica dioica 19- C Bor. **Jenny reekie** a hollow cabbage stalk packed with tow, used to blow smoke into a house as a Halloween prank 19- NE T C. **Jenny speeder** = Jennie-lang-legs 20- SW Bor. **Jenny spinner** = Jennie-lang-legs 19- N NE SW Bor. **Jenny Wullock** 1 a hermaphrodite; an effeminate man la19- C. 2 a castrated farm animal; an farm animal with undescended testicles la20- C. [familiar form of the personal names Jennifer, Jane, Jean and Janet]

Jenuar, Jenvarie see JANUAR

†**jeopard, juperd** v to risk, venture 16. [shortened form of JEOPARDIE[1.2]]

jeopardie[1.1]**, jeopardy,** NE **jipperty,** †**juparty,** †**iuperdy,** †**jeperte** /'dʒɛpərdi; NE 'dʒɪpərti/ n 1 danger, peril; risk, chance la14-. 2 a daring exploit, a feat of arms; a battle or raid la14-e19. 3 pl risks, difficulties 15-e19. 4 valour, prowess la15-e16. 5 a stratagem, a trick la14-e16. [ME juparti]

†**jeopardie**[1.2] v to venture, risk 16. [see the noun]

jerarche see CHERARCHY

jerb see JARBE

jereflour see GERAFLOUR

jerg see JIRG[2.1]

jerk see JIRG[1]

jerker, Bor **yerker** /'dʒɛrkər; Bor 'jɛrkər/ n a white oatmeal pudding 20- NE T Bor. [perhaps Eng jerk, from their motion when cooking]

†**jerkin**[1] n 1 merrymaking; a party taking place on a ship's leaving port 19. 2 the departure of a ship la19. [unknown]

jerkin[2]**,** †**girkin** /'dʒɛrkɪn/ n 1 a close-fitting, sleeveless garment for the upper body 16-. 2 a bodice worn by women 18-e19. †**jerkenet, jirkinet, girkienet** a bodice worn by women la17-18. [unknown]

jerr see JIRR

Jerusalem haddie, Jerusalem haddock /dʒərusələm 'hadi, dʒərusələm 'hadək/ n the opah or kingfish Lampris guttatus la19- Ork N NE T EC. [from the name of the city + HADDIE]

Jerusalem traveller /dʒərusələm 'travələr/ n a louse, an insect of the order Phthiraptera 20- Ork NE T. [from the name of the city + traveller (TRAIVEL[1.2])]

jesing see JIZZEN

jesp[1]**, jisp** /dʒɛsp, dʒɪsp/ n 1 a small gap or opening; a crack; a flaw in the weave of a fabric; a broken thread la18-. 2 a stain, speck, blemish 19- SW Bor. [unknown]

†**jesp**[2]**, jasp** n jasper, the precious stone 15-e17. [Fr jaspe]

Jessie /'dʒɛsi, 'dʒɛse/ n derogatory an effeminate man or boy; a cowardly person (of either sex) 20-. **Jessie Ann** = JESSIE 20- NE. **Jessie Fisher** = JESSIE 20- NE T. **jessypunt** a sycophantic person la20- EC. [from the personal name]

jest see JEEST[1.1], JEEST[2.1], JEEST[2.2]

jester see GESTER

Jethart, Jeddart, Jedburgh, †**Jedwart,** †**Gedward** /'dʒɛðərt, 'dʒɛdərt, 'dʒɛdbʌrə/ n Jedburgh, the town in the Borders la11-. **Jeddart callant, Jethart callant** one of the main male participants in the Jedburgh Callants Festival la19-. **Jeddart cast** = Jeddart justice 17-19, 20- historical.

Jeddart justice, Jedburgh Justice, Jethart Justice precipitate or arbitrary justice, condemnation without a hearing *la17-*. **Jeddart law, Jethart law** = *Jeddart justice 18-19, 20- historical*. **Jeddart snails, Jethart snails** a kind of toffee from Jedburgh *20-*. **Jeddart staff, Jedburgh staff, †Jedwart staff, †gedward staf** a weapon similar to a bill or halberd, originally from Jedburgh (represented on Jedburgh's coat of arms) *16-18, 19- historical*. [the river name *Jed* + OE *worþ* an enclosure]

jeualrie *see* JOWEL

jeuk *see* DEUK, JOUK[1.1], JOUK[1.2]

jeukery-packery *see* JOUKERIE-PAWKERIE

†jevel, ievell, javell *n* a ruffian, a rascal *16-19*. [unknown]

jevellour *see* JAVELOR

jevill *see* JAVELL

Jew, †Jow /dʒu/ *n* **1** a person of Hebrew descent, a follower of Judaism *la14-*. **2** a term of abuse for an unbeliever or infidel *e16*. **Jew's loaf** a small loaf rounded on top with a brownish glaze *la19- WC SW*. **Jew's roll** = *Jew's loaf*. [ME *Jeu*, Lat *Jūdaeus*]

jewel *see* JOWEL

jewkry-pawkry *see* JOUKERIE-PAWKERIE

jeyner *see* JINER

jeyole *see* JILE[1.1]

Jhone *see* JOHN

jib /dʒɪb/ *v* to milk a cow to the last drop *18- WC SW Bor*. **jibbings** the strippings from a cow's udder *19- WC SW Bor*. [unknown]

jibber, *NE* **jebber** /ˈdʒɪbər/; *NE* ˈdʒɛbər/ *n* silly talk, idle chatter *19-*. [onomatopoeic]

jibbery *see* GIBBERY[1]

jibble[1.1] /ˈdʒɪbəl/ *n* **1** a small or unsatisfactory quantity of a liquid (especially to drink) *19-*. **2** a splash, the splashing or lapping of a liquid *20-*. [unknown; compare JABBLE[1.1]]

jibble[1.2] /ˈdʒɪbəl/ *v* to spill a liquid by agitating its container *19-*. [see the noun]

jice, joice, juice, †jise, †jus, †juce /dʒɪs, dʒʌɪs, dʒɔɪs, dʒus/ *n* extracted liquid, juice *16-*. [MFr *jus*]

jick[1.1] /dʒɪk/ *n* **1** the act of eluding *19- C Bor*. **2** a sudden jerk *19- Bor*. **play the jick** to play truant *20- C Bor*. [variant of JINK[1.1]; compare JOUK[1.1]]

jick[1.2] /dʒɪk/ *v* **1** to elude, dodge, evade *19- C Bor*. **2** to jerk away suddenly; to tug or pull smartly *19- C Bor*. **jicker** to move, walk or ride quickly *la18- EC Bor*. [see the noun]

jidge *see* JUDGE[1.1], JUDGE[1.2]

jidgement *see* JUDGEMENT

jiff /dʒɪf/ *n* a person of doubtful reputation *20- NE*. **jiffer** = JIFF. [perhaps variant of CHUFF]

jig *see* JEEG[1.1], JEEG[1.2]

jigger *see* JEEGER

jiggle *see* JEEGLE[1.1], JEEGLE[1.2]

jile[1.1], **jyle, jail, †jeyole, †jayle, †gyel** /dʒʌɪl, dʒel/ *n* a prison, a jail *la14-*; compare JAVELL. **jiler, jailer, †geyler, †jylour, †jaylour** a prison warder, a gaoler *la14*; compare JAVELOR. **get the jile, get the jail 1** to be sent to prison *la19-*. **2** to be severely punished *la20-*. [ME *gaiol*]

jile[1.2], **jyle** /dʒʌɪl/ *v* to send to prison *la19-*. [see the noun]

jillet, †gillet /ˈdʒɪlət/ *n* a flighty girl, a flirtatious girl *la18-19, 20- SW*. [familiar form of the personal names *Jill* and *Gillian*]

jilly *see* GILLIE[2]

jilp[1.1], *EC* **jilt** /dʒɪlp; *EC* dʒɪlt/ *n* **1** a splash, a spurt; a small quantity of liquid splashed or spilt *19- NE T EC*. **2** a meagre quantity of liquid, a thin or insipid drink *la19- NE T EC*. [onomatopoeic; compare JAUP[1.1]]

jilp[1.2], **gilp**, *EC* **jilt** /dʒɪlp; *EC* dʒɪlt/ *v* **1** to splash or spill liquid; to move a container so that the contents spill *19- NE* *T C*. **2** *of a liquid* to splash about or over *19- Sh NE T*. [see the noun]

jilt[1] /dʒɪlt/ *n* **1** a jilt, a woman who jilts a lover *la18-*. **2** a contemptuous term for a girl or young woman *la18-19, 20- Bor*. Compare JILLET. [reduced form of JILLET]

jilt *see* JILP[1.1], JILP[1.2]

jimmy *see* GIM

Jimmy, Jimmie /ˈdʒɪme/ *n* **1** a white pudding or oatmeal pudding *20-*. **2** an informal form of address to a man (usually a stranger) *la20-*. **Mealie Jimmie** *see* MEALIE. [familiar form of the personal name *James*]

†jimp[1], **iymp, gymp** *n* a subtle or trifling point; a quirk *la15-16*. [perhaps related to JIMP[2.2]]

jimp[2.1] /dʒɪmp/ *v* **1** to curtail, restrict; to stint, keep in short supply *19-*. **2** to give a short or scant measure *la19-*. **jimpit, †gimpit** short, stunted *19-* [unknown]

jimp[2.2], **gimp, †gymp, †jump** /dʒɪmp/ *adj* **1** *of people* slender, small, graceful, neat, dainty *16-*. **2** *of measure or quantity* scanty, sparing, barely adequate *17-*. **3** *of clothes* close-fitting, tight *19-*. **jimpie, jimpy 1** small, slender *19-*. **2** scanty, barely sufficient *19-*. **jimp o** lacking, short of *20- NE T EC*. [unknown]

jimp[2.3] /dʒɪmp/ *adv* barely, scarcely *la18-*. **jimply** barely, scarcely *la18-* [unknown]

†jimp[3], **jump** *n* a strip or sliver of leather (used to build up the heel of a shoe) *la17-e19*. [perhaps related to JUMP]

jimp[4], **†jump** /dʒɪmp/ *n* a woman's bodice *la18-19, 20- NE*. **jimpie, †jampy** a woman's bodice *18-19, 20- NE*. [OFr *juppe* a tunic, compare EModE *jump*]

jimp *see* JUMP

jine[1.1], **join** /dʒʌɪn, dʒɔɪn/ *n* **1** the clubbing together of several people to buy drink; a social gathering or outing *la19-*. **2** an association of neighbours for some communal task *19- Uls*. [see the verb]

jine[1.2], **jyne, join, †jone, †june, †joyn** /dʒʌɪn, dʒɔɪn/ *v* **1** to fasten together, attach; to unite or combine *15-*. **2** to become a communicant of (a particular religious denomination) *19-*. **3** to begin work *la19-*. **a jined member** Presbyterian Church a communicant *19-*. [ME *joinen*]

jiner, jyner, jeyner, joiner; *N* **chiner** /ˈdʒʌɪnər, ˈdʒɛnər, ˈdʒɔɪnər;* N* ˈtʃʌɪnər/ *n* **1** a woodworker, carpenter *17-*. **2** a sharer; a partner or confederate *la17*. **joinery, jinery 1** woodworking, carpentry *la18-*. **2** a joiner's workshop *20-*. [JINE[1.2], with agent suffix]

jing[1] /dʒɪŋ/ *interj* a mild expletive *la18-*. **jings** a mild expletive *20-*. **by jing** = *jings*. **by jings** = *jings*. [unknown; compare Eng *jingo*]

jing[2] /dʒɪŋ/ *v* to ring, jingle *19, 20- T*. [onomatopoeic]

jing-bang, *H&I* **jeeng-bang** /dʒɪŋˈbaŋ; *H&I* dʒɪŋˈbaŋ/ *n* a considerable number, a lot *19-*. **the hail jing-bang, the whole jing-bang** the whole lot, the entire company, the whole affair *19-*. [unknown]

jingle *see* CHINGLE

jingo-ring /ˈdʒɪŋɡo rɪŋ/ *n* a children's singing game, where the players hold hands and dance in a ring *19-*. [unknown first element + RING[1.1]]

jinipperous, jinniprous /dʒəˈnɪpərəs, dʒəˈnɪprəs/ *adj* spruce, trim; finicky, over-particular, stiff *19- NE*. [perhaps JENEPERE juniper]

jink[1.1] /dʒɪŋk/ *n* **1** the act of dodging or eluding someone; a dodge, a trick *la18-*. **2** a quick or sudden movement, a jerk, a turn *la19-*. **3** a playful trick or frolic *19, 20- Sh NE H&I Uls*. **4** a coil, a twist, a kink *la19- Sh NE WC*. **jinkie** a chasing game; hide-and-seek *19-*. **jinks** = *jinkie*. **high jinks** lively or boisterous sport, unrestrained merrymaking, originally a drinking game *18-*. [onomatopoeic]

jink[1,2] /dʒɪŋk/ *v* **1** to jaunt, frolic; to flirt *18-*. **2** to turn quickly, spin, to move or dodge nimbly or swiftly, slip in or out *la18-*. **3** to dart, zigzag; to make sudden or jerky movements *la18-*. **4** to evade, elude; to cheat or trick *la18-*. **5** to play truant *la20- N T EC*. **6** to dance or play the violin jerkily or briskly *18-19*. **jinker** a pleasure-seeker; a libertine, a wanton; a dodger or trickster *18-19, 20- NE*. **jinkers** a game involving the catching or dodging of a ball thrown at a wall *20-*. [see the noun]

jink[2] /dʒɪŋk/ *n* a chink, a crack *19- C*. [variant of Eng *chink*]

Jinken's hen see JENKIN'S HEN

jinkie[1] /ˈdʒɪŋki/ *adj* a nonsense word in nursery rhymes *la19- Ork NE*.

jinkie[2.1] /ˈdʒɪŋki/ *adj* jaunty *20- NE*. [reduced form of PERJINK[1.1]]

jinkie[2.2] /ˈdʒɪŋki/ *adv* jauntily *20- NE*. [see the adj]

Jinny see JENNY

jinsh /dʒɪnʃ/ *n* a small piece of something *19- NE*. [compare KINSH[2]]

jint[1.1], **jynt**, **joint** /dʒɪnt, dʒʌɪnt, dʒɔɪnt/ *n* the place where things join; the point at which two bones meet *16-*. **joint girse** horse-tail *Equisetum 20- Ork*. [ME *joint*, EModE *joint*]

jint[1.2], **jynt**, **joint** /dʒɪnt, dʒʌɪnt, dʒɔɪnt/ *v* to provide or fasten with joints; to separate at the joint, cut (meat) into joints *18-*. [see the noun]

jint[1.3], **jynt**, **joint** /dʒɪnt, dʒʌɪnt, dʒɔɪnt/ *adj* joined, fastened; shared, common; united in a group *15-*. Compare JUNCT. **jointly**, **jintly**, †**juntly** in conjunction or combination, together *la14-*. **jointure**, †**jointour 1** the estate settled on a widow *16-*. **2** a metal link or connecting piece of a harness *e16*. **joint adventure** *law* a limited partnership undertaken for a specific purpose and restricted as regards to liability *la18-*. †**joint-feftment**, **junt-feftment** *law* infeftment made to two people jointly *15*. [see the noun]

jipperty see JEOPARDIE[1.1]

jirble[1.1], *Bor* **jairble** /ˈdʒɪrbəl; *Bor* ˈdʒɛrbəl/ *n* **1** a small quantity of liquid poured out; a drop; a drip, a splash *19- C Bor*. **2** *pl* spillings; dregs *19- EC Bor*. [perhaps onomatopoeic]

jirble[1.2], *Bor* **jairble** /ˈdʒɪrbəl; *Bor* ˈdʒɛrbəl/ *v* **1** to splash, slop (liquid) *la18-*. **2** to pour out unsteadily in small quantities *19-*. [see the noun]

jird see JIRT[1.1], JIRT[1.2]

jirg[1.1] /dʒɪrg/ *n* a squelching sound *19- NE*. [onomatopoeic]

jirg[1.2], *NE* **jirje**, *NE T* **jerk** /dʒɪrg; *NE* dʒɪrdʒ; *NE T* dʒɛrk/ *v* **1** to make a squelching or splashing sound *la18- NE T EC SW*. **2** to wash clothes in water (with a squelching or splashing sound); to shake liquid violently up and down *20- NE Bor*. [see the noun]

jirg[2.1], **jerg**, **jirk** /dʒɪrg, dʒɛrg, dʒɪrk/ *n* a creaking or grating sound *la18-*. **jargle** clamour, noise *20- T EC Bor*. [onomatopoeic]

jirg[2.2], **jirk**, *Bor* **jarg**, *Bor* **jairg**, †**girg**, †**jark** /dʒɪrg, dʒɪrk; *Bor* dʒarg; *Bor* dʒɛrg/ *v* **1** to creak, make a grating sound; to jar *16-*. **2** to grate or grind the teeth *19, 20- N H&I Bor*. **3** to hesitate, waver or flinch *e17*. **jargle** to make a sharp, shrill or harsh sound; to argue *19- T EC Bor*. [see the noun]

jirje see JIRG[1.2]

jirk, *Ork N* **cherk**, †**girke** /dʒɪrk; *Ork N* tʃɛrk/ *n* **1** a sharp sudden movement, a jerk *la18-*. **2** a smart blow *17-19, 20- NE T*. **jirkie** changeable *19- NE T C*. **in a jirk** in an instant *la19- N NE T EC*. [onomatopoeic]

jirk see JIRG[2.1], JIRG[2.2]

jirp /dʒɪrp, tʃɪrp/ *v* to make a squelching noise when wet; to become sodden *20- Ork*. [compare JIRG[1.2]]

jirr, **jerr** /dʒɪr, dʒɛr/ *n* a fit of temper *la19- NE*. †**jirrings** quarrels *e18*. [onomatopoeic]

jirt[1.1], *Sh* **jird** /dʒɪrt; *Sh* dʒɪrd/ *n* a sudden or sharp blow, squeeze or push, a jerk, a jolt *la17-19, 20- Sh EC*. [variant of CHIRT[1.1]]

jirt[1.2], *Sh* **jird** /dʒɪrt; *Sh* dʒɪrd/ *v* to jerk; to move jerkily, dart *20- Sh EC Bor*. [see the noun]

jise see JICE

jisp see JESP[1]

jist[1.1], **juist**, **just** /dʒɪst, dʒʊst, dʒʌst/ *adj* **1** equitable, fair; lawful, justified *la15-*. **2** exact, precise; correct, accurate *16-*. [ME *just*]

jist[1.2], **juist**, **joost**, **just**, *Ork N* **chist**, *NE* **jeest**, *H&I* **deest**, *H&I WC* **chust**, *SW* **doost**, *Bor* **duist** /dʒɪst, dʒʊst, dʒʌst; *Ork N* tʃɪst; *NE* dʒist; *H&I* dist; *H&I WC* tʃʌst; *SW Bor* dust/ *adv* **1** exactly, accurately, correctly, directly *la15-*. **2** at this time, just now, precisely *la17-*. **3** only, merely; barely *18-*. **4** frequently following the word or phrase it modifies really, quite, absolutely, simply, indeed, truly ◊*I took a dram, for I was geeled juist la18-*. **jist that**, **juist that** quite so, precisely *la19-*. [see the adj]

jittle see JUITLE[1.2]

jivvle /ˈdʒɪvəl/ *n* a bare, uncomfortable apartment, a cell-like place; a jail *20- NE*. [compare JAVELL]

jiz see GIZZ

jizzen, **gissan**, †**jesing**, †**gesyne**, †**gising** /ˈdʒɪzən/ *n* childbed *15-17, 18- literary*. [ME *gesin*]

jo, **joe** /dʒo/ *n* **1** a term of endearment for someone considered precious or dear *16-*. **2** a sweetheart, a (male) lover *17-*. **3** joy, happiness *16*. [MFr *joie*]

joabby see JOBBY

joattur see JOTTER[1.1]

job[1.1], **joab**, **jobe**, *Ork* **chob** /dʒɔb, dʒob; *Ork* tʃɔb/ *n* a piece of work; a task, a deed; regular paid employment, an occupation *18-*. [unknown]

job[1.2] /dʒɔb/ *v* **1** to do a job or task, undertake (casual) work *la18-*. **2** to give or receive a position or post corruptly; to abuse a public office or position of trust for personal gain *18-19*. **3** to have illicit sexual intercourse *18-e19*. [unknown]

job[2.1], *T* **jobe** /dʒɔb; *T* dʒob/ *n* a light prick; a prickle *19, 20- Sh NE T EC*. **jobbie**, **joby** prickly *19- Sh NE T EC*. **jobbie nettle** the stinging nettle *Urtica dioica 20- NE T*. [variant of JAB[1.1]]

job[2.2] /dʒɔb/ *v* to jab, pierce, stab; to prick (with a pin or thorn) *18-19, 20- Sh Ork NE T EC*. [see the noun]

†**job**[3] *v of a horse* to go at an easy pace, jog, amble *la16*. [unknown]

jobby, **jobbie**, **joabby** /ˈdʒɔbi, ˈdʒobi/ *n* **1** a task, a small piece of work *19-*. **2** a bowel movement; a lump of excrement *la20-*. **3** a contemptuous term for a person *la20-*. **4** any nonsense *la20-*. [JOB[1.1] + -IE[1]]

jobe see JOB[1.1]

job-trot /ˈdʒɔb trɔt/ *n* a slow, monotonous or easy-going pace; the settled or routine way of doing things *la17-19, 20- NE T*. [unknown; compare Eng *jog-trot*]

Jock, †**Jok** /dʒɔk/ *n* **1** a generic male personal name (frequently used as a reference to the common man) *16-*. **2** a male country-dweller; a farmworker *16-*. **3** a nickname for a Scotsman *17-*. **4** the male of a bird or animal *19-*; compare BUBBLY-JOCK. **5** an oatmeal pudding, a haggis *la19-*. **6** *mining* an iron rod attached to the rear of a train of hutches as a safety mechanism in the event of a rope breaking *la19-*. **7** a nickname for a soldier in one of the Scottish regiments *20-*. **8** a lump of stone in coal *20-*. **Jock-brit** a contemptuous term for a miner *20- C*. †**jock-fellow-like**, **joke-fellow-like** intimate, familiar *17-e19*; compare *jakfallow lyk* (JACK[1]).

Jock Hack a ploughman, a countryman *la19- NE*. **Jock Muck** = *Jock Hack*. **Jock Scott** angling an artificial fly, named after its inventor *19-*. †**Jok upaland** a rustic person, a country-dweller *la16-e17*; compare *Johne Upaland* (JOHN). **afore ye could say Jockamanorie** in a short time, very quickly *20- NE*. †**afore ye could say Jock Morrison** = *afore ye could say Jockamanorie 19*. **the deil's gane ower Jock Wabster** a proverbial expression indicating that things are in a mess or out of control *18-19, 20- N NE T*. **Jock the laird's brither** a proverbial expression describing a person treated with familiarity or little respect *la17-19, 20- historical*. **Jock Tamson's bairns** the human race, common humanity; a group of people united by a common sentiment or interest *19-*. **play Jock needle Jock preen** to play fast and loose, act in a double-dealing or shifty way *la19- NE*. [familiar form of the personal name *John*]

Jockie /'dʒɔke, 'dʒɔki/ *n* **1** a male personal name, frequently used as a generic term for a man *la16-*. **2** a familiar companion; a fellow Scot *la17-*. **3** a vagrant, a gipsy *la17-19, 20- Bor*. **4** a horse-dealer; a postilion *18-19*. **Jockie blindie** the game of blind-man's buff *la19- T*. **Jockie-blind-man** = *Jockie blindie 19-*. **Jockey coat** a greatcoat *18-*. **Jockie an his owsen** notches cut on a cowherd's stick, representing the method of yoking of an ox-plough team *e20, la20- historical*. [JOCK + -IE¹]

jockteleg, jocktaleg, †**jock the leg,** †**jocteleg,** †**jackteleg** /'dʒɔktəlɛg/ *n* a large clasp or pocket knife *17-* [probably JOCK + LEG¹·¹]

joco /dʒəˈko/ *adj* jovial, merry, cheerful; pleased with oneself *la19-*. [reduced form of Eng *jocose*]

joctibeet /dʒɔktəˈbit/ *n* the wheatear *Oenanthe oenanthe la19- N*. [probably onomatopoeic]

†**joculatour** *n* an entertainer, a jester *la15*. [Lat *joculātor* a joker, a jester]

joe see JO

joell see JOWEL

jog¹·¹ /dʒɔg/ *n* a jab, a prick *20- NE T EC*. [compare JAG¹·¹]

jog¹·², **joog** /dʒɔg, dʒug/ *v* to prick, pierce *18-*. [see the noun]

jog see JOUG²

joggill see JOOGLE¹·²

John, †**Johne,** †**Jhone** /dʒɔn/ *n* a generic male personal name (frequently prefixed to an epithet to form a nickname) *16-*. **Johndal, Jondal** a term of contempt for a young ploughman *la19- N*. **John Barleycorn** the personification of barley as the grain from which malt liquor is made; ale or whisky *la18-*. **John Gunn** a privy, a latrine *20- NE*. **John o Groat's buckie** the cowrie shell *Trivia monacha 18-*. **John o Groat's nightcap** a cap-shaped seashell *Capulus ungaricus 20- Ork N*. **John Thomson's man, John Tamson's man** a hen-pecked husband *16-19, 20- historical*. †**Johne Upaland, Johane Upponland** a rustic person, a country-dweller *16*. [from the personal name]

Johnny, Johnnie /'dʒɔni/ *n* a diminutive form of JOHN, frequently used to form nicknames *17-*. **Johnnie a'thing, Johnnie aathins** the owner of a small general store; a shop with a variety of merchandise *la19-*; compare *Jenny a'thing* (JENNY). †**Johnnie Ged's Hole** the grave *la18*. **Johnny Groatie** = *Johnnie Groats buckie 20- NE*. **Johnnie Groats buckie** the cowrie shell *Trivia monacha la18-*. **Johnnie Groat's House** a house on the North-Eastern tip of Canisbay parish in Caithness, proverbially the most northerly and remotest part of the Scottish mainland *19-*. **Johnny mainland** the angler fish *Lophius piscatorius 20- Ork*. [from the personal name]

Johnsmass, Johnsmas, †**Jonesmes** /'dʒɔnzməs/ *n* St John the Baptist's day, celebrated on the 24th of June *17- Sh Ork*. **Johnsmass floor, Johnsmas flooer** the ribwort plantain *Plantago lanceolata 20- Sh*. **Johnsmas Foy** a celebration held on St John's Day, coinciding with the arrival of the Dutch herring fleet in Lerwick Harbour *la19- Sh*. [from the name of the saint + MASS² denoting an ecclesiastical festival]

joice see JICE

join see JINE¹·¹, JINE¹·²

joiner see JINER

joint see JINT¹·¹, JINT¹·², JINT¹·³

joip see JUPE¹

joiter see JOTTER¹·¹

jok see JOUG²

Jok see JOCK

joke /dʒok/ *v* **1** to tease, poke fun at *18-*. **2** to jest, make a joke *20-*. **jokie** jocular, fond of a joke *19-*. [Lat *jocāri* to jest]

joke-fellow-like see JOCK

jokkis see JOUGS

jole, djoll /tʃɔl/ *n* a clumsy lump, a thick or heavy piece of wood, a chunk of meat *la19- Sh Ork*. [variant of DOLL¹]

jolesy see JEELOUS

jolious see JOLLY

jollisie see JALLISIE

jolly, †**joly** /'dʒɔli/ *adj* **1** merry, joyful; pretty, bright, resplendent *la14-*. **2** *of female dogs* in season *16-17*. †**jolious** jolly, merry, joyful *la16*. [ME *joli, joli*]

jonator see JANITOR

Jondal see JOHN

jone see JINE¹·²

†**jonet, jenet** *n* a small Spanish horse *16*. [MFr *genet*]

†**jonet flour, janet flour** *n* a variety of yellow flower *la16-17*. [compare FLOURE JONET]

jonick¹·¹, **jennock** /'dʒɔnək, 'dʒɛnək/ *n* fair play, justice *20-*. [unknown]

jonick¹·², **gennick** /'dʒɔnək, 'dʒɛnək/ *adj* genuine, honest, fair, just *la19-*. [unknown]

joob, jube /dʒub, tʃub/ *n* deep mud or mire; a very deep place (in a bog); a deep part of the sea *Sh*. [ON *djúp* a deep place]

joodge see JUDGE¹·¹, JUDGE¹·²

joodgment see JUDGEMENT

joog see JOG¹·², JOUG¹·¹

joogle¹·¹ /'dʒugəl/ *n* a shaking or rocking motion *19-*. [see the verb]

joogle¹·², †**jougle,** †**jaugle,** †**joggill** /'dʒugəl/ *v* to shake or jog repeatedly, rock; to wrestle (with) *16-*. [perhaps frequentative form of Older Scots *jog* to shake, nudge]

joogle² /'dʒugəl/ *v* to juggle *20-*. [OFr *jogler* to perform as an entertainer]

jook see DEUK, JOUK¹·¹, JOUK¹·², JOUK²

jookerie-packerie, jookery-paukery see JOUKERIE-PAWKERIE

joop see JUPE¹

joost see JIST¹·²

joot, *NE* **jeet,** *Bor* **jut,** †**jute** /dʒut; *NE* dʒit; *Bor* dʒʌt/ *n* **1** insipid drink, dregs; weak tea *19-*. **2** *derogatory* a tippler, a drunkard *la18-19, 20- NE*. **3** weak or sour ale; inferior whisky *18-19, 20- Ork*. **jooter** a mess *20- Ork*. **jooterie** *of a sore* festering *20- Ork*. †**jutor, jutter** a tippler, a drunkard *la16-17*. [ME *joute* a soup or pottage made of boiled vegetables or herbs]

jooter /'dʒutər/ *v* to saunter, totter *20- EC Bor*. [probably onomatopoeic]

†**jordan, jurdane, jairdine** *n* a chamber-pot, a urinal *la15-18*. [unknown]

jorg, *Sh* **gurg,** *EC* **jork** /dʒɔrg; *Sh* gʌrg; *EC* dʒɔrk/ *v* **1** to make a squelching sound *la19- Sh EC SW Bor*. **2** to make a grating sound *19- EC*. [variant of CHORK]

jornal see JOURNAL¹
jorney see JOURNEY¹·¹
jorram see IORRAM
jorrie see JAURIE
jose see JOYSE
joskin, *NE T* **geeskin** /ˈdʒɔskən; *NE T* ˈdʒiskən/ *n* a country bumpkin; a farmworker *la19-*. [perhaps derivative of JOSS]
†**joss** *v* to jostle *e19*. [variant of DOSS⁴]
jossle /ˈdʒɔsəl/ *v* to shake, totter *la19-*. [EModE *iustle* to joust]
jot¹·¹, †**jott**, †**jote** /dʒɔt/ *n* **1** a whit, an iota; the least part of something *la15-*. **2** a small or occasional piece of work, an odd job *16-19, 20- NE*. **jotterie** odd jobs, dirty work *19- Bor*. [Lat *iōta* the name of the Greek letter *i*]
jot¹·² /dʒɔt/ *v* **1** to write down hastily or briefly, make a short note of *18-*. **2** to do light work, potter about *la19- NE*. **jotting** a note, a memorandum; an excerpt *18-*. [see the noun]
jotter¹·¹, **joattur**, **joiter** /ˈdʒɔtər, ˈdʒotər, ˈdʒʌɪtər/ *n* **1** a person who takes notes *la18-*. **2** a rough notebook, a school exercise book *19-*. **3** an odd-job man; an inefficient worker, a dawdler *la19, 20- EC*. **get yer jotters** to get the sack, be dismissed *la20-*. [derivative of JOT¹·²]
jotter¹·² /ˈdʒɔtər/ *v* to do odd jobs or light menial work; to work in a dilatory fashion *la19-*. [frequentative form of JOT¹·²]
jottle /ˈdʒɔtəl/ *v* to appear busy without achieving much *19- EC*. **jottler** an odd-job man *19, 20- Uls*. [frequentative form of JOT¹·²]
joug¹·¹, **joog**, **jug**, †**juig** /dʒug, dʒʌg/ *n* **1** a pitcher *la16-*. **2** a mug or drinking vessel *17-*. **3** a drink of alcohol *la20-*. **4** a vessel kept as the standard measure of the pint in Scotland, the *Stirling jug la16-e19*. **Stirling jug** the vessel kept in Stirling as the main example of the standard measure of the pint in Scotland, about three imperial pints (1.7 litres) *la16-e19, 20- historical*. [unknown]
joug¹·², **jug** /dʒug, dʒʌg/ *v* **1** to put in a jug; to measure capacity with a jug; to stew or boil in a jug *la17-*. **2** to tipple, drink *16-17*. [unknown]
joug², †**jog**, †**jok**, †**jug** /dʒug, dʒʌg/ *v* to put in the JOUGS *la16-19, 20- historical*. [from the noun JOUGS]
jougal, **juckel**, **deugle** /ˈdʒugəl, ˈdʒʌkəl, ˈdjugəl/ *n* a dog *20-*. [Sanskrit *çgāla-* a jackal]
jouggis see JOUGS
jougle see JOOGLE¹·²
jougs, †**jouggis**, †**jokkis**, †**juggs** /dʒugz, dʒʌgz/ *npl* an instrument of public punishment consisting of a hinged iron collar attached by a chain to a wall or post and locked round the offender's neck *la16-e19, la19- historical*. [OFr *joug*, Lat *iugum* a collar attached as a mark of slavery, an arched device under which the defeated had to pass as a sign of submission; the plural form apparently refers to the construction in hinged halves]
jougs see JUGS
jouk¹·¹, **jook**, **jeuk** /dʒuk/ *n* **1** a quick ducking or dodging movement *16-*. **2** a trick *la16-19, 20- T SW Bor*. **3** a bow or curtsy, a gesture of deference, a nod of the head *la16-19, 20- T*. **4** a bend, a meander, a loop of a river *la19- WC SW Bor*. **joukie**, **jooky** evasive, elusive, sly *19-*. [unknown]
jouk¹·², **jook**, **juke**, **jeuk**, †**jowke**, †**juck** /dʒuk/ *v* **1** to trick, cheat, deceive *la15-*. **2** to duck or dodge a blow or missile *16-*. **3** to hide, skulk, duck out of sight *16-*. **4** to evade, elude, to avoid (someone or something); to shirk, flinch *18-*. **5** to play truant from school *19-*. **6** to dodge in and out, dart, flicker *19-*. **7** to cower, crouch *la19-*. **8** to bow deferentially; to humble oneself, show deference *16-19, 20- T EC*. **9** to soak, drench with water *20- Ork*. **jouker**, †**jucur** **1** a slippery or evasive character; a trickster *la15-*. **2** a truant *la19-*. **jouking**, **jeuking** **1** the action of the ducking *16-*. **2** dodging, shiftiness, dissembling *la16-*. **jouk an let the jaw gae by** to give way prudently in the face of overwhelming force, submit to the force of circumstance *18-*. **jouk under** to be subservient to *la19- NE T EC*. **juke yer heid** to duck *19-*. [unknown]
jouk², **jook**, **juke**, †**deuk** /dʒuk/ *n* a shelter; a sheltered spot, a nook; a place of concealment *la18-*. **up yer jook** (stashed) up your jumper or shirt *la20-*. **up yer jouks** = *up yer jook*. [perhaps JOUK¹·²; compare OFr *jouc* a perch for hens]
joukerie, **joukery**, †**joukrie** /ˈdʒukəri/ *n* trickery, deceit, roguery *la14-19, 20- C*. [JOUK¹·², with noun-forming suffix -ERIE]
joukerie-pawkerie, **jookery-paukery**, **jeukery-packery**, **jookerie-packerie**, **jukery-pokery**, *Ork* **chukery-packery**, †**jewkry-pawkry** /ˈdʒukəri pɔkəri, ˈdʒukəri pakəri, ˈdʒukəri pokəri; *Ork* ˈtʃukəri pakəri/ *n* a clever trick; roguery, trickery *la17-*. [JOUKERIE + *pawkrie* (PAWK)]
joukery, **joukrie** see JOUKERIE
Joun see JUNE
joundie see JUNDIE¹·²
joup see JUPE¹, JUPE²
journal¹, †**journall**, †**jornal**, †**jurnal** /ˈdʒʌrnəl/ *n* **1** a (published) daily record of events; a diary; originally a daily account book *la15-*. **2** a daily newspaper *18-*. **3** a register of the Justiciary Court or the Justice Aire *15-16*; compare ADJOURNAL. **4** *coinage* a single minting or portion of work *17*. [ME *journal*]
journal² /ˈdʒʌrnəl/ *n* the part of a shaft or axle which rests on the bearings *19-*. [unknown]
journey¹·¹, †**journee**, †**journay**, †**jorney** /ˈdʒʌrne/ *n* **1** the act of travelling, a spell of travelling; originally a day's travel *la14-*. **2** a stage or portion of a journey at the end of which new horses were provided *la16-17*. **3** *coinage* one minting or portion of work, originally a day's work; the quantity of coins so produced *la16-17*. **4** a travelling cloak worn over armour *la15-e16*. **5** a day's performance in battle or tournament; a warlike expedition; a feat of arms *la14-16*. †**journey hors** a post-horse *17*. †**jorney maister** the master of a posting-station *17*. [ME *journei*]
journey¹·², †**journay** /ˈdʒʌrne/ *v* **1** to make a journey, travel *la15-*. **2** to cite or summon to appear in court on an appointed day *la15-e17*. [ME *journeien*, OFr *journoyer*]
jow¹·¹ /dʒʌu/ *n* **1** a single peal or stroke of a bell; the ringing or tolling of a bell *16-*. **2** a swing or act of swinging *la19- EC*. [see the verb]
jow¹·² /dʒʌu/ *v* **1** to ring or toll a bell; *of a bell* to ring or toll *16-*. **2** to move with a rocking motion, swing; to jostle, jog *19-*. **jow yer ginger** to feel bothered, become flustered *la19- NE T*; compare *jee yer ginger* (JEE¹·²). **jow yer jundie** = *jow yer ginger*. [unknown; compare JOWL¹·²]
jow²·¹ /dʒʌu/ *n* the surge or swell of water or waves *19-*. [see the verb]
jow²·² /dʒʌu/ *v* **1** to spill a liquid from a container (by rocking it) *19- C*. **2** *of a boat* to rock, toss; *of a body of water* to surge, roll *19-*. **jow-boat** a swing at a fair *la19- T*. [compare JAW¹·²]
jow see JAA, CHAW¹·¹, CHAW¹·²
Jow see JEW
jowall see JOWEL
jowcat /ˈdʒʌukət/ *n* a liquid measure less than a pint (0.57 litre); a gill *la16-19, 20- historical*. [unknown]
jowel, **jewel**, †**jowall**, †**juell**, †**joell** /ˈdʒʌuəl, ˈdʒuəl/ *n* a precious stone, a jewel; an ornament or adornment (made of precious stones); treasure, a treasured possession *la14-*.
jowlry, †**jowelry**, †**jeualrie** jewellery, precious objects

15-. **jewel coal**, †**jewell coall**, †**jowall coall** a high-grade coal with a jewel-like surface *la17-*. [ME *jeuel*]

jowke *see* JOUK[1,2]

jowl[1.1] /dʒʌul/ *n* the knell or clang of a bell *19, 20- literary*. [unknown]

jowl[1.2] /dʒʌul/ *v of a bell* to toll, knell *19- EC SW Bor*. [unknown]

jowler /ˈdʒʌulər/ *n* a heavy-jawed hunting dog *la18-19, 20- historical*. [EModE *jowler*]

jowp *see* JUPE[1]

joy[1.1], †**ioy** /dʒɔɪ/ *n* **1** happiness, rejoicing *la14-*. **2** a term of endearment to a child or sweetheart, or a friendly address between women *la14-19, 20- Sh*; compare JO. [ME *joi*]

†**joy**[1.2], **ioy** *v* to rejoice, delight in, enjoy *la14-e18*. [ME *joien*]

joyn *see* JINE[1.2]

†**joyse, joys, jose** *v* **1** *law* to enjoy or have the use of, be in occupation or possession of (lands, an office or rights) *la14-e19*. **2** to have or obtain a spouse *la15-16*. **3** to take pleasure, rejoice in *la16-e17*. [ME *joissen*]

jube *see* JOOB

jubish, *WC Uls* **jubous** /ˈdʒubɪʃ; *WC Uls* ˈdʒubəs/ *adj* dubious, suspicious *la19-*. [altered form of Eng *dubious*]

juce *see* JICE

juck *see* CHUCK[2], DEUK, JOUK[1.2]

juckel *see* JOUGAL

judge[1.1], **jidge**, *Ork* **chudge**, *NE* **jeedge**, *SW* **joodge**, †**juge**, †**iuge** /dʒʌdʒ, dʒɪdʒ; *Ork* tʃʌdʒ; *NE* dʒidʒ; *SW* dʒudʒ/ *n* **1** *law* the officer of the crown who hears and tries cases in a court of justice *la14-*. **2** an adjudicator or arbiter; a person who makes a judgement *la14-*. †**Judge Ordinar, Juge Ordinar** a judge with a fixed and regular jurisdiction in all actions of the same general nature *15-e19*. **Judge Ordinary 1** a *Judge Ordinar la17-*. **2** a Sheriff-substitute; a Lord Ordinary *18-e20, la20- historical*. †**juge subdelegat** a deputy or assistant judge *la15-e16*. **judge of the roup** a person appointed as arbiter in any dispute arising from buying or selling at auction *18-*. [ME *juge*]

judge[1.2], **jidge**, *Ork* **chudge**, *NE* **jeedge**, *SW* **joodge**, †**juge** /dʒʌdʒ, dʒɪdʒ; *Ork* tʃʌdʒ; *NE* dʒidʒ; *SW* dʒudʒ/ *v* **1** to make a judgement, act as judge; *law* to try in court *la14-*. **2** to swear, curse; to express displeasure *19- NE*. [ME *jugen*]

judgement, jidgement, *NE C* **jeedgement**, *SW* **joodgment**, †**jugement**, †**jugisment** /ˈdʒʌdʒmənt, ˈdʒɪdʒmənt; *NE C* ˈdʒidʒmənt; *SW* ˈdʒudʒmənt/ *n* **1** *law* an act of judging; a decision in a court case *la14-*. **2** a decision; an opinion *15-*. **3** discernment, good sense; reason, wits, sanity *la15-*. **4** the extent or territory of judicial authority; jurisdiction *la15-e17*. **judgement-like** characteristic of divine displeasure, appearing to threaten divine retribution, awful *la17-*. †**furth of judgement** *law* out of or outside the court *la15-17*. †**in face of jugement** *law* during the formal course of proceedings in court, before a court of law, in court *15-17*. **out of your judgement** lacking sanity or rationality; distraught *la17-*. [ME *jugement*]

judicative /ˈdʒudɪkətɪv/ *adj* judicial *la15-*. [Lat *jūdicāt-*, ptp stem of *jūdicāre* to judge]

judicatory, †**judicatorie** /dʒuˈdɪkətɔri/ *n* **1** a court of judicature in church or state, a tribunal having judicial authority *la16-*. **2** judicature, jurisdiction; the judiciary *la16-*. [Lat *jūdicātōria* a court of law]

†**judicatour** *n* judicature *la16-e18*. [EModE *judicature*]

judicatum solvi /dʒudɪˈketəm solvi/ *adj law* (of a security) pledged for the payment or satisfaction of a judgement *16-*. [Lat *jūdicātum solvi* that which has been awarded by the court should be paid]

judicial /dʒuˈdɪʃəl/ *adj law* of or pertaining to judgement or the judicature *la16-*. **judicially**, †**judiciallie 1** by way of legal judgement, by decision of a court of law *la16-*. **2** during the formal course of proceedings in court *la16-17*. **judicial factor** a person appointed by the Court of Session or Sheriff Court to administer the property of a person unable to administer it himself *la18-*. [ME *judicial*, EModE *judicial*]

judicio sisti /dʒuˈdɪʃɪo sɪsti/ *adj law* relating to an undertaking that a debtor will appear in court to answer a claim *16-*. [Lat *jūdiciō sisti* that one be made to appear in court]

juell *see* JOWEL

juffle /ˈdʒʌfəl/ *v* **1** to scuffle, fumble *16-19, 20- Bor*. **2** to shuffle, walk painfully or awkwardly *19, 20- EC Bor*. †**juffler** an awkward or clumsy person *e16*. [unknown]

jug *see* JOUG[1.1], JOUG[1.2], JOUG[2]

juge *see* JUDGE[1.1], JUDGE[1.2]

jugement *see* JUDGEMENT

juggins *see* DEUGS

juggis *see* JUGS

juggs *see* JOUGS

jugisment *see* JUDGEMENT

†**jugs, juggis, jougs** *npl* swill, dregs, foul or waste liquid *16-e19*. [unknown]

juice *see* JICE

juig *see* JOUG[1.1]

juist *see* JIST[1.1], JIST[1.2]

juitle[1.1], **jeetle** /ˈdʒutəl, ˈdʒitəl/ *n* a dash or small quantity of liquid *19- NE SW*. [perhaps derivative of JOOT]

juitle[1.2], **jittle, jeetle, geetle** /ˈdʒutəl, ˈdʒɪtəl, ˈdʒitəl/ *v* **1** to tipple *19, 20- SW Bor*. **2** to spill, splash, overflow *19- NE C SW*. [see the noun]

juke *see* CHOWK, JOUK[1.2], JOUK[2]

jukery-pokery *see* JOUKERIE-PAWKERIE

Julie, July, †**Julii**, †**Jully**, †**Jule** /ˈdʒuli, dʒuˈlae/ *n* the seventh month of the year *la14-*. [Lat *Jūlius*]

Julius Hoff, †**Iulius Hoif** /ˈdʒulɪəs hɔf/ *n* the name for a round building that stood near the River Carron *16- historical*. Compare ARTHURIS HUFE. [from the name of the Roman emperor + OE *hof* a house, hall; compare ARTHURIS HUFE]

Jully, July *see* JULIE

jum *see* JAMB

jummle, jummil, *Ork* **chummle** /ˈdʒʌməl; *Ork* ˈtʃʌməl/ *v* **1** to jumble, mix up, confuse *16-*. **2** to agitate, shake, churn *16-*. **3** to make a churning, clunking or confused noise *19, 20- Sh*. **jummlie**, †**jumly** turbid, muddy *19-*. [probably imitative]

jump, jimp, *Ork* **chump** /dʒʌmp, dʒɪmp; *Ork* tʃʌmp/ *v pt* **jumped, jamp**, *EC SW Bor* **jampt 1** to leap, spring, bound *17-*. **2** to coincide *17*. **jumpin-jack 1** a dancing doll, a puppet *20-*. **2** a child's toy made from the wishbone of a fowl *la18-20, 21- historical*. **jumpin-rope** a skipping rope *19-*. **jump the dyke** to defect, become a turncoat *la20-*. [EModE *jump*]

jump *see* JIMP[2.2], JIMP[3], JIMP[4]

†**junct** *adj* joined, assembled *la14-17*. Compare JINT[1.3]. [Lat *junctus*]

juncture, †**junctour** /ˈdʒʌŋktʃər/ *n* **1** (the act of) fastening or joining together; a joint (of the body) *16-*. **2** a coming together or conjunction of events or circumstances *la17-*. **3** a metal link or connecting piece of a harness *16*. [Lat *junctūra*]

jund, chund /dʒund, tʃund/ *n* a heavy blow, a jolt *la19- Ork*. [unknown]

jundie[1.1], **jundy**, *NE* **junny** /ˈdʒʌndi; *NE* ˈdʒʌni/ *n* **1** a push (with the elbow), a shove, a jolt, a blow *18-*. **2** a trot, an even steady pace *la19- T*. [unknown]

jundie[1,2], **jundy**, *NE* **junny**, †**joundie** /ˈdʒʌndi; *NE* ˈdʒʌni/ *v* **1** to push; to jostle, elbow *la17-*. **2** to irritate, provoke anger *20- NE*. †**jundy on** to jog along *e19*. [unknown]

june *see* JINE[1,2]

June, *NE* **Jeen**, †**Joun** /dʒun; *NE* dʒin/ *n* the sixth month of the year *15-*. Compare JUNY. **the lang eleeven o June** 11 June (Old Style), the longest day of the year *la19- T Uls*. [Lat *Jūnius*]

Junii *see* JUNY

junior /ˈdʒunjər/ *adj* younger; lower in rank or class *la16-*. **junior secondary school 1** a state secondary school in a remote or rural area offering only four years of secondary education rather than six *20-*. **2** a state secondary school providing less academic courses than the *senior secondary school* (SENIOR[1,2]), attended by pupils who were not successful in the qualifying examination *20, 21- historical*. [Lat *jūnior*]

junk /dʒʌŋk/ *n* **1** a chunk, a lump; a joint of meat *la18-*. **2** a shapeless block of quarry stone not suitable for dressing *20- NE*. **3** a stout, stocky person *20- Ork*. [variant of Eng *chunk*]

junner[1,1] /ˈdʒʌnər/ *n* something ramshackle or badly made *20- SW*. [see the verb]

junner[1,2] /ˈdʒʌnər/ *v* to jolt, bump against; to spill, break *20- SW*. †**chunnery** fragments, smithereens *la19*. [frequentative form of JUNDIE[1,2]]

junny *see* JUNDIE[1,1], JUNDIE[1,2]

junrells /ˈdʒʌnrəlz/ *npl* debris, ruins *19- SW*. [derivative of JUNNER[1,1]]

junt /dʒʌnt/ *n* **1** the place where things join; the point at which two bones meet *16-*. **2** a large lump of something; a joint or chunk of meat; a chunk of bread *18-19, 20- NE Uls*. **3** a squat, clumsy person *la18- NE T*. **4** a large quantity of liquid *19- SW*. [compare JINT[1,1]]

junt-feftment *see* JINT[1,3]

juntly *see* JINT[1,3]

†**Juny, Junii** *n* June *15-e17*. Compare JUNE. [Lat *Jūnius*]

jup *see* JUPE[1]

juparty *see* JEOPARDIE[1,1]

jupe[1], *Sh* **joop**, *Ork* **choop**, *NE* **jeep**, *WC SW* **gipe**, †**jup**, †**joup**, †**joip**, †**jowp** /dʒup; *Sh* dʒøp; *Ork* tʃup; *NE* dʒip; *WC SW* dʒʌɪp/ *n* **1** a jacket, short coat or loose tunic worn by men *la16-19, 20- Ork EC Bor*. **2** a woman's jacket or smock, originally also a bodice or kirtle *la16-19, 20- NE C Bor*. **3** a child's smock *18- Ork Bor*. **4** a fisherman's short canvas smock *20- Sh*. **5** a loose-fitting garment; a wrap *20- NE*. **jupie**, *Sh* **joopie 1** a woollen shirt or singlet *20- Sh*. **2** a man's short jacket or loose tunic *20- Bor*. **jupsie** *of a garment* ill-fitting, loose or bulky *la19- Ork*. [OFr *jupe, gipe*]

jupe[2], **joup** /dʒup/ *v* to play truant from school *la20- N H&I*. [unknown]

jupe *see* CHOOP

juperd *see* JEOPARD

†**jurament, jurement** *n* an oath *la15-19*. [Lat *jūrāmentum*]

jurant[1,1] /ˈdʒurənt/ *n* a person taking an oath, originally of abjuration (in favour of William and Mary, Anne or the House of Hanover) *18, 19- historical*. **non jurant** a person refusing to take an oath (of abjuration) *18, 19- historical*. [see the adj]

jurant[1,2] /ˈdʒurənt/ *adj* taking an oath (originally of abjuration in favour of William and Mary, Anne or the House of Hanover) *18-e19, la19- historical*. **non jurant** refusing to take an oath *18, 19- historical*. [Lat *jūrānt-*, presp stem of *jūrāre* to swear]

juratory caution /ˈdʒurətəre ˈkɔʃən/ *law* inadequate security allowed in some civil cases where no better security is available *la18-*. [Lat *jūrātōrius* confirmed by oath + CAITION[1,1]]

jurdane *see* JORDAN

†**jure**[1] *n* **1** the science of law, jurisprudence *la15-16*. **2** substantiating evidence or grounds supporting a claim *la15-16*. **3** a title, a legal right, a privilege *16*. [Lat *jūr-*, oblique stem of *jūs* law, right]

jure[2], **djur** /tʃur, dʒur/ *n* an animal, a creature; cattle that are not housed *19- Sh*. [ON *dýr*]

jurer *see* JUROR

jurmummle /dʒərˈmʌməl/ *v* **1** to mess or mix up; to confuse *19- Bor*. **2** to disfigure, crush *19- Bor*. [perhaps onomatopoeic]

jurnal *see* JOURNAL[1]

juror, †**jurer** /ˈdʒurər/ *n* **1** a member of a jury *18-*. **2** a person taking an oath of allegiance *18, 19- historical*. **3** a profane swearer *la17*. **non-juror** a person refusing to take an oath of allegiance *18-19, 20- historical*. [AN *jurour*]

†**jurr** *n derogatory* a servant-girl *la18-19*. [shortened form of Eng *journey-woman* a daily help]

jus *see* JICE

jus devolutum /dʒus dɛvɔˈljutəm/ *n in church law* the right of presenting a minister to a congregation, which falls to the Presbytery if the charge has remained vacant for six months *18-*. [Lat *jūs dēvolūtum* a right which has devolved]

jus mariti /dʒus maˈriti/ *n law* the right of a husband on marriage to ownership of his wife's non-heritable property except for some personal effects (such as clothing and jewellery and their receptacles) *18-19, 20- historical*. [Lat *jūs marītī* the right of the husband]

jus quaesitum tertio /dʒus kweˈsitəm tɛrʃio/ *law* a contractual right of one party, arising out of a contract between two others, to which the first is not a party *la17-*. [Lat *jūs quaesītum tertiō* a right sought by a third person]

jus relictae, jus relicti /dʒus rəˈlıkte, dʒus rəˈlıkti/ *n law* the share of a deceased spouse's moveable goods to which the surviving wife (relictae) or husband (relicti) is entitled: one third if there are surviving children, one half if there are none *18-*. [Lat *jūs relictae* the right of the female survivor, *jūs relictī* the right of the male survivor]

just /dʒʌst/ *v* to ascertain the accuracy of a weight or measure, correct to the standard *la16-19, 20- Sh Ork*. [ME *just*]

just *see* JIST[1,1], JIST[1,2]

jus tertii /dʒus ˈtɛrʃiae/ *n law* the right of a third party (when it is denied that a person has the right he alleges, though it might properly be claimed by another, the third party) *18-*. [Lat *jūs tertiī*]

justery, justry /ˈdʒʌstəri, ˈdʒʌstri/ *n* **1** the office or jurisdiction of a Justice *la15-19, 20- historical*. **2** the Justiciary as an official body *la15-e16*. **3** justice, the administration of the law *la15*. **4** a Justice Aire or other justice court *e15*. **5** one of the districts into which the country was divided for administration of the law by the Justices *la14-e15*. [perhaps JIST[1,2], with noun-forming suffix *-ery*]

justice, †**justis**, †**iustice** /ˈdʒʌstɪs/ *n* **1** (maintenance of) fairness, equity or rightness *15-*. **2** *law* judicial proceedings; legal redress; the punishment of crime *15-*. **3** a judge in the Scottish legal system, especially the supreme criminal judge, originally one of the officers of state charged with the holding of a *Justice Aire* or a *Justice Court* as presiding judge *15-*. **4** *law* the Scottish Court of Justiciary *la15-e17*. **Justice Aire, Justice Ayre** *law* the circuit court of a Justice *la14-19, 20- historical*. **Justice Clerk** *law* the principal clerk of justiciary, latterly, one of the principal judges and vice president of the Court of Justiciary, but originally the officer of state who officiated as clerk of the *Justice Court* or *Justice Aire la15-19, 20- historical*; compare LORD JUSTICE CLERK. **Justice Court 1** *law* the Scottish Court of Justiciary *la17-19, 20- historical.* **2** *law* a court presided over by a Justice or Justices *la15-17.* **Justice Depute**, †**justice deput** *law* a deputy for a Justice or for the *Justice General la15-17, 19- historical.* **Justice General** *law* the principal Justice or Justiciar, latterly the president of the Court of Justiciary *la15-19, 20- historical*; compare LORD JUSTICE GENERAL. †**Justice Principall** *law* = *Justice General 16.* †**Justice in that part** *law* a person who has been granted particular rights of justiciary usually over a particular area *la16-17.* [ME *justice*]

justiceman /ˈdʒʌstɪsmən/ *n mining* a checkweighman *18- T C.* [JUSTICE + MAN]

justicery *see* JUSTICIARY

justiciar, †**justicier** /dʒʌˈstɪʃɪər/ *n* **1** *law* a high-ranking officer entrusted by the crown with judicial or administrative functions within a specific region (historically either north or south of the River Forth respectively) *la16-e18, la18- historical.* **2** *law* a judge or magistrate *17-19, 20- literary.* †**justitiars aire** a circuit court *e17.* [Lat *justitiārius*]

justiciary, †**justicery** /dʒʌˈstɪʃəri, dʒʌˈstɪʃɪəri/ *n* **1** the office or jurisdiction of a Justice or Judge *15-.* **2** the judicature as an official body *la15-.* **3** a (circuit) court *15-18.* [Lat *justitiāria*]

justicoat /ˈdʒʌstɪkot/ *n* a jacket or sleeved waistcoat *la17-19, 20- historical.* [Fr *justaucorps* a close-fitting coat, with inflection from *coat*]

justify, **justifee**, †**iustify** /ˈdʒʌstɪfae, ˈdʒʌstɪfi/ *v* **1** to prove right or reasonable; to corroborate, verify, vindicate *15-.* **2** to judge, administer justice; to convict, condemn; to execute a criminal *15-19.* †**justify to the dede** to put (a criminal) to death *la15-16.* [ME *justifien*]

justis *see* JUSTICE

justry *see* JUSTERY

jut, jute *see* JOOT

Juteopolis /dʒuˈtɔpəlɪs/ *n* a nickname for the city of Dundee *la19-.* [Eng *jute* a fibre obtained from the bark, with noun-forming suffix *-opolis*, so named because of the city's famous jute industry]

jyle *see* JILE[1.1], JILE[1.2]

jylour *see* JILE[1.1]

jyne *see* JINE[1.2]

jyner *see* JINER

jynt *see* JINT[1.1], JINT[1.2], JINT[1.3]

K

ka *see* KAE[1.1]
kaak *see* CAUK[1.1]
kaavie[1.1], **caavie** /ˈkɑvi/ *n* a heavy fall of snow; a blizzard *la19- Sh.* [Norw dial *kave*]
kaavie[1.2] /ˈkɑvi/ *v of snow* to fall heavily and in drifts *la19- Sh.* [see the noun]
kaavie[2], **kavi** /ˈkɑvi/ *n* 1 a rock, a boulder; a stone used for ballast, the sinker of a fishing-line *la19- Sh.* 2 land; the low land visible from a boat at sea *la19- Sh.* [KAV + -IE[3]]
kab *see* CAB
kabbelow /ˈkabəlʌu/ *n* 1 cabbage, potatoes and butter mashed together *19- T EC.* 2 a milling crowd, an untidy place *20- Sh.* [extended sense of CABELEW]
kabbilow *see* CABELEW
kabby *see* CABBIE
kabe, †cabe /keb/ *n* the thowl pin on a boat (used to keep the oar steady) *19- Sh.* [ON *keipr* a rowlock]
kaber *see* CABER
kabill *see* CABLE
kace *see* CASE[2]
kach *see* CACK[1.2]
kachepele *see* CATCHEPOOLE
kaddie /ˈkadi/ *n* an ill-natured or mischievous person; a spoilt child *la19- Sh Ork.* [variant of CADDIE[1.1]]
kadel *see* CADDEL[2.1], CADDEL[2.2]
kae[1.1], *NE SW* **kyaw, †ka, †kay, †caa** /ke; *NE SW* kjɔ/ *n* 1 the jackdaw *Corvus monedula la15-.* 2 the call of the jackdaw *la19, 20- T.* 3 a foolish person *la18-19.* **kae-witted** foolish *la18- T EC.* [ME *co*; compare MDu *ca*, Norw *kaie, kå*]
kae[1.2] /ke/ *v of a jackdaw* to caw *la19- NE T.* [see the noun]
kae[2] /ke/ *interj* an expression of disapproval, contempt or incredulity *la18-19, 20- NE.* [compare MDu *ke*]
kaen /ken/ *v* to split cod *20- N.* [named from the short piece of cane used to keep the split cod open when drying]
kaeper *see* CAPER
kaff *see* CAFF
kag /kjag/ *v* to grieve, vex oneself *la19- Sh.* [Norw dial *kjaka* to wrangle, harass]
kahute *see* CAHUTE
kaichpellar *see* CATCHEPOOLE
kaid *see* KED
kaif *see* KAV
kaig *see* CAG
kail, kale, *Sh* **kell, †cale, †keill** /kel; *Sh* kel/ *n* 1 cole, brassica, especially the curly variety *Brassica oleracea Acephala*; cabbage *la14-.* 2 broth or soup (in which colewort, borecole or cabbage is the main ingredient) *la14-.* 3 a dish made of mashed kail, milk, butter and seasoning *18-.* 4 a main meal, lunch or dinner *la17-19, 20- NE T EC Bor.* **kail bell, kale bell** the dinner-bell; a call to dinner *la17-19, 20- NE T.* **kail-blade** a leaf of kail *la18-.* **kail broo, kail bree** the juice of boiled kail *la19, 20- Sh Ork N NE.* **kail brose** brose made with the liquid from boiled kail *la18-19, 20- N NE T WC.* **kail gullie, kale gully** a blade fixed at right angles to the end of an upright handle, used for cutting and chopping kail stems *18-19, 20- Ork N NE T Uls.* **kail-kenny, kail kennin** a dish of cabbage and potatoes mashed together *19-.* **kail-ladle** a tadpole *20- T EC SW.* **kail root** the stump left after the head of the kail has been cut *la19-.* **kail runt, kale runt** 1 the stalk of the kail plant *17-.* 2 a contemptuous term for an old woman *la19- T EC SW.* **kail stock** 1 the stalk of the kail plant; compare CASTOCK *17-.* 2 a full grown kail plant *la17-.* **†kail-supper, kale sipper** a person who is fond of soup; a nickname for an inhabitant of Fife *la18-19.* **kail time, kale time** dinner time *la18-19, 20- T C.* **kail-wife** 1 a woman who sells vegetables and herbs *la16-19, 20- NE WC.* 2 a scold, a coarse brawling woman *17-18.* **kail worm** a caterpillar *la18-.* **get saut tae yer kail** to make a living *18-.* **get yer kail het** = *get yer kail through the reek la19, 20- NE T.* **get yer kail through the reek** to get a severe scolding *la18-.* **mak saut to yer kail** = *get saut tae yer kail la19-.* [ON *kál*]
kailie *see* CEILIDH[1.1], CEILIDH[1.2]
kailyard, kailyaird, †kailʒard, †cailʒard /ˈkeljard, ˈkelʒerd/ *n* 1 a cabbage garden, a kitchen-garden *16-.* 2 the name of a type of sentimental Scottish fiction popular in the late 19th and early 20th centuries dealing with rural domestic life and containing dialect speech *la19-.* **kailyardism** sentimentality *la20-.* [KAIL + YAIRD[1.1]]
kailyee *see* CEILIDH[1.1]
kaim *see* KAME[1.1], KAME[1.2]
kaimer /ˈkjemər/ *v of a horse* to rear up *20- Ork N.* [frequentative form of KAME[1.2]]
kain, kane, cain, cane, †can, †kean, †cayne /ken/ *n* 1 an exaction; a payment in kind, such payments collectively; originally a portion of the produce of a tenancy payable as rent *12-.* 2 the produce with which rent is paid; a quantity of cheese (of approximately 3 tons) *18- H&I WC SW.* **†canage** the payment of goods in kind; the volume of produce paid *14-16.* **kenner, †kainer, †kaner, †caner** 1 an overseer of (salmon) fishing; originally someone with responsibility for overseeing the payment of fish as KAIN *16- N NE.* 2 a dairy farmer who paid his rent in cheese *la19.* **†cane cheis** cheese paid as rent by a tenant *16.* **kain fowl, †caine foul** a fowl or poultry paid as rent *la15-19, 20- historical.* **†pay the kain** to pay the reckoning or the penalty *18-e19.* [Gael *càin* tribute, a fine, IrGael *cáin* a law, a penalty]
kaip *see* CAIP[1.1], KEP[2.2]
kaird *see* CAIRD[1.1]
kairdique *see* CARDIQUE
kairn *see* CAIRN[1.1]
kairt *see* CAIRD[4]
kairy *see* CAIRIE[1.2]
†kaisart, kesart *n* a cheese-vat *la17-e19.* [Flem *kaeshorde*; compare CHESSART]
kaishin, caishin /ˈkeʃən/ *n* occasion; reason, cause *20- Sh N.* [aphetic form of OCCASION]
kaitchpull *see* CATCHEPOOLE
kake *see* CAKE
kale *see* KAIL
kalends, †calendis /ˈkaləndz/ *n* calends, the first day of the month in the Roman calendar *la14-.* **the cauld kalends** *weather* a cold spell at the beginning of one of the spring months, especially March or May *la19- NE T.* [Lat *kalendae*]
kalk *see* CAUK[1.1], CAUK[1.2]
kallavine *see* KEELYVINE
kallow *see* CALLOW

kame[1.1], **kaim, comb**, †**kem**, †**keam**, †**came** /kem, kom/ *n* **1** a comb for hair or wool *la14-*. **2** a bird's crest *la15-*. **3** a long narrow steep-sided ridge, the crest of a hill or ridge; frequently in place-names *16-*. **4** a combing; the act of combing *20-*. **5** a small peninsula, a narrow isthmus *20- N*. **6** a honeycomb *e16*. **claw yer kaim** to beat or thrash a person *19- EC*. **get an ill kaim for yer heid** to bring misfortune upon oneself *18-19, 20- EC*. [OE *camb*]

kame[1.2], **kaim, comb**, †**came**, †**kem** /kem, kom/ *v* **1** to arrange or smooth hair with a comb; to tease wool with a comb *la14-*. **2** to rake loose hay or straw from a stack; to rake stones from a field *20-*. **3** *of a child* to climb or clamber up; to be eager *20 Ork N NE*. **4** to scold *20- NE WC*. **5** *of a horse* to rear *19, 20- Ork N*. †**kaming claith** a cloth put over the shoulders while the hair is combed *16-e18*. †**kaming stock, keming stock** a support to which carding- or rippling-combs were fixed *16-e18*. **kaim against the hair** to ruffle, irritate *la18- NE EC*. **kaim someone's head for him** to scold someone *la19-*. [see the noun]

†**kamester, combster, kemstar** *n* a wool-comber *15-e18*. [KAME[1.1], with agent suffix]

kammik *see* CAMACK

kamshell, camshell /ˈkamʃɛl/ *n* the bone or gladius of the cuttlefish *Sepia officinalis la17- Sh Ork*. [perhaps CAM[1.1] pipeclay, from its resemblance to the calcified bone]

kan *see* CAN[1], CAN[2.1]

Kandelmes *see* CANDLEMAS

kaner *see* KAIN

kanker *see* CANKER[1.1]

kankyrryt *see* CANKERT

kannie, canny /ˈkɑni/ *n* the stern compartment in a rowing boat; the skipper or steersman's seat *la19- Sh*. [compare Icel *kani* a projection, the beak of a boat]

kanny *see* CANNY[1.1]

kant, cant /kɑnt/ *n* **1** state, humour; manner, behaviour *20- Sh Ork*. **2** opportunity, occasion *20- Ork*. [figurative meaning of Older Scots *kant* an edge, a slope]

kant *see* CANT[4]

kanteelam, canteelim /kanˈtiləm/ *n* ill-natured gossip *la19- Ork*. [unknown]

kape *see* CAIP[1.1]

kappernoitit *see* CAPERNOITED

kar *see* CAR[1]

kard *see* CAIRD[1.1], CAIRD[2.1]

kark *see* CARK[1.1]

karkage, karkish *see* CARCAGE

karle *see* CARLE[1.1]

karling *see* CARLINE

karm /kɑrm/ *n* a (poor) state or condition; a disorderly heap *la19- Sh Ork*. [unknown]

karp *see* CARP

karriewhitchit /kariˈʍɪtʃət/ *n* term of endearment for a child or young animal *19- NE T*. [unknown]

kart *see* CAIRT[1.1], CAIRT[1.2]

kartie *see* CART

kase *see* COOSE[1.2]

kassen *see* CAST[1.2]

kast *see* CAST[1.1], CAST[1.2]

kastik *see* CASTOCK

Kate Kennedy /ket ˈkɛnədɪ/ *n* a mythical personage in whose honour a historical pageant is performed annually in spring by the students of St Andrews University *19-*. [from the personal name *Kate* and the surname *Kennedy*]

katherane *see* CATERAN

Katie, Katy /ˈketi/ *n* **1** a diminutive form of the name Katherine *16-*. **2** a woman of bad character *e16*; compare KITTIE[1]. **katie beardie, katie bairdie 1** the name of a popular song *17-*. **2** the stone loach *Barbatula barbatula 20- T EC SW Bor*. **3** a woman with a beard or moustache *20- N NE T*. **kaite leelie, katie lailie** a daddy-long-legs *20- H&I*. †**katie unsell** a girl or woman of bad character *e16*; compare KITTIE[1]. **katie wren** the wren *Troglodytes troglodytes la19- NE EC Bor*. [a familiar form of the personal name *Katherine*; compare KITTIE[1]]

katmogit, catmoagit /katˈmogɪt/ *adj of animals* having a light-coloured body with dark legs and belly *la19- Sh*. [ON *köttr* a cat; second element unknown]

katogle, †**katyogle** /katˈogəl/ *n* an owl *la19- Sh Ork*. [Norw *kattugle*]

katt *see* CAT[1]

kattaklu *see* CATTICLOO

Katy *see* KATIE

katy-handed *see* KETACH

katyogle *see* KATOGLE

kauch, kiaugh, kyaucht /kjɔx, kjɔxt/ *n* care, worry; trouble or hassle *la18- WC SW*. [perhaps Gael *ceath* an expression of disgust]

kav, kaif /kav, kef/ *v of a stormy sea* to foam as it breaks, throw up a spray *20- Sh NE*. [ON *kafa* to dive under water]

kavie *see* CAVIE[1.1], CAVIE[1.2]

kavill *see* CAVEL[1.1], KEVEL[3]

kavvel[1.1], **cavil** /ˈkavəl/ *n* the rear section of a boat where fish are brought on board *la19- Sh*. **kavvelin-tree, kavlin tree** a cylindrical piece of wood inserted into the mouth of a fish to extract the hook *20- Sh*. [Norw *kavle* a cylinder]

kavvel[1.2], **cavil** /ˈkavəl/ *v* to take a fish off the hook by means of a notched wooden stick *la19- Sh*. [see the noun]

kay *see* KAE[1.1]

keam *see* KAME[1.1]

kean *see* KAIN

kearn *see* CAIRN[1.1]

keave *see* CAVE[2]

keavie, †**keavy**, †**cavey** /ˈkivi/ *n* a species of crab *la17- EC*. [unknown]

keb[1.1] /kɛb/ *n* **1** a ewe that has given birth to a dead lamb or failed to rear a live one *16-19, 20- C SW Bor*. **2** a stillborn or premature lamb *la19- SW Bor*. **keb hoose, keb house 1** a shelter for young lambs in the lambing season *la19- SW Bor*. **2** a small shed or shelter where a ewe that has lost her lamb is confined while being made to adopt another *la19- Bor*. **keb yowe, keb ewe** a ewe that has lost her lamb *la16-19, 20- EC SW Bor*. [unknown]

keb[1.2] /kɛb/ *v* **1** *of a ewe* to give birth prematurely, or to a dead lamb *19- WC SW Bor*. **2** *of a ewe* to lose a lamb by early death *19- EC SW Bor*. **kebbed ewe** a ewe that has lost her lamb *19- SW Bor*. [unknown]

keb *see* COB[1.1], COB[1.2], KED

kebar, kebber *see* CABER

kebbag *see* KEBBOCK

†**kebbie** *n* a stick, a staff *e19*. Compare NIBBIE. [unknown; compare ON *keppr* a cudgel]

kebbie-lebbie *see* CABBY-LABBY[1.1]

kebbock, kebbuck, *N* **kebbag**, †**kebbok**, †**cabok** /ˈkɛbək; *N* ˈkɛbəg/ *n* **1** a (whole) cheese; sometimes made with ewe-milk or skimmed cow's milk *la15-*. **2** the moon *la20- literary*. **kebbock heel** the hard end-piece of a cheese *la18-*. **a kebbuck o cheese**, †**ane kebbok of cheis** a whole cheese *la15-*. [perhaps Gael *càbag*, although that may itself be a borrowing from Scots]

kechepule *see* CATCHEPOOLE

kecher *see* KICHER[1.2]

kechin *see* KITCHEN[1.1]

keck¹·¹ /kɛk/ *v* to cackle, cluck; to chuckle *19*, *20- NE WC*. [see the interj]
keck¹·² /kɛk/ *interj* **1** an imitation of the cluck made by a hen *la18-19*, *20- SW*. **2** an imitation of the caw made by a jackdaw *e16*. [onomatopoeic]
keckle¹·¹ /ˈkɛkəl/ *n* a cackle; a chuckle; laughter *la19-*. **2** talk, chatter *la19*, *20- Uls*. [see the verb]
keckle¹·², *NE EC* **caikle**, †**kickle**, †**kekkill**, †**kekle** /ˈkɛkəl; *NE EC* ˈkekəl;/ *v* **1** to laugh (noisily); to giggle, cackle; to express unrestrained delight *la15-*. **2** *of birds* to cackle, cluck *16-*. [onomatopoeic; compare Du *kakelen*]
ked, **keb**, †**kaid** /kɛd; kɛb/ *n* the sheep-tick *Melophagus ovinus 17-*. [unknown]
keddie *see* CADDIE², CUDDIE¹
keech¹·¹, **kich** /kix/ *n* **1** (a lump of) excrement; filth or dirt *la19-*. **2** nonsense *la20-*. **keechie** filthy, nasty *20-*. **keech-catchers** plus-fours *la20-*. [altered form of CACK¹·¹]
keech¹·², **kich** /kix/ *v* to defecate *la19-*. [see the noun]
keech¹·³, **kich** /kix/ *interj* an exclamation of disgust or disbelief; a warning to a child not to touch something dirty or undesirable *19-*. [see the noun]
keechan *see* CAOCHAN
keechle¹·¹ /ˈkixəl/ *n* a short laugh, a giggle *20- EC SW*. [onomatopoeic; compare KECKLE¹·¹]
keechle¹·² /ˈkixəl/ *v* to giggle, titter *la19-*. [see the noun]
keed *see* COOD¹
keeger¹·¹, **kwigger**, **quigger** /ˈkigər, ˈkwɪgər/ *n* a mess, an untidy mixture, muddle *20- NE*. [perhaps euphemistic form of KEECH¹·¹]
keeger¹·², **kweecher**, **quigger** /ˈkigər, ˈkwixər, ˈkwɪgər/ *v* to mix up messily, mess about, work in a slovenly or ineffective way *20- NE*. [see the noun]
keehoy, †**keehow** /kiˈhɔi/ *n* the call to searchers in the game of hide-and-seek; the game itself *la19-*. [compare CAHOO]
keek¹·¹, **kiek**, †**keik** /kik/ *n* **1** a peep, a glance, a look *la16-*. **2** a very short visit *20- Sh Ork N*. **keek o' day** sunrise, dawn *la19- NE T EC*. **keek o' noon** mid-day *20-*. [see the verb]
keek¹·², †**keke**, †**keik** /kik/ *v* to peep, glance; to look hastily or furtively *la15-*. **keeker 1** an eye *19-*. **2** a person who watches surreptitiously, a peeping Tom *la19-*. **3** a black eye *la19-*; compare *blue keeker* (BLUE¹·²). **keeking glass** a mirror *la16-*. **keek-hole** a chink or peep-hole *19-*. **keek and hide** the game of peek-a-boo *20- Ork NE*. **keek in** to make a very brief visit *20-*. [ME *kiken*; compare MLG *kiken*, Du *kijken*]
keek² /kik/ *n* **1** a cunning, sly or malicious person *19- NE*. **2** a contemptuous term for a young woman *20- NE*. [unknown]
†**keek³** *n* a linen cap for the head and neck *la18-e19*. [perhaps KEEK¹·², from the difficulty of seeing sideways out of the bonnet]
keek *see* KICK¹·¹, KICK¹·²
keek bo¹·¹ /ˈkik bo/ *n* the game of peek-a-boo *18-*. **keekie-bo** the game of peek-a-boo *20-*. [compare Du *kiekeboe*, LG *kike-ba*]
keek bo¹·² /ˈkik bo/ *interj* a shout used in the game of peek-a-boo (when the player in hiding has been seen) *19-*. **keekie-bo** a shout used in the game of peek-a-boo *la19-*. [see the noun]
keeker *see* KIEGER
keel¹·¹, †**keill** /kil/ *n* **1** an owner's red mark made with ruddle on sheep *la15-*. **2** ruddle, red ochre (used for marking sheep) *17-*. **3** *weaving* the mark made with ruddle by the warper at each end of his warp to ensure that the weaver returns the correct amount of woven yarn *19*, *20- C Bor*. **4** an identifying mark made on a person *e16*. **keelie** marked with ruddle; reddish in colour *19- SW Bor Uls*. †**keelman** a supplier of ruddle *la18-e19*. [unknown]
keel¹·², **kele**, †**keill** /kil/ *v* to mark (sheep) with ruddle; to stain or blemish *la16-*. [unknown]
keel²·¹, †**kele**, †**keyll** /kil/ *n* **1** the keel of a ship *la15-*. **2** *colloquial* the buttocks, the backside *18-19 20- Bor*. **3** the (small of the) back *19- Sh Ork N*. **keel draucht** an iron or wooden covering on the outside of a boat's keel to protect it when the boat is being drawn *la19- Sh Ork N NE Uls*. **keel up** a heavy fall on one's back *20- Sh Ork NE T*. [probably ON *kjǫlr*]
keel²·² /kil/ *v* to overturn, upset, throw someone down onto their back *19-*. [see the noun]
keel³ /kil/ *n* a coloured crayon or pencil *la19- NE T C Bor*. [reduced form of KEELYVINE]
keelick /ˈkilək/ *n* a blow, a stroke *19- NE T EC*. **keelakin** a thud, a hard blow *la19- NE*. [unknown; compare *keel up* (KEEL²·¹)]
keelie¹ /ˈkili/ *n* the kestrel *Falco tinnunculus 19- EC SW Bor*. **keelie-hawk** a kestrel *la19- EC SW Bor*. [onomatopoeic]
keelie² /ˈkili/ *n* **1** a rough criminal living in a city (especially Glasgow) *19-*. **2** a hooligan, a street-urchin *19-*. Compare GLESCA KEELIE. [Gael *gille* a lad, a young man]
keelie³ /ˈkili/ *n* a game of marbles *20- Ork*. [perhaps Gael *gille* a lad, a young man, or Gael *cill* a graveyard]
keelie⁴, *SW* **kullie** /ˈkili; *SW* ˈkʌli/ *n* a lead pencil, a crayon or coloured pencil *20 EC SW Bor*. [reduced form of KEELYVINE]
keelie *see* KEEL¹·¹
keelin, **keeling**, †**keling**, †**killing** /ˈkilɪn, ˈkilɪŋ/ *n* **1** a fully-grown or large cod *Gadus morhua la14-*. **2** a newly-spawned or partly-grown cod *20- NE EC*. †**keeling sound**, **killing sound** the swimming bladder of the cod, used for glue *16*. [unknown, perhaps related to ON *keila* a type of large cod]
keelivine *see* KEELYVINE
keelup /ˈkiləp/ *n* a heavy blow *19- NE*. [unknown; compare *keel up* (KEEL²·¹)]
keelyvine, **keelivine**, *Sh* **kallavine**, *N* **callivan**, *SW* **kulivin**, †**killavyne** /ˈkilivʌin; *Sh* ˈkaləvʌin; *N* ˈkaləvən; *SW* ˈkʌləvən/ *n* **1** a lead pencil, a crayon or coloured pencil *18-*. **2** black lead, graphite *la17*. **keelievine pen** a lead pencil *17-*. [unknown; compare Eng *killow* graphite]
keen, †**kene**, †**keyn** /kin/ *adj* **1** eager, enthusiastic *15-*. **3** *of prices* highly competitive *la19-*. **4** avaricious, driving a hard bargain *20-*. **5** lively, brisk, with renewed vigour after an illness *20-* **6** *of animals* spirited *20-*. **7** *of a curling rink* crisp, smooth *19*, *20- WC*. **8** brave, fierce, valiant *la14-16*. **9** savage, cruel, violent, terrible *la14-16*. **keen of** eager for, fond of *la19-*. [OE *cēne* bold]
keeng, **keng** /kiŋ, keŋ/ *v* to mend broken crockery with a clasp or rivet *la19- Sh*. [Norw dial *kjeng* a small iron clamp]
keeng *see* KING
keep¹·¹, †**kepe**, †**keip** /kip/ *n* **1** charge, custody *la15-*. **2** (the cost of) board and lodging; maintenance *la19-*. **3** heed, care, regard *la14-19*. **keeps**, **keepies** a game of marbles in which the winnings are kept *20-*. **keep house** a storeroom, originally a strongroom or prison *la17-19*, *20- historical*. **keep up** upkeep, the cost of maintenance *20-*. [see the verb]
keep¹·², †**kepe**, †**kyp**, †**keip** /kip/ *v pt*, *ptp* **kepit**, **kept**, **keip**, †**keiped**, †**keipt 1** to hold, retain; to conserve, store *la14-*. **2** to observe, comply with, to adhere to, practise *la14-*. **3** to tend, take care of; to guard *la14-*. **4** to carry on, conduct (a business); to maintain (animals) *16-*. **5** *of health* to fare *la19-*. **6** to sustain, keep up (talk, noise or an activity) *la19- NE*. **7** to give careful attention to *15-16*. **8** to meet *la14-15*. **keeping 1** observing, maintaining *la14-*. **2** providing with food and shelter *15-*. **keepie-in** a pupil detained after school as a punishment *la19- NE T SW*. **keepie-up** a game of

keeping a ball in the air by means of the feet, knees or head *20-*. **keepin aff** except, not counting *la19- T C*. **keep aff o anesel** to act defensively in fighting; to stand up for oneself *la19-*. **keep a stack** to trim a hay- or corn-stack while it is being built *20- H&I WC SW*. **keep the heid** to stay calm, keep one's temper *la20-*. **keep in aboot** to restrain, keep in order *la19-*. **keep in guid wi** to keep on good terms with *20-*. **keep in yer hand 1** to restrain yourself, refrain from violence *la19- NE EC*. **2** to be stingy *la19- NE EC*. **keep me** may God keep me *19-*. †**keep the mell in the shaft** to keep in a good state of order, health or prosperity *19*. **keep oot o langour** to entertain, amuse; to cheer up *18-19, 20- Sh NE*. †**keep short by the head** to curb a person's spending *e19*. **keep steeks**, †**keep stitches** to keep pace, keep up (with) *la18-19, 20- T SW Bor*. **keep tack till** to keep pace with, keep up with *20-*. **keep tae yer threep** to maintain one's opinions despite all opposition or contradiction *la18-19, 20- N NE Bor*. †**kepe tathe** to adhere to the local regulations regarding manuring of land *17*. **keep tee** to keep up (with), keep abreast (of) *20- NE T*. **keep up 1** to stay awake *la19-*. **2** *of weather* to stay fine *20-*. **3** to store or hoard (grain) *la16-17*. **keep up yer rig** to maintain the same rate of corn cutting as the others in the harvest field *la19- C SW*. **keep wide** *as a command to a sheepdog* to keep some distance from the flock so as not to disturb the sheep *la19-*. **keep yer ain fish guts for yer ain sea maws** to take care of those closest to you before concerning yourself with others *18-19, 20- N NE*. **keep yer breath to cool yer parritch** to keep silent; to mind your own business *19-*. **keep yer pooch** to provide with pocket money *20-*. **keep yer tongue aff** to refrain from scolding *la19-*. **keep yer tongue ahint yer teeth** to keep silent *la19, 20- Sh Ork N NE EC*. **keep yer tung** to keep a check or guard on your tongue *15-*. †**upon their keping** in hiding, on the run *e17*. [OE *cēpan*]

keeper, †**kepar**, †**keipar** /'kipər/ *n* **1** a guard, a defender; a watchman; a supervisor, a guardian *la14-*. **2** one who has the charge of animals; a herdsman *15-*. **3** the custodian of a seal or other symbol of (royal) authority *15-*. **4** an adherent *la15-*. **5** a catch or clasp *16-*. **6** the owner of a business; the organizer of a fair *17-*. **7** a store animal, one kept for fattening *20- NE*. **8** a person who conducts or is present at a conventicle *la17*. [KEEP[1.2], with agent suffix]

Keeper of the Privy Seal /'kipər əv ðə prɪve sil/ *n* the official in charge of the Privy Seal and its use *15-*. [KEEPER + PRIVY[1.2] + SEAL[1.1]]

Keeper of the Records /'kipər əv ðə rɛkərdz/ *n* **1** the official responsible for the preservation of the public registers, records and rolls of Scotland *20-*; compare Keeper of the Registers. **2** the official responsible to the Lord Clerk Register for custody of the public records of Scotland *la17-e18*. [KEEPER + RECORD[1.1]]

Keeper of the Registers /'kipər əv ðə rɛdʒɪstərz/ *n* **1** the official responsible for framing the registers of sasines and deeds *20-*. **2** the official responsible to the Lord Clerk Register for custody of the public records of Scotland *la17-e18*. [KEEPER + REGISTER[1.1]]

Keeper of the Signet /'kipər əv ðə sɪgnət/ *n* a title or office of the Lord Clerk Register; originally the custodian of the SIGNET[1.1] (sense 2) *16-*. [KEEPER + SIGNET[1.1]]

keer *see* CURE[1.1], CURE[1.2]

keerate *see* CURATE

keerie[1.1], **keero** /'kiri, 'kiro/ *n* the native sheep of Orkney *la19- Ork*. Compare CAIRIE[1.1]. [Gael *ciridh* a pet name for calling sheep]

keerie[1.2] /'kiri/ *interj* a call to a lamb or sheep *20- T C SW Uls*. [see the noun]

keeriosity, **queeriosity**, **curiousity**, †**curiousitie** /kiri'ɔsɪte, kwiri'ɔsɪte, kjurɪ'ɔsɪte/ *n* **1** inquisitiveness, the desire for information *la16-*. **2** an unusual object or eccentric person; something strange *18-*. **3** refinement, elegance, fastidiousness *16*. **4** over-refinement or subtlety of thought *la16*. [ME *curiousitie*, EModE *curiositie*]

keerious, **kwerious**, **curious**, *Sh* **kurrious**, †**querious**, †**curyus**, †**curius** /'kiriəs, 'kwiriəs, 'kjurɪəs; *Sh* 'kørɪəs/ *adj* **1** eager to know or learn; inquisitive *la14-*. **2** strange, unusual, peculiar *19-*. **3** ready, desirous, keen, anxious *la16-e17, 20- Sh*. **4** skilful, painstaking; careful, studious *la14-16*. **5** *of words or sounds* elaborately expressed; artificial *15-16*. **6** elegant, beautiful *16*. [ME *curious*]

keero *see* KEERIE[1.1]

keeroch[1.1], **queeroch** /'kirəx, 'kwirəx/ *n* an unsightly mess; an untidy person *19- NE*. [unknown]

keeroch[1.2], **kweerich** /'kirəx, 'kwirəx/ *v* to stir or poke about messily; to work awkwardly *la19- NE*. **kweerichin**, **queerachin** awkward and unskilful *20- NE*. [unknown]

keers /kirz/ *n* weak porridge; a thin gruel given to feeble sheep in the spring *19- Bor*. [unknown]

keeslip, †**kislip** /'kizlɪp/ *n* the stomach of an animal (used as a source of rennet) *18- SW Bor*. [unpalatalized form of OE *cȳslybb* rennet; compare MDu *kaeslibbe*]

keeso /'kiso/ *n* a bulky item; a large or lazy person *20- Ork*. [ON *keis* a round belly]

keessar /'kisər/ *n* a large woman; a big cow *la19- NE*. [unknown]

keest /kist/ *n* sap, pith, substance *19- EC Bor*. **keestless 1** tasteless, insipid *19- SW Bor*. **2** lacking in substance or spirit *e19*. **keistie**, **keesty** *of a person* lecherous; *of an animal* on heat *19- C SW Bor*. [MDu *keest* a kernel]

keester /'kistər/ *n* an unpleasant trait *20- Ork*. [unknown]

keetchin *see* KITCHEN[1.1]

keething *see* KYTHE

keevee, **quivvy** /ki'vi, 'kivi, 'kwɪvi/ *n* attention, alertness, vigilance *19-*. **on the kevee** on the lookout, on the alert; in high spirits; worked up *20-*. [Fr *qui vive* who should live?]

keg *see* CAG

kegel /'kɛgəl/ *v* to twist or tangle; to sprain *20- Sh*. [Norw dial *kjegla* to wind slowly, twist]

keiching *see* KITCHEN[1.1]

keik *see* KEEK[1.1], KEEK[1.2]

keild *see* KILL[2.2]

keiler /'kʌɪlər/ *n* **1** a person who coils ropes in the bottom of a boat *20- N NE*. **2** a useless or insignificant person *20- N NE*. [altered form of Eng *coiler*]

keill *see* KAIL, KEEL[1.1], KEEL[1.2], KILL[2.2]

keind *see* KIND[1.1], KIND[1.2]

keing *see* KING

keip *see* KEEP[1.1], KEEP[1.2]

keipar *see* KEEPER

keiped, **keipt** *see* KEEP[1.2]

keir[1] /kir/ *n* an ancient fortification; frequently in place-names *la16-*. [British or Pictish **cair* fort, possibly by way of a Gaelic cognate]

†**keir**[2] *adj of horses* dun, dark brown or grey *16-17*. **keir black** dark-coloured *la16-e18*. [Gael *ciar*]

keir *see* CAIR

keist *see* KIST[1.1]

keistie *see* KEEST

†**keith** *n in Perthshire* a bar across a river to prevent salmon from mounting further *la18-e19*. [Gael *cuidh, cuith* an enclosure]

keith *see* KYTHE

keizie *see* CASSIE

keke *see* KEEK[1,2]
kekkill, kekle *see* KECKLE[1,2]
kekle, keksi *see* KEX
†**kelchyn** *n law* a fine paid to the kinsmen of a murder victim *15-e17.* [unknown]
keldi, †**keld,** †**kell** /'kɛldi/ *n* a spring, a fountain; a well; frequently in place-names *13-19, 20- Sh Ork.* **kell head** a fountainhead, a wellspring *16-.* [ON *kelda*]
kele *see* KEEL[1,2], KEEL[2,1], KILL[2,2]
keling *see* KEELIN
kell /kɛl/ *n* **1** a woman's ornamental hairnet or cap; the headdress of a young, unmarried woman *14-19, 20- Ork.* **2** an incrustation of scab, scurf or dirt (on the skin) *19- C SW Uls.* **3** a shroud *e19.* **kellt, kelled** covered with dirt or scurf *20- WC SW.* [MFr *cale*]
kell *see* KAIL, KELDI, KILL[1,1]
kellach /'kɛləx/ *n* a large, conical wicker basket or pannier (with a lid) used for carrying dung to the fields or transporting corn on horseback *la18-19, 20- N.* [Gael *ceallach*]
kelly /'kɛle/ *n* sherbet *20- T.* [perhaps related to Eng *alkali* a soda-like substance]
kelpie[1] /'kɛlpi/ *n in mythology* a water demon, usually in the form of a horse, said to haunt rivers and lochs and lure the unwary to their deaths *la17-.* [probably Gael *cailpeach, colpach* a bullock, a colt]
kelpie[2] /'kɛlpi/ *n* **1** a big, raw-boned youth *la18- NE T.* **2** a mischievous young person *19- Bor.* [variant of GILPIE]
kelshie *see* CALSHIE
Kelso convoy /kɛlso 'kɔnvɔɪ/ *n* the accompanying of a guest (all or part of the way) on their journey home *19, 20- historical.* Compare *a Scots convoy* (CONVOY[1,1]). [from the place-name + CONVOY[1,1]]
Kelso Laddie, Kelsae Laddie /kɛlso 'ladi, kɛlse 'ladi/ *n* the leading male participant in the Kelso Riding of the Marches *20-.* [from the place-name + LADDIE]
kelt[1] /kɛlt/ *n* a salmon or sea-trout (in poor condition) on its way back to the sea after spawning *16-.* **kelted** having spawned; emaciated *19- EC SW Bor.* [unknown]
†**kelt**[2] *n* a coarse, homespun grey or black cloth (used for outer garments) *16-19.* [unknown; compare Gael *cealt* clothes; coarse cloth]
kelter[1] /'kɛltər/ *n* a coarse, homespun grey or black cloth (used for outer garments) *16-18, 20- Ork.* [perhaps Gael *cealtar* coarse cloth, compare KELT[2]]
kelter[2,1] /'kɛltər/ *n* a fall (head over heels); a tumble *19- SW Bor.* [probably frequentative form of KILT[2,1]]
kelter[2,2] /'kɛltər/ *v* **1** to tumble, fall (head over heels); to stumble or totter *19, 20- Ork.* **2** to overturn, upset *la18-19, 20- T.* **3** to wriggle, undulate, struggle *19, 20- literary.* [see the noun]
keltie *see* KELTY
Kelton Hill Fair /'kɛltən hɪl fer/ *n* a rumpus, a noisy uproar *20- SW.* [from the Kirkcudbrightshire place-name + FAIR[2]]
†**kelty, keltie** *n folklore* the name of a legendary figure believed to have been victorious in a drinking challenge against a King's trooper *la18-19.* **Keltie's Mends** an (unwanted) extra drink (imposed as a punishment) *la18-19.* **gie somebody kelty** to force a large alcoholic drink on a person who has tried to avoid drinking *la17-19.* [unknown]
Kelvinside /kɛlvɪn'sʌɪd/ *n* an affected pronunciation of Scottish English *20-.* [from the name of Glasgow district]
kem *see* KAME[1,1], KAME[1,2]
kemel *see* CAUMEL
kemerel *see* CAMERAL
kemp[1,1] /kɛmp/ *n* **1** a champion; a professional fighter *16-18, 19- literary.* **2** a contest (to finish first in the harvest field) *la18- Ork N NE Bor.* **3** *pl* a children's game played with plantain stalks in which each contestant tries to decapitate his opponent's stalks *19- Bor.* **4** crested dog's-tail grass *Cynosurus cristatus 20- N.* **5** a stalk of ribwort plantain *Plantago lanceolata la16-19.* **kempoo** marsh ragwort *Jacobaea aquatica 20- Ork.* [OE *cempa,* ON *kempa* a champion, Norw dial *kjempe* the plantain, its stalks]
kemp[1,2], †**camp** /kɛmp/ *v* **1** to compete in the completion of a piece of work; especially in the harvest field *18-.* **2** to contend or strive; to busy oneself *16-19, 20- Sh.* **3** to compete in eating; to eat hurriedly *18-19, 20- EC.* **kemper** a person who strives or contends, a fighter, a keen worker *17-19, 20- Sh EC Bor.* [see the noun; compare MDu, MLG *kempen*]
kempie[1,1], *Bor* **campie** /'kɛmpi; *Bor* 'kampi/ *n* **1** a bold person; a champion, a fighter *16-19, 20- NE EC Bor.* **2** a lively child *20- NE.* [KEMP[1,1] + -IE[1]]
kempie[1,2], **campy** /'kɛmpi, 'kampi/ *adj* bold, energetic; quick-tempered, brisk *19- WC Bor.* [see the noun]
†**kempit** *n* the pith of hemp, or of a wild carrot or parsnip, dried and used as a candle *e19.* [unknown]
kemple, kimple, †**kimpill** /'kɛmpəl, 'kɪmpəl/ *n* **1** a bundle of straw (of a certain measure) *16-.* **2** a lump or chunk (of food); a fragment, a piece broken off *la19- NE.* **3** a truss of straw prepared for thatch *20- N.* **4** an untidy mass; a stout person *20- N.* [ON *kimbill* a little trunk, a bundle; compare Gael *ciomboll*]
kemstar *see* KAMESTER
ken[1,1] /kɛn/ *n* knowledge, acquaintance, comprehension, insight *16-.* [see the verb]
ken[1,2] /kɛn/ *v* **1** to understand or perceive; to have knowledge of *la14-.* **2** to recognize, identify; to be aware of or acquainted with *la14-.* **3** *law* to acknowledge a person as legal successor to an inheritance (especially a widow) *la15-.* **4** *used as a tag question* do you know, do you understand: ◊*I've seen it afore, ken? 20-.* **5** to make known; to inform or tell; to teach *la14-18.* **6** *law* to ascertain authoritatively and point out the limits of a landholding; to assign property to a person in this way *la15-17.* **7** to show or point out the way *la14-16.*
kenable obvious, easily recognizable *la19, 20- Sh NE Bor.* **kens faar** goodness knows where *20- NE.* **kennawhat** a nondescript or unidentifiable thing *19-.* **ken o mysel'** to be aware consciously or intuitively, have instinctive knowledge (of) *la19-, Sh NE.* **ken o't** to know by dire experience, suffer for one's actions *20-.* **ken the richt side o a shillin** to get value for money *la19-.* **kens whan** goodness knows when *20- NE T EC Bor.* **kens what** goodness knows what *19- NE T EC Bor.* **ye ken** *used as a tag question* do you know, do you understand: ◊*she's pretty game, ye ken? la18-.* [OE *cennan* to make known, declare, ON *kenna* to know, teach, tell]
kench *see* KINCH[1,1], KINCH[1,2], KINCH[2]
kend *see* KENT[1]
†**kendalye, kendely** *n* Kendal cloth, a coarse, green, woollen cloth *la15-16.* [a derivative form of the English place-name]
kendill, kendle *see* KENNLE
kene *see* KEEN
keng *see* KEENG
†**kenkynolle** *n* (the office of) a clan chief *la14-e16.* [Gael *ceann-cineil;* compare *hede o kyn* (HEID[1,1])]
kenmark /'kɛnmark/ *n* a distinguishing mark; a mark of ownership on an animal, a brand *la19- Sh N NE T EC.* [ON *kennimark*]
kenned *see* KENT[1]
kennel /'kɛnəl/ *n* a water channel, a street gutter *18-19, 20- WC SW.* [ME *chanel, canel*]
kennel-coal *see* CANDLE COAL

kenner see KAIN

kennill see KENNLE

kennin, kenning /ˈkɛnɪn, ˈkɛnɪŋ/ *n* **1** recognition; acquaintance; knowledge *15-*. **2** teaching, understanding, comprehension *la15-*. **3** a small quantity, a trifle *la18-*. **4** the distance from anything which is the limit at which it can be seen at sea *la16-e17, 20- historical*. **kenning to the terce** *law* the ascertainment by a sheriff of the just proportion of a husband's estate belonging to the widow in virtue of her TERCE *la17-20, 21- historical*. [verbal noun from KEN[1,2]]

kennit see KENT[1]

kennle, kinnle, kendle, kindle, †kennill, †kendill, †kyndill /ˈkɛnəl, ˈkɪnəl, ˈkɛndəl, ˈkɪndəl/ *v* to set fire to; to catch fire, ignite; to inflame or excite *la14-*. **kennlin, kinlin**, †**kendling** kindling material; wood, live coals or peat used as kindling *15-*. [derivative of ON *kynda*]

kensie see KENSY[1]

kenspeckle[1.1] /ˈkɛnspɛkəl/ *n* a distinguishing mark *la19- NE C*. [unknown]

kenspeckle[1.2], †**kenspekill** /ˈkɛnspɛkəl/ *adj* easily recognizable, conspicuous, familiar *16-*. **kenspeckled** familiar, recognizable *la17-*. [unknown]

†**kensy**[1], **kensie** *n* a kind of woollen cloth *la16-e17*. [compare KENTSHIRE]

†**kensy**[2], **kenzie** *n* a term of abuse for a man *16-e19*. [unknown]

kent[1.1], **kenned**, †**kend**, †**kennit** /kɛnt; kɛnd/ *adj* **1** known, familiar *15-*. **2** having a certain fame or reputation *la15-*. †**be it kend** *as a formula in legal documents* let it be known *la14-18*. †**be it made kend** = *be it kend 15-e16*. †**make kend** to make known, declare *15-16*. [ptp of KEN[1,2]]

kent[1.2] /kɛnt/ *see* KNAW[1]

kent[2.1] /kɛnt/ *n* a long staff or pole (for leaping ditches); a punt-pole (for propelling a boat) *17-19, 20- SW Uls*. [unknown]

†**kent**[2.2] *v* to propel a boat with a punt-pole; to convey *19*. [unknown]

Kentshire, †**Kentschire** /ˈkɛntʃər/ *n* the English county of Kent *la15-*. †**Kentschyre claith** a Kentish cloth *la16-e17*. [an alternative name for the English county]

Kent Star /kɛnt ˈstar/ *n* the name of a Glasgow gang, active in the inter-war years *e20, la20- historical*. [unknown]

kenzie see KENSY[2]

keo see KIOW-OW[1.1], KIOW-OW[1.2]

kep[1.1], **caip, cap** /kɛp, kep, kap/ *n* **1** a garment for covering the head; a cap *la15-*. **2** a woman's head-covering *la19- SW Bor*. [OE *cæppe*]

kep[1.2], **caip, cap** /kɛp, kep, kap/ *v* **1** to confer a degree on a graduand by touching his or her head with a cap *la19-*. **2** to cover with a cap *la18*. [see the noun]

kep[2.1] /kɛp/ *n* **1** the act of catching, a catch *20-*. **2** a contrivance for checking, stopping or holding (doors or windows) *18-19, 20- SW*. **3** the heading off or intercepting of animals *20- NE WC*. **4** *pl mining* moveable rests or supports for the cage at the top of the pit shaft; = SHUT *la19, 20- C*. **5** a chance, an opportunity *la18- WC Bor*. **keppies** a ball game in which a circle of players throw a ball to one another *20- N T SW*. [see the verb]

kep[2.2], †**kaip** /kɛp/ *v* **1** to catch (a falling object); to catch (liquid) in a vessel *la15-*. **2** to intercept; to stop, head off; to ward off (a blow) *16-*. **3** to keep or contain; to restrain or guard; to catch hold of (an animal) *la16-*. **4** to meet, encounter *la18-19, 20- NE T*. **5** *of hair* to hold (up) with a band or comb *19, 20- N SW*. **6** *of a train or bus* to connect with another *20- NE T*. **7** to direct the passage of animals *la20- WC SW Bor Uls*. Compare KEEP[1.2]. **kepper 1** a person who is good at catching *20-*. **2** *sport* a ball which is easy to catch *20- C*. **3** *pl* a catching game *la19- C SW*. **4** a landing net for fish *la20- Sh*. **5** a keeper (of a building) *la15-16*. **kep-a-gush** a splay-footed person *20- Bor*. **kepping kame** a large comb used to hold up a woman's hair on the back of the head *19, 20- N*. **kep a catch** to bridge a gap, serve a turn, be useful in the interim *20-*. **kep again** to check, intercept, turn back *20- N NE EC SW*. **kep a slap** = *kep a catch 19-*. **kep gushes** to dam the water in a street gutter with the feet *20- Bor*. **kep skaith** to suffer harm *16-19, 20- literary*. [variant of KEEP[1.2]]

kepar see KEEPER

kepe see KEEP[1.1], KEEP[1.2]

kepit see KEEP[1.2]

kepp see KIP[1]

kepper see KEP[2.2]

keppies see KEP[2.1]

kepping kame see KEP[2.2]

kepsweevle /kəpˈswivəl/ *v* to tilt or topple; to capsize *la19- Sh Ork*. [perhaps a conflation of Eng *capsize* with Eng *swivel*]

kept see KEEP[1.2]

ker see CAR[2]

kercake see CARCAKE

kerdikew see CARDIQUE

kerk see CARK[1.2]

kerkage see CARCAGE

kerl see CARLE[1.1]

kerlin, kerlyng see CARLINE

kern see KIRN[1.1]

kernel, kirnel, †kirnell, †chirnel /ˈkɛrnəl, ˈkɪrnəl/ *n* **1** the central edible part of a fruit, nut or grain *la15-*. **2** a lump under the skin (in the neck); a swollen gland, a boil *19-*. **kirnels** animal glands used as food, lamb's fry, lamb's testicles *18-19, 20- SW Bor*. [OE *cyrnel*]

kerr see CAR[1], CARE[1.1], CARE[1.2]

kerridge see CAIRRAGE

kerro /ˈkɛro/ *n fisherman's taboo* a spinning-wheel *20- Sh*. [perhaps onomatopoeic]

kers, kerse see CARSE[1], CARSE[2]

kerseckie see CARSACKIE

kert see CAIRD[3]

kerter see CAIRTER

kesart see KAISART

kesh see KEX[1]

kess see CASE[1]

Kessock herring /ˈkɛsək hɛrɪŋ/ *n* a small variety of herring caught in the Inner Moray Firth *la18- N NE T*. [from the place-name + HERRIN]

kest see CAST[1.1], CAST[1.2], COOSE[1.1], COOSE[1.2], KIST[1.1]

ket[1] /kɛt/ *n* carrion, tainted (animal) flesh *19- Bor*. [ON *kjöt* meat, flesh]

ket[2.1], †**cot** /kɛt/ *n* **1** a matted fleece *la14-19, 20- C*. **2** a spongy, fibrous kind of peat *19- SW Bor*. **3** couch grass *Elymus repens 19- Bor*. **ketty** *of turf* matted, lumpy *19- WC Bor Uls*. [AN *cot*]

ket[2.2] /kɛt/ *adj* irascible, quick-tempered *19- SW*. [see the noun]

ketach, caitach /ˈkɛtax, ˈkɛtəx/ *n* **1** the left hand *la19- H&I*. **2** a left-handed person *20- H&I WC*. **kittagh-handed, katy-handed** left-handed *19- WC Uls*. [Gael *ciotag* the left hand, *ciotach* left-handed]

ketch see CATCH[1.2], KEYTCH[1.1], KEYTCH[1.2]

†**kethat** *n* a large-skirted coat; an overgarment *e16*. [unknown]

kethie, kithie, *NE* **kethrie** /ˈkɛθe, ˈkɪθe; *NE* ˈkɛθri/ *n* the angler fish *Lophius piscatorius 19- NE EC Bor*. **kethock**, *N* **kyathack** = KETHIE *19- N NE WC SW*. [unknown]

kettell see CATTLE

ketter /'kɛtər/ *n* a mean, heartless person; a miser *20- Ork.* [perhaps related to CATOUR]
ketterel *see* KITERAL
ketterine *see* CATERAN
kettle, †**kettill** /'kɛtəl/ *n* **1** a large cooking pot; a cauldron; a fish-kettle *15-.* **2** a container used for boiling water, a kettle *18-.* **3** a riverside picnic (on the Tweed) at which newly-caught salmon are cooked on the spot *la17-19, 20- EC Bor.* **4** a cooking pot used on a rowing boat *20- Sh.* **5** *mining* a cylindrical or barrel-shaped vessel of wood or iron used to raise and lower materials and men during the sinking of a pit *la19- C.* **kettlie** the game of hopscotch *20- N NE T H&I.* **kettle-bellied** pot-bellied *la19, 20- N SW.* **kettle biler**, **kettle boiler** *derogatory* a house-husband *20- T.* **kettle brod** a wooden pot-lid *20- Sh N.* **kettle drum** a large bowl-shaped drum *la17-.* [OE *citel*]
kettle *see* KITTLE[2.2]
kettlin *see* KITTLIN
keuch[1.1] /kjʌx/ *n* a troublesome, persistent, tickling cough *19, 20- NE Bor.* [probably variant of COAF[1.1]]
keuch[1.2], **kyoch**, *Sh* **kjüff** /kjʌx, kjɔx; *Sh* kjøf/ *v* to cough persistently from a tickling in the throat *19-, 20- Sh Bor.* [see the noun]
kev *see* KYAUVE[1.2]
kevel[1] /'kɛvəl, 'kɛvəl/ *v* **1** to hold oneself awkwardly, stumble *19- SW Bor Uls.* **2** to botch a job, work clumsily *20- Sh.* [perhaps frequentative form of CAVE[2]]
†**kevel**[2], **cavill** *v* to scold, wrangle; to find fault *la16-e19.* [EModE *cavil*]
kevel[3], †**cavell**, †**kavill** /'kɛvəl, 'kɛvəl/ *n* a large hammer used in quarrying and stone-breaking *16-19, 20- Bor.* **kevel-hammer** a large hammer *la16-19, 20- Bor.* **kevel-mell** a large hammer *17-19, 20- Bor.* [unknown]
kevel[4.1], †**cavell** /'kɛvəl, 'kɛvəl/ *n* **1** a wooden bit inserted into the mouth to prevent a horse from eating or a lamb from sucking *18- Sh Ork.* **2** a twitch or rope-bit (for a difficult horse) *19- Bor.* **3** a gag for a scold *16-19.* [see the verb]
kevel[4.2], †**cavill** /'kɛvəl, 'kɛvəl/ *v* **1** to fit a wooden bit into the mouth of a lamb to prevent it from sucking *19- Sh.* **2** to gag *e16.* [ON *kefla*]
kevel *see* CAVEL[2]
kevil *see* CAVEL[1.1]
kewrne *see* QUERN
kex, *Bor* **kesh** /kɛks; *Bor* kɛʃ/ *n* the cow parsnip *Heracleum sphondylium la18-19, 20- Sh Ork N Bor.* †**kekle** = KEX *la18.* **keksi** = KEX *20- Sh.* [compare Norw dial *-kjeks* in various plant names of the *Apiaceae* family]
key[1.1], †**kye** /ki/ *n* **1** a device for operating a lock *la14-.* **2** *music* a system of related notes *la16-.* **3** mood, humour, frame of mind *19-.* **4** *pl, in children's games* a state of or a call for truce *20-.* **5** *pl* an edible seaweed *19- Ork N.* **6** an accessory part of a wool-comb *la16-e17.* **keysies** *in children's games* a state of or a call for truce *la20-.* **seek for a key that is in the lock** to waste one's time, do something futile *la19- C.* **use the king's keys**, †**use the kingis keyes** to force entry by virtue of a legal warrant *la16-e19, 20- historical.* [OE *cǣg*]
key[1.2] /ki/ *v* to fasten with a key, lock up *19, 20- Sh Uls.* [see the noun]
†**keyheid** *n* the westernmost or most inland part of the quay of Aberdeen *16-17.* [ME *keie* + HEID[1.1]]
keyll *see* KEEL[2.1]
†**key-maister** *n* an officer in charge of the quays in the harbour of a seaport *la16-17.* [EModDu *kayemeester*]
keyn *see* KEEN

keytch[1.1], **caitch**, †**ketch** /kɛtʃ/ *n* a toss, a jerk, a heave *18-19, 20- Bor.* [perhaps variant of CADGE[2.1]]
keytch[1.2], **caitch**, †**kytch**, †**ketch** /kɛtʃ/ *v* to overturn; to pitch or toss around; to hitch up *18-19, 20- Bor.* [see the noun]
kiarr *see* KYAR
kiaugh *see* KAUCH
kibbie *see* KIBBY
kibble /'kɪbəl/ *adj* well-built; active, agile *la18- NE T.* [unknown]
kibbling /'kɪblɪŋ/ *n* **1** a beating *la20- SW Bor.* **2** a cudgel, a rough stick *e19.* [derivative of ME *kible*]
kibby, **kibbie** /'kɪbi/ *adj* **1** nimble, active *la19- Sh.* **2** eager, anxious *la19- Sh.* [Norw *kipen* lively, restless, merry]
kich *see* KEECH[1.1], KEECH[1.2], KEECH[1.3]
kiche *see* KITCHIE[1.1]
kicher[1.1] /'kɪxər/ *n* a short, sharp cough *20- NE T C.* [onomatopoeic]
kicher[1.2], **kecher** /'kɪxər, 'kɛxər/ *v* to have a short, persistent, tickling cough *19- NE T C SW.* [see the noun]
kicher[2.1] /'kɪxər/ *n* a titter, a giggle *20- NE T.* [onomatopoeic; compare Ger *kichern*]
kicher[2.2] /'kɪxər/ *v* to titter, giggle *19- Sh NE T Uls.* [see the noun]
kiching *see* KITCHEN[1.1]
kick[1.1], *Sh Ork* **keek** /kɪk; *Sh Ork* kik/ *n* **1** a blow with the foot; the act of kicking *18-.* **2** a novelty, a new (clothing) fashion; something newfangled *19- Sh Ork NE.* **3** a trick, a caper *19- NE EC.* **4** a habit, a whim *20- NE T.* **5** *pl* airs, manners *19, 20- Sh NE.* **kicky 1** showy, dandified *la18-19, 20- NE T SW.* **2** provocative, teasing *la19- NE.* [unknown]
kick[1.2], *Sh Ork* **keek** /kɪk; *Sh Ork* kik/ *v* **1** to strike out with the foot *la16-.* **2** to show off; to walk haughtily or strut *la19- N NE T.* **kick ba 1** a football *19-.* **2** the game of football *la19-.* **kick the block** a game in which a player has to hunt for other hidden players while preventing any of them creeping out to kick a block of wood *la19-.* **kick-bonnety** a game played by kicking a cap or bonnet until the owner can substitute another which is in turn kicked *la19- N T EC.* **kick the can** = kick the block *20-.* **kick ower the theats** to act in an unrestrained manner *20- NE T;* compare *loup the theats* (LOWP[1.2]). **kick wi the wrong foot** *derogatory* to be a Roman Catholic *la20-.* [unknown]
kicker[1] /'kɪkər/ *n* a person or an animal that kicks *19-.* **sit the kicker** to resist; to refuse to budge or be disturbed *19- NE.* **stand the kickers** = sit the kicker *20- NE.* [KICK[1.2], with agent suffix]
kicker[2] /'kɪkər/ *n* a tedder, a machine for spreading out new-mown hay *la19-.* [KICK[1.2], with agent suffix]
kickle *see* KECKLE[1.2]
kickmaleerie /kɪkməˈliri/ *n* a flimsy trifling thing; an ornament or adornment *19- T EC Bor.* [KICK[1.1] + *-maleerie* a fanciful ending as in WHIGMALEERIE]
†**kid** *v* to flirt *19.* [unknown]
kid *see* KYTHE
kidgie *see* CADGY
kieger, **keeker** /'kigər, 'kikər/ *n* **1** a crick in the neck *20- Sh.* **2** a twist in a rope *la19- Sh.* [frequentative form of Norw *kikk* a dislocation, a sprain]
kiek *see* KEEK[1.1]
kiest *see* CAST[1.1], CAST[1.2]
kiffle *see* KIGHLE
kig *see* CAG
kiggle-caggle, **kiggle-kaggle** /'kɪɡəl kaɡəl/ *v* to cause a curling stone to make a succession of zigzag movements

between other stones to reach its objective *19-*. [probably reduplicated compound based on COGGLE]

kighle, *Bor* **kiffle** /ˈkɪxəl; *Bor* ˈkɪfəl/ *n* a short, tickling cough *20- T EC Bor*. [onomatopoeic]

kilbern *see* KILL[1.1]

kilch[1.1], **kiln**, †**kell** /kɪltʃ/ *n* an unexpected blow, a push, a shove *19- SW Bor*. [conflation of KEYTCH[1.1] with KILT[2.1]]

kilch[1.2], †**kilsh** /kɪltʃ/ *v* to push, shove; to jerk or ram *19- SW Bor*. [see the noun]

kilchan, **calchen**, **coulichin** /ˈkɪlxən, ˈkalxən, ˈkulɪxən/ *n* a rack hung in the chimney for drying fir candles *19- NE*. [compare Gael *cealaich* the fireplace of a kiln]

kilches *see* CALSHES

Kilde *see* CULDEE

kilfuddoch /kɪlˈfʌdəx/ *n* a meeting and discussion, a debate, a dispute *19, 20- literary*. [altered form of CURCUDDOCH]

kilhailie /kɪlˈheli/ *n* a somersault, a fall *20- N*. [perhaps related to Scots *keelhaul* to be 'laid out' with a drink]

kill[1.1], **kiln**, †**kell** /kɪl, kɪln/ *n* **1** a furnace or oven (for drying grain or calcinating lime); a kiln *la15-*. **2** the wooden tripod (for ventilation) round which a stack of hay or corn is built *19-*. **3** a kiln-shaped chasm in the rocks connecting with the sea; frequently in place-names *19- Sh Ork N*. **4** *humorous* a whisky still *20- EC SW*. **kill barn**, **kiln barn**, †**kilbern** a barn attached to or containing a kiln *la16-19, 20- Ork NE*. **kill beddin**, **kiln beddin** the packed straw on the drying floor of a kiln, over which the grain was spread *la18-*. **kill cast**, **kiln cast** the quantity of oats taken to the mill at one time to be ground into meal for household use *19- EC SW*. **kill crack** a trivial blemish *la19-*. **kill crackit** *of the glazing of pottery* cracked by cooling at an uneven temperature *la19-*. †**kill croft**, **kiln croft** the piece of ground occupied by or attached to a kiln *la15-19*. **kill door**, **kiln door** the steps up to the entrance to a kiln *la19- Sh NE*. **kill ee** the open space in front of a kiln fireplace *20- NE Bor*. **kill head**, **kiln head** the roof of a kiln, also forming the floor of the drying chamber on which the grain is spread to dry *la18-19, 20- Sh Bor*. **kill man**, **kiln man** the man in charge of a corn-kiln *17-*. **kill plate** one of the perforated metal plates forming the surface of the drying floor in modern kilns *la20- Ork N EC SW*. **kiln pot** the heating chamber under a corn-kiln *18-19, 20- T SW Uls*. **kill rib** one of the bars laid across the kiln joists to support the bed of straw on the drying floor *la17-19, 20- Sh Uls*. **kiln stead** = *kill croft la15-19, 20- Sh*. **kiln stick** one of the beams which support the drying floor *la17-19, 20- Sh Ork Bor*. **kill tree**, **kiln tree** = *kiln stick 16-19, 20- Sh Ork*. **fire the kill** to start trouble, raise a commotion *18- Sh EC Uls*. **the kill's on fire** there is a state of tumult or excitement *16-19, 20- T EC Uls*. **set the kill on fire** = *fire the kill la17-19, 20- Sh Uls*. [OE *cylen*]

kill[1.2], **kiln** /kɪl, kɪln/ *v* **1** to place in a kiln; to heat or dry (grain) in a kiln *16-*. **2** to disinfect clothes in a kiln *e17*. [see the noun KILL[1.1]]

kill[2.1] /kɪl/ *n* the act of killing; something killed *la19-*. **get yer kill** laugh uproariously *20-* **laugh yer kill** = *get yer kill 20- NE T*. [see the verb]

kill[2.2], †**kele**, †**keill** /kɪl/ *v pt, ptp also* **kilt**, †**keild** **1** to put to death, deprive of life *15-*. **2** to thrash, beat; to hurt badly; to cause to suffer *16-*. **3** to exhaust, overwork *la19-*. **kill the coo** a serious matter; bother or trouble *19- H&I SW Bor*. [ME *killen*]

killavyne *see* KEELYVINE

killick /ˈkɪlɪk/ *n* **1** a leading seaman in the Navy, the anchor badge on his sleeve being likened to a pickaxe *20- WC*. **2** the 'mouth' of a pickaxe *18-e19*. [variant of *gellock* (GAVELOCK)]

killicoup *see* KILLIECOUP

Killie /ˈkɪli, ˈkɪle/ *n* **1** a nickname for the town of Kilmarnock *la18-*. **2** a nickname for Kilmarnock Football Club *20-*. [shortened form of KILMARNOCK]

killiecoup, †**killicoup** /kɪliˈkʌup/ *n* a tumble head over heels; a somersault *19, 20- Bor*. [COWP[1.1], with intensifying prefix]

killieleepie /kɪliˈlipi/ *n* the common sandpiper *Actitis hypoleucos 19-*. [onomatopoeic]

†**killiemankie** *n* (a garment made from) calamanco, a woollen cloth *17-e19*. [altered form of EModE *calamanco*; compare Du *kalamink*]

killieshangie *see* COLLIESHANGIE

killing *see* KEELIN

killing time /ˈkɪlɪŋ tʌɪm/ *n* a name for the period of the greatest persecution of the Covenanters in 1685, later extended to cover the period 1679-1688 *la17, 18- historical*. [presp of KILL[1.2] + TIME]

killogie, **kiln-logie**, †**killogy** /kɪˈlogi, kɪlnˈlogi/ *n* **1** the lower part of a kiln, underneath the drying chamber; the kiln itself *16-*. **2** the fire or fireplace of a kiln *la18-19, 20- Sh Ork NE H&I*. **3** the covered space in front of the fireplace of a kiln *19, 20- historical*. [KILL[1.1] + LOGIE]

killum-kallum *see* GILLIE[1.1]

killyvie /kɪliˈvi/ *n* a fuss, a disturbance *19- WC*. [unknown]

killywimple /kɪliˈwɪmpəl/ *n* **1** the undulating flight of a bird *20- literary*. **2** a trill or affectation in singing *19*. [intensifying prefix *killy-* + WIMPLE[1.1]]

Kilmares *see* KILMAURS

Kilmarnock /kɪlˈmarnək/ *n* **1** a broad, flat, woollen bonnet of blue, black or red *19-*. **2** a knitted, woollen, conical skull-cap worn as a nightcap or by indoor workers such as weavers *la19-*. **Kilmarnock bonnet** a broad, flat, woollen bonnet *la18-*. **Kilmarnock hood** a knitted woollen skull-cap *la18-19, 20- NE T*. †**Kilmarnock knives** knives manufactured in Kilmarnock *la17*. **Kilmarnock shot** games a safe shot, put deliberately wide or out of play; any kind of unsporting play *20-*. †**Kilmarnock stockings** stockings manufactured in Kilmarnock *17-e19*. [from the name of the town in Ayrshire]

Kilmaurs, †**Kilmares** /kɪlˈmɔrz/ *n* a town in Ayrshire (noted for its cutlery) *la17-*. **Kilmaurs kail** a strong, hardy variety of kail mainly used for feeding cattle *la18-19, 20- WC*. **Kilmaurs measure** a generous measure *20- NE WC SW*. **gleg as a Kilmaurs whittle** quick-witted *la18- WC SW*. **sharp as a Kilmaurs whittle** = *gleg as a Kilmaurs whittle la19- WC SW*. [from the name of the town in Ayrshire]

kiln *see* KILL[1.1], KILL[1.2]

kiln-logie *see* KILLOGIE

kilsh *see* KILCH[1.2]

kilt[1.1] /kɪlt/ *n* a kind of skirt, usually of tartan cloth, reaching to the knee and thickly pleated at the back, commonly worn as part of modern male Highland dress *18-*. **kilted** wearing a kilt *19-*. **help my kilt!** an expression of surprise *20-*. [see the verb]

kilt[1.2] /kɪlt/ *v* **1** to tuck up one's clothes or skirt round the body *16-*. **2** to lift up, suspend something; to hang a person *la17-*. **3** to travel lightly or quickly *19*. **kilting 1** a pleated frill on a petticoat *20-*. **2** the lap of a woman's petticoat *17-e19*. **high kiltit**, **high kilted** having the skirts well tucked up; immodest, indecent *la18-*. [ON *kelta*, *kjalta* a lap, ON *kilting* the lap of a garment]

kilt[2.1] /kɪlt/ *n* **1** *masonry* the slope of a stone to allow water to run off *19- EC Bor*. **2** a tilt; an overturn, an upset *19- Bor*. [unknown]

kilt[2.2] /kɪlt/ *v* to overturn, upset; to tilt *19- EC SW Bor*. [unknown]

kilt³ /kɪlt/ *n* the proper way or knack of doing something *19- SW*. [probably extended sense of KILT²·¹]
kilt *see* KILL²·²
kiltie¹·¹, **kilty** /ˈkɪlte, ˈkɪlti/ *n* a wearer of the kilt; a soldier in a Highland regiment; a Scot *19-*. **kiltie cauld bum** a disparaging taunt addressed to a kilt wearer *la20-*. [KILT¹·¹ + -IE¹]
kiltie¹·², **kilty** /ˈkɪlte, ˈkɪlti/ *adj derogatory* Scottish *19-*. [see the noun]
kilya /ˈkɪljə/ *n* (the call of) a gull *20- Sh*. [onomatopoeic]
kim¹ /kɪm/ *adj* 1 spirited, frolicsome, lively *19 20- NE*. 2 spruce, nimble *19- NE*. [unknown]
kim² /kɪm/ *n* a bed *20- Ork*. [unknown]
kimmer¹·¹, **gimmer**, †**cummer**, †**cumar**, †**commere** /ˈkɪmər, ˈgɪmər/ *n* 1 a female intimate or friend; a gossip *15-*. 2 a married woman, a wife *18-*. 3 a girl, a lass *la18-*. 4 a godmother *la16-19, 20- Sh*. 5 a midwife *la16-19, 20- Sh*. 6 a witch *18-e19*. †**cummerfealls** an entertainment at the birth of a child *19*. [ME *commare*]
†**kimmer**¹·², **cummer** *v* to gossip *la17-e19*. [see the noun]
kimmerin, †**cummering** /ˈkɪmərɪn/ *n* a feast given to celebrate the birth of a child *la17-19, 20- literary*. [derivative of KIMMER¹·¹]
kimmin, †**cummen**, †**cumming**, †**kymmond** /ˈkɪmɪn/ *n* a tub, a pail (used in brewing) *16-19, 20- EC*. [unknown]
†**kimming** *n* cumin, the spice *16-e17*. [ME *comin*]
kimpill *see* KEMPLE
kimpkin *see* KINKEN
kimple *see* KEMPLE
kims /kɪms/ *v* to toss the head or jerk the body *20- Sh Ork*.
kimsey haughty *20- Ork*. [Norw *kimse*]
kin /kɪn/ *n* 1 relatives; a family, a clan, a race *la14-*. 2 kinship, family relationship, ancestry *la14-*. 3 a family member, a relation *la15-*. **kinless** without (noble or influential) relatives *la17-*. **of kin** related to *la14-*. [OE *cynn*]
kin *see* KIND¹·¹, KIND¹·³, KIND¹·⁴
kinallie *see* CANALLY
kinboot, †**kinbutte**, †**kynbute** /ˈkɪnbut/ *n* compensation paid for manslaughter by the slayer to the kindred of the slain; ASSYTHMENT *15-18, 19- historical*. [KIN + BUIT²·¹]
kinch¹·¹, †**kench** /kɪnʃ/ *n* 1 a twist or doubling in a rope, a kink; a loop, a noose, a running knot *19-*. 2 a sudden twist or jerk in wrestling *19-*. 3 a predicament, a difficult problem *20- NE EC*. **kincher** a puzzle or predicament *20- NE*. [altered form of KINK¹·¹]
kinch¹·², **kench** /kɪnʃ, kɛnʃ/ *v* 1 to twist a loop in a rope with a stick in order to tighten it *19-*. 2 to tie up a bundle *19- WC SW*. 3 to twitch a horse *la19- NE C*. 4 *weaving* to fasten loops on to bridles *19, 20- WC*. **kinch pin** a pin or rod used for twisting ropes *19- C SW*. [see the noun]
kinch², †**kench** /kɪnʃ/ *n* 1 an (unexpected) advantage or opportunity *17-19, 20- NE Uls*. 2 a division of land (decided by the casting of lots) *la18*. 3 one's lot or fortune *la16-e17*. 4 the fall of the dice *la15*. †**count your kinch** to reckon up your score, appreciate your true condition *la16-e17*. **keep kinches** to serve a turn, be useful in an emergency; to fall in with the plans or ways of another *19, 20- SW*. [OFr *cheance* the fall of the dice; compare Du, MLG *kanse, kan(t)ze*]
kinch³ /kɪnʃ/ *v* to throw a stone in a particular way; to make a flat stone skip on the surface of water *20- EC Bor*. [unknown]
kind¹·¹, **keind**, **kin'**, †**kynd** /kʌɪnd, kʌɪn/ *n* 1 a category, a group, a division (of things) *la14-*. 2 a group of people sharing a common origin, a family; a species of animal *la14-*. 3 innate nature or character *la14-*. 4 inherited character *15-*. 5 the physical nature or constitution of a person or animal *la14-16*. **in a kind** after a fashion *la19- NE EC*. **kin-a-wise**, **kinnaweys** somewhat, rather *la19- C Bor*. **kind of**, **kinna**, **kinnae** kind of *15-*. **not a kind** not any, not a single one ◊*out she ran with not a shawl kind on her 20-*. **of kind** by birth or descent; by native constitution, naturally *15-e19*. **out of your kind** at variance with or contrary to one's inherited rank or character *16-*. **yon kin**, **yon kind** not quite normal or proper; not worth or up to much, in indifferent health *20-*. [OE *cynd*]
kind¹·², **keind** /kʌɪnd/ *v* 1 to resemble, take after *20- Bor*. 2 to sort, arrange in kinds *20- EC Bor*. [see the noun]
kind¹·³, **kin'**, †**kynd** /kʌɪnd, kʌɪn/ *adj* 1 kindly, benevolent; generous, considerate *la15-*. 2 native (to a place) *la14-19, 20- Sh*. 3 belonging to one by birth or inheritance; lawful, rightful *la15-e18*. 4 *of a bondman or tenant* belonging by birth to the lands specified or to a particular lord *la14-e16*. 5 well-bred, noble *15-16*. 6 related, of one's kin *16*. **kindlike** †**kyndlik** kindly, considerate; natural *la14-*. †**kynd born** *of a bondman* belonging by birth to a particular lord *e15*. [OE *gecynde*]
kind¹·⁴, **kin'** /kʌɪnd, kʌɪn/ *adv* somewhat, rather: ◊*an odd kind chiel la18-*. [see the adj]
kindle /ˈkɪndəl/ *v of rabbits* to produce young *20-*. [derivative of KIND¹·¹]
kindle *see* KENNLE
kindly, †**kyndlie** /ˈkʌɪndle/ *adj* 1 generous, benevolent, thoughtful *16-*. 2 natural, normal; characteristic, congenial *la14-19, 20- Ork*. 3 native, indigenous; true-born, rightful *16-19, 20- Sh Ork*. 4 of a good or excellent nature or quality, thriving *la18-19*. 5 *of a possession or right* belonging to one by right of birth or heredity *16-17*. 6 *of lands or tacks* belonging to a person as the KINDLY TENANT *16-17*. 7 *of a place* native to one, which one belongs *la16-17*. 8 related, of one's kindred *la16*. 9 *of a tenant or tacksman* having a right to the tenancy or tack in consequence of its long continued occupation *16*. 10 having the right of a KINDLY TENANT to (the land specified) *16*. †**kindliness**, **kyndelynes** the right of a KINDLY TENANT *17-18*. **kindly sheep** native Shetland sheep *la18- Sh Ork*. [KIND¹·¹, with adj-forming suffix]
kindly tenant, †**kyndlie tenent** /ˈkʌɪndle tɛnənt/ *n law* a person holding lands by right of long-standing or hereditary occupation rather than by charter or other written tenancy agreement *16-19, 20- historical*. **the King's Kindly Tenants of Lochmaben** tenants holding lands by right of long occupation in the villages around Lochmaben *19-20, 21- historical*. †**maist kyndlie tenent** best-entitled tenant *la16*. [KINDLY + TENANT]
kindness, **kin'ness** /ˈkʌɪndnəs, ˈkʌɪnnəs/ *n* 1 benevolence, generosity; a kind act *15-*. 2 affection, friendship, amity; neighbourliness *15-*. 3 the right of a KINDLY TENANT to his holding or tack *16-e19*. 4 kinship, relationship by birth *15-e17*. 5 permission to occupy a holding with the friendly consent or goodwill of the landlord *16-17*. 6 prescriptive or hereditary right or title *16-e17*. [KIND¹·³, with noun-forming suffix]
kindred¹·¹, †**kinrede**, †**kynrayd** /ˈkɪndrəd/ *n* 1 kinsfolk, relatives; a family, a clan, a race *16-*. 2 kinship, family relationship, ancestry; affinity *la16-*. [ME *kinrede*]
kindred¹·² /ˈkɪndrəd/ *adj* related by blood; existing between relatives; similar, cognate *la16-*. [see the noun]
king, **keeng**, **keing** /kɪŋ, kiŋ/ *n* 1 a male sovereign or monarch, the ruler of a kingdom *la14-*. 2 the title conferred on the boy who gave the highest gratuity to the schoolmaster at Candlemas; compare *Candlemas King* (CANDLEMAS) *18-20, 21- historical*. 3 *in cock-fighting* the winning cock or its owner *la19- NE Bor*. †**kingis** *of commodities* of royal or excellent quality, of the finest sort *16*. **kinglike**, †**kinglyke**

kingly, befitting a king *15-*. **king alison, king ellison** the ladybird, a beetle of the family *Coccinellidae la19- NE T*. **king ba** a children's game in which a ball is caught between the fists *20- T C*. **king-coll-awa** the ladybird, a beetle of the family *Coccinellidae la19- NE*. **king's chair** a seat formed by two children each of whom grasps one of his own wrists and the opposite wrist of the other child *la19- NE T*. **king's cushion** = *king's chair 19- EC Uls*. †**king's freemen** men who by virtue of services rendered by themselves or their family in the military had a statutory right to exercise trades as freemen without becoming members of their particular trade incorporation *la18-19*. **king's hood,** *NE* **king's heed 1** the second of the four stomachs of a ruminant *19-*. **2** *humorous* the human stomach *la18*. **be a king tae** to surpass, be superior to *la19-*. **king across the ditchie** a children's game *20- N T*. **the King's ellwand 1** *astronomy* Orion's Belt *19- N Bor*. **2** the foxglove *Digitalis purpurea la19- Bor*. **king of the herrings** the Arctic chimaera *Chimaera monstrosa la19- Sh NE T*. **king of the midden** a self-important person; a petty tyrant *la20-*. †**King's Own Borderers** an earlier name for the *King's Own Scottish Borderers 19*. **King's Own Scottish Borderers** the Scottish regiment first raised in 1689, and known by this designation from 1887 onwards *la19-20, 21- historical*. †**the kingis pese** the protection afforded to those living within the law under the king's jurisdiction *15-e17*. [OE *cyning*]

kingdom /ˈkɪŋdəm/ *n* a country or nation subject to a king (or queen) *15-*. **the Kingdom** = *the Kingdom of Fife 20-*. **the Kingdom of Fife** Fife (from its self-contained situation) *la17-*. [OE *cynedōm*]

kingle /ˈkɪŋəl/ *n* a type of very hard sandstone *19- C SW*. [unknown]

kingrik *see* KINRICK

kink[1.1] /kɪŋk/ *n* **1** a bend, a loop *la19-*. **2** a crease, a fold *la19-*. [probably Du *kink*]

kink[1.2] /kɪŋk/ *v* to bend, twist; to warp *la19-*. [probably Du *kinken*]

kink[2.1], †**kinke** /kɪŋk/ *n* **1** a convulsive catching of the breath (in whooping-cough); a fit of coughing *la17-*. **2** a violent and irrepressible fit of laughter *la17-*. [see the verb]

kink[2.2] /kɪŋk/ *v* **1** to gasp or choke convulsively or spasmodically; to cough uncontrollably; to suffer an attack of whooping-cough *la18-*. **2** to choke with laughter *19-*. **kinkers** whooping cough *20- NE T EC*. **kink cough** whooping cough *18-19, 20- SW Bor Uls*. Compare CHINCOUGH. **kink hoast, kink host** whooping-cough *la16-*. [OE *cincian*; compare LG *kinken*]

†**kinken, kinkin, kimpkin** *n* a keg, a small barrel *la15-19*. [MDu *kinnekijn*]

kin-kind /kɪnˈkaɪnd/ *n* a kind or type (of something) *la18-19, 20- NE*. [altered form of *a'kin kind* (A'KIN)]

kinnen, *Sh* **kyunnen,** *Ork* **kunnin,** †**cuning,** †**conyng,** †**kinning** /ˈkɪnən/; *Sh* ˈkjʌnən; *Ork* ˈkʌnən/ *n* a rabbit, a cony *15-19, 20- Sh Ork EC*. [ME *coning*]

kin'ness *see* KINDNESS

kinnle *see* KENNLE

kinrede *see* KINDRED[1.1]

†**kinrent** *n* kindred *15-16*. [altered form of KINDRED[1.1]]

kinrick, kinrik, kingrik /ˈkɪnrɪk, ˈkɪŋrɪk/ *n* a kingdom, a realm; kingship *la14-*. [OE *cynerīce*]

kinsh[1] /kɪnʃ/ *n* a lever used in quarrying stones *19- EC SW Bor*. [unknown]

kinsh[2] /kɪnʃ/ *n* a small quantity, a pinch *20- NE EC*. [perhaps altered form of Older Scots *pincshe* a pinch]

kintra, kintry, countra, coontra, country, *NE* **quintra,** *NE* **quintry,** *NE* **cwintry,** *NE* **kwintry,** *Bor* **cuintrie,** †**contre,** †**cuntre,** †**countre** /ˈkɪntrə, ˈkɪntre, ˈkʌntrə, ˈkuntrə, ˈkʌntre; *NE* ˈkwɪntrə; *NE* ˈkwɪntre; *Bor* ˈkuntre/ *n* **1** a nation, a country *la14-*. **2** a district; a tract of land; the territory of a clan; the inhabitants of a district *la14-*. **countryfeed** countrified *la19, 20- NE T C*. **country clash, kintra clash** the gossip of the district *19-*. **country Jock** *derogatory* a farmworker, a country-dweller *la19- NE T EC*. [ME *contre*]

Kintyre pursuivant, †**Kintyre pursevant** /kɪnˈtaer ˈpʌrswɪvənt/ *n* one of the Scottish pursuivants *la15-*. [from the place-name + ME *pursevaunt*]

†**kinvaig** *n* a small woollen plaid *19*. [unknown]

kiow-ow[1.1]**, kyow, keo** /ˈkjʌu ʌu, kjʌu, kjo/ *n* **1** a thing of no importance; silly chatter *19- N T C SW*. **2** a trick, a ploy, a carry-on *la19- T SW Uls*. [perhaps onomatopoeic]

kiow-ow[1.2], *SW* **keo** /ˈkjʌu ʌu; *SW* kjo/ *v* to talk or act frivolously, caper about, play the fool *la19- N NE T SW Uls*. **kiow-owin** tattling, frivolous *19- N NE T SW*. **kyow-owy** fussy, pottering *la19- T*. [see the noun]

kip[1], *Bor* **kype,** †**kepp** /kɪp; *Bor* kʌɪp/ *n* **1** a jutting or projecting point on a hill; the summit of a sharp-pointed hill; frequently in place-names *la16-*. **2** a turned-up tip or nose *19- EC Bor Uls*. **3** the projecting cartilage on the lower jaw of the male salmon at spawning time *la19- SW Bor*. **kippie** *n* a small hill *la17- T C SW Bor*. **kippie** *adj* **1** *of cattle* having upturned horns *19- NE Bor*. **2** *of a person* having an upturned nose *20- EC Bor*. **kippit 1** *of a hill* peaked; having jutting outcrops of rock or boulder; frequently in place-names *la14-*. **2** *of horns* turned up *la16-*. **3** *of the nose* upturned *la19- SW Bor*. †**kip-headed, kip-hedit** *of cattle* having upturned horns *la16-e18*. **kip nose** a nose turned up at the tip *19- Bor*. [MLG *kippe* a point, a peak]

kip[2.1] /kɪp/ *n* a truant *la19- T C Bor*. **play the kip** to play truant *la19- T C Bor*. [unknown]

kip[2.2] /kɪp/ *v* to play truant from school *19, 20- EC Bor*. [unknown]

kip[3.1] /kɪp/ *n* **1** a quantity of fish *20- Ork*. **2** a bundle of grass; a tuft of hair *20- Ork*. **3** a bundle or pack containing a specific quantity of goods *16-17*. **kippek** a bundle of fish (tied together) *la19- Sh*. [MDu, MLG *kip*, ON *kippa* a bundle, *kippi* a sheaf]

kip[3.2] /kɪp/ *v* to tie up (hides or fish) in a bundle *15-e16, 20- Sh*. [EModDu *kippen* to put (fish) into kips]

kip[4] /kɪp/ *n* **1** haste, hurry *19- T Bor*. **2** a state of great excitement; a fit of anger *20- NE Bor*. [probably reduced form of KIPPAGE]

kipill *see* COUPLE[1.1]

kippage, †**quippage** /ˈkɪpədʒ/ *n* **1** disorder, confusion; a state of excitement or anger *19-*. **2** a person of unsightly appearance *la19- NE EC*. **3** mood or condition *20- N SW*. **4** the crew of a ship *16-e17*. Compare EQUIPAGE. [MFr *esquipage* crew]

kipper[1.1] /ˈkɪpər/ *n* **1** a smoke-dried herring, originally also a salmon *la18-*. **2** a male salmon in the spawning season *la15-19*. [unknown]

kipper[1.2] /ˈkɪpər/ *v* to smoke-dry a fish; to expose to a hot, stifling atmosphere *la18-*. [unknown]

kipper[2] /ˈkɪpər/ *n* a large bowl; a large quantity (of food) *la19- NE*. [compare KYPE]

kipper[3] /ˈkɪpər/ *v* to pile or stack (carelessly) *20- NE*. [derivative of KIP[1]]

kippie[1.1] /ˈkɪpe/ *n* **1** a left-handed person *la19- T C*. **2** the left hand *20- T EC*. [unknown]

kippie[1.2] /ˈkɪpe/ *adj* left-handed *la19- T EC*. [unknown]

kippie, kippit *see* KIP[1]

kipple *see* COUPLE[1.1], COUPLE[1.2]

kirdandy /kɪrˈdandi/ *n* a row, an uproar *la19- WC SW Uls*. [shortened form of the name *Kirkdamie Fair*, a fair in Ayrshire held on the last Saturday of May]

kire *see* QUEIR

kirk[1.1], †**kyrk** /kɪrk, kʌrk/ *n* **1** a building used for public worship, a church; frequently in place-names *la12-*. **2** a local church congregation *16-*. **3** the CHURCH OF SCOTLAND *la16-*. **4** the Christian church; the Roman Catholic Church *la14-e17*. **5** the ruling body or *kirk-session* of a local church *la16-e17*. **6** the General Assembly of the Church of Scotland *la16-e17*. **kirkie** *n* a church *la19, 20- NE*. **kirkie, kirky** *adj* enthusiastically devoted to church affairs *20-*. **kirkless 1** *of a minister* without a church *19-*. **2** *of a layman* not attending or not a member of a church *19, 20 NE SW*. **kirk beadle**, †**kirk bedell** a church officer, an official charged with keeping order in the church and parish, attending the *kirk-session* and carrying out its edicts *17-*. **kirk book** an official record book of a church *16-*. **kirk box** the box containing church funds or the fund for the parish poor; a church collection box *17-19, 20- historical*. **kirk claes** Sunday clothes *la19-*. **kirk cough** a low, smothered cough such as might be heard in church *20- SW*. **kirk door**, †**kirk dure** the outer door of a church, the public place where baptisms and marriages were traditionally celebrated, offerings collected, proclamations read, and acts of repentance were carried out *la15-*. **kirk folk, kirk fowk 1** churchgoers, frequenters of the church; the congregation *la19-*. **2** church officials, ecclesiastics *19*. **kirk greedy** zealous in attendance at church *19-*. **kirk hoast** = *kirk cough 20- Ork*. †**kirk hole** the grave *la18-19*. **kirk house** a house belonging to or adjoining a church *16-19, 20- historical*. **kirk ladle** a small box on the end of a long handle for taking the collection *19-*. **kirkland** land belonging to the church, a glebe *la15-*. **kirkman 1** an ecclesiastic *la14-19, 20- Sh Ork*. **2** a regular churchgoer *la17-19, 20- Sh NE*. **kirk master 1** the official charged with the upkeep of the church buildings *la15-20, 21- historical*. **2** a church treasurer or deacon *la16-19, 20- historical*. **3** the officer of a guild responsible for the upkeep of the fraternity's altar and chaplaincy in the parish church *la15-18*. **4** a paid kirk officer appointed by the burgh *la16-e17*. **kirk mense** wearing clothing suitable for church *19- WC SW Bor*. **kirk officer**, †**kirk officiar** = *kirk beadle la16-*. **kirk reekit** bigoted *19, 20- SW*. **kirk road** a road or path used by parishioners going to the parish church, and constituting a right of way *18-*. **kirk session** *Presbyterian Church* the lowest court, consisting of the minister and the elders of the congregation and exercising its functions of church government within a parish *17-*. **kirk shot** a place near a church where fishing nets are shot *19, 20- literary*. **kirk shune** shoes kept for churchgoing *la19-*. **kirk skail** the dispersal of the congregation after a church service *19-*. **kirk stile** a stile or narrow entrance to a churchyard (used as a meeting place), where announcements were made and the bier was received into the churchyard at funerals *15-20, 21- historical*. **kirktoun, kirkton** a town or village situated by a church; the hamlet in which the parish church of a rural parish is located; a farm adjacent to a church; frequently in place-names *12-*. **kirk work**, †**kyrkwerk** building work on a church *15-20, 21- historical*. **at the kirk door** openly or in the public gaze; shamelessly *19, 20- NE T EC*. **Auld Kirk 1** the Church of Scotland (as opposed to other Presbyterian denominations) *19-*. **2** *humorous* whisky *la19-*. **come into the body of the kirk** to join the main company *20-*. **gie claes kirk mense** to wear a new garment at church for the first time *20- SW Bor*. **keep the kirk** to retain one's membership on the Communion Roll (of a particular church) though living outside its parish boundaries *19, 20- NE T*. **kirk and market**, †**kirk and mercat** in public, in a public place *la15-*. †**the kirk malignant** the Roman Church *16*. **Kirk of Scotland** the post-Reformation Presbyterian church in Scotland; the CHURCH OF SCOTLAND *la16-*. †**the kirk triumphant** *Christian Church* the community of Christian souls in heaven (considered to have conquered the world) *la15-e17*. **maister of the kirkwerk** *in Aberdeen* the official charged with the upkeep of the church buildings *15-19, 20- historical*. **mak a kirk or a mill o** to do whatever one wishes; to make the best or worst of a situation *18-*. †**man of kirk** an ecclesiastic *la15-16*. **neither big kirks nor place ministers** to be engaged in some questionable activity *la19- NE*. [ON *kirkja*; compare OE *cirice*]

kirk[1.2] /kɪrk, kʌrk/ *v* **1** *of a woman* to attend church for the first time after giving birth *15-*. **2** *of a newly married couple* to attend church, be received at church *la17-*. **3** *of a civic or academic body* to attend or be received at church together (soon after election) *la19-*. [see the noun]

kirk[2.1] /kɪrk, kjɪrk/ *n* a tug; a jerk *20- Ork*. [see the verb]

kirk[2.2] /kɪrk, kjɪrk/ *v* to tug or jerk (something heavy) *20- Ork*. [Norw *kjergja* to struggle with something difficult to move]

Kirkcaldy stripe /kərˈkɔdi straɪp/ *n* a type of cloth made in Kirkcaldy featuring a distinctive stripe; the pattern itself *la19- NE T C Bor*. [from the place-name *Kirkcaldy*, the Fife coastal town + STRIPE[1]]

kirkin, kirking /ˈkɪrkɪn, ˈkɪrkɪŋ/ *n* a ceremonial attendance at church *la17-*. **kirkin feast, kirking feast** a celebration held after the KIRKIN *la15-19, 20- Ork*. **kirkin time** the time of a church service *19- Ork NE SW Bor*. **kirking o the cooncillors** the first church service after the election of a local council *la20-*. **kirking of the parliament** the first church service after the election of a Scottish Parliament *la20-*. [KIRK[1.1], with *-ing* suffix]

kirknin /ˈkɪrknɪn/ *n* a ceremonial attendance at church *20- Sh*. [derivative of KIRK[1.1]]

kirkyaird, kirkyard, †**kyrkȝard**, †**kyrkyharde** /ˈkɪrkjerd, ˈkɪrkjard/ *n* a churchyard *la14-*. **kirkyard cough** = *kirkyaird hoast 20-*. **kirkyard deserter** an elderly or sickly-looking person *19, 20- NE*. **kirkyaird hoast** *humorous* a cough which sounds likely to prove fatal *la19-*. [KIRK[1.1] + YAIRD[1.1]]

kirmash /kərˈmaʃ/ *n* a crash; noise and confusion, hullabaloo *19- Ork SW*. [Du *kermis*, MDu *kerck-misse* the mass celebrated on the anniversary of the dedication of a church, later the fair held on this occasion]

kirn[1.1], *Ork* **kern**, *N H&I EC* **curn** /kɪrn; *Ork* kern; *N H&I EC* kʌrn/ *n* **1** a churn; a churnful *la15-*. **2** a natural feature resembling a churn; frequently in place-names *la16-*. **3** a churning motion, a confused stirring *la19-*. **4** milk in the process of being churned; buttermilk *19, 20- Sh NE T EC*. **5** a sloppy mess; wet mud; a distasteful mixture of food or liquid *19- Sh NE EC*. **6** a muddle, a jumble, confusion *20- NE T EC SW*. **7** a confused stir or uproar; a throng *20- NE T*. **8** work done in a lazy, slovenly or dirty way *la19- NE*. **9** a rummaging or pottering; an aimless trifling *la19- NE*. **kirnie** milk being churned, buttermilk *la19- T Bor*. **kirnkorses** = *kirn-staff 20- Sh*. **kirn-milk** buttermilk; curds made from buttermilk *16-*. **kirn-staff** (the handle of) the plunger of an upright churn *17-19, 20- Sh Ork NE*. **kirnstick** = *kirn-staff la19- NE WC*. **stannin kirn** an upright churn worked by a plunger *20- NE EC SW*. **the kirn's broken, the kirn's brokken** the milk is beginning to form into butter *la19-*. [ON *kirna*]

kirn[1.2] /kɪrn/ *v* **1** to churn (butter) *la16-*. **2** to stir, mix together *la17-19, 20- Sh NE T*. **3** to splash about (with the hands) lazily or ineffectively; to work in a slovenly manner, mess around *19- Sh NE T EC*. **4** to rummage, search through or poke about *la19- Sh NE T*. **5** *of a crowd* to swarm or mill about *20- Sh NE T C SW*. **6** to wind up or rotate machinery *20- SW Bor*. **7** to fuss over, show affection towards, mollycoddle *la18- NE*. **8** to bore with a drill or circular chisel *la19- EC*. **kirnin** footling, inefficient *20- NE T*. [see the noun]

kirn², *Uls* **churn** /kɪrn; *Uls* tʃʌrn/ *n* **1** a celebration marking the end of the harvest; a harvest feast *la16-19, 20- C SW Bor*. **2** the last sheaf or handful of corn of the harvest, frequently plaited and ornamented for display *19- SW Bor Uls*. **kirn baby**, †**kern baby** a corn-dolly (made from the last sheaf or handful of corn to be cut) *19, 20- NE Bor*. **kirn cut** the last handful of corn to be cut *19- T SW Bor*. **kirn dollie** = *kirn baby 19, 20- NE T C Bor*. **kirn supper** the celebration held when the last corn is cut *19- NE T EC SW Bor Uls*. [unknown; compare CURN¹]

kirnel, kirnell *see* KERNEL

†**kirnell, kyrnell** *n* **1** a crenel, an indentation in battlements *la14-17*. **2** *pl* battlements *16*. [ME *carnel, kernel*]

kirnin, kirning /'kɪrnɪn, 'kɪrnɪŋ/ *n* **1** the action of churning; one complete act of churning *17-*. **2** the quantity of milk required for one churning *20-*. **3** the quantity of butter produced at a churning *20-*. **kirnin day, kirning day** the day on which the churning is done *la19-*. **kirnan rung** the plunger of a churn *la18- WC SW*. **kirknin water** hot water used to mix the buttermilk in a churn *la19- Sh*. [verbal noun from KIRN¹˒²]

kirr¹ /kɪr/ *adj* **1** cheerful, lively, brisk; self satisfied *la18- C SW*. **2** amorous, wanton *19- WC SW*. [unknown]

kirr²·¹ /kɪr/ *v* to hush or silence; to scare away *20- Sh*. [ON *kyrr* quiet, still]

kirr²·² /kɪr/ *interj* a command for silence or expression of dismissal *la19- Sh Ork*. [imperative of the verb]

kirrie dumplin /'kɪre dʌmplɪn/ *n* the flower cluster of the drumstick primula, *Primula denticulata 20- T*. [a shortened form of the place-name *Kirriemuir* + DUMPLIN]

kirroo *see* CURROO

kirsen¹·¹, **kirsten**, **christen**, *N* **cursen**, †**cristin** /'kɪrsən, 'kɪrstən, 'krɪsən; *N* 'kʌrsən/ *v* **1** to baptize; to sponsor at baptism *la16-*. **2** to dilute spirits (with water) *e19*. **3** to convert to Christianity *la14-e16*. **kirsened**, †**kirsint** decent, proper *19- Sh Ork*. [OE *cristnian* to make Christian]

kirsen¹·², **kirsten**, **christin**, †**cristyn** /'kɪrsən, 'kɪrstən, 'krɪsən/ *adj* **1** decent, clean, proper, fit (to eat or wear) *19- Sh*. **2** Christian *la14-16*. [OE *cristen*, Lat *christiānus*]

kirsenin, christening, *N* **cursnin**, †**crystynnyng** /'kɪrsənɪn, 'krɪsənɪŋ; *N* 'kʌrsnɪn/ *n* (a ceremony of) baptism *la15-*. **christening bit** an offering of food made to the first person to see a baby either before or after christening; compare BABY'S PIECE *la19- EC SW*. **christening piece** = *christening bit la19- T EC*. [verbal noun from KIRSEN¹·¹]

†**kirsp** *n* a fine fabric, a kind of gauze or crepe; crisp *la15-e16*. [metathesis of Older Scots *crisp*]

kirsten *see* KIRSEN¹·¹, KIRSEN¹·²

kirsty /'kɪrsti, 'kɪrste/ *n* a whisky jar *20 NE EC Bor*. [from the female personal name]

Kirsty kringlik /'kɪrsti krɪŋlɪk/ *n* a long-legged spider; a crane-fly *20- Ork*. [unknown]

kis *see* CAUSE²

kishie, kishielepp *see* CASSIE

kislip *see* KEESLIP

kiss, †**kis**, †**kys** /kɪs/ *v* to touch with the lips, kiss *la14-*. **kiss-my-luif** a fawner, sycophant; an effeminate person *la19-*. **kiss my erse** an expression of abusive contempt *16-*. [OE *cyssan*]

kist¹·¹, **chist, chest**, *Sh* **kjist**, †**kest**, †**keist** /kɪst, tʃɪst, tʃɛst; *Sh* kjɪst/ *n* **1** a chest, a trunk, a large box *la14-*. **2** a coffin *la14-*. **3** the chest, the thorax *la19-*. **4** a rocky, box-like chasm in a river *la19- NE*. **5** a kind of fish-trap used on the lower Ness *la16-18*. **6** a case for storing or transporting certain kinds of dry goods or merchandise; a packing case *la15-e17*. **kist locker** a small compartment in a trunk for keeping money and valuables *la18-*. **kist-neuk** a corner of a chest reserved for money or valuables *la18-*. **kist o drawers** a chest of drawers *la19-*. **kist o whistles 1** *derogatory* a church organ *18-*. **2** *humorous* a wheezy chest *la20- N T*. **kistfu o whistles** = *kist o whistles*. **flit yer kist-neuk** to move from your accustomed place *20- NE*. [ON *kista*]

kist¹·² /kɪst/ *v* **1** to put or enclose in a coffin *la17-*. **2** to place or pack in a box or chest; to store, save or put by *la19-*. **kistin, kisting, chesting** the (ceremony of) laying of a corpse in its coffin on the night before the funeral *19-*. [see the noun]

kist²·¹ /kɪst/ *v* to drive off a cat *la19- Sh*. [see the interj]

kist²·² /kɪst/ *interj* a sound made to scare off a cat *la19- Sh Ork*. [natural utterance]

kist *see* CAST¹·²

kit¹·¹ /kɪt/ *n* **1** a small (wooden) tub or box *la14-*. **2** personal belongings, a set of articles or tools; a soldier's equipment *19-*. **3** a fair amount of something, a large quantity of food *la19, 20- Bor*. [MDu *kitte* a scuttle, a pouring vessel]

†**kit¹·²** *v* to place or pack in a wooden vessel *18-e19*. [see the noun]

kitchen¹·¹, *Sh* **keetchin**, *Ork* **kitcheen**, †**kiching**, †**kechin**, †**keiching** /'kɪtʃən; *Sh* 'kitʃən; *Ork* 'kɪtʃɪn/ *n* **1** a place where food is cooked *la14-*. **2** something savoury added to plain food to make it more tasty *la15-*. **3** an allowance of food (from the kitchen); provisions or perquisites given to (farm) servants *la14-19, 20- EC SW*. **4** a money allowance (given to servants) in lieu of food *la18-e19*. **5** a tea-urn *la18-19*. **6** (the supply of) provisions for a kitchen *la16-17*. **kitchenless** lacking anything that will give taste or savour *19, 20- Sh*. **kitchen fee** tallow; dripping (formerly the perquisite of the cook) *la15-*. †**kitchine meit** something savoury added to plain food to make it more tasty *la16*. [OE *cycene*]

kitchen¹·² /'kɪtʃən/ *v* **1** to flavour, season; to render more palatable *18-*. **2** *of foodstuffs* to spin out, use sparingly *18-*. [see the noun]

kitchie¹·¹, †**kiche** /'kɪtʃe, 'kɪtʃi/ *n* **1** a kitchen *16-*. **2** something savoury added to plain food to make it more tasty *la19- Sh N NE T*. **kitchie deem** a kitchen maid; a domestic servant on a farm *20- NE*. **kitchie lass** = *kitchie deem*. [reduced form of KITCHEN¹·¹]

kitchie¹·² /'kɪtʃe, 'kɪtʃi/ *v* **1** to flavour, season; to render more palatable *la19- Sh N NE*. **2** *of farmworkers* to take one's meals in the farm-kitchen; to live in (rather than living in a bothy or cot-house) *20- NE*. [see the noun]

kite¹·¹, **quoit**, †**cuit** /kʌɪt, kwʌɪt/ *n* a curling stone, a game of curling *19-*. [extension of the English game of *quoits*]

kite¹·², **quoit**, *WC* **cute**, †**coit** /kʌɪt, kwʌɪt; *WC* kjut/ *v* to play the game of curling; to play a curling stone *19-*. †**quoitin stane, coitin stane** a curling stone *19*. [see the noun]

kite *see* KYTE

kiteral, †**kytrall**, †**ketterel** /'kɪtərəl/ *n* a term of abuse for a person *la16-19, 20- NE*. [unknown]

kith /kɪθ/ *n* **1** acquaintances, neighbours; kinsfolk *la14-*. **2** one's native country or district; a country or nation *la15-e17*. [OE *cȳþþ*]

kith *see* KYTHE

kithan /'kɪθən/ *n* **1** a rascal, a trickster *20- N*. **2** *derogatory* a girl, a woman *20- N*. **kithag** *derogatory* a girl, a woman *20- N*. [unknown]

kithie see KETHIE
kitlin, kitling see KITTLIN
kittagh-handed see KETACH
kittick see KITTOCK²
kittie¹, kitty /ˈkɪte, ˈkɪti/ n **1** a girl or young woman; a giddy, skittish woman *16-19, 20- NE*. **2** a woman of doubtful character *la19- Sh NE*. **3** the jack in the game of bowls *la19- NE T C*. **4** a name for a pet animal *19- Sh SW*. **5** the wren *Troglodytes troglodytes la18-19, 20- Bor*. **kitty cat** the ball in the game of shinty *19- Bor*. **kitty neddie, kitty needy** the common sandpiper *Actitis hypoleucos la19, 20- NE*. †**kittie unsell** a girl or woman of bad character *la16*; compare *katie unsell* (KATIE). **kitty wren** the wren *19- C Bor*; compare *cutty wran* (CUTTY¹·³). [familiar form of *Katherine*; compare KATIE]
kittie², kitty /ˈkɪte/ n a prison, a jail; the village lock-up *la19- EC SW Bor Uls*. [unknown]
kittie³ /ˈkɪti/ n a kittiwake *la19, 20- Sh NE T EC*. [shortened form of KITTIWAKE]
kittill see KITTLE¹·¹, KITTLE¹·², KITTLE¹·³
kittiwake, †**kittiwaik** /ˈkɪtiwek/ n a gull *Rissa tridactyla la17-*. [onomatopoeic of the bird's cry]
kittle¹·¹, †**kittill** /ˈkɪtəl/ n **1** a tickle *19-*. **2** a pleasurable excitement, a stimulus *19-*. **3** an irritation (of the throat) *la19-*. **4** a stir or a poke of a fire *20-*. **5** a difficult feat *20- EC SW Bor*. **6** a polish, a shine *20- NE*. [see the verb]
kittle¹·², *Sh Ork* **kyittle,** *WC SW* **cuittle,** †**kittill** /ˈkɪtəl/ *Sh Ork* ˈkjɪtəl; *WC SW* ˈkutəl/ v **1** to tickle *16-*. **2** to stimulate, excite or rouse *16-*. **3** to commence playing a musical instrument; to tune up; to strike up a tune *la18-*. **4** to provoke or annoy; to tease *la19-*. **5** curling to give speed to a stone by sweeping the ice in front of it *la19-*. **6** to stir up a fire *20-*. **7** *of the wind* to rise up; to blow more strongly and gustily *19- NE EC Bor*. **8** to chide or reprove *la19- NE EC*. **9** *of people* to become angry; *of horses* to become restive *la19- NE T*. **10** to puzzle, perplex, nonplus *19- EC Bor*. **11** *of health or circumstances* to improve *20- NE T*. **kittlesome** difficult, intractable; tricky, puzzling *la19-*. **kittlie, kittly** *of things* tickly, causing a tickling sensation; *of people* itchy, ticklish *19-*. **2** troublesome, difficult, precarious; obscure, difficult, puzzling *19- NE C SW*. **3** sensitive; easily roused or provoked *19, 20- EC*. †**kittlie-cout** a children's game similar to hunt-the-thimble *19*. [probably ON *kitla*]
kittle¹·³, †**kittill** /ˈkɪtəl/ adj **1** ticklish, tickly *la16-*. **2** easily upset or offended, difficult to deal with; unreliable, fickle *la16-*. **3** *of a task or problem* hard to deal with, intractable, tricky, puzzling *la16-*. **4** *of an angle or bend* awkward, difficult to negotiate *19-*. **5** cunning, skilful *19- NE T WC*. **6** liable, inclined (to) *la18- SW*. **7** *of written texts* difficult to comprehend, obscure *18-19*. **kittle cattle** people or animals who are unmanageable, capricious or difficult *19-*. **kittle in the trot** quick-tempered, irritable *la19- NE*. [see the verb]
kittle²·¹ /ˈkɪtəl/ n the unborn young of small animals *20- NE*. **be in kittle** *of cats or other small animals* to be pregnant *20- NE SW*. [see the verb]
kittle²·², *Sh* **kettle** /ˈkɪtəl; *Sh* ˈkɛtəl/ v **1** *of cats or other small animals* to give birth; to have a litter *la18-*. **2** *derogatory of a woman* to give birth *19, 20- Sh NE*. **3** *of an idea* to come into being *e19*. [probably back-formation from KITTLIN]
kittlin, kitlin, *Sh* **kettlin,** †**kitling** /ˈkɪtlən; *Sh* ˈkɛtlən/ n **1** a kitten *la16-*. **2** the young of other small animals *la18-19, 20- NE WC*. **3** a brat, a whelp *16- e17*. [ON *ketlingr* a kitten]
†**kittock¹, kittok** n term for a woman or girl of low rank or character; a prostitute *la15-16*. [familiar form of *Katherine*; compare KITTIE¹]

kittock², kittick /ˈkɪtək/ n the kittiwake *la19- Ork*. [diminutive form of KITTIWAKE]
kitty see KITTIE¹, KITTIE²
kivel see CAVEL²
kivver see COVER¹·¹, COVER¹·²
kizen /ˈkɪzən/ v to dry up; to wither, shrivel or shrink from exposure to sun or drought *la18- WC SW*. [unvoiced form of GIZZEN¹·¹]
kizzen, cousin, *Sh* **kushin,** †**cusine,** †**cosing,** †**cousing** /ˈkɪzən, ˈkʌzən; *Sh* ˈkøʃən/ n a cousin; a relative, a kinsman *la14-*. Compare CUSINES. [ME *cosin*]
kjaebin see CAIBIN
kjirp see CARP
kjist see KIST¹·¹
kjnee see KNEE¹·¹
kjöl see QUEEL
kjüff see KEUCH¹·²
kjursald /ˈkjørsəld/ n a young horse *la19- Sh*. [variant of Scots COOSER]
klag see CLAAG¹·²
klaitchie see CLATCH¹·¹
klak /klak/ n **1** a rocky fishing ground near the shore *19- Sh Ork*. **2** a stony piece of ground *20- Sh*. [Norw *klakk* a small heap, a sandbank, Icel *klakkr* an upstanding rock]
klave /klev/ n **1** the bottom corners of a herring net *20- N*. **2** the angle formed between the back-rope and the gevel-rope on a fishing-net *20- Ork*. [ON *klafi* a forked stick]
kleeber, kleber, †**claber** /ˈklibər, ˈklebər/ n steatite, soapstone *la18- Sh*. [Norw *kleber* a stone used for the weights of a loom]
kleepie, kleepo, kleebo, †**cleepie** /ˈklipi, ˈklipo, ˈklibo/ n a severe blow; a (corrective) smack to the head *19, 20- Ork*. [compare CLYPE⁴]
kleevins see CLEAVE¹·²
klemmel, †**clemel,** †**clamel** /ˈklɛməl/ n steatite, soapstone *la18- Sh Ork*. [unknown]
klepp see CLAP¹·², CLEP²
klett see CLAT¹·¹, CLAT¹·², CLETT
kletter see CLATTER¹·¹
klevi see KLIVVY
kley see CLAY
klibba-taings, klibbi-tengs /ˈklɪbətɛŋz, ˈklɪbitɛŋz/ npl a pair of (wooden or iron) tongs *la19- Sh*. [ON *klýpitöng* a smith's tongs or pincers]
klibber see CLIBBER
klick-mill, clack mill /ˈklɪkmɪl, ˈklak mɪl/ n a type of watermill *20- Ork*. [MILL¹·¹, with imitative first element]
kliksi see CLICKSIE
klimse see CLUMPSE
kline, cline /klʌɪn/ v to smear or spread butter *la19- Sh Ork*. **clinoo, klino** a slice of bread thickly spread with butter *20- Ork*. [ON *klína* to smear]
kliver see CLIVER¹
klivvens see CLEAVE¹·²
klivvy, klevi, clavey; *Ork* **clivoo** /ˈklɪvi, ˈklevi; *Ork* ˈklɪvu/ n **1** a steep or difficult path (on a cliff) *20- Sh Ork N*. **2** barren, rocky ground *20- Sh*. [ON *kleifa* a cliff, a rocky ascent]
klokk¹·¹ /klɔk/ n the leaf or frond on a seaweed tangle *20- Ork*. [unknown]
klokk¹·² /klɔk/ v to strip the leaves off seaweed tangles *20- Ork*. [unknown]
klondyke /ˈklɔndʌɪk/ v to export fresh herring packed in salt and ice by fast steamer to Continental Europe *20, 21- historical*. [from the place-name *Klondike*, a region of Canada, in reference to its being a centre for gold-mining, the export practice being much more profitable than salt curing]

klondyker /ˈklɔndʌɪkər/ n **1** a factory ship used for processing and transporting herring and mackerel (to the Continent) 20-. **2** an exporter of fish to Continental Europe 20, 21- historical. [KLONDYKE, with agent suffix]

klondyking /ˈklɔndʌɪkɪŋ/ n **1** the processing of fresh mackerel or herring on factory ships sited on the fishing grounds la20-. **2** the preparation for speedy export of fresh herring by sprinkling them with salt and ice 20, 21- historical. [verbal noun from KLONDYKE]

klonger, klunger /ˈklɔŋər, ˈklʌŋər/ n the dog rose, the wild brier *Rosa canina* 20- Sh. [ON *klungr*]

kloor see CLOOR[1.1]

klov see CLIV

klovgeng see CLOWGANG

klow see CLOW[3]

kludet /ˈkludət/ adj of socks knitted from tie-dyed wool; variegated 20- Sh. [altered form of Eng *clouded*]

klug see CLOG

kluir see CLOOR[1.2]

klumbung /klʌmˈbʌŋ/ n a clumsy person; an ill-shaped object la19- Sh Ork. [Norw *klump* a heap + ON *bunga* a protuberance]

klumper, clumper /ˈklʌmpər/ n a boulder, a large fragment of rock 20- Sh Ork. [Norw *klump* a heap, a lump, Icel *klumbr* a heap]

klunger see KLONGER

klunk see CLUNK[1.2]

klurt see CLART[1.1], CLART[1.2]

klush see CLOUSH

klype see CLYPE[1.1]

klyster see CLEESTER[1.2]

knab[1] /nab, knab/ n a knot or root of fir 20- NE. [altered form of Scots *knob*]

knab[2], **nabb** /knab, nab/ n a person of importance, prestige or moderate wealth; a person with social pretensions, a snob la17-. **knabbery, nabbery, knabry** gentry 19-. †**knabbie** having rank, means or position; genteel, pretentious la18-19. [unknown]

knab see KNAP[2.1], KNAP[2.2], NABB

knabb see NABB

knabbie see KNAB[2]

knablick[1.1], **knablich** /ˈnablɪk, ˈnablɪx/ n **1** a knot or root of fir 19- NE. **2** a boulder; a rough hillock 19- NE. [diminutive form of KNAB[1]]

knablick[1.2], **knablich, †knabliech** /ˈnablɪk, ˈnablɪx/ adj irregularly shaped; rough, knotty 18- NE. [see the noun]

knack[1.1], †**knak** /nak, knak/ n **1** a sharp clicking, breaking or striking noise; a sharp blow, a crack la18-. **2** a mocking retort; a gibe la15-16, la19- NE. **3** pl a throat disease of poultry; *humorous* any complaint characterized by wheezing 19, 20- EC Bor. **4** a trick 17. [onomatopoeic]

knack[1.2], †**knak** /nak, knak/ v **1** to make a sharp, cracking noise; to snap the fingers 18-. **2** to break or snap with a sharp sound la19-. **3** to strike or slash sharply la19- Sh NE T. **4** to make fun of; to deride 15-e16, la19- WC SW. **5** to chatter away la19- NE Uls. **knack aff** to strike or knock off (with a sharp implement) 20- Sh NE. [see the noun]

knackatt see NACKET[2]

knacker's midden /ˈnakərz mɪdən/ n **1** a mess, a shambles 20- C Bor. **2** a glutton 20- C Bor. [probably altered form of ANNACKER'S MIDDEN, with influence from Scots *knacker* a slaughterman]

knackie, nacky /ˈnaki, ˈnake/ adj **1** deft, ingenious, skilful 18-. **2** witty, facetious; pleasant in conversation 18-. **3** nimble, smart; trim, neatly built, spruce la19-. [Eng *knack* a skilful way of doing something + -IE[2]]

knafe see KNAVE

knag[1], **nag** /knag, nag/ n **1** a knot or spur projecting from a tree la18-. **2** a (wooden) peg used for hanging things up 16-19, 20- T EC SW. **at the knag an the widdie** at variance, at loggerheads la19- NE. [MLG *knagge*]

knag[2], **knog** /knag, nag, knɔg, nɔg/ n **1** a keg, a small cask 16-19, 20- N NE Uls. **2** a small, wooden dish with one stave extended to form the handle la18-19, 20- Bor. **knaggie, noggie** = KNAG[2]. [unknown]

knaif see KNAVE

knaip see KNAPE

knak see KNACK[1.1], KNACK[1.2]

knap[1], †**knop**, †**knup** /nap, knap/ n **1** a rounded knob, a lump or bump; a protuberance 15-19, 20- Sh Ork NE. **2** a tassel (on a hat or cap) la15-e18, 20- Sh Ork T. **3** the point of the elbow la16-19, 20- Sh Bor. **4** a shin of beef la17-19, 20- C. **5** the kneecap 19, 20- Sh NE T EC Bor. **6** a hillock or knoll, a mound 19- Sh Ork NE T C. **7** a steep headland or promontory 18- Sh Ork. **8** a rock in the sea 20- NE. **9** an ornamental knob, boss or stud la15-e18. **10** a jewelled, pendant ornament la15-e17. **11** the bud or compact head of a flower 16. †**knappit, knoppit** 1 ornamented with knobs or tassels la15-e17. **2** having buds or knotty protuberances e16. **knapplach, knaplich** a lump, a large protuberance, a rough projection la19- NE. **knappy 1** friable; crisp, brittle la18- T EC Uls. **2** lumpy, bumpy 19- Ork NE. **knap-bane** *in cattle* the knee or knuckle-joint 20-. **knapdarloch 1** a knot of dung or matted hair hanging from the coat or tail of an animal la19-. **2** *derogatory* an undersized, dirty, cheeky person 20- NE. †**knap silk button** a knob-shaped button e17. **knap tang** the seaweed *Ascophyllum nodosum* 19- Sh. [Ger *Knopf*, MLG *knoppe*, ON *knappr*]

knap[2.1], †**knab** /nap, knap/ n a sharp knock or blow; a rap, a tap 16-. [onomatopoeic]

knap[2.2], †**knab, †nab** /nap, knap/ v **1** to knock, strike sharply, rap la15-. **2** to break stones for building or road-making 17-. **3** to break sharply, snap 19-. **4** to strike the heels on the ground when walking; to walk briskly la19- Ork T EC. **knapper 1** a small hammer used by stone breakers la18-. **2** a person who works as a stone breaker la19-. [see the noun]

knap[3] /knap/ n a sturdy lad; a chap 19, 20- Ork N NE. **knappy, nappie** stout, sturdy, strong 19, 20- Ork. [perhaps extended sense of KNAP[1]]

knap[4.1], NE **gnap** /knap; NE gnap/ n **1** a snap (with the teeth), a bite la19, 20- Sh Ork NE. **2** a morsel, a bite of food la18-19, 20- Sh NE EC. **3** a sharp or biting remark la18- NE. Compare KNIP[3.1]. [see the verb]

knap[4.2], Ork N NE **gnap**, Ork N **nap** /knap; Ork N NE gnap; Ork N nap/ v **1** to bite or gnaw; to break or snap with the teeth; to munch, eat greedily 16-. **2** to speak in an affected manner la16-19 20- Sh NE T EC. **3** *of horses* to nibble one another in a friendly way 20- Sh Ork N. †**knappar, gnappar** one who bites or snaps; a ruffian e16. **knap-at-the-wind, gnap-at-the-wind 1** a mere bite; a morsel la19- Ork NE. **2** thin oatcakes, light bread, insubstantial food 20- NE. **knapper-knytlich, knipperknatlich** short-tempered; mean 20- NE. **in gnapping earnest** in dead earnest la18- NE. [Norw *knapa* to gnaw quickly and noisily]

knap see NAP[1]

†**knapburd, knaphard, knappart** n clapboard la16-17. [altered form of EModE *clapboorde* with influence from KNAPPEL]

knapdarloch see KNAP[1]

†**knape, knaip** n a lad, an attendant la15-e17. [OE *cnapa*]

knaphard see KNAPBURD

knapholt see KNAPPEL

knaplich see KNAP¹
knappart see KNAPBURD
knapparts, knapperts, †gnapperts /'napərts, 'knapərts/ *npl* **1** the bitter vetch or heath pea *Lathyrus linifolius 19- NE*. **2** the acorn *la17-e18*. [KNAP¹ + reduced form of Older Scots *wort*; compare Norw *knappurt*, MLG *knópwort* as names of various herbs]
knappel, *Sh* **knappild, †knapholt, †knappett, †knappald** /'napəl; *Sh* 'napəld/ *n* clapboard, split oak smaller than wainscot, often used as barrel-staves and as panelling or boarding *la15-19, 20- Sh NE*. Compare KNAPBURD. [MLG, MDu *klapholt*]
knapper-knytlich see KNAP⁴˙²
knapperts see KNAPPARTS
knappett see KNAPPEL
knappie see NAP¹
knappild see KNAPPEL
knappiskaw see KNAPSCALL
knapplach see KNAP¹
knappy see KNAP¹, KNAP³
†knapscall, knapska, knappiskaw *n* a metal helmet or skullcap (worn under a bonnet); the helmet and bonnet together *la15-e17*. **knapscall bonnet** a bonnet for covering a KNAPSCALL; latterly the shell and bonnet together *la16-e17*. [unknown]
knapscap /'napskap/ *n* = KNAPSCALL *19, 20- historical*. [KNAPSCALL, with substitution of *cap*]
knapska see KNAPSCALL
†knapwood *n* clapboard *la17-e18*. [compare KNAPBURD, KNAPPEL]
knar, knarr /knar, nar/ *n* **1** a knot in wood *19, 20- NE*. **2** a burly, stockily-built person *20- NE*. **3** a knot in thread *la16*. [Du *knar*, LG *knarre*]
†knarholt, knorhald *n* clapboard *la14-e16*. Compare KNAPPEL. [MLG, MDu *knarholt*; compare KNAPPEL]
knark¹˙¹, *Ork* **knirk** /knark; *Ork* knɪrk/ *n* **1** a creaking noise *la19- Sh Ork*. **2** a bite, a snap with the teeth *20- Sh*. [see the verb]
knark¹˙², *Ork* **knirk** /knark; *Ork* knɪrk/ *v* to make a crunching or gnawing noise; to squeak or creak *19- Sh Ork*. [Norw dial *knarka* to creak, Swed dial *knarka* to chew audibly]
knave, †knafe, †knaif, †kneff /nev, knev/ *n* **1** a rogue *la15-*. **2** the jack in a pack of cards *18-*. **3** a male servant, attendant or groom; a menial *la14-e19*. **4** a miller's assistant *17-e19*. **5** a woman's lover *la16-e18*. **6** a male child *la14-15*. **†knaveship, knaifschip, knaschip 1** a small quantity of corn or meal in addition to the multure levied on each lot of corn ground at a mill, as payment for the miller's servants *14-19*. **2** the office of under-miller or miller's assistant; the perquisites of this office *16-17*. **†knave bairn, knaf barn** a male child *la14-e19*. **†knaif child** a male child *la14-16*. [OE *cnafa*]
knaw¹, know /nɔ, no/ *v ptp* **knawn, †knawin 1** to be aware of, be familiar with; to perceive or recognize *la14-*. **2** to have knowledge of; to remember; to understand *la14-*. **3** *law* to make judicial inquiry into; to take legal cognizance of *15-e17*. **I kent his faither** a dismissive comment regarding a successful person, whose background is well known *20-*. **knowin** a small amount *la19- SW Uls*. **that is to knaw** that is to say *e16*. [OE *cnawan*]
†knaw² *v* to gnaw *16-e17*. [ME *knauen*]
knawledge¹˙¹**, knowledge** /'nɔlədʒ/ *n* **1** recognition or awareness of, familiarity with (something) *la14-*. **2** information, that which is known; experience, skill *la14-*. **3** *law* judicial or authoritative knowledge; formal investigation to obtain this; legal cognizance *la14-*. [probably KNAW¹, with noun-forming suffix]

†knawledge¹˙²**, knawlege** *v* **1** to acknowledge *15-16*. **2** *law* to make judicial inquiry into; to decide judicially *e17*. [ME *knoulechen*]
kne see KNEE¹˙¹
kned /knɛd, nɛd/ *v* **1** to knead *la16-19, 20- T EC SW Bor*. **2** to tire out, exhaust *20- T*. **3** *of animals* to breathe with effort, pant *20- N*. [ptp of ME *knede*]
knee¹˙¹, *Sh* **kjnee, †kne, †knie** /ni; *Sh* kni/ *n* **1** the joint at the bend of the leg *la14-*. **2** the lap of a seated person *la14-*. **3** a bend in a coulter-stem *20- EC*. **4** a bend in a part of a plough, as in the plough-beam *20- Sh*. **5** a piece of naturally bent wood used in ship-building *16-e17*. **†kneed, kneit** *of a metal bar or band* having an angular bend *la16-e19*. **knee breeks** knee-breeches *19-*. **knee head** a piece of naturally-bent timber used to secure together parts of a ship *la15-19, 20- Sh*. **knee hicht** a small child, one no higher than the knee *la19- Sh Ork SW*. **knee ill** a disease affecting the knee-joints of cattle *19, 20- T WC SW*. **knee lid** the kneecap *19-*. **knee shall, kjnee shall** the kneecap *la19- Sh*. **knee tea** a meal in which cup and plate are held on the knee *la19- NE*. **knee wife** a midwife *20- H&I*. **knee woman** a midwife *la20- H&I*. **knee buks** to strike or hold with the knee *20- Sh*. [OE *cnēow*]
knee¹˙² /ni/ *v* **1** to bend so as to form a knee-shaped angle *19-*. **2** to mark the ear of a sheep with a slanting cut *la19- Sh*. [see the noun]
kneebie, neebie /'nibi/ *n* one of the wooden arms of a pack-saddle *la19- Sh*. [Norw dial *knipa* a steep-sided hilltop]
kneef, knief, *Sh* **kniff,** *Ork* **niff** /knif; *Sh* knɪf; *Ork* nɪf/ *adj* **1** alert, agile; lively, keen *18- Sh Ork N NE T*. **2** fit, in sound health; well-recovered *20- N NE T*. [unknown]
kneel, †knele /nil/ *v* **1** to rest on the knees *la14-*. **2** to receive Communion *17-e19*. [OE *cnēowlian*]
kneep /knip, nip/ *n* a lump *la19- NE*. **kneeplach** a large lump or piece *la19- NE T*. **kneeple** = *kneeplach*. [unknown]
kneetle see KNUITLE
kneevle /'knivəl/ *n* a bit, a lump *la18-19, 20- NE*. **kneevlick** a big lump (of cheese); a fair quantity *la19- NE*. [unknown; compare LG *knevel* a lump]
kneff see KNAVE
kneggum /'knɛgəm, 'nɛgəm/ *n* a pungent, disagreeable taste or flavour; an after-taste, a lingering bad smell *la18-*. [probably Norw *knaga* to gnaw; compare KNAG¹]
kneip see KNIP², KNYPE¹
kneit see KNEE¹˙¹
knele see KNEEL
knell¹˙¹, *NE* **knyell** /knɛl, nɛl; *NE* knjɛl/ *n* **1** the sound of a bell being struck *16-*. **2** a shot or explosion, a loud echoing boom; a crack, a thud *la19- NE*. [OE *cnyll*]
knell¹˙² /knɛl, nɛl/ *v* **1** *of a bell* to ring, toll *la15-*. **2** to strike with a resounding blow, knock *16-*. [OE *cnyllan*]
knep, nyep /knɛp, nɛp, njɛp/ *v* **1** to clasp the hands, clench the fist *19- Sh*. **2** to tie or gather a bag or bundle *la19- Sh*. **3** to purse the lips *la20- Sh*. [ON *kneppa* to button, add studs]
knetting see KNIT
knevel see NEVEL¹˙²
knewel, †knewill /'knuəl/ *n* **1** a cross-bar or toggle of wood or metal; the wooden pin on the end of a rope or halter *la16- NE T EC*. **2** the tag put through the ring on the rope or chain for tethering cattle in a stall *19- NE EC*. [MLG, Du *knevel*, ON *knefill*]
knib see GNIB
knibloch, kniblock, †knublock /'knɪbləx, 'knɪblək/ *n* **1** a small rounded stone, a hard clod of earth *18-*. **2** a lump, a chunk *19-*. [diminutive form of KNAB¹]

knicht[1.1], **knight**, †**knycht** /nɪxt, nʌɪt/ *n* **1** a man of the rank of knight; a mounted soldier, a champion *la14*-. **2** a chesspiece *la15*-. †**knichtheid**, **knychthede** knighthood *la14-17*. †**knycht preceptor** the Preceptor (of Torphichen) *e16*. [OE *cniht* a boy, a youth]

knicht[1.2], **knight** /nɪxt, nʌɪt/ *v* to confer a knighthood on *16*-. **knichtit 1** made a knight *la16*-. **2** highly gratified (by an honour or favour); delighted with oneself *20*- *NE*. [see the noun]

knick[1.1], **nick** /knɪk, nɪk/ *n* a click; a cracking or rapping sound *la19*- *Sh Ork NE T*. [see the verb]

knick[1.2], **nick**, *NE* **gnick** /knɪk, nɪk; *NE* gnɪk/ *v* **1** to make a cracking, clicking or ticking sound *18*-. **2** to break, snap *19*-. **3** to flick a marble *19*-. **4** to crack or click the fingers *19, 20*- *NE T*. **nicker** *n* a marble used for striking another *la19*-. **nicker** *v* **1** to make a cracking or clicking sound *20*- *Sh NE*. **2** to propel a marble *la20*- *NE*. [onomatopoeic; compare MLG *knicken*, Du *knikken*, Norw *knekkja* and KNACK[1.2]]

knickle *see* KNUCKLE[1.1], KNUCKLE[1.2]

knidge *see* KNITCH[1.1]

knie *see* KNEE[1.1]

knief *see* KNEEF

knife, †**knyfe** /nʌɪf/ *n* **1** a bladed cutting implement *la14*-. **2** a small knife worn with a sword or WHINGER *16-17*. **knifie** a boys' game in which each player tries to stick an open knife into the ground by sliding or tossing it from different parts of the arms and body *e20, la20*- *historical*. [OE *cnīf*]

kniff /knɪf/ *n* a bad smell *20*- *Sh N*. [onomatopoeic]

kniff *see* KNEEF

knight *see* KNICHT[1.1], KNICHT[1.2]

knip[1] /knɪp/ *n* a small, mischievous child *la19*- *N NE T*. [perhaps altered form of KNAP[1]]

knip[2], †**kneip** /knɪp/ *n* **1** a small bundle or cluster *17, la19*- *Sh N*. **2** a string of fish *la19*- *Sh N*. [Norw *knippe* a bundle]

knip[3.1], **gnip** /knɪp, gnɪp/ *n* **1** a sharp, breaking noise, a crack or snap; a biting sound *la18-19, 20*- *literary*. **2** a morsel, a bite of food *la19*; compare KNAP[4.1]. **gnipper and gnapper**, †**kniper and knaper** every scrap of food *18-19, 20*- *NE*. **gnipper for gnapper** bit by bit, piece by piece *19*- *NE*. [see the verb]

knip[3.2], **gnip**, †**gnyp** /knɪp, gnɪp/ *v* **1** to pull to pieces, break off, snap *20*- *Sh NE SW*. **2** to talk sharply, bitingly or affectedly *la19*- *NE*. **3** to bite, nip; *of animals* to crop grass *15-e19*. Compare KNAP[4.2]. [onomatopoeic; compare Norw dial *knippa* to snap, Du, LG *knippen* to clip, snip]

knip, knipe *see* KNYPE[1]

knipperknatlich *see* KNAP[4.2]

knir *see* KNUR

knirdge /knɪrdʒ/ *v* to squeeze, crush; to crunch *20*- *Sh Ork*. [intensive variant of NIDGE[1.2]]

knirk *see* KNARK[1.1], KNARK[1.2]

knit /nɪt, knɪt/ *v* **1** to tie or fasten; to unite, fix together *la14*-. **2** to knit a garment *la17*-. **3** to join in alliance; to combine in military formation *la14-e17*. **4** to join in marriage *16*. **knit 1** knitted *la16-18*. **2** *of a joiner's or smith's work* secured by a joint, welded *e17*. **nittle**, †**knittal** a cord, a fastening *16, 19*- *NE T*. **knittin, knitting**, †**knetting 1** (a piece of) tape, string, or cord; a lace *la16*-. **2** the action of knitting *17*-. **knittins** details, particulars, items of news *20*- *NE*. **knit up 1** to fasten, tie *la16*-. **2** to conclude, make firm *16*. [OE *cnyttan* to tie]

knitch[1.1], **knidge**, *Ork* **neitch** /nɪtʃ, nɪdʒ; *Ork* nitʃ/ *n* **1** a bundle; a bale of straw *la16-19, 20*- *Ork N NE*. **2** a sturdy person or animal *20*- *N NE*. **knidgel** a (short) sturdy person *20*- *N*. **knitshel**, †**knitschell** a small bundle *16-19, 20*- *Sh EC*. [OE *gecnycc* a bond]

knitch[1.2] /nɪtʃ/ *v* to make into a bundle or bale *la19*- *Ork NE EC*. [see the noun]

knite *see* KNOIT[1]

knock[1.1], †**knok** /nɔk, knɔk/ *n* **1** a rap (on a door), a resounding blow *15*-. **2** a wooden mallet for beating linen after bleaching *18-e19*. **3** a knocker on a door or gate *la16-17*. [see the verb]

knock[1.2], †**knok** /nɔk, knɔk/ *v* **1** to rap (on a door); to strike *la14*-. **2** to beat or pound (flax or cloth) *la15-19, 20*- *literary*. **3** to bruise or husk barley *la16-19, 20*- *N NE*. **knocking mell** a mallet for pounding barley *la18-19, 20*- *Ork*. **knocking-stane 1** a hollowed-out stone in which to pound barley *la16-19, 20*- *Sh Ork N EC*. **2** a flat stone on which to beat linen after bleaching *17-19*. **knocking trough** = *knocking-stane la17-19, 20*- *Bor*. †**knockit barley** barley ground in a *knocking-stane e19*. †**knockit bear** = *knockit barley la16-e19*. [OE *cnucian*]

knock[2], **nock**, †**knok**, †**nok** /nɔk/ *n* a clock *15*-. †**knock house, knok hous** the part of a building in which a public clock was placed; a steeple *la16-19*. †**knock keeper** a person appointed to attend to a clock *la16-17*. **knock laft** a clock loft or gallery in a church *18-19, 20*- *EC*. †**knocksmith** a clock-maker *la17*. †**knok maker** a person who built or repaired clocks *16-17*. †**knokman** = *knock keeper 17*. [altered form of MDu, MLG *klocke*]

knock[3], †**knok** /nɔk/ *n* a hill, a hillock; frequently in place-names *14*-. [Gael *cnoc*]

knockit *see* NACKET[1]

knockle *see* KNUCKLE[1.1]

knog *see* KNAG[2]

knoilt, knuilt /knɔɪlt, nɔɪlt, knult, nult/ *n* a sharp blow (with the knuckles) *la19*- *Sh*. **nooltie** a sharp blow *20*- *Ork*. [Norw dial *knolta* to push]

knoit[1], *NE* **knite** /knɔɪt, nɔɪt; *NE* knʌɪt/ *n* **1** a large piece, a lump *19*- *N NE T WC*. **2** a knob, a bump; a bunion *la19*- *NE WC SW Uls*. [altered form of KNOT[1.1]]

knoit[2.1], †**knyte** /knɔɪt, nɔɪt/ *n* a sharp blow, a knock *la18*-. **cry knoit** to make a sharp sound in striking or being struck *la18*- *NE*. **play knoit** = *cry knoit 19*- *SW*. [unknown]

knoit[2.2] /knɔɪt, nɔɪt/ *v* **1** to knock, beat, strike sharply *18-19, 20*- *NE Bor*. **2** to hobble, walk stiffly and jerkily *19, 20*- *EC*. **3** *of the knees* to knock together *18-19*. [unknown]

†**knok** *n* a bundle of hemp or flax *la16-17*. **knok lint** = KNOK *e17*. [MLG *knocke*]

knok *see* KNOCK[1.1], KNOCK[1.2], KNOCK[2], KNOCK[3]

knoll, noal /nɔl, nol/ *n* a large piece, a lump (of food) *la18*-. [MDu, MLG *knolle*]

knoll *see* KNOWE

knool, knoll, noll /nul, nɔl, nol/ *v* **1** to beat, strike, knock *la18-19, 20*- *Sh*. **2** to knead dough *19, 20*- *T*. **knoolt, knuled** crushed, dispirited *la19*- *SW Bor*. [perhaps OE *cnyllan* ON *knylla* to beat, strike]

knoose *see* KNUSE

knoost, *N* **knoush** /nust; *N* nuʃ/ *n* a large lump, a hunk *18-19, 20*- *N NE SW*. [LG *knuust*, MDu *knoest* a knot in a tree]

knop, knoppit *see* KNAP[1]

knorhald *see* KNARHOLT

knorl *see* KNURL

knot[1.1], †**knout** /nɔt/ *n* **1** a looped fastening (in string, thread or rope); a knot *la15*-. **2** a group or cluster of people *16*-. **3** a node or joint in a tree or plant *16*-. **4** a lump, a broken-off chunk; a substantial amount *19*-. **5** a lump in porridge *20*-. **6** a flowerbed, a formal garden *16-19, 20*- *N EC SW Uls*. **7** a sturdy, thickset person or animal *la19*- *Sh N NE*. **8** the cloudberry *Rubus chamaemorus 19, 20*- *Bor*. **knot berry**, †**knout berry** the cloudberry *la18-19, 20*- *Bor*. **knot grass**

a variety of grass with nodes on the stem or rhizome *la18*-. **King's Knot** the grassy mound laid out as an ornamental garden below Stirling Castle *la18- EC*. **affen the knot** crazed, distraught *la18- NE Uls*. **a knot in the puddin** a strangulated hernia *la19- C SW Bor*. **the knot o yer craig** the Adam's apple *19- NE T*. **the knot o yer thrapple** = *the knot o yer craig*. [OE *cnotta*]

knot¹,² /nɔt/ *v* **1** to tie in a knot *la16-*. **2** *of porridge or sowans* to form lumps *19-*. **3** *of arthritic joints* to swell, gnarl *20-*. **4** *of turnips* to suffer from finger-and-toe disease *20-*. **knotting sowans** sowans made thick and only half-boiled so as to form lumps *19- NE*. **knottit sowans** = *knotting sowans*. **knottit ream** clotted cream *20- NE*. [see the noun]

knotless /'nɔtləs/ *adj* futile, aimless, ineffective *la17-*. **a knotless threid 1** a thread that has no knot and tends to slip out of the needle *la18-*. **2** an aimless, useless person or a useless thing *la18-*. [KNOT¹,¹, with adj-forming suffix]

knotty¹, **knottie** /'nɔti/ *adj* full of lumps or knobs *la15-*. **knotty meal** the earth-nut or pig-nut *19- N NE*. **knotty tam, knottie tam** a dish of oatmeal and hot milk or water formed into partially cooked lumps *la19- N NE*. [KNOT¹,¹ + -IE²]

knotty², **notty** /'knɔti, 'nɔti/ *n* **1** the game of shinty *18- N*. **2** the ball used in shinty or football *20- Sh Ork N*. [ON *knöttr*]

knoud, noud /nʌud/ *n* the grey gurnard *Eutrigla gurnardus 19- H&I WC SW Uls*. [Gael *cnòdan*]

knoush see KNOOST

knout see KNOT

know see KNAW¹

knowe, know, knoll /nʌu, nol/ *n* a (small) rounded hill, a fairy hill; a hillock, a mound; frequently in place-names *13-*. **know heid, knowe head** a hilltop *la16-*. [OE *cnoll*]

knowledge see KNAWLEDGE¹,¹

knowll see KNULE

knowpert /'knʌupərt/ *n* the crowberry *Empetrum nigrum la19- NE*. Compare CROUPERT. [perhaps derivative of *knop* (KNAP¹), with influence from CROUPERT]

knub¹,¹ /knʌb/ *n* a thump, a blow; a bump or bruise *19- Sh*. [see the verb]

knub¹,² /knʌb/ *v* to thump, batter, bruise *19- Sh*. [Norw dial *knubba* to push, press, Dan *knubbe* to strike]

knublock see KNIBLOCH

knuck, nock /nʌk, nɔk/ *n* a number of bundles of wool carded and tied together for spinning *la19- Sh Ork*. [LG, Du *knocke* a bundle of flax]

knuckle¹,¹, **nockle, knockle, nickle, knickle, †knuckil** /'nʌkəl, 'nɔkəl, 'nɪkəl/ *n* **1** a protuberant bone at a finger-joint *la16-*. **2** the length of the second finger from tip to knuckle (used as a measurement) *la19- Sh Ork Uls*. **3** the flicking of a marble (to make it strike another); the striking marble itself *la19- NE*. **4** the protuberant bone at the joint of the knee, wrist or ankle *20- N NE SW*. **knucklie 1** a game played with marbles *20-*. **2** *pl* the game of knucklebones or chuckie-stanes *20-*. [ME *knokel*; compare OFris *knokele*, MLG *knokel*]

knuckle¹,², **knickle, nickle** /'nʌkəl, 'nɪkəl/ *v* **1** to submit, yield *19-*. **2** to measure in lengths of the second finger from tip to knuckle *la19- Sh N Uls*. **3** to flick or propel a marble *19- NE SW*. **knuckler, knickler, nickler** a marble used to strike another *la19-*. **knuckled cake** cakes pressed out with the knuckles (rather than a rolling pin) *19- Ork T EC Bor*. **knickle deid** to play a marble with the knuckles firmly on the ground *la19- T C*. **knuckle in** to play in a marble from wherever it lies *20- T SW Bor Uls*. [see the noun]

†knuife, noof *v* to converse familiarly *la18-e19*. [unknown]

knuilt see KNOILT

knuitle, *NE* **kneetle** /'nutəl; *NE* 'nitəl/ *v* to strike, beat (with the knuckles); to squeeze or pummel; to press down *19, 20- Sh NE*. [perhaps frequentative form of KNOIT²,², with influence from KNUCKLE¹,¹]

knule, nool, †knowll /knul, nul/ *n* **1** a lump, a knob, a swelling *19- T C SW Bor*. **2** a small horn found on the head of certain kinds of cattle *19- C SW Bor*. **nuiled, neulled** *of cattle* having short or stumpy horns *19- WC SW Bor*. **knule kneed** having swollen or enlarged knee-joints; knock-kneed *la18-19, 20- SW Bor*. **†knowll-ta** a toe swollen at the joints *e16*. [Ger *Knolle*, LG *knolle, knul(le)*]

knuled see KNOOL

knup see KNAP¹

knur, †knir, †nir /knʌr, nʌr/ *n* **1** a lump, a bump, a weal *19- Ork NE*. **2** an enfeebled or stunted person *19, 20- Bor Uls*. **†knurlin** a small or stunted person *la18-19*. [MDu, MHG *knorre*]

knurl, knorl, norl /knʌrl, knɔrl, nɔrl/ *n* **1** a lump, a bump, a protuberance *la19-*. **2** a stunted person *la18-19, 20- SW*. **norlick, knorlick** a swelling, a cyst *la18-19, 20- NE*. **knorlie, norlie** lumpy, knobbly, gnarled *la19, 20- N*. [diminutive form of KNUR]

knuse, Ork nizz, †knoose, †noose /nuz; *Ork* nɪz/ *v* to squeeze, press down, bruise; to pummel or cuddle roughly *18-19, 20- Sh Ork SW Bor*. **noozle** to press, crush *19, 20- Bor*. [compare Norw *knuse* to crush, squeeze]

knycht see KNICHT¹,¹

knyell see KNELL¹,¹

knyfe see KNIFE

knype¹, **knipe, kneip, knip** /knʌɪp, knɪp/ *v* **1** to knock, strike sharply *la19- NE Uls*. **2** to keep on, work away *20- NE T*. [probably onomatopoeic]

knype² /knʌɪp/ *v* to tie boats together in harbour *20- EC*. **knypin, gnepin** a short rope used for lashing boats together *20- NE EC*. [perhaps Norw dial *kneppa, knippa* to tie or bind tightly together]

knyte see KNOIT²,¹

ko see QUO

koddi see CUDDIE³

koillet, kulliet /'kɔɪlət, 'kʌljət/ *adj of a cow* having no horns, polled *la19- Sh*. [ON *kollóttr* hornless]

kok see COCK¹,¹

†koken *n* a rogue *e16*. [OFr *coquin* a beggar, a rogue]

kolkoom see COLLCOOM

koly see COLLIE²

koly-ho /'koli ho/ *n* the dogfish *Scyliorhinus canicula 20- Ork*. [COLLIE² + HOE]

kooerly see COORLY

koog see COAG

kooks /kuks/ *v* to coax *la19- Sh*. [altered form of Eng *coax*]

koom see COOM¹,¹

koos see COOSE¹,¹

koosh, kosh /kuʃ, koʃ/ *interj* a call to scare birds or animals *la19- Sh*. [compare Norw *kyss* a threatening cry]

kop see COUP¹,²

korkalit see CORKLIT

kornal see CORNEL

†korp *n* in Shetland the croak of a raven *19*. [compare ON *korpr* a raven]

kos see COSE¹,²

†kosch, cosche *adj* hollow *e16*. [compare Gael *còsach* cavernous, full of holes]

kosh see KOOSH

køtel see CUTTLE¹,¹

kouhuby see COWHUBY

kow see COO, COW³

†Kowanday *n* St Congan's Day (13 Oct), when one of Turriff's two fairs was held *16-e17*. [from the name of the saint + DAY]

kowda *see* CUDDOCH

†kowisworth, cowsworth *n in Orkney* a unit of land of the rental value of one cow *la16-e19*. [compare ON *kýrverð* the value of a cow]

kowth *see* COUTH

koy *see* COY, QUEY

kraang *see* CRANG

kram, cram /kram/ *v of a cat* to scratch *la19- Sh*. [Norw dial *krama* to grab, snatch]

krampis, krampies /ˈkrampɪs, ˈkrampiz/ *n* oatmeal kneaded into a dough with melted fat or raw fish livers and boiled *la19- Sh Ork*. [Norw dial *krampa* to press]

kranset /ˈkransɪt/ *adj of livestock* having a head or face of a different colour to the body *20- Sh*. [Norw dial *kransut*]

kransi, †cranzie /ˈkransi/ *n* the common coralline, a type of seaweed *19- Sh*. [ON *kranz* a wreath]

krappen *see* CRAPPIN²

kreest[1.1] /krist/ *n* a groan, a grunt; a moan or whine *la19- Ork*. [see the verb]

kreest[1.2] /krist/ *v* **1** to grunt, moan or whimper *la19- Ork*. **2** to squeeze or press down *20- Ork*. **3** to exert oneself *20- Sh*. [ON *kreista* to press, force, compel]

kreill *see* CREEL[1.1]

krekin, cracken /ˈkrɛkɪn, ˈkrakɪn/ *n fisherman's taboo* a whale; a large sea creature *la18- Sh EC*. [Norw dial *krake* a huge sea monster]

krekks *see* CREX[1.2]

kreppo /ˈkrɛpo/ *n* an oatmeal bannock *20- Ork*. [ON *kreppa* to squeeze]

krib *see* CRIB³

krimchie *see* CRUMCH

kring *see* CRING[1.1]

kringle /ˈkrɪŋəl/ *n* **1** a low stool made out of coiled straw or heather *la19- Ork*. **2** a rounded hillock *20- Ork*. **3** a halter; a metal loop in a rope for carrying straw *20- Sh*. Compare CRING[1.1]. **kringly** wrinkled *20- Ork*. **kringly-headed** confused *20- Ork*. [ON *kringla* a circle]

kro *see* CRO²

kröl, crül /krøl/ *n* an oatmeal or barley-meal cake or scone *la19- Sh*. [Norw *krull* a curl, Norw dial *kryl* a hump]

krolkit /ˈkrølkət/ *adj* crooked; hump-backed *20- Sh*. [Norw dial *kryl* a hump]

krom *see* CROAM

kromack *see* KRUMMICK

krug *see* CROOG

kruggle, cruckle /ˈkrʌgəl, ˈkrʌkəl/ *v* **1** to crouch, stoop; to bend with a heavy burden *la19- Sh Ork*. **2** to huddle or cower *20- NE*. [frequentative form of CROOG]

kruggset *see* CRUGSET

krul *see* CRÖL

krummick, *Ork* kromack, *N* cromag, *N* gromack /ˈkrʌmək; *Ork* ˈkromək; *N* ˈkroməg; *N* ˈgromək/ *n* **1** the fingertips; a clutched hand *la19- Sh Ork N*. **2** a small measure, a pinch, a handful *la19- Sh Ork N*. **cromags fu** (as much as can be held between) the tips of the fingers and the thumb together; a handful *20- Sh Ork N*. **set a cromag, set a kromack** to bring the fingertips and thumb together *20- Sh Ork N*. [ON *krumma* a paw]

krunk /krʌŋk/ *n* constipation *la20- N H&I*. [unknown]

kruttle *see* CRUTTLE[1.1], CRUTTLE[1.2]

kubby, kubi *see* CUBBIE

kucher *see* KYUCKER

kugl *see* COGGLE

kuiller *see* CEULER

kuir *see* CURE[1.1], CURE[1.2]

kuithe *see* CUITHE

kuithin *see* COOTHIN

kuitle *see* CUITTLE

kuivy, cuvy /ˈkøvi/ *n* something stumpy, docked or squat in appearance *19- Sh Ork*. [Norw dial *kuv* a rounded top]

kuke *see* CUIK[1.1]

kukk *see* CACK[1.1]

kukker *see* KYUCKER

kul *see* CEUL

kulivin *see* KEELYVINE

kullie *see* KEELIE⁴

kulliet *see* KOILLET

kullyak *see* COLLIK

kuner *see* CUN

kungle *see* CUNGLE

kunnin *see* KINNEN

†kurchie, curchay, courchay *n* a kerchief *16-e19*. [altered form of CURCHEFFE]

kure *see* CURE[1.2]

kurn *see* CURN¹

kurrie *see* CURRIE²

kurrious *see* KEERIOUS

kus *see* COOSE[1.2]

kushin *see* KIZZEN

kussie *see* CUSSIE

kut *see* CUT[1.2]

kuttack *see* CUTTACK

kuttanoy *see* CUTTANOY

kutty *see* CUTTY[1.1]

kuythe *see* CUITHE

kwak *see* QUACK³

kwal *see* QUALL[1.1]

kwark[1.1]**, quark, kwerk** /kwark, kwɛrk/ *n* **1** the throat *19- Sh*. **2** a gulp, a swallow *20- Ork*. **3** a hollow of the body, an armpit or the groin *20- Sh*. **kwarkabus** a disease of sheep characterized by a swelling of the throat *19- Sh*. [ON *kverkr* the throat, the gullet; plural form of *kverk* the angle below the chin]

kwark[1.2]**, kwerk, *Sh* whirk, *Ork* whark** /kwark, kwɛrk; *Sh* мɪrk; *Ork* мark/ *v* **1** to swallow with difficulty, gulp; to cough or splutter *la19- Ork*. **2** to croak, speak hoarsely *20- Sh*. [Norw dial *kverka* to choke]

kweecher *see* KEEGER[1.2]

kweerich, kweerichin *see* KEEROCH[1.2]

kwerious *see* KEERIOUS

kwerk *see* KWARK[1.1], KWARK[1.2]

kwern *see* QUERN

kwigger *see* KEEGER[1.1]

kwintry *see* KINTRA

kyaard *see* CAIRD[1.1], CAIRD[1.2]

kyar, kiarr /ˈkaeər, kaɪˈɑr/ *n* coconut fibre used for making ropes *la19- Sh*. [altered form of Eng *coir*]

kyaucht *see* KAUCH

kyauve[1.1] /kjav/ *n* a struggle, exertion; turmoil *la19- NE T*. [Norw *kav*; there may be some confusion in usage with TYAUVE[1.1]]

kyauve[1.2]**, *Sh* kev** /kjav; *Sh* kev/ *v* **1** to toil, wrestle laboriously, struggle with *20- Sh NE*. **2** to move or toss restlessly; to tumble about; to wrestle in fun *la19- Sh NE*. **3** to knead *19- N NE*. [variant of CAVE², Norw *kava* to wrestle, ON *kafa* to plunge, dive]

kyaw *see* KAE[1.1]

kye, †ky, †kyne /kae/ *npl* cows, cattle *la14-*. Compare COO. **kye-time** milking-time *20- NE SW Bor Uls*. [OE *cȳ* cows]

kye see KEY[1.1], KYTHE
kyeuk see CUIK[1.1], CUIK[1.2]
kyittle see KITTLE[1.2]
kyle[1] /kʌɪl/ *n* a narrow strait or arm of the sea or a narrow part of a river; frequently in place-names *16-*. [Gael *caol*]
kyle[2.1] /kʌɪl/ *n* **1** *pl* the game of skittles or ninepins *la16-*. **2** a skittle or ninepin *la17-19, 20- EC*. **3** a chance, an opportunity *la18- NE EC*. **4** a game where a metal ball is rolled through a hoop *la19- EC*. **the kyles** the game of skittles or ninepins *15-*. [MDu *keghel*, MFr *quille*]
kyle[2.2] /kʌɪl/ *v of the metal ball used in skittles* to reach the point aimed at *la19- EC*. [see the noun]
kyle see COLE[1.1], COLE[1.2]
kyloe, kylie /ˈkʌɪlo, ˈkʌɪli/ *n* one of a breed of small Highland cattle *la18-*. †**kyle nolt** = KYLOE *la16*. [Gael *Gàidhealach* Gaelic, Highland]
kymmond see KIMMIN
kynbute see KINBOOT
kynd see KIND[1.1], KIND[1.3]
kyndill see KENNLE
kyndlie see KINDLY
kyne see KYE
kynrayd see KINDRED[1.1]
kyoab[1.1] /kjob/ *n* **1** a gift or bribe; a reward or recompense *19- Sh*. **2** a kiss *20- Sh*. [ON *kaup* wages]
kyoab[1.2] /kjob/ *v* to bribe, induce; to ingratiate oneself with a gift *19- Sh*. [see the noun]
kyoch see KEUCH[1.2]
kyoder /ˈkjodər/ *v* to caress; to show fondness (insincerely) *la19- Sh*. [altered form of CUITER]
kyow see KIOW-OW[1.1]
kyp see KEEP[1.2]

kype /kʌɪp/ *n* **1** a game in which a marble or ball is aimed at a hole in the ground *17- N NE*. **2** a (scooped-out) hollow in the ground, used as the target in a game of marbles *19- NE T*. **kypie 1** a hollow used in a game of marbles *19- NE*. **2** a game of marbles *la19- N NE*. probably [OE *cȳpa* a basket]
kype see KIP[1]
kyrk see KIRK[1.1]
kyrkyharde, kyrkʒard see KIRKYAIRD
kyrnell see KIRNELL
kys see KISS
kytch see KEYTCH[1.2]
kyte, kite /kʌɪt/ *n* the stomach, the belly *16-*. †**kytefu, kyteful** a bellyful *19*. **kytie** corpulent, fat *19-*. †**kyte clung** emaciated, starving *19*. **up the kyte** pregnant *la20- EC*. [compare MDu *kuyt* a fleshy part of the body, MLG *kút* entrails]
kythe, *Sh Ork* **kye,** †**keith,** †**kith** /kaeð; *Sh Ork* kae/ *v ptp* **kythed** †**kid 1** to show, display; to reveal or make manifest *la14-*. **2** to show or present oneself, make an appearance, become manifest *la14-*. **3** to exhibit a sign or marvel; to perform a miracle *la14-e17*. **4** to turn out or prove to be *la15-e17*. **5** to make a formal appearance in a court of law *e17*. †**kid** renowned; notorious *la14-e17*. **kything, keething** appearance, manifestation *18-*. †**kythesome** pleasant, prepossessing *19*. **kythe to** to take after, accord with; to be attracted to *la19- NE WC SW Bor*. [OE *cȳþan* to make known]
kytrall see KITERAL
kyucker, *Sh Ork* **kukker,** *Ork* **kucher** /ˈkjukər, ˈkjʌkər, ˈkukər, ˈkʌkər; *Ork* ˈkʌxər/ *v* **1** to fondle, coddle, fuss over *20- Sh*. **2** to improve in health, recover *19- Sh Ork WC*. **3** to cheer up, comfort; to revive *20- Sh*. [altered form of Eng *cocker*]
kyunnen see KINNEN

L

la see LIE[1.2]
laa see LAW[1.1]
laach see LAUCH[1.1], LAUCH[1.2]
laad see LAD
laag see LAIG[1.1], LAIG[1.2]
laager /ˈlɑɡər/ *n fisherman's taboo* the halibut *Hippoglossus hippoglossus* 19- *Sh*. [Norw *lege* a big fish that lies for a while in the same fishing ground]
laar /lɑr/ *n* a gentle breeze *la19- Sh*. [Dan *laring*]
laav[1.1], **lav** /lav/ *n* 1 something which hangs down or droops 20- *Sh*. 2 the flower of the tormentil *Potentilla erecta* 20- *Sh*. [see the verb]
laav[1.2], **lav** /lav/ *v* 1 *of a bird* to hover 19- *Sh*. 2 *of a person* to hang about *la19- Sh*. **laavie-luggit, lavilugget** having drooping ears 19- *Sh*; compare LAVE-LUGGIT. **laavin-luggid** = *laavie-luggit* 20- *Sh*. [ON *lafa* to hang, dangle]
lab[1], *T* **lob**, †**lub** /lab; *T* lɔb/ *n* a lump; a portion, a bit; a shred 19- *T EC Bor*. [perhaps onomatopoeic]
lab[2] /lab/ *n* 1 a game of marbles *la19-*. 2 a blow, a stroke 19, 20- *Bor*. 3 a throw; a tossing movement 19. [extended meaning of LAB[1]]
lab see LAIB[1.2]
labber see LABOUR[1.2], LAIB[1.2]
labbich see LAIB[1.1]
laberlethin /lɛbərˈlɛθən/ *n* a long rambling discourse *la19- NE T EC*. [unknown]
†**labie, laby** *n* the flap or skirt of a man's coat or shirt *la15-19*. [unknown]
laborious, †**laboryus,** †**laborus,** †**lauborus** /ləˈbɔrɪəs/ *adj* 1 industrious, hard-working *la15-*. 2 toilsome, involving considerable time or effort 16-. 3 belonging to the peasant or artisan class 16-19. [ME *laborious*, Lat *labōriōsus*]
labour[1.1], *NE* **lawbour,** †**laubour** /ˈlebər/; *NE* ˈlɔbər/ *n* 1 work, toil; exertion; effort; a task, a job of work 15-. 2 agricultural work, tillage *la15-*. 3 the use of persuasion, solicitation or influence *la15-e17*. [ME *labour*, Lat *labor*]
labour[1.2], **labber,** *NE* **lawbour** /ˈlebər, ˈlabər/; *NE* ˈlɔbər/ *v* 1 to work, toil; to strive 15-. 2 to till, cultivate 15-. 3 to work a quarry or mine; to work at wool or leather 15-. 4 to beat, thrash 19-. 5 to exert persuasion; to negotiate 16. 6 to suffer (an illness) 16-17. **labourer,** †**labourar** (a manual) worker 15-. †**labourer of the ground** a cultivator, a landworker *15-e18*. **labouring** 1 performance of work, toil, exertion 15-. 2 tillage *la15-19*, 20- *Sh*. 3 a farm or holding; arable ground 17-19. [ME *labouren*, Lat *labōrāre*]
labrod, lawboard 19- /ˈlabrod, ˈlɔbord/ *n* a board laid across the knees for working on (used especially by tailors) 19, 20- *Ork NE EC*. [Scots *lap* + BROD[2.1]]
lab-sided /labˈsʌɪdəd/ *adj* unevenly balanced, leaning to one side *la19-*. [altered form of Eng *lop-sided*]
labster see LAPSTER
laby see LABIE
lace[1.1], †**las** /les/ *n* 1 a cord, a string; a ribbon 15-. 2 an openwork fabric *la17-*. 3 a noose or snare *la14-16*. [OFr *las*]
lace[1.2], †**las** /les/ *v* 1 to fasten with a lace 15-. 2 to trim with lace *la16-17*. [OFr *lacier*]
lacer /ˈlesər/ *n* a lace, especially a bootlace *la19-*. [LACE[1.2], with agent suffix]
lach see LAICH[1.2], LAUCH[1.1], LAUCH[1.2], LATCH[3]

lache see LAICH[1.3], LAISH, LASH[3]
lachet see LATCHET
†**lachfasting** *n in Orkney* the preservation of property against encroachment *e16*. [ON *lög-festing* claiming as lawful property and forbidding another any use]
lachter[1], **lauchter** /ˈlaxtər, ˈlɔxtər/ *n* 1 the total number of eggs laid by a fowl in a season; a single clutch on which a hen broods *la18-*. 2 a hatch or brood of chickens 19-. [ON *látr* a lair, a place where something is laid]
lachter[2], **lochter,** *SW Uls* **luchter,** †**lochtir** /ˈlaxtər, ˈlɔxtər; *SW Uls* ˈlʌxtər/ *n* 1 *in reaping corn* the amount grasped and cut in one stroke; the last sheaf cut in a harvest; a handful (of hay or straw) 19, 20- *N T SW Uls*. 2 a lock of hair; a tuft of grass *la14-19*. [ON *lagðr* a lock of wool]
lachter, lachtter see LAUCHTER
lack[1.1], †**lak,** †**lake,** †**laik** /lak/ *n* 1 want, deficiency *la13-*. 2 disgrace *la14-e19*. 3 a fault or failing such as to bring shame or disgrace *la15-16*. 4 offence, injury; insult 15-16. 5 blame, censure *la14-16*. †**but lak** without fault, blamelessly *la15-e16*. †**think lak** see THINK. †**to lak** at fault; blameworthy, despicable *la14-16*. [compare MLG *lak*, MDu *lac*]
lack[1.2], †**lak** /lak/ *v* 1 to be wanting or absent; to be deficient *la15-*. 2 to censure, blame; to disparage *la15-19*. †**lacklicht** *in Shetland* without light, dull *la19*. [see the noun]
†**lack**[1.3], **lak** *adj* deficient in quality, inferior *15-e19*. [compare ON *lakr*]
lackanee /lakəˈniː/ *interj* an expression of dismay 19-. [aphetic form of *alakanee* (ALACK)]
lackie /ˈlaki/ *n* 1 the third stomach of a ruminant; sheep entrails 19- *Sh Ork*. 2 the lap or bosom *la19- Sh Ork*. [ON *laki* the third stomach]
lacreische, lacrissye see LICKERY
lad, laad, lawd, laud, †**laid** /lad, lɔd/ *n* 1 a male servant; a groom *la14-*. 2 a boy, a (young) man 15-. 3 a son 16-. 4 a male sweetheart 19-. 5 a man showing certain strong character traits 20-. 6 the central male participant in Riding of the Marches celebrations 20-. 7 a bachelor 19, 20- *N*. †**ladry** base conduct or talk, ribaldry *15-16*. †**lad bairn** a son *la18-19*. †**lads love** southernwood *Artemisia abrotanum* 19. **the auld Lad** the Devil *la19, 20- EC Uls*. **lad and lass** boyfriend and girlfriend *la18-*. **lad o pairts** a promising, talented boy or young man *la19-*. [unknown]
ladder see LEDDER[1.1]
laddie, laudie, *NE T EC* **lathie** /ˈladi, ˈlade, ˈlɔdi; *NE T EC* ˈlaði/ *n* 1 a young man *la16-*. 2 a male child 17-. 3 a male sweetheart 18-. 4 *in Kelso* the leading male rider and standard-bearer in the Riding of the Marches celebrations 20- *Bor*. †**laddie bairn** a son *la18-19*. **laddie wean** a boy 19-. [LAD + -IE[1]]
laddle see LADLE[1.1]
lade, lead, †**leid** /led/ *n* a channel bringing water to a mill; a mill-race 15-. [OE *lād* a watercourse, a channel]
lade see LAID[1.1], LAID[1.2]
ladill see LADLE[1.1]
ladin see LAID[1.2], LAIDEN
ladinar see LAIDNER
ladle[1.1], †**ladill,** †**laddle,** †**laidle** /ˈledəl/ *n* 1 a deep-bowled, long-handled spoon-like implement, used for conveying liquids *la15-*. 2 *Presbyterian Church* a box fixed on the end of

ladle a long handle, used for taking a collection *19-*. **3** a tadpole *19- N NE*. **4** a ladle used as a standard measure for measuring the duty on foodstuffs at a burgh market; the duty itself *la16-18*. **ladleful**, †**laidle-full 1** as much as can be contained and carried in a ladle *16-*. **2** an amount levied as duty on dry goods *la16-e17*. **aneath somebody's ladle** dependent on or subject to someone *20- NE*. [OE *hlædel*]

ladle[1,2], †**laidil** /'ledəl/ *v* **1** to convey with a ladle; to ladle out *la19-*. **2** *in Glasgow* to exact duty on grain or other dry goods *la17-e18*. †**laddillar** a collector of duty on grain *17*. [see the noun]

ladner *see* LAIDEN
ladrone *see* LAITHERIN
lady *see* LEDDY
Lady Muck /lede 'mʌk/ *n* a woman with aspirations beyond her status *20-*. **Lady Muck fae Stoorie Castle** = LADY MUCK *la20- EC*. **Lady Muck and Glabber** = LADY MUCK *la20- WC*. [LEDDY + MUCK[1,1]]
laeffe *see* LAVE[1]
laega /'lega/ *n* an anchorage *la19- Sh*. [ON *lega*]
laekly *see* LIKELY[1,1], LIKELY[1,3]
laem /lem/ *n* a half-loft made by laying planks over the crossbeams of the living room of a cottage, used for storage *la19- Sh*. [ON *hlemmr* a trapdoor]
laen *see* LEN[1,1]
laesir *see* LEISURE
laest *see* LEAST[2,1], LEAST[2,2]
laeve *see* LEAVE[1]
lafe *see* LAVE[1], LOAF
laft[1,1], **loft** /laft, lɔft/ *n* **1** an attic, a room made under the roof of a house or tenement *la14-*. **2** the upper storey of a two-storey building *15-*. **3** a gallery in a church *16-*. **4** *golf* the act of striking the ball so as to make it rise; the slope on the face of the golf club which causes this *la19-*. **5** a joisted boarded ceiling *la15-19*. **6** the deck of a ship *la15*. **7** one of the storeys of a building *16*. **lafting**, **lofting 1** a joisted ceiling *16-*. **2** boarding *16-*. **3** an upper storey *17*. **loft house** an attic or upper storey *la15-19, 20- Uls*. †**on loft, upon loft 1** in or into the air *la14-e16*. **2** loudly *15*. **3** *of a person's spirits* raised, high *16*. [ON *loft* the air, the sky, an upper room]
laft[1,2], **loft** /laft, lɔft/ *v* **1** to create an upper room by flooring the roof joists of a building *la15-*. **2** to (cause to) rise off the ground *19-*. **3** *golf* to strike the ball so as to make it rise high *la19-*. **4** to furnish a boat with a deck *la17-e18*. **lofted** *of a golf club* having a face sloping forward from the sole so as to make the ball rise *la19-*. [see the noun]
lag[1,1] /lag/ *n* **1** a delay, an interval *19-*. **2** the last in a series; a person who finishes last in a game *la19-*. [unknown]
lag[1,2] /lag/ *adj* lingering, tardy, slow *18-*. [unknown]
lag[2] /lag/ *n* a call to a goose to come and be fed; the goose itself *19- SW*. **laggie** = LAG[2]. [unknown]
lag[3] /lag/ *n* **1** a catch of fish *la19- Sh*. **2** humour, mood *la19- Sh*. **3** *of fish* an inclination to bite *la19- Sh*. [ON *lag* mood]
lag[4] /lag/ *v* **1** to spread or pour in layers *la19- Sh*. **2** to tug, pull or drag a short distance at a time *la19- Sh*. [ON *laga*]
lag[5] /lag/ *v* *spinning* to draw out a tuft of wool *20- Sh*. [ON *lagðr* a lock of wool]
lag *see* LAIG[1,2]
lagalloun *see* LEGLEN
lagamachie *see* LEGAMACHIE
laget /'lagət/ *n* **1** a strip of cloth tied to an animal's fleece or hair for identification *19- Sh*. **2** a shred of wool or hay *la19- Sh*. [ON *lagðr* a tuft of wool]
laggen, leggin, †**laigen,** †**laggyne** /'lagən, 'lɛgən/ *n* **1** the projection of the staves beyond the bottom of a barrel *16-*. **2** *pl* the edge or rim of a hill; frequently in place-names *19-*. **3** the angle inside a vessel or dish where sides and bottom meet *la18-19, 20- Sh NE Uls*. **4** the welt of a shoe *20- Bor*. **5** the horizon, the edge of the sky *20- Bor*. **6** the bottom hoop or base of a barrel *19*. **laggin gird 1** the hoop at the bottom of a cask *19, 20- Sh*. **2** the edge, the rim, the brink of something *19, 20- Sh*. [ON *lǫgg* the rim at the bottom of a cask]

lagger[1,1] /'lagər/ *n* mire, mud *la19- N NE EC*. **laggery** muddy *19- T H&I*. [see the verb]

lagger[1,2], **laiger** /'lagər, 'lɛgər/ *v* **1** to smear with something; to bespatter or dirty *18-*. **2** to sink in or be encumbered by soft ground or snow; to walk with difficulty *18-19, 20- Ork NE EC*. **laggert,** †**laggerit** made wet or muddy; besmeared, bespattered *16-*. [perhaps frequentative form of ME *laggen* to soil, make dirty]

laggyne *see* LAGGEN
lagman *see* LAWMAN
laib[1,1] /leb/ *n* **1** a mouthful (of liquid) *19-*. **2** an untidy, ill-fitting piece of clothing *la19- NE*. **3** a rambling or incoherent discourse *la19- NE*. **lebbach, labbich 1** a mouthful (of liquid) *la19- NE*. **2** a rambling or incoherent discourse *la19- NE*. [voiced variant of LAIP[1,1]]
laib[1,2], **leb, lab** /leb, lɛb, lab/ *v* to lick up, lap or gobble *18-19, 20- NE T Uls*. **laibach** to babble, chatter *la19- NE*. **labber, laiber** to beslobber; to bespatter with food *19- Bor*. [see the noun]
laich[1,1], †**lauch** /lex/ *n* **1** the low side or lowest part of anything *16-19, 20- NE EC SW*. **2** a stretch of low-lying ground *la14-e19*. [see the adj]
laich[1,2], †**lach** /lex/ *v* **1** to humble a person *19-*. **2** to reduce in value *la18-e19*. **3** to reduce in height *e16*. **laichen** to humble; to reduce *19-*. [see the adj]
laich[1,3], **laigh,** †**lache,** †**lauch,** †**leauch** /lex/ *adj* **1** not tall, lofty or high; flat *la14-*. **2** occupying a low or lower situation; situated in the lower part of a building (in the ground floor or basement) *16-*. **3** of humble rank, level or consequence; inferior, less *la16-19*. †**laigh bigging** a low building; an outbuilding *17-e18*. **laich country** the lowland parts of Scotland, outside the Highlands *la16-*. **laich hoose, laigh house,** †**laich hous 1** a one-storey building; a rural cottage *18-*. **2** a room or rooms in the lower part of a building; a cellar *la16-19, 20- NE T EC*. **3** a lower building, frequently one of a group, attached to a main building of several storeys; *pl* outbuildings *la16-e18*. †**laich kirk, laigh kirk** a church which is not the chief church in a town *la16-19*; compare **high kirk** (HEICH[1,3]). **laich road, laigh road 1** the lower of two roads leading to the same place *19-*. **2** an underground road along which the dead were believed to travel *19, 20- literary*. **laigh room** a room or rooms in the lower part of a building; a cellar *18-*. **laigh set** squat, stocky *la19, 20- SW*. **laigh shop** a cellar in a shop; a basement shop *la18-19, 20- NE EC*. [ON *lágr*]
laich[1,4], †**lauch,** †**leauche** /lex/ *adv* **1** in or to a less high or inferior position; close to the ground *15-*. **2** in a low rank or condition, humbly *la16-e17*. **laich doun** in a low voice *19- NE T EC*. **laich in** under one's breath *19- N EC*. [see the adj]
laich *see* LAUCH[1,1], LAUCH[1,2], LATCH[2]
laichen *see* LAICH[1,2]
laichly, *Bor* **leuchly** /'lexle; *Bor* 'ljuxle/ *adv* in or into a low position *la15-*. [LAICH[1,3], with adv-forming suffix]
laichy braid /'lexe bred/ *n* a short stocky person or animal *la19- NE*. [LAICH[1,3] + BRAID[1,2]]
laid[1,1], **lode, load,** *Ork* **led,** †**lade,** †**leid** /led, lod; *Ork* lɛd/ *n* **1** a pack or burden *la14-*. **2** a measure of quantity, the amount of a commodity in a pack *la15-*. **3** a (large) amount of alcoholic drink, as much as a person can consume *19- EC Bor*. **4** a severe head cold: ◊*Ah've goat sic a load Ah*

cannae breathe la19, 20- Sh N EC. †**lade hors** a packhorse *la15-e17.* †**lademan, loadman 1** a man in charge of a packhorse *la14-19.* **2** the miller's assistant who collected and delivered corn and meal *la17-19.* †**ladesaidle, lodesaidell** a packsaddle *la14-e18.* **laid-tree** the centre rail of a frame laid on a hay cart to enable it to take a heavier load *19- EC Bor.* [see the verb]

laid[1.2]**, load,** †**lade** /led, lɒd/ *v pt* **load** †**lade,** *ptp also* **load, ladin,** †**lade,** †**loaden 1** to pack or prepare goods or cargo for transport *15-.* **2** to ship or convey goods *la15-.* **laidin, laiding 1** a consignment of goods to be transported *18-.* **2** a ship's cargo *la16-e19.* **3** the action of putting the cargo on board a ship *la15-16.* **loaded wi the cauld** having a severe head cold *la20-.* [OE *hladan*]

laid *see* LAD, LEID[2]

laidder *see* LEATHER[1.1], LEATHER[1.2], LEDDER[1.1]

laiden, †**ladin** /'lɛdən/ **1** to pack or prepare goods for transport; to load cargo onto a ship *16-19, 20- C.* **2** to overwhelm, oppress a person *la16-17.* †**ladner, laidner** a shipper *la16-e17.* †**ladining, laidning 1** the loading of cargo onto a ship *16-18.* **2** a ship's cargo *la16-e18.* [OE *hladan*]

laidgalloun *see* LEGLEN

laidil *see* LADLE[1.2]

laidle *see* LADLE[1.1]

laidly *see* LAITHLY[1.1]

laidner, †**ladinar,** †**lardener,** †**lairdner** /'lɛdnər/ *n* a storeroom for meat and provisions *la14-e18, 20- historical.* †**laidner mart** a fattened ox or cow killed and salted for winter provisions *la15-17.* †**laidner mart cow** = *laidner mart 17-18.* †**laidner time** the season when a fattened ox or cow was killed and cured *18-19.* [ME *lardiner*]

laidner *see* LAIDEN

laidnert /'lɛdnərt/ *adj* stocked, supplied with provisions *20- T.* [LAIDNER + -IT[2]]

laidron *see* LAITHERIN

laif *see* LOAF

laifie *see* LUIFFIE

laig[1.1]**, lig,** *Sh* **laag,** *NE* **lyaag** /leg, lɪg; *Sh* lɑg; *NE* ljag/ *n* a noisy, unintelligible babble; gossip *19, 20- Sh NE.* **lig-lag, leg-laig** noisy, incoherent speech *19, 20- Sh NE.* [see the verb]

laig[1.2]**, lig, lag,** *Sh* **laag,** *NE* **lyaag** /leg, lɪg, lag; *Sh* lɑg; *NE* ljag/ *v* to gossip, chatter *la19, 20- Sh NE T.* **lig-lag** to chatter noisily or incoherently *la19, 20- Sh NE T.* [Norw dial *laga*]

laig *see* LEG[1.1]

laigen *see* LAGGEN

laiger *see* LAGGER[1.2]

laigh *see* LAICH[1.3]

laik[1.1]**, lake** /lek/ *n* **1** a marble used as a stake in a contest *19, 20- NE T WC.* **2** sport; (a stake wagered on) a contest *la15-16.* [ON *leikr*]

†**laik**[1.2] *v* to sport, amuse oneself *15-16.* [ON *leika*]

laik *see* LACK[1.1], LAKE[1], LAKE[2], LAKE[3], LECK[1.3]

laikage *see* LECK[1.1]

laikwake *see* LYKE

lailly *see* LAITHLY[1.1]

lain *see* LAYNE[1.1], LAYNE[1.2], LIE[1.2]

lainch *see* LENCH

laing *see* LANG[1.1]

laip[1.1]**, lape, lap** /lep, lap/ *n* **1** the act of lapping liquid *19-.* **2** a mouthful or small amount (of liquid) *19-.* **3** a perfunctory wash *20-.* [see the verb]

laip[1.2]**, lape, lap,** *Sh Ork* **lep** /lep, lap; *Sh Ork* lɛp/ *v* **1** to take up liquid with the tongue *15-.* **2** *of water* to move upon the shore with a rippling sound *15-.* [OE *lapian*]

lair[1.1]**,** †**layer** /ler/ *n* **1** a person's bed *15-.* **2** a burial place or grave; a burial space reserved by a person or family in a graveyard or church *15-.* **3** a place where animals lie down; a fold or enclosure *16-.* **4** a site for temporary storage *la16-.* **5** a patch of ground on which cut peats are laid to dry *17- NE.* **6** the overnight grazing of livestock amongst another person's crops *16-17.* **7** the floor of the trench from which peats have been cut *17.* †**lair-silver** the price charged for a burial place *16-e18.* **lair-stane** a gravestone *la16- NE Bor.* [OE *leger* a place to lie, or Gael *lár* ground]

lair[1.2] /ler/ *v* **1** to bury a person *la18-.* **2** to lay a millstone in position *20- NE T.* **3** to drive animals to an enclosure *17-18.* **4** *of animals* to be at rest in an enclosure *16.* [see the noun]

lair[2.1] /ler/ *n* **1** mud, muck *17-.* **2** a mire, a swamp *17-19, 20- NE.* **lairy** miry, muddy *19, 20- NE T Bor.* [ON *leir*]

lair[2.2] /ler/ *v* to sink or stick in soft or boggy ground; to become bogged down (in mud or snow) *la16-.* [see the noun]

lair[3]**, lear,** †**lare** /ler, lir/ *n* **1** the act of teaching; education, tuition or instruction *la14-.* **2** learning, knowledge; religious doctrine; a branch of study *la14-.* †**at the lair** under instruction, at school *la14-16.* [OE *lār*; pronunciation also influenced by LEAR]

lairag *see* LAVEROCK

lairbair *see* LARBAR[1.2]

laird[1.1]**, lard,** †**leard** /lerd, lard/ *n* **1** a landowner having tenure directly from the Crown *la14-.* **2** Christ or God *la14-.* **3** the landlord of landed property or an estate *15-;* compare *landislaird* (LAND[1]). **4** the chief of a Highland clan *la16-.* **5** an owner of property, especially a houseowner *19-.* **6** a jocular term of address for a male person *20-, NE T EC.* **7** a prince, chief or lord *la14-19, 20- literary.* **lairdie 1** a laird *19-.* **2** *derogatory* a pretentious landowner, king or person in a position of power *19-.* **lairdly** lordly, aristocratic; lavish, extravagant *la19- NE.* **lairdship 1** a barony, a landed estate, especially that of a small freeholder *la14-.* **2** the dignity or rank of laird *la15-19, 20- historical.* **3** a term of address to a nobleman *19, 20- C Bor;* compare *lordship* (LORD). **auld laird** *see* AULD[1.2]**. young laird** *see* YOUNG. †**laird in the Abbey** a debtor *18-e19;* compare *Abbey Laird* (ABBEY). [OE *hláford*]

laird[1.2] /lerd/ *v* to possess (an estate) *la19.* **laird it** to rule tyrannically (over); to domineer *la19-.* [see the noun]

lairdner *see* LAIDNER

lairge[1.1]**, large, lerge,** †**larg,** †**lairg** /lerdʒ, lardʒ, lɛrdʒ/ *adj* **1** ample in quantity, plentiful *la14-.* **2** generous; lavish *la14-.* **3** big, substantial *15-.* **4** wide-ranging, comprehensive *15-.* **5** *of speech* voluble, unrestrained *la15-19.* **6** of fully or more than fully the measure indicated *la16-e17.* **lairgely, largely 1** for the most part *15-.* **2** generously *14-16.* **3** without restraint *15-16.* **at large 1** at liberty, unhindered *la15-.* **2** at length, in full *la15-17.* **3** profusely *16.* **lairge in** having an abundant supply (of) *19- NE T.* [OFr *large*]

†**lairge**[1.2] *adv* **1** *of distances or length* fully, quite *15-e18.* **2** abundantly *la15-17.* **3** generously, lavishly *la16.* [see the adj]

lairgis /'lergɪs/ *n* a wet lump, a mess *la19- Ork NE.* [altered from pl of SLAIRG[1.1], with possible influence from LAIR[2.1]]

lairn *see* LEARN

lairock *see* LAVEROCK

lairoo /'leru/ *n* a layer, a coating *20- Ork.* [altered form of Scots *layer*]

†**laish, lasche, lache** *adj* **1** relaxed, limp; lacking energy *16-e18.* **2** slack, negligent *la15-17.* [OFr *lasche*]

†**laist**[1.1]**, lest, last** *n* the last day (of a month) *la16-17.* **at the last** in the end, finally *la14-17.* [see the adj]

laist[1.2]**, lest, last** /lest, lɛst, last/ *adj* **1** describing the final one of a series *la14-.* **2** belonging to the end or final stage

laist *15-.* **3** most recent *15-.* **†the last day** the previous day, yesterday, the other day *la18-19.* **†the last heir** *law* the Crown as heir in the case of intestacy *16-e19*; compare ULTIMUS HAERES. [OE lætest, superlative of læt late]

laist[1,3], **lest**, **last** /lest, lɛst, last/ *adv* **1** most recently *la14-.* **2** latest, after all others, finally *15-.* **†last bypast** *of a date* most recently *16-e18.* **†last wes** *of a date* most recently *16-e17.* [see the adj]

laist *see* LEST[1.1], LEST[1.2]

lait[1], **†late** /let/ *n* **1** *pl* manners, behaviour *15-19, 20- literary.* **2** outward appearance, bearing *la14-15.* **ill laits** *see* ILL[1.3]. [ON lǽti manners; plural form of *lát*]

†lait[2] *v* to seek, look for *15.* [ON leita]

lait *see* LATE

laiteran *see* LATERAN

laith[1.1], **†leth**, **†loath** /leθ/ *n* **1** ill-will, hatred; revulsion, scorn *la15-19, 20- Ork.* **2** harm, injury *la14-15.* [OE lāþ]

laith[1.2], **†loth** /leð/ *v* to detest *la14-.* [OE lāþian]

laith[1.3], *Sh* **leath**, **†lathe**, **†leth**, **†loith** /leθ; *Sh* liθ/ *adj* **1** unwilling, reluctant; reluctantly done or said *la14-.* **2** repulsive; abhorrent *la14-16.* **laithfu**, **†leethfu** **1** reluctant *18-.* **2** bashful *la18-.* **3** disgusting, filthy *19- NE T EC.* **laithiement** a surfeit *19- NE T EC.* **laithsome** disgusting, hateful *la16-.* **laeth apo** tired of, surfeited with *la19- Sh.* [see the noun]

laith *see* LATH

laither *see* LEATHER[1.1]

laitherin, **†laithron**, **†laidron**, **†ladrone** /'leðərən/ *n* a lazy, loutish person, a loafer *16-19, 20- SW.* [OFr ladron, Lat latro a robber]

laithly[1.1], **†lathly**, **†laidly**, **†lailly** /'leðle/ *adj* loathsome, hideous *la14-.* [OE lāþlic]

†laithly[1.2], **lathly** *adv* foully, horribly *la14-e16.* [OE lāþlīce]

laithron *see* LAITHERIN

Laitin[1.1], **Latin**, **†Latyn**, **†Latein** /'letɪn, 'latɪn/ *n* **1** the Latin language *la14-.* **2** an inhabitant of ancient Latium *la15-16.* [see the adj]

Laitin[1.2], **Latin**, **†Lating**, **†Latyn** /'letɪn, 'latɪn/ *adj* **1** of the Latin language *la14-.* **2** of the people or country of ancient Latium *15-e16.* [Lat Latīnus]

laitit, **†lated**, **†latit** /'letɪt/ *adj of metal* softened or weakened by heating or rust *16-19, 20- NE.* [unknown]

lait-wak *see* LATEWAKE

laive *see* LEAVE[1]

lak *see* LACK[1.1], LACK[1.2], LACK[1.3]

lakay *see* LECKIE

lake[1], **†laik** /lek/ *n* **1** a substantial body of landlocked water *17-;* compare LOCH. **2** a pool left at ebb-tide, used as a fish trap *17- SW.* **3** a stagnant pond, a pool *la14-19.* **4** a swamp *e16.* [OFr lac, Lat lacus]

†lake[2], **laik** *n* fine bleached linen *la15-e17.* [MDu, Flem laken (linen) cloth]

†lake[3], **†laik** *n* the flowing water of a river or stream *la15-16.* [OE lacu]

†lake[4] *interj* an expression of dismay *19.* [aphetic form of alake (ALACK)]

lake *see* LACK[1.1], LAIK[1.1], LECK[1.1], LECK[1.2], LIKE[2]

laldie, **laldy** /'lalde, 'laldi/ *n* a beating; punishment *la19-.* **get laldie** to be punished; to attract severe punishment *la19- C SW Bor.* **gie laldie** to punish (someone) severely *la19-.* **gie it laldie** to do something vigorously or exuberantly *20-.* [unknown]

lall /lɑl, lal/ *n* a toy, a plaything *19- Sh Ork.* **lallie** = LALL. [imitative of childish speech]

Lallan[1] /'lalən/ *n* = LALLANS *la19-.* [altered form of LAWLAND[1.1]]

lallan[2], **lalland** /'lalən, 'lalənd/ *adj* of or pertaining to the language of the Scottish Lowlands *la18-.* [altered form of LAWLAND[1.2]]

Lallans, **Lawlans** /'lalənz, 'lɔlənz/ *npl* **1** the language of the Scottish Lowlands *la19-.* **2** the literary Scots used by writers of the Scottish Renaissance movement *20-.* [altered form of LAWLANDS]

lamb[1.1], **lam**, **†lame** /lam/ *n* **1** the young of a sheep *la14-.* **2** an affectionate term of address *19-.* **lammie**, **lambie** an affectionate term of address *17-.* **lammit** an affectionate term of address *la19- Sh.* **lamb bed** the uterus of a ewe *19- Ork N SW.* **lamb's ears** the hoary plantain *Plantago media 20- EC SW Bor.* **lamb-hoose**, **laamoose** a house or shelter for lambs *la19- Sh.* **lamb's lugs 1** = *lamb's ears 20- NE T EC.* **2** lamb's ear or woolly betony *Stachys byzantina 20-.* **lammie-meh** a pet name for a lamb *20-.* **lammie sourocks** sheep's sorrel *Rumex acetosella 19- Bor.* **lamb's tongue** field mint *Mentha arvensis 19-.* [OE lamb]

lamb[1.2] /lam/ *v of a sheep* to bear a lamb; *of a person* to assist at the birth of a lamb *19-.* **lambing-stick** a shepherd's crook used for catching ewes by the neck at lambing-time *20- WC Bor.* **lambing-storm** a period of severe weather, usually in March around the time when lambs are born *20- N.* [see the noun]

lamber *see* LAMMER

Lambes *see* LAMMAS

lambleck *see* LAMP-BLACK

Lambmes *see* LAMMAS

lame[1.1], **loam**, *Sh* **lem**, *Ork* **leam** /lem, lom; *Sh* lɛm; *Ork* lim/ *n* **1** earth, soil *la14-.* **2** earthenware, china *16-19, 20- Sh N NE.* **3** a piece of broken crockery, especially one used as a toy *la19- Sh N NE WC.* [OE lām clay]

lame[1.2], *Ork* **leam**, **†lime** /lem; *Ork* lim/ *adj* made of earthenware or china *16-19, 20- Sh Ork N NE.* [see the noun]

†lame[2.1] *n* lameness, infirmity *15-e16.* [see the adj]

lame[2.2] /lem/ *v* to cripple or maim *la14-.* [see the adj]

lame[2.3] /lem/ *adj* crippled, disabled *16-.* [OE lama]

lame *see* LAMB[1]

†lamen, **lemman** *n* a sweetheart; a lover or mistress *14-17.*

lamenry, **lemanrye** illicit or profane love *la15-16.* [ME lemman]

lament[1.1] /lə'mɛnt/ *n* **1** lamentation *16-.* **2** a song mourning or commemorating a death, an elegy, a dirge; the air to which such a song is sung or played *la17-.* **lamentable**, **†lamentabill 1** pitiable, deplorable *la16-.* **2** mournful, sorrowful *la15-16.* [Lat lāmentum]

lament[1.2] /lə'mɛnt/ *v* **1** to grieve, mourn *16-.* **2** to complain of, state as a grievance *la16-.* **3** *of seabirds* to cry *la19- Sh.* [Lat lāmentāri]

lamentation, **†lamentatioun** /lamən'teʃən/ **1** the expression of grief, the act of mourning *la14-.* **2** a song or poem expressing grief *la15-e16.* [Lat lāmentātio]

lameter *see* LAMIT

lamgabblich /lam'gablɪx/ *n* a long rambling discourse *20- NE.* [altered form of LAGAMACHIE, with infl from *gabble*]

lamit, **lamed** /'lemɪt, lemd/ *adj* crippled, disabled *15-.* **lameter**, **†lamiter** a lame or crippled person or animal *18-.* [ptp of LAME[2.2]]

Lammas, **†Lammes**, **†Lambmes**, **†Lambes** /'laməs/ *n* the first of August, a Scottish quarter day *la14-.* **Lammas drave** the summer herring fishing on the Fife coast *la17- NE T EC.* **Lammas Fair** a fair held at Lammas in various places *17-.* **Lammas flude** a flood caused by a period of heavy rain about Lammas *la18-.* **Lammasman** a young salmon trout which begins its journey upriver from the sea for the first time about the beginning of August *la19-.*

Lammas market a fair held at Lammas, especially one held in Kirkwall or St Andrews *19-*. **Lammas spate** = *Lammas flude 19-*. **Lammas stream** a high and strong tide occurring about Lammas *la19- Ork N NE EC*. [OE *hlāfmæsse* loaf mass, originally a harvest festival]

lammer, laumer, †**lamber** /ˈlamər, ˈlɔmər/ *n* amber *16-*. **lammer bead, laumer bead,** †**lamber beid** an amber bead, frequently used as a charm or amulet *16-19, 20- Sh NE EC*. [OFr *lambre*, Arabic *al anbar*]

†**Lammermuir lion** *n humorous* a sheep *18-19*. [from the name of a range of hills in southern Scotland + LION]

lamp[1] /lamp/ *n* **1** a device providing a source of illumination *la15-*. **2** one of the heavenly bodies supplying light, the sun or a star *la15-e19*. **3** a shining light or example, a paragon *16*. †**lamp of licht** a person of extreme excellence or beauty *la15-16*. [OFr *lampe*]

lamp[2.1] /lamp/ *n* a long firm stride *la19- WC SW Bor*. [see the verb]

lamp[2.2] /lamp/ *v* **1** to stride along; to take long springing steps *17-*. **2** to limp, hobble *19-*. [unknown; compare Norw dial *lampa* to stride, trudge]

lamp[3] /lamp/ *v* to beat, thrash; to defeat *19-*. [unknown]

lamp[4] /lamp/ *n* a ledge on a cliff-face *la19- Sh*. [unknown; compare Swed dial *lampa* a ledge fitted to a bed]

lamp-black, †**lambleck** /ˈlamp blak/ *n* fine black soot from a candle or oil lamp; pigment made from soot *la17-*. [LAMP[1] + BLECK[2.1]]

lampeekoo /lamˈpiku/ *n* a variation of hide-and-seek *20- NE T*. [unknown; compare PEE-COO]

lamper eel, †**lamper ele,** †**lamper eil** /lampər ˈil/ *n* a lamprey *16-*. [ME *laumprei* + EEL]

lampet *see* LEMPIT

lan *see* LAND[1.1], LAWN

lance[1.1], †**lans** /lans/ *n* **1** a weapon consisting of a long wooden shaft with a pointed iron or steel head; a spear or pike *15-*. **2** a pointed surgical instrument, a lancet *16-*. †**lance staff** a lance or pike *16-e17*. [OFr *lance*]

lance[1.2] /lans/ *v* **1** to pierce or cut (with a lance or lancet) *la16-*. **2** to hurl, launch or shoot *la17-*. **3** to bound or spring *la14-e19*. [OFr *lancier*]

lanche *see* LENCH

land[1.1], **lan** /land, lan/ *n* **1** the solid part of the earth's surface as opposed to sea or water; the shore *la14-*. **2** a country, region or territory *la14-*. **3** ground or territory viewed as property or a commodity *la14-*. **4** ground or soil used for cultivation; arable land; the fields of a farm as opposed to the buildings *la14-*. **5** a holding of land in a burgh or town (available for building); a building site; a tenement or building erected on a holding of land *15-*. **6** the country as opposed to the town; the rural parts of a place *15-*. **7** an S-hook attaching the yoke to the muzzle of a plough *la17-*. **8** the soil which has still to be turned over by the ploughshare; the width of the cut made by the plough in the soil *la18-*. **9** one of the cultivated strips of the runrig system, a rig *la15-17*. **lander** *in a plough-team* the left-hand horse, which walks on the unturned earth *20-*. **landit, landed** possessing land; belonging to the class of landowning proprietors *la15-*. **landless,** †**landles** not possessing land, having no landed property *16-*. **lan afore** *in a plough-team* the left-hand horse which is in front in a four-horse team *la18-*. **lan beast** *in a plough-team* the left-hand horse, which walks on the unturned earth *20-*. **land birst,** †**land bryst** the breaking of waves on the shore, surf *la14-19, 20- N*. †**land breach** = *land birst la18*. **Land Court** = *Scottish Land Court* (SCOTS[1.2]). **land end 1** the end of a furrow, where the plough turns *19-*. **2** the end of a rig *16-17*. †**land feaver** a disease *17*. **land fell** the rising or inflowing tide *19- Sh*. †**land flesche mercat** a market for selling meat brought into a burgh from the surrounding countryside by those not belonging to an incorporation or guild *la16-17*. †**land flescheour** a butcher or seller of meat from the country using the *land flesche mercat 16*. †**land gate, land gates 1** landwards, in the direction of the country *la18-19*. **2** by land, overland *la15-16*. **land horse** *in a plough-team* the left-hand horse, which walks on the unturned earth *19, 20- H&I WC SW*. †**land ill** a disease, such a epilepsy *16-19*. **land labourer** a person who works on the land as a casual labourer *la17-*. **landlady 1** a proprietrix of land or houses; the hostess of an inn or boarding-house *la17-*. **2** the mistress of a house where one is a guest *19-*. **landslady,** †**landislady** a proprietrix of land or houses; the hostess of an inn or boarding-house *la16-19, 20- T*. **landlord 1** the proprietor of a landed estate; an innkeeper; the owner of accommodation to let *la17-*. **2** the head of the family where one is a guest *19, 20- Ork SW*. †**landislord, landislaird** the landlord of an estate or rented house *16-17*. †**land lowper** *derogatory* an idler; a vagabond *la16-19*. †**land lyar** a small boat for going ashore from a larger vessel *la16-e17*. **land mail, land maill 1** rent or formerly feu duty paid by tenants of crown, church or udal lands *16- Sh Ork*. **2** *in Lanark* the rent paid by the tenants of the common land of the burgh *la16-e18*. †**land master** a landowner *la18-19*. †**land meither** *in Glasgow* a person appointed to inspect and settle the boundaries of property *la17-e18*; compare LANIMER. †**land meithing** *in Glasgow* the inspection and fixing of boundaries *la17-e18*. †**land mercat, land market** = *land flesche mercat 16-e18*. **land mouse** the field vole *20-, C SW*. **land plate** the side-plate on the left-hand side of a plough *20- H&I EC SW Uls*. †**land raip** a rope passing from the end of a drag-net to the shore *17-18*. **land rent** revenue or income from land *la16-*. **land sea** heavy surf, indicating a storm *20- Sh Ork N*. †**land settertoun** a fee or fine for letting or re-letting land *la16*. **land setting** the letting of land and farms to tenants *17-*. **land side** the left-hand side of the plough *la18-*. †**land skuld** *in Orkney and Shetland* rent payable on land *16*. †**land stale, land stool** the foundation on land of the pier of a bridge or weir *la15-19*. **land stane, land stone** a loose stone in the soil turned up in digging or ploughing *la18-19, 20- Ork SW Uls*. **land tow, laand tow** a cable for mooring a boat *la19- Sh*. **land and tenement** land in a burgh, held in tenure and usually built on *15-16*; compare *tenement of land* (TENEMENT). **the Land o Cakes** a nickname for Scotland (from the importance of oatcakes in the Scottish diet) *la17-*. **the Land o the Leal** the land of the faithful, Heaven *la18-*. [OE *land*]

land[1.2] /land/ *v* **1** to come or bring to land; to disembark *16-*. **2** to arrive at a place; to arrive at a conclusion or termination *18-*. **3** to be born *la19-*. **lander** a fall on the ground *20-*. **landing 1** the action of coming to land; disembarkation *16-*. **2** the journey of a plough from one side of a field to another and back again *19- EC SW Bor*. [see the noun]

land[2] /land/ *v* to encumber or burden a person (with a responsibility or obligation) *20-*. [perhaps a variant of LANT[1.2]]

landart *see* LANDWARD[1.3]

landimare, landimere, landimure *see* LANIMER

†**landward**[1.1] *n* the country as opposed to the town; the rural area in the neighbourhood of a town; the rural part of a district or parish *15-18*. [LAND[1.1], with suffix denoting a specified direction]

landward[1.2], **lannart** /ˈlandwərd, ˈlanərt/ *adj* **1** rural, in or of the country as opposed to (a particular) town; in or of a rural part of a parish or district *16-*. **2** rustic, awkward, uncouth *16-19, 20- C*. [see the noun]

landward[1,3], **landwart**, **landart** /'landwərd, 'landwərt, 'landərt/ *adv* in or towards the direction of the country as opposed to (a particular) town *19-*. †**landwardis** in the direction of the country *15-17*. [see the noun]

lane[1] /len/ *n* a marshy meadow; a slow-moving, winding stream *la17- SW*. [Gael *lèan(a)*, IrGael *léana* a marshy meadow]

lane[2,1], **lone** /len, lon/ *n* solitude *la16-19, 20- literary*. **its lane 1** without a mate or companion *la16-*. **2** unaided, especially of a child learning to walk *18-*. **my lane 1** on one's own, solitary *la16-*. **2** unaided, especially of a child learning to walk *18-*. **3** ownself, ownselves: ◊ *to his lane by oor lanes 18-*. [see the adj]

lane[2,2], **lone** /len, lon/ *adj* solitary *la14-*. **lanesome**, **lonesome** lonely, alone *la18-*. [aphetic form of ALANE[1,1]]

lane *see* LAWN, LAYNE[1,1], LAYNE[1,2], LEN[1,1], LEN[1,2].

lanely /'lenle/ *adj* solitary, alone *la17-*. [LANE[2,2], with adj-forming suffix]

lanerly, *Sh* **lennerlie** /'lenərle; *Sh* 'lɛnərli/ *adj* lonely, alone; reserved in manner *19-*. [LANE[2,2], with adj-forming suffix]

lang[1,1], **long**, †**laing** /laŋ, lɔŋ/ *adj* **1** great, large; lengthy *12-*. **2** tall, high *la15-*. **3** large in amount *la18-19, 20- NE*. **langsome**, †**langsum 1** lengthy, tedious *la14-*. **2** *of people* sluggish, slow, dilatory *16-19, 20- Sh Ork EC SW*. **3** lonely, forlorn; bored *la19- Sh NE T EC*. †**langsumly** for long *la15-e17*. **lang ale** a soft drink *20- NE*. **lang band** the crossbeam or purlin of a roof *la19- Sh*. **lang bed** a makeshift or shake-down bed *la19- Sh*. †**lang board** a long table at which master and servants sat together *la18-19*. **lang cairt**, **long cart** a two-wheeled cart with a long body and sparred sides *19-*. †**lang carriage** the feudal duty of carting goods over long distances *16-18*. **lang chafted**, **long chafted** long in the jaw, lantern-jawed *19, 20- NE T*. **lang chair** a bench *19- SW Bor*. †**lang drauchtit**, **lang draughted** scheming, cunning *19*. **lang game**, **long game** *golf* the part of a round played from the tee and along the fairway *la19-*; compare *short game* (SHORT). †**lang gown** a judge, advocate or counsel *e19*. **lang hat** a top hat *20-*. **lang heid** shrewdness; a shrewd or sagacious person *19-*. **lang heidit**, **lang heided**, **long headed** shrewd, sagacious *19-*. †**lang helter time** the time of year when livestock was turned out to graze on the harvested fields *19*. **lang ingans** a version of the game of leapfrog *20- NE*. **lang kail**, **long kail** great or Scotch kail, a variety with less wrinkled leaves and purplish in colour *18-19, 20- literary*. **lang kent** familiar *20-*. **lang leeks** = *lang ingans 20- NE T*. **lang lie**, **long lie** a period of staying in bed beyond the usual time *19-*. **lang lip** a sulky expression *la19- NE Uls*. **lang luggit 1** having long ears or sharp hearing; given to eavesdropping *19-*. **2** shrewd *20- T C*. **lang lugs 1** a person or animal with long ears, especially a donkey *18-*. **2** a hare *20- N WC Bor*. **lang nebbit 1** having a long nose, snout or beak *19-*. **2** inquisitive, critical *19-*. **3** *of things* long, tapering or pointed *19-*. **4** *of words* polysyllabic; learned, pedantic *19-*. **5** astute, having an eye to one's own advantage *18-19, 20- T C SW Bor*. **6** gnome-like, elfin in appearance; supernatural in origin *18-19, 20- Ork Uls*. **lang sandy** the heron *20- NE*. **lang shankit 1** long-legged *la19-*. **2** having a long shank or handle *18-19, 20- NE SW*. †**lang sheep**, **long sheep** a South Country Cheviot sheep *la18-19*. †**langspiel** a harp or stringed instrument associated with Shetland *e19*. **lang teem whaup** = *lang whaup*. **lang teethed**, **long teethed** long-established, of an old family; aged *20- NE T*. †**lang-time** for, during or since a long time *la14-e17*. **Lang Whang 1** the part of the old Edinburgh to Lanark road (A70) between Balerno and Carnwath *19-*. **2** *golf* the name given to a particularly long hole on some golf courses, such as the 8th at Kelso *20-*. **lang whaup** a tall scrawny person *la19-*. **lang wund** involved *19- Sh SW Uls*. †**at the lang** fully; finally *la16-e17*. **at the lang lenth** at long last, finally *la19-*. **at the lang an last lenth** at long last, finally *19, 20- Sh Ork NE*. **at the lang run** in the end, finally *18-19, 20- Sh N EC SW*. **i the lang lenth** at long last, finally *la19- Sh NE*. **the lang day, the long day** the Day of Judgement *18-*. **lang drink o water, long drink o water** a tall lanky person *la19-*. **lang in the horn** advanced in years and experience; wise *la20- T C SW*. †**lang o** taking a long time, dilatory *la18-19*. †**the lang sands** a lengthy (legal) process *la17-e19*. †**lang time** for a long time; a long time since *la14-e17*. **mak a lang airm** to stretch out and help oneself *20-*. †**of lang time** for, during or since a long time *la15-16*. [OE *lang*]

lang[1,2], **long** /laŋ, lɔŋ/ *adv* for a long time *la14-*. **lang back** long ago *19-*. †**lang ere**, **langer**, **langeir** before, formerly *la14-16*. **lang may yer lum reek** a proverbial expression wishing enduring prosperity *20-*. [OE *lange*]

lang[2], **long** /laŋ, lɔŋ/ *v* to want, feel a strong desire; to be impatient; to yearn *la15-*. [OE *langian*]

†**lang**[3] *v* **1** to pertain or relate to; to be the property or right of *la14-e16*. **2** *of things* to be an appurtenance or accessory of *la15-e16*. **3** *of people* to belong, as a member of a family, or as an adherent or dependent *15-e16*. [OE *gelang* belonging, dependent]

†**lang**[4] *prep* along *la15-19*. **langis**, **langgis** along *la15-e17*. [aphetic form of ALANG[1,2]]

langage *see* LANGUAGE

langal *see* LANGLE[1,2]

langald *see* LANGLE[1,1]

langamachie *see* LEGAMACHIE

langer *see* LANGOUR

langett *see* LANGLE[1,1]

langfad *see* LYMPHAD

langidge *see* LANGUAGE

langis, **langgis** *see* LANG[4]

langle[1,1], †**langald**, †**langett** /'laŋəl, 'laŋgəl/ *n* a hobble, a tether to prevent an animal from straying *la15-19, 20- N NE SW Uls*. Compare LINGLE[2,1]. [Lat *lingula* a thong]

langle[1,2], †**langal** /'laŋəl, 'laŋgəl/ *v* **1** to hobble an animal *la15-18, 19- Ork N NE SW Uls*; compare LINGLE[2,2]. **2** to encumber, hamper, frustrate *la17-19, 20- NE*. [see the noun]

langlins[1,1] /'laŋlənz/ *adv* lengthwise *20- Sh NE*. [LANG[1,1] + -LINS]

†**langlins**[1,2], **langlines** *prep* along *la16-18*. [see the adv]

langour, **languor**, **langer** /'laŋgər, 'laŋər/ *n* **1** boredom, low spirits *la15-*. **2** longing for someone to do something *la16-17*. **3** prolonged or chronic illness; distress, grief, misery *la14-16*. **langersome** boring, tedious *la19- Sh Ork N Uls*. [ME *langour*, Lat *languor*]

lang reed, **lang reid** /'laŋ rid/ *n* a period of dearth in late winter *la15- Ork*. [ON *langa* long + *hríð* a storm, snow-storm]

lang-settle, **long-saddle**, †**langsadill**, †**langsattill** /'laŋ sɛtəl, 'lɔŋ sadəl/ *n* a long wooden bench with a back and arms or sides (with a chest below the hinged seat), often convertible into a bed *la15-19, 20- SW*. †**langsaill bed**, **longsaddle-bed** a wooden bench convertible into a bed *16-e18*. [LANG[1,1] + SATTLE[1,1]]

lang syne[1,1] /laŋ 'sʌɪn/ *n* old times, memories of the past; old friendship *la18-*; compare AULD LANG SYNE. [LANG[1,2] + SYNE[2,1]]

lang syne[1,2] /laŋ 'sʌɪn/ *adj* ancient; relating to long ago *la18-*. [see the noun]

lang syne[1,3], **long syne** /laŋ 'sʌɪn, lɔŋ 'sʌɪn/ *adv* long ago, long since *15-*. **lang-frae-syne** long ago, long since *19- Sh NE EC*. **lang sin-syne** = *lang-frae-syne*. [see the noun]

language, **langidge**, †**langage** /ˈlaŋwɪdʒ, ˈlaŋɪdʒ/ *n* **1** a system of communication; the speech of a particular nation *la14-*. **2** speech, words; discourse; a manner of speaking *la15-*. [AN, OFr *language*]

languor *see* LANGOUR

lanimer, †**landimere**, †**landimare**, †**landimure** /ˈlanɪmər/ *n* **1** *pl* boundaries of land *15-*. **2** the annual ceremony of inspecting the boundaries of Lanark and Linlithgow *15-*. **3** a person who inspected and adjusted boundaries within a burgh *17-18*. **Lanimer Day**, †**landsmark day** the celebrations accompanying the annual riding of the marches in Lanark and Linlithgow *la18-*. **Lanimer Queen** the girl chosen as chief female participant in the Lanimer Day celebrations *20-*. [OE *landgemǣre*; compare OUTLANDIMER]

lank /laŋk/ *n* **1** a spent herring *la19- NE*. **2** a lean, skinny person *20- Uls*. [OE *hlanc* lean]

lannart *see* LANDWARD[1.2]

Lanny /ˈlane, ˈlani/ *n* a nickname for Lanliq, a proprietary brand of inexpensive fortified wine *20-*. [*Lang's liqueur* imported from South Africa to Glasgow]

lant[1.1] /lant/ *n* the card game loo *18-19, 20- Sh*. [reduced form of Eng *lanterloo*]

lant[1.2] /lant/ *v* **1** to put in a dilemma *19, 20- Sh*. **2** to mock *19- NE*. [see the noun]

lantern, **lantren** /ˈlantərn, ˈlantrən/ *n* **1** a case containing a source of light, a lamp *la14-*. **2** the sun, the moon or a star *la15-16*. [Lat *lanterna*]

lap[1.1] /lap/ *n* **1** a flap, a fold; a fold forming a pouch *15-*. **2** a wrapping round, a coil *la19-*. **3** a small truss of hay *la19- N Uls*. **4** a lobe (of the liver or of the ear) *la17-19, 20- Sh*. **5** a sheepmark made by slitting the ear so as to make a flap *18-19, 20- Ork*. **6** a patch *la19, 20- Sh*. **7** a small amount *20- Sh Uls*. **lap cock** a small truss of hay *la18- C*. **lap cole** = lap cock *20- Uls*. [OE *læppa*]

lap[1.2] /lap/ *v* **1** to fold or wrap; to parcel up *la15-*. **2** to patch, mend *la19, 20- Sh NE T SW*. **3** to fold up newly-woven linen for storage or dispatch *18-19*. **4** to press round in a hostile way; to hem in or surround *15-16*. **5** to embrace *la15-e16*. [see the noun]

lap, **lape** *see* LAIP[1.1], LAIP[1.2], LEAP

†**lapidar** *n* a jeweller; a connoisseur of precious stones *16-e17*. [OFr *lapidaire*]

lapper[1.1], **lopper** /ˈlapər, ˈlɔpər/ *n* **1** a clot, coagulated matter; clotted milk or blood *19-*. **2** sour, thick milk *19-*. **3** cream cheese *20- NE*. **4** slushy snow *19- SW Bor*. **lapper milk** thick sour milk *19-*. [see the verb]

lapper[1.2], †**lopper** /ˈlapər/ *v* **1** *of blood or milk* to clot or curdle *16-*. **2** *of water* to freeze *la18- NE T SW Bor*. **3** to smear with or become covered with blood *18-19, 20- literary*. **4** *of soil* to dry out in a caked or lumpy state *la19- NE*. **lappert milk** thick sour milk *17-19, 20- NE EC SW Bor*. **lappering tub** a container used for curdling milk *20- NE EC Bor*. [perhaps ON *hlaup* coagulation]

lapper[2.1] /ˈlapər/ *n* a lapping sound or motion *20- NE T EC*. [frequentative form of Scots *lap*]

lapper[2.2] /ˈlapər/ *v of water* to lap, ripple *la19-*. [see the noun]

lappie /ˈlapi/ *n* a small pool of water, a puddle *19-, T*. [Scots *lap* + -IE[1]]

laproun *see* LEPRONE

lapster, **labster**, **lobster**, †**lapstar**, †**lopstar** /ˈlapstər, ˈlabstər, ˈlɔbstər/ *n* a large marine crustacean of the *Nephropidae* family *16-*. **labster creel**, **lobster creel** a lobster trap *19-*. **lapster kist** a box floated in water in which lobsters are kept alive until sent to market *20- Ork N T*. [OE *loppestre*]

lapt *see* LEAP

larach, **laroch**, †**lerroch** /ˈlarəx/ *n* **1** a site, a stance; the foundation of a building *16-*. **2** the ruins of a building *la16-*. **3** the foundation of a haystack or corn-stack *19, 20- NE T*. [Gael *làrach*, IrGael *láithreach*]

†**larbar**[1.1] *n* an impotent man *16-e17*. [unknown]

†**larbar**[1.2], **lairbair** *adj* exhausted, impotent *16-e17*. [unknown]

lard *see* LAIRD[1.1]

lardener *see* LAIDNER

†**lardon** *n* a gibe, a piece of sarcasm *la16*. [MFr *lardon*]

lare *see* LAIR[3]

larg *see* LAIRGE[1.1]

large *see* LAIRGE[1.1]

largesse, †**larges**, †**lerges** /larˈdʒes/ *n* **1** liberality, the lavish bestowal of gifts *la14-*. **2** the ceremonial bestowal of gifts on a special occasion, originally on New Year's Day *16-*. †**at his larges** at liberty, free *la14-16*. [MFr *largesse*]

larick /ˈlarək/ *n* the larch tree *18-*. [Lat *larix*]

larick *see* LAVEROCK

larkie /ˈlarki/ *n* the game of hide-and-seek *20- C*. [Eng *lark* a frolic + -IE[1]]

laroch *see* LARACH

larrie, **lorry** /ˈlare, ˈlari, ˈlɔri/ *n* a large vehicle for transporting goods by road; a truck or wagon used on railways *la19-*. [unknown]

lary, †**laurye**, †**lawry** /ˈlare/ *n* the laurel *16-19, 20- SW*. [ME *lauri*]

larycht aithe *see* LAWRICHT-AITH

†**las** *interj* alas *la18-e19* **las-a-day** an expression of sorrow or regret *la18-e19*. [aphetic form of Older Scots *alas*]

las *see* LACE[1.1], LACE[1.2], LASS

lasch *see* LASH[1.1], LASH[1.2], LASH[3]

lasche *see* LAISH

lase *see* LASS, LESS[3]

laser *see* LEISURE

lash[1.1], †**lasch** /laʃ/ *n* **1** a blow (with a whip) *16-*. **2** a great splash of water, a heavy fall of rain *19-*. **3** a large amount, an abundance (of people or things) *la19-*. **lashangallaivie** abundance *19- EC Bor*. [see the verb]

lash[1.2], †**lasch** /laʃ/ *v* to strike a blow; to whip; to move quickly or dash; to indulge in excess *15-*. **lashins and lavins** abundance *20- N SW Uls*. [OFr *lascher* to let go]

lash[2] /laʃ/ *n weaving* a looped string fastened so as to raise groups of warp-threads in a loom together; the knotting together of the threads forming one colour in a pattern *19-*. [unknown; compare LATCH[1]]

†**lash**[3], **lasch**, **lache** *adj* slack, negligent, relaxed *la15-e19*. [OFr *lasche*]

lasie *see* LAZY[1.2]

laskit[1.1], **lesteek** /ˈlaskɪt, ˈlɛstik/ *n* elastic *19-*. [altered form of Eng *elastic*]

laskit[1.2], **lesteek** /ˈlaskɪt, ˈlɛstik/ *adj* elastic *19-*. [see the noun]

lass, †**las**, †**lase** /las/ *n* **1** a girl *la14-*. **2** a woman *16-*. **3** a maidservant *16-*. **4** a sweetheart *la16-*. **5** a female child, a daughter *la16-*. **6** an unmarried woman *18-*. **7** the chief female participant in various local festivals such as the Riding of the Marches *20-*. **lassickie**, *N* **lassigie** a girl or young woman *la19- N NE T EC*. **lassock** a girl or young woman *la18-19, 20- NE*. **lass bairn** a female child, a daughter *17-*. [unknown]

lassie /ˈlasi, ˈlase/ *n* **1** a girl *18-*. **2** an unmarried woman *la18-*. **3** a sweetheart *la18-*. **4** a maidservant *19-*. **5** a female child, a daughter *la19-*. **lassielike** girlish, like a girl *19-*. **lassie bairn** a female child, a daughter *17-*. **lassie boy** an effeminate boy *20-*. **lassie wean** a female child, a daughter *19-*. [LASS + -IE¹]

last¹ /last/ *n* **1** a denomination of weight, capacity or quantity *15-*. **2** a unit of measurement of a ship's burden *la16-e18*. **3** *in Shetland* a unit of valuation of land equal to 18 merks *la16-18*. **4** *in Orkney* the largest denomination of weight or quantity equal to 24 meils *16-17*. †**lastage 1** a port-duty levied on the cargo of a ship *15-17*. **2** the cargo of a ship measured in lasts *16-e17*. [OE hlæst]

last²·¹ /last/ *n in shoemaking* a wooden model of the foot used in shaping footwear *16-*. †**nevir a last** = *nocht a last*. †**nocht a last** not a trace, nothing *la14-e15*. [OE lāst a footstep, a trace]

†**last²·²** *v* to put a shoe on a wooden last *17-19*. [see the noun]

last *see* LAIST¹·¹, LAIST¹·², LAIST¹·³, LEST¹·¹, LEST¹·²

lat, let, †**latt** /lat, lɛt/ *v pt* **lat, luit, loot,** *Sh* **löt,** *NE* **leet,** †**leit,** †**lute,** *ptp Sh NE* **latten, letten, luitten, loot,** †**lattyn 1** to allow, permit; to cause, make happen *la14-*. **2** to act or initiate an action: ◊*he let skelp wi a stick la14-*. **3** to lease, hire out *15-*. **4** to think or expect something of a person *la14-16*. **5** to consider or suppose *la14-15*. **6** to declare, avow *la14-15*. †**let a-be, let a-bee** forbearance, compromise *la18-19*. **lat at** to hit out at; to make a sarcastic thrust at *18-*. **let bat** to acknowledge, show interest in *20- Sh NE Bor*. **let dab** *see* DAB¹·². **lat doon, let down 1** to lower *la14-*. **2** to disappoint or betray; to fail to support or maintain *la15-*. **3** *of a cow* to yield milk *la17-*. **4** to lower a price *19-*. **5** to swallow *20- NE T EC*. **6** *in knitting* to drop a stitch *19, 20- NE*. **7** to bleed meat before sale *16-e18*. **lat doon on** to stop teasing or reproaching (a person) *20- NE*. **lat intil** to strike or attack violently *la19- N NE*. **lat ken, let ken** to make known *18-*. **lat licht** to divulge; to admit *19- NE*. †**lat of** to disparage *15-16*. **lat oot, let oot 1** to release or allow to go *la14-*. **2** to lengthen or expand *la14-*. **3** to allow a fire to go out *18-*. **lat see 1** to show, reveal *15-*. **2** to pass, hand over *la19-*. **lat sing** *see* SING¹·². **lat sit** to leave things as they are *la19- NE*. †**lat to borch** *see* BORROW¹·¹. **lat wi** to concede; to indulge *19- NE*. **lat wit, let wit** to make known; to let it be known *la14-19, 20- NE*. [OE lǣtan]

lat *see* LATE, LATH, LET¹·¹, LET¹·²

lat be, let be /lat 'bi, lɛt 'bi/ *v* to leave alone or undisturbed; to desist *la14-*. **let-be for let-be** to leave alone; to tolerate *la19-* [LAT + BE]

latch¹ /latʃ/ *n* **1** a door catch *19-*. **2** a loop or catch for a mechanism *la18-19, 20- N NE EC Bor*. [probably OFr *lache* lace; compare LATCHET]

latch², †**leche,** †**laich** /latʃ/ *n* **1** a mire, a bog or piece of boggy ground; frequently in place-names *13-19, 20- NE*. **2** a stream (flowing through boggy ground); frequently in place-names *13-19, 20- EC*. [OE *lacu* a stream, and OE *leccan* to moisten]

latch³, †**lach,** †**leth** /latʃ/ *v* to be slow or dilatory; to procrastinate, delay *16-19, 20- NE*. †**lacheand, leithand, lathand** lagging, negligent *la14-16*. **latchie, latchy** slow, dilatory *20- NE*. **latchin** slow, tardy, lazy *la19- NE*. †**lething, lathin** tardiness, loitering *la15-16*. [OFr *lascher*; compare LAISH]

latchet, †**lachet** /'latʃət/ *n* **1** a loop of string or fabric (used as a fastening) *16-*. **2** a shoelace *17-19, 20- N*. **3** a strip of metal; the wire or metalwork for a window lattice *17-e18*. [OFr *lachet*]

late, †**lait,** †**lat,** †**leat** /let/ *adj* **1** of an advanced hour *la14-*. **2** after the expected time; deferred or delayed *15-*. **3** former; belonging to the recent past *15-*. **4** deceased *la15-*. †**late and sune** early and late, at all times *la18-19*. **late of** tardy in: ◊*he was late of arriving la18-*. [OE lǣt]

late *see* LAIT¹
lated *see* LAITIT
Latein *see* LAITIN¹·¹

lateran, letteran, lettern, laiteran, lectern, †**lettroun,** †**lattroun,** †**lectroun** /'latərən, 'lɛtərən, 'lɛtərn, 'letərən, 'lɛktərn/ *n* **1** a support for a book, a stand at which something is read or sung *la15-*. **2** *Presbyterian Church* the desk of the reader or precentor *la16-*. **3** a lawyer's desk *la17-18*. **4** a writing desk in a private house *la15-e18*. †**go to the lettron** to pursue legal studies *la17-18*. [OFr *lettrun* a reading desk]

latewake, †**lait-wak** /'letwek/ *n* a vigil kept over a corpse until burial, a wake *la17-19, 20- historical*. [altered form of *leek-waak* (LYKE)]

lat flee, let fly, †**let fle** /lat 'fli, lɛt 'flae/ *v* **1** to discharge missiles *la14-*. **2** to attack violently *la15-*. **3** to set to vigorously *la15-*. [LAT + FLEE]

lath, lat, †**laith,** †**lauth** /laθ, lat/ *n* a thin strip of wood; sarking for a roof *la15-*. †**lathing, lauthing** roof-boarding; sarking *16-e18*. †**lathbrod, lathburd 1** lath-nails *la15-16*. **2** lath-boarding, laths collectively *e16*. [ME *latthe*]

lathand *see* LATCH³
lathe *see* LAITH¹·³
lathie *see* LADDIE

†**lathly** *v* to despise, detest *e16*. [compare OE *lāðlic*, ME *loðlic*]

lathly *see* LAITHLY¹·¹, LAITHLY¹·²
Latin *see* LAITIN¹·¹, LAITIN¹·²
lating *see* LAWTHING
Lating *see* LAITIN¹·²
latit *see* LAITIT
lat on *see* LET ON

lat ower¹·¹ /lat 'ʌur/ *n* **1** the act of swallowing *19- NE T*. **2** appetite *19, 20- NE*. [see the verb]

lat ower¹·² /lat 'ʌur/ *v* to swallow *19- NE T EC*. [LAT + OWER¹·³]

latrine, lettrin, †**latrin,** †**lettrin,** †**lettron** /lə'trin, 'lɛtrɪn/ *n* a privy *17-*. [Fr *latrine*, Lat *lātrīna*]

latt, latten *see* LAT

latter, †**letter** /'latər/ *adj* **1** recent; nearer the end *la14-*. **2** the last in a series, the second of two *16-*. **latter fair 1** a fair held towards the end of the year; the last or most recent of a series of fairs *la16-19, 20- historical*. **2** a horse fair held in Dundee on *Latter Maryday la16-19, 20- historical*. **Latter Maryday** the Nativity of the Virgin Mary (8 Sep), observed as a fair day *16-19, 20- historical*. †**latter-meat, letter-meat** left-over food (given to the servants) *16-18*. †**latter-meat room** a larder for storing food already cooked *17-18*. †**latter mynd** a person's intention as to the disposal of his property after death; a will *16*. †**latter will, letter will** a person's will or testament *16-18*. [OE lǣtra, comparative of *lǣt* late]

lattit *see* LET¹·²
lattroun *see* LATERAN
lattyn *see* LAT

†**latuce** *n* lettuce *16-e17*. [ME *letuse*]

Latyn *see* LAITIN¹·¹, LAITIN¹·²
lauborus *see* LABORIOUS
laubour *see* LABOUR¹·¹

lauch¹·¹, lach, laach, laugh, *Sh Ork* **laich** /lɔx, lax, laf; *Sh Ork* lex/ *n* laughter; a laugh *la18-*. [see the verb]

lauch¹·², lach, laach, laugh, *Sh Ork* **laich,** †**lawch** /lɔx, lax, laf; *Sh Ork* lex/ *v pt* **laucht, leuch,** †**lowche** †**luche,** *ptp* **laucht, leuchen,** *NE* **lauchen** to express amusement, laugh *la14-*. **come lauchin hame** *of something borrowed* to be returned to the lender with a gift in recompense *18-19, 20- Sh Ork NE*. **lauchin rain** an unexpected shower of rain from a clear sky *la19, 20- T Uls*. [OE *hliehhan*]

†lauch² *n* a reckoning; a bill in a tavern *la15-e17*; compare LAWIN. **†fre lauch, frie lach** free entertainment or provisions *16-e17*. [compare ON *lag*, MDu, MLG *lach*]

lauch *see* LAW¹·¹, LAICH¹·¹, LAICH¹·³, LAICH¹·⁴

lauchen, laucht *see* LAUCH¹·²

†lauchtane *adj* **1** *of a garment* dull-coloured, grey *la14-16*. **2** *of the skin* livid, discoloured *la14-16*. [Gael *lachdunn*]

lauchter, lachter, †lawchtir, †lachtter /ˈlɔxtər, ˈlaxtər/ *n* laughter, the action of laughing *15-*. [OE *hleahtor*]

lauchter *see* LACHTER¹

†laud *n law* a finding in a case of arbitration *16*. [ME *laude*]

laud *see* LAD

laugh *see* LAUCH¹·¹, LAUCH¹·²

laun *see* LAWN

launch *see* LENCH

†laurean, lawrean *n* laurel *Laurus nobilis la14-16*. [variant of ME *laurel* or *laurer*]

†laureate¹·¹ *v* **1** to confer a university degree on *17-e18*. **2** to be admitted to a university degree, graduate *16-e18*. **3** to crown or be crowned with a laurel wreath *la15-e17*. [see the adj]

laureate¹·², **†laureat, †lawriate** /ˈlɔrɪət, ˈlɔrɪet/ *adj* **1** *of a person* worthy of being crowned with laurel; *of a poet* supreme, pre-eminent *la15-*. **2** *of writing or speech* excellent, eloquent; worthy of a laurel wreath *16-*. **3** holding a degree; having graduated *17*. [Lat *laureātus* crowned with laurel]

laureation /lɔrɪˈeʃən/ *n* **1** university graduation; the act of receiving a degree *17-*. **2** the complimentary speech with which honorary graduates are promoted *la19-*. [LAUREATE¹·¹, with noun-forming suffix]

Laurence, Lawrence, †Lowrence /ˈlɔrəns/ *n* **1** the name of a saint *16-*. **2** a name given to a fox *15-16*. **Laurencemas** the feast of St Laurence *la19- Sh*. **St Laurence Fair, †Sanct Lowrence fair** a fair held St Laurence Day (in mid-August) in various towns *la16-*. [from the personal name Lat *Laurentius*]

laurye *see* LARY

lauteth *see* LAWTITH

lauth *see* LATH

lav *see* LAAV¹·¹, LAAV¹·²

†lavatoure *n* **1** a place for washing; a vessel for ceremonial or ritual washing *e16*. **2** the spiritual cleansing of baptism *e16*. [Fr *lavatoire* washing, place for washing]

lave¹, †lafe, †laeffe, †leife /lev/ *n* the rest, the remainder; what is left *la14-*. **an a the lave o't** and all the rest of it *la18-19, 20- NE*. **ane amang the lave** one among many *19, 20- NE*. [OE *lāf*]

lave², †lawe, †leave /lev/ *v* **1** to bale or empty out water with a bucket or scoop *16-*. **2** to wash, bathe *la16-19, 20- literary*. [OE *lafian*]

lave *see* LEAVE¹

lavell *see* LEVEL¹·¹, LEVEL¹·²

lavellan /ləˈvɛlən/ *n* the water-shrew *Neomys fodiens la17- N*. [Gael *la-bhallan*]

lave-luggit, †leave-lugged, †lave-lugged /levˈlʌɡɪt/ *adj* having drooping ears *la17-18, 19- Bor*; compare *laavie-luggit* (LAAV¹·²). [ME *lave* drooping (of the ears) + LUG¹]

laven *see* LEAVEN

laverock, larick, lairock, *Ork* **laveroo**, *N* **lairag**, *NE* **livrock, †laverok** /ˈlavərək, ˈlɛvrək, ˈlarək, ˈlerək; *Ork* ˈlavəru; *Ork* ˈlevru; *N* ˈlerəɡ; *NE* ˈlɪvrək/ *n* the skylark *Alauda arvensis 15-*. [OE *lāwerce*]

lavie /ˈlavi/ *n on St Kilda* the guillemot *Uria aalge* or razorbill *Alca torda la17-19, 20- historical*. [Gael *làmhaidh*, ON *langvé*]

lavilugget *see* LAAV¹·²

lavish *see* LOVISH

lavvy, lavvie /ˈlavi, ˈlave/ *n* a lavatory *20-*. **lavvy diver** a plumber *la20-*. **lavvy heid** a term of abuse for a person *21-*. [reduced form of Eng *lavatory*]

law¹·¹, **laa, †lauch** /lɔ, la/ *n* **1** the (body of) statutory or customary rules of a state or community *la14-*. **2** judicial action, enforcement of the law *la14-*. **lawfu, lawful, †lauchfull** permitted or recognized by law *la14-*. **lawyer, lawer, laawer,** *SW* **lawvyer, †lawwer, †lawier 1** a person trained in the law; a solicitor or advocate *la16-*. **2** a university professor of law *la16-e19*. **3** *pl* specific points of law cited in support of a plea; the legal basis of a case *la15-e16*. **law agent** a solicitor *la18-*. **†law-biding** submitting to the law *la16-17*. **†law day** a day on which courts could be lawfully held *15-16*. **lawful day** a day on which it is permissible to transact business; a day on which a court is in session *16-*. **†lawfere** a lawful partner, a person in partnership with another by legal agreement *e17*. **law lord** one of the judges of the Court of Session, to whom the courtesy title of lord is given *18-*. **law-paper** a legal document *19, 20- Ork WC*. **law plea** a lawsuit, a process of litigation *la18-*. **law sovertie** surety that a person would not injure another *16-17*. **†law-wark, law-work** theology based on Mosaic law, implying formal morality rather than evangelical religion *17-19*. **†the law of Clan Macduff** a privilege granted to the kin of the Earls of Fife of remission of the penalty of slaughter, on payment of compensation by the slayer *15-16*. [OE *lagu* law]

law¹·² /lɔ/ *v* **1** to go to law, litigate; to pursue in court, sue *19, 20- Ork NE SW*. **2** to control or determine *la18-e19*. [see the noun]

law² /lɔ/ *n* **1** an isolated or conspicuous rounded or conical hill; frequently in place-names *12-*. **2** a mound of earth and shingle on a riverbank to which salmon nets are brought ashore *la16-e19*. **3** an artificial mound or hillock; a gravemound *la16-e19*. [OE *hlǣw*]

law *see* LOW¹·¹, LOW¹·², LOW¹·³

lawage *see* LOVISH

lawboard *see* LABROD

†law-borch, law-borgh *n* a person who stood surety for someone that they would not injure another *la15-16*. Compare LAWBURROWS. **draw oneself law-borgh** to pledge oneself not to injure another *la15*. [LAW¹·¹ + OE *borg* a guarantee of security]

lawbour *see* LABOUR¹·¹, LABOUR¹·²

lawburrows, †law-borowis /lɔˈbʌroz, ˈlɔbʌrəs/ *npl* **1** law security required by or given by a person that they will not injure another *15-*. **2** an injunction; a strict condition *20- Ork*. Compare LAW-BORCH. **letters of lawburrows, †letters of lawborrowis** the warrant charging a person to give security against injuring another *16-20, 21- historical*. [LAW¹·¹ + OE *borgas* guarantees of security]

lawch *see* LAUCH¹·²

lawchtir *see* LAUCHTER

lawd *see* LAD, LAWIT

lawe *see* LAVE²

†lawic *adj* lay, not of the clergy *la15-e17*. [altered form of LAWIT]

lawid *see* LAWIT

lawin, lawing /ˈlɔən, ˈlɔɪŋ/ *n* **1** a bill for food and drink supplied in a public house; a person's share of the reckoning *16-*. **2** retribution, consequences *la18-19, 20- literary*. **3** a contribution towards the refreshments at a wedding *17-19*. **4** a drinking party (in a tavern) *16-17*. [derivative of LAUCH²]

†lawit, lawid, lawd *adj* **1** lay, secular *la14-e17*. **2** unlearned; unpolished *la14-16*. Compare LEWD. [OE *lǣwede*; compare LAWIC]

Lawland[1.1], **Lowland** /'lɔlənd, 'loländ/ *n* **1** the Scottish Lowlands (east and south of the Highland line) *la15-*. **2** low-lying land *la15-*. [LOW[1.1] + LAND[1.1]]

Lawland[1.2], **Lowland** /'lɔlənd, 'loländ/ *adj* belonging to or characteristic of the Lowlands of Scotland *16-*. **Lowland Bagpipe** a bagpipe in which the air is supplied by a set of bellows *la19-*. **Lowland Scots** the variety of the Scots language spoken to the south and east of the Highland line *18-*. [see the noun]

Lawlander, Lowlander /'lɔləndər, 'oländər/ *n* a native or inhabitant of the Scottish Lowlands *17-*. [LAWLAND[1.1], with agent suffix]

Lawlands, Lowlands /'lɔləndz, 'oländz/ *n* **1** the Scottish Lowlands (east and south of the Highland line) *la15-*. **2** a low-lying area, low-lying lands *17-*. Compare LAWLAND[1.1]. [LOW[1.2] + LAND[1.1]]

Lawlans see LALLANS

lawman, †**lagman** /'lɔmən/ *n in Shetland and Orkney* the president and legal assessor of the LAWTHING and other courts *14-16, 19- historical*. [ON lögmaðr; compare Norw *lagmann*]

lawn, †**laun**, †**lane**, †**lan** /lɔn/ *n* a fine fabric, originally linen *15-*. [perhaps from the French place-name *Laon*]

lawpell /lɔˈpɛl/ *n* a loose tuft of wool on a sheep's fleece *la19- Sh*. [LAGET + PELL[1]]

lawrean see LAUREAN

Lawrence see LAURENCE

lawriate see LAUREATE[1.2]

†**lawricht-aith, larycht aithe** *n in Shetland* an oath sworn by an accused person as to his innocence, and by two witnesses as to his character *la16-e17*. [ON lýritar-eiðr]

†**lawrichtman, lawrightman, lawrikman** *n* **1** *in Shetland* the official in charge of weights and measures *la15-19*. **2** *in Orkney* an official who served as a local delegate to the central court and acted as chancellor of the assize and legal assessor in the parish courts; a local peace-officer *15-e19*. [ON lögréttumaðr]

lawry see LARY

lawthing, †**lawting**, †**lating** /'lɔθɪŋ/ *n in Orkney and Shetland* the supreme court of judicature *la15-19, 20- historical*. [ON lögþing]

lawtith, lawtie, †**lauteth,** †**leaute** /'lɔtɪθ, 'lɔti/ *n* **1** loyalty; integrity, honourable behaviour *la14-19, 20- literary*. **2** the truth *la14-15*. [OFr *leaute*]

lax, lox /laks, lɔks/ *n* a salmon *la14-*. **lax fisher** a salmon fisherman *14-*. **lax net** salmon-net *la15-*. [ON *lax*]

lay[1.1] /le/ *n* **1** the act of lying down or resting; a rest *19-*. **2** the re-steeling of the cutting edge of an implement *la18-*. [see the verb]

lay[1.2] /le/ *v* **1** to place or set down; to set in position; to lie flat *la14-*. **2** to set a table; to spread a tablecloth *la14-*. **3** to put down a foundation; to build or construct; to establish *la14-*. **4** to re-steel an iron implement *la16-*. **5** to flatten crops by wind or rain *la18-*. **6** to play a curling stone *la19-*. **7** to make a rope or cord by twisting strands together *15-19, 20- NE*. **8** to smear a sheep's wool with butter and tar as a winter protection *la17-19, 20- N*. **9** to plant a hedge *la18- EC SW Bor*. **10** to silence or check speech or noise *16-e19*. **11** to set aside; to put out of action *15-e17*. **12** to deliver or supply *la16-17*. **13** to audit accounts *16-17*. **14** to wager *la15-16*. **15** to allot land *la14-e17*. **16** to pay out money *la15*. **lay-bag** the ovary of a fowl *19-*. **laid drain** a field drain formed by stones laid on each side and flat stones laid above these *19-*. **lay pock, lay pyock** = *lay-bag 19- Sh N NE*. †**laid wark** couched work, embroidery where thread was laid flat on the surface and then held in place by stitches *17*. **laid wool** wool from sheep which have been smeared with butter and tar *17-19, 20- historical*. **be laid aff yer feet** to be incapacitated by illness *la19-*. **lay aboot, lay about** to turn a boat around *la19-*. †**lay anker** to drop anchor *15-e17*. **lay aside** to put out of the way; to get rid of *16-*. **lay at 1** to strike at, beat *la19-*. **2** to act with vigour; to work hard *20- Sh Ork*. **3** to keep a rowing-boat stationary *20- Sh*. **lay awa** *of a fowl* to lay eggs away from the usual nest *19-*. **lay by 1** to discard, set aside *la14-*. **2** to store away, retain *16-*. **3** to discourage; to desist *18-*. **4** to incapacitate through illness *la18-*. **lay doon** to bury *19-*. **lay doon a mooth upon** *of an animal* to graze *20- Sh*. **lay frae you 1** to hit out in all directions *19-*. **2** to set aside; to take off clothing *la14-17*. †**lay furth** to remove furniture from a house (in evicting a tenant) *16*. †**lay furth on breid** to extend, spread out *16*. **lay in 1** to put in place *16-*. **2** to set to work energetically *la19-*. **3** to fold over; to turn up a hem *19-*. **4** *forestry* to hack a tree around the trunk before felling (to prevent it splitting) *20-*. **5** to stock up *20-*. **6** *knitting* to decrease *20- Sh*. **7** to pay in kind *16-17*. **8** to build a dam; to dam or bank up a river or pond *la16-17*. **9** to supply building materials *la17*. **10** to restore a piece of ground to the common land from which it had been taken *e17*. **lay into, lay intil** to eat greedily *la19-*. **lay on 1** to beat, strike *la14-*. **2** *of rain or snow* to fall heavily *15-*. **3** to work hard; to apply energy *19-*. **4** to eat heartily *la19-*. **5** to charge with a responsibility; to place confidence in *la14-e17*. **lay out** to spread out or unfold *la15-*. **lay ower 1** to turn over a furrow in ploughing *20-* **2** to paint *16-e17*. **lay past** to discard or put away *20-*. **lay till, lay tae 1** to beat *19-*. **2** to set to; to work vigorously *la19-*. **3** to start to eat *la18-19, 20- Sh Ork N Uls*. **4** to close a door *la19- Sh Ork N NE*. †**lay to se, lay to the se** to put ships to sea *e15*. **lay up 1** to heap or pile up; to assemble or make ready *la19- Sh Ork*. **2** *knitting* to cast on *20- Sh Ork*. **3** to put a load on a horse's back *20- Sh*. **lay up guddicks** see GUDDICK. †**lay up mittens** to kill a person *la18-e19*. **lay wi** to work hard, exert oneself strenuously *la19- Sh Ork*. [OE lecgan]

lay[2] /le/ *n* **1** *weaving* the framed part of a loom which strikes home each successive weft thread; the batten *la16-*. **2** a turning lathe *20-*. [MDu *laey*]

†**lay**[3.1] *n* an alloy *la14-17*. **layit** alloyed; *of coinage* debased *16-17*. [aphetic form of OFr *alay*]

†**lay**[3.2] *adj of coinage* made of alloy, debased *la16-17*. [see the noun]

†**lay**[4] *n* delay *15-e16*. [aphetic form of Eng *delay*]

lay[5] /le/ *n* mood, disposition *la19- Sh Ork EC*. [perhaps Norw *lag*]

lay[6] /le/ *n* **1** a lull between breakers during which a boat may dart through the surf to the beach *la17- Sh Ork N*. **2** a wave, a breaker *20- Sh*. **laebrack, laybreak** the surf, the breaking of waves on the beach *la19- Sh*. [ON *lag* a lull between breakers]

lay see LEY[1.1], LEY[1.2], LIE[1.2]

lay aff[1.1] /le af/ *n* a harangue, a rigmarole *20-*. [see the verb]

lay aff[1.2] /le 'af/ *v* to recount fluently; to talk volubly and confidently *la19-*. [LAY[1.2] + AFF[1.3]]

layer see LAIR[1.1]

†**layit** *adj* of or relating to the laity *16*. Compare LAWIC, LAWIT. [altered form of ME *laic*]

laylock /'lelək, 'lelɔk/ *n* lilac *Syringa vulgaris la18-*. [altered form of Eng *lilac*]

†**layne**[1.1], **lane, lain** *n* concealment *15-16*. **but lane** without concealment, in truth *15-16*. [ON *leyni*]

layne[1.2], †**lain**, †**lane**, †**len** /len/ *v* to conceal; to remain silent about; to suppress the truth *la14-19, 20- literary*. [ON *leyna* to hide, keep secret]

lay-on /'le ɔn/ *n* a hearty meal; a surfeit *la19-*. [LAY[1.2] + ON[1.1]]

laytil see LITTLE[1,2]

†**lazarus, lazarous** *n* a leper *la15-16*. [from the biblical name *Lazarus*, the patron saint of lepers]

lazy[1.1] /'leze, 'lezi/ *n* a fit of laziness *20-*. [unknown]

lazy[1.2], †**lasie** /'leze, 'lezi/ *adj* **1** idle, slothful *la16-*. **2** *of land* uncultivated, fallow *18-*. **lazy bed** an undug strip of soil on which potatoes or seeds are laid and covered over with manure and sods from an adjacent trench *18- H&I Uls*. [unknown]

†**le, lie, ly** *def art preceding vernacular forms in Latin texts* the: ◊*Piscaria de le Redhowch la12-19*. [AN *le*, OFr *li*; compare LEZ]

le see LEE[1.1], LEE[1.2], LEE[2.1], LEE[2.2], LEY[1.1]

lea see LEAVE[1], LEY[1.1], LEY[1.2]

lead[1.1] /lid/ *n* **1** the act of leading; direction or guidance *la18-*. **2** *curling* the first player on each side *19, 20- WC SW*. **3** *curling* the course or rink *19*. **follow yer ain lead** to do as you please *20-*. [see the verb]

lead[1.2], †**lede,** †**leid** /lid/ *v pt, ptp* **led** †**leid 1** to conduct, escort, guide *la14-*. **2** to command, rule, govern *la14-*. **3** to convey; to cart; to transport *la14-*. **4** to spend one's life *la14-*. **5** *of a road or way* to go somewhere *la14-*. **6** to carry harvested grain or hay from the field to the stackyard; to bring home peats from the moss *la14-*. **7** *law* to call or produce evidence, testimony or witnesses *15-*. **8** *curling* to lead off for one's side, play first *19-*. **9** *law* to conduct legal proceedings, hold a court; to bring an action or deliver a judgement *15-19*. **10** to guide another's hand in writing *16*. **led farm** a smaller or outlying farm managed through an employee *la18-*. **lead by the neb** to have a person under total control *20-*. [OE *lǣdan*]

lead see LADE, LEID[2]

leader, †**ledar** /'lidər/ *n* **1** a person or thing that leads, guides or directs *la14-*. **2** a carter or carrier of goods *la15-19, 20-historical*. **3** a tributary of a stream *la19-*. **4** a tendon, a sinew *la19-*. **5** an extension in a salmon-net to lead the fish into the main trap *20- N NE SW Bor*. **6** *law* a person who administered the law *la15-16*. [OE *lǣdere*]

leaf, †**lefe,** †**leif** /lif/ *n pl* **leafs,** †**levis,** †**leiffis 1** an item of foliage, a leaf of a plant *la14-*. **2** a page of a book; a sheet of paper *la15-*. **3** a section or hinged flap of a table or door *16-*. **4** a segment of an orange *20-*. [OE *lēaf*]

leaf see LEIF[1.2], LOAF

league, †**lege,** †**lig,** †**lieg** /lig/ *n* **1** an alliance; an association *la15-*. **2** The Solemn League and Covenant *17-*. [MFr *ligue*, Lat *liga*]

leak see LECK[1.1], LECK[1.2]

leal[1.1], †**lele,** †**leill** /lil/ *adj* **1** loyal, faithful *la14-*. **2** honest, honourable, law-abiding *la14-*. **3** true, accurate; genuine; legally valid *la14-*. **4** *of a measure* fair, exact *15-19, 20- historical*. **5** *of a woman* chaste, pure *18-19*. **6** faithful in religion; Christian *la14-15*. **lealty** loyalty *19-*. **leal-heartit** faithful, sincere *18-*. **bear leal and soothfast witness,** †**bere lele and suthefast witnes** to give a truthful testimony *la14-*. [OFr *leel, leal*]

†**leal**[1.2], **lele** *adv* **1** loyally, honestly, sincerely *15-e19*. **2** truly, accurately, thoroughly *15-e19*. **leal becumit** lawfully obtained, honestly earned *17*. **leil won** honestly gained *la15-16*. [see the adj]

leam[1.1], **leme** /lim/ *n* a gleam or ray of light; radiance *la14-19, 20- literary*. [OE *lēoma*]

leam[1.2], **leme** /lim/ *v* to shine, glitter, flash; to glow or gleam with light *la14-19, 20- literary*. [see the noun]

leam[2] /lim/ *v* to take a ripe nut from its husk; *of a nut* to drop out of its husk when ripe *19- SW Bor*. **leamer, leammer** a ripe nut *19, 20- SW Bor*. [unknown]

leam see LAME[1.1], LAME[1.2], LOOM[2]

lean[1.1] *n* a rest; a resting-place, a seat *la18-19, 20- T EC*. [see the verb]

lean[1.2], *Sh* **lin,** †**lene** /lin; *Sh* lɪn/ *v* **1** to incline or bend *la14-*. **2** to recline, lie down; to rest, take a seat *la14-*. [OE *hlinian*]

lean see LEN[1.2]

leap, †**lepe** /lip/ *v pt* **leapt,** †**lap, lape, lapt,** *Sh Ork* **lep,** *ptp* **leapt, luppen,** †**loppin 1** to jump, bound, spring *la14-*. **2** to rush, dash or dart *la14-*. **3** *of things* to spring forth, fly apart *la14-*. **4** *of frost* to thaw *19-*. **5** *of potatoes being boiled in their skins* to burst open *20- EC SW*. **6** *of the face* to flush, blush; to erupt with a rash *20- Sh Bor*. **7** to emerge; to escape *la14-19*. **8** *of animals* to mount, copulate with *16*. †**leaping-on-stone** a mounting-block *la17-19*. **luppen sinnen** a ganglion, a swelling or tumour *la19- C SW Uls*. †**lepe abak, lepe back** to back out of an agreement *16-e17*. [OE *hlēapan*; compare LOWP[1.2]]

leap see LEEP[1.1]

lear, leir, †**lere** /lir/ *v* **1** to teach or instruct *la14-*. **2** to acquire knowledge, ascertain *la14-*. **leared,** †**lerit** educated; belonging to the clergy *15-19, 20- literary*. †**leir a lesson** to follow advice or an example *15-16*. [OE *lǣran* to teach]

lear see LAIR[3]

leard see LAIRD[1.1]

learn, lairn, *NE* **leern,** †**lerne** /lɛrn, lern; *NE* lirn/ *v* **1** to acquire knowledge, ascertain *la15-*. **2** to teach *la15-*. [OE *leornian*]

lease[1.1] /liz/ *n* **1** *weaving* the division of the threads in a warp before it is put on the loom *19, 20- WC*. **2** a coherent train of thought; a clear understanding of a story or idea: ◊*I lost the lease o't la19, 20- C SW Uls*. [see the verb]

lease[1.2] /liz/ *v* **1** *weaving* to separate or sort out the yarn for the warp threads *19- C Bor*. **2** to arrange in order; to sort; to disentangle or tidy up *19- SW Bor*. [OE *lesan* to glean, gather]

lease[2], †**leese** /liz/ *v* to tell lies; to slander *18- literary*. [compare LEIZED]

lease[3], †**lese** /lis/ *v* to release *17-19, 20- literary*. [aphetic form of *release*]

lease see LESS[3]

leaser see LEISURE

leash[1.1], †**lesch,** †**leich** /liʃ/ *n* **1** a lead or thong for securing a dog (or other animal) *la14-*. **2** a long piece of string, rope or thread *19-*. **3** a whip, a lash; a stroke of a whip *16-19, 20- Sh EC*. **4** a long distance; a large amount *19, 20- NE*. **5** a set of three hounds *16*. [OFr *lesse, laisse*]

leash[1.2], **leesh,** †**lesch** /liʃ/ *v* **1** to lash or tie together *la19-*. **2** to whip, flog *16-19, 20- Sh*. **3** to move or work quickly or energetically *18-19 , 20- Sh NE Bor*. **4** *of rain* to fall in torrents *20- Sh T*. [see the noun]

leasing, †**lesing,** †**leising,** †**lesine** /'lizɪŋ, 'lisɪŋ/ *n* **1** the act of lying or slandering *la14-*. **2** a lie, a piece of slander *15-e19*. **leasing-maker,** †**lesing maker** a person guilty of slander likely to cause sedition; a liar *15-19, 20- historical*. **leasing-making** *law* the making of slanderous statements which could prejudice relations between a monarch and his or her subjects; verbal sedition *la16-19, 20- historical*. [OE *lēasung*] .

least[1], **lest,** †**leist** /list, lɛst/ *conj* for fear that, in case *la16-*. †**least that, leist that** for fear that *la16-e19*. [OE *þy lǣs þe*]

least[2.1], *Sh Ork* **laest,** *Sh* **leste** /list; *Sh Ork* lest/ *adj* smallest; slightest; lowest *la14-*. **leastest** the very least or smallest *la19- Sh NE T H&I*. **leastways, leastwise** at least *la19-*. [OE *lǣst*]

least[2.2], *Sh Ork* **laest**, †**lest** /list; *Sh Ork* lest/ *adv* **1** in the lowest degree, to the smallest extent *la14-*. **2** at least *19, 20- Ork*. [see the adj]
leasure *see* LEISURE
leat *see* LATE
leath *see* LAITH[1.3]
leather[1.1], **laither**, *Sh Ork NE* **ledder**, *NE* **laidder**, †**lether**, †**leddir** /ˈlɛðər, ˈlɛðər; *Sh Ork NE* lɛdər; *NE* ˈlɛdər/ *n* **1** tanned animal skin *15-*. **2** human skin; the hide of an animal *16-*. **3** a heavy blow *20-*. **leadern**, *NE* **leddern**, †**ledderin**, †**letherin** made of leather *la15-*. [OE *leþer*]
leather[1.2], *Sh Ork NE* **ledder**, *NE* **laidder**, †**lether** /ˈlɛðər; *Sh Ork NE* lɛdər; *NE* ˈlɛdər/ *v* **1** to beat, thrash *la18-*. **2** to do something fast and energetically; to work hard *19-*. **3** to hurry, walk briskly *19- NE EC Bor*. **4** *of a hound* to tear the skin of its quarry *16*. [see the noun]
leauch *see* LAICH[1.3]
leauche *see* LAICH[1.4]
leaute *see* LAWTITH
leave[1], **laive**, **lave**, **leve**, **lea**, **lee**, *Sh* **laeve**, †**lefe** /liv, lev, li; *Sh* ˈleəv/ *v pt* **left**, *NE* **leeft 1** to depart, go away *la14-*. **2** to allow to remain (in the same place or condition) *la14-*. **3** to cease, desist, discontinue *la14-*. **4** to bequeath (in a will) *15-*. **5** to accompany or escort someone (home) *20- H&I Uls*. **leavins**, †**levyngis** left-overs *16-*. †**left** abandoned by God *18-e19*. **leaving certificate** *see* CERTIFICATE. **leave aside** putting aside; not counting: ◊*leave aside this cup, I've drunk nae tea the day la19-*. **leave me alone for** trust me to complete or deal with *19-*. **left to yersel** misguided, led astray *18-*. [OE *lǣfan*]
leave[2.1], †**leve**, †**lefe** /liv/ *n* **1** permission, dispensation *la14-*. **2** dismissal (from a job); notice to quit *la15-*. **3** approval for a pupil to leave the classroom during a school lesson *20-*. **4** the playtime interval in school *20-*. **leave taking** the action of taking leave or saying farewell *la14-*. †**get one's leave** to be discharged or dismissed *17-19*. [OE *lēaf*]
leave[2.2], †**leve**, †**lefe** /liv/ *v* to permit, allow *la14-*. [see the noun]
leave *see* LAVE[2]
leave-lugged *see* LAVE-LUGGIT
leaven, †**laven** /ˈlɛvən/ *n* **1** yeast; fermenting dough *16-*. **2** oatmeal and water made up as a dough for oatcakes or as food for young poultry *18-19, 20- Sh N NE T EC*. †**laventub** the vessel in which dough is mixed and leavened *16*. [MFr *levain*]
leave-o /ˈlivo/ *n* a children's game of capture and release *20-*. [from a call made in the game, reduced from Eng *relieve-o*]
leb *see* LAIB[1.2]
lebbach *see* LAIB[1.1]
lecence *see* LEESHENCE[1.1]
lecent *see* LICENT
lecentiat *see* LICENTIATE[1.1]
leche *see* LATCH[2]
lecher, †**lichour**, †**lechour** /ˈlɛtʃər/ *n* a lewd or lustful man *la14-*. **lechery**, †**lichory** lewdness; excessive lust *la14-*. [OFr *lecheor, liceour*]
lechful *see* LEFUL
lechour *see* LECHER
leck[1.1], **leak**, †**lake**, †**lek** /lɛk, lik/ *n* **1** an unintended hole (through which liquid passes), a leak *16-*. **2** a container with a means of drawing off tanning liquid (from steeping bark) *18-19*. †**lekkage**, **laikage** wastage of imported wine by leaking from the barrels; an allowance made for this in charging duty *16-e17*. **leaky tide** a tide in the upper part of the Firth of Forth which appears to lose water temporarily before the full tide, and gain it before the ebb *18- EC*. [Ger *Leck*, MDu, LG *lek*]

leck[1.2], **leak**, †**lake**, †**lek** /lɛk, lik/ *v* **1** *of liquid, light or gas* to escape, flow out (through a hole) *la15-*. **2** *of a ship* to let in water; *of a container* to let water escape *16-*. **3** *of rain* to fall in intermittent showers *17-19, 20- Sh Ork EC Bor Uls*. [see the noun]
†**leck**[1.3], **lek**, **laik** *adj of a ship* leaky *16-17* [see the noun]
leck[2], †**lek** /lɛk/ *n* **1** a flat stone or slab; a flat rock or rocky ledge in the sea; frequently in place-names *19, 20- NE SW*. **2** an igneous rock which breaks into slabs; a piece of this used as an oven-slab *17-19*. †**leckstone**, **lek stain** an oven-slab *17-19*. [Gael *leac* a slab, a ledge of rock]
leckerstane, **lickarstane**, †**likarstane** /ˈlɛkərsten, ˈlikərsten/ *n* a large conspicuous stone or stone-heap, traditionally associated with burials; frequently in place-names *15-19, 20- historical*. [unknown first element + STANE[1.1]]
†**leckie**, **lakay** *n* a lackey *la16-e18*. Compare ALLEKAY. [ME *lakey*]
lectern *see* LATERAN
†**lection**[1] *n* a university lecture; a lesson *la16-17*. [Lat *lectio* a lesson, a lecture]
†**lection**[2] *n* election *la15-17*. [OFr *lectiun*]
lector, †**lectour** /ˈlɛktər/ *n* **1** a reader *la15-*. **2** a lecturer in a university *la16-19*. **3** a pupil learning to read *16-e18*. **4** a clerk, a scribe *la16-e17*. †**lector schole** an elementary school *la16-e17*. [Lat *lector*]
lectroun *see* LATERAN
lecture[1.1] /ˈlɛktʃər/ *n* **1** a lesson or discourse on a given subject (in a university or college) *la15-*. **2** *Presbyterian Church* a reading of a passage of scripture (with commentary) *la16-19*. [Lat *lectūra*]
lecture[1.2] /ˈlɛktʃər/ *v* **1** to deliver a lecture *18-*. **2** *Presbyterian Church* to deliver a scriptural reading with commentary *18-e19*. [see the noun]
lecturi /ˈlɛktəri/ *numeral in sheep-counting* seven *20- SW*. [nonsense word derived from a system of counting of sheep]
led *see* LAID[1.1], LEAD[1.2], LEDE[1], LID
ledar *see* LEADER
ledd *see* LEID[2]
ledder[1.1], **ladder**, **lether**, *NE* **laidder** /ˈlɛdər, ˈladər, ˈlɛðər; *NE* ˈlɛdər/ *n* a runged structure (for climbing), a ladder *la14-*. [OE *hlǣder*]
†**ledder**[1.2], **leddir** *v* to set a ladder to a wall; to scale with a ladder *15-e18*. [see the noun]
ledder *see* LEATHER[1.1], LEATHER[1.2]
leddir *see* LEATHER[1.1], LEDDER[1.2]
leddy, **lady**, *Ork* **lethy** /ˈlede, ˈlede; *Ork* ˈlɛði/ *n* **1** a gentlewoman; a woman of rank or title *la14-*. **2** the Virgin Mary *la14-*. **3** the title prefixed to the name of an estate and to a female landowner or wife of a landowner *la15-*. **ladyness** the quality or character of a lady *19, 20- Ork T EC Uls*. **lady's beds** lady's bedstraw *Galium verum la19-*. **leddy body** a ladylike woman *20- Ork NE T*. **lady-bracken**, **lady-breckan** the lady fern *Athyrium filix-femina 19- NE SW Bor Uls*. **lady's clover** wood sorrel *Oxalis acetosella la19- T Uls*. **lady's fingers** the cowslip *Primula veris la19- EC*. **lady's gairtens**, **lady's garters 1** the striped ribbongrass *Phalaris arundinacea picta la19-*. **2** the blackberry *Rubus fruticosus la18-e19*. †**lady's gown** *law* a gift made by a buyer to the seller's wife on her renouncing her liferent in the seller's estate *18-e19*. **lady's hen** the skylark *Alauda arvensis 18- Sh Ork Bor*. **lady lander**, †**leddy-launners**, the ladybird *Coccinella 19- T C Bor*. **lady limpet** the blue-rayed limpet *Patella pellucida 20- Ork*. **lady's meat** the young leaves and buds of the hawthorn *19, 20- N SW*. †**lady**

mes a mass celebrated in honour of the Virgin Mary *15-16*. **lady-nit** the greater plantain *Plantago major 20- Bor*. **lady provost 1** the courtesy title of the wife of a lord provost *20-*. **2** a female lord provost *la20-*. **lady's purse** shepherd's purse *Capsella bursa-pastoris 20- N SW Bor Uls*. †**lady tercer** a widow possessing an inherited liferent *la16-e19*. **ladies' thimbles 1** the foxglove *Digitalis purpurea la19-*. **2** the harebell *Campanula rotundifolia la19, 20- Uls*. **leddie wylk** a species of mollusc, *Gibbula cineraria*, with a bluntly conical striped shell *20- Sh*. **ladies from hell** a nickname for kilted Scottish soldiers (originally applied to the Black Watch by the Germans during WWI) *20-*. **ladies in their carriages** monkshood *Aconitum napellus 20- T Uls*. †**lady of terce** a widow possessing an inherited liferent *16*. **lady o the meadow** meadowsweet *Filipendula ulmaria 19- N SW*. **Our Lady's Ellwand** Orion's Belt *18-19, 20- Ork*. [OE *hlǣfdige*]

†**lede¹, leid, led** *n* a person; a man *la15-e17*. **all leidis** all people, everyone *la15-e16*. **all levandleid** all living people *16-e17*. [OE *lēod* a man, a prince]

†**lede²**, **leid** *n* a nation; people *la14-16*. [OE *lēode* people]

lede *see* LEAD¹,², LEID¹, LEID²

ledge¹ /lɛdʒ/ *n* **1** a raised edge or projection; a shelf of rock *17-*. **2** a narrow horizontal surface *19-*. †**ledging** the parapet of a bridge *17-e19*. **ledgit** the top of the lower sash of a window *la19- NE*. [ME *legge*; compare LAY¹,²]

†**ledge²** *v* to assert, declare; to accuse *19*. [aphetic form of ALLEGE]

lee¹·¹, lie, †ley, †le /li, lae/ *n pl* †**lyis 1** a falsehood *la15-*. **2** a false or inaccurate statement (made by mistake) *20-*. **lee-like** false, lying; fictional *19, 20- SW Bor*. **leesome** incredible; shocking *la19- C SW Bor*. **leesome-like** incredible, implausible *19- WC SW Bor*. [OE *lyge*]

lee¹·², lie, †ley, †le /li, lae/ *v* **1** to tell lies *la14-*. **2** to say something in error (without intention to deceive) *la19-*. †**lee in your throat** to lie unashamedly *17-19*. **lie on** to tell lies about, slander *la14-*. [OE *lēogan*]

lee²·¹, †le /li/ *n* shelter; the sheltered side; a sheltered place or state *la14-*. [OE *hlēo*]

lee²·², †le /li/ *adj* sheltered (from the wind) *la15-*. **lea-laik** sheltered *19- WC SW*. **lee-gaw** a sign of bad weather in the leeward part of the sky *20- N NE*. **lee-side** the side of a pot boiling less fiercely *18-19, 20- Ork SW*. [see the noun]

lee *see* LEAVE¹, LEIF¹·¹, LEIF¹·², LUIF, LYE

leebel *see* LIBEL¹·¹, LIBEL¹·²

leeberal, leibral, liberal /'lɪbərəl, 'lɪbrəl, 'lɪbərəl/ *adj* **1** generous; broad-minded *la14-*. **2** *of offspring* legitimate *16*. [ME *liberal*, Lat *līberālis*]

leeberty /'lɪbərte/ *n* liberty *19-*. [AN, MFr *liberté*]

leebral *see* LEEBERAL

leebrary, library, †**liberary** /'lɪbrəre, 'laebrəre/ *n* a repository of books *la16-*. [MFr *librairie*]

leecure, leeker, †**licour,** †**liquour** /'lɪkər/ *n* **1** a liquid or fluid; a beverage *15-*. **2** alcohol, spirits; a liqueur *la18-*. [altered form of ME *licour*]

leed *see* LEID¹, LEID²

leeft *see* LEAVE¹

leefu, †**leful** /'lifu/ *adj* **1** solitary *19-*. **2** kind-hearted, considerate, compassionate *18-19*. **3** willing, ready *la15-16*. **yer leefu lane** all by oneself, solitary *18-*. [LEIF¹·¹, with *-fu* suffix]

leek, †**leke** /lik/ *n* **1** a vegetable of the onion family *Allium porrum la14-*. **2** something of little value *la14-e17*. [OE *lēac*]

leek *see* LYKE

leeker *see* LEECURE

leelang /'lilaŋ/ *adj* of a long duration; whole, entire *la18-19, 20- literary*. **the leelang day** the whole day *la18-19, 20- literary*. †**the leelang nicht** the whole night *la18-19*. [LEIF¹·² + LANG¹·¹]

leem *see* LUME

leemit¹·¹, limit /'limit, 'lɪmɪt/ *n* a boundary or margin; the furthest point or extent (of something) *15-*. [ME *limite*, Lat *līmes*]

leemit¹·², limit /'limit, 'lɪmɪt/ *v ptp also* †**limit** †**lemit 1** to restrict or confine; to set bounds or a boundary *16-*. **2** to ordain or designate (a time or place); to appoint (a person) *la14-17*. [AN *limeter*, Lat *līmitāre*]

leemon, lemon, †**limon** /'lɪmən, 'lɛmən/ *n* a citrus fruit, a lemon *la16-*. **leemonade** lemonade *la19-*. [MFr *limon*]

leen /lin/ *n* a meadow, a pasture *la18- N*. [ON *læna* a hollow or valley or Gael *lèana* a meadow]

leen *see* LIN

leenge /linʒ/ *v* to slouch in walking *19- EC Bor*. [unknown]

†**leengyie, lignie, lenʒe** *adj* fine; thin; slender *la14-e19*. [OFr *ligne*]

leep¹·¹, leap /lip/ *n* a state of great heat; sweltering weather *19- Sh Ork N*. [see the verb]

leep¹·², †**lepe** /lip/ *v* **1** to heat partially; to parboil *16-*. **2** to become excessively hot *20- Sh Ork N*. **leepit 1** warmed up; parboiled; scalded *18-*. **2** fond of warmth, self-indulgent *18-*. [perhaps OE **hlīepan*; compare ON *hleypa* to cause to leap or rush; to curdle (milk) as by heating it]

Lee-penny /'li pɛni/ *n folklore* a healing talisman in the form of a small stone set in a groat of Edward IV of England, owned by the Lockharts of Lee *19- historical*. [from the name of the barony + PENNY]

leepie *see* LIPPIE

leerie /'liri/ *n* **1** a lamplighter *19-20, 21- historical*. **2** a lamp; the light from a lamp or a candle *la19- literary*. **leerie pole** the pole used by lamplighters *20, 21- historical*. [compare Eng *leer* a furnace used in glassmaking]

†**leerie-la¹·¹** *n* (the call of) a cock *19*. [onomatopoeic]

leerie-la¹·² /'lirila/ *v of a cock* to crow *20- NE T EC*. [see the noun]

leern *see* LEARN

leerup /'lirəp/ *n* a smack; a lash with a whip *19- Ork N NE T* [unknown; compare Du *lerpen, larpen* to whip]

leese *see* LEASE²

leesh *see* LEASH¹·²

leeshence¹·¹, leesense, licence, †**lecence** /'lɪʃəns, 'lɪsəns, 'laesəns/ *n* **1** permission *15-*. **2** an official document granting permission *16-*. **3** *Presbyterian Church* permission (for a probationer) to preach *18-*. **4** a university degree above that of bachelor *la16*. [MFr *licence*, Lat *licentia*]

leeshence¹·², license, †**licence** /'lɪʃəns, 'laesəns/ *v* **1** to grant permission *16-*. **2** *Presbyterian Church* to grant a licence to preach *18-*. [see the noun]

leesome¹ /'lisəm/ *adj* **1** pleasant, lovable *la18-*. **2** *of weather* fine, mild, bright *la18- NE*. **leesome lane** absolutely alone *19-*. [LIEF, with adj-forming suffix]

leesome², †**lessum,** †**lesum,** †**levesum** /'lisəm/ *adj* lawful, permissible; right, just *la15-*. [ME *lefsom*; compare OE *lēaf*, LEAVE²·¹, LEFUL]

leesome *see* LEE¹·¹

leet¹·¹, †**leit,** †**lite** /lit/ *n* **1** a list of selected candidates for a post or office *la16-*. **2** a select or prizewinning animal at an agricultural show *20- SW*. **3** *pl* the nominated candidates for a post or office *la16-17*. **long leet** a first list of selected candidates, to be further selected into a *short leet 18-*. **short leet** the final list of candidates for a post *la18-*. [MFr *liste* a strip, a band; compare MFr dialectal *lite*]

leet[1,2], †**leit**, †**lite** /lit/ v to list or nominate a person as a candidate *la16-*. [see the noun]

leet[2], †**leit** /lit/ n **1** a stack of peats or coal of a specific size *la16-*. **2** a division in an oblong stack of grain or beans *17-19, 20- C*. **leet peats** a quantity of peats delivered as part of a farm tenant's rent *17-19, 20- historical*. [OE *hlīet*, ON *hleyti* a share]

leet[3], †**leit** /lit/ v **1** to make mention; to pass on information *la19-*. **2** to make a sign of acknowledgement; to pay attention, heed *la18-19, 20- Sh Ork N NE*. **3** to pretend *la15-e19*. [OE *lǣtan* to allow; compare LAT]

leet *see* LAT

leetany /ˈlitəni/ n a long rambling story, a rigmarole *19- Sh NE*. [altered form of Older Scots *litanie*]

leetera, **leetery** /ˈlitərə, ˈlitəre/ numeral children's rhymes six *la19-*. [nonsense word derived from a system of counting of sheep]

leeterary, **literary** /ˈlitərəre, ˈlɪtərəre/ adj relating to literature or formal writing; versed in literature *la18-*. [Lat *litterārius*]

leeteratur, **leetratur**, **literature**, †**leteratoure** /ˈlitərətʃər, ˈlitrətʃər, ˈlɪtrətʃər/ n written works; scholarship, learning (on a specific subject) *la14-*. [Lat *litterātūra*]

leeve, **leve**, **live**, †**lefe**, †**lif**, †**luf** /liv, lɪv/ v to be alive; to survive; to continue to spend one's life; to reside *la14-*. **leevin 1** a living being *19-*. **2** food *19-*. †**the langar levand, the langast levand** the survivor *la14-17*. †**the langar levar, the langast levar** = *the langar levand la14-17*. **live aff** to live on *20-*. **livin like** lively, in good health *la19-*. [OE *lifian*]

leever *see* LEIF[1,2]

leeze me *see* LEIF[1,1]

leezure *see* LEISURE

lefe *see* LEAF, LEAVE[1], LEAVE[2,1], LEAVE[2,2], LEEVE, LEIF[1,1]

left /lɛft/ adj the opposite of right *15-*. **left-fitter** derogatory a Roman Catholic *20- C*. **left-hand man** one of the two chief supporters of the cornet or standard-bearer in various Riding of the Marches festivals *20- EC SW Bor*. [ME *lift*]

left *see* LEAVE[1]

†**leful**, **levefull**, **lechful** adj permissible; right, honest, proper *la14-e17*. [ME *lefful*; compare OE *lēaf*, LEAVE[2,1], LEESOME[2]]

leful *see* LEEFU

leg[1,1], **laig**, **leig**, **lig** /lɛg, leg, laeg, lig, lɪg/ n **1** a lower limb, a leg *la14-*. **2** a measure of land relating to a sixteenth of a ploughgate or a quarter of a horsegang *16-*. **3** a support, a prop *la16-19*. **4** = *leg dollor la17*. **leg bail** retreat, flight *la18-*. †**leg dollor**, **leggit dollor** a Dutch silver coin, so called from the device on its reverse *la17-e18*. †**leg sok** a long sock or stocking *la16-e17*. **gie a stane legs** curling to accelerate the pace of a stone by sweeping the ice in front of it *la19-*. **on leg**, **upon leg** on the move, gadding about *19-*. **put legs and airms tae** to add to or embellish (an anecdote) *la19-*. **tak legs** to run off *la18-*. [ON *leggr*]

leg[1,2] /lɛg/ v to walk quickly, run or hurry on foot *la18-*. **leg aff** to set off, depart *la19-*. **leg on** n speed and energy in walking or working *la19-*. **leg on** v to walk or work energetically or quickly *la19-*. [see the noun]

legacy /ˈlɛgəse/ n **1** a bequest, a will or testament *la15-*. **2** a delegation *la14-16*. [OFr *legacie*]

legal[1,1] /ˈligəl/ n law the time allowed for redeeming an inheritance used as security for a debt *17-*. [shortened form of *legal reversion* (LEGAL[1,2])]

legal[1,2] /ˈligəl/ adj **1** of or relating to the law *15-*. **2** *Presbyterian Church* emphasizing the Old Testament doctrine of salvation by good deeds rather than faith alone *18-19, 20- historical*. †**legal reversion** the term fixed by law for redeeming an inheritance used as security for a debt *17*.

legal rights the claims which the surviving spouse and issue have to share in a deceased's estate, whether or not there is a will *la19-*; compare *prior rights* (PRIOR[2]). [Lat *lēgālis*]

legamachie, **lagamachie**, **langamachie** /ləˈgaməxi, laŋˈgaməxi/ n a long-winded, rambling story *19- NE*. [Greek *logomachía* a battle of words]

legate /ləˈget/ v law to bequeath *la16-*. **legator** a person to whom a legacy is left, a legatee *la16-*. **legatrix** a female legatee *17-19*. [Lat *lēgāt-*, ptp stem of *lēgāre*]

†**Legavrik** n in Inverness a fair held on the first of February *la16-17*. [Gael *leth-gheamhradh* the winter half of the year]

lege *see* LEAGUE

lege poustee *see* LIEGE POUSTIE

leggin *see* LAGGEN

leggums /ˈlɛgəmz/ npl leggings *19- T EC Bor*. [altered form of Eng *leggings*]

legitim /ˈlɛdʒɪtɪm/ n law the share of a person's moveable estate due to their children *la17-*. [Lat *lēgitima* (*pars*) the lawful share]

legitimation, †**legitimatioun** /lədʒɪtəˈmeʃən/ n **1** law the act of rendering legitimate *la15-*. **2** legitimacy *la15-17*. [MFr *legitimation*]

leg-laig *see* LAIG[1,1]

leglen, †**lagalloun**, †**laidgalloun** /ˈlɛglən/ n a wooden (milk) pail *15-19, 20- literary*. [LAID[1,2] + GALLON]

leibult *see* LIBEL[1,1]

leich *see* LEASH[1,1]

leid[1], **leed**, **lede** /lid/ n **1** language, speech; a national tongue *la14-*. **2** a constant or repeated theme; a long rambling story *19- NE T*. **3** a formula or refrain, the format of a rhyme or song *la18-19*. **4** a manner of speaking or writing; style, diction *la15-18*. [shortened form of *leden*, from OE *lǣden* language]

leid[2], **leed**, **ledd**, **lead**, †**lede**, †**laid** /lid, lɛd/ n **1** a heavy base metal *la14-*. **2** lead sheeting on a roof *16-*. **3** a clock weight *la19-*. **4** a vat used in brewing or dyeing *15-e18*. **lead-ie** a handmade lead marble, or a lead counter used in a game played with buttons *la19, 20- SW Bor*. **leid draps** small shot used in fowling *19, 20- SW*. **leid stane** fishing a lead-sinker for a handline *16-*. †**leid ure** lead-ore *la15-17*. †**under the lede** under the (lead) seal of a papal bull *la15-e16*. [OE *lēad*]

leid *see* LADE, LAID[1,1], LEAD[1,2], LEDE[1], LEDE[2], LID

leif[1,1], †**lee**, †**lefe** /lif/ adj **1** dear, beloved; agreeable *la14-19, 20- literary*. **2** in ballads solitary, desolate, eerie *la18-19*. **3** pleased, willing *15*. **leeze me**, †**leis me** dear to me *16- literary*. [OE *lēof*]

leif[1,2], **leaf**, **lief**, **lee**, †**lieve** /lif, li/ adv rather *la15-*. **leever**, †**levar**, †**lourd 1** (would) rather *la14-*. **2** entirely, absolutely *la18-*. **liefest** most willingly, most gladly *la19-*. [see the adj]

leif *see* LEAF

leife *see* LAVE[1]

leiffis *see* LEAF

leig *see* LEG[1,1]

leill *see* LEAL[1,1]

leink *see* LINK[1,1]

leinth *see* LENTH[1,1]

leippie *see* LIPPIE

leir *see* LEAR

leish /liʃ/ adj active, athletic, supple *19- SW Bor Uls*. [unknown]

leising *see* LEASING

leisk *see* LISK

leis me *see* LEIF[1,1]

leispund, **leischpund** *see* LISPUND

leist *see* LEAST[1]

leister[1.1] /ˈlistər/ *n* a pronged salmon-fishing spear *la16-*. [ON *ljóstr* a fish-spear]
leister[1.2] /ˈlistər/ *v* to catch fish with a salmon spear *19-*. [see the noun]
leisure, leezure, *Sh* **laesir, †leaser, †leasure, †laser** /ˈlɛʒər, ˈliʒər; *Sh* ˈlaeʒər/ *n* 1 free or spare time; freedom *la14-*. 2 leisureliness, deliberation *16*. **†laserit** having the opportunity or free time to do something *16-e17*. [OFr *leisir*]
†leit *v* to linger, tarry *la15-16*. [unknown]
leit *see* LAT, LEET[1.1], LEET[1.2], LEET[2], LEET[3]
leithand *see* LATCH[3]
†Leith-ax *n* a long-handled battle-axe or halberd *e16*. [from the name of the port + AIX]
leit of *see* LET AFF[1.2]
leized, †lesed /lizd/ *adj* 1 *law* injured in regard to one's rights, interest, property or reputation *la17-18, 20- historical*. 2 impaired, injured *e18*. **†the party lesed** the injured party *la17-e18*. [Lat *laesus*, ptp of *laedere* to hurt; compare LESE-MAJESTY, LESION]
lek *see* LECK[1.1], LECK[1.2], LECK[1.3], LECK[2], LIKE[1.2]
leke *see* LEEK
lekly *see* LIKELY[1.3]
lele *see* LEAL[1.1], LEAL[1.2]
lely *see* LILY[1.1], LILY[1.2]
leme *see* LEAM[1.1], LEAM[1.2]
†Lemistar blak, Lymmester blak *n* a type of expensive fine black cloth (used for hose) *e16*. [from the place-name *Leominster* + BLACK[1.1]]
lemit *see* LEEMIT[1.2]
lemman *see* LAMEN
lemon *see* LEEMON
lempit, *Ork N* **lemped,** *EC Bor* **lempeck, †lempet, †lampet** /ˈlɛmpɪt; *Ork N* ˈlɛmpəd; *EC Bor* ˈlɛmpək/ *n* 1 a limpet, a mollusc of the genus *Patella la12-*. 2 a nickname for a native of Stronsay parish *20- Ork*. [OE *lempedu*]
lemse /lɛms/ *adj* stiff, feeble *20- Sh*. **lemsket** = LEMSE. [Norw dial *lemster* stiff, feeble, Norw dial *lamsen* heavy, slouching]
len[1.1], **lane, lend, laen, †lene** /lɛn, len, lɛnd/ *n* a loan *la14-*. **†in len, in lain** on loan *la16-e18*. **tak the len o** to take advantage of, impose upon *la19-*. [see the verb]
len[1.2], **lane, lend, †lean** /lɛn, len, lɛnd/ *v* 1 to make a loan *la14-*. 2 to deal a blow *la16-19*. 3 to give or bestow *la14-e17*. **len an ear to** to listen to *la14-*. **†len a lift to** to aid or support *la16-17*. [OE *lǣnan*]
len *see* LAYNE[1.2]
lenage *see* LINAGE
lench, launch, †lanche, †lainch /lɛnʃ, lɔnʃ/ *v* to put a ship or boat to sea, launch *la16-*. [OFr *lancher, lancier* to throw (a spear), let fly]
†lend[1], **leynd** *n* the loin, the buttock *la14-16*. [OE *lendenu*]
†lend[2], **leynd** *v ptp* **lent, lende** 1 to be present; to have come *la14-16*. 2 to dwell; to sojourn; to remain *la14-16*. 3 *of the affections* to have lighted upon; to be set or fixed on *15-e16*. [OE *lendan*, ON *lenda*]
lend *see* LEN[1.1], LEN[1.2]
lende *see* LEND[2]
lendie /ˈlɛndi/ *n* nothing *20- Ork*. [reduced form of *ill-end* (ILL[1.3])]
lene *see* LEAN[1.2], LEN[1.1]
length *see* LENTH[1.1], LENTH[1.2]
lennerlie *see* LANERLY
lenocinium /linoˈsɪnjəm/ *n law* the connivance of a spouse in the adultery of the other (constituting a bar to divorce) *la16-*. [Lat *lēnocinium* pandering, procuring]

†lent *adj* 1 slow *la16-e18*. 2 *of a fever* lingering *la17-e18*. [MFr *lent*, Lat *lentus*]
lent *see* LEND[2], LENTH[1.1]
lentell *see* LINTEL
lenth[1.1], **linth, length,** *Sh Ork* **lent, †leinth** /lɛnθ, lɪnθ, lɛŋθ; *Sh Ork* lɛnt/ *n* 1 extent, breadth *la14-*. 2 long duration *la14-*. 3 distance; amount *15-*. 4 a person's height *15-*. **at lang lenth** at long last *la19-*. **at lenth an lang** at last, in the end *la18- Sh NE T EC*. **gae a bonnie length** to let oneself go; to follow one's inclinations *la19-*. **gae aw yer length** = *gae a bonnie length*. **gae yer lenth,** *Sh* **get yer lent** to fall on your face *15-*. **†in lenth and brede** over the whole area or extent *15-16*. **†on lenth** extended, spread out *la15-16*. [OE *lengþu*]
†lenth[1.2], **length, lynth** *v* to lengthen, prolong *15-e17*. [see the noun]
lentren, †lentrin, †lentron /ˈlɛntrən/ *n* Lent *la14-19, 20- literary*. **†lentrin kail** soup made without meat; cabbage boiled in water and then served in milk *19*. **†lentrinware, lentrounwair** a kind of lambskin *15-17*. [ME *lenten* Spring, Lent]
lenʒe *see* LEENGYIE
leo *see* LEW
Leonis canves *see* LYOUNS CANUES
lep *see* LAIP[1.2], LEAP
lepe *see* LEAP, LEEP[1.2]
leper *see* LIPPER[2.1], LIPPER[2.2], LIPPER[2.3]
leprone, lipperan, †laproun /ˈlɛpron, ˈlɪpərən/ *n* a young rabbit *16-19, 20- Sh*. [OFr *laperel*]
lerb[1.1] /lɛrb/ *n* a lick, a mouthful of liquid *20 NE*. [see the verb]
lerb[1.2] /lɛrb/ *v* to lap, slobber *19- NE*. [compare LAIB[1.2] and Du *lerpen*]
lere *see* LEAR
lerge *see* LAIRGE[1.1]
lerges *see* LARGESSE
lerne *see* LEARN
lerroch *see* LARACH
les *see* LESS[1.2], LESS[1.3], LESS[1.4], LEZ, LISS[1]
†lesart, lesard *n* 1 a lizard *la15-17*. 2 a lizard-skin *e16*. [OFr *lesard*]
lesch *see* LEASH[1.1], LEASH[1.2]
†lese *v ptp* **lesit, lorn** 1 to cease to possess; to lose *la14-e17*. 2 to be lost or destroyed; to perish *la15-e17*. [OE *lēosan*]
lesed *see* LEIZED
lese-majesty, †lese-majeste /ˈliz madʒəsti/ *n* 1 treason *la15-*. 2 disloyalty to religious belief *la16-17*. [MFr *lese majesté*, Lat *laesa mājestās*; compare LEIZED, LESION]
lesine, lesing *see* LEASING
lesion, †lesioun /ˈliʒən/ *n* 1 hurt, injury *la15-*. 2 *law* detriment to a person in respect of property or rights *la16-*. [MFr *lesion*, Lat *laesio*; compare LEIZED, LESE-MAJESTY]
lesit *see* LESE
lesour *see* LIZOUR[1.1]
less[1.1] /lɛs/ *n* a lesser thing or state *15-*. **frae less tae mair** from one thing to another, from bad to worse *la18-*. **†less and mair** people of both lower and higher rank *la14-16*. [see the adj]
less[1.2], **†les** /lɛs/ *adj* 1 smaller in quantity, amount or size; fewer *la14-*. 2 lesser in degree, quality or effect *la14-*. 3 of lower rank *la14-e16*. **†les age** minority, the state of being under the legal age of majority *16-e17*. **†les and mair** lesser and greater; everyone, everything *la14-16*. **†les or mair** of lesser or greater amount *la14-17*. **†less or mair** of lesser or greater magnitude or consequence *la14-e16*. [OE *lǣssa*]

less¹·³, †**les** /lɛs/ *adv* to a lesser extent, in a lesser degree *la14-*. [OE *læs*]

less¹·⁴, †**les** /lɛs/ *conj* **1** in case of, for fear that *16-*. **2** unless *la15-19, 20- N NE T*. †**les na** unless *la15*. †**les nor** unless *16*. †**les than** unless *la14-e16*. [see the adv]

less² /lɛs/ *interj* an expression of dismay *19, 20- Sh*. [aphetic form of ALESS]

less³, **lease**, †**lase** /lɛs, lis/ *n* a tenancy, a lease *la16-*. [AN *les*]

lesson, †**lessoun** /'lɛsən/ *n* **1** (a period of) instruction; a school exercise; something to be learned or memorized *la14-*. **2** an instructive example from which one may learn; a rebuke aimed at preventing a repetition of an offence *15-*. **3** the public discourse which followed the examination for admission as an advocate *17-e18, 20- historical*. **4** the action of reading or study *la14-16*. †**leir a lesson** to follow advice or an example *15-16*. [OFr *lecon*]

lessum see LEESOME²

lest¹·¹, **laist**, **last** /lɛst, lest, last/ *n* continuance, duration; durability, permanence *la14-19, 20- Sh NE T EC*. [see the verb]

lest¹·², **laist**, **last**, **last** /lɛst, lest, last/ *v* **1** to endure, continue *la14-*. **2** to extend in space; to reach *la15-e16*. **lastie**, **lestie** lasting *15-*. †**lesting** continuance, duration, permanence *la14-15*. [OE *læstan*]

lest see LAIST¹·¹, LAIST¹·², LAIST¹·³, LEAST¹, LEAST²·², LIST¹·²

leste see LEAST²·¹

lesteek see LASKIT¹·¹, LASKIT¹·²

lesu see LIZOUR¹·¹

lesum see LEESOME²

lesure see LIZOUR¹·²

let¹·¹, †**lat** /lɛt/ *n* **1** a hindrance, an obstacle *la14-*. **2** a hurdle blocking a gap in a hedge or wall *20- SW*. **3** hesitation *la14-e17*. †**letles** without hindrance *la14*. [see the verb]

†**let**¹·², **lat** *v pt, ptp* **let**, **lettit**, **lattit 1** to hinder or prevent *la14-e19*. **2** to neglect; to refrain or desist; to hesitate *la14-16*. [OE *lettan*]

let see LAT

letacamp see LET-DE-CAMP

let-aff¹·¹, **let-off** /'lɛt af, 'lɛt ɔf/ *n* **1** a show of ostentation *19-*. **2** a reduction of rent *la19-*. [LAT + AFF¹·³]

let aff¹·² *v pt* †**leit of** /lɛt 'af/ *v* to break wind, fart *16-*. [see the noun]

let be see LAT BE

†**let-de-camp**, **letacamp**, **littigant** *n* a camp-bed *16-e17*. **lettgant bed**, **liticampt bed**, **lettdecamp bed** a camp-bed *la15-e17*. [OFr *lit de camp*; compare EModDu *lit de camp*, *lidecant*]

leteratoure see LEETERATUR

let fle, **let fly** see LAT FLEE

leth see LAITH¹·¹, LAITH¹·³, LATCH³, LITH¹·¹

lether see LEDDER¹·¹

lethy see LEDDY

letle see LITTLE¹·²

let-off see LET-AFF¹·¹

let on, **lat on** /lɛt 'ɔn, lat 'ɔn/ *v* **1** to impart information; to show interest in *la16-*. **2** to pretend *la16-*. [LAT + ON¹·¹]

lett /lɛt/ *n* a small amount of liquid, a drop *la19- Sh*. Compare LETTO. [unknown]

letten see LAT

letter /'lɛtər/ *n* **1** an alphabetical character *la14-*. **2** a piece of correspondence *la14-*. **3** *law pl* a writ or warrant in missive form (issued by the High Court of Justiciary or by the Court of Session) *la14-*. **4** a missive from the sovereign to intervene by prerogative in the processes of the courts or crown offices, or to issue commands *la15-e17*. †**letters conform**, †**letters conformand** *law* a warrant issued by the supreme court to render effective the judgements of inferior courts *la15-e19*. †**letter obligatour** a written contract or bond embodying a legally-binding undertaking *la14-e17*. †**letters ordinar** a decree from an ordinary court *la15-16*. **letters patent** an open letter or document issued by the crown or other authority recording the terms of a grant, appointment or concession *la14-*. †**letters in the first, secund, thrid, and ferd form** warrants issued by the Council for giving up to four successive charges, issued as the first step in a process of diligence against a person for debt, on eventual pain of being treated as a rebel *la15-e17*. †**letters in the four forms**, **letters of four forms** *law* warrants giving up to four successive charges *16-17*. **letters of arrestment** *law* a writ to attach property for debt *la16-*. †**letters of caption** *law* a warrant for the arrest of a person for debt *la15-18*. †**letters of cursing** a warrant issued by a decree of the pre-Reformation church courts excommunicating a rebellious offender *16-19*. **letters of fire and sword** *law* a warrant from the Privy Council to enforce court decrees of removing and ejection *la17-19, 20- historical*. **letters of horning** *law* a warrant charging the person named to pay a debt (originally under the penalty of being put to the horn) *16-20, 21- historical*. **letters of inhibition** *law* **1** a warrant prohibiting a debtor from burdening or alienating his heritage to the prejudice of his creditor *16-*. **2** a prohibition issued formally by an authority *la15-e17*. †**letters of intercommuning** a writ issued by the Privy Council prohibiting any communication with the people named in it *17-18*. †**letters of manrent** a written contract of manrent *la15*. **letters of open doors** *law* a warrant authorizing the forcing open of lockfast places containing goods to be impounded *18-e20, la20- historical*. †**letters of panis** a missive containing a royal command or summons and specifying the penalties for the recipient in the event of failure to comply *e16*. †**letters of presentation** the writ by which a presentation is intimated to the superior *15-18*. †**letters of procuratory** written authorization for one person to act on behalf of another *la15-e17*. †**letters of slains** *law* a writ subscribed by the kin of someone killed in a private feud, acknowledging payment of compensation, stating there is no further liability for the crime, and requesting the sovereign to grant remission *la15-18*. **letters of supplement** *law* a warrant from the Court of Session enabling an inferior judge to summon a defender to appear when they do not live in the jurisdiction *la18-*. †**run one's letters** to await trial *18-19*. [ME *lettre*]

letter see LATTER

letteran see LATERAN

lettergae /'lɛtərge/ *n* the precentor in a church *18-19, 20- literary*. [agent noun from *let gae* (LAT) to strike up a tune]

lettern see LATERAN

lettit see LET¹·²

letto /'lɛto/ *n* an insignificant person, an animal of low value *20- Ork*. **oh letto** an expression of commiseration or disparagement *20- Ork*. Compare LETT. [Norw dial *læta*]

lettrin, **lettron** see LATRINE

lettroun see LATERAN

leuch, **leuchen** see LAUCH¹·²

leuchen see LAUCH¹·²

leuchly see LAICHLY

leuk¹·¹, **look**, †**luik**, †**luke** /luk/ *n* **1** an act of looking, a glance *la14-*. **2** personal appearance *la15-*. **a leuk o, a look til, a look tae** a look or visit for the purpose of seeing or examining *la19-*. [see the verb]

leuk¹·², **luik**, **look**, **luk**, †**luke**, †**luck** /luk, lʌk/ *v* **1** to direct one's gaze *la14-*. **2** to inspect, examine or consult *la14-*. **3**

to seek or search for *la15*-. **4** to expect *la16*-. **leuk aboot, look aboot** to attend to *20- Sh*. **leuk at the mune till ye fa in the midden** to lose touch with reality *18*-. †**leuk doun** to be melancholy or downcast *16*. **leuk doon on** to regard with disfavour, hold in contempt *16*-. **leuk efter, look after** to take notice of, respect *19- NE*. **leuk the gate o** to heed; to visit *la18*-. **look like Watty to the worm** to look disgusted or reluctant; to look with loathing *la15- N NE*. **leuk near, look near** to heed; to visit *19*-. **leuk on, look on** to attend a deathbed *la18-19, 20- Bor*. **leuk oot** to seek or search for *la16*-. **leuk ower 1** to look after, watch over *la18*-. **2** to overlook, forgive *la19*-. **leuk ower the door** to go outside *19*-. **leuk ower the windae** to lean over the sill and look out of the window *17*-. **leuk see, look see** look here *la19*-. **leuk till, look tae** to look at, observe or behold *la14-19, 20- Sh NE*. **lucks-tu, luksto** look here *19, 20- Ork*. **leuk up** to be alive *la19*-. **never leuk ower yer shooder** to improve steadily, not fail or relapse *20*-. **yer lookin een** your very eyes *19*-. [OE *lōcian*]

leuman see LOWMON
levage see LOVAGE
leval see LEVEL[1.2]
†**Levand** *adj* coming from the Levant *16*. [from the name of the Mediterranean region]
levar see LEIF[1.2]
leve see LEAVE[1], LEAVE[2.1], LEAVE[2.2], LEEVE
levefull see LEFUL
†**leve-gard, loveguard** *n* a bodyguard of soldiers; a lifeguard *17*. [compare LG *liivgarde*, Du *lijfgarde*]
level[1.1], †**lavell** /ˈlɛvəl/ *n* **1** a horizontal surface or plane *16*-. **2** a measuring instrument, a spirit level *la16*-. **3** *mining* a water-level, a passage for drainage *16-18*. [OFr *livel*]
level[1.2], †**leval**, †**lavell** /ˈlɛvəl/ *v* **1** to make level *15*-. **2** to ascertain whether something is level *17*-. **3** to aim at (with a weapon) *la17*-. [see the noun]
Leveller /ˈlɛvələr/ *n* one of a body of peasants in Galloway who had been dispossessed by the enclosure system, who organized themselves in 1724 to knock down the walls built around fields *e18, 19- historical*. [LEVEL[1.2], with agent suffix]
lever see LIVER[1]
levery see LIVERY
levesum see LEESOME[2]
levetenand see LIEUTENANT
†**leviat** *v ptp* **leviat** to enlist troops; to levy taxes *la16-e17*. [compare EModE *leviation*]
levin see ANE LEVIN
levis see LEAF
†**lew, leo** *n* a Flemish or Dutch gold coin *la15-16*. [MDu, Flem *leeuwe* a lion]
lew see LOO[1.1], LOO[1.2], LOO[1.3]
lewd, †**lewit** /ljud, lud/ *adj* **1** lascivious, unchaste *la16*-. **2** evil, wicked *la16-e18*. **3** common, base, vulgar *la15-17*. Compare LAWIT. [OE *lǣwde*]
lewder see LOWDER[1.1]
lewer see LOWER, LURE
lewit see LEWD
lewyne see ELEEVEN
lewzerne see LUCERVE
ley[1.1], **lea**, †**le**, †**lay** /le, lae, li/ *n* **1** a tract of open grassland, a meadow, a pasture; a clearing in a wood; frequently in place-names *la12*-. **2** uncultivated ground, fallow land (originally part of the outfield); frequently in place-names *16*-. **3** oats grown on ploughed-up grassland *la17*-. **4** second-year or older pasture following hay *20*-. [OE *lēah*]
ley[1.2], **lea**, †**lay** /le, lae, li/ *adj of land* fallow, unploughed; barren, unproductive *15*-. **lea arnit, ley arnit** *humorous* a small stone *19- NE*. **lea break** fallow ground or old pasture due to be ploughed up in rotation *20*-. **ley corn** oats grown on ploughed-up grassland *20*-. **ley crap** oats grown on ploughed-up grassland *la18*-. **lea field, ley field** a field of old or established grass *20*-. **ley fur, lea furrow** a ploughing of old grassland *la19*-. **ley girse, ley grass** established pasture, grassland not recently ploughed *20*-. **lea ground, lay ground** ground not recently ploughed *la19*-. **ley hay** hay cut from old pasture *18*-. **lea land, ley land** land left unploughed *la16-19, 20- Sh NE*. **lea oats** oats grown on ploughed-up grassland *20*-. **ley park** a field of old or established grass *la19*-. **lea rig, ley rig** a grass field or strip of grass left untilled in a ploughed field *16*-. †**lie ley, lie lea** to lie fallow *16-19*. [see the noun]

ley see LEE[1.1], LEE[1.2], LYE
leynd see LEND[1], LEND[2]
†**lez, les** *def art in Latin texts preceding plural nouns in the vernacular* the *15-e16*. [MFr *les*; compare LE]
†**li., lib** *n pl* also **libs** a pound (of money or weight) *15-e16*. [abbreviation of Lat *lībra* a pound (of money or weight)]
liable /ˈlaebəl/ *adj* legally bound or responsible *17*-. **liable in law** subject to, liable to or for *la17*-. [EModE *lyable*]
†**liart** *n* a small French coin, a quarter of a sou *16-17*. [MFr *liard*; compare LYART]
liart see LYART
lib[1] /lɪb/ *v* **1** to castrate (farm animals) *16*-. **2** to grope in the soil and remove growing potatoes without disturbing the tops *19*-. **3** to mutilate; to curtail or deprive *18-19, 20- SW*. [ME *libbing*; compare MDu *lubben* to geld]
†**lib**[2.1] *n* a (healing) charm *la16-17*. [OE *lybb*]
†**lib**[2.2] *v* to cure (with a charm) *la15-17*. [see the noun]
lib see LI.
†**libber-lay** *n* a cudgel *la15-e16*. [unknown]
libel[1.1], **leebel**, *Bor* **leibult** /ˈlaebəl, ˈlibəl; *Bor* ˈlʌɪbəlt/ *n* **1** a scurrilous, defamatory or treasonable publication *la15*-. **2** *law* a formal statement of the grounds on which a suit or prosecution is brought *la15*-. **3** a piece of writing, a declaration or missive *la15-19, 20- NE C Bor*. **4** *Presbyterian Church* a charge against a clergyman in an ecclesiastical court *18-20, 21- historical*. **5** a little book, a short treatise *15-16*. [OFr *libel*]
libel[1.2], **leebel** /ˈlaebəl; ˈlibəl/ *v* **1** *law* to specify in an indictment; to state as grounds for a suit or prosecution *la15*-. **2** to defame falsely in writing *19*-. **3** *Presbyterian Church* to make a formal charge against *la17-19, 20- historical*. †**libellat** specified in an indictment *16*. [see the noun]
liberal see LEEBERAL
liberary see LEEBRARY
†**liberate, liberat** *adj* set at liberty, released *17*. [Lat *līberātus*, ptp of *līberāre*]
libertie see LUBBERTIE
libertine /ˈlɪbərtɪn/ *n* **1** a person who who leads a licentious life *la16*-. **2** a student in King's College Aberdeen with no bursary or scholarship *la18-19*. [ME *libertin*, EModE *libertine*, Lat *lībertīnus* a freed man]
†**librar**[1], **librall**, **librell** *n* a library *15-e17*. [MFr *librairie*]
†**librar**[2] *n* a bookseller *la16-e17*. [MFr *libraire*]
library see LEEBRARY
librell see LIBRAR[1]
libs see LI.
licence see LEESHENCE[1.1], LEESHENCE[1.2]
license see LEESHENCE[1.2]
†**licent, lecent** *v* to permit, authorize *16-e17*. [perhaps altered form of *licence* (LEESHENCE[1.2]) by analogy with verbs *absent, present* from corresponding nouns in *-ence*]

licentiate[1.1], †**licentiat**, †**lecentiat** /lae'sɛnʃɪet/ *n* **1** a person licensed to preach; a probationer *19-*. **2** a holder of the university degree of licence *la15-16*. [Lat *licentiātus*]

†**licentiate**[1.2], **licentiat** *v ptp* **licentiat** to authorize, permit *la16-e18*. [Lat licentiāt-, ptp stem of *licentiāre*]

lichory, lichour *see* LECHER

licht[1.1], **light** /lɪxt, lʌɪt/ *n* **1** a source of illumination; daylight *la14-*. **2** a window or opening in a wall to admit light *la14-*. **3** mental or spiritual enlightenment *15-*. **4** *law* a servitude binding one owner of property not to build or plant on it so as to obstruct the light of their neighbour *la17-*. **5** candle-wax tallow *17*. **lichtie** a phosphorescent light, a will-o'-the-wisp *20- NE*. **Lichties 1** a nickname for the natives or inhabitants of Arbroath *la19- T*. **2** a nickname for Arbroath Football Club *20-*. **licht coal** splint coal (used for illumination as well as heat) *la18-19, 20- C*. **between the lights** twilight *20- NE EC*. **canna see the licht o day tae** to be blind to the faults of a person *19- NE EC Bor*. †**sit in yer own licht** to obstruct yourself *16-e17*. [OE *lēoht*]

licht[1.2], **light** /lɪxt, lʌɪt/ *v pt, ptp* **lichtit, lit**, †**licht 1** to set light or fire to *la14-*. **2** to illuminate; to enlighten *la14-*. [OE *līhtan*]

licht[1.3], **light** /lɪxt, lʌɪt/ *adj* bright, shining; not dark *la14-*. **lichten 1** to make light or bright *15-*. **2** to illuminate or enlighten *15-*. **the Light Blues** a nickname for Glasgow Rangers Football Club *la19-*. [see the noun]

†**licht**[1.4], **light** *adv* brightly *la15-16*. [OE *lēohte*]

licht[2.1], **light** /lɪxt, lʌɪt/ *npl* **1** the lungs *la15-*. **2** the light parts of corn seed separated out by winnowing and sifting *19-*. [see the adj]

licht[2.2], **light** /lɪxt, lʌɪt/ *v pt, ptp* **lichtit, lit 1** to reduce in weight *la14-*. **2** to ease, mitigate *la15-19, 20- T SW*. **3** to dismount or alight; to land; to arrive *la14-e19*. **4** to be degraded or humiliated *15-16*. **5** *of a blow* to strike in a particular place *la14-16*. **licht on, light on** to set upon; to attack *16-*. **licht to, licht til** to set upon; to upbraid *20-*. [OE *līhtan*]

licht[2.3], **light** /lɪxt, lʌɪt/ *adj* **1** not heavy *la14-*. **2** agile, nimble *la14-*. **3** cheerful, free from care *15-*. **4** underweight; below the standard or legal weight *la15-*. **5** easily digested *la15-*. **6** slight, trivial *la15-*. **7** *of beer* low-gravity *20-*. **8** dizzy, light-headed *20- C*. **9** delivered of a child *20- Ork*. **10** frivolous; promiscuous *la14-e19*. **11** unladen, unhampered *la15-e17*. **12** *of conflicts* involving small numbers or few casualties *16-e17*. **13** mentally unstable *la16-17*. **lichter** *of a woman* delivered of a child *15-19, 20- N*. **lichtsome 1** carefree, light-hearted *la15-*. **2** cheering, pleasant *18-*. **3** nimble, agile *la19-*. **light farrant** frivolous, flighty *la16-19, 20- NE SW*. **licht fit** light-footed, nimble *la16-*. **licht heidit** frivolous; unreliable *15-*. †**licht horseman** a mounted raider or reiver *la16-e17*. **licht in the heid** dizzy, light-headed *20-*. **licht on** abstemious, temperate in the use of *20-*. †**set licht** to despise; to undervalue *la15-16*. [OE *lēoht*]

licht[2.4], **light** /lɪxt, lʌɪt/ *adv* lightly, nimbly *la15-*. **light-set** light-footed, nimble *19-*. [OE *lēohte*]

†**lichter** *n* a loading boat *la16-e17*. [EModE *lighter* or Du *lichter*]

lichtlifee *see* LICHTLYFU

lichtlify, lightlafee /'lɪxtləfåe, 'lʌɪtləfi/ *v* to scorn, disdain or disparage *19, 20- NE T*. [LICHTLY[1.3], with causative suffix]

†**lichtly**[1.1], **lightly** *n* a slight, an insult *la16-19*. [see the adj]

lichtly[1.2], **lightly** /'lɪxtli, 'lʌɪtli/ *v* to make light of; to disparage or insult *la14-*. [see the adj]

†**lichtly**[1.3], **lightly** *adj* slighting, contemptuous, scornful *la15-18*. **lichtlines** arrogance, contempt; an insult *15-16*. [OE *lēohtlic*]

lichtly[1.4], **lightly** /'lɪxtli, 'lʌɪtli/ *adv* **1** not heavily, with little force *la14-*. **2** readily, easily *la14-*. **3** flippantly, contemptuously *la14-*. **4** nimbly *la14-*. **5** briefly, superficially *15-*. [OE *lēohtlīce*]

lichtlyfu, lichtlifee /'lɪxtlifu, 'lɪxtlifi/ *adj* slighting, contemptuous *la16, la19- NE*. †**lichtlifullie** slightingly, contemptuously *la16-e17*. [LICHTLY[1.1], with adj-forming suffix]

lichtnin, lightnin, †**lychtnyng** /'lɪxtnɪn, 'lʌɪtnɪn/ *n* **1** (a flash of) electricity discharged in the atmosphere, lightning *16-*. **2** dawn *20- Sh SW*. [ME *lyghtnyng*]

lick[1.1], †**lik** /lɪk/ *n* **1** an act of licking; a taste *17-*. **2** a small amount, the least particle *17-*. **3** a smack; *pl* a thrashing *18-*. **4** a smart pace, a burst of speed *19-*. **5** a small measure of meal given to the under-miller as a gratuity *la17-e19*. †**lick of goodwill** meal given as a gratuity *18-e19*. [see the verb]

lick[1.2], †**lik** /lɪk/ *v* **1** to pass the tongue over *la14-*. **2** to hurry *la19-*. **3** to take a pinch of snuff *19, 20- Uls*. **lick lip** fawning, wheedling *la19- WC Uls*. **lick penny** a greedy or dishonest person *19, 20- T EC SW*. **lick spit** a sycophant *19, 20- N EC*. **lick want** famine, hunger *20- NE T EC*. **lick an skail** abundance, extravagance *20- NE T EC*. **lick ma dowp** an obsequious person *18-19, 20- T EC*. **lick thoums** to confirm a bargain by licking and joining thumbs *17-19, 20- SW*. †**lick a whipshaft** to suffer humiliation or defeat *18-e19*. **lick the white oot o yer ee** to cheat; to take advantage of *18-19, 20- WC*. †**lick yer winnins** to make the best of a bad job *la18*. [OE *liccian*]

lick[1.3] /lɪk/ *adv* with a heavy thud *la19-*. [see the verb]

lickarstane *see* LECKERSTANE

lickery, liquorie, †**lacrissye,** †**lacreische,** †**licorese** /'lɪkəre, 'lɪkəri/ *n* liquorice *la15-*. **lickery stick** liquorice root *la19- WC*. [AN *lycorys*; compare ALICREESH]

licour *see* LEECURE

lid, led, †**leid** /lɪd, lɛd/ *n* **1** a moveable cover *la15-*. **2** an eyelid *la16-*. **3** one of the boards of a large book *20-*. **4** a door of a box bed or cupboard; a shutter *la16-19, 20- NE T*. **5** *mining* the cover or flap of a valve; a flat piece of wood on the top of a prop *la19, 20- EC*. †**the lid of the knee** the kneecap *la16-17*. [OE *hlid*]

lidder *see* LITHER

Liddisdale drow /'lɪdɪsdel 'drʌu/ *n* a thick drizzle *19- Bor*. [from the name of the valley + DROW[1.1]]

lidgait, lidyate *see* LIGGATE

lie[1.1], **lye** /lae/ *n* **1** the act of lying; a rest or sleep *18-*. **2** *golf* the position of the ball; the spot on which it lies *la18-*. **3** a place where a person lies; a bed or couch *19-*. **4** a railway siding (within a coal-mine) *la19-*. **5** the inclination of the face of a golf club as held by the player *19*. [see the verb]

lie[1.2], †**ly,** †**lay** /lae/ *v pt* **lay,** †**la,** *ptp* **lain,** *NE* **lien,** †**lyne,** †**lyin 1** to be recumbent or prostrate; to lay flat *la14-*. **2** to extend lengthwise; to be situated *la14-*. **3** to be; to remain *la14-*. **4** to be confined to bed *15-*. **5** *of the tongue* to be still; *of the voice* to be silent *19-*. **6** to lodge, stay; to reside; *of an army* to be encamped *la14-17*. **7** to have sexual intercourse *la14-17*. **8** to lurk; to lie in wait *la14-16*. **9** to be in residence as an ambassador *16-e17*. †**lyage** the storage of goods at a port until collected by the consignee; a charge made for this *la18*. †**lyer, lyar 1** the bottom millstone *la16-18*. **2** a carpet, a rug, a coverlet *la15-e16*. **lie day 1** a day of LYING TIME *la19- C*. **2** one of the days allowed for loading and unloading a ship *16-18*. †**lying dog** a setter *17*. **lyin money** ready money *la16-*. †**lying pelf** = *lyin money e18*. **lyin siller** ready money *la19-*. **lying storm** a fall of snow which remains for a while on the ground before melting *la18-*. **lie time** = LYING TIME *la19- C*. **lie aff** a command to a sheepdog to keep at a distance from the sheep *20-*. **lie by** *v* to hold back, remain inactive or uncommitted *la16-19, 20- Sh T EC*. **lie by** *n* **1** a person who stands aside or remains uncommitted *la16-19, 20- Uls*. **2** a siding at the roadside used for storing road-metal *20- C SW Bor*. **3** arrears *20- NE*. **lie doon** to take to bed with illness *20-*. †**ly furth** to delay entering into possession of inherited property *16-e17*. **lie lown 1** to lie quietly, comfortably or snugly *18-19, 20- literary*. **2** to lie low, keep out of trouble *18-19, 20- literary*. **lie on** *mining* to work an extra shift, do overtime *20- EC*. **lie oot, lie out 1** *of cattle* to remain unhoused *17-*. **2** to delay entering into possession of inherited property *16-18*. **3** to withhold allegiance *la16-e17*. **4** *of a debt* to remain unpaid *17*. **lie ower 1** to remain unpaid *20-*. **2** to be postponed *la16-19*. **lie tae, lay till** to feel or show affection *la18-*. †**ly upon** to exact accommodation from *15-e17*. †**lie wrang** *of a woman* to lose her chastity *la18-19*. **lie yont** to shift over in bed *19-*. [OE *licgan*]

lie *see* LE, LEE[1.1], LEE[1.2]

lief *see* LEIF[1.2]

lieg *see* LEAGUE

liege poustie, †**lege poustee** /ˈliʤ pusti/ *n law* soundness in mind and body *la14-*. [OFr *lige poeste*]

lien *see* LIE[1.2]

lieutenant, †**lieutenand,** †**lutenand,** †**levetenand** /luˈtɛnənt, ləfˈtɛnənt/ *n* **1** a deputy, a person wielding delegated authority *la14-*. **2** an army officer, next in rank below captain *16-*. †**lieutenantry, leveteinendrie** the office or (area of) jurisdiction of a lieutenant *16-17*. **lieutenant general 1** a high-ranking army officer *la17-*. **2** a viceregent or army commander second after the sovereign *15-e18*. [OFr *lieutenant*]

lieve *see* LEIF[1.2]

liewer *see* LURE

lif *see* LEEVE

life, †**lyve,** †**lyf** /lʌɪf/ *n* the condition of being alive, the period between birth and death *la14-*. **lifie** full of life, lively *la18-*. **lifieness** vivacity, vigour *la19, 20- Sh Ork EC*. †**liflade, lyflede 1** means of living, maintenance *la14-e17*. **2** property as a means of support *la15*. **in life** alive *la14-19, 20- Sh EC*. **living and lifelike** hale and hearty *18-*. **leevin and life-thinking** = *living and lifelike 18-19, 20- Sh*. †**lyvis fude** a livelihood *15-16*. †**on life, on lyiff** alive *la14-e19*. †**out of lyfe** lifeless *15-16*. [OE *lif*]

liferent /ˈlʌɪfrɛnt/ *n law* **1** a right to receive the revenue of a property till death without the right to dispose of the capital *la14-*. **2** the right to reside in a property during one's life *la15-*. **3** the revenue of escheated property *16-e18*. **liferented** *of property* possessed in liferent *la17-*. **liferenter** a person who enjoys liferent *16-*. **lifrentrix** a woman who enjoys liferent *la16-*. [LIFE + RENT[2]]

lift[1] /lɪft/ *n* the sky, the heavens *la14-*. **drap frae the lift** to fall from the sky; to appear from nowhere *la19- NE T EC*. **fa frae the lift** to come or happen suddenly or unexpectedly *la19- NE T EC*. [OE *lyft*]

lift[2.1], *C* **luft** /lɪft/ *C* lʌft/ *n* **1** an act of lifting; a load *16-*. **2** help, relief, encouragement *la16-*. **3** the carrying a corpse for a funeral *la17-*. **4** a large amount *la18-*. **5** a rising swell in the sea *19-*. **6** a theft; something stolen *19-*. **7** the uneven rising step of a person who has one leg shorter than the other *la19-*. **8** the amount of fish that can be lifted aboard by hand in the net *20-*. **9** the rounding-up and moving of sheep by a sheep-dog *19-*. **10** *piping* a special emphasis produced by the use of cut notes *20-*. **11** a layer or course in a dry-stone wall *19- Sh SW*. **12** a card trick *la18-19, 20- WC SW*. **13** a collection, a whip-round *20- WC SW*. **14** *mining* the first seam of coal removed from a mine; a slice taken off a pillar of coal *la19, 20- EC*. **15** a social evening, a party *20- Sh*. **gie a lift tae** to give a helping hand to; to promote or encourage *la16-*. **tak the lift o** to make a fool of *20- NE T*. **tak a lift wi** to help or encourage *19, 20- Uls*. [see the verb]

lift[2.2], *C* **luft** /lɪft/ *C* lʌft/ *v* **1** to raise or move upwards; to take or pick up *la14-*. **2** to uplift money or rents *15-*. **3** to raise the spirits, elate *la15-*. **4** to collect or gather up; to remove *la16-*. **5** to drive animals to market *la16-*. **6** to carry a corpse out for burial; to start a funeral procession *la17-*. **7** *golf* to pick up the ball *19-*. **8** to take possession of money due; to withdraw money from a bank *19-*. **9** to stand up and depart *19-*. **10** to take out of the ground; to harvest a crop *19-*. **11** to gather scythed corn into a sheaf for binding *la19-*. **12** to mention a person's name *la19-*. **13** to take a woman up to dance *la19-*. **14** *of a sheep-dog* to round up sheep and move them forward *20-*. **15** to hear; to understand *20-*. **16** *of the police* to arrest, take into custody *20-*. **17** to serve a dish at the table *20- NE T EC*. **18** to strike up a tune; to lead the singing *17-19, 20- EC Bor Uls*. **19** to steal cattle in a raid *la17-19, 20- historical*. **20** *of the chest* to heave from difficulty in breathing *la19, 20- C SW Bor*. **21** to raise troops *la16-17*. **22** to move a military camp; to decamp *la16-17*. **lifters** *in the Secession Church* the group which approved of the minister raising the communion elements before consecrating them *la18, 19- historical*. **liftit** cheered up *19-*. **a-liftin,** *Sh* **in lifteen** *of livestock* in a very debilitated state; needing assistance to stand up *17-*. **as fast as legs can lift** at full speed *la18-19, 20- SW Uls*. **lift a leg 1** to move; to run or gallop *18-*. **2** to have sexual intercourse *18-*. **lift and lay** to pick something up and lay it down again *la19- C Uls*. **lift yer feet** to show great activity *la19, 20- EC Bor*. **lift yer hand tae** to hit *19-*. **lift yer lines** *Presbyterian Church* to withdraw formally from the communicant membership of a congregation *la19-*. [ON *lypta*]

lig[1], **ligg** /lɪɡ/ *v* **1** to lie in a bed *16-*. **2** to lie down; to recline or rest *15-19, 20- literary*. **3** to remain; to be situated *15-19, 20- literary*. **4** to have sexual intercourse *la15-19*. **5** to lie in the grave, be buried *la16-e17*. **6** to lodge or camp *la15-17*. †**ligg at wait** to lie in ambush *e16*. [ON *liggja*]

†**lig**[2] *n* a league, the measure of distance *la15-17*. [ME *lege*]

lig *see* LAIG[1.1], LAIG[1.2], LEAGUE, LEG[1.1]

ligg *see* LIG[1]

liggate, liggat, ligget, †**lidgait,** †**lidyate** /ˈlɪɡet, ˈlɪɡət/ *n* a self-closing gate, frequently one shutting off pasture from arable land *la12-19, 20- SW*. [OE *hlidgeat* a folding door, a hinged gate]

†**ligger**[1], **liggar** *n* a military camp; a siege *17-e18*. **ligger lady** a female camp-follower *la17-19*. [Du *leger* a camp]

ligger[2] /ˈlɪɡər/ *n* **1** a newly-spawned salmon *19- SW*. **2** a salmon that has stayed too long in fresh water *19- SW*. [LIG[1.2], with agent suffix]

ligget *see* LIGGATE

light *see* LICHT[1.1], LICHT[1.2], LICHT[1.3], LICHT[1.4], LICHT[2.1], LICHT[2.2], LICHT[2.3], LICHT[2.4]

lightlafee *see* LICHTLIFY

lightly *see* LICHTLY[1.1], LICHTLY[1.2], LICHTLY[1.3], LICHTLY[1.4]

lightnin *see* LICHTNIN

lignage *see* LINAGE

lignie *see* LEENGYIE

lignott *see* LINGOTT

lik *see* LICK[1.1], LICK[1.2], LIKE[1.2], LIKE[2]

likarstane *see* LECKERSTANE

like[1.1] /lʌɪk/ *n* **1** the same kind of thing *la14-*. **2** *golf* an equal number of strokes on both sides; a stroke which makes the scores even *19-*. †**the like** that very thing, indeed *la19*. **no the like** nothing of the sort, not at all: ◊*Ye're sleepin.—I'm no the like. la19.* [see the adj]

like¹·², **lik**, *Sh N* **lek** /lʌik, lɪk; *Sh N* lek/ *adj* **1** similar, analogous *la14-*. **2** about to, on the point of *la14-*. **3** likely, probable *la15-*. **liker 1** more like: ◊*he's liker his mither than his faither la14-*. **2** more apt or appropriate for: ◊*a worset goon's the liker you la19-*. **be like yer meat** to look well-nourished *19-*. **be like yersel 1** to be unchanged in appearance *19-*. **2** to act up to one's reputation *20-*. **like wha but him** in a grand or confident manner *19, 20- NE*. **mair liker** more like *la19- N EC*. [OE *gelīc*]

like¹·³ /lʌik/ *adv* **1** after the manner of *la15-*. **2** likely, probably *la15-*. **3** about, approximately *la18-*. **4** so to speak, so as to let you understand: ◊*juist for the day like 19-*. **like sae**, †**lyksay** likewise, similarly *17-*. **like as 1** in the same way, to the same extent *15-*. **2** similarly, furthermore *la15-*. [see the adj]

like¹·⁴ /lʌik/ *prep* after the manner of *la15-*. **like linkie** at once, at top speed *20-*. **like spottie** = like linkie *19- NE T*. [see the adj]

like², **lik**, *H&I* **lake** /lʌik, lɪk; *H&I* lek/ *v* **1** to find agreeable *la14-*. **2** to love; to have a strong affection for *18-*. **3** to be pleasing or agreeable to: ◊*it likis me la14-19, 20- literary*. **liking**, †**lyking 1** preference, inclination, fondness *la14-*. **2** happiness, contentment; pleasure, satisfaction *la14-*. **3** a much-loved person *la15-e17*. **as ye like** as you can imagine: ◊*as impident as ye like la19-*. **come what likes** come what may *la18-*. **I dinna like** I hesitate; I am embarrassed: ◊*I can't accept it. It's too generous. I dinna like. 19-*. [OE *līcian*]

-like /lʌik/ *suffix* having the qualities of the root noun or adjective *15-*. [LIKE¹·³, LIKE¹·⁴]

likely¹·¹, *Sh* **laekly** /ˈlʌikle, ˈlʌikli; *Sh* ˈlekli/ *n* **1** likelihood, probability, chance *18-*. **2** an exact resemblance: ◊*da very laekly o her midder 20- Sh*. [see the adj]

likely¹·², **likly**, †**lykely** /ˈlʌikle, ˈlʌikli, ˈlikle/ *adj* **1** probable *la14-*. **2** capable; competent *la14-*. **3** *of things* appearing to be suitable (for some purpose) *15-*. †**liklynes 1** probability *la14-e17*. **2** semblance, feigned or superficial appearance *la14-e17*. **3** similarity *la14-15*. **be liklynes** to all appearances, apparently *la14-15*. †**the liklyest** the best prospect *la14-16*. [ON *líkligr*]

likely¹·³, *Sh* **laekly**, *N* **lekly**, †**lykely** /ˈlʌikle, ˈlʌikli; *Sh N* ˈlekli/ *adv* probably *la17-* [see the adj]

liken¹, **likkin** /ˈlʌikən, ˈlikən/ *v* **1** to compare *la14-*. **2** to associate or connect *19-*. [LIKELY¹·², with verb-forming suffix]

liken² /ˈlʌikən/ *adj* likely to be or do: ◊*I was liken to dee la16-19, 20- Sh Ork C Uls*. [LIKE¹·², with adj-forming suffix *-en*]

likkin *see* LIKEN¹

†**likly** *v* to make a rhyme true *e16*. [from the adj LIKELY¹·²]

likly *see* LIKELY¹·²

†**Lilias-day** *n* a July holiday and fair in Kilbarchan, Renfrewshire *la19*. [from the name of the Spanish saint *Liliosa*, whose day is 27 July + DAY]

†**lill** *n* a hole in a flute or in the chanter of a bagpipe *18-19*. [probably Du *lul*; compare LILT¹·¹]

†**Lilles**, **Lyllis** *n* worsted cloth (made in Lille) *16-e17*. [from the French place-name]

†**lill for lall**, **lill for law** *n* tit-for-tat *15-e16*. **play lill for law** = quit lill for lall. **quit lill for lall** to requite *15-e16*. [OE *lǣl* wið lǣle* weal for weal; compare Lat *līvōrem pro līvōre*]

lillie *see* LILY¹·¹, LILY¹·²

†**lillikinis** *npl* lace trimmings *la16-e17*. [EModDu *leliekijn* a lily, lily of the valley]

lillilu /ˈlilɪlu/ *n* a lullaby; a meaningless refrain *19, 20- Sh Ork NE EC*. [onomatopoeic]

lilly /ˈlile, ˈlili/ *adj* lovely, beautiful *la18- literary*. [OE *lēoflic*, perhaps with influence from LILY¹·¹]

lilt¹·¹ /lɪlt/ *n* **1** a lively or cheerful song or tune *17-*. **2** rhythm, cadence *19-*. **3** a dance *la19-*. [see the verb]

lilt¹·² /lɪlt/ *v* **1** to sing cheerfully; to strike up a song *la16-*. **2** to dance; to skip or leap about *la18-*. **3** to move jerkily; to limp *19*. **4** to sound an alarm, raise a loud cry *e16*. **lilter** a singer *19, 20- literary*. †**lilt pipe** a musical pipe *la15*. **The Liltin** the old setting of the lament *The Flowers o the Forest la18- Bor*. **lilt it** to dance; to leap about *18-19, 20- N*. †**lilt up** to strike up a tune or a song *18-e19*. [compare Du, LG *lul* a pipe]

lily¹·¹, †**lillie**, †**lely** /ˈlili/ *n* **1** a plant or flower of the genus *Lilium la14-*. **2** a plant or flower of the genus *Narcissus*, a daffodil *la19-*. **3** a heraldic lily or fleur de lis *16-e17*. [OE *lilie*, Lat *līlium*]

lily¹·², †**lillie**, †**lely** /ˈlili/ *adj* lily-like, white *la15-*. [see the noun]

lilyoak /ˈlileok/ *n* the common lilac *19-*. [altered form of LAYLOCK, by association with LILY¹·¹ and *oak*]

limb, †**lim** /lɪm/ *n* **1** an arm or leg *la14-*. **2** an organ of the body *la14-e17*. **3** a joint of meat *la15-e16*. **limb o the deil** a wicked or mischievous person or animal *la19-*. [OE *lim*]

lime¹·¹, †**lyme** /lʌim/ *n* **1** mortar, cement *la14-*. **2** quicklime *15-*. **3** birdlime *16-*. **lime-coal** coal used for burning lime *la17-19, 20- WC SW*. **lime-craig**, **lymecraig** (the working face of) a limestone quarry *17-19, 20- EC*. †**lyme fald** a place for storing lime *e16*. †**lyme hoill**, **lym holl** a tanner's lime-pit *la16-17*. †**lime pot**, **lyme pott** a tanner's lime-pit *16-17*. †**lyme quarrell** a limestone quarry *17*. **lime shells** the unground lumps produced by burning limestone *la18-*. **limestane**, †**lymestane 1** limestone *16-e17*. **2** *pl* pieces of limestone *16-e17*. †**lyme wand** a stick smeared with bird-lime for trapping birds *la15-16*. **lime-wark** a place where lime is worked and burned, a limekiln *19, 20- WC SW*. **lime and stane** masonry *la14-*. [OE *līm*]

lime¹·², †**lyme** /lʌim/ *v* **1** to dress land with lime *la17-*. **2** to steep skins in a solution of lime *17*. [see the noun]

lime *see* LAME¹·²

limfad *see* LYMPHAD

limit *see* LEEMIT¹·¹, LEEMIT¹·²

†**limitate** *v* to circumscribe; to delimit *16-17*. **limitat** *adj* **1** circumscribed within a boundary; territorially delimited *16-17*. **2** restricted in scope, powers or action *la16-17*. [Lat *līmitāt-*, ptp stem of *līmitāre* to limit]

limmer, †**lymmar**, †**lymare**, †**lymber** /ˈlɪmər/ *n* **1** a wicked man, a criminal *15-*. **2** a woman considered to be promiscuous; a mistress or a prostitute *16-*. **3** an impudent or exasperating woman *18-*. **4** a mischievous child *19-*. **5** a female animal *la18-19, 20- T Bor*. †**lymmerie** villainy *16*. [unknown]

limn¹·¹ /lɪm/ *n* a portrait, a likeness; a photograph *20- Ork WC SW*. [see the verb]

†**limn**¹·², **lymn** *v* **1** to paint a portrait *17-19*. **2** to illuminate a manuscript *e16*. [altered form of OFr *lumine* to light up]

limner /ˈlɪmnər/ *n* **1** a title given to the royal portrait-painter, as an officer of the monarch's household in Scotland *la16-*. **2** a portrait-painter *la17-19*. [LIMN, with agent suffix]

limon *see* LEEMON

†**limp** *n* a lumpfish *17-e18*. [MLG *lumpen*, from its appearance]

lin, †**leen** /lɪn/ *v* to pause, desist, cease *17-19, 20- Sh Ork SW*. [OE *linnan*, ON *linna*]

lin *see* LINE²·¹, LINN¹, LINN²

†**linage**, **lenage**, **lignage** *n* **1** ancestry, kinship *15-e17*. **2** progeny *la14-e16*. [OFr *lignage*]

linally *see* LINEALLY

†**lincome twine**, **linkome twine**, **lincum twyne** *n* twine or thread made at Lincoln *la16-e19*. [from the place-name + TWINE¹·¹]

linder *see* LINNER

line¹·¹ /lʌin/ *n* 1 a long mark or stroke *la14-*. 2 a continuous extent or length *la14-*. 3 a line of family descent; lineage *la14-*. 4 a line of writing; a portion of text or its content *la14-*. 5 a rope, cord or string; a fishing line *16-*. 6 written authorization *la17-*. 7 a prescription *la19-*. 8 a note to a teacher explaining a child's absence from school *la19-*. 9 an account with a shop; a bill *20-*. 10 a shopping list *20-*. 11 a betting slip *20-*. 12 a line of verse or psalm read in a church service *la16-19, 20- historical*. 13 a bar or sandbank in a river or harbour *16*. **lines** 1 writing, a written message *la16-*. 2 a certificate of church-membership *la19-*. **liney** marbles a game where the target is a scored line *20- T C*. **gie somebody a line o yer mind** to give someone a piece of your mind *la19- NE EC*. **give out the line** to read or intone a line of a psalm before it is sung by the congregation *19- historical*. **lift yer lines** *see* LIFT²·². †**read the line** = give out the line *la17-e19*. [OE *līne*, MFr *ligne*, ON *lína*]

line¹·², †**lyne** /lʌin/ *v* 1 to mark out with lines *15-*. 2 to trace out property boundaries *15-e18*. †**lineatioun** the measuring and settlement of boundaries *17*. **liner**, **lyner** 1 an official appointed to measure out and fix property boundaries within a burgh *15-19, 20- historical*. 2 *in Glasgow* a member of a Dean of Guild Court supervising the erection or alteration of buildings *16-20, 21- historical*. 3 a line-fishing boat *la19-*. **lining** 1 permission to proceed with building after due inspection of the boundaries *la18-20, 21- historical*. 2 the measuring and settlement of boundaries *15-e17*. 3 a stone or post set in position or marked as a boundary by officials *la15-e16*. **lynster** a member of a Dean of Guild Court who supervised the erection or alteration of buildings *e17*. **breve of lining** *see* BRIEF¹·¹. [see the noun]

†**line**²·¹, **lin**, **lyne** *n* 1 linen thread or cloth *la14-e19*. 2 the flax plant *la15-e17*. [OE *līn*]

line²·² /lʌin/ *v* 1 to apply a lining to *la15-*. 2 to thrash *19, 20- N NE*. **line someone's luif** to bribe *la19-*. [see the noun]

lineally, †**lineallie**, †**linally** /ˈlɪniəli/ *adv* 1 by lineal descent *15-*. 2 in a straight line *la15-*. [derivative LINE¹·¹]

lineatioun *see* LINE¹·²

linen¹·¹, †**linin**, †**lynnyng** /ˈlɪnən/ *n* cloth woven from flax *la15-*. [see the adj]

linen¹·², †**linin**, †**linning** /ˈlɪnən/ *adj of cloth* made from flax *la14-*. †**lynning clathis** 1 linen garments or underclothes *la14-e17*. 2 penitential garments *la15-e17*. [OE *līnen*]

linens, **linins**, †**linningis** /ˈlɪnənz/ *npl* 1 a shroud *18-19, 20- N T SW*. 2 linen shirts or undergarments *la16-19, 20- Sh*. 3 penitential garments *17-19*. [plural of LINEN¹·¹]

ling¹·¹ /lɪŋ/ *n* a line; a rope, cord or string *la15-19, 20- literary*. **lingtow** a long rope used by smugglers for carrying their goods *la19, 20- literary*. **lingtowmen** smugglers *19, 20- historical*. †**in a ling**, **intill ling** 1 in a straight line, in a direct course *la14-e16*. 2 straight away, immediately *la14-e16*. [OFr *lingne*, *ligne*]

ling¹·² /lɪŋ/ *v* to rush forward *la14-19, 20- Bor*. **lingit** thin, lean *19, 20- Bor*. [see the noun]

ling² /lɪŋ/ *n* 1 heather *Calluna vulgaris la15-*. 2 harestail cotton-grass *Eriophorum vaginatum* or deergrass *Trichophorum cespitosum la17- C Bor*. †**pull ling** harestail cotton-grass *la18-19*. [ON *lyng* ling, heather; the whortleberry]

lingal *see* LINGLE²·¹

lingan, **lingel** *see* LINGLE¹

linget /ˈlɪnʒət, ˈlɪŋət/ *n* the seed of flax, linseed *la15-19, 20- NE*. **linget oil** linseed oil *la15-19, 20- NE*. †**linget seed** flax seed *la15-e19*. †**olye linget** = *linget oil 16*. [unknown]

linget *see* LINGLE²·¹

lingie /ˈlɪŋi/ *n* a long rambling story, a rigmarole *20- NE EC SW*. [altered form of Eng *lingo*]

lingle¹, **lingel**, *NE EC* **lingan**, †**linyel** /ˈlɪŋəl, lɪŋˈɛl; *NE EC* lɪŋən/ *n* shoemakers' waxed thread *17-*. **lingle backit** having a long narrow back *la19- SW Bor*. **lingle en**, **lingel end** the tip of the shoemakers' thread (to which the birse is attached for threading it through the leather) *19- C SW Bor*. **lingel tailed** 1 having a long, thin tail or long, narrow, trailing skirts *18-19, 20- EC SW Bor*. 2 narrow-hipped *18-19, 20- EC SW Bor*. [OFr *lignoel*, *ligneul* a cobbler's thread]

lingle²·¹, **lingal**, **linget**, †**lynʒell** /ˈlɪŋəl, ˈlɪŋəl, ˈlɪŋət/ *n* 1 a rope for hobbling or fettering an animal *16-19, 20- NE T EC*. 2 a strap, thong or looped cord *la18-19, 20- NE EC Uls*. 3 a long, drawn-out discourse *la19- N NE*. 4 a tall lanky person *la19- N NE*. [AN **lengle*, Lat *lingula*, *ligula*; compare LANGLE¹·¹]

lingle²·² /ˈlɪŋəl, ˈlɪŋəl/ *v* to hobble a horse (or other animal) by tying its legs *la19- NE*. [see the noun; compare LANGLE¹·²]

†**lingot**, **lignott**, **lingnot** *n* 1 an ingot of precious metal *la15-17*. 2 an ingot mould *16-17*. [MFr *lingot*]

linin *see* LINEN¹·¹, LINEN¹·²

linins *see* LINENS

link¹·¹, †**leink** /lɪŋk/ *n* 1 a link of a chain *la15-*. 2 a wide bend in a river; the land enclosed by a loop of a winding river *la18-*. 3 *pl* a string of sausages or black puddings *19-*. 4 a link in the chain from which the pot-hook hung in the fireplace *la16-20, 21- historical*. 5 a joint of the body; a vertebra *la17-19, 20- Sh SW*. 6 a lock of hair, a curl *la18-19, 20- Sh*. 7 a straw rope used to hold down a thatch *20- Sh*. 8 a fetter *la15-16*. **link stane** a stone on the end of a straw rope used to hold down thatch *20- Sh*. [ON *hlekkr*]

link¹·² /lɪŋk/ *v* 1 to connect or join with a link *la15-*. 2 to go arm in arm *19-*. 3 to lift a pot on or off a pot-hook *18-20, 21- historical*. 4 to tie down thatch with a straw rope *20- Sh*. 5 to beat or thrash *20- Ork*. 6 to work ploughed land with a chain-harrow *20- NE*. 7 to chain up; to bind *la16-17*. [see the noun]

link² /lɪŋk/ *v* 1 to move fast or easily; to walk briskly *18-*. 2 *of spinning* to act with speed and energy; to work vigorously *18-19, 20- N NE EC*. 3 to skip or dance about *19- NE*. **linkie** 1 a mischievous, playful person *19- SW Bor*. 2 a deceitful, untrustworthy person *19- SW Bor*. **linking** active, agile, brisk *la18-19, 20- C SW*. **like linkie** *see* LIKE¹·⁴. **link it** to take oneself off quickly *20- NE*. [unknown; compare Norw *linka* to toss or bend the body, fling, drive]

linkis *see* LINKS

linkome twine *see* LINCOME TWINE

links, †**linkis**, †**linx** /lɪŋks/ *npl* 1 a stretch of undulating sandy ground near the seashore, covered with turf, bent-grass or gorse; frequently in place-names *la15-*. 2 a golf-course *la16-*. **Links Market** an annual fair held in Kirkcaldy *19-*. [OE *hlincas* ridges, slopes, banks]

Linlithgow /lɪnˈlɪθɡo/ *n* a unit of dry measures *17-e19, la19- historical*. **Linlithgow measure** one of the standard dry measures (which were committed to the custody of the burgh 1617-1824) *18-e19, la19- historical*. [from the name of the town in West Lothian]

linn¹, †**lin** /lɪn/ *n* 1 a waterfall, a cataract *la15-*. 2 a deep, narrow gorge *la18- SW Bor*. [OE *hlynn* a torrent, or Gael *linne* a pool, a waterfall]

linn², **lin** /lɪn/ *n* a pool below a waterfall *la16-*. [Gael *linne* a pool]

linn³ /lɪn/ *n in Ayrshire* a kind of fireclay used as slate-pencils *19-20, 21- historical*. [from the name of the Linn Bed seam of coal near Kilmarnock]

linn⁴ /lɪn/ *n* **1** a plank in a rowing-boat used as a seat or a foot-rest *la19- Sh Ork*. **2** a wooden plank or runner laid under the keel of a boat for launching and beaching *20- Sh Ork N*. [ON *hlunnr*]

lin-nail, †**lyn nail** /'lɪn nel/ *n* a linch-pin *la15-19, 20- Ork EC Bor*. [OE *lynis* an axle-tree + NAIL¹·¹]

linner, linder /'lɪnər, 'lɪndər/ *n* **1** a woollen or flannel undershirt *la18- NE*. **2** a woollen jacket or cardigan *la18-e19*. [perhaps ON *lindi* a belt, a girdle, a binder]

linning *see* LINEN¹·²

linningis *see* LINENS

lin-pin /'lɪn pɪn/ *n* a linch-pin *16-19, 20- Ork EC Bor*. [OE *lynis* a linch-pin + *pin* (PEEN¹)]

-lins /lɪnz/ *suffix* in the manner or direction of *18-*. [OE *ling* + *-s*]

linsey-winsey, linsie-winsie /'lɪnse wɪnse/ *n* linsey-woolsey, a type of fabric *la16-19, 20- NE EC Bor Uls*. [rhyming compound from ME *lindesie* a coarse fabric]

lint¹ /lɪnt/ *n* **1** scraped linen cloth or flax waste *la14-*. **2** flax in the process of manufacture for spinning *15-*. **3** the flax plant *la15-*. **4** linen thread used by shoemakers to make waxed thread *20-*. **lint-beet** a bundle of flax cut and ready for processing *19, 20- WC Uls*. **lint-bell** the flower of the flax plant *19, 20- Uls*. **lint bow**, †**lynt boll** the seed pod of flax *la15-19, 20- Uls*. **lint-dresser** a flax-dresser *18-19, 20- WC*. **lint-hole** a pond for steeping flax *la19-*. **lint mill** a flax-factory or its machinery *la18-*. **lint pot** a pond for steeping flax *la19, 20- NE EC*. **lint tap 1** the bundle of dressed flax put on a distaff for spinning *18-19, 20- historical*. **2** very fair or grey hair *18-19, 20- NE*. **lint-wheel** a spinning wheel for flax *17-19, 20- Uls*. **lint-white** *of hair* white as flax, flaxen-blond *la18-*. [ME *linet*, MFr *linette*]

lint² /lɪnt/ *v* to rest or recline *19, 20- Ork Bor*. [pt of Older Scots *lin* to rest, pause]

lintel, †**lentell**, †**lyntell** /'lɪntəl/ *n* **1** a horizontal support over a door or window *16-*. **2** a mantelpiece *la18-*. **3** the threshold of a door *la19-*. **lintel ale**, †**lintel aill**, **lintill eall** a drink given to masons at a building job when the door-lintel was put on *17-e18, 20- historical*. [OFr *lintel* a threshold]

linth *see* LENTH¹·¹

lintie /'lɪnti/ *n* **1** the linnet *Linaria cannabina 18-*. **2** an animated, happy girl *20-*. **3** the twite *Linaria flavirostris la19- Sh*. **lintick** the linnet *la19- Ork*. [shortened form of LINT-WHITE, with diminutive suffix]

lintie pipes /'lɪnti pʌɪps/ *n in riddles* a lamb *20- Sh*. Compare *rantie-pipes* (RANT¹·¹). [unknown]

†**Linton** *n* a variety of blackfaced hill-sheep bred in the Tweed region *la18-19*. [from the place-name *West Linton*]

lintwhite, †**lintquhite** /'lɪntʍʌɪt/ *n* the linnet *Linaria cannabina 16-19, 20- literary*. [OE *līnetwīge*]

linx *see* LINKS

linyel *see* LINGLE¹

lion, †**lyoun** /'laeən/ *n* **1** a wild animal of the cat family *Panthera leo la14-*. **2** the royal emblem of Scotland (adopted by William the Lion in place of the earlier dragon) *la14-*. **3** a copper or mixed metal coin first issued in 1555 *la16, la19- historical*. **4** a gold coin issued under Robert III and James II *15*. †**lyoun nobill** a gold coin issued from 1584 to 1588 *la16*. †**lyoun pece** = *lyoun nobill la16-e17*. **Lion Rampant** the device on the royal standard of Scotland *18-*. [ME *lioun*; compare LYON]

Lion *see* LYON

lip¹·¹ /lɪp/ *n* **1** one of the fleshy edges of the mouth *la14-*. **2** the rim of a vessel *la16-*. **3** the edge or brink of a stream or pool; frequently in place-names *19-*. **4** the edge or brim of a hat *la16-19, 20- T EC SW*. **5** a notch in the edge of a knife-blade or sword-blade *20- EC Bor*. **lippie** a glass full to the brim with liquid *19- WC SW*. **lip-fu, lip-foo** completely full, brimming over *la19, 20- Sh NE T*. **lip labour** empty or useless talk; prattle, chatter *17-19, 20- Sh*. **let down the lip** to look dismayed *20-*. **pit down the lip** to pout, scowl *20-*. [OE *lippa*]

lip¹·² /lɪp/ *v* **1** to be full to the brim or overflowing, brim over *18-*. **2** to touch with the lips, taste *la19-*. **3** to break, notch or chip a blade *19, 20- EC Bor*. **4** to point a wall *19*. [see the noun]

lipe /lʌɪp/ *n* **1** *mining* a small intrusion or irregularity in the joints of a coal-seam *18- C*. **2** the upturned edge of a peat spade *19- Bor*. **lipey** *of a coal-seam* intersected by small, irregular, glazed joints *18- C*. [compare OFr *lippe* a portion, a slip]

lippen¹, lippin, †**lipne** /'lɪpən/ *v* **1** to trust, depend or rely on; to confide in *la14-*. **2** to entrust (something); to put in someone's charge *la14-*. **3** to expect; to count on; to look forward to *15-*. **4** to begin to understand *20- Ork*. **lippen tae 1** to trust in, depend on *la16-*. **2** to look forward to; to expect *16-17*. **no tae lippen tae** untrustworthy *19-*. [unknown]

lippen² /'lɪpən/ *v* to chance upon, come across by accident *19, 20- Sh Ork*. [unknown]

lipper¹·¹ /'lɪpər/ *n* a ripple; a choppy sea *e16, 19- Sh Ork N H&I*. [see the verb]

lipper¹·², †lopper /'lɪpər/ *v* **1** *of water* to ripple or be ruffled (by the wind or tide) *16-19, 20- Sh Ork N NE*. **2** to be full to overflowing, be brimming over *19, 20- Sh Ork NE EC*. [probably frequentative form of LIP¹·²; compare LAPPER²·²]

lipper²·¹, *N NE* **lyper**, †**leper** /'lɪpər; *N NE* 'lʌɪpər/ *n* **1** a large, festering sore or mass of sores, a scab *20-*. **2** leprosy *15-17*. [ME *lepre*, Lat *lepra*]

lipper²·², **leper**, *N NE* **lyper** /'lɪpər, 'lɛpər; *N NE* 'lʌɪpər/ *n* **1** a leprous person *la15-*. **2** a derogatory term for a person or animal *la19- Sh*. **lipper-fat, lyper fat** bulging with fat, excessively fat *19- NE Bor*. [from LIPPER²·¹ and perhaps AN *lepre*]

lipper²·³, **leper** /'lɪpər, 'lɛpər/ *adj* **1** pestilential; diseased; mottled *18-19, 20- Sh*. **2** leprous *16-e19*. **lipperous, leprous 1** affected by leprosy *15-*. **2** afflicted with a disease (resembling leprosy) *la17-*. †**lipper folk, leper folk** lepers *15-e17*. †**lipper-hous, leiper hous** an asylum for lepers *la16-17*. †**lipper man, lepir man** a leper *15-17*. [see the noun]

lipperan *see* LEPRONE

lippie, *NE* **leepie**, †**leippie** /'lɪpi; *NE* 'lipi/ *n* **1** a dry measure varying in weight according to district and commodity; a quarter of a Scots peck *16-19, 20- N T EC*. **2** a (wooden) box-shaped measure of this size (for measuring a horse's feed) *17-19, 20- N NE*. **lippie's bound** an allotment, originally the amount of ground seeded by a measure of seed *la19- T EC*. [perhaps diminutive form of OE *lēap* a basket, a measure]

lippie *see* LIP¹·¹

lippin *see* LIPPEN¹

liquid /'lɪkwɪd/ *adj of debt or due payment* assessed and fixed in advance; specified exactly (in a contract) *16-*. [Lat *liquidus* clear, evident, certain]

liquidate, †**liquidat** /'lɪkwɪdet/ *adj of debt or due payment* assessed and fixed in advance; specified exactly (in a contract) *16-*. **liquidate damages** *law* damages stipulated by a penalty clause in a contract *19-*. [Lat *liquidāt-*, ptp stem of *liquidāre*]

†liquidatioun *n law* judicial valuation or ascertainment of the amount of a debt, rent or payment due, or of the monetary equivalent of a service or payment in kind *la16-17*. [Lat *liquidāt-*, ptp stem of *liquidāre*, with noun-forming suffix]

liquorie *see* LICKERY

liquour *see* LEECURE

lire¹, †lyre /laer/ *n* **1** *in a carcass of beef* the slice of meat near the sternum, the upper portion of brisket *18-*. **2** flesh *la15-18, 19- historical*. **†lyre and bane** flesh and bone *la14-16*. [OE *lira*]

†lire², †lyre *n in poetry* the complexion *15-19*. [ON *hlýr* cheek]

lirk¹·¹, lurk /lɪrk, lʌrk/ *n* **1** a wrinkle in the skin *la17-*. **2** a crease, rumple or fold in cloth or paper *18-*. **3** a fold or hollow in a hill, a crevice, a ravine *19-*. **4** the angle of the elbow or knee *la19, 20- SW Bor*. **5** an unusual trait of character, a mental twist *la17-19, 20- NE*. [compare Norw *lyre* protruding crease or fold in the skin]

lirk¹·², **lurk** /lɪrk, lʌrk/ *v* to crease, wrinkle *la17-*. [see the noun]

lirk², **lurk** /lɪrk, lʌrk/ *v* **1** to loiter or act furtively; to keep out of sight *la14-*. **2** to live quietly or out of the public eye *la14-17*. **3** to shrink, cower or cringe *la15-16*. [LOUR¹·², with frequentative -*k*]

lis *see* LISS¹

lisk, †leisk /lɪsk/ *n* the groin or flank *16-*. [compare Dan *lyske*, MDu, Flem *liesche*]

lispund, †leispund, †leischpund /ˈlɪspʌnd/ *n* a unit of weight used originally in the Baltic trade and later in Shetland and Orkney (for measuring butter, oil, malt and grain) *16-18, 19- historical*. [LG, Du *lispund* a Livonian pound]

liss¹, †lis, †les /lɪs/ *v* **1** *of pain* to cease or abate *19, 20- Uls*. **2** to relieve a person of pain or suffering *la14-16*. **lissens, lissance** respite *19, 20- Bor*. [OE *lissian*, perhaps also with influence from LESS¹·²]

†liss², lissis *npl* lists (for jousting) *la15*. [OFr *lisse*]

list¹·¹ /lɪst/ *n* **1** appetite, inclination *16-19, 20- EC*. **2** pleasure, enjoyment, delight *la15-16*. **†at list** at one's pleasure, according to one's will *15-16*. [see the verb]

list¹·², **†lest** /lɪst/ *v* to wish, desire *la14-19, 20- N*. **†me list** it pleases me, I desire *la14-e16* [OE *lystan*]

list² /lɪst/ *v* **1** to make a list *la17-*. **2** to enlist people into the army; to recruit soldiers *la17-*. **3** to enlist oneself as a soldier *la17-*. [Older Scots *list* a roll, a catalogue]

†listly *adv* skilfully, deftly *la14-e16*. [OE *listelīce*]

lit¹·¹, †litt, †lyt /lɪt/ *n* a dye, dyestuff; a colour or tint *15-19, 20- Sh N*. **†lit-house, litt-house, lithous** a dye-works *la16-19*. [ON *litr* colour]

lit¹·², **†litt** /lɪt/ *v* to colour; to dye or stain *15-19, 20- Sh N*. [ON *lita* to dye]

lit *see* LICHT¹·², LICHT²·²

lite *see* LEET¹·¹, LEET¹·²

†literatorie *adv* by letter; in writing *16-e17*. [Lat *litterātōriē*]

literature *see* LEETERATUR

lith¹·¹, †leth /lɪθ/ *n* **1** a joint in a limb; a joint in a finger or toe *la14-*. **2** a segment of an orange or apple *19-*. **3** a section of something; a part of a book *17-19, 20- H&I*. **4** a limb *19*. **lith and limb, †lith and lyme** all parts of the body *la14-19, 20- NE T*. **†out of lithe** out of joint, dislocated *la16-e17*. [OE *liþ*, ON *liðr*]

lith¹·² /lɪθ/ *v* to disjoint or dislocate; to wring the neck of a hen *la19- NE T*. [see the noun]

lithe *see* LYTHE¹·¹, LYTHE¹·², LYTHE¹·³

lither, †lidder /ˈlɪðər/ *adj* lazy, lethargic, slow *la15-19, 20- SW Bor*. **†lidder speid** slowly *e16*. [OE *lýþre* bad, base]

Lithgae /ˈlɪθge/ *n* **1** a nickname for the town of Linlithgow in West Lothian *20-*. **2** a nickname for Linlithgow Rose Football Club *la20-*. [reduced form of the place-name *Linlithgow*]

†lithry *n* a (disreputable) crowd *la18-e19*. [altered form of LIVERY a collection of uniformed servants]

litigious /lɪˈtɪdʒəs/ *adj* **1** *of people* inclined towards legal action *la17-*. **2** *of property* subject to litigation (and which therefore cannot be sold or otherwise alienated) *17-*. **3** vindictive, spiteful *19- NE*. [Fr *litigieux*]

litill *see* LITTLE¹·¹, LITTLE¹·², LITTLE¹·³

litiscontestation /ˌlʌɪtɪskɔntesˈteʃən/ *n law* the stage at or after which an action in court begins to be contested *la15-*. [Lat *lītis contestātio* the formal entry into a lawsuit by the calling of witnesses]

litster, †litstar, †littistar /ˈlɪtstər/ *n* a dyer of cloth *la14-19, 20- historical*. [LIT¹·¹, with agent suffix]

litt *see* LIT¹·¹, LIT¹·²

littigant *see* LET-DE-CAMP

littistar *see* LITSTER

little¹·¹, †litill /ˈlɪtəl/ *n* a small amount, quantity or degree; a short period of time *la14-*. [see the adj]

little¹·², †litill, †letle, †laytil /ˈlɪtəl/ *adj* **1** small in quantity or size *la14-*. **2** *of two places of the same name* smaller or less important; frequently in place-names *la14-*. **3** cherished, dear *la15-*. **littler** smaller *la16-*. **littlin, little ane, little one** a child, an infant *la16-*. **little body** a child, an infant *la19-*. **little boukit, little buikit 1** small in body or bulk, shrunken *la18-*. **2** of little importance, insignificant; deflated in esteem *la19- NE*. **little folks, little foukies** the fairies *18-*. **little guid**, *NE* **little gweedie** the sun-spurge *Euphorbia helioscopia 19-*. **†Little Guid, Little Gude** the Devil *e19*. **little house** a privy *la16-*. **†little man** a junior or adolescent male farm worker *la17-e19*. **little-thing, †lytill thing** a small matter, a trifle: ◊*the loss was little-thing to what it might have been la14-19, 20- NE T*. **little wee** very small, tiny *17-*. **little-worth**, *Sh* **little wirt** feeble; worthless *19-*. **a little wee** (to) a small extent, a little; a small amount; a short distance *la14-*. **little wee man** a very small or tiny man *19-*. **tae little maitter** to little purpose, with small advantage *la18- Sh NE T*. [OE *lȳtel*]

little¹·³, †litill /ˈlɪtəl/ *adv* **1** to a small extent, not much *15-*. **2** not at all: ◊*he fearit him litill la14-e17*. [see the adj]

liv *see* LUIF

live *see* LEEVE

liver¹, †lever, †luffyr /ˈlɪvər/ *n* an organ of the body *15-*. **liver-drink** a fatal blow *la19- Sh*. **liver head** a fish head stuffed with fish livers and boiled *la19- Sh*. **†luffyr ill** sickness of the liver *16-17*. **liver muggie** a cod's stomach stuffed with fish livers and boiled *19- Sh*. **liver-rock** a rock of homogeneous sandstone *19-*. [OE *lifer*]

liver² /ˈlɪvər/ *v* **1** to deliver goods to the shore; to unload a ship *17-19, 20- N NE T H&I*. **2** *of a ship* to discharge its cargo *17-18*. **3** to deliver, hand over *15-e16*. [ME *liveren*]

liver³ /ˈlɪvər/ *v* to thicken soup (with meal or flour) *19- Sh Ork N*. **liverie** *of soup* thickened *20- SW*. **liverin** thickening (for soup) *19- Sh N*. [Norw dial *levra*, *livra*]

livery, †levery, †luveray, †lovery /ˈlɪvəre/ *n* a uniform for a manservant; originally food or clothing given as a gratuity *la14-*. **†livery-meal** meal given in lieu of board *la18-e19*. [ME *livere*]

livrock *see* LAVEROCK

lizour¹·¹, †lizar, †lesour, †lesu /ˈlɪzər/ *n* (a strip of) grazing, a meadow or pasture *15-19, 20- WC*. [OE *lǣs* pasture]

†lizour¹·², lesure *v* to pasture or graze livestock *la15-19*. [OE *lǣswian*]

†lizure, lizzar *n* the selvage of a piece of cloth *la18-e19*. [OFr *lisiere*]

lö /lø/ *v* to listen intently; to eavesdrop *19- Sh*. [ON *hlýða*]

loacher *see* LOGGER

load *see* LAID[1.1], LAID[1.2]

loaden *see* LAID[1.2]

loaf, laif, *Sh* **lof, †lafe, †leaf** /lof, lef; *Sh* lɔf/ *n pl* also **laifs, †laves, †leaves 1** a shaped mass of bread baked as a single piece *la14-*. **2** a moulded mass of sugar *la16-*. **loafie 1** a kind of currant bun *la19- NE T*. **2** a loaf of bread made with wheat flour *20- NE T*. **loaf breid, loaf bread, †leaf bread** bread made with wheat flour *18-*. [OE *hlāf*]

loam *see* LAME[1.1]

loan[1.1]**, lone, †loyne** /lon/ *n* **1** an unpaved or grassy track for livestock (leading to common grazing); frequently in place-names *15-*. **2** a lane, street or road *19-*. **3** the farm roadway leading to the farmhouse; the ground adjoining a farmhouse *19, 20- NE T H&I*. **loanin, loaning, †lonyng 1** an enclosed track for animals through cultivated land; a grassy strip serving as a milking place; frequently in place-names *14-*. **2** the right of passage for animals by way of a track or passage *la15-17*. **loan heid, lone heid, loan head** the higher or outer end of a loan *la16-*. **†commoun lone** a public or communal cattle-track or milking area *16-17*. [OE *lanu*]

†loan[1.2]**, lone, loyne** *v* **1** *of cattle* to pass along a grassy track *la15-e18*. **2** to drive cattle along a grassy track *17-e18*. [see the noun]

†loan[2]**, lone** *n* provisions for a military campaign *16-e18*. [Gael *lòn*, IrGael *lón* food, provisions]

loard *see* LORD

loass *see* LOSS[1.1], LOSS[1.2]

loast *see* LOSS[1.2]

loat *see* LOT[1.1]

loath *see* LAITH[1.1]

lob *see* LAB[1]

lobba *see* LUBBA

lobster *see* LAPSTER

†loca *n fisherman's taboo* a chest *e19 Sh*. [ON *lok*]

local[1.1] /ˈlokəl/ *v* to apportion the liability for payment among the heritors and assign (a stipend) out of the teinds of a parish *la16-e20, la20- historical*. [see the verb]

local[1.2] /ˈlokəl/ *adj* **1** pertaining to a particular place *la16-*. **2** *of parochial stipends* assigned parish by parish out of the teinds of lands within each parish *la16-17*. **3** *of troops' quarterings* allocated to a specified district *17*. [MFr *local*, Lat *locālis*]

locality /ləˈkalɪti/ *n* **1** a place or district *la18-*. **2** the revenues of a certain piece of land allocated to an individual or corporate body as (part of) his or their income; the land in question *17-e20, la20- historical*. **3** (the apportioning of) liability for payment of a minister's stipend among the possessors of the teinds of lands lying within a parish *17-e20, la20- historical*. **4** a levy for maintaining troops within a parish *17-e19*. **5** a minister's or schoolmaster's stipend *17*. **6** the district allocated to troops to provide their maintenance *17*. **decree of locality** the decision of the Commission of Teinds confirming the allocation of liability for a minister's stipend *18-e20, la20- historical*. **†decreet of locality** = *decree of locality 17-18*. [Fr *localité*]

locastry, †lockerstrae /lokəˈstri/ *n* a small reed or straw pointer, used in teaching children to read or to keep one's place on a page when reading aloud *19- NE*. [**locus strae* a straw for indicating the position of the word or letter]

locate /ləˈket/ *v pt, ptp* **†locat 1** to situate, establish in a place *la16-*. **2** to identify or discover the location of (something or someone) *la18-*. **3** to let out on hire or lease *16-19*.

location, †locatioun *n* **1** a place of settlement or activity; the fact or condition of being placed *la16-*. **2** *law* the action of hiring out or renting *la16-*. **locator** *law* a person who leases out goods or property, or offers services for hire *la17-*. [Lat *locāt-*, ptp stem of *locāre* to let for hire]

loch, †louch, †lowch, †low /lɔx/ *n* **1** a (natural) lake; an inlet of the sea; frequently in place-names *14-*. **2** a small pool or puddle *20-*. **3** a discharge of urine *20- Ork NE T*. **loch fit, loch foot** the lower end of a loch; frequently in place-names *la18-*. **loch-head, †locheid** the upper end of a loch; frequently in place-names *16-*. **loch leech, †lochleiche 1** the leech *Hirudo medicinalis la16-19, 20- historical*. **2** a parasite, a rapacious person *la16-e18*. **loch maw, loch maa** the common gull *Larus canus 17-19, 20- Sh N*. **loch-reed** the common reed *Phragmites australis 18-19, 20- historical*. **lochside, †louchside** the side of a loch; the district round a loch *la14-*. **loch trout** a trout which feeds in a loch, usually larger than a river-trout *19-*. [Gael *loch*]

Lochaber axe /lɔxˈabər aks/ *n* a kind of long-handled battle-axe, still carried as ceremonial arms by the attendants of Edinburgh's Lord Provost *16-*. [from the name of the region + AIX]

lochan /ˈlɔxən/ *n* a small loch *la17-*. [Gael *lochan*]

Lochgelly /lɔxˈgɛli/ *n* a leather strap for punishing school children (manufactured in Lochgelly, Fife) *20, 21- historical*. **Lochgelly tawse** = LOCHGELLY *la20- historical*. [from the place-name]

Lochiel's lantern /lɔxˈilz ˈlantɛrn/ *n* the moon (the light of which was used for cattle-raiding) *la19, 20- historical*. Compare *MacFarlane's Bowat* (BOWET). [from the name of the chief of Clan Cameron + LANTERN]

Lochleven trout /lɔxˈlivən ˈtrʌut/ *n* a variety of trout peculiar to Lochleven *la18-*. [from the name of the loch + TROOT]

loch-liver /lɔx ˈlɪvər/ *n* a jellyfish *19- NE*. **loch-lubbertie** = *loch-liver*. [unknown]

†locht, lucht *n* **1** a boatload (of a commodity) *la16-17*. **2** a whole cargo *la14*. [IrGael *lucht* contents, a batch, Gael *luchd* a cargo]

lochter, lochtir *see* LACHTER[2]

lock[1.1]**, lok** /lɔk/ *n* **1** a mechanism for fastening or securing (by means of a key) *la14-*. **2** an enclosed section of a canal with gates at either end *18-*. **lockit, †lokkit** furnished with a lock or locks *15-*. **lockit book** an official register of a guild or craft (fitted with clasps and locks) *16-19, 20- T*. [OE *locc*]

lock[1.2]**, lok** /lɔk/ *v* **1** to secure with lock and key *15-*. **2** to embrace *19- Sh T*. **3** *of snow or mist* to make a place impassable or impenetrable *la19, 20- T*. **4** to entrap, imprison *la15-e18*. **lockit, †lokkit 1** locked up, fastened with a lock *la14-*. **2** kept secure or hidden *16-*. [see the noun]

lock[2]**, lok,** *N* **lowk, †luik** /lɔk; *N* lʌuk/ *n* **1** a tress of hair *la15-*. **2** a small quantity; a handful or a pinch (of meal or salt) *la16-*. **3** a large quantity or number (of anything); an abundance *la18-*. **4** a bundle or handful; an armful of hay *18-19, 20- Sh Ork N SW Uls*. **5** *law* a small quantity of meal exacted as one of the perquisites of the miller's servant *17-19, 20- historical*. **lock and gowpen** *law* a small quantity of meal exacted as one of the perquisites of the miller's servant *la18-19, 20- historical*. [OE *loc*]

†lockanties *interj* an expression of surprise or disappointment *la18-e19*. [compare LOVENANTY]

lockart *see* LOKKAT

locker, †lokker /ˈlɔkər/ *v* to bend or twist; *of hair* to curl *la15-19, 20- literary*. **†lokkerit** curled, curly *e16*. [probably from the noun LOCK[2]]

Lockerbie lick /ˈlɔkərbi lɪk/ *n* a gash or wound in the face; a beating or a defeat *la18-19, 20- WC SW Bor*. [from the name of the town in Dumfriesshire + LICK[1.1]]

lockerstrae *see* LOCASTRY

lockfast /ˈlɔkfast/ *adj* fastened by a lock; shut and locked; secured under lock and key against interference *la15-*. [LOCK[1.1] + *fast* (FEST[1.1])]

lockie *see* LOKE

lockman, †**lokman** /ˈlɔkmən/ *n* a public executioner *la15-19, 20- historical*. [unknown]

†**locumtenant** *n* a lieutenant *la15-e16*. [Lat *locumtenens*]

locus /ˈlokəs/ *n* a place, site or position *18-*. **locus poenitentiae** *law* the opportunity given to a person to withdraw from an agreement before he has confirmed it in law *18-*. [Lat *locus*]

Lod /lɔd/ *interj* a euphemism for God *la19-*. [altered form of LORD]

lodberrie /ˈlɔdbɛri/ *n* a flat rock forming a natural landing-place; a private pier; a house which combines pier, court-yard, warehouse and dwelling-house *la18- Sh Ork*. [ON *hlaðberg* a projecting pier, a rock where ships are loaded]

lode *see* LAID[1.1]

lodesman, †**lodisman** /ˈlɔdzmən/ *n* a guide; a pilot or steersman *16-19, 20- Sh*. [altered form of OE *lādmann*]

lodge *see* LUDGE[1.1], LUDGE[1.2]

lodgin, lodging *see* LUDGIN

lodie /ˈlodi/ *n* a space in the corner of the living-room in which potatoes are stored *la19- Sh*. [ON *hlaða* a storehouse]

lodisman *see* LODESMAN

lodomy /ˈlɔdəmi/ *n* laudanum *19, 20- NE T EC*. [altered form of Eng *laudanum*]

loe *see* LUVE[1.2]

loesome *see* LUVESOME

lof *see* LOAF

lofe[1.1], †**lof** /lof/ *n* 1 an offer (to sell or to buy something at a certain price) *la16-19, 20- SW Bor*. 2 praise, honour, glory *la14-16*. [see the verb]

†**lofe**[1.2], **lof, love** *v* 1 to haggle over, set a price on; to offer wares at a specific price *la16-e19*. 2 to praise or honour; to value highly *la14-e17*. **lovabill, loffabill** 1 *of laws or customs* laudable, acceptable; respected, established *15-17*. 2 *of people* praiseworthy, honourable; satisfactory, acceptable *15-16*. **lovage** praise, honour *la15-e16*. **loving** 1 praise, commendation; an act of praising *la14-e18*. 2 honour, credit; fame, glory *la14-16*. [OE *lofian* to praise, value]

loft *see* LAFT[1.1], LAFT[1.2]

lofting *see* LAFT[1.1]

logage *see* LOVISH

logan[1.1], **loggin** /ˈlɔgən/ *n* a selection of small articles, coins or marbles (scattered for children to scramble for) *19- NE*. [OFr *lagan* flotsam and jetsam, jettisoned cargo]

logan[1.2], **loggin** /ˈlɔgən/ *v* to scatter coins or marbles *19- NE*. [see the noun]

loge *see* LUDGE[1.1], LUDGE[1.2]

loggage, luggage /ˈlɔgədʒ, ˈlʌgədʒ/ *n* baggage *17-*. [Scots *lug* to pull, with noun-forming suffix]

†**loggars, logouris** *npl* a kind of hose; stockings without feet *la15-e19*. [unknown]

logger, loacher /ˈlɔgər, ˈloxər/ *v* to drench, soak or besplatter; to slobber (food) *19, 20- N*. [unknown; compare LAGGER[1.2]]

†**loggerand** *adj* bandy, crooked *la15*. [unknown]

loggin *see* LOGAN[1.1], LOGAN[1.2]

logie, loggie /ˈlogi, ˈlɔgi/ *n* 1 the fireplace or KILLOGIE of a kiln *la16-19, 20- historical*. 2 the outer opening of a ventilation funnel in a corn-stack *la18-19, 20- T*. [probably Gael *logan, lagan* a hollow, a pit]

logive *see* LOVISH

logouris *see* LOGGARS

logyng *see* LUDGIN

†**loik-hertit, luik-hertit** *adj* warm-hearted *e16*. [perhaps ME *leuk* warm]

lois *see* LOS

loist *see* LOSS[1.2]

loit[1.1] /lɔɪt/ *n* 1 a (semi-liquid) mass of something filthy or disgusting; a lump of faeces *19, 20- Sh NE T*. 2 a small quantity of liquid *19, 20- Sh N*. [perhaps onomatopoeic]

loit[1.2] /lɔɪt/ *v* to defecate; to vomit *19- NE T SW*. [see the noun]

loith *see* LAITH[1.3]

lok *see* LOCK[1.1], LOCK[1.2], LOCK[2]

loke, †loks, †lockie /lok/ *interj* an expression of surprise or glee *la18-19, 20- Bor*. [probably altered form of LORD; compare LOCKANTIES]

†**lokkat, lockart** *n* a metal crossbar in a window *16-e17*. [OFr *locquet*]

lokker *see* LOCKER

†**lokkeris** *npl* curly locks of hair *e16*. [from the verb LOCKER]

lokkin *see* LOUK

lokman *see* LOCKMAN

loks *see* LOKE

loll[1] /lɔl/ *n* a pampered, lazy person *18-19, 20- NE*. [Eng *loll* to hang, droop]

loll[2] /lɔl/ *v* to howl like an animal; to caterwaul *19- Bor*. [onomatopoeic; compare Du *lollen*]

Lombard, †Lumbard, †lumbart /ˈlɔmbard/ *n* 1 a native of Lombardy *la14-*. 2 a style of sleeve from Lombardy *16*. [from the name of the region of northern Italy]

lomo /ˈlomo/ *n* a (large or clumsy) hand; a paw *19- Ork*. **lomick** a hand *19- Sh Ork*. [ON *lámr* a hand]

lomon *see* LOWMON

lomp *see* LUMP

lomvie *see* LONGVIE

lonchard *see* LUNCART

London, Londoun *see* LUNNON

lone *see* LANE[2.1], LANE[2.2], LOAN[1.1], LOAN[1.2], LOAN[2]

lone *see* LOAN[1.1], LOAN[1.2]

long *see* LANG[1.1], LANG[1.2], LANG[2]

longart *see* LUNCART

longavil *see* LONGUEVILLE

long-saddle *see* LANG-SETTLE

longsoucht *see* LUNGASUUT

long syne *see* LANG SYNE[1.3]

†**longueville, longavil** *n* a variety of pear *la17-19*. [from the French place-name]

longvie, longie, longwee, †lomvie, †lungie /ˈlɔŋvi, ˈlɔŋi, ˈlɔŋwi/ *n* the guillemot *Uria aalge la18- Sh*. [ON *langvé*]

lonnach, lonnack /ˈlɔnəx, ˈlɔnək/ *n* 1 couch grass *Elymus repens* (heaped for burning) *la18-19, 20- NE T Bor*. 2 a long rope *la19- NE*. [unknown]

Lon'on *see* LUNNON

loo[1.1], **lew** /lu/ *n* a warmth, a slight rise in temperature (of the interior of haystacks) *19-*. [see the verb]

loo[1.2], **lew** /lu/ *v* to make tepid, heat slightly; to become warm *la19, 20- Sh Uls*. [OE *hlēowan* to warm]

loo[1.3], **lew** /lu/ *adj* lukewarm, tepid *18-*. **loo warm, †lew warm** lukewarm *16-*. [OE *hliēwan* to warm]

loo *see* LUVE[1.2]

looch, louch /lux/ *adj* depressed or ill *20- NE C*. **loochy** *of an illness* severe, debilitating *20- NE EC*. [unknown; compare LOUGH]

lood[1.1], **loud**, †**lowd** /lud, lʌud/ *adj* strongly audible; noisy, clamorous, loud-voiced *la14-*. [OE *hlūd*]

lood[1.2], **loud**, †**lowd** /lud, lʌud/ *adv* **1** with a loud noise or voice; aloud *la14-*. **2** flagrantly, openly *16*. **loud-spoken**, **lood-spoken** having a loud or domineering voice *la19-*. †**loud na still** in every respect, entirely *la14-15*. **loud out** aloud, in a loud voice *19-*. [OE *hlūde*]

looder *see* LOWDER[1.1]

looder-horn /ˈludərhɔrn/ *n* a bullock's horn used as a trumpet on fishing-boats for signalling in fog or darkness *la19- Sh*. [ON *luðr* + HORN]

loof *see* LUIF

loofie *see* LUIFFIE

loog *see* LUG[1]

look *see* LEUK[1.1], LEUK[1.2]

loolie /ˈluli/ *n in Inverness* a child's word for a lamplighter *la19-e20, la20- historical*. [altered form of LEERIE]

loom[1.1] /lum/ *n* the indistinct appearance of something seen through a haze or at a great distance; a haze or fog *19-*. [see the verb]

loom[1.2] /lum/ *v* to appear indistinctly; *of a ship* to appear on the horizon *19-*. [Eng *loom* (of a ship) to move slowly up and down; compare Fris *lômen*, Swed dial *loma* to move slowly]

loom[2], *NE* **leam** /lum; *NE* lim/ *n* **1** the red-throated diver *Gavia stellata* or the great northern diver *Gavia immer 19- Sh Ork NE*. **2** the guillemot *Uria aalge 20- Sh Ork*. [ON *lómr*]

loom, loomb *see* LUME

loon, loun, †**lown** /lun/ *n* **1** a young man; a boy or youth *la15-*. **2** a young farm worker; a farm-boy who does the odd jobs *19-*. **3** a male child, a son, a baby boy *19-*. **4** a nickname for a native of Forfar *la19-*. **5** a mischievous rogue, a young scamp *17-19, 20- T EC*. **6** a rough or dishonest man *la15-19, 20- T C Bor Uls*. **7** a sexually immoral person *la16-19, 20- EC*. **loun-like** disreputable, shabby, scruffy *17-19, 20- T*. †**lounrie, lownrie 1** baseness; villainy *16-e19*. **2** sexual wickedness, fornication *la16-e18*. **the Loons** a nickname for Forfar Athletic Football Club *20-*. **loon-lookin** rough-looking, villainous *la19, 20- literary*. †**loun minister** a name applied by the Covenanters to a minister who accepted the episcopalian and royalist regime *17*. **play the loon 1** to behave unchastely; to have sex *la16-19, 20- EC*. **2** to misbehave; to cheat *la16-e17*. [unknown]

†**loonder, lounder, lundyr** *v* to idle or skulk *la16-19*. [Du *lunderen*]

loonder *see* LOUNDER[1.1], LOUNDER[1.2]

loonge *see* LUNGE

loop, †**loup,** †**lowp** /lup/ *n* **1** a bend in a river; the winding of a river or its valley *la15-*. **2** a piece of string or rope doubled back on itself, a coil or bend *16-*. **3** *in knitting* a stitch *la18-*. **loopie, loopy** deceitful, shifty, crafty *la18-*. †**louping, luping** cord or braid consisting of loops (used as fastening or trimming on garments) *la16-e18*. **loopit** coiled, looped, intertwined *16-*. **tak a loop** to take up one's knitting; to knit *la19-*. [unknown]

loopick, lupik /ˈlupɪk/ *n* **1** a horn spoon with a short or broken-off handle *19- Sh Ork*. **2** (the shell of) a small crab of the family *Lithodidae la19- Sh*. [unknown]

loorach /ˈlurəx/ *n* **1** an ungainly or untidy person *20- N NE T H&I*. **2** a tattered or trailing garment or piece of cloth; an untidy or ragged piece of rope or string *20- N NE H&I*. **3** a much-worn coat *20- NE*. **loorachy, lourichy 1** in poor health or condition *la20- NE T*. **2** dirty or dishevelled *la20- NE*. [Gael *lùireach* a trailing, untidy garment; a lanky, clumsy person, Lat *lōrīca* a coat-of-mail]

†**loose** *v pt, ptp* **loosed** to lose *17*. [OE *losian*; compare LOSS[1.2]]

loose *see* LOUSE, LOWSE[1.1], LOWSE[1.2]

loosen *see* LOWSEN

loosie *see* LOUSE

loosome *see* LUVESOME

†**loot** *n* a lout *la19*. [variant of Eng *lout*]

loot *see* LAT, LOUT[1.2]

loove *see* LUVE[1.1]

loozie *see* LOUSE

lope *see* LOWP[1.2]

loppend /ˈlɔpənd/ *adj of the hands* numb with cold, without power or feeling *20- Ork*. [Icel *loppinn*, Norw dial *loppen*]

lopper *see* LAPPER[1.1], LAPPER[1.2], LIPPER[1.2]

loppin *see* LEAP

lopstar *see* LAPSTER

†**lorane** *n* a silver coin, a testoon *la16*. [perhaps from the name of the duchy or the cross of *Lorraine*]

lord, loard /lɔrd, lord/ *n* **1** a master, a ruler *la14-*. **2** a formal title applied to various officers of state *la14-*. **3** a nobleman or magnate *la14-*. **4** the landowner or proprietor of a landed estate *la14-*. **5** Christ or God *la14-*. **6** a judge of the Court of Session or the High Court; *pl* the court itself *la15-*. **Lord sake** an expression of surprise or protest *19-*. †**Lordis auditoris** the judicial committees of Parliament *la15*. †**the Lord's mornin** Sunday morning *la19*. **the Lord's nicht** Sunday night *la17-19, 20- historical*. †**Lords of the clergie** the Bishops in the post-Reformation parliament *la17*. †**lord of one's awin** a person who had full or independent ownership or control of his property *15*. †**the Lordis Saboth** Sunday *e17*. [OE *hlāford*; compare LAIRD[1.1]]

Lord Advocate /lɔrd ˈadvəkət/ *n* the principal law officer of the Crown in Scotland *la16-*. [LORD + ADVOCATE[1.1]]

†**Lord chalmerlane** *n* one of the chief officers of the royal household *la15-16*. [LORD + CHAMBERLAIN]

†**Lord Chancellour** *n* the highest officer of the Crown and chief legal authority *la15-17*. [LORD + CHANCELLOR]

†**Lord Chief Baron of Exchequer** *n* the president of the Court of Exchequer which was set up in 1707 and then abolished in 1856 *18-19*. Compare BARONS OF EXCHEQUER. [LORD + CHIEF[1.1] + BARONS OF EXCHEQUER]

Lord Clerk Register, †**Lord Clerk of Register** /lɔrd clark ˈrɛdʒɪstər/ *n* **1** the Clerk of Parliament; the officer of state responsible for compiling, and custodian of, the public and governmental registers and records *la16-19, 20- historical*. **2** a titular office giving the holder precedence after the LORD JUSTICE GENERAL *19-*. [LORD + *Clerk of the Register* (CLARK[1.1])]

Lord Commissioner /lɔrd kəˈmɪʃənər/ *n* **1** the representative of the monarch in the General Assembly of the Church of Scotland *17-*. **2** the representative of the monarch in the Scottish Parliament *17-e18*. [LORD + COMMISSIONER]

Lord Commissioner of Justiciary /lɔrd kəˈmɪʃənər əv dʒʌˈstɪʃəre/ *n* a judge of the High Court *la17-*. Compare LORD OF JUSTICIARY. [LORD + COMMISSIONER + JUSTICIARY]

†**Lord Conservator** *n* an officer based at Campvere, Holland, appointed to protect the rights of the Scottish merchants and settle their disputes *17-18*. [LORD + CONSERVATOR]

Lord Cornet /lɔrd ˈkɔrnət/ *n* the chief rider and standard-bearer of the burgh in ceremonies of Riding of the Marches *20-*. [LORD + CORNET]

Lord High Admiral /lɔrd hae ˈadmɪrəl/ *n* the commander-in-chief of the navy *18-19, 20- historical*. [LORD + HEICH[1.3] + ADMIRAL]

Lord High Commissioner /lɔrd hae kəˈmɪʃənər/ *n* the representative of the monarch in the General Assembly of the Church of Scotland *18-*. Compare Lord Commissioner. [Lord + heich¹·³ + Eng *commissioner*]

Lord High Constable /lɔrd hae ˈkɔnstəbəl/ *n* one of the chief officers of the royal household *17-*. [Lord + High Constable]

Lord High Steward of Scotland /lɔrd hae stuərd əv ˈskɔtlənd/ *n* the chief officer of the Royal Household *17, 18- historical*. [Lord + heich¹·³ + reduced form of Great Steward of Scotland]

†**Lord High Treasurer, Lord High Thesaurer** *n* the chief financial officer of Scotland *17-e18*. Compare Lord Treasurer [Lord + High Thesaurer]

†**Lordis of the Thre Estatis** *npl* the members of Parliament collectively, the Three Estates in Parliament *la15-e16*. [Lord + *The Three Estates* (three)]

Lord Justice Clerk /lɔrd dʒʌstɪs ˈklark/ *n* one of the principal judges and vice president of the High Court of Justiciary; originally the principal clerk of justiciary, the officer of state who officiated as clerk of the justice court *la16-*. [Lord + *Justice Clerk* (justice)]

Lord Justice General /lɔrd dʒʌstɪs ˈdʒɛnərəl/ *n* the principal justice and President of the High Court of Justiciary *la16-*. [Lord + *Justice General* (justice)]

Lord Lyon /lɔrd ˈlaeən/ *n* the chief officer of arms of Scotland and head of the Lyon Court *la16-*; compare Lyon. **Lord Lyon King at Arms** an alternative designation for the Lord Lyon (which is not officially approved) *la17-*. **Lord Lyon King of Arms** an alternative designation for the Lord Lyon *la16-*. [from the armorial bearing of the Kings of Scotland, the lion rampant, which is worn on his robes]

Lord of Erection /lɔrd əv əˈrɛkʃən/ *n* a layman to whom the Crown transferred the title to church lands after the Reformation *17-18, 19- historical*. [Lord + erection]

Lord of Justiciary /lɔrd əv dʒʌˈstɪʃəre/ *n* a judge of the Court of Justiciary *la17-19, 20- historical*. [Lord + justiciary]

Lord of Parliament /lɔrd əv ˈparləmənt/ *n* a member of the lowest rank of the Scottish peerage, a baron below the rank of earl or viscount; originally the lowest rank of those required to attend parliament by personal summons *15-*. [Lord + parliament¹]

†**Lord of Plat** *n* a commissioner for administrating the territorial organization of parishes, supply of ministers and provision of stipends *17*. [Lord + plat¹]

Lord of Regality /lɔrd əv rɪˈgaləti/ *n* a person to whom rights of jurisdiction almost co-extensive with that of the Crown were entrusted *15-e18, la18- historical*. [Lord + regality]

Lord of Register *see* Lord Register

†**Lord of Sanct Johnis** *n* Preceptor of the Knights Hospitallers of St John *la15-16*. [Lord + the name of the saint]

Lord of Seat, †Lord of Sete /lɔrd əv ˈset/ *n* a judge in the Court of Session *la15-16, 19- historical*. [Lord + seat]

Lord of Session /lɔrd əv ˈsɛʃən/ *n* a judge of the Court of Session; a member of the College of Justice *la15-*. Compare Lords of Council and Session. [Lord + session¹·¹]

†**Lord of the Counsail** *n* **1** a member of the sovereign's Council in any of its various advisory, judicial, auditorial or executive capacities *la15-e17*. **2** a judge of the Court of Session; a member of the College of Justice *16-e17*; compare Lords of Council and Session. [Lord + *counsale* (cooncil)]

Lord Ordinary /lɔrd ˈɔrdənəre/ *n* one of the judges of the Court of Session who sit on cases of first instance in the Outer House, originally a judge with a regular and fixed jurisdiction *la16-*. [Lord + *ordinary* (ordinar¹·²)]

Lord President /lɔrd ˈprɛzɪdənt/ *n* the president of the Court of Session and head of the Scottish judiciary *la16-*. [Lord + president]

Lord Privy Seal /lɔrd prɪve ˈsil/ *n* the keeper of the Privy Seal of Scotland, which was latterly a titular office and now entirely abolished *la15-e20, la20- historical*. [Lord + Privy Seal]

†**Lord Probationer** *n* a newly-appointed judge of the Court of Session after he had presented his letter of appointment and before he took the oath *la18-e19*. [Lord + Eng *probationer*]

Lord Provost /lɔrd ˈprɔvəst/ *n* a courtesy title given to the provosts of Scottish cities *la15-*. [Lord + provost]

Lord Rector /lɔrd ˈrɛktər/ *n in Scottish Universities* the elected representative of the student body on the University Court, in post for three years, originally the elected head of the University, subordinate only to the chancellor *16-*. [Lord + rector]

Lord Register, †Lord of Register /lɔrd ˈrɛdʒɪstər/ *n* an officer of state who had custody of the national records and registers *17-19, 20- historical*. Compare Lord Clerk Register. [Lord + register¹·¹]

lordschipe, lordschype *see* lordship

Lord Secretary /lɔrd ˈsɛkrətəre/ *n* the Secretary of State and assistant to the Lord Chancellor *16-e18, 19- historical*. [Lord + *secretary* (secretar)]

lordship, †lordschipe, †lordschype /ˈlɔrdʃɪp/ *n* **1** the authority and function of a lord; dominion, sovereignty *la14-*. **2** the land belonging to a lord; the territory under his jurisdiction; originally an estate or estates held as a single unit by a feudal lord *la14-*. **3** a royalty payable on sales (of minerals or books) *18-e20, la20- historical*. [Lord, with *-ship* suffix]

Lords of Council and Session, †Lordis of Council and Sessioun /lɔrdz əv ˈkʌunsəl ənd sɛʃən/ *npl* the judges of the Court of Session; the College of Justice *16-*. [Lord + *council* (cooncil) + session¹·¹]

Lords of the Articles /lɔrdz əv ðə ˈartɪkəlz/ *npl* the parliamentary committee responsible for drafting and preparing legislation *la15-17, 18- historical*. [Lord + airticle]

Lord Steward of Scotland /lɔrd stuərd əv ˈskɔtlənd/ *n* the chief officer of the Royal Household *17, 18- historical*. Compare Lord High Steward of Scotland. [Lord + stewart + Scotland]

Lord Treasurer, †Lord Thesaurer /lɔrd ˈtrɛʒərər/ *n* the chief financial officer of Scotland, latterly an honorary office *16-*. [Lord + thesaurer]

loren, lorin /ˈlɔrən/ *n* the cormorant *Phalacrocorax carbo la18- Sh*. [derivative of Norw *lår*, ON *lár*]

lorie /ˈlɔri/ *interj* a euphemism for God *19, 20- Sh Ork N NE*. [altered form of Lord]

lorimer, †lorimar /ˈlɔrɪmər/ *n* a maker of the metal parts of a horse's harness; a maker of small iron-ware *la12-18, 19- historical*. [OFr *loremier*]

lorin *see* loren

lorn *see* lese

Lorne sausage /lɔrn ˈsɔsɪdʒ/ *n* square-shaped sausage-meat cut into flat slices *la19-*. Compare sliced sausage. [perhaps from the name of the Scottish district + Eng *sausage*]

lorne shoe /lɔrn ˈʃu/ *n* a kind of shoe in which the upper and tongue are cut as one piece and stitched to the rest of the shoe *la19- Sh NE T EC Bor*. [a proprietary trade name in honour of the Marquis of Lorne + shae¹·¹]

lorry /ˈlɔri/ *v* to spatter with mud or dirt *20- Ork*. [unknown]

lorry *see* larrie

†**los, lose, lois** *v pt, ptp* **lossit, lost** to unload a ship; *of a ship* to discharge its cargo *15-e17*. [MDu *lossen* to free, redeem, unload a ship, MLG *lossen* to unload a ship]
los *see* LOSS^(1.1), LOSS^(1.2), LOWSE^(1.2)
losane *see* LOZEN^(1.1)
lose *see* LOS, LOSS^(1.1), LOSS^(1.2)
†**losel** *n* a lazy or dishonest person *la18-19*. [probably altered form of *losen*, ptp of LESE to lose]
losenge *see* LOZENGE
†**losengeour** *n* **1** a liar, a flatterer *la14-e16*. **2** a lazy person *16*. [OFr *losengeour*]
losengit *see* LOZEN^(1.2)
losh /lɔʃ/ *interj* a euphemism for God *la18-*. †**loshins** good gracious *la19*. **losh me** goodness me *19-*. [altered form of LORD]
losin *see* LOZEN^(1.1)
losit *see* LOSS^(1.2)
loss^(1.1), **loass**, †**los**, †**lose**, †**loys** /lɔs, los/ *n* **1** the fact of losing; that which is lost *la15-*. **2** detriment or disadvantage; misfortune or ruin *la16-*. [see the verb]
loss^(1.2), **loass**, **lose**, †**los** /lɔs, los, luz/ *v pt, ptp* **lost**, *C* **loast**, †**losit**, †**lossit**, †**loist 1** to misplace or lose possession of; to be deprived of *la14-*. **2** to suffer defeat, be unsuccessful *la14-*. **3** to cause to perish, destroy *la14-*. **4** to waste or squander *16-*. **loss the heid, lose the heid** to lose one's temper; to become over-excited *20-*. **lose mind** to forget *20-*. **lose yer puggie** to lose one's temper *la20- C Bor*. [OE *losian*]
lost *see* LOS, LOSS^(1.2)
losynnit *see* LOZEN^(1.2)
lot^(1.1), **loat** /lɔt, lot/ *n* **1** assignment by chance selection; one of a group of objects used to make this assignment *la12-*. **2** an allotted share or portion *la16-*. **3** fate, fortune, destiny *la16-*. **4** a large number or amount *19-*. **5** a piece of land allotted to a particular tenant *17-e19*. **6** an allowance of corn paid to the thresher *la17-18*. †**lotman** a corn-thresher *la18-19*. **lot and scot** *see* scot and lot (SKATT^(1.1)). [OE *hlot*]
lot^(1.2) /lɔt/ *v* **1** to assign or allocate by lot *17-*. **2** to contribute a proportionate or allotted share to a common (municipal) payment *la15-19, 20- historical*. [see the noun]
löt *see* LAT
†**lotch** *n* a plump lazy person *e19*. [perhaps LATCH³]
loth *see* LAITH^(1.2)
Lothian, Louden, Lowden, †**Lowthiane** /'loðɪən, 'lʌudən/ *n* an area in East-Central Scotland *16-*. **The Lothians** the name for the (former) counties of East Lothian, Midlothian and West Lothian collectively (with or without the City of Edinburgh) *20-*. **Lothian Region** a local government area formed from the former counties of the City of Edinburgh, East Lothian, Midlothian and West Lothian *la20, 21- historical*. [unknown]
louch *see* LOCH, LOOCH, LOUTCH^(1.2)
loud *see* LOOD^(1.1), LOOD^(1.2)
louder, looder, †**lowther** /'lʌudər, 'ludər/ *v* **1** to walk wearily, plod; to move clumsily or lazily *la18- NE T H&I EC*. **2** to loiter; to laze about *19- NE EC*. [probably Du *leuteren* to linger, dally, MDu *loteren* to sway about, hesitate]
louder *see* LOWDER^(1.1)
lough /lʌux, lux/ *v of the wind* to die down *20- T*. [perhaps based on LAICH and SOUCH; compare LOUCH]
†**louk, luk, lowk** *v ptp* **lowkit, lukkin, lokkin 1** to close, shut *16-e17*. **2** to draw together or form a close mass *16*. **3** to enclose, surround or entrap *15-e16*. **lowkyt** *of flower-buds* closed, compact *e16*. **loukit kaill** cabbage *la16-17*. [OE *lūcan* to close, lock; compare LUCKEN^(1.3)]
loun *see* LOON

lounder^(1.1), **loonder, lunder, lunner,** †**lundyr** /'lʌundər, 'lundər, 'lʌndər, 'lʌnər/ *n* a heavy blow *18-*. [unknown]
lounder^(1.2), **loonder, lunder, lunner** /'lʌundər, 'lundər, 'lʌndər, 'lʌnər/ *v* **1** to beat, thrash; to pound or batter *la18-*. **2** to move or work with energy and speed; to speak vehemently *la19, 20- Sh Ork NE*. **loundering,** †**lund'ring** *n* a beating *la17-*. **loundering** *adj of a blow* resounding, severe *18-*. [unknown]
lounder *see* LOONDER
†**lounge** *v* to belabour, beat *19*. [altered form of LUNGE]
lounge *see* LUNGE
lounkart *see* LUNCART
loup *see* LOOP, LOWP^(1.1), LOWP^(1.2)
lour^(1.1), **lower** /lur, lʌur/ *n* **1** a gloomy or threatening sky *19- literary*. **2** a gloomy or sullen look *e19*. [see the verb]
lour^(1.2) /lur/ *v* **1** *of weather* to look threatening, become overcast *19-*. **2** to lie low; to skulk; to cower or crouch *15-e19*. **3** to grovel, submit *16-e17*. **lourin** threatening *20-*. **loury, lowry** *of the sky* dull, overcast; threatening rain *19-*. **loorbrow** a frowning aspect *20- T EC Bor*. **lour-shouthered** round-shouldered, stooping *19- Bor*. [perhaps MDu *loeren* to frown; to lie in wait]
†**lourd** *adj* sluggish, heavy, stupid *15-17*. [MFr *lourd*]
lourd *see* LEIF^(1.2)
lourdie, lourdy /'lurdi/ *adj* heavy; sluggish, slow *la18-19, 20- literary*. [derivative of LOURD]
lous *see* LOUSE, LOWSE^(1.2)
louse, loose, luce, †**lous** /lʌus, lus/ *n pl* **lice,** †**lyse** an insect of the order *Phthiraptera*, a louse *15-*. **loosie, loozie,** †**lowsy 1** infested with lice *16-*. **2** filthy, vile *la16-*. **lucy arnut, lousy arnut** the earthnut *Bunium bulbocastanum* or *Conopodium majus 19-*. [OE *lūs*]
louse *see* LOWSE^(1.2)
lout^(1.1), **lut** /lʌut, lut/ *n* the act of bending or bowing; a stoop, a hunched posture *la16-19, 20- Sh*. [see the verb]
lout^(1.2), **loot,** †**lowt** /lʌut, lut/ *v* **1** to bend, stoop or duck *la14-*. **2** to submit, yield *la15-*. **3** to bend or bow (a part of the body); to lower the head *la18-*. **4** to humble oneself *16-19*. **loutit** bent with age; round-shouldered *20-*. [OE *lūtan*, ON *lúta*]
lout^(1.3), **lut** /lʌut, lut/ *adj of the shoulders* bent, stooping, round *16-19, 20- Sh*. [see the verb]
loutch^(1.1) /lutʃ, lʌutʃ/ *n* a slouching gait, a stoop *20- NE EC*. [see the verb]
loutch^(1.2), †**louch** /lutʃ, lʌutʃ/ *v* to stoop, slouch *la16-19, 20- NE T EC SW*. [probably conflation of LOUT^(1.2) with SLOOCH^(1.2)]
louther *see* LOWDER^(1.1)
lovage, †**luffage,** †**levage** /'lʌvədʒ/ *n* the herb *Levisticum officinale la15-*. [AN *luvasche*]
lovage *see* LOVISH
love *see* LOFE^(1.2), LUVE^(1.1), LUVE^(1.2)
loveguard *see* LEVE-GARD
lovenanty, lovanentie, lovananty /lovə'nanti, lovə'nɛnti/ *interj* an expression of surprise or protest *la19-*. [perhaps from Scots *Lord defend thee*; compare LOCKANTIES]
lovery *see* LIVERY
lovey-dickie /lʌvi'dɪki/ *interj* an expression of surprise or protest *la19- T EC Bor*. [compare Eng *love-a-duck* and LOVENANTY]
lovey-ding /lʌvi'dɪŋ/ *interj* an expression of surprise or protest *la19- N EC*. [compare LOVEY-DICKIE and LOVENANTY]
lovie *see* LUVE^(1.1)
lovish, lavish, *EC* **logage,** †**lovage,** †**logive,** †**lawage** /'lɔvɪʃ, 'lavɪʃ; *EC* 'lɔgədʒ/ *adj* unrestrained, extravagant *16-*. [MFr *lavasse* a deluge, *lavage* a washing]
lovit *see* LUVIT

†**low**[1.1], **law** *v* to lower; to bring low; to overthrow *la14-e18*. [see the adj]

low[1.2], **law** /lo, lɔ/ *adj* **1** not high; low in height *la14-*. **2** occupying a low or lower position *la14-*. **3** *of ground* low-lying *la14-*. **4** base; humble *la14-*. **low door** (on) the ground floor *20-*. **low road** the lower of two roads (connecting two places) *19-*. [ON *lágr*]

low[1.3], **law** /lo, lɔ/ *adv* in or into a low position *15-*. [see the adj]

low *see* LOCH, LOWE[1.1], LOWE[1.2]

†**lowance, lowins** *n* an allowance (of food or money given to a beggar or pensioner) *la16-19*. [aphetic form of *allowance* (ALLOOANCE)]

†**lowand-ill, lowing-ill** *n* a disease of cattle characterized by prolonged or continuous lowing or bellowing *la16*. [presp of Older Scots *low* to bellow, moo + ILL[1.1]]

lowch *see* LOCH

lowche *see* LAUCH[1.2]

lowd *see* LOOD[1.1], LOOD[1.2]

lowden[1.1] /'lʌudən/ *v* to diminish in intensity *19, 20- literary*. [see the adj]

†**lowden**[1.2], **lowdin** *adj* subdued, mute *la16-e18*. [metathesis of *lownd* (LOWN[1.3])]

Lowden *see* LOTHIAN

lowder[1.1], **louder**, *Sh Ork* **looder**, *NE* **louther**, †**lewder** /'lʌudər; *Sh Ork* 'ludər; *NE* 'lʌuðər/ *n* **1** a heavy wooden bar used as a lever, especially for lifting millstones *la16-19, 20- NE T Uls*. **2** a stout stick *18- NE T Uls*. **3** a heavy blow *19- NE T Uls*. **4** the wooden base of a hand-mill *la19- Sh Ork*. [ON *luðr* the stand of a hand mill]

lowder[1.2], *Uls* **ludher** /'lʌudər; *Uls* 'ludər/ *v* to hammer; to thrash or beat *la19- NE Uls*. [see the noun]

lowdin *see* LOWDEN[1.2]

lowe[1.1], **low** /lʌu, lo/ *n* **1** a fire, a blaze; a flame *la14-*. **2** a state of passion or excitement *15-*. **3** a glow, radiance *19-*. **in a lowe** on fire, alight, glowing *16-*. **2** in a state of emotion or excitement *la16-*. Compare ALOW[2]. **tak low** to catch fire, go up in flames *la17-*. [ON *logi* a flame]

lowe[1.2], **low** /lʌu, lo/ *v* **1** to burn; to blaze *17-*. **2** to be in a state of passion or desire *18-*. **3** to gleam, glow or flare *19-*. **get yer lowin laid** to have one's enthusiasm dashed; to be put in one's place *la18- NE*. [ON *loga* to blaze]

lower[1], †**lewer** /'lʌuər/ *n* a lever *19- SW Bor*. [altered form of Eng *lever*]

Lower[2.1] /'loər/ *n education* a secondary school examination grade sat as part of the Scottish Leaving Certificate, abolished in 1962 *la19-20, 21- historical*. Compare HIGHER[1.2]. [shortened form of *Lower Grade of the Scottish Leaving Certificate*]

Lower[2.2] /'loər/ *adj* **1** lesser; less high; situated further down (than something or somewhere else) *16-*. **2** *in secondary education* at a less advanced or difficult level: ◊*Lower French la19-*. [LOW[1.2], with comparative adj-forming suffix *-er*]

lower *see* LOUR[1.1]

lowg *see* LUG[1]

lowie /'lʌui/ *n* money, bank notes *la19- SW*. [Travellers' language, from Romany]

lowing-ill *see* LOWAND-ILL

lowins *see* LOWANCE

lowk *see* LOCK[2], LOUK

lowkit *see* LOUK

Lowland *see* LAWLAND[1.1], LAWLAND[1.2]

Lowlands *see* LAWLANDS

lowmon, lomon, †**lowman,** †**leuman** /'lomən/ *n* the leg, the foot *la18, 19- NE*. [unknown]

lown[1.1] /lʌun/ *n* **1** a peaceful, sheltered spot; the lee side *la18-19, 20- T C*. **2** calm, unclouded weather *19, 20- WC*. **3** tranquillity, silence *19, 20- literary*. [ON *logn* calm weather]

lown[1.2] /lʌun/ *v* **1** to shelter *la14-*. **2** *of windy or stormy weather* to moderate, become calm *15-*. [see the adj]

lown[1.3], †**lowne,** †**lowyn,** †**lownd** /lʌun/ *adj* **1** calm, still, quiet *la15-*. **2** humble, unassuming; subdued, restrained *la15-*. **3** *of a place* sheltered, snug *la16-*. [ON *lygn* calm]

lown[1.4] /lʌun/ *adv* **1** quietly, gently; calmly, peacefully *la16-19, 20- literary*. **2** in a sheltered position, snugly *18-19, 20- C*. **3** softly, in a low voice *19, 20- EC SW*. [see the adj]

lowne *see* LOWN[1.3]

lowp[1.1], **loup** /lʌup/ *n* **1** a leap, a jump, a bound *la14-*. **2** *folklore* a leaping-place; a point at which a river or gorge is believed to have been crossed by leaping; frequently in place-names *17-*. **3** a shelf in a river-bed over which water cascades, or over which fish may leap up-river *la18-*. **4** a throb, a start *20-*. **loup hunt** an (amorous) adventure *la19- NE T*. [ON *hlaup*]

lowp[1.2], **loup, lope** /lʌup, lop/ *v ptp* **lowpit, lowpen** **1** to leap, jump, vault; to spring forward; to leap up and down *la14-*. **2** *of things* to spring or fly (apart or away); to jump out of place *la14-*. **3** to start with pain, surprise or shock *la16-*. **4** *of the heart or blood* to throb, race *la16-*. **5** to spring to one's feet; to run off; to jump to attention *18-*. **6** *of water* to cascade, roll *19-*. **7** *of frost* to thaw, break *19- NE*. **lowpin** **1** infested (with vermin) *la20-*. **2** throbbing with pain *la20-*. **3** stinking, disgusting; awful *la20-*. **loupin' an leevin** *of fish* fresh, newly caught; *of people* hale and hearty *la19, 20- T EC*. **loup-coonter** *derogatory* a male shop-assistant *la19-*; compare *coonter louper* (COONTER[1]). **loup the cuddy** leapfrog *20-*; compare *cuddy-lowp, cuddy-loup-the-dyke* (CUDDY). **louper dog** the porpoise *Phocoena phocoena la19- N NE T*. **loup-the-dyke** undisciplined, wayward *19-*. **louping ill** a tick-borne viral disease of sheep, ovine encephalomyelitis *la18-*. **lowpin mad** enraged *la20-*. **loupin-on-stane** a mounting-block *17-*. **loup aff** **1** to dismount from a horse *la19-*. **2** to change the subject abruptly *la19-*. **3** to set off at a run *20- Sh*. †**lowp back** to withdraw (from a promise), back out *18-e19*. **loup the country** to flee the country; to emigrate *19- NE*. **loup dykes** to thrive, succeed; to overcome difficulties *la18-*. **loupy for spang** with a leap and a bound; at a gallop *la19- NE*. **loup a gutter** to avoid or overcome a difficulty or loss *la19-*. **loup on, lowp on** **1** to mount (a horse) *la15-*. **2** to copulate with *la16-18, la20- literary*. **lowp ower** to go beyond, transgress *18-*. **loup the stank** to avoid or overcome a difficulty or loss *la19- NE*. **loup the theats** to break free of restraints *la19- NE T*. **lowp up** to raise one's price suddenly when making a bargain *19-*. **loup up at** to flare up angrily at; to chide sharply *20-*. [ON *hlaupa*]

†**lowp**[2] *n* a basket for catching fish *16-17*. [ON *laupr* a box or basket]

lowp *see* LOOP

lowpen, lowpit *see* LOWP[1.2]

Lowrence *see* LAURENCE

Lowrie, Lowry /'lʌuri, 'lʌure/ *n* **1** a name for a fox *la15-19, 20- literary*. **2** a name given to the great bell of certain churches *la19-*. **3** a name for a crafty person *la19-*. **Lowrin Fair** the name of two fairs held in Rayne, Aberdeenshire and Laurencekirk, Kincardineshire in mid August, dedicated to St Lawrence *18-*. [a pet form of the personal name LAURENCE]

lowrie-towe /'lʌuri 'tʌu/ *n nautical* a rope with a hook on the end for hauling *20- Sh NE T*. [unknown]

lowse[1.1], **lows, loose** /lʌuz, lʌus, lus/ *v* **1** to release, set free; to absolve or acquit *la14*-. **2** to untie or unfasten; to become loose or unfastened *la14*-. **3** *law* to withdraw an arrestment on goods held for debt *15*-. **4** to unyoke a horse, ox or other draught animal from a plough or harness *la15*-. **5** to (cause to) stop work or other activity *la17*-. **6** to express anger or rage *la18*-. **7** to set to with vigour *la19*-. **8** to unfasten a sheaf of corn (before feeding it into a threshing mill) *20*-. **9** *of frost or snow* to thaw *16-19, 20- Sh Ork*. **10** *of a cow's udder* to swell with milk *19- SW*. **11** *of perspiration* to break out *la19- Sh*. **12** *law* to free (property) from encumbrance *15-e19*. **13** *law* to revoke a legal restraint *la15-17*. **14** to open one's wallet; to spend *la15-17*. **15** to procure, purchase *la15-17*. †**lowsance** release *18-e19*. **lowsed 1** finished working; having completed a task *la17*-. **2** tired, weary *la19*-. **lowser** the person who opens up the sheaves and feeds them to the threshing mill *20*-. **lowsin loft** the loft onto which sheaves are thrown for threshing *20*-. **lowsin time** time to stop work, the end of the working day *la18*-. **lowse doon 1** to undo and let down (clothing or hair) *16*-. **2** *of a cow* to show signs of calving *20- Ork*. [see the adj]

lowse[1.2], **louse, loose,** †**lows,** †**lous,** †**los** /lʌus, lus/ *adj* **1** unfastened, hanging loose; loose fitting; insecurely fixed, not secured *15*-. **2** at liberty, unrestrained *la15*-. **3** dissolute, immoral; dishonest, lawless *la15*-. **4** *of weather* unsettled *la19- Sh Ork N SW*. **5** without fixed employment or accommodation *la16-18*. **6** released from an obligation; absolved *la14-e17*. **7** *of goods* moveable, transportable *16-e17*. †**lows butter** *in Orkney* butter in small packets rather than in barrels *la16-e17*. **lowse-fittit** free to travel *18*-. [ON *lauss* loose]

lowse[1.3], †**lows** /lʌus/ *adv* unrestrainedly, freely *la15*-. [see the adj]

lowsen, loosen /ˈlʌuzən, ˈlusən/ *v* to become loose; to slacken, unfasten *17*-. [LOWSE[1.3], or ON *losna* to become loose]

lowt *see* LOUT[1.2]

Lowthiane *see* LOTHIAN

lowyn *see* LOWN[1.3]

lox *see* LAX

loyne *see* LOAN[1.1], LOAN[1.2]

loys *see* LOSS[1.1]

lozen[1.1], †**losin,** †**losane** /ˈlɔzən/ *n* **1** a diamond-shaped figure *la15*-. **2** a pane of glass (originally a diamond-shaped pane) *la16*-. **3** a diamond or criss-cross pattern on clothes *16*. [MFr *loseingne*; variant of *losange, losenge*; compare LOZENGE]

lozen[1.2] /ˈlɔzən/ *v ptp also* †**losynnit,** †**losengit 1** to pattern with diamond-shapes; to criss-cross *la15*-. **2** to glaze a window *20*-. [see the noun]

lozenge, †**losenge,** †**lozange** /ˈlɔzəndʒ/ *n* a diamond shape, a rectilineal figure *la15*-. †**lozange armes** funeral hatchments *la17*. †**lozenge lion** a gold coin with the lion rampant in a diamond-shaped shield on the obverse *19*. [OFr *losange* a lozenge-shape, a window-pane]

lozenger /ˈlɔzəndʒər/ *n* a flavoured sweet, originally diamond-shaped *la19*-. [derivative of LOZENGE]

lub *see* LAB[1]

lubba, lobba /ˈlubə, ˈlʌbə, ˈlobə/ *n* coarse vegetation; rough grazing on mossy or boggy ground *18- Sh Ork*. [unknown]

lubbard, lubbert /ˈlʌbərd, ˈlʌbərt/ *n* a lout *la16-19, 20- SW Bor*. [derivative of EModE *lubber*]

lubbertie, *T* **libertie** /ˈlʌbərti; *T* ˈlɪbərti/ *n* a jellyfish *20- NE T*. [compare LOCH-LIVER]

luce *see* LOUSE, LUSS

†**lucerne** *n* a light; a lamp or lantern *la15-e16*. [ME *lucerne*]

†**lucerve, lewzerne** *n* a lynx; lynx skin or fur *16-e17*. [OFr *loucervier*]

luche *see* LAUCH[1.2]

lucht *see* LOCHT

luchtach /ˈluxtəx/ *n* the retinue or bodyguard of a Highland chief *18, 19- historical*. [Gael *luchd-taighe*]

luchter *see* LACHTER[2]

†**Lucine, Lucyne** *n* the moon *16*. [Lat *Lūcīna* the goddess of childbirth]

luck[1.1], **luk** /lʌk/ *n* **1** chance *la15*-. **2** a piece of luck or good fortune; a useful or valuable object come upon by chance *la16*-. **luckpenny, luck's penny** money given for luck; a sum returned by the seller to the buyer as a discount *18*-. **upon luck's heid** on the chance of success, on chance; for luck *17-19, 20- Sh Ork*. [LG *luk*]

luck[1.2], †**luk** /lʌk/ *v* **1** to fare, prosper; to turn out well or ill *16*-. **2** to have good fortune; to succeed *la16*-. [see the noun]

luck *see* LEUK[1.2]

lucken[1.1] /ˈlʌkən/ *n* a half-split haddock for drying or smoking *19- NE*. [see the adj]

†**lucken**[1.2], **lukkin** *v* to close, draw together; to form a compact mass *16-19*. [see the adj]

lucken[1.3], †**lukkin** /ˈlʌkən/ *adj* **1** closed tight, clenched; having the sinews contracted *la15-19, 20- Bor*. **2** *of a haddock or whiting* gutted, but not split right down to the tail *19, 20- NE*. **3** *of a hand or foot* webbed *la15-19*. **4** *of leather* consolidated and thickened by tanning and hammering *18*. †**lucken gowan** the ox-eye daisy *18-19*. [ptp of LOUK]

luckenbooth, †**lukkin-buth** /ˈlʌkənbuθ/ *n* a booth or covered stall which could be locked up *la15-19, 20- historical*. **luckenbooths** a row of luckenbooths in the High Street of Edinburgh, which were demolished in 1817 *la15-e19, la19- historical*. [LUCKEN[1.3] + BUITH]

luckenbooth brooch /ˈlʌkənbuθ brotʃ/ *n* a silver brooch in the shape of a heart or two hearts entwined *20*-. [LUCKENBOOTH + BROACH[1.1]]

lucky[1.1], **luckie** /ˈlʌki/ *n* **1** a familiar term for an elderly woman, frequently prefixed to a surname *17*-. **2** a landlady, the hostess of a pub *18*-. **3** a midwife *19, 20- WC*. **4** a grandmother *18-19, 20- NE*. **5** a wife, a married woman *la18-19, 20- NE T*. **6** a witch *19*. **luckie-daddie** a grandfather *18-19, 20 NE T*. **luckie minnie** a grandmother *la18*-. **lucky minny's lines** the seaweed *Chorda filum la19, 20- Sh Ork*. **lukki minnie's oo** bog cotton *Eriophorum angustifolium 19- Sh*. [see the adj]

lucky[1.2], **luckie, lukkie** /ˈlʌki/ *adj* **1** fortunate, bringing luck *16*-. **2** full, ample, more than the standard or stipulated amount *17*-. **lucky-box** a child's savings-bank *20*-. **lucky midden** discarded waste in which something salvageable may be found *20- WC*. **lucky penny** money given for luck; a sum returned by the seller to the buyer as a discount *18*-. **lucky-pock** a lucky bag; a lucky dip or lottery *la19*-. **lucky tattie** a candied confection covered in cinnamon powder with a small novelty inside *la20*-. [LUCK[1.1] + -IE[2]]

lucky[1.3], **luckie** /ˈlʌki/ *adv* abundantly, plentifully *la18-19, 20- Sh NE*. [see the adj]

lucrative /ˈlukrətɪv/ *adj* **1** financially profitable *18*-. **2** *law* gratuitous, granted as a free gift *17*. **luctrative successor** an heir-apparent who accepts part of an estate as a gift before the death of the grantor (thereby accepting liability for prior debts) *la17*-. [Lat *lucrātīvus*]

†**lucrie** *n* gain, pecuniary advantage *la16*. [MFr *lucre*, Lat *lucrum*]

Lucyne *see* LUCINE

ludder /ˈlʌdər/ *n* broken water or a surge created by a boat in heavy seas *la19- Sh*. [ON *lauðr*]

lude *see* LUVE[1.2]

ludge[1.1]**, lodge, †luge, †loge** /lʌdʒ, lɔdʒ/ *n* **1** a (temporary) dwelling or shelter; a workman's hut *la14-*. **2** a porter's lodge *15-*. **3** a local branch of freemasons, originally a society or incorporation of masons *16-*. **4** a fisherman's bothy *19- Sh T*. **5** *mining* a pithead shed or shelter *la17-19*. **6** a mason's shed or workshop *la15-18*. **7** a storage shed *la16-17*. **8** a person's residence or lodgings *16*. [OFr *loge* an arbour, a hut]

ludge[1.2]**, lodge, †luge, †loge** /lʌdʒ, lɔdʒ/ *v* **1** to accommodate; to quarter (troops); to dwell, have (temporary) residence, stay *la14-*. **2** *law* to leave pleadings in the custody of the clerk of court *19-*. **3** to harbour thoughts, ideas or expressions *16*. **4** to be located in a place; to lie (on the ground) *e16*. **†lodgeable** habitable *18-e19*. **lodgement** *mining* an underground reservoir or water store *la19, 20- EC*. **ludger, lodger, †lugear 1** a paying guest in another person's house *la17-*. **2** a person who provided temporary accommodation; a host *16*. [OFr *logier*]

ludgin, lodgin, lodging, †lugeing, †logyng /'lʌdʒɪn, 'lɔdʒɪn, 'lɔdʒɪŋ/ *n* **1** a temporary residence *la14-*. **2** provision of accommodation or sleeping quarters *la14-*. **3** a dwelling-house, a residential building *15-*. **4** *mining* a pithead shed or shelter *la17*. **5** an animal's lair *e16*. [verbal noun from LUDGE[1.2]]

ludher *see* LOWDER[1.2]

†ludibry *n* (an object of) mockery *17-e18*. [Lat *lūdibrium*]

†ludifie *v* to ridicule *17*. [Lat *lūdificāre*]

luf *see* LEEVE

luf-blenk *see* LUVE[1.1]

lufe *see* LUIF, LUVE[1.1], LUVE[1.2]

†luff, lufe *n* **1** (the sheet on) the weather or windward side of a fore-and-aft sail; the windward side of a ship *16-e17*. **2** a contrivance for altering a ship's course *e15*. [OFr *lof*]

luffage *see* LOVAGE

luffer /'lʌfər/ *n* a lull or quieter period in a gale or storm *20- Ork NE*. [unknown]

luffyr *see* LIVER[1]

lufsum *see* LUVESOME

luft *see* LIFT[1.1], LIFT[1.2]

lug[1], *N* **loog,** *EC* **lowg** /lʌg; *N* lug; *EC* lʌug/ *n* **1** an ear *la15-*. **2** a projecting part of an object (by which it may be handled or lifted) *la15-*. **3** the flap of a cap or bonnet *la15-*. **4** the handle of a cup, bowl, dish or pot, frequently one of a pair *la16-*. **5** a flap of a shoe *17-*. **6** a hidden recess from which one might overhear the conversation in a room *19-*. **7** the pectoral fin of a fish *19-*. **8** one of the wings on a wing-chair *20-*. **9** one of the hand grips at the top of a full sack *20-*. **10** a part of the muzzle of a plough *20-*. **11** the chimney corner *la18-19, 20- NE EC Uls*. **12** the corner of a herring-net *19, 20- NE T Uls*. **13** a projecting flange or spike on an iron instrument (such as a spade) *18, 20- NE*. **14** a loop on the end of a fishing-line *la19- Sh*. **luggie** a person with characteristic ears; also used as a nickname *la17-19, 20- N NE EC*. **luggit, luggid,** *N* **loogard** *n* a blow to the ear *la19- Sh Ork N H&I*. **luggit** *adj* **1** having an ear or ears (of a specified nature) *la15-*. **2** *of laces or braids* having ornamental loops *16-e17*. **lug bane** the bone behind the pectoral fin of a fish *la19, 20- Sh Ork*. **lug-chair** a wing-chair *la19-*. **lug-hole** an earhole *la20-*. **lug mark** *n* **1** an earmark on a sheep *la17-*. **2** an identifying mark or feature *19-*. **lug mark** *v* to mark the ear of *17-*. **lug stane** one of a series of stones attached to the lower corners of a herring-net or salmon-weir to make it hang vertically in the water *18-19, 20- N NE*. **about yer lugs** all around you *16-*. **at your lug** close by, in close contact with *la16-*. **†at the lug o the law** at the centre of affairs, in close touch with authority *18-19*. **by the lug and the horn** by force *19, 20- SW*. **frae lug to laggan** from top to bottom, all over *la19- SW*. **get yer heid in yer hands and yer lugs tae play wi** *see* HEID[1.1]. **get yer lug in yer luif** to be severely taken to task *18-19, 20- T*. **hae the wrang soo by the lug** to have misunderstood, have come to a wrong conclusion *18-*. **lauch on the ither side o your lug** to laugh on the other side of your face *la19, 20- Sh T SW*. **lay yer lug** to wager that *19, 20- Sh T*. **lay yer lug into** to eat or drink heartily *18-19, 20- N C*. **lay oor lugs thegither** to lay our heads together *la19-*. **ower the lugs** in over your head; inundated or immersed *18-19, 20- NE T*. **tak someone by the lug** to take someone by the ear; to force someone to do something *la16-*. **up to the lugs** = *ower the lugs 19-*. [unknown; compare Swed *lugg* the forelock]

lug[2] /lʌg/ *n* a clumsy person *19, 20- WC Uls*. [unknown]

luge *see* LUDGE[1.1], LUDGE[1.2]

lugear *see* LUDGE[1.2]

lugeing *see* LUDGIN

luggage *see* LOGGAGE

luggie[1] /'lʌgi/ *n* **1** a small, wooden dish with one or two handles (used for serving milk with porridge) *18-*. **2** a wooden milking-pail *la19, 20- T C SW Bor*. [LUG[1] + -IE[1]]

†luggie[2] *adj of crops* overgrown, top-heavy *18-19*. [unknown]

luggie *see* LUG[1]

lug in /'lʌg ɪn/ *v* to eavesdrop *20-*. [LUG[1] + IN[1.3]]

luid *see* LUVE[1.2]

luif, loof, lufe, liv, lee, leef /luf, lɪv, li, lif/ *n pl* **luifs, loofs, luives, looves 1** the palm of the hand *la15-*. **2** an animal's foot *la18-19, 20- SW*. **livfu, loofu** a handful *16-*. **aff loof** offhand, without premeditation or preparation *18-19, 20- C*. **†clap loofs together** to shake hands *19*. **crack lufes** to shake hands in friendship *18-19, 20- N*. **the ootside o the luif** an expression of defiance or derision *19, 20- SW*. [ON *lófi*]

luiffie, loofie, *T* **laifie** /'lufi; *T* 'lefe/ *n* **1** a stroke with a strap or cane on the palm of the hand *19-20, 21- historical*. **2** a flat, handleless curling stone with indentations for the thumb and fingers *19, 20- historical*. **3** a mitten *19, 20- SW*. **4** a kind of flat bread roll *20- T*. [LUIF + -IE[1]]

luik *see* LEUK[1.1], LEUK[1.2], LOCK[2]

luik-hertit *see* LOIK-HERTIT

luindge *see* LUNGE

luit, luitten *see* LAT

luk *see* LEUK[1.2], LOUK, LUCK[1.1], LUCK[1.2]

luke *see* LEUK[1.1], LEUK[1.2]

†Lukismes, Luxmes *n* the festival of St Luke, 18 Oct, a customary date for payment of debts and dues; the date of one of the annual fairs in Rutherglen *15-17*. [from the name of the saint + MASS[2]]

lukkie *see* LUCKY[1.2]

lukkin *see* LOUK, LUCKEN[1.2], LUCKEN[1.3]

lukkin-buth *see* LUCKENBOOTH

lum, lumb /lʌm/ *n* **1** a chimney, a smoke-vent or flue; a chimney-stack *17-*. **2** a fireplace; a chimney-piece and chimney-corner *17-*. **3** the funnel of a ship or steam train *20-*. **4** a wooden canopy above a fire or wood-lined opening in the ridge of the roof for light and ventilation *17-19, 20- Sh Ork NE*. **5** a funnel-like passage through a cliff; a rock chimney *la18-19, 20- NE T SW*. **6** a top-hat *la19, 20- H&I WC*. **7** a pie-funnel *e18, 20- T SW*. **lummie** a chimney on fire *20- T EC*. **lum-can** a chimney-pot *19- Sh NE T*. **lum-cheek** the chimney-corner; the fireside *la19, 20- Sh T SW*. **lum hat** a top-hat *la19-*. **lum-heid, lumbhead** the chimney top, the part of the chimney rising above the roof *la17-*. **lum-pig** a chimney-pot *19- WC SW*. **lum tap** the top of a chimney or funnel *19-*. [unknown]

Lumbard /ˈlʌmbərd/ *adj* of Lombardy *la15-*; compare LOMBARD. †**Lumbart paper, Lumbard paper** an expensive kind of paper used for both cartridges and books *16-17*. †**Lumbard sleve** a style of sleeve believed to have originated in Lombardy *16-17*. [from the name of the region of northern Italy]

Lumbard, lumbart *see* LOMBARD

lumber[1.1] /ˈlʌmbər/ *n* a casual pick-up, a date *la20-*. [unknown]

lumber[1.2] /ˈlʌmbər/ *v* to chat up; to have sex or a casual relationship with *la20-*. [unknown]

lume, loom, *N NE* **leem,** †**lwme,** †**loomb** /lum; *N NE* lim/ *n* **1** a weaving-loom *16-*. **2** an instrument or tool of any kind *la14-19, 20- N NE SW*. **3** a receptacle, vat or tub; a basin or bowl *la15-19, 20- Sh N NE*. **4** the penis *15-e19*. †**loomefull** a dry measure, for which Linlithgow held the standard *e17*. **leems** crockery *19- N NE*. [OE *lōma*]

lumfad *see* LYMPHAD

luminar, †**lumynar** /ˈlumɪnər/ *n* **1** *fisherman's taboo* a light *la19- Sh*. **2** a luminary, a source of light *la15-16*. [Lat *lūmināre*]

luminator /ˈlumɪnetər/ *n in St Andrews University* a student who was paid to take responsibility for the heating and lighting in a lecture-room *la17-e19, la19- historical*. [Lat *lūminātor* a giver of light]

†**luming** *n* a stone building component *e17*. [unknown; compare LUM]

lummed /lʌmd/ *adj* thwarted, frustrated, baffled *20- SW*. [unknown]

lump, †**lomp** /lʌmp/ *n* **1** a shapeless mass, a mound *la14-*. **2** a protuberance or swelling on the body *la15-*. **3** a large amount or portion *20-*. **4** a piece or share or land *la16-18*. **5** a mass of iron in the process of manufacture *16-e17*. **6** a lifeless or soulless person *15-e17*. **the lump of someone's death** the chief cause of or an important factor in someone's death *la18-19, 20- Sh SW*. [ME *lumpe*]

lumynar *see* LUMINAR

luncart, lounkart, *T* **lonchard,** †**longart** /ˈlʌŋkərt, ˈlʌŋkərt; *T* ˈlɔnʃərd/ *n* **1** a temporary shelter or hunting-lodge *la14-18, 20- T*. **2** a large nodule of one mineral in the layers of another *19- C*. **3** a hole made in a wall to allow sheep to pass through, or a stream to flow under *19- H&I SW*. **4** an open-air fireplace (made of sods with an iron bar across the top from which to hang a pot) *la19-e20, la20- historical*. [Gael, IrGael *longphort* a harbour; a camp; a residence, a dwelling]

lunch /lʌnʃ/ *n* **1** a (midday) meal; a sandwich or packed meal *19-*. **2** a lump, a chunk *la18-19, 20- T*. [EModE *lunch* a thick piece]

lunder *see* LOUNDER[1.1], LOUNDER[1.2]

lundyr *see* LOONDER, LOUNDER[1.1]

lungasuut, †**lungasüte,** †**lunsaucht,** †**longsoucht** /ˈlʌŋɡasøt/ *n* a lung disease in cattle and sheep *15-16, la19- Sh*. [OE *lungen* a lung + ON *sótt* disease]

lunge, loonge, luindge, lounge, †**lunsh** /lʌnʒ, lunʒ, lundʒ, lʌundʒ/ *v* to slouch; laze about *16-*. **lounger,** †**loungeour** an idle person *16-*. [unknown]

lungie /ˈlʌŋɡi/ *n* the intestines of a sheep (used for puddings or sausages) *20- Sh*. [Icel, Faer *langi* the long gut]

lungie *see* LONGVIE

lunk[1] /lʌŋk/ *adj* **1** *of weather* humid, sultry *19- C Uls*. **2** *of food or drink* tepid, lukewarm *19, 20- literary*. **lunkie** *of weather* humid, sultry *19, 20- WC*. †**lunkit** *of food or drink* tepid, lukewarm *19*. [compare Norw dial *lunka* to warm slightly]

lunk[2] /lʌŋk/ *v* to walk with an uneven gait *la19- Sh*. [Norw dial *lunka* to go with short steps]

lunkie /ˈlʌŋki/ *n* a hole in a wall made to allow sheep to pass through, or a stream to flow under *19- H&I WC SW Bor*. **lunkie hole** = LUNKIE *19- SW Bor*. [compare LUNCART]

lunner *see* LOUNDER[1.1], LOUNDER[1.2]

Lunnon, Lon'on, London, †**Londoun** /ˈlʌnən, ˈlʌndən/ *n* the city of London *19-*. **Londoner,** †**Londiner** a native of London *la16-*. **Londoners** a skipping game with two ropes being simultaneously turned in opposite directions *20- Sh NE T*. **londies** = *Londoners 20- Sh NE*. **London bun** a glazed bun with currants and orange peel, sprinkled with crystallized sugar *la19-*. †**Lunnon candy** a kind of sweetmeat *19*. †**Lundoun claith** cloth made in or imported from London *la16-17*. **London ropes** = *Londoners la20- NE EC*. [Lat *Londinium*]

lunsaucht *see* LUNGASUUT

lunsh *see* LUNGE

lunt[1.1] /lʌnt/ *n* **1** a match, a fuse *16-*. **2** a puff of smoke or steam *la18-*. †**luntstaff** a staff for holding a lighted match *17*. **set lunt to** to set fire to *19-*. †**with lunt werk** *of firearms* having a matchlock *e17*. [Du *lont* a match]

lunt[1.2] /lʌnt/ *v* **1** to catch fire; to burn, blaze *la18-*. **2** to smoke; to emit smoke; to smoke a pipe *la18-*. **3** to set fire to, kindle *la19- SW Bor*. [see the noun]

lunt[2] /lʌnt/ *v* to walk with a springy step; to walk briskly *19- SW Bor*. [compare Norw dial *lunta* to stroll, Swed *lunte* to hop]

lunyie, †**lunzie,** †**lunʒie** /ˈlʌnji/ *n* the loin *16-19, 20- Bor*. **lunyie bane, lunzie-bane** the hip-bone *la17-19, 20- Ork*. [OFr *loigne*]

lupik *see* LOOPICK

luppen *see* LEAP

luppie, loopie /ˈlʌpi, ˈlupi/ *n* a round barrel-shaped basket *19- Sh Ork N*. [diminutive form of ON *laupr* a box, a basket]

lurdan[1.1], †**lurdane** /ˈlʌrdən/ *n* **1** a rough person; a lazy or stupid person *15-*. **2** a woman perceived to be promiscuous; a prostitute *la14-17, 20- SW*. **3** a criminal *la14-e16*. †**lurdanry** villainy *e16*. [OFr *lourdin* a dullard]

†**lurdan**[1.2] *adj* heavy, dull; wretched, mean *la16-19*. [see the noun]

lure, †**lewer,** †**liewer** /lur/ *n* the udder of a cow or other animal *la17-19, 20- Ork N EC*. [unknown]

lurk *see* LIRK[1.1], LIRK[1.2], LIRK[2]

†**luschbald** *n* a term of abuse for a person *e16*. [unknown]

luss, luce /lʌs, lus/ *n* scurf, dandruff *19, 20- Sh SW*. [unknown]

†**luster** *v ptp* **lustart** to put a glaze on *la16-e17*. [MFr *lustrer*]

lusty /ˈlʌsti/ *adj* **1** vigorous, robust, healthy *la15-*. **2** lustful *la15-*. **3** cheerful, pleasant; beautiful, handsome *la15-e19*. **4** gallant, valiant *la15-17*. [ME *lusti*; compare ON *lostigr*]

lusum *see* LUVESOME

lut *see* LOUT[1.1], LOUT[1.3]

lute *see* LAT

lutenand *see* LIEUTENANT

†**luttard** *adj* bowed, bent *e16*. [compare LOUT[1.2]]

luve[1.1], **love,** †**lufe,** †**loove** /lʌv/ *n* **1** a feeling of deep affection or romantic attachment *la14-*. **2** a sweetheart, lover *la14-*. **3** a kind of crepe or gauze used for mourning *17*. **lovie 1** a sweetheart, a lover *20-*. **2** a child's word for a hug *20-*. **luve bairn** a love-child *20-*. **luve blink,** †**luf-blenk** a loving or amorous glance *16-19, 20- SW*. **love-darg** a piece of work or a service done as a favour to a friend *la18-19, 20- NE T C*. †**luf drowry** a love-token *15-e16*. **love lozenger** a sweet with a motto inscribed on it *20-*. †**lufe rent 1** love, affection, friendship *la14-16*. **2** lust *la15-16*. †**for love and**

favour *law* a formula in documents relating to gifts and donations *18-e19*. [OE *lufu*]

luve[1,2], **love**, **loo**, **loe**, †**lufe** /lʌv, lu, lo/ *v pt, ptp* **luved**, **looed**, †**lude**, †**luid** **1** to have deep affection for or romantic attachment to *la14-*. **2** to cherish, hold dear; to take pleasure in, enjoy *la14-*. [OE *lufian*]

luveray *see* LIVERY

luvesome, **loosome**, **loesome**, †**lufsum**, †**lusum** /ˈlʌvsəm, ˈlusəm, ˈlosəm/ *adj* **1** lovable; friendly, affectionate *la15-19, 20- literary*. **2** beautiful *la15-19, 20- literary*. †**loosomely**, **lufsumly** affectionately, cordially *la14-19*. [OE *lufsum*]

†**luvit**, **lovit** *adj pl* **lovittis**, **lovitis** beloved, dear *la14-17*. [ptp of LUVE[1,2]]

Luxmes *see* LUKISMES

luxury, †**luxurie**, †**luxure** /ˈlʌkʃəri/ *n* **1** indulgence; a delicacy *la16-*. **2** lasciviousness, lechery *la15-e16*. [OFr *luxurie*, Lat *luxuria*]

lwme *see* LUME

ly *see* LE, LIE[1,2]

lyaag *see* LAIG[1,1], LAIG[1,2]

†**lyam** *n* a rope, a thong, a leash *16-19*. [OFr *liem*]

lyart, **liart** /ˈlaeərt/ *adj* **1** *of hair* streaked with white; grizzled, silvery *15-*. **2** *of landscape or vegetation* variegated, multi-coloured, streaked with different colours *la18-19, 20- literary*. **3** *of a horse or cow* dappled, streaked or spotted *la15-18*. [OFr *liart*]

lychtnyng *see* LICHTNIN

lyde *see* LYTHE[1,2], LYTHE[1,3]

lye, †**lee**, †**ley** /lae/ *n* water made alkaline by salts from wood ashes *17-*. [OE *lēag*]

lye *see* LIE[1,1]

lyf *see* LIFE

lyin *see* LIE[1,2]

lying time /ˈlaeəŋ tʌɪm/ *n* a period of time worked by an employee for which they are not immediately paid, either at the beginning of a new job, or between the closing of the books for the week's work and the payment of wages, payment being retained until the person leaves the employment *la19-*. [presp of LIE[1,2] + TIME]

lyis *see* LEE[1,1]

lyke, *Sh Ork N* **leek** /lʌɪk; *Sh Ork N* lik/ *n* **1** an (unburied) corpse *la15-19, 20- Sh Ork NE T EC*. **2** a vigil kept over a corpse until burial, a wake; the gathering on such occasions *la16-19, 20- Sh N NE*. †**likis** funeral rites *e16*. **lykehouse** a mortuary; a house where a corpse awaited burial *18-19, 20- historical*. **leek-steen** a stone on which a coffin is rested *20- Sh*. **leek-strae** the straw from a deathbed (burned at the funeral) *la19- Sh*. **lykewake**, *Sh Ork* **leek-waak**, †**lykewalk**, †**laikwake**, †**leikwake** a vigil kept over a corpse until burial, a wake *la16-*; compare LATEWAKE. [OE *līc*, ON *lík* a body, a corpse]

lykely *see* LIKELY[1,2], LIKELY[1,3]

Lyllis *see* LILLES

lymare *see* LIMMER

†**lymbe** *n* limbo *la15-e17*. [Lat *limbus* a border, an edge]

lymber *see* LIMMER

lyme *see* LIME[1,1], LIME[1,2]

lymmar *see* LIMMER

Lymmester blak *see* LEMISTAR BLAK

lymn *see* LIMN[1,2]

lymphad, †**limfad**, †**lumfad**, †**langfad** /ˈlɪmfad/ *n* a West Highland (or Irish) galley *la16-17, 19- historical*. [Gael, IrGael *long fhada* a long ship]

lyne *see* LIE[1,2], LINE[1,2], LINE[2,1]

lyn nail *see* LIN-NAIL

lynnyng *see* LINEN[1,1]

lyntell *see* LINTEL

lynth *see* LENTH[1,2]

lynȝell *see* LINGLE[2,1]

lyog, **lyoag** /ljog/ *n* **1** *fisherman's taboo* the sea; the seabottom *la19- Sh*. **2** a boggy hollow in the hills; a small morass *19- Sh*. [Norw dial *log* water, a stream]

Lyon, †**Lyoun**, †**Lion** /ˈlaeən/ *n* the chief officer of arms of Scotland, the LORD LYON *la16-*. **Lyon Clerk** the clerk of the *Lyon Court la17-*. **Lyon Court** the Court of Heralds in Scotland *18-*. **Lyon herald 1** an alternative name for the Lyon *la15-19, 20- historical*. **2** a Scottish herald, a member of the *Lyon Court 17-e18*. †**Lyon herald King of Arms** an alternative name for the Lyon *16-17*. **Lyon King at Arms** an alternative name for the Lyon *17-*. **Lyon King of Arms** an alternative name for the Lyon *la15-*. [shortened form of *Lord Lyon King of Arms* (LORD LYON)]

lyoun *see* LION

†**Lyouns canues**, **Lyonis cammes**, **Leonis canves** *n* a strong, coarse cloth from Lyons in France *16-e17*. [from the French place-name + CANNAS]

lyper *see* LIPPER[2,1], LIPPER[2,2]

lyre *see* LIRE[1]

lyse *see* LOUSE

lyt *see* LIT[1,1]

lythe[1,1], **lithe** /laeð/ *n* shelter, protection from the weather; a sheltered spot, the lee side of something *la18-19, 20- N NE T*. [see the verb and adj]

lythe[1,2], **lithe**, **lyde** /laeð, lʌɪd/ *v* **1** to thicken soup, gravy or porridge *17-*. **2** to shelter *la18-19, 20- NE*. **lithin** a thickening agent *17-19, 20- NE SW*. **lyelicks**, †**lythocks** a gruel of fine oatmeal boiled in buttermilk *18-19, 20- C SW*. †**lithely** readily, cheerfully *19*. **lithy** *of soup* thick, smooth and palatable *la18-19, 20- C*. [OE *līþigian* to make mild]

lythe[1,3], **lithe**, **lyde** /laeð, lʌɪd/ *adj* **1** *of a place* sheltered, snug *la15-19, 20- N NE T*. **2** *of people* kindly *19- NE*. **lythesome** gentle, kindly, pleasant *la19-*. [OE *līþe*]

lythe[2] /laeθ/ *n* the pollack *Pollachius pollachius 16-*. [ON *lýr*]

lyve *see* LIFE

M

ma, my, me, mi, *T* **meh,** †**may** /ma, mae, mi, mɪ, mə; *T* mɛ/ *adj* my, belonging or relating to me: ◊*I'm going to ma bed la14-*. [reduced form of MINE²]
ma *see* MAE¹·¹, MAE¹·², MAK¹·², MAW¹, MAY², ME
-ma-, †**me-** /mə/ *affix* a nonsense syllable added to certain words: ◊*magowk* ◊*hochmagandie la17-*. [unknown]
maa *see* MAE²·¹, MAE²·², MAW⁴, MAW⁶
maak /mak/ *n* the milt of a fish 20- *N*. [related to Norw *melke*, although the vowel is problematic; cf Dan *malk* milk]
maak *see* MAIK²·¹
maalin *see* MERLIN
maamie *see* MAUMIE
maasguum, marsgum, *N* **mersgim,** *NE* **mursgan** /ˈmɑsgum, ˈmɑrsgum; *N* ˈmɛrsgəm; *NE* ˈmʌrsgən/ *n* the angler or monkfish *Lophius piscatorius 19- Sh Ork N NE*. [Norn *marsgum*; perhaps from ON *marr* sea + *gumi* a man]
maat *see* MATE¹
maber *see* MAIRBLE¹·¹, MAIRBLE¹·²
Mac, †**Mack** /mak/ *n* **1** a nickname for a person or clan whose surname has the prefix *Mac- la17-*. **2** a familiar form of address to a male stranger *20-*. [Gael *Mac-*; prefix forming a patronymic, corresponding to the suffix *-son*]
macalive *see* MAKHELVE
macallum /məˈkaləm/ *n* a vanilla ice-cream served with raspberry sauce *20-*. [from the surname *MacCallum*]
MacClarty /məˈklɑrti/ *n* a nickname for a slovenly or untidy person *20-*. **Mrs MacClarty** a nickname for a dirty or slovenly housewife *19-*. [from the surname of the *MacClarty* family in E Hamilton's *Cottagers of Glenburnie*, with a pun on CLARTY]
macer, †**masar,** †**messer** /ˈmesər/ *n* **1** an official who keeps order in a court of law; an usher in the Court of Session *la15-*. **2** an officer of the crown, under the authority of the Lord Lyon King of Arms, who delivered royal commands and summonses, and uttered public proclamations *15-17*. [ME *macere*, OFr *maissier*]
MacFarlane's Bowat *see* BOWET
mach *see* MAICH, MATCH¹·¹, MATCH¹·²
machair /ˈmaxər/ *n* low-lying land adjacent to the sand of the seashore (used for rough grazing) *18-*. **the Machairs** the rough grazing land bordering the Solway Firth and Luce Bay *la18-*. [Gael *machair*]
machine /məˈʃin/ *n* **1** a mechanical contrivance or apparatus *16-*. **2** a motor vehicle *20-*. **3** a horse-drawn passenger vehicle; a trap or carriage *la19-20, 21- historical*. **machinery 1** the mechanism of a machine *18-*. **2** a factory which operated or manufactured machines *la18-19, 20- historical*. [MFr *machine*, Lat *māchina*]
machreach, michrach /məˈxriəx, məˈxrax/ *n* a fuss, an outcry, a row *la20- NE*. [altered form of Gael *mo chreach* my ruin!, alas!]
macht *see* MAUCHT
†**macis, meassis** *n* an aromatic spice, mace *15-17*. [ME *macis*, OFr *macis*]
mack, †**makke** /mak/ *adj* neat, tidy; suitable *la17-19, 20- Bor*. **macklike 1** neat, seemly, apt *la17-19, 20- Bor*. †**makly** *adj* seemly, well-proportioned *e18*. †**makly** *adv* evenly, moderately, aptly *e16*. [ON *makr* comfortable, becoming, suitable, ME *mak* or OE *mæc* equal, agreeable]

mack *see* MAK¹·²
Mack *see* MAC
mackallow *see* MAKHELVE
Mackay /məˈkae/ *n* a common Scottish surname *14-*. **the real Mackay** the genuine article *la19-*. [Gael *mac* and the Gaelic personal name *Aodh*]
mackerel, †**makrell** /ˈmakrəl, ˈmakərəl/ *n* a type of fish *Scomber scombrus 16-*. **as clean as a mackerel** completely, effectively, entirely *la19- T C*. [OFr *maquerel*, ME *makerel*, EModE *macquerell*]
macky *see* MAKKY
Macmillanite /məkˈmɪlənʌit/ *n* Presbyterian Church a follower of Reverend John MacMillan of Balmaghie, Kirkcudbrightshire *18-19, 20- historical*. [derived from the surname *MacMillan* + *ite*]
Macpherson's Law /məkˈfɛrsənz lɔ/ *n* the principle that the worst things befall the people who least deserve it *la20-*. [originally humorously propounded by Wilfred Taylor in *The Scotsman* (27/2/1952), using an illustrative incident which befell the Clan *Macpherson*]
MacTavish /məkˈtavɪʃ/ *n* a familiar form of address to a male stranger *la20-*. [from the surname]
†**maculat** *adj* stained, defiled *la15-e16*. [Lat *maculātus*, ptp of *maculāre*]
†**macull** *n* a spot, a blemish *16*. [MFr *macule*, Lat *macula*]
Macwhachle /məkˈʍaxəl/ *n* a familiar form of address to a male stranger *20- WC*. **wee Macwhachle** a familiar term of address to a toddling infant *20- WC*. [a spurious surname from MAC + WAUCHLE¹·²]
mad¹·¹, †**made** /mad/ *adj* **1** mentally ill *la14-*. **2** confused, disturbed; foolish, irrational *la14-*. **3** angry, furious *15-*. **4** dismayed, sorrowful *15-16*. [OE *gemād* foolish, senseless, mad]
mad¹·² /mad/ *adv* extremely: ◊*mad keen la19-*. **mad for** extremely eager for or desirous of *la19-*. [see the adj]
mad *see* MAUD
madam, madame, †**madem** /ˈmadəm/ *n* **1** a form of polite address used to a woman *la14-*. **2** a term of address used by servants to their mistress *16-20, 21- historical*. **3** a woman or rank; the lady of a house *la14-e19*. [OFr *madame*, ME *madam*]
madder, †**mader,** †**mather,** †**maither** /ˈmadər/ *n* the root of the plant *Rubia tinctorum* used to make a red dye; the dye or red colouring itself *15-*. [OE *mæddre*]
madderam, madrim /ˈmadərəm, ˈmadrəm/ *n* **1** madness; a tantrum or rage *la19- Sh Ork N*. **2** fun, hilarity *la19- Sh Ork N*. [modelled on *wuddrum* with substitution of MAD for WUD¹·¹]
made, †**maid** /med/ *adj* **1** manufactured, produced *15-*. **2** prepared, finished, ready for use *15-*. **3** invented, fictitious *17-*. **4** distressed, harassed, overworked *la19- NE*. **made-like** feigned, assumed *19, 20- Sh*. **made diet** a cooked meal *la19- Sh NE T*. **made lee** a deliberate falsehood *19, 20- Sh NE EC*. **made tie** a man's bow-tie sold with the bow ready tied *20- Sh C*. **made up wi** pleased, elated with *la19-*. [ptp of MAK¹·²]
made *see* MAD¹·¹, MAK¹·²
madem *see* MADAM
mader *see* MADDER

madgie *see* MATTIE¹
madin *see* MAIDEN
madin-land *see* MAINLAND²
madrim *see* MADDERAM
mae¹·¹, †**ma**, †**mo** /me/ *n* **1** a greater number or amount; a larger quantity *15-19, 20- SW Bor*. **2** people or items in addition to those already mentioned *la14-e18*. [see the adj]
mae¹·², †**ma**, †**mo**, †**mea** /me/ *adj* **1** greater in quantity or amount *la16-*. **2** more numerous *la14-19, 20- EC SW Bor*. **3** additional to those already mentioned; extra *15-19*. **4** several, many *15-e16*. **be at ane mae wi't** to be unable to cope; to be at the end of life *19- Bor*. [OE *mā*]
mae¹·³ /me/ *adv* more; again *la14-*. [see the adj]
mae²·¹, **meh**, **maa** /me, mɛ, ma/ *n* the bleat of a sheep or lamb; the sound of bleating *18-*. [onomatopoeic]
mae²·², **meh**, **maa** /me, mɛ, ma/ *v of sheep or goats* to bleat *18-*. [see the noun]
maegins, **megins** /ˈmɛɡɪnz/ *npl* the middle of a period of time *la19- Sh*. **da megins o de night** the depths of night *20- Sh*. [ON *megin* the chief part of something]
maen *see* MANE¹·²
Maes *see* MES
maeshie *see* MAISE²
maet *see* MEAT¹·¹
maffling /ˈmaflɪŋ/ *n* procrastination; blundering or bungling *19- SW*. [MDu, EModDu *maffelen* to stammer, mumble]
Mag *see* MEG
magan-land *see* MAINLAND²
magdom *see* MAKDOM
magell *see* MAGGLE
mager, **mooger** /ˈmɑɡər, ˈmuɡər/ *adj* **1** emaciated *la19- Sh*. **2** scanty *20- Sh*. **maegerdom** a state of weakness *20- Sh*. [ON *magr* meagre, lean]
mager *see* MAUGRE¹·¹, MAUGRE¹·³
†**magg** *v of a carter* to pilfer coal for resale *la18-e19*. †**mag wood** *n* an inferior variety of coal *la17*. [perhaps shortened form of Eng *magpie*]
maggie¹ /ˈmaɡi, ˈmaɡe/ *n* a magpie *20-*. [shortened dim form of Eng *magpie*]
maggie² /ˈmaɡi, ˈmaɡe/ *n mining* an inferior quality ironstone *la18- C*. [unknown]
Maggie³, **Meggie** /ˈmaɡi, ˈmɛɡi/ *n* a girl's name *17-*. Compare MEG. **meggie-lickie-spinnie** a spider *19- NE T*. **Maggie Mulloch** *folklore* a spirit traditionally associated with the family of Grant of Tullochgorum in Strathspey *la19- NE*. **meggie spinnie** a spider *19- NE T*. **meggie wi the mony feet**, **maggie wi the mony feet** a centipede *la18-*. [shortened dim form of the personal name *Margaret*]
maggle, †**magill**, †**magell**, †**maigle** /ˈmaɡəl/ *v* **1** to spoil food by overhandling *20- N H&I SW*. **2** to botch a job *16-19, 20- Uls*. **3** to maim or mutilate *la15-e19*. **maggled**, †**magglit**, **maglit 1** botched, bungled *la16-19, 20- Uls*. **2** maimed, mutilated *la15-e17*. [perhaps a variant of Eng *mangle*]
maggot /ˈmaɡət/ *n* **1** a grub, a larva *18-*. **2** a whim, a fancy *18-19, 20- literary*. **maggotive**, **mageteeve**, †**maggative** capricious, perverse *la19, 20- NE*. **maggoty**, **maggotty** capricious, perverse *19-*. [extended sense of Eng *maggot* a fly larva]
maggs, **mags** /maɡz/ *npl* a gratuity, a tip *la18- C*. [perhaps shortened form of Eng *magpie*]
magill *see* MAGGLE
magink /məˈɡɪŋk/ *n* a strange-looking object or animal *20- Sh NE T*. [MA- + US *gink* a fellow]
magirkie, **magirky** /məˈɡɪrki/ *n* a headdress of woollen material which also protected the throat *la17-19, 20- historical*. [unknown]

magister /ˈmadʒɪstər/ *n* a master; a teacher or lecturer *la15-19, 20- historical*. [Lat *magister*]
magistrand /ˈmadʒɪstrand/ *n* a fourth- or final-year undergraduate *17-*. **magistrand class** the class in Natural and Moral Philosophy which was usually taken by university students in their final year *17-e20, la20- historical*. [Lat *magistrandus*]
magistrate /ˈmadʒɪstret/ *n* **1** a civil administrator of the law *la16-*. **2** a provost or bailie who holds administrative and judicial powers; a stipendiary magistrate *la16-*. **3** a smoked herring *la19- WC*; compare GLASGOW MAGISTRATE. [Lat *magistrātus*]
maglit *see* MAGGLE
magnum /ˈmaɡnʌm/ *n* a bottle of twice the standard size, originally containing two quarts of wine or spirits *la18-*. [shortened form of MAGNUM BONUM]
†**magnum bonum** *n* = MAGNUM *la18-e19*. [Lat *magnum bonum* a large good thing]
magowk¹·¹ /məˈɡʌuk/ *n* an April Fool *20-*. **magowk's day** April Fool's Day *20- WC SW*. [MA- + GOWK¹]
magowk¹·² /məˈɡʌuk/ *v* to make an April Fool of *20-*. [see the noun]
magrame *see* MEGRIM
magre *see* MAUGRE¹·¹, MAUGRE¹·³
magryme *see* MEGRIM
mags *see* MAGGS
Mahoun /maˈhun/ **1** the prophet Muhammad *la15-16*. **2** a nickname for the Devil *la15-19, 20- WC SW*. [ME *Mahoun*, shortened form of *Mahomet*]
†**maich**, **mauch**, **mach** *n* a male connection by marriage; a son-in-law or a brother-in-law *la14-17*. [ON *mágr* a son-, brother-, father-in-law]
maid /med/ *n* **1** a young girl; a virgin *la15-*. **2** a female servant *la15-*. **3** a daughter *la14-17*. **4** a lady-in-waiting *la15-16*. **maid in the mist** navelwort, wall-pennywort *Umbilicus rupestris 19- SW Bor*. **the maid of Lorne** an informal title given to the eldest daughter of the chief of the clan MacDougall *19-*. [ME *maid*, reduced form of MAIDEN]
maid *see* MADE, MAITHE¹·¹
maiden, †**maidin**, †**madin** /ˈmedən/ *n* **1** a girl or young woman *la14-*. **2** a virgin; the Virgin Mary *la14-*. **3** an unmarried female *la15-*. **4** the last corn cut in the harvest-field; the harvest-home feast and celebrations *18-*. **5** a maidservant, a female attendant *la14-19, 20- T EC Bor*. **6** an unmarried heiress; the eldest or only daughter of a landowner or farmer *15-19, 20- N NE*. **7** one of the upright posts of a spinning-wheel supporting the yarn spindle *19, 20- Sh Uls*. **8** an instrument similar to the guillotine used for beheading criminals *la16-18, 19- historical*. **9** a daughter *la14-17*. **10** *folklore* a position held by one of the younger witches at a meeting of witches *17*. **maidenheid**, **maidenhood 1** the state of being a virgin *la14-*. **2** the hymen *la15-*. **3** the last handful of corn cut at harvest *20- WC*. †**madin bairne**, **madyne barne** a female child *la14-e17*. **maiden castle**, †**madin castell** an alternative name for Edinburgh Castle *15-16, 17- historical*. †**maiden child** a female child *la14-e17*. **maiden clyack** the last corn cut in the harvest-field *20- NE*. †**maiden cummer**, **maiden kimmer** a young woman who acted as attendant to the mother at a christening *18-e19*. **maiden hair 1** a type of fern *16-*. **2** a kind of fabric *la16*. **maidens hair** the coarse sinews in certain cuts of boiled beef *19, 20- NE Bor*. †**maiden skate** a young specimen of the thornback ray or skate *la18-19*. [OE *mǽden, mǽgden*]
maidwyfe *see* MIDWIFE
maieste, **maiestie** *see* MAJESTY

maig¹·¹, meg /meg, mɛg/ *n* **1** a large ungainly hand *19- Sh N WC Bor*. **2** the flipper of a seal *19- Sh Ork N*. [Gael màg a soft plump hand, a paw]

maig¹·² /meg/ *v* to spoil by overhandling; to dirty with the fingers *19- Bor*. [see the noun]

maigle *see* MAGGLE

maigriment *see* MEGRIM

Maii *see* MEY

maijesty *see* MAJESTY

maik¹ /mek/ *n* a halfpenny *19-20, 21- historical*. **daft as a maik watch** *see* DAFT. [unknown]

maik²·¹, *NE* **maak**, †**make**, †**mak** /mek; *NE* mak/ *n* **1** the equal or peer of a person or thing *la14-*. **2** a spouse; the mate of an animal or bird *la14-19*. **3** a close friend or companion *16-19*. †**the maik** the equivalent *16*. [OE *gemǽcca* a mate, an equal, ON *maki* a match, a mate]

†**maik²·²** *v* to mate; to pair, match *16-e17*. [see the noun]

maik *see* MAK¹·²

maikless, †**maikles** /ˈmekləs/ *adj* matchless, peerless *15-19, 20- literary*. [MAIK²·¹, with adj-forming suffix]

mail¹, maill, †**male**, †**mal**, †**meal** /mel/ *n* rent *la14-*. **mailer**, †**malar**, †**mailler** a tenant; a tenant farmer; a cottar *la14-19, 20- historical*. **mailing 1** a tenant farm *15-*. **2** rent *18-*. **3** the action of letting or renting *la14-17*. †**mailings** duties, compliments *e18*. †**mail duties, maill dewtie** rent *17-e19*. †**male fre** rent-free *la15-17*. **mail garden** a market garden *la18-19, 20- Bor*. †**mail gardener** a market gardener *la18-19*. †**mail man** a tenant *15-17*. †**mail mart** an ox or cow paid as part of rent *15-18*. **mail payer** a tenant *la16-e19*. **mails and duties** the rents of an estate *16-19, 20- historical*. [ON *mál* speech, agreement]

mail², †**mailʒe**, †**malʒe**, †**melʒe** /mel/ *n* **1** body armour composed of metal rings; chain-mail *la14-*. **2** a metal eye through which the warp thread passes in a loom *19, 20- C*. **3** the shell of a crustacean *la19*. **4** a small metal ring or eyelet on a garment *la15-e17*. **mailed**, †**malyt** covered or armed with mail armour *16-*. †**mailless** unprotected by armour *e19*. **mail coat** a suit of chain-mail *la16-*. **mailed cod** the roundnose grenadier *Coryphaenoides rupestris 20-*. [OFr *maille*, ME *maille*]

mail³ /mel/ *n* a stain *19- EC Bor*. †**mailed** stained *e19*. [OE *māl* a spot, a mole]

mail⁴, †**male**, †**meal** /mel/ *n* **1** letters or packages delivered by post *18-*. **2** a travelling bag, a trunk *la15-19, 20- literary*. †**mail pillion 1** a bag for carrying luggage behind the saddle *la17-e19*. **2** a pad or cushion to carry a rider or a store a portmanteau *la17-e19*. [ME *mal*, EModE *mail*]

mail *see* MEAL²

mail eys *see* MALESE

†**maill** *n in the Hebrides* a measure of land equal to one forty-eighth of a TIRUNG *la17*. **mail-land** = MAILL *la17*. [perhaps ON *mǿlir* a land-measure]

maill *see* MAIL¹, MAILʒE, MEAL¹·¹, MELL¹·¹

maillie, mallie /ˈmele, ˈmali/ *n* a ewe; a pet name for a favourite ewe *19- SW*. [variant of the personal name *Molly*]

maillyer *see* MELDER

†**mailʒe, maill, melʒie** *n* a French copper coin of low value *la15-16*. [MFr *maille*]

mailʒe *see* MAIL²

maimory *see* MEMORY

main¹·¹, †**mayn**, †**mane** /men/ *n* physical strength or force *la14-*. [OE *mægen*]

main¹·², †**mayn**, †**mane**, †**mean** /men/ *n* **1** the principal part of anything *la16-*. **2** the mainland (of a country) *la16-*. **3** the open sea *16-*. **mains** a principal water channel or conduit for water, gas or electricity *17-*. [see the adj]

main¹·³, †**mayn**, †**mane** /men/ *adj* **1** largest, greatest, principal *la15-*. **2** big, strong, great *la15-19, 20- Ork N Uls*. **3** unmitigated *19- T EC*. **mainly** very *18, 20- SW*. **main coal** the principal or best seam of coal *la18- C*. **main door** a door giving access to a *main door flat*, as opposed to a common entrance to a block of flats *19-*. **main door flat, main door house** a ground-floor flat in a block of flats, which has its own door direct from the street *20- C Bor*. †**main sea** the open sea *16-e17*. **main tree** the ridge-beam of a house *la19- Ork*. [ME *main*, partly ON *megn* strong, powerful, partly OE *mægen*]

main¹·⁴ /men/ *adv* exceedingly, very *la18-*. [see the adj]

main² /men/ *n* self-restraint, patience *20- Ork*. **mainless** impatient, impetuous *la19- Sh Ork*. [back-formation from MENSE¹·¹]

main *see* MEAN³

mainage *see* MANAGE

†**maine, mayne, mane** *n* white bread of the finest quality *15-16*. **mayne breid, mane breid** = MAINE. [ME *maine*, shortened form of *(pain) demeine*]

mainer *see* MANURE¹·¹, MANURE¹·²

maingie *see* MENYIE

mainis *see* MAINS

mainland¹ /ˈmenlənd/ *n* **1** the principal land mass of a territory, originally especially Scotland *la14-*. **2** the Lowlands of Scotland *16*. **3** low-lying fertile land *16*. [MAIN¹·³ + LAND¹·¹]

mainland², †**madin-land**, †**magan-land** /ˈmenlənd/ *n* the largest island of Shetland or Orkney *16-*. [ON *megin-land*]

mainner, manner, *NE* **menner**, †**maner** /ˈmenər, ˈmanər; *NE* ˈmɛnər/ *n* **1** a way, fashion or mode (of procedure, living or behaving); usage, custom *la14-*. **2** the way in which a thing is executed or made, its nature, character or style *la14-*. **3** a species, a sort, a kind *15-*. **manners**, †**maneris** decorous, polite behaviour, moderation *15-*. †**for maneris sake** for the sake of appearances *la16*. †**in maner as** as *la14-e17*. [ME *maner*, AN *manere*]

mains, †**mainis**, †**maynis**, †**manys** /menz/ *n* **1** the home farm of an estate; frequently in place-names *la14-*. **2** the outbuildings of a farm *18-*. **3** a name for the farmer of a particular farm, in accordance with the custom of calling a farmer by the name of his farm *19- NE*. †**in maining** *of land* farmed by the proprietor himself rather than leased to tenants *e17*. [aphetic form of the plural of DEMAIN]

mains *see* MAIN¹·²

†**mainschoitt, manshote** *n* a roll or loaf of the finest wheat flour *la16-e17*. Compare MAINE. [compare ME *mainchet*]

maintain, manteen, †**maintene**, †**manteme** /menˈten, mənˈtin/ *v* **1** to (cause to) continue *la14-*. **2** to keep in good repair or governance *la14-*. **3** to uphold, support *la14-*. **4** to advance an argument or claim *la14-*. [ME *maintenen*]

maintenance, †**mantenance**, †**mentenance** /ˈmentənəns/ *n* **1** support, protection for a person or activity *15-*. **2** the keeping of an institution or custom vigorous or unharmed *la15-*. **3** (the provision of) financial or material support; livelihood *la16-*. **4** the abetting of wrongdoing *la15-16*. **5** the monthly pay due to serving troops, originally the troops of the Army of the Covenant; the tax to provide this, first imposed on the Scottish shires and burghs in 1645 *17*. **6** support with the hands, physical support *la15*. [ME *maintenaunce*]

maintene *see* MAINTAIN

†**mainʒie¹·¹, manʒie, menʒie** *n* **1** a disabling wound or injury, a mutilation *la15-16*. **2** a defect or flaw *la15-17*. [OFr *mahaigne*]

†**mainʒie¹·²**, **menʒe** *v* to maim, mutilate, disable *la14-e17*. [OFr *mahaignier* or from the noun]

mair¹·¹, **more**, †**mare**, †**mar**, †**meir** /mer, mor/ *adj* **1** larger in physical size *la14*-. **2** greater in quantity or amount *la14*-. **3** additional in quantity or number, further *la14*-. **4** greater in degree, quality or effect *la14-18*. **5** of greater importance, superior *la14-e16*. [see the adj]

mair¹·², **more**, †**mare**, †**mar** /mer, mor/ *adv* **1** to a greater extent, in a greater degree *la14*-. **2** more: ◇*mair sonsie la14*-. **3** *with a comparative adjective or adverb*: ◇*mair aulder la14*-. **4** in addition; besides *la14*-. **5** any longer, again *la14*-. **mairattour** besides, over and above *15*-. **mair liker** more like, similar to *18*-. **mairower** besides, over and above *la15*-. [see the adj]

mair¹·³, **more**, †**mare**, †**mar** /mer, mor/ *pron* **1** a greater amount or number *15*-. **2** something else, something in addition *la14*-. **3** he who, or that which, is greater *la14-16*. **the mair** although, in spite of the fact that *19- T SW*. **mair by token 1** moreover, in addition *18-19, 20- NE T SW*. **2** especially, in particular *19, 20- NE EC SW*. **mair for token** moreover, in addition *la18- SW Uls*. **the mair mean taikin** more particularly, especially *19- NE*. †**the mair o** any the more because of *la18-19*. †**with sum mair** *added to expressions of quantity, number* indicating that the actual amount or figure is larger than that stated *la14-17*. [OE *māre*]

mair², **mayor**, †**mare** /mer, 'meər/ *n* **1** *law* an officer with executive function or subordinate jurisdiction in a sheriffdom or regality *la13-19, 20- historical*. **2** the chief officer of the municipal government of an English town or city; occasionally the provost of a Scottish burgh or city *15*-. †**mair of fee** a mayor holding office by hereditary right *15-e18*. [AN *mair, maiur*]

mair *see* MUIR

mairble¹·¹, **marble**, †**marbill**, †**marbre**, †**maber** /'merbəl, 'marbəl/ *n* **1** recrystallized limestone often used in sculpture or architectural decoration, marble *la14*-. **2** a piece or block of marble, a marble slab *la14*-. **3** *children's games* a small round ball originally made of marble *19*-. †**marbill-stane** marble stone *15-16*. [ME *marble*, OFr *marbre*]

mairble¹·², **marble**, †**marbill**, †**marbre**, †**maber** /'merbəl, 'marbəl/ *adj* made of, or of the colour of, marble *16*-. [see the noun]

Mairch¹, **Merch**, **March** /mertʃ, mertʃ, martʃ/ *n* the third month of the year *15*-. [ME *march*, Lat *Martius* of Mars]

mairch²·¹, **march** /mertʃ, martʃ/ *n* **1** an act or instance of marching, especially military; a procession *17*-. **2** a tune or musical composition designed for marching *18*-. [see the verb]

mairch²·², **merch**, **march** /mertʃ, mertʃ, martʃ/ *v* **1** *of persons, especially travelling in company* to journey on foot at a regular pace *16*-. **2** *of troops* to proceed on foot with a regular measured tread; to advance *la16*-. [EModE *march*]

mairch *see* MARCH¹·¹, MARCH¹·²
mairchant *see* MERCHANT¹·¹, MERCHANT¹·²
maircheant *see* MERCHANT¹·¹
mairiage *see* MAIRRIAGE
mairk *see* MARK¹·¹, MARK¹·², MERK
mairmalade *see* MARMALADE

mairriage, **marriage**, **merriage**, **merridge**, †**mariage**, †**mairiage**, †**meriage** /'merɪdʒ, 'marɪdʒ, 'mɛrɪdʒ/ *n* **1** the state of being married, matrimony; the action of getting married; the wedding ceremony; a particular matrimonial alliance or union *la14*-. **2** the feudal right of a superior with regard to the succession and marriage of an unmarried minor succeeding as his vassal *15-e18, la18- historical*. **3** a large gathering of birds, especially rooks *20- NE T EC*. **4** a dowry *la15*. **mairriage braws** wedding clothes *la19- NE C*. †**mariage gere** a dowry *la15-16 Ork N NE*. **mariage gude** a dowry *la15-16*. **marriage lintel** the lintel stone of a door bearing the initials of a couple and a (usually 17th- or 18th-century) date of the marriage *20- EC SW*. **marriage stone** = *marriage lintel NE EC*. [ME *mariage*, AN, OFr *mariage*]

mairry, **marry**, **merry**, †**mary** /'mere, 'mare, 'mɛre/ *v* to enter into matrimony, become a wife or husband; to join, give, take in marriage *la14*-. **mairry on** to marry to *16*-. †**mairry upon** to marry to *15-18*. **mairry wi** to marry; to be married to *18*-. †**mairry with** to marry to *14-18*. [AN, OFr *marier*]

mairt *see* MART¹, MART²
Mairtimas *see* MARTINMAS
mairtin *see* MARTIN

mairtyr¹·¹, **martyr**, **merter**, *N* **myarter**, †**martir**, †**marteir**, †**marthyr** /'mertər, 'martər, 'mertər; *N* 'mjartər/ *n* **1** one who suffers for a cause; originally in the Christian Church a believer who suffers death for his or her faith *la14*-. **2** one who suffers acute pain, unhappiness or emotional torment *la14*-. **3** one of those who suffered death in the 17th century in the cause of spiritual independence as set forth in the National Covenant or in the Solemn League and Covenant *18*-. **4** a disgusting mess, a dirty confusion *20- N NE T*. **martyrdom 1** *in the Christian Church* the suffering and death of a martyr for his or her beliefs *la14*-. **2** the act of killing or suffering death for a cause, originally for the independence of Scotland *la15*-. **3** protracted suffering, torment *la15*-. **4** slaughter *la14-15*. **martyr stone**, **martyr's stone** a stone marking the grave of a martyr *19*-. [Lat *martyr* a witness, a martyr]

mairtyr¹·², **martyr**, **merter**, *N* **myarter**, †**martir** /'mertər, 'martər, 'mertər; *N* 'mjartər/ *v* **1** to put to death as a martyr *la14*-. **2** to kill in a merciless or brutal fashion *la15*-. **3** to cover with dirt *19*-. **4** to hurt or wound severely, inflict pain or torment on *16-19, 20- Sh*. [OE (*ge*)*martyrian*, and see the noun]

mairvel¹·¹, **mervel**, **marvel**, †**mervell**, †**mervaill** /'mervəl, 'mervəl, 'marvəl/ *n* **1** an astonishing or wonderful thing *la14*-. **2** a miracle *la14-e17*. **3** astonishment, admiration, wonder *la15-e19*. **mervellous 1** amazing, wonderful; miraculous *15*-. **2** amazingly large in degree or size; huge, tremendous *la15-e17*. [ME *merveille*,]

mairvel¹·², **mervel**, **marvel**, †**mervaill**, †**merwall** /'mervəl, 'mervəl, 'marvəl/ *v* **1** to feel surprise or astonishment at something; to be amazed *la14*-. **2** to feel astonishment or wonder, gaze at, reflect on in wonder *la15*-. **3** *with interrogative pronoun* to express curiosity and amazement *la15*-. †**mervaill of** to be amazed at *la14-16*. [ME *merveillen*]

mairyguild *see* MARIGOLD
mais *see* MESS¹·¹

maise¹, †**meaze**, †**mease** /mez/ *n* **1** a quantity of 500 fish, usually herring *14- WC SW*. **2** *in Orkney* a quantity of dried fish *16-e17*. [OFr *mese, maise*, MDu *mese* a barrel for keeping fish]

maise², †**maze**, †**mease** /mes/ *n* a large mesh basket *18- Sh Ork N*. **maeshie**, **meshi** = MAISE² *19- Sh Ork NE*. [ON *meiss*]

maisic *see* MUSIC
maisie *see* MEY

maisle, **measle**, *N* **mizzle** /'mezəl, 'mizəl; *N* 'mɪzəl/ *v* to redden, scorch or blotch the skin of the legs by sitting too near a fire *18-19, 20- N H&I Uls*. **mizzle-shinned**, †**misle-shinn'd** having scorched or blotched legs *18*-. [from the noun MAISLES]

maisles, **measles**, *NE EC* **mizzles**, †**mesillis**, †**missellis** /'mezəlz, 'mizəlz; *NE EC* 'mɪzəlz/ *npl* an infectious disease characterized by a red skin rash *la16*-. [ME *maseles*]

†**maison** *n* a house; a household, a family *la16-e17*. [Fr *maison*]

†**maisoun-deu, mason-dew, mayson diew** *n* an almshouse *15-e17*. [ME *mesondeu*, AN *maisun Deu*]

maisser *see* MASER

maissoun *see* MASON

maist[1.1], **most,** †**mast,** †**maste,** †**moist** /mest, most/ *adj* **1** largest, greatest; very great *la14-*. **2** *of persons* chief, most powerful or important, greatest *la14-19, 20- SW Bor*. **3** *of things* chief, principal *la14-*. **maist han** in greatest measure, almost entirely *la19 Sh NE*. [see the adj]

maist[1.2] /mest/ *adv* **1** to the greatest extent, in the highest degree *la14-*. **2** very *la14-*. **3** *with an adjective or adverb to form the superlative* most: ◊*maist sonsie la14-*. **4** *with a superlative adjective or adverb*: ◊*the maist hardest thing la16-*. **5** mainly *15-19, 20- Sh NE T*. **maistlins** almost, nearly *19, 20- Sh Ork T*. **maistly 1** most of all, especially *la18-*. **2** almost, nearly *19-*. [see the adj]

maist[1.3] /mest/ *pron* the greatest amount, the largest number, the majority *la14-*. [OE *mǣst*, OE *māst*]

maist[2] /mest/ *adv* almost *16-*. [aphetic form of AMAIST]

maist *see* MAST[1.1]

maister[1.1], **master, mester** /'mestər, 'mastər, 'mɛstər/ *n* **1** a person having authority or control, a leader, a ruler, a chief, a magnate; the person who has the power or ability to control, use or dispose of something *la14-*. **2** a schoolmaster *la14-*. **3** as a mode of address, prefixed to the personal name or surname of a man, originally mainly of a Master of Arts, frequently a clergyman or schoolmaster *la14-*. **4** a person whose superior skill or authority is acknowledged by disciples or followers *la14-*. **5** the captain of a ship *la14-*. **6** a skilled tradesman, qualified to carry on business on his own account, employ others and train apprentices; originally as a member of a trade incorporation *15-*. **7** an employer *15-*. **8** the head of a society or government department *15-*. **9** the heir to an earldom or lordship *15-*. **10** the person in charge of an animal *la15-*. **11** a landlord or proprietor *16-*. **12** a feudal superior *16-*. **13** the manager or supervisor in a business or works *15-19*. **14** a scholar of authority, an expert in a particular field, a person particularly skilled in something *la14-17*. **15** a holder of a master's degree from a university *la14-17*. **16** a teacher in a university *la15-17*. **maisterfu 1** powerful; big, strong *la15-19, 20- Sh Ork NE T*. **2** *of robbers, beggars or their actions* threatening, using violence *15-e19*. **3** *of a storm* violent *e16*. **maisterie,** †**maistry,** †**mastry 1** (the exercise or display of) power, authority or skill *la14-*. **2** ascendancy, victory *la14-*. **3** force, violence *la14-e16*. **maistership 1** control, rule *16-*. **2** influence, patronage *la15-17*. **3** the office, function or dignity of maister *la15-16*. **4** as a mode of address *16-e17*. †**maistrice, mastris** might, force; skill; ascendancy *la14-16 literary*. **maister hoosal** the master of ceremonies at a wedding *20- Ork*. **maister man 1** a master of a craft; a foreman or overseer *17-19, 20- Bor*. **2** a chief or leader, a mighty man *la14-e17*. †**maister-tree** the main swingle-tree immediately attached to the plough *19*. **maister wood** the principal beams of wood in a tenant's house-roof *19- N*. **maister and mair** an autocratic, domineering master *19- EC Bor*. †**master of mortifications** a member of the Town Council of Aberdeen appointed to administer the city's mortified property *17-e19*. †**Maister of the Revills** *see* REVEL[1.1]. †**master of wark** an official, usually of a municipality, in charge of building operations *15-19*. [ME *maister*, Lat *magister*]

maister[1.2], **master** /'mestər, 'mastər/ *v pt, ptp* also †**maistrit** to gain control; to overcome, defeat; to attain expertise *la14-*. [see the noun]

maister *see* MESTER

†**maister stik, maisteris steik, masterstick** *n* the piece of work produced by a craftsman to prove himself qualified for acceptance as a MAISTER[1.1] (sense 6) *16-17*. [EModDu *meesterstuck*]

maistress, mistress, †**mistres,** †**maistres,** †**mastres** /'mestrəs, 'mɪstrəs/ *n* **1** a woman who has control, a female ruler, patron or muse, a woman having the care and tutelage of someone *la14-*. **2** a term of polite address to a woman *la15-*. **3** prefixed in full to the name of a married woman, Mrs *16-*. **4** a female employer *la16-*. **5** an extramarital female lover *la16-*. **6** a protective covering for a miner working in a wet shaft or for a miner's lamp *la19, 20- EC*. **7** the wife or widow of the heir-apparent of an earldom or lordship *16-e17*. **the mistress 1** the female head of a household or family *la16-*. **2** the wife of a person of standing in the community, such as a farmer, minister or shopkeeper *la18-*. [ME *maistres*]

maistrice *see* MAISTER[1.1]

maistrit *see* MAISTER[1.2]

maistry *see* MAISTER[1.1]

mait *see* MATE[1], MATE[2.1], MATE[2.2], MEAT[1.1], MEAT[1.2]

maiter *see* MAITTER

maithe[1.1], **maid,** *Sh* **med,** †**meith** /mеð, med; *Sh* mɛd/ *n* a maggot *15-19, 20- Sh Ork N T*. **maidie,** †**mathie,** †**meithie** maggoty *la16-17, 20- Sh*. [OE *maþa*]

maithe[1.2] /með/ *v* to become infested with maggots *19- NE*. [see the noun]

maither *see* MADDER

maitter, matter, metter, †**mater,** †**maiter** /'metər, 'matər, 'mɛtər/ *n* **1** material, substance *la14-*. **2** basis, ground, source, origin *la14-*. **3** the subject, the theme (of a literary work or discourse) *la14-*. **4** an undertaking, a course of events, a state of affairs; a concern, a business, an issue *15-*. **there is nae maitter** it doesn't matter *la18-*. [ME *mater*, Lat *māteria*]

maitterie /'metəre/ *adj* septic, festering *20- NE T C*. [MAITTER + -IE[2]]

majesty, *NE Bor* **maijesty,** †**maieste,** †**majeste,** †**maiestie** /'madʒəste; *NE Bor* 'medʒəste/ *n* **1** the dignity or authority of a sovereign; the glory or greatness of a deity *la14-*. **2** the personality of a sovereign or deity, especially as a mode of address *15-*. **3** splendour, magnificence; royal dignity *15-*. [ME *mageste*, OFr *magesté*, Lat *mājestās*]

major[1.1] /'medʒər/ *n* the military rank above captain *17-*. **major-mindit** haughty, commanding *19, 20- C Bor*. [from the adj MAJOR[2]]

†**major**[1.2] *v* to walk about with a military air, strut *e19*. [see the noun]

major[2] /'medʒər/ *adj* **1** greater, larger, more important *15-*. **2** *law, of a person* no longer a minor, of full legal age *la16-*. [ME *majour*, Lat *māior*]

majority /mə'dʒɔrɪte/ *n* **1** *law* the state of being of full legal age, no longer a minor *la16-*. **2** the larger number or part, a number more than half the total *la18-*. [EModE *maioritie*]

mak[1.1], **make** /mak, mek/ *n* **1** form, shape; a (distinctive) style of manufacture *la14-*. **2** the action or process of manufacturing (an object) or developing (a character) *17-*. **3** manner, style of behaviour *la14-16*. [see the verb]

mak[1.2], **mek, make,** †**maik,** †**mack,** †**ma** /mak, mɛk, mek/ *v pt* **made, med, meed, makkit, makit,** *ptp* **made** †**med,** †**meed,** †**makit 1** to manufacture; to produce, bring about, create; to devise, organize; to compose; to appoint, institute, enact, give rise to, cause to be or become *la14-*. **2** to compel someone to do something *la14-*. **3** to perform a task, deliver a speech, utter words *la14-*. **4** *law* to execute a deed, conclude a contract *la14-*. **5** to be the material or components of, go to form *15-*. **6** to fix a price *15-*. **7** to prepare to go, set out, proceed *15-*. **8** to draw up a document *la15-*. **9** to earn, gain money, win something *16-*. **10** to prepare a bed for use *16-*. **11** to draw a distinction, raise a difficulty *la16-*. **12** *of food or drink* to thicken, set, infuse *la19-*. **13** *of the weather* to produce or threaten a particular condition *20- Sh Ork N NE SW*. **14** *of dung* to mature *20- N NE T EC*. **15** to prepare ground for sowing *17-19, 20- Ork NE T*. **16** *mainly negative or interrogative* to matter, be of consequence, avail ◊ *it disna mak a fig la15-19, 20- N NE*. **17** to think, consider *la19- Sh*. **18** to knit *20- Sh*. **19** *of a wave* to break *20- Sh*. **20** *of cattle* to put on weight or condition *20- Ork*. **21** to cure and pack fish *16-17*. **22** to prepare or exert oneself to do something or for an action *15-17*. **23** to pretend, make as if to do or to be something *15-e17*. **24** to defray expenditure *la15-e17*. **25** to make over land or money to a person *15-16*. **26** to commit a crime or fault *la15-16*. **makk-but** *fisherman's taboo* a boat *20- Sh*. **makdoon** a garment altered to suit a smaller wearer *20- Sh N NE T EC*. **mak on** a pretence; an imposter *20- Sh NE*. **mak aboot 1** to be in the process of preparing *20- Sh*. **2** to change places *20- Sh*. **mak better** to improve, get better *la19, 20- Sh*. **mak a better o** to improve upon, do better with *la19-*. **mak by 1** to overtake, excel *la19- T C SW Uls*. **2** to make money or gain advantage by, profit by *la19, 20- Ork NE*. **mack ceremony** to stand on ceremony; to fuss, scruple *18- T Uls*. **mak-a-deu, mak-a-dü** *n* a pretence *la19- Sh Ork*. **mak-a-deu, mak-a-dü** *v* to make a pretence *la19- Sh Ork*. **mak doon 1** to dilute (spirits) *19-*. **2** to prepare a bed by turning down the bedclothes *19-*. **3** to grind, crush *la18- Sh NE T SW*. †**mak dwelling 1** to take up or have one's residence *la14-16*. **2** to remain in a place *la14-15*. †**mak faith** to possess credence, be valid or trustworthy *la16-e17*. **mak fashion** to pretend *19, 20- Sh NE EC Bor*. **mak a fend** to attempt, try *18-*. **mak for 1** to favour *15-*. **2** to proceed in a direction *la15-*. **3** to prepare for, be on the point of *20-*. **4** *of weather* to show signs of impending snow or rain *20-*. †**mak furth** to finish; to complete (preparation or equipping) *la14-e17*. †**mak gait** to make one's way *la15-e17*. †**mak in** intervene *e19*. **mak intae** to make or force one's way into *la19-*. **mak in wi** to ingratiate oneself *19, 20- Sh Ork N C Uls*. **mak it up 1** to plan, contrive, arrange *19-*. **2** to plan to get married *la19-*. †**mak mair fit** to hurry *e19*. **mak a maitter, mak maitter** to make a fuss *la19-*. **mak a mane, mak mane 1** to lament, mourn *la14-*. **2** to complain, grumble *la18-*. **mak a maucht, mak mauchts** to make a move or effort to do something *la19- T*. **mak a mean** to make an attempt *la16-19, 20- Sh*. †**mak mening** to lament *la14-15*. †**mak a mow** to pull a face (in derision) *la15-e17*. †**mak murther** to murder *la15-16*. **mak nae mane for** to show no sympathy towards *la19-*. **mak naething o it 1** to fail to comprehend something *20-*. **2** *of an ill person* to fail to show signs of improvement *20-*. **mak o** to fuss over, make much of *18-*. **mak on 1** to pretend, feign *la19-*. **2** to build and kindle a fire *la14-18*. **mak oot 1** to achieve, accomplish, manage *18-*. **2** to discern *la18-*. **3** to produce in writing *19-*. **4** to make up weight *20-*. **5** to make a living, succeed *19, 20- Sh NE T Uls*. **6** to acquire *la19- Sh*. **7** to set out on a journey *19, 20- SW*. **8** to make up a total *la16-e17*. **9** to confirm, prove an assertion *la17*. **mak oot ower** to send a sheepdog round a flock to gather them up *20- Sh*. **mak or meddle** to interfere *la18-*. **mak or mell** to interfere *la18-*. **mak ower** to refurbish *la16-*. **mak a prayer** to say or recite a prayer *la14-*. **mak rich** to become rich, make money *la18- EC SW*. †**mak saill** to set sail *16-17*. **mak tae** to go towards *la15-*. **mak through wi** (to struggle to) bring to an end *19, 20- N*. **mak till** to go towards *la15-*. †**mak to** to set to work, set to *la16-e17*. **mak up 1** to make good, compensate; to contribute to; to invent, concoct; to draw up a list; to become reconciled *17-*. **2** to make a bed *19-*. **3** to enrich, establish successfully in life *16-19, 20- Ork NE T Uls*. **4** *fisherman's taboo* to break *la19- Sh*. **5** *law* to complete, establish fully a title *18-19*. **6** to build, erect; to rebuild, repair *15-17*. **mak up for** to proceed in a direction *20- Ork NE T*. **mak up on** to catch up with, overtake *20-*. **mak way** to set about, prepare *20- Sh Ork NE*. **make weel** to make good, succeed *20- Ork C*. †**mak yer ain of** to arrest *e19*. **no mak muckle o't** to show little improvement *la19- Sh NE T EC*. **not make much of it** to show little improvement *20-*. [OE *macian*]

mak *see* MAIK[2,1]

makar, maker /'makər/ *n* **1** a person who makes something; an author *la14-*. **2** God, nature *la14-*. **3** a person who performs an action *15-*. **4** a poet, originally especially one of the Scottish poets of the 15th or 16th century *la15-*. [MAK[1,2], with agent suffix]

makdom, *Sh Ork* **magdom**, †**makdome** /'makdəm; *Sh Ork* 'magdəm/ *n* **1** a person's build or appearance *la15-19, 20- Ork NE*. **2** a trace, a vestige *20- Ork*. **3** pleasing appearance, beauty *16-e17*. [probably MAK[1,1], with *-dom* abstract suffix]

make *see* MAIK[2,1], MAK[1,1], MAK[1,2]

maker *see* MAKAR

†**makhelve, mackallow, macalive** *n in the Highlands and Islands* a portion or endowment in cattle for a child put to fosterage *la16-18*. [Gael *macaladh* fostering]

makine *see* MAUKIN

makit *see* MAK[1,2]

makke *see* MACK

makkit *see* MAK[1,2]

†**makky, macky** *n* a variety of cloth *la16*. [perhaps from the surname *Mackie, Mackay*]

makly *see* MACK

makrell *see* MACKEREL

mal *see* MAIL[1]

†**mala fama, mallyfamie** *n Presbyterian Church* a report of bad behaviour; especially in cases of church discipline *18-e19*. [Lat *mala fāma* bad reputation, evil rumour]

malafooster /malə'fustər/ *v* to destroy, wreck, ruin *20-*. [HibEng *mallafooster* to beat mercilessly, IrGael *malafúster*]

malagarouse, malagroose *see* MALAGRUIZE

†**malagrugrous** *adj* grim, forbidding; gloomy, melancholy *19*. [AN *mal-* + ALAGRUGOUS]

malagruize, malagroose, malagarouse /malə'gruz, maləgə'ruz/ *v* **1** to dishevel, disarrange, spoil *la19- NE T EC*. **2** to injure, hurt with physical violence *20- NE H&I WC*. [AN *mal-* + GROZE]

malancolious *see* MELANCHOLIOUS

malancoly *see* MELANCHOLY[1,1], MELANCHOLY[1,3]

†**malapert, malapart** *adj* presumptuous, audacious, impudent *la15-e19*. [ME *malapert*]

malasche *see* MOLASS

malashes *see* MOLASSES

male *see* MAIL[1], MAIL[4], MEAL[1,1], MEAL[2]

†**malese, malice, mail eys** *n* physical or mental unease or distress; a disease or sickness *la14-e16*. [ME *males*]

malesoun *see* MALISON[1,1]

†**malewrus, malheurius** *adj* unfortunate, ill-fated *16-19*. [EModE *malerous*]

maleys *see* MALICE

†**mal-grace** *n* disfavour, disgrace *la16-17*. [ME *male grace*]

malheurius *see* MALEWRUS

malice, †**malyce**, †**maleys** /'malıs/ *n* **1** ill-will, rancour *15-*. **2** wickedness *la14-17*. **3** a hostile act, a grudge *la15-e17*. [ME *malice*]

malice *see* MALESE

malicious, †**malitious**, †**malitius** /mə'lıʃəs/ *adj* motivated by ill-will, spiteful, ill-tempered, cruel *la15-*. [ME *malicious*, Lat *malitiōsus*]

malignancy /mə'lıgnənse/ *n* **1** ill-will, malevolence *20-*. **2** *applied by the Covenanters to their adversaries* anti-Covenanting sympathy or adherence *17*. [MALIGNANT[1,2], with noun-forming suffix]

†**malignant**[1.1] *n* a person ill-disposed to established religion, a malcontent *17*. [see the adj]

malignant[1.2] /mə'lıgnənt/ *adj* **1** *of a disease* virulent, highly contagious or infectious *la16-*. **2** *of people* wicked, baleful, harmful *la18-*. **3** rebellious, used especially by the early Protestants and the Covenanters of their adversaries *16-17*. †**malignant kirk** applied to the Roman Catholic Church by the early Protestants *16*. [Lat *malignant-*, presp stem of *malignāre* to act maliciously]

malison[1.1], *Sh* **mellishon**, †**malisoun**, †**malesoun** /'malısən; *Sh* 'mɛlıʃən/ *n* **1** a malediction, a curse *la14-*. **2** an accursed person; a torment; the Devil *la15-19, 20- Sh N*. **3** a mischievous child *20- Sh N*. [ME *malisoun*]

†**malison**[1.2] *v* to curse *la16-17*. [see the noun]

malisoun *see* MALISON[1.1]

malitious, **malitius** *see* MALICIOUS

malkie[1.1] /'malke/ *n* an open razor used as a weapon; a weapon in general *20- C*. [rhyming slang; reduced form of *Malky Fraser* razor; *Malkie* being a shortened form of *Malcolm*]

malkie[1.2] /'malke/ *v* **1** to slash (someone) with an open razor *20- C*. **2** to injure someone violently *20- C*. [see the noun]

malkin *see* MAUKIN

mall *see* MELL[1.1]

mallash *see* MOLASS

mallduck /'maldʌk/ *n* the fulmar *Fulmarus glacialis 19- Sh Ork*. [altered form of MALLIMOKE, with influence from Eng *duck*]

mallie *see* MAILLIE

mallimoke /'malımok/ *n* the fulmar *Fulmarus glacialis 19- Sh Ork N NE H&I EC*. **mallie** the fulmar *Fulmarus glacialis 20- Sh NE H&I*. [Du *mallemok*]

malloch *see* MOW[1]

mallock /'malək/ *n* grass wrack, sea grass *Zostera marina 19- Ork*. Compare MARLIK. [Norw *marlauk*]

mallyfamie *see* MALA FAMA

malmy *see* MAUMIE

malt *see* MAUT

†**maltalent**, **matalent** *n* ill-will, malice *la14-e19*. [ME *maltalent*]

malten *see* MAUTEN

malvader /məl'vadər/ *v* **1** to punch, beat *19-*. **2** to become dazed or confused *19-*. [HibEng *mulvather* to confuse, bamboozle]

malversation /malvər'seʃən/ *n* corrupt behaviour in a position of trust *19-*. [MFr *malversation*]

†**malverse**[1.1] *n* a breach of trust, a piece of grave misconduct *18*. [see the verb]

†**malverse**[1.2] *v* to betray the trust attaching to an office by acting dishonestly, corruptly or oppressively *17-e18*. [MFr *malverser*]

malvis *see* MAW[2]

malvoisie, **malvesy**, †**mavasy** /'malvɔızı, 'malveze/ *n* a type of white wine, malmsey *15-*. [ME *malvesi*]

malyce *see* MALICE

malʒe *see* MAIL[2]

mam /mam/ *n* **1** mother, mum *la18-*. **2** grandmother *la19- Sh*. [shortened form of MAMMIE]

mament *see* MOMENT

mamick /'mamık/ *n fishing* a female ling with fully-developed roe *la19- Sh*. [MAM + -OCK]

mammie /'mame/ *n* **1** a child's word for mother *la17-*. **2** a wet-nurse *17-e19, la19- Sh*. **3** a midwife *la16-19*. **mammie keekie** a spoilt child *20- WC SW Bor*. **mammy daddy** an exclamation of fear, panic or excitement *20- C*. [infantile reduplication of syllables]

mamp *see* MUMP[1.2]

man, **maun**, **mon**, **min** /man, mɔn, mən, mın/ *n* **1** an adult male human being *la14-*. **2** mankind, humanity *la14-*. **3** a husband or lover *la14-*. **4** a dependent or protégé; the vassal or liegeman of a lord *la14-*. **5** *as a term of address* a meaningless tag or expressing surprise, remonstrance or irony: ◊*Jock, man, I'm dumfounert 15-*. **6** a manservant or assistant workman *la15-*. **7** a male child *la16-*. **manfully** bravely, resolutely *la14-*. **manheid 1** the state of being an adult male; the qualities of a man, manliness, courage, prowess, strength *15-19, 20- NE*. **2** the state of being a human being, humanity, human nature *la14-e17*. **manly** *adj* **1** having the qualities associated with a man *la14-*. **2** human *la15-e17*. **manly** *adv* in a manly fashion *15-*. **men** people; *used as an indefinite pronoun* one *la14-*. **man bairn** a male child *la16-*. **men's ba** = *hand-ba* **2** (HAND) *20- Ork Bor*. **man big** grown to manhood, adult *la19- N EC Bor Uls*. **man body** an adult man *19-*. **man child** a male child *16-*. **menfolk** men, the adult males of a particular family, the male workers on a farm *19-*. **man grown** grown to manhood, adult *la19-*. **man-keeper 1** the newt or water-lizard *Lissotriton vulgaris la19- H&I SW Bor Uls*. **2** the common lizard *Zootoca vivipara 19- SW Bor Uls*. **man-length** grown to manhood, adult *la19, 20- C SW*. †**man miln** a handmill *16-17*. **man-muckle** grown to manhood, adult *19- EC SW Bor*. †**manslayar**, †**manslaar** a murderer *la14-16*. **be man o yer meat** to have a healthy appetite and digestion *la19, 20- T C*. †**man and knaf** every man, all of them *la14*. †**man and lad** every man, all of them *e16*. †**man and mither's son** every man, all of them *16-*. †**man and page** every man, all of them *la14-e16*. †**man and syre** every man, all of them *16-*. **man in black** a minister, a clergyman *20-*. **man of business** a lawyer *la14-*. **a man o his mind** a person who thinks and acts for himself, a self-reliant person *20- T WC*. †**man of main** a strong or powerful man *la14-e19*. **man of war**, †**man of wer 1** a fighting man, a soldier *15-*. **2** a warship *16-*. **the men** = *menfolk*. †**the Men** Presbyterian Church a group of extremely strict spiritual leaders in a parish *19*. **the Men's day** Presbyterian Church the Friday preceding the half-yearly Communion service, used by *the Men* for religious exhortation *la19-*. [OE *mann, monn*]

man *see* MAUN[1.2], MAUN[3]

manage, **mainage**, **manish**, †**menadge**, †**minnage** /'manıdʒ, 'menıdʒ, 'manıʃ/ *v* **1** to take charge of, control, direct *la16-*. **2** to succeed in reaching a destination or achieving an outcome *la19-*. **3** to keep a person supplied; to be sufficient, last *la19, 20- Sh*. Compare MENAGE. [Ital *meneggiare* to be able to use skilfully, MFr *mesnager* to manage, administer (a house, finances etc)]

manager, †**menagier** /'manədʒər/ *n* **1** a person who organizes or directs an enterprise *18-*. **2** a member of a board of management of the temporal affairs of certain Presbyterian churches *la18-*. **3** a member of the governing body of a small burgh where there is no popularly elected town council *la19-*. [MFr *mesnagier*, MANAGE with agent suffix]

manco *see* MANKIE

mand see MAUN²

mandate¹, †**mandat** /ˈmandet/ *n* **1** a command, an injunction *16-*. **2** *law* a formal warrant authorizing one person to act on behalf of another (without payment); a commission of attorneyship or proxy *16-*. **mandant** *law* a person who gives a mandate *la17-*. †**mandatar** *law* a person to whom a mandate is given *la17-e18*. †**mandator** = *mandant la17-18*. [Lat *mandātum*]

mandate² /ˈmandet/ *v* to learn by heart, memorize *18-*. [Lat *mandāt-*, ptp stem of *mandāre*; as in *memoriae mandāre* to commit to memory]

mandement see MANDMENT

mandill see MANTLE

†**mandment, mandement** *n* **1** a command *la14-e16*. **2** *law* a formal warrant authorizing one person to act on behalf of another (without payment); a commission of attorneyship or proxy *15-17*. [ME *maundement*]

†**mandrag, mandrak** *n* **1** the mandrake *Mandragora officinarum 16*. **2** an unpleasant or poisonous person *16*. [shortened form of Lat *mandragora*]

mane¹·¹, moan, mean, †**mene,** †**mone** /men, mon, min/ *n* **1** lamentation, (the expression of) grief or sorrow, complaining *15-*. **2** a voiced complaint, a grievance, a grouse *15-*. **3** any mournful sound *19-*. [unknown]

mane¹·², maen, mean, mene, meen, †**meyn** /men, min/ *v* **1** to mourn, lament; to bemoan, bewail, express sorrow, loss or regret *la14-*. **2** to pity, show sympathy *15-*. **3** to utter a moaning or mournful sound *19-*. **4** to indicate pain or injury (by flinching or by ostentatiously nursing the affected part) *la18-19, 20- NE EC SW Uls*. **5** to present formally as a grievance, make a formal complaint *la15-18*. **6** to complain of: ◊ *my broder was menand him self not to be weill 15-16*. †**mening** mourning, lamentation *15-16*. **mak mane 1** to lament, mourn *la14-*. **2** to complain, grumble *la18-*. **mak nae mane aboot** to show no sympathy towards *la19-*. **mak nae mane for** to show no sympathy towards *la19-*. **to mane** to be pitied: ◊ *they're no to mean 16-*. [unknown]

mane² /men/ *n* **1** a person's (long) hair *la14-*. **2** long hair on the top of the neck of an animal *15-*. **3** the top of a sheaf of oats *la19- Sh*. [OE *manu*]

mane see MAIN¹·¹, MAIN¹·², MAIN¹·³, MAINE

maner see MAINNER, MANOR

maneswere see MANSWEAR

manfierdie /ˈmanfiərdi/ *adj of a woman* of marriageable age, ready for marriage *la19- Sh Ork*. [perhaps MAN + Norw *ferdig* ready]

mang¹ /maŋ/ *v* **1** to be extremely eager or anxious, long for *la19- NE*. **2** to err; to become perplexed, distracted or frantic *la15-19*. **3** to bewilder, perplex; to stupefy; to lead astray *la15-16* †**mangit** confused, crazed *16-e19*. [unknown]

mang² /maŋ/ *v Travellers' language* to talk, ask, boast *19-*. **mang the can, mang the cant** to speak Romany or Travellers' language *20-*. [Romany *mang-* to want, beg]

†**mangery, mangeory, maniory** *n* a banquet, feasting *la14-e16*. [ME *maungeri*]

maniest see MONIEST¹·²

manifest¹·¹ /ˈmanɪfɛst/ *n* a public proclamation, a manifesto *17-*. [EModE *manifest*]

manifest¹·² /ˈmanɪfɛst/ *v* to show plainly, demonstrate, reveal; to attest *15-*. [ME *manifesten*, Lat *manifestāre*]

manifest¹·³ /ˈmanɪfɛst/ *adj* **1** clearly revealed, plainly evident, obvious *la15-*. **2** visible, in public view *la15-17*. [ME *manifest*, Lat *manifestus*]

†**manifest¹·⁴** *adv* clearly; palpably *15-e16*. [see the adj]

manifold see MONIEFAULD¹·², MONIEFAULD¹·³

maniory see MANGERY

manish see MANAGE

manishee /ˈmanɪʃi/ *n Travellers' language* a woman *20- Bor*. [Sanskrit *mānusi*]

manjuggel, manyogl /manˈjʌɡəl, manˈjɔɡəl/ *v* to juggle; to struggle with something awkward *20- Sh*. **manyugilti** juggling, magic tricks *la19- Sh*. [Norn *manjugl*]

mank¹·¹ /maŋk/ *n* **1** a fuss *19- C Bor*. **2** a flaw, a fault; a deficiency, a lack *16-e19*. [MFr *manc, manque*, or from the adj]

mank¹·² /maŋk/ *v* **1** to mutilate, deface, spoil, botch *15-*. **2** to be deficient or wanting *la16-e18*. **mankit** mutilated, maimed; *of a text* corrupted *15-*. [MDu *manken* to injure]

†**mank¹·³** *adj* deficient, defective; botched, ill-made *16-e18*. [MDu, OFr *manc*, Lat *mancus* having a useless hand, maimed]

†**mankie, manky, manco** *n* calamanco, a glossy woollen material *18-19*. [shortened form of Eng *calamanco*]

mankind /manˈkʌɪnd/ *n* **1** the human race *la14-*. **2** human nature *la14-16*. **3** the male sex *la15-e17*. [OE *mancynn*]

manky see MANKIE

mannace, mannance see MENACE¹·¹, MENACE¹·²

manndrid, manndird /ˈmandrɪd, ˈmandɪrd/ *n* manliness, strength, courage *la19- Sh*. [ON *manndýrðir* manly qualities]

manner see MAINNER, MANURE¹·¹, MANURE¹·²

mannie /ˈmane/ *n* **1** a man *la17-*. **2** a term of affection for a small boy *la19-*. **3** the one who is 'it' in a game *la19- NE*. **4** a skipper *20- NE*. **sic mannie, sic horsie** one is influenced by one's superiors *la19- NE*. [MAN + -IE¹]

mannour see MANURE¹·¹, MANURE¹·²

manor, †**maner,** †**manure** /ˈmanər/ *n* a large country house, the chief dwelling-house of an estate; a landed estate *la14-*. †**maner place** a manor-house *la14-e18*. [ME *maner*]

manrent, †**manred,** †**manreid** /ˈmanrɛnt/ *n* **1** the sworn undertaking to support a patron or be his man; homage *la14-17, 18- historical*. **2** persons from whom manrent was due, vassals collectively, vassalage *16*. †**manrentschip** = MANRENT *la15*. [OE *manrǣden* the condition of being subordinate, with metathesized suffix]

manse /mans/ *n* **1** a dwelling-house for ecclesiastics, especially the one provided for a parish minister *16-*. **2** a house reserved for the occupants of particular chairs at Aberdeen University *17-*. **3** a large or stately dwelling, a mansion; the principal residence of an estate with its attached outbuildings and land *la15-17*. **4** a measure or piece of land *la16-17*. [Lat *mansus* a dwelling, a quantity of land considered sufficient to support a family]

manshote see MAINSCHOITT

mansion, †**mansioun** /ˈmanʃən/ *n* **1** a large and imposing dwelling-house, the principal dwelling of an estate *15-*. **2** an abode, a dwelling-place *la15-16*. **3** *astrology* a house of the Zodiac *la15-16*. [ME *mansioun*]

†**mansuet, manswete** *adj* gentle, mild *15-e17*. [ME *mansuet*, OFr *mansuete*]

†**mansuetude** *n* gentleness *la15-16*. [ME, MFr *mansuetude*, Lat *mansuētūdō*]

manswear, †**maneswere,** †**mensweir** /ˈmanswer/ *v pt* **manswore**, *ptp* **mansworn, mansweirt 1** to swear falsely, commit perjury, perjure oneself, break an oath *la14-*. **2** to swear falsely or blasphemously by (a god) *la15-16*. **3** to refuse or cease to acknowledge, especially on oath; to disavow, abjure *16-e17*. **4** to quit (a place) on oath not to return within the time stated *16*. **mansworn, mansweirt 1** *of persons* forsworn, perjured *la14-e18, la18- literary*. **2** *of oaths* sworn falsely, perjured *la15-e17*. [OE *mānswerian*]

manswete see MANSUET

mansworn see MANSWEAR

mant[1.1] /mant/ *n* a speech impediment, a stammer, a stutter *19-*. [see the verb]
mant[1.2] /mant/ *v* to have a speech impediment, stammer, stutter *16-*. [Gael *mannt* to lisp, stammer]
mantea, manteau see MANTIE
manteel see MANTLE
manteen see MAINTAIN
mantele see MANTLE
manteme see MAINTAIN
mantenance see MAINTENANCE
mantie, †manteau, †mantea /ˈmante, ˈmanti/ *n* a woman's loose gown; a shawl *la17-*. **mantie-maker** a dressmaker *la18-19, 20- Sh NE Bor*. [Fr *manteau* a coat; *mantea* influenced by the place-name *Mantua*]
mantle, manteel, †mantill, †mantele, †mandill /ˈmantəl, manˈtil/ *n* 1 a loose sleeveless cloak or wrap *la14-*. 2 a covering, especially a bedcover *la14-*. 3 a natural covering of any sort; the green covering of plants *la15-*. 4 the plaid worn as their principal garment by Highlanders and Irishmen *16-e17*. 5 a set of skins of fur, enough to line a mantle *la15-e17*. **†mantilling** 1 the action of lining a mantle with fur *e16*. 2 a kind of cloth *la16-e17*. **†mantill wall** a curtain wall, or outer wall, a rampart, a screen wall *16-e17*. [ME *mantel*]
†manufactor[1] *n* industrial production; a factory *17*. [Fr *manufacture*]
†manufactor[2] *n* a craftsman, especially one employed in a large workshop *17-18*. [obsolete Fr *manufacteur*]
manufactory /manjuˈfactəre/ *n* 1 industrial production *17-*. 2 a factory *17-*. [Lat *manūfactus*, with *-ory* suffix]
manumission /manjuˈmɪʃən/ *n* 1 liberation from bondage or slavery *15-*. 2 *Scottish Universities* the conferring of a university degree, graduation *17*. [ME *manumissioun*, Lat *manūmissio* the act of freeing a slave]
manure[1.1], *Sh WC SW* **manner**, *Bor* **mainer, †mannour** /məˈnjur; *Sh WC SW* ˈmanər; *Bor* ˈmenər/ *n* 1 (organic) material used to fertilize land, dung *la17-*. 2 the utilizing or cultivation of land *la16-e17*. [see the verb; compare Lat *manūra* tillage]
manure[1.2], *Sh WC SW* **manner**, *Bor* **mainer, †mannour** /məˈnjur; *Sh WC SW* ˈmanər; *Bor* ˈmenər/ *v* 1 to fertilize with manure *19-*. 2 to cultivate, till, tend *15-19, 20- Sh WC SW Uls*. 3 to occupy; to have the use of land *15-e17*. [ME *mainouren*]
manure see MANOR
many see MONIE[1.2]
†manyment *n* management *la16-e17*. [AN, MFr *maniement*]
manyogl see MANJUGGEL
manys see MAINS
manyugilti see MANJUGGEL
manʒie see MAINʒIE[1.1]
maormor see MORMAER
map[1] /map/ *v* to nibble with twitching of the lips (as a rabbit or sheep does) *19-*. **map-map** a pet name for a rabbit; a call to a rabbit *19-*. [imitative, compare EModE *moppe* to move the lips]
map[2] /map/ *v* 1 to be listless or sorry for oneself *20- T*. 2 *of a bitch* to be in heat *18*. **mappit** stupid *20- NE T*. [perhaps related to Eng *mope*; compare Du *moppen* to sulk, pull faces]
†mappamound *n* the globe, the world *la15-16*. [ME *mappemounde*, Lat *mappa mundī*]
mappat see MOPPAT
mappie /ˈmape/ *n* 1 a pet name for a rabbit *la19-*. 2 a call to a rabbit *19-*. [MAP[1] + -IE[1]]
mappie-mou /ˈmape mu/ *n* a name for various plants, especially of the figwort family, which have blossoms in the shape of a rabbit's mouth, such as antirrhinum, calceolaria, foxglove *la19, 20- NE T EC*. [MAPPIE + MOOTH[1.1]]
mar[1.1], **†marr** /mar/ *n* a hindrance, an obstruction *17-19, 20- Sh WC*. [see the verb]
mar[1.2], **mer** /mar, mer/ *v* 1 to obstruct, hinder, intercept, stop *la14-*. 2 to impair, damage, ruin; to injure, harm *la14-*. 3 to confuse, perplex or annoy *la14-19, 20- Ork N WC*. 4 to confound or astonish *la14*. [OE *mierran*]
mar[2] /mar/ *n* the open sea, the ocean; deep-sea fishing grounds; the ocean floor *20- Sh*. **mar-bank** the continental shelf *20- Sh*. **marfloo** a crustacean of the family *Talitridae la19- Sh*. [ON *marr*]
mar[3] /mar, mar/ *n* clay; mud *20- Sh Ork*. **mar-pow** a pool where a fine bluish or whitish clay is found *20- Ork*. [unknown; compare Eng *marl*, Faer *marra*]
mar see MAIR[1.1], MAIR[1.2], MAIR[1.3]
marackel see MIRACLE[1.2]
†marais, marras, merres *n* a marsh, a swamp *14-17*. [OFr *marois*]
marakkel see MIRACLE[1.1]
marbill see MAIRBLE[1.1], MAIRBLE[1.2]
†marble *n* a kind of soil, a loose, earthy deposit of clay mixed with calcium carbonate, marl *la17-19*. **marblie** *of soil* marly *la17*. [altered form of Eng *marl* with influence from MAIRBLE[1.1]]
marble, marbre see MAIRBLE[1.1], MAIRBLE[1.2]
march[1.1], **merch, mairch** /martʃ, mertʃ, mertʃ/ *n* 1 the Anglo-Scottish Border; the region of the Borders *la14-*. 2 the boundary or frontier of a country or district, the land near a border *15-*. 3 the boundary-line of a property or of lands belonging to a community *15-*. 4 the limit of a working in a coal-mine *la17-19*. 5 a boundary-marker, a landmark *la15-e18*. 6 a natural frontier or limit of a stretch of land or water *15-16*. **†marchar** a Borderer *la14-e15*. **Marches, †marchis** a boundary area; the Borders *15-*. **march bauk** a strip of land dividing two properties *la16-19, 20- NE EC*. **march ditch** a ditch marking a boundary *19-*. **march dyke** a boundary wall *la15-*. **march fence** a boundary fence *19-*. **†marchman** a Borderer; a fighting man from the region of the Borders *la14-19*. **mairch roadie** a path between boundaries *20- NE*. **march stane** a stone marking a boundary *16-*. **mairch stank** = *march ditch la19, 20- Sh SW*. **†march treason** an offence against the law of the marches between Scotland and England *e19*. **riding of the marches** see RIDING. [ME *march*]
march[1.2], **merch, mairch** /martʃ, mertʃ, mertʃ/ *v* 1 to have a common boundary with; to border, adjoin; to form the boundary of *la14-*. 2 to fix and mark a boundary *la15-19, 20- EC*. [ME *marchen*]
march see MAIRCH[2.1], MAIRCH[2.2]
March see MAIRCH[1]
marchand see MERCHANT[1.1], MERCHANT[1.2]
marciall see MARTIAL
marcie see MERCY[1.1]
mardle[1], **merdle, †merdale** /ˈmardəl, ˈmɛrdəl/ *n* 1 a large number, a crowd, a heterogeneous collection *19- NE*. 2 camp-followers *la14-e15*. [MFr *merdaille* a worthless rabble, *merde* a turd]
mardle[2.1] /ˈmardəl/ *n* derogatory a fat, clumsy, lazy person *19- Sh NE T*. [unknown]
mardle[2.2] /ˈmardəl/ *adj* heavy, clumsy, corpulent; lazy *19- Sh NE T C*. [unknown]
mare /ˈmeər, ˈmɛər/ *n* a nightmare *16, la19- Sh*. [OE *mare*]
mare see MAIR[1.1], MAIR[1.2], MAIR[1.3], MAIR[2], MEAR[1]
mareel /maˈril/ *n* phosphorescence seen on the sea *la19- Sh*. [Norn *marelde*, ON *mörueldr*]

margelene see MARJORAM
margent see MARGIN¹·¹
margh see MARRA
margin¹·¹, **mergin**, †**margent** /ˈmardʒɪn, ˈmɛrdʒɪn/ n an edge, a border, originally of a printed page 16-. [ME *margin*]
†**margin**¹·², **mergin** v to annotate; to note or specify in the margin *la16-17*. **margening** annotating in the margin; marginal annotations *la16*. [OFr *margier*, MFr *marger* to form a border]
margorie see MARJORAM
†**margullie**, **murgully** v to mangle, hack about; to besmirch, debase, abuse *18-e19*. [OFr *margoillier* to dirty]
mariage see MAIRRIAGE
Maries see MARYS
marigold, †**mairyguild**, †**mariguld** /ˈmarəgold/ n a plant with yellow flowers, the corn-marigold or marsh-marigold *16-*. [ME *marigold*]
†**marikine**, **meroquin** n leather, originally goatskin, as manufactured in Morocco *16-18*. [MFr *maroquin*; ultimately from *Morocco*]
†**marinall**, **marinell** n a sailor, a seaman *la15-17*. [ME *marinel*]
mariner, †**marinar**, †**marynar** /ˈmarɪnər/ n a sailor, a seaman *la15-*. [ME *mariner*]
mariolyne see MARJORAM
marischal see MARSHAL¹·¹
marjoram, †**mariolyne**, †**margelene**, †**margorie** /ˈmardʒərəm/ n a herb of the genus *Origanum 16-*. [MFr *marjolaine*, MDu *margelleine*]
mark¹·¹, **merk**, **mairk** /mark, mɛrk, merk/ n 1 a visible trace; a distinguishing feature; a criterion; a sign made for identification *la14-*. 2 a conspicuous object serving to mark a boundary or position, a landmark *15-*. 3 a target *la15-*. 4 a prominent person *la19- Sh*. 5 an insensitive spot supposedly placed on the body of a witch by the Devil as a sign of his possession *la16-e18*. 6 a stone or cluster of stones made into a string or chain of jewels *la16*. **markstane** a boundary stone *16-19, 20- Sh*; compare *march stane* (MARCH¹·¹). [OE *mearc*]
mark¹·², **merk**, **mairk** /mark, mɛrk, merk/ v 1 to trace, plot, indicate (a boundary) with landmarks *la14-*. 2 to identify with a sign or writing, designate *15-*. 3 to notice; to point out *16-*. 4 to note down, make a written note of *17-*. 5 to take aim *la15-19, 20- C*. 6 to purpose, intend *la15-16*. 7 to hit *la15-e16*. 8 to direct one's way, proceed *la15-16*. **marked**, **mairked**, **markit** 1 identified or distinguished by a mark *la16-*. 2 *of persons* notable, distinguished *la19-*. 3 *of a stroke in fencing* kept tally of, scored *16*. **mark a finger on** to harm in any way *la19- NE Uls*. **mark a finger upon** = *mark a finger on*. **mark a foot to the ground** to set foot on the ground, stand *la18-19, 20- SW Uls*. [OE *mearcian*]
mark see MERK, MIRK¹·³
markal, †**mercal** /ˈmarkəl/ n a single-stilted wooden plough *la18- Sh Ork*. [perhaps ON *mergr* marrow + ON *kólfr* bolt]
market see MERCAT
marl /marl/ n 1 a patch or blotch of mixed colours, a mottled or veined pattern *18-*. 2 mottled yarn *20-*. **marlie** mottled or variegated in pattern or colour *19-*. [probably back-formation from MARLIT]
marled see MARLIT
marlee see MARLIK
marless see MARROW¹·¹
marleʒon see MERLIN
marlik, **marlee** /ˈmarlɪk, ˈmarli/ n seaweed *Zostera marina la19- Sh*. Compare MALLOCK. [Norw *marlauk*]

marlit, **marled**, †**merlit** /ˈmarlɪt, ˈmarəld/ adj chequered, variegated, mottled, veined, streaked *16-*. [perhaps reduced form of *marble* (MAIRBLE¹·¹) + -IT²]
marmaid see MERMAID
marmaiden, **marmadyn** see MERMAIDEN
marmalade, **mairmalade**, †**marmalad**, †**marmalit** /ˈmarməled, ˈmɛrməled/ n a preserve, a thick fruit jam or jelly, usually of (bitter) oranges or other citrus fruit, originally of quinces *la16-*. [Port *marmelada*]
†**marmor**, **marmore**, **marmour** n marble *la14-e17*. Compare MAIRBLE¹·¹. [Lat *marmor*]
maroc see MIRAC
marool /məˈrul/ n the angler or monkfish *Lophius piscatorius la19- Sh*. [Norw *marulk*]
maroonjeous, **maroongeous** /məˈrundʒəs/ adj wild, obstreperous; surly, obstinate *la19, 20- NE*. [unknown]
Maroons /məˈrunz/ npl a nickname for Heart of Midlothian Football Club *20-*. [metonymy from the colour of their strip]
marr see MAR¹·¹
marra, **marrow**, *Sh* **mergh**, †**margh**, †**merch** /ˈmarə, ˈmaro; *Sh* merk/ n 1 the soft, fatty material present in the cavities of bones, marrow *la14-*. 2 the core substance or most essential part of something *la15-*. 3 a variety of vegetable squash *la18-*. †**merchie** full of substance, effective *la17*. **mergie**, **merky** marrow *la19- Sh Ork*. **mervy** 1 *of food* savoury, agreeable *19-*. 2 *of soil* friable *20- Ork*. 3 *of fruit or vegetables* ripe *19*. [OE *mearg*; Sh form also from ON *mergr*]
marra see MARROW¹·¹, MARROW¹·²
marras see MARAIS
marriage see MAIRRIAGE
marrot /ˈmarət/ n the common guillemot; the razorbill *18-19, 20- NE EC*. [probably onomatopoeic; compare MURR¹·¹, MURR¹·²]
marrow¹·¹, **marra**, **morrow** /ˈmaro, ˈmarə, ˈmɔro/ n 1 a match, an equal *16-*. 2 another of the same kind, a counterpart; one of a pair *18-*. 3 a marriage-partner, a spouse *la16-17, 18- literary*. 4 a comrade, a companion, a friend; a colleague or associate or partner in business *la15-19, 20- Sh T EC SW*. 5 an opponent *16-17*. **marrowless**, **marless** 1 *of items normally found as a pair* odd, not matching *18-*. 2 unmarried *19- NE T EC*. 3 matchless, unequalled *17-19, 20- EC*. **marrows**, †**marrowis** a matching pair *16-*. †**marrowship** partnership; partners, associates *15-e16*. [unknown]
marrow¹·², **marra**, **morrow** /ˈmaro, ˈmarə, ˈmɔrə/ v 1 to associate, enter into partnership, combine *15-*. 2 to marry *16-*. 3 to match, equal *la16-*. 4 *of small farmers* to cooperate with neighbours in certain tasks *la18-*. **marra wi'**, **marrow with** to marry *17-*. [unknown]
†**Marrow**² n an abbreviation of the title of E Fisher's book *The Marrow of Modern Divinity*, whose strongly Calvinistic doctrines were condemned by the GENERAL ASSEMBLY in 1720, a prolonged controversy ensuing *e18*. [*marrow* (MARRA)]
marrow see MARRA
marry see MAIRRY
marschall see MARSHAL¹·¹
marsgum see MAASGUUM
marshal¹·¹, **marischal**, †**marschall** /ˈmarʃəl/ n 1 an official, originally a household officer, who superintends events and ceremonies *la14-*. 2 the hereditary title of a high officer of state *la12-e18, 19- historical*. 3 the title of the hangman in various burghs *la17-e18*. 4 the title of a low-ranking regimental officer of regiments of foot *17*. **Marischal College** a college in the University of Aberdeen, founded in 1593 by

the fifth *Earl Marischal* (EARL) *la16-*. [AN, OFr *mareschal* a farrier, a person who tends horses]

marshal[1,2] /'marʃəl/ *v* **1** to arrange, organize participants or events; originally, to determine the order of precedence at a ceremony *la15-*. **2** to take care of, tend to the feet of (horses) *la15-e16*. [see the noun]

mart[1], **mairt** /mart, mert/ *n* **1** a market, especially of livestock or agricultural equipment *la18-*. **2** a building used for agricultural auctions *la18-*. [MDu *mart*]

mart[2], **mairt, mert** /mart, mert, mert/ *n* **1** an ox or cow fattened for slaughter *14-*. **2** any other (farm) animal or bird salted or dried for winter provision *17-*. **3** a fat, well-fed cow *20- Sh*. **4** a fat, lazy (wealthy) person *16-19, 20- NE*. †**mairt cow** a fat cow intended for slaughter *la16-17*. †**mart scheip** a sheep intended for slaughter *17-19*. †**mert silver** a money payment as feu duty in lieu of a payment in cattle *16-e18*. [Gael *mart* a cow]

†**Mart**[3] *n* Mars *la14-e16*. [Lat *Mart-*, oblique stem of *Mars*]

marteir, marthyr *see* MAIRTYR[1,1]

martial, †**marciall,** †**merciall** /'marʃəl/ *adj* relating to or appropriate for war, military; apt for combat; brave, valiant *16-*. [ME *mercial*, EModE *marcial*, Lat *mārtiālis*]

Martimes *see* MARTINMAS

martin, mairtin, †**mortoun,** †**martoune** /'martın, 'mertın/ *n* a bird of the swallow family *la15-*. [probably backformation from MFr *martinet* a martin, a swift]

Martin Bullion's Day, *Sh* **Martabolimas day,** †**Martinabullimus dae** /'martın bulıənz de; *Sh* martaˈbɒlıməs de/ *n* the Feast of the translation of St Martin, 4 July (Old Style), 15 July (New Style); St Swithin's day *19, 20- Sh NE*. [Fr *Saint Martin le Bouillant* St Martin the Boiling, Lat *Martinus bulliens*, so called because this feast occurred during the heat of the summer]

Martinmas, Mertinmas, Mairtimas, †**Martinmes,** †**Martimes,** †**Mertimes** /'martınməs, 'mertınməs, 'mertıməs/ *n* the feast of St Martin, 11 Nov; *law* a Scottish quarter day, one of the term days *la14-*. **Martinmas term 1** the Martinmas term day *la14-*. **2** *Scottish universities* the autumn term in the Universities of St Andrews and Glasgow *20-*. [from the saint's name *Martin* + MASS[2]]

martir *see* MAIRTYR[1,1], MAIRTYR[1,2]

martoune *see* MARTIN

martrik, martrix *see* MERTRICK

martyr *see* MAIRTYR[1,1], MAIRTYR[1,2]

marvel *see* MAIRVEL[1,1], MAIRVEL[1,2]

mary *see* MAIRRY

†**Maryday** *n* one of the festival days of the Virgin Mary *la15-e18*; compare *first Maryday* (FIRST), *Latter Maryday* (LATTER). [from the name *Mary* + DAY]

Maryhill Magyars /'merehıl magjarz/ *n* a nickname for Partick Thistle Football Club *20-*. [equating the artistry of the team, based in Maryhill, Glasgow, with that of the highly-regarded Hungarian national side of the 1950s]

Marymas, Marymass, †**Marymes** /'mereməs, 'merıməs/ *n* one of the festival days of the Virgin Mary *la15-*. **Marymass Fair, Marymas Fair** a local Fair or festival held (originally at MARYMAS) in August *19-*. [from the name *Mary* + MASS[2]]

marynar *see* MARINER

Marys, Maries /'merez/ *npl* **1** ladies-in-waiting, originally the four ladies-in-waiting of Mary Queen of Scots, all of whom were called Mary *la16- historical*. **2** female attendants, maids of honour *17-19*. [from the personal name *Mary*]

mas *see* MASS[1,1]

masar *see* MACER, MASER

maschle, meeschle /'maʃəl, 'mıʃəl/ *n* a mixture, a muddle, a mess *la19- NE*. [probably related to Eng *mash*, with frequentative suffix, but cf also OSc MASHLUM]

mascorn *see* MOSS[1,1]

masel, mysel, myself, †**my seluin,** †**me self** /ma'sɛl, mae'sɛl, mae'sɛlf/ *pron* me, I (personally) *la14-*. [ME + SEL[1,1], with alteration of ME on analogy with HERSEL]

maser, mazer, †**masar,** †**maisser** /'mezər/ *n* **1** a drinking cup or bowl *la15-17, 18- historical*. **2** a variety of wood, usually maple, used to make drinking bowls *la15-16*. †**maser tree** the maple *Acer campestre la16-e17*. [ME *maser*]

mash /maʃ/ *n* a heavy two-faced hammer, used for stonebreaking *la17-*. **mash hammer** = MASH *la18-*. [probably Fr *masse* a sledgehammer]

mash *see* MASK[2,1], MASK[2,2]

mashacker *see* MASSACRE[1,2]

mashie /'maʃi/ *n golf* an iron-headed club used for lofting or for medium distances; a number 5 iron *la19-e20, la20- historical*. **mashie niblick** *golf* a type of iron-headed club which combines the features of a MASHIE and a NIBLICK, a number 7 iron or occasionally a number 6 iron *20- historical*. [probably MASH + -IE[1]]

mashlach, mashlo *see* MASLOCH

mashlum[1,1] /'maʃləm/ *n* (flour, bread or baked goods made from) mixed grains or grains and pulses *15-*. [AN *mestilun*, OFr *mesteillon*]

mashlum[1,2] /'maʃləm/ *adj* muddled, confused *la18-*. [with extended sense from the noun]

mask[1,1] /mask/ *n* **1** a brew or infusion, especially of tea; a pot of tea *la17-*. **2** a (large) quantity or amount *la19- NE T*. **3** *brewing* the mixture of malt and hot water used in making wort *16-e18*. **4** a mixture of malt or draff with hot water as a feed for a farm animal *16-e18*. †**mask fat** a vat for steeping malt *la13-e18*. †**mask rudder** the paddle used to stir steeping malt *la16-e18*. [variant of Eng *mash*; compare Norw *mask*]

mask[1,2] /mask/ *v* **1** to make or infuse tea; *of tea* to brew *la18-*. **2** *brewing* to mix (malt) with hot water to make wort; to brew (ale or beer) *15-19, 20- Ork*. **3** *of a storm* to threaten, brew up *17-19*. [see the noun]

mask[2,1], **mash,** †**mast,** †**mass** /mask, maʃ/ *n* the mesh of a net *la15-*. [OE *max*, ON *möskvi*]

mask[2,2], **mash,** *Uls* **mast** /mask, maʃ; *Uls* mast/ *v of fish* to catch in a net; to be trapped in a net *19-*. [see the noun]

mask[3,1] /mask/ *n* **1** a covering or disguise for the face *la16-*. **2** a pretence *20-*. **3** a masked entertainment *la16*. †**maskery** a masked entertainment *16*. **masking** a masked entertainment *16-*. [EModE *mask*]

mask[3,2] /mask/ *v* to disguise, hide, conceal; to conceal with a mask *la16-*. [see the noun]

maskin, masking /'maskın, 'maskıŋ/ *n* **1** the action or process of brewing; a quantity brewed *17-*. **2** an infusion or pot of tea *19-*. †**masking fat** a vat for steeping malt *la15-e19*. **masking pat, maskin-pat** a teapot *la18- T WC*. [verbal noun from MASK[1,2]]

†**masloch, mashlach, mashlo** *n* (flour, bread or baked goods made from) mixed grains or grains and pulses *15-19*. [altered form of MASHLUM[1,1]]

mason, †**masoun,** †**maissoun,** †**meassone** /'mesən/ *n* **1** a builder or worker in stone *la13-*. **2** a person who has been admitted to the freedom of the mason's incorporation or craft, a Freemason *la17-*. †**masoner** a stonemason *17*. **masonry 1** stonework *18-*. **2** the work of a mason *la14-e18*. **mason's bread** a mixture purporting to be oatcake given as a joke to an apprentice on becoming a journeyman *20- Ork T*. **mason's ghost** the robin redbreast *20- T Bor*. **mason-ludge**

1 a Freemasons' meeting place *18-*. 2 a mason's workshop *16*. **mason's mear** a wooden trestle used to support scaffolding *20- NE*. **mason's mell** a whisky bottle or decanter shaped like a mason's hammer *20-*. †**mason-werk** 1 the craft and skills of building in stone *la15-17*. 2 stonework *la16-17*. **the masons,** †**the masonis** 1 the incorporation of workers in stone *la14-*. 2 the society of Freemasons *19-*. **the mason word, the mason's word** *freemasonry* the secret word given to a masonic initiate *17-*. [AN *mason*]

mason-dew *see* MAISOUN-DEU

masoun *see* MASON

mass[1.1], †**mas** /mas/ *n* 1 a coherent, undivided or solid body; a large, heavy or dense object *15-*. 2 an amorphous body of a substance or substances, a lump of raw material *la15-*. 3 a large quantity of anything, originally referring to a quantity or bundle of letters or papers *la15-*. 4 solid bulk *19-*. 5 a large number of people closely packed or crowded together *19-*. **massily,** †**massely** massively, bulkily *16-*. [ME *masse*]

mass[1.2] /mas/ *v* to assemble or gather into a mass, collect together *16-*. [see the noun (sense 5)]

mass[2], †**mess,** †**mes** /mas/ *n* the celebration of the Eucharist in some Christian churches *la14-*. †**mes buik** a missal *15-e18*. †**mes-clathis** vestments *15-e17*. †**mes-mongar** contemptuous a Roman Catholic *la16*. †**mes-priest** a Roman Catholic priest, a personal chaplain *la16-17*. [OE *mæssa*, ME *messe*]

mass *see* MASK[2.1]

massacre[1.1], *Sh* **misacker,** *NE* **missaucre,** †**massacker,** †**massacar** /'masəkər; *Sh* mə'sakər; *NE* mə'sɔkər/ *n* 1 the merciless slaughter of large numbers of people *la16-*. 2 severe injury; destruction *la19-*. [OFr *massacre*]

massacre[1.2], *Sh* **misacker,** *NE* **missaucre,** †**mashacker,** †**massacar** /'masəkər; *Sh* mə'sakər; *NE* mə'sɔkər/ *v* 1 to kill people, animals or birds indiscriminately in large numbers *17-*. 2 to spoil by mishandling or rough treatment *la18-*. 3 to maul, mutilate, bruise, beat *19-*. [MFr *massacrer*]

massie *see* MASSY

massinmore, †**massymore** /'masınmor/ *n* the dungeon of a castle *la18- literary*. [Spanish *mazmorra*]

massy, massie, mawsie /'mase, 'mɔze/ *adj* 1 solid, substantial, weighty; ponderous; bulky *la14-*. 2 *of a person* bulky, large *la16-*. 3 proud, self-important, conceited *18-C Bor*. 4 *of a garment* thick, warm, comfortable *la19- NE*. [MASS[1.1] + -IE[2]]

massymore *see* MASSINMORE

mast[1.1], *NE* **most,** †**maist** /mast; *NE* most/ *n* 1 an upright pole supporting the sails (of a ship) *la14-*. 2 an upright pole for supporting flags or other equipment *16-*. 3 a pole suitable for use as a mast *16*. **masten** a mast *la19- Sh*. **mast hoop** the hoop binding together the timbers of a mast *20-*. **to the mast-heid** to the fullest possible extent *19-*. [OE *mæst*]

mast[1.2] /mast/ *v* to equip a ship with masts *16-*. [see the noun]

mast *see* MAIST[1.1], MASK[2.1], MASK[2.2]

maste *see* MAIST[1.1]

masten *see* MAST[1.1]

master *see* MAISTER[1.1], MAISTER[1.2], MESTER

masterstick *see* MAISTER STIK

mastiff, †**mastive,** †**mastis,** †**mastishe** /'mastɪf/ *n* a breed of large dog used for fighting or as a watch dog *15-*. **mastifflike,** †**mastewlyk,** †**mastive lyk** like a mastiff in behaviour or appearance *16-*. [Lat *mastivus*]

mastres *see* MAISTRESS

mastris, mastry *see* MAISTER[1.1]

mat[1] /mat/ *n* 1 a woven floor covering, a rug; a similar item used on furniture *15-*. 2 an underlay for a bed *16-*. 3 a (quilted or thick woollen) covering for a bed *16-19*, *20- C Bor*. 4 a sack made of matting *17-18*. [Lat *matta* a rush mat, a bedcover]

mat[2], †**mot,** †**mote** /mat/ *v* 1 may, might *la14-*. 2 must *la15-16*. [OE *mōtan*]

mat *see* MAUT

matalent *see* MALTALENT

matash *see* MOUSTACHE

match[1.1], †**mach** /matʃ/ *n* 1 an equal *la15-*. 2 an opponent *16-*. 3 a (sporting) contest *la16-*. 4 a spouse *la16-*. 5 *following a verbal noun* a bout or fit of some activity: ◊ *a greetin match 19-*. **match-play** *golf* a game scored on the number of holes won by each side rather than the total number of strokes *la19-*. [OE *gemæcca*]

match[1.2], †**mach** /matʃ/ *v* 1 to provide with a companion, partner or spouse *la15-*. 2 to be placed in an encounter or contest with *la15-*. 3 to meet in combat, fight *la15-16*. [see the noun]

mate[1], *Sh* **maat,** †**mait** /met; *Sh* mɑt/ *n* 1 a companion, a fellow-worker; a close friend *16-*. 2 *on a ship* a fellow member of the crew, a shipmate *16-*. 3 *on a ship* the chief assistant to the boatswain or master, the first or second officer in command of a ship *17-*. 4 an equal, a match *17-*. [MLG *māt*, Du *maat*]

mate[2.1], †**mait** /met/ *n* checkmate *15-*. [ME *mat*, Arabic *al-shāh-māta* the king is dead]

mate[2.2], †**mait,** †**mete** /met/ *v* 1 to checkmate; to be checkmated *15-*. 2 to vanquish, overcome; to frustrate; to exhaust *15-16*. **mated** exhausted, spent *la19- NE*. **mated oot** exhausted, spent *19- Bor*. [ME *maten*]

mate[2.3] /met/ *adj* 1 *chess* checkmated *15-*. 2 defeated; exhausted; dejected *la14-16*. [see the noun]

†**mater** *n* mother *e16*. [Lat *māter*]

mater *see* MAITTER

materes *see* MATTRESS

material[1.1] /mə'tɪrɪəl/ *n* a physical substance, a substance or component from which something is made *la15-*. **materials,** †**materiallis** equipment, implements, tools *17-*. [Lat *māteria* stuff, matter]

material[1.2] /mə'tɪrɪəl/ *adj* 1 relating to or consisting of physical substance or matter *la15-*. 2 pertinent, relevant *15-*. [Lat *māteriālis* formed of matter]

†**matern** *adj* 1 that is a mother *e16*. 2 related on the mother's side *e17*. [Lat *māternus*]

maternal /mə'ternəl/ *adj* like a mother *16-*. **maternal tongue** mother tongue, native language *la15-*. [EModE *maternal*; compare Fr *langue maternelle*]

matfull /mat'fʌl/ *n* a sexually mature herring *la19-*. [MATTIE[1] + *full* (FOU[2.1])]

mather *see* MADDER

mathie *see* MAITHE[1.1]

†**matin**[1.1], **matyn** *n* = MATINS *la14-e16*. **matin buke** a book of hours or primer *la15-16*. [reduced form of MATINS]

†**matin**[1.2], **mattyn** *adj* at the time of matins, of or belonging to the early morning *la14-e19*. [see the noun]

matins, †**matynis,** †**matynnis** /'matınz/ *npl* 1 *Roman Catholic Church* the early morning office, the public service preceding the first mass of the day *la14-*. 2 the Little Office of Our Lady *e16*. [ME *matin*]

matkie *see* MATTIE[1]

matlo /'mɑtlo, 'matlo/ *n* the housefly *Musca domestica 19- Sh Ork*. [uncertain, compare ON *maðkr* a maggot, and see MAITHE[1.1]]

matriculate, †**matriculat** /mə'trɪkjulet/ *v* 1 *heraldry* to record (arms) in the official register of the Lord Lyon King of

Arms *la16-*. **2** to enrol (as a university student) *la17-*. [Lat *matriculat-*, ptp stem of *mātrīculāre* to enrol]

matrimonial, †**matrimoniall** /matrɪˈmonɪəl/ *adj* **1** of or relating to marriage *la16-*. **2** deriving by marriage *la16-e17, 18- historical*; compare *croun matrimonial* (CROON¹·¹). [EModE *matrimoniall*, Lat *mātrimōniālis*]

matron /ˈmetrən/ *n* **1** a senior, respectable married woman *la14-*. **2** a chaperone *19*. **3** as the distinctive designation of a married female saint, especially St Anne *e16*. [AN, MFr *matrone*, Lat *mātrōna*]

†**matronize, matronise, matroneeze** *v* **1** to act as a matron or married woman of standing *e19*. **2** to chaperone *e19*. **3** *humorous* to patronize *19*. [MATRON, with verb-forming suffix]

matsill /məˈtsɪl/ *n* an affectionate form of address to a child *20- NE*. [MA + *tsill* (CHILD) a child]

mattent, †**mautent** /ˈmatənt/ *adj* lazy, weary, lethargic *18- NE T*. [participial adj from MAUTEN to sprout, germinate]

matter *see* MAITTER

mattie¹, *NE* **madgie**, †**matkie** /ˈmate, ˈmati; *NE* ˈmadʒi/ *n* a young maiden herring with the roe not fully developed *18-*. [Du *maatjes*]

mattie² /ˈmati/ *n* a maternity hospital *la20- Ork NE H&I*. [reduced form of Eng *maternity*]

Mattismess /ˈmatesmes, ˈmatesmɛs/ *n* St Matthew's day, 21st September *20- Sh*. [Norw *Mattismesse*]

mattle /ˈmatəl/ *v* to nibble *19-*. [onomatopoeic]

mattress, mattrass, †**materes** /ˈmatrəs, məˈtrɛs, məˈtras/ *n* a fabric casing filled with some material to provide comfortable support, usually as part of a bed *la14-*. [ME *materas*]

mattyn *see* MATIN¹·²

†**matutine, matutyne** *adj* of the morning *16*. [Lat *mātūtīnus* belonging to the early morning]

†**matutines** *npl* = MATINS *la15-16*. [Lat *mātūtīnae*]

matutyne *see* MATUTINE

matyn *see* MATIN¹·¹

matynis, matynnis *see* MATINS

mauch *see* MAICH, MAUK

mauchle /ˈmɔxəl/ *v* to botch, act or work clumsily; to exert oneself to no purpose *la16-19, 20- SW Bor*. [perhaps a variant of MAGGLE]

maucht, maught, mought, macht /mɔxt, maxt/ *n* physical strength or force, capability, physical or mental power *la14-*. **mauchtless, mauchless**, *Ork* **mouchless** feeble, powerless *la16-*. **mauchtly** *of wind* strong *la19- Sh*. **maughty** powerful *la18-*. [probably ON *máttr, *mahtr*]

maud, †**mad** /mɔd/ *n* a checked plaid or wrap, used as a bed-covering or worn by shepherds *la17-19, 20- Ork C Bor*. [unknown]

mauger *see* MAUGRE¹·¹, MAUGRE¹·², MAUGRE¹·³

maught *see* MAUCHT

maugre¹·¹, **mauger, magre, mager** /ˈmɔgər, ˈmagər/ *n* **1** ill-will, displeasure, spite *la14-19, 20- NE*. **2** odium, the state of being regarded with ill-will *15-16*. **magerfu, magerful** domineering, wilful *la19, 20- literary*. **maugersome** stubborn; spiteful *20- NE*. **in mauger o** in spite of *15-19, 20- NE*. [ME *maugre*, OFr *maugré*]

maugre¹·², **mauger** /ˈmɔgər/ *v* **1** to act in despite of, defy; to master; to spite *19- NE*. **2** to harm *20- NE*. [see the noun]

maugre¹·³, **mauger**, *N* **meagre**, †**magre**, †**mager** /ˈmɔgər; *N* ˈmigər/ *prep* in spite of, notwithstanding *la14-*. **maugre a person's heid** in spite of a person's opposition or resistance *15-*. **maugre a person's neck** = *maugre a person's heid*. **magre of** in spite of *la15-19, 20- N*. [see the noun]

mauk, mauch /mɔk; mɔx/ *n* a maggot *16-*. **mauk flee** a bluebottle *19- C Bor*. **as deed as a mauk** completely lifeless *la18-*. [ME *mauke*, ON *maðkr*]

maukie /ˈmɔke/ *adj* **1** maggoty *la18-19, 20- T EC Bor*. **2** filthy *19, 20- N EC*. **maukie fly** a bluebottle *20- Bor*. [MAUK + -IE²]

maukin, *NE* **myawkin**, †**mawkin**, †**makine**, †**malkin** /ˈmɔkɪn; *NE* ˈmjɔkɪn/ *n* **1** the hare *Lepus europaeus* or *Lepus timidus 18-*. **2** an awkward, ungainly girl *18-*. **3** a maidservant *18-*. **4** a feeble person, a weakling *20- NE Uls*. **5** the female pudenda *16-18*. [ME *Malkin*, a pet-form of *Maud* with diminutive suffix]

maukit, mawkit, mockit /ˈmɔkɪt/ *adj* **1** *of sheep* infested with maggots *19-*. **2** putrid; filthy *la20-*. **3** exhausted *20- Bor*. [MAUK + -IT²]

mauley *see* MIAUL

†**maument, mawment** *n* an idol *la14-16*. [ME *maumet*; compare *Muhammad*]

maumie, malmy, *Sh NE* **maamie** /ˈmɔme, ˈmalme; *Sh NE* ˈmami/ *adj* **1** mellow, pleasant *18-*. **2** *of fruit and vegetables* ripe, mellow *la19- NE WC*. **3** *of a liquid* thick and smooth; full-bodied *la18-19, 20- NE*. **4** *of weather* soft, mild *20- NE*. **5** *of a solid substance* crushed to powder *la19- Sh*. [ME *malm*, OE *mealm-* soft rock, light soil, ON *málmr* sand + -IE²]

maun¹·¹ /mɔn/ *n* compulsion, necessity *la18-*. [see the verb]

maun¹·², **mon, man** /mɔn, mən/ *v auxiliary verb* must; *with omission of a verb of motion* must go: ◊*I maun awa la14-*. **maunna, mustna** must not *18-*. **maun-be** an unavoidable necessity *19-*. [ON *man*, 1 and 3 pers sing present indicative of *muna*]

maun², †**mand** /mɔn/ *n* **1** a basket made of wicker or wooden slats *la15-*. **2** a platter for oatcakes usually made of wooden slats *la17-19 NE*. [ME *maund*]

maun³, **man** /mɔn/ *v* **1** to manage, succeed *la18-19, 20- WC SW*. **2** to master, control, domineer *19- Sh NE WC*. [ON *magna* to grow strong]

maun *see* MAN

maunder *see* MAUNNER

maundrels /ˈmɔndrəlz/ *npl* nonsense, idle tales *la18-*. [*maunder* (MAUNNER), with *-rel* diminutive, derogatory suffix]

maunna *see* MAUN¹·²

maunner, maunder /ˈmɔnər, ˈmɔndər/ *v* **1** to talk in a rambling fashion *la18-*. **2** to grumble *19-*. [EModE *maunder*]

Maunsemas /ˈmɔnsməs/ *n* the feast of St Magnus, Earl of Orkney, 16th April or 13th December *20- Sh Ork*. [from the name *Magnus* + MASS²]

maut, malt, †**mat** /mɔt, mɔlt/ *n* **1** grain, usually barley, prepared for brewing or distilling by steeping, germinating and kiln-drying; spent grain after it has been used for brewing *la14-*. **2** whisky; ale *16-*. **mautman 1** a maker of malt, a maltster *16-19, 20- N NE EC*. **2** a kind of cloth *la16*. †**malt silvir** a payment to a maltster for making grain into malt *la16-e17*. **malt whisky** whisky distilled from malted barley in a pot-still *19-*. **the maut's abune the meal** *of a person* drunk *17-*. **maut and meal** = *meal and maut* (MEAL¹·¹). [OE *mealt*]

†**mauten, malten** *v of grain or seeds* to germinate, sprout; to become malt *la18-19*. [from the noun MAUT]

mautent *see* MATTENT

mauvie /ˈmɔvi/ *n* the stomach *20- N*. [Eng *maw* + -IE¹; compare *myave* (MAW³)]

mavasy *see* MALVOISIE

maveis *see* MAVIS

mavie /ˈmeve, ˈmevi/ *n* the song thrush *la19-*. [reduced form of MAVIS]

mavie *see* MOVE

mavis, †**maveis** /'mevɪs/ *n* the song thrush *Turdus philomelos 15-*. [ME *mavis*]

†**mavite, mawyte** *n* wickedness, treachery *la14-e15*. [AN *malveisté*]

maw¹, ma /mɔ, ma/ *n* mother *20-*. **yer maw** an exclamation of dismissal or disbelief *la20- C*. [reduced form of MAMMIE]

maw² /mɔ/ *n pl* **maws** †**mawis**, †**malvis** the mallow *Malva sylvestris 15-19, 20- Bor*. [ME *malwe*; compare OE *mealwe*]

maw³ /mɔ/ *n* the belly or stomach of a person, animal or fish, the crop of a bird; also the jaws, mouth or gullet of a voracious animal or person *la14-*. **myave** the stomach, *la19- NE*; compare MAUVIE. [OE *maga*]

maw⁴, *Sh Ork* **maa** /mɔ; *Sh Ork* mɑ/ *n* a gull, especially the common gull *Larus canus 16-*. [ON *máv-* oblique stem of *már*]

maw⁵·¹ /mɔ/ *n* a miaow, the cry of a cat *19- SW Bor*. **mawie** a name for a cat *20- Ork*. [onomatopoeic]

maw⁵·² /mɔ/ *v of a cat* to mew *la18-19, 20- Bor*. [see the noun]

maw⁶, *Sh Ork T* **maa** /mɔ; *Sh Ork T* mɑ/ *v pt* **mawit, mawed**, *SW Bor* **meuw**, *ptp* **mawn** to cut grass or crops, mow, originally with a scythe *15-*. **mawer**, †**mawar** a mower *la15-18, 19- SW*. **mawster** a mower *19- SW*. **maain girse** meadow hay *20- Sh T*. [OE *māwan*]

mawed, mawit *see* MAW⁶

mawkin *see* MAUKIN

mawkit *see* MAUKIT

mawment *see* MAUMENT

mawn *see* MAW⁶

mawsie /'mɔzi/ 1 a warm woollen jersey *la19- NE T*. 2 an amply-proportioned, motherly-looking woman *la18-19*. [perhaps from *Mause*, a form of *Mary*]

mawsie *see* MASSY

mawster *see* MAW⁶

mawyte *see* MAVITE

maxie /'maksi/ *n* a gross error in a Latin translation, entailing the highest deduction of marks *la19- NE*. [shortened form of Lat *maximus error*]

†**may¹** *n* a maiden, a young woman *la14-19*. [perhaps ON *mær*]

may², †**ma** /me/ *v pt* **micht, might**, †**mocht** 1 *as an auxilliary verb* expressing possibility, capacity, or ability; having good cause or permission to do something *14-*; compare MICHT². 2 to possess, exert power, might *la14-15*. †**mayfall** perhaps, perchance *la14-e15*. [OE *magan*]

may *see* MA

May *see* MEY

mayan *see* MOYEN²·²

maybe¹·¹ /'mebi/ *n* a possibility *18-*. **a maybe is not aye a honey bee** a mere possibility guarantees no beneficial outcome *19- proverbial*. [see the adverb]

maybe¹·², **mebbe, mibbe, mibby** /'mebi, 'mebe, 'mɛbi, 'mebe, 'mɪbi, 'mɪbe/ *adv* 1 perhaps, possibly *la18-*. 2 *of quantity or measurement* approximately *la19-*. 3 then, that being so, in that case: ◊*whaur dae ye come fae maybe? 20- NE WC*. **maybe aye and maybe hooch aye** an expression of uncertainty or disbelief *20-*. [shortened form of Eng *it may be*]

maybes, mebbes, mibbes /'mebiz, 'mɛbiz, 'mɪbiz/ *adv* perhaps, possibly *19-*. [MAYBE¹·² + -s]

mayn *see* MAIN¹·¹, MAIN¹·², MAIN¹·³

mayne *see* MAINE

maynis *see* MAINS

mayntym *see* MEANTIME¹·¹

mayor *see* MAIR²

mayson diew *see* MAISOUN-DEU

maze¹·¹ /mez/ *n* a state of amazement, perplexity *19-*. [perhaps from the verb]

maze¹·² /mez/ *v* to amaze *la19- EC Bor*. [aphetic form of Eng *amaze*]

maze *see* MAISE²

mazer *see* MASER

me, mi, †**ma** /mi/ *pron* 1 myself, me *la14-*. 2 I *la18-*. [OE *me*]

me *see* MA

me- *see* MA-

mea *see* MAE¹·²

mead¹, †**meid** /mid/ *n* an alcoholic liquor made from fermenting honey and water *15-*. [OE *medu*]

mead², †**mede**, †**meid** /mid/ *n* a meadow, a grassy ground *13-*. [OE *mǣd*]

mead *see* MEITH¹·¹

meadow *see* MEEDIE

meagre, †**megir** /'migər/ *adj* 1 fine, delicate; thin, emaciated; narrow *16-*. 2 inferior, inadequate, deficient *19-*. **meagreness**, †**megirnes** thinness; timidity; scantiness *16-*. [ME *megre*]

meagre *see* MAUGRE¹·³

meal¹·¹, **male**, †**mele**, †**meill**, †**maill** /mil, mel/ *n* grain or pulses ground to a powder or granules; oatmeal *la14-*. **meal ark** a chest for storing oatmeal *16-19, 20- C SW Uls*. **meal-belly** an inhabitant of the island of Sanday *e18, 20- historical*. **meal-bowie** a barrel for storing oatmeal *19- NE T*. **mealcorn** grain in general; food, sustenance *la16, la18- Sh Ork N NE*. **meal-girnel** = *meal ark 16-*. †**meal kail** broth made with oatmeal and kail *18-19*. **meal-kist** = *meal ark la16-*. †**mealmaker** a miller; also a person who buys grain to sell as meal *la15-18*. †**meleman** a dealer in meal *16-e18*. †**meill-mercat** the burgh market where oats or oatmeal was sold *la15-18*. †**meal mob** rioters protesting against shortages and high prices of oatmeal *la18-19*. **Meal Monday** a Monday holiday in February in the Universities of St Andrews, Edinburgh and Glasgow *la19-*. †**meal-monger** = *meleman la17-19*. **meal-poke** a bag for holding oatmeal *la16-*. **meal-seeds** the husks of oats, used for making sowans *19- Sh Ork N T EC*. **meal an ale** 1 a dish made with oatmeal, ale and whisky and eaten at harvest-home celebrations *la19- NE T*. 2 the harvest-home celebration; a meal held to raise money for charity *la20- NE T*. **meal an bree** BROSE *la18-19, 20- Uls*. †**meal an kail** = *meal kail la17-19*. **meal and maut** food and drink *16-19, 20- NE T*. †**meal an thrammel** meal moistened with water or ale, eaten between meals *la18-e19*. [OE *melu*]

meal¹·² /mil/ *v* 1 *of grain* to yield or turn into meal when ground *la18-*. 2 to add meal to (soups or stews) *19- N T*. **meal yer kail** to be a source of profit *20- N*. [see the noun]

meal², **male**, †**mail** /mil, mel/ *n* 1 a time or occasion for taking food; the food offered or eaten *la15-*. 2 a single milking of a cow or cows *la17-*. **male o meat** meal-time, food offered or eaten *la17- SW Bor*. [OE *mǣl*, MDu *male* a fixed time]

meal *see* MAIL¹, MAIL⁴

meal-an-folly, †**merefow** /'mil ən 'fɔle/ *n* common yarrow *Achillea millefolium 17- Ork*. [altered form of ME *milfoil*, EModE *milfoil*]

mealie, mealy, †**meillie** /'mili, 'mile/ *adj* 1 of or related to meal *17-*. 2 of the consistency of meal, floury, powdery; *of soil* friable *19-*. 3 of the colour of meal, brownish, beige or speckled with brown and beige *19-*. †**mealy-bag** a bag for holding oatmeal *18-19*. **mealie creeshie, meelacrusha** oatmeal fried in fat *la19- WC SW Uls*. **mealie drink** water sprinkled with oatmeal *20- Ork NE T*. **mealie dumpling** a round pudding of oatmeal and fat with seasoning, boiled or

steamed 20-. **mealie jerker** a white oatmeal pudding *20-NE T*. **mealie-Jimmie** a white pudding or oatmeal pudding *20*-. **mealie-mou'd, mealie-moothed** ingratiating, hypocritical *20*-. †**meillie poke** = *mealy-bag 17-19*. **mealie-pudding** a pudding similar to a white pudding but usually made with coarser oatmeal and less suet *20*-. [MEAL¹·¹ + -IE²]
meall *see* MOOL¹·¹
meally *see* MELLAY¹·²
mealock *see* MOOL¹·¹
mealy *see* MEALIE
mean¹·¹, †**mene**, †**mein** /min/ *n* **1** something intervening or intermediate, a middle point between extremes *14*-. **2** a method, an agency, an instrument; an opportunity *la14-19*. **3** resources, possessions, means of support *la16-19*. **4** influence, credit *16*. **5** trickery, a trick, a plot *16-e17*. **means 1** a method, an agency, an instrument; an opportunity *16-*. **2** resources, possessions, means of support *la16-*. [AN *mene, mean* middle, intermediary, and MEAN¹·³]
†**mean¹·²**, †**mene**, †**meyne** *v* to mediate, settle by mediation; to arrange *16-e17*. [perhaps from the noun]
mean¹·³, †**mene**, †**meyn** /min/ *adj* middle, intermediate; intermediary *la14-*. †**in the meyn sessone** in the meantime *la15-e17*. [ME *mene*]
mean², **mene**, †**mein** /min/ *v pt, ptp* **meant** †**meanit**, †**meaned**, †**ment 1** to intend *la14-*. **2** to signify, portend *la14-*. **3** to convey in words, declare, say *la14-18*. **4** to believe, have in mind, remember; to reckon, plan *la14-17*. [OE *mǣnan*]
mean³, †**mene**, †**mein**, †**main** /min/ *adj* **1** *of rank, status, value* low, inferior; unimportant, trivial; *of prices, ability, provision* moderate, poor, inadequate; *of height, stature* rather small *16-*. **2** *of farmland and facilities shared by several tenants* possessed jointly or in common *la16-*. **3** *of an animal* in poor condition, thin *la19- Sh N T Uls*. †**in meanis** in common, as a joint possession or undertaking *la16-17*. [OE *gemǣne* in common]
mean *see* MAIN¹·², MANE¹·¹
meanjie, minjy /'mɪndʒi, 'mɪndʒi/ *adj* mean, stingy *20- C*. [probably Eng *mingy*, a conflation of Eng *mean* = MEAN³ and *stingy*]
meant *see* MEAN²
meantime¹·¹, †**mene time**, †**mayntym**, †**myntyme** /'mɪntʌɪm/ *n* an intervening period, the time being, present *la14-*. **in the meantime** during an intervening period, for the time being, at present *la14-*. **in the mids of the meantime** = *in the meantime 19-*. [MEAN¹·³ + TIME]
meantime¹·², †**mein tym** /'mɪntʌɪm/ *adv* **1** during an intervening period *la16-*. **2** for the time being, at present *20-*. [see the noun]
meanwhile, †**meyne-quhile**, †**meyn quhile** /'mɪnʍʌɪl/ *n* an intervening period, the time being, present *15-*. [MEAN¹·³ + WHILE]
mear¹, **meer, mare**, †**mere**, †**meir** /mir, mer/ *n* **1** a female equine, especially a horse *15-*. **2** a trestle used to support scaffolding *la17-19, 20- NE*. **3** an inhabitant of the parish of Rousay *la19- Ork*. **4** the beam which supports the waterwheel of a horizontal mill *20- Sh*. **5** a bricklayer's hod *la16-19*. **6** a woman *16-e17*. **7** a wooden frame on which wrongdoers, especially soldiers, were made to 'ride' as a public punishment *17*. **mearie, meerie**, †**meiry** a mare *la17-*. [OE *mearh* a horse, *mȳre* a mare]
mear²·¹, †**mere**, †**meir** /mir/ *n* a boundary *la14-17, 20- Uls*. [OE *gemǣre* a boundary]
mear²·², †**mere**, †**meir** /mir/ *v* to border, form a boundary *la14-17, 20- Uls*. [see the noun]

mearing, mering, merin /'mirɪŋ, 'mirɪn/ *n* (a strip of uncultivated land marking) a boundary; the ridge between cultivated strips *la16- N NE*. [verbal noun from MEAR²·²]
mease, †**mese**, †**meis**, †**meys** /miz/ *v* **1** to pacify, calm (a person), ease (strife) *la15-*. **2** to calm (the weather) *la14-16*. **3** to quench (a fire); to cool (something hot) *la14-16*. **4** to mitigate, soothe (pain) *e16*. [aphetic form of AMES]
mease *see* MAISE¹, MAISE²
measle *see* MAISLE
measles *see* MAISLES
meassis *see* MACIS
meassone *see* MASON
measure¹·¹, **meisure**, *Sh NE* **mizzer**, †**mesure**, †**missour**, †**mussour** /'mɛʒər, 'miʒər; *Sh NE* 'mɪzər; *Sh NE* 'mɪʒər/ *n* **1** dimension, size, quantity *la14-*. **2** a quantity (of something) determined according to an agreed standard *la14-*. **3** due proportion, what cannot or ought not to be exceeded, bounds, limits; moderation *la14-*. **4** a standard system of determining capacity or dimension, originally as used for particular commodities *15-*. **5** a standard instrument for determining capacity or dimension, a vessel of a standard capacity, a rod of a standard length *15-*. **6** the relative duration of notes in music; regular time or rhythm in music or poetry; a melody; a dance *la15-*. **7** a plan, a course of action; a legislative proposal or enactment *18-*. †**by mesure** by measuring (out), as determined by measurement *15-17*. [ME *mesure*]
measure¹·², **meisure**, *Sh NE* **mizzer**, †**mesure**, †**missure** /'mɛʒər, 'miʒər; *Sh NE* 'mɪzər; *Sh NE* 'mɪʒər/ *v* **1** to determine size or capacity by comparison with a standard; to apportion *la14-*. **2** to moderate; to limit *la14-*. **3** to appraise, assess, estimate *la15-*. **4** to adjust to a particular size, curtail *e16*. [ME *mesuren*]
meat¹·¹, **mait, maet**, †**mete**, †**meit**, †**met** /mit, met/ *n* **1** food of any sort *la14-*. **2** food prepared or served, a meal *la14-*. **3** animal flesh as food *la14-*. **4** produce (animal or cereal) while still alive or growing *16-17*. **5** a livelihood, a living *la14-17*. **maetly** well nourished *20- Sh*. **meatrife** plentifully supplied with food *19, 20- Bor*. †**mete-almery** a food cupboard *la15-e17*. †**mete-burde** a dining-table *la15-e17*. †**meit-butter** better quality butter, fit for consumption as food *la16-18*. †**mete-fisch** freshly-caught fish *16-17*. **meat-hail** having a healthy appetite *la18-19, 20- Sh NE EC*. **meat-midder** the mistress of a house, a housewife or hostess *19- Sh*. †**meit-scheip** a sheep intended for slaughter as food *16-17*. **meat-tea** high tea, often associated with funerals *20- C Uls*. **a good meat hoose** *see* GUID¹·³. **meat-like and claith-like** well-fed and well-dressed *la17-*. [OE *mete*]
meat¹·², **mait**, †**mete** /mit, met/ *v* **1** to provide food for, feed *la16-19, 20- Sh Ork NE EC*. **2** to eat a meal, be provided with food *la16-19, 20- Sh NE*. **3** *of ears of corn* to swell *20- Sh Ork*. [see the noun]
meath *see* MEITH¹·¹
meaul *see* MIAUL
meaze *see* MAISE¹
mebbe *see* MAYBE¹·²
mebbes *see* MAYBES
mecanyk *see* MECHANIC¹·²
mechanic¹·¹, †**mechanick** /mə'kanɪk/ *n* **1** a person who assembles or repairs machines *19-*. **2** a manual workman, craftsman or artisan *la16-19*. [see the adj]
mechanic¹·², †**mecanyk** /mə'kanɪk/ *adj* **1** of or relating to manual labour or the work of a craftsman or artisan *16-*. **2** *of a person* that performs manual labour *16*. [MFr *mecanique* characterized by the use of tools or the hands, Lat *mēchanicus*]
mechanick *see* MECHANIC¹·¹

med see MAITHE[1.1], MAK[1.2], MID[1.2]

medal, †**medal3ie** /'mɛdəl/ *n* **1** a metal object of the shape and form of a coin given as a prize or commemoration *la16-*. **2** *golf* a competition scored according to the total number of strokes played, not the number of holes won in a round (originally played for the prize of a medal or medallion) *la19-*. **medalist, medallist 1** *golf* the winner of a medal competition or a round in a competition played according to medal play *20-*. **2** an expert in medals *e19*. **medal competition** *golf* a competition played according to the rules of medal play *la19-*. **medal play** *golf* stroke play as used in competitions where a prize, originally a medal, is offered *la19-*; compare *stroke play* (STRAIK), *match play* (MATCH[1.1]). [MFr *medaille*]

meddill see MIDDLE[1.2], MIDDLE[2]
meddle see MIDDLE[2]
mede see MEAD[2], MEED
medeator see MEDIATOR
medecyne see MEDICINE[1], MEDICINE[2]

mediate, †**mediat** /'midiət/ *adj* **1** *of a person* intermediary, intervening; that acts for another *16-*. **2** *of an heir* not lineal, collateral *la15-16*. [Lat *mediātus*]

mediator, †**mediatour**, †**medeator** /'midiətər/ *n* an intermediary, intercessor or go-between *la14-*. [ME *mediatour*, Lat *mediātor*]

†**mediatrice** *n* a female mediator *la14-e16*. [Lat *mediātric-*, oblique stem of *mediātrix*]

mediatrix /'midiətriks/ *n* a female mediator *la15-*. [Lat *mediātrix*]

medicin see MEDICINE[2]
medicinar see MEDICINER

†**medicinary** *n* the art or practice of medicine; medical treatment; a medical practitioner *16*. [MEDICINE[1], MEDICINE[2], with noun-forming suffix *-ary*]

medicine[1], †**medecyne** /'mɛdəsɪn/ *n* **1** a substance or preparation used as a remedy or treatment for disease *la14-*. **2** healing, medical remedies or treatments *15-*. **3** a spiritual or psychological remedy, a cure *15-*. [ME *medicin*, Lat *medicīna*]

†**medicine**[2], **medecyne**, **medicin** *n* a doctor *15-17*. [MFr *medecin*]

mediciner, **medicinar** /mə'dɪsɪnər/ *n* **1** a medical practitioner, a doctor, a healer *la14-*. **2** (the title of) the Professor of Medicine at King's College, Aberdeen *la16-e19*. **3** a healer of spiritual or emotional sicknesses *la15-17*. [MEDICINE[2] + -ER]

medick, **methick** /'mɛdɪk, 'mɛθɪk/ *n* the dandelion *Taraxacum officinale 20- NE*. [transferred use of Eng *medick* a plant of the genus *Medicago*, especially lucerne, from Lat *Mēdica*]

medie /'midi, 'mide/ *n* a less serious error in Latin translation *la19- NE*. Compare MAXIE. [shortened form of Lat *medius error*]

medling see MIDDLIN[1.1]
medow see MEEDIE
medwyfe see MIDWIFE

meechie /'mixi, 'mixe/ *adj* mean, stingy *20-*. [unknown]

†**meed**, **meid**, **mede** *n* **1** reward, recompense; remuneration, payment; a bribe *la14-e19*. **2** the quality of deserving well, merit, worth *la14-18*. **3** assistance, support *15-e17*. [OE *mēd*]

meed see MAK[1.2], MEITH[1.1], MUID

meedie, **meeda**, **meedow**, **meadow**, *Sh* **möddoo**, †**medow** /'midi, 'midə, 'mido, 'mɛdo; *Sh* 'mødu/ *n* **1** a piece of permanent grassland or a grass field, cut for hay or used as pasture *la12-*. **2** marshy grassland where the natural coarse grasses are often cut for hay *16-*. **meadow queen** meadow-sweet *Filipendula ulmaria 20- Ork*. [OE *mæd*]

meef see MOOTH[2]

†**meek**[1.1], **meke** *v* to humble, mollify, tame *la14-18*. [see the adj]

meek[1.2], †**meke**, †**meik** /mik/ *adj* mild; humble; submissive *la14-*. **meek-taestit** pleasant, mild-flavoured *la19- Sh*. [ON *mjúkr* soft, pliant, gentle]

meelackie see MOOL[1.1]
meelacrusha see MEALIE
meelie see MOOL[2], MOOLIE[1.1]
meen see MANE[1.2], MUNE

meenie, **minnie** /'mini, 'mɪni/ *n* a fine awl *20- N*. [Gael *minidh* an awl]

meeninit see MINNONETTE

meenister[1.1], **minister** /'minɪstər, 'mɪnɪstər/ *n* **1** *Christian Church* a member of the clergy (having charge of a church), an ecclesiastic *la14-*. **2** *Roman Catholic Church* the title of the superior of a house of the Trinitarian Order *14-*. **3** an attendant; a person who acts under the authority of another, an executive, an agent *la14-*. **4** the executive officer in charge of a government department, originally an executive officer of the Crown *la14-*. **5** *pl* grains of barley burnt in preparing BURSTEN *20- Ork*. **6** a black rabbit *20- Ork*. **minister's man** the manservant of a member of the clergy; a church officer or beadle *19-*. **minister's mark** a method of identifying sheep by cutting off both ears *la19- Sh*. **minister of the Kirk** a member of the clergy *17-*. [ME *ministre*, Lat *minister* a servant, a priest's attendant, a priest]

meenister[1.2], **minister** /'minɪstər, 'mɪnɪstər/ *v* **1** to furnish, supply, impart *la14-*. **2** to execute, dispense (justice) *15-*. **3** to serve or officiate (as a clergyman) *15-*. **4** *Christian Church* to dispense (a sacrament) *la15-*. **5** to serve, officiate in an office *la15-16*. [ME *ministren*]

meenistry, **ministry**, †**ministerie**, †**ministrie** /'minɪstrɛ, 'mɪnɪstrɛ/ *n* **1** executive officers of government viewed collectively; a department of government headed by a minister *15-*. **2** *Christian Church* the work, vocation or office of a clergyman *la16-*. **3** the spiritual service of a minister of religion *la16-*. **4** the pastorship of a particular congregation or parish *la16-*. **5** a religious house under the superiority of a clergyman *16-19*. **6** *Presbyterian Church* the kirk session *la16-e17*. [Lat *ministerium*]

meenit[1.1], **minute**, **minent**, †**minut**, †**menwt** /'minət, 'mɪnət, 'minənt/ *n* **1** a sixtieth part of an hour or degree *la15-*. **2** *law* a summary or draft of the contents of a deed or warrant presented for registration *16-*. **3** a written record of proceedings; originally a note of the events and proceedings of a legal action *la16-*. **4** a memorandum *la16-*. **5** *law* an original document setting out the terms of a contract *la16-e18*. **meenits**, **minutes 1** a written record of proceedings *la16-*. **2** *in a school* a period of recreation; *in a factory* a tea-break *la19- NE T*. **mintie**, **minitie** a minute, a short time *20-*. **minute-book** a record book containing the transactions of a society, club or other organization, originally especially those of a notary or court *la16-*. **at the meenit** instantly, without hesitation *la19-*. **at the meenitheid** = *at the meenit*. **a wee minute** a moment, a short space of time *20-*. **in a minute** readily, without a second thought *20-*. **on the minute-heid** punctually, at the precise moment *20-*. [ME *minut*, Lat *minūtum*]

meenit[1.2], **minute**, †**minut** /'minət, 'mɪnət/ *v* to record proceedings (in a register or record book) *la16-*. [MFr *minute* an original document from which copies are made]

meenlicht see MUNELICHT
meer see MEAR[1], MUIR

meerswine see MERE
meeschle see MASCHLE
meese see MESS[1.2]
meeser see MISERT[1.1]
meeserable, miserable, †**miserabill** /ˈmɪzərəbəl, ˈmɪzərəbəl/ *adj* **1** wretched, unhappy, lamentable *la15-*. **2** despicable, contemptible *la15-*. **3** mean, stingy, miserly *la19-*. **4** poverty-stricken *la15-17*. [MFr *miserable*]
meesery, misery, †**miserie,** †**meserie** /ˈmɪzəre, ˈmɪzəre/ *n* wretchedness, distress, unhappiness, frequently caused by poverty *la15-*. [ME *miseri*]
meesick see MUSIC
meet[1], †**mete** /mit/ *v* **1** to encounter, by chance or arrangement *la14-*. **2** *of a group meeting by arrangement* to assemble, convene *la14-*. **3** to encounter (an enemy), engage in battle; to combat, counter (something non-material) *la14-*. **4** *of non-material things or events* to unite; to occur or exist simultaneously *16-*. **5** to respond to, offer a rejoinder to *15-e17*. **6** *law* to provide an adequate answer to contrary allegations *la16-e17*. **meet in wi** to meet a person or persons *19-*. **meet wi yer merchant** to meet your match *19- C*. [OE *mētan*]
meet[2.1], †**mete,** †**meit,** †**meyit** /mit/ *adj* **1** well-fitting, of the right dimensions *la14-*. **2** suitable, fitting, appropriate, apt *15-*. [OE *gemǣte*]
†**meet**[2.2] *adv* **1** closely, neatly fitting *16-e17*. **2** appropriately, fittingly *la15-16*. [see the adj]
meeth see MOOTH[2]
meeting, meetin, †**meting,** †**meiting** /ˈmitɪŋ, ˈmitɪn/ *n* **1** the action of encountering (a person) *la14-*. **2** the action of engaging an enemy or opponent in battle or a (sporting) contest; a fight, a contest *la14-*. **3** *of a group* the action of assembling or convening for some common purpose; (the members of) an assembly *la14-*. **meeting-house** a building, other than a church, for religious meetings or for other meetings such as town council meetings *la17-*. **meeting-place** a place at which a meeting occurs, a place of trysting or mustering *la16-*. [verbal noun from MEET[1]]
meeve see MOVE
meffin /ˈmɛfɪn/ *n* the act of warming oneself at the fire by sitting in front of it with the legs apart *20- T*. [unknown]
meg see MAIG[1.1]
Meg, †**Mag** /mɛg/ *n* **1** an unsophisticated country girl *16-*. **2** a large cannon *la16-e17*; compare MONS MEG. **Meg's hole** a break in the clouds to the south-west, foretelling clearer weather *20- C*. **Meg Mulloch** a familiar spirit traditionally associated with the Grants of Tullochgorum in Strathspey *la17- NE*. **Meg o mony feet** a centipede *e19*. [familiar forms of *Margaret*]
Meggie see MAGGIE[3]
megins see MAEGINS
megir see MEAGRE
megrim, †**magrame,** †**magryme,** †**migramme** /ˈmigrəm, ˈmɛgrəm/ *n* **1** a whim, a preposterous notion *19-*. **2** a migraine, a severe headache; dizziness; earache *16-19, 20- NE*. **maigriment** agitation, restlessness; an illness *20- Sh Ork*. [ME *migrain, migrem*]
megstie, mexty /ˈmɛgsti, ˈmɛksti, ˈmɛxti/ *interj* in expressions of surprise, distress or disapproval, goodness me *19-*. **megstie me** goodness me *19-*. [altered form of MICHTY[1.4]]
meh see MA, MAE[2.1], MAE[2.2]
meid see MEAD[1], MEAD[2], MEED, MEITH[1.1], MID[1.2]
meidwif see MIDWIFE
meik see MEEK[1.2]
meikle see MUCKLE[1.1], MUCKLE[1.2], MUCKLE[1.3]

meil, †**mele** /mil/ *n weights and measures* a unit of weight, especially for dry goods *la12-19, 20- historical*. [ON *mælir* a measure]
meill see MEAL[1.1], MELL[1.1]
meillie see MEALIE
mein see MEAN[1.1], MEAN[2], MEAN[3]
meine see MIEN
mein tym see MEANTIME[1.2]
meinʒe see MENYIE
meir see MAIR[1.1], MEAR[1], MEAR[2.1], MEAR[2.2]
meis see MEASE, MESS[1.1]
meisure see MEASURE[1.1], MEASURE[1.2]
meit see MEAT[1.1], MEET[2.1], METT[1.2]
meith[1.1], *Sh* **meid,** *Sh* **mead,** *Sh* **meed,** †**methe,** †**meath,** †**mithe** /miθ, mið; *Sh* mid/ *n* **1** a distinguishing feature; a landmark, especially as used by sailors to steer by; a point of reference, an indication, a guide *16-*. **2** a boundary, a boundary marker *15-19, 20- Sh Bor*. **3** a sea-mark, (a barrel used as) a marker in the estuary of the River Tay *la16-17*. **4** a turning-post; a terminus *e16*. **5** a course *e16*. [ON *mið* a fishing-bank marked by landmarks, and from the verb]
meith[1.2], †**meth,** †**mith** /miθ, mið, mid/ *v* **1** to navigate by reference to prominent landmarks *la19- Sh*. **2** to settle and mark boundaries *la15-18*. [ON *miða* to mark the position of something]
meith see MAITHE[1.1]
meiting see MEETING
mek see MAK[1.2]
meke see MEEK[1.1], MEEK[1.2]
mekill see MUCKLE[1.2], MUCKLE[1.3]
melancholious, †**malancolious,** †**melancolious,** †**molloncholious** /mɛlənˈkoliəs/ *adj* **1** characterized by melancholy, gloomy, sad; resentful *la15-19, 20- literary*. **2** causing, consisting of or of the nature of the humour of melancholy *la15-e17*. [ME *malencolious*]
melancholy[1.1], †**milankily,** †**malancoly,** †**melancoly** /ˈmɛlənkəli/ *n* **1** deep dejection, sadness *la15-*. **2** mischief, devilment *la19 Sh*. **3** yarrow, milfoil *Achillea millefolium 20- Sh*. **4** anger, sullenness *la14-16*. **5** (the condition resulting from an excess of) the humour black bile *la15-e17*. [ME *malencoli*]
†**melancholy**[1.2] *v* to feel sadness or resentment *e15*. [OFr *melancolier* to be sad]
melancholy[1.3], †**malancoly** /ˈmɛlənkɔli/ *adj* gloomy, dejected; overly serious, pensive *la15-*. [see the noun]
melancolious see MELANCHOLIOUS
melancoly see MELANCHOLY[1.1]
melder, *NE* **maillyer,** †**meldir,** †**meller** /ˈmɛldər; *NE* ˈmeljər/ *n* **1** a quantity of grain ground at one time *la17-*. **2** the occasion of grinding one quantity of corn *la18, 19- NE*. **3** the meal ground from the corn which formed part of a farm-servant's wages *19*. **4** = *salt melder* (SAUT[1.1]) *e16*. **meldered** *of grain* kiln-dried in preparation for grinding *20- Ork*. **meldering** the meal produced in a melder *la18-19, 20- NE*. [ON *meldr* grist, flour]
meldrop /ˈmɛldrəp/ *n* a drop of mucus from the nose *la15-19, 20- Bor*. [OE *mǣldropa* phlegm, saliva, mucus, ON *méldropi* the saliva from a horse's bit]
meldy /ˈmɛldi/ *n* corn-spurry *Spergula arvensis 19- Sh*. [Norw *melde* weeds among corn]
†**mele, mell** *v* **1** to speak, tell *la14-16*. **2** *of a bird* to sing *15-16*. [OE *mǣlan*, ON *mæla*]
mele see MEAL[1.1], MEIL
melg /mɛlg/ *n* milt, the sperm of a male fish *la16- N NE*. [Gael *mealg*]

meliorate, meliorat /ˈmiliəret/ *v of a tenant* to improve buildings or land occupied *la16-*. **melioration, †melioratioun** *law* an improvement to property made by a tenant for which compensation would be paid by the proprietor *la15-*. [Lat *meliorat-*, ptp stem of *meliorare*]

mell[1.1], **maill**, *Sh* **mall**, **†meill** /mɛl, mel; *Sh* mal/ *n* **1** a heavy hammer; a club; originally also a mace *15-*. **2** a heavy blow, as struck by a large hammer *la17-*. **3** a mallet awarded to the last in a race *la17-19*. **4** a clenched fist *la19*. **mell hammer** a mallet *20-*. **mell-heid** a stupid person, a blockhead *20- Bor*. **mell-heidit** stupid *16, 19- Bor*. [ME *mal*]

mell[1.2] /mɛl/ *v* **1** to strike with a heavy hammer *18-*. **2** to strike heavily, thrash; to trounce *la18-*. [see the noun]

mell[2] /mɛl/ *v* **1** to mix, mingle, combine, blend *la14-*. **2** to concern or busy oneself (with), meddle, interfere *la14-*. **3** to associate, have dealings with *16-*. **4** to come together, engage in combat, fight *la14-e19*. **5** to have sexual intercourse (with) *la14-e17*. **6** to engage in an exchange of insults, flyte *la16*. **melled yowe** a ewe mated to a ram of a different breed *la19, 20- N Bor*. [ME *medlen, mellen*]

mell *see* MELE

mellay[1.1], **†melle, †mella, †mellie** /ˈmɛle/ *n* **1** (a battle involving) hand-to-hand fighting; combat between individuals; a closely packed mass of fighting men *la14-*. **2** cloth of a mixed weave or a mixture of colours *16-17*. [ME *mele*, AN *mellé*, OFr *meslée*]

†mellay[1.2], **meally, mella** *adj of cloth* of mixed weave or colour, variegated *la16-e17*. [see the noun]

melle *see* MELLAY[1.1]
meller *see* MELDER
mellie *see* MELLAY[1.1]

†mellifluate, mellifluat *adj* honeyed, mellifluous *la15-16*. [Lat *mellifluus*, with *-ate* suffix]

mellishon *see* MALISON[1.1]

mell moorin /ˈmɛl murən/ *n* a blizzard of powdery snow *la19- Sh*. [ON *mjöll* + MOOR[2.1], with *-ing* suffix]

melmot, melmet /ˈmɛlmət/ *n* juniper *Juniperus communis 17- NE*. [unknown]

melody /ˈmɛləde/ *n* **1** tuneful music; pleasant sound, harmony; a tune or song *la14-*. **2** rejoicing, joy *15-e16*. **melodious** tuneful *la15-*. [ME *melodi*]

melt[1.1], **milt** /mɛlt, mɪlt/ *n* **1** the spleen *la15-*. **2** the semen or testes of a male fish *16-*. **3** the tongue *la19-*. [OE *milte*]

melt[1.2] /mɛlt/ *v* to fell a person or animal with a blow near the spleen; to thrash *la16-19, 20- C*. [probably from the noun]

melt[2] /mɛlt/ *v* to bruise, crush *la19- Sh*. [ON *melta* to dissolve; compare Faer *melta* to squeeze (a limb) too hard]

melt[3] /mɛlt/ *v pt* **meltit,** *ptp* **meltit, molten, †moltin, †meltyne** to liquefy, dissolve *la14-*. Compare MOUTEN. [OE *meltan*; compare Faer *melta* to squeeze (a limb) too hard]

meltith, †melteth, †meltit, †meltyd /ˈmɛltɪθ, ˈmɛltɪð/ *n* **1** a meal *la15-*. **2** a single milking; the quantity of milk from a single milking *la16-e19*. [OE *mǣltid*, ON *máltíð*; compare MEAL[2]]

meltyne *see* MELT[3], MOUTEN

†melvie *v* to cover with meal or flour *la18-e19*. [perhaps OE *melw-*, oblique stem of *melu* MEAL[1.1]]

melʒe *see* MAIL[2]
melʒie *see* MAIL3E

mem[1.1] /mɛm/ *n* Madam, usually a term of address; also a married woman, a schoolteacher *19-*. [altered form of Eng *ma'am* madam]

mem[1.2] /mɛm/ *v* to address as 'Mem', ingratiate oneself in this way *la19-*. [see the noun]

member /ˈmɛmbər/ *n* **1** a person as a component of a society, group or club *la14-*. **2** *law* a subordinate official of a court *la15-*. **3** a limb or bodily part, especially the penis *15-*. **†members** male and female genitals *15-17*. [ME *membre*, Lat *membrum*]

memor *see* MEMORY

†memorance *n* memory, remembrance *la15-17*. [aphetic form of ME *rememoraunce*, OFr *rememorance* or reduced form of MEMORY with *-ance* suffix]

memorandum /mɛməˈrandəm/ *n* **1** a reminder or record of events *la15-*. **2** a memento, a souvenir *la19-*. [Lat *memorandum* (it is) to be remembered]

memore *see* MEMORY

memorial /məˈmoriəl/ *n* **1** a commemoration of a person or event; a monument; an observance or custom intended as a reminder of a past occasion; a reminder, a memento *15-*. **2** *law* a document prepared by a solicitor for counsel supplying facts and circumstances and indicating the question on which counsel's opinion is sought *la18-*. **3** *law* a statement of facts submitted to the Lord Ordinary in the Court of Session as a preliminary to a hearing *18-19*. **4** posthumous reputation, fame *la15-17*. **5** a memorandum of instructions or proposals *16-17*. **6** a register, an inventory *la16-17*. **7** remembrance, recollection *15-16*. **8** a record, chronicle or tale *15-16*. [Lat *memoriālis* relating to memory]

memory, maimory, †memore, †memor, †memour /ˈmɛməri, ˈmemərɛ/ *n* **1** the faculty or capacity for remembering *la14-*. **2** the fact or state of being remembered, especially after death *la14-*. **3** the time over which human remembrance extends *la15-*. **4** a commemoration, a record, a memorandum, a memoire *la14-e18*. **5** the mental faculty, the mind or wits *15-e16*. **6** one who, or that which, serves as a reminder *e16*. [ME *memori*, Lat *memoria*]

men *see* MAN, MEND, MIEN

menace[1.1], **†minace, †mannace, †mannare** /ˈmɛnəs/ *n* **1** a threat *la14-*. **2** a hint *la19-*. [ME *manace*]

menace[1.2], **†minace, †mannace, †mannare** /ˈmɛnəs/ *v* to threaten, utter threats *la14-*. [ME *menacen*]

menadge *see* MANAGE

menage, menodge /məˈnadʒ, məˈnɔdʒ, məˈnodʒ/ *n* a neighbourhood savings club to which members contribute a fixed weekly sum for a stated period *19- C Bor*. Compare MANAGE. **couldnae run a menage** *of people or organizations* to be incapable of performing the simplest tasks, be incompetent *20- WC*. [from the verb MANAGE]

menagier *see* MANAGER
mence *see* MENSE[1.1]
mencioun *see* MENTION

mend, men /mɛnd, mɛn/ *v* **1** to repair something broken; to make good a defect *la14-*. **2** to add fuel to a fire *la14-*. **3** *of a person* to reform; to improve oneself, one's character or faults; to remedy an evil *la14-*. **4** to restore a person to health, heal; to recover from an illness *la14-*. **5** *of a wound, disease* to get better *16-*. **6** to fatten, cause to grow plump *19- SW Bor Uls*. **7** to emend, correct writing or verse *15-17*. **8** to compensate for an injury by paying damages; to make amends or reparation *15-e17*. **9** *in negative and interrogative, frequently impersonal* to avail, profit, advantage a person *la15-16*. **10** to improve something in quality, ameliorate; to better oneself or one's situation; to supplement income or resources *la14-17*. **11** to assist the poor *la14-16*. **mending, mendin 1** repair; healing *la14-*. **2** amends, redress *15-16*. **3** reformation; assistance *la14-16*. **there's no ane o them tae mend anither** they're all equally bad *19- C Bor*. [aphetic form of AMEND]

mendiment *see* MENIMENT
mendis *see* MENDS
mendment *see* MENIMENT

mends, mens, mense, †**mendis** /mɛndz, mɛns, mɛns/ *n* **1** compensation, reparation; atonement *15-*. **2** healing, a remedy *la15-e17*. **3** improvement, betterment in morals or fortune *la15-e17*. **a mends, ane mendis** compensation, reparation; atonement *15-*; compare AMENDS. **nae mens** no harm done, never mind *20- Sh*. [aphetic form of AMENDS]

mene *see* MANE[1.1], MANE[1.2], MEAN[1.1], MEAN[1.2], MEAN[1.3], MEAN[2], MEAN[3]

meneer *see* MINEER[1.2]

mene time *see* MEANTIME[1.1]

meng *see* MING[2.2]

meniment, †**mendment,** †**mendiment** /ˈmɛnɪmənt/ *n* amendment; correction *15-*. [ME, AN *mendement*; disyllabic aphetic form of *amendment*]

menis *see* MINIS

mennen *see* MINNON

menner *see* MAINNER

menodge *see* MENAGE

menorite *see* MINORITY

menoun *see* MINNON

mens *see* MENDS

mensal /ˈmɛnsəl/ *adj* describing a church or benefice, the revenues of which, during pre-Reformation or Episcopal times, were taken to meet the expenses of the bishopric *la17- historical*. [Lat *mensa* a table]

mense[1.1], †**mence,** †**mensk** /mɛns/ *n* **1** dignity; moderation; courtesy, hospitality *la16-*. **2** common sense, intelligence *18-*. **3** honour, credit *la14-19, 20- SW Bor*. **4** something which brings a person credit or honour *19, 20- EC SW Bor*. **5** a reward, a prize *e19*. [ON *mennska* humanity]

mense[1.2], †**mensk** /mɛns/ *v* to do honour to; to grace, adorn; to honour with one's presence *la14-19, 20- WC SW*. **menseful 1** *of persons* good-mannered, polite; sensible; honourable, noble *la15-*. **2** *of things* seemly, proper *19-*. **menseless,** †**mensles 1** unmannerly, objectionable in behaviour *la15-*. **2** *of prices* inordinate, extortionate *la18-*. **3** stupid, foolish *19-*. **4** greedy, grasping *18-19, 20- EC SW Bor*. [see the noun]

mense[2] /mɛns/ *n* a large amount *la19- Sh NE T Uls*. [perhaps aphetic form of Eng *immense*]

mense *see* MENDS

mensioune *see* MENTION

mensk *see* MENSE[1.1], MENSE[1.2]

menstraill, menstral *see* MINSTREL

menstralcy, menstralsy *see* MINSTRELSY

mensweir *see* MANSWEAR

ment *see* MEAN[2]

mentenance *see* MAINTENANCE

†**mentenant** *n* a dependant *16-17*. [back-formation from MAINTENANCE]

mention, †**mentioun,** †**mencioun,** †**mensioune** /ˈmɛnʃən/ *n* **1** the action of remarking on, referring to in speech or writing, originally calling to mind *la14-*. **2** a trifle, a trace, a particle *la19- Sh Ork Uls*. [ME *mencioun*]

†**mentionat** *v ptp* **mentionat** to specify, designate *16-e18*. [Lat *mentionāt-*, ptp stem of *mentionāre*]

mentioun *see* MENTION

mento *see* MINTA

menwt *see* MEENIT[1.1]

menyie, maingie, †**menȝe,** †**menȝie,** †**meinȝe** /ˈmɛɲi, ˈmɛɲji, ˈmɛɲi, ˈmeni/ *n* **1** a herd or flock of animals *la18-*. **2** a crowd, a multitude; a rabble *la14-19, 20- NE EC*. **3** a festive gathering, a party *la19- Ork EC*. **4** a large or diverse collection of things *la18-19, 20- NE*. **5** a family, a household *la14-19*. **6** a body of retainers or followers, a retinue *la14-19*. **7** a body of troops *la14-e18*. **8** a tribe, a race, a nation *la15-e16*. [ME *meine*]

menȝe *see* MAINȜIE[1.2], MENYIE

menȝie *see* MAINȜIE[1.1], MENYIE

meout *see* MYOWT

mer *see* MAR[1.2]

meracle *see* MIRACLE[1.2]

mercal *see* MARKAL

mercat, market, †**merket** /ˈmɛrkət, ˈmarkət/ *n* **1** (a place set aside for or the occasion of) the buying and selling of commodities of all sorts; a gathering of persons engaged in buying and selling *la14-*. **2** the action or business of buying and selling; a commercial transaction *la15-18, 20- SW*. **3** a gift given at a market or fair, a fairing *la19- NE T*. **4** the business of finding a husband or wife *la17-19*. **5** the Forum of Rome *15-e16*. †**mercat-like** fit for the market, marketable *la15-e16*. **mercat cross** a cross erected in and marking the centre of a marketplace; originally the place where public proclamations were made and other public acts carried out *15-*. **mercat-day 1** the day of the week on which a market is regularly held *15-*. **2** a regular marker of periods and changes of fortune over time *17-e19*. †**mercat-gate 1** a street in a town where a market is held, frequently in place-names *14-17*. **2** the main road leading to a marketplace *15-e17*. †**mercat-met** measured by the standard measures used in a public market *16*. **market mixtures** sweets commonly sold at markets *20- T EC*. **mercat-place** the location of a market *16-*. **market-stance** the site where a market or fair is held *19, 20- Sh Ork NE T*. †**mercat-steid** a marketplace *16*. **mercat-street** = *mercat-gate 16-*. †**mak mercat 1** to buy or sell a commodity, do business *la15-17*. **2** to find a husband or wife, become engaged to be married *la17-19*. †**mak mercat of** to offer for sale, sell *la15-17*. [OE *market*]

merceabill *see* MERCIABLE

mercement *see* MERCIMENT

merch *see* MAIRCH[2.2], MARCH[1.1], MARCH[1.2], MARRA

Merch *see* MAIRCH[1]

merchant[1.1], **mairchant, merchan,** †**marchand,** †**merchand,** †**maircheant** /ˈmɛrtʃənt, ˈmɛrtʃənt, ˈmɛrtʃən/ *n* **1** a person who buys and sells goods for profit, a trader *la14-*. **2** a shopkeeper, especially of a grocery and general store *15-*. **3** a member of the guild of merchants of a burgh *15-*. **4** a customer, buyer *18-*. **5** an itinerant salesman, a packman *la16-18*. **marchandise 1** goods bought or for sale, marketable commodities *la14-*. **2** the occupation or business of a merchant; the process of buying or selling, commerce, trading, business *15-*. †**marchandrise** = *marchandise la14-e17*. †**marchand-buith** a shop or stall kept by a merchant *16-17*. †**merchant-geir** merchandise *16-e17*. †**merchant-gude, merchand-gudes** (saleable, satisfactory) merchandise *15-17*. †**marchand·man** = MERCHANT[1.1] (sense 1) *15-17*. †**merchand-ware, merchand-waris 1** = *merchand-gude la15-17*. **2** the goods sold in a general store *18-19*. [ME *marchaunt*]

merchant[1.2], **mairchant, merchan,** †**marchand,** †**merchand** /ˈmɛrtʃənt, ˈmɛrtʃənt,ˈmɛrtʃən/ *adj* **1** of, relating to or for the purpose of trading *la14-*. **2** *of a commodity* that is bought or sold; that is marketable *16-e17*. [see the noun]

†**merciable, merciabill, merceabill** *adj* merciful, compassionate *la15-16*. [ME *merciable*]

merciall *see* MARTIAL

merciment, †**mercement,** †**merciament** /ˈmɛrsɪmənt/ *n* **1** mercy *la16-*. **2** a fine imposed by a court *15-17*. **3** the condition of being liable to a fine at the discretion of a court *15-17*. [ME *merciment*, Lat *merciamentum*]

mercy[1.1], †**marcie** /ˈmɛrse/ **1** clemency, compassion, forgiveness, forbearance *la14-*. **2** an act of divine mercy; circumstances for which special thankfulness is due; a good thing received from God *la16-*. **3** = MERCIMENT (sense 2), (sense 3) *15-17*. **merciful**, †**mercyfull**, †**mercifull 1** forbearing, forgiving *la14-*. **2** *of the weather* temperate, favourable *la19- Sh Ork*. **merciless**, †**mercyles**, †**merciles 1** showing no mercy, pitiless *16-*. **2** receiving no mercy, unpitied *la16-*. **the mercies** alcohol, strong drink, especially whisky *19- NE WC*. **take tae mercy** to pardon *e19*. [ME *merci*]

mercy[1.2] /ˈmɛrse/ *interj* in exclamations of surprise or alarm *la19-*. **mercy bliss dee** an exclamation of surprise or alarm *Sh Ork la19-*. **mercy me** an exclamation of surprise or alarm *la19-*. [see the noun]

merdale *see* MARDLE[1]

merdistinkel /ˈmɛrdɪstɪŋkəl/ *n* an extreme state of exasperation or noisy complaining *la19- Sh*. [perhaps Norw *mord* extreme effort, used as an intensifying prefix; for second element, compare Swed dial *stinka* to rush off]

merdle *see* MARDLE[1]

mere /mir/ *n* a body of water, the sea, an estuary, a lake *15-*. †**mereswyne**, **meerswine**, **merswyne** a dolphin or porpoise *15-e19*. [OE *mere*]

mere *see* MEAR[1], MEAR[2.1], MEAR[2.2]

merefow *see* MEAL-AN-FOLLY

mereit *see* MERIT

mereswyne *see* MERE

mergh, **mergie** *see* MARRA

mergin *see* MARGIN[1.1], MARGIN[1.2]

meriage *see* MAIRRIAGE

meridian[1.1] /məˈrɪdɪən/ *n* **1** *astronomy* an imaginary line around the globe passing through the north and south poles *16-*. **2** a midday drink, especially a dram of whisky *la18-*. **3** a midday rest or siesta *e19*. **4** the mid point (of life) *e19*. [Lat *merīdiānus*]

meridian[1.2] /məˈrɪdɪən/ *adj* **1** of or relating to midday, noon *16-*. **2** southern *16*. [ME *meridian*, EModE *meridian*, Lat *merīdiānus*]

merin, **mering** *see* MEARING

merit, †**merite**, †**mereit** /ˈmɛrɪt/ *n* **1** the condition or fact of deserving well, of being entitled to reward or gratitude; excellence, worth *la14-*. **2** the condition or fact of deserving more or less well *15-*. **3** a quality or defect, a good or bad point of anything, the intrinsic rights and wrongs of a matter *la15-*. †**meritable**, **meritabill**, **merytabil** worthy of reward or praise *15-16*. †**meritor**, **meritour** serving to earn reward from God, meritorious *15-e16*. †**meritory** = *meritor*. [ME *merit*, Lat *meritum*]

merk, **mark**, †**mairk** /mɛrk, mark/ *n* **1** a unit of weight, mainly of gold, silver and bread, usually 8 ounces (226.8 grams) *15-e17*. **2** a unit of weight of commodities, especially butter or oil, originally probably half a Norwegian pound, one twenty-fourth of a setten *la16-19, 20- Sh Ork historical*. **3** a monetary unit equivalent in value to two-thirds of a pound Scots; corresponding to the English mark, but of lower value after the devaluation of Scottish currency in the 14th century, and depreciating thereafter to reach a value of thirteen and a third pence sterling at the time of the Union in 1707 *la14-19, 20- historical*. **4** a coin of the value of a mark *la18-19, 20- historical*. **5** = merkland **1** *18-e19*. **6** *in Shetland and Orkney* = merkland **2** *la15-19*. **merkland 1** a measurement of land, originally the area of which the annual rental value was one merk, frequently in place-names *la15-19, 20- historical*. **2** a measurement of land, of which originally the capital value was one merk for its arable part *16-19, 20- Sh Ork*. †**mark-pece** = MERK (sense 3) *la16-17*. **markis worth 1** *of land* assessed as yielding the specified number of merks in annual rent *la14-e17*. **2** *of land or possessions* valued at the specified number of merks *15-e17*. [ON *mörk*]

merk *see* MARK[1.1], MARK[1.2], MIRK[1.3]

merket *see* MERCAT

merkis-day /ˈmɛrkɪs de/ *n* a fair day, festival or holiday *20- Sh*. [MERK + DAY]

merkister /ˈmɛrkɪstər/ *n* a strip of grassland between areas of cultivated land *18- Ork*. [Norn *merkister*]

merky *see* MARRA

merl *see* MIRL[2.2]

merle, †**merl** /mɛrl/ *n* the blackbird *Turdus merula 15-* literary. [AN, MFr *merle*]

merle *see* MIRL[2.1], *blue merle* (BLUE[1.2])

merlin, *Sh* **maalin**, †**merlʒeoun**, †**marleʒon** /ˈmɛrlɪn; *Sh* ˈmalɪn/ *n* **1** a small falcon *Falco columbarius la15-*. **2** a hawk of any sort *la19- Sh*. **3** erroneous = MERLE *19*. [ME *merlioun*]

merlingoe /mərˈlɪŋgo/ *n* a brightly-coloured bird *20- SW*. [unknown; compare PAPINGO]

merlit *see* MARLIT

merlʒeoun *see* MERLIN

mermaid, †**marmaid** /ˈmɛrmed/ *n* a mythical sea creature with the head and torso of a woman and the tail of a fish *la16-*. **mermaid's glove** a sponge or other marine organism resembling a glove *la18-*. **marmaid's purse** the egg-case of a ray, skate or dogfish *18-*. [OE *mere* the sea + MAID]

mermaiden, †**marmaiden**, †**marmadyn** /mɛrˈmedən/ *n* a mermaid or siren *16-*. [OE *mere* the sea + MAIDEN]

meroquin *see* MARIKINE

†**meroure** *n* a mirror *la14-15*. [ME *mirour*]

†**merrans**, **merrens** *n* an obstruction, an impediment *la15-16*. [OFr *marance* an affliction, a fault]

merres *see* MARAIS

merriage, **merridge** *see* MAIRRIAGE

merry, †**mery**, †**mirrie** /ˈmɛri/ *adj* **1** *of people* cheerful, happy, carefree *la14-*. **2** *of events, pastimes or stories* pleasurable, amusing *la14-*. **3** *of music and birdsong* delightful, joyful *16-*. **4** *of a time or place* that gives pleasure; when or where a person is free from care; devoted to jollity, festivity or fun *15-*. **5** boisterous and cheerful from drinking alcohol, slightly drunk *la16-*. **6** *of light* bright *e19*. **merrily 1** cheerfully, joyfully; in a delightful manner *la15-*. **2** energetically *e19*. **merriness**, †**merynes 1** merrymaking; fun *la15-*. **2** joyfulness *16*. **merry-begotten** conceived out of wedlock, illegitimate *la15-*. **merrycourant** a riotous revel; a sudden unceremonious dismissal *la19- SW Uls*. **merry dancers 1** the aurora borealis, northern lights *la17-*; compare *pretty dancers* (PRETTY). **2** a nickname for the inhabitants of Stenness *20- Ork*. **merry-ma-tanzie** (part of) the refrain of a children's ring game *19-*. †**merry-meat** a meal to celebrate the birth of a child *19*; compare *blithemeat* (BLITHE[1.2]). [OE *myrge*]

merry *see* MAIRRY

†**mers**, **merse** *n nautical* a round-top on the masthead of a ship *la15-e16*. [MDu *merse* a crow's-nest, a basket]

merse, †**mers**, †**mersk** /mɛrs/ *n* **1** the district of Berwickshire lying between the Lammermuirs and the Tweed; also the whole of Berwickshire *13-*. **2** the flat alluvial land bordering the Solway *16- SW Bor*. **3** marsh land or bog *15-17 NE*. **The Merse** = MERSE (sense 1). [OE *mersc* a marsh]

merse *see* MERS

mersgim *see* MAASGUUM

mersk *see* MERSE

merswyne *see* MERE

mert *see* MART[2]

merter *see* MAIRTYR¹·¹, MAIRTYR¹·²
Mertimes, Mertinmas *see* MARTINMAS
†**mertrick, mertrik, martrik** *n pl* also **martrix** the pine marten; its fur *15-e19*. [back-formation from Lat *martrix*, fem form of *martor*, but in Scots re-analysed as a plural]
mervaill, mervel *see* MAIRVEL¹·¹, MAIRVEL¹·²
mervell *see* MAIRVEL¹·¹
mervy *see* MARRA
merwall *see* MAIRVEL¹·²
mery *see* MERRY
merytabil *see* MERIT
mes *see* MASS², MESS¹·¹
†**Mes, Mess, Maes** *n of a clergyman* holding the degree of Master of Arts *17-19*. **Mes John** *humorous* a name for a (mainly Presbyterian) minister or for ministers as a group *la17-19*. [shortened form of MAISTER¹·¹]
meschant¹·¹, **mischant** /ˈmɛʃənt, məˈʃant, ˈmɪʃənt/ *n* **1** *pl* evil-doers *20-*. **2** a wicked person, a villain *16-e17*. [see the adj]
meschant¹·², **mischant** /ˈmɛʃənt, məˈʃant, ˈmɪʃənt/ *adj* **1** wicked, bad *16-*. **2** spiritless, feeble, weak, stupid *16-17*. **mischantly 1** wickedly; wrongfully *la16-*. **2** miserably; feebly, cowardly *la16-e17*. **mischantness** (an act of) villainy, wickedness *la16-*. [ME *mischaunt*, EModE *meschant*]
mese *see* MEASE
me self *see* MASEL
mesell *see* MISELL
meserie *see* MEESERY
meshi *see* MAISE²
mesillis *see* MAISLES
meslin stane *see* MYSLIN
mesmerise¹·¹ /ˈmɛzməraez/ *n* a surprise *20-*. [see the verb]
mesmerise¹·² /ˈmɛzməraez/ *v* to surprise, astound, dumbfound *20-*. [from the name Friedrich Anton Mesmer, in relation to his theory of hypnosis]
mess¹·¹, *NE* **meis**, †**mes**, †**mais** /mɛs; *NE* mes/ *n* **1** a serving of food; a course or prepared dish at a meal *15-*. **2** a group of diners, people regularly dining together *16-*. **3** an untidy, dirty or disordered state of affairs *la19-*. **4** a plate, a platter, a dish *16-17*. **5** the provision or supply of food for a person's or household's meals *la15-e17*. [ME *mes*]
mess¹·², *NE* **meese** /mɛs; *NE* mis/ *v* **1** to measure out (a portion for a meal, an ingredient in cooking) *19- NE*. **2** to interfere (with); to provoke *20-*. †**mess and mell** to interfere; to mix or have dealings (with) *19*. **mess up** to spoil, dirty, untidy (things) *20-*. **nae messin** do not interfere (with a person) *20-*. [see the noun]
mess *see* MASS²
Mess *see* MES
messagate *see* MESSIEGATE
message /ˈmɛsədʒ/ *n* **1** a communication delivered by a messenger or envoy *la14-*. **2** business entrusted to a messenger or envoy; an errand of any sort *15-*. **3** a person or party of persons conveying a communication; an envoy, an ambassage *la14-16*. **messages** purchases, shopping *20-*. **message bag** a shopping bag *20-*. **message-bike** a type of bike with a basket on the front for delivering shopping, used by grocers and butchers *20-*. **message boy** an errand-boy *la19-*. **go a message** to run an errand *la19-*. **go the messages** to do one's shopping *20-*. †**mak a message** to carry out an errand, deliver a message *15*. [ME *message*]
messager *see* MESSENGER
messan, messin, †**messen** /ˈmɛsən/ *n* **1** a contemptuous term for a person *la16-*. **2** a contemptuous term for a dog *la18-19, 20- C SW*. **3** a small pet dog, a lapdog *la15-e18*.

messan-dog a small dog *16-*. †**messan-tyke** a small dog *16-19*. [Gael *measan* a small dog, a lapdog]
messenger, †**messingere,** †**messengere,** †**messager** /ˈmɛsəndʒər/ *n* **1** someone who carries messages, a courier or envoy *la14-*. **2** = *messenger-at-arms*. **3** a precursor, a harbinger *la15-*. **4** an agent *15-e16*. †**messingery** the office of *messenger-at-arms 16-18*. **messenger-at-arms** an officer of the Court of Session with authority to travel throughout Scotland to serve documents and enforce court orders, originally a messenger of the Scottish Crown under the authority of the Lord Lyon King of Arms and appointed by the Lord Lyon on the recommendation of the Court of Session *15-*. [ME *messager, mesanger*]
messer *see* MACER
messiegate, messagate /ˈmɛsiɡɛt, ˈmɛsəɡɛt/ *n* a path through arable land, originally to the church *la19- Ork*. [ON *messa* mass + ON *gata* a road]
messin *see* MESSAN
messingere *see* MESSENGER
mester, maister, †**master** /ˈmɛstər, ˈmestər/ *n* stale urine, used as a cleaning agent *la16-19, 20- NE T*. [Gael *maistir* urine prepared for dyeing]
mester *see* MAISTER¹·¹
mestris *see* MYSTERY
mesure *see* MEASURE¹·¹, MEASURE¹·²
met¹·¹, **mett** /mɛt/ *n* **1** a boundary marker *19- Sh Ork*. **2** a pressure mark, an imprint *20- Sh*. **3** a boundary *15-e17*. [perhaps MDu *met* a measure of land, or ON *met* weights; compare METT¹·¹]
†**met**¹·² *adj* measured *la14-e18*. [probably from weak ptp of METT¹·²]
met *see* MEAT¹·¹, METT¹·¹, METT¹·²
metal, †**mettall** /ˈmɛtəl/ *n* **1** a hard solid substance, metal *15-*. **2** rock broken up and used in road-making *la18-*. **3** a geological stratum in which minerals occur *18-19, 20- EC*. **4** metallic ore *la15-17*. **5** *heraldry* either of the tinctures or and argent *la15*. [ME *metal*]
†**mete** *v* to dream *la15-16*. [OE *mǣtan*]
mete *see* MATE²·², MEAT¹·¹, MEAT¹·², MEET¹, MEET²·¹, METT¹·¹, METT¹·²
meth *see* MEITH¹·²
methe *see* MEITH¹·¹
methery /ˈmɛθəre/ *numeral in children's rhymes* the number four *20-*. [nonsense word derived from a system of counting sheep]
methick *see* MEDICK
meting *see* MEETING
mett¹·¹, **met,** †**mete** /mɛt/ *n* **1** a measure, measurement; a standard or system of measurement (only of quantity or dimension, not weight) *la15-*. **2** a unit of measurement of capacity; a specific quantity measured out in accordance with this *la15-*. **3** a unit of measurement for coal *la16- NE T*. **4** a standard instrument for measuring capacity *la15-e18*. **5** a quantity of herring *18*. †**mete-lume** a standard instrument for measuring capacity *16-e17*. †**met-stick** a measure used in making a shoe; a piece of wood cut to the length of a person's foot *19*. [OE *met*; compare MET¹·¹]
mett¹·², **mete,** †**met,** †**meit** /mɛt, mit/ *v* **1** to measure as to quantity or dimension *15-*. **2** to make a mark or imprint *20- Sh*. **3** to compose poetic measures *la18*. †**metster, metstar** an official authorized to measure saleable goods or land *la16-e19*. †**mettage 1** the official measurement of goods *16-e17*. **2** the duty payable for measuring goods *16-e17*. **3** the measuring of land, mainly for the settling of boundaries *la16-17*. †**metter, mettar** = *metster la15-18*. [OE *metan*; compare MET¹·¹, MET¹·²]
mett *see* MET¹·¹

mettall *see* METAL, METTLE[1.1]
mettell *see* METTLE[1.1]
metter *see* MAITTER
mettick /'mɛtək/ *n* a soft crab *19- NE*. [unknown]
metticks *see* METTOOS
mettin /'mɛtɪn, 'mɛtɪn, 'mɛtɪn/ *n* **1** an ear or grain (of corn or barley) *20- Sh Ork*. **2** a morsel (of food) *20- Sh Ork*. [verbal noun from Norn *met* to feed, form seed]
mettle[1.1], **†mettell**, **†mettall** /'mɛtəl/ *n* a person's character, temperament *16-*. **mettalled** *of a person or horse* spirited *la16-*. [figurative use of METAL]
mettle[1.2] /'mɛtəl/ *adj* spirited, mettlesome *la18-*. [see the noun]
mettoos, metticks /'mɛtuz, 'mɛtəks/ *npl* a plant growing in sand dunes, perhaps *Carex arenaria 20- Ork*. [unknown]
meubles *see* MOBILL
meuggle /'mjugəl, 'mjʌgəl/ *v* to bespatter with dirt *20- N*. [frequentative form of ON *myki*, Norw *myk* muck, dung with *-le* suffix]
meuw *see* MAW[6]
meve *see* MOVE
†mewt *v of a cat* to mew *17-e18*. [onomatopoeic ME *meuten*]
mexty *see* MEGSTIE
Mey, May, †Maii /mae, me/ *n* the fifth month of the year *la14-*. **meysie, maisie** the primrose *Primula vulgaris la19-*. **May-bird** the whimbrel *Numenius phaeopus la18-19, 20- H&I Uls*. **May-flood** a high tide occurring in May *la19-* mainly *Ork*. **may-flooer** = *meysie 20- Sh Ork Uls*. **May-spink** = *meysie la19- NE T*. [ME *Mai*, Lat *Māius*]
meyit *see* MEET[2.1]
meyn *see* MANE[1.2], MEAN[1.3], MIEN
meyne *see* MEAN[1.2]
meyne-quhile, meyn quhile *see* MEANWHILE
meys *see* MEASE
mi *see* MA, ME
miaul, meaul /mɪ'ɔl/ *v of a cat (also of a person)* to mew, yowl *la18-*. **mauley** a name for a cat, puss *20- Sh*. [onomatopoeic, perhaps related to Fr *miauler*]
miauve[1.1] /'mjav/ *n* the cry or mew of a cat *19- NE*. [imitative, altered form, of *miaow*]
miauve[1.2] /'mjav/ *v of a cat* to mew *19- NE*. [see the noun]
mibbe *see* MAYBE[1.2]
mibbes *see* MAYBES
mibby *see* MAYBE[1.2]
mice *see* MOOSE
miceling *see* MYSLIN
†mich, myche, myth *v* to pilfer *la15-e16*. Compare MITCH[2]. [ME *michen*]
michael, mickey /'mɪxəl, 'mɪke/ *n* **1** a chamber-pot *la19-*. **2** a privy *la19- C*. [perhaps connected to Eng *micturate*]
michael *see* MICHEL
Michael Fair /'mɪxəl fer, 'mʌɪxəl fer/ *n* a fair or market held in October *19- NE T*. [from the name of Saint *Michael* + FAIR[2]]
Michaelmas, †Michaelmes /'mɪxəlməs, 'mɪkəlməs/ *n* the feast day of St Michael, 29 September *15-*. **†Michaelmas heid court** the annual meeting of the freeholders of a county, held at Michaelmas, at which the voters' rolls were made up and the county assessments fixed, originally the first meeting of a burgh, sheriff or baron court after Michaelmas *17-19*. **†Michaelmas moon** the harvest moon; the booty from Highland or Border raids carried out at the time of the full moon in autumn *18-e19*. [from the name of Saint *Michael* + MASS[2]]
†michane, mychane *n* the belly *e16*. [probably Gael *maothain* soft parts, the abdomen]

Michel, †Michell, †michael /'mɪxəl/ *n* a person of lowly rank, a rustic; a country bumpkin *16- NE*. [from the personal name]
michrach *see* MACHREACH
micht[1], **might, †mycht** /mɪxt, mʌɪt/ *n* **1** ability, capacity; strength; power, efficacy, virtue; authority, dominion; wealth *la14-*. **2** oppressive force, violence *la15-*. **†michtful** powerful *15-19*. **michtily, †michtyly, †michtely** powerfully; abundantly; greatly *la14-*. **†michts, mychtis** divine powers or influence *la14-e18*. [OE *meaht*]
micht[2], **might, †mocht, †mytht, †miht** /mɪxt, mʌɪt/ *v* **1** as past tense of MAY[2] *la14-*. **2** *as an auxiliary verb* = MAY[2] *la14-*. **3** expressing a wish: ◊*might she be struck dumb! 15-*. [OE *meahte, mihte*, pt of *magan*]
micht *see* MAY[2]
michty[1.1], **†myghty** /'mɪxte, 'mɪxti/ *n* a powerful or important person; *collectively* powerful, clever, influential people *la15-*. **the Michty** the Almighty, God *la19, 20- Sh SW*. [see the adj]
michty[1.2], **mighty, †mychty, †myghti** /'mɪxte, 'mɪxti/ *adj* **1** powerful; important; rich *la14-*. **2** physically powerful, strong *la14-*. **3** *of things* of great size, amount or strength; sumptuous *15-*. **4** *of characteristics or qualities* present in a high degree; *of sound* loud; *of alcohol* strong *la15-*. **5** greatly given to or having great ability in the practice specified *16-*. **6** disgraceful, scandalous *la19- NE T*. [OE *mihtig*]
michty[1.3] /'mɪxte/ *adv* greatly, thoroughly, drastically *la19- T*. [see the adj]
michty[1.4] /'mɪxte/ *interj* expressing surprise or exasperation; God almighty *la19-*. **Michty be here** expressing surprise or exasperation *la19-*. **Michty me** expressing surprise or exasperation *la19-*. **Michty on's** expressing surprise or exasperation *la19-*. [compare *the Michty* (MICHTY[1.1])]
micken /'mɪkən/ *n* spignel *Meum athamanticum la18-19, 20- NE T*. [Gael *muilceann*]
mickey *see* MICHAEL
Mick Jagger /mɪk 'dʒagər/ *n* lager *la20- C*. [rhyming slang]
mickle *see* MUCKLE[1.1], MUCKLE[1.2], MUCKLE[1.3]
mid[1.1], **†myd** /mɪd/ *n* **1** the middle, the midst *la14-*. **2** a lamb of middle quality or growth *19-*. [OE *midde*]
mid[1.2], **†myd, †meid, †med** /mɪd/ *adj* **1** central, middle *la14-*. **2** situated in the intermediate floors of a building *16-17*. **3** of medium size, quality or age *16-e17*. **4** equal in amount *la14-16*. **5** *astronomy* mean, equidistant *16*. **†midwart, midward** the middle of something; in the middle *la14-e19*. **†mid-age** middle-age *la15-e17*. **†mid-aged** middle-aged *la19*. **mid couple 1** *law* a piece of evidence linking a claimant with the right claimed *la17-*. **2** a link or fastening, a ligament connecting the two parts of a flail *la16-19, 20- Uls*. **midday** noon *la14-*. **midfield 1** the middle part of an open space, frequently of a sports field or football pitch *la15-*. **2** the centre division of an army *16*. **mid-finger** the middle finger *15-19, 20- Sh SW Uls*. **†midgate** halfway *16-17*. **†midgates** halfway *la19*. **mid-house 1** the small middle room of a *but and ben* (BUT[1.1]) *la19- NE*. **2** the central floor or floors of a building *16-e17*. **mid-impediment** *law* any event happening between two others which prevents the last event from becoming effective *la18-*. **†mid-lentroun** the middle of Lent *15-e17*. **†midman** a mediator *la15-17*. **midnicht** the middle of the night, twelve o'clock at night *la14-*. **†mid persoun** = *midman 16-e17*. **mid-place** = *mid-house* **2** *la19, 20- NE*. **mid-rig** ploughing the dividing furrow between two ridges *18-*. **mid-room** the middle compartment in a six-oared fishing-boat *la19- Sh*. **†midschip** the middle part of a vessel *la15-16*. **midsimmer, †midsumer** June 24, St John the Baptist's Day, the period after that date *la14-*.

†**mid-superior** *law* a person who holds an intermediate position of superiority in the occupancy of land between a superior and a vassal or series of vassals *19-*. †**in the midtime** in the meantime *15-17*. [see the noun]

midden[1.1], †**midding** /ˈmɪdən/ *n* **1** a dunghill, a compost heap, a refuse heap *la14-*. **2** a dirty, slovenly person *19-*. **3** a muddle, a shambles, a mess *20-*. **4** a domestic ash-pit *20-*. **5** a gluttonous person or animal *19- NE T*. **6** a dustbin; a place where dustbins are kept *la19- C*. **midden böl** a dunghill *la19- Sh*. **midden bree** the effluent from a midden *20- NE*. **midden cock** a barnyard cockerel *19, 20- SW Uls*. †**midden dub** the pool of effluent from a dunghill *la18-e19*. **midding feals** turfs laid on a dunghill to aid the maturing process *la17-19, 20- Ork*. **midden flee** a dung-fly *18, 20- T Bor*. **midden fowl** a barnyard fowl *la17-*. **midden-heap** a domestic ash-pit or refuse heap *la19- N C*. **midden heid** the top of a dunghill; figuratively, a person's home territory *la17-*. **midden-hole** the excavated site of or pool of effluent from a dunghill *la18-*. **midden mavis** *humorous* a female *midden-raker la19-*. **midden pow** = *midden dub la19- Sh Ork*. **midden-raker** a searcher of refuse heaps *la19, 20- T WC*. **midden-stance** the place in a field where manure is put before spreading *19, 20- Sh*. **midden-stead 1** the site of a dunghill *la16-*. **2** a person's home territory *19-*. **midden tap** = *middenheid la18-19, 20- T*. †**midding tyk** a farmyard dog *e16*. **midden weed 1** white goosefoot *Chenopodium album 20- EC Bor*. **2** knotgrass *Polygonum 19 WC*. **in the midden** *of the moon* surrounded by a lunar bow, foretelling a storm *20- NE*. [ME *midding*, ON *mykidyngja*, Norw dial *mykjadyngja* a muck heap]

†**midden**[1.2], †**midding** *v* to heap into a dunghill *la16-e19*. [see the noun]

midder *see* MITHER
middest *see* MIDS
middill *see* MIDDLE[1.1], MIDDLE[1.2], MIDDLE[2]
midding *see* MIDDEN[1.1], MIDDEN[1.2]
middis *see* MIDS

middle[1.1], †**middill**, †**myddil**, †**mydle** /ˈmɪdəl/ *n* **1** the middle of the body, the waist *15-*. **2** the centre, the central portion or intermediate position in relation to a thing or things *17-*. **midled** *of a sheep* marked for identification with an incision from the top to the middle of the ear *la19- Sh*. [OE *middel*]

middle[1.2], †**middill**, †**meddill** /ˈmɪdəl/ *adj* **1** equidistant from the extremes, intermediate, central *12-*. **2** the second of three *15-*. †**middill erd** the world, regarded as halfway between heaven and hell *16-19*. †**middill world** = *middill erd e19*. [see the noun]

middle[2], **meddle**, †**middill**, †**meddill**, †**mydle** /ˈmɪdəl, ˈmɛdəl/ *v* **1** to mix, mingle, combine *16-*. **2** to interfere with, bother, harm *16-*. **3** to associate with *la16-*. **4** to engage in combat, join battle *16-17*. **5** to unite sexually *16-17*. [ME *medlen*]

middlin[1.1], †**midling**, †**medling** /ˈmɪdlɪn/ *adj* **1** intermediate in size, quality, grade or value; medium *la15-*. **2** fair, tolerable *19-*. **middlin way** the middle course *la15*. [perhaps MIDDLE[1.1], with -*in* suffix]

middlin[1.2] /ˈmɪdlɪn/ *adv* fairly, tolerably *19-*. [see the adj]

†**middrit**, **mydred**, **mitherit** *n* **1** the diaphragm, the midriff, the omentum *la15-e19*. **2** the skirt of a bullock used as food *17-19*. **middrits** the heart and skirt of a bullock used as food *la18-19*. [OE *midhriþre*]

midge, *H&I* **mudge**, †**mige** /mɪdʒ; *H&I* mʌdʒ/ *n* **1** a very small flying, frequently biting, insect commonly found in swarms near water *la15-*. **2** a small insignificant person or animal *la18-*. **midgie**, *Sh Ork* **mudjick**, *NE* **midjick** an insect *la19-*. [OE *mycg*]

midge *see* MUDGE[1.2]

midgie /ˈmɪdʒe/ *n* a rubbish dump; a dustbin *20- WC*. **midgie man** a refuse collector *la20- WC*. **midgie-motor** a refuse lorry *la20- WC*. **midgie-raker** a person who takes things from rubbish dumps, dustbins or skips *la20- C*. [altered form of MIDDEN[1.1]]

midgie, midjick *see* MIDGE
midled *see* MIDDLE[1.1]
midling *see* MIDDLIN[1.1]
†**midlings** *npl* goods of an intermediate sort *16-e18*. [plural noun from MIDDLIN[1.1]]

mids, **midst**, †**middis**, †**myddis**, †**middest** /mɪdz, mɪdst/ *n* **1** the middle, the centre *la14-*. **2** a middle course, a compromise *la15-19, 20- NE Bor*. **3** *ploughing* the dividing furrow between two ridges *18- NE*; compare *mid rig* (MID[1.2]). **4** a means of doing something *la16-e18*. **5** *logic* the grounds from which a conclusion follows *17*. **in the mids o the meantime** meanwhile; at present *la19- NE*. [ME *middes*; compare MID[1.1], MID[1.2]]

midwife, †**medwyfe**, †**meidwif**, †**maidwyfe** /ˈmɪdwʌɪf/ *n* a person, usually a woman, who assists women in childbirth *la14-*. [OE *mid* with + WIFE]

mien, †**men**, †**meyn**, †**meine** /min/ *n* bearing, manner, appearance *16-*. [probably aphetic form of ME *demeine*]

miene *see* MOYEN[1.1]
mige *see* MIDGE
might *see* MAY[2], MICHT[1], MICHT[2]
mighty *see* MICHTY[1.2]
mignard *see* MIN3ARD
migramme *see* MEGRIM
miht *see* MICHT[2]

†**mik** *n* a support for a gun; possibly a support used to keep part of a clock in place *la15-16*. [MDu *mik* a forked prop]

mikill *see* MUCKLE[1.2]
milankily *see* MELANCHOLY[1.1]

mild /mʌɪld/ *n* a species of fish, the gilt-head bream *Sparus aurata la18- Ork*. [unknown]

milds *see* MYLES

mile, †**myle**, †**myll**, †**mylne** /mʌɪl/ *n* **1** a unit of distance of 1,760 yards (approximately 1,609 metres) *la14-*; compare *Scots mile* (SCOTS). **2** a great distance *15-*. **gae yer mile 1** to go as far as a person dares (in wild conduct) *20-*. **2** to lose one's temper *20-*. **gae yer miles** = *gae yer mile*. [Lat *mille*; shortened form of *mille passūs* 1000 paces]

miles *see* MYLES
milgruel *see* MILK[1.1]

militant /ˈmɪlɪtənt/ *adj* engaged in warfare, warlike, combative *la15-*. [ME *militaunt*]

militate, †**militat** /ˈmɪlɪtet/ *v* **1** *originally of a legal decision, statute or argument* to have effect, carry weight, operate (against a person) *la16-*. **2** to contend, strive *17-*. [Lat *mīlitāt-*, ptp stem of *mīlitāre* to serve as a soldier, wage war and, in post-classical Latin, to dispute]

milk[1.1], **mulk** /mɪlk, mʌlk/ *n* **1** the white liquid secreted by female mammals for the nourishment of their young, used as food *la14-*. **2** an annual entertainment in a school, when the pupils presented a small gift or sum of money to the teacher and were given a treat of curds and cream *la17-e19*. **milkness**, †**milknes** the aggregate yield of milk of a cow or ewe or of a herd of dairy animals over a period; milk and dairy products *la15-*. **milk-beal** a whitlow *20- WC SW Bor Uls*. **milk-bealin** = *milk-beal*. **milk-bowie** a wooden milk bucket *18-19, 20- NE T*. **milk-boyne** a broad, shallow vessel for holding milk to let the cream rise *19- C SW*. **milk-brose**

milk 415 **mince**

oatmeal mixed with boiling milk *la19-*. **milk-broth** a dish made with barley and milk *19- NE*. **milk-cellar** a small room used as a dairy *la18- Ork NE*. **milk-cow** a cow (kept for) giving milk *la15-*. †**milk ewe** a ewe giving milk *16-17*. **milgruel** porridge made with milk *la19- Sh*. **milk-house** a dairy *la17-*. **milk kirn** a churn for milk *la15-*. **milk-lue** moderately warm, tepid *la19- Sh Ork N*. **milk-meat** a dish of milk and meal or bread; broth made with skimmed milk *17-19, 20- NE*. **milk-porridge** porridge made with milk *la16-*. **milk pot** a milk jug *la19, 20- Ork*. **milk-pottage** = *milk-porridge la16, la19- NE*. **milk-saps** bread soaked in hot sweetened milk *la19-*. **milk-sile**, †**milsie** a milk strainer *la18- SW Bor*. **milk-soup** soup made with milk, frequently including eggs or fish *la18-19, 20- N NE*. **milk white**, †**milk quhite** the opaque white or bluish white of milk *la14-*. †**milk-wife** a wet nurse *e16*. †**milk woman** = *milk-wife e17*. **milk and breid** oatcakes crumbled in milk *la18-*. †**milk and watter** bluish-white; a cloth of this colour *16*. [OE *meolc*]

milk[1,2], **mulk** /mɪlk, mʌlk/ *v* **1** to draw milk from *la15-*. **2** to add milk to (tea) *20-*. **3** *of a cow or ewe* to yield milk (well or badly) *19-*. **4** to exploit (resources); to elicit information *18-*. **milk dry** to drain completely, exploit to exhaustion *19-*. [OE *melcan, meolcian*]

milky, mulky, †**mylky** /ˈmɪlke, ˈmʌlke/ *adj* **1** *of cows, goats or sheep* giving milk, in milk *la15-*. **2** of milk, consisting of or made with milk; like milk *16-*. **milky thrissle** the milk-thistle *20-*. [MILK[1,1] + -IE[2]]

mill[1,1], **mull**, †**miln**, †**mylne**, †**mylve** /mɪl, mʌl/ *n* **1** (a building containing) machinery for grinding grain, traditionally worked by water- or wind-power, a corn-mill *13-*. **2** a building with machinery for carrying out manufacturing processes, such as fulling cloth, breaking stone, stamping coins or smelting metal *la16-*. **3** a hand-operated machine for grinding spices *la16-*. **4** a snuffbox, originally incorporating a grinder *17-*. **5** machinery for threshing grain crops, a threshing-mill *la18-*. **6** a tin box or canister with a lid *19, 20- NE*. **mill-bannock** a large round oatmeal cake baked at a mill *18-*. †**mill-bitch** a bag into which the miller secretly diverted some of a customer's meal *19*. **mill-caul**, †**mill-call** a mill-dam or weir *17- SW Bor*. **mill-clap** the mechanism in a corn-mill for striking or shaking the hopper to cause the grain to move down to the millstones *la16-*. †**mill-closse** the sluice of a mill *la16-e19*. **mill-coorse** the circular path trodden by the horses driving a threshing-mill *20- Ork NE*. **mill-dam** a weir controlling the flow of water to a corn-mill *15-*. †**miln-damheid** the embankment of a mill-dam *la16-e18*. †**mill-ee 1** the opening through which meal came from the millstones *la18-19*. **2** the profits of a corn-mill *17 NE*. **mill-fish** the turbot *Scophthalmus maximus la19- Sh*. **mill-gang** the five- or six-sided building housing the driving apparatus of a horse-driven threshing-mill *20- N EC Bor, historical*. **mill-groot** stone suitable for making millstones *20- Sh*. **mill-happer** the cone-shaped vessel from which the grain about to be ground passes to the millstones *16-19, 20- Sh Ork NE SW*. †**mill-house** the building housing a mill; the dwelling-house of a mill *15-*. †**miln-knave** an undermiller *la14-e18*. **mill-lade** the channel bringing water to a corn-mill *15-*. **mill-lavers** the beams to which the horses driving a threshing-mill were harnessed *la19-20, 21- Ork NE, historical*. **mill-pick** a tool for roughening the surface of a millstone *16, 20- Ork*. †**mill-reek** lead poisoning *la18-e19 C*. **mill-rind 1** the iron fitting supporting the upper millstone of a corn-mill *la15-*. **2** the name of a number of coins, perhaps because of their bearing an impression resembling a mill-rind *17*. †**mill-ring** the space between the millstones and the surrounding kerb; the meal remaining there *19, 20- historical*. **mill-rink** = *mill-gang 20- historical*. **mill-seeds** husks of corn with meal adhering to them *19, 20- Ork SW*. **mill-stane 1** a millstone *la14-*. **2** stone from which millstones are made *19-*. **mill-toon, Milton**, †**milnetun** the buildings comprising a mill, the adjacent farm or hamlet *13-*. †**mill trow** a wooden conduit carrying water to a mill-wheel *18*. **mill-wheel**, †**mill-quheill** a water-driven wheel used to drive a corn-mill *16-*. **mill-yins** factory workers *20- EC Bor*. **like a mill sheeling** at a quick, steady pace; volubly *19, 20- NE SW*. **through the mill** through an ordeal, under a searching examination *19-*. [OE *mylen*]

mill[1,2], †**miln** /mɪl, mʌl/ *v* to grind (grain) in a mill; to process (cloth) mechanically; to stamp (coins) *16-*. [see the noun]

millar *see* MILLER

millart, †**milnward**, †**milware** /ˈmɪlərt/ *n* the person in charge of a corn-mill, a miller *16- NE*. †**millart word** a secret password, supposedly current among millers, believed to confer supernatural powers *19 NE*. †**millarrt's word** = *millart word*. [MILL[1,1] + OE *weard* a keeper]

millen *see* MOOL[1,2]

miller, †**milnar**, †**millar** /ˈmɪlər/ *n* the person in charge of a corn-mill *14-*. **miller's lift** an upward thrust with the handle of a crowbar, as in setting a millstone *la19, 20- N C*. † **miller's word** a secret password, supposedly current among millers, believed to confer supernatural powers *la19-*. [MILL[1,1], with agent suffix]

miln *see* MILL[1,1], MILL[1,2]

milnar *see* MILLER

milnward *see* MILLART

milsie *see* MILK[1,1]

milt *see* MELT[1,1]

milware *see* MILLART

mim[1,1] /mɪm/ *v* to behave in a prim, affected way *la19-*. [see the adj]

mim[1,2] /mɪm/ *adj* prim, restrained in manner or behaviour, especially in a prudish or affected way *16-*. **mim-moued** affectedly prim or demure in speaking or eating *18-*. **mim-spoken** prim or shy in speech *la19-*. **as mim as a Mey puddock** very demure and staid (the frog supposedly remaining silent from May till the end of summer) *la18-*. [perhaps imitative of pursing the mouth; compare MUM[1,2]]

mim[1,3] /mɪm/ *adv* primly, affectedly *la18-*. [see the adj]

mimp /mɪmp/ *v* **1** to speak or act affectedly *la19- NE EC SW Bor*. **2** to eat with the mouth nearly closed *20- Ork EC SW Bor*. [perhaps imitative of pursing the mouth]

†**min, myn** *adj* lesser *la14-16*. **mare and min** *of persons* greater and lesser; greater and smaller, to a greater or smaller extent, altogether, entirely *la14-16*. [ON *minni*]

min *see* MAN, MUNE

minace *see* MENACE[1,1], MENACE[1,2]

mince[1,1], **minch** /mɪns, mɪnʃ/ *n* **1** minced meat *18-*. **2** nonsense *la20-*. **3** any unpleasant substance *la20-*. **minschie** a crumb, a morsel *la19- NE T*. **mince pie 1** a pie made with finely-chopped meat *20-*. **2** a pie made with dried fruit and suet *20-*. **mince round** a large round pie with mince and gravy encased in flaky pastry *20-*. **mince and tatties 1** a dish of minced meat, gravy and potatoes *20-*. **2** something typical of working-class Scottishness *la20-*. [see the verb]

mince[1,2], **minch**, †**minsch** /mɪns, mɪnʃ/ *v* **1** to chop up; to subdivide *17-*. **2** to minimize, disparage, water down; to prevaricate, quibble *17-*. **3** to cut short, diminish, remove a part (from) *16-e19*. **minced collops** minced steak cooked with oatmeal, onion, carrot and or other vegetables *18-*. †**minced pie, mincht pey 1** a pie made with finely-chopped meat *la17-19.* **2** a pie made with dried fruit and suet *18-e19.* [ME *mincen*, EModE *mince*]

mind[1.1], **mine**, †**mynd**, †**myne** /mʌɪnd, mʌɪn/ *n* **1** the memory, the capacity to remember *la14-*. **2** an act of commemoration, the state of being remembered, a memorial *la14-*. **3** a memory, a recollection, something remembered *15-*. **4** the mental or cognitive faculty, (the seat of) reason, sanity; wish, purpose, intention; disposition, attitude, feelings *la15-*. **5** an opinion, a judgement, a decision *15-19*. **mindful, mindfu 1** heedful *16-*. **2** desiring, intending *la16-*. **mindless**, †**myndles** senseless, insane; forgetful, oblivious *16-*. **a mind tae** with the intention to *la18- Sh WC SW Uls*. **hae mind** to take heed of, bear in mind, remember *15-*. **keep mind** to bear in mind, take heed (of) *la18-*. **of mind to** with the intention to *16-*. **out of mind, out of your mind** forgotten *la15-*. [OE *mynd*]

mind[1.2], †**mynd**, †**myne** /mʌɪnd, mʌɪn/ *v* **1** to remind (a person) (of something) *16-*. **2** to remember, recollect, call to mind *la17-*. **3** to recall (one person to another) by conveying greetings *la17-*. **4** to remember (a person) in a will, give (someone) a small gift *18-*. **5** to mention in one's prayers, pray for *la17-19, 20- Sh NE T*. **6** to have in mind, intend, desire *16-19*. **minding 1** a small gift made by way of remembrance, a token of goodwill *19-*. **2** a memory, recollection *20-*. **mind o, mind on, mind upon** to remember, recollect *18-*. [see the noun]

mine[1.1], †**mind**, †**mynd** /mʌɪn/ *n* **1** an excavation made for the extraction of minerals *15-*. **2** a passageway or tunnel running from the surface to a mine-working or connecting one underground working with another; a drift, a level *17-*. **3** an excavation made for military purposes (to raise a siege) *la15-18*. [ME *min*]

mine[1.2], †**mind** /mʌɪn/ *v* **1** to tunnel; to undermine *la14-*. **2** to make a passageway by tunnelling, often for the extraction of minerals *la17-*. **miner**, †**minour**, †**mynour 1** a person who extracts materials, originally metal, by digging *la15-*. **2** a person who digs mines for military purposes *la14-*. [ME *minen*]

mine[2] /mʌɪn/ *pron* **1** of or belonging to me *la14-*. **2** my *la14-19*. **mines** mine, my one *17-*. **mine ain, mine own** my own *la15-*. [OE *mīn*]

mine *see* MIND[1.1]

mineer[1.1] /mɪˈnir/ *n* an uproar, a noisy gathering, a tumult, a fuss *la19- NE*. [see the verb]

mineer[1.2], **meneer** /mɪˈnir/ *v* to make a din; to stupefy with noise *la19- NE*. [aphetic form of DOMINEER]

minent *see* MEENIT[1.1]

mineral[1.1], †**mynerall**, †**mynorall** /ˈmɪnərəl/ *n* **1** a substance obtained by mining, an ore or metal *la16-*. **2** a mine, a deposit of ore or metal, mine workings *la15-17*. [Lat *minerāle*]

mineral[1.2], †**minerall** /ˈmɪnərəl/ *adj* **1** *of water or a spring* containing (a large proportion of) minerals in solution *la16-*. **2** of, deriving from or related to a mineral *17-*. [Lat *minerālis*]

mines *see* MINE[2]

ming[1] /mɪŋ/ *n* **1** a smell *20-*. **2** a disgusting mess *la20-*. **minger** an unattractive person *la20-*. [unknown]

ming[2.1] /mɪŋ/ *n* a mixture or compound for smearing on sheep *20-*. [see the verb]

ming[2.2], †**meng** /mɪŋ/ *v* **1** to mix, blend; to mix up, confuse *la14-19*. **2** to mix (tar) for marking sheep or applying to wounds during sheep-shearing *19- Bor*. [OE *mengan*]

mingin /ˈmɪŋɪn/ *adj* **1** having a bad smell, stinking *la20-*. **2** very drunk *la20-*. **3** low quality, inferior, distasteful *la20-*. [unknown]

mingse, minkse /mɪŋs, mɪŋks/ *v* to mix *la19- Sh Ork*. **minkster, minxter** a mixture *la19- Sh Ork*. [MING[2.2] with ending after Norse verbs in *-sa*]

minion, †**minȝeoun**, †**munȝoun** /ˈmɪnjən/ *n* **1** a person dependent on a patron's favour, a hanger-on, a servile person, an underling *la15-*. **2** a small cannon *la16-17*. **3** a sweetheart or favourite *16*. **minions of the law** police officers *la18-*. [MFr *mignon*]

†**minis, minish, mynnis, menis** *v* to lessen *15-e19*. [ME *minishen*]

minister *see* MEENISTER[1.1], MEENISTER[1.2]

ministerie *see* MEENISTRY

†**ministrate, ministrat** *v* = MEENISTER[1.2] *la15-19*. [Lat *ministrāt-*, ptp stem of *ministrāre*]

ministrie, ministry *see* MEENISTRY

minitie *see* MEENIT[1.1]

minjy *see* MEANJIE

mink[1], **munk** /mɪŋk, mʌŋk/ *n* **1** a noose, a loop *19- N NE*. **2** a cow's tether; a horse's halter *19- NE T EC*. **3** figuratively, an entanglement, a snare; matrimony *la19- NE T*. [Gael *muince* a collar; compare Gael *muinghiall* a halter]

mink[2] /mɪŋk/ *n* a dirty or disgusting person; a person of low social status or poor taste *la20-*. **minker** = MINK[2] *20-*. [perhaps a conflation of *minger* (MING[1]) and TINK[1]]

minkse *see* MINGSE

minkster *see* MINGSE

minn /mɪn/ *n* **1** a bay, an inlet of the sea *la18- Sh*. **2** the mouth of a person *20-*. [ON *minni*]

minnage *see* MANAGE

minnie[1.1], †**mynnye** /ˈmɪne/ *n* **1** *of people* a familiar term for a mother *16-*. **2** a grandmother, an older woman *la19- Sh Ork*. **3** *of animals* a mother, a dam *la18-19*. **minnie's bairn** a child particularly favoured by his or her mother, a mother's pet *18-19, 20- T*. [perhaps a variant of MAMMIE]

†**minnie**[1.2] *v of a young animal* to run back to its mother; *of a shepherd* to put a lamb to its mother *la18-e19*. [see the noun]

minnie *see* MEENIE

minnon, *Bor* **mennen**, †**menoun** /ˈmɪnən; *Bor* ˈmɛnən/ *n* a small freshwater fish of the carp family, especially *Phoxinus phoxinus la14-*. [probably related to Eng *minnow*]

minnonette, *NE* **meeninit** /ˈmɪnənɛt; *NE* ˈmɪnɪnɪt/ *n* the garden plant mignonette *Reseda odorata la19- NE T SW*. [altered form of Eng *mignonette*]

minor[1.1], †**minour** /ˈmʌɪnər/ *n* a person under 21 or (from 1969) 18 years of age; *law* a male over 14 years or a female over 12, the legally recognized age of puberty, and under 18 or 21 *16-*. Compare PUPIL. [see the adj]

minor[1.2] /ˈmʌɪnər/ *adj* below the age of adulthood *la15-*. [Lat *minor*]

minority, †**menorite** /mʌɪˈnɔrəte/ *n* the state of being under the recognized age of adulthood *la15-*. **minority and lesion** the grounds on which contracts by a minor may be avoided *la15-*. [MFr *minorité*]

minour *see* MINE[1.2], MINOR[1.1]

minsch *see* MINCE[1.2]

minstrel, †**menstral**, †**menstraill**, †**minstral** /ˈmɪnstrəl/ *n* a professional entertainer, especially a musician or singer *14-*. **minstrelly** = MINSTRELSY *la14-e17*. [AN *menestral*]

minstrelsy, †**menstralsy**, †**menstralcy** /ˈmɪnstrəlse/ *n* **1** musical entertainment *la14-*. **2** (a collection of) minstrel poetry or song *19-*. [ME *minstralsi*]

mint[1.1] /mɪnt/ *n* **1** an attempt, effort, intention *16-*. **2** a threatened blow, a feint *16-19, 20- NE*. **3** a physical movement towards doing something *16-e17*. [see the verb]

mint[1.2], †**mynt** /mɪnt/ *v* **1** to intend, attempt, aim, aspire (at, to) *la14-*. **2** to mention, speak of, utter *la18-*. **3** to insinuate, hint (at), suggest *la18-19, 20- Ork NE EC*. **4** to make a threatening movement, feint *15-19, 20- N NE*. **5** to brandish a weapon, aim a blow; to threaten a person *la16-19, 20- N NE*. **6** to plan, scheme, attempt something *19, 20- NE*. [OE *myntan*]

mint[2] /mɪnt/ *n* a tiny being or object *20- Sh*. [Norn *mint*]

minta, †**mento** /'mɪntə/ *n* obligation or control (of a person or thing) *19- NE*. †**oot o mento** free from obligation or control *19*. [unknown]

mintie *see* MEENIT[1.1]

minut, minute *see* MEENIT[1.1], MEENIT[1.2]

†**minuwae** *n* an elegant or stately dance, a minuet *la18-19*. [Fr *menuet*]

minxter *see* MINGSE

†**minȝard, mignard** *adj* dainty, mincing, effeminate *la16-17*. [MFr *mignard*]

minȝeoun *see* MINION

mir *see* MYRRH

mirac, maroc /mɪˈrak maˈrok/ *adj* drunk; stupefied *20- NE T C*. [reduced form of MIRACULOUS]

miracklous *see* MIRACULOUS

miracle[1.1], *Sh* **marakkel**, †**mirakle** /'mɪrəkəl; *Sh* məˈrakəl/ *n* **1** an event viewed as outside natural agency and ascribed to divine intervention *la14-*. **2** a spectacle, something to wonder at, an oddity *la19- Sh*. **3** a disabled person *20- Sh*. [ME *miracle*, Lat *mīrāculum*]

miracle[1.2], **meracle**, *Sh* **mirakle**, *Sh* **marackel** /'mɪrəkəl, 'mɛrəkəl; *Sh* mɪˈrakəl; *Sh* məˈrakəl/ *v* **1** to marvel, wonder, be astonished *19-*. **2** to hurt, injure, cause physical disability *la19- Sh*. [see the noun]

miraculous, miracklous /mɪˈrakjuləs, mɪˈrakəlʌs, məˈrakləs/ *adj* **1** of the nature of a miracle, ascribable to a miracle; resembling a miracle *la16-*. **2** having the power to work miracles or do something amazing *la16-*. **3** very drunk *la19-*. **4** clumsy, loutish *20- N NE*. [EModE *miraculus*]

mirakle *see* MIRACLE[1.1], MIRACLE[1.2]

mird /mɪrd/ *v* **1** to meddle, have dealings or association with; to sport, dally, be intimate with *17- N NE T EC SW*. **2** to venture, dare, attempt *18-19*. [unknown]

mire[1.1], †**myre** /maer/ *n* **1** wet or swampy ground, a bog; a puddle *13-*. **2** wet mud, filth *16-*. **3** a peat bog *16-*. **miredrum** the bittern *Botaurus stellaris la19-*. **mire-duck** the wild duck, the mallard *Anas platyrhynchos 19-*. **mire snipe** the common snipe *Gallinago gallinago la15-19, 20- N NE SW*. **miretigs** a marshy piece of land *20- Sh*. †**meet with a miresnipe** to meet with a misfortune *la17-e19*. [ON *mýrr*]

mire[1.2], †**myre** /maer/ *v* **1** to fall or plunge in a bog; to cast into mud or mire *la15-*. **2** to bespatter with mud or filth, soil, defile *16-*. **3** to involve in difficulties, hamper, bog down *16-*. [see the noun]

mirk[1.1], **murk** /mɪrk, mʌrk/ *n* darkness, night, twilight *la15-*. [see the adj]

mirk[1.2], **murk**, †**myrk** /mɪrk, mʌrk/ *v* to darken, make or grow dark, obscure, blacken; to besmirch *la15-*. **mirking** dusk, nightfall *la18-*. [see the adj]

mirk[1.3], **murk, merk**, *NE* **mark**, †**myrk** /mɪrk, mʌrk, mɛrk; *NE* mark/ *adj* **1** *of night, a place* dark, black, gloomy, obscure *la14-*. **2** *of things, situations* obscure, difficult to comprehend *la14-*. **3** *of persons, states of mind* gloomy, depressing *la16-*. **4** *of weather, the air* dull, murky, lowering *la14-19*. **5** *of persons* in spiritual or intellectual darkness, unenlightened, deluded *la15-e19*. **mirkness**, †**mirknes 1** darkness, gloom *la14-*. **2** blindness *la14-19*. **3** spiritual darkness, unenlightenment *la14-16*. **4** obscurity, secrecy *15-16*. **mirksome** dark, gloomy *la19-*. †**mirk Monanday, mirk Monday** Monday, 29 March 1652 (Old Style), on which occurred a total eclipse of the sun *la18-19*. **mirk nicht** the dead of night *la14-19, 20- T WC*. †**a mirk mirrour** something difficult to comprehend *la15-e17*. [ON *myrkr*]

mirkabrod /'mɪrkəbrɒd/ *n* patchy hill mist *20- Sh*. [ON *myrkr* + Norw *brot* a broken piece]

mirken, †**mirkn**, †**myrkn** /'mɪrkən/ *v* **1** to darken, obscure *15-e16, la20- Sh NE*. **2** to grow dark *16-19, 20- Sh*. **mirkenin** late twilight *la18-19, 20- Sh*. [ON *myrkna*, or MIRK[1.3] with verb-forming suffix]

mirkie *see* MIRKY[2.1]

mirkle /'mɪrkəl/ *n* the radical or basal leaves of the seaweed *Alaria esculenta 19- Ork*. [perhaps Gael *mircean*; compare also Faer *mirkjallur*]

mirkn *see* MIRKEN

mirky[1], **murky** /'mɪrki, 'mʌrke/ *adj* **1** dark, sombre; *of the atmosphere, a place* obscure, impenetrable; gloomy *la18-*. **2** obscured by dirt, dirty *19-*. [MIRK[1.1] + -IE[2]]

mirky[2.1], **mirkie** /'mɪrki, 'mʌrke/ *adj* merry, cheerful, mischievous *la18- N NE T EC Bor*. [perhaps Gael *mireagach* merry, playful]

mirky[2.2] /'mɪrki, 'mʌrke/ *adv* cheerfully, pleasantly, merrily *19- NE*. [see the adj]

mirl[1.1] /mɪrl/ *n* a quivering motion *20- Sh*. [see the verb]

mirl[1.2] /mɪrl/ *v* **1** to move quickly and lightly, twirl, whirl *19- Sh*. **2** to mill about, swarm *20- Sh*. **mirliecog** a spinning top *20- Sh*. [frequentative form of MIRR[1.2], influenced by Eng *twirl, whirl* etc]

mirl[2.1], **merle** /mɪrl, mʌrl, mɛrl/ *n* a speckled, marbled or variegated appearance *19-*. [back-formation from MIRLIE]

mirl[2.2], **merl** /mɪrl, mʌrl, mɛrl/ *v* to mottle, speckle, become blotched *19-*. [see the noun]

mirl *see* MURL[1.1], MURL[1.2]

mirles *see* MIRRLES

mirlie /'mɪrlɪ, 'mʌrle/ *adj* **1** mottled or variegated in pattern or colour *la18-*. **2** *of the colour of birds and animals* mottled, streaked; speckled; dappled; roan *19-*. **3** *of wool or knitted garments* flecked, mottled *la18-, 20- Ork SW*. **mirlie-backs** cirro-cumulus cloud formations, mackerel clouds *19- Ork NE SW*. [MFr *merellé*, from *merelier* chequer board]

mirliecog *see* MIRL[1.2]

mirligoes /'mɪrlɪgoz/ *npl* vertigo, dizziness, light-headedness *la18-*. **in the mirligoes** light-headed, confused *19-*. **on the mirligoes** = *in the mirligoes*. [mirled (MARLIT), with -*igo* from Eng *vertigo*]

mirr[1.1] /mɪr/ *n* a quivering, especially the shimmering of the air on a hot day *la19- Sh Ork*. [see the verb]

mirr[1.2] /mɪr/ *v* to tingle, quiver, tremble *la19- Sh Ork*. [Norw dial *mirra* to tingle]

mirrie *see* MERRY

mirrles, mirles /'mɪrəlz/ *npl* measles *19- NE T*. [plural of MIRL[2.1]]

†**mis** *adv* wrongly, mistakenly *15-16*. **ga mis** to be mistaken *la15-e16*. [aphetic form of Eng *amiss*]

mis *see* MISS[1.1], MISS[1.2]

misaander /məˈsɑndər/ *v* to wander aimlessly *20- Sh*. [perhaps conflation of Eng *meander* and *saunter*]

misacker *see* MASSACRE[1.1], MASSACRE[1.2]

misanswer /mɪsˈansər/ *v* to disobey; to give a rude answer *20- NE Uls*. [*mis*- prefix + ANSWER[1.2]]

misanter *see* MISHANTER[1.1]

†**misbeet** *v of yarn* to become crossed or tangled in weaving *19*. [*mis*- prefix + BEET[1]]

misbegowk /mɪsbəˈgʌuk/ *n* a disappointment *la19, 20- Bor*. [*mis*- prefix + BEGOWK]

misbehauden, misbehadden, †misbehalding /mɪsbəˈhɔdən, mɪsbəˈhadən/ *adj* disrespectful, indiscreet, impolite *17-19, 20- Sh Ork NE*. [EModE *misbeholden*]

misca, miscall /mɪsˈka, mɪsˈkɔ, mɪsˈkɔl/ *v* **1** to abuse verbally, speak ill of, slander, disparage *la16-*. **2** to mispronounce (a word) in reading *19-*. [ME *miscallen*]

miscairry, miscarry, †miscary /mɪsˈkeri, mɪsˈkare/ *v* **1** to come to harm, be harmed, spoiled, ruined; to go astray; to spoil, botch *la15-*. **2** to fail to obtain one's desire *18-*. **3** to be pregnant when unmarried *18-19, 20- Sh*. **4** to behave badly, misbehave *17*. **†miscarrying** erring, blundering *17*. [ME *miscarien*]

miscall *see* MISCA
miscarry, miscary *see* MISCAIRRY
mischaip *see* MISCHAPE
†mischancit, myschancit *adj* unlucky, ill-omened *la15-16*. [EModE *mischaunced*]

mischancy, †myschancy /mɪsˈtʃansi/ *adj* **1** unlucky, ill-omened *16-*. **2** risky, dangerous *19-*. [EModE *mischance* bad luck, with adj-forming suffix *-y*]

mischant *see* MESCHANT[1.1], MESCHANT[1.2]
†mischape, mischaip *adj* given a wrong or ugly shape *e16*. [ptp of ME *misshapen*]
mischeifaislie *see* MISCHIEVOUS
mischeiff, mischeve *see* MISCHIEVE
mischevous *see* MISCHIEVOUS

mischief, †myscheif, †myschefe /ˈmɪstʃɪf, ˈmɪstʃif; *Sh Ork* mɪsˈʃif/ *n* **1** harm, (an) injury, (a) wrong; wrongdoing *la15-*. **2** a physical injury; bodily harm *la18-*. **3** an evil plight, misfortune, trouble; military disadvantage or loss *la14-19, 20- Sh Ork T Uls*. **4** strife, discord *la16-e17*. [ME *mischef*]

mischieve, †mischeve, †mischeiff /mɪsˈtʃiv; *Sh* mɪˈʃiv/ *v* **1** to injure physically, give a beating to, treat cruelly *la15-19, 20- Sh NE T*. **2** to harm, damage; to inflict injury or loss upon; *in passive* to suffer hurt or misfortune, come to grief *16-19*. [ME *mischeven*, EModE *mischeve*]

mischievous, mischievious, †mischevous /ˈmɪstʃɪvəs, mɪsˈtʃivəs/ *adj* **1** inflicting, producing or entailing harm or damage, having harmful effects or intent *16-*. **2** characterized by playful pranks and naughtiness without real intention to harm; *of a young woman* roguish *18-*. **3** calamitous, disastrous *16*. **mischievously, †myschewsly, mischeifaislie 1** harmfully, hurtfully; teasingly *16-*. **2** disastrously; wickedly *16*. [ME *mischevous*, EModE *mischevous*]

miscomfit /mɪsˈkʌmfɪt/ *v* to displease, offend *20- NE*. [ME *miscomfort* conflated with Eng *misfit*]
†misconstruct *v* to misinterpret *17-e19*. [*mis-* prefix + Lat *construct-*, ptp stem of *construere* to construct]
†miscontent[1.1] *n* discontent, dissatisfaction *17*. [see the adj]
†miscontent[1.2] *v* to displease *la16-e17*. [see the adj; compare MFr *mescontenter*]
†miscontent[1.3] *adj* discontented, annoyed *16-e17*. [*mis-* prefix + CONTENT[1.1] or MFr *mescontent*]

miscontentit, miscontented /mɪskənˈtɛntɪt, mɪskənˈtɛntəd/ *adj* discontented, dissatisfied *16-19, 20- NE*. [*mis-* prefix + ME *contenten* or participial adj from MISCONTENT[1.2]]

†miscontentment *n* **1** discontent, displeasure, resentment; a grievance *la16-17*. **2** mutual bad feeling, discord *17*. [*mis-* prefix + Eng *contentment* or MFr *mescontentement*]

†miscook, miscuke *v* **1** to spoil food in cooking, cook badly *16-19*. **2** to bungle, mismanage *16-19*. [*mis-* prefix + CUIK[1.2]]

†misdeme *v* to misjudge *la14-e17*. **misdemyng** the action of misjudging *15-e16*. [*mis-* prefix + OE *dēman*]

misdo /mɪsˈdu/ *v* **1** to do, perform badly or wrongly *la14-*. **2** to do wrong, transgress; to harm *la14-15*. **misdoer, †misdoar** a wrongdoer *la14-*. **misdoing, †mysdoing, †mysdoyng** wrongdoing *15-*. [*mis-* prefix + OE *dōn*]

misdoot[1.1], **misdoubt** /mɪsˈdut, mɪsˈdʌut/ *n* (a) doubt, suspicion, fear *19, 20- N T SW*. see the verb

misdoot[1.2], **misdoubt** /mɪsˈdut, mɪsˈdʌut/ *v* **1** to distrust, doubt, disbelieve *17-*. **2** to presuppose, suspect, be afraid (that) *17-19, 20- Sh NE SW Uls*. [*mis-* prefix + DOOT[1.2]]

misdoubt *see* MISDOOT[1.1], MISDOOT[1.2]
†misell, mesell *adj* **1** leprous *la14-e17*. **2** *of fish and swine* infected, tainted *16*. [variant of MAISLE]
miser *see* MISERT[1.1]
miserabill, miserable *see* MEESERABLE
†misericorde[1.1] *n* compassion, mercy *la15-e17*. [ME *misericord*, Lat *misericordia*]
†misericorde[1.2] *adj* compassionate, merciful *la15-16*. see the noun
miserie *see* MEESERY

misert[1.1], **meeser, miser** /ˈmaezərt, ˈmizər, ˈmaezər/ *n* **1** a mean, grasping person, a hoarder *la16-*. **2** a wretched person *la16-*. **misert-pig** a child's (earthenware) moneybox *la19, 20- Sh*. [see the adj]

misert[1.2] /ˈmaezərt/ *adj* avaricious *19- Sh T SW*. [Lat *miser* wretched]

misery *see* MEESERY

misfa, †misfall /mɪsˈfa/ *v pt* **misfell**, *ptp* **misfallin** to suffer misfortune, come to grief; *of an event* to turn out badly *la14-17, 20- literary*. [OE *mis-* + FA[1.2]; compare MDu *misvallen*]

misfare, *Sh* **misfure**, *Sh* **misföre, †misfair, †mysfare** /mɪsˈfer; *Sh* mɪsˈfur; *Sh* mɪsˈfør/ *v pt Sh* **misföre †mysfur**, *ptp* **misforne †misfarne 1** *of a boat* to be lost or wrecked *la19- Sh Ork*. **2** to come to grief, go wrong, fail to prosper *la14-19, 20- Sh*. **3** to impair, bring to ruin; to mismanage *la15-16*. [OE *misfaran*, ON *misfara*]

misfare *see* MISFURE
misfarne *see* MISFARE
†misfashion, misfasson, misfason *v* to make badly; to dishonour (oneself) *16-e19*. **misfashioned, misfassonit** misshapen, badly formed *16-e19*. [*mis-* prefix + FASHION[1.2]]

misfaul /mɪsˈfɔl/ *v of a boat* to capsize, be wrecked *la19- Sh*. [perhaps conflation of MISFARE with *misfall* (MISFA)]

misfell *see* MISFA
misfit[1.1] /ˈmɪsfɪt/ *n* **1** *of clothes* a failure to fit *19-*. **2** *of people* an inability to interact harmoniously *20-*. [*mis-* prefix + EModE *fit*]

misfit[1.2] /mɪsˈfɪt/ *v* **1** to fail to measure or fit correctly, fit badly *19-*. **2** to offend, displease *la19- NE*. [*mis-* prefix + ME *fitten*]

misföre, misforne *see* MISFARE
misfortoun *see* MISFORTUNE
misfortunate, *NE* **misfortinit, †misfortunat, †mysfortunat** /mɪsˈfɔrtʃənət; *NE* mɪsˈfɔrtənət/ *adj* unfortunate, unlucky *la15-19, 20- N NE WC Uls*. **†misfortunatly** unfortunately *la17-19*. [*mis-* prefix + FORTUNATE]

misfortune, †misfortoun /mɪsˈfɔrtʃən/ *n* **1** (a piece of) bad luck *la15-*. **2** pregnancy outside marriage, (the birth of) an illegitimate child *la18-*. **misfortunit, misfortoun'd** unfortunate, ill-fated *la15-e17*. [*mis-* prefix + FORTOUN]

misfure, †misfare /mɪsˈfør/ *n* **1** a disaster, particularly the loss of a boat at sea *la19- Sh*. **2** a misfortune *15-19*. [from the verb MISFARE]

misfure *see* MISFARE
misgae /mɪsˈge/ *v* **1** to go wrong, fail, miscarry *18-19, 20- NE T*. **2** to go astray *15-e19*. [*mis-* prefix + GAE]

misgide *see* MISGUIDE

misgie, misgive /mɪsˈgi, mɪsˈgɪv/ v 1 to (cause to) fail, let a person down *19, 20- Sh WC*. 2 to fail, go wrong; *of crops* to give a poor yield, fail to grow *la16-e19*. 3 to blame oneself, regret *la15*. 4 *of a gun* to fail to go off, misfire *la16-18*. [*mis-* prefix + GIE]

misglim, misglam /mɪsˈglɪm, mɪsˈglim, mɪsˈglam/ v to neglect, forget; to ill-treat, fail to care for *20- Sh Ork*. [ON *misgleyma*]

misgoggle *see* MISGUGGLE

misgrown /mɪsˈgron, mɪsˈgrʌun/ *adj* stunted, deformed *la18-19, 20- Sh*. [OE *mis-* + GROWE[1.2]]

†**misgruggle** v to spoil by rough handling, crumple *la18-e19*. [*mis-* prefix + GRUGGLE[1.2]]

misguggle, misgoggle /mɪsˈgʌgəl, mɪsˈgɔgəl/ v to handle roughly or clumsily; to rumple; bungle; to hack *la18-*. [*mis-* prefix + GUGGLE[1.2]]

misguide, †**misgide**, †**misgyde** /mɪsˈgʌɪd/ v 1 to lead astray, mislead *16-*. 2 to treat badly, neglect; to bring up badly or cruelly; to misgovern *16-*. 3 to waste, squander, mismanage *16-19, 20- Sh Ork NE T*. [*mis-* prefix + GUIDE[1.2]]

mishandle, †**mishandil** /mɪsˈhandəl/ v 1 to ill-treat; to handle wrongly or ineffectively *la16-*. 2 to mangle, maim, knock about *la19, 20- Sh Uls*. [*mis-* prefix + HANLE[1.2]]

mishanter[1.1], *Sh Ork* **misanter** /məˈʃantər; *Sh Ork* məˈsantər/ *n* 1 a mishap, a disaster; a misfortune *la18-*. 2 a physical hurt or injury *la19, 20- Sh NE T*. 3 a name for the Devil used as a swear-word *19*. †**the Mishanter** = MISHANTER[1.1] (sense 3) *la18-e19*. [reduced form of Eng *misadventure*]

mishanter[1.2] /məˈʃantər/ v to hurt, injure *la19- NE*. [see the noun]

mish-mash[1.1] /ˈmɪʃmaʃ/ v to mix up, throw together confusedly or in a muddle *la18-*. [EModE *mishmash*]

mish-mash[1.2] /ˈmɪʃmaʃ/ *adj* confused, muddled *19-*. [see the verb]

misk /mɪsk/ *n* a damp, boggy, low-lying stretch of grassland *18- WC*. [unknown]

misken, †**myskene** /mɪsˈkɛn/ v 1 to be ignorant or unaware of, not know *la14-*. 2 to fail to recognize or identify *16-19, 20- Sh N NE*. 3 to have mistaken ideas of one's own importance, get above oneself *la14-19, 20- N NE*. 4 to refuse to recognize, spurn, ignore, disdain *la15-e19*. 5 to leave off doing something, desist *e19*. 6 to misunderstand, mistake *la14-e17*. [ON *miskenna*]

misknaw, misknow /mɪsˈnɔ, mɪsˈno/ v 1 to be ignorant or unaware of *15-*. 2 to misunderstand, misjudge *la14-*. 3 to fail to recognize or identify *la14-e19*. 4 to repudiate, ignore, disavow *la15-e17*. 5 to be unfamiliar with, be unversed in *la14-16*. 6 to have an exaggerated opinion of oneself *16*. [perhaps by analogy with MISKEN; but compare ME *misknouen*]

†**mislabour** v to impoverish (land) by overcropping and bad husbandry *la17-18*. [*mis-* prefix + LABOUR[1.2]]

mislear, misleir /mɪsˈlir/ v 1 to misinform, misguide, lead astray *17-*. 2 to hurt, abuse, maltreat; to vilify *17-e19*. [*mis-* prefix + LEAR]

misleared, misleert, mislaird, †**misleirit** /mɪsˈlird, mɪsˈlirt, mɪsˈlerd/ *adj* 1 unmannerly, rude *la16-*. 2 misinformed, mistaken, erroneous *19-*. 3 excessively selfish, greedy *19, 20- NE T EC*. [OE *mislǽran*]

†**mislearnit, mislearned** *adj* unmannerly, rude; abusive *e17*. [OE *mis-* + LEARN + -IT[1]; compare MISLEARED]

misleir *see* MISLEAR

misle-shinn'd *see* MAISLE

misleving *see* MISLIVING

mislike, *Sh N* **mislek** /mɪsˈlʌɪk; *Sh N* mɪsˈlek/ v 1 to dislike *la16-*. 2 to displease *la14-e17*. [OE *mislīcian*]

†**mislikely** v to make unlikely; to depreciate; to smirch *19*. [OE *mis-* + LIKELY[1.1]]

†**misliken** v to speak ill of, disparage; to undervalue *e19*. [OE *mis-* + LIKEN[2]]

mislippen, mislippin /mɪsˈlɪpən/ v 1 to neglect, overlook *la16-*. 2 to deceive, lead astray *19-*. 3 to distrust, doubt, suspect *19-*. 4 to defraud, disappoint *la16-17*. [OE *mis-* + LIPPEN[1]]

misliving, †**misleving** /mɪsˈlɪvɪŋ/ *n* evil or sinful living *la15-*. [ME *misliving*]

misluck[1.1], †**misluk** /mɪsˈlʌk/ *n* bad luck, misfortune *la16-*. [OE *mis-* + LUCK]

†**misluck**[1.2] v to meet with bad luck; to miscarry *17-19*. [see the noun]

misluckit /mɪsˈlʌkət/ *adj* dogged with bad luck, unfortunate *la19- NE*. [MISLUCK[1.1] + -IT[2]]

misluk *see* MISLUCK[1.1]

mislushious /mɪsˈlʌʃəs/ *adj* malicious, ill-intentioned *18-*. [altered form of MALICIOUS, with influence from Eng prefix *mis-*]

†**mismade** *adj* misshapen, deformed *la14-16*. [ME *mismad*]

mismade *see* MISMAK

†**mismaggle** v to disarrange, interfere with; to spoil *la18-e19*. [*mis-* prefix + MAGGLE]

†**mismaid** *adj* discouraged or upset *e16*. [probably ptp of MISMAY]

mismak, mismake /mɪsˈmak, mɪsˈmek/ v *pt, ptp* **mismade** 1 to trouble oneself, become disturbed or upset, show concern *19- C Bor Uls*. 2 to prepare or cook food badly *19, 20- Sh T*. 3 to make badly, misshape *16-e19*. 4 to unmake, destroy *la16-e17*. [ME *mismaken*]

misman /mɪsˈman/ v to frighten badly, unman *20- Sh*. **mismanned** weakened, exhausted *20- Sh*. [*mis-* prefix + MAN]

mismar /mɪsˈmar/ v to spoil, tangle, disarrange *19- Sh NE*. [*mis-* prefix + MAR[1.2]]

mismarrowed, *Sh Uls* **mismorrowed** /mɪsˈmarod; *Sh Uls* mɪsˈmɔrod/ *adj* mismatched, ill-assorted *la18-*. [*mis-* prefix + MARROW[1.2] + -IT[1]]

mismay /mɪsˈme/ v to trouble, bother, upset *15-*. [probably altered form of Eng *dismay*, ME *dismaien*]

mismorrowed *see* MISMARROWED

mismuive /mɪsˈmuv/ v to trouble, disturb; to alarm *19-*. [*mis-* prefix + MOVE]

†**misnortourit, misnorturit, misnurtured** *adj* badly brought up, unmannerly *la16-e17*. [*mis-* prefix + NORTER[1.2] + -IT[1]]

†**misperson, mispersoun** v to treat (a person) with indignity; to abuse verbally *15-e17*. [apparently variant of DISPERSON]

misred /mɪsˈrɛd/ *adj* tangled, involved, confused *la18-19, 20- Sh N SW*. [*mis-* prefix + REDD[1.3]]

†**misregard**[1.1] *n* disregard, failure to heed or respect *17*. **misregardful** heedless, neglectful *17*. [see the verb]

†**misregard**[1.2] v to treat with disrespect, slight; to ignore *la16-e18*. [*mis-* prefix + REGAIRD[1.2]]

misremember /mɪsrəˈmɛmbər/ v to forget; to remember incorrectly *19, 20- SW Uls*. [*mis-* prefix + REMEMBER]

misrestit /mɪsˈrɛstɪt/ *adj* suffering from loss of sleep *20- Sh NE SW*. [*mis-* prefix + REST[1.2] with *-it* suffix]

miss[1.1], †**mis** /mɪs/ *n* 1 a failure to hit a target *la17-*. 2 a loss, a want, a cause for regret or mourning *la19-*. 3 wrongdoing; sin, (an) offence or fault; harm, injury *la14-e19*. 4 a mistake *la15-17*. [from the verb and ON *missa* loss, also ON *á mis* so as to miss]

miss[1.2], †**mis** /mɪs/ v *pt, ptp* also **mist** 1 to fail to hit a target *la14-*. 2 to fail (to achieve or obtain), go without, be deprived of something desirable *la14-*. 3 to notice the absence or loss

of *la14-*. **4** to lose, suffer the loss of *la14-*. **5** to regret the absence of, feel the want of *la14-*. **6** to fail to intercept *la15-*. **7** to avoid, escape *16-*. **8** to fail to obtain footing on (a step) *16-*. **9** to fail to see, perceive or notice *16-*. **10** to fail to keep a promise or appointment *la16-*. **11** to fail to happen *la17-*. **12** to pass over, skip in reading *19-*. **13** *of crops* to fail to germinate or grow; *of a breeding animal* to fail to conceive *la19-*. **14** *reflexive* to fail to experience something good or entertaining by being absent: ◊*ye fair missed yersel 20-*. **15** *of a thing* to lack something; to be lacking or wanting *17-e19*. †**in missing** absent, lost, lacking *la16-e17*. **miss a fit** to trip, stumble *la18-*. †**miss but** to fail to *la16-e19*. †**miss stays** *nautical* to fail in an attempt to go from one tack to another *19*. [OE *missan*]
missate *see* MIS-SET
missaucre *see* MASSACRE[1.1], MASSACRE[1.2]
missell *see* MUZZLE[1.1]
missellis *see* MAISLES
missellit *see* MUZZLE[1.2]
†**misseme, mysseme** *v* to be unbecoming or unbefitting *16-e19*. [ME *misseeme*]
mis-set, †**misset**, †**missate** /mɪsˈsɛt/ *v* **1** *of clothes* to be unbecoming *20- Sh*. **2** to displease *la14-19*. [*mis-* prefix + SET[1.2]]
missie /ˈmɪse, ˈmɪsi/ *n* the eldest unmarried daughter of a farmer *20- NE EC Uls*. [Eng *miss* with diminutive suffix *-ie*]
missionar /ˈmɪʃənər/ *n* an itinerant evangelical preacher; a member of a non-Presbyterian or dissenting church *19, 20- NE T Uls*. [Lat *missionārius*]
missionary /ˈmɪʃənre, ˈmɪʃənəre/ *n* **1** a person engaged in a religious mission or supplementing the work of the minister in a parish *19-*. **2** a lay preacher, especially in the Free Kirk and the Free Presbyterian Kirk *20- H&I*. **3** an emissary *e19*. [Lat *missionārius*]
missive /ˈmɪsɪv/ *n* **1** a (formal) letter; an authoritative or official communication in the form of a letter *16-*. **2** *law* a document in the form of a letter exchanged by the parties to a contract *16-*. **3** the official letter sent to each of the members of the Convention of Burghs announcing a meeting and listing the agenda *la16-e17*. †**missive bill** = MISSIVE (sense 1) *16-e17*. **missive dues** the proportion of administrative expenses allocated to each member of the Convention of Burghs *la17-*. †**missive letter** = MISSIVE *la16-18*. †**missive writing** = MISSIVE *16*. **missive of lease** a lease drawn up in the form of a MISSIVE (sense 2) *19-*. †**missive of tack** a tack drawn up in the form of a MISSIVE (sense 2) *e19*. [EModE *missive*]
missly, mistlie /ˈmɪsle, ˈmɪstle/ *adj* **1** alone, lonely through absence of a usual companion *19, 20- Uls*. **2** missed, regretted owing to being absent *19, 20- Uls*. [probably from the ptp of MISS[1.2], with adv-forming suffix]
missour *see* MEASURE[1.1]
missure *see* MEASURE[1.2]
†**misswear** *v* to swear falsely, perjure oneself *la19*. [*mis-* prefix + SWEER[1.2]]
†**missworn, missworne** perjured, forsworn *la16-e19*. [*mis-* prefix + ptp of SWEER[1.2]]
mist *see* MISS[1.2]
mistak[1.1] /mɪsˈtak/ *n* **1** a misconception, an error; a misunderstanding *la17-*. **2** an unintended pregnancy (outside marriage), the birth of an illegitimate child *20-*. **in a mistak 1** mistaken, labouring under a misapprehension *18-*. **2** in error, by mistake *18-*. **nae mistak but** without doubt, certainly *la19-*. [see the verb]
mistak[1.2], **mistake** /mɪsˈtak, mɪsˈtek/ *v pt* also **misteuk 1** to misapprehend, misunderstand; to estimate wrongly *la16-*. **2** to do wrong, transgress *la14-19, 20- Ork T*. **mistaen, mistaken 1** misunderstood, wrongly conceived; *of persons* under a misapprehension *20-*. **2** *of a remark* taken amiss, misunderstood *20- Sh Ork N EC SW*. **3** overcome with, under the influence of (drink) *18*. **mistak yersel** to make a mistake, go wrong *la17-*. [*mis-* prefix + TAK[1.2]; compare ON *mistaka*]
mistell /mɪsˈtɛl/ *v* to misinform *20- EC Bor*. [EModE *mistell*]
†**mistemper** *v* to disturb, upset *la15-e17*. **mistemperance** overindulgence, excess *la15-e16*. [*mis-* prefix + TEMPER[1.2]]
mister[1.1], †**myster** /ˈmɪstər/ *n* **1** need, necessity; pressure of circumstances *la14-*. **2** an emergency, a crisis, a plight *la14-e19*. **3** needy circumstances, destitution, poverty *la14-e19*. **4** want, lack *la14-16*. **5** a craft, a trade, employment *la14-15*. †**misterful 1** needy, impoverished *la14-17*. **2** necessary *15*. **misters** requirements, needs *la15-e17*. [ME *mister*]
†**mister**[1.2] *v* **1** to require, need *15-e18*. **2** to be in want *la15-16*. **3** to be necessary, be needful *la14-16*. **4** *of things* to be lacking in some respect, be faulty *la16-e17*. [see the noun]
mistery *see* MYSTERY
misteuk *see* MISTAK[1.2]
misthrive /mɪsˈθraev/ *v* to fail to prosper, do badly *la16-17, 18- Sh NE T*. **misthriven** not prosperous; undernourished *la18- Sh NE T*. [*mis-* prefix + THRIVE[1.2]]
mistime /mɪsˈtaɪm/ *v* to keep irregular hours, depart from routine in sleeping and eating *19, 20- N NE T*. **mistimeous** irregular, unpunctual, slovenly *20- N NE*. [*mis-* prefix + TIME]
mistlie *see* MISSLY
†**mistoneit** *adj* discordant, out of tune *16*. [*mis-* prefix + TONE[1] + -IT[2]]
mistres, mistress *see* MAISTRESS
mistrue, †**mistrow** /mɪsˈtru/ *v* to disbelieve, distrust, doubt *la14-15, la19- Sh*. [ME *mistrouen*, ON *mistrúa*]
mistryst /mɪsˈtraɪst/ *v* **1** to fail to meet, let down, break faith with; to seduce *la17-19, 20- NE Bor*. **2** to delude, perplex, dismay *e19*. [*mis-* prefix + TRYST[1.2]]
mitch[1] /mɪtʃ/ *n* the crutch or rest in which the top of a mast lies when lowered *20- N EC*. [EModE *miche*; compare MIK]
mitch[2] /mɪtʃ/ *v* to play truant *la20- Uls*. [perhaps related to MICH]
mite, †**myte** /mʌɪt/ *n* **1** a coin of low value, originally a Flemish copper coin; a very low monetary value *15-*. **2** a small but valuable contribution, what could be afforded *16-*. **3** a small clay marble *la19- NE T*. **4** the smaller size of button used in the game of *buttony* (BUTTON) *20- T EC*. **5** an undersized potato *20- Sh*. **mites** the game of *buttony* (BUTTON) *20-*. **mitie** small, tiny *20- Sh*. **a mite** a jot *15-16*. [MDu *mite* a small copper coin; a little bit, a jot]
mith *see* MEITH[1.2]
mithe *see* MEITH[1.1]
mither, mother, *Sh moder*, *Sh NE* **midder**, †**mothir**, †**muder** /ˈmɪðər, ˈmʌðər; *Sh* ˈmodər; *Sh NE* ˈmɪdər/ *n* **1** a female parent *la14-*. **2** an abbess, the Mother Superior of a convent *la16-*. **3** an originator or source *15-*. **4** anything large of its kind *la19- Sh Ork*. **5** an ancestress, especially referring to Eve *15-19*. **motherie** a small delicately-coloured shell used for making necklaces *20- N NE T*. **mither's bairn** a spoilt, indulged child *la19-*. †**moder brother** a maternal uncle *la15-17*. **moder dy** a shoreward current or underswell in the sea *20- Sh*; compare DY. **mither's pet** the youngest child of a family *19-*. **mither-side** the maternal line of descent *la16-*. †**moder sister** a maternal aunt *16-e17*. **modersook** a shoreward current *20- Sh*. **mother tongue**, †**mother toung**, †**moder thowng** a person's native language;

frequently, Scots *15-*. †**gud mither douchter** *with unmarked possessive* the daughter of a good mother *la15-e17*. [OE *mōdor*]

mitherit *see* MIDDRIT

mitre, †**myter**, †**mytir** /ˈmaetər/ *n* **1** the headdress of a bishop *la15-*. **2** a paper hat worn as a punishment, usually inscribed with the nature of the offence *la16-17*. [ME *mitre*]

mittane *see* MITTEN[1.1], MITTEN[2]

mitten[1.1], †**mittane** /ˈmɪtən/ *n* **1** any kind of glove, with or without separate compartments for the fingers and thumb *la15-*. **2** a small squat person or child *19- NE T*. **right i dy mittens** in your usual good health and spirits *la19- Sh*. [ME *mitain*]

mitten[1.2] /ˈmɪtən/ *v* to grab hold of, seize *la19- Sh NE T*. [see the noun]

†**mitten**[2], **mittane** *n* a bird of prey; the male hen-harrier *16-19*. [unknown]

mittle /ˈmɪtəl/ *v* to do bodily harm to, mutilate *19, 20- Ork NE T*. [altered form of Eng *mutilate*]

mix /mɪks/ *v pt, ptp* **mixt**, **mixit**, **mixed 1** to mingle, blend, combine; to prepare by mixing or stirring *16-*. **2** *of greying hair* to become mixed in colour *20-*. **mix yer moggans** to have sexual intercourse; to marry *18-*. [back-formation from MIXT]

mixed *see* MIXT

mixie-maxie *see* MIXTER-MAXTER[1.1], MIXTER-MAXTER[1.2]

mixt, **mixed**, **mixit** /mɪkst, ˈmɪksɪt/ *adj* **1** *of people* mingled, associated, in company *la15-*. **2** mingled, blended *16-*. **3** mentally confused, muddled with drink *19*. **4** *of cloth* woven with more than one colour of yarn, variegated *17-18*. **5** *of wine* adulterated *la15-17*. **6** *of water* turbid *e16*. **mixt meal** flour made from several varieties of grain *la18-19, 20- Sh*. [ME *mixt*, Lat *mixtus*]

mixter, **mixture**, †**mixtour** /ˈmɪkstər, ˈmɪkstʃər/ *n* an act of mixing, blending, compounding; a blend, a compound, an alloy *la15-*. †**without mixture** unadulterated, pure *16-17*. [Fr *mixture*, Lat *mixtūra*]

mixter-maxter[1.1], **mixtie-maxtie**, **mixie-maxie** /ˈmɪkstərˈmakstər, ˈmɪksteˈmakste, ˈmɪkseˈmakse/ *n* a jumble of objects, a mixture, a confusion *19-*. [reduplicative form of MIXT, MIXTER]

mixter-maxter[1.2], **mixtie-maxtie**, **mixie-maxie** /ˈmɪkstərˈmakstər, ˈmɪksteˈmakste, ˈmɪkseˈmakse/ *adj* heterogeneous; jumbled; in a state of confusion *la18-*. [see the noun]

mixtour, **mixture** *see* MIXTER

mizzer *see* MEASURE[1.1], MEASURE[1.2]

mizzle /ˈmɪzəl/ *v* to vanish, melt away *la19- NE T Bor Uls*. [Shelta *misli* to go]

mizzle *see* MAISLE, MUZZLE[1.1]

mizzles *see* MAISLES

mo *see* MAE[1.1], MAE[1.2]

moabill *see* MOVABLE[1.2]

moadern, **modren**, **modern**, †**moderne** /ˈmɔdərn, ˈmɔdrən, ˈmɔdərn/ *adj* in existence at this time, current, present, contemporary; originally of persons, now living; currently holding a position or title *la15-*. [MFr *moderne*]

moan, **mon** /mon/ *v imperative* come on *la20- C*. [reduced form of Eng *come on*]

moan *see* MANE[1.1]

moarnin *see* MORNIN

moat *see* MOTE[1]

mob[1.1] /mɔb/ *n* an unruly crowd *18-*. [shortened form of Lat *mōbile vulgus*]

mob[1.2] /mɔb/ *v* to crowd round, throng, attack or surround in a mob *la18-*. **mobbing** *law* riotous or intimidatory behaviour committed in the pursuit of a particular end *la18-*. **mobbing and rioting** *law* the joining together of a number of people to act in a way which is against peace and good order *la19-*. [see the noun]

†**mobil**, **moble** *adj of goods or property* capable of being moved; not heritable *la14-15*. [ME *moeble*, Lat *mōbilis*]

†**mobill**, **moble** *n pl* **moblys meubles** property; possessions, wealth *la14-16*. [ME *moeble*, Lat *mōbilis* easy to move]

moch[1.1] /mɔx/ *n* a moth *17-*. **mochie** full of moths, motheaten *19- Sh N NE T WC*. **moch-eaten 1** damaged by moths *la19- Sh Ork N NE T EC*. **2** (as if) damaged by woodworm *la19 NE*. [ME *motthe*]

moch[1.2] /mɔx/ *v ptp* **mocht** to be moth-damaged *20- NE*. [see the noun]

moch[2.1] /mɔx/ *n* a warm moist atmosphere, close misty weather *la19*. [unknown]

moch[2.2] /mɔx/ *v of food* to become tainted, fusty or rotten *17- NE*. [unknown]

moch[2.3] /mɔx/ *adj* **1** *of weather* humid; muggy *16-*. **2** *of food* impaired by damp, mouldy *19- NE*. **mochie 1** *of weather* humid; misty and oppressive, muggy *la18-*. **2** *of stored articles* impaired by damp, mouldy *19- NE*. **muchtie** = *mochie* (sense 1) *NE*. [unknown]

mocher /ˈmɔxər/ *v of cows* to feed well, especially on the best pasture; to pamper *la18- N*. [unknown]

Mochrum elder /ˈmɔxrəm ɛldər/ *n* the cormorant *la19- SW*. [named after *Mochrum*, a coastal parish in Wigtownshire]

mocht *see* MAY[2], MICHT[2], MOCH[1.2]

mock[1.1], †**mok** /mɔk/ *n* **1** an act of mockery or derision, a derisive utterance *la15-*. **2** an object of derision; a joke *16-*. **3** the very small egg sometimes laid by a hen and regarded as an omen of misfortune *la19- EC SW Bor*. **mockrife** scornful, mocking *19-*. [see the verb]

mock[1.2], †**mok** /mɔk/ *v* **1** to ridicule, deride, make fun of; to scoff, jeer *la15-*. **2** to delude, deceive *la15-16*. [ME *mokken*]

mockit *see* MAUKIT

mod[1] /mɔd/ *n in Gaelic-speaking areas* a council or parliament *19, 20- historical*. **the Mod** the annual Gaelic festival of music and literature first held at Oban in 1892 *la19-*. [Gael *mòd* a meeting, an assembly]

mod[2] /mɔd/ *n* a small object, a quantity of small objects or creatures *la19- Sh*. [ON *moð* the refuse of hay]

mød *see* MU

möddoo *see* MEEDIE

model[1.1] /ˈmɔdəl/ *n* **1** a design, a pattern, a representation, a mould *17-*. **2** an exact likeness *19-*. [EModE *model*]

model[1.2] /ˈmɔdəl/ *v* **1** to design, fashion *la17-*. **2** to organize (a military body) *la17-e18*. [see the noun]

model[2] /ˈmɔdəl/ *n* a hostel for single men; a hostel for the homeless *la19-*. **modeller** a person who lives in a MODEL[2] *la19- historical*. [reduced form of Eng *model lodging house*]

moder *see* MITHER

moderate[1.1] /ˈmɔdərət/ *n* a member of the moderate party in the Church of Scotland *19, 20- historical*. [see the adj]

moderate[1.2], †**moderat** /ˈmɔdəret/ *v* **1** to control, regulate so as to lessen something excessive *la16-*. **2** *Presbyterian Church* to preside over or chair a church court *17-*. **3** to preside over, chair (a discussion) *17*. **moderate in a call**, †**moderate a call** *of a presbytery* to preside over the election and induction of a minister to a vacant charge *la17-*. [Lat *moderāt-*, ptp stem of *moderārī*; compare MFr *moderer* for Presbyterian Church use]

moderate[1.3], †**moderat** /ˈmɔdərət/ *adj* **1** not excessive or extreme *16-*. **2** *Presbyterian Church* applied to the less rigorously Calvinist party *18-e19*. [Lat *moderātus*]

moderation, †**moderatioun** /mɔdəˈreʃən/ *n* **1** regulation, abatement of severity or excess *16-*. **2** the authority to

moderator 422 **molocate**

moderate in a call (MODERATE[1.2]) *18-.* **3** *Presbyterian Church* (the principles of) the MODERATE[1.3] (sense 2) party *18-e19.* **4** the office of MODERATOR (sense 1) *la16-e17.* [ME *moderacioun*, EModE *moderation*, Lat *moderātio*]

moderator, †**moderatour** /ˈmɔdəretər/ *n* **1** *Presbyterian Churches* the minister who presides over a church court *la16-.* **2** the chairman of the High Constables *17-.* **3** the chairman of the *Convention of Burghs* (CONVENTION) *la16-e17.* **4** a chairman, a president, an umpire *17-.* **the Moderator** *Presbyterian Church* **1** the minister chosen to preside over congregational meetings or kirk sessions *16-.* **2** the minister chosen to preside over the General Assembly of the Church of Scotland for one year *20-.* [ME *moderatour*]

modern, moderne *see* MOADERN

modern studies /ˈmɔdərn ˈstʌdiz/ *n in secondary schools* the study of local, national, international and political issues from a social and economic perspective *la20-.* [*modern* (MOADERN) + Eng *studies*]

modewarp, modewart *see* MOWDIEWORT

modify /ˈmɔdəfae, ˈmɔdɪfi/ *v* **1** to change so as to make less severe or extreme, abate *la17-.* **2** *law* to specify the exact amount of a payment or fine, assess at a precise sum *15-19.* **3** *Presbyterian Church* to determine the amount of a parish minister's stipend *la16-19.* **4** to determine and decree the nature and extent of a penalty or punishment *la15-e18.* **5** to award a payment *la16-e17.* †**modifiar** the person who prescribed the amount of a minister's stipend *la16-e17.* **modification**, †**modificatioun 1** alteration *19-.* **2** the assessment of a minister's stipend *la16-19.* **3** the assessment of a payment or penalty *la15-17.* [ME *modifien*, Lat *modificāre*]

modren *see* MOADERN

modywarp hyll *see* MOWDIEWORT

mofe *see* MOVE

Moffat measure /ˈmɔfət mɛʒər/ *n* a liberal amount of anything *la19- SW Bor.* [from the town in Dumfriesshire, once noted for the amount of ale brewed]

moger[1.1] /ˈmogər/ *n* a muddle, a mess; a bungle *19- N T WC SW.* [unknown]

moger[1.2], *N* **mooger**, *N* **myogre** /ˈmogər; *N* ˈmugər; *N* ˈmjogər/ *v* to work in a slovenly or messy way, botch a piece of work *20- N NE T WC SW.* [unknown]

moggan, moggin, *N* **moogan** /ˈmɔgən; *N* ˈmugən/ *n* **1** a woollen stocking; a stocking foot worn over the shoe to prevent slipping in wet or frosty weather *la18- Ork N NE T.* **2** the leg of a stocking; a coarse footless stocking; a protective covering for the legs made of sacking or straw ropes, worn for farm work *la18- N NE H&I.* **3** a mitten, a glove with one compartment for the thumb and another for the fingers *20- Ork N T.* **4** an old stocking leg used as a purse; a hoard of money *19- NE.* **mix yer moggans** *see* MIX. [unknown]

mogs /mogz/ *v* to trudge, struggle (through snow) *20- Ork.* [perhaps related to MOGGAN]

moich /mɔɪx/ *adj Travellers' language* silly, foolish, easily taken advantage of *la20-.* [unknown]

moidert, moidered /ˈmɔɪdərt/ *adj* confused, dazed *19- WC SW Bor Uls.* [unknown; compare Eng *moithered*]

moiety, †**moietie**, †**moyetie** /ˈmɔɪəte, ˈmɔɪəti/ *n* **1** an instalment (of a total payment); a share (in income); a small remuneration *la17-.* **2** a part, a portion *18-.* [ME *moite*, EModE *moietie*]

Moir *see* MOOR[1]

mois *see* MOSS[1.1]

moist *see* MAIST[1.1], MUIST[1.1], MUST[1.2]

moister, moisture, †**mosture**, †**moistour** /ˈmɔɪstər, ˈmɔɪstʃər/ *n* **1** liquid, water, especially as vapour or condensation; rain, tears *15-.* **2** *in medieval physiology* the property of humidity *la15-17.* [ME *moistur*]

†**moistify** *v humorous of drinking alcohol* to moisten, wet *la18-19.* [apparently coined by Robert Burns from Eng *moist*]

moistour, moisture *see* MOISTER

moit *see* MOTE[1]

moith *see* MOTH

mok *see* MOCK[1.1], MOCK[1.2]

†**molass, malasche, mallash** *n* alcohol distilled from molasses; whisky adulterated with this *la16-19.* **molassed** drunk on cheap alcohol *la18-e19.* [back-formation from MOLASSES, construed as pl]

molasses, †**malashes** /məˈlasɪz/ *n* raw sugar syrup, treacle *la17-.* Compare TRAICLE. [probably Port *melaços* or Spanish *melazos*]

mold *see* MOOL[1.1], MOOL[2]

mole[1.1], †**mold**, †**moll** /mol/ *n* a small burrowing mammal with dense dark fur and powerful forelimbs adapted for digging, *Talpa europaea 17-.* **molie** a mole-catcher *la19- N NE C.* **moleskin** *n* **1** a garment (especially trousers) made of shaved cotton fustian *19-.* **2** something true or reliable *20- NE.* **moleskin** *adj* true or reliable *20- NE T C SW.* [Fris, MDu *moll*]

mole[1.2] /mol/ *v* to loiter about, wander idly *20- NE.* [see the noun]

mole *see* MULL[1]

molendinar /mɔlənˈdʌɪnər/ *adj* belonging or relating to a mill or miller; frequently in place-names *la12-.* **molendinary** *n* a mill *e19.* **molendinary** *adj* = MOLENDINAR *19.* [Lat *molendīnārius*; adopted by Sir Walter Scott]

†**molest**[1.1] *n* harm, affliction *la14-16.* [ME *molest*]

molest[1.2] /məˈlɛst/ *v* to interfere with, attack; to distress, vex *la15-.* [ME *molesten*]

molestation, †**molestatioune** /mɔləˈsteʃən/ *n* **1** hostile interference, harassment *la15-.* **2** *law* the troubling or disturbing of a holder or occupier of lands in his legal possession *15-19, 20- historical.* [ME *molestacioun*]

molich *see* MOLLACH

moll *see* MOLE[1.1], MOW[1]

mollach, molich /ˈmɔləx, ˈmɔləx/ *v* to loiter about, wander idly *20- NE.* [intensive form of MOLE[1.2]]

mollacher /ˈmɔləxər/ *n* something impressively big *la20- C.* [unknown]

†**mollet** *n* a severe bit for an unruly horse, perhaps spiked or studded *16.* **mollet-bit** = MOLLET. [probably a variant of MULLET]

mollet *see* MULLET

mollicate *see* MOLOCATE

molliegrunt *see* MOLLIGRANT[1.2]

molligrant[1.1], **mullygrumph** /ˈmɔlegrant, ˈmʌlegrʌmf/ *n* a complaint; a state of dissatisfaction, a fit of sulks *19- Ork NE T EC Bor.* **molligrants** a fit of sulks *19- EC Bor.* [conflation of MOLLIGRUPS with *grant*, *grumph* to grunt]

molligrant[1.2], **molliegrunt** /ˈmɔlegrant, ˈmɔlegrʌnt/ *v* to complain, grumble *la19- NE T C.* [see the noun]

molligrups, mooligrubs /ˈmɔlegrʌps, ˈmulegrʌbz/ *n* a fit of melancholy or sulks; stomach-ache, colic *18-.* [altered form of Eng *mulligrubs*; also, compare MOULIE and *grups* (GRIP[1.1] (sense 3))]

molloncholious *see* MELANCHOLIOUS

mollop /ˈmɔləp/ *v* to be disdainful; to give oneself airs *19- Bor.* [unknown]

mollops /ˈmɔləps/ *npl* airs, antics, capers *19- Bor.* [unknown]

molocate, mollicate /ˈmɔloket, ˈmɔlɪket/ *v* to beat up, destroy *la20- C.* [unknown]

molten, moltin see MELT³, MOUTEN

moment, †mament /'momənt/ n **1** a very short time, an instant 15-. **2** importance, weight la16-. **moment-hand** the second hand of a watch or clock 19, 20- T EC. [ME moment, Lat mōmentum]

mon /mɔn/ prep among 20- NE T. [aphetic form of amon (AMANG)]

mon see MAN, MAUN¹·², MOAN

monacord see MONOCORD

Monanday see MONDAY

monarchy /'mɔnərke/ **1** a state governed by a king or queen; a system of government headed by a king or queen 15-. **2** a group of nations or states under the dominion of a single nation or its ruler, an empire la16. [ME monarchi]

mond see MUIND

Monday, Monanday, †Monounday, †Munonday, †Mounday /'mʌnde, 'mʌnənde/ n the day that comes after Sunday la14-. **Monday's haddie** a fish that has lost its freshness la19, 20- NE T Bor. [OE Mōnandæg]

mone see MANE¹·¹, MONEY, MUNE

†mones, monys, monish v pt, ptp **monest, monyst, monist** to urge, exhort; to warn; to remind; to reprove la14-e17. [perhaps altered form of ME monesten, AN monester]

monet see MONEY

moneth see MONEY, MONTH¹

money, †mone, †moneth, †monet /'mʌne/ n **1** wealth la14-. **2** coinage; currency la14-. **3** pl a sum or quantity of money 18-. **†the mone** the Scottish mint 15. [ME monei]

monie¹·¹**, mony** /'mone, 'mʌne, 'mɔne/ n a large number la14-. [see the adj]

monie¹·²**, mony, many** /'mone, 'mʌne, 'mɔne, 'mɛne/ adj **1** as a determiner designating a large indefinite number la14-. **2** with plural or collective nouns big, great, considerable la18-19, 20- Sh T. **†monyway** in many ways, many times over la14-16. **†monywise** = monyway. **for monie lang** = monie a lang. **many a, †many ane** a large indefinite number la14-. **monie a lang** for a long (time), for many (years) la18-19, 20- NE T. **monie a lang day** = monie a lang 19-. **mony a mickle maks a muckle** small quantities add together to make a lot; every little helps 20-. **mony a mony** very many 19- NE T SW. **†mony ane 1** following a noun many, in great number la14-e19. **2** many a person la14-19, 20- Sh NE. **monie a year and day** see YEAR. **many's the** many a la18-. [OE manig]

mönie /'møni/ n the spinal cord 20- Sh. [ON mæna the spinal marrow]

moniefauld¹·¹ /'monefɔld/ n the third stomach of a ruminant la18-; compare MONIPLIES (sense 2). **moniefaulds** the intestines 19- NE T. [MONIE¹·² + FAULD¹·¹]

moniefauld¹·²**, manifold** /'monefɔld, 'manəfold/ adj numerous and varied, occurring many times 15-. [OE manigfeald]

moniefauld¹·³**, manifold** /'monefɔld, 'manəfold/ adv many times over, in many and various ways 15-. [see the adj]

†moniest¹·¹**, monyast** n the greatest number, the majority 16-e19. [see the adj]

†moniest¹·²**, maniest** adj most 16-e18. [superlative of MONIE¹·²]

moniment, monument /'monɪmənt, 'monjəmənt/ n **1** a structure erected to commemorate something, a memorial la16-. **2** an object of ridicule or distaste, a laughing-stock; a rogue; a fool la18- Sh N NE T Bor. **3** a written record of the past; a relic; an antiquity la14-17; compare MUNIMENT. [Lat monimentum, monumentum]

moniplies /monɪ'plaez/ npl **1** a tortuous argument or statement 18-. **2** the third stomach of a ruminant 19, 20- EC; compare MONIEFAULD¹·¹. [MONIE¹·² + plies (PLY¹·¹)]

monish, monist see MONES

monition, †monitioun /mə'nɪʃən/ n **1** admonition, warning, instruction la14-. **2** Christian Church a formal charge, injunction or warning by an ecclesiastical authority 15-16. [AN monicion, MFr monition]

monk, †munk, †mounk /mʌŋk/ n **1** a member of a religious order la12-. **2** a monkfish la20- Sh. [OE munuc]

monkey, monke /'mʌŋke, 'mʌŋki/ n **1** a primate or other similar animal la16-. **2** a tool with a ratchet for tensioning fencing wire 20- C Bor. **monkey-chip** a variety of the game of marbles 20- NE WC. [unknown]

†monocord, monycord, monacord n a single-stringed musical instrument la15-17. [ME monocorde]

monopoly, †monopolie, †monopole, †monopol /mə'nɔpəle/ n **1** the exclusive right to control of the trade in a commodity 17-. **2** the exclusive right to or possession of anything 19-. **3** a seditious faction; a conspiracy 16-e17. [Lat monopōlium the exclusive right to control of the trade in a commodity, EModE monopoly]

Monounday see MONDAY

†Mons, Mounts n = MONS MEG la15-e17. [from the city of Mons in Belgium]

Mons Meg /mɔnz 'mɛg/ n a large 15th-century cannon, probably cast at Mons in Flanders, and now at Edinburgh Castle 17-. [MONS + MEG]

monstroasity /mon'strɔsəte/ n something which is outrageous or ridiculous la20-. [altered form of Eng monstrosity]

mont see MONTH², MOUNT, MUNT¹·²

montane see MOUNTAIN

†monter, munter, mounter n a watch la16-17. [MFr montre a clock face]

month¹**, Sh Ork munt, †moneth** /mʌnθ; Sh Ork mʌnt/ n **1** frequently uninflected following a plural numeral each of the twelve conventional, named divisions of the year; a period of approximately 30 days la14-. **2** following the name of a particular month: ◊December month already 19- T. **a month o munes** a month of Sundays, an impossibly long time, an eternity la19- Sh NE T Uls. [OE mōnaþ]

month²**, mounth, †mont, †mount** /mʌnθ, mʌnθ/ n a stretch of hilly or high ground; a mountain, a hill, a moor; frequently in place-names la12-17, 18- historical. **month-grass** cotton-grass la19 T. **the Mounth** the mountains of the eastern Highlands, the eastern Grampians of Angus and Kincardineshire south of the Dee la14-. [Gael monadh a hill, a moor, a range of hills, with influence from MOUNT]

monument see MONIMENT

mony see MONIE¹·¹, MONIE¹·²

monyast see MONIEST¹·¹

monycord see MONOCORD

monys, monyst see MONES

monzie see MUNSIE

moo see MOU¹·¹

mood see MUID

moodge see MUDGE¹·²

moog see MUG¹

moogan see MOGGAN

moogard see MUGGART

mooger see MAGER, MOGER¹·²

moogildin /mu'gɪldɪn/ n food a young coalfish or saithe roasted with the liver inside or stuffed with fish livers and roasted 19- Sh Ork. [unknown]

moogins see MUGGINS

mool¹·¹, **mould**, *NE* **meall**, †**muild**, †**mulde**, †**mold** /mul, muld, mold; *NE* mil/ *n* **1** the earth of the grave, the grave itself *15-*. **2** earth, soil, the surface of the earth *la15-*. **3** soil broken up in the process of cultivation, loose soil, lumps of earth *16-*. **4** *with reference to witchcraft* earth as the remains of a buried corpse *16-17*. **meelackie** = *mealock la19-*. **muilder** crumbled fragments of oatcake *la19- Sh Ork Uls*. **mealock**, **moolock 1** a crumb, a small fragment *la19-*. **2** a small wisp of straw *20- Sh N*. **mools** = MOOL¹·¹. **moolbred** *farming* the board or metal plate on a plough which turns the soil and makes the furrow *la14-*. **mould fur** the last furrow of a rig, ploughed on soil from which the sod has already been turned over *la19, 20- Ork NE T*. †**mulde-meyt** *in a funeral* grave food, a sacrificial roasting of meat as part of the ceremony *e16*. **abune the mool** alive, in this world *20- Sh Ork NE*. [OE *molde*]

mool¹·², **moul**, †**mule** /mul/ *v* **1** to make into crumbs, reduce to fragments *18-19, 20- NE T*. **2** *of persons* to mix well together, fraternize or associate; to co-operate; to curry favour *18-19, 20- NE Bor*. **3** to crumble (one substance with another) *la16-19, 20- NE*. **4** to bury, inter *19- Uls*. **mooler**, **muller**, *Ork* **mulder** to crumble into dust, decay *18-*. **moolin**, **millen** a crumb, a fragment *18-*. **mool in** = MOOL¹·² (sense 3) *la16-19, 20- Ork NE EC*. [see the noun]

mool², **mule**, **mould**, †**muild**, †**muld**, †**mold** /mul, muld, mold/ *n* **1** a pattern; a matrix; a template *la15-*. **2** a buttonmould of bone or metal; a button made of such a mould covered with cloth; a flat linen-covered button *18-*. †**muldry** moulded work, moulding; ornamental masonry, ornamentation in wood *16-17*. **meelie** = MOOL² (sense 2) *20- NE*. [ME *mold*]

moolet /'mulət/ *v* to whimper, whine *19- WC*. [unknown]

moolie¹·¹, **meelie**, *Sh* **müldie** /'mule, 'mili; *Sh* 'møldi/ *n* **1** *children's games* a marble made of burnt clay *la19, 20- N NE WC*. **2** dry crumbs of peat *20- Sh*. [MOOL¹·¹ + -IE¹]

moolie¹·², **mooly**, *Sh* **müldy** /'mule, 'muli; *Sh* 'møldi/ *adj* **1** earthy, deep in the soil *19-*. **2** *of earth* crumbled, finely broken up *19, 20- Sh Ork*. **3** liable to crumble, crumbling *la19- C*. [see the noun]

mooligrubs *see* MOLLIGRUPS

moolkin /'mulkɪn/ *n* a beating *20- WC*. [verbal noun from Gael *mulc* to push, butt]

moolly *see* MOULIE

moolock *see* MOOL¹·¹

mooly /'mule/ *n* a term of affection, usually to a child *20- N H&I EC*. [Gael *m'ulaidh* my treasure]

mooly *see* MOOLIE¹·²

moon *see* MUNE

moonlight *see* MUNELICHT

moontain *see* MOUNTAIN

moop *see* MOUP¹·²

Moor¹, †**More**, †**Moir** /mur/ *n* **1** a native of ancient Mauretania; a person with dark skin *16-*. **2** a person dressed up as a Moor *la16*. †**moris**, **moreis**, **morys** Moorish *16*. [ME *more*, EModE *more*]

moor²·¹ /mur/ *n* dense, powdery snow *la19- Sh Ork*. **moorie** = MOOR²·¹ *20- Sh Ork*. [see the verb]

moor²·² /mur/ *v* **1** *of snow* to fall densely, pile up in drifts *la19- Sh Ork*. **2** *of a person* to be choked with a cold *20- Ork*. [probably back-formation from MOORCAVIE; in sense 2, perhaps also influenced by SMORE¹·²]

moor *see* MUIR

mooratoog /'murətug, 'mørətug/ *n* an ant *19- Sh*. [ON *maurr* an ant + TOOG]

moorcavie, **mooriekaavie** /'murkavi, 'murikavi/ *n* a blinding snowstorm *la19- Sh*. [Norn *murkavi*; compare Faer *murrakàvi*]

moorit¹·¹ /'murɪt/ *n* a reddish-brown coloured Shetland sheep or its wool *19- Sh Ork*. [see the adj]

moorit¹·² /'murɪt/ *adj* reddish-brown, describing one of the traditional colours of a Shetland sheep or its wool *la18- Sh Ork*. [ON *mórauðr*]

moorment *see* MUIRMENT

moose, **mouse**, †**mous**, †**mows** /mus, mʌus/ *n pl* **mice** †**myse**, †**myce 1** a small rodent, a mouse *15-*. **2** a small lead weight tied to a cord, used by tradesmen to guide cords into sash and case windows or to drop wires behind plaster *20-*. **3** the lump of flesh or tissue at the end of a leg of mutton *la18-e19*. **mouse-cheep** the squeak of a mouse *la19-*. **mouse dirt**, †**mysdirt** mouse excrement *la15-*. **mouse-fa**, †**mouse-fall** a mousetrap *la17-19, 20- Sh EC*. **mouse grass** the silver hair-grass *Aira caryophyllea 20- Sh NE*. **moosie hawk** the kestrel *Falco tinnunculus la19- Ork*. **mouse moulding** a narrow strip of wood shaped to fill the angle between floor and skirting board or wall to prevent the passage of mice *20-*. **mouse pea**, †**mouse pease** (one of) various species of vetch *la16-19, 20- Sh Ork N SW*. **mousewab**, †**mouswob** a spider's web, a cobweb *la16-*. **mouse weasel** a small female weasel *20- N NE SW*. **mak mice feet o**, **mak like mice feet** to reduce to fragments, destroy; to confound *18- Sh NE*. **the mouse in the meal girnel** a children's game *20- Ork*. [OE *mūs*]

moosh¹·¹ /muʃ/ *n* crumbly material *20- N*. [see the verb]

moosh¹·² /muʃ/ *v* to crumble away, decay *20- N*. ? [perhaps altered form of Gael *muisean* a dirty thing]

moosh¹·³ /muʃ/ *adj* crumbly, rotten, mouldy *20- N*. [see the verb]

moosin *see* MOZE¹·²

moosk *see* MUSK

mooskin *see* MOSKIN

moost /must/ *v* to smell, become mouldy *la19- NE*. [probably a conflation of MOOSH¹·² or Eng *must* with FOOST¹·²]

moot¹·¹ /mut/ *n* a whisper, a hint *19, 20- Sh N NE*. Compare MUTE. [see the verb]

moot¹·², †**mute**, †**mwte** /mut/ *v* **1** to speak, discuss; to say, utter, divulge; to hint, insinuate *la14-*. **2** to argue, plead, protest; to take an action or person to court, litigate *la14-17*. Compare MUTE. [OE *mūtian*]

moot² /mut/ *n* a tiny creature, a child *19 Sh N*. **mootie** diminutive, tiny *la19- Sh*. [Norn *mutt*]

moot *see* MOUT¹·¹, MOUT¹·²

mooth¹·¹, **mou**, **mouth**, **mow**, †**mowth** /muθ, mu, mʌuθ, mʌu/ *n* **1** the outfall of a river, frequently in place-names *la11-*. **2** the oral orifice, or the cavity immediately behind this opening *la14-*. **3** the open end or entrance of a cave, a passage, a container, a tract of country or a harbour *la14-*. **4** a spokesperson *la16-*. **5** a mouthful, something to eat or drink *19-*. **6** a garrulous, boastful person *la19-*. **7** the blade (of a shovel or spade) *19- Sh Ork NE T EC SW*. **8** the beginning (of a season, day or event) *19- NE T SW*. **9** the open top of a shoe *20- Ork NE SW*. **10** a speech, an utterance *la18, 20- WC SW*. **11** the end of a peat-stack from which peats are taken for use *la19- NE*. **mou'd**, †**mouthit**, †**mowit**, **mowitt** having a mouth of the sort specified *16-*. **moothfu**, †**moothful** a quantity that fills the mouth *la15-*. **mou bag** a horse's nosebag *la19-*. **mou-band** *v* to utter, express, mention *la17- NE WC*. †**mou-band** *n* conversation, a gossip *19*. **mow-bund** tongue-tied; unable to master a pronunciation *20-*. †**mouth-cloth** a cloth for wiping the mouth, a facecloth *17-e18*. **mouth cord** the rope linking the inner

bit rings of a pair of horses to keep them together *20- WC*.
mou-poke = *mou bag 19-*. †**mouth thankles** the pudenda *16-e17*. **in the mooth o the poke** at the outset, barely started *19- NE T C*. **pit oot o mooth** to dismiss as a topic of conversation *20- Sh*. **tak a moothfu o** to enunciate deliberately or emphatically *20- Sh Ork N C*. **wi mooth and een** in a gaping, staring manner, very close-up *la19, 20- NE*. [OE *mūþ*]

mooth[1,2], **mouth, mou** /muθ, mʌuθ, mu, mʌu/ *v* to tell, utter, mention *19, 20- Sh C*. [see the noun]

mooth[2], *Sh Ork Bor* **muif**, *Sh Ork N* **meef**, †**meeth** /muθ; *Sh Ork Bor* muf; *Sh Ork N* mif/ *adj* **1** *of the atmosphere* oppressively close and humid *la18-, 20- N*. **2** *of persons* oppressed or exhausted by heat *la18-19, 20- N*. **3** cheerful *la18-e19*. **müffin** *of weather* close and sultry *20- Sh*. **moothlie** in a soft, smooth way *19-*. **meethness** an oppressively hot and humid atmosphere *la18- NE WC Bor*. **moothy** = MOOTH[2] (sense 1) *20- Ork C Bor*. [ON *móða* condensed vapour, mist]

moothie /ˈmuθi, ˈmuθe/ *n* a mouth-organ *20-*. [MOOTH[1,1] + -IE[1]]

moot-hill, †**mute-hill**, †**mwtehill** /ˈmuthɪl/ *n* a hill on which assemblies were held *15-e17, 19- historical*. [MUTE + HILL[1]]

mooze *see* MOZE[1,1], MOZE[1,2]

mop-mop *see* MOUP[1,1]

†**moppat, moppet, mappat** *n* a mop, an implement for applying, cleaning, sealing or applying fluids to metal (gun barrels or wheels) or wood, frequently a sheepskin or waste cloth *16-e17*. [unknown; compare MFr *mappe* a napkin]

moppie *see* MOUP[1,1]

mora /ˈmɔrə/ *n law* a delay in asserting a right or claim which, when coupled with prejudice to the defender, may prevent the pursuer from succeeding *18-*. [Lat *mora* a delay]

Moray /ˈmʌre/ *n* the ancient northern Scottish province, originally extending from the rivers Nairn to Deveron, and now comprising geographically the counties of Elgin and Nairn. †**Moray coast** a hard subsoil found along the coast of the Moray Firth *la18-e19*. **Moray pan** = *Moray coast 19-*. [Gael *Moireabh* sea-settlement]

more *see* MAIR[1,1], MAIR[1,2], MAIR[1,3], MUIR

More, moreis *see* MOOR[1]

morg *see* MURG

morgeoun *see* MURGEON[1,2]

morgeown *see* MURGEON[1,1]

morie *see* MORRA

morkin /ˈmɔrkən/ *n* a sheep that has died of natural causes *la18- SW Bor*. [ME *mortkin*]

mormaer, †**maormor** /ˈmɔrmer/ *n* a high steward of one of the ancient Celtic provinces of Scotland *19- historical*. [Gael *mórmhaor*]

morn, †**morne** /mɔrn, morn/ *n* the early part of the day, the (early) morning *la14-*. **the morn** tomorrow, the following morning or day *la14-*. **the morn-come-never** the morrow that never comes, the end of time *19- C Bor*. †**the morne day** the following day *la14-15*. †**the morne eftir** the day following *la14-e17*. **the morn's efternuin** tomorrow afternoon *la19-*. **the morn's morn** tomorrow morning *20-*. **the morn's morning** tomorrow morning *19-*. **the morn's nicht** tomorrow night *la17-*. †**the morne nixt eftir** the day following *la14-e17*. [OE *morgen*]

mornin, moarnin, morning /ˈmɔrnɪn, ˈmornɪn, ˈmɔrnɪŋ/ *n* **1** the early part of the day *la14-*. **2** the early part of the following day, tomorrow morning *la14-*. **3** a glass of spirits or a snack taken before breakfast; a mid-morning drink or snack *17-*. **morning-blink** the first glimmer of daylight *la17-19, 20- Sh*. **morning drink** a drink taken in the forenoon or during the mid-morning break from work *la16-*. †**morning gift** = *morrowing gift* (MORRA) *16*. **morning piece** a snack taken during the mid-morning break from work *la19-*. **morning roll** a bread roll *la19-*. **in the mornings** in the morning *la19, 20- Sh Ork NE EC*. [ME *morning*]

Morningside /ˈmɔrnɪŋsʌɪd/ *n* a very over-refined pronunciation of Scottish English *20-*. **Morningside speed** *slang* cocaine *la20- EC*. [from the name of a district of Edinburgh]

morra, morie, morrow, †**morow** /ˈmɔrə, ˈmɔrə, ˈmore, ˈmɔro/ *n* **1** tomorrow *la15-*. **2** the morning *15-e17*. †**morrowing** morning *16 literary*. †**morrowing gift, morwyngift** a settlement or endowment of money or property made (usually) by the husband to the wife on the morning after their marriage *15-16*. **the morra** tomorrow *17-*. **the morrow's morning, the morrow morning, the morrow's morn** the following morning, tomorrow morning *la17-, 20- C Uls*. [ME *morwe*]

morrow *see* MARROW[1,1], MARROW[1,2], MORRA

morrowing gift *see* MORRA

†**mors** *v* to prime (a gun) *16-e17*. **mozing hole, motion hole** the touch-hole of a gun *la18-e19*. **morsing powder** priming powder *la16-19*. [aphetic form of MFr *amorcer* to prime (a gun)]

mort[1], †**morth** /mɔrt/ *n* **1** a dead body *la15-19, 20- literary*. **2** the skin of a sheep that has died of natural causes *19, 20- Bor*. †**mort batell** a fight to the death *16*. **mort-bell** a bell rung at funerals *la16-19, 20- historical*. **mort brod** a wooden memorial plaque *20- Ork*. **mort cauld** a severe head cold *18-19, 20- Sh*. †**mort charge** freight with a high weight-to-bulk ratio which paid lower freightage *16-e17*. **mortclaith, mortcloth**, †**mortclathe 1** a pall covering a coffin on its way to the grave *la15-*. **2** the fee paid to the kirk session for the hire of a cloth to cover a coffin *17-19, 20- historical*. †**mortcloth money** money paid for the hire of a cloth to cover a coffin *17-18*. †**mortfundyit** deadly cold *e16*. **mort head 1** a representation of a skull *la16-19, 20- literary*. **2** a turnip lantern representing a skull *19- NE*. **3** a human skull *17-19*. **mort kist**, †**mort chest**, †**mort chist** a coffin *la16-*. **mort lambskin** the skin of a sheep or lamb that has died of natural causes *la17-19, 20- Bor*. **mort safe** an iron grid placed over a grave or coffin to deter body snatchers *19, 20- historical*. †**mort stand** a set of ecclesiastical vestments or altar-cloths used for funeral services *16*. **yer morth o cauld** your death of cold *19- SW Uls*. [ME *mort* death]

mort[2] /mɔrt/ *n* a girl or woman; a wife *19, 20- NE T EC SW*. Compare MOT. [unknown; used in Travellers' language]

mortal[1,1], †**mortall** /ˈmɔrtəl/ *n* a living being *la16-*. †**aganis all mortall** *of a legal agreement* against all people *la15-17*. [see the adj]

mortal[1,2], †**mortall**, †**mortale**, †**mortell** /ˈmɔrtəl/ *adj* **1** subject to death; transitory *15-*. **2** deadly, fatal, lethal *la15-*. **3** *of war or combat* fought to the death *15-*. **4** completely intoxicated *19-*. **mortalled** completely intoxicated *la20-*. **mortally** exceedingly, completely: ◊*he was mortally fond of her la18-*. **mortal end** the end of everything *20-*. [ME *mortal*]

mortal[1,3] /ˈmɔrtəl/ *adv* exceedingly; completely: ◊*he was getting mortal angry 19-*. **mortal drunk** completely intoxicated *19-*. **mortal fou** completely intoxicated *19-*. [see the adj]

mortale *see* MORTAL[1,2]

mortall *see* MORTAL[1,1], MORTAL[1,2]

mortancestor, mortancestry *see* BRIEF[1,1]

mortar stane /ˈmɔrtər sten/ *n* a hollowed stone used as a mortar for pounding barley *16-19, 20- historical*. [OE *mortere*, Lat *mortārium*]

mortell *see* MORTAL[1,2]

†**mortercheyn, mortichein** *n* glanders, a disease of horses *17-19*. [perhaps Fr *mort d'échine* spinal death]
mortfundyit *see* MORT¹
morth *see* MORT¹
mortichein *see* MORTERCHEYN
mortifee *see* MORTIFY
mortification, †**mortificatioun** /mɔrtəfɪ'keʃən/ *n* **1** the action of controlling lust by self-denial or physical discipline *la15-*. **2** extreme embarrassment *18-*. **3** *law* the assignment of land, property or money to an ecclesiastical or charitable body; the document embodying a deed making such an assignment *la15-19, 20- historical*. [ME *mortificacioun*]
mortify, mortifee, †**mortifie** /'mɔrtəfae, 'mɔrtəfi/ *v* **1** to bring oneself under control by self-denial, abstinence or discipline *la15-*. **2** to embarrass, shame or humiliate *18-*. **3** *law* to bequeath land, property or money to an ecclesiastical body or charitable institution in perpetuity *la15-e19, la19- historical*. **mortifier** the donor of a lands, property or money for religious or charitable purposes *17-e19, la19- historical*. [ME *mortifien*]
mortis causa¹·¹ /'mɔrtɪs 'kɔzə/ *adj of a deed or bequest* taking effect on the death of the grantor *la19-*. [Lat *mortis causā* by reason of death]
mortis causa¹·² /'mɔrtɪs 'kɔzə/ *adv law* by reason of the death of the grantor *la19-*. [see the adj]
mortoun *see* MARTIN
morwyngift *see* MORRA
morys *see* MOOR
mos *see* MOSS¹·¹
mosh /mɔʃ/ *n in marbles* a hollow scooped in the ground in which the target marble is placed *20- C*. **moshie** a game of marbles involving three hollows scooped in the ground *20- C*. [unknown]
mosie /'mozi/ *adj* the name applied to a coal seam of variable thickness in the Clackmannanshire coalfield *la18- T EC*. Compare *coal mosie* (COAL). [unknown]
mosin *see* MOZE¹·²
moskin, mooskin /'mɔskɪn, 'muskɪn/ *adj* rotting, decayed; musty *20- Sh*. [Norw dial *mausken*; but compare MUSKANE]
moss¹·¹, †**mos,** †**mois** /mɔs/ *n* **1** boggy ground, moorland *13-*. **2** a peat bog; a stretch of moorland allocated to tenants for cutting fuel *13-*. **3** a plant of the class *Musci 19-*. **4** moss-like plants used as fodder *la16-19, 20- N WC Bor*. **5** turf or soil from a bog *16-19*. **mosser 1** a person who cuts and dries peats *la19-*. **2** a Border cattle reiver *la17, la19- historical*. **mossing 1** peat cutting *19-*. **2** a crop of cotton grass *la19- N*. **mossy** boggy, peaty *16-*. **moss aik, moss oak** the wood of ancient oak trees preserved in peat bog *la18-*. **moss bank** a place where peats are cut *la18-*. **moss bluiter** the common snipe *Gallinago gallinago 19- SW Bor*. **moss cheeper** the meadow pipit *Anthus pratensis la17-*. **moss corn, mascorn** silverweed *Argentina anserina*; its edible root *19-*. **moss crop** cotton grass *la17-*. **moss duck** the mallard *Anas platyrhynchos 19-*. **moss fir** the wood of ancient fir trees preserved in peat bog *18-19, 20- T*. **moss flow** a wet peat bog *19- T C SW Bor*. **moss grieve** the estate official in charge of the rights of peat-cutting in a moss *la17- N NE T*. **moss ground 1** boggy ground; a peat bank *18-*. **2** soil, turf or peat from a bog *17*. **moss hag 1** dangerous boggy moorland *18-*. **2** a pit in moorland where peats have been cut *20- C Bor*. **moss hole** dangerous boggy moorland *la17-*. **moss laird** a tenant given an area of moorland rent-free or at reduced rent in return for draining and cultivating it *la18-19, 20- historical*. †**moss leave, mos leive** the right or permission to cut peats in a moss *la16-e18*. **moss mail,** †**mos maill** rent paid for the right of cutting peats in a moss *16-19, 20- NE*. †**moss mingin, moss mining** the cranberry *Vaccinium oxycoccos 19*. **moss pot** a water-filled pit in a peat bog *18- NE*. **moss road** a track to a peat bog *19-*. †**moss room** a portion of a peat bog assigned to a tenant for his own use *16-19*. **moss trooper,** †**mos trouper** a Border cattle reiver *17-19, 20- historical*. **Moss o' Byth** the ace of spades *20-*. [OE *mōs* a bog]
moss¹·² /mɔs/ *v* to cut peats in a peat bog *19- NE EC Uls*. [see the noun]
most *see* MAIST¹·¹, MAST¹·¹, MUST²
moste *see* MUST²
mosture *see* MOISTER
møsty *see* MUST¹
mot /mɔt/ *n* a wife *20- NE*. Compare MORT². **motie 1** a wife *20- NE*. **2** an easy-going person *20- NE*. [perhaps a variant of MORT²]
mot *see* MAT²
mote¹, **moat,** †**mott,** †**moit** /mot/ *n* **1** a natural or man-made mound or hillock; an embankment *15-*. **2** a ditch; a tidal moat *la16-17*. **motehill,** †**mothill,** †**moathill** a mound, a hillock *la15-*. [ME *mote*]
mote²·¹ /mɔt/ *n* **1** a particle of dust *la14-*. **2** a speck, a fragment, a crumb *16-19, 20- Sh Ork EC Bor*. **3** a flaw, a blemish; a fault *la16-19, 20- NE Bor*. **moty, motty** flecked with specks of dust *la16-* [OE *mot* an atom, a particle]
mote²·² /mɔt/ *v* **1** to remove pieces of fluff from cloth *la17-19, 20- NE SW*. **2** to clear of specks or particles *19, 20- NE*. **3** to criticize; to find fault *16-19*. [see the noun]
mote *see* MAT², MUTE
moth, †**moith** /mɔθ/ *n* **1** an insect of the order *Lepidoptera*, a clothes moth *la15-*. **2** something which erodes or diminishes happiness or wealth *la17-18*. Compare MOCH¹·¹. [OE *moþþe*]
mother, mothir *see* MITHER
mothy /'mɔθi/ *adj* unaired, damp *18-19, 20- Bor*. [probably a variant of *mochie* (MOCH²·³)]
motif *see* MOTIVE
motion hole *see* MORS
motive, †**motif** /'motɪv/ *n* an incentive or reason to act *15-*. †**of your awin fre motive** *law* freely, without coercion *la15-e18*. [ME *motif*]
mott /mɔt/ *n* a mark or target in quoits or marbles *19, 20- EC Bor*. [probably Fr *motte* a small heap of earth or MOTE¹]
mott *see* MOTE¹
mottoune *see* MUTTON
mou¹·¹, **moo, mow** /mu, mʌu/ *n* **1** a heap of unthreshed grain or hay (in a barn) *la14-*. **2** a recess in a barn where unthreshed grain is heaped *la19-*. **3** a large vertical section of a haystack *20- NE SW*. **4** a pile or stack of peats *la18-19*. **5** a stack of wood *e16*. [OE *mūga* a heap (of hay etc)]
mou¹·² /mu, mʌu/ *v* to pile up unthreshed grain or hay in a barn *19- SW Bor*. [see the noun]
mou *see* MOOTH¹·¹, MOOTH¹·², MOW²·¹
mouchless *see* MAUCHT
moud /mʌud/ *n* a clothes moth *19- Bor*. Compare MOCH¹·¹, MOTH. [Eng *mowt*]
mou'd *see* MOOTH¹·¹
mouden *see* MOUTEN
moudie *see* MOWDIE
moudyskin *see* MOWDIE
mouf *see* MUFF
mought *see* MAUCHT
mougre /'mugər/ *v* to cast a shadow over; to create gloom or despondency *19- H&I*. [Gael *mùig* to suppress; to become gloomy]
†**moul**¹·¹, †**mowle** *v* to grow mouldy *la16-e19*. [ON *mygla*]

moul[1,2], †**mowld**, †**mowlit** /mul/ *adj* mouldy *15-19, 20- NE T EC*. [see the verb]

moul[2], †**mowl** /mul/ *n* a chilblain (on the heel) *16-19, 20- Sh N WC*. **moolie heel** a heel affected with chilblains *la18-19, 20- N H&I EC Bor*. [ME *mule*]

moul *see* MOOL[1,2]

mould *see* MOOL[1,1], MOOL[2]

moulie, **moolly**, †**moulyie** /'muli, 'mule/ *adj* 1 mouldy *la16-19, 20- N NE T C*. 2 parsimonious, avaricious *19, 20- C Bor*. 3 *of money* long-hoarded, carefully guarded *19, 20- C Bor*. [MOUL[1,1] + -IE[2], ME *mouli*]

Mounday *see* MONDAY

mounk *see* MONK

mount, **munt**, †**mont** /mʌunt; *C* mʌnt/ *n* 1 a mountain *la14-*. 2 a low tree-covered hill *la19- C*. 3 high land, moorland *la16-e17*. Compare MONTH[2]. [OE *munt*]

mount *see* MONTH[2], MUNT[1,1], MUNT[1,2]

mountain, **moontain**, **muntain**, †**montane** /'mʌuntən, 'muntən, 'mʌntən/ *n* a landmass rising to great height above its surroundings; a large hill *la14-*. **mountaineer** 1 a mountain dweller *19-*. 2 a person who climbs mountains *la19-*. 3 a persecuted Covenanter *18-19*. **mountain dew** (illicitly distilled) whisky *19, 20- literary*. **Mountain-men** a group of persecuted Covenanters who took refuge in the mountains of Galloway *18-e19, 20- historical*. [ME *mountain*]

mounter *see* MONTER

mounth *see* MONTH[2]

Mounts *see* MONS

moup[1,1] /mʌup/ *n* 1 a child's word for a rabbit *20- N SW Bor*. 2 the antirrhinum *20- SW Bor*. **moppie** a child's word for a rabbit *20- NE T Bor*. **mop-mop** a child's word for a rabbit *20- WC SW Bor*. Compare MAP[1], MAPPIE, MAPPIE-MOU. [onomatopoeic]

moup[1,2], **mowp**, †**moop** /mʌup/ *v* 1 to twitch the lips; to nibble or munch *16-19, 20- C SW Bor*; compare MAP[1]. 2 to consort or live with *la18-19, 20- SW*. 3 to mumble *19, 20- Bor*. [see the noun]

mourie *see* MOWRIE

mourn *see* MURN[1,1], MURN[1,2]

mournin *see* MURNIN

mous, **mouse** *see* MOOSE

mouser, **mowser** /'mʌusər, 'mʌuzər/ *n* a moustache *20-*. [Eng *mouser* cat, in relation to its whiskers]

moust *see* MUIST[1,1]

moustache, **moutash**, **moutache**, **matash** /mə'staʃ, mu'taʃ; *Sh T* mə'taʃ/ *n* a strip of hair growing above the upper lip *la16-*. [EModE *mustaches*, Fr *moustache*]

mout[1,1], **moot** /mʌut, mut/ *n* the process or period of moulting in birds *19- C Bor Uls*. [see the verb]

mout[1,2], **moot**, †**mowt** /mʌut, mut/ *v* 1 *of a bird* to moult *la15-19, 20- C SW Bor*. 2 to crumble, fall into decay *19, 20- Sh EC Bor*. 3 to squander, dissipate *19, 20- Sh Bor*. †**mout-it** decayed, worn away; shabby *16-19*. **mootnafeed** worn away, crumbled into decay *20- Sh*. [Lat *mūtāre* to change]

moutache, **moutash** *see* MOUSTACHE

mouten, **molten**, *NE* **mouden**, †**moltin**, †**meltyne** /'mʌutən, 'mɔltən; *NE* 'mʌudən/ *adj* 1 *of metal* liquefied by heat; melted and solidified again *la14-*. 2 *of fat* clarified *la19- NE*. [ptp of MELT[3]]

mouter *see* MULTURE[1,1]

mouth *see* MOOTH[1,1], MOOTH[1,2]

moutoun *see* MUTTON

movable[1,1], **moveable**, †**movabill** /'muvəbəl/ *n* law personal property as opposed to heritable property *la16-*. [see the adj]

movable[1,2], **moveable**, †**movabill**, †**moabill**, †**mufabill** /'muvəbəl/ *adj* 1 transportable *15-*. 2 *of personal property* not heritable and thus passing to the next of kin instead of to the heir-at-law *15-*. 3 *of a tenant* without security of tenure; not entered on a rental *la17*. [ME *mevable*, OFr *movable*]

move, **muve**, *NE* **meeve**, †**mufe**, †**mofe**, †**meve** /muv; *NE* miv/ *v* 1 to go or proceed; to change position *la14-*. 2 to advance or progress; to incite or instigate *la14-*. 3 to arouse emotion *la14-*. 4 *of inherited property* to derive from a predecessor *la15*. **movement**, **muvement** 1 the process or manner of moving *la15-*. 2 an urge, an impulse, an inclination *la15-*. †**meevie nor mavie** *in the North East* not a movement or sound *19*. [ME *meven*, *mōven*, OFr *movoir*]

moveable *see* MOVABLE[1,1], MOVABLE[1,2]

†**movir**, **mure** *adj* quiet, gentle, mild *15*. [ME *mure*; for *-v-* compare SOVER[1,2]]

†**mow**[1], **moll** *n* dust, mould; crumbled fragments *la14-18*. **mulloch**, **malloch** the crumbled refuse of peat *19*. [ME *mol*; compare Flem, Du *mol* dust]

†**mow**[2,1], **mou** *n* 1 a derisive grimace *la15-e17*. 2 a joke, a prank; a piece of fun *16-e17*; compare MOWS[1,1]. **mowar** a person who mocked or joked *la15-e16*. [ME *moue*]

†**mow**[2,2] *v* 1 to mock or deride *la15-e17*. 2 to joke or fool around *16*. [see the noun]

mow[3] /mʌu/ *v* to have sex with, to copulate *16-19, 20- literary*. [probably euphemistic use of MOW[2,2]]

mow *see* MOOTH[1,1], MOU[1,1]

mowar *see* MOW[2,1]

mowdie, **moudie** /'mʌudi, 'mʌude/ *n* 1 a mole *Talpa europaea* *la18-*. 2 a mole-catcher *la19- C Bor*. **mowdie-hill**, **moudiehill** a molehill *18-19, 20- literary*. **mowdiehillock**, **moudie hillock** a molehill *la17-19, 20- WC SW*. **mowdieman** a mole-catcher *19- C SW Bor*. **mowdieskin**, **moudie skin** the skin of a mole *19, 20- NE SW*. [reduced form of MOWDIEWORT]

mowdiewort, †**modewarp**, †**modewart** /'mʌudiwɔrt, 'mʌudiwʌrt/ *n* 1 a mole *Talpa europaea* *la15-*. 2 an underhand person; a spy or informer *19, 20- C*. 3 a reclusive or retiring person *la19- NE T EC*. 4 a mole or wart on the skin *20- WC SW*. 5 a small dark child with a lot of hair *la16-19*. **mowdiewort hill**, †**modywarp hyll** a molehill *16-*. [OE *molde* earth + OE *weorpan* to throw]

mowdy /'mʌudi 'mʌude/ *v* to loiter; to prowl furtively *20- WC*. [probably figurative use of MOWDIE]

mowl *see* MOUL[2]

mowld *see* MOUL[1,2]

mowle *see* MOUL[1,1]

mowlin *see* MOYLIE

mowlit *see* MOUL[1,2]

mowp *see* MOUP[1,2]

mowrie, †**mourie** /'mʌuri/ *n* 1 gravel mingled with sand; shingle *la17- NE*. 2 a gravelly beach *la19- NE*. [Gael *morfhaich* land liable to flooding by the sea; compare also Gael *morghan* gravel, shingle beach]

mows[1,1] /mʌuz/ *npl* banter, fun; a joke *la15-19, 20- NE*. †**in mows** in jest; as a joke *16-e18*. **nae mows** no laughing matter; a serious situation *16-19, 20- NE T EC*. [plural form of MOW[2,1]]

mows[1,2] /mʌuz/ *adj* safe, harmless, circumspect *la19- NE*. [see the noun]

mows *see* MOOSE

mowser *see* MOUSER

mowt *see* MOUT[1,2]

mowth *see* MOOTH[1,1]

†**moy** *adj* demure, prim, meek *15-e18*. [probably MDu *mooy* elegant, handsome]

moyen[1.1], **myen**, †**myane**, †**miene** /ˈmɔɪən, ˈmaeən/ *n* **1** power; influence; mediation, intercession *15-19, 20- NE.* **2** foreknowledge *la19- NE.* **3** a means, an agency *15-17.* **4** resources, funds *16-17.* **5** an agent or intermediary *la16-e17.* [ME *mene*, MFr *moyen*; compare MYANCE]

moyen[1.2] /ˈmɔɪən/ *v* **1** to bring about; to contrive or arrange; to persuade or induce *la16-19, 20- NE T.* **2** to recommend a person *la19- NE T.* [see the noun]

†**moyen**[2.1], **myon**, **myane** *n* a medium-sized culverin *16-e17.* [probably shortened form of MFr *coulevrine moyenne*]

†**moyen**[2.2], **myane**, **mayan** *adj of a culverin* medium-sized *16.* [MFr *moyenne*, as in *coulevrine moyenne*]

moyetie *see* MOIETY

moy-foy /ˈmɔɪ fɔɪ/ *n* **1** a perishable or decaying object; a state of ruination *20- Ork.* **2** *pl* mischief, pranks *20- Sh.* [Norw *måfå* something useless or meaningless]

moylie, **mowlin** /ˈmɔɪle, ˈmʌulən/ *n* **1** a hornless cow or bullock *19- SW.* **2** a hornless wild goat *20- SW.* [HibEng *moyley, moileen*]

moyn *see* MUNE

moze[1.1], *Sh N* **mooze** /moz; *Sh N* muz/ *n* decay, dampness, dry rot *la19- Sh Ork*; compare MOSKIN. **mozie**, **moozy** decayed, damp, mouldy *la19- Sh Ork WC.* [Norn *mos* a state of decomposition]

moze[1.2], *Sh N* **mooze** /moz; *Sh N* muz/ *v* to decay, to become musty or mouldy *20- Sh Ork N*; compare MOSKIN. **mosin**, **moosin 1** musty, mildewed *la19- Sh Ork N.* **2** numb *la19- Sh.* [see the noun]

mozing hole *see* MORS

mu /mu/ *n* a wasting disease of sheep, sheep-rot *19- Sh.* **mød** affected with sheep-rot *20- Sh.* [Norn *mu* a wasting away]

much *see* MUTCH

muchin, **muchkin** *see* MUTCHKIN

muchtie *see* MOCH[2.3]

muck[1.1], †**muk**, †**mwk** /mʌk/ *n* **1** dung, farmyard manure *la15-.* **2** dirt, filth; refuse, rubbish *la15-.* **muckafy** to make dirty *la19- Sh.* †**muck-bell** a silver bell given annually in Dumfries to the winner of the horse-race in which the town's refuse-collectors participated *la17-e18.* †**muck-creel** a pannier or hamper used for taking dung to the fields *la15-e19.* †**muck-fail**, **muck feal** turf mixed with dung to form a manure or compost *17-19.* **muck flee** a bluebottle; a dung-fly *20-.* **muck-hack** a pronged muck-rake *la18-19, 20- EC Bor.* **muck kishie** = *muck-creel la19- Sh.* **muckman** a refuse-collector and street cleaner *la16-19, 20- historical.* **muck-midden**, †**muk-mydding** a dunghill *la16-.* **muck rotten** rotten to the point of decomposition *la19- Sh.* **muck-a-byre**, **muck-the-byre** a derogatory term for a farmer *la18-19, 20- NE T.* [ME *muk*, ON *myki* dung]

muck[1.2], †**muk** /mʌk/ *v* **1** to clear of dirt; to clean out *la14-.* **2** to scrape dung out of a byre or stable *16-.* **3** to spread with dung; to fertilize *16-.* **4** to clutter up *20- Sh NE.* [see the noun]

muckie, **muckack** /ˈmʌki, ˈmʌkək/ *n* a rose-hip *20- N.* [Gael *mucag*]

muckle[1.1], **mickle**, **meikle**, †**mykil** /ˈmʌkəl, ˈmɪkəl, ˈmikəl/ *n* a large quantity, a great deal *la14-.* **I wadna muckle say but** I wouldn't be surprised if *19, 20- Sh NE.* [see the adj]

muckle[1.2], **mickle**, **meikle**, †**mekill**, †**mikill**, †**mukill** /ˈmʌkəl, ˈmɪkəl, ˈmikəl/ *adj* **1** large in size or extent; big, bulky *la14-.* **2** designating the larger of two farms or estates of the same name *14-.* **3** numerous, abundant *la14-.* **4** full-grown, adult *17-19, 20- Sh Ork NE SW.* **5** of high rank or social standing; self-important *la18-19, 20- Sh NE T EC.* **6** *of letters of the alphabet* capital *la19- Sh NE.* **muckledom**, **mickledom** size, bulk *la16-.* **Mucklie 1** the fair held on Muckle Friday *la19- historical.* **2** a present brought from the fair *la19- historical.* **muckle boat** *fishing* a decked herring-boat *20- Sh.* **muckle-bookit**, **muckle-boukit 1** broad or burly in physique *19-.* **2** pregnant *19- N NE T Bor.* **muckle-chair**, †**meikle chair** a large armchair *18-.* **muckle-coat** an overcoat *18-19, 20- Sh NE EC.* **muckle deil** the Devil *17-19, 20- Sh NE T EC SW.* **muckle feck** the greater part, the largest share *la19- NE EC.* **Muckle Friday** the Friday on which the half-yearly hiring market was held; the hiring market itself *la19-e20, la20- historical.* **muckle furth** the open air, the outdoors *la18- NE.* **muckle hammer** a heavy hammer for stone-breaking *19, 20- Sh.* **muckle hell** the depths of Hell *la19, 20- Sh.* **muckle kirk**, **meikle kirk** the parish church; the Church of Scotland *19, 20- Sh Ork N NE.* **muckle-kited** pot-bellied *e17, 20- NE EC.* **muckle kokkeluri** the scentless mayweed *Tripleurospermum inodora* or the ox-eye daisy *Leucanthemum vulgare 20- Sh.* **muckle maister** the Devil *20- Sh.* †**muckle maun** great, large, big *18-e19.* **muckle-moued**, **mickle mouth'd**, †**meikle mouthed** having an unusually large mouth *18-19, 20- Sh Ork NE T EC.* **muckle pot** the largest size of cooking pot, a cauldron *la18-19, 20- Sh Ork NE.* **muckle preen** a large pin used to fasten a shawl *20- Ork N.* **muckle scorie** the glaucous gull *Larus hyperboreus 20- Sh.* **muckle chield**, *Sh* **muckle sheeld 1** a well-grown boy *la19- Sh EC.* **2** the Devil *la19- Sh.* **muckle-supper** a harvest-home feast *20- Ork.* **muckle tae** the big toe *la16-.* †**mekill thing** a great deal *la14-16.* **muckle tohoi**, **muckle tae hae** a foolish or frivolous man *20- T Bor.* **muckle wheel**, †**meikle wheel** a spinning wheel consisting of a large hand-turned wheel connected by a band to the spindle *18-19, 20- Sh N.* †**mekillwort** deadly nightshade *Atropa belladonna 16-e17.* **an as muckle** and the same again *la19- Ork NE T.* **muckle an nae little** no small amount *19, 20- NE.* **the Muckle Toun** a nickname for Langholm in Dumfriesshire *20-.* [OE *micel*, ON *mikill*]

muckle[1.3], **meikle**, **mickle**, †**mekill**, †**mykil** /ˈmʌkəl, ˈmikəl, ˈmɪkəl/ *adv* to a large extent or degree *la14-.* **muckle aboot it** much the same, without change *la19, 20- Sh.* [see the adj]

mud[1], †**mude** /mʌd/ *n* wet earth or soil; dirt *15-.* **mud fish** codfish preserved with salt and packed in brine *17- Sh Ork N NE.* [ME *mud*]

mud[2] /mʌd/ *n* a small-headed stud for the heels of boots or shoes *19, 20- Sh T.* [unknown]

mud[3.1] /mud/ *n* ground loosened up in preparation for planting *20- Sh.* [see the verb]

mud[3.2] /mud/ *v* to loosen up soil in preparation for planting *20- Sh.* [Norw *modda* to root about in hay, straw etc]

muddle /ˈmʌdəl/ *v* to root about in soil; to work potatoes away from the root of a plant leaving the stem undisturbed *19, 20- Sh WC.* [perhaps frequentative form related to MUD[3.2]]

mude *see* MUD[1], MUID

muder *see* MITHER

mudge[1.1] /mʌdʒ/ *n* **1** a movement *19-.* **2** a sound, a whisper; a rumour *19- N NE T C.* [perhaps back-formation from MUDGINS or from the verb]

mudge[1.2], **midge**, *EC* **moodge** /mʌdʒ, mɪdʒ; *EC* mudʒ/ *v* to move or stir; to shift position *la18-.* [see the noun]

mudge *see* MIDGE

mudgins, †**mudgeounes** /ˈmʌdʒɪnz/ *npl* face-pulling, grimacing *la16-19, 20- NE T.* [perhaps a variant of EModE *motion*]

mudjick *see* MIDGE

mufabill *see* MOVABLE[1.2]

mufe *see* MOVE

muff, †**mouf** /mʌf/ *n* **1** a tubular covering for the hands *16-*. **2** a bird with distinctive throat markings or raised feathers around its neck *17-e19*. **3** a muffler or scarf *16*. †**muffed** *of a domestic fowl* having a crest or tuft of feathers *18-e19*. [Du *mof* a mitten]

†**muffell** *n* a muffler or chin-cloth *16-e17*. [perhaps a specific use of MUFFLE, or from the Eng verb or noun *muffle*]

muffie, mufty /'mʌfi, 'mʌfti/ *n* **1** a crested or tufted breed of fowl *19-*. **2** a woolly variety of moth *19- C Bor*. **3** the whitethroat *Sylvia communis 20- EC*. **muffi-legged** *of a hen* having thick plumage on the legs *20- Sh*. [MUFF + -IE¹]

müffin *see* MOOTH²

muffle, †**muffill** /'mʌfəl/ *n* a mitten *la16-19, 20- Ork N H&I*. [MFr *moufle*]

mufty *see* MUFFIE

mug¹, *N NE* **moog** /mʌg; *N NE* mug/ *n* **1** a drinking vessel *la18-*. **2** an earthenware container or jar *16-19*. **mugger 1** a tinker who sold articles made of earthenware *19-e20, la20- historical*. **2** earthenware *la19- NE EC Bor*. [unknown; compare Du *mok*, Norw, Dan *mugge*]

mug² /mʌg/ *n* **1** a hole in the ground used as a target in marbles *19- WC Bor*. **2** a hole on a golf course *20- WC*. **3** a mark where the batsman stands in rounders *20- Sh*. **muggie** a game of marbles *la19- WC SW*. [perhaps an extension of MUG¹]

mug³·¹ /mʌg/ *n* drizzling rain accompanied by mist or fog *19- Sh NE T*. [ON *mugga* drizzling mist]

mug³·² /mʌg/ *v* to drizzle, *19- Sh NE T*. **muggle** to drizzle *19- Sh NE*. [see the noun]

mug⁴ /mʌg/ *n* a breed of extremely woolly sheep imported from England to improve the quality of wool in the Scottish breeds *la18- SW Bor*. [perhaps reduced form of EModE *mugged* hornless]

muggart, moogard, mugwort, †**muguart** /'mʌgərt, 'mugərd, 'mʌgwɔrt/ *n* a tall perennial plant *Artemisia vulgaris 16-*. **muggart kail** a dish of boiled mugwort *19- N NE T*. [OE *mucgwyrt*]

mugger *see* MUG¹

muggerafeu, muggro-fue /'mʌgərəfø, 'mʌgrofø/ *n* mist, drizzle *20- Ork*. [MUG³·¹; the second element may be from Norw dial *fuka* sea fog]

muggi *see* MUGGY

muggie /'mʌgi/ *n* **1** the stomach of an animal or fish (stuffed with meat or other food and eaten) *19- Sh Ork*. **2** rennet made from a calf's stomach *20- Sh*. **3** the contents of a limpet shell *20- Sh*. [ON *magi* stomach]

muggie *see* MUG²

muggin /'mʌgən/ *n* corporal punishment; a beating *la19-e20, la20- historical*. [verbal noun from Eng *mug* to strike on the face]

muggins, moogins /'mʌgɪnz, 'mugɪnz/ *n* mugwort *Artemisia vulgaris la19- NE H&I WC SW Uls*. [shortened form of MUGGART, with *-in(g)* suffix 'of the kind of' and pl ending]

muggle *see* MUG³·²

muggro-fue *see* MUGGERAFEU

muggy /'mʌgi/ *adj* drizzling, misty *19- Sh Ork NE Uls*. [MUG³·¹ + -IE²]

muguart, mugwort *see* MUGGART

muid, mood, *NE* **meed,** †**mude** /mud; *NE* mid/ *n* **1** spirit, disposition; state of mind *la14-*. **2** a fit of temper; a state of sulkiness *la15-*. **3** courage, valour *la14-e16*. †**mudie, mudy** brave, bold *la13-18*. [OE *mōd* mind, spirit]

muif *see* MOOTH²

muil *see* MULE

muild *see* MOOL¹·¹, MOOL²

muind, mond /mønd, mɔnd/ *n* **1** a short period of time *la19- Sh*. **2** stormy weather, a squall *la19- Sh*. [ON *mund* a short period of time in which something happens]

muinlicht *see* MUNELICHT

muir, moor, *NE* **meer,** *C* **mair,** †**mure,** †**more** /mjur; *NE* mir; *C* mer/ *n* **1** a tract or expanse of heath; barren open country *la14-*. **2** rough, uncultivated land belonging to an individual proprietor or estate *la15-*. **3** unenclosed uncultivated ground; the common land belonging to a burgh (used as a marketplace or drying ground) *la12-20, 21- historical*. **4** peat or peaty soil; a layer of peat *la18-19, 20- Sh Ork*. †**muirish** consisting of or abounding in moorland *17-e19*. **muir band, moor band** a hard subsoil of sand and clay with embedded stone which is impervious to water *19, 20- EC Bor*. **muir burn,** †**mureburne 1** the controlled burning of the heather on heathland to clear the way for new growth *15-*. **2** a violent row; an outburst of temper *18-19*. **moorcheeper** the meadow pipit *Anthus pratensis 20- T C Bor*. **muircock,** †**murcoke** the male red grouse *Lagopus lagopus 15-*. **muir duck** the wild duck, the mallard *Anas platyrhynchos la19- NE EC SW*. **muirfowl,** †**mure foule** the red grouse *Lagopus lagopus 16-*. **muirhen,** †**mure hen** the female of the red grouse *Lagopus lagopus 16-*. **muir-ill, moor ill,** †**mure ill** a name for various diseases of cattle, including red water (bovine babesiosis), enteritis and a type of dysentery *la16-*. **muirland,** †**mureland** *n* land consisting of moor; rough unenclosed land useful only for grazing *16-*. **muirland, muirlan** *adj* **1** relating to moorland; *of people or animals* raised upon or inhabiting moorland *16-19, 20- literary*. **2** *of people* rustic, uncouth *16-19, 20- literary*. **muirpoot,** †**mure-powt** a young red grouse *Lagopus lagopus 16-19, 20- Bor*. **muir road** a road passing through moorland *18-*. **muir stone, moor stone** the stone quarried from outcrop rock on moorland *la18-19, 20- NE*. †**tak the muir** to take refuge on moorland *e19*. **throu the muir** a severe scolding; a violent quarrel *19- NE T*. [OE *mōr*]

†**muirment, murmunt, moorment** *n* stones and rubbish which blocked up the workings of a colliery *la17-18*. [AN, MFr *murement* the act of building walls]

†**muist**¹·¹, **muste, moist** *n* **1** musk *la15-e19*. **2** hair powder *la18-e19*. **mustit** perfumed with musk; containing musk *la16-e17*. **muste ball** a pomander *la15-e18*. †**must-cat** a musk-deer or a civet cat *e16*. [OFr *musc* musk]

†**muist**¹·², **moust** *v* to apply hair powder; to powder a wig *la18-e19*. [see the noun]

muk *see* MUCK¹·¹, MUCK¹·²

mukill *see* MUCKLE¹·²

mulberry /'mʌlbəri/ *n* **1** a tree of the genus *Morus la17-*. **2** the whitebeam *Sorbus aria la19- NE T EC*. [ME *mulberi*]

mulctur *see* MULTURE¹·¹

muld *see* MOOL²

mulde *see* MOOL¹·¹

mulder *see* MOOL¹·²

müldie *see* MOOLIE¹

muldoan /'mʌldon, mʌl'don/ *n* the basking shark *Cetorhinus maximus 20- NE WC*. [unknown]

müldy *see* MOOLIE¹·²

mule, †**muil,** †**mull** /mjul/ *n* a kind of soft shoe or slipper *la16-*. [EModE *moyle*]

mule *see* MOOL¹·², MOOL², MULL¹

mülick *see* MULLYO

mulk *see* MILK¹·¹, MILK¹·²

mulky *see* MILKY

mull¹, †**mule,** †**mole** /mʌl/ *n* a promontory, a headland *14-*. [Gael *maol* a bare hill, a headland, ON *múli* a muzzle, a snout; a projecting mountain]

mull[2.1] /mʌl/ *n* **1** the mouth or muzzle of an animal; *pl* the lips of an animal *16, la19- Sh Ork N EC*. **2** the sulky lip of a person *20- Ork EC*. **3** the point of a fishing-rod to which the line is attached *20- Sh*. †**mullis, mwlls** the labia of the vulva *16*. [ON *múli* the muzzle]

mull[2.2] /mʌl/ *v* **1** to munch or chew; to eat with relish *la19- Sh N*. **2** *of animals* to move food about with the lips *20- Sh Ork*. **3** to kiss *la19- Sh*. **4** to shape the toe of a knitted stocking by decreasing to a point *20- Sh*. [see the noun]

mull see MILL[1.1], MULE

mullach /'mʌləx/ *n* an affectionate term of address *20- N*. [Gael *muileach* dear]

†**muller, mullour, mullar** *n* a (wooden) frame or ornamental moulding *16-19*. **mullorit** furnished with a moulding or ornamental framing *la16-17*. [MFr *moulure*]

muller see MOOL[1.2]

mullet, †**mollet** /'mʌlət/ *n* **1** *heraldry* a star with five straight points, representing the rowel of a spur *la15-*. **2** the rowel of a spur *la15*. Compare MOLLET. [ME *molet*]

mulloch /'mʌləx/ *n* a hornless cow *19- WC SW*. [Gael *maolag*]

mulloch see MOW[1]

mullour see MULLER

mullygrumph see MOLLIGRANT[1.1]

mullyo, *Sh* **mülick** /'mʌljo; *Sh* 'mølək/ *n* a bundle of gleaned stalks *19- Sh Ork*. [unknown]

multi /'mʌlti, 'mʌlte/ *n* **1** a multistorey block of flats *la20-*. **2** a flat in a multistorey block of flats *la20-*. [reduced form of Eng *multistorey*]

multiplepoinding /'mʌltəpəlpɔɪndɪŋ, 'mʌltəpəlpɪndɪŋ/ *n law* an action brought by or in the name of the holder of a fund or property to determine which of several claimants has preferential right to it or in what proportions it should be divided *17-*. [Fr *multiple* + verbal noun from POIND[1.1]]

†**multiplie** *n* a large number or quantity *la15-16*. [reduced form of MFr *multiplicité* or noun derived from OFr *multiplier*]

multure[1.1]**, mouter,** †**mutter,** †**mulctur** /'mʌltʃər, 'mutər/ *n* **1** a toll or duty of a proportion of the grain or meal ground at a mill *15-19, 20- historical*. **2** the right of the proprietor or tenant of a mill to collect duty on grain or meal *la16-19, 20- historical*. **3** a kiss *20- Ork*. [ME *multur*]

multure[1.2] /'mʌltʃər/ *v* to pay or levy multure *15-19, 20- historical*. †**multurer** a collector of multure *14-19*. [MFr *moulturer* to grind, exact toll on grain ground, or from the noun]

mum[1.1] /mʌm/ *n* the slightest utterance, a murmur *la16-19, 20- literary*. [onomatopoeic; compare MIM[1.2]]

mum[1.2] /mʌm/ *v* to utter the least sound; to mutter, mumble *la16-19, 20- literary*. [see the noun]

mumble see MUMMLE

mumchance see MUMSCHANCE

mummle, mumble, †**mummill** /'mʌməl, 'mʌmbəl/ *v* to speak indistinctly, to mutter *16-*. **mumbler** an implement for breaking clods, a kind of heavy harrow *20- EC Bor*. [onomatopoeic]

mump[1.1] /mʌmp/ *n* **1** a complaining person, a grumbler *la20-*. **2** a word, a whisper; a hint or suggestion *19- NE WC*. **3** a toothless person *e18*. [onomatopoeic]

mump[1.2]**,** †**mamp** /mʌmp/ *v* **1** to mumble or mutter *19-*. **2** to grumble, to complain peevishly *19-*. **3** to sulk or mope; to loaf about *19-*. **4** to chew like a rabbit *18-19, 20- NE C SW Bor Uls*. **5** to communicate by gesture or grimace *18-19, 20- NE T WC*. **mump and moan** to grumble and complain *la20-*. [see the noun]

mump[1.3] /mʌmp/ *adj* depressed, sullen *la19- NE C Bor*. [see the noun]

mumpy /'mʌmpe/ *adj of people* surly, cross *la20- C*. [perhaps MUMP[1.1] + -IE[2]]

†**mumschance, mumchance** *n* a masquerade; mumming *la16*. [Ger *Mummenschanz*, MDu *mommecanse*]

mun[1.1] /mon, mun/ *n* a change; an improvement *la19- Sh*. [ON *munr* the turn of the balance]

mun[1.2] /mon, mun/ *v* **1** to change; to increase *la19- Sh*. **2** to move a cow to fresh pasture *20- Sh*. [ON *muna* to move]

mun[2] /mʌn/ *n* the jaws, the mouth *19, 20- NE T H&I SW Bor*. [Eng *mum*, LG, Du *mond* the mouth, ON *munnr*; associated with Travellers' language]

†**mundiall** *adj* worldly *la15-16*. [MFr *mondial*]

mundy /'mʌnde/ *n* a kind of heavy hammer used by shipwrights *20- C*. [probably from the name of the firm of shipsmiths, J *Mundy* of Partick]

mune, moon, min, *NE* **meen,** †**mone,** †**moyn** /mun, mɪn; *NE* min/ *n* **1** the earth's satellite, the moon *la14-*. **2** the mechanical depiction on a clock or watch of the phases of the moon *16-*. **3** a very long period of time *la18-*. **4** the period from new moon to new moon, a lunar month *la15-19, 20- Bor*. **5** the goldcrest *Regulus regulus la19- Bor*. **muneless,** *NE* **meenless,** †**moneles** without light from the moon *16-*. **moon-bow** a halo round the moon, believed to be a sign of an approaching storm *la19-*. **munebroch, moonbroch** = *moon-bow*. **muneshine, moonshine** moonlight *19, 20- NE Bor*. †**the monys cruke** the waning moon *e16*. [OE *mōna*]

munelicht, muinlicht, moonlight, *NE* **meenlicht** /'munlɪxt, 'munlʌɪt; *NE* 'mɪnlɪxt/ *n* the light of the moon *18-*. **munelicht flit** = *munelicht flitting 20-*. **munelicht flitting, moonlight flitting** a secret removal during the night, usually to avoid paying debts *la18-*. [MUNE + LICHT[1.1]]

†**munge**[1] *n* a heap; a mixture *e16*. [unknown]

munge[2] /mʌndʒ/ *v* to grumble; to sulk *la18-19, 20- EC Bor*. [perhaps onomatopoeic]

muniment /'mjunɪmənt/ *n law* a document establishing a legal right *la15-*. [ME *muniment*]

munk see MINK[1], MONK

munn /mʌn/ *n* a short-handled horn spoon *18-19, 20- SW*. [probably MUN[2] the mouth, perhaps originating among Travellers, who made horn spoons]

munnvik /'mʌnvɪk/ *n* the corner of the mouth *20- Sh*. [ON *munnvik* the corners of the mouth (pl)]

Munonday see MONDAY

Munro /mən'ro/ *n* a name for any Scottish peak of 3000 feet (914.4 metres) or more *la19-*. **Munroist** a person who has climbed all of the Munros *la20-*. **Munro bagger** a person who participates in *Munro bagging la20-*. **Munro bagging** the climbing of Munros, with the aim of completing them all *la20-*. Compare CORBETT and DONALD[2]. [named after Sir Hugh *Munro*, who published the first list of the mountains in 1891]

munsie, †**monzie** /'mʌnsi/ *n* **1** an odd-looking or ridiculously-dressed person; a person inviting ridicule or contempt *19- NE Bor*. **2** the jack or knave in a set of playing cards *19- NE*. **3** a person in a run-down or sorry condition *la19- NE*. **4** a derogatory term for a Frenchman *la17-e19*. **mak a munsie o** to reduce to a ridiculous or sorry state; to spoil or botch *la19- NE*. [altered form of Fr *monsieur*]

munt[1.1]**, mount** /mʌnt, mʌunt/ *n* **1** a fitting, a decoration; ornamental metalwork added to a piece of wooden furntiure *la19-*. **2** a horse used for riding *20-*. [see the verb]

munt[1.2]**, mount,** †**mont** /mʌnt, mʌunt/ *v* **1** to ascend *la15-*. **2** to climb onto or sit on something *16-*. **3** to set up a gun or cannon; to launch an attack *la16-*. **4** to fit out; to furnish or equip; to clothe *17-*. **5** to adorn or trim *17-*. **6** to prepare to

set off; to depart *la18- NE*. **7** to amount to; to equal *15-16*.
munting 1 equipment, dress; a bride's trousseau *la19, 20- C SW Bor*. **2** trimmings *C SW Bor*. [ME *mounten*]
munt see MONTH¹, MOUNT
muntain see MOUNTAIN
munter /'mʌntər/ *n derogatory* an unattractive person *la20-*. [perhaps from Travellers' language *munt* to cry]
munter see MONTER
munʒoun see MINION
mup-mup see MOUP¹·¹
†**muralʒe** *n* a defensive wall *e16*. [EModE *muraill*]
murder see MURTHER¹·¹, MURTHER¹·³, MURTHER¹·⁴
†**murdris, murthrys** *v pt, ptp* **murdrist, murdreist, murdressit 1** to slay or kill; to commit murder *la14-17*; compare MURTHER¹·³. **2** to torment *e16*. **murderissar, murthorsar, murdresar** a murderer *15-e17*. **murdreis hoill** a loophole in a fortification for the defenders to shoot through *la16-e17*. [AN *murdriss-*, lengthened stem of *murdrir*]
mure see MOVIR, MUIR
murg, morg /mʌrg, mɔrg/ *n* **1** a mess, a mass of dirty material *20- Sh*. **2** a heavy fall of snow *20- Sh*. [Norn *morg*, Norw *morke* a mass]
murgeon¹·¹, †**murjin**, †**murgeoun**, †**morgeown** /'mʌrdʒən/ *n* a bodily contortion; a facial grimace *16-19, 20- NE*. [altered form with intrusive *-r-* of MUDGINS]
†**murgeon¹·²**, **morgeoun** *v* **1** to mock or mimic; to grimace or posture *la16-19*. **2** to mutter or complain *e19*. [see the noun]
murgis /'mʌrgɪs/ *n* **1** an uproar, a turmoil *la19- Sh Ork*. **2** a mess; soft mud *20- Sh Ork*. **3** a dense crowd *20- Sh*. [probably MURG + -IS³]
murgully see MARGULLIE
murjin see MURGEON¹·¹
murk see MIRK¹·¹, MIRK¹·², MIRK¹·³
murken¹·¹ /'mʌrkən/ *v of hay* to become musty or mouldy *20- Sh Ork*. [ON *morkna* to become rotten]
murken¹·² /'mʌrkən/ *adj of hay* musty, mouldy *19- Sh Ork*. [see the verb]
murky see MIRKY¹
murl¹·¹, mirl /mʌrl, mɪrl/ *n* a crumb, a fragment; a small piece of oatcake *la19- NE T EC*. **murlack, murlick** a crumble, a fragment *la19- NE*. **murlie, murly** crumbly, friable *19, 20- NE EC Bor*. [unknown]
murl¹·², mirl, †**murle** /mʌrl, mɪrl/ *v* to crumble; to decay; to reduce to fragments *la15-19, 20- Ork NE T EC*. **murlin** *n* a crumb, a fragment *la19- N NE T EC*. **murlin** *adj* crumbling, mouldering *20- NE T EC*. **murl doun** to decay or fall apart *la19- NE T EC*. [unknown]
†**murle** *v* to murmur; to babble *19*. [frequentative form of MURR¹·²]
murle see MURL¹·²
murlin /'mʌrlɪn/ *n* a round narrow-mouthed basket used mainly by fishermen *la18- N NE T EC*. [Gael *mùrlainn*]
murly /'mʌrli/ *adj* tiny *20- Ork*. [unknown]
†**murmell¹·¹** *n* an expression of discontent *e16*. [see the verb]
murmell¹·², †**murmill** /'mʌrməl/ *v* to grumble; to mumble *16-19, 20- Ork WC*. [probably OFr *mormeler*]
murmichan /'mʌrmɪxən/ *n folklore* a monster or wicked fairy used to frighten children *20- T EC*. [unknown]
murmill see MURMELL¹·²
murmunt see MUIRMENT
murmur, †**mvrmour,** †**mwrmwr** /'mʌrmʌr/ *v* **1** to speak quietly or indistinctly *15-*. **2** to grumble or complain *15-*. **3** to criticize, to accuse; to calumniate *15-*. **murmuration,** *Sh* **murmurashen,** †**murmuratioun 1** murmuring, low noise; complaining, grumbling *la15-*. **2** the action of spreading a rumour *la15-17*. **murmur the judge** *law* to cast reflection on the character or integrity of a judge *la17-*. [ME *murmuren*]
murn¹·¹, mourn /mʌrn, mɔrn, morn/ *n* **1** a low moaning sound; an audible expression of grief *la19-*. **2** the sound of running water *19*. **mak murn for** to lament *la19, 20- NE*. **mak a murn ower** to lament *la19, 20- NE*. [see the verb]
murn¹·², mourn, †**murne** /mʌrn, mɔrn, morn/ *v* **1** to feel or express grief or sorrow *la14-*. **2** to grumble or complain; to show resentment *la19-*. [OE *murnan*]
murnin, mournin, †**mvrnyng,** †**mwrning** /'mʌrnɪn, 'mɔrnɪn, 'mornɪn/ *n* **1** the (conventional or ceremonial) manifestation of grief or sorrow *la14-*. **2** *pl* the black garments worn to convey grief *la16-*. **murnin hem** *humorous* the inner rim of a tea-cup visible between the tea and the lip of the cup (implying that not enough tea has been served) *la20- C*. **murnin letter** a black-edged letter of invitation to a funeral *20-*. †**mournin string** a black sash or a black streamer worn as a sign of mourning *la17-e19*. †**murning weid, mourning weids** mourning clothes *16-17*. †**mak murning** to express grief audibly *la14-16*. [verbal noun from MURN¹·²]
murr¹·¹ /mʌr/ *n* a purring or murmuring sound *19, 20- Sh*. [onomatopoeic]
murr¹·² /mʌr/ *v* **1** *of a cat* to purr *19, 20- Sh N NE*. **2** to make a continuous murmuring or vibrating sound *20- Sh N*. [see the noun]
murr²·¹ /mʌr/ *n* a fragment or morsel; a small or undersized object *la19- Sh Ork*. [Norn *murr* a collection of small things; compare Icel *mor* particles, dust, mud]
murr²·² /mʌr/ *v* to smash into fragments *20- Sh*. [see the noun]
murr³ /mʌr/ *n* fine rain or drizzle *19- Sh Ork*. [Norw dial *myrre* fog, mist]
murr⁴ /mur/ *n* silverweed *Argentina anserina* *19- Sh Ork N*.
murrik an edible tuber *la19- Sh*. [ON *mura*]
mursgan see MAASGUUM
murt see MURTO
murther¹·¹, murder, †**murthir,** †**murthour** /'mʌrθər, 'mʌrdər/ *n* **1** the deliberate and unlawful killing of a person *13-*. **2** mass slaughter; a massacre *15-16*. [OE *morþor*]
†**murther¹·²** *n* a murderer *la14-17*. [OE *myrþra*]
murther¹·³, murder, †**murthour,** †**murthur,** †**mwrdir** /'mʌrθər, 'mʌrdər/ *v* **1** to kill unlawfully with premeditation *15-*. **2** to harass, torment or distress *19- Sh NE T Bor Uls*. **murtherer, murderer,** †**murtherar 1** a person who commits murder *la14-*. **2** a device for catching deep-sea fish *la19-*. [ME *morther*, probably an aphetic form of OE *āmyrþran* and also loss of prefix in OE *formyrþrian* and *ofmyrþrian*]
murther¹·⁴, murder, †**murthour** /'mʌrθər, 'mʌrdər/ *interj* an expression of alarm or fear; a warning of danger *la15-*. **murder polis** *interj* a humorous expression of alarm, irritation or disgust *la20-*. **murder polis** *adj humorous* bad, dreadful: ◊*It's murder polis in the shops afore Christmas la20-*. [see the noun]
murther² /'mʌrθər/ *v of a child* to murmur; to whimper or sob quietly *19, 20- NE*. [onomatopoeic]
murthir see MURTHER¹·¹
murthorsar see MURDRIS
murthour see MURTHER¹·¹, MURTHER¹·³, MURTHER¹·⁴
murthrys see MURDRIS
murthur see MURTHER¹·³
murto, murt /'mʌrto, mʌrt/ *n* **1** an undersized or underdeveloped creature *19- Sh*. **2** a small object *19- Sh*. [ON *murta* a small fish]
musche see MUSH³

muschit *adj of taffeta or ermine* spotted *la16*. [MFr *mouchette* a small piece of cloth or fur decorating a costume]

muscle *see* MUSSEL

muscovy cat /'mʌskəve kat/ *n* a tortoiseshell cat *20- SW*. [unknown]

†muse *n* a room used for meditation or study *la17*. [Fr *musée*, Lat *mūseum* a place dedicated to the pursuit of learning]

mush[1] /mʌʃ/ *n* the mixture of oak sawdust and chips burned when smoking herring to make kippers *20- Sh NE*. **mush-och** a heap of straw or grain *18- SW*. **mush-house** a store for oak sawdust and chips *20- Sh NE*. [compare MASCHLE]

†mush[2] *n* a whisper, a sound *19*. [onomatopoeic]

mush[3], **†musche** /mʌʃ/ *v in needlework* to gather, flounce, or scallop; to cut into a pattern with a stamp *17-19, 20- NE EC*. **†musche taffetie** patterned or ornamented taffeta *la16*; compare MUSCHIT. [MFr *moucher* to cut, trim a candle]

music, musick, maisic, *NE* **meesick** /'mjuzık, 'mezık; *NE* 'mızık/ *n* a tune; musical art, composition or performance *15-*. **musicker** a musician *19, 20- Bor*. **†music-bells** a set of bells or carillon in a church *18-e19*. [ME *musik*]

musicianer /mju'zıʃənər/ *n* a musician *16-19, 20- NE WC SW Uls*. [Older Scots *musician* with agent suffix]

musick *see* MUSIC

musie /'mjuzi/ *n* a muse *la18-19, 20- literary*. [MFr *muse*, Lat *mūsa* + -IE[1]]

musk, moosk /mʌsk, musk/ *n weather* a haze, a mist *la19- Sh*. **muski** hazy *20- Sh*. [Norn *musk*; compare Norn *muska* to rain finely]

muskan, muskin /'mʌskən/ *n* a razorfish *Xyrichtys 19- SW*. [Gael *mùsgan*]

†muskane *adj* rotting, decayed; musty *e16*. [probably Gael *mosgain*; but compare MOSKIN]

musken *see* MUTCHKIN

muskin *see* MUSKAN

muslin, †musseline /'mʌzlən/ *n* **1** a lightweight cotton fabric *la17-*. **2** a fine linen fabric *18*. **muslin kail** a thin soup made from barley and vegetables without any meat-stock *la18-19, 20- Bor*. [Fr *mousseline*]

mussel, †mussill, †muscle /'mʌsəl/ *n* an edible bivalve mollusc *16-*. **mussel brose** mussels boiled in their own juice which is then stirred into oatmeal *la18-19, 20- historical*. **mussel-draig** a rake for gathering mussels *la19- Sh*. **mussel-ebb** mussel-beds exposed at ebb-tide *19- Sh H&I T C Bor*. **mussel-midden** a refuse heap where mussel-shells are thrown *19- N NE T EC*. **mussel picker** the oystercatcher *Haematopus ostralegus la19- N EC Uls*. **mussel-scaup, †mussill scap** a mussel-bed *la15-19, 20- Sh N NE T C*. [OE *muscelle*]

musseline *see* MUSLIN

mussell *see* MUZZLE[1.1], MUZZLE[1.2]

mussill *see* MUSSEL

mussour *see* MEASURE[1.1]

must[1] /'møst/ *n* a bad smell *19- Sh*. **møsty** smelly *20- Ork*. [Norw dial *must* vapour, a smell]

must[2], *Sh* **most, †moste, †moist** /mʌst; *Sh* most/ *v* to have to; to be obliged to *la15-*. Compare MAUN[1.2]. [OE *mōste*, pt of OE *mōtan*]

mustart, mustard, †mustar /'mʌstərt, 'mʌstərd/ *n* a condiment made from the mustard plant *15-*. **†mustard-stane** a stone on or with which mustard was pounded *16-e19*. [ME *mustard*]

muste *see* MUIST[1.1]

mustna *see* MAUN[1.2]

mutch, †much /mʌtʃ/ *n* **1** a close-fitting linen or muslin cap worn mainly by (married) women *la16-e20, la20- historical*. **2** a nightcap (worn by men) *la15-e20, la20- historical*. **3** an old woman *20- C SW*. **mutch-string** the string for tying a mutch under the chin *la19-e20, la20- historical*. [MDu *mutsche*]

mutchkin, *SW* **musken, †muchkin, †muchin** /'mʌtʃkın; *SW* 'mʌskən/ *n* a measure of capacity for liquids, a quarter of a Scottish pint (0.43 litre); a container of this capacity used as a measure for spirits *15-19, 20- historical*. [EModDu *mudseken, mutskena*]

†mute, mote *n* **1** a formal meeting to discuss and transact official or legal business *15-e16*. **2** an action at law; a plea *15-e17*. **3** litigation *15-e17*. Compare MOOT[1.1], MOOT[1.2]. [OE *mōt*, ON *mót*]

mute *see* MOOT[1.2]

mute-hill *see* MOOT-HILL

mutilate, †mutilat /'mjutəlet/ *v pt, ptp* also **†mutilate †mutilat, †mutilit** **1** to maim or disfigure; to deprive of a limb or organ *16-*. **2** to render a book incomplete by cutting out pages or defacing the text *la16-*. [Lat *mutilāt-*, ptp stem of *mutilāre*]

mutilation, †mutilatioun /mjutə'leʃən/ *n* **1** the action of maiming or disabling a person *16-*. **2** the defacement of a text; the excision of text from a book *17-*. **3** *law* the crime of wounding and causing serious bodily harm *16-19, 20- historical*. [AN *mutilacion*, Lat *mutilātio*]

mutilit *see* MUTILATE

mutter *see* MULTURE[1.1]

muttie /'mʌti/ *n* a measure for grain, originally a third or a quarter of a peck (approx 9 litres); the vessel containing this amount *la17- N NE*. [unknown; compare Du *mudde*, Ger *mutt(e)*, both some kind of dry measure]

muttle /'mʌtəl, 'motəl/ *n* a small knife *19- Sh*. [Norw *mutel*]

mutton, †muttoun, †mottoune, †moutoun /'mʌtən/ *n* **1** the flesh of sheep used for food *la14-*. **2** the carcasses of sheep or a sheep; a sheep intended for slaughter *15-17*. **3** sheepskin *la16*. **†moutoun-bowk, mutton-bouk** the carcass of a sheep *16-e18*. **†mutton-ham** a leg of mutton cured in the same way as a ham *19*. **sic a mutton's on a hen** an expression of surprise at an incongruous or incredible situation *20- Sh NE*. [ME *motoun*]

mutuum /'mjutjuʌm/ *n law* a contract by which the borrower of goods for consumption agrees to repay a like quantity of the same goods instead of the actual goods borrowed *la17-e20, la20- historical*. [Lat *mūtuum* a loan]

muve *see* MOVE

muzzle[1.1], **mizzle, †mussell, †missell** /'mʌzəl, 'mızəl/ *n* **1** the nose and mouth of an animal *la15-*. **2** a restraint fixed to an animal's face *la15-*. **3** the opening at the end of the barrel of a gun *la16-*. **4** the bridle of a plough; the piece of metal on the end of the plough-beam to which tackle or traces are attached *16-19, 20- C Uls*. **5** a piece of cloth worn so as to cover the lower part of the face *16-e17*; compare MUFFELL. [ME *mosel*]

muzzle[1.2], **†mussell** /'mʌzəl/ *v* **1** to muzzle an animal *la16-*. **2** to silence a person *la16-*. **†mussellit, missellit** having the lower part of the face covered; masked or veiled *la15-e17*. [see the noun]

mvrmour *see* MURMUR

mvrnyng *see* MURNIN

mwk *see* MUCK[1.1]

mwrdir *see* MURTHER[1.3]

mwrmwr *see* MURMUR

mwrning *see* MURNIN

mwte *see* MOOT[1.2]

mwtehill *see* MOOT-HILL

my *see* MA

†**myance, myanis, myans** *n* means *16*. Compare MOYEN[1.1]. [from the plural of *myane* (MOYEN[1.1])]
myane *see* MOYEN[1.1], MOYEN[2.1], MOYEN[2.2]
myarter *see* MAIRTYR[1.1], MAIRTYR[1.2]
myave *see* MAW[3]
myawkin *see* MAUKIN
myce *see* MOOSE
mychane *see* MICHANE
myche *see* MICH
mycht *see* MICHT[1]
mychty *see* MICHTY[1.2]
myd *see* MID[1.1], MID[1.2]
myddil *see* MIDDLE[1.1]
myddis *see* MIDS
mydle *see* MIDDLE[1.1], MIDDLE[2]
mydred *see* MIDDRIT
myen *see* MOYEN[1.1]
myghti *see* MICHTY[1.2]
myghty *see* MICHTY[1.1]
mykil *see* MUCKLE[1.1], MUCKLE[1.3]
myle *see* MILE
myles, miles, milds, †**myldis** /ˈmʌɪlz, ˈmʌɪldz/ *n* any of several edible plants of the goosefoot family *Chenopodiaceae*, especially the common orache *Atriplex patula 16-19, 20- SW Bor Uls*. [OE *melde*]
mylky *see* MILKY
myll *see* MILE
mylne *see* MILE, MILL[1.1]
mylve *see* MILL[1.1]
†**mymmerkin, mymerken** *n* a malformed or stunted person *e16*. [unknown]
myn *see* MIN
mynd *see* MIND[1.1], MIND[1.2], MINE[1.1]
myne *see* MIND[1.1], MIND[1.2]
mynerall *see* MINERAL[1.1]
mynnis *see* MINIS
mynnye *see* MINNIE[1.1]
mynorall *see* MINERAL[1.1]
mynour *see* MINE[1.2]
mynt *see* MINT[1.2]
myntime *see* MEANTIME[1.1]
myogre *see* MOGER[1.2]
myon *see* MOYEN[2.1]

myowt, myout, meout /mjʌut/ *n* a sound or whisper; a murmur of complaint or protest *la19- NE H&I Uls*. [onomatopoeic]
myr *see* MYRRH
myre *see* MIRE[1.1], MIRE[1.2]
myrk *see* MIRK[1.2], MIRK[1.3]
myrkn *see* MIRKEN
myro, myroo /ˈmaero, maeru/ *n* an ant *20- Ork*. [perhaps shortened form of PISMIRE, with *-o* suffix; compare Sw *myra* ant]
myrrh, †**mir,** †**myr** /mɪr/ *n* **1** a bitter, aromatic gum resin exuded by trees of the genus *Commiphora la14-*. **2** a tree or shrub that exudes myrrh *15-*. [Lat *myrrha*]
myschancit *see* MISCHANCIT
myschancy *see* MISCHANCY
myschefe, myscheif *see* MISCHIEF
myschewsly *see* MISCHIEVOUS
mysdoing, mysdoyng *see* MISDO
myse *see* MOOSE
mysel, myself, my seluin *see* MASEL
mysfare *see* MISFARE
mysfortunat *see* MISFORTUNATE
mysfur *see* MISFARE
myskene *see* MISKEN
myslin, †**miceling** /ˈmaeslɪn/ *n* a poor quality coal *la18- EC*.
meslin stane = MYSLIN *20- EC*. [altered form of MASHLUM[1.1]]
mysseme *see* MISSEME
myster *see* MISTER[1.1]
mystery, †**mistery** /ˈmɪstre, ˈmɪstəre/ *n pl also* †**misteris** †**mestris 1** *Christian Church* a religious truth known or understood only by divine revelation *la15-*. **2** something beyond comprehension or explanation *16-*. **3** a technical or trade secret; a masonic secret or ritual *la17-*. **4** a medieval miracle play *la16-e19*. **5** a religious rite or sacrament *la16-17*. [Lat *mystērium*]
myte *see* MITE
myter, mytir *see* MITRE
†**myth** *v* to indicate; to reveal or show *la15-16*. [ON *miða*; compare MEITH[1.2]]
myth *see* MICH
mytht *see* MICHT[2]

N

na[1.1], **naa**, **naw** /na, nɔ/ *adv* no, the negative response *la14*-. Compare NAE[1]. [specific use of NA[1.2]]

†**na**[1.2], **ne** *adv* in no way, by no means *la14-e16*. [OE *nā*]

na[1.3], †**nay**, †**ne**, †**no** /na/ *conj* **1** than *la14*-. **2** nor *la14-16*. [specific use of NA[1.1]]

†**na**[1.4] *conj* but (that), other than, unless *la14-16*. **na had nocht bene** had it not been; but for *la14-e15*. **na war it** were it not *la14-e15*. [specific use of NA[1.1]]

na[1.5] /na/ *interj* an expression of surprise, incredulity or dismay *18-19*, *20- Sh NE*. [specific use of NA[1.1]]

na[2], **nae**, *NE* **no**, *NE* **ni** /na, ne; *NE* no; *NE* nɪ/ *adv* in questions now, then: ◊*fat kin o' dog wid ye ca' that, ni? 19-.* [unstressed form of NOO]

na see NAE[1]

-na, **-nae**, †**-ne** /na, nə, ne/ *adv* not, no ◊*she cannae* ◊*ye needna la16*-. [reduced form of NOCHT[1.2]]

naa see NA[1.1]

naar see NAR[1.2], NAR[1.3]

nab /nab/ *n* a peg or nail on which to hang things *18*-. Compare KNAB[1]. [probably Norw dial *nabb* a peg, a nail]

nab see KNAP[2.2], NABB

nabal[1.1], **nabble**, *Sh* **nibald** /'nabəl; *Sh* 'nɪbəld/ *n* a miser *la18-19*, *20- Sh Ork NE SW*. [from the name of the biblical character *Nabal*]

nabal[1.2] /'nabəl/ *adj* grasping, churlish *la19*, *20- Sh Ork NE*. [see the noun]

nabb, *Sh Ork* **knab**, *Sh Ork* **knabb**, †**nab** /nab; *Sh Ork* knab/ *n* a hillock, a summit; a rocky protuberance, a promontory *19*, *20- Sh Ork*. [Norw dial *nabb*, *knabb*]

nabb, **nabbery** see KNAB[2]

nabbie, **nabby** /'nabi/ *n* a type of herring-fishing boat *la19*-. [unknown]

nabble /'nabəl/ *v* **1** to nibble *20*-. **2** *in weaving* to work with speed and deftness *20- T*. [Du *knabbelen*, Ger *knabbern*, LG *knabbeln*]

nabble see NABAL[1.1]

nabby see NABBIE

nace, **ness** /nes, nɛs/ *adj* pitiable, destitute *la18- NE EC*. [ON *neiss*]

nacked see NAKIT

nacket[1], *Sh* **knockit**, *WC* **nockit**, †**nakket** /'nakət; *Sh WC* 'nɔkɪt/ *n* **1** a packed lunch, a snack *19*-. **2** a type of small, fine loaf; a cake or biscuit *la16-19*, *20- NE Bor*. [unknown]

nacket[2], †**knackatt** /'nakət/ *n* **1** a small, neat person *la18*-. **2** a little ball *19*-. **3** a pert or precocious child *la19*, *20- Sh Ork NE*. **4** a cook's boy or a miller's boy *17-e18*. **5** a ball boy (in tennis) *e16*. **nackety** neat *la18-19*, *20- NE T*. [MFr *naquet* the ball boy in tennis]

nacky see KNACKIE

nadir see NEDDER[1.1]

nae[1], **no**, †**na**, †**nay**, †**ne** /ne, no/ *adj* no, not any *la14*-. **nae ane** no one *la18*-. **naebody**, **neebody**, †**na body** no one *la15*-. **naegate**, †**na gait** in no way *la16*-. **nae place** nowhere *la19*-. **nae road** by no means, in no possible way *20*-. **naewey** nowhere *la19*-. **naewhere**, †**no quhar** nowhere *16*-. †**be na kin way**, **be na kin wys** by no means, in no way *15-e16*. †**na ma**, **na mae** *n* no more *la14-e17*. †**na ma** *adj* no greater in number, no further *15-16*. **nae mare** *n* nothing more, nothing else *15*-. †**nae mare** *adj* no further, no other *la14-16*. **nae mare** *adv* **1** no longer, not again; never again *la14*-. **2** in no greater degree, to no greater extent *15*. **nae sma saut** of considerable importance *20- T EC*. **nae weys** in no way, by no manner of means *19*-. [OE *nān*]

nae[2] /ne/ *adv* nay, no, the negative response *19*-. Compare NA[2]. [ON *nei*]

nae see NA[2], NO

-nae see -NA

naeder see NAITHER[1.3]

nael see NAVEL

naesay see NA-SAY[1.1], NA-SAY[1.2]

naether see NAITHER[1.2], NAITHER[1.3]

naething, **naethin**, **nithin**, †**nathing** /'neθɪŋ, 'neθɪn, 'nɪθɪn/ *n* not anything, nothing *la14*-. [OE *nān þing*]

naffle see NEVEL[1.2]

nag, *Uls* **niag** /nag; *Uls* njag/ *n* a hard ball used in shinty or hurling *la19*-. [variant of KNAG[1]]

nag see KNAG[1], NAIG

nage see NAIG

†**nags** *npl* marbles a game in which the loser was struck on the knuckles by the other players' marbles; the blows so struck *19*. [perhaps altered form of KNACK[1.1]]

†**nagus** *n* a stingy person *e16*. [unknown]

naider see NAITHER[1.2]

naig, **nag**, †**nage** /neg, nag/ *n* **1** a horse *18*-. **2** a small horse or pony *la15-17*. **naigie** a small horse or pony *18-19*. [unknown]

naikit see NAKIT

nail[1.1], †**nale** /nel/ *n* **1** a metal pin or spike (for hammering) *la14*-. **2** a fingernail or toenail; a claw *15*-. **3** the length of the middle finger from the knuckle to the tip *20- Ork*. **4** a measure of cloth, a sixteenth of an ell *16-17*. **5** a Flemish unit of wool (of 6 pounds) *15*. †**nail string** the iron rod from which nails were cut *18-19*. **aff at the nail** deranged *18*-. [OE *nægl*]

nail[1.2] /nel/ *v* **1** to fix or attach with a nail *la14*-. **2** to hit, to strike down, to kill *la18*-. **3** to clinch an argument or bargain *la18*-. **4** to beat; to scold *la19- Bor*. [OE *næglian*]

nain[1.1] /nen/ *n* what is one's own, one's due *19*-. [see the adj]

nain[1.2], †**nane** /nen/ *adj* own *la14*-. **yer nain** yourself *19*, *20- Ork NE*. [wrong division of *mine ain*]

naince see NANES

nainsell /nen'sɛl, 'nɛnsɛl/ *pron* own self *la19*-. **her nainsell** *pron* a way of referring to oneself (associated with Highlanders) *la17*-. **her nainsell** *n* humorous a Highlander *18*-. [NAIN[1.2] + SEL[1.2]]

†**naiphouse**, **nepus** *n* a dormer *17-e19*. [KNAP[1] + HOOSE[1.1]]

naipkin, **napkin**, **nepkin**, *EC* **neepyin** /'nepkɪn, 'napkɪn, 'nɛpkɪn; *EC* 'nipjɪn/ *n* **1** a pocket-handkerchief; a neckerchief *15*-. **2** a small cloth to wipe the lips and protect clothes at the table *la17*-. [ME *napkin*, OFr *nappe* a cloth and diminutive suffix *-kin*]

naiproun see APRIN

nair see NAR[1.3]

nairra, **narra**, **nerra**, **narrow**, *Ork N* **nerro**, †**naro**, †**narow** /'nera, 'nara, 'nɛra, 'naro; *Ork N* 'nɛro/ *adj* **1** not broad or wide; limited in extent *13*-. **2** parsimonious, mean *la15*-. **3** strict, illiberal *e16*. **nairrowly**, **narrowly 1** scarcely, barely *la14*-. **2** closely, intently *la14*-. **nairra begaun** miserly *19*-.

nairra boukit thin, lean *20- NE T.* **narrow nebbit 1** sharp-nosed *19, 20- Uls.* **2** bigoted, strict *19, 20- Uls.* †**narrow seis** straits, narrows *16-17*. [OE *nearu*]
naische *see* NESCHE
naisty *see* NESTY[1,2]
†**nait**[1,1], **nate** *n* purpose *la15-e16.* [ON *neyti*]
†**nait**[1,2] *adj* deft *16.* [ON *neytr*]
naither[1,1], **naether, neither, naider,** †**nather** /ˈneðər, ˈniðər, ˈnedər/ *adv* **1** also not *la16-.* **2** indeed not: ◊*I widnae dae it, naither I wid 19-.* **naitherins, nedderins** either: ◊*na, nae him nedderins 19, 20- NE.* **naithers** either ◊*the bairns wasna nae great shake naithers 19-.* [altered form of NOWTHER[1,1], by analogy with AITHER[1,2]]
naither[1,2], **naether, nather, neither,** *Sh* **nedder,** *NE* **naeder** /ˈneðər, ˈnaðər, ˈniðər; *Sh* ˈnɛdər; *NE*ˈnedər/ *pron* not the one or the other *la15-.* **naitherins** either: ◊*A dinna like naitherins o' them 19-.* [see the adv]
naither[1,3], **nather, neither** /ˈneðər, ˈnaðər, ˈniðər/ *adj* not one or the other *17-.* [see the adv]
naitional, national /ˈneʃənəl, ˈnaʃənəl/ *adj* relating to a nation *la16-.* **National Archives of Scotland** the name for the Scottish archives since the merger of the General Register Office for Scotland and the National Records of Scotland in 2011 *21-.* [MFr *national*]
naitral *see* NATURAL[1,2]
naitur *see* NATURE
naitural *see* NATURAL[1,2]
nakit, naked, *NE* **nyakit,** †**naikit,** †**nacked** /ˈnekɪt, ˈnekɪd; *NE* ˈnjakɪt/ *adj* **1** unclothed; partially clad, wearing only an undergarment *la14-.* **2** *of land* devoid of vegetation, bare, barren; frequently in place-names *16-.* **3** mere; simple; frank *la16-.* **4** *of an alcoholic drink* neat *19, 20- EC SW.* **5** thin, lean, emaciated *20- T C.* **6** destitute *15-17.* **7** exposed to attack *15-17.* **8** *of a weapon* unsheathed *15-17.* **9** *of a promise or allegation* unsupported by documentation or evidence *15-17.* [OE *nacod*]
nakket *see* NACKET[1]
nale *see* NAIL[1,1]
nam[1] /nam/ *v* to seize, to grab *19- Sh Bor.* [perhaps pt of OE *niman*]
nam[2], *Sh NE* **nyam** /nam; *Sh NE* njam/ *v* to eat up greedily *19- Sh NE Bor.* [perhaps onomatopoeic]
name *see* NEM[1,1], NEM[1,2]
named *see* NEM[1,2]
namely[1,1] /ˈnemle/ *adj* noted, famed; of good repute *17-.* [NEM[1,1], with adj-forming suffix; translating Gael *ainmeil* famous]
namely[1,2] /ˈnemle/ *adv* **1** specifically, that is to say *16-.* **2** particularly, especially *la14-e19.* [NEM[1,1], with adv-forming suffix *-ly*]
namit, nammit *see* NEM[1,2]
nane[1,1], **none** /nen, nʌn/ *adv* **1** not at all, in no way: ◊*she slept nane 15-.* **2** not any, no *15-e16.* [OE *nān*]
nane[1,2], **none,** *NE* **neen** /nen, nʌn; *NE* nin/ *pron* **1** no one, not any, not one *la14-.* **2** neither (of two) *19-.* **nane o the twa** neither *19-.* [see the adv]
nane *see* NAIN[1,2]
nanes, naince, †**nanis** /nens/ *n* **1** certainly, indeed *la14-19, 20- literary.* **2** a joke *20- N.* **3** for that very purpose, expressly *16.* **for the nanes** certainly, indeed *la14-19, 20- literary.* [ME *nones*]
nap[1], †**knap** /nap/ *n* a bowl, a drinking vessel *18-19, 20- SW.* **nappie,** †**knappie** a small pot *18-19, 20- Sh.* [OE *hnæpp*]
nap[2] /nap/ *n* a jibe *la19- EC.* **tak the nap aff** to make fun of, to mock *la19-.* [probably a variant form and extended usage of KNAP[2,1]]

nap *see* KNAP[4,2]
nap bed, nape bed *see* NOP BED
†**nape** *n* an ape *la15-17.* [wrong division of Eng *an ape*]
naperie, napery, †**napry** /ˈnapəri/ *n* (table) linen *la15-.* **napery press** a linen cupboard *17-.* [ME *naperi*]
naperon *see* APRIN
†**Napillis, Naplis** *n* Naples *la15-e17.* †**Napillis taffetie** Naples taffeta *la16-e17.* [Lat *Neāpolis*]
napkin *see* NAIPKIN
nappie[1,1] /ˈnapi/ *n* (strong) ale *la18-19, 20- literary.* [see the adj]
nappie[1,2] /ˈnapi/ *adj* **1** *of ale or beer* foaming, strong *18-19, 20- literary.* **2** *of people* slightly intoxicated, happy *la18-19.* [EModE *nappy*]
nappie *see* KNAP[3], NAP[1]
nappis *see* NOPPIS
napry *see* NAPERIE
napsek *see* NOPSEK
nar[1,1], **naur** /nar, nɔr/ *v* to approach *20- Sh SW.* [see the adj]
nar[1,2], **naar, naur,** †**ner** /nar, nɔr/ *adj* **1** near, close *17-.* **2** the near side or left-hand side *17-.* **3** nearer, closer to the speaker *20-.* Compare NEAR[1,2]. **narlins** almost *19, 20- Sh Ork.* **narrer,** †**nerrar** nearer *la14-.* **narrest, nerrest** nearest *15-.* [ON *nær* near, nearer, ON *nærri* comparative of *nær*]
nar[1,3], **naar, naur,** †**ner,** †**nair** /nar, nɔr/ *adv* **1** nearer, closer *la14-.* **2** close by, nearby *15-.* **3** nearly, almost *19-.* Compare NEAR[1,3]. †**narby** *adv* nearby *16-19.* †**narby** *prep* nearby *la16-19.* **nar hand** nearby *16-.* [see the adj]
nar[1,4], **ner, nerr, naur** /nar, nɛr, nɔr/ *prep* close to, beside *la14-.* [see the adj]
nar *see* NYARR, NOR[1,2]
nare *see* NEER
narg[1,1] /narg/ *n* nagging *19, 20- Sh.* [altered form of NYAAG[1,1] with epenthetic *r*]
narg[1,2] /narg/ *v* to keep grumbling, to nag *19- Sh Ork N NE SW.* [see the noun]
naro, narow, narra *see* NAIRRA
narr *see* NYARR
narrate /nəˈret/ *v* **1** to relate, to recount *la17-.* **2** *law* to set forth the relevant facts in a document *la17-18.* [Lat *narrāt-,* ptp stem of *narrāre*]
narration[1], †**narratioun** /nəˈreʃən/ *n* **1** the act of recounting, a narrative *16-.* **2** *law* the act of reporting an accusation or complaint; a report or accusation *16-17.* **3** *law* a statement of alleged facts as the basis of a legal action *16-17.* [EModE *narracion* from oblique stem of Lat *narrātio*]
narration[2] /nəˈreʃən/ *n* an uproar, a fuss, a clamour *la19-.* [wrong division of Eng *an oration*]
narrative /ˈnarətɪv/ *n* **1** an account of events; the action of relating *la16-.* **2** *law* the part of a legal deed which states the relevant essential facts *17-.* **3** *law* a statement of alleged facts as the basis of a legal action *la16-17.* **4** *law* that part of a legal document which contains the statement of the alleged facts on which the plea is based *16-e17.* [MFr *narrative*]
narrow *see* NAIRRA
na-say[1,1], **naysay, naesay** /ˈna se, ˈne se/ *n* a refusal, a denial *la16-.* [NA[1,1] and NAE[2] + SAY[1,1]]
na-say[1,2], **naysay, naesay** /ˈna se, ˈne se/ *v* to refuse, to deny *18-.* [NAE[2] + SAY[1,2]]
nasche *see* NESCHE
nash[1], **gnash** /naʃ, gnaʃ/ *n* impudent or caustic talk *18-19, 20- SW Bor.* **nashgab** garrulous or impudent talk *19- WC Bor.* [probably onomatopoeic; compare SNASH[1,1]]
nash[2] /naʃ/ *v Travellers' language* to hurry *20-.* [originally Romany]
nashag *see* GNASHACK

nastie see NESTY¹·².
nasty see NESTY¹·¹, NESTY¹·².
nat /nat/ *n* a small, sharp-tempered person *la19- Sh NE Uls*. [perhaps figurative use of Eng *gnat*]
nat see NAUCHT
natch¹·¹ /natʃ/ *n* **1** a notch or indentation *18-*. **2** *curling* a cut made in the ice to hold a player's foot when delivering the stone *19-*. **3** small scissors used by tailors *18-e19*. [altered form of Eng *notch*]
natch¹·² /natʃ/ *v* to make a notch or incision *18- Sh NE EC*. [see the noun]
nate see NAIT¹·¹, NETT
nather see NAITHER¹·¹, NAITHER¹·², NAITHER¹·³, NETHER²
nathing see NAETHING
natie see NETT
nation, †**natioun** /'neʃən/ *n* **1** the people of a country; a political state *la14-*. **2** one of the regional divisions of the student body in the older Scottish Universities *la15-*. **3** one of the privileged bodies of foreign nationals trading in continental towns *16-e17*. **4** birth; breed, race *la14-16*. [ME *nacioun*]
national see NAITIONAL
National 5, Nat 5 /'naʃənəl 'faev, 'nat 'faev/ *n* a certificate, examination or course awarded to pupils in secondary schools *la20-*.
native¹·¹ /'neɪtɪv/ *n* **1** a person born in or indigenous to a place *la17-*. **2** the district of one's birth *19, 20- NE T SW*. **3** a serf or bondman; a servant or tenant of long standing *la14-17*. [see the adj]
native¹·² /'neɪtɪv/ *adj* **1** belonging by birth, origin or heredity *la15-*. **2** inborn, innate, natural *la16-*. **3** *of land* belonging by right *16-17*. **4** belonging by kinship *16*. †**natif bond** a bondman or bond tenant *15*. **native born** born in a country or place; having a certain status by virtue of birth *la15-*. †**native man, natiff man 1** a person's servant or tenant of long standing or from birth *la16-e17*. **2** a KINDLY TENANT *16*. **3** a bond tenant *15*. †**native servant** a servant of long standing *la16-e17*. †**native tenant** a KINDLY TENANT *la16-e17*. [ME *natif*, Lat *nātīvus*]
natter¹·¹, **nyatter** /'natər, 'njatər/ *n* **1** grumbling talk; aimless chatter *la19-*. **2** a nagging, grumbling person; a chatterer *20-*. **natterie, nyatterie 1** peevish, bad-tempered *la19-*. **2** *of weather* drizzly, windy, showery *20- Sh Ork*. **nitteret** ill-natured *la19, 20- Sh Ork*. [perhaps frequentative of NAT]
natter¹·², **nyatter** /'natər, 'njatər/ *v* **1** to chatter; to nag, to grumble *19-*. **2** *of weather* to be windy and drizzly *20- Ork N*. [see the noun]
nattle, nyattle /'natəl, 'njatəl/ *v* **1** to nibble, to chew awkwardly *19- Sh SW Bor*. **2** to mumble; to nag *19- Sh SW Bor*. [altered form of NATTER¹·²]
†**natural**¹·¹, **naturel** *n* **1** innate disposition or temperament; inherent character *la16-17*. [see the adj]
natural¹·², **naitural, naitral,** †**naturell** /'natʃərəl, 'netʃərəl, 'netrəl/ *adj* **1** existing in or formed by nature *15-*. **2** physical, bodily *la15-*. **3** native-born *la15-*. **4** *of offspring* related by blood *la15-*. **5** sagacious *16-*. **naturality 1** innate ability or intelligence *16-*. **2** human sympathy, natural humanity *16-19*. **3** the rights or position of a native-born subject *16-e17*. **naitral hertit** kindly, affectionate *la19, 20- Uls*. **natural philosophy** the study of natural phenomena, the physical sciences *15-*; compare *philosophour naturall* (PHILOSOPHER). **natural possession** *law* owner-occupancy of a property *17-*. **natural science** physics *la15-*. [ME *nātural*, Lat *nātūrālis*]
natural¹·³ /'natʃərəl/ *adv* in a fashion according to nature *la16-*. [see the adj]

nature, naitur /'netʃər, 'netər/ *n* **1** the physical world *la14-*. **2** the inherent qualities of a person or thing *la14-*. **3** physical constitution *la15-*. **4** semen *la15-17*. **5** the substance of a statute or written agreement *15-17*. **naitur grass** grass which grows wild and luxuriantly *18-19, 20- NE T*. [ME *natur*, Lat *nātūra*]
nauchle see NOCHT¹·².
naucht see NOCHT¹·¹, NOCHT¹·²
nauchtie see NOCHT¹·²
†**naufrage** *n* a shipwreck *la16-17*. [EModE *naufrage*, Lat *naufragium*]
naught see NOCHT¹·²
naur see NAR¹·¹, NAR¹·², NAR¹·³
†**nave** *n* a fist *la14-e17*. Compare NIEVE¹·¹. [ON *hnefi*, perhaps with influence from Norw dial *nava*]
navel, nael, †**nyvle,** †**navill** /'nevəl, nel/ *n* **1** the umbilicus *la18-*. **2** the hub of a wheel *15-e16*. [OE *nafela*]
navis-bore /'navəsbor/ *n* a knot-hole in wood *19- NE*. [ON *nafarr* an auger + Norw dial *bore* a hole]
†**navyne** *n* a fleet, a naval force *la14-e16*. [AN *navein* a boat]
naw see NA¹·¹
nay see NA¹·², NAE¹
naym see NEM¹·¹
naysay see NA-SAY¹·¹, NA-SAY¹·²
ne see NA¹·¹, NA¹·², NAE¹, NIGH
-ne see -NA
neam see NEM¹·¹
neap see NEEP¹·¹
near¹·¹, †**nere** /nir/ *v* to draw near, to approach *16-*. [see the adv]
near¹·², †**nere** /nir/ *adj* **1** closely related by blood or kinship *la14-*. **2** close, nearby *15-*. Compare NAR¹·¹. **nearlins** almost *la18-19, 20- Sh NE*. †**neirnes** closeness of kinship *15-e17*. **near cut** a short cut *la18-*. **at the nearest** by the shortest or quickest way *18-*. [see the adv]
near¹·³, †**nere** /nir/ *adv* **1** close by, within a short distance *la14-*. **2** close in time or relation *la14-*. **3** nearly, almost *la14-*. **4** narrowly, only just *19-*. Compare NAR¹·³. **nearabout, nearabouts** *prep* close by, in the vicinity of *15-*. **nearabout, nearabouts** *adv* almost, by and large *la19-*. **nearbegaun** miserly *19-*. †**near besyde** *adv* close, adjacent *la14-17*. †**near besyde** *prep* near *la14-17*. **nearby** *adv* **1** close at hand *la14-*. **2** nearly *la15-*. **nearby** *prep* near, beside *la14-*. **neargaun** miserly *la18-*. **as near** nearly, near enough *la18-*. †**nere thareby 1** near at hand, close by *la14-16*. **2** approximately *15-e16*. [OE *nēar*, compare ON *nǣr*]
near¹·⁴, †**nere** /nir/ *prep* **1** close to *la14-*. **2** closely related to or associated with *la14-16*. Compare NAR¹·⁴. **nearhand** *adv* **1** near at hand, close by *la14-*. **2** almost, all but *la14-*. **nearhand** *adj* close, near, neighbouring *la18-*. **nearhand** *prep* near, close to *la14-*. **nae near a yonner** lacking in intelligence *20- NE*. **near the bane** miserly *la19-*. **near the bit 1** quite accurate or near the mark *20- Sh NE EC*. **2** miserly *20- WC SW*. †**nearhand beside** near *15-16*. †**nearhand by** *adv* close, neighbouring *la14-18*. †**nearhand by, neirhand by** *prep* near *la14-e16*. **near hand cut** a short cut *la18-*. [see the adv]
†**near**², **nere, neir** *adv* nearer, more closely *la14-e19*; compare NAR¹·². **near and near** nearer and nearer, ever closer *la14-e19*. [comparative of NIGH]
neat¹·¹, †**nete** /nit/ *adj* **1** efficient, tidy *la17-*. **2** exact, precise *la17-*. **3** trim, smart, elegant *18-*. **4** clean, unsullied *la15-16*. Compare NETT. [EModE *neat*]
neat¹·² /nit/ *adv* exactly, precisely *19-*. [see the adj]

neath, †**nethe**, †**neth** /niθ/ *prep* beneath *17- literary*. [aphetic form of ANEATH¹·²]
neathmaist, **neithmost**, *NE* **nyowmost**, †**nowmost** /'niθmest, 'niθmost; *NE* 'njʌumost/ *adj* undermost *la15-*. [OE *niþemest*]
neb¹·¹, **nib** /nɛb, nɪb/ *n* **1** a bird's beak *la14-*. **2** a nose; a snout; a face *17-*. **3** the nib of a pen *la18-*. **4** a projecting piece of land or rock *19-*. **5** the point of a pin, knife or pencil *19-*. **6** the prow of a boat *la19-*. **7** a prying look *la20-*. **8** a nosy person *la20-*. **9** the toe of a shoe *la19*. **10** sharpness, pungency *19*. **11** a projecting part of the human body; the fingers, toes or tongue *la16-19*. **nebbie 1** brusque *la19, 20- C SW Bor Uls*. **2** biting, sharp *la19- C SW*. **3** cheeky, impertinent *la19- C SW*. **4** inquisitive, nosey *20- C Uls*. **nebbit 1** sharp, pointed *la16-*. **2** having a beak, nose or point of a specified kind: ◊*reid-nebbit la16-*. **nebfu 1** a beakful *19-*. **2** a small quantity; a drop of alcohol *19-*. **nebsie** impudent *20- EC Bor*. **neb end** the tip of the nose *20- C SW Bor*. **see far afore yer neb** to have foresight *19, 20- Sh Ork T*. [OE *neb*]
neb¹·² /nɛb/ *v* **1** *of a bird* to tap with the beak *19-*. **2** to put a point on a quill-pen or pencil *la19-e20, la20- historical*. **3** to be inquisitive; to pry *la20- C*. [see the noun]
nebert /'nɛbərt/ *n fisherman's taboo bait 19- Sh*. [compare Icel *niðrburðr* a quantity of bait lowered into the sea]
nece *see* NIECE
necessar /'nɛsɛsər/ *adj* **1** essential, requisite *la14-*. **2** determined by circumstance *la15-17*. **3** profitable, useful; appropriate, convenient *16-17*. **4** *of people* giving useful service *16-17*. [OFr *necessaire*, Lat *necessārius*]
necessars, †**necessaris**, †**necessairs** /'nɛsɛsərz/ *npl* **1** essentials, requisites *la14-19, 20- Sh*. **2** necessary work or business *16-e17*. **3** necessary rights of property access *16*. [substantive use in plural of NECESSAR]
necessitate¹·¹, †**necessitat** /nə'sɛsətet/ *v* to oblige, to compel *17-*. [from the adj, perceived as a participial adj]
necessitate¹·², †**necessitat** /nə'sɛsətet/ *adj* **1** obliged, compelled by circumstance *la16-18, 20- NE*. **2** unavoidable *17*. [Lat *necessitāt-*, ptp stem of *necessitāre*]
nechbour *see* NEEBOR¹·¹
nechbourret *see* NEEBORHOOD
†**neche**, **neych**, **nich** *v* to approach *la14-16*. [OE *genēahian*]
nechyr *see* NICHER¹·²
neck¹·¹, **nek**; *NE* **naick** /nɛk; *NE* nek/ *n* **1** the part of the body connecting head and trunk *la14-*. **2** the collar of a garment *16-*. **3** the throat, the gullet *20-*. **4** *mining* the upper part of a shaft, above the coal *18- EC*. †**nekkit** having a flap or flaps covering the neck *la15-e16*. **neck band** a loop used to tether an animal by the neck *20- Sh Ork*. †**neck-break** downfall, ruin; a stumbling block *la17*. †**nekhering 1** a blow to the nape of the neck *la15-17*. **2** a variety of herring, the shad *la15*. **in spite o yer neck** in defiance of your efforts or wishes *19-*. **mak a lang neck** to stretch the neck to reach or see *la18-19, 20- T*. †**strike in the neck** *of disaster* to overtake a person *e16*. [OE *hnecca* the back part of the neck]
neck¹·² /nɛk/ *v* **1** to embrace or caress *19-*. **2** to break a person's neck *19, 20 SW*. **3** to break the neck of a bottle *19, 20 SW*. [see the noun]
nedder¹·¹, †**nadir** /'nɛdər/ *n* an extension placed below a beehive to give extra room for breeding *19, 20- WC SW*. [specific sense of NETHER²]
nedder¹·², †**neider** /'nɛdər/ *v* to place an extension below a beehive *la19-*. [see the noun]
nedder *see* NAITHER¹·³, NETHER²
neddermest *see* NETHERMAIST
neddyr *see* NETHER¹
nede *see* NEED¹·¹, NEED¹·²

nedenaill *see* NEED-NAIL
nedill, **nedling** *see* NEEDLE¹·¹
nedirmair *see* NETHERMAIR
neebie *see* KNEEBIE
neebor¹·¹, **neibour**, **neighbour**, *NE* **neiper**, †**nychtbur**, †**nechbour**, †**nybour** /'nibər, 'nɛbər; *NE* 'nipər/ *n* **1** someone who lives nearby, a neighbour *la14-*. **2** a workman's mate, a fellow-worker *la17-*. **3** a match, one of a set or pair *la18-*. **4** a husband or wife, a partner *la19-*. **5** a fellow-inhabitant of a burgh; a fellow-member of a community *15-17*. **6** a person admitted to full citizenship of a burgh; a burgess *la15-17*. **neebourless**, **neibourless** *of one of a pair* lacking the other *la19-*. **neebourlike**, **neighbourlike**, †**nychbourlyk 1** neighbourly *la15-*. **2** striving to emulate one's neighbours *18-19, 20- Sh C Uls*. †**nychtbourschip** the fact of being a neighbour; neighbourly relations *la15-16*. **neepertie**, **neeportrie** neighbourliness *17- NE*. †**ane lawful nichbour** a good citizen or neighbour *15-17*. **ane sufficiand nichbour** a good citizen or neighbour *15-17*. **be neebors tae 1** to be next to, be adjacent to *15-*. **2** to have a person as neighbour *19-*. **be neibours wi** to have a person as neighbour *19-*. **Guid Nychburris** the Dumfries festival of the Riding of the Marches *20-*. †**hald nichtbourschip to** to act as a good neighbour towards *la16*. [OE *nēahgebūr*]
neebor¹·², **neibour** /'nibər, 'nɛbər/ *v* **1** to co-operate with one's neighbours (in agricultural jobs) *la18-*. **2** to be near or adjacent to *19-*. **3** to associate or consort with *la19-*. **4** to match, to form a set with *20-*. [see the noun]
neebor¹·³, †**nethbour** /'nibər/ *adj* **1** between neighbours *la14-*. **2** neighbouring *la15-*. **3** *of enmity* internal, domestic *la15-e17*. [see the noun]
neeborhood, **neighbourheid**, *Sh* **neebrid**, †**nechbourret**, †**nychburhede**, †**nichtburhed**, /'nibərhod, 'nɛbərhid; *Sh* 'nibrəd/ *n* **1** good relations or conduct within a community; the mutual obligations of the members of a community *15-*. **2** friendly relations between neighbours *16-*. **3** the local area, the vicinity *17-*. **4** (the boundary in) a dispute between neighbours over property rights *la15-17*. †**act of nychtborheid** a formal agreement for the regulation of boundary disputes *la16-17*. †**aith of neibourhede** the oath sworn by a person on becoming a burgess *la16-e17*. [NEEBOR¹·¹, with *-heid* suffix]
need¹·¹, †**nede**, †**neid** /nid/ *n* **1** a necessity *la14-*. **2** a difficulty or emergency, a situation requiring help *la14-*. **3** necessary business *la14-19*. **needfu**, †**neidfull 1** requisite, necessary *la14-*. **2** *of a person* poor, needy *la14-*. **needfus** necessities *la18-*. †**nedilingis** necessarily *la14-e16*. †**neidway** necessarily *la14*. †**neidwayis** necessarily *la14-e16*. **needy 1** poor, destitute *16-*. **2** parsimonious, avaricious *la15-16*. **needfire**, †**neidfyre 1** fire produced by the friction of dry wood (sometimes reputed to have magical or prophylactic properties) *17-19, 20- historical*. **2** a warning beacon, a bonfire *19, 20- literary*. **3** spontaneous combustion *16-e19*. **hae mair need tae dae** would be better employed doing *20-*. **not out of the need o** still in need of *la19-*. **of neidforce** of necessity *la15-e17*. †**on neidforce** on compulsion *la15-e17*. [OE *nīed*]
need¹·², †**nede**, †**neid** /nid/ *v* **1** to require *la14-*. **2** to have to be; to be of necessity: ◊*are ye a guid driver? - A wad need la19-*. **3** ought to be: ◊*this lock needs sortit 20-*. **what needs?** there is no need *la15-*. **winna need tae** would be better not to *la19-*. [OE *nīedan*]
needcessity, †**neidcessitie** /nid'sɛsəte/ *n* **1** necessity, need *la16-*. **2** *pl* the necessities of life *la19, 20- Uls*. [conflation of NEED¹·¹ with Eng *necessity*]
needfire *see* NEED¹·¹

needle[1.1], †**nedill**, †**nidle** /'nidəl/ n **1** an instrument for sewing la15-. **2** a brooch or ornamental pin la16-17. **3** a spar used as a support in scaffolding 16-17. **needlach, needlack** a young eel la19- N. †**nedling** the setting up of transverse supports la16-17. **the needle ee** a children's game 19-. **needle naked** stark-naked 20- Sh N NE. [OE nædl]

needle[1.2] /'nidəl/ v **1** to move like a needle, to penetrate or slip quickly through 19, 20- Sh NE. **2** to interlace ropes on a roof or cornstack to hold the thatch down 20- Sh Ork. [see the noun]

†**need-nail, nedenaill** v to fasten securely; to nail up with clinched nails 16-e19. [LG neednagel a clinched nail]

neef /nif/ n difficulty, bother 18- NE. [unknown]

neeger /'nigər/ v to head a football 20- EC. [unknown]

neem see NEM[1.1]

neen see NANE[1.2], NUNE

neep[1.1], **neap, neip,** †**nepe,** †**nip** /nip/ n **1** a turnip; a swede la15-; compare TURNEEP. **2** a humorous term for the head la19-. **3** a large oversized watch la19-. **4** a stupid person 20-. **neep brose** brose made with the liquid in which turnips have been boiled la19, 20- NE T Uls. **neep cleek** a hooked implement for pulling up turnips 20- NE T EC SW. **neep cutter** a turnip slicer la19-. **neep grund** ground prepared for turnips 20- Sh Ork NE. **neep hack** a two-pronged iron implement for pulling turnips out of frozen ground 19, 20- WC. **neep heid** a stupid person 19-. **neep land** ground from which a crop of turnips has been taken la19- Sh Ork NE. **neep lantern** a turnip-lantern (used at Halloween) la19- Sh Ork N NE T EC. **neep machine** a horse-drawn machine for sowing turnips la19- NE T. **neep muck** manure for putting on turnip ground 20- Sh NE. **neep reet, neep ret** land from which a turnip crop has been taken, and still so called under the subsequent corn-crop la19- NE. **neep seed 1** turnip seed la19-. **2** the time for sowing turnips la19- NE. **neep shawin 1** the removal of turnip or swede tops 20- Ork NE T. **2** turnip sowing 20- NE. **neepy candle** = neep lantern 20- NE. **the neeps** the time of the year when turnips are hoed la19- Sh NE T. [OE næp from Lat napus]

neep[1.2] /nip/ v **1** to feed cattle with turnips la19- Sh Ork NE EC. **2** to sow land with turnips 20- NE EC. [see the noun]

neepyin see NAIPKIN

neer, nare, †**neir,** †**nere** /nir, ner/ n a kidney; a loin la14-. **near leather** a strap in a horse's harness passing over the loins 20-; compare EAR LEATHER. **near strap** a strap in a horse's harness passing over the loins la19-. [perhaps MDu niere or MLG nēre, compare Ger Niere]

neer see NEVER

Ne'erday see NEW-YEAR

neese[1.1], **neeze** /niz/ n a sneeze 18-19, 20- Sh Ork NE. [see the verb]

neese[1.2], **neeze,** †**neys** /niz/ v to sneeze 16-. [compare ON hnjósa, MLG neysen, nêsen, MDu niesen]

neesick /'nisɪk/ n a porpoise Phocoena phocoena 19- Sh. [ON hnísa, with diminutive suffix -ick]

neester /'nistər/ v to creak, to squeak 19- Sh Ork. [Norw dial gnistra]

neet, †**neit** /nit/ adv nor yet la18- NE. [ne (NA[1.1]) + Eng yet]

neet see NIT[2]

neeze see NEESE[1.1], NEESE[1.2]

neffie, nevy, †**nevoy,** †**nevo,** †**nepho** /'nɛfi, 'nɛvi/ n **1** a nephew la14-. **2** a grandson; a great-grandson 15-e17. **3** a granddaughter; a niece 16-e17. **4** a descendant e16. [ME neveu, OFr nevo]

negart see NIGGART

†**negative** adv law in the negative, by way of denial 16-19. [Lat negātīvē negatively]

Negative Confession /nɛgətɪv kənˈfɛʃən/ n Presbyterian Church the King's Confession, or Second Confession of Faith (1580-1) la16-17, 20- historical. [NEGATIVE + Eng confession]

negleck[1.1], **neglect,** †**neglek** /nəˈglɛk, nəˈglɛkt/ n (an act of) negligence 17-. [Lat neglēctus]

negleck[1.2], **neglect,** †**neglek** /nəˈglɛk, nəˈglɛkt/ v to ignore, to disregard; to leave unattended or uncared for; to fail 16-. [Lat neglēct-, ptp stem of neglegere]

neibour see NEEBOR[1.1], NEEBOR[1.2]

neid see NEED[1.1], NEED[1.2]

neider see NEDDER[1.1]

neifar see NIFFER[1.2]

neiff see NIEVE[1.1], NIEVE[1.2]

neighbour see NEEBOR[1.1]

neighbourheid see NEEBORHOOD

neip see NEEP[1.1]

neiper see NEEBOR[1.1]

neir see NEAR[2], NEER, NEVER

neis see NESS

neist[1.1], †**neste,** †**neyst** /nist/ adj next, nearest la14-. †**neisten** next, nearest e19. **neistmost** the next again la19- Sh NE. [OE nīehst]

neist[1.2], †**neste** /nist/ adv next la14-. [see the adj]

neist[1.3], †**neste** /nist/ prep next to la14-. [OE nīehst]

neit see NEET, NIT[2]

neitch see KNITCH[1.1]

neither see NAITHER[1.1], NAITHER[1.2], NAITHER[1.3], NETHER[2]

neithmost see NEATHMAIST

nek see NECK[1.1], NICK[1.1], NICK[1.2]

nem[1.1], **name,** Sh Ork N neem, †**neam,** †**naym** /nɛm, nem; Sh Ork N nim/ n **1** an appellative or designation; a proper noun la14-. **2** reputation, renown, fame la14-. **3** those bearing a particular name; a family or clan 16-. **4** a title of rank or dignity; the authority or state which a title conveys 15-17. **name bairn** a child who has been called after someone 20- Sh. **name dochter** a girl who has been called after someone 19, 20- Sh Ork. **name faither** the man after whom someone is named la17-. **name mother** the woman after whom someone is named la18-. **name son** a boy who has been called after someone la18-19, 20- Sh Ork. **ca someone out of his name 1** to miscall, to speak to the detriment of 19-. **2** to give a nickname to la19-. **get the name** to have a child named after oneself la19- NE T. **gie a bairn its name 1** to christen a child 20-. **2** to legitimize a child (by the marriage of its parents) 20-. **gie in the names, gie up the names** to supply the names for the proclamation of marriage banns 19-. **in the name o a'!** an expression of surprise, disgust or exasperation la19-. **in the name o the wee man!** an expression of surprise, disgust or exasperation la20-. [OE nama]

nem[1.2], **name** /nɛm, nem/ v pt also **named** †**namit,** †**nemmyt,** †**nammit 1** to give a name to; to identify or mention by name la14-. **2** to specify as to amount or value 15-16. **namie** one of the two chief players in a children's guessing game la19- Sh Ork NE. **namer** = namie. †**above nemmit** above mentioned la15-16. †**als wele nemmit as nocht nemmyt** a legal formula allowing for the inclusion of people or property not specifically listed in a document la14-16. †**als wele unnemmyt as nemmyt** = als wele nocht nemmyt. **canna name** to be unable to call by the correct name la17-. **name for** to call a child after a particular person la19-. **be named for** to have the reputation for la15, 20- Sh. **name tae** to associate or connect the names of two people (as a couple) *la19- NE Uls.* **name wi, †nem with** to connect the names of two people *la16-19, 20- SW.* [OE *namian*]

†nemmin, nemyn *v* to give a name to, to name *la14-15.* [OE *nemnan*, ON *nefna*]

nemmyt *see* NEM[1.2]

†nepe *v of a ship* to be stranded at neap tide *16.* [OE *nēpflōd* a neap tide]

nepe *see* NEEP[1.1]

nepho *see* NEFFIE

nepkin *see* NAIPKIN

†nepote, nepot *n* a grandson; a nephew *16-e17.* [Lat *nepōt-*, oblique stem of *nepos*]

nepus *see* NAIPHOUSE

ner *see* NAR[1.2], NAR[1.3], NAR[1.4]

nere *see* NEAR[1.1], NEAR[1.2], NEAR[1.3], NEAR[1.4], NEAR[2], NEER

nerice *see* NOURICE[1.1]

nerr *see* NAR[1.4]

nerra, nerro *see* NAIRRA

nerve[1.1] /nɛrv/ *n* **1** a sinew or tendon; a fibre in the body *16-.* **2** a band of material used to decorate a garment *e16.* [Lat *nervus*]

†nerve[1.2] *v* to decorate with threads or bands of material *e16.* [MFr *nerver*]

nervish /'nɛrvɪʃ/ *adj* excitable, anxious *19-.* [NERVE[1.1], with adj-forming suffix]

nes *see* NESH, NESS

nesch *see* NESH

†nesche, nasche, naische *n* soft ground, a bog *la15-e17.* [from the adj NESH]

nescok *see* ESSCOCK

nese *see* NESS, NIZ

†nesethrill *n* a nostril *la14-e17*; compare NOSETHIRL. [*nese* (NIZ) + THIRL[1.1]]

nesh, †nesch, †nes /nɛʃ/ *adj* soft, tender; fragile, delicate *la14-19, 20- literary.* [OE *hnesce*]

ness, nes, †nese, †neis /nɛs/ *n* a headland or promontory; frequently in place-names *la12-.* Compare NIZ. [OE *næs*, ON *nes*]

ness *see* NACE

nest /nɛst/ *n* a place where birds or animals rear their young, a nest *15-.* **look ower the nest** *of a young person* to begin to act independently *la19- WC SW Bor.* [OE *nest*]

neste *see* NEIST[1.1], NEIST[1.2], NEIST[1.3]

†nestreis *npl* latrines, privies *la16.* [probably the stem of NESTY[1.1] with the derogating suffix *-ry*]

nesty[1.1]**, nasty** /'nɛsti, 'nasti/ *v* to dirty, to befoul *18-.* [see the adj]

nesty[1.2]**, naisty, nasty, †nastie** /'nɛsti, 'nesti, 'nasti/ *adj* dirty, foul; offensive, unpleasant *la16-.* [unknown; compare Du *nestig*]

net /nɛt/ *n* openwork fabric made of twine or cord (used for catching fish); a piece of meshed fabric *la14-.* [OE *net(t)*]

net *see* NETT

nete *see* NEAT[1.1]

neth, nethe *see* NEATH

nethbour *see* NEEBOR[1.3]

nether[1]**, †neddyr** /'nɛðər/ *n* an adder *Vipera berus la15, 19- N T EC Uls.* Compare ETHER. [OE *nædre*]

nether[2]**, nedder, †nethir, †nather, †neither** /'nɛðər, 'nɛdər/ *adj* **1** lower, under *la14-.* **2** *in place-names* the lower situated of two farms or roads of the same name *la14-.* **3** *of a building* downstairs; in the basement or cellar *la15-17.* **nether end** the posterior, the buttocks *17-.* **†nether part** the posterior, the buttocks *la15-e17.* [OE *niþera*]

nether *see* NITHER

†nethermair, nethir mare, nedirmair *adv* further down *la15-e16.* [NETHER[2] + MAIR[1.2]]

nethermaist, nethermost, †neddermest /'nɛðərmest, 'nɛðərmost/ *adv* lowest, furthest down *la16-.* [NETHER[2] + MAIST[1.2]]

nethir *see* NETHER[2]

nett, net, *Bor* **nate** /nɛt; *Bor* net/ *adj* **1** exact, precise; free from further deduction *la15-.* **2** clean, unsullied *la15-.* **3** smart, elegant *17-.* Compare NEAT[1.1]. **†nettie, natie** sheer, unmitigated *la18-e19.* [MFr, Du *net*]

nettercap /'nɛtərkap/ *n* **1** a spider *la19- NE T EC.* **2** a crane-fly *20- T.* **netterie** a spider *la19- NE T.* [wrong division of *an* ETTERCAP]

nettie *see* NETT

nettle, †nettill /'nɛtəl/ *n* a stinging plant *Urtica dioica la15-.* **nettle brose** brose made with the juice of boiled young nettle-tops *19- NE T.* **nettle broth** broth made from nettle-tops *19, 20- SW Uls.* **†nettill claith** a type of cloth *la16-e17.* **nettle creeper, nettlie creeper** the whitethroat *Sylvia communis la19- C.* **†nettle kail, netl caill** = *nettle broth la16-19.* **on nettles** on tenterhooks; impatient, ill-humoured *la19-.* [OE *netel*]

nettle-earnest /'nɛtəlvɛrnəst/ *n* dead earnest *19- Bor Uls.* [wrong division of *in ettle earnest* (ETTLE[1.1])]

neuk, nook, †nuke /njuk, nuk/ *n* **1** a corner, an angle *la14-.* **2** a corner or angle of a piece of land *la14-.* **3** a headland, a promontory *la14-.* **4** an external angle of a building; the corner of a street *15-.* **5** an outlying or remote place *16-.* **6** the angle of a stream; an inlet *16-.* **7** a corner made in a fold of a garment or napkin *la16-17.* **neukit 1** having corners or angles *16-.* **2** cantankerous *20- NE.* **the East Neuk** the eastern corner of Fife *la17-.* **in his ain neuk** under strict control *19- Sh NE T.* **†in the nuke, in nwikis** clandestinely *16.* [unknown]

neutral /'njutrəl/ *adj* **1** impartial *la15-.* **2** *in grammar* neuter *16-e17.* **†neutrallie** uncommitted, impartial *la16-17.* [ME *neutral* not taking sides, Lat *neutrālis* neither masculine nor feminine]

nev, neve *see* NIEVE[1.1]

nevel[1.1]**, †nevell** /'nɛvəl/ *n* a punch, a blow *16-19, 20- N SW Bor.* [see the verb]

nevel[1.2]**,** *EC* **naffle, †knevel** /'nɛvəl; *EC* 'nafəl/ *v* **1** to punch or pummel; to batter *la16-19, 20- Sh N SW Bor.* **2** to squeeze, to pinch, to knead *la18-19, 20- Sh Ork EC.* [frequentative form of NIEVE[1.1]]

never, nivver, neer, *N* **noor, †niver, †neir** /'nɛvər, 'nɪvər, nɛr, nir; *N* nur/ *adv* at no time; not at all *la14-.* **†neer-do-gude** a dishonest or unsuccessful person *e19.* **neer-do-weel, †never-do-well** a dishonest or unsuccessful person *la17-.* **nevermass** a time that never comes *18-19, 20- literary.* **†never-the-latter** nevertheless *15.* **never a** not a single, absolutely none: ◊*there's never a Scot shall set them free la15-.* **never a bit** an expression of surprise or disbelief *20- NE T.* **†never nane** no one, none at all *15-e16.* **never out o your road** always able to turn things to your own advantage; not easily upset *19, 20- NE.* [OE *næfre*]

†nevin, nevyne *v* to name, to mention, to declare *la14-16.* [ON *nefna*]

nevo, nevoy, nevy *see* NEFFIE

nevyne *see* NEVIN

†new[1.1] *v* to renew, to restore; to recommence, to revive *la14-15.* [see the adj]

new[1.2]**,** *NE* **nyow, †now, †nue** /nju; *NE* njʌu/ *adj* **1** recent, not seen or known before *12-.* **2** fresh, not stale or damaged; not used or worn *15-.* **3** additional; renewed; different *15-.* **4** restored, as new *la15-16.* **newlins, †newlingis 1** newly, recently *la14-19*, *20- NE*. **2** anew *15-16*. **3** at once *la14*. **newly 1** recently *la15-*. **2** anew, again *la14-e17*. **3** for the first time, without precedent *la15-16*. **new cheese** a dish made from the cream of a newly-calved cow's milk *19- NE*. †**newcorne** harvest-time *la16-17*. **new extent** the Scottish land valuation made in 1474 *16- historical*; compare *auld extent* (AULD¹·²). **new farrant** novel, modern *20- NE*. † **new bod, new shod** a fresh attempt at something *16-19*. **of new, of the new 1** again, afresh *la14-19*, *20- WC SW Bor Uls*. **2** lately, recently *la14-16*, *20- WC SW Bor Uls*. **3** newly, for the first time *15-16*. †**on new** afresh, anew *la14-e16*. [OE *nīwe, nēowe*]

new¹·³ /nju/ *adv* **1** newly, recently, just *la14-*. **2** anew, afresh, again *15-19*. **new calfit**, †**new calffit**, †**new ca'd** *of cows* recently calved, in milk *la15-*. [see the adj]

†**new²** *v* **1** to oppress *la18-19*. **2** *in falconry* to drive waterfowl into the water *e16*. [AN, OFr *enewer* to water, waulk]

newance *see* NEWINS

newfangle¹·¹ /nju'faŋgəl/ *n* novelty, innovation *la18-19, 20- Sh T*. [see the adj]

†**newfangle**¹·², **newfangill** *adj* **1** *of a person* fond of novelty; inexperienced *16-19*. **2** *of things* novel, new *18-19*. [ME *neuefangel*]

newin, newing /'njuɪn, 'njuɪŋ/ *n* the working of yeast in the making of ale *la16-*. [compare NEWINS]

newins, newance, †**newingis** /'njuɪnz, 'njuəns/ *n* **1** a novelty, an innovation *la16-19*, *20- N SW Uls*. **2** news, information *la19- Uls*. [NEW¹·¹, with noun-forming and plural suffix, later reconstrued as singular]

newis *see* NEWS¹·¹

New Lichts /'nju lɪxts/ *npl* **1** the moderate or more latitudinarian element of the Church of Scotland *18-e19, 20- historical*. **2** one of the two corresponding groups which split both branches of the Secession Church, the Burghers in 1799 and the Antiburghers in 1806, the New Lichts from both combining in 1820 to form the United Secession Church *la18-e19, 20- historical*. Compare AULD LICHTS. [NEW¹·² + LICHT¹·¹]

New Register House /nju rɛdʒɪstər 'hʌus/ *n* the building which houses the court of the Lord Lyon and General Register House in which the Scottish registers or records are kept *la19-*. Compare REGISTER HOUSE. [NEW¹·¹ + REGISTER HOUSE]

news¹·¹, †**newis** /njuz/ *n pl* also †**newses 1** a report of recent occurrences; a piece of information *la15-*. **2** a conversation; gossip *la19- Sh N NE*. **3** *pl* novelties, wonders *16*. **newsie** gossipy, talkative *19- N NE T*. [specific use of noun from NEW¹·¹, after MFr *nouvelles*]

news¹·² /njuz/ *v* to chat, to gossip *19- Sh N NE T EC*. **newser** a person who likes to chat; a talkative child *20- Sh N NE T*. [see the noun]

newses *see* NEWS¹·¹

New Town /'nju tʌun/ *n* the area of central Edinburgh to the north of the Castle ridge, planned and built between 1766 and 1850 *la18-*. Compare AULD TOON. [NEW¹·¹ + TOUN]

New-year, †**New-ȝere** /nju'jir/ *n* **1** the year just begun or about to begin; the first days of January *la15-*. **2** a New-year's gift; food or drink given in hospitality at New Year *la19-*. **New-year's day, Ne'erday**, *Sh* **Newerday**, †**Noor's Day**, †**Nurday 1** the first day of the New Year *la15-*. **2** a New-year gift; food or drink given in hospitality at New Year *la19-*. †**New-year's even, newyere even** New Year's Eve *16-e18*. **New-year gift**, †**new-ȝeir gift**, †**Nuregift** a gift given at New Year *16-*. **Neuersmas, newer's mas**, †**newermes** (a mass performed on) New-year's Day *la15-19, 20- Sh*. [NEW¹·¹ + YEAR]

next *see* NIXT¹·¹, NIXT¹·², NIXT¹·³

neyce *see* NIECE
neych *see* NECHE
neys *see* NEESE¹·²
neyst *see* NEIST¹·¹
ni *see* NA²
niag *see* NAG
nib *see* NEB¹·¹, NIP¹·¹
nibald *see* NABAL¹·¹
nibbie /'nɪbi/ *n* **1** a walking stick; a shepherd's crook *19- C SW Bor*. **2** a projecting knob *20- Sh*. **nibbie staff** a walking stick *la19- Bor*. [*nib* (NEB¹·¹) + -IE¹]
†**nibbit** *n* an oatcake sandwich *la18-19*. [unknown]
nibble, †**nybbill** /'nɪbəl/ *v* **1** to take small bites; to bite repeatedly *16-*. **2** to fiddle with *19-*. [unknown; compare MLG *nibbeln* to eat in small bites]
niblick /'nɪblɪk/ *n* a golf club corresponding to the No 8 or 9 iron *la19-e20, la20- historical*. [diminutive derived from *nib* a bird's beak, from the hooked appearance of the club]
nice, †**nyce**, †**nys** /nʌɪs/ *adj* **1** pleasant, agreeable *la18-*. **2** fine, dainty, refined *la18-*. **3** fastidious *la18-*. **4** disdainful, haughty *la15-17*. **5** precise, intricate *la15-16*. **6** ridiculous, absurd *la15-e17*. **7** lascivious *16*. **8** strange, astonishing *16*. †**nycenes** hauteur; reserve, caution *la16-e17*. †**nycete, nycetee** folly *la14-e16*. **nice gabbit** fussy or fastidious about food *19, 20- NE*. **aw the nice** a sentimental expression of approval *la20-*. [ME *nice*]
nich *see* NECHE
†**nichell** *n* nothing *la15-16*. [altered form of Lat *nihil*]
nicher¹·¹, **nicker** /'nɪxər, 'nɪkər/ *n* **1** a whinny, a neigh *la18-*. **2** a snigger *19-*. **nickerers** new shoes *19- Bor*. [see the verb]
nicher¹·², **nicker**, †**nikkir**, †**nechyr** /'nɪxər, 'nɪkər/ *v* **1** to whinny, to neigh *16-*. **2** to snigger *19-*. [compare Norw dial *knikra*]
nicht¹·¹, **night**, †**nycht** /nɪxt, nʌɪt/ *n* the period of darkness after sunset, the night-time *la14-*. †**nicht-at-een** evening *la19*. **night clock** a night-flying beetle *19- Sh SW Uls*. †**nycht glass** an hourglass used on a ship to time the night watches *16-e17*. **nicht mutch** a nightcap *la16-19, 20- Ork N*. †**nycht season** night time *la16-17*. †**nycht waker, nicht walkar 1** a person who stays up late engaged in revelry *16-17*. **2** a law-breaker who goes about at night *16-17*. †**nicht waking, nycht walking** staying up late to engage in revelry or riotousness *la15-e18*. †**nicht walk** a wake held at night *la15-17*. †**be nichtirtale, on nychterertale** by night *la14-15*. †**on nychterertale** by night *15*. **the nicht, the night** tonight *la15-*. **the nicht afore the morn** the eve of the Common Ridings in the Borders or the Lammas Fair in Kirkwall *la19- Ork Bor*. †**under nicht** at night *16-17*. [OE *niht*]
nicht¹·², **nycht** /nɪxt/ *v* **1** to be overtaken by night *la16-19, 20- NE*. **2** to spend the night *17, 20- NE*. **3** *of night* to fall *15-e16*. [see the noun]
nichtburhed *see* NEEBORHOOD
nick¹·¹, **nik**, †**nek** /nɪk/ *n* **1** a notch, an incision *17-*. **2** a narrow gap in a range of hills; frequently in place-names *17-*. **3** one of the notches or growth-rings on an animal's horns *la18-*. **4** a broken-off fragment, a scrap *17-19, 20- Sh Uls*. **5** a prison; a police station *19-*. **6** a sprocket *16-19*. **7** a notch in a stick used as a means of reckoning *la17-e19*. **nickie** an oatcake or bun with an indented edge *la19- C Bor*. **nick stick** a tally; a reckoning stick *la17-19, 20- Bor*. **a nick in yer horn** a year of one's life *19-*. †**nicks in yer horn** age or experience *19*. [ME *nik*]
nick¹·², †**nik**, †**nek** /nɪk/ *v* **1** to catch with a knife; to cut a notch in *la15-*. **2** to cut off, to sever *18-*. **3** to catch, to seize *la18-*. **4** to cheat, to trick *19-*. **5** to imprison *20-*. **6** to go

somewhere quickly *la*20-. **nickit** notched *la*16-. **as auld farrant as a nickit bake** *of a child* old-fashioned, quaint 20- *EC SW*. **as auld farrant as a nickit bap** = *as auld farrant as a nickit bake* 20- *NE*. **nick aboot wi** to keep company with *la*20-. †**nick the threed** to kill *la*18-19. [see the noun]

Nick /nɪk/ *n* a nickname for the Devil *18*-. †**nickie** a scamp, a mischievous boy *19*. **Nickie-ben** a nickname for the Devil *la18-*. [shortened form of *Auld Nick* (AULD[1.2])]

nick *see* KNICK[1.1], KNICK[1.2]

nicker *see* KNICK[1.2], NICHER[1.1], NICHER[1.2]

nickerers *see* NICHER[1.1]

nickie-tams /ˈnɪki ˈtamz/ *npl* straps tied round farmworkers' trousers below the knees *20*-. [shortened form of Eng *knickerbocker* + TOME]

nickle *see* KNUCKLE[1.1], KNUCKLE[1.2]

nickle naething /ˈnɪkəl ˈneθɪŋ/ *n* the term represented by the letter N on the side of a spinning top *la19*- *NE T*. [NICHELL + NAETHING]

nickler *see* KNUCKLE[1.2]

nick-nacket /ˈnɪkˈnakət/ *n* a knick-knack *la18-19, 20*- *NE EC*. [reduplicative compound based on KNACK[1.1]]

nickum /ˈnɪkəm/ *n* a scamp, a mischievous boy *19- NE*. [NICK, with diminutive suffix *-um*]

nidder *see* NITHER

niddle /ˈnɪdəl/ *v* **1** to work quickly or perseveringly with the fingers *19, 20- NE EC Uls*. **2** to fiddle about, to toy with *19, 20- Ork NE Bor*. [unknown]

nidge[1.1], **nudge**, *Sh* **nodge**, *Ork* **knudge**, *N NE* **knidge**, †**gnidge** /nɪdʒ, nʌdʒ; *Sh* nɔdʒ; *Ork* knʌdʒ; *N NE* knɪdʒ/ *n* **1** a push or prod (with a knee or an elbow); a shove *19*-. **2** a forceful squeeze, a pressing down; a bruise *la19- Sh Ork N NE*. [see the verb]

nidge[1.2], **nudge**, *Sh* **nodge**, *Ork* **knudge**, *N NE* **knidge**, †**gnidge** /nɪdʒ, nʌdʒ; *Sh* nɔdʒ; *Ork* knʌdʒ; *N NE* knɪdʒ/ *v* **1** to poke, to push; to jog or jostle *19*-. **2** to rub, to squeeze; to press, to bruise *18-19, 20- Sh Ork N NE*. [unknown; compare Norw *nugge* to push, OE *gnīdan* to rub, grind together, crumble, Norw *gnida* to squeeze, crush]

nidge[2] /nɪdʒ/ *v* to dress a stone roughly, by picking with a sharp-pointed hammer *19, 20- NE*. [voiced variant of NITCH]

nidle *see* NEEDLE[1.1]

nie *see* NIGH

niece, *NE* **niesh**, †**nece**, †**neyce** /nis; *NE* niʃ/ *n* **1** the daughter of a sibling *15*-. **2** a female relative, a granddaughter *15-17*. **3** a nephew *15-e17*. [ME *nece*]

nieve[1.1], *Sh* **nev**, †**nive**, †**neve**, †**neiff** /niv; *Sh* nɛv/ *n* **1** a fist *la14*-. **2** *pl* fisticuffs *la18-19, 20- Sh Ork*. **3** a fistful *la19- Sh Ork*. **4** the handgrip of an oar *la19- Sh Ork*. **5** a measure of a hand's breadth *la17-e18*. **6** grasp, possession *16*. **nievefu**, *Sh* **nevfoo**, †**neifu** a fistful, a handful *la14*-. **nievie-nievie-nicknack** (the first line of a rhyme in) a children's guessing game *18*-. [ON *hnefi* a fist]

†**nieve**[1.2], †**neiff** *v* **1** to guddle fish *e19*. **2** to strike with the fists *e17*. [see the noun]

niff *see* KNEEF

niffer[1.1] /ˈnɪfər/ *n* an exchange or barter *15*-. [probably NIEVE[1.1] + FARE[1.1]]

niffer[1.2], †**neifar** /ˈnɪfər/ *v* to barter, to trade; to haggle, to bargain *16*-. [see the noun]

niffler /ˈnɪflər/ *n weaving* a comb-like instrument between whose teeth the web was spread on the loom *la18-19, 20- historical*. [NEVEL[1.2], with agent suffix]

niffnaff[1.1] /ˈnɪfnaf/ *n* a small or insignificant person or object *19, 20- Sh Ork NE WC Uls*. [see the verb]

niffnaff[1.2] /ˈnɪfnaf/ *v* to waste time; to speak or act frivolously *18-19, 20- Sh T Uls*. [perhaps a reduplicated formation; compare NYAFF[1.1]]

nigg, nyig /nɪg, njɪg/ *v* **1** to nag, to pester *la19- Sh*. **2** *of a fish* to tug at the bait *la19- Sh*. **3** to work ineffectually *20- Sh*. [unknown]

niggart, †**negart** /ˈnɪgərt/ *n* a miser *la16-19, 20- T SW Uls*. [ME *nigard*]

nigh, †**ne**, †**nie** /nae/ *adv* **1** near *15*-. **2** nearly, almost *la17*-. **nigh hand 1** nearby *19*-. **2** nearly, almost *19*-. [OE *nēah*]

night *see* NICHT[1.1]

nig nay[1.1] /ˈnɪg ne/ *n* a knick-knack *la17-19, 20- SW*. [unknown]

nig nay[1.2] /ˈnɪg ne/ *v* to fuss, to potter about *la19, 20- SW*. [unknown]

nik *see* NICK[1.1], NICK[1.2]

nikkir *see* NICHER[1.2]

nimble *see* NIMMLE

nimious /ˈnɪmiəs/ *adj law* excessive, ureasonable *la17*-. **nimious and oppressive** excessive and burdensome *20*-. [Lat *nimius*]

nimm /nɪm/ *interj* an expression of pleasure (by or to a child) at something good to eat *20*-. [onomatopoeic]

nimmle, nimble, †**nymmill** /ˈnɪməl, ˈnɪmbəl/ *adj* agile, quick *la15*-. [OE *numel*; from *nim* take, with *-le* suffix]

nimp /nɪmp/ *n* a morsel, a fragment *19, 20- NE C SW Uls*. [unknown]

nimsh, imsh /nɪmʃ, ɪmʃ/ *n* a tiny piece *20- N NE T*. [unknown]

†**nine**[1.1], **nyne** *adj* ninth *la14-e17*. Compare NINTH. [use of the cardinal as an ordinal as if NINTH]

nine[1.2], **nyne** /nʌɪn/ *numeral* the cardinal number after eight *la14*-. **ninesie** the ninth movement in the game of chuckies *20- T H&I Uls*. †**nine-eyed-eel** the lamprey *19*. **nine holes** the cut of beef below the breast *19*-. **tae the nines** to perfection *18*-. [OE *nigon*]

nineteen[1.1] /nʌɪnˈtin/ *n* a lease of a farm for nineteen years *19*-. [specific use of the numeral]

nineteen[1.2], †**nyntene**, †**nynteine** /nʌɪnˈtin/ *adj* nineteenth *16-19, 20- NE*. [see the numeral]

nineteen[1.3], †**nyntene**, †**nynteine** /nʌɪnˈtin/ *numeral* the cardinal number after eighteen *la14*-. **nineteen canteen** a long time ago; an indeterminate time in the past *la20*-. **nineteen oatcake** = *nineteen canteen la20*-. [OE *nigontēne*]

nineteent, nineteenth, †**nynetende** /nʌɪnˈtint, nʌɪnˈtinθ/ *adj* the ordinal number after eighteenth *15*-. [NINETEEN[1.3], with (altered) *-th* ordinal suffix]

Ninety Twa /nʌɪnte ˈtwa/ *n* a name for the 92nd Regiment of Foot, which later became the the *Gordon Highlanders* (GORDON) *19, 20- historical*. [specific use of the numeral]

ninth, *NE T* **nint** /nʌɪnθ; *NE T* nʌɪnt/ *adj* the ordinal number after eighth *la14*-. [NINE[1.2], with *-th* suffix]

nip[1.1], **nib**, †**nipp** /nɪp, nɪb/ *n* **1** a pinch *la16*-. **2** a fragment, a piece *17*-. **3** a sheepmark, a notch cut in the ear *la18*-. **4** pungency, sharpness of flavour *19*-. **5** an advantage in bargaining *la19*-. **6** a cigarette end *la20*-. **7** *mining* an interruption in a seam of coal *19*. **nip of hunger** the effect of hunger on farm stock *20- Bor*. [see the verb]

nip[1.2] /nɪp/ *v* **1** to seize, to grip; to catch; to pinch *la15*-. **2** *of clothes* to fit tightly *16*-. **3** to tingle, smart or sting *16*-. **4** to snatch or steal *la18*-. **5** *of food* to taste sharp or pungent *19*-. **6** to be sarcastic or hurtful *la19*-. **7** to get the better of, to cheat *la19*-. **8** *in baking* to make indentations around the edges of pastry *20*-. **9** to put out a cigarette by compressing the end *la20*-. **nippit 1** tight-fitting; too small *16*-. **2** stingy *19*-. **3** curt, bad-tempered *la19*-. **4** hungry, badly fed *la19*-. **5** bigoted *la19*-. **nippity** with short sharp movements *20*-.

†**nipcaik** a miser *e16*. **nip-lug** backbiting, squabbling *19, 20- NE T*. **Nip-nebs** a nickname for Jack Frost *la19-*. **nip-scart** a stingy person *19, 20- SW Bor*. [unknown; compare MDu *nipen*, LG *nippen* to sip, MLG *knipan* to pinch]
nip *see* NEEP[1.1]
nippy /'nɪpi, 'nɪpe/ *adj* **1** sarcastic, bitter; curt, snappish *la19-*. **2** sharp, stinging *la19-*. **3** *of food* hot, spicy *la20-*. **4** miserly, greedy *19*. **nippy sweetie, nippie sweetie 1** a sharp-tasting sweet *20-*. **2** a curt or disapproving person *la20-*. **3** a nip of whisky *la20-*. [NIP[1.1] + -IE[2]]
†**nipschot** *n* a misdirected shot *16-e17*. **play nipschot** to shoot amiss; to make a mistake *16-e17*. [unknown]
nir *see* KNUR, NOR[1.2]
nirl[1.1], **nurl** /nɪrl, nʌrl/ *n* **1** a fragment, a crumb; a small object *19, 20- literary*. **2** a cold, biting wind *20- Sh*. **nirlie 1** stunted, shrivelled *19, 20- Sh Ork*. **2** *of cold* pinching, nipping *la19, 20- Sh T EC*. **the nirls** a rash; chickenpox or measles *la16-*. [variant of KNURL]
nirl[1.2], **nurl**, *Sh* **nyurl** /nɪrl, nʌrl; *Sh* njʌrl/ *v* **1** to shrink, to shrivel; to stunt in growth *19-*. **2** to pinch with cold *19-*. **3** to complain *la20- Sh*. [see the noun]
nise *see* NIZ
nit[1], **nut** /nɪt, nʌt/ *n* **1** a kernel enclosed in a hard shell, a nut *15-*. **2** a metal nut for screwing on a bolt *16-*. **3** a part of a gun *16*. †**nute gall** an oak-gall, used to make dye-stuff *la16*. [OE *hnutu*]
nit[2], **neet**, †**neit** /nɪt, nit/ *n* (the egg of) the head louse *la16-*. **neetie** *n* a greedy or disobliging person *19, 20- NE C*. **neetie** *adj* parsimonious *19, 20- C Bor*. †**nitty now, neitie now** infested with nits *la16-e18*. [OE *hnitu*]
nitch /nɪtʃ/ *n* a notch, a small incision *e18, 20- Sh Ork T*. [unknown; compare Eng *niche, notch*, NICK]
nither, nidder, †**nether** /'nɪðər, 'nɪdər/ *v* **1** to oppress; to distress *15-*. **2** to pinch with cold or hunger *18-*. **3** to stunt or shrivel, to check in growth *18-*. **4** to make low, to abase *la15-e17*. **5** to constrict or confine *16-e17*. [OE *niþerian*, ON *niðra* to bring low]
nithin *see* NAETHING
Nithsdale measure /'nɪθsdel mɛʒər/ *n* a measure of capacity about one-tenth larger than the standard Scots equivalent *18-e19, la19- historical*. [from the name of the valley in Dumfriesshire + MEASURE[1.1]]
nitteret *see* NATTER[1.1]
nittle *see* KNIT
nitty now *see* NIT[2]
nive *see* NIEVE[1.1]
niver, nivver *see* NEVER
nixt[1.1], **next** /nɪkst, nɛkst/ *adj* **1** nearest, closest; adjacent to; *15-*. **2** immediately following *15-*. **3** *of days or months* the next but one *18-*. Compare NEIST[1.1]. †**nextan, nextin** *in ballads* next *la18-e19*. †**nixt hand, next hand** nearest to, immediately following; second only to *15-e16*. [OE *nīehst*]
nixt[1.2], **next** /nɪkst, nɛkst/ *adv* in the next place, immediately afterwards *la14-*. Compare NEIST[1.2]. †**nixt adjacent** next to, beside *la16-17*. †**nixtcumis** = *nixt-to-cum la15-16*. **nixt efter, next efter** next in a sequence *la14-*. †**nixt-to-cum, next to come** immediately following, next: ◊*on Monunday nixtocum 15-e18*. [see the adj]
nixt[1.3], **next** /nɪkst, nɛkst/ *prep* beside, nearest to; following closely on from *la14-*. Compare NEIST[1.2]. [see the adj]
niz, †**nese**, †**nise** /nɪz/ *n* **1** the nose *la14-*. **2** a promontory, a headland *la13-e16*. **3** the crown of a tooth *e18*. **nizzin 1** a sharp reproof *la19- Ork NE EC*. **2** a buffeting from the weather *la19- NE*. **nizwise** perceptive *17- NE*. [ME *nese*; compare NOSE]
nizz *see* KNUSE

no, nae /no, ne/ *adv* **1** not *la15-*. **2** not at all, quite the opposite of *19-*. **nae a bit** an expression of amazement *20- NE*. **nae bit**, †**no but** no more than, only just *17-19, 20- NE*. **nae handy** excessive: ◊*at a rate nae handy 20- NE*. **nae ilka body** not everybody, no ordinary person *19- N NE T*. **nae in, no in** abstracted, daydreaming *la19-*. **nae that ill** *adv* not so badly, quite well *19-*. **nae that ill** *adj* not so bad, good enough *20- Sh NE EC*. †**no utherwayis** in no other way *15-17*. **nae weel** ill, in poor health *20-*. [OE *nā, nō* or altered form of ME *noth* a variant of *nought*; compare NOCHT[1.2]]
no *see* NA[1.2], NA[2], NAE[1]
noal *see* KNOLL
nob[1] /nɔb/ *n* **1** the nose *la18-19, 20- NE*. **2** the toe of a shoe *19, 20- EC*. [specific senses of Eng *knob*]
†**nob**[2] /nɔb/ *n* an interloper; a blackleg in a strike *19*. [reduced form of Eng *knobstick*]
nobile officium /nobɪle oˈfɪʃiəm/ *n law* the Court of Session's power of equitable jurisdiction in cases where the law itself does not provide a clear remedy *la18-*. [Lat *nōbile officium* noble duty]
†**nobilitate** *v pt, ptp* **nobilitat nobilitated 1** to raise to the rank of titled nobility *la16-18*. **2** to bring renown to, to make illustrious *la16-e18*. [Lat *nōbilitāt-*, ptp stem of *nōbilitāre*]
noble[1.1], †**nobill** /'nobəl/ *n* **1** a person of noble birth, a member of the nobility *la14-*. **2** a gold coin *la14-e18, 19- historical* **3** a person of distinction or renown *la15-e16*. †**the nine nobles** the nine worthies (of ancient and medieval history and legend) *la15-e16*. [see the adj]
noble[1.2], †**nobill** /'nobəl/ *adj* **1** of high rank or title *la14-*. **2** excellent, admirable *la14-*. †**noble part** a vital bodily organ *la16-e17*. [ME *noble*]
nocht[1.1], **nauchle, naucht**, *NE* **noth**, †**noucht** /nɔxt, 'nɔxəl, nɔxt; *NE* nɔθ/ *n* nothing, nought *la14-*. [OE *nōwiht*]
nocht[1.2], **naucht, not**, †**naught** /nɔxt, nɔt/ *adv* not at all, in no way *la14-*. **nochtie**, †**nauchtie 1** *of things* small, worthless, unfit for use *16-*. **2** *of people* underachieving, insignificant *19-*. **nochtify** to belittle *la19- Sh T*. **nochtless** worthless *19, 20- Sh Bor*. †**nochtagaynstandand** notwithstanding, nevertheless *la14-15*. †**nochtgaynstanding** notwithstanding, nevertheless *la14-e16*. †**nocht-obstant, not-obstant** notwithstanding, nevertheless *la15-e17*. †**nocht than** nevertheless *la14-15*. †**nocht-the-les, not-the-les** nevertheless *la14-17*. **notwithstanding**, †**nochtwithstanding** *adv* nevertheless *15-*. **notwithstanding**, †**nochtwithstanding** *prep* despite *15-*. †**notwithstanding, nochtwithstanding** *conj* though *15-17*. †**notwithstanding of** in spite of *16-17*. †**nocht to seik** not hard to find, present in abundance *15-16*. [compare NOCHT[1.1], NO]
nock *see* KNOCK[2], KNUCK
nockit *see* NACKET[1]
nockle *see* KNUCKLE[1.1]
†**nocturne** *adj* nocturnal *16*. [MFr *nocturne*]
nod /nɔd/ *v* to incline the head briefly *la15-*. **nid nodding** nodding while dozing *la18-19, 20- literary*. [unknown]
noddy /'nɔdi/ *n* a light two-wheeled carriage *19-e20, la20- historical*. [perhaps from the verb NOD with *-y* suffix]
noggie *see* KNAG[2]
nois *see* NOSE
†**noisome** *adj* noisy, rowdy *19*. [Eng *noise*, with adj-forming suffix *-some*; compare *dinsome* (DIN[1.1])]
noisthirl *see* NOSETHIRL
†**nok**[1] *n* the tip of a yardarm *16*. [MDu *nocke*, Fris, LG *nok*]
†**nok**[2] *n* a hook which held the thread in a distaff *la15-16*. [uncertain ME *nok*; compare Norw *nokke* a hook on a spindle]
nok *see* KNOCK[2]
†**nold** *v* would not, did not *e16*. [OE *nolde*]

nolder see NOWTHER[1.1], NOWTHER[1.3]
noll see KNOOL
nolt see NOWT[1]
nomber see NUMMER[1.1], NUMMER[1.2]
nominal raiser see RAISER
nominate /'nɔmɪnet/ *adj* **1** *law* nominated or appointed to an office or title *la17-*. **2** *law* named and appointed in the will of the testator *la18-*. [Lat *nōminātus*, ptp of *nōmināre*]
Non /nɔn/ *n Presbyterian Church* a person who opposed the introduction of a minister to a charge against the wishes of the congregation *la19, 20- historical*. Compare INTRUSION. [shortened form of Eng *non-intrusionist*]
none see NANE[1.1], NANE[1.2], NUNE
†non-entres, non-entress *n* **1** non-entry into possession of a property *la15-17*. **2** failure to appear in court *la15-e16*. [prefix *non-* + ENTRESS]
non-entry, †non-entre /'nɔn ɛntre/ *n law* **1** the failure of an heir to a deceased vassal to renew investiture; the fee payable to the superior in the case of such failure *la15-19, 20- historical*. **2** failure to present oneself or another at a court of law for trial *la15-16*. [*non-* + ENTRY]
†noneschankis, noynsankys *n* a light meal taken in the afternoon *la14-16*. [altered form of ME *nonschenches*; compare *nuncheon*]
non-implement /'nɔn ɪmpləmənt/ *n law* the non-fulfilment of a contract *18-*. [prefix *non-* + IMPLEMENT[1.1]]
non jurant see JURANT[1.1], JURANT[1.2]
non-juror see JUROR
†non-so-prettie *n* a kind of cloth *e17*. [NANE[1.2] + SAE[2.1] + PRETTY]
†nonsunt *n* the twelve-penny groat coined under Francis and Mary *la16*. [from the Lat inscription on the reverse of the coin *iam nōn sunt duo sed ūna caro* now they are not two but one flesh]
noo, nou, now /nu, nʌu/ *adv* **1** at this time, at present; immediately or next *la14-*. **2** under the present circumstances, in view of these facts *15-*. **nooadays** at the present time *la18-*. **†now-on-dayes** = *nooadays la15-e16*. **†as now 1** for the time being *15*. **2** immediately, at once *15*. **the noo, the now 1** just now, at present; just a moment ago *18-*. **2** in a moment, soon *la19-*. **noo an than, noos an thans** now and then, from time to time *18-*. **†noo as then** *law* for all time *15-e17*. **noo nae, noo na** an expression of sympathy or mild remonstrance *19- C Bor*. **than as noo** for all time *15-16*. [OE *nū*]
noof see KNUIFE, NUIF
nook see NEUK
nool see KNULE
nooltie see KNOILT
noon see NUNE
noop /nup/ *n* the cloudberry *Rubus chamaemorus la19- N Bor*. **nub-berrie, nup-berry** the cloudberry *la18- Bor*. [unknown]
noop see NOUP
noor see NEVER
noose see KNUSE
noozle /'nuzəl/ *n* one of the short cords by which the meshwork of a herring-net is attached to the head-rope *20- N EC Bor*. Compare OSEL. [OE *nostle* a band]
noozle see KNUSE
†nop *v* to have a short sleep *la15-16*. **nop and nod** to sleep *la15-16*. [altered form of Eng *nap*]
†nop bed, nap bed, nape bed *n* a flock mattress *la15-e17*. [reduced form of NOPPIS + BED[1.1]]
nopesek see NOPSEK

†noppis, nappis *npl* wool flock *la14-17*. [MDu *noppe* wool flock, nap of cloth]
†nopsek, nopesek, napsek *n* a flock mattress *la15-16*. [reduced form of NOPPIS + SECK[1.1]]
nor[1.1] /nɔr/ *adv* indeed not: ◊*is it sore? no, nor sore 20-*. [probably from the conj]
nor[1.2], *NE* **nir,** *NE Bor* **nar** /nɔr; *NE* nɪr; *NE Bor* nar/ *conj* **1** than *15-*. **2** and not *la15-*. **3** (but) that: ◊*nae wonder nor you're thin la15-*. [ME *nor*]
nor[2] /nɔr/ *adv* if, although; would that *la15-*. [unknown]
noraleg /'nɔralɛg/ *n* a needle, a large pin; an awl *la19- Sh*. [unknown]
nordern see NORTHERN
norie /'nɔri/ *n* the puffin *Fratercula arctica la18-19, 20- Sh*. [perhaps onomatopoeic of its cry; compare *tammie norrie* (TAMMIE)]
norl see KNURL
norland[1.1]**, norlan, †northland** /'nɔrlənd, 'nɔrlən/ *n* **1** the north and north-east of Scotland *la15-*. **2** a person from the north or north-east of Scotland *la18-19, 20- EC*. **3** a Highland cow *e19*. [shortened form of Eng *northland*]
norland[1.2]**, norlan, †northland** /'nɔrlənd, 'nɔrlən/ *adj* coming from the north or north-east of Scotland *la15-*. [see the noun]
Norn /nɔrn/ *n* the Norse language of Shetland and Orkney *la15-19, 20- historical*. [ON *Norræna*]
norrie /'nɔri/ *n* **1** a whim, a notion *la18- C SW Bor*. **2** cheap ornaments, knick-knacks *20- C*. [possibly from wrong division of *an* ORRA[1.2] odd (notion, thing)]
Norroway, †Northway /'nɔrəwe/ *n* Norway *16-19, 20- Sh Ork NE*. **†Norowayis** Norwegians *15-e16*. [OE *Norþweg*]
norter[1.1]**, nurture** /'nɔrtər, 'nʌrtʃər/ *n* **1** upbringing, education; encouragement, care *la14-*. **2** rigorous discipline; rough treatment *20- NE*. **3** good manners, courtesy *la15-16*. [ME *norture, nurtur*]
norter[1.2]**, nurture** /'nɔrtər, 'nʌrtʃər/ *v* **1** to bring up, to educate; to encourage, to care for *la15-*. **2** to discipline, to chastise, to punish *16-19, 20- NE*. [see the noun]
north[1.1] /nɔrθ/ *n* **1** a cardinal point of the compass; the northerly part of a place *12-*. **2** the northern and north-eastern parts of Scotland *16-*. **3** a northerly wind *la18-*. **northart,** *Sh* **nordert,** *NE* **norrit** *adv* northward, to the north *16-*. **†northart** *n* the north; a northerly direction *17-19*. [see the adv]
north[1.2] /nɔrθ/ *adj* in or belonging to the north; northerly *13-*. **norther** the more northerly of two places of the same name *16-*. **northerly, †northerlie** from, towards or in the north *16-*. **northlins, norlins** towards the north, in a northerly direction *18-*. **†north cuntre** the north and north-east of Scotland *la14-17*. **north part** the northern part of a place *la15-*. **†north partis** the north and north-east of Scotland *15-16*.**†on north half** on the north side, to the north *la14-15*. **the North Isles 1** the Orkney and Shetland Islands *la18-*. **2** the northern Hebrides *16-e17*. [see the adv]
north[1.3] /nɔrθ/ *adv* northwards *la14-*. **northmost, northmast, †northmest** most northerly *16-*. **nort ower, †northour** northwards *16-19, 20- Sh*. [OE *norþ*]
northern, *Sh* **nordern** /'nɔrðərn; *Sh* 'nɔrðərn,/ *adj* northerly; belonging to or in the north *la16-*. **the Northern Isles** the Orkney and Shetland Islands *19-*. **Northern Meeting 1** a formal ball held in Inverness in late summer *la18-*. **2** a piping competition held in Inverness in early September *19-*. [OE *norþerne*]
northland see NORLAND[1.1], NORLAND[1.2]
†Northman, nortman *n* a Norman *16*. [NORTH[1.2] + MAN]
Northway see NORROWAY

nose, †**nois** /noz/ *n* **1** the organ of smelling *la15-*. **2** *mining* coal left protruding where it has been inadequately stripped *la19, 20- EC*. **nosie** a throw in the game of knifie *20- NE T C*. [OE *nosu*]

nosethirl, †**noisthirl**, †**nosthril** /ˈnozθɪrl/ *n* a nostril *la14-e17, 18- Sh N*. Compare NESETHRILL [NOSE + THIRL[1.1]]

not *see* NOCHT[1.2], NOTE[1.1]

†**notar** *n* **1** *law* a notary or notary public *la14-18*. **2** *law* a clerk of court *la15-e17*. **3** a scribe *16-e17*. [AN *notarie*]

notarial, †**notorial** /noˈtɛrɪəl/ *adj law* executed by a notary *la17-*. **notarial instrument** *law* a formal document made out by a notary *la18-*. **notarial protest** *law* a *notarial instrument* in which the notary protests that a debtor shall be liable on non-payment to the consequences set forth in the instrument *la18-*. [NOTAR, with adj-forming suffix *-ial*]

†**notarie** *n* a notary public *la15-16*. **office of notarie** the profession of notaryship *la15-e17*. [Lat *notāria* the office of a notary]

note[1.1], **not**, **nott** /not, nɔt/ *n* **1** a musical note, a tune *la14-*. **2** a sound or cry *la15-*. **3** *law* a formal record, especially in a court register *la15-*. **4** a written statement or list of particulars; an informal jotting, a memorandum *la16-*. **5** a distinguishing mark or characteristic; something noteworthy *la16-*. **6** a banknote *la18-*. **7** *law* the procedure in the Inner House for making an incidental application *19-*. **8** *law* an appendix to a decree in which a judge gives the reasons for his decision *20-*. [Lat *nota*, AN, OFr *note*]

note[1.2] /not/ *v* **1** to make a written note *la14-*. **2** to observe, to detect *la14-*. **3** to mark out from others, to specify *15-*. **notit** distinguished, celebrated *16-*. [OE *genotian* to make a note, Lat *notāre* to mark, signify]

†**note**[2] *n* **1** a task, a duty *la14-e16*. **2** behaviour, actions *la14-e16*. [OE *notu*]

note *see* NOTT

noth *see* NOCHT[1.1]

nother *see* NOWTHER[1.3]

notice[1.1], **notish**, *Ork* **notteece** /ˈnotɪs, ˈnotɪʃ; *Ork* ˈnɔtɪs/ *n* **1** an announcement; information *la15-*. **2** observation, attention, heed *la15-*. **3** care, attentive help *19- Sh NE*. [AN, OFr *notice*]

notice[1.2], **notish** /ˈnotɪs, ˈnotɪʃ/ *v* **1** to see, to observe; to take heed of *la17-*. **2** to watch over; to tend or take care of *la17- Sh Ork NE*. [see the noun]

notion /ˈnoʃən/ *n* **1** a concept, an idea *16-*. **2** a liking or affection *la18-*. **notionate** full of whims, obstinate *la19, 20- WC SW Uls*. **a notion o** a liking for *la18-*. [Lat *nōtio*]

notish *see* NOTICE[1.1], NOTICE[1.2]

notorial *see* NOTARIAL

notoriety, †**notoriete**, †**notorite** /notəˈraeəte/ *n* the fact of being well known (for something bad) *la16-*. [MFr *notorieté*]

†**notory** *adv* openly *la15-e16*. [from the adj NOTOUR]

notour /ˈnotər/ *adj* **1** *of wrongdoers* notorious *15-*. **2** *law* publically known, openly admitted *la15-*. **3** famous, celebrated *17-*. †**notourly** notoriously, openly or publicly known *15-19*. †**make notour** to make known, to declare *17*. [AN *notoire*]

nott, **not**, †**note**, †**noyt** /nɔt/ *v ptp* **nott** to make use of; to need *la15-19, 20- NE*. [OE *notian* to make use of]

nott *see* NOTE[1.1]

notteece *see* NOTICE[1.1]

notty *see* KNOTTY[2]

nou *see* NOO

noucht *see* NOCHT[1.1]

noud *see* KNOUD

noumer *see* NUMMER[1.1], NUMMER[1.2]

noup, **noop** /nup/ *n* **1** a knob or protuberance; the elbow *19-*. **2** a jutting or overhanging crag or mountain-top; a steep headland or promontory; frequently in place-names *18- Sh Ork*. [ON *gnúpr*]

nourice[1.1], **nerice**, †**nurys**, †**nurisch** /ˈnʌrɪs, ˈnɛrɪs/ *n* a nurse for a child; a wet-nurse or foster-mother *la14-19, 20- NE*. †**nurisch father**, **nurisfader** a foster-father *la16-e17*. †**nourice fee** the wages given to a wet-nurse *la18-e19*. †**nourice-ship**, **nurischip** the occupation or post of child's nurse or wet-nurse *la16-e19*. [ME *norice*]

nourice[1.2], †**nureis** /ˈnʌrɪs/ *v* to nourish, to feed; to encourage, to foster or promote *la14-19, 20- literary*. [ME *norishen*]

novation, †**novatioun** /noˈveʃən/ *n* **1** an (undesirable) innovation *16-*. **2** *law* the substitution of a new debt or debtor for a former one *la17-*. **3** *law* the alteration of a legal obligation or status *16-17*. **4** innovation in religious doctrine or polity *la16-17*. **5** the wrongful appropriation of common land; the land appropriated *la16-17*. **6** a new tax *la16*. [MFr *novation*, Lat *novātio* an innovation]

†**novator** *n* an innovator *17*. [Fr *novateur*, Lat *novātor*]

novelle, **novell** /nɔˈvɛl/ *n* a novel, a work of fiction *la18-*. [Ital *novella*]

novodamus /novəˈdeməs, novəˈdaməs/ *n law* the formal renewal of a grant in order to alter or correct a former grant *17-*. [Lat (*dē*) *novō dāmus* we grant anew]

†**now** *n* the head *16-e18*. [OE *hnoll*]

now *see* NEW[1.2], NOO

nowder *see* NOWTHER[1.1]

nowmost *see* NEATHMAIST

nowt[1], †**nolt** /nʌut/ *n pl* **nowt** †**nolt 1** *pl* cattle *la14-*. **2** one head of cattle, an ox, steer *15-*. **3** a large, awkward person *la18-*. **nowt beast**, †**nout beas** a bovine animal *la17-*. **nowt foot**, †**nolt fute** jellied cow's foot *16-19, 20- Sh WC*. †**nolt price**, **noltis price** payment due for cattle *la16-17*. [ON *naut* cattle; the *-l-* forms are scribal, by analogy with words where an original *-l-* is vocalized, such as COWT]

nowt[2] /nʌut/ *n* **1** nothing *19- SW Bor*. **2** *pl* a shout in a game of marbles limiting a player's choice of position *20- SW Bor*. [variant of NOCHT[1.1]]

†**nowther**[1.1], **nowder**, **nolder** *adj* neither, not any *la14-e16*. [see the adv]

nowther[1.2] /ˈnʌuðər/ *adv* neither *la14-19, 20- literary*. [OE *nowþer*]

†**nowther**[1.3], **nother**, **nolder** *pron* neither, none *15-19*. [see the adv]

†**noy**[1.1] *n* **1** vexation, harm *la14-19*. **2** *pl* wrongs, injuries *la14-17*. [aphetic form of ENNOY and ME *noi*]

†**noy**[1.2] *v* **1** to hurt, to harm; to annoy or irritate *la14-e19*. **2** to be troubled; to be angry *la14-e19*. [aphetic form of Eng *annoy* and ME *anoien*]

noynsankys *see* NONESCHANKIS

†**nub** *n* a club-footed person *18-e19*. [MLG *knubbe* a knot, a knob]

nubby /ˈnʌbe/ *adj* club-footed *20- Bor*. [NUB, with adj-forming suffix *-ie*]

nue *see* NEW[1.2]

nug[1.1] /nʌg/ *n* a nudge, a jerk, a tug *20- Sh*. [Norw dial *nugg* rubbing, scraping]

nug[1.2] /nʌg/ *v* to nudge, to jerk; to nod the head *la19- Sh*. [Norw dial *nugga* to shove]

nuif, **noof** /nuf/ *adj* neat, snug; comfortably off *la18- SW*. [unknown]

nuke *see* NEUK

†**nulay** *n in Shetland or Orkney* the lowest division of a run-rig field *17*. [unknown]

null /nʌl/ *adj* **1** *law* without legal force, void, invalid *16-*. **2** without value or significance; amounting to nothing *la18-*. †**nulling** rendering null, cancellation *16-e17*. †**null defence** non-defence; lack of defence *la15-e19*. [AN, MFr *nul*, Lat *nullus*]

nullity, †**nullite** /ˈnʌlɪte/ *n law* the fact of being legally null or invalid; a cause of legal invalidity *16-*. [MFr *nullité*]

number, numbir *see* NUMMER[1.1], NUMMER[1.2]

†**numerat** *adj* counted out, paid in cash *la15-17*. [Lat *numerāt-*, ptp stem of *numerāre* to count or Lat *numerātio* a counting out]

numeration /ˈnjuːməreʃən/ *n* **1** counting, tallying *16-*. **2** a counting out in cash; payment in cash *la16-17*. [MFr *numeration*, Lat *numerātio*]

nummer[1.1], **number**, †**noumer**, †**numbir**, †**nomber** /ˈnʌmər, ˈnʌmbər/ *n* **1** a sum or quantity; one of a series *la14-*. **2** a numeral, an arithmetical symbol *la14-*. [ME *nombre*]

nummer[1.2], **number**, †**noumer**, †**numbir**, †**nomber** /ˈnʌmər, ˈnʌmbər/ *v* **1** to count, to enumerate; to amount to *la14-*. **2** to count out money, to pay in cash *la15-e17*. **numberable**, †**noumerable 1** countable *la15-*. **2** numerous *la16-17*. [from the noun and ME *nombren*]

numpty[1.1] /ˈnʌmpti/ *n* a foolish person *la20-*. [unknown; compare Eng *numps* a silly or stupid person]

numpty[1.2] /ˈnʌmpti/ *adj* foolish *la20-*. [unknown]

nune, noon, *N NE* **neen**, †**none** /nun; *N NE* nin/ *n* midday *la14-*. [Lat *nōna (hōra)* the ninth hour of the day]

nureis *see* NOURICE[1.2]

nurisch *see* NOURICE[1.1]

nurl *see* NIRL[1.1], NIRL[1.2]

nurr[1.1] /nʌr/ *n* a growl or snarl; grumbling *19-*. [see the verb]

nurr[1.2], *Sh Ork N* **nyirr** /nʌr; *Sh Ork N* njɪr/ *v* **1** to growl, to snarl; to grumble *19-*. **2** to purr *19, 20- Sh*. [onomatopoeic]

nurture *see* NORTER[1.1], NORTER[1.2]

nurys *see* NOURICE[1.1]

nut *see* NIT[1]

nyaag[1.1] /njag/ *n* **1** a nagging ache *20- Sh*. **2** a sour, mouldy taste *20- Sh*. **3** painful, laborious toil *20- Sh*. [see the verb]

nyaag[1.2] /njag/ *v* **1** to gnaw or chew *la19- Sh Ork*. **2** to toil laboriously *la19- Sh Ork*. **3** to taste sour or mouldy *20- Sh Ork*. **4** to ache *20- Sh*. [ON *gnaga* to gnaw]

nyaarm *see* NYARM

nyaff[1.1], **gniaf**, †**gnaff** /njaf/ *n* **1** a diminutive or insignificant person *19-*. **2** a contemptible or conceited person *19-*. **3** a small or insignificant object *19, 20- NE*. [see the verb]

nyaff[1.2] /njaf/ *v* **1** *of a dog* to yelp or yap *19-*. **2** to talk senselessly or irritatingly *19-*. **3** to quarrel, to talk snappishly *19-*. **nyaffin 1** yelping, yapping *19-*. **2** idling, wasting time *19-*. [onomatopoeic]

nyakit *see* NAKIT

nyam *see* NAM[2]

nyarb /njarb/ *v* to be discontented; to complain *19- NE*. [onomatopoeic]

nyarm, nyaarm /njarm/ *v of an animal* to bleat *20- Sh Ork*. [onomatopoeic]

nyarr, narr, †**nar** /njar, nar/ *v* **1** to snarl; to growl *16-19, 20- NE Bor Uls*. **2** to be peevish, to fret *19, 20- N NE*. Compare NURR[1.2]. [onomatopoeic]

nyatter *see* NATTER[1.1], NATTER[1.2]

nyattle *see* NATTLE

nyauve *see* GNYAUVE

nybour, nychtbur *see* NEEBOR[1.1]

nyce *see* NICE

nychburhede *see* NEEBORHOOD

nycht *see* NICHT[1.1], NICHT[1.2]

nyep *see* KNEP

nyig *see* NIGG

nyiggle /ˈnjɪɡəl/ *v* to cut ineffectually, to hack at *la19- Sh*. [unknown; compare NIGG, *niggle*]

nyirr *see* NURR[1.2]

nymmill *see* NIMMLE

nyne *see* NINE[1.1], NINE[1.2]

nynetende *see* NINETEENT

nynteine, nyntene *see* NINETEEN[1.2], NINETEEN[1.3]

nyoag[1.1] /njoɡ/ *n* a moan; a lowing sound *la19- Sh*. [unknown]

nyoag[1.2], **nyog** /njoɡ/ *v* **1** to moan; to whine *la19- Sh*. **2** to complain, to scold *20- Sh*. [unknown]

nyod /njɔd/ *interj* an alteration of the word 'God' *la19, 20- NE*. [euphemistic alteration of GOD]

nyog *see* NYOAG[1.2]

nyow *see* NEW[1.2]

nyowl /njʌul/ *v* to howl or cry like a cat *20- Sh NE*. [onomatopoeic]

nyowmost *see* NEATHMAIST

nys *see* NICE

†**nyte** *v* to deny; to refuse *la14-16*. [ON *níta*]

nyuggel /ˈnjʌɡəl/ *n folklore* a water-spirit in the form of a horse *19- Sh Ork*. [ON *nykr*, OE *nicor* a water-demon]

nyurl *see* NIRL[1.2]

nyvle *see* NAVEL

O

o¹, †**oe** /o/ *n* **1** something shaped like an O *16-*. **2** the looped brass fitting for raising a window sash *la19- T WC*. **3** a circular window *16-19*. [from the shape of the letter]

o², **of**, **a**, **ay**, †**off** /o, ɔv, a, e/ *prep* **1** out of *14-*. **2** belonging to *la14-*. **3** *in titles* indicating that a person is the clan chieftain, proprietor or principal tenant: ◊*Macleod of Macleod* ◊*Tam o Shanter la14-*. **4** (some) of: ◊*a wee drap o' parritch 16-*. **5** for; on account of; in return for: ◊*he's nane the waur o that 18-*. **6** about, concerning: ◊*ye mind o her 18-*. **7** with: ◊*pourin o rain 18-*. **8** in, in respect of, in the matter of: ◊*she was blin o an ee* ◊*a big boy of his age 18-*. **9** as regards, about, as far as concerns: ◊*he is ill to please o worldly bliss la18-*. **10** some of, a few of; a number or quantity of: ◊*o them fought, o them fled 19-*. **11** from: ◊*he takes that o his mither 19-*. **12** with, in consequence of, as a result of: ◊*the lassie's greetin o hunger 19-*. **13** *of time* to, before: ◊*quarter of eleven 20- Sh NE EC Uls*. **14** during, in the course of: ◊*the pain is warst o the nicht 19, 20- NE EC*. **15** at, in respect of: ◊*guid o the science 19, 20- NE*. **16** concerning, in regard to: ◊*we forbid you of it 18-19*. **17** *in taxation* indicating the unit on which payment is levied: ◊*of ilk skin a halfpeny 15-e17*. **o' a faimly** having children of a given number: *fower o a faimly la18-*. [OE *of*; reduction in form of of (AFF¹·⁴) and ON¹·² leads to confusion and transference of usage]

o³, **oh** /o/ *interj* **1** an expression of surprise or pain *15-*. **2** *in verse* an extra syllable added to the rhyme-word at the end of a line or half-line *18-*. [a natural utterance]

o *see* A¹, ON¹·², OY

O *see* ORDINARY GRADE

-o¹ /o/ *suffix in verse* an extra syllable added to the rhyme-word at the end of a line or half-line *20-*. [O³]

-o² /o/ *suffix* an addition forming nouns and adjectives from truncated forms *20-*. [unknown]

oabject *see* OBJECT¹·¹, OBJECT¹·²

oabvious *see* OBVIOUS

oaffen *see* AFFEN

oaffer *see* OFFER¹·¹, OFFER¹·²

oaffice *see* OFFICE

oafficer *see* OFFICER

oaften *see* AFFEN

oag, **og** /og, ɔg/ *v* **1** to move slowly; to wriggle or crawl *19- Sh*. **2** to be infested with vermin *la19- Sh*. [Norw dial *oka*, aka to move]

oagly *see* UGLY¹·²

oak *see* AIK

oam *see* YOAM¹·¹, YOAM¹·²

oan *see* ON¹·¹, ON¹·²

oanshach /'onʃəx/ *n* a foolish person; a person with learning difficulties *20- NE H&I*. [Gael *oinnseach* a foolish woman]

oany *see* ONIE¹·¹, ONIE¹·²

oanybody *see* ONIEBODIE

oar *see* AIR³

oarange *see* ORANGE¹·¹, ORANGE¹·²

oarder *see* ORDER¹·¹, ORDER¹·²

oary *see* ORRA¹·²

oary boat /'ore bot/ *n* a rowing boat *20-*. [AIR³, with adj-forming suffix *-y* + BOAT¹·¹]

oat *see* AIT

oath *see* AITH

oaven, **une**, **oven**, *C* **ine**, †**ovin**, †**oyne**, †**oon** /'ovən, un, 'ɔvən; *C* ʌɪn/ *n* **1** an enclosed compartment for cooking food and baking bread, an oven *la14-*. **2** a large shallow pan set among the glowing embers of a fire *la19- WC SW*. **3** a furnace *la14-e16*. †**oon-cake**, **oen-cake**, **een-cake** a thick bun made from oatmeal and yeast and baked in the oven *19*. **une pan** = *oon pot 20- Bor*. **oon pot**, **une pot** a pot or saucepan used in the oven *20-*. [OE *ofen*]

obay *see* OBEY

obder, **obdor** /'ɔbdər/ *n* a small porch; a wooden lintel or shelf above a door *19- Sh*. [ON *ofdyri* a lintel]

obedience /ə'bidjəns/ *n* submission to authority *la14-*. †**do obedience** to render obedience or dutiful service; to submit *la15-17*. **mak obedience** to do ceremonial reverence; to show respect by a curtsy or bow *la14-*. †**obedience of** compliance with or performance of a command *la15-17*. [ME *obedience*]

obedienciall *see* OBEDIENTIAL

†**obedient¹·¹** *n* an obedient or dutiful person; a person who is subject to authority *16-17*. [see the adj]

obedient¹·² /ə'bidiənt/ *adj* submissive to authority *15-*. [ME *obedient*]

obediential, †**obedienciall** /obidi'ɛnʃəl/ *adj* **1** of an obligation imposed by law rather than arising from a contract *la17-*. **2** relating to or characterized by obedience *la15-e17*. [Lat *obēdientiālis*]

obefore *see* OF-BEFORE

obeis *see* OBEY

obeisance, †**obeysaunce** /ə'besəns, ə'bisəns/ *n* obedience *la15-*. †**at obeysance** obedient *e16*. [ME *obeisauce*]

obeit *see* OBIT

ober /'obər/ *n* **1** responsibility, liability; power, influence *20- Ork*. **2** impudent self-confidence *20- Ork*. [ON *ábyrgð*]

oberin, **obran** /'obərɪn, 'obrən/ *n pl also* **obrance 1** odds and ends, scraps *la19- NE Uls*. **2** a hint, a rumour *19*. [altered form of *overins* (OWRINS)]

obey, †**obay**, †**obeis**, †**obeys** /o'be/ *v* to submit, to comply *14-*. †**obeyand** submitting, obedient or subject to *la15-e16*. †**obey till** to submit to, to comply with *la14-16*. [ME *obeien*, *obeishen*]

obeysaunce *see* OBEISANCE

†**obit**, **obite**, **obeit** *n* **1** a person's death; the anniversary of a death *la14-17*. **2** a memorial service *15-17*. **3** payment for an annual memorial service; the revenue intended for such provision *16-17*. **obit silver** payment for an annual memorial service *16-17*. [AN, OFr *obit*, Lat *obitus*]

object¹·¹, **oabject**, **objeck** /'ɔbdʒɛkt, 'ɔbdʒɛkt, 'ɔbdʒɛk/ *n* **1** a material thing *la16-*. **2** the person or thing to which thought or action is directed; a goal or purpose *la16-*. **3** a person with medical problems or learning difficulties; someone deserving of pity *18-*. **4** a person with an unattractive or ridiculous appearance *la20-*. [Lat *objectum* something presented to the senses]

object¹·², **oabject**, **objeck** /əb'dʒɛkt, ob'dʒɛkt, əb'dʒɛk/ *v* **1** to express opposition or protest *la15-*. **2** to reproach; to mock or disparage *16*. [probably Lat *objectāre* and Lat *object-*, ptp stem of *ōbicere*]

objection, †**objectioune** /əbˈdʒɛkʃən/ *n* **1** a feeling or expression of opposition *16-*. **2** a barrier, an obstacle *16*. [ME *objeccioun*, EModE *objection*]

obleege, oblige, †**oblis,** †**obleis,** †**oblish** /oˈblidʒ, əˈblaedʒ/ *v* **1** to compel or constrain; to legally or morally bind *la14-*. **2** to pledge oneself; to be bound or contracted *15-*. **3** to be in debt; to be under obligation to make payment *16-*. †**be obleidged in** to be obligated for a sum of money *la14-e17*. [ME *obligen*]

obleegement, obleissment *see* OBLIGEMENT

obligant /ˈɔblɪgənt/ *n law* a person who is legally bound by a contract or bond *la16-*. [Lat *obligant-*, presp stem of *obligāre* to bind, oblige]

obligation, †**obligatioun,** †**obligacioun** /ɔblɪˈgeʃən/ *n* **1** a commitment or duty; a legal or moral constraint *la14-*. **2** *law* (a document expressing) a binding agreement or formal contract *la14-*. **3** the action of binding oneself legally or morally *la14-e18*. [ME *obligacioun*, Lat *obligātiō*]

†**obligatour**[1.1] *n* a written contract or bond embodying a legally-binding undertaking *la16-17*. [shortened form of *letter obligatour* (LETTER)]

†**obligatour**[1.2] *adj* legally or morally binding *17*. [Lat *obligātōrius*]

oblige *see* OBLEEGE

obligement, obleegement, †**oblisment,** †**obleissment** /əˈblaedʒmənt, oˈblidʒmənt/ *n* **1** a formal contract or agreement (to pay a sum of money) *la15-*. **2** an act of kindness, a favour *18-*. [MFr *obligement*]

oblis, oblish *see* OBLEEGE

oblisment *see* OBLIGEMENT

†**oblissing** *n* **1** a binding contract or oath; the document expressing this *15-16*. **2** the fact of having pledged or committed goods as security *la15-16*. [altered form of Older Scots *obliging*, verbal n from OBLEEGE]

†**obolus** *n* a halfpenny *15-16*. [Lat *obolus*, originally a Greek coin]

obran, obrance *see* OBERIN

obregd, oobregd, obrigd /ˈobrɛg, ˈubrɛgd, ˈobrɪgd/ *n* an additional differentiating mark put in a sheep's ear when the animal is sold *19- Sh*. [probably related to Norw dial *bragd* sheep-mark, *åbregde* alteration]

obreption /oˈbrɛpʃən, ɔˈbrɛpʃən/ *n law* the obtaining of a gift or dispensation by false statement *la17-*. [Fr *obreption*, Lat *obreptio* a creeping up on unawares]

obrigd *see* OBREGD

obscure[1.1], †**obscuir** /əbˈskjur/ *v* **1** to darken, to dim; to become dark *la15-*. **2** to conceal *la16-*. [ME *obscuren*]

obscure[1.2] /əbˈskjur/ *adj* **1** dark, dim; unclear, indistinct *la15-*. **2** hidden, concealed *la16-*. [ME *obscure*]

observe[1.1] /əbˈzɛrv/ *n* an observation; a remark, comment *la17-*. [see the verb]

observe[1.2] /əbˈzɛrv/ *v* **1** to adhere to a custom; to celebrate a rite or festival *la15-*. **2** to preserve something intact, to maintain in good order *la15-*. **3** to pay attention to, to notice or take note of *la16-*. [ME *observen*]

observer, †**observar** /əbˈzɛrvər/ *n* **1** a person who follows a law, religion or custom; an adherent *17-*. **2** a person who watches closely, a spectator *18-*. **3** *in a penalty clause of a contract* the party who kept the terms of the contract, as against the party who failed to do so *17*; compare PARTY OBSERVER. [OBSERVE[1.2], with agent suffix]

†**obstant** *adj* opposing, resistant, adverse *la15-16*. [Lat *obstāns*]

obstene *see* ABSTEEN

obtain, obteen, †**obtene,** †**optene,** †**uptene** /əbˈten, əbˈtin/ *v* **1** to acquire *15-*. **2** to be the case, to hold true *19-*. **3** to achieve or attain an objective *16-17*. **4** to take a person into custody *la16*. **5** *law* to be successful, to win an action *15-16*. **6** to conquer *15-16*. [AN *obtenir, optiner*, MFr *obtenir, optenyr*]

obtemper /ɔbˈtɛmpər/ *v law* to comply with or submit to; to obey a court order *16-*. †**obtemperance** compliance; obedience *la16-e17*. [EModE *obtemper*, Lat *obtemperāre* to obey]

†**obtemperate, obtemperat** *v* to obey; to comply with *la17-19*. [Lat *obtemperāt-*, ptp stem of *obtemperāre*]

†**obtend** *v* to put forward as an argument; to pretend, allege or maintain *la16-e17*. [Lat *obtendere*]

obtene *see* OBTAIN

obvious, oabvious /ˈɔbviəs, ˈobviəs/ *adj* perceived or understood; clear *19-*. [Lat *obvius*]

ocarist *see* EUCHARIST

†**occanʒe, okkenʒe** *adj of gloves* made of goose skin *la16*. [OFr *ocagné*]

occasion, †**occasioun,** †**occation** /əˈkeʒən/ *n* **1** an opportunity; a reason, a pretext *la14-*. **2** a particular time or circumstance; an eventuality *16-*. **3** *Presbyterian Church* the celebration of the Lord's Supper; the periodical Communion Service *17-*. [AN, MFr *occasion*, Lat *occāsiō*]

†**occident** *adj* situated in the west; western *16-17*. [ME *occident*, Lat *occidēns*]

†**occisioun** *n* **1** slaughter, mass killing *la14-16*. **2** the killing of a single person, a murder *la15-e16*. [AN *occisiun*, Lat *occīsiō*]

occour *see* OCKER

occupation, †**occupatioun,** †**occupacioun** /ɔkjuˈpeʃən/ *n* **1** the act of taking possession; holding, tenure *15-*. **2** engagement or employment in an act or business; a task, a job *la15-*. **3** the body of those following a particular trade or occupation, a craft incorporation *16*. [ME *occupacioun*, Lat *occupātio*]

occupy, occupee, †**occupe** /ˈɔkjupae, ˈɔkjupi/ *v* **1** to take or hold possession of territory by conquest or settlement *la14-*. **2** to employ or make use of; to be busy with *la14-*. **3** to usurp the possession of; to appropriate for personal use *la14-16*. [ME *occupien*, Lat *occupāre*]

occur, †**accur** /əˈkʌr/ *v* **1** to happen, to take place *la15-*. **2** to come to mind *la15-*. **3** to meet or encounter; to appear or arrive *16-17*. [Lat *occurrere*]

och /ɔx, ox/ *interj* **1** an expression of exasperation or weariness *16-*. **2** an expression of sorrow, pain or regret *16-*. Compare OCHONE. **och aye the noo** an expression of affirmation freq. used as a humorous marker of Scottish speech *la20-*. [Gael *och*]

-och /əx/ *suffix* an additional syllable with reiterative or intensive force *16-*. [Gael *-ach* suffix forming adjs and nouns]

ochane, ochanee *see* OCHONE

ochiern *see* OGTHIERN

ochone, †**ochane** /əˈxon, ɔˈxon/ *interj* an expression of sorrow *la15-*. **ochanee, ochone-a-me,** *Ork* **whan awhan** an expression of sorrow *la19-*. [Gael *ochòin*]

ocht[1.1], **oucht, aucht,** *Ork Bor* **owt** /ɔxt; *Ork Bor* ʌut/ *pron* anything *la14-*. [see the adj]

†**ocht**[1.2], **oucht** *adj* any *19*. [OE *āwiht*]

ocht[1.3], **ought** /ɔxt, ɔt/ *adv* **1** somewhat, rather *la14-*. **2** to any extent *la14-16*. [see the adj]

ocht[2], **aucht, ought** /ɔxt, ɔt/ *v* **1** to be under obligation to do something *la14-*. **2** to have a claim or right, to be entitled *la14-*. [pt of AWE]

ocht *see* AWE

ochtlins[1.1] /ˈɔxtlɪnz/ *n* anything *18-19, 20- Bor*. [see the adv]

ochtlins[1.2] /ˈɔxtlɪnz/ *adv* in any way, in the least degree *18-19, 20- literary*. [OCHT[1.1], with adv-forming suffix *-lins*]

-ock, -ick, -ack, -ach, -ag, -og /ək, əx, əg/ *suffix* an extra syllable forming diminutives from nouns and verbs *16-*. [OE *-oc*; often confused or conflated with Gael *-ag, -óc*]

†**ocker, okker, occour** *n* **1** usury, the lending of money at (excessive) interest *la15-e18*. **2** interest; a rate of interest *la14-e17*. **ockerer, ockarar** a usurer *15-19*. [ON *okr*]

ock-name /'ɔknem/ *n* a nickname *la19- Sh*. [ON *auki* increase + *name* (NEM[1.1])]

Octavians /ɔk'teviənz/ *npl* a committee of eight members appointed by James VI in 1595-6 to control Crown revenues and the exchequer *la16, 17- historical*. [Lat *octāvus* eighth]

†**octo** *n* in Caithness and Sutherland a measure of arable land; a half farthingland, the eighth part of a pennyland *18-19*. [Gael *ochdamh* an eighth of a davach or an ounceland]

od, odd, odds /ɔd, ɔdz/ *interj* an expression of surprise or distress *la18- Sh NE EC*. **odd saffs** God save us *19, 20- Sh*. **od sake, odd sakes** for God's sake *la19, 20- NE C*. [aphetic form of GOD]

od *see* ODD[1.2]

odal *see* UDAL

odd[1.1] /ɔd/ *n golf* the handicap given to a weak opponent by deducting one stroke from their total at every hole *la19-*. **play the odd** to play one more stroke than an opponent *la19-*. [singular form of ODDS]

odd[1.2], †**od**, †**ode** /ɔd/ *adj* **1** *of a number* not even *la14-*. **2** additional, extraneous, unattached *16-*. **3** out of the ordinary *la16-*. **4** unique *la14-16*. †**odland** land additional to, or not forming part of, a main body of land *15-16*. †**for od or evin** on any account *la14-15*. [ME *odde*; compare Norw *odde*]

odd *see* OD

oddes, oddis *see* ODDS

oddisman *see* ODMAN

oddle /'ɔdəl/ *n* a gutter, a drain; a sewer *19- Sh Ork N*. [altered form of ADDLE with influence from OLLER]

odds, †**oddis**, †**oddes** /ɔdz/ *npl* **1** a small surplus sum or number in addition to that specified; an indefinite additional amount *16-*. **2** a difference, a disparity, inequality: ◊*forty years makes a great odds of a girl la16-*. **3** the ratio between stakes in a bet; the balance of probability *la18-*. **4** *golf* the handicap given by a strong player to a weaker in a single match *19-*. **mak the odds even 1** to equalize or level inequalities *16-*. **2** to atone for transgressions, to remit someone's shortcomings *16*. **odds and evens** a children's guessing game *la19-*. **the odds of** more than: ◊*there was the odds of forty head of cattle on the land 19- Sh NE Uls*. [from the adj ODD[1.2]]

odds *see* OD

oddsman *see* ODMAN

ode *see* ODD[1.2]

oder *see* ITHER[1.1], ITHER[1.3]

odere *see* ODOUR

odger *see* OGEOUR

odious[1.1], †**odius** /'odiəs/ *adj* **1** hateful, detestable *la15-*. **2** extremely large; excessive, intense *19, 20- Sh Uls*. **3** full of hate; hostile *15-16*. [ME *odious*, Lat *odiōsus*]

odious[1.2] /'odiəs/ *adv* **1** very, exceedingly *la19- Sh SW*. **2** with great aversion *la15*. [see the adj]

odius *see* ODIOUS[1.1]

†**odman, oddsman, oddisman** *n* **1** a neutral arbiter given the casting vote *15-18*. **2** *pl* arbitrators *16-17*. Compare ODPERSOUN. [ON *oddamaðr*]

odorne *see* ADORN

odour, †**odor**, †**odyes**, †**odere** /'odər/ *n* **1** scent, smell *la14-*. **2** a sweet-smelling substance or plant *16-e17*. [ME *odour*, Lat *odor*]

†**odpersoun** *n* a neutral arbiter given the casting vote *16*. [altered form of ODMAN]

odyre *see* ODOUR

oe *see* O[1], OY

†**oeconomus, iconumus, economist** *n* **1** the keeper of student lodgings at a university *la16-18*. **2** the steward or manager of property and finances at a religious house or a college *16-e18*. [Lat *oeconomus* a steward]

†**oecumenick** *adj* ecumenical *16-17*. [MFr *œcumenique*, Lat *oecumenicus*]

oen-cake *see* OAVEN

o'er *see* OWER[1.3], OWER[1.4]

o'ercome *see* OWERCOME[1.1]

o'erpit *see* OWERPIT

o'ers *see* OWRES

of *see* AFF[1.3], AFF[1.4], O[2]

†**of-before, obefore, abefore** *adv* earlier, previously, formerly *la14-18*. [*of* (O[2]) + Older Scots *before*]

off *see* AFF[1.1], AFF[1.2], AFF[1.3], AFF[1.4], O[2]

offcast *see* AFFCAST

offcasting *see* AFFCASTIN

offcome *see* AFFCOME

offeecial *see* OFFICIAL[1.1], OFFICIAL[1.2]

offeecious *see* OFFICIOUS

offend, †**offen** /ə'fɛnd/ *v* **1** to cause resentment in, to wound the feelings of *15-*. **2** to commit a crime, sin or fault; to transgress *15-*. **3** to feel resentful *la15-17*. **4** to harm or injure; to sin against *15-e17*. **offend against**, †**offend aganis** to sin against *16-*. [ME *offenden*, Lat *offendere*]

offer[1.1], **oaffer** /'ɔfər, 'ofər/ *n* **1** a proposal, a tender *la15-*. **2** an attempt or gesture; a feeble effort *19-*. †**in your offer** at one's disposal; for the taking *la18-19*. [ME *offre*]

offer[1.2], **oaffer**, †**offir** /'ɔfər, 'ofər/ *v* **1** to tender, to propose, to present *la14-*. **2** to make an attempt or show of intention, to endeavour *la17-*. **3** to indicate or suggest; to appear to be the case *la17-*. **4** to present oneself to the service of a superior authority *la14-16*. **5** to put oneself forward in combat *la15-16*. **offering 1** a contribution, a donation, an oblation *la15-*. **2** the act of proposing or showing an intention *la15-*. **3** a small quantity; a feeble attempt *20- Sh NE WC*. [OE *offrian*]

†**offerand, offrand** *n* **1** an oblation, a religious offering *la14-16*. **2** church offerings forming part of the regular income of a church or benefice *la15-16*. **3** the Presentation of Christ in the Temple, as celebrated at Candlemas *15*. [ME *offrende*]

off fallings *see* AFF FA'INS

off-go *see* AFFGO

offgoing *see* AFFGAUN[1.1]

off-going *see* AFFGAUN[1.2]

offhand *see* AFF-HAND[1.1], AFF-HAND[1.2]

office, oaffice /'ɔfəs, 'ofəs/ *n* **1** a position of duty or authority *la14-*. **2** the celebration of a religious service; a liturgy *la14-*. **3** a room used as a place of business *17-*. **4** a workshop, a factory, a shop *la18-19*. †**office house** a workshop, an outbuilding *la15-17*. †**office man** an officer, an official *la15-17*. †**office of arms** the business or science of heraldry; the corporate body of Scottish heralds *la15-16*. [ME *office*, Lat *officium*]

officer, oafficer, offisher, †**officher**, †**officiar** /'ɔfəsər, 'ofəsər, 'ɔfəʃər/ *n* **1** an administrative or executive functionary *la14-*. **2** an official of a legal, municipal or ecclesiastical court whose duty is to keep order at meetings and to deliver messages or summonses *15-*. **3** a person holding a military commission *16-*. **4** a servant or attendant *16-*. **officership** the position and functions of an officer *la16-*. †**officer corn**

grain paid by tenants towards the emoluments of the officer of a Baron-court *17-18*. †**officer of armes** a herald or pursuivant under the authority of the Lord Lyon King of Arms *la15-16*. **officer of state** one of the important officials of state in Scotland *17-*. [ME *officer*, Lat *officiārius*]

official[1.1], **offeecial**, †**officiale**, †**officiall** /əˈfɪʃəl, əˈfiʃəl/ *n* **1** a person holding public office; an officer *17-*. **2** the presiding officer or judge in the court of an archbishop, bishop or archdeacon *15-16, 17- historical*. [ME *official*, Lat *officiālis*]

official[1.2], **offeecial** /əˈfɪʃəl, əˈfiʃəl/ *adj* pertaining to duties or services *la16-*. **Official Report** the verbatim written record of the proceedings of the Scottish Parliament *la20-*. **Official Reporter** a person who writes the *Official Report la20-*. [Lat *officiālis*]

officiar *see* OFFICER

officiary, †**officiarie** /əˈfɪʃəre/ *n* **1** a division in a large Highland estate, under the care of a ground officer *la16-e20, la20- historical*. **2** the position and functions of a ground officer or factor of a large estate *la16-17*. **3** the position and functions of an officer of a burgh, barony or craft *la16-17*. [OFFICER, with *-ie* suffix]

officious, **offeecious** /ɔˈfɪʃəs, əˈfiʃəs/ *adj of a person* asserting authority in an excessive or fussy way *la19-*. [Lat *officiōsus*]

offie[1] /ˈɔfi/ *n* a privy, a dry closet *19- T H&I Bor*. [reduced form of (*house of*) OFFICE]

offie[2] /ˈɔfi, ˈɔfe/ *n* an off-licence shop *la20-*. [shortened form of Eng *off-licence*]

offir *see* OFFER[1.2]

offisher *see* OFFICER

offlet *see* AFF-LAT

off-loof *see* AFF-LOOF

offpit, **offput** *see* AFF-PIT

offputting *see* AFF-PITTIN[1.1], AFF-PITTIN[1.2]

offrand *see* OFFERAND

offreis, **offrez** *see* ORPHUS

offset *see* AFFSET

offspring, †**ofspryng** /ˈɔfsprɪŋ/ *n* **1** progeny; descendants *la14-*. **2** ancestry; lineage, race *la14-16*. [OE *ofsprinc*]

offtakin *see* AFFTAKIN[1.2]

offtaking *see* AFFTAKIN[1.1]

ofputting *see* AFF-PITTIN[1.1]

ofspryng *see* OFFSPRING

oft *see* AFT[1.1], AFT[1.2]

often, **ofen** *see* AFFEN

†**oftsyse**, **oftsis** *adv* often, repeatedly; frequently, commonly *la14-16*. [ME *oftsithes*]

og *see* OAG

-og *see* -OCK

ogadoo *see* OKERDU

†**ogang** *n in Shetland and Orkney* a court held at the site for settling boundary disputes; a court of perambulation *16-e17*. [related to ON *ganga* walking]

†**ogart**, **ogert** *n* pride, arrogance, presumption *la14-e17*. [ME *angart*, *ongart*; compare ON *ágirnd* ambition, greed, ON *ágjart*, variant of *ágjarn* ambitious, impetuous]

†**ogeour**, **odger** *n* an ogee arch; a stone cut for an arch *16-e17*. [perhaps altered form of Fr *ogive*]

ogert *see* OGART

ogertfu, **ogertfow** /ˈɔgərtfu, ˈɔgərtfʌu/ *adj* dainty, affected, fastidious *18-19, 20- historical*. [OGART, with adj-forming suffix *-fu(l)*]

†**ogie** *n* the fireplace in a kiln; an opening before a kiln *19*. [aphetic form of LOGIE, by wrong division of KILLOGIE]

O Grade *see* ORDINARY GRADE

ogsome *see* UGSOME

†**ogthiern**, **ochiern** *n law* a person who ranked with the son or grandson of a thane *13-19*. [Gael *òg-thighearna* a young lord, a chief's son]

oh *see* O[3]

oh-yah *see* OOYAH

oil *see* ILE[1.1], ILE[1.2]

oilger *see* OLGER

†**oint**, **oynt** *v* to anoint *la14-17*. [aphetic form of ANOINT]

ointment *see* EYNTMENT

oire *see* AYRE

ois *see* USE[1.1], USE[1.2]

oise *see* OYCE

oismont *see* OSMOND

oist *see* HOST[1.1], HOST[1.2]

oix *see* OX

oken *see* AIKEN

okerdu, **ogadoo**, **ooka-doo** /ˈɔkərdu, ˈɔgədu, ˈukədu/ *n* one of a number of plants (such as hemp nettle, dead nettle or bugle) found among corn *la19- Sh*. **ooga-tooga** thin grass; sparse hair *20- Sh*. [probably ON *akrdái*]

okkenʒe *see* OCCANʒE

okker *see* OCKER

old *see* AULD[1.1], AULD[1.2]

oldar *see* AULDER

older *see* OWTHER[1.2]

old farrant *see* AULD-FARRANT

Old Firm /ˈold fɪrm/ *n* a collective term for Rangers and Celtic Football Clubs *20-*. [perhaps referring to the popularity of these teams as a regular fixture]

old long syne *see* AULD LANG SYNE

old man *see* AULD MAN

Old Town *see* AULD TOON

old wifie *see* AULD WIFE

oleit *see* OLITE

olger, **oilger** /ˈɔlgər, ˈɔɪlgər/ *n* liquid manure in a byre *20- Sh*. [unknown]

olif *see* OLIVE

†**oliphant**, **olyfant** *n* **1** an elephant *15-16*. **2** ivory *la15*. [ME *olyphaunt*, OFr *olifant*]

olite, **oleit** /ˈolʌɪt/ *adj* **1** eager, willing; cheerful *la16-19, 20- literary*. **2** active, energetic, nimble *la16-19*. [reduced form of ON *ofléttr* prompt, ready]

olive, †**olif** /ˈɔləv/ *n* an evergreen tree of the genus *Olea*; the fruit of this tree *15-*. [ME *olive*]

oller, †**ullier** /ˈɔlər/ *n* **1** the drainage channel behind cattle in a byre *19- Sh*. **2** liquid manure; mud *la19- Sh*. [perhaps Norw dial *åle* cattle urine, with *-er* suffix; compare OLGER]

ollick /ˈolək/ *n* a young ling *Molva molva 19- Sh*. [perhaps Norw *ål* an eel, with diminutive suffix *-ock*]

olyfant *see* OLIPHANT

olʒe *see* ILE[1.1]

ombekend *see* UNBEKENT

omberaucht *see* UMBERAUCH

ombesege *see* UMBESEGE

ombeset *see* UMBESET[1.2]

ombethynk *see* UMBETHINK

ombyschew *see* UMBESCHEW

omdo *see* UNDO

ome *see* YOAM[1.1]

†**omnigaddrum**, **omnigatherum** *n* **1** a miscellaneous collection of things; a miscellaneous gathering of people *16-e19*. **2** *in Stirling* a miscellaneous group of crafts, not incorporated separately, and treated for certain purposes as a single unit *17-e18*. [Lat *omni-* all + GAITHER, with Latinate suffix *-um*]

on[1.1], **oan** /ɔn, on/ *adv* **1** in action, in operation *la14-*. **2** expressing advancement or continuation *la14-*. **3** expressing contact with and support from (a surface) *la14-*. **on a, on an, on o, on on, on upon** onto, to, upon *la18-19, 20- N EC*. **on for** keen on, in favour of, taken up with *la19-*. **on tae, on til 1** onto *19-*. **2** approaching, getting on for *19-*. **on wi** = *on for la19-*. [OE *on*]

on[1.2], **oan**, **o** /ɔn, on, o/ *prep* **1** positioned above and attached to *la14-*. **2** about, concerning: ◊*dae ye mind on thon? la14-*. **3** at, near, beside, by: ◊*dinnae sit on the door in the cald souch* ◊*Perth is on the Tay la14-*. **4** supported by, by means of, with: ◊*gae on a walkin stick la14-*. **5** in *la14-*. **6** at (a particular time or date), during *14-*. **7** to: ◊*cry on yer sister an tell her tae come in til her tea 15-*. **8** for: ◊*wait on a reply 20-*. **9** to *19-*. **10** of *la16-19*. **11** per: ◊*1000 on ell 19*. Compare O[2]. **on fit** afoot *20- Ork T SW*. †**on na way, on-na-wayis, on-na-wise** in no way or manner, on no account *15-17*. **on yersel** on one's own account, independently *la19-*. [see the adv]

on *see* ANE[1.1], ANE[1.2]
on- *see* UN-
onabasit *see* UNABASIT
onabill *see* UNABLE
†**onamovit** *adj* unmoved *e16*. [participial adj from *un-* + AMOVE[1]]
†**on-ane, onone, anone** *adv* **1** forthwith, straight away *la14-16*. **2** continuously *la15-e16*. **sone on-ane** immediately, quickly *la14-15*. [OE *on āne* in one]
onawarnyst *see* UNWARNIST
†**onbeast, unbeist** *n* **1** a monster or wild beast; a frightening animal *la14-e19*. **2** an objectionable person *la15-e19*. **3** toothache *e19*. [ON[1.1] + BEAST[1.1]]
onbegrave *see* UNBEGRAVE
onbet *see* UNBET
onbodeit *see* UNBODYIT
onbraw *see* UNBRAW
onbydrew *see* UMBDRAW
oncairry[1.1], **oncarry**, *Sh* **onkerry** /ɔnˈkere, ɔnˈkare; *Sh* ɔnˈkeri/ *n* a fuss, a turmoil; rowdy behaviour *19- Sh T EC*. [see the verb]
oncairry[1.2], **oncarry** /ɔnˈkere, ɔnˈkare/ *v* to behave rowdily, to cause a fuss *18-19, 20- NE*. [ON[1.1] + CAIRRY[1.2]]
oncallyt *see* UNCA'D
oncanny *see* UNCANNIE
oncarry *see* ONCAIRRY[1.1], ONCAIRRY[1.2]
oncasin *see* UNCASSEN
oncast[1.1] /ˈɔnkast/ *n knitting* the first row of stitches *la19- Sh Ork T H&I WC*. [see the verb]
oncast[1.2] /ˈɔnkast/ *v knitting* to cast on the first row of stitches *la19, 20- Ork*. [ON[1.1] + CAST[1.2]]
oncast[2] /ˈɔnkast/ *n* a sudden attack of illness or disaster *20- Sh*. [ON[1.1] + CAST[1.1]]
†**onca wark** *n* in *Orkney* services required of tenants as part of their rent *la18-19*. [ON[1.2] + CA[1.1] + WARK[1.1]]
once *see* AINCE[1.1], AINCE[1.2]
oncle *see* UNCLE
oncome /ˈɔnkʌm/ *n* **1** a heavy fall of rain or snow *19-*. **2** the approach or beginning of something; development or progress *19- Sh NE T*. **3** *building* the corbelling at the gathering of a flue above the fire-opening; funnel-shaped pieces of fireclay between the fireplace opening and the fireclay lining of a smoke flue *20-*. **4** an attack of a disease of unknown origin; a sharp attack of illness *19- Bor*. Compare INCOME[1.1]. [ON[1.1] + COME[1.1]]
oncomin /ˈɔnkʌmɪn/ *adj* friendly, amicable, cordial *20-*. [participial adj from ON[1.1] + COME[1.2]]

oncorn *see* UNCORN
oncost, †**uncost** /ˈɔnkɔst/ *n* **1** additional expenses, incidental costs; overheads *15-*. **2** *mining* a timeworker *la19*. **oncost men** employees hired in additional to the regular miners; those paid fixed wages for time worked rather than by the amount of coal produced *la17-20, 21- historical*. [MDu *onkosten* expenses]
oncum *see* UNCUM
ondacent *see* UNDECENT
ondag /ˈɔndag/ *n* a downpour, a heavy fall of rain *20- NE T*. [ON[1.1] + DAG[1.1]]
ondali, undali /ˈondali, ˈʌndali/ *adj* strange, peculiar; eerie *19- Sh*. [ON *undrligr*]
ondantit *see* UNDAUNTIT
ondeemous *see* UNDEEMOUS
ondegest *see* UNDEGEST
ondemandit *see* UNDEMANDIT
ondepe *see* UNDEIP
onder *see* UNDER[1.1], UNDER[1.2]
onderlowt *see* UNDERLOUT[1.2]
onderly *see* UNDERLIE
onderspecifeit *see* UNDERSPECIFEIT
onderstand *see* UNDERSTAND[1.2]
ondertak *see* UNDERTAK
onding[1.1] /ˈɔndɪŋ/ *n* **1** a heavy continuous fall of rain or snow *la18-*. **2** an attack or assault; an outburst of noise *la19, 20- literary*. [ON[1.1] + DING[1.1]]
onding[1.2] /ˈɔndɪŋ/ *v* to rain or snow heavily *19, 20- NE EC*. [see the noun]
ondocht *see* UNDOCHT
on-draw /ˈɔndrɔ/ *n* a garment worn only on occasion or when going outside *20- Sh*. [ON[1.1] + DRAW[1.2]]
†**ondreyd** *adj* not dreaded *e16*. [ptp of *un-* + DREID[1.2]]
ondyrtakyn *see* UNDERTAK
†**one** *indef art* an *15-17*. [literary quasi-anglicization of *ane* (AN[1]), by analogy with ANE[1]]
one *see* ANE[1.1], ANE[1.2]
one- *see* UN-
onely *see* ANELY[1.2]
oner *see* WANNER[2.1], WANNER[2.2]
†**oneratioun** *n* a financial burden or charge; a written statement of a charge *16*. [Lat *onerātio* the action of taking on a load]
oneresonabile *see* UNREASONABLE
onerie *see* ANE[1.1]
onerous /ˈonərəs/ *adj* **1** *law* involving payment; granted or created in return for money or services received *17-*. **2** burdensome *la17-*. **onerosity** *law* the fact of requiring payment *la17-19, 20- historical*. [ME *onerous*, EModE *onerous*, Lat *onerōsus*]
onerstan *see* UNDERSTAND[1.2]
onest *see* HONEST
oneth *see* UNEIS
one to *see* ONTO[1.1]
oneto *see* ONTO[1.2]
onevyn *see* UNEVEN[1.1]
onevynly *see* UNEVENLY
onfa, †**onfall** /ˈɔnfa, ˈɔnfɔ/ *n* **1** a heavy fall of rain or snow *19-*. **2** an attack of a disease (of unknown origin) *19- Bor*. **3** the fall of evening *19- Bor*. **4** a military attack *la17-19*. [OE *onfeall* an attack of disease or other calamity]
onfald *see* UNFAULD
onfall *see* ONFA
onfarrant *see* UNFARRANT
onfeel *see* UNFEEL
onfery *see* UNFEARY

onforleit *see* UNFORLEYT
onfrend *see* UNFRIEND
onfylit *see* UNFYLET
ongae, ongo /ɔnˈge, ɔnˈgo/ *n* **1** movement, progress *17-*. **2** uproar, strife *la19- Sh NE Bor.* [ON¹·¹ + GAE]
ongaein, ongoing, ongaun /ɔnˈgeən, ɔnˈgoɪŋ, ɔnˈgɔn/ *n* a proceeding, an event *la17-*. [ON¹·¹ + verbal noun from GAE]
ongang /ˈɔŋgaŋ/ *n* **1** rowdy or unrestrained behaviour *la19, 20- Sh NE Bor.* **2** the starting up or setting in motion of mill machinery *la19- NE.* [ON¹·¹ + GANG¹·¹]
ongaun *see* ONGAEIN
ongo *see* ONGAE
ongoing *see* ONGAEIN
onhabill *see* UNABLE
onhanger /ˈɔnhaŋər/ *n* a follower or dependant *19, 20- EC Uls.* [ON¹·¹ + *hang* (HING¹·²), with agent suffix]
onhing /ˈɔnhɪŋ/ *n* the act of waiting; a tedious delay *la19- NE T.* [ON¹·¹ + HING¹·¹]
onie¹·¹, **ony, oany,** †**onne** /ˈɔni, ˈɔne, ˈone/ *adj* any *la14-*. **onyane** anyone *16-*. †**onykin, onykyne** of any kind or sort *la14-e15.* **onyplace** anywhere *la18-*. **onywey, oniewey, onyway** anyhow, in any way *la14-*. **onyweys, onyways,** †**onywise** anyhow, in any way, anywhere *la14-*. **ony ither wey** anyhow; anywhere else *la19-*. [OE *ǣnig*]
onie¹·², **ony, oany,** †**onne** /ˈɔni, ˈɔne, ˈone/ *adv* **1** in any degree, to any extent *15-*. **2** in any way, at all: ◊*can ye fish ony? la18-*. [see the adj]
onie¹·³, **ony** /ˈɔni, ˈɔne, ˈone/ *pron* any *la14-*. **onie o the twa** either *19-*. [see the adj]
oniebodie, onybody, ony-buddy, oanybody, emdie, emdy /ˈɔnibədi, ˈɔnebədə, ˈɔnebʌde, ˈonebəde, ˈɛmdi, ˈɛmde/ *n* anybody *la16-*. [ONIE¹·¹ + BODY]
onis *see* AINCE¹·¹
onkend, onkent *see* UNKENT
onkerry *see* ONCAIRRY¹·¹
onkill *see* UNCLE
onkouth *see* UNCOUTH¹·¹
onlay¹·¹ /ˈɔnle/ *n* **1** a heavy fall of snow or rain *19- Sh.* **2** an extended period of bad weather *20- Sh.* [ON¹·¹ + LAY¹·²]
onlay¹·² /ˈɔnle/ *v* to lay on, to superimpose *la16-19, 20- Sh.* [see the noun]
onleif *see* UNLEIF
onleill *see* UNLELE
on-leping *see* ONLOWPING
onles *see* UNLESS¹·¹, UNLESS¹·²
onless *see* UNLESS¹·¹
onlesum *see* UNLEISUM
onlie *see* ANELY¹·¹
†**on loft** *adv* aloft *la14-16.* [ON¹·² + ON *lopt* the sky, the air, an upper room]
onlookin /ˈɔnlukɪn/ *adj* fit to be seen, presentable *20- Sh.* [ON¹·¹ + participial adj from *look* (LEUK¹·²)]
†**onlowping, on-leping** *n* the act of mounting a horse to depart *la15-e17.* [ON¹·¹ + verbal noun from LOWP¹·²]
only *see* ANELY¹·¹, ANELY¹·²
onlykly *see* UNLIKELY
onmark *see* ANMARK
onn *see* OON
onne *see* ONIE¹·¹, ONIE¹·²
onone *see* ON-ANE
onpit¹·¹, **onput** /ˈɔnpɪt, ˈɔnput/ *n* **1** clothing, a garment *la19- WC Bor.* **2** pretence, insincere behaviour *20- Sh Bor.* **3** a faker or pretender *20- Bor.* [ON¹·¹ + ptp of PIT²]
†**onpit**¹·², **onput** *v* to put into position; to install *16-17.* [ON¹·¹ + PIT²]
onplane *see* UNPLANE

onplast, †**umplist** /ˈɔnpləst/ *n* a sudden fierce gale *la19- Sh.* [probably ON¹·¹ + ON *blástr* a blast, a breath]
onplayn *see* UNPLANE
onpossible, unpossible, *Sh* **oonpossible,** †**unpossibill** /ɔnˈpɔsəbəl, ʌnˈpɔsəbəl; *Sh* unˈpɔsəbəl/ *adj* impossible *la15-*. [*un-* prefix + POSSIBLE¹·¹]
†**onprisit, unprisit** *adj* untested as to quality or value; unpriced *15-16.* [*un-* prefix + MFr *priser*]
onprofitabil *see* UNPROFITABLE
onprovisitly *see* UNPROVISIT
onput *see* ONPIT¹·¹, ONPIT¹·²
onputting /ˈɔnputɪŋ/ *n* **1** appearance, manner *la19- Bor.* **2** the action of putting on or installing *16-17.* [ON¹·¹ + verbal noun from PIT²]
onressonabill *see* UNREASONABLE
onrest *see* UNREST
†**onrestles** *adj* restless *e16.* [*un-* prefix + ME *restles*]
onrude *see* UNRUDE
onrycht *see* UNRICHT¹·¹, UNRICHT¹·², UNRICHT¹·³
ons *see* OUNCE
onset¹ /ˈɔnsɛt/ *n* **1** a beginning; an attack or onslaught *16-*. **2** a scolding *la18-19, 20- NE.* **onsetter 1** *mining* the person who loads the hoist at the pit bottom *20- C.* **2** an assailant *la16-e17.* [ON¹·¹ + SET¹·²]
onset² /ˈɔnsɛt/ *n* a dwelling-site, a steading with a dwelling-house and outhouses built on it; a small cluster of houses *15-19, 20- Uls.* [ON¹·¹ + OE *set* or ON *setr* a habitation, a dwelling]
†**onsetting** *n* **1** the action of setting or fixing *16-e17.* **2** the action of attacking or assailing *la16.* [ON¹·¹ + verbal noun from SET¹·²]
onsilly *see* UNSEELY
onslaucht, onslaught, †**anslacht,** †**unsolt** /ˈɔnslɔxt, ˈɔnslɔt/ *n* a violent attack *17-*. [ON¹·¹ + ME *slaht* slaughter]
onspoken *see* UNSPOKEN
†**onspulȝeit, unspuilȝeit** *adj* unspoiled *16-17.* [*un-* prefix + ptp of SPULYIE¹·²]
onstandin /ɔnˈstandɪn/ *adj* determined, unyielding, obstinate *la19- Sh.* [ON¹·¹ + verbal noun from STAND¹·²]
onstead, †**onsted,** †**onsteid** /ˈɔnstɛd/ *n* a steading *la16-19, 20- Bor.* [ON¹·¹ + STEID¹·¹]
onsure *see* UNSURE
ontak /ˈɔntak/ *n* **1** the taking on of a task or responsibility; a big or difficult job *20- Sh NE T.* **2** a fuss or state of excitement *20- Sh.* [ON¹·¹ + TAK¹·¹]
ontake /ˈɔntek/ *v* to undertake a task; to accept a debt or liability *la17-19, 20- Sh NE.* **ontaker** an irresponsible and untrustworthy person; a person who runs up debt *20- T.*
†**ontakin** buying on credit; being untrustworthy *la19.* [ON¹·¹ + TAK¹·¹]
ontaking /ˈɔntekɪŋ/ *n* **1** the start of an undertaking *18-19, 20- Sh NE T.* **2** an attack of pain; an onset of bad weather *20- Sh.* **3** enlistment as a soldier; engagement to a post *la17-e18.* [ON¹·¹ + verbal noun from TAK¹·²]
†**on-takis-man** *n* a person who did not hold a tack of part of the common in Inverurie *e17.* [*un-* prefix + *tacksman* (TACK²)]
onthrift *see* UNTHRIFT
ontil *see* UNTIL¹·¹
onto¹·¹, **unto,** †**one to** /ˈɔntu, ˈʌntu/ *prep* **1** towards, to *la14-*. **2** similar to *15-16.* **4** until, up to *15-16.* [by analogy with UNTIL¹·¹ by substitution of to (TAE³·²) for TILL²·²]
†**onto**¹·², **oneto** *conj* until *la15-16.* [see the prep]
ontyne *see* HUNT¹·²
onvart *see* ONWART¹·¹
onvsyt *see* UNUSED

onwait¹·¹, **onwyte** /'ɔnwet, 'ɔnwʌɪt/ *n* 1 the act of waiting; a long wait *la19- NE*. 2 a person requiring constant attention; a person who causes a long wait *20- NE*. [ON¹·¹ + WAIT¹·¹]

onwait¹·², **onwyte** /'ɔnwet, 'ɔnwʌɪt/ *v* to wait for; to tend or attend to *la16-19, 20- NE*. †**onwaiter** 1 a person who waited or was kept waiting *17*. 2 an attendant or servant *17*. **onwaiting**, †**unwaiting** 1 prolonged or patient waiting *la16-19, 20- literary*. 2 attendance or service *la16-17*. [see the noun]

onwal *see* ANNUAL¹·¹, ANNUAL¹·²

onwarnyst *see* UNWARNIST

†**onwart**¹·¹, **onvart** *n* advance payment *la15-e16*. **in onwart of payment** made in advance *la15-e16*. [see the adv]

†**onwart**¹·² *adv* further on, onward *15-e16*. [ME *onward*]

onwaschin *see* UNWASHEN

onweel *see* UNWEEL

onwrokyn *see* UNWROKIN

onwyte *see* ONWAIT¹·¹, ONWAIT¹·²

ony *see* ONIE¹·¹, ONIE¹·², ONIE¹·³

onybody, ony-buddy *see* ONIEBODIE

onygate, ony gait /'ɔneget/ *adv* 1 anyway, anyhow *la18-*. 2 anywhere *20- SW*. **onygates** anyway, anyhow *19-*. [ONIE¹·¹ + GAIT³]

onyrkyt *see* UNIRKIT

ony road /'ɔne rod/ *adv* anyway, anyhow *20-*. [ONIE¹·¹ + ROAD¹·]

onȝeon *see* INGAN

oo¹, **ool, wool, woo**, †**oull**, †**woll**, †**wow** /u, ul, wul, wu/ *n* the fleece of sheep; wool *la13-*. **ooen, woollen**, †**woon** made or consisting of wool *la15-*. †**woolster** a wool-stapler *la16*. **oother, ouder** 1 fluff from wool or cotton when it begins to fray *19- Bor*. 2 a light morning mist or haze; a heat haze *e19*. **ooy** woolly, covered with wool *la18-*. †**wollbutter** butter used in the processing of wool *e17*. **woo card** the spiked board used for teasing wool *la16-19, 20- Sh Ork*. **oo mill** a tweed mill *la19- NE WC*. †**woo wheel** a spinning wheel *17-19*. [OE *wull*]

oo², †**ow**, †**wow**, †**wooe** /u/ *v* to court, to make romantic advances *15-*. [OE *wōgian*]

oo *see* CALLER¹·², OY, WE

oobit, oubit, *SW* **wubbit**, †**wobat**, †**wobart** /'ubɪt; *SW* 'wubɪt/ *n* a caterpillar; the larva of the tiger moth *la16-*. **hairy oobit** a hairy caterpillar *19- EC Bor*. [ME *welbode*, first element apparently from *wool*]

oobregd *see* OBREGD

ooch *see* OUCH²

oodby *see* OUTBY¹·¹

oof¹·¹, **wolf**, †**wowf** /uf, wulf/ *n* 1 a wild carnivore related to the dog *Canis lupus*, a wolf *13-*. 2 the angler-fish *Lophius piscatorius la19- NE*. [OE *wulf*]

oof¹·², **wolf, woof, wowff** /uf, wulf, wuf, wʌuf/ *v* 1 *of a grain crop* to grow leaves profusely without producing seed-heads *la19- NE T C*. 2 to consume ravenously *20- NE C*. [see the noun]

ooga-tooga *see* OKERDU

oogly *see* UGLY¹·²

ook *see* WEEK²

ooka-doo *see* OKERDU

ookly *see* WEEKLY¹·¹, WEEKLY¹·²

ool¹·¹, **owl**, †**oule**, †**howle** /ul, ʌul/ *n* 1 a nocturnal bird of prey of the order *Strigiformes*, an owl *la15-*. 2 a term of abuse for a person *16-e17*. Compare HOOLET¹·¹. [OE *ūle*]

ool¹·², †**owle** /ul/ *v* 1 to treat harshly, to ill-use *19, 20- Sh Uls*. 2 to be dejected or subdued *20- Sh Uls*. **oold, oolt** downcast, subdued, bewildered *20- Ork NE Bor*. [see the noun]

ool *see* OO¹

ooler /'ulər/ *n* an undersized potato *20- Ork*. [unknown]

oolet *see* HOOLET¹·¹

oomik, umik /'umək/ *n* 1 a small quantity, a handful *19- Sh*. 2 a small, weak creature *la19- Sh*. 3 *taboo* a mouse *la19- Sh*. [ON *úmagi* one incapable of looking after himself]

oomin, oomund /'umɪn, 'umənd/ *n* an indistinct image; a sensation or suspicion *19- Sh Ork*. [perhaps altered form of HUM² with confusion with *omen*]

oon, onn, won /un, ɔn, wɔn/ *n* 1 the strip of ground reaped or dug by one worker *20- Sh Ork*. 2 a company of three shearing with hooks *20- Ork*. [Norw dial *one* a strip of woodland, or of a field which is to be mown]

oon *see* OAVEN, WOUND¹·¹, WOUND¹·²

oon- *see* UN-

oonchancy *see* UNCHANCY

oonder *see* UNDER¹·¹, UNDER¹·²

oon-egg *see* WIND¹·¹

ooner *see* UNDER¹·²

oonerstan, oonersteed *see* UNDERSTAND¹·²

oonherty, †**unhearty** /un'hɛrti/ *adj* listless, dispirited, melancholy *la17-19, 20- Sh*. [*un-* prefix + HERTY]

oonken *see* UNKEN

oonkent *see* UNKENT

oonless *see* UNLESS¹·¹

oonnaitral *see* UNNATURAL

oonpossible *see* ONPOSSIBLE

oonrizzonable *see* UNREASONABLE

oonweel *see* UNWEEL

oop *see* UP¹·², UP¹·³

oopie stiffie /'upi stɪfi/ *interj* an encouragement a child to get to its feet *20- NE T WC*. [HOOPS² + STIFF¹·² + -IE¹]

oopsie doopsie /'upsi dupsi/ *interj* = OOPIE STIFFIE. [rhyming compound from HOOPS² + -IE¹]

oor¹, **hoor, hour**, †**our**, †**howre** /ur, ʌur/ *n* 1 sixty minutes *la14-*. 2 *pl* o'clock: ◊*twa oors 15-19*. [ME *houre*]

oor² /ur/ *v* 1 to crouch or shiver with cold; to huddle *la19, 20- literary*. 2 to creep; to droop *la19- Sh*. 3 to doze, to dream *20- Sh Ork*. **oorit** 1 cold, shivery, hunched up with cold or discomfort *la19-*. 2 tired or ailing-looking, miserable, dejected *la19- C SW Bor*. **oorlich, oorlick** 1 *of people* miserable-looking, shivery *la18- NE*. 2 *of the weather* damp, bleak *19- NE*. [unknown]

oor³, **our, wir, wer, wur**, *NE T* **weer**, †**ouer**, †**owr** /ur, ʌur, wɪr, wər, wʌr; *NE T* wir/ *possessive pron* 1 belonging to or pertaining to us *la14-*. 2 belonging to the immediate family: ◊*it's oor Ann at the door. 20-*. 3 *in royal or noble usage* my: ◊*we the Earl of Crawford decree this to be done in our name la14-e17*. **oors, ours**, †**ouris**, †**owris** which belongs to us *la14-*. **oorsel, wirsel, oursell**, †**ourself** a reference to self *la14-*. **oorsels, wirsels, oursels, ourselves**, †**ourselfis**, †**ourselffis** a reference to self or selves *16-*. **wur ain** our own *20-*. [OE *ūre*, ON *várr*]

oor *see* IVER

oorie, ourie /'uri/ *adj* 1 dismal, gloomy, miserable-looking *18-*. 2 *of weather* dull and chilly, raw *19-*. 3 eerie, uncanny, disquieting *la19-*. 4 uneasy, apprehensive *la19- Sh*. **oorichie, oorickie** *of a child* wise, solemn *la19- NE T C*. Compare OOR². [ON *úr* drizzle]

oorlich, oorlick *see* OOR²

oorsel, oorsels *see* OOR³

oose, oos /uz, us/ *n* woollen fluff; fluff from cotton *19-*. **oosie, oozy** fluffy; covered with fluff; having a good nap or pile *18-*. [plural of OO¹]

ooster *see* OWSE

oot¹·¹, **out** /ut, ʌut/ *n* 1 something that is outside or external *la18-*. 2 *in children's games* a player with a particular role *19-*. **oot aboot** business transacted away from home;

an outing *la19- NE*. **outs and ins**, **oot and ins** details, ramifications *la18-*. [see the adv]

oot[1,2], **out** /ut, ʌut/ *v* **1** to eject or turn out; to expel or dismiss from office *15-*. **2** to exhibit or reveal; to divulge *la16-*. **3** to spend money *la16-e19*. **4** to issue or circulate counterfeit money *la16-e17*. **5** to put up for sale; to sell *la16-e17*. [see the adv]

oot[1,3], **out** /ut, ʌut/ *adj* **1** not within; outside or outlying *la14-*. **2** *of farmworkers* working out of doors or in the fields *la18-*. **3** *of a fire* extinguished, burned out: ◊*I came home til an oot fire and a caul hoose 19-*. **4** belonging to or occurring in a separate place *la15-16*. **oot aboot** outside, outdoors *19-*. **oot and in** *of neighbours* paying frequent short calls; accustomed to dropping by *la19- T WC*. [see the adv]

oot[1,4], **out** /ut, ʌut/ *adv* **1** out, outwards; away from the interior *la14-*. **2** completely, fully *la14-*. **3** *of a container or its contents* emptied, drained, consumed: ◊*is your cup out? la15-*; compare *cap out* (CAP[1]). **4** referring to the Jacobite Risings of 1715 or 1745 in arms against the Hanoverian government *la18- historical*. **5** *of a gathering* over, concluded: ◊*the school was out la16-*. **6** *of churchgoers or schoolchildren* dismissed and out of the building, dispersed *19-*. **7** omitting verb of motion (to go) out: ◊*the dog needs oot la19-*. **8** *in golf* over the first nine holes of an 18-hole course *la19-*. **9** referring to the Disruption of 1843 as a seceder from the established Church to the Free Kirk *la19- historical*. **oot aboot** out of doors, at some distance from home; in an isolated spot *la18-*. **oot amang**, **oot amo**, **out amon** out of, away from *la19-*. **oot at** out of; out via a door or window *la15-*. **ut efter** from beginning to end *20- Sh*. **oot and in 1** in and out, inwards and outwards, inside and out *la15-*. **2** all over, throughout, entirely *la15-16*. [OE ūt]

oot[1,5], **out** /ut, ʌut/ *prep* **1** out of, from *la14-*. **2** beyond, outside, not in *la15-*. **3** along, away, outward: ◊*out the way homeward 16-*. **oot aboot** out towards, in the vicinity of *20-*. **oot the game** unable to continue, out of action *la20-*. [see the adv]

oot[1,6], **out** /ut, ʌut/ *interj* an expression of indignation or disapproval; an expression of dismissal *15-*. [see the adv]

oot-[1,1], **out-** /ut, ʌut/ *prefix with nouns* outer, external *la14-*. [OOT[1,3]]

oot-[1,2], **out-** /ut, ʌut/ *prefix with verbs* outwards, beyond; surpassing, exceeding *la14-*. [OOT[1,4]]

oota, **ootay** *see* OOT O
ootbreak *see* OUTBREAK[1,1]
ootbye *see* OUTBY[1,1], OUTBY[1,2], OUTBY[1,3]
ootcast *see* OUTCAST
ootcome *see* OUTCOME[1,1]
ootdichtins *see* OUT-DICHTINGS
ootding *see* OUTDING
ooten, **oot on**, **oot on** /'utən, 'ut ɔn, 'ʌut ɔn/ *prep* out of *la19-*. Compare OOT O. [perhaps OE ūtan outside of or OOT[1,3] + ON[1,2], with confusion in the reduced forms between ON[1,2] and O[2]]
ooter, **outer**, †**utter**, †**uter**, †**vtyr** /'utər, 'ʌutər/ *adj* external, further away *la15-*. Compare UTTER. **outerlin** the weakling of a brood; the black sheep of a family *la19-*. **Outer Isles** the Outer Hebrides *20-*; compare OOT ISLE. [variant of UTTER and comparative of OOT[1,3]]
ooterly, **outerly**, *Sh* **uterly**, †**vtterlie** /'utərle, 'ʌutərle; *Sh* 'utərli/ *adj* **1** *of wind* blowing offshore *17-19*, *20- Sh N*. **2** far out at sea *20- Sh*. **outerly folk** strangers *20- SW*. [OOTER, with adj-forming suffix *-ly*]
ootfa *see* OUTFA
ootferm *see* OUT-FARM
ootfield *see* OUTFIELD[1,1], OUTFIELD[1,2]
ootgae *see* OUTGAE

ootgaen, †**outgane**, †**outgone** /ut'gen/ *adj* past, overtaken, beyond *la14-19*, *20- Sh*. [OOT[1,4] + ptp of GAE]
ootgaet *see* OUTGATE
ootgane *see* OUTGAE
ootgang *see* OUTGANG[1,1], OUTGANG[1,2]
ootgaun *see* OUTGAE
ootheady *see* OUT-HEIDIE
oother *see* OO[1]
ootin *see* OUTING
oot isle, †**out ile** /'ut ʌɪl/ *n* **1** an outlying or more distant island *20- Sh Ork*. **2** *pl* islands lying away from the mainland (in the Hebrides, Shetland or Orkney) *la14-e17*. Compare *Outer Isles* (OOTER). [OOT[1,4] + ISLE]
ootland *see* OUTLAND[1,1], OUTLAND[1,2]
ootlat *see* OUTLAT
oot-lattin *see* OUTLATTING
ootlaw[1,1], **outlaw**, †**utlaw**, †**wtelau**, †**wtlaw** /'utlɔ, 'ʌutlɔ/ *n law* a person declared to be outside the law and deprived of its benefits and protection *la14-19*, *20- historical*. [OE *utlaga*]
ootlaw[1,2], **outlaw**, †**vtlaw** /'utlɔ, 'ʌutlɔ/ *v* to declare someone an outlaw; to make something illegal *15-*. [see the noun]
ootlay *see* OUTLAY[1,1], OUTLAY[1,2]
ootler *see* OUTLER
ootleuk, **ootluik**, **outlook** /'utluk, 'ʌutluk/ *n* **1** a view, a prospect *la19-*. **2** mental attitude *20-*. [OOT-[1,2] + LEUK[1,1]]
ootlier *see* OUTLIER
ootlin *see* OUTLAND[1,1], OUTLAND[1,2]
ootlive *see* OUTLIVE
ootluik *see* OOTLEUK
oot-lye *see* OUTLIE
ootlying /ut'laeɪŋ/ *adj of animals* not housed in winter *la19-*. [OOT-[1,2] + participial adj from LIE[1,2]]
ootmaag, **outmag** /'ut'mag, ʌut'mag/ *v* to exhaust, to weaken *la19- Sh*. Compare OOTMOUCHT. [perhaps OOT-[1,2] + a reduced form of Norw *makt* strength]
ootmaist, **outmost**, †**outmest** /'utmest, 'ʌutmost/ *adj* **1** most extreme or most important; utmost, last *la14-*. **2** outermost, most remote *15-*. Compare UTMAIST. †**dae yer outmost** to do one's utmost *la17-19*. [ME *outmost*]
ootmoucht /ut'mɔxt/ *adj* exhausted, worn out *la19- Ork*. Compare OOTMAAG. [OOT-[1,2] + MAUCHT]
oot o, **oota**, **ootay**, †**owte off** /'ut o, 'utə, 'ute/ *prep* **1** out of, from *la14-*. **2** expelling or excluding from: ◊*to put the King out of his estait la14-*. **3** deriving or originating from *la16-*. **oot-a-daeks** outside the dyke which cuts off the hillgrazing from the cultivable ground or home pasture *la19- Sh Ork*. **oota a face** without restraint *20- Ork H&I*. **oot o ither** disjointed; disintegrated, fragmented *la19- N NE T*. **oot o't 1** mistaken, in error *20-*. **2** in an exalted state of mind *20- NE*. **3** *of a person* impaired by alcohol or drugs *la20-*. **oot yer heid** greatly distressed or confused *la19-*. **oot yourself** greatly upset *18- EC SW*. Compare OOTEN. [OOT[1,4] + O[2]]
oot on *see* OOTEN
oot ower[1,1], †**out-our**, †**out-over** /'ut ʌuər/ *adv* **1** throughout, all over; completely *18-*. **2** at a distance; aside; apart *la18-*. **3** out of bed, up *la19- Sh NE T*. **4** across, outwards *la14-16*. **by and outowre** *see* BY[1,1]. [see the prep]
oot ower[1,2], †**out-our**, †**out-over** /'ut ʌuər/ *prep* **1** *of motion* over the top of; over to the side of, across *la14-*. **2** *of position* above, on top *la14-*. **3** bent over; involved or engaged with *18-*. **4** on the other side of, on either side of *la18-*. **5** more than, in excess of, beyond *la14-e19*. **oot ower the door** out of doors; over the doorstep *18-*. **oot ower the head** above the head *la18-19*, *20- NE*. **oot ower the lugs** over

the ears *la18-19, 20- NE*. Compare ATOUR[1.2] and INOWER[1.2]. [OOT[1.4] + OWER[1.4]]

ootpit *see* OUTPUT

ootpoor *see* OUTPOUR

ootrage, outrage, †**outraige,** †**utterage,** †**oultrage** /ˈutredʒ, ˈʌutredʒ/ *n* **1** wrongful conduct, a violation of morality *la14-*. **2** lack of moderation; intemperance, extravagance *la14-*. **3** anger, rage *15-*. **ootrageous, outrageous,** †**owtrageous** *adj* **1** extreme, excessive *la14-*. **2** violent, offensive *15-*. **outrageous** *adv* extremely; excessively *la14-17*. [ME *outrage*]

ootraik *see* OUTRAIK

ootral *see* OUTRAL

oot-relation /utrəˈleʃən/ *n* a distant relative *19, 20- Ork NE*. [OOT[1.1] + RELATION]

ootricht, outricht /ˈutrɪxt, ˈʌutrɪxt/ *adv* entirely; all at once *19-*. [ME *outriʒt*]

ootrig[1.1]**, outrig** /ˈutrɪɡ, ˈʌutrɪɡ/ *n* **1** equipment, dress; outward appearance *la19, 20- Sh T*. **2** the act of fitting out a vessel or equipping troops *17*. [see the verb]

ootrig[1.2]**, outrig** /utˈrɪɡ, ˈʌutrɪɡ/ *v* to fit out or equip; to get ready, to prepare *18-19, 20- C*. **outrigging,** †**outriging** supplying, fitting out *la16-19, 20- NE*. [OOT-[1.2] + RIG[1.2]]

oot-rin *see* OUTRUN[1.1], OUTRUN[1.2]

oot-room *see* OUTROOM

ootrun *see* OUTRUN[1.1], OUTRUN[1.2]

ootseam *see* OUTSEAM

ootset *see* OUTSET[1.1], OUTSET[2]

ootshot *see* OUTSHOT[1.2]

ootsider, outsider /utˈsʌɪdər, ʌutˈsʌɪdər/ *n* **1** a person who does not belong to a particular group *la19-*. **2** the end slice of a loaf of bread *20- C Uls*. [Older Scots *outside*, with agent suffix]

ootstandin *see* OUTSTANDING

ootstreekit *see* OUTSTREEKIT

oot-tak *see* OUT-TAK[1]

oot-takin *see* OUT-TAKIN[1.1]

oot-turn *see* OUT-TURN

ootwaal *see* OUTWALE[1.1]

ootward[1.1]**, outward,** †**outwart,** †**outwert,** †**utward** /ˈutwərd, ˈʌutwərd/ *adj* **1** outside, outer, external *la14-*. **2** cold, aloof, reserved *17-19, 20- Bor*. [OE *ūtanweard, ūteweard, ūtweard*]

ootward[1.2]**, outward,** †**outwart** /ˈutwərd, ˈʌutwərd/ *adv* away from; on the outside, externally *la14-*. [see the adj]

ootwick *see* OUTWICK[1.1], OUTWICK[1.2]

ootwilins *see* OUTWALE[1.2]

ootwin *see* OUTWAN

ootwinter *see* OUTWINTER

ootwith *see* OUTWITH[1.1], OUTWITH[1.2], OUTWITH[1.3]

ootyoke *see* OUT-YOKE

ooy *see* OO[1]

ooyah, oh-yah, owyah /ˈuja, ˈoja, ˈʌuja/ *interj* a cry of pain *20-*. [an involuntary utterance]

†**oozlie** *adj* untidy, unkempt, dirty *19*. [unknown; compare ON *úsæll* wretched, *úsælligr* joyless, ill-favoured]

opeenion, opinion, †**opingan,** †**opunyone** /əˈpinjən, əˈpɪnjən/ *n* **1** belief, considered view *la14-*. **2** personal attitude or appraisal; esteem *la14-*. [ME *opinioun*]

open[1.1]**,** †**opyn,** †**oppin** /ˈopən/ *n* an opening, a gap, a space; the countryside *la15-*. **the open o the heid** the front suture of the skull, the fontanelle *la18-19, 20- Sh*. [see the adj]

open[1.2]**, apen,** *Bor* **wuppen,** †**opin,** †**oppin,** †**apin** /ˈopən, ˈepən/; *Bor* /ˈwʌpən/ *v* **1** to make or become open *la14-*. **2** to initiate a proceeding or business; to raise a matter *la15-*. **3** to make available, to grant *la15-16*. **open on** *of a door* to face onto or towards a place or direction *la15-*. **open to** = *open on*. [OE *openian*]

open[1.3]**, apen,** †**opin,** †**oppin,** †**appin** /ˈopən, ˈepən/ *adj* **1** unclosed, allowing access *la14-*. **2** unconcealed, evident *la14-*. **3** free, available; otherwise unoccupied *20- EC Bor*. **4** *of female animals* bearing or ready to bear young; not sterilized *la18-19*. **open account** *law* a debt entered in a book, not constituted by voucher or decree (for goods supplied by shops) *18-*. **open cast** *mining* a method of excavating coal from the surface *17-*. †**oppin gate** the public street; a free or open access road *la15-16*. **open steek** *needlework* a kind of openwork stitch *19, 20- Ork*. †**opin voce 1** *of the voice* audible and public *la15-16*. **2** by public fame or rumour *16-e17*. **the apen furth, the open furth** out of doors *19, 20- NE*. [OE *open*]

opgester, uppgester, †**upgaster,** †**upgaister** /ˈɔpɡɛstər, ˈʌpɡɛstər/ *n* **1** *in Shetland* a person who transfered ownership of property in return for lifelong maintenance *16-e19, la19-historical*. **2** *in Shetland* a person who stayed for a lengthy period as a guest at another person's house *20, 21- historical*. [Norn *uppgester*]

opgestrie, †**upgaistrie** /ˈɔpɡɛstri/ *n in Shetland* the transfer of the ownership of property in return for maintenance *e17, 19- historical*. [Norn **uppgestrie*]

opin *see* OPEN[1.2], OPEN[1.3]

opingan, opinion *see* OPEENION

oppin *see* OPEN[1.1], OPEN[1.2], OPEN[1.3]

†**oppone, appone** *v* **1** *law* to oppose by argument, to produce evidence to the contrary of *la15-18*. **2** to dispute *16-17*. [Lat *oppōnere*]

opporchancity /ɔpərˈtʃansɪte/ *n humorous* an opportunity *la20-*. [conflation of Scots *opportunity* and CHANCE[1.1]; coined by comedians Rikki Fulton and Jack Milroy]

opposeetion, opposition /ɔpəˈzɪʃən, ɔpəˈzɪʃən/ *n* **1** contrary or hostile argument or action; resistance *15-*. **2** astronomical opposition *16*. [ME *opposicioun*, Lat *oppositio*]

oppugn, †**oppung** /əˈpjun/ *v* to oppose, to dispute *la16-*. [EModE *oppugn*, Lat *oppugnāre*]

oprisin *see* UPRISE

opstander *see* UPSTANDER

optene *see* OBTAIN

opunyone *see* OPEENION

opyn *see* OPEN[1.1]

or[1.1] /ɔr/ *prep* **1** before *la14-*. **2** until *19-*. [ME *ar*, ON *ár*]

or[1.2]**,** *Sh* **ir** /ɔr; *Sh* ɪr/ *conj* **1** before; until *la14-*. **2** sooner than, rather than *la14-*. **3** than *16-18, 19- Sh Ork*. **or a be dune** before it's all over *la19- Ork NE T*. **or ever** before ever, even before *la14-*. †**or lang gae** before long *la18-19*. [see the prep]

ora *see* ORRA[1.1], ORRA[1.2]

oraisoun *see* ORISON

orange[1.1]**, oarange,** †**orenge,** †**oringe** /ˈɔrəndʒ, ˈorəndʒ/ *n* **1** a large reddish-yellow citrus fruit *16-*. **2** the colour of this fruit *la16-*. [ME *orange*, EModE *orange*]

orange[1.2]**, oarange,** †**oringe,** †**orinche** /ˈɔrəndʒ, ˈorəndʒ/ *adj* orange in colour *16-*. [see the noun]

Orange[2] /ˈɔrəndʒ/ *adj* **1** of or relating to the Orangemen and their Order *la18-*. **2** *derogatory* Protestant *20-*. **Orange lodge** a club or branch of the Orange Order *19-*. **Orangeman** a member of the Orange Order *la18-*. **Orange Order** a political society promoting Protestant and Loyalist principles, founded in Northern Ireland in 1795 and originally known as the Orange Society *la19-*. **Orange walk** a parade held by Orange communities during the marching season *la19-*. **Orangewoman** a female member of the

Orange Order *la19-*. [named after William of *Orange*, a principality of The Netherlands]

oranger, †**orenger**, †**oringer** /'ɔrəndʒər/ *n* an orange *la16-*. [MFr *oranger* an orange tree]

orator, †**oratour**, †**orter** /'ɔrətər/ *n* **1** a speechmaker, a public speaker *la15-*. **2** a person whose duty or employment it is to pray on another's behalf; a chaplain *la15-e17*. [ME *oratour*, Lat *ōrātor*]

oratory /'ɔrətre, 'ɔrətəre/ *n* **1** a small chapel for private prayer *la15-*. **2** a study *15-e16*. **3** an inner shrine of a temple, as the seat of an oracle *e16*. [ME *ōrātori*]

†**oratour** *n* = ORATORY *la14-e17*. [AN *oratoire, oratur*]

oratour *see* ORATOR

orchard, *Bor* **wortchat**, †**orchat**, †**orchart**, †**orcheard** /'ɔrtʃərd; *Bor* 'wɔrtʃət/ *n* a piece of enclosed land for the cultivation of fruit trees *15-*. [OE *ortgeard*]

†**orchard-litt**, **orcheart lit**, **orchetlit** *n* the name of a dye *la16-17*. [EModE *orchell* red or violet dye + LIT[1.1]]

ordeen, **ordain**, *NE* **urdeen**, †**ordine** /ɔr'din, ɔr'den; *NE* also ʌr'din/ *v pt* also †**ordand**, †**ordoned** **1** to appoint; to invest or confer holy orders upon *la14-*. **2** to decree or command; to order, arrange or assign *la14-*. **3** *Presbyterian Church* to admit an elder or deacon to office *la16-*. **4** to prepare for battle, to marshal troops *la14-15*. †**ordinar** a person who made a decree; a person who ordained an ecclesiastic *la16-17*. [ME *ordeinen*]

order[1.1], **oarder**, †**ordour** /'ɔrdər, 'ɔrdər/ *n* **1** rank, class, grade *la14-*. **2** a monastic society *la14-*. **3** a fraternity of knights; the badge or insignia of a military group *la14-*. **4** control, discipline *15-*. **5** a sequence; a methodical arrangement *la15-*. **6** established practice *la15-*. **7** decency, propriety *la15-*. **8** a command, an instruction; an authoritative direction or mandate *la16-*. **9** *pl* requirements or gear; all that is needed for a purpose *la18-*. **10** *Reformed Church* a scheme for territorial reorganization or for the regular and settled provision of ministers' stipends *la16*. †**as the order is usit** according to the law, in regular legal form *la14-e15*. †**ordour of table** *law* a list giving the sequence in which causes were to be called *16*. †**per ordour** in order, in proper sequence *la14-e16*. †**tak ordour** to give directions, to impose order; to make arrangements *la16-17*. **tak order with** to arrange, to resolve *la16-19, 20- NE*. **tak an order o** = *tak ordour la19- NE*. [ME *ordre*]

order[1.2], **oarder**, †**ordour** /'ɔrdər, 'ɔrdər/ *v* **1** to arrange in a particular position; to assign a place, to organize *16-*. **2** to direct, regulate or manage; to control or rule *16-*. **3** to issue a directive, instruction or command *16-*. [see the noun]

Order of the Thistle /ɔrdər əv ðə 'θɪsəl/ *n* the senior order of chivalry in Scotland *la17-*. [named from the insignia of the order]

ordinance, †**ordonnance**, †**ordines** /'ɔrdənəns/ *n* **1** arrangements, provisions, preparations *la14-*. **2** a decision; a ruling or settlement *la14-*. [ME *ordinaunce*]

ordinar[1.1], **ordnar**, **ordinary** /'ɔrdənər, 'ɔrdnər, 'ɔrdənəre/ *n* **1** an ecclesiastical dignitary with spiritual authority and jurisdiction over a region *15-*. **2** the usual state of things; what is customary or habitual *17-*. **3** one of a series of sermons given by a minister on one text *la17-19, 20- NE*. **4** a person's regular allowance or share; a fixed portion or permitted serving *16-19*. **5** one of the judges of the Court of Session who sit on cases of first instance in the Outer House *la16-19*. **6** an officer with a regular or permanent appointment; a permanently engaged gunner *la16-17*. **7** a judge with a regular and fixed jurisdiction *15-17*. **8** a regular reading from the Bible within a household *la17*. †**ordinaris lettres** letters from an ecclesiastical ordinary *la15-e16*. **aff ordinar** out of the ordinary; extraordinary *la19-*. **for ordinar** normally, usually *17-*. **nae ordinar** unusually, extraordinarily *la19-*. **past ordinar** extraordinary *la19-* [ME *ordiner, ordinārī*, MFr *ordinaire*]

ordinar[1.2], **ordnar**, **ordinary** /'ɔrdənər, 'ɔrdnər, 'ɔrdənəre/ *adj* **1** usual, normal *la15-*. **2** *of a judge* having a fixed and regular jurisdiction in all actions of the same general nature *15-*. **3** *Scottish Universities* applied to the general courses in any particular subject, passes in a certain number of which lead either to an Ordinary Degree or to the higher classes of an Honours course *la19-*. **4** regular or frequent in attendance *la16-17*. **5** applied to the regular lords of session (as distinct from the extraordinary and supernumerary lords) *la16-e17*. **6** applied to the lord of session taking his turn of sitting separately on cases of first instance *la16-e17*. **Ordinary Degree** an academic degree gained by a number of passes in ordinary courses, according to varying regulations *la19-*. †**ordinar letters** a decree from an ordinary court, including an ecclesiastical court *la15-16*; compare *letters ordinar* (LETTER). †**ordinar pure** people who were officially registered as parish poor, who received aid from parish funds *la16-17*. [ME *ordinari*, MFr *ordinaire*]

ordinar[1.3], **ornar**, /'ɔrdənər, 'ɔrnər/ *adv* usually, in the usual way; somewhat, to a certain extent *la16-*. [see the adj]

ordinar *see* ORDEEN

†**Ordinar Lord of the Session**, **Ordinary Lord of Session** *n* a judge of the Court of Session with a regular and fixed jurisdiction *la16-17*. Compare LORD ORDINARY. [ORDINAR[1.2] + LORD OF SESSION]

ordinary *see* ORDINAR[1.1], ORDINAR[1.2]

Ordinary Grade, **O Grade** /'ɔrdənəre gred, 'o gred/ *n* **1** *secondary education* a state examination at a less advanced level; the course leading such an examination *la20, 21- historical*. [ORDINAR[1.2] + Eng *grade*]

ordine *see* ORDEEN

ordines *see* ORDINANCE

ordnance /'ɔrdnəns/ *n* ammunition; artillery *16-*. [variant of ORDINANCE]

ordnar *see* ORDINAR[1.1], ORDINAR[1.2]

ordoned *see* ORDEEN

ordonnance *see* ORDINANCE

ordour *see* ORDER[1.1], ORDER[1.2]

ore *see* AIR[3]

ored *see* ORRET

oreeginal *see* ORIGINAL[1.1], ORIGINAL[1.2]

orenge *see* ORANGE[1.1]

orenger *see* ORANGER

†**orenʒe** *n* an orange *16*. [ME *orenge*, OFr (*pomme d'*)*orenge*]

orfant *see* ORPHANT

organ, †**orgain** /'ɔrgən/ *n* a musical instrument consisting of pipes sounded by compressed air *la15-*. **organ loft** a gallery in a church or other building in which an organ is placed *16-*. [ME *organ*]

†**orgement**, **orge mounde** *n* boiled barley; barley soup or porridge *la16-e18*. [MFr *orge mondé*]

†**orguillous**, **orgulous**, **orguellous** *adj* proud, arrogant *la15-e19*. [ME *orguillous*]

original[1.1], *NE* **oreeginal** /ə'rɪdʒənəl; *NE* ə'rɪdʒənəl/ *n* **1** a source; something in its first uncopied form *15-*. **2** origin, birth, descent *15-19, 20- NE*. **3** birthplace *17-19, 20- NE*. [see the adj]

original[1.2], *NE* **oreeginal**, †**originale** /ə'rɪdʒənəl; *NE* ə'rɪdʒənəl/ *adj* **1** pertaining to the origin; initial, first, earliest *15-*. **2** new, fresh; not copied or derivative *15-*. **3** *of a history text* describing the origins or the earliest era of a country *e15*. †**originale justice** an innate sense of justice *la15*.

Original Seceder a member of the church formed in 1842 by the reuniting of the Burgher and Antiburgher elements in the Auld Lichts church, now merged with the Church of Scotland *19, 20- historical.* [ME *original,* Lat *orīginālis*]
orinche *see* ORANGE¹·²
oringe *see* ORANGE¹·¹, ORANGE¹·²
oringer *see* ORANGER
orishon /'ɔrɪʃən/ *n derogatory* an odd-looking or insignificant person *19- SW.* [unknown]
orison, *Ork* **eerison,** †**orisoun,** †**oraisoun,** †**urison** /'ɔrəsən; *Ork* 'irəsən/ *n* **1** a prayer *la14-19, 20- literary.* **2** a formal written discourse or address; an oration *16-e17.* **3** *grammar* a sentence *16-17.* [ME *orisoun*]
†**orkie** *n* a Dutch or Flemish coin worth two doits *17-19.* [reduced form of Du *oortken,* diminutive of *oort*]
Orkney, †**Orknay,** †**Orkynnay** /'ɔrkne/ *n* the Orkney islands *la15-.* **Orkney chair** a wooden armchair with a high curved back made of woven straw or bent grass *la19-.* **Orkney cheese** cheese made in Orkney using the Dunlop method *la18-.* **Orkney herald,** †**Orknay herauld** the designation of one of the Scottish heralds *la16-.* [ON *Orkneyjar*]
orloge, †**orlage,** †**horologe** /'ɔrlɔdʒ/ *n* a clock; the dial of a clock or sundial *la15-19, 20- T.* [ME *orloge*]
orloppin *see* OWERLEAP
ormal, urmal, hirmal /'ɔrməl, 'ørməl 'hɪrməl/ *n* a scrap, a fragment *19- Sh Ork.* [ON *örmul*]
Ormond /'ɔrmənd/ *n heraldry* one of the Scottish pursuivants *la15-.* [named after the Marquis of *Ormonde,* the title of the second son of James III]
ornament, †**ournement** /'ɔrnəmənt/ *n* **1** embellishment *15-.* **2** *in weaving* the last part of a piece of cloth, often coarser than the rest *20- WC.* **3** *pl* insignia, regalia *la15-17.* [ME *ournement,* Lat *ōrnāmentum* equipment, circumstance conferring honour]
†**ornar** *see* ORDINAR¹·³
orp, *Sh Ork* **irp,** *Bor* **wurp,** †**erp,** †**orpe** /ɔrp; *Sh Ork* ɪrp; *Bor* wʌrp/ *v* to grumble, to complain peevishly *la16-;* compare NYARB, YARP. **orpit,** *Sh Ork* **irped** fretful, discontented, peevish *la15-.* [unknown]
orphaling *see* ORPHELINE
orphant, orfant, orphan /'ɔrfənt, 'ɔrfən/ *n* a child whose parents are dead *la15-.* [Lat *orphanus*]
orpheist *see* ORPHUS
†**orpheline, orphaling** *n* an orphan *16-17.* [ME *orphelin,* EModE *orphelyn*]
†**orphus, offreis, offrez** *n* an ornamental band or border on ecclesiastical vestments or draperies, an oprhrey *16.* **orpheist, orpheoust** adorned with an orphrey; bordered with rich material *la16.* [AN *orfreis*]
orpie, orpy, wurpie /'ɔrpi, 'wʌrpi/ *n* orpine, one of the stonecrops *Hylotelephium telephium la15-19, 20- SW Bor.* [OFr *orpin*]
orra¹·¹, †**ora** /'ɔrə, 'orə/ *n* what is left over; an article not in immediate use *la18-.* **orral** a scrap, a fragment, a remnant; *pl* odds and ends; leftovers *19- NE T.* [see the adj]
orra¹·², **ora,** *T* **oary,** †**orray,** †**orrow** /'ɔrə, 'orə; *T* 'ore/ *adj* **1** *of a person* unoccupied; unemployed; superfluous *17-.* **2** *of an object* spare, extra; mismatched, not one of a pair *18-.* **3** *of events* occasional, coming at irregular or infrequent intervals *la18-.* **4** *of a job* casual, unskilled *19-.* **5** *of items* miscellaneous, nondescript *19-.* **6** *of a person* doing casual or unskilled work; *of an animal* being used for odd jobs *la19-.* **7** *of events* strange, uncommon, abnormal *la19-.* **8** *of people or things* dirty, shabby, disreputable *17-19, 20- NE T.* **9** *of women* unmarried, unattached *la16-17.* **orraster 1** an extra hand, a casual labourer *20- NE.* **2** a disreputable or untrustworthy person *20- NE.* **orra beast** a horse kept for odd jobs; not one of a pair *19- NE.* **orra billie** a man or boy who does odd jobs (on a farm) *20- NE.* **orra horse** a horse kept for odd jobs; not one of a pair *19- NE.* **orra loon** = *orra billie.* [probably reduced form of OWER¹·⁴ + *a'* (AW¹·¹)]
orral *see* ORRA¹·¹
orraman /'ɔrəmən/ *n* **1** a person who undertakes general duties (on a farm) *19-.* **2** any mechanical contrivance used by a person working single-handed *20- NE.* [ORRA¹·² + MAN]
orraster *see* ORRA¹·²
orray *see* ORRA¹·²
orret, ored /'ɔrət, 'ɔrəd/ *n* a small wedge driven into a wooden peg to expand it and prevent it from slipping *20- Sh Ork.* [Norw dial *årette*]
orrow *see* ORRA¹·²
orry *see* AURRIE
ort¹·¹ /ort/ *n* **1** *pl* refuse, leavings; leftover food *la16-.* **2** feed for farm animals *19.* [MDu *orte,* MLG *ort*]
ort¹·² /ort/ *v* **1** to reject, to throw away *19, 20- EC Bor.* **2** to waste food *19, 20- Ork SW Bor.* [see the noun]
†**ort**² *n* a sector of a dollar which had been cut in four; a coin valued at a quarter-dollar *16-17.* [MDu *oord*]
ort³ /ɔrt/ *n* a brood, a litter; a large family of children *19- Sh.* [ON *verpa* to throw, lay eggs; compare Faer *urt* a clutch of eggs]
orter *see* ORATOR
ös *see* USE¹·¹
Oscar Slater /'ɔskər 'sletər/ *adv rhyming slang* later *20- WC.* **Oscar** = OSCAR SLATER. [from the name of the defendant in a notorious Glasgow trial; Slater was convicted of murder but the conviction was later quashed]
osel, ozel, ozzel /'ɔsəl, 'ozəl/ *n* one of the short cords by which the mesh-work of a herring-net is attached to the head-rope *la18-.* [wrong division of *a nosel,* OE *nostle* a band]
†**osill, oswald, oswat** *n* a blackbird or ring-ouzel *la15-18.* [OE *ōsle*]
oslin /'ɔzlɪn/ *n* a variety of apple cultivated in Scotland, the Arbroath Pippin *19-.* [unknown]
osmal, usmal /'ɔsməl, 'ʌzməl, 'øsməl/ *adj* **1** grim, sinister; evil-looking *la19- Sh Ork.* **2** dark, dusky, grey *la19- Sh.* [unknown]
†**osmond, oismont** *n* a superior quality of imported iron *15-e17.* [OSw *osmunder,* meaning uncertain]
osmond stone /'ɔzmənd ston/ *n* a very hard stone used in parts of western and central Scotland for the floors of ovens *la18-20, 21- historical.* [OSMOND + STANE¹·¹]
Osnaburg, †**ozenbrigs** /'ɔznəbərg/ *n* **1** a kind of coarse linen *17-19, 20- historical.* **2** a strong coarse cotton (used to make overalls or sacking) *18-19, 20- T EC.* [named from the German city *Osnabrück,* where the fabric was originally made]
ospital, ospittall *see* HOASPITAL
ossigar /'ɔsigər/ *n of poultry* in a state of moulting *la19- Sh Ork.* [unknown]
ossiltree *see* ASSLE-TREE
ost /ɔst, øst/ *v* to curdle milk by adding sour milk or buttermilk and heating *19- Sh.* **ostin, eusteen** curdled milk (used as a poultice) *20- Sh.* [Norw *ysta*]
ost *see* HOST¹·¹
ostel *see* HOSTEL
†**ostend** *v ptp* also **ostensit 1** to show, exhibit *la15-e17.* **2** *law* to exhibit or present a document for scrutiny *la15-16.* [Lat *ostendere*]
†**ostensioun** *n* **1** manifestation, demonstration *la15-16.* **2** *law* presentation of a document for scrutiny *la15-e16.* **3**

the action of presenting a hand whilst taking an oath *16*. [EModE *ostencion*, Lat *ostensio*]

†**ostentive** *adj* ostentatious *17-e18*. [Lat *ostent-*, ptp stem of *ostendere*, with adj-forming suffix *-ive*]

ostillary *see* HOSTELRY
ostin *see* OST
ostlaire, ostler *see* HOSTLER
öswal *see* USUAL
oswald, oswat *see* OSILL
ote *see* AIT
othe *see* AITH
other *see* ITHER[1.1], ITHER[1.2], ITHER[1.3], OWTHER[1.2]
otter /'ɔtər/ *n* **1** an aquatic mammal *Lutra lutra la13-*. **2** a piece of fishing-tackle used by poachers of salmon or trout *19-*. **3** the barb of a fishing-hook or fishing-spear *la19, 20- Bor*. [OE *oter*]
otterline cow *see* ETTERLIN
ou, ow /o, u, ʌu/ *interj* an expression of surprise or vexation *la18-*. **ou ay, ow ay** an expression of affirmation *19-*. [probably onomatopoeic]
oubit *see* OOBIT
ouch[1] /ux/ *interj* an involuntary sound expressing exertion or disgust *la19-*. [compare OCH, ACH]
ouch[2], **ooch** /ʌutʃ, utʃ/ *interj* an expression of pain or surprise *20-*. **oucha, ootcha** an expression of pain *la20-*. [onomatopoeic]
ouch *see* UCHE
oucht *see* OCHT[1.1], OCHT[1.2]
ouder *see* OO[1]
ouer *see* OOR[3]
ouerly *see* OVERLY[1.1], OVERLY[1.2]
ouersale *see* OURSAILE
ouf /uf, ʌuf/ *n* **1** a small or insignificant person *19, 20- literary*. **2** a stupid or ineffectual person *19, 20- NE*. [variant of Eng *oaf*, compare ON *álfr* an elf]
ought *see* AUCHT[2], OCHT[1.3], OCHT[2]
ouipstander *see* UPSTANDER
ouirfret *see* OWER-FRET
ouirpas *see* OVERPAS
ouirput *see* OWERPIT
ouirword *see* OWERWORD
ouk *see* WEEK[2]
ouklie *see* WEEKLY[1.3]
oukly *see* WEEKLY[1.2]
ould *see* AULD[1.2]
oulder *see* AULDER
ouldest *see* AULDEST
oule *see* OOL[1.1]
ouler *see* ALLER
oulk *see* WEEK[2]
oull *see* OO[1]
oultrage *see* OOTRAGE
ounce, unce, †**ons** /ʌuns, ʌns/ *n* a unit of weight equal to one sixteenth of a pound (approx 28.35 grams) *15-*. **ounceland** a measure of land (in Orkney, Shetland, Caithness and western Scotland) consisting of eighteen or twenty pennylands, on which a feu duty of one ounce of silver or one eighth of a mark was paid *17-19, 20- historical*; compare URISLAND; TIRUNG. [ME *ounce*]
oup *see* UP[1.2]
oupe-standeng *see* UPSTANNIN[1.1]
our *see* OOR[1], OOR[3], OWER[1.1], OWER[1.2], OWER[1.3], OWER[1.4]
-our *see* -ER
†**our-alquhare, over-allquhair** *adv* everywhere, all over *la14-16*. [OWER[1.3] + A'WHERE]
ourance *see* OWRANCE

†**our-ane** *adv* in one, together *e16*. [OWER[1.3] + ANE[1.1]]
ourblaw *see* OWERBLAW
our-burd *see* OWERBOARD
ourcast *see* OWERCAST[1.1], OWERCAST[1.2]
ourcled *see* OWERCLAD
ourcum *see* OWERCOME[1.1], OWERCOME[1.2]
ourdrive *see* OVERDRIVE
oureche *see* OWERREACH
oure-sey *see* OWERSEA[1.2]
oureswak *see* OWERSWAK
ourevolve *see* OURVOLVE
oure-yhude *see* OWERGAE
ourflete *see* OWERFLEETE
ourfret *see* OWER-FRET
ourga, ourgaan *see* OWERGAE
ourgang *see* OWERGANG[1.1], OWERGANG[1.2]
ourget *see* OWERGET
†**ourgilt, ovirgilt, owergilt** *v pt* **ourgilt, ourgiltit, overgilt** to overlay with gold *la15-e17*. [OWER[1.3] + GILT[3]]
ourgive *see* OWERGIE
ourgo *see* OWERGAE
ourhale *see* OWERHAIL
ourhand *see* OWERHAN
ourharl *see* OWERHARL
ourheid *see* OWERHEID[1.2]
†**ourhele, ourhelde** *v* to cover over *la15-16*. [OWER[1.3] + OE *helian*]
†**ourhip, overhip** *v* to pass over; to skip or omit *16*. [OWER[1.4] + HIP[2.2]]
ourhye *see* OWERHIE
ourie *see* OORIE
ouris *see* OOR[3], OWRES
ourisman *see* OWERSMAN
ourlap *see* OWERLEAP
ourlard *see* OVERLORD
ourlay *see* OWERLAY[1.1], OWERLAY[1.2]
ourleff *see* OVERLEVE
ourlepe *see* OWERLEAP
ourleve *see* OVERLEVE
†**ourloft, overloft** *n* a gangway, a raised half-deck *la15-e17*. [altered form of OURLOP by conflation with loft (LAFT[1.1])]
†**ourlop, overlope, owirlupe** *n* a raised gangway; a platform covering the hold of a ship (and forming the lowest deck) *la15-17*. [MDu *overlopen*]
ourlord *see* OVERLORD
ourloupe *see* OWERLOUP
ourluke *see* OWERLEUK
†**ourman, overman, owirman** *n* **1** a person in authority, a ruler; the head of an institution *la14-16*. **2** a craftsman appointed to supervise his colleagues and their work *la15-e16*. **3** the provost of Prestwick and Wigtown *la15-e16*. **4** one of the leading officials of a burgh; a magistrate *16*. **5** a chief arbiter; a chief and arbitrating executor *15-e17*. Compare OWERSMAN. [OWER[1.2] + MAN]
ourmare *see* OVERMARE
ournement *see* ORNAMENT
ourpas *see* OVERPAS
†**ourquhare** *adv* everywhere *la14-e16*. [OWER[1.3] + WHAUR[1.1]]
ourquhelm *see* OWERWHELM
ourreke *see* OWERREACH
ourrin *see* OWERRIN
ours *see* OOR[3]
†**oursaile, ouersale** *v* to cross water in a ship *la14-e16*. [OWER[1.3] + SAIL[1.3]]
†**ourscalit** *adj* sprinkled, scattered *e16*. [OWER[1.3] + ptp of SKAIL[1.2]]

†**ourschine, overshyne** *v pt* **ourschane** to shine over; to illuminate *15-e16*. [OWER¹·³ + SHINE¹·²]
our-se *see* OWERSEE
ourself *see* OOR³
ourselfis, ourselffis *see* OOR³
oursell *see* OOR³
oursels, ourselves *see* OOR³
ourset *see* OWERSET¹·¹, OWERSET¹·²
oursey *see* OWERSEA¹·¹
oursicht *see* OWERSICHT
oursie *see* OWERSEE
oursile *see* OVERSILE
ourslide *see* OVERSLIDE
oursman *see* OWERSMAN
oursowme *see* OWERSOUM
†**ourstrenkle** *v* to sprinkle or besprinkle *la15*. [OWER¹·³ + STRINKLE¹·²]
oursyll *see* OVERSILE
ourta, ourtak, ourtane *see* OWERTAK
ourthraw *see* OWERTHRAW¹·¹, OWERTHRAW¹·²
ourthroe *see* OWERTHRAW¹·²
ourthrow *see* OWERTHRAW¹·¹
ourthwort *see* OVERTHORT¹·¹, OVERTHORT¹·²
†**ourtirve, overtyrve, ourtirf** *v* to overturn; to overthrow *la14-15*. **ower-tirvie** to overthrow *e19*. [unknown]
ourtre *see* OWERTREE
†**ourtummyll, overtumble** *v* to tumble over, to capsize, to fall down; to cause to fall *la14-e17*. [OWER¹·⁴ + TUMMLE]
ourturn *see* OWERTURN¹·²
†**ourvolve, ourevolve** *v* to turn over; to lay aside *e16*. [OWER¹·³ + VOLVE]
ourwalter *see* OURWELTER
†**ourwelt, overwelt** *v* to turn over; to throw over or down *e16*. [OWER¹·⁴ + WALT²]
†**ourwelter, overwelter, ourwalter** *v* to roll over *e16*. [OWER¹·⁴ + WELTER²·²]
ourword *see* OWERWORD
ourȝeid *see* OWERGAE
our-ȝeir *see* OWERYEAR
ous *see* US
ouse *see* OWSE
oussen *see* OX
out *see* OOT¹·¹, OOT¹·², OOT¹·³, OOT¹·⁴, OOT¹·⁵, OOT¹·⁶
out- *see* OOT-¹·¹, OOT-¹·²
outainsell *see* UTENSIL
†**outawing** *adj of a debt* owing, outstanding *17*. [OOT¹·⁴ + participial adj from AWE]
outband, outbound, outbond /ˈutband, ˈʌutbʌund, ˈʌutbɔnd/ *n* a stone with its long side along a wall face, a quoin or jamb stone *la18-*. **out and in bond** stones or bricks laid in alternate positions in the angles of walls *la19-*. [OOT¹·³ + BAND¹·¹]
outbirst *see* OUTBURST
outbond, outbound *see* OUTBAND
†**out-braid** *v* to break into speech; to blurt out *16-e17*. [OOT¹·⁴ + BRAID²·²]
outbreak¹·¹, ootbreak, outbreck, †**outbrek** /ˈʌutbrɛk, ˈutbrɛk, ˈʌutbrɛk/ *n* wasteland reclaimed as arable, marginal land *16- Sh Ork N*. [see the verb]
†**outbreak¹·², outbreke** *v* to reclaim marginal land *e16*. [OOT¹·⁴ + BRAK¹·²]
†**outbreak², outbreke** *v* to break out *la15-e16*. **outbreaking 1** an outburst of sin or rebellion; a bout of disorderly behaviour *17-e19*. **2** the flooding of a river or stream *la17*. [unknown]
outbrist *see* OUTBURST

†**out-burges** *n* a burgess resident outside the burgh *la15-16*. [OOT¹·³ + BURGESS¹·¹]
†**outburst, outbirst, outbrist** *v* to burst out, to give forth *15-19*. [OOT¹·⁴ + BIRST¹·²]
outby¹·¹, ootbye, *Sh* **oodby** /ˈʌutˈbae, utˈbae; *Sh* ˈudbae/ *adj* **1** outlying, distant, away from the main or central part *19-*. **2** *of farmland* away from the steading *19-*. **3** *of a farm* in an upland or more pastoral area *19-*. **4** out of doors, out in the fields *19-*. **oot-bye worker** a field labourer *la19-*. [see the adv]
outby¹·², ootbye /ˈʌutˈbae, utˈbae/ *adv* **1** outwards; a little way off, at a distance *17-*. **2** out of doors, out in the fields *17-*. **3** away from home; not at hand *19-*. **4** away from the shore, out at sea *19-*. **5** in an upland district *19- SW Bor*. **6** towards the outer part of a room; away from the fire, nearer the door *la18-19, 20- Sh Ork*. [OOT¹·⁴ + BY¹·¹]
outby¹·³, ootbye /ˈʌutˈbae, utˈbae/ *prep* **1** outside, beyond *19-*. **2** on the outskirts of; in the neighbourhood of *20- NE Uls*. [see the adv]
outcast, ootcast /ˈʌutkast, ˈutkast/ *n* a quarrel *17-*. [OOT¹·³ + CAST¹·¹]
outcome¹·¹, ootcome, †**outcum** /ˈʌutkʌm, ˈutkʌm/ *n* **1** an appearance or emergence; an escape; an eruption *la14-*. **2** the time of year when the days begin to lengthen *la17-*. **3** a result; an effect or consequence *la18-*. **4** the difference in cost between raw material and manufactured article; profit or surplus *19-*. **outcoming 1** issuing forth, emergence *la15-*. **2** profit, gain; a worthwhile result *19-*. †**outcummit, outcomed** *of a sheep* with young *la16-17* [OOT¹·⁴ + COME¹·²]
†**outcome¹·², outcum** *adj* **1** *of goods* manufactured, produced; residual, surplus *la18-19*. **2** *of a sheep* with young *la16-17*. [see the noun]
out-dichtings, ootdichtins, †**out-dichtynnis** /ˈʌutdɪxtənz, ˈutdɪxtənz/ *npl* refuse of threshed grain; the sweepings from a mill *16-19, 20- Bor*. [OOT¹·³ + verbal noun from DICHT¹·²]
outding, ootding /ˈʌutdɪŋ, ˈutdɪŋ/ *v* to beat, to exceed, to surpass *19-*. [OOT¹·⁴ + DING¹·²]
†**outdraucht** *n* an extract, abstract or partial copy of a record or account *16*. [OOT¹·³ + DRAUCHT¹·¹]
†**outdraw** *v* to pull out; to extract *16*. [OOT¹·⁴ + DRAW¹·²]
†**outdwelland** *adj* living outside the burgh *15-16*. [OOT¹·⁴ + participial adj from DWALL¹]
outdwellar /ˈʌutdwelər/ *n* a person who lived outside the burgh; a stranger, an outsider *15-16, 20- historical*. [OOT¹·⁴ + DWALL¹, with agent suffix]
outen, out on /ˈutən, ˈʌutən/ *prep* **1** outside *la19-*. **2** without, lacking *20- literary*. [reduced form of *withoutin* (WITHOOT¹·²), perhaps conflated with *out on*]
†**outer, utter** *v* to swerve; to balk *16*. [unknown]
outer *see* OOTER, UTTER
Outer House, †**Utter Hous** /ˈʌutər hʌus/ *n law* the part of the Court of Session in which cases of first instance are heard *la16-*. Compare *Inner House* (INNER). [*outer* (OOTER) + HOOSE¹·¹]
outerly *see* OOTERLY
outfa, ootfa, outfall /ˈʌutfɔ, ˈutfɔ, ˈʌutfɔl/ *n* **1** a quarrel *17-19, 20- Sh N Uls*. **2** a sortie; a raid *17-e19*. [OOT¹·³ + FA¹·²]
†**outfang** *n law* theft committed ouside of a lord's jurisdiction *la16-e19*. Compare INFANG. [reduced form of OUTFANGTHIEF]
outfangthief, outfangandthef, †**outfangand-thefe** /ˈʌutfaŋθif, ˈʌutfaŋəndθɛf/ *n* **1** *law* the right of a lord to pursue a thief outside his own jurisdiction and to bring him back for trial or to try a thief coming from outside his jurisdiction *la14-e18, la18- historical*. **2** *law* a thief from outside

a lord's jurisdiction but apprehended within his jurisdiction *la14-e18, la18-* historical. Compare INFANGTHIEF. [OE *ūtfangeneþēof*]

out-farm, ootferm /'ʌutfarm, 'utfɛrm/ *n* an outlying farm; a farm worked by a manager or subtenant *la18-*. [OOT-[1.3] + FERM[1.1]]

outfield[1.1]**, ootfield, †outfeild** /'ʌutfild, 'utfild/ *n* **1** the more outlying and less fertile parts of a farm *16-19, 20-* historical. **2** a poorer outlying patch of ground which was previously uncultivated *20- Sh*. [OOT-[1.3] + FIELD[1.1]]

outfield[1.2]**, ootfield, †outfeild** /'ʌutfild, 'utfild/ *adj* outlying, remote; out of doors *16-*. [see the noun]

outgae, ootgae /ʌut'ge, ut'ge/ *v presp* **outgaun, ootgaun, outgoing,** *ptp* **outgane, ootgane** to go out, to depart *19-*. **outgaun, ootgaun** *n* departure, leaving *19-*. **outgaun, ootgaun** *adj* **1** outgoing *19-*. **2** *of the tide* ebbing *20- Sh T SW*. Compare OUTGANG[1.2]. [OOT[1.4] + GAE]

outgane *see* OOTGAEN, OUTGAE

outgang[1.1]**, ootgang, ootgan** /'ʌutgaŋ, 'utgaŋ, 'utgan/ *n* **1** a way out, a means of getting out *16-*. **2** an open pasture for cattle *19-*. **3** a departure at the end of a season or year; removal from a tenancy *la19-*. **4** expense, outlay *la19-*. **5** the exportation of goods; export duty *15-16*. [OOT[1.4] + GANG[1.2]]

outgang[1.2]**, ootgang** /ʌut'gaŋ, 'utgaŋ/ *v* **1** to go out, to issue forth *15-*. **2** to surpass, to outstrip *la17-*. **outganging, ootgangin** exit, departure *15-*. [see the noun]

outgate, ootgaet, †outget /'ʌutget, 'utget/ *n* **1** a way out, an exit; an outlet *16-*. **2** a market, a sale; a means of disposal of merchandise *la19, 20- Sh*. **3** a solution to a problem *la15-19*. **4** an outcome of events *la16-17*. [OOT-[1.3] + GAIT[3]]

outgaun *see* OUTGAE

outget *see* OUTGATE

†outgie, utgie, outgif *v* **1** to issue, to pay out *la15-e19*. **2** to give out as judgement *la15-e17*. **outgiving 1** delivering, issuing *la16-*. **2** *pl* disbursements, payments *la17-*. [OOT[1.4] + GIE]

outgoing *see* OUTGAE

outgone *see* OOTGAEN

†outh[1.1]**, owth** *adv* above *la14-15*. **at outh** in authority *15*. [unknown]

†outh[1.2]**, owth** *prep* above, over *la14-e15*. [unknown]

†out-haiffin, owthawyng *n* taking out, exporting *la15-16*. [OOT-[1.1] + HAE[1.2]]

†outhald *v* **1** to withstand *la15-e17*. **2** to extend, to hold out *16*. **outhalding** holding back or keeping out *la15-e17*. [OOT-[1.2] + HAUD[1.2]]

out-hand /'ʌuthand, 'uthand/ *adv curling* with the stone directed outwards from the hand, so as to give it a bias from right to left *20-*. [OOT-[1.1] + HAN[1.1]]

out-heidie, ootheady /ʌut'hidi, ut'hidi/ *adj* headstrong, rash *la19- NE T*. [OOT-[1.1] + HEIDIE[1.3]]

outher *see* OWTHOR

†out-horn *n* a horn blown by officers of the crown to give an alarm *15-16*. [OOT-[1.1] + HORN]

†out-hound, outhund *v* **1** to incite or instigate violence or crime *la17-18*. **2** to set a dog to attack or chase; to steal cattle using a dog *18*. **outhounder** an instigator, an inciter *la16-18*. [OOT-[1.2] + HOOND[1.2]]

out ile *see* OOT ISLE

outing, ootin /'ʌutɪŋ, 'utɪn/ *n* **1** an expedition, a trip *la14-*. **2** expulsion, rejection; issuing or venting *la16-*. **†in outing** abroad or away from home *la16-e17*. [OOT[1.2], with noun-forming suffix *-ing*]

outintoun, †outtintoun /'ʌutəntun, 'utəntun/ *adj* coming from outside the boundaries of a town or from outside the sucken of a mill *la16-19, 20-* historical. **†outintounis** coming from outside the town or estate *la16-18*. **†outtintounisman** a man from outside the town *la16-17*. **†outtintounis multure** multure payable on corn brought in from outside the sucken of a mill *17*. [OE *ūtan* from outside + TOUN; compare OUT-TOUN[1.2]]

†outjet *n* a projection; a jutting-out part of a building *la17-e19*. **outjetting** jutting out *la17*. [OOT-[1.2] + AN, MFr *jetter* to throw]

outland[1.1]**, ootland, ootlin, outlan** /'ʌutlənd, 'utlənd, 'utlən, 'ʌutlən/ *n* **1** an outsider, a stranger, an outcast *la18-*. **2** rough ground on the edge of arable land; outlying or marginal land *la18- NE*; compare OUTFIELD[1.1]. **3** land held in addition to but lying outside the principal holding or estate *16-e17*. **outlander** an outsider, a stranger, an outcast *17-*. **†outlandis** coming from outside, not belonging to or residing in the burgh *15-e17*. **outlandish, †outlandisch 1** foreign, unfamiliar; peculiar, strange *la16-*. **2** from outside of the burgh *17*. [OE *ūtlenda*, ON *útlendingr*]

outland[1.2]**, ootland, ootlin, †outlan, †utland** /'ʌutlənd, 'utlənd, 'utlən/ *adj* **1** strange, foreign; remote, distant *15-19, 20-* literary. **2** from or living outside the bounds of a town or district; coming from a remote place *16-19, 20-* literary. [OE *ūtlende*, ON *útlendr*]

†outlandimer, outlandemer *n in Glasgow* a person appointed to perambulate and survey land boundaries *la16*. [OOT-[1.1] + LANIMER]

outlat, ootlat /'ʌutlat, 'utlat/ *n* an outlet *20-*. [OOT-[1.2] + LAT to allow]

outlatting, †oot-lattin /'ʌutlatɪŋ/ *n* **1** *knitting* the increase in the stitches in the heel of a stocking *la19- Sh NE Bor*. **2** letting out *la16-17*. [OOT-[1.2] + verbal noun from LAT to allow]

outlaw *see* OOTLAW[1.1], OOTLAW[1.2]

outlay[1.1]**, ootlay** /'ʌutle, 'utle/ *n* **1** expenditure, the laying out of money *la18-*. **2** a thing that lies outside or away from a place *la16*. [see the verb]

outlay[1.2]**, ootlay** /ʌut'le, ut'le/ *v* **1** to expend money *19-*. **2** *of a hen* to lay away from the regular nest *la19*. **outlaying** *n* **1** the laying out or expenditure of money or goods *17-*. **2** the eviction or ejection of a tenant *e16*. **outlaying** *adj* **1** *of a hen* laying away from the regular nest *la19*. **2** *of land* remote *20-*. [OOT-[1.2] + LAY[1.2]]

outleeve, ootlive, outlive, †outleve /ʌut'liv, ut'lɪv, ʌut'lɪv/ *v* to live longer than another person *la16-*. [OOT-[1.2] + LEEVE]

outler, ootler /'ʌutlər, 'utlər/ *n* a farm animal which remains outside during the winter *la18-19, 20- literary*. [probably altered form of OUTLIER]

outleve *see* OUTLEEVE

outlie, oot-lye /'ʌutlae, 'utlae/ *n* **1** money put out on loan or on mortgage *19-*. **2** an outlying piece of ground *20- NE*. [OOT-[1.2] + LIE[1.2]]

outlie *see* OUTLY

outlier, outlyer, ootlier /'ʌutlaeər, 'utlaeər/ *n* **1** a farm animal which remains outside during the winter *18-*. **2** a person from a different or remote district, or from outside the burgh *18-19, 20- Sh*. **3** a detached boulder, a free-standing stone; a rock in the sea *19, 20- Sh*. **4** *pl* stones found above ground rather than quarried *la18-19*. **5** an absentee from church *e17*. [OOT-[1.2] + LIE[1.2], with agent suffix]

outlive *see* OUTLEEVE

†outliveray *n pl* bounty given to servants *la16*. [OOT-[1.1] + LIVERY]

outlook *see* OOTLEUK

†outlordschip *n* patronage or support from a lord or magnate from outside the burgh *la15-16*. [OOT-[1.1] + LORDSHIP]

†outly, outlie *adv* fully, completely *17-19*. [OE *ūtlice*]

outlyer *see* OUTLIER

†outlying *n* absence from church services or the kirk-session *e17.* [OOT-^{1,2} + verbal noun from LIE^{1,2}]
outmag *see* OOTMAAG
†outman *n* a man who came from outside the community or burgh; an outsider *la15-16.* [OOT-^{1,1} + MAN]
†out-marchis *npl* the outer borders of a country *la15-e16.* [OOT-^{1,1} + pl of MARCH^{1,1}]
outmest, outmost *see* OOTMAIST
†outmyln, outmyll *n* a mill outside of a town; a mill other than those to which townspeople were astricted *16-17.* [OOT-^{1,1} + MILL^{1,1}]
out on *see* OUTEN
out-our *see* OOT OWER^{1,1}, OOT OWER^{1,2}
outouth *see* OUTWITH^{1,3}
out-over *see* OOT OWER^{1,1}, OOT OWER^{1,2}
outow *see* OUTWITH^{1,2}, OUTWITH^{1,3}
outowthe *see* OUTWITH^{1,1}
†out-parochine, outparish *n* a part of a burgh parish lying outside the burgh itself; the rural part of a burgh parish *la16-e17.* [OOT-^{1,1} + PAROCHIN]
†outpassage *n* a means of exit or escape; the act of going out *15-16.* [OOT-^{1,1} + PASSAGE^{1}]
†outpassing *n* **1** going out, departure *la15-e17.* **2** expiry *la15-e17.* **3** the exportation of goods *la15-16.* **4** retirement from office *16.* [OOT-^{1,2} + PASSING^{1}]
outpatt *see* OUTPUT
†outpay *v* to pay in full, to settle a debt *e16.* [OOT-^{1,2} + PEY^{1,2}]
†outpenny *n* a penny paid to the bailie by an outgoing property owner in token of resignation of the property *la15-e16.* [OOT-^{1,1} + PENNY]
outpour, ootpoor /'ʌutpor, 'utpur/ *n* a heavy fall of rain, a downpour *la19- Ork NE.* [OOT-^{1,2} + POUR^{1,2}]
output, ootpit /ʌut'put, ut'pɪt/ *v pt* also **†outpatt 1** to put or send out; to supply *la15-.* **2** to evict or eject; to discharge or dismiss *16-.* **3** to issue false coinage *la16-e18.* **†outputtar, outputter 1** a person who conveyed stolen goods away from a district *15-e17.* **2** a person who issued or circulated coinage unlawfully *la16-e17.* **3** a person who was responsible for finding and equipping men for military service *17.* **outputting 1** expulsion, ejection; banishment *la15-.* **2** the finding and equipping of men for military service *17-e18.* **3** the issuing of false coin *la16-e18.* **4** the conveying of stolen goods out of the district *la15-e17.* **ootpittins** excretions *20-.* [OOT-^{1,2} + PIT^{2}]
outquat, outqueit *see* OUTQUIT
†outquent, owt quent *adj* extinguished *e16.* [OOT-^{1,2} + ptp of Eng *quench*]
†outquit, outquite *v ptp* also **outqueit, outquat** law to free land or property from encumbrance by payment of a debt *15-17.* **outquiting** redemption from attachment or pawn of property *la15-e18.* [OOT-^{1,2} + QUIT^{1,1}]
outrad *see* OUTRED^{1,1}, OUTRED^{1,2}
outrage, outraige *see* OOTRAGE
outraik, ootraik /'ʌutrek, 'utrek/ *n* **1** an extensive grazing area *19- Bor.* **2** scope, opportunity; conduct, behaviour *19 Bor.* [OOT-^{1,1} + RAIK^{1,1}]
outral, ootral /'ʌutrəl, 'utrəl/ *n* a person from a different country, district or family; a stranger or incomer *la19-.* [OOT-^{1,1}, with diminutive suffix *-rel*]
outreche *see* OUTREIK^{1,1}, OUTREIK^{1,2}
Outrecht *see* UTTRECHT
outred^{1,1}, **†outrad, †outterd** /'ʌutrəd/ *n* **1** profit; return on an investment *20- Sh.* **2** the settlement of a debt; the conclusion of business *la15-18.* **3** the equipping or outfitting of a ship *la15-e17.* **4** the completion of a piece of work *la16-e17.* [see the verb]

†outred^{1,2}, **outrad, outreid** *v pt* **outred 1** to settle by payment; to discharge a debt *la15-e18.* **2** to redeem lands or property from a pledge by due payment *la15-e18.* **3** to equip or fit out a ship; to equip or provision troops *la16-e18.* **4** to complete a piece of work *16-17.* **† outredder, outreddar** a person who equipped a ship for a voyage *la16-e17.* [OOT-^{1,2} + REDD^{1,2}]
outreek *see* OUTREIK^{1,2}
outreid *see* OUTRED^{1,2}
†outreik^{1,1}, **outrick, outreche** *n* **1** the equipping of a person for an expedition or a special occasion *17-19.* **2** the finding and equipping of troops or their horses; a tax raised for the finding or equipping of troops *17-e18.* **3** the equipping or outfitting of a ship *la16-e18.* [see the verb]
†outreik^{1,2}, **outreek, outreche** *v* **1** to equip or supply a ship *la16-e18.* **2** to provide and equip men for military or naval service *la16-17.* **outreiker** a person who found and equipped a man for military service *17.* [OOT-^{1,2} + REIK]
outricht *see* OOTRICHT
outrick *see* OUTREIK^{1,1}
outrig *see* OOTRIG^{1,1}, OOTRIG^{1,2}
outring /'ʌutrɪŋ/ *n* **1** a method of striking one curling stone with another on its outer edge so as to drive it towards the tee *19-.* **2** the side of the curling stone away from the tee *20-.* Compare INRING. [OOT-^{1,1} + RING^{1,1}]
†outriving *n* unauthorized cultivating of another person's land *la15-17.* [OOT-^{1,2} + verbal noun from RIVE^{1,2}]
outroom, oot-room /'ʌutrum, 'utrum/ *n* **1** an outer room attached to a house, but entered from the outside by a separate door *la17-19, 20- NE T C.* **2** a piece of land rented collectively by sub-tenants or employees *la18-19.* [OOT-^{1,1} + ROOM^{1,1}]
outrun^{1,1}, **ootrun, oot-rin** /'ʌutrʌn, 'utrʌn, 'utrɪn/ *n* **1** an area of outlying grazing land on an arable farm *la19-.* **2** the outward run of a dog to gather sheep *20- Ork SW Bor.* [OOT-^{1,1} + RIN^{1,1}]
outrun^{1,2}, **ootrun, oot-rin** /ʌut'rʌn, ut'rʌn, ut'rɪn/ *v* **1** to outpace at running, to leave behind *la20-.* **2** to run out, to flow out *16-e19.* **3** *of time* to run out; *of a contract or lease* to expire *la15-17.* **outrunning 1** *pl* digressions in storytelling *20- Sh.* **2** the running out of an hourglass *la16-e19.* **3** the expiry of a contract or lease, or of a set period of time *la15-17.* [see the noun]
†outschot *adj of goods* of inferior quality, rejected *la16-e17.* [perhaps MDu *uteschot* cullings, refuse]
outschot *see* OUTSHOOT, OUTSHOT^{1,1}
outschute *see* OUTSHOOT
outseam, ootseam /'ʌutsim, 'utsim/ *n* an outside seam *la17-.* **†outseamed** *of gloves* sewn on the outside *la17.* **ootseam awl** an awl for sewing shoes from the outside *la19- Sh NE T.* [OOT-^{1,1} + SEAM^{1,1}]
outset^{1,1}, **ootset** /'ʌutsɛt, 'utsɛt/ *n* **1** ornament, embellishment; an advantageous display or arrangement *la16-19, 20- Uls.* **2** the issue of a book *17-e19.* **3** a start in life; the provision made for a child leaving home *e19.* **4** the payment of a promised sum *la15.* [OOT-^{1,1} + SET^{1,1}]
†outset^{1,2} *v* to set forth or display advantageously *16.* [see the noun]
outset^{2}, **ootset, †owtseit** /'ʌutsɛt, 'utsɛt/ *n* **1** a patch of reclaimed and newly-cultivated or newly-inhabited land, frequently taken in from moorland *16-18, 19- Sh.* **2** a piece of land detached from the main estate or holding to which it belongs *16-17.* **3** a steading with a dwelling-house and outhouses built on it *16-e17.* [OOT-^{1,1} + OE *set* or ON *setr* a habitation, a dwelling]
outsetting /'ʌutsɛtɪŋ, 'utsɛtɪŋ/ *n* **1** setting out, departure *la17-19, 20- Sh NE.* **2** making publicly known by publication

or proclamation *la16-e17*. **3** the letting out of land on lease or feu *17*. **4** the performing of a show *la16*. **5** support or maintenance; equipping or provisioning *la16*. [OUTSET¹·¹, OUTSET², with *-ing* suffix]

outshoot, †**outschute** /ʌutˈʃut/ *v pt* †**outschot 1** to outdo, to get the better of *la16-*. **2** to shoot outwards or forwards *la15-e17*. **3** to overreach, to go too far *la16-17*. [OOT-¹·² + SHUIT]

outshot¹·¹, †**outschot** /ˈʌutʃɔt/ *n* a projecting part of a wall or building; an extension built onto the side of a building *la16-*. [OOT-¹·¹ + OE *scot*]

outshot¹·², **ootshot** /ʌutˈʃɔt, utˈʃɔt/ *adj* projecting, protruding, bulging *19, 20- EC Bor.* [see the noun]

outsicht *see* OUTSIGHT

outsider *see* OOTSIDER

†**outsight**, **outsicht** *n* livestock or equipment kept out of doors *la15-e19*. Compare INSICHT¹. [by analogy with and coupled with INSICHT¹]

out-stair /ˈʌutster, ˈutster/ *n* an exterior stair on a house, giving separate access to an upper flat *la18-*. [OOT-¹·¹ + STAIR¹]

outstanding, **ootstandin** /ˈʌutstandɪŋ, ˈutstandɪn/ *adj* **1** of a debt unpaid, unsettled *17-*. **2** noteworthy, remarkable *19-*. **3** *Presbyterian Church* resisting the National Covenant *17*. [OOT-¹·² + participial adj from STAND¹·²]

†**outstead**, **outsted**, **outsteid** *n* a settlement or farm at or near the edge of an estate; a secondary house on a farm property *la16-19*. [OOT-¹·¹ + STEID¹·¹]

outsteading /ˈʌutstedɪŋ/ *n* an outbuilding on farm land (used to house workers); a secondary house on a farm property *19, 20- N NE T C.* []

outsted, **outsteid** *see* OUTSTEAD

outsteiks /ˈʌutstiks, ˈutstiks/ *npl* shoes with the soles stitched from the outside *18- Bor.* [OOT-¹·¹ + STEEK²·¹]

outstreekit, **ootstreekit** /ʌutˈstrikət, utˈstrikət/ *adj* outstretched *19- Sh NE T SW.* [OOT-¹·² + ptp of STREEK¹·²]

†**outstrikeing** *n* the creation of an opening for a door or window *la16-e18*. [OOT-¹·² + verbal noun from STRIK¹·²]

outstriking, **oot-strikkin**, †**outstricking** /ˈʌutstrɪkɪŋ, ˈutstrɪkɪn/ *n* an eruption of the skin; a rash *la17-19, 20- T.* [OOT-¹·² + verbal noun from STRIK¹·²]

outsucken, †**outsuckin** /ˈʌutsʌkən, ˈutsʌkən/ *n law* multure payable on corn brought in from outside the sucken of a mill *la16-19, 20- historical.* **outsuckner**, **outsuckiner** a person from outside a sucken *la17-18.* **outsucken multure** = OUTSUCKEN. [OOT-¹·¹ + SUCKEN¹·¹]

out-tak¹, **oot-tak** /ˈʌuttak, ˈuttak/ *n* **1** lasting quality, durability *la19- Sh Ork.* **2** yield, profit *la19- Sh Ork.* **3** expenses, outlay *la19- Sh.* [OOT-¹·¹ + TACK²]

†**out-tak**²·¹ *v* **1** to extract or remove *15-16*. **2** to exclude or except *15-16*. **out-takand** excepting, not counting *la14-15*. [OOT-¹·² + TAK¹·²]

†**out-tak**²·² *prep* except, leaving aside *la14-e16*. [see the verb]

out-takin¹·¹, **out-taking**, **oot-takin** /ˈʌuttakɪn, ˈʌuttakɪŋ, ˈuttakɪn/ *n* the action of taking or lifting out; a removal *15-19, 20- Ork.* [verbal noun from OUT-TAK²·¹]

†**out-takin**¹·² *prep* excepted, besides *la14-e19*. [pres ppl of OUT-TAK²·¹]

†**out-tane**¹·¹, **owtane** *adj* excluded, excepted *la14-e16*. [ptp of OUT-TAK²·¹]

†**out-tane**¹·², **owtane** *prep* except for, with the exception of *la14-e16*. [see the adj]

†**out-tane**¹·³, **owtane** *conj* except that *la14-15*. [see the adj]

outterd *see* OUTRED¹·¹

†**out-thraw** *v pt* **out-threw** to thrust outwards; to billow forth *la15-e16*. [OOT-¹·² + THRAW¹·²]

out-through¹·¹, †**out-throw**, †**out-throuch** /ʌutˈθru/ *adv* right through, throughout *la14-*. [OOT-¹·² + THROU¹·²]

out-through¹·², **out-throw**, †**out-throuch** /ʌutˈθru, ʌutˈθro/ *prep* **1** throughout, right across: ◊*the news spread out-through the toun la14-*. **2** from one side to another of: ◊*they ran out-through the field 16*. **3** right through: ◊*the arrow pierced him out-throw the heart la15-17*. [see the adv]

outtintoun *see* OUTINTOUN

out-toll /ˈʌuttol/ *n* a penny paid to the bailie by an outgoing property owner in token of resignation of the property *la13-e18, la19- historical.* [OOT-¹·¹ + TOLL]

†**out-toun**¹·¹ *n* **1** an outlying field on a farm *17-e19*. **2** an outlying estate detached from the main property *la17*. [OOT-¹·¹ + TOUN]

†**out-toun**¹·² *adj* coming from outside the boundaries of a town or from outside the sucken of a mill *la16-e19.* **out-tounis**, **uttounes** coming from outside the town or estate *la15-e17.* **out-tounisman** a man from outside the town *16.* **out-toun multure** multure payable on corn brought in from outside the sucken of a mill *18-e19.* [see the noun]

out-turn, **oot-turn** /ˈʌuttʌrn, ˈuttʌrn/ *n curling* the playing of the stone with the handle outwards so that it travels in an inward arc *la19-.* [OOT-¹·¹ + TURN¹·¹]

oututh *see* OUTWITH¹·²

†**out-wach**, **outwatch** *n* an outlying watch or watchmen; guards placed outside the body of an army or town *la15-e17*. [OOT-¹·¹ + WATCH¹·¹]

outwale¹·¹, **outwail**, **outwyle**, *Ork* **ootwaal** /ˈʌutwel, ˈutwel, ˈʌutwʌɪl; *Ork* ˈutwɑl/ *n* **1** the remainder, the surplus; *pl* rejects, refuse *la16-*. **2** an outcast, an excluded or rejected person *la15-e17*. [OOT-¹·¹ + WALE¹·¹]

outwale¹·², **outwyle** /ˈʌutwel, ˈutwel, ˈutwʌɪl/ *v* **1** to reject, to pick out for rejection *la16-19, 20- Sh NE.* **2** to choose, to handpick *la16.* **outwalins**, **ootwilins** the leavings; the refuse *la19, 20- Sh N NE.* [see the noun]

outwan, **ootwin** /ˈʌutwən, ˈutwɪn/ *adv* outwards *la19, 20- NE EC.* [OOT-¹·⁴ + -WAN]

outward, **outwart** *see* OOTWARD¹·¹, OOTWARD¹·²

outwatch *see* OUT-WACH

outwert *see* OOTWARD¹·¹

outwick¹·¹, **ootwick** /ˈʌutwɪk, ˈutwɪk/ *n in curling* a shot which strikes an already-played stone on the outside at such an angle as to drive it towards the tee *19-*. [see the verb]

outwick¹·², **ootwick** /ˈʌutwɪk, ˈutwɪk/ *v in curling and bowls* to play a shot which strikes an already-played stone or bowl on the outside at such an angle as to drive it towards the tee or jack *19-*. [OOT-¹·² + WICK⁴·²]

outwinter, **ootwinter** /ʌutˈwɪntər, utˈwɪntər/ *v* to keep livestock out of doors throughout the winter *la18-*. [OOT-¹·² + WINTER¹·²]

outwith¹·¹, **ootwith**, †**outowthe** /ʌutˈwɪθ, utˈwɪθ/ *adj* outer; outermost, outlying *la16-19, 20- NE.* [see the adv]

outwith¹·², **ootwith**, †**oututh**, †**vtouth**, †**outow** /ʌutˈwɪθ, utˈwɪθ/ *adv* outside; out of doors; outwards *la14-19, 20- NE.* [OOT-¹·⁴ + WI]

outwith¹·³, **ootwith**, †**outouth**, †**outow**, †**utouth** /ʌutˈwɪθ, utˈwɪθ/ *prep* **1** outside of, beyond *la14-*. **2** out of the control of; away from *la14-*. [see the adv]

†**outwitten** *adv* unknown, unaware *la18-e19.* **outwitten o**, **outwittens o** unknown to, without the knowledge of *la18-e19.* [perhaps OOT-¹·¹ + WITTIN]

outwyle *see* OUTWALE¹·¹, OUTWALE¹·²

out-yoke, **ootyoke**, †**outʒok** /ˈʌutjok, ˈutjok/ *n in Shetland* the yoke carried by the outer two oxen in a ploughing team consisting of four animals *17-20, 21- historical.* [OOT-¹·¹ + YOKE¹·¹]

ouverture see OVERTURE¹·¹
oven see OAVEN
over, hovery /'ovər, 'hovəri/ *numeral in children's rhymes* a nonsense word originally representing a number *la19-20, 21- historical*. [nonsense word derived from a system of counting sheep]
over see OWER¹·¹, OWER¹·², OWER¹·³, OWER¹·⁴
over-allquhair see OUR-ALQUHARE
overance see OWRANCE
overblaw see OWERBLAW
overboard, over-burde see OWERBOARD
overby see OWERBY
overcast see OWERCAST¹·²
overcled see OWERCLAD
overcome see OWERCOME¹·²
overcum see OWERCOME¹·¹, OWERCOME¹·²
overdrive, †ourdrive /ovər'draev/ *v pt also* **-drafe**, *ptp* **-drevin 1** to work a person or animal too hard; to drive an animal too far *la18-*. **2** to come through difficulties; to survive or endure *la14-17*. **3** to spend or occupy time *la14-e17*. **4** to allow time to pass or elapse; to be inactive *la14-16*. **5** to be brought to an end; to have passed away *la14-e16*. **6** to cover, to overspread *la15-16*. [OWER¹·³ + DRIVE¹·²]
overeengie see AIPPLERINGIE
over-end see OWEREND¹·¹
overflete see OWERFLEETE
overga see OWERGAE
overgang see OWERGANG¹·²
overget see OWERGET
overgilt see OURGILT
overgive see OWERGIE
overgo see OWERGAE
overhale see OWERHAIL
overhand see OWERHAN
overharle see OWERHARL
overhede, overheid see OWERHEID¹·²
overhing see OWERHING
overhip see OURHIP
overhye see OWERHIE
overins see OWRINS
overlay see OWERLAY¹·¹, OWERLAY¹·²
†overledder *n* the upper of a shoe *16-e17*. [ME *overlether*; compare MDu *overleder*]
overlepe see OWERLEAP
†overleve, ourleve, ourleff *v* to outlive, to survive *15-e17*. [OWER¹·³ + LEEVE]
overloft see OURLOFT
overlope see OURLOP
overlord, †ourlord, †ourlard /'ovərlərd/ *n* a feudal superior *la14-19, 20- historical*. [OWER¹·² + LORD]
overloup see OWERLOUP
overluke see OWERLEUK
overly¹·¹, ouerly /'ovərli, 'ʌuərli/ *adj* **1** superficial, casual, careless *la17-19, 20- N NE Bor*. **2** excessive, exaggerated; unconventional, unusual *19, 20- Sh*. **†overliness** superficiality *17*. [OWER¹·³, with adj-forming suffix *-ly*]
overly¹·², ouerly /'ovərli, 'ʌuərli/ *adv* **1** excessively, too much, in the extreme *19-*. **2** superficially, in a casual manner, by chance *17-19, 20- NE Bor*. [OE *oferlīce*]
overman see OURMAN
†overmare, ourmare *adv* farther over, farther away *la14-e15*. [OWER¹·³ + MAIR¹·²]
†overpas, ourpas, ouirpas *v* **1** to travel throughout, to go across *la14-16*. **2** to exceed, to go beyond *15-17*. **3** to neglect to dwell on, to omit to mention *15-17*. **4** *of time* to elapse *16*. **5** to pass away, to depart; to come to an end *la14-e17*. **6** *of an emotion* to affect a person temporarily *16*. [OWER¹·³ + PASS¹·²]
overplus see OWERPLUS
overquhelme see OWERWHELM
overrin see OWERRIN
†oversailyie¹·¹ *n* the bridging of a close by an overhead passage joining the two sides, the structure itself *la17*. [see the verb]
†oversailyie¹·² *v* to bridge over a close or alley; to overhang or project *la17*. [OWER¹·³ + MFr *saillir*]
over-se see OWERSEA¹·²
oversee see OVERSEE
overset see OWERSET¹·²
overshyne see OURSCHINE
oversicht see OWERSICHT
†oversile, oursile, oursyll *v* **1** to cover; to obscure or conceal *la15-16*. **2** to impair the sight of *16-e17*. **3** to deceive or delude a person *16-e17*. [OWER¹·³ + SILE¹]
†overslide, ourslide *v* **1** *of an event or action* to pass unnoticed *la15-e17*. **2** *of time* to pass or elapse *16*. **3** to glide over; to slide across *16*. [OWER¹·³ + SLIDE¹·²]
oversman see OWERSMAN
oversoum see OWERSOUM
overstap see OWERSTAP
overstentit see OWERSTENT
overta, overtak, overtane see OWERTAK
†overthort¹·¹, ourthwort *adv* from one side to the other, across *la14-17*. [see the prep]
†overthort¹·², ourthwort, overwhart *prep* **1** from side to side of, across *15-17*. **2** all over, throughout *15-e16*. [ME *ouerthwart*]
overthraw see OWERTHRAW¹·¹, OWERTHRAW¹·²
overtour see OVERTURE¹·²
overtree see OWERTREE
overtumble see OURTUMMYLL
overture¹·¹, †ouverture /'ovərtjur/ *n* **1** a suggestion, a recommendation *la16-*. **2** a proposal drawn up for the consideration of a legislative body; a bill placed before the Scottish parliament or Convention of the Estates for enactment *la16-*. **3** *Presbyterian Church* a call for legislation brought before a higher church court by a lower body, usually made by a presbytery to the General Assembly *la16-*. [ME *overtur*, EModE *overture*]
overture¹·², †overtour /'ovərtjur/ *v* to submit as a proposal to a legislative or deliberative assembly; to propose a motion formally *la17-*. [see the noun]
overturn see OWERTURN¹·²
overtyrve see OURTIRVE
overwelt see OURWELT
overwelter see OURWELTER
overwent see OWERGAE
overwhart see OVERTHORT¹·²
overwhelm see OWERWHELM
overyear see OWERYEAR
ovey, ovie /'ovi/ *n* a piece or pieces of old wood laid across the purlins in a roof under the thatch *19- Sh*. **ovy daek** a dam in a stream made by placing a piece of wood across it *20- Sh*. [Norw dial *åved*]
ovin see OAVEN
ovirgilt see OURGILT
ovirmast see OWERMAIST
ovy daek see OVEY
ow see AWE, OO², OU
owder see OWTHER¹·², OWTHER¹·⁴
owdience see AUDIENCE

owdny /'ʌudni/ *n* something larger than normal; a large object *20- Ork.* [unknown]
owdyr *see* OWTHER¹·³
owe *see* AWE²
owen *see* AWN²
ower¹·¹, †**owre**, †**our**, †**over** /ʌur, 'ʌuər/ *v* to overpower, to take control; to regulate or manage oneself *la15-.* [see the adv]
ower¹·², **owre**, **over**, **iver**, †**uver**, †**our**, †**ever** /ʌur, 'ʌuər, 'ovər, 'ɪvər/ *adj* **1** upper, higher; *in place-names* the upper or higher of two places of the same name *la14-.* **2** *of ropes* going across or over *la20-.* **3** *in a building* on a higher floor; upstairs *la15-17.* [OE *uferra*]
ower¹·³, **owre**, **over**, †**our**, †**o'er** /ʌur, 'ʌuər, 'ovər/ *adv* **1** above, covering; downward (over) *la14-.* **2** across, sideways *la14-.* **3** overmuch, excessively *la14-.* **4** from beginning to end, throughout *14-.* **5** off to sleep *la18-.* **6** *of time* well on, late, far advanced *la18- Sh NE.* **7** quite, rather *19- Sh Ork.* **ower and abune** over and above, as well *la17-.* **ower weel** in very good health *la19- Sh Ork N Uls.* [OE *ofer*]
ower¹·⁴, **owre**, **over**, †**our**, †**o'er** /ʌur, 'ʌuər, 'ovər/ *prep* **1** above, across *la14-.* **2** down from, out of, out at *la16-.* **3** beyond the control or capabilities of; too much for *la19- Sh NE T.* **ower all 1** all over, everywhere *la14-.* **2** above all else, most of all *la15-.* **ower the door** outside, out of the house *18-.* **ower the heid o**, **ower yer heid 1** at the expense of, in spite of *la15-.* **2** without a person's knowledge or permission *la15-.* **tak over his heid** to dispossess or undercut a person *la15-e17.* [see the adv]
owerance *see* OWRANCE
†**owerblaw**, **overblaw**, **ourblaw** *v* to cover (with snow or sand); to blow over *16-e19.* [OWER¹·³ + BLAW¹·²]
owerboard, **overboard**, †**owerbuird**, †**over-burde**, †**our-burd** /'ʌurbord, 'ovərbord/ *adv* over the side of a boat; away from or beyond a boat *15-.* [OE *ofer bord*]
owerby, **overby** /ʌur'bae, ovər'bae/ *adv* over, across; at a short distance away *la17-.* [OWER¹·³ + BY¹·¹]
owercap /ʌur'kap/ *v* **1** to be superior to; to beat or surpass *la19, 20- Sh.* **2** to overlap *e19.* [OWER¹·³ + Eng *cap*]
owercassin *see* OWERCAST¹·²
owercast¹·¹, †**ourcast** /'ʌurkast/ *n* **1** a layer of cloud covering the sky *18-.* **2** an outcast, an orphan *la19.* **3** the action of casting something over or down *la15.* [OWER¹·³ + CAST¹·²]
owercast¹·², **overcast**, †**ourcast** /ʌur'kast, ovər'kast/ *v ptp* also **owercassin 1** to spread, to cover over; *of the sky* to cloud over, to darken *la15-.* **2** to recover from or to throw off an illness *la18-.* **3** *of the stomach* to be upset *16.* **4** to look over, to inspect; to read through *la16.* [see the noun]
owerclad, **overcled**, †**ourcled** /ʌur'klad, ovər'klɛd/ *adj* clothed or clovered over *la15-19, 20- Sh.* [OWER¹·³ + ptp of CLEED]
owercome¹·¹, **o'ercome**, †**overcum**, †**ourcum** /'ʌurkʌm/ *n* **1** a sudden attack of illness *19-.* **2** a refrain or a chorus; a repeated phrase *19-;* compare OWERWORD. **3** a surplus or excess *15-19.* [see the verb]
owercome¹·², **overcome**, †**overcum**, †**ourcum** /ʌur'kʌm, ovər'kʌm/ *v* **1** to overpower; to prevail over *la14-.* **2** to revive or recover *la14-.* †**overcoming** a crossing; a journey *la15-19.* [OWER¹·³ + COME¹·²]
owercoup /ʌur'kʌup/ *v* to overturn, to upset *18-.* [OWER¹·³ + COUP¹·²]
owercroon, **owrecrown** /'ʌurkrun, 'ʌurkrʌun/ *n* a peaked mutch worn by married women *19, 20- historical.* **owercroun mutch** = OWERCROUN. [OWER¹·⁴ + CROON¹·¹]

owerday /'ʌurde/ *n* the previous day *la18-19, 20- Sh NE EC Bor.* **owerday's breid** bread which has been kept for more than one day *20- Sh NE EC Bor.* [OWER¹·² + DAY]
owerend¹·¹, †**over-end** /ʌur'ɛnd/ *v* to turn or set on end, to tip up or flip over *17-.* [see the adj]
owerend¹·² /ʌur'ɛnd/ *adj* standing up *20- Sh.* [OWER¹·² + EN¹·¹]
owerfa /ʌur'fa/ *v* to fall over *20- NE T.* **at the owerfa'in** on the point of collapsing or disintegrating *20- NE T.* [OWER¹·³ + FA¹·²]
owerfammer /ʌur'famər/ *v* to knock over; to render helpless *20- Ork.* [unknown]
†**owerfleete**, **overflete**, **ourflete** *v pt* **owerflet** to overflow; to flood or flow over *15-19.* [OWER¹·³ + FLEET¹·²]
†**ower-fret**, **ourfret**, **ouirfret** *v ptp* **ourfret** to decorate or adorn all over *la15-e19.* [OWER¹·³ + Eng *fret* to adorn richly]
owergae, †**overga**, †**ourga**, †**ourgo** /ʌur'ge/ *v pt* also †**ourʒeid** †**oure-yhude**, †**overwent** *ptp* **owergane**, **owergaun**, *Sh N* **owergeen 1** *of time* to pass, to elapse *la14-.* **2** to overflow or cover over; to overrun or infest *15-.* **3** to overpower or overwhelm; to oppress; to surpass *la14-19, 20- Sh.* **4** to overstep or transgress, to become unruly *20- Sh Ork.* **5** to go over; to pass through, to cross *la14-19.* **owergaeing**, **owre-gaun**, **ourgaan 1** a crossing; a way across *la16-.* **2** the act completing a task *la19-.* **3** a severe reproof *20- Sh NE T.* †**owregauns** transgressions *19.* **owrgaun rapes** ropes which go vertically over the thatch on a corn-stack *19, 20- C SW.* **in the owergaun** in crossing, on the way across *la19, 20- NE.* †**lat overgo**, **lat ourgo** to let pass; to omit *la15-17.* [OWER¹·³ + GAE]
owergaff /ʌur'gaf/ *v of the sky* to become overcast after a clear morning *19- Bor.* [unknown]
owergane *see* OWERGAE
owergang¹·¹, †**ourgang** /'ʌurgaŋ/ *n* **1** a going over, an application of something to a surface *20- Sh NE SW.* **2** a severe scolding *20- Sh NE SW.* **3** the right of going across a body of water to fish *la16.* **4** the extent of a town *16.* [see the verb]
owergang¹·², †**overgang**, †**ourgang** /ʌur'gaŋ/ *v* **1** to exceed, to surpass *18-.* **2** to overcome, to oppress, to dominate *la15-19, 20- Sh.* **3** to spread across; to overrun or infest *la16-e19.* **4** to oversee, to superintend *la19.* [OWER¹·³ + GANG¹·²]
owergaun, **owergeen** *see* OWERGAE
†**owerget**, **overget**, **ourget** *v* to overtake, to catch up with *15-19.* [OWER¹·³ + GET¹·²]
owergie, †**overgive**, †**ourgive** /ʌur'gi/ *v* to give up or renounce; to resign, to surrender property *15-19, 20- literary.* [OWER¹·³ + GIE]
owergilt *see* OURGILT
owergrip¹·¹ /'ʌurgrɪp/ *n* a sprain *20- Sh Ork.* [see the verb]
owergrip¹·² /ʌur'grɪp/ *v* to sprain *20- Sh Ork.* [OWER¹·³ + GRIP¹·²]
†**owerhail**, **overhale**, **ourhale** *v* **1** to overtake *16-e18.* **2** to oppress, to overthrow *la15-e17.* **3** to disregard, to overlook *la16.* **4** to consider, to survey *e15.* [OWER¹·³ + HALE¹·²]
owerhan, †**overhand**, †**ourhand** /ʌur'han/ *n* the upper hand; mastery, victory *la14-19, 20- Sh NE T SW.* [OWER¹·² + HAN¹·¹]
†**owerharl**, **overharle**, **ourharl** *v* **1** to oppress or overwhelm; to overpower, to handle roughly *la15-19.* **2** to consider, to relate *la15.* [OWER¹·³ + HARL¹·²]
owerhaul /ʌur'hɔl/ *v* to drive a screw or bolt too tightly, so that the thread is damaged *19, 20- N NE T.* [OWER¹·³ + HAUL¹·²]
owerheid¹·¹ /ʌur'hid/ *adj* untidy, slovenly; sloppy, careless *la19- Sh Ork NE.* [see the adv]
owerheid¹·², †**overhede**, †**ourheid** /ʌur'hid/ *adv* **1** at an average rate per item *la15-.* **2** in gross, overall *16-.* **3** above the head; in the air *19-.* **4** in a commotion or

confusion; in an untidy manner *16-19, 20- Sh Ork NE*. [OE *oferhēafod*]

†owerhie, overhye, ourhye *v* to overtake, to catch *la14-19*. [OWER¹·³ + HEY⁴]

owerhing, †overhing /ʌurˈhɪŋ/ *v* to overhang *17-*. [OWER¹·³ + HING¹·²]

†owerhip *adv of hammering* with great force; done overhand with a swing starting at the hip *la18-19*. [OWER¹·⁴ + HIP¹]

owerlair *see* OWERLAY¹·²

owerlay¹·¹, overlay, †ourlay /ˈʌurle, ˈovərle/ *n* 1 a hem in which one part of the cloth is folded or laid over the other *19-*. 2 a necktie, a cravat, a scarf *18-19, 20- C Bor*. 3 a collar, a neckband *la16-17*. [see the verb]

owerlay¹·², †ourlay, †overlay /ʌurˈle/ *v* 1 to sew a hem in which one part of the cloth is folded or laid over the other *19, 20- Sh Ork T*. 2 to cover over; to paint *la16-19*. 3 to oppress *la16-e17*. **†overlayer, owerlair** a neckband, a cravat *la16-18*. [OWER¹·³ + LAY¹·²]

†owerleap, overlepe, ourlepe *v pt* also **ourlap**, *ptp* **orloppin** to jump over; to traverse *la15-19*. [OWER¹·³ + LEAP]

owerleuk, owerlook, †overluke, †ourluke /ʌurˈluk/ *v* 1 to fail to observe; to disregard or fail to act upon *16-*. 2 to survey, to view from above; to afford a view *la16-*. [OWER¹·³ + LEUK¹·²]

†owerloup, overloup, ourloupe *n* 1 an encroachment by farm animals onto neighbouring land *18-e19*. 2 the right of occasional grazing on a neighbour's land *la17-18*. 3 the spring tide at the change of the moon *18*. [OWER¹·³ + LOWP¹·²]

owermaist, †ovirmast, †uvirmest /ˈʌurmest/ *adj* 1 uppermost *16-*. 2 farthest off or over *19- Sh NE*. [ME *overmost*]

owermaister /ʌurˈmestər/ *v* to conquer, overpower *17-19, 20- NE*. [OWER¹·³ + MAISTER¹·²]

†owerpit, ouirput, o'erpit *v* to survive a hardship or difficulty; to recover; to triumph *la16-e19*. [OWER¹·³ + PIT²]

owerplus, owerplush, †overplus /ˈʌurplʌs, ˈʌurplʌʃ/ *n* a surplus, an excess; what is left over *la17-*. [ME *overplus*]

owerpooer /ʌurˈpuər/ *v* to subdue by force, to dominate *la19-*. [OWER¹·³ + POOER¹·¹]

ower-rax, owerrack /ʌurˈraks, ʌurˈrak/ *v* 1 to stretch or reach over, to overreach *la19-*. 2 to sprain, to overstrain *la19- Sh Ork*. [OWER¹·³ + RAX¹·²]

†owerreach, oureche, ourreke *v* 1 to overtake, to catch up with *la15-19*. 2 to outmanoeuvre; to overpower or vanquish *la15-16*. [ME *overrechen*]

owerrin, †overrin, †ourrin /ʌurˈrɪn/ *v* 1 to invade, to ravage; to overwhelm *la15-*. 2 *of liquid* to flow over, to engulf *la15-*. 3 to overtake, to outstrip *la16-*. 4 to exceed a boundary or limit *la16-*. 5 to knock down, to run over a person *la16-19, 20- Ork*. 6 *of time* to run out *la14-e15*. [ME *overrennan*]

owersea¹·¹, †owersie, †oursey /ʌurˈsi/ *adj* 1 foreign, from over the sea *la16-*. 2 far-fetched *17*. [see the adv]

†owersea¹·², over-se, oure-sey *adv* on or across the sea *la14-17*. [OE *ofer sǣ*]

owersee, oversee, †our-se, †oursie /ʌurˈsi, ovərˈsi/ *v* 1 to survey, to inspect *16-*. 2 to tend to animals; to superintend or manage *la15-19, 20- Sh Ork NE*. 3 to permit, to condone; to ignore or disregard *16-17*. 4 to misjudge, to act in error *la16-e17*. [OE *ofersēon*]

owerset¹·¹, †ourset /ˈʌursɛt/ *n* 1 a translation *la20-*. 2 a disorder of the stomach *la17*. 3 defeat; subjugation *la15-e16*. [see the verb]

owerset¹·², †overset, †ourset /ʌurˈsɛt/ *v pt* **owerset** 1 to overpower, to defeat, to oppress *la14-*. 2 to upset, to overturn; to knock over *16-*. 3 to translate *la20-*. 3 to recover, to prevail *la15-16*. 4 *of a storm* to overwhelm *la15-16*. [OE *ofersettan*]

owersicht, oversicht, †oursicht /ˈʌursɪxt, ˈovərsɪxt/ *n* 1 negligence *la16-*. 2 supervision, management, care *la16-*. 3 licence, indulgence; allowance, permission *la16-e17*. [OWER¹·² + SICHT¹·¹]

owersie *see* OWERSEA¹·¹

owersman, oversman, †ourisman, †oursman /ˈʌurzmən, ˈovərzmən/ *n* 1 *law* a chief arbiter appointed to have the final decision in the event of deadlock; the chief and arbitrating executor of a will *16-*. 2 a manager or inspector in a coalmine *la17-19, 20- C*. 3 a foreman, an overseer *16-18*. 4 a craftsman appointed as a supervisor *16-e18*. 5 the provost of Prestwick and Wigtown *la15-16*. [altered form of OURMAN, with insertion of genitive ending]

†owersoum, oversoum, oursowme *n* (the keeping of) animals in excess of the alloted soum of a piece of pasturage *la15-e19*. [OWER¹·² + SOUM¹·¹]

owerstap, †overstap /ʌurˈstap/ *v* to overstep; to step over or across *17, 20- NE T*. [OWER¹·³ + STAP¹·²]

ower-steer /ʌurˈstir/ *adj* immoderate, excessive; slipshod *20- Sh*. [OWER¹·⁴ + STEER¹·¹]

†owerstent, overstentit *adj of tax* assessed at too high a rate, excessive *la17-19*. [OWER¹·⁴ + STENT²·¹]

†owerswak, ourswak *n* the dashing of waves on a beach *16-19*. [OWER¹·² + SWACK¹·¹]

owertak, overtak, †ourtak, †ourta, †overta /ʌurˈtak, ovərˈtak/ *v ptp* **ourtane, overtane, owertaen** 1 to catch up with and pass *la14-*. 2 to tackle, to deal with; to accomplish a task *la14-*. 3 to capture or seize, to arrest *la14-17*. 4 to be found guilty in a court of law; *of an offence* to be proven against a person *la14-16*. 5 *of a body of people* to occupy or fill a space *la14-e15*. **owertaen, overtaken** 1 drunk, intoxicated *17-*. 2 passed or surpassed *18-*. [OWER¹·³ + TAK¹·²]

owerthraw¹·¹, †overthraw, †ourthraw, †ourthrow /ˈʌurθrɔ/ *n* defeat, destruction, ruin *la15-*. [see the verb]

owerthraw¹·², †overthraw, †ourthraw, †ourthroe /ʌurˈθrɔ/ *v* 1 to defeat, to depose *la15-*. 2 to capsize or overturn; to demolish *la15-*. [OWER¹·³ + THRAW¹·²]

ower-tirvie *see* OURTIRVE

owertree, †overtree, †ourtre /ˈʌurtri/ *n* a crossbeam, a lintel *16-19, 20- NE WC*. [OWER¹·² + TREE¹·¹]

owerturn¹·¹ /ˈʌurtʌrn/ *n* 1 the resale of goods *la19-*. 2 the chorus of a song; a repetition of a story *19*. [see the verb]

owerturn¹·², overturn, †ourturn /ʌurˈtʌrn, ovərˈtʌrn/ *v* 1 to turn or tip over; to upend *15-*. 2 to reverse, to reinstate *15-*. 3 to overthrow, to overwhelm *la15-*. [OWER¹·³ + TURN¹·²]

owerwhelm, overwhelm, †overquhelme, †ourquhelm /ʌurˈmɛlm, ovərˈmɛlm/ *v* to overpower, to overthrow; to engulf or inundate *la15-*. [ME *overwhelmen*]

owerword, †ourword, †ouirword, †owr vord /ˈʌurwərd/ *n* the refrain of a poem or song; a repeated phrase *16-19, 20- literary*. [OWER¹·² + WORD¹·¹]

oweryear, overyear, †our-ʒeir /ʌurˈjir, ovərˈjir/ *adj* 1 *of animals* left or kept over from the previous year *16-*. 2 *of old stock* antiquated, superannuated *16-17*. [OWER¹·⁴ + YEAR]

owin *see* AIN¹·¹

owirlupe *see* OURLOP

owirman *see* OURMAN

owl *see* OOL¹·¹

owld *see* AULD¹·²

owld man *see* AULD MAN

owle *see* OOL¹·²

own *see* AIN¹·¹, AIN¹·², AWN²

ownar *see* AWN²

owne *see* AWE

owr *see* OOR³

owrance, owerance, †overance, †ourance /ˈʌurəns, ˈʌuərəns/ *n* control, mastery; superiority *la16-*. [OWER[1.1], with noun-forming suffix *-ance*]

owre *see* OWER[1.1], OWER[1.2], OWER[1.3], OWER[1.4]

owrecrown *see* OWERCROON

owre-gaun, owregauns *see* OWERGAE

†owres, o'ers, ouris *npl* excesses, extremes *la16-e18*. [substantive use of OWER[1.2]]

owrgaun rapes *see* OWERGAE

owrins, overins /ˈʌurɪnz, ˈovərɪnz/ *npl* 1 odds and ends, remnants *19- C Bor.* 2 trivial activities; surplus money *19- Bor.* [perhaps OWER[1.4] + *anes* (ANE[1.1]) or as if forming a pl verbal noun from OWER[1.4] = *to be over and above, surplus*]

owris *see* OOR[3]

owr vord *see* OWERWORD

ows *see* USE[1.2]

owse, ouse /ʌuz, uz/ *v* 1 to scoop up water; to empty by baling *19- Sh Ork N.* 2 to draw water in a pail *20- Sh.* 3 *of rain* to pour down in torrents *20- Sh.* 4 to pour or ladle out food *20- Sh.* **owser** a scoop for baling a boat *20- Sh Ork N.* **owster, ooster** the act of baling *19- Sh.* **owse-room** the space in a boat from which the bilge-water is baled out *la19- Sh.* **owseskerri** a scoop for baling a boat *19- Sh.* [ON *ausa* to sprinkle, pour]

owse, owsegate, owsen *see* OX

owser, owster *see* OWSE

owsteran *see* AUSTERN

owt *see* OCHT[1.1]

owtane *see* OUT-TANE[1.1], OUT-TANE[1.2], OUT-TANE[1.3]

owte off *see* OOT O

owth *see* OUTH[1.1], OUTH[1.2]

owthall *see* UDAL

owthawyng *see* OUT-HAIFFIN

owther[1.1], †owthyre /ˈʌuðər/ *adj* either *la14-19, 20- SW Bor.* Compare AITHER[1.1]. [ME *owðer*]

owther[1.2], †owder, †other, †older /ˈʌuðər/ *adv* either *la14-19, 20- SW Bor.* [OE *ōþer*]

†owther[1.3], owdyr *pron* one or other of two, either *la14-e16*. [OE *owðer*]

†owther[1.4], owder, authir *conj* or *la14-e17*. [see the pron]

owthor, owthir, owther, outher, author, †authour, †autour, †auctour /ˈʌuθər, ˈoθər, ˈɔθər/ *n* 1 a writer; an authority in writing *15-*. 2 an inventor or creator; an instigator *la14-*. 3 *law* a person from whom another derives their title *18-*. 4 an ancestor *e17*. [ME *auctour*]

owthyre *see* OWTHER[1.1]

owt quent *see* OUTQUENT

owtrageous *see* OOTRAGE

owtseit *see* OUTSET[2]

owyah *see* OOYAH

ox, †oix, †hox /ɔks/ *n pl* **owsen oxin, oussen** 1 a bovine draught animal; a castrated male bovine *la12-*. **owse** an ox *la18-19, 20- NE.* **†oxine** an ox *la15-16.* **oxin bow, owsen bow, †oussen bow** a curved wooden collar for a draught ox *la15-19, 20- NE.* **ox-ee** 1 the great tit *Parus major 16-19, 20- T C.* 2 the blue tit *Parus caeruleus la18-19, 20- T C Bor.* **oxgang, oxingang** a measure of land equivalent to one eighth of a ploughgate; frequently in place-names *14-19, 20- historical.* **oxgate, oxingate, owsegate** = *oxgang la16-19, 20- historical.* **†ox-gers** the extent of pasturage suitable for one ox *16.* **†oxin tilth** a measure of land *e16.* [OE *oxa*]

oxter[1.1], †oxster /ˈɔkstər/ *n* 1 the armpit; the under part of the upper arm *15-*. 2 the underside of an animal's shoulder joint *la16-*. 3 the armhole of a garment *la19-*. **oxterfu** an armful; as much as one can hold in the crook of an arm *18-*. **oxter cog** to help a person to walk by supporting them under the arm *la19- Uls.* **oxter lift** as much as can be carried under the arm or in the arms *19- Sh NE.* **oxter pickle** the small grain frequently attached to the full one within the husk in oats *19- NE.* **oxter pooch** a breast pocket *la18-*. **oxter staff** a crutch *19- NE.* **gie an oxter** to lend an arm to assist someone to walk *la19-*. **†in oxteris** arm in arm *16.* **†in utheris oxteris** in one another's arms *16.* **in your oxter** in your armpit; in your arms *la16-*. **under your oxter** under your arm; in your armpit *la15-*. 1 up to your armpits *20-*. 2 bogged down, encumbered *la20-*. 3 deeply implicated or embroiled in something *la20-*. **wi your airms in your oxters** with your arms folded *20-*. [ME *oxtere*]

oxter[1.2] /ˈɔkstər/ *v* 1 to lead or support by the arm *la18-*. 2 to hold or carry under the arm *la18-*. 3 to take someone's arm; to go arm in arm *la18-*. 4 to elbow, shove or jostle *la19-*. 5 to embrace, to cuddle *la19- NE T EC WC.* [see the noun]

oy, oye, oe, †o, †oo /ɔɪ, o/ *n* 1 a grandchild *la15-*. 2 a nephew *la16-19, 20- Sh Ork N.* 3 a niece *la16-e17.* [Gael *ogha* a grandson, a descendant]

oyas *see* HOYES[1.2]

oyce, oyse, †oise /ɔɪs, øs/ *n* an inlet of the sea (which is almost cut off by a bar of shingle) *la15- Ork N.* [ON *óss*]

oye *see* OY

oyes *see* HOYES[1.1], HOYES[1.2]

oyesis *see* HOYES[1.1]

oyll *see* ILE[1.1]

oyne *see* OAVEN

oynment *see* EYNTMENT

oynt *see* OINT

oyntment *see* EYNTMENT

oys *see* USE[1.2]

oyse *see* OYCE

ozel *see* OSEL

ozenbrigs *see* OSNABURG

ozzel *see* OSEL

P

pa see PALL², PAW², PEY¹·²
paa see PAW³
paal see PALL¹·¹, PALL¹·²
paam see PAM¹
paat see PAWT¹·²
Pace, Pasch, Peace, Pess, *Sh Ork N* **Paes,** †**Pask,** †**Pax** /pes, paʃ, pis, pɛs; *Sh Ork N* pez/ *n* **1** the festival of Easter *la14-*. **2** the Jewish festival of Passover *15-16*. †**Pasch Court** the Easter session of the Head Court of each burgh *18*. **Pasch Day,** †**Pace Day 1** Easter Sunday *la14-19, 20- Sh Ork N NE*. **2** Easter Monday *20- Sh Ork*. **Pace egg, Paes egg, Pess egg** a hard-boiled egg with a decorated shell, rolled down a hill by children at Easter *19-20, 21- historical*. **Pace egg day** Easter Monday *20- Bor*. †**Pasch Fair** a fair held at Easter *18-e19*. †**Pasche fyne** a payment made at Easter in certain churches, forming part of the fees of the vicar or incumbent *16*. **Pasch market,** †**Pasche mercat** a market held at Easter *la15-19, 20- historical*. **Pace-yaud** a person who fails to observe the custom of wearing something new for Easter *19- T*. [ME *pask*]
pace see PAISE¹·², PEACE¹·¹, PASS¹·¹
pacey whin see PEASIE
pacife, pacify see PECIFY
pack¹·¹, †**pak** /pak/ *n* **1** a bundle or bale of goods or possessions; a backpack used to transport goods *15-*. **2** a gang of people; a group of wild animals *15-*. **3** a group of people crowded together; a crush, a squeeze *20-*. **4** sheep owned by a shepherd, which are allowed to graze alongside his employer's flock *19, 20- N T C Bor*. **5** worldly goods; property or fortune *16-19, 20- NE T Bor*. **6** a measure of wool (usually 12 stones Scots in weight) *16-19*. **7** an initial stock of merchandise; a means of setting up in business *16-17*. **pack merchant 1** a pedlar, an itinerant seller of goods *19- N NE*. **2** a cloud formation which resembles a man with a pack on his back *la19- N NE*. †**beir a pak** to be a pedlar *16*. **bring yer pack to the pins** to squander your wealth and resources *18-19, 20- NE T*. †**mak thair paks thin** to reduce to poverty; to impoverish *e16*. [ME *pak*, MDu *pac*]
pack¹·² /pak/ *v* **1** to put goods into a container or parcel; to fill, cram or press tightly *la15-*. **2** to fill oneself with food, eat to excess *la16-*. **3** *in ploughing* to lay the furrows close together *la19-*. **4** to burden, lay heavily upon *la19- Sh*. **pack and peel,** †**pak and pele 1** to pack and unpack bulk merchandise; to act as a wholesale merchant in the export and import trade *la15-e18, 19- historical*. **2** to deal or associate with unprivileged merchants by allowing them the rights of trade belonging to the guilds *la16-e19, la19- historical*. **pack someone up** to end a romantic relationship with a person *la20- C*. †**pack up** to bring a dispute to an amicable agreement *la16-e17*. [see the noun]
†**pack²**, **pak** *n* in Shetland and Orkney a quantity of woollen cloth, equivalent to 60 cuttells or Scottish ells *16-19*. [ON *pakki* a pack, a bundle]
pack³ /pak/ *n* an agreement; a plot or conspiracy *la16-19, 20- SW Uls*. **in pack** in collusion *la19, 20- SW Uls*. [perhaps Eng *pact*]
pack⁴ /pak/ *adj* on intimate and friendly terms; in league *18-19, 20- T C SW Bor Uls*. [perhaps PACK¹·¹ or PACK³]

packet, †**pakket,** †**packed,** †**pacquett** /'pakət/ *n* **1** a small package or parcel; a bundle of goods or letters *16-*. **2** a pannier, a saddle for carrying loads *18-19, 20- NE*. [probably MFr *paquet* or EModE *pacquet*]
packhouse, †**pakhouse** /'pakhʌus/ *n* a warehouse for storing (perishable) merchandise *la16-19, 20- NE T EC*. [Du *pakhuis*]
packie¹ /'pake/ *n* a pedlar, an itinerant seller of goods *19, 20- Sh N EC SW*. **packieman** a packman *19, 20- Sh T*. [PACK¹·¹ + -IE¹]
packie², pakkie /'paki/ *n* a quantity of fishing-line *19- Sh*. **a packie o towes** a bundle of fishing-lines *19- Sh*. [Norn *pakki* a collection of fishing-lines constituting a long-line, ON *pakki* a pack, bundle]
packman, †**pakman** /'pakmən/ *n* **1** a pedlar, a travelling merchant *la16-20, 21- historical*. **2** a cloud formation which resembles a man with a pack on his back *la19- Sh NE WC SW*. [PACK¹·¹ + MAN]
paco see PEACOCK
pacok see PEACOCK
pacquett see PACKET
paction¹·¹, †**pactioun** /'pakʃən/ *n* **1** an agreement, bargain or understanding *16-*. **2** *law* an unofficial agreement as distinct from a legally binding contract *16-*. **3** a conspiracy, a plot; collusion, fraud *16-e18*. [EModE, MFr *paction*, Lat *pactio*]
†**paction¹·²** *v* to make an agreement or bargain; to enter into a compact *la17-e19*. [see the noun]
pactioun see PACTION¹·¹
pad¹ /pad/ *n* **1** a cushion; a mass or wad of soft material *18-*. **2** a soft stuffed saddle *17-19*. [unknown]
pad²·¹ /pad/ *n* **1** a footpath; a narrow, unsurfaced track *18-*. **2** a route over a natural obstacle, a pass through hills; frequently in place-names *19- C*. [EModE *pad*]
pad²·² /pad/ *v* **1** to travel on foot; to walk steadily *la18-*. **2** to move about quietly or furtively *19-*. **3** to depart; to leave a job *la19, 20- NE*. **paddered** trampled, well-trodden *la18-19, 20- Uls*. **paddit, padded** trampled, well-trodden *20- Sh NE SW*. **pad the road** to trudge around (in a search for work) *19, 20- NE*. [see the noun]
pad³ /pad/ *v* to inform; to warn; to drop a hint *la19- Sh*. [Norn *pad*; compare ON *pati* a rumour]
paddill see PAIDLE³
paddle see PAIDLE¹·¹, PAIDLE¹·², PAIDLE²·¹, PAIDLE³
paddo see PADDY²
paddock, †**paddok** /'padək/ *n* **1** a small enclosed field *16-*. **2** a small farm *19- SW Bor*. [EModE *paddock*, OE *pearroc* a fence enclosing a piece of ground]
paddok see PADDOCK, PUDDOCK¹·¹
†**paddok-lok, padlok lok, patlok lokk** *n* a portable lock; a padlock *16-17*. [unknown first element + LOCK¹·¹]
Paddy¹ /'padi, 'pade/ *n* **1** a short form of the of the personal name Patrick *18-*. **2** a nickname for an Irishman *19-*. **paddy barrow** a barrow without sides (used for carrying large stones) *20- Ork N NE T C*. **Paddy's Market 1** a former street market in Glasgow *la19-20, 21- historical*. **2** a confused scene; an untidy room *20- T C*. **Paddy's Milestone** a nickname for Ailsa Craig in the Firth of Clyde, which was originally a conspicuous landmark for Irish immigrants sailing to Scotland *la19-*. **come the Paddy ower** to outwit,

trick or confuse *19, 20- T*. [diminutive of Ir *Pádraig*, Ireland's patron saint]

paddy[2], †**paddo** /'pade, 'padi/ *n* a frog or toad *la14-*; compare PUDDOCK[1.1]. **paddy ladle** a tadpole *la19, 20- Bor*. **paddy's rhubarb** the butterbur *Petasites hybridus la20- EC Bor*. [Eng *pad* a frog, a toad, with diminutive suffix]

paddy *see* PATTY

padgean *see* PAGEANT

padill *see* PAIDLE[2.1], PAIDLE[4]

padlok lok *see* PADDOK-LOK

†**paduasoy, pudosoye, poyl-de-soy** *n* a corded silk fabric *la16-e19*. [EModE *paduasoy*]

padʒane *see* PAGEANT

paece *see* PEACE[1.1]

paeck *see* PECK[1.1]

paedagogue *see* PEDAGOGUE

paek *see* PECK[1.2]

paekie *see* PECK[1.1]

Paes *see* PACE

paewae /'pewe/ *adj of a person* pallid, sickly; spiritless *18-19, 20- Sh NE EC Bor*. [probably imitative of a plaintive sound with influence from WAE[1.1], WOW[2]; compare PEELIE-WALLY]

paffle, poffle, †**poffill,** †**pofle** /'pafəl, 'pɔfəl/ *n* a small piece of land, a croft, an allotment; frequently in place-names *la13-19, 20- EC Bor*. [perhaps OE **pofel* a piece of low-lying sandy ground]

pagan[1.1], †**paian** /'pegən/ *n* a person not subscribing to a major or dominant religion *la14-*. [see the adj]

pagan[1.2], †**pagen,** †**payane,** †**paian** /'pegən/ *adj* not subscribing to a particular religion *la14-*. [Lat *pāgānus* heathen, as opposed to Christian or Jewish]

page, †**pege,** †**paige** /pedʒ/ *n* **1** a boy, a youth; a servant or attendant *la14-19, 20- historical*. **2** a youth being trained for knighthood *la14-17*. [ME *page*]

pageant, †**padgean,** †**padʒane** /'padʒənt/ *n* a play, a performance; a parade or procession *16-*. [ME *pagent*, EModE *pageaunt*]

pagen *see* PAGAN[1.2]

pagger[1.1] /'pagər/ *n* a fight *20- NE T EC Bor*. [Travellers' language]

pagger[1.2] /'pagər/ *v* to fight *20- NE T EC Bor*. **pagart, pagard** exhausted *20- NE T EC Bor*; compare PUGGLED. [see the noun]

paian *see* PAGAN[1.1], PAGAN[1.2]

paich *see* PECH[1.2]

paichled *see* PECHLT

paidle[1.1], **paddle** /'pedəl, 'padəl/ *n* the act of wading in shallow water *la19-*. [see the verb]

paidle[1.2], **paddle** /'pedəl, 'padəl/ *v* **1** to wade in shallow water or mud *la18-*. **2** to shuffle or toddle along; to walk slowly or aimlessly *la18-*. **3** to trample, to tread down *la18-19, 20- Ork EC SW Uls*. [EModE *paddle*]

paidle[2.1], **paddle,** †**padill** /'pedəl, 'padəl/ *n* a hoe; a long-handled tool used for weeding, for scraping earth from a hard surface or for clearing the coulter of a plough in the furrow *la16-*. [variant of PATTLE[1.1]]

paidle[2.2] /'pedəl/ *v* to work with a hoe; to clean or clear by means of a hoe *la16-19, 20- EC Bor*. [see the noun]

paidle[3], **paddle,** †**paddill** /'pedəl, 'padəl/ *n* the lumpfish or lumpsucker *Cyclopterus lumpus 16-19, 20- Sh Ork N NE EC*. **paidle cock,** †**paddle cock** the male lumpfish *la19, 20- NE T SW*. [unknown]

paidle[4], †**padill** /'pedəl/ *n* **1** a small leather bag or wallet; a flat leather pouch *la16-19, 20- historical*. **2** the pocket or trap in a fishing-net, especially in the small stake-net used for catching flounders *19- SW*. **paidle net** a fishing-net containing a pocket or trap *la19- SW*. [perhaps diminutive form of EModE *pad* a pannier, a basket]

paidling, paidlin /'pedlɪŋ, 'pedlɪn/ *adj* aimless, irresponsible *la18-19, 20- NE SW*. [presp of PAIDLE[1.2]]

paidmint, †**pathment,** †**paithment** /'pedmənt/ *n* a pavement *la14-19, 20- T*. [PATH, with noun-forming suffix]

paige *see* PAGE

paigle[1.1] /'pegəl/ *n* rough or menial housework; a dirty household task *19, 20- Ork*. [unknown]

paigle[1.2] /'pegəl/ *v* to undertake dirty or menial household tasks *la19, 20- Ork*. [unknown]

paik[1.1] /pek/ *n* **1** a blow, a beating; punishment or chastisement *16-*. **2** *derogatory* a disreputable or insignificant person; an animal of little value *19, 20- Bor*. **get yer paiks** to be duly punished *16-19, 20- Sh SW*. **gie a person their paiks** to punish a person *la16-19, 20- EC*. [unknown]

paik[1.2] /pek/ *v* **1** to beat, punish *16-*. **2** to trudge or tramp along *19, 20- Bor*. [unknown]

paik *see* PAWK, PECK[1.2]

paikin, *Sh* **paiksin,** *Sh* **pexin** /'pekən; *Sh* 'peksɪn; *Sh* 'peksɪn/ *n* a thrashing, a beating; punishment *la19-*. [probably verbal noun from PAIK[1.2], perhaps influenced by the noun PAIK[1.1]]

pail, †**paill,** †**peal** /pel/ *n* **1** a hearse *19, 20- Bor*. **2** a cloth for draping a coffin, a funeral pall *16-e19*. **3** a canopy, a decorative hanging *16-17*. [OFr *paile*, Lat *pallium*]

pail *see* PALE[3]

pailace *see* PALACE

pailin[1.1], **palin, pailing,** †**pealling** /'pelɪn, 'pelɪŋ/ *n* **1** a fence made of posts *16-*. **2** a fence post *19-*. **pailined** enclosed with a fence or posts *20-*. **pailing stab** a fence post *la20-*. [PALE[2], with *-ing* noun suffix]

pailin[1.2], **palin** /'pelɪn/ *v* to enclose with a fence made of pales *20-*. [see the noun]

pailister /'pelɪstər/ *n* the game of quoits *18- H&I WC*. [Gael *peilistear* a quoit, flat stone]

paill *see* PAIL, PALE[2]

paillag *see* PELLOCK

pailʒoune *see* PAVILION

paiment *see* PAMENT[1.1]

pain[1.1], †**pane,** †**payne** /pen/ *n* **1** physical or mental suffering *la14-*. **2** exertion or effort *la14-*. **3** a penalty or punishment; a fine *la14-19, 20- historical*. **painful 1** causing or suffering pain *la15-*. **2** difficult, exacting, laborious *la14-*. **3** *of a person* laborious, assiduous, diligent *la16-17*. **the painless** an anaesthetic *20- Sh*. **the pains** rheumatism, rheumatic twinges *la18-*. [ME *pein*]

pain[1.2], †**payn,** †**pane** /pen/ *v* **1** to exert oneself, strive *la14-*. **2** to cause or inflict pain *15-*. **3** to suffer pain *la15-*. [see the noun; also ME *peinen*, OFr *peinir*]

pain *see* PEEN[2]

painch, pench, paunch, †**panche** /penʃ, penʃ, pɔnʃ/ *n* **1** the stomach; a large or protruding belly *la14-*. **2** *pl* the entrails of an animal used as food; tripe *16-*. **3** *pl* the bowels or intestines of a person or animal *la17-19, 20- WC SW Uls*. †**paunching** the procedure of puncturing the stomach of a ruminant to allow accumulated gases to escape *19*. **paunchings,** *Sh* **penshins** the part of a cow's stomach from which tripe is made *la19, 20- Sh*. [ME *paunch*]

paint *see* PENT[1.1], PENT[1.2]

paintit *see* PENTIT

†**paintrie, payntry** *n* **1** a painting; painted pictures or designs *15-e17*. **2** paint or pigment *16-e17*. [MFr *peintrerie*]

paip, †**pape** /pep/ *n* **1** the stone or kernel of a fruit, a pip *18-19, 20- T EC Bor*. **2** a dried cherrystone used as a counter and as currency in children's games *19, 20- EC SW Bor*. **the**

paips a game played with cherrystones *19, 20- SW Bor.* [AN *pepin* with influence from Eng *pip*]

paip see PAPE

paiper see PAPER[1.1]

pair[1], **perr**, †**pare**, †**peare** /per, pɛr/ *n* **1** a set of two related objects; two matching or corresponding components *la14-*. **2** a set of more than two related objects *la15-*. **3** two lovers, a couple; two mated animals *la15-*. **4** a single object viewed as a collection of its component parts: ◊ *a pair o breeks la16-*. **5** a team of two horses for ploughing and other farm jobs *la19-*. **6** the distance between a set of two archery targets *17*. **an ae pair place** a farm with one team of horses *20- NE*. **a fowre-pair-horse ferm** a farm requiring four pairs of horses for its cultivation *la19- NE EC*. **pair of arrows** a set of three arrows or darts *18-*. **pair of bagpipes** a set of bagpipes *la17-19, 20- Sh T*. **pair of beads**, †**pair of bedis** a string of beads; a rosary *la15-*. **pair o blankets** a large blanket used folded in two *16-*. †**pair of buttis** the distance between a set of two archery targets *la16-17*. **pair of cards** a pack of cards *la16-19, 20- NE C Bor*. †**pair of knyffis** a pair of knives kept in a single sheath *la15-e17*. **pair o questions** the Shorter Catechism *20- NE T WC*. †**pare of schetis** a large sheet used folded in two *la15-e18*. **pair of shears** a pair of scissors *la15-*. †**pair of twises** a set of small instruments *la17*; compare TWYS. [ME *paire*]

pair[2], **pare** /per/ *v* to weaken or impair; to diminish; to deteriorate *15-19, 20- Sh*. [aphetic form of APPAIR]

pair see PUIR[1.3]

paircel, **parcel**, †**persell**, †**parcell**, †**parcial** /'persəl, 'parsəl/ *n* **1** a portion or division; an instalment of a payment *la16-*. **2** a piece of land; a batch of a commodity *la16-*. **3** a package *18-*. **4** a small company or collection of people or animals; a group, herd or flock *la17-19, 20- Sh SW Uls*. [ME *parcel*, EModE *parcelle*]

pairchment, **parchment**, †**perchment** /'pertʃmənt, 'partʃmənt/ *n* **1** an animal's skin prepared for writing on *la15-*. **2** a certificate issued to qualified teachers in state schools on which comments on their proficiency were annually recorded by the School Inspectorate and which served as an authorization to teach *19-e20, la20- historical*. **3** a certificate given to a qualified teacher on satisfactory completion of a probation period *19-20, 21- historical*. [ME *parchemin, parchement*]

pairhoose see PUIR[1.1]

pairin-flooer, **pairing-meal** see PARE

Pairis see PARIS

Pairis bun see PARIS BUN

Pairiser /'perɪsər/ *n* a sweet, sugar-topped, sponge-like bun *la19-*. [shortened form of PARIS BUN + -ER]

pairish, **perish**, **parish**, †**pareis**, †**paroche**, †**parioch** /'perɪʃ, 'perɪʃ, 'parɪʃ/ *n* **1** the area committed to the care of a priest or minister; an area of jurisdiction for civil administration *la16-*. **2** the inhabitants of a parish *la16-*. **3** curling the ring surrounding the tee *la19, 20- WC*. **parish kirk**, **pairish kirk** the church serving a parish *la14-*. **parish priest** a priest serving a parish *la14-*. **parish school** a school established by the Church of Scotland to provide instruction in the rudiments of education and in Latin, and to equip promising pupils for University entrance *la17-19, 20- historical*. [ME *parish*]

pairk see PARK[1.1]

pairlament see PARLIAMENT[1]

pairling see PEARL[2]

pairls, **perils**, †**parleis**, †**perrillis** /perlz, 'perəlz/ *n* paralysis; a paralytic tremor or weakness *la14-19, 20- Bor*. [reduced form of PARALSIE]

pairlt, **perelt** /'perlt, 'perəlt/ *adj* affected with paralysis or a paralytic tremor *19, 20- Bor*. [back-formation from PAIRLS]

pairple, †**parpall**, †**perpell** /'perpəl/ *n* a partition *la16-19, 20- Bor*. †**pairple wall**, **parpall wall**, **perpell wall** a partition wall *la15-e18*. [variant of PARPEN[1]]

pairse see PIERCE

pairt[1.1], **part**, **pert** /pert, part, pɛrt/ *n* **1** a portion or division of a larger whole *la14-*. **2** a side; a direction *la14-*. **3** a person's role or way of life *15-*. **4** a limb or organ; the genitalia *15-*. **5** an attribute of the mind, a talent *15-*. **6** a place, area or neighbourhood *15-19, 20- Sh Ork NE*. **7** a site, a clearly defined spot *19, 20- Sh T SW Uls*. **8** a person's allotted portion; a contribution; a dowry *15-19*. **9** a subdivision of an estate held by a smaller landowner; one of a number of pieces of land into which an estate might be divided for separate disposition *la14-17*. †**pairtie** a small farm *19*. †**partisman** a person who shared or took part in an undertaking; a partner *la15-16*. †**partlyik** proportionally *16-e17*. †**partlingis** in part; partly *la16*. **for that pairt o** in regard to, concerning *la19-*. **be guid yer part** to be consistent with your duty; to behave appropriately *18-19, 20- NE*. **be ill yer part** to behave inappropriately *18-19, 20- NE*. **in that part 1** *law* by special appointment and with jurisdiction limited either to particular matters or with respect to time or place *la15-*. **2** on or concerning that point; in that respect *la15-e17*. **keep yer ain pairt** to look after one's own interests *19, 20- Ork NE T*. †**kepe a gude pairt to** to behave well towards *la15-16*. †**pairt and pairtlik** in fair or equal shares *16-e17*. **parts and pertinents** *law* everything forming part of lands being conveyed (except rights held by the crown) that is not specially reserved *16-*. **parts and pendicles** = *parts and pertinents 16-19, 20- historical*. †**parts, pendicles and pertinents** = *parts and pertinents 16-19*. †**part of orisoun** part of speech *16*. [ME *part*]

pairt[1.2], **part**, **pert** /pert, part, pɛrt/ *v* **1** to divide into two or more parts *la14-*. **2** to separate or depart from; to relinquish *la14-*. **3** to divide into portions and distribute, to share out *15-*. **4** to leave a place *14-19, 20- Uls*. **5** to separate from a person; to part with something *la14-19, 20- Uls*. **6** *of money or goods* to be divided or divisible *19, 20- Sh NE T*. **7** to serve food at a table *20- NE*. **pairt wi bairn**, **part wi bairn** to give birth to a premature or stillborn baby; to suffer a miscarriage *la15-19, 20- Sh NE Uls*. †**part with** to leave one's spouse after being authorized to do so; to be separated formally from one's spouse *la15-16*. [ME *parten*]

pairt see PERT

pairtie see PAIRTY[1.1]

pairtiner see PAIRTNER

pairtisay, **pairtisie** /'pertəse, 'pertəsi/ *n* a thing done by or belonging to more than one person, a joint venture or possession *19-20, 21- historical*. [perhaps related to Fr *partager* to share]

pairtissing see PARTISING

pairtner, **pertner**, †**partiner**, †**pairtiner** /'pertnər, pɛrtnər/ *n* a partner *la14-*. **pairtnery** partnership *15-*. [ME *partener*]

pairtrick, **paitrick**, **partrik**, †**pertrik**, †**perdrix** /'pertrɪk, 'petrɪk, 'partrɪk/ *n* a partridge *Perdix perdix la14-*. [AN *partriz, perdix*, ME *partrich*]

pairt-tak, **partake**, †**part-tak** /pert'tak, par'tek/ *v* **1** to share; to participate *17-*. **2** to support; to side with or defend *16-19*. [back-formation from PAIRT-TAKAR or PAIRT-TAKING]

pairt-takar, **partaker**, †**part-takar** /pert'takər, par'tekər/ *n* **1** a partner, a participant *16-*. **2** a supporter, an ally; an accomplice *16-18*. [PAIRT[1.1] + Eng *taker*]

pairt-taking, **partakin**, †**part-taking** /pertˈtakɪŋ, parˈtakɪn/ *n* **1** sharing; participating *16-*. **2** aiding and abetting *16*. [PAIRT[1.1] + Eng *taking*]

pairty[1.1], **pairtie**, **perty**, †**partie** /ˈperte, ˈperti, ˈperte/ *n* **1** a division, a side or faction; a body of supporters *la14-*. **2** *law* a litigant; the opposing litigant; a party to a contract or dispute *la14-*. **3** a social gathering *20-*. **4** a match, an equal *16*. **5** a lover; a spouse *la15-e17*. **6** an antagonist, an adversary *la15-17*. **7** a part or portion; a share; a quantity *la14-e17*. †**pairtie failʒear** a person who failed to perform an obligation, a defaulter *la16-e18*. [ME *parti*]

†**pairty[1.2]** *v* **1** to take sides; to make common cause *la16-18*. **2** to support; to take the part of *la16-17*. [see the noun]

pairty[1.3], **party** /ˈperte, ˈparte/ *adj* **1** held in common, shared *18-*. **2** antagonistic, hostile *la16-e17*. **3** parti-coloured, variegated *la15-e16*. **4** actively concerned, personally involved *la15*. [AN, MFr *parti*, ptp of *partir* to share, divide]

†**pais**, **pase** *n* pasteboard *la16*. [shortened form of PAISBUIRD]
pais *see* PAISE[1.1], PASS[1.1]

†**paisbuird**, **paisboard**, **paseboord** *n* board made by pasting sheets of paper together *17*. [EModE *pasteboard*]

paise[1.1], †**pais** /pes/ *n* **1** *in weaving* one of the weights in the pulley which controls the tension of the warp threads *19-20, 21- historical*. **2** one of the weights of a weight-driven clock *la16-e19*. **3** the weights and prices of different kinds of bread as laid down by the magistrates of burghs; the official list or table of these *15-17*. **4** a standard weight *15-16*. **5** charge, responsibility *la15-e16*. †**of pais** conforming to the prescribed or standard weight *la15-e16*. [ME *peis*]

†**paise[1.2]**, **pace**, **pease** *v* **1** to assess weight by feel; to estimate weight or condition *16-19*. **2** to deliberate upon or consider *16-e17*. **3** to measure the weight of goods using a balance *la15-17*. [ME *peisen*]

paisey whin *see* PEASIE

Paisley /ˈpezle/ *adj* **1** originating in or manufactured in Paisley *19-*. **2** *of textiles* having a characteristic pattern associated with Paisley *19-*. **Paisley pattern** an elaborate colourful design based on Hindu and Arabic motifs *20-*. **Paisley shawl** a shawl of the Paisley pattern made of cashmere and wool or silk, or cotton and wool, and in former times frequently acquired by a woman on marriage *19-*. [from the place-name]

Paisley Buddy, **Paisley bodie** /ˈpezle bʌde, ˈpezle bɔdi/ *n* a nickname for a native of Paisley *la17-*. Compare *the Buddies* (BODY). [from the place-name + BODY]

Paisley screw /ˈpezle skru/ *n* a screw driven home with a hammer instead of a screwdriver (implying laziness) *20- WC*. **Paisley screwdriver** a hammer *20- C*; compare GLASGOW SCREWDRIVER. [from the place-name + Eng *screw*]

†**pais-penny** *n* a coin found as treasure-trove *la15-e16*. [perhaps altered form of POSE[1.1], but the vowel change is unexplained]

†**paitclaith** *n* a garment worn over the neck and upper part of the chest *la16-e17*. [variant of PATELET, with the final syllable reformed as CLAITH]

paiter *see* PATTER[1.1], PATTER[1.2]
paith *see* PETH
paithment *see* PAIDMINT, PATHEMENT[1.1]
paitlat *see* PATELET
paitrick *see* PAIRTRICK
paittel *see* PATTLE[1.2]

paittern, **pattren**, **pattern**, †**patron**, †**patroun** /ˈpetərn, ˈpatrən, ˈpatərn/ *n* **1** a model or exemplar; a prototype *la14-*. **2** a repeated decorative design *19-*. [ME *patron*]

pak *see* PACK[1.1], PACK[2]
pakhouse *see* PACKHOUSE

pakie *see* PAWKIE[1]
pakkald *see* PAUCHLE[1.1]
pakket *see* PACKET
pakkie *see* PACKIE[2]
pakman *see* PACKMAN

palace, **pailace**, †**palyce**, †**palis** /ˈpalɪs, ˈpelɪs/ *n* **1** the residence of a ruler *15-*. **2** a mansion *la15-*. **3** an official residence of the Scottish sovereign; the precinct of such a residence *la15-*. [ME *palais*]

palaiver[1.1], **palaver** /pəˈlevər, pəˈlavər/ *n* **1** idle talk *19-*. **2** fussy or ostentatious behaviour *la19-*. **3** a foolishly ostentatious person; an extremely fussy person *la19-*. [probably West African Pidgin, originally Port *palavra* word, speech]

palaiver[1.2], **palaver** /pəˈlevər, pəˈlavər/ *v* **1** to waste time; to make a great deal of a small task *19-*. **2** to behave in a silly or ostentatious way *la19-*. [see the noun]

paldie *see* PALLALL

pale[1.1] /pel/ *n* a small scoop for taking samples (of cheese) *19, 20- SW*. [Fr *pelle* a shovel]

pale[1.2] /pel/ *v* to pierce cheese with a small scoop to remove a sample *18-19, 20- SW*. [see the noun]

pale[2], †**paill**, †**peal** /pel/ *n* **1** a pointed stake used in fencing; a fence *la15-*. **2** *in heraldry* a vertical stripe *la15-*. **3** a peg used as a stopper *16-e19*; compare *cock and pail* (COCK[1.1]). [ME *pal*, Lat *pālus* a stake]

pale[3], †**pail** /pel/ *adj* lacking colour; dim *15-*. **pale ale** a kind of low-gravity beer *20-*. **India Pale Ale** = *pale ale*. [ME *pal*]

paleʒoun *see* PAVILION

†**palice**, **palyce** *n* a palisaded park or town *e16*. [MFr *palis* a fence of pales, an enclosure]

palie[1.1] /ˈpali/ *n* **1** a lethargic or feeble person *19-*. **2** an undersized, ailing lamb *19, 20- SW Bor*. [probably related to PALE[3]]

palie[1.2], **pallie**, †**paulie** /ˈpali/ *adj* **1** thin, pallid, listless *19-*. **2** *of a child* stunted in growth; delicate *19-*. **3** *of a young lamb* undersized, not thriving *19-*. **4** *of a person* incapacitated, lame *la18- T C Bor*. **5** *of a limb* injured; paralysed *19, 20- T EC Bor*. [see the noun]

palin *see* PAILIN[1.1], PAILIN[1.2]

palinode, †**palinod** /ˈpalɪnod/ *n law* a formal retraction of a defamatory statement which a pursuer could demand of the defender as part of the damages in a libel action; an apology *17-19, 20- historical*. [Fr *palinodie*]

palis *see* PALACE

pall[1.1], **pawl**, *Ork* **paal** /pal, pɔl; *Ork* pal/ *n* **1** a pole, a stout post; a beam, a mooring post for ships *18-19, 20- N SW*. **2** a prop or stay; a support, a fulcrum *19, 20- Ork*. [variant of Eng *pawl* a bar used to lock a capstan]

pall[1.2], **paal**, **pawl** /pal, pɔl, pɑl/ *v* **1** to puzzle or perplex; to thwart *19, 20- Sh Ork N*. **2** to surprise or astonish *20- Sh Ork NE*. **3** to brace oneself against something *19- Sh Ork*. **paul a'** to exceed or surpass *la19- Sh Ork NE*. [see the noun]

pall[2], †**pa** /pɔl/ *n* **1** rich cloth *la14-17, 18- historical*. **2** a robe or cloak *la14-e16*. [OE *pæll*]

pallack *see* PELLOCK

pallall /paˈlal/ *n* **1** hopscotch *la18-*. **2** the counter with which the game of hopscotch is played *la19- T*. **3** the name of one of the squares, usually the seventh, on which hopscotch is played *la19- T EC*. **pallie**, *T EC* **paldie** **1** hopscotch *la19- T EC*. **2** the counter with which the game of hopscotch is played *la19- T EC*. **pallalls** hopscotch *19-*. [probably shortened and reduplicated form of Fr *palet* a stone used to throw at a target in various games]

pallat *see* PALLET
pallawa *see* PALLIE

pallet, *N* **pellad**, †**pallat** /ˈpalət; *N* ˈpɛləd/ *n* **1** a ball; a float on a fishing net *19- NE EC Bor.* **2** a tadpole *20- N.* **3** *derogatory* the head *16-19.* [ME *palet*]

palliasse, †**palʒas**, †**pallʒeis**, †**palliess** /ˈpalıas, ˈpaljəs/ *n* a straw mattress *16-.* [MFr *paillasse*]

pallie, **pallawa** /ˈpale, ˈpaləwɔ/ *n* a small edible crab, frequently used for bait *19- EC.* [unknown]

pallie *see* PALIE[1.2], PALLALL

palliess *see* PALLIASSE

pallion, **pullion**, †**pallioun** /ˈpaljən, ˈpʌljən/ *n* **1** *pl* rags; ragged or worn-out clothing *19-.* **2** a rough person; a tall skinny person *20- NE.* **3** a cloak, a mantle *la15.* [ME *pallioun* a cloak]

pallion *see* PAVILION

pallioun *see* PALLION

pallo *see* PELLOCK

pally-fittit /ˈpale-fıtıt/ *adj* **1** having a damaged or useless foot *20- C Bor.* **2** splay-footed, flat-footed *la18-e19.* [PALIE[1.2] + FIT[1.1], with adj-forming suffix]

pally-handit /ˈpale-handıt/ *adj* **1** having a damaged or useless hand *20- C Bor.* **2** left-handed *la20- T EC.* [PALIE[1.2] + HAN[1.1], with adj-forming suffix]

pallʒeis *see* PALLIASSE

palm[1] /pam/ *n* **1** the palm of the hand *15-.* **2** *pl* the grippers or claws of a pair of tongs *19, 20- Ork Uls.* **3** the blade of a baker's shovel *19.* **4** the hand of a clock *17-19.* **5** the blade of an oar *16.* [ME *paum, palm*, Lat *palma*]

palm[2], †**palme** /pam/ *n* **1** a piece of a willow or other tree used to represent the palm on Palm Sunday *la14-.* **2** a tropical tree *15-.* †**palm fair** an annual two-day fair beginning on the fifth Monday in Lent *la16-18.* **palm tree**, †**palme tre** a tropical tree; a native tree used to represent a palm tree *la14-.* [OE *palm*, Lat *palma*]

palmer[1.1], **paumer**, †**palmere** /ˈpamər, ˈpɔmər/ *n* **1** a pilgrim *13-.* **2** the cormorant *Phalacrocorax carbo la19- Ork.* **3** something large or outstanding of its kind *20- Ork.* **palmer scarf** the guillemot *Uria aalge la19- Ork N.* [AN *palmer, paumer*]

palmer[1.2], **paumer** /ˈpamər, ˈpɔmər/ *v* **1** to walk aimlessly; to saunter *19, 20- NE.* **2** to move clumsily or noisily; to stamp around *la19, 20- NE.* [see the noun]

palmere *see* PALMER[1.1]

palmie[1.1], **pawmie** /ˈpami, ˈpame, ˈpɔme/ *n* a stroke with a strap or cane on the palm of the hand as a punishment to schoolchildren *la18-20, 21- historical.* [perhaps PALM[1] + diminutive suffix -*ie* or reduced form of Lat *pande palmam* hold out your hand]

palmie[1.2] /ˈpami, ˈpame/ *v* to administer a stroke with a strap or cane on the palm of the hand as a punishment to schoolchildren *19-20, 21- historical.* [see the noun]

palp *see* PAP[1]

†**palsify** *v* to afflict with palsy, to paralyse *la19.* [Eng *palsy*, with verb-forming suffix]

palt *see* PELT[1.1]

palyce *see* PALACE, PALICE

†**palʒardrie**, **palʒardy** *n* deception; treachery *16.* [MFr *paillardie*]

palʒas *see* PALLIASSE

pam[1], **paam** /pam/ *n* **1** the knave in any suit of cards *19, 20- Sh NE.* **2** the knave of clubs *e19.* **pawmie** the knave of clubs *la19, 20- Sh.* [Fr *Pamphile* the name of a card game, and of the knave of clubs]

pam[2] /pam/ *numeral in children's counting rhymes* five *20- Ork.* [altered form of BAOMBE or OWelsh *pimp*, from the numerals used for counting sheep]

†**pament**[1.1], **paiment** *n* paving; a pavement *16-17.* Compare PATHEMENT[1.1]. [variant of Eng *pavement*]

†**pament**[1.2] *v* to pave *la16-e17.* [see the noun]

pament *see* PEYMENT

†**pamphelet** *n* a woman considered to be promiscuous *e16.* [OFr *Panfilés*, translated title of Lat *Pamphilus, de amore* 12th-century love poem or comedy]

pan[1.1], **paun**, †**pane** /pan, pɔn/ *n* **1** a broad, shallow cooking vessel, a pot *la14-.* **2** an industrial container used to heat substances *la14-.* **3** *pl* a group of salt pans or the site occupied by them; a salt works of this kind; frequently in place-names *la15-19, 20- historical.* **4** the receptacle in a commode; the bowl of a toilet *17-.* **5** a hard and impermeable substratum of the soil *la18-.* **6** the skull, the cranium *19-.* **7** the epidermis of a sheep which separates with the old wool when the new fleece has started to grow *20- Ork.* **8** a dense shoal of small fish *20- Sh.* **9** a conveyor in a coal or shale-mine *la20- EC.* **10** the bowl containing the fuel and wick of a lamp; a lamp *16-17.* **panner** a heavy catch of herring *20- N.* **pannie** kindling, firewood *20- NE T EC.* **pan breid**, **pan bread** *n* bread baked in a pan or tin *20-*; compare PAN LOAF. **pan breid** *adj rhyming slang* deid *la20-.* †**pan coal** small coal or dross (used as fuel for salt pans) *la18-19.* †**pan cratch** a precipitate of lime forming on the sides of salt pans, used for rendering or harling walls *17-18.* **pan haggis** fried oatmeal (mixed with scraps of meat or other leftovers) *la20- C SW Bor.* **pan jotral 1** a hotchpotch of food; leftovers *19, 20- NE Bor.* **2** a cake made from the leftovers of other cakes (with the addition of fruit) *20- NE.* †**pan kail** boiled, mashed kail *18-19.* **pan scone** a pancake, a drop scone *20- SW Bor.* **pan wood**, †**pan wod 1** small coal or dross (used as fuel for salt pans) *16-19, 20- historical.* **2** a measure of coal or dross (enough fuel to maintain the furnace of a salt pan for a week) *la17.* **caw yer pan in** to work very hard, to exert yourself to the point of exhaustion *20- C.* **caw yer pan oot** = *caw yer pan in la20- C.* [OE *panne, ponne*]

pan[1.2] /pan/ *v* **1** *of soil* to form into a layer impervious to rainwater *la19-.* **2** to tie a pan or kettle to a dog's tail, especially to make it go home *la19-20, 21- historical.* [see the noun]

pan[2.1] /pan/ *n* a purlin, a horizontal beam running the length of a roof from gable to gable attached to the main rafters *16-19, 20- SW.* **pan raip 1** a rope for securing thatch *19, 20- NE.* **2** a rope for trapping birds *20- Sh.* **pan tree 1** a beam running across the top of the walls of a house from which to suspend the chains for cooking pots; a similar shorter beam across the chimney opening *20- Ork.* **2** a horizontal roof-beam *la16-18.* [ME *panne*, EModE *pan*, Lat *panna*]

†**pan**[2.2] *v* to fit or furnish with beams *la15-17.* **pan and ruif** to build a roof *la15-17.* [see the noun]

pan *see* PAND

pancake /ˈpankek/ *n* **1** a small cake made with batter, a drop scone *20-.* **2** a children's game *la20- C.* [PAN[1.1] + CAKE]

panche *see* PAINCH

pand, **pawn**, **pan**, **pond**, †**pend** /pand, pɔn, pan, pɔnd/ *n* a valance *la16-.* [OFr *pante, pente* a bed hanging]

pand *see* PAWN[1.1], PAWN[1.1]

pander /ˈpandər/ *v* to wander about aimlessly *19- WC SW Bor.* [perhaps conflation of PALMER[1.1] with Eng *wander* or Sc DANDER]

pandie[1.1] /ˈpandi, ˈpande/ *n* a stroke with a leather strap or cane on the palm of the hand; a beating from a schoolteacher *19-20, 21- historical.* **get a pandie** to be beaten with a strap or cane *19-20, 21- historical.* [Lat *pande palmam, pande manum* stretch out your hand]

pandie[1,2] /'pandi, 'pande/ *v* to beat on the palm of the hand with a strap or cane; to punish schoolchildren *la19-20, 21- historical*. [see the noun]

†pandirt *n in Shetland* a state of excitement or panic; a muddle *la19*. [unknown, compare PANSHIT]

pandoor, **†pandore** /'pandor/ *n* **1** a large succulent type of oyster found in the Forth, especially around Prestonpans *la18-19, 20- EC*. **2** the entrance to or environs of a salt pan *la18*. **pandoor oyster** an oyster found in the Forth *18-19, 20- EC*. [PAN[1.1] + DOOR]

pandrap *see* PAN DROP

pan drop, pandrap /'pan drɔp, 'pandrap/ *n* a hard round peppermint-flavoured sweet, a mint imperial *la19-*. [PAN[1.1] + DRAP[1.1]]

pane *see* PAIN[1.1], PAIN[1.2], PAN[1.1], PEEN[2]

panel[1.1], **†pannell**, **†pennall** /'panəl/ *n* **1** *law* a person or people indicted before a criminal court, the accused *la16-*. **2** the children's panel *la20-*. **3** the place of arraignment in a court; the dock or the bar *17-19*. **4** *in Shetland and Orkney* a convicted person, a condemned criminal *17*. **†enter in panel** *law* to present for trial *la16-e17*. **†on the panel** *law* on trial for a criminal offence, arraigned *16-e17*. [perhaps ME *panel* a slip of parchment containing the jury list, AN *panel* list from which jurors are chosen]

panel[1.2], **†pannell** /'panəl/ *v* **1** *law* to bring before a court; to indict *la16-*. **2** to beat up; to thrash *la20- C*. [see the noun]

panel[2] /'panəl/ *n* a list of general practitioners registered as accepting patients under the National Health Service; a list of patients registered with a general practitioner on this list or with a medical practice *20-*. **on the panel 1** on the list of patients of a medical practitioner *20-*. **2** certified by a medical practitioner to be unfit for work because of illness *20-*. [related to PANEL[1.1]]

panel[3], **†pannell** /'panəl/ *n* **1** the padded underside of a saddle; a cloth or pad placed under a saddle *15-*. **2** a piece of embroidery *la15-*. **3** a section of wood fitting into a larger framework *16-*. **4** a rectangular pane of glass in a mullioned window *16-*. **5** a prefabricated section of wooden walling making up part of a wall *la16-*. **panelling** wooden panels or panel-work; a surface composed of panels *17-*. [ME *panel*, Lat *panellus* pad or lining of a saddle]

†panetar, paniter *n* the officer of a household in charge of the pantry *la14-16*. [ME *paneter*]

pang[1.1] /paŋ/ *v* **1** to pack a receptacle tightly; to cram or stuff *16-*. **2** to cram the stomach with food; to eat to excess *17-19, 20- NE*. **panged** pressed together, packed closely side by side *19, 20- EC*. **pang'd-fu** stuffed, full to overflowing *19, 20- NE Bor*. [unknown]

pang[1.2] /paŋ/ *adj* completely filled; overflowing *la16-*. **pang fu** stuffed, crammed *19-*. [unknown]

pani /'pani, 'pane/ *n* **1** water; rain *20- T EC Bor*. **2** a waterhen *20- Bor*. [Romany *pani*; compare Hindi *pānī*, *panee*, Sanskrit *pānīya* water, liquid]

paniter *see* PANETAR

pan loaf /'pan lof/ *n* **1** a loaf of bread with a hard smooth crust, baked in a pan or tin *la19-*. **2** an accent or way of speaking perceived as affected or over-refined *20-*. **pan loafy 1** *of accents* affected, over-refined *la20-*. **2** *of people* snobbish, having airs and graces *la20-*. [PAN[1.1] + LOAF]

pannell *see* PANEL[1.1], PANEL[1.2], PANEL[3]

panne velvet, †pan-velvot /'pan vɛlvət/ *n* **1** a fabric similar to velvet finished to give a high shine *la18-*. **2** a plush fabric similar to velvet but with a longer nap *la16-e17*. [MFr *panne (de velours)*]

Pans /panz/ *n* a nickname for Prestonpans, East Lothian *20-*. **the Pans** = PANS. [shortened form of *Prestonpans*]

†panse, pans *v* **1** to dress a wound *la16-18*. **2** to care for a person medically or surgically *la16-17*. **3** to pay heed; to care about *la16-e17*. **4** to think about; to consider *la15-17*. [OFr *panser*]

panshit, *Sh Ork* **panshite**, *NE* **panshine** /'panʃit; *Sh Ork* 'panʃʌit; *NE* 'panʃʌin/ *n* a state of excitement; a panic or muddle *19, 20- Sh Ork NE*. [unknown, compare PANDIRT]

pant[1] /pant/ *n* a public well or fountain *18- Bor*. **pant well** a public well *19- Bor*. [unknown, but compare PANI]

pant[2] /pant/ *n* a prank, a piece of fun *la19-*. [reduced form of Eng *pantomime*]

pant *see* PINT[2.1]

pantin, †pantoun /'pantən/ *n* a soft shoe or slipper *la15-17, la19- Sh*. [perhaps related to PANTOUFLE]

pantit *see* PENTIT

pantoufle, †pantoffil /pan'tufəl/ *n* a slipper *la15-19, 20- SW*. [MFr *pantoufle*]

pan-velvot *see* PANNE VELVET

pap[1], **†pape, †paup, †palp** /pap/ *n* **1** a nipple or breast *la14-*. **2** a conical hill; frequently in place-names *la15-*. **3** the sea anemone *Metridium dianthus* *18- NE EC*. **4** *fishing* a piece of whalebone attaching the weight to the hooked lines *19- Sh*. **5** a segment of an orange *20- NE*. **6** the teat of a female animal *la15-17*. **†pap bairn** a child at the breast, a baby *la18-19*. **pap milk** breast-milk *la19, 20- Sh*. **†pape in the craig** the uvula *17-e18*. **pap o the hause** the uvula *18-*. **pap o the throat** the uvula *la20- N NE*. [perhaps Lat *papilla* nipple]

pap[2] /pap/ *n weaving* a paste or dressing of flour and water used to give body to cloth *19, 20- C Bor*. **pappin, poppin** a paste used by weavers *19- Bor*. **†the pap of praise** recognition easily acquired but lacking value or substance *e19*. [Eng *pap* a semi-liquid food; compare MDu *pap* gruel; Ger *pappe* paste, glue]

pap[3.1] /pap/ *n* a tap or rap; a blow *19-*. [see the verb]

pap[3.2], **pop** /pap, pɔp/ *v* **1** to touch or strike lightly; to tap or rap on a surface *18-*. **2** to aim an object, to throw or shoot a missile *18-*. **3** to make a rapping, tapping or plopping sound *la18-*. **4** to beat; to thrash *19-*. **5** to fall or drop lightly; to plop down *19-*. **6** to strike a target; to pelt with missiles *la19-*. **7** to sound a car horn *20-*. **8** to go in or out; to make a brief visit *la20-*. **†pappin** a beating *la19*. **†pap-in** a drink made of light ale and oatmeal with a small quantity of whisky or brandy *18-19*. [onomatopoeic]

paparap /'papərap/ *n fishing* hooks lashed together and fastened to a weighted string, used when poaching to drag a line out of a river *19- NE*. [perhaps PAP[3.2], as in *popper up*]

Pape, paip /pep/ *n* **1** the Pope *la14-*. **2** *derogatory* a member of the Roman Catholic Church *20-*. **papery** Roman Catholicism *la16-*. [Lat *pāpa*]

pape *see* PAIP, PAP[1]

papejay *see* PAPINGO

paper[1.1], **peyper, pipper, pepper, †peper, †paiper, †peaper** /'pepər, 'pɪpər, 'pɛpər/ *n* **1** a material made in thin sheets from fibrous matter *la14-*. **2** a piece of paper; a document *16-*. **3** the paper to which pins, needles or buttons are secured for sale *la16-*. **4** a printed or written proclamation or notice *la16-19, 20- Sh*. **†paper buke** a notebook *la16-17*. **†paper crier** a newspaper vendor *18*. **paper lead** lead foil *la19, 20- Sh*. **†paper minister** *derogatory* a clergyman who read out his sermon (viewed as a sign of a lack of inspiration or real conviction) *19*. **paper note** a (one-pound sterling) banknote *la19-*. **†paper priest** = *paper minister la18*. **paper pound** a one-pound sterling banknote *la19-20, 21- historical*. **†the paper** the manuscript of a sermon *18-19*.

work on paper to deal in or live on credit *la19- NE*. [ME *papir*]

paper¹·² /'pepər/ *v* to insert a notice in a newspaper concerning a person or thing (such as an accusation of fault or repudiation of debts) *la19-20, 21- historical*. [see the noun]

papingo, †**papingay**, †**papejay**, †**popinjay** /'papɪŋgo/ *n* **1** a parrot *16-19, 20- literary*. **2** a representation of a parrot used as a target in archery *la16-19, 20- WC*. [ME *papejai*, OFr *papegai*]

papish¹·¹ /'pepɪʃ/ *n derogatory* a Roman Catholic *la16-*. †**papisher** a Roman Catholic *e19*. [see the adj]

papish¹·² /'pepɪʃ/ *adj* Roman Catholic *la16-*. [PAPE + adj-forming suffix]

pappin *see* PAP², PAP³·²

†**papple**¹·¹, **popill** *n* **1** a bubble in boiling liquid *e19*. **2** a bulge (caused by a bubble) *17*. [see the verb]

papple¹·², †**popill**, †**pople** /'papəl/ *v* **1** to boil or bubble up; to seethe *15-*. **2** *of cooking fat* to sizzle or splutter *19-*. **3** *of people* to be too hot; to be extremely excited *19*. [onomatopoeic]

†**papple**³ *n* the corncockle *Agrostemma githago 18-19*. [Eng *popple*]

parad, **parade** *see* PARAUD

Paradise, †**Paradis** /'parədʌɪs/ *n* **1** Heaven *la14-*. **2** a nickname given by fans of Celtic Football Club to Celtic Park football stadium in Glasgow *20-*. [ME *paradis*, Lat *paradīsus*]

paraffin /'parəfɪn/ *n* **1** a flammable fuel from coal or shale *19-*. **2** a smart, flashy appearance; stylish clothing *20-*. **paraffin ile** *n* an oily flammable liquid used as fuel *la19-*. **2** *rhyming slang* style *20-*. [Ger *paraffin*]

†**paraffle** *n* a flourish, an ostentatious display *e19*. [Fr *paraphe* a flourish added to a signature]

†**parage** *n* **1** noble lineage *la15-e16*. **2** equality in rank *16*. [ME *parage*]

parala *see* PUREALE

†**paraling**, **parralling**, **perrelling** *n* **1** equipment, furniture *la15-e17*. **2** an ornamental trimming for clothing *la16-e17*. **3** a wall-hanging *la15-e16*. [aphetic form of APPARELLING]

†**paralsie**, **paralisie**, **parlesy** *n* paralysis, palsy; a paralytic tremor or weakness *la14-19*. [ME *paralisi*]

†**paraphernals**, **paropharnalis** *npl law* the personal effects of a married woman, which remained her own property after her marriage *16-19*. [Lat *paraphernālia* married woman's property]

paraphrase, †**perraphrasis**, †**parapris** /'parəfrez/ *n* **1** a free rendering or rewording of something written or spoken *la16-*. **2** *Presbyterian Church* a collection of metrical versions of scriptural passages used for congregational singing *18-*. [Lat *paraphrasis*]

paraud, **parawd**, **parade**, **parad** /pə'rɔd, pə'red, pə'rad/ *n* **1** a procession, a march *la17-*. **2** a mustering of troops *la17-*. **3** an ostentatious display *la18-*. [Fr *parade*]

†**parcage** *n in documents concerning disputes on the Anglo-Scottish border* the act of enclosing stray cattle or sheep; the fine payable to obtain their release *la15-16*. [MFr *parcage*; compare PARK¹·¹]

parcel, **parcell** *see* PAIRCEL

parch *see* PERCH

parchment *see* PAIRCHMENT

parcial *see* PAIRCEL

parciall *see* PARTIAL

parciounar *see* PORTIONER

pardoos /pər'dus/ *n* a thump; a resounding blow, a violent fall *la19, 20- Sh*. [intensifying prefix *per* + DOOSE¹·¹]

pare /per/ *v* **1** to cut away the outside or excess; to trim or peel *la14-*. **2** to destroy pasture by overgrazing or arable land by overcropping *20- Sh*. **3** to pine; to become emaciated *20- Sh*.

†**pairin-flooer** a coarse meal or flour made from the husks of the grain *la19*. †**pairing-meal** = *pairin-flooer 19*. †**pare and burn** to burn the top layer of vegetation cut from a field before ploughing, the ashes being used as manure *18-e19*. [ME *paren*]

pare *see* PAIR¹, PAIR²

pareeshioner, †**parochinar**, †**parischinar** /pə'rɪʃənər/ *n* a parishioner, a member or inhabitant of a parish *la15-*. Compare PAIRISH, PAROCHIN. [PAROCHIN + agent suffix]

paregale *see* PEREGALL¹·²

pareis *see* PAIRISH

Pareis *see* PARIS

parent, **pawrent** /'perənt, 'pɔrənt/ *n* a person's father or mother *la15-*. [ME *parent*, Lat *parens*]

parewsse *see* PERUSE

†**pargen**, **pergen** *v* to roughcast, to plaster *e16*. **pargenar** a plasterer *16*. [OFr *pargeter*; compare SPARGEN]

parioch *see* PAIRISH

Paris, **Pairis**, †**Pareis** /'parɪs, 'perɪs/ *n* the capital city of France *la15-*. [MFr *Paris*]

†**Paris black** *n* a black fabric used for making clothes *16-e17*. [PARIS + BLACK¹·¹]

Paris bun, **Pairis bun** /'parɪs bʌn, 'perɪs bʌn/ *n* a sweet, sugar-topped, sponge-like bun *20-*. Compare PAIRISER. [PARIS + BUN]

parischin *see* PAROCHIN

parischinar *see* PAREESHIONER

parish *see* PAIRISH

parishen *see* PAROCHIN

Parisian barm /pə'rɪzɪən barm/ *n* flour, malt and water stocked or stored with mature or old barm and used as a medium for the growth of yeast *20-*. [Eng *Parisian* + BARM¹·¹]

park¹·¹, **pairk**, **perk**, **paurk** /park, perk, pɛrk, pɔrk/ *n* **1** an enclosed piece of land, a forest or woodland used for hunting *12-*. **2** land set aside for recreation; gardens; a recreation-ground *16-*. **3** a meadow, grazing-land; an area of enclosed farm-ground, a field *la16-*. **parkie** a nickname for the keeper or attendant of public recreation grounds or gardens *20-*. **park dyke** a field wall *16-*. **park lamb** a lamb reared in a field as opposed to open hill pasture *19-*. [OFr *parc*]

park¹·² /park/ *v* **1** to enclose (forest) land; to form land into fields *16-19, 20- Sh*. **2** to rear animals in a field or enclosure instead of on free range *la18-19, 20- Sh*. **3** to drive animals out to pasture *20- NE*. **4** to lodge troops in a camp or fortification *e16*. [see the noun]

parkin *see* PERKIN

†**parks**, **parques** *npl* the Fates *la16*. [Lat *Parcae*]

parl, **parle** /parl/ *n* a ring fixed to the mast of older types of fishing-boat to control the raising and lowering of the sail *la19- Ork NE*. **parly** a boat using this type of rig *la19- Ork*. [Eng *parrel*]

parleis *see* PAIRLS

parlesy *see* PARALSIE

parley¹·¹, **parlie** /'parle/ *n* **1** a discussion between opposing armies; a truce arranged for this purpose *17-*. **2** *children's games* a state of neutrality, a period of truce *18- N NE T EC*; compare BARLEY². **3** *children's games* neutral ground, 'home' *la19, 20- Uls*. [EModE *parley*]

parley¹·² /'parle/ *interj children's games* a call for a truce or pause *18-*. [see the noun]

parliament¹, **pairlament**, **perlament** /'parləmənt, 'pɛrləmənt, 'pɛrləmənt/ *n* **1** a formal assembly or council summoned by a monarch *la14-*. **2** the legislative assembly of Great Britain which replaced the parliament of Scotland by the Act of Union in 1707 *18-*. **3** (the buildings housing) the Scottish Government, the legislative body

parliament which has devolved powers from the British Parliament at Westminster, originally as the Scottish Executive *la20-*. **4** the original parliament of Scotland, abolished by the Act of Union in 1707 *la14-e18*. **5** a convention, conference or council *16-e17*. **parliamenter** a member of Parliament *la17-19, 20- Sh T*. †**parliamentin, parliamenting** a discussion, a conversation *la16-e19*. **Parliament Hall 1** the hall of Parliament House in Edinburgh, the meeting place of the Scottish Parliament from 1639 to 1707 and thereafter the anteroom to the Court of Session *e18, la18- historical*. **2** apartments in Edinburgh and Stirling Castles where the medieval Scottish Parliament met *20- historical*. **Parliament House 1** the building in Edinburgh housing the Court of Session *18-*. **2** the building in the High Street of Edinburgh where the original Scottish Parliament met *la16-e18*. **parliament man** a member of Parliament; an experienced parliamentarian *17-*. [ME *parlement*]

†**parliament**[2] *n* a part of a cloak or gown *e16*. [perhaps aphetic form of Eng *apparelment*]

parliamentary /parləˈmɛntəri/ *adj* of or relating to a parliament *la17-*. **parliamentary church** a QUOAD SACRA church especially in the Highlands and Islands, created by Acts of Parliament in 1810 and 1824 by dividing up large parishes *19, 20- historical*. **parliamentary road** a road built and maintained jointly by the government and local landowners under the Highland Roads and Bridges Act of 1803 *19, 20- historical*. **Parliamentary school** a parish school connected to a parliamentary church *19, 20- historical*. [PARLIAMENT[1] + adj-forming suffix]

Parliamo Glasgow /parliˈamo glazgo/ *n* a type of speech supposedly used on the streets of Glasgow *la20-*. [from a series of sketches created by the comedian Stanley Baxter]

parlie[1] /ˈparle, ˈparli/ *n colloquial* a name for the Scottish Parliament *la20-*. [shortened form of PARLIAMENT[1.1]]

parlie[2] /ˈparle, ˈparli/ *n* a crisp, rectangular, ginger biscuit *19-*. **parlie biscuit** a ginger biscuit *la20-*. **parlie cake** a ginger biscuit *la20-*. [shortened form of Eng *parliament-cake*]

parlie *see* PARLEY[1.1]

paroche *see* PAIRISH

parochial /pəˈroxɪəl/ *adj* of or concerning a parish *16-*. †**parochial board** an elected body set up in each parish by the Poor Law Amendment (Scotland) Act of 1845, responsible for the Poor Law provisions and much of the parish administration *19*. †**parochial school** one of the schools set up by the Church of Scotland *la18-19*. †**parochial visitation** a periodical inspection by the Presbytery of the religious affairs of a parish *18-19*. [ME *parochial*, Lat *parochiālis*]

parochin, †**parishen**, †**parischin**, †**prochin** /ˈparəʃɪn/ *n* **1** the inhabitants or members of a parish *la15-*. **2** a parish district *15-19, 20- literary*; compare PAIRISH. †**toun and parochin** *see* TOUN. [ME *parishen*]

parochinar *see* PAREESHIONER

†**parokett** *n* a parrot *16-17*. [MFr *perroquet, paroquet*]

paropharnalis *see* PARAPHERNALS

parpall *see* PAIRPLE

parpen[1], †**parpan** /ˈparpən/ *n* **1** a stone which passes through the entire thickness of a wall *la15-*. **2** the parapet of a bridge *19-*. **3** a partition wall *la16-19, 20- Bor*. †**parpenwall** a partition wall *16-e19*. [ME *perpen*]

parpen[2] /ˈparpən/ *adj of a door or window frame* in exact alignment; exactly parallel or perpendicular *la19- NE*. [probably reduced form of Eng *perpendicular*]

parquere *see* PERQUEIR[1.2]

parques *see* PARKS

parr /par/ *n* a young salmon with dark stripes on its side, at the stage before it becomes a SMOUT *la18-*. [unknown]

parralling *see* PARALING

parrat *see* PARROT

parreck *see* PARROCK[1.1]

parritch, parridge, porridge, purritch, †**porritch** /ˈparɪtʃ, ˈparɪdʒ, ˈpɔrɪdʒ, ˈpʌrɪtʃ/ *n* **1** rolled oats or oatmeal boiled in salted water or milk; food in general *la18-*. **2** a thick soup *17*. †**parritch-cap** a wooden porridge-bowl *la18-e19*. **parritch-spurtle** a stick used for stirring porridge *la18-*. **parritch-stick** = *parritch-spurtle 19-*. [altered form of POTTAGE]

parrock[1.1], **parreck, parroch,** †**parrok** /ˈparək, ˈparəx/ *n* **1** an enclosure or paddock *la13-*. **2** a sheep-pen used at lambing time *19- SW Bor*. **3** a group of people, animals or objects closely packed or huddled together *19- NE T*. [OE *pearroc* a fence or enclosure]

parrock[1.2] /ˈparək/ *v* to confine or enclose; to herd together; to crowd *la18-19, 20- Bor*. [see the noun]

parrot, †**parrat** /ˈparət/ *n* = PARROT COAL *17-*. [unknown]

parrot coal /ˈparət kol/ *n* cannel coal, a highly volatile bituminous coal which ignites easily and is much used in the maufacture of coal oil and gas *la16-*. [unknown first element + COAL]

parry /ˈpare/ *v* **1** to turn aside; to ward off a blow *19-*. **2** to waste time, to dawdle; to equivocate *la19- T EC Bor*. **parry wi** to meddle with; to have dealings with *19- NE T C*. [Fr *parer*]

parrymauk, parrymyawk, peeriemyak /pariˈmɔk, pariˈmjɔk, piriˈmjak/ *n* an exact replica, a duplicate *20- NE T*. [perhaps Eng *par, peer* equal + MAKE or MAIK]

Pars /parz/ *n* a nickname for Dunfermline Athletic Football Club *20-*. [unknown]

parsell *see* PERSEL

parsenere *see* PORTIONER

parsment *see* PARTIMENT

parson, †**parsone,** †**persoun,** †**person** /ˈparsən/ *n Christian Church* a rector, vicar or other clergyman *la14-*. **parson gray** a dark shade of grey, the grey worn by a clergyman *19-*. [Lat *persōna*]

parson *see* PERSON

parsonage, †**personage** /ˈparsənədʒ/ *n* the benefice or living of a parson *la15-*. †**parsonage teinds** the tithe of grain given to a parson *la16-17*. [ME *personage*]

parsone *see* PARSON

part *see* PAIRT[1.1], PAIRT[1.2]

partake *see* PAIRT-TAK

partaker *see* PAIRT-TAKAR

partakin *see* PAIRT-TAKING

partan, †**pertane** /ˈpartən/ *n* **1** a crab, especially the common edible crab *Cancer pagurus 15-*. **2** an unattractive, bad-tempered or foolish person *la19-*. **partan cairtie** a toy cart made from a crab's shell *la19- Ork NE EC*. **partan bree** crab soup *20-*. **partan pie** a dish of seasoned crab meat cooked and served in its shell *18-*. **partan tae, partan's tae** a crab's claw *16-*. **partan-taed** pigeon-toed *la20- Sh NE T*. **as fu as a partan** brimful *la19- Ork NE*. [Gael *partan* a small crab]

parteecular, parteeklar *see* PARTICULAR[1.1], PARTICULAR[1.2], PARTICULAR[1.3]

partial, †**parciall,** †**pertiale** /ˈparʃəl/ *adj* **1** unduly favouring one party *la15-*. **2** of or relating to a part rather than the whole; particular, individual *16-*. **partial counsel** *law* advice or information given improperly to a witness in a case by a judge, juror, witness or other member of the court and constituting a ground for excluding this evidence as biased *16-19, 20- historical*. [ME *parcial*, Lat *partiālis*]

partibus /ˈpartɪbʌs/ *n law* a note written in the margin of a Court of Session summons listing the contestants in a case and their counsel and solicitors *18-*. [Lat *partibus* the parties being]

†**particate, particat** *n* **1** a measure of length, six ells (approximately 5.64 metres) *la15*. **2** a square measure of land consisting of 1/4 of a Scots acre; a piece of land of this size *la16-18*. **particate-man** *in the Borders* the owner or tenant of a particate of land *18-19*. [Lat *particāta*; compare Lat *pertica* a measuring rod]

particular[1.1]**, particler, parteecular, parteeklar** /pərˈtɪkjulər, pərˈtɪklər, parˈtɪkjulər, parˈtɪklər/ *n* a detail; an individual person or thing; a private concern *la16-*. [see the adj]

particular[1.2]**, particler, parteecular, parteeklar,** †**particular** /pərˈtɪkjulər, pərˈtɪklər, parˈtɪkjulər, parˈtɪklər/ *adj* **1** specific to an individual person or thing; separate; detailed *15-*. **2** private, personal, not public; confidential *15-19, 20- Sh Ork N EC*. **3** remarkable, exceptional; odd, peculiar *16-19, 20- Sh Ork T*. **4** clean, hygenic *20-*. †**particularie** individually, in detail *la15-e17*. **in particular** especially; individually *la15-*. [ME *particuler*, Lat *particulāris*]

particular[1.3]**, particler, parteecular, parteeklar** /pərˈtɪkjulər, pərˈtɪklər, parˈtɪkjulər, parˈtɪklər/ *adv* **1** particularly, markedly, especially *la19-*. **2** individually, separately *la16*. [see the adj]

particularity /partɪkjuˈlarɪte/ *n* **1** a detail, a particular; an idiosyncrasy *la16-19, 20- Sh T*. **2** self-interest, private advantage; a private grievance or feud *16-e17*. [EModE *particularitie*]

†**particule** *n* a small part of anything, a detail, a particle *16-e18*. [MFr *particule*, Lat *particula*]

partie *see* PAIRTY[1.1]

†**partiment, parsment** *n* a division or company *e16*. [Lat *partimentum*]

partiner *see* PAIRTNER

†**partisan** *n* a long-handled spear *17-e19*. **partisan staff** = PARTISAN *17*. [EModE *partisan*, Ital *partigiana*, the weapon used by partisans]

†**partising, pairtissing** *n* **1** a formal division of land or goods into shares or portions *la14-e17*. **2** *law* a legal separation or divorce *la15-e17*. [AN *partisun* partition, separation with verbal noun suffix]

partle /ˈpartəl/ *v* to waste time; to work in a half-hearted way *la18-19, 20- WC*. [perhaps variant of PAWT[1.2] with frequentative suffix]

partrik *see* PAIRTRICK

part-tak *see* PAIRT-TAK

part-takar *see* PAIRT-TAKAR

part-taking *see* PAIRT-TAKING

party *see* PAIRTY[1.3]

†**party observer** *n law* the party who kept the terms of a contract, in penalty clause of contract, as against the party who failed to do so *17-18*. [Eng *party* + OBSERVER]

pas *see* PASS[1.1], PASS[1.2]

Pasch *see* PACE

pase *see* PAIS

paseboord *see* PAISBUIRD

pash[1] /paʃ/ *n* the head, the brain *la17-19, 20- literary*. [unknown]

pash[2] /paʃ/ *v* to smash or crush *la17-19, 20- literary*. [onomatopoeic]

Pask *see* PACE

pasment, †**passment,** †**pesment,** †**passement** /ˈpasmənt/ *n* decorative edging; trimming or braid *16-19, 20- literary*. †**pasmentit** trimmed with braid or other material *16-19*. [MFr *passement*]

†**pasneip** *n* a parsnip *la16-e18*. [ME *passenepe*]

pasper, †**paspier** /ˈpaspər/ *n* the plant samphire *Crithmum maritimum 17- SW*. [MFr *passe pierre, percepierre* samphire, saxifrage]

†**paspie** *n* = PASPER *la16-17*. [reduced form of PASPER + -IE[1]]

paspier *see* PASPER

pass[1.1]**, pace,** †**pas,** †**pais,** †**pays** /pas, pes/ *n* **1** a step; a way of walking, a rate of progression *la14-*. **2** a narrow passage, a defile *la14-*. **3** a measure of distance or height *15-*. **4** a predicament; a critical position *15-*. **5** the act of passing, passage *la15-*. **6** written permission to go to or from a place *la16-*. **7** a passage between looms in a weaving shop or machines in a factory; a team of weavers or other workers *la18-19, 20- WC SW*. **8** an indoor passage or corridor *la18-19, 20- Uls*. **9** the passage between the pews in a church, an aisle *la19, 20- NE*. **10** a passage of writing *15-e17*. †**on pace** quickly *la15*. †**the pace of Calies** the Straits of Dover *16*. **the pace** = *the pace of Calies*. [AN *pas*, ME *pas*]

pass[1.2]**,** †**pas** /pas/ *v* **1** to go or proceed; to depart; to travel; to cross *la14-*. **2** *of time* to elapse; *of a person* to spend time *la14-*. **3** to surmount or go beyond; to surpass or exceed; to excel; to transcend *la14-*. **4** *of an action, activity or event* to take place, to happen *la14-*. **5** to come to an end; to die *la14-*. **6** *of a route or boundary* to lead or run from one place to another *15-*. **7** to attain a required standard; to be found acceptable or be approved *la15-*. **8** to transmit *la15-*. **9** to give up or abandon *18-*. **10** to serve or sit on a jury *15-e20, la20- historical*. **11** to overlook or disregard; to pardon or waive *15-19*. **12** *law* to issue or execute a grant or warrant; *of a grant or award* to be issued *la14-17*. **13** *of an inquiry or decision* to take place; to be put into effect *la15-17*. **passer** a large iron hoop for holding the staves of a barrel in position during construction *20- NE*. †**passit by, past by** gone by, at an end, finished *15-16*. †**pass gilt** money acceptable as currency *la17*. **pass key** a key which operates a particular lock or any one of a set of locks *17-*. **pass lock** one of a set of locks operated by the same key *17-19, 20- N EC*. **pass-remarkable** too quick to make personal comments *20-*. **it passes me** it is beyond my comprehension *la19-*. †**pass upon 1** *of an adjudicator or judge* to proceed to give judgment on *la15-e17*. **2** *of a grant, award or decree* to be issued or given effect *la15-e17*. **3** to make an attack on *16*. †**pass fra** to renounce or abandon a right *15-17*. †**pass the irnis** *of an issue of coins* to be struck and put into circulation *la16-17*. **pass our 1** to cross a stretch of water *15-*. **2** *of time, an occasion or event* to run its course, to come to an end *la15-*. **pass the great seal** to be authenticated by the attachment of the great seal with the authority of the Chancery of Scotland or of the Court of Session *16-*. †**pass the seals** to be authenticated by being sealed with the appropriate seal *16-18*. **pass the word to** to talk or converse with *la19- Sh N*. **pass water** *of a bucket* to leak *la19, 20- EC*. [ME *passen*]

passage[1] /ˈpasadʒ/ *n* **1** the action or fact of going; a journey, travel; departure *la14-*. **2** the means of passing freely; leave to proceed; unimpeded progress *15-*. **3** a way or route; a crossing, ferry or ford *15-*. **4** a corridor or a tunnel *la15-*. **5** a water course, gutter or conduit *16-17*. **6** money which was current or generally acceptable; currency *la15-17*. **7** a military or naval expedition *la15-e16*. †**have passage** *of legal documents* to become legal; to pass into law *16-e17*. †**lang passage** prolonged time, a long distance *la15-e16*. [ME *passage*]

†**passage**[2] *n* dice *e16*. [ME *passage*, EModE *passage* the name of a game of dice]

passager *see* PASSENGER
passand *see* PASSING²
passement *see* PASMENT
passenger, †passinger, †passager /'pasəndʒər/ *n* 1 a person conveyed in a vehicle or a ship *la16-*. 2 a passing traveller, a passer-by *16-19*. 3 a ferry-boat *16-e17*. [ME *passager*]
passing¹ /'pasɪŋ/ *n* 1 the action of going or proceeding *la14-*. 2 death *15-*. 3 the action of sanctioning *la15-*. 4 the act of crossing; a crossing-place; the right to cross *15-17*. [verbal noun from PASS¹,²]
passing², **†passand** /'pasɪŋ/ *adj* 1 extreme, excessive *la15-*. 2 *of money* legally current *la17*. [participial adj from PASS¹,²]
passinger *see* PASSENGER
passion, patience, patients, †passioun /'paʃən, 'peʃəns, 'peʃənts/ *n* 1 pain, suffering; religious martyrdom *la14-*. 2 strong emotion, vehemence, ardour *la15-*. 3 an attack of disease, a fit *la15-16*. **ma patience!** an exclamation expressing wonder, disbelief or exasperation *la19, 20- Sh NE T Uls*. **patient of death, †patients o dead, †passioun of dede** the agony of death, death throes *15-19, 20- Uls*. [Lat *passio*, ME *passioun*; *patient* and *patience* forms by erroneous association]
passit *see* PAST¹,¹, PAST¹,³
passive /'pasɪv/ *adj of a legal heir* liable for the debts of an estate *la16-*. **†passive debt** *law* a debt owed to another *e18*. **passive title** the title or right of succession to an inherited estate which carries with it liability for the debts of the granter *la17-*. [ME *passif*, EModE *passif*]
passment *see* PASMENT
passover, pass-over /'pasovər/ *n* an intentional omission; something overlooked or misunderstood *19, 20- NE T Uls*. [PASS¹,² + OWER¹,³]
past¹,¹, **†passit** /past/ *adj* 1 gone by, at an end *la15-*. 2 *after a date* last, preceding: ◊*I haena seen him for a year past 20-*. 3 having reached a specified age on one's last birthday: ◊*Wee Rab's nine past 20-*. [from ptp of PASS¹,²]
past¹,² /past/ *adv* 1 so as to go by *la18-*. 2 on one side, out of the way *19-*. 3 over, done with *19-*.
past¹,³, **†passit** /past/ *prep* beyond *15-*. **not to be able to see past someone** to be obsessed with someone's virtues or merits; to favour someone to the exclusion of all others *la20-*. **past a'** unspeakable, unbelievable, intolerable: ◊*thae loons, they're jist past a' la19, 20- Sh N EC*. **past memory of man** from time immemorial *la15-*. **past ordinar** outstanding, remarkable, exceptional *19, 20- Uls*. **past yersel** beside oneself with fury *20-*. [see the adj]
†pastance, pastans *n* recreation, pleasure *16*. [MFr *passe temps, passetans*]
paster¹, **†pasture** /'pastər/ *n* the pastern of a horse (between the fetlock and the hoof) *la15-*. **†pasturit, pastered** having pasterns of a specified sort *la15-e18*. [OFr, MFr *pasture* shackle for a horse's foot]
paster²,¹, **pasture, †pastour** /'pastər, 'pastjər/ *n* grass or herbage used as grazing for livestock; the right to grazing *la14-*. **pasturage** 1 grazing, pastureland *16-*. 2 the action, occupation or practice of allowing grazing animals to feed on grass *16-*. 3 *law* the right of pasturing livestock on another's land *la16-*. **†pasturall** pastureland; grazing *la16*. [ME *pastur*, Lat *pāstūra* place suitable for grazing animals, action of feeding animals]
paster²,², **pasture, †pastour** /'pastər, 'pastjər/ *v* to graze, to feed on grassland *15-*. [see the noun]
pat, pot, poat, pote, †pott, †poit /pat, pɔt, pot/ *n* 1 a vessel, container or cooking-pot *la14-*. 2 the flat stone or counter used in the game of hopscotch *la19- N NE*. 3 a kind of whisky still in which heat is applied directly to the pot; originally one made by adding an attachment to a cauldron-type cooking pot *la18-19*. **pottle** a potful *la18- NE T*. **pottie heid** meat from the head of a cow or pig, boiled, shredded and served cold in jelly made from the stock; compare POTTED HEID *la19- WC SW*. **pot-barley** barley from which the outer husk has been removed in milling, used for making broth *la18-*. **pot-black** very black or dirty *20- C Uls*. **pot-bool, †pot boul** a device for lifting or hanging a pot *la16-17, 20- Ork N*. **pat -brod** a (wooden) pot-lid *17- Sh T EC*. **pat-brose** a kind of porridge boiled very briefly *la19- NE*. **†pot-clip** = *pot-bool la16-e18*. **pot fit** one of the legs or feet of a cauldron pot *20- NE*. **†pot-head** *in Shetland* the caaing whale, the long-finned pilot whale *Globicephala melas la19*. **pot-lid** *curling* a shot which exactly covers the tee; the tee itself *19-*. **pot lug** the ear or loop by which a pot is suspended *18, 20- Sh Ork*. **†pot pece** a gun with a large bore; a mortar *la16-17*. **potsker, pottskerd** a broken pot (kept to hold the oil from fish-livers) *20- Sh Ork*. **pot-stick** a stick for stirring food in cooking, a spurtle *19- SW Uls*. **pot-still** a whisky still *la18-*. **pot-tastit** tasting of the pot; stale, unpalatable *la19, 20- Ork NE*. **†gar the pat play broon** to provide food; to support a person *19*. **gin I be pottie ye're pannie** you are as bad as I am, you are in no position to criticize *la19- NE*. **†mak the pat play** to provide food, to support (a person)*18-19*. **out like a pot fit** *of people* in a state of discord, not on speaking terms *la20- NE*. **stick out like a pot fit** to be very noticeable *20- NE*. [OE *pott*]
pat *see* PATE, PIT²
patatie *see* PITAWTIE
pate, †pat /pet/ *n* 1 a person's head, brain or intellect *17-*. 2 the skin of a calf's head *la17*. [unknown]
pate *see* PEAT¹,¹
†patelet, patlet, paitlat *n* a covering for the neck and upper chest worn by women *16-17*. Compare PAITCLAITH. [MFr *patelette* a band of stuff]
patent¹,¹ /'petənt/ *n* a document conferring a right, appointment or concession for the development of a trade or occupation *la14-*. **patenter, †patentar** a person who has been granted a patent *17-*. [shortened form of Eng *letters patent* or ME *patent* open; compare AN *lettres patent*]
patent¹,² /'petənt/ *adj* 1 clear, evident *la15-*. 2 *of a door* wide open, unobstructed *la15-e19*. 3 *of a building or route* open to all, generally accessible *16-e19*. 4 of open aspect, exposed *la15-17*. 5 liable to harm *16*. **†make patent doors** *of a messenger-at-arms* to force an entry with the authority of a warrant in an action of poinding *la16-e18*. **†the most patent door** the main door of a church or other public building where public proclamations were made *la16-19*. [EModE *patent*]
patent *see* POTENT²
patesar *see* PATISAR
†path *v* to pave *16-18*. **pathit, paithit** paved *la15-e19*. [from the noun PETH]
path *see* PETH
†pathement¹,¹, **paithment** *n* a surface paved with stones or tiles; the stones or tiles used for paving *15-17*. [PETH with noun-forming suffix -*ment*, analogous to Eng *pavement*]
†pathement¹,² *v* to pave *e17*. **pethmentit, pedmented** paved *la16-e17*. [see the noun]
pathment *see* PAIDMINT
patie /'peti/ *n* the puffin *Fratercula arctica 19- WC*. [diminutive form of *Peter* or *Patrick*]
patience, patients *see* PASSION
patill *see* PATTLE¹,¹, PATTLE¹,²

†**patisar, patesar, pottisear** *n* a pastry-cook *16-e17*. **patisserie, potissarie** pastries *la16*. [MFr *pasticier, pasticerie*]
Pat Lally /pat 'lale/ *n* an alcoholic drink *la20-*. [rhyming slang using the name of a former Glasgow Lord Provost in place of the word SWALLIE[1.1]]
patlet *see* PATELET
patlok lokk *see* PADDOCK-LOK
†**Patrickmes** *n* **1** the feast of St Patrick, 17 March *la15-e18*. **2** the date of one of the annual fairs in Dumbarton *17*. [the name of the saint *Patrick* + MASS[2]]
patrimonial /patrɪˈmonɪəl/ *adj* **1** *law* referring to property or money; pecuniary *la18-*. **2** constituting part of the patrimony of a bishopric *17*. [EModE *patrymonyall*, Lat *patrīmōniālis*]
†**patrociny, patrocine** *n* patronage *la16-e18*. [Lat *patrōcinium*]
patron[1], †**patroun**, †**pawtron** /ˈpatrən, ˈpetrən/ *n* **1** a protector; a guardian saint or deity *15-*. **2** *Christian Church* a person holding the right of presentation to a church benefice *15-*. **3** a (regular) customer *la19-*. **4** the master of a ship *la15-16*. [ME *patroun*]
†**patron**[2], **patroun** *n* a paper container for the charge of a cannon or pistol; a paper cartridge *16-17*. [Ger *Patrone*, MLG *patrone* a cartridge]
patron *see* PAITTERN
†**patrontash, patrontasche** *n* a pouch or case for holding cartridges and other ammunition *la17-e18*. [Du *patroontasch* Ger *patronentasche*]
patroun *see* PATRON[1], PATRON[2]
patter[1.1], **paiter** /ˈpatər, ˈpetər/ *n* fast, fluent talk (intended to impress) *19-*. **gie's yer patter** give me your news *20-*. [see the verb]
patter[1.2], **paiter** /ˈpetər, ˈpatər/ *v* **1** to repeat prayers rapidly or mechanically *16-19, 20- historical*. **2** to talk in a persistent or monotonous way; to chatter on endlessly *19, 20- C Bor*. [shortened form of Lat *pater noster* Our Father]
patter[2] /ˈpatər/ *v* to trample ground *la19, 20- NE WC*. [perhaps a frequentative of PAWT[1.2], with influence from Eng *pat* to beat gently]
patter *see* PAITER
pattern *see* PAITTERN
pattle[1.1], **pettle**, †**patill** /ˈpatəl, ˈpɛtəl/ *n* a small spade-like tool, used especially for clearing the mould board of a plough *la14-*; compare PAIDLE[3]. **pattle shaft** the handle of a spade-like tool *la19, 20- Sh*. **pattle tree 1** the handle of a spade-like tool *19- Sh Ork*. **2** a notched wooden stick for removing a hook from a fish's throat *20- Sh Ork*. [unknown; compare later PAIDLE[1.2]]
pattle[1.2], †**patill**, †**paittel** /ˈpatəl/ *v* **1** to poke or dabble in water or mud *la19, 20- Sh Ork*. **2** to toddle, to take short steps *20- Sh Ork*. **3** to trample ground *20- Ork*; compare PATTER[2]. **4** to scrape with a small spade-like tool *la16*. [see the noun]
pattren *see* PAITTERN
patty, *Ork* **paddy**, *N* **potye** /ˈpati; *Ork* ˈpadi; *N* ˈpɔtji/ *n* a (young) pet or domesticated pig *19- Sh Ork N*. **paddy tang** the seaweed *Pelvetia canaliculata* eaten by pigs *20- Sh Ork*. [unknown; compare Dan *pattegris* a sucking pig, from *patte* a teat]
pauchle[1.1], **pochle**, **pockle**, **poackle**, †**pechle**, †**pauchald**, †**pakkald** /ˈpɔxəl, ˈpɒkəl, ˈpokəl/ *n* **1** a small bundle or parcel; a load of goods or merchandise *16-19, 20- EC Bor Uls*. **2** a small quantity of something taken by an employee from their employer, either furtively or as a perquisite; goods or money acquired dishonestly *20- EC Bor*. **3** the personal belongings of a person living and working away from home *20- T EC*. **4** a swindle, a piece of trickery *la20- C*. **5** a packet of letters *16-17*. [derivative of PACK[1.1] with unexplained ending]
pauchle[1.2], **pochle**, **pockle** /ˈpɔxəl, ˈpɒkəl/ *v* **1** to steal or pilfer; to embezzle *20-*. **2** to cheat; to rig an election or game *20-*. **3** to shuffle playing cards *20- WC*. **pochler 1** a pedlar, an itinerant handyman or tinker *19, 20- literary*. **2** a cheat, a swindler *20-*. [see the noun]
pauchle[2.1] /ˈpɔxəl/ *n* **1** a chaotic, disorganized state *la20- N EC Uls*. **2** an elderly, frail or feeble person *19- SW Uls*. [see the verb]
pauchle[2.2] /ˈpɔxəl/ *v* **1** to struggle or strive; to move feebly; to shuffle or hobble *la19-*. **2** to work ineffectually *20- C*. **pauchled** worn out, exhausted *20-*. **pauchler** a clumsy, unskilful person *20-*. [perhaps related to PAUCHLE[1.2] *ie* to walk as if with a burden; compare also BAUCHLE[1.1]]
pauchtie, paughty /ˈpɔxti, ˈpɔxte/ *adj* **1** conceited, haughty or arrogant; insolent *la16-*. **2** stout-hearted, spirited, gallant *la18-e19*. [unknown; compare Eng *paughty, pafty*]
pauk *see* PAWK
pauky *see* PAWKIE[1]
paul a' *see* PALL[1.2]
paulie *see* PALIE[1.2]
paumer *see* PALMER[1.1], PALMER[1.2]
paun *see* PAN[1.1]
paunch *see* PAINCH
paup *see* PAP[1]
pauper /ˈpɔpər/ *n* **1** a very poor person *19-*. **2** a school pupil who received free education in return for various janitorial duties *19-e20, la20- historical N*. †**pauperte** poverty *la15*. [Eng *pauper*]
paurk *see* PARK[1.1]
paut *see* PAWT[1.2]
†**pautener, paytener** *adj of a person* cruel; deadly *la14-e15*. [ME *pautener*]
pavee[1.1], **pavie**, *Uls* **pa-veaze** /ˈpevi, ˈpeve; *Uls* ˈpaviz/ *n* **1** a fuss about nothing, a commotion; a great state of excitement *19- T EC SW Bor*. **2** a bodily contortion; a flamboyant or affected gesture; a stately or strutting bearing *la16-19*. **3** a trick, a practical joke *17-e19*. [unknown]
pavee[1.2], **pavie**, *Uls* **pavise** /paˈvi; *Uls* paˈviz/ *v* **1** to adopt an exaggerated bearing; to strut or parade about *19, 20- NE SW Uls*. **2** to frisk about; to move in a quick, light way *19*. [perhaps from the noun, or sense 1 may be related to Eng *pavane* a stately dance; compare also PAW[1.1]]
pavey-waveys /ˈpeve ˈwevez, ˈpevi ˈweviz/ *n* a skipping game in which the rope is made to wave either horizontally or vertically on the ground, the object being to jump over it without touching it *la20- C*. [Eng *pavement* + Eng *wave*]
pavie *see* PAVEE[1.1], PAVEE[1.2]
pavilion, †**pallion**, †**paleʒoun**, †**pailʒoune** /pəˈvɪljən/ *n* **1** a large and stately tent *la14-*. **2** *pl* the tented encampment of an army *la14-e16*. **3** a canopy and curtains of a bed *16*. **4** a flag or banner *la16*. [ME *paviloun*]
paving stone /ˈpevɪŋ ston/ *n* a type of flat, iced cake *20- T EC*. [Eng *paving stone*]
†**pavis, pavys** *n* a shield; a defensive screen or testudo; a protection *la15-e17*. [ME *pavis*, MFr *pavais*, apparently from Ital *Pavese* relating to Pavia]
pavise *see* PAVEE[1.2]
paw[1.1], *Sh* **pjaw** /pɔ; *Sh* pjɔ/ *n* a slight movement; a feeble gesture or motion *18-19, 20- Sh*. **no play paw** to make the slightest movement; to show no signs of life *la18- Bor*. †**play a paw** to play a trick *la16-17*. [unknown]
paw[1.2], *Sh* **pjaw**, *Bor* **pawl** /pɔ; *Sh* pjɔ; *Bor* pɔl/ *v* **1** to make a slight movement; to work feebly or half-heartedly *19- Sh Bor*. **2** to play with one's food *19- Bor*. [unknown]

paw², **pa** /pɔ, pa/ *n* term of address for a male parent *la19- T C*. [reduced form of Eng *papa*; compare PAWPIE]

paw³, *NE* **paa** /pɔ; *NE* pa/ *n* **1** the paw of an animal *la15-*. **2** *humorous* the hand of a person *la20-*. [AN *powe*, MFr *poe*]

†pawk, **pauk**, **paik** *n* a trick, a stratagem *16-e19*. **pawkrie**, **pawkery** trickery, slyness *e19*; compare JOUKERIE-PAWKERIE. [unknown]

pawkie¹, **pawky**, **pauky**, **†pakie** /ˈpɔki, ˈpɔke/ *adj* **1** wily, crafty; shrewd, astute *17-*. **2** stubborn *17-*. **3** having a sly wit; sardonic *19-*. **4** roguish; flirtatious; lively, merry *18-19, 20- SW*. **5** humorously critical, having a sly, quiet wit *19-*. **6** quaint, fantastic, amusing *19, 20- N*. **pawkie-witted** wily, crafty; shrewd *18-*. [PAWK with adj-forming suffix]

pawkie² /ˈpɔki, ˈpɔke/ *n* a mitten *19-*. [unknown]

pawl *see* PALL¹·¹, PALL¹·², PAW¹·²

pawmie *see* PALMIE¹·¹, PAM¹

pawn¹·¹, **pawnd**, **†pand** /pɔn, pɔnd/ *n* **1** a pledge; something held in surety against a debt or service *15-*. **2** the state of being pawned; the action of pawning *19-*. **3** a pawnshop *la19-*. **4** *pl* a sum of money deposited with the kirk session by a couple as a guarantee of their intention to marry within forty days and of their chaste conduct in the interval *la16-e19*. **lay doon the pawns** to make official notification of one's intention to marry, to arrange for the proclamation of banns *18-19, 20- historical*. **†lay in pand** to put in pawn; to lay down as a pledge or security *15-17*. [OFr, MFr *pan*; compare MDu *pant*]

pawn¹·², **†pand** /pɔn/ *v* to pledge or wager; to deposit an article as security against a sum of money *la16-*. **pawn on to** to foist on to, to palm off on *19- NE EC Bor*. [see the noun]

pawn *see* PAND, POWNE

pawnd *see* PAWN¹·¹

pawpie /ˈpɔpi/ *n* a child's word for a grandfather *19-*. [altered form of Eng *papa*]

pawrent *see* PARENT

pawt¹·¹, **powt** /pɔt, pʌut/ *n* **1** a stamping, heavy step; a kick *18-19, 20- Sh N NE*. **2** a poking or prodding movement, a thrust *19, 20- Bor*. [see the verb]

pawt¹·², **powt**, *Sh* **paat**, **†paut**, **†pout**, **†polt** /pɔt, pʌut; *Sh* pɑt/ *v* **1** to stamp the foot in rage; *of a horse* to paw the ground *la17-*. **2** to walk in a heavy way; to stamp around angrily *la19- Sh N NE Uls*. **3** *of an animal* to prod with the head or horns *16-19, 20- Bor*. **4** to poke or prod (with a stick) *19, 20- NE*. **pout net** a stocking-shaped net fastened to poles, used to force out or catch fish resting under projecting riverbanks *la17-19, 20- Bor*. **†pout staff** the pole of a *pout net la15-e19*. **pawt at** to touch or feel with the hand *la18-19, 20- WC*. [variant of ME *poten*, OE *potian* push, strike]

pawtron *see* PATRON¹

Pax *see* PACE

pay *see* PEY¹·¹, PEY¹·²

payane *see* PAGAN¹·²

payment *see* PEYMENT

payn *see* PAIN¹·²

payne *see* PAIN¹·¹

paynt *see* PENT¹·²

payntit *see* PENTIT

payntry *see* PAINTRIE

pays *see* PASS¹·¹

paysie /ˈpezi/ *n* a peahen *la20- NE*. [shortened form of Eng *peahen* with familiar *-sie* suffix]

paytener *see* PAUTENER

pe *see* PEE²

pea¹, **pey** /pi, pe/ *n* **1** a seed of the leguminous plant *Pisum sativum*, a pea *la17-*. **2** *pl* a grade of very small coal *la19- EC*. **pea bree**, **pea brae** the liquid in which peas have been boiled; pea soup *20- T C*. **pea cod** a pea-pod *18-19, 20- T*. **pea huil**, **pea hool** a peapod *18- EC Bor*. **pea-shaup** a peapod *19, 20- C*. **pea-splittin** petty, fussy; mean *la19- SW Uls*. **pea-tree** the laburnum *19, 20- Bor*. [back-formation from PEASE¹ which was erroneously interpreted as a plural]

pea² /pi/ *n* a small marble *la19-*. **peaser**, **peezer** a small marble *20- T EC*. **peasie** a small marble *20-*. **peesil** a small marble *20- EC*. [PEA¹]

peace¹·¹, **pace**, *Sh* **paece**, **†pese**, **†peax**, **†pece** /pis, pes; *Sh* pez/ *n* **1** cessation of hostilities; freedom from strife or commotion; amity *la14-*. **2** a truce or peace treaty *la14-*. **3** the protection of the monarch extended to law-abiding people; public order *la14-*. **4** tranquillity of mind *la15-*. **5** an outlaw's pardon; his re-admission to allegiance *16-17*. **†peace-warning** a notice to a tenant to quit *la19*. **be at peace** a command to sit still *19-*. **gie me peace** a request for peace *20-*. **haud yer peace**, **†hald yer pese** to be or keep quiet *16-*. **†in pese** in peacetime *la14-e17*. **†in tyme of pese** in peacetime *15-17*. **I wish to peace** I wish to goodness *la19- WC SW Bor*. **†peace of the fair** the special protection granted to merchants and traders travelling to or from a fair *15-16*. **peace be here** a request for quietness and order *18-19, 20- literary*. **sit at peace** a command to sit still *la19-*. **wi peace** peacefully; without disturbance *la19, 20- Sh Ork NE*. [ME *pes*, MFr *pais*]

†peace¹·² *v* **1** to be silent; to reduce to silence *16*. **2** to end hostilities, to reconcile; to moderate or pacify *la14-15*. [see the noun]

peace¹·³ /pis/ *interj games* a call for a truce *la19- T EC Bor Uls*. [see the noun]

Peace *see* PACE

peachie *see* PEEDGIE

peacock, **†pacok**, **†pecok**, **†paco** /ˈpikɔk/ *n* the male peafowl *Pavo cristatus 14-*. [OE *pēa*, *pawa* + *cocc*]

peak /pik/ *n* **1** a sharply projecting point of rock; a mountain *19-*. **2** a type of lace with a pointed, scalloped edge *19- Ork Bor*. **peakie** a pointed heap of stones used for target-practice *la19- Sh Ork*. **peakit 1** pointed, peaked *20-*. **2** *of lace* having a scalloped or frilled edge *20- Ork EC SW*. [Eng *peak*; compare PIKE¹·¹]

peak *see* PEEK⁴

peaker *see* PIKE⁴

peakit, **peekit** /ˈpikɪt/ *adj of people* having a thin, gaunt, sickly appearance *20-*. [variant of Eng *peaky* with substitution of *-it* adj-forming suffix]

peakrie *see* PIKE⁴

peal *see* PAIL, PALE²

pealling *see* PAILIN¹·¹

peaper *see* PAPER¹·¹

pear *see* PEER²

peare *see* PAIR¹

pearl¹, **†perle**, **†perll**, **†peirle** /pɛrl/ *n* **1** a lustrous, white ball formed in some oysters and other shellfish *15-*. **2** a greatly valued or esteemed person *16-*. **3** a small piece of coal one size larger than dross *20-*. **4** a cataract on the eye *la16-19, 20- Uls*. **pearlins 1** a string of pearls *19, 20- literary*. **2** dewdrops *19, 20- literary*. **pearlit**, **†perlit** set or adorned with pearls *16-*. **pearly**, **†perly** *of dewdrops or tears* resembling a pearl *16-*. [ME *perl*]

pearl², **†perle** /pɛrl/ *n* **1** *knitting* a purl stitch *19-*. **2** embroidery or edging (of loops of twisted gold or silver wire) *16*. **pearlit**, **pearled**, **†perlit** edged with embroidery; ornamented with a knitted border *la16-19, 20- Uls*. **pearlin**, **perlin**, **†perling**, **†peirling**, **†pairling** lace or other ornamental trimming *la16-19, 20- NE*. [variant of Eng *purl*]

pease, pizz, †**pese,** †**pise,** †**peis** /piz, pɪz/ *n* **1** pea plants; pea seeds, peas *15*-; compare PEA¹. **2** something insignificant *la15-16*. **pease-bannock** a round flat cake or scone made of pea flour and baked *18*-. †**pease-bogle** a scarecrow *19*; compare *tattie-bogle* (TATTIE). **pease-brose** a dish made of pea flour and boiling water stirred to a paste *19*-. †**pease-clod** a roll or loaf made of pea flour *la18*. †**pease-kill 1** peas roasted whole in their pods in hot ashes or in a kiln *17-19*. **2** a scramble for enjoyment or gain; a state of confusion *la18-e19*. **pease-meal,** †**pease-maill** pea flour *17*-. **pease-pistils** = *pease-brose* 20- *WC*. †**pease-scone** a scone made of pea flour *18-19*. **pease-strae,** †**peis stra** the stalks and foliage of the pea plant used as fodder or bedding for animals *la16-19, 20- SW*. **Pease Strae** a Scottish country dance *la19*-. **pease-wisp** a small quantity of pea straw; a small bundle of anything thrown together *la19*-. [Lat *pisa* a variety of pea; compare PEA]
pease see PAISE¹,²
pease cod /ˈpizkɔd/ *n* a peapod *la17-19, 20- N*. †**peasecod tree** the laburnum *la17-e19*. [PEASE + COD²]
†**peaser** *n* a draught of liquor, especially whisky *la19*. [aphetic form of Eng *appease* assuage, satisfy + agentive suffix *-er*]
peaser see PEA²
peasie /ˈpizi, ˈpizɛ/ *adj* made of or like pease meal *20- EC Bor*. **peasy-bannock** a round flat cake or scone made of pea flour and baked *20- EC SW Bor*. **peasie whin, pacey whin, paisey whin** a type of (granite) stone with a marled granular surface *la18- NE*. [PEASE with *-ie* adj-forming suffix]
peasie see PEA²
peat¹,¹, **pate,** †**pete,** †**pett,** †**pit** /pit, pet/ *n* **1** (a piece of) semi-carbonized decayed vegetable matter found under the surface of boggy moorland (dried for use as fuel) *la14*-. **2** earth or turf turned over by a plough or spade *la19- Sh Ork*. **peatery** a peat bog or moss belonging to a landed estate; the right to cut peats from this *19-e20, la20- historical*. †**peating, peting** the action of getting peat, the right to cut peats *la15-17*. **peaty** of the nature of or containing peat; *of water or whisky* affected by peat in colour or taste *la18*-. **peat-bank** the bank or vertical face from which peats are cut *la19*-. **peat-barra** a flat barrow with a high end and no sides used for carrying peats *20*-. **peat-bing** a stack of peats *20- Sh NE WC*. **peat-bog** a boggy place where peats are cut; a bog composed of peat *la16*-. **peat-bree** the water which drains from peaty soil *19- NE SW*. **peat cassie** a straw or rush basket for carrying peats on a person's back *la19- Sh Ork SW Uls*. **peat-caster** a person who cuts peats and lays them out to dry *17*-. **peat-castin** the action of cutting peats and laying them out to dry *la17*-. **peat-clod** a single piece of peat *19- Sh N SW Uls*. **peat-coom** peat dust or crumbs *la19- N SW Bor*. **peat-creel** a straw or rush basket for carrying peats *la16- NE H&I C Uls*. **peat-crue, paet-kro** a storage place for peats *la19- Sh*. †**peat-gate** the track, road or right-of-way leading to a *peat-bog 17-19, 20- historical*. **peat grieshoch** a red-hot smouldering peat; a peat fire or embers *la19- NE SW*. **peat-hag** a hole or pit left in a peat bog from cutting peats *19*-. **peat-hill 1** boggy ground, moorland *la19- Sh Ork SW*. **2** a place where peats were stacked *17-18*. **peat-hole** = *peat-hag la17-19, 20- Uls*. **peat-house** an outhouse used for storing peat or other fuel *16-19, 20- Sh NE SW*. **peat-lair** the area of moor on which newly cut peats are laid out to dry *20- Sh N T SW*. **peat larroch** = *peat lair 20- T*. †**peat-leading** the transport of cut and dried peats *la16-18*. **peat-leave** the right to cut peats *18, 20- Sh*. **peat lowe** a peat fire, the glow from a peat fire *19, 20- NE*. †**peatman** an estate servant in charge of the supply of peats; an itinerant peat merchant *18-19*. **peat-meshie** a large pannier for transporting peats *20- Sh*. **peat-moss 1** a peat-bog *16*-. **2** peat *18*-. **peat muild 1** peat dust or crumbs *la19*-. **2** peaty soil *20- SW*. **peat-muir** peaty soil *20*-. †**pete myre** = *peat-bog 15-e17*. **peat-neuk** a corner or alcove (in the kitchen) used for storing peats for immediate use *18*-. †**peat-pot** = *peat-hag 15-e19*. **peat-ree** an enclosed recess, either inside or outside, for storing peats *20*-. **peat-rickle** a small heap of three or four peats set on end to dry *19, 20- NE*. **peat-rivvie** a straw or rush basket for carrying peats *20- Sh*. **peat-ruig** an unstacked heap of peats *20- Sh N*. **peat-skyo** a wall protecting a peat stack *20- Sh*. **peat-spade** a specially-shaped spade used for cutting peats *la15*-. **peat-stack** = *peat-bing la16*-. **fit the peats** to set peats on end to dry *la20- Uls*. **a peat o sape** a bar of soap *19, 20- NE SW*. **the peats** the work of digging and preparing peats for fuel *20*-. [unknown]
†**peat**¹,² *v* to fuel with peat *la17-18*. [unknown]
†**peat**², **pete** *n* a gable stone supporting a coping-stone *16-18*. [reduced form of PEAT STANE]
peat³, †**pete** /pit/ *n* **1** term of endearment (for a child) *la19, 20- NE*. **2** term of reproach or scorn for a woman *19*. **3** an advocate reputed to be the protégé of a particular judge *la17-19*. **prood peat** a vain woman *19, 20- WC*. [EModE *peat*; compare MDu *pete* godmother]
†**peatches, piatches** *npl* a colonnade, an arcade *la17-e18* [EModE, Ital *piazza* a public square]
peat reek /ˈpit rik/ *n* **1** the pungent smoke from a peat fire *la18*-. **2** Highland whisky whose characteristic flavour is supposedly from the smoke of the peat fire used to dry the malt *la18*-. **peat reek whisky** Highland whisky *la18*-. [PEAT¹,¹ + REEK¹,¹]
peat stane, peet-stane, †**pete stane** /ˈpit sten/ *n* a gable stone supporting a coping-stone; a coping-stone or keystone of an arch *16*-. [unknown first element + STANE¹,¹]
peaver see PEEVER¹
peax see PEACE¹,¹
pebble see PEEBLE
pece see PEACE¹,¹, PIECE
pech¹,¹ /pɛx/ *n* **1** a laboured breath; a pant or a gasp *16*-. **2** a sigh of weariness, relief or satisfaction *19*-. **3** an asthmatic wheeze; a breathless cough *la19- NE C*. **pechie, pechy** short-winded; asthmatic, wheezy *20*-. **get ower something wi a pech** to get something done by dint of great effort *20- N NE T SW*. **out o' pech** short of breath *20*-. **a sair pech** an exhausting struggle *20*-. [onomatopoeic]
pech¹,², **paich,** †**peich** /pɛx, pex/ *v* **1** to breathe hard; to puff, pant or gasp for breath *16*-. **2** to move or work so as to pant or gasp with the exertion *la18*-. **3** to sigh or groan *la18*-. **4** to cough in an asthmatic way *la20*-. [see the noun]
Pech see PICT
†**pechan, peghan** *n* the stomach, the belly *la18-19*. [unknown]
pechar see PITCHER
pechle see PAUCHLE¹,¹
pechlt, paichled /ˈpɛxəlt, ˈpexəlt/ *adj* out of breath, exhausted *19- NE EC Bor*. [perhaps ptp of PECH¹,¹ + *-le* suffix]
Pecht see PICT
Pechtis see PICTISH
Pechtland see PICTLAND
pecify, pecifee, pacify, †**pacife** /ˈpɛsɪfae, ˈpɛsɪfi, ˈpasɪfʌɪ/ *v* to bring to a state of peace; to calm or subdue *la15*-. [EModE *pacyfy*, Lat *pācificāre*]
peck¹,¹, *Sh* **paeck** /pɛk; *Sh* pek/ *n* **1** what can be held in a bird's beak; a scrap of food *la19*-. **2** the first grass in the spring *la19- Sh*. **paekie** a morsel *20- Sh*. [see the verb]

peck[1,2], *Sh* **paek**, †**paik**, †**pekke** /pɛk; *Sh* pek/ *v of a bird* to strike with the beak *18-*. **peckin** a small quantity, a bite of food *la19- Sh*. †**pekke mod** to become angry *e14*. [perhaps MDu *pecken* See also PICK]

peck[2], †**pek**, †**pect**, †**peick** /pɛk/ *n* **1** a measure for dry goods, a quarter of a firlot *15-e20, la20- historical*. **2** a small plot of land requiring a peck of oat seed to sow it *19*. **3** a vessel used as a measure for dry goods *15-e19*. †**peck of land in** *Ross-shire* a measurement of approximately three acres of land *17-18*. [ME *pek*]

pecok *see* PEACOCK

pect *see* PECK[2]

†**pecuniars** *npl* a person's financial state *e19*. [EModE *pecuniar*, OFr *pecuniaire* relating to money]

pedagogue, †**pedagoge**, †**pedagog**, †**paedagogue** /ˈpɛdəɡɔɡ/ *n* **1** a teacher, a tutor *la16-*. **2** the science of teaching *la15-e17*. **3** a place of learning *16*. [MFr *pedagogue* schoolmaster, school]

pedagogy /ˈpɛdəɡɔdʒi, ˈpɛdəɡɔɡi/ *n* **1** the science of teaching *19-*. **2** a university; a university building or faculty *15-17*. [Lat *paedagōgium* a place of instruction]

peddar *see* PEDDER

peddell *see* BEDDAL

pedder, pether, †**peddar**, †**pethar** /ˈpɛdər, ˈpɛðər/ *n* **1** a pedlar, a packman *la15-19, 20- SW Bor*. **2** a maker of baskets *20- NE EC*. [ME *pedder*]

pedell *see* BEADLE

pedmented *see* PATHEMENT[1,2]

†**pedral, pedderell** *n* a packman *16*. [metathesized form of Eng *pedlar*]

pee[1,1] /pi/ *n* urine; the act of urinating *19-*. [see the verb]

pee[1,2] /pi/ *v* to urinate; to wet with urine *la18-*. **peeins** urine *la20- NE T EC*. **pee-the-bed** the dandelion *20-*. [from the initial letter of *piss*]

†**pee**[2], **pe, pey** *n* an outer garment of coarse woollen material, a riding jacket *la15-17*. [Late MDu *pie* coat of coarse woollen stuff]

peeack *see* PEEK[4]

pee-ay *see* PREE[2]

peeble, pebble /ˈpibəl, ˈpɛbəl/ *n* **1** a small smooth rounded stone *18-*. **2** a semi-precious stone (of agate or rock-crystal) found in streams and rocks (set in silver to make a distinctive type of jewellery) *18-19, 20- historical*; compare *Scots pebble* (SCOTS[1,2]). [eME **pibel*, OE *papolstān, popelstān*]

†**pee-coo** *n in Angus* a game resembling hide-and-seek *19*. [Compare LAMPEEKOO]

peedgie, peachie /ˈpidʒi, ˈpitʃi/ *n* a small glass marble *20- N NE T*. [perhaps reduplication of PEA[2]]

peedie /ˈpidi/ *adj* small *20-*. [perhaps variant of Sh PEERIE[3]]

peefer, †**pifer** /ˈpifər/ *v* to complain peevishly *19- SW Bor*. †**peeferin** trifling, feckless, ineffectual *19*. [probably onomatopoeic]

peegril *see* PEGRAL

peek[1,1] /pik/ *n* **1** the cry of a small animal or bird; a quiet or insignificant sound *la19- NE T Uls*. **2** a person with a weak voice; an unimpressive or insignificant individual *la19- NE T*. [onomatopoeic]

peek[1,2] /pik/ *v* **1** *of a bird* to cheep or chirp; *of an animal* to cry feebly *19- Sh NE Uls*. **2** *of a person* to complain or grumble; to whine or whimper *19- NE T*. [see the noun]

peek[1,3], **peak**, †**peeack** /pik/ *interj* a sound representing the cry of a small animal or bird, or the shrill voice of a child *la19- NE T Uls*. **peak-peak** a call to chickens *la19- NE EC*. [see the noun]

peek[2] /pik/ *n* a small point of light; a small flame *19-*. **peekie** a flame or point of light *19, 20- NE*. **a peek o licht a** blink of light, a small flame *19, 20- NE*. [probably from the Eng noun *peek* a furtive look, by analogy with PEEP[1]]

peek *see* PICK[3,2]

peekie /ˈpiki/ *n* **1** a type of knitting needle (formerly used to knit Ayrshire bonnets) *la19- WC SW*. **2** a knitted bonnet *la19, 20- historical*. [related to PIKE[1,1]]

peekit *see* PEAKIT

peel[1,1] /pil/ *n* **1** the skin or rind of a fruit or vegetable *18-*. **2** a small crab which has newly cast or is about to cast its shell and is therefore suitable for bait *20- NE*. †**in peel** *of fish* not packed *16-e18*. [probably ME *pil* and PEEL[9]]

peel[1,2], †**pele**, †**pill** /pil/ *v* **1** to strip the skin off fruit or vegetables *15-*. **2** to rub or scrape skin off; to skin *19-*. **3** to plunder or rob; to cheat *la15-19*. **4** to unpack or unwrap bulk goods; to separate goods into smaller packages for retailing *16-e17*; compare *pack and peel* (PACK[1,2]). **peeler** a small crab which has newly cast or is about to cast its shell and is therefore suitable for bait *la19- NE T Uls*. **peelock** a potato cooked and served in its skin *19- SW*. †**pelour** a robber, a thief *la15-16*. **peel yer wands** to begin a new enterprise or way of life (such as married life or an apprenticeship) *20- Bor*. [probably ME *pilen*]

peel[2,1], **pele** /pil/ *n* **1** a defensive palisade or stockade; the ground enclosed by such defences *la14-19, 20- historical*. **2** a fortified house or small defensive tower, originally one built within a palisade (in the Border counties); frequently in place-names *la14-19, 20- historical*. **peel house** a fortified dwelling or refuge *la14-19, 20- historical*. **pilmuir** a piece of common land enclosed by a fence and cultivated as arable ground *18-19, 20- EC Bor*. [ME *pel*]

†**peel**[2,2] *v* to support or protect by means of stakes *la16-18*. [see the noun]

peel[3], †**peill** /pil/ *n* a small, compressed ball of medicine, a pill *la17-*. [ME *pile*]

peel[4] /pil/ *n* a particle, a scrap *la19- Sh*. [Norn *pil*]

peel[5] /pil/ *n* a pail, a bucket *20- Ork*. [Eng *pail*; compare AN *paele* a frying pan]

peel[6] /pil/ *n* an equal, a match; something comparable *18-19, 20- C SW Bor*. [from the verb PEER[1]]

peel[7] /pil/ *v in curling and bowling* to tie a match; to have equal scores *18-19, 20- C SW Bor*. [perhaps variant of Eng *peer* to equal]

peel *see* PUIL[1,1]

peel-an-eat[1,1] /piləˈnit/ *n* (a meal of) potatoes cooked in their skins *la18-19, 20- NE C SW Bor*. [PEEL[9] + EAT[1,2]]

peel-an-eat[1,2] /piləˈnit/ *adj* unhealthy-looking, delicate, sickly *19, 20- NE Bor*. [see the noun]

peeled, †**pelit**, †**peld**, †**peild** /pild/ *adj* **1** stripped of an outer layer, bare *la15-*. **2** stripped of possessions, destitute *la15-*. **3** *of fish* unsmoked and bulk packed *la16-e17*. [ptp of PEEL[9]]

peelick /ˈpilək/ *n* a blow, a smack *la19- T*. [diminutive form Eng *peal* strike, batter]

peelie-wally /ˈpili-wale/ *adj* sickly, feeble; pallid, thin and ill-looking *19-*. [reduplicative formation with variation of initial consonant and vowel; compare PALIE[1,1]]

peelie-wersh /ˈpili-wɛrʃ/ *adj* sickly, delicate; insipid, nondescript *19-*. [from the first element of PEELIE-WALLY + WERSH]

peels /pilz/ *adj of the contestants in a game* having equal scores, tied, drawn *la19- C SW Bor*. [from the noun PEEL[6]]

peen[1,1], **pin**, †**pyn**, †**pine** /pin, pɪn/ *n* **1** a peg or bolt *15-*. **2** a thin fastener (of steel wire) with a sharpened point *15-*. **3** a mood, a frame of mind *19-*. **4** a miner's tally used to label the hutches of coal he had filled *la19-e20, la20- historical*. **5** *golf* the flagpole marking each hole *20-*. **6** as much washing as would go through a mangle at one time *20, 21- historical*.

7 a small, neat person or animal; a small child *la19- NE*. **8** a kind of door-knocker *16-18, 19- historical*. **9** the latch of a door *e19*. **10** the peg over which the rope was slung on a gallows; the gallows itself *16-e17*. **pins** small stones wedged into the crevices between larger stones in a wall to consolidate it *la19-*. **peen-heid 1** a stupid person *20- C SW*. **2** the young fry of the minnow or stickleback *20- EC Bor*. **3** a person or animal with a small head *20- T EC*. **pin-leg** a wooden leg *20-*. **pin reel** a dance in which one unpartnered person dances alone in the centre of a ring of dancers *20- Sh Ork NE*. **pin stones** small stones wedged into the crevices between larger stones in a wall to consolidate it *la19-*. **pin-head oatmeal** oatmeal ground to a particular coarseness *20-*. **full pin** at full speed *la19- Sh N T EC*. **†in a merry pin** in a happy mood *la18-19*. **in a pin** in a bad temper *20- Sh Ork*. **pit in the pin** to give up drinking *19-*. [OE *pinn*; compare PREEN¹·¹]

peen¹·², **pin** /pin, pɪn/ *v* **1** to fasten with a pin or peg *la15-*. **2** to consolidate masonry with pins *la16-*. **3** to grab, grasp at or seize; to understand *la19-*. **4** , to hit with a sharp quick blow; to strike with a missile or pelt with stones *19- Sh Ork NE T C*. **5** to move with speed and vigour *19, 20- Ork N NE*. **6** to beat or thrash *la19, 20- N Bor*. **7** *mining* to put a pin on a hutch of coal; to substitute one's own pin for that of the rightful owner *20- historical*. **peened, pinned** *of a person* tied down to work, not having a moment's leisure *20- NE*. **peener, pinner 1** an unscrupulous or opportunistic person *la19- NE Bor*. **2** a large quantity of alcohol; a heavy drinking bout *19, 20- Uls*. **3** (the missile used in) a children's throwing game *20- T*. **4** a piece of wood used to fasten or stabilize a structure *la16-e17*. **pinning, pinnin, pinnan 1** the act of consolidating masonry with small stones *la16-*. **2** *pl* small stones used in consolidating masonry *la16-19, 20- Sh Ork NE*. **3** a beating or scolding *la19, 20- SW Bor*. **pin in** to rush a task *20- NE*. **pin-the-widdie** a small unsplit haddock which is hung in the smoke of the chimney to cure *19, 20- NE*. **pin yer lugs back** an instruction to listen carefully *20-*. [see the noun]

peen², **pane**, **†pain**, **†peyn** /pin, pen/ *n* **1** a sheet of glass *18-*. **2** a piece of richly decorated cloth; an ornamental bedcovering *la15-e16*. **3** a piece or portion of something *16*. [ME *pan*, Lat *pannus* a (piece of) cloth]

peen³·¹, **piend**, *Sh* **pin** /pin, pind; *Sh* pɪn/ *n* **1** the pointed or chisel end of a mason's hammer, the bevelled or tapered face used for dressing stone *19-*. **2** one of the sloping ridges at the corner of a roof where two adjacent sloping surfaces meet *la18-19, 20- NE C*. **3** a peak or apex, a point; a coping *18- Sh NE T SW*. **peen hammer** a mason's hammer *20- NE T EC*. **piend roof** a hipped, ridged or pavilion roof *la19, 20- N EC*. [ON; compare Norw dial *penn* the pointed end of a hammer]

peen³·², **†pene** /pin/ *v* **1** to bring to a point; to taper *la19-*. **2** to hammer out or beat metal flat and thin *e16*. **peener** a mason's hammer *la20- N EC*. [ON; compare Swed dial *pena* to beat with a hammer]

peenge¹·¹ /pinʒ, pindʒ/ *n* a feeble, sickly-looking person; a fretful child *20- EC Bor*. [see the verb]

peenge¹·², **pinge** /pinʒ, pindʒ/ *v* **1** to droop, pine or mope; to look cold and miserable *18-*. **2** to whine, complain or whimper *la18-*. **peengin, peengein 1** ailing, pinched and cold-looking *18-*. **2** mean, grudging *19, 20- EC*. [onomatopoeic with influence from WHINGE¹·¹, PEEK¹]

peengie /ˈpinʒi, ˈpinʒe, ˈpindʒi, ˈpindʒe/ *adj* **1** sickly-looking, puny; in poor health *19-*. **2** *of a child* peevish, fractious *20- NE C Bor*. [from the verb PEENGE¹·² with adj-forming suffix -IE¹]

peenie /ˈpini/ *n* **1** an apron; a woman's cross-over overall *la19-*. **2** a child's word for the stomach *20- C*. [reduced form of Eng *pinafore*]

peenish *see* PUNISH

peeoy /piˈɔi/ *n* a home-made firework *19-e20, la20- historical*. [onomatopoeic]

peep¹·¹ /pip/ *n* **1** a quick glance *19-*. **2** a small light or flame (from a lamp or gas jet) *la19-*. **3** a small opening, a narrow aperture or crack *19, 20- Sh T Uls*. **pit the gas at a peep** to reduce the pressure of a gas jet on a hob (or formerly on a lamp) to the lowest point at which it will remain alight *20-*. **put someone's gas at a peep** to reduce a conceited person's self-esteem *20-*. [unknown, compare PEEK²]

peep¹·², **†peip**, **†pipe** /pip/ *v* **1** to squint or glimpse; to look quickly or slyly *16-*. **2** *of light* to appear *16-*. [unknown]

peep²·¹, **†pepe**, **†peip** /pip/ *n* **1** a squeak; a cheep *la15-*. **2** the slightest sound *19-*. [onomatopoeic]

peep²·², **†peip**, **†pype**, **†pipe** /pip/ *v* **1** *of an animal* to squeak; *of a bird* to cheep *la16-*. **2** *of a person* to whine or complain *la16-19, 20- Sh NE*. **3** *of music* to sound shrilly *e16*. **peep sma** an insignificant person *18-19, 20- Bor*. **†pipe up** *of a breeze* to begin to blow *e16*. [see the noun]

peep³ /pip/ *n* a small marble *la19- EC*. [unknown; compare PAIP]

peer¹, **†pere**, **†peir** /pir/ *n* **1** a person's equal in rank or before the law *la14-*. **2** a member of the (titled) nobility *15-*. **3** an equal in gifts, abilities or characteristics *la15-*. **4** a companion or playmate; a spouse or mate *la15-18*. **peerless**, **†peirles** unequalled, incomparable *la14-*. **†peir and peir** as equals or associates *la14-e15*. [ME *per*]

peer², **pear, perr**, **†pere** /pir, per, per/ *n* **1** the fruit of the pear tree, a pear *15-*. **2** a pear tree *la17-*. **3** something of little value *15-16*. [ME *pere*, OE *peru*, Lat *pēra*]

peer³ /pir/ *v* to look narrowly or with difficulty *17-*. [unknown]

†peer⁴, **†pere, peyr** *v* to pour in drops; to allow to trickle *16-e18*. [unknown; compare Norw dial *pira* trickle]

peer *see* PUIR¹·¹, PUIR¹·³

peerie¹, **peery**, **†pirie** /ˈpiri, ˈpire/ *n* **1** a child's spinning-top *la17-*. **2** a fir cone *20- Bor*. **3** *mining* a surveyor's large brass plumb-bob *20- EC*. **4** a small stone marble *20- NE*. **peerie cord** the string with which a spinning top is set in motion *19-*. **peerie heel, peery heel** a stiletto heel *la20-*. **peerie heidit** in a state of mental confusion *20-*. **traicle peerie** *see* TRAICLE. **sleep like a peerie** to sleep soundly *19-*. [PEER² + dim suffix -IE¹]

peerie², **peery** /ˈpiri, ˈpire/ *n* a trickle *19- WC*. [from the verb PEER⁴ with adj-forming suffix -*ie*]

peerie³ /ˈpiri, ˈpire/ *adj* small, little, tiny *la19-*. **peerie breeks 1** a child or a person with short legs *la19- Sh Ork*. **2** a haddock roe *20- Sh*. **peerie flitter** the wren *Troglodytes troglodytes 20- Sh*. **peerie folk** *folklore* fairies *20- Sh Ork*. **peerie guiser** a child masquerader at UP-HELLY-AA *20- Sh*. **peerie hawk** the merlin *Falco columbarius la19- Sh*. **peerie hoosie** a game where children pretend to live in a house like adults *20- Sh Ork*. **peeire laird** a small landowner *la19- Sh Ork*. **peerie pinkie** the little finger *20- Sh Ork N*. **peerie start** a moment, a short period *la19- Sh*. **peerie summer** a spell of warm weather in autumn *la19- Sh Ork*. **peerie tenant** a tenant with a holding of 10-50 acres *la19- Ork*. **peerie whaup** the whimbrel *Numenius phaeopus la19- Sh Ork*. **peerie winkie** *in nursery rhymes* the little finger or toe *la19- Sh Ork WC*. **peerie writ** handwriting *20- Sh*. **peerie wyes** with small tentative movements; hesitantly *20- Sh*. [probably Norn related to Norw dial *piren* niggardly, sickly, feeble, spindly; compare PEEDIE]

peeriemyak see PARRYMAUK
peerie-wearie see PEERY
peerie-weerie[1.1] /ˈpiri wiri/ *n* a tiny creature *19- Sh T WC*. [see the adj]
peerie-weerie[1.2] /ˈpiri wiri/ *adj* small, little, tiny *19- Sh Ork T WC*. [reduplicative form of PEERIE[3]]
peertith see PUIRTITH
peery /ˈpiri/ *adj* inclined to peer; inquisitive, nosey *19, 20- Uls*. **peerie-wearie 1** strained or short-sighted-looking *19- C*. **2** shrewd *e19*. [from the verb PEER[2] + adj-forming suffix *-ie*]
peery see PEERIE[1], PEERIE[2]
peeryorie /piriˈjɔre/ *n* in Edinburgh a street-cry term for a potato *19, 20- historical*. [altered form of PITAWTIE]
peesie /ˈpizi/ *adj* excellent, splendid *20- C*. [altered form of BEEZER]
peesie see PEESWEEP
peesie-weesie /ˈpiziˈwizi/ *adj of people* gaunt, ailing; shrill-voiced, complaining *19, 20- NE EC SW*. [perhaps derivative of PEESWEEP]
peesil see PEA[2]
peesk see POOSK[1]
peester[1.1] /ˈpistər/ *n* a cheep, a squeak, a whimper *la19- Sh*. [Norn *pister*; compare Norw *pister*]
peester[1.2] /ˈpistər/ *v* to cheep, squeak or whimper *la19- Sh*. [Norn *pister*; compare Norw *pist(r)a*]
peesweep, peewee, peesie /ˈpizwip, ˈpiwi, ˈpizi/ *n* the lapwing *Vanellus vanellus la18-*; compare PEEWEET. **peesie's eggs** the fritillaria, from its speckled flowers *20- T*. **peesweep grass** a type of rush *Luzula campestris la19- Bor*.
†**peesweep-lookin** sharp-featured; gaunt, ailing *19*. [imitative of the bird's cry]
peet-stane see PEAT STANE
peety[1.1], **pity**, †**peté**, †**pité**, †**piete** /ˈpiti, ˈpɪte/ *n* **1** compassion, sympathy; clemency, mercy *la14-*. **2** a cause for compassion or regret *la14-*. **peetifu**, **pityful 1** compassionate *la16-*. **2** *of a person* deserving of compassion *la16-*. **piteous**, †**peteous**, †**petuous**, †**pieteous 1** deserving of compassion; mournful *15-*. **2** compassionate *16-*. **it's a peety o 1** it's a pity about *19-*. **2** it will be the worse for you; it will serve you right *20- Sh N T*. **peety me** an expression of surprise, disapproval or disgust *19-*. [ME *pite*, Lat *pietās*; compare PIETY]
peety[1.2], **pity**, †**pete**, †**pite** /ˈpiti, ˈpɪte/ *v* to feel or show compassion or clemency *la16-*. [see the noun]
peeve[1.1] /piv/ *n* an alcoholic drink *20- NE T EC*. **on the peeve** engaged in a bout of drinking alcohol *la20- EC*. [Travellers' language *peeve*; compare Rom *péava* to drink]
peeve[1.2] /piv/ *v* to drink alcohol *20- NE T EC*. [see the noun]
peever[1], **peaver** /ˈpivər/ *n* the flat stone or counter used in the game of hopscotch *19- T C Uls*. **peever beds** the game of hopscotch *20- C*. [unknown]
peever[2] /ˈpivər/ *n* a very small marble *la19- NE EC*. [unknown]
peevers /ˈpivərz/ *n* hopscotch *la19- T C Bor*. [PEEVER[1]]
peevie beds see PEEVER[1]
peewee see PEESWEEP
peeweet /ˈpiwit/ *n* a miner's blue-grey vest *20- EC*. [from the colour of a lapwing's wings]
peezer see PEA[2]
peg[1.1] /pɛg/ *n* **1** a (wooden) pin used for fastening or adjusting *la18-*. **2** a policeman *la19- NE C*. **3** a thrusting blow *17-18*. [MDu *pegge* a plug, a small wooden pin]
peg[1.2] /pɛg/ *v* **1** to fasten together with pegs; to hang out a washing with pegs *19-*. **2** to whack or beat *la19- C SW Bor*. [see the noun]

pege see PAGE
peggie /ˈpɛgi, ˈpɛge/ *n* a stick for stirring and pounding clothes in a wash-tub *20, 21- historical*. [familiar form of the the name Margaret]
peggin /ˈpɛgɪn/ *n* a beating, a thrashing *20- EC Bor*. [from the verb PEG[1.2]]
peghan see PECHAN
pegral, peegril, †**pegrall** /ˈpɛgrəl, ˈpigrəl/ *adj* **1** mean, greedy, miserly *la19- NE Bor*. **2** petty, paltry *16*. [altered form of PEDRAL]
†**pegy-mast** *n* a top-mast or a small mast or yard for a pennant on a ship *la15-e16*. [perhaps related to MDu *pegge* + MAST[1]]
peh see PIE[1]
peich see PECH[1.2]
Peicht see PICT
peick see PECK[2]
peiffer see PIFER
peik see PICK[4], PICK[5.1]
peild see PEELED
peill see PEEL[3]
peip see PEEP[2], PEEP[3], PEEP[5]
peir see PEER[1], PERE
peirche-tre see PERCH
peirk see PIRK[1.2]
peirle see PEARL[1]
peirling see PEARL[2]
peirse see PIERCE
peirt see PERT
peis see PEASE, PIECE
peist /pʌɪst/ *v* **1** to work in a lethargic half-hearted way *la19- NE SW*. **2** to struggle along, to have difficulties *20- NE*. **peister** to struggle along, to have difficulties *20- NE*. [unknown]
pek see PECK[2]
pekcaman see PICK[2.1]
pekke see PECK[1.2]
pekyllyn see PICKLIN
pelcher /ˈpɛltʃər/ *n* the grey mullet *Chelon labrosus la19- N*. [with transference of meaning from Eng *pilchard*]
peld see PEELED
pele see PEEL[2], PEEL[9]
pelf /pɛlf/ *n* **1** wealth, possessions *15-19, 20- literary*. **2** booty *15-17*. [ME *pelf*]
pelit see PEELED
pell[1] /pɛl/ *n* **1** matted hair; an animal with matted hair *20- Sh Ork N NE*. **2** *pl* rags; ragged garments *19- Sh Ork N*. **3** a dirty, slovenly person, a reprobate *19- Sh Ork*. **4** a broken or shabby object *la19- Sh*. **5** a scrap, a trace *la19- Sh*. **pelly** ragged, tattered *20- Sh Ork N*. [probably Du *pel* skin, fleece or Norw dial *pela* to strip, pluck, skin; compare also Lat *pellis* skin, hide]
pell[2] /pɛl/ *n* buttermilk *19- SW Bor*. **as soor as pell** see SOOR. [unknown]
pellack see PELLOCK
pellad see PALLET
peller see PILLAR
pellet[1] /ˈpɛlət/ *n* a pelt; a sheepskin *15-19, 20- Bor*. [AN *pellet* skin of a small animal]
pellet[2] /ˈpɛlət/ *n* **1** a piece of (small) shot *la16-*. **2** a handbow or crossbow for shooting small shot *la16-e17*. Compare PELLOK. †**pellet bow** a hand-bow *17*. [ME *pelot* a small ball, pill, cannon-ball, EModE *pellet*]
pellet[3], **pellit** /ˈpɛlət, ˈpɛlɪt/ *adj* **1** *of an animal's coat* matted, caked with dirt *19- Sh Ork*. **2** *of a garment* ragged, tattered *20- Sh Ork*. [from the noun PELL[1] + adj-forming suffix -IT[2]]

pellile /pəˈlil/ *n* the redshank *Tringa totanus la19- NE*. [perhaps imitative of its call]

pellit *see* PELLET³

pellock, pellack, pallack, *Ork* **pallo,** *N* **paillag,** †**pellok,** †**pelok** /ˈpɛlək, ˈpalək; *Ork* ˈpalo; *N* ˈpeləg/ *n* **1** the porpoise *Phocoena phocoena*; originally also the dolphin *14-*. **2** something bulky and clumsy; a short overweight person *la18- Sh Ork NE*. **pellack whale** a porpoise *17- Sh Ork*. [unknown]

†**pellok** *n* a piece of shot fired from a crossbow or gun; a bullet or cannonball *15-e16*; compare PELLET². **pellok bow** a hand-bow or crossbow which shot pellets *16-e17*. [probably altered, by substitution of Scots dim suffix, from ME *pelot*]

pellok *see* PELLOCK

pelloo /ˈpelu/ *n* a peat with a grassy surface *20- Ork*. [formation in -o from Norw dial *pela* to pare turf with a spade; compare PELL¹]

pelok *see* PELLOCK

pelour *see* PEEL⁹

pelsh /pɛlʃ/ *n* a drenching shower of rain, a downpour *20- NE*. [perhaps altered form of *pelt* to rain heavily, conflated with such words as *blash, plash*]

pelt¹·¹, †**palt** /pɛlt/ *n* a hard blow or stroke *la15- Ork T Uls*. [probably EModE *pelt*]

pelt¹·² /pɛlt/ *v* **1** to strike repeatedly; to deliver repeated blows or missiles *16-*. **2** to work energetically, to exert oneself *la19- Sh Ork NE Uls*. [probably EModE *pelt* from a variant of ME *piltan*]

pelt² /pɛlt/ *n* **1** ragged clothes; coarse cloth or sacking used to protect the clothes *la16-19, 20- historical*. **2** a low-grade type of coal containing a lot of stone, shale and slate *19, 20- C*. **3** a ragged person *20- Sh*. **4** trash, rubbish *16-19*. [perhaps related to Norn *pjol* a worn out garment, a rag; compare EModDu *palt* piece, fragment, patch]

peltag *see* PILTOCK

pelter /ˈpɛltər/ *n* **1** a state of great excitement or agitation *la19, 20- Sh NE*. **2** a violent shower of rain *20-*. **get pelters** to receive abuse *la20-*. **give pelters** to give abuse *la20-*. **receive pelters** to receive abuse *la20-*. [from PELT¹·² with frequentative suffix *-er*]

peltie /ˈpɛlti/ *n* a shipyard hammer *20- WC*. [from PELT¹·²]

peltin-pyock, piltin-pyock /ˈpɛltɪnpjɔk, ˈpɪltɪnpjɔk/ *n* **1** a rough garment worn as protective clothing for rough work *la19- NE T*. **2** clothes ruined by misuse *la19- NE T*. [PELT² + POKE¹·¹]

†**peltry**¹·¹ *n* worthless objects; trash, rubbish *la16-19*. [related to PELT²; compare the adj and Norw dial *pjaltra* rags]

peltry¹·² /ˈpɛltri/ *adj* **1** worthless, trashy *la16-19, 20- NE*. **2** *of food* unpalatable; *of weather* unpleasant *la18- NE*. [see the noun]

pen¹·¹ /pɛn/ *n* **1** a writing implement *la14-*. **2** a bird's feather; the quill or barrel of a feather *la15-*. **3** literary activity, the work of an author *la15-*. **4** the stalk of a plant or vegetable, a stalk of straw *la18-*. **5** a small spoon (originally for taking snuff) *la18- Ork NE EC*. **6** a penis *16*. †**pen ball** a kind of golf ball stuffed with feathers *la16-e17*. **pen nibs** rhyming slang Hibs, Hibernian Football Club *20-*. [ME *penne*, Lat *penna*]

pen¹·² /pɛn/ *v* to write down *16-*. [see the noun]

pen² /pɛn/ *n* a pointed conical hill *la18- Bor*. [OWelsh *penn* a head, top]

pen *see* PEND¹·¹

pence *see* PENNY

pench *see* PAINCH

pencil, †**pensell,** †**pensall,** †**pinsell** /ˈpɛnsəl/ *n* **1** a small pennon or streamer; a standard *la15-19, 20- historical*. **2** the standard carried at the celebration of the Common Riding in Hawick *e18*. [ME *pencel*]

pencil *see* PINCIL

pend¹·¹, **pen,** †**penn** /pɛnd, pɛn/ *n* **1** an arch, a vault; the arch of a bridge or gateway *la15-*. **2** a covered, vaulted or arched passageway through a building or buildings *16-*. **3** a covered drain or sewer, the entrance to or grating over a drain or sewer *19- SW Bor*. **4** the vault of the heavens, the sky *la16-19*. **5** the stonework of an arch or vault *16-e17*. **pend close** a covered passageway through a building or buildings *19-*. †**Pen' Folk** a small religious sect which took its name from its meeting-house in a *pend close* in the High Street of Paisley *la19*. **pend gate 1** a gate closing the entrance to a covered passageway through a building or buildings *la19- T EC*. **2** an arched gate *e17*. **pend mouth** the entrance to a covered passageway through a building or buildings *la19- NE T WC*. †**pend stane** a stone shaped for building into an archway *la16-e19*. [see the verb]

†**pend**¹·² *v* to build as or furnish with an arch or vaulting; to arch, to vault *15-e19*. [AN *apentiz*, ME *pentis*]

pend *see* PAND

pendakill *see* PENDICLE

†**pendice, pendas, pendes** *n* **1** an ornamental hanging on the end of a strap or belt *la15-e19*. **2** an earring *18*. [MFr *appendice* something attached or appended with noun-forming suffix *-ice*]

pendicle, †**pendakill** /ˈpɛndɪkəl/ *n* **1** a piece of land or property regarded as subsidiary to a main estate *15-*. **2** *of trade incorporations* a specialized craft or trade regarded as a subdivision of a general craft *17-e20, la20- historical*. **3** *of trade incorporations* a tradesman not fully incorporated and having limited rights *la18-19, 20- historical*. **4** a small piece of ground forming part of a larger holding or farm and frequently let to a sub-tenant *la18-19, 20- T C Bor*. **5** a subsidiary part or aspect of a process, situation or story *la15-e19*. **6** an ecclesiastical dependency, a daughter church *16-18*. **7** a place or district regarded as a detached portion of a larger territory or administratively dependent on another area *16-e18*. **8** a hanging ornament or attachment, a pendant *la16-17*. **9** a hanging cloth; a valance *la15-e17*. **pendicler** the tenant of a a small piece of ground subdivided from a farm; a smallholder *la18-19, 20- historical*. **pairts and pendicles** *see* PAIRT¹·¹. [Lat *pendiculum*, Lat *pendēre* hang]

pendle /ˈpɛndəl/ *n* **1** the pendulum of a clock *18-19, 20- Ork NE*. **2** a pendant earring *e19*. [Fr *pendule*]

pene *see* PEEN⁵

†**penetrive, penitrif, penetryve** *adj* penetrating, piercing; keen, sharp *la15-16*. [probably shortened form of MFr *penetratif*]

penga /ˈpɛŋga/ *n* money, cash *la19- Sh*. [Norn *penga*, ON *penningr* a penny]

pen-gun /ˈpɛŋɡʌn/ *n* a toy gun made from a quill; a popgun or peashooter *18-e20, la20- historical*. **like a pen-gun** *of speech* continuous, chattering *19, 20- NE C*. [PEN¹·¹ + Eng *gun*]

penitent¹·¹ /ˈpɛnɪtənt/ *n* a repentant sinner *la15-*. †**penitent stuil** in St Andrews Kirk the seat occupied by a person undergoing public penance *la16*; compare *stuil of repentance* (STUIL). [see the adj]

penitent¹·² /ˈpɛnɪtənt/ *adj* **1** repentant *la14-*. **2** dissatisfied *16*. [ME *penitent*]

penitrif *see* PENETRIVE

penkel /ˈpɛŋkəl/ *v* to twinkle *la19- Sh*. [Du *pinkelen*]

penn *see* PEND¹·¹

pennall *see* PANEL¹·¹

pennar *see* PENNER

penne *see* PENNY

penner, †**pennar**, †**pennerth**, †**penneth** /ˈpɛnər/ *n* **1** a pencase *la15-19, 20- NE*. **2** a top-hat *la19- NE*. **3** a case for keeping small objects; a needle case *16-17*. †**pennar inkhorn** a pen-case and inkhorn combined *la16-17*. [from PEN¹·¹]

penny, †**penne**, †**penney**, †**peny** /ˈpɛne, ˈpɛni/ *n pl* **pence** †**pens**, **pennies**, †**pennyis 1** money, cash; wealth; a sum of money *la15-*. **2** a Scottish coin of the value of 1/12 of a Scottish shilling and 1/240 of a Scottish pound *la14-17, 18- historical*. **3** a British coin of post-Union currency worth 1/240 of a pound sterling *18-20, 21- historical*. **4** a British coin worth 1/100 of a pound sterling *la20-*. **5** a contribution, a payment *la14-17*. **6** a symbolical payment indicating contractual agreement in property transactions *15-17*. **pennybook** a child's first school primer, originally costing a penny; the first class in a primary school *la19-e20, la20- historical*; compare *tippeny book* (TIPPENY). **penny bookie** = *penny-book*. †**penny bridal** = *penny wedding la16-19, 20- literary*. **penny-buff** a child's first school reading book (originally with a buff cover) *e20, la20- historical*. **penny chap** a game of dominoes in which a forfeit of a penny is paid when a player cannot play *20-*. **penny dainty** a large toffee sweet *20-*. †**penny-dog** a dog devoted to its master; a sycophantic person, a toady *18-19*. **penny-fee** cash, wages, earnings *la18- literary*. †**pennyfull** *of the moon* round, full *la15*. **penny geggie** a travelling theatrical show originally costing a penny for admission *la19-e20, la20- historical*. **penny-jo** a prostitute *la19- C*. †**penny-mail** rent paid in cash *la15-e18*. **penny mob** a Glasgow gang which charged a penny membership fee so that the members' fines could be paid *la19, 20- historical*. **penny-pig** a money-box *17-*. †**penny-purs** a purse for small change *e16*. **penny-rattler** a shop selling small cheap goods *20- NE*. †**penny-reel** a dance at which a dancer paid a penny each time he took the floor *19*. **penny Scots** Scottish coin of the value of 1/12 of a Scottish shilling *la15-17, 18- historical*. †**penny siller** money *la18-19*. †**pennystane** a round flat stone used as a quoit; the game of quoits *la16-e19*. †**pennystane-cast** the distance to which a pennystane quoit could be thrown, a stone's throw *la14-19*. **penny-thing** a fancy cake or biscuit (originally costing a penny) *20- T C*. **penny-wabble** a thin weak ale *la19- NE*. **penny-wedding** a wedding at which guests contribute money or food and drink towards the entertainment, the surplus being given to the couple as a gift *la17-19, 20- historical*. †**penny-whaup** = *penny-wabble la18-19*. **a bonnie penny** a considerable sum of money *19-*. **a braw penny** a considerable sum of money *19-*. **a gey penny** a considerable sum of money *la19-*. **hae een like penny bowls** to have a startled wide-eyed expression *la19- Ork T SW*. †**mak penny of** realise as negotiable funds; convert into cash *la15-17*. †**penneis and pennyworthis** cash and its equivalent *16-17*. [OE *pening, penig*]

pennyland /ˈpɛnɪland/ *n* **1** *in the Norse system of taxation* a division of land (whose size varied by region) on which a tax of one penny was owed to the overlord; frequently in place-names *16-19, 20- historical*. **2** land having a rental value of one penny; frequently in place-names *16-17*; compare *merkland* (MERK) and *pundland* (PUND¹). [PENNY + LAND¹·¹]

pennyworth, **pennysworth** /ˈpɛnewʌrθ, ˈpɛnezwʌrθ/ *n* **1** as much as can be bought or sold for a penny *15-*. **2** a very small amount; a contribution *15-*. **3** value for money; a bargain *16-19*. **4** *pl* equivalent payment or value *15-17*. **5** *pl* retail merchandise; goods or wares *15-e17*. **6** land having a rental value of one penny *la15-e16*. **get yer pennyworth oot o** to revenge oneself on; to get the better of *20-*. **hing in pennyworths** *of the hair* to hang down in lank tangles *la18-19, 20- SW*. [PENNY + WORTH¹·¹]

pens *see* PENNY, PENSE²
pensall *see* PENCIL
†**pense**¹ *n* a spell of study; a school exercise *17-e18*. [Lat *pensum* a piece of work assigned]

†**pense**², **pens** *v* to think or ponder; to call to mind *la15-16*. **pensit** arrogant *16*. [MFr *penser* to think, Lat *pensāre* to weigh, ponder]

pensefu /ˈpɛnsfu/ *adj* thoughtful, meditative, pensive *la19-*. [compare PENSE²]

pensell *see* PENCIL

pensie, **pensy** /ˈpɛnse, ˈpɛnsi/ *adj* **1** self-important, affected, pompous *18-19, 20- NE*. **2** sensible, respectable, fastidious *18-19, 20- NE*. [compare PENSE²]

pensile *see* PINCIL

pension, †**pensioun** /ˈpɛnʃən/ *n* **1** a regular payment for past or present services; a stipend or allowance *la14-*. **2** *Christian Church* a fixed payment from the revenues of an ecclesiastical benefice *15-e17*. **3** a tax or tribute *15-16*. **pensioner**, †**pensionar 1** the recipient of a pension *16-*. **2** a mercenary; a hired soldier *16-e17*. †**pensionary** an ecclesiastical benefice paying a fixed revenue *16*. [ME *pensioun*, Lat *pensio*]

pensy *see* PENSIE

pent¹·¹, **pint**, **paint** /pɛnt, pɪnt, pent/ *n* **1** a mixture of pigment, paint *la18-*. **2** the painted woodwork of a room or building, the paintwork *20-*. [see the verb]

pent¹·², **pint**, **paint**, †**paynt** /pɛnt, pɪnt, pent/ *v* **1** to represent or portray in lines and colour *la14-*. **2** to adorn with colour; to apply pigment *la14-*. [ME *peinten*]

pentit, **pintit**, **paintit**, †**payntit**, †**pantit** /ˈpɛntɪt, ˈpɪntɪt, ˈpentɪt/ *adj* **1** depicted in colour or paint; coloured or decorated with paint *15-*. **2** *of a person* having the face or body coloured or tattooed; wearing (a lot of) cosmetics *la15-*. **3** *of speech* feigned, deceitful, insincere *16*. **4** *of glass* coloured with pigment or tinted with metal oxides *e16*. †**paintit werk** stained glass *e16*. [ME *painted*]

†**penty** *v* to punch or tap *e18*. [unknown]

†**penult**¹·¹ *n* the second last day of a month *la16-17*. [see the adj]

†**penult**¹·² *adj* last but one, penultimate (with reference to the second last day of the month) *la15-e19*. [written abbreviation of Lat *paenultima*]

penure pig *see* PINNER PIG

penurious, **perneurious** /pəˈnjurɪəs, pərˈnjurɪəs/ *adj* **1** *of a child* bad-tempered, whining *20- NE*. **2** *of a person* painstaking, scrupulous, fastidious *20- NE*. [Eng *penurious*, Lat *pēnūriōsus* needy, poor]

†**penuritie**, **penurite** *n* **1** destitution, poverty *la15-16*. **2** deficiency, scarcity *16*. [Lat *pēnūria* with *-ity* suffix]

peny *see* PENNY
peonar *see* PIONEER

people¹·¹, †**pepill**, †**pupil**, †**peopill** /ˈpipəl/ *n* **1** human beings; a community, nation or race *la14-*. **2** employees, followers, subjects or laypeople *la17-*. [ME *peple*]

people¹·², †**peple** /ˈpipəl/ *v* to furnish with inhabitants; to populate *la15-*. [see the noun]

peowl *see* PEWL¹·¹
pepe *see* PEEP²
peper *see* PAPER¹·¹, PEPPER
pepher *see* PIFER
pepill *see* PEOPLE¹·¹
peple *see* PEOPLE¹·²

pepper, †**peper**, †**piper** /ˈpɛpər/ *n* a hot spice *15-*. †**peppercurn**, **pepir quern** a pepper-mill *16-e19*. †**pepper dilse**

a pungent edible seaweed, jagged fucus *Osmundea pinnatifida la18-e19*. **pepper and mustard breed** a Dandie Dinmont (from its brindled grey or yellow colour) *19-20, 21- historical*. **pepper and mustard terrier** = *pepper and mustard breed*. [OE *pipor*, Lat *piper*]

pepper *see* PAPER[1.1]

peppin, peppint /ˈpɛpɪn, ˈpɛpɪnt/ *adj* spoiled, pampered *19- NE*. [derivative of Eng *pap* soft baby or invalid food with verb-forming suffix *-en*]

†**perambule, perambill, peramble** *v* **1** to walk round boundaries or through a piece of land to confirm, designate or formally acknowledge extent or ownership *la15-e17*. **2** to walk about a place *e16*. [Lat *perambulāre*]

†**perbrakit** *adj* breached, holed *la15-16*. [participial adj from ME *parbraken*]

perceive, †**persave,** †**persaif** /pərˈsiv/ *v* to apprehend; to comprehend or discern *la14-*. [ME *perceiven*]

perception, †**perceptioune** /pərˈsɛpʃən/ *n* **1** *law* the collection or levying of rents *la15-*. **2** the process of becoming aware; awareness *19-*. **3** *Christian Church* the receiving of the sacrament *la16*. [ME *percepcioun*]

perch, †**parch** /pɛrtʃ/ *n* **1** piles of stones used to guide navigation in the Firth of Clyde *18, 19- historical*. **2** a pole or bar set up in a seaway to guide ships *17*. †**peirche-tre** a stake set up in a harbour or estuary to guide ships *la16*. [MFr *perche* pole]

perchment *see* PAIRCHMENT

percill *see* PERSEL

perconnon, precunnance, †**percunnand** /pɛrˈkʌnən, prɪˈkʌnəns/ *n* proviso, understanding *15-19, 20- NE*. **on perconnon that** on the understanding that, on condition that *15-19, 20- NE*. [OFr intensive particle *par* + OFr *connoissance* knowledge, understanding, ME *cunnand* skillful]

perdrix *see* PAIRTRICK

perduellion /pɛrdjuˈɛliən/ *n law* high treason *16-18, 19- historical*. [Lat *perduellio* treason]

†**pere, peir** *adj* equal (to) *la14-16*. Compare PEER[1]. [ME *per*]

pere *see* PEER[1], PEER[2], PEER[4]

†**peregall**[1.1] *n* an equal or match *la15-16*. [see the adj]

†**peregall**[1.2]**, paregale** *adj* fully equal *15-16*. [ME *paregal*]

pereis *see* PERISH

perel *see* PERIL

perelt *see* PAIRLT

peremptor[1.1]**,** †**peremptour** /pəˈrɛmtər/ *n* **1** *law* the appointed day and time of a court action *la15-16, 19- historical*. **2** *law* a defence put forward by a litigant which, if proved, annulled further proceedings forever *16-e18*. †**on your peremptors** conforming to rigid social attitudes, behaving in an overly formal manner *e19*. [see the adj]

peremptor[1.2]**, peremptory,** †**peremptour** /pəˈrɛmtər/ *adj* **1** *of the date or time of a court case* precisely specified, without possibility of postponement *la14-*. **2** *of a person* excessively careful, fussy *19- Sh*. **3** *of matters* urgent; unavoidable; conclusive *16-18*. **4** *of a person* imperious; resolute, certain *17-18*. **5** *of a plea* functioning (if accepted) to quash further action *la14-17*. **peremptory defence** *law* a defence put forward by a litigant which, if proved, annuls further proceedings forever *16-*; compare *dilatory defence* (DILATOR). †**peremptory exception** = *peremptory defence la15-e17*. [MFr *peremptoire*, Lat *perēmptōrius*]

†**peremptorie** *adv* at the specified appointed *la16-17*. [EModE *peremptorie*]

peremptorily /pəˈrɛmtrəli/ *adv* **1** resolutely; imperiously *la17-*. **2** *law* on the date or within the time appointed *16-e18*. [from the adj PEREMPTORIE with *-ly* suffix]

†**peremptorly, peremptourly** *adv* **1** conclusively, decisively; categorically *17-e19*. **2** *law* on the date or within the time appointed *15-e18*. **3** by way of peremptory exception or defence *la16-e17*. [from the adj PEREMPTOR[1.2] with *-ly* suffix]

peremptory *see* PEREMPTOR[1.2]

peremptour *see* PEREMPTOR[1.1], PEREMPTOR[1.2]

perfain *see* PROFANE

perfeck[1.1]**, perfect** /ˈpɛrfək, ˈpɛrfəkt/ *adj* flawless, complete *16-*. **perfect age** *law* the age at which a person is considered mature or adult; the age of legal competence or majority *la15-19, 20- historical*. [Lat *perfectus*; compare earlier PERFIT[1.2]]

perfeck[1.2]**, perfect** /pərˈfɛk, pərˈfɛkt/ *v* **1** to make flawless *la15-*. **2** to finish or complete; to accomplish *la16-*. [see the adj]

perfeet *see* PERFIT[1.2]

perfervid, †**praefervid** /pərˈfɛrvɪd/ *adj* **1** ardent, impassioned, enthusiastic *la17-*. **2** enthusiastically patriotic *20-*. [Lat *praefervidus*, Lat *perfervidus*]

perffyt *see* PERFIT[1.1]

perfit[1.1]**, perfeet,** †**perfite** /ˈpɛrfɪt, ˈpɛrfɪt/ *adj* **1** flawless; excellent; complete, exact *la15-19, 20- Bor*. **2** *of a musical note* three times the length of a note of the next lower denomination *la16*. †**perfytly** completely; flawlessly; unmistakably *15-19*. †**perfiteness** flawlessness *16-19*. †**perfyt age** *law* the age at which a person was considered mature or adult, the age of legal competence or majority *la15-e17*. [ME *parfit*; compare later PERFECT[1.2]]

†**perfit**[1.2]**, perffyt** *v* **1** to complete, finish or accomplish *la16-19*. **2** to make a person fully accomplished or knowleable *la18-e19*. **3** to make flawless; to bring to perfection *la15-17*. [see the adj]

perfit[1.3] /ˈpɛrfɪt/ *adv* faultlessly; completely, absolutely *la15-19, 20- literary*. [see the adj]

perfite *see* PERFIT[1.2]

perform /pərˈfɔrm/ *v* **1** to carry out or bring about; to complete or accomplish *16-*. **2** to construct *la15-e17*. [ME *performen*]

performis *see* PERFURNIS

†**perfunctorious** *adj* perfunctory, offhand *la16-17*. [Lat *perfunctōrius*]

†**perfurnis, perfornis, perfurmis** *v* **1** to bring to completion; to accomplish *la14-16*. **2** to complete a payment; to make up a required total *15-16*. **3** to provide or supply *16*. [ME *perfurnishen*]

perfyt age, perfytly *see* PERFIT[1.2]

pergaddis, †**pergaddus** /pərˈɡadɪs/ *n* a heavy blow or thump; a bang or clatter *19- NE T EC*. [unknown]

pergen *see* PARGEN

peril, †**perill,** †**perel,** †**perrell** /ˈpɛrəl/ *n* **1** danger *la14-*. **2** responsibility for loss or damage to goods bought or borrowed *15-17*. [ME *peril*, Lat *perīculum*]

perils *see* PAIRLS

perish, †**peris,** †**pereis,** †**perych** /ˈpɛrɪʃ/ *v* **1** to die *la14-*. **2** to be ruined; to be demolished or destroyed *la14-*. **3** to destroy or wreck; to squander *la15-*. **4** to finish completely, to consume entirely *la18-*. **5** to kill a person; to commit suicide *la15-19*. †**perishment** piercing cold *la19*. †**perish the pack** to squander money and possessions *19*. [ME *perishen*]

perish *see* PAIRISH

perished, †**perist** /ˈpɛrɪʃt/ *adj* **1** dead; decayed or ruined *la14-*. **2** extremely cold *la18-*. [participial adj from PERISH]

perjink[1.1] /pərˈdʒɪŋk/ *adj* **1** trim, neat; smart in appearance *la18-*. **2** prim, strait-laced *la18-*. **3** exact, precise, scrupulously careful *la18-*. **perjinkety 1** prim, strait-laced *la19-*. **2** exact, precise *la18-*. [DINK[1.2], JINK with intensifying prefix

perjink[1,2] /pər'dʒɪŋk/ *adv* primly, fastidiously; carefully *20-*. [see the adj]
perjinks /pər'dʒɪŋks/ *npl* fussy details, niceties *19-*. [from the adj PERJINK[1,1]]
†**perjure**[1,1] *n* perjury *la15-16*. [Lat *perjūrium*]
perjure[1,2] /'perdʒər/ *v* to commit perjury *16-*. [EModE *periure*, Lat *perjūrāre*]
†**perjure**[1,3] *adj* guilty of perjury *la16-e17*. [ME *perjur*]
perk[1,1] /pɛrk/ *n* **1** a wooden pole or rod projecting from a wall or window on which to dry clothes; an indoor drying rail or rope *17-*. **2** a linear measure of varying extent *19- WC SW*. **3** a pole or perch *la14-e19*. [ME *perk*]
†**perk**[1,2] *v* to perch *16-e17*. **perk tree** a post to support a clothes-line *la14-19*. [MFr *percher, perquer*]
perk see PARK[1,1]
perkin, parkin /'pɛrkɪn, 'parkɪn/ *n* a hard ginger-flavoured biscuit made of oatmeal, flour and treacle *la19-*. [unknown, compare PARLIE[2]]
perlament see PARLIAMENT[1]
perle see PEARL[1], PEARL[2]
perlicket /pər'lɪkət/ *n* a trace, a scrap *20- N NE*. [perhaps intensifier prefix *per-* + LICK[1,1] + dim suffix *-et*]
perling see PEARL[2]
perlit see PEARL[1]
perll see PEARL[1]
perlyaag, pirlyaag /pər'ljag, pɪr'ljag/ *n* **1** rubbish; a worthless object *20- NE*. **2** insubstantial, trashy food *20- NE*. [unknown]
perma see PIRR[1]
permansible /pər'mansɪbəl/ *adj* enduring *e16, 20- literary*. [Lat *permansibilis*]
permission, †**permissioun** /pər'mɪʃən/ *n* consent *15-*. [ME *permissioun*]
permutation /pɛrmju'teʃən/ *n* **1** alteration from one state to another; transformation *la15-*. **2** *law* an exchange of one thing for another *15-*. [ME *permutacioun*, Lat *permūtātio*]
perneurious see PENURIOUS
pernick /per'nɪk/ *n* a fussy person, a perfectionist *la19- C*. [back-formation from PERNICKETY]
pernickety, †**pirnickitie** /pər'nɪkɪti, per'nɪkəte/ *adj* **1** *of a person* very precise, obsessed by detail, fussy *19-*. **2** *of a person* cantankerous, touchy, bad-tempered *19-*. **3** *of a task* requiring close attention or great care, troublesome *19-*. [unknown]
pernikkerous /pər'nɪkərəs/ *adj* malicious, bad-tempered *20- Sh*. [from Norn *pernitret*. Form influenced by PERNICKETY]
pernim, pernyim /pər'nɪm, pər'njɪm/ *adj* **1** prim, priggish *20- Sh*. **2** cheeky, impudent *20- Sh*. [unknown]
peroffer see PROFFER[1,1], PROFFER[1,2]
†**peronall** *n* a young woman; a prostitute *e16*. [apparently ME *pernel* shortened from the personal name *Petronilla*]
perpell see PAIRPLE
perpetual, †**perpetuall,** †**perpetuale** /pər'pɛtʃuəl, pər'pɛtʃəl/ *adj* **1** permanent, everlasting *la14-*. **2** continuous, without interruption, constant *16-*. †**in perpetuale, in perpetuall** in perpetuity *la15-16*. [ME *perpetuel*, Lat *perpetuālis*]
perplexit, †**proplexit** /pər'plɛksɪt/ *adj* confused, muddled *la15-*. [Lat *perplexus* with *-it* suffix]
perqueer see PERQUEIR[1,2]
perqueir[1,1]**, prequier** /pər'kwir, prə'kwir/ *adj* **1** clearly seen, distinctly visible *20- Ork*. **2** *of a person* thoroughly-versed; expert, knowledgeable *16-18*. **3** *of language* clear, distinct *la18*. **4** *of objects* skilfully made, elaborate *la18*. [see the adv]

perqueir[1,2]**,** †**perqueer,** †**perquire,** †**parquere** /pər'kwir/ *adv* **1** by heart, from memory; perfectly, exactly *la14-19, 20- literary*. **2** with visual clarity, distinctly *20- Ork*. **3** certainly, without doubt *16-17*. †**perqueerly** clearly, accurately *la18-e19*. †**live perquire** to be short of money; to live in poverty *la16-17*. [OFr *par cuer* by heart]
perr see PAIR[1], PEER[2]
perraphrasis see PARAPHRASE
perrell see PERIL
perrelling see PARALING
perrillis see PAIRLS
pers see PIERCE
persaif, persave see PERCEIVE
perschew see PURSUE
persecute /'pɛrsəkjut/ *v* to harass or oppress *la15-*. **persecuting time** the worst period of the persecution of the Covenanters *19- historical*; compare KILLING TIME. [EModE *persecute*, Lat *persecūt-*, ptp stem of *persequi*]
persecution, †**persecutioun** /pɛrsə'kjuʃən/ *n* **1** harassment, oppression *la14-*. **2** legal prosecution; an action at law; a legal claim *la15-e19*. [ME *persecucioun*]
†**persel, percill, parsell** *n* parsley *16-e19*. [ME *perseli* AN *persil, percil*]
persell see PAIRCEL
persevere, †**perseweir** /pɛrsə'vir/ *v* to continue steadfastly, persist; to last or remain *la14-*. [AN, MFr *perseverer*, Lat *perseverāre*]
persew see PURSUE
persewant see PURSUIVANT
persewar see PURSUER
perseweir see PERSEVERE
persewt see PURSUIT
perskeet, pirskeet /pər'skit/ *adj* **1** fastidious, precise, over-particular *19- Sh*. **2** prudish; strait-laced *19- Sh*. [unknown]
person, †**persoun,** †**parson** /'pɛrsən/ *n* **1** a human being *la14-*. **2** nature, personality *la14-*. **3** the body, the physique *15-*. [ME *persoun*]
person see PARSON
personage see PARSONAGE
personal, †**personall** /'pɛrsənəl/ *adj* **1** pertaining to a person; individual, private *15-*. **2** pertaining to the body, physical *la15-*. **3** *law* done in person, not by proxy *la15-*. **personal bar** *law* an impediment to a legal right or action due to a person's own previous statements or behaviour *20-*. †**personal diligence** *law* the procedure of imprisonment for debt *18-19*. †**personal execution** = *personal diligence la18-e19*. **personal exception** = *personal bar 20-*. †**personal objection** = *personal bar e19*. [ME *personal*, Lat *persōnālis*]
persoun see PARSON, PERSON
persuade, *NE* **perswad,** †**persuaid** /pər'swed; *NE* pər'swad/ *v* **1** to win over by argument; to convince *16-*. **2** to advise; to commend *la15-16*. [EModE *perswade*, Lat *persuādēre*]
persuasion, *NE* **perswashin,** †**perswasioun** /pər'sweʒən; *NE* pər'swaʃɪn/ *n* the action of convincing by argument *la14-*. [ME *persuasioun*, Lat *persuāsio*]
persuit, persute see PURSUIT
perswad see PERSUADE
perswashin, perswasioun see PERSUASION
pert, pairt, †**peirt** /pɛrt, pert/ *adj* **1** clever, sharp *15-*. **2** cheeky; presumptuous *16-*. **3** quick to act *la16-17*. **4** bold, daring *la14-16*. **5** expert, skilled *15-16*. †**in pert** openly, in public *15-16*. [aphetic form of APERT]
pert see PAIRT[1,1], PAIRT[1,2]

pertain, **perteen**, †**pertene**, †**pertein** /pərˈten, pərˈtin/ v 1 to belong to; to be connected to *la14-*. 2 *law* to come under the jurisdiction of *la14-*. 3 to be fitting, suitable or appropriate to *la15-*. 4 to be relevant or relate to *16-*. **pertain tae** to belong to *15-*. [ME *pertenen*]
pertane *see* PARTAN
perteen, pertein *see* PERTAIN
pertenance *see* PERTINENCE
pertene *see* PERTAIN
pertiale *see* PARTIAL
particular *see* PARTICULAR[1,2]
†**pertinence, pertinens, pertenance** *n* 1 accessories, fittings; belongings *la15-17*. 2 *law* something connected with or forming part of a piece of land or heritable property *la14-16*. 3 accompaniments to a main dish *16*. [ME *purtenaunce*, Lat *pertinentia*]
pertinent[1.1] /ˈpɛrtɪnənt/ *n* 1 *law* something connected with or forming part of a piece of land or heritable property (except the rights of the crown) not specially reserved, such as buildings on the land or a right of pasturage *15-*. 2 *pl* accessories, fittings; additional requirements *16-19, 20- Ork*. [ME *pertinent*, Lat *pertinentia*]
pertinent[1.2] /ˈpɛrtɪnənt/ *adj* belonging or relevant to; appropriate *15-*. [see the noun]
pertner *see* PAIRTNER
pertrik *see* PAIRTRICK
†**pertrubill, pertrubbil, perturbill** *v* to disturb greatly; to cause disorder *16-e19*. [OFr *pertroubler*]
†**pertrublans** *n* disturbance *e16*. [OFr *pertroubler*]
perty *see* PAIRTY[1.1]
peruse, †**parewsse**, †**pervys** /pəˈruz/ *v* 1 to examine; to scrutinise *16-*. 2 to prowl about *20- T*. [EModE *peruse*]
†**pervene, pervein** *v* to reach; to haunt *la16-18*. [Lat *pervenīre*]
perverse, †**pervers**, †**perverst**, †**perversit** /pərˈvɛrs/ *adj* 1 wicked *la15-*. 2 obstinate, unreasonable *16-*. [MFr *pervers*]
pervoo /pərˈvu/ *v* 1 *of a bird* to abandon its nest *20- NE*. 2 *of a person* to stop keeping regular company with an acquaintance, to drop a friend *20- NE*. [variant of FORHOO]
pervys *see* PERUSE
perych *see* PERISH
pesane *see* PISSAN
pese *see* PEACE[1.1], PEASE
pesel *see* PIZZLO
pesment *see* PASMENT
Pess *see* PACE
pest[1.1] /pɛst/ *n* 1 a troublesome or annoying person or animal; a nuisance *16-*. 2 a deadly epidemic disease; bubonic plague *la15-19, 20- historical*. 3 a harmful plant or insect *19-*. [MFr *peste*, Lat *pestis* plague]
pest[1.2] /pɛst/ *v* to trouble or annoy *18-*. [see the noun]
pester /ˈpɛstər/ *v* 1 to annoy persistently *la18-*. 2 to encumber or obstruct *17-19, 20- T SW*. [EModE *pester*]
pestilentious /pɛstɪˈlɛnʃəs/ *adj* 1 tending to produce an epidemic disease *16-*. 2 morally pernicious *16*. [MFr *pestilencieux*]
pestole, pestolet *see* PISTOLL
pet[1.1], †**pett** /pɛt/ *n* 1 a hand-reared lamb or sheep; a domesticated animal treated with affection *16-*. 2 an indulged or spoiled child; a person treated with favour *16-*. 3 a term of affectionate address used to a child *la18-*. 4 a day of sunshine in the middle of a spell of bad weather *19- H&I WC*. **pet day** a sunny day during a spell of bad weather *19- C SW Bor Uls*. [Gael *peata* a domesticated animal]
pet[1.2] /pɛt/ *v* 1 to treat with special favour, to spoil; to stroke or caress *17-*. 2 to rear an animal by hand *18-*. **pettle** to fondle or pamper; to treat with favour *la18-19, 20- SW Bor*. [see the noun]
pet[1.3] /pɛt/ *interj* a call to a sheep or lamb *20- N T SW*. [see the noun]
pet[2.1], **pett** /pɛt/ *n* ill-humour *la16-*. **in a pet** in a fit of sulks *20-*. **tak the pet**, †**take the pett** to sulk *la16-*. [unknown]
pet[2.2] /pɛt/ *v* 1 to take offence, to sulk *18-*. 2 to offend; to anger or upset *18-*. [unknown]
†**pet**[3], **pett** *n* a fart *16*. [MFr *pet*]
pet *see* PIT[2]
pete *see* PEAT[1.1], PEAT[2], PEAT[3], PEETY[2]
peté *see* PEETY[1]
peteous *see* PEETY[1]
peter /ˈpitər/ *n* a restraint or check *la19-*. **come the peter ower** to act in a domineering way; to dictate to *20-*. **pit the peter on** to put a sudden stop to; to bring up short *la19-*. [unknown; compare English slang *peter* to stop, leave off]
†**peter bowie** *n* a wedge or stick used by shoemakers for rubbing the seams of shoes before sewing *19*. [from the personal name; second element unknown]
peter dick *see* PETERY DICK
Peter Fair /ˈpitər fɛr/ *n* a summer fair held in Buckie (and originally in Fyvie as well) *18- NE*. [from the name of Saint *Peter* + FAIR[2]]
Petermass, †**Petermes** /ˈpitərmas/ *n* the feast of St Peter and St Paul (on 29th June), or the feast of St Peter ad Vincula (on 1st August) *16-17, 18- historical*. **Petermass Fair**, **Petermas Fair** a fair held in Thurso at the end of June or in early July *18-e20, la20- historical*. †**Petermass Market** a market held in Thurso in the summer *18-19*. [from the name of Saint *Peter* + MASS[2]]
Peter's mark /ˈpitərz mark/ *n* one of the black marks behind the gills of a haddock *19, 20- N NE C*. [from the name of saint *Peter* + MARK[1.1]]
Peter's plough /ˈpitərz plʌu/ *n* the constellation *Ursa Major 19, 20- T*. [from the name of Saint *Peter* plough (see PLOO[1.1])]
Peter's thoom /ˈpitərz θum/ *n* one of the black marks behind the gills of a haddock *la20- Sh Ork N WC*. [from the name of Saint *Peter* + THOOM[1.1]]
petery dick, peterie dick, peter dick /pitəri ˈdɪk, pitər ˈdɪk/ *n* 1 a rhythmic pattern of two or three short beats followed by one long one; a dance step which followed this pattern *19-20, 21- historical*. 2 a child's toy used to beat out a rhythm *20- NE*. [onomatopoeic with influence from the male personal names *Peter* and *Dick*]
pete stane *see* PEAT STANE
peth, path, paith /pɛθ, paθ, peθ/ *n* 1 a steep track or road leading down into a ravine and up the other side, a cleft running up the slope of a steep hill; frequently in place-names *12-*. 2 a footpath *16-*. †**the peths, the pethis** a name for the ravines crossing the coastal route from Scotland to England near Cockburnspath *16-e17*. [OE *pæþ* track, valley]
pethar, pether *see* PEDDER
pethmentit *see* PATHEMENT[1.2]
peticott *see* PETTICOAT
petie custom *see* PETTY
petition, †**petitioune**, †**peticioun** /pəˈtɪʃən/ *n* 1 the action of supplicating; an entreaty or prayer *15-*. 2 a formal request to an authority to grant a privilege or redress a wrong *la15-*. 3 *law* one of the methods by which proceedings can be brought before the Court of Session or the High Court of Justiciary *19-*. 4 *law* an application to a court submitting an issue to its jurisdiction and requesting a decision *la15-17*. **petition and complaint** 1 *law* an application to the Court of Session for redress of complaints of professional misconduct brought against magistrates *19-*. 2 *law* the form for

bringing under review by the Court of Session the actions of a freeholder or magistrate of a royal burgh at their head court *e19*. [ME *peticioun*]

†**petitor**[1.1] *n* a petitioner in a law suit *la16-e18*. [see the adj]

†**petitor**[1.2], **petitour** *adj* characterized by a legal claim; petitionary *la15-17*. [shortened form of PETITORY]

petitory /ˈpɛtɪtəri/ *adj law* relating to an action, claim or judgement enacted by means of a petition in which the court is asked to order the defender pay money or deliver goods *15-*. [Lat *petītōrius* of or concerning a claim to ownership]

petitour *see* PETITOR

petrie-ball /ˈpitri bɔl/ *n* a shoemaker's tool *la19- NE EC*. [variant of PETER BOWIE]

Petronella /pɛtrəˈnɛlə/ *n* the name of a lively Scottish country dance *19-*. [perhaps from the personal name]

pett *see* PEAT[1.1], PET[1.1], PET[2.1] PET[3]

petted lip /ˈpɛtəd lɪp/ *n* **1** a protruding lower lip, a pout *la20-*. **2** a sulky mood *la20-*. [back-formed from the noun PET[2.1]]

petticoat, †**petticote**, †**peticott**, †**pittiecoit** /ˈpɛtɪkot/ *n* **1** a woman's underskirt or undergarment *16-*. **2** a derogatory term for a woman *20-*. **3** the skirt of a woman's riding habit *e19*. **4** a kilt *e19*. **5** a man's under-coat, worn under a doublet *la15-17*. **pettitcoat tails** triangular shortbread biscuits cut from a round, with the outer edge scalloped like a petticoat frill *19-*. [ME *peticote*]

pettie *see* PETTY

pettle *see* PATTLE[1.1], PET[1.2]

petty, †**pettie**, †**pety**, †**pittie** /ˈpɛti, ˈpɛte/ *adj* **1** of less size or importance; minor, smaller, inferior *15-*. **2** insignificant, inconsequential *17-*. **3** *of a person* small-minded, spiteful *18-*. †**pitte commounis** an allowance of food or money assigned to a member of a society *la16-e17*. **petty customs**, †**petie customes**, †**pittie customes** a tax levied on goods entering a burgh for sale in its market *la15-e20, la20- historical*. †**petty pan** a small metal pan or mould used for pastry *18-e19*. **petit point**, †**pettie point** a type of embroidery stitch *17-*. [MFr *petit* small]

petuous *see* PEETY[1]

petuus *see* PIETY

pety *see* PETTY, PIETY

peuch[1.1] /pjux/ *n* a puff of wind or breath *19, 20- Sh NE*. [onomatopoeic; compare PECH[1.1]]

peuch[1.2], **pioch** /pjux, pjɔx/ *v* to exhale; to sigh *la19- Sh T WC Uls*. [see the noun]

peuch[1.3], †**peugh** /pjux/ *interj* **1** a noise imitating the sound of the wind or breath *la19- NE EC Bor*. **2** an expression of impatience, disgust or disbelief *19, 20- Sh T*. [see the noun]

peuch *see* PLOO[1]

peucher /ˈpjuxər/ *n* a persistent choking cough *20- NE SW*; compare PYOCHER. [onomatopoeic]

peucher *see* PYOCHER

peuchle /ˈpjuxəl/ *v* **1** to cough or wheeze; to repeatedly clear the throat *20- Sh NE T C*. **2** to puff or pant *20- Sh T*. **3** to work ineffectually *19- Bor*. [onomatopoeic]

peuchtie, **pituchtie** /ˈpjuxti, pɪˈtjuxti/ *n* a young saithe or coalfish *Pollachius virens* 20 *H&I WC*. [perhaps altered form of Gael *piocach* with dim ending]

peugh *see* PEUCH[1.3]

peumonie /pjuˈmoni/ *n* pneumonia *20- Ork N T C*. [reduced form of Eng *pneumonia* in jocular usage]

peur *see* PUIR[1.3]

peurl *see* PEWL[1.1], PEWL[1.2]

peuther *see* PEWTER, PUTHER

†**pevagely** *adv* in a careless or hasty manner *e16*. [from a variant of the adj PEVYCH]

†**pevych**, **pevach** *adj* perverse, malignant, devious *e16*. [unknown, but a variant of EModE *pievish*]

pew[1.1], **pue**, **pju** /pju/ *n* **1** a gasp; the sound made by exhaling *18-19, 20- Sh Ork*. **2** a small quantity; a slight trace *19- Sh SW*. **3** a puff of smoke; a breath of wind *19- SW*. †**not play pew** to stop breathing; to have no effect *18-e19*. [onomatopoeic]

pew[1.2] /pju/ *v* **1** *of smoke or vapour* to rise, to disperse *19- SW*. **2** to breathe; to show signs of life *20- Sh*. [see the noun]

†**pew**[2.1] *n* the cry of a kite or other bird *la15-16*. [onomatopoeic]

†**pew**[2.2] *v of a bird* to cry *e16*. [see the noun]

pewder *see* PEWTER

pewl[1.1], *Sh* **peurl**, *NE* **peowl** /pjul; *Sh* pjurl; *NE* pjʌul/ *n* **1** a shriek or cry; a grumble or complaint *20- NE T*. **2** a thin curl or wisp of smoke or vapour *19- SW Bor*. **3** the herring gull *Larus argentatus 19- NE*. **4** a morsel or bite of food *19- SW*. **5** *pl* a nickname for the inhabitants of the villages of Gamrie and Pennan *20- NE*. [onomatopoeic]

pewl[1.2], **pule**, *Sh* **peurl**, *NE* **pyowl** /pjul; *Sh* pjurl; *NE* pjʌul/ *v* **1** to whine or cry; to grumble or complain *19, 20- Sh NE T Bor*. **2** *of animals* to be in a weakened state, to pine *19, 20- NE T Bor*. **3** *of people* to scrape a meagre living *19- T*. **4** *of snow or rain* to fall lightly or intermittently *19- Bor*. **pewl amang yer food** to eat listlessly and without appetite *18-19, 20- NE Bor*. [see the noun]

pewter, †**pewther**, †**pewder**, †**peuther** /ˈpjutər/ *n* an alloy of tin and lead *la14-*. [ME *peutre*]

pewter *see* PUTHER

pewther *see* PEWTER

pexin *see* PAIKIN

pey[1.1], **pay** /pae, pe/ *n* **1** a payment; a wage *15-*. **2** *pl* a beating; punishment *la14-19, 20- Ork T EC*. †**peymaister**, **paymaister** a person made responsible for discharging a debt or refunding a loss to another *17*. **pey line** a wage slip *la20-*. **pey-poke** a wage packet *20-*. [AN *paie*, *pay* payment, settlement, a blow]

pey[1.2], **pye**, **py**, **pay**, †**pa** /pae, pe/ *v* **1** to make payment; to recompense; to clear a debt *15-*. **2** to beat; to punish *15-*. **3** *of a source of income* to yield or provide a return *15-*. **4** to pay for: ◊*it'll help tae pey the coal 19-*. **5** to satisfy or gratify *la14-15*. **pay wedding** a wedding at which guests contribute money or food and drink towards the entertainment, the surplus being given to the couple as a gift *19- C SW*. **pey aff**, **pay aff** to pay for others' drinks or entertainment *20- T C*. **pey alang** to go quickly, to hurry *19- NE*. †**pay someone hame** to take revenge on a person *la16-e19*. **pay someone's skin** to thrash or punish a person *18-19, 20- Sh*. **pey up** to do something with energy and application *la19- NE*. [AN *paier* to satisfy someone, to give what is due, to inflict a blow, to settle]

pey *see* PEA[1], PEE[2], PIE[1]

peyment, **payment**, †**pament** /ˈpaemənt, ˈpemənt/ *n* **1** the act of paying; money paid *la14-*. **2** punishment; a beating *la14-19, 20- NE*. **3** currency *15-16*. †**payment making**, **peyment macking** the action of paying *la16-e17*. [AN, MFr *paiement*]

peyn *see* PEEN[2]

peyper *see* PAPER[1.1]

peyr *see* PEER[4]

phanatik *see* FANATIC[1.1], FANATIC[1.2]

phane *see* FANE

pharie *see* FAIRY

†**pharmacian** *n* a pharmacist, an apothecary *la17-e18*. [Fr *pharmacien*]

phary *see* FAIRY

pheare *see* FERE[1]

pheasant, phesand *see* FEESANT
pheesic *see* PHYSIC
phese *see* VICE²
philabeg *see* FILLEBEG
†philagram *n* delicate lace-like work which was crafted by using strands of silver or gold *la17*. [Fr *filigramme*]
philamort *see* FEILAMORT
philarge *see* VOLAGE
philosopher, †philosophour /fəˈlɔsəfər/ *n* a person who studies philosophy; a lover of wisdom or learning *la15-*. **†philosophour naturall** a student of natural phenomena *la15-e16*; compare *natural philosophy* (NATURAL¹·²). **†the Philosopher** Aristotle *la15-e16*. [MFr *philosophe* with agent suffix *-ER*]
philosophy, †philosophie /fəˈlɔsəfi/ *n* **1** knowledge; learning; the study of morality or ethics *15-*. **2** *in Scottish Universities* the courses in Ethics, Physics and Metaphysics; the Arts course as a whole *e18*; compare *natural philosophy* (NATURAL¹·²). **3** *in medieval universities* the advanced courses which followed on the preparatory study of the liberal arts *la14-17*. **4** knowledge of the occult *16*. [MFr *philosophie*]
phinoc *see* FINNOCK
phiscall *see* FISCAL
phise *see* VICE²
phisickis *see* PHYSICS
phisik *see* PHYSIC
phisikis *see* PHYSICS
phitones *see* PYTHONESS
phrase¹·¹, fraise, †phrais /frez/ *n* **1** a small group of words expressing a single idea *16-*. **2** elaborate or gushing speech; flattery, insincerity *18-*. **3** a fuss, a commotion *la18-19, 20- NE T*. **4** a pretence, a delusion *la19- NE T*. **phrasie, fraisie, fraisy 1** gushing, grandiloquent *20- NE T WC Bor*. **2** fussy, fastidious *20- NE*. **haud a phrase wi** to flatter, to cajole *la18-19, 20- NE T*. **mak a phrase wi 1** to make a fuss or outcry *17-19, 20- NE T C*. **2** to boast or brag; to exaggerate *18-e19*. [Lat *phrasis* diction, style, expression]
phrase¹·², **fraise** /frez/ *v* **1** to express in words *18-*. **2** to flatter, to praise insincerely *la18-19, 20- NE SW Bor*. **†faizle** to flatter, to fawn *19*. **phraser, fraiser** a wheedler, a sycophant *19, 20- NE*. **phrasing** *n* flattery *19, 20- NE C Bor*. **phrasing** *adj* ingratiating or insincere in speech *19, 20- NE C*. **fraise wi** to speak grandiloquently *20- NE*. [see the noun]
phtisik *see* TEESICK
physic, pheesic, feesick, †feisik, †phisik /ˈfɪzɪk, ˈfizɪk/ *n* **1** medicine; medical care *la15-*. **2** knowledge of the phenomenal world; natural science *la15-16*. **†under phisik** under medical care, receiving medical treatment *17*. [ME *phisik*, Lat *physicum*]
physics, †phisickis, †phisikis /ˈfɪzɪks/ *n* natural science; the science that deals with the nature of matter and energy *la16-*. [from the obs Eng adj *physic* + pl ending, after Lat *physica* neut pl of *physicus*]
physiognomy, †physinomie, †fysnomy, †visnomy /fɪziˈɔnəmi/ *n* **1** the study of the features of the face (as indicative or character or destiny) *la15-*. **2** the facial features, the countenance *la15-*. **†phisnamour, physnymour** a person skilled in physiognomy *la15*. [ME *phisonomi*, Lat *physiognōmia*]
piaavan *see* PYAUVIN
piaavie *see* PYAUVIE
piatches *see* PEATCHES
pibroch /ˈpibrɔx/ *n* the classical music of the Scottish bagpipes *18-*. [Gael *piobaireachd* piping]
piccataurie *see* PICTARNIE
pice *see* PIECE

pichar *see* PITCHER
picher¹·¹ /ˈpɪxər/ *n* **1** a state of confusion; an excited or overwrought state of mind *la19- NE T Uls*. **2** a disorganized or ineffective person *la19- NE*. [unknown]
picher¹·² /ˈpɪxər/ *v* to work in a disorganized way; to muddle along *la19- NE Uls*. **picherin** ineffectual, unmethodical *la19- NE*. **pichert** perplexed, unable to cope *20- NE*. [unknown]
picht *see* PITCH¹·²
Picht *see* PICT
Pichtis *see* PICTISH
Pichtland *see* PICTLAND
pick¹·¹, **pike** /pɪk, pʌɪk/ *n* **1** a bite of food, a morsel; a snack *18-*. **2** unrestricted choice; a choice article, the best or choicest *la18-*. **3** a small quantity; a trace or scrap *20-*. **pick and dab** a light meal; a snack of potatoes dipped in salt *19, 20- Uls*. **hae a pickie say** to have a certain amount of authority or responsibility *20- NE*. **pickie-say** a narrow-brimmed tweed hat (worn as a badge of authority by the foreman on a farm) *20- NE*. **no a pick on** *of a person or animal* extremely thin *20- C*. **the pick an wale** unrestricted choice; the best or choicest *la18-19, 20- Sh NE WC*. [see the verb]
pick¹·², **†pik**, **†pyke** /pɪk/ *v* **1** to peck *la14-*. **2** to choose, to select *la14-*. **3** to question; to interrogate *20- Ork NE T Bor*. **4** *weaving* to finish cloth by removing loose or faulty threads *la18*. **picker 1** *weaving* a person employed to trim loose threads from the web *19- C*. **2** *in a sawmill* the man who arranges the sawn timber according to size *la20- NE T*. **picket** meagre, scraggy, shrunken *la18-19, 20- NE*. **pickie** a person who picks at their food, a poor eater *la20- C Bor*. **pickin** a mouthful of food, a frugal meal *19-*. **†pickle, pik-ill** *of a bird* to peck; *of a person* to eat in a sparing way; to nibble *16-e19*. **†pick one's lane** to be self-reliant *19*. **pick oot, †pyke out** to select *la16-*. **pick someone up** to understand someone, to get someone's meaning *la19-*. **†pickle in one's ain pock-neuk** to be self-reliant *17-e19*. **†pickle oot o ae pock** *of a group of people* to share a common means of livelihood; to live together *la18-19*. [PIKE⁴; compare ON *pikka* to pick, prick; Du *pikken* to pick, peck]
pick²·¹, **†pik** /pɪk/ *n* **1** a pickaxe; a tool for breaking up hard ground *la14-*. **2** a chap or crack in the skin *20- Ork NE*. **3** (the sound of) a light stroke or tap *16- Sh Ork*. **pikki, picko 1** a tapping sound or action *20- Sh Ork*. **2** a game of tig *20- Sh Ork*. **pickieman, pickman, †pikeman, †pekcaman 1** a miner, a coal hewer *17-19, 20- historical*. **2** a man who dressed millstones with a mill pick *la16-19, 20- historical*. **pickieturd** *in children's rhymes* the magpie *Pica pica 20- Ork*. **pick and mell** with utmost vigour *la19, 20- SW*. [PIKE¹·¹]
pick²·² /pɪk/ *v* **1** to pierce with a pick or sharp instrument *17-*. **2** to make a tapping or knocking sound *la19- Sh Ork*. **picker** *mining* a sharp piece of metal used to trim the wick of a miner's lamp *19, 20- historical*. **pickit 1** *of a surface* roughened, pitted, uneven *la19- Sh NE EC*. **2** *of the skin* rough, chapped *20- Ork NE*. **pick on** to make an impression on; to affect *19- SW*. **pick upo da kirn** to churn milk with a light tapping motion *la19- Sh*. [ON *pikka* to pick, peck, tap, stab; compare Du *pikken* to pick, peck]
pick³·¹ /pɪk/ *n* **1** *farming* a miscarried animal *20- WC SW Bor Uls*. **2** a marble thrown or pitched at the other marbles in a game instead of being rolled *20- NE T*. **tak a pick** to throw a marble at another marble instead of rolling it *20- NE T*. [see the verb]
pick³·², **peek** /pɪk, pik/ *v* **1** to throw, pitch or hurl; to thrust or drive *19, 20- WC Uls*. **2** *of a female animal* to abort her young, to give birth prematurely *19- NE C SW Bor Uls*. **3**

weaving to throw the shuttle across the loom *la20- T C Uls*. †**picker, peeker** *weaving* a mechanism for shooting the shuttle across the loom *19*. **picker stick** = *picker 20- C*. **pick calf** *of a cow* to miscarry its young *la18- WC SW Bor Uls*. **pick lamb** *of a sheep* to miscarry its young *la18- WC SW Bor Uls*. **pick on** to happen on; to fix on *19-*. [ME *picchen* to thrust, throw; to build; to adorn]

pick[4], †**pik**, †**peik** /pɪk/ *n* pique, animosity, ill-feeling *la16-*. **pickant** sharp, keen, biting *la16-19, 20- NE*. **hae a pick at** to have or form a dislike for; to bear someone a grudge *18-*. [MFr *pique* a minor quarrel]

pick[5.1], †**pik**, †**peik** /pɪk/ *n* pitch, bitumen *la14-*. †**pikky, pykky** like pitch; dark, gloomy *e16*. **picky-fingered** given to stealing *19, 20- T EC*. **pick black** pitch-dark *la18-19, 20- NE*. †**pick mirk** pitch-dark *la18-e19*. **pick tar** pitch, bitumen *20- Sh NE*. [ME *pich*, OE *pic*]

†**pick**[5.2] *v* to smear with pitch *la14-e19*. [see the noun]
pick[6] /pɪk/ *n in playing cards* a spade *19- NE*. [Fr *pique*]
pick *see* PIKE[1.1], PIKE[4]
Pick *see* PICT
pickalty *see* PICKLETY
†**pickand, pikant** *n* a prickle; a thorn; a spike *la15*. [MFr *piquant*]
picken *see* PICKIE
pickerel, †**pikkerel** /'pɪkərəl/ *n* the dunlin *Calidris alpina*; any small wading bird *la17-*. [PICK[1.1] with *-rel* dim suffix]
picket *see* PICK[1.2]
pickie, T H&I picken /'pɪke, 'pɪki; T H&I 'pɪkən/ *n* the young of the saithe *Pollachius virens*, any small fry of fish *la19, 20- T H&I WC*. [Gael *piocach*; compare PEUCHTIE]
pickie-maw *see* PICKMAW
pickill *see* PICKLE[2]
†**pickindail, pikindaill** *n* a piccadill, a decorative collar *17-e18*. [Fr *peccadille* a minor sin]
pickle[1], †**pikkill** /'pɪkəl/ *n* 1 a liquid for preserving food; the food so preserved *la16-*. 2 a predicament *19-*. 3 an elaborate and demanding piece of work; a fiddling, awkward job *la20- C SW*. [MDu *pēkel*]
pickle[2], **puckle**, †**pickill**, †**pikle** /'pɪkəl, 'pʌkəl/ *n* 1 a grain of oats, barley or wheat *la16-*. 2 a small particle or grain of salt or meal; a granule, a speck *17-*. 3 a small or indefinite amount of something, an unspecified number *17-*. [unknown]
pickle *see* PICK[1.2]
picklety, pickalty /'pɪkəlti/ *n* a predicament *19-*. [from PICKLE[1]]
picklin, †**pekyllyn** /'pɪklɪn/ *n* putting in brine *la15-*. [MDu *pēkelen*]
pickloo /'pɪklu/ *n* a predicament *20- Ork*. [probably PICKLE[1]]
pickmaw, †**pikmaw** /'pɪkmɔ/ *n* the black-headed gull *Chroicocephalus ridibundus la15-19, 20- SW Bor*. **pickiemaw** = PICKMAW *20- Bor*. [perhaps PICK[5.1] from its colour + MAW[2]]
pickthank *see* PIKE-THANK[1.1], PIKE-THANK[1.2]
Pict, Pecht, Picht, Pech, Pick, †**Peicht** /pɪkt, pɛxt, pɪxt, pɛx, pɪk/ *n* 1 one of a Brythonic people who inhabited Scotland north of the Forth before the foundation of the kingdom of Alba *la14- historical*. 2 a small undersized person, animal or object *17-19, 20- Sh NE*. **Picts' house** an underground dwelling, an earth house, mainly dating from the first two centuries AD *18- Sh Ork N*. [ME *Peght*, OE *Peoht*, *Piht*, Lat *Pictī* apparently from *pingere* to paint]
pictarnie, piccataurie /'pɪktarni, 'pɪkətɔri/ *n* 1 the common tern *Sterna hirundo* or arctic tern *Sterna paradisaea la18-*. 2 the black-headed gull *Chroicocephalus ridibundus 18-19, 20- N NE T*. 3 a thin, wretched-looking person *19, 20- NE*.

4 a bad-tempered person *20- N*. [first element of PICKMAW + Eng *tern*]

picter, †**pictour** /'pɪktər/ *n* 1 a picture; a portrait or likeness *16-*. 2 an effigy used in witchcraft to harm the person represented *la16-17*. **picter hoose** a cinema *20-*. **the big picter** the main film shown during the programme at a *picter hoose 20-*. **the picters** the cinema a film *20-*. [EModE *picture*, Lat *pictūra*]
Pictish, †**Pichtis**, †**Pechtis** /'pɪktɪʃ/ *adj* of or relating to the Picts or their language *la16- historical*. [PICT + Eng *-ish* adj suffix]
Pictland, †**Pichtland**, †**Pechtland** /'pɪktlənd/ *n* the territory of the Picts *16- historical*. [PICT + LAND[1.1]]
pie[1], *T* **peh, pey**, †**py** /pae; *T* pɛ/ *n* 1 a baked pastry dish *16-*. 2 an affair, a scheme; an escapade *la19, 20- NE*. †**mak a pie 1** to make an agreement *la18*. **2** to set up a trap for a person *la16-e17*. [ME *pī*]
pie[2] /pae/ *v* to peer closely; to squint *la15-19, 20- Sh NE C*. **pie-eyed** cross-eyed, having a squint *la20- NE C*. [perhaps related to SPY]
†**pie**[3] *n* an eyelet *la16-19*. Compare PIE-HOLE [unknown]
pie *see* PY, PYE
piece, †**pece**, †**peis**, †**pice** /pis/ *n* 1 a part, a portion; an item *la14-*. 2 a distance: ◇*Ah'll chum ye a piece doon the road 15-*. 3 a bite of food; a snack *17-*. 4 a contemptuous term for a person *18-*. 5 a slice of bread; a sandwich *20-*. 6 a packed lunch *20-*. 7 a portion or space of time *19- NE*. 8 a head of cattle *la15-e18*. 9 an area of land; a stretch of water; a district or territory *la15-17*. 10 a (silver) goblet *la15-17*. 11 *law* a writ establishing a right or title *la16-e17*. 12 a container used for collecting church offerings *la16*. **piecie** a child's word for a sandwich or snack *19-*. **piece box** a box in which a (lunchtime) snack is carried *20-*. **piece denner** a lunchtime meal of sandwiches *la20- NE EC Bor*. **piece poke** a bag in which a snack is carried *20- NE T EC SW*. **piece time** a break for a meal or snack during working or school hours *la19-*. **a piecie** a little, somewhat: ◇*it's a piecie cauld 20- Sh N NE EC*. **piece and jeelie** bread and jam *20-*; compare JEELIE PIECE. †**piece and piece** little by little, gradually *16-18*. **piece on jam** a jam sandwich *20-*. **piece on sausage** a sausage sandwich *20-*. **the piece** each, apiece *18-*. [ME *pece*]
pie-hole /'paehol/ *n* an eyelet *18-19, 20- Sh EC*. [PIE[3] + HOLE[1.1]]
piend *see* PEEN[3]
pierce, †**pers**, †**peirse**, †**pairse** /pirs/ *v* to penetrate, to perforate; to break through or into *la14-*. **piercing-shot** *mining* a blast of explosive in the roof or brushing, designed to bring down an increasing thickness of stone *la19, 20- EC*. [ME *percen*]
piet *see* PYET[1.1], PYET[1.2]
piete *see* PEETY[1], PIETY
pietie *see* PIETY
piety, †**piete**, †**pietie**, †**pety** /'paeəti/ *n* 1 godliness, devoutness, reverence *la15-*. 2 dutifulness; patriotism *16*. †**pietefull, petyfull** pious, dutiful *e16*. †**petuus, piteous** godly, dutiful *16*. [ME *piete*, Lat *pietās*; compare PEETY[1]]
†**pifer, pepher, peiffer** *n* a fife or other wind instrument *la16-17*. 2 a player on the fife *la16*. **piferer** a fife-player *la16-e17*. [Ital *piffero*, Lat *piffarus*]
pifer *see* PEEFER
pig[1] /pɪɡ/ *n* 1 a swine *la15-*. 2 *in the Borders* a small, stunted lamb fattened for the market instead of being kept for breeding *e19*. **pig crue** a pigsty *la19- T Uls*. **pig hoose** a pigsty *20-*. [perhaps from an unattested OE form **picga* or **pigga*]
pig[2], †**pigg** /pɪɡ/ *n* 1 an (earthenware) container; a pot or jar *la15-*. 2 *pl* crockery *la15-*. 3 an earthenware hot-water

bottle *la19-*. **4** a fragment or shard of earthenware (used in children's games) *la16-20, 21- historical*. **5** an earthenware chimney pot *la17-19, 20- WC*. **6** a flower vase *18-19, 20- NE T EC*. **7** an earthenware money box (shaped like a pig) *19-e20, la20- historical*. **8** a chamberpot *19, 20- NE T EC*. **9** a cinerary urn *e16*. **pigger 1** a dealer in earthenware; a maker or seller of crockery *17-19, 20- NE T*. **2** an earthenware or clay marble *la19- NE T*. **pigfu** a quantity filling an earthenware container, a dishful *la16-19, 20- NE*. **piggery** crockery, dishes *19- NE T*. **pig cart** the cart carrying a crockery-merchant's stock *la19-e20 la20- historical*. **piggie bank** a money box (made of earthenware) *20-*. **piggie money** *children's games* broken bits of earthenware used as pretend money *la20- historical*. **piggy bool** a clay marble *20- NE T EC*. †**pig maker** a potter, a maker of coarse pottery *16-e18*. **pig man** an (itinerant) pottery merchant *la17-e20, la20- historical*. **pig shop** a stall or shop selling cheap crockery; a china shop *la19- EC*. **pig wife** a female crockery-seller (going from door to door giving pottery in exchange for rags) *19-20, 21- historical*. **pig-an-ragger** a travelling hawker giving crockery in exchange for rags *la19, 20- historical*. †**pigs and whistles** odds and ends; fragments *la17-e19*. **to pigs and whistles** to pieces, to ruin *la18-*. [unknown]
pigg /pɪg/ *v* to scold; to criticise *20- Sh*. [Norn *pigge* to prod, pierce]
†**pigge** *n* a top-mast or a small mast for a pennant on a ship *e16*. [shortened form of PEGY-MAST]
piggin /ˈpɪgɪn/ *n* a wooden tub-shaped container with one stave extended to form a handle (used as a milk pail or feeding dish) *la18-19, 20- Sh NE Uls*. [unknown]
pight *see* PITCH[1.2]
pik *see* PICK[1.2], PICK[2.1], PICK[4], PICK[5.1], PIKE[1.1]
pikant *see* PICKAND
†**Pikcardie** *adj of hemp* of or from Picardy *la16-e17*. [from the name of the French province]
pike[1.1], †**pyke**, †**pik**, †**pick** /pʌɪk/ *n* **1** a shafted weapon with a pointed metal head *16-*. **2** a pointed tip or end; the spike of a railing *la15-19, 20- Ork NE EC Bor*. **3** a thorn or prickle on a plant; a spine or quill of an animal *la15-19, 20- Ork EC*. **4** the pin on the sternpost of a boat *20- NE*. **5** a long piece of lead for ruling paper; a slate pencil *19*. **6** a pickaxe *la18-19*. **pikie** spiked, jagged, barbed *19- NE T EC*. **pike spade** an iron-shod wooden spade *20- NE*. †**pike staff** a long walking-stick with a spike on the lower end *la15-e19*. **ding on puir men an pike staves** to rain heavily *19, 20- NE T*. **rain auld wives an pike staves** to rain heavily *19, 20- N NE T*. [ME *pik*, OE *pīc* a point, pointed instrument, pike]
pike[1.2] /pʌɪk/ *v* **1** to pick, probe or prod with a pointed instrument *la14-*. **2** *of farm animals* to nibble, to graze *la18-*. **3** to scold, beat or chastise *19-*. **4** *of illness or hunger* to make a person or animal thin and emaciated *la19-*. **5** to shoe a horse with sharps to give grip on icy roads *19, 20- NE*. **a pike-at-yer-meat** a poor or fussy eater *20-*. **pike at** to pick at food *la19-*. **pike oot** to peck; to pick with a sharp implement *la15-*. †**pike on the wind** to sail close to the wind *e17*. †**pike up the cost** to sail close to the coast *e16*. [perhaps from unattested OE *pīcian*; compare OFr *piquier*]
pike[2], †**pyke** /pʌɪk/ *n* a freshwater fish *Esox lucius la15-*. [perhaps related to PIKE[1.1] with reference to the fish's pointed jaw]
pike[3.1] /pʌɪk/ *n* a round, conical-topped hayrick for drying hay before stacking *19, 20- H&I SW Bor Uls*. [PIKE[1.1] compare regional Norwegian *pik* peak, summit]
pike[3.2] /pʌɪk/ *v* to build hay into a rick *19- SW Bor*. **piker** a person who builds hay into ricks *20- Bor*. [see the noun]

pike[4], **pick**, †**pyke** /pʌɪk, pɪk/ *v* to steal, rob or pilfer *la15-19, 20- literary*. †**picker, pikar, peaker** a thief, a pilferer *la14-e18*. **pikery**, †**pykrie**, †**peakrie 1** petty theft, pilfering *la15-19, 20- historical*. **2** stolen goods *16-e17*. †**piking** the action of stealing, petty theft *la15-18*. †**pyking** engaged in petty theft; dishonest *17-19*. †**pikkillar** a petty thief or pilferer *la16*. †**pyke purse** a pickpocket, a thief *16-17*. [MFr *piquer* to pierce, pilfer]
pike *see* PICK[1.1]
piked *see* PIKIT
pike-thank[1.1], **pickthank**, †**pykthank** /ˈpʌɪkθaŋk, ˈpɪkθaŋk/ *n* a sycophant; a tell-tale *16-19, 20- N NE*. [PIKE[4] + Eng *thank*]
pike-thank[1.2], **pickthank** /ˈpʌɪkθaŋk, ˈpɪkθaŋk/ *adj* ungrateful *19- NE*. [see the noun]
pikill *see* PICK[1.2]
pikindaill *see* PICKINDAIL
pikit, piked /ˈpʌɪkɪt, ˈpʌɪkd/ *adj* **1** pointed; spiked or spiky *16-*. **2** *of a person or animal* having a gaunt emaciated appearance, thin and unhealthy-looking *la19, 20- EC Bor*. **piket-like** looking thin or unhealthy *la19, 20- EC*. **pikit weir** barbed wire *20- NE T*. [from the noun PIKE[1.1]]
pikkerel *see* PICKEREL
pikkifild *see* PINKIEFIELD
pikkill *see* PICKLE[1]
pikkillar *see* PIKE[4]
pikle *see* PICKLE[2]
pikmaw *see* PICKMAW
†**pikoneir** *n* a soldier armed with a pike *16-17*. [MDu *pikenier*, MFr *piquenaire*]
pilch *see* PILSH
†**pild, pyllit** *adj of velvet* having a nap of a specified length *e17*. [from the noun PILE[4]]
†**pildagerst, pilligrast** *n* the groats from the naked oat or barley *17*. [perhaps EModE *pilled* peeled + GIRST]
pile[1] /pʌɪl/ *n* **1** a blade of grass *16-*. **2** a pointed stake *17-*. **3** a grain of corn; a leaf of tea *la18- WC Uls*. **4** a pellet of shot *la19- WC Uls*. **5** a snowflake *20- WC Uls*. **6** an unbarbed arrow *e15*. [OE *pīl* a pointed object, a spike; hairs of plants, Lat *pīlum* javelin]
pile[2.1] /pʌɪl/ *n* **1** a heap, a stack *la16-*. **2** a series of weights fitting within or upon each other *la16-17*. [ME *pil*, Lat *pīla* pillar, pier]
pile[2.2] /pʌɪl/ *v* **1** to form into a heap; to create a pile *la18-*. **2** to increase the motion or the speed of a scooter by moving the body or feet *la20- NE T C*. [see the noun]
†**pile**[3] *n* the lower part of a minting apparatus which struck the back of the coin *la16-e17*. [ME *pil*, EModE *pyll*]
pile[4], †**pyle**, †**poill** /pʌɪl/ *n* **1** the nap on cloth *la16-*. **2** the layer of scum or fat that accumulates on the surface of boiling liquid when meat is cooked *19- Sh*. **3** hair *e16*. †**pylie gray, pyle gray, pylygray** gray cloth with a pronounced coarse or hairy nap *16*. [EModE *pile* hair, Lat *pilus*]
piler /ˈpʌɪlər/ *n* a home-made cart, propelled by hands or feet *la20- H&I C*. [PILE[2.2] with *-er* suffix]
pilgate *see* PILGET[1.1], PILGET[1.2]
pilget[1.1], **pilgate** /ˈpɪlgət, ˈpɪlget/ *n* **1** a state of distress or excitement *la19- Ork NE T*. **2** a quarrel or disagreement; a struggle against the odds *la18- NE T*. [perhaps Eng *pell* to hurry, to strike + AGAIT in motion]
†**pilget**[1.2], **pilgate** *v of children* to quarrel or bicker *19*. [see the noun]
pilget *see* PIL3ET
pilgrim, †**pilgrym**, †**pilgrame** /ˈpɪlgrɪm/ *n* a person who travels to a sacred place as an act of religious devotion *la14-*. **pilgrimer** a pilgrim *16-17, 19- literary*. [ME *pilgrim*, Lat *peregrīnus*]

piling, pilin /ˈpʌɪlɪŋ, ˈpʌɪlɪn/ *n* **1** a paling, a fence *19- SW Bor*. **2** the action of driving in stakes (to indicate the limits of mineral workings) *la16-18*. **pilin lett** a slat of wood in a fence *la20- SW Bor*. [PILE¹]

pilk¹·¹ /pɪlk/ *n* **1** a husk, an empty shell; a morsel or scrap *20- Sh NE*. **2** a rod with a hook on the end for catching fish or lifting them out of the water *20- Sh*. **3** an uncooperative cow *20- SW*. [see the verb]

pilk¹·² /pɪlk/ *v* **1** to pick out; to shell or peel *18-19, 20- Sh N NE*. **2** to pilfer, to steal *la18- Sh NE EC*. **3** to feel or handle; to touch *20- Sh*. **4** to strike or beat; to deliver a blow *20- Sh*. **5** to catch fish with a rod with a hook on the end *20- Sh*. **6** to tickle *20- Sh*. **7** to milk a cow completely; to strip of milk *19*. [ME *pilken* to strike, pick clean; to deprive; Shetland usages from Norn *pilk* to pick, prick]

pill see PEEL⁹

pillae, pillow /ˈpɪle, ˈpɪlo/ *n* a soft bag filled with down or feathers, a pillow *16-*. **pillowbere**, †**pillowber** a pillowcase *16-19, 20- Bor*. **pillow slip** a pillowcase *19-*. [ME *pillow*]

pillage /ˈpɪlədʒ/ *n* **1** loot, the spoils of war *la15-*. **2** the share of the contents of a prize-ship due by law to the ordinary members of the ship's company which made the capture *la16-e17*. [ME *pilage*]

pillan see PILLER

pillar, †piller, †peller, †pyler /ˈpɪlər/ *n* **1** a tall vertical support or ornament for a building; a tall vertical monument *la14-*. **2** a pillar in a church or post in the street used as a place of public repentance or punishment; a raised platform on which those convicted of minor offences were publicly displayed *la15-18*. [ME *piler*, Lat *pīlāre*]

piller, pullar, pillan /ˈpɪlər, ˈpulər, ˈpɪlən/ *n* a small crab which has just cast or is about to cast its shell and is used for bait *18- Ork NE T EC*. [perhaps Norw dial *pilla* to peel]

piller see PILLAR

pillersho /ˈpɪlərʃo/ *n* a young trout *20- Ork*. [perhaps Norw dial *pilar* a small fish + Norw dial *kjøe* trout]

†**pillery** *n* pillage, plundering *la15-16*. [ME *pillerie*]

pilleurichie /pɪˈlurəxe/ *n* a fuss or commotion; an uproar *la19- NE*. [onomatopoeic]

pillie¹ /ˈpɪli/ *n* the penis *la16-19, 20- Sh Ork WC SW Uls*. †**pillie wantoun** an amorous, lecherous person *e16*. [probably related to Norw *pill* penis]

†**pillie**², **pilʒe** *v* to rob or plunder a ship; to seize goods by piracy *16-e17*. [MFr *piller*]

pillie see PULLEY

pilliedacus /pɪleˈdakəs/ *n* the person in charge *la19- NE T EC*. **the heid pilliedacus** a boss; a self-important employer or leader *la19- NE T EC*. [perhaps BILLY + a mock Latin element. The first element may also refer to PILLIE¹]

†**pilliewinkis** *n* an instrument of torture for squeezing fingers *la16-17*. [altered form of ME *pirewinkes*]

pilligrast see PILDAGERST

pillion, †pilʒane /ˈpɪljən/ *n* **1** the passenger seat of a motorcycle *20-*. **2** a pad or a light saddle used by a woman, or attached behind a normal saddle for a second rider or for carrying luggage *16-e19*. [Gael *pillean*, Lat *pellis* a skin, pelt]

†**pillok** *n* the penis *e16*. [PILLIE¹ + -OCK]

pillow see PILLAE

pilmuir see PEEL²

pilpert /ˈpɪlpərt/ *n* a badly-fed, cold-looking child *20- NE*. [unknown]

pilsh, †pilch /pɪlʃ/ *n* **1** a rough or heavy man *19- NE T*. **2** an ill-fitting or unattractive garment *la19- NE T*. **3** a piece of thick cloth; a rag *la19- NE*. **4** a triangular piece of material bound over a baby's nappy to keep it in place *e20, la20- historical*. **5** an outer garment of animal skin with the fur used as a lining *e16*. **pilshach** an ill-fitting or ugly garment *19- NE*. [OE *pylece*, Lat *pellicia*]

piltin-pyock see PELTIN-PYOCK

piltock, piltick, *N* **peltag** /ˈpɪltək; *N* ˈpɛltəɡ/ *n* the coalfish *Pollachius virens* in its early stages, usually in the second year of life *la17- Sh Ork N*. **piltock band** a cord of piltocks strung together by the heads *20- Sh*. **piltock eela, piltick eela** rod-fishing for piltocks *20- Sh*. **piltock flee, piltik flee** the fly used in piltock fishing *20- Sh*. **piltock fleet** a line, with up to a dozen hooks, dragged under water for piltock fishing *20- Sh*. **piltock tom** a fishing-line used for catching piltocks *20- Sh*. **piltock waand** the rod used in fishing for piltocks *20- Sh Ork N*. [ON *piltr* a boy + -OCK]

pilty-cock /ˈpɪltekək/ *n* an early form of curling stone with indentations for the fingers and thumb instead of a handle *19- historical*. [unknown]

pilʒane see PILLION

pilʒe see PILLIE²

†**pilʒet, pilget** *n* a light saddle used by a woman *16-e17*. [altered form of PILLION]

pin see PEEN¹, PEEN³, PEEN⁴

pinch¹·¹ /pɪnʃ/ *n* **1** a critical point, a crisis *la16-*. **2** a pointed iron rod or bar for levering or making post holes, a crowbar *la17-*. [see the verb]

pinch¹·², †**pinsch** /pɪnʃ/ *v* **1** to spend or give meanly; to be excessively economical *la16-*. **2** to move a heavy object by levering it *la18-*. **3** to put into difficulty; to bring to a standstill *la18-19*. **pincher 1** *pl* a tool for pinching; tweezers or pliers *la18-*. **2** a crowbar *la18-*. **3** a blunt chisel used for chipping the edge of a squared-off stone *la19-*. **pinching bar** a crowbar *la18-*. [ME *pinchen*, EModE *pinch*]

pincil, pencil, †pinsell, †pensile /ˈpɪnsəl, ˈpɛnsəl/ *n* **1** a writing implement *16-*. **2** a paint brush *la16-17*. **3** the penis *la16*. [ME *pencel*]

pind see POIND¹·²

pinding /ˈpɪndɪŋ/ *n* a bowel disorder affecting lambs fed on over-rich milk *19- Bor*. [OE *gepyndan* to enclose, stop up]

pine¹·¹, **pyne** /pʌɪn/ *n* **1** a disease of sheep or cows due to a mineral deficiency *19-*. **2** punishment or torture; the pains of Hell *la14-17, 18- literary*. **3** physical pain; mental *la14-19, 20- Sh Ork NE T*. **4** hardship, effort *la14-16*. [OE *pīn*, ON *pina*]

pine¹·² /pʌɪn/ *v* **1** to languish from grief *la15-*. **2** *of animals* to waste away from disease; to become exhausted or emaciated *la16-*. **3** *of fish* to shrink in the curing process *la16-19, 20- Sh NE*. **4** to cause pain and suffering; to torment or torture *la14-19*. †**pined, pynit, pynd 1** in pain; tortured, tormented *16-19*. **2** emaciated, reduced to skin and bone *16-19*. †**pining** a disease of sheep *19*. **pine awa** to languish; to waste away *16-*. [see the noun]

pine see PEEN¹

piner¹ /ˈpʌɪnər/ *n* **1** an animal suffering from a disease; an animal or person that is not thriving *19-*. **2** a strong wind from the north or north-east that dies away by degrees *la19- NE*. **piner wind** a strong wind *20- NE*. [from the verb PINE¹·² + -ER]

piner², **pynour, †pinour** /ˈpʌɪnər/ *n* **1** a porter; *in Aberdeen* a member of a society of porters *15-19, 20- historical*. **2** a labourer; a turf-cutter *15-19, 20- N*; compare PIONEER. †**pynourschip** the office or duties of a labourer or porter *16*. [perhaps MDu *piner* a labourer]

pinge see PEENGE²

pingill see PINGLE¹·²

pingle¹·¹ /ˈpɪŋəl/ *n* **1** an effort, a struggle *18-19, 20- NE C*. **2** a contest; a disagreement or quarrel *la16-e19*. †**pingling** contention, exertion *la16-19*. [see the verb]

pingle[1,2], †**pingill** /ˈpɪŋəl/ v **1** to struggle or strive, to exert oneself; to work hard with little result *16-*. **2** to contend or compete; to quarrel or disagree *16-19, 20- Bor*. **3** to work in a lazy, ineffectual way *19, 20- Bor*. **pingled** harassed, oppressed; exhausted *18-19, 20- literary*. †**pingling** contention, exertion; labour with little success *la16-19*. [unknown; compare Du *pingelen* to haggle, chaffer, Swe dial *pyngla* to work ineffectively]

pingle[2] /ˈpɪŋəl/ n a small, shallow metal cooking-pan (with a long handle); a saucepan *19- C SW Bor*. **pingle pan** a small pan, a shallow cooking-pot *la18-19, 20- NE SW Bor*. [unknown]

pingling /ˈpɪŋlɪŋ/ adj **1** *of people* painstaking, meticulous *19-*. **2** *of people* lacking character or energy *19-*. **3** *of work* fiddling, tedious, demanding *la19- Sh WC Bor*. [from the verb PINGLE[1,2]]

pinish *see* PINNISH

pink[1] /pɪŋk/ n a garden flower, the primrose or primula *19-*. Compare PINKIE[2]. [unknown]

†**pink**[2.1] n a decorative hole or eyelet in a garment *e16*. [unknown]

pink[2.2] /pɪŋk/ v **1** to ornament cloth with slashing or scalloping; to cut cloth decoratively *16-*. **2** to strike with a small object so as to make a tiny sharp sound *19-*. **3** to impel or catapult a small object through the air *19-*. **4** to adorn, to dress up *la19-*. **5** *of drops of moisture* to drip or fall (with a sharp, tinkling sound) *la18-19, 20- Ork NE*. **pinkin** a beating, a thrashing *la20- Bor*. **pinkle** *of hunger pangs* to produce a prickling or tingling sensation *19, 20- Bor*. [unknown]

†**pink**[3] n a small creature or thing *la16-19*. [unknown; compare Du *pink* the little finger]

†**pink**[4] v **1** to narrow the eyes; to blink or peer *19*. **2** *of stars* to twinkle *19*. [probably EModDu *pinken* to blink]

pinkafil *see* PINKIEFIELD

pinkie[1.1], **pinky** /ˈpɪŋki, ˈpɪŋke/ n **1** the little finger *19-*. **2** something small or insignificant; a tiny hole; a particle of light *19, 20- literary*. [PINK[3] with dim suffix -IE]

pinkie[1.2] /ˈpɪŋki, ˈpɪŋke/ adj tiny, minute *19- C Bor*. [see the noun]

pinkie[2] /ˈpɪŋki, ˈpɪŋke/ n the primrose *la18- NE T WC*. [unknown, perhaps related to PINK[2.1]]

†**pinkie**[3] n weak beer *e19*. [reduced form of INKIE PINKIE]

†**pinkie**[4] adj *of the eyes* narrowed, peering, blinking *18-e19*. [from the verb PINK[4]]

pinkiefield, **pinkafil**, **pikkifild** /ˈpɪŋkifild, ˈpɪŋkəfɪl, ˈpɪkifɪld/ n a quarrel, disagreement or dispute *19- Sh*. [unknown]

pinky *see* PINKIE[1.1]

pinner pig, †**penure pig** /ˈpɪnər pɪg/ n an earthenware money box *la18- WC*. Compare *penny pig* (PENNY). [perhaps reduced form of Eng *penury* or alteration of *penny pig* (PENNY)]

†**pinnet** n a small flag, a ship's ensign; a streamer *18-19*. [altered form of Eng *pennant*]

pinni /ˈpɪni/ n *fisherman's taboo* a term used in Shetland for a fishing-buoy made from an inflated animal skin *20, 21- historical*. **pinnek**, **pinnock** a small fishing-buoy *20, 21- historical*. [ON *pinni* a pin]

pinnish, **pinish**, **pinnis** /ˈpɪnɪʃ, ˈpɪnɪs/ v to suffer pain or discomfort (from cold or hunger) *20- Sh*. **pinishin** a bitter, biting cold *20- Sh*. [Norn *pinnis*, ON *pínask* to be tormented]

pinno /ˈpɪno/ n a point or pinnacle of rock *20- Ork*. [Norw *pinne* a pin, point or stump]

pinour *see* PINER[2]

pinsch *see* PINCH[2]

pinsell *see* PENCIL, PINCIL

pint[1], **pynt**, †**point** /pʌɪnt/ n **1** a liquid measure equivalent to just over half a litre *19-*. **2** a unit of liquid capacity equivalent to three imperial pints (used as the basis of the measures for dry goods) *la14-19, 20- historical*. **3** a vessel or measure containing a pint *la15-e17*. **pint stowp** a drinking vessel or measure containing a pint *16-19, 20- literary*. **Scotch pint** a measure of capacity equal to three British imperial pints (used latterly in the bakery trade) *la17-19, 20- historical*. [OFr *pinte*]

pint[2.1], **pynt**, **point**, †**poynt**, †**punct**, †**pant** /pʌɪnt, pɔɪnt/ n **1** a sharp end or tip *la14-*. **2** a tagged length of leather or cord used for fastening; a shoelace or bootlace *la15-*. **3** a tapering piece of land, a promontory *16-*. **4** the leading member of a team of reapers, the man at the front left-hand-side of the team *19, 20- NE Uls*. **5** the tapering part of a field which is not completely rectangular; the furrows shortened because of this *la20- NE EC SW*. **6** a feat of arms; a military venture *la14-e15*. [OFr *pointe*]

pint[2.2], **pynt**, **point** /pʌɪnt, pɔɪnt/ v **1** to indicate by pointing *15-*. **2** to provide with a point *la15-*. **3** *building* to pack the spaces between stones with mortar with the point of a trowel *16-*. **4** *building* to indent a stone face with a pointed tool *la20- NE T*. **pint oot**, **point out** to indicate *la16-*. [ME *pointen*]

pint[3], **point**, †**poynt** /pʌɪnt, pɔɪnt/ n **1** a detail, a particular; a mark or characteristic *la14-*. **2** a specific moment in time *la14-*. †**at point**, **at poynt 1** properly, fitly, aptly *la14-16*. **2** in full readiness *la15-16*. †**put to ane poynt** to bring to a settlement *16-17*. †**put to poynt** to put in good order *la15-16*. [ME *pointe*]

pint *see* PENT[1.1], PENT[1.2]

pinted *see* POINTIT

pintit *see* PENTIT

pintitly *see* POINTIT

pintle, †**pintill** /ˈpɪntəl/ n a penis *15-*. †**pintle fish**, **pintill fisch** a sand eel *la16-e18*. [OE *pintel*]

†**pinto** n *weaving* a pin or bolt used as a handgrip for turning the beam in a loom *e19*. [variant of PINTLE]

piob mhor /pib ˈvɔr/ n the large Scottish bagpipes or great Highland pipes *19-*. [Gael *pìob mhòr*]

pioch *see* PEUCH[1.2]

pioneer, †**pioner**, †**peonar** /paeəˈnir/ n **1** a military construction worker *16-*. **2** an explorer *19-*. **3** a porter, a labourer *16-17*. [OFr *peonier* a foot soldier, MFr *pionnier*]

pipar *see* PIPER

pipe[1.1], †**pype** /pʌɪp/ n **1** a musical instrument *15-*. **2** a cylindrical pipe or tube *16-*. **3** a tobacco-pipe *17-*. **4** a large ripe acorn with its stalk *20- Bor*. **5** the Scottish bagpipes *16-17*. **pipie** a pipe major *20-*. **pipe band** a military or marching band made up of pipers and drummers with a drum-major *20-*. **pipey-dottle** the plug of tobacco and ash in a half-smoked tobacco-pipe *la20-*. **pipe major** the leader of a pipe band; a military title equivalent to a regimental bandmaster *la19-*. **pipe riper** a pipe-cleaner *la19- Sh NE C*. **pipe shank** the stem of a tobacco-pipe *la19-*. **pipe shankit** *of people or animals* having long, thin legs *la19- C Bor Uls*. **pipe stapple 1** the stem of a tobacco-pipe *la18-19, 20- SW Bor*. **2** a large ripe acorn with its stalk *20- Bor*. **the great pipe** the Scottish bagpipes *la16-*. [OE *pīpe*]

pipe[1.2] /pʌɪp/ v **1** to pipe; to play a tune on a pipe or bagpipes *15-*. **2** to flute cloth; to frill with an iron *la19-*. **3** *of the wind* to make a piping sound; to rise audibly *la15-19*. [Lat *pīpāre*]

†**pipe**[2] n a large cask *15-17*. [ME *pipe*]

pipe *see* PEEP[3], PEEP[5]

piper, †**pipar**, †**pyppar** /ˈpʌɪpər/ n **1** a bagpipe player; a person who plays on a pipe *la15-*. **2** a military title given

piper see PEPPER

pipes /pʌɪps/ *npl* Scottish bagpipes *la16-*. **pipes and drums** the pipers and drummers making up a pipe band *20-*. †**tune yer pipes** to start to cry; to wail like the sound of bagpipes being tuned *la17-19*. [pl of PIPE¹·¹ or reduced from pl of BAGPIPE]

†**pippane** *n* a reel containing a standard length of thread *la15-16*. [unknown]

pipper¹·¹ /ˈpɪpər/ *n* a trembling, excited state; a frightened condition *20- Sh*. [see the verb]

pipper¹·² /ˈpɪpər/ *v* to tremble or quiver with fear or cold *19- Sh*. **pipperation** a fit of trembling *20- Sh*. [Norn *pipper* to tremble, ON *pipra*]

pipper see PAPER¹·¹

pipsyllis /ˈpɪpsɪlɪs/ *n* a disease; malingering, feigned illness *20- NE*. [probably altered form of Eng *epilepsy*]

pirg /pɪrg/ *v* to jibe, taunt or insinuate *20- Sh*. Compare PIRK¹·². [Norn *pirk* to curl, to cause to bristle, Norw *pirka* to poke]

pirie see PEERIE¹

pirk¹·¹ /pɪrk, pirk/ *n* a sharp point; a thorn or prickle *la19- Ork N*. **pirkle** *pl* a spiked nose-band used to prevent a calf sucking *la20- N NE WC*. [see the verb; compare PIRG]

pirk¹·², **peirk** /pɪrk, pirk/ *v* **1** *of hair or fibres* to bristle or stick up *19- Sh*. **2** *of people* to dress in a precise, careful manner *20- Sh*. [Norn *pirk* to curl, to cause to bristle, Norw *pirka* to poke; compare PIRG]

pirkas /ˈpɪrkəs/ *n* **1** something of value, a lucky acquisition *20- N*. **2** a difficult situation, a predicament *20- N*. [reduced and altered form of Eng *perquisite*]

pirket /ˈpɪrkət/ *adj* **1** rough-looking, pointed *20- Sh*. **2** *of the features* shrunken, sharp, aquiline *20- Sh*. **3** over-dressed *20- Sh*. [Norn *pirket* shrivelled, lean; Compare Swed *perket* slender, frail]

pirl¹·¹, †**purll** /pɪrl/ *n* **1** a curl, twist or coil *16- C Bor*. **2** hair twisted into a knot or bun *la20- T EC SW*. **3** an eddy or swirl in water; a gentle breeze *19- NE Bor*. **4** a snowflake *20- C Bor*. [see the verb]

pirl¹·², **purl** /pɪrl, pʌrl/ *v* **1** to manoeuvre a small object by poking it *la18-*. **2** *of snow or wind* to swirl; *of water* to ripple *la18-*. **3** to twist, coil or curl (hair or wool) *19-*. **4** to cause to rotate; to spin or whirl *19-*. **5** to mess about; to work half-heartedly *la19- Sh NE EC*. **6** to poke a fire *19- Sh NE*. **7** to work potatoes out of the ground without disturbing the stems *19- Sh*. **8** *in football or hockey* to drive the ball with quick light strokes or kicks *20- NE*. **9** to thrust or poke *la15*. [probably onomatopoeic; compare PEARL², PURL¹·², BIRL¹·²]

pirl see PURL¹·¹

pirlag see PURL¹·¹

pirlicue¹·¹ /ˈpɪrlɪkju/ *n* **1** a flourish or ornament at the end of a handwritten word *19, 20- NE SW*. **2** a resumé, a conclusion *19, 20- SW*. **3** *Presbyterian Church* the summary of sermons preached during the Communion season by visiting ministers, delivered by the parish minister *19, 20- historical*. [perhaps PIRLIE¹·² The second element may represent *cue* a tail]

pirlicue¹·² /ˈpɪrlɪkju/ *v Presbyterian Church* to deliver the summary of sermons *19, 20- historical*. [see the noun]

pirlie¹·¹, **purlie** /ˈpɪrli, ˈpʌrli/ *n* **1** something very small *19, 20- Ork T*. **2** a small twisted sweet *20- WC SW*. **3** the little finger *19, 20- T*; compare PIRLIE-WINKIE. [PIRL¹·¹ + *-ie* diminutive-forming suffix]

pirlie¹·² /ˈpɪrli, ˈpʌrli/ *adj* curly, curled; twisted *19- Bor*. [PIRL¹·¹ + *-ie* adj-forming suffix]

pirlie pig, †**pirrell pig** /ˈpɪrli pɪg/ *n* **1** a (circular) earthenware money box with a coin-slot *la17-*. **2** the box used by the Town Council of Dundee for collecting fines from absentee members *19-20, 21- historical*. [PIRL¹·² + PIG²]

pirlie-winkie /ˈpɪrliwɪŋki/ *n* the little finger *19-*. Compare PINKIE¹ (sense 2). [PIRLIE¹·¹ + WINKIE]

pirlyaag see PERLYAAG

pirm see PIRN¹·¹

pir maw see PIRR¹

pirmet, †**pirned**, †**pirnit** /ˈpɪrmət/ *adj* striped, variegated; woven in different colours *la15-19, 20- Sh*. [PIRN¹·¹, from the Sh variant]

pirn¹·¹, **purn**, *Sh Ork* **pirm** /pɪrn, pʌrn; *Sh Ork* pɪrm/ *n* **1** a spool of sewing thread; a reel for thread *la15-*. **2** a spool for holding the weft yarn in a shuttle *17-*. **3** the reel of a fishing rod *la18-*. **4** the amount of yarn that can be wound on a reel *la15-19, 20- NE EC Bor*. **5** something trivial or of little value *la19- Sh T*. **6** *mining* a disc on which flat ropes are wound *la18-19, 20- SW*. **7** a twitch for quietening a horse *20- Bor*. **8** a stripe or band in a piece of cloth of a different colour or texture from the rest; an irregularity or flaw *la17-e18*. **pirn mill** a mill where weavers' bobbins are made *20- T*. †**pyrne satine** satin variegated with a contrasting thread *16-e17*. **pirn taed** hen-toed *20- Sh NE T*. **purny-taed** hen-toed *20- Sh NE T*. **pirn taes** toes which turn inwards *20- NE*. **pirn wheel** a wheel for winding yarn on to bobbins *16-*. †**pirn winder** the person who loaded a weaver's bobbins with yarn *la18-19*. **fill a pirn** to wind yarn on to a weaver's bobbin *la18-19, 20- T*. **a ravelled pirn** a confused or complicated matter *la18-19, 20- NE*. [unknown]

pirn¹·² /pɪrn/ *v* to wind yarn; to reel a line *19-*. **pirn in** to reel in a fishing-line *la19- SW Bor*. **pirn out** to allow a fishing-line to unwind *la19- SW Bor*. [unknown]

pirned see PIRMET

pirnickitie see PERNICKETY

pirnie¹·¹ /ˈpɪrni/ *n* a striped woollen hat (originally a nightcap) made in Kilmarnock *19- C SW Bor*. [PIRN¹·¹]

†**pirnie**¹·² *adj* variegated, striped; uneven or irregular in weave *la16-e19*. **pirnie plaid** a plaid with a stripe instead of the usual checked pattern *la17-19*. [see the noun]

pirnit see PIRMET

pirr¹, **purre** /pɪr, pʌr/ *n* the common tern *Sterna hirundo 19-*. **pir maw**, *Uls* **perma 1** the black-headed gull *Chroicocephalus ridibundus 19- C SW Uls*. **2** the roseate tern *Sterna dougallii 18-19*. [onomatopoeic of the bird's cry]

pirr²·¹, †**pirrhe** /pɪr/ *n* **1** a fit of temper, a sudden rage *la19- Sh Ork NE Bor*. **2** an over-excited state of mind; a panic *la19- Sh Ork NE*. **3** a sudden sharp breeze; a gentle breath of wind *17-19, 20- Sh NE*. **pirrie 1** *of a person* quick-tempered *19- Bor*. **2** *of a person* unpredictable, unreliable *20- Sh*. [probably onomatopoeic, but compare BIRR¹·¹]

pirr²·² /pɪr/ *v* **1** *of liquid* to ripple; to flow *19-*. **2** *of a breeze* to blow gently *19- Sh EC*. **3** *of a person* to tremble with anger *20- Sh Ork Bor*. [see the noun]

pirr³ /pɪr/ *n* a young cod *19- Sh*. [Norn *pirr* a small fish]

pirr⁴ /pɪr/ *n* a hot drink made with oatmeal, cream of tartar and sugar (used as a cold remedy) *20- Sh*. [perhaps from the verb PIRR²·¹ as a jocular reference to the effervescence of the drink]

pirrell pig see PIRLIE PIG

pirren /ˈpɪrən/ *n* a (small) child *19- Sh Ork*. [perhaps Norn *pirrena* a sickly child]

pirrhe see PIRR²·¹

pirrivee, pirwee /pɪri'vi, pɪr'wi/ *n* a state of excitement or rage *20- Ork N*. [conflation of PIRR[2,1] and TIRRIVEE]
pirskeet *see* PERSKEET
pirwee *see* PIRRIVEE
piscence *see* PUISSANCE
pische *see* PISH[1,2]
pise *see* PEASE
pisert /'paezərt/ *n* a miser, a skinflint *19- Sh Bor*. [unknown]
pish[1,1] /pɪʃ/ *n* **1** urine *la17-*. **2** rubbish, nonsense *20-*. **3** a badly performed job or action *la20-*. **pish oot** a heavy downpour of rain *20- NE SW*. **pish pot** a chamber pot *19-*. **a long streak o pish** a contemptuous term for a person *la20-*. **on the pish** on a drinking binge *la20-*. **rip the pish oot o** to make a fool of; to humiliate *la20-*. [see the verb]
pish[1,2], †**pische** /pɪʃ/ *v* **1** to urinate *16-*. **2** *of water* to gush or splash; *of rain* to pour down *la18-*. **pished** drunk *la20-*. **pish yersel** to wet yourself (with fear or laughter) *la20-*. [probably altered form of *piss* from MFr *pisser*]
pish[1,3] /pɪʃ/ *adj of a person or situation* bad, of poor quality *la20-*. [see the verb]
pish-minnie /'pɪʃ mɪni/ *n* an ant *19- SW Bor*. [PISH[1,1] + MINNIE]
pish-mither /'pɪʃ mɪðər/ *n* an ant *19- SW Bor*. [PISH[1,1] + MITHER]
pishmool, †**pismuill** /'pɪʃmul/ *n* an ant *17- WC Uls*. [PISH[1,1] + unknown second element]
pish-the-bed /'pɪʃ ðə bɛd/ *n* the dandelion *Taraxacum officinale la19-*. Compare *pee-the-bed* (PEE[1,2]). [from the diuretic properties of the plant]
pisk /pɪsk/ *n* a cheeky, precocious child *20- Sh*. **piskabel** = PISK. [Norn *pisk*; compare Swed dial *pyske* a dwarfish person, a gnome]
piskie[1] /'pɪski, 'pɪske/ *n* a member of the Scottish Episcopal Church *la19-*. [reduced form of Eng *Episcopalian*]
piskie[2] /'pɪski, 'pɪske/ *adj of grass or hair* dry, withered, shrivelled *19- SW*. [unknown]
pismire, †**pismore** /'pɪsmaer/ *n* an ant *la15- C SW Bor Uls*. [ME *pissemire*]
pismire *see* BISMAR
pismuill *see* PISHMOOL
piss[1] /pɪs/ *interj* a call to a cat or kitten *19- Sh N*.
piss[2] /pɪs/ *v* to incite a dog to attack *20- N NE WC*. [unknown]
†**pissan, pesane** *n* a piece of armour to protect the upper chest and neck *la15-e16*. [ME *pisan*]
pissance *see* PUISSANCE
pissant *see* PUISSANT
pissle[1,1], **pissell** /'pɪsəl/ *n* **1** something insignificant *20- Sh*. **2** *pl* odd jobs *20- Sh*. [Norn *pisl*]
pissle[1,2] /'pɪsəl/ *v* **1** to shell; to remove a husk from a seed *20- Ork*. **2** to work in an ineffectual manner *20- Ork*. [Norw dial *pusla* to fiddle, to shell, peel]
pisslin /'pɪslɪn/ *adj of people* useless, ineffectual *20- Ork*. [adj ppl from the verb PISSLE[1,2]]
pistack /'pɪstak/ *v* **pistack it!** a cry to chase off a cat or dog *19, 20- WC*. [uncertain, compare Norw dial *piis, pise* petname for a cat, related to Du *poes* a cat, call-name for a cat]
pistill *see* PYSTLE
pistoll, †**pestole** /'pɪstɒl/ *n* a gold coin *la16-17, 18- historical*. **pistolet**, †**pistolat**, †**pestolet** a type of foreign gold coin *la16-e17, la17- historical*. [EModE *pistole*]
pit[1,1], **pitt** /pɪt/ *n* **1** a hole in the ground (made by digging) *la14-*. **2** Hell *la15-*. **3** a coal mine *16-*. **4** a hole marking a boundary *la16-18*. **5** a dungeon *15-17*; compare POT[1,1]. **pit bing** a slag heap from a coal mine *20- C*. **pit bottomer mining** the person who loaded the hoist at the pit bottom *la19-e20, la20- historical*. †**pit stone** a boundary stone *la17-e19*. **pit and gallows** a right of jurisdiction over criminals found within baronial lands (translating Latin *furca et fossa*) *15-e18, la18- historical*. [OE *pytt*]
pit[1,2] /pɪt/ *v* **1** to dig holes in; to fill with holes *la14-*. **2** to make holes in the ground to indicate a boundary *la18-e19*. [see the noun]
pit[2], **put, pet,** †**pitt** /pɪt, pʌt, pɛt/ *v, pt* **pit, pat, put, pot,** *ptp* **pit, put, putten, pitten, potten 1** to place in a specified place or position *la14-*. **2** to put cattle or sheep on or to a place of grazing *la15-*. **3** to set a person on their way: ◊*Ah'll pit ye up the road la15-*. **4** to accuse or charge with a crime *15-*. **5** to install a person in an office or tenancy *la15-*. **6** to cause to be or become *17-*. **7** to put forward as a pledge, representative or substitute for a person or thing *la15-17*. **8** to add a person's name to a list *17*. **9** to implant or instill a quality *la15-16*. **pit aboot 1** to cause inconvenience or distress; to upset oneself *19-*. **2** to wrap oneself up well; to wrap up a parcel *la19- Sh Uls*. **pit aff, put off 1** to remove clothing *15-*. **2** to waste time; to postpone or delay *la16-*. **pit afore** to put an apron on *20- Sh*. **pit again** to set oneself against; to oppose or forbid *20- Sh*. **pit apo yer feet** to put on your shoes *19- Sh*. **pit at 1** to take action against, to attack *16-*. **2** *law* to prosecute *16-19, 20- historical*. **3** to influence *la16-17*. †**pit at under** to disadvantage; to discomfit *la14-16*. **pit awa 1** to abolish or cancel; to renounce *la14-*. **2** to put away or lay aside *15-*. **3** to banish a person; to dismiss from employment *15-*. **4** to do away with; to clear away *la15-*. **5** to bury *la19-*. **6** *reflexive* to commit suicide *la19-*. **7** to dispose of or alienate property *15-16*. **pit-by 1** something saved for later use *la19-*. **2** a snack, a light meal *20-*. **pit by 1** to set aside; to get rid of *la15-*. **2** to while away or spend time; to postpone; to remain *la15-*. **3** to store or stow away *16-*. **4** to make do with: ◊*Ye maun pit by wi that 19-*. **5** to bury *19- WC SW Uls*. **6** to avert blame *15-17*. **pit somebody by the door** to turn away or reject a person *20-*. **pit doon**, †**put doun 1** to depose or demote; to discredit *la15-*. **2** to overthrow, defeat or suppress *la15-*. **3** to kill, to put to death *la15-*. **4** to suffocate bees with sulphur (to reach the honey) *19-*. **5** to inter, to bury *la19- N NE Uls*. **6** to set potatoes or other plants in the ground *20- N Uls*. **7** to go or send to a place: ◊*she pit doon tae Glasgow for her new pans 20- NE*. **8** to demolish *la15-16*. **pit frae, put from 1** to expel, exclude or dismiss; to dispossess *la15-*. **2** to prevent or hinder *16-*. **3** to dissuade or discourage *la19, 20- NE Uls*. **4** to liberate *la15-16*. †**pit handis in** to attack or kill a person *la15-e18*. †**pit hand tae, put hand to** to lay hands on; to take or steal *la15-19*. **pit hand tae anesel** to commit suicide *la16-19, 20- literary*. **pit in yer han** to help yourself *la19-*. †**pit in memory, put in memorie** to record in writing *la15-16*. **pit intae, put into** to insinuate or suggest to, to impose an idea on *la19- NE T*. **no pit it by someone** *derogatory* to believe a person capable of a certain action or behaviour *20-*. **pit on** insincerity, pretence, falseness *20- Sh NE T*. **pit on 1** to put on, to affix *la15-*. **2** to dress, to put on clothes *la15-*. **3** to impress; to impose on *20- N NE T EC*. **pit oot, put out 1** to expel; to evict a tenant *15-*. **2** to fit out with clothes *17, 20- Sh NE*. **3** to enlist or supply troops *17*. **pit oot somebody's pipes** to put someone in their place, to thwart a person *18-19, 20- NE*. **pit oot the line** *of a precentor* to sing the line of a psalm for the congregation to repeat *20- H&I*. **pit oot yer han** to help yourself *la19-*. **pit somebody past something** to put a person off something *la19-*. **pit-ower 1** a snack, a makeshift meal *la19, 20- NE*. **2** a temporary expedient *20- Sh*. **pit ower, put over 1** to accomplish; to have done with *la18-*. **2** to defer or postpone *19-*. **3** to consume; to wash down, to swallow *la19-*. **4** to last out, to survive, to make do *19, 20- N NE T*. **5** to spend or

pass time *16-19, 20- Sh NE*. **pit-past** *n* a snack, a makeshift meal *20-*. **pit past** to put away, to set aside for later use *19-*. **pit speech upon** to speak to someone *20- Sh N*. **pit ye through** to make something clear *19- Sh N NE T*. **pit tae, put to 1** to close a door (over) *la15-*. **2** to kindle or set alight a fire *20- NE WC*. **3** *law* to affix a seal or signature to a document to authenticate it *la14-e16*. **pit sombody to** to set a person to work *16-*. **pit to the horn, put to the horn** to declare a person outlaw *la14-19, 20- historical*. **pit somebody to the school** to send someone to be educated *la16-20, 21- historical*. **pit yer tongue till** to divulge; to mention *la19-*. †**put to the war** to defeat *15-16*. **pit up, put up 1** to lift up; to put in a raised position *la15-*. **2** to construct a building *16-*. **3** to vomit, to bring up *la19-*. [OE *pȳtan* to push, poke, thrust, put out]

pitato *see* PITAWTIE

pitawtie, potottie, potato, †**pitato,** †**patatie** /pəˈtɔte, pəˈteto/ *n* **1** an edible tuber, a potato *la17-*. **2** a word used in a children's counting rhyme: ◊*one pitawtie, two pitawtie, three pitawtie, four 20-*. **pitawtie bogle** a scarecrow *19-*; compare *tattie bogle* (TATTIE). **potato scone** a dough of flour, milk and mashed potato, rolled out thinly and baked on a girdle; compare *tattie scone* (TATTIE) *20-*. [EModE *potato*]

Pitcaithly bannock /pɪtˈkeθle banək/ *n* a round flat cake of thick shortbread containing chopped almonds and citron peel *19-*. [from the place-name + BANNOCK]

pitch[1.1] /pɪtʃ/ *n* the act of pitching; the highest point *17-*. [see the verb]

pitch[1.2], †**picht,** †**pight** /pɪtʃ/ *v* **1** to set up a tent *la15-*. **2** to throw or toss *18-*. **3** to establish or locate *la15-e17*. **4** to select *la17*. **5** to set with jewels *la15-16*. **pitcher, pecher 1** the flat counter used in the game of hopscotch *la19-e20, la20- historical*. **2** the game of hopscotch *la19- N NE*. **3** a marble thrown rather than rolled *la19- NE T*. **pitchie** the flat counter used in the game of hopscotch *20- NE*. [unknown, compare PICK[3.2]]

pitcher, †**pichar,** †**pechar** /ˈpɪtʃər/ *n* **1** a container for liquids *la15-*. **2** the quantity of ale contained in a pitcher *la15-17*. [ME *picher*]

pite *see* PEETY[2]
pité *see* PEETY[1]
piteous *see* PIETY

pith /pɪθ/ *n* **1** strength, vigour *la14-*. **2** the strength-giving quality of food or drink *la15-17*. **3** virility *16*. **pithy 1** strong, solid; robust, powerful *la16-*. **2** *of words* forceful; convincing; to the point *la16-*. **a yer pith** with all your energy *la19, 20- Ork N*. †**the pith o maut** whisky *e19*. [OE *piþa*]

pithonesse *see* PYTHONESS

pit-mirk[1.1] /ˈpɪt mɪrk/ *n* pitch darkness *18-19, 20- literary*. [PIT[1.1] + MIRK[1.1]]

pit-mirk[1.2] /ˈpɪt mɪrk/ *adj* pitch dark, dark as a pit *la18-19, 20- literary*. [see the noun]

pitt *see* PIT[1.1], PIT[2]

†**pittance-silver, pittane-silver** *n* a bequest or endowment (given to a religious house for food or wine on special occasions) *16-e17*. [Older Scots *pittance* + SILLER[1.1]]

pitte commounis *see* PETTY
pitten *see* PIT[2]
pitten tae /pɪtən ˈte/ *adj* in difficulties *19-*. [PITTEN, ptp of PIT[2]]

†**pitter-patter** *v* to repeat words or prayers rapidly and mechanically *17-e19*. [imitative; reduplication with vowel variation; perhaps originally from *paternoster*]

pittie *see* PETTY
pittiecoit *see* PETTICOAT

†**pittie-pattie** *adv* with a rapid fluttering motion *18-e19*. [onomatopoeic]

pituchtie *see* PEUCHTIE
pity *see* PEETY[1], PEETY[2]
pizen *see* PUSHION[1.1]
pizened *see* PUSHIONT
pizz /pɪz/ *v* to sizzle or fizz *20- Ork*. [onomatopoeic]
pizz *see* PEASE
pizzlo, pesel /ˈpɪzlo, ˈpesəl/ *n* a twisted or knotted length of string; a tangle *20- Sh Ork*. [Norn *pesel*]
pjaw *see* PAW[1.1], PAW[1.2]
pju *see* PEW[1.1]

placard[1.1], **plaicaird,** †**placad,** †**placatt** /ˈplakard, ˈplekerd/ *n* **1** a poster, a public notice *la16-*. **2** a summons, a call *la18-e19*. **3** a licence or warrant to buy horses *la16-17*. [EModE, Fr *placard* Compare also Du *plakkaat*]

placard[1.2], **placad** /ˈplakard, plaˈkad/ *v* **1** to publish in a public notice *la17-*. **2** to utter derogatory statements about; to gossip about *18-19, 20- Sh H&I*. [see the noun]

place[1.1], **pliss,** †**plais** /ples, plɪs/ *n* **1** room, space, ground *la14-*. **2** a particular location; an area or building used for a particular purpose *la14-*. **3** a town or village; a residence or house; a holding of land; an estate, farm or croft *la14-*. **4** a position or office, employment; a function *16-*. **5** the section of a coalface assigned to each miner *la19- C SW*. **6** a passage from the Bible *16-17*. **placie 1** a small farm or croft *la19- Ork NE EC*. **2** a location, an area; a building *20- NE T EC*. †**place haldar** a deputy *la16-e17*. †**place of repentance** the area of a church where penitents stood to be rebuked *la16-19*. **have place 1** to occupy a position *la15-*. **2** *of a procedure* to have credence or validity *la15-e17*. **3** to have a right to do something *la15-16*. **the place of** the mansion-house of a particular estate *15-19, 20- historical*. [OE *plæce*]

place[1.2], †**plais** /ples/ *v, pt, ptp* **plaist 1** to locate; to site *16-*. **2** to install in a locality or position *16-*. **3** *Presbyterian Church* to induct a minister to a new charge *la16-*. **4** *Presbyterian Church* to settle a probationer in their first charge *18-20, 21- historical*. **5** to order according to rank *la16*. **placed minister** *Presbyterian Church* a clergyman responsible to a parish or congregation *18-*. [see the noun]

plack, †**plak** /plak/ *n* **1** money, cash; wealth or fortune *19-*. **2** something of little value or significance *16-19, 20- NE T*. **3** a small sum; a coin of low value *17-18*. **4** a small Scottish copper coin worth four pennies *la15-e17*. **plackless** penniless; short of money *la18-19, 20- Bor*. †**plack bill** *law* a letter issued under the signet; the summons or warrant presented to a debtor in small civil actions *la18-e19*. †**plack pie** a pie costing a small amount *la17-e19*. †**a plack's worth** a very small amount, as much as could be bought for a small amount *17-18*. †**catch the plack** to make money; to increase one's wealth *la18-e19*. †**mak yer plack a bawbee** to make money; to profit from something *18-19*. †**plack an bawbee** *of a payment* to the last penny; made in full *19*. †**plack an farthin** = *plack an bawbee*. †**twa an a plack** an ironic term for a considerable sum of money *la17-19*. [MDu *placke*]

plad *see* PLAID[1.1]
pladding *see* PLAIDING
pladge *see* PLEDGE[1.1]
plading *see* PLAIDING
plag /plag/ *n* a garment *19- Sh*. [Norn *plagg*]
†**plage** *n* **1** a region; a district within a burgh *15-e16*. **2** a point of the compass *16*. [ME *plage*, MFr *plage*]
plage *see* PLAGUE[1.1]
plagium /ˈpledʒɪʌm/ *n law* kidnapping, child-stealing *19-*. [Eng *plagium*]

plague[1.1], †**plage**, †**plaig**, †**pleague** /pleg/ *n* **1** an epidemic; pestilence *la15-*. **2** an affliction, a calamity *la15-*. [ME *plage*, Lat *plāga* stroke, wound]
plague[1.2] /pleg/ *v* to inflict with calamities; to punish or oppress *la16-*. **plagued 1** afflicted, tormented *la16-*. **2** confounded, damned *18-e19*. [see the noun]
plaicaird *see* PLACARD[1.1]
plaid[1.1], †**plad**, †**plyd**, †**pled** /pled/ *n* **1** a length of twilled (tartan) woollen cloth, originally worn an outer garment by men and women, and now surviving as part of full ceremonial Highland dress *16-*. **2** the woollen cloth of which a plaid is made *16-*. **3** a plaid or tartan cloth used as a blanket or bed-covering *la16-*. **plaidie** a plaid garment or blanket; a shawl or stole *19-*. **plaid neuk** a fold or flap in a plaid used as a pocket *la16-e20, la20- historical*. [perhaps a ptp of PLY[1.1]; Gael *plaide* is a borrowing from Scots]
plaid[1.2] /pled/ *v* to dress or wrap oneself in a plaid; to carry a child in a plaid *19, 20- literary*. [see the noun]
plaidge *see* PLEDGE[1.1]
plaiding, **plaidin**, †**plading**, †**pladding**, †**pledding** /ˈpledɪŋ, ˈpledɪn/ *n* the material from which a plaid is made *16-*. **plaidin market** *humorous* a bed *20- NE SW*. [PLAID[1.1] + -IN]
plaig *see* PLAGUE[1.1], PLAYOCK
plaik *see* PLAYOCK
plain[1.1], †**pleyn** /plen/ *n* **1** a tract of flat, open country *la14-*. **2** a small or limited stretch of level ground, a flat space *la15-e16*. [see the adj]
plain[1.2], **plenn**, †**plean**, †**plane** /plen, plɛn/ *adj* **1** apparent, unmistakable; clear *la15-*. **2** without elaboration; simple; candid, forthright *la14-*. **3** *of ground* open; flat; free from hills, woods or bodies of water *la14-19, 20- Sh*. **4** *of a surface* flat, smooth, level *la15-19, 20- Sh*. **5** *of a road or passage* unobstructed, open *la15-19*. **6** clearly visible or audible; in the public view *la14-16*. **plain bread** bread baked as a *plain loaf 20- T*. **plain Geordie** the flat bottom crust of a loaf of bread *20- T*. **plain loaf** a flat-sided white loaf with a hard black crust on top and a floury brown crust at the bottom; a batch loaf *20-*; compare PAN LOAF. **plain soled** flat-footed *19-*. **plain stanes**, **plain stones 1** a pavement; a paved area (surrounding a mercat cross or Town House) *17-*. **2** flat stones used for paving *17-*. **as plain as parritch** self-evident *la18-19, 20- C*. †**in plain** openly, publicly; frankly; truly *15-e17*. [ME, *plain*]
plain[1.3] /plen/ *adv* **1** simply, straightforwardly; wholly *la14-*. **2** clearly, audibly *15-e16*. [see the adj]
plain[2], **pleen**, †**plene**, †**pleyne** /plen, plin/ *v* **1** to complain; to lament *la15-19, 20- literary*. **2** to make a formal complaint *la14-17*. Compare PLAINYE[1.2]. [ME *pleinen*]
plainen /ˈplenən/ *n* coarse linen *la18- Ork NE T*. [probably Eng *plain* a rough, hardwearing cloth + adj-forming suffix *-en*]
plainie /ˈplene, ˈpleni/ *n* the simplest manoeuvre in various children's games *20-*. [PLAIN[1.2] + -IE[2]]
plainies, **plennies** /ˈpleniz, ˈplɛniz/ *npl* paving stones; a pavement *la19- T*. [shortened form of *plain stanes* (PLAIN[1.2])]
plaint[1.1], †**plent** /plent/ *n* **1** a complaint, a protest; an expression of distress or grief *la14-19, 20- NE T*. **2** *law* the feudal right to hear and judge complaints *15-17*; compare *court plaint* (COORT[1.1]). [ME *pleint*]
†**plaint**[1.2] *v* to complain; to find fault with *16-e19*. [see the noun]
plaint *see* PLANT[1.1]
plaintwis *see* PLENTUOUS
plainye[1.1], †**plenzie** /ˈplenji/ *n* a complaint, an objection *19, 20- literary*. [see the verb]

plainye[1.2], †**plenzie**, †**plenʒe**, †**pleinʒe** /ˈplenji/ *v* **1** to complain; to lament *la14-19, 20- literary*. **2** to make a formal complaint *la14-16*. Compare PLAIN[2]. [ME *pleint*]
plaip /plep/ *v* to flap; to make a slapping noise *la19- NE T*. [onomatopoeic]
plais *see* PLACE[1.1], PLACE[1.2], PLEASE[1.2]
plaist *see* PLACE[1.2]
plaister[1.1], **plester**, **plaster** /ˈplestər, ˈplɛstər, ˈplastər/ *n* **1** a medicinal substance applied to a wound *la14-*. **2** lime and other materials used for making casts and applied as a finishing surface to walls *15-*. **3** a fawning person; a flatterer *20-*. **4** an unskilled, clumsy job; a mess *20-*. **5** excessive adornment *la19- T WC Uls*. **6** a beating; a reprimand *la18, 20- Sh N*. **7** cursing, swearing *20- Sh*. [OE *plaster*]
plaister[1.2], **plester**, **plaster** /ˈplestər, ˈplɛstər, ˈplastər/ *v* **1** to overlay with plaster *16-*. **2** to work in a slovenly or slapdash way; to mess around *la19-*. **3** to make an unwanted fuss; to fawn or be over-attentive *20-*. **4** to curse or swear *20- Sh*. [see the noun]
plait *see* PLAY[1.2]
plaite *see* PLAT[1.1]
plait slevis *see* PLATE
plak *see* PLACK
plan[1.1] /plan/ *n* **1** a design; a proposal *18-*. **2** a plot of ground, an allotted rig on the runrig system; a croft *18-e19*. [Eng *plan*]
plan[1.2] /plan/ *v* **1** to intend or propose to do something *la18-*. **2** to make provision for; to arrange or design *20-*. [see the noun]
plane[1] /plen/ *n* the sycamore *Acer pseudoplantanus la16-*. **plane tree** the sycamore *la16-*. [AN, OFr *plane* sycamore]
plane[2.1], **plain** /plen/ *n* a joiner's plane *la16-*. [EModE *plane*]
plane[2.2] /plen/ *v* **1** to make smooth or level *la15-*. **2** to use a joiner's plane *la19-*. **3** to make plain; to demonstrate or declare *la15-16*. [ME *planen*, MFr *planer*]
†**plane**[3] *v of a bird* to glide *e16*. [MFr *planer*]
plane *see* PLAIN[1.2]
planet, **plenit** /ˈplanət, ˈplɛnət/ *n* **1** a rocky or gaseous body revolving around a star *la14-*. **2** a heavy localized shower of rain *20- Bor Uls*. **3** an area of ground *19*. [ME *planet*, Lat *planēta*]
plank[1.1] /plaŋk/ *n* **1** a long, narrow, flat piece of timber *15-*. **2** a plot of agricultural land *17- Sh Ork N*. **3** a hidden hoard; a hiding place *la20-*. [ME *plank*]
plank[1.2] /plaŋk/ *v* **1** to add strips of agricultural land together to form a plot *la16- Sh Ork N*. **2** to set down; to place in a decisive or emphatic way *la19-*. **3** to hide or stow away *la19-*. [see the noun]
†**plank**[2] *n* a small coin of low value *la15*. [apparently altered form of PLACK, perhaps influenced by MFr *blanc* a coin of low value; compare Gael *plang*]
planner /ˈplanər/ *n* **1** a person who plans or arranges something; something which facilitates planning *20-*. **2** a landscape gardener *la18-19*. [PLAN[1.2] + agent suffix]
planschour *see* PLENSHER
plant[1.1], †**plaint** /plant/ *n* **1** an organism growing in the ground *15-*. **2** a perfect specimen, a paragon *16*. **plant taft** an enclosed vegetable plot *la18- N*. [AN *plante*, MFr *plante*]
plant[1.2] /plant/ *v* **1** to place a seed in the ground so that it can grow *la14-*. **2** to stock or cover an area with plants *la15-*. **3** to furnish a place with inhabitants; to populate *la15-*. **4** *of people* to settle or camp *la15-*. **5** to place or install; to erect or establish *16-*. **6** *joinery* to attach a piece of moulding *la19-*. **7** to provide a church with a minister; to appoint a minister to a charge *la16-19*. †**plant doun** to place or erect *la15-16*. [AN, MFr *planter*]

plantation /planˈteʃən/ *n* **1** the action of planting trees; a place where trees are planted *la15-*. **2** colonisation; a colony *17-*. **3** the appointment of a minister or schoolmaster; the supplying of a church or school with a minister or schoolmaster *la16-e18*. [ME *plantacioun*]

planteous *see* PLENTUOUS

planticruive, planticru, plantie-krob, plantie crib, planticrub /ˈplanti krøv, ˈplanti krø, ˈplanti krɪb, ˈplanti krʌb/ *n* a small walled enclosure on open ground or moorland used for propagating seedlings in protected conditions *la19- Sh Ork N*. [Norn, ON *planta* + ON *kró* a small pen, fence, *v* form influenced by CRUIVE[1.1]]

plantin, planting /ˈplantɪn, ˈplantɪŋ/ *n* **1** a plantation of trees, a woodland *la16-*. **2** something to be planted; young trees or seedlings *16-18*. [PLANT[1.2] + *-in* suffix]

plap *see* PLOWP[1.2], PLOWP[1.3]

plapper /ˈplapər/ *v* **1** to splash about in water *la19- NE*. **2** *of boiling liquid* to bubble noisily *20- NE*. Compare PLOWP[1.2]. [onomatopoeic]

plasch *see* PLASH[1.1], PLASH[1.2]

plase fluik *see* PLASH FLUKE

plash[1.1], **†plasch** /plaʃ/ *n* **1** a splash, the noise made by something falling into water *16-*. **2** a sudden sharp downpour of rain *19-*. **3** an insipid or tasteless drink or broth *19- NE T Uls*. **4** a muddy puddle *19*. Compare BLASH[1.1]. **†plash mill** a fulling mill driven by a water-wheel *la18-19*. Compare *waulk mill* (WAULK). [onomatopoeic, MLG *plaschen*, MDu *plassen*]

plash[1.2], **†plasch** /plaʃ/ *v* **1** to work messily; to mess about in water *la19-*. **2** to splash through water; to squelch through mud *la17-19, 20- Sh Ork NE T SW*. **3** to soak; to drench *la18-19, 20- Sh Ork*. **4** *of rain* to fall in torrents *19, 20- NE C*. Compare BLASH[1.2]. **plashin** soaking wet *19, 20- NE T C*. **plashy 1** rainy, showery *la18-19, 20- NE*. **2** causing a splash *19*. **3** waterlogged *19*. [see the noun]

plash[1.3] /plaʃ/ *interj* splash *19 Sh NE T*. [see the noun]

plashack, plashach /ˈplaʃək, ˈplaʃəx/ *n* the plaice *Pleuronectes platessa 20- N NE*. [perhaps a variant of Eng *plaice* + *-ack* diminutive suffix; compare PLASH FLUKE]

plash fluke, †plase fluik /ˈplaʃ flukˈ/ *n* the plaice *Pleuronectes platessa la16-19, 20- NE*. [probably a variant of Eng *plaice* + FLEUK; compare Eng *plaice-fluke*]

plaster *see* PLAISTER[1.1], PLAISTER[1.2]

plat[1.1], **plot, †platt, †plaite** /plat, plɔt/ *n* **1** a scheme; a conspiracy *16-*. **2** a map, a plan *16-*. **3** a piece of ground *la16-*. **4** a sequence of events in a story *la16-*. **5** *Presbyterian Churches* a scheme for the territorial organisation of parishes, supply of ministers and provision of stipends *la16-19, 20- historical*. **6** *Presbyterian Churches* the body which implemented and administered the organisation of the Presbyterian system *la16-e17*. [see the verb]

plat[1.2], **plot** /plat, plɔt/ *v* to plan; to devise a scheme *17-*. **plotter, †platter** a conspirator *la16-*. [EModE *plot*]

plat[2.1] /plat/ *n* **1** a platform; a landing (on a stair) *17-19, 20- Sh T SW*. **2** a mat or flat basket used by fishermen *20- N NE*. **3** a flat surface, a rocky ledge *20- Sh*. [see the adj]

plat[2.2], **plet** /plat, plɛt/ *v* **1** to turn over the points of the nails attaching the shoe to a horse's hoof *19- Sh EC Bor*. **2** to place or set something down flat; to put in place *15-19, 20- Sh*. **3** *of a person* to fall or lie down flat *16*. [see the adj]

plat[2.3], **plet** /plat, plɛt/ *adj* **1** direct, clear, plain *la14-19, 20- literary*. **2** flat, level, even; low-lying *la15-19, 20- Sh*. **plat fittit** flat-footed *19- WC Bor*. **†plat fute** the name of a dance and its tune *16*. **plat and plain** direct, clear, plain *la14-19, 20- Sh*. [ME *plat*; compare also MDu *plat*]

plat[2.4], **†platt** /plat/ *adv* **1** flat; flat on the ground *15-19, 20- Sh*. **2** exactly, directly; in a straight direction *16-19, 20- Sh*. **3** in a blunt or straightforward manner *16-19, 20- Sh*. [see the adj]

plat *see* PLATT

platch[1.1], **plotch** /platʃ, plɔtʃ/ *n* **1** a splashing in water or mud; a splash *la19-*. **2** a patch of cloth or land *la19, 20- Sh Bor*. **3** a piece of wet ground *19- Bor*. **platchie** wet, muddy *19- NE Bor*. [probably variant of PLASH[1.1]]

platch[1.2] /platʃ/ *v* **1** to splash *19- Sh NE Bor*. **2** to walk through mud or mire *19- Sh EC Bor*. **3** to work in a sloppy or ineffectual way *19- Sh T Bor*. **platchin** soaking wet *19- Bor*. [see the noun]

platch[1.3] /platʃ/ *adv* with a splash *20- Sh Bor*. [see the noun]

platch[2.1] /platʃ/ *v* to walk in a heavy, flat-footed manner *19- Sh Bor*. [unknown]

platch[2.2] /platʃ/ *n* a foot with a fallen arch *19- Sh Bor*. [unknown]

plate, †platt, †plet, †pleitt, †pleat /plet/ *n* **1** a sheet of metal; precious metal or bullion *la14-*. **2** a shallow dish, a piece of tableware *la15-*. **3** a silver or gold trophy as the prize for a horse race; the race itself *la17-*. **†platit** covered with plates of metal *15-e16*. **†plat copper** sheet copper *16-e17*. **†plate glufe** a glove reinforced by plate-armour *la16-e17*. **†plet jack** a short coat of mail or plate-armour *18-e19*. **†plet leid** sheet lead *16*. **plait slevis, plate-sleeves** sleeves consisting of or reinforced by plate-armour *la16-e19*. [ME *plat*, Lat *plata*]

platform[1.1], **pletform, †platfurme** /ˈplatfɔrm, ˈplɛtfɔrm/ *n* **1** a raised level stage *16-*. **2** a scheme for government or administration, a prescribed procedure or form of words *la16-*. **3** *mining* a junction of two or more lines in a hutch railway, originally laid on a raised board *la19- EC*. **4** *Presbyterian Churches* the drawing by churches of an equal level of income from the Sustentation Fund *la19-e20, la20- historical*. **5** a flat roof; a partially flat roof serving as a walk on top of a building *16-17*. **†platform roof, plateforme ruif** a flat roof (with a roof walk) *16-17*. [MFr *plateforme*]

†platform[1.2], **platforme** *v* to provide a building with a flat roof or roof walk *la16-e17*. [see the noun]

platfurme *see* PLATFORM[1.1]

†platis *n* a public square *e16*. [probably MDu *plaetse*]

†platt, plat *n* a blow, a stroke *16-e19*. [probably MDu *plat*]

platt *see* PLAT[1.1], PLAT[2.4], PLATE

platter *see* PLOWTER[1.2]

plausible, †plausibill, †plausable /ˈplɔzəbəl/ *adj* **1** winning approval; agreeable *la16-*. **2** having the appearance of being acceptable or trustworthy *la16-*. [Lat *plausibilis* ptp of *plaudere*; compare MFr *plausible*]

play[1.1], **pley** /ple, plae/ *n* **1** exercise, activity; pleasure; fun *la14-*. **2** a game, a sport or pastime; a trick *15-*. **3** a dramatic performance; a dramatic composition *la15-*. **4** a musical performance *la19-*. **5** a country fair or festival *la15-19*. **†playrife** playful, light-hearted *19*. **the play** time off school for recreation; a holiday from work, school or college *17-19, 20- NE Bor*. **†the play be ended** the matter is concluded *la15-17*. [see the verb]

play[1.2], **pley** /ple, plae/ *v, pt, ptp also* **†plait 1** to amuse oneself, to have sport *la14-*. **2** to have sexual intercourse *la14-*. **3** *of a liquid* to boil *15-*. **4** to participate in a game; to bet on a game *15-*. **5** to play a trick *la15-*. **6** to perform on a musical instrument *la15-*. **7** to act; to perform a play *la15-*. **8** to make a noise: ◊*the door played clink la18-*. **9** to move briskly *15-17*. **†play club** *golf* a wooden-headed club for driving the ball a long distance *la17-19*. **†play cote** a coat or garment worn by a player in a performance *16*. **†play

day 1 a day on which a play or pageant was performed; a day of recreation *la16-17*. **2** a holiday from school *la16-17*. †**play feild** an open space for public festivities or performances *la16-17*. **play fere**, **play fare 1** a plaything, a toy *la18-19, 20- Sh Ork*. **2** a playmate; a jester *16-e19*. †**playfuil** a jester *16-e18*. **playgin** a plaything, a toy *19- Bor*. †**play Saturday** a Saturday holiday, fair or festival *la18-19*. †**play Sunday** a Sunday holiday, fair or festival *la18-19*. **play a rig**, **play the rig** to play a trick on; to make fun of *la19, 20- NE*. **play yersel** to amuse yourself, to play *la14-*. **away and play yersel** an expression of dismissal or disbelief *20-*. **go and play yersel** an expression of dismissal or disbelief *20-*. †**play the wort** to prepare the wort for beer or whisky making before adding the yeast *la16-17*. **play lick** to fall heavily *la19-*. **play the loon 1** to be promiscuous; to have sex *la16-19, 20- EC*. **2** to misbehave *la16-e17*. **play up wi** to harm, spoil or destroy *la19- Sh NE T*. †**play your pageant** to perform your role; to live your life *16*. †**play whiltie-whaltie** see WHILTIE-WHALTIE. [OE *plegan, plegian*]

play see PLEA[1.1]

playock, **plaig**, †**playok**, †**plaik** /'pleək, pleg/ *n* **1** a plaything, a toy *15-*. **2** a game, a pastime *19*. [PLAY[1.1] + -ock diminutive suffix]

play piece /'ple pis/ *n* a snack for breaktime at school *20-*. [PLAY[1.1] + PIECE (sense 2)]

playrife see PLAY[1.1]

plea[1.1], **pley**, **plie**, †**play** /pli, plae/ *n* **1** *law* an allegation or pleading by or on behalf of a litigant *15-*. **2** *law* an action at law, a lawsuit; litigation *la15-*. **3** a quarrel or disagreement; strife or enmity *16-19, 20- Ork NE T*. †**pleyabill, pleabill** *law* **1** subject to litigation *la15-16*. **2** *of a dispute* argued and decided by a legal process *16*. †**pleyar** *law* a litigant; a disturber of the peace *la16-e17*. **plea in bar of trial** *law* a statement or objection by the counsel for the accused, giving reasons why judgement should not be passed or why criminal proceedings should be dropped *20-*. **plea in law** *law* a proposition at the end of a pleading indicating the relief sought and why *19-*. **the pleas of the Crown** *law* criminal cases on murder, robbery, rape and arson, which could only be heard in the Court of Justiciary (although since 1975 the crimes of robbery and arson can be tried in a Sheriff Court) *17-*. [ME *ple*]

plea[1.2], **pley**, †**plie** /pli, plae/ *v* **1** *law* to litigate; to put forward a plea or make a formal allegation *la15-*. **2** to quarrel, disagree or argue *la15-19, 20- T*. **3** to sue a person *15-17*. [see the noun]

†**plead**[1.1], **plede**, **pleid** *n* **1** *law* a court action, litigation *la14-15*. **2** an allegation, a claim *la15-e17*. **3** contention, opposition *la15-16*. [see the verb]

plead[1.2], †**plede**, †**pleid** /plid/ *v, pt* **pled 1** *law* to put forward and argue a case in court *15-*. **2** to implore or entreat *15-*. **pleader**, †**pledar 1** *law* a person who pleads in a law court; an advocate *la16-*. **2** a litigant *17*. [ME *pleden*]

pleague see PLAGUE[1.1]

plean see PLAIN[1.2]

pleasance, †**plesance**, †**plesans**, †**pleasants** /'plɛzəns/ *n* **1** a pleasure-ground or park (attached to a castle); frequently in street-names and place-names *16-19, 20- historical*. **2** the feeling of pleasure or happiness; satisfaction *15-19*. **3** the action or quality of pleasing *la14-16*. **4** *pl* a source of pleasure *la14-16*. [ME *plesaunce*]

†**pleasant**[1.1] *n* a jester, a fool, a clown *la16-17*. [see the adj]

pleasant[1.2], **pleasant**, †**plesand** /'plɛzənt, 'plizənt/ *adj* **1** agreeable, pleasing *la14-*. **2** *of a person* humorous, witty, merry *la19-*. **pleasantly 1** agreeably *la15-*. **2** *of a payment* made satisfactorily; made in full *16-17*. **3** good humouredly; without resentment *la15-17*. [ME *plesaunt*]

pleasants see PLEASANCE

please[1.1], †**pleis** /pliz/ *n* pleasure *16-19, 20- NE T*. **nae hae a please** to be incapable of being pleased; to be perpetually dissatisfied *19- NE T*. [see the verb]

please[1.2], **plais**, †**ples**, †**plese** /pliz, plez/ *v* **1** to give pleasure or satisfaction *la14-*. **2** to be inclined, to see fit *la15-*. **3** to like or approve of; to be pleased or satisfied with *la15-e18*. **4** to satisfy a person by payment of compensation or a debt *la15-e17*. †**pleis madame** a type of dye; the colour obtained by its use, or a cloth of this colour *la16-e17*. †**plesit** may it please *la15-e16*. [ME *plesen*]

pleasure[1.1], **pleesure**, †**plesour**, †**pleseir**, †**pleassour** /'plɛʒər, 'pliʒər/ *n* **1** (a source of) enjoyment or delight *la15-*. **2** a good turn, a favour; a payment made in good-will; a benefaction *16-e17*. **3** the inclination to please; courtesy *16-e17*. [ME *plesir*]

pleasure[1.2], **pleesure** /'plɛʒər, 'pliʒər/ *v* to please; to give pleasure to; to satisfy *la16-*. [see the noun]

pleat /plit/ *n* **1** a fold or series of folds in cloth *20-*. **2** a pigtail, a plait *20-*. Compare PLET[1.1] [Eng *pleat*]

pleat see PLATE

pled see PLAID[1.1], PLEAD[1.2]

pledding see PLAIDING

plede see PLEAD[1.1], PLEAD[1.2]

pledge[1.1], *Sh* **plaidge**, †**plege**, †**pladge** /plɛdʒ; *Sh* pledʒ/ *n* **1** a solemn vow *16-*. **2** *law* (a person or thing held as) surety; a hostage *15-19, 20- historical*. †**plege chalmer** = *plege house la16-e17*. †**plege house** the place in Dumfries where hostages or sureties were kept; a debtor's prison *17-e18*. †**upon plegis** in return for or after receipt of sureties *16-e17*. [ME *plegge*]

pledge[1.2] /plɛdʒ/ *v* to guarantee; to assert *la15-*. [ME *pleggen*]

plee /pli/ *n* **1** a seagull; a young gull before it changes its first plumage *la19, 20- Sh NE EC*. **2** the thin piping cry of a seagull or other bird *la19- Sh Ork*. [onomatopoeic]

pleen see PLAIN[2]

pleengie /'pliŋi/ *n* a seagull; a young herring gull *19- NE*. Compare PLEE. [onomatopoeic]

pleenk /pliŋk/ *n* weak beer *la19- Ork*. Compare PINKIE[3]. [unknown]

pleenkie see PLINK[1.2]

pleep[1.1] /plip/ *n* **1** the oystercatcher *la19- Sh NE Bor*. **2** a wading bird of the snipe family *la19- Ork NE T*. **3** the high-pitched cry of a seabird *la19- Sh Ork*. **4** a complaint; a whine *20- Sh Ork*. [onomatopoeic]

pleep[1.2] /plip/ *v* **1** *of birds* to utter a shrill, high-pitched cry *la19- Sh N T*. **2** to complain; to whine *la19- Sh Ork*. **pleep-sit** peevish, whining *20- Sh*. [see the noun]

pleesant see PLEASANT[1.2]

pleester /'plistər/ *v* to whimper or whine; to complain *20- Ork*. [probably onomatopoeic; compare Norw dial *plystra* to whistle, pipe, Norw *pist(r)a* to squeak, whimper]

pleesure see PLEASURE[1.1], PLEASURE[1.2]

pleet see PLUIT[1.1], PLUIT[1.2]

plege see PLEDGE[1.1]

pleid see PLEAD[1.1], PLEAD[1.2]

pleinʒe see PLAINYE[1.2]

pleis see PLEASE[1.1]

pleiter see PLOWTER[1.1], PLOWTER[1.2]

pleitt see PLATE

plencheoun-nail see PLENSHIN-NAIL

plene see PLAIN[2]

plenis see PLENISH[1.2]

†**plenish**[1.1] *n* furniture, household equipment *18-19*. [see the verb]

plenish[1.2], *Sh NE* **plinish**, †**plenis** /ˈplɛnɪʃ; *Sh NE* ˈplɪnɪʃ/ *v* **1** to furnish a house *16-*. **2** to provide; to fulfil *la15-19*. **3** to stock land with trees, plants or livestock *la15-18*. **plenishment** furniture, household equipment *la17-19*, *20- Sh Uls*. [AN *pleniss-* extended stem of *plenir* to fill]

plenishing /ˈplɛnɪʃɪŋ/ *n* **1** furniture, household equipment (brought by a bride to her new home) *la16-*. **2** goods, provisions or accessories *16-17*. [verbal noun from PLENISH[1.1]]

plenit *see* PLANET

plenn *see* PLAIN[1.2]

plennies *see* PLAINIES

†**plensher, plenschour, planschour** *n* a flooring nail *16-e18*. [reduced form of PLENSHER-NAIL]

†**plensher-nail** *n* a flooring nail *la15-18*. [AN, MFr *plancher* flooring, planking + NAIL[1.1]]

†**plenshin, plenshion** *n* a flooring nail *17-e18*. [reduced form of PLENSHIN-NAIL]

plenshin-nail, †**plencheoun-nail** /ˈplɛnʃɪn nel/ *n* a flooring nail *la16-19*, *20- Sh*. [AN, MFr *plancher* flooring, planking + NAIL with influence from EModE *planching* planking, boarding]

plent *see* PLAINT[1.1]

plente *see* PLENTY

†**plentuous, plaintwis, planteous** *adj* having a grievance *la14-e17*. **be plantous of** to have a grievance about; to make a formal complaint *la15-e17*. **be plenteus on** = *be plantous of*. [PLAINT[1.1] + adj-forming suffix *-eous*]

plenty, plinty, †**plente** /ˈplɛntɪ, ˈplɛnte, ˈplɪnte/ *n* **1** abundance *la14-*. **2** a great number; a large proportion *19-*. [ME *plente*]

plenʒe *see* PLAINYE[1.2]

plenzie *see* PLAINYE[1.1], PLAINYE[1.2]

plert[1.1], **plirt** /plɛrt, plɪrt/ *n* a heavy fall; a splash or splat *la19- Ork SW Uls*. [probably onomatopoeic]

plert[1.2] /plɛrt/ *v* to plod, to splash *20- Sh Ork*. [see the noun]

plert[1.3], **plirt** /plɛrt, plɪrt/ *adv* with a splash or plop *20- Ork*. [see the noun]

ples *see* PLEASE[1.2]

†**plesable** *adj* agreeable, pleasing *16-e17*. [ME *plesable*]

plesance *see* PLEASANCE

plesand *see* PLEASANT[1.2]

plesans *see* PLEASANCE

plese *see* PLEASE[1.2]

pleseir *see* PLEASURE[1.1]

plesit *see* PLEASE[1.2]

plesour *see* PLEASURE[1.1]

plester *see* PLAISTER[1.1], PLAISTER[1.2]

plet[1.1], †**plett** /plɛt/ *n* **1** a plait or braid of hair *16-*. **2** a pleat or fold in a garment; a crease *16-19*, *20- Sh N NE T*. **3** a predicament, a quandary *20- Bor*. **4** an intertwining of strands *16*. [ME *pleit*]

plet[1.2] /plɛt/ *v* **1** to fashion by plaiting, intertwining or interweaving *la15-*. **2** to cross or twist together the limbs *la15-*. **3** to fold cloth or other material *18-*. **4** to walk in an unsteady way; to stagger drunkenly *20-*; compare PLAIT[2], PLEAT[1]. **plettin-house** *in Orkney* a building where workers would plait straw for making bonnets *20- historical*. †**plet in your arms** to embrace *15-16*. [see the noun]

†**plet**[1.3], **plett** *adj* **1** intertwined, interwoven, pleated *16-17*. **2** clasped, fixed closely *16*. **3** *of metal bars* criss-crossed, interwoven *16-e17*. **yplet** *of hair* braided *e16*. [see the noun]

plet *see* PLAT[2.2], PLAT[2.3], PLATE

platform *see* PLATFORM[1.1]

plett *see* PLET[1.1], PLET[1.3]

plettie /ˈplɛte/ *n* a landing on a tenement stair *20- T*. **plettystanes** a pavement *la20- T EC*. [variant of PLAT[2.1] + -IE[1]]

pleuch *see* PLOO[1.1]

pleugh *see* PLOO[1.1], PLOO[1.2]

pleuran /ˈplurən/ *adj* wailing, crying *20- Ork*. [probably onomatopoeic]

plever *see* PLIVER

plew *see* PLOO[1.1], PLOO[1.2]

pley *see* PLAY[1.1], PLAY[1.2], PLEA[1.1], PLEA[1.2]

pleyn *see* PLAIN[1.1]

pleyne *see* PLAIN[2]

plicht[1], **plight**, †**plite**, †**plyte** /plɪxt, plʌɪt/ *n* an unfortunate state or condition *la14-*. [OE *pliht*, AN *plite*]

†**plicht**[2.1] *n* **1** responsibility; risk, danger *15-16*. **2** wrongdoing, sin, crime *la14-e16*. [OE *pliht*]

plicht[2.2] /plɪxt/ *v* to pledge *15-19*, *20- literary*. **plicht your troth**, †**plicht your treuth** to engage yourself to marry; to become betrothed *16-*. [see the noun]

†**plicht**[3] *n* a support or refuge in a crisis *16*. [reduced form of PLICHT-ANKIR]

†**plicht-ankir, plight-anchor** *n* a support or refuge in a crisis *16*. [probably MLG *plichtanker* the main anchor of a ship]

plie *see* PLEA[1.1], PLEA[1.2]

plight *see* PLICHT[1]

plight-anchor *see* PLICHT-ANKIR

plinish *see* PLENISH[1.2]

plink[1.1] /plɪŋk/ *n* the sound made by the strings of a musical instrument when plucked *la19-*. [onomatopoeic]

plink[1.2] /plɪŋk/ *v* **1** to pluck the strings of a musical instrument *la19-*. **2** *of light* to glint or twinkle *20- Sh Ork*. **pleenkie** a method of shooting a marble so that it makes a sharp, tinkling noise *20- Ork*. [see the noun]

plinkie, *Sh* **blinkie** /ˈplɪŋki; *Sh* ˈblɪŋki/ *n* an electric torch *la20- Sh Ork*. [PLINK[1.2] + -IE[1]]

plinkin /ˈplɪŋkɪn/ *adj of a liquid* tinkling, pattering *la19-*. [presp of PLINK[1.2]]

plinty *see* PLENTY

plirt *see* PLERT[1.1], PLERT[1.3]

†**plish-plash**[1.1] *n* a splashing noise or motion *17-19*. [onomatopoeic]

†**plish-plash**[1.2] *v of a liquid* to splash or cascade *19*. [see the noun]

plish-plash[1.3] /ˈplɪʃ plaʃ/ *adv* with a splashing noise *la19- Sh NE T*. [see the noun]

†**plisk** *n* a practical joke, a trick; an escapade *e18*. [unknown]

pliskie[1.1] /ˈplɪski/ *n* **1** a practical joke, a trick; an escapade *18-*. **2** a plight or predicament; a sorry state *19*, *20- Sh EC*. **3** a wild idea, an extravagant notion *la19- NE EC*. **play someone a pliskie** to play an unpleasant trick on someone *la18-*. [PLISK + -IE[1]]

pliskie[1.2] /ˈplɪski/ *adj* mischievous, full of tricks, wily *la19*, *20- T SW Uls*. [see the noun]

pliss *see* PLACE[1.1]

plite *see* PLICHT[1]

pliver, plover, †**pluvar**, †**plever** /ˈplɪvər, ˈplovər/ *n* a game bird of a number of shore or grassland species, a plover *15-*. [ME *plover*]

pliver's page, plover's page, †**plover page** /ˈplɪvərz pedʒ, ˈplovərz pedʒ/ *n* the dunlin *la19- Sh Ork N*. [possessive form of PLIVER + PAGE from the bird's habit of flying with the PLIVER]

plodge, plotch /plɔdʒ, plɔtʃ/ *v* to walk on muddy or waterlogged ground, to squelch along slowly or heavily *19- EC Bor*. Compare PLATCH[1.2]. [perhaps a blend of Eng *plod* and *trudge*]

ploiter *see* PLOWTER[1.1], PLOWTER[1.2]

ploitery see PLOWTERY
plome see PLUME
plompe see PLUMP¹
ploo¹·¹, **plew, plu, pleugh, pleuch, plooch, plough, plow, peuch,** *C* **pue,** †**pluch,** †**pluich,** †**plouch** /plu, plux, plʌu, pjux; *C* pju/ *n* **1** an implement for turning the soil, a blade used to turn the soil in preparation for planting *la14-*. **2** the constellation *Ursa Major 16-*. **3** a team of plough-horses or oxen *la17-*. **4** an area of land which could be tilled by an eight-oxen plough in a year *15-18, 19- historical*. **5** the people working a plough; the tenants of a *ploughgate la15-17*. **pleuchie, peuchie** a ploughman; a country person *la19, 20- T EC*. †**pleuch feast** a ritual entertainment given at the first ploughing of the new season *la16-19*. **plough-gang** a measure of arable land, sometimes equated with the *ploughgate 16-19, 20- historical*. **ploughgate** an area of land which could be tilled by an eight-oxen plough in a year, usually taken to be 104 Scots acres (as used for tax assessment) *17-19, 20- historical*; compare DAVACH. †**pleuch graith** the movable fittings and attachments of a plough *16-e19*. †**pleugh guids** the oxen used for ploughing, a plough-team *la16-17*. **plew irons, ploo airns** the metal parts of a plough, especially the coulter and share *15-*. **ploughland 1** an area of land, sometimes equated with the *ploughgate*; frequently in place-names *la14-19, 20- historical*. **2** land suitable for ploughing, arable land *la19-*. **plewman, plooman** a farmworker specialising in ploughing *la15-*. **plooman's love** southernwood *Artemisia abrotanum la20- NE T EC*. **ploo rynes** the reins used for a plough team *la19- NE SW*. **pleuch slings** the hooks connecting the swingle-trees to the plough *19, 20- NE T*. **plough soam** the rope or chain by which horses or oxen are yoked to the plough, the traces *la17-19, 20- SW*. **plough sock** a ploughshare *la17-*. **plew stilt, pleugh stilt 1** *pl* the shafts or handles of a plough *la16-*. **2** a unit of land measurement equal to half a *ploughgate la16-e18*. **ploo theats** the plough-traces *la18-19, 20- NE*. **gie a ploo gurr** to cut a furrow deeper than usual and at a slant *la20- NE*. **haud the pleugh** to drive a plough; to be a working farmer *18-*. **pick something up at the ploo** to learn something from observation of life rather than by formal instruction *la20- WC*. [OE *plōg*]
ploo¹·², **plough,** †**pleugh,** †**plew,** †**plow** /plu, plʌu/ *v* to till the ground with a plough in preparation for planting *16-*. [see the noun]
plooch see PLOO¹·¹
plooching, plooking /ˈplutʃɪŋ, ˈplukɪŋ/ *n* a thrashing, a beating; punishment *20- N H&I*. **ploocherin** = PLOOCHING. [Gael *plùc* beat, thump + -*ing*]
plood see PLOWD¹·²
plooder see PLOWDER
plook, plouk, pluke, *Sh* **pluk,** †**plowk,** †**pluck** /pluk; *Sh* plʌk/ *n* **1** a pimple or boil; a swelling, a growth *la16-*. **2** a small protuberance near the rim of a container marking the level of a standard measure *la16-19, 20- historical*. **3** a pointed rock or stone; an area of rough rocks on the sea-bed *20- Sh*. **plookit** covered with pimples, spotty *la19-*. **plooky** covered with pimples, spotty *16-*. [ME *plouke*]
plooking see PLOOCHING
ploom, plum, †**ploum** /plum, plʌm/ *n* **1** the edible fruit of the tree *Prunus domestica*, a plum *la15-*. **2** a plum tree *16-*. **3** the fruit of the potato-plant *la18-*. [ME *plum*]
ploom-damas, †**plum-damas,** †**ploum-damas** /ˈplum daməs/ *n* a damson plum or damson; a dried plum or prune *16-19, 20- Bor*. [PLOOM + *Damas* Damascus]
ploot, plut /plut/ *n* a foot *la19- Sh Ork*. **pluttick** a foot *19- Sh*. [probably, related to PLOOTSH]

plooter see PLOWTER¹·¹
plootsh, plootch, ploots /plutʃ, pluts/ *v* **1** to walk in a flat-footed or clumsy way; to plod *la19- Sh*. **2** to dabble in water *20- Sh Ork*. [probably onomatopoeic; compare PLATCH¹·²]
plop see PLOWP¹·¹, PLOWP¹·², PLOWP¹·³
plosible, plowsible /ˈplozəbəl, ˈplʌuzəbəl/ *adj* agreeable, friendly, likeable *la19- Ork T*. [Eng *plausible*]
plot¹·¹ /plɔt/ *n* **1** a scalding; an immersion in boiling water *la19-*. **2** an overheated or sweaty state *la19- Sh EC*. [see the verb]
plot¹·², **plowt** /plɔt, plʌut/ *v* **1** to immerse the carcass of an animal in boiling water to facilitate plucking or scraping *la17-*. **2** to scald with boiling water to clean or sterilise *18-*. **3** to bathe a sore in very hot water to encourage the expulsion of poison *19-*. **4** *of a person* to swelter with heat *19-*. **5** to pluck wool from a sheep or feathers from a bird *19-*. **6** to overheat; to burn; to roast; to boil for an extended period *17-19, 20- NE T EC Bor*. **plottin het** scalding hot *19-*. [probably Du *ploten* to remove wool from a fleece, especially by immersion in a hot alkaline solution]
plot see PLAT¹·¹, PLAT¹·², PLOWT¹·²
plotch see PLATCH¹·¹, PLODGE
Plotcock, †**Plotcok** /ˈplɔtkɔk/ *n* a name for the devil *la16-18, 19- historical*. [probably *Pluto* the Roman god of the underworld + hypocoristic suffix -*cock*]
†**plotter** *n weaving* a person who trimmed the nap on woollen cloth *17*. [Du *ploter, plooter* a fleece or wool cutter; compare PLOT¹·²]
plotter see PLOWTER¹·²
plottie /ˈplɔti/ *n* hot toddy; mulled wine *18-*. [PLOT¹·² + noun-forming -*ie* suffix]
plottit /ˈplɔtɪt/ *adj* bare, despoiled; having a miserable or sickly appearance *19- Bor*. [PLOT¹·¹ + adj-forming -*it* suffix]
plouch see PLOO¹·¹
†**ploud** *n* a green sod, a thick piece of turf *16-e19*. [unknown]
plough see PLOO¹·¹, PLOO¹·²
plouk see PLOOK
plouking see PLUKING
ploum see PLOOM
ploum-damas see PLOOM-DAMAS
plounge see PLUNGE¹·²
plout see PLOWT¹·¹, PLOWT¹·²
plover see PLIVER
plover page, plover's page see PLIVER'S PAGE
plow see PLOO¹·¹, PLOO¹·²
plowd¹·¹ /plʌud/ *n* **1** a heavy ungainly carriage or walk, a waddle *la19- NE*. **2** a heavy fall, a thud, a bump *la19- NE*. [see the verb]
plowd¹·², **plood** /plʌud, plud/ *v* **1** to waddle or plod *19- N NE H&I Bor*. **2** to work perseveringly; to strive painstakingly *20- Sh NE*. **pludisome** dogged, persevering, painstaking *20- Sh NE*. [onomatopoeic; compare PLOWT¹·², perhaps influenced by Eng *plod*]
plowder, plooder /ˈplʌudər, ˈpludər/ *v* to walk in a heavy-footed way (through water or mud); to paddle around in water *19- NE H&I Bor*. [PLOWD¹·² + frequentative suffix]
plowk see PLOOK
plowp¹·¹, **plop** /plʌup, plɔp/ *n* a hollow sound of something falling (into water) *19-*. [onomatopoeic; compare earlier Eng *plop*]
plowp¹·², **plop, plap** /plʌup, plɔp, plap/ *v* to make a hollow sound (of something falling into water) *19-*. [see the noun]
plowp¹·³, **plop, plap** /plʌup, plɔp, plap/ *adv* with a hollow sound *19-*. [see the noun]
plowsible see PLOSIBLE

plowster[1.1] /ˈplʌustər/ *n* **1** a mess; a muddle *19- Bor*. **2** an incompetent, messy worker *19- Bor*. [see the verb]

plowster[1.2], **pluister** /ˈplʌustər, ˈplustər/ *v* to work in messy or muddy conditions; to flounder about *19- NE EC Bor*. [onomatopoeic; compare PLOWTER[1.1], PLAISTER[1.2], SLAISTER[1.2]]

plowt[1.1], **plout** /plʌut/ *n* **1** a heavy shower, a downpour of rain *18-*. **2** a noisy fall or plunge (into water); a splash or plop *19-*. **3** a clumsy, blundering person or animal *20- NE EC Bor*. **4** a dull blow, a punch or thump *20- Sh NE*. [onomatopoeic; compare PLOWD[1.1]]

plowt[1.2], **plout**, *Sh* **plot** /plʌut; *Sh* plɔt/ *v* **1** to fall heavily (into liquid) *la19- NE T H&I SW Uls*. **2** to walk through water or over wet ground; to squelch along *19- Sh NE T*. **3** *of rain* to fall with a splash; to hit the ground with force *la19, 20- Sh NE T*. **4** to plunge something into a liquid *la18- N C*. **5** to hit heavily; to punch *20- Sh NE*. **6** to set down suddenly and heavily *la19, 20- NE*. **plowt kirn** a churn operated by a plunger *18-19, 20- Ork*. †**ploot staff** the plunger of a *plowt kirn e18*. **plot yersel doon** to sit down heavily *20- Sh*. [see the noun; compare PLOWTER[1.2]]

plowt[2] /plʌut/ *n* a dish made of meat boiled and set in jelly; potted head *20- EC*. [compare PLOT[1.1]]

Plowt[3] /plʌut/ *n* a nickname for Fleshmarket Close in Edinburgh, originally the site of the meat market and slaughterhouse *20-*. [unknown]

plowt *see* PLOT[1.2]

plowter[1.1], **ploiter**, **plooter**, *NE* **pleiter** /ˈplʌutər, ˈplɔitər, ˈplutər; *NE* ˈplʌitər/ *n* **1** the act of working or walking in water or mud, a splashing about *19-*. **2** a splash or splashing of liquid *19-*. **3** a difficult, disagreeable or messy task; a botched job *19-*. **4** a wet or sticky mess of food *la19-*. **5** a messy inefficient worker, a muddler *20- T C SW Bor*. **6** a wet, muddy spot; a bog, a mire *19, 20- NE*. [see the verb]

plowter[1.2], **ploiter**, *Sh NE EC* **platter**, *NE* **pleiter**, *WC Bor* **plotter** /ˈplʌutər, ˈplɔitər; *Sh NE EC* ˈplatər; *NE* ˈplʌitər; *WC Bor* ˈplɔtər/ *v* **1** to dabble with the hands or feet, usually in a liquid; to splash aimlessly in mud or water; to wade messily through wet ground *19-*. **2** to work or act idly or aimlessly, potter or fiddle about *19-*. **3** to fumble about, rummage or grope in the dark *20-*. **4** to make a mess of, spoil (especially a piece of land by bad cultivation) *19- Sh NE SW*. [PLOWT[1.2] + frequentative suffix; compare Du *ploeteren* to drudge, plod, wade through mud]

plowtery, **ploitery** /ˈplʌutərɪ, ˈplɔitərɪ/ *adj of the weather* wet, showery, rainy, causing muddy wet conditions *la19- NE*. [PLOWTER[1.1] + adj-forming suffix]

ploy[1] /plɔi/ *n* **1** a venture, an undertaking; a piece of business, a scheme *la17-*. **2** a piece of fun, a trick, a practical joke *18-*. **3** a social gathering, a party *la18-19, 20- Sh*. [perhaps shortened form of Eng *employ* an occupation, activity]

ploy[2] /plɔi/ *n* a legal action; a quarrel *la16-*. [probably a variant of PLEA[1.1]]

ployk *see* PLUYK

plu *see* PLOO[1.1]

pluch *see* PLOO[1.1]

pluck[1.1] /plʌk/ *n* **1** the liver, lungs and heart or other viscera of an animal, *18-*. **2** a mouthful of grass or other fodder taken by or available to an animal as food *la17-19 Sh NE SW Uls*. **3** a moulting state in fowls or animals *20- Ork N NE SW*. **4** the action of seizing or gaining a prize, a bonus or something in demand *la19- NE T WC*. **5** a two-pronged, mattock-type implement used for taking turnips out of hard ground or forking dung *19, 20- NE*. **be in the pluck** to moult *20- Ork N*. **go in the pluck** = *be in the pluck*. [see the verb]

pluck[1.2], †**pluk** /plʌk/ *v* **1** to pull, tug; to pick (fruit); to remove (hair, wool or feathers) by pulling or picking *15-*. **2** to take (turnips) out of the ground with a pronged tool *la20- NE*. **3** to steal (livestock); to rob (a person); to pillage *16-17*. **plucker** *joinery* a tool for smoothing a curved surface *la19, 20- NE*. †**play pluck at the craw** to play a game in which one player is pulled about by the others; to grab what one can get *16*. [ME *plukken*]

pluck *see* PLOOK

plucker, **plukker** /ˈplʌkər/ *n* **1** a type of coastal fish, also known as the father-lasher or sea scorpion *19- Sh N*. **2** a type of coastal fish, also known as the angler or fishing frog *la19- Sh*. [Norn *plukker* an angler fish, sea scorpion; compare GUNPLUCKER]

pluck-up, †**pluk-up** /ˈplʌkʌp/ *n* a scramble; a commodity in demand *la19-*. †**pluk-up fair** a sale or general scramble in which each person tries to get as much as they can *la16-17*. [PLUCK[1.2] + UP[1.2]]

pludisome *see* PLOWD[1.2]

pluff[1.1] /plʌf/ *n* **1** a mild explosion, a whiff or puff of air, smoke or gunpowder *la17-*. **2** a firework, a squib *la19-*. **3** padding in a garment; a pad *18-19, 20- NE SW*. **4** a tube used as a peashooter or as a simple form of bellows *la17-19, 20- Sh*. **5** a powder puff *18-e19, 20- Ork*. **6** a small quantity, a pinch of powder or dust *19, 20- Sh*. **7** a handgun *16-e17*. **pluff gun** a tube used as a pea-shooter *la19, 20- Sh*. **pluff-a-tootie** a thick jam sandwich *20- Sh*. [onomatopoeic]

pluff[1.2] /plʌf/ *v* **1** to discharge (smoke or breath) with a small explosion, puff (something) out in a cloud *17-*. **2** to become inflated, swell up, puff out *20-*. **3** to explode, go up in a puff of smoke *20- Sh NE Bor*. **4** to have a puffy appearance *19, 20- Sh NE*. †**pluffing** firing, shooting (a gun) *17-e19*. **pluffings** the refuse of corn, husks, chaff *19- Bor*. **pluff oot** to extinguish, blow out with a puff of air *19-*. [see the noun]

pluff[1.3] /plʌf/ *adv* with a puff *la19, 20- Sh NE T*. [see the noun]

pluffer /ˈplʌfər/ *n* a peashooter *la19-*. [PLUFF[1.2] + agent suffix]

pluff grass, **pyuff girse** /ˈplʌf gras, ˈpjʌf girs/ *n* a type of grass, Yorkshire fog *Holcus lanatus* *19- NE*. [PLUFF[1.1] + GIRSE[1.1] because of the lightness and fluffiness of its seeds]

pluffy[1] /ˈplʌfɪ/ *adj* plump, chubby; puffy, fleshy; fat *19-*. [PLUFF[1.1] + adj-forming suffix]

pluffy[2] /ˈplʌfɪ/ *n* a kind of toffee made fluffy and brittle by the addition of bicarbonate of soda; puff candy *20- T EC Bor*. [PLUFF[1.1] + adj-forming suffix]

pluffy[3] /ˈplʌfɪ/ *n* a porpoise *Phocoena phocoena* *20- NE*. Compare PUFFY DUNTER. [PLUFF[1.2] + adj-forming suffix, because the animal puffs air through its blowhole]

plug[1] /plʌg/ *v mining* to blast rock by means of a PLUG SHOT *la19, 20- EC*. [shortened form of PLUG SHOT]

plug[2] /plʌg/ *v* to play truant *20- C Bor*. [perhaps a variant of PLUNK[2]]

plug shot /ˈplʌg ʃɔt/ *n mining* a charge placed in a small hole in a rock of moderate size to break it up *la19, 20- EC*. [PLUG[1] + SHOT[1.1]]

pluich *see* PLOO[1.1]

pluister *see* PLOWSTER[1.2]

pluit[1.1], *Ork* **pleet** /pløt; *Ork* plit/ *n* a cry or wail *20- Sh Ork*. †**pleeter** a mournful whimpering sound *la19*. [onomatopoeic; compare PLUIT[1.2], Norw *plyta* a small flute]

pluit[1.2], *Ork* **pleet** /pløt; *Ork* plit/ *v* to cry; to complain *la19- Sh Ork*. [see the noun]

pluk *see* PLOOK, PLUCK[1.2]

pluke *see* PLOOK

†**pluking**, **plouking** *n* the action of stopping up a barrel with a plug or wedge *16*. [probably LG *pluck*, *plock* to plug, bung + -IN[1]; compare later Eng *plugging*]

plukker *see* PLUCKER

pluk-up *see* PLUCK-UP

plum see PLOOM

plumb[1.1] /plʌm/ *n* **1** a ball of lead, used as a bullet or as the weight attached to a plumb line *la15-*. **2** a deep underwater pool or hole *la18-19, 20- WC Bor*. **3** a deep hole used as a privy *e16*. †**plum dental** *in Shetland* perpendicular, upright; sensible, sane *la19*. †**plum jurdane** a deep hole used as a privy *e16*. †**plumb lede** unworked or untreated lead; the colour of this *la15-16*. [ME *plum, plumb*]

plumb[1.2] /plʌm/ *v* **1** to measure (a depth) *la16-*. **2** to seal with lead *la17-*. [see the noun]

plum-damas see PLOOM-DAMAS

plum dental see PLUMB[1.1]

plume, †**plome** /plum/ *n* **1** a bird's feather; plumage *16-*. **2** a quill pen *16-*. [ME *plum*, MFr *plume*, Lat *plūma*]

plum jurdane see PLUMB[1.1]

plummet, †**plwmet** /ˈplʌmət/ *n* **1** a piece of lead, attached to a line, used to measure the depth of water, a sounding lead *16-*. **2** a plumb line *18-*. **3** the pommel on the hilt of a sword, frequently weighted with lead *15-18*. [ME *plumet*]

†**plump**[1], **plompe** *n* a compact body, a cluster, a clump; a group or band *la16-19*. [ME *plump*]

plump[2.1] /plʌmp/ *n* **1** a heavy fall *la16-*. **2** a heavy downpour of rain *19-*; compare *thunner plump* (THUNNER[1.1]). **plump hasher** a heavy implement for slicing turnips *20- NE*. **plump kirn** a churn worked by moving a plunger up and down *20- NE*. †**plump shower** a heavy downpour of rain *la17-e18*. **play plump** to plunge, dive *20- Sh T WC*. [onomatopoeic]

plump[2.2] /plʌmp/ *v* **1** to drop or land heavily; to come abruptly into a place *19-*. **2** *of rain* to fall heavily, pour *19-*. **3** *of a boiling liquid* to make a loud bubbling or plopping noise *la18-19, 20- Uls*. **plumper** the plunger of a churn *la19- NE*. [see the noun]

plumrose /ˈplʌmros/ *n* a primrose *la18-*. Compare PRIMROSE. [variant of Eng *primrose*]

plunge[1.1] /plʌnʒ, plʌndʒ/ *n* **1** an act of diving or becoming immersed in liquid *16-*. **2** a heavy fall of water, a downpour of rain *la18-19*. †**plunge churn** a churn worked by moving a plunger up and down *19*. [see the verb]

plunge[1.2], †**plounge** /plʌnʒ, plʌndʒ/ *v* **1** to immerse (a person or thing) into a liquid *la14-*. **2** to throw oneself violently forward *la14-*. **3** to thrust (a person) into an undesirable situation *la15-*. [AN *plunger*]

plunk[1.1] /plʌŋk/ *n* **1** a heavy fall or plunge; the sound of this *19-*. **2** the sound of a cork being drawn from a bottle; a popping sound *19-*. **3** a sharp jerk or thrust used to propel a marble forward; the game played in this way *la19-*. [onomatopoeic]

plunk[1.2] /plʌŋk/ *v* **1** to fall into water; to drop (an object) into water *19-*. **2** to put (something) down with a thump *19-*; compare PLANK[1.2] (sense 2). **3** *children's games* to propel (a marble) with a flick; to pitch; to throw *19-*. **4** to hit with a thump *20-*. **5** to pluck (the strings of a musical instrument) to make a popping or twanging noise *19- WC SW Bor*. **6** to make a plopping or gurgling noise as when drawing a cork or swallowing *19, 20- T SW*. **plunker** a heavy marble designed to be flicked or tossed *la19-*. [see the noun]

plunk[1.3] /plʌŋk/ *adv* with a dull, heavy sound suddenly, quickly *la19-*. [see the noun]

plunk[2] /plʌŋk/ *v* to play truant *19- C Bor*. **plunker** a truant *19- C Bor*. [unknown]

plunkie[1] /ˈplʌŋki/ *n* a practical joke; a trick *19- Sh Ork*. [unknown]

plunkie[2] /ˈplʌŋki/ *n* **1** the game of marbles *20-*. **2** toffee cooled after boiling by dropping in cold water *la19- NE*. [PLUNK[1.2] + noun-forming suffix]

plurality, pluralitie, †**pluralite** /ˈplurəlɪte, ˈpluralɪti/ *n* **1** the state or condition of being more than one *la15-*. **2** the act of holding more than one church benefice *16-*. **3** the greater number (of the whole), the majority *la16-*. [ME *pluralite*]

plut, pluttick see PLOOT

pluvar see PLIVER

†**pluyk, ployk** *n* a club, a cudgel *la14-e15*. [perhaps Gael *ploc* a block of wood, tree stump; a club, bludgeon; genitive form *pluic*]

plwmet see PLUMMET

ply[1.1] /plae/ *n* **1** a fold, a layer or thickness of material *15-*. **2** condition, state *15-*. **3** a strand or twist of rope, wool or thread *la16-*. **4** *mining* a thin layer of hard rock separated by a softer one from another hard layer, a rib *la18- C*. **in ply** in good condition *la15-*. **oot o' ply** in bad condition *la15-*. [AN *pli, plei*, MFr *pli, ply*]

ply[1.2] /plae/ *v* **1** to bend; to be pliable *la15-*. **2** to provide a lining for or reinforce a garment *17*. **3** to fold or double over (cloth or paper) *la14-15*. †**plying** providing a garment with lining; pleating, pleats; a type of (pleated or lining) material *la17-e19*. **plying hammer** a heavy double-faced hammer (used in shipyards) *la19- WC*. [ME *plien*, AN *plier*, OFr *plier*]

ply[2] /plae/ *v* **1** to sail or move on (a course), to voyage; to tack, to sail obliquely against the wind *17-*. **2** to apply (oneself) to a task, work hard and perseveringly *la15-19*. [ME *plien*]

plyd see PLAID[1.1]

plype[1.1] /plaɪp/ *n* (the sound of) a sudden squirt or rush of water; a sudden heavy shower of rain; (the noise of) a fall into water *la19- NE T Bor*. [onomatopoeic]

plype[1.2] /plaɪp/ *v* **1** to drop suddenly into water, plunge or splash into mud or water *19- NE T*. **2** to dabble or work messily in a liquid or wet material *19- NE T*. **3** to walk on wet or muddy ground, squelch along *la19- NE T*. **plyper** to work messily or carelessly in liquid *la19- NE T*. [see the noun; compare PLAIP]

plyte see PLICHT[1]

plyven /ˈplaevən/ *n* the flower of the white clover or red clover *19-*. [unknown]

pneumatics, †**pnewmaticks** /njuˈmatɪks/ *n* **1** *in Scottish Universities* pneumatology, a branch of metaphysics concerned with the science, doctrine or theory of spirits or spiritual beings *la17-19, 20- historical*. [Eng *pneumatic*; Lat *pneumat-* (from Greek πνεῦμα air, spirit) + *-ics* suffix from earlier names of sciences]

'po see UPON

poach[1.1] /potʃ/ *n* a wet, muddy area of ground, a puddle; a disordered state of affairs, a shambles, a mess *la19- NE*. [perhaps related to Eng *poach* to churn up soft ground with one's feet]

poach[1.2], *NE* **potch** /potʃ; *NE* pɔtʃ/ *v* **1** to catch game illegally *19-*. **2** to stir or poke with a stick, to push, prod, thrust *19- NE Bor*. **3** to pound or stamp on clothes in washing *20- NE T*. **4** to reduce (food in a dish) to mush by over-handling, mess about with *19- NE*. **5** to work in an aimless or messy way *la19, 20- Bor*. [unknown]

poach[2], †**poch** /potʃ/ *n* the armed bullhead or pogge, the fish *Agonus cataphractus la16-19, 20- T*. [unknown]

poacket see POCKET

poackle see PAUCHLE[1.1]

poak, poag /pok, pog/ *v* to walk slowly and deliberately, to march around in a purposeful way *20- Sh Ork*. [unknown]

poakit see POCKET

poan[1.1], **pone** /pon/ *n* a thin strip of green turf used under the thatch in the roofing of houses or to cover peat-stacks *19- Sh Ork*. [Norn *pon* a piece of green turf for thatching, ON *spánn* shingle for thatching]

poan[1,2] /pon/ *v* **1** to strip off a thin layer of turf *19- Sh Ork.* **2** to cover a roof with strips of turf *19-.* **pon de bank** *in peat-cutting* to pare off a layer or layers of turf or rooty material prior to reaching the peat *20-.* [Norn *pon* to cut green turf for thatching]

poast *see* POST[2.1]

poat *see* PAT

pob /pɔb/ *n* **1** *of flax or jute* the refuse, waste; any fibrous or dusty waste material *18, 19- NE T EC.* **2** rope or twine teased into fibres *20- NE.* **pob tow** = POB. [unknown; compare Gael *pab* shag, rough hair; oakum]

pobie, †**pobe** /ˈpobi/ *n* foster-father *la17- Sh.* [ON *papi* pope, priest, anchorite]

poch /pɔx/ *adj of people* slightly unwell, out of sorts *20- NE.* [perhaps onomatopoeic suggesting exhaustion. Compare PECH[1.1]]

poch *see* POACH[2]

pochle *see* PAUCHLE[1.1], PAUCHLE[1.2]

pock, †**poke**, †**polk** /pɔk/ *n* an eruption or pustule on the skin *16-.* **pock arred**, **pockard** pockmarked, having a scarred or pitted skin *19, 20- WC Bor Uls*; compare ARR. **pockyawrd** = *pock arred.* **the pock** a disease characterized by pustules (such as chickenpox or smallpox) *19-.* [OE *pocc*]

pock *see* POKE[1.1]

pocked *see* POKED

pocket, **poacket**, **poakit**, †**poket** /ˈpɔkət, ˈpokət/ *n* **1** a pouch in a garment *17-.* **2** a bag *15-19, 20- historical*; compare POKE[1.1] (sense 1). †**pocket fish** the cuttlefish *Sepia officinalis.* **pocket naipkin** a handkerchief *19-.* [ME *poket*]

pocket *see* POKED

pockie *see* POKIE

pockle /ˈpɔkəl/ *n* a bagful *19- T.* [reduced form of POKE[1.1] + Eng *-ful*; see also POKEFU]

pockle *see* PAUCHLE[1.1], PAUCHLE[1.2]

pockmantie, **pokmantie**, **poikmantie**, **pockmantle** /pɔkˈmanti, pokˈmanti, pɔkˈmantəl/ *n* a travelling-bag, a portmanteau *la16-19, 20- historical.* [altered form of MFr *portemanteau* with influence from POKE[1.1]]

pocky cloud /ˈpɔki ˈklʌud/ *n* a pouched or bag-like cumulous cloud *19- Ork.* [POKE[1.1] + CLOOD[1.1]]

pod *see* PUD[1]

poddock *see* PUDDOCK[1.1]

podlie, **podley**, †**podlok**, †**podlo**, †**podler**, †**podline** /ˈpɔdli, ˈpodle/ *n* **1** the young of the coalfish at the second stage of its development; the pollack *Pollachius virens*, the LYTHE[2] *16-.* **2** a tadpole *19, 20- T EC.* **3** an affectionate term for a child *la19- NE T.* **4** a red-breasted minnow *20- EC Bor.* [perhaps a variant of POLLACK]

poffill, poffle *see* PAFFLE

pofle *see* PAFFLE

pogo /ˈpogo/ *n* a child's toy made of feathers tied together at the quills so that the tips radiate out in all directions *20- Ork.* [unknown]

poik *see* POKE[1.1]

poikful *see* POKEFU

poikmantie *see* POCKMANTIE

poill *see* PILE[4]

poind[1.1], †**poon** /pɔɪnd, pɪnd/ *n* **1** impounded goods or livestock *15-.* **2** the seizure of goods for debt *19.* **3** an animal or cattle seized as plunder *15-16.* †**poind fauld, pund fauld, pundfall** an enclosure in which impounded livestock was kept, a pound *la13-19.* †**pundlan** the fine payable before impounded livestock was released *la13-e16.* †**poindlaw, punlaw** = *pundlan 16.* †**poind-money** the money realized on distrained goods *la18-19.* †**drive poinds** to exact goods for money owed, originally to seize and drive off distrained livestock *16-e19.* †**tak poinds** = *drive poinds la14-e17.* [see the verb]

poind[1,2], †**pund**, †**pind**, †**pound** /pɔɪnd, pɪnd/ *v* **1** *law* to seize and sell the goods of a debtor; to impound (goods); to distrain upon a person (for debt, unpaid rent, taxes or fines) *15-.* **2** to distrain or impound stray livestock as surety for damage committed by them *la15-19, 20- N EC Bor.* **poindable**, †**poindabill** liable to be distrained *16-.* **poinder**, †**poyndlar 1** a debt collector *la16-.* **2** a forester *19, 20- NE.* **3** a person authorized to impound straying animals *la15-e19.* **poind the ground** to take the goods on land such as furniture or farm equipment) in enforcement of a real BURDEN[1.1] possessed over the land *la18-20, 21- historical.* [OE *gepyndan*]

†**point, poynct, punt** *v* to appoint, arrange *la15-17.* [aphetic form of APPOINT]

point *see* PINT[1], PINT[2.1], PINT[2.2], PINT[3]

†**pointal, puntell** *n* **1** a pointed weapon *15-e16.* **2** a plectrum *e16.* [PINT[2.1] with diminutive suffix]

pointed *see* POINTIT

point game, points game /ˈpɔɪnt gem, ˈpɔɪnts gem/ *n curling* a game played by an individual as opposed to a team, points being awarded for particular skills demonstrated *19-.* [PINT[3] + Eng *game*]

pointie /ˈpɔɪnti/ *n* a throw in the game of *knifie* (KNIFE) *20-.* [PINT[2.1] + with diminutive suffix]

pointit, pointed, pinted /ˈpɔɪntɪt, ˈpɔɪntəd, ˈpʌɪntəd/ *adj* **1** sharp or angular *16-.* **2** *of persons* precise, over-attentive to detail, demanding; punctual, exact *18-.* **pointitly, pintitly** accurately, punctiliously, punctually, immediately *19- T C.* [PINT[2.1] with participial adj-forming suffix]

points /pɔɪnts/ *n curling* a game played by an individual as opposed to a team, points being awarded for particular skills demonstrated *20-.* Compare POINT GAME. [PINT[3]]

points game *see* POINT GAME

pois *see* POSE[1.1], POSE[2]

poison *see* PUSHION[1.1]

poist *see* POST[1], POST[2.1]

poit *see* PAT

poke[1.1], **pock, pok,** *NE* **pyock,** †**poik,** †**polk** /pok, pɔk; *NE* pjɔk/ *n* **1** a bag or pouch, a sack *15-.* **2** a beggar's bag used for collecting meal or other food given in charity *16-.* **3** a hood or hat *17-.* **4** a pouch-like swelling under the jaw of a sheep caused by sheep rot; the disease itself *la18-.* **5** a shopkeeper's paper bag *la19-.* **6** a kind of fishing-net *la16-18, 19- Sh Ork N SW Bor.* **7** *humorous* the human stomach *20- N SW.* **8** the udder of a milch animal *la19, 20- SW.* **9** the stomach of a fish *20- N.* **10** an appendage to a hat *17.* †**poik braik, polkbreik** a bag for supplies *16-e17.* †**pokman, polkman** a porter *la16-17.* **poke net, pock net** a kind of fishing-net *la17-.* †**pock neuk** the bottom or corner of a bag, especially one used to hold money *la16-19.* **pock puddin 1** *derogatory* a nickname for an Englishman *18-.* **2** a dumpling or pudding steamed in a bag *la17-19, 20- WC.* **poke shakings, pock shakings 1** the last child of a large family *19-.* **2** the smallest pig in a litter *19-.* **gang wi the pock** to go about begging; to seek funding *la18-.* †**lowse yer pock** to tell your news, give a full account of something *18-19.* **on yer ain pock** reliant on your own resources *19- WC SW.* [ME *poke*]

poke[1,2] /pok/ *v* to fish with a poke net *la16- Sh Ork SW.* †**poke up** to put away into store; to save, hoard *la16-18.* [see the noun]

poke *see* POCK

†poked, pocked, pocket *adj of sheep* having a swelling under the jaw, infected with sheep-rot *la17-19*. [POKE¹·¹, with adj-forming suffix]

pokefu, †poikful /ˈpokfu/ *n* a bagful *la16-*. [POKE¹·¹ + -FUL]

poket *see* POCKET

pokey-hat /ˈpoke hat/ *n* an ice-cream cone *20- C Uls*. [perhaps Eng *hokey-pokey* ice-cream + Eng *hat* from its shape, or perhaps an alteration of Ital *ecco un poco* shouted by Italian ice-cream vendors]

pokie, pockie /ˈpoki, ˈpɔki/ *n* a woman's handbag *20- Ork*. [POKE¹·¹ with diminutive suffix]

pokmantie *see* POCKMANTIE

pol *see* POWL¹·¹

polacie *see* POLICY

pole *see* POLL¹·¹, POW¹

polece *see* POLIS¹·¹

poleist *see* POLISH

policat *see* PULLICATE

police *see* POLICY, POLIS¹·¹, POLIS¹·²

policy, †policie, †polacie, †police /ˈpɔlɪse, ˈpolɪse/ *n* **1** government, administration, regulation of public affairs *la15-*. **2** *pl* the enclosed grounds of a large house, the park of an estate *18-*. **3** *pl humorous* the garden of an ordinary house *la20-*. **4** the improvement or development of a town or landed estate by the erection or improvement of buildings, plantation of parks and provision of amenities; the buildings involved in this *15-e18*. **5** refinement, cultivation, civilization *16-e17*. [ME *policie*]

polis¹·¹, police, †polece /ˈpolɪs, pəˈlis/ *n* **1** the official body enforcing law and order *la18-*. **2** a policeman; a policeofficer *20-*. **3** the civil administration and organization of a community, the public services *la15-e19*. **4** the improvement or development of a town or landed estate (with buildings, parks and amenities) *la15-16*; compare POLICY (sense 4). **Police burgh** a burgh set up under various public Acts, in which magistrates and police commissioners were elected with powers similar to those of the councils of the older burghs *19, 20- historical*. **Police commissioner** = Commissioner of Police (COMMISSIONER) *20-*. **†police dung** dung and waste material collected in the streets of a city *19*. **polisman, policeman 1** a member of the police force *19-*. **2** *mining* a movable guard over or round a pitmouth or at mid-workings; safety gates *la19, 20- EC*. **poliswumman, policewoman** a female police officer *20-*. [MFr *police*]

polis¹·², police /ˈpolɪs, pəˈlis/ *v* **1** to control, regulate, keep in (civil) order *19-*. **2** to improve or develop (land) by cultivation and planting *16*. [Fr *policer*]

polish, †polise /ˈpɔlɪʃ, ˈpolɪʃ/ *v* to make clean, smooth or shiny by friction *15-*. **polished,** *Sh Uls* **polist, †poleist 1** made clean, smooth or shiny by friction *la14-*. **2** complete, utter, out and out *19, 20- Sh Uls*. **3** bright, beautiful; adorned, embellished *la14-e16*. [ME *polishen*]

†politik, pollutick *adj* **1** relating to government or politics; public, civic, secular *la15-17*. **2** refined, cultured, polished *la16*. [ME *politik*; sense 2 erron for Lat *polītus*]

polk *see* POCK, POKE¹·¹

poll¹·¹, pole, polie /pɔl, pol/ *n* a haircut *20- N EC Bor*. [see the verb]

poll¹·² /pɔl, pol/ *v* **1** to cut hair *la16-*. **2** to impoverish, exploit, overcharge *16-e17*. [*poll* (POW¹)]

poll *see* POW¹, POW², POWL¹

pollach *see* PULLOCH

†pollack *n* a freshwater whitefish; the POWAN *18-e19*. [Gael *pollag*, IrGael *pollóg*]

pollutick *see* POLITIK

pollywag /ˈpɔlewag, ˈpolewag/ *n* a tadpole *la19- T C*. [ME *polwigle*]

polonie /ˈpoləni, pəˈloni/ *n* **1** a loose ill-fitting garment; a clumsy, outlandish article of dress *20- Sh NE*. **2** an oddly-dressed person, an oddity *19- Sh*. **3** a kind of loose-fitting gown or coat worn by women or young boys; a greatcoat for older boys or men *18-19*. [Fr *Pologne*, Lat *Polonia* Poland]

polt *see* PAWT¹·², PULT

†pomate¹·¹ *n* a pomade, a scented ointment for dressing the hair or skin *16-e19*. [MFr *pommade*, Lat *pomata*]

†pomate¹·² *v* to dress the hair or skin with scented ointment *la18-e19*. [see the noun]

†pome *n* **1** an apple *la15*. **2** a globe *la15-16*. **3** a pomander *16*. [ME *pome*]

pomp *see* PUMP¹·¹

pond *see* PAND, PUND¹

†pone *v* to vow, to swear *19*. [aphetic form of DEPONE]

pone *see* POAN¹·¹

poney *see* POWNIE²

†pong *n* = PONG-PONG. [Fr *pompon*]

†pong-pong *n* an artificial flower or rosette for a woman's dress or hat *la18*. [Fr *pompon*; Compare Eng *pom-pom*]

Pontius Pilate's Bodyguard /ˈpɔnʃʌs paelə ts bɔdegard/ *n* a nickname for the Royal Scots Regiment *la19-*. [in reference to the regiment's seniority in the British Army and a tradition that Pontius Pilate was born in Fortingall, Perthshire]

pony *see* POWNIE²

poo /pu/ *n* the common edible crab *Cancer pagurus 19- EC Bor*. [unknown]

pooch¹·¹, pouch, †putch /putʃ, pʌutʃ/ *n* **1** a pocket in a garment *16-*. **2** a pouch, a small bag *la16-*. **3** one's money or cash; one's purse or finances *la17-*. **4** a deep hole in the bed of a river *la20- C*. **lauch like a pooch on pey day** to laugh heartily *la19- T EC*. [AN *pouche*, ME *pouch*]

pooch¹·², pouch /putʃ, pʌutʃ/ *v* **1** to put something into one's pocket, to take something either legitimately or dishonestly; to steal, pocket *18-*. **2** to eat something greedily and with relish, gulp down *la19- NE T*. [see the noun]

poochle, puchal /ˈpuxəl/ *adj* proud, self-assured, cocky *19- NE*. [unknown]

pooder¹·¹, pouder, poother, pouther, †pulder, †puther, †pudder /ˈpudər, ˈpuðər/ *n* **1** powder, gunpowder *la14-*. **2** *curling* the force or strength behind the delivery of a stone, the impetus with which a stone is played *19-*. **pouthery, poothery** like powder; charged with powder *la18-*. **†paudir lumbard** a spice *la14*. **†powdir myll** a mill for making gunpowder, or pulverizing stone *16-17*. **†poudir violet** a powder made from violets, used as a perfume *16*. **lat oot the pouther** to reveal a secret *la19- NE*. [ME *poudre*]

pooder¹·², pouder, pouther, powder, †pulder /ˈpudər, ˈpuðər, ˈpʌudər/ *v* **1** to preserve (food) with salt or spices *la15-*. **2** to sprinkle with powder; to scatter with small particles, frequently as decoration *16-*. [ME *poudren*]

pooer¹·¹, power, poor, †powar, †pouer /ˈpuər, ˈpʌuər, pur/ *n* **1** ability, capacity *la14-*. **2** power of control, jurisdiction, command *la14-*. **3** an armed force; the main body of an army *la14-*. **4** authority *la14-*. **†at your power** *in the subscription of a letter* to the best of your ability *la14-17*. **†be power by force** *15-e16*. **†power of** ability to control *la18-e19*. **†to your power** = at your power *la16-17*. **†with all power** by force *15*. [ME *pouer*]

†pooer¹·² *v* to exert authority over, command *e18*. [see the noun]

poogs /pugz/ *npl* worn, shabby clothes *20- Ork*. [unknown]

pook *see* POUK¹·², POWK¹·²

pooky /ˈpuki/ *n* a young baby, an infant *19- Sh*. [Norn *púki* an unbaptized child, ON *púki* an imp]

pool *see* PUIL¹·¹

poolicks /ˈpulɪks/ *npl* **1** old clothes, rags, tatters *19, 20- T.* **2** one's best clothes; evening dress *20- EC.* [perhaps altered form of Gael *pùrlag* a rag, tatter + pl suffix]

poon *see* POIND[1.1]

poopit *see* PUPIT

poor *see* POOER[1.1], POUR[1.2], PUIR[1.1], PUIR[1.3]

poorie, purri /ˈpuri, ˈpʌri/ *interj* a call to a cat *20- Sh.* [Norn *purri* a call or pet name for a cat]

poortith *see* PUIRTITH

poose *see* POSE[1.1], POSE[1.2]

pooshin *see* PUSHION[1.1]

poosie *see* PUSSY

poosie knickle, poosie knuckle, pussy-knuckle /pusi ˈnɪkəl, pusi ˈnʌkəl/ *n in a game of marbles* a faulty shot in which the marble is lobbed rather than flicked *20-.* [POUSS + KNUCKLE[1.1]]

poosk[1], **pusk, peesk** /pusk, pisk/ *v* **1** to search, poke around or hunt for something, specifically vermin *19-.* **2** to pilfer *20-.* **3** to drift about doing odd jobs; to fidget aimlessly *20-.* **4** *of the wind* to blow in gusts of increasing violence *20-.* **pusker** a storm, bad weather *20-.* **poosk girs** to look for a human hair in a handful of grass as a form of divination *20-.* [unknown]

poosk[2] /pusk/ *n* a state of excitement or confusion *20-.* [Norn *pusk* great anger or excitement]

poost *see* POUST

pooster, †pouster, †powster /ˈpustər/ *n* physical strength; the physical capacity or use of (a part of) the body *la16-19, 20- Sh.* Compare POUSTIE (sense 4), POUSTIT. [POUSTIE with *-er* suffix after *power*. Sh examples may be influenced by Norn *puster*]

poot[1.1] /put/ *n* a sulky expression, a pout *20-.* **pootie** sulky *20- NE.* **pootsie** sulky *20- Ork.* **i the poots** sulking *20- Sh Ork.* [see the verb]

poot[1.2] /put/ *v* to sulk, to pout *20-.* [Eng *pout*]

poot[2.1] /put/ *n* **1** a young pig *20- Ork.* **2** a young cat, a kitten *20- Sh Ork.* **pooty** a kitten *20- Sh Ork.* [Norn *putti* a cat, a small animal]

poot[2.2] /put/ *interj* a call to a pig *20- Ork.* [see the noun]

poot[3], **pout, powt** /put, pʌut/ *n* a small haddock *19-.* [cognate with MDu *puut* frog; compare MDu *pudde* a fish]

poother *see* POODER[1.1]

pootin *see* POUTING

pootrums /ˈputrəmz/ *n* diarrhoea *la20- N H&I.* [unknown; compare Southern US Eng *poot* to defecate]

poots /puts/ *v* to sulk *20- Ork.* [from the phrase *i the poots* (POOT[1.1])]

pootsie *see* POOT[1.1]

pop /pɔp/ *n* a small round sheep mark made by dabbing on the marking substance with a stick *la19- SW Bor.* [imitative of the action]

pop *see* PAP[3.2]

popill *see* PAPPLE[1.1], PAPPLE[1.2]

popinjay *see* PAPINGO

pople *see* PAPPLE[1.2]

†poplexy, poplesy *n* a stroke of apoplexy *16-e19.* [aphetic form of ME *apoplexie*]

poppy *see* PUPPIE[1]

†popular[1.1] *n* **1** the general population *la16.* **2** a pawn in chess *la15.* [see the adj]

popular[1.2] /ˈpɔpjələr/ *adj* of the population in general *16-.* **†popular sermon** the sermon preached to the people of a parish by a probationer as part of his trials for entry to the ministry *la17-e18.* [Lat *populāris*]

†porciunkle *n in Ayrshire* a small portion of land *la15-e16.* [MFr *portioncule*, Lat *portiuncula*]

pore /por/ *n* a tiny aperture in the skin *15-.* **pory** spongy, porous in texture *19, 20- Sh.* [ME *pore*]

pore *see* PORR[1.2]

pork[1], **purk** /pɔrk, pʌrk/ *n* **1** the flesh of a pig *16-.* **2** a pig *la15-16.* [MFr *porc*, Lat *porcus*]

pork[2.1] /pɔrk/ *n* a prod, a poke *20- SW Bor.* [see the verb]

pork[2.2] /pɔrk/ *v* to prod, poke, push *la19- NE SW Bor.* [perhaps conflation of Eng *poke*, PORR[1.2]]

porr[1.1] /por, pɔr/ *n* **1** a thrust or stab, a poke or prod *17-19, 20- SW.* **2** a thorn, a prickle; a thistle *20- N.* **3** a poker; compare PORRING IRON *17-e18.* [see the verb]

porr[1.2], **purr, †pore** /por, pʌr/ *v* **1** to prod, poke, thrust at *la16-19, 20- Sh Ork SW.* **2** to prick, stab *19- N SW.* [ME *porren*; compare Du *porren* to poke, thrust]

porridge *see* PARRITCH

†porring iron, porring irne a poker *la16-e19.* [verbal noun from PORR[1.2] + IRON]

porritch *see* PARRITCH

port[1.1] /port/ *n* **1** an opening in the side of a ship *15-.* **2** a gateway or entrance (of a walled town or a castle) *15-18, 19- historical.* **3** the road passing through or leading to a gateway; the adjacent area *17-18, 19- historical.* **4** a piece of open ground near a town gate used as the site of a hiring market, especially for farmworkers; the market itself *la18-20, la20- historical.* **5** an opening in a beehive through which bees can fly *la20- NE Uls.* **6** *in curling and bowls* a narrow passage between two stones or bowls through which a third can be aimed *la18-.* **7** *pl* the limits or boundaries (of a town or property) *16.* **†port boulls** *in Elgin* the game of bowls *la16-e17.* [MFr *porte*, Lat *porta*]

†port[1.2] *v in curling or bowls* to send a curling stone or bowl between two stationary stones or bowls lying close together *19.* [see the noun]

port[2] /port/ *n* a tune; a theme tune associated with a person or family, especially played on the bagpipes *18-19, 20- N NE H&I.* [Gael *port*]

port[3] /port/ *n* a harbour or harbour town *la14-.* [AN, MFr *port*]

port-a-beul /porʃtə ˈbiəl/ *n* a fast tune, usually a reel to which Gaelic words of a repetitive nature have been added to make it easier to sing, sometimes used as an accompaniment to dancing in the absence of instrumental music *20-* [Gael *port à beul* music from mouth]

†portabill, portable *adj* that is, or has, to be borne *la15-17.* **portabill burdin** a service that must be rendered by those liable *la17.* **portable chargeis** a payment that must be paid by those liable *la15-17.* [ME *portable*, Lat *portābilis*]

†portar *n* a citizen of a Flemish city *16.* [reduced form of Flem *porterie*]

portar *see* PORTER[1], PORTER[2]

†portary *n* citizenship or burghership in a Flemish or Dutch city, and its rights and privileges *la16.* [Flem *porterie*]

†portative[1] *n* a portable organ *15-16.* [MFr (*orgue*) *portative*]

†portative[2] *adj* navigable *la16-17.* [Lat *portātīvus* capable of carrying]

porteous, †portous, †portuis, †porteus /ˈportɪəs/ *n* **1** an official list of names; *law* a list of persons to be indicted or otherwise proceeded against *15-19, 20- historical.* **2** a portable breviary *la15-e19.* **†Porteous clerk** *law* one of a number of legal officers who investigated the circumstances of crimes to be prosecuted in the circuit courts *e18.* **porteous roll** *law* a list of persons drawn up by the Justice Clerk for indictment before the Circuit Court of Justiciary *la17-19, 20- historical.* [ME *porthors*]

porter[1], **†portar** /ˈportər/ **1** a person employed to carry burdens; a ferryman *16-.* **2** *weaving* a section of the reed in a loom containing 20 interstices through which the warp threads are passed *18-*. [ME *portour*, EModE *porter*]

†**porter**², **portar** *n* a gate- or door-keeper *la14-17*. [ME *porter*]

porter *see* PORTURE

porterage *see* PORTRIDGE

porter biscuit /ˈpɔrtər ˈbɪskət/ *n* a large round flattish bun resembling a roll in texture *20- C*. [apparently from Eng *porter* the dark ale with which these were commonly eaten]

porteus *see* PORTEOUS

portion, †**portioun** /ˈpɔrʃən/ *n* **1** a piece, a share *la14-*. **2** a passage from the Bible chosen for reading, especially at family worship *la18-19*, *20- NE*. †**portionat** provided with a portion of an inheritance *la16*. †**portion natural** *law* a child's share of heritable property *la16-19*. [ME *porcioun*]

portioner, †**portionar**, †**parciounar**, †**parsenere** /ˈpɔrʃənər/ **1** the proprietor of a small estate or piece of land once part of a larger estate *la15-*. **2** *law* a joint (female) heir, or her successor; a joint proprietor *la15-*; compare *heir portioner* (HEIR¹·¹). **3** a person who shares or participates with another in a joint venture or jointly-owned commercial property, a partner *la14-e17*. [PORTION with *-er* suffix]

portioun *see* PORTION

portous *see* PORTEOUS

portrait, †**portract**, †**pourtrait** /ˈpɔrtret/ *n* a likeness or representation of a person or object *la16-*. †**portrature**, **portratour**, **portratur 1** portraiture *la14-17*. **2** external appearance; physique; physical beauty *la14-e17*. [OFr *portrait*, *portraiture*]

portray, †**portra** /pɔrˈtre/ *v* **1** to represent, depict *la14-*. **2** to shape, form or fashion *la14-e16*. [ME *portraien*]

portridge, **portridg**, †**porterage**, †**potridge** /ˈpɔrtrɪdʒ/ *n* a likeness, a depiction *19- Sh*. [altered form of PORTRAIT]

portuis *see* PORTEOUS

†**porture**, **porter** *v ptp* **porturit**, **porturat 1** to represent, depict *e16*. **2** to shape, form or fashion *la14-e16*. [perhaps a syncopated form of ME *portraiture* as a verb, or a blend of this noun with the verb PORTRAY]

†**port-youl** *n* a mournful tune; a sad outcry *la17-19*. **sing port-youl** to cry, lament *la17-19*. [PORT² + probably Eng *yowl*, in reference to PORT-A-BEUL]

pos, **pus** /pos, pus, pʌs/ *n* a swelling, a boil *20- Sh*. **possic**, **possick**, **posic 1** a gathering of pus *20- Sh*. **2** a poultice *20-*. **3** a quantity of some messy substance *20- Sh*. [Norn *pos* a swelling, a boil]

pose¹·¹, *Bor* **poose**, †**pois** /poz; *Bor* puz/ *n* a collection of money or valuables kept safely or hidden away, a fund or stock of money; a hoard; savings *16-*. †**in pose** *of money or valuables* in safe keeping; set aside, yet quickly accessible, available *la15-17*. [MFr *pose* the action of depositing]

pose¹·², *Bor* **poose** /poz; *Bor* puz/ *v* to place; to hide (something) *la19- N NE T EC Bor*. **pose by** to set aside *20- N NE T*. **pose up** to save up (money) *la19- N NE T*. [Fr *poser* lay down]

†**pose**², †**pois** *v ptp* **posed**, **posit**, **poissit** *Presbyterian Church* to interrogate, question *la16-e18*. [aphetic form of EModE *appose*, *oppose*]

posel, **posil** /ˈpozəl, ˈposəl/ *n* a heap, a collection *19- T*. **poselie** = POSEL *20- T*. [POSE¹·¹ + *-el* diminutive suffix]

posh¹ /poʃ, pɔʃ/ *n* a child's word for porridge *la19-*. **posh-ie** = POSH¹. [perhaps onomatopoeic or a child's form of Eng *porridge*, perhaps with influence from Eng *posh* a soft pulpy mass]

posh² /pɔʃ/ *n* a type of violin made in Shetland (suitable for a child) *19- Sh*. [Fr *pochette* a kit or small fiddle which a fiddler could carry in his pocket]

posie /ˈpoze, ˈpozi/ **1** a collection of money or valuables *la19-*. **2** a heap, a collection of objects or of children *la19*, *20- NE T*. [POSE¹·¹ + -IE¹]

posil *see* POSEL

positive¹·¹ /ˈpɔzətɪv/ *adj* **1** *grammar* the basic form of an adjective or adverb, without qualification or comparison *16-*. **2** explicitly stated; free from reservation; precise, absolute *17-*. **3** *of people* determined, adamant, obstinate *18-*. **4** *law* formally and explicitly laid down and enacted by man, not proceeding from divine ordinance or the natural order *la15-e17*. [MFr *positif*, Lat *positīvus*]

†**positive**¹·² /ˈpɔzətɪv/ *adv* explicitly; affirmatively *17*. [see the adj]

posonit *see* PUSHIONT

poss /pɔs/ *v* **1** to press, squeeze down, pound *19- Bor Uls*. **2** to knead or press down clothes in washing; to trample a washing to extract the dirt *19- T Bor*. **3** to strike; to hit with the knees or feet; to knee; to kick; to trample *16-e17*. **posser** a stick used to pound clothes in the wash-tub *la18-19*, *20- SW Bor*. **possing tub** a wash-tub *19*, *20- SW Bor*. **poss stick** = *posser 20- NE Bor*. [unknown;]

†**possede**, **posseid** *v* to possess *la14-e17*. [Lat *possidēre* to possess, *possīdere* to take possession of]

possess, †**posses** /pəˈzɛs/ *v* **1** to have, enjoy or control anything *15-*. **2** to take possession of by force *16-*. **3** *law* to give a person possession or occupancy of property *15-17*. **4** to take or be in possession or occupancy of property as owner or tenant *16-18*. **5** *in the Borders* to cause (land) to be occupied by cattle *16*. [ME *possessen*]

possession, †**possessioun** /pəˈzɛʃən/ *n* **1** occupancy, ownership, control *la14-*. **2** a property enjoyed or occupied though not necessarily owned; a tenancy; a piece of ground or small farm held under lease *la14-19*. [ME *possessioun*, Lat *possessio*]

possessor, †**possessour** /pəˈzɛsər/ *n* an owner or occupier *15-*. [ME *possessour*]

possessory, †**possessoury** /pəˈzɛsəre/ *adj of a legal claim or entitlement* founded on possession or occupancy *15-*. **possessory judgment** *law* the rule by which an occupant of at least seven years standing cannot be dispossessed by a rival claimant except by a court action of reduction *17-*. [ME *possessorie* relating to possession]

†**possessour** *adj* = POSSESSORY *la15-e17*. [altered form of POSSESSORY]

†**posset** *n* **1** a drink made of hot milk curdled with ale or wine, sometimes with sugar and spices *16-17*. **2** a poisonous drink *la16-17*. [unknown]

possibility, **possibilitie**, †**possibilite** /pɔsəˈbɪləti/ **1** the fact of being possible *la14-*. **2** capacity, power, means *la14-e17*. [AN *possibileté*, MFr *possibilité*]

possible¹·¹, †**possibill** /ˈpɔsəbəl/ *adj* capable of occurring, being done *la14-*. †**all possibill** the greatest possible, the utmost *la15-17*. [ME *possible*]

†**possible**¹·², †**possibill** *adv* possibly *la16-17*. [see the adj]

possic, **possick** *see* POS

†**possodie** *n* **1** term of endearment *e16*. **2** a poisonous drink *la16*. [unknown; compare POSSET and POWSOWDIE]

post¹, †**poist** /post/ *n* **1** a pillar; an upright of timber or other solid material *15-*. **2** *in mining or quarrying* a vertical mass of rock available for quarrying; a thick layer or seam of stone, usually sandstone or limestone; the working face in a granite quarry *la17-19*, *20- NE T C*. **post stone** a very hard, fine-grained sandstone *20- EC*. [OE *post* a post, a pillar, a doorpost, Lat *postis*]

post²·¹, †**poist**, †**poast** /post/ *n* **1** a means of delivering despatches by relay at pre-arranged places; one of a series of relay stations *16-*. **2** a postal or courier service *la17-*. **3** a postal delivery *la17-*. **4** a Royal Mail postman *19-*. **5** an official letter-carrier, a courier carrying mail or packages *16-e19*. **6** a message bearer (on a single occasion) *la16-e17*. **7** one of a series of stations where post-horses were kept for relays, a stage *17*. **postie** a letter-carrier; a Royal Mail postman *17-*. †**generall postmaister** = *postmaister generall e17*. **postcaird** a postcard *20-*. **postmaister 1** the officer in charge of a post or of a local post office *17-*. **2** a person licensed to hire out horses to Travellers *17*. **postmaister generall, post master general** the person having overall authority over local postmasters *17-20, 21- historical*. **post office** the local office conducting postal business *17-*. †**at post 1** *of a message or messenger* as or by express courier; at express speed *16-e17*. **2** *of a person* by relays of horses at post-stages; at great speed *16*. †**at the post** = *at post*. †**rin the post** to be an express messenger or despatch rider, perhaps using relays of horses; to travel at express speed *16*. †**ride the post** = *rin the post la16*. [MFr *poste*]

post[2.2] /post/ *v* **1** to travel with despatches; to send a courier *16-*. **2** to travel at speed or post-haste *la16-*. **3** to send a letter or parcel; to send a message by courier or postal service *17-*. **4** to act as a postman *la20- NE*. [see the noun]

†**post**[2.3] *adv* at great speed *la16-17*. [see the noun]

post[3] /post/ *v* to knead or press down (clothes) when washing, to trample (a washing) to extract the dirt *19- NE T H&I*. [Gael *post*, borrowed into Gael from POSS]

post[4] /post/ *n* a piece of lead shot *20- Sh*. [unknown]

†**postillat, postyllat, postulat** *n* a coin, originally the debased gulden of bishop Rudolph of Diepholt *la15*. [Fris *postulatus gelden*, MFr *postulat* a coin from Liège, Lat *postulātus*; compare POSTULAT]

postour *see* POUSTER

postpone /pəsˈpon/ *v* **1** to defer, delay, put off till later *la15-*. **2** *law* to relegate the claims of a creditor by giving others priority of repayment, demote in the ranking of creditors *18-*. **3** to keep a person waiting for something promised or due *16-17*. **4** to set aside; to disregard; to quit *la15-16*. **5** to subordinate (one thing to another); to treat as of lesser importance; to esteem less *16-e17*. [Lat *postpōnere*]

†**postrum**[1], **postrome, postroun**, *n* a postern, a door or gate other than the main entrance *15-16*. **postrum yett** a back or side gate *la15-16*. [altered form of ME *postern*]

†**postrum**[2] *n* an abscess *16-e17*. [aphetic form from MFr *apostume*; compare APOSTEME]

†**postulat** *n Roman Catholic Church* a person nominated to a bishopric, although canonically disqualified, while awaiting a papal dispensation of the impediment *la15-e17*. [Lat *postulātus*]

postulat *see* POSTILLAT

†**postule** *v Roman Catholic Church* to nominate a canonically disqualified person in the expectation of papal dispensation *e15*. [Lat *postulāt-*, ptp stem of *postulāre*]

posture *see* POUSTER
postyllat *see* POSTILLAT

posy /ˈpozi/ *n* **1** a small bunch of flowers *la15-*. **2** term of endearment for a child or woman, a sweetheart *19, 20- WC SW*. [a variant of EModE *poesie* a bunch of flowers, MFr *poesie* a poem]

pot[1.1], †**pott** /pot/ *n* **1** a pit or hole in the ground; an excavation *13-*. **2** a deep hole in the bed of a river, a pool in a river or stream *la15-*. **3** a pit from which peats are dug *la15-19, 20- SW Bor*. **4** a coal mine; a mine shaft *16-19*. **5** a tanner's pit for bark or lime; compare *barkpot* (BARK[2]), *limepot* (LIME) *15-17*. **6** the chasm or abyss of Hell *la15-17*; compare PIT[1.2]. **pot hole 1** a puddle-hole *18-*. **2** a pool in rocks on the seashore *20-*. **3** a small depression in a field which is difficult to drain *20-*. **pot and gallows** = *pit and gallows* (PIT[1.1]). [unknown]

pot[1.2] /pot/ *v* **1** to dig pits in the ground, to fill an area with pits *la14-*. **2** to dig holes to indicate a boundary; to erect a boundary-stone (by putting its base in a hole); to delimit land in this way *16-e18*. **3** to dig holes in a moss to extract peat *la16-19*. [unknown]

pot *see* PAT, PIT[2]
potage *see* POTTAGE
potato *see* PITAWTIE
potch *see* POACH[1.2]

potch potch, potchie potchie /ˈpɒtʃ pɒtʃ, ˈpɒtʃi pɒtʃi/ *interj* a call to a pig *20- N*. [Gael *poitidh poitidh*]

pote *see* PAT
potegar *see* POTHECAR
potegary *see* POTICARY

†**potent**[1.1] *n* powerful people, a powerful person *la16-e17*. [see the adj]

potent[1.2] /ˈpotənt/ *adj* powerful, having great power *15-*. [Lat *potent-*, presp stem of *posse* to be able]

†**potent**[2], **patent** *n* **1** a staff, crozier, crutch *la14-16*. **2** a gibbet; a gibbet-like structure for tilting at *16*. [ME *potent*]

potestater, Sh pottersta /pɒtəˈstatər; Sh ˈpɒtərsta/ *n* expectation; anticipation, a state of waiting *la19- Sh NE*. **in one's potestater** at the height of one's career and influence, in a state of full well-being and prosperity, in one's prime *la19- Sh NE*. [from the Sc legal phr Lat *in ligiā potestāte* sound in body and mind; compare LIEGE POUSTIE]

†**pothecar, poticar, potegar** *n* an apothecary *la15-17*. Compare POTTINGAR, APOTHICAR, APOTHECARIE, POTICARY and IPOTINGAR. [aphetic form of APOTHICAR]

†**poticary, potegary** *n* an apothecary *la15-19*. Compare POTTINGAR, APOTHICAR, APOTHECARIE, POTHECAR and IPOTINGAR. [aphetic form of APOTHECARIE]

potingar *see* POTTINGAR
potingary *see* POTTINGARY
potissarie *see* PATISAR
potottie *see* PITAWTIE
potridge *see* PORTRIDGE
potsker *see* PAT
pott *see* PAT, POT[1.1]

pottage, pottitch, †**potage** /ˈpɒtədʒ, ˈpɒtɪtʃ/ *n* **1** a vegetable broth *15-*. **2** oatmeal porridge; breakfast; food in general *la17-19, 20- NE*. Compare PARRITCH. [OFr *potage* vegetable soup]

potted heid /ˌpɒtəd ˈhid/ *n* **1** meat from the head of a cow or pig, boiled, shredded and served cold in jelly made from the stock *la19-*. **2** *rhyming slang* DEID[1.2] (sense 1) *la20- EC*. [from ptp of Eng POT + HEID]

potted hoch /ˌpɒtəd ˈhɒx/ *n* a similar dish to POTTED HEID but made of meat from the shin of a cow or pig *la19-*. [from ptp of Eng POT + HOCH]

potten *see* PIT[2]

potterlow /ˈpɒtərˌlʌu/ *n of food spoilt in cooking* a broken or ruined condition, smithereens, pulp *20- NE*. **tae potterlow** *of food* reduced to pulp or fragments, completely spoilt; *of persons or circumstances* in an unhealthy or degraded condition *la19- NE*. [unknown; compare Eng *go to pot*]

potterneeshin /ˌpɒtərˈniʃən/ *n* **gae to potterneeshin** to become ruined or destroyed *20- NE*. [conflation of POTTERLOW with CROCKANITION infl by a play on *pot* and *crock*]

pottersta *see* POTESTATER

pottie[1.1] /ˈpɒte/ *n* putty, cement used to fix panes of glass or repair wood *18-*. [Fr *potée*]

pottie[1,2] /ˈpɔte/ *v* to apply putty *la18*-. **it winna pottie** *of a story or plan* it will be unworkable, it won't function adequately *la19*-. [see the noun]

pottie[2] /ˈpɔti/ *n games* a marble made of fine clay or earthenware *la19*- *NE*. **pottie bod** = POTTIE[2] *20- NE*. [synecdoche from PAT]

pottingar, †**potingar**, †**pothecar**, †**potegar** /ˈpɔtɪndʒər/ *n* an apothecary, a pharmacist *la15-19, 20- historical*. [altered aphetic form of APOTHICAR]

†**pottingary**, **potingary** *n* **1** the art or practice of an apothecary, pharmacy *la15-e17*. **2** the drugs or medicines of an apothecary *la15-e16*. **3** an apothecary *la15-16*. [from the noun POTTINGAR, compare POTICARY]

†**pottinger** *n* a bowl for soup or porridge, a porringer *18-e19*. [POTTAGE + *-er* suffix, with alteration of the stem]

pottisear *see* PATISAR
pottitch *see* POTTAGE
pottskerd *see* PAT
potye *see* PATTY

pou, **pow**, **pu**, **pull** /pʌu, pu, pul, pʌl/ *v* **1** to remove forcibly, pluck (hair or feathers) *15-*. **2** to pick, gather (fruit, flowers or produce) *15-*. **3** to drag, haul along *la15-*. **4** to draw or extract (a tooth) *19-*. **5** *of a vent or chimney* to have a strong draught, to draw *20-*. **pull doon** to destroy, demolish *16-*. †**pull his ear** to nag, demand to be heard *16*. †**pou stalks** to pluck stalks of corn or cabbage plants for use in divination (at Halloween) *la18*. **like pullin teeth** extremely difficult to obtain (money or a response) *20-*. †**pull up sails** to hoist sail; to get on with life *16*. [ME *pullen*]

pouch *see* POOCH[1,1], POOCH[1,2]

poud /pʌud/ *v* to bump, swing or jostle (a person or thing) from side to side *20- NE*. [unknown; compare *showdie-powdie* a see-saw, from SHOWD[1,2]]

pouder *see* POODER[1,1], POODER[1,2]

†**poudir violet**, **powdir wiolet** *n* a powder made from violets, probably as a perfume *16*. Compare POODER[1,1]. [AN *pudre de violets* a powder soaked in oil of violets]

pouer *see* POOER[1,1], POUR[1,2]

pouk[1,1] /puk/ *n* **1** a plucking motion, a twitch, a tug, a sharp pull *la18- T C SW Bor Uls*. **2** a small quantity *la19- WC SW Uls*. **3** what has been or is to be plucked (off), a picking, frequently tufts of wool from a sheep, fluff, a tuft of hair; a mouthful or bite *19, 20- T SW*. **4** *of birds* the moult *19- T C*. **5** the feathers of a bird, when they begin to grow after moulting *19- SW Bor*. **poukie** *of persons* dejected-looking, thin and unhealthy-looking *la19- WC SW Uls*. **in the pouk 1** *of birds* moulting *la19- C*. **2** *of persons* not very well, below par *19-*. **play pouk at** to clutch at, try to grasp or tug *19- SW*. [unknown]

pouk[1,2], **pook**, †**puke**, **puik** /puk/ *v* **1** to pull out the loose hay at the foot of (a stack) to let air in *19- T C SW*. **2** to pluck, twitch, tug, pull sharply *17-19, 20- C Bor*. **3** to pluck (a fowl) *19- C SW*. **4** *in card games* to take a card or cards from the pack when unable to play from one's hand *la20- C SW*. **pookin**, **pouking** *of birds* the period of moulting *la19- C*. **poukit** *of birds* plucked; *of persons or things* having a miserable, emaciated appearance; shabby, threadbare *19- C SW Bor*. **pouk at** to pluck or tug at, pull at sharply; to annoy, harass; to criticize *19, 20- SW*. [unknown]

poulie /ˈpuli/ *n* a louse *19- C*. [unknown]

poullie /ˈpuli/ *n* a young domestic fowl, a young hen, especially one intended for consumption, a pullet *19, 20- Uls*. [Fr *poulet* a chicken]

poulse *see* PULS
poultry *see* POUTRIE
poun *see* POWNE, PUND[1]

pounce *see* PUNCE[1,1]

pound, *Sh* **pund** /pʌund; *Sh* pʌnd/ *n* **1** an enclosed stretch of water, a pond, pool, reservoir *la16-19, 20- C SW Bor*. **2** a semi-enclosed piece of water, a bay, a bight *la20- Sh*. Compare PUND[2]. [ME *pound, pund*]

pound *see* POIND[1,2]
poundland *see* PUND[1]
pouny *see* POWNIE[1]

pour[1,1] /por, pur/ *n* **1** a heavy shower of rain, a downpour *la18-*. **2** a small quantity of a liquid, a drop *19, 20- C Uls*. **pour out** the scattering of coins to children by members of a wedding party (usually the groom or the bride's father); a cry raised by children in the hope of a scattering of coins *19, 20- C Bor*; compare SCATTER[2] (sense 2). [see the verb]

pour[1,2], **poor**, †**powre**, †**pouer** /por, pur/ *v* **1** to empty liquid from its container *16-*. **2** to empty a container by pouring out its contents *16-*. **3** to drain potatoes or other vegetables *la19-*. **4** to smear sheep with an oily compound as a protection against insects and wet *la19*. **pourin** a small quantity of a liquid, a drop *19, 20- Sh T Bor Uls*. **pour on** to hurry *la19- Ork*. [ME *pouren*]

pourie /ˈpure, ˈpuri/ *n* **1** a vessel with a spout for pouring, a jug, especially a cream jug *la18-19, 20- T C Bor*. **2** a small oil can with a spout *la19, 20- C SW Bor*. **3** a small quantity of a liquid, a drop *la19, 20- NE T Bor*. [POUR[1,2] with *-ie* noun-forming suffix]

pourins /ˈpurənz/ *npl* **1** the liquid strained off anything that has been soaked or boiled *20-*. **2** the last drops of liquid left in a container, the dregs *19- NE Uls*. **3** the liquid strained off sowans after their fermentation *19, 20- NE*. [pl verbal noun from POUR[1,2]]

pours *see* PURSE[1,1]
pourtrait *see* PORTRAIT
pouse *see* POUSS, PUSS

pouskered /ˈpuskərd/ *adj of persons* exhausted, worn-out *la20- T WC*. [perhaps altered form of POUSTIT]

pouss, **push**, †**pouse**, †**pusche** /pʌʃ, puʃ/ *v* **1** to push, shove; to cause to move (forward) *la16-*. **2** to incite, urge, encourage *la16-*. **3** to poke or thrust (a stick); to prod; to punch *17-e19*. †**pouss one's fortune** to engage in improving one's fortune or finances *17-19* [MFr *pousser*; the Sc form retained unpalatalized /s/, but *push* was adopted later from Eng]

pouss *see* PUSH
poussie *see* PUSSY

poussie hander /pusi ˈhandər/ *n* = POOSIE KNICKLE *20- T*. [POUSS + HAND with *-er* suffix]

poust, **poost** /pʌust, pust/ *n* strength, vigour, power, force *19-*. [shortened form of POUSTIE]

pouste *see* POUSTIE

pouster, **posture**, †**postour** /ˈpustər, ˈpʌustər, ˈpɔstjər/ *n* **1** the disposition, state or circumstances of anything *17-*. **2** a state of military preparedness *17-*. **3** physical situation, location; pose, posture *17-*. †**in posture** in a suitable frame of mind *17*. [Fr *posture*]

pouster *see* POOSTER

poustie, †**pouste**, †**powste** /ˈpusti/ *n* **1** power, strength, force, authority, control *la14-*. **2** physical strength; the physical capacity or use of (a part of) the body *16-*. **3** ability to do or effect something, capacity, might *la14-e15*. **4** sound physical health; compare LIEGE POUSTIE *la14-e15*. [ME *pouste*, OFr *poesté*]

poustit /ˈpustɪt/ *adj* drained of strength or virtue, powerless; not in one's normal state of health or mind; suffering sickness or pain *19-*. **ill-pousted** in a bad temper *20- Ork*.

[probably related to Norn *puster* vital power, capacity for work + -IT³; compare POOSTER]

pout, powt /put, pʌut/ *n* **1** a poult, a young game-bird *16-19, 20- N NE EC SW*. **2** affectionate term for a child or young person; a sweetheart *18- Ork NE T EC*. [ME *polet*]

pout *see* PAWT¹·², POOT³

pouther *see* POODER¹·¹, POODER¹·²

pouting, pootin /'pʌutɪŋ, 'putɪn/ *n* the hunting of game-birds; a shoot *la17-*. [POUT with -*ing* suffix]

poutrie, poultry, †pultrie, †powtry /'putre, 'poltre/ *n* farmyard fowls *la15-*. [ME *pultrie*]

pover *see* PUIR¹·³

povereese /'pɔvəriz/ *v* to reduce to a condition of poverty; to exhaust (land) by overworking; to over-exploit *la19-*. [perhaps variant of ME *poverish* or aphetic form of Fr *appauvriss-*, extended stem of *appauvrir* to impoverish]

povily /'pɔvəli/ *adj* feeble, spiritless, lacking in energy *20- Ork*. [unknown]

pow¹, poll, †pole /pʌu, pol/ *n* **1** a person as a unit in a list *15-*. **2** *of a human being or animal* the head; the crown of the head; the scalp; the skull *la15-*. **3** the blunt or rounded part of an axe-head or hammer *la19- Sh NE SW*. **powie** a blacksmith's hand-hammer which has both striking faces rounded off *20- T EC*. **†poll axe, pow ax** a battle-axe *15-e19*. **†poll money, pole money** a capitation tax, poll tax *17*. **†poll penny** a charitable offering made at a funeral *la15-e16*. **†by the poll** *of voting or taxation* according to the number of heads *15-17*. [MDu *pol*]

pow², poll /pʌu, pol, pɔl/ *n* **1** a slow-moving stream or ditch flowing through carseland *14-*. **2** a (shallow or marshy) pool of water *18-19, 20- Sh Ork N SW*. **3** a puddle, a pothole in the street *20- Sh Ork N*. **4** a sea-pool in the rocks *20- Sh NE*. **5** an inlet serving as a landing-place for small vessels *16-19, 20- SW*. **6** *in Orkney* a marshy, low-lying field *18*. [Gael *poll* a pit, mire, pool, gulf; cognate with PUIL¹·¹ from OE *pōl*]

pow *see* POU

powan /'pʌuən/ *n* a freshwater whitefish *Coregonus clupeoides*, found only in Scotland in Loch Lomond and Loch Eck *17-*. [Gael **pollan*; compare POLLACK]

powar *see* POOER¹·¹

powart, powat *see* POWHEID

powder *see* POODER¹·²

powdir myll *see* POODER¹·¹

powdir wiolet *see* POUDIR VIOLET

power *see* POOER¹·¹

powheid, †powart, †powat /'pʌuhid/ *n* a tadpole *17- NE C SW Bor*. **powie** = POWHEID *19- T EC*. [POW¹ + HEID]

powin *see* POWNE, PUND¹

powk¹·¹ /pʌuk/ *n* a hole or hollow in the ground, usually waterlogged or marshy *la18- NE T*. [see the verb]

powk¹·² /pʌuk, puk/ *v* **1** to poke *la19-*. **2** to dig or excavate in a careless, clumsy way *18- NE*. **3** to shove or kick *20- Sh Ork*. **pookin** a beating, punishment *20- Ork*. [Eng *poke*, the vowel perhaps infl by HOWK¹·²]

powk² /pʌuk/ *v* to walk with a heavy or exhausted step *19- NE*. [perhaps onomatopoeic with infl from POWK¹·² and POWT]

powl¹·¹, †pol, †poll /pʌul/ *n* **1** a pole, a long, thin, round shaft of wood *la15-*. **2** a walking stick, a stilt, a crutch *la19-*. [Eng *pole*]

powl¹·² /pʌul/ *v* **1** to move along rapidly at a walk or jog *la19- H&I WC SW Bor*. **2** to propel oneself with the aid of a crutch *19- SW*. [see the noun]

powne, pownie, †powin, †poun, †pawn /pʌun, 'pʌune/ *n* a peacock *15-19, 20- literary*. [OFr *poün*, Fr *paon*]

pow-net, Sh bow-net /'pʌu nɛt; Sh 'bʌu nɛt/ *n* the net closest to the buoy used to position a series of nets shot from a herring-boat *20-*. [variant of BOW⁴ a buoy, perhaps with influence from POW¹ (sense 3), + NET,]

pownie¹, †pouny /'pʌune/ *n* **1** a pony, a small horse *la17-*. **2** a carpenter's trestle for supporting planks of wood for cutting *20- N EC Uls*. [probably MFr *poulenet* a little foal]

†pownie², pony, poney *n* a turkey, especially the female *18-e19*. **pownie cock** a turkey cock *18-e19*. [POWNE; the turkey was freq confused with the peacock]

pownie *see* POWNE

powowit /pʌu'wʌuit/ *n* = POWHEID *la18- EC Bor*. [extended form of *powat*]

powpet *see* PUPIT

powre *see* POUR¹·²

powsowdie, powsodie /pʌu'sʌudi, pʌu'sodi/ *n* **1** broth or thick soup made from a sheep's head *la17-*. **2** a mixture of various ingredients, a messy hotchpotch, a mush *19-*. [probably POW¹ + SOWDIE; compare POSSODIE]

powste *see* POUSTIE

powster *see* POOSTER

powt *see* PAWT¹·¹, PAWT¹·², POOT³, POUT

†powter¹·¹ *n* (the noise made by) a poking or prodding movement, stirring, prod or thrust *19*. Compare PAWT¹·¹. [see the verb]

powter¹·² /'pʌutər/ *v* **1** to poke or prod repeatedly *16-*; compare PAWT¹·². **2** to poke into, interfere *19-*. **3** to work ineffectually or fecklessly, to potter *19-*. **4** to paddle or poke about in a liquid, make a noise in a liquid *la19, 20- T H&I SW*. [PAWT¹·² with -*er* frequentative suffix]

powtry *see* POUTRIE

pox /pɔks/ *v* **1** *masonry* to spoil a stone by bad cutting *20- NE SW*. **2** to botch a job, ruin a peice of work *la20- NE*. [Eng *pox* to infect with the pox]

poyl-de-soy *see* PADUASOY

poynct *see* POINT

poyndlar *see* POIND¹·²

poynt *see* PINT²·¹, PINT³

poysonit *see* PUSHIONT

poysoun *see* PUSHION¹·¹, PUSHION¹·²

pozie /'pozi/ *n* a narrow alleyway or passage between buildings, a close *20- NE*. [unknown]

praan *see* PRAWN

pract *see* PRET¹·²

practeeze *see* PRACTISE

practeis *see* PRACTICE, PRACTISE

practic, practick, prattick, *N NE* **prottick, †prettik, †practique** /'praktɪk, 'pratɪk; *N NE* 'protɪk/ *n* **1** a way of doing things; established custom, usage *15-*. **2** an action or activity belonging to the practice of a craft or profession *la15-*. **3** an escapade, especially a discreditable one; a piece of mischief *18-19, 20- NE*. **4** skill nefariously applied; trickery; a stratagem *la15-19, 20- NE*. **5** a commercial scheme or venture, an undertaking *20- NE*. **6** a display of skill, a feat of physical skill or daring *16-19*. **7** *law* customary usage or procedure, the usual practice *16-e19*. **8** *law* a recorded decision of a court cited as a precedent *la16-18*. **9** a precedent *16-17*. **10** the action of practising, practice as opposed to theory *15-e17*. **11** proficiency or skill gained by practice *la15-16*. Compare PRACTICK¹·¹. [ME *practik*, AN *practik*, Lat *practica*]

†practicate *adj* **1** *of a procedure* practised (as the usual way of doing something) *16-17*. **2** experienced, skilled *la16*. [Lat *practicāt-*, ptp stem of *practicāre* to practise]

practice, †practise, †practeis, †practize /'praktɪs/ *n* **1** established method, usage or custom *la15-*. **2** the fact of putting something into action *la16-*. **3** a way of acting; conduct, an action *la16-*. **4** *law* a legal precedent *la16-e18*. **5** conspiracy, intrigue; a plot *la16-e17*. [from the verb PRACTISE]

practice-chanter /ˈpraktɪs tʃantər/ *n* a pipe of lower pitch than a chanter, with a softer reed used for learning and practising bagpipe fingering *20-*. Compare CHANTER (sense 2). [Eng *practice* + CHANTER]

practician /prakˈtɪʃən/ *n* a practitioner of an art or profession; a practical man as opposed to a theorist, a doer *la15-*. [MFr *practicien*]

†**practick**[1.1], **pratik**, **prettik** *v pt, ptp* also **pratik, practit** 1 to practise as an established usage or normal procedure *la15-16*. 2 to carry out an action *15-16*; compare PRACTISE (sense 1). 3 to come to pass; to be proved true in practice *e16*. 4 to acquire or verify (knowledge) by experience *16*. 5 to cause (a person) to act in an underhand way; to suborn *16-e17*. [MFr *practiquer, pratiquer*]

†**practick**[1.2] *adj* requiring skill, difficult *16-17*. [ME *practik*, EModE *practik*]

practick *see* PRACTIC

practicks, †**practiques** /ˈpraktɪks/ *npl* a compendium of recorded court decisions, especially the decisions of the Court of Session, forming a system of case-law *16-19, 20- historical*. [plural of PRACTIC]

†**practikis**, †**prettikkis** *npl* trimming for garments *la16*. [perhaps related to Lat *praetexere* to weave in front of, edge, border]

practique *see* PRACTIC

practiques *see* PRACTICKS

practise, **practeeze**, †**practize**, †**practeis** /ˈpraktɪs, prakˈtiːz/ *v* 1 to perform, carry out (actions) *16-*. 2 to exercise (a vocation or way of life) *16-*. 3 to bribe, suborn *16-17*. 4 to use as established usage or normal procedure *la16-e17*. 5 to plot *16-e17*. Compare PRACTIC. †**practiser** 1 a schemer, plotter *la16-17*. 2 a person who practises witchcraft *la16-e17*. **practeezing** a dancing class *18-19, 20- Ork*. [EModE *practise*, Lat *practizāre*]

practise *see* PRACTICE

practize *see* PRACTICE, PRACTISE

prae- *see* PRE-

praecipuum /priˈsɪpjuʌm/ *n law* an indivisible right to a peerage or mansion-house which went to the eldest and not jointly to all heirs portioners *18-*. [Lat *praecipuum* that which is taken from an inheritance before the general distribution begins]

praedial *see* PREDIAL

praefervid *see* PERFERVID

praepositura /pripɔzɪˈtjurə/ *n law* the right of a wife to incur debts on behalf of her husband for food and household requirements *la18-*. [Lat *praeposita negōtiīs* in the position of a wife) set over the management (of a household)]

praescrive *see* PRESCRIBE

prain *see* PRAWN

prain-fluke /ˈpren fluk/ *n* the flounder *la19- NE*. [PRAWN + FLEUK from its diet of prawns]

praisant *see* PRESENT[2]

praise[1.1], †**prayis**, †**prase** /prez/ *n* 1 credit, honour, eulogy; the condition of receiving or deserving praise *la16-*. 2 a euphemism for God *la19-*. **Praise be blest** an expression of relief or joy *18-*. [see the verb]

praise[1.2], †**prase**, †**pryce** /prez/ *v* to hold in honour, extol or commend *la14-*. [ME *preisen, prīsen*]

praise *see* PRICE[1.1], PRICE[1.2]

praisent *see* PRESENT[1.2], PRESENT[1.3], PRESENT[2]

pram[1.1] /pram/ *n* oatmeal mixed with buttermilk, milk or cream *19- Sh*. **burstin pram** = PRAM[1.1]. [see the verb]

pram[1.2] /pram/ *v* 1 to stuff (a receptacle) with something, press (an object) into a small area *19- Sh NE T*. 2 to press down, squeeze; to exert pressure or force on *19- Sh NE*. 3 of *people* to crowd, throng *20- Sh Ork*. [MLG, MDu *prammen*, *pramen* press, squeeze]

†**prame** *n* a flat-bottomed boat *la15-e17*. [MDu *praem*; compare ON *prámr*, Fr *prame*]

pran /pran/ *v* 1 to bruise, beat, punish *18- NE*. 2 to crush, pound, trample *19- NE*. [Gael *pronn, prann* to pound, mash, grind; compare PRON]

prane *see* PRAWN

prang /praŋ/ *n* a prong, a spike *19, 20- NE T*. [Eng *prong*]

prank[1] /praŋk/ *n* a trick, a practical joke *18-*. [EModE *prank* a trick]

prank[2] /praŋk/ *v* 1 to play tricks or practical jokes; to meddle, interfere; to act in a lighthearted or careless way *19- NE T Bor*. 2 to play, amuse oneself *la19*. 3 to behave ostentatiously *16-17*. [conflation of EModE *prank* to prance, caper with EModE *prank* to play a trick]

prap[1.1], **prop**, †**prope** /prap, prɔp/ *n* 1 a post or stake (used as a prop) *la15-*. 2 a stone or heap of stones or a pole used as a boundary marker *la15-*. 3 a memorial or gravestone *19-*. 4 *ploughing* a guide to mark the course and end of the first furrow of the rig *la19- Ork NE*. 5 a target *la15-19, 20- NE*. 6 *pl* a throwing or shooting contest *la15-e19*. 7 a woman viewed as a sexual target *16*. [unknown]

prap[1.2], **prop**, †**prope** /prap, prɔp/ *v* 1 to support (with a prop) *la16-*. 2 to mark (a boundary) by means of posts or stones *la15-19, 20- NE*. 3 to set up a target *19, 20- Sh*. 4 to aim or throw (missiles) at a target *19*. 5 to erect (a boundary marker) *15-16*. [unknown]

prase *see* PRAISE[1.1], PRAISE[1.2]

prat *see* PRET[1.1], PRET[1.2]

pratik *see* PRACTICK[1.1]

pratt *see* PRET[1.1]

prattick *see* PRACTIC

pratty *see* PRETTIE, PRETTY

†**pravitie** *n* depravity *la15-16*. [Lat *prāvitās* crookedness, distortion, perverseness, depravity]

prawn, *NE* **praan**, †**prain**, †**prane** /prɔn; *NE* pran/ *n* 1 a shrimp, a prawn *16-*. 2 a langoustine *Nephrops norvegicus 20-*. Compare PRAIN-FLUKE. [unknown]

prayis *see* PRAISE[1.1]

pre-, **prae-** /pri, pre/ *prefix* 1 before, previously, in advance; anterior to; (occurring) prior to *16-*. 2 superior to, greater than, beyond; exceedingly *la16-*. [Lat *prae-, pre-*]

preach, †**preche**, †**preiche** /pritʃ/ *v* 1 to expound on religious topics *la14-*. 2 *of a Presbyterian minister* to officiate as a preacher (as distinct from a reader) to a congregation *la16-*. **preacher**, †**prechar**, †**prechour** 1 a person who expounds on religious topics *la14-*. 2 *Presbyterian Church* a minister licensed to preach *la16-e17*. **preach in** to conduct a service to welcome (a minister) to a new charge after their induction *20-*. [ME *prechen*]

preaching /ˈpritʃɪŋ/ *n* 1 the action of expounding on religious topics *la14-*. 2 the delivery of a sermon or moral discourse *15-*. 3 *Presbyterian Church* a religious service including a sermon, specifically one on the days leading up to and following the communion service *la16-*. †**preaching day** *Presbyterian Church* a day devoted to preaching *la16-19*. [verbal noun from PREACH]

preas *see* PRESS[1.2]

prebend /ˈprɛbənd/ *n Roman Catholic Church* the portion of revenues of a cathedral going to support a canon *la15-19, 20- historical*. [ME *prebend*]

prebender, †**prebendar** /ˈprɛbəndər/ *n* the holder of a PREBEND *15-17, 20- historical*. **prebendary**, †**prebendry** the benefice supporting a PREBENDER *la15-*. [probably AN *prebender* also perhaps PREBEND + -AR]

†**precable** *adj law* that may be asked or demanded by the authority from a subject *la16*. [stem of Lat *precārī* to ask, request + *-able*]

†**precare** *adj* revocable at the will of the granter *la15*. [MFr *precaire*, Lat *precārius*]

†**precarie** *n law* the fact of being granted on request, revocable at the will of the granter *la16*. [Lat *precārium*]

precarious /prəˈkeriəs/ *adj* risky, perilous *18-*. †**precarious loan** = PRECARIUM *la18*. [Lat *precārius* given as a favour, depending on the favour of another, uncertain]

precarium /prəˈkeriʌm/ *n law* a loan revocable at the will of the granter *la17-*. [Lat *precārium*]

precede /priˈsid/ *v* **1** to come before in time, antedate, anticipate *la15-*. **2** to have priority or precedence *la15-*. **3** to surpass; to exceed *la14*. †**precedand, precedant** *of dates* preceding, past, before *la15-16*. [MFr *preceder*]

precedent *see* PRESIDENT

preceese[1.1]**, preceeze,** †**preceis** /prəˈsis, prəˈsiz/ *adj* **1** exact *la16-*. **2** particular, special, noteworthy *e19*. **3** strict in observance, punctilious; over-strict *la16-17*. **preceesely 1** exactly; scrupulously, punctiliously *la16-*. **2** at an exact time, punctually *la16-*. [EModE *precise*, MFr *precis*]

preceese[1.2]**,** †**preceis** /prəˈsis/ *adv* exactly, specifically *la15-*. [Lat *praecīsē*]

preceeze *see* PRECEESE[1.1]

preceid *see* PRESIDE

†**preceidings** *npl* **1** earlier or previously mentioned events *la16*. **2** payments due for earlier periods *la17*. [pl verbal noun from PRECEDE]

preceis *see* PRECEESE[1.1], PRECEESE[1.2]

precent /priˈsɛnt/ *v* **1** *Presbyterian Church* to lead the singing of the congregation, to act as PRECENTOR *la17-*, **2** to sing (a line of a psalm) as a lead to a church congregation *18-19, 20- H&I Uls*. [back-formation from PRECENTOR]

precentor, †**presenter** /priˈsɛntər/ *n Presbyterian Church* the person appointed by the Kirk Session to lead the singing by singing the line for the congregation to repeat, usually in those denominations where instrumental music is not used *17-*. [Lat *praecentor*]

precept, †**precep** /ˈprisɛpt/ *n* **1** *law* a document instructing or authorizing a certain action, a warrant *la14-*. **2** a command, instruction or injunction *15-*. **3** *law* a writ ordering the formal giving of possession of heritable property to an heir or successor *15-19*. **4** *law* a written order from a judge or court instructing an inferior officer to put a DECREET[1.1] into effect *la15-e19*. **5** *law* a summons *16-18*. **6** a payment made by a Kirk Session to the needy *18*. **7** a written order or warrant authorizing a payment *la15-e18*. **8** a warrant instructing a debtor to pay a debt *17-e18*. **9** *law* a warrant issued at the stages of a royal grant's passing the seals *la15-17*. **10** a summons to attend Parliament, the Exchequer or a justice aire *15-16*. **precept of clare constat** *law* a precept of sasine by which an heir is recognized by the superior, so called from the opening wording of the document in Latin (it is clearly established) *la16-*. †**precept of poinding** a warrant authorizing a poind *la16*. †**precept of ramuving** = *precept of warning la16-e17*. **precept of sasine** *law* the mandate by which the superior authorized his agent to give possession *la15-19, 20- historical*. †**precept of warning** *law* a formal notice to quit from landlord to tenant *16-18*. [Lat *praeceptum*]

preceptor, †**preceptour** /priˈsɛptər/ *n* **1** the head of a collegiate church or alms-house *la15-17, 18- historical*. **2** the superior of a collegiate church or alms-house *la16-17*. **3** a teacher *16-e17*. †**preceptory** the superiority of a collegiate church or alms-house; such an institution, its property and revenues *16-17*. [Lat *praeceptor*]

precess *see* PRESES

preche *see* PREACH

precinct, †**precink** /ˈprisɪŋkt/ *n* **1** a delimited area *la16-*. **2** an administrative district, after 1656, with regard to the Scottish excise *17*. [Lat *praecinctus*]

†**preclare,** †**preclair** *adj* **1** *of places* splendid, fine *16-e17*. **2** *of things that shine* bright, lustrous *16*. **3** *of persons and their actions* illustrious, renowned; excellent, noble *16*. **4** *of a voice* sounding loudly and clearly *e16*. [Lat *praeclārus* very bright]

†**precogitate** *adj* thought of in advance, premeditated *la16-17*. [Lat *praecōgitāt-*, ptp stem of *praecōgitāre*]

precognition /prɛkɔgˈnɪʃən/ *n law* the process of preliminary examining witnesses; a statement made by a witness during this investigation *la17-*. [MFr *precognition* foreknowledge]

precognosce /priˈkɔgnos/ *v law* to examine witnesses or other persons concerned with a case to detemine whether there is a case to answer and make it possible to prepare a charge and defence; to examine a witness in preparation for a trial *la17-*. [PRE- + COGNOSCE with infl from PRECOGNITION]

†**precordial** *adj* warm; sincere; comforting or cheering the heart *16*. [Lat *precordiālis* cardiac, heartfelt]

precunnance *see* PERCONNON

predial, †**praedial** /ˈpridɪəl/ *adj of a jurisdiction* heritable *17-*. **predial servitude** *law* a servitude attached to land or other heritable property; any servitude other than LIFERENT *la17-*. [Lat *praediālis* relating to land, farms]

predikanter /ˈpredɪkantər/ *n fisherman's taboo* a clergyman *20- Sh*. [Du *predikant* a preacher]

†**pree**[1.1] /pri/ *n* an experiencing or sampling of something, a tasting or testing; a small quantity tested or tried, a sample *19*. [see the verb]

pree[1.2]**,** †**prie** /pri/ *v* **1** to try by tasting; to taste *17- literary*. **2** to have experience of, try out, sample *19, 20- N NE T Bor*. **preein, preeing 1** a small quantity of something, a sample *19, 20- NE T*. **2** a taste, a tasting *19, 20- T EC*. **pree the nets** to make a test haul to find out if the fishing area is a productive one *19-*. **pree someone's lips** to kiss a person *18-*. **pree someone's mou** = *pree someone's lips*. [by v-deletion from **preeve** (PRUIVE)]

pree[2] /pri/ *interj* a word used to call cattle *20-*. **preeay, preea, pee-ay** = PREE[2] *20-*. **pree leddy** = PREE[2] *20- NE H&I C*. [unknown; compare PROO]

preef *see* PRUIF

preek *see* PRICK[1.2]

preen[1.1]**, prin,** †**prene,** †**prein** /prin, prɪn/ *n* **1** a metal pin *la14-*. **2** a pin as a symbol of something of very little value *la15-*. **3** a fishing-hook *la15, la19- Sh*. **4** *pl* a game played with pins or in which pins were the stakes *19*. **preenack,** †**preinak** a pine-needle *la16- NE*. **preen cod 1** a pincushion *la16-19, 20- Ork N T EC*. **2** a woman's genitalia *e16*. **preen heid 1** a pin-head; something of very little value or consequence *17-19, 20- Sh NE T*. **2** the fry of the minnow *la19- C Bor*. **preen hook** a fishing-hook *20- Sh*. **preen heidit** *of persons* stupid *la19- NE T EC*. **preen tail day** 2nd April, when children fix paper tails to unsuspecting victims *20- Bor*. **be sittin on preens** be in a very nervous, apprehensive state, be on tenterhooks *la19-*. [OE *prēon* a pin, a brooch; compare PIN]

preen[1.2]**,** †**prene,** †**prine** /prin/ *v* to fasten with a pin *16-*. **preen yer lugs back** listen carefully, pay attention *la20-*. **preen something tae yer sleeve** to make a special effort to remember something, take a mental note of something

20- *NE.* **preen tae 1** an illicit sexual partner, a mistress 20- *C.* **2** a person or thing attached to another *la20- EC.* [see the noun]
preese *see* PRESS[1.1], PRESS[1.2]
preeve *see* PRUIVE
†**preface** *v of a Presbyterian minister* to preach; to deliver a paraphrase of, or commentary on, a scriptural reading or psalm to be sung by the congregation *18-19.* [EModE *praeface*]
†**prefacioun, prefatioun** *n Roman Catholic Church* the prelude to the central part of a Eucharistic service *la14-e16.* [ME *prefacioun*]
prefatioun *see* PREFACIOUN
prefer /prəˈfɛr/ *v* **1** to favour, regard more highly *15-.* **2** to be preferable to; to surpass, excel *16.* †**preferable** *law* given priority; assigned before other rights are considered *la17.* †**preference** *law* prior or privileged claim to payment *17.* [ME *preferren*]
†**prefixt, prefixit, profixit** *adj* settled, determined *la15-17.* [ME *prefixed*].
preiche *see* PREACH
preif *see* PRUIF, PRUIVE
preik *see* PRICK[1.2]
prein *see* PREEN[1.1]
preis *see* PRESS[1.1], PRESS[1.2], PRICE[1.1], PRICE[1.2]
preist *see* PRIEST
†**prejudge**[1.1] *n* harm *16-17.* [see the verb]
prejudge[1.2], †**prejuge** /priˈdʒʌdʒ/ *v* **1** *law* to pass judgement in advance of trial; to take a prior or premature decision on *la16-.* **2** to cause harm or financial or other loss to; to affect unfavourably *16-e18.* **3** to damage or injure physically; to impede *la17-18.* [PRE- + JUDGE[1.1] after Lat *praejūdicāre* and MFr *prejuger*]
†**prejudicate** *adj* prejudiced *la17-e19.* [Lat *praejūdicāt-*, ptp stem of *praejūdicāre*]
prejuge *see* PREJUDGE[1.2]
preke *see* PRICK[1.2]
prelacy /ˈprɛləsi/ *n* **1** the status, benefice or see of a a bishop, abbot or prior *la15-.* **2** *derogatory* church government by bishops, episcopacy *17.* [ME *prelaci*]
prelate, †**prelat,** †**prelot,** †**prelait** /ˈprɛlət/ *n* **1** an ecclesiastical dignitary of high rank, a bishop, abbot or prior *15-.* **2** *pl* the spiritual estate of the Scottish Parliament *15-e17.* **3** the Scottish bishops, the leading representatives of the Episcopalian party *17.* [ME *prelat*]
†**prelation** *n* **1** preferment, promotion; pre-eminence *la16-e17.* **2** privileged right of payment before others; prior claim to payment *17.* [ME *prelacion*, EModE *prelation*, Lat *praelātio*]
prelim /ˈprɪlɪm/ = a *preliminary examination* (PRELIMINARY) *20-.* [shortened form of *preliminary examination* (PRELIMINARY)]
preliminaries /prəˈlɪmɪnərez/ *npl in a church service* the hymns preceding the sermon *20-.* [Lat *praelimināria* introductory measures]
preliminary /prəˈlɪmɪnəre/ *adj* preparatory, introductory *18-.* **preliminary defences** *law* a defence based on the relevancy of an action rather than its merits *19-*; compare DILATORY DEFENCE. **preliminary examination 1** an examination set by a school to assess what results the prospective candidates for an award bearing examination are likely to achieve *20-.* **2** *Scottish Universities* the entrance examination set annually by each of the Universities *la19-20, 21- historical.* Compare PRELIM. [Lat *praelimināria* introductory measures]
†**prelimit** *v* restrict in advance; confine within limits previously fixed *17.* **prelimiting** = *prelimitation e17.*

prelimitation *Presbyterian Church* the imposition of restrictions in advance on what might be discussed *17.* **prelimiting** = *prelimitation la17.* [PRE- + Eng *limit*; compare Lat *prelimitāre*]
prelocutor *see* PROLOCUTOR
prelot *see* PRELATE
†**premonish, premoneis** *v* **1** *law* to give an official notification or warning with a fixed period of notice *la16-17.* **2** *law* to warn a creditor to appear and receive payment *la17.* **3** to give a prior warning *la16.* [Lat *praemonēre* to forewarn, foreshow]
premonition, †**premunitioun** /prɛməˈnɪʃən/ *n* **1** prior notice or warning *la15-.* **2** *law* an official notification or warning, with a fixed period of notice after which some legal action is required *la15-18.* Compare *instrument of premonition* (INSTRUMENT[1.1]). [ME *premunicion*, Lat *praemonitio*]
prence *see* PRINCE
prencipal *see* PRINCIPAL[1.1]
prencipall *see* PRINCIPAL[1.2]
prene *see* PREEN[1.1], PREEN[1.2]
prent[1.1] /prɛnt/ *n* **1** the imprint on a coin, the printing of letters on paper, a trace *15-.* **2** a pat of butter imprinted with a decorative motif *19- NE C Uls.* **3** (the engraving on) a stamp or die *la15-e17.* **4** likeness, form, appearance *la15-e16.* **5** a pattern of excellence *la15-e16.* **6** a batch or impression of coins *16.* **prent buik** a printed book *la16-19, 20- NE.* **printfield** a cotton printing works, originally established on a bleaching field, frequently in place-names *18-.* [ME *prent*]
prent[1.2] /prɛnt/ *v ptp* **prent** to print *la15-.* **prenter,** †**prentar 1** a printer *16-.* **2** a workman in the mint *la15-e17.* [ME *prenten*]
prentice[1.1], †**prentis,** †**prenteis,** †**printeis** /ˈprɛntɪs/ *n* **1** an apprentice (of a trade or craft); a learner *la14-.* **2** a disciple, a follower *la14-16.* **prenticeship,** †**prentischip 1** an apprenticeship *16-19, 20- NE.* **2** = *prentice fee la15-e18.* **entered prentice** *freemasonry* a person who has passed his first DEGREE *18-19, 20- historical.* †**prentice fee** the fee paid to be taken on as an apprentice *la16-17.* †**prenteis siller** = *prentice fee 16.* †**be booked prenteis** to enter into an agreement to serve a master as an apprentice *la16-17.* †**be band prenteis** = *be booked prenteis la15-e17.* †**becum prenteis** = *be booked prenteis la15-16.* †**enter prenteis** = *be booked prenteis 16-e17.* [ME *prentis*]
prentice[1.2] /ˈprɛntɪs/ *v* to apprentice to a trade or craft; to indenture or bind as an apprentice *la18- NE T EC.* [see the noun]
prentis *see* PRENTICE[1.1]
prepair *see* PREPARE[1.2]
preparation /prɛpəˈreʃən/ *n* **1** the action of preparing *la15-.* **2** *Presbyterian Church* preparation for the communion service *la16-17.* †**preparation day** the day preceding the communion service when special services of preparation were conducted *17-e18.* **preparation Saturday** = *preparation day 19-.* †**preparation sermon** a sermon preached on a *preparation day la17-19.* [MFr *preparation*, Lat *praeparātio*]
preparative /prəˈpɑrətɪv/ *n* **1** preparation *16-.* **2** a precedent, an example *16-e18.* [ME *preparatif*]
preparatory /prəˈpɑrətəre/ *adj* in preparation *17-.* **preparatory service** *Presbyterian Church* a church service in preparation for communion *20-.* †**preparatory sermon** *Presbyterian Church* a sermon in preparation for communion *17*; compare *preparation sermon* (PREPARATION). [Lat *praeparātōrius*]
†**prepare**[1.1] /prəˈper/ *n* preparation *16-e19.* [see the verb]
prepare[1.2], †**prepair** /prəˈper/ *v* **1** to make ready *16-.* **2** to make, form or process *la16-.* **3** to draw up (a writing or

document) *la16-17*. †**preparatour** a preparatory act or thing *15*. [MFr *preparer*]

†**prepone** *v* to put first, prefer *la15-16*. [Lat *praepōnere*]

prepone see PROPONE

†**prepositor** *n law* a person who employs an agent to manage an enterprise, the principal in a business negotiation or undertaking *la17-e19*. [Lat *praeposit-*, ptp stem of *praepōnere* to place in front, set in authority + *-or* suffix]

prequier see PERQUEIR[1.1]

prerogative /prəˈrɔɡətɪv/ *adj* held or enjoyed by privilege *15-*. [AN *prerogatif*, Lat *praerogātīvus*]

pres see PRESS[1.1], PRESS[1.2]

presand see PRESENT[2]

presandlie see PRESENTLY

presbyter /ˈprɛzbɪtər/ *n* **1** *Presbyterian Church* a minister or ruling elder who is a member of a presbytery *la16-*. **2** *Presbyterian Church* a member of a congregation elected and ordained to take part in church government *la16-17*. [Lat *presbyter* elder]

presbyterial see PRESBYTERY

Presbyterian[1.1] /prɛzbəˈtɪrɪən/ *n* a member or supporter of a Presbyterian church or political grouping *la17-*. [see the adj]

Presbyterian[1.2] /prɛzbəˈtɪrɪən/ *adj* **1** of or pertaining to the system of church government adopted by the post-Reformation Scottish church in which the church is governed by elders *17-*. **2** describing the views or attitudes of a member or supporter of a Presbyterian church or political grouping *la17-*. [Lat *presbyterium* reformed with *-an* adj-forming suffix]

presbytery /ˈprɛzbətre/ *n* **1** *Presbyterian Church* the ecclesiastical court above the kirk session and below the synod, consisting of the minister and (at least) one ruling elder from each parish or congregation within a designated area *la16-*. **2** the area represented by and under the jurisdiction of a presbytery, one of the units of organization in the Church of Scotland *la16-*. **presbyterial 1** of or belonging to a presbytery or its functions *17-*. **2** organized according to Presbyterian principles *17*. †**Presbytery of Relief**, **Presbytry Relief** = the Relief Church (RELIEF) *la18-e19*. [Lat *presbyterium*]

prescribe, †**prescrive**, †**praescrive** /prəˈskrʌɪb/ *v* **1** to restrict *la15-*. **2** *of an action or a right* to become invalid through the passage of time, lapse *la15-*. **3** *of a debt or crime* to be immune from prosecution through lapse of time *la15-*. **4** to order the use of a remedy or medicine *la16-*. **5** to lay down a rule or direction to be followed; to ordain or appoint *la16-*. **6** to render invalid by the passage of time *18-e19*. **7** to have authority *e16*. [Lat *praescrībere*, MFr *prescriv-* stem of *prescrire*]

prescription /prəˈskrɪpʃən/ *n* **1** *law* the lapse of time after which a right is either established or rendered invalid, or a debt is annulled if unchallenged or unclaimed *15-*. **2** (the title acquired by) uninterrupted possession *15-*. **3** a regimen; a written direction for a medicine *17-*. [ME *prescripcioun*, Lat *praescrīptio*]

prescriptive /prəˈskrɪptɪv/ *adj of ownership or title* arising from possession *19-*. **prescriptive title** *law* title acquired by continuous possession *19-*; compare PRESCRIPTION (sense 1). [Lat *praescrīpt-*, ptp stem of *praescībere* + *-ive* suffix; compare Lat *praescrīptīvus* relating to a legal exception]

prescrive see PRESCRIBE

presedent see PRESIDENT

presence, †**presens**, †**presentis** /ˈprɛzəns/ *n* **1** the state of being present; the fact of being in the same place as another *la14-*. **2** access to or audience with (a sovereign) *la15-*. **hearing in presence** the hearing before an enlarged court a case in which the judges of the Inner House have been unable to reach a verdict *18-*. †**in presence** the impressive appearance or bearing of an important person *15-16*. [ME *presence*]

present[1.1] /ˈprɛzənt, ˈprɛzənt/ *n* the present time *la14-*. †**at that present** at the time at which the events narrated took place *la16*. †**at this present** at the present time *la16-17*. **for the present** at or during the present time *la16-*. †**this present** this (actual) document *la14-17*. [ME *present*, PRESENT[1.2]; compare Lat *praesentes* the present document]

present[1.2], **praisent** /prəˈzɛnt, prɛˈzɛnt/ *v* **1** to introduce (a person) *la14-*. **2** to hand over, proffer (formally) *la14-*. **3** *of a person* to come into the presence of another or others, or a particular place (in a formal manner) *la14-*. **4** *Christian Church* to recommend a clergyman to a benefice or vacant charge *la14-*. **5** to offer a child for baptism *la16-*. **6** *Presbyterian Church* to put forward the name of a licensed probationer or minister to the presbytery for approval *la16-*. **7** to attend (a venue) *16-17*. **8** to bring a wrongdoer before a court (or other authority) *15-e17*. **9** to nominate a person as a candidate for an appointment *15-17*. **10** *law* to lay (a writ) before a court *15-17*. **11** to represent *la15-e17*. †**present one's face** to come into someone's presence *e16*. †**be presentit to the mercat** *of goods* to be offered for sale at a public market *15-17*. †**present the mercat 1** *of goods* to be offered for sale at a public market *16-17*. **2** *of a person* to use a public market for the sale of goods *16-17*. †**present to** to aim (a firearm) at *la16-e17*. [ME *presenten*, Lat *praesentāre* to place before, exhibit, but also in Lat meaning to give as a gift. Compare PRESENT[2]]

present[1.3], **praisent** /ˈprɛzənt, ˈprɛzənt/ *adj* **1** in the place specified; here, there *la14-*. **2** existing, occurring at the present moment, current, actual *15-*. **3** instantaneous; immediate *la16-17*. [ME *present*]

present[2], **praisent**, †**presand**, †**praisant** /ˈprɛzənt, ˈprɛzənt/ *n* **1** a gift or offering *la14-*. **2** a white speck on the fingernail, commonly believed to presage the arrival of a gift *la19- Ork NE C*. **3** a payment in addition to rent *la16-18*. [ME *present*]

presentation /prɛzənˈteʃən, prɪzənˈteʃən/ *n* **1** the (formal or ceremonial) handing over of something *la15-*. **2** the nomination of a person to a secular office or bursary *16-*. **3** *Presbyterian Church* the action of presenting a probationer minister to a congregation *la16-*. **4** a deed presenting the named person to a benefice or parish *la15-17*. **5** *Roman Catholic Church* the right or act of presenting a clergyman to a benefice *15-16*. **6** *law* the granting by the Sovereign to a donatory of heritage acquired by the Crown by escheat; the writ recording the grant *16-18*. **7** a representation or likeness *la15-16*. **bond of presentation** *law* a written obligation binding the obliger to produce a person freed from custody for debt at a particular time and place; a bail-bond *18-*. †**letters of presentation** a deed presenting the named person to a benefice or parish *15-18*. [ME *presentacioun*, Lat *praesentātio*]

presenter see PRECENTOR

presentis see PRESENCE

presently, †**presandlie** /ˈprɛzəntli/ *adv* **1** in the immediate future, forthwith; soon, after a short time *16-*. **2** at this time, at present *16-*. **3** recently, newly, only just *16-17*. [PRESENT[1.3] + *-ly* suffix]

preserve /prəˈzɛrv/ *v* to keep safe, guard, protect *la14-*. **God preserve us** an invocation or expressing surprise or dismay *la15-*. **preserve us** = God preserve us *la18-*. [MFr *preserver*, Lat *preservāre*]

preserves /prəˈzɛrvz/ *npl* weak spectacles intended to preserve the sight *la17*-. [from the verb PRESERVE]

preses, †**precess** /ˈprisɪz/ *n* **1** the chairman or president of a meeting; the spokesman or leader of a group *17*-. **2** *Presbyterian Church* chairperson of the board of managers in the United Presbyterian Church, or in those churches of the Church of Scotland which were United Presbyterian before 1929 *20*-. [Lat *praeses* a president, chief, guardian]

preside, †**preceid** /prəˈzʌɪd/ *v* to act as chairperson, hold the office of president at a meeting *la17*-. [Fr *présider*, Lat *praesidēre*]

president, †**presedent**, †**precedent** /ˈprɛzɪdənt/ *n* **1** a person who presides over a country, institution or meeting; originally a person deputed to rule *la14*-. **2** the member of the Court of Session appointed or elected to preside in the absence of the Chancellor *la15-e18*. **3** a person appointed or elected to preside in the council as deputy of the provost in Edinburgh and Elgin *la15-16*. **4** the member of the Privy Council who deputized for the Chancellor *17*. **5** the chief official of a court or of the Convention of Burghs *la15-17*. **6** a presiding (female) deity, a patroness *e16*. †**preceidencie** presidentship, chairmanship (of a meeting) *la17*. [MFr *president*, Lat *praesidēns* pres ppl of *praesidēre* to sit in front of]

presome *see* PRESUME[1.2]

presoun *see* PRISON[1.1]

press[1.1], **preese**, †**pres**, †**preis** /prɛs, prɪs/ *n* **1** a tightly-packed crowd *la14*-. **2** hand-to-hand fighting *15-e16*. **3** a dangerous or difficult situation *la14-e17*. **4** pressure, force, strength *15-e17*. **5** haste, urgency *16*. **6** an apparatus for applying pressure *16*-. **7** an unsuccessful attempt to defecate *19- Ork NE T EC*. †**the press** the throng, the crowd *la14-16*. [ME *presse*]

press[1.2] /prɛs/ *n* **1** an apparatus for applying pressure *16*-. **2** an unsuccessful attempt to defecate *19- Ork NE T EC*. [ME *presse*, EModE *presse*, PRESS[1.1]]

press[1.2], **preese**, †**pres**, †**preis**, †**preas** /prɛs, prɪs/ *v* **1** to apply pressure, strain, squeeze *la16*-. **2** to attack, harass *la14-16*. **3** to crowd, throng *la14-e17*. **4** to hasten; to strive to move *la14-e17*. **5** to attempt, endeavour *la14-e17*. **6** to persuade, urge *16-e17*. **7** to constrain, compel *la16-e17*. †**pressit** *of cloth* pressed to give a particular finish *16*. †**pressing paper** paper used in cloth manufacture to produce a particular finish *la17-e18*. [ME *pressen*; also partly from the noun]

press[2] /prɛs/ *n* **1** a (large) cupboard, sometimes shelved, also one built into a recess in a wall *la15*-. **2** a lidded chest or chest of drawers *la15-16*. †**pres almerie** a (kitchen) cupboard *la15-17*; compare AUMRY (sense 1). **press bed** a bed that can be enclosed in a chest or cupboard when not in use or built into a recess in the wall and shut off from the room by wooden doors *la17*-; compare BOX-BED. [ME *presse*; compare PRESS[1.1], derived from the same word]

prest *see* PRIEST

prestable /ˈprɛstəbəl/ *adj* **1** *of actions or transactions* able to be carried out, practicable, enforceable *17*-. **2** *of money or payments* able to be paid out, liable to be exacted; transferable *la17*-. [Lat *prestābilis* that may be lent]

prestation /prɛˈsteʃən/ *n law* a payment due by law or custom; (liability for) the performance of an obligation or duty *la17*-. [Lat *praestātio* payment]

prestingolva /ˈprɛstəŋɡɔlvə/ *n taboo* a clergyman *19- Sh*. [ON *prestinn*, variant of *prestr* priest; the second element is obscure]

†**presume**[1.1] *n* anticipation, expectation *la15-e16*. [see the verb]

presume[1.2], †**presome** /prəˈzum/ *v* **1** to take it upon oneself; to assume (a role) without adequate authority *la14*-. **2** *law in official prohibitions* to take the liberty (to do something) *15-17*. [AN, MFr *presumer*]

presumption /prəˈzʌmʃən/ *n* **1** overweening self-confidence, arrogance *la14*-. **2** assumption (of guilt) *la14*-. **3** *law* an assumption or ground for belief admissible in legal proof based on inference from nature or from the circumstances of a particular case *15*-. †**violent presumption** *see* VIOLENT[1.2]. [ME *presumpcioun*, Lat *praesumptio*]

presumptive /prəˈzʌmtɪv/ *adj* **1** giving reasonable grounds for presumption *la16*-. **2** inferred, presumed *19*-. [Lat *praesumptīvus*]

†**presuppone** *v* to presuppose; to prejudge *la15-17*. [Lat *praesuppōnere*]

pret[1.1], **prat**, *N* **prot**, †**pratt** /prɛt, prat; *N* prɔt/ *n* **1** a practical joke *18-19, 20- Sh N*. **2** a trick; a deceitful scheme *16-19*. **3** an act of disobedience or a bad habit in a horse *18-19*. †**tak the prat** *of a horse* to be disobedient, refuse *18-e19*. [OE *prætt* a trick, guile, ON *prettr*]

pret[1.2], **prat**, *N* **prot**, †**pract** /prɛt, prat; *N* prɔt/ *v* **1** *of a horse* to be disobedient, refuse *19*-. **2** to meddle or interfere with, tamper or fiddle with *la19*-. **3** to play tricks, fool around *la15-e19*. [see the noun]

pretence, †**pretens** /prəˈtɛns/ *n* **1** outward appearance, a (false) show *la15*-. **2** (a false) assertion of a claim to authority, a pretext, an intention *16*-. **3** a claim or aspiration to a possession, a right, a privilege *la16*-. [ME *pretens*]

pretend /prəˈtɛnd/ *v* **1** to make believe; to allege, assert or contend *la14*-. **2** to represent, mean, betoken *la14-e16*. **3** *law* to bring (an action), to lay (an accusation) *la14-16*. **4** to form a hostile design or attempt, to plot (against) *16-e17*. †**pretendit** **1** alleged *la15*-. **2** professed falsely, feigned *la15-e16*. [ME *pretenden*]

pretens *see* PRETENCE

†**preter** *prep* in addition to *e16*. [Lat *praeter*]

†**pretermitt** *v* **1** to omit; to neglect; to overlook *la15-e17*. **2** to leave off for a time, suspend *16-17*. [Lat *praetermittere*]

†**pretor** *n* the council-chamber of a burgh *la15-e16*. [MFr *pretoire*]

†**prettie**, **protty**, **pratty** *adj* mischievous, naughty, restive *la17-e19*. [PRET[1.1] with adj forming *-ie* suffix]

prettik *see* PRACTIC, PRACTICK[1.1]

prettikin /ˈprɛtɪkɪn/ *n* **1** an exploit *la19- Sh Ork*. **2** an escapade, a piece of mischief *19- Sh Ork*. [perhaps PRET[1.1] with dim suffix]

prettikkis *see* PRACTIKIS

pretty, **pratty**, *NE* **protty**, †**pritty** /ˈprɪte, ˈprate; *NE* ˈprɔte/ *adj* **1** ingenious, skilful; fine, pleasing *la15*-. **2** *of things* cleverly made, of good quality or finish, attractive *la15*-. **3** *of a woman* comely, bonny; well-built, buxom *la15*-. **4** *of a person* attractive, fine; having an impressive and dignified bearing *la16*-. **5** *of a man* courageous, gallant, manly *17- Sh NE T Bor*. **6** *of animals* well-grown, sturdy, well-bred, in good condition *20- Sh NE*. **7** small, inconsiderable; *of time or distance* short, of no great duration or extent *la16-17*. **8** mean, petty, insignificant *e16*. **prettily**, †**prattelie** prettily, skilfully *16*-. **pretty dancers** the aurora borealis, the northern lights *18*-; compare *merry dancers* **1** (MERRY). [variant of PRETTIE; compare Du *prettig* pleasant, nice, MDu *pertich* cunning, quick]

prevag /prəˈvag, ˈprɛvag/ *n* a joke, a prank *20- Ork*. [unknown]

prevail, †**prevale**, †**prevele** /prəˈvel/ *v* **1** to predominate, be victorious *la15*-. **2** to surpass (another) *la15-16*. [ME *prevaile*]

prevat *see* PRIVATE[1.2]

preve see PRIVY¹·², PRUIVE

†preveen, prevene, provene *v* **1** to avert (harm or danger) *la15-18*. **2** to forestall (a person) *15-17*. **3** to influence in advance, prejudice *16-17*. **4** *of death* to overtake (a person) prematurely *16-17*. **5** *of God* to go before (a person) with spiritual guidance *la15-e17*. **6** *of a court or judge* to exercise a prior right of jurisdiction, by carrying out the first judicial act *17*. **7** to arrive before, precede *16-e17*. **8** to come before in merit, surpass *16-e17*. [Lat *praevenīre* to come before, anticipate, hinder]

prevele see PREVAIL

prevely see PRIVY¹·²

prevene see PREVEEN

prevention /prəˈvɛnʃən/ *n* **1** avoidance by forethought, anticipation *la16-*. **2** *of a court or judge* the privilege of exercising a prior right of jurisdiction, by carrying out the first judicial act *la17*; compare PREVEEN (sense 6). [MFr *prevention*, Lat *praeventio*]

†prevento *n law* a mechanism for shortening a TERM *la17*. [shortened form of Lat *praeventō terminō* the term (having been) anticipated, by anticipation of the term or limiting date]

†prevert *v* to go beyond, outstrip *e16*. [Lat *praevertere*]

previe writting see PRIVY¹·²

previlege see PRIVILEGE¹·¹

pricat see PRICKET

price¹·¹, **†prise, †preis, †praise** /prʌɪs/ *n* cost, value *la14-*. **†prise-corn** corn that has been officially valued, frequently for compensation for damage *17*. **be the price o someone** to serve someone right, be just what someone deserves *20-*. **†brek the price** see BRAK. **†mak price** to agree a price *16-17*. **twa, three prices** two or three times the market value or former price *19-*. [ME *pris*]

price¹·², **prize, †prise, †preis, †praise** /prʌɪs, prʌɪz/ *v* **1** to prize, esteem highly; to extol, commend, praise *14-*. **2** to reckon at a particular (frequently low or zero) value *la14-*. **3** to set or agree a price; to fix the official price of (goods) *15-*. **4** to value, put a monetary value on (land or goods) *la15-*. **5** to evaluate (the quality of a thing or a person) *la15-e19*. **6** to value (land or goods) for the purpose of distraint, to apprise (to a creditor for a debt) *15-16*. **†prisar, prysar 1** a valuer *15-e18*. **2** the official appointed to prescribe the price of goods for sale *16-17*. **3** a judge of literary merit *e16*. **†prisit corn** = *prise-corn* (PRICE¹·¹) *16-e17*. [OFr *prisier, prise* to value, to praise; spelling and sense influenced by PRICE¹·¹]

price see PRIZE

prick¹·¹, **†prik** /prɪk/ *n* **1** something of little consequence, a dot, a small puncture *16-*. **2** something that pierces, goads or spurs *16-*. **3** a skewer or pin for fixing thatch or fastening clothes *16-18*. **4** a knitting-needle *16-e18*. **5** an upright spike for impaling something *16-17*. **6** a gnomon, an indicator on a sundial *la16-e17*. **7** the central supporter of the cross-bar of the standard firlot *la16-17*. **8** a spire or pinnacle *16-17*. **9** a pointed weapon *15-e16*. **pricky** having sharp points or spines, prickly *la19-*. **†prick firlot** = *prick mett*. **†prick mett** the standard measure for grain or PEASE, especially the Linlithgow firlot *17*. **†prick measure** = *prick mett*. **†prick stockens** knitted stockings *la17-e18*. **†prik hois** = *prick stockens e17*. **†prik hornit** *of cattle* having erect horns, like spikes *16-18*. [ME *prik*, OE *prica*]

prick¹·², **preek, †prik, †preke** /prɪk, prik/ *v* **1** to cause pain or injury to *la14-*. **2** to spur on a horse; to advance at speed on horseback *la14-*. **3** to pierce with something pointed *la15-*. **4** *of grazing cattle* to run from the stings of insects *18- NE*. **5** *mining* to pierce rock with the point of a pick *la19- EC*. **6** to slaughter a cow by cutting the spinal cord at the back of the neck *la19- Sh*. **7** *mining* to cut into a layer of soft fireclay at the bottom of a seam by hand *20- EC*. **8** to fasten with a pin *la16-e19*. **9** to pierce a person suspected of witchcraft with a pin to find the devil's mark *la16-17*. **10** to pin out and so stretch (an animal skin) *la16-17*. **11** *boatbuilding* to secure (the timbers) with pegs *la17*. **12** to write down music by means of notes or small holes pricked out *la16-17*. **13** to designate (a person) to an office by marking a name on a list *17*. **14** to affect with a feeling of guilt or shame; to reproach *la15-16*. **pricker, †prikar 1** *mining* a thin stratum suitable for piercing *la19- EC*. **2** a light horseman, a skirmisher, a reiver *la15-19*. **3** a person who pricks suspected witches with a pin *17*. **pricking 1** a sensation of being pricked *15-*. **2** fast riding *la15-16*. **3** a skirmish *15-16*. **4** the action of piercing a person suspected of witchcraft *la17*. **†pricklous** = *prick the louse e16*. **†prick nott** a mark indicating a musical note *17*. **†prick and prin** to dress oneself up, take excessive pains with one's appearance *la18*. **†prik on** to attack on horseback *la14*. **†prick the louse** a contemptuous term for a tailor *la18-19*. [ME *priken*, OE *prician*]

pricket, †pricat, †prikkat /ˈprɪkət/ *n* **1** a spire, pinnacle or pointed finial *la16-*. **2** a candle for a candlestick with a spike *la15-e17*. [PRICK¹·¹ + *-et* dim suffix]

prickle¹·¹ /ˈprɪkəl/ *n* a prickling or stinging sensation *la19-*. [see the verb]

prickle¹·², **†pricle, †prikill** /ˈprɪkəl/ *v* **1** to stimulate, goad *16-*. **2** to stand on end, stick up *19-*. **3** to irritate, annoy *e16*. [PRICK¹·² + *-el* frequentative suffix]

prick-me-dainty¹·¹ /ˈprɪk mi ˈdɛnti/ *n* an affected, self-conscious person; a dandy *19, 20- NE*. [compare *prick and prin* (PRICK¹·²)]

prick-me-dainty¹·² /ˈprɪk mi ˈdɛnti/ *adj* over-refined, mannered *19, 20- NE WC Bor*. [see the noun]

pride¹·¹, **†pryde** /prʌɪd/ *n* **1** self-esteem; arrogance; conceit; vanity *la14-*. **pridefu, †pridefull 1** haughty, arrogant, snobbish, vain *la15-*. **2** self-assured; smug *19-*. **pridefully** arrogantly *16-*. **†prydles** shameless *16*. **†pridy** characterized by pride, proud *la15*. [ME *prid*, OE *prȳt*, from the adj *prūd*]

pride¹·² /prʌɪd/ *v* **1** to fill (oneself) with pride *la14-*. **2** to take pride in, feel proud of, to be or become proud or vain *la15-e19*. [see the noun]

prie see PREE¹·²

prief see PRUIF

priest, †prest, †preist /prist/ *n Roman Catholic Church* a clergyman *la14-*. **†be someone's priest** to cause someone's death, be the death of *la18-e19*. **priest and devil** a shoemaker's last *20- T Uls*. [OE *prēost*]

prieven, prieving see PRUIVE

prig, †prigg /prɪɡ/ *v* **1** to haggle, bargain *la16-*. **2** to plead (with); to beseech, *18-*. **prig doon** to beat down (a price) *la17-19, 20- NE WC Bor*. **†prig penny** to haggle over pennies *e16*. [perhaps Du *prigen* to strive, exert oneself, resist, stand against]

prik see PRICK¹·¹, PRICK¹·²

prikkat see PRICKET

†priksang *n* (music sung from) written or pricked notation *16*. [PRICK¹·¹ + SANG]

primacy, †primacie /ˈprʌɪməsi/ *n* **1** pre-eminent authority *la16-*. **2** the province or see of an ecclesiastical primate *16-e19*. [ME *prīmaci*, EModE *primacie*]

†primar *n* **1** the PRINCIPAL¹·¹ of a college or university *17-e18*. **2** a university student of the first grade in social rank, the son of a nobleman, who paid higher University fees than the

Seconders (SECOND¹·²) and TERNARS and wore a better-quality gown *la17-e19*. [Lat *prīmārius* a principal]

†**prime**¹·¹ *n weights and measures* in Scots Troy (SCOTS¹·²) a unit of weight for gold and silver consisting of 1/24 of a grain *17-e18*. [see the adj]

prime¹·², †**pryme** /prʌɪm/ *v* **1** to prepare; to load, fill or stuff full; to charge *16-*. **2** to bring a pump into operation by charging it with water *19-*. †**prime-gilt** a customary allowance originally paid to the master and crew of a ship for the loading and care of the cargo and perhaps donated by them to charitable use; a levy (for charitable use) by an authority on the masters and crew of ships unloading at a port *16-e19*. [perhaps from the adj]

prime¹·³ /prʌɪm/ *adj* **1** first in rank or importance; leading *la16-*. **2** *of a plotter or claimant* principal, main *17*. [MFr *prime* first, Lat *prīmus*]

†**primineary, primonire** *n* a dilemma or predicament *e19*. [Eng *praemunire* a writ charging a sheriff to summon a person accused of asserting papal jurisdiction in England, the trouble one might get into for this offence. Shortened from Lat *praemūnīre faciās*]

primp¹·¹ /prɪmp/ *n* a strait-laced and self-conciously correct person; a show-off *la19- NE Bor*. [probably from the adj]

primp¹·² /prɪmp/ *v* **1** to dress or arrange in a stiff or affected way *la16-*. **2** to behave in an affected or conceited manner *la16- NE Bor*. **primped, primpit** stiff, formal, over elaborate, correct; *of people* affected; elaborately and formally dressed *19- NE Bor*. [probably from the adj; compare PROMP]

primp¹·³ /prɪmp/ *adj* closed up; fastidious, strait-laced; haughty, conceited *la16-19, 20- Sh NE Bor*. [unknown; compare PROMP and Eng *prim*]

primsie /ˈprɪmzi/ *adj* self-consciously correct, demure and strait-laced *la18-19, 20- Sh Ork NE T*. [Eng *prim* + *-sie* suffix]

Primus /ˈprʌɪməs/ *n Episcopalian Church* the bishop chosen by his colleagues to be the president of their episcopal meetings, but without metropolitan or special authority *18-*. [Lat *prīmus* first]

prin *see* PREEN¹·¹

prince, †**prence** /prɪns/ *n* **1** a king, a monarch; a prince *la14-*. **2** the heir to the Scottish throne and, after the Union of the Crowns in 1603, that of the united kingdoms of Scotland, England and Wales *la15-*. **Prince of Scotland 1** a formal title of PRINCE used only in connection with the lands of the *Principality of Scotland* (PRINCIPALITY) *la18-*. **2** title of the eldest son of the Sovereign before the Union of the Crowns *16-e17*. **Prince and Stewart of Scotland** = *Prince of Scotland* **2**. **Prince Charlie's rose, Prince Charlie rose** the rose *Rosa 'Alba Maxima'*; the emblematic *white rose* (WHITE¹·²) *la19-*. [ME *prince*]

principal¹·¹, †**prencipal** /ˈprɪnsɪpəl/ *n* **1** a chief, the leading person, a leader *la14-*. **2** *law* the principal piece of property or sum of money involved in a transaction, claim or dispute *la14-*. **3** *law* the original of a document *la15-*. **4** the academic head of a university or college *la16-*. **5** *law* the person primarily liable or chiefly responsible for a crime or a debt, a person for whom another is surety, or as party in a lawsuit or the execution of a legal action *la15-17*. **6** in *pl* the chief persons of a family or clan *la16*. [see the adj]

principal¹·², †**prencipall** /ˈprɪnsɪpəl/ *adj* **1** chief, first in importance, main *la14-*. **2** *law of a document* original, not a copy *la15-*. **3** excellent, first-rate, outstandingly good *19, 20- Sh NE*. **4** applied to a main residence, especially of an estate *la14-e17*. **5** applied to the *sheriffdom* (SHERIFF) of Edinburgh as distinguished from its dependent CONSTABULARY of Haddington *16*. **principally,** †**principaly** chiefly, especially, particularly *15-*. [ME *principal*, Lat *principālis*]

†**principal**¹·³ *adv* principally *15-16*. [see the adj]

principality /prɪnsəˈpalɪti/ *n* **1** a state or region held or governed by a prince *la16-*. **2** the office of principal of a college or university *e17*. **the Principality of Scotland** the lordship of certain lands in Scotland, especially those held as of right by the eldest son of the Sovereign as Prince and Stewart of Scotland and failing him, by the Crown itself *la15-*. [ME *principalite*]

prine *see* PREEN¹·²

pringle *see* PRINKLE²

prink, *Sh Ork* **prunk** /prɪŋk; *Sh Ork* prʌŋk/ *v* **1** to make smart or pretty *17-*. **2** to strut, walk with a swagger, walk in a jaunty, self-conscious way *la19- Ork T*. [probably a variant of EModE *prank*, Du *pronken* to decorate, show off, Ger *prunken*; *Sh Ork* direct from Du, Ger]

prinkie /ˈprɪŋki/ *adj* over-meticulous in dress or appearance, fussy over details; ostentatious; conceited *19-, 20- Ork NE*. Compare PRUNK. [PRINK + *-ie* adj-forming suffix]

prinkle¹ /ˈprɪŋkəl/ *n* a young coalfish *19- NE*. [unknown]

prinkle², **pringle** /ˈprɪŋkəl, ˈprɪŋɡəl/ *v* **1** to twinkle, glitter, sparkle; *of a boiling pot* to bubble, simmer *18-*. **2** to have the sensation of pins and needles, to tingle, thrill, prickle *18-19, 20- NE T SW Bor*. **3** to cause to tingle, set pricking; to jab with a pin *la19, 20- NE T*. **prinkly** prickly, tingling *20- Bor*. [apparently variant of PRICKLE¹·² perhaps infl by *twinkle* and *tingle*]

printeis *see* PRENTICE¹·¹

prior¹, †**priour** /ˈpraeər/ *n* **1** the male head of a religious house or order *la14-*. **2** the supervisor of the leper hospital of Kingcase in Prestwick, Ayrshire *la15-e17*. **priory, priorie** a monastery or nunnery governed by a prior or prioress *la14-*. [OE *prior*, AN *priour*, Lat *prior* an ancestor, predecessor, in post-classical Latin also a great man, the head of a religious house]

prior² /ˈpraeər/ *adj* having precedence; former, earlier *17-*. **prior rights** the statutory rights of the spouse of a person dying intestate to the deceased's dwelling-house with furnishings and plenishings and a financial provision out of the remaining estate *la20-*. [Lat *prior* previous, former, elder, more important]

prioress /ˈpraeərəs/ *n* the female head of a religious house or order *la14-*. †**prioressie** a nunnery or convent presided over by a prioress *la16-e17*. [ME *priores*]

priour *see* PRIOR¹

prip-tail /ˈprɪptel/ *n* a swaggering conceited person, a braggart *la20- Ork*. [perhaps variant of PRIMP¹·³ + TAIL]

prise¹·¹, †**pryse** /praez/ *n* an instrument used for levering, a lever *16-19, 20- T SW Bor*. [ME *prise*]

prise¹·² /praez/ *v* to lever, to move by leverage *la16-*. [probably from the noun although attested earlier than the noun]

prise *see* PRICE¹·¹, PRICE¹·², PRIZE

prison¹·¹, †**presoun,** †**prisoun** /ˈprɪzən/ *n* imprisonment; a jail *la14-*. [ME *prisoun*]

prison¹·² /ˈprɪzən/ *v* to imprison *la14-19, 20- Sh Ork*. [see the noun]

pritty *see* PRETTY

†**private**¹·¹, **privat** *v pp* and *pt* **privat** to deprive, to dispossess (of something) *la15-17*. [Lat *prīvāt-*, ptp stem of *prīvāre*]

private¹·², †**privat,** †**prevat** /ˈpraevət/ *adj* **1** not public or official; not done openly; clandestine *la15-*. **2** *of a person* not holding public office *16-*. **private school** Edinburgh University, St Andrews University a seminar or tutorial as opposed to a public lecture *17-e18*. †**private writing** a personal letter or document from the sovereign intervening in normal legal or official processes or existing rights *la16-e17*; compare *privy writing* (PRIVY¹·²). [Lat *prīvātus*]

privative /'praevətɪv/ *adj* **1** *of an authority, right or obligation* exclusive *la17-*. **2** *law of the jurisdiction of a court* exclusive, not shared or exercised by others *la17-*. [Fr *privatif*, Lat *prīvātīvus*]

privein *see* PRUIVE

prively *see* PRIVY¹·²

privilege¹·¹, †**previlege**, †**privelege** /'prɪvəlɪdʒ/ *n* **1** special advantage or immunity *la14-*. **2** the area over which the immunities of a BURGH extended *16-e18*. **3** a document conferring a right *la15-16*. **4** the right of absence *la16-e17*. **5** the right of sanctuary *16*. [ME *privilege*]

privilege¹·² /'prɪvəlɪdʒ/ *v* to grant a right or immunity (to someone); to exempt (from something) *la15-*. **privileged**, †**privilegit**, †**previlegit 1** invested with or enjoying a privilege *15-*. **2** *law of certain actions in the Court of Session*, especially *privileged summons*, exempted from the usual rules of hearing, heard in less time than usual *16-*. **privileged debt** *law* a debt owed by the estate of a deceased person, *eg* for funeral expenses, which takes precedence over debts to ordinary creditors *la18-*. †**privileged deed** *law* a deed which does not require the signatures of witnesses to validate it, *eg* on the grounds of necessity or expediency *e19*. **privileged summons** *law* a summons in which the normal period of 27 days between the citation of a person and his appearance in court is shortened *la16-*. †**privileged writing** *law* = privileged deed *e20, la20- historical*. [ME *privilegen*, MFr *privilegier*, Lat *prīvilēgiāre*]

privy¹·¹ /'prɪvi, 'prɪve/ *n* a latrine, a toilet *la14-*. [see the adj]

privy¹·², †**preve** /'prɪvi, 'prɪve/ *adj* **1** hidden, secret; sharing in the knowledge of something private *la14-*. **2** intimate, familiar *la14-e15*. †**prively**, **prevely 1** privately, secretly, discreetly *la14-17*. **2** *of speech* so as to remain private, in a whisper *la14-16*. †**privy censures** *Presbyterian Church* a meeting of a kirk session or presbytery at which each member was examined separately and questions were put to his fellow-members about his church duties and his behaviour in his private life *17-19*. **Privy Council** the official body consisting of high officers of state and other magnates presided over by the Chancellor, which, nominally subject to Parliament, exercised judicial, legislative and executive power *16-e18, la18- historical*. †**privy inquest** an inquiry into the behaviour and honesty of the inhabitants of a place with a view to banishment of those found unworthy *la16-e17*. †**privy writing**, **previe writting** a personal letter or document from the sovereign intervening in normal legal or official processes or existing rights *la16*; compare *private writing* (PRIVATE¹·²). †**in previe or in apert** *law* in secret or openly *15-16*. [ME *prive*, Lat *prīvātus*]

†**privy**¹·³ *adv* privately, secretly *la15-16*. [see the adj]

privy² /'prɪvi/ *n* privet, a semi-evergreen shrub *Ligustrum vulgare la18-*. [variant of Eng *privet*, origin unknown]

Privy Seal /'prɪvi sil/ *n* **1** the seal used to authenticate various classes of crown letters or grants, also required on a PRECEPT as a step in the process of obtaining the *Great Seal* (GREAT¹·²); it was not abolished by the Act of Union but continued subject to regulations made by ensuing Parliaments and is still in existence although no longer a requirement *15-*. **2** the authority or office of the PRIVY SEAL *la14-16*. **3** a writ under the PRIVY SEAL *e16*. Compare KEEPER OF THE PRIVY SEAL, LORD PRIVY SEAL. [PRIVY¹·² + SEAL¹·¹]

prize, †**prise**, †**price** /praez/ *n* seizure, something seized or captured *la15-*. †**blaw the prys** to sound a blast on a hunting horn to signal that the quarry is taken *e16*. [AN, OFr *prise* the action of taking, capture; compare AN, OFr *corner la prise* = *blaw the prize*]

prize *see* PRICE¹·²

pro- /pro, prɔ/ *prefix* **1** on behalf of *la17-*. **2** *of kinship terms* two generations removed (used in place of 'grand') *15-e17*; compare PRONECE, PRONEVOY. [Lat *prō-*]

proablem *see* PROBLEM

proadge /prodʒ/ *v* to make poking or prodding movements with a long instrument *19- Sh SW*. [variant of Eng *prod*]

proag *see* PROG¹·¹, PROG¹·²

prob¹·¹ /prɔb/ *n* **1** an instrument used to penetrate and examine something *19-*. **2** a sharp-pointed instrument for piercing the swollen stomach of cattle in order to release the accumulated gas *20- Ork NE*. **3** a prod, poke or jab *19- NE EC*. [ME *probe, probe*]

prob¹·² /prɔb/ *v* **1** to explore or examine with a probe *19-*. **2** to prod, poke, jab or stab *19- Sh NE T EC*. **3** to release gas from the stomach of (cattle) by piercing *20- NE*. [see the noun]

probation /proˈbeʃən/ *n* **1** testing, a trial *la15-*. **2** *law* the hearing of evidence in court before a judge; evidence, proof and the procedure for demonstrating it *la15-*. **3** the act of proving, a demonstration *la15-19*. **4** that which constitutes proof; (a piece of) demonstrative evidence *la15-16*. **probationary** relating to a *probationer* **1** *18-e20, la20- historical*. **probationer 1** *Presbyterian Church* a student minister during the period between his licensing and his ordination *la17-*. **2** *law* a newly-appointed judge of the Court of Session after he has presented his letter of appointment and before he takes the oath *la18-e20, 20- historical*; compare LORD PROBATIONER. **conjunct probationer** *see* CONJUNCT. [MFr *probation*, Lat *probātio* from Lat *probāre* prove, test]

probative /'probətɪv/ *adj of a legal document* containing its own evidence of validity or authenticity *la17-*. [Lat *probātīvus* pertaining to proof]

problem, **proablem** /'prɔbləm, 'probləm/ *n* **1** a difficulty or dilemma; a challenging or puzzling question (for academic or scholastic discussion) *la15-*. **2** a comparison or analogy *la15-e17*. [MFr *probleme*, Lat *problēma* a question proposed for academic discussion]

proceed, †**procede**, †**proceid** /proˈsid/ *v* **1** to advance, progress, move forward *la14-*. **2** *of a judge* to conduct or continue legal proceedings; to execute a legal procedure against a person *la14-*. **3** *of a legal procedure or writ* to take effect; to be carried out *la14-*. **4** *of a litigant* to take legal action *la15-*. **proceeding 1** *law* the fact or manner of conducting legal proceedings or taking legal action *la15-*. **2** an event or course of action; the fact or manner of taking action *la16-*. †**procede agane** to take hostile action against *15-16*. **procede in** *of a quality, course of action* to advance, make progress *15-*. [OFr, MFr *proceder*, Lat *prōcēdere*]

proceedings /prəˈsidɪŋz/ *npl* the transactions or deliberations of a court or assembly; a series of actions or events *la16-*. [pl of verbal noun from PROCEED]

proceid *see* PROCEED

process¹·¹, †**proces** /'prosɛs/ *n* **1** progress, course, passage (of time); a sequence (of events) *la14-*. **2** a series of prescribed ceremonial or official actions constituting a recognized procedure *15-*. **3** litigation, legal proceedings, a legal action or case; trial; a judgement; also, occasionally, the sentence *15-*. **4** legal procedure, the style or manner of proceeding in a particular case or court *15-*. **5** the legal papers on which an action is based, and which are lodged in court prior to the hearing *la16-*. **6** *law* a documentary record of a case *la14-17*. **7** the mandate, summons or writ formally initiating a legal action *la15-e17*. **8** *law* the passage of legal business through the prescribed steps of a legal procedure *la15-17*.

†**no-process** *law* the legal judgement that there is no case to answer *la17-e19*. **process of law** formal legal proceedings *la14-*. †**under process** involved in legal proceedings; under trial, judgement or sentence *la15-17*. †**in process** = *under process*. [ME *proces*, Lat *prōcessus*]

process[1,2] /ˈprɔsɛs/ *v* **1** to take action on, put into effect *17-*. **2** to proceed against in law, sue, bring to trial *la15-19*. [see the noun]

prochin *see* PAROCHIN

†**proclaim**[1.1] *n* the action of proclaiming, a proclamation *la15-e16*. [see the verb]

proclaim[1.2], †**proclame** /proˈklem/ *v* **1** to make an official announcement, announce *15-*. **2** to read, publish; to read the banns of, to announce the forthcoming marriage of *la16-*. **3** to denounce publicly *16*. [ME *proclamen*]

proclamation /prɔkləˈmeʃən/ *n* **1** a public announcement *la15-*. **2** the publication of marriage banns *la16-*. [ME *proclamacioun*, Lat *prōclāmātio*]

proclame *see* PROCLAIM[1.2]

procuir *see* PROCURE

†**procurage** *n* Roman Catholic Church a payment from a parish for entertainment of a visiting bishop or other dignitary *16*. [Lat *prōcūrāgium*]

procuration /prɔkjuˈreʃən/ *n* **1** care, protection; acquiring; acting as PROCURATOR or agent *la15-*. **2** management for another, stewardship, government *la16-17*. **3** nefarious contriving, scheming *15-16*. **4** Roman Catholic Church a payment from a parish for entertainment of a visiting bishop *la15-16*; compare PROCURAGE. **5** the collection of voluntary contributions *la15-16*. **6** *law* the action of acting as PROCURATOR on behalf of another *16*. [ME *procuracioun*, Lat *prōcūrātio*]

pro-curator /proˈkjurətər/ *n law* a guardian or CURATOR who has not been legally appointed *la17-20, 21- historical*. [Lat *prō-* in place of + CURATOR]

procurator, procurature /ˈprɔkjuretər/ *n* **1** a person authorized to act on behalf of another, especially an agent or manager *la14-*. **2** a legal representative; a solicitor or lawyer practising before the lower courts *15-*. **3** *Presbyterian Church* an ADVOCATE[1.1] (sense 1) appointed as official advisor in legal matters to the GENERAL ASSEMBLY *18-*. **4** *Aberdeen University* a student representative appointed by each NATION to preside over it and to vote on its behalf in *Rectorial* (RECTOR) elections *la17-20*. **5** the law-agent or legal representative of a burgh, = PROCURATOR FISCAL (sense 1) *15-e17*. **6** *Glasgow University* a student representative appointed by each NATION to preside over it in *rectorial* (RECTOR) elections *la15-19*. **7** *St Andrews University* = PROCURATOR (sense 6) *18-19*. [ME *procuratour*, Lat *prōcūrātōr*]

procurator fiscal, †**procuratour fischall**, †**procurator phiscall** /prɔkjuretər ˈfɪskəl/ *n* **1** the public prosecutor, appointed formerly by the SHERIFF or magistrates, now by the LORD ADVOCATE, who initiates the prosecution of crimes, and carries out to some extent the duties of an English coroner *la16-*. **2** the law-agent and collector of a commissary court or COMMISSARIAT *la16-17*. **3** = PROCURATOR (sense 3) *la16-17*. [PROCURATOR + EModE, MFr *fiscal*]

procuratory /prɔkjuˈretɔre, ˈprɔkjurətəre/ *n law* **1** the mandate or authorization by which a person is formally made the procurator of another, *eg* a factor or, mainly, a legal representative; the authority delegated *la15-*. **2** authorization delegated to another to resign a property or right to the SUPERIOR[1.1] (sense 2) for reconveyance *la15-19*. **procuratory of resignation** *law* = PROCURATORY (sense 2) *la16-19*. **procuratory to resign** = *procuratory of resignation 15-17*. [Lat *prōcūrātōrium*]

procuratour fischall *see* PROCURATOR FISCAL

†**procuratrix, procuratrice** *n* a female PROCURATOR or agent *la16-19*. [Lat *prōcūrātrīx* feminine form of *prōcūrātor*]

†**procurature, procuratour, procurator** *n* the mandate or authorization by which a person is formally made the procurator of another, *eg* a factor or, mainly, a legal representative; the authority delegated *15-e17*. Compare PROCURATORY. [Lat *prōcūrāt-*, ptp stem of *prōcūrāre* to take care of + *-ure* suffix]

procurature *see* PROCURATOR

procure, †**procuir** /proˈkjur/ *v* **1** to bring about, achieve *la14-*. **2** to obtain (a person's) services *la14-*. **3** to prevail upon, induce or persuade (a person) (to do something criminal) *19-*. **4** to obtain in response to a petition, mainly by formal application *la14-17*. **5** to petition, plead (for), to make supplication *la16-17*. **6** to collect (alms) *la15-16*. **7** *law* to appear (for) another as his representative or PROCURATOR (sense 2), to plead or serve as an advocate or attorney *16-e17*. **procurer,** †**procurour 1** a person who makes arrangements or brings something about *la14-*. **2** a person who speaks for another in litigation, a PROCURATOR (sense 2) *la15-16*. †**procure the seal** to obtain the use of (someone's) seal *la14-e16*. [OFr, MFr *procurer*, Lat *prōcūrāre* to take care of, manage, act as procurator]

prod[1.1] /prɔd/ *n* **1** a wooden pin or skewer; a thatching-pin *18- N NE T*. **2** a thorn, a prickle *19- SW*. **3** a prick or stab; the sting of an insect *19, 20- SW*. [see the verb]

prod[1.2] /prɔd/ *v* to poke, prick or stab *17-*. [unknown]

prod[2] /prɔd/ *n* a lazy creature; a foolish person *la19- T C*. [shortened form of Eng *prodigal*]

Prod[3] /prɔd/ *n derogatory* a Protestant *20-*. **Proddie, Proddy** *derogatory* a Protestant *20-*. [shortened form of *Prodistan* (PROTESTANT)].

proddled /ˈprɔdəld/ *adj* poked, stirred up, jabbed at; pricked by a thorn *la19- SW Uls*. [ptp formation from PROD[1.2] + *-le* frequentative suffix]

†**prodie** *n* a trinket, plaything *19*. [probably shortened form of PRODIGY]

†**prodig** *adj* wasteful, lavish *16-e17*. [MFr *prodigue*]

prodigy, prodigie, †**prodige** /ˈprɔdɪdʒi/ *n* an extraordinary phenomenon; an omen, portent *16-19, 20- historical*. [Lat *prōdigium*]

Prodistan *see* PROTESTANT

produce /prəˈdjus/ *v* **1** to bring into being; to bring about *la15-*. **2** *law* to present as evidence in a court *la15-*. [Lat *prōdūcere* to lead or bring forth, bring before (a court), beget]

production /prəˈdʌkʃən/ *n* **1** the act of producing; something which has been produced *la15-*. **2** *law* the presentation of evidence in court *la15-*. **3** *law* an article or document produced as evidence, an exhibit *19-*. **4** *of time* extending or lengthening *e16*. **to satisfy production** *law* to produce a document when challenged to do so in a court of law *19-*. [EModE *produccion* or ME *produccioun*]

proem, †**proheme** /ˈproəm/ *n* an introductory discourse or prologue; a preface *la15-*. [ME *proheme*, Lat *prohoemium*]

profane, *Sh* **perfain,** †**prophane** /proˈfen; *Sh* pərˈfen/ *v* **1** to treat (something sacred) with irreverence, contempt or neglect; to desecrate or defile *16-*. **2** to speak profanely, to swear *la19 Sh*. **profaner,** †**prophanar** a defiler of sacred things *la16-*. [ME *prophanen*, EModE *prophane*]

profer *see* PROFFER[1.2]

profession /prəˈfɛʃən/ *n* **1** a professional occupation *la14-*. **2** the religion a person professes, a religious system or sect, a vocation *la16-*. **professional examination** one of a series of degree examinations, called the First Professional Examination, Second Professional Examination, etc, taken by students of medicine and veterinary medicine *la19-*. [ME *professioun*, Lat *professio*]

professor /prəˈfɛsər/ *n* **1** a teacher of the highest rank (in a university or college) *la15-*. **2** a person who makes open profession of religious faith, an acknowledged adherent of a religious doctrine *la16-19, 20- literary*. [ME *professour*, Lat *professor* a public teacher]

proffect, proffeit *see* PROFIT¹·¹

proffer¹·¹, †**proffir,** †**peroffer** /ˈprɔfər/ *n* an offer or proposal *la14-*. [AN *profre, profer*, OFr *poroffre*]

proffer¹·², †**profer,** †**peroffer** /ˈprɔfər/ *v* to present, tender, offer; to show; to propose *la14-*. [AN *profrer*, OFr *poroffrir, paroffrir*]

profit¹·¹, †**proffit,** †**proffect,** †**proffeit** /ˈprɔfɪt, ˈprɔfɪt/ *n* **1** benefit, advantage *la14-*. **2** revenue from produce or exploitation of natural resources; the milk yield of a cow *la14-*. **3** financial gain; wealth, monetary return *la15-*. **4** interest on capital lent *la16-*. **5** a source of revenue *15-16*. †**put to profit 1** to make (land or wealth) profitable or productive *la15-e17*. **2** to put (a person) to a remunerative employment *la15-16*. **tak the profit of a person's milk** *witchcraft* to spoil a cow's milk yield by a spell *17- Sh Ork historical*. †**upon profit** at interest *la16-e17*. **profitable,** †**proffitabill 1** yielding profit or advantage; beneficial, useful, fruitful, valuable *15-*. **2** *of a person* useful, diligent *la15-e17*. [ME *profit*]

profit¹·² /ˈprɔfɪt, ˈprɔfɪt/ *v* **1** to benefit, gain *15-*. **2** to make progress (in knowledge) *la15-17*. [ME *profiten*; also from the noun]

profite /proˈfʌɪt/ *adj* proficient, skilful, expert *19, 20- NE*. [perhaps altered form of PERFIT¹·² with infl from Eng *proficient*]

profixit *see* PREFIXT

prog¹·¹, **progue, proag,** *N* **proug** /prɔg, prog; *N* prʌug/ *n* **1** a stab, thrust or poke, the act of pricking or stabbing *19-*. **2** a thorn, spine or prickle *la19- C SW*. **3** a piercing weapon or instrument, a barb, dart or arrow *la18-19, 20- Sh Ork N*. [perhaps a conflation of PROD¹·¹ + BROG]

prog¹·², **proag,** *N* **proug** /prɔg, prog; *N* prʌug/ *v* **1** to stab, pierce, prick; to prod, jab *18-*. **2** to make poking, prodding movements, poke around *la19- Sh T*. **progger** a long spike or rod with a transverse handle used when searching for drains *la20- C*. [see the noun]

prog² /prog/ *n* fish-liver oil; fish and potatoes with fish-liver oil *20- Sh*. [unknown; compare Eng *prog* a meal, food, especially provisions for a journey]

†**progenitrys** *n* a female ancestor, an ancestress *la15*. [Lat *prōgenitrix*]

proget *see* PROJECT¹

prognostic /prɔgˈnɔstɪk/ *n* **1** a prediction or omen *19-*. **2** an almanac *19, 20- NE*. [shortened form of PROGNOSTICATION, also Eng *prognostic*]

prognostication, †**pronosticatioun** /prɔgnɔstɪˈkeʃən/ *n* **1** a prediction or omen, a prophecy, a forecast *la15-*. **2** an almanac *la16-18*. Compare PROGNOSTY [ME *pronosticacioun*, Lat *prognosticātio* a portent, prediction]

prognosty /prɔgˈnɔsti/ *n* an almanac *19- NE*. [shortened form of PROGNOSTICATION]

program /ˈprogram/ *n* a public notice, official notification or advertisement; a scheme of intended proceedings *17-*. [Lat *programma*]

progress, †**progres,** †**progresse** /ˈprogrɛs/ *n* **1** the course or process of an activity, or of time *la16-*. **2** *law* an unbroken series of possessors or incumbents over a considerable period; the demonstration or proof of the existence of such a series, *la16-17*. †**air by progress** a person who is an heir or successor as part of a series *la16-17*. †**charter by progress** a *feu charter* (FEU) repeating or confirming a grant of land as distinct from that conveying the original grant *18-19*. **mak progress** advance, proceed *16-*. **progress of title** the series of title-deeds, extending over at least ten years, which constitute a person's title to land *la17-*. **progress of title-deeds** = *progress of title*. [Lat *prōgressus* forward movement, advance]

progression, †**progressioun** /proˈgrɛʃən/ *n* (the action of advancing in) a sequence of steps *la15-*. †**be progressioun** by a series of steps, in succession *e16*. [ME *progressioun*, Lat *prōgressio*]

progue *see* PROG¹·¹

†**prohemiate** *v* to compose a proem *la16*. [Lat *prooemiāt-*, ptp stem of *prooemiāri*]

proil¹·¹, **proll** /prɔɪl, prol/ *n* spoils, loot, booty; odds-and-ends, clutter *la19- Sh Ork*. **proly** a windfall, a secret feast *20- Ork*. [probably Du *prul* trash, rubbish]

proil¹·² /prɔɪl/ *v* to go in search of prey, prowl *20- Sh*. [see the noun]

project¹, **projeck,** †**proget** /ˈprɔdʒɛkt, ˈprɔdʒɛkt/ *n* **1** a plan, an endeavour *la16-*. **2** an effort, an undertaking, a feat; an escapade *la19- Sh*. [MFr *projet*, Lat *prōjectum*]

project² /prəˈdʒɛkt/ *v* to protrude, jut; to cast or throw *la17-*. [Lat *prōject-*, ptp stem of *prōicere*]

proke /prok/ *v* to poke about, make a poking movement *19, 20- SW Uls*. **proker** a poker *19, 20- Uls*. [ME *prokien* probably from Eng perhaps via Ireland]

†**prolixt, prolixit** *adj* lengthy; long-winded *la15-17*. **prolixitnes** excessive wordiness *e16*. [MFr *prolixe*, Lat *prōlixus* with ptp suffix]

proll *see* PROIL¹·¹

†**prolocutor, proloquitor, prelocutor** *n* **1** *law* a spokesman in court, an advocate or forspeaker *la15-e18*. **2** a person appointed to act as spokesman for a group or body of which he is a member *16*. [Lat *prōlocūtor*, agent-noun from *prōloquī* to speak out]

†**prolong**¹·¹ *n* delay, procrastination; *law* a dilatory plea *la15-e17*. [MFr *prolong, prolongue* a fixed date, an adjournment]

prolong¹·² /prəˈlɔŋ/ *v* **1** to draw out, extend in duration *la15-*. **2** *law* to adjourn a court hearing until a later date *15-e17*. [MFr *prolonger*]

proloquitor *see* PROLOCUTOR

proly *see* PROIL¹·¹

promeis *see* PROMISE¹·¹, PROMISE¹·²

†**promene**¹·¹ *n* a royal tour *la16*. [see the verb]

†**promene**¹·², **promine** *v* to walk at leisure, take a walk *la16-e17*. [MFr *promener*]

promes *see* PROMISE¹·¹, PROMISE¹·²

promis *see* PROMISE¹·¹

†**promiscue** *adv* indiscriminately *e17*. [Lat *prōmiscuē*]

promiscuous /prəˈmɪskjuəs/ *adj* indiscriminate *17-*. †**promiscuouse dancing** mixed dancing, men with women *17*. [Lat *prōmiscuus*]

promise¹·¹, †**promis,** †**promes,** †**promeis** /ˈprɔmɪs, ˈprɔmɪs/ *n* **1** an agreement to undertake a particular course of action *la15-*. **2** *law* a contractual undertaking or obligation; the document recording it *la15-e17*. †**promys of marriage** a handfasting or agreement to marry *la16-e17*. [ME *promis*]

promise¹·², †**promes,** †**promeis** /ˈprɔmɪs, ˈprɔmɪs/ *v* to agree to undertake, vow; to propose; to threaten *15-*. †**promissioun** the action of promising, a promise *15-16*. [see the noun]

†**promit**¹·¹ *n* a promise; a contractual undertaking *la15-16*. [see the verb]

†**promit**[1,2] *v* **1** to promise, agree to undertake *la15-e18*. **2** to promise a woman in marriage to a man *la15-16*. [ME *promitten*]
†**promontour** *n* a headland *16-e17*. [Lat *prōmontōrium*]
promote /prə'mot/ *v* **1** to advance the cause or interests of (a person); to confer a higher rank or office on someone *15-*. **2** *curling* to cause a stone to move forward by striking it with another stone *20- NE EC SW*. **promoter**, †**promotour** **1** a person who furthers, advances or supports *la14-*. **2** an agent employed to promote Scottish interests at the Papal Court *16*. **promotor** *universities* the official, usually a senior member of the academic staff, who presents students for their degrees at graduation ceremonies *la17-*. [Lat *prōmōt-*, ptp stem of *prōmovēre*]
promotion, †**promotioun** /prə'moʃən/ *n* **1** advancement, preferment *la15-*. **2** *in universities* academic advancement, graduation *la16-e17*. [ME *promocioun*]
†**promove** *v* **1** to advance, promote; to support, foster *15-e18*. **2** *in universities* to advance a student to a higher class or allow to graduate *la15-e17*. **promoval** furtherance, advancement *la17*. [ME *promoven*]
†**promp** *v* to behave in an affected manner *la15*. [perhaps related to PRIMP[1,2]]
promys of marriage *see* PROMISE[1,1]
pron /pron/ *n* the residue of oat husks and oatmeal remaining from the milling process, bran seeds *18- N NE*. [Gael *pronn* the coarsest part of oatmeal with the seeds left in sifting; food]
pronack, **prontag**, **pronach** /'pronək, 'prontəg, 'pronəx/ *n* a crumb, a fragment, a splinter; mush, a mess, a hotchpotch *19- N NE T*. [Gael *pronnag* a crumb]
†**pronece** *n* a grand-niece *e16*. Compare PRONEVOY. [PRO- + Eng NIECE]
†**pronevoy**, †**pronevow** *n* a great-grandson *15-e17*. Compare PRONECE. [PRO- + Eng *nevoy* variant of *nephew*]
pronoonce *see* PRONOUNCE
pronosticatioun *see* PROGNOSTICATION
pronounce, **pronoonce**, †**pronunce** /prə'nʌuns, prə'nuns/ *v* **1** to declare solemnly, announce officially; to articulate clearly *la14-*. **2** *law* to promulgate an act or statute by proclaiming it formally *la15-e16*. [ME *pronouncen*, Lat *prōnuntiāre*]
prontag *see* PRONACK
pronunciation, †**pronunciacioune** /pronʌnsi'eʃən/ *n* **1** the uttering of a word or words; the manner in which a word is articulated *16-*. **2** *law* the official announcement of the sentence or decree of a court *la15-17*. [Lat *prōnuntiātio*]
proo, †**prow** /pru/ *interj* **1** a call to cattle *la17-19, 20- H&I EC*. **2** a command to a horse to stop *19, 20- Bor*. **proo-yae** a call to cattle *19- Sh H&I*. **proo-leddy** a call to cattle *20- C Bor*. [unknown; compare PREE[2]]
proochie, †**prutchie** /'prutʃi/ *interj* a call to cattle *19-*. **pruitchie-leddy** a call to cattle *19- C*. [variant of PROO]
prood, **prude**, **proud**, †**prowd** /prud, prʌud/ *adj* **1** noble, gallant; stately; arrogant, haughty *la14-*. **2** *of persons* pleased, gratified, glad *16-*. **3** *of an object or surface* set higher than, not on the same level as its immediate surroundings *19-*. **4** *of fish* slow to take the bait, difficult to catch *la19- NE SW*. **5** *of growing crops* well grown, (too) luxuriant for the season *la18-19, 20- Sh NE*. **6** *of the sea or a river* running high, swollen *17-18, 19- NE*. **prouden** to make (someone) proud *la20- NE EC*. **proodfu** haughty *la16-19, 20- NE T EC SW*. †**proudnes** excessive self-satisfaction; arrogance, insolence *16*. [ME *proud*, OE *prūd*, ON *prúðr*]
proof *see* PRUIF

prop /prop/ *n* a plug, a wedge *16, la19- Sh*. [Du *prop*, MDu *proppe* a broach, skewer, plug]
prop *see* PRAP[1,1], PRAP[1,2]
†**propale** *v* to make public, divulge, publicize or announce *16-e19*. [Lat *prōpalāre* to make public, Lat *prōpalam* openly]
prope *see* PRAP[1,1], PRAP[1,2]
propel /pro'pɛl/ *v* **1** to move (something) forward; to urge on *la16-*. **2** *of an heir of entail* to anticipate the succession of one's heir apparent by giving them enjoyment of the entailed property before their succession *19-*. [Lat *prōpellere* to drive forward]
†**propense** *adj* subject or susceptible (to illness or infection) *la16-e17*. [Lat *prōpensus*]
†**proper**[1,1] *n* private property, possession *la14-17*. [see the adj; compare Lat *proprium*, Fr *propre* own]
proper[1,2], †**propir** /'propər/ *adj* **1** belonging to one as a property; special, particular *la14-*. **2** correct, true, fitting; genuine *15-*. †**proper improbation** *law* the setting aside or discrediting of a document on the grounds of its falsity or the fact that it has been forged *la18*; compare *reduction-improbation* (REDUCE). †**proper jurisdiction** *law* the authority of a judge when acting in his own person as distinct from the authority delegated by him to a deputy *la18-e19*. †**proper wadset** *law* a mortgage of property which allowed the creditor to take as interest whatever income derived from the property *17-e19*; compare *improper wadset* (IMPROPER). [MFr *propre*, Lat *proprius*]
†**proper**[1,3] *adv* excellently, finely; correctly *la15-e16*. [see the adj; compare MFr *propre* properly]
properly /'propərli/ *adv* **1** correctly, appropriately; literally *la14-*. **2** (belonging to someone) as personal or private property; particularly; individually *15-*. **3** in accordance with reality; accurately *la14-17*. [PROPER[1,2] + *-ly* adv-forming suffix]
property, †**properte**, †**propyrte** /'propərti/ *n* **1** ownership *la14-*. **2** goods, wealth or land under ownership *la14-*. **3** a (distinguishing) attribute or quality *la14-*. **4** congruence with reality, truth, correctness *e15*. **5** particularity of diction *e16*. [ME *proprete*]
prophane *see* PROFANE
†**propiciant** *adj* propitious, well-disposed *16*. [Lat *propitiant-*, presp stem of *propitiāre*]
†**propine**[1,1] *n* **1** a gift *15-19*. **2** an offering or dedication, especially a poem or writing *16-e19*. [MFr *propine* gratuity, Lat *propīna*]
†**propine**[1,2] *v* **1** to give a person a gift; to present a person (with something) *16-19*. **2** to offer or give to drink, present with drink *la16-e18*. **3** to offer or dedicate a work of literature (to someone) *la16-17*. **4** to propose an idea, state something *la16*. [see the noun]
propir *see* PROPER[1,2]
proplexit *see* PERPLEXIT
propone, **propound**, †**propoun**, †**prepone** /prə'pon, prə'pʌund/ *v* **1** to set forth for consideration; to suggest *la14-*. **2** *law* to put forward or state (a plea) in a court *15-*. **3** to propose as a candidate *16-e17*. **4** to utter *16*. **5** to set down in writing *la16*. **6** to offer as a prize or reward *16*. **7** to put forward as a model or example *la16-17*. **8** to intend (to do something) *15-e18*. †**propone defences** *law* to state or move a defence *17-18*. [Lat *prōpōnere* to announce, propose, intend]
†**proport** *v of legal documents* to convey meaning, signify, purport *la14-e18*. [OFr *porporter, proporter* to purport]
proportion, †**proportioun** /prə'porʃən/ *n* **1** a part, a share; a contribution *15-*. **2** *music* harmony *16-*. **3** *Presbyterian Church* the district assigned to an elder for visiting, a quarter *18-e19*. **4** *military* the number of troops to be raised by an administrative district as a fraction of the national army *17*.

5 a tune *e16*. **proportional** corresponding in size, degree or amount *la16-*. **proportionally 1** by equal or commensurate proportions *la14-*. **2** correspondingly *la16-*. **proportionate 1** similar in proportion; well-proportioned *la15-*. **2** *music* having or depending upon specific intervallic relationships *la15-16*. **proportionit** in proportion, harmonious *15-*. [ME *proporcioun*, Lat *prōportio*]
propose *see* PURPOSE¹·¹
propoun, propound *see* PROPONE
propriete *see* PROPRIETY
proprietor, †proprietar /proˈpraeətər/ *n* someone with the exclusive right to the use or disposal of a thing; an owner *la15-*. [MFr *proprieteur*]
propriety, †propriete /proˈpraeəti/ *n* **1** conformity to accepted standards of behaviour *la18-*. **2** goods, wealth or land under ownership *15-16*. **3** a (distinguishing) attribute or quality *la15-16*. [MFr *propriété*, Lat *proprietās*]
propulsion /prəˈpʌlʃən/ *n* **1** the action of moving (something) forward; the condition of being driven onward *17-*. **2** *law* the act of anticipating the succession of one's heir apparent by giving them enjoyment of the entailed property before their succession *la19-*. [Lat *prōpulsio* the action of urging on, Lat *prōpuls-*, ptp stem of *prōpellere*]
propyrte *see* PROPERTY
†pro-rector *n* in St Andrews University the vice-rector *19*. [PRO- + RECTOR]
pro re nata /pro re ˈnata/ *adv* as the occasion requires; for an unforeseen contingency *la16-*. [Lat *prō rē nātā* for the matter which has arisen]
prorogate, †prorogat /ˈprorəget/ *v, ptp* **prorogate 1** *law* to extend in time, prolong (especially of a lease) *16-*. **2** *law* to extend the jurisdiction of a judge or court to a case which would otherwise be ruled outside their competence *la17-*. **3** *law* to defer, postpone *16-e19, la19- historical*. **4** *law* to adjourn a sitting of Parliament *la14-e18*. [Lat *prōrogāt-*, ptp stem of *prōrogāre*]
prorogation, †prorogatioun /prorəˈgeʃən/ *n* the action of extending or lengthening (the duration of something); prolongation; continuance *15-*. [ME *prorogacioun*]
prosecute, †prosequute /ˈprɔsəkjut/ *v ptp* **†prosecute 1** to persist in (a course of action); to persevere; to fulfil (an aim) *la16-*. **2** to engage in (an activity) *la16-*. **3** *law* to arraign before a court *la16-*. **4** to pursue (a person) with hostile or punitive intent *la16*. **prosecuting 1** the action or process of a prosecution *la16-*. **2** the action of seeking to obtain or secure *17-*. [Lat *prōsecūt-*, ptp stem of *prōsequī*]
prosecution, †prosequutione /prɔsəˈkjuʃən/ *n* **1** the carrying out of a plan, or performance of an activity *la16-*. **2** seeking to gain possession of something by legal means *la16-*. **3** the action of pursuing with hostile intent *la15-e17*. [EModE *prosecution*, Lat *prosecutio*, from Lat *prōsequī* to pursue]
prosequute *see* PROSECUTE
prospect, prospeck /ˈprɔspɛkt ˈprɔspɛk/ *n* **1** an (extensive) view from a specific location *la16-*. **2** a spyglass, telescope *17-e19*. **prospect glass** a spyglass *17-19*. [Lat *prōspectus* a look out, view]
†prosper, prospir *adj* **1** successful *la15-e16*. **2** favourable, auspicious *e16*. [Lat *prosper*]
prosperity, †prosperite, †prosperitie /prɔˈspɛrəti/ *n* the condition of being successful; good fortune, success *la14-*. [ME *prosperite*, Lat *prosperitās*]
pross /pros, prəs/ *v* to put on airs, show off; to gossip *19, 20- WC Bor*. [unknown]
†prostern *v* to cast down; to prostrate (oneself) *16-e17*. [MFr *prosterner*, Lat *prōsternere*]

prot *see* PRET¹·¹, PRET¹·²
proteccioun *see* PROTECTION
proteck, protect /proˈtɛk, proˈtɛkt/ *v* to defend; to afford immunity from harm *la16-*. [Lat *prōtect-*, ptp stem of *prōtegere*]
protecteris *see* PROTECTRICE
protection, †proteccioun /prəˈtɛkʃən/ *n* defence or preservation from harm *la14-*. [ME *proteccioun*, Lat *prōtectio*]
protector, †protectour /proˈtɛktər/ *n* **1** a person who provides defence against injury or harm; a patron *la14-*. **2** the viceroy or regent of Scotland during periods of invasion or minority *la15-16*. **†Protectour of Ingland** an English viceroy *16*. [MFr *protecteur*, Lat *prōtector*]
protectrice, †protecteris /proˈtɛktrɪs/ *n* a protectress *la14-*. [MFr *protectrice*]
†protectrix *n* a protectress *la15-19*. [Lat *prōtectrix*]
†proterve *adj* wayward, perverse *la16*. [ME *proterve*, Lat *protervus* reckless, impudent]
protest¹·¹ /ˈprotɛst/ *n* **1** an objection; *law* a (formal) complaint or instrument *18-*. **2** a demand for legal redress *17*; compare PROTESTATION. [see the verb]
protest¹·² /proˈtɛst/ *v* **1** to assert (the opposite), declare; to object, disagree *15-*. **2** *law* to put forward a PROTESTATION to safeguard one's interests; to make a demand (for the measure requested) *15-*. **3** to stipulate, demand, insist *16*. **4** to put in a claim (for something) *16-17*. **†Protesters** the name given to those Presbyterians who opposed union with the Royalist party in 1650 *la17*. [AN, MFr *protester*, Lat *prōtestārī*]
Protestant, *WC Uls* **Prodistan, †Protestane** /ˈprɔtəstənt; *WC Uls* ˈprɔdəstən/ *n* a member or adherent of one of the Protestant churches or bodies *la16-*. [apparently Lat *prōtestāns* probably after Ger *protestieren* or *protestierend*]
protestation, †protestatioun /prɔtəˈsteʃən/ *n* **1** a solemn affirmation of a fact or belief; a declaration of dissent or objection *16-*. **2** *law* the procedure by which a defender in the Court of Session compels the pursuer to proceed with his action or to end it *18-*. **3** *law* a stipulation or demand to a court by a party to a lawsuit for the safeguarding of his interests in the face of the decisions of the court; the instrument in which it was recorded *la14-17*. **protestation for remeid of law** an appeal from a decision of the Court of Session to the Scottish Parliament *18-19, 20- historical*; compare *remeid of law* (REMEID). **†protestation for remeid in law** = *protestation for remeid of law*. [ME *protestacioun*, Lat *prōtestatio*]
†prothogoll *v* to set down as a note or minute of a transaction; to engross in a protocol book *16-e17*. [from the noun PROTOCOL]
protocol, †prothogoll /ˈprotəkɔl/ *n* **1** the original note or minute of a transaction, drawn up by a notary or clerk of court *la15-*. **2** the register in which a notary recorded the details of transactions or other legal proceedings *la16-e19*.
protocol book a book in which a notary recorded the details of transactions or other legal proceedings *la15-e19, la19- historical*. [ME *prothogol*, Lat *prōtocollum* the first leaf of a papyrus-roll (6th century), public notary's protocol (10th century)]
prottick *see* PRACTIC
protty *see* PRETTIE, PRETTY
pro-tutor /proˈtjutər/ *n* a person who acts as guardian of a pupil without being legally appointed in that capacity *la17-*. Compare PRO-CURATOR. [PRO- + TUTOR]
†pro-tutrix *n* a female PRO-TUTOR *18*. [PRO- + TUTRIX]
proud *see* PROOD
proug *see* PROG¹·¹, PROG¹·²
provay *see* PURVEY¹·²
prove *see* PRUIF, PRUIVE
proveist *see* PROVOST

proven, †**provin** /ˈprovən, ˈpruvən/ *adj* shown to be as stated; demonstrated *16-*. **proven rental** *law* a scheme of a minister's rental proved in a process of AUGMENTATION *la18-*. **not proven** *law* a verdict in a criminal trial when it is found that although there is a suspicion of guilt, the case against the accused has not been proved beyond reasonable doubt; the accused is then unconditionally discharged *17-*. [from the strong ptp of *preve* = PRUIVE]

provene *see* PREVEEN

proves, provest *see* PROVOST

†**proviance** *n* provision; providence *la14-16*. [OFr *porveance*]

†**proviant** *n* provisions; food supply for an army *e17*. **proviant master** the officer in charge of providing food and other supplies for an army *e17*. [Du *proviand*, Ger *proviant* imported by soldiers serving in the Thirty Years' War]

providand *see* PROVIDING[1,2]

provide /proˈvʌɪd/ *v* **1** to arrange; to furnish; to supply; to equip *la15-*. **2** *law* to make provision for *la15-*. **3** *law* to contractually prearrange for the delivery of property (to a person) after one's death *la16-17*. **4** to foresee *15*. †**provyd of** to provide or supply with *la15-e17*. †**provid in** = *provyd of la16-18*. [Lat *prōvidēre*]

providence /ˈprɔvɪdəns/ *n* **1** provision; preparation *la15-*. **2** foresight; prudent regard to the future *la15-*. **3** an instance of very good (or very bad) fortune, an event brought about by natural forces (which is attributed to God) *16-*. [ME *providence*, Lat *prōvidentia*]

providing[1.1] /prəˈvʌɪdɪŋ/ *n* **1** provision of necessities or equipment *17-*. **2** the household articles traditionally collected by a young woman to supply her needs as a married woman *la18-*. [verbal noun from PROVIDE]

providing[1.2], †**providand** /prəˈvʌɪdɪŋ/ *conj* on condition, provided (that) *16-*. [presp of PROVIDE]

providit /prəˈvʌɪdɪt/ *adj* **1** prepared, (made) ready *16-*. **2** furnished with what is necessary, equipped *la16-*. **3** *of a person* having sufficient means *la15-16*. **4** *of a church* supplied with an incumbent; *of an incumbent* installed, appointed *la16*. [participial adj from PROVIDE]

provin *see* PROVEN

provincial /prəˈvɪnʃəl/ *n* **1** *Christian Church* the superior member of a religious order in a district *15-*. **2** *Presbyterian Church* a provincial synod *la16-17*. †**provincial assembly** a provincial synod *la16-17*. [ME *provincial*, Lat *prōvinciālis* relating to an ecclesiastical province]

†**provinsellis** *npl* hose or breeches *la16*. [MFr *provençales*]

provision /prəˈvɪʒən/ *n* **1** the act of providing; foresight; providence *15-*. **2** a supply or stock of provisions *la15-*. **3** an order or rule prescribing action or conduct in possible future circumstances; a stipulation, reservation *la16-*. **4** *Roman Catholic Church* a papal document of appointment to a clerical vacancy *la15-e16*. **5** *Presbyterian Church* the appointment of a minister to a kirk *la16-e17*. †**bond of provision** a legally binding agreement by which certain stipulations are made on behalf of the children of the party concerned *la17*. **mak provision** to make ready; to make advance arrangements; to cater to the needs of *la15-*. [ME *provisioun*, Lat *prōvīsio*]

provisor, †**provisour** /prəˈvaezər/ *n* **1** the title of the steward of the Students' Union at the University of Aberdeen *20-*. **2** the steward, purveyor or treasurer of a community or college *la15-18*. **3** the official responsible for the provision of supplies to the royal household *16-17*. [ME *provisour* a manager, a purveyor, Lat *prōvīsor* a person who takes forethought for, a caterer, an administrator]

provocation, *Sh* **provokshin**, †**provocatioun** /prɔvəˈkeʃən, prəˈvokʃən/ *n* incitement; incentive, temptation *15-*. [MFr *provocation*, Lat *prōvocātio* an appeal at law, an excitation]

provoke[1.1] /prəˈvok/ *n* **1** a person or thing which causes annoyance, a nuisance, pest *la19-*. **2** a provocation, challenge, invitation, summons *la18-e19*. [see the verb]

provoke[1.2] /prəˈvok/ *v* **1** to invoke, incite *la15-*. **2** to challenge (a person to combat) *la15-*. **3** *law* to challenge a right by putting forward an appeal *la15-*. [ME *provoken*]

provost, †**provest**, †**proveist**, †**proves** /ˈprɔvəst/ *n* **1**, a superintendent, a head, the chief dignitary; a person in authority *la14-*. **2** the head of a Scottish municipal corporation or burgh, who was the civic head and chairman of the town or burgh council and the chief magistrate, corresponding to English *mayor*; since 1975 used only as a courtesy title in some authorities *la14-*; compare LORD PROVOST. **3** *Scottish Episcopal Church* the minister of a cathedral church *la19-*.

†**provostry** **1** the office of provost of a collegiate corporation of clergy or the revenues attached to it *la15-19, 20- historical*. **2** the office or jurisdiction of a provost of a Scottish burgh *16-e19*. **provostship**, †**prowestschipe** the office or jurisdiction of a provost *16-*. [OE *prafost*, AN *provost*]

prow *see* PROO

prowd *see* PROOD

prowly /ˈprʌuli/ *n* a scolding, a telling-off, a punishment *la19- Ork*. [unknown]

pruch[1.1] /prʌx/ *n* goods or benefits received at (or obtained from) work in addition to pay, perquisites *20- WC*. [unknown]

pruch[1.2] /prʌx/ *v* to hunt for cheap goods or a bargain; to scrounge *20- WC*. [unknown]

prude *see* PROOD

prudence /ˈprudəns/ *n* **1** practical wisdom; discretion *la14-*. **2** a woollen wrap for the head worn by women, especially in winter *20- NE WC Bor*. [ME *prudence*, Lat *prūdēntia*]

pruf *see* PRUIF

prufe *see* PRUIVE

pruif, proof, prief, preef, †pruf, †prove, †preif /pruf, prif/ *n* **1** confirmation by experience or examination; sufficient or certain evidence verifying an alleged fact *la14-*. **2** *law* establishment of the facts in a court by evidence *15-*. **3** *law* (a piece of) evidence *15-*. **4** submission of something to a trial, test *la15-*. **5** the ability to withstand assault; impenetrability *la15-*. **6** the method by which the disputed facts in a case are judicially determined, including the taking of evidence by a judge or by a commissioner appointed by the Court, to determine the issues on which trial will take place; also trial before a judge only *18-*. **7** *agriculture* a sample consisting of a proportion of a stack or crop of corn tested to estimate quality and yield; the yield of the sample or the estimated total yield; the action of such testing *la15-19, 20- N Uls*. **8** *Presbyterian Church pl* scriptural texts used to illustrate the doctrines in the catechisms, especially those of the Shorter Catechism printed as a schoolbook *18-19*. **9** a person who gives evidence; a witness *la15-16*. **10** *metallurgy* a test of a sample of ore or metal to determine its quality *la16*. **11** *law* the giving of evidence in court, the action of serving as a witness *15*. **prief barley** the grain selected as a sample for assessment *la16-19, 20- NE T*. **prief corn** the grain selected as a sample for assessment *la16-19, 20- NE T*. †**proof man** the person appointed to assess grain *la16-e19*. †**proof of lead** a supposed magic protection from bullets *la17-e19*. †**proof-a-shot** = *proof of lead e18*. [ME *profe*, *prēve*, OFr *prouve*]

pruitchie-leddy *see* PROOCHIE

pruive, prove, preeve, †preve, †prufe, †preif /pruv, priv/ *v, ptp also* **proven 1** to attempt; demonstrate, display, make manifest *la14-*. **2** to establish the worth or quality of a person or thing by experience, try out, test, sample *la14-*. **3** to establish the truth, substantiate, verify *la14-*. **4** *law* to establish or verify evidence in court, especially as to quantity or value; to prove a case *la15-*. **5** to assess the quality and content of (a given quantity of grain) by examining a random sample *la15-19, 20- Ork NE SW*. **6** to try the productivity of a fishing ground by making a test haul *e19*; compare *pree the nets* (PREE¹·²). **7** to put into action, perform, accomplish *la14-17*. **8** *law* to establish ownership *la15-e16*. **9** to discover, ascertain *la14-e17*. **preevin**, †**prieven**, †**privein**, †**prieving** a taste; a sample; a kiss *17-19, 20- Sh*; compare PREE. **prove the tenor** *law* the process or legal action by which the substance of a lost document is established by witnesses or proofs *17-*. [ME *proven, prēven*, OFr *prover, pruever*]

†**prundamas** *n* a damson plum; a prune *la15-e17*. Compare PLOOM-DAMAS. [MFr *prune de Damas, prune damascene* plum of Damascus]

prune, †**prunʒe** /prun/ *v* **1** *of a bird* to preen *16-*. **2** to dress or adorn oneself or one's hair *16-19*. Compare PREEN¹·². [AN *proign-* pres ppl stem of *proindre*]

prunk /prʌŋk/ *adj* smart in appearance, well-dressed *19- Sh*. **prunkly** in a smart, well-presented manner *20- Sh*. [from the verb *prunk* (PRINK)]

prunk *see* PRINK

prunʒe *see* PRUNE

†**prunʒeand** *adj* piercing; sharp *e16*. **prunʒeandlie** sharply *la16*. [perhaps altered form of *punʒeand* (PUNʒE²) after PREEN¹·¹]

prutchie *see* PROOCHIE

†**pruts, prutish** *interj* an expression of scorn or defiance *la18-e19*. **pruts no** = PRUTS. [a natural utterance]

pry¹ /prae/ *v* to move by leverage *20-*. Compare PRISE¹·². [back-formation from PRISE¹·²]

†**pry**² *n* one of various species of sedge (*Carex*) common in southern Scotland, used for feeding sheep *la18-19*. [unknown; compare Eng *pry grass*]

pryce *see* PRAISE¹·²

pryde *see* PRIDE¹·¹

pryme *see* PRIME¹·²

prysar *see* PRICE¹·²

pryse *see* PRISE¹·¹

psalm¹·¹, †**pschalme**, †**salm**, †**saum** /sam/ *n* **1** *Christian Church* one of the songs contained in the Book of Psalms in the Old Testament and Hebrew Scriptures; a paraphrase of one of these, sung or spoken during worship *15-*. **2** *Presbyterian Church* the metrical version of the Psalms adopted from French Protestant usage, the 1650 version being regularly used in congregational praise *la16-*. **psalm buik** a book of psalms, especially metrical psalms *16-*. [ME *psalm*, OE *sealm*, ON *psalmr*]

psalm¹·² /sam/ *v* to recount (a story) at great length and in monotonous detail, to reel (off) endlessly in a monotonous whining voice *20- NE*. [see the noun]

pschalme *see* PSALM¹·¹

ptarmigan *see* TARMAGAN

pu *see* POU

public¹·¹ /'pʌblɪk/ *n* **1** the community or nation as a corporate authority; the commonwealth, the state; the interest of the community *la17-*. **2** duties on property payable to the community or state *la17*. [see the adj]

†**public**¹·² *v* to make publicly or generally known (by proclamation or official pronouncement) *15-16*. [see the adj]

public¹·³, †**publik**, †**publict** /'pʌblɪk/ *adj* pertaining to, serving or open to the community or nation as a whole *la15-*. **public burdens** taxes as they affect land; rates and taxes *18-*. †**public right** *law* a heritable right acquired when the purchaser of a property completes his feudal title with the seller's superior, originally a distinct procedure but latterly merely formal in conveyancing practice *la18-e19*. **public room** a room in a dwelling in which visitors are received; a sitting room, a dining room *19-*. **public school 1** a state-controlled school run by the local education authority and supported by contributions from local and national taxation *la17-*. **2** a school open to the whole community *la19-*. [ME *publik*, MFr *public*]

publican /'pʌblɪkən/ *n* **1** a person who owns or manages a public house or bar *18-*. **2** a reprobate, a spiritual outcast, a villain *la14-17*. [ME *publican*, Lat *pūblicānus*]

publication, †**publicatioun** /pʌblɪ'keʃən/ *n* **1** the process of publishing something; a book, journal or newspaper *16-*. **2** *law* disclosure of depositions of witnesses in court *16-17*. [ME *publicacioun*, OFr *publication*]

publict, publik *see* PUBLIC¹·³

publish, †**publis**, †**publisch** /'pʌblɪʃ/ *v ptp also* †**publist 1** to make publicly or generally known (by proclamation or formal announcement) *15-*. **2** *law* to make the depositions of witnesses, or parties to the case, known in court *e16*. [ME *publishen*]

†**publy** *adv* publicly, by public proclamation *e15*. [AN, MFr *publier*, perhaps after ME *puplen* to make known publicly, reveal]

puchal *see* POOCHLE

puckle *see* PICKLE²

puckles /'pʌkəlz/ *adv* occasionally, now and then *la20- NE*. [perhaps pl of *puckle* (PICKLE²) applied to periods of time, with development to adverb]

pud¹, **pod** /pʌd, pɔd/ *n* **1** a term of endearment for a child or small squat animal *la19- C*. **2** a small, neat, usually plump person or animal *18-19, 20- Uls*. **3** a pigeon *20- T*. [shortened form of PUDDIN]

pud² /pʌd/ *n* an ink-holder, an ink-pot *19, 20- Bor*. [unknown]

pudder *see* POODER¹·¹

puddie /'pʌde/ *n* a pigeon *20- Bor*. **pud-doo, puddie-doo** a tame pigeon *19, 20- T EC*. [PUD¹ + -IE¹]

puddill *see* PUDDLE¹·¹

puddin, pudding /'pʌdɪn, 'pudɪn, 'pudɪŋ/ *n* **1** a kind of sausage or haggis made from the stomach or intestines of a sheep or pig stuffed with various mixtures of oatmeal, onions, suet, seasoning and blood, boiled and stored for future use *la15-*; compare *black puddin* (BLACK), *mealie puddin* (MEAL¹), *white puddin* (WHITE). **2** *pl* entrails, viscera, guts (of persons or animals) *16-*. **3** a sweet dish made with flour, milk and sugar and often served as a dessert *17-*. **4** a stupid or clumsy person *20-*. **puddin bree**, †**pudding broo** the water in which a savoury pudding has been boiled *18- Ork NE T*. †**pudding fillar** a glutton; a person who stuffs guts, a sausage maker, a person of low social status *e16*. **puddin lug 1** one of the projecting ends of a savoury pudding *la19- NE*. **2** an exclamation expressing impatience *la19- NE*. **3** an ear which has swollen as the result of a blow *la20- WC*. **puddin market**, †**pudding mercat 1** *humorous* the stomach *la20- Ork NE T*. **2** the market (in Edinburgh) where savoury puddings were sold *la16-17*. **puddin supper, pudding supper** a savoury pudding served with chips *20-*. **haud the puddin reekin** keep an activity going with vigour *19- C*. **keep the puddin boilin** = *haud the puddin reekin*. [ME *poding*, AN *bodin*]

puddle¹·¹, †**puddill** /'pʌdəl/ *n* **1** a small pool of (dirty or muddy) liquid *16-*. **2** a street gutter *20- NE*. **3** an untidy or disorganized worker, a muddler, a bungler *19, 20- T*. **4** a state of disorder, a muddle, a mess, confusion *16-19*. [EModE *puddle*; compare MDu *poedel*]

puddle¹·² /'pʌdəl/ *v* **1** to work in a muddling, inefficient way, muddle along, mess about *la16-*. **2** to walk with short steps, plod; *of the feet* to work up and down *19, 20- Bor*. †**puddlit, pudlid** covered in mud; thrown into a muddy puddle *16-e18*. [see the noun]

puddock¹·¹, **paddok**, *NE* **poddock** /'pʌdək, 'padək; *NE* 'podək/ *n* **1** a frog or toad *14-*. **2** *agriculture* a flat, wooden, usually triangular platform (shaped rather like a frog) used to transport heavy loads *18-*. **3** a spiteful or arrogant person *19-*. **4** a clumsy, ungainly or ugly person *19, 20- NE*. **5** *pl* a game similar to cricket, with local variations *la19- N T EC*. **paddock barrow** a platform used to transport heavy loads *19-, 20- N NE*. **puddock cruds** frogspawn *la19-, NE SW*. **puddock hair** the down or fluff growing on very young creatures, especially birds *19, 20- H&I Bor*. **puddock pipes** a kind of grass, the marsh horse-tail *17-*. **puddock pony** a tadpole *20- T*. **puddock redd** frogspawn *18-19, 20- EC SW Bor*. **puddock rude** frogspawn *16-19, 20- N Bor*. **puddock's spindle** the spotted orchid *la19, 20- H&I SW*. **puddock spit** cuckoo-spit, a frothy secretion produced by certain insects, such as the frog-hopper, to protect their larvæ *la19-*. †**puddock stane, paddok stane** a toadstone, a stone object popularly believed to be produced by toads, and often credited with magical or healing properties *la15-e18*. **puddock stool** a toadstool or mushroom; any fungus (with a stalk) *la16-*. **be in the puddock hair** *of persons or animals* be very young, be an infant *e19*. [ME *paddok* a frog, a toad]

puddock¹·² /'pʌdək/ *v* to move (gravel or stone) by means of a wooden platform *la19- NE*. [see the noun]

†**puddy** *n* a kind of cloth *e18*. [probably shortened form of *pudosoye* (PADUASOY)]

pudge /pʌdʒ/ *n* a small, plump, thickset person or animal *la19-*. **pudget** = PUDGE *la19-*. **pudgie** = PUDGE *la18-*. **pudgle** = PUDGE *19, 20- NE Bor*. [perhaps a variant of PUD¹]

pudosoye *see* PADUASOY

pue *see* PEW¹·¹, PLOO¹·¹

puff¹·¹ /pʌf/ *n* **1** a small exhalation of breath; a tiny burst of air, vapour or smoke *16-*. **2** a belch or fart *e16*. **puffie** a porpoise *20- NE T EC*; compare *puffy dunter*, PLUFFY³. **in yer puff** in your life (while you have drawn breath) *la20-*. [see the verb]

puff¹·² /pʌf/ *v ptp also* **puft 1** to emit a small amount of breath, wind, vapour or smoke at one time *la16-*. **2** to swell (up), to inflate with vanity or pride *la15-*. **3** to boast, brag *19-*. **4** to break wind *e16*. [onomatopoeic]

puff candy /pʌf 'kandi/ *n* a type of hard, honeycombed candy made by adding bicarbonate of soda to a boiling mixture of sugar and water *la19-*. [PUFF¹·² + CANDY¹·¹]

puffer /'pʌfər/ *n* a small steamboat used to carry cargo around the west coast of Scotland and the Hebrides *la19-20, 21- historical*. [PUFF¹·² + *-er* agent suffix]

puffy dunter /'pʌfe dʌntər/ *n* a porpoise *la19- NE Bor*. Compare PLUFFY. [PUFF¹·¹ + -Y + DUNTER (sense 1) from its quick breathing on surfacing]

pug¹ /pʌg/ *n* a small locomotive *la19-*. **puggie** a small locomotive *la19-*. **puggy line** informal name for the Lochaber narrow-gauge railway built for the construction of the tunnel from Loch Treig to Fort William *20-*. [EModE *pug* monkey, ape + -IE¹; perhaps compare Du *pug* small; a person of small stature]

pug² /pʌg/ *v* to pull, tug *la17-*. [unknown]

puggie¹·¹, **puggy** /'pʌge, 'pʌgi/ *n* **1** a monkey *la17-*. **2** an ugly, unpleasant person *la19, 20- T WC*. **puggy bun** a bun consisting of a treacle sponge mixture in a pastry case, and bearing a resemblance to a monkey's face *la20- T EC*. **puggy pipe** the cup and stalk of the acorn, resembling a pipe *la20- EC*. **get yer puggy up** lose your temper *la19- C*. [EModE *pug* monkey, ape + -IE¹; perhaps compare Du *pug* small; a person of small stature]

puggie¹·² /'pʌge, 'pʌgi/ *adj* ugly, monkey-like *18-*. [see the noun]

puggie² /'pʌge, 'pʌgi/ *n* **1** stomach *20-*. **2** a one-armed bandit; a fruit machine *la20-*. **3** an automatic telling machine *la20-*. **4** *children's games* a hole into which marbles are rolled *la20- C Bor*. **5** *games* the bank, kitty, jackpot or pool in a game of cards *la20- T WC*. **puggie machine** a fruit machine *la20-*. **as fou as a puggie 1** extremely drunk *20- N T C Bor*. **2** very full because of overeating *la20- C*. [variant of *bogie* a leather bag; compare Norn *paggi* a stuffed stomach, OIcel *poki* a pouch, bag]

puggled, puggelt /'pʌgəlt/ *adj* **1** overcome due to exhaustion, heat or frustration; very tired; at the end of one's resources *20-*. **2** very drunk *20-*. [unknown; probably from Travellers' language rather than Eng army slang. Compare PAGGER¹·²]

pugs /pʌgz/ *npl mining* a stratum of hard coal in a free coal seam *la19- C*. [probably plural of Eng *pug* loam or hard pounded clay used to make bricks etc]

puidge /pudʒ/ *n* **1** a small enclosure, pen or sty; a hut, a hovel *19-*. **2** a mess, a muddle *20- Bor*. **3** a small enclosure used for fattening cattle *la20- Bor*. [unknown; compare Eng *pudge* a muddy puddle or ditch]

puik *see* POUK¹·²

puil¹·¹, **pool**, *N NE* **peel**, †**pule** /pul; *N NE* pil/ *n* a pool, a body of water; frequently in place-names *la12-*. **peel rushich** a heavy shower, a downpour; a torrent *20- NE*. [OE *pōl*]

puil¹·² /pul/ *v mining* to make a hole in (stone), to undercut (coal) *18-*. [see the noun]

puir¹·¹, **poor**, *NE* **peer** /pur; *NE* pir/ *n* **1** poor people; the poor collectively *la14-*. **2** a poor person, a pauper, someone receiving charity *15-e19*. †**poor's box** a collecting box for poor relief kept by the kirk session; the poor fund itself *la16-18*. **puirshouse, pairshouse** a poorhouse, a workhouse *la18-19, 20- historical*. **puir's inspector** a colloquial term for the Inspector of Poor, an official appointed to a parish in accordance with the 1845 Act, who investigated cases of poverty and paid out poor relief *19-20, 21- historical*. **poor's rates** a rate or assessment for the relief or support of the poor, administered by a parish *la18-e20, la20- historical*. **poor's roll 1** a list of paupers in a parish who received poor relief *la17-20, 21- historical*. **2** *law* a roll of persons officially recognized as qualifying because of poverty for free legal aid under the Act of 1424 *17-20, 21- historical*. [see the adj]

†**puir**¹·² *v* to make poor, to impoverish *15-16*. [see the adj]

puir¹·³, **poor, pair**, *NE* **peer**, †**pure**, †**peur**, †**pover** /pur, per; *NE* pir/ *adj* **1** lacking in wealth or resources, impoverished, needy *la14-*. **2** *with self-deprecating force* humble, modest, insignificant *15-*. **3** *followed by a person's name* indicating that that person had been given free legal aid because their name was on the poor roll *la18-e20, la20- historical*. †**puiranis** 'poor ones', poor people *la16-17*. **puir bodie** a needy, sickly or unfortunate person; a beggar *15-*. **puir John** a cod or ling found in shallow water in poor condition *la19- Sh*. †**poor man** a dish made from the remains of a shoulderbone of mutton *18-19*. †**pure men** the tenant-farmers of a rural estate *la15-16*. **peer page** a kindle of candlestick *19- NE*. **puir sowl**, *NE* **peer sowl** = *puir bodie 20-*. **puir man's clover** self-heal, a type of plant (or plants) believed to have healing properties *la20- NE T*. **ding on puir men and pike staves** to rain heavily, pour with rain *19- NE*. **mak a puir mou** to plead poverty as an excuse for meanness, to complain of one's poverty, exaggerate one's need *19-*. **rain puir men and pike staves** = *ding on puir men and pike staves*. [ME *povre*]

puir see PURE[1.1]

puirtith, poortith, *NE* **peertith, †purteth, †puirteith** /'purtɪθ; *NE* 'pirtɪθ/ *n* poverty; the condition of being poor *16-*. [OFr *povretet, pouretet* with alteration of final consonant]

puissance, †piscence, †pusiance, †pissance /'pjusəns, 'pwisəns/ *n* **1** capacity, ability; physical strength *la15-*. **2** authority, influence *16*. **3** supernatural power *16*. **4** military or financial resources *16*. [ME *puissaunce*]

puissant, †pissant, †pussant /'pjusənt, 'pwisənt/ *adj* powerful; strong *la15-*. [MFr *puissant*]

puist[1.1] /pust/ *v* to cram, stuff full; to cram (the stomach or oneself) with food *19, 20- Bor*. [unknown; perhaps compare POSS, POUSS]

puist[1.2] /pust/ *adj of people* in easy circumstances, comfortably off *19- SW Bor*. [see the verb]

puist[2] /pust/ *v* to urge forward, push, impel; to attack by pushing or punching; to criticize *19- SW Bor*. [unknown; compare PUIST[1.1]]

puke see POUK[1.2]

puldary see BALDERRY

pulder see POODER[1.1], POODER[1.2]

pule see PEWL[1.2], PUIL[1.1]

pull see POU

pullach /'puləx/ *n* a species of cod *la19- NE*. [Eng *pollack* a type of marine fish, perhaps via Gael *pollach*; compare POLLACK, PODLIE]

pullar see PILLER

pulley, †pillie, †pulle /'pule, 'pulɪ/ *n* **1** a mechanical device by which a weight or object may be lowered or raised *la15-*. **2** an apparatus for drying clothes which consists of a series of wooden rods within a metal frame, suspended from the ceiling, and can be lowered and raised *20-*. **pulleyshee, †pille scheif 1** a pulley, especially a rope on a pole, used to hang clothes out of a window to dry *18-19, 20- T C*. **2** the sheave or grooved roller over which a rope runs in a pulley-block *16-17*. [ME *puli*]

†pullicate, policat *n* a coloured, frequently checked, gingham-type cotton produced in Scotland; a handkerchief of this fabric *18-19*. [named after *Pulicat* in S India, where handkerchiefs of this material were first made]

pullie /'pule/ *n* a turkey *19- N NE Uls*. [unknown; Gael *pulaidh* is a borrowing from Scots]

pullion see PALLION

†pull-ling, purlaing *n* the harestail cotton-grass *la18-19*. [POU + LING[2]]

pulloch, pollach /'pʌləx, 'pulax, 'pɔləx/ *n* a small edible crab *18-19, 20- NE T*. [unknown; compare PILLER]

pulpet see PUPIT

†puls, poulse *v* **1** to strike violently; *of a bell* to toll *la16*. **2** to urge, incite *16*. [EModE *pulse*, Lat *pulsāre*]

pult, *Ork* **polt** /pʌlt; *Ork* pɔlt/ *n* a short stout person *19, 20- Ork T Uls*. [unknown]

pulter /'pultər/ *n* a rough stormy state of the sea *20- Sh*. [compare Norw dial *poltra* to bubble, well up]

pultice /'pʌltɪs/ *n* a poultice *la19-*. [Eng *poultice*]

pultrie see POUTRIE

pump[1.1], **†pomp** /pʌmp/ *n* a device used to draw water (from a well or mine) with a piston or plunger operated in a pipe or cylinder *la15-*. [MDu *pompe*]

pump[1.2] /pʌmp/ *v* to move (liquid or gas) by means of a pump *16-*. **pumped** *of a tree* affected by pumping or heart-rot, having a hollow stem or trunk *la19- NE SW*. **pumping** a disease affecting trees, a form of heart-rot which leaves the stem hollow like a pump shaft *la19-*. **†pump staff** a pump-rod *la16-17*. [see the noun]

pump[2.1] /pʌmp/ *n colloquial* a breaking of wind *19-*. [probably from the verb]

pump[2.2] /pʌmp/ *v colloquial* to break wind *19-*. [perhaps related to PUMP[1.2]]

pumpet see PUPIT

pumphal[1.1], **pumphel** /'pʌmfəl/ *n* **1** an enclosure for livestock *la17-18, 19- NE*. **2** a kind of square church pew, with a seat or bench round the inside, entered by a door or gate and with a small table in the centre *17-18, 19- NE*. [*poind fauld* (POIND[1.1])]

pumphal[1.2] /'pʌmfəl/ *v* to shut up (livestock) in an enclosure *la19- NE*. [see the noun]

pun see PUND[1]

punce[1.1], **pounce, †punse** /pʌns, pʌuns/ *n* **1** the talon of a bird of prey *16-*. **2** a light blow with the elbow or foot, a nudge, poke, thrust *19-*. [probably shortened form of PUNCHIOUN[1]]

punce[1.2] /pʌns/ *v* **1** to poke or jog with the foot or elbow (when lying in bed) *19-*. **2** to punch or kick; to strike with the knee *16-17*. [see the noun]

punch /pʌntʃ/ *n* a short, stout person or animal *la19, 20- NE*. **punchie** = PUNCH. **punchikie** = PUNCH. [unknown; perhaps shortened form of PUNSCHIOUN[2]]

punchbowl /'pʌntʃbol/ *n* a large bowl for (making and) serving punch *la18-*. **bottom of the punchbowl** a Scottish dance tune and country dance *20-*. **round about the punchbowl** a children's game *la19, 20- Uls*. [Eng *punch* an alcoholic drink made with fruit + BOWEL]

punchie, punchy /'pʌnʃi, 'pʌnʃe/ *adj of persons or animals* thickset and short *19, 20- NE*. [PUNCH]

†puncis, punsis *npl* a pulse, the beat of a person's blood *16-e17*. [ME *pous*]

punct see PINT[2.1]

pund[1], **poun, pun, powin, †pond** /pʌnd, pund, pʌun, pun, pʌn, 'pʌuən/ *n* **1** a monetary unit (originally the same value as the English pound) *la14-*. **2** a measure of weight; originally a measure varying in value according to whether the standard was the Scots Troy or TRON *15-*. **pundland, poundland** a measure of land, originally assessed at the annual value of one pound in the extent, fixed at half a ploughgate; frequently in place-names *16-19, 20- historical*. **pund Scots** a monetary unit officially abolished in 1707 *16-18, 19- historical*. [OE *pund*]

pund[2] /pʌnd/ *n* an enclosure for animals *17- Sh SW*. [ME *pund*]

pund see POIND[1.2], POUND

pundar see PUNDLER

pundfall, pund fauld see POIND[1.1]

pundie /'pʌndi, 'pʌnde/ *n* **1** a strong type of beer; liquor in general *19- NE EC Bor*. **2** a measure of beer given free to brewery workers *la20- EC Bor*. [unknown]

pundlan see POIND[1.1]

†pundlane, pundlene *n* the due payable for the release of animals impounded for trespass *la13-e16*. [POIND[1.1] + LEN[1.1]]

pundler, pundar /'pʌndlər, 'pʌndər/ *n* a large weighing beam, typically used in a steelyard *la16- Sh Ork N SW*. [ON *pundari* a steelyard]

†punge *v* to pierce, prick; to sting *15-e16*; compare PUNƷE[2]. **pungitive** hurtful, sharp, stinging *la15-16*. [Lat *pungere*; compare ME *pingen*]

Punic, †**punik**, †**punyk** /ˈpjunɪk/ *adj* **1** Carthaginian, of or relating to ancient Carthage in North Africa *16-*. **2** bright red or reddish-purple *e16*. [Lat *Pūnicus*]

punish, *N* **peenish**, †**punis**, †**puneis**, †**punisch** /ˈpʌnɪʃ; *N* ˈpinɪʃ/ *v* **1** to penalise for an offence *la14-*. **2** to stint, limit; to reduce (a stone) in size by cutting and dressing *19- N NE*. [ME *punishen*]

punkies /ˈpʌŋkiz/ *npl* a game of marbles played using three holes in the ground; the holes themselves *la19- N H&I*. [probably a variant of PLUNKIE²]

punlaw *see* POIND¹·¹

†**punsche**, **puntch** *n* a puncheon, a large cask *la16-e17*. **punschie** = PUNSCHE *la16-17*. [shortened form of PUNSCHIOUN²]

†**punschioun¹**, **punsion** *n* **1** a pointed weapon or tool *la14-e17*. **2** a punch for stamping letters; *coining* an engraved stamp used for impressing a design or figure on metal *15-17*. [ME *punchoun*]

†**punschioun²**, **punsioun** *n* a large cask *la15-17*. [EModE *poncheon*]

punse *see* PUNCE¹·¹
punsion *see* PUNSCHIOUN¹
punsioun *see* PUNSCHIOUN²
punsis *see* PUNCIS

†**punsit** *adj of metal work* embossed by hammering the under side so as to raise the surface *e16*. [PUNCE¹·² + -IT²]

punt /pʌnt/ *v* to assist someone to lift themselves to a higher position or over a wall by pushing from below *20- C*. **punt up** = PUNT. **puntie up** = PUNT. [unknown; compare Eng *punt* to kick, propel]

punt *see* POINT
puntch *see* PUNSCHE
puntell *see* POINTAL
punyk *see* PUNIC

†**punʒe¹** *n* a small number of soldiers, a small force *e16*. [ME *poine*]

†**punʒe²** *v* to pierce *la14-15*. [AN *puign-*, stem of *poindre* to prick]

pup /pʌp/ *n* a brick smaller in width and depth than usual *la20- C Bor*. [Eng *pup* a young dog]

pupil, †**pupill** /ˈpjupəl/ *n* **1** *law* a child under the legal age of puberty (12 for girls and 14 for boys), a minor *la15-*. **2** a schoolchild, a student *la16-*. †**pupillar** *law* of a minor *la16-18*. **pupillaritie** *law* the state of being a minor *la16-*. [ME *pupille*, Lat *pūpillus*, *pūpilla* an orphan, a ward]

pupil *see* PEOPLE¹·¹
pupill *see* PUPIL

pupit, **poopit**, **pulpet**, †**powpet**, †**pumpet** /ˈpupɪt, ˈpʌlpɪt/ *n* **1** *Christian Church* a pulpit, the location from which preaching takes place *15-*. **2** the poop of a ship *e16*. [ME *pulpit*, Lat *pulpitum* a scaffold, a stage]

puppie¹, **poppy** /ˈpʌpe, ˈpɔpe/ *n* **1** a young dog *15-*. **2** a doll, a puppet *17*. †**puppie play** = *puppie show la17-e18*. **puppie show** a puppet show, a Punch-and-Judy show *la18-*. **mak a puppie show o** make a fool of, make an exhibition of *19- NE C*. [MFr *poupee* a doll, a plaything]

puppie² /ˈpʌpe/ *n* the poppy *Papaver rhoeas 18- Ork WC SW Bor*. [Lat *papāver*]

†**puray**, **pure**, **pur** *n* fur; pure white miniver *15-e16*. [AN *puree*]

purchase¹·¹, †**purchas**, †**purches** /ˈpʌrtʃəs/ *n* **1** acquisition *la14-*. **2** gains, winnings *15-19*. **3** supporters, backers *15-e16*. **4** *Roman Catholic Church* a dispensation *15-e16*. **5** effort, contrivance, machination *la14-15*. †**in purches** out of wedlock *la15-e16*. †**on your purchase** by what one can get by any means, on one's own resources *la15-e19*. †**off purchas** = *in purches e15*. [ME *purchas*]

purchase¹·², †**purchas**, †**purches** /ˈpʌrtʃəs/ *v* **1** to buy *la17-*. **2** to acquire, obtain, gain possession of *la14-19, 20- Uls*. **3** to acquire land other than by inheritance *la14-17*. **4** to obtain by request or formal application *la14-17*. **5** to bring about or procure an outcome; to manage or arrange to do something *la14-e17*. **6** to raise an army; to obtain backing or support *la14-e17*. **7** to induce or prevail upon a person to do something *15-e16*. †**purches lordschip** to obtain patronage *la15-17*. [ME *purchacen*]

pure¹·¹, †**puir** /pjur/ *adj* **1** free from impurities; perfect *la14-*. **2** faultless, guiltless; chaste *la15-*. **3** *law* with no condition attached *15-e17*. **4** *Christian Church of religious doctrine* free from corruption, error or imperfection *la15-e17*. **purely 1** *law* unconditionally, absolutely *15-*. **2** *Presbyterian Church of religious doctrine* without corruption or error *la16-17*. **purely and simply** *law* unconditionally, absolutely *15-*. [ME *pur*]

pure¹·² /pjur/ *adv* absolutely, completely *20-*. **pure dead brilliant** absolutely, very good *la20-*. [see the adj]

pure *see* PUIR¹·³, PURAY

†**pureale**, **parala** *n law* a perambulation to determine boundaries *15*. [ME *purale*]

†**pured** *adj of fur* trimmed to show one colour only *16*. [participial adj of a verb *pure*, formed from either the adj PURE¹·¹ or from ME *puren*, OFr *purer*]

purfeit *see* PURFLED

†**purfell¹·¹** *n* a border (of a garment) *la15-e16*. [ME *purfil*]

†**purfell¹·²**, **purfill**, **purphal** *v* **1** to ornament with a border *la15-16*. **2** to decorate, beautify *la15-16*. [see the noun]

purfled, **purfl't**, †**purfeit** /ˈpʌrfəld, ˈpʌrfəlt/ *adj* fat and wheezing, short of breath *18-19, 20- Bor*. [unknown, perhaps from a frequentative form of PUFF¹·², with epenthetic *r*]

purge /pʌrdʒ/ *v* **1** *law* to clear (oneself or another) of the imputation of guilt (by oath or bearing witness) *15-*. **2** to cleanse; to evacuate; to remove by cleansing *la15-*. **3** *law* to eliminate the consequences of a failure to comply with some condition by complying *la16-*. **4** *Presbyterian Church* to correct or verify (the roll of communicants in a congregation) by removing the names of lapsed members *la19-*. **5** *law* to clear an offence by atonement *16-e18*. **purgation 1** the cleansing of waste material from the body; excretion; a purgative *la14-*. **2** *law* the act of clearing (oneself or another) of the imputation of guilt (by oath); an affirmation of innocence made upon oath *15-17*. **3** the cancellation of an offence by the establishment of innocence or by atonement *la16*. †**purgit of partial counsail** *of a judge or witness* cleared of the possibility of partiality, having sworn as to their impartiality *16*. [ME *purgen*]

purify /ˈpjurɪfae/ *v* **1** to rid of impurities, cleanse *la15-*. **2** *law* to fulfil (a condition), so as to bring an agreement into operation *la17-*. [ME *purifien*, MFr *purifier*]

purk *see* PORK¹

purl¹·¹, **pirl** /pʌrl, pɪrl/ *n pl* a small ball of dung, especially as excreted by sheep *18-*. **pirlag** a small ball of dung *20- Ork N*. **purlack** = *pirlag 20- T*. [unknown; compare Norn *parle*, *pirle* gritty excrement as from sheep, *purle* a small thing]

purl¹·² /pʌrl, pɪrl/ *v of animals* to defecate *19, 20- Sh*. **purling** a ball of horse dung *20- Sh Ork*. [see the noun]

purl *see* PIRL¹·²
purlack *see* PURL¹·¹
purlaing *see* PULL-LING
purlie *see* PIRLIE¹·¹
purll *see* PIRL¹·¹
purn *see* PIRN¹·¹

purphal see PURFELL[1.2]

purpie[1.1] /ˈpʌrpi/ n the colour purple *la18-19, 20- Ork NE EC*. [see the adj]

purpie[1.2] /ˈpʌrpi/ adj purple *la17-19, 20- T C*. †**purpie fever** a disease accompanied by a purplish rash, perhaps typhus *la17-e19*. [reduced form of PURPURE[1.2]]

†**purpie**[2] n a plant, probably purslane *Portulaca oleracea la15-e18*. [MFr *pourpié* purslane]

purpose[1.1], †**purpos**, †**purpois**, †**propose** /ˈpʌrpəs/ n 1 an objective, an intention; a proposition *la14-*. 2 efficiency, neatness, tidiness *la19- Ork WC Uls*. 3 a plan or design for a literary work *la14-16*. **purpose-like**, †**purposlyk** *of persons* neat, tidy, methodical, efficient *la15-*. †**bring to purpos** to bring to a conclusion, achieve success *15*. †**tak purpos** to resolve, determine *la14-16*. †**tak to purpos** = *tak purpos la14-e16*. [ME *purpos*]

purpose[1.2], †**purpos**, †**propois** /pʌrˈpoz/ v pt **purpost** to set as an objective, to intend, resolve *la14-*. [ME *purposen*]

purpose[1.3] /ˈpʌrpəs/ adj well-ordered, tidy, methodical; tidy-looking *19- Sh N NE EC Uls*. [see the noun]

purpour see PURPURE[1.1], PURPURE[1.2]

†**purpris**[1.1] n a precinct, enclosure *15*. [AN *purpris*, OFr *porpris*]

†**purpris**[1.2] v *law* to enclose or encroach upon land illegally *la15-e17*. [from the noun, also AN *purpris*, ptp of *purprendre* to seize illegally]

†**purprision**, **purprusioun** n *law* illegal enclosure of or encroachment on royal or common land *15-e19*. [MFr *porprison* enclosed land, Lat *porprensio* occupation, usurpation]

†**purpure**[1.1], **purpour** n 1 the colour purple *la15-e17*. 2 purple cloth *la14-16*. [OE *purpure*, Lat *purpura*]

†**purpure**[1.2], **purpour** adj purple *la14-17*. **purpurat** purple-coloured; splendid *la15-16*. **purpurit** purple-coloured; dressed in purple *la16-17*. [OE *purpuren*, Lat *purpureus*]

purr see PORR[1.2]

purre see PIRR[1]

purri see POORIE

purritch see PARRITCH

purry /ˈpʌre/ n a savoury dish of oatmeal brose with chopped kail stirred into it *la18-19, 20- historical*. [Fr *purée* a broth of mashed vegetables]

purse[1.1], †**purs**, †**pours** /pʌrs/ n a pouch for carrying money; the pouch and its contents *15-*. †**purs maister** a purse-bearer, a treasurer, a bursar *la15-17*. **purse mou** a cloud shaped like the opening of a purse, said to presage high wind *la19- T*. **purse penny** a coin, usually of high value, kept for luck *17-*. **purspike, purspyk** a pickpocket *16-e17, la20- T*. [ME *purs*]

†**purse**[1.2] v to put into a purse *la16-e18*. [see the noun]

pursevant see PURSUIVANT

purspike, purspyk see PURSE[1.1]

pursue, †**persew**, †**perschew** /pərˈsu/ v 1 to follow, chase *15-*. 2 *law* to seek to obtain a right or possession by legal or other action *15-*. 3 to continue in a course of action *la15-*. 4 *law* to prosecute, sue (a person) *la15-*. 5 *law* to carry on an action, prosecute a case, to claim damages *la15-*. 6 to importune or beg a person persistently for favours; to pay suit as a lover *la15-19, 20- SW*. 7 to try to attain an end *la15-16*. 8 to attack, assail, besiege *la15-17*. 9 to make one's way to a place *la15-e16*. 10 to commit (oneself) to battle *la15-e16*. [ME *purseuen*]

pursuer, †**persewar** /pərˈsuər/ 1 *law* the active party in a civil action, the plaintiff, a prosecutor *15-*. 2 a hunter; a persecutor *16-*. 3 an assailant, a besieger *la16-e17*. [ME *purseuere*]

pursuit, †**persuit**, †**persute**, †**persewt** /pərˈsut/ n 1 the action of following aggressively; a chase *la15-*. 2 *law* the action of prosecuting or bringing a suit; a prosecution *la14-18*. 3 an attack *16-17*. 4 a siege *la16-17*. 5 harassment; ill-treatment; persecution *la16-17*. [AN *pursuit, pursute*; compare AN *pursure* to pursue]

pursuivant, †**pursevant**, †**persewant**, †**pursyfant** /ˈpʌrswɪvant, ˈpʌrsɪvant/ n 1 a heraldic officer below the rank of herald, a member of the Lyon Court *15-*; compare BUTE PURSUIVANT, CARRICK PURSUIVANT, KINTYRE PURSUIVANT, SLAINS PURSUIVANT. 2 an attendant on the CORNET at the Riding of the Marches ceremony at Dumfries *20-*. 3 an attendant *e16*. [ME *pursevaunt*]

purt /pʌrt/ n mud; a quagmire *20- Sh*. [Norn *purt* stagnant pool perhaps from ON *pyttr* pool, with metathesis of *r*]

purteth see PUIRTITH

purvay see PURVEY[1.2]

purvey[1.1] /ˈpʌrve/ n the food and drink supplied for a social gathering *20- C*. [see the verb]

purvey[1.2], †**purvay**, †**provay** /pərˈve/ v to provide *la14-*. [ME *purveien*]

pus, puss /pʌs, pus/ n the mouth or face *20-*. [perhaps Gael *bus* the mouth or US *puss*, IrGael *pus*]

pus see POS

pusche see POUSS, PUSH

push, †**pouss**, †**pusche** /puʃ/ n a thrust, a prod, a blow, a stroke, a knock, a push *17-*. [from the verb POUSS]

push see POUSS

pushin see PUSHION[1.1]

pushined see PUSHIONT

pushion[1.1], **pooshin, pushin, pysen, pizen, poison**, †**pusion**, †**pusoun**, †**poysoun** /ˈpuʃən, ˈpʌɪzən, ˈpɔɪzən/ n 1 a substance capable of bringing on illness or death; a drink containing such a substance, poison *la14-*. 2 an unpleasant or detestable person or thing *la19- Sh N*. **pooshinous, pysenous** 1 poisonous *19-*. 2 unpleasant, detestable, horrible *20- Sh N EC*. **pushion berry** the woody nightshade *Solanum dulcamara la19- WC Bor*. [northern ME *puson*, ME *poisoun*]

pushion[1.2], **pysen**, †**poysoun** /ˈpuʃən, ˈpaezən/ v 1 to poison *la14-*. 2 to taint, make unpleasant, spoil; to make (food) unpalatable *la15-*. **pushionable**, †**poysounable** poisonous; corrupting; unpleasant *la15-*. [from the noun or ME *poisonen*, northern ME *puson*]

pushion[1.3], **pysen** /ˈpuʃən, ˈpaezən/ adj unpleasant, detestable, foul *19-*. [see the noun]

pushiont, pushined, pysened, pizened, †**poysonit**, †**posonit** /ˈpuʃənt, ˈpaezənt/ adj 1 affected by or imbued with poison; poisonous *16-*. 2 *of persons* unpleasant, spiteful, malicious *16-*. 3 unhealthy or unwholesome-looking, dingy, discoloured *19, 20- Bor*. 4 *of things* tending to corrupt *la16*. [participial adj from PUSHION[1.2]]

pusiance see PUISSANCE

pusion see PUSHION[1.1]

pusk see POOSK[1]

puslick /ˈpʌʃlək/ n the (dried) dung of cattle or sheep *19, 20- N NE*. [unknown]

pusoun see PUSHION[1.1]

puss, †**pouse** /pus/ n 1 (a call to) a cat *la17-*. 2 a hare *la18-19, 20- NE Uls*. [EModE *pus, pusse*]

puss see PUS

pussant see PUISSANT

pussy, poussie, poosie /ˈpusi, ˈpuse/ n 1 (a call to) a cat *la18-*. 2 a hare *la18-19*. **pussy-baudrons** an affectionate name for a cat *la19-*. [PUSS + diminutive suffix]

pussy-knuckle see POOSIE KNUCKLE

put see PIT², PUTT¹·², PUTT²
putch see POOCH¹·¹
put doun see PIT²
puther, †**peuther**, †**pewter** /ˈpuθər/ v 1 to fuss about achieving nothing, to make a great show of working *19- Ork T Uls*. 2 to importune in a fussy and ingratiating way, to bustle about trying to win favour; to canvass for votes using flattery *18-19, 20- Ork*. [unknown]
puther see POODER¹·¹
put off see PIT²
put out see PIT²
put over see PIT²
putt¹·¹ /pʌt/ n 1 *golf* the tapping stroke used to move the ball across the green and into the hole *18-*. 2 the thrusting movement by which a putting stane or weight is propelled *19-*. 3 a (gentle) touch or push; a butt from an animal; the recoil from a gun *15-19, 20- Sh NE SW*. **mak yer putt guid** to succeed in a venture, gain one's object *la17-19, 20- WC SW Bor*. **putt an row** with utmost endeavour *la18-19, 20- Sh NE SW*. [see the verb]
putt¹·², **put** /pʌt/ v 1 *games* to throw a stone or heavy metal ball *la16-*. 2 *golf* to strike the ball on the green with a tapping stroke *la17-*. 3 to push, shove, thrust; to nudge, prod; *of an animal* to butt with the head or horns, *15-19, 20- Sh Ork NE*. 4 to pulsate, throb *la19, 20- Bor*. [variant of PIT², differentiated by pronunciation and in modern Scots by the regular use of the weak conjugation, e.g. *puttit* versus *pat*; compare Norn *putt* push, nudge]
putt², **put** /pʌt/ n 1 a jetty or stone buttress projecting from a river bank, used to alter the current or protect the bank *la17- Bor*. 2 a piece of masonry supporting a wall, a buttress *16-e19*. 3 a buttress of a bridge *e17*. **putt stone** a copingstone *la19- Ork N NE EC*; compare PEAT STANE. [unknown]
puttar see PUTTER
putten see PIT²
putten till /ˈpʌtən tɪl/ adj in difficulties *la18-*. Compare PITTEN TAE. [ppl adj from PUTT¹·² + TILL²·¹]
putter, †**puttar** /ˈpʌtər/ n 1 *in athletics* a person who putts a stone *la16-*. 2 *mining* a person whose job it is to push a loaded hutch from the coalface to the pit bottom *la18-*. 3 *golf* the club used for putting *18-*. 4 *golf* a person who putts *19-*. **driving putter** see DRIVE¹·². [PUTT¹·² + agent suffix]
putting /ˈpʌtɪŋ/ n 1 the action of tapping a golf-ball with a light stroke (towards the hole) *la16-*. 2 a game played with a golf ball and putter over (usually) eighteen very short holes *la19-*. **putting cleek** a cleek used for putting *la19-*. **putting club** a putter *la17*. **putting green** 1 the area of close-cut turf surrounding the hole on a golf course *19-*. 2 a series of short holes used for putting practice or for recreational putting *la19-*. †**puttin' stane** *games* a heavy stone thrown as part of a contest *la18-19*. [verbal noun from PUTT¹·²]
put to see PIT²
puttock /ˈpʌtək/ n the buzzard *Buteo buteo la19- SW*. [Eng *puttock* red kite or buzzard]
put up see PIT²
†**py, pie** n the magpie *16*. [ME *pi*, OFr *pie*]
py see PEY¹·², PIE¹
pyag /pjɑg/ v to work laboriously; to move painfully *la19- Sh*. [Norn *pjag*]
pyat see PYET¹·¹, PYET¹·²

pyauvie, piaavie /ˈpjɔvi, ˈpjavi/ n an attack of sickness or faintness, a fit of nausea *20- N NE*. [N form of PAW¹·¹ with extension of meaning]
pyauvin, piaavan /ˈpjɔvɪn, ˈpjavɪn/ adj sickly, ailing; suffering from heat *20- N NE*. [verbal noun from otherwise unattested verb]
pye, pie /pae/ n *in children's games* a counting out rhyme *la20-*. **count a pye** see COONT¹·². [unknown]
pye see PEY¹·²
pyet¹·¹, **pyot**, **pyat**, †**piet** /ˈpaeət/ n 1 the magpie *Pica pica la14-*. 2 a nickname for a person, sometimes applied to a family or social group *la14-*. 3 *contemptuous* a chattering, irresponsible person *la18-*; compare *tale pyet* (TALE) and *tell piet* (TELL). 4 a bird with black and white plumage *19-*; compare *sea pyet* (SEA) and *water pyet* (WATTER¹·¹). 5 a piebald horse *la17-19, 20- NE EC*. 6 a farmhand who stands on a corn stack and passes the sheaves from the forker to the builder *la19- NE*. [ME *piot* a magpie; a chattering woman, OFr *piot* a young magpie]
pyet¹·², **pyot**, †**pyat**, †**piet** /ˈpaeət/ adj 1 marked with more than one colour; *of a horse* piebald *16-*. 2 *of speech* loud, empty, voluble *la16-*. [PY, + adj-forming suffix]
pyke see PICK¹·², PIKE¹·¹, PIKE², PIKE⁴
pykky see PICK⁵·¹
pykthank see PIKE-THANK¹·¹
pyle /pʌɪl/ v to steer, pilot; to direct (a person) *la19- Sh*. [perhaps shortened form of Eng *pilot*]
pyle see PILE⁴
pyler see PILLAR
pyllit see PILD
pynd see PINE¹·²
pyne see PINE¹·¹
pynit see PINE¹·²
pynour see PINER²
pynt see PINT¹, PINT²·¹, PINT²·²
pyocher, *Uls* **peucher** /ˈpjɔxer; *Uls* ˈpjuxər/ v 1 to cough asthmatically or chokingly *20- Sh NE T Bor Uls*; compare PEUCHLE, PEUCHER. 2 to puff, pant *20- Sh NE T*. 3 to fuss, work ineffectually *20- Sh NE*. [onomatopoeic]
pyock see POKE¹·¹
pyogie /ˈpjogi/ n a short, fat person *19- Sh*. [Norn *pjogi* a small, insignificant person]
pyot see PYET¹·¹, PYET¹·²
pyow /pjʌu/ n an unpleasant, domineering woman; a self-important woman *20- N NE*. [unknown]
pyowl see PEWL¹·²
pype see PEEP³, PIPE¹·¹
pyppar see PIPER
pyrne satine see PIRN¹·¹
pysen see PUSHION¹·¹, PUSHION¹·², PUSHION¹·³
pysened see PUSHIONT
†**pystle, pistill** n 1 a letter *la15-18*. 2 a letter from an apostle, a New Testament epistle *la14-e16*. [OE *pistol*, aphetic form of OFr *epistle*]
pythoness, †**pithonesse**, †**phitones**, †**fetonas** /paeθəˈnɛs/ n a female soothsayer, a witch *la14-*. [MFr *pythonisse*]
pyuff girse see PLUFF GRASS

Q

qua *see* QUAW, TWA
quaa *see* QUAW
quach *see* QUAICH
quack[1.1], *Ork* **whaak**, †**quaick**, †**quake** /kwak; *Ork* ʍak/ *n* **1** the noise made by a duck *la18-*. **2** a stammer, a stutter *20- Ork*. [onomatopoeic]
quack[1.2], *Sh* **whaak**, *NE* **quake**, †**quaik** /kwak; *Sh* ʍak; *NE* kwek/ *v* to make the characteristic quacking noise of a duck *19-*. [see the noun]
quack[1.3], †**quaick** /kwak/ *interj* the noise made by a duck *16-*. [see the noun]
quack[2] /kwak/ *n* a moment *la19- Ork*. [imitative of a short sharp sound]
quack[3], **quag**, *Ork* **kwak**, †**quaig** /kwak, kwag; *Ork* kwak/ *n* **1** a quagmire; a marshy or boggy place *la16-*. **2** a seething mass, an infestation *20- Ork*. [unknown; compare Eng *quag*]
quackie /ˈkwaki, ˈkwake/ *n* a duck *19, 20- NE EC Bor*. [QUACK[1.2] + -IE[3]]
quad *see* QUED
quader /ˈkwɔdər/ *v* **1** to make square, quadrate *19- NE*. **2** to correspond, agree *16, 19- NE*. [Lat *quadrāre*]
quadrant /ˈkwɔdrənt/ *n* **1** an instrument for making angular measurements *la15-*. **2** a farthing *15-e17*. [ME *quadrant*]
quadriennium utile /kwɔdrienɪəm ˈjutʌɪl/ *n law* the first four years of a person's majority (from age 21 to 25) during which acts done during their minority could be revoked *la17-20, 21- historical*. [Lat *quadriennium ūtile* the useful period of four years]
†**quadrulapse**, **quadrilapse** *n Presbyterian Church* a fourth offence against church discipline *17-19*. [Lat *quadru-* four- + Eng *lapse*; compare DULAPSE]
†**quadruplat** *adj music* quadruple; based on a ratio of 1:4 *la15*. [Lat *quadruplāt-*, ptp stem of *quadruplāre* to multiply by four]
quadruple /kwɔˈdrupəl/ *v* to multiply by four *la14-*. [MFr *quadrupler*, Lat *quadruplāre*]
quadruply[1.1] /ˈkwɔdrəplae/ *n law* a fourth answer, made by the defender in reply to the TRIPLY of the pursuer *17-*. [see the verb]
†**quadruply**[1.2] *v law* to answer a fourth time *16-e18*. [MFr *quadrupliquer*, Lat *quadruplāre*; compare DUPLY[1.2]]
quaeit *see* QUAIT[1.4]
quaestor, †**questor** /ˈkwɪstər/ *n in St Andrews University and Glasgow University* the chief financial officer of the University, the University Treasurer *16-*. [Lat *quaestor* one of the financial officers of the Roman state]
quaet *see* QUAIT[1.1], QUAIT[1.3]
quafe *see* QUEFF
quag *see* CAG, QUACK[3]
quaich, †**quach**, †**queich**, †**queff** /kwex/ *n* a shallow, bowl-shaped (silver or wooden) drinking cup, with two ears or handles *16-*. [Gael, IrGael *cuach* a cup, a bowl]
quaick *see* QUACK[1.1], QUACK[1.3], QUEY
quaid *see* QUED
quaif *see* QUEFF
quaig *see* QUACK[3], QUEY
†**quaik**, **quak** *n* an inarticulate cry *la15-e16*. [perhaps related to QUACK[1.3]]
quaik *see* QUACK[1.2], QUAK, WHEEK[1.1]
quail, †**quaill**, †**quailʒe**, †**qualʒe** /kwel/ *n* **1** a small game bird of the family *Phasianidae*, similar to a partridge *15-*. **2** the corncrake *Crex crex la15*. [ME *quail*]
quail *see* QUALL[1.2]
quailʒe *see* QUAIL
quaint, *Ork* **whint**, **quint**, †**quent**, †**quaynt** /kwent; *Ork* ʍɪnt; *Ork* kwɪnt/ *adj* **1** strange, unfamiliar; odd, curious; weird, uncanny; old-fashioned *15-*. **2** crafty, cunning, sly; subtle, insidious *16-e17, 20- Ork*. **3** *of the senses* keen, sharp *20- Ork*. **4** clever, ingenious, skilfully made; beautiful *la15-16*. **5** valiant, brave *e15*. [AN *queint, quaint*]
quair, †**quare** /kwer/ *n* **1** a literary work, a writing or treatise *la15-19, 20- literary*. **2** a quire, a number of sheets of paper *la15-19*. **3** an unbound gathering of pages; notes or a notebook *16-e18*. [ME *quaier*]
†**quaird**, **querd**, **quear** *n* a stage in the rotation of crops; a division of the infield land on a farm, used for crop rotation *la16-18*. [perhaps altered form of Eng *quart* a quarter, as sometimes the infield was divided into four parts for manuring; but compare also Gael *cuiart* a cycle, a round]
quaisteen *see* QUESTION
quait[1.1], **quaet**, **quate**, **quiet**, †**quyet**, †**quyt** /ˈkweət, kwet, ˈkwaeət/ *n* **1** peace, absence of strife *la14-*. **2** peacefulness, quietness, repose, peace of mind *15-*. **3** privacy, seclusion *16-e17*. **4** a person who brings solace *e16*. †**at quiet** at peace *16-19*. †**in quiet** = *at quiet la14-16*. [see the adj]
quait[1.2], **quate**, **quiet**, †**quyet** /ˈkweət, kwet, ˈkwaeət/ *v* to quieten, pacify; to keep quiet *la16-*. [see the adj]
quait[1.3], **quaet**, **quate**, **quiet**, *Sh Ork* **whiet**, †**quyet**, †**quiete** /ˈkweət, kwet, ˈkwaeət/ *Sh Ork* ˈʍʌɪət/ *adj* **1** peaceful, inactive, unaggressive *la15-*. **2** secret, private *16-*. **3** remote, secluded *16-*. **4** *of weather* windless, still, calm *la16-*. **5** modest in numbers or cost *16-17*. **quaitlike** in a quiet fashion *la15-*. **quiet as pussy** in a quiet, tranquil way *19-*. **quait wi ye!** a command for silence *la19-*. [ME *quiet*]
quait[1.4], **quaeit**, **quate**, **quiet**, †**quyet** /ˈkweət, kwet, ˈkwaeət/ *adv* stealthily; unobtrusively *la16-*. [see the adj]
quak, *Sh* **whaak**, *Ork* **whack**, †**quaik** /kwak; *Sh Ork* ʍak/ *v pt also* †**quouk**, †**quoik**, †**qwoyk**, †**quuik** **1** to shake or tremble; to shiver *la14-*. **2** to swarm; to be infested with vermin *20- Ork*. **quakin aish** the aspen *Populus tremula la18-*. **quakin bog** a quagmire *la19-*. †**quack esp**, **quaik asp** the aspen *17-e18*. †**qaukin esp**, **quakin asp** the aspen *16-19*. **quakkin moss** a quagmire *la19-*. **quakin qua**, **quakin qua**, **quaakin qua** a quagmire *19- C SW Uls*. **quakin trei** the aspen *20- Bor*. [OE *cwacian*]
quak *see* QUAIK
quake *see* QUACK[1.1], QUACK[1.2], WHEEK[1.1]
qual *see* TWAL
qualefeit *see* QUALIFIED
quali *see* QUALLIE
qualife *see* QUALIFY
†**qualificate** *adj* suitably qualified, circumscribed by appropriate reservations *17-e18*. [Lat *quālificātus*]
qualified, †**qualefeit** /ˈkwɔləfaed/ *adj* **1** possessed of the required skill, capable, competent; suitable *16-*. **2** *of a statement or oath* modified by additions or reservations *la17*. **qualified chapel** an Episcopalian place of worship whose

members had renounced allegiance to the Jacobite monarchy *la19- historical*. †**qualified-meeting-house** = *qualified chapel e18*. **qualified oath** *law* an oath modified by reservations or relevant additions *la17-e19*. [ptp of QUALIFY]

qualify, †**qualefie,** †**qualife** /'kwɔləfae/ *v* **1** to modify, limit; to specify or define *la16-*. **2** *law* to substantiate, establish a claim, accusation or argument *16-*. **3** to pass the *qualifying examination* for admission to secondary education *20, 21- historical*. **4** *of a person* to achieve the necessary skills or qualifications for a particular trade, profession or other office; to fulfil conditions to be eligible (for something) *la17-*. **5** to acquire or give legal sanction to by the taking or administration of an oath (in regard to the Scottish Episcopalians); to swear allegiance *18*. **qualifying examination** = QUALLIE *20, 21- historical*. [EModE *qualify*]

quality[1.1], *Sh Ork* **whality,** †**qualite,** †**qualitee** /'kwɔləti; *Sh Ork* 'mɔləti/ *n* **1** a desirable attribute; excellence of character; a positive characteristic *15-*. **2** an outstanding or exceptional thing *la20-*. **3** *law* a proviso or qualification *17-18*. **4** high social standing *15-e19*. [ME *qualite*]

quality[1.2] /'kwɔləti/ *adj* good, excellent *la20-*. [see the noun]

quall[1.1], *Sh* **kwal** /kwɔl; *Sh* kwal/ *n* a lull in wind or weather *20- Sh NE*. [see the verb]

quall[1.2], **quail** /kwɔl, kwel/ *v* **1** to decline, fail or become feeble *la16-*. **2** *of wind or weather* to abate or become calm *19, 20- Sh NE*. [altered form of QUELL]

quallie, quali /'kwɔle, 'kwɔli/ *n* an examination at the end of primary education which decided which type of secondary education pupils should attend *la20, 21- historical*. **quallie dance** a party for pupils in their last year at primary school *la20-*. [shortened form of *qualifying examination* (QUALIFY)]

†**qualm, quhalm, qwalm** *n* **1** mortality, pestilence *e15*. **2** disaster, calamity *e16*. [OE *cwealm*]

qualʒe *see* QUAIL

quam *see* WHAM[4]

quantity, †**quantitie,** †**quantete** /'kwɔntəti/ *n* **1** amount *la14-*. **2** a number or numbers *la14-*. **3** size, dimensions *la14-17*. **4** value, worth *la16-e17*. [ME *quantite*, Lat *quantitās*]

quare *see* QUAIR

quarel *see* QUARREL[3]

quark *see* KWARK[1.1]

quarnat *see* CORNET

†**quarnell, quernell** *n* a corner *16*. **quernallit, quarnelt** squared; having corners *16-e19*. [perhaps ME *cornel* a corner, angle; compare KIRNELL]

quarrel[1], †**quarrell,** †**querrell,** †**correll** /'kwɔrəl/ *n* **1** a stone-quarry *14-19, 20- T SW*. **2** the stone or coal taken from a quarry *15-19, 20- N NE T*. †**quarrell coall** coal from an open-cast working; outcrop coal *17*. †**querrel heuch** = *quarell hole e17*. †**quarell hole** a quarry, a pit or excavation resulting from quarrying *16-e19*. †**quarrell mell** a large sledgehammer used in quarries *16-17*. †**quarrell pick** a pickaxe *16-17*. [OFr *quarriere*]

quarrel[2.1], *Sh* **wharl,** †**querrell** /'kwɔrəl; *Sh* мarl/ *n* a (cause for) complaint, a dispute; a state of enmity, feud *15-*. **2** *law* a complaint, charge, accusation, legal plea *15-17*. [ME *querele*]

quarrel[2.2], *Sh* **wharl,** †**querel** /'kwɔrəl; *Sh* мarl/ *v* **1** to dispute with a person; to engage in a quarrel with (someone) *la16-*. **2** to dispute (a fact or claim); to challenge the truth or validity of; to take objection to *la16-*. **3** to find fault with (a person); to reprove, rebuke, abuse *la16-*. †**quarrellable** disputable *17*. [from the noun and ME *querelen*, EModE *quarrell*]

quarrel[3], †**quarrell,** †**quarel,** †**querral** /'kwɔrəl/ *n* a crossbow bolt or arrow *16-*. [ME *quarrel*]

quarrew, quarrey, quarroue *see* QUARRY

quarrour *see* QUEREOUR

quarry, *Sh Ork* **wharry,** †**quarrey,** †**quarroue,** †**quarrew** /'kwɔri; *Sh Ork* 'мɔri/ *n* a surface excavation where stone is or has formerly been extracted *la16-*. **quarry hole** a quarry, a pit or excavation resulting from quarrying *16-*. †**quarry mell** a sledgehammer *la17-e18*. **wharry pick** a pickaxe *20- Sh*. [ME *quarrei*]

quart /kwɔrt/ *n* **1** a measure of capacity, a quarter of a gallon; a vessel with the capacity of a quart *la15-*. **2** the fourth part of the great tithes *e17*. [ME *quart*]

quartar *see* QUARTER[1.1]

quarten /'kwɔrtən/ *n* a quarter (of something) *la18-20, 21- historical*. **quarten loaf** a quartern loaf, a four-pound loaf *la18-*. [AN *quartron*]

quarter[1.1], *Sh* **wharter,** *NE* **corter,** †**quartar** /'kwɔrtər; *Sh* 'мartər; *NE* 'kɔrtər/ *n* **1** a fourth part (of something) *la14-*. **2** a fourth part of a territory, estate or tract of land; frequently in place-names *la14-*. **3** the fourth part of a year; a school term or rental term *15-*. **4** a locality, a district *16-*. **5** accommodation, originally for troops *la17-*. **6** the fourth part of a round of oatcakes or scones *la18-*. **7** a quarter-pound *la19-*. **8** one of the areas into which burghs and parishes were divided for administrative purposes *16-19*. **9** the assembling for military service according to district *16*. **quarterly** *n* an examination held at the end of a school term *18-20, 21- historical*. **quarterly** *adj* **1** produced or occurring every quarter of a year *la16-*. **2** *heraldry* arranged in the four divisions of a heraldic shield; placed in diagonally opposite quarters of a shield or standard *la15-e17*. **quarterly** *adv* **1** every quarter, once a quarter *16-*. **2** by or through each quarter (of a town) *16-e17*. †**quarter caik** *in Paisley and Kirkcudbright* a quarter of a round loaf of bread *la16-17*. **quarterland** land equivalent to a quarter of a unit of land-measurement, such as the davach or ploughgate *la16-19, 20- historical*. **quarterman 1** a farmworker who does miscellaneous jobs and errands *la19- EC*. **2** *in Shetland* a pauper, housed in turn by people in a district *20- historical*. **quartermaster, quartermaister 1** a ship's officer below the rank of skipper or mate *16-*. **2** a military officer charged with arranging the billeting and supplying of troops *17-*. **3** an official of a trade incorporation appointed to assist the deacon *la16-e18*. **4** an official in a burgh, a person appointed to have charge of one of the subdivisions of the burgh *la15-17*. **quarter-moon** the crescent moon *17-*. †**quarter pennies** the sum of money contributed per quarter by each member of an incorporated trade *18-19*. **quarter seal,** †**quarter sele** a Chancery seal (consisting of a replica of the upper half of the great seal, obverse and reverse) *la15-*. †**Quarter sessions** *law* a court of review and appeal held quarterly by the Justices of the Peace *17-19*. **quarter-sponge** the first stage of breadmaking in which a quarter of the water required has been used *20-*. **quarter-wife** *in Shetland* a female pauper, housed in turn by people in a district *la19- historical*. [ME *quarter*]

quarter[1.2], *Sh* **wharter** /'kwɔrtər; *Sh* 'мartər/ *v* **1** to cut the body of a person (such an executed criminal) into quarters *15-*. **2** to provide accommodation; to billet troops; to lodge *17-*. **3** to subdivide (a burgh or piece of land) into quarters or parts *la15-16*. **quarterer 1** a poor person who is given temporary lodgings by way of charity *19, 20- historical*. **2** one who provides accommodation for troops *la17*. [from the noun and ME *quarteren*]

quasi-delict /'kwezae 'dilɪkt/ *n law* an act of negligence not motivated by criminal intent but making a person liable to an action for damages *19-*. [Lat *quasi* almost + Lat *dēlictum* an offence, a petty crime; compare DELICT]

quastion *see* QUESTION

quat, quet, †**quate** /kwat, kwɛt/ *v* **1** to cease, desist or stop *la18-*. **2** to leave or forsake; to give up or release *17-19, 20- C SW Uls*. **3** to repay *la16-19*. Compare QUIT. **quattin time** time to stop work, the end of the working day *19- WC SW*. [new formation from pt of QUIT]

quat *see* QUIT[1.1], QUIT[1.2], WHIT[1.3]

quate *see* QUAIT[1.1], QUAIT[1.2], QUAIT[1.3], QUAIT[1.4], QUAT, QUIT[1.1]

†**quatorzeim, quatorziem** *n* a quatorzain, a fourteen-line piece of verse *17-e18*. [Fr *quatorzaine* a group of fourteen items, possibly influenced by *quatorzième* fourteenth]

†**quaver, quavyr, caver** *n* a quiver, a case for arrows *16-17*. [variant of Eng *quiver*]

quaw, qua, †**quaa** /kwɔ/ *n* a bog, a quagmire *15-*. [unknown; compare QUACK[3], first element of EModE *quallmire*]

quay *see* COME[1.2], QUOY

quayf *see* QUEFF

quaynt *see* QUAINT

quayntis *see* QUENTIS

queak /kwik/ *v* to make a weak, squeaking noise; to cheep *la19, 20- NE*. [onomatopoeic]

quean *see* QUINE

quear *see* QUAIRD

†**qued, quaid, quad** *adj* vile, bad *16-19*. [OE *cwēad* dung; compare OFris *quád* dung, vile]

queef /kwif/ *n* a trick, a sleight of hand *20- NE Bor*. [unknown]

queel, *Sh* **kjöl,** †**cule** /kwil; *Sh* kjøl/ *n* a cooling, a chill; a cool breeze *la16-19, 20- Sh NE*. [OE *cōl*]

queel *see* CUIL

queem[1.1] /kwim/ *v* **1** to join or fit closely *e16, 19- WC*. **2** to smooth out *20- WC*. [OE *cwēman* to please, satisfy]

†**queem**[1.2], **queme, quim,** *adj* **1** close- or well-fitting, snug, neat *16-19*. **2** friendly, intimate *la17-19*. **3** quiet, still *la14-e16*. **4** fitting, suitable, right *la14*. **quemful** pleasant, agreeable *la14*. [OE *cwēme* pleasing, satisfying]

queem[1.3] /kwim/ *adv* **1** smoothly *la19, 20- SW*. **2** fittingly; so as to fit snugly *la14-e18*. [see the adj]

queen, *Sh* **wheen,** †**quene,** †**quein,** †**queyn** /kwin; *Sh* ʍin/ *n* **1** a female monarch; the wife or consort of a king *la14-*. **2** a woman of pre-eminent rank or status, originally especially the Virgin Mary; a chief female character (in a festival) *la14-*. **3** something supreme or pre-eminent in its class or kind *la14-*. †**queneist** a partisan of Mary, Queen of Scots *la16*. **Queen Anne** a long-barrelled, large-bore flintlock musket *19-*. **queen's cake** a queen cake, a white, sweet cake *19, 20- Ork*. **queen's chair** a method of carrying a girl seated on the crossed and joined arms of two bearers *20- Ork NE EC Bor*. **Queen Mary** a girls' ring dance accompanied by a song beginning with these words *la19-*. **Queen's and Lord Treasurer's Remembrancer** the general administrator of Crown revenues in Scotland *19-*. †**quene of the Canongait** the nickname of a local character *e16*. **Queen of the South 1** a nickname for the town of Dumfries *la19-*. **2** a football team that plays in Dumfries *20-*. **3** the schoolgirl chosen as the festive queen of the Riding of the Marches *20-*. **queen o the meeda** meadowsweet *Filipendula ulmaria 19-*; compare *meedie-queen* (MEEDIE). **The Queen's Own Cameron Highlanders** the name given by Queen Victoria in 1881 to the regiment originally raised in 1793 as the 79th or Cameronian Volunteers *la19-20, 21- historical*. **Queen's Own Highlander** a soldier in the *Queen's Own Highlanders (Seaforth and Camerons) la20-*. **Queen's Own Highlanders (Seaforth and Camerons)** the regiment formed in 1961 by the amalgamation of the Seaforth Highlanders and *The Queen's Own Cameron Highlanders la20-*. [OE *cwēn*; compare QUINE]

queeple /ˈkwipəl/ *v* to peep; to quack in a squeaking high-pitched tone like a duckling *la19- NE T*. [onomatopoeic; compare WHEEPLE[1.2]]

queer[1.1], *Sh Ork* **wheer,** †**queir,** †**qweir** /kwir; *Sh Ork* ʍir/ *adj* **1** strange, peculiar, odd, untrustworthy *16-*. **2** considerable, very great; of a large quantity or number *20-*. **3** amusing, funny, entertaining *la18-e19*. **queerways** in not quite a normal state, slightly unwell *19- Ork C SW*. **queery** *n* an oddity, a queer thing or person *19- T C*. **queery** *adj* rather strange, somewhat odd *la19- T*. **a queer lot** a large amount, a considerable quantity *20-*. [unknown]

queer[1.2] /kwir/ *adv* in an odd or peculiar manner; very *la19-*. [unknown]

queer *see* QUEIR

queerachin *see* KEEROCH[1.2]

queerin *see* QUERN

queeriosity *see* KEERIOSITY

queern *see* QUERN

queeroch *see* KEEROCH[1.1]

queesitive, †**quesitiue** /ˈkwisətɪv/ *adj* inquisitive *la16, la19- Sh NE T*. [aphetic form of Eng *inquisitve*]

queet, †**coot** /kwit/ *n* the guillemot *Uria aalge la17- NE*. [ME *cote*; compare Du *koet*]

queet *see* CUIT

queeth *see* CUITHE

queetikins *see* CUITIKINS

queff, †**quaif,** †**quayf,** †**quafe** /kwɛf/ *n* a close-fitting cap *15-19, 20- NE*. [OFr *coife*]

queff, queich *see* QUAICH

quein *see* QUEEN

queir, quhair, choir, *Sh* **whire,** *NE* **kire,** *Bor* **queer,** †**quere,** †**quire** /kwer, kwaer; *Sh* ʍaer; *NE* kaer; *Bor* kwir/ *n* **1** the chancel of a church, the part of a church building eastward of the nave, originally used by the singers *la14-*. **2** a body of singers, originally in a church *15-*. **3** (part of) the ruins of a pre-Reformation church *19-*. **4** the body of clergy of a cathedral or collegiate church *15-e19*. [ME *quer*]

queir *see* QUEER[1.1]

queirn *see* QUERN

†**queith** *n* a speech (in honour of a dead person) *e16*. [ME *queth*]

quek *see* QUICK[1.2]

quel *see* TWAL

quell, †**qwel** /kwɛl/ *v* **1** to overcome, suppress or crush; to oppress *la15-*. **2** to kill *la14-16*. **3** to knock down or strike *16*. †**quelling** killing, slaughter *e16*. [OE *cwellan*]

queme, quemful *see* QUEEM[1.2]

quene *see* QUEEN, QUINE

quenry *see* QUINE

quenster *see* CUN

†**quent** *adj* well acquainted, familiar *e16*. [aphetic form of *acquent* (ACQUANT[1.2])]

quent *see* QUAINT

†**quentance, quyntans** *n* **1** acquaintance, familiarity, personal knowledge *la14-e17*. **2** people with whom one is acquainted *la14-e17*. [aphetic form of Eng *acquaintance*]

†**quentis, quayntis, qwyntis** *n* **1** cunning; cleverness; a skill, a device, a trick *la14-15*. **2** a coat of arms, a heraldic device by which a person could be recognized *la14-e15*. [ME *queintis*, AN *queintise*; compare QUAINT]

querche *see* CURCH

querd *see* QUAIRD

quere *see* QUEIR

querel *see* QUARREL[2.2]

†**quereour, quarrour, qwarear** *n* a quarrier, a person who quarries stone *la14-17*. [ME *quarriour*]
querious *see* KEERIOUS
quern, kwern, *NE* **queern, queerin,** †**queirn,** †**curn,** †**kewrne** /kwɛrn; *NE* kwirn; *NE* ˈkwirɪn/ *n* **1** a hand-mill (for grinding corn, oats, pepper and snuff) *16-*. **2** the stomach or gizzard of a fowl *19- N NE*. [OE *cweorn*]
quern *see* CURN[1]
quernell *see* QUARNELL
querral *see* QUARREL[3]
querrell *see* QUARREL[1], QUARREL[2.1]
†**quert** *adj* alive and well; in good health *la14-15*. **querty** vivacious, active, in good spirits; full of fun or mischief *la18-19*. **in quert** alive and well; in good health *15-e16*. **with quert** = *in quert la16*. [ME *quert*; compare ON *kyrt*, variant of *kyrr*, quiet, at rest]
quesitiue *see* QUEESITIVE
question, quaisteen, queystion, *Sh* **whestin,** †**quastion** /ˈkwɛstʃən, ˈkwɛstɪn, ˈkwɛstʃən/ *Sh* ˈʍɛstɪn/ *n* **1** investigation, inquiry into a matter; uncertainty; a (legal) dispute, litigation *la14-*. **2** a query; a problem or issue (requiring an answer) *15-*. **3** *Presbyterian Church pl* (the questions and answers making up) the Shorter Catechism *la17-*. **4** an expression of doubt or wonder *20- WC SW Bor*. **questionable,** †**questionabill** open to dispute or litigation *15-*. †**question book** the Shorter Catechism *18-19*. †**questionarie tryall** *Presbyterian Church* an oral examination undergone by a candidate for the ministry in the North-East and Perthshire *la17*. [ME *questioun*]
questor *see* QUAESTOR
quet *see* QUAT
quetance *see* QUITTANCE
†**quething-word** *n* a farewell speech to one who has died *e16*. [verbal noun from ME *quethen* to speak + WORD[1]]
quey, *Sh* **whaig,** *Sh* **quaig,** *Ork* **why,** *NE* **quaick,** †**quy,** †**quoy,** †**koy** /kwae, kwe; *Sh* ʍeg; *Sh* kweg; *Ork* ʍae; *NE* kwek/ *n* a heifer *15-*. **queyock,** *Sh* **quoyach,** †**quyok,** †**quoyok,** †**quyach** a heifer *la15-*. [ON *kvíga*]
queyn *see* QUEEN, QUINE
queyock *see* QUEY
queystion *see* QUESTION
quha *see* WHA
quhail, quhaill *see* WHAAL
quhaip *see* WHAUP[1.1]
quhair *see* QUEIR, WHAUR[1.1], WHAUR[1.2]
quhais *see* WHASE
quhale *see* WHAAL
quhalm *see* QUALM
quhalp *see* WHALP[1.1]
quham *see* WHAM[4]
quhame *see* WHAM[1]
quhan *see* WHAN[1.1], WHAN[1.2]
quhang *see* WHANG[1.1]
quhap *see* WHAUP[3]
quhape *see* WHAUP[1.1]
quhar *see* WHAUR[1.2]
quhare *see* WHAUR[1.1], WHAUR[1.2]
quhasa *see* WHA
quhase *see* WHASE
quhasill *see* WEASEL
quhat *see* WHIT[1.1], WHIT[1.2], WHIT[1.3], WHIT[1.4]
quhattin *see* WHATTEN
quhawme *see* WHAM[1]
quhawpe *see* WHAUP[1.1]
quhay *see* WHA, WHEY
quhayng *see* WHANG[1.1]

quhedir *see* WHIDDER[1.2]
quheil *see* WHEEL[1.1], WHEEL[1.2]
quheip *see* WHUP[1.2]
quheit *see* WHEAT, WHEET
quhele *see* WHEEL[1.1], WHEEL[1.2]
quhelm *see* FOLM[1.2]
quhelp *see* WHALP[1.1]
quhen *see* WHAN[1.1], WHAN[1.2]
quhence *see* WHENCE[1.1], WHENCE[1.2]
quhene *see* WHEEN[1.1], WHEEN[1.2]
quhens *see* WHENCE[1.1], WHENCE[1.2]
quhere *see* WHAUR[1.1]
quhet *see* WHAT, WHET
quhete *see* WHEAT
quhete brede *see* WHITE BREID
quhether *see* WHITHER[2], WHIDDER[1.2]
quhethir *see* WHITHER[1.1], WHITHER[1.2]
quhetstane *see* WHET
quhew *see* WHEUGH, WHEW
quhey *see* WHEY
quheyne *see* WHEEN[1.1]
quhi *see* WHY[1.2]
quhich *see* WHILK[3.1], WHILK[3.2]
quhidder *see* WHITHER[2], WHIDDER[1.1], WHIDDER[1.2]
quhigg *see* WHIG[3]
†**quhile, quhill, quhyle** *adv* **1** at times *la14-16*. **2** for a time, temporarily, meanwhile *la14-e16*. **3** formerly, once, before *la14-15*. [OE *hwīle*]
quhile *see* WHILE[1.1], WHILE[1.2]
quhilis *see* WHILES[1.1], WHILES[1.2]
quhilk *see* WHILK[3.1], WHILK[3.2]
quhill *see* WHILE[1.1], WHILE[1.2], WHILE[1.3], QUHILE
†**quhillylillie, quhillelille, quhillie lillie** *n* **1** the penis *e16*. **2** an attack of sickness, a spasm *e16*. Compare WHILLILU. [unknown]
quhilom *see* WHILOM[1.1], WHILOM[1.2]
quhilum *see* WHILOM[1.1], WHILOM[1.2]
quhimper *see* WHIMPER[1.2]
quhin *see* WHIN[1], WHIN[2]
quhingar *see* WHINGER
quhinge *see* WHINGE[1.1], WHINGE[1.2]
quhingear, quhinȝar *see* WHINGER
quhip *see* WHUP[1.1], WHUP[1.2]
quhir *see* WHIRR[1.1], WHIRR[1.2]
quhirl *see* WHURL[1.1], WHURL[1.2]
quhirr *see* WHIRR[1.1]
quhisilar *see* WHUSTLER
quhisk *see* WHISK[1.1], WHISK[1.2]
quhisle *see* WHUSTLE[1.2]
quhisper *see* WHUSPER[1.1], WHUSPER[1.2]
quhissill *see* WHUSTLE[1.1], WHUSTLE[1.2]
†**quhit, quytt** *n* in Shetland, Orkney and the North-East a small Danish coin *16*. [ON *hvítr penningr*]
quhit *see* WHEET, WHITE[1.1], WHITE[1.2]
quhite *see* WHEAT, WHITE[1.1], WHITE[1.2], WHITE[2]
quhithir *see* WHITHER[1.1]
quhiting *see* WHITIN
quhitred, quhitret *see* FUTRET
quhit-stane *see* WHET
quhitt breid *see* WHITE BREID
quhitter *see* WHITTER[4.2]
quhittil *see* WHITTLE[1.1]
quho *see* WHA
quhois *see* WHASE
quhole *see* HAIL[1.1], HAIL[1.2]
quholp *see* WHALP[1.1]

quhom see WHAM⁴
quhomle see WHUMMLE¹·²
quhone see WHAN¹·¹, ¹·²
quhorle see WHURL²
quhow see HOO¹
quhoyn see WHEEN¹·¹, WHEEN¹·²
†**quhryne**¹·¹ *n* a squeal, a whine *e16*. [see the verb]
†**quhryne**¹·², **cwhryn, quhryn, quhrine** *v* to whine, squeal; to complain *la15-16*. [ON *hrína*]
quhuir see WHIRR¹·²
quhy see WHY¹·¹, WHY¹·², WHY¹·³
quhyd see WHID¹·¹
quhyle see QUHILE
quhylis see WHILES¹·¹
quhylum see WHILOM¹·³
quhymper see WHIMPER¹·²
quhyn see WHIN⁴
†**quhyne** *adv* whence *la14-e16*. [reduced form of ME *whethen*, ON *hvaðan*]
quhynge see WHINGE¹·²
quhyp see WHUP¹·¹
quhyr see WHIRR¹·²
quhyt see QUITE, WHITE¹·²
quhyte see WHITE¹·¹
quhyte breid see WHITE BREID
qui see QUOY
quick¹·¹, †**quik**, †**quyk** /kwɪk/ *n* **1** the living; living people *la14*-. **2** the sensitive part of a foot, finger or organ; the tender part of a sore *la15*-. [see the adj]
quick¹·², †**quik**, †**quyk**, †**quek** /kwɪk/ *adj* **1** living, alive *la14*-. **2** speedy, prompt, keen, sharp; lively, alert, vigorous *la15*-. **3** swarming, infested *20- Sh Ork Uls*. **4** *of representations* lifelike *16-e17*. †**quik gudis** livestock, cattle *15-17*. †**quick moss** a moss which trembles or in which a person can sink *la18-e19*. †**quik-sichtit** sharp-sighted *17*. **quick water** the current of a river, running water *20- SW Bor*. **quick and quidder** swiftly, quickly *la19- Sh*. †**quyk and quidderful** alive and full of vigour *15-e17*. [OE *cwic* living, alive]
quicken, †**quikkin**, †**quykkyn** /ˈkwɪkən/ *v* **1** to (cause to) re-animate, revive; to come to life *la14*-. **2** to arouse, inspire *la15*-. **3** to ferment *la16*. †**quickenin** yeast, a fermenting agent *17-e19*. †**quikener, quyknar** a life-giver *15-e17*. [QUICK¹·², with verb-forming suffix]
quickens /ˈkwɪkənz/ *n* couch grass *Elymus repens la17-19, 20- EC SW*. [OE *cwice*, from *cwic* living, alive; compare Eng *quitch* (grass)]
quickreich see QUIGRICH
quid see CAN²·², COOD¹, COOD²
quiet see QUAIT¹·¹, QUAIT¹·², QUAIT¹·³, QUAIT¹·⁴
quiete see QUAIT¹·³
†**quietie, quiete** *n* quietness, peace, privacy *la15-e17*. Compare QUAIT¹·¹. [AN, MFr *quieté*]
quiff see WHIFF¹·¹
quigger see KEEGER¹·¹, KEEGER¹·²
quigrich, coygerach, †**quickreich** /ˈkwɪgrɪx, ˈkɔɪɡərəx/ *n* the name given to the pastoral staff of St Fillan *15*-. [Gael *coigreach* a stranger, a foreigner; so called because it was carried to distant places as a symbol of authority for the recovery of stolen property]
quik see QUICK¹·¹, QUICK¹·²
quikkin see QUICKEN
quile see COAL, COLE¹·¹, COLE¹·²
quilk see WHILK¹·¹
quilt see TWILT¹·¹, TWILT¹·²
quim see QUEEM¹·²

quine, quean, queyn, *T* **coin**, †**quyne**, †**quene**, †**qwene** /kwʌɪn, kwen; *T* kɔɪn/ *n* **1** a young (unmarried) woman, a wench, a girl *15*-. **2** a female child, a schoolgirl *19- N NE T*. **3** a female sweetheart *19- literary*. **4** a daughter *20- NE T*. **5** a maidservant *19, 20- NE*. **6** a bold, impudent woman *15-19, 20- NE*. **7** a mistress, a concubine *19*. **quinie** = QUINE.
†**quenry, quenerie** associating with prostitutes *la16*. [OE *cwēn* a woman, a noblewoman, a wife, a queen, *cwene* a woman, a wife, a mistress, a queen]
quinie see CUNYIE¹·¹
quink /kwɪŋk/ *n* the brent goose *Branta bernicla* or the greylag goose *Anser anser la16, 19- Ork*. **quink goose** = QUINK *19- Ork*. [perhaps onomatopoeic; compare Norw dial *kvinka* to wail, whine]
quinkins /ˈkwɪŋkɪnz/ *npl* **1** a fry-up, titbits; dregs, leavings or traces of food left in a saucepan *19, 20- NE T*. **2** an insignificant or inconsequential thing *19- NE*. [perhaps altered from KIN-KIND from A' KIN O', A' KIND O' every kind, with pl ending]
quint see QUAINT
†**quinta essencia** *n* **1** *in alchemy* (the process of or equipment used in making) a quintessence *e16*. **2** a nickname of the alchemist John Damian *e16*. [Lat *quinta essentia* fifth essence]
quinter see TWINTER
quintra, quintry see KINTRA
†**quintulapse** *n* *in the North-East* (a person guilty of) a fifth lapse or occasion of sinning *la17*. [Lat *quintu-* five- + Eng *lapse*; compare DULAPSE]
quintuply¹·¹ /ˈkwɪntjuplae/ *n law* a fifth answer, made by the pursuer in reply to the QUADRUPLY of the defender *17*-. [Lat *quintu-* five-, by analogy with QUADRUPLY¹·¹ etc]
†**quintuply**¹·² *v law* to answer for the fifth time *la17-18*. [see the noun]
quippage see KIPPAGE
quire see QUEIR
quirk¹·¹ /kwɪrk, kwʌrk/ *n* **1** a trick, an oddity *la18*-. **2** a riddle, a catch question, an arithmetical problem *20- Sh NE T*. **quirky 1** intricate, twisted, complicated *la19- NE T H&I*. **2** cunning, resourceful, tricky *19, 20- N NE T*. [unknown]
quirk¹·² /kwɪrk, kwʌrk/ *v* to trick or cheat *la18-19, 20- NE T H&I*. [unknown]
†**quisquis, quisquous, quiscos** *adj* perplexing, debatable, dubious *la17-19*. [perhaps Lat *quisquis* whoever, whatever, hence uncertain, undefined]
quissan see CUSHIN
quit¹·¹, *Sh* **whet**, *Ork* **quite**, †**quyt**, †**quyte** /kwɪt; *Sh* mɛt; *Ork* kwʌɪt/ *v pt* **quat, quit**, *NE T* **quate**, *NE* **quittit**, †**quite 1** to relinquish or abandon; to leave *15*-. **2** to cease an activity; to give up, stop: ◊*he quat drinkin la16*-. **3** to free, exonerate or acquit *15-19, 20- Sh*. **4** to repay, discharge a debt, return a favour or fulfil a promise; to pay back a wrong *la14-17*. **5** to remit a payment due; to release from an obligation *la16-17*. Compare QUAT. †**quite out** to recover, redeem (a possession) *15-e17*. [ME *quiten*]
quit¹·², **quat**, †**quite** /kwɪt, kwat/ *adj* **1** free, liberated, rid of, discharged from, released *la14*-. **2** deprived of; excluded from; lacking *15-16*. **3** cleared, acquitted; innocent *15-e17*. **4** done or made away with, lost *la15-16*. †**ga quyte** to run into loss or ruin, be done away with or lost *e16*. †**mak quyte of** to get rid of; to divorce; to make a clearance *15-17*. [ME *quite*]
quit see WHIT¹·³
quite, †**quyte**, †**quhyt** /kwʌɪt/ *adv* **1** completely, totally, absolutely *la14*-. **2** fairly, reasonably *la18*-. [ME *quit*; compare MFr *quittes* totally]

quite *see* COAT, QUIT[1.1], QUIT[1.2]
quittance, cuttance, cuttans, †quetance /ˈkwɪtəns, ˈkʌtəns, ˈkʌtənz/ *n* **1** encouragement *la19-*. **2** an account, news, an explanation (of events) *la18-19, 20- Sh NE WC*. **3** the discharge of a debt or obligation; a receipt for payment *la15-e19*. **4** *law* the act of clearing oneself of a charge *la14-e17*. [AN *quitance*, MFr *quittance* acquittal, discharge (of a debt)]
quitter *see* WHITTER[4.2]
quittit *see* QUIT[1.1]
quivvy *see* KEEVEE
quiz, *Sh* **whiss**, *Ork* **whizz** /kwɪz; *Sh* ᴍɪs; *Ork* ᴍɪz/ *v* to question inquisitively; to interrogate *la19-*. [unknown]
quo, co, ko, †quod /kwo, ko/ *v* **1** *used to report direct speech* quoth, said *la14-*. **2** *used at the end of a piece of writing* written by *16-18*. [OE *cweþan*]
quoad /ˈkwoad/ *prep law* so far as, as much as *la17-*. [Lat *quoad*]
quoad omnia /ˈkwoad ɔmnɪə/ *adj* **1** applied to a parish which combined secular as well as ecclesiastical functions *19-*. **2** *of a church constitution* in which the kirk session is responsible for all matters and which does not allocate secular functions to a congregational board *19-*. [Lat *quoad omnia* as regards all matters]
quoad sacra /ˈkwoad sakrə/ *adj* applied to a parish which functions for religious purposes only, created by statute because the existing parish became too large for a single minister; the original parish remained the unit for civil administration until such matters were transferred to other local government bodies *18-*. [Lat *quoad sacra* as regards sacred matters]
quoad ultra /ˈkwoad ʌltrə/ *adj law* used in the written pleadings of an action to indicate the point beyond which the defender makes no further admission of the allegations of the pursuer *la19-*. [Lat *quoad ultra* as regards the rest]
quod *see* QUO
quoddoch *see* CUDDOCH
quoik *see* QUAK
quoil *see* COLE[1.1]
quoit *see* KITE[1.1], KITE[1.2]
quoniam attachiamenta, †quoniam atachiamenta /ˈkwonɪəm atatʃɪəˈmentə/ *n law* a name given, from its opening words, to an ancient (now thought to be late 14th-century) work of Scots Law *15, 18- historical*. [Lat *quoniam attachiamenta* since arrestments]
quorill *see* WHURL[2]
quorum, *NE* **coarum, †coram** /ˈkworəm; *NE* ˈkorəm/ *n* **1** the number required to be present for a session of a committee or other group to be able to enact business *17-*. **2** a gathering, especially of friends for social purposes, a company *la17-19, 20- NE*. [EModE *quorum* a select body of justices of the peace, every member of which had to be present to constitute a deciding body]
†quosche, cosche *n* a hollow or valley suitable for grazing *16-e17*. Compare KOSCH. [Gael *còs* a hollow]
quoss *see* COSE[1.2]
†quot, quote, cote *n law* the proportion of a deceased person's moveable estate payable to the bishop of the diocese for confirmation of the testament *16-19*. **quottar** a collector of the QUOT *la16*. **quot silver, cott silver** = QUOT *la16-e18*. [AN, MFr *cote, quote* a contribution or share of tax]
quouk *see* QUAK
quow *see* COO
quoy, quay, why, †quy, †qui /kwae, kwi, kwe, ᴍᴀɪ/ *n* **1** a piece of land (originally part of the common pasture) which had been enclosed and cultivated as part of a farm; cultivated land not attracting skatt *la15- Sh Ork*. **2** *in an older church building* a humorous name for the enclosed pew below the pulpit in which the elders sit at Communion *20- Ork*. **quoyland, †quyland** enclosed (cultivated) land *16- Sh Ork*. [ON *kví* an enclosure]
quoy *see* QUEY
quoyach, quoyok *see* QUEY
quuik *see* QUAK
quy *see* QUEY, QUOY
quyach *see* QUEY
quyet *see* QUAIT[1.1], QUAIT[1.2], QUAIT[1.3], QUAIT[1.4]
quyk *see* QUICK[1.1], QUICK[1.2]
quykkyn *see* QUICKEN
quyn *see* TWINE[1.1]
quyne *see* QUINE
†quynkill *v of a light* to go out *e16*. [perhaps related to OE *ācwincan* to go out, be extinguished]
quyntans *see* QUENTANCE
quyok *see* QUEY
quyschile *see* WHUSTLE[1.1]
quyt *see* QUAIT[1.1], QUIT[1.1]
quyte *see* QUIT[1.1], QUITE
quytie *see* WHEETIE[1.1]
quytt *see* QUHIT
quytter *see* WHITTER[4.2]
qwalm *see* QUALM
qwarear *see* QUEREOUR
qweir *see* QUEER[1.1]
qwel *see* QUELL
qwene *see* QUINE
qwhylum *see* WHILOM[1.2]
qwis *see* WHISS[1]
qwoyk *see* QUAK
qwyntis *see* QUENTIS

R

ra[1.1] /ra/ *n* the shortening of a tether or line by doubling it back and knotting it *20- Sh*. **get a ra on yer tedder** *of people* to have their abilities constrained *20- Sh*. [Norn *ra*]

ra[1.2] /ra/ *v* to shorten an animal's tether with a knot; to shorten a rope *la19- Sh*. [see the noun]

ra *see* RAE[1], RAE[2], RAW[2.2], THE[1.2]

raa *see* RAE[1]

raab[1.1] /rab/ *n* **1** a fall of rock from a cliff face, an avalanche; falling rock *19- Sh*. **2** a crashing or rumbling noise (from falling rock) *19- Sh*. [see the verb]

raab[1.2] /rab/ *v of a mass of rocks* to fall from the face of a cliff *19- Sh*. **raubit** ruinous, tumbledown *la19- Sh*. [Norn *rab*, ON *hrapa* to fall down; compare RAB[1.2]]

raad[1.1] /rad/ *n* **1** prudence, economy *la19- Sh*. **2** orderliness, tidiness *20- Sh*. Compare REDD[1.1]. [see the verb]

raad[1.2] /rad/ *v* **1** to regulate, arrange in an orderly fashion, set to rights *la19- Sh*. **2** to economize *20- Sh*. Compare REDD[1.2]. [Norn *rad*]

raag *see* RAG[4]

raaga, raga, †ragha /ˈragə/ *n* wreckage, driftwood *18- Sh*. **raga banes** a carcase; the disintegrated remains of a dead animal *19- Sh*. **raaga tree** a tree or branch washed up as driftwood *19- Sh*. [Norn *raga* driftwood]

raam /ram/ *n* lanolin *20- Sh*. [unknown]

raami /ˈrami/ *n fisherman's taboo* a cat *la19- Sh*. [Norn *rami* provided with claws]

raan /ran/ *n* a disease of turnips *la20- NE SW*. **raaned** affected with raan *la20- NE SW*. [perhaps RAWN fish roe from a supposed similarity in appearance]

raan *see* RAWN

raas /ras/ *adj of fabrics* coarse, loosely knit or woven *20- Sh*. [perhaps Du *ras* a kind of coarse cloth or Dan *rask* a thin coarse woollen cloth]

raaz *see* RAZE

rab[1.1] /rab/ *n* idle talk, nonsense *20- Sh*. [ON *rabba*]

rab[1.2] /rab/ *v* to talk nonsense, prattle *la19- Sh*. [Norn *rab*, ON *rabba* to babble, to talk nonsense; compare RAAB[1.2]]

Rab, Rob /rab, rɔb/ *n* familiar forms of the personal name Robert *la18-*. [variants of short form of the personal name]

†rabat, rebat *n* a kind of collar *la16-17*. [Fr *rabat*]

Rabbie-rin-the-hedge, Rabbierinniehedge /rabɪrɪnðəˈhɛdʒ, rabɪrɪnɪˈhɛdʒ/ *n* goosegrass *Galium aparine la19-*. [familiar form of the name *Robert* + RIN[1.2] + THE[1.2] + HEDGE]

rabbill *see* RAIBLE[1.1]

rabbit, †rabat /ˈrabɪt/ *n* a small long-eared mammal *la16-*. **rabbit fish** a name for various fish, mainly the arctic chimaera, *Chimaera monstrosa la19- Sh NE*. **rabbit's sugar** the seeds of the common sorrel, *Rumex acetosa 20- NE*. **rabbit thissle** the sowthistle, *Sonchus oleraceus 20- EC Bor*. [EModE *rabet, rabbyt*]

rabblach /ˈrabləx/ *n* **1** a disorderly outpouring of words or noises; nonsensical talk *la19- NE Uls*. **2** a carelessly erected building, something ruinous or dilapidated *la19- Sh NE*. [RAIBLE[1.1] + -ACH]

rabble *see* RAIBLE[1.1], RAIBLE[1.2]

rabel *see* REBEL[1.1]

rabell *see* REBEL[1.1], REBEL[1.3]

rabet *see* RYBAT

Rab Ha /rab 'hɔ, rab 'ha/ *n* a glutton, a voracious eater *la19- WC SW*. [from the name of a vagrant, Robert Hall, noted for his gastronomic feats]

rabiator, †rubeatour /ˈrabietər/ *n* a violent, ruthless person; a boorish or domineering person *16-19, 20- SW Bor*. [perhaps Medieval Lat *robiātor* a robber]

rable *see* RAIBLE[1.1]

rabous *see* REBOUS

Rabs /rabz/ *npl* Kirkintilloch Rob Roy Football Club *la20- WC*. [familiar form from the first name of the historical figure *Robert Roy MacGregor*]

rabut *see* REBUT[1.2]

race[1.1], **†rase, †rais, †rays** /res/ *n* **1** a run, a journey at speed; the act of running *la14-*. **2** a contest of speed *16-*. **3** *mining* a group or train of hutches coupled together *19-*. **4** a passage where sheep are graded or separated *20- NE T EC*. **5** a full load of water or coal transported in one journey *19- EC*. **6** a row, a number of units in a line *20- Sh*. **7** a section of a harvest field cut by three reapers working abreast *20- Ork*. **8** a charge or attack (in battle); a course (in a tournament) *15-16*. **9** a journey, especially a (trading) voyage or expedition by sea *15-e16*. **10** the course or path followed by a runner or other moving body *16-e18*. **11** the course (of life or events) *16-17*. **race by** a short visit *la20- Ork EC*. **†race-ca** in Orkney a shout indicating the start of a contest of speed *la19*. **race in** = race by *la20- EC*. **in a race** hurriedly, as quickly as possible *la14-*. **†intill a rays** = *in a race 16*. **†rew a race** to regret one's course of action *la15-16*. **tak a race** to move or work quickly *20-*. **†with a rase** = *in a race la14-e16*. [ON *ras*]

race[1.2] /res/ *v* to run, to travel at speed *la15-*. **†racer** a promiscuous woman *la18*. [see the noun]

race[2], **†raice, †rais** /res/ *n* **1** a group of people connected by common descent or origin *la16-*. **2** a set of articles used together *19- NE*. [MFr, Fr *race*]

race[3] /res/ *n* a group of peats, turves or sheaves propped up to dry *la19- Sh Ork*. [Norn *res*]

rachan *see* RAUCHAN

rache[1.1], **ratch** /ratʃ/ *n* a gundog or hound which hunts by scent *la15-19, 20- historical*. [ME *racch*]

rache[1.2], **ratch** /ratʃ/ *v* to range about ravenously; to prowl *19- EC Bor*. [see the noun]

†rachel saut, ratchell salt, rochell salt *n* coarse-grained salt *la16-la19*. [probably named after the French port *La Rochelle*, a major exporter of salt from the Middle Ages, but the later occurrences are more probably associated with RATCHELL]

rachle *see* RAUCHLE, RAUCLE

rach-ma-reeshil /ˈraxməˈriʃəl, ˈrakməˈriʃəl/ *adj* confused, mixed-up, jumbled *19, 20- T EC*. [unknown]

rachtir *see* RAGHTER

racionabil *see* RATIONABLE

rack[1], **†rake, †rak, †reik** /rak/ *n* **1** a framework or set of bars for support or display *17-*. **2** a frame of spars on a wall for holding crockery and cutlery *la17-*. **3** a spar, a stay; a post intended to form part of a framework *16-e17, la20- NE T EC*. **4** a set of bars used to support a roasting spit or other cooking utensil *la15-17*; compare RAX[2]. [ME *rak*, MDu *rek*, *rak*, MLG *rek*]

rack²·¹ /rak/ n **1** an instrument of torture on which a victim was stretched *la16-*. **2** a sprain, a wrench, a dislocation *la18-*. **3** *in textiles* a frame for stretching wet cloth in the process of fulling *19, 20- T Bor*. **rack pin** a stick used to tighten a rope or chain (on a loaded cart) *19-*. **rack stock 1** an instrument of torture on which a victim was stretched *17, 18- historical*. **2** a piece of equipment used in shoemaking, a last or a mechanism for stretching leather *la16-19*. **rack strap** a strap used by a shoemaker *20- NE*. **tak owre the rack stock** to take severely to task *la19- NE*. [ME *rak*]

rack²·² /rak/ v **1** to wrench, dislocate, tear, twist *15-*. **2** to stretch; to pull; to increase in length *la15-*. **3** to reach, to extend *la19- WC SW Bor*. **4** to worry needlessly, to be over-anxious *20- SW Bor*. **5** to stretch (the neck); to hang, be hanged *19*; compare RAX¹·². †**rak sauch** to be put to death by hanging *16*. [see the noun]

rack³ /rak/ n **1** a stretch or reach of a river devoted to (salmon) fishing; one of a series of such divisions *la18-19, 20- T*. **2** a ford in a river, a ridge of gravel or a shallow place *la17-19, 20- SW*. **3** a path, a track *la20- T*; compare RAIK¹·¹. **4** *curling* the ice forming the area of play *la18- WC*. **5** *curling* a team; the number of players required for a team *la18-19*. **rack ban** the chain connecting the bridle of a plough with the swingle-tree *la19- NE*. [variant of RAKE² with short vowel]

rack⁴·¹ /rak/ n **1** driving mist or fog *16-18, 19- NE T EC*. **2** a rush or onset; a heavy blow, a crash, a shock; a series of explosions *15-19*. **3** a rush of wind; a gale, a storm *e16*. [see the verb]

rack⁴·² /rak/ v **1** *of clouds* to fly before the wind, clear away *19, 20- historical*. **2** to cause a noisy blast; *of a gun* to go off, fire *e16*. **racking** *of clouds* flying before the wind; *of wind* driving *19, 20- T Bor*. **rack up** *of weather* to clear *19, 20- T C Bor*. [perhaps related to ON *reka* to drive; compare RAIK²·² and OE *racu* a storm]

rack see WRACK¹·¹

†**rackabimus** n a sudden jolt or fall *e19*. [perhaps related to RACK⁴·¹]

rackel see RAUCLE

racket¹, †**rakket**, †**rakcat** /'rakət/ n **1** a bat, a racket *16-*. **2** a violent stunning blow, a thump, a stroke *18-19, 20- Sh*. **3** the game of rackets *16*. **rackets** the game of rackets *18-*. [probably MFr *raquette*]

racket² /'rakət/ n a rocket, a firework; a missile *19-*. [Eng *rocket*, Ital *rocchetta*; for *-a-* form, compare Du *raket*]

rackie see RAKKI¹·¹

rackle, †**rakkill** /'rakəl/ n **1** a chain *17-19, 20- literary*. **2** a small chain attached to a pipe stem, which holds the lid and a pin for clearing out the pipe *la19- NE*. **3** the rattling or jingling noise made by a chain *la19- NE*. [perhaps related to Eng *reckon* a chain, with influence from *shackle* and *rattle*]

rackle see RAUCLE

rackless see RECKLESS

rackon see RECKON

racks

rackses see RAX²

racord see RECORD¹·¹, RECORD¹·²

racunnys see RECOGNISE

rad, †**red**, †**redd**, †**raid** /rad/ adj frightened, alarmed; apprehensive *la14-19, 20- SW Bor*. †**radnes** fear, fright, apprehension *la14-e15*. †**radour, raddour** fear, terror, dread *la14-e16*. [ON *hræddr*]

rad see REDE¹·¹, REDD³·²

radcoll see REDCOAL

raddy see READY¹·²

rade, raid, †**rode,** †**raed,** †**reid** /red/ n **1** an anchorage *15-18, 20- Ork*. **2** one of a series of deep-sea fishing grounds allocated to crews of fishermen; a fishing-ground marked out with two meiths *19- Sh NE*. [a specialized sense of OE *rād* a riding, a mounted foray]

rade see RAID, REDD¹·¹, RIDE¹·²

rademe see REDEEM

radge¹·¹ /radʒ/ n **1** a promiscuous woman *20-*. **2** a wild obstreperous person or animal *20-*. **3** a foolish person *la20-*. **radger** a wild, intractable person or animal *la19- T*. **take a radge** to fly into a rage *la20- C*. [probably Fr *rage*]

radge¹·², †**rage** /radʒ/ adj **1** mad, violently excited, furious, wild *16-*. **2** sexually excited *20-*. **3** silly, weak-minded *20-*. [see the noun]

radgie¹·¹ /'radʒe/ n a foolish person *la20-*. **take a radgie** to fly into a rage *la20- T EC*. [RADGE¹·¹]

radgie¹·² /'radʒe/ adj angry, excited *20- NE*. [see the noun]

radical¹·¹ /'radɪkəl/ n **1** a supporter of any thorough political or social change; a member of the extreme section of a political party; a member or supporter of a radical movement; a revolutionary *19-*. **2** a wild, unruly person, a rogue, a rascal *19, 20- Sh NE EC*. [see the adj]

radical¹·² /'radɪkəl/ adj **1** inherent, fundamental *la15-*. **2** original, primary *la16-*. **3** thorough, involving the root or origin; acting upon what is essential and fundamental *19-*. **4** revolutionary, progressive, unorthodox *20-*. **radical right** *law* the ultimate proprietary right of a person establishing a trust, which survives if the fulfilment of the trust purposes does not exhaust the whole estate *19-*. [Lat *rādicālis* relating to or forming the root, original, fundamental]

radical basket see RETICULE BASKET

†**radicate** adj firmly established; deeply implanted *la15-16*. [Lat *rādīcāt-*, ptp stem of *rādīcāre* to take root]

†**radious, radius** adj **1** emitting rays of light; shining brightly *16*. **2** *of precious stones* sparkling, glittering *e16*. [MFr *radieux*, Lat *radiōsus*]

radnes see RAD

†**radot** v to mutter disconnectedly *la16*. **radotage** disconnected mutterings *e19*. [MFr *radoter*]

radoun see REDOUND

radres see REDRESS¹·¹, REDRESS¹·²

rae¹, **ray, roe,** †**ra,** †**raa,** †**ro** /re, ro/ n the roe deer *Capreolus capreolus la14-*. **rae buck** a roebuck, the male of the roe deer *15-*. †**rafell, raphell** the hide of the roe deer *la15-e18*. [OE *rā*]

rae², †**ra,** †**ray,** †**row** /re/ n a sail-yard, the yard or spar on which a boat's sails are spread *la15-19, 20- Sh*. **raeband** the rope attaching the sail to the yard *16-19, 20- Sh N*. †**tak the sails from the rae** to immobilize a ship by removing its sails *16-18*. [MDu *ra* a pole, a stake ON *rá* a sail-yard, a pole]

raed see RADE

raeffle see RAIVEL¹·²

raek see REAK¹·¹, REAK¹·²

rael¹·¹, **real,** †**reall** /rel, ril/ adj **1** actual, physical; originally of the possession of property in a legal sense *15-*. **2** true, genuine *16-*. **3** of a substantial amount *20-*. **4** *of character* honest, forthright, genuine *la17-19, 20- Sh T SW*. **5** *of money* cash or coin *la16-17*. [ME *real*]

rael¹·², **rale, real** /rel, ril/ adv very, extremely *19-*. [see the adj]

rael see RAIVEL¹·²

raem see REAM¹·¹

raemikle /'remɪkəl/ n a round wooden tub used in a dairy; a pail *la19- Sh* [Norn *rømikoll* with substitution of REAM¹·¹ for the first element]

raep see RAIP¹·¹, REAP

raevl see RAIVEL¹·¹

raew /re'u/ *n* the cry of a cat in pain or on heat *20-* Ork. [onomatopoeic]

rafert *see* REEFORT

raff¹, *SW* **raft** /raf; *SW* raft/ *n* **1** plenty, abundance; a large number, a crowd *la18- NE SW*. **2** *of plants* overgrown, growing quickly and abundantly *19- NE*. **raffie 1** abundant, generous, well-supplied *la19-, NE*. **2** *of crops or animals* thriving, flourishing *20- NE*. [shortened form of ME *rif* and *raf*, AN *rifraf*, MFr *rif et raf* altogether, completely]

raff², *Ork* **rav** /raf; *Ork* rav/ *n* a short sharp shower accompanied by gusts of wind *la18-19, 20- Ork NE T SW*. [unknown]

raffan, †**raffin** /'rafən/ *adj* merry, boisterous *18-19, 20- T WC*. [perhaps extended sense of RAFF¹]

raffle *see* RAIVEL¹·¹, RAIVEL¹·²

raft /raft/ *n* **1** a beam, a rafter *la16-19, 20- Bor*. **2** a tall thin person *la19- Sh Uls*. [ME *raft*, ON *raptr* a rafter]

raft *see* RAFF¹

rag¹·¹ /rag/ *n* **1** a shred, a scrap (of fabric) *la14-*. **2** a thin animal or fish *la19-*. **3** a rough projection on a surface, after sawing, filing *20-*. **4** the poorest pig in a litter *20- SW Bor*. **5** a partial winnowing of corn *la18-19*. **ragger** a person who collects rags *20- N NE EC*. †**rag fallow** multiple ploughings and manuring of grassland as preparation for sowing wheat *la18-19*. †**rag fauch** = *rag fallow la18*. **rag pock** a bag for holding rags or old clothes *la19-*. **rag weed** ragwort *Jacobaea vulgaris la18-*. **rag wheel** a sprocket wheel, a wheel with projecting struts that interlock with a similar wheel in order to turn it *la17-*. **rag-a-tag** ragged robin, the plant *Lychnis flos-cuculi 20- Sh*. **lose your rag, lose the rag** to lose your temper *20-*. [ME *rag*, ON *rögg* a tuft of fur]

†**rag¹·²** *v* **1** to winnow corn partially, remove rough fibrous material *19*. **2** *of oats* to reach the stage of growth where the grain begins to appear *e19*. [see the noun]

rag²·¹ /rag/ *n* **1** a disturbance, a noisy dispute *19-*. **2** a scolding *19*. **hae a rag oot o** to enjoy a joke at the expense of another *la19-*. **tak the rag o** to make fun of, make a fool of *20-*. [unknown]

rag²·² /rag/ *v* to scold, to reproach severely *19-*. [unknown]

rag³ /rag, rɑg/ *n* a wet mist or drizzle *20- Sh Ork NE*. **raggle** a wet mist or drizzle *20 NE*. [Norn *rag*]

rag⁴, **raag** /rɑg/ *v* to catch a fish by striking it with a fishing hook *20- Sh*. [Norn *rag* to hook a fish anywhere but the mouth]

rag⁵ /rag/ *n* a whetstone *la19- EC SW Bor*. [Eng *rag* a kind of hard stone]

rag⁶ /rag/ *n* the top layer of stones on a dyke, forming the coping *20- Ork*. [perhaps RAG¹·¹ from the ragged appearance of the coping stones; compare Eng *rag(stone)* a piece of rough stone]

†**rag⁷** *v of a wall* to develop cracks and bulges; to come out of alignment *18-e19*. [perhaps variant of RACK²·²]

raga *see* RAAGA

ragabash¹·¹, †**ragabrash** /'ragəbaʃ/ *n* **1** a lazy, feckless person; a scruffy person *18-19, 20- T SW Bor*. **2** a rough or unruly group *19- SW*. [unknown]

ragabash¹·² /'ragəbaʃ/ *adj* **1** rough, uncouth *19- T EC SW Bor*. **2** useless *19*. [unknown]

ragall *see* RAGGLE¹·²

ragbild /'ragbɪld/ *n* a raggedly-dressed person; a lazy or aimless person *la19- Sh*. [Norn *ragbelt*; compare RAGABASH¹·¹. The second element may be Norn *pelt* a rag or ragged person.]

rage¹·¹, †**raige**, †**rege** /redʒ/ *n* **1** violent anger; fury *la14-*. **2** madness, frenzy *16-*. **3** passion, lust *la15-16*. **on rage** on heat, sexually aroused *16*. [ME *rage*]

rage¹·² /redʒ/ *v* **1** to be extremely angry; to behave riotously or destructively *la15-*. **2** to scold, berate; to vent one's fury (at or on a person) *16-*. **3** to spread widely, increase in influence and intensity *16-*. **4** to act in a frenzied manner; to be or become mad *15-*. **5** to behave promiscuously *16*. †**rageand** furious, violent; frenzied; turbulent, boisterous *16*. **raging 1** violent activity; anger, frenzy *la15-*. **2** a scolding *20-*. **3** sexual intercourse *la15-e16*. †**ragit** enraged *e16*. [ME *ragen*]

rage *see* RADGE¹·²

ragger /'ragər/ *n fisherman's taboo* a knife *la19- Ork*. [Eng *rag* to make ragged; with agent suffix]

ragget, raggety *see* RAGGIT

raggie¹ /'ragi/ *adj* ragged *19-*. **raggie biscuit** a biscuit with an uneven edge, made in St Andrews *la20- T EC*. [RAG¹·¹ + -IE²]

raggie² /'ragi/ *n* a person who collects rags, a ragman *la19- Sh*. [RAG¹·¹ + -IE³]

raggie³ /'ragi, 'rage/ *n* a (diseased) salmon *la19- Bor*. [RAG¹·¹ + -IE²]

raggie Willie /ragi 'wɪli/ *n* ragged robin, the plant *Lychnis flos-cuculi 20- Sh*. [RAG¹·¹ + -IE² + *Willie*, shortened form of *William*, as found in several plant names]

raggit, †**ragget** /'ragɪt/ *adj* **1** *of people* wearing ragged clothes *la14-*. **2** *of material* ragged, in tatters *la15-*. **raggety** in rags, tattered *la19-*. [RAG¹·¹ + -IT²]

raggle¹·¹ /'ragəl/ *n* a groove cut in stone or wood to receive another stone or board *19-*. [unknown]

raggle¹·², †**ragall**, †**regale** /'ragəl/ *v* **1** to cut a groove in stone or wood (so that another piece of stone or wood can be inserted), *eg* in the edge of a roof, the steps of a stair; to join such elements in this way *16-*. **2** *mining* to cut into the coalface *la19- EC*. **raglet** a groove cut in stone to receive another stone or a spout *19-*. [unknown]

raggle² /'ragəl/ *v* **1** to make an uneven or ragged cut (in something), cut jaggedly *la18-19, 20- Sh SW*. **2** to throw out of alignment, disorder *19*. **ragglish** erratic; *of weather* uncertain, gusty with rain; *of people* wild, unreliable *19- NE*. **raggly** with an uneven edge *20- Ork*. [from the noun RAG¹·¹ with frequentative suffix]

raggle³·¹ /'ragəl/ *n* a dispute, an argument *la19- NE*. [perhaps from the verb or RAG²·¹ with frequentative suffix]

raggle³·² /'ragəl/ *v* **1** to wrangle, to dispute *la19- NE*. **2** to haggle *19*. [perhaps conflation of Eng *wrangle* and Eng *haggle*; also, compare RAG²·² to dispute]

ragglin, raglin, †**ragaling**, †**ragglyne** /'raglɪn/ *n* **1** a groove cut in stone; the space for the edges of the slates under the coping-stones of a gable *16-*. **2** *mining* a groove cut into the side of a mine to act as a ventilation shaft *19, 20- EC*. [verbal noun from RAGGLE¹·²]

ragglish *see* RAGGLE²

ragha *see* RAAGA

raghter, †**rachtir**, †**rawchtir** /'raxtər/ *n* a plank or beam of wood; a rafter *15-19, 20- C*. [MDu *rachter*]

raglet *see* RAGGLE¹·²

raglin *see* RAGGLIN

ragman, †**ragmen**, †**ragment** /'ragmən/ *n* **1** the document recording the oath of fealty sworn by the Scottish nobles in 1291, accepting Edward I of England as their overlord, later returned by Edward III in 1328 in recognition of Scotland's independence *la14-16, 17- historical*. **2** a long rambling discourse *16*. **3** a list *e16*. [unknown]

ragnail /'ragnel/ *n* a torn piece of skin or broken nail at the side of a fingernail, a hangnail *la19-*. [RAG¹·¹ + NAIL¹·¹]

raible¹·¹, **raibble, rabble**, †**rabill**, †**rable**, †**reeble** /'rebəl, 'rabəl/ *n* **1** *derogatory* people or communities regarded as having no valid principle of organization or unity *la16-*. **2** a disorderly outpouring of words or noises; nonsensical talk *la16-*. **3** *derogatory* the population at large; a mixed, confused or disorderly crowd *17-*. **4** a carelessly erected building, something ruinous or dilapidated *la19- Sh NE*. **5** a (noisy) group; a straggling line *e16, la19- C*. **rabblement** a riot, a noisy mob *18- literary*. [ME *rabel*; compare Du *rabbelen* to speak indistinctly]

raible[1,2], **rabble**, †**reeble** /'rebəl, 'rabəl/ *v* **1** to mob, assault with overwhelming numbers (specifically by a hostile Presbyterian congregation against an Episcopalian clergyman, after the Revolution settlement of 1688-89) *la17-18, 19- historical*. **2** to utter (a torrent of words), speak or read hastily and indistinctly *la18-19, 20- Sh SW*. **rabble out** to drive (an Episcopalian clergyman) from his charge in the sense of RAIBLE[1,2] (sense 1) *19*. [ME *rablen*; compare Du *rabbelen* to speak indistinctly]

raice see RACE[2]

raid, †**road**, †**rade**, †**red** /red/ *n* **1** an armed incursion; a warlike expedition (originally on horseback); a sudden or surprise attack *15-*. **2** *humorous* an outing taken for pleasure *e19, 20- EC*. **3** a journey made on horseback; a ride; a procession *la15-e17*. **4** the assembling of a force in the service of the king to carry out a military operation; the force assembled *16-e17*. **5** the act of mounting for sexual intercourse; copulation *16*. [OE *rād* a riding, a mounted foray]

raid see RAD, RADE, REDD[1,2], REDD[2,1] RIDE[1,2]

raif see RAVE[1,2], RIVE[1,2], REIF, REIVE

raiffell see REVEL[1,2]

raige see RAGE[1,1]

raigler see REGULAR[1,2]

raik[1,1], **rake** /rek/ *n* **1** a route; a journey; a long or tiring walk; a stroll *15-*. **2** a journey made for a specified purpose *la16-*. **3** as much as can be carried in one load *17-*. **4** a roving person or animal, especially a person who wanders about in search of gossip or entertainment *19-*. **5** an area of pasture for cattle or sheep *15-19, 20- C Bor*. **6** *mining* a train of loaded hutches *la19- C*. **7** *of food* a spoonful; a helping *20- T EC Bor*. [ON *reik* a stroll]

raik[1,2], †**rake** /rek/ *v* **1** to travel; to proceed slowly or aimlessly; to walk, stroll; to wander, roam *la14-*. **2** *of grazing animals* to roam in search of pasture *la15-*. **3** to take (the road); to range over or wander through (the streets or fields) *15-*. **raiker** a traveller; a wanderer; a vagrant *la16-*. [ON *reika*]

raik[2,1] /rek/ *n* speed, pace, rate *la18-19, 20- NE Bor*. [see the verb]

raik[2,2], **rake** /rek/ *v* **1** to move, travel with speed, cover the ground quickly *14-19, 20- NE T WC Bor*. **2** to work energetically and speedily *la19- NE*. [OE *racian* to proceed at speed]

raik see RAKE[1,1], RAKE[1,2], RAKE[2], REAK[1,1], REAK[1,2]

rail[1] /rel/ *n* **1** a (horizontal or sloping) wooden or metal bar on which something may be hung, or by which something may be supported *18-*. **2** a row of protective studs in the sole of a boot or shoe *la18-19*. **3** a temporary barricade of nets *e16*. [ME *raile* AN *raille*; compare RAVEL[1,1]]

†**rail**[2] *n* a woman's short-sleeved front- or over-bodice, worn on formal dress occasions *18-19*. **railie** = RAIL[2] *19*. [ME *rail* a kind of neckcloth, OE *hrægel* a garment, a mantle]

railing, **railin** /'relɪŋ, 'relɪn/ *n* **1** a hand-rail *18-*. **2** a fence made of upright iron rods *19-*. [RAIL[1] + *-ing* suffix]

rail stair /'rel ster/ *n* a stair fitted with a hand-rail *la16-19, 20- NE T C*. [RAIL[1] + STAIR[1]]

raim see RAME[1,1], RAME[1,2]

rain[1,1], †**rayn** /ren/ *n* condensed water vapour falling from the atmosphere *la14-*. **rain goose** the red-throated diver *Gavia stellata 18- Sh Ork N*. **rain thraw**, **rain traa** a change of wind direction, accompanied by rain *20- Sh T EC*. **rain tree** **1** a humorous term for an umbrella *la19- Sh*. **2** a bevelled wooden bar along the foot of a door to deflect rain from the threshold *20- Sh*. [OE *regn*]

rain[1,2], †**rayn**, †**rane** /ren/ *v* **1** *of rain* to fall; *of an agent* to pour down, let fall (rain) *la14-*. **2** *in assaying silver* to produce water during the process of cupellation *la17*. †**rain Jeddart staves** to rain heavily *e19*. **rain puir men and pike staves** to rain heavily *20- NE T*. [OE *regnian*]

raing see REENGE[1,1], RING[1,1]

raintter see RANTER[1,1]

raip[1,1], **rope**, *Sh* **raep**, †**rape** /rep, rop; *Sh* 'reəp/ *n* **1** a length of strong line or cord, usually made of twisted strands of fibrous material *la14-*. **2** the ropes securing thatch on a roof or on a corn-rick *la18-*. **3** a strong cord made of straw or hay *19-*. **4** a clothes-line *19-*. **5** a straw band for a sheaf of corn *19- NE EC Bor*. **6** a rope six ells in length for measuring land *16-17*. **7** a string of onions or garlic *15-16*. **raipfu** **1** a quantity that can be secured by a rope *19, 20- Sh*. **2** a person who deserves to be, or has been hanged *la16-19*. **ropes** the game of skipping using ropes *20- C*. †**trail the raip** *folklore* to carry out the practice of attempting to conjure bad luck by twisting a straw rope and trailing it around an object in an anticlockwise direction *19*. [OE *rāp*]

raip[1,2] /rep/ *v* **1** to tie, bind with a rope or ropes *la19-*. **2** to secure the thatch of (a corn-rick) with a network of (straw) ropes *la19-*. **3** to fix a fishing-net to a rope *20- Sh*. **4** to coil, wind (up) into a ball *la19- Sh NE*. **5** to hang like a rope or a clothes-line *20- Sh*. **6** to sew roughly in making a temporary repair *20- Sh N*. **raepin band** a rope laced through the top of a straw basket or creel to keep it closed *20- Sh*. **raepin string** = *raepin band 20- Sh*. [see the noun]

raip see REAP, RIP[1,2]

rair[1,1], **roar**, †**rare**, †**royr**, †**reire** /rer, ror/ *n* **1** a loud call, cry or shout; *of people* usually an expression of grief, pain or anger *15-*. **2** a loud report; a belch *19- NE T*. **3** a call of greeting or acknowledgement to someone in passing *20- C*. **roarie**, **rory** **1** *of colours* garish, loud *la19-*. **2** *of colours* bright, showy *20-*. **3** loud, noisy, roaring *20-*. **4** drunk *la19, 20- Sh T WC*. **roaring** crying out, shouting *la14-*. [see the verb; *-o-* forms may be related to Du *roere*]

rair[1,2], **roar**, †**rare**, †**roir** /rer, ror/ *v* **1** to call or cry loudly, *of people* to weep *la14-*. **2** to make a loud noise or din *16-*. **3** to summon with a loud shout; to greet or acknowledge someone loudly (in passing) *la19- Sh H&I C SW*. **4** *curling of a stone* to make a roaring noise as it moves rapidly on the ice *19- T C SW Bor*. **5** *of breaking ice* to make a resounding, cracking noise *la18-e19 SW*. **roarin buckie** the whelk, *Buccinum undatum* the shell of which when held to the ear seems to make a roaring sound like that of the sea *19- NE T EC*. **roaring game** the game of curling *la19-*. **roar and greet** to weep *18-*. [OE *rārian*]

rair see RARE[1,1]

raird, see REIRD[1,1], REIRD[1,2]

rais see RACE[1,1], RACE[2]

raise[1,1] /rez/ *n* a state of extreme bad temper, a frenzy *la19- T EC*. [see the verb; compare *raise on*]

raise[1,2], †**rease** /rez/ *v* **1** to lift (something) up, move to a higher position, elevate; to exalt *la14-*. **2** to help or make (a person) stand up *la14-*. **3** to restore to life *la14-*. **4** to bring (a siege) to an end; to adjourn, prorogue (a meeting); to cause (an army) to move *la14-*. **5** to levy (taxes or troops) *la14-*. **6** to utter (a cry), produce (a loud noise); to sing (a song) *la14-*. **7** to make higher; to increase *15-*. **8** to arouse, rouse from sleep *15-*. **9** to lift, remove, dig up *15-*. **10** to originate; to construct; to cause to appear or come into existence *15-*. **11** to arouse (people) to common action *15-*. **12** *law* to have (a legal document) drawn up as evidence or grounds for an action *la15*-. **13** to incite, stir up, enrage, drive into a frenzy *16*-. **14** to bring (a thing) to an upright position *16*-. **15** *law* to bring (an action) *16*-. **16** *curling* to strike and move forward (another stone of one's own side) towards the TEE[1] *19*-. **17** to set up (peats) on end to dry *la19- Sh Ork*. **18** to remove (property) from the possession of a tenant *16-17*. **19** *law* to set up (a court or inquest) *15-16*. †**raise net** a fixed fishing-net which rises and falls with the level of the tide *la16-e19*. **raise a reek** to make a great fuss or cause a commotion *la18-19, 20- Sh C*. **raise on** to turn on in anger, attack *19- NE T C*. †**raise the psalms** *Presbyterian Church* to lead the singing of psalms *17*. †**raise the song** to begin to sing *19*. [ON *reisa*]

raise *see* RAZE, RISE[1.2]

raised, †**raisit** /rezd/ *adj* infuriated, wild, overexcited *17*-. [participial adj from RAISE[1.2]]

raiser /'rezər/ *n* **1** *law* the person who brings an action in court *la16*-. **2** *law* the holder of the disputed property in a MULTIPLEPOINDING *19*-. **nominal raiser** = RAISER (sense 2) when a claimant initiates proceedings *20*-. **real raiser** the holder of the disputed property in a multiplepoinding when the holder himself initiates proceedings *la19*-. [RAISE[1.2] + *-er* agent suffix]

raisin, †**rasing**, †**resing**, †**reasing** /'rezən/ *n* **1** a dried grape, a raisin *15*-. **2** a grape *la15-16*. †**raisin kail** broth with raisins added, a traditional dish at weddings *19*. **Raisin Monday** *St Andrews University* **1** a Monday in the winter term when senior students demanded of first-year students a pound of raisins in return for their protection *la19-20, 21- historical*. **2** a weekend-long celebration at the end of which the students cover themselves in foam from aerosol cans *20*-. **raisin weekend** = **raisin Monday 2**. †**raisings of cure** currants *16-e17*. †**raisings of Corinth** currants *16-e17*. †**raisings of the sone** sun-dried raisins *la16-e17*. [ME *raisin*]

†**raisit** *adj of fabric* perhaps woven with a looped pile, or a velvet finish *16-e17*. **raisit werk 1** a decorative pattern in relief on wood, stone or metal *16-e17*. **2** a pattern embroidered in relief on cloth *la15-17*. [participial adj from RAISE[1.2]]

raisit *see* RAISED

raison *see* REASON[1.1], REASON[1.2]

raith, †**rath**, †**reath** /reθ/ *n* **1** a quarter of a year; a period of three months *la14*-. **2** a school term *17*-. [Gael *ràithe*]

raith *see* REDD[3.1], REDD[3.2]

raither, rether, rather, *Sh NE* **redder** /'reðər, 'rɛðər; *Sh NE* 'rɛdər/ *adv* rather, sooner, more truly *15*-. **ratherly** rather *19, 20- N Uls*. [OE *hraþor*]

raivel[1.1], **ravel,** *Sh* **raevl,** *Ork* **raffle** /'revəl; *Sh also* 'refl; *Ork* 'rafəl/ *n* **1** a muddle, a tangle, a confusion *la19*-. **2** a broken or frayed thread, a loose end *19, 20- T Uls*. [see the verb]

raivel[1.2], **ravel, reavel, raffle,** *Sh* **raeffle,** *T* **rowl,** *SW* **rael,** *SW* **rile,** *SW Bor* **reul** /'revəl; 'rafəl; *Sh also* 'refəl; *T also* rʌul; *SW* rɛil; *SW Bor* rjul/ *v pt, ptp* **raveled, ravelt,** †**raivlit 1** to get into a state of confusion, muddle or disorder *la15*-. **2** to entangle (yarn) *18*-. **3** *of yarn* to unwind from a reel *la18*-. **4** to speak incoherently, ramble, be delirious *la19*-. **5** to confuse, perplex *la19*-. **6** to confuse or outwit *20- Sh Ork NE*. †**travelment** a confusion, a tangle *e19*. **get raffled** an expression of dismissal *la20*-. **go an raffle yersel** an expression of dismissal or contempt *la20*-. [Du *ravelen, rafelen* to tangle, fray out]

raivelled, ravelled, raivelt, *Sh* **reffelled** /'revəld, 'revəlt *Sh* 'refəld/ *adj* **1** tangled, confused, in difficulties *la16*-. **2** confused in mind; rambling, delirious *la19*-. **3** *of hair* dishevelled, unkempt *20- NE EC SW*. **raivelled hesp** a tangled skein; an intricate problem, a state of confusion *17-19,* *20- Sh*. **raivell'd pirn** = *raivelled hesp 19*-. **raivelled skein** = *raivelled hesp la19*-. [participial adj from RAIVEL[1.2]]

rak[1] /rak/ *n* an emaciated creature *20- Sh*. **rakkie** skinny, in poor condition *20- Sh*. [perhaps ON *hrak-* in compounds, denoting wretched]

rak[2] /rak/ *v* to roam *20- Sh*. [Norn *rak*]

rak *see* RACK[1], RECK[1.1], RECK[1.2]

rakcat *see* RACKET[1]

rake[1.1], †**raik** /rek/ *n* **1** a raking tool *la15*-. **2** a very thin person *la16*-. **3** a grasping, hoarding person *20*-. **4** an accumulation, a hoard *la19- NE T EC*. [ME *rake*, OE *raca*]

rake[1.2], †**raik** /rek/ *v* **1** to rake, gather together (hay or straw) with a rake *17*-. **2** to cover (a fire) with small coal or ashes so that it will not go out overnight *16*-. **3** to turn over and smooth out (seaweed) in the last stages of kelp-burning *la19- Sh Ork N Uls*. **4** to search (a person) *19- NE C Bor*. **5** to rub (the eyes); to scratch *18-19, 20- Sh NE*. **6** to drag *20- Sh*. **raker 1** a person who cleans or gathers (something) by raking *la16*-. **2** the person on a farm who rakes up the straw left after the sheaves are tied *19-e20, la20- historical*. **3** a large lump of coal put on a fire to keep it burning through the night *20- H&I C*. **rakyt** *of a fire* covered (for the night) *e16*. **rakin coal** a lump of coal put on a fire to keep it burning *19- WC SW Bor*. [from the noun or ON *raka* to rake]

†**rake[2], raik, reik** *n* a stretch of water *17*. **the Rake** a stretch of river, mainly the Dee or Don, devoted to salmon fishing *la14-17*. [OE *rǣcan* to stretch, extend, ON *rák* a streak, a stripe]

rake *see* RACK[1], RAIK[1.1], RAIK[1.2], RAIK[2.2], RICK[1.2]

rakket *see* RACKET[1]

rakki[1.1], rackie /'raki/ *n ships* the mechanism used to raise or lower the yard of a lugsail *la19- Sh*. [Norn, ON *rakki*]

rakki[1.2] /'raki/ *v ships* to hoist or lower the mainsail *la19*-. [see the noun]

rakki[2] /'raki/ *n fisherman's taboo* a dog *20*-. [Norn, ON *rakki* a dog]

rakkill *see* RACKLE

rakkin *see* RECKON

rakles *see* RECKLES, RECKLESS

raklie *see* RAUCLE

rakster *see* REKSTER

rale *see* RAEL[1.2]

ralliach *see* ROIL

rally[1.1] /'rale/ *n* a disorderly crowd; a piece of boisterous fun *19, 20- Sh*. [see the verb]

rally[1.2], ralyie /'ralɪ, 'raljɪ/ *v* to crowd or bunch together; to play around together in a boisterous manner *la19, 20- Sh*. [Eng *rally*, MFr *rallier* to reassemble, regroup]

rally[2.1] /'rale/ *n* a quarrel, a row *20- Sh Ork*. [see the verb]

rally[2.2] /'rale/ *v* to scold, speak angrily to (a person) *la19- Sh NE T Bor*. **rally on** = RALLY[2.2] *la18- Sh NE T Bor*. [Fr *railler* to mock]

rally[3], rullye /'ralɪ, 'rʌljɪ/ *n* a sudden movement, a lurch *la19- Sh Ork*. [Norn *ralli*]

ralyie *see* RALLY[1.2]

ralzy *see* RELY

ram[1], †**rame** /ram/ *n* **1** a male sheep, a ram *la15*-. **2** a battering-ram *16-e17*. **3** a ramrod *e16*. **ramhorn spoon** a spoon made from the horn of a ram *la16*-. **ram race 1** a headlong rush *16-19, 20- Sh WC Bor*. **2** heedless, impetuous activity *la18-19, 20- Sh WC Bor*. **3** a short burst of speed to gain impetus *19- Sh WC Bor*. **ram reel** a reel danced by men only (especially by freemasons) *19- N NE T Bor*. †**ram stick** a ramrod *e17*. [OE *ramm*]

ram[2] /ram/ *v* **1** to stuff with food or drink *18*-. **2** to push, shove, clear one's way by pushing and shoving *la19*-. **3** to punish by bumping the buttocks against a wall or by caning the soles of the feet *la19-*. **ram-full** crammed full (of food or drink) *20-*. [probably from the noun RAM¹]

ram-, rum- /ram, rʌm/ *prefix intensifier* prefixing words implying force, vigour or disorder, *eg* RAMFEEZLE, RAMSCOOTER, RUMGUMPTION *18-*. [unknown; there may be some influence from RAM¹]

ramage *see* RAMMAGE¹, RAMMAGE²

ramagiechan /ramə'gixən/ *n* a big, awkward, impetuous person *19- NE T*. [unknown]

ramail *see* RAMMEL

†**ramas** *v* to gather or add together; add up *la16-17*. [MFr *ramasser*]

ramayn *see* REMAIN¹·¹, REMAIN¹·²

rambaleugh *see* RUMBALLIACH

ramble *see* RAMMEL, RAMMLE¹·²

†**rambooze** *adv* suddenly, headlong *la19 Sh*. [RAM- + BOOSE²·¹, BOOSE²·²]

†**ramburse, remburse** *v* to repay (money); to reimburse *la16-17*. [MFr *rembourser*]

rambust /ram'bʌst/ *adj* boisterous, rough *19- NE Bor*. [altered form of Eng *rumbustious*, with possible influence from RAM-]

rame¹·¹, †raim /rem/ *n* a phrase, a remark repeated over and over *la16-*. [see the verb] .

rame¹·², raim, rhame, †raym, †ream /rem/ *v* 1 to cry aloud, shout or roar *16*. 2 to repeat, recite something; to drone on monotonously *18-19, 20- Uls*. 3 to dwell on (something), complain at length about *la19- Bor*. 4 to talk nonsense, rave *19- Sh Ork EC Bor*. 5 to obtain (something) by repeated requests *e16*. [ON *remja* to roar]

rame *see* RAM¹

ramember, ramemmor *see* REMEMBER

rames *see* RAMMISH¹·¹

ramfeezle, ramfoozle /ram'fizəl, ram'fuzəl/ *v* to muddle or confuse; to exhaust *la18-19, 20- NE T C Bor*. [apparently coined by Burns, with possible influence from RAM-]

ram-gam /'ram'gam/ *adj* precipitate, rash, heedless *20- Ork*. [perhaps RAM- + GAMS²]

ramgunshoch /ram'gʌnʃəx/ *adj* bad-tempered, rude, boorish *18-19, 20- NE SW Bor Uls*. [unknown; first element may refer to RAM¹; compare also GANSH¹·²]

ramiegeister, †rammyjeester /ramɪ'dʒistər/ *n* a sharp blow; something that causes a shock *19- NE*. [unknown]

ramised /'ramɪst/ *adj* 1 dazed from being woken up or from lack of sleep *la19- Sh*. 2 stupid *la19 Sh*. [Norn *ramist*, Norw *romsen*; vowel influenced by Scots RAMMISH¹·²]

rammack, †rammock /'ramək/ *n* 1 a big rough piece of wood, a stick; a worthless object *la19- NE*. 2 a big, coarse person; a large, worthless animal *19- NE*. [perhaps related to Gael *ramachdair* a coarse, vulgar person]

rammage¹, †ramage /'raməɡʒ/ *adj* 1 *of people* violent, wild, unruly, frenzied *la15-*. 2 *of animals or birds* especially *hawks* wild, untamed, unruly *la15-e17*. Compare RAMMISH¹·². [ME *ramage* MFr *ramage* wild, unkempt]

†**rammage², ramage** *adj of velvet or taffeta* patterned with a representation of branches and foliage *la16-e17*. [OFr, MFr *ramage* full of branches, living in the woods]

rammall *see* RAMMEL

rammatrek /'ramətrɛk, 'ramətrɛk/ *n* 1 badly spun yarn, stuff spoiled in the manufacturing process *la19- Sh*. 2 rubbish *20- Sh*. 3 a poor or damaged corn crop *20- Sh*. 4 an unruly crowd *20- Sh*. [Norn *ramatrag*]

rammel, †ramble, †rammall, †ramail /'raməl/ *n* 1 branches *20-*. 2 small branches, thin timber or cut brushwood suitable for fences or fuel *la13-19*. 3 brushwood, undergrowth *16*. [OFr *ramaille* branches]

rammie *see* RAMMY

rammish¹·¹, †rames, †rammise /'ramɪʃ/ *v* to rush about frantically; to become frenzied *la15-17*. **rammish to deid** to die as a result of furious activity or a frenzy *17, 20-* literary. [back-formation from the adj]

rammish¹·², †ramsh, Ork †ramse /'ramɪʃ/ *adj of people or animals* wild, unruly; deranged *la15-19, 20- Ork NE*. **rammsie** *of children* boisterous *20- Ork*. [probably altered form of RAMMAGE¹]

rammle¹·¹ /'raməl/ *n* noisy or riotous behaviour; a noisy drinking bout *18- NE C SW Bor*. **on the rammle** drinking heavily *la19- EC Bor*. [unknown]

rammle¹·², ramble /'raməl, 'rambəl/ *v* 1 to wander, travel *19-*. 2 to wander about aimlessly, especially under the influence of drink *18- NE T SW Bor Uls*. **rammel't** drunk *20- EC Bor*. [altered form of Eng *ramble*]

rammy, rammie /'rame/ *n* a free-for-all, a violent disturbance, a scuffle *20-*. [unknown]

rammyjeester *see* RAMIEGEISTER

ramp¹·¹ /ramp/ *n* 1 an outburst of temper, a violent mood *la19- NE T*. 2 a romp, a scuffle *19, 20- NE*. [see the verb]

ramp¹·² /ramp/ *v* 1 *of horses or lions* to rear, stand on the hindlegs with forelegs raised in a threatening posture *la15-*. 2 to play boisterously *19- NE T EC SW Uls*. 3 to stamp, beat the floor with the feet *la18- C SW Bor Uls*. 4 *of plants* to climb, ramble *la20- NE Uls*. 5 *of people* to act in a fierce manner, rampage *la15-17*. [ME *raumpen*]

ramp² /ramp/ *adj* 1 strong or coarse in flavour or smell *19, 20- Uls*. 2 wild, unruly, disorderly *la17-e19*. [probably altered form of Eng *rank*]

†**ramp³** /ramp/ *v of milk* to become glutinous *19*. [perhaps RAMP²]

rampage¹·¹ /'rampedʒ/ *n* an outburst of rage or fury; violent, disorderly behaviour; riotous living *19-*. **on the rampage** rampaging *la19-*. [see the verb]

rampage¹·² /ram'pedʒ, ram'padʒ/ *v* 1 to rage or rush about furiously *la17-*. 2 to play roughly or boisterously *la19-*. [RAMP¹·² + noun-forming suffix -*age*]

rampant, †rampand /'rampənt/ *adj* 1 *heraldry of a lion* standing facing left on the left hindleg with both forelegs raised, the right above the left, and the head in profile *15-*. 2 fierce, wild, unrestrained *la15-*. [ME *raumpaunt*]

ramper eel /'rampər 'il/ *n* 1 the sea lamprey *Petromyzon marinus* or river lamprey, *Lampetra fluviatilis*; any large eel *la18-*. [altered form of LAMPER EEL]

rampis *see* RAMPS

rample /'rampəl/ *v* to play roughly, sport *19-*. [frequentative form of RAMP¹·²]

ramps, †rampis /ramps/ *n* wild garlic *Allium ursinum 16-19, 20- Bor Uls*. [OE *hramsa*]

ramscallion /ram'skalɪən, ram'skʌlɪən/ *n* a rascal *la19-, 20- Uls*. [EModE *rapscallion*]

ramscooter /ram'skutər; *NE* ram'skwitər/ *v* to beat, batter or trounce *la19-*. [unknown; the first element is perhaps RAM-]

ramse /'rams/ *adv* vigorously, furiously *20- Ork*. [RAMMISH¹·²]

ramse *see* RAMMISH¹·², RAMSH²

ramsh¹, ransh /ramʃ, ranʃ/ *v* to munch, crunch and chew vigorously *19- NE T C*. [onomatopoeic]

ramsh², ramse /ramʃ, rams/ *adj* 1 *of food or drink* unpalatable, coarse or having a strong flavour *19, 20- Sh Ork NE T EC*. 2 *of people* brusque, impatient *la19- NE*. 3 *of yarn* rough, coarse-textured *20- Ork NE T EC*. [perhaps ON *ramr* bitter, strong]

ramsh *see* RAMMISH¹·²

ramshackle *see* RANSHACKLE

ram-stam[1.1], **ram-tam** /'ramˈstam, 'ramˈtam/ *n* **1** a headstrong, impetuous person or action *la18-*. **2** the strongest kind of ale, drawn from the first mash *la18-e19*. [see the adj]

ram-stam[1.2] /'ramˈstam/ *v* to rush or blunder about in a headlong, impetuous way *19-*. [see the adj]

ram-stam[1.3] /'ramˈstam/ *adj* headstrong, heedless *18-*. **ram-stamphish** rough, unrefined *19-*. [probably RAM[1] or RAM- + STAM[2]]

ram-stam[1.4] /'ramˈstam/ *adv* headlong, without forethought *18-*. [see the adj]

ramstoorie /ramˈsture, ramˈsturi/ *adj of a worker* vigorous but careless, rough-and-ready *20- NE T EC*. [RAM- + STOOR[1.2] + -IE[2]] check hw form

ramstougar /ramˈstugər/ *adj* rough, disorderly *19-*, *20- WC*. **ramstougerous** = RAMSTOUGAR. [unknown; first element is probably RAM-]

ram-tam *see* RAM-STAM[1.1]

ran *see* RAND, RIN[1.2]

rance[1.1] /rans/ *n* **1** a prop, a wooden support, stay or strut *la18-*, *20- NE*. **2** the stretcher of a table or chair *19- NE T SW*. **3** a bar for securing a door *la19- EC SW*. **4** a prop to strengthen a wall of coal or the roof of a working in a mine; a pillar of coal left for this purpose *19- C*. **5** the crossbar or wire of a fence *la18- NE Bor*. †**rannsett** the stretcher of a table or chair *la17*. **rance piller** a prop, a wooden support, stay or strut *e17*. †**rance wall** *mining* a wall of coal supporting the roof of a working *18*. [MFr *rance* a wooden prop]

rance[1.2] /rans/ *v* **1** to prop up, brace (a building or mine) *la17- C Bor*. **2** to make fast, close up, especially by wedging a bar across an opening, fasten firmly to prevent motion *19*, *20- EC*. [see the noun]

rancell *see* RANSEL

†**rancie** *adj* ruddy-complexioned *e19*. [unknown]

ranclit *see* RANKLED

†**rancounter**[1.1], **rencounter**, **ranconter**, **rencontre** *n* **1** a hostile encounter, a battle, a skirmish, a duel *la16-19*. **2** a chance meeting *16-19*. **3** a dispute *17*. **4** *law* an unpremeditated combat *la17*. [see the verb]

†**rancounter**[1.2], **rencounter**, **ranconter**, **rencontre** *v* **1** to encounter by chance *16-19*. **2** to engage in combat, attack; to meet in battle *la16-17*. **3** to challenge (an action) *17*. **rancounter with** to come upon, fall in with *17*. [MFr *rencontrer*]

rand, **ran** /rand, ran/ *n* **1** a border, an edge *18-19*, *20- Sh*. **2** a strip, a narrow section *19*, *20- T*. **3** a stripe or section of a different colour or texture *la18- SW Bor*. [MDu *rand* a margin, a border, a strip]

rander[1.1] /'randər/ *n* **1** senseless, incoherent talk *19-*, *20- N Bor*. **2** a talkative person *19- Bor*. **randers** senseless, incoherent talk *19-*, *20- N Bor*. [see the verb]

rander[1.2] /'randər/ *n* order, regulation, restraint *la18- NE*. *19-*, *20- N Bor*. [see the verb]

rander[1.3], **render** /'randər, 'rɛndər/ *v* **1** to hand over (a person or thing) (to another); to surrender *la14-*. **2** to give back or restore (a thing); to give (thanks) *16-*. **3** to repeat words; to emit sounds *16-*. **4** to produce or bring forth (fruits or feelings) *16-*. **5** to cause to become *16-*. **6** to discharge pus from a wound *la19-*. **7** to talk idly or nonsensically, ramble *19*, *20- Sh N Uls*. †**rander compt**, **rander count** to give (an account) of, justify, especially one's faith *la16-e17*. [ME *rendren*]

rander *see* RANTER[1.1], RANTER[1.2]

randevous, **randezvous** *see* RENDEZVOUS[1.1]

randevouze, **randezvouse** *see* RENDEZVOUS[1.2]

randibow /'randibo/ *n* an uproar; a wild party *20- Sh*. [Eng *rantipole*]

randie[1.1] /'rande, 'randi/ *n* **1** a beggar woman; any foul-mouthed, brawling, bad-tempered woman *la18-*. **2** a loose or dissolute woman *19-*. **3** a (usually rude or quarrelsome) beggar, a ruffian *18-19*, *20- N EC SW*. **4** a boisterous, mischievous person *20- NE SW Bor Uls*. **5** an escapade *la19- NE Uls*. [see the adj]

†**randie**[1.2] *v* to behave in an abusive, belligerent manner *19*. [see the adj]

randie[1.3], **randy** /'rande, 'randi/ *adj* **1** wild, unruly, dissipated *18-*. **2** *of a woman* loud-voiced, coarse and aggressive *19*. **3** *of language* coarse, uncouth; obscene *la19-*. **4** lecherous, lustful; sexually excited *20-*. **5** rough, belligerent, riotous, aggressive, *la18-19*, *20- Sh C*. [probably RANT[1.2] + -IE[2]]

randit /'randɪt/ *adj* striped or streaked with different colours *19- SW Bor*. [RAND + -IT[2]]

randle *see* RANTLE

†**randoun**, **randon** *n* a straight course or line *la14-16*. **at randon** quickly; heedlessly *17*. **in a randoun** at speed; directly *la14-16*. **in randoun** = *in a randoun*. [ME *randoun*]

randy *see* RANDIE[1.3]

randyvoo *see* RENDEZVOUS[1.1]

rane[1.1], *T* **rone** /ren; *T* ron/ *n* a constant refrain, a prolonged or repeated utterance, frequently a complaint or demand *15-19*, *20- NE T H&I*. **rennie**, **ronnie** = RANE[1.1] (sense 1) *la19- T EC*. †**in a rane** continuously, without stopping *la14-16*. [probably Gael *rán* shout, roar; also compare RAME[1.1]]

rane[1.2], *T* **rone** /ren; *T* ron/ *v* **1** to utter a continuous noise; to keep on repeating; to complain; to ask persistently *15-19*, *20- T EC*. **2** to recite (a song, ballad) monotonously *19- T H&I C*. **ronnie on** = RANE[2] *la19- T*. [perhaps from the noun; also compare RAME[1.2]]

rane *see* RAIN[1.2]

ranegill, †**renigald** /'ranəgɪl/ *n* a rough character, a renegade, especially a Tinker *16*, *19- NE Bor*. Compare RANGLE. [conflation of EModE *renegade* with *rangaill* (RANGLE)]

rang *see* REENGE[1.1], RING[2.2], RING[3.2]

rangaill *see* RANGLE

rangald, **rangale** *see* RANGLE

rangat *see* RANGIT

range *see* REENGE[1.1], REENGE[1.2], REENGE[2.1], REENGE[2.2]

rangiebus *see* REGIBUS

rangit, †**rangat** /'raŋɪt/ *n* **1** a rabble (especially of soldiers); a crowd, a group *17*, *20- NE*; compare RANGLE (sense 1). **2** disorder, commotion *e16*; compare RANGLE (sense 3). [variant of RANGLE with altered ending]

rangle, †**rangaill**, †**rangale**, †**rangald**, †**ringald** /'raŋəl/ *n* **1** a rabble (especially of soldiers); a crowd, a group *la14-19*, *20- NE*. **2** camp followers *la14-e15*. **3** disorder, commotion *la15-16*. [OFr *ringaille* the lowest ranks of an army, camp followers]

Ranish *see* RINS

rank[1.1] /raŋk/ *n* **1** a row or line (especially of soldiers) *16-*. **2** people from a particular social class *la16-*. **3** *St Andrews University* a division in the order of merit awarded to students at the end of the class work of the academic year (before the degree examinations) *la19-*. **4** a group (of people) belonging to a trade *17*. [EModE *rank*]

rank[1.2], *NE* **runk** /raŋk; *NE* rʌŋk/ *v* **1** to draw up in a line; to put in order; to classify *la16-*. **2** *law* to place (a creditor) in his due place on the list of accredited claimants to the realized estate of a bankrupt; *of a creditor* to be placed thus *18-*. **3** to get ready, prepare, especially dress before going out *la19- NE*. **ranking 1** putting in order *la16-*. **2** *law* the formation of a list of accredited claimaints *la17-*. **ranking**

and sale *law* the process whereby a bankrupt estate is sold and the price divided among the creditors *18-*. **rank oot** to prepare for use *19- NE*. [see the noun]

rank[1,3] /raŋk/ *adj* **1** downright, absolute *la15-*. **2** abundant, copious; thick, dense *la15-*. **3** noxious *16-*. **4** strong, formidable *16-e19*. **5** swift, impetuous *16-e19*. Compare RONK. [OE *ranc* proud, arrogant]

rank[2] /raŋk, raŋk/ *adj of a boat* top-heavy, unstable *la19- Sh Ork*. [Norn *rank*, Norw *rank*]

rankle *see* RINKLE

rankled, †**rankild**, †**ranclit** /'raŋkəld/ *adj* embittered *16-*. [ptp of Eng *rankle*]

ranksman /'raŋksmən/ *n* (a member of another crew of) a boat fishing in collaboration with another boat and sharing the price of their catches *la19- Sh*. [RANK [1,1] + MAN]

rannegald *see* RINAGATE

rannle *see* RANTLE

rannle bauk /'ranəl bɔk/ *n* a bar of wood or iron fixed across the chimney from which the chain and hook for holding cooking utensils is suspended *19- Ork EC Bor*. [RANTLE + BAUK[1,1]]

rannoch /'ranəx/ *n* fern, bracken *20- H&I*. [Gael *raineach*]

ranowne *see* RENOWN[1,1]

ransel, †**ransell**, †**rancell** /'ransəl/ *v* to make an official search for stolen property *17- Sh Ork*, *20- historical*. †**ranseler** = *ranselman 17-e19 Sh Ork*. **ranselman**, †**rancelman** the official charged with searching for stolen property *17- Sh Ork*, *la20- historical*. [unknown; the first element is probably from ON *rann* a house]

ransh *see* RAMSH[1]

ranshackle, **ranshaikle**, **ramshackle** /ran'ʃakəl, ran'ʃekəl, ram'ʃakəl, ram'ʃekəl/ *v* to search, ransack *19- Bor Uls*. [EModE *ransackle*, from *ransack + -le* frequentative suffix]

ransom[1,1], †**ransoum**, †**ransoun** /'ransəm/ *n* **1** a sum or price paid or demanded for the release of a prisoner or the restoration of captured property; the action of paying such a sum *la14-*. **2** an exorbitant price or rent *19-*. [ME *raunsoun*]

ransom[1,2], †**ransoun**, †**ranson** /'ransəm/ *v* **1** to redeem *la14-*. **2** to set free on payment of ransom *la14-*. [from the noun or ME *raunsounen*]

rant[1,1] /rant/ *n* **1** a long angry speech, a tirade *18-*. **2** a lively tune or song, especially one suitable for an energetic dance; frequently in titles of dance tunes *18-*. **3** an extravagant celebration, a festive gathering with music and dancing *la17-19*, *20- Sh Ork NE*. **4** boisterous or riotous merrymaking, (an occasion of) excess especially in drinking *la17-19*, *20- NE*. †**rantie** frolicsome, full of boisterous fun *la18-19*. **rantie-pipes** *in the answer to a riddle* **1** a lamb *20- Sh*. **2** a duck *20- Ork*. [see the verb]

rant[1,2] /rant/ *v* **1** to be uproariously merry, indulge in boisterous fun; to behave riotously *18-19*, *20- Sh NE T C*. **2** to make a great noisy fuss, complain at length *la19- N SW Uls*. **3** to play or sing a lively tune, especially for a dance *la18-19*. **ranter 1** a person who declaims with passion and at length, originally especially on religious subjects *la19-*. **2** a dissolute, riotous person *la18-19*. **3** a person who played for dancers, a strolling minstrel *la18-e19 literary*. **rantin 1** roistering, merry, uproarious *18-*. **2** *of a fire* burning strongly, blazing *18-19*. **rantinlie** merrily, uproariously *18-*. [Du *ranten* to talk foolishly, rave]

ranter[1,1], *N* **rander**, †**raintter** /'rantər; *N* 'randər/ *n* **1** a rough, hasty stitching or sewing *20-*. **2** a scrawl, a scribble *20- N*. **3** (neat) sewing *17*, *20- EC*. [see the verb]

ranter[1,2], *N* **rander** /'rantər; *N* 'randər/ *v* **1** to sew together, darn, mend neatly *17-19*, *20- Sh Ork N EC Bor*. **2** to mend or stitch hastily or roughly *19*, *20- EC*. **3** to work in a careless, hasty manner *la19- NE*. [Fr *rentraire* to darn, mend]

ranter[2,1] /'rantər/ *n* order, tidiness *20- NE*. [see the verb]

ranter[2,2] /'rantər/ *v* to tidy (up); to set (out) in order *20- NE*. [perhaps RANTER[1,2] with reference to sense 1]

†**rantie-tantie**, **ranty-tanty** *n* **1** a reddish-leaved plant found in cornfields, formerly eaten as a vegetable, probably the common sorrel *Rumex acetosa la17-19*. **2** a drink distilled from heath and other vegetable substances *19*. **3** fornication *18*. [unknown; sense 3 possibly associated with RANT[1,2]]

†**rantle**, **rannle**, **randle** *n* = RANTLE-TREE *la17*. [reduced form of RANTLE-TREE]

rantle-tree, *Ork N* **rantree** /'rantəl'tri; *Ork N* 'rantri/ *n* **1** a thin, stick-like person or thing *19-*. **2** a bar across a chimney from which pots were suspended *la18- NE T C SW Bor*. **3** a roof-beam, a rafter *la18-e19*. [compare Norw dial *randa-tre*]

ranty-tanty *see* RANTIE-TANTIE

rap[1,1] /rap/ *n* **1** (the noise made by) a blow; a sharp knock (at a door) *15-*. **2** an instant, a moment *18-*. **in a rap** = RAP[1,1] (sense 2) [probably onomatopoeic]

rap[1,2] /rap/ *v* **1** to (cause to) strike sharply or violently; to fall with a sharp thud *16-*. **2** to knock, bang at (a door); to cause (a knocker stick or door) to make a banging noise *16-*. **3** *of rain or arrows* to fall rapidly in a shower or in drops *16-19*, *20- Sh Ork*. **4** *of the penis* to function adequately *e16*. **5** to give evidence, inform *e19*. **rap aff** to cause (a gun) to fire repeatedly *19-*. †**rap furth** to emit (thunder) with a clap *e16*. **rap to** to slam (a door) *17- Sh NE*. **rap up** to rouse by knocking *la19*, *20- Sh N SW*. [see the noun]

rap[2] /rap/ *n* an ineffectual person or a cheat *19- N EC SW Uls*. [probably Eng *rap* a good-for-nothing from Ir *rapaire* a counterfeit coin; compare Gael *rap* a bad coin and *raipaire* a worthless fellow]

rap[3] /rap/ *n pl* oilseed rape *Brassica napus 18-19*, *20- SW*. [perhaps Du *raap*]

rape *see* RAIP[1,1]

raperee, **roparie** /'repəri, 'ropəri/ *n* a ropeworks *19-*. [RAIP[1,1] with *-ery* suffix]

raploch[1,1], †**roploch** /'raplɔx/ *n* coarse, homespun, undyed, woollen cloth; a garment made of this *16-*. **raploch grey** = RAPLOCH[1,1]. [unknown; compare the Stirling place-name *Raploch*, though no specific connection is established]

raploch[1,2], †**rapplach** /'raplɔx/ *adj* **1** *of persons* ordinary, undistinguished; without manners *la19- NE T H&I*. **2** made of RAPLOCH[1,1], coarse, homespun, undyed *18-e19*. **3** homemade, unrefined, rough-and-ready *la18-19*. [see the noun]

raport *see* REPORT[1,2]

rapplach *see* RAPLOCH[1,2]

rapple /'rapəl/ *v* **1** to grow rapidly, shoot up *19-*. **2** to make or mend hurriedly and roughly *19-*. [probably frequentative form of ME *rapen* to hasten]

†**rapt** *n* **1** abduction or violation by force, rape *16-17*. **2** the violent seizure (of goods) *la16-e17*. **3** a forcible movement, a carrying away *e17*. **4** robbery, plunder *e17*. [Lat *raptus* a carrying off by force]

rapture /'raptʃər/ *n* **1** (a fit of) ecstasy or delight *la17-*. **2** a paroxysm or fit of rage *19- C SW Bor*. [EModE *rapture*]

raquer *see* REQUIRE

raquest *see* REQUEST[1,1]

rare[1,1], *WC* **rerr**, †**rair** /rer; *WC* rer/ *adj* **1** uncommon, scarce *la16-*. **2** unusually excellent, admirable *la16-*. **3** exceptional, extreme *20-*. **4** *of a number of people* small; *of a gathering* sparsely attended *la16-17*. **5** odd, strange *17*. [MFr *rare*, Lat *rārus*]

rare[1,2] /rer/ *adv* to an exceptional degree *la16-*. [see the adj]

rare see RAIR¹·¹, RAIR¹·²

rarity /'rerətɪ/ n **1** a thing of exceptional excellence *la17-*. **2** something of great scarcity *la18-*. **3** fewness of numbers; sparseness of attendance (at a meeting) *16-17*. [MFr, Fr *rareté*, Lat *rāritās*]

rascal, †**rascall**, †**rascaille** /'raskəl/ n **1** a rogue *la16-*. **2** (one of) the common people or a riotous group of people *la16-19*. **Rascal Fair** a hiring market for the employment of men who had failed to get employment at a regular market *la19- NE*. **rascal knot** a kind of knot tied on the straw bands of corn sheaves *20- NE Bor*. [ME *rascaile, raskaille*, AN, OFr *rascaille*]

rasch see RASH¹, RASH²·¹

rasche see RASH²·², RASH²·³

†**rase** v pres **rasys** to growl, bark furiously *e16*. [MDu *rāsen* to rage, also (of a dog) to be rabid]

rase see RACE¹·¹, RAZE

raser see RIZZAR

rash¹, **resh**, **rush**, *EC Bor* **thresh**, *WC* **thrash**, †**rasch**, †**resch**, †**ris** /raʃ, reʃ, rʌʃ; *EC Bor* also θreʃ; *WC* also θraʃ/ n **1** a plant of the order *Juncaceae*, which grows in marshy ground *la15-*. **2** the pith of a rush, a peeled rush used for a lamp wick *19- N*. **rashen** made of rushes *la18-*. **rasher** = RASH¹ (sense 1) *la19- Bor*. **rashie 1** = RASH¹ (sense 1) *19-*. **2** made of rushes; overgrown with rushes *18-*. **Rashiecoat** the name of the heroine of the Scottish version of *Cinderella*, who wore a coat of rushes *20-*. **rash buss** a clump of rushes *16- NE SW*. **the rash buss keeps the cow** referring to a time of peace and security from marauders *16-17, 18- literary*. **rush corn** inferior oats fed unthreshed to livestock *18*. [ME *rishe*]

rash²·¹, †**rasch** /raʃ/ n **1** (the noise of) a violent impact, a crash *la15-e16*. **2** a sudden downpour of rain or hail *19-*. **3** a sudden stabbing pain *20- Sh*. [see the verb]

rash²·², †**rasche** /raʃ/ v **1** to produce a stabbing or searing pain; to throb *la19-*. **2** to rain heavily *19, 20- Ork N*. **3** to rush violently or hastily *16-e19*. **4** to cast or pour out hurriedly *16-e18*. **5** to bang together, with violence or force *16-17*. **6** to smash or break with violence *e16*. [ME *rashen*]

rash²·³, †**rasche** /raʃ/ adj **1** impetuous, hasty, headstrong *la15-*. **2** *of speech* ill-considered *la16-*. **3** active, agile, vigorous *19- SW Bor*. [ME *rash*]

rask /rask/ n rank, luxuriant growth *20- Sh*. **raskit** having excessive leaf growth *20- Sh*. [unknown; compare ROOSK, also Dan, Swe *rask* vigorous]

rasour see RAZOR

rasp /rasp/ n **1** the fruit or plant of the raspberry *Rubus idaeus 18-*. **2** a mole; a red-coloured birthmark *20- EC*. [unknown]

rasys see RASE

rat¹, †**ratt** /rat/ n a rodent of the genus *Rattus la16-*; compare RATTON. **rat tail**, **rat's-tail** the seed-head of the greater plantain *Plantago major la19-*. [OE ræt]

rat²·¹ /rat/ n a rut or groove; a deep scratch *16-19, 20- Bor Uls*. [unknown]

rat²·² /rat/ v to score or scratch; to make a rut or groove (in) *16-*. [unknown]

†**ratann** n a drumming, a quick succession of taps *la18*. [onomatopoeic; compare Fr *rataplan* a military drum-roll]

†**ratch¹**, †**roch**, †**rotche** n the barrel of a gun *la16-e18*. [shortened form of Fr *rochet* a lancehead; a spool]

ratch²·¹ /ratʃ/ n a scratch, a line *la19, 20- SW Bor*. [see the verb]

ratch²·² /ratʃ/ v to damage by rough handling; to tear or scratch *19- Bor*. [perhaps onomatopeoic or conflation of RAT²·² + Eng *scratch*]

ratch see RACHE¹·¹, RACHE¹·²

†**ratchell** n a hard stony crust under the soil, a gravelly subsoil *la18-19*. [probably Fr *rochaille* an agglomeration of small stones]

ratchell salt see RACHEL SAUT

rate, †**rait** /ret/ n **1** an amount, a value; a standard valuation, a fixed charge, a price *la15-*. **2** a code of conduct or behaviour *la16-17*. **at nae rate** not under any circumstances, by no means *la18-19, 20- T*. [Fr *rate*, Lat *rata*]

rath /raθ/ n a circular earthwork, a defensive homestead or settlement; frequently in place-names *15-*. [Gael *ràth*, IrGael *ráth*]

rath see RAITH, REDD³·¹, REDD³·²

rather see RAITHER

Rathven Market /'rafən 'markət/ n a horse fair held in the town of Buckie, Banffshire *la19-*. Compare PETER FAIR. [from the name of a village near Buckie + MERCAT]

†**ratihabit** v *law* to express approval of; to sanction (a crime or criminal) *la17-e18*. [Lat *ratihabēre*]

†**ratihabition**, **ratihabitioun** n *law* approval, approbation or a sanction *16-e18*. [Lat *ratihabitio*]

†**rationable**, **rationabill**, **racionabil** adj reasonable, just, right *la14-16*. [Lat *ratiōnābilis*]

†**rat rane** /'rat ren/ n a string of meaningless words; a rigmarole, a tedious repetition; a piece of doggerel verse *16-*. [unknown first element + probably Gael *rán* shout, roar]

rat-rhyme, †**rat-rime** /'rat rʌɪm/ n a string of meaningless words; a rigmarole, a tedious repetition; a piece of doggerel verse *16-*. [unknown first element + RHYME¹·²]

†**ratt**, **rot** n a line (of soldiers) *17*. [Du *rot*]

ratt see RAT¹

ratten see RATTON

rattill see RATTLE¹·¹, RATTLE¹·²

†**rattis** npl a wheel used as an instrument of torture and execution *16-e17*. [MDu *rat*]

rattle¹·¹, †**rattill** /'ratəl/ n **1** something that makes a rattling sound, a toy *la17-*. **2** a rapid succession of percussive sounds, a banging or clashing sound *16-*. **3** a sharp blow, a thump, a crash *17-*. **4** a strong uvular r, a burr in speech *18-19, 20- NE*. †**rattle bag** a bag filled with small stones on the end of a stick, used to make a rattling noise *la18-e19*. **rattle head** *mining* a suction pipe *la19, 20- EC*. †**rattle scull** a thoughtless, empty-headed person *18-19*. **rattle stane**, **rattle steen** in a children's rhyme a hailstone *la19- NE T WC SW*. [probably onomatopoeic; compare Du *ratel*]

rattle¹·², †**rattill** /'ratəl/ v **1** to make a rapid series of short sharp noises *la15-*. **2** to strike or beat repeatedly, (cause to) hit, crash noisily *19, 20- Sh N T*. **3** to pronounce a strong uvular r, speak with a burr *la18-*. **4** to do (something) with great haste *20-*. **5** to chatter; to talk (nonsense) *16-*. **rattle someone's jaw** to strike someone, not necessarily on the face *la20-*. **rattle up** to make (something) speedily and not too carefully *19-*. [probably onomatopoeic; compare Du *ratelen*]

ratton, **ratten**, **rottan**, †**rattoun** /'ratən, 'rɔtən/ n **1** a rat *15-*. **2** a nickname, a contemptuous term or term of endearment for a person *la16-*. †**ratton fa** a rat-trap *la17-e19*. **ratton's nest** a state of perpetual unrest and bustle *19-*. [OFr *raton* a young rat]

rauchan, **rachan** /'rɔxən 'raxən/ n a plaid or wrap, traditionally worn by shepherds; a rough garment *la17-19, 20- T*. Compare MAUD. [Gael *rachdan* a tartan plaid worn as a cloak]

rauchle, **rachle** /'rɔxəl, 'raxəl/ n a loose, untidy heap of objects; something ramshackle or dilapidated *la19-*. [perhaps variant of RUCKLE = RICKLE with influence from RAUCLE]

rauchle see RAUCLE

raucht see REAK¹·²

rauck see RAUK[2.2]
raucky /'rɔke/ *adj* scratchy *20- SW*. [RAUK[1.1], RAUK[1.2] + -IE[2]]
raucle, rackle, rauchle, rachle, †rackel /'rɔkəl, 'rakəl, 'rɔxəl, 'raxəl/ *adj* **1** *of persons*, rough, crude, tough, uncouth *la18-*. **2** *of speech* rough, unpolished, blunt to the point of rudeness *la18-*. **3** strong, sturdy, robust *19-*. **4** hard, stern, grim, unbending *19-*. **5** bold, impulsive, rash *la17-, 20- EC*. **rachlie** dirty and disorderly *19-*. **†raklie** rapidly, impetuously *la15*. **rackle-handed 1** bold, impetuous *la17-*. **2** strong and sturdy *19-*. **3** having powerful hands *la19-*. [ME *rakel*]
rauk[1.1] /rɔk/ *v* to clear the chest or throat of phlegm, hawk *la19- T EC*. [probably from the adj]
†rauk[1.2], **rawk** *adj* hoarse, raucous *la15-19*. [OFr *rauque*, Lat *raucus*]
†rauk[2.1] *n* a scratch; a scratching sound *la19*. [see the verb]
†rauk[2.2], **rauck** *v* **1** to grope; to rummage *la18-19*. **2** to scratch *e19*. [altered form of RAKE[1.2]]
rauk see ROUK[1]
raux see RAX[1.2]
rav see RAFF[2]
rave[1.1] /rev/ *n* **1** a person who talks volubly and incoherently *20-*. **2** a vague rumour, an unlikely story *19*. [see the verb]
rave[1.2], **†raif** /rev/ *v* to talk wildly or foolishly; to behave delusionally or confusedly *15*. [ME *raven*]
†rave[2] *v* to wander, stray or roam *la16-19*. [ME *raven*; compare Icel *ráfa*; later occurrences may be altered form of Eng *rove*]
rave see RIVE[1.2]
ravel[1.1], **revil, †reavil, †ravil** /'revəl/ *n* **1** a rail, a railing; a balustrade; a bridge parapet *16-*. **2** the horizontal beam in a byre fixed to the tops of the stakes for the attachment of cows' tethers *18-*. **3** a plank or beam *la16*. **†traveling** railing; railings *17-19*. **ravel tree, realtree** = RAVEL[1.1] (sense 2) *la17, 18- SW Bor Uls*. [compare Faer *revil* a fillet of wood, Du *ravel* a plank, a beam, a rafter]
†ravel[1.2] *v* to enclose with a railing *17-19*. [see the verb]
ravel see RAIVEL[1.1], RAIVEL[1.2]
ravelled see RAIVELLED
raven, †travin, †rawine, †revin /'revən/ *n* a large black bird of the crow family *Corvus corax la14-*. [OE *hræfn*]
ravenous, †rawenous, †revanus /'ravənəs/ *adj* **1** predatory, voracious; rapacious *la15-*. **2** famished *20-*. **3** *of a river* fast-flowing *e16*. [OFr *ravinos* impetuous]
raverie, reverie, †revery /'revəre/ *n* **1** noise, din *e16*. **2** a fanciful notion, a fantasy *17-*. **3** a rumour, a piece of gossip *la18-*. **4** madness, raving; furious or deranged speech; nonsense, foolish talk *la16-19, 20- NE*. **5** wantonness, wildness, an instance of this *15-e16*. [OFr *raverie*]
ravest see REVEST
ravil see RAVEL[1.1]
ravin see RAVEN
ravish, †travis, †trevis, †trevisch /'ravɪʃ/ *v* **1** to seize and carry off by force; to rape *la14-*. **2** to transport, carry away with feeling, fill with rapture *la15-*. **3** to carry from earth to heaven, transport spiritually *la14-e17*. [ME *ravishen*]
ravsay /'ravsi, 'ravzi/ *adj* unkempt, slovenly *la19- Ork*. [unknown]
raw[1.1], **row** /rɔ, ra, ro/ *n* **1** a row of houses, usually of a uniform construction with common gables, frequently applied to miners' or farmworkers' cottages; a street of such houses *13-*; *in street-names 13*. **2** a line *la14-*. **3** a ring of people, especially children *19, 20- SW Bor*. **4** a collection of persons or things of a particular kind; a bank of oarsmen *16*. **†on raw 1** in a line *la14-16*. **2** in order, in succession, one after another *la14-16*. **†on raws** in lines *la15-e16*. [OE *ræw*]

raw[1.2], **row** /rɔ, ra, ro/ *v* **1** to arrange in a line *19- Ork C SW*. **2** *of root crops* to plant, come up in lines or drills *19, 20- SW*. **3** to drive (sheep) in single file, especially bring (late lambing ewes) in single file off the hill to a place suitable for lambing *la19- SW Bor*. [see the noun]
raw[2.1] /rɔ/ *n* neat whisky *19, 20- Sh N*. [see the adj]
raw[2.2], *Sh Ork NE* **ra** /rɔ, ra/ *adj* **1** *of food* uncooked *15-*. **2** *of yarn or textiles especially silk* unprocessed; *of cloth* unfulled *16-*. **3** *of persons, birds* immature *la16-*. **4** *of corn-sheaves* damp, not fully dried out *la19, 20- Sh NE*. **5** *of grain* undried (in a kiln) *16-e17*. **raw gabbed** voluble in an ill-informed way *la19- Sh*. **raw leaven** uncooked oatcake dough *20- Sh NE*. **raw sowens**, *NE* **rawsins**, *N* **rawins** unboiled SOWANS *19, 20- Sh Ork N NE*. **†raw mowit** = *raw gabbed e16*. [OE *hrēaw*]
raw[3] /rɔ/ *v of grain* to absorb moisture, grow mouldy *la19- Sh*. [probably related to Norw *roste* to mash]
rawenous see RAVENOUS
rawine see RAVEN
rawk see RAUK[1.2]
rawn, rowan, *Sh Ork N* **raan, †rown, †roan, †roun** /rɔn, 'rʌuən; *Sh Ork N* rɑn/ *n* **1** the roe of a fish *16-*. **2** the turbot *Scophthalmus maximus la18-19, 20- NE*. **rawner** an unspawned salmon *19-*. **rawn fleuk** = RAWN (sense 2). [ME *roune*; compare Dan *raun*, ON *hrogn*]
rawsins see RAW[2.2]
rax[1.1], *Sh Ork* **rex, †wrax** /raks; *Sh Ork* rɛks/ *n* **1** the act of stretching, a pull, a stretch *la18-*. **2** a strain, a sprain *la19-*. **3** the act of reaching; reach *19-*. [see the verb]
rax[1.2], *Sh Ork* **rex, †raux, †wrax** /raks; *Sh Ork* rɛks/ *v* **1** to stretch *la14-*. **2** to make a great effort; to overexert, strain a part of yourself; to rouse yourself *16-*. **3** to deal (a person) a blow *18-*. **4** to lengthen by stretching, pull out; to extend something to its full reach or capacity; to be flexible or accommodating *16-*. **5** to hang a person *16-*. **6** to reach out or over the hand or arm; to give a person your hand *17-*. **7** to extend, raise up the head or eyes in order to look or listen; to crane the neck *19-*. **8** to hand a person down or over an object *19-*. **9** to sprain a limb *la19-*. **10** to reach for, stretch out to take or grasp something; to help yourself to food *20-*. **11** to extend in distance from one point to another, reach *20-*. **12** to grow, develop *la18-19*. **13** to expand your power; to rule *15-16*. **rax oot** *of day length* to increase *la19- Sh NE T*. [OE *raxan* to stretch; REX forms perhaps by conflation with Norn *rekk*]
†trax[2], **racks** *n pl* **raxes rackses, raxis** a set of bars used to support a roasting spit or other cooking utensil *16-e19*. [plural of RACK[1]]
rax see REX
†tray[1.1] *n* **1** clothes *la14-15*. **2** order of battle *la15-16*. [aphetic form of Eng *array*]
†tray[1.2] *v* to draw up in order of battle *la14-e17*. [see the noun]
†tray[2] *n* a king; a man *e16*. [ME *roi* or variant *rai*]
ray see RAE[2]
raym see RAME[1.2]
rayn see RAIN[1.1], RAIN[1.2]
raynge see REENGE[1.2]
rays see RACE[1.1], RISE[1.2]
rayson see REASON[1.1]
raze, *Sh* **raaz, †trase, †traise** /rez; *Sh* rɑz/ *v* **1** to demolish or level *la17-*. **2** to pare, shave *la16-*. **3** to gash, cut or tear *la14-19, 20- Sh*. **4** to erase writing; to alter by erasure *15-19*. [ME *rasen*]
razor, razzor, †rasour /'rezər, 'razər, 'rɔzər/ *n* **1** an implement designed for shaving *la14-*. **2** a bivalve mollusc of the family *Solenidae*, having a long narrow shell, a razor fish

20-. **Razor Kings** a Glasgow gang of the 1920s and 30s *20, 21- historical*. [ME *rasour*]

†**reabill, reable, rehabile** *v* to restore to a former state or position; to legitimize *16-17*. [re- + MFr *habiler* to make appropriate to a function]

reach /ritʃ/ *v* to retch, try to vomit *la19-*. [OE *hrǣcan* to bring up (blood or phlegm)]

reach see RIACH

read[1.1] /rid/ *n* **1** an act or spell of reading; something read *20-*. **2** a loan (of a book) for the purpose of reading it *19-*. [see the verb]

read[1.2], †**rede**, †**reid**, †**red**, †**ride** /rid/, *v pt, ptp* **read** †**red**, †**rede**, †**reid 1** to understand the meaning of written matter *la14-*. **2** to foretell the future by interpreting (dreams, riddles, playing cards or tea cups) *15-*. **3** *of a preacher* to read a sermon, rather than preach extempore *la18-*. **4** to speak or tell (of) *la14-15*. **5** to teach a particular subject *la16-e17*. **reader**, †**readar 1** a person who reads written matter; a student *la15*. **2** a person who reads and expounds to students, a teacher; a lecturer of the highest grade below professor *16-*. **3** *Presbyterian Church* the person appointed to read Scriptures in the absence of a minister *la16*. **reading 1** the action of looking at written matter with comprehension *la15-*. **2** the ability to read *la16-*. **3** the action of uttering (written matter) aloud, especially of the reading of prayers or Scriptures by a reader during church services *16-*. **4** the formal uttering aloud of (a particular portion of) written matter *15-*. **5** *Presbyterian Church* a passage from the Bible read aloud, especially in family worship *la16-*. **6** the foretelling of the future *19, 20- Ork SW*. **readin-med-aisy**, **reediemadeasy** a first school reading book *19-*. **readin sweetie** a piece of confectionery with a motto written on it, a conversation lozenge *20-*. †**read richt** to have or take a correct view *16*. **read up** to read aloud *19, 20- EC SW*. **read someone their character** to tell (a person) what you think of them *la19- Sh*. [OE *rǣdan*]

ready[1.1], †**redy**, †**reddy** /ˈrɛde/ *v* **1** to make ready, prepare *la14-*. **2** to cook (food), prepare (a meal) *la17*. [see the adj]

ready[1.2], †**redy**, †**reddy**, †**raddy** /ˈrɛde/ *adj* **1** *of persons* in a state of preparedness, willing *la14-*. **2** *of things* immediately available, convenient; direct *la14-*. **3** *with infinitive or verbal noun* apt, liable, likely to: ◇*ready makin mistakes la16-*. **readily**, †**reddily**, †**reddilie 1** promptly, willingly, without delay; easily *la14-*. **2** probably; naturally, in the normal course of events *17-19*. **as ready tae row as rin** *of a very fat person* as capable of moving by rolling as running *20- Ork NE*. [ME *redi*]

reaff see REIF

reak[1.1], *Sh* **raek**, *Ork SW* **raik**, †**reyk**, †**rike** /rik/; *Sh* rɛk; *Ork SW* rek/ *n* ability or power to reach *16-19,20- Sh Ork SW*. [see the verb]

reak[1.2], *Sh* **raek**, *Ork SW* **raik**, *SW* **reek**, †**reke**, †**reyk**, †**rike** /rik/; *Sh* rɛk; *Ork SW* rek/ *v pt, ptp* **reakit, rauchit 1** to extend; to stretch out yourself or a limb; to hand, proffer something *la14-*. **2** to reach for, grasp *la14-19, 20- Sh Ork SW*. **3** to deliver (a blow), wound *la14-19, 20- Sh SW*. **4** to stretch or extend between two points or to a point, attain *la14-19, 20- Sh*. **5** to pass round wine; *of wine* to circulate *la15-e17*. **6** to grant, bestow *la15-16*. **7** *of money* to suffice *15-16*. **reekim, rickam** a sharp blow, a quarrel *19-*. [perhaps MDu *reiken*, OE *rǣcan*, ON *rekkja*]

real see RAEL[1.1], RAEL[1.2]

reall see RAEL[1.1], ROYAL[1.2]

real raiser see RAISER

realte see ROYALTY

realtree see RAVEL[1.1]

ream[1.1], *Sh* **raem**, †**reme** /rim; *Sh* rem/ *n* **1** cream *la15-*. **2** the froth on top of beer *la18-19, 20- NE EC Uls*. **reamy 1** of a creamy consistency; consisting of or made with cream *19-*. **2** frothing *19, 20- NE*. **ream breid** oatcakes made with cream *20- NE*. **raem calm** a sea as still as the surface of cream *la19- Sh*. **ream cheese** cheese made from cream *la18-19, 20- NE*. **ream pig** a jug for holding cream *la19-*. **ream stoupie** = *ream pig 20- NE*. [OE *rēam*]

ream[1.2] /rim/ *v* **1** to skim the cream off milk *18-*. **2** *of beer or soapy water* to form a froth or foam *18-*. **3** *of alcohol* to confuse the mind *la18-*. **4** *of milk* to remain still till the cream rises *la19-*. **5** *of a person* to be filled with an emotion *la19-*. **6** to sprinkle a surface thickly *la19- Sh*. **reamer** a shallow dish for skimming cream off milk *19-*. **reamin**, †**reamand** *of a vessel* full to the brim of a frothy liquid; *of beer* frothy, overflowing with froth *16-*. †**reaming dish** = *reamer 18-e19*. **reamin fou** full of frothy liquid *la18-*. **ream ower** to overflow, run over *la18-*. [see the noun]

ream see RAME[1.2]

reap, raep, †**raip** /rip, rep/ *v* to reap, harvest crops; to derive advantage, benefit from *la16-*. [ME *repen*]

rear, †**reir** /rir/ *n* the back; back part *la15-*. †**on reir** back; in the background *la15*. [probably aphetic form of AREAR]

rease see RAISE[1.2]

reasing see RAISIN

reason[1.1], **raison, rizzon**, †**resoun**, †**ressoun**, †**rayson** /ˈrizən, ˈrɛzən, ˈrɪzən/ *n* **1** mental faculty; the power of thinking *la14-*. **2** a statement, fact or circumstance advanced in support of a contention, an argument; an explanation; a legal plea; a justification or proof *la14-*. **3** that which is right, propriety *la14-e17*. **4** justice; satisfaction *15-e17*. **5** a statement, report, speech or writing; a legend; a motto; a notice *15-e17*. **6** a moderate or settled way of life *la15-16*. **oot o rizzon** *of prices* unreasonable, exorbitant *19-*. **oot o yer reason** mad *la19, 20- Sh NE T*. **rizzon or nane** with or without reason on one's side; obstinately *la19, 20- NE*. [ME *resoun*]

reason[1.2], **raison, rizzon**, †**resoun** /ˈrizən, ˈrɛzən, ˈrɪzən/ *v* to discuss rationally; to question; to persuade by argument *15-*. [ME *resounen* and from the noun]

reath see RAITH

reave see REIVE

reavel see RAIVEL[1.2]

reavel-ravel see REVIL-RAILL

reavil see RAVEL[1.1]

reawté see ROYALTY

reb see RIB[1.1]

rebaghle /rəˈbaxəl, rəˈbɔxəl/ *n* disparagement, reproach *19-*. [probably altered form of REBALK]

rebak see REBALK

rebald see RIBALD[1.1], RIBALD[1.2]

rebalddaill see RIBALDAILE

†**rebalk, rebak** *v* to abuse, reproach *la15-16*. [unknown]

reban see RIBBON

rebat /rəˈbat/ *v* to give a curt, brusque or discouraging reply *la19- NE*. [perhaps Eng *rebate* to repress, diminish or REBUT[1.2]]

rebat see RABAT

†**rebegeastor** *n* a stroke with a stick *la16*. [unknown; compare RAMIEGEISTER]

rebel[1.1], †**rebell**, †**rabel**, †**rabell** /ˈrɛbəl/ *n* **1** a person who disregards or flouts authority; a person in opposition to any established system *14-*. **2** a person who engages in armed resistance against an established authority *16-*. **3** *law* a lawbreaker, latterly a debtor, declared outside the law by being put to the horn *14-19, 20- historical*. [see the adj]

rebel[1,2], †**rebell** /rəˈbɛl/ v to oppose or resist established authority; to refuse allegiance; to disobey a lawful superior *la14-*. †**rebeller, rebellour, rebellar** a person who rebels against lawful authority *la14-e19*. [ME *rebellen*, Lat *rebellāre*]

rebel[1,3], †**rebell**, †**rabell** /ˈrɛbəl/ *adj* 1 refusing obedience or allegiance; offering armed resistance to authority *la14-*. 2 declared outside the protection of the law, outlawed *16-e19, 20- historical*. [ME *rebel*, Lat *rebellis*]

rebellion, †**rebellioun** /rəˈbɛljən/ *n* 1 an act of resistance to established government; an insurrection *15-*. 2 an act of disobedience to or defiance of any superior or authority *15-*. 3 *law* failure to obey a legal command or summons; (the penalty of) public denunciation as a rebel *15-17*. [ME *rebellioun*, Lat *rebellio*]

rebet *see* RYBAT

rebeuk *see* REBUKE[1,2]

rebig /rɪˈbɪɡ/ *v* to rebuild *la17- Sh Ork N NE*. [re- + BIG[1]]

rebook *see* REBUKE[1,1], REBUKE[1,2]

rebound[1,1], *NE* **reboun**, †**rebund** /rəˈbʌund, rəˈbund; *NE* rəˈbun/ *n* 1 the action of bouncing back *20-*. 2 a loud explosive noise as of gunshot, a reverberation *la19- NE EC*. 3 a reprimand, a severe rebuke *20- NE T EC*. 4 a violent impact *e16*. [19 and 20 Sc occurrences from Eng *rebound*, and from the verb; e16 occurrence from EModE *rebound* or MFr *rebond*]

rebound[1,2], †**rebund** /rəˈbʌund, rəˈbund/ *v* 1 to spring back, start away, usually from a stimulus *la15-*. 2 *of sounds* to reverberate; *of places* to re-echo *e16*. [ME *rebounden*]

†**rebous, rebouris, rabous** *n* 1 a contrary movement; movement back *e16*. 2 threatening speech or behaviour *e16*. **at rebouse** in the wrong or opposite direction; amiss, perversely, through perversity *la14-15*. **but rebous** without fuss or objection *e16*. [MFr *rebous*]

reboyt *see* REBUT[1,2]

rebuke[1,1], †**rebuik**, †**rebook** /rəˈbjuk/ *n* 1 a reprimand *la16-*. 2 shame, disgrace *16*. †**but rebuik** without check, incessantly *e16*. [see the verb]

rebuke[1,2], **rebook**, †**rebeuk**, †**rebuik** /rəˈbjuk, rəˈbuk/ *v* to criticize, admonish *la16-*. [ME *rebuken*, EModE *rebuke*]

rebund *see* REBOUND[1,1], REBOUND[1,2]

rebut[1,1], †**rebute** /rəˈbʌt/ *n* a repulse or check; a rebuff, a rebuke, a reproach *la15-*. [see the verb]

rebut[1,2], †**rebute**, †**reboyt**, †**rabut** /rəˈbʌt/ *v* 1 to repel, repulse *la14-*. 2 to revile, rebuke or reproach *la14-19*. 3 *curling* to play a very forceful shot in the late stages of a game *19*. 4 to repel, reject (something offered) *la15-16*. 5 to deprive (of something) *e16*. [ME *rebouten*]

reca, recall /rəˈka, rəˈkɔl/ *v* 1 to remember; to recount *la16-*. 2 to call back, cause or require to return or be returned *17-*. [re- + CA[1,2]]

receed, receid *see* RESIDE

receipt, †**recept**, †**reset**, †**ressait** /rəˈsit/ *n* 1 the action or fact of receiving *15-*. 2 the action or fact of receiving a person into shelter, accommodation or custody *la15-*. 3 written acknowledgement of something received *la16-*. 4 the instructions for making something; a recipe *19-*. 5 a (medical) prescription or preparation *16-19, 20- T SW Uls*. 6 amounts of money or goods received; a written record of these *la15-17*. Compare RECIPE[1,1]. [ME *receit*]

receive, †**resave**, †**ressave** /rəˈsiv/ *v* 1 to accept; to take possession of; to take on; to be the recipient of *la14-*. 2 to meet, welcome a person; to admit; to accept as a member; to harbour, shelter; to take under control *la14-*. 3 to undergo *la14-*. 4 *of a thing* to admit, accommodate *la15-*. 5 *in imprecations* to obtain possession of, seize, carry off: ◊*God receive me 16-19, 20- Sh Uls*. [ME *receiven*]

recent /ˈrisənt/ *adj* 1 that has happened in the immediate past; originating lately; belonging to the immediate past *16-*. 2 undiminished by the passage of time, in full vigour; fresh, unspoiled *la15-e17*. [MFr *recent*, Lat *recens*]

recepe *see* RECIPE[1,1]

recept *see* RECEIPT, RESET[1,1] RESET[1,2]

†**recheng, rechene** *n* rechange, the re-exchange of a bill *la15*. [re- + *change* (CHYNGE[1,1])]

rechnie *see* REECHNIE

recipe[1,1], †**recepe** /ˈrɛsəpe/ *n* 1 the instructions for preparing food *19-*. 2 a formula for a medical prescription *16-19, 20- T SW Uls*. 3 a procedure or plan for attaining a particular result *19-*. Compare RECEIPT [Lat *recipe* a formula for a medical preparation]

†**recipe**[1,2] *v as an instruction in a list of ingredients* to take *la15*. Compare RECEIPT. [Lat *recipe*, imperative singular of *recipere* receive]

†**reck**[1,1], **rek, rak** *n* heed, care *la15-19*. [see the verb]

†**reck**[1,2], †**rek**, †**trak** *vpt* **reckit, roucht, rocht** 1 to heed, have regard for, care about *la14-19*. 2 to reckon, consider or think *la18-19*. [OE *reccan*]

†**reckles, rakles** *v* to neglect; to be negligent or heedless *la16*. [OE *rēcelēasian*]

reckless, rackless, †**rekles**, †**rakles** /ˈrɛkləs, ˈraklǝs/ *adj* 1 heedless of consequences, rash, negligent *la14-*. 2 accidental, unintentional *16-19*. **racklessly, recklessly** 1 heedlessly, rashly *la14-*. 2 through carelessness; accidentally *la14-17*. [OE *rēcelēas*]

reckon, rackon, †**trekkin, trakkin** /ˈrɛkən, ˈrakən/ *v* 1 to compute, count, calculate; to include in a count or reckoning *la14-*. 2 to list, mention one after another, name serially *la14-*. 3 to hold or consider as being of a certain worth, importance or character; to regard *15-*. 4 to draw up an account or financial statement *la15-e17*. 5 to place or name according to a specified order; to work out a genealogy *15-e16*. **reckoning**, †**rekning**, †**raknyng** 1 calculation, computation, enumeration *la14-*. 2 a mode or method of numbering or computation *la14-*. 3 the action of rendering an account to another person; an account so rendered *14-*. 4 an account to be given of one's actions *14-*. 5 a bill, an account of charges due *15-*. †**compt and rekkin** to draw up an account or financial statement *la15-17*. †**to compt and rekkining** pending settlement of what is due; on account *la15-16*. [OE *recenian*]

reclaim[1,1], †**reclame** /rəˈklem/ *n* 1 the claiming back of a thing *20-*. 2 a protest or objection *16*. [ME *reclaim*, EModE *reclaim*]

reclaim[1,2], †**reclame**, †**recleme** /rəˈklem/ *v* 1 to claim back; to claim again *la16-*. 2 to protest, object, be in opposition *16-*. 3 *law* to appeal a judgement, especially to another court, in recent times from the Outer House to the Inner House of the Court of Session *la16-*. 4 to recall or bring back from error to a better state *la15-17*. 5 to train (a hawk) *e19*. **reclamation** 1 the action of claiming back *17-*. 2 *law* an appeal *la16-e17*. **reclaiming motion** *law* the procedure by which an appeal is made from the Outer to the Inner House of the Court of Session *20-*. †**reclaiming note** = *reclaiming motion la19*. †**reclaiming petition** = *reclaiming motion 18-19*. [ME *reclaimen*, Lat *reclāmāre*]

reclead /rəˈklid/ *v* to reclothe *la19- Sh T WC*. [re- + CLEED]

recleme *see* RECLAIM[1,2]

recognition, †**recognitioun** /rɛkəɡˈnɪʃən/ *n* 1 the act of identifying or acknowledging *18-*. 2 *law* the resumption of land by a superior, originally due to failure to observe the conditions of tenure; specifically when a vassal had sold half or more of it without the superior's consent *la15-e18*, *la18- historical.* **3** an inquiry or investigation by a jury, an inquest *15-17.* [AN, MFr *recognition,* Lat *recognitio*]

recognize, †recognis, †reconis, †racunnys /'rɛkəgnaez/ *v* **1** to identify, acknowledge *16-.* **2** to repossess land or rights *la14-e17.* [AN *reconis-,* pl stem of *reconoistre,* influenced by Lat *recognōscere*]

recognosce /rɛkəg'nos, rɛkəg'noz/ *v* **1** *law of a feudal superior* to resume possession of property *15-e18, la18- historical.* **2** to verify, affirm as authentic *la15-e17.* **3** to recognize, identify *16-17.* **4** to acknowledge; to admit *16-e17.* **5** to revise, amend *la16-18.* [Lat *recognōscere*]

recoil, †recule, †recull /rə'kɔɪl/ *v* **1** to start back, retreat *la14-.* **2** *of an action* to come back on, rebound *20-.* [ME *recoilen*]

recoird *see* RECORD[1.1]

recollect, †recolleck /rɛkə'lɛkt/ *v* **1** to remember *la18-.* **2** to collect, gather together *e16.* [Lat *recollect-,* ptp stem of *recolligere*]

†recomfort, reconfort *v* to strengthen, inspire; to console *la14-16.* [AN *recomforter,* OFr *reconforter*]

recommend /rɛkə'mɛnd/ *v* **1** to put forward, mention an idea *la15-.* **2** to commit or consign oneself to another or to God *la14-.* **3** to direct (an employer) to a person suitable for employment *19- NE T.* **4** to commend, praise a person *la14-16.* **5** to commend, convey one's service to another *16.* [ME *recommenden,* Lat *recommendāre*]

recompans *see* RECOMPENSE[1.1]
recompanse *see* RECOMPENSE[1.2]
recompence *see* RECOMPENSE[1.1], RECOMPENSE[1.2]

†recompensation, recompensatioun *n* **1** compensation; reward (for an outlay or effort); atonement *la14-16.* **2** *law* a counterclaim of compensation raised by a pursuer in an action for debt where the defender has pleaded compensation as a defence *la17-19.* [ME *recompensacioun,* Lat *recompensātio*]

recompense[1.1]**, †recompens, †recompence, †recompans** /'rɛkəmpɛns/ *n* **1** compensation; return, reward *la15-.* **2** *law* a non-contractual obligation by which a person is obliged to restore a benefit derived from another's loss *la17-.* **3** a counterclaim *19.* **4** retribution, revenge *la15-16.* **5** atonement *la15-16.* [AN, MFr *recompense,* Lat *recompensa*]

recompense[1.2]**, †recompens, †recompence, †recompanse** /'rɛkəmpɛns/ *v* **1** to compensate for, make good loss, damage or expenses; to make restitution for (sin) *la15-.* **2** to reward effort or service *16-.* **3** *law* to put forward a counterclaim in a debt action *e18.* **4** to repay a person, retaliate, take revenge; to repay by retaliation *la15-16.* [ME *recompensen,* re- + Lat *compensāre*]

reconcile, †reconsal, †reconsel, †recounsell /'rɛkənsʌɪl/ *v* **1** to restore (a previous state or relationship); to readmit a person into the church; to restore to favour; to settle a quarrel; *of estranged persons* to come together again *la14-.* **2** to render compatible or consistent *la16-.* [ME *reconcilen*]

reconis *see* RECOGNISE
reconter *see* RECOUNTER[1.2]
recontre *see* RECOUNTER[1.1]
recontyr *see* RECOUNTER[1.2]

reconvention, †reconventioun /rikən'vɛnʃən/ *n law* the right to sue a person who has brought an action against one, even if that person lives in another country and is thus in another jurisdiction *la15-.* [MFr *reconvention,* Lat *reconventio*]

recooorse *see* RECOURSE[1.1]

record[1.1]**, †recoird, †racord** /'rɛkərd/ *n* **1** a written, or otherwise preserved, account or attestation *la15-.* **2** *law* the official report of the proceedings in a court of law, including the judgement given *15-.* **3** *law* a document consisting of the pleadings of the parties to an action and interlocutors pronounced in it *la15-.* **4** repute, account *15-19.* **5** *law* an attestation by an officer of a court that he has served a summons or other writ *la15-e17.* **6** a statement; a reply *15-16.* **7** testimony, witness; proof *la14-16.* [ME *record*]

record[1.2]**, †racord** /rə'kɔrd/ *v* **1** to relate, narrate or mention in writing or another permanent form; to give a written account of or put on record *la14-.* **2** to relate orally, say, tell, speak of *la14-e17.* [ME *recorden*]

†recounter[1.1]**, recontre** *n law* the action of offering a counter-pledge or security *15-16.* [see the verb]

†recounter[1.2]**, reconter, recontyr** *v* **1** to engage in combat; to attack *15-16;* compare RANCOUNTER[1.2]. **2** to meet by chance, come across *la15-17.* **3** *of a defender in a lawsuit* to oppose the giving of a pledge by offering a counter-pledge *15-17.* [re- + Eng *counter* or MFr *rencontrer*]

recourse[1.1]**, recoorse** /rə'kors, rə'kurs/ *n* **1** the action of resorting or turning to (a means of support) *la16-.* **2** *law* the right of the assignee to claim compensation from the assignor, especially in the case of failure to honour a bill of exchange or in the case of eviction *18-.* **have recourse to 1** to resort to, turn to (for resolution); to apply for advice or assistance to a person or institution *15-.* **2** to have access to; to choose to go to a place *15-19.* **3** *law* to have the right to bring a cause back before a court *la15-17.* [ME *recours,* Lat *recursus*]

recourse[1.2] /rə'kors/ *v* to return; to resort or turn to *la15-.* [see the noun]

recreant, †recreand, †recryand, †recryant /'rɛkrɪənt/ *adj* cowardly; treacherous *la14-.* [ME *recreaunt*]

recreate, †recreat /'rɛkriet/ *v* **1** to refresh, divert, amuse oneself *16-.* **2** to refresh, reinvigorate the mind *la15-19.* [Lat *recreāt-,* ptp stem of *recreāre*]

recreit *see* RECRUIT
recrew *see* RECRUE

recrimination /rəkrɪmə'neʃən/ *n* **1** an accusation or reproach *17-.* **2** *law* a counter-charge on grounds of adultery in a divorce action *la18-.* **3** *law* the action of bringing a counter-charge in a legal action *la17.* [MFr *recrimination*]

†recrue, recrew *n* a body of troops (providing reinforcement) *17.* [Fr *recrue*]

recruit, recreit, †recrute /rə'krut, rə'krit/ *n* **1** a newly-enlisted soldier *18-.* **2** a body of troops (providing reinforcement) *la17-.* [altered form of RECRUE; compare Du *recruut*]

rector, †rectour /'rɛktər/ *n* **1** *in Scottish Universities* the elected representative of the student body on the University Court, in post for three years, originally the elected head of the University, subordinate only to the chancellor *16-;* compare LORD RECTOR. **2** the incumbent of a parish; a clergyman in charge of a full congregation of the Scottish Episcopal Church *la16-.* **3** the title of the headteacher of some secondary schools *18-.* **4** a ruler *la15-16.* **†Rectorate, †Rectorat** the office of university rector *17-19.* **rectorial 1** of a rector *18-.* **2** the canvassing and ceremonial connected with the election and inauguration of a university rector *la19-.* **Rectorship** the office of a rector *la16-.* [Lat *rector* a ruler, one who guides]

recuir *see* RECURE[1.1], RECURE[1.2]
recule, recull *see* RECOIL

recur, †ricur /rə'kʌr/ *v* **1** *of an event* occur repeatedly *16-.* **2** *law* come back (on), have legal recourse to *16-.* **3** go back, resort or have recourse to *la17-.* [Lat *recurrere* to run back]

†recure[1.1]**, recuir** *n* remedy *la14-16.* [see the verb]

†**recure**¹·², **recuir** *v* to cause to recover; get back; to redress *la15-17*. [Lat *recūrāre* and altered form of Eng *recover*]

red /rɛd/ *n* the track on a beach up which boats are pulled above high water level *20- Ork N*. [unknown]

red *see* RAD, RAID, READ¹·², REDD¹·¹, REDD¹·², REDD¹·³, REDE¹·¹, REDE¹·², REED³, REID¹·¹, REID¹·², RIDE¹·²

redargue /rəˈdargju/ *v* **1** *law* to refute; to cast doubt on; to disprove an argument or statement *la17-*. **2** to prove a person wrong by argument *la17-e18*. **3** to blame, reprove *la16-17*. [MFr *redarguer*, Lat *redarguere*]

red biddy /rɛd ˈbɪdɪ/ *n* a mixture of cheap red wine and methylated spirit or other alcohol *20-*. [REID¹·¹ + familiar form of the personal name *Bridget*]

Redcap /ˈrɛdkap/ *n folklore* a fairy or goblin said to haunt old buildings *19-*. [REID¹·¹ + shortened form of CAPIDOSE]

redcoal, redcoll, †**radcoll** /ˈrɛdkol, ˈrɛdkɔl/ *n* the horseradish *Armoracia rusticana 16-*. [EModE *redcole*; perhaps ME *red* rapid + *cole*]

Redcoat, Reidcoat /ˈrɛdkot, ˈrɪdkot/ *n* **1** a soldier in the British army *la17-*. **2** a ladybird *19- SW Bor*. [REID¹·¹ + Eng *coat*]

redcoll *see* REDCOAL

redd¹·¹, **red,** †**rade,** †**rede,** †**reid** /rɛd/ *n* **1** the act of clearing away or tidying up; a putting in order; a cleaning, a tidying *la15-*; compare RAAD¹·¹. **2** rubbish or rubble which has been or is to be cleared away *16-*. **3** waste material from a coalpit or quarry *18-*. **4** a combing and arranging of the hair *la19, 20- Sh NE T EC*. **5** the power to clear or sweep aside obstacles; energy, drive *la19- Sh Ork NE*. **6** the payment of (debts), the setting in order of (finances, affairs); the buying of (things) *la15-19*. **7** the curvature of a ploughshare which helps keep it clear of obstructions *la18-19*. **8** the act of completing (a job); fitting out (a ship) *la15-e16*. **redd bing** a heap of waste at the surface of a mine or quarry *la19, 20- EC*. **redd box** *mining* a truck for carrying rubbish to the pithead *la19- EC*. **redsman** *mining* the person who keeps the passages in a pit clear of debris *la17- EC*. **mak red** to make progress or headway in business *la16-19, 20- Sh Ork NE*. [see the verb]

redd¹·², **red, rid, raid,** †**rede** /rɛd, rɪd, red/ *v pt* **redd red** †**reddit 1** to put things in order, tidy up (a room or building) *16-*; compare RAAD¹·². **2** to clear a space, the way or a passage, make room, remove obstructions *15-*. **3** to clear land by reaping or ploughing *18-*. **4** to clear away, remove (a thing or person); to depart *la15-*. **5** to save, rescue *la15-*. **6** to free, relieve another or oneself of *la15-*. **7** *mining* clear ground or a site, clear out a ditch or channel, remove debris, rubbish or silt *15-*. **8** to clear (a fireplace or tobacco pipe) of ashes, poke up or out *la19-*. **9** to disentangle, unravel, sort out thread, yarn, ropes, fishing-lines or nets *16-*. **10** to separate combatants; to put an end to fighting *la15-*. **11** to tidy one's clothes or oneself *la16-*. **12** to comb hair *18-*. **13** to arrange; to settle affairs; to clear up, sort out problems or difficulties *15-*. **14** to fix exactly, verify or determine (boundaries) *15-*. **15** *law* to vacate a property, cause a property to be vacated, leave a house ready for the next occupant *la15-*; compare *void and redd* (VOID). **16** to clean the intestines of a slaughtered animal of fat *20- Sh Ork Bor*. **17** to clear the throat, nose or stomach *19- N NE*. **18** to save from burning; to put out a fire; to make haste ◊*fleein like tae redd fire la14-18, la19- NE*. **19** to clean out and renew the bedding of a housed animal *19, 20- NE*. **20** to pay money due, settle an account, clear a debt; to reimburse a person; pay for (a thing) *la15-17*. **21** to bring animals or people under control *la16*. **redder,** †**reddir 1** a comb *la19- Sh Ork N*. **2** a person who intervenes to stop a fight or quarrel *la15-19, 20- Sh*. **redding-up 1** a scolding,

a rebuke *la18-*. **2** a tidying *la19-*. **redment, reddiment 1** a settlement of affairs *19-*. **2** a tidying-up *20- Bor*. †**redder's lick** a blow received by a person trying to stop a fight *19*. **redder's straik** = *redder's lick 20-*. **redd kame, reddin kame** a comb for the hair *19-*. **reddin straik 1** = *redder's lick 18-*. **2** a severe blow (of fate) *17, 20- Sh*. **redd yer crap** to get something off your chest *la19- NE*. **redd yer fit** to clear the way for action or progress, extricate oneself from some difficulty *19-*. **redd the hoose** *curling* to clear the tee of stones with a fast, forceful shot *20-*. **redd the ice** = *redd the hoose 19-*. †**redd the marches** to go round the boundaries of a burgh or parish to verify that all is in order *la15-19*; compare RID, RIDE. **redd roads** to scythe corn round the edges of a field to allow space for a reaping machine *20, 21- historical NE*. **redd up** = *redding-up*. **redd oot** to make clean and tidy *20- T EC*. **redd oot kin** to trace lineage *19-*. **redd up relations** = *redd oot kin 20-*. [OE *hreddan* to rescue, MLG, MDu *reden* to put in order; compare ON *ryðja* to clear land]

redd¹·³, **red, rid,** †**reid** /rɛd, rɪd/ *adj* **1** *of land or fields* cleared of its crop, bare after cropping or ploughing *la15-*. **2** clear (of impediments, obstructions, rubbish; occupiers), unencumbered *la16-*. **redd-han, red-han** a freeing, a clearance, a free hand *la19-*. **redland oats** a crop of oats sown after a cleaning crop (such as turnips) *20- WC SW*. [ptp of REDD¹·²]

redd²·¹, *N* **rodd,** †**raid,** †**reid,** †**rod** /rɛd; *N* rɔd/ *n* **1** fish- or frog-spawn, *la15-*. **2** the rut in a riverbed made by salmon for spawning in *19-*. [unknown]

redd²·², *N* **rodd** /rɛd; *N* rɔd/ *v of fish* to spawn *18-*. **redding,** *N* **rodding,** †**roding** spawning *la15-*. [unknown]

†**redd**³·¹, **rath, raith** *adj* quick, hasty, eager; prepared, willing *la15-19*. **redd handit** quick and skilful with one's hands *la18-19*. [OE *hræd*]

redd³·², †**rad,** †**rath,** †**raith** /rɛd/ *adv* immediately, promptly, quickly, readily *la14-*. †**rathly** promptly, quickly *la14-e17*. **as redd as** as soon as, readily *20- NE*. [OE *hrede, hræde*]

redd *see* RAD, REDE¹·²

reddendo /rəˈdɛndo/ *n law* the duty or service to be paid by a vassal to a superior as set out in a feu charter; the clause in which this is set out *17-*. [Lat *reddendō* by giving in return]

redder *see* RAITHER

reddicle basket *see* RETICULE BASKET

reddie, redie, ruddy /ˈrɛdɪ, ˈrʌdɪ/ *n games* a red clay marble *la19- H&I WC*. [from the adj REID¹·¹]

reddin, redding /ˈrɛdɪn, ˈrɛdɪŋ/ *n* **1** the action of clearing, tidying; verifying (boundaries); separating (combatants); settling (disputes); removing (from a place) *la15-*. **reddins, reddings, reddance 1** rubble, debris *17-*. **2** the fat removed from an animal's intestines and used for making puddings *la19, 20- Sh Ork SW*. **3** clearance, riddance *19*. [verbal noun from REDD¹·²]

Reddshank *see* REDSHANK

reddy *see* READY¹·¹, READY¹·²

rede¹·¹, *Sh Ork* **rad,** †**red,** †**reid** /rid; *Sh Ork* rad/ *n* **1** advice, counsel *la14-19, 20- historical*. **2** a tale, a narrative *la14-e19*. **3** a course of action, a plan *la14-e17*. **4** reason, judgement *la14-e17*. **raddman, raadman** a councillor *19- Sh Ork*. [OE *ræd*]

rede¹·², †**redd,** †**red,** †**reid** /rid/ *v pt* **rede** *ptp* **redd,** †**rede 1** to advise or counsel; to warn *la14-*. **2** to interpret, explain *18-*. **3** to think, consider, reckon *la18-19*. **4** to guard, protect *la14-15*. [OE *rædan*]

†**rede**² *n* a sound, noise or commotion *la15-e16*. [unknown; compare REIRD¹·¹]

rede *see* READ¹·², REDD¹·¹, REDD¹·², REID¹·²

redeem, †**rademe**, †**redeme** /rəˈdim/ v **1** to repurchase a former possession; to buy back *15-*. **2** to free land from a bond by payment of the sum due; to rescue or deliver from captivity or sin *la15-*. [ME *redemen*]

Red etyn, †**Reid etin** /rɛd ˈɛtɪn/ n a mythical giant *16-*. Compare ETIN. [REID¹·² + ETIN]

red face *see* REID FACE

red fish /ˈrɛdfɪʃ/ n **1** a male salmon of the distinctive orange-red colour associated with spawning *15-*. **2** a red or pink fleshed fish; salmon or trout *16-*. **redfisher** a person who fishes for RED FISH *la16-*. †**redfishing** a salmon fishing ground *16-19*. [REID¹·² + Eng *fish*]

red hand¹·¹ /rɛd hand/ n in the act of committing a crime, or with the evidence still on the person or in the possession of the perpetrator *15-19, 20- historical*. **the Red Hand of Ulster** *heraldry* the arms of Ulster, a red left hand cut off squarely at the wrist *la18-19, 20- historical*. †**with red hand** in the act of committing a crime *15-e17*. [REID¹·² + HAN¹·¹]

red hand¹·² /rɛd hand/ adj **1** *of a crime* committed so recently that the perpetrator still bears clear evidence of its commission *15-*. **2** *of a person* in the act of committing a crime, or still bearing evidence of having just committed a crime *la16-*. **red handit, red handed** bearing evidence of having committed a crime *19-*. [see the noun]

redie *see* REDDIE

Red Lichtie, Reid Lichtie /rɛd ˈlɪxti, rɪd ˈlɪxti/ n **1** a nickname for a native or inhabitant of Arbroath *la19-*. **2** *pl* a nickname for Arbroath Football Club *20-*. [from the red light in the harbour]

redloon /ˈrɛdlun/ n a kind of moss which leaves red ashes when burned, peat of this sort *20- Ork*. [REID¹·² + Norn *lon* a piece of home pasture]

redment *see* REDD¹·²

red neb *see* REID NEB

redomyt *see* REDYMYTE

redoubted, †**redoutit** /rəˈdʌutəd/ adj feared; respected, distinguished *la14-*. [ME *redouted* and/or infinitive *redouten*]

redound, †**radoun** /rəˈdʌund/ v **1** to accrue to a person *la15-*. **2** to surge up, overflow *la15-16*. **3** to come back, return; to rebound; to resound *la15-16*. **4** to penetrate *16*. **5** to refund (money or costs) *16*. [ME *redounden*]

Red Rab /rɛd ˈrab/ n the robin redbreast, *Erithacus rubecula 20- C Bor*. [REID¹·² + familiar form of *Robert*]

redress¹·¹, †**redres**, †**radres** /rəˈdrɛs/ n **1** reparation, compensation *la14-*. **2** reformation; restoration; correction *la16-*. [AN *redresse* and from the verb]

redress¹·², †**redres**, †**radres** /rəˈdrɛs/ v **1** to right a wrong, remedy discord or trouble *la14-*. **2** to restore, give back; to make good a bill *16*. [ME *redressen*]

†**redschip**, **reidschip** n tackle, the equipment of a ship *la16-e17*. [MLG *rēdeschap* or Du *reedschap*]

Redshank, †**Reddshank** /ˈrɛdʃaŋk/ n **1** a Highlander *16-19, 20- historical*. **2** a wading bird *Tringa totanus 16-*. **3** a name for various weeds with red stems or seed spikes, especially the common sorrel *Rumex acetosa* and the the broad-leaved dock *Rumex obtusifolius 19, 20- H&I C SW Bor*. [REID¹·² + SHANK¹·¹]

reduce /rəˈdʒus/ v **1** *law* to annul, set aside by legal process *la15-*. **2** to bring down in size, value or extent *la16-*. **3** to return to a previous condition *16-17*. **4** to recall, bring to mind *15-16*. **5** to take back into one's possession, regain control of property *la15-16*. **6** to translate a text *e16*. **reducible**, †**reduceabill** *law* of a deed, contract or decree capable of being annulled by a court *la16-*. [MFr *reducer*]

reduction, †**reductioun** /rəˈdʌkʃən/ n **1** the act of reducing; the state of being reduced *16-*. **2** *law* the process of annulling a deed *16-*. **3** the bringing back (of money) to the mint again *la16*. **reduction improbation** *law* a reduction sought on grounds of forgery *la18-*. **reduction reductive** *law* the annulment of an improperly-obtained reduction *19-*. [MFr *reduction*]

†**red wamb, red waimb** n the char *Salvelinus alpinus 17-18*. [REID¹·² + WAME¹·¹]

red ware, red waur, reed ware, *Sh* **ridwir** /ˈrɛdwər, ˈrɛdwɔr, ˈrɛdwar, ˈrɪdwer; *Sh* ˈrɪdwɪr/ n a red seaweed *Laminaria digitata la18- Sh Ork N NE T EC*. **redware codling** a young inshore cod *19- Sh Ork N EC*. [REID¹·² + WARE]

†**red-wat** adj blood-stained *19*. **red-wat-shod** up to the ankles in blood *la18-e19*. [REID¹·² + *wat* (WEET¹·³)]

red waur *see* RED WARE

redy *see* READY¹·¹, READY¹·²

†**redymyte, redomyt** adj wreathed, crowned; adorned, beautiful *e16*. [Lat *redimītus*]

ree¹, *NE H&I C Bor* **reeve**, *T C* **reed**, †**rie** /ri; *NE H&I C Bor* riv; *T C* rid/ n **1** a walled enclosure or pen for livestock, frequently made of stone and often with a covered area *la17-*. **2** a yard or enclosure in which coal for sale is stored *18- H&I C SW*. **3** a prehistoric hill-fort *la18-19*. [unknown]

ree²·¹ /ri/ n a state of great excitement or frenzy *18-19, 20- Uls*. [unknown]

ree²·² /ri/ v to become extremely excited; to fly into a rage *la19- Ork NE EC*. [unknown]

ree²·³ /ri/ adj **1** tipsy, befuddled with drink *la18-19, 20- Ork N*; *compare* REEZIE¹. **2** over-excited, delirious, mentally unstable *la18-19, 20- Uls*. [unknown]

ree³·¹ /ri/ n a medium-sized sieve or riddle for cleaning grain, peas, or beans *18-19, 20- C Bor*. [unknown]

ree³·² /ri/ v to clean grain, grass-seed, peas or beans by sieving *la18- C SW Uls*. [unknown]

ree⁴·¹ /ri/ n a period of stormy weather *19- Sh*. [ON *hríð*]

ree⁴·² /ri/ adj *of weather* stormy *20- N*. [see the noun]

reeb¹·¹, *Ork* **reep** /rib; *Ork* rip/ n a narrow strip *la19- Sh Ork N*. **reebie** in strips, streaked *20- Sh*. [Norw dial *rip*]

reeb¹·², *Ork* **reep** /rib; *Ork* rip/ v **1** *of water* to run in streams, drip in a continuous flow *20- Sh Ork*. **2** *of colour* to be streaked *20- Sh*. **reebin** the uppermost plank in the side of a boat, the sheerstrake *la19- Sh*. [see the noun]

reebal, reebald *see* RIBALD¹·¹

reebin *see* RIBBON

reeble *see* RAIBLE¹·¹, RAIBLE¹·²

reechmaraw /ˈrixməˈrɔ/ n a swelling of the lips *20- WC SW*. [unknown]

reechnie, rechnie /ˈrixni, ˈrɛxni/ n a rough, uncouth person *la19- NE*. [unknown]

reed¹·¹ /rid/ n **1** the direction of the grain in wood, stone or metal *la18-*. **2** *mining* the line in a coal seam along which the strata split off *la18- C*. **3** a longitudinal defect in a lead pipe *20-, WC*. **reedie** *of a lead pipe* liable to split longitudinally *20- C*. [unknown]

reed¹·² /rid/ v *of a lead pipe* to split longitudinally *20- WC*. [unknown; see the noun]

reed², †**reid** /rid/ n **1** the fourth stomach of a ruminant *la18-*. **2** the stomach of an animal *la15*. [OE *rēada*]

reed³, †**red, †reid** /rid/ n **1** a plant of the genus *Phragmites*, the stalk or stem of the plant (used as a musical instrument); a cane; a reed-bed *la15-*. **2** part of the mouthpiece of a musical instrument, used to make a vibration *16-*. **3** *weaving* an instrument for separating the threads of the warp and beating up the weft; the quality of the cloth produced *la16-e19, 20- historical*. [OE *hrēod*]

reed *see* REE¹, REID¹,², RUID
reediemadeasy *see* READ¹,²
reed ware *see* RED WARE
reef, *Sh* **ruff**, †**reif** /rif; *Sh* rʌf/ *n* a skin disease producing scabs; a rash; an incrustation; an itch *la16-19, 20- Sh*. [OE *hrēof* rough, scabby, leprous]
reef *see* REEVE, RUIF¹,¹
reefort, **rifart**, †**rafert** /'rifərt/ *n* a radish or horseradish *la16-19, 20- WC*. [OFr *reffort, riffort*]
reeg *see* RIG¹,¹
reeho /'riho/ *n* a state of excited impatience, a stir *20- NE*. [perhaps onomatopoeic; compare REE²,²]
reein *see* REEN¹,¹, REEN¹,²
reek¹,¹, *NE* **rick**, †**reke**, †**reik** /rik; *NE* rɪk/ *n* **1** smoke from burning matter; a cloud or column of such smoke *la14-*. **2** vapour, steam; a fume or odour *la16-*. **3** the act of smoking a pipe, a smoke, a whiff, a puff *la19-*. **4** mist, especially a morning mist rising from the ground *la18, 20- Sh NE Uls*. **5** a house with a fire burning on the hearth, an inhabited house *la16-19, 20- Sh Ork*. **6** tumult, commotion; a dispute *16-e17*. **reeky, reekie,** †**reky 1** smoky, emitting smoke; smoke-filled; blackened or begrimed by smoke *16-*. **2** of or like smoke; misty, damp *16-e19*. **reekie-mire** a hollowed cabbage-stalk packed with oily waste, used to blow smoke into a house as a prank *la19- NE*. †**reekie Peter** an open lamp burning with a wick *la19 NE*; compare CRUISIE. †**reek fowl, reek hen** a chicken paid as part of the rental for every house with a hearth *16-19*. **reek house** an inhabited house *16-19, 20- Sh*. **a reek in the house** a bad atmosphere at home *18-19, 20- NE*. †**a sour reek in the hoose** = *a reek in the house 18-19*. [OE *rēc* smoke, ON *reykr* smoke, steam]
reek¹,², *NE* **rick**, †**rek**, †**reik** /rik; *NE* rɪk/ *v* **1** *of something burning* to emit smoke *16-e19*. **2** *of a house* to have smoke coming out of the chimney *la16-*. **3** *of a chimney* to emit smoke *19-*. **4** *of a chimney* to fail to emit smoke properly, sending it back into the room *17-*. **5** *of a person* to smoke a pipe *20-*. **6** *of hot liquid, damp hay or corn* to emit vapour or steam *16-*. **7** to show anger or fury *la19, 20- WC*. **8** *of a place* to be filled with smoke *16*. **9** *of dry ground* to send up dust *e16*. **reeking** inhabited *la18-19, 20- Sh Ork*. **reekin hot** *of a bowl or quoit* delivered at great speed *la19- EC*. **a reekin lum 1** an inhabited house *la20-*. **2** a chimney which allows smoke to come into the room, hence a source of annoyance *20-*. **reekit 1** blackened with smoke or soot, sooty *la18-*. **2** *of food* smoke-cured; tainted with or tasting of smoke *16-*. [OE *rēcan*]
reek², †**reik** /rik/ *n* a wild, irresponsible trick, a subterfuge *19- EC Bor*. [EModE *reak*]
reek *see* REAK¹,² REIK
reel¹,¹, †**reill** /ril/ *n* **1** a device on which yarn or thread is wound *16-*. **2** a whirling movement *la16-*. **3** a traditonal Scottish dance with four or more dancers *la16-*; compare *foursome reel* (FOWER), *eightsome reel* (ECHTSOME). **4** the music to which a reel is danced *la16-*. **5** a noise, a crash, a peal *la16-19, 20- Sh N EC*. **6** a noisy commotion, a disturbance *16-e18*. **7** a violent rush forward; a rapid careless delivery (of a speech) *16*. **reel foot, reel fit** a club-foot *la19-*. **reel footed** having a club-foot *la19-*. **oot o reel, oot o the reel** out of step or tune, astray, disarranged *la19- NE*. **Reel of Tulloch,** †**Tullich Reel 1** a tune of uncertain origin used for dancing a reel *18-*. **2** a Highland dance performed by four people *19-*. [OE *hrēol*]
reel¹,², †**trele**, †**reill** /ril/ *v* **1** to turn with a circular motion, whirl or spin around *16-*. **2** to dance a reel; to execute a figure-of-eight travelling movement *16-*. **3** to wind yarn on a reel; to fill a spool with thread *la16-*. **4** *of the head or senses* to be in a whirl; to become confused *la18-*. **5** to stagger *19-*. **6** to roll the eyes in an expression of excitement or greed *16-19, 20- NE T*. **7** to rush about in a furious or violent way; to behave in a loud manner *la14-19*. **8** *of an army* to waver, give way *16-e19*. **9** to make a great noise, clamour or clatter *18-19*. [see the noun]
reel² /ril/ *n* a mason's hammer of medium weight with two oblong faces *la19-*. [unknown]
reel-rall¹,¹ /'ril rɔl/ *n* a state of confusion, turmoil; a muddle of objects, sounds or words *18-*. [altered form of REVIL-RAILL]
reel-rall¹,² /'ril rɔl/ *adj* confused, disorganized, higgledy piggledy *19-*. [see the noun]
reel-rall¹,³ /'ril rɔl/ *adv* in a confused way, higgledy piggledy *19-*. [see the noun]
reemage¹,¹, **rummage**, *NE T* **reemish** /'riməʤ, 'rʌməʤ; *NE T* 'rimɪʃ,/ *n* **1** a careful, thorough search *la19-*. **2** a commotion, a great noise *19*. **3** a payment made for the arrangement of cargo in the hold of a ship *17*. †**rumiger** the person who arranges the cargo in a ship *la16-17*. [MFr *arrumage* the arranging of cargo]
reemage¹,², **rummage**, *NE T* **reemish** /'riməʤ, 'rʌməʤ; *NE T* 'rimɪʃ,/ *v* to search or investigate thoroughly *19-*. [see the noun]
reemish¹,¹, **reemis** /'rimɪʃ, 'rimɪs/ *n* **1** a resounding crash or rumble *la18- NE*. **2** *of a lighter sound* a scuffle, a din, a clatter *19, 20- NE*. **3** a heavy stroke, blow or beating *la18- NE*. [unknown]
reemish¹,² /'rimɪʃ/ *v* to move about noisily; to jolt *20- NE*. [unknown]
reemish *see* REEMAGE¹,¹, REEMAGE¹,²
reemle /'riməl/ *v* to make a sharp, tremulous noise; to make a lot of noise *la19- NE*. [altered form of RUMMLE¹,²]
reemock /'riməк/ *n* couch grass *Elymus repens*; its roots *19- NE*. [unknown]
reen¹,¹, **reein** /rin, 'riən/ *n* a squealing or screeching noise *19- Sh Ork*. [see the verb]
reen¹,², **reein** /rin, 'riən/ *v* to squeal or screech *la19- Sh Ork*. [ON *hrína* to squeal like a pig]
reen *see* REIN¹,¹, REIN¹,², RIND¹
reenge¹,¹, **range**, †**trang**, †**traing** /rinʒ, renʒ/ *n* **1** a line, file or row *la14-*. **2** a clattering, ringing noise *19-*. **3** a stroll, walk *la19- NE T EC*. **4** the area round or seats immediately below the pulpit in a Presbyterian church *la17- NE EC*. **5** a thorough search, a tour of inspection *16-19, 20- NE C*. **6** a stretch of countryside with definable limits; distance, bounds *la16-19, 20- NE*. **7** a strip or fold of cloth *16-e18*. [ME *raunge*]
reenge¹,², **range**, *C* **ringe**, †**traynge** /rinʒ, renʒ; *C* rɪnʒ/ *v* **1** to draw up soldiers; to arrange *la14-*. **2** to traverse or wander over; to travel through *la16-*. **3** to clear out the ashes from between the bars of a grate *19- T C Bor*. **4** to agitate water to drive fish from a hiding place *19- Bor*. **5** to search a place widely and thoroughly *la16-19*. **6** to make a clattering or rumbling noise *19*. **reenge the ribs** to clear out the ashes from between the bars of a grate *la18-*. [MFr *ranger* (to set in) line or rank]
reenge²,¹, **range**, **rinse**, †**ringe** /rinʒ, renʒ, rɪns/ *n* **1** a pot scourer made of heather twigs *18-20, 21- historical*. **2** an act of cleaning or rinsing *la19-*. [see the verb]
reenge²,², **range**, **rinse**, †**ringe**, †**rinche** /rinʒ, renʒ, rɪns/ *v* **1** to clean or soak; to rinse out *la16-*. **2** to clean by scraping or scrubbing, scour *la19-*. **3** to wash down a meal with liquor *19- NE T EC*. **reenger**, **ranger** a pot scourer *18-19, 20- WC Bor*. [ME *rincen*, EModE *rinse*]
re-enter, †**re-entir** /ri'ɛntər/ *v* **1** to enter again into a place or circumstance *16-*. **2** to put a person in a place of custody

again *la16*. [ENTER, AN, MFr *rentrer*, with prefix denoting repetition]

reep /rip/ *n derogatory* a person *19 NE*. [unknown]

reep see REEB¹·¹, REEB¹·²

reerd see REIRD¹·¹

reerie /'riri/ *n* a noisy quarrel or disturbance, a row, an uproar *19- NE*. [unknown]

ree-ruck /'ri rʌk/ *n* a small rick of corn set up to aid drying *19- Bor*. [RUCK¹·¹, with unknown first element]

reese see RUISE¹·¹, RUISE¹·²

reeshle see REESLE¹·¹, REESLE¹·²

reesk, reisk, †**resk,** †**risk** /risk/ *n* **1** moorland or marshy ground covered with coarse grass or sedge; unproductive land; frequently in place-names *la15-19, 20- N NE*. **2** a growth of natural coarse grasses, sedges or rushes on rough, waste or marshy ground *18-19, 20- NE*. **reeskie** *of ground* marshy, moorish, growing only coarse grass and sedges *17- NE*. [Gael *riasg* sedge-grass, land covered with this]

reesle¹·¹, reestle, reeshle, rustle /'risəl, 'riʃəl, 'rʌsəl/ *n* **1** a rustling sound *la19-*. **2** an involuntary shiver or shudder *la19-*. **3** a shake producing a rattling or jingling sound, a jolt, a jerk *19- Sh NE T EC*. **4** a loud clattering, knocking or banging noise *17-19, 20- Sh N EC*. **5** a heavy blow or stroke *19, 20- Sh NE EC Bor*. **6** a large crowd or amount *20- Sh NE*. **7** something which clatters or rattles by being loose or unstable, something rickety or likely to collapse *la19- T*. **8** a spell of bad weather, especially windy weather at harvest-time *20- N*. [see the verb]

reesle¹·², reestle, reeshle, rissle, rustle, †**reishle** /'risəl, 'riʃəl, 'risəl, 'rʌsəl/ *v* **1** to make a soft rustling sound; to rustle *la16-*. **2** *of wind* to whistle *la19-*. **3** *of doors or crockery* to clatter or rattle *19-*. **4** *of people or animals* to move about noisily or with a clatter; to crash or stomp about *19-*. **5** to move or shake an object so as to make it rustle or rattle *la19-*. **6** to shake, stir or agitate; to sieve grain or ashes *20-*. **7** to go through with a scuffling noise; to rummage through *20- NE T EC*. **8** to beat or thrash *18-19, 20- T H&I C*. **9** to shiver or shudder *la19- Sh H&I*. **10** to chase out or away by making a noise *la19- Sh T*. [probably imitiative; compare MDu *rysselen*]

reesle¹·³ /'risəl/ *adv* with a rustling noise; with a clash or clatter *la19- Sh NE T*. [see the verb]

reest¹·¹ /rist/ *n* a wood or rope framework on which fish or meat is smoked *19- Sh Ork NE H&I*. [unknown; compare Norw, Dan *riste* to broil, grill, Icel, Norw *rist* a gridiron]

reest¹·², †**treist** /rist/ *v* to cure food by drying or smoking; to be cured by smoking *la16-*. **reestit, reested 1** *of food* smoked, cured *16-*. **2** *of a person* shrunken, wizened *16-e19*. [see the noun]

reest²·¹, †**rest,** †**reist** /rist/ *n* **1** a halt, a stay; cessation *la14-*. **2** a device for halting movement; a support, a prop *la15-*. **3** *of horses* the act of stopping and refusing to move *19, 20- EC*. **4** a fixture on a saddle for holding the butt end of a lance *la15-16*. **5** the arrest (of people); the attachment (of goods) *16*. **tak the reest** *of a horse* to jib *19- WC Bor Uls*. [aphetic form of ARREIST¹·²]

reest²·², rest, rist, reist /rist, rɛst, rɪst, rʌɪst/ *v* **1** to halt, stop, pause *la14-*. **2** to stop and refuse to move; to come to a sudden halt; to become rooted to the spot *la18-*. **3** to cover or damp down a fire for the night *la18-*. **4** to arrest or seize goods for debt; to impound *16-19, 20- NE Bor*. **5** to bring to a halt; to arrest the motion or action of *16-19, 20- NE T SW*. **reester** a jibbing horse; a stubborn person *la19- H&I WC*. **reestie** *of a horse* inclined to jib; *of a person* recalcitrant, obstinate *18- C SW Bor Uls*. **ristin clod** a turf laid over a fire to keep it burning slowly all night *la19- Sh NE*. **restin peat** a peat laid over a fire to keep it burning slowly all night *la19- Sh NE*. [see the noun]

reest³·¹, wrest /rist, rɛst/ *n* the mouldboard of a plough *18-19, 20- NE C SW Uls*. [OE *rēost*]

reest³·² /rist/ *v* to tilt a plough to the right (the mouldboard side) *20- H&I C*. [see the noun]

reest see ROOST¹

reestle see REESLE¹·¹, REESLE¹·²

reet see RUIT¹·¹, RUIT²

reeto /'rito/ *n* a thin scraggy animal *20- Sh*. **reetowy** scraggy, emaciated *20- Ork*. [unknown]

†**reeve, reef** *v* to chatter or babble *19*. [perhaps AN *rever* to wander in one's mind; compare RAVE¹·²]

reeve see REE¹, RIVE¹·²

reevick /'rivək/ *n* a very thin, flimsy piece of cloth; muslin cheesecloth *19- Bor*. [perhaps dim of obs or dial Eng *reeve* a long narrow strip of cloth]

reezie¹ /'rizi/ *adj* windy, blowy; gusty *19- EC*. [unknown]

reezie² /'rizi/ *adj* light-headed, tipsy *19, 20- Bor*. [unknown]

refar see REFER¹·², REIVER

refase see REFUSE¹·²

refe see REIF

refeese see REFUSE¹·²

†**refer¹·¹, referr** *n* (a written statement of) a matter referred for consideration *17*. [see the verb]

refer¹·², *NE T* **refar** /rə'fɛr/; *NE T* rə'far/ *v* **1** to submit a matter to a higher authority *15-*. **2** *law* to submit a fact at issue to proof by the oath of one of the parties in the case, especially in a case concerning debt *la15-*. **3** to postpone to a later time; to delay, put off making a decision *la15-*. **4** *of a boundary line* to relate to identifying markers *la15-e16*. **reference 1** the act of submitting a matter to an authority for settlement *la16-*. **2** *law* the act of submitting a fact at issue to proof by oath *la18-*. **referrer** *law* a person who submits a fact at issue to proof by oath *la17-*. [ME *referren*]

†**refete** *v* **1** to refresh *la14-e15*. **2** to recover, recuperate *la15*. [ME *refeten*]

reffell see REVEL¹·¹

reffelled see RAIVELLED

reffus see REFUSE¹·²

reffuse see REFUSE²

refleck, reflect, †**reflecke** /rə'flɛk, rə'flɛkt/ *v* to cast back heat or light; to cast discredit on someone or something *la17-*. [MFr *reflectir*]

refond see REFUND

reform, †**refourm,** †**refurm** /rə'fɔrm/ *v* **1** to alter or improve; to correct; to eliminate (something undesirable) *15-*. **2** to redress a wrong; to make reparation for damage *15-*. **3** to rebuild or repair a building *la14-17*. **Reformation,** †**reformatioun** the movement leading to the sweeping away of the religious doctrines and practices of the Roman Catholic Church and the establishment of the Presbyterian Church in Scotland *la16-17, 18- historical*. **reformer,** †**reformar 1** one of the leaders of the Reformation *la16-*. **2** a reformado, a military officer left without a command but retaining his rank and receiving full or half pay *e17*. **3** a member of the *Reformed Presbyterian Church 18-*. **reformed, reformit 1** *of the Protestant religion* purified of errors or abuses *16-*. **2** altered, improved; amended *la16-*. **Reformed kirk, Reformed Church,** †**reformit kirk** a Protestant church, especially the Church of Scotland *la16-*. **Reformed Presbyterian Church** the church descending from those Covenanters who continued to oppose the Revolution Settlement after 1688 *18-*. [ME *reformen*]

refound /rɪ'fʌund/ *v* to found again; to re-establish *16-*. [OFr *refonder*]

refound *see* REFUND

refourm *see* REFORM

refrain, †**refrene**, †**refreyn**, †**refrane**, †**refrenʒe** /rəˈfren/ *v* **1** to abstain *la15-*. **2** to keep oneself from *16-*. **3** to hold back or restrain oneself or another *la14-*. **4** to avoid something undesirable *la16*. [ME *refreinen*]

refresh, †**refresche**, †**refres** /rəˈfreʃ/ *v* **1** to renew, revive *la14-*. **2** to restore or renovate a building *la14-*. **3** to furnish supplies or reinforcements *15-*. †**refreshfull** supplying, full of refreshment *17*. [ME *refreshen*]

refreyn *see* REFRAIN

†**reft, reift** *n* robbery; stolen goods *la15-e18*. [altered form of REIF, after ptp of REIVE]

reft *see* REIVE

refuis *see* REFUSE[2]

refuise *see* REFUSE[1.1], REFUSE[1.2]

refund, †**refound**, †**refond** /rəˈfʌnd/ *v* **1** to reimburse; to compensate a person *15-*. **2** to make good, repair; to redress an injury or loss *la15-17*. **3** to cast the blame of something onto a person or thing *la17*. [probably AN *refundre*, Lat *refundere* to cause to flow back]

refurm *see* REFORM

refuse[1.1], **refuise** /rəˈfjuz/ *n* a refusal, rejection *la15-*. [MFr *refus* refusal]

refuse[1.2], **refuise, refase,** *NE* **refeese,** †**refuys,** †**reffus** /rəˈfjuz, rəˈfez; *NE* rəˈfiz/ *v* **1** to decline to accept; to reject *la14-*. **2** to deny an allegation *la16-18*. [ME *refusen*]

†**refuse**[2], **reffuse, refuis** *adj* refused, rejected, discarded *16*. [MFr *refus* waste, dross, rubbish]

†**refute**[1] *n* shelter, protection; a refuge *la15-e16*. [AN, OFr *refuite*]

refute[2] /rəˈfjut/ *v* **1** to disprove *20-*. **2** to reject or refuse *la16-17*. **3** to repel an attack; to foil a plan *17*. **refutation,** †**refutatioune 1** the confutation (of an argument) *la16-*. **2** the military repulse of an attacker *la16*. [EModE *refute*]

refuys *see* REFUSE[1.2]

regaird[1.1], **regard** /rəˈgerd, rəˈgard/ *n* **1** attention, consideration, heed; respect *la15-*. **2** concern, care *la15-*. **regairdless,** †**regardles 1** heedless, uncaring *17-*. **2** heedless of religious practices, irreligious *la19- Sh Ork N EC.* †**in regard of** in comparison with *la14-17*. [AN *regard*, OFr *regart*]

regaird[1.2], **regard** /rəˈgerd, rəˈgard/ *v* to notice or heed; to take into account; to respect *16-*. [MFr *regarder*]

regal, †**regale,** †**regall** /ˈrigəl/ *adj* of or pertaining to a king or queen; royal *16-*. [ME *regal*, AN *regal*, Lat *rēgālis*]

regale *see* RAGGLE[1.2], REGALL

regalia /rəˈgelja/ *n* **1** the insignia of royalty *17-*. **2** *law* rights held by the Crown *17-*. **regalia majora** *law* rights held by the Crown which are inalienable *18-*. **regalia minora** *law* rights held by the Crown which may be conveyed to subjects by royal grant *la19-*. [Lat *regālia*]

regality, †**regalite,** †**regalitie** /rəˈgalǝte/ *n* a jurisdiction almost co-extensive with that of the Crown, granted by the sovereign to a powerful subject; land or territory subject to this jurisdiction; a particular area under this jurisdiction *la14-e18, la18- historical.* **regality court** a court held by a lord of regality *16-e18, 20- historical*; compare *court of regality* (COORT[1.1]). [AN, OFr *regalité*, Lat *rēgālitās*]

†**regall, regale** *n* = REGALITY *la14-e18*. [from the adj REGAL]

regall *see* REGAL

regard *see* REGAIRD[1.1], REGAIRD[1.2]

rege *see* RAGE[1.1]

regemen *see* REGIMEN

regement *see* REGIMENT

regent[1.1] /ˈridʒənt/ *n* **1** a governor, especially one invested with royal authority to rule during a minority or absence *la15-*. **2** *in Scottish Universities* a teacher who took a class of students through the full four-year Arts course in language, physics and philosophy *16-18, 19- historical.* **3** *in the Universities of St Andrews and Aberdeen* a lecturer who acts as adviser and consultant to students assigned to them *20-*. †**regentrie** the office or function of a regent *la16-e17*. [Fr *regent*, Lat *regent-*, presp stem of *regere*]

regent[1.2] /ˈridʒənt/ *v* to act as a regent in a university *17-*. **regenting** a system of university teaching by a regent *la19- historical.* [see the noun]

regester *see* REGISTER[1.1], REGISTER[1.2], REGISTER[2]

regibus, rangiebus /ˈrɛdʒɪbəs, ˈrɛndʒɪbəs/ *n* a boys' game, usually involving one side trying to capture the caps of the other side *19- NE*. [Lat *rēgibus*, dative pl of *rex* a king]

regimen, †**regemen** /ˈrɛdʒəmən/ *n* **1** the regulation of diet or health *19-*. **2** government, rule *la15-e16*. [Lat *regimen*]

regiment, †**regement,** †**regment** /ˈrɛdʒəmənt/ *n* **1** rule, government *la15-*. **2** a unit of an army *la16-*. **3** a reign, a term of office *la16-e17*. **4** rules to govern conduct or diet *la15-16*. [ME MFr *regiment*]

regimentals /rɛdʒəˈmɛntəlz/ *npl* the uniform of a regiment; formal dress or livery; a person's best clothes *la19, 20- NE EC*. [REGIMENT + *-al* + plural suffix]

regin *see* REGYNE

region, †**regioun** /ˈridʒən/ *n* **1** a realm; a country; an area, a district; a part of the world, universe or heavens *la14-*. **2** one of the nine larger units into which mainland Scotland was divided for local government purposes 1974-1995 *la20, 21- historical.* **regionalization** the reorganization of Scotland into local government areas or regions *la20, 21- historical.* [ME *regioun*]

register[1.1], †**regester** /ˈrɛdʒɪstər/ *n* **1** a collection of State and official papers, including parliamentary and judicial records and private deeds *14-*. **2** a written record of events or details, such as school attendance *la15-*. **3** a registrar, an official responsible for the state registers and records *la17-e18*. †**registrie, registri** a collection of official papers *16*. †**register buik, register buke** a book used for keeping records *16-e17*. [OFr *registre*, AN *regestre*, Lat *registrum, regestrum*]

register[1.2], †**regester** /ˈrɛdʒɪstər/ *v* to set down information formally; to record in a register *15-*. [OFr *registrer, regestrer,* Lat *registrāre*]

†**register**[2], **regester** *n* a registrar, a chronicler *16-17*. [EModE *register*]

Register House /ˈrɛdʒɪstər hʌus/ *n* the building in Edinburgh in which the Scottish registers or records are kept *16-*. Compare NEW REGISTER HOUSE. [REGISTER[1.1] + *house* (HOOSE[1.1])]

Register Office /ˈrɛdʒɪstər ɔfɪs/ *n* = REGISTER HOUSE *la18-19, 20- historical*. [REGISTER[1.1] + OFFICE]

Register of Sasines, †**Register of Seasings** /ˈrɛdʒɪstər əv sezɪnz/ *n* the record of documents concerning transfer of ownership (usually a sale or an inheritance) of a piece of land or of a building *la16-*. [REGISTER[1.1] + SASINE]

Register of the Great Seal /ˈrɛdʒɪstər əv ðɪ grɛt sil/ *n* a collection of charters issued under the Great Seal, mainly of royal grants of lands and confirmations *14-*. [REGISTER[1.1] + *Great Seal* (GREAT[1.2])]

Register of the Privy Council /ˈrɛdʒɪstər əv ðɪ prɪve kʌunsəl/ *n* the records of the Privy Council *16-*. [REGISTER[1.1] + *Privy Council* (PRIVY[1.2])]

Register of the Privy Seal /ˈrɛdʒɪstər əv ðɪ prɪve sil/ *n* the records of writs passed under the Privy Seal *la15-*. [REGISTER[1.1] + PRIVY SEAL]

†registrate, registrat *v ptp* **registrate, registrat 1** to enter in a register or record *15-19*. **2** to cause to be remembered *la16-17*. [Lat *registrat-*, ptp stem of *registrāre*]

registration, †registratioun /redʒəˈstreʃən/ *n* an act of registering or recording *la16-*. [Lat *registrātio*]

reglar *see* REGULAR[1,2]

regment *see* REGIMENT

regne *see* RING[3,2]

regour *see* RIGOUR

regrait, regrate *see* REGRET[1,1], REGRET[1,2]

regress, †regres /rəˈgrɛs/ *n* **1** the act of going back, a return *la14-*. **2** *law* an obligation by a superior to re-admit a vassal to land which he had conveyed in WADSET[1,1], once he was able to redeem it *15-18*. **3** the right of passage to property; access *16*. **†haf regres** *law* to have the right to seek compensation *la15-16*. [Lat *regressus*]

regret[1,1], †regrate, †regrait /rəˈgrɛt/ *n* **1** lamentation; an expression of grief, sorrow or disappointment *la14-*. **2** an expression of discontent; a formal complaint *la16-e18*. [OFr *regrat, regret*]

regret[1,2], †regrate, †regrait /rəˈgrɛt/ *v* to lament; to feel or express sorrow; to complain about; to mourn a death *la14-*. [OFr *regrater, regreter*]

regular[1,1], †reguler /ˈrɛgjulər/ *n* **1** a person who does something or attends a place on a regular basis *20-*. **2** a regulating power or principle, a standard *e16*. [see the adj]

regular[1,2], reglar, raigler /ˈrɛgjulər, ˈrɛglər, ˈrɛglər/ *adj* **1** recurring at set intervals *16-*. **2** trained, professional; *of soldiers* full-time, constituting part of the standing army *la17-*. **3** conforming to a rule, originally of a monastic order *15-19*. [OFr *reguler*, Lat *rēgulāris*]

regulate, †regulat /ˈrɛgjəlet/ *v* to control, to govern or direct *la15-*. [Lat *regulāt-*, ptp stem of *regulāre*]

regulation /rɛgjəˈleʃən/ *n* a means of control; a rule *la17-*. **†Regulation Roll** *law* a roll of the Court of Session listing jury cases or those where no appearance had been made for the defender *e19*. [Lat *rēgulātio*]

reguler *see* REGULAR[1,1]

†regyne, regin *n* a queen *e16*. [Lat *rēgīna*]

rehabile *see* REABILL

rehabilitate, †rehabilitat /riəˈbɪlətet/ *v* **1** to re-establish reputation or health; to restore a person to former privileges, rank and possessions *la16-*. **2** to legitimize a bastard *la16*. [Lat *rehabilitāt-*, ptp stem of *rehabilitāre*]

rehabilitation, †rehabilitatioun /riəbɪləˈteʃən/ *n* **1** the act of restoring someone to their former rank or privileges *la15-*. **2** the act of legitimizing *la16-e17*. [Lat *rehabilitātio*]

†rehator, rahatour *n* a term of abuse for a person *e16*. [unknown; compare ME *rehetour* a bad sort of servant, also Lat *reātus* condition of being accused of an offence]

†rehearse[1,1], †rehers *n* a repetition, a recitation, a recounting; an account or report *la14-16*. [see the verb]

rehearse[1,2], †rehers, †reheirs /rəˈhɛrs/ *v* to recite; to repeat; to express in words; to list *la14-*. **rehearsal, †reheirsall** repetition; the act of recounting, setting down or listing *la15-*. [OFr *rehercer*]

reid[1,1], rid, red /rid, rɪd, rɛd/ *v* to redden; to make or become red *la19-*. [see the adj]

reid[1,2], reed, rid, red, rud, †rede /rid, rɪd, rɛd, rʌd/ *adj* **1** *colour* of a red or reddish hue *la14-*. **2** heated to redness, red hot *la14-*. **3** violent, bloody, resulting in bloodshed *la16-19*. **4** mad, furious *19*. **5** *of grain or crops* dried up and discoloured by overheating *16-17*. **6** golden *e16*. **red-avised** having a ruddy complexion, red-faced *20- Sh Bor*. **red brae** the gullet, the throat *20-*. **red fish** salmon in general; the male salmon at spawning time *la15-19, 20- WC SW* **reed flannen** red flannel, a warm comforting material *20- NE*. **red friar, †rede frere** a Templar *16-e17, 18- historical*. **red gown 1** the scarlet gown worn (on certain occasions) by undergraduates of the Universities of Aberdeen, Edinburgh, Glasgow and St Andrews *la18-*. **2** the scarlet gown worn by a judge of the Court of Session in his capacity as a Lord of Justiciary dealing with criminal cases *17-18*. **†red hawk, reid haulk 1** the kestrel *Falco tinnunculus la19*. **2** the merlin *Falco columbarius la14-e16*. **†Red-head tax** a freight tax on coal carried by sea further north than Red-Head, a promontory in Angus *la18*. **red-heidit** having red hair or a red head or top; excitable, impetuous, hot-tempered *la16-*. **reid horn mad** furiously angry *20- Ork N*. **Red Hose Race** an annual foot-race at Carnwath in Lanarkshire, for the prize of a pair of red stockings *19- WC*. **red kail** great or Scotch kail, a less curly, purplish variety of kail *la16-19*. **rid lane** the gullet, the throat *20- C*. **red-legged crow** the chough *Pyrrhocorax pyrrhocorax la18-*. **red loanin** the gullet, the throat *la19- Ork SW Uls* **red mad, reed mad** furiously angry, demented *19, 20- Sh N*. **reid nakit** stark naked *la19- NE T*. **red road** the throat *20-*. **red sodger** a red-coloured spider *la19, 20- EC*. **†red smeddum** red precipitate of mercury used as an insecticide *la18*. **red wud, †rede wod** beside oneself with rage; wild with passion; raving mad *16-*. **†full reid and sweit** *of salmon* mature and ready for consumption *15-e17*. **†reid and quhyt** fresh, young, lovely *e16*. [ME *red*, OE *rēod*]

reid *see* RADE, READ[1,2], REDD[1,1], REDD[1,3], REDD[2,1], REDE[1,1], REDE[1,2], REED[2], REED[3]

Reidcoat *see* REDCOAT

reid-ersie /rid ˈɛrse/ *n* a bee with red markings on the back of its abdomen *19, 20- NE T*. [REID[1,1] + ERSE[1,1]]

Reid etin *see* RED ETYN

reid face, rid face, red face /rid ˈfes, rɪd ˈfes, rɛd ˈfes/ *n* a blushing face, as a sign of embarrassment or shame *19-*. **get a red face** to feel very embarrassed *19-*. **gie someone a red face** to cause someone extreme embarrassment *19-*. [REID[1,1] + FACE[1,1]]

reid-gibbie /rid ˈgɪbi/ *n* a stickleback *20- T*. [REID[1,1] + familiar form of *Gilbert*]

Reid Lichtie *see* RED LICHTIE

reid neb, rid neb, red neb /rid ˈnɛb, rɪd ˈnɛb, rɛd ˈnɛb/ *n* **1** a red nose *17-*. **2** the oystercatcher *Haematopus ostralegus 20- NE*. **3** a variety of potato with red markings at one end *la18-e19*. **red-nebbit pussy** the puffin *Fratercula arctica 20- NE*. [REID[1,1] + NEB[1,1]]

reidschip *see* REDSCHIP

reif, rief, raif, †refe, †reyf, †reaff /rif, ref/ *n* **1** the act or practice of robbery, plundering; a robbery *la14-19, 20- WC Bor*. **2** plunder, booty *la14-e19*. **3** rapacity, greed *15-e16*. **of reif** *of a bird or animal* predatory *la15-16*. [OE *rēaf*]

reif *see* REEF, REIVE

reiffar *see* REIVER

†reiffelled gun *n* a rifle *la17*. [participial adj from OFlem *rijffelen* to scratch + GUN[1,1]]

reift *see* REFT

reign *see* RING[3,1], RING[3,2]

rei interventus /re ɪntərˈvɛntəs/ *n law* conduct by one party to an uncompleted and informal contract with the knowledge and permission of the other party, which makes the contract binding *la18-*. [Lat *rēī interventus*]

reik, reek, †reke /rik/ *v* to fit out; to equip *la16-19, 20- NE T WC*. [perhaps MDu *rēken*]

reik *see* RACK[1], REEK[1,1], REEK[1,2], RAKE[2]

reill *see* REEL[1,1], REEL[1,2]

rein[1.1], **rine**, †**renʒe**, †**renyie**, †**reen** /ren, rʌin/ *n* **1** part of a bridle, one of the leather straps attached to each side of the bit by which the horse or other animal is controlled and guided *la14*-. **2** a means of control or restraint *16*-. [ME *rein*]

rein[1.2], **rine**, †**renʒe**, †**reen**, †**reyn** /ren, rʌin/ *v* **1** to control a horse by use of a rein *15*-. **2** to restrain or control a person *la15*-. [see the noun]

reing *see* RING[1.1]

reir *see* REAR

reird[1.1], **raird**, **reerd**, †**rerd** /rerd, rird/ *n* **1** a roar; an uproar or clamour; a din, a loud noise *15*-. **2** a loud outburst (of laughter or scolding) *18*-. **3** a noisy breaking of wind *18-19, 20- NE*. [OE *reord* voice, cry]

reird[1.2], **raird**, †**rerd** /rerd/ *v* **1** to make a loud crashing or cracking noise; to resound *la15-19, 20- SW Bor*. **2** to scold loudly *19*-. **3** to break wind *19- EC*. **4** to shout, to roar *15-e19*. [see the noun]

reis *see* RICE

reishle *see* REESLE[1.2]

reisk *see* REESK

reist *see* REEST[1.2], REEST[2.1], REEST[2.2], WREST[1.2]

reiterate, †**reiterat** /riˈitərɛt/ *v* **1** to repeat an action or utterance *la16*-. **2** to renew an appointment or agreement *la16-e17*. [Lat *reiterāt*-, ptp stem of *reiterāre*]

†**reithe**[1.1], **rethe** *adj* **1** zealous, keen *e19*. **2** wild, furious; violent; terrible *15*. [OE *rēþe* fierce, cruel, savage, ON *reiðr* wrathful, angry]

†**reithe**[1.2], **rethe** *adv* furiously, violently, wildly *e15*. [see the adj]

reive, **reave**, †**reif**, †**reve**, †**raif** /riv/ *v ptp* **reived**, **reft** **1** to rob, to plunder or pillage, especially as a raid across the Scottish-English Border *la14*-. **2** to take away; to steal and remove by theft or pillage *la14-19, 20- NE T*. **3** to despoil; to rob a person *la14-19*. **4** to carry off a person by force; to rescue a person by carrying off *la14-e17*. [OE *rēafian* to plunder]

reiver, †**reiffar**, †**refar**, †**revar** /ˈrivər/ *n* **1** a plunderer, a robber, a cross-border raider *la14-19, 20- historical*. **2** the chief male participant in the annual festival at Duns, Berwickshire *20- Bor*. **3** a pirate *la14-18*. **Reiver's Lass** the female partner of the reiver at the Duns festival *20- Bor*. [from the verb REIVE or OE *rēafere*]

rejeck, **reject** /rəˈdʒɛk, rəˈdʒɛkt/ *v* **1** to refuse to accept; to set aside *16*-. **2** to repel or rebuff; to dismiss a person from one's presence or mind *16*-. **3** to refer something to another person for decision *16-17*. [ME *rejecten*, Lat *reject*-, ptp stem of *rēicere* to throw back]

rejoice, †**rejois**, †**reiois**, †**reiose** /rəˈdʒɔis/ *v* to feel or express joy; to make joyful; to enjoy *la15*-. †**rejoisit**, **rejosyt** glad, joyful *e16*. [OFr *resjouir*, AN *rejoicer* to enjoy the use of]

rek *see* RECK[1.1], RECK[1.2], REEK[1.2]

reke *see* REAK[1.2], REEK[1.1], REIK

rekill *see* RICKLE[1.1], RICKLE[1.2]

rekkin *see* RECKON

rekles *see* RECKLESS

rekster, **rakster** /ˈrɛkstər, ˈrakstər/ *n* **1** a long journey or drive, sometimes implying fruitless effort; a period of hard work *la19- Sh*. **2** a stretch or extent of land *20- Sh Ork*. **3** a punishment *20- Sh Ork*. **4** confusion, a mess *20- Ork*. **rekster dyke** an enclosed track for managing sheep *la19- Sh*. [ON *rekstr* a driving, a way along which cattle are driven]

relacion *see* RELATION

†**relapse**[1.1], **relaps** *n* the committing of a sin for which one has already been reprimanded *la16-e18*. [Lat *relapsus* a relapsed heretic]

†**relapse**[1.2], **relaps** *n* **1** *Presbyterian Church* a person who has offended twice against church discipline, especially in fornication *la16-e18*. **2** *Roman Catholic Church* a person who has left the faith *16*. [Lat *relapsus* a relapsed heretic]

relapse[1.3] /rəˈlaps/ *v* to fall back into a former state of error or wrongdoing, originally of heresy *la16*-. [Lat *relaps*-, ptp stem of *relābī*]

†**relapse**[1.4], **relaps** *adj Presbyterian Church* of a person that has fallen again into wrongdoing or offended twice against church discipline *la16-e18*. [from the noun RELAPSE[1.1]]

relation, †**relatioun**, †**relacion** /rəˈleʃən/ *n* **1** the action of giving an account or narration; a recital, a report *la14*-. **2** a relationship, correspondence or connection *la15*-. **3** a person with whom there is a family connection *17*-. **4** *law* a statement by a witness *15-e17*. [ME *relacioun*]

relax /rəˈlaks/ *v* **1** to free from anxiety, to calm down *16*-. **2** *law* to release from a legal process, sentence or penalty, especially from outlawry; to set free from confinement *16-18*. **3** to free goods that have been arrested *16*. **relaxation 1** release from ordinary tasks or cares, recreation *la16*-. **2** *law* release from a judicial penalty or restriction *la15-18*. [Lat *relaxāre*]

rele *see* REEL[1.2]

release[1.1], †**releis**, †**relesch** /rəˈlis/ *n* **1** deliverance; discharge; freeing *15*-. **2** a variety of the game of tig in which players who have been touched by the catcher may be released by the touch of an uncaught player *20- NE T C*. [ME *reles*]

release[1.2], †**relese**, †**relesch** /rəˈlis/ *v* **1** to set free, to deliver from restraint; to discharge from a legal process or obligation *la15*-. **2** to relinquish a claim; to remit a payment; to revoke a punishment *la14-17*. [ME *relesen*]

releegion, **religion**, †**religioun**, †**relygyowne** /rəˈlidʒən, rəˈlidʒən/ *n* **1** a system of faith; a belief in God or gods *15*-. **2** a life bound by monastic vows *15*-. **3** members of a religious order *la14-16*. †**the religion** the Reformed religion, Protestantism *la16-e17*. [AN *religiun*]

releegious, **religious** /rəˈlidʒəs, rəˈlidʒəs/ *adj* **1** devout, pious, God-fearing *la14*-. **2** bound by monastic vows; belonging to a religious order *la14*-. **3** of or relating to religion, originally especially monastic life *15*-. [ME *religious*, Lat *religiōsus*]

relefe *see* RELIEF

releif *see* RELIEF, RELIEVE,

releis *see* RELEASE[1.1]

releisch *see* RELESCHE

relesch *see* RELEASE[1.1], RELEASE[1.2]

†**relesche**, **releisch** *v of birds* to sing *e16*. **relesching** music-making *e16*. [EModE *relish* to sing, warble, a musical embellishment]

relese *see* RELEASE[1.2]

relevant, †**relevand** /ˈrɛləvənt/ *adj* **1** pertinent *la16*-. **2** *law* pertinent, sufficient to justify the appropriate penalty or remedy, if the alleged facts are proved *16*-. **relevancy** *law* the state of being relevant *la16*-. [Lat *relevans*]

releve *see* RELIEF, RELIEVE

relevis *see* RELIEF

relic, †**relik**, †**relique**, †**relict** /ˈrɛlɪk/ *n* **1** something left over from the past *la14*-. **2** the remaining portion of anything, a remnant; something surviving from the past *la16*-. **3** a reliquary *la15-16*. **4** a precious or valuable thing, a sacred ornament *la15-16*. †**relics**, **relikis** the remains of a dead person *16-e19*. [ME *relik*]

relict, †**relik** /ˈrɛlɪkt/ *n* **1** a widow *la15*-. **2** a widower *17*-. **3** a holy relic *16-17*. [Lat *relicta*]

relict *see* RELIC

relief, †**relefe**, †**releif**, †**releve** /rəˈlif/ *n pl* †**relevis** **1** *law* a payment made by the heir of a deceased vassal to the superior for his recognition as lawful successor *la14-*. **2** aid in time of danger *15-*. **3** assistance to the poor; ease from physical pain or illness *16-*. **4** *law* the right of a person standing security for a debt to reclaim payment from his principal or from his fellow cautioners if he has paid more than his share *la16-*. **5** *in the game of tig* a call by which an uncaught player may release one who has been touched by the catcher and made to stand still *20- NE C*. **6** freedom from ecclesiastical oppression, especially with reference to the 18th-century controversy in the Church of Scotland concerning the right of a congregation to elect its own minister *la18-e19*. **7** *law* (the right of an obligant to) reimbursement for payments made or expenses incurred in carrying out an obligation properly imposed or undertaken *la15-17*. **8** the release of a person from restraint or captivity or a bad situation; an order of release *la15-17*. **the Relief Church** the ecclesiastical body formed in the wake of the 18th-century controversy led by Thomas Gillespie claiming the right of a congregation to elect its minister *la18-e19, la19- historical*. **the Relief Kirk** = *the Relief Church*. [ME *relef*]

relieve, †**releve**, †**releif** /rəˈliv/ *v* **1** to rescue; to assist; to mitigate (need) *la14-*. **2** to set free from captivity or punishment *16-*. **3** *law* to release from a legal obligation; to reimburse a cautioner or guarantor *la15-e19*. **4** to recover, to regain property *la16*. **5** to exalt; to raise in rank or standing *15-16*. **6** to advance or return (to battle); to rally *la15-16*. **reliever 1** a member of the Relief Church *la19 historical*. **2** a variety of the game of tig *20- NE T H&I C*. [OFr *relever*, Lat *relevāre*]

religion, religioun *see* RELEEGION

religious /rəˈlɪdʒəs/ *n* a person bound by monastic vows or dedicated to a religious life; a member of a religious order *la14-*. [from the adj *religious* (RELEEGIOUS)]

religious *see* RELEEGIOUS

relik *see* RELIC, RELICT

relique *see* RELIC

rely, †**ralzy** /rəˈlae/ *v* **1** to depend on; to have confidence in *la17-*. **2** to make one's home with *20- NE*. **3** to assemble *la14-e18*. **rely tae** to make one's home with *20- NE*. **rely til** = *rely tae*. [AN *relier* to rally, reassemble; in sense 3, possible association with Fr *rallier* to reassemble, regroup]

relygyowne *see* RELEEGION

remain[1.1], †**remane**, †**ramayn** /rəˈmen/ *n 1 pl* the remainder, the rest, what is left *15-*. **2** *pl* the surviving members of a group *la15-e17*. **3** the unpaid balance of an amount due *16-e18*. **4** a remnant (of cloth) *la16-e17*. [MFr *remain*]

remain[1.2], †**remane**, †**remayn**, †**ramayn** /rəˈmen/ *v* **1** to be left after everything else has gone *la14-*. **2** to continue *la14-*. **3** to stay; to live or dwell *la15-*. †**remanand, remaynand** the rest, the remainder *la14-17*; compare REMNANT[1.1]. **remainder 1** what is left *la17-*. **2** a remnant of cloth at the end of a bale *20-*. **remainder sale** a sale of remnants of cloth or other left-over goods at reduced prices *20-*. †**remane fra** to stay away from, not attend *la15-e17*. †**remane on** to wait for *la15-e17*. [AN *remaner*, *remaindre*, *remanant*]

remanent *see* REMNANT[1.1], REMNANT[1.2]

remark[1.1] /rəˈmark/ *n* **1** a comment *18-*. **2** a token *la19*. **in remark** notable, remarkable *20- Sh*. [see the verb]

remark[1.2] /rəˈmark/ *v* **1** to observe, to take note of *la16-*. **2** to comment on *19-*. †**remarkin** observation, notice; a spectacle *la18-19*. [MFr *remarquer*]

remayn *see* REMAIN[1.2]

remburse *see* RAMBURSE

reme *see* REAM[1.1]

remead *see* REMEID[1.1], REMEID[1.2]

remede *see* REMEID[1.2]

remeeve *see* REMOVE[1.2]

remeff *see* REMOVE[1.2]

remeid[1.1], **remede**, †**remead** /rəˈmid/ *n* **1** remedy, redress, relief; (a) cure *la14-*. **2** *law* redress by appeal to a higher court *15-*. **3** the margin by which coins were allowed to deviate from standard fineness or weight *16-17*. [AN *remeide*, AN, MFr *remede*]

remeid[1.2], **remead**, †**remede** /rəˈmid/ *v* **1** to remedy, redress; to rectify, amend; to cure *la14-19, 20- NE SW Bor*. **2** *law* to redress (a grievance) *16-e17*. [from the noun or reduced form of AN *remedier*]

remember, †**ramember**, †**rememor**, †**ramemmor** /rəˈmɛmbər/ *v* **1** to recollect, bear in mind *15-*. **2** to bring to mind; to commemorate *la15-*. **3** to remind a person (of or about something) *16-19, 20- C*. **4** to record, mention *la16-17*. †**be rememberit** to be mindful; to remember (that) *16-e17*. **remember of** to have, retain a memory of, recollect *la15-19, 20- Sh H&I C*. **remember on** = *remember of*. **remember it to you** to remember to repay, requite, make good: ◊*I'll remember it to you on term day la19-*. †**remembering prayer** *Presbyterian Church* the intercessory prayer *e19*. [ME *remembren*]

remission, †**remissioun** /rəˈmɪʃən/ *n* **1** forgiveness *15-*. **2** *law* a formal pardon; a document conveying this *la15-18*. †**tak remissioun** *of a defendant* to appeal, have recourse to a pardon *la15-17*. †**without remissioun** not letting a person off a payment due *la14-e16*. †**allege ane remissioun** *see* ALLEGE. [ME *remissioun*]

remit[1.1] /ˈrimɪt/ *n* **1** the referring of a matter to another authority for opinion, information or execution; *law* the transfer of a case from one court to another; the terms and limits of such a reference *la17-*. **2** the action of releasing a person from paying a debt *la15-e17*. **3** remission, pardon; (a document conveying) a formal pardon *15-17*. [see the verb]

remit[1.2] /rəˈmɪt/ *v* **1** to forgive, pardon (an offence) *la14-*. **2** *law* to refer (a matter or person) to another court, authority or justice *la15-*. **3** to set aside, renounce (something one has a right to); to let (a person) off (something owed); to cancel (a punishment) *15-17*. **4** to refer (a person) to a book or other source or information *15-e17*. **5** to transmit, send (money) *16-e19*. **6** to postpone; to end *la16-17*. [Lat *remittere* to send back]

remmick /ˈrɛmək/ *n fisherman's taboo* an oar *19- Sh*. [unknown, but *rem-* most likely corresponds to Lat *rēmus* oar, borrowed into a number of both Germanic and Romance languages; compare Du *riemen*, Ger *Riemen*].

remnant[1.1], †**remanent**, †**remnand** /ˈrɛmnənt/ *n* **1** the remainder, the rest; something left over *15-*. **2** a left-over piece of cloth, a part-bale sold cheaply *la17-*. **3** a name (used by themselves) for the extreme Covenanters who refused to accept the Revolution Settlement of 1688 *18-e19*. [ME *remenaunt*]

remnant[1.2], **remanent** /ˈrɛmnənt, ˈrɛmənənt/ *adj* **1** left over; surviving; additional; remaining *16-*. **2** *of an amount of money due* still to be paid, outstanding *la15-16*. [see the noun]

remofe *see* REMOVE[1.2]

†**remonstrance** *n* **1** a written representation or statement concerning a matter of public importance *la17*. **2** a statement drawn up in Dumfries in 1650 in which a Presbyterian group declared its opposition to co-operation with the King's party *la17*; compare REMONSTRATOR, RESOLUTION. **western remonstrance** = REMONSTRANCE (sense 2). [MFr **remonstrance*]

†**Remonstrator** *n* an extremist Presbyterian, especially one involved in the *western remonstrance* (REMONSTRANCE) *la17*. [EModE *remonstrate* with agent suffix]

†**remord** *v* **1** *of thought* to afflict (a person) with remorse or painful feelings *16-e17*. **2** to examine (one's conscience) in a penitent spirit *la15-16*. **3** to recall to mind with remorse or regret *la15-16*. **4** to feel remorse *la15-e17*. [ME *remorden*, Lat *remordēre* to bite back]

remorse[1.1], †**remors** /rəˈmɔrs/ *n* a feeling of compunction or regret *la16-*. [ME *remors*, EModE *remorss*]

remorse[1.2] /rəˈmɔrs/ *v* to express regret or remorse; to repent *la19- NE*. [see the noun]

remove[1.1], †**remuf** /rəˈmuv/ *n* **1** the action of removing, eliminating or departing *16-*. **2** the action of removing a horse's shoe to trim the hoof; a shoe so removed and re-used *16-*. [see the verb]

remove[1.2], **remuve**, *NE* **remeeve**, †**remufe**, †**remofe**, †**remeff** /rəˈmuv; *NE* rəˈmiv/ *v* **1** to cause (a person) to move or depart; to take away (a thing) *la14-*. **2** *of a tenant* to quit a property *la14-*. **3** to dismiss from office, to depose *15-*. **4** to take (oneself) off, to depart *15-*. **5** to dismiss (an interested party) from a court *la15-*. **6** to put an end to; to banish (a feeling) *la15-*. **7** *of a landlord* to compel (a tenant) to quit his holding *16-*. **8** *of a thing* to disappear *15-16*. **removal**, †**removeall 1** the action of removing, eliminating or departing *16-*. **2** flitting *17-*. **removing 1** *law* the action of a landlord compelling a tenant to quit *16-*. **2** the action of sending away, expelling, dismissing or departing *la16-*. **removal term** the days on which contracts of employment (on farms) began and ended, the dates on which flittings from tied houses take place *la19-*. [ME *remeven* or variant of *remouven* or Lat *removēre*]

renaig, **renegue**, **reneeg** /rəˈneg, rəˈnig/ *v* to refuse to do work; to shirk; to shy away from a responsibility, engagement or challenge *20-*. [Lat *renegāre* to deny, reject]

renchel /ˈrɛnʃəl, ˈrɛnʃəl/ *n* a thin, spindly thing or person *19- Bor*. [perhaps transferred sense of RANCE[1.1] with diminutive ending]

rencontre, **rencounter** *see* RANCOUNTER[1.1], RANCOUNTER[1.2]
rendal *see* RIN[1.2]
render *see* RANDER[1.2]
rendezvous[1.1], **randyvoo**, †**rendevouse**, †**randezvous**, †**randevous** /ˈrɔndəvu, ˈrandɪvu/ *n* **1** an arrangement to meet *17-*. **2** a muster of the militia *17-19*. **3** a meeting of a Covenanter's field conventicle *la17*. [EModE *rendevous*, MFr *rendez-vous*]

rendezvous[1.2], †**randezvouse**, †**randevouze** /ˈrɔndəvu/ *v* to assemble at the place appointed (for the muster of the militia) *17-*. [see the noun]

reneeg *see* RENAIG
renegade, **renegate**, *see* RINAGATE
renegue *see* RENAIG
renew /rəˈnju/ *v* **1** to repair, renovate, refresh; to reinforce; to replace or replenish *15-*. **2** to grant afresh; to extend the validity, application or period of (a lease); to revive, reawaken (a feeling); to bring back (a custom); to resume (an activity) *15-*. **3** to repeat, to announce *la15-e17*. [re- + Eng *new* or AN *renuer*]

reng *see* RING[3.2]
renigald *see* RANEGILL
renk *see* RINK[1.1], RINK[1.2], RINK[2]
rennglit *see* RINGL'D
rennie *see* RANE[1.1]
rennish /ˈrɛnɪʃ/ *n* a sudden crashing or clanging noise *19- SW*. [perhaps a variant of REEMISH[1.1]]
†**renomme** *n* renown *la14-*. [OFr *renomee*]

renone *see* RENOWN[1.1]
renoun *see* RENOWN[1.1], RENOWN[1.2]
renounce, *NE* **renunce**, †**renuns** /rəˈnʌuns; *NE* rəˈnʌns/ *v* **1** to give up, to resign; to surrender (a privilege); to repudiate; to reject, abandon *la14-*. **2** *law* to surrender (a lease or inheritance) *la15-*. **renunciation**, †**renunciatioun 1** a repudiation, rejection *15-*. **2** *law* the action of formally surrendering (a lease, inheritance) or resigning (office) *la15-*. [ME *renouncen*]

renounit *see* RENOWNED
renovation, †**renovatioune** /rɛnəˈveʃən/ *n* **1** the action of restoring, refreshing or repairing *19-*. **2** the renewal or resumption (of an agreement, state of affairs or action) *16*. **3** the action of replacing something with a fresh substitute *la15*. [AN, MFr *renovation*]

†**renove**, **renow** *v* to renew *16-e17*. [OFr *renover*, Lat *renovāre*]

renown[1.1], †**renoun**, †**renone**, †**ranowne** /rəˈnʌun/ *n* **1** celebrity, fame; reputation *la14-*. **2** rumour *la14-15*. †**of renoune**, **of renowne** famous, celebrated; of distinction *la14-16*. [ME *renoun*]

†**renown**[1.2], **renoun** *v* to make famous; to record *15-17*. [AN *renouner* and from the noun]

renowned, †**renownit**, †**renounit** /rəˈnʌund/ *adj* famous; distinguished *la14-*. [ptp of RENOWN[1.2]]

†**renownye**, **renownee** *n* renown *la14-e16*. [conflation of RENOWN[1.1] with RENOMME]

Rens *see* RINS
rent[1.1] /rɛnt/ *n* **1** a tear, a laceration *la16-*. **2** a breach, dissension between people *18-e19*. [see the verb]
rent[1.2] /rɛnt/ *v* to rend, to tear, to crack or split; to lacerate *16-*. [OE *rendan*]
rent[1.3] /rɛnt/ *adj* ripped, torn, lacerated; ragged, scruffy *la14-*. [ptp of RENT[1.2], *rend*]
rent[2] /rɛnt/ *n* **1** (property as) a source of income or wealth *la14-*. **2** payment made by a tenant for the use of property *la14-*. **3** income, revenue; wealth; profit, value *15-17*. **4** interest *17*. †**rent maister 1** a treasurer; the burgh treasurer of Lanark *la15-e17*. **2** the High Treasurer of Denmark *la16*. [ME *rent*]

rentaill *see* RENTAL[1.2]
rental[1.1], †**rentale**, †**rentall** /ˈrɛntəl/ *n* **1** the amount paid or received as rent *15-*. **2** a rent-roll, a register of the rent due by tenants *15-19, 20- historical*. **3** a kind of lease granted on favourable terms by a landlord to a KINDLY TENANT *16-19*. **4** an extract from a rental book or a document confirming a rental lease *la16-e17*. **rentaller** a person who held land by being entered in a favourable lease; a KINDLY TENANT *la16-19, 20- historical*. †**rentall buik**, **rentale buke**, **rental book** a rent-roll, a register of the rent due by tenants *16-e19*. [ME *rental*]

rental[1.2], †**rentaill** /ˈrɛntəl/ *v* **1** to enter a person in a rent-roll, grant a person a (favourable) lease *la15-16, 20- historical*. **2** to record details of a piece of land, a lease or rent in a rent-roll; to lease, rent land *16-19, 20- historical*. [see the noun]

renunce, **renuns** *see* RENOUNCE
renye /ˈrɛnji/ *v* to writhe in pain *19- Ork*. [ON *rengja* to twist, distort]

renyie *see* REIN[1.1]
renʒe *see* REIN[1.1], REIN[1.2]
repair[1.1], †**repare**, †**repar** /rəˈper/ *n* **1** the action of coming or going; habitual or continual going (to and from a place or among people) *la14-*. **2** the action of meeting; a meeting-place, a rendezvous, a dwelling-place *la14-*. **3** a gathering or concourse of people; extensive resort of people to a place *la15-19*. **4** access (to) or association, residence (with)

another *15-16.* †**out of repair** away from people *la15-16.* [ME *repair*]

repair[1,2], †**repare** /rəˈper/ *v* **1** to resort, to go habitually or frequently; to return to (people or a place) *la14-.* **2** to be present, temporarily or habitually; to dwell (in a place) *la14-16.* [ME *repairen*]

repair[2,1], †**repare** /rəˈper/ *n* **1** the mending or restoration (of a thing) *la16-.* **2** provision (of a person's sustenance and upkeep) *15-e16.* [see the verb]

repair[2,2], †**repare**, †**repar** /rəˈper/ *v* **1** to mend, to restore; to renew; to improve; to ornament *la15-.* **2** to remedy, to compensate, to make amends *la15-.* [ME *reparen*]

repar *see* REPAIR[1,1], REPAIR[2,2]

†**reparal**, **reparrell** *v* to repair; to equip *15-16.* [ME *repareilen*]

reparation, †**reparatioun** /rɛpəˈreʃən/ *n* **1** the action of repairing or restoring; *pl* repairs, improvements *15-.* **2** amends, compensation *15-.* **3** *law* the redress of a civil wrong, usually by award of damages *la17-.* **4** *Roman Catholic Church* the upkeep of or provision for an altar *la14-16.* **5** furniture, furnishings *la15-16.* [ME *reparacioun*]

repare *see* REPAIR[1,1], REPAIR[1,2], REPAIR[2,1], REPAIR[2,2]

reparrell *see* REPARAL

†**repater** *v* to feed *e16.* [MFr *repaistre*]

repay *see* REPEY

repeat, †**repete**, †**repeit** /rəˈpit/ *v* **1** to say over again; to reiterate *la14-.* **2** to do (something) again *la16-.* **3** *law* to repay, to refund, to make restitution *17-.* **4** *law* to claim back (money or goods); to claim restitution *la16-17.* **5** to recite; to enunciate formally or in public; to relate or recount *la14-15.*
repetition, †**repetitioun 1** *law* restitution, repayment *la15-.* **2** the action of saying something again; recitation *16-.* [MFr *repeter*]

repel, †**repell** /rəˈpɛl/ *v* **1** to drive back, to repulse; to send away *la15-.* **2** *law of a court* to reject (a plea or submission); to overrule (an objection) *16-.* **3** to debar, to disqualify *la15-e17.* **4** to reject (an argument, doctrine or custom) *la16.* [Lat *repellere*]

repent /rəˈpɛnt/ *v* to feel or express contrition and regret (for something) *la14-.* †**repenting stool** = *repentance stool* (REPENTANCE) *la16-e19.* [ME *repenten*]

repentance /rəˈpɛntəns/ *n* the act of repenting; sorrow or regret for wrongdoing; an action performed as an outward sign of repentance *la14-.* **repentance stool** a seat in a prominent place in a church, usually in front of the pulpit, on which offenders sat to be rebuked *la16-19, 20- historical.*

place of repentance *see* PLACE[1,1] [ME *repentaunce*]

repet *see* RIPPET

repete *see* REPEAT

repetition, repetitioun *see* REPEAT

repey, **repay** /rəˈpe, riˈpae/ *v* to pay back, refund; to compensate; to make restitution *la16-.* **repayment** the act of paying back again *la15-.* [EModE *repay*]

repledge, **replege** /rɪˈplɛdʒ/ *v* **1** *law* to transfer (a cause) from one jurisdiction to another, mainly that of the defender's feudal superior *la15-e18, la18- historical.* **2** *law* to take back or take over (something forfeited or impounded) on proper security *la16-e17.* **3** to become security for (a person); to redeem *la15-16.* [AN, MFr *repleger*]

†**repledgiation**, †**replegiatioun** *n* the action of repledging *16-e18.* [Lat *replegiātio*]

replege *see* REPLEDGE

†**replegiate** *v ptp* **replegiate** *law* to transfer (a cause) from one jurisdiction to another, mainly that of the defender's feudal superior *16.* [back-formation from Lat *replegiāt-*, ptp stem of *replegiāre*]

replegiatioun *see* REPLEDGIATION

replenish /rɪˈplɛnɪʃ/ *v* **1** to fill up again, restock *la18-.* **2** to repair; to rehabilitate *la19, 20- Sh.* **replenishit**, †**replenischit 1** (well) stocked or provided *15-.* **2** filled, imbued with a quality *la15-e17.* [AN, MFr *repleniss-*, stem of *replenir*]

reply[1,1] /rəˈplae/ *n* **1** a response *la17-.* **2** *law* a counter-answer by the pursuer to the answer of the defender in the argument of a lawsuit; sometimes this was called the answer and the reply was the second rejoinder by the defender *la16-e19.* [see the verb]

reply[1,2] /rəˈplae/ *v* **1** to answer, respond; to make counter-answer in a formal argument *la15-.* **2** *law* to answer the plea of a defender *la15-e17.* [ME *replien*]

repoirt *see* REPORT[1,1], REPORT[1,2]

repois *see* REPOSE[2,2]

repone[1,1] /rəˈpon/ *n* an answer, a reply *19-.* [see the verb]

repone[1,2] /rəˈpon/ *v* **1** *law* to restore a defender to his right to defend his case, especially after judgement has been given against him in his absence *la16-.* **2** to give as a reply; to answer *17-.* **3** to restore to office or to rights previously held, reinstate *16-19.* **4** *Presbyterian Church* to restore a deposed minister to his charge *la16-19.* **5** to put a person or thing back (in a place) *16-e17.* [Lat *repōnere* to replace, restore]

report[1,1], †**repoirt** /rəˈport/ *n* **1** an account, a formal statement; a rumour *la15-.* **2** a written record of proceedings *la16-.* **3** *law* the act (by a judge) of remitting a case *17-.* [AN, MFr *report* and from the verb]

report[1,2], †**repoirt**, †**raport** /rəˈport/ *v* **1** to give an account of, to relate (something); to convey, to communicate (a message); to record *la15-.* **2** to render a formal account; to notify *la16-.* **3** *of a judge of first instance* to remit (a case or part of it) to a body of one's colleagues for decision *la17-.* **4** to bring (something) in return or as a result obtain for oneself, get (a reward or profit) *la15-17.* **5** to have recourse, appeal, apply (for help or funding) to *15-e16.* **reporter**, †**reportar 1** a narrator or recounter (of events) *la15-.* **2** *law* the officer responsible for bringing a case before a children's hearing *la20-.* **3** *law* a judge who remitted a case for review or decision *17.* **Reporter to the Children's Panel** *law* the officer responsible for bringing a case before a children's hearing *la20-.* [ME *reporten*]

repose[1] /rəˈpoz/ *v* **1** to place, put; to deposit *15-.* **2** to give as a reply; to answer *la16-17.* **3** *law* to restore (a defender) to his right to defend his case, especially after judgement has been given against him in his absence *e17.* [re- + EModE *pose*; after Lat *repōnere*]

repose[2,1] /rəˈpoz/ *n* **1** rest *la15-.* **2** relief from worry or care *la16-.* [EModE *repose*]

repose[2,2], †**repois** /rəˈpoz/ *v* **1** to take rest; to refresh oneself *la15-.* **2** to depend or rely on *la16-e17.* [ME *reposen*]

repossess, †**reposses** /ripoˈzɛs/ *v* **1** to restore or reinstate a person (to or in property) *la16-.* **2** *of property* to regain or recover possession; to reoccupy *la19-.* **repossession 1** recovery (of property) *la16-.* **2** restoration to a possession or charge *la16-e17.* [re- + Eng *possess*]

repree *see* REPROVE

repreif *see* REPROOF, REPROVE

represent /rɛprəˈzɛnt/ *v* **1** to bring vividly or clearly before the mind *la14-.* **2** to denote, stand for, symbolize *la15-.* **3** to substitute for another; to be a representative for someone or something *la15-.* **4** to describe as having a particular function or character *16-.* **5** to impersonate, act the part of; to reproduce by performance *16-.* †**representing days** the 20 days from the pronouncement of a Court of Session judgement during which an appeal against it might be lodged *la18-e19.* [AN *representer*]

representation /rɛprəzɛnˈteʃən/ *n* **1** an image, a symbol *la15-*. **2** *law* the right to succeed to heritable property because one represents a deceased direct heir (such as a grandson succeeding his grandfather) *la17-*. **3** *law* the right to inherit an estate which carries with it liability for the debts of one's predecessor *18-*. **4** *law* an appeal against the decision of a judge of the Court of Session presented in the form of written pleadings *19-*. **5** the fact of being represented *20-*. [MFr *representation*, Lat *repraesentātiō*]

reprise /rəˈpriz, rəˈpraez/ *n* **1** a resumption, a renewal; a fresh attempt *la17-*. **2** *building* a part of a structure jutting out, a moulding; the foot of a window worked on the same stone as the sill *e16*. [ME *reprise*, EModE *reprise*]

reproach[1.1], †**reproche** /rəˈprotʃ/ *n* **1** shame, censure *la15-*. **2** a source of blame *16-*. **3** a rebuke *la16-*. [AN, MFr *reproche*]

reproach[1.2], †**reproche** /rəˈprotʃ/ *v* **1** to blame, censure, upbraid *16-*. **2** to bring or cast up (a fault) to a person as an admonishment *la15-16*. [EModE *reproche*]

reprobate /ˈreprobet/ *v* **1** to reject, exclude *la15-*. **2** *law* to show evidence to be invalid or inadmissible; to reject an instrument or deed *17-*; compare APPROBATE[1.1]. †**reprobator** *law* an action challenging the impartiality or honesty of a witness *17-e19*. [Lat *reprobāt-*, ptp stem of *reprobāre*]

reproche *see* REPROACH[1.1], REPROACH[1.2]

reproof, †**repreif**, †**reprufe**, †**repruif** /rəˈpruf/ *n* **1** censure; a rebuke, a reprimand *15-*. **2** shame, disgrace; a cause for censure, fault *la14-e17*. **3** abusive language *15-16*. [ME *repreve*, OFr *reprueve*]

reprove, †**repree**, †**repreif**, †**reprufe** /rəˈpruv/ *v* **1** to censure; to rebuke, reprimand *la14-*. **2** to refute *la15-16*. [ME *repreven*, OFr *repruever*]

reprufe, repruif *see* REPROOF

†**repudie** *n* rejection, dismissal; divorce *la15-16*. [MFr *repudie*]

repugnant /rəˈpʌɡnənt/ *adj* **1** distasteful, objectionable *20-*. **2** contrary; inconsistent, incompatible *la15-e17*. **3** opposing, hostile *la15-16*. [ME *repugnaunt*]

repute, †**reput** /rəˈpjut/ *v pt* **repute, reputit, reputed**, †**reput 1** to consider a person or thing as being or to be something *la14-*. **2** to take (for), regard (as) *la15-*. **3** to impute, assign, attribute *la15-e16*. †**repute and halden** reputed, considered, reckoned *16-e19*; compare HABIT AND REPUTE[1.1]. [AN, OFr *reputer*, Lat *reputāre*]

requair, requare *see* REQUIRE

requeesht *see* REQUEST[1.2]

requeist *see* REQUEST[1.1], REQUEST[1.2]

requere *see* REQUIRE

request[1.1], †**requeist**, †**raquest** /rəˈkwɛst/ *n* an act or instance of asking for something; a petition, an application *la14-*. †**Maister of Requestis** the member of the Privy Council who dealt with petitions *la16-18*. [ME *request*]

request[1.2], †**requeesht**, †**requeist** /rəˈkwɛst/ *v* to ask for *16-*. **request of** to ask, beg of (a person) *la15-*. [AN, MFr *requester*]

require, *NE* **requair**, †**requare**, †**requere**, †**raquer** /rəˈkwaer/; *NE* rəˈkwer/ *v* **1** to ask, to request; to command, demand; to want, to need *la14-*. **2** to render necessary, be requisite; to conform with a principle, law or regulation; to make or be appropriate *la14-*. [AN *requere, require*, Lat *requīrere*]

requisition, †**requisitioun** /rɛkwəˈzɪʃən/ *n* **1** the action of requesting or requiring; a request; a demand *16-*. **2** *law* a demand by a creditor for repayment of a debt *la16-*. **3** the state of being pressed into service or use *la18-*. **4** *law* the action of formally requiring a person to carry out an action, fulfil an obligation *la15-e17*. [MFr *requisition*, Lat *requisītiō*]

†**requite**[1.1], **requit** *n* requital, compensation *la18-19*. [see the verb]

requite[1.2], †**requit** /rəˈkwʌɪt/ *v* to return (a favour); to repay (a person) *la16-*. [ME *requiten*]

rerd *see* REIRD[1.1], REIRD[1.2]

rerr *see* RARE[1.1]

rerr terr /ˈrɛr tɛr/ *n* **1** a good time; a wild party or gathering *20- WC*. **2** a witty, amusing person; a larger-than-life character *20- WC*. [RARE[1.1] + TEAR[2.1]]

resait *see* RESET[1.2]

resave *see* RECEIVE

resch *see* RASH[1]

rescind, †**reshind** /rəˈsɪnd/ *v* to annul, revoke, repeal, cancel *16-*. [Lat *rescindere*]

rescission, †**rescissioune** /rəˈsɪʒən/ *n* annulment *17-*. [Lat *rescissio*]

rescissory, †**rescissorie** /rəˈsɪsəre/ *adj law* **1** of a legal action purporting to declare (a deed or illegal act) void *la17-*. **2** of an Act of the Scottish Parliament of 1661 acting to rescind the acts passed since 1633 in favour of episcopacy *la17*. [Lat *rescissōrius*]

rescue[1.1], †**reskew**, †**rescours** /ˈrɛskju/ *n* the act of saving, freeing; deliverance *la14-*. [see the verb]

rescue[1.2], †**reskew**, †**rescours**, †**recours** /ˈrɛskju/ *v* to save, to free; to bring help; to regain, to deliver *la14-*. [ME *rescouen*]

reset[1.1], †**resset**, †**ressait**, †**recept** /ˈriset/ *n* **1** *law* the action or practice of receiving stolen goods *16-*. **2** (a place of) refuge used by or offered to fugitives, criminals and undesirables *la15-e19*. **3** *law* the receiving or harbouring of criminals *la15-e19*. **4** a person who shelters a fugitive or criminal *la15-e17*. **5** a harbour for ships *15-16*. **6** a place of accommodation, a residence, a place of shelter or refuge *la14-16*. **reset of theft** the receiving of stolen goods *16-*. [ME *recet*]

reset[1.2], †**resset**, †**recept**, †**resait** /rɪˈsɛt ˈrisɛt/ *v pt* **reset 1** to receive; to give shelter or protection to (a criminal or fugitive) *la14-*. **2** to receive stolen goods, usually with the intention of reselling *la14-*. **resetter**, †**resettour** a person who harbours criminals or receives stolen goods *15-*. [OFr *receter*]

reset *see* RECEIPT

resh *see* RASH[1]

reshind *see* RESCIND

reside, †**receed**, †**receid** /rəˈzʌɪd/ *v* to dwell, settle, remain (in a place); to take up residence (to carry out an employment) *la15-*. [AN *resider*]

residence, †**residens** /ˈrɛzədəns/ *n* **1** the act or fact of living, dwelling or having one's usual abode *la14-*. **2** the place where a person resides or dwells *16-*. **3** attendance required of a judge at a sitting or the Court of Session *la16-e17*. †**mak residens 1** to stay at or in a place for a certain time *la14-e17*. **2** to stay or be in attendance at a place to carry out duties *15-16*. [ME *residence*]

resident[1.1] /ˈrɛzədənt/ *n* **1** a person settled or dwelling in a place *la19-*. **2** a diplomatic representative residing in a foreign country *17-18*. [see the adj]

resident[1.2] /ˈrɛzədənt/ *adj* **1** staying in a place in performance of a duty *la15-*. **2** dwelling, residing in a place *16-*. [ME *resident*]

residenter /rɛzəˈdɛntər/ *n* a resident, inhabitant, especially one of long standing *17-*. [RESIDENT[1.2], with *-er* suffix]

†**residenting** *adj* residing, dwelling *la17-e19*. [RESIDENT[1.1], with *-ing* suffix]

residew *see* RESIDUE

residuary /rəˈzɪdjure/ *adj* **1** of the nature of what remains, remaining *19-*. **2** pertaining to the established Church of

Scotland remaining after the breakaway of the Free Kirk in 1843 *19, 20- historical*. [RESIDUE with adj-forming suffix]

residue, †**residew** /'rɛzədju/ *n* **1** the remainder, the rest *16-*. **2** *law* the remainder of an estate after all charges, debts and bequests have been paid *19-*. [ME *residue*, EModE *residue*]

resign, †**resing**, †**ressyng** /rə'zaɪn/ *v* **1** to relinquish, to surrender, to give up; originally *of a vassal* to surrender property or rights held by feudal tenure to his superior *la14-*. **2** to consign to (the attention of) another *16*. [ME *resignen*]

resignation, †**resignatioun** /rɛzɪg'neʃən/ *n* **1** the action of relinquishing or resigning *17-*. **2** *law* the way in which a vassal relinquished a feudal tenure *la14-19, 20- historical*. [AN *resignacion*, *resignacioun*, MFr *resignation*]

resile, †**reseill** /rə'zʌɪl, rə'sʌɪl/ *v* **1** to draw back, withdraw (from an agreement or undertaking) *la16-*. **2** to recoil (from something), shrink away in distaste or disgust *la16-*. [MFr *resilir*, Lat *resilīre* to jump back, recoil]

resing *see* RESIGN

resist /rə'zɪst/ *v* **1** *of a person* to oppose, withstand; to stand against, make opposition to; to prevent *la14-*. **2** *of a thing* to stop, hinder, withstand, be proof against *16-*. [ME *resisten*]

resistence, †**resistens** /rə'zɪstəns/ *n* the action of opposing, withstanding *la14-*. †**mak resistens** to resist, oppose *la14-16*. [ME *resistence*]

resk *see* REESK

reskew *see* RESCUE[1.1], RESCUE[1.2]

resolution, †**resolutioun** /rɛzə'luʃən/ *n* **1** the solving of a doubt or difficulty; (a) solution; clarification *16-*. **2** a formal decision by an assembly to resolve an outstanding problem *la16-*. **3** an act of deciding; a decision; firm purpose *la16-*. **4** *of the body* a state of weakening or wasting; a paralysis or stroke *16*. **Resolutioner** *Presbyterian Church* one of the party which supported an accommodation with Charles I *la17, 18- historical*. [ME *resolucioun*, EModE *resolucion*, Lat *resolūtio*]

resolutive /rɪ'zɔljutɪv, rɛzə'ljutɪv/ *adj law* that provides for nullification of an agreement if certain conditions specified in it are contravened *la17-*. **resolutive clause** *law* a clause in a deed which is resolutive *la17-*. [Lat *resolūtīvus*]

resolve /rə'zɔlv/ *v* **1** to expound (an argument); to solve (a problem) *la15-*. **2** to take a firm decision; to settle upon, decide *la16-*. **3** *law* to make or become void, (cause to) lapse *la18-e19*. **4** to free (a person) of doubt; to inform, convince, assure (a person) of something *la16-e17*. **5** to separate; to dissolve *la15-e17*. **resolvit**, **resolved**, *Sh* **rezold**, **1** reduced into elements or components *16-*. **2** *of a person* determined, decided, of settled purpose; satisfied, contented, calm *la16-*. [Lat *resolvere*]

resort[1.1] /rə'zɔrt/ *n* **1** the habit or opportunity of going to a place or meeting with others *16-*. **2** a place of repair; a residence *la16-*. [ME *resort*, EModE *resorte* and from the verb]

resort[1.2] /rə'zɔrt/ *v* **1** to return, to revert; to go (regularly or frequently) to; to have recourse to *la14-*. **2** to stay in a place *16-e17*. [ME *resorten*]

resoun *see* REASON[1.1], REASON[1.2]

respeck[1.1], **respect** /rə'spɛk, rə'spɛkt/ *n* **1** heed, consideration, concern; reference or regard *la15-*. **2** (deferential) regard, affectionate esteem; partiality, favour *16-*. **3** something taken into account, a consideration *la16-*. [ME *respect*, Lat *respectus*]

respeck[1.2], **respect** /rə'spɛk, rə'spɛkt/ *v* **1** to consider, to take into account *la16-*. **2** to regard affectionately, to esteem *la16-*. [Lat *respectāre*, Lat *respect-*, ptp stem of *respicere*]

respect *see* RESPECT[1.1], RESPECT[1.2]

respective[1.1] /rɪ'spɛktɪv/ *adj* **1** properly pertaining to, particular *17-*. **2** attentive, careful *la16-e17*. [Lat *respectīvus*]

†**respective**[1.2] *adv* respectively *16-e18*. [Lat *respectīvē*]

respit[1.1], †**respet**, †**respyt**, †**respect** /'rɛspɪt/ *n* **1** an extension of time granted, a postponement, delay *la14-*. **2** an interval of rest, a temporary cessation; a truce *la15-*. **3** a privilege granted only under the royal prerogative allowing postponement of a legal action; the document granting this delay *15-17*. †**but respyt** without delay *la14-16*. [ME *respit*, Lat *respectus*]

†**respit**[1.2], **respyt**, **respect** *v* **1** to postpone; to delay, adjourn (a legal action) *15-18*. **2** to allow (a person) a respite *la15-e19*. **3** to grant (a person) an adjournment of a legal action *e16*. [ME *respiten*, Lat *respectāre*]

†**resplait**[1.1], **respleit** *n law* adjournment, postponement *la15-e17*. [see the verb]

†**resplait**[1.2], **resplate** *v law* to adjourn (a cause or judgement); to defer (consideration or payment of something); to release (from prosecution or punishment) *15-16*. [AN, MFr *respleiter*]

†**responde** *n law* **1** a receipt book in which NON-ENTRY and relief duties due by heirs were recorded *16-e17*. **2** a record book in which decrees and acts were entered by the Clerk of the Session for the charging of fees *e18*. **3** a single entry in a receipt book *la16-17*. **responde book** a receipt book in which NON-ENTRY and relief duties due by heirs were recorded *la17-e19*. [Lat *respondē*, 2nd sing imperative of *respondēre* to reply, the first word of each article in the book]

responsabill, **responsable** *see* RESPONSIBLE

†**responsall**[1.1], **responsaill** *n* a reply; a (divine) answer *la15*. [Lat *responsāle*]

†**responsall**[1.2], **responsale** *adj* **1** answerable, financially responsible or trustworthy; financially liable, acting as guarantor *la15-e18*. **2** able to meet financial obligations, solvent; well-off *16-e18*. **3** willing to answer a legal charge *la16-e17*. **4** *of a pledge, caution* sufficient *16-17*. [AN, MFr *responsal*]

response, †**respons** /rə'spɒns/ *n* **1** an answer, a verbal reaction to something *la15-*. **2** an answer attributed to a divine source *la15-17*. [AN, OFr *respons*, Lat *responsum*]

responsible, †**responsabill**, †**responsable** /rə'spɒnsəbəl/ *adj* **1** answerable, accountable, liable (for something) *16-*. **2** trustworthy, reliable *la16-*. **3** *of a task* requiring reliability *19-*. **4** able to meet financial obligations, well-off *la16-17*. [AN, MFr *responsable*]

†**responsioune** *n* **1** an answer, a verbal reaction to something *la15*. **2** an answer attributed to a divine source *e16*. [AN, MFr *responsion*, Lat *responsio*]

respyt *see* RESPIT[1.1], RESPIT[1.2]

ressait *see* RECEIPT, RESET[1.1]

ressave *see* RECEIVE

resset *see* RESET[1.1], RESET[1.2]

ressoun *see* REASON[1.1]

ressyng *see* RESIGN

rest[1.1], *NE* **rist** /rɛst; *NE* rɪst/ *n* **1** repose; freedom from exertion or trouble; a place of rest; abiding, residence *la14-*. **2** *music* a measured interval of silence, a pause *16-*. **3** a support for a firearm to ensure accuracy of aim *16-*. **4** death; eternal life *la15-e17*. **5** the socket in which the bolt of a door rests *e16*. [OE *rest*]

rest[1.2], *NE* **rist** /rɛst; *NE* rɪst/ *v* **1** to take repose, continue in a state of tranquillity; to remain *la14-*. **2** to be situated or supported, lean on something *16-*. **3** *of arable land* to lie fallow *la18- Sh N NE T EC*. †**resting bed** a day bed *la17*. **resting chair** a chair on which a person can lie; a settle *17-19, 20- Sh*. **resting stane** a stone used as a resting place; a stone on the road to a churchyard where the coffin was laid while the bearers rested *la19-*. [OE *restan*]

rest[2.1], †**rist** /rest/ *n* **1** the remainder; a remnant *15-*. **2** *pl* sums of money due, arrears *16-e18*. **the auld rest** = arrears *la15-e16*. [AN, MFr *reste*]

rest[2.2], †**rist** /rest/ *v* **1** to continue, maintain *la15-*. **2** to remain, be left over *16-*. **3** *of a sum of money* to remain due or unpaid, be overdue *la15-19, 20- Sh Ork*. **4** *of a person* to owe (someone something) *16-19, 20- Sh*. **5** *law of a legal action* to remain in suspension; to be abandoned *16-e17*. **resting**, †**restand** the outstanding amount (of a debt) *la16-*. [ME *resten*]

rest *see* REEST[2.1], REEST[2.2]

†**restagn, restagne** *v* **1** to overflow as a consequence of being dammed up *e17*. **2** to dam up *e18*. [OFr *restagner*, Lat *restagnāre*]

†**restagnate, restagnat** *v ptp* **restagnat 1** *of flowing water* to overflow as a consequence of being dammed up *la17*. **2** to dam up, cause (water) to cease to flow *e18*. [Lat *restagnāre*]

restagne *see* RESTAGN
restaur *see* RESTORE
restauration, restauratioun *see* RESTORATION
restoir *see* RESTORE

restoration, †**restauration,** †**restauratioun** /rɛstəˈreʃən/ *n* **1** the restoring of something to an earlier or better condition; repair; improvement *la16-*. **2** the return (of something) to a previous owner, the restitution of stolen goods *16-17*. **3** the reinstatement of the human race in divine favour *la14-15*. [AN, MFr *restauration*]

restore, †**restoir,** †**restaur** /rəˈstor/ *v* **1** to give back; to bring back to a condition previously enjoyed, repair; to bring back to health; to reinstate; to re-establish; to redeem *la14-*. **2** to make good (loss, damage); to make amends; to compensate *15-e17*. **3** *law* to put (a litigant) back in the situation prevailing before a legal act in consequence of which they suffered harm *la16-17*. [ME *restoren*, Lat *restaurāre*]

restreen, restrain, †**restrenȝe** /rəˈstrin, rəˈstrɛn/ *v* **1** to prevent; to keep under control *la14-*. **2** to limit, moderate *la15-*. **3** to suppress; to forbid *la14-e17*. [ME *restreinen*]

restrenȝe *see* RESTREEN

restrick, restrict, †**restrik** /rəˈstrɪk, rəˈstrɪkt/ *v* **1** to confine, limit *16-*. **2** to bind by a legal or moral obligation *16-e17*; compare ASTRICT (**sense 2**). [Lat *restrict-*, ptp stem of *restringere* confine]

resume /rəˈzum/ *v* **1** to take or get back; to take or start up again *la15-*. **2** *of a landlord* to repossess part of a piece of land which has been let in accordance with the terms of the lease *la18-*. **resumptions** *law* the act of repossessing (property which has been let) *la18-*. [AN, MFr *resumer*, Lat *resūmere*]

†**resurs, resours** *v* to rise again *la15-e16*. [AN *resurs-*, MFr *resours-*, pt stem of *resourdre*]

retain, †**retene** /rəˈten/ *v* **1** to keep from, hold back; to restrain *16-*. **2** to keep; to confine *la16-*. **retainer,** †**reteener** a dependent; a servant *16-*. [ME *reteinen*, EModE *reteyne*]

reteir *see* RETIRE
retene *see* RETAIN

retention, †**retentioun** /rəˈtɛnʃən/ *n* **1** the action of keeping or withholding; confinement *la16-*. **2** *law* the right not to fulfil one's own part of a contract until the other party has fulfilled theirs (including the right not to deliver goods until the buyer has paid for them) *17-*. [ME *retencioun*, EModE *retention*]

retere *see* RETIRE
rethe *see* REITHE[1.1], REITHE[1.2]
rether *see* RAITHER

†**rethore** *n* a teacher of rhetoric, a master of eloquence *16-e17*. [Lat *rhētor*]

†**rethoreis** *n* rhetoric *la15-e16*. [Lat *rhētoricē*]

rethorie *see* RETHORY

†**rethorik** *adj* rhetorical *e16*. [ME *rethorik*]

rethorik *see* RHETORIC

†**rethory, rethorie** *n* rhetoric; eloquence *la15-e16*. [RETHORE + -IE[3]]

reticule basket, radical basket, reddicle basket /ˈrɛtɪkəl baskət, ˈradɪkəl baskət, ˈrɛdɪkəl baskət/ *n* a woven bag for carrying on the arm *la19- N NE SW*. [Fr *réticule* + Eng *basket*]

retire, †**reteir,** †**retere** /rəˈtaer/ *v* **1** to withdraw, retreat; to leave a job *16-*. **2** to go back, return (home); to depart; to move back *la16-*. **3** to recover, take back (a document setting out an obligation), usually on fulfilment of the obligation *17-e18*. **4** to withdraw from currency, pay up (a bill of exchange) when due *la17-e19*. **5** *of a debtor* to seek sanctuary (in the Abbey of Holyroodhouse in Edinburgh) *18-e19*. **retiral** retirement from office or other commitment *20-*. **retiring collection** *Christian Church* an extra collection for some special purpose taken as the congregation leaves *20-*. [MFr *retirer*]

retorik *see* RHETORIC
retorn *see* RETURN[1.1] RETURN[1.2]

retour[1.1] /rəˈtur/ *n* **1** *law* the return or extract of a decision sent to chancery by a jury or inquest, especially one declaring a successor heir to his ancestor; the record of such a return, especially one specifying the annual taxable value of the land *la15-*. **2** a round, a turn, a bout; a second helping of food or round of drinks *la19- NE*. **3** the act or right of returning; a return *la14-19*. **4** a return journey at reduced rates in a carriage or on a horse hired by another for the outward journey *18-e19*. †**retour duty** the amount of tax payable based on the value recorded in the official return *la16-19*. †**retour maill** = *retour duty la16-17*. [ME *retour*]

retour[1.2] /rəˈtur/ *v* **1** *law* to make a return to chancery, especially one declaring a person heir; to declare the annual taxable value of (the land concerned) on such a return *la15-*. **2** to return; to revert to; to come back again *15-17*. **retourable** *of a brief* returnable to the authority issuing it *la17-19, 20- historical*. [see the noun]

retoured, †**retourit** /rəˈturd/ *adj* **1** *of land* subject to an official return and valued at the sum declared in it *la16-*. **2** *of a person* declared heir in a an official return *18-*. †**retoured duty** the amount of tax payable based on the value recorded in the official return *la16-19*. [ptp of RETOUR[1.2]]

retourn *see* RETURN[1.1], RETURN[1.2]

†**retractatioun** *n law* amendment, revocation or withdrawal of legal decisions *16*. [Lat *retractātio*]

retrait *see* RETREAT[1.1], RETREAT[1.2]

retreat[1.1], †**retrete,** †**retrait** /rəˈtrit/ *n* **1** a signal to retreat *la14-*. **2** the act of retreating; a withdrawal *la16-*. **3** a place of retreat or resort, a refuge *la16-*. [ME *retret*]

retreat[1.2], †**retrete,** †**retrait** /rəˈtrit/ *v* **1** to go back, withdraw, retire *la15-*. **2** to rescind (a decision, sentence) *15-17*. **3** to retract (a charter or right previously granted) *la15-16*. [AN *retreiter*, MFr *retraiter*]

retrete *see* RETREAT[1.1], RETREAT[1.2]

†**retrocess** *v law* to restore a right temporarily assigned to another, reinstate a person in a post or office *la17-18*. [probably back-formation from RETROCESSION]

retrocession, †**retrocessioun** /rɛtroˈsɛʃən/ *n law* a returning of a right to the person who granted it *la16-*. [MFr *retrocession*]

rett /rɛt/ *n* an enclosure for animals *20- Sh.* [ON *rétt* a communal sheep fold]

return[1.1], †**retourn**, †**retorn** /rəˈtʌrn/ *n* **1** the action of coming or going back; a withdrawal, a retreat *15-* **2** the sending back, after due processing, of a document *la17-*. **3** an answer *17.* [ME *return* and from the verb]

return[1.2], †**retourn**, †**retorn** /rəˈtʌrn/ *v* **1** to come or go back; to turn round, retreat *la14-*. **2** *of property or legacy* to go back to a previous owner or another legatee *15-*. **3** to revert to a previous state; to change or turn into *la15-*. **4** to send back *la16-*. **5** to turn (something) back on to someone, blame *la15.* **6** restore (a state) *16.* **7** to turn (the head or eyes) *16.* [ME *returnen*]

†**returne** *n* the return or extract of a decision sent to chancery by a jury or inquest *e16.* [OFr *retournee*]

reuall *see* ROWEL

reubarb *see* RHUBARB

reul *see* RAIVEL[1.2]

reule *see* RULE[1.1], RULE[1.2]

reult *see* RULT[1.1], RULT[1.2]

reume *see* RHEUM

reuth[1.1], **ruith** /røð/ *n* a small seed, especially of wild mustard *Sinapis arvensis la19- Ork N.* **reuthie breid** bread made from wild mustard seed *la19- Ork.* [Norw *ryd* discarded waste]

reuth[1.2] /røð/ *v of words* to gush, pour out profusely *la19- Ork.* [see the noun]

revanus *see* RAVENOUS

revar *see* REIVER, ROVER[2]

revatwirie *see* RIVATWARI

reve *see* REIVE

reveal, †**revele**, †**reveil** /rəˈvil/ *v* **1** to disclose, to make known *la14-*. **2** to divulge; to inform on; to identify *la15-*. **3** to show, make visible *16-*. †**revelar**, **revealer** an informer *la15-17.* [AN, OFr *reveler*]

revel[1.1], †**reffell** /ˈrɛvəl/ *n* noisy merrymaking; festivity *la15-*. †**Maister of the Revills** a title held jointly by the brothers Edward and James Fountain who arranged various entertainments *la17.* [AN, MFr *revel*]

revel[1.2], †**raiffell** /ˈrɛvəl/ *v* to make merry, play sports or games *la15-*. [AN, MFr *reveler*]

†**revel**[2] *n* a severe blow *17-e19.* [unknown]

†**revelayk**, **reyflake**, **reylock** *n* robbery *15.* [REIF + ME -*laik*, OE -*lāc*, noun-forming suffix expressing action]

revell *see* ROWEL

revelyn *see* RULLION

revenge[1.1] /rəˈvɛndʒ/ *n* **1** the action of taking revenge, retaliation; an instance of revenge *15-*. **2** *law* (the exacting of) satisfaction for crime, wrongdoing or injury, retribution *la16-e17.* **3** punishment *la15-16.* [MFr *revenge*]

revenge[1.2] /rəˈvɛndʒ/ *v* **1** to avenge oneself, take revenge; to take countermeasures against a threat *la14-*. **2** to avenge an injury, exact retribution; to take countermeasures; to vent anger *la14-*. **3** to avenge (a person) *la15-*. †**revengeabill** vengeful; seeking retribution *16.* †**revengeance**, **revengeans** revenge, vengeance *la14-15.* [AN, MFr *revenger*]

rever *see* ROVER[2]

reverence, †**reverens** /ˈrɛvərəns/ *n* **1** respect; veneration; deference *la14-*. **2** a gesture indicative of respect or deference *la15-*. **3** the condition of being revered; that which inspires respect *la15-*. †**in reverens** in honour of a person *e16.* **in someone's reverence** under an obligation to; in the power or at the mercy of (someone) *la16-e19, la19- H&I.* †**out of the reverence of** not under an obligation; not in the power or at the mercy of *la17-19.* [ME *reverence*, Lat *reverentia*]

reverend /ˈrɛvərənd/ *adj* deserving respect, deference or veneration *la14-*. [ME *reverent*, MFr *révérend*, Lat *reverendus*; in later use perhaps Eng *reverend*]

reverens *see* REVERENCE

reverie *see* RAVERIE

reverse, †**revers** /rəˈvɛrs/ *v* **1** to overthrow, overturn *la14-*. **2** to abrogate, annul *15-*. **3** to invert, turn upside down *16-*. **reverser** *law* a person who borrows money on security of land but retains the right to redeem the land, a mortgager *17-.* [ME *reversen*]

reversion, †**reversioun** /rəˈvɛrʃən/ *n* **1** *law* (the right of) redeeming mortgaged lands *la15-*. **2** remains, left overs *e19.* [ME *reversioun*, Lat *reversio*]

revert /rəˈvɛrt/ *v* **1** to restore, return to a former state *15-*. **2** to recover (health, vitality, consciousness) *16-e19.* **3** *of a plant* to sprout or flower again *16.* **4** *of property* to return to a former owner *15.* **5** to improve; to make or become better *la15-16.* [ME *reverten*]

revery *see* RAVERIE

†**revest**, **ravest** *v* to clothe *15-e16.* [ME *revesten*]

revestre *see* REVESTRY

†**revestry**, **revestre** *n* **1** the vestry of a church (used as a place for official meetings) *la15-17.* **2** a room for privacy *e16.* [AN *revestrie*]

revil *see* RAVEL[1.1]

†**revil-raill**, **reavel-ravel** *n* rambling speech *la15-17.* Compare REEL-RALL[1.1]. [reduplicative compound based on RAIVEL[1.1]]

revin *see* RIVE[1.2]

revis, **revisch** *see* RAVISH

revoke, †**revoik** /rəˈvok/ *v* **1** to rescind; to withdraw *15-*. **2** to summon back, recall *la15-16.* **3** to recant; to make a recantation *15-16.* [ME *revoken*, Lat *revocāre*]

revolve, †**rewoll** /rəˈvɔlv/ *v* **1** to turn over in the mind, consider *la15-*. **2** to spin, rotate *la16-*. **3** to read through, search (a book) *la15-16.* **4** to spin out, unroll a destiny *e16.* [MFr *revolver*, Lat *revolvere*]

revyn *see* RIVE[1.2]

†**rew**, **rue** *n* a street *la14-16.* [AN *rew*, AN, OFr *rue*]

rew *see* RUE[1.1], RUE[1.2]

rewaird[1.1], **reward** /rəˈwɛrd, rəˈwɔrd/ *n* recompense; remuneration; requital; repayment for wrongdoing *la14-*. [ME *reward*]

rewaird[1.2], **reward**, †**ryward** /rəˈwɛrd, rəˈwɔrd/ *v* to repay, recompense *la14-*. [ME *rewarden* and from the noun]

reward *see* REWAIRD[1.1], REWAIRD[1.2]

rewburd *see* RHUBARB

rewill, **rewle** *see* RULE[1.1], RULE[1.2]

rewine *see* RUIN[1.1], RUIN[1.2]

rewme *see* RHEUM

rewoll *see* REVOLVE

rewyne *see* RUIN[1.1]

rex, **rax** /rɛks, raks/ *n* a children's chasing game *la19- NE T H&I.* [Lat *rex* a king]

rex *see* RAX[1.1], RAX[1.2]

reyf *see* REIF

reyflake, **reylock** *see* REVELAYK

reyk *see* REAK[1.1], REAK[1.2]

reyn *see* REIN[1.2]

rhame *see* RAME[1.2]

rhetoric, †**rethorik**, †**retorik** /ˈrɛtərɪk/ *n* **1** the art or study of the use of language for the purpose of persuasion *15-*. **2** eloquent, elegant or ornate language, language designed to persuade *la15-*. **3** (the title of) a treatise on rhetoric *la15-e17.*

rhetorical, †**rethoricall** dealing with questions about rhetoric; elegant; eloquent *16-*. [ME *rethorik*, Lat *rhētoricē*, *rhētorica*]

rheum, †**rhewme**, †**reume**, †**rewme** /rum/ *n* **1** watery matter secreted by the mucous glands, mucus; a head cold; catarrh *16-*. **2** *pl* rheumatic pains *la16-19, 20- NE T SW*. **3** noxious moisture *e16*. [ME *reume*, EModE *rewme*]

rheumaticals /ruˈmatɪkəlz/ *npl* = RHEUMATICS *19-*. [altered form of RHEUMATICS]

rheumaticks *see* RHEUMATICS

rheumatics, rheumaticks, roomatics /ruˈmatɪks/ *npl* rheumatism *la18-*. [AN *reumatike, reumatique*, MFr *rhumatique* Lat *rheumaticus*]

rheumatise, *Sh* **roomatis**, *Ork* **rumateese** /ˈrumataez/; *Sh* ˈrumatɪs; *Ork* ˈrumatɪz/ *n* rheumatism *19-*. [Eng *rheumatise*, apparently altered form of *rheumatism*]

rhewme *see* RHEUM

Rhinns, †**Rinnis** /rɪnz/ *npl* an area of land only connected to the mainland by a narrow isthmus *15-*. **the Rhinns of Galloway** the western peninsula of Wigtownshire *la17-*. **the Rhinns of Islay** a peninsula on the western coast of Islay; originally one of the administrative divisions of the island *la16-*. [Gael, IrGael *rinn* a promontory, a headland]

rhone *see* RONE[1]

rhubarb, rewburd, *N H&I* **roobrub**, †**reubarb** /ˈrubarb, ˈrubʌrd; *N H&I* ˈrubrʌb/ *n* one of the perennial plants of the genus *Rheum la15-*. **gie somebody rhubarb** to give someone a beating *20-*. [ME *rubarbe*]

rhyme[1.1], †**rime**, †**ryme** /rʌɪm/ *n* **1** *in verse* a pattern in the terminal sounds of lines *la14-*. **2** a (rhyming) poem or verse *la15-*. **rhymeless** without reason, meaningless; *of persons* irresponsible, reckless, ineffective *19- NE*. [ME, *rīm*]

rhyme[1.2], †**rime**, †**ryme** /rʌɪm/ *v* **1** *of verse* to have rhyming endings to lines *la15-*. **2** to write poetry; to compose in verse *16-*. **3** to repeat, to drone monotonously; to talk nonsense *la19-*. **rhymer**, †**rymour** a poet; a bard, a strolling performer *la13-*. **rhyming**, †**rymming** the art of using rhyme; composing in rhyme *15-*. [AN, OFr *rimer*]

riach, †**reach** /ˈriəx/ *adj of homespun cloth* greyish-white, drab, brindled *la17- Sh Ork N NE*. [Gael *riabhach*]

rial *see* ROYAL[1.2], RYAL

riall *see* ROYAL[1.1]

rialte *see* ROYALTY

rib[1.1], †**reb** /rɪb/ *n* **1** one of the curved bones forming the ribcage in vertebrates *la14-*. **2** a spar of wood in the framework of a boat *16-*. **3** *pl* the bars of a grate *la17-*. **4** a horizontal roof-timber joining rafters *16-19, 20- NE EC*. **5** *mining* a wall of solid coal or other mineral *la19, 20- EC*. **6** *in ploughing* a ridge left unploughed *18-e19*. **7** a horizontal timber supporting a floor *16-e18*. **8** one of the strips of wood laid across supporting beams to form the latticed floor of the drying chamber of a kiln *la15-17*. [OE *rib*]

rib[1.2], †**ribb** /rɪb/ *v* **1** to plough every alternate furrow, turning the soil over onto the adjacent unploughed strip *la18-*. **2** to furnish horizontal timbers to support a floor *la17*. **ribbit, ribbed** marked with ribs or ridges *la16-*. **deep ribbit** large-chested *la19-*. **rib-side** *mining* a face of solid mineral left projecting beyond the next face *la19, 20- EC*. [see the noun]

ribald[1.1], *Sh Ork* **reebald**, †**reebal**, †**rebald** /ˈrɪbəld; *Sh Ork* ˈribəld/ *n* **1** a scoundrel; a ruffian *la15-19, 20- Sh Ork*. **2** a fornicator, a loose woman, a prostitute; a dissolute person or one who used indecent or blasphemous language *la15-e17*. **3** a retainer or soldier of the lowest class; a person of low birth *la14-e17*. **ribaldry 1** obscene language, low or debauched behaviour *15-*. **2** rough, unpolished verse *e16*. [see the adj]

ribald[1.2], †**rebald** /ˈrɪbəld/ *adj of persons* lecherous, licentious; *of writing* abusive, scurrilous *la15-*. [AN *ribald*]

†**ribaldaile, rebalddaill** *n* the lowest class of retainers or soldiers; a rabble; low company *la14-e16*. [OFr *ribaldaille*]

ribb *see* RIB[1.2]

ribban, ribband *see* RIBBON

ribbit *see* RYBAT

ribble-rabble[1.1], †**rible rable** /ˈrɪbəl rabəl/ *n* a disorderly crowd *la17-19, 20- T*. [reduplicative compound of *rabble* (RAIBLE[1.1])]

ribble-rabble[1.2] /ˈrɪbəl rabəl/ *adj* disorderly *19-*. [see the noun]

ribble-rabble[1.3] /ˈrɪbəl rabəl/ *adv* in a state of great confusion *la19-*. [see the noun]

ribbon, ribband, *Sh NE* **reebin**, †**ribban**, †**reban**, †**ruban** /ˈrɪbən, ˈrɪbənd, rɪˈband; *Sh NE* ˈribən/ *n* a narrow strip of fine, decorative woven material; a length of this used for tying (parcels or hair) *la15-*. **ribboned, ribbonit**, †**ribband 1** adorned with ribbons *la15-*. **2** like a ribbon *la19-*. [AN *ribane*, MFr *riban*]

ribe /rʌɪb/ *n* a long-legged, thin person; an emaciated animal *19, 20- SW Uls*. [unknown]

rible rable *see* RIBBLE-RABBLE[1.1]

rice, rys, reis, †**ryce** /rʌɪs/ *n* **1** twigs or small branches, brushwood *la15-*. **2** a branch, a twig; a stick *16-*. [OE *hrīs*]

†**rich**[1.1] *v* **1** to become rich *la15-e18*. **2** to make oneself or another rich, enrich *la14-16*. [see the adj]

rich[1.2], †**ryke**, †**rik** /rɪtʃ/ *adj* **1** *of a person* wealthy, opulent; well-off, substantial *la14-*. **2** *of a thing* valuable; costly; splendid; sumptuously decorated *la14-*. **3** *of a person* powerful, mighty; *a of thing* powerful, strong *15-*. **4** abundant, fertile, flourishing *la15-*. **5** *of wine* of the best quality, choice; strong *16-* **richly** sumptuously; expensively; splendidly; lavishly; abundantly *la14-*. [OE *rīce*]

rich *see* RASH[1]

riches, †**ryches**, †**richesse**, †**ritches** /ˈrɪtʃɪz/ *n* wealth; money, valuables *la14-*. [ME, *riches*]

richt[1.1], **right**, †**rycht**, †**recht** /rɪxt, rʌɪt/ *n* **1** that which is morally just or equitable; just treatment, fairness, justice *la14-*. **2** a justifiable or legally proper title or claim *la14-*. **3** that which a person may justly claim as their due, an amount due *15-*. **4** law *15-16*. **5** a document substantiating a claim or title *la15-17*. †**at all richt** at every point *la14-15*. †**at richt, at rychtis** properly, aright *la14-e16*. **hae richt** to have a justifiable moral or legal claim to own or be something *la14-*. **the richt** that which is right; justice; truth *15-*. †**richt and roth** *in Shetland and Orkney* the unchallengeable title to ownership of land enjoyed under the udal system by all the legitimate descendants of an earlier udal proprietor *16*. †**right by progress** a right established under charter by progress *18-e19*. [see the adj]

richt[1.2], **right**, †**rycht** /rɪxt, rʌɪt/ *v* to straighten, to correct, to heal, to mend *la14-*. [OE *rihtan*]

richt[1.3], **right**, †**rycht**, †**ryght** /rɪxt, rʌɪt/ *adj* **1** straight; direct *la14-*. **2** properly pertaining or belonging to a person *la14-*. **3** lawful, rightful; legitimate *la14-*. **4** on the right side of the body *la14-*. **5** correct, true; genuine, veritable *15-*. **6** in one's right mind; sane *15-*. **7** in accordance with justice or equity *la15-*. **8** fitting, appropriate *la15-*. **9** sober, living in a sober, well-behaved way *la19-*. **richtify** to put to rights, set right *20- NE C*. **rightlins** rightly *la19- Sh NE*. **richtlike** just, fair, equitable *la19- NE T*. **richtly**, †**rythly 1** properly; correctly *16-*. **2** justly, fairly *16-*. **3** directly, straight *15*. **richt an** very, completely *la18- NE SW Bor Uls*. **the richt gate 1** the correct way to behave or do anything *la14-*. **2** in no uncertain manner, thoroughly, properly *la19- NE*. **the richt wey o** a correct understanding of, the hang of *20-*. **the**

richt wey o't the true account or story, the genuine version *la19-*. [OE *riht*].

richt¹,⁴, **right**, †**rycht** /rɪxt, rʌɪt/ *adv* **1** straight, directly; precisely, exactly *la14-*. **2** very, exceedingly *la14-*. **3** appropriately; in the required manner *15-*. **4** adequately, satisfactorily *la18-*. **5** thoroughly, very much, very well *la19- NE T*. **6** righteously; uprightly *la15-16*. **7** in accordance with the facts, accurately, truly *la15-16*. **8** rightly, by right *e16*. **richt eneuch** comfortably off, well provided for *la19, 20- Ork N NE C*. **richt noo** immediately *la19-*. **richt oot** outright, unequivocally *20-*. [OE *rihte*]

richteous, **righteous**, †**richtwis**, †**rychtwis** /ˈrɪxtjəs, ˈrʌɪtjəs/ *adj* **1** *of a person* virtuous; just; morally upright *la14-*. **2** *of conduct* just; fair *la14-*. **3** rightful, lawful, legitimate *la14-18*. **4** *of the pertinents or boundaries of property* correctly determined, recognized or sanctioned in law *14-17*. **5** *of a claim, plea* legitimate, legally justified *la14-15*. **6** *of a judgement, law* just *15-16*. **7** *of weights and measures* in accordance with the standard set, correct *16*. [OE *rihtwīs*]

rick *see* REEK¹·¹, REEK¹·²

rick¹·¹, **rik** /rɪk/ *n* a sharp upward jerk, a sudden pull *la19- Sh Ork*. [ON *rykkr*]

rick¹·², **rik**, **rake** /rɪk, rek/ *v* to strike with or as with a fish hook or spear, to hook a fish *19- Sh Ork*. [ON *rykkja*]

ricket /ˈrɪkət/ *n* a noisy disturbance, a racket, a row *19, 20- T*. [probably onomatopoeic; compare RICKLE²·¹]

ricketie /ˈrɪkəti/ *n* **1** a wooden rattle consisting of a small frame whirled round on wooden ratchets *la18-19, 20- C*. **2** a ratchet brace or drill *la19, 20- C*. [onomatopoeic; compare RICKET]

rickety buckie /ˈrɪkəti bʌki/ *adj* a snail or snail shell *20- Ork*. [Eng *rickety* affected by rickets + BUCKIE¹, because they were believed to cure rickets]

rickietickie /rɪkiˈtɪki/ *n* a button on a thread, used by children to rattle on a window *20- NE C*. [onomatopoeic]

rickle¹·¹, **ruckle**, †**rekill** /ˈrɪkəl, ˈrʌkəl/ *n* **1** a heap or pile of things loosely or carelessly thrown together *la16-*. **2** a small heap of peats or turfs, stacked loosely for drying *la16-*. **3** an old, mean or dilapidated building *la18-*. **4** an emaciated, broken-down person or animal *la18-*. **5** an untidy collection or huddle of buildings *19-*. **6** a ramshackle or disintegrating object *la19-*. **7** a dry-stone wall; a layer of small stones placed on top of larger stones as a coping to such a wall *la18-19, 20- Ork NE T EC*. **8** a small temporary stack of grain or seed-hay *la18-19, 20- WC SW*. **a rickle o banes** an emaciated, broken-down person or animal *la18-*. [probably conflation of ON *hraukr* a small pile (of peats) and ON **rykla* a small, loose heap; compare Norw *rygla*]

rickle¹·², **ruckle**, †**rekill** /ˈrɪkəl, ˈrʌkəl/ *v* **1** to pile together loosely; to construct loosely or insecurely *la16-*. **2** to build without mortar; to build a dry-stone wall *la18-*. **3** to stack peats loosely for drying *la18-*. **4** to build grain into small temporary ricks *la18- WC SW*. **ricklie** badly-constructed, ramshackle, rickety *18-*. **rickle up** to build a dry-stone wall *la16- EC*. [from the noun or ON **rykla*]

rickle²·¹ /ˈrɪkəl/ *n* a clatter; a succession of sharp noises *e16, 20- NE EC*. [onomatopoeic]

rickle²·² /ˈrɪkəl/ *v* to rattle, move with a rattling or clattering sound, come down, fall with a clatter *la17, 20- NE EC*. [see the noun]

rickling *see* RIGLEN

rickmatick /ˈrɪkməˌtɪk/ *n* a related group of any sort *la19-*; compare *the hale rickmatick* (HAIL¹·²). [altered form of Eng *arithmetic*]

ricur *see* RECUR

rid *see* REDD¹·², REDD¹·³, REID¹·¹, REID¹·², RIDE¹·²

rid-baa /rɪd ˈbɑ/ *n* the yolk of an egg *20- Sh*. [REID¹·¹ + BA¹]

ridden *see* RIDE¹·²

riddil *see* RIDDLE²

riddill *see* RIDDLE¹·¹, RIDDLE¹·²

riddin *see* RIDE¹·²

riddle¹·¹, †**riddill** /ˈrɪdəl/ *n* **1** a coarse sieve *16-*. **2** a measure of claret, thirteen bottles arranged round a MAGNUM (from the practice of carrying it in at ceremonial dinners in a riddle) *19-*. [OE *hriddel*]

riddle¹·², †**riddill** /ˈrɪdəl/ *v* to sift by passing through a riddle *16-*. **riddlings** coarser elements remaining in the riddle *16-*. **riddling heids** the refuse of corn left after riddling *20- N SW*. [see the verb]

riddle², †**riddil**, †**ryddill**, †**rydle** /ˈrɪdəl/ *n* an enigma, a puzzle *15-*. [OE *rǣdels*]

riddle³, *Ork* **rittle** /ˈrɪdəl/ *v* to chatter, prattle; to tattle *20- Sh Ork*. [unknown]

riddy /ˈrɪdi/ *n* a red face as a sign of extreme embarrassment *20-*. [reduced form of REID FACE]

ride¹·¹ /rʌɪd/ *n* **1** an episode of riding; a journey (on horseback or by ship) *19-*. **2** *in curling* a forceful shot played to dislodge a stone blocking passage to the tee *la19-*. [see the verb]

ride¹·², †**tryd** /rʌɪd/ *v pt* **rade**, **rode**, *Sh Ork N T* **red**, **raid**, †**rid**, *ptp* **ridden**, *SW* **rid** †**riddin**, †**ridin**, †**rode** **1** to travel on an animal's back; to travel on or in a vehicle (originally as drawn by a horse) *la14-*. **2** *of a ship* to lie at or on anchor; to rest motionless in a harbour *15-*. **3** to cross a stretch of water on horseback, ford a river *16-*. **4** to have sexual intercourse with *16-*. **5** *in curling and bowls* to play a stone with such force that it moves an opponent's stone which was blocking its path to the tee *19-*. **6** *mining* to travel up and down the shaft in a cage *la19- C*. **7** *farming of a harrow* to override another being drawn alongside it and become interlocked with it *la18-19, 20- SW*. **8** to go on horseback on a hostile expedition, take part in a foray *15-e17, 19- historical*. **9** *of a river* to be fordable on horseback *18-19*. **10** to ride in a ceremonial procession *la15-17*. **ride-out** one of a series of rehearsal rides of a section of the boundaries in the weeks before the Riding of the Marches *20- SW Bor*. †**ride at the ring** to take part in a competition in which a rider tried to spear and carry off a small ring suspended from an overhead crossbar *18*. **ride on the riggin o** to be completely preoccupied with; to be very officious about *18-*. †**ride or gang** **1** to take part in a procession on horseback or on foot *15-16*. **2** to (commit oneself to) go with a feudal superior on a military expedition or raid *la15-e17*. †**ride the fair** to open a fair or market with a ceremonial procession of magistrates and council *la17-18*. **ride the marches** to verify (boundaries); to perform the ceremony of Riding of the Marches *la16-*. †**ride the market** = *ride the fair 18*. †**Ride the Parliament** to open Parliament with a ceremonial procession *la16-e18*. **ride the shaft** *mining* to go down the pit by sliding down the shaft rope *la19, 20- WC*. †**ride the stang** to suffer the punishment of being mounted on a pole and displayed in public *18-e19*. †**ride the stang on** to deal out the punishment of riding the stang to an effigy of, or someone impersonating the offender; to hold up to public ridicule *18-e19*. **ride the tow** = *ride the shaft*. **no tae ride the water on** not to be depended on, unreliable, untrustworthy *la18-19, 20- NE T Bor*. [OE *rīdan*]

†**ride**² *adj of blows* violent, severe *la14-15*. [perhaps aphetic form of ME *unride* violent, causing grave injury]

†**ride**³ *v* mark during perambulation the boundaries of land or the teinds payable on growing crops *la15-17*. **ride out** = RIDE³ *la18-*. [probably REDD¹·² confused with RIDE¹·², as the inspection was usually carried out on horseback]

ride see READ¹·²

rideeculas, ridiculous /rəˈdikjuləs, rəˈdɪkjuləs/ *adj* ridiculous *la17-*. [Lat *rīdiculōsus*]

rider /ˈrʌɪdər/ *n* **1** a person who rides a horse, animal, bicycle, motorcycle *la15-*. **2** *in curling and bowls* a forceful shot played that moves an opponent's stone which was blocking its path to the tee *la19-*. **3** a gold coin current in Flanders and Holland; a Scottish gold coin with the figure of the king on horseback on the obverse *la15-e18, la19-* *historical*. **4** *law* a person who makes a liquid claim upon a claimant *19-*. **5** a mounted trooper; a raider or reiver *16-e19*. **6** a tall standard fruit tree used to fill space on a high wall *19*. [RIDE¹·², with agent suffix]

rid face see REID FACE

riding /ˈrʌɪdɪn, ˈrʌɪdɪŋ/ *n* **1** the action or fact of sitting or travelling on horseback *la15-*. **2** the action of riding ceremonially or in procession *la16-*. **3** an episode of riding, especially as a feudal servitude; a foray on horseback *la15-17, e19* *historical*. **riding claim** *law* a LIQUID claim on a claimant in a MULTIPLEPOINDING which may be lodged in the MULTIPLEPOINDING itself *20-*. **riding claimant** a person who makes a *riding claim 20-*. **riding commission** *Presbyterian Church* a committee appointed to examine the causes of rejection of a candidate by a presbytery or congregation, and to override these if they are found to be insufficient *18*. **riding committee** = *riding commission 18-20 historical*. **riding interest** = *riding claim 19-*. †**riding money** a charge or payment to maintain mounted troops *la17*. **riding season** the breeding season of animals *la17-19, 20- Ork*. †**riding time** = *riding season 18*. **Riding of the Marches** the traditional ceremony of riding round the boundaries of common land to inspect landmarks and boundary stones *20-*; the focus of an annual local festival in certain, especially Border, towns *la16-*; compare *redd the marches* (REDD¹·²), RIDE³. [verbal noun from RIDE¹·²]

rid neb see REID NEB
ridwir see RED WARE
rie see REE¹
rief see REIF
rif see RIVE¹·²
rifart see REEFORT

†**rife**¹·¹, †**ryf** *n* abundance, plenty *la16-e18*. [see the adj]

rife¹·², †**ryf** /rʌɪf/ *adj* **1** widespread, prevalent *la15-*. **2** plentiful, abundant, numerous *la14-*. **3** having plenty of, well supplied with, rich in *la16-*. **4** quick, ready, eager (for) *la16, la19- Sh Ork NE*. **5** *of information* widely known; *of a term or phrase* frequently employed *la14-16*. [OE *ryfe*]

rife¹·³, †**ryf** /rʌɪf/ *adv* plentifully, abundantly *la14-*. [see the adj]

-rife /rʌɪf/ *suffix* **1** *with nouns* having an abundance of, notable for, liable to, *eg cauldrife* (CAULD¹·¹) *16-*. **2** *with verbs* liable to, likely to, having a tendency to, *eg* WAUKRIFE *la15-*. **3** *with adjs* sometimes with intensive force, *eg wildrife* (WILD¹·¹) *la19-*. [probably RIFE¹·²] .

riff see RUIF¹·¹

†**riffell gun, rifle gun** *n* a rifle *la17-e19*. [altered form of EModE *rifle* to cut spiral grooves + GUN¹·¹]

riffle see RUFFLE¹·¹, RUFFLE¹·², RUFFLE²·²

rift¹·¹, †**ryfft** /rɪft/ *n* **1** a breaking of wind, a belch, a fart *15-*. **2** an exaggerated account; a boast *19- NE*. **3** a lively chat *19*. **hae the rift o** to have (food) repeating *la19- T*. [see the verb]

rift¹·² /rɪft/ *v* **1** to belch; to break wind *la15-*. **2** to exaggerate, brag *18-19, 20- N NE*. **riftin fou** *of a person* very full of food or alcoholic drink *19-*. †**rift out** *(of the effects) of alcohol* to cause unpleasant memories to rise up (as from the stomach) *e17*. †**rift up** = *rift out*. [ON *rypta*]

rift²·¹, †**ryft** /rɪft/ *n* **1** a break, a split, a crack; a gap *16-*. **2** a cleft or fissure in a rock *15-19, 20- Sh NE T*. **3** a slit in the ear of a sheep indicating ownership *18- Sh Ork*. [ON *ript*]

†**rift**²·² *v* **1** *in Shetland* to mark a sheep with a slit in the ear *la19*. **2** to split, crack *la16*. [ON *ripta*]

rig¹·¹, *Sh N* **reeg**, †**tryg** /rɪg; *Sh* rig/ *n* **1** a ridge of high ground, a long narrow hill, a hill-crest, frequently in place-names *la12-*. **2** an extent of land, long rather than broad *15-*. **3** one of the divisions of a field ploughed in a single operation *16-*; compare RUNRIG. **4** each separate strip of ploughed land, raised in the middle and sloping gradually to a furrow on either side, and usually bounded by patches of uncultivated grazing; cultivated land; a field *18-*. **5** *pl* the arable land belonging to one farm or proprietor *18- literary*. **6** a strip of ground leased for building in a Scottish burgh, usually with a narrow street frontage and a considerable extension backwards *16-18, 20- historical*. **7** a piece of land planted with a crop or being harvested *17-19, 20- Ork NE T*; compare *corn rig* (CORN¹·¹). **8** the back or backbone of a person or animal *15-19, 20- Sh N*. **9** a (frequently white) strip running along the back of an animal *la19- Sh Uls*. **10** a measure of land, usually fifteen feet wide and varying in length *la15-19, 20- H&I*. **11** a team of reapers *la16-19*. **12** *weaving* the centre line of a web of cloth along which it is folded, the folded edge *la15-17*. † **rigget** an imperfectly castrated male animal; a male animal with an undescended testicle, a rig *la16*. †**riggit 1** *especially of cows* having a stripe of a different colour along the back *la16-e18*. **2** *of cloth* striped *la16*. **riglin** a male animal or sometimes a man with one testicle undescended *la16-*. **riggy, rigga** name for a cow with a stripe marking on the back *la18-19, 20- Sh Uls*. **rig-back** the back or backbone *la16-19, 20- Sh*. **rig-bane** the backbone, the spine *la15-19, 20- Sh N EC*. **rig-breist** = *rig-heid 20- Sh*. †**rig-end** the land at the end of a furrow on which the plough is turned *19*; compare *endrig* (EN). **rig-fit** the foot or lower end of a RIG¹·¹ (sense 4) *20-*. **rig-heid** the crown or high part of a RIG¹·¹ (sense 1) *la19, 20- Sh*. **rig-lenth** the length of a RIG¹·¹ (sense 2) as a measurement of distance *17-19, 20- Sh*. **rigged and furred** ribbed *la18-*. **rig-aboot** the system of land tenure whereby different strips were allotted to tenants annually *19, 20- Sh Ork N NE historical*; compare RUNRIG. †**rig and baulk** arable strips of land separated by uncultivated strips onto which stones and rubbish from the cultivated strips were cleared *e19, la19- historical*. **rig and fur, rig and furrow** *of the pattern on a ploughed field* also *of knitting* corrugated, ribbed *la18-*. **rig and rendal**, †**rig rendale** = *rundale* (RIN¹·²) *16- Sh Ork N*. [perhaps ON *hryg-gr*; compare OE *hrycg*]

rig¹·² /rɪg/ *v* **1** to plough (land) in strips *la18- C SW Uls*. **2** to provide a roof with a ridge or a building with a roof or roof-ridge *la15-17*. [see the noun]

rig² /rɪg/ *n* mischief, a trick or prank *la18-*. **on the rig** out for fun or mischief *19-*. [unknown]

rig³ /rɪg/ *n* the smallest animal or weakling of a litter *la19-*. [unknown; compare RIGLEN]

rig aboot /rɪg əˈbut/ *v* to tidy up, set to rights *20- Sh*. [unknown first element + ABOOT¹·¹; compare Eng *rig* to prepare a boat or ship for sea]

rigbody, rigbuddy see RIGWIDDIE¹·¹

rigga see RIG¹·¹

rigger worm /ˈrɪgər wʌrm/ *n* a marine worm used as bait *20- T EC Bor*. X [unknown first element + Eng *worm*]

riggin¹, †**triggyng** /ˈrɪgɪn/ *n* **1** the roof-ridge or roof of a building; the structural materials employed in its construction *16-*. **2** the highest part of anything; the top of a stretch of high ground; a high ridge of land, especially running along the side of a plain, frequently in place-names *16-*. **3** = RIG[1.1] (sense 8) *16-19, 20- Ork NE EC*. **4** the crown of a road *la17-19, 20- Sh*. **5** the action of ridging a roof or roofing a building *16-17*. **6** loft or attic space *la16-17*. **7** shelter, a roof over one's head *e19*. **riggin-bane** = *rigbane* (RIG[1.1]) *la18-19, 20- Ork*. **riggin divot** a turf used as a ridge coping for a thatched roof *la17- NE*. **riggin-heid** the ridge of a roof *20- NE T C SW*. †**riggin-loft** = RIGGIN[1.1] (sense 6) *e19*. **riggin stane** a stone used as a ridge stone or structural element of a roof *la15-19, 20- NE C*. **riggin tree** the ridge beam of a roof *la16-19, 20- Sh T*. **the riggin o the nicht** the middle of the night *la19- NE*. [RIG[1.1], with -*ing* suffix]

riggin² /ˈrɪgɪn/ *n* a tall ungainly person; originally a woman *la19- Sh*. [unknown]

riggyng *see* RIGGIN[1]

right *see* RICHT[1.1], RICHT[1.2], RICHT[1.3], RICHT[1.4]

righteous *see* RICHTEOUS

riglen, rickling, †**wregling** /ˈrɪglən, ˈrɪklɪŋ,/ *n* **1** the smallest animal in a litter *la19- T EC SW*. **2** an undersized or weak animal or person *18-19, 20- EC SW*. [perhaps diminutive form of RIG³]

riglin *see* RIG[1.1]

rigmarie /ˈrɪgməˌri/ *n* **1** something of little or no value *la17-19*. **2** a frivolous gathering, a frolic *19-*. [the name attributed to low-value coins of Queen Mary's reign, supposedly bearing the inscription *Reg[ina] Maria*; but no known coin fits the description]

rigour, †**regour** /ˈrɪgər/ *n* **1** harshness, severity (of weather) *15-*. **2** excessive strictness, harshness (of those in authority) *15-*. **3** strict accuracy; legalistic exactitude *la15*. †**the rigour of law** the strict interpretation of the terms of the law applied without mitigation *la15-17*. [ME *rigour*, Lat *rigor*]

rigwiddie[1.1], *T* **rigbuddy,** *H&I EC* **rigbody,** †**rigwoodie** /ˈrɪgˌwɪdi/; *T* rɪgˈbʌdi; *H&I EC* rɪgˈbɒdi/ *n* a band passing over the back of a carthorse and supporting the cart-shafts *16-*. [RIG[1.1] + WIDDIE]

rigwiddie[1.2], †**rigwoodie** /ˈrɪgˌwɪdi/ *adj* **1** *of a person* stubborn, obstinate; perverse *19-*. **2** *of an old woman or witch* wizened, gnarled, tough and rugged-looking, misshapen; ill-favoured *la17-19*. [see the noun]

rik *see* RICH[1.2], RICK[1.1], RICK[1.2]

rike *see* REAK[1.1], REAK[1.2]

rile *see* RAIVEL[1.2]

rill /rɪl/ *v* to chatter, babble, prattle *20- Ork*. [unknown; compare Norw *røla*]

rilling *see* RULLION

rim¹ /rɪm/ *n* **1** a circular edge *16-*. **2** the driving wheel of a spinning-wheel *19, 20- Sh*. **3** a circle or ring of light, a halo *la19- Sh*. **rim fu** full to the brim *20- Sh NE*. **rimmer** a hoop or band of metal or wood used to protect the runner-stone of a mill or to shape a cheese *18-*. **rimmin** brimming over, overflowing *20- Sh NE*. **rimwale** a board round the gunwale of a boat *20- Sh EC*. [OE *rima* a border, a rim, ON *rim* a rail]

rim² /rɪm/ *n* a rocky ridge or reef, a strip of rocky ground *la18- Ork*. [ON *rimi* a strip of land]

†**rim³,** †**ryme** *n* **1** a membrane, skin *e16*. **2** the peritoneum *la16-e19*. **rimcrackin** a large meal *20- Ork*. **rimfu** = *rimcrackin 20- SW Uls*. **rimrax, rimraxin** = *rimcrackin 20- NE*. **rim-side** the flesh-side of a skin *la15-17*. [OE *reōma*]

rimburst /ˈrɪmbʌrst/ *n* a rupture, a hernia *la16-19, 20- Ork N T*. **rimbursin,** †**rumbursin** = RIMBURST *15-19, 20- Bor*. **rimburstinnes, rimburstenness** = RIMBURST *la16-17*. [RIM³ + BIRST[1.2]]

rimcrackin *see* RIM³

rime, †**ryme** /rʌɪm/ *n* **1** hoar-frost *16-*. **2** a frosty haze or mist *16-19, 20- Sh Ork T*. **rimie** frosty *20-*. [OE *hrīm*]

rime *see* RHYME[1.1], RHYME[1.2]

rimfu *see* RIM³

rimle /ˈrɪməl/ *v mining* to probe or stir *la19, 20- EC*. [perhaps frequentative form of Eng *ream* to widen a hole, excavate]

rimpin /ˈrɪmpən/ *n* a miserable or annoying person or animal, *eg* a mean old woman *19- SW Bor*. [unknown]

rimple /ˈrɪmpəl/ *n* a wrinkle; a ripple *19, 20- Ork T*. [ME *rimpil*]

rim-ram /ˈrɪm ram/ *adj* confused, higgledy-piggledy, disordered *19, 20- NE*. [onomatopoeic]

rimrax, rimraxin, rimside *see* RIM³

rin[1.1], **run** /rɪn, rʌn/ *n* **1** an unbroken period of time *la18-*. **2** a journey; a trip taken for pleasure *la18-*. **3** a sequence of similar events or states *la18-*. **4** a flow of water *19-*. **5** a restricted and safe place for animals to move or exercise in *20-*. **6** *in golf* a stroke in which the ball is made to run along the ground *20-*. **7** the course of a river or stream, frequently with the lands bordering it, a river valley *la18-19, 20- NE Bor*. **8** a strong current or tide; the heavy surge of rollers *19, 20- Sh*. **9** a fast-flowing stretch of river *20- N*. **10** the overflow of a body of water, a stream, a rivulet, a water channel *la16-19*. **11** the action of or a spell of running *la17*. **rundie** a little or short run *20- Sh*. **hae the run o** to be allowed access to all parts of (something) without restriction *la19-*. **run o the rig** the direction or angle at which a field has been ploughed *20- T H&I C Bor*. [see the verb]

rin[1.2], **run,** †**ryn** /rɪn, rʌn/ *v pt* **ran** †**rane,** †**ryne,** †**run,** *ptp* **run** †**runnyn 1** to move on foot at a faster pace than walking; to go about unrestrainedly, rush about; *of animals* to be at liberty; to go quickly, hasten; to pass rapidly into a different situation, *eg* rin intae debt *la14-*. **2** to go, make a journey on foot; to follow a route or cover distance by running *la14-*. **3** *of water, fluids* to flow; *of a solid body, vehicle, mechanical device, ship* to move or function swiftly, smoothly, easily; *of rumour, noise* to spread quickly *la14-*. **4** to run away, take flight *15-*. **5** to continue; to remain in operation; to prevail, have effect *15-*. **6** to go quickly or frequently *la15-*. **7** to cause (horses, dogs) to run, gallop, race, take exercise *16-*. **8** *in bowls* to drive away (another bowl or the jack) with a strong shot *18-*. **9** *baking* to put (a batch of loaves) in the oven for baking *20-*. **10** to hold (the hands) under running water, swill, rinse *20-*. **11** to be covered with water, mud, be awash; to leak, stop being watertight *19- Sh N T*. **12** *of milk* to coagulate, curdle *19, 20- Sh Ork*. **13** *of a dog* to move sheep at a brisk pace, range out in herding sheep *20- SW Bor*. **14** *of a wall* to collapse *20- Sh*. **15** to draw (liquor); to distil (whisky) *18-19*. **16** to ride swiftly on horseback, especially in jousting, compete *15-16*. **17** to cause to flow, serve, sell (wine) *16-17*. **18** melt or smelt (metal) *17*. **19** *of money* to have currency *la14-15*. **rinner, runner,** †**rinnar 1** a messenger, courier *la15-*. **2** someone who runs; a competitor in a footrace *la16-*. **3** a thin cut of meat from the forepart of the flank *18-*. **4** a narrow strip of carpet *19-*. **5** a small water-channel, a ditch, runnel, a small stream *la16-19, 20- Ork EC SW*. **6** the upper millstone of a mill *la16-e17*. **7** a tapster *e17*. **rundale,** *Sh Ork* **rendal** a landholding system similar to RUNRIG[1.1] but involving larger portions of (mainly OUTFIELD[1.1]) land *15-*. †**run deil** an out-and-out rogue *la18-19*. †**run-joist** a beam running along the side of a roof across the rafters to support the thatch, a purlin *la18-e19*. **run-knot** a slip-knot which has been pulled tight *la19- Sh NE C SW*. **run lime** mortar poured liquid into the crevices of stonework *19- NE*. †**run-line** the singing of a psalm by a congregation in two or more continuous lines, instead of the earlier practice of one line at a time after the precentor had read or intoned it *19*. †**rin-met** = *rinning met* (RINNING[1.2]) *la16-17*. †**rin-roof, renrouf 1** the roof over the main part of a building *16-e19*. **2** a projecting roof or canopy; a lean-to; a dormer roof *16-17*. **run soil** alluvial soil *la18, 20- Ork*. †**runtree** a continuous horizontal beam or bar, mainly one which holds vertical posts firm, *eg* in a fence, byre *la18-e19*. †**run-wall** a light partition wall from one side of a house to the other *la18-e19*. **rin-water** a natural flow of water, especially one which will drive a millwheel without a dam *20- NE*. **rinaboot 1** roving *la19-*. **2** a vagabond, rover; a restless person, a gadabout *19-*. †**be run** expired, come to an end *la14-17*. **rin ahin 1** to run close behind or at the heels of *la19-*. **2** to be in arrears, fall into debt *la19, 20- NE C*. **rin-a-mile** games a variation on hide-and-seek *20- NE WC*. **run (somebody) a message** to run an errand for someone *la20-*. **rin awa wi the harras** to talk in a dogmatic, assertive or exaggerated way *la17-, 20- T EC*. **rin the cutter** to evade the revenue cutter when smuggling; *humorous* to bring home liquor unobserved *la19-*. **rin doon wi 1** to pour milk down the throat of an animal being hand-reared *20- Sh*. **2** to pour medicine down an animal's throat *20- Ork*. †**run a heat** = *run wi the heat la18-19*. **rin in by** to pay a short call on (a person) *la19-*. **rin in the nicht** to spend the night courting *20- Ork*. **rin in to** = *rin in by*. **rin neep dreels** to hoe between rows of turnips with a horse-hoe *20- NE EC*. **rin neeps** = *rin neep dreels*. **rin oot, run oot 1** *of a vessel* to leak *18-*. **2** to fill (a receptacle by pouring from another *la19- Sh*. **3** *in kelp-burning* to draw off the ash *20- Ork*. †**rin a spere** to use, make a thrust with a spear *la15-16*. **rin stockings** to strengthen stocking heels by darning them with a running stitch *19- NE C SW Bor*. **rinthereoot** a vagrant, a wandering person *e19, la19- NE T*. **rin the hills** to roam about in a wild, unrestrained way, rush about *19- NE T*. **rin the rigs** to run riot, have a wild time, have fun *la18-*. †**run the rig on** to hoax, trick *la18-19*; compare *play a rig on* (PLAY). †**rin at the ring** = *ride at the ring* (RIDE[1.2]) *la16*. **rin up, run up** to fill (a receptacle) with liquid *la19- Sh*. **rin upon, run upon 1** to drip (liquid) on *20- Sh*. **2** to depend on *16-17*. **run wi the heat, run o the heat** *of cattle* to run about in hot weather when tormented by flies *20- N NE SW*. **rin wud** to behave wildly and recklessly; to run out of control; to go mad; to become wild or savage *15-*. [OE *rinnan*, ON *renna*]

rin *see* RUIND

rinagate, renegade, †**rinigat,** †**renegate,** †**rannegald** /ˈrɪnəgɛt, ˈrɛnəged/ *n* **1** a scoundrel, a rascal *la16-*. **2** a deserter; an apostate; a turncoat *la15-*. **3** a vagabond, a wanderer *17*. [MFr *renegat*, Lat *renegātus*]

rinche *see* REENGE[2.2]

rind[1], *N* **reen,** †**rynd** /raɪnd/; *N* rin/ *n* **1** the whole bark or the inner bark of a tree; the hard outer integument, shell or peel of a plant, insect, fruit *16-*. **2** a strip or slat of wood, a thin piece cut off the edge of a board, a piece of beading *18- Sh Ork N NE T EC SW*. **3** the edge (of a strip of cultivated land or a peat-bank) *18-19, 20- NE*. **4** skin *e16*. [OE *rind*]

rind[2.1] /raɪnd/ *n* melted fat or tallow *la18- H&I WC*. [see the verb]

rind[2.2], †**rynd,** †**rand** /raɪnd/ *v* to melt down, render (fat, tallow), clarify (butter) *16-*. **rander** clarified fat, dripping *la19, 20- Ork T*. **rinder** a person employed to render tallow *la16-e19*. [MFr *rendre*]

rind[3] /raɪnd/ *n* hoar-frost *e16, 19- EC SW Bor*. [probably altered form of RIME]

†**rind[4]** *n* the iron fitting supporting the upper millstone of a mill *la15-17*; compare *millrind* (MILL[1.1]). [MDu *rijn*, MLG *rín*]

rine *see* REIN[1.1], REIN[1.2]

ring[1.1], *NE* **raing,** †**ryng,** †**reing** /rɪŋ; *NE* ren/ *n* **1** a small circlet of usually (precious) metal mainly for wearing on the finger *la14-*. **2** a group of people formed into a circle for a game or dance *la15-*. **3** *marbles* a circle on the ground used as a target; the game itself *19-*. **4** a circular ditch and rampart of a prehistoric hill-fort, especially of the early Iron Age *la18-e19*. **5** a traditional dance of circular formation *16-e19*. **6** the meal which falls into the space between a millstone and its casing, regarded as the miller's perquisite *15-e19*. **ringie** *marbles* a circle on the ground used as a target; the game itself *la19-*. †**ring bear** the meal which falls into the space between a millstone and its casing, regarded as the miller's perquisite *la15-e19*. **ring cutter** *curling* an instrument for marking the circles round the tees *la18-*. †**ring-dans** a traditional dance of circular formation *e16*. †**ring-eyed** wall-eyed *la17*; compare RINGLE EE. **ring fowlie** the reed-bunting *19, 20- NE*. †**ring gang** *agriculture* the topmost circle of sheaves in the vertical wall of a stack, made to project as eaves *la18-19*. **ringnet 1** a herring net suspended between two boats which gradually sail closer to one another with a circular sweep until the net closes and traps the fish *la19-*. **2** a type of salmon-net *16-e17*. **ringnetter** a boat used in ringnet fishing *20-*. **ringnetting** fishing with a ringnet *20-*. †**ring sang** a song sung by the dancers of a traditional dance of circular formation *e16*. **the ring 1** *marbles* a circle on the ground used as a target; the game itself *19-*. **2** a circlet of metal suspended from a post which each of a number of riders attempts to carry off on the point of a lance *la16-19, 20- historical*. [OE *hring*]

ring[1.2] /rɪŋ/ *v* **1** to supply with a ring or rings *16-*. **2** to put a metal tyre round the rim of a wheel *la19- Ork NE T SW*. **3** to put a ring in the nose of a pig *la15-17*. **ringer** *in curling* a stone which lies within the ring surrounding the tee *19-*. **ringit,** †**rynggyt 1** *of the eye* having a white circle round the iris; walleyed *19, 20- Sh T SW*. **2** *of animals* having white hair round the eye *20- Sh*. **3** *of a piece of common land* enclosed, fenced *17-e19*. **ringing bed** a base of stone or a metal plate on which a red-hot metal rim is placed on a wheel and shrunk to fit it *20- N NE T EC*. **ring the mill** to provide the first grain for a mill to grind after the millstones have been picked; keep someone going *19-*. [see the noun]

ring[2.1] /rɪŋ/ *n* **1** the ringing of a bell *la16-*. **2** the striking of a clock *la19-*. **3** a resounding blow, especially on the ear or head *la19-*. [see the verb]

ring[2.2], †**tryng** /rɪŋ/ *v pt* **rang** †**rong,** *ptp* **rung** †**trong 1** *of a bell or other metallic object* to give out a clear, resonant sound when struck; to cause a bell to give out such a sound *la14-*. **2** *of a place* to re-echo, resound with a sound or sounds; *of a sound* to resonate *16-*. **3** *of ice or frosty ground* to make a ringing sound under impact or friction *19-*. **4** to give a resounding blow to (especially the ear, the head) *20-*. **5** to announce by ringing a bell; to proclaim, make known *15-16*. **ringer** a resounding blow, especially on the ear or head *20-*. **ringin frost** a hard, prolonged frost *19-*. **ring in 1** *of church bells* to increase in tempo before stopping or reducing to a single bell as a sign that a service is about to begin *19, 20- NE T EC*. **2** to give way, abandon an effort or struggle; to be near the end of one's powers of endurance; to be at death's door *19, 20- NE T EC*. [OE *hringan*]

ring[3.1], reign, †**tryng,** †**tregne** /rɪŋ, ren/ *n* **1** the period of a sovereign's rule *15-*. **2** regal power, rule; dominion, sway *la15-*. **3** a kingdom, realm; the kingdom of heaven *la15-17*. [ME *regne*]

ring[3.2], reign, †**tryng,** †**tregne,** †**treng** /rɪŋ, ren/ *v pt* **reigned** †**trang,** †**trong,** †**tringit,** *ptp* **rung** †**trungyn 1** to rule as a monarch; to predominate or prevail *la14-*. **2** *of a person* to enjoy eternal life (in heaven) *la15-*. **3** to continue, endure; to exist *la15-*. **4** to rant, storm, behave in a domineering way *19*. **ringin 1** domineering *19-*. **2** out-and-out, downright *19- N NE C*. **3** forcefully, with ease *la19- NE*. [ME *regnen*, Lat *regnāre*]

ringald *see* RANGLE

ringalodie /ˌrɪŋəˈlodi/ *n fisherman's taboo* a cooking pot with a hooped handle *la19- Sh*. [unknown]

ringe *see* REENGE¹,², REENGE²,¹, REENGE²,²

ringit *see* RING³,²

ringl'd, rennglit /ˈrɪŋəld, ˈrɛŋlɪt/ *adj of clothes* having horizontal stripes *la19- Sh NE EC*. [RINGLE² + -IT²]

ringle¹ /ˈrɪŋəl/ *n* a ringing, jingling sound *20-*. [RING²,¹, with frequentative *-le* suffix]

†**ringle²** *n* a circular stripe *19*. [RING¹,¹, with diminutive *-le* suffix]

ringle ee /rɪŋəl ˈi/ *n* **1** a walleye *18-*. **2** a circle of white hair around the eye of an animal *20- Sh*. **ringle eed, ringle eyed,** †**ringill eit** *of an animal* having an eye surrounded by white hair *la16-*; compare *ringit* 2 (RING¹,²). [RINGLE² + EE¹]

ringlie /ˈrɪŋli/ *adj of clothes* striped *Sh Ork*. [RINGLE² + -IE²]

rinigat *see* RINAGATE

rink¹,¹, †**renk,** †**rynk** /rɪŋk/ *n* **1** *in games* the marked-out area of play *la18-*. **2** *in games* the team forming a side in a game *la18-*. **3** *in games* a game; one of a series of games constituting a match *19-*. **4** a stretch of ice, a smooth surface for skating *la19-*. **5** a ranging up and down, a restless, especially noisy, prowling or hunting *la19- NE*. **6** a rattling noise *la19- NE*. **7** a battleground; an open space in a battle; a piece of ground marked out for a joust; an arena *15-19*. **8** the course or route of a person or thing; a journey *la15-e17*. **9** a straight line; a line of demarcation or division, especially the boundary between Scotland and England *la18-19*. **10** the course marked out for a race or contest *16-e17*. **11** a row of fighting men *e15*. **renkie** *in various games* the marked-out area of play *20- Sh*. **rinker** a round woollen cap of the type worn by curlers *20- Sh NE T C*. **rink game** *curling* a game played by a team of four players *20-*. [MFr *renk* a space for jousting]

rink¹,², †**renk** /rɪŋk/ *v* **1** to range or prowl about restlessly and noisily *18- NE T*. **2** to search thoroughly, rummage (in) *la19- NE*. **3** to climb, clamber *la19- NE*. [see the noun]

†**rink²**, **renk** *n* a (fighting) man, a warrior *la15-e16*. [OE *rinc*]

rinkle, †**rankle** /ˈrɪŋkəl/ *v* to make a tinkling, jingling or rattling sound *20- Sh*. [Norw *ringla, rangla*]

rinkum /ˈrɪŋkʌm/ *n* a blow, a thump *20- NE*. [RING²,¹]

†**rin mairt, rynmart** *n* an ox or cow handed over as payment in kind of rent due to a feudal superior *la15-16*. [MART²; first element unknown]

rinnal, runnel, †**rinel** /ˈrɪnəl, ˈrʌnəl/ *n* a small watercourse or stream *la15-*. [ME *rinel*]

rinning¹,¹, **rinnin, running,** †**rynnyng** /ˈrɪnɪŋ, ˈrɪnɪn, ˈrʌnɪŋ/ *n* **1** the action or fact of running (a course); running as a sport or exercise *15-*. **2** the act of riding as a participant in various sports *la16-*. **3** *pl* the main points of a story, sermon, the outline, gist *la19- NE*. **4** a raid or foray *la14-17*. **5** horse racing *16*. **6** the action of melting down (wax, metal) *16-17*. **7** the action of drawing (wine, beer) for retail sale *la16-e17*. †**rinning hound** a hunting dog *16-e17*. **running stock farming** a system of stock-management whereby all stock is sold at regular intervals, and breeding stock is bought in when required *la18- WC SW*. †**rinning of the spear** jousting with spears *e16*; compare *speir rinning* (SPEAR). [verbal noun from RIN¹,²]

rinning¹,², **rinnin, running,** †**rinnand** /ˈrɪnɪŋ, ˈrɪnɪn, ˈrʌnɪŋ/ *adj* **1** *of water* flowing *15-*. **2** that which moves swiftly, smoothly or easily *16-*. **3** *of a person* moving swiftly, carrying out their duties on foot *la16-*. **4** *of grain* measured by *rinand met la16-e17*. **5** *of Parliament* current, liable to be summoned to meet during the period for which currency was given *16-17*. †**rinand met, rynnand met** a standard measuring vessel for dry goods *16-e17*. [participial adj from RIN¹,²]

Rinnis *see* RHINNS

rinrig *see* RUNRIG¹,¹, RUNRIG¹,²

†**Rins, Rens, Ranish** *adj of wine* Rhenish *la15-17*. [named after the River Rhine]

rinse *see* REENGE²,¹, REENGE²,²

rint /rɪnt/ *n* a rag *20- Sh*. **rintie-pells** tatters *20- Sh*. [Norw *rind* a stripe in cloth]

riot¹,¹, †**ryot** /ˈraeət/ *n* **1** a violent disturbance of the peace by a crowd of people *la14-*. **2** revelry, debauchery; extravagance *la15-*. **3** unlawful bodily harm or violence to another person, assault and battery *17-18*. [ME *riot*]

riot¹,², †**ryot** /ˈraeət/ *v* **1** to engage in violent disturbance or assault *19-*. **2** to ravage, harry (a country) *la14-e15*. **rioting 1** violent disorder *la19-*. **2** revelry *la16-e17*. [AN, OFr *rioter* to argue or dispute]

riot *see* ROYET¹,²

riotous, †**ryatous,** †**ryotus** /ˈraeətəs/ *adj* **1** uncontrolled, immoderate, extravagant; licentious; wanton; lecherous *16-*. **2** stubborn, obstinate *15-16*. [ME *riotous*]

rip¹,¹, †**ripe** /rɪp/ *n* **1** a tear, rent *20-*. **2** the act of sawing wood along the grain *20-*. **3** a slit cut in the ear of a sheep as an identifying mark *18- Ork*. **4** speed *la19- Sh*. [see the verb]

rip¹,², *NE* **raip** /rɪp; *NE* rep/ *v* **1** to cut, tear (up) *17-*. **2** to undo knitting *la19-*. **3** to strip off turf before digging *la18- Sh SW*. **4** to move with speed and vigour, rush *20- Sh*. **ripper** a method of fishing; a heavy metal bar fitted with hooks and attached to a fishing-line *20- Sh Ork N NE T EC*. [unknown; compare MDu *rippen*, MLG *reppen*]

rip² /rɪp/ *n* **1** a wisp of hay or handful of stalks of unthreshed grain *17-*. **2** an amount of hay or grain used to feed animals *la18-19, 20- Uls*. **3** a single stalk of unthreshed grain *la19- Sh Ork N*. **4** *law* a sample of a crop carried to the market cross as a symbol of the right to point it, and as a sample of its quality *la17-18*. [perhaps altered form of REAP]

rip³ /rɪp/ *n* a round wicker (or straw) basket used for carrying fish, eggs or fishing-lines *la16- NE T EC*. **rippie** a kind of circular net used in crab-fishing or salmon-poaching; a tadpole net *la19- NE*. [ON *hrip*]

rip *see* RIPE¹,²

ripe¹,¹ /rʌɪp/ *n* a poke to clear an obstruction *la19-*. [see the verb]

ripe¹,², **rype,** †**rip** /rʌɪp/ *v* **1** to search thoroughly, rummage; to examine (for stolen property or evidence) *15-*. **2** to pick (a pocket), plunder *17-*. **3** to clean (ash) out of a pipe *la19-*. **4** to clear the bars of a fireplace of ash *20-*. **5** to dig or plough up ground *la14-e16, la19- SW Bor*. **6** to dig up potatoes *la19- Sh*. **7** to strip berries from a bush *20- Sh NE*. †**rype furth** to bring to light; to reveal *16-e17*. †**rype out** = *rype furth*. **ripe the ribs** to clear (the bars of a fireplace) of ash *19-*. [OE *rīpan* plunder]

ripe *see* RIP¹,¹

riples *see* RIPPLES

rippek *see* RITTOCK

rippet, †**repet,** †**tryppet** /ˈrɪpət/ *n* **1** a noisy disturbance; the sound of boisterous merrymaking *16-*. **2** a row, a quarrel *19, 20- NE C*. †**trippetting** a noisy disturbance *19*. [perhaps onomatopoeic or altered form of REPEAT]

rippill *see* RIPPLE

rippillis *see* RIPPLES

ripple, **rippill** /'rɪpəl/ *v* to remove the seeds from flax *la15-*. †**rippling comb**, **rypling came** a comb for removing the seeds of flax from the stem *la16-19*. [compare MDu, MLG *repelen*]

ripple-grass, †**ripplegirse** /'rɪpəl gras/ *n* the ribwort plantain; the greater plantain *19-*. [Eng *ripple* a cut, scratch (for which the leaves were used) + GIRSE[1.1]; compare Norw *ripla* to scratch]

ripples, †**trippillis**, †**riples** /'rɪpəlz/ *npl* **1** a disease affecting the back and loins, a venereal disease *16-*. **2** a dance or dancing step performed originally to the song in the *Merry Muses* beginning 'I rede you beware o' the ripples' *la17-*. [unknown]

ris *see* RASH[1], RISE[1.2]

rise[1.1], †**trys** /raez/ *n* **1** an increase *la17-*. **2** a piece of fun at someone's expense, a joke, hoax *18-*. **3** the act of getting out of bed in the morning *20-*. **4** the layer of new wool next to the skin of a sheep at shearing time which represents the growth of the new coat *19- C Bor*. [see the verb]

rise[1.2], †**trys**, †**tris**, †**tryis** /raez/ *v pt also* **raise**, *WC SW* **ris**, †**trays**, *ptp* **risen** †**trissin** **1** to stand up, become upright; to recover, flourish, grow *la14-*. **2** to get out of bed in the morning *la14-*. **3** to ascend, move upwards, take flight; to mount, climb up *la14-*. **4** to advance in power; to attain rank or wealth *15-*. **5** *of the sun or other heavenly body* to appear above the horizon *15-*. **6** to cause to rise up; to lift up, raise *la15-*. **7** to increase *la15-*. **8** *of a court or assembly* to adjourn *16-*. **9** *of a body part* to swell; *of the penis* to become erect *la15-17*. **riser 1** a person who gets out of bed *la19-*. **2** the vertical part of a step *la19-*. **3** a stone which reaches to the full height of the rubble wall *20-*. **rising**, †**trysing 1** resurrection *la14-*. **2** the action of getting up, getting out of bed; advancement *15-*. **3** beginning, growth *la15-*. **4** rebellion *16-*. **5** *of a period of time* approaching: ◊*it's rising fower o'clock la19-*. **rise band** *masonry* a vertical joint rising through several courses without bonding *la18- C*. [OE *risan*]

risk[1] /rɪsk/ *v* to make a ripping, tearing sound *la16-19, 20- SW*. [imitative or perhaps altered form of RISP[1.2]]

risk[2.1] /rɪsk/ *n* a tug, pull (on coarse grass) *la19- Sh*. [see the verb]

risk[2.2] /rɪsk/ *v* **1** to cut with a sickle or tear up (coarse grass) *la19- Sh*. **2** to stab or rip, especially with a hooked implement *20- Sh*. [Norw dial *ryskja*]

risk *see* REESK

risp[1.1] /rɪsp/ *n* **1** a coarse file or rasp *16-*. **2** a door-knocker, a vertical serrated metal rod fixed to the door and a ring which was drawn up and down it to produce a rattling noise *19-*. **3** a harsh grating sound *la19, 20- Sh NE T*. **4** a scrape, a filing or sharpening *20- Sh*. [see the verb]

risp[1.2] /rɪsp/ *v* **1** to file, smooth off with a file; cut or saw roughly *la16-*. **2** to make a harsh, grating sound *la17-*. **3** to make a grating noise with a file *19-*. **4** to grind (two surfaces) together; grind (the teeth) *la17-19, 20- NE*. [ON *rispa* scratch, score]

risp[2], †**trysp** /rɪsp/ *n* a species of sedge or reed *16-*. **rispgrass** = RISP[2]. [unknown]

rissert *see* RIZZAR

rissin *see* RISE[1.2]

rissle *see* REESLE[1.2]

rissom /'rɪzəm/ *n* a particle, a small particle *19-*. [ME *rison*; compare Swed *ressma* an ear of grain, especially oats]

rist *see* REEST[2.2], REST[1.1], REST[1.2], REST[2.1], REST[2.2]

ristle /'rɪsəl/ *n* a small plough with a sickle-shaped coulter for cutting a narrow deep rut through roots *18-e19, la19- historical*. [Gael *risteal*, ON *ristill* a ploughshare; compare REEST[3.1]]

rit[1.1] /rɪt/ *n* **1** a scratch, a score, a groove *18-*. **2** a sheepmark in the form of a slit in the ear (or nostril) *19- Sh Ork SW*. **3** the shallow preliminary cut or furrow made in ploughing or draining *19, 20- N*. [see the verb]

rit[1.2], **rut**, †**tritt** /rɪt, rʌt/ *v* **1** to scratch, score, groove *19-*. **2** to mark with a shallow trench or furrow as a guide (in ploughing or draining) *la14-19, 20- Sh Ork N SW Bor Uls*. **3** to slit (a sheep) in the ear for identification *19- Sh Ork SW Bor*. **4** to thrust (a sword) through, stab; *of cattle* to gore *e18, 20- Sh N*. **rutter** a marker on a drill plough, which cuts the line of the next drill *20-*. **ritting spade** a double-handled spade for making the first cuts in draining *19, 20- N WC SW Bor*. †**tritting irne** a turf-cutter *la17*. †**trytt irne** = *ritting irne la16*. [probably from an unattested OE verb; compare Ger *ritzen*]

rit *see* RUIT[1.1]

ritches *see* RICHES

rither *see* RUDDER

ritt *see* RIT[1.2]

rittle *see* RIDDLE[3]

rittock, *Sh* **rippek** /'rɪtək; *Sh* 'rɪpək/ *n* **1** a gull; the tern, kittiwake or black-headed gull *la18- Sh Ork N*. **2** a spiteful, waspish woman *20- Sh*. [ON *rytr* a kind of gull]

rittocks /'rɪtəks/ *npl* the refuse of melted lard or tallow *19- SW Bor*. [unknown]

riv /rɪv/ *v* to sew, knit, tie loosely or coarsely; to make or mend roughly *19- Sh*. **rivva kishie** a woven basket *la19- Sh*. [ON *rifa* to sew]

riv *see* RIVE[1.1], RIVE[1.2]

riva /'rɪvə/ *n* a cleft, fissure; slit *19- Sh*. **rivvik** = RIVA *la19- Sh*. [ON *rifa* a cleft]

rivatwari, †**trevatwirie** /'rɪvətwari/ *n* an auger; a large nail *la19- Sh*. [Norn *rivatwari*]

rive[1.1], *Sh* **riv**, †**tryw** /rʌɪv; *Sh* rɪv/ *n* **1** a tear, rip, scratch (in cloth or the skin) *la17-*. **2** a bite, a large mouthful; a good feed *la18-*. **3** an uprooting, severance, a break *19-*. **4** a pull, a jerk, a wrench, a grab; a hug *19-*. **5** energy in working, vigorous activity *la19, 20- Sh*. **6** a split, crack, fissure *19, 20- Sh*. **7** a large quantity or company *19, 20- NE*. **8** a tearing hurry *20- Sh*. [see the verb]

rive[1.2], *Sh* **riv**, *Ork NE* **reeve**, †**tryve**, †**trif**, †**tryfe** /rʌɪv; *Sh Ork NE* rɪv/ *v pt* **rave**, **rived**, †**traif**, *ptp* **riven**, **rivend**, †**trevin 1** to tear, rip, lacerate *la14-*. **2** to tear the hair in grief or anguish *la14-*. **3** to tear at, maul; to wrench, pull apart, break up (into pieces) *la14-*. **4** *of a thing* to burst, crack, split *la14-*. **5** *of the stomach* to fill to bursting from eating and drinking *la14-*. **6** to pull or tug roughly or vigorously *la15-*. **7** *of the head or heart* to burst with pain or anguish *la15-*. **8** to burst with laughing *18-*. **9** to work hard or laboriously; toil *19-*. **10** to eat voraciously, tear into food *19-*. **11** *of cloud* to break up, disperse *la19- Sh NE EC SW*. **12** to break up (untilled ground) with the plough; to cultivate (common land or moorland) *16-19, 20- N NE T*. **13** *of wind* to blow violently so as to do damage *16-19, 20- Sh N NE*. **14** to work with a tugging or tearing motion *la18-19, 20- Sh NE*. **15** to whet, sharpen *la19- Sh*. **16** to tear up a document in order to destroy or cancel it *la15-e18*. **17** to pierce with a pointed weapon *16*. **reevin** *of a fire* blazing, burning ferociously *20- NE*; compare ROVIN. **rivin storm** weather capable of doing damage to buildings, ferocious wind or storm; a high gusty wind *la19- Sh Ork N*. **rivin win** = *rivin storm 20- NE*. **rive at** to eat voraciously *19-*. *da rivin o da dim* dawn *la19- Sh*. **rive something fra out of** to tear (a thing) off, from its place *la14-*. **rive oot 1** to tear, wrench or pluck from a location, remove by force *16-*. **2** to break up untilled ground *16*. **rive through** to force a way forward *19, 20- EC*. **rive up** to pull up (by the roots);

to remove by force, tear off, wrench up; to dig up *16-*. **rive someone's bonnet** to excel or go one better than someone, especially said of children excelling their parents *19-*. **riv wi da lasses** to romp, play boisterous courting games *la19- Sh.* [ON *rífa*]

rived *see* RIVE[1,2]
riveling *see* RULLION
riven, rivend *see* RIVE[1,2]
rivlin *see* RULLION
rivvle /'rɪvəl/ *n* a mess, a state of confusion or dishevelment *20- Ork.* **rivly** *of clothes* shabby, worn out *20- Ork.* [probably altered form of RAIVEL[1,1]]
riwell *see* ROWEL
rizzar, russle, †**rizer,** †**raser,** †**rissert** /'rɪzər, 'rʌsəl/ *n* the redcurrant *Ribes rubrum 17-19, 20- NE T C SW Bor.* †**rizer berries** redcurrants *la16-e18.* †**black rizzar** *see* BLACK[1,2]. [perhaps altered from MFr *roussel* reddish or OFr *rousor* reddish colour]
rizzered /'rɪzərd/ *adj* **1** dried, parched; *of haddock* sun-dried *18-19, 20- NE T EC Bor Uls.* **2** *of clothes* dried out of doors, thoroughly aired *19- EC Bor.* [perhaps Fr *ressoré* dried up, shrivelled]
rizzon *see* REASON[1,1], REASON[1,2]
ro[1] /ro/ *n* a poor, feeble or emaciated animal; a carcass of a diseased animal *la19- Sh.* [ON *hrae* a carcass]
†**ro**[2,1], **ruve, rufe** *n* rest, peace *la14-16.* [OE *rōw*]
ro[2,2], †**ruve,** †**rufe** /ro/ *v* to take a rest, rest (in one place) *la16, 20- Sh.* [see the noun]
ro *see* RAE[1]
road[1,1], *Sh* **rod,** †**rode** /rod; *Sh* rɔd/ *n* **1** a (wide) route between places; a track; a path *13-*. **2** a way, direction, course, route: ◊*what road are you going? la14-*. **3** *mining* an excavated passageway *la17-*. **4** a way, method, manner: ◊*that's nae the road to dae it la17-*. **5** a hand-cut path round a grain field to clear the way for a reaping machine *la19-20, 21- historical.* **6** a condition, state *20- NE H&I.* **roadie** a path *la18- N NE.* **road board** a local government committee which supervised the making and repair of roads in a county *la19-*. **road coal** coal cut from the face at road level *19- EC.* **road-end, roaden** the junction where a side road meets a main road; frequently in place-names *la19-*. **road harl** a scraper for removing mud from a road *20- EC.* **roadhead** *mining* the end of an underground passage at the working face *la19, 20- C.* **roadman** a mine official responsible for the making and maintenance of haulage roads *la19, 20- C.* †**road money** a tax levied on the inhabitants of a district for the upkeep of roads *la18-19.* **a roads** everywhere *la19-*. **a the road** all the way, during the whole extent of a journey *la19-*. **get the road** to be dismissed from a job *20- T WC SW.* **hae yer ain road** to follow one's own inclination, go your own way *20-*. **in the road** in the way, causing inconvenience *19-*. **on the road** *of a woman* pregnant *20-*. **oot o the road** out of the or one's way *la17-*. **oot o the road o** unaccustomed to, out of the way of *18-*. **tae the road** recovered after an illness, able to be about again *la19- NE T.* **tak in the road** to travel along the road, cover the distance, especially at speed *20 NE T.* **tak the road** to set off (on a journey) *la18-*. [Early forms in *o* imply an origin distinct from OE *rād*, the source of Eng *road* and Sc RADE; later forms may be influenced by or correspond to Eng *road*]
road[1,2], †**rodd** /rod/ *v* **1** to travel on a road, set out on a journey *la19- NE T.* **2** to send a person off (on an errand or in a particular direction) *20- NE T.* **3** to make a pathway by constant passage *la17-19.* **4** to dismiss (an employee) *la17.* **roadit** on the road, off on a journey; *of a child* able to walk *la19- NE T.* [see the noun]
road *see* RAID
roan[1], **ron** /ron/ *v* to rob (birds' or bees' nests) *la19- Sh.* [ON *rán*]
roan[2], †**roweing,** †**ruan** /ron/ *adj of an animal's coat* having a predominant colour intermingled with white *17-*. **roant, roaned** of a roan or variegated colour *20- NE SW.* **ronemoose** the shrew *Sorex araneus la19- Ork.* [MFr *roan*]
roan *see* RAWN, RONE[1]
roar *see* RAIR[1,1], RAIR[1,2]
roarin fu /rorɪn 'fu/ *adj* very drunk *la18-.* [*roaring* (RAIR[1,2]) + FOU]
roast[1,1], †**rost,** †**roist** /rost/ *n* a piece of meat that has been roasted or is intended for roasting; roast meat *la15-.* [ME *rost*]
roast[1,2], †**rost,** †**roist** /rost/ *v ptp* **roastin, rossin 1** to cook by exposure to dry heat (originally that of an open fire) *la14-*. **2** to pester, annoy *20-*. **3** *witchcraft* to expose a wax or clay image of a person to heat intending to cause harm to the person *16-17.* **4** to torture a person by exposure to heat *la14-e17.* **roastit 1** cooked by roasting *15-*. **2** *of a person* uncomfortably warm *la16-*. **3** *of cheese* toasted *la18-*. **roastin, rossen, roassen 1** cooked by roasting *la16-*. **2** excessively hot; overheated *la16-*. †**rosting irne** a gridiron *15-17.* †**rost-irne** = *rosting irne la14-e17.* [ME *rosten*]
rob, rub /rɔb, rʌb/ *v* **1** to steal; to plunder; to despoil; to commit theft *15-*. **2** to take away a person's power or ability *e16*. **robbers and rangers** a kind of hide-and-seek *la19- T WC.* [ME *robben*]
rob *see* ROBE
Rob *see* RAB
Robbie Burns /'rɔbɪ 'bʌrnz/ *n* an old-fashioned plough with wooden stilts and beam and an iron body, without a coulter *20- NE C.* [from the name of the poet]
Robbie Dye /'rɔbɪ 'daɪ/ *n* an extreme enthusiast for the town of Hawick, especially for its Rugby team *la20- Bor.* [from the nickname of one such]
Robbie-rin-oot /rɔbɪ'rɪnut/ *n* diarrhoea *19- Sh.* [diminutive form of *Robert* + *rin oot* (RIN[1,2])]
robe, *Sh* **rob** /rob; *Sh* rɔb/ *n* a long loose-fitting outer garment (worn as a token of occupation, office or rank) *15-*. **robecoat** a loose outer garment formerly worn by women; an overdress *18, 20- Sh Ork.* †**rob royall** the robe worn by a monarch in token of their office *la15-17.* [ME *robe*]
Rob Gibb's contract /rɔb gɪbz 'kɔntrakt/ *n as a motto or toast* disinterested love and loyalty *e18, 20- historical.* [from a Master of Horse to King James V who, on being asked by the king why he served him, replied 'for stark love and kindness']
robin /'rɔbɪn/ *n* **1** the robin redbreast *Erithacus rubecula 16-.* **2** the wren *Troglodytes troglodytes 19- Sh.* **3** a child's word for the penis *20-*. **Robin Hood,** †**Robin Hude 1** the English outlaw (presented as a leader of May Day revelry) *15-*. **2** a mummer's play with Robin Hood as the leading character *la16.* **Robin-a-ree, Robin-a-reerie** a name for a burning stick used in a children's game *19- T SW.* **Robin-rin-the-hedge, Robin-roond-the-hedge** goosegrass *Galium aparine la19- WC SW Bor.* **Robin redbreast,** †**Robene reidbreist** a robin *la15-.* [diminutive form of *Robert*]
Rob Roy /rɔb 'rɔɪ/ *n* a red and black checked pattern in cloth *19-*. **Rob Roy tartan** = ROB ROY. [from the nickname of Robert MacGregor of Glengyle (1671-1734), the protagonist of Walter Scott's novel *Rob Roy*, published 1818.]

Rob Sorby /rɔb 'sɔrbe/ *n* a sharp-edged tool such as a scythe or saw *la19- NE T.* [named after Robert Sorby, a Sheffield edge-tool manufacturer]

roch *see* RATCH¹, ROCHE, ROUCH¹·³

†**roche, roch** *n* **1** a rocky eminence; a cliff; a crag; a reef *la14-e17*; compare ROCK (sense 1). **2** a boulder *e16*. [ME *roche*]

rochell salt *see* RACHEL SAUT

rochian /'rɔxɪən/ *n* a ruffian *20- NE T.* [conflation of ROUCH¹·³ with Eng *ruffian*]

rocht *see* RECK¹·²

rock¹, roke, †**rok** /rɔk, rok/ *n* **1** a rocky eminence; a cliff; a crag; a reef; a large stone *15-*; compare ROCHE (sense 1). **2** the common edible crab *Cancer pagurus la19-*. **3** a curler's name for a curling-stone *20-*. **rocklie** pebbly *19- EC SW Bor.* **rocky-on** a pile of stones built by children against the incoming tide *20- NE.* **rock bool** a round, hard, candied-sugar sweet *20- EC Bor.* **rock cod** a kind of cod, *Gadus morhua callarias*, which lives among rocks *19-*. **rock codfish** = *rock cod*. **rock codling** = *rock cod*. **rock-halibut** the coalfish *Pollachius virens 20- NE T.* **rock herring** the allis or twait shad *Alosa alosa 19, 20- NE.* **rock lintie** the twite *Linaria flavirostris*; the rock pipit *Anthus petrosus la19- N NE T.* **rock partan** the common edible crab *Cancer pagurus la19-*. **rock sole** the Dover sole *Solea solea la19- N NE.* **rock turbot** the flesh of the catfish or wolf-fish *Anarhichus lupus 20- NE T Bor.* [ME *rok*]

rock², †**rok** /rɔk/ *v* **1** to (cause to) move back and forwards *la14-*. **2** to stagger or reel in walking *18, 19- Sh NE SW.* **rocker,** †**rokkar 1** a thing which rocks; originally a cradle *la16-*. **2** a nurse or attendant whose duty it was to rock a child in its cradle *16-e17*. **rockie** with a rocking or rolling motion *19, 20- EC SW.* **rocketie-row** = *rockie*. [OE *roccian*]

rock³, †**rok** /rɔk/ *n* **1** a distaff *la14-18, 19- literary.* **2** a distaff with the wool or flax attached; the quantity of wool or flax placed on a distaff for spinning *16-19*. **3** something extremely thin and rodlike *e16*. †**rockin** a gathering of women from neighbouring houses to spin and chat together; any convivial gathering of neighbours *la18-19*. [MDu, MLG *rocke*]

rocket, †**rokkat,** †**rocquet** /'rɔkət/ *n* a bishop's surplice *la15-19, 20- historical.* [ME *roket*]

rocketie-row *see* ROCK²

rocquet *see* ROCKET

röd¹·¹ /røøː/ *n* drizzle; mist *la19- Sh.* **rödin** drizzling *20- Sh.* [see the verb]

röd¹·² /røøː/ *adj* misty; wet *20- Sh.* [ON *hrjóta* to drizzle]

röd²·¹, rüd, †**rod** /røøː, rud/ *n* **1** rubbish, refuse *16, la19- Sh.* **2** nonsense; rambling talk *la19- Sh.* [Norw dial *ryd* refuse]

röd²·², rüd /røøː, rud/ *v* **1** in winnowing grain to remove (broken straw) *la19- Sh.* **2** to talk nonsense; to rave; to mumble *la19- Sh.* [ON *ryðja* to clear and from the noun]

rod *see* REDD²·¹, ROAD¹·¹, RÖD²·¹

rodd *see* REDD²·¹, REDD²·², ROAD¹·²

rodden, roddin, †**rodding** /'rɔdən/ *n* the berry of the rowan *Sorbus aucuparia*; sometimes the tree itself *la16-*. **rodden tree** the rowan tree *16-*. **nae to care a rodden** not to care in the least *20- NE T.* **have had roddens tae yer supper** to be in a sour or surly humour *20- NE.* **as soor as roddens** very sour or bitter *la19-*. [compare Norw dial *raudn*]

rodden fleuk /'rɔdən fluk/ *n* the turbot *la18-*. Compare *rawn fleuk* (RAWN). [pres ppl of *rod* to spawn, of unknown origin + FLEUK]

roddikin, †**rodykyn** /'rɔdəkɪn/ *n* the fourth stomach of a ruminant; tripe *16-19, 20- EC Bor.* [Du *roodeken*]

roddin, rodding *see* RODDEN

rodding /'rɔdɪŋ/ *n* a narrow track or path, a track made by sheep *16-19, 20- Uls.* [unknown]

roddit *see* ROAD¹·²

roddle /'rɔdəl/ *v* to rock, shake; to totter *la19- WC.* [unknown]

rode *see* RADE, RIDE¹·², ROAD¹·²

rodykyn *see* RODDIKIN

roe *see* RAE¹

†**roebuck berry** *n* (the fruit of) the stone bramble *Rubus saxatilis la18-19*; compare *rae buck* (RAE¹). [RAE¹ + BERRY¹]

rog /rog/ *n* a stripe or streak *la19- Sh.* [Norw dial *råk*]

rogue, †**roge** /rog/ *n* a dishonest person *la16-*. †**rogue-money** a local tax levied for the expenses of arrest and detention of criminals *18-19*. [unknown]

roid *see* RUDE¹

roil /rɔɪl/ *n* a storm, a heavy sea *la19- H&I.* **ralliach** choppy, stormy *la19- H&I.* [perhaps Gael *roithleach* rolling, tossing]

roilt *see* RULT¹·¹

roin /'rɔɪn/ *adj of a sow* in season *la19- Sh.* [unknown]

roir *see* RAIR¹·²

rois *see* ROSE

roising *see* ROSE

roist *see* ROAST¹·¹, ROAST¹·²

roiter *see* ROYET¹·¹

roith *see* ROTH

rok *see* ROCK¹, ROCK², ROCK³

roke *see* ROCK¹, ROUK¹

†**rokelay** *n* a short cloak *18-e19*. [altered form of Fr *roquelaure*, from the Duc de Roquelaure (1656–1738)]

rokkat *see* ROCKET

rokkis *see* ROCK¹

roll /rol/ *n law* a list of persons or cases set down for hearing in court *15-*. **the Rolls** documents dealing with royal or state business *la15-e17, 19- historical.* †**the Kingis Rollis** = *the Rolls la14-e17*. [ME *rolle*]

roll *see* ROW¹·¹, ROW¹·², ROW³, ROW²

rolment *see* ROW³

rolp *see* ROUP²·²

†**romany buge** *n* lambskin furs of Greek origin used for lining garments *la15-e16*. [perhaps from Romano di Lombardia, in the Bergamo region of Italy + ME *bouge* sheepskin]

†**Rome raiker, Rome raker** *n Roman Catholic Church* a cleric constantly travelling to Rome in the hope of advantage *16-18*. [from the name of the city + RAIK²·², with agent suffix]

ron *see* ROAN¹, RONE²

rone¹, roan, rhone /ron/ *n* **1** the horizontal gutter for rainwater running along the eaves of a roof; sometimes the downpipe *18-*. **2** *mining* a wooden water-channel *la19, 20- EC.* **3** the pipe of a boat's pump *la16-e18*. **ronepipe, roanpipe** the downpipe for draining water from the gutter; the gutter itself *20-*. [compare Norw dial *run, rån*]

rone², †**ron** /ron/ *n* a thicket of brushwood or thorns; a patch of dense stunted woodland *15-19, 20- Uls.* [ME *ron*; compare MLG, ON *rein*]

rone³ /ron/ *n* **1** a strip or patch of ice on the ground *la18-*. **2** children's ice slide *16-e19, la19- NE.* [unknown]

rone *see* RANE¹, RANE², ROWAN¹

rong *see* RING²·², RING³·²

röni /'røøni/ *n* **1** a heap of stones *19- Sh.* **2** an outcrop of rock *20- Sh.* [ON *hraun*]

†**ronk** *adj* plentiful, dense in growth *e16*. Compare RANK¹·³ (sense 2). [variant of RANK¹·³]

ronnachs /'ronəxs/ *npl* couch grass *19- NE.* [altered form of LONNACH]

ronnie *see* RANE¹·¹

roo¹, †**row** /ru/ *v* **1** to strip the fleece (from a sheep) by plucking *17- Sh Ork*. **2** to clip (sheep) *20- Sh*. **get yer lugs tae roo** to get into serious trouble *20- Sh*. [Norw dial *rua*]

roo²·¹ /ru/ *n* a heap or pile (of peats) *19- Sh Ork*. [reduced form of ROOG¹·¹]

roo²·² /ru/ *v* to pile in heaps *19- Sh Ork*. [see the noun]

roobrub *see* RHUBARB

rood *see* RUID

rooder /'rudər/ *n* a barnacle *19- Sh*. **roodery** scab on potatoes *la19- Sh*. **ruder pecker** the purple sandpiper *Calidris maritima 20- Sh*. [ON *hrúðr* a crust, scab]

rood-goose /'rød gøs/ *n* the brent goose *la18- Sh Ork N*. [probably ON *hroðgás*; compare Norw *rotgås*, Du *rotgans*]

roof *see* RUIF¹·¹, RUIF¹·²

roog¹·¹ /rug/ *n* **1** a heap or pile, especially of peats *la19- Sh*. **2** a big clumsy person *la19- Sh*. **3** a mound, cairn, barrow *20- Sh*. [see the verb]

roog¹·² /rug/ *v* to pile into heaps, especially stack peats *la19- Sh*. [ON *hrúga*]

roog *see* RUG¹·²

rook¹·¹, †**ruke**, †**ruik** /ruk/ *n* **1** a black, raucous-voiced bird of the crow family *Corvus frugilegus 15-*. **2** *marbles* a complete loss of what one has *la19- C Bor*. **3** a term of abuse for a thief or cheat *16-19*. [OE *hrōc*]

rook¹·², †**truck** /ruk/ *v* **1** to defraud, cheat *la17-*. **2** to plunder, clean out; to remove by theft *18-*. **3** to rob a bird's nest of eggs *19-*. **4** *marbles* to win (all an opponent's marbles) *la19-*. **rookie** *marbles* a game in which the winner takes all *20-*. [see the noun]

rook² /ruk/ *n* **1** a quarrel, uproar, fuss *19, 20- T*. **2** a noisy group of people *la19, 20- T*. [unknown]

rook³ /ruk/ *n* an animal whose bones are showing *la19- Sh*. [unknown]

rook⁴ /ruk/ *v* to smoke a pipe *20- Sh*. [Du *rooken*]

rook *see* ROUK¹

rooketty-coo¹·¹, **ruckity-coo** /rukəti 'ku, rʌkəti 'ku/ *n* the call of a pigeon *20-*. [onomatopoeic]

rooketty-coo¹·², **ruckity-coo** /rukəti 'ku, rʌkəti 'ku/ *v* **1** *of lovers* to talk affectionately, bill and coo *19-*. **2** *of a pigeon* to coo *20-*. [see the noun]

rookety-doo /rukəti 'du/ *n* a tame pigeon *la19- C*. [onomatopoeic + DOO]

rookle *see* RUGGLE

rool *see* RŪL

roolyie, †**trulʒe**, †**royhl** /'rulji/ *v* to rumble or stir noisily; to move about vigorously *e15, 20- N*. [perhaps OFr *roillier*, related to *roelle* a wheel]

room¹·¹, †**troum**, †**trowme**, †**trum** /rum/ *n* **1** (availability of) space, a particular space or area *la14-*. **2** a chamber or apartment *16-*. **3** the apartment of a but and ben not used as the kitchen; a sitting-room, best room *la18-*. **4** a piece of rented land, farm, a croft, frequently in place-names *la15-19, 20- historical*. **5** the distance between ships at sea or boats fishing *e16, 20- Sh NE*. **6** *mining* the working space left between supporting pillars of coal *17-19, 20- C*. **7** the compartment or space between the thwarts of a boat *la18- Sh*. **8** *pl* domains, territories; estates *la15-16*. **9** the space in a mill necessary for storing a person's grain awaiting grinding; a person's turn for grinding *15-e17*. **10** authority; an office or function; an appointment *la15-17*. **11** a place in a series, logical sequence, or queue: ◊*in the first room 16-18*. **12** a place, position; the space in a market where stalls are set up *la16-17*. **13** a seating space in a church *la16-e18*. **room-end** the end of a but and ben away from the kitchen *19-*. †**roum free** not incurring the payment levied on corn for occupying space in a mill while awaiting grinding *la12-e17*. **in room of** in place of *16-*. †**on rowme** at a distance, apart *e16*. **room and kitchen** a dwelling, usually a flat, consisting of a kitchen/living-room and another room *19-*. **room and rance** *mining* a method of working coal by leaving pillars of coal to support the roof *19-*. [OE *gerūma*]

room¹·², †**troum**, †**trowm** /rum/ *v* **1** to move aside in order to make room *la18, 20- Ork*. **2** to hollow out *20- Sh*. **3** to clear (space); to vacate *15-e16*. **4** to install (a person in an office) *la16-17*. **rouming** *see* souming and rouming (SOUM¹·²). [see the adj]

room¹·³, †**troum**, †**trowm** /rum/ *adj* **1** roomy, spacious, wide *15-19, 20- Sh*. **2** *of the wind* favourable *17, 18- Sh Ork*. **3** empty, unobstructed, clear *la15-e19*. †**the rowm se** the open sea *15-e17*. [OE *rūm*]

roomatics *see* RHEUMATICS

roomatis *see* RHEUMATISE

roon *see* ROOND¹·¹, ROOND¹·³, ROOND¹·⁴, RUIND

roond¹·¹, **roon**, **roun**, **round** /rund, run, rʌun, rʌund/ *n* **1** movement in a circle; a ring dance; a patrol *16-*. **2** a song sung by two or more singers taking up the tune successively *16-*. **3** *golf* a complete circuit of the course in which all the holes are played *la18-*. **4** the correct sequence; one's turn in a sequence of activities *la18-*. **5** a cut of meat, especially beef, taken from the hindquarter *19-*. **6** a round turret; a rounded recess in a room *16-19, 20- historical*. **7** a circular sheepfold *19- SW Bor*. **8** *farming* a single circuit in ploughing a piece of ground *20- Ork NE*. **9** a strip or quantity of cloth *la17*. **10** a circular window *e16*. **round steak** a cut of meat, especially beef, taken from the hindquarter *19-*. **the round** the surrounding country, neighbourhood *19- Sh Ork EC*. **the roond o the clock** a complete circuit of the hour-hand of a clock, twelve hours: ◊*he slept the roond o the clock la19-*. [ME *round*, EModE *rownde* and from the adj]

roond¹·², **round** /rund, rʌund/ *v* **1** to make round or curved *17-*. **2** to cut (a person's hair) close to the head *e16*. [see the adj]

roond¹·³, **roon**, **roun**, **round**, †**rownd** /rund, run, rʌun, rʌund/ *adj* **1** circular, spherical *la14-*. **2** sizeable, big *15-*. **3** *of a quantity, usually a dozen* complete, entire, full *la16-*. **4** *of flour or oatmeal* coarsely ground *la16-19, 20- NE*. **5** *of cloth* made of thick thread, coarse *la15-e18*. **6** *of speech or behaviour* honest, plain *15-16*. **7** *of a man's bonnet or cap* covering and encircling the head *la15-17*. **roun croon** a woman's bonnet with a round crown *19, 20- Ork*. **roundheid** *fisherman's taboo* a seal *20- Sh*. **round o 1** a circular window *16-19*. **2** a nonentity *la19-*. **roun soun** complete, whole: ◊*a roun soun dizzen 19- SW*. †**round sele** one of the seals of a bishop *15-16*. [ME *round*]

roond¹·⁴, **roon**, **roun**, **round** /rund, run, rʌun, rʌund/ *adv* **1** with a circular course *la15-*. **2** to each in turn, successively *la18-*. **3** in the neighbourhood, round about *la18*. **4** on completing a circuit *e16*. [see the adj]

roond aboot¹·¹, **round aboot**, **round about** /'rundəbut, 'rʌundəbut, 'rʌundəbʌut/ *n* **1** a road junction consisting of a central island around which traffic moves in one direction *20-*. **2** a circular prehistoric fort *la18- SW Bor*. **3** a circular roll made of coarse flour; a circular oatcake *19-, 20- NE*. [see the adverb]

roond aboot¹·², **round about** /'rundəbut, 'rʌundəbʌut/ *adv* **1** on all sides, all round *la15-*. **2** (so as to move) in a circle; in a circuitous fashion *16-*. **3** in the vicinity *18-*. [ROOND¹·⁴ + ABOOT¹·¹]

roond aboot[1,3], **round about** /ˈrundəbut, ˈrʌundəbʌut/ *prep* on all sides of; (in a ring) around; so as to move or pass round *16-*. [see the adverb]

roop *see* ROUP[1.1], ROUP[1.2], ROUP[2.2], ROUP[3], ROUP[6]

roose *see* ROUSE[1], ROUSE[2], RUISE[1.1], RUISE[1.2]

rooshel /ˈruʃəl/ *v* to hustle *20- NE T*. [form of Eng *rush* + diminutive suffix *-le*]

rooshie-doo *see* RUSH[1.1]

rooshter *see* ROOSTER

roosk, rusk /rusk/ *n* a thick or luxuriant growth, usually of hair *20- Sh*. **rooskie** *of hair* tousled, unkempt *20- Sh*. **ruskit** *of hair* frizzy or tousled *la19- Sh*. [Norw dial *ruskut* disorderly]

roost[1], *NE* **reest**, †**rust**, †**ruist** /rust; *NE* rist/ *n* **1** a place where poultry roost *la16-*. **2** the open cross-joists of a cottage living-room *la17-19, 20- Sh*. [OE *hrōst*]

roost[2.1], **rust**, †**roust**, †**rowst** /rust, rʌst/ *n* **1** corrosion (formed on the surface of iron or steel); anything corrosive or damaging *la15-*. **2** *in negative constructions* not a penny *20-*. **3** moral corruption *la15-16*. **4** rancour *16-17*. **roostie 1** affected by rust *la15-*. **2** *of the throat or voice* rough, dry; hoarse, raucous *18-*. **3** morally corrupt *la15-e17*. **4** *of non-metallic things* deteriorated, decayed *16-17*. **5** *of sexual performance* clumsy; impotent *e16*. **roostie nail** a dram of whisky *20- NE C SW*. [OE *rūst*]

roost[2.2], **rust**, †**roust** /rust, rʌst/ *v* to become rusty; to deteriorate *16-*. **roostit 1** rusty *15-*. **2** *of the throat* rough, dry; hoarse, raucous *la18-*. [see the noun]

roost[3] /rust/ *n* drizzle, mist *19- Sh EC*. [unknown]

roost[4], †**roust** /rust/ *n* a turbulent stretch of sea caused by a strong current in a restricted passage or by a meeting of conflicting currents *la17- Sh Ork*. [Norw dial *røst*]

rooster, rooshter /ˈrustər, ˈruʃtər/ *n* useless rubbish *19- NE*. [perhaps altered from TROOSHTER or *roostie* (ROOST[2.1])]

root *see* ROUT[1.1], ROWT[1.2], RUIT[1.1], RUIT[1.2], RUIT[2]

rooth *see* RUTH

roove *see* RUIVE[1.1], RUIVE[1.2]

ropach /ˈropəx/ *adj* untidy, dirty, slatternly *20- T H&I*. [Gael *ropach*]

roparie *see* RAPEREE

rope *see* RAIP[1.1], ROUP[1.1]

roploch *see* RAPLOCH[1.1]

rør /rør/ *n* the common reed *Arundo*; canary grass *Phalaris arundinacea 20- Sh*. [Norw *rør*]

rorie /ˈrori/ *n* something large of its kind; a large turnip *la19- NE*. [unknown]

ros *see* ROSE

rosat *see* ROSET[1.1], ROSET[1.2]

rose, †**ros**, †**rois**, †**roys** /roz/ *n* **1** the flower or the plant of the genus *Rosa la14-*. **2** an artefact in the shape of a rose; a representation of a rose *la15-*. **3** the crown end of a potato tuber *19*. **4** an example of something excellent, supreme, beautiful or red; applied to a woman, especially the Virgin Mary *la14-16*. **5** the golden rose, an ornament blessed by the Pope and sent to someone as a mark of favour *15-16*. **rosie, rosy** *adj* full of or abounding in roses; of the colour of a rose *16-*. **rosie, rosy** *n in children's games* a reddish marble *la19- NE*. †**roising** rosy *la15*. †**rosyne** a rose, a title of the Virgin Mary *e16*. †**rose end** the crown end of a potato tuber *19*. **rose lintie 1** the male linnet (which has bright red plumage during the breeding season) *Linaria cannabina 19, 20- Ork N H&I EC Uls*. **2** the lesser redpoll *Acanthis flammea cabaret la19, 20- H&I*. †**rose noble**, **ros nobill 1** a gold coin stamped with a rose design *la15-17*. **2** *law* a pre-arranged token payment for the redemption of wadset land *la16-17*. **rosy-posy** a term of endearment *la19- NE T EC*. [Lat *rosa*, AN, OFr *rose*]

†**roseegar, roseager** *n* darnel *Lolium tremulentum la17-e18*. [variant of Eng *rosaker* realgar, red arsenic, altered form of *resalgar* with influence from *rose* due to the red colour of the mineral's crystals]

†**rosere, roseir** *n* a rosebush *la14-16*. [ME *roser*]

roset[1.1], †**rosat** /ˈrozət/ *n* resin, rosin *la15-*. **rosety, rosetty** of, full of or covered with resin *19-*. **roset en** a resined thread, used for sewing leather *19-*. **rosety-en** a shoemaker's thread *la19- NE C*. **rosety ruits** fir-roots used as fuel *la19- NE T*. [altered form of ME *rosin*]

roset[1.2], †**rosat** /ˈrozət/ *v* to rub with resin; to rub a fiddle-bow with rosin *16-*. [see the noun]

roset[1.3] /ˈrozət/ *adj* resinous *la19- Sh N NE T*. [see the noun]

rosidandrum /roziˈdandrəm/ *n* rhododendron *20-*. [altered form of Eng *rhododendron*]

ross[1] /rɔs/ *n* a knot in a line made to exclude any damaged part *20- Sh*. **rossik** = ROSS[1] *la19 Sh*. [unknown]

ross[2] /rɔs/ *v* to run a fishing-line down to the sea bottom then move it up to keep it clear of the bottom; to move a line to attract fish *20- Sh*. [unknown]

rossan /ˈrɔsən/ *n* a thicket *19- SW*. [Gael *rosan*, IrGael *rosán*]

rosshole /ˈrɔshol/ *n* the openings under the timbers of a boat which allow the water to run freely along the keel *la19- Sh*. [Norw dial *ræsehol*]

rossin *see* ROAST[1.2]

rost *see* ROAST[1.1], ROAST[1.2]

rot[1.1], †**rott** /rɔt/ *n* decay, putrefaction; a disease causing putrefaction *16-*. **rottack** an old, discarded, decayed object, a piece of rubbish *19- NE*. [see the verb]

rot[1.2], †**rott** /rɔt/ *v* to decompose, decay *la14-*. [OE *rotian*]

rot *see* RATT

rotche *see* RATCH[1]

†**roth, roith** *n* **1** *in Shetland and Orkney* the unchallengeable title to ownership of land enjoyed under the udal system by all the legitimate descendants of an earlier udal proprietor *la15-17*. **2** the right of an heir to redeem alienated udal land *la15-16*. **roth land** udal land *e16*. [ON *ráð* advice]

rothick /ˈrɔðək/ *n* a young edible crab *Cancer pagurus 19- N NE*. [Gael *ru(a)dhag* a crab (little red one)]

rothie /ˈroθi/ *n* **1** a tumult, an uproar; a tangle, a muddle *19- NE*. **2** a rude, coarse person *20- NE*. [unknown]

†**rothman** *n in Shetland and Orkney* a landowner with the hereditary privilege of sitting on the head court of Kirkwall; an heir who inherited the right to redeem alienated udal land *16*. [ON *ráðmaðr* councillor]

rott *see* ROT[1.1], ROT[1.2]

rottack *see* ROT[1]

rottan *see* RATTON

rotten, †**rottin** /ˈrɔtən/ *adj* **1** decayed; corrupt *la14-*. **2** *of rock* crumbling *la18-*. **3** drunk *20-*. **4** *law* not in accordance with the truth, corrupt *15*. **rotten drunk** very drunk *20-*. †**rotten grass** one of several grasses supposed to be poisonous to sheep *la18-19*. [ON *rotinn*]

rouch[1.1], **rough** /rɔx, rʌx, rʌf/ *n* **1** rough ground *la15-*. **2** something harsh or unpleasant *17-*. **3** the major part of something *19-*. **4** higher, thicker grass along the edges of a golf course *20-*. **5** *farming* land in an unimproved, virgin condition *20-*. [see the adj]

rouch[1.2], **rough** /rɔx, rʌx, rʌf/ *v* to provide a horse with frost-nails *19, 20- SW Uls*. [see the adj]

rouch[1.3], **ruch, rugh, rough, roch**, †**rowch**, †**rwch** /rɔx, rʌx, rʌf, rox/ *adj* **1** *of ground or a surface* uneven, broken *la15-*. **2** wild, lacking refinement or acceptable social behaviour; uncivil; harsh *la15-*. **3** coarse-textured, shaggy; hairy *16-*. **4** *of materials or manufactured articles* crude, unrefined; not well finished *16-*. **5** *of weather or the sea* turbulent, stormy *16-*. **6** *of grass or crops* strong, luxuriant, dense *la16-*. **7** lewd, foul-mouthed, indecent *19-*. **8** *of sheep* unshorn *la15-e19, la19- SW Bor*. **9** abundant; plentifully supplied, especially with good plain fare: ◊*a guid rouch hoose 18-19, 20- C SW*. **10** *of a bone* having meat on it *la18-19, 20- C*. **11** *of hides* undressed, untanned (with the hair still on) *la14-e18*. **ruchie** *n* **1** the long rough dab *Hippoglossoides platessoides19- NE*. **2** a wild rough boy *20- N*. **3** a rough, coarse woman *20- NE*. **ruchie** *adj* **1** hairy, shaggy, unkempt *la19- Ork N*. **2** curly-haired *20- Ork*. **roughsome** unrefined, uncouth, unpolished, crude; uneven *la17-19, 20- WC SW*. **roughback** the long rough dab *Hippoglossoides platessoides la18- NE*. **rough bear** an inferior variety of barley *la17-*. **rough blade** the mature leaf of a plant (as opposed to the seed leaf) *20-*. **the rough bounds** the mountainous region in the West Highlands from Loch Sunart (Argyllshire) to Loch Hourn (Inverness-shire) *19-*. **rough coal** a kind of inferior coal *la18-19, 20- C*. **rough dram** enough alcohol to cause drunkenness *la19- N*. **rough-head 1** a turf or peat with the surface grass still attached, originally used as the head of a brush *17-19, 20- Uls*. **2** a brush *17-e18*. **ruchstane** a natural boulder *20- T C SW*. **ruchstane dyke** a dry-stone wall *20- NE T EC*. **ruch and right 1** entirely, taking everything into consideration *la18- NE T*. **2** rough and ready, having somewhat uncouth manners, blunt *la19-*. †**rough and round** simple, homely; *of food* plain but substantial *e19*. [OE *rūh*]

rouch[1.4], **rough**, †**ruch** /rɔx, rʌx, rʌf/ *adv* **1** *of how a task is performed* crudely but adequately *16-*. **2** in a rough or rude manner, uncivilly *la16-*. **3** in a comfortable or well-supplied state *la19- T SW*. **rouch-living** *of a man* living in a dissolute, debauched or immoral way *19, 20- Sh NE T*. **rough-spun** coarsely made; *of manners* rough, crude, unpolished *la18-19, 20- T EC Uls* [see the adj]

rouchle /'rɔxəl/ *v* to toss about, shake roughly, tousle *19- H&I*. [perhaps ROUCH[1.3], with *-le* suffix]

roucht *see* RECK[1.2]

roudes *see* RUDAS[1.1], RUDAS[1.2]

rough *see* ROUCH[1.1], ROUCH[1.2], ROUCH[1.3], ROUCH[1.4]

roughie *see* RUFFIE[1]

rouk[1], **rook**, **rauk**, †**roke** /ruk, rɔk/ *n* **1** mist, fog; drizzle *16-*. **2** a cloud *e16*. **roukieie**, **rawky** misty, damp, drizzly; muggy *18-*. [ON **raukr*; compare Swed *rauk*, Du *rook* smoke]

†**rouk**[2] *v* to crouch, huddle *la15-16*. **rouk and roun** to huddle together, talk intimately or secretly *la15-16*. [perhaps ME *rouken* crouch, huddle together]

rouk *see* RUCK[1.1], RUCK[1.2]

roule *see* RULE[1.1], RULE[1.2]

roum *see* ROOM[1.1], ROOM[1.2], ROOM[1.3]

roun, **round** /run, rʌun, rʌund/ *v* to converse in whispers, tell (something) or talk quietly or privately *la14-*. †**rounar**, **roundar** a talebearer, gossip *la15-e17*. [OE *rūnian*]

roun *see* RAWN, ROOND[1.1], ROOND[1.3], ROOND[1.4]

rounall *see* ROUNDEL

round *see* ROOND[1.1], ROOND[1.2], ROOND[1.3], ROOND[1.4]

round aboot *see* ROOND ABOOT[1.1]

round about *see* ROOND ABOOT[1.1], ROOND ABOOT[1.2], ROOND ABOOT[1.3]

roundel, **rounall**, †**roundall**, †**roundail** /'rʌundəl, 'rundəl, 'runəl,/ *n* **1** a circular object, a disc *16-*. **2** a round turret *18-19, 20- T EC SW*. **3** a circular sheepfold *20- N T WC Bor*. **4** a round heap *20- NE T EC*. **5** a circular patch of grass worn smooth by cattle *19- C SW*. **6** a cask *15-17*. **7** a poem; a rondeau; a verse epigram *16-17*. **8** a small round table *la15-16*. **9** a circle *15*. †**roundell burd** a small round table *la16-e17*. [ME *roundel*]

rounge *see* RUNDGE

rountrie *see* ROWAN[1]

roup[1.1], *Sh Ork* **roop**, †**rowp**, †**rope** /rʌup; *Sh Ork* rup/ *n* a sale or let by public auction *la17-*. [see the verb]

roup[1.2], *Sh Ork* **roop**, †**rowp**, †**rope** /rʌup; *Sh Ork* rup/ *v* **1** to sell or let by public auction *la15-*. **2** to sell up; to evict (a bankrupt) and sell their effects *19-*. **rouper** a person who puts up goods for sale by auction; an auctioneer *la16-*. **rouping** a selling or letting by public auction; an auction *16-*. **rouping clerk** an auctioneer's clerk *la19- N WC*; compare *clerk of the roup* (CLERK). **rouping roll** a record of transactions at an auction sale *e18, 20- N WC SW Bor*. **rouping wife** a woman who buys and resells second-hand furniture; a female auctioneer *la18-*. **roup bill** a list of items for sale at an auction *la19, 20- Sh N T*. **roup roll** = *rouping roll la18-*. **bring to the roup** to bring to bankruptcy, ruin *20- C*. **put to the roup** to offer for sale or let to the highest bidder *la18, 20- Sh N T*. **roup oot** to evict (a bankrupt) and sell their effects *20-*. [specific use of ROUP[2.2]]

roup[2.1] /rup, rʌup/ *n* **1** hoarseness, huskiness, any inflamed condition of the throat *la16-*. **2** a catarrhal disease of the mouth or throat in poultry *19-*. **roupie** hoarse, rough, husky *la18-*. **roupit** hoarse, rough, raucous *la18-19, 20- T C SW Bor*. **the roup** hoarseness, huskiness *18-19, 20- N NE T EC*. [probably from the verb; compare AN *rupie* nasal mucus]

roup[2.2], **roop**, †**rowp**, †**rolp** /rʌup, rup/ *v* **1** to cry, shout raucously, roar, proclaim loudly; to clamour for; *of a raven or crow* to croak, caw *15-19, 20- NE WC Bor*. **2** to invoke (a deity) loudly *e16*. [ON *raupa* to boast]

roup[3], **roop** /rup/ *v* **1** to plunder, rob, deprive of everything *19, 20- NE T EC SW Bor*. **2** to prune (a hedge or bush) very severely *20- T EC*. **3** to take (the marbles of a defeated opponent) in a game of *roopie 20- Ork T EC*. **roopie** a game in which the winner claims all the loser's marbles *20- Sh Ork*. [perhaps a variant of ROOK[1.2]]

roup[4] /rʌup/ *v* to vomit *la19- NE*. [probably onomatopoeic]

roup[5] /rʌup/ *npl* the stems of the seaweed, oarweed *Laminaria digitata la19- NE*. [unknown]

roup[6], **roop** /rup/ *n* a dense mist *la19- SW Bor*. [perhaps altered form of ROUK[1]]

rouse[1], **roose** /rʌuz, ruz/ *v* **1** to wake from sleep, stir up, become active *17-*. **2** to become agitated, excited or enraged *la19- NE T C SW Bor*. **3** to move with violence or speed, rush *la19- Sh Ork NE*. **rousie 1** *of the wind* tempestuous *20- Ork*. **2** *of an animal* restless, easily excited *20- Bor*. **rousing bell** *Presbyterian Church* a bell rung to let distant worshippers know it is time to get up for church *la19- EC*. **rouse on** to become enraged at *20- NE T EC*. [unknown]

rouse[2], **roose** /rʌuz, ruz/ *v* **1** to sprinkle (fish) with salt to cure them *18-19, 20- Sh Ork N NE EC*. **2** to sprinkle with water; to water with a watering-can *la19- NE T*. **rouser** a watering-can *la18- Ork NE T C*. [aphetic form of OFr *arrouser* bedew; sprinkle]

roust *see* ROOST[2.1], ROOST[4], ROWST[1.1], ROWST[1.2]

†**rout**[1.1], **rowt**, **root** *n* a loud crashing noise (of the sea or thunder) *16-19*. [see the verb]

rout[1.2], †**rowt** /rut, rʌut/ *v* **1** *of wind or water* to roar loudly *la14-*. **2** *of rocks* to resound, re-echo *e16*. **routing**, †**rowtand** roaring, rumbling; frequently in place-names *la13-*. [OE *hrūtan* to make a noise, rumble, rattle]

†**rout²**, **rowt** *n* a (heavy) blow, stroke, a buffet *la14-19*. [ME *route* a blow]

†**rout³,¹**, **rowt** *n* **1** a detachment of soldiers; a fighting force; an assemblage or company of persons *la14-16*. **2** a confused mêlée in a battle *15-16*. **3** a flock, herd, a swarm (of animals or insects) *la15-e16*. [AN, OFr *route* company, armed band]

†**rout³,²**, **rowt** *v* to join or go about in an armed group or band *la14-e16*. [see the noun]

†**rout⁴** *n* a species of wild goose *la16-17*. Compare ROOD-GOOSE. [unknown]

rout see ROWT¹,¹, ROWT¹,², ROWT², ROWT³

routh¹,¹ /rʌuθ/ *n* **1** plenty, abundance, profusion *la17-*. **2** a large amount or extent *20- Ork*. **routhie** abundant, plentiful *la18-*. [unknown]

routh¹,² /rʌuθ/ *adj* plentiful, abundant, profuse, well-endowed *la18-*. [unknown]

routh, routht see RUTH

rovack /'rovək/ *n* **1** the buttocks; the anus *19- Sh*. **2** the tail of a fish, especially the dried strip along the back of a dogfish *20- Sh*. [Norw dial *rove*, with diminutive suffix]

rove¹,¹ /rov/ *n* a ramble or wandering *19, 20- Sh T EC*. [from the verb]

rove¹,² /rov/ *v* **1** to move about freely, wander *la16-*. **2** to wander in thought or speech, be delirious, rave *la17-19, 20- Sh Ork N T*. [EModE *rove*, origin unknown; compare RAVE², RAVE¹,²]

rove see RUIVE¹,¹

rover¹ /'rovər/ *n* a large blazing fire *20- Sh N*. [unknown; compare EModDu *roef* roof of a fireplace]

rover², †**revar**, †**rever** /'rovər/ *n* archery a mark selected at random *la16-*. †**at rovers** without definite aim, at random, haphazardly *e18*. [an early sense of ROVE¹,² with noun-forming suffix; compare RAVE²]

roverous /'rovərəs/ *adj* obstreperous, clamorous *20- Sh*. [perhaps adj from altered form of RAVERIE in sense 4]

rovin /'rovɪn/ *adj of a fire* blazing *la19- NE*. [unknown; compare EModDu *roef* roof of a fireplace and *reevin* (RIVE¹,²)]

rovin fu /'rovɪn fu/ *adj* full to the brim *la19- T EC*. [perhaps, as intensifier, extended use of ROVIN + FOU²,³]

row¹,¹, **roll**, †**rowll** /rʌu, rol/ *n* **1** a piece of parchment or paper (containing the written record of official business) an official record *15-*. **2** a register, a catalogue, a list *16-*. **3** a quantity of tobacco leaves formed into a cylindrical mass *17-*. **4** a small loaf of bread *17-*. **5** a quantity of cloth, yarn or wool rolled into a cylinder or onto a spool *la15-19, 20- Sh*. **6** the high-water mark on a beach; a mass of seaweed along this line *20- N NE*. **7** a plump person; an untidy or lazy person *20- SW*. **8** a term used in reckoning the score in Orkney football *20- Ork*. **9** a rounded stick or roller for levelling grain in a measure *la15-19*. **10** *in mining* a winch or windlass *17*. **11** a pad worn round the waist to give fuller dimensions to a skirt *e17*. **rowie 1** a flaky bread roll made with a large percentage of butter *20- NE T*. **2** a roll of tobacco *la17*. †**roll of sute of court** a register of the names of those bound to attend the courts of sheriffs *15-17*. †**in roll** in writing *15-17*. [ME *rolle*]

row¹,², **roll** /rʌu, rol/ *v* **1** to move by rolling, turn over and over; to rotate *la14-*. **2** to move with a rolling or staggering gait, waddle, lurch or stumble along *la15-*. **3** to turn over (an idea) in the mind or memory, consider; *of thoughts* to revolve in a person's mind *16-*. **4** *of the eyeballs* to (cause to) move from side to side *16-*. **5** *of time or the seasons* to pass *16-*. **6** *of a sound* to re-echo *16-*. **7** to wind, twist, twine *la16-*. **8** to move about, fidget, toss and turn restlessly *la16-*. **9** to wrap up, envelop in, wrap around *la16-*. **10** to wind up (a clock or other mechanism) *la17-*. **11** to convey in a wheeled vehicle, wheel *18-*. **12** *of bowls* to roll towards the jack *18-19, 20- NE T EC SW*. **13** to play (a bowl or curling-stone) *la18-19, 20- NE T SW*. **14** *of a sheep* to roll over on to its back *20- T C*. **15** to form (cotton or carded wool) into a roll before it is spun *15-19*. **16** to shape or smooth (metal) with a roller or revolving tool; perhaps to cut a gemstone *la15-17*. **17** to abound (in riches, passion) *la15-16*. **18** to ride, travel in, drive (a cart or chariot) *la15-e16*. **19** *of a building* to tumble down *e16*. **roller**, †**rollar 1** a cylinder used for rolling or flattening *la15-*. **2** a (ribbed or grooved) rolling pin used in making oatcakes *19, 20- NE SW*. **3** a rounded stick for levelling grain in a measure *18, 20- N*. **4** a roll of carded wool ready for spinning *la19- Sh Ork N*. **rowing, rowan** a roll of carded wool ready for spinning *18-19, 20- WC SW Uls*. **rollie-pin** *games* a rolling action of the hands between the bouncing and catching of a ball *20-*. †**rowbowlis, rollboull** bowls *16-e17*. **row-heid** the end of a mill-trough where the water falls on to the wheel *20- Ork NE*. **row-shoudert** round-shouldered *20- NE T*. **row a gird** *games* to bowl a hoop *19-*. **be rowed intae** to be involved or embroiled in *la18- T C SW Bor*. [ME *rollen*]

†**row¹,³**, **roll** *v* **1** to write, include (a name) in a list or register, enrol *15-17*. **2** *law* to enter (a contract, action or judgement) in the records of a court *15-17*. **3** *law* to enter (a person) in a list of those to be charged in court *e16*. **rolment** *law* a record of the proceedings of a court hearing; an extract from the record of a particular action *15-17*. [from ROW¹,¹ or ME, *rollen* to record in a roll or register]

row², †**roll** /rʌu, ro/ *v* **1** to propel a boat with oars; to travel in a boat propelled by oars *la14-*. **2** *of a boat* to move along in the water easily or smoothly *la18-19, 20- Sh NE T*. **3** to put to sea in a fishing boat *19- Sh NE*. **4** to cross (a stream) using the feet as if they were oars *la15*. †**rowage** rowing dues or charges *la16-17*. **rowboat**, †**row boit**, †**roll bote** a rowing boat *16-*. [OE *rōwan* go by water]

row see RAE², RAW¹,¹, RAW¹,², ROWE, ROO¹

rowan¹, **rone** /'rʌuən, ron/ *n* **1** the fruit of the mountain ash *la16-*. **2** the mountain ash *17-*. **rowanberry** the fruit of the mountain ash *18-*. **rowanbuss** the mountain ash *17-*. **rowan jelly** a sharp-tasting preserve made from rowanberries, and served with game or meat *la19-*. **rowantree**, †**rountrie**, †**rantre** the mountain ash *17-*. [ON *reynir*]

†**rowan²** *adj of cloth or other goods* imported from Rouen *la15-e18*. [from the name of the French city]

rowan see RAWN

rowch see ROUCH¹,³

row-chow¹,¹ /'rʌu tʃʌu/ *v of children at play* to roll, tumble *20- T C SW*. [reduplicative compound based on ROW¹,²; or second element may be altered form of JOW¹,²]

row-chow¹,² /'rʌu tʃʌu/ *adj* rolling, revolving; mixed up, tangled *la19, 20- C SW*. **row-chow tobacco** a game in which a chain of boys coils round a large boy and all sway to and fro shouting the name of the game until they fall in a heap *19- T C SW Bor*. [see the verb]

†**rowe**, **row** *n* the wheel, an instrument of torture *la16-e17*. [MFr *roue*]

roweing see ROAN²

rowel, †**revell**, †**reuall**, †**riwell** /'rʌuəl/ *n* **1** a small wheel on a spur *la16-*. **2** something circular, a wheel-shaped ornament *15*. [ME *rouel*]

rowl see RAIVEL¹,²

rowlie-powlie /'rʌuli pʌuli/ *n* **1** a game of chance involving the rolling of a ball, skittles or ninepins played at fairs *19-*. **2** a fairground stallholder in charge of a game of chance *19*. [reduplicative compound based on ROW¹,², corresponding to Eng *roly-poly*]

rowll see ROW¹·¹
rowm see ROOM¹·², ROOM¹·³
rowme see ROOM¹·¹
rown see RAWN
rownd see ROOND¹·³
rowp see ROUP¹·¹, ROUP¹·², ROUP²·²
rowst¹·¹, †**roust** /rʌust/ *n* a shout, roar, bellow; the act of roaring or bellowing *la15-19, 20- NE T*. [ON *raust*]
rowst¹·², †**roust**, †**rust** /rʌust/ *v* to shout, roar, bellow *la15-19, 20- T*. **rousting** *of weather* windy, blustery *20- NE T EC*. [ON *reysta*]
rowst² /rʌust/ *v* to arouse, stir to action, rout out *la19, 20- NE T EC SW*. [unknown]
rowst see ROOST²·¹
rowt¹·¹, †**rout**, †**root** /rʌut/ *n* 1 bellowing or lowing, especially of cattle; the act of bellowing *16-*. 2 a shout, outcry, clamour, fuss *16-19*. 3 the noise of birds *e16*. [see the verb]
rowt¹·², **rout**, **Ork root** /rʌut; *Ork* rut/ *v* 1 *of cattle* to bellow, roar, low *la15-*. 2 *of a person* to shout, make a great deal of noise *15-19, 20- Ork T WC SW*. 3 *of wild animals* to roar, cry *la16-18, 20- T C Bor*. 4 *of a person* to play (on a horn); *of a horn* to blast, sound *19*. [ON *rauta* bellow]
†**rowt²**, **rout** *v of a person* to snore *la14-e19*. [OE *hrūtan*, ON *hrjóta*]
rowt³, †**rout** /rʌut/ *v* to belch, break wind *16-19, 20- C*. [MFr *router*]
rowt see ROUT¹·¹, ROUT¹·², ROUT², ROUT³·¹, ROUT³·²
rowth see RUTH
†**roy¹** *n* a prince, a sovereign *la15-e17*. [ME *roi*]
†**roy²** *v* to talk nonsense *e16*. [ME *roien*]
roy³ /rɔɪ/ *n* a variety of trunk rot in conifers, especially the larch *la18- NE*. **royed** affected with rot *la19- N NE*. [Gael *ruaidhe* redness; a defect in fir timber]
royal¹·¹, †**riall** /'rɔɪəl/ *n* a member of a royal family *15-*. [see the adj]
royal¹·², †**rial**, †**ryall**, †**reall** /'rɔɪəl/ *adj* 1 relating to royalty *la14-*. 2 of the office, symbols, place or residence of royalty *15-*. 3 kinglike or queenlike *la14-16*. 4 *of literary style* elevated *e16*. **royally**, †**royallie**, †**royaly** in a manner befitting a king or queen; splendidly *15-*. †**royal bounty** an annual payment made by the Crown to the Church of Scotland for the promotion of religion in the Highlands and Islands *18-19*. **royal burgh** a burgh deriving its charter and its lands and privileges directly from the Crown *17-e20, la20- historical*. **Royal Company of Archers** the Sovereign's bodyguard in Scotland *18-*. **The Royal Highland and Agricultural Society of Scotland** a society formed to inquire into the state of the Highlands and Islands *20-*. **Royal Highland Show** = *Highland Show* (HIELAND¹·²) *20-*. **Royal Mile** the street in Edinburgh extending from the Castle to the Palace of Holyroodhouse *20-*. **Royal Scots** a regiment, originally raised in 1633 as a regiment in the French service; so called since 1812 *la19-20, 21- historical*. [AN, OFr *roial*]
royalty, †**realte**, †**rialte**, †**reawté** /'rɔɪəlte/ *n* 1 the status, office or rank of a king or queen *la14-*. 2 a district directly under the sovereign *15-19, 20- historical*. 3 the condition of being directly subject to royal administration *15-16*. 4 kinglike pomp or magnificence *la14-16*. 5 a kingdom, realm *la14-15*. [AN, MFr *roiauté*]
royd see ROYET¹·²
royet¹·¹ /'rɔɪət/ *n* 1 an unruly, troublesome, bad-tempered person *19- C SW*. 2 a troublesome animal *18-e19*. **royter**, **roiter** talk nonsense, babble, rave *19- C*. [unknown]
royet¹·², **royt**, †**royd**, †**riot** /'rɔɪət, rɔɪt/ *adj* 1 disorderly, incoherent, undisciplined, turbulent *16-19, 20- NE*. 2 *of children* wild, unruly, mischievous *18-19, 20- Sh NE T EC*. 3 *of weather* wild, stormy, variable *la19- NE*. †**royetnes**, **royitnes** wildness *e16*. [unknown]
royhl see ROOLYIE
roylock /'rɔɪlək/ *n* a large bulky object, a big stout person *la19- Sh*. [Norw dial *rull* a round log, anything round and thick, with noun-forming suffix *-lock*]
†**royn** *adj* red, vermilion *e16*. [unknown]
royr see RAIR¹·¹
roys see ROSE
royt see ROYET¹·²
ruan see ROAN²
rub¹·¹, †**rubb** /rʌb/ *n* 1 an act or spell of rubbing *19-*. 2 *golf* an accidental factor affecting the resting place of the ball in play for which the player receives no compensation *19-*. 3 a slight jibe, reproof or teasing *la19-*. 4 an obstacle, impediment *17-e19*. [see the verb]
rub¹·², †**rubb** /rʌb/ *v* 1 to subject to a degree of friction and pressure by movement to and fro *la15-*. 2 to apply (ointment or polish) by rubbing *la16-*. 3 *in bowls and curling* to move (a bowl or stone) aside by knocking gently against it with another *19-*. 4 to grind (grain or peas) into meal *16-17*. **rubber**, †**ruber** a brush or cloth for rubbing or scrubbing to clean or polish; a scrubbing-brush *16-19, 20- WC*. **rubbins** liniment, embrocation *20- Sh Ork*. **rubbing bottle** a bottle of liniment or embrocation *20-*. **rubbin stane** pipeclay used to whiten doorsteps *20- Ork C Bor*. **rubbing stick** a stick used by shoemakers to rub leather smooth *20- Ork*. **rubbing stock** a post in a field for cattle to rub themselves against *18- Ork NE T*. **rubbin tub** a vat used for cleaning the husks off corn *20- Sh*. **rub aff o** to rub, wipe *la19- Sh Ork*. **rub fra** to remove by rubbing *16-*. †**rub on** to shame; to imply evil of, accuse; to impinge on *17*. **rub oot o** = *rub aff o*. [ME *rubben*; compare LG *rubben*, Norw *rubba*]
rub see ROB
ruban see RIBBON
†**rubber**, **rubbour** *n* a cask, barrel *la14-e18*. [unknown; compare Lat *robur* a kind of hard oak; oaken or made of a hard wood]
rubbish, **rubbage** /'rʌbɪʃ, 'rʌbədʒ/ *n* 1 *in mining and building* waste material (of stone, lime or wood) *17-*. 2 domestic waste; a brokendown object or person *18-*. 3 stones or weeds cleared from farmland *19-*. 4 a thing of little value; nonsense *19-*. [ME *robous*; compare AN *rubbouse*]
rubeatour see RABIATOR
ruch see ROUCH¹·³, ROUCH¹·⁴
ruck¹·¹, †**ruk**, †**ruik**, †**rouk** /rʌk/ *n* 1 a stack of hay or corn *16-*. 2 a small temporary haystack made in the field during the drying process *19-*. 3 a heap of anything *la19- NE*. 4 a stack or heap of fuel, especially peats *16-19, 20- NE*. **ruck foun** a foundation of stones on which a stack is built *20- NE T EC SW*. **ruck heid** the tapering top of a stack *20- NE T EC SW Uls*. **ruck tow** the rope used to bind the thatch on a stack *20- NE T*. [ON *hraukr* a small stack]
ruck¹·², †**rouk** /rʌk/ *v* to pile up, stack up, build (hay or corn) into a stack *17-*. [see the noun]
ruck see ROOK¹·²
ruckie /'rʌke/ *n* a stone; a marble *20- Bor*. [probably diminutive form of Eng *rock* perhaps with influence from *yuckie*, diminutive of YUCK]
ruckity-coo see ROOKETTY-COO¹·¹, ROOKETTY-COO¹·²
ruckle¹·¹, *Sh* **rukkle** /'rʌkəl/ *n* a rattling or gurgling sound; a death rattle *19, 20- Sh SW Bor*. [compare Norw dial *rukl* a death rattle]

ruckle[1,2] /'rʌkəl/ *v presp* †**ruclande** to make a harsh rattling, gurgling or roaring sound, especially of the breathing of a dying person *16-*. [compare Norw dial *rukla* to make a rattling sound in the throat]

ruckle[2,1], *Sh* **rukkle** /'rʌkəl/ *n* **1** a wrinkle, fold, crease *la19-*. **2** a swell in the sea *20- Sh.* **ruckly** wrinkled, corrugated, uneven *20- Sh Ork.* [from the verb or, especially Sh and Ork, Norw dial *rukle*]

ruckle[2,2] /'rʌkəl/ *v* to wrinkle, crease, work into folds *la19-*. [EModE *ruckle*]

ruckle *see* RICKLE[1,1], RICKLE[1,1]

ruclande *see* RUCKLE[1,2]

ruction /'rʌkʃən/ *n* **1** a disturbance, a row *19-*. **2** a tumult in the sea *20- Sh.* [HibEng *ruction*, apparently from *insurrection*]

rud *see* REID[1,2], RUDE[2]

rüd *see* RÖD[2,1], RÖD[2,2]

rudas[1,1], †**roudes** /'rʌdəs/ *n* a coarse or masculine-looking woman; a bad-tempered woman *18-19, 20- NE.* **auld rudas** = RUDAS[1,1]. [unknown]

rudas[1,2], †**roudes** /'rʌdəs/ *adj* **1** *of a woman* ugly; cantankerous *19-*. **2** wild, undisciplined, irresponsible *la19-*. **3** *of a man* cantankerous, stubborn, rough-mannered *e19.* [unknown]

rudder, *EC SW* **rither**, †**ruddyr**, †**ruther** /'rʌdər; *EC SW* 'rɪðər/ *n* the steering mechanism of a ship *15-*. [OE *rōþor*]

ruddick /'rʌdɪk/ *n* a furrow or single strip dug across a field *la19- Sh.* [Norw *rodde* a row + -OCK]

ruddie[1,1] /'rʌdi/ *n* a loud, reverberating, frequently repeated, noise *19, 20- NE T.* [unknown; compare ROTHIE]

ruddie[1,2] /'rʌdi/ *v* to make a loud, repeated noise; to beat noisily on *19- N NE T.* [see the noun]

†**ruddoch** *n* term of contempt for a (bad-tempered) old person *la18-19.* [unknown; compare RUDAS[1,1]]

ruddy *see* REDDIE

ruddyr *see* RUDDER

rude[1], †**ruid**, †**roid** /rud/ *adj* **1** roughly or hurriedly made, not well-finished, coarse; uncultivated, wild *la14-*. **2** violent, rough; uncivil, discourteous *la14-*. **3** unlearned, unskilled; unrefined; inelegant *la14-16.* [ME *rude*]

†**rude**[2], **rud** *n* a pink or reddish complexion *la15-e19.* [OE *rudu*]

†**rude** *see* RUID

rudge[1,1] /rʌdʒ/ *n* a heap (of objects, originally stones) *20- Sh.* [see the verb]

rudge[1,2] /rʌdʒ/ *v* to gather (stones) from land and pile in heaps; to clear (pasture of dung) *19- Sh.* [ON *hryðja* to clear land]

rudge[2] /rʌdʒ/ *v* to rattle, grate *20- Ork.* [Norw dial *ryda* to cough, gurgle, Icel *hryðja* to cough up phlegm]

rue[1,1], **rew** /ru/ *n* regret, sorrow, compassion *16-*. **ruefu 1** pitiable, doleful *la16-*. **2** terrible, dreadful *19.* **tak the rue**, *EC SW* **mak a rue 1** to repent, regret; to change one's mind *la18-*. **2** to take offence or a dislike *20- SW Bor.* [OE *hrēow*]

rue[1,2], **rew** /ru/ *v* **1** to regret *la14-*. **2** to regret a promise or bargain; to withdraw from a bargain or contract *la16-19, 20- N T SW.* **3** to pity; to have pity on *la14-19, 20- T EC.* **4** to repent *16-e17.* **rue-bargain** money given as compensation for breaking a bargain or withdrawing from an agreement *19, 20- SW Bor Uls.* [OE *hrēowan* to rue, grieve, *hrēowian* to repent]

rue[2] /ru/ *v* to drizzle; to talk in a rambling manner *20- Ork.* [Norw dial *rjoa, ry* to drizzle, chatter]

rue[3] /ru/ *v* to sway; to move jerkily *20- Ork.* [Norw dial *ro* to rock, swing]

rue *see* REW

ruf *see* RUIF[1,1]

rufe *see* RO[2,1], RO[2,2], RUIF[1,1], RUIVE[1,1]

ruff[1,1] /rʌf/ *n* **1** a drumming on the floor with the feet to indicate approval or applause *19, 20- N NE.* **2** the beating of a drum, a drum-roll preceding a proclamation *la18-e19.* [probably imitative of a drum-roll]

ruff[1,2] /rʌf/ *v* **1** to beat (a drum); to beat a roll on (a drum); *of a drum* to sound a roll *18-19, 20- NE EC.* **2** to applaud or show approval by stamping the feet *la18-19, 20- NE C.* **3** to show disapproval, silence (a speaker) by stamping or shuffling with the feet *la18-19, 20- NE EC.* **ruff doon** to show disapproval, silence (a speaker) by stamping or shuffling with the feet *la19, 20- NE EC.* [see the noun]

ruff[2] /rʌf/ *v* to rumple, ruffle (the hair) *20- Sh.* [probably back-formation from RUFFLE[1,2]]

ruff *see* REEF

ruffie[1], †**roughie** /'rʌfe/ *n* a torch or light, a fir-brand, a wick of rag smeared with tallow; a torch used when fishing for salmon at night *la18-*. [unknown; compare ME, EModE *ruff* candle, candle wick]

ruffie[2], **ruffy** /'rʌfe/ *n* **1** the Devil *19, 20- EC SW Bor.* **2** a devil or fiend *la15-16.* **3** a ruffian *16.* **4** a person playing the part of a fiend in the St Nicholas Day festivities *e16.* [reduced form of *Ruffin* the name of a demon]

ruffle[1,1], †**ruffill**, †**riffle** /'rʌfəl/ *n* **1** a flounce or frill *la17-*. **2** a superficial injury; damage; impairment *15-e17.* [unknown;]

ruffle[1,2], †**riffle** /'rʌfəl/ *v* **1** to throw into disarray or disorder *la14-*. **2** to confuse, bewilder, trouble, vex *la15-*. **3** to spoil the smoothness (of cloth, feathers or hair) *la16-*. **4** to damage, break *la17-e18.* [unknown]

†**ruffle**[1,3] *n* a skirmish; a setback, a defeat *la16-e18.* [see the verb]

†**ruffle**[2], **riffle** *v* to sack, pillage; to plunder, loot *15-e18.* [unknown; compare Du *roffelen* to thrash, seize;]

ruffy *see* RUFFIE[2]

rug[1,1], **rugg** /rʌg/ *n* **1** a pull, a rough, hasty tug *15-*. **2** a tug on a fishing-line when a fish has been hooked, a bite *la19- Sh Ork N NE T C.* **3** a strong undercurrent in the sea, a strong tide *la19- Sh NE T EC.* **4** a bargain, especially one which takes unfair advantage of the seller; an unreasonably high profit *18-19, 20- NE T H&I C.* **5** a twinge or pang of nerves or emotions *la19- NE T C.* **6** *of grazing animals* a bite of grass, a feed *la18-19, 20- NE SW.* **7** a knot or tangle of hair *20- Ork NE.* **8** a share, portion, especially of an abstract quality *19, 20- N.* **9** a good match, a catch *e18.* **ruggie** *of hair* tangled, difficult to comb; *of a situation* difficult *la19- NE T C Bor.* **nae great rug** not much of a catch, no great shakes *la18, 20- Ork.* [see the verb]

rug[1,2], *N* **roog** /rʌg; *N* rug/ *v* **1** to pull vigorously or forcibly, tug, drag, draw down, out, up or at *la14-*. **2** *of pain, hunger, an empty stomach* to gnaw, ache, nag *18-19, 20- NE T Uls.* **3** to break or tear off *la14-17.* **4** to tear apart *la15-17.* **5** to take without consent, remove forcibly or violently *la16-17.* **rug-saw** a two-handed or cross-cut saw *la16-18, 20- WC.* †**rug and reive** to rob *la15-16.* **rug and rive** to tear at, rend; to pull or tug vigorously; to struggle, tussle *19-.* **rug awa i the face o'd** to work persistently at a tedious task *20- Ork.* [compare Norw *rugga*, Faer *rugga* rock]

rug[2] /rʌg/ *n* mist, drizzle *18- Sh Ork.* [compare Dan *rug*]

†**ruge** *n* roaring *e16.* [Lat *rugīre* to roar]

rugfis, †**rugfus**, †**rugface** /'rʌgfəs/ *adj* rough *19- Ork.* [unknown]

rugg *see* RUG[1,1]

ruggie /'rʌgi/ *n* **1** an undersized, old or thin cod *19- Sh Ork.* **2** an inhabitant of North Sanday *20- Ork.* [unknown; compare Norn *rag* an emaciated or miserable creature]

ruggle, rookle /ˈrʌɡəl, ˈrukəl/ *v* to shake, rock *la19- Sh.*
ruglie, ruckly unsteady, insecure *la19- Sh.* [Norw dial *rugga* to rock]

ruggy *see* RUGSIE

rugh *see* ROUCH¹·³

rugsie, ruggy /ˈrʌɡzi, ˈrʌɡi/ *adj* loutish; ramshackle *20- Ork.* [Norw dial *rugga* to rock]

ruid, rood, rude, *NE SW* **reed** /rud; *NE SW* rid/ *n* **1** the cross on which Christ was crucified *la14-.* **2** a piece of ground measuring a ruid in area; land measured in terms of ruids; sometimes cultivated land belonging to a burgh, frequently in place-names *13-.* **3** a measurement of area equal to 36 square ells (approx 36 m²) *15-19, 20- NE T.* **4** a linear measure, 6 ells (approx 6 metres) *la14-e19.* **5** *building as a measurement of work done* an area of 36 square ells or yards of walls built, slates laid, roads made *la15-19.* **6** a measurement of area equal to 40 square ells (approx a quarter of an acre or a tenth of a hectare) *15-e19.* **7** a measure of timber *la15-16.* **8** a crucifix *la13-16.* †**rude altar** an altar of the Holy Cross *15-e17.* **Ruid-day 1** the day of the Exaltation of the Cross, 14 September *la15-.* **2** the day of the Invention of the Cross, 3 May *la16-19, 20- N NE.* †**Ruid even 1** the eve of *Ruid-day* (sense 2) *17- NE.* **2** the eve of *Ruid-day* (sense 1) *la14-19.* **Ruid fair** a fair or market held on *Ruid-day 16-19, 20- SW.* **Rudemass,** †**rudemes** = *Ruid-day 16-.* **Reed-Day in barlan** = *Ruid-day* (sense 2) *20- N.* **Reed-day in hairst,** †**Rude-day in harvest** = *Ruid-day* (sense 1) *16-.* †**the Rude** a chapel, altar, church, endowment so named *la15-e16.* [OE *rūd*]

ruid *see* RUDE¹

ruif¹·¹, **roof,** *Sh* **ruf,** *NE* **reef,** *EC* **riff,** †**rufe** /ruf; *NE* rif; *EC* rɪf/ *n* **1** the permanent exterior upper covering of a building *la14-.* **2** the ceiling of a room or other covered area *la15-.* **3** the wooden substructure supporting the exterior covering of a building *la15-18.* **4** a canopy, tester *la15-17.* **rooftree 1** the main beam or ridge of a roof *16-.* **2** a house, home *18-.* [OE *hrōf*]

ruif¹·², **roof** /ruf/ *v* to furnish with a RUIF¹·¹ *17-.* [see the noun]

ruif *see* RUIVE¹·²

ruik *see* ROOK¹·¹, RUCK¹·¹

ruin¹·¹, †**rewine,** †**rewyne** /ruən/ *n* **1** (an agent of) destruction; a state of collapse; a decline, a downfall *la14-.* **2** the remains of a decayed or fallen building *la16-.* [ME *ruin*]

ruin¹·², †**rewine,** †**ruyne** /ruən/ *v* to destroy, defeat; to come or reduce to ruin or disaster *la16-.* **ruinage** destruction, spoiling, ruination *20- Sh NE.* †**rewinate** bring to ruin, destroy, demolish; impoverish *la16-17.* [MFr *ruiner*]

ruind, rin, †**rund,** †**roon** /rʌɪnd, rɪn/ *n* **1** the border or selvage of a web of cloth; a strip of cloth *la17-.* **2** any thin strip of material, a shred, fragment *la18-e19.* **ruind shune** shoes made of strips of selvages of cloth *19-.* [unknown; compare Norw dial *rune* threadbare garment]

ruise¹·¹, **roose,** *NE* **reese,** †**ruse,** †**ruys** /ruz; *NE* riz/ *n* praise, commendation, flattery; boasting; a boast *la14-.* [ON *hrós*]

ruise¹·², **roose,** *NE* **reese,** †**ruse,** †**ruys** /ruz; *NE* riz/ *v* **1** to praise; to flatter *15-19, 20- Sh Ork N NE SW Bor.* **2** to boast *15-17.* [ON *hrósa*]

ruist *see* ROOST¹

ruit¹·¹, **root, rit,** *Sh* **röt,** *N NE* **reet,** †**rute** /rut, rɪt; *Sh* røt; *N NE* rit/ *n* **1** the underground part of a plant or tree *la14-.* **2** the embedded or basal part of the nails, hair or teeth; the part of anything by which it is joined to something else *15-.* **3** a source or foundation *15-.* **4** a person's lineage *la15-.* **5** the root of a plant used as food or medicine *16-.* **6** a dried tree root used as firewood, especially one dug up from a bog *19-.* **7** the bottom of a hedge *19-.* **8** the base of a wall *16-e17.* **at the root o yer tongue** *of a thing* almost but not quite remembered, on the tip of one's tongue *la19-.* †**the rute of your hert** the essential part of one's being, the bottom of one's heart *16.* **the reet and the rise o** the source and every aspect of (something) *la19- NE.* †**rute and ryne of** the complete or perfect manifestation of (something) *e16.* [ME *rote*, ON *rót*]

ruit¹·², **root,** †**rute** /rut/ *v* **1** to implant, establish *la14-.* **2** to remove (by force or effort); eradicate, wipe out *la15-.* [see the noun]

ruit², **root,** *N SW* **reet** /rut; *N SW* rit/ *v* **1** *of a pig* to dig with the snout *la16-.* **2** to poke about, rummage, search; to leave things in confusion as a result of searching *la19- Sh Ork N SW.* **3** to work in a clumsy, ineffective way *20- N.* **reet and fyke** = RUIT² (sense 3). [OE *wrōtan*]

ruith *see* REUTH¹·¹

ruive¹·¹, **roove,** †**rufe,** †**rove** /ruv/ *n* especially *boat-building* a burr, a metal washer on which the point of a nail or bolt can be clinched; a rivet *la15-.* [ON *ró*]

ruive¹·², **roove,** †**ruif** /ruv/ *v* to rivet, clinch (a nail or bolt); to fix firmly *la16-.* [see the noun]

ruk *see* RUCK¹·¹

ruke *see* ROOK¹·¹

rukka /ˈrʌkə/ *n* a long period of absence; a long journey *20- Sh.* [Norw *ruke* a period of time]

rukkle *see* RUCKLE¹·¹, RUCKLE²·¹

rūl, *Ork* rool /røl/ *n* a young horse, a pony *19- Sh Ork.* [reduced form of Norw *ruvel* a shaggy little creature]

rule¹·¹, *NE* **roule,** †**reule,** †**rewill,** †**rewle** /rul; *NE* rʌul/ *n* **1** a regulation or principle *la14-.* **2** authority or government *la15-.* **3** a measuring rod; a line *16-.* †**reulie** orderly *la15.* [ME *reule*]

rule¹·², *NE* **roule,** †**reule,** †**rewill,** †**rewle** /rul; *NE* rʌul/ *v* **1** to control, guide, direct *15-.* **2** to curb, restrain (behaviour or oneself) *la15-.* **3** to wield (power or authority); to govern *la15-.* **4** to take charge of; to manage; to keep (*eg* a clock) in good order *la15-e17.* **5** *of prices* to be at a certain rate, be current *17.* **6** to arrange, set in order *la15-e17.* **ruling elder** *Presbyterian Church* a person who has been ordained as a church elder; a governing or lay elder as opposed to a teaching elder or minister *17-.* [ME *reulen*]

rullion, *Sh Ork* **rivlin,** *N* **rilling,** †**riveling,** †**revelyn,** †**ryllyng** /ˈrʌljən; *Sh Ork* ˈrɪvlɪn; *N* ˈrɪlɪŋ/ *n* **1** a coarse, ungainly, rough-looking person or animal *19-.* **2** a shoe of undressed hide *15-19, 20- Sh Ork N historical.* **3** *pl* rags, tatters, cheap cloth *19-, 20- N.* [OFr *revelin*]

rullye *see* RALLY³

rult¹·¹, *Sh* **roilt,** *Ork* **reult** /rʌlt, rult; *Sh* rɔɪlt; *Ork* rølt/ *n* **1** a slouching, rolling gait; a lurch, roll *20- Sh Ork.* **2** an awkward, shapeless object *20- Sh.* [Norw dial *rult* one who walks in a flat-footed way]

rult¹·², *Ork* **reult** /rʌlt, rult; *Ork* rølt/ *v* to walk with a slouching, rolling gait *la19- Sh Ork.* [Norw dial *rulta* to fall, tumble]

rulʒe *see* ROOLYIE

rum¹ /rʌm/ *adj* boorish, coarse in manner or speech *20- NE WC SW.* [extended sense of Eng *rum* bad, suspect]

†**rum**² *n pl mining* an inferior bituminous shale; a bend or dislocation in a stratum *19.* [unknown]

rum *see* ROOM¹·¹

rum- *see* RAM-.

rumateese *see* RHEUMATISE

rumballiach, rambaleugh /rəmˈbaljəx/ *adj* tempestuous, stormy *19- Bor.* [unknown]

rumble see RUMMLE[1.1], RUMMLE[1.2], RUMMLE[1.3]

rumbledethump, rumeltythump, rumelythump /ˈrʌmbəldəθʌmp, ˈrʌməltiθʌmp/ n **1** mashed potatoes with milk, butter and seasoning *19, 20- WC SW*. **2** mashed potatoes with cabbage (or turnip) *19, 20- T EC*. **3** oatmeal and onions fried in fat *20- T* [RUMMLE[1.2] + *de* + THUMP[1.1]]

rumbursin see RIMBURST

rumburst /ˈrʌmbʌrst/ v to rupture *20- Ork Uls.* [RIM[3] + *burst* (BIRST[1.2])]

rumfording, rumfoordin /rʌmˈfɜrdɪn/ n a metal lining for the back of a fireplace *20- T Bor.* [from Count von Rumford (1753-1814) who suggested this method of improving smoky chimneys; compare Eng *rumfordize*]

rumgumption /rʌmˈgʌmʃən/ n common sense, understanding, shrewdness *la17-*. [unknown; compare RUMMLEGUMPTION]

rumle see RUMMLE[1.2]

rummage see REEMAGE[1.1], REEMAGE[1.2]

rummill see RUMMLE[1.1], RUMMLE[1.2]

†**rummis, rummish** v **1** to roar, bellow; to (cause to) make a rumbling, crashing noise *la15-e19*. **2** to protest loudly, make an uproar *e16*. [unknown]

rummle[1.1], **rumble,** †**rummill,** †**rummyll** /ˈrʌməl, ˈrʌmbəl/ n **1** a severe blow *la14-*. **2** a deep continuous grumbling sound like distant thunder *16-*. **3** a sudden impetus, a rush *la19- Sh NE WC*. **4** a mixture, concoction; something confused or disordered *19, 20- Sh EC Bor*. **5** a rough knocking or beating *19-, 20- NE WC*. **6** a movement causing a rumbling sound; a commotion, tumult; a vigorous stir, a rough jolting *la17, 20- Sh C*. **7** a badly built piece of masonry, a ruin; something ugly or dilapidated *la19- Sh NE*. **8** *derogatory* a large clumsy person; a rough reckless person *20- WC SW*. [see the verb]

rummle[1.2], **rumble,** †**rummill,** †**rumle,** †**rummyll** /ˈrʌməl, ˈrʌmbəl/ v **1** to make a low continuous rumbling sound *16-*. **2** to stir or shake vigorously; to mash (potatoes), scramble (eggs) *18-*. **3** to toss about restlessly in bed *20- NE T WC SW Bor*. **4** to clear (a narrow passage, especially a tobacco pipe) with a rod or wire *la19, 20- NE T WC SW*. **5** to strike or beat severely; jolt, handle roughly *la19- C SW Bor*. **6** to feel (in one's pocket) for something *20- C Bor*. **7** to knock violently or throw stones (at a door) as a prank *20- NE WC*. **8** *of a building* to collapse *20- Sh NE*. **9** to pick (someone's pocket), rob *e19*. **10** to make a noise or disturbance; move about noisily or riotously *la16-19*. **rummlin 1** *of a person* boisterous, full of mischief; slapdash *19-*. **2** *of a drain* filled with loose stones *la18-19*. **rummlin kirn** a deep narrow gully on the seashore where the tide makes a loud rumbling noise *19- SW*. **rummlegarie 1** a wild, reckless, or thoughtless person *la18-*. **2** a nonsensical speech *20- Uls*. **3** wild and unruly *18-e19*. **rummilskeerie** a wild reckless person *la19- C*. **rumble tumble** (full of) noisy confusion *la19- T C Bor*. **rummle up** *football* to jostle, charge (one's opponent); to play a rough attacking game *20-*. [MDu, MLG *rummelen*]

rummle[1.3], **rumble** /ˈrʌməl, ˈrʌmbəl/ adj *of a drain* filled with loose stones *18-19, 20- N WC SW*. [see the verb; compare *rummlin* **2** (RUMMLE[1.2])]

rummlegumption /rʌməlˈgʌmʃən/ n **1** understanding, common sense, level-headedness *la18-*. **2** *humorous* frequently *pl* wind in the stomach, flatulence *la19, 20- WC SW*. **3** courage, pluck *20- NE*. [unknown; compare RUMGUMPTION]

rummlie /ˈrʌmle/ adj **1** *of soil* rough and stony; hence loose and crumbly *20- NE SW*. **2** *of a person* disordered, jumbled; untidy *20- Sh NE*. **rummlieguts** *derogatory* a voluble, senseless talker, a windbag *20- EC SW Bor*. [RUMMLE[1.1] + -IE[2]]

rummyll see RUMMLE[1.1], RUMMLE[1.2]

rumour /ˈrumər/ n **1** general or widespread talk or report, hearsay; an instance of this *15-*. **2** noise, din, outcry *la15-19*. **3** the crying or noise made by birds or animals *16*. [ME *rumour*]

rump[1.1] /rʌmp/ n **1** the part of the body (in an animal or bird) where the tail starts; the posterior, the buttocks *19-*. **2** a hind-quarter cut of beef, *round-steak* (ROUND) *la19-*. **3** *derogatory* a person or animal *16-19*. **rumpie** a small crusty loaf or roll *19-*. **rumpie-pumpie** sexual intercourse; copulation *la20-*. **rump steak** = RUMP[1.1] (sense 2). **rump and stump** completely, to the very last piece or fragment *19-*; compare *stump and rump* (STUMP[1.1]). [ON *rumpr*]

rump[1.2] /rʌmp/ v **1** to cut, clip or crop very short *la18-*. **2** to eat down to the roots *la19- T SW Bor*. **3** to plunder, expropriate, win (all a person's money or belongings); to make bankrupt *19- NE T EC Bor*. **4** *marbles* to win all a person's marbles *20- T C*. **5** to dock (a horse's tail) *la17-e18*. [see the noun]

†**rumpill** n a fold, pleat *e16*. [MDu *rompel*, MLG *rumpel*]

rumple, †**trumpill** /ˈrʌmpəl/ n **1** the tail, hindquarters, haunches (of an animal or fish) *15-19, 20- Sh N*. **2** the buttocks, seat (of a person) *la16-19, 20- Sh*. **rumple-bane** the coccyx *la18-*. [RUMP[1.1], with -*le* suffix]

rumption /ˈrʌmʃən/ n a state of noisy, bustling disorder, an uproar *19-*. [perhaps conflation of Eng *rumpus* and RUCTION]

rumse[1] /rʌms/ v to move uneasily, stir, toss about during sleep *20- Sh Ork*. [Norw dial *romsa*]

rumse[2], **rumps** /rʌms, rʌmps/ v to rummage; to make a disturbance *20- Sh Ork*. [unknown; compare OIcel *runsa* to turn inside out, ransack]

run see RIN[1.1], RIN[1.2]

runch[1], †**runsch** /rʌnʃ/ n a weed found in cornfields, generally identified as the wild radish *Raphanus raphanistrum la16-*. **runchick, runchech,** †**ruinscheoch** = RUNCH[1] *la16-19, 20- Sh Ork*. **runchie,** *Ork* **runsho** = RUNCH[1] *19, 20- Sh Ork*. [unknown]

†**runch**[2.1] n a crunching, grinding *19*. [see the verb]

runch[2.2] /rʌnʃ/ v to crunch, grind, crush *la19-, 20- WC*. [perhaps a variant of RUNDGE to chew with influence from *crunch*]

runch see WRANCH[1.1], WRANCH[1.2]

runchie, runsheoch, runcy /ˈrʌnʃe, ˈrʌnʃɔx, ˈrʌnse/ n a coarse raw-boned person *19- NE EC*. [unknown]

rund see RUIND

rundge, †**rounge,** †**runge** /rʌndʒ/ v **1** to devour, swallow up *18-*. **2** to chew, gnaw, champ *e16*. **3** to clip (coins) *16-17*. [ME *roungen*, EModE *rounge*]

rundie see RIN[1.1]

rune /run/ n **1** a Germanic character or letter shape *19-*. **2** a cryptic rhyme or incantation; an incantatory noise *20-*. [ON *rún*]

rung[1.1], †**roung,** †**rong** /rʌŋ/ n **1** a spoke, tread of a ladder, rail or crossbar *16-*. **2** a stout stick; a cudgel *la15-19, 20- N NE SW Uls*. **3** a blow with a stick; a thump, whack *la19- Sh NE T EC*. **4** *derogatory* a bad-tempered person; a large, ugly person or animal; a thin, scraggy animal *19- NE Bor*. **rung-backed** *of a chair* having a back of wooden spokes or spars *20- Sh Ork N SW*. †**rung cart** a primitive cart constructed from the trunks of saplings and stout sticks *la18-19*. [OE *hrung*]

rung[1.2] /rʌŋ/ v **1** to make or fit (eg a ladder, cart, chair) with spars or rungs *16-*. **2** to beat with a stick, cudgel *19, 20- Sh NE T*. [see the noun]

rung[2.1] /rʌŋ/ n a hollow ringing sound *la19- Sh*. [see the verb]

rung[2.2] /rʌŋ/ v **1** to resound, reverberate, boom *la19- Sh*. **2** to play (a fiddle) *la19- Sh*. [Norw *runge*]

rung see RING[2.2], RING[3.2]

rungyn see RING[3.2]
runk[1] /rʌŋk/ n **1** a cabbage-stalk, especially when hard and withered *20- N NE*. **2** an emaciated, worn-out person, animal or thing *19, 20- Sh N NE*. **3** *derogatory* a bad-tempered woman *20- NE*. [altered form of RUNT[1], perhaps by association with RUNKLE[1.1]]
runk[2] /rʌŋk/ v to deprive (a person) of all his money or possessions, bankrupt *19, 20- NE T EC*. [unknown]
runk[3.1] /rʌŋk/ n a clearing-up, a lull *20- Sh*. [see the verb]
runk[3.2] /rʌŋk/ v *of weather* to clear up; *of rain* to stop *la19- Sh*. [probably altered form of Norn *lunk*]
runk[4] /rʌŋk/ n anything large or bulky *20- Sh Ork*. [unknown]
runk see RANK[1.2]
runker /'rʌŋkər/ n **1** the lumpfish *Cyclopterus lumpus la19- N NE*. **2** a species of wrasse, the goldsinny *Ctenolabrus rupestris*, the rock cook *Centrolabrus exoletus* or the ballan wrasse *Labrus bergylta 20- NE*. [unknown]
runkle[1.1], †**runcle**, †**runkill** /'rʌŋkəl/ n a wrinkle, crease, ridged indentation *16-*. **runkly** wrinkled *la18-*. **runkillit** wrinkled, creased, furrowed *la15-*. [unknown; compare Norw dial *rukle*]
runkle[1.2], †**runkill** /'rʌŋkəl/ v **1** to wrinkle *19-*. **2** to crease, rumple, crush *18-*. **3** to gnarl, twist, distort, curl *18-19, 20- T C*. [see the noun]
runnalan /'rʌnələn/ n an open drain or gutter *19- Sh*. [derivative of Eng *runnel*]
runnel see RINNAL
runnick /'rʌnək/ n an open drain or gutter *19- Sh Ork*. [diminutive form of Norw *renne* a ditch]
†**runnie** n *in Shetland* a male pig, a boar *19*. [ON *runi*]
running see RINNING[1.1], RINNING[1.2]
runnyn see RIN[1.2]
runrig[1.1], †**rinrig** /'rʌnrɪg/ n a system of joint landholding by which each tenant had several detached strips or rigs of land allocated in rotation by lot each year, so that each would have a share in turn of the more fertile land; such a portion of land *15-18, 19- H&I historical*. [RIN[1.2] + RIG[1.1]]
runrig[1.2], †**rinrig** /'rʌnrɪg/ adj *of land* divided up and cultivated under the runrig system *16-18, 19- historical*. [see the noun]
†**runsy** n a riding horse *la15-e16*. [ME *rounci*]
runt[1] /rʌnt/ n **1** an old or decayed tree or tree-stump *16*. **2** the hardened, withered stem of a cabbage or kail plant *17-*. **3** a short, thickset person; an undersized or dwarfish person or animal *20-*. **4** the smallest pig in a litter *20- Ork T C SW Bor Uls*. **5** *derogatory* a coarse, gnarled, ill-natured person, especially an old woman; a general term of contempt for a person or thing *la16-19, 20- Sh NE T EC Uls*. **6** the tail of an animal; the rump, the upper part of the tail *la18- SW*. **runtit 1** stunted *la18- SW*. **2** completely deprived of one's possessions; made bankrupt *la19- NE SW*; compare RUNK[2]. [unknown]
runt[2] /rʌnt/ n an ox or cow for fattening and slaughter, a store animal, frequently a Highland cow or ox; an old cow (past breeding and fattened for slaughter) *18-*. [unknown; compare MDu *runt* ox, cow]
rur, rhur /rur/ n a barnacle *20- Sh*. [reduced form of ROODER]
rural, †**rurall** /'rurəl/ adj **1** living in, characteristic of, the country, pastoral; simple, unsophisticated *la15-*. **2** *law of a lease* relating to land as opposed to buildings (whether in the country or in the town) *la17-*. [MFr *rural*, Lat *rūrālis*]
rus, N **roos** /rus/ n **1** great activity or bustle, a hurry *la19- Sh*. **2** a storm, bad weather *20- Sh N*. **3** a blazing fire *la20 Sh*. [Norw dial *rusk* bustle, windy weather]
ruse see RUISE[1.1], RUISE[1.2]

rush[1.1], †**rusch** /rʌʃ/ n **1** a sudden violent movement; a violent impact *15-*. **2** the rash, associated with scarlet fever *18-*. **3** a luxuriant growth of vegetation or hair *20- Sh Ork T*. **4** dysentery, especially in sheep or cattle *la18-e19*. **5** a crashing noise *la15-e16*. **rushie** a noisy squabble or scramble *19, 20- EC*. **rooshie-doo** = *rushie la19, 20- NE*. **rush fever** scarlet fever *la18-19, 20- C*. [see the verb]
rush[1.2], †**rusch** /rʌʃ/ v **1** to move with speed, force or urgency *la14-*. **2** to force (an opponent) to move by the application of force or violent impetus; to move in this way *la14-*. **3** to flirt with, court (a girl) *20-*. **4** *especially of sheep or cattle* to suffer from dysentery *20- N EC Bor*. **5** to fall quickly or violently *la14-e16*. [perhaps AN *russher* or AN, OFr *ruser* to push back]
rush see RASH[1]
rushyroo /'rʌʃiru/ n the shrew *Sorex araneus 20-*. [altered form of Eng *earthshrew*]
rusk see ROOSK
ruskie[1] /'rʌske/ n **1** a straw basket *la17-*. **2** a basket for holding meal or seed-corn *18-19, 20- T H&I*. **3** a straw beehive *la19- NE T EC Bor*. **4** *in the Borders* a straw sunbonnet *19*. [Gael *rùsgan* a kind of basket; a kind of dish used to measure meal]
†**ruskie**[2] adj strong, vigorous, rough *19*. [unknown; compare Gael *rùsgaire* a strong, brawny person]
†**russet, russat** n a (coarse or cheap) woollen cloth *14-e19*. [AN *russet*]
russie /'rʌsi/ n a stallion *20- Sh*. **russie-foal 1** a foal with a matted shaggy coat *20- Sh*. **2** a native of Fetlar *la19- Sh*. [ON *hross* a horse]
russle see RIZZAR
rust see ROOST[1], ROOST[2.1], ROOST[2.2], ROWST[1.2]
†**rusticate** adj countrified, boorish *la15*. [Lat *rusticātus*]
rustle see REESLE[1.1], REESLE[1.2]
rut see RIT[1.2]
rute see RUIT[1.1]
ruth, rooth, †**routh**, †**routht**, †**rowth** /ruθ/ n **1** a reinforced part of the gunwale where the oar rests *19- Sh Ork N NE*. **2** (a long spell of) rowing *15-e16, 19- Sh*. **3** a stroke of the oars *e16*. [ON *róðr* an act of rowing]
ruther /'rʌðər/ n **1** turmoil, chaos, ruin *20- NE*. **2** an outcry, uproar *la18-19*. [unknown]
ruther see RUDDER
ruve see RO[2.1], RO[2.2]
ruyne see RUIN[1.2]
ruys see RUISE[1.1], RUISE[1.2]
rwch see ROUCH[1.3]
ryal, †**rial**, †**ryall** /'raeəl/ n a gold or silver coin *la15-e19, la19- historical*. [OFr *rial* royal]
ryatous see RIOTOUS
rybat, *H&I EC* **ribbit**, †**rabet**, †**rebet** /'raebət; *H&I EC* 'rɪbət/ n the reveal or side of the jamb of a door or window *15-*. [ME *rabet*]
ryce see RICE
ryches see RICHES
rycht see RICHT[1.1], RICHT[1.2], RICHT[1.3], RICHT[1.4]
rychtwis see RICHTEOUS
ryd see RIDE[1.2]
ryddill, rydle see RIDDLE[2]
ryf see RIFE[1.1], RIFE[1.2], RIFE[1.3]
ryfe see RIVE[1.2]
ryfft see RIFT[1.1]
ryft see RIFT[2.1]
ryg see RIG[1.1]
ryis see RISE[1.2]
ryllyng see RULLION

ryme see RHYME[1.1], RHYME[1.2], RIM[3]
ryn see RIN[1.2]
rynd see RIND[1], RIND[2.2]
ryne see RIN[1.2]
ryng see RING[1.1], RING[2.2], RING[3.2]
rynggyt see RING[1.2]
rynk see RINK[1.1]
rynmart see RIN MAIRT
rynnyng see RINNING[1.1]
ryot see RIOT[1.1], RIOT[1.2]

ryotus see RIOTOUS
rype see RIPE[1.2]
ryppet see RIPPET
rys see RISE[1.1], RISE[1.2]
rysing see RISE[1.2]
rysp see RISP[2]
ryve see RIVE[1.2]
ryw see RIVE[1.1]
ryward see REWAIRD[1.2]

S

-s, **†-is** /s/ *suffix forming adverbs* having some quality of the root noun *16-*. [from the genitive singular inflection of nouns]

sa *see* SAE[1], SAE[2.1], SAY[1.2], SEE

saam *see* SAME[1]

saat *see* SAUT[1.1], SAUT[1.2], SAUT[1.3]

sab[1.1], **sob** /sab, sɔb/ *n* **1** a convulsive sound; a sob *la15-*. **2** the noise made by the wind or the sea *19-*. [see the verb]

sab[1.2], **sob** /sab, sɔb/ *v* to weep noisily, to wail *la14-*. [ME *sobben*, probably onomatopoeic]

sab[2] /sab/ *v* to soak, saturate *la19- Sh Ork*. [Swed dial *sabba*]

†sab[3] *v* to subside or sink; to sag or droop *18-e19*. [unknown]

Sabbath, **Sawbath**, **†Saboth** /ˈsabəθ, ˈsɔbəθ/ *n* the seventh day of the week (as a day of rest and religious observance); Sunday *la14-*. **†sabbathly**, **sabothlie** *adv* every Sunday *17-e19*. **†sabbathly** *adj* recurring every Sunday *17-e19*. [Lat *sabbatum*]

sable, **†sabill** /ˈsebəl/ *n* **1** black *la15-*. **2** blackness, darkness *16*. [MFr *sable* black tincture in heraldry]

†Sabot *n* God *e16*. [Lat *Sabaōth* literally (Lord) transliterated from Greek *kyrios sabaōth* lord of hosts (as adopted from Hebrew), misunderstood as a name of God]

Saboth *see* SABBATH

sack *see* SECK[1.1], SECK[1.2]

sacket, **†saket** /ˈsakət/ *n* **1** a small sack or bag; a satchel *la15-19, 20- SW*. **2** a mischievous or impudent person *la19- T*. [OFr *saquet*]

sackless *see* SAKELESS

sacrament, **saicrament** /ˈsakrəmənt, ˈsekrəmənt/ *n* **1** *Christian Church* a solemn religious ceremony or act *la14-*. **2** *Christian Church* the Eucharist, the Lord's Supper or Holy Communion *la14-*. **3** *Christian Church* the consecrated elements used in religious ceremonies *la15-*. **4** *Presbyterian Church* the period from Thursday to the following Monday including Communion and the other services *18-19, 20- Sh N H&I SW*. **†sacrament hous** a tabernacle *16*. **Sacrament Sabbath** = *Sacrament Sunday 19-*. **Sacrament Sunday** the Sunday of the Communion service *la18-*. [OFr *sacrement*, Lat *sacrāmentum*]

†sacre *v* **1** to perform a sacred office; to dedicate something to a deity *la14-e16*. **2** to invest a person in a sacred office *la14-e16*. [OFr *sacrer*]

sacreit *see* SECRET

†sacrify *v* **1** to consecrate *e19*. **2** to sacrifice; to offer as a sacrifice *la14-16*. [OFr *sacrifier*]

†sacring bell, **sacryne bell**, **secrrind bell** *n Roman Catholic Church* a small bell rung at the elevation of the host during the mass *la15-16*. [verbal noun from SACRE + BELL[1.1]]

sacrist /ˈsakrɪst/ *n* the chief porter and mace-bearer of King's College and Marischal College in Aberdeen *17- NE*. [OFr *sacriste*, Lat *sacrista*]

sad[1.1] /sad/ *n* a thud, a thump; a heavy-pressing downward movement *19-*. [see the adj]

sad[1.2] /sad/ *v* **1** to become or make solid or firm *la16-*. **2** to compress or compact; to sink or settle down *la16-*. **3** to sadden *la16-e17*. **sadden** to make solid or firm *la18-19, 20- WC SW*. **saddit 1** *of bread* heavy, not fully baked *20- C SW Bor*. **2** *of earth* beaten hard, hard-packed *18- NE T WC*. **3** confirmed, strengthened *e16*. [see the adj]

sad[1.3], *NE* **sod** /sad; *N* sɔd/ *adj* **1** sorrowful, mournful, melancholy *la14-*. **2** causing sorrow, distressing, lamentable *la14-*. **3** *of bread or pastry* not risen, heavy *19-*. **4** remarkable, outstandingly good *la18- NE T*. **5** *of material objects* solid, dense; compact, firm *16-19, 20- WC SW*. **6** *of people* grave, sedate *la14-19*. **7** *of a blow* heavy, vigorous *la14-17*. **8** *of colour* dark, sombre *la15-17*. **9** *of people* steadfast, resolute, reliable *la14-16*. **10** *of people* weary, exhausted *la14-e16*. [OE *sæd* sated with, weary of, filled]

†sad[1.4] *adv* **1** having a severe or heavy effect *la15-19*. **2** firmly fixed *la15*. [see the adj]

sad *see* SAY[1.2]

saddle *see* SAIDLE[1.1], SAIDLE[1.2]

†sade *n* a turf, a sod *e19*. [MLG *sade*]

sadell *see* SAIDLE[1.1]

sadill *see* SAIDLE[1.1], SAIDLE[1.2], SATTLE[1.1]

sae[1], **sey**, **†sa**, **†say** /se/ *n* **1** a wooden tub used for transporting water *la14-19, 20- Sh Ork N NE SW*. **2** *in Glasgow and Paisley* a tub used as a measure for tanner's bark *17*. **sae-fu**, **seyfull**, **†safull** the fill of a tub *e16, 20- Sh Ork N*. **sae-tree** a pole by which a tub can be carried between two people *la19- Ork N*. [ON *sár* a cask]

sae[2.1], **say**, **so**, **†sa**, **†swa**, **†sua** /se, so/ *adv* **1** thus, in this manner *la14-*. **2** to such an extent or degree *la14-*. **3** in consequence *la14-*. **4** provided that, on condition that *la14-*. **5** indeed, actually: ◊*this is braw, so it is* ◊*you're a wee dodger, so you are 19- WC SW Uls*. **sae as** in order that *la19-*. **sae comin** characteristic *20- Ork*. **sae fer**, **sae far** to such an extent; to the extent that *15-*. **†sagat**, **swagate** thus *la14-e15*. **sae like** much the same as, in a similar manner *16-*. **sae muckle**, **†samekill 1** so much; to such an extent *la14-*. **2** equally, as much *15-*. **†sa done** extremely *16-e17*. **†gif sa beis** if it is so *la15-16*. **sae be**, **say be** it being the case that, provided that *la18-*. **sae bein**, **so-bein**, **†sa beand** that being so; provided that *16-*. [OE *swā*]

sae[2.2], **so** /se, so/ *interj* **1** an expression of resignation, satisfaction or approval *20- Sh Ork*. **so so 1** well then; very well *19, 20- Sh*. **2** no more; that is enough *20- Sh Ork*. [see the adv]

saed *see* SAY[1.2]

saep *see* SAIP

saf *see* SAUF

safe *see* SAUF, SAVE[2.1], SAVE[2.2], SAVE[2.3]

safer *see* SAUFEY

safety, **†savite**, **†safity**, **†salfty** /ˈsefte, ˈsefti/ *n* **1** security, freedom from danger *la14-*. **2** preservation, protection, keeping safe *la14-*. [AN *saufte*, AN, MFr, *savete*, *salvete*]

saff *see* SAVE[2.1]

safity *see* SAFETY

saft[1.1], **soft** /saft, sɔft/ *n* a thaw; rain, moisture *la19- T WC*. [see the adj]

†saft[1.2], **soft** *v* **1** to soothe or assuage *la14-e16*. **2** to mollify or appease *la15-16*. **3** to calm or restrain oneself *la15-e16*. **4** to weaken or diminish *la15-e16*. [see the adj]

saft[1.3], **soft** /saft, sɔft/ *adj* **1** not hard or sharp; yielding, flexible, malleable *la14-*. **2** soothing, gentle, smooth *la14-*. **3** *of ground* spongy, boggy; frequently in place-names *la14-*. **4** *of weather* mild, pleasant; in a state of thaw *15-*. **5** *of people* lenient, moderate; weak, easily imposed on *16-*. **6** *of*

saft *weather* wet, rainy, damp *19-*. **saften, †softine 1** to make soft or softer; to soothe or mitigate *la14-*. **2** to thaw *19, 20- NE*. **saftie, softie 1** a person with learning difficulties *la19-*. **2** a timid or effeminate male *la19-*. **3** a soft bread roll *20-*. **4** an edible crab which has cast its shell *la19- NE T EC*. **5** a soft carpet-slipper *20- NE T WC*. **saftick** an edible crab *la19- NE*. **saftly, saftlie, softly, †softlie 1** gently, tenderly; carefully, gradually *la14-*. **2** quietly, in a low voice *la15-*. **saft biscuit, soft biscuit** a plain floury bun or roll with an indentation in the middle *la19- Ork N NE T*. **saft mark, soft mark** a person who is easily imposed on *20-*. **hae a saft side tae** to have a special liking for; to be well disposed towards *20-*. [OE *sōfte*]

saft[1.4] /saft/ *adv* **1** quietly; gently *15-*. **2** easily, comfortably *la15-*. [OE *sōfte*]

sag /sag/ *v of the tide* to cease to flow; to be at the turn *la19- Sh*. [Eng *sag* to subside, sink; compare Norw dial *sagga* to go slowly]

sagan, saigen /ˈsagən, ˈsegən/ *n* a surly, rough or clumsy person *20- NE*. [perhaps euphemistic form of SAWTAN[1]]

sagat *see* SAE[2.1]

saich *see* SICH[1.2]

saicont *see* SECOND[1.2]

saicrament *see* SACRAMENT

saicret[1.1], **secret, †secreit** /ˈsekrət, ˈsikrət/ *n* something kept hidden; a mystery *la15-*. [MFr *secret*, Lat *sēcrētum*]

saicret[1.2], **secret, †secreit** /ˈsekrət, ˈsikrət/ *adj* **1** concealed, hidden, out of sight *la15-*. **2** private, secluded *la15-*. **3** discreet, confidential; clandestine *la15-*. **†Secret Counsall** a body of advisers; the Privy Council *la15-17*. **†secret members** the genitals *16-17*. **†secret seal** a lesser seal of a burgh *15-e17*. **†in secret wyse** secretly, clandestinely *la15*. [see the noun]

said *see* SAY[1.2]

saide *see* SAITHE

saidle[1.1], **seddle, saddle, †sadill, †sadell** /ˈsedəl, ˈsɛdəl, ˈsadəl/ *n* **1** a seat for a rider or support for a pack; the part of the harness that lies across a draught animal's back *la14-*. **2** *in Fife* the part of a stall on which an animal stood *19*. **3** *nautical* a block of wood fastened to a spar to take the bearing of another spar attached to it *16*. **saidle crub** the steel groove in the saddle of a cart horse in which the back-chain works *20- NE WC*. **†saddle lap** the side flaps of a saddle *e19*. [OE *sadol*]

saidle[1.2], **saddle, †sadill** /ˈsedəl, ˈsadəl/ *v* to fit or equip a horse with a saddle *la14-*. [OE *sadelian*]

saif *see* SALVE, SAUF, SAVE[2.1], SAVE[2.2], SAVE[2.3]

saiffing *see* SAVAND, SAVING

saige *see* SIEGE[1.1]

saigen *see* SAGAN

saik *see* SAKE, SECK[1.1]

saikles, saikless *see* SAKELESS

sail[1.1], *Sh* **sell, †saill, †sale** /sel; *Sh* sɛl/ *n* **1** a canvas sheet used to catch the wind and propel a boat *la14-*. **2** a boat, a ship *la15-17*. **3** a voyage, a maritime expedition *la14-*. **4** a ride in a cart or other vehicle; a ride on horseback *19-*. **5** a banner, placard or screen *la15-17*. **†sailrif** abounding in sails *e16*. **sailman** the man in charge of the sails in a fishing-boat *20- Sh*. [OE *segl*]

sail[1.2], *N* **seil, †saill, †sale** /sel; *N* sʌɪl/ *v* **1** to travel by boat; to journey by sea *la14-*. **2** to be flooded or inundated with liquid *18-*. **3** to ride or drive in a vehicle *20-*. **†sailage** *of a ship* the action of or ability to sail *la15-e17*. **sailor, †sailar 1** a person who travels by sea *la15-*. **2** a seaman, a mariner *la16-*. **3** a swimmer *e16*. [OE *seglan*]

†sail[2], **sale, saill** *n* a hall, a spacious chamber *la15-e17*. [OE *sæl*]

saill *see* SELL[2]

†sailyie[1.1], **sailȝe, sailzie** *n* **1** an assault *la15-e19*. **2** a projecting part of a building *16*. [OFr *saillie*]

sailyie[1.2], **†sailȝe, †sailzie, †saill** /ˈselji/ *v* **1** to assault or attack *la14-19, 20- literary*. **2** to add a projecting part to a building *la16-17*. [OFr *saillir*]

saim *see* SAME[1]

sain[1.1] /sen/ *n* a blessing; a gesture or invocation of goodwill and good fortune *19-*. [from the verb, ultimately from Lat *signum* a sign]

sain[1.2], **sane, †sayn** /sen/ *v* **1** to bless; to confer or invoke a blessing *la14-*. **2** to protect from harm by making the sign of the cross or reciting a prayer *la14-*. **3** to offer good wishes; to inaugurate with an act or ceremony *la18-19, 20- NE*. **4** to heal or cure *20- literary*. **God sain** God bless *18-19, 20- literary*. [OE *segnian* to make the sign of the cross]

sain *see* SAY[1.2]

saint[1.1], **saunt, sant, †sanct** /sent, sɔnt, sant/ *n* **1** a canonized person *la14-*. **2** a person of exemplary holiness or goodness *16-*. **3** *Presbyterian Church* one of the elect, an adherent of the reformed church *16-e19*. [OFr *saint*, Lat *sanctus*]

saint[1.2], **sant, †saunt, †sanct** /sent, sant/ *v* **1** to canonize *la14-*. **2** to disappear, vanish (in a sudden or mysterious manner) *18-19, 20- Sh Bor*. **3** to cause to vanish quickly or inexplicably; to spirit away *19, 20- Sh*. [see the noun]

saint[1.3], **sanct, †sant** /sent, sənt/ *adj* **1** holy, sanctified *la14-*. **2** *of a church* dedicated to a saint *la14-*. **St Andrew's Cross, †Sanct Androis Croce** the Scottish flag; the diagonal cross particular to Saint Andrew *16-*. **†St Faith's cattle** cattle collected from Galloway into one large herd and driven to St Faith's Market, near Norwich *la18-e19*. **†St Faith's drove** = *St Faith's cattle la18-e19*. **†Sanct Innocentis bishop** the boy elected to play the lead role of bishop in the revelries centred on Holy Innocents' Day *la15-e16*. **St John's nut** a double hazelnut (which was believed to be a charm against witchcraft) *la16-19, 20- SW*. **St Michael's bannock** a bannock baked on Michaelmas Eve *20- H&I*. **St Michael's cake** a cake baked on Michaelmas Eve *18-19, 20- H&I*. **St Mungo** a nickname for the city of Glasgow (of which St Mungo is patron) *la18-*. **†Sanct Nicholas bischop** the boy elected to play the lead role of bishop in the revelries centred on St Nicholas' Day *la15-e16*. **†Sanct Nicholas mett** a duty on salt used for the upkeep of St Nicholas' Church in Aberdeen *16*. **St Peter's Mark** *see* PETER'S MARK. **the Saints** a nickname for St Johnstone or St Mirren Football Club *20-*. [see the noun]

saip, saep, soap, †sape, †sope /sep, sop/ *n* a substance used for cleaning *15-*. **soapery, †soparie** a soap factory *la17-*. **saip bells, soap bells** soap bubbles *18-19, 20- T EC*. **saep blotts** soapsuds *la19- Sh N*. **saip graith** soapy lather *la19- T C SW Bor*. **†saipman** a soapmaker, a soap-boiler *17-e19*. **saip sapples** soapsuds *19- T C SW*. **saipy suds** soapy lather *la19-*. **†soapwork** the manufacture of soap *17-18*. **soapworks** a soap factory *17-*. [OE *sāpe*]

sair[1.1], **sore, †sare** /ser, sor/ *n* **1** an injury, a wound; an affliction or disease *la14-*. **2** sorrow or grief; anguish or sadness *15-*. **3** physical pain or suffering *la14-e17*. [OE *sār*]

†sair[1.2], **sare** *v* to wound, injure or hurt *15-16*. [see the adj]

sair[1.3], **sare, sore, †sayr, †soir** /ser, sor/ *adj* **1** *of a part of the body* suffering, in pain *la14-*. **2** sorrowful, sad *la14-*. **3** harsh, severe *la14-*. **4** *of weather* severe, stormy, cold *la14-*. **5** causing or involving distress or grief, unhappy, unfortunate *15-*. **6** *of hardship or difficulty* hard, fierce *15-*. **7** *of afflictions* pressing hard upon one, hard to bear, oppressive *la15-*. **8** *of a task* involving physical effort, causing physical strain *la15-*. **9** *of the head* aching *16-*. **10** *of something unpleasant* serious, considerable, thoroughgoing *la18-*. **11** *of a person* injured, hurt *la14-17*. **sair face, sore face 1** a beating, not necessarily just on the face *20-*. **2** a pathetic expression assumed to elicit sympathy *20- Sh NE T*. **sair hand, sore hand 1** a mess, a piece of unskilled workmanship *20- SW Uls*. **2** a large thick slice of bread with butter or jam (which looks like a bandaged hand) *20- C*. **sair heid 1** a headache *16-*. **2** a small plain sponge cake with a paper band round the lower part of it *20- NE T EC*. **sair heidie** a small plain sponge cake *20- NE T EC*. **sair hert, sore heart** a sad or sorrowful state of mind; a cause for grief, a great disappointment *18-*. **sair wye** badly, seriously *20- Sh*. **sair yin, sair wan, sore one** (the result of) a violent blow *20-*. **lay aside fur a sair fit** to save for a time of need or difficulty, keep for an emergency *18-19, 20- Uls*. **lay up fur a sair leg** = *lay aside fur a sair fit 18-19, 20- T*. **a sair wame** colic, stomach-ache *19, 20- N NE T EC*. **it's a sair fecht** life is a struggle *20-*. **it's a sair fecht for a half loaf** it's a hard struggle for little reward *20- NE EC*. **sair on** destructive, harmful, giving hard wear or usage to: ◊*she's sair on her claes 20-*. [OE *sār*]

sair[1,4], **sare, sore** /ser, sor/ *adv* **1** severely, harshly, so as to cause great pain or suffering *la14-*. **2** *of weeping, sorrow* in a distressed manner, bitterly, intensely *la14-*. **3** with vehemence or intensity, with all one's strength or feeling *la18-*. **4** very, very much, greatly extremely *la14-*. **5** hard, with great exertion, laboriously *la16-19, 20- NE T*. **6** with expressions *of fear* dreadfully, terribly *la14-17*. **7** fiercely, ferociously *la14-16*. **sair aff** badly off, very poor *19-*. **sair done** *of meat* well done, overcooked *19, 20- NE*. †**sair herted** sad at heart *la16-19*. **sair made** sorely harassed, oppressed, hard put upon *19- Sh T*. **sair not** badly needed *la19- NE*. **sair pit 1** in difficulties *20-*. **2** ill, suffering from an illness *20- N T*. **sair awa wi't** *of persons or things* far gone, worn out by illness, hard usage etc *la19- NE T EC*. **sair pit on** suffering from an illness *20- N T*. **sair pit tae** in severe difficulties *20-*. †**sit someone sare** to distress someone *la15-16*. [OE *sāre*]

sair *see* SAUR[1.1], SAUR[1.2], SER, SAIRVE

sairgeant, sergeant, †**sergeand,** †**seriand** /'sɛrdʒənt, 'sɛrdʒənt, 'sardʒənt/ *n* **1** a soldier of the rank immediately above corporal *16-*. **2** a burgh official whose responsibilities included power of arrest and issuing writs *la14-17*. **3** an attendant or servant *la14-16*. **4** an official of a craft incorporation *16*. **5** a foot soldier *15*. [OFr *sergent*]

sairie, sorry, †**sary,** †**sory** /'sere, 'sɔre/ *adj* **1** regretful, repentant *la14-*. **2** sad, sorrowful; distressed, unhappy *la14-*. **3** in a poor state; hapless, pitiable, wretched *15-*. **4** serious, solemn *19*. [OE *sārig*]

sairious, serious /'sɛrɪəs, 'sɪrɪəs/ *adj* **1** *of a person* earnest, sincere; sombre *la17-*. **2** *of a matter* important, grave *la17-*. [ME *serious*, AN *serious*, Lat *sēriōsus*]

sairly, sorely /'sɛrle, 'sorle/ *adv* **1** grievously, painfully; bitterly, sadly *la15-*. **2** greatly, severely *la16-*. [OE *sārlīce*]

sairmon *see* SERMON[1.1]

sair's, sirse, †**sirs** /sɛrs, sɪrs/ *interj* an expression of surprise or alarm *18-19, 20- N NE T H&I C*. [aphetic form of Older Scots *preser* + us]

sairvant, servant, *NE* **servan,** †**servand,** †**sarvand** /'sɛrvənt, 'sɛrvənt; *NE* 'sɛrvən/ *n* **1** a domestic or personal servant, an employee *la14-*. **2** a person holding office under or engaged in service for a monarch, magnate or governement; a retainer or dependent *15-*. **3** *Christian Church* a priest, minister or ecclesiastic *la15-*. **4** a person who assists a craftsman or member of a profession in their work; an assistant, apprentice or clerk *15-e18*. **5** a slave or serf *la14-e17*. **6** a disciple, a believer, a worshipper *la14-e17*. **7** a lover, paramour *16*. **servan chiel** a young male servant *la19- N NE*. **servan lass, servant lass** a maidservant *17-20, 21- literary*. **servant man,** †**servand man** a male servant *15-20, 21- historical*. **servant woman,** †**servand woman** a female servant *16-20, 21- historical*. [OFr *servant*]

sairve, serve, ser, sair, †**serf,** †**sarve,** †**sar** /sɛrv, sɛrv, sɛr, sɛr/ *v* **1** to perform the functions and duties of a servant; to render service *la14-*. **2** to supply with goods or services; *of a waiter* to supply food to a table *la14-*. **3** to treat or behave towards in a certain way: ◊*to sair a bairn like that! la14-*. **4** *in religion* to be a devotee or worshipper; to worship *la14-*. **5** *of a thing* to be of use, have a function or purpose; to supply a need; to suffice, be adequate *la14-*. **6** *law* to carry out the legal process of petition to a sheriff required to declare a person heir to an estate *la15-e20, la20- historical*. **7** *of clothes* to fit, suit *18-19, 20- NE T*. **8** to satiate, sate *la18-19, 20- N*. **9** to give money, food or drink to a beggar *19*. **10** *law* to complete the process finding a widow entitled to her terce *16-e17*. **saired** satisfied, replete *la18-*. **server 1** a person who hands round refreshments at a funeral; originally a waiter *e16, la19- WC SW*. **2** a salver, tray *la17-19, 20- NE T C*. **sairin 1** one's fill, especially of food *la18-19, 20- Sh NE T WC*. **2** a thorough beating or trouncing *19, 20- NE*. **serving lass** a maidservant *la17-*. †**serve a brieve** *of a judge or sheriff* to investigate the claim made in a writ issuing from Chancery *15-16*. [OFr *servir*, Lat *servīre*]

sais *see* SEIZE

saison[1.1]**, season,** *NE* **sizzon,** †**sesoun,** †**sesson,** †**sasoun** /'sezən, 'sizən; *NE* 'sɪzən/ *n* **1** a period or time of the year *la14-*. **2** a time of ripeness and maturity *la15-*. **3** taste, flavour *la15-e16*. **seasonable,** †**sessonabill 1** appropriate to the season; warm, pleasant *la15-*. **2** timely, opportune; convenient *17-*. [OFr *seson*]

saison[1.2]**, season,** *NE* **sizzon,** †**seson,** †**sasoun** /'sezən, 'sizən; *NE* 'sɪzən/ *v* to adjust the flavour of food by adding seasoning *la14-*. [OFr *saisonner*, and from the noun]

sait *see* SEAT

saithe, *Sh* **saide,** †**seath** /seθ; *Sh* sed/ *n* the full grown coalfish *Pollachius virens* in its third or fourth year *16-*. [ON *seiðr*]

saitin, †**satyne,** †**saiting,** †**salting** /'setɪn/ *n* a glossy silk fabric, satin *la14-*. [MFr *satin*]

saitisfaction, satisfaction, †**satisfaccione** /setəsˈfakʃən, satəsˈfakʃən/ *n* **1** compensation, repayment or reimbursement; restitution or reparation *la14-*. **2** gratification, pleasure; fulfilment of a desire or need *la16-*. **3** *Presbyterian Church* the performance of an act of public penance *la15-17*. [MFr *satisfaction*, Lat *satisfactiōn-*]

saitisfee, satisfy, †**satify** /'setəsfi, 'satəsfae/ *v* **1** to remunerate or reimburse; to compensate *la15-*. **2** to comply with a request; to fulfil a need *16-*. **3** to assure or convince *16-*. †**satisfy the kirk** to atone for an offence (by public repentance) *la16-e17*. [MFr *satisfier*]

saiven *see* SEEVEN

sak *see* SECK[1.1]

sake, †**saik,** †**sayk** /sek/ *n* **1** in the interest of (something or someone); on a person's account *la14-*. **2** (accusation of) guilt; fault *la14-16*. **for ony sake!** for Heaven's sake! *19-*. **sakes me** an exclamation of surprise *la19-*. [OE *sacu* conflict, fault]

sakeless, saikless, sackless, †**saikles,** †**sakles** /'sekləs, 'sakləs/ *adj* **1** innocent; not guilty *la14-*. **2** inoffensive, harmless, guileless *la16-*. **3** foolish, careless, apathetic *19, 20- SW Bor*. **4** unafflicted; unchallenged *16-e19*. **5** *of an action*

perpetrated against an innocent victim *16-17*. †**saiklesly** innocently; without just cause *la14-e17*. [OE *sacleas*]
saket see SACKET
sakles see SAKELESS
salamonicall see SOLOMONICAL
sald see SELL[1]
sale see SAIL[1.1], SAIL[1.2], SAIL[2]
salerife see SELL[1]
salf see SAUF
salff see SEL[1.1]
salfty see SAFETY
†**salineer stones** *npl* grit occurring with deposits of gold *16-17*. [perhaps Fr *salinière* a place where salt is made + *stone* (STANE[1.1])]
Salisbury crag /sɔlzbʌri 'krag/ *n* rhyming slang skag, heroin *20-*. *EC*. [from the name of the cliffs in Holyrood Park in Edinburgh]
salist, solist /sə'lɪst/ *v* to pause, rest or desist *la19-* *Sh*. [Eng *solace* †to take recreation, infl in form by *solist* (SOLICIT[2])]
sall, shall, †**schall** /sal, ʃal/ *v pt* **sud, suld, should 1** will have to, must *la14-*. **2** desire to, intend to *la14-*. Compare SUD. **sanna, shanna** shall not *la18-*. **I'se warrant** I am sure, I would bet *19-*. †**I'se uphaud** I have no doubt *19*. [OE *sceal*, 1st and 3rd person sing present tense of *sculan*]
sall see SOWL[1.1]
saller see CELLAR[2]
salm see PSALM[1.1]
salmon, salmond, salmont, salmound see SAUMON
†**salrar, sallarar, sellerar** *n* the cellar-keeper in a religious house *15-e16*. [ME *celerer*, AN *selerer*, Lat *cellerārius*]
sals see SAUCE
salsar see SAUCER
†**salt** *n* an assault or attack *la14-16*. [aphetic form of Older Scots *assalt*, OFr *assaut*]
salt see SAUT[1.1], SAUT[1.2], SAUT[1.3]
salteye see SAUTIE[1.2]
salting see SAITIN
saltire, †**saltoire** /'sɔltaer/ *n* St Andrew's cross; the flag of Scotland *17-*. [OFr *saultoir*]
Saltoun barley /'sɔltun barle/ *n* fanner-dressed pot barley *18-* historical. [named after Andrew Fletcher of *Saltoun* in East Lothian, who introduced the process + BARLEY[1]]
saltpetre, †**salt petir,** †**salpeter,** †**salpetir** /salt'pitər/ *n* potassium nitrate *16-*. [ME *salpetre*, OFr *salpetre*, Lat *salpetra*, with influence from salt (SAUT[1.1])]
salty see SAUTIE[1.1], SAUTIE[1.2]
†**salus**[1.1] *n* a salutation; greetings *15*. [ME *salus*, OFr *salus* inflected form of *salu*]
†**salus**[1.2], **saluse** *v* to salute, greet *la14-16*. [from the noun]
†**salutaire, salutar** *adj* health-giving, healing, beneficial *la15-17*. [MFr *salutaire*, Lat *salūtāris*]
†**salutary** *adj* = SALUTAIRE *la16*. [MFr *salutaire*, Lat *salūtāris*]
†**Salvatour** *n* Christ *la15-16*. [Lat *salvātor* saviour]
†**salvatrice** *n* the Virgin Mary *e16*. [Lat *salvatric-* saviour (fem)]
salve, †**sawe,** †**saif** /salv/ *v* to anoint with ointment; to soothe; to heal *la14-*. [OE *sealfian*]
salve see SAUF, SAVE[2.1], SAW[3]
salvendo see SOLVENDIE
†**Salviour, Saluyour, Saweoure** *n* Christ *la14-e17*. [AN *salveour, sauveour* literally saviour]
sam see SAME[2.1], SAME[2.2]
same[1], *Sh Ork N* **saam,** †**saim,** †**seam** /sem; *Sh Ork N* sɑm/ *n* the fat of pigs; grease, lard *15-*. [ME *saime*, OFr *saim*]
same[2.1], *Sh* **sam,** †**samin,** †**sammyn** /sem; *Sh* sɑm/ *n* that same person or thing; the aforesaid person or thing *la15-*.

sammas as if *20-* *Sh*. **the same as** in the same way as, just as if *19-*. [see the adj]
same[2.2], *Sh Ork N* **sam,** *NE* **samen,** †**samin,** †**sammyn** /sem; *Sh Ork N* sɑm; *NE* 'semən/ *adj* identical with, unchanged *la14-*. †**samelike** the same as, just like *la14-19*. [ON *samr*, with influence from the adv form *samin* (SAME[2.3])]
same[2.3], †**samin,** †**sammyn** /sem/ *adv* **1** in the same way; all the same *la15-*. **2** together; in company; mutually *la14-e16*. †**samelike** in the same way *la16*. [OE **samen*, with influence from the adj form SAME[2.2]]
samekill see SAE[2.1]
samen see SAME[2.2]
samin see SAME[2.1], SAME[2.2], SAME[2.3]
sammyn see SAME[2.1], SAME[2.2], SAME[2.3]
†**samyng** *n* in Shetland and Orkney a term in the TENENDAS clauses of conveyances; the rights of possession as joint-proprietor *16*. [compare ON *sam-eiginn* common, ON *sam-eiga* joint possession]
sanct see SAINT[1.1], SAINT[1.2], SAINT[1.3]
sanctitude /'saŋktətjud/ *n* holiness, sanctity *la15-*. [Lat *sanctitūdo*]
Sanct Maruifis fair see SUMMEREVE'S FAIR
sanctuary, †**sanctuar** /'saŋktʃuri/ *n* **1** a holy or consecrated place; the inner part of a church or temple or the area round the altar in a Christian church *la14-*. **2** a sacred place in which fugitives were immune from arrest; a place of safety *la15-18, 19-* historical. [Lat *sanctuārium*]
sand[1.1] /sand/ *n* **1** granules of rock (finer than gravel) *la14-*. **2** an expanse of sandy ground, a beach *la14-*. **sandy, sannie** consisting of or covered in sand *la15-*. **sannie** a sandshoe *20- T C SW Bor*. **sand bed 1** a stretch of sand by the sea or a river; a sandbank *16-*. **2** a very heavy drinker, a drunkard *19, 20- EC*. **san' blin'** short-sighted (due to albinism) *la15-19, 20- Sh N*. **sand bunker** a hazard on a golf course consisting of a natural or artificial hollow filled with sand *19-*. **sand-dab** a species of small flatfish *Limanda limanda 20-*. **san' dorbie** the sandpiper *Actitis hypoleucos 20- NE*. **sand-eel, sandal, sanle, sannal,** †**sandele,** †**sandell** an eel-like fish *Ammodytes*, found on sandy shores *la16-*. **sand fleuk** the smear-dab *Microstomus kitt 19- NE T EC*. **sand-glass** an hourglass *16-*. **sand iron** *golf* the sand wedge, the club designed to hit the ball out of bunkers *la19-*. **sand-jumper** a sand flea *Orchestia gammarellus 20- NE SW*. **sand-laverock** the sandpiper *Actitis hypoleucos la19- Ork N SW*. **sandlin** a sand-eel *19- NE T*. **sinloo** the ringed plover *Charadrius hiaticula la19- Ork*. **sand-lowper** a sand flea *18- N T EC SW*. **sandshoe** a gym shoe, a plimsoll *20-*. **sandy eel** a sand-eel *20- Sh*. **sandy-giddock** a sand-eel *20- Sh*. **sandy laverock** the ringed plover *Charadrius hiaticula 19, 20- N H&I*. **sandy lowper** a sand flea *la19- EC*. †**sanny mill** a sandcastle *la18-19*. **sandy swallow** the sand martin *Riparia riparia la19-*. **the sands,** †**the sandis** a particular stretch of sandy ground *la14-*. [OE *sand*]
sand[1.2] /sand/ *v* **1** to cover or sprinkle with sand; to be inundated or damaged by sand *16-*. **2** to smooth or polish with sandpaper *20-*. **3** *of a fish* to bury itself in sand (for concealment) *20- Bor*. **4** to run a ship ashore on sand *16-e19*. **5** to adulterate a coin with sand in the smelting *18*. [see the noun]
Sandemanian /sandə'meniən/ *n* a member of a religious body deriving from the Glasites *19-e20, la20-* historical. [named after Robert Sandeman, with noun-forming suffix *-ian*]
Sandy, Sandie, Sawnie, Sanny /'sandi, 'sɔni, 'sani/ *n* **1** a diminutive form of the name Alexander *la18-*. **2** a young man (from the country); a Scotsman *la18-19*. **3** a nickname for the Devil *la18-e19*. †**Sannock 1** a diminutive form of

the name Alexander *la18-*. **2** a young man, a yokel *la18-19*. **Sandie Campbell** a pig; pork or bacon (in allusion to the boar's-head crest on the Campbell coat-of-arms) *la19-*. **Sandy oat** a variety of oat *19- NE*. [shortened form of the personal name *Alexander*]

sane *see* SAIN[1,2], SAY[1,2]

sang[1], **song** /saŋ, sɔŋ/ *n* **1** singing; something sung *la14-*. **2** the musical utterance of birds *15-*. **3** a fuss, a clamour, an outcry *18-*. **4** the noise of the sea breaking on the shore *la19- Sh NE*. **5** poetic composition *15-16*. **sang buik** a book of songs *la15-*. **sangschaw** a song festival, by analogy with WAPPENSHAW *20-*. **sang scule** a school attached to a church, for the teaching of singing and music *16-e17, 20- historical*. **sangster** a singer *la15-*. **an auld sang** an old story or saying, a proverb *la19-*. **mak a sang aboot** to make a fuss *19-*. [OE *sang*]

sang[2] /saŋ/ *interj* an expression of surprise or fright *la19-*. **by my sang** an expression of surprise or fright *la18-*. **by sang** = *by my sang*. **my sang** = *by my sang*. [Fr (*par le*) *sang* (*de Dieu*) (by God's) blood]

sang *see* SING[1,2], SING[2,2]

†**sangler, sanglier** *n* a wild boar *la15-e17*. [OFr *sangler, sanglier*]

sanguine, †**sangwyne**, †**sanguane** /'saŋgwɪn/ *adj* **1** sanguine of complexion or temperament *e16-*. **2** blood-red *la15-e17*. **3** clever; optimistic; cheerful *19-*. †**sanguinolent** blood-red *e16*. [ME *sanguin*, OFr *sanguin*, Lat *sanguineus* bloody]

sanle *see* SAND[1,1]
sanna *see* SALL
sannachie *see* SHENACHIE
sannie *see* SAND[1,1]
Sannock, Sanny *see* SANDY

Sanquhar /'saŋkər/ *n* a town in Dumfriesshire formerly noted for its knitting industry *la15-*. **Sanquhar gloves** gloves knitted in various ornamental patterns with a double thread *la18- SW*. **Sanquhar hose** stockings knitted in various ornamental patterns *la18-20, 21- historical*. **Sanquhar knitting** garments knitted in the Sanquhar patterns *21-*. [named after the town in Dumfriesshire, Gael *seann cathair* old fort]

†**sans** *prep* without *16-e19*. **sans faill** without doubt *e16*. **sans phrase** without saying more *e19*. [ME *sans*, OFr *sans*]

sanshach /'sanʃəx/ *adj* **1** wily, shrewd *19- NE*. **2** disdainful, haughty *19- NE*. **3** over-precise, irritable *19- NE*. **4** pleasant, genial *20- N NE*. [compare Gael *sònasach* easily annoyed, Gael *sonasach* happy, fortunate]

sant *see* SAINT[1,1], SAINT[1,2], SAINT[1,3]

San Toy /'san tɔɪ/ *n* a name of a Glasgow gang active in the 1920s and 1930s *20, 21- historical*. [from the name of a musical comedy first performed in 1899, used as rhyming slang for BOY]

sap[1], †**sop** /sap/ *n* **1** the juice or fluid of plants *15-*. **2** vital energy *la16-*. **3** a quantity of liquid, usually for drinking with food *la18-*. **sap-money** money given to workers in lieu of a milk or ale allowance *la18- NE*. **sap spail** the sap wood of a tree *19, 20- NE T*. [OE *sæp*]

sap[2,1], **sop** /sap, sɔp/ *n* **1** a piece of bread soaked in wine or other liquid *la14-19, la20- EC*. **2** a term of endearment *16*. †**sop of sorrow** (a person) deep in sorrow *la15-16*. †**soppis** a term of endearment *16*. [OE *sopp*]

sap[2,2], **sop**, †**soup** /sap/ *v* to soak, steep, saturate *16-19, 20- NE*. **sappit** soaked (with seawater) *20- Sh N NE T*. [OE *soppian*]

sape *see* SAIP
sapling *see* SIPLING

†**sapour** *n* **1** flavour, taste *la15-16*. **2** sap; juice *16*. [Lat *sapor*]

sappie, sappy, †**soppy** /'sapi, 'sape/ *adj* **1** full of moisture; wet, sodden, soppy *la15-*. **2** *of meat or fish* juicy, succulent *16-*. **3** *of food* soft, soggy *la19-*. **4** plump, fat; fleshy *19- NE EC SW*. **5** given to drinking too much *19- WC SW Bor*. **6** *of a kiss* soft, long-drawn-out *la18-19, 20- Ork NE SW*. **7** *of a bed* soft, yielding, comfortable *la18-19*. **8** profitable, favourable *19*. **9** pious, smug *19*. **sappy-heidit** simple-minded, silly, foolish *la19- T*. [SAP[1] + -IE[2]; some senses influenced by SAP[2,1]]

sapple[1,1] /'sapəl/ *n* soapsuds, lather for washing *19-*. [see the verb]

sapple[1,2] /'sapəl/ *v* to soak, saturate; to steep laundry in soapy water *19- C SW Uls*. [frequentative form of SAP[2,2]]

sappy *see* SAPPIE

saps /saps/ *npl* pieces of bread soaked or boiled in milk (as food for children or invalids) *la17-*. **sapsy** *n* a foolish, weak-willed or characterless person *20- C*. **sapsy** *adj* foolish, sloppy; effeminate *20- C SW*. [plural of SAP[2,1]]

sar *see* SARR, SAUR[1,1], SAUR[1,2], SAIRVE

sarbit *see* SWARBIT

sardonyx, †**sardonice**, †**sardanis** /sar'dɒnɪks/ *n* a semi-precious stone *16-*. [ME *sardonix, sardonyse*, Lat *sardonyx*]

sare *see* SAIR[1,1], SAIR[1,2], SAIR[1,3], SAIR[1,4]

sark[1,1], **serk** /sark, sɛrk/ *n* **1** a (man's) shirt *la14-*. **2** a woman's shift or chemise *la15-*. **3** a surplice *19*. **sarket** an undershirt, a woollen vest *la19- NE*. **sarkless** without a shirt or shift *la18-*. **sark alane** wearing only a sark *16-*. **sark neck** the collar or collar-band of a shirt *la16-*. **sark tail, serk tail** the back part of a shirt *18-*. **a sarkfu o sair banes** a person stiff or sore from hard labour or from a beating *17-*. †**sark of God** a penitential shirt *e18*. [OE *serc*, ON *serkr*]

sark[1,2], **serk** /sark, sɛrk/ *v* **1** to cover the rafters of a roof with wooden boards onto which the slates may be fixed *la16-*. **2** to clothe in or provide with a shirt *18-*. [see the noun]

sarking, serking /'sarkɪŋ, 'sɛrkɪŋ/ *n* **1** shirting, originally enough material to make a sark *la16-*. **2** (the furnishing of) roof boarding to which slates or thatch may be fixed *16-*. [derivative of SARK[1,1]]

†**sarr, sar** *v* to grip tightly *e16*. [OFr *serrer*]

sartie *see* CERTIE
sarvand *see* SAIRVANT
sarve *see* SAIRVE
sary *see* SAIRIE

sasine, †**sesin**, †**seisin**, †**sessing** /'sesɪn, 'sezɪn/ *n* **1** *law* the act or procedure of giving possession of feudal property, originally by a symbolic handing over of earth and stones *la14-*. **2** *law* the document attesting possession of feudal property *15-19, 20- historical*. **3** possession *13-16*. †**sesing ox, sasine ox** an ox due as a perquisite to the person conferring sasine *la15-17*. [OFr *saisine*, Lat *sasina*]

sasoun *see* SAISON[1,2]

Sassenach[1,1] /'sasənax/ *n* **1** an English person *18-*. **2** a Scottish Lowlander *la18-19, 20- literary*. [Gael *Sasannach* Saxon, English]

Sassenach[1,2] /'sasənax/ *adj* **1** English-speaking; English *18-*. **2** of the Scottish Lowlands *19*. [see the noun]

sassenger /'sasənʒər/ *n humorous* a sausage *19, 20- Ork N WC*. [altered form of Eng *sausage*]

sasser *see* SAUCER, SAUSTER
saster *see* SAUSTER
sat *see* SIT[1,2]
Satan *see* SAWTAN[1]
sate *see* SEAT
Sathan, Sathanis *see* SAWTAN[1]
satisfaccione, satisfaction *see* SAITISFACTION
satisfy *see* SAITISFEE

satt see SIT¹,²
Satterday see SETERDAY
sattil see SATTLE¹,²
sattle¹·¹, settle, †sadill /'satəl, 'sɛtəl/ *n* **1** a seat, a bench *16-*. **2** a ledge or raised platform in a byre where the cattle stand *19- T SW Bor*. **settle bed** a wooden bed which can be folded up to form a seat during the day; a divan bed *19- C SW Uls*. [OE *setl*]
sattle¹·², settle, †sattil /'satəl, 'sɛtəl/ *v* **1** to sink down *la15-*. **2** to come or bring to order; to decide, resolve or reconcile *la16-*. **3** to establish a person in an office; to install a minister in a charge; to provide a vacant parish with a minister *la16-*. **4** to cause troops to fall back; to yield ground *16-e17*. **†satlingis** sediment, lees *la15-17*. **settlement 1** an act of settling; an arrangement or adjustment *la17-*. **2** *law* the disposition of property by will, a testament *18-*. **3** *Presbyterian Church* the placing of a minister in a charge *18-*. **settleder** more settled *19- NE T*. [OE *setlan*]
Saturday, Saturnday see SETERDAY
satyne see SAITIN
sauce, †sawce, †sals /sɔs/ *n* **1** a flavoured liquid or creamy preparation accompanying food; meat juice or gravy *la14-*. **2** bitter treatment *16-e17*. **saucy, †sawsy 1** covered in sauce; soaked in spices; pickled *16-*. **2** impudent, cheeky; forward *la16-*. **3** vain, conceited *la18-*. **4** fastidious about food or dress *20- WC SW Bor*. **5** scornful, contemptuous *la18-19, 20- Bor*. [OFr *salce, sausse*, Lat *salsa*]
saucer, sasser, †sauser, †salsar /'sɔsər, 'sasər/ *n* **1** a round shallow vessel placed under a cup *19-*. **2** a dish or deep plate used to hold sauces or condiments *la15-17*. **3** *in Aberdeen* a representation of a saucer engraved on a stone used as an official boundary mark *la16-17*. [ME *saucer*, OFr *saussier*]
saucer see SAUSTER
sauch, saugh /sɔx/ *n* **1** (the wood of) the willow *Salix la14-*. **2** a rope of twisted willow withes *16*. **sauchie** made of willow; abounding in willows *19-*. **saugh buss, saugh bush** a willow tree *la16-*. **saugh tree** a willow tree *16-*. **sauch wand** a twig or branch of willow *la18-*. **sauch willie** the willow *20-*. [OE *salh*]
sauch see SEE
sauchen, saughen /'sɔxən/ *adj* **1** made of willow; covered with willow trees *la16-*. **2** *of people* tough, resilient; dour, stubborn and sullen *17-19, 20- NE*. **3** soft, yielding, lacking in energy or spirit *18- NE*. [SAUCH, with adj-forming suffix]
saucht¹·¹, †saught /sɔxt/ *n* peace, quiet *la16-*. [OE *seht*, ON **sæht*]
†saucht¹·² *v* to become reconciled *la14-e15*. **sauchtnyng, sauchnyng, sawchnyng** reconciliation; an agreement *la14-e16, e19*. [OE *sehtian*, ON *sætta*]
†saucht¹·³ *adj* in agreement, at peace, reconciled *la14-16*. [OE *seht*, ON **sáhtr*]
sauf, safe, save, †saf, †saif, †salve /sɔf, sef, sev/ *adj* **1** not in danger, free from harm, secure *15-*. **2** without prejudice to, with due respect to *15-*. **3** dependable, reliable *la15-*. **4** having escaped from harm; intact, undamaged *16-*. **safe lintel** a wooden lintel placed for additional support behind the stone lintel of a door or window *18-*. [AN *salf, sauf*, OFr *salve*]
sauf see SAVE²·¹, SAVE²·², SAVE²·³
†saufey, safer, sawfa *n* a reward paid for recovering lost property *la16-19*. **safer silver** = SAUFEY *17*. [ME *salfay*, perhaps related to Lat *salvus* safe]
sauffand see SAVAND
sauffing see SAVING
saugh see SAUCH
saughen see SAUCHEN

saughrin see SOCHER
saught see SAUCHT¹·¹
saul see SOWL¹·¹
sauld see SELL¹
saull see SOWL¹·¹
sault see SAUT¹·¹, SAUT¹·³
saum see PSALM¹·¹
saumon, salmon, †salmond, †salmound, †salmont /'sɔmən, 'samən/ *n* a fish of the genus *Salmo*, a salmon *la14-*. **salmon coble, †saumont-coble** a flat-bottomed boat used in salmon fishing *la18-*. **salmon cruive** a trap in a river used to catch salmon *la18-*. **salmon lowp, sawmon loup 1** a salmon leap *20-*. **2** a kind of leapfrog *20- NE T WC*. **sawmon rae** salmon roe *19, 20- SW*. [AN *samoun*, with influence in spelling from Lat *salmo*]
saunt see SAINT¹·¹, SAINT¹·²
saur¹·¹, sar, savour, †sair /sɔr, sor, sar, 'sɛvər/ *n* **1** a smell, an (unpleasant) aroma *la14-*. **2** flavour, taste *la15-*. **3** a slight wind, a gentle breeze *19- H&I WC*. **saurless, †savirles 1** tasteless, insipid *la16-*. **2** lacking in wit, spirit or energy *19- NE*. **†savorous** of good savour *la15-e16*. [AN *saver*]
saur¹·², sar, savour, †sair, †sawr, †savor /sɔr, sar, 'sɛvər/ *v* **1** to have a certain taste or odour; to smell of *la14-*. **2** to show traces or characteristics of *la15-*. **3** to perceive *la14-16*. **4** to add flavour *e16*. **saurin 1** a taste; a tasting *la16-*. **2** a relish or liking for something *20- N*. **†savoryng** something that conveys a flavour or idea of *e16*. **†sar out** to ferret out *e18*. [AN *savurer*]
†sauser, sawser, sasser *v in Aberdeen* to mark boundary stones with a saucer-like mark *la16-17*. [from the noun SAUCER]
sauser see SAUCER
sauster, saster, *Sh* saucer, †sawster, †sasser /'sɔstər, 'sastər; *Sh* 'sɔsər/ *n* a sausage *la16-19, 20- Sh SW*. [reduced form of ME *saucister*, altered form of *sausige*]
saut¹·¹, salt, *Sh NE* saat, †sault /sɔt, sɔlt; *Sh NE* sat/ *n* **1** sodium chloride, salt *13-*. **2** a saltcellar *17-*. **salter, sauter** a dealer in salt; a worker in a salt pan *la15-*. **saut backet** a salt box *18-19, 20- NE T EC*. **†saltcot** a salt-house, a saltworks *13-e17*. **saat cuddie** a receptacle for salt *la19- Sh*. **saut dish** a saltcellar *19-*. **saut fat, saltfat, †saltfit, †saltfoot** a saltcellar or salt dish *15-19, 20- Sh Ork N T EC*. **sautman** an itinerant seller of salt *19, 20- historical*. **†saltmaster** a collector of salt-duty *la17*. **†salt melder** meal mixed with salt, sprinkled over sacrifices *e16*. **salt pan** a shallow vessel in which brine is evaporated to make salt; a saltworks *la16-*. **saut willie** a salt jar *20- EC*. **lay in saut** to pickle; to lay aside; to keep in reserve (for use in revenge) *la18-19, 20- Sh*. **the Saut burgh** a nickname for Dysart in Fife, once a centre of the salt trade *20 historical*. **as saut as lick** very salty *19, 20- C SW*. [OE *sealt*]
saut¹·², salt, *Sh NE* saat /sɔt, sɔlt; *Sh NE* sat/ *v* **1** to preserve with salt *la14-*. **2** to add salt; to sprinkle with salt *la16-*. **3** to punish, take revenge on; to snub; to treat severely *la18-*. **4** to overcharge *la19- literary*. **sauter, salter, †saltar 1** a saltmaker; a salt-worker; a dealer in salt *14-*. **2** a shrew, a termagant *la19- NE T*. **3** harsh or severe punishment *la19- NE T*. **†sautit** made bitter *la18*. [OE *sealtan*, and from the noun]
saut¹·³, salt, *Sh NE* saat, †sault /sɔt, sɔlt; *Sh NE* sat/ *adj* **1** preserved or cured with salt *la14-*. **2** saturated with salt, salty, saline *la15-*. **3** *of prices* overly expensive *18-*. **4** *of speech or manner* harsh, unkind *la19-*. **5** *of experience* painful, bitter *la15-19, 20- SW*. **†saltly 1** bitterly, fiercely, severely *la16*. **2** dearly *la17*. **saut-bree** seawater; water in which salt has been mixed or boiled *la18- Sh NE*. **†salt faill** seaside turf *la17-18*. **†salt girs** grassland close to the sea

la16-e17. **saut scone** a cause of grief *20- SW*. **saut water 1** seawater, the sea *15-*. **2** the seaside (as a place for holidaying or recuperation) *19*. [see the noun]

sautie[1.1], **salty** /ˈsɔti, ˈsɔlti/ *n* the dab *Limanda limanda 19- NE EC*. [short for *sautie-fleuk*, SAUTIE[1.2] perhaps from the adj]

sautie[1.2], **salty**, †**salteye** /ˈsɔti, ˈsɔlti/ *adj* impregnated with or tasting of salt; made with or containing salt *la16-*. **sautie backit** a salt box *20- Ork NE*. **sauty bannock** an oatmeal bannock made with a greater than usual amount of salt, baked on Shrove Tuesday *19, 20- historical*. [SAUT[1.1] + -IE[2]]

savage[1.1], †**savich** /ˈsavədʒ/ *n* a wild or uncivilized person *la16-*. [see the adj]

savage[1.2], †**savich** /ˈsavədʒ/ *adj* **1** fierce, cruel, ferocious *15-*. **2** untamed; uncultivated *16-*. **3** intrepid, valiant *la15*. [AN *savage*]

†**savand**, **saiffing**, **sauffand** *conj* except (that) *la14-16*. [presp of SAVE[2.1]]

savand *see* SAVING

save[1] /sev/ *n* heather-shoots used in brewing *la19- Ork*. [Norw dial *save* sap, wort]

save[2.1], **sauf**, **safe**, †**saif**, †**salve**, †**saff** /sev, sɔf, sef/ *v* **1** to keep safe; to rescue or protect from harm; to salvage *la14-*. **2** to preserve; to accumulate; to set aside for later use *la16-*. **3** to draw a boat up on the shore for the winter *la19- N*. **saving stone** a stone built over a lintel to distribute the load of the wall above onto the jambs *20- T WC*. **sauf us** an exclamation of surprise, apprehension or protest *19- Ork NE T*. **save yer braith tae cool yer parritch** to mind your own business, be quiet *19-*. [AN *saver, sauver, salver*]

save[2.2], †**safe**, †**saif**, †**sauf** /sev/ *prep* **1** except *15-*. **2** with due respect to *la15-*. [see the verb]

save[2.3], †**safe**, †**saif**, †**sauf** /sev/ *conj* except that *15-*. [see the verb]

save *see* SAUF

savich *see* SAVAGE[1.1], SAVAGE[1.2]

saving, †**savand**, †**saiffing**, †**sauffing** /ˈsevɪŋ/ *prep* **1** except for, excepting only *la14-*. **2** reserving, without prejudice to *15-16*. **3** with due respect to *16*. **4** not to mention *la16*. [presp of SAVE[2.1]]

†**saving-tree** *n* an evergreen shrub *Juniperus sabina* which produces an abortifacient drug *17-e19*. [presp of SAVE[2.1] + TREE[1.1]]

savite *see* SAFETY

savor *see* SAUR[1.2]

savour *see* SAUR[1.1], SAUR[1.2]

Savoy Arcadians /saˈvɔɪ arˈkediənz/ *n* a Glasgow gang of the 1920s and 1930s *20, 21- historical*. [perhaps named after the former *Savoy Theatre Arcade* in Hope Street, Glasgow]

saw[1], **sow**, *NE SW* **shaw**, *NE* **shaave** /sɑ, so; *NE SW* ʃɑ; *NE* ʃɑv/ *v pt* **sawed**, *NE* **sew**, *Sh NE* **schew** *ptp* **sawn**, **sawed 1** to scatter (seed), plant (a crop); to scatter, disperse, distribute (anything); to disseminate, spread; to foment (beliefs) *la14-*. **2** to scatter seed on land; to plant (land) with seed; *of seed* to be sufficient for (an area of land) *15-*. **3** to throw out (a fishing-line) from a boat, shoot (a line) *20- NE*. **sawin**, **sawing 1** the action, fact or period of the year of planting (seed, a crop) *la14-*. **2** the action of planting (land) *la15-*. **3** a quantity of seed planted or required to be planted to produce a particular crop; the resulting crop; an area of land in terms of the seed required to plant it *la15-17*. **sawin happer** a canvas sheet from which seed was broadcast *e20, la20- Ork NE WC historical*. **sawin sheet** = *sawin happer 16-20, 21- historical*. **sawin time** seed-time *la16, 20- NE*. **saw doun** to plant (land) with grass *la18-*. [OE *sāwan*]

saw[2.1] /sɔ, sɑ/ *n* a tool, a metal plate or strip with a toothed edge used for cutting *16-*. **saw-neb** the goosander *Mergus merganser*; the red-breasted merganser *Mergus serrator la19- N NE*. **sastik**, **sawstock** a log of undressed timber *18- Sh Ork*. [OE *sagu*]

saw[2.2], †**schaw** /sɔ, sɑ/ *v pt* †**sew** *ptp* †**sawin** †**sawyn** to cut (timber) with a saw *15-*. **sawins** sawdust *19, 20- NE WC*. [see the noun]

saw[3], **salve** /sɑ, salv/ *n* **1** ointment *la14-*. **2** a remedy *la15-e17*. [OE *sealf*]

saw *see* SAY[1.1], SEE

Sawbath *see* SABBATH

sawce *see* SAUCE

sawe *see* SALVE

sawfa *see* SAUFEY

sawin *see* SAW[2.2]

sawl *see* SOWL[1.1]

Sawnie *see* SANDY

sawr *see* SAUR[1.2]

sawser *see* SAUSER

sawster *see* SAUSTER

Sawtan[1], **Sathan**, **Satan**, †**Sathanis** /ˈsɔtən, ˈseθən, ˈsetən/ *n* the Devil *la14-*. [OE *Satan*, Lat *Sātān*]

sawtan[2], **sawtie** /ˈsɔtən, ˈsɔte/ *n* a small light shooting marble *20- WC*. [extended sense of SAWTAN[1], due to the mischief it can cause another player's marbles]

sawyn *see* SAW[2.2]

sax, **six**, †**sex** /saks, sɪks/ *numeral* the cardinal number next after five *la14-*. **sickie** sixpence *la19- NE T EC*. **sixsie** a move in the game of *chuckies* (CHUCK[2]) *20-*. **saxsome**, †**sex sum** a group of six people *la14-*. **saxteen**, **sixteen 1** the cardinal number next after fifteen *la14-*. **2** = *saxteenth 15-17*. **saxteenth**, †**sextend**, †**saxteint** the ordinal number corresponding to sixteen *15-*. **saxtie**, **saxty** the cardinal number coming after fifty-nine *la14-*. **sixern**, **sixareen**, †**sex-airring** a six-oared boat; *of a boat* six-oared *la16- Sh Ork*. **sax-month**, **sixmonth** a period of six months *20- Sh T*. †**sax pairt** a sixth *la15-17*. **saxsome reel** a reel danced in sets of three couples *19- Sh Ork*. **the saxteen** the sixteen representatives of the pre-Union peerage of Scotland elected from their own number after each general election (until 1963) to sit in the House of Lords *la18-20*. **sixteensome** a reel danced in sets of eight couples *20-*. **six and sax**, **sixes and saxes** very much alike, six and half a dozen *20-*. †**six knocks** *law* the procedure required in the serving of a summons: six blows on the door of the principal dwelling-place *16-e18*. [OE Northumb dial **sæx*, OE *six, sex*]

saxt, **sixth**, **sax**, †**sext**, †**sixt** /sakst, sɪksθ/ *adj* the ordinal number corresponding to the cardinal number six, the sixth in order *la14-*. [OE *sexta, sixta*]

†**saxter-aithe** *n in Shetland* the 'sixfold oath' required of a person accused of a serious crime or of a second offence *e17*. [calque of ON *séttar-eiðr*]

say[1.1], †**saw** /se/ *n* **1** something spoken or written; a remark, a piece of gossip; talk, speech; an opinion *la14-19, 20- Sh NE T C*. **2** a saying, a proverb *la14-16, la18- Sh Ork N NE*. **3** *law* a claim, an assertion, an agreement, a statement; a person's word *15-e17*. **4** a prophecy *la14-e16*. [see the verb]

say[1.2], †**sa** /se/ *v pt* **said** †**sad**, †**saed** *ptp* **said**, *Sh T* **sain**, †**sad**, †**sane**, †**sene 1** to utter, pronounce, articulate (words); to declare, state in speech or writing; to recommend, instruct; to tell; to recite *la14-*. **2** to talk, speak *la14-19, 20- C SW Bor*. **sayer**, †**sayar 1** a person who says something *la18-*. **2** a narrator or author *la15-e16*. **3** a person who says or celebrates the Roman Catholic mass, a celebrant *la16-e17*. **saying 1** the action of uttering; an utterance, pronouncement; a wise or authoritative precept *la15-*. **2** a proverb *la16-*. **said wird** a saying, proverb *la19- Sh.* **I winna say but, I winna say but what, I widna say** I dare say, I won't deny (that) *la19-*. **say ae wey, say ae wey wi** to agree, be in harmony (with) *20- NE T WC*. **say awa 1** to hold forth, speak one's mind *19-*. **2** to say grace before a meal *19, 20- Ork NE T*. **say for** to vouch for *17-*. **say ower** to recite, repeat from memory *la19-*. **say thegither** to agree, be of one mind; to be on good terms *20- NE T EC*. **say wi** to agree, concur with *20-*. **say (a body) wrang** to speak ill of (someone) *la19-*. [OE *secgan*]

say *see* SAE¹, SAE²·¹, SEY¹·¹, SEY¹·², SEY², SEY³

sayawa, seawa /seə'wa/ *n* **1** a long rambling discourse, a rigmarole *19-*. **2** a loquacious person *20- NE Bor.* [SAY¹·² + AWA¹·¹]

sayk *see* SAKE
sayn *see* SAIN¹·²
saynd *see* SEND¹·¹
sayr *see* SAIR¹·³
sca *see* SCAW
scaad *see* SCAWD

scab¹·¹ /skab/ *n* **1** a crust formed over a wound or sore *la16-*. **2** a skin disease affecting horses or sheep *la15-*. **3** one of the umbelliferae, *eg* hemlock *20- Bor.* **4** a skin disease in people, probably including scabies or syphilis; an associated pock or pustule *15-17*. **scabbert 1** scabbed, bare *19-*. **2** a bare, stony piece of land *20- NE.* **3** a person suffering from SCAB¹·¹ (sense 4); *derogatory* a person *19*. **scabbit 1** suffering from SCAB¹·¹ (sense 2) *la15-*. **2** *of a person* mean, worthless *18-*. **3** *of land* bare, infertile *la19, 20- Sh N T*. **4** suffering from SCAB¹·¹ (sense 2) *16-17*. [ON **skabbr*]

scab¹·² /skab/ *v* to form a scab or scabs on (skin or a wound) *17-*. [see the noun]

scabbie, scabby /'skabe/ *adj* covered with scabs; dirty, shabby, disreputable *18-*. **scabby-heid** a derogatory term for a person implying they have head lice *20- C*. **I could eat a scabby-heidit wean** I'm indiscriminately hungry *C la20-*. **I could eat a scabby dug** = *I could eat a scabby-heidit wean*. [SCAB¹·¹ + -IE²]

scabrous /'skabrəs/ *adj* **1** *of ground* rough, uneven; *of poetry or writing* crude, unpolished *la16-*. **2** *of questions* difficult to resolve *17-*. [Lat *scabrōsus*]

scad /skad/ *n* a hurry, a flurry, a fluster, haste, a bustling crowd *la19- Sh.* [perhaps an extended sense of SCAUD¹·¹]

scad *see* SCAUD¹·¹, SCAUD¹·², SCAWD

scaddin /'skadın/ *n* **1** a thin flaky turf, the top paring of peat from a bog; a peat turf used for thatching *18- NE T.* **2** a lean, emaciated person or animal *la19- NE.* **3** *derogatory* a person or thing; sometimes the lowest playing card in a game *la19- NE.* [unknown; perhaps related to SCAW]

scaddit /'skadıt, 'skɔdıt/ *adj* **1** boiled, boiling; made using boiling water *19-*. **2** *of cloth, clothing and footwear* faded or shabby *la19-*. **scaddit scone** a scone of barley- or wheatmeal mixed with hot milk or water *20- NE WC SW.* †**scaddit wine** mulled wine *19.* [ptp of SCAUD¹·²]

scaddow *see* SHADDA¹·¹
scadlips *see* SCAUD¹·²

scaff¹·¹ /skaf/ *n* **1** a term of contempt for a person *la20-*. **2** the action of going about idly, roaming in search of amusement or on the scrounge *la19- N NE T.* **3** food, provisions *la18-19, 20- Sh Ork.* **4** booty, things appropriated or acquired by scrounging *20- Ork N.* **5** (worthless) rubbish *19.* **scaffie** of poor quality, shabby *la20-*. †**scauff and raff, scaff raff** riff-raff *e19.* [see the verb]

scaff¹·², **scoff, scouf,** †**skaff** /skaf, skɔf, skʌuf/ *v* **1** to steal, plunder, sponge, scrounge (especially food); to go about looking for what may be picked up *16-19, 20- N NE T EC Bor.* **2** to wander about *la19- NE.* **3** to eat or drink greedily or quickly *19-*. †**scaffar** a parasite, a sponger; an extortioner *16-e17.* †**scafferie, skafrie** extortion *la16-e17.* [compare Du, Ger *schaffen* to procure (food)]

scaff², *NE* **scaith,** †**skaff,** †**skaif** /skaf; *NE* skeθ/ *n* a light boat, skiff *la14-17, la18- Ork N NE.* [OFr *scaphe*, Lat *scapha*]

scaffie /'skafe/ *n* a street-sweeper, a refuse-collector *la19-*. **scaffy cairt** a refuse-collector's cart or lorry *la19-*. [shortened form of Eng SKAFFINGER + -IE¹]

scag¹·¹ /skag/ *n* a putrid fish *la19- Sh N NE.* [perhaps from the verb]

scag¹·² /skag/ *v* **1** *of the human face* to become wrinkled, lose its bloom *20- N.* **2** *of fish* to become rotten by exposure to sun or air *e19.* [perhaps Gael *sgag* to crack, split, become weather-beaten]

scail *see* SKAIL¹·²

scailie, scallie, skylie, skeely, †**scailӡe,** †**scailyie** /'skele, 'skale, 'skʌıle, 'skili/ *n* **1** (a) slate *la15-*. **2** a slate pencil *19-*. †**scailie brod** a slate for writing on *17-e19.* [MDu *schaelie* a slate, OFr *escaille* a fish-scale, a lamina]

scaill *see* SKAIL¹·¹
scailyie, scailӡe *see* SCAILIE
scaip *see* SCAPE
scair *see* SKAIR¹·²
scairsment *see* SCARCEMENT
scait *see* SKATE
scaith *see* SCAFF²
scal *see* SCAULD¹·²
scald *see* SCAUD¹·¹, SCAUD¹·², SCAULD¹·¹, SCAULD¹·², SCAWD

scaldie /'skɔlde/ *n* a non-Traveller; a person from the settled community, a house-dweller *20-*. [Travellers' language]

scalding *see* SKALDING

scale¹, †**skale,** †**skail** /skel/ *n* **1** *pl* (part of) an instrument for weighing things, (the pan of) a balance *la14-*. **2** a shallow drinking bowl; a shallow dish for skimming milk *16-19, 20- Ork WC Bor.* [ON *skál* a bowl, in pl weighing scales]

†**scale²** *n* **1** a ladder *la15-16.* **2** a straight (as opposed to a spiral) flight of steps *la16-17.* [Lat *scāla*]

scale³, †**skale** /skel/ *n* **1** a thin membranous growth on the surface of fish *la15-*. **2** a sixpence *20- NE WC.* **3** a thin plate of wood or metal *la16-e17.* **4** a particle of skin, scurf, dandruff *la16-17*; *compare* SCAW. [OFr *escale* fish-scale]

scale *see* SKAIL¹·²
scaledrake *see* SKELLDRAKE

scale stair /'skel ster/ *n* a straight (as opposed to a spiral) flight of steps *17-*. [SCALE² + STAIR¹]

scalie *see* SKELLIE
scall *see* SCAW

scallag, †**scoloc** /'skalək/ *n* a farm labourer; a boy *la14- H&I.* [Gael *sgalag* a bond-servant; IrGael *scológ* a manservant, a farm servant]

scallie *see* SCAILIE

scallion /'skaljən/ *n* a spring onion, originally perhaps also a leek *19- C SW Uls.* Compare SYBOW. [Eng *scallion*]

scalp *see* SCAUP¹·¹, SCAUP¹·²

scam¹·¹ /skam/ *n* **1** a burn, a singe; its mark or effect *19-*. **2** a film of vapour, a haze *19-*. **3** a spot, a blemish, a crack, an injury *19, 20- Sh Ork NE T EC.* **4** a withering or scorching of plants by frost or other weather *20- N NE T.* **5** a hurt to one's feelings, a wound, a cause of suffering *la19- NE.* [see the verb]

scam¹·², scaum /skam, skɔm/ *v* **1** to burn slightly, scorch, singe; to damage *17-*. **2** to cover with a film of moisture or haze *19-*. **3** *of frost* to scorch, wither (plants) *la19, 20- N NE*

T. **4** to scold severely *20- NE T.* [unknown; compare Swed *skämma* to spoil, disfigure]

†**scamble, skemmill** *v* to sponge, scrounge *la16-17*. [from the noun SKEMMEL[1.1]]

scambler, skemler, †**scamler,** †**skamelar** /'skamlər/ *n* a sponger, a parasite *16-18, 20- N.* [SCAMBLE, with agent suffix]

scamp /skamp/ *v* to go, wander about, frequently intending trouble *la19, 20- NE.* [Eng cant *scamp, schampen* to decamp, run away]

scamp *see* SKEMP

scance[1.1], /skans/ *n* **1** a quick (appraising) look, a cursory survey *la18-*. **2** a gleam (of light), a glimpse (of something), a tinge (of colour) *19-*. [see the verb]

scance[1.2], †**scanse** /skans/ *v* **1** to scrutinize, examine critically *la16-*. **2** to gleam, glitter, shine *la18-*. **3** to criticize, reproach *19, 20- N SW.* **4** to scan, analyse the metre of (verse) *la16*. **5** to give the appearance of *la15-*. **6** to ponder, think deeply about, reflect (upon *or* about); to wonder *la16-e19*. **7** to talk pompously, exaggerate *e19*. [Lat *scans-*, ptp stem of *scandere* to scan metrically]

scandal /'skandəl/ *n* **1** discredit, damage done originally to religion; disgrace; an (unfounded) imputation of bad conduct; open or flagrant sin *17-*. **2** *law* an actionable report defaming a person's character, defamation *18-19*. **scandaleese, scandalize 1** to discredit, shame; to shock *la16-*. **2** to attack verbally; to insult; to slander *la17-*. [EModE *scandal*, Lat *scandalum* cause of moral stumbling]

scangie *see* SKAINIE

scanse *see* SCANCE[1.2]

scant[1.1], †**skant** /skant/ *n* short supply, scarcity (of provisions or people); lack of the necessities *la15-19, 20- Ork N C.* [see the adj]

†**scant**[1.2] /skant/ *v* **1** to stint, limit (a supply); *of supplies* to become scarce *la15-17*. **2** *of wind* to become slight or unfavourable *17-19*. [see the adj]

scant[1.3], †**skant** /skant/ *adj* **1** in short supply, scarce; hard to obtain *15-*. **2** *of a measure* less than appropriate or necessary; deficient or barely correct; only just *16-*. **scantlins** scarcely, hardly *la18-*. **scantly 1** scarcely, hardly, barely *la14-*. **2** with difficulty *la14-16*. **scantness,** †**scantnes** insufficiency; shortage; scarcity *15-*. **scant of** lacking in; poorly supplied with *la15-*. †**scant-o-grace** a reprobate *18-19.* †**scant weill** inadequately *e16.* [ON *skamt*, neuter of *skammr* short, brief]

scant[1.4], †**skant** /skant/ *adv* **1** scarcely, hardly; barely *la14-*. [see the adj]

scant[2] /skant/ *n* a type or size of slate *20- NE T.* [reduced form of Eng *scantle*]

scantack /'skantək/ *n* in Morayshire a hooked and baited line fixed along a shore or in a stream frequently by poachers *19-*. [unknown]

scantlins *see* SCANT[1.3]

scap *see* SCAUP[1.1]

scape, †**scaip,** †**schaip** /skep/ *v* to escape *15-*. [ME *scape*, northern OFr *escaper*]

scar *see* SCARE[1.1], SCARE[1.3], SCAUR[1]

†**Scarborough warning, Skairsbrugh warning** *n* very short notice; no warning at all *la16-e19*. Compare SKYREBURN WARNING. [from the name of the town in Yorkshire]

scarce[1.1], †**scars,** †**skars,** †**skerche** /skers/ *adj* **1** in short supply, short of, deficient in *16-*. **2** *of a person* stingy, mean *15-16*. **scarcelins** scarcely *20- Sh C SW.* **scarcely 1** barely; only just; not quite *la14-*. **2** inadequately, sparingly *16.* **3** with difficulty *16-e17*. [ME *scarse*, OFr *scars*]

scarce[1.2], †**scars,** †**skars** /skers/ *adv* **1** barely, hardly; only just *16-*. **2** just, with difficulty *e16*. [see the adj]

scarcement, †**scarsment,** †**skarsment,** †**scairsment** /'skersmənt/ *n* **1** *building* a horizontal ledge serving as the base of a wall or support for cross-beams *16-*. **2** the edge of a ditch cut to form a ledge on which plants may be planted *la18-*. [SCARCE[1.1] or verb therefrom, with noun-forming suffix]

scare[1.1], *Ork SW* **scar,** *N* **skerr,** *Uls* **scaur,** †**skyre** /sker; *Ork SW* skar; *N* skɛr; *Uls* skɔr/ *n* **1** (a) fright *17-*. **2** something that causes or a reaction to fright or fear, an alarm *la16-19*. [see the verb]

scare[1.2], **scaur, sker, skeer,** †**skar,** †**skyre** /sker, skɔr, skɛr, skir/ *v* **1** to frighten; to terrify *la14-*. **2** to frighten away, drive off; to deter from by arousing fear or apprehension *la15-*. **3** to take fright (at), run, shy away in fear *la15-*. **scare-craw** a scarecrow *17-*. [ON *skirra*]

scare[1.3], *Sh* **sker,** *Ork* **skar,** *N* **skerr,** *NE T EC* **skeer,** *WC* **scaur,** †**scar,** †**skyre** /sker; *Sh N*sker; *Ork* skar; *NE T EC* skir; *WC* skɔr/ *adj* **1** *especially of animals* timid, shy, nervous, easily frightened or alarmed; wild *16-19, 20- Ork WC.* **2** *of girls* flighty, skittish, wild *19, 20- N.* **3** *in Shetland, of sheep* wild *17-e18.* **skeery,** *Ork* **skirry,** †**scaury 1** fearful, nervous *19-*. **2** *of young people* indulging in wild or crazy behaviour *19-*. [ON *skjarr* timid, with influence from SCARE[1.2]]

scare *see* SKAIR[1.1]

scarf /skarf/ *n* the cormorant *Phalacrocorax carbo*; the shag *Phalacrocorax aristotelis la17, 18- Sh Ork N NE Uls.* Compare SCART[2]. [ON *skarfr*]

scargivenet /skər'gɪfnət/ *n* a skinny adolescent *19-*. [unknown]

scarnach /'skarnəx/ *n* **1** heaps of loose stones on hillsides, scree, detritus *la18-e19.* **2** a great number or crowd of things or people *19-.* [Gael *sgàirneach* scree]

scarp *see* SKARP

scarrow /'skaro/ *n* **1** a shadow, shade *19- SW Bor.* **2** a faint light or reflection of light *la18- SW.* [altered form of Eng *shadow*]

scars *see* SCARCE[1.1], SCARCE[1.2]

scarsment *see* SCARCEMENT

scart[1.1], **skart,** *NE C* **scrat,** †**scarth** /skart; *NE C* skrat/ *n* **1** a scratch, a slight wound; the noise made by scratching *16-*. **2** a mark or scrape of a pen, a scribble *la18-*. **3** a furrow or mark on the ground *20-*. **4** the smallest quantity of something, a grain, a trace *19- T C SW Bor.* **scart free** unscathed, scot free *la17-19, 20- EC.* **scart hale** = *scart free la19- T EC.* [see the verb]

scart[1.2], *NE C* **scrat,** †**skrat** /skart; *NE C* skrat/ *v* **1** to scratch, scrape with the nails or claws *la14-*. **2** to scrape or gather together in a parsimonious and acquisitive way; to scrape a living *la16, la19- NE T C SW Bor.* **3** to scrape or scratch (the ground) *la16-*. **4** to scrape with a spoon, take the last bit of food from (a dish) *18-*. **5** to strike (a match) *la19-*. **6** to mark (a surface) with a scratch or incision *19-*. **7** to mark (a paper) with a pen; to write, especially carelessly; to scribble (a note etc) *19-*. **8** to make a scraping, grating, or rasping noise *20-*. **skratter** a small brush or scrubber *20- Ork.* **scrat aff** to mark out with shallow furrows the rigs to be ploughed in (a field) *20- Ork NE T.* **scart somebody's buttons** to run one's fingers down another's jacket buttons, as a challenge to fight *19, 20- Bor.* [ME *scratten*]

scart[2], *NE* **scrath,** †**scarth,** †**skarth** /skart; *NE* skraθ;/ *n* the cormorant *Phalacrocorax carbo*; the shag *Phalacrocorax aristotelis la15- NE T C SW Uls.* [variant of SCARF]

scart[3], *NE T* **scrat,** †**scarth,** †**skarth** /skart; *NE T* skrat/ *n* **1** a hermaphrodite; an animal of indeterminate sex *la16, 20- Bor.* **2** a puny, shrunken person or animal; *derogatory* a contemptible, mean person *19-*. **3** a monster *e16*. [ME *scrat*, ON *skratte* goblin, monster]

scarth *see* SCART¹·¹, SCART², SCART³

scartle¹·¹ /ˈskartəl/ *n* a scraper, hoe or rake *19- EC Bor.* [see the verb]

scartle¹·² /ˈskartəl/ *v* to scrape together in little bits; to make little scratching movements *19- WC Bor.* [diminutive form of SCART¹·²]

scash¹·¹ /skaʃ/ *n* a quarrel, a dispute, a brawl *la18 NE.* [unknown]

scash¹·² /skaʃ/ *v* **1** to quarrel, squabble *19- NE.* **2** *of feet or gait* to twist, turn to one side; to shuffle along with the toes turned out *la19- NE.* [unknown]

scash¹·³ /skaʃ/ *adj of the feet or mouth* twisted, turned to one side *la19- NE WC.* [unknown]

scashle¹·¹ /ˈskaʃəl/ *n* **1** a quarrel, a dispute, a brawl *19- NE.* **2** an untidy or slovenly person or garment *la19- N T.* [frequentative of SCASH¹·¹]

scashle¹·² /ˈskaʃəl/ *v* to quarrel, squabble *la19- NE.* [frequentative of SCASH¹·²]

scat *see* SKATT¹·¹, SKATT¹·²
scate *see* SKATE
scathald *see* SKATTALD
scathe *see* SKAITH¹·¹, SKAITH¹·²
scathold, scattald *see* SKATTALD

scattan, †scatyin /ˈskatən/ *n* a herring *19- NE H&I WC.* [Gael *sgadan*]

scattel *see* SKUTTEL

scatter¹·¹ /ˈskatər/ *n* the scattering of money etc on a festive or celebratory occasion *20- C Bor.* [see the verb]

scatter¹·², †scattir, †skattir, †skatyr /ˈskatər/ *v* **1** to disperse, spread, strew; to distribute *e16-.* **2** *at a wedding or celebration* to throw handfuls of coins or sweets in the street for children to scramble for *20- C Bor.* **scatterment** a scattering, dispersal; a rout *la19- NE SW.* **scatter-wit** a person incapable of coherent thought, a scatterbrain *la19- NE T EC SW Bor.* [ME *scateren*]

scatyin *see* SCATTAN

scaud¹·¹, scad, scald /skɔd, skad, skɔld/ *n* **1** a burn caused by hot liquid or steam *19-.* **2** tea *19-.* **3** a faint appearance of colour or light; a reflection *17-19, 20- T C Uls.* **4** a sore caused by chafing of the skin *18-19, 20- C Bor.* **5** a cause of grief or annoyance; vexation *18-19, 20- NE.* [see the verb]

scaud¹·², scad, scald, †skald, †schald /skɔd, skad, skɔld/ *v* **1** to burn or injure with hot liquid or steam *16-.* **2** *of a liquid* to boil or froth as if boiling *16-.* **3** to cleanse or sterilize with boiling water; to make tea with boiling water *la16-.* **4** to cause grief or pain to; to punish *19, 20- T H&I C SW.* **5** to (cause to) feel strong emotion or desire *la14-e16.* **scaudin, †scaldand 1** very hot; (capable of) burning *la15-.* **2** *of desire* burning, fervent *la14-16.* **scalder** a jellyfish *la19- N NE SW.* **†scadlips** broth made with a small amount of barley *la17-19.* **scaud yer lips wi ither folk's kail** to interfere, meddle *la16-.* **scaud yer tongue wi ither folk's kail** to interfere, meddle *la18-.* [OFr *escalder, escauder*]

scauld¹·¹, scaul, scold, †skald, †scald, †scawl /skɔld, skɔl, skold/ *n* **1** a vituperative, abusive person; a foul-mouthed quarrelsome person *la15-.* **2** jeering, abuse; the act of scolding *la17-.* [ON *skáld* a poet]

scauld¹·², scald, scaul, scold, *NE* **skaal, †scal, †skald** /skɔld, skald, skɔl, skold; *NE* skal/ *v* **1** to use abusive language; to quarrel noisily *la16-.* **2** to rebuke angrily *17-.* **scaulin pyock** a loose fold of skin under the jaws of a fat person *20- NE.* [see the noun]

scaum *see* SCAM¹·²

scaup¹·¹, scalp, †scap, †skap /skɔp, skalp/ *n* **1** the top or crown of the head; the skull, the cranium *la15-.* **2** a bank in the sea supporting a colony of shellfish, especially mussels or oysters *la15-.* **3** thin shallow soil; a piece of infertile, stony ground; a small bare hill or piece of rock *16-19, 20- Sh NE.* **4** the shellfish found on rocks between high and low tide *19, 20- N.* **†scalpie, scappy** bare and exposed; *of soil* thin and shallow *18.* [ME *scalp*; compare ON *skálpr* a sheath]

scaup¹·², scalp /skɔp, skalp/ *v* to pare off the topsoil from a piece of ground; to denude soil *19- Sh.* [see the noun]

scaur¹, scar, †skar /skɔr, skar/ *n* a sheer rock, a precipice; a steep, eroded hill; frequently in place-names *16-.* [ON *sker* a reef; compare SCORE]

scaur²·¹ /skɔr/ *n* a mark left by a wound or sore; a blemish *la16-.* [OFr *escare*]

scaur²·² /skɔr/ *v* to wound, gash or disfigure *la17-.* [see the noun]

scaur *see* SCARE¹·¹, SCARE¹·², SCARE¹·³

scaw, †sca, †scall /skɔ/ *n* **1** (a disease causing) a scaly or scabby skin *la14-19, 20- Ork NE WC.* **2** a barnacle; a mass of barnacles *19- Ork N NE.* [ON *skalle* a bald head]

scawanger *see* SKAFFINGER

scawd, scad, scaad, †scald, †skade, †skawd /skɔd, skad/ *adj* **1** diseased, affected with scab, itch or ringworm; scabby *16-19, 20- N NE H&I WC.* **2** spoiled in appearance; shabby, faded, scruffy *la18-19, 20- NE T WC SW.* **3** *of rocks* covered with barnacles or shellfish *la19- Ork N NE.* **4** foul; mean, contemptible *17-19, 20- NE.* **scawdit, †scaldit 1** scabbed, scabby; contemptible *16-19, 20- NE C.* **2** chaffed, scuffed *20- NE T EC.* **scaadman's heid** a sea-urchin of the genus *Echinus 19, 20- Sh Ork N.* [participial adjective from SCAW, with adj-forming suffix]

scawl *see* SCAULD¹·¹
sceldrick *see* SKELDOCK
scelet *see* SKELET

scent, sint, †sent /sɛnt, sɪnt/ *n* **1** a smell or odour; perfume; the smell by which prey is pursued *la14-.* **2** a small quantity; a drop, a pinch *19-.* [AN *sente* the odour including the trail of an animal]

schabill *see* SHABLE
schad *see* SHADE
schaddow *see* SHADDA¹·¹
schade *see* SHED¹·¹
schadov *see* SHADDA¹·²
schadow *see* SHADDA¹·¹
schaem *see* SHAME¹·¹
schaffron *see* CHAFFERON
schaft *see* CHAFT¹
schaiff *see* SHAVE, SHEAVE¹·¹
schaik *see* SHAK¹·², SCHALK
schaikin *see* SHAK¹·²
schaim *see* SCHEME¹·²
schaip *see* CHAPE¹·¹, SCAPE, SHAPE¹·¹, SHAPE¹·²
schairp *see* SHAIRP¹·³
schairping *see* SHARPING
schak *see* SHAK¹·¹, SCHALK
schakar *see* SHAKER
schake *see* SHAK¹·²
schakill *see* SHACKLE¹·¹
schakin *see* SHAK¹·²
schalaw *see* SCHALLOW
schald *see* SCAUD¹·², SHAULD¹·¹, SHAULD¹·²

†schalk, schaik, schak *n* a servant; a man *la15-e16.* [OE *scealc*]

schall *see* SALL
schallop *see* SHALLOP

†**schallow, schalaw** *n* a drove, a flock *15-16*. [Gael *sealbh*]
schalm *see* SHALM
schalmer *see* CHAUMER
schame *see* SHAME[1.1], SHAME[1.2], SCHEME[1.1]
schamenlo, schamloch *see* SHAMLOCH
schammoy *see* SHAMBO
schamyll *see* SKEMMEL[1.1]
schandellar *see* CHANDLER
schane *see* SHINE[1.2]
schank *see* SHANK[1.1]
schanker *see* CANKER[1.1]
schap *see* CHAPE[1.2], SHAPE[1.2]
schape *see* SHAPE[1.1], SHAPE[1.2]
schapell *see* CHAIPEL
schapen *see* SHAPE[1.2]
schapio, schappeo *see* CHAPEAU
schaplane *see* CHAPLAIN
schapman *see* CHAPMAN
schappin *see* SHAPE[1.2]
schar *see* SHEAR[1.2]
schare *see* SHEAR[1.2], SKAIR[1.1], CHARE
scharge *see* CHAIRGE[1.1], CHAIRGE[1.2], SHARG[1]
scharny *see* SHARN[1.1]
scharp *see* SHAIRP[1.2], SHAIRP[1.3]
scharpe *see* SHAIRP[1.4]
scharpentyn *see* SERPENTINE
schau *see* SEE, SHAW[1.2]
schavyn *see* SHAVE
schaw *see* SAW[2.2], SHAW[1.1], SHAW[1.2], SHAW[2]
schawe *see* SHAVE
schawin *see* SHAW[1.2]
schawm *see* SHALM
schayme *see* SHAME[1.1]
schear *see* SCHEIR
scheat *see* SHETH
scheckle *see* SHACKLE[1.2]
sched *see* SHED[1.1], SHED[1.2]
schedule, †**sedule**, †**sedull**, †**cedull** /ˈʃɛdjul, ˈskɛdjul/ *n* 1 a written statement of details; a notice or memorandum *la15-*. 2 *law* a supplementary statement accompanying or appended to a document *17-*. 3 a timetable or plan *la20-*. [ME *cedule*, OFr *cedule*, Lat *schedula*]
schefe *see* SHAIF, SHEAVE[1.1]
scheid *see* SHED[1.1], SHED[1.2]
scheidmaker *see* SHEATH
scheif *see* SHAIF
scheiftane *see* CHIEFTAIN
scheik *see* CHEEK[1.1]
scheil *see* SHEEL[1.2]
scheild *see* SHIEL[1.1], SHIELD[1.1], SHIELD[1.2]
scheill *see* SHIEL[1.1]
scheillik *see* SHEEL[1.2]
scheilling *see* SHEELING, SHIELING
scheillit *see* SHEEL[1.2]
scheip *see* SHEEP
scheipheird *see* SHEPHERD
†**scheir, schere, schear** *n* the groin or pubis *15-e17*. [OE *scearu*]
scheir *see* SHEAR[1.1], SHEAR[1.2], SHIRE[1]
scheir dawark *see* SHEAR[1.2]
scheis *see* CHEESE[1], CHUSE
scheit *see* CHEAT[1.2]
scheith *see* SHEATH
Scheitland *see* SHETLAND
scheker *see* CHEKKER
scheld *see* SHIELD[1.1], SHIELD[1.2]

schelde *see* SHIELD[1.1]
schele *see* SHIEL[1.1]
scheling *see* SHIELING, SHILLING
scheling siedes *see* SHEELING
schell *see* SHELL[1.1]
†**schelm, schellam** *n derogatory* a rogue, a scoundrel *la16-17*. Compare SKELLUM. [Ger *schelm*]
scheltie *see* SHELTIE
scheme[1.1], **skaim**, †**schame**, †**skeme** /skim, skem/ *n* 1 a plan; a design or diagram *la17-*. 2 a local-authority housing estate *20-*. 3 *derogatory* a person from a housing scheme *la20-* C. **schemie, schemo** *n* 1 *derogatory* an inhabitant of a housing scheme *la20-* C. 2 a scruffy or contemptible person *la20-* C. **schemie** *adj* 1 from a housing scheme *la20-* C. 2 scruffy; contemptible *la20-* C. [EModE *scheme*, Lat *schēma*]
scheme[1.2], **skaim**, †**schaim** /skim, skem/ *v* to plan or plot; to devise a scheme *19-*. [see the noun]
schenachy *see* SHENACHIE
schene *see* SHEEN[1.1], SHEEN[1.2], SHEEN[1.3]
schent *see* SHENT[1.2], SHENT[1.3]
schepe *see* SHEEP
schepehird *see* SHEPHERD
scheptour *see* CHAIPTER
scher *see* SHEAR[1.2]
scherald *see* SHIRREL
†**Scherand** *adj of wine* from the Gironde area of France *16*. [from the name of the River *Gironde*]
scherar *see* SHEARER
scherard *see* SHIRREL
schere *see* SCHEIR, SHEAR[1.1]
scheresmyth *see* SHEAR[1.1]
scheret *see* SHIRREL
schering *see* SHEARING
scherp *see* SHAIRP[1.2], SHAIRP[1.3], SHAIRP[1.4]
schervitour *see* SERVITOR
schet *see* SHITE[1.1], SHUIT, SHUT[1.2]
schete *see* SHEET[1], SHEET[2]
scheth *see* SHETH
scheverone *see* CHEVERON
schevin *see* SHAVE
schew *see* SAW[1], SHAW[1.2], SHEW[1.2]
schewd *see* SHOWD[1.2]
schewe *see* SHOO[1.2]
schewill *see* SHEVEL[1.3]
schewre *see* SHEAR[1.2]
scheyn *see* SHEEN[1.3]
scheyne *see* SHEEN[1.1]
†**schide**[1.1], **schyde** *n* a split piece of wood, kindling; a firebrand *15-e16*. [OE *scīd*]
†**schide**[1.2] *v* to cleave or split *e16*. [see the noun]
schif *see* SHEAVE[1.1]
schift *see* SHIFT[1.1], SHIFT[1.2]
schill *see* CHILL, SHEEL[1.2]
schilling *see* SHILLING
schilling hill *see* SHEELING
schilwing *see* SHELVIN
schimlay *see* CHIMLEY
schimmeis *see* CHEMOIS
schin *see* SHIN
schinder *see* CINNER
schinit *see* SHINE[1.2]
schip *see* SHIP[1.1], SHIP[1.2]
Schipka Pass *see* SHIPKA PASS
schippart *see* SHEPHERD
schir *see* SIR

schire see SHIRE¹, SHIRE²·², SHIRE²·³
schirefe see SHERIFF
schitt see SHITE¹·¹, SHITE¹·²
schiver see SHIVER²
schiveron see CHEVERON
schlorach see SLORACH¹·¹, SLORACH¹·²
scho see SHAE¹·¹, SHAE¹·², SHE
schod see SHOD¹·³
schog see SHOG¹·²
schogg see SHOG¹·¹
schoir see SCHORE, SHORE¹, SHORE²·¹, SHORE²·²
schoke see SHOCK
schokle see SHOCKLE
scholar, †scolar, †scoller, †schooler /ˈskɔlər/ *n* **1** a school pupil; a university student; a learner *la14-*. **2** a learned person, an academic *15-*. **3** the pupil or follower of a particular teacher, master or doctrine *15-*. [OE *scōlere*]
schone see SHAE¹·¹
school see SCHULE
schooler see SCHOLAR
schop see CHOP¹·²
schoppin see CHOPIN
schor see SCHORE, SHORE¹
schorchat see SCORCHET
†schore, schor, schoir *adj* steep, precipitous; rough, jagged *la14-16*. [perhaps related to SHEAR¹·²]
schore see SHAIR²·¹, SCORE¹·¹
schorling see SHORELING
schorne see SCORN¹·¹, SHEAR¹·²
schort see SHORT¹·¹, SHORT¹·², SHORT¹·³, SHORT¹·⁴
schort-breid see SHORTBREAD
schot see SHOT¹·¹, SHOT¹·³, SHOT³, SHOTT², SHUIT
schote see SHOT¹·¹
schothouis see SHOT¹·³
schotquhap see SHOT WHAIP
schot starne see SHOT¹·³
schott see SHOT¹·²
schottill see SHOTTLE, SHUTTLE¹·¹
schour see SHOOER¹·¹
schout see SHOUT¹·¹, SHOUT¹·²
schove see SHOO¹·¹
schow see SHOO¹·¹, SHOO¹·²
schowr see SHOOER¹·¹
schowt see SHOUT¹·¹, SHOUT¹·²
schoys see SHAE¹·¹
schred see SHRED
schrenk see SHRINK
schrine see SCREEN¹·²
schrink see SHRINK
schro see SCREW¹
schroud see SHROOD¹·¹, SHROOD¹·²
schrowd see SHROOD¹·¹, SHROOD¹·²
schrunk see SHRINK
schrynk see SHRINK
schudder see SHIDDER¹·²
schuif see SHAVE
schuik see SHAK¹·²
schuir see SHEAR¹·²
schuk, schuke see SHAK¹·²
schuld see SUD
schulder see SHOODER¹·¹, SHOODER¹·²
schuldir see SHOODER¹·¹
schule, scuil, skuil, school, skeel, *NE* **skweel,** *NE* **squeel, †scule, †scoul** /skul, skɪl; *NE* skwil/ *n* **1** an establishment in which children are taught; a school building; the pupils (and teachers) of a school *la14-*. **2** a faculty of a university or college *15-*. **3** the teaching or beliefs of a particular person or group of people; followers of such teaching *la15-*. **4** the place where an ancient Greek or Roman philosopher taught *la14-e16*. **†scolladge, scolage** school fees *la15-e18*. **school bairn** a schoolchild *la20- Sh EC*. **†school board 1** an elected body set up in each parish or burgh by the Education Act of 1872 to provide universal elementary education, but later abolished by the Education Act of 1918 *la19-e20, la20- historical*. **†school doctor, scholdoctour** an assistant master in a school *17-e18*. **school house, †scolehous** a school building *la16-*. **schule maister, skuil maister, school master,** *NE* **skeelmaister 1** the head of a school; a male teacher in a school *la15-*. **2** a private tutor *16-17*. **†scool meall, schole maill** rent paid for premises used as a school *16-17*. **†schule paet** *in Shetland and Orkney* a peat brought every morning for the school fire by each pupil as part of their school fees *la19*. **school piece** a child's mid-morning or lunchtime snack at school *20-*. **†school wages** school fees *17-19*. **schule wean** a schoolchild *19- WC SW*. **learn the schule** to be a pupil at school *19, 20- NE T EC*. [Lat *schola*]
schule see SHUIL¹·¹, SHUIL¹·²
schunder see SINDER¹·²
schupe see SHAPE¹·²
schurge see SCOURGE¹·¹
schut see SHUT¹·²
schutt see SHOT¹·²
schuttis see SHUIT
schwne see SHAE¹·¹
schyde see SCHIDE¹·¹
schyld see CHIEL
schyn see SHIN
schyne see SHINE¹·¹, SHINE¹·²
schynnie see SHINTY
schyre see SHIRE¹, SHIRE²·³
science, †sciens /ˈsaeəns/ *n* **1** knowledge; learning; a particular body of knowledge or branch of learning *la14-*. **2** a practical skill; a craft, trade or occupation *16-*. [AN *science*, Lat *scientia* knowledge]
†scientive *adj* knowledgeable, learned *la16*. [MFr *scientif*]
scilence see SEELENCE¹·¹
scillop, scullop, †skelup /ˈskɪləp, ˈskʌləp/ an auger with a rounded tapering blade (used in barrel-making) *la18-*. [compare Du *schilp, schulp, schelp* a gouging chisel, literally a scallop shell]
scion, †syon /ˈsaeən/ *n* **1** an heir or descendant *la16-*. **2** a shoot, a twig; a sapling *la15-e16*. [ME *sioun*, AN *cioun*]
scip see SKIP¹·²
scipe see SKYBE
scirhe see SKYRE
scission, †scissione /ˈsɪʒən/ *n* division; schism *15-*. [MFr *scission*, Lat *scission-*]
scitell see SUBTLE
sclaff¹·¹ /sklaf/ *n* **1** a slap, a blow with something flat; a thud *la19-*. **2** *golf* a shot where the club grazes the ground before hitting the ball *la19-*. **3** a light loose-fitting shoe or slipper; an old worn-down shoe *la19- NE T EC*. **4** a thin flat piece of something *la19, 20- NE*. [see the verb]
sclaff¹·² /sklaf/ *v* **1** to slap; to strike with something flat *la19-*. **2** *golf* to graze the ground with the club when striking the ball; to hit the ball in this way *la19-*. **3** to walk in a flat-footed or shuffling way *la19-*. **sklaff-fittit** flat-footed *20-*. [onomatopoeic]
sclaffarde see SCLAFFERT
sclaffer¹·¹ /ˈsklafər/ *n* **1** a big clumsy flat-footed person; a flat-foot *la19- NE T EC*. **2** a loose-fitting shoe or slipper;

an old worn-out shoe *la19- NE T EC.* **3** *golf* a clumsy, inept player *la20-.* [SCLAFF[1.2], with agent suffix]

sclaffer[1.2] /'sklafər/ *v* to walk in a flat-footed or shuffling way *la19, 20- NE H&I.* [frequentative form of SCLAFF[1.2]]

sclaffert, **†sclaffarde** /'sklafərt/ *n* **1** a slap, a blow with something flat *16-19, 20- N NE.* **2** a clumsy flat-footed person *20- NE.* [SCLAFF[1.2], with noun-forming suffix]

sclaik *see* SLAKE[2]

sclair *see* SLAIR

sclaiver /'sklevər/ *v* to gossip; to spread a malicious rumour; to slander a person *la19- NE.* [altered form of CLAVER[1.2]]

sclak *see* SLACK[1.2]

sclam *see* SCLIM[1.2]

sclammer[1] /'sklamər/ *v* to climb, scramble *19-*. [altered form of CLAMMER]

sclammer[2.1] /'sklamər/ *n* an outcry, a din *20 NE T.* [altered form of Eng *clamour*]

sclammer[2.2] /'sklamər/ *v* to cry; to make a raucous noise *20- NE.* [see the noun]

sclander[1.1], **slander**, **†sklander** /'sklandər, 'slandər/ *n* **1** a false or malicious statement *15-*. **2** the uttering of false statements, defamation *la15-*. **3** disgrace; ill-repute *la14-17.* **4** a discreditable act; a crime; a source of shame *15-e17.* [OFr *esclandre*]

sclander[1.2], **slander**, **†sklander** /'sklandər, 'slandər/ *v* **1** to defame by spreading untrue or malicious rumours *la14-.* **2** to bring shame or disgrace on; to censure; to criticize harshly *la14-17.* **3** to accuse or suspect a crime or wrongdoing; to condemn by public consensus *la15-17.* [OFr *esclandrer*]

sclap[1.1] /sklap/ *n* a heavy blow, a hard smack (with something flat) *la19- N NE.* [altered form of SLAP[1.1]; compare SCLAFF[1.1]]

sclap[1.2] /sklap/ *v* to walk in a flat-footed or shuffling way *20- NE.* [see the noun]

sclatch[1.1] /sklatʃ/ *n* **1** a large smudge or smear; a daub of something wet or dirty *19- Sh NE T EC.* **2** a mess; a botch or bungle *19- NE T EC Bor.* **3** a heavy fall (into water or mud) *19- NE T Bor.* **4** a slap, a smack; a slapping or crashing noise *19- NE T Bor.* Compare SLATCH[1.1]. [altered form of CLATCH[1.1]]

sclatch[1.2] /sklatʃ/ *v* **1** to smear or cover with a wet or messy substance *la19-.* **2** to walk in an ungainly, slovenly way; to shuffle *19, 20- N NE T EC.* **3** to work messily; to use carelessly; to construct clumsily or untidily *19, 20- NE T EC.* Compare SLATCH[1.2]. [see the noun]

sclate[1.1], **slate**, **†sklait**, **†skleat** /sklet, slet/ *n* **1** a thin piece of of readily-split stone; slate or flagstone (used for roofing) *la15-*. **2** a flat piece of hardwood nailed on to the underside and foreside of an oar to prevent wear *20- Sh Ork.* **sclateband** a type of rock *19- C SW.* **slate diamond** iron pyrites *19- T WC Bor.* **slate hoose** a house with a slate roof *15-19, 20- Sh T Uls.* **sclate stane** a piece of slate or slate-like stone; false or worthless currency *18-.* [ME *sclate*, OFr *esclate*]

sclate[1.2], **sklait**, **slate**, **†skleat** /sklet, slet/ *v* to roof or cover with slates *16-.* [see the noun]

sclater, **slater**, **†sclatter**, **†sklaitter**, **†skletter** /'skletər, 'sletər/ *n* **1** a person who fixes slates onto roofs *la14-.* **2** the woodlouse *Oniscus asellus la17-.* [SCLATE[1.2], with agent suffix]

sclave[1.1] /sklev/ *n* a gossip, a scandalmonger *20- NE.* [see the verb]

sclave[1.2] /sklev/ *v* to gossip; to spread a malicious rumour; to slander a person *19- NE.* [probably back-formation from SCLAIVER]

sclave *see* SLAVE[1.1], SLAVE[1.2]

sclender *see* SKLENNER

sclent *see* SKLENT[1.1], SKLENT[1.2]

sclenter /'sklentər/ *n* loose stones, scree; a stony hillside *la18- C SW Bor.* [perhaps altered form of SLIDDER[1.1]]

scleve *see* SLEEVE[1.2]

sclew *see* SLAY[1]

sclice[1.1], **slice**, **†sklyse** /sklʌɪs, slʌɪs/ *n* **1** a (thin) piece of something *16-.* **2** a splinter, a sliver *15-e17.* [ME *sclyce*, OFr *esclice*]

sclice[1.2], **slice**, **†sklisse** /sklʌɪs, slʌɪs/ *v* to cut piece by piece; to cut in slices *17-.* [ME *skłyce*, OFr *esclicer*]

sclidder *see* SLIDDER[1.1], SLIDDER[1.2]

scliff *see* SKLIFF[1.2]

sclim[1.1] /sklɪm/ *n* a climb *la19- C Bor.* [see the verb]

sclim[1.2], **sklim** /sklɪm/ *v pt* **sclimmed**, **sclam** to climb *la19-.* [altered form of CLIM]

sclinder *see* SKLENNER

sclit, **†sklut** /sklɪt/ *n* slaty or fissile coal, coaly blaes; a clayey stratum *la18-19, 20- C.* [altered form of SCLATE[1.1]]

sclither *see* SLIDDER[1.1], SLIDDER[1.2]

scloister *see* SLAISTER[1.2]

sclore[1.1] /sklor/ *n* inconsequential chatter, a long rambling story *la19- T H&I EC.* [unknown]

sclore[1.2] /sklor/ *v* to chat or gossip; to prattle *la19, 20- Bor.* [unknown]

scloy *see* SCLY[1.2]

sclunsh /sklʌnʃ/ *v* to walk with a slow heavy tread; to stump along *la19- NE T EC.* [probably onomatopoeic]

sclushach /'sklʌʃəx/ *n* a crab that has cast its shell *20- NE.* [probably altered form of CLOSHACH]

sclutter *see* SLUTTER[1.2]

scly[1.1], **sly**, **sloy** /sklae, slae, slɔɪ/ *n* **1** a strip of ice used as a slide *19- C SW Bor.* **2** the act of sliding on ice *la19- WC SW Bor.* [see the verb]

scly[1.2], **sly**, **scloy** /sklae, slae, sklɔɪ/ *v* to slide or skate on ice *19- C SW Bor.* **†sklire** to skate on ice *e19.* [perhaps altered and reduced form of ME *slīthen* to slide]

sclype *see* SLYPE[1.1], SLYPE[1.2]

scoarn *see* SCORN[1.1], SCORN[1.2]

Scoatch *see* SCOTS[1.1], SCOTS[1.2]

Scoatland *see* SCOTLAND

Scoats *see* SCOTS[1.1]

Scoattish *see* SCOTS[1.2]

scob[1.1], **scobe** /skɔb, skob/ *n* **1** a twig or cane of willow or hazel (bent over to fasten down thatch or make baskets) *16-19, 20- SW Bor Uls.* **2** a slat of wood used as a splint for broken bones or repairing a wooden shaft *la19, 20- NE T SW.* **3** *in weaving* a defect in which the shuttle passes on the wrong side of the warp threads *19- T C Bor.* **4** something thrust into the mouth, a gag *la17-18.* **5** a rod of wood or metal *la18-e19.* [Gael *sgolb*, IrGael *scolb* a splinter, a thatching rod, a thin stick]

scob[1.2], **scobe** /skɔb, skob/ *v* **1** *in weaving* to miss threads, to allow the weft to miss the warp *la19- T C SW Bor.* **2** to put a broken bone in splints *19, 20- NE T.* **3** to close or obstruct the mouth with a gag *la17-e18.* [see the noun]

scob[2] /skɔb, skob/ *v* **1** to scoop out, hollow; to gnaw out with the teeth *la19- C SW Uls.* **2** to remove pieces or quantities from the inside of a heap, leaving the outside undisturbed *la19- C SW.* [Gael *sgob* to snatch, scoop out, nibble, peck]

scobe *see* SCOB[1.1], SCOB[1.2]

scodge[1.1], **scudge** /skɔdʒ, skɔdʒ, skʌdʒ/ *n* **1** a servant who does rough or dirty work; a drudge or menial; an odd-job man *la18-.* **2** a rough apron worn for dirty work; compare *scodgie brat* (SCODGIE) *20- EC Bor.* [unknown]

scodge[1.2], **scudge** /skɔdʒ, skɔdʒ, skʌdʒ/ *v* **1** to do rough menial work *19, 20- C Bor.* **2** to act slyly; to sneak idly about

scodgebell see COACHBELL

19- N EC SW. **scodgie** to do rough menial work *la19- N NE T C.* [unknown]

scodgie, scudgie /ˈskɔdʒi, ˈskɔdʒi, ˈskʌdʒi/ *n* **1** a servant who does rough or dirty work; a drudge or menial; an odd-job man *la18-*. **2** a rough apron worn for dirty work *20- EC Bor.* **scodgie brat** a rough apron worn for dirty work *20- EC Bor.* **scodgie claes** a person's second-best or working clothes *20- NE T.* [SCODGE[1.1] + -IE[1]]

scoff /skɔf/ *v* to dodge or avoid doing something; to play truant *20- NE.* [perhaps altered form of SCUFF[1.2]]

scoff see SCAFF[1.2], SCOWP[1.2]

scog see SCUG[1.2]

scoir see SCORE[1.1], SCORE[1.2]

scolar see SCHOLAR

scold see SCAULD[1.1], SCAULD[1.2]

scoll see SKOL[1.1], SKOL[1.2]

scoller see SCHOLAR

scoloc see SCALLAG

scomfish[1.1], **scumfish** /ˈskʌmfɪʃ/ *n* a suffocating atmosphere; a state of suffocation *19, 20- Ork.* **get a scumfish at** to be disgusted at *la19, 20- Sh NE T.* **tak a scumfish at** to take a strong dislike to *20- Sh NE T.* [see the verb]

scomfish[1.2], *Sh* **skunfish**, †**scumfit** /ˈskʌmfɪʃ; *Sh* ˈskʌnfɪʃ/ *v* **1** to suffocate, choke; to overpower with heat *la18-*. **2** to disgust, sicken *la19- Sh N NE T EC.* **3** to defeat *la14-15.* †**sconfyste** defeated *la14.* [shortened form of DISCOMFISH]

scon see SCONE[1.1]

sconce[1.1], †**skons** /skɔns/ *n* **1** protection, shelter *la16-19, 20- literary.* **2** a protective screen, partition or wall; a firescreen *16-19, 20- N.* **3** a shelter, a shed *la17-e19.* **4** a parapet or palisade *la16-17.* [Du *schans*]

sconce[1.2] /skɔns/ *v* to protect; to fend off; to shelter or conceal *17-19, 20- literary.* [see the noun]

sconce[2] /skɔns/ *v* to cheat; to obtain something by false pretences *la18-19, 20- T.* [unknown; compare Oxford University slang *sconce* to fine someone a tankard of ale or the like]

sconce[3] /skɔns/ *v* to settle oneself; to take up one's position *la19- NE.* [shortened form of Eng *ensconce*]

scondies see SCONE[1.1]

scone[1.1], **scon** /skɔn/ *n* **1** a large, flat round wheat or barleymeal cake (baked on a girdle), cut into four three sided pieces; a similar small round individual-sized cake *16-*. **2** a slap or smack *19- NE T C.* **3** an oatcake *18, 19- Sh.* **4** a cow-pat *la19- Ork.* **scondies** a child's word for a smack or a spanking *20- NE.* **scone bonnet** a broad, flat, woollen bonnet *19, 20- T C SW Bor.* **scone cap** = *scone bonnet.* **sconeface** a nickname for a person or object with a round flat face *20- T C.* **a scone o the day's baking** one of the same kind as others, an average or typical person *la19-*. **my wee scone 1** a term of endearment (to a child) *20- C.* **2** an object of pity *la20- EC.* **who stole yer scone?** why do you look so unhappy? *20-*. [perhaps MDu *schoonbrot* fine bread, a kind of flat loaf]

scone[1.2] /skɔn/ *v* **1** to strike a surface with a flat object; to crush flat with a slap *19-, Ork N NE T C.* **2** to slap or smack; to spank a child *18-19, 20- NE T C SW.* [extended sense of the noun]

sconner see SCUNNER[1.1], SCUNNER[1.2]

scoo see SCULL[1]

scooby /ˈskubi/ *n* rhyming slang a clue: ◊*he's no got a scooby la20-*. **scoobied** exhausted; disoriented because of alcohol or drugs *la20-*. [from *Scooby Doo*, a cartoon character]

scooder see SCOWDER[1.2]

scoog see SCUG[1.2]

scoonrel, scoondrel, scoundrel /ˈskunrəl, ˈskundrəl, ˈskʌundrəl/ *n* a dishonest or unscrupulous person *18-*. [unknown]

scoop see SCOPE, SCOWP[1.2], SCUIP[1.1], SCUIP[1.2]

scoor see SCOUR[1], SCOUR[2.1], SCOUR[2.2], SCOUR[3.1], SCOUR[3.2]

scoort see SKURT

scoosh see SKOOSH[1.1], SKOOSH[1.2]

scoot see SCOUT[1.1], SCOUT[1.2], SCOUT[3.1], SCOUT[4], SCOUT[5]

scooth see SCOWTH

scootie see SCOUT[1.1], SCUITIE

scootie-alan, skootieallan, †**scoutiaulin** /skutiˈɑlən/ *n* the Arctic skua *Stercorarius parasiticus 18- Sh Ork.* [SCOUT[1.2] + ALAN]

scoove see SCOVE

scope, scowp, scoup, †**scoop** /skʌup; *Sh* skup/ *n* **1** a mark for shooting at; an end, aim, goal *la16-17* **2** the intended meaning of a speaker of writer *la16-17* **3** freedom or space for action *17-*. [Ital *scopo* aim, purpose, Greek *skopós* a mark for shooting at]

scor see SCORE[1.2]

†**scorchet, schorchat, skorchett** *n* a sweetmeat made of sugar flavoured with rosewater *15-e17.* [SUCCAR + *rosat* from OFr *rosat*, Lat *rosātus* oil of roses]

scord, skord /skɔrd, skɔrd/ *n* a deep indentation or fissure in the skyline of a hill *19- Sh.* [ON *skarð*, perhaps with influence from SCORE [2]]

score[1.1], †**scoir,** †**skoyr,** †**schore** /skɔr/ *n* **1** a set of twenty *la14-*. **2** a mark or line indicating a boundary; a starting line or finish-line *16-*. **3** a line or stroke drawn; a mark scoring out a word *la16-*. **4** a notch or incision *la16-*. **5** a wrinkle or furrow on the skin; a scratch or cut; a scar left by a wound *16-19, 20- Sh N NE C.* **6** a parting in the hair *20- C.* **7** a debt, a bill *la16-17.* **scorie,** †**skorie 1** scratched, notched, incised *la16-19, 20- NE Bor.* **2** *of skin* wrinkled, scarred *19, 20- NE Bor.* [ON *skor*]

score[1.2], †**scor,** †**scoir** /skɔr/ *v* **1** to keep a tally or account; to keep a record of points scored *la15-*. **2** to mark with cuts; to make incisions; to scratch *16-*. **3** to draw a line through writing *la16-*. **4** to earn points in a game or contest *19-*. **5** to break apart a ship *la15-16.* **scurrit, skurd** *of an ox* marked in some way *16 NE.* †**score abune the breath** *folklore* to make a scratch on the forehead of a suspected witch as a means of thwarting her power *18-19.* **over the score** beyond the bounds of reason or moderation *18-*. **score oot, score oot** to draw a line through writing to cross it out or cancel it *17-*. [ON *skora*]

score[2] /skɔr/ *n* a crevice, a cleft; a gully in a cliff-face, frequently in place-names *19, 20- Sh N EC.* Compare SKUR[1]. [a specialized usage of SCORE[1.1]]

scorie, skorie, scorrie, *NE* **scurrie** /ˈskɔre, ˈskɔri; ˈskʌri/ *n* **1** a young gull *la18- Sh Ork N NE.* **2** an avaricious, quarrelsome person *20- N.* **3** an inhabitant of Papa Stour in Shetland or Wick in Caithness *20- Sh N.* [Norw *skåre*]

scorn[1.1], **scoarn,** †**scoarn,** †**skorn,** †**schorne** /skɔrn, skɔrn/ *n* **1** derision, mockery, contempt *la14-*. **2** a snub, a rejection (of a would-be lover) *la14-19.* **3** something worthy of contempt *la14-16.* [OFr *escarn*]

scorn[1.2], **scoarn,** †**scorne,** †**skorn** /skɔrn, skɔrn/ *v* **1** to mock, ridicule *la14-*. **2** to disdain, reject *la14-*. **3** to imitate, lampoon *20- Sh Ork.* **4** to deceive *la14-e17.* **scorn at** to jeer or scoff at *18-*. †**scorn wi** to tease a girl about a lover *la18-19.* [OFr *escarnir*]

scorp see SKIRP[1.2]

scorrick see SKOURICK

scorrie see SCORIE

scoskie /'skɔski/ *n* the starfish *Asterias rubens la19- N NE.* [altered form of Gael *crosgag, crosgan*]
Scot /skɔt/ *n pl* also †**Scottis 1** a member of the Gaelic-speaking people originating in the west of Scotland *la12-15, 16- historical.* **2** a native of Scotland *la14-.* [Lat *Scōtus* in earliest use, a native of Ireland]
scot *see* SKATT[1.1], SQUAT[1.1], SQUAT[1.2]
scot and lot *see* SKATT[1.1]
Scotch *see* SCOTS[1.1], SCOTS[1.2]
Scotia /'skoʃə/ *n* an alternative name for Scotland *16-18, 19- literary.* [Lat *Scōtia* in earliest use, Ireland]
Scotland, Scoatland, †**Skotland,** †**Scottland** /'skɔtlənd, 'skotlənd/ *n* a country in the northern part of Britain *la14-.* [SCOT + LAND[1.1]]
Scots[1.1], **Scoats, Scotch, Scoatch,** †**Scottish,** †**Scottis** /skɔts, skots, skɔtʃ, skotʃ/ *n* **1** the Scots language, the Germanic language spoken in Scotland *la15-.* **2** the Scottish Gaelic language *15- historical.* [see the adj]
Scots[1.2], **Scottish, Scoattish, Scotch, Scoatch,** †**Scottis** /skɔts, 'skɔtɪʃ, 'skotɪʃ, skɔtʃ, skotʃ/ *adj* **1** of or pertaining to Scotland; deriving from or made in Scotland *la14-.* **2** of Scottish nationality *la14-.* **3** speaking or expressed in the Scots language *16-.* **4** of or belonging to the Scottish legal system *16-.* **5** *of a regiment* raised in Scotland; composed of Scottish troops *la16-.* **6** *in the Northern Isles* of or pertaining to the Scottish mainland *20-.* **7** of or pertaining to the the Scottish-Gaelic speakers who originated in the west of Scotland *16- historical.* **8** *of coins* minted in Scotland; *of currency* having a value specific to Scotland *la15-19, 20- historical.* **9** *of a unit of weight or measurement* having a value specific to Scotland *18-19, 20- historical.* **Scots acre** an area of 5760 square ells *la18-19, 20- historical.* **Scottish antisyzygy** the presence of duelling polarities within one entity, considered to be characteristic of the Scottish temperament *la20-;* compare *Caledonian antisyzygy* (CALEDONIAN[1.2]). **Scots blanket** a blanket of a hard, unbrushed texture *la17-20, 21- historical;* compare *Ayrshire blanket* (AYRSHIRE). **Scotch broth** a thick soup made from mutton, barley and root vegetables *la18-.* **Scotch bun** a rich spiced fruit cake, baked in a pastry crust and traditionally eaten at Hogmanay *la19-.* **Scots collops** thin slices of meat stewed with stock and flavouring *la17-.* **Scots Confession** the 1560 Confession of Faith of the reformed Scottish Church, the first published document of the Scottish Reformation *la16-17, 18- historical;* compare *Negative Confession* (NEGATIVE). **Scotch convoy** the accompanying of a guest a part or all of the way back to their home *19-.* **Scotch cousin** a distant relative *la19, 20- NE T C SW.* **Scotch craa** the rook *Corvus frugilegus la19- Sh.* **Scotch cuddy** a pedlar, a travelling packman or draper *20- WC SW.* **Scots dyke** a linear earthwork constructed in 1552 between the rivers Esk and Sark to settle the border between Scotland and England *18-.* †**Scots ell** the Scottish yard of 37 inches (940 mm) *la17-19.* **Scottish Episcopal,** †**Scots Episcopal** a member of the Scottish Episcopal Church *la18-.* **Scotch flummery, Scots flummery** a dish in which oatmeal, wine, dried fruit and milk or cream are steamed *la18-.* **Scotch gravat** a hug, a cuddle *20- NE T C SW Bor.* **Scots Greys** a former Scottish cavalry regiment *18-20, 21- historical;* compare *Royal Scots Greys* (ROYAL). **Scotch hands** a pair of bats for making pats or rolls of butter *la19-.* **Scotch horses** *games* a formation of children running or skating with arms linked behind their backs *20-.* **Scots law** the legal system of Scotland, so entitled after the Act of Union *18-.* **Scotch mahogany** the wood of the alder, which turns red when exposed to light and weather *la19- WC SW.* **Scotsman,** †**Scottis man** a male native of Scotland *la14-.* **Scots mile 1** a distance of around 1980 imperial yards *la16-.* **2** a long distance *la18- literary.* **Scotch muffler** an alcoholic drink, especially whisky *20- NE T C.* **Scotch nightingale** the sedge warbler *Acrocephalus schoenobaenus la19, 20- C.* **Scots pebble** a semi-precious stone found on hills or streams in Scotland *18-.* **Scotch pie** a small round pie of cooked mutton or beef, with the rim raised to retain the filling *19-.* **Scots pint, Scotch pint** a Stirling jug, formerly the standard measure of the pint in Scotland, equating to around three imperial pints *17-.* **Scots plough** a swingless or wheelless plough *17-19, 20- historical.* **Scots sea, Scottish Sea,** †**Scottis see** the Firth of Forth, the Forth estuary *la14-18, 19- historical.* **Scots thistle** the cotton thistle *Onopordum acanthium* adopted as the national emblem of Scotland *la18-.* **Scottish Traveller** a person from a legally recognized group of Gipsy or Traveller communities *la20-;* compare TINKER. **Scots Troy,** †**Scots Troyes** a standard measure of weight *la17-19, 20- historical;* compare TROIS. **Scotswoman,** †**Scottis woman** a female native of Scotland *16-.* †**old Scots Episcopal** an adherent of that branch of the Scottish Episcopal Church which had been proscribed for its Jacobitism *18-e19.* **Scotch and English** a children's game in which two opposing sides tried to capture one another or an seize an object *19, 20- historical.* **Scottish Certificate of Education** *see* CERTIFICATE. **Scottish Land Court** a court set up by statute in 1911 with a chairman who has the same authority as a Court of Session judge and members with agricultural expertise; its jurisdiction covers the various forms of agricultural tenancy *20-.* [SCOT with adj-forming suffix. *Scots* (the descendant of the historical form *Scottis*) survived until the nineteenth century only in certain locutions, but has gradually re-established itself as preferable to *Scotch* in general contexts. *Scottish* was first used in general contexts by anglicizing *Scots,* then retained in formal contexts stressing national or historical aspects *eg* 'Scottish burgh'. *Scotch* (the prevailing form in England) was adopted into Scots and was the prevailing form in the nineteenth century but is now acceptable in Eng only in certain compounds *eg* 'Scotch whisky']
Scotticism /'skɔtəsɪzəm/ *n* a Scots word or expression (in an English-language text) *la17-.* [Lat *Scotticus,* with noun-forming suffix]
Scottis *see* SCOT, SCOTS[1.1], SCOTS[1.2]
Scottish *see* SCOTS[1.1], SCOTS[1.2]
Scottish Certificate of Education *see* CERTIFICATE
Scottland *see* SCOTLAND
scouf *see* SCOWP[1.2], SCAFF[1.2]
scoug *see* SCUG[1.1], SCUG[1.2]
scouk[1.1], **skulk,** *N NE* **skook,** †**skolk** /skʌuk, skʌlk; *N NE* skuk/ *n* **1** a skulking, cowardly person *17- Sh N NE.* **2** a furtive look; a frown *18-19, 20- NE T.* [see the verb]
scouk[1.2], **skulk,** *N NE* **skook,** †**scowk** /skʌuk, skʌlk; *N NE* skuk/ *v* **1** to conceal oneself, lurk; to sneak about, move stealthily *la14-.* **2** to scowl, frown *18-19, 20- N NE EC.* **3** to play truant *20- Ork NE T.* **4** to shun or avoid *17-e19.* [compare Norw *skulka*]
scoul[1.1], **scowl** /skul, skʌul/ *n* an angry or malevolent look *16-.* [see the verb]
scoul[1.2], **scowl** /skul, skʌul/ *v* to look angry or sullen *16-.*
scoul-horned *of a cow* having horns pointing downwards over the forehead *la17-19, 20- WC.* [unknown; compare Dan *skule*]
scoul *see* SCHULE
scoundrel *see* SCOONREL

scoup see SCOPE, SCOWP[1.1], SCOWP[1.2], SCUIP[1.1]

scour[1], **scoor** /skʌur, skur/ *n* a gusty or squally shower of rain *la18*-. **scourie, scoorie, scowrie** *of weather* blustery with rain; wet and squally *la18*-. [ON *skúr* a shower]

scour[2.1], **scoor** /skur/ *n* a run; a dash, quick pace *la18-19, 20- N*. [see the verb]

scour[2.2], **scoor** /skur/ *v* **1** to go rapidly; to rush about *la14*-. **2** to search thoroughly *la15*-. [unknown; compare Norw *skura* to rush]

scour[3.1], **scoor** /skʌur, skur/ *n* **1** the act of scouring *19*-. **2** a purging of the bowels; diarrhoea *19, 20- Ork NE T*. **3** an apparatus for washing gold-bearing soil *17-e19*. **4** a large alcoholic drink *la17-e19*. **5** a blow or stroke *la19- NE*. **6** a cutting remark, a rebuke *19- NE WC*. **scoor oot 1** a thorough cleaning *20*-. **2** the scattering of coins at a wedding for children to scramble for *20- T EC*. [see the verb]

scour[3.2], **scoor** /skʌur, skur/ *v* **1** to purge or clear out the stomach or bowels; to suffer from diarrhoea *la14*-. **2** to scrub; to cleanse with detergent; to polish *la15*-. **3** to reprimand severely *19- Sh WC*. **4** to drain a glass of alcohol *15-19*. **scourins** coarse woollen cloth; coarse blankets *la16-19, 20- N*. **scoorin blot** soap suds *20- Sh Ork*. **scoorin bootie** a shawl or headscarf of coarse woollen cloth *la19- Ork*. **scourin clout** a rough cloth for washing floors *20*-. **scoorda-buggie, †skur-de-bogi** the youngest child in a family *19- Sh*. [MDu, MLG *schuren*]

scourge[1.1], **†scurge, †schurge** /skʌrdʒ/ *n* **1** a whip or lash *la14*-. **2** a person who inflicts punishment; a cause of suffering or calamity *la15*-. **3** a domineering woman *la19*-. **4** the whip of a spinning top *la19- WC*. [AN *escorge*]

scourge[1.2], **†scurge, †skurge** /skʌrdʒ/ *v* **1** to flog, whip *15*-. **2** to punish; to cause to suffer *16*-. **3** to exhaust the fertility of land *la18-19*. [OFr *escorgier*]

scourie[1.1], **scowrie** /ˈskuri, ˈskʌuri/ *n* a scruffy, disreputable-looking person *18-19, 20- WC*. [unknown]

scourie[1.2], **scowrie, †skowry** /ˈskuri, ˈskʌuri/ *adj* **1** *of a person* scruffy, disreputable-looking; *of an object* shabby, dilapidated *16-19, 20- C*. **2** *of an area of the sea* over-fished *20- Sh*. **3** *of clothing* shabby, threadbare *19*. [unknown]

scoury see SCURRY

scout[1.1], **scoot** /skʌut, skut/ *n* **1** a sudden gush or flow of water from a spout *19*-. **2** a waste pipe *19*-. **3** a contemptible, ineffectual person *19*-. **4** diarrhoea; watery excrement *la19*-. **5** a syringe *19, 20- T C Bor*. **6** a peashooter *la19, 20- C Uls*. **scootie 1** small, insignificant *la19*-. **2** scruffy, disreputable *la19*-. [see the verb]

scout[1.2], **scoot** /skʌut, skut/ *v* **1** to squirt or spurt liquid; *of liquid* to gush or squirt out *19*-. **2** *of a person* to suffer from diarrhoea *19*-. **3** *of a bird* to excrete *20- Sh*. **scooter 1** a syringe *la19*-. **2** a peashooter *20*-. **3** *pl* diarrhoea *20*-. **scoot gun** a syringe *19, 20- T EC Bor*. [probably ON *skjóta* to shoot]

scout[2] /skut/ *n* the guillemot *Uria aalge* or the razorbill *Alca torda 16-19, 20- historical*. [perhaps SCOUT[1.2]]

scout[3.1], **scoot** /skut/ *n* **1** a reconnoiterer; a look-out *15*-. **2** a member of the Scouting Association *20*-. [OFr *escoute*]

scout[3.2], **†skout** /skʌut/ *v* to act as a scout; to spy on; to reconnoitre *la16*-. [see the noun]

†scout[4], **scowt, scoot** *n* a small flat-bottomed boat; a yawl *15-19*. [MDu *schute*]

scout[5], **scoot** /skʌut, skut/ *n* a disreputable person; a loiterer *la16-19, 20- Ork*. [perhaps ON *skúta* a taunt]

scouth see SCOWTH

scouther see SCOWDER[1.1], SCOWDER[1.2]

scoutiaulin see SCOOTIE-ALAN

†scove, scoove *v of a bird* to fly smoothly; to glide *la18-19*. [perhaps altered form of SKIFF[1.2] or SCUFF[1.2]]

scow[1] /skʌu/ *n* a flat-bottomed boat; a lighter or barge *19*-. [Du *schouw*]

scow[2.1], **skow** /skʌu/ *n* **1** a strip of wood, a barrel stave; a thin plank *la15-19, 20- Sh N*. **2** *pl* splinters or slivers of wood *19, 20- Ork N*. **3** *pl* fragments, shattered pieces *la19- Ork N SW*. **4** a long, thin, bony person or animal *la19- Sh Ork*. **ding tae scows** to smash to pieces *19, 20- Ork N*. [Du *schooven* sheaves of corn, bundles of staves]

scow[2.2], **skow** /skʌu/ *v* to break in pieces; to smash *19- Sh*. [see the noun]

scow[3], **scrow** /skʌu, skrʌu/ *n* a sudden, heavy, squally shower of rain *19, 20- NE T H&I Bor*. [unknown]

scow[4] /skʌu/ *v* to examine a hen to see if she is about to lay *20- Sh*. [compare Norw dial *skoa* to examine]

scowder[1.1], **scouther** /ˈskʌudər, ˈskʌuðər/ *n* **1** a scorch, a burn; the mark of a burn *la18*-. **2** a slight shower of rain or snow *19*-. **3** a jellyfish *19- H&I WC*. **4** a toasted oatcake *19- Uls*. **5** a naive or inexperienced person *19- Uls*. **scowthery** beginning or threatening to rain or snow *la18-19, 20- WC Bor*. [see the verb]

scowder[1.2], **scouther**, *Sh* **scooder, †skolder** /ˈskʌudər, ˈskʌuðər; *Sh* ˈskudər; *Ork* ˈskʌðər/ *v* **1** to burn, scorch or singe; to overcook *16*-. **2** *of frost or rain* to wither or blight foliage *la18-19, 20- T C SW Bor*. **3** to rain or snow slightly *la19- Ork NE Bor*. **4** *of the skin* to become wrinkled *16-17*. **†scoutherin** reproving, chastising *19*. **scoudrum** chastisement *19- NE*. [perhaps altered form of *northern* Eng *scalder*; SCAUD[1.2] with intensifying suffix]

scowf see SCOWTH

scowk see SCOUK[1.2]

scowl see SCOUL[1.1], SCOUL[1.2]

scowner see SCUNNER[1.1], SCUNNER[1.2]

†scowp[1.1], **scoup** *n* a skip or bounce; a thump *16-e19*. Compare SKIP[1.1]. [see the verb]

scowp[1.2], **scoop**, *NE* **scouf**, *NE* **scoff, †scoup** /skʌup, skup; *NE* skʌuf, skɔf/ *v* to bound, dart; to skip about *16-19, 20- NE WC*. **†scowper, scoupar** a dancer *la16*. [perhaps ON *skopa* (*skeið*) (to take a) run; compare SKIP[1.2]]

scowp see SCOPE

scowrie see SCOURIE[1.1], SCOURIE[1.2]

scowt see SCOUT[4]

scowth, scouth, scooth, scowf /skʌuθ, skuθ, skʌuf/ *n* **1** freedom; scope; liberty *la16*-. **2** abundance, plenty *19*-. **3** opportunity, the chance to improve or prosper *20*-. **scowthie, scouthie** capacious, bulky, big *la19- NE*. **scowth and rowth 1** freedom, room to range *19, 20- NE EC*. **2** plenty, abundance *19, 20- NE EC*. [perhaps altered form of *scowp* (SCOPE)]

scra see SCRAE[2.1]

scraap see SCRAPE[1.2]

scrab[1], *WC* **scribe** /skrab; *WC* skrʌib/ *n* **1** the crab-apple *Malus sylvestris 16-19, 20- C SW Uls*. **2** a gnarled or shrivelled tree or plant *la18- NE*. **3** a stunted person or animal *la19- NE*. [ME *scrab*; compare Swed dial *skrabba*]

scrab[2] /skrab/ *v* to scratch, scrape *la19- H&I Uls*. [EModE *skrab*, Du *schrabben*]

scrae[1] /skre/ *n* **1** a stunted or underdeveloped person or animal *19, 20- NE WC*. **2** a shrivelled dried-up object *18-19, 20- N*. **3** an ill-natured person; a miser *la19, 20- N*. [ON *skrá* a piece of dried skin or parchment]

scrae[2.1], **†scra** /skre/ *n* dried fish *la16- Ork N*. **scrae-fish** dried fish *la16- Sh Ork N*. [ON *skreið*; perhaps with influence from SCRAE[1]]

scrae² /skre/ *v* to preserve fish by drying *la19- N*. [from the noun]

scraffle, *Sh Ork* **skravle** /'skrafəl; *Sh Ork* 'skravəl/ *v* to scramble; to claw about with the hands *19- Sh Ork N SW Bor*. [onomatopoeic; perhaps with influence from Eng *scrabble*]

scrag see SCROG

scraible¹·¹ /'skrebəl/ *n* a perk or concession (gained in an underhand manner) *20- C*. [extended meaning; see the verb]

scraible¹·² /'skrebəl/ *v* to scramble; to claw about with the hands *20-*. [Eng *scrabble*]

scraich see SKRAICH¹·¹, SKRAICH¹·²

scraik see SKRAICH¹·¹

scrail see SKRELL

scraip see SCRAPE¹·²

scraive see SCREEVE¹·²

scrammle¹·¹ /'skraməl/ *n* 1 a rough climb; a disorderly struggle *19-*. 2 the scattering of coins to children at a wedding *19-*. [see the verb]

scrammle¹·² /'skraməl/ *v* 1 to clamber; to climb quickly or awkwardly *19-*. 2 to struggle; to move hurriedly *19-*. 3 to jumble or muddle *19-*. [EModE *scramble*]

scran¹·¹, *NE* **scraun** /skran; *NE* skrɔn/ *n* 1 food *19-*. 2 scraps or leavings of food (acquired by begging) *19- Ork NE C*. 3 refuse or rubbish picked up by a beggar *20- NE H&I C*. 4 odd fish (such as mackerel amongst herring) claimed by the crew of a boat *20- NE*. **scran bag 1** a bag in which a beggar collected scraps of food *19, 20- historical*. 2 a storage receptacle for food; a bread bin *20- Sh* **on the scran** scrounging food or picking up discarded odds and ends *20-*. [unknown]

scran¹·², *NE* **scraun** /skran; *NE* skrɔn/ *v* 1 to scavenge for food *19-*. 2 to save or scrape together frugally *19-*. 3 to glance at a text; to look through a newspaper *la20-*. 4 to take the odd fish found in a catch as a bonus *la19- NE EC*.

scranner 1 a scavenger, a beggar *20-*. 2 a fishing boat which makes surreptitious catches within the three-mile limit *20- NE*. [unknown]

scranch /skrantʃ, skranʃ/ *v* to crush with a grating noise; to crunch *la18-19, 20- Uls*. [perhaps Du, Flem *schrantsen* to grind with the teeth, crush, with influence from Eng *crunch*]

scrape¹·¹ /skrep/ *n* 1 a scratch, a slight wound *la16-*. 2 a hasty piece of writing; a quickly-written letter *17-*. 3 a difficult situation *18-*. 4 an amount applied by scraping; a small amount *20-*. 5 *in ploughing* the shallow first furrow made in commencing a rig *20- WC SW*. **a scrape of a pen** a hasty piece of writing; a quickly-written letter *la17-*. [see the verb]

scrape¹·², **scrap**, **scraap**, **scrawp**, †**scraip** /skrep, skrap, skrɔp/ *v* 1 to clean by scraping; to rub or scratch with something sharp; to erase or eradicate *la14-*. 2 to scratch around; to acquire or accumulate with difficulty *la15-*. **scraper 1** an implement for scraping *la16-*. 2 a frugal or avaricious person *19, 20- Bor*. 3 *golf* a club used for getting the ball out of hazards *la17*. **scrapie** a sheep disease causing itching *20-*. †**scraping club** *golf* a club used for getting the ball out of hazards *19*. **scrapit face** a person with a thin, pinched face *la19- Sh*. [ON *skrapa*]

scrat see SCART¹·¹, SCART¹·², SCART³

scratch /skratʃ/ *n* 1 a slight wound; superficial damage *la17-*. 2 mashed potatoes mixed with suet and oatmeal *la19*. [EModE *scratch*]

scratcher /'skratʃər/ *n* 1 a bed (originally one in a public lodging-house) *20-*. 2 a trawler which fishes close to the shore *20- NE*. [Eng *scratch*, with agent suffix]

scrath see SCART²

scrauch see SKRAUCH¹·²

scrauchle /'skrɔxəl/ *v* to scramble with hands and feet; to clamber hastily and clumsily *19- H&I C SW Bor*. [altered form of SCRAFFLE, perhaps with influence from SPRAUCHLE¹·²]

scraun see SCRAN¹·¹, SCRAN¹·²

scraw /skrɔ/ *n* a thin turf or sod, especially as used for roofing *la18-19, 20- H&I SW Uls*. [Gael *sgrath*, IrGael *scraith*]

scrawp see SCRAPE¹·²

scree¹ /skri/ *n* a mass of loose stones on a steep hillside *19-*. [compare OIcel *skriða* a landslide]

scree²·¹ /skri/ *n* 1 a riddle or sieve; a box-shaped riddle, for sifting grain, sand or coal *la18-*. 2 an arrangement of parallel bars for riddling coal at a pit-head *la19-*. [perhaps reduced form of Eng *screen*]

scree²·² /skri/ *v* to riddle, sift (coal) *20- H&I C*. [see the noun]

scree³, **skri** /skri/ *v* to manage, cope, get by *la19- Sh*. [Norw dial *skria* to glide]

screebie see SCREEVIE

screechim see SCREIGHIN

screed¹·¹, †**screid**, †**skreid** /skrid/ *n* 1 a long narrow piece of cloth, twine, paper etc; a torn piece, shred *16-*. 2 *frequently disparaging* a long discourse or piece of writing *la18-*. 3 a strip of land; a large or appreciable distance or area *la19- NE T SW*. 4 a tear, gash, slash; a scratch *18-19, 20- T EC*. 5 the sound of tearing; a grating, scraping noise; *humorous* a tune on the fiddle *la18-19, 20- WC Uls*. 6 a bout of drinking *19, 20- SW*. 7 a substantial quantity of something *19, 20- Uls*. [ME *screde*, OE *scrēad*; compare SHRED]

screed¹·² /skrid/ *v* 1 to tear, rip; to come apart *la18-*. 2 to compose (a piece of writing) rapidly and lengthily; to write rapidly *19-*. 3 to make a shrill or screeching noise; to play (a tune) on a fiddle or bagpipe *18-19, 20- Uls*. **screed aff** to read volubly, recite fluently, reel off *la18-*. [see the noun]

screef see SCRUIF¹·¹, SCRUIF¹·²

screel, **skreel** /skril/ *v* to scream, screech *la19-*. [onomatopoeic; compare SKIRL¹·²]

screen¹·¹, †**scrine**, †**screinge** /skrin/ *n* 1 a piece of furniture consisting of one or more rectangular leaves covered or hung with cloth and used to ward off heat or afford privacy *la16-*. 2 a shawl, headscarf *18-19*. [ME *screne*, AN *escrien*]

screen¹·², †**schrine** /skrin/ *v* to furnish with screens or curtains *la17-*. **screener** *in the manufacture of linen* a person who examines cloth for flaws and faults *20- T EC*. [see the noun]

screenge¹·¹, †**scringe** /skrindʒ, skrinʒ/ *n* 1 a rubbing, a scrubbing, a scouring *la19 NE T*. 2 a lash of a whip, a beating *19, 20- NE Uls*. 3 a prowler *la19- WC Uls*. 4 a large tract or extent of land *la19- NE*. [see the verb]

screenge¹·², **scringe** /skrindʒ, skrinʒ, skrindʒ/ *v* 1 to rub or scour energetically *19-*. 2 to search eagerly or inquisitively *19-*. 3 to fish the sea bottom inshore with a small net *19-*. 4 to whip, flog *la18-19, 20- NE T Uls*. 5 to prowl about, wander about aimlessly *la19- NE*. **screenger 1** a person who hunts about to pick up or find things *la19-*. 2 (a person who fishes with) a *screenge net la19- H&I EC*. **screenge net** a small seine net used as in SCREENGE¹·² (sense 3) *la19, 20- H&I WC*. [perhaps onomatopoeic]

screenge² /skrindʒ/ *v* to shrink, contract *20 SW Bor*. [altered form of CREENGE]

screevie¹·¹ /skriv/ *n* 1 a large scratch; an abrasion of the skin; a mark or tear *19-*. 2 a scraping or grating sound; the sound made by tearing cloth *20- T WC Bor Uls*. **screevie** a slate pencil *20- EC SW*. [perhaps conflation of SCREED¹·¹ and SCRIEVE²·²]

screeve¹·², **scraive** /skriv, skrev/ *v* 1 to graze (the skin), peel or tear off (a surface), scratch, scrape *19-*. 2 to make a scraping motion or sound; to draw an object over another with a screeching noise, especially a bow over fiddle strings; to play a tune on a fiddle *19-*. **screever** a pancake or segment of a scone cooked on a girdle *20- T WC Bor*. [see the noun]

screeve see SCRIEVE²·²

screevie, †screebie, †scrubie, †scruby /'skrivi/ *n* scurvy *17-19, 20- NE*. **†screebie girss, scrubie grass** the plant *Cochlearia officinalis* believed to have anti-scurvy properties *19*. [EModE *scruby*, metathesis of *scurvy*]

†screich, skreigh *n* whisky *19*. [unknown]

screid see SCREED¹·¹

screigh see SKRAICH¹·¹

screighin, screechim /'skrixən, 'skrixəm/ *n* whisky *20- Sh*. [unknown; compare SCREICH]

screinge see SCREEN¹·¹

screke see SKRAICH¹·¹

screw¹, shrew, shirrow, †sheroo, †skrow, †schro /skru, ʃru, ʃə'ru/ *n* **1** a small insectivorous land mammal *Sorex araneus*, resembling a mouse *la16-*. **2** *derogatory* a scoundrel, a wretch; a coarse woman *la14-*. [OE *scrēawa*]

screw², †scrow /skru/ *n* a freshwater shrimp *la17-19, 20- WC Bor*. [compare Fr *escrouelle*]

screw see SCROO¹·¹, SCROO¹·²

screwtap /'skru tap/ *n* a bottle of beer or wine with a screw-on top *20-*. [Eng *screw* + TAP¹·¹]

scrib see SCRIBE¹·¹

scribble, †scrible, †scruble /'skrɪbəl/ *v* to card or tease (wool) mechanically *la17-*. **†scribbler, scrubler** a person who cards wool *la17-18*. [LG *schrubbeln*]

scribe¹·¹, †scrib /skrʌɪb/ *n* **1** a writer, author *la16-*. **2** a secretary in the service of a court, council or other official body *16-e17*. **3** a mark made with a pen; a piece of writing, a letter *la16-19, 20- Sh SW Uls*. [Lat *scrība*]

scribe¹·² /skrʌɪb/ *v* to write, set down in writing *la16-*. [Lat *scrībere*]

scribe see SCRAB¹

scrible see SCRIBBLE

†scriddan *n* (rocks and gravel brought down by) a mountain stream or torrent *la18-e19*. [Gael *sgriodan*]

scrieve¹·¹ /skriv/ *n* **1** a long animated story or chat; a harangue *19-*. **2** a long solo performance on a musical instrument *20- Ork*. [see the verb]

scrieve¹·² /skriv/ *v* **1** to move, glide along, speed on smoothly *la18-*. **2** to talk fluently, recite at length; to reel off a long story *19-, 20- Sh T SW*. **†scrieve aff** = SCRIEVE¹·² (sense 2) *la19*. [perhaps ON *skrefa* to stride]

scrieve²·¹, †scryve /skriv/ *n* **1** a piece of writing; a letter or its contents; a document *la16-*. **2** *in thieves' slang* a banknote, especially a pound note *la18-e19*. [see the verb]

scrieve²·², screeve, †scrive /skriv/ *v* **1** to write, especially easily and copiously *la15-*. **2** to scratch or incise a mark on (wood), *eg* to show the shape in which something is to be made *la19, 20- WC SW*. [Lat *scrībere* to write; with influence from DESCRIVE and compare SCREEVE¹·²]

scriever, scriver /'skrivər/ *n* **1** *often derogatory* a writer, a scribbler *17-*. **2** a scribe or secretary in the service of a military company or a troop of soldiers *17*. [SCRIEVE²·², with agent suffix]

scriff see SCRUIF¹·¹, SCRUIF¹·²

scrift¹·¹ /skrɪft/ *n* a long account, a long passage of prose or verse recited or read *la18-19, 20- NE T*. [compare Norw *skrift* written text, Du *schrift* writing]

scrift¹·² /skrɪft/ *v* to recite, declaim, reel *la18-19, 20- NE*. [see the noun]

†scrim¹, skrym, skirm *v* **1** to dart, rush; to skirmish *la14-e16*. **2** to beat, strike vigorously *la18-19*. **skirmage** rubbing, searching noisily *19-*. [OFr *escremir, eskermir*]

scrim²·¹ /skrɪm/ *n* a kind of thin coarse linen or canvas, made in narrow widths *la18-*. [unknown]

scrim²·² /skrɪm/ *v building, in plastering* to fill (a crevice or joint) with SCRIM²·¹ *20-*. [unknown]

scrime see SKRIME

scrimp¹·¹, †scrimpt /skrɪmp/ *v* **1** to restrict in supplies, stint *la17-*. **2** to restrict or cut down in amount; to use or consume frugally or meanly *la18-*. **3** to economize, be parsimonious *20-*. **scrimpit** scanty; restricted; undersized; mean *18-*. **scrimpy** *adj* scanty, inadequate *20-*. **scrimpy** *n* a scanty measure *la19-*. [see the adj]

scrimp¹·² /skrɪmp/ *adj* **1** scant, in short supply *la17-*. **2** parsimonious, ungenerous, sparing *18-*. **3** *of clothes* short, constricted *18-19, 20- Sh Ork NE T EC*. **4** *of persons* having a scanty supply, in want *la18- Sh NE T EC*. **5** *of numbers* limited, bare *18*. **scrimpness** scantiness, deficiency, especially in wits *20-*. [uncertain; compare Swed *skrympa* to shrink, MDu *schrimpen* to shrivel]

scrimp¹·³ /skrɪmp/ *adv* scarcely, almost but not quite; parsimoniously *la18-*. [see the adj]

scrimpt see SCRIMP¹·¹

scrine see SCREEN¹·¹

scringe see SCREENGE¹·¹, SCREENGE¹·¹

scrip see SKIRP¹·¹, SKIRP¹·²

scrit see SKRIT¹·¹, SKRIT¹·²

scrive see SCRIEVE²·²

scriver see SCRIEVER

scroatch see SCROOCH

scroban /'skrobən/ *n* the crop of a fowl; the human gullet or chest *la19- N H&I*. [Gael *sgrobán*]

scrocken, scrochen, *Sh* **skurken, †skruken** /'skrɔkən, 'skroxən; *Sh* 'skʌrkən/ *v* to dry out (especially peats); to shrink or shrivel up with heat or drought *la17-19, 20- Sh NE*. [compare Norw dial *skrokken* shrivelled]

scrockle = SCROCKEN *20- NE*. [altered form of SCROCKEN]

scrog, scrag, scrug, *N* **skroug** /skrɔg, skrag, skrʌg; *N* skrʌug/ *n* **1** (an area of) brushwood or undergrowth, a thicket (of bushes) *13-*. **2** a stunted or crooked bush or tree; a gnarled or crooked tree stump *18-*. **3** the crab-apple (tree) *la19- EC Bor*. **4** a dried-up or shrivelled thing; a lean scraggy animal or person *20- N H&I*. **scroggie** covered with undergrowth; *of trees* stunted, crooked, spindly; growing densely, forming thickets *la15-*. [unknown]

scrog see SCRUG

scroll¹·¹, †scrow, †skrow /skrol/ *n* **1** a piece of paper or, originally, parchment; a writing-pad usually for rough drafts or notes *la15-19, 20- Ork NE T*. **2** a crowd, mob; originally a list of people *la16-19, 20- SW*. **3** a rough draft or copy; a draft of a legal or official transaction prior to its being entered into the official register *la16-19*. **4** a piece of writing, a list or account, a relation (of events), a story *16-19*. **5** damaged skins of parchment, strips or scraps of skin or hide used to make glue *16-19*. **scrow-buik 1** a school rough notebook *20- EC*. **2** a book in which drafts or copies of documents are written *la16-19*. [ME *scrow*, AN *escrowe*]

†scroll¹·², †scrow *v* **1** to draw up, draft (a document); to record *17*. **2** to make a copy of (a document) *18-19*. [see the noun]

scronach¹·¹, scrunnich /'skronəx, 'skrʌnəx/ *n* a shrill cry, outcry, loud lamentation *la18- NE*. [altered form of CRONACH¹·²]

scronach¹·², scronnach /'skronəx, 'skrɔnəx/ *v* **1** to shriek, yell, cry out *19- NE T*. **2** to make a great outcry or fuss, grouse *la19- NE T*. [see the noun]

scroo¹·¹, screw, †scrow, †skrow /skru/ *n* a stack of corn or hay *17- Sh Ork N NE*. [Norw dial *skruv*]

scroo[1.2], **screw**, †**scrow** /skru/ *v* to build (corn) into stacks *17- Sh Ork NE*. [see the noun]

scrooch, †**scrotch**, †**scroatch** /skrutʃ/ *v especially of sun or wind* to scorch, burn; to shrivel, wither *17-18, 20- SW*. [metathesis of Eng *scorch*]

scroosh /skruʃ/ *n frequently derogatory* a large number of people, especially children *20- N H&I*. [perhaps altered form of colloquial Eng *scrouge*]

scrotch *see* SCROOCH

scrow *see* SCOW[3], SCREW[2], SCROLL[1.1], SCROLL[1.2], SCROO[1.1], SCROO[1.2]

scrub[1.1] /skrʌb/ *n* 1 a pot-scrubber *19, 20- NE C*. 2 a mean avaricious person, a hard bargainer *la18-19, 20- Uls*. 3 *pl* the husks of grain *la19- Ork*. **scrubby** sordid, mean, parsimonious *la19, 20- Ork NE EC Uls*. [see the verb]

scrub[1.2] /skrʌb/ *v* 1 to clean by rubbing *19-*. 2 to beat down in bargaining, treat meanly *19*. 3 to keep (plants) clean, weeded, tilled *la15*. **scrubber** an implement for cleaning pots *19-*. [MDu, MLG *schrubben* to scratch in the ground]

scrubie *see* SCREEVIE

scruble *see* SCRIBBLE

scruby *see* SCREEVIE

scrufe, **scruff** *see* SCRUIF[1.1], SCRUIF[1.2]

scruffle *see* SKROVLE[1.1], SKROVLE[1.2]

scrug, †**scrog** /skrʌg/ *v of a man* to pull (a cap) forward over the brow to appear jaunty or bold *18-19, 20- T H&I WC*. [unknown; compare Dan *skrugge* to stoop]

scrug *see* SCROG

scruif[1.1], **scruff**, **scriff**, *NE* **screef**, †**scrufe**, †**scroof** /skruf, skrʌf, skrɪf; *NE* skrif/ *n* 1 scurf, dandruff; an incrustation on the skin; a scab, a piece of encrusted skin, hair or dirt *17-*. 2 a thin surface layer, a film, crust or rind *la16-19, 20- Sh Ork N NE Uls*. 3 the layer of vegetation on the surface of the ground *la16-19, 20- Sh N NE*. 4 the surface of water or the sea *19- Sh Ork N NE*. 5 the skin, the epidermis *la16-19*. 6 *mining* refuse, debris *la15-16*. 7 debased coinage; the refuse deriving from minting copper or base-metal coins; money regarded as debased, filthy lucre *la16-17*. 8 the outward aspect or the superficial appearance of a thing *la16-17*. **scruiffy** filthy, caked with dirt *19- WC Bor*. [ME *scruffe*, metathesis of OE *sceorf*]

scruif[1.2], **scruff**, **scriff**, **screef**, †**scrufe** /skruf, skrʌf, skrɪf, skrif/ *v* 1 to loosen topsoil, skim off weeds, hoe *19-*. 2 to crust over, cover with a thin crust or layer; to gloss or skim over, treat superficially *17-19, 20- Sh NE*. 3 to brush or scrape against; to scrape off the surface of, graze, skin *la16-19, 20- T*. **scriffin** a thin crust or covering; the face of the earth *19-*. **scruiffin** a thin paring or scraping *20- C*.

scriffle = SCRUIF[1.2] (sense 3) *20- EC*. [see the noun]

scrump[1] /skrʌmp/ *n* something crisp and hard; a crust, a hard surface layer *la19- NE*. **scrumpie** baked hard and crisp *la19- NE*. **scrumpit**, **scrumplit** = *scrumpie 19- NE EC*. [unknown; compare Norw dial *skrump* crisp, hard meat, Dan *skrumpen* shrivelled]

scrump[2] /skrʌmp/ *v* to crunch, munch, chew (something hard and crisp) *la19- NE T*. [altered form of CRUMP with influence from SCRUMP[1]]

†**scrumpill**, **skrumple** *n* a wrinkle, crease *e16*. [see the verb]

scrumple, †**scrumpill**, †**skrimple** /'skrʌmpəl/ *v* to crumple, crush, wrinkle; originally to shrivel with heat, crinkle *16-*. [altered form of EModE *crumple*]

scrunnich *see* SCRONACH[1.1]

scrunt[1] /skrʌnt/ *n* 1 something shrunken or worn down by use or age *16-*. 2 a person shrunken or withered by age or illness, a thin scraggy person; a poorly-developed animal or plant *19-*. 3 a mean, miserly person *19-*. **scruntit**,

†**scrountit** shrivelled, shrunken, stunted in growth *la16-*. **scrunty** 1 stunted, shrivelled, stumpy, wizened *19-*. 2 mean, parsimonious *19-*. [unknown]

scrunt[2.1] /skrʌnt/ *n* 1 the act of planing roughly; a thick or rough shaving of wood *la19- NE C*. 2 a harsh grating sound made by scraping on wood or a fiddle *19-*. [see the verb]

scrunt[2.2] /skrʌnt/ *v* 1 to scrape, scrub, scratch, grind *19- T C*. 2 to plane (a board) roughly to remove a thick shaving; to rough down (pointing) with a handpick *20- NE C*. 3 to produce a harsh sound by scraping; to scrape a tune on a fiddle *la18-19*. [probably onomatopoeic with influence from SCRUNT[1]]

scry[1.1] /skrae/ *n* 1 a public proclamation, especially one made by a town-crier ringing a hand-bell in a public place *la18-NE*. 2 outcry, clamour, din; a cry of alarm or acclamation; a shout *15-e19*. [see the verb]

†**scry**[1.2] *v* 1 to cry out *15-e17*. 2 to proclaim, make known by public proclamation *18-19*. [OFr *escrier*]

scryve *see* SCRIEVE[2.1]

scud[1.1] /skʌd/ *n* 1 brisk movement *la16-*. 2 a blow, a smack; a stroke with a strap or cane *19-*. 3 a belt or tawse for punishing schoolchildren *20, 21 NE historical*. 4 a turn at doing something, a shot or go *20- N H&I WC*. 5 cider *la20- WC*. 6 a jinx *20- Uls*. 7 *pl* foaming ale; beer with a head *18-e19*. **scuddie** a game resembling shinty or hockey; the club or the ball used in it *la19-*. [see the verb]

scud[1.2] /skʌd/ *v* 1 to move, travel quickly (over or through a place) *17-*. 2 to beat with the open hand or a strap; to smack, spank *19-*. 3 to throw (a flat stone) so as to make it skip over water *la19-*. 4 to slide or skate on ice *20- T EC*. 5 to drink copiously *e18*. **scudder** *n* a driving shower of rain or snow *20- NE*. **scudder** *v of wind* to sweep along in rainy gusts *la19, 20- NE*. **scuddrie** with cold driving showers *la19-NE*. [EModE *scud*]

scud[2] /skʌd/ *n* the bare skin, a state of nudity; a naked person *20-*. **scud mag** a pornographic magazine *21-*. **in the scud** naked *21-*. [shortened form of SCUDDIE[1.1]]

scudda, **scud** /'skudə, skud, skʌd/ *n* the undergrowth of wool on a sheep *la18- Sh historical*. **scudda muild** ground from which the turf has been removed *20- Sh*. [perhaps ON *skot-* shooting, springing]

scuddie[1.1] /'skʌdi/ *n* 1 the bare skin, a state of nudity; a naked person *19- NE T C SW*. 2 a nestling, a young unfledged bird *la19- WC*. [unknown]

scuddie[1.2] /'skʌdi/ *adj* 1 naked, without clothes *19-*. 2 mean, scruffy, shabby-looking *la19- NE WC*. 3 stingy, penurious; insufficient, too small *la19- NE*. **scuddie naked** completely naked *20-*. [unknown]

scuddie *see* SCUD[1.1]

scuddle[1], †**scudle** /'skʌdəl/ *v* 1 to wash (dishes); to work in a sloppy or disorganized way; to do odd jobs *la16-*. 2 to make (clothes) dirty, shabby or shapeless by rough usage *19-NE T EC*. **scuddlin claes** second-best clothes *20- Ork N NE T*. [back-formation from SCUDDLER]

scuddle[2] /'skʌdəl/ *v of persons or animals, especially dogs* to scurry, roam about, sneak about; to dodge, shirk work *la19, 20- N*. [probably frequentative form of SCUD[1.2]]

scuddler, †**scudler**, †**scudlar** /'skʌdlər/ *n* 1 a maid-of-all-work; a scullion, a kitchen-boy; a servant who carries out the most menial tasks in a kitchen *la15-19, 20- NE*. 2 the leader of a band of masqueraders who performed at festive events *19- Sh historical*. 3 a worthless, idle person; a wastrel *16-e17*. [OFr **escudeler*, Lat *scutella* a dish, a pan]

scuddrie *see* SCUD[1.2]

scudge *see* SCODGE[1.1], SCODGE[1.2]

scudlar, **scudler** *see* SCUDDLER

scudle *see* SCUDDLE[1]

scuff[1.1], **skuff** /skʌf/ *n* **1** a glancing or brushing stroke of the hand, a slight touch in passing, a hasty wipe *19-*. **2** a slight passing shower of rain *19-*. **3** disreputable people *19-*. **scuffy 1** shabby, worn, tarnished, mean-looking *la19-*. **2** parsimonious *20- NE*. [see the verb]

scuff[1.2], **skuff**, †**scuffe**, †**skoof** /skʌf/ *v* **1** to touch lightly in passing; to draw one's hand quickly over; to brush off or away *18-*. **2** to shuffle with the feet; to draw the feet over (the ground) lightly but noisily; to scuffle *la18-*. **3** to wear away (clothes) with hard usage, make worn and shabby; to tarnish *la18-*. **4** to hit, strike with a glancing blow *19- Bor Uls*. **5** to slur over; to evade *la16*. **scuffin** *of clothes* second-best *la19- C SW*. **scuffle** to graze, rub slightly; to wear away; to tarnish *la19- NE T*. [perhaps onomatopoeic]

scuff[1.3] /skʌf/ *adv* with a whizzing or scuffling noise; so as to graze or touch (a surface) lightly as it passes *la19- NE T*. [see the verb]

scuffe *see* SCUFF[1.2]

scuffet *see* SKIVET[2]

scuffle /'skʌfəl/ *n* a bakers' swab for cleaning out ovens *la19-*. [EModE *scovell*, Fr *escouvelle*]

scuffle *see* SCUFF[1.2]

scug[1.1], **skog**, **scoug**, **skoog**, †**skugg**, †**skowg** /skʌg, skɔg, skʌug, skug/ *n* **1** shelter, protection, defence *la15-19, 20- Sh NE T EC Bor*. **2** a pretence, a pretext, a hypocritical excuse *la16-19, 20- Sh NE*. **3** shadow; gloom; shade (as a means of concealment) *16-e19*. †**skugry** shadowy places; concealment *la15*. †**skuggy** shady; sheltering *16-e19*. [ON *skugge* shadow]

scug[1.2], **skug**, **scog**, **scoug**, **scoog**, *Sh* **skjoag**, †**skowg** /skʌg, skɔg, skʌug, skug; *Sh* skjog/ *v* **1** to conceal, screen; to shade, darken with shadow *16-*. **2** to shelter, shield, protect *19-*. **3** to take shelter or refuge (from); to avoid or evade (bad weather etc); to hide, sulk *18-19, 20- Sh NE T EC*. [see the noun]

scuif /skuf/ *n* a scoop, a small hand shovel *20- EC Bor*. [altered form of SCUIP[1.1]]

scuil *see* SCHULE

scuill *see* SCULE

scuip[1.1], **scoop**, **skip**, †**scoup**, †**skowp**, †**skupe** /skup, skɪp/ *n* **1** a utensil for bailing out, ladling or skimming liquids; a concave shovel-like tool *16-*. **2** a hat or bonnet with a protruding brim *19-*. **3** *mainly* **skip** the front brim of a hat, the peak of a cap *20- N C SW*. **skippit bunnet** a cloth cap with a peak *19-*. [ME *scope*, MLG *schōpe*]

scuip[1.2], **scoop**, **scoup**, *Sh* **skjüp** /skup, skʌup; *Sh* skjup/ *v* to take herring out of a net with a scoop; to catch herring which have fallen through the mesh of a net *la19- Sh*. †**scoup aff** to drink (alcohol) in a single motion *19*. †**scoup up** = *scoup aff*. [see the noun]

†**scuir**, **sgoor** *n* a skewer *18*. [EModE *scure*, *skewer* variant of EModE *skiver*; compare SKIVER[2]]

†**scuitie**, **skutie**, **scootie** *n* a shallow, wooden, scoop-shaped drinking cup *e19 Bor*. [altered form of SCUIP[1.1]]

scuitifu, **skuittie-fih**, **scootifu** /'skutefu/ *n* the fill of a SCUITIE *19- Bor*. [SCUITIE, with *-ful* suffix]

†**sculding** *v in Orkney and Shetland* a procedure for dealing with minor offences *la16*. **skuld**, **skuild** to accuse (someone) of wrongdoing under the procedure of *sculding e17*. [perhaps ON *sculd* debt + ON *þing* a court]

sculduddery, †**skulduddery**, †**sculdudry** /skʌl'dʌdəre/ *n* **1** fornication, unchastity *la17-*. **2** obscenity, indecency; obscene language *19-*. [unknown]

scule, †**scuill** /skul/ *n* **1** a shoal (of fish) *la16-*. **2** a flock (of birds) or herd (of cattle) *la16-17*. [ME *scole*, MDu *schōle*]

scule *see* SCHULE

scull[1], *Ork N NE* **scoo**, †**skull**, †**skill** /skʌl; *Ork N NE also* sku/ *n* **1** a large shallow, scoop-shaped basket *la15-*. **2** a shallow drinking vessel or ladle *e16, 20- Ork*. **scull-gab** a cloud formation thought to resemble such a basket and indicating the likely wind direction *la19- NE*. [unknown]

scull[2] /skʌl/ *v* to (cause to) move with a zig-zagging motion; to skim a stone across water *la19- Sh Ork*. [ME *skull* an oar]

scull *see* SKULL

scullop *see* SCILLOP

scullrow /'skʌlro/ *n* a notch in the stern of a boat used as a kind of rowlock when the boat is propelled by a single oar *19- WC SW*. [SCULL[2] + ROW[2]]

scully-boat /'skʌlibot/ *n* a small boat, a light skiff *20- Sh*. [SCULL[2], with adj-forming suffix *-y* + BOAT[1.1]]

scult[1.1] /skʌlt/ *n* a blow with the flat of the hand, a slap; a stroke of the cane or strap on the hand *la18-*. [onomatopoeic]

scult[1.2] /skʌlt/ *v* **1** to strike with the palm of the hand, slap, smack *18-19, 20- NE T Bor*. **2** to strike on (the palm); to strap, cane *19- Bor*. [see the noun]

scum[1.1], *Sh Ork* **skoom** /skʌm; *Sh Ork* skum/ *n* **1** froth, foam; matter floating on the top of a liquid *16-*. **2** persons regarded as worthless; a disreputable person *17-*. **3** a thin layer of ice *20- N SW*. **4** dross (from melted metal); (a layer of) refuse *la16-19*. **scoomy**, **skoomi** *of the sky, clouds* hazy *la19- Sh*. [ME *scome*, MDu, MLG *schūme*]

scum[1.2], *Sh Ork* **skoom** /skʌm; *Sh Ork* skum/ *v* **1** to skim (cream); to remove (surface material, debris or dirt) *la16-*. **2** to catch with a small round net on a long pole (any herring fallen back into the sea as the nets are hauled aboard) *la19- N*. **3** to graze, touch lightly in passing *20- Sh*. **4** to strike with the hand across (the cheek), slap (someone's face) *18-e19*. **5** to skim, fly closely above without touching; to fly or sail swiftly or effortlessly *16*. **scummer**, †**scummar 1** a sea rover, a pirate *la14-*. **2** a ladle or shallow dish for skimming *14-19, 20- N T EC*. **3** *on a fishing boat* the crew member who uses the *scumming net la19- Sh N NE*. **scum-milk** skimmed milk *19-*. **scumming net** a scoop-net for catching salmon in rivers or herring dropped from the net of a fishing boat *la18-*. **scum net** = *scumming net*. [see the noun]

scumfish *see* SCOMFISH[1.1]

scumfit *see* SCOMFISH[1.2]

scuncheon, †**skonschon** /'skʌnʃən/ *n building* the inner edge of a window or door jamb; the open finished end of a wall *la16-*. [ME *sconchon*, MFr *escoinson*]

scunder *see* SCUNNER[1.1], SCUNNER[1.2]

scunge[1.1], *NE* **squeenge** /skʌndʒ; *NE* skwindʒ/ *n* a scrounger, a sponger, a prowler after food *20-*. [unknown]

scunge[1.2], *NE* **squeenge** /skʌndʒ; *NE* skwindʒ/ *v* **1** to prowl or slink about (in search of something); to sponge, scrounge *19-*. **2** to rummage *20- NE*. **scunger** a prowler, a moocher *20- NE*. [unknown]

scunner[1.1], *N Uls* **scunder**, †**skunner**, †**sconner**, †**scowner** /'skʌnər; *N Uls* 'skʌndər/ *n* **1** a feeling of disgust, loathing, nausea or surfeit; repugnance, distaste, dislike, loss of interest or enthusiasm *16-*. **2** a thing or action which causes loathing, aversion or disgust; a nuisance *19-*. **3** a person who causes disgust or dislike, a troublesome or objectionable person *la18-*. **4** a shudder *la19-*. **scunnerfu** disgusting, nauseating, objectionable *la19-*. **scunnerous**, **scunneris** = *scunnerfu la19- Sh Ork H&I EC*. **scunnersome** = *scunnerfu la19-*. **tak a scunner at** to become disgusted, nauseated or bored by; to develop an intense dislike of *16-*. **tak a scunner against** = *tak a scunner at la17-*. [unknown]

scunner[1,2], *N Uls* **scunder**, †**skunner**, †**sconner**, †**scowner** /ˈskʌnər; *N Uls* ˈskʌndər/ *v* **1** to feel aversion, disgust or loathing; to feel nauseated or surfeited *la14*-. **2** to shrink back, flinch; to hesitate *la14*-. **3** to cause a feeling of repulsion, aversion or loathing; to nauseate; to surfeit; to make bored, uninterested or antipathetic *19*-. **scunner at** to feel disgust for, be sickened, bored or repelled by *la16*-. **scunner wi** = *scunner at la14-19, 20- T.* [unknown]

scunneration /skʌnəˈreʃən/ *n* an object of dislike or disgust, an offensive sight *la19*-. [SCUNNER[1,2], with noun-forming suffix]

scups /skʌps/ *npl* the male genitals *20- Ork.* [perhaps ON *skop* pl noun]

scur[1.1] /skʌr/ *n* **1** a scab or scar which forms over a healing sore or wound *19- NE*. **2** a rudimentary, loosely-attached horn in polled or hornless cattle *19, 20- SW*. **3** a despicable person, a rascal, an old fellow *19*. **4** a sheriff officer or his assistant *19.* **scurl** = SCUR[1.1] (sense 1) *19- NE T Bor.* [see the verb]

scur[1.2] /skʌr/ *v of a wound or sore* to form a scab, crust over in healing *la19- NE*. [perhaps shortened form of Eng *scurf*]

scur[2] /skʌr/ *n* the mayfly immediately after its larval stage, frequently used as an angler's bait *19- WC.* [unknown]

scurdie, †**skurdy** /ˈskʌrdi/ *n* whinstone or basalt *la18- N NE T*. [probably from Scurdy Ness, near Montrose, which is formed of such rock]

scurl *see* SCUR[1.1]

†**scurr**[1] *n* a buffoon, a jester *la16*. [Lat *scurra*]

scurr[2] /skʌr/ *v* to slither, slide, skate, skid *20- NE*. [variant of SKIRR[1]]

scurrie *see* SCURRY

†**scurriour**, **scurrour** *n* a reconnoitrer, a scout *la14-e17*. [aphetic form of *discurriour* (DISCOVER)]

scurrit *see* SCORE[1.2]

†**scurrour**, **skurriour** *n* a buffoon, a jester *e16*. [Lat *scurra*, with *-(i)our* suffix; compare SCURR[1]]

scurry, *NE* **squeerie**, **scoury**, †**scurrie** /ˈskʌri, ˈskʌre; *NE* ˈskwiri, ˈskuri/ *v* **1** to reconnoitre *la16*. **2** to roam about, wander idly, prowl about *la19- NE*. **skurrieman** a wanderer, a vagabond *19, 20- T.* [back-formation from SCURRIOUR]

scurryvaig[1.1], †**scurryvage** /skʌriˈveg/ *n* a vagabond; an idle, unkempt, or slatternly person; a lout; a scullion *16-19, 20- Bor.* [perhaps Lat *scurra vagus* wandering buffoon]

scurryvaig[1.2] /skʌriˈveg/ *v* to range or roam about or aimlessly; to live in idleness and dissipation *19*-. [see the noun]

scush[1.1] /skʌʃ, skuʃ/ *n* (the noise of) shuffling with the feet *19, 20- NE*. **scushle** an old worn-down shoe *19- NE T.* [onomatopoeic]

scush[1.2], *NE* **skish** /skʌʃ, skuʃ; *NE* skɪʃ/ *v* to shuffle, walk with a shambling gait *19- N NE*. **scushle** = SCUSH[1.2] *19, 20- N NE*. [see the noun]

†**scutarde** *n derogatory* a person who defecates, one prone to diarrhoea *e16*. [perhaps SCOUT[1.2] or SKITTER[1.2] with agent suffix]

†**scutch**[1.1] *n* the stick used for beating flax, a swingle; the corresponding part in a machine *la18-19*. [OFr *escouche*]

scutch[1.2] /skʌtʃ/ *v* **1** to dress (especially flax) by beating *la16*-. **2** to strike off (the ears of corn) from the stalk with a stick *la18-e19.* **scutcher** = SCUTCH[1.1] *la18-19, 20- T.* [OFr **escoucher*]

scutch[2.1] /skʌtʃ/ *n* **1** a thin layer or covering; a small quantity *20- Ork N.* **2** the act of skimming or grazing a surface; a grazing or scuffling movement or sound; a swift light motion over a surface *la19, 20- N.* [see the verb]

scutch[2.2] /skʌtʃ/ *v* **1** to skim or graze the surface of one object with another; to flick, sweep or hoe, especially perfunctorily *la19- N NE.* **2** to walk quickly with a light scuffling step *la19- N NE.* **3** to slide on ice, skate, sledge *20- NE*. [perhaps onomatopoeic; compare SKETCH[1.2]]

scutch[3.1] /skʌtʃ/ *n* a slash, a cutting of twigs or thistles, the trimming of a hedge *la19, 20- SW.* [see the verb]

scutch[3.2] /skʌtʃ/ *v* **1** to dress (stone) roughly with a pick *19*-. **2** to cut or shear with a hook or knife, slash, trim (a hedge) *la19, 20- C SW*. **3** to make a vertical cut in a coalface with a pick *la19, 20- EC.* [altered form of Eng *scotch* to cut, gash]

scutch[4] /skʌtʃ/ *n* a wedge put under a wheel to prevent it slipping *20- C Bor.* [altered form of Eng *scotch* an obstruction]

scuttall hoill *see* SCUTTLE HOLE

scutter[1.1] /ˈskʌtər/ *n* **1** the doing of work awkwardly or dirtily, a botch, a bungle; a time-consuming and irritating occupation *la19*-. **2** a person who works in an ineffective, muddled or dirty way *la19- N NE T.* **scutterie** troublesome; *of a job* time-wasting, muddling *la19- NE.* [see the verb]

scutter[1.2] /ˈskʌtər/ *v* **1** to do something in a slovenly or bungling way, make a mess (of); to spill or splash about *19*-. **2** to be engaged in troublesome, time-wasting, pointless work; to fiddle about aimlessly or confusedly, dawdle *la19*-. **3** to hinder with something unimportant, detain through some needless or annoying cause *la19- NE T.* [perhaps altered form of SKITTER[1.2] with extension of meaning]

†**scuttle** *v* to serve on a plate, dish up (food); to pour (liquid) from one container to another; to spill in so doing *e19*. [OE *scutel* a dish]

scuttle hole, †**scuttall hoill**, †**scutter hole** /ˈskʌtəl hol/ *n* a sewage pit, a drain *16- NE T.* [EModE *skottelle* a small hatchway on a ship, MFr *escoutille* a hatch(way) + HOLE[1.1]]

scuvatt *see* SKIVET

scythe, †**sith**, †**syth** /saeθ/ *n* **1** an implement with a long, slightly curved blade for hand-cutting grass or crops *la15*-. **2** a mower, a scytheman *20- NE.* **scyther** = SCYTHE (sense 2) *19*-. **scythe-sned** the curved wooden handle or shaft of a scythe *19, 20- NE T.* **scythe-straik** a scythe sharpener *19, 20- NE SW.* [OE *sīðe*]

se *see* SEA, SEE

sea, **sey**, †**se**, †**sie** /si, se, sae/ *n* a large body of salt water *la14*-. **seaward**, †**seywart** towards the sea *16*-. **sea-biddie** *fisherman's taboo* bread or oatcakes for eating at sea *la19- Sh.* **sea-box 1** the provisions locker on a fishing-boat *la19- Sh.* **2** a mariner's friendly society, so called from the box in which the funds were kept *17-19.* **sea-breed** = *seabiddie 20- Sh Ork.* **sea breeks**, †**se brekis** trousers for use at sea; a fisherman's waterproof or canvas trousers *16, la19- Sh.* †**se-breve**, **sey-breif** an official document or pass specifying the nature of the business authorized to the ship; a letter of marque, a licence allowing reprisals at sea *16-17.* †**se burd** at sea, seaborne *16.* †**sea-car** an embankment against the sea, a sea wall *18-e19.* **sea-cat** the wolf-fish *Anarhichas lupus 16-.* †**sea craig** a rock by or in the sea *la16.* **sea craw** the razorbill *Alca torda 19- Sh.* **sea-cubbie** a woven straw basket *la19- Ork.* **sea-daisy** thrift or the sea pink *19, 20- Ork.* **sea-dog 1** the dogfish *Squalus acanthias la17-.* **2** a mythical beast *e16.* **sea-doo** the black guillemot *Cepphus grylle la19, 20- H&I.* **sea-ferdy** seaworthy *20- Sh Ork.* †**sea-fire** sea phosphorescence *19.* **sea-flech** a sand flea *20- Sh NE T.* †**se-flude** the sea as ebbing and flowing, the tidal waters of the sea *16-17.* †**sea-fyke** a powder made from the crushed dried egg-capsules of the whelk *Buccinum undatum*, which causes skin irritation *la18-e19.* **sea-geese** barnacles *Lepas anatifera 20- Ork.* **sea-goo** a seagull *la19- NE.* †**sea-green** land partially reclaimed from the sea, but still flooded by spring tides *18-19.* †**se-grund**, **se-ground** the bottom of the sea *la14-17.* **sea-gust** salt spume driven by wind onto the land *17- Sh Ork*. **sea-haar, sea-haur** a sea fog *19-*. **sea-lark 1** the dunlin *Calidris alpina la19, 20- T.* **2** the ringed plover *Charadrius hiaticula la17-19*. **sea lintie** the rock pipit *Anthus petrosus la19, 20- WC*. **sea loch** a sea inlet, especially one long and narrow in shape *17-*. **sea-maw** a seagull *la15-*. **sea-meath** a landmark *la19, 20- Sh*. **sea-pap** a sea anemone *la19- NE EC Bor*. **sea-pyot** the oystercatcher *Haematopus ostralegus 18-*. †**se-reiver, se-rever, se-revar** a pirate *16-e17*. †**sea-sleach, sea-sletch** mud formed by a tidal river or estuary *18-19*. **sea-soo** the small-mouthed wrasse *Centrolabrus exoletus 19, 20- NE WC*. †**sea-swine** the porpoise *Phocaena phocaena*. **sea-toun** a seaport town or village; the area of a town nearest to the harbour, frequently in place-names *la16-*. **sea-tow** a mooring rope attached to the stern of a boat *la19- Sh*. **sea-ware** seaweed, especially the coarse kind washed up by the tide and used as manure *la16-19, 20- Sh Ork NE*. †**sea-wrack 1** = *sea-ware la17-e19*. **2** wreckage cast up by the sea *16-17*. [OE *sǽ*]

Seaforth /'sifɔrθ/ *n* a soldier in the regiment raised in 1778 by the Earl of Seaforth; a *Seaforth Highlander la18-20, 21- historical*. **Seaforth Highlander** a soldier in the *Seaforth Highlanders la19-20, 21- historical*. **Seaforth Highlanders** the name given to the regiment formed in 1881 by amalgamation of the 72nd Duke of Albany's Own Highlanders (raised by the Earl of Seaforth in 1778) and the 78th Highlanders, Ross-shire Buffs (raised in 1793 by Colonel Francis Humberston MacKenzie); (since 1961) amalgamated with The Queen's Own Cameron Highlanders to form the Queen's Own Highlanders (Seaforth and Camerons) *la19-20, 21- historical*. [from the name of the Earl of Seaforth]

seal[1.1], †**sele**, †**seill**, †**seel** /sil/ *n* **1** an emblematic or heraldic device impressed in wax; the wax impressed with a device and attached to a document as an attestation of authenticity and guarantee of reliability *14-*. **2** a sealing device, a closure of wax or metal which must be broken to gain access to a document *la14-*. **3** a stamp or seal attached to cloth to indicate quality and origin *16-e18*. **4** a branding-iron used to mark containers or measures as of the correct standard; the mark so made *15-17*. **5** *pl* the process of authentication, by affixing one or more seals, undergone by a document; the government department concerned with this *15-17*. **pass the seals** to be authenticated by being sealed with the appropriate seal *16-18*. **seal of cause 1** a charter granted by a town council to a body of craftsmen, forming them into an INCORPORATION *la16-19, 20- historical*. **2** the seal of a burgh, used to authenticate an act of incorporation or other documents *la15-e17*. †**sele of office** the seal of a corporate body, court or incorporation *la15-e17*. †**under a (person's) seal** authenticated or secured by a seal *la14-e17*. [OFr *seel*]

seal[1.2], †**sele**, †**seill** /sil/ *v* **1** to ratify or authenticate by affixing a seal *la14-*. **2** to block, close up (a cave or passage) *la14-*. **3** to fasten, secure or enclose with a seal *la14-*. **4** to impress or mark (a measuring vessel) with a stamp of authenticity *15-17*. **5** to attach (a seal) to cloth as a proof of quality *16-e17*. **sealing ordinance** *Presbyterian Church* the sacrament of the Lord's Supper or baptism *17-*. [OFr *seeler*]

seal see SELCH, SELL[2]

sealy see SEELY

seam[1.1], †**seme** /sim/ *n* **1** the (stitched) join between two pieces of material *15-*. **2** a geological stratum containing mineral or ore deposits *la16-*. **3** sewing, needlework *18-*. **4** any task or piece of work *la19- T C SW Bor*. **5** the parting of the hair *20- Sh Ork T EC*. **6** a row of natural or, more usually, artificial teeth *20- NE T*. **7** the join between the planks of a ship *16-e17*. †**seme byttar** a tailor *e16*. **a seam o teeth** = SEAM[1.1] (sense 6) *la19, 20- NE T*. [OE *sēam*]

seam[1.2], †**seem** /sim/ *v* to fit one edge of (a plank) to another; to rivet the planks of a boat together using SEAM[2] nails *19, 20- Sh N*. †**seming** the fitting of one edge of a plank to another *la16-17*. †**seamit, seamed** *of (the construction of) a ship* fastened with seams *16-e17*. [see the noun; compare SEAM[2]]

seam[2], *Sh* **sem** /sim; *Sh* sɛm/ *n* a nail used to fix together the planks of a clinker-built boat, riveted by a RUIVE[1.1] *la15-18, 19- Sh*. [compare Norw *søm* a nail, probably cognate with SEAM[1.1]]

seam see SAME[1]

†**seand**[1], **sein** *adj* appropriate, fitting, proper; valid *la15-17*. [OFr *seant*]

†**seand**[2.1] *prep* considering, with reference to *e16*. [presp of SEE]

†**seand**[2.2] *conj* considering; because *16-17*. [see the prep]

seann triubhas see SHANTREWS

sear see SEER

search[1.1], †**serche** /sertʃ/ *n* **1** an examination, an inquiry, an investigation *16-*. **2** an investigation into the Register of Sasines, in order to discover the nature of the title, details of the *burdens* (BURDEN[1.1] (sense 3)), which affect a property offered for sale *la18-*. [ME *serch*, AN *serche*]

search[1.2], †**serche**, †**sers**, †**cerse** /sertʃ/ *v* to examine, peruse; to ransack; to investigate; to seek to discover, inquire *15-*. **searcher**, †**serchour 1** someone who searches *la16-*. **2** *Presbyterian Church* an official appointed to look for and report to the kirk session any absences from church services, or disorderly behaviour *la16-e19*. **3** a royal or burghal officer, an inspector of markets or ships, especially for dutiable or contraband articles *15-17*. **4** an official of an incorporation required to enforce regulations and maintain quality *la15-18*. **5** a person who tracks down (criminals) *16-e17*. †**serchery, sercherie** the office of *searcher* **3**, especially a customs-officer *16-e18*. [ME *serchen*, OFr *cerchier*]

search[2.1] /sertʃ/ *n* a sieve, a strainer, a riddle *18-19, 20- NE T*. [ME *sarce*, OFr *saas*]

search[2.2] /sertʃ/ *v* to sieve, sift, strain *18-19, 20- NE T*. [see the noun]

season see SAISON[1.1], SAISON[1.2]

seat, sate, seit, †**sete**, †**set**, †**sait** /sit, set/ *n* **1** a place or thing on which to sit; a chair *la15-*. **2** a place of residence; a dwelling-house; a location, site, also in place-names *la12-*. **3** *in place-names* a high, conspicuous and often saddle-shaped hill, such as *Arthur's Seat 16-*. **4** a fishing-ground *la19- Sh*. **5** a court the Court of Session; a kirk session *la15-17*. **6** a sitting, session or diet of a court *la15-19*. **7** the chair, throne or place reserved for a person of authority or dignity *15-e17*. **8** a bishop's see; the papal see *la14-17*. **9** a base, a foundation *la16-17*. †**sete-burd** a table at which people sat *la15-16*. **seat-rent** the rent paid for the use of a seat in a church at services *la17-*. †**seat-tree** the weaver's seat in a handloom *la18-19*. [ON *sǽti*]

seater /'sitər/ *numeral in children's rhymes* seven *20-*. [nonsense word derived from a system of counting sheep, compare Welsh *saith* seven]

seath see SAITHE, SEYTH

sebow see SYBOW

secede /sə'sid/ *v* to withdraw formally from an institution or alliance, primarily in reference to the withdrawal of a group of ministers from the Church of Scotland *la17-*; compare SECESSION (sense 2). **Seceder 1** a member of any of the branches of the *Secession Church* (SECESSION) *18-*. **2** a member of the Free Presbyterian Church *20- H&I*. [Lat *sēcēdere* to withdraw]

secession, †**secessioun** /sə'sɛʃən/ n 1 the withdrawal of a dissenting group 16-. 2 *Presbyterian Church* the departure of ministers from the established church; most notably the withdrawal in 1732 of a group of ministers led by Ebenezer and Ralph Erskine *la17-*. **Secession Church** the church formed by the dissenting ministers after their departure *19-*; compare *United Secession Church* (UNITED). [MFr *sécession*, Lat *sēcessiōn-*]

sech *see* SICH[1.1], SICH[1.2]

seck[1.1], **sack**, †**sek**, †**saik**, †**sak** /sɛk, sak/ n 1 a large rectangular bag of coarse material for carrying grain or coal *la14-*. 2 a sackful *15-*. 3 a dry measure of oatmeal; compare BOLL *20- NE C*. 4 sacking worn as a sign of mourning or penitence *la15-e17*. **seckin, secking,** †**sacken** material used for making sacks, sackcloth *17-*. **seckclaith** 1 *Presbyterian Church* sacking worn as a symbol of penitence especially by a person undergoing church discipline *la16-19, 21- historical*. 2 a garment made of sacking *la15-17*. †**seck goun, seck gown** a penitential garment made of sacking *17-e19*. **give someone a seckfu o sair banes** to give someone a beating *la19-*. [ON *sekkr*, OE *sacc*]

seck[1.2], **sack** /sɛk/ v to put in a bag *18-*. [see the noun]

†**seck**[2], **sect** n a category or sex of persons, male or female *e19*. [ME *secte*, Fr *secte*, with influence from *sex*]

†**seck**[3] n a class of white wines imported from Spain and the Canaries *17-e18*. [shortened form of SECK WYNE]

seckie /'sɛki, 'sekə/ n a linen overall jacket worn by foremen in a weaving factory *20- N WC*. [aphetic form of *kerseckie* (CARSACKIE)]

†**seck wyne, wyne seck** n dry white wine *la16-17*. [MFr *vin sec*]

second[1.1], †**secund** /'sɛkənd/ n 1 the next person, thing, day etc after the first *16-*. 2 a backer or supporter *16-*. †**secundis in degreis of consanguinitie** *law* first cousins *la16-e17*. †**secund of kin** = *secundis in degreis of consanguinitie*. †**secunds in blood** = *secundis in degreis of consanguinitie la18*. †**secunds and thirds** people related at two or three removes from a common ancestor *la16-17*. [see the adj]

second[1.2], **saicont, secont,** †**secund,** †**secound** /'sɛkənd, 'sekənt/ adj 1 next in a sequence (rank, importance or quality) after the first *la14-*. 2 other, another, additional to the first *la14-*. 3 applied to the storey immediately above the ground floor of a building *la18-20*. †**Seconder** *in St Andrews and Glasgow Universities* a student of social rank just below a nobleman, who had special privileges and paid higher fees *17-e19*; compare PRIMAR, TERNAR. **second-handed** second-hand, not new, deriving from a previous owner or owners *la18-*. **second pair** the pair of horses worked by the second or assistant horseman on a farm *la19- N SW*. **second-sight,** †**second-sicht** the faculty or power of seeing future, distant or supernatural events as if they were actually present; the image thus seen; the ability to foretell future events; telepathic powers *la16-*. **second-sighted** having this faculty *la17-*. †**secund teind** the tithe deriving from legal transactions *la15-16*. [OFr *second*, Lat *secundus*]

seconder *see* SECUNDAR

secont, secound *see* SECOND[1.2]

secours *see* SUCCOUR[1.1]

†**secre**[1.1] n something intended to be kept hidden or private, a secret *la14-16*. [see the adj]

†**secre**[1.2] adj 1 *of a person* trusted; intimate *15-e16*. 2 concealed, hidden; *of a place* secluded *15-16*. [ME *secre*, OFr *secré*]

secreit *see* SAICRET[1.1], SAICRET[1.2]

†**secret, sacreit** n a coat-of-mail designed to be worn concealed under the outer clothes *16-e17, e19 historical*. [MFr *secrète* a skullcap worn under the helmet]

secret *see* SAICRET[1.1], SAICRET[1.2]

secretar /'sɛkrətər, 'sekrətər/ n 1 a person employed to do various sorts of office work, originally to write letters or draft documents *la15-*. 2 the person in charge of a department of government, a Secretary of State; originally the secretary of the sovereign, the royal officer in charge of the royal signets and responsible for writs passing the signet *la15-*. 3 a person who performs confidential services for another; a person entrusted with secrets, a confidant *15-17*. [MFr *secrétaire*, Lat *sēcrētārius*]

†**secretary** n the royal secretariat, the office presided over by the royal secretary *16-e17*. [Lat *sēcrētāria*]

secrrind bell *see* SACRING BELL

sect *see* SECK[2]

secund *see* SECOND[1.1], SECOND[1.2]

†**secundar, seconder** adj secondary, of second quality or of the second size, secondary *la15-16*. [Lat *secundārius*]

sedarin *see* SEDERUNT

seddle *see* SAIDLE[1.1]

sede *see* SEED[1.1], SEED[1.2]

sederunt, *NE* **sedarin** /sə'dɛrənt, 'sɛdərənt; *NE* sə'dɛrən/ n 1 in minutes of deliberative bodies, used to introduce the list of those present at a meeting; the list itself; the persons who attended *la16-*. 2 a meeting of a deliberative or judicial body, originally of the Court of Session or of a kirk session *la16-*. 3 a meeting of an informal or social nature *18-*. 4 an unpleasant interview, a scolding *19, 20- NE T*. 5 remuneration for attendance at a day's sitting payable to a Lord of Session *e17*. †**sederunt buik** a minute book *la16-e19*. †**sederunt day** a day appointed for a sitting of the Court of Session *la17-e19*. **Act of Sederunt** an ordinance regulating the procedure of a deliberative body, especially the Court of Session *la17-*. **Buik of Sederunt** 1 the records of the Court of Session, including the *Acts of Sederunt 17-*. 2 the list of people attending a meeting; the persons who attended *la16-*. [Lat *sēdērunt* they sat down]

sedule, sedull *see* SCHEDULE

see, *Bor* **sei,** †**se,** †**sie,** †**seyne** /si; *Bor* sae/ v *pt* **saw, seed,** †**sa,** †**schau,** †**sauch** *ptp* **seen** †**sene,** †**sein** 1 to perceive by the eye, look at; to examine *la14-*. 2 to see to it, ensure, take measures or steps, contrive *la18-*. 3 *in imperative* hand or pass, give into a person's hand, let (a person) have: ◊*see me the teapot 19-*. 4 emphasizing or pointing something out ◊*come awa, noo see, Marget la19- NE T*. 5 introducing a person or thing about to be discussed observe, take note of: ◊*see him, he canny drive 20- C*. 6 to reveal *16*. †**seen, sene, seyn** 1 visible *15-19*. 2 manifest, evident *la15-17*. 3 expert, knowledgeable *la16-e18*. **seeing glass** a mirror *20- NE T C*. **I think I see ...** *ironic* there is no chance *la19-*. **I've seen as muckle as** I wouldn't be surprised if *la19-*. **I've seen myself, I've seen me** I can remember, I have often (done something) *20-*. **see about** to look after, enquire about (a person) *la18, 20- NE T C*. **see her ain** *of a female* to menstruate *20- EC*. **see a stime** *mainly in negative* to catch the least glimpse, see any trace *la15-*. **see at 1** *imperative* look at, observe *la19- NE T*. 2 to consult, inquire of *la19- NE T C*. †**see between the een** to meet *19*. **see day aboot wi** to be even with, get one's own back on *19- N EC Bor*. **see efter 1** to look after (a person), attend to the wants of *la19-*. 2 to take steps to obtain, make enquiries for *20- NE T H&I C*. **see someone far enough** expressing annoyance to wish that someone were out of the way or had not appeared *la19-*. †**se for 1** to look for, try to find *la15*. **2**

to make arrangements, take steps to deal with; to provide for *15-16*. †**se on** to look on, look at *la14-e16*. †**se our** to read, study (a book) *15-e16*. **sees** give me (a thing) *la19-*. **sees a haud o, see haud o** give me (a thing) *la19-*. **seestu 1** you understand, let me tell you *19- Sh Ork WC SW*. **2** a nickname for the town of Paisley (because once considered to be characteristic of Paisley speech) *19-20, 21- WC historical*. **seestuna** *expressing admiration* would you have thought it! *la19- Sh Ork*. **see thegither** to see eye to eye, agree *20-*. **see yer thoum** *negative* to see ahead of one (in the dark) *la19- Sh N T*. **see till, seetle** to look at, observe *19, 20- Sh Ork NE T EC*. **see to 1** to attend to, take care of *15-*. **2** to look at, observe *la18-e19*. **3** = SEE (sense 3) *la18-19, 20- Ork NE T*. [OE *sēon*]

seeck[1.1], **sick**, †**seke**, †**seik** /sik, sɪk/ *n* **1** *pl* ill people, the unwell *la15-*. **2** an ill or unwell person *la14-17*. [see the adj]

seeck[1.2], **seek, sick,** †**seke,** †**seik** /sik, sɪk/ *adj* **1** ill, unwell *la14-*. **2** *of ground* not productive; out of condition *16-*. **sickrife,** †**seke-ryf 1** slightly ill; not thriving *19, 20- literary*. **2** sickening, nauseating; tiresome *la19- T EC*. **3** ill or susceptible to illness *la15*. **sick-laith** extremely unwilling, very reluctant *la18- EC Bor*. **sick-sairt, sick-sair** thoroughly sated or bored, sick to death *19- Ork NE T*. **sick-sorry 1** very sorry *la19- Ork N H&I EC*. **2** = *sick-sairt 19- Bor*. **seik-stawed, seek-stawed** = *sick-sairt 20- EC Bor*. **seeck-tired, sick-tired** = *sick-sairt 19-*. **seek fed up** = *sick-sairt 20-*. [OE *sēoc*]

seed[1.1], †**sede,** †**seid** /sid/ *n* **1** a plant's unit of reproduction *la14-*. **2** semen *la14-*. **3** a line of descent *la14-*. **4** the initial germ of growth or development; the animating principle or soul *la14-*. **5** an individual grain of seed *la15-*. **6** a progenitor, an ancestor *20- N Uls*. **7** progeny; a people, a race *15-17*. †**seedie** full of oat husks *18-e19*. **seed-bird** the wagtail *Motacilla la18-19, 20- Bor*. **sids** particles of bran, especially oat bran, used as food, frequently used to make SOWANS *16- Sh Ork N T*. **seed-faerdy** *of grain* fit for sowing *la19- Sh*. **seed-fur 1** the furrow into which grain is to be sown and harrowed *18, 20- N*. **2** a shallow furrow to mark where a hand-sower should spread the seed *20- Ork SW historical*. †**seed-furrow, seed-fur** to plough (land) with furrows to receive seed *la17-e19*. **seed-lady** the pied wagtail *Motacilla alba la19, 20- WC*. **seed-like** *of soil* ready for sowing *la19- N NE*. **lat sid, say sids** *in negative constructions* never to say a word, never to make the least remark *20- NE*. **a seed in yer teeth** something irritating or annoying *la18-19, 20- Bor*. [OE *sǣd*]

seed[1.2], *Sh* **sid,** †**sede** /sid/ *v* **1** to originate, develop *la15-*. **2** *of fine rain* to drip *la19- Sh*. **3** to weave a pattern of spots, resembling seeds, in a piece of muslin or linen *19*. [see the noun]

seed *see* SEE

seedge *see* SIEGE[1.1]

seefer *see* CEEPHER

seek[1], **sik,** †**sek,** †**seke,** †**seik** /sik, sɪk/ *v pt ptp* **socht, soucht 1** to search for, look for; to hope or intend to obtain or accomplish *la14-*. **2** to search (a place); to look through, examine, scrutinize (the mind) *la14-*. **3** to discover by inquiry, investigate, ascertain *la14-*. **4** to approach with a request or petition, ask for, request; to intend to purchase or hire; to beg *la14-*. **5** to make an attempt or request to go or come *la15-*. **6** to request in marriage, ask for the hand of, propose to (a woman) *la16-*. **7** to ask for, require as a price, wages or payment *17-*. **8** to invite (a farmworker) to remain for the next half-year *18-*. **9** to wish, desire *la19-*. **10** to ask, tell (a person) (to come, to do) *la19-*. **11** to require, demand, expect as one's right or due *la16-19, 20- N T*. **12** to bring, fetch *20- Bor*. **13** to attack, assail, pursue with hostile intent *la14-17*. **14** to practise (a trade, skill) *15-e17*. **15** to visit, go to (a place, person), in a direction *la14-17*. **16** to intend, aim, attempt to do or to be something *la14-e17*. **socht** exhausted *19, 20- NE T*. **seek-an-hod** hide-and-seek *19- T*. †**seke in** to try to get or acquire *la17-e18*. †**seke on** to attack *15*. **seek to** to resort or apply to, have recourse to, strive for *la14-19*. †**sek up for** *nautical* to bear up for, sail towards *e17*. **seek up on** to gain on *20- Sh*. [OE *sēcan*]

seek[2] /sik/ *v* to percolate, soak, ooze *la19- NE T WC SW*. [perhaps extended sense of SEEK[1]]

seek *see* SEECK[1.2]

seel, seil, †**sele,** †**seill,** †**seyll** /sil/ *n* happiness, bliss, prosperity, good fortune *la14-19, 20- literary*. **seelfu** happy, lucky; pleasant *la15-*. [OE *sǣl*]

seel *see* SEAL[1.1]

seeldams *see* SELDOM[1.2]

seelence[1.1], **silence,** †**scilence,** †**silens,** †**seilence** /ˈsɪləns, ˈsaɪləns/ *n* **1** absence of speech or other noise; refusal, unwillingness or failure to speak *la14-*. **2** *with possessive adjective* failure to speak or provide information by way of speech or writing *16-*. **3** absence or omission of mention in written material *la16-*. **putting to silence** *law* the court action to prevent someone from putting about an unfounded claim to be married to some person *19-*. †**under silence of nicht** *of mainly criminal activity* carried out in secrecy, under cover of darkness *la15-e17*. [OFr *silence*]

seelence[1.2], **silence** /ˈsɪləns, ˈsaɪləns/ *v* **1** to (cause to) become silent; to suppress sound *la16-*. **2** *Presbyterian Church* to cause (a minister) to cease preaching; to deprive (a minister) of his or her charge *la17*. [see the noun]

seelent, silent /ˈsɪlənt, ˈsaɪlənt/ *adj* keeping silence, without speaking; noiseless; unexpressed *la16-*. [Lat *silēns*]

seely, sealy, †**silly** /ˈsɪli/ *adj* **1** blessed, lucky, happy *la14-*. **2** holy, innocent *15-17*. †**seely court** *folklore* the court of the fairies *la18-e19*. **seely-hoo, ceeliehoo** a caul on the head of a newborn child, thought to be very lucky *18- NE EC*. †**seely wight** a fairy *e19*. [OE *sǣlig*]

seem[1.1], **seim** /sim/ *n* outward appearance or semblance, image *18-*. [see the verb]

seem[1.2], †**seme,** †**seim** /sim/ *v* **1** to appear to be, give the appearance of (what is expressed in the complement) *la14-*. **2** to look becoming in (a piece of clothing) *20- Bor*. **3** *of dress* to suit, be becoming *20- Sh*. **4** to be appropriate, suitable *15-16*. **5** to pretend to be (something) *la14-16*. **6** to be seen, manifest or evident *la14-e16*. **7** to appear to exist, be present; to be apparent *16*. **it seems** apparently, seemingly *la14-*. [ON *sœma* to honour, conform to]

seen *see* SEE, SEEVEN, SUNE[1.2], SYNE[2.1]

seendil, sinnle, †**seldin,** †**sendle,** †**seindill** /ˈsɪndəl/ *adv* rarely, infrequently *la14-17, 18- literary*. †**seldin times** = SEENDIL *la15-e18*. [metathesis of OE *seldan* seldom]

seenie *see* SINNIE[1]

seep *see* SYPE[1.1], SYPE[1.2]

seer, †**sear** /sir, siər/ *n* **1** a person who sees visions or has second sight *la16-*. **2** an overseer; an inspector *la15-e17*. [SEE, with agent suffix]

seerup, syrup, †**serop,** †**syrop** /ˈsɪrəp, ˈsaɪrəp/ *n* a concentrated solution of sugar, a thick, sweet liquid used as a vehicle for medicine or in food *la15-*. [ME *syrope*, OFr *sirop*]

seestu *see* SEE

seet *see* SUIT[2]

seetuate, situate, †**cituat,** †**sitwat,** †**sitevate** /ˈsɪtɪət, ˈsɪtjuət/ *adj* located, situated *la15-*. [Lat *situāt-*]

seetuation, situation, †**sitivation,** †**situacioun** /sɪtiˈeʃən, sɪtjuˈeʃən/ *n* position, locality; placing, positioning *la15-*. [MFr *situation*]

seeven, seven, seen, *N* **siven,** *NE* **saiven,** †**sevin,** †**sevyn,** †**seveyne** /ˈsivən, ˈsɛvən, sin; *N* ˈsɪvən; *NE* ˈsɛvən/ *numeral* **1** the cardinal number next above six *la14-*. **2** *in rugby football* a team of seven players only *20-*. **3** seventh *la14-16*. **sevens** a rugby competition among teams of seven players each, originally from various Border towns *20-*. **sevensie** the seventh game in the series at *chuckies* (CHUCKIE) *20-*. **sevensome,** †**sevin sum** seven in all, a group of seven *la15-*. **seevent** the ordinal number corresponding to the cardinal number seven, next after sixth *la14-*. **seeventeen,** †**sevintene** **1** the cardinal number next above sixteen *la14-*. **2** seventeenth *la14-*. **seeventy,** *WC* **sinty** the cardinal number next above sixty-nine *la14-*. **sevenicht,** †**sennicht,** †**se'ennight,** †**sevenycht** a period of seven nights, a week *la14-*. †**be sic sevin** seven times more *e16*. **seven-a-side(s)** a rugby game with seven players on each side *20-*. **seven lang and seven short** a long time *la19- Sh Ork*. **the Seven Sisters 1** the Pleiades *20-*. **2** seven similar cannon used at the Battle of Flodden *la16, e19 historical*. †**the seven starns** the Pleiades *16-e19*. [OE *seofon*]

seg¹, segg /sɛg/ *n* **1** sedge *15-*. **2** the yellow flag iris *Iris pseudacorus 18-*. **3** a float made of bundles of sedge used in learning to swim *19*. **segging** a disease of oat-plants *19-*. **seggy** sedgy, covered in or bordered with sedges; marshy *12-*. [OE *secg* sedge]

seg² /sɛg, sɛg/ *v* to sink, subside, collapse *la17-*. [MLG *sacken* to subside, Norw dial *sagga* to walk heavily]

seg³ /sɛg, sɛg/ *v of the acidity in sour fruit* to set (the teeth) on edge *la18- C SW Bor*. [extended sense of Eng *sage* to saw]

†**sege** *n* a man, a fellow *la15-16*. [OE *secg* a man]

sege *see* SIEGE¹·¹, SIEGE¹·²

†**segg** /sɛg/ *n* an animal, especially a bull, which has been castrated when fully grown *la18-e19*. [compare Dan *seg* a castrated boar]

segg *see* SEG¹

seggan, *H&I WC* **sheggan** /ˈsɛgən; *H&I WC also* ˈʃɛgən/ *n* **1** the yellow flag iris *Iris pseudacorus 19- H&I WC SW Uls*; compare SEG¹ (sense 2). **2** the stinking iris *Iris foetidissima la18- WC*. [probably derivative of SEG¹]

sei *see* SEE
seich *see* SICH¹·¹, SICH¹·²
seid *see* SEED¹·¹
seif *see* SIEVE¹·¹
seige *see* SIEGE¹·¹, SIEGE¹·²
seignet *see* SIGNET¹·¹
seik *see* SEECK¹·¹, SEECK¹·², SEEK¹
seil *see* SAIL¹·², SEEL, SILE²·²
seilence *see* SEELENCE¹·¹
seill *see* SEAL¹·¹, SEAL¹·², SEEL, SELL²
seim *see* SEEM¹·¹, SEEM¹·²
sein *see* SEAND¹, SEE
seindill *see* SEENDIL
seinyie *see* SENƷE
seinʒe *see* SINNON
seip *see* SYPE¹·²

†**seir, sere** *adj* various, many; separate, distinct, different *la14-16*. [ME *ser* different, various, diverse, extraordinary, ON *sér* for oneself, separately]

seisin *see* SASINE
seit *see* SEAT, SET¹·²
seith *see* SEYTH

seize, †**ses,** †**seys,** †**sais** /siz/ *v* **1** to take possession of (by force); *originally of a feudal superior* to confiscate; to arrest; to capture *la14-*. **2** to put (a person) in possession of (a feudal holding) *15-20, 21- historical*. **3** to put, settle, establish in a place *la15-16*. **seizer 1** *Presbyterian Church* an official appointed to look for and report to the kirk session any absences from church services or disorderly behaviour *la18- historical*. **2** a person authorized to confiscate certain goods or cattle *la17-18*. †**sessonar** a lawful possessor (of lands) *la15*. [OFr *saisir*]

sek *see* SEEK¹, SECK¹·¹
seke *see* SEECK¹·¹, SEECK¹·², SEEK¹
sekir *see* SICCAR¹·²
sekyre *see* SICCAR¹·¹

sel¹·¹, self, †**salff,** †**selwyn** /sɛl, sɛlf/ *n* **1** a person's own or intrinsic being *la16-*. **2** the person's or thing's (own) self or (very) being; also used to emphasize the excessive presence of the thing mentioned in some context, *eg* **saut's sel** salt itself; very or excessively salty *la15-19, 20- SW Bor*. †**the self** itself *la14-17*. †**be the self** on its own, separately *la14-17*. †**in the self** in itself, intrinsically *la14-17*. [OE *self*]

sel¹·², self /sɛl, sɛlf/ *pron* **1** *coming immediately before or after a noun in apposition, in emphatic use* himself, herself, itself *la14-17*. **2** *with personal pronoun eg* **himsel** alone, by himself *la19-*. **selly,** †**selfie** *adj* selfish *17-*. **selly** *n* selfishness *18-*. **the sell o'm, the sell o ye, the sel o't** *used for the emphatic or reflexive pronoun* himself, yourself or itself *19, 20- NE T H&I*. [see the noun]

selch, *NE* **sulch, seal,** †**selich,** †**selk** /sɛlx; *NE* ˈsʌlx, sil/ *n* **1** a grey seal, the animal *12-*. **2** a fat clumsy person *la19- NE*. [OE *seolh*]

selchie *see* SELKIE

†**selcouth, selkouth** *adj* strange, unusual; marvellous *la14-19*. [OE *seldan* seldom + OE *cūð* known]

seldin *see* SEENDIL

seldom¹·¹ /ˈsɛldəm/ *adj* scanty, poor in quantity *20- NE Bor*. [see the adv]

seldom¹·², *Ork* **seeldams** /ˈsɛldəm; *Ork* ˈsildəmz/ *adv* infrequently *la16-*. Compare SEENDIL. [OE *seldan*]

sele *see* SEAL¹·¹, SEAL¹·², SEEL

†**self, selfin** *adj* same *la14-e17*. **the self** the same (thing) *15-16*. [OE *self*]

self *see* SEL¹·¹, SEL¹·²

self and same /ˈsɛlf ən ˈsem/ *adj* identical *19, 20- Ork Bor*. [SELF + SAME²·²]

self-contained /sɛlfkənˈtend/ *adj* **1** *of accommodation, especially a flat, originally of a house* restricted to the use of one household, not shared *la18-*. **2** complete in itself *19-*. [SEL¹·¹ + ptp of *contain* (CONTEEN)]

selfin *see* SELF
selich *see* SELCH
selie *see* SILLY
seling *see* SYLING
selk *see* SELCH
selkhorn *see* SHILCORN

selkie, *Sh N* **silkie,** †**selchie** /ˈsɛlki; *Sh N* ˈsɪlki/ *n* **1** a seal *17- Sh Ork N NE*. **2** a native of North Ronaldsay, Orkney *20- Ork*. **selkie folk** *folklore* seals with the power to transform themselves into human shape *la19- Sh Ork*. [SELCH + -IE¹]

Selkirk bannock, Selkirk bannie /ˈsɛlkɪrk ˈbanək, ˈsɛlkɪrk ˈbane/ *n* a kind of rich fruit loaf, made as a speciality by Selkirk bakers *19-*. [from the place-name + BANNOCK]

Selkirk grace /ˈsɛlkɪrk gres/ *n* a rhymed grace before meals (often wrongly ascribed to Burns) *19-*. [from the place-name + GRACE]

selkouth *see* SELCOUTH

sell¹ /sɛl/ *v pt, ptp also* **selt, sauld,** *Sh* **sald 1** to dispose of (goods or merchandise) for money; to deal in, put up for sale on a regular basis; *of a commodity* to find a buyer, fetch a price *la14-*. **2** to give up treacherously, betray *la14-*. †**sellrif, selrife, salerife** *of goods* saleable, easy to sell *16-e19*. **to sell,** †**to be sauld** for sale *15-*. [OE *sellan*]

sell[2], **seal,** †**saill,** †**seill** /sɛl/ *n* the rope, iron loop or chain by which cattle are fastened in their stalls *la16- N NE H&I*. [OE *sāl* a string, a line]

sellack, sellag *see* SILLOCK
sellar *see* CELLAR[1.1], CELLAR[1.2]
seller *see* CELLAR[2]
sellok *see* SILLOCK
selt *see* SELL[1]
selwyn *see* SEL[1.1]
sem *see* SEAM[2]
semat *see* SEMMIT
sembill *see* SEMMLE
†**sembland, semlant** *n* **1** appearance *la14-e16*. **2** likeness *e16*. [OFr *semblant*]
†**semble, semle, semblie** *n* **1** a meeting (of people), an assembly *la14-16*. **2** a hostile meeting, the assemblage of people fighting *la14-e16*. [aphetic form of ASSEMBLY]
semble *see* SEMMLE
semblie *see* SEMBLE
seme *see* SEAM[1.1], SEEM[1.2]
semi /'sɛmɪ/ *n* in the universities of Aberdeen and St Andrews, originally also Edinburgh and Glasgow a second-year student *17-*. †**semi-class** *in a Scottish university* the second-year class *la17-18*. [shortened form of SEMI-BAJAN]
semi-bajan *n* = SEMI *17-*. [Lat *sēmi* half + BEJAN]
semle *see* SEMBLE, SEMMLE
semmit, simmit, simit, †**semat** /'sɛmɪt, 'sɪmɪt/ *n* **1** an undershirt or vest *la19-*. **2** a (Roman) tunic *la15*. [unknown; compare OFr *samit* a silk fabric]
semmle, †**semble,** †**sembill,** †**semle** /'sɛməl/ *v* **1** to come or be brought together, assemble (as a group); to fit together (components) *la14-e16, 20- Sh Ork*. **2** to gather (things) together in order to make a selection or choose *20-*. **3** to meet in conflict; to attack *15-16*. [aphetic form of ME *assemblen*, OFr *assembler*]
sempill, semple *see* SIMPLE
†**sempiterne**[1.1] *n* a hard-wearing fabric *17*. [see the adj]
†**sempiterne**[1.2] *adj* everlasting *la15-e16*. [ME *sempiterne*, OFr *sempiterne*, Lat *sempiternus*]
sen *see* SEND[1.2], SYNE[2.1], SYNE[2.2], SYNE[2.3]
senate /'sɛnət/ *n* **1** a gathering with deliberative and legislative functions; a governing body, especially that of ancient Rome *la14-*. **2** = SENATUS *20-*. **3** a Scottish deliberative body, a town council or synod; the College of Justice; parliament *la16-e18*. [Lat *senātus*]
senator, †**senatour** /'sɛnətər/ *n* **1** a member of a senate, originally of ancient Rome, Jerusalem and Tyre *la14-*. **2** = *Senator of the College of Justice 16-17*. **Senator of the College of Justice** the official title of a judge of the Court of Session *16-*. [Lat *senātor*]
senatus /sə'netəs/ *n* = *Senatus Academicus la19-*. **Senatus Academicus** *in the universities of Aberdeen, Edinburgh, Glasgow and St Andrews* the body which superintends and regulates the teaching and discipline of the university *17-*. [Lat *senātus*]
sence *see* SENS, SINSE
send[1.1], †**saynd** /sɛnd/ *n* **1** *at a wedding* a messenger sent ahead of a bridegroom to summon the bride *la18-*. **2** a messenger, an embassy *la14-16*. **3** a message, summons or intimation sent *16-19*. **4** God's ordinance or dispensation *15-16*. [from the verb and OE *sand* the act of sending]

send[1.2], **sen** /sɛnd, sɛn/ *v* **1** to cause to go or be taken, dispatch (a message); to direct (a person to go somewhere or do something); to convey; to transport *la14-*. **2** to export (commodities) *15-16*. †**send eftir** to send a message; to summon *la14-15*. **send to** to make contact with (someone), inquire concerning *la14-*. **a sent errand** a commission entrusted to another *20- Sh*. [OE *sendan*]
sendle *see* SEENDIL
sene *see* SAY[1.2], SEE, SYNE[2.1], SYNE[2.2], SYNE[2.3]
senior[1.1], †**seniour** /'sinjər/ *n* **1** an older person, a more advanced student *20-*. **2** *Presbyterian Church* a church elder *la16*. **3** *Christian Church* an elder in the early church *16*. [see the adj]
senior[1.2] /'sinjər/ *adj* older, more advanced *18-*. **senior secondary school** a state secondary school providing more academic courses than the *junior secondary school* (JUNIOR), attended by pupils who were successful in the *qualifying examination* (QUALIFY) *20-, 21- historical*. [EModE *senior*, Lat *senior*]
sennachie *see* SHENACHIE
sennicht *see* SEEVEN
sennon *see* SINNON
†**sens, sence, cense** *n* **1** incense *la14-e16*. **2** perfume *e16*. [aphetic form of ME *encence*, OFr *encens*]
sense /sɛns/ *n* the essential part of something; goodness, juice *la19- NE T*. [aphetic form of Fr *essence*]
†**sensement, censement, sensyment, sensment** *n* a decision, a judgement, a verdict *15-17*. [OFr *sensement*]
sensuality, †**sensualitie,** †**sensualitee,** †**sensualite** /sɛnʃu'alɪte, sɛnsju'alɪte/ *n* **1** preoccupation with sensual needs or desires; ((excessive) indulgence in) the pleasure of the senses *la15-*. **2** sexual appetite, lust *la15-16*. **3** the part of human nature concerned with the senses *la15-e16*. [OFr *sensualité*, Lat *sensuālitas*]
sensyment *see* SENSEMENT
sensyne *see* SINSYNE
sent *see* SCENT, SEND[1.2]
sentence, †**sentens** /'sɛntəns/ *n* **1** an opinion; judgement, decision; condemnation; punishment, retribution *la14-*. **2** a short stretch of text functioning as a grammatical unit *la16-*. **3** the meaning or significance (of a word or passage) *la14-16*. **4** the content, subject-matter or theme (of a work of literature); a text or book; a wise saying, maxim; something written or said *15-16*. †**sentence-money, sentence-silver** *law* a court fee payable when sentence was given, assessed at a fixed rate on the basis of the sum awarded *la16-e18*. [OFr *sentence*]
sentiner *see* CENTINER
sentreis *see* SENTRICE
sentrell *see* CENTRELL
sentrice, †**centries,** †**sentreis,** †**centreis** /'sɛntrɪs/ *n* **1** *building* a timber framework supporting the construction of a bridge or an arch *15-*. **2** (part of) the framework of a doorway *la17-e18*. [plural of Fr *cintre*]
†**senȝe, senȝie, seinyie** *n* **1** a distinguishing mark *15*. **2** a battle-cry, a rallying cry, a call to battle *15-16*. **3** a signboard *la16-e17*. [aphetic form of ENSENYIE]
†**senȝeour** *n* **1** a lord, master, ruler *la15-16*. **2** *as a title or mode of address* especially used to represent Italian *Signor* and French *Seigneur la15-16*. **3** an old man *la15*. **senȝeoury, signorie** the status, authority or territory of a lord *la14-e17*. [ME *seignour*, AN *segnour*]
†**septuply** *v law, of the pursuer* to make a seventh answer, in reply to the SEXTUPLY of the defender *la18*. [formed on Lat *septem* seven, by analogy with QUADRUPLY[1.1] etc]

†sepulture, sepultur, sepultour *n* **1** interment, burial *la14-16*. **2** a place of interment or burial, a grave, tomb *la14-17*. **3** *Roman Catholic Church* a repository for the sacrament *la15-16*. [OFr *sepulture*, Lat *sepultūra*]

sequel /'sikwəl/ *n* **1** *law* the perquisites given to a miller's servants for each consignment of grain ground *la15-18, 19- historical*. **2** an event following after another *19-*. **3** a consequence or repercussion *la15-16*. [OFr *sequelle*, Lat *sequēla*]

sequestrate /'sikwəstret/ *v* **1** to confiscate *17-*. **2** *law* to put (the property of a bankrupt) into the hands of a trustee for division among the creditors; to make a person bankrupt *18-*. **3** to remove, separate, set aside *16-19*. **4** *law* to divert (the income of an estate) to someone other than the owner *la16-17*. **5** *law* to place (lands or other heritable property) under a factor or trustee appointed by the Court of Session to administer the property and rents from it, usually while the ownership is the subject of a legal action *18-19*. [Lat *sequestrāt-*, ptp stem of *sequestrāre*]

sequestration, †sequestratioun /'sikwəstreʃən/ *n* **1** seizure of income or assets for non-fulfilment of an obligation; especially that of a bankrupt for distribution among the creditors *la15-*. **2** confiscation of possessions by a government *la16-e19*. [Lat *sequestrātiōn-*]

ser, sair /sɛr, ser/ *n* one's fill, enough, satiety *19, 20- NE T Bor*. [variant of SAIRVE]

ser *see* SAIRVE

serche *see* SEARCH[1.1], SEARCH[1.2]

sere *see* SEIR, SHAIR[2.1]

serefe *see* SHERIFF

serene /sə'rin/ *adj* **1** calm, untroubled *16-*. **2** *of the sky* clear, not cloudy *16-e19*. **3** *as an honorific title* kingly, queenly, noble *16*. [Lat *serēnus* calm (of weather)]

serf *see* SAIRVE

†serge *n* a wax candle *la14-e17*. [OFr *cerge*]

sergeand, sergeant, seriand *see* SAIRGEANT

serious *see* SAIRIOUS

†serjeandrie, sergeandry *n* an attendant, servant *la15-e18*. [OFr *sergenterie*]

serk *see* SARK[1.1], SARK[1.2]

serking *see* SARKING

sermon[1.1]**, sairmon, †sermoun** /'sɛrmən, 'sermən/ *n* **1** a discourse, a conversation, something said; a discourse on a religious or moral theme *la14-*. **2** the part of a religious service in which preaching takes place; divine service, an act of church worship *la16-*. [AN *sermun*, Lat *sermōn-*]

†sermon[1.2] *v* to address (an audience); to deliver (an address), make (an announcement) *15-17*. **sermoning** talk, discourse, conversation; preaching *la14-17*. [OFr *sermouner*]

†sero[1.1] *n* lateness, latecoming *17-e18*. [see the adj]

†sero[1.2] *adj* late *17-e18*. [Lat *sērō*]

serop *see* SEERUP

†serpentine, scharpentyn *n* a kind of (ship's) cannon *la15-16*. [OFr *serpentine*]

sers *see* SEARCH[1.2]

sertan *see* CERTAIN[1.2]

sertane *see* CERTAIN[1.1]

serty *see* CERTIE

seruyabill, servable *see* SERVEABILL

seruyce *see* SERVICE

servan, servand, servant *see* SAIRVANT

†serve *v* to deserve *la14-18*. [aphetic form of ME *deserven*, OFr *deservir*]

serve *see* SAIRVE

†serveabill, seruyabill, servable *adj* willing to serve, obedient *la15-e17*. [ME *serviable*, OFr *serviable, servable*]

serviat *see* SERVIETTE

service, †servyis, †seruyce, †siruice /'sɛrvəs/ *n* **1** (an act of) ministration or assistance rendered to another *la14-*. **2** a church service *la14-*. **3** the act of serving food or drink; the food served *la14-*. **4** the condition or action of serving another as an employee; the duties attached to an employment *15-*. **5** military service *15-*. **6** *Presbyterian Church* the serving of the elements at Communion *la16-*. **7** *law* the procedure for transmitting heritable property *la16-20, 21- historical*. **8** compulsory or forced labour as a penalty for crime, penal servitude *la18*. **9** *building* the assistance of workmen by labourers, labouring or unskilled work *16-18*. **10** the condition or action of serving a superior in a feudal relationship; allegiance; fealty *la14-e17*. **11** the duty, especially military service, in return for which land was held; something done in return for a benefit *la14-17*. **12** the office of a miller or his assistant *15-e17*. **general service** *law* the procedure by which a person establishes their right of succession to a deceased person *la16-20, 21- historical*. **†service man** an assistant workman *la16-e18*. **special service** *law* the procedure by which a person establishes their rights as heir with reference to a particular property *la16-20, 21- historical*. [OFr *service*]

servient /'sɛrvɪənt/ *adj law, of persons or property* subjected to a SERVITUDE *la16-*. [Lat *servient-*, presp stem of *servīre* to serve]

serviette, *N C* **servit, †serviet, †serviat, †serviot** /sɛrvɪ'ɛt; *N C* 'sɛrvɪt/ *n* **1** a small towel or table napkin *la15-*. **2** a small tray *19*. **†serviting** material for serviettes *17*. [MFr *serviette*]

servitor[1]**, †servitour, †serviture, †schervitour** /'sɛrvətər/ *n* **1** a (male) servant *la15-*. **2** *at Edinburgh University* a janitor or attendant *la19-*. **3** an apprentice to a craftsman *la15-17*. **4** a clerk or secretary *16-17, e19 historical*. **†your servitour** *a deferential form of address* your humble servant *la15-18*. [ME *servitour*, OFr *servitor*, Lat *servītor*]

servitor[2]**, †servitour** /'sɛrvətər/ *n* a table napkin or hand towel *16-19, 20- WC*. [conflation of *servit* (SERVIETTE) with SERVITOR[1]]

†servitrice, servitrix, servetrix *n* a female servant *la15-18*. [Lat *servītrīce-*]

servitude, †servitute /'sɛrvətjud/ *n* **1** slavery, bondage *15-*. **2** *law* an obligation attached to a piece of property limiting the owner's use of it or permitting others to exercise particular rights over it *16-*. **3** subjection to feudal overlordship, vassalage *la15-17*. [MFr *servitude, servitute*, Lat *servitūdo*]

†serviture *n* service *e16*. [Lat *servītūra*]

serviture *see* SERVITOR[1]

servyis *see* SERVICE

ses *see* SEIZE

sesin *see* SASINE

seson *see* SAISON[1.2]

sesoun *see* SAISON[1.1]

†sesque altra *n music* an interval of a fifth; 3:2 time *16-17*. [Lat *sesquialter* once and a half]

sess *see* CESS[1.1], CESS[1.2]

sessing *see* SASINE

session[1.1]**, †sessioun, †cessioun** /'sɛʃən/ *n* **1** a court; a diet of a court or parliament *la15-*. **2** *law* the supreme civil judicature in Scotland, originally a court of justice consisting of the Chancellor and other persons chosen by the king, which determined causes previously brought before the king and his council; a particular diet of the Court of Session *15-*. **3** *Presbyterian Church* the governing council or court at parish level, consisting of elders and minister *la16-*. **4** the part of the year during which teaching is carried on in the Scottish universities *18-*. **5** a meeting of a kirk session *la16-17*. **sessional** coming from, relating to or administered by a kirk session *17-*. **sessioner 1** a member of the Court of Session *la16-17*. **2** a member of a kirk session *la16-17*. **church session** *Presbyterian Church* the lowest court, consisting of the minister and the elders of the congregation and exercising its functions of church government within a parish *17-*. **session-buik** the minute-book and register of a kirk session *17-*. **session-box** (the box or chest containing) the church funds, especially those to be distributed as charity *la17-*. **session-clerk** the clerk or secretary of a kirk session *la16-*. **session-house 1** the room in or attached to a church, in which the kirk session meets *17-*. **2** the building where the Court of Session was held *17-e18*. †**on the Session** in receipt of poor relief *19*. [MFr *session*, Lat *sessiōn-*]

session[1.2] /ˈsɛʃən/ *v* **1** to summon or take before the kirk session for offences against church discipline *la19-*. **2** *of a betrothed couple* to be called before the kirk session to record their intention to marry and to deposit their earnest money *18-19*. [see the noun]

sesson *see* SAISON[1.1]

sesters /ˈsɛstər/ *n* the drainage channel in a byre *20- Ork*. [plural of Norw dial *sesse-tre* a plank behind the stall on which a milking-stool (sess) rests]

set[1.1], **sett** /sɛt/ *n* **1** a person's attitude, disposition, manner *15-*. **2** a young plant or cutting for planting *16-*. **3** the way in which a tune is arranged, the setting of a piece of music *la16-*. **4** *law* an estimate of the value of a ship *la17-*. **5** a checked pattern in cloth, especially (the arrangement of) the squares and stripes in a tartan, the pattern of tartan associated with a particular clan *18-*. **6** (part of) a potato used for planting *la18-*. **7** *of a person* build, physique, kind *19-*. **8** a dispute, a wrangle, a fuss *la19-*. **9** the constitution or form of organization of a burgh *17-e19, la19- historical*. **10** a joke, a piece of fun *la19, 20- H&I WC SW Bor*. **11** the manner or position in which a thing is set, fixed or arranged; the way in which a thing goes or works; a condition, a state (of affairs) *17-19, 20- Sh Ork N T C*. **12** the action of letting or leasing; a lease *15-19, 20- NE T SW*. **13** a twist or warp in a piece of wood *la19, 20- WC SW*. **14** a check or stoppage, as in growth; a setback, a disappointment *la17, 18- NE T*. **15** a feeling of disgust or repulsion *la18- NE T*. **16** a whetstone *19- EC Bor*. **17** the layer of skin on a sheep which loosens when the new fleece starts to grow *20- Ork*. **18** an arrangement or contract for regular supply from a producer, especially of milk, a standing order; the amount supplied *18-19*. **19** an amount or batch of a commodity *16-17*. **20** a body of procedures, regulations *la15-17*. **21** a disposition of hunters; an area to be hunted; a trap *la14-16*. **22** an attack or onset *la15-19*. **23** a setting for a gem *16*. **action of set and sale** an action in which a part-owner of a ship seeks to buy out or be bought out by his partners or to have the ship sold *la18-*. **tak a set o land** to take one's bearings *20- NE T EC*. [see the verb]

set[1.2], **sett**, †**seit** /sɛt/ *v ptp NE* **setten 1** to lease (property), hire out; *of property* to be be leased, hired out, fetch a rent *14-*. **2** to cause or make to sit, seat, place on a seat *la14-*. **3** to appoint (a time); to lay down (a limit) *la14-*. **4** to assign (a person) a function or office *la14-*. **5** to put (a thing, (part of) a person) in a place or situation; to serve (food) *la14-*. **6** to put in position, arrange, fix *la14-*. **7** to ornament, decorate, inlay *la14-*. **8** to be seemly or suitable for, become, suit, fit: ◊*it sets us to be dumb a while la15-*. **9** to burn, set (fire) to; to light (a fire) *16-*. **10** *of a person* to look becoming in *19-*. **11** to dislocate (the neck) *20-*. **12** to leave (milk) standing for the cream to rise *20-*. **13** *of plants and animals* to stop growing, suffer a check in growth *19, 20- Ork NE T WC*. **14** to bring (a mill) to a stop by diverting the water from the wheel *17-19, 20- NE T Bor*. **15** *of a horse* to refuse to move *la19- NE T SW*. **16** to cause to pass or go to a place, send (a person or thing) *la14-19, 20- T WC Bor*. **17** to disgust, nauseate *19, 20- NE T*. **18** to start off, set out, make one's way *la14-19, 20- Sh Ork*. **19** to accompany, escort, convey (a person on a journey, frequently home) *18-19, 20- SW Bor*. **20** to lay or shoot (fishing-lines or nets) *la19- Sh N*. **21** to direct or guide in; to decide on a certain course *la14-19, 20- NE T*. **22** to stack (peats) in piles to dry *20- NE*. **23** to arrange, hold (a market, fair or wedding) *la15-17*. **24** to found (a town); to erect (a building, boundary markers); to establish (a boundary); to identify with (a mark) *15-17*. **25** to put down in writing *15-16*. **26** to put (something) into effect *la14-16*. **27** to convene (a deliberative or judicial body) *la14-16*. **28** to gamble, wager *16*. **set aff 1** to mark out, separate, make distinctive *17-*. **2** to sack (an employee) *19-*. **3** to cause to explode, let off an explosive charge or shot *la19-*. **4** to plant out *19- Sh N T*. **5** to dawdle, be dilatory *19- NE SW*. **6** to stop the working of (a mill) *18-19*. †**set apon sys** to take risks, act recklessly *e16*. **set at** to attack (a task) with energy *la19- Sh*. **set awa** a fuss; a row, scolding; a send-off *20- NE T Bor* **set awa** to set off, start on a journey *19-*. **set by 1** to lay aside, clear away, set aside for future use *la18-*. **2** to provide with sustenance *17-19*. † **set caution** to put down a pledge *la16-17*. **set doon**, **set down** a formal meal *20-*. **set doon, set down**, †**set doun** *ptp* **setten doon** †**settin down 1** to put down, lay down, deposit (on the ground) *15-*. **2** to cause to sit down, especially at a table for a meal *la14-*. **3** to go bankrupt *20- NE SW*. **4** to provide for (a home) *20- Sh*. **5** to cause (a judicial body) to sit *16-17*. **6** to cause (something) to start up *la15-17*. **7** to put down, quell *16*. **set doon** *of a meal* formally served at table *20- NE T C*. **settin doon** provision (for married life) *19- T EC*. **set du at** to relax *20- Sh*. **set efter** to pursue, follow *la19, 20- Sh N T C*. **set for 1** to send for, summon *20- T EC*. **2** to make for *la18*. **set frae du** to set to work, go at with vigour *la19- Sh*. **set in 1** to put in place *16-*. **2** to bring in (a meal), lay (a table for a meal) *19, 20- Sh NE T*. **set on 1** to set in motion, start off (a mill etc) *17-*. **2** to make and kindle (a fire) *la16-*. **3** to rear (a lamb or calf) over winter *la19-*. **4** to put (an unweaned animal) to suckle, especially to put a lamb to a ewe that has lost her own *la19- WC Bor*. **5** to set to work, begin in earnest *la19, 20- Sh*. **6** to put on, fix, attach *la16-17*. **set oot, set out** a display, a show, a turn-out *la19-*. **set oot, set out 1** to place, put in a position *16-*. **2** to send out, eject forcibly *la19, 20- T*. **3** to cause (a building) to project onto public ground *e17*. **set ower** to ferry across (a body of water) *la15, 20- Sh*. **set a scull** to arrange baited fish-lines in a basket *20- NE*. **set to**, *Sh* **set till 1** to put in position; to close (a gate) *la14-*. **2** to begin with energy and determination; to get to work *la16-*. **3** to set upon, attack *19- NE C Bor*. **set up 1** to put in a prominent or upright position; erect, build; to fix in position *la14-*. **2** to cause kindling to catch fire, encourage (a fire); to set (a chimney) on fire *la16-*. **3** to display (a notice, food for sale) *la16-*. **4** to put into operation; to establish (an enterprise) *16-*. **5** to make (an implement or mechanism, eg a fishing-line, plough, clock) ready for use *la16-*. **6** to earth up (a plant) *la18-*. **7** to arouse, stir up; to incite *19, 20- Sh Ork Bor*. **8** *of rain, a shower* to develop, build up *20- Sh*. **9** *of a horse* to become difficult *e19*. †**set upon sex and sevin** to hazard, wager; to act recklessly *16*. **set up yer gab** to utter impudent remarks *19-*. †**set up a face** to assume an appearance, pretend *la18*. **set you up** *derogatory of a person who seems to be conceited* what a cheek, the impudence! *18-*. [OE *settan*]

set¹·³ /sɛt/ *adj* **1** *of a time or place* appointed, prescribed *la14-*. **2** *of a person* having a particular character, disposition or inclination *la15-*. **3** *of a liturgy or prayers* laid down, prescribed *17-*. **4** pleased *20- NE*. **5** let, leased *16-e18*. **6** *of cloth, especially tartan* having a certain pattern of colours or embroidery, especially in squares and checks *16-e18*. **7** *of a horse's tail* stiffened or cocked up *la18*. †**set battell** pitched battle *la14-e17*. **set-in** inserted, inset *16-*. **set-on 1** equipped, dressed, fed *19- Sh NE T WC*. **2** attached or constructed in a particular fashion *la15-17*. **setten on** frizzled, shrivelled; puny *19, 20- WC SW Bor*. **set stane** a whetstone *19-*. †**set time** a fixed or allotted duration *la17*. **set-up** conceited *la19-*. †**of set purpose** deliberately *la15-17*. [ptp of SET¹·²]

†**set**¹·⁴, **sett** *conj* although *la14-16*. [extended use of the verb or adj]

set² /sɛt/ *n* **1** a number of persons or things associated in some way *la17-*. **2** a team to build corn-stacks; the number of rigs reaped at one time by a band of reapers *19- EC SW Bor Uls*. **3** a sect *e16*. [ME *sette* a sect, OFr *sette* a sect]

set, sete *see* SEAT

seteesh /səˈtiʃ/ *n* a schottische *20- Ork NE*. [altered form of Eng *schottische*]

Seterday, Setturday, Saturday, †**Satterday,** †**Saturnday** /ˈsɛtərdɛ, ˈsatərdɛ/ *n* the day following Friday *la14-*. **Saturday's penny** pocket money *la19-*. **Seterday's slap** the period from Saturday night till Monday morning, fixed by law for the free passage of fish upriver *15-*; compare SLAP²·¹ (sense 2). [OE *sæterndæg*]

setnin /ˈsɛtnɪn/ *n* a lamb that is kept under cover over the winter *la19- Sh*. [Norw dial *setning*, derivative of *setja på* to hand feed, literally to set up]

sett *see* SET¹·¹, SET¹·², SET¹·⁴, SIT¹·²

setten, †**setting** /ˈsɛtən/ *n* **1** a unit of weight mainly for dry goods and meat *15-19, 20- Ork historical*. **2** a rental valuation of land *la16-19 Ork*. [ON *séttungr* a sixth part]

setter¹, †**settar** /ˈsɛtər/ *n* **1** *in baking bread* a strip of wood supporting the row of end- or side-loaves in a batch in the oven *19-*. **2** a horse that stops and refuses to go forwards *20- NE T*. **3** a large lump of coal put on to keep a fire going *20- C*. **4** a person who lets or gives out on lease *la15-e19*. [SET¹·², with agent suffix]

setter² /ˈsɛtər/ *n* (summer) pasture; a meadow; frequently in place-names *19- Sh*. **setter-land** = SETTER² *la18*. [ON *sætr* mountain pastures]

setterel /ˈsɛtrəl/ *adj* **1** small and thickset *la18- NE*. **2** short-tempered, sarcastic *la19- NE*. [SET¹·³ + with *-rel* derogative diminutive suffix]

settin¹·¹ /ˈsɛtɪn/ *n* a young plant; the quantity of potatoes planted as seed *la19-*. †**settin stik** a dibber *e17*. **settin tree** a dibber *20- Sh*. [verbal noun from SET¹·²]

settin¹·² /ˈsɛtɪn/ *adj* fit, suitable, becoming; *of a person* attractive in looks or manner *la18-19, 20- NE T*. [presp of SET¹·²]

settin *see* SIT¹·²
setting *see* SETTEN
settle *see* SATTLE¹·¹, SATTLE¹·²
seuch *see* SHEUCH¹·¹, SOUCH¹·¹
seue *see* SIEVE¹·¹, SIEVE¹·²
seuerall *see* SEVERAL
seur *see* SHAIR²·¹
seure *see* SHAIR²·²
seven *see* SEEVEN

sevendle, sevendable, *Ork* **sevaandal** /səˈvɛndəl, səˈvɛndəbəl;* Ork* səˈvandəl/ *adj* **1** thorough, out-and-out, extreme; forceful *19-*. **2** strong, firm, securely made, built or fixed *19- Bor*. **sevaandaly, sevendibly** forcefully; thoroughly; awfully *20- Ork Uls*. [altered form of SOLVENDIE]

sever, †**sypher** /ˈsɛvər/ *v* **1** to separate, set apart, cut off *la15-*. **2** *of persons* to part; to depart *la15-18*. [ME *severen*, AN *severer*]

sever *see* SURE

several, siveral, †**seuerall** /ˈsɛvrəl, ˈsɪvərəl/ *adj* **1** *of a number* few, some *17-*. **2** separate, distinct; different; diverse, sundry *15-17*. **3** *of property* private *15-16*. [ME *several*, AN *several*]

severals /ˈsɛvrəlz, ˈsɪvərəlz/ *npl* several persons or things *la17-19, 20- Sh N NE EC Bor*. [substantive use of SEVERAL]

severance /ˈsɛvrəns, ˈsɪvərəns/ *n* **1** separation *la19-*. **2** difference, distinction *e16*. [ME *severance*, AN *severance*, OFr *sevrance*]

seveyne, sevin, sevyn *see* SEEVEN
sew *see* SAW¹, SAW²·², SHEW¹·², SUE
sewat *see* SHUET
sewch *see* SHEUCH¹·¹, SHEUCH¹·²

†**sewe** *n* a thick soup or stew *la15*. [ME *sewe* broth, OE *sēaw* juice]

sex *see* SAX
sext *see* SAXT

†**sextulapse** *n Presbyterian Church* a sixth lapse into fornication *17*. [Lat *sextu-* six- + Eng *lapse*; compare DULAPSE]

†**sextuply** *v law, of the defender* to make a sixth reply in answer to the QUINTUPLY¹·¹ of the pursuer *18*. [formed on Lat *sextus* sixth, by analogy with QUADRUPLY¹·¹ etc]

†**sey**¹·¹, **say** *n* **1** a try, a test; originally in combat *la15-e19*. **2** a sample-piece submitted as proof of competence for entry to a trade incorporation *la16-e19*. **3** a sample of a precious metal kept as a record of its fineness *16-e17*. **4** the testing of metals to ascertain their standard of purity *la16-e17*. **5** tasting of food or drink *la15*. **say box** the chest in which samples of precious metals were kept *16-e17*. **say-drink** one of the charges levied on a newly admitted entrant to a trade *la16-e18*. †**say master 1** an officer appointed by a burgh to assay coin or metal *17*. **2** a master of a craft appointed to examine the work of applicants for admittance to the craft *17*. **sey-piece** something chosen as an example of excellence; a sample piece submitted as proof of competence for entry to a trade incorporation *16-e19*. **sey tas** a cup or goblet made of precious metal of a particular fineness *la16-e17*. [aphetic form of ASSAY]

sey¹·², †**say** /saɪ/ *v* **1** to attempt (something difficult) *la16-19, 20- literary*. **2** to test, try out, make trial of *15-19*. **3** to discover by trial, examination or search *16-17*. [see the noun]

†**sey**², **say** *n* a woollen cloth similar to serge *la15-19*. **say-bumbacie, sey-bombasie** a type of bombasine, finely woven like serge *la16-e17*. [ME *say*, AN *say*]

sey³, †**say** /se, saɪ/ *n* **1** *sewing* the armhole of a sleeve *18-*. **2** a cut of beef from the shoulder to the loin *la16-e19*; compare BACKSEY, FORESYE. [compare ON *segi* a strip or slice of flesh]

sey *see* SAE¹, SEA, SYE¹·²
seyl *see* SILE²·¹
seyll *see* SEEL
seynd *see* SYNE¹·²
seyne *see* SEE
seyp *see* SYPE¹·²
seys *see* SEIZE

†**seyth, seith, seath** *v* to boil, cook by boiling *la14-e19*. [OE *sēoðan*]

sgian *see* SKEAN
sgian dubh *see* SKEAN DHU
sgoor *see* SCUIR

sha /ʃa/ *interj* a call to a dog to chase prey *19- H&I SW Bor.* [Gael *seo* here!]

shaa *see* SHAW[1.2]

shaag /ʃag/ *v* to exhaust, wear out with drudgery *la19- Sh.* [uncertain; compare Norn *shag* to chew, gnaw]

shaald *see* SHAULD[1.1], SHAULD[1.2]

shaav[1.1] /ʃav/ *n* a botched job (of cutting) *20- Sh.* [unknown]

shaav[1.2] /ʃav/ *v* to hack, cut inexpertly *20- Sh.* [unknown]

shaave *see* SAW[1]

shab /ʃab/ *v* to get rid of (a person), remove, evict; to slink away, sneak off *19- SW.* [EModE *shab*, compare Ger *schaben*]

†**shabble** *n* a small, insignificant person or thing *e19.* [perhaps related to SHAB]

shabble *see* SHABLE

shabby /'ʃabi/ *adj* 1 mean, ungenerous *la18-*. 2 dingy, scruffy *19-*. 3 unwell, in poor health *20- EC Bor.* [EModE *shabby*, compare Ger *schäbig*]

shable, †**shabble**, †**schabill** /'ʃabəl/ *n* a curved sword, a sabre, cutlass *17-19, 20- literary.* [compare Ger dial *schabel*, Polish *szabla*]

shachle *see* SHAUCHLE[1.1], SHAUCHLE[1.2]

shack *see* SHAK[1.1]

shackle[1.1], **sheckle**, *NE* **shaikle**, †**schakill** /'ʃakəl, 'ʃɛkəl; *NE* 'ʃekəl/ *n* 1 a fetter *la16-*. 2 a coupling for a plough or wagon *la16-*. 3 the wrist *la16, 20- T C.* 4 the hinge of a flail *la16, 20- NE.* 5 the afterbirth of an animal *20- Ork.* 6 a hobble or tether for an animal *16-17.* **shackle-bane, sheckle-bane** the wrist *la16-*. [OE *sceacel*]

shackle[1.2], †**scheckle** /'ʃakəl/ *v* to fasten (a prisoner) with shackles *la17-*. **shacklin** a hobble for an animal *la19- Sh.* [see the noun]

shadda[1.1], **shaddae, shaddie, shedda, shadow,** *Bor* **scaddow,** †**schadow,** †**schaddow** /'ʃadə, 'ʃade, 'ʃɛdə, 'ʃado; *Bor* 'skado/ *n* 1 shade, darkness; shelter (from the sun) *la15-*. 2 a reflected image; a dark shape projected by a body blocking the light *la15-*. 3 a phantom, an apparition *la14-*. 4 an outward pretence *la15-*. 5 the shaded or western part of a piece of land *la14-19.* †**shadow-half** = SHADDA[1.1] (sense 5) *16-19.* †**schadow land** = *shadow-half la16-18.* †**schadow pleuch** = *shadow-half 16-17.* [OE *scead(u)we* oblique case of *sceadu*]

shadda[1.2], **shadow,** †**schadov,** †**schaddow** /'ʃadə, 'ʃado/ *v* to cast a shadow; to conceal; to protect *16-*. [OE *sceadwian*]

shaddae, shaddie *see* SHADDA[1.1]

shade, †**tschad** /ʃed/ *n* 1 (a place of) shelter from the sun *17-*. 2 a shadow, a spirit *la16-*. 3 a shed, a roofed structure used as a shelter or store *18-e19.* [OE *scead* shade, shelter]

shade *see* SHED[1.1], SHED[1.2]

shadow *see* SHADDA[1.1], SHADDA[1.2]

shae[1.1], **shoe,** *NE* **shee,** †**scho** /ʃe, ʃu; *NE* ʃi/ *n pl* also **shune shoon, shin,** *NE SW* **sheen,** †**schone,** †**schwne,** †**schoys** 1 an article of footwear, a shoe *la14-*. 2 a horseshoe *15-*. 3 the chute carrying grain from the hopper to the millstone *la19- Sh Ork N NE T SW.* 4 the plate or iron strip attached as a protector on the underside of a wooden plough or a wheel rim *16-18.* **shoonless,** †**scholes** without shoes *la14-*. †**shoe-clouter, scho cluitter** a mender of shoes, a cobbler *la16-e18.* **shae-head** the top or upper edges of a shoe *la19-*. **shoe-horn,** †**schone horne** an implement used to help the putting on of shoes *la16-*. **shoe-latch** a shoelace *la19, 20- NE.* †**shoe-lachet** = *shoe-latch e17.* **shae-pint** a shoelace *20- NE.* [OE *scōh*]

shae[1.2], **shoe,** *NE* **shee,** †**scho** /ʃe, ʃu; *NE* ʃi/ *v* 1 to provide with shoes *16-*. 2 to shoe a horse's feet *15-*. 3 to fit with metal rims, studs or tips; to hobnail (shoes) *la15-18, 20- T EC SW.* **shaein-box** the box in which a blacksmith keeps his smaller tools *la19- NE SW.* **shaein-shed** a shed, as part of a smithy, in which horses are tied up to be shod *20- Ork NE SW.* [OE *scōgan*]

shaed *see* SHEATH

shael /ʃel/ *n* a perch for poultry *la19- Sh.* [Norw dial *sjell* scaffolding, a loft]

shaela *see* SHAILA

shaetry *see* CHEATRY

shafs *see* JAFS[1.2]

shaft /ʃaft/ *v* to brandish, shake (a weapon or fist) *18- Ork.* [unknown]

shaft *see* CHAFT[1]

shag[1] /ʃag/ *n* the refuse of oats, barley or other cereals *18-19, 20- NE T.* [ME *shoggen* to shake]

shag[2] /ʃag/ *n* an ox or bull which has been castrated incompletely or when fully grown *18-19, 20- N.* [probably a variant of SEGG]

shaggle[1] /'ʃagəl/ *v* to hack, cut clumsily or unevenly; to gnaw, bite roughly *la19- Sh.* [compare Faer *sjagla*]

shaggle[2] /'ʃagəl/ *v* to waddle, shamble *20- Ork.* [probably a variant of SHAUCHLE[1.2]]

shaif, sheaf, *N T* **shave,** †**schefe,** †**scheif,** †**sheave** /ʃef, ʃif; *N T* ʃev/ *n* 1 a quantity of the stalks of reaped grain tied in a bundle for drying and storage prior to threshing *15-*. 2 a bundle of twenty-four arrows *15-17.* 3 a bundle of iron or steel rods or bars *15-16.* 4 a quantity of timber; a number of logs bound together *la17.* **shafe-laft** a barn loft where sheaves are stacked before being threshed *20- Ork N NE SW.* [OE *scēaf*]

shaikle *see* SHACKLE[1.1]

shaiky *see* SHAKKY

shaila, †**shaela** /'ʃela/ *n* 1 hoar-frost *la19- Sh.* 2 a steely grey; the colour of the wool of Shetland sheep *19- Sh.* [Norw *hela* hoar frost]

shair[1] /ʃer/ *v* to grind, grate (the teeth) *la19- Sh Ork.* [Norw *skjære* to grind (the teeth)]

shair[2.1], **sure, suir, seur,** *NE* **sheer, sere,** †**suyr,** †**schore** /ʃer, ʃur; *NE* ʃir, sir/ *adj* 1 efficacious, effective *15-*. 2 safe, secure; strong, reliable *la15-*. 3 accurate, true; assured, convinced *16-*. **shairly** 1 securely, safely *la14-*. 2 with assurance, certainty or conviction; undoubtedly *15-*. 3 effectively, with legally binding force *la16.* [AN *sur*]

shair[2.2], **sure,** †**seure,** †**sur** /ʃer, ʃur/ *adv* 1 surely, indeed, for certain *16-*. 2 safely, securely *15-e17.* [see the adj]

shair *see* CHEER[1]

shaird, shard, sherd /ʃerd, ʃard, ʃɛrd/ *n* 1 a fragment of broken pottery *la16-*. 2 *fisherman's taboo* a boat *20- Sh.* 3 a puny or deformed person or animal; a bad-tempered or malicious person *la18- NE Uls.* 4 broken, decayed remains (of something); a scrap or remnant *18-19.* [OE *sceard*]

shairin *see* SHEARING

shairn *see* SHARN[1.1], SHARN[1.2]

shairp[1.1], **sherp, sharp** /ʃerp, ʃɛrp, ʃarp/ *n* 1 *music* a note raised half a tone above the natural pitch *la16-*. 2 the act of sharpening (an implement) *19- Sh NE SW.* 3 a frost-nail on a horse's shoe *20- N NE C Uls.* [see the adj]

shairp[1.2], **sherp, sharp,** †**scharp,** †**scherp** /ʃerp, ʃɛrp, ʃarp/ *v* 1 to sharpen *la14-*. 2 to render (the mind or feelings) more acute *la15-*. 3 to prepare for icy ground, especially to provide (a horseshoe) with frost-nails *la19-*. 4 to make (the sea) rough *e16.* **sherpit** sharpened to a point *16-*. [OE **scierpan*]

shairp[1.3], **sherp, sharp,** †**scharp,** †**schairp,** †**scherp** /ʃerp, ʃɛrp, ʃarp/ *adj* 1 having a keen edge or fine point; rough, jagged *la14-*. 2 *of a person* quick, intelligent, alert *la14-*. 3 *of soil* containing sand and grit, gravelly, open and loose *19-*. **4** *of a taste or smell* pungent, acid, sour *16-*. **5** *of emotions* keen, ardent *la14-*. **sharp-nibbit, sharp-nebbit** having a pointed nose or tip *la16-19, 20- Sh NE*. **sharp-set** keen, eager, especially for food or sex *la18-19, 20- NE WC*. †**be scharp to, be scharp upon** to be hard or severe on *16*. [OE *scearp*]

shairp[1,4], **sharp,** †**scherp,** †**scharpe** /ʃerp, ʃarp/ *adv* in a sharp manner; briskly, eagerly; abruptly *15-*. [OE *scearpe*]

shak[1,1], **shake,** *Sh* **shack,** †**schak** /ʃak, ʃek/ *n* **1** the action of shaking *16-*. **2** the loss of grain by wind damage *la18-19, 20- Sh Ork N*. **3** *in wrestling* a twist or throw, a bout *19*. [see the verb]

shak[1,2], **shake,** *Ork* **shack,** †**schaik,** †**schake** /ʃak, ʃek/ *v pt* **shuk, shuke, shakit,** †**schuke,** †**schuik,** †**schuk,** *ptp* **shakken, sheuken, shakit,** *C* **shucken, shooken,** *WC SW* **shook,** †**schakin,** †**schaikin 1** to (cause to) vibrate, tremble, move irregularly, quake *la14-*. **2** to weaken (a person's faith) *la14-*. **shakkins** herring which have to be shaken out of the net and are thus damaged, inferior herring *20- Sh N*. **shak-doon** a makeshift or temporary bed *18-*. †**shake-fork** a pitchfork; *heraldry* a Y-shaped charge *la17-19*. †**shake-wind** a strong blustery wind which shakes off ripe ears of corn *la18-19*. **shak aff o me** to leave (quickly and without ceremony) *20- Sh*. **shak-and-trumble** quaking grass *la19- NE T*. **shak a fa** to have a wrestling bout or tussle *18-* mainly *NE*. **shak yer feet 1** to wipe your feet *19- Sh NE*. **2** to dance *la18-*. **shakings of the pot** = *shakkins o the poke*. **shakkins o the poke, shakkins o the pyoke** the last remnants; the youngest of a family *20-*. [OE *sceacan*]

shake see SHAK[1,1], SHAK[1,2]

shaker, *Ork NE* **shakker,** †**schakar** /ʃekər; *Ork NE* 'ʃakər/ *n* **1** mainly *pl* the moving racks in a threshing mill *19-*. **2** a fit of shaking, from disease or fear; a state of terror or intimidation *la19, 20- Sh Ork N NE C*. **3** quaking-grass *Briza media la19, 20- EC SW Bor*. **4** *pl* a dress trimming of thin metal plates which vibrated as the wearer moved *16-17*. **5** something hanging from a plant and vibrating, dewdrops *e16*. [SHAK[1,2], with agent suffix]

shakie see SHAKKY
shakit, shakken see SHAK[1,2]
shakker see SHAKER
shakky, shakie, †**shaiky** /ˈʃaki, ˈʃeki/ *adj* trembling, unsteady *la16-*. **shakie-tremlie** *adj* wobbly, insecure; giddy *la19- NE T*. **shakie-tremlie** *n* mainly *pl* quaking-grass *Briza media la19- NE T*. [SHAK[1,2] + -IE[2]]

shalder, chalder, chaldroo /ˈʃɑldər, ˈtʃaldər, ˈtʃaldru/ *n* the oystercatcher *Haematopus ostralegus la18- Sh Ork*. Compare SKELDRO. [compare Faer *tjaldur*]

shall see SALL, SHELL[1,1], SHELL[1,1]
shallop, †**schallop,** †**challop** /ˈʃaləp/ *n* a seagoing vessel, a sloop; a large fishing boat; a dinghy *16-*. [MFr *chaloupe*]
†**shalm, schalm, schawm** *n* a medieval woodwind instrument *la15-e19*. [ME *shalme*, erroneous singular of ME *shalmuse*, AN *chalmus*]
shalt see SHELTIE
shalter see SHELTER
shaltie see SHELTIE
sham[1] /ʃam/ *n* the leg *19, 20- NE*. [Fr *jambe*]
sham[2], *Bor* **shan** /ʃam; *Bor* ʃan/ *v* to make a wry face, grimace *19, 20- Sh*. [probably back-formation from SHAMMLE]
shamble see SHAMMLE, SKEMMEL[1,1]
†**shambo, schammoy, chammoy** *n* chamois leather, goatskin *la16-e19*. [MFr *chamois*]
shame[1,1], **shemm,** *Ork* **sheem,** †**schame,** †**schayme,** †**schaem** /ʃem, ʃem; *Ork* ʃim/ *n* self-reproach, disgust; a sense of morality or propriety; disgrace, loss of self-esteem; what is morally disgraceful *la14-*. **shamefu, shameful 1** full of shame; overcome by shame; causing shame, disgraceful, degrading *la14-*. **2** modest, bashful *15-18*. **shamefully 1** in a manner that causes shame or disgrace *la14-*. **2** shamefacedly, modestly *la14-e16*. †**schamelie** disgracefully, shamefully; in shame or disgrace *la14-16*. †**shame-dance** = *shame-reel 19*. †**schamous dance** = *shame-reel la15*. †**shame-reel** the first dance at a wedding (danced by the bride and best man, and the bridegroom and bridesmaid) *19*. **shame-spring** the tune played for the *shame-reel 19- NE*. †**shame is past the shed of your hair** you have lost all sense of shame *la16-e18*. [OE *scamu*]

shame[1,2], *Ork* **sheem,** †**schame** /ʃem; *Ork* ʃim/ *v* to (cause to) feel shame; to be ashamed; to put to shame, subject to dishonour or indignity, disgrace *la14-*. **shamit reel** the first dance at a wedding *19- N NE*. [OE *scamian*]

shamell see SHAMMLE, SKEMMEL[1,1]
sham-gabbit, shan-gabbit /ˈʃamɡabɪt, ˈʃaŋɡabɪt/ *adj* having the lower jaw protruding beyond the upper, with a projecting lower lip *19-*. [SHAM[2] + *gabbit* (GAB[1,1])]
shamlich see SHAMMLE
†**shamloch, schamloch, schamenlo** *n* a cow that has not calved for two years *16-e19*. [Gael *seamlach* a cow that gives milk without having a calf beside her]
shammie-leggit /ˈʃaməlɛɡɪt/ *adj* bandy-legged *20- T C*. [SHAM[2] + LEG[1,1] + -IT[2]]
shammle, shamble, †**shamell** /ˈʃaməl, ˈʃambəl/ *v* **1** to walk with an uneven, rolling gait *19-*. **2** to strain, dislocate, distort; to twist (the face), grimace *18-*. **shammelt** *especially of teeth* twisted, crooked, out of alignment *20- NE*. **shamlich** a weak, puny, or slovenly person or animal *la19- NE*. †**shammel-shanks** a bandy-legged person *la18-19*. [EModE *shamble*]

shan[1,1], †**shand** /ʃan/ *n* **1** inferior or damaged loaves, usually sold at a discount *20-*. **2** counterfeit money *e19*. **shan shop** a shop selling discount bakery goods *la20-*. [see the adj]
shan[1,2] /ʃan/ *adj* **1** of poor quality, bad, shabby *18-19, 20- NE T EC Bor*. **2** *of treatment of others* unfair; unjustifiable *NE EC Bor*. **3** affected by illness; suffering *20- EC Bor*. **4** bashful, timid, frightened *19, 20- N Bor*. [perhaps Gael *sean* old; in recent use via Travellers' language]
shan see SHAM[2]
shance see CHANCE[1,1], CHANCE[1,2]
shand see SHAN[1,1]
shan-gabbit see SHAM-GABBIT
shangan, shannag, shonnag /ˈʃaŋən, ˈʃanəɡ, ˈʃonəɡ/ *n* an ant *20- N*. [Gael *seangan*]
shangie[1,1], †**shangan,** †**shanie** /ˈʃaŋe/ *n* **1** *pl* manacles, handcuffs *19- NE T EC*. **2** *mining, shipbuilding* a washer put round a drill or bolt to prevent leakage *la19, 20- Ork NE WC*. **3** *nautical* a loop of rope used as a support for an oar *la19- Ork N*. **4** a forked stick used to make a catapult *20- NE T SW Bor*. **5** *building* a tie-bar, eg in the shuttering for concrete *20- Sh*. **6** a cleft stick or tin can put on a dog's tail *la17-19*. [uncertain, perhaps a variant of CHENƷE[1,1]]
shangie[1,2], †**shangan** /ˈʃaŋe/ *v* to put a cleft stick on (a dog's tail); to tie; to restrain, curb, control *la18-19, 20- T*. [see the noun]
shangie[2] /ˈʃaŋe/ *n* a row, disturbance, fight *20-*. [shortened form of COLLIESHANGIE]
†**shangie**[3] *adj* thin, scraggy, gaunt *19*. **shangie-moud** with gaunt cheeks, lantern-jawed *18*. [Gael *seang*]
shanie see SHANGIE[1,1]
shank[1,1], †**schank** /ʃaŋk/ *n* **1** the leg between the knee and the ankle; the shin *la14-*. **2** the stem or shaft of an implement

or object *la15*-. **3** a stocking, especially in the process of being knitted or woven *16*-. **4** the stem or stalk of a plant or fruit, the trunk of a tree *16*-. **5** a leg of meat *19*-. **6** the lower part or sides of a cornstack *la19*-. **7** a downward spur or slope of a hill *14-19, 20- T Bor*. **8** a chimney-stack *20- WC*. **9** the vertical shaft of a mine *17-19, 20- EC*. **10** the shaft of a nail; a headless nail *16-e17*. **shankie** a small cooking pan with a long handle *19- EC SW Bor*. **shankit** having shanks or legs of a particular sort *16*-. **shanks' naigie** one's own legs as a means of travel *18*-. **shanks' pownie** = *shanks' naigie 20- Ork N Bor*. [OE *scanca*]

shank[1.2] /ʃaŋk/ *v* **1** to walk, travel on foot *18*-. **2** to send off on foot, dismiss *18-19, 20- WC Bor*. **3** to knit (stockings) *19- NE T*. **4** to sink (a shaft) *18-19, 20- C*. **shank it** to travel on foot *la18*-. [see the noun]

shanker /'ʃaŋkər/ *n* **1** a knitter (originally weaver) of stockings *17*-. **2** a gadabout; a (young) active person *19- NE*. **3** a mine or well sinker *la19*. **shanker's naigie** one's own legs as a means of travel *20- T C*. [SHANK[1.1], with agent suffix]

shankie *see* SHUNKY

shanna *see* SALL

shannack, sownack /'ʃanək, 'sʌunək/ *n* a bonfire, originally especially at Halloween *19- NE T EC*. **shanacle** = SHANNACK. [Gael *samhnag* a Halloween bonfire]

shannag *see* SHANGAN

shannel *see* CHANNEL[1.1]

shanner /'ʃanər/ *n* **1** an inferior or dilapidated vehicle *21- WC*. **2** something shabby or undesirable *21- C*. **3** an unfair or undesirable situation *la20- C*. [SHAN[1.2], with -*er* suffix]

shantie *see* CHANTY

shantrews, seann triubhas, †shantruse /ʃan'truz, ʃɒn'truz/ *n* a solo Highland dance; the tune played for it *la18*-. [Gael *seann triubhas* old trousers]

shap *see* CHAP[3.1], CHAP[3.2], SHAUP[1.1], SHOP

shape[1.1], **†schape, †schaip, †schap** /ʃep/ *n* **1** a contour, an outline; image; appearance *la14*-. **2** an attitude, a posture; conduct, manner *la19*-. **3** a dressmaking pattern, a pattern piece *20*-. **4** an oddly shaped or droll figure *20- C SW Bor*. **5** a poor specimen *la19- Sh*. **6** the fashion or cut of a garment *la14-e16*. **shapely** well-formed, elegant *15*-. **mak a shape** to make an effort (at), do (something) well *la19*-. [OE *sceap*]

shape[1.2], **†schape, †schaip, †schap** /ʃep/ *v pt* also **†schupe** *ptp* also **†schapen †schappin, †yschappit** **1** to create; to form, alter, fashion; to give, have, take on a shape *la14*-. **2** to turn out, show promise; to adapt oneself (to) *la18*-. **3** *sewing* to cut (cloth) according to a pattern *la15-19, 20- Sh Ork N*. **4** to direct one's course or efforts (to), set out for; to go (away) *la14-19, 20- N WC*. **5** to attempt, endeavour, contrive; to set about, prepare oneself (to do); to make preparations; to devise (a plan) *la14-19, 20- N*. **6** to destine, decree *15-e16*. **†schapin, schaip** naturally fitted (for) *la14-17*. **shapins** scraps of cloth left over after sewing *19- NE*. **shape and sew** to cut out and make up (clothes) *la15-19, 20- Sh Ork N*. [ME *shapen*, OE *scieppan*]

shape *see* CHAPE[1.2]

shapin *see* CHOPIN

shapper *see* CHAPPER

shard *see* SHAIRD

share /ʃer/ *v ptp* **shorn** *of milk* to curdle *19- Sh Ork* [Norw *skjera*]

share *see* SHEAR[1.2], SHIRE[2.1], SKAIR[1.1], SKAIR[1.2]

†sharg[1], **scharge** *n* a puny, sickly child *17-19*. [Gael *searg* a puny creature]

sharg[2.1] /ʃarg/ *n* nagging, grumbling *la19- Sh*. [compare Swed dial *sarga* to nag]

sharg[2.2] /ʃarg/ *v* to argue; to grumble *la19- Sh Ork*. [see the noun]

shargar, sharger /'ʃargər/ *n* **1** a puny, weak person *18-19, 20- NE T*. **2** the weakest of a brood or litter *la19- NE*. [altered form of SHARG[1]]

shargart /'ʃargərt/ *adj* stunted *la19- NE*. [SHARGAR + -IT[2]]

sharger *see* SHARGAR

sharl-pin /'ʃarl pɪn/ *n* the pivot on which the loop of a hinge turns *la19- Sh Ork*. [shortened form of *charnle-pins* (CHARNEL)]

sharn[1.1], **shairn, shern** /ʃarn, ʃern, ʃɛrn/ *n* excrement; cattle-dung *la16*-. **sharn bree** the ooze from farmyard manure *la19- NE*. **sharn midden** a dung heap *19- NE*. **sharny, †scharny** dirty or smeared with dung *la16*-. **sharny flee** a dung-fly *20*-. [OE *scearn*]

sharn[1.2], **shairn** /ʃarn, ʃern/ *v* to smear or soil with cattle-dung *la19- NE*. [see the noun]

sharp *see* SHAIRP[1.1], SHAIRP[1.2], SHAIRP[1.3], SHAIRP[1.4]

sharping, †schairping, †sherping /'ʃarpɪŋ/ *n* the action of making sharp *16*-. **sharping-corn** an annual payment (in the form of stooks of corn) to the blacksmith for sharpening agricultural implements *la17-19, 20- Bor historical*. **sharping stane** a whetstone *la17*-. [from the verb SHAIRP[1.2]]

sharrie[1.1] /'ʃare/ *n* a quarrel, row *la19- NE*. [unknown; compare SHIRRAMUIR and Eng *charivari*]

sharrie[1.2] /'ʃare/ *v* to quarrel, fight *la19- NE*. [see the noun]

sharrow /'ʃaro/ *adj* bitter to the taste *19, 20- Ork N*. [Gael *searbh*]

shaskit /'ʃaskət/ *adj* tired, worn-out *la19- Sh*. [shortened form of DISJASKIT]

shass *see* CHESS

shaste *see* CHASE[1.2]

shat *see* SHITE[1.2]

shathmont /'ʃaθmənt/ *n* the distance from the knuckle of the little finger in the clenched fist to the tip of the extended thumb, approximately six inches (150 mm) *la18*-. [altered form of Eng *shaftment*]

shatter /'ʃatər/ *v* to chatter, chirp, rattle *la17, 20- N*. [ME *chateren*]

shatters *see* CHATTERS

shauch /ʃɔx/ *adj* awry, askew, twisted *19*-. [perhaps back-formation from SHAUCHLE[1.2]]

shauchle[1.1], **shochle, shachle** /'ʃɔxəl, 'ʃaxəl/ *n* **1** a shuffling, shambling gait *19*-. **2** an old and worn-out article of footwear *19*-. **3** a weak, stunted, or deformed person or animal *19, 20- NE T H&I*. **shauchlie** unsteady on one's feet *19*-. [see the verb]

shauchle[1.2], **shochle, shachle** /'ʃɔxəl, 'ʃaxəl/ *v* **1** to shuffle, shamble, walk clumsily *18*-. **2** to cause footwear to distort, become out of shape by wear or rough usage *19, 20- WC SW*. **shachled** = *shauchlin* **1** *19, 20- T C Bor*. **shauchlin** **1** unsteady or weak on one's feet, shuffling; knock-kneed; wearing worn-out shoes *19*-. **2** *of shoes* out of shape, down at heel and worn, badly-fitting *19*-. **shauchle aff** to shuffle or shake off, get rid of *20- NE*. [probably onomatopoeic]

shauld[1.1], **shaul**, *Sh* **shaald, †schald** /ʃɔld, ʃɒl; *Sh* ʃald/ *n* a shallow part in the sea or a river, a shoal *la14*-. [see the adj]

shauld[1.2], **shaul**, *Sh* **shaald, †schald** /ʃɔld, ʃɒl; *Sh* ʃald/ *adj* **1** shallow *la14*-. **2** shallow in character or intellect, empty-headed *17-19, 20- Sh*. **3** *of sand, ground* covered shallowly by water *16-e17*. [OE *sceald*]

shaup[1.1], **†shap** /ʃɔp/ *n* **1** the seed husk of a leguminous plant; a peapod *18-19, 20- T C Uls*. **2** usually *pl* fragments, broken pieces *la19- NE*. **3** an empty-headed, frivolous person *18-e19*. **shaupie** lanky, not plump *19, 20- WC*. [perhaps related to ON *hjúpa* a scabbard, or OE **hjúpa* a rosehip]

shaup[1,2] /ʃɔp/ *v* to shell (peas), take (peas) from the pods *la19- C.* [see the noun]

shave, †**schawe**, †**schaiff** /ʃev/ *v pt* also †**schuif**, *ptp* also †**schavyn** †**schevin** to remove (hair) with a razor or knife *la14-.* †**shavie** a trick, a prank, a swindle *18-19.* **tae a shavin** exactly, precisely *19- N C.* [OE *scafan*]

shave *see* SHAIF, SHEAVE[1,1]

shavel *see* SHEVEL[1,2]

shaviter /'ʃevətər/ *n* a slovenly, disreputable-looking character *19- Bor.* [probably altered form of Eng *shaver* a rogue]

shavs *see* JAFS[1,2]

shaw[1,1], **show**, †**schaw** /ʃɔ, ʃo/ *n* **1** the action of displaying or exhibiting something; external aspect or appearance; an appearance intended to impress; a pretence *la16-.* **2** a spectacle, an entertainment, a public performance *17-.* **3** *pl* mainly **shaws**, *Sh* **shows** the stalks and leaves of potatoes or root vegetables *18-.* **show-buik** a child's picture-book *20- C Bor.* **the shows** a funfair, a fairground *20-.* [see the verb]

shaw[1,2], **show**, *Sh* **shaa**, †**schaw**, †**schau** /ʃɔ, ʃo; *Sh* ʃa/ *v pt* also *Sh* **shew** †**schew**, *ptp* also *Sh* **shawn** †**schawin 1** to reveal, display, make visible; to produce, exhibit for inspection, submit evidence; to expound, explain, teach; to prove, demonstrate *la14-.* **2** to present a good appearance, make a good show *la14-.* **3** to cut off the leafy tops (sometimes also the roots) of turnips or other root vegetables *la19-.* **4** *imperative* give, hand over *20- Ork N.* **5** to display, unfurl (a banner) *la15-e19.* **6** *law* to plead, allege; to decree, declare formally *la14-17.* **shewer** *law* a person appointed by a court to show a jury property which is the subject of litigation *19-.* **it shaws on** *impersonal* it appears *20- Sh Ork.* **shaw respeck** to attend a funeral *la19-.* †**schaw the richt** to provide that justice is seen to be done *la15-16.* [OE *scēawian* to look]

shaw[2], †**schaw** /ʃɔ/ *n* a small, especially natural wood, a thicket *la12-.* [OE *sceaga*]

shaw *see* SAW[1]

shawlie /'ʃɔli, 'ʃole/ *n* **1** a piece of fabric worn by women over the shoulders or head *la19-.* **2** an urban working-class woman or girl *20- NE C Uls.* **shawlie wifie**, **shawlie wife** = SHAWLIE (sense 2). **shawlie wumman**, **shawlie woman** = SHAWLIE (sense 2). [Eng *shawl* + -IE[3]]

shawn *see* SHAW[1,2]

†**shayth** *n* reason, what is reasonable; (a person's) rights *16-e17.* [perhaps Gael *seadh* cause, reason]

she, *Sh Ork* **sheu**, *Sh* **shö**, †**scho** /ʃi; *Sh Ork* ʃø/ *personal pron used as subject* **1** she *la14-.* **2** used by a husband of his wife or by a servant of his or her mistress *la19-.* **3** referring to an inanimate object *la14-.* **4** *Highland* I *la15-19.* †**scho and he**, **he or scho** this one or that, everyone *16.* [OE *hēo*]

sheaf *see* SHAIF

sheal *see* SHIEL[1,2]

sheall *see* SHIEL[2]

shealling *see* SHIELING

shear[1,1], †**schere**, †**scheir**, †**cheir** /ʃir/ *n* **1** the act of cutting, especially corn *18-19, 20- Sh NE.* **2** a cut edge, especially the cut end of a sheaf of corn *20- NE.* **3** a shorn animal *la17.* **4** *pl* scissors, shears, clippers for shearing sheep *la14-.* **5** mainly *pl* a piece of metal in which the axle-ends of a wheel or roller turn; the beam of a farm cart between which the shafts are placed *la17-19, 20- Ork T SW.* **6** mainly *pl* a contrivance for attaching coal hutches to the haulage rope *19, 20- EC.* **7** *pl* a representation of a pair of shears as the symbol of the incorporation of waulkers and shearers *16.* †**shear-grinder** a person who grinds shears *la17-19.* †**shear-smith**, **scheresmyth** a maker of shears and scissors *la14-e18.* [OE *scēar*]

shear[1,2], **share**, †**scher**, †**scheir**, †**schar** /ʃir, ʃer/ *v pt* also *Sh* **shure** †**schuir**, †**schewre**, †**schare**, *ptp* also **shorn** †**schorne 1** to cut; to wound; to rend, tear; to carve, slice, chop; to cut off, sever, divide *la14-.* **2** to reap (corn), cut (crops) with a sickle *la14-.* **3** to shape, carve (wood, stone), pierce or engrave (metal) *la16-e18.* **4** to cut (a person) as part of a surgical procedure *la14-e17.* **5** to cut off the superfluous nap from woollen cloth *15-e17.* †**shear-darg**, **scheir dawark** a day's work at reaping or shearing (as a feudal service to a landlord) *16-18.* †**sheareman** a person who removes the excess nap from cloth *la17.* **shear-mark** a V-shaped notch cut out of the ear of a sheep for identification *18- Sh Ork.* **shear-moose** the shrew *Sorex araneus la19- Ork N T WC.* †**schorne werk** carved or engraved wood or metal work *16.* †**shear shope** a place where cloth is manufactured *la17.* †**schorne of the stane** operated on to remove a gall-stone *la15-e17.* [OE *scieran*]

shearer, †**scherar** /'ʃirər/ *n* **1** a person who reaps corn, a harvester *16-.* **2** a person who removes the excess nap of cloth by shearing *14-e17.* **shearer's bannock** a large bread roll or bun eaten on the harvest field *la19- T EC Bor.* **shearer's scone** = *shearer's bannock 20-.* †**sheraris darg** a day's work at reaping or shearing *la16-17.* [from the verb SHEAR[1,2], with agent suffix]

shearing, *Ork* **shairin**, †**schering**, †**sheiring** /'ʃirɪŋ; *Ork* 'ʃerɪn/ *n* **1** the action of cutting or filing *15-.* **2** the action of cutting grass or corn, reaping; harvest *la15-.* **3** a division, a parting *15-e16.* **4** *mining* a preliminary vertical cut *la18-19.* **5** the action of cutting the excess nap on cloth *la15-17.* †**schering darg** a day's work at reaping or shearing *la6.* †**shearing silver** money paid by a tenant in lieu of service at harvest time *la16-18.* [verbal noun from SHEAR[1,2]]

sheath, †**shaed**, †**scheith**, †**scheth** /ʃiθ/ *n* **1** a case enclosing the blade of a sword, dagger or other sharp implement *la15-.* **2** a pad on a belt used to hold knitting needles when not in use *la18-19, 20- Sh N NE T C.* †**schethemakar**, **scheidmaker**, **chifmakir** a manufacturer of sheaths *16-17.* [OE *scēað*]

sheave[1,1], **shave**, *Bor* **shive**, †**schefe**, †**schaiff**, †**schif** /ʃiv, ʃev; *Bor* ʃʌɪv/ *n* **1** a slice (of bread or cheese) *la14-.* **2** a pulley(-wheel) *la15-;* compare CHEEVE. [OE **scife* a slice of bread, and MDu *schive* a disc, a pulley, a wheel]

sheave[1,2] /ʃiv/ *v* to cut into slices *19, 20- Sh NE.* [see the noun]

sheave *see* SHAIF

sheckle *see* SHACKLE[1,1]

shed[1,1], **shade**, *Ork N NE T* **sheed**, *N* **sheyd**, †**sched**, †**scheid**, †**schade** /ʃɛd, ʃed; *Ork N NE T* ʃid; *N* ʃeɪd/ *n* **1** the parting of the hair on the head or the wool on a sheep's back; the place on the head where the hair parts *la14-.* **2** the act of sorting out sheep, frequently as a test in sheepdog trials *20-.* **3** an opening or gap, especially between the two sets of threads in a loom *la18-19, 20- C Bor.* **4** a strip of land, a distinct or separate piece of (mainly arable) ground *12-19, 20- Ork N.* **5** a slice, a lump, a piece divided off *16-19, 20- T.* **6** a quantity (of blood) *16-19, 20- T.* [OE *scēad* separation]

shed[1,2], **shade**, †**sched** /ʃɛd, ʃed/ *v pt* **shed** †**sched**, †**scheid 1** to part or comb (the hair or a sheep's fleece) to one side or the other; *of hair* to be combed or parted *la15-.* **2** to cause bloodshed; to cleave with a weapon *la14-.* **3** to separate, split; to divide (lambs from ewes); to be dispersed or scattered *la15-.* **4** to emit, spill, pour; to dispose of, discharge *la15-.* **5** *of birds, fish* to cleave (the air, water) *la15-16.* **shedder 1** a pen for sorting sheep *20-.* **2** one who sheds blood *la16-17.* **shedding 1** the act of separating sheep *la17-.* **2** the action of causing blood to flow, bloodshed *la14-*. **3** a departure; a parting of the ways; a fork in the road or crossroads *la17-19, 20- C*. †**shed the shanks** to spread the legs (prior to copulation) *la16*. [OE *scēadan* to divide]

shedda see SHADDA[1.1]

shee see SHAE[1.1], SHAE[1.2]

sheed see SHED[1.1]

sheek see CHEEK[1.1]

sheeks[1.1] /ʃiks/ *n* (insincere) chatter *la19- Sh*. [perhaps altered from plural of CHEEK[1.1]]

sheeks[1.2] /ʃiks/ *v* to chatter, *la19- Sh*. [probably from the noun]

sheel[1.1], **sheil** /ʃil/ *n* the act of husking corn; the act of turning something out of its container, a throwing about; dismissal from a job *20 NE*. [see the verb]

sheel[1.2], **shiel**, **shill**, †**scheil**, †**schill** /ʃil, ʃɪl/ *v* **1** to take (peas, grain or flax seeds) out of the husk or pod *la15-*. **2** to cut (a mussel or other shellfish) from its shell *19-*. **3** to pay (money) *19, 20- Sh N NE T*. **4** *in gambling* to take everything, win a person's entire stake *la19, 20- NE SW*. **5** to throw, scatter *20- NE*. **sheelit**, **shilled**, †**scheillit** that has had the husk, pod or shell removed *16-*. **sheelock**, †**scheillik** the small or light grains of corn; husks; chaff and broken straw *17- NE*. **shiel-blade** a knife for scooping mussels out of the shell *20- NE EC*. **sheel oot** = SHEEL[1.2] (sense 5). [OE **scielian, scilian*]

sheel see SHUIL[1.1], SHUIL[1.2]

sheeld see CHIEL

sheelder see CHEELDER

sheeling, **shilling**, †**scheilling** /'ʃilən, 'ʃɪlən/ *n* **1** the action of separating grain from husks or peas from pods; shelling *la16-*. **2** grain removed from the husk by milling; the husks removed from grain or bran *16-*. **sheelin-hill**, †**schilling hill** a piece of rising ground where grain was winnowed by the wind *16-19, 20- historical*. **sheeling-seeds**, †**scheling siedes** the husks removed from the grain in the first process of milling *17-19, 20- N NE*. **sheelin-stane** a millstone set to remove the husks in the first process of milling *la18-19, 20- EC*. [verbal noun from SHEEL[1.2]]

sheem see SHAME[1.1], SHAME[1.2]

sheemach, **sheemich**, *NE* **shoomach** /'ʃimax; *NE* 'ʃumax/ *n* **1** a tangled or matted mass of hair *la19- NE*. **2** a pad or woven covering, used as a saddle; a kind of pack-saddle *19- NE*. **3** *derogatory* a worthless or worn-out thing, a puny person or animal *19- N NE*. [unknown Gael *seam* a small object; compare Gael *sioman* a straw rope, Gael *sumag* a pack-saddle]

sheen[1.1], †**schene**, †**scheyne** /ʃin/ *n* **1** brightness, shining *la18-*. **2** the pupil (of the eye) *16-e19*. **3** a beautiful woman, a maiden *la14-16*. [see the adj]

sheen[1.2], †**schene** /ʃin/ *v* to shine, gleam, glisten *la14-*. [see the adj]

†**sheen**[1.3], **schene**, **scheyn** *adj* beautiful, bright *la14-e19*. [OE *scīene*]

sheen see SHAE[1.1], SUNE[1.2]

sheep, †**schepe**, †**scheip**, †**cheip** /ʃip/ *n* a sheep, a ruminant of the genus *Ovis 12-*. **sheepie 1** = SHEEP *la19-*. **2** the cone of the Scots pine *20- NE*. **sheep bag** the stomach of a sheep used as the container for haggis *20-*. **sheep-bucht** a sheep pen, especially at a market or for milking-ewes *18-*. †**sheep-cot** a shelter for sheep, a sheep house *15-18*. **sheep-crue** a sheep pen *20- Sh N*. **sheep drain** an open or surface drain in pasture land *la19-*. **sheep-eik** the natural grease in a sheep's wool *19- SW Bor*. **sheep-fank** an enclosure for sheep *19-*. **sheep-fauld**, †**scheipfald** an enclosure for sheep *la15-*. **sheep-gang** a sheep pasture, an area of hill-grazing *la18- EC Bor*. **sheep-gate** a path made by sheep in grazing; the marks of scissors on hair after unskilful hairdressing *20- Sh*. **sheep's heid**, **sheep heid** a sheep's head, especially used to make soup *16-*. †**schepis hew** of the colour of undyed wool *la16-e17*. **sheepman 1** a man appointed to superintend the keeping of sheep on common land *20- Ork*. **2** a sheepstealer, a rogue *e17*. **sheepie meh** *child's word* **1** a sheep, so called from its bleat *20-*. **2** the flower of the wild white clover *Trifolium repens 20- N NE H&I EC*. **sheep-money** a yearly payment to a farmworker in lieu of pasturing a few of his own sheep *la18-19, 20- Bor historical*. **sheep-net** a net on stakes used to confine sheep on a turnip field *19-*. **sheep's purls** sheep-dung *20-*. **sheep-raik** a path or strip of ground trodden by grazing sheep *la18-19, 20- Bor*. **sheep-ree** an enclosure for sheep *la18- SW Bor*. **sheep-rodding** a sheep-track *19, 20- Uls*. **sheep siller** white mica, especially in small scales *19- N NE T*. **sheepie's silver** = *sheep siller*. **sheep-stell** an enclosure for sheep *19- N Bor*. **sheep-taid** a sheep-tick *19- WC Bor*. **shee tief** a nickname for an inhabitant of the island of Yell *20- Sh*. **sheep-troddles** sheep-dung *20- WC SW Bor*. **nae sheep shank** a person of some importance *la18-19, 20- C Bor*. **sheep's heid broth** soup made using a sheep's head as the main ingredient *18-*. [OE *scēap*]

sheer see SHAIR[2.1], SHIRE[2.1]

sheer dog /'ʃir dɔg/ *adj* the Portugal shark *Squalus cornubicus*; the smooth dogfish *Galeus canis 19, 20- NE*. [Eng *sheer + dog* (DUG)]

sheet[1], †**schete** /ʃit/ *n* **1** a large, broad piece of cloth or canvas used for covering, wrapping; a bedsheet *la14-*. **2** a piece of paper *la16-*. **3** a sheet of canvas folded into a pouch to hold corn-seed when sowing *la18-19, 20- N*. **4** a large canvas sheet made into a pocket for holding wool; the amount it contains, 240 lb (108 kg) *la19, 20- N*. **5** a winding-sheet, a shroud *15-17*. **6** the garb worn for public penance *e17*. **sheet shaking** *in Aberdeen* the remains of ground grain shaken from the sheet in which it has been transported *16*. [OE *scȳte*]

sheet[2], †**schete** /ʃit/ *n nautical* a rope attached to the lower corner of a sail to extend the sail or alter its direction *16-*. **gie sheet** to go at full speed, bolt *20- Sh*. **tak sheet** = *gie sheet Sh NE*. [OE *scēata* the lower corner of a sail]

sheet, **sheetit** see SHUIT

sheggan see SEGGAN

sheil see SHEEL[1.1]

sheiling see SHIELING

shein, **shine** /ʃʌin/ *v* to throw with force or violence, pitch, fling *la19- Bor*. [unknown; compare Eng *shy*]

sheir see SHEAR[1.1]

sheiring see SHEARING

shelband /'ʃɛlbən/ *n* a framework of movable boards used to extend the sides of a cart permitting transport of higher loads *19- SW*. [reduced form of SHELVIN + BAND[1.1]]

shelf see SKELF[1]

shell[1.1], *Sh Ork N NE* **shall**, †**schell** /ʃɛl; *Sh Ork N NE* ʃal/ *n* **1** the hard covering of a mollusc or crustacean, a seashell or snail-shell *la14-*. **2** a scale or pan of a weighing balance *la16-*. **3** *pl* the lumps of burnt limestone before it is slaked, unground quicklime *18-19, 20- NE T WC*. **4** a saucer *la19- NE*. **5** *pl* fragments, sherds *la16-18, 19- Sh*. **6** the patella or kneecap *la19- Sh*. **7** a teapot *la15-16*. **8** a metal vat or tank used in salt-making or brewing *16-17*. **9** a metal helmet *la16*. **10** the bowl or pan which holds the oil in a CRUISIE lamp *la19*. **shelly-coat 1** *folklore* a water-sprite wearing a shell-covered coat *la17-*. **2** a sheriff-officer or bailiff *la18*. †**shell-paddock** a tortoise *la16-17*. [OE *sciell*]

shell[1.2], *Sh Ork N* **shall** /ʃɛl; *Sh Ork N* ʃal/ *v* **1** to take (peas, grain, flax seeds) out of the husk or pod *18-*; compare

shellwing

SHEEL[1.1]. **2** *of sheep or their wool* to become caked with snow *la18-19*. **shelling** husked grain; chaff *17-*. **shelling-seeds** bran *18-*. [see the noun]
shellwing see SHELVIN
shelmont, shillment, †shelvement, †shilmine /ˈʃɛlmənt, ˈʃɪlmənt/ *n* a framework of movable boards used to extend the sides of a cart permitting transport of higher loads *18- T C Bor*. [reduced form of SHELVIN with noun-forming suffix]
shelter, *Sh N* **shalter** /ˈʃɛltər; *Sh N* ˈʃaltər/ *n* refuge, protection *la17-*. **†shelterage** a place of shelter *17-e19*. [EModE *shelter*]
sheltie, *Ork* **sholtie,** *NE* **shult,** *NE* **shalt,** *NE* **shaltie, †scheltie** /ˈʃɛlti; *Ork* ˈʃɔlti; *NE* ʃʌlt, ʃalt, ʃalti/ *n* **1** a Shetland pony, one of a breed of very small horses, originally native to Shetland *17-*. **2** a pony, usually a Highland pony or garron *la18-*. **3** a Shetland sheepdog *20-*. **4** *humorous* a Shetlander *16- Sh Ork N*. **5** the black flea or sandhopper of the genus *Orchestia 20- Ork*. [from the place-name *Shetland* + -IE[1]]
shelve see SKELF[1]
shelvement see SHELMONT
shelvin, *NE, Sh Ork N* **shellwing, †shilvin, †schilwing** /*NE* ˈʃɛlvən; *Sh Ork N* ˈʃɛlwɪŋ/ *n* usually *pl* a framework of movable boards used to extend the sides of a cart permitting transport of higher loads *17-*. [verbal noun from EModE *shelve*]
shemm see SHAME[1.1]
shenachie, sennachie, †schenachy, †sannachie /ˈʃɛnəxi/ *n* a teller of traditional Gaelic heroic tales; originally a professional recorder and reciter of family history and genealogy *la15-*. [Gael *seanachaidh*]
†shent[1.1] *n* disgrace *la14-15*. [see the verb]
†shent[1.2], **schent** *v* **1** to kill, injure, punish; to destroy, ruin *la14-e17*. **2** to humiliate, shame; to rebuke; to upset, distress *la14-17*. [OE *scendan*]
shent[1.3], **†schent** /ʃɛnt/ *adj* put to shame, disgraced, ruined *la16-*. [participial adj from SHENT[1.2]]
shepherd, †schepehird, †scheipheird, †schippart /ˈʃɛpərd/ *n* **1** a person who looks after sheep *la14-*. **2** Christ as the protector of the Church; a pastor as the protector of his congregation *16-*. **3** the chief male participant in the Moffat Gala *la20-*. **shepherd's check, shepherd-check** = *shepherd-tartan la19-*. **†shepherd's club** the common mullein *Verbascum thapsus 18*. **shepherd's lass** the chief female participant in the Moffat Gala *20-*. **shepherd's plaid** a plaid worn by shepherds, especially one in *shepherd-tartan 19-*; compare MAUD. **shepherd's stirk** a calf reared by a shepherd as one of his perks *20- WC SW*. **shepherd-tartan, shepherd's tartan** (a cloth of) black and white checks *la19-*. [OE *scēaphyrde*]
sherd see SHAIRD
sheriff, shirra, sherra, †shirref, †schirefe, †serefe /ˈʃɛrəf, ˈʃɪrə, ˈʃɛrə/ *n* **1** a legal officer who performs judicial duties and certain administrative duties, some of the latter delegated by the *sheriff principal 18-*; compare *sheriff-substitute*. **2** the chief judge of a *sheriffdom 18-*. **3** the (hereditary) chief officer of a shire or county, responsible to the sovereign for peace and order, and having civil and criminal jurisdiction *13-e18*. **sheriffdom 1** the area under the jurisdiction of a sheriff; a group of regions or a division of a region *la14-*. **2** = *sheriffship 15-e17*. **sheriffship, †schirefschip** the office of sheriff *la15-*. **†schirefis buikis** the record of proceedings of the sheriff court *16-17*. **sheriff-clerk, †schiref clerk** the clerk of the *Sheriff Court*; originally the clerk of the court of a sheriffdom *la14-*. **Sheriff Court, †schiref court** the court presided over by a SHERIFF (sense 2) *15-*. **†sheriff-depute 1** the lawyer appointed to perform the judicial duties of the chief officer of a shire or county *15-e18*. **2** the chief judge of a sheriffdom *18-e19*. **†sheriff-fee** a fee payable to the SHERIFF (sense 3) *la16-18*. **†sheriff's fiars** the price of (each variety of) grain fixed for the year by the local sheriff in the Fiars Court (used to determine ministers' stipends) *la17-18*. **†sheriff's gloves, sheriff gloves** a perk of the SHERIFF levied at a fair *16-17*. **†sheriff-mair** = *sheriff-officer la16-e19*. **sheriff-officer** an official or messenger who carries out the warrants of a SHERIFF (sense 1), enforces DILIGENCE (sense 2), and serves writs *la16-*. **sheriff principal 1** = SHERIFF (sense 2) *18-*. **2** = SHERIFF (sense 3) *16-e18*. **sheriff-substitute** = SHERIFF (sense 1) *18-*. **sheriff in that part** a person appointed to substitute for the sheriff in a particular assignment *la15-*. [OE *scīrgerēfa*]
shern see SHARN[1.1]
sheroo see SCREW[1]
sherp see SHAIRP[1.1], SHAIRP[1.2], SHAIRP[1.3]
sherping see SHARPING
sherra see SHERIFF
sherrack[1.1], **shirrak** /ˈʃɛrək, ˈʃɪrək/ *n* a noisy squabble, a rumpus *19- WC*. [unknown]
sherrack[1.2], **shirrak** /ˈʃɛrək, ˈʃɪrək/ *v* to raise a riot about (a person), incite a mob against (a person) by publicly reviling and denouncing them *20- NE WC*. **sherracking** a public dressing-down *20-*. [unknown]
shess see CHESS
sheth, †scheth, †scheat /ʃɛθ/ *n* **1** a crossbar, especially a spar in the frame or sides of a cart *la15-18*, *19- T EC Bor*. **2** a connecting bar or strut in a plough *16-19*, *20- H&I Bor*. **3** a division of land *e15*. [perhaps OE *sceaþa* a nail]
Shetland, †Scheitland /ˈʃɛtlənd/ *n* the name of the most distant group of islands off the north coast of Scotland *12-*. **Shetland herring** herring caught in Shetlandic waters *la16-*. **†Shetland hose** stockings made of Shetland wool *19*. **Shetland shawl** a kind of very fine lacework shawl made of Shetland wool *la19-*. **Shetland sheep** a breed of small sheep native to Shetland *la18-*. **Shetland wool** originally wool from Shetland sheep; now used as a general term for pure wool of a similar quality *la18-*. [place-name; see also ZETLAND]
sheu see SHE
sheuch[1.1], **sheugh, shough, shuch, †souch, †sewch, †seuch** /ʃux, ʃʌx/ *n* **1** a narrow trench or ditch, for drainage or fortification; an open drain *16-*. **2** a narrow ravine, gap or passageway; an abyss *16-*. **3** a temporary trench or furrow for plants *19-*. **4** (the cleft of) the buttocks *la20-*. **5** a furrow made by a plough *16-19*, *20- WC Bor*. **6** a street gutter *la19- T C*. **the Sheuch** the North Channel in the Irish Sea *20-*. **in a sheuch** in a state of squalor or misery *la19*, *20- H&I WC SW*. [ME *sogh* a boggy place; compare Flem *zoeg* a meadow ditch]
sheuch[1.2], **sheugh, †souch, †sewch** /ʃux, ʃʌx/ *v* **1** to dig, trench, make a ditch or furrow *16-*. **2** to plant, especially to lay (a plant or seedlings) in a temporary trench *18-*. **3** to bury, cover with earth *la18-*. [see the noun]
sheugh see SHEUCH[1.1], SHEUCH[1.2], SHOO[2]
sheuken see SHAK[1.2]
sheul see SHUIL[1.2]
sheumid see SHOLMIT
shevel[1.1], **†shile, †shoul** /ˈʃɛvəl/ *n* **1** a wry smile, a grimace *la19- SW*. **2** a distortion *la19- NE*. [unknown]
shevel[1.2], *N NE T* **showl,** *SW* **shile, †shavel** /ˈʃɛvəl; *N NE T* ʃʌul; *SW* ʃʌɪl/ *v* to twist out of shape; to distort (the mouth), screw up (the face); to grimace, become distorted *la16-*. **†sheveling-gabbit** wry-mouthed *18-e19*. [unknown]

†shevel[1.3], **schewill** *adj of the mouth* distorted, twisted *16-19*. **sheaval-gabbit** wry-mouthed *la18-19*. **shaivle-moot** = *sheaval-gabbit*. [unknown]

shever *see* SHIVER[2]

shew[1.1] /ʃu, ʃo/ *n* the act of sewing; a spell of needlework *20- Bor*. **shew-up** the closure or shutting-down of a business, bankruptcy *20- T C SW Bor*. [see the verb]

shew[1.2], **sew**, *T* **shoe**, **†schew** /ʃu, ʃo, so/ *v pt, ptp* also **shewed** to stitch, embroider; to make or attach by sewing *15-*. **shewster, shooster** a seamstress, a needlewoman *16-19, 20- NE T C*. **†sewing gold** gold thread *16-e17*. **†sewing silver** silver thread *16-e17*. [OE *sīwian*]

shew *see* SHAW[1.2]

shewet *see* SHUET

sheyd *see* SHED[1.1]

shiak /ˈʃaeak/ *npl* a kind of grey striped black oats *18-19, 20- NE*. [unknown]

shicavy /ʃəˈkavi/ *n* a tumult, turmoil *20- Sh*. [unknown]

shick *see* CHEEK[1.1], CHEEK[1.2]

shicken *see* CHUCKEN

shid *see* SUD

shidder[1.1], **shudder** /ˈʃɪdər, ˈʃʌdər/ *n* an act of shuddering *18-*. [see the verb]

shidder[1.2], **shudder**, **†schudder** /ˈʃɪdər, ˈʃʌdər/ *v* to tremble convulsively, make a convulsive movement *15-*. [ME *shoderen*, MLG *schodderen*, MDu *schuderen*]

shidder *see* SHOOTER[1.1]

shiel[1.1], **†schele**, **†scheill**, **†scheild** /ʃil/ *n* **1** a temporary or roughly-made hut or shed, frequently one used by (salmon) fishermen or shepherds (and their animals) *la12-*; compare SHIELING (sense 2). **2** a small house, a hovel; a summer or country retreat in the hills (occupied by the gentry) *la16-*. **3** a summer pasture (with a shepherd's hut or huts) *16-19*. **sheally hut** = *shiel-hoose 18-*. **shiel-hoose** a shepherd's or fisherman's hut *la16-*. [ME *shele*, OE **scēla*]

†shiel[1.2], **sheal** *v* to build or live in a hut or bothy on summer pasture; to herd (sheep and cattle) at a shieling *la17-e19*. [see the noun]

†shiel[2], **sheall** *n* in the Highlands and Islands son of a person, sometimes used with a clan name *la16-17*. [Gael *sìol* progeny]

shiel *see* SHEEL[1.2], SHUIL[1.1], SHUIL[1.2]

shield[1.1], **†scheld**, **†schelde**, **†scheild** /ʃild/ *n* **1** a piece of defensive armour carried in the hand or on the arm *la14-*. **2** *heraldry* an escutcheon *15-*. **3** a privy *15-16*. **4** a metal plate over a keyhole; a protective plate *la16-e17*. **†under scheld** prepared for or engaged in warlike action, under arms *15-16*. [OE *scield*]

shield[1.2], *NE* **shiel**, **†scheld**, **†scheild** /ʃild; *NE* ʃil/ *v* to protect, shelter *la14-*. [OE *scieldan*]

shieldo /ˈʃildo/ *n* a porch *20- Ork*. [perhaps Norw dial *skjœle* a lean-to, with influence from SHIELD[1.2]]

shieling, sheiling, †scheling, †scheilling, †shealling /ˈʃilɪŋ/ *n* **1 a** an upland or outfield pasture to which livestock was driven in the summer months *la12-18, 19- historical*. **2** a roughly-made hut, a temporary shelter, especially one for shepherds and dairymaids on a SHIELING (sense 1) *17-19, 20- historical*. **†scheling place** = SHIELING (sense 1) *la16-18*. [derivative of SHIEL[1.1]; in Lat (late 12th century) *scalinga*]

shiffel *see* SHUIL[1.1]

shiffle *see* SHUFFLE

shift[1.1], **†schift** /ʃɪft/ *n* **1** a plan, an expedient, a course of action *la15-*. **2** a changeover of workmen; the length of time worked by a crew of workmen *la16-*. **3** a change of situation, abode or employment; dismissal from work *la19-*. **4** each successive crop in a system of crop-rotation; the land or field on which this is grown *18-*. **5** a change of clothing *19-*. **6** a move in the game of draughts *la19-*. **7** a subterfuge, an evasion; a sophistical argument *la16-17*. **8** a way of earning a living *16-18*. [see the verb]

shift[1.2], **†schift** /ʃɪft/ *v* **1** to get rid of, shed *16-*. **2** to move (to another place), drive, convey *la16-*. **3** to change, alter; to replace *la16-*. **4** to change (one's own or another person's clothing or shoes); to put on clean clothes; to provide (someone) with (fresh) clothes *la18-*. **5** to change places (with) *la18-19, 20- NE T*. **6** *in jute and linen spinning* to change the bobbins on a spinning frame *20- C*. **7** to make a move in the game of draughts *la19-*. **8** to escape, evade, dodge; to turn aside, put off, defer *la16-18*. **9** to appoint, arrange *la14*. **shiftin claes** clothes put on when changing from working clothes *la19- C*. **shift yer feet** to change one's shoes and stockings *20-*. [OE *sciftan* to divide]

shig /ʃɪg/ *n* a small temporary hay- or cornstack *20- SW*. [HibEng *shig*, IrGael *síog*]

shiggerie, shoggerie /ˈʃɪgəri, ˈʃɔgəri/ *n* hard, unremitting work *20- Sh*. [unknown]

shiggle *see* JEEGLE[1.1], JEEGLE[1.2]

shilagie /ʃɪˈlagi/ *n* the coltsfoot *Tussilago farfara*, especially its leaves used as a substitute for tobacco *la19, 20- T C*. [shortened form of TUSHILAGO]

shilcorn, †selkhorn /ˈʃɪlkɔrn/ *n* a pimple, a blackhead *la17-19, 20- C SW Bor Uls*. [unknown]

shile *see* SHEVEL[1.1], SHEVEL[1.2]

shilfa, shilfie, chilfie, †shoulfall /ˈʃɪlfə, ˈʃɪlfe, ˈtʃɪlfe/ *n* the chaffinch *Fringilla coelebs la17-19, 20- N H&I C Bor*. **shilly, shully** = SHILFA *la19, 20- EC*. [unknown]

shill[1.1] /ʃɪl/ *adj* high-pitched, shrill; resounding *16-19, 20- T*. [OE **sciell*]

†shill[1.2] *adv* shrilly, resonantly *la15-18*. [see the adj]

shill *see* CHILL, SHEEL[1.2]

shilling, †schilling, †scheling, †syllyn /ˈʃɪlɪn/ *n* **1** a money of account, of the value of twelve pennies, a twentieth of a pound; a coin of this value *15-20, 21- historical*. **2** a denomination of weight, a twentieth of a pound *15-e17*. **forty-shilling ale** (usually **40/-**) a very light beer, originally in the classification of the strength of beer from the price per barrel *la19-*. **shilling-land** of which the annual product was valued at a shilling, 2.6 Scots acres *la15-19, 20- historical*; compare *Scots acre* (SCOTS[1.2]). [OE *scilling*]

shilling *see* SHEELING

shillment *see* SHELMONT

shilly *see* SHILFA

shilmine *see* SHELMONT

shilp /ʃɪlp/ *adj* sour, sharp, acid *20- N*. [back-formation from SHILPIT]

shilpie /ˈʃɪlpi/ *adj* thin, puny, pinched-looking *19, 20- WC*. [altered form of SHILPIT]

shilpit /ˈʃɪlpət/ *adj* **1** mainly *of persons* thin, puny, shrunken, sickly, of starved or drawn appearance *17-*. **2** *of wine* insipid, thin *la17-19, 20- Sh Ork*. **3** sour, bitter; no longer fresh *19, 20- Sh Ork N*. [probably altered form of SHIRPIT]

shilvin *see* SHELVIN

shim[1.1] /ʃɪm/ *n* a horse-hoe, a kind of small plough for weeding and earthing up *19- NE*. [unknown]

shim[1.2] /ʃɪm/ *v* to use a horse-hoe, weed with a SHIM[1.1] *la19- NE*. [unknown]

shimee, †shimal /ˈʃɪmi/ *n* a straw rope *la17, 20- N*. [altered forms of Gael *sìoman*]

shimley *see* CHIMLEY

shimmer *see* SKIMMER[1.1], SKIMMER[1.2]

shimmie *see* SHINTY

shin, †**schin**, †**schyn** /ʃɪn/ *n* **1** the front part of the leg between the knee and ankle; the edge of the shank bone *la15-*. **2** a ridge or steep hill-face, a projecting part of a piece of high ground *19- NE C Bor*. **the shin o the brae** = SHIN (sense 2) *20- NE*. [OE *scinu*]

shin *see* SHAE[1.1], SUNE[1.2]

shine[1.1], †**schyne** /ʃʌɪn/ *n* **1** brightness, radiance *la16-*. **2** a stir, a turmoil, a row *la19, 20- Sh Ork N NE T*. **3** a social gathering, a tea party *19- NE WC*. [see the verb]

shine[1.2], †**schyne** /ʃʌɪn/ *v pt also* †**schane**, †**schinit**, †**shined** to emit or reflect light, glow, glisten; to be resplendent *la14-*. Compare SHEEN[1.2]. [OE *scīnan*]

shine *see* SHEIN

shinner *see* CINNER

shinnon *see* SINNON

shinty, shimmie, *Uls* **shinny,** †**schynnie** /ˈʃɪnte, ˈʃɪme; *Uls* ˈʃɪne/ *n* **1** a game in which two teams of 12 players aim to hit a ball into a goal with a curved stick *la16-*. **2** a caman, the stick used in the game of shinty *la17-*. **3** the ball used in the game of shinty *19*. [perhaps from the cry *shin (to) ye* used in the game]

ship[1.1], †**schip**, †**schepe**, †**scip** /ʃɪp/ *n* a seagoing vessel *la14-*. †**ship-brokin** shipwrecked; ruined by shipwreck *la14-17*. **ship-wrack** severe damage or destruction suffered by a ship; the wreckage of a ship *la16-19, 20- Sh*. †**mak ship-wrack of** to suffer the loss of *e17*. [OE *scip*]

ship[1.2], †**schip** /ʃɪp/ *v* **1** to transport by ship; cause to embark *la14-*. **2** *of a ship* to take in water over the sides *16-*. [OE *scipian*]

Shipka Pass, Schipka Pass, Skipka Pass /ˈʃɪpkə pas, ˈskɪpkə pas/ *n* the nickname of a street which runs under the viaduct between London Road and the Gallowgate in Glasgow, once noted for being home to many people of East European origin, destroyed by fire February 2011 *20- WC*. [from the name of a pass in the Balkans which came to prominence in the Russo-Turkish War of 1877]

shire[1], †**schire**, †**schyre**, †**scheir** /ʃəɪr/ *n* **1** a county, an administrative district; originally a district governed by an appointee of the monarch, usually a sheriff, this unit being based on a subdivision of the royal demesne *la11-*. **2** a district or area more generally *16-19, 20- Sh NE*. **3** a nickname for East Stirlingshire Football Club *20-*. **the Shire** the county of Wigtownshire *la19- SW*; compare *stewartry* (STEWART). [OE *scīr*]

shire[2.1], *WC* **sheer,** *SW Uls* **share** /ʃəɪr; *WC* ʃir; *SW Uls* ʃer/ *v* **1** to skim liquid; to allow the dregs to settle, separate from the dregs *la16-*. **2** to separate into curds and whey; *of milk* to curdle *la17*. **3** *of the mind* to (allow to) become clear *la19- H&I Uls*. **sheerings, shirins** liquid which rises to the top and is poured off *19, 20- N Bor Uls*. [see the adj] [OE *scīran* to make clear, ON *skíra* to cleanse, purify]

shire[2.2], †**schire** /ʃəɪr/ *adj* **1** bright, glowing *15-e18, 20- literary*. **2** thin; watery; sparse *16-19, 20- Bor*. **3** *of liquid* clear, unclouded *15-e18*. **4** complete, sheer, utter *16-e19*. **shirely** brightly *15*. [OE *scīr*]

†**shire**[2.3], **schire, schyre** *adv* **1** brightly, clearly *la14-e16*. **2** sheer or straight down *e16*. [see the adj]

shire *see* CHEER[1]

shirf *see* SHURF

shirins *see* SHIRE[2.1]

shirk, shurk /ʃɪrk, ʃʌrk/ *n* a shark *la19- Sh*. [variant of Eng *shark*]

shirmuffet *see* CHURR MUFFIT

†**shirp** *v* to wither, shrivel *17-e19*. [unknown, perhaps variant of *sherp* (SHAIRP[1.2])]

shirpit /ˈʃɪrpət/ *adj* thin, shrunken, with sharp, drawn features *19- C*; compare SHILPIT. [participial adj from SHIRP]

shirra *see* SHERIFF

shirrak *see* SHERRACK[1.1], SHERRACK[1.2]

shirramuir, *NE* **shirrymeer** /ˈʃɪrəmjur; *NE* ˈʃɪremir/ *n* a noisy row, a rumpus; a dressing-down *19, 20- NE*. †**the Shirramuir** the Jacobite rising of 1715 which ended in the battle of Sheriffmuir, near Stirling *la18-19*. [from the place-name *Sheriffmuir*]

shirre *see* SKYRE

shirref *see* SHERIFF

shirrel, †**scherald,** †**scherard,** †**scheret** /ˈʃɪrəl/ *n* a sod or turf *16-19, 20- NE*. [probably derivative of SHEAR[1.1], SHEAR[1.2]]

shirrow *see* SCREW[1]

shirrymeer *see* SHIRRAMUIR

shissors *see* CHIZORS

shite[1.1], **shit,** †**schitt,** †**schet** /ʃʌɪt, ʃɪt/ *n* **1** excrement; diarrhoea *la16-*. **2** a derogatory term for a person *16-*. **shitebag** a derogatory term for a person *la20-*. [OE *scitte*, with influence from the verb]

shite[1.2], **shit,** †**schitt** /ʃʌɪt, ʃɪt/ *v pt* **shat 1** to excrete, void excrement *16-*. **2** to defile with excrement *la16-*. [OE *bescītan*]

shither[1] /ˈʃɪðər/ *npl* people; natives of a particular district; kinsfolk *20- N*. [variant of *childer* (CHILD)]

shither[2] /ˈʃɪðər/ *v* to shiver, shudder *19, 20- EC Bor*. [perhaps variant of SHIDDER[1.2], with influence from SHIVER[1]]

shittle *see* SHUTTLE[1.1]

shiv *see* SHOO[1.2]

shive *see* SHEAVE[1.1]

shiver[1], †**chiver,** †**chyvir,** †**cheuer** /ˈʃɪvər/ *v* to tremble with cold or fear *la14-*. **shivering bite** food taken after bathing to allay shivering *la19- WC Bor*; compare *chitterin bit* (CHITTER). **shivery bite** = *shivering bite la19- NE T C SW Bor*. [ME *chiveren*]

shiver[2], †**shever,** †**schiver** /ˈʃɪvər/ *n* a fragment, a splinter *15-*. [ME *shiver*]

shiver[3] /ˈʃɪvər/ *n* a blister in or near the mouth caused by the herpes simplex virus; a cold sore *20- T EC*. [perhaps related to SHIVER[2]]

shivereens /ʃɪvərˈinz/ *npl* fragments, small bits *la19-*. [conflation of SHIVER[2] and Eng *smithereens*]

shivvel *see* SHUIL[1.1]

shö *see* SHE

shoag *see* SHOG[1.2]

shoap *see* SHOP

shoar *see* SHORE[1]

shoart *see* SHORT[1.3]

shoat *see* SHOT[1.1]

shochle *see* SHAUCHLE[1.1], SHAUCHLE[1.2], SHOCKLE

shock, †**schoke,** †**chok** /ʃɒk/ *n* **1** a violent impact; an upset or surprise *la16-*. **2** a (paralytic) stroke, a cerebral haemorrhage or thrombosis *la19-*. [MFr *choc* a clash of troops]

shockle, shochle, *Bor* **shaikle,** †**shoggle,** †**schokle** /ˈʃɒkəl, ˈʃɒxəl; *Bor also* ˈʃekəl/ *n* an icicle, a chunk of ice *la16-*. [shortened form of *ice schockle* (EESHOGEL)]

shod[1.1] /ʃɒd/ *n* **1** an iron tip on a (usually wooden) object to prevent wear; the metal tyre of a cartwheel *19-*. **2** a metal plate on the toe or heel of a shoe; a hobnail *19, 20- N NE SW Uls*. **3** a shoe, especially a child's shoe; a horseshoe *la17-19*. [see the adj]

shod[1.2] /ʃɒd/ *v pt* **shod, shoddit, shodit 1** to furnish with shoes; to shoe (a horse) *19-*. **2** to fit (a bootlace, spade, or cartwheel) with a metal tip or rim *18-*. **3** to put iron toe- and heel-pieces on (a shoe), cover (the soles of shoes) with studs *la19, 20- Sh NE WC*. **shodding 1** metal tips or edging *19-*. **2** boots and shoes, footwear *18-19*. [from the ptp of SHAE[1.2]]

shod[1,3], †**schod** /ʃɔd/ *adj* **1** provided with, wearing shoes *la16-*. **2** *of a wheel* furnished with an iron rim or tyre *16-e18*. †**schod shuil** a wooden shovel with a metal rim *16-e18*. [participial adj from SHAE[1,2]]

shoddie /'ʃɔdi/ *n* a natural building stone, used roughly dressed *20- N NE H&I C*. [unknown; compare Eng *shoad* loose fragments of ore]

shoe see SHAE[1,1], SHAE[1,2], SHEW[1,2]

shog[1,1], †**schogg** /ʃɔg/ *n* **1** a jog, a shake, a nudge *18-*. **2** the act or motion of swinging or rocking; a swinging-rope; a child's swing *la19-*. **3** a shaky, unstable state *la16*. [see the verb]

shog[1,2], **shug**, **shoog**, †**shoag**, †**schog** /ʃɔg, ʃʌg, ʃug/ *v* **1** to shake, jog, (cause to) swing, sway or rock, wobble *la15-*. **2** to proceed at a leisurely but steady pace, jog along, keep going *18-19, 20- Sh NE Uls*. **shog-bog** a soft watery bog, a quagmire *19-*. **shoggin boat** a swing-boat at a funfair *la19-*. [ME *shoggen*; compare MLG *schocken*]

shoggerie see SHIGGERIE

shoggie[1,1] /'ʃɔgi/ *n* **1** a jolt, a nudge *20-*. **2** the act of swinging or rocking; a child's swing *20- T C SW Bor*. [SHOG[1,1] + -IE[1]]

shoggie[1,2], **shuggie** /'ʃɔgi, 'ʃʌgi/ *v* to swing, rock *19-*. [see the noun]

shoggie[1,3], **shoogie** /'ʃɔgi, 'ʃugi/ *adj* shaky, unsteady, wobbly *la19- NE T WC*. **shoggie-boat** a swing-boat at a funfair *la19-*. **shoggie-bog** a marsh, a quagmire *20- WC SW*. [SHOG[1,1] + -IE[2]]

shoggie-shoo[1,1], †**shoggy-shou** /'ʃɔgi ʃu/ *n* **1** a seesaw, the game of seesawing *la17-*. **2** a swing *19, 20- T C SW Bor*. [SHOGGIE[1,1] + SHOO[1,1]]

shoggie-shoo[1,2] /'ʃɔgi ʃu/ *v* to seesaw; to sway, wobble *19- WC SW Bor*. [see the noun]

shoggle see SHOCKLE, SHOOGLE[1,1], SHOOGLE[1,2]

shogglie see SHOOGLY

shoggy-shou see SHOGGIE-SHOO[1,1]

shokk see SHUG[1]

shöll see SHUIL[1,2]

sholmark /'ʃɔlmɑrk/ *n* an abnormal birthmark on an animal *la19- Sh*. [perhaps Norw *hjelm* a helmet + MARK[1,1]]

sholmit, *Ork* **sheumid** /'ʃɔlmət; *Ork* 'ʃømət/ *adj of a cow* having a white face *19- Sh Ork*. [Norw dial *hjelmutt* literally helmeted]

sholtie see SHELTIE

shon, **shun**, **chun** /ʃɔn, ʃʌn, tʃʌn/ *n* a small loch or pool *la18- Sh Ork N*. [perhaps Norw dial *tjørn* a tarn, with influence from Norw dial *sjo* a lake]

shonnag see SHANGAN

shoo[1,1], **shue**, **shuve**, **shove**, †**schow**, †**schove** /ʃu, ʃuv, ʃʌv/ *n* **1** a hard push, a shove *la15-*. **2** a rocking motion; a swing, a seesaw *17-19, 20- WC*; compare SHOGGIE-SHOO[1,1]. **3** an attack; a strong forward movement *la15-e17*. **shooer**, **sjuer** a push, a shove *20- Sh*. [see the verb]

shoo[1,2], **shue**, **shuve**, **shiv**, **shove**, †**schow**, †**schewe**, †**shuff** /ʃu, ʃuv, ʃɪv, ʃʌv/ *v* **1** to push, thrust forcefully, press on *15-*. **2** to launch or propel a boat; to row backwards *16-19, 20- Sh Ork N Uls*. **3** to swing, rock or sway backwards and forwards; to swing on a rope, gate, or seesaw *19, 20- C Bor*. †**schowar**, **schovar** a person who pushes himself forwards, a pushy person *e16*. **shove-by** a hastily-prepared or makeshift meal *la19-*. **shue shuggie** something said when dandling a child *20-*. Compare SHOGGIE-SHOO[1,2]. [OE *scúfan*]

†**shoo**[2], **sheugh** *interj* expressing rejection rubbish, nonsense *la18-19*. [instinctive utterance]

shooder[1,1], **shouder**, **shoother**, **shouther**, **shoulder**, *NE* **showder**, *T* **shidder**, †**schulder**, †**schuldir** /'ʃudər, 'ʃuðər, 'ʃoldər; *NE* 'ʃʌudər; *T* 'ʃɪdər/ *n* **1** the joint which attaches the arm to the body *la14-*. **2** the part of a garment covering the shoulder *la15-*. **3** a rounded flat ridge below the summit of a hill *16-*. **4** the foreleg and adjacent parts of an animal prepared as a joint of meat *la16-*. **5** the swelling part of a wave rising to the crest *20-*. **6** *pl* a coathanger *20- C*. **7** the dome-shaped upper part of the pot of a whisky-still *la18-19, 20- NE*. **8** (a projection at) the upper part of the blade of a sword *17*. **shouderie 1** a shawl for covering the shoulders *20-*. **2** a ride on someone's shoulders *la20-*. **shooder-cleek** the hook on a cart-shaft to which the shoulder-chain is attached *20- C Bor*. **shoother-heid** the socket of the shoulder bone; the shoulder joint *la19- NE T EC Bor*. **shoulder-lire** a cut of beef from the upper foreleg *18-*. **shoother-pick** a pickaxe which is wielded over the shoulder *la19- NE*. [OE *sculdor*]

shooder[1,2], **shouder**, **shoother**, **shouther**, **shoulder**, †**schulder** /'ʃudər, 'ʃuðər, 'ʃoldər/ *v* **1** to push aside *la16-*. **2** *building* to point (the inside joints of) slating) with mortar *20-*. **3** to walk heavily, plod *la19- NE T*. †**schulderar** a person who pushes forward *e16*. †**schulderinglie** in a forceful, thrusting manner *la16*. **shouder-the-win** (having) a deformity in which one shoulder is higher than the other *20-*. [see the noun]

shooer[1,1], **shour**, **shower**, †**schour**, †**schowr** /ʃur, ʃuər, 'ʃʌuər/ *n* **1** a downfall of rain or hail; a copious fall of objects *la14-*. **2** a pang or paroxysm of pain, death, illness, childbirth or jealousy *la14-19, 20- Sh*. **a shower in the heids** a fit of weeping *19, 20- EC Bor*. [OE *scūr*]

shooer[1,2], **shour**, **shower** /ʃur, ʃuər, 'ʃʌuər/ *v* to fall in a shower *17-*. [see the noun]

shoog see SHOG[1,2]

shoogie see SHOGGIE[1,3]

shoogle[1,1], **shoggle**, **shuggle** /'ʃugəl, 'ʃɔgəl, 'ʃʌgəl/ *n* **1** a jog, jolt, shake *19-*. **2** the act of swinging on a rope or tree-branch *la20- T C*. [see the verb]

shoogle[1,2], **shoggle**, **shuggle** /'ʃugəl, 'ʃɔgəl, 'ʃʌgəl/ *v* **1** to (cause to) sway, rock, wobble, swing; to shake, joggle *18-*. **2** to jog along, move with little unsteady jerks; to shuffle *19, 20- Sh N NE*. [frequentative form of SHOG[1,2]]

shoogly, **shooglie**, **shogglie** /'ʃugli, 'ʃɔgle/ *adj* shaky, unsteady, tottery, insecure *19-*. **shoogly jock** brawn in jelly *20- H&I C*. **yer jaiket's oan a shooglie nail** you are in a precarious position; you are likely to lose your job *la20-*. [SHOOGLE[1,2] + -IE[2]]

shooi /'ʃui/ *n* the Arctic skua *Stercorarius parasiticus 19- Sh*. [unknown]

shook see SHAK[1,2], SHUG[2]

shooken see SHAK[1,2]

shool see SHUIL[1,1], SHUIL[1,2]

shoom[1,1] /ʃum/ *n* a low buzzing or humming sound *20- NE*. [onomatopoeic]

shoom[1,2] /ʃum/ *v* to make a low buzzing or humming sound *20-*. [onomatopoeic]

shoomach see SHEEMACH

shoon see SHAE[1,1]

shoop see SOUP

shoopiltie see SHOUPILTIN

shoormil /'ʃurməl/ *n* the foreshore, the water's edge *19- Sh*. [compare Faer *sjóvarmáli*]

shooskie /'ʃuski/ *n* **1** a name for the Devil; a rascal, a scamp *19- Sh*. **2** *taboo* a clergyman *la19- Sh*. [compare Faer *tjóvsk* thievish]

shooster see SHEW[1,2]

shoot see SHOT[1,1], SHUIT[1,2], SHUT[1,2], SUIT[1,1]

shoother see SHOODER[1,1], SHOODER[1,2]

shop, **shoap**, *NE* **chop**, *NE T* **tchop**, *Uls* **shap**, †**schop** /ʃɔp, ʃop; *NE T* tʃɔp; *Uls* ʃap/ *n* a place where goods are sold;

shopman *see* CHOPMAN

a workshop *la15-*. **shoppie, choppie,** *NE T* **tchoppie** = SHOP *la19-*. **shop-door** the front flap or fly of trousers *la19-*. †**chop-keiper** a shopkeeper *17*. **shop-lassie** a female shop assistant *la19, 20- NE*. [OE *sceoppa*]

shopman *see* CHOPMAN

shord[1.1] /ʃord/ *n* a prop (for a boat), a stay or support *la19- Sh*. [conflation of Norw *skorda* with Eng *shore* a prop]

shord[1.2] /ʃord/ *v* to prop up, support *19- Sh Ork*. [see the noun]

shore[1], †**schor**, †**schoir**, †**shoar** /ʃor/ *n* **1** land bordering a stretch of water *la15-*. **2** a quay, a landing-place, a harbour *la15-19, 20- Ork N NE T EC*. **shore bretsch** breaking waves, the surf *20- Sh*. †**shore dues, shoir dews, shoar deues** a levy payable for making use of the harbour *17-19*. **shore heid** the ground on the upper or land side of a quay or harbour *la16, 19- EC*. †**schore mail** harbour-dues *e17*. †**shore-master** a harbour master *17-19*. †**schore silver** harbour-dues *la16-17*. [MLG *schore*]

†**shore**[2.1], †**schoir** *n* threatening behaviour, threats, menaces *la14-18*. [unknown]

shore[2.2], †**schoir** /ʃor/ *v* **1** to scold, upbraid *la18-19, 20- Sh Bor*. **2** to threaten, menace *la14-19, 20- Bor*. **3** *weather* to indicate or threaten (rain or snow) *18-19*. **4** to urge on, incite *19*. **5** to offer as a mark of favour *la18-19*. †**shoring** the action of threatening; a threat, threats *la16-e18*. [unknown]

†**shoreling, schorling** *n* (the skin of) a recently-shorn sheep *14-e19*. [*shorn* (SHEAR[1.2]), with *-ling* suffix]

shorie /'ʃore/ *n* a variety of the game of marbles *la19- T EC*. [unknown]

shorn *see* SHARE, SHEAR[1.2]

short[1.1], †**schort** /ʃort/ *n* **1** something short *la16-*. **2** a short time, an instant *la18- NE*. **3** *pl* the refuse of flax tow after carding or of hay or straw from threshing *la18-19, 20- SW Bor*. †**short ruid** a linear measure of 6 ells (approx 6 m) or square measure of 36 ells (approx 6 m2) *18-e19*; compare RUID (sense 4). **the short and lang o it** the entirety or sum total of something, the upshot *la19, 20- NE T*. †**at schort 1** briefly, concisely *la15-16*. **2** in a short time, quickly *16-e17*. [see the adj]

†**short**[1.2], †**schort** *v* **1** to cut short, shorten *la15-e17*. **2** to make time or a journey seem shorter; to amuse, entertain (a person) *15-19*. [OE *scortian* to grow short]

short[1.3], **shoart**, †**schort** /ʃort, ʃort/ *adj* **1** small, not long; brief; near; abrupt, succinct; substandard *la12-*. **2** *of food* crumbly, friable *17-*. **3** *of black-face sheep* relatively short in the body (compared with the Cheviot) *la18-19*. **shortie** = SHORTBREAD *la19-*. **shortsome** *of people or situations* lively and entertaining, cheerful, making time pass quickly *18-19, 20- N NE T*. **short butter** butter which is soft and crumbly from being churned too hot *20- NE SW*. **short coal** coal with wide cleavages in the seam *20- EC*. **shortcome** = *short-coming la18-*. **short-coming** a deficiency, shortage; a fault in character or conduct *17-*. †**schort days** in a short time *16*. †**schort-ended** short-winded *la16*. **Shorter Catechism** *Presbyterian Church* the shorter of two instruction manuals in the principles of the Christian religion approved by the General Assembly in 1648 *17-*. **short-game** *golf* the playing of short strokes when approaching the hole and putting *la19-*. **short goon 1** a woman's long loose blouse worn over other clothes for protection *la18- T H&I C Bor*. **2** a man's short, loose upper garment *la15-16*. †**schort hose** knee-breeches *la15-17*. †**short-hought** stocky-legged *18-e19*. †**short hour** an early hour (of the morning) *la18-e19*. **short-set** small and stockily-built *la19- Sh Ork N NE T C*. **short sword** a short-bladed sword; a dagger *la15-19, 20- historical*. †**short time** = *schortwhile la14-16*. †**schortwhile** (during, for) a short time *la14-e19*.

short in the pile = *short in the trot la19- SW*. **short in the trot** in a bad temper, curt and uncivil *la19- NE*. [OE *scort*]

short[1.4], †**schort** /ʃort/ *adv* for a brief while; in a brief space of time, soon *la15-*. **shortlins 1** a little while ago, recently *la18-*. **2** soon *19-*. **short ago** a short time ago *20- Sh Ork N NE T*. **short and lang** in brief, summarily *19, 20- WC SW Uls*. **short syne** a short time ago, recently *la16-19, 20- Sh N T C*. [see the adj]

shortbread, shortbreid, †**schort-breid** /'ʃortbred, 'ʃortbrid/ *n* a biscuit made by mixing butter, sugar and flour *la16-*. [SHORT[1.3] + BREID]

shot[1.1], **shoat, schote,** †**schot,** †**shoot** /ʃot, ʃot/ *n* **1** the action or act of shooting; a projectile *la14-*. **2** the range of a shot *16-*. **3** the action of shooting a fishing-net into the water and hauling it in; the haul of fish taken *la16-*. **4** *curling* the playing of a stone towards the tee; the score awarded to any stone nearer the tee than its opponents; a stone so played *la17-*. **5** a brief loan; a temporary use (of something); a turn or go *20-*. **6** a discharge, flow (of blood or other fluid) from the body *16-19, 20- NE SW*. **7** *weaving* a single movement of the shuttle carrying the weft across the web *la18-19, 20- T C*. **8** the place from which fishing-nets are shot; a stretch of river or fishing ground *15-19*. **9** a rush, a dash *la14-e15*. **10** a shooting pain *la15-17*. **11** a push, a shove, a blow *la16-19*. **12** *folklore* a disease caused by a shot from an elf or fairy arrow *16-e17*; compare ELF-SHOT[1.1] (sense 2). **13** a payment, a contribution *la15-e19*. **shottie** a loan (of something) or a turn (at something) *20-*. [OE *scot* the action of SHUIT]

shot[1.2], *Sh Ork* **shut,** †**schott,** †**schutt** /ʃot; *Sh Ork* ʃʌt/ *v* **1** to discharge a weapon *la16-19, 20- Sh Ork N NE T EC*. **2** *fishing* to cast (lines or nets) *la16- NE EC*. Compare SHUIT. [see the noun]

shot[1.3], †**shote,** †**schot** /ʃot/ *adj of plants* run to seed *18-*. **shot-blade,** †**shot bled** the leaf enclosing the corn-stalk and ear *17-*. †**shot brae** a landslip, an avalanche *e19*. **shot-cock** a young cockerel, to be kept for breeding *20- NE*. †**schot frie** safe from being shot at *la16-17*. †**shot heuch, schothouis** a landslip *la16-e19*. **shot joint** a joint deformed by rheumatism *20-*. †**shot star, schot starne 1** a shooting star, a meteor *18-19*. **2** jelly-like algae found in pastures after rain (formerly thought to be the remains of a shooting star) *17-e19*. **shot o** rid of, free from *18-*. [participial adj from SHUIT]

shot[2] /ʃot/ *n* mainly *pl* wooden shutters used to close a window or opening in the wall of a house; the window itself *16-19, 20- historical*. **shot hole** a small opening in the wall of a house *19, 20- historical*. **shot window** a window with shutters *16-19, 20- historical*. [compare MDu *schotdore* a sliding door]

shot[3], †**schot** /ʃot/ *n* a piece of ground, especially one cropped rotationally; a smallholding *la16-*. [perhaps related to OE *scēat* a corner of land]

shot[4], **shott** /ʃot/ *n fishing* the stern compartment in a rowing boat used to hold the catch *19- Sh*. [LG *schot* a partition separating off the hold of a boat]

shot[5] /ʃot/ *interj* a warning among children of the approach of a policeman, teacher or other figure of authority *20- EC*. **shottie, shoatie** = SHOT[5]. **keep shot** to act as a lookout *20- EC*. **keep shottie** = *keep shot*. [compare SHOT[1.1] (sense 9)]

shot *see* SHUIT

shott[1], **shot** /ʃot/ *n* an inferior sheep; a reject *18-*. [substantive use of participial adj from SHUIT]

shott[2], †**schot** /ʃot/ *n* a young pig after weaning *la16-*. [ME *shot*; compare Du *schote*]

shott *see* SHOT[4]

shotten /ʃɔtən/ *adj of a fish* newly spawned *19-*. [participial adj from SHUIT]

shotten *see* SHUIT

shottle, shuttle, †schottill, †chottill /'ʃɔtəl, 'ʃʌtəl/ *n* a small compartment at the top of a trunk or chest, usually with a lid or drawer; a drawer, frequently one of a set of drawers in a cabinet or cupboard intended for storage or safekeeping of small items; a portable case or container for documents *16-*. [compare LG *schot* a drawer]

†shot whaip, schotquhap *n* perhaps a kind of curlew *16-e17*. [unknown first element + WHAUP[1.1]]

shouder *see* SHOODER[1.1], SHOODER[1.2]

shough *see* SHEUCH[1.1]

shoul *see* SHEVEL[1.1]

should *see* SUD

shoulder *see* SHOODER[1.1], SHOODER[1.2]

shoulfall *see* SHILFA

†shoupiltin, shoopiltie *n in Shetlandic folklore* a water-sprite or demon *18-19*. [ON *sjór* sea + ON *piltr* a boy, with ON article suffix *-inn*]

shour *see* SHOOER[1.1], SHOOER[1.2]

shout[1.1], †schout, †schowt /ʃut, ʃʌut/ *n* a loud cry or call, a noise; an alarm, a disturbance *la14-*. **†schout and cry** hue and cry *la16-e17*. **†schout and hoyes** = *schout and cry e17*. [ON *skúta* a taunt]

shout[1.2], †schout, †schowt /ʃut, ʃʌut/ *v* **1** to utter a loud cry, at (someone), call out (a warning), greet with shouts; to make a shouting sound *la14-*. **2** *of a woman* to be in labour; to give birth *19- WC SW Bor*. **shoutin 1** the action of shouting; a shouting noise *16-*. **2** (a celebration of) childbirth *19- C Bor*. [see the noun]

shouther *see* SHOODER[1.1], SHOODER[1.2]

shove *see* SHOO[1.1], SHOO[1.2]

shove-by *see* SHOO[1.2]

shovel, shovell *see* SHUIL[1.1], SHUIL[1.2]

show /ʃo, ʃʌu/ *n* **1** the refuse of flax stems broken off in scutching *la18-19, 20- WC Bor Uls*. **2** the awns of barley *20- Ork*. [EModE *shove*]

show *see* CHAW[1.1], CHAW[1.2], SHAW[1.1], SHAW[1.2]

showd[1.1] /ʃʌud/ *n* **1** a rocking, swaying motion; a waddling gait; the act of swinging or dangling *19- N NE*. **2** a child's swing *19- N NE*. **3** a ride in a cart or barrow *20- N*. **showdie** = SHOWD[1.1] *la19- N NE*. [see the verb]

showd[1.2], †schewd /ʃʌud/ *v* **1** to swing to and fro, rock; to have a rocking, waddling gait *la16- N NE*. **2** to cause to sway or rock; to swing, dandle (a child) *19- NE*. **showdin boat** a swing-boat at a fair *20- NE*. [unknown; compare MLG *schudder* to shake, wag]

showder *see* SHOODER[1.1]

shower *see* SHOOER[1.1], SHOOER[1.2]

showl *see* SHEVEL[1.2]

shows *see* CHOWS

shred, NE shreed, †schred /ʃred; NE ʃrid/ *n* a strip, a small piece, a scrap of cloth, a remnant or fragment *15-*. [OE *scrēad* a cutting, a scrap]

shrew *see* SCREW[1]

shrink, †schrink, †schrenk, †schrynk /ʃrɪŋk/ *v* **1** to fail in courage; to hesitate *la15-*. **2** to draw back from physical contact or pain, recoil; to avoid, shun *la15-*. **3** to contract, reduce in size *17-*. Compare SKRINK[1.2]. [OE *scrincan*]

shrood[1.1], shroud, †schroud, †schrowd /ʃrud, ʃrʌud/ *n* **1** the sheet in which a corpse is laid for burial *19-*. **2** clothing, a garment; an outfit; protective clothing, armour *la15-16*. **3** *pl* protective boards for a mill-wheel *la16*. [OE *scrūd* clothing]

shrood[1.2], shroud, †schroud, †schrowd /ʃrud, ʃrʌud/ *v ptp* **†schrowd, †yschrowdyt 1** to screen, shade, envelop; to conceal, protect *la15-*. **2** to seek shelter; to conceal oneself *16-17*. **3** to clothe, dress, adorn well or richly *la14-e16*. [see the noun]

shroud *see* SHROOD[1.1], SHROOD[1.2]

shrunkled /'ʃrʌŋkəld/ *adj* shrunken, shrivelled *la19- NE T EC Bor*. [conflation of SKRUNKLE with SHRINK]

shuch *see* SHEUCH[1.1]

shucken *see* SHAK[1.2]

shud[1] /ʃʌd/ *n* a lump of coagulated blood, ice or earth *19- Bor*. [perhaps altered form of SHED[1.1] sense 5, sense 6]

shud[2] /ʃʌd/ *n* a dull thudding, trampling or shuffling noise *19- Sh*. [onomatopoeic]

shudden /'ʃʌdən/ *n* a small loch or pool *20- Sh*. [variant of SHON]

shudder *see* SHIDDER[1.1], SHIDDER[1.2]

shue *see* SHOO[1.1], SHOO[1.2]

shuet, suet, †shewet, †sewat /'ʃuət, 'suət/ *n* hard animal fat; suet *16-*. [ME *seuet*, AN *suet]

shuff *see* SHOO[1.2]

shuffle, †shiffle /'ʃʌfəl/ *v* **1** to move awkwardly, scramble; to move without lifting the feet *17-*. **2** to treat (a matter) equivocally or manipulatively, cheat, smuggle *la16-18*. **shuffle-the-brogue** *games* hunt-the-slipper *19- SW Uls*. [LG *schuffeln*]

shuffle *see* SHUIL[1.1], SHUIL[1.2]

shug[1], shokk /ʃʌg, ʃɔk/ *n* drizzle, mist *la19- Sh Ork N*. [probably Norw dial *tjukka* an overcast sky]

shug[2], shook /ʃʌg, ʃuk/ *interj* a call-word to a horse *la19- Sh Ork N*. **shuggie, shookie** = SHUG[2] *20-*. [Gael *siuc*]

Shug[3] /ʃʌg/ *n* familiar form of Hugh *20-*.

shug *see* SHOG[1.2]

shuggar *see* SUGAR

shuggie *see* SHOGGIE[1.2]

shuggle *see* SHOOGLE[1.1], SHOOGLE[1.2]

shuil[1.1], shule, shool, shuffle, shovel, *Sh* **shivvel,** *Ork* **sheul,** *N NE* **shiffel,** *N NE* **shiel,** *NE* **sheel, †schule, †shovell, †chuffell** /ʃul, 'ʃʌfəl, 'ʃʌvəl; *Sh* 'ʃɪvəl; *Ork* ʃøl; *NE* 'ʃɪfəl, ʃil/ *n* **1** a shovel *la14-*. **2** an act of shovelling *la18- NE T C Bor*. **3** mainly **shiel**, a peat-cutting spade with a long, narrow blade *20- N*. **4** a slit or crescent-shaped earmark on sheep *la19- Sh*. **shuilfu** a shovelful *la19- Ork T EC Bor*. **shuily** *of the feet* like a shovel, flat and splayed out *20- Ork H&I WC*. **shuil-bane** the shoulder blade *la19- Sh Ork*. **shuil-feeted** shuffling *20- Ork*. **shuil-fit** a person with flat shuffling feet *20- C Bor*. [OE *scofl*]

shuil[1.2], shuffle, shovel, *Sh* **shöll,** *Ork* **sheul,** *N NE* **shiel,** *NE* **sheel, †shool, †schule, †shovell** /ʃul, 'ʃʌfəl, 'ʃʌvəl; *Sh Ork* ʃøl; *N NE* ʃil/ *v* **1** to dig, clear or lift with a shovel *la15-*. **2** to take away (someone's) store of something, clean (a person) out *la19-*. **3** to shuffle, slide (along) *19, 20- T Bor*. **4** to cut the top turf of a peat-bank *20- N*. **shool-the-board** a kind of draughts where the winner is the first to get all his men off the board *19- Sh NE T Bor*. **2** shovel-board *la16-17*. [see the noun]

shuit, shoot, *N* **sheet, †schute, †schote, †schet** /ʃut; *NE* ʃit/ *v pres* **shot †schuttis,** *pt* **shot,** *NE* **sheetit, †schot, †schote,** *ptp* **shot,** *NE* **shotten,** *NE* **sheetit, †schot, †schote 1** to discharge a missile; to fire a gun; to wound, kill by shooting *la14-*. **2** to move rapidly, rush *la14-*. **3** to emit (flames or rays) swiftly and forcibly *la14-*. **4** to position (a fishing-net) in water *15-*. **5** *of plants* to sprout, bud *la16-*. **6** *of plants* to go to seed; *of grain* to come into ear *la17-*. **7** to push, shove, thrust *la14-19, 20- Sh Ork N NE*. **8** to reject (for retention or purchase) the bad specimens of cattle or sheep *la18- WC SW Bor*. **9** *of a bank, wall or snow* to protrude, bulge; to collapse, avalanche *la16-19, 20- Ork*. **10** *folklore* to cause illness, injury or death by shooting the

victim with an *elf-arrow* (ELF) *la16-19*. **11** to launch (a boat) *la14-17*. **12** *of blood or tears* to stream out *la15-17*. **13** to force (a lock), break open (a door) *la16-e17*. **14** to void excrement *la15-e16*. **15** to vomit *e16*. **16** to overshoot (a space) *e16*. **shuit-aboot** a makeshift meal *la19- NE T*. **shoot-by** to manage, get by with makeshift facilities *la18-19, 20- T EC*. †**schute a day** to postpone, put off till a later date *la14-16*. †**schute doun** to throw or pull down (a wall); *of a wall* to fall down *la15-16*. †**schute furth** to drive out or away, expel *16*. †**schute oot yer fit** to give a convulsive kick, as in dying; to die *la18-19*. **shuit ower** to last over (a period); to tide (someone) over *18-19, 20- EC*. **shoot the crow, shoot the craw** to run away, abscond; to depart without paying *la19-*. †**schute to dead, schute o dead** *folklore* to kill or harm with an *elf-arrow* (ELF); to die suddenly (due to supernatural causes) *la16-19*. †**schute upon** to assault violently *la14-e16*. [OE *scēotan*]
shuit *see* SUIT[1.1]
shuk, shuke *see* SHAK[1.2]
shuld *see* SUD
shule *see* SHUIL[1.1]
shully *see* SHILFA
shult *see* SHELTIE
shun *see* SHON
shunder *see* CINNER
shune *see* SHAE[1.1], SUNE[1.2]
shunky, shunkie, shankie /'ʃʌnke/ *n* a lavatory, a privy, a dry toilet *20- C SW*. [from the personal name *Shanks* and Co., Barrhead, manufacturers of lavatory fittings]
shunner *see* CINNER
shure *see* SHEAR[1.2]
shurf, shirf /ʃʌrf, ʃɪrf/ *n derogatory* an insignificant person *19- Bor*. [ME *schroff* rubbish for burning, OE *sceorf* scurf]
shurg /ʃʌrg/ *n* wet, gravelly subsoil *la19- Sh*. [perhaps onomatopoeic]
shurk *see* SHIRK
shusy, †**susy** /'ʃuzi/ *n* **1** a corpse for dissection *19*. **2** *derogatory* a (silly, empty-headed) woman *20- NE EC*. [from the personal name *Susie*]
shut[1.1] /ʃʌt/ *n* **1** a window shutter *la18-19, 20- Uls*. **2** *mining* one of the sliding or hinged boards on which the cage rests at the pithead *la19, 20- EC*. [see the verb]
shut[1.2], †**schut,** †**schet,** †**shoot** /ʃʌt/ *v ptp* **shut**, *NE* **shuttit 1** to close or fasten (a door); to prevent access to a place *16-*. **2** to break off (a conversation) *e15*. **shut-day** a holiday on which shops are shut for the whole or part of the day, an early-closing day *20- C*. **shut tae** to close or fasten (a door) *la19-*. [OE *scyttan*]
shut *see* SHOT[1.2]
shūta /'ʃøtə/ *interj* a coaxing call to a cow or calf *20- Sh Ork*. [Norw dial *søta* sweet one]
shute *see* SUIT[2]
shuttit *see* SHUT[1.2]
shuttle[1.1], †**shittle,** †**schottill** /'ʃʌtəl/ *n weaving* the mechanism by which the thread of the weft is passed to and fro between the threads of the warp *la16-*. **shuttle-gab, shittle-gab** a misshapen mouth, with one jaw protruding beyond the other, especially of an animal *20- N*. **shuttle-gabbit** having a *shuttle-gab 20- Bor*. [OE *scytel* a dart, an arrow]
shuttle[1.2] /'ʃʌtəl/ *v* **1** to move to and fro like a shuttle *19-*. **2** to weave; to drive the shuttle in a loom *la19- T C*. **shuttler, shittler** a weaver; a boy who fills carriages and bobbins in a lace factory *la19- T C*. [see the noun]
shuttle[2] /'ʃʌtəl/ *adj* quick, active, making sudden hasty movements *la19, 20- NE*. [perhaps related to SHUIT or from SHUTTLE[1.1]]

shuttle *see* SHOTTLE
shuynd-bill /'ʃøndbɪl/ *n in udal law in Shetland* a deed confirming a testament or settling an inheritance dispute *16-19, 20- historical*. [ON *sjaund* a funeral feast + BILL[1]]
shyve /ʃʌɪv/ *v* to throw, fling (a rope) *20- NE*. [perhaps Eng *shy* to throw, with influence from *shuve* (SHOO[1.2])]
sib[1.1] /sɪb/ *n* mainly *pl* kindred, relatives *la14-*. **sib or fremd** relatives and strangers, everyone *la14-19, 20- Sh NE*. [OE *sibb*]
sib[1.2] /sɪb/ *adj* **1** related by blood (or marriage) of the same kindred or lineage *la14-*. **2** closely akin, allied with, of the same sort, similar *16-*. **3** likely to inherit or acquire; having a claim to, especially by right of kinship *18-19*. **sib-like** friendly, like members of the same family *19, 20- SW*. **sibness,** †**sibnes 1** kinship, relationship by common descent *16-*. **2** closeness, intimacy, affinity *la16-*. **sibred,** †**sibrend,** †**sibrent** kinship, kinfolk *e15, 20- Sh Ork*. †**sibman** a kinsman *la14-15*. †**as sib as sieve to riddle** identical, as alike as two peas *la15-e19*. [OE *sibb*]
sibbens *see* SIVEN
sic[1.1], **sich, such,** †**sik,** †**syk,** †**swilk** /sɪk, sɪx, sʌx/ *adj* such; of the sort described; that same one; such as; to such an extent *la14-*. **sic-an-sae** alike, similar, much of a muchness *la19- WC Bor*. **sic-sey** = *sic-an-sae 20- NE*. **sic-an-sic** such-and-such, so-and-so *18-*. **sic-an-siclike** = *sic-an-sae 19-, 20- Sh Ork NE T*. **sic-sam** = *sic-an-sae 20- Sh*. **sic-a,** †**sic ane 1** such a one, a person or thing of the kind mentioned *la15-*. **2** *with pl noun* what a lot of *20-*. **sic a like 1** such, of the sort described *la15-*. **2** *in exclamations* what a ... *19-*. **sic a bodie** so-and-so, such a person *20-*. †**be sic thre** three times better *16*. †**be sic sevin** seven times more, seven times better *e16*. †**sic thre** three of that kind *la15-16*. [OE *swilc*]
sic[1.2], **sich, such** /sɪk, sɪx, sʌx/ *adv* **1** so, such, in such a way *19-*. **2** *in exclamations* how: ◊*sic bonnie she is! 20- NE*. [OE *swilce*]
sic[1.3], **sich, such,** †**sik** /sɪk, sɪx, sʌx/ *dem pron* **1** a person or persons like those mentioned *la14-*. **2** the person or thing just mentioned *15-*. [see the adj]
sic *see* SICK[1.2]
siccan[1.1], †**sykkyn,** †**sikkynd** /'sɪkən/ *adj* **1** such, of such a kind, of a sort already mentioned *16-*. **2** *in exclamations* what (a)... *19-*. **siccan like** similar *19-*. **siccan-a-like yin** so-and-so *20- EC SW Bor*. **sicna** a, such a *20-*. [SIC[1.1] + KIN]
siccan[1.2] /'sɪkən/ *adv in exclamations* how: ◊*siccan cauld it was! 19-*. [see the adj]
siccar[1.1], **sicker,** †**sekyre** /'sɪkər/ *v* **1** to assure *la14-*. **2** to fix firmly, establish; to make firm and secure *la15-*. [see the adj]
siccar[1.2], **sicker,** †**sikker,** †**sekir,** †**sicir** /'sɪkər/ *adj* **1** safe, secure *la14-*. **2** firmly fixed, strongly built, stable; securely under control, held firm *15-*. **3** prudent, cautious; stingy, wary *la17-*. **4** reliable, loyal, trustworthy; steadfast, resolute; steady, sure *la14-19, 20- NE T SW Bor*. **5** assured, convinced, certain; inevitable *la14-19, 20- Sh NE SW*. **6** *of a blow* hard and effective, telling *la15-19, 20- Sh Ork Bor*. **7** bad-tempered *20- Sh Ork*. **8** harsh, rigorous *19, 20- Ork*. **9** *in legal contexts* legally binding, trustworthy, sworn *la14-e17*. **10** skilled, expert *la15-16*. **11** confident, having a sense of security *la14-15*. **sickerly, siccarlie 1** safely, securely; firmly, steadily *la14-*. **2** reliably; certainly, assuredly; bindingly *la14-*. **3** sharply, severely *15-*. **4** prudently, cautiously; meanly *18-*. **5** accurately; painstakingly *15-*. **sickerness 1** safety, security; stability, permanence; certainty; assurance; caution, prudence; safe custody *la14-*. **2** security for the payment of a debt *15-16*. **mak sicker 1** to make sure or certain

15- **2** *law* to assure possession of property or a position by legal means *la14-e17*. [OE *sicor*]

siccar[1,3], **sicker**, †**sickir** /ˈsɪkər/ *adv* **1** safely, securely, firmly, stably; strongly, tightly *15-19, 20- NE T EC*. **2** as a matter of fact, certainly *e16*. **3** straight, true; accurately, precisely *la16-19*. **4** hard, forcefully *la15-18*. [see the adj]

†**sice, sys** *n games* the six on a dice; a throw of six *la15-16*. [ME *sis*, OFr *sis* six]

sich[1,1], **sigh**, *NE* **sech**, *Sh* **seich**, †**sych** /sɪx, sae; *NE* sɛx; *Sh* sɛx/ *n* an audible exhalation expressing weariness or unhappiness *15-*. [see the verb]

sich[1,2], **seich**, **saich**, **sech**, **sigh**, †**sicht** /sɪx, sex, sɛx, sae/ *v* to utter a sigh *la14-*. [OE *sīcan*]

sich *see* SIC[1,1], SIC[1,2], SIC[1,3]

sicht[1,1], **sight**, †**sycht** /sɪxt, sʌɪt/ *n* **1** the ability to see, eyesight, the field of vision, a thing seen, a spectacle; a look, view or glimpse *la14-*. **2** the act of seeing, a close look, an examination; supervision *la14-*. **3** judgement, opinion; outlook *15-*. **4** the reading of a document *la15-*. **5** *pl* those features of a place considered interesting for a visitor to see *17-*. **6** the pupil (of the eye) *19, 20- Sh T C*. **7** the eyes *la14-16*. **8** a place on a riverbank from which salmon can be watched *la18*. **sichtless**, †**sichtles 1** blind *la16-*. **2** out of sight *17-e19*. †**sichty** visible, easily seen, conspicuous *e16*. †**at one sicht** in a single look *la15-e17*. †**at the sicht of** under the supervision or scrutiny of *la15-e19*. **a sicht for sair een** a welcome or pleasing sight *19-*. [OE *gesiht*]

sicht[1,2], **sight**, †**sycht** /sɪxt, sʌɪt/ *v* **1** to view; to catch sight of *17-*. **2** to examine, scrutinize, inspect; to investigate *16-*. **3** to inspect (a newborn animal) to determine its sex *20- Sh Ork NE EC*. **4** to scrutinize (a person) indecently *la20-*. [see the noun]

sicht *see* SICH[1,2]

†**sichtis, sychtis** *npl* the armholes of a garment *e16*. [unknown]

sicir *see* SICCAR[1,2]

sick[1,1] /sɪk/ *n* a hand-reared lamb *20- NE*. **sickie, siccie** = SICK[1,1]. **sick lamb** = SICK[1,1]. [see the interj]

sick[1,2], **sic** /sɪk/ *interj* a call to a lamb or calf to come to be fed *20- NE T*. **siccie** = SICK[1,2]. [probably altered form of SOOK[1,3]]

sick *see* SEECK[1,1], SEECK[1,2]

sicker *see* SICCAR[1,1], SICCAR[1,2], SICCAR[1,3]

sickie *see* SAX

siclike[1,1], †**siclik**, †**syklyke** /ˈsɪklʌɪk/ *adj* **1** of the same or similar kind *15-*. **2** *of health or quality* unchanged; so-so, indifferent *20-*. [SIC[1,1] + -LIKE[2]]

siclike[1,2], †**syklyke** /ˈsɪklʌɪk/ *adv* **1** similarly, in like manner *la15-*. **2** *introducing a further member of a list* likewise, also *18*. [see the adj]

siclike[1,3], †**siclyk** /ˈsɪklʌɪk/ *pron* **1** of that kind, the like *la15-*. **2** *pl* people of that sort *la15-*. [see the adj]

siclyk *see* SICLIKE[1,3]

†**sic wise, syk wys** *adv* in such a way, to such an extent; in this way, in the same way *e16*. [SIC[1,1] + OE *wīse* manner]

sid *see* SEED[1,2], SUD

sidderwud *see* SITHERWOOD

siddle /ˈsɪdəl/ *v* to sidle; to slip *la19- T*. [variant of Eng *sidle*]

side[1], **syde**, †**syd**, †**syid** /sʌɪd/ *n* **1** a lateral surface, an edge; one half or part; a division, a faction *14-*. **2** *in place-names* a slope, a hillside *la11-*. **3** a district or region *16-*. **4** *pl* the female body in pregnancy or childbirth *15-16*. **side-band** *in a turf wall* a sod laid longitudinally *la18, 20- Sh*. †**side-bar** the bar or barrier in the Outer House of the Court of Session at which the rolls of the Lords Ordinary were called *la17-e19*. †**side-burd** a table placed at the side of a room *16-e17*. **side-casting** the act of ploughing along the side of a slope *20- T H&I SW*. †**side-ill** a paralytic disease of sheep *18-e19*. **side-legs** sidesaddle *19-*. **side-plough** *in Orkney* a plough with only one stilt *18, 19- historical*. **sidereps**, †**sydrapis** the traces used to harness a horse to a cart or plough *16-17, 18- Sh Ork N*. **side-schuil** a subsidiary school, especially in a remote part of a parish *19, 20- historical*. **i'da nicht side** during the night *la19- Sh*. **i'da saison side** in the course of the season *la19- Sh*. **nae sides tae no affectation** about; no airs and graces to *la20-*. †**on side** to one side, aside *la14-16*. **sidie for sidie** side by side, step for step *19*. **this side of time** in this world, while life lasts *17-*. [OE *sīde*]

side[2,1], †**syde** /sʌɪd/ *adj* **1** *especially of clothes or hair* long, hanging low *la14-19, 20- T WC*. **2** *of the lips* pendulous, wide *la15*. †**side-coat** a long coat with a long frock or tails, a greatcoat *18-19*. †**side-tailed** having a long tail or tails *18-e19*. **side upon** hard or severe on *19- NE*. **side and wide** extending in every way, long and large *19, 20- WC*. [OE *sīd* ample, wide]

side[2,2] /sʌɪd/ *adv* **1** *especially of clothing* low down, towards or on the ground *la15-19, 20- SW*. **2** proudly, boastfully *e16*. [OE *sīde* amply, widely]

sideleens *see* SIDELINS[1,3]

sidelins[1,1], **sidlings**, †**sidlens** /ˈsʌɪdləns, ˈsɪdləŋz/ *n* a sloping piece of ground, a hillside *la17-19, 20- NE C SW Bor*. [see the adverb]

sidelins[1,2], †**sidling** /ˈsʌɪdlənz/ *adj* **1** sidelong, oblique, moving or glancing sideways *la15-19, 20- Sh NE SW Bor*. **2** sloping, on an incline *19, 20- Ork NE SW*. [see the adverb]

sidelins[1,3], *Sh* **sideleens**, †**sidlings**, †**sidling** /ˈsʌɪdlənz; *Sh* ˈsʌɪdlɪnz/ *adv* **1** sideways, side on, to one side, side by side *15-*. **2** *of speech or look* indirectly, obliquely *la18-*. [SIDE[1], with suffix *-ling* and adv-forming suffix *-s*]

†**sidelins**[1,4], **sydelingis**, **sidling** *prep* at, from, along the side of *la15-e16*. [see the adv]

sidieweys, sidiewyse /ˈsʌɪdewez, ˈsʌɪdewaez/ *adv* sideways *19-*. [SIDE[1] + -IE[2] + *weys* (WEY[1])]

sidlens *see* SIDELINS[1,1]

sidling *see* SIDELINS[1,2], SIDELINS[1,3], SIDELINS[1,4]

sidlings *see* SIDELINS[1,1], SIDELINS[1,3]

sie *see* SEA, SEE, SYE[1,2]

-sie /zi, si, ze, se/ *suffix* **1** *with nouns* used as an endearment, especially with (diminutives of) proper names, *eg* Maisie, and in children's language in names of figures in chuckstones and hopscotch, *eg twosie* (TWA) *18-*. **2** *with adjs and nouns* forming an adjective with altered force, *eg bigsie* (BIG), *japsy* (JAUP[1,1]) *la18-*. [extended sense of -IE[1]]

siege[1,1], *NE* **seedge**, †**sege**, †**seige**, †**saige** /sidʒ/ *n* **1** *military* the blockade of a town or castle by an army to bring about its surrender *la14-*. **2** *building* the bench on which stones or slates are prepared *la18-*. **3** a seat; (the power or status of) a throne; the residence, authority, territory or jurisdiction of a bishop, a bishopric *la14-e17*. **4** a school or college class *la16-e17*. **5** a place where something is set or fixed; the berth of a boat in a harbour *15-16*. **6** a privy or latrine *16*. [OFr *siege* a seat]

siege[1,2], †**sege**, †**seige** /sidʒ/ *v* **1** to scold severely, berate *20- NE*. **2** to besiege *la14-e19*. **3** to set, install, place (a stone) *15-e16*. [see the noun]

sieth *see* SUITH[1,3]

sieve[1,1], †**siff**, †**seue**, †**seif** /sɪv/ *n* **1** a utensil for separating fine from coarse particles or straining liquids *15-*. **2** a sieve allegedly used by witches as a boat *la16-e19*. †**siff-wricht** a maker of sieves *16-17*. [OE *sife*]

sieve[1,2], †**siff**, †**seue** /sɪv/ *v* to sift, strain, pass through a sieve *la16-*. [see the noun]

siff see SIEVE[1.1], SIEVE[1.2]
siffer see SUFFER
sigg[1.1], *Ork* **sikk** /sɪg; *Ork* sɪk/ *v* to incite a dog to attack *20- Sh Ork N.* [see the interj]
sigg[1.2] /sɪg/ *interj* an exclamation to incite a dog to attack *la19- Sh T.* [altered form of SEEK[1]]
sigg[2] /sɪg/ *n* a callus *la19- Sh Ork.* [Norw dial *sigg* pig-skin, bacon-rind]
sigh see SICH[1.1], SICH[1.2]
sight see SICHT[1.1], SICHT[1.2]
sign[1.1], †**sing**, †**syng**, †**syne** /sʌɪn/ *n* 1 an identifying mark, symbol, emblem or banner *15-*. 2 a gesture, a signal, an omen *la14-*. 3 a (legal) signature *15-e17*. [AN *seigne*]
sign[1.2], †**sing** /sʌɪn/ *v* to make a sign, signal, indicate; to confirm with a signature *la15-*. [AN *seigner* or from the noun]
signakle see SINACLE
signature, †**signatour**, †**signator** /'sɪgnətʃər/ *n* 1 a person's name handwritten as a means of authentication *19-*. 2 *law* a document presented to the Baron of Exchequer as the ground of a royal grant to the person in whose name it was presented; originally (before 1603) a warrant signed by the monarch *la15-19*. [MFr *signature*, Lat *signātūra*]
signet[1.1], †**seignet** /'sɪgnət/ *n* 1 a small seal, especially one fixed in a finger-ring *la14-*. 2 one of the Crown seals of Scotland, originally the small seal of the sovereign used mainly for private correspondence *15-*. 3 a signet-ring *la15-*. 4 the seal of the Court of Session *17-*. 5 the wax impression of a signet *la15-e17*. [AN *signet*]
signet[1.2] /'sɪgnət/ *v* 1 to stamp (a letter or document) with a SIGNET[1.1] (sense 5) *la15-*. 2 the symbol of the authority of the Court of Session *17-*. 3 *law* to stamp a document or letter with a signet *la15-17*. [see the noun]
sik see SIC[1.1], SIC[1.3], SEEK[1]
sike see SYKE
sikk see SIGG[1.1]
sikker see SICCAR[1.2]
sikkynd see SICCAN[1.1]
silder see SILLER[1.1]
†**sile**[1], **syle** *v* to cover (the eyes or sight), hide, conceal; to deceive, mislead *la15-17*. [OFr *ciller* to blink; to sew up a hawk's eyes; compare Fr *cil* an eyelash]
sile[2.1], †**seyl** /sʌɪl/ *n* a sieve, especially for milk *la19- WC SW Bor.* [ME *syle*, ON **síl*]
sile[2.2], **seil** /sʌɪl/ *v* to pass (a liquid, especially milk) through a sieve *18-*. [compare Norw *sila* or from the noun]
sile[3], **sill** /sʌɪl, sɪl/ *n* the newly-hatched young of fish, especially herring *18-*. [ON *síld* herring, and compare Swed dial *sil* the young of fish]
sile[4], †**sill**, †**syl** /sʌɪl/ *n* a wooden beam, a roof rafter, usually one of a pair *14-19, 20- Bor.* [probably OE *sȳl* a pillar, a column]
sile[5], **syle** /sʌɪl/ *n* a bar fixed across the eye on the underside of an upper millstone and fitted on top of the spindle of the lower stone *la19- Sh Ork.* **aff o da sile** out of sorts *20- Sh.* [Norw dial *sigle*]
sile[6], **syle**, **soil**, †**sulȝe**, †**suilȝe**, †**sol** /sʌɪl, sɔɪl/ *n* 1 an area, a region; the source of a people, a place, a (native) country *16-*. 2 the (vegetative) surface of the ground; earth, soil *15-*. 3 (the whole extent) of the lands or acreage of an estate or community; sometimes the land (arable or grazing) in contradistinction to the buildings *la14-17*. 4 the land belonging to an individual *15-e17*. [AN *soil*]
silence see SEELENCE[1.1], SEELENCE[1.2]
silens see SEELENCE[1.1]
silent see SEELENT
siling see SYLING

silkie see SELKIE
sill see SILE[3], SILE[4]
sillab see SYLLAB[1.1]
siller[1.1], **silver**, **silder**, †**siluer**, †**syluyr** /'sɪlər, 'sɪlvər, 'sɪldər/ *n* 1 silver, the precious metal; silver bullion; articles made of silver *la14-*. 2 money; cash; funds; wealth; originally, silver coin *la14-*. 3 the colour silver; *heraldry* the tincture argent *15-*. †**siller-bridal**, **siller-brydell** a wedding at which the guests pay for their entertainment as a contribution towards the new home *17-e19*. Compare *penny bridal* (PENNY). **Silver City** a nickname for Aberdeen *la19-*. **silver darlings** herring *20-*. †**siluer seik** penniless *la15*. [OE *seolfor*]
siller[1.2], **silver** /'sɪlər, 'sɪlvər/ *v* to pay, give money *20- Sh.* **sillered**, †**silverit** 1 decorated or covered with silver *la15-*. 2 *of hair* turned white or grey *19-*. 3 monied, wealthy *19, 20- NE C.* [see the noun]
siller[1.3], **silver**, †**sylver**, †**siluyr** /'sɪlər, 'sɪlvər/ *adj* 1 made or consisting of or having the colour or lustre of silver *la14-*. 2 *of payments, rents or duties* made or levied in money (rather than goods) *16-e19*. **siller-fish** the bib or pout *Trisopterus luscus la19- NE.* **siller gun** a small silver replica of a gun used as a shooting trophy, especially that presented to the Incorporated Trades of Dumfries and Kirkcudbright by James VI *la16- SW.* **siller shakers** quaking-grass *Briza media 19- EC SW Bor.* **silverwark**, **silverwork** articles made of silver *la15-*. **silver wullie** the pyramid shell *Gibbula cineraria 19, 20- Ork NE EC Bor.* [see the noun]
Sillerton Loon /'sɪlərtən 'lun/ *n* 1 nickname for one of the destitute boys who attended Robert Gordon's Hospital *18-19, 20- NE, historical*. 2 a student at Robert Gordon's College *la19- NE.* [after one of the school houses named in recognition of Robert Gordon of Silverton]
sillick see SILLOCK
sillie see SILLY
sillock, *Sh* **sillick**, *Ork* **sillo**, *N* **sellag**, **sellack**, †**sellok**, †**silluk** /'sɪlək; *Ork* 'sɪlo; *N* 'sɛləg, 'sɛlək/ *n* the coalfish *Pollachius virens* in its first year of life *16, 17- Sh Ork N.* **sillock bru** coalfish soup *20- Sh.* **sillo heuk** a bait-hook for sillocks *20- Ork.* **sillock oil** oil made from sillock livers *la19- Sh Ork.* †**sillock pock** a net bag for catching sillocks *la19.* †**sillock-pocker** a maker of sillock pocks *la19.* [probably SILE[3] + -OCK]
silly, †**sillie**, †**selie** /'sɪle/ *adj* 1 lacking physical strength or endurance, weak, feeble, delicate, sickly *la15-*. 2 foolish, lacking intelligence or sophistication *16-*. 3 *of things* weak, shaky, insubstantial; paltry, insignificant *la15-*. 4 having learning difficulties *17-*. 5 helpless, defenceless, unable to fend for oneself *15-19, 20- T C Bor.* 6 *of ground* unfertile; *of soil* poor in quality; frequently in place-names *la17-*. 7 deserving of pity or sympathy; suffering undeservedly *16-19.* 8 *of a person* humble, lowly, *la16-17.* **silly cuddies** the game of leapfrog *20- WC.* [variant with extended sense of SEELY]
silly see SEELY
silour see SYLOUR[1.1]
silt /sɪlt/ *v* to crave (a particular food) *20- Ork.* [compare Norw dial *sylt* hunger]
siluer see SILLER[1.1]
siluyr see SILLER[1.3]
silver see SILLER[1.1], SILLER[1.2], SILLER[1.3]
simit see SEMMIT
simmen[1.1], **simmon**, **simmond**, *Sh* **simmint** /'sɪmən, 'sɪmənd; *Sh* 'sɪmənt/ *n* a rope made of straw, heather or rushes, originally mainly used to hold down thatch *17- Sh Ork N.* **simmon clew** a ball of straw rope *la19- Sh Ork.* [ON *síma* a rope, a cord with -ing suffix or influence from Gael *sìoman*]

simmen¹·² /ˈsɪmən/ v to tie down thatch with straw ropes *la18- Ork N*. [see the noun]

simmer¹·¹, **summer**, †**somer**, †**somir**, †**symmer** /ˈsɪmər, ˈsʌmər/ n summer, the season between spring and autumn *la14-*. **simmer and winter** all year round *la15-*. [OE *sumor*]

simmer¹·², **summer**, †**sommer** /ˈsɪmər, ˈsʌmər/ v to spend the summer *la19-*. **simmer and winter** to adhere to, be faithful to; to go into at length and in great detail, discuss in all aspects; to be long-winded in telling a story *17-*. [see the noun]

simmer¹·³, **summer**, †**somer**, †**symmyr** /ˈsɪmər, ˈsʌmər/ adj belonging or relating to, occurring in, appropriate to, characteristic of summer *la15-*. **simmer blink** a momentary gleam or short spell of sunshine *17-19, 20- Sh T*. **simmer cloks** shimmering sun-beams *la19- Sh*. **simmer-cowts** a heat haze, the shimmering of the air on a hot day *la18-*. **simmer-dim** summer twilight when the sun barely sets before rising again *la19- Sh*. **simmer meill** oatmeal kept for use until harvest gave a new supply *16*. **simmer-mal** the first day of summer *la19- Sh*. **simmer-side** the summer season *20- Sh SW*. **simmer-snawdrap** the summer snowflake *Leucojum aestivum la19- Ork Bor*. †**simmer tre** a flower-bedecked pole erected during summer games *la16*. **summer-weed** bovine mastitis *20- NE C SW*. [see the noun]

†**simmer**², **sommer**, **summer** n 1 a packhorse *la14-e16*. 2 a main beam *la14-18*. 3 the central beam in the drying-floor of a kiln *la15-e19*. [AN *sumer*]

simmerset /ˈsɪmərsɛt/ n a somersault *la19- NE SW*. [EModE dial *simmerset*, altered form of Eng *somersault*]

Simmie see SYMIE

simmint see SIMMEN¹·¹

simmish /ˈsɪmɪʃ/ v to astonish; to bemuse *la19- Sh*. [unknown]

simmit see SEMMIT

simmon, **simmond** see SIMMEN¹·¹

simple, **semple**, †**simpill**, †**sempill** /ˈsɪmpəl/ adj 1 honest; of humble origins, lowly; modest *la14-*. 2 uneducated, illiterate; stupid *la14-*. 3 law involving no complication or further legal process; no more than the thing mentioned *15-18*. †**simple ward** law the oldest form of feudal land tenure, *ie* by military service, with various rights and obligations, especially that of the superior to uphold and draw the rents of the lands of a deceased vassal while the heir was not infeft or was a minor, as recompense for the loss of military services during this period *la17-18, 19 historical*. [OFr *simple*]

simpliciter /sɪmˈplɪsətər/ adv law simply, unconditionally, without reservation; absolutely *16-*. [Lat *simpliciter*]

simulate, †**simulat** /ˈsɪmjulət/ adj feigned, pretended based on false premises *la15-*. **simulately** deceitfully, fraudulently *la16-e18*. [Lat *simulāt-*, ptp stem of *simulāre* pretend]

sin¹, **son**, †**sone**, †**soune**, †**sonne** /sɪn, sʌn/ n a male child in relation to his parents; Christ, as the son of Mary or God; *as a mode of address* a young man *la14-*. **son-afore-the-father** a plant whose flowers appear before its leaves, mezereon *Daphne mezereum, Anemone hepatica*, flowering currant *Ribes 19, 20- NE Bor*. †**sonis of God Christian Church** believers *la15-16*. †**sonis of haly kirk Roman Catholic Church** baptized believers *15-16*. **son of the manse** a son of a Presbyterian minister *19-*. **the Sons of the Rock** 1 the natives of Dumbarton or Stirling *19- C*. 2 a nickname for Dumbarton Football Club *20-*. **the Sons** = *the Sons of the Rock* 2. [OE *sunu*]

sin²·¹, †**syn**, †**syne** /sɪn/ n 1 an action or behaviour seen as offensive to God; (a) violation of moral or religious principles or law *la14-*. 2 pity, a sense of sympathy or shame *la14-*. **hae nae sin o** to bear no blame or reproach for *la19, 20- Sh NE*. [OE *synn*]

sin²·², †**syn** /sɪn/ v to commit sin, act sinfully *la14-*. **sin yer soul** to incur the guilt of sin (especially by telling lies) *la19-*. [OE *syngian*]

sin see SUN¹·¹, SUNE¹·², SYNE²·¹, SYNE²·², SYNE²·³

†**sinacle**, **signakle** n 1 the sign of the cross *e16*. 2 an indication, vestige, trace *la18*. [ME *signacle*, AN *signacle*, Lat *signāculum*]

sincesyne see SINSYNE

sinder¹·¹, **sinner**, **sunner** /ˈsɪndər, ˈsɪnər, ˈsʌnər/ v 1 to separate, split, divide; to (cause to) break or burst apart *la15-*. 2 to part company, be divided; to part with (something) *16-*. 3 to hoe out overcrowded seedlings *20- NE*. **sindering** separating, parting, splitting up *la15-*. [OE *syndrian*]

†**sinder**¹·², **sounder**, **schunder** adj separate, various *la14-16*. **in sinder**, **in to sondir**, **ysundir** apart, asunder, in pieces *la14-e17*. [OE *onsundran* asunder, OE *sundor* separately]

sindie /ˈsɪndi, ˈsɪndɛ/ v colloquial to exclude for an indefinite period *la20-*. [reduced form of Lat *sine diē*]

sindra see SINDRY¹·²

sindrins, **sinerance** /ˈsɪndrɪnz, ˈsɪnərəns/ n the parting of roads, a fork in a road *19-*. [plural of the verbal noun from SINDER¹·¹]

sindry¹·¹, **sinnrie**, **sundry** /ˈsɪndri, ˈsɪnri, ˈsʌndri/ n several people; a number of persons or things indiscriminately *la14-*. **a an sindry**, **all and sindry** one and all, all collectively and severally *la14-*. [from the adj]

sindry¹·², **sundry**, **sindra**, †**syndry** /ˈsɪndrɛ, ˈsʌndrɛ, ˈsɪndrə/ adj 1 various, diverse; several *la14-*. 2 separate, distinct, apart and by itself *la14-*. [OE *syndrig*]

sindry¹·³, **sundry**, **sinnery**, **sinry** /ˈsɪndrɛ, ˈsʌndrɛ, ˈsɪnərɛ, ˈsɪnrɛ/ adv 1 separately, severally *la14-*. 2 asunder, apart, in or to pieces *la15-*. [OE *syndrige*]

sine see SYNE¹·¹, SYNE¹·²

sine quo non /ˈsʌɪnɛ ˈkwo ˈnon/ n law an indispensable person *la17-19*. [Lat *sine quō nōn* without whom not, after *sine quā nōn* without which not]

sinerance see SINDRINS

sing¹·¹ /sɪŋ/ n a whizzing blow, a wallop, a smack *20- NE Bor*. [see the verb]

sing¹·², †**syng** /sɪŋ/ v pt **sang**, ptp **sung**, †**song** to use the voice musically, sing; *Roman Catholic Church* to chant, intone mass *la14-*. **singin cake** a sweet biscuit given to children on Hogmanay in return for a song *la19- EC*. **singin e'en** Hogmanay, when children went from house to house singing songs for cakes or treats *19- T EC*. **lat sing** to let fly, hit out *20- NE T SW*. †**sing dool** to lament, bewail one's luck *la18-19*. **sing dumb** to keep silent *18-*. **sing sma** to adopt a deferential or submissive tone or attitude *19-*. **sing thrums**, **sing gray thrums** *of a cat* to purr *19- NE T WC*. [OE *singan*]

sing²·¹ /sɪŋ/ n the act of singeing or burning, a scorch, a burn *19- NE T WC*. [see the verb]

sing²·² /sɪŋ/ v pt **singit**, T **sang**, NE **sung** ptp **singit**, **sung** to singe; to cleanse, prepare for cooking *16-*. **singit** 1 scorched, burned *la16-*. 2 stunted, shrivelled, puny *la18-19, 20- T*. [OE *sengan*, confused with SING¹·²]

sing see SIGN¹·¹, SIGN¹·²

singlar see SINGULAR¹·¹

single¹·¹, **singel**, †**singill** /ˈsɪŋəl, ˈsɪŋɡəl/ n 1 a single thing or person *la19-*. 2 a handful or small bundle of gleaned corn *16-19, 20- WC Bor*. 3 the one-stone-thick upper part of a dry-stone wall *20- SW*. **singloo** = SINGLE¹·¹ (sense 2) *20- Ork*. [see the adj]

single¹·², **singel** /ˈsɪŋgəl, ˈsɪŋəl/ v **1** to separate; to select *17-*. **2** to thin out (seedlings, especially turnips) *19-*. **singling** *piping* the form in which a ground (theme) or variation is first played *20-*. **singlins** gleaned corn *la19- C Bor*. [see the adj]
single¹·³, **singel**, †**singill**, †**syngill** /ˈsɪŋəl, ˈsɪŋgəl/ adj **1** only one *la14-*. **2** not served with chips, by itself: ◊*single fish* ◊*single pudding 20-*. **3** unmarried; simple, plain, without specified status *la16-*. **4** scantily or thinly clad *20- Sh*. **5** *military* of the lowest rank *18-19*. **singly 1** separately, one by one *la18-*. **2** simply *la16*. **3** only, merely *17*. **4** sincerely, honestly *17-e18*. †**singill avail** *in feudal obligations* the payment exacted when heirs married without the consent of their superiors *16*. **single catechism**, **single carritch**, †**singill catechis**, †**singill cattichisholm** *Presbyterian Church* the Shorter Catechism without the scripture-proofs appended to each question *la16-*. **single-end** a one-roomed house or flat (within a tenement) *la19-*. **single escheat** *law* the forfeiture of movables to the Crown on conviction for murder, originally also for other crimes *17-*. **single-horse-tree** a swingletree of a plough to which the traces of a single horse are attached *la18- T SW Bor*. **single note** a one-pound banknote *19-*. †**single-soled**, †**singill-solit** *of footwear* with a single thickness of material in the sole *16-e19*. [OFr *single*]
singular¹·¹, †**singlar**, †**singuler**, †**singulair** /ˈsɪŋjələr, ˈsɪŋgjulər/ adj remarkable, exceptional; unique, individual; particular *la15-*. †**singular batell** = *singular combat la15-e17*. †**singular combat** single combat *la16-e19*. **singular successor** *law* a person who acquires heritable property, otherwise than by inheritance, *eg* by purchase *17-*. [ME *singuler*, OFr *singuler*, Lat *singulāris*]
†**singular**¹·² adv especially, exceptionally *la15-16*. [see the adj]
singuler *see* SINGULAR¹·¹
†**sinistrous** adj **1** designed to deceive or mislead; malicious, prejudiced; false *la16-17*. **2** evil, corrupt *la16-e18*. [EModE *sinister* with *-ous* suffix]
sink¹·¹ /sɪŋk/ n **1** a cesspit; a drain, a sewer *16-*. **2** a pit-shaft, a coal-pit *la16-*. **3** a basin with pipework allowing the supply and drainage of water *19-*. **4** a hollow, low-lying area, a marsh or bog *la16-19, 20- Sh*. [see the verb]
sink¹·², †**synk** /sɪŋk/ v *ptp* **sunk**, †**sonkyn 1** to become submerged; to descend, subside; to lower or immerse *la14-*. **2** to penetrate the mind or heart *la15-*. **3** to excavate a well or mineshaft *la16-*. **4** to imprecate, swear; to curse *la19- Sh SW Bor*. **5** to engrave a pattern on a die or stamp *16-17*. **sinker**, †**sinkar 1** a weight attached to the rope of the head-collar worn by a stalled horse *19-*. **2** a weight attached to the lower corners of a herring-net to make it sink *19- N NE*. **3** *coining* an engraver of designs of dies *16-17*. **4** a lead weight used on a stocking-frame *la17*. **sinksman**, †**synkeman** a person who excavates pit-shafts or wells *la17- EC*. **sinking sand**, †**sinkand sand** quicksand *16-*. †**sinking paper**, **sinkand paper** absorbent paper which allowed the ink to run or spread *la16-17*. **sunk-raip** the sole or messenger rope of a herring drift net *20 NE EC*. [OE *sincan*]
sinna, **sunna** /ˈsɪnə, ˈsʌnə/ n one of several varieties of seaside grass *la17, 19- Sh Ork*. **sinna-girse**, **sinny girse** long grass by the sea shore; couch grass *20- Sh Ork*. **sinna-peat** a fibrous, grassy peat *la19- Sh*. [Norw dial *sinegras*]
sinner *see* SINDER¹·¹
sinnery *see* SINDRY¹·³
sinnie¹, *WC* **seenie**, †**synny** /ˈsɪne; *WC* ˈsine/ n senna, (the dried leaves of) a shrub of the genus *Senna*, used medicinally *la16-*. [OFr *séné*, Lat *senna*]

sinnie² /ˈsɪni/ n a small kiln for drying corn *la19-*. [perhaps a variant of SORNIE]
sinnie *see* SINNON
sinnle *see* SEENDIL
sinnon, **shinnon**, †**sinnie**, †**sennon**, †**seinʒe** /ˈsɪnən, ˈʃɪnən/ n a sinew or tendon *la14-*. [altered form of OE *seonowe* oblique case of *seono*]
sinnrie *see* SINDRY¹·¹
sinry *see* SINDRY¹·³
sinse, **sense**, †**sence** /sɪns, sɛns/ n (a faculty of) perception, feeling or reason; understanding; meaning *la15-*. [ME *sens*, AN *sens*, Lat *sensus*]
sinsyne, †**sensyne**, †**synsyne**, †**sincesyne** /sɪnˈsʌɪn/ adv **1** since then, from or after that time *la14-*. **2** ago *la16-*. [SYNE²·² + SYNE²·¹]
sint *see* SCENT
sinty *see* SEEVEN
sip /sɪp/ v to eat in spoonfuls or in large mouthfuls *la18-19, 20- N NE T*. [perhaps extended sense of Eng *sip* or altered form of SUP¹·²]
sipe *see* SYPE¹·¹
sipher *see* CEEPHER
†**sipling**, **sipplyn**, **suppline**, **sapling** n **1** a young tree *16-*. **2** a length of wood, a staff *la15-17*. [SAP¹ with *-ling* suffix, perhaps with influence from OFr *souplin* a shoot of a tree]
sippe *see* SIP
sipper *see* SUPPER¹·¹
sipple *see* SIRPLE¹·¹, SIRPLE¹·²
sipplyn *see* SIPLING
sir, †**schir** /sɪr/ n **1** a title of a knight or nobleman *la14-*. **2** *term of address* used between men of equal rank *la14-*. [variant of OFr *sire*]
siree *see* SWARREE
†**sirken**, **sirkent** adj fond of one's comforts, coddling oneself *19*. [unknown]
sirname *see* SURNAME
sirp /sɪrp/ n a soggy, wet condition *la19- Sh Ork*. **sirpan** soaking wet *20- Sh Ork*. [Norw dial *surp* slush, a wet mass]
†**sirple**¹·¹, **sipple** n a tipple *19*. [see the verb]
sirple¹·², †**sipple** /ˈsɪrpəl/ v to sip continuously, go on drinking in small quantities, tipple *17-19, 20- EC Bor*. [frequentative form of SIP]
sirs, **sirse** *see* SAIR'S
siruice *see* SERVICE
sis, **sise** *see* SIZE
†**sissok** n a woman of low character, a concubine, a mistress *la15*. [unknown]
sist¹·¹ /sɪst/ n *law* a stay or suspension of a proceeding; an order by a judge to stay judgement or execution *la17-*. [see the verb]
sist¹·² /sɪst/ v **1** *law* to stop, stay or halt (a legal process or procedure) by judicial decree *17-*. **2** *law* to present oneself before a court, appear for trial or as a litigant; to summon or cite to appear in a court case *17-*. **3** to stop, end; to come or bring to a standstill; to desist *17-19*. [Lat *sistere* to make to stand or stop]
sistance /ˈsɪstəns/ n the smallest possible quantity (of food) *20- Ork N*. [aphetic form of Eng *subsistence* or reduced form of *sustenance*]
sistentation *see* SUSTENTATION
sister¹, †**cister** /ˈsɪstər/ n **1** a female sibling *la14-*. **2** a female (person or thing) related in some way; a fellow female, a nun *la14-*. **sister bairn** the child of a parent's sister, a cousin; a sister's child *la16-17, la18- Sh N*. †**sister-dochter** a niece *15-17*. †**sister-germane** a full sister, a sister by both parents *16-17*. **sister-part** a daughter's share of heritable

property (half that of a son) *16- Sh Ork.* **sister son, sister's son** a nephew *la14-19, 20- Sh Ork.* [OE *sweostor*]

†**sister**² *n* a musical instrument, perhaps stringed and played with a plectrum or quill *16.* [perhaps Lat *cithara*]

sistie-moose /ˈsɪstəmus/ *n* a bird; in some areas, the wren *20- Sh.* [unknown; perhaps confusion of Eng *titmouse* and TITTIE]

sit¹·¹ /sɪt/ *n* **1** a period or occasion of sitting *17-.* **2** a subsidence of land or property, frequently due to mining work *la17-19, 20- NE C.* [see the verb]

sit¹·², †**syt**, †**sitt**, †**sett** /sɪt/ *v pt* **sat**, *WC SW Uls* **sut**, †**satt**, *ptp* also *Sh Ork N NE T C* **sitten**, *NE WC SW Bor* **sutten**, **sat**, †**settin**, †**syttyn**, †**yset 1** to be or remain seated; to remain, stay *la14-.* **2** to suit, fit, be appropriate *la14-.* **3** to remain in occupation (of a tenancy); to take up residence; to dwell *15-.* **4** to consider, arbitrate, come to a decision; *of a judge, meeting* to convene, be in session *la15-.* **5** *of a bird* to perch, roost *la15-.* **6** *of a doctor* to be available for consultation *20-.* **7** *of plants* to stop growing or developing, be stunted *18-19, 20- NE T SW.* **8** to ignore (a demand) *la15-19.* **9** to fail to act, delay; to wait *la15-e18.* **10** to occupy the papal or an episcopal see *15-17.* **11** to press on (a person), oppress, be a burden to *la15-16.* †**sitter** a person who regularly occupies a seat in a church *19.* †**sit-house, sitt-house, sait hous** a dwelling-house *15-e19.* **sitsicker** a species of crowfoot, especially *Ranunculus acris 19, 20- NE.* †**ewill sittin** having a bad seat on horseback *la16.* **sit at peace** to sit still *19-.* **sit awhile** to pay a social visit *20- Ork N.* **sit below** to attend the church of, listen to the preaching of (a particular minister) *19, 20- T SW.* †**sit by** to wait *e16.* **sit doon 1** to be seated, seat oneself *la14-.* **2** to settle in a place or situation, make one's home *la15-.* **3** to become bankrupt *la19- NE EC.* **4** *of a court, school, meeting etc* to convene, begin its session *la15-e19.* **5** *of the wind* to drop, moderate *la16-19.* **6** *of a ship* to sink *16-e17.* **7** *of sheep or horses* to come to the end of their useful life, break down *16.* **sit doon on yer knees** to kneel *la14-.* **sitten doon 1** *of an illness* persistent, chronic *19, 20- C Bor.* **2** sunk, subsided *20- Ork.* **sit in** to draw your chair in or towards; to take a seat at table, participate in a meal *19-.* **sit in aboot** = *sit in 19- NE T.* **sit in the britchins** *see* BRITCHIN. **sit intae** to pull a chair towards a fire *la19-.* **sit on 1** to stay on, remain; *of a tenant at the end of a lease* to remain in occupation of the place leased *la19, 20- Sh NE T.* **2** *of food* to stick to the bottom of the pan; to become singed *19, 20- T WC SW Bor.* **sit on someone's coat-tails** to depend on or make use of someone else; to sponge *la18-.* **sit on yer knees** = *sit doon on yer knees* †**sit on your owne cott taill** to pay your own way *la16.* **sit tae** to sit at a table to eat *20-.* **sit tae yer meat** to sit at a table to eat *18-.* †**sit with** to put up with, tolerate *la15-e18.* **sit up 1** to stay up late or overnight *la15-.* **2** to watch over a corpse before burial *20- EC SW Bor.* **3** to come to a halt (in an endeavour) *la17.* **sutten on** stunted, dwarfed *19- SW Bor.* †**weill sittin** having a good seat on horseback *e16.* [OE *sittan*]

sit *see* SUIT²

sit-doon¹·¹ /sɪtˈdun/ *n* **1** a chance or spell of being seated, a seat *20-.* **2** a home, a (marriage) settlement, a situation or position (in life) *la19- NE T.* [see the verb]

site *see* SYTE¹·¹

sitevate *see* SEETUATE

sitfast¹·¹, †**sitt-fast** /ˈsɪtfast/ *n* **1** a stone deeply and firmly embedded in the earth *19- N SW Bor.* **2** a tenacious plant which is hard to eradicate, *eg* the creeping crowfoot *Ranunculus repens la18- C SW Uls.* **3** a deeply embedded, recalcitrant attitude *la17.* [SIT¹·² + FEST¹·²]

†**sitfast**¹·² *adj* (firmly) seated; *especially of stones* firmly embedded in the earth *la18-19.* [see the noun]

†**sith**¹, **syith** *n pl* also **syis sys 1** a time, an occasion *la14-16.* **2** *pl expressing multiplication* times *15-e17.* [OE *sið*]

†**sith**²·¹ *prep* since *16.* [reduced form of OE *siððan*]

sith²·² /sɪθ/ *conj* since, considering (that) *15-.* [see the prep]

sith *see* SCYTHE, SUITH¹·³

sithe /saɪð/ *n* a chive *Allium schoenoprasum 20- C SW Bor.* [ME *sive*, MFr *cive*]

sithean /ˈʃiən/ *n* a natural or artificial mound, frequently a prehistoric burial place; a fairy hill or mound; frequently in place-names *la19-.* [Gael *sìthean*]

sithement *see* SYTHMENT

sitherwood, sidderwud /ˈsɪðərwud, ˈsɪdərwud/ *n* southernwood *Artemisia abrotanum la19- WC SW Bor.* [altered form of Eng *southernwood*]

sitivation *see* SEETUATION

sitooterie /sɪˈtutərə/ *n humorous* an area where people can sit outside; a patio, conservatory; originally an alcove or recess where people might sit out at a dance *20-.* [SIT¹·² + OOT¹·⁴ with noun-forming suffix]

sitten, sutten, †**sittin** /ˈsɪtən, ˈsʌtən/ *adj* **1** *of an egg on which a bird has been sitting* with a developed chick inside, near to hatching *20-.* **2** *of tea* stewed, strong and bitter *20- N.* [participial adjective from SIT¹·²]

sitten *see* SIT¹·²

sitt-fast *see* SITFAST¹·¹

sittin doon /ˈsɪtən ˈdun/ *n* **1** a settlement in marriage *20- N T C SW.* **2** a bankruptcy *la19- NE T.* [verbal noun from SIT DOON¹·²]

situacioun *see* SEETUATION

situate, sitwat *see* SEETUATE

siven, sivven /ˈsɪvən/ *n* the wild raspberry *Rubus idaeus 19, 20- NE SW.* †**sivvens, sibbens** a venereal disease characterized by raspberry-like sores *la18-19.* [Gael *suibhean* variant of *suibheag* a raspberry; a venereal sore]

siven *see* SEEVEN

siver *see* SYVER

siveral *see* SEVERAL

sivven *see* SIVEN

six, sixareen, sixmonth *see* SAX

sixt, sixth *see* SAXT

size, †**sise,** †**sis** /saez/ *n* **1** dimensions, magnitude *16-.* **2** a jury *la14-17.* **3** a duty on imported goods *la16-18.* **4** an assize, a judicial inquiry *la15-17.* †**size boll** an amount or measure of duty payable *la16-18.* †**syse hering** *fishing* a royalty of herring due to the Crown *15-e17.* Compare *assise herring* (ASSIZE). [extended senses of OFr *sise* an assize]

sizzie *see* SUSSIE¹·¹

sizzon *see* SAISON¹·¹, SAISON¹·²

sjuer *see* SHOO¹·¹

skaab /skɑb/ *n* bare, stony ground; a flat rock in the sea; the bottom of the sea *la19- Sh.* [variant of SCAUP¹·¹]

skaal *see* SCAULD¹·²

skaave /skɑv/ *v* to scrape, shave, scratch, abrade; to hoe *20- Sh Ork.* **skaavins** *food* the scrapings from the bottom of a pot *la20- Sh.* Compare SKOVINS. [Norw dial *skava*]

skade *see* SCAWD

skae /ske/ *v* to happen, come to pass *la19- Sh.* [Norw, Dan *ske*, MLG *schen*]

skaed *see* SKAITH¹·²

skaerd *see* SKAIR²·¹, SKAIR²·²

skaff *see* SCAFF¹·², SCAFF²

†**skaffinger, scawanger** *n* a street-sweeper or rubbish collector *la15-e18.* Compare SCAFFIE. [altered form of ME *scavager*, AN *scawager*]

skaich see SKECH¹·²
skaichen see SKEICHEN¹·¹, SKEICHEN¹·²
skaid see SKAITH¹·¹
skaif see SCAFF²
skaigh see SKECH¹·¹
skaik¹·¹ /skek/ *n* a smear, a daub, a streak *20- NE T.* [unknown]
skaik¹·² /skek/ *v* to smear, plaster with a soft wet substance, streak, blotch *19- NE T.* [unknown]
skaiken see SKEICHEN¹·²
skaikit, skawkit, †skeikit /ˈskekət, ˈskɔkət/ *adj* streaked, striped; daubed, besmirched *la16-19, 20- NE T.* [unknown; compare SKAIK¹·²]
skail¹·¹, †scaill /skel/ *n* 1 the dismissal or dispersal of a group of people *17-.* 2 a strong, scattering or driving wind *la18-.* 3 a dispersed company *la14.* [see the verb]
skail¹·², skale, skyle, †skell, †scail, †scale /skel, skʌɪl/ *v* 1 to scatter, throw, distribute *la14-.* 2 to disperse, discharge, dismiss; *of a group* to separate, break up, depart *la14-.* 3 *military* to rout, disband, scatter, put to flight; to raise a siege *la14-.* 4 to dispose of possessions *la15-.* 5 to pour (out), spill (liquid); to shed (tears or blood); *of liquid* to spill, overflow, leak; *of rain* to fall *la15-.* 6 to come apart, become detached, be dispersed *la16-.* 7 to waste, squander *17-.* 8 *farming* to spread seed, manure or peats *19-.* 9 *farming* to plough ground in order to flatten rigs *la18- N NE T C SW.* 10 to burst (a garment) at a seam *la18- N NE T.* 11 to spread rumours or news, disseminate information *la14-e16.* 12 to remove (a responsibility), annul (a proclamation), change (a decision) *16.* 13 to spread out sails *e16.* 14 to let hair hang loose *e16.*
skailwin, skilewin 1 a scattering wind, a hurricane *la19, 20- H&I.* 2 a spendthrift *20- H&I.* [perhaps related to ON *skilja* to separate, divide]
skail see SCALE¹
skaildrake see SKELLDRAKE
skaill see SKEEL²
skaim see SCHEME¹·¹, SCHEME¹·²
skainie, *N* **skeany,** *N NE* **scangie,** *SW* **skeenie, †skenʒe, †skainye** /ˈskeni; *N SW* ˈskini; *N NE* also ˈskanji/ *n* (a quantity of) thread or string; coarse yarn; pack-thread; twine *la15-.* [MFr *escaigne*]
skair¹·¹, share, †scare, †schare /sker, ʃer/ *n* 1 a portion, a part *la15-.* 2 a part of a business venture owned or invested in by a number of people in common; originally a portion of the cargo of a ship *la15-.* 3 a portion of the common land let or feued *la15-e19 SW.* [ME *shar* a portion, a share; perhaps with influence from MDu *scare* a share in common grazing ground, and compare SKAIR¹·²]
skair¹·², skare, share, †scair /sker, ʃer/ *v* to divide, distribute, possess or participate in equally; to share *la15-.* [from the noun, perhaps with influence from ON *skera* to cut]
skair²·¹, *Sh* **skaerd, †skayr** /sker; *Sh* skerd, skjard/ *n* 1 the joint at the end of the shaft of a golf club where the head is fixed *la19-.* 2 a splice or scarf-joint joining two pieces of wood *la16- Sh N NE T EC.* 3 a section of a fishing rod *19- Sh N T EC.* 4 a thumb-knot join in a fishing line between the *tippin* (TIP¹·²) and the SNOOD¹·¹ (sense 2) *20- NE.* [ON *skar-* a score, a notch, an incision, with influence from Norw dial *skar* a scarf-joint, and Norw *skard* a cut]
skair²·², *Sh* **skaerd** /sker; *Sh* skerd, skjard/ *v* 1 to splice (two pieces of wood etc) *la18-19, 20- Sh Ork N.* 2 to splice (a golf club) *la19- EC.* 3 to join the *tippin* (TIP¹·²) to the SNOOD¹·¹ (sense 2) of a fishing line with a thumb-knot *20- NE.* [see the noun]
Skairsbrugh warning see SCARBOROUGH WARNING
Skairsburn warning see SKYREBURN WARNING

skair scone /ˈsker ˈskɔn/ *n* a scone made of oatmeal, flour, beaten egg and milk *19- NE SW.* [altered form of *care* as in CARCAKE, to alliterate with SCONE¹·¹]
skait see SKAITH¹·²
†skaitbird *n* a bird, possibly the Arctic skua *Stercorarius parasiticus 16.* [probably; the noun corresponding to SKITE¹·² + BIRD¹]
skaitch see SKETCH¹·¹
skaith¹·¹, skaid, scathe, †skath, †skeath /skeθ, sked/ *n* 1 damage, hurt, injury, harm *la14-.* 2 damage for which compensation is sought; damages including the costs of legal action *la14-.* 3 damage to property caused by trespassing animals; the act or offence of trespass *15-19.* 4 a cause of harm; a matter for regret *15-19.* 5 harm or injury attributed to witchcraft or the evil eye *17-19.* 6 financial loss; loss of profits *15-17.* 7 (a liability for) compensation paid for a person's trouble or services *18.* **†scatheful, scathefu** harmful, injurious *la14-19.* **†scatheless, scatheles** unharmed; not subject to financial loss or penalty *la14-e19.* **†quhat skath** how dreadful *e16.* [ON *skaðe*]
skaith¹·², †scathe /skeð/ *v ptp* **†skait †skaed** 1 to harm, injure, damage *la14-.* 2 to subject to financial loss, penalize, fine *la14-e19.* [ON *skaða* to hurt, be the source of pain]
skaivie see SKAVIE¹·¹, SKAVIE¹·²
skaken see SKEICHEN¹·³
skald see SCAUD¹·², SCAULD¹·¹, SCAULD¹·²
skalder¹·¹ /ˈskɑldər/ *n* a loud shrill laugh *la20- Sh.* Compare SKILDER¹·¹. [see the verb]
skalder¹·² /ˈskɑldər/ *v* to laugh *20- Sh Ork.* Compare SKILDER¹·². [Norw dial *skaldra*]
†skalding, scalding *n* (the skin or carcass of) a type of sheep *la14-17.* [perhaps *scald* (SCAWD), with noun-forming suffix]
skaldock see SKELDOCK
skale see SCALE¹, SCALE³, SKAIL¹·²
skallet /ˈskɑlət/ *adj* bald, hairless *20- Sh.* [Norw dial *skollutt*]
skalva /ˈskɑlvə/ *n* soft flaky snow *la19- Sh.* [Norw dial *skavl* a snowdrift]
skambill see SKEMMEL¹·¹
skamelar see SCAMBLER
skant see SCANT¹·¹, SCANT¹·³, SCANT¹·⁴
skap see SCAUP¹·¹
skape see SKEP¹·¹
skar, scaar /skar/ *n* 1 the remains of a candle wick *la19-e20 Sh.* 2 a small quantity *la19- Sh.* [Norw *skar*]
skar see SCARE¹·², SCARE¹·³, SCAUR¹
skare /sker/ *n* a swathe of hay, the amount cut by a sweep of the scythe *20- Ork N.* [probably ON *skári*]
skare see SKAIR¹·², SKIRE¹·²
skarie /ˈskere/ *n* a type of scone *20- NE.* [shortened form of SKAIR SCONE + -IE¹]
skarp, scarp /skɑrp/ *n* a bare barren piece of ground *20- Sh Ork.* **skarpy** *of ground* bare, barren *20- Ork.* **skarpid, skarpit** *of ground* grazed bare *20- Sh.* [compare Norw *skarp* barren]
skarrach /ˈskɑrəx/ *n* a gusty shower of rain; a light fall of snow *19- T EC SW.* [unknown; perhaps related to SCOUR¹]
skarrik, skorek /ˈskɑrək, ˈskorək/ *n* a gap or cleft in rocks *la19- Sh.* [Norw *skar* with -OCK suffix]
skars see SCARCE¹·¹, SCARCE¹·²
skarsment see SCARCEMENT
skart see SCART¹·¹
skarth see SCART², SCART³
skat see SKATT¹·¹, SKATT¹·²
skate, †scate, †scait /sket/ *n* 1 a fish of the genus *Raja 16-.* 2 *derogatory* a stupid or objectionable person *18-.*

skate

†**skatebread** a kind of very small fish *la17*. **skate bree** the water in which skate has been boiled, skate soup, said to have aphrodisiac and curative properties *la19, 20- SW*. **skate-bubble** a jellyfish *20- H&I EC*. **skate-purse** the ovarium of a skate *19-*. †**skate-rumple** the part of the backbone of a skate above the root of the tail *16-19*. [ON *skata*]
skate *see* SKEET[4.1], SKEET[4.2]
skater, N skeeter /'sketər, 'skitər/ *n* a water beetle *20-*. [Eng *skate* to glide on ice, with agent suffix]
skath *see* SKAITH[1.1]
skathie, †**skethie** /'skaðe/ *n* a rough shelter, especially a fence or wall used as a windbreak in front of a door *e17, 19-NE Bor*. [Gael *sgàth* a wattle fence or door , a shelter + -IE[1]]
skatt[1.1]**,** †**skat,** †**scat,** †**scot** /skat/ *n* **1** a land tax levied on udal property *la15- Sh Ork N*. **2** a tax or exaction *16-e17*. **3** a charge made on merchant ships to cover communal losses *la16-e17*. **4** a municipal tax levied on burgesses to defray communal expenses *la16*. **skattland** *in Shetland and Orkney* **1** quarter of an URISLAND *la15-17, 20- historical*. **2** land on which SKATT[1.1] (sense 1) is payable *16-*. †**scat and lot, scot and lot, skott and lott** = SKATT[1.1] (sense 4) *la15-17*. [ON *skattr*]
skatt[1.2]**,** †**skat,** †**scat** /skat/ *v* **1** to assess udal land for tax, impose a tax on udal land *16- Sh Ork*. **2** to exact (a bribe or payment); to oppress by exactions *la15-16*. **3** to contribute to local taxes on burgesses or on shipping *la16-17*. †**scat and lot, scot and lot** to pay the contribution required of burgesses or shipping *la15-17*. [see the noun]
skattald, †**scattald,** †**scathald,** †**scathold** /'skatəld/ *n* **1** the common pasture-land of a community *la16- Sh Ork*. **2** *in Shetland and Orkney* a group of townships and the land belonging to them; the members of such a community *la16-e18*. [derivative of SKATT[1.1]]
skattir, skatyr *see* SCATTER[1.2]
skav /skav/ *n* an overhanging rock, a concave cliff-face *20- Sh*. †**scaavie** = SKAV *la19*. [compare ON *skafa* to shave, pare]
skave /skev/ *adj* squint, askew *la19- Sh*. [Norw dial *skeiv*]
skavie[1.1]**, skaivie** /'skeve/ *n* **1** a trick, a piece of mischief *19- NE*. **2** a mishap, an accident; a disappointment *la19- NE*. [unknown]
skavie[1.2]**, skaivie,** †**skeevie** /'skeve/ *v* to rush about; to swan around in an idle, silly or ostentatious way; to roam *la19- NE*. [unknown]
skavle /'skevəl/ *v* **1** to twist; to knock awry or out of shape *la19- Sh*. **2** to walk with a crooked, twisting gait; to totter, reel *la19, 20- Ork N*. [frequentative verb from SKAVE]
skawd *see* SCAWD
skawkit *see* SKAIKIT
skayr *see* SKAIR[2.1]
skean, skeen, sgian, *Sh* **skune,** *Sh* **skoan,** †**skene** /skin, 'skiən; *Sh* skøn; *Sh* skon/ *n* a Highlander's short-bladed black-hilted sheath-knife or dagger *la16-*. **skunie** a knife *19- Sh*. †**skeen occle** a knife concealed in the upper part of the sleeve under the armpit *18-e19*. [Gael, IrGael *sgian*]
skean dhu, sgian dubh /skiən 'du/ *n* a short-bladed knife usually worn in the stocking as part of male Highland dress *19-*. [Gael *sgian dubh* black knife]
skeany *see* SKAINIE
skeath *see* SKAITH[1.1]
skeb *see* SKEP[1.1]
skech[1.1]**, skaigh** /skex/ *n* **1** the act of scrounging, pilfering; what has been obtained in this way *la19- NE C SW*. **2** a scrounger, a sponger *la19- NE C*. **on the skaigh** on the prowl, scrounging *20-*. [perhaps altered form of ME *skek* a raid, AN *eskek* booty, plunder]

skeet

skech[1.2]**, skaich** /skex/ *v* **1** to obtain in an underhand way, by wheedling or stealing; to scrounge; to frequently wander about in search of (food), scrounge (a meal) *19-*. **2** to go about in a silly, vain, idle way *la19- NE*. **skaicher** a scrounger *19- NE T WC*. [see the noun]
skechan *see* SKEICHEN[1.3]
skeechan /'skixən/ *n* an intoxicating malt liquor produced in the later stages of brewing and formerly used by bakers instead of yeast; sometimes mixed with treacle etc and sold as a kind of beer *19-*. [altered form of *keechan* (CAOCHAN)]
skeeg[1] /skig/ *n* the smallest amount (especially of liquid), the least drop *la18- T C Uls*. **skeegle** a small drop *20- T WC*. [unknown]
skeeg[2.1] /skig/ *n* a blow, a smack, a spanking *19- NE*. [see the verb]
skeeg[2.2]**,** †**skeyg** /skig/ *v* **1** to whip, strike, slap, spank *la18- NE*. **2** to hurry, stride along *19*. [probably onomatopoeic]
skeel[1.1]**, skill** /skil, skɪl/ *n* **1** (practical) knowledge and ability, expertise, discrimination, experience *la14-*. **2** skill in the art of healing, frequently of a non-professional (originally supernatural or illicit) kind *la16-*. **3** reason; what is reasonable or just; a reason or cause *la14-16*. **hae skeel o** to be experienced in, have practice in; to have a liking for or favourable opinion of *la18-*. **man of skill** = *person of skill 19-*. **person of skill** an expert in a subject, especially one called in by a court *19-*. **woman of skill** = *person of skill 18-*. [ON *skil* distinction]
skeel[1.2]**, skill** /skil, skɪl/ *v* **1** to scan expertly, investigate; to determine the weather from observable signs *20- NE*. **2** to show skill in, understand, explain *15-17*. [ON *skilja* to distinguish]
skeel[2]**,** †**skeil,** †**skaill** /skil/ *n* a tub or bucket, frequently with handles formed by elongated staves; a scoop *16-19, 20- NE T EC*. [ME *skele* a pail, ON *skóla* a pail]
skeel *see* SCHULE, SKYLE[1.2]
skeeling-goose, †**skilling-guis** /'skilɪŋ gus/ *n* the shelduck *Tadorna tadorna la16-19, 20- Sh Uls*. [unknown; compare SKELLDRAKE]
skeely, skilly, †**skillie** /'skili, 'skɪle/ *adj* **1** skilled, experienced, practised *la16-*. **2** having real or supposed skill in the art of healing *19, 20- NE EC*. **skeeliest,** †**skilliest** one who is the most skilled (at something) *17-*. **skilly man** a man credited with healing abilities *19, 20- N NE*. **skeely wife** a woman credited with great or supernatural healing powers, especially one called to emergencies or confinements *la18-*. [SKEEL[1.1] + -IE[2]]
skeely *see* SCAILIE
skeen *see* SKEAN
skeenie *see* SKAINIE
skeen occle *see* SKEAN
skeepack, †**skippack** /'skipək/ *n* the children's game of tig *la19- N*. Compare SKIPPIE. [Gael *sgiabag* a hasty touch]
skeer *see* SCARE[1.2], SCARE[1.3], SKIRE[1.3]
skeerock *see* SKOURICK
skeet[1.1] /skit/ *n* a squirt of liquid; an ejaculation of semen *20- Sh*. [see the verb]
skeet[1.2] /skit/ *v* **1** to squirt, eject (liquid) in a jet or stream *la19- Sh Ork N*. **2** to tease *20- Ork*. **skeeter** the squid *20- N*. **skeeto 1** a water-pistol *20- Ork*. **2** a cuttlefish or squid *20- Ork*. **skeetik** *1* a cuttlefish or squid *la19- Sh*. **2** a nickname for a native or inhabitant of Lerwick *20- Sh*. [Norw *skyte* to shoot]
skeet[2] /skit/ *n* diarrhoea *20- Sh N*. Compare SKIT[2.1]. [Norw dial *skita* excrement]

skeet³ /skit/ *n* the pollack *Pollachius pollachius 20- N NE*. [unknown; perhaps from SKEET⁴·² on account of its rapid movements]

skeet⁴·¹, **skate** /skit, sket/ *n* an ice-skate *19-*. [see the verb Du *schaats* a skate]

skeet⁴·², **skate** /skit, sket/ *v* 1 to glide over ice on skates; to slide *19-*. 2 to make (a stone) skim over water *la19- Sh Ork N WC*. 3 to hurry; to dart about *la19- Sh.* **skeetle** to scurry *20- Sh.* [perhaps altered form of Eng *skate* with influence from SKEET¹·²]

skeet *see* SKITE¹·²

skeetch *see* SKETCH¹·¹, SKETCH¹·²

skeeter *see* SKATER

skeevie *see* SKAVIE¹·²

†**skeevy**, **skivie** *adj* harebrained, mad, mentally deranged *19*. [unknown; compare SKAVE, SKAVIE¹·²]

skeg /skɛg/ *n fisherman's taboo* the sail of a boat *19- Sh*. [Faer *skeki* a rag]

skegg /skɛg/ *n* an awn of barley *20- Ork.* **skegg peat** the outermost peat in a peat-bank *20- Ork*. [Norw dial *skjegg* awnsa beard]

skeggle /ˈskɛgəl/ *v* to slip, lose balance *la19- Sh*. [Norw dial *skjegla* to go awry]

skeich¹·¹, **skeigh** /skix/ *v originally of horses* to shy, take fright *e16, 20- N WC*. [see the adj]

skeich¹·², †**skeigh** /skix/ *adj* 1 *of horses* inclined to be shy, restive, frisky, spirited *16-*. 2 *of people* high-spirited; haughty; coy; befuddled *la16-*. **skakesem** coy, shy *la19- Ork*. [related to OE *scēoh* shy, fearful]

†**skeich**¹·³, **skeigh** *adv* in a shy, coy manner, skittishly, spiritedly *la18-19*. [see the adj]

skeichen¹·¹, **skaichen** /ˈskixən, ˈskɛxən/ *n* fastidiousness, fussiness, disgust or nausea about food *19- NE*. [see the verb]

skeichen¹·², **skaichen**, **skaiken** /ˈskixən, ˈskɛxən, ˈskɛkən/ *v* to disgust, nauseate; to be disgusted or nauseated *la19- NE*. [SKEICH¹·², with verb-forming suffix]

skeichen¹·³, **skechan**, **skaken** /ˈskixən, ˈskɛxən, ˈskɛkən/ *adj* 1 timid, nervous *la19- NE*. 2 fastidious about food, easily upset or nauseated *20- NE*. [see the verb]

skeigh *see* SKEICH¹·¹, SKEICH¹·², SKEICH¹·³

skeikit *see* SKAIKIT

skeil *see* SKEEL²

skeirie *see* SKYRIE

†**skekel**¹·¹ *n* a guiser, traditionally dressed in a straw costume *19 Sh*. [unknown]

†**skekel**¹·² *v* to go guising *19 Sh*. [unknown]

skekler /ˈskɛklər/ *n* a guiser, traditionally dressed in a straw costume *la19- Sh*. [SKEKEL¹·² with agent suffix]

skelb¹·¹ /skɛlb/ *n* 1 a thin flake, sliver or splinter of wood, stone or metal *la16-19, 20- NE T EC Uls*. 2 a thin slice or sliver of anything *la19- NE*. Compare SKELF²·¹, SKELP². [Gael *sgealb*, IrGael *scealb*]

skelb¹·² /skɛlb/ *v* to cut or break into flakes or splinters *19- NE T EC*. Compare SKELF²·², SKELP². [see the noun]

skelder /ˈskɛldər/ *n* thin, flaky stones unsuitable for use in building *20- Sh Ork*. [perhaps altered form of *skelfer* (SKELF²·¹)]

†**skeldock**, **sceldrick**, **skaldock** *n* wild mustard *Sinapis arvensis* or wild radish *Raphanus raphanistrum 17-e19*. Compare SKELLOCH². [metathesis of ME *kedloc* charlock, wild mustard, OE *cedelc* applied to various cruciferous weeds]

skeldro, **skeldroo** /ˈskɛldru/ *n* the oystercatcher *Haematopus ostralegus 20- Ork*. [perhaps altered form of SHALDER]

†**skelet**, **scelet**, **skellat** *n* a skeleton *17-e19*. [Fr *squellette*]

skelf¹, **shelf**, **shelve** /skɛlf, ʃɛlf, ʃɛlv/ *n* 1 a flat piece of wood or metal fixed horizontally to hold objects; a shelf *la15-*. 2 a ledge of rock (in the sea); a hidden source of danger *17-*. 3 a shelf above a BOX-BED, frequently used as a bed for young children; a bunk *18-19, 20- Ork T EC*. **skelvy** *of a river bank* shelving *la18-19, 20- Sh*. [MLG *schelf*]

skelf²·¹, **skelve** /skɛlf, skɛlv/ *n* 1 a thin flat fragment or slice, a flake; a splinter or small chip of wood *17-*. 2 a small thin insignificant person *20- WC Bor*. 3 a wedge of wood *20- WC*. **skelfer** a lamina or flake of stone *20- Ork*. [probably Du *schelf* a flake, a spinter of wood]

skelf²·², **skelve** /skɛlf, skɛlv/ *v* 1 to take off (as) in flakes, slice *20- Sh T WC*. 2 to flake, break into flat slices *19- Ork N T*. [see the noun]

skell /skɛl/ *v* to squint; to have a squint *20- Sh*. [Norw *skjela* or back-formation from SKELLY¹·²]

skell *see* SKAIL¹·²

†**skellach** *n* a small bell; a handbell, such as one used by a public crier *la17-19*. [altered form of SKELLET¹]

skellach *see* SKELLOCH²

skellat *see* SKELET, SKELLET¹

skelldrake, †**scaledrake**, †**skaildrake** /ˈskɛldrek/ *n* the sheldrake *16-19, 20- Sh Uls*. [variant of ME *sheldrake*, perhaps MDu *schillede* variegated + ME *drake*]

skellet¹, †**skellat**, †**skillet** /ˈskɛlət/ *n* a small bell; a handbell, such as one used by a public crier *16-19, 20- Ork*. †**skellat bell** = SKELLET¹ *la16-e19*. †**skellat bellman** a bellman, public crier *18-e19*. [OFr *escalete*]

skellet², **skillet**, †**skellit** /ˈskɛlət, ˈskɪlət/ *n* 1 a pan, a skillet *17-*. 2 a tin water-scoop *la19, 20- N NE*. [ME *skellet*; compare OFr *escuelete* a small plate]

skellie, **scalie** /ˈskɛle, ˈskɛle/ *n* wild mustard *Sinapis arvensis 19, 20- T H&I Bor*. [reduced form of SKELLOCH² + -IE¹]

skellie *see* SKELLY¹·¹, SKELLY¹·², SKELLY¹·³, SKELLY²

skellie bell /ˈskɛle bɛl/ *n* a small bell; a handbell, such as one used by a public crier *20- WC*. [reduced form of SKELLET¹ + -IE¹ + BELL¹·¹]

skellit *see* SKELLET²

skelloch¹·¹ /ˈskɛləx/ *n* a scream, a screech, a shrill cry *19-*. [see the verb]

skelloch¹·², *NE* **skyallach** /ˈskɛləx; *NE* ˈskjaləx/ *v* to shriek, scream, cry shrilly *19-*. Compare SQUALLOCH¹·¹. [probably onomatopoeic with frequentative -OCH suffix]

skelloch², **skellach** /ˈskɛləx/ *n* frequently *pl* wild mustard *Sinapis arvensis la17-*. [perhaps SKELDOCK via borrowing into Gael as *sgeallag*]

skellum /ˈskɛləm/ *n derogatory* a rogue, a scoundrel; *latterly* a young boy, a scamp *la16-*. Compare SCHELM. [Du *schelm*]

skelly¹·¹, **skellie** /ˈskɛle/ *n* 1 a squint in the eye; a sidelong glance; a quick look *la18-19, 20- T C SW Bor Uls*. 2 an error, an unsuccessful or misdirected aim or attempt *20- SW Uls*. [see the verb and adj]

skelly¹·², **skellie** /ˈskɛle/ *v* 1 to squint, be cross-eyed; to look askance *la15-*. 2 to make a mistake in a statement, exaggerate *la18- SW*. [ON *skelgjask* to squint, come askew]

skelly¹·³, **skellie** /ˈskɛle/ *adj* 1 squinting, having a squint in the eye *19-*. 2 lop-sided; awry *20- C Bor*. **skellie e'ed**, **skelly eyed** squint-eyed *la18-*. [ON *skjalgr* wry, oblique, squinting]

skelly², **skellie** /ˈskɛle/ *n* a ridge of rock running out to sea, usually covered at high tide, a reef, frequently in place-names *16-19, 20- NE T EC*. [perhaps altered form of SKERRY, and compare IrGael *sceilg* a rock]

skelly³ /ˈskɛle/ *n* the chub *Squalius cephalus la18- SW Bor*. [perhaps derivative of Eng *scale* or ON *skel* a scale]

skelp[1.1] /skɛlp/ *n* **1** a stroke, a blow, a smack, a slap *16-*. **2** a blow of misfortune *la18-*. **3** the sound of a blow, a crack *19-*. **4** an attempt, a try *20-*. **5** an indirect satirical reference, a hit (at someone) *20- NE C*. **6** a long piece of recital, a screed *19, 20- EC*. **7** a blast of wind, a squall, a downpour of rain; a splash of liquid *19, 20- NE*. [see the verb]

skelp[1.2], *NE* **skilp** /skɛlp; *NE* skɪlp/ *v* **1** to smack, slap; to hit, strike; to hammer, beat; to drive with blows *la16-*. **2** to throb, pulsate; *of a clock* to tick *18-*. **3** to run, move, travel at great speed, scamper, gallop *18-*. **4** to work with energy or gusto, be vigorously busy *la18-*. **5** *of water, rain or hail* to (cause to) splash, spatter; to pelt *la19-*. **6** *of (the blows of) misfortune or fate* to hit, strike *19-*. **7** to do (a piece of work) vigorously; to reel or rattle off (poetry) *19, 20- EC SW*. **skelping** big of its kind, of striking size *la18-*. **skelpit leathering** a thrashing, a spanking *20- T WC*. **skelp at** = SKELP[1.2] (sense 4). [probably onomatopoeic]

skelp[1.3] /skɛlp/ *adv* with a smack or crack, vigorously *la18-*. [see the noun]

skelp[2] /skɛlp/ *n* **1** a long strip or expanse, especially of ground, an indefinite area *la19-*. **2** a large person, a large slice or chunk, a slab *20-*. **3** a splinter, a flake of wood or stone *la16-18, 20- N NE WC*. [probably variant of SKELB[1.1]]

†**skelpie**[1.1] *n* a naughty, mischievous girl *19*. [reduced form of *skelpie limmer* (SKELPIE[1.2])]

†**skelpie**[1.2] *adj* naughty *la19*. **skelpie-limmer** a naughty, mischievous girl *la18-*. [SKELP[1.1] + -IE[2]]

skelter /'skɛltər/ *v* to scurry, scamper, rush headlong *la19-*. [probably *-skelter*, as in Eng *helter-skelter*]

skelup *see* SCILLOP

skelve *see* SKELF[2.1], SKELF[2.2]

skelvy *see* SKELF[1]

skeme *see* SCHEME[1.1]

skemler *see* SCAMBLER

skemmel[1.1], **shamble**, †**shamell**, †**skambill**, †**schamyll** /'skɛməl, 'ʃambəl/ *n* mainly *pl* **1** a shambles, a slaughterhouse; a meat or fish market *16-*. **2** a place of death or carnage; a state or scene of total disorder, ruin or mess *la16-*. **3** a peat bank, a bench-like area or hag left in a moss from which peats have been cut *20- SW*. **4** a bench or table for displaying meat or fish for sale *15-17*. †**skemmel maill** rent for (stalls in) the meat or fish market *16*. [OE *scamol* a footstool, table, counter, ON *skemill* a footstool]

skemmel[1.2], **skemmle** /'skɛməl/ *v* to move awkwardly; to scramble *19, 20- Bor*. [probably from the noun; on account of the splayed legs of a bench]

skemmill *see* SCAMBLE

skemmle *see* SKEMMEL[1.2]

skemp, **scamp** /skɛmp, skamp/ *n* a rascal, a rogue *19-*. [variant of Eng *scamp*]

skene *see* SKEAN

skenk *see* SKINK[1]

skenʒe *see* SKAINIE

skeo, **skio** /skjo/ *n* **1** a dry-stone shed for wind-curing meat or fish; a larder *17- Sh Ork*. **2** a badly constructed dwelling house *20- Sh*. †**skewhowse** *in Orkney* = SKEO (sense 1) *la16*. [Norw dial *skjå* a drying house]

skeomet, **skjomet** /'skjomət/ *adj* pale, sickly-looking, sallow *19- Sh*. [Norw dial *skjåmut* dark in colour]

skep[1.1], *Sh* **skeb**, †**skape** /skɛp; *Sh* skeb/ *n* **1** a large wickerwork or straw basket *13-*. **2** a beehive *la16-*. **skeppie** = *skep-bee*. **skep-bee** the hive- or honey-bee *20- NE T EC*. [ON *skeppa* a basket]

skep[1.2] /skɛp/ *v* to put (a swarm of bees) into a hive *19-*. **skep-pit** put to bed, tucked up for the night *la18, la19- WC Bor*.

†**skep in wi** to share accommodation with, live or associate with *la18-19*. [see the noun]

sker *see* SCARE[1.2], SCARE[1.3]

skerche *see* SCARCE[1.1]

†**sker-handed** *adj* left-handed *19*. [altered form of *car-handit* (CAR[2])]

skerp /skɛrp/ *n* a rip, tear *20- Ork*. [altered form of SKERT]

skerr *see* SCARE[1.1], SCARE[1.3]

skerry, **skerrie** /'skɛri/ *n* a reef, a rocky islet or stretch of rocks often covered at high tide; frequently in place-names *16-*. [ON *sker* + -IE[1]]

skerry-handit /'skɛre'handɪt/ *adj* left-handed *19- Bor*. [altered form of *caurry-handit* (CORRIE[2])]

skert, **skirt** /skjɛrt/ *n* a sheep-mark made by cutting and notching the ear *el9- Ork*. [compare Norw *skjerding*]

sketch[1.1], *Sh* **skitch**, *NE* **skeetch**, †**skaitch** /skɛtʃ; *Sh NE* skitʃ/ *n* **1** the upright part of a ladder; a scaffolding pole; two poles crossed near the upper end; a sawyer's trestle *16-17, 20- Sh NE*. **2** the act of skating, a turn or spell of skating *la19- Sh T*. **3** an ice-skate *19, 20- T*. [OFr *escache* a wooden frame, a stilt]

sketch[1.2], **skytch**, *T* **skeetch** /skɛtʃ, skʌɪtʃ; *T* skitʃ/ *v* **1** to skate *la18-19, 20- NE SH T EC*. **2** *of a stone* to skim along the surface of water; to skim (a stone) along the surface of water *20- N EC*. Compare SCUTCH[2.2]. **sketcher 1** the flat object kicked in the game of hopscotch; *pl* the game of hopscotch *20- N NE EC*. **2** a stone suitable for skimming along the surface of water *20- N NE EC*. **3** a skater *20- Sh T EC*. **4** an ice-skate *19, 20- T WC*. [see the noun]

sketch[2] /skɛtʃ/ *n* **1** a drawing; a design *19-*. **2** a brief period of time *20- Bor*. [extended sense of Eng *sketch*]

skeugh *see* SKEW[2.1], SKEW[2.2], SKEW[2.3], SKEW[2.4]

skew[1], †**sqway** /skju/ *n* **1** (a stone forming part of) the coping of the sloping part of a gable *16-*. **2** *mining* a piece of rock slanting upwards and overhanging a working place *la18-*. **3** *in building work* a board or beam used in some fashion obliquely; an oblique or sloping element *16-el7*. **skew corbel** the lowest stone in a gable coping *la19-*. †**skew peit** = *skew corbel el7*. **skew putt** = *skew corbel*. **skew stone** = *skew corbel 19, 20- NE SW*. [ME *scue*, OFr *escu*]

skew[2.1], *NE* **skyow**, *NE* **skeugh** /skju; *NE* skjʌu, skjux/ *n* **1** a twist, a turn, a sideways movement *la19-*. **2** a squint, a sidelong glance *20- NE*. **3** a quarrel, a row *20- NE*. [see the verb]

skew[2.2], *NE* **skyow**, *NE* **skeugh** /skju; *NE* skjʌu, skjux/ *v* **1** to twist, turn sideways or to one side, distort; to screw up (the face) *16-*. **2** *of the eyes* to squint due to an astigmatism; to look obliquely *la19-*. **3** to go obliquely or off the straight, move sideways; to sway (affectedly or drunkenly); to swagger *la15-19, 20- NE*. **4** *of the feet, legs or gait* to splay, turn outwards *la19- NE*. **5** to quarrel, disagree *20- NE*. [OFr *eskuer*]

skew[2.3], *NE* **skyow**, *NE* **skeugh** /skju; *NE* skjʌu, skjux/ *adj* **1** oblique, slanted, squint *20-*. **2** *of the feet* splayed *20- NE*. **skyow-fittit** splay-footed *la19- NE T WC*. **skew-whiff** awry, at a rakish angle *la18-*. [see the verb]

skew[2.4], *NE* **skeugh** /skju; *NE* skjux/ *adv* at a slant, askew, at an oblique angle or angles *la19, 20- Sh NE*. [see the verb]

skewl[1.1] /skjul/ *n* a turning aside, a twist *la19, 20- Bor*. [see the verb]

skewl[1.2], *NE T* **skyowl** /skjul; *NE T* skjʌul/ *v* **1** to turn aside, deflect *19, 20- T Bor*. **2** to screw up, twist (the mouth) *19*. **3** to wear down (shoes) on one side *19-*. [altered form of SKEW[2.2]]

skey *see* SKY[1.1]

skeyg *see* SKEEG[2.2]

ski *see* SKY[2]

skibbie *see* SKIPPIE

skibby /ˈskɪbe/ *adj* left-handed *20- WC.* [perhaps altered form of KIPPIE]

skibo /ˈskɪbə, ˈskɪbo/ *n* a type of Highland cattle *19- T.* [from the place-name, the Skibo estate in Sutherland]

skice /skʌɪs/ *v* to make off quickly and unobtrusively, clear out *la19- NE.* [EModE *skice*]

skiddle¹·¹ /ˈskɪdəl/ *n* 1 an insipid liquid; weak tea *la19- H&I WC.* 2 a mess, a muddle, a confusion *20- T H&I C.* 3 *derogatory* a small thing, matter, person or animal *19, 20- SW.* 4 a messy, inept or clumsy person *20- T.* [see the verb]

skiddle¹·², **skittle** /ˈskɪdəl, ˈskɪtəl/ *v* 1 to splash, spill, play with (liquid) *19- NE T C SW*; compare SKEDADDLE. 2 to dabble, potter *20-.* **skiddler** a minnow or stickleback, a tiddler *20- T.* **skiddling, skittling** insubstantial, insipid *20- WC.* [variant of SCUDDLE¹]

skiddle² /ˈskɪdəl/ *v* to move rapidly and lightly *20- C SW Bor.* [variant of SCUDDLE²]

Skiers Thursday *see* SKIRE THURSDAY

skiff¹·¹ /skɪf/ *n* 1 a slight touch or graze in passing, an abrasion *la19-.* 2 a slight gust of wind *19-.* 3 a slight or flying shower of rain or snow, a light drizzle, a fleeting patch of wet mist *19-.* 4 a slight touch (of an illness) *la19, 20- N T WC.* 5 a thin slice *20- EC Bor.* [see the verb]

skiff¹·² /skɪf/ *v* 1 to move lightly, skim, glide, skip *18-.* 2 to rain or snow very slightly *la19-.* 3 to touch lightly in passing, brush, graze; to brush, flick off *19-.* 4 to propel (an object) along a surface; to skip (a stone) over water; to slide (a small stone or other object) over the ground in the game of PEEVERS *19-.* **skiffer** a flat stone suitable for skipping over water *20- C Bor.* **skiffin** a slight fall of snow *la19-.* **skiff by** to do work carelessly or superficially *la19- Sh N NE T.* **skiff ower** = *skiff by.* [onomatopoeic; compare SCUFF¹·², SKIFT¹·²]

skiff², **skift** /skɪf, skɪft/ *n* a type of small sea-going fishing boat with oars and a lugsail *la17-19, 20- N NE H&I C.* [EModE *skiffe*, Fr *esquif*]

skiffin /ˈskɪfən/ *n* a thin partition or screen *20- NE T C.* [variant of SKIFTING]

skiffle¹·¹ /ˈskɪfəl/ *n* a slight shower of rain *20- NE T WC SW Bor.* [SKIFF¹·¹, with diminutive suffix]

skiffle¹·² /ˈskɪfəl/ *v* to skip or skim across a flat surface, *eg* of a stone on water *20- N SW Bor.* **skiffler** a flat stone used for skipping across water *20- N SW Bor*; compare *skiffer* (SKIFF¹·²). **skifflers** the action of skipping stones over water *20- N SW Bor.* [SKIFF¹·¹, with frequentative suffix]

skiffle² /ˈskɪfəl/ *v* to raise or produce (sparks) by scuffling the feet *20- WC Bor.* [altered form of Eng *scuffle*]

skift¹·¹ /skɪft/ *n* 1 a light shower of rain or snow *la19-.* 2 a hurried or cursory dusting *20- T C Bor.* 3 a thin strip of wood-shaving *20- Sh.* [see the verb]

†**skift**¹·² *v* 1 to move lightly, skim, skip *la16-e19.* 2 *of rain or snow* to fall lightly *19.* [variant of SKIFF¹·²]

†**skift**² *n* a share or division (of land) *16-e18.* [ON *skipti* division, sharing]

skift *see* SKIFF²

skifter /ˈskɪftər/ *n* 1 a light shower of rain or snow *20- Sh N NE T EC.* 2 *pl* the action of skipping a stone over water *18- N NE EC.* [derivative of SKIFT¹·²]

skiftin /ˈskɪftən/ *n* a light fall or sprinkling of snow *20- NE T C Bor.* [verbal noun from SKIFT¹·²]

skifting /ˈskɪftɪŋ/ *n* a narrow piece of boarding, especially skirting-board *la18- C SW Bor.* **skifting board** = SKIFTING. [verbal noun from SKIFT¹·²]

skik¹·¹ /skɪk, skik/ *n* order, good management, thrift *20- Sh.* [Norw *skik*]

skik¹·² /skɪk, skik/ *v* to be thrifty or economical *19- Sh.* [Norw *skikke* to put in order, Du *schikken* to put in order]

skilder¹·¹ /ˈskɪldər, ˈskjɪldər/ *n* 1 a clatter, a crash *la19- Sh Ork.* 2 a shrill, noisy laugh; laughter and shouting *20- Sh.* **skilters** smithereens *20- Ork.* [see the verb]

skilder¹·² /ˈskɪldər, ˈskjɪldər/ *v* to make a loud high-pitched noise, laugh, shout *la19- Sh Ork.* [variant of SKALDER¹·²]

skilderin /ˈskɪldərən/ *n* a smooth glazed surface; enamel *la19- Sh.* [derivative of Norw dial *skjøldra* a breast-plate, armour plating]

skilewin *see* SKAIL¹·²

skill *see* SCULL¹, SKEEL¹·¹, SKEEL¹·²

skillet *see* SKELLET¹, SKELLET²

skillie *see* SKEELY

skilling-guis *see* SKEELING-GOOSE

skilly *see* SKEELY

skilm /ˈskɪləm/ *n* a deposit of milk or cream on the inside of an unwashed pail *la19- Sh.* [conflation of SKIM with Norw *skimmel* mould]

skilp *see* SKELP¹·²

skilt¹·¹ /skɪlt/ *n* a flighty, giddy young person, a gadabout *19, 20- SW.* [see the verb]

skilt¹·² /skɪlt/ *v* to go, gad about; to dart, skip *la17-19, 20- Bor.* [probably onomatopoeic]

skim /skɪm/ *n* scum on milk *20- Sh.* [Eng †*skim* and Norw dial *skim*]

skime¹·¹ /skʌɪm/ *n* 1 a glance or flash of the eye, a quick (sideways) look *19- SW.* 2 a gleam of light, flash; a brief glimpse or appearance *19-.* [ON *skími* a gleam of light or from the verb]

skime¹·² /skʌɪm/ *v* 1 to glance, shine with reflected light, gleam *19-.* 2 to glimpse, see indistinctly *20- Sh.* [EModE *skime* to squint, compare ON *skima* to peer, look about]

skimmer¹·¹, **shimmer** /ˈskɪmər, ˈʃɪmər/ *n* 1 a flicker or glimmer of light *19-.* 2 a light sprinkling of snow or rain *la19- Sh NE T C.* [see the verb]

skimmer¹·², **shimmer** /ˈskɪmər, ˈʃɪmər/ *v* 1 *of light or a bright object* to shine, glitter, twinkle, gleam *la18-.* 2 to glide along easily and quickly *la18-.* **skimmering** a light sprinkling (of snow) *la19- Sh NE T.* [OE *scimerian*, MLG *schemeren*]

skimmin /ˈskɪmɪn/ *n* a sprinkling *la19- Sh NE.* [verbal noun from Eng *skim*]

skimp¹·¹ /skɪmp/ *n* banter, mockery, sarcasm *la19- Sh.* [see the verb]

skimp¹·², **skjimp** /skɪmp, skjɪmp/ *v* to poke fun at, tease, ridicule *19- Sh Ork.* [Icel *skimpa* to scorn]

skim-the-milk /ˈskɪmðəmɪlk/ *n* a figure in the game of *chucks* (CHUCK² (sense 2)) *20- N H&I WC.* [Eng *skim* + THE + MILK¹·¹]

skin¹·¹, †**skyn** /skɪn/ *n* 1 the natural outer covering of the body of a vertebrate; the skin *la14-.* 2 a hide, pelt, fur *la14-.* 3 the peel, rind (of fruit) *la17-.* 4 a robbery or what has been stolen; a petty scam or swindle; a small amount of cash retained from a common fund for private use *la19- C.* 5 a sheet of gold leaf *16.* **skin-bare** naked *la19, 20- Sh.* **skin-bowe** a Shetland reel *20- Sh.* **skin-claes** waterproof clothing *la19- Sh.* **skinjup** a jerkin or pullover made of skin *la19- Sh.* **skin-naked** completely naked *la19, 20- Sh.* **at the skin** soaked through to the skin *la19- Sh NE.* †**skin and birn** 1 the skin (usually of a sheep) with the identifying brand *la16-17.* 2 the totality of something; all and sundry *18-e19.* **skin-for-skin** *mining, of props* set so close as to be touching *la19, 20- EC.* [ON *skinn*]

skin¹·², †**skinne** /skɪn/ *v* 1 to strip the skin from, flay *17-.* 2 to pare the surface layer of soil off (land) *20- N NE T H&I C.* **skinnin** a small amount; a piece of petty economy or profit *la19- NE T EC SW Bor.* **skin-the-cuddy** *games* a kind of leapfrog *20- NE C*. **skin the schule** to play truant *20- Ork*. [see the noun]

skindrin /'skɪndrɪn/ *n* a small quantity, a thin layer *la19- Sh*. [derivative of Norw *skind* a surface layer]

skineemelink *see* SKINNYMALINK

skinger /'skɪŋər/ *n* a thin layer or spread *20- Sh*. [perhaps derivative of SKIN[1.1]]

skink[1], *Sh* **skenk** /skɪŋk; *Sh* skɛŋk/ *n* a soup, originally made from a shin of beef *16-*. Compare CULLEN SKINK. [MDu *schenke* a shin, a hough, a ham]

skink[2.1] /skɪŋk/ *n* **1** alcoholic drink, especially of a weak, insipid kind *19-*. **2** a thin oatmeal and water gruel *la19, 20- Uls*. [see the verb]

skink[2.2], †**skynk** /skɪŋk/ *v* **1** to pour (a small amount of liquid) from one container to another; to mix (liquids or ingredients) by repeating this process *18-19, 20- SW Uls*. **2** to behave lavishly *e17, la19- NE T*. **3** to pour out, serve (alcohol); to fill (a glass) with alcohol *16-19*. **4** to give as a gift; to hand *16-e17*. †**skinking** *of liquid or soup* easily poured, thinly diluted, lacking substance *la18-19*. †**skink over** to renounce *16-e17*. [probably MDu *schenken* to make a present of]

skink[3] /skɪŋk/ *v* to crush, squash *19-*. [unknown]

skinkle[1] /'skɪŋkəl/ *v* to glitter, gleam, sparkle *la18-*. **skinklin** sparkling, shining *la18-*. [perhaps variant of EModE *scintill*, Lat *scintillāre*]

†**skinkle**[2.1] *n* a very small quantity *19*. [diminutive form of SKINK[2.1]]

†**skinkle**[2.2] *v* to sprinkle, scatter, spray, or spill in small quantities *19*. [see the noun]

skinne *see* SKIN[1.2]

skinny[1] /'skɪne/ *n* a bread roll, especially a breakfast roll *20- Bor*. [unknown]

skinny[2] /'skɪne/ *adj* thin, scrawny *18-*. **skinnybreeks** the shellfish *Mya arenaria 20- Ork*. [SKIN[1.1] + -IE[2]]

skinnymalink, *Ork* **skineemelink** /'skɪnemǝlɪŋk; *Ork* 'skɪnimǝlɪŋk/ *n* an excessively thin person or animal *la19-*. **skinnymalinky** = SKINNYMALINK *20-*. [extended sense of SKINNY[2], with -MA-]

skinny tattie /'skɪne tati/ *n* a potato boiled in its skin *la20- C SW Bor*. [SKIN[1.1] + -IE[1.12] + TATTIE]

skint[1.1] /skɪnt/ *n* a very small amount, a drop or splash *20- Ork N*. [altered form of SKINK[2.1]]

skint[1.2] /skɪnt/ *v* to splash, bespatter *20- N*. [see the noun]

skint[2] /skɪnt/ *v* to hurry *20- Ork*. [Norw *skynde*]

skintie /'skɪnte/ *adj* small, meagre, scanty *20- C Bor*. [perhaps conflation of Eng *skimpy* with Eng *scanty*]

skio *see* SKEO

skip[1.1], †**skyp** /skɪp/ *n* a bounding or leaping movement *la15-*. [see the verb]

skip[1.2], †**scip**, †**skyp** /skɪp/ *v* **1** to spring, leap, move by skips or bounds; to hurry away, abscond *la15-*. **2** *of the nose* to turn up *e16*. **skippie** *of roads* slippery, icy *20- NE T*. **skip-rape** a skipping rope *la19- T EC SW*. [ME *skippen*; probably ON, compare Swed *shuppa*]

skip[2.1] /skɪp/ *n* curling *or* bowls the team captain and director of play *19-*. [shortened form of SKIPPER]

skip[2.2] /skɪp/ *v* to captain a team *20-*. [see the noun]

skip *see* SCUIP[1.1]

Skipka Pass *see* SHIPKA PASS

skippack *see* SKEEPACK

skipper, †**skippar**, †**schippar** /'skɪpǝr/ *n* the captain or master of a ship *15-*. [MDu, MLG *schipper*]

skippie, **skibbie** /'skɪpe, 'skɪbi/ *n* the game of tig *la19- N*. **skippie-lickie** = SKIPPIE *20-*. [SKIP[1.2] + -IE[3]]

skippit bunnet *see* SCUIP[1.1]

skire[1.1], **skyre** /skaer/ *v* to shine brightly, glitter; to be gaudy; to wear gaudy, garish clothes *la17-19, 20- Ork NE*. **skyrin** bright; gaudy in colour, garish *18-19, 20- Sh Ork NE*. Compare SKYRIE. [see the adj]

skire[1.2], *Ork* **skare**, †**skyre** /skaer; *Ork* sker/ *adj* of light or flames clear; bright, pure *la16, 19- Ork NE*. [ON *skírr*]

†**skire**[1.3], **skeer**, **skyr** *adv* absolutely, utterly, altogether, completely *la16-19*. **skeer nakit** completely naked *la18-19*. [see the adj]

Skire Thursday, *Sh* **Skir-Furisday**, †**Skyre Thursday**, †**Skiers Thursday**, †**Skir-Thurisday** /'skaer 'θʌrzde; *Sh* 'skør'fʌrɪsde/ *n* Maundy Thursday; a fair or market held on that day *15-19, 20- Sh*. [SKIRE[1.2] + THURSDAY]

skirfen *see* SKIRVIN

skirl[1.1] /skɪrl/ *n* **1** a scream or shriek of pain, anguish or fear *15-*. **2** a shriek of laughter or excitement *18-*. **3** the loud cry, wail, or whistle of a bird *19-*. **4** (the high-pitched sound of) a strong wind; stormy weather *19-*. **5** the shrill sound of bagpipes; a wrong note accidentally played *la19-*. **6** a screeching, whirring or whistling noise made by something mechanical *la19-*. **7** a flurry of snow or hail *19- NE T*. **skirlie o' snaw** a flurry of snow *la19-*. **skirlo** a propeller *20- Ork*. **skirly wheeter 1** the oystercatcher *Haematopus ostralegus 20- NE*. **2** an unhealthy-looking animal; a young person *20- Ork*. [see the verb]

skirl[1.2] /skɪrl/ *v* **1** to scream, cry out with fear, pain or grief *16-*. **2** *of birds* to call, scream, screech *la16-*. **3** to utter with a high-pitched discordant sound, cry or sing shrilly, raise a clamour *17-*. **4** to cause (bagpipes or a fiddle) to make their characteristic shrill sound; to make this sound on the bagpipes *17-*. **5** to shriek with excitement or laughter *la18-*. **6** to creak; to make a crackling, screeching, or whistling sound *19-*. **7** *of food frying* to sizzle, crackle, sputter *19-*. **8** *of the wind* to blow with a shrill noise, whistle *la19-*. **skirl-in-the-pan** a fried dish of oatmeal and onions *20- N T*. [metathesis of ME *skrillen*; compare Norw dial *skryla*]

skirlie, **skirly** /'skɪrle/ *n* a fried dish of oatmeal and onions *20-*. [shortened form of *skirl-in-the-pan* (SKIRL[1.2]) + -IE[1]]

skirl naked /'skɪrl 'nekǝd/ *adj* stark naked *19- T EC Bor*. [variant of *skeer nakit* (SKIRE[1.3]), confused in form with SKIRL[1.2]]

skirly *see* SKIRLIE

skirm *see* SCRIM[1]

skirp[1.1], †**scrip** /skɪrp/ *n* **1** a small drop, splash, or spurt of liquid; a slight shower or spot of rain *la19- NE EC*. **2** a drop of alcohol, a dram *19- NE*. **3** a fragment of metal or stone; a pellet; a splinter *20- NE*. **4** only **scrip** a scornful grimace *la15*. [see the verb]

skirp[1.2], †**skrip**, †**scrip**, †**scorp** /skɪrp/ *v* **1** *of water or mud* to splash, fly up in small drops; *of rain* to spit *la19- Ork NE*. **2** to sprinkle (liquid), splash in small drops or squirts *19, 20- NE*. **3** to mock, jeer, scoff (at) *la15-18*. [ME *skirpen* to mock, ON *skirpa* to spit]

skirr[1] /skɪr/ *v* to scurry about, rush, whizz, slide, skate; *of sleet or snow* to be driven by the wind *19, 20- Ork*. [onomatopoeic; compare EModE *skyr* to run away, rush about]

skirr[2], **skorr** /skɪr, skør/ *v* to scare, chase off (poultry) *20- Sh*. [Norw dial *skirra*]

skirt[1.1], †**skyrt** /skɪrt/ *n* **1** the lower part of a gown, coat or dress; a separate garment, covering the body from the waist down *15-*. **2** the outlying part; the lower slopes of a hill; the foot of a rock *la15-17*. †**skirts of** the outlying part of a place *la15-17*. [ON *skyrta* a shirt]

skirt[1.2] /skɪrt/ *v* **1** to run away, decamp; to elope *19-*. **2** to elude, evade; to lurk, skulk; to truant *la19-*. [see the noun]

skirvin, †**skirfen** /ˈskɪrvɪn/ *n* **1** a thin covering of soil or snow *19- Bor.* **2** a crust *e17.* [metathesis of *scriffin* (SCRUIF¹,²)]

skish *see* SCUSH¹,²

skit¹,¹ /skɪt/ *n* **1** a trick, hoax *19-.* **2** a squirt of water, a jet; a sharp, short shower *la19-.* **3** a frivolous, vain woman *la16, e19.* [see the verb]

skit¹,² /skɪt/ *v* to squirt, spray, splash (water) *la19, 20- Sh N.* [perhaps a variant of SKITE¹,²]

skit²,¹ /skɪt/ *n* **1** diarrhoea *20-.* **2** *especially of a woman* an arrogant or disagreeable person *19, 20- Sh.* [ME *skit*; compare Norw *skit* dirt, and SKITE²,²]

skit²,² /skɪt, skit/ *v* to defecate *20- Sh.* Compare SKITE²,². [see the noun]

skitch *see* SKETCH¹,¹

skite¹,¹ /skʌɪt/ *n* **1** a sudden sharp glancing blow *la18-.* **2** a hasty rub; a superficial cleaning: ◊*gie the flair a quick skite 20-.* **3** a high-spirited, boisterous party or gathering *la19-.* **4** a slip, a slither, a skid *19-.* **5** a small amount of water; a short, sharp shower of rain *19-.* **6** the act of squirting liquid; a squirt, a syringe *19, 20- N NE.* **7** a small amount of alcohol, a dram *la19- NE T.* **8** the yellowhammer *Emberiza citrinella 19-.* **gie somebody a skite** to deal unfairly or deceitfully with someone *la18-.* **on the skite** engaged in a period of high-spirited, sometimes drunken, enjoyment *la19-.* **play somebody a skite** = *gie somebody a skite 19-.* [see the verb]

skite¹,², *Sh Ork* **skeet** /skʌɪt; *Sh Ork* skit/ *v* **1** to dart through the air suddenly, forcibly and frequently obliquely *18-.* **2** to rebound, ricochet *19-.* **3** to throw suddenly and forcibly; to send flying, make (something) shoot off at an angle; to cause (a stone) to skip over the surface of water *19-.* **4** to cause a spray or splash of liquid; to squirt, splash *19-.* **5** to slip, slide on a slippery surface *la19-.* **6** to skate *la19-*; compare SKATE. **7** to act wildly or boisterously; to drink freely *20- T WC Bor.* **8** to strike, hit (a person) *20- N T C SW.* **skiter** a squirt, a syringe, an instrument for spraying; a pea- or water-shooter *la19- Sh NE T.* **skitie** slippery *20-.* [ON *skýt-*; stem of *skjóta* to shoot, propel, dart]

skite¹,³ /skʌɪt/ *adj* mad, crazy *20-.* [see the verb]

skite¹,⁴ /skʌɪt/ *adv* with a sharp rap or blow, forcibly and with a rebound *19, 20- NE T EC.* [see the verb]

skite²,¹ /skʌɪt/ *n* a nasty or objectionable person *19-.* [see the verb]

skite²,² /skʌɪt/ *v presp* †**skyttand** to have diarrhoea; to soil with excrement; to defecate *16-19, 20- NE EC*; compare SKIT²,². **skiter** *derogatory* a person *la19- NE.* [ME *skiten*, ON *skíta*]

skitten /ˈskɪtən/ *adj* fastidious, squeamish; delicate, sickly *20- NE.* Compare SKEICHEN¹,³. [altered form of *skaken* (SKEICHEN¹,³)]

skitter¹,¹ /ˈskɪtər/ *n* **1** diarrhoea, liquid excrement *la16-.* **2** anything dirty or disgusting, a mess, rubbish *19, 20- Sh N NE T.* **skitterie**, **skittery 1** trifling, contemptibly small or inadequate *20-.* **2** *of excrement* loose, fluid *la17-.* **3** *of a task* fiddly, time-consuming *20- C SW Bor.* **skitter broltie** the corn bunting *Emberiza calandra la19- Ork.* **skittery feltie** the fieldfare *Turdus pilaris 20- C SW.* **skitterie winter** the last person to arrive for or leave work on Hogmanay *20- WC.* **the skitters**, †**the skitter** diarrhoea, the ailment *la16-.* [see the verb]

skitter¹,² /ˈskɪtər/ *v* **1** to have diarrhoea, void liquid excrement *la16-.* **2** to waste time doing trivial jobs, potter about aimlessly *20-.* **skitterin**, †**skitterand 1** insignificant *20-.* **2** suffering from diarrhoea *16-.* **skitter the slaps**, **skitterida slaps** to take home the last load of corn at harvest time *20- Sh Ork.* [frequentative form of SKITE²,²]

skitter² /ˈskɪtər/ *v* to slither, slip *la19, 20- NE T.* [frequentative form of SKITE¹,²]

skittle, **skittling** *see* SKIDDLE¹,²

skittling *see* SKIDDLE¹,²

skive¹ /skaev/ *v* **1** to roam, prowl *la19-.* **2** to avoid work, play truant, evade a duty *la20-.* **skiver 1** one who avoids work, a truant *la20-.* **2** a prowler, a prying person *la19, 20- WC SW.* [perhaps Eng dial *skive* to dart about, or slang *skive* to evade a duty from Fr *esquiver* to evade, dodge]

skive² /skaev/ *v* **1** to shave, pare, scrape, slice off a thin layer *20- NE T C.* **2** to whittle wood *20- Ork.* [ON *skífa*]

skived /skaevd/ *adj* tilted, askew *20- Ork NE EC SW.* [compare SKAVE]

skiver¹ /ˈskɪvər/ *n* a splinter of wood in the skin *20- Ork NE T C.* [compare SKIVER² and SKIVE²]

skiver², **skivver** /ˈskɪvər/ *v* to pierce, stab, skewer *19, 20- WC.* [compare EModE *skiver* a skewer]

skivet¹ /ˈskɪvət/ *n* a sharp hard blow *19- Bor.* [unknown; compare SKIFF¹,¹ and SCUFF¹,¹]

†**skivet**², **scuffet**, **scuvatt** *n* a tool used in a forge, probably a spade or shovel *16-e19.* [MFr *escouvette* a brush or mop used by smiths to sprinkle water on the fire]

skivie *see* SKEEVY

skivver *see* SKIVER²

skjimp *see* SKIMP¹,²

skjoag *see* SCUG¹,²

skjöll *see* SKULE

skjomet *see* SKEOMET

skjüp *see* SCUIP¹,²

sklaik *see* SLAIK¹,²

sklait *see* SCLATE¹,¹, SCLATE¹,²

sklaitter *see* SCLATER

sklander *see* SCLANDER¹,¹, SCLANDER¹,²

sklant *see* SKLENT¹,³, SKLENT³

sklaterscrae *see* SKRATTISKRAE

sklatter /ˈsklatər/ *n* an untidy splash, a daub *20- NE T.* [probably onomatopoeic]

skleat *see* SCLATE¹,¹, SCLATE¹,²

skleesh *see* SLEESH

skleet *see* SKLUTE¹,²

skleff /sklɛf/ *adj* **1** *of a dish* shallow, flat *19, 20- EC Bor.* **2** thin and flat; *of persons* thin; flat-chested *19-.* **3** equal, even (in a competition) *20- Bor.* **the skleff** flat, level ground *20- Bor.* [onomatopoeic; compare SCLAFF¹,¹]

skleg *see* SLIG

sklenner, **sklinner**, †**sclender**, †**sklender**, †**sclinder** /ˈsklɛnər, ˈsklɪnər/ *adj* **1** thin; slim, skinny *la15-.* **2** deficient; limited; slight; of little importance or strength *16-.* [ME *sclendre*]

sklent¹,¹, †**sclent** /sklɛnt/ *n* **1** a slope, an incline *la18-.* **2** a sidelong glance; a squint *19-.* **3** *of wind or rain* a slanting motion *la19-.* **4** a sideways movement or change of direction; a twist *la18-19, 20- Sh.* **5** a flash of light *20- NE.* **6** a cut made off the straight *la16.* †**a sclent** following a slanting course, obliquely; deviating from a straight line or path; awry, devious *la15-e17.* **on the sclent** on a slope, in a slanting direction, squint *19- EC SW.* [see the verb]

sklent¹,², **sklint**, †**sclent** /sklɛnt, sklɪnt/ *v* **1** to move obliquely, turn sideways, curve, zigzag *15-.* **2** *of light* to shine in a slanting direction *la18-.* **3** to slope, slant, lie to one side *la18-.* **4** to glance, cast (the eyes) sideways, look askance, squint *19-.* **5** to aim (something) obliquely or sideways *la16-19, 20- Sh C.* **6** to deviate from the truth *la16-19.* **7** to reflect sarcastically on, hint at, allude to indirectly or by insinuation *17-19.* [altered form of SLENT²]

sklent¹·³, *H&I* **sklant** /sklɛnt; *H&I* sklant/ *adj* **1** slanting, to one side, oblique *19*-. **2** *of a look or glance* sidelong *19, 20- Sh.* **3** inaccurate; devious, dishonest *e17, 20- NE.* **sklent-weys, sclant-weys** in an oblique or approximate fashion *20-.* [see the verb]

sklent¹·⁴ /sklɛnt/ *adv* at a slant, off the straight, obliquely *20-.* [see the verb]

sklent¹·⁵ /sklɛnt/ *prep* across, athwart *19- EC SW Bor.* [see the verb]

sklent²·¹ /sklɛnt/ *n* a rip, a tear *la19- Sh NE.* [see the verb]

sklent²·² /sklɛnt/ *v* to split, tear *19-.* [altered form of SLENT¹]

sklent³, *Sh* **sklant** /sklɛnt; *Sh* sklant/ *n* a chance, an opportunity *20- Sh NE Uls.* [altered form of *slant*; compare SKLENT¹·¹]

skletter see SCLATER

skleush¹·¹ /skluʃ/ *n* a trailing, shuffling, heavy-footed gait *la19- N NE.* [onomatopoeic; compare SLUSH¹·¹]

skleush¹·² /skluʃ/ *v* to walk in a clumsy, shuffling or leg-weary manner *la19- N NE Bor.* [see the noun]

skleuter see SLUTTER¹·²

skliff¹·¹, **skloof** /sklɪf, skluf/ *n* **1** (the sound of) a slap, a swipe in passing *19-.* **2** (the sound of) a shuffling, trailing way of walking *la19, 20- NE T C SW Bor.* **3** a clumsy, worn-out shoe *la19-, 20- NE C SW Bor.* **4** a thin slice; a segment (of the moon or an orange) *20- Sh T H&I C SW.* **skliffer** a flake, thin sheet or layer *19- WC SW.* [onomatopoeic; compare SKIFF¹·¹]

skliff¹·², **scliff, skluif, skloof** /sklɪf, skluf/ *v* **1** to walk with a heavy, shuffling step, drag the feet, scuffle *19-.* **2** to cut away the upper surface or covering of, pare, slice *20-.* **3** to strike with a glancing blow, scuff, rub against *la19, 20- C SW Bor.* [see the noun]

skliff¹·³ /sklɪf/ *adv* with a heavy sound *la19-.* [see the noun]

sklim see SCLIM¹·²

sklinner see SKLENNER

sklint see SKLENT¹·²

sklinter /ˈsklɪntər/ *v* to splinter, break off in fragments or flakes *19-.* [altered form of Eng *splinter*]

sklisse see SCLICE¹·²

skloit see SKLYTE¹·²

sklone /sklon/ *n* a large amount of any soft plastic substance, a pancake-like mass *la19- NE.* [probably altered form of SCONE¹·¹]

skloof see SKLIFF¹·¹, SKLIFF¹·²

skluif see SKLIFF¹·²

sklut see SCLIT

sklute¹·¹ /sklut/ *n* a heavy shuffling tread *19, 20- Bor.* [onomatopoeic]

sklute¹·², *N* **skleet** /*Bor* sklut; *N* sklit/ *v* to set the feet down clumsily in walking, walk in a flat-footed, shuffling, or splay-footed way *19- N Bor.* [see the noun]

sklyse see SCLICE¹·¹

sklyte¹·¹ /sklʌɪt/ *n* **1** (the sound of) a heavy fall, a thud *la19- NE T EC.* **2** a soft, wet, semi-liquid mass *la19- NE T.* **3** a big, clumsy, slovenly person or animal *20- NE.* **4** a large portion or slice *20- NE.* **5** a broken-down object, especially a worn-out shoe *19.* **sklyter** = SKLYTE¹·¹ (sense 3). [onomatopoeic]

sklyte¹·², **skloit** /sklʌɪt, sklɔɪt/ *v* **1** to fall with a thud; to slip, slither or clatter *20- NE T.* **2** to slop, splash, splatter (liquid) *la19- NE T.* **3** to work messily or clumsily *20 T EC.* **sklyter** = SKLYTE¹·². [see the noun]

sklyte¹·³ /sklʌɪt/ *adv* with a thud or plump, especially into something soft or wet *la19- NE T.* **sklyter** = SKLYTE¹·³. [see the noun]

skoag /skog/ *n* a fishing-line, a rod of whalebone with cord and hooks attached to each end *19- Sh.* [Norw dial *skåk* a swingle-tree, from the similarity of structure]

skoan see SKEAN

skobb see SKUB¹·¹

skog see SCUG¹·¹

skoil see SQUEEL¹·¹, SQUEEL¹·²

skoit¹·¹ /skɔɪt/ *n* **1** a peep, an inquisitive or surreptitious look *la19- Sh.* **2** (range of) sight *la19- Sh.* [see the verb]

skoit¹·² /skɔɪt/ *v* to peer, pry, peep *19- Sh.* [compare Dan *skotte*, Norw dial *skyttra*]

skol¹·¹, †**skoll**, †**scoll** /skɔl/ *n* a toast, a drink taken to wish a person good health *la16-.* [Norw, Dan *skål* your health!]

†**skol**¹·², **scoll** *v* to drink toasts; to drink freely *la16-e18.* [see the noun]

skolabrod /ˈskɔləbrɔd/ *n* a broken wooden object *20- Sh.* [Norw *skålbrott* a fragment of a wooden bowl]

skolbrøl¹·¹ /ˈskɔlbrøl/ *n* a bellow made by a cow or ox *la19- Sh.* [skoil (SQUEEL¹·¹) + BRÖL¹·¹]

skolbrøl¹·² /ˈskɔlbrøl/ *v of animals* to bellow or roar *la19- Sh.* [see the noun]

skolder /ˈskɔldər/ *n* **1** an outburst, torrent (of words); a clatter *20- Ork.* **2** a strong dry wind, a breeze *20- Ork.* [compare Norw dial *skaldra* to rattle]

skolder see SCOWDER¹·²

skolk see SCOUK¹·¹

skoll see SKOL¹·¹

skolp see SKULP

skolt see SKULT

†**skomer, skummer, skymmer** *v* to defecate *16.* [ME *scombren*, OFr *descombrer* to relieve of a load]

skons see SCONCE¹·¹

skonschon see SCUNCHEON

skoof see SCUFF¹·²

skoog see SCUG¹·¹

skook see SCOUK¹·¹, SCOUK¹·²

skoolm see SKUML¹·²

skoolt see SKULT

skoom see SCUM¹·¹, SCUM¹·²

skoosh¹·¹, **scoosh** /skuʃ/ *n* **1** a splash, a spurt, a jet (of liquid) *20-.* **2** a carbonated flavoured drink *la20- C.* **3** something done with ease *la20- C.* **skooshy cream** cream in an aerosol *la20- C.* [onomatopoeic]

skoosh¹·², **scoosh** /skuʃ/ *v* **1** *of liquids* to (cause to) gush in spurts or splashes, squirt *la19-.* **2** *of a moving object, especially a vehicle* to glide, move rapidly (with a swishing sound) *la19-.* **skoosher** a device for sprinkling or spraying, a sprinkler *20-.* **skoosh-car** a tramcar *20- WC historical.* **skoosh it** to do (something) with ease *la20-.* [see the noun]

skoosh¹·³, **scoosh** /skuʃ/ *adv* with a splash or swish *20- NE C.* [see the noun]

skoot¹ /skut/ *v* to project at an angle *20- Sh Ork.* **skootie** *of feet* big, splayed *20- Ork.* [Norw dial *skuta* to project]

skoot² /skut/ *v* to look about one attentively or cautiously *20- N NE.* [compare SCOUT³·²]

skootieallan see SCOOTIE-ALAN

skorchett see SCORCHET

skord see SCORD

skorek see SKARRIK

skorie see SCORIE

skorm see SKURM

skorn see SCORN¹·¹, SCORN¹·²

skorr see SKIRR²

skort see SKURT

Skotland see SCOTLAND

skottel see SKUTTEL, SKUTTLE

skourick, *Uls* **scorrick**, †**skeerock** /ˈskurək; *Uls* ˈskɔrək/ *n* **1** a minute amount; mainly *in negative constructions* not a scrap, not a bit *19, 20- Sh N.* **2** *pl* odds and ends *20- Uls.* [unknown]

skout *see* SCOUT[3.2]

skovins /ˈskovɪnz/ *npl* **1** the scrapings of a pot *19- Sh.* **2** large snowflakes *20- Sh.* Compare *skaavins* (SKAAVE). [compare Norw dial *skova* pot-scrapings]

skow *see* SCOW[2.1], SCOW[2.2]

skowg *see* SCUG[1.1], SCUG[1.2]

skowk *see* SCOUK[1.2]

skowp *see* SCUIP[1.1]

skowry *see* SCOURIE[1.2]

skoyr *see* SCORE[1.1]

skraable /ˈskrɑbəl/ *v* to rustle, crackle *20- Sh Ork.* [variant of SKRAVLE; compare Swed dial *skrabba* to creak]

skraal /skrɑl/ *n* a large number, quantity *20- Sh Ork.* [Norw dial *skroll* a heap]

skraich[1.1], **scraich, skraigh, screigh, †screke, †scraik, †skryke** /skrex, skrix/ *n* **1** a shriek, screech, a shrill strident sound *16-.* **2** a puny, shrill-voiced person *la19- NE.* [see the verb]

skraich[1.2], **scraich, skraigh, skreich, skraik, skreek, †screek** /skrex, skrix, skrek, skrik/ *v* to screech, shriek, scream *la15-.* **skraiching, †skryking** shrieking *16-.* [onomatopoeic; compare ME *skriken*, Norw *skrika*, ON *skrækja*]

skrank /skraŋk/ *adj* thin, skinny *19-.* [back-formation from SKRANKIE]

skrankie /ˈskraŋke/ *adj* thin, scraggy; meagre; shrivelled *18-19, 20- Sh Ork C.* [compare Norw dial *skrank* a thin, raw-boned figure, with -IE[2] suffix]

skrat *see* SCART[1.2]

skrattiskrae, sklaterscrae /ˈskrɑtɪskre, ˈskletərskre/ *n* **1** *derogatory* a talkative ignorant person *la19- Sh.* **2** a swarm of insects or vermin *20- Sh.* [unknown]

skrauch[1.1] /skrɔx/ *n* a shriek, a screech, a shrill or harsh discordant sound *19, 20- Ork N NE T EC Bor.* [see the verb]

skrauch[1.2], **scrauch** /skrɔx/ *v* to scream, shriek, screech *19, 20- N NE EC Bor.* Compare SKRAICH[1.1]. [onomatopoeic]

skravle /ˈskravəl/ *v* to rustle; to make a crackling or scraping sound *20- Sh.* Compare SKRAABLE. [compare Swed *skrafla*]

skravle *see* SCRAFFLE

skreed[1.1] /skrid/ *n* a swarm, a shoal, a pack, a crowd *19- Sh Ork N.* [Norw dial *skreid* a shoal]

skreed[1.2], *Ork* **skrythe** /skrid; *Ork* skraeð/ *v* to swarm, teem, crowd; to infest *19- Sh Ork N.* [see the noun]

skreek, skreigh /skrik, skrix/ *n* first light, the crack of dawn *19-.* **skreek o day** = SKREEK *la18-.* **skreek o dawn** = SKREEK *20- EC Uls.* [variant of CREEK[2], with influence from forms of SKRAICH[1.1]]

skreek *see* SKRAICH[1.2]

skreel *see* SCREEL

skreich *see* SKRAICH[1.2]

skreid *see* SCREED[1.1]

skreigh *see* SCREICH, SKREEK

skrell, scrail /skrɛl, skrel/ *n* a crash, a crack *20- Sh.* Compare SKROIL. [Norw dial *skrell*]

skreppo /ˈskrɛpɔ/ *n* a heap; a ruin *20- Ork.* [unknown]

skri *see* SCREE[3]

skrift /skrɪft/ *n* a very thin person, animal or object; a thin slice or fragile object *la19- Sh Ork T.* **skrifty** lean, spare *20- Ork.* [compare Swed dial *skrift* a skeleton, an emaciated person]

skrime, scrime /skrʌɪm/ *v* **1** to distinguish with difficulty, see indistinctly *19- Sh Ork.* **2** to peer, look closely *la19- Sh Ork.* [Norw dial *skrima* to have weak eyesight]

skrimple *see* SCRUMPLE

skrink[1.1] /skrɪŋk/ *n* a wrinkled, bad-tempered person *20- Bor.* **skrinkie** = SKRINK[1.1] *19- Bor.* [see the verb]

skrink[1.2] /skrɪŋk/ *v* to shrink, shrivel up *19, 20- EC Bor.* [compare Swed *skrynka* to wrinkle]

skrinkie /ˈskrɪŋke/ *adj* thin, wrinkled, shrivelled *19- Bor.* **skrinkie-faced** with a wrinkled, bad-tempered face *19- NE Bor.* [SKRINK[1.1] + -IE[2]]

skrip *see* SKIRP[1.2]

skrit[1.1], **scrit** /skrɪt/ *n* a scraping sound; a tear *la19- Sh.* [see the verb]

skrit[1.2], **scrit** /skrɪt/ *v* to scratch, scrape; to write *la19- Sh.* [onomatopoeic; compare *scrat* (SCART[1.2])]

skrivlin /ˈskrɪvlɪn/ *n* a small stack of hay *19- Sh.* [derivative of Norw dial *skryva* to stack, with diminutive suffix *-lin*]

skroil /skrɔɪl/ *n* a crash; fragments *la19- Sh.* [unknown; compare SKRELL]

skröl *see* SKRUIL[1.1]

skrottie /ˈskrɔti/ *n* lichen, especially *Parmelia saxatilis*, used as a dye; brownish red or orange *19- Sh.* [perhaps altered form of CROTTLE[2] with -IE[1] suffix]

skrovle[1.1], **scruffle** /ˈskrɔvəl, ˈskrɔfəl/ *n* a scraping, scrabbling noise; the sound of waves breaking on the shore *20- Sh Ork.* [see the verb]

skrovle[1.2], **scruffle** /ˈskrɔvəl, ˈskrɔfəl/ *v* to rustle, crackle; to scratch, grope, scrabble *la19- Sh.* [frequentative form of Norw dial *skråva* to make a rustling noise]

skrow *see* SCREW[1], SCROLL[1.1], SCROO[1.1]

skruddack /ˈskrʌdək/ *n* a crack, a fissure, a cleft *la19- Sh.* [Norw dial *skrote* with -OCK diminutive suffix]

skrue /skrø/ *n* fragments *20- Ork.* [perhaps Norw dial *skrue* a landslide]

skrüid /skrød/ *n* a landslide, an avalanche; a steep eroded slope *20- Sh.* [Norw dial *skrida* a landslide]

skruil[1.1], **skröl** /skrøl/ *n* a roar, a bellow; a screeching noise *la19- Sh.* [see the verb]

skruil[1.2] /skrøl/ *v* to roar, bellow, howl *19- Sh.* [Norw dial *skryla* to wail]

skruken *see* SCROCKEN

skrult[1.1] /skrʌlt/ *n* a grating noise, a scraping sound *la19- Sh Ork.* [see the verb]

skrult[1.2] /skrʌlt/ *v* to make a scraping noise; to scrape, grate *la19- Sh Ork.* [probably onomatopoeic]

skrumple *see* SCRUMPILL

skrunkit /ˈskrʌŋkɪt/ *adj* shrunk, shrivelled *la19, 20- NE.* [probably altered form of SKRINK[1.2]]

skrunkle /ˈskrʌŋkəl/ *v* to shrink, shrivel, crumple, become hard *20- NE T EC.* **†skronklit** wrinkled *la16.* [probably altered and frequentative form of SKRINK[1.2]]

skryke *see* SKRAICH[1.1]

skrym *see* SCRIM[1]

skrythe *see* SKREED[1.2]

skub[1.1], **skobb** /skʌb, skob/ *n* fine rain, drizzle, mist *19- Ork.* [unknown]

skub[1.2] /skʌb, skub/ *v* to rain, drizzle *20- Sh.* [unknown]

skuchle /ˈskʌxəl/ *v* to shuffle; to walk clumsily *20- Ork.* [perhaps a variant of SHAUCHLE[1.2], with influence from Norw dial *skokla*]

skuff *see* SCUFF[1.1], SCUFF[1.2]

skug /skʌg/ *n* a light passing shower *20- Sh Ork.* [Norw dial *skuggi* fog]

skug *see* SCUG[1.2]

skugg *see* SCUG[1.1]

skuil *see* SCHULE

skuild *see* SCULDING

skuill *see* SKULE

skuittie-fih *see* SCUITIFU

skuk see SCOUK[1.2]
skuld see SCULDING
skulduddery see SCULDUDDERY
skule, *Sh* **skjöll**, *Ork* **skull**, *NE* **skweel**, †**skuill** /skul; *Sh* skjøl; *Ork* skʌl; *NE* skwil/ *n* an inflammatory disease of the gums and palate of a horse *la17-19, 20- Sh Ork N NE*. [Norw dial *skjøl*]
skulk see SCOUK[1.1], SCOUK[1.2]
skull, †**scull** /skʌl/ *n* **1** the cranium *la16-*. **2** a tight-fitting cap worn out of doors or by children *la18-19, 20- Ork*. **skull-davie** a large (woman's) hat *20- NE*. [ME *sculle*, ON *skoltr*]
skull see SCULL[1], SKULE
skulp, skolp /skʌlp, skolp/ *n* **1** a jellyfish *la19- Sh*. **2** a dried-up jellyfish membrane *20- Sh*. [perhaps Dan dial *skulp* the tremulous movement of a liquid]
skult, skolt, †**skoolt** /skʌlt, skɔlt, skolt/ *n* the skull, the head *la19- Sh Ork*. [Norw *skolt*]
skuml[1.1] /'skʌməl/ *n* a sidelong or furtive glance *la19- Sh*. [see the verb]
skuml[1.2], **skoolm** /'skuməl, skulm/ *v* to scowl, squint *20- Sh*. [Norw dial *skumla* to scowl]
skummer see SKOMER
skumpik see SKYUMPACK
skunfish see SCOMFISH[1.2]
skunge /skʌndʒ/ *v* to thrust, chase out, clear away *la19- Sh*. [Norw dial *skunsa*]
skunk /skʌŋk/ *n* the sole or messenger rope of a herring drift net *la18- H&I WC*. [unknown; possibly altered form of *sunk* as in *sunk-raip* (SINK[1.2])]
skunner see SCUNNER[1.1], SCUNNER[1.2]
skupe see SCUIP[1.1]
skur[1] /skʌr/ *n* a deep chasm in the sea-bed where there are good fishing grounds; originally a fissure in rocks *19- Sh Ork*. [Norw *skor* a cleft, ON *skör* a rim, an edge]
skur[2] /skʌr/ *n* the boundary between two inshore fishing-grounds *20- Sh*. [compare ON *skǫr* an edge]
skurd see SCORE[1.2]
skurdy see SCURDIE
skurge see SCOURGE[1.2]
skurken see SCROCKEN
skurm, skorm /skʌrm, skorm/ *n* a hard shell, an egg-shell; a rind, a crust *19- Sh Ork*. [Norw dial *skurm* a shell]
skurriour see SCURROUR
skurt, skort, scoort /skʌrt, skɔrt, skurt/ *n* **1** an armful *la19- Sh Ork N*. **2** the space enclosed by the body and folded arms or clasped hands *19- Sh Ork*. [probably Norw *skjød* the lap, the bosom]
skut /skʌt/ *n* a cigarette end *20- C*. [perhaps Eng *scut* a rabbit's tail; compare DOWP[1.1]]
skutamilliescroo /'skʌtəmɪlə'skru/ *n* hide-and-seek played among cornstacks *20- Sh*. [Norw dial *skjota imillom skruver* to dart between corn stacks]
skutfast[1.1] /'skʌtfast/ *n* a mooring or anchor rope at the stern of a boat *20- Sh*. [Norw *skut* the stern of a boat + FAST]
skutfast[1.2] /'skʌtfast/ *v* to moor (a boat) *20- Sh*. [see the noun]
skuther /'skʌðər/ *n* a brief gale, a passing shower *20- Ork*. [variant of *scudder* (SCUD[1.2])]
skutie see SCUITIE
skuttel, skottel, †**scattel** /'skʌtəl, 'skotəl/ *n* a wedge-shaped board in the floor of a boat in the stern or stem *la18- Sh*. [perhaps derivative of Norw *skut* the stern or stem of a boat]
skuttle, skottel /'skʌtəl, 'skotəl/ *n* an (empty) eggshell *20- Sh Ork*. [Norw dial *(eggja) skutl* (egg)shell]
skweel see SCHULE, SKULE
sky[1.1], †**skey** /skʌɪ, skae/ *n* **1** the heavens, the firmament *la15-*. **2** daylight, the light of the sun, especially at dawn or sunset *la16-19, 20- Bor*. **3** *in Aberdeenshire* the outline of a hill as seen against the sky, the skyline *la16-19*. †**sky-break** daybreak *la17-19*. †**sky-breaking** = *sky-break 17-e18*. **sky-set** nightfall *la17-19, 20- NE*. †**sky-setting** = *sky-set la17-e19*. [ON *ský* a cloud]
sky[1.2] /skʌɪ, skae/ *v* **1** to shade (a patch of water) so as to see the bottom *la19- NE T*. **2** to look towards the horizon, shading the eyes with the hand *la19- NE*. **3** to look about *20- NE T*. [see the noun]
sky[2], **ski** /skae/ *n in Shetland and Orkney* a board on a single-stilted plough equivalent to the mouldboard *18-19, 20- historical*. [Norw dial *skjei* the upright part of a plough]
sky[3.1] /skae/ *n* courtship; fun *19- Ork*. [see the verb]
sky[3.2] /skae/ *v* to court *20- Ork*. [shortened form of slang *skylark* to frolic]
†**sky**[4] *n Dumfriesshire and Galloway* some sort of cloth *la16-e17*. [perhaps referring to cloth the colour of the SKY[1.1]]
skyallach see SKELLOCH[1.2]
skybald[1.1], **skypal**, †**skybell** /'skaebəld, 'skaepəl/ *n* **1** a rascal, a rogue *la16-*. **2** a poor wretch; a ragged, unkempt person *la17-*. **3** something worthless *20- N*. [unknown]
skybald[1.2], **skypal** /'skaebəld, 'skaepəl/ *adj* **1** rascally, disreputable, worthless; tattered, ragged *la16-*. **2** not having or providing enough, needy; stingy *la19- NE*. [unknown]
skybe, scipe /skʌɪb, skʌɪp/ *n* a mean rogue, a bad-mannered or worthless person; an oaf *18-19, 20- T EC SW Bor*. **skypie** = SKYBE *20- NE*. [shortened form of SKYBALD[1.1]]
skybell see SKYBALD[1.1]
skyle[1.1] /skʌɪl/ *n* a screen on the windward side of a chimney to prevent smoke from blowing down *19- Sh*. [Norw dial *skyle* a cover over a chimney]
skyle[1.2], *N* **skeel** /skʌɪl; *N* skil/ *v* **1** to shelter, deflect wind or rain from (a chimney or building) *la19- Sh Ork N*. **2** to shade (the eyes); peep, peer *la19- Sh*. [Norw dial *skyla* to shelter]
skyle see SKAIL[1.2]
skylie see SCAILIE
skymmer see SKOMER
skyn see SKIN[1.1]
skyow see SKEW[2.1], SKEW[2.2], SKEW[2.3]
skyowl see SKEWL[1.2]
skyp see SKIP[1.1], SKIP[1.2]
skypal see SKYBALD[1.1], SKYBALD[1.2]
skyr see SKIRE[1.3]
†**skyre, scirhe, shirre** *n* an unsightly physical mark, perhaps a lump, tumour, scar or scab *16*. [unknown; compare Lat *scirros* a hard swelling]
skyre see SCARE[1.1], SCARE[1.2], SCARE[1.3], SKIRE[1.1], SKIRE[1.2]
Skyreburn warning, †**Skairsburn warning** /'skaerbʌrn 'wɔrnɪŋ/ *n* no warning at all (of an event or a sudden disaster) *la17- SW*. [altered form of Eng *Scarborough warning* with reference to the Skyre Burn in Kirkcudbrightshire]
Skyre Thursday see SKIRE THURSDAY
skyrie, skeirie /'skaeri, 'skere/ *adj* bright; gaudy in colour, garish *20- Ork NE*. Compare *skyrin* (SKIRE[1.1]). [SKIRE[1.2] + -IE[2]]
skyrt see SKIRT[1.1]
skytch see SKETCH[1.2]
skyttand see SKITE[2.2]
skyumpack, skumpik /'skjʌmpək, 'skʌmpək/ *n* the edgepeat, a large, badly-shaped peat *la19- Sh*. [Dan *skumpe* the turf on the top of a peat moss with -OCK diminutive suffix]
sla see SLAE[1], SLAY[1]
slaa see SLAW[1.1]
slab[1] /slab/ *n* **1** a flat, thick piece of something solid *la19-*. **2** the first slice cut off a loaf, with one side crusty *20- T C*. **3** a thin person with a broad frame *la19- NE T*. [ME *slabbe*]

slab² /slab/ *v* to wet with saliva, beslobber; to stain (one's clothes) with saliva or with food when eating *18-*. **slab up** to eat or drink noisily, messily or greedily *la18- NE T*. [probably MDu, MLG *slabben*]

slab³ /slab/ *n* tea *20-*. [Travellers' language]

slabber¹·¹ /ˈslabər/ *n* **1** a greedy or noisy mouthful *la19- NE T EC*; compare SLUBBER¹·¹. **2** a slovenly, slack-lipped person, a slobberer *19- T C SW*. **3** something liquid or messy, especially food *20- NE T EC*. **4** frequently *pl* senseless or foolish talk, idle chatter *20- C SW*. **5** mud; muddy, trampled soil *la19, 20- NE EC*. **slabbery** *of roads* waterlogged, muddy *la19- WC*. [see the verb; compare Dan †*slabber* muddy ground]

slabber¹·² /ˈslabər/ *v presp* †**slabring 1** to slaver, dribble; to eat or drink noisily *17-*; compare SLUBBER¹·². **2** to wet with a messy, semi-liquid substance *19-*. **3** to wet with saliva, beslobber; to stain (one's clothes) with saliva or with food when eating *18-19, 20- N T C SW*. **4** to make a snorting, bubbling sound as in weeping or sleeping *19, 20- WC SW*. **5** to work carelessly, messily or with something wet or messy *19, 20- SW*. **6** to talk drivel, babble *20- C*. [Du *slabberen*, LG *slabbern*]

slachter see SLAUGHTER¹·¹

slack¹·¹ /slak/ *n* **1** a slackening or loosening *la19-*. **2** the loose part of anything, anything loose *la19-*. **3** negligence, carelessness *la16*. [see the adj]

slack¹·², †**slak**, †**sclak** /slak/ *v* **1** to release (tension), slacken, loosen *16-*. **2** to slacken off, become less tense or active, grow flaccid *la18-*. **3** to release, let out (sail, a horse's reins) to gain speed *e16*. [see the adj]

slack¹·³, †**slak** /slak/ *adj* **1** idle, negligent, lacking firmness or diligence *la15-*. **2** loose *19-*. **3** *of a ewe* past breeding age *la18-*. **4** *of money* scarce; *of persons* short of money *la18-19, 20- T C*. **5** *of a building* untenanted, thinly occupied, not busy *e19*. [OE *sleac*]

slack¹·⁴ /slak/ *adv* **1** loose *la18-*. **2** scarcely, loosely *e15*. [see the adj]

slack², †**slak**, †**slaik** /slak/ *n* **1** a hollow, a boggy valley between hills, a saddle in a hill-ridge, a pass; frequently in place-names *la14-*. **2** a pit, a hole; a gap *15-16, 20- Sh*. **3** a bog, boggy ground; a marsh *la16-19, 20- Bor*. [ON *slakki* a shallow dell, in some place-names perhaps SLOCK²]

slack³ /slak/ *n* aptitude, skill *20- Ork*. [perhaps altered form of Norw (*ha godt*) *lag* (*med*) (to have) the knack (of)]

†**slacky** *n* a kind of sling or catapult *la17-e19*. [unknown]

slade see SLAID, SLED, SLIDE¹·²

slae¹, **sloe**, †**sla**, †**slo** /sle, slo/ *n* (the fruit of) the blackthorn *Prunus spinosa la16-*. [OE *slāh*]

slae² /sle/ *n* the slow-worm *Anguis fragilis 19- H&I SW Bor*. [shortened form of OE *slāwyrm*]

slag¹·¹ /slag/ *n* a large blob of something wet, soft or messy *la18-19, 20- T*. [probably onomatopoeic; compare SLAG²]

†**slag**¹·² *v* to mess about with food, gobble up in large spoonfuls *e19*. [see the noun]

slag² /slag; *Sh* slɑg/ *n* a marshy place, morass *19- Sh Bor*. [compare ME *slag* muddy, ON *slagi* dampness]

slag³·¹ /slag/ *n* **1** a slap, a swinging blow *la19- Sh*. **2** a heavy clumsy person, a hulking object *20- Sh Ork*. **3** a heavy swell in the sea *20- Ork*. [Norw *slag* a blow]

slag³·² /slag/ *v* to hit with a swinging blow, slap *la19- Sh*. [see the noun]

slag see SLAKE¹

slaich see SLAIK¹·²

†**slaid**, **slade** *n* a glade, a dell, a valley; frequently in place-names *la12-e16*. [OE *slæd*]

slaid see SLIDE¹·²

slaiger¹·¹, *NE* **slagger** /ˈslegər; *NE* ˈslagər/ *n* **1** a wet, soggy, or slimy mess, a daub, a smear of sloppy food *la18-*. **2** the act of bedaubing; slovenly work *la19, 20- C Bor*. [derivative of SLAG¹·¹]

slaiger¹·² /ˈslegər/ *v* **1** to smear with something soft and wet, daub with mud *la19-*. **2** to eat or drink messily *19-*. **3** to walk messily in mud; to plod wearily or carelessly *19, 20- WC Bor*. **slaigerin** dirty, slovenly, slatternly *la19-*. **slaiger on** to smear or daub (a soft, wet substance) on or over a surface *20- N EC*. [see the noun]

slaik¹·¹ /slek/ *n* **1** the act of daubing or smearing; something soft, wet, or messy which has been smeared on *19-*. **2** a lick with the tongue, a slobbering lick or kiss *18-19, 20- T C SW Bor*. **3** a careless or slatternly wash, a hasty clean or wipe; a dirty, messy way of working *la19, 20- T WC SW*. **4** a person who eats or drinks excessively *20- T C Bor*. [see the verb]

slaik¹·², **slake**, **slaich**, *NE* **sklaik** /slek, slex; *NE* sklek/ *v* **1** to besmear, bedaub, streak *la18-*. **2** to lick, smear with the tongue, beslobber *16-19, 20- T C SW Bor*. **3** to kiss, caress, fondle sloppily; to fawn, behave obsequiously *la16-19, 20- T C*. **4** *especially of a pet animal* to lick (dishes) or consume (food) on the sly; to scrounge *19, 20- WC*. [ME *slaken* to lick, ON *sleikja* to lick]

slaik see SLACK², SLAKE¹

slain, **slaine** see SLAY¹

slaip, **slape** /slep/ *adj* slippery, smooth, sleek *19, 20- Bor*. [Eng *slape*, ON *sleipr*]

slair, *NE T* **sclair** /sler; *NE T* skler/ *v* to smear, cover (with something soft, wet or messy) *la18-*. [probably onomatopoeic]

slairg¹·¹ /slerg/ *n* a quantity of something messy or semi-liquid, a dollop, a smear *19, 20- EC SW Bor*. [see the verb]

slairg¹·², **slairk**, †**slerg** /slerg, slerk/ *v* **1** to smear, bespatter (with something wet and dirty) *19- SW Bor*. **2** to smear (a substance) on or into something *18-19, 20- SW*. **3** to sup liquid noisily, slobber at one's food *19- Bor*. [probably onomatopoeic]

slairy¹·¹ /ˈslere/ *n* a smear, daub, a lick of paint *la19-*. [see the verb]

slairy¹·², **slerry** /ˈslere/ *v* to smear, cover (with something soft, wet, messy) *la18-*. [altered form of SLAIR]

slairy¹·³ /ˈslere/ *adj* slovenly in one's eating habits *20- C*. [see the verb]

slaister¹·¹, *Sh Ork* **slester** /ˈslestər; *Sh Ork* ˈslɛstər/ *n* **1** a state of wetness and dirt, a splashy mess; dirty water, slops *la18-*. **2** a slovenly, dirty worker; a messy person, especially a messy eater *19-*. **3** a state of confusion *la19-*. **4** a small amount of something either solid or liquid *20-*. **5** an unpalatable or nauseating mixture of foods *la18-*. **6** unskilful work *20- Ork*. **7** an unskilful worker *20- Ork*. **slaistery** wet and dirty, muddy, slimy *19-*. [see the verb]

slaister¹·², *Sh Ork NE* **slester**, *N Bor* **slyster**, *N* **sleester**, *T* **scloister** /ˈslestər; *Sh Ork NE* ˈslɛstər; *N Bor* ˈslʌɪstər; *N* ˈslɪstər; *T* ˈsklɔɪstər/ *v* **1** to work messily or splash the hands about in a liquid; to work awkwardly, clumsily or ineffectively *la18-*. **2** to eat or drink messily or greedily *19-*. **3** to make messy, smear *la18-*. **4** to smear (a substance) on a surface, spread or scatter messily *20-*. **5** to idle, slack, loaf about *20- N EC*. **6** to wade in mud or water *19, 20- Sh N*. **slesterin** untidy, slovenly *la19-*. **slaister-kyte** a messy eater; a glutton *la18-*. [probably onomatopoeic]

†**slait¹**, **slate** *n* derogatory a dirty, slovenly or nasty person *18-e19*. [unknown]

†**slait²** *v pt* **slatit** to incite or set (a dog) on *la14-16*. [ON **sleita*]

slaive see SLEEVE¹·¹

slaiver see SLAVER¹·¹, SLAVER¹·²
slak see SLACK¹·², SLACK¹·³, SLACK², SLAKE¹
slake¹, sloke, *Ork* **slag, †slaik, †slawk, †slak** /slek, slok; *Ork* slag/ *n* one of various species of edible fresh- and saltwater algae *la15-19, 20- Sh Ork N NE H&I*. **†slawkie** covered with algae, slimy; smooth, soft and flabby *19*. [Gael *slòcan, slabhagan,* IrGael *sleabhac, sleabhcán*]
slake², †sclaik /slek/ *v* **1** to appease, satisfy (an appetite or desire, frequently thirst) *la15-*. **2** *of activity* to lessen, moderate, diminish; *of a person, animal* to become less active; to stop work or activity; to weaken *la15-17*. **3** to assuage, mitigate, moderate (pain, sorrow, a penalty) *la14-17*. [OE *sleacian* to slacken, become less active]
slake see SLAIK¹·²
slammach /ˈslaməx/ *n frequently in pl* gossamer, spiders' webs *19- NE*. [SLAUM¹·¹, with -OCH suffix]
slamp /slamp/ *adj* slim, lithe, supple *19- N NE T*. [unknown]
slamp see SLUMP¹·¹
slander see SCLANDER¹·¹, SCLANDER¹·²
slane see SLAY¹
slang¹ /slaŋ/ *n Travellers' language* a field *20- SW Bor*. [Eng *slang* a long strip of land]
†slang², slung *n* a type of cannon *16-17*. [MDu, MLG *slange*]
slang see SLING¹·²
slap¹·¹, *Sh* **slep,** *N* **slop** /slap; *Sh* slɛp; *N* slɔp/ *n* **1** a smack, a blow *la17-*. **2** a large quantity, a dollop *la19, 20- Sh T*. **3** a stamp with the foot *la19- Sh*. **4** a hearty, loud kiss *20- Sh*. [LG *slapp*]
slap¹·² /slap/ *v* **1** to smack, hit *19-*. **2** to exceed, beat, go beyond *la19, 20- N C SW*. [see the noun]
slap²·¹, slop /slap, slɔp/ *n* **1** a gap or opening in a wall, fence or hedge *la14-*. **2** an opening left temporarily in a salmon weir to allow the fish to swim up-river to spawn *15-*. **3** a pass or shallow valley between hills; frequently in place-names *18-*. **4** a hole, a missing part, a break in continuity; a lack, a want *17-19, 20- Sh T SW*. **5** a narrow passage or lane between houses *la19- NE*. **6** a gap or breach in the ranks (of an army) *la15-19*. **7** a gash or wound *la14-17*. **8** a gap to let water into or out of a dam, drain or ditch *18-e19*. **9** a stone, perhaps as cut for use in a door or window aperture *la16-e17*. **†slap-riddle** a wide-meshed riddle for separating grain from broken straw *18-e19*. [MDu, MLG *slop* a gap, a narrow entrance, Flem *slop* an opening in a dam]
slap²·², †slop /slap/ *v* **1** to make a gap or break in (a wall); *building* to make an aperture for a door or window *16-*. **2** to open a gap in a salmon weir or net to allow fish to pass through *20-*. **3** to thin out (seedlings) *20- NE*. **4** to make breaks or breaches in (a body of troops) *la15-e16*. **5** to wound, pierce (a person) *e16*. **slapped** notched, roughened at the edge *18- Sh NE*. [see the noun]
slap³, †sloap /slap/ *n* **1** mainly *pl* sloppy food, dregs *19-*. **2** a careless or dirty person *19- C SW*. **slap-bowl** a basin for collecting waste liquids *la18-*. [probably Eng *slop*]
slape see SLAIP
slarrie see SLAURIE¹·²
slash¹·¹ /slaʃ/ *n* a violent dash or clash, especially of something wet, a splash; a large mass of sloppy food *19, 20- Sh N NE T Uls*. [perhaps OFr *esclache* a splash]
slash¹·² /slaʃ/ *v* **1** to throw (liquid) with a splash; to strike with something wet *la19-*. **2** to rush violently, dash forward *19, 20- Sh T*. [see the noun]
slash¹·³ /slaʃ/ *adv* with a clash or splash, with violence *20- Sh T WC*. [see the noun]
slasy gawsy see SLAWSY

slatch¹·¹ /slatʃ/ *n* **1** a messy, dirty worker; a dirty, coarse woman *19- WC Bor*. **2** a resounding blow, a heavy thud *la19- Sh N Bor*. **3** a wet and muddy place *20- Bor*. Compare SCLATCH¹·¹. [perhaps onomatopoeic]
slatch¹·² /slatʃ/ *v* **1** to work in something messy; to potter or dabble in mud *19- Bor*. **2** to walk or splash through mud, wade about messily *19- Bor*. **3** to smack, slap hard *20- Bor*. Compare SCLATCH¹·². [see the noun]
slate see SCLATE¹·¹, SCLATE¹·², SLAIT¹, SLIT¹·²
slater see SCLATER
slather /ˈslaðər/ *n* a smear, a slobber, a quantity of any messy substance *20-*. [probably onomatopoeic]
slattyvarrie /slatəˈvare/ *n* the edible seaweed *Laminaria digitata 19- H&I*. [Gael *slat-mhara*]
slauch see SLOCH²·¹
slauchter¹·¹, slaughter, †slauchtir, †slawchtir, †slachter /ˈslɔxtər, ˈslɔtər/ *n* **1** the killing of a person as a criminal act; murder; assassination *la14-*. **2** the indiscriminate killing of large numbers of people in battle; carnage, massacre *la14-*. **3** the butchering of domestic animals for food *15-*. **4** the (usually criminal) killing of an animal or animals *la15-*. **†slauchtir scheip** sheep earmarked for or having been butchered for food *la16-17*. **†slauchtir skynis** the skins of (newly) slaughtered animals *16-e18*. [ON *slátr* butcher meat]
slauchter¹·², slaughter /ˈslɔxtər, ˈslɔtər/ *v* to kill; to massacre; to butcher *17-*. [see the noun]
slauer see SLAVER¹·²
slaum¹·¹ /slɔm/ *n* slime, something slimy or oozy *20- NE*. [MLG *slamm* mud]
slaum¹·², †slawm /slɔm/ *v* to slobber *la18-*. [see the noun]
slaurie¹·¹ /ˈslɔre/ *n* a smear, a smudge, a daub of something soft and sticky *la19- C SW*. [ME *slori* mud, slime]
slaurie¹·², slarrie /ˈslɔre, ˈslare/ *v* to daub or splash with mud; to dirty (one's clothes) *19-*. [ME *slorryed* bedaubed with mud, muddy]
slave¹·¹, *NE* **sclave** /slev; *NE* sklev/ *n* **1** a person who is the property of another; a servant who has no personal rights or freedoms; a serf *la15-*. **2** a person or animal submissive to or dominated by another person, feeling or habit *16-*. **3** a person of low birth; a menial; a drudge *16-19, 20- NE*. [ME *sclave,* OFr *esclave,* Lat *sclavus*]
slave¹·², *NE* **sclave** /slev; *NE* sklev/ *v* **1** to work like a slave, drudge *20-*. **2** to enslave *la17*. [see the noun]
slaver¹·¹, slaiver, *NE* **sliver** /ˈslevər; *NE* ˈslɪvər/ *n* **1** saliva, drool *la17-*. **2** chatter, drivel *la19-*. **3** slime, exudation, sticky moisture *20- Ork NE T*. **4** fine rain, drizzle *20- C SW*. **slavery** *weather* wet, rainy *la19- N WC SW*. **slavers 1** saliva, drool *la18-*. **2** foolish talk *la19-*. **slavery-buckie 1** the whelk *Colus islandicus 20- NE T*. **2** the whelk *Buccinum undatum 20- Ork*. [ME *slavere,* compare Icel *slafur*]
slaver¹·², slaiver, *NE* **sliver, †slauer** /ˈslevər; *NE* ˈslɪvər/ *v* **1** to allow saliva to fall from the mouth, drool *la15-*. **2** to talk nonsense, chatter in a silly way *la19-*. **3** to fondle, cuddle, kiss amorously *20- C SW*. [ME *slaveren,* compare Icel *slafra*]
slaw¹·¹, slow, *Sh Ork* **slaa** /slɔ, slo; *Sh Ork* sla/ *adj* not fast; dilatory; tardy; sluggish; lacking energy or willingness *15-*. **slow-thooms** a slow-moving person, a slow worker *19- Bor*. [OE *slāw*]
slaw¹·², slow /slɔ, slo/ *adv* slowly, tardily; in a leisurely way *16- literary*. [see the adj]
slaw see SLAY¹
slawchtir see SLAUCHTER¹·¹
slawk see SLAKE¹
slawm see SLAUM¹·²
†slawsy, slasy gawsy *n a term of endearment* addressed to a man *e16*. [unknown]

slay¹, †**sla** /sle/ *v pt* **slew**, †**slaw**, †**sleuch**, †**sclew**, *ptp* **slain**, †**slane**, †**slaine**, †**slayne** **1** to kill by striking violently; to put to death *la14-*. **2** to eradicate (a fault or quality); *law* to extinguish (a claim or right) *la14-16*. **3** to destroy (vegetation) *la15-e19*. **4** to strike fire from flint *la14-e16*. **5** *of a thing* to cause (a person) to die *15-17*. **slay doun** to kill, strike down, annihilate *15-16*. [OE *slēan* to strike, smite]

†**slay²** *n weaving* an instrument used to beat up the weft *16-17*. Compare REED³ (sense 3). [OE *slege* a stroke]

slayne *see* SLAY¹

sle *see* SLEE¹·²

sleb¹·¹ /slɛb/ *n* the underlip, especially as protruded in a pout *la19- Sh*. **slebset** with a sulky expression *20- Sh*. **hing a sleb** to pout, assume a sulky expression *20- Sh*. [probably altered form of Norw *lepe* a (hanging) lip]

sleb¹·² /slɛb/ *v* to pout *20- Sh*. [see the noun]

sleband *see* SLEEBAND

slebs *see* SLEPSE

sled, †**slade** /slɛd/ *n* **1** a sledge; a drag or slide-car used for the transport of (heavy) goods *la14-*. **2** a child's cart, usually made of short planks on the chassis of a disused pram *20- T C*. †**sledder** a man who drives or uses a sled *16-18*. [MDu, MLG *sledde*]

sled *see* SLIDE¹·²

slee¹·¹, *Sh* **sley** /sli; *Sh* sle/ *v* to go or come silently or slyly *la18-19, 20- Sh*. [see the adj]

slee¹·², **sly**, †**sle**, †**sley**, †**slie** /sli, slae/ *adj* **1** cunning; deceitful *la14-*. **2** *of persons* skilled, clever, expert; wise *la14-*. **3** *of things* well-made; demonstrating the skill of their creator or user *la14-*. [ON *slœgr* clever, cunning]

slee¹·³ /sli/ *adv* slyly, cunningly, stealthily *19-*. [see the adj]

slee *see* SLEIVE

†**sleeband**, **sleband** *n* an iron ring round the beam of a wooden plough to strengthen it where the coulter was attached *16-e19*. [perhaps reduced form of SLEEVE¹·¹ + BAND¹·¹]

sleech *see* SLEEK²

sleek¹·¹, †**slieck** /slik/ *n* **1** flattery *la19- Sh Ork*. **2** a measure of capacity, especially of grain or fruit *la17-19, 20- WC*. [probably shortened form of *sleek measure*; compare SLEEK¹·²]

sleek¹·², †**sleke** /slik/ *v* **1** to smooth, give the appearance of smoothness *19-*. **2** *weights and measures* to level off (goods) at the top of a container; *of a substance or commodity* to fill (a container) *la15-*. **3** to walk or move smoothly or furtively, slink, sneak *19-*. **4** to flatter, wheedle, ingratiate oneself *la18- C SW Bor*. [ME *sliken, sleken* to smooth, polish]

sleek¹·³, †**sleik** /slik/ *adj* **1** smooth and glossy *16-*. **2** fawning and deceitful; cunning, self-seeking, sly *la18-*. **sleekie 1** sleek, smooth, slippery *la16-*. **2** fawning, deceitful, sly *la18-*. **3** concealed *20- Sh*. †**sleik-stane** a stone for smoothing or sharpening *la16-19*. [see the verb; compare ME *slike*]

sleek², *T EC SW* **sleech**, *EC* **slike**, †**slik**, †**slyke** /slik; *T EC SW* slitʃ; *EC* slʌɪk/ *n* alluvial mud deposited by the sea or a river, silt; bog mud, boggy ground *la14-19, 20- T EC SW*. [compare MDu *slijc*, MLG *slick* mud]

sleekie /ˈsliki/ *n* a conger eel *20- Sh*. [SLEEK¹·³ + -IE³]

sleekit, †**slekit**, †**slekyt** /ˈslikət/ *adj* **1** smooth, having an even surface or glossy skin; slippery *16-*. **2** smooth in manner, plausible; sly, cunning, not to be trusted *15-*. **3** *of weather* deceptive *20-*. **sleekitness** speciousness, slyness, obsequiousness *19-*. [participial adj from SLEEK¹·²]

sleep¹·¹, †**slepe**, †**sleip** /slip/ *n* **1** slumber, the state of being asleep *la14-*. **2** the repose of death *16-*. **sleepery, sleepry 1** sleepy; characterized by drowsiness *16-19, 20- Bor*. **2** sleep-inducing *16*. †**sleepies** the smooth rye brome-grass *Bromus secalinus e19*. †**sleipryfe** sleep-inducing *e16*. **sleepy mannies** the specks of matter which form in the corners of the eyes during sleep *20- NE EC*. **sleepy men** = *sleepy mannies 20- WC*. **sleepy motes** = *sleepy mannies 20- EC*. **sleepy things** = *sleepy mannies 20- T*. [OE *slǣp*]

sleep¹·², †**slepe**, †**sleip** /slip/ *v pt* **sleepit**, †**slept 1** to slumber, be asleep; to fall asleep *la14-*. **2** *of a top* to spin so fast and so smoothly as to appear motionless *19, 20- N NE C*. **3** *law, of an action* to be in abeyance, lie dormant; to lapse *16-, 20-*. **be sleepit oot** to have slept one's fill *20-*. **sleep as sound as a horn** to sleep very soundly *20- Sh N SW*. **sleep in** to oversleep *19-*. **sleep thegither** to share a bed, sometimes implying sexual intimacy *la15-*. †**sleipand and walkand** incessantly, day and night *la15-e16*. †**sleyping, walking** = *sleipand and walkand e16*. **sleep with** = *sleep thegither 16-*. [OE *slǣpan*]

sleesh, *NE* **skleesh** /sliʃ; *NE* skliʃ/ *n* **1** a slice *la19- Sh NE*. **2** a swipe, a cutting stroke; a lash, as with a whip *20- Ork Bor*. **sleeshack** a dish of potatoes fried in slices *20- N NE*. **sleesher** something outstanding of its kind *20- Bor*. [altered form of *slice* (SCLICE¹·¹)]

sleester *see* SLAISTER¹·²

†**sleeth** *n in the North-East* a slow, lazy person; a worthless person *18-e19 NE*. [variant of SLOUTH¹·¹]

sleeve¹·¹, *T* **slaive**, †**slefe**, †**sleve**, †**sleif** /sliv; *T* slev/ *n* the part of a garment that covers (some part of) the arm *la14-*. **sleeve-poultice** *humorous* a sweetheart *la20- Ork*. [OE *slīefe*]

sleeve¹·², †**scleve**, †**slewe** /sliv/ *v* **1** to go arm-in-arm with, keep company with, court *20- T C SW*. **2** to fit a garment with a sleeve *16-e17*. [see the noun]

slefe *see* SLEEVE¹·¹

slefset /ˈslɛfsət/ *adj* dirty, untidy, slovenly *20- Sh*. [Norw dial *slafsut* dirtied, soiled]

sleif *see* SLEEVE¹·¹

sleik *see* SLEEK¹·³

sleip *see* SLEEP¹·¹, SLEEP¹·²

†**sleive**, **sleve**, **slee** *v* to slip (something) out of or over *15-19*. [OE *slēfan* to slip (clothes) on]

sleke *see* SLEEK¹·²

slekit, slekyt *see* SLEEKIT

slemmer *see* SLIM¹·¹

†**slent¹** /slɛnt/ *v* to split, cleave *17*. [unknown]

slent² /slɛnt/ *v* to slant, move obliquely *17-*. Compare SKLENT¹·². [ON **slenta* to slant]

slep *see* SLAP¹·¹

slepe *see* SLEEP¹·¹, SLEEP¹·²

slepse, slebs /slɛps, slɛbs/ *v* to salivate, slaver, dribble *la19- Sh*. [altered form of Norw dial *lepja* to lap]

slerg *see* SLAIRG¹·²

slerp¹·¹ /slɛrp/ *n* **1** a spoonful of liquid taken with a slobbering sound *20- SW Bor*. **2** an untidy, slovenly person *19- T EC*. **3** a blob, a smear, a lump of something wet or messy *20- Ork*. **4** a wet smacking blow, a slap *20- Ork*. **5** a wet kiss *20- Ork*. [see the verb]

slerp¹·² /slɛrp/ *v* **1** to consume noisily or messily *20- C SW Bor*. **2** to salivate or slobber, splutter messily, spit *20- Ork EC Bor*. **3** to smear with something wet or messy *20 Ork Bor*. **4** to kiss clumsily *20- Ork*. [variant of SLORP¹·²]

slerpy /ˈslɛrpe/ *adj* slovenly, messy *20- Ork EC*. [SLERP¹·¹ + -IE²]

slerry *see* SLAIRY¹·²

slester *see* SLAISTER¹·¹, SLAISTER¹·²

sleuch *see* SLAY¹

sleug /slug/ *n* an ugly or ungainly person; an unpleasant person *19-*. [unknown]

sleugh *see* SLUCH

†sleuth¹, sloith *n* a track or trail (of a person or animal) *la14-e17*. **sleuth-dog, slough dog** a bloodhound used for hunting or tracking *17-e19*. [ON *slóð* a path, a trail]
†sleuth² *adj* slothful *16-19*. [from the noun *sleuth* (SLOUTH¹·¹)]
sleuth *see* SLOUTH¹·¹, SLOUTH¹·²
sleuther *see* SLUTTER¹·²
sleuth hound, *SW* **slowan, †slow hound, †slough hound, †slewthound** /'sluθ hʌund; *SW* 'sluən/ *n* a bloodhound used for hunting or tracking *la14-*. [SLEUTH¹ + HOOND¹·¹]
sleve *see* SLEEVE¹·¹, SLEIVE
slew *see* SLAY¹
slewe *see* SLEEVE¹·²
slewie /'slui/ *v* to walk with a heavy swinging or swaying gait *la19- NE*. [altered form of Eng *slew* to swing round]
slewth *see* SLOUTH¹·¹, SLOUTH¹·²
slewthound *see* SLEUTH HOUND
sley *see* SLEE¹·¹, SLEE¹·²
slibbery /'slɪbəre/ *adj* slippery *la18-19, 20- T*. [ME *slibbri*, MLG *slibberig*]
slice *see* SCLICE¹·¹, SCLICE¹·²
sliced sausage /slʌɪst 'sɔsɪdʒ/ *n* sausage-meat cut into flat slices and cooked *la20-*. **slicing sausage** = SLICED SAUSAGE. Compare LORNE SAUSAGE. [SCLICE¹·² + Eng *sausage*]
slicht¹·¹, †slycht /slɪxt/ *n* **1** cunning, craftiness, guile, trickery; deceitfulness *la14-*. **2** knowledge, wisdom, ability, method or knack (of doing something) *la14-19, 20- T EC*. **†slicht-full** crafty, cunning *15-e16*. **†slichtfully** cunningly, deceitfully *la14*. [ON *slœgð*]
†slicht¹·², slycht *adj* crafty, cunning; deceitful; skilful; requiring dexterity, cunning or deceit *16*. [see the noun]
slicht²·¹ /slɪxt, slʌɪxt/ *v* to treat with indifference or disdain; to neglect, ignore; to use disrespectfully, fritter away, waste *17-*. [see the adj]
slicht²·², slight /slɪxt, slʌɪxt/ *adj* **1** small, insubstantial; trivial, lacking substance *16-*. **2** smooth, level; *of the sea* unruffled, calm *la19- Sh Ork*. **3** *of women* of loose moral character *la17-18*. **4** *of commodities* inferior; ordinary *16-17*. **5** *of coins* light in weight *16-17*. **6** *of persons* of little account; disreputable *la16-17*. **†slightly** without proper attention, seriousness or respect, slightingly *la16-19*. **slight-a-face** coming directly; bit by bit, in sequence *20- Ork*. [ME *slight*, ON **sleht-* smooth]
†slicht³, slight *v* to raze to the ground, demolish *17-19*. [LG *slichten*]
slichten, slychten, slighten /'slʌɪxtən/ *v* to smooth, level *20- Sh*. [SLICHT²·², with verb-forming suffix]
slid, †slide, †slyde /slɪd/ *adj* **1** *of surfaces* slippery, smooth *16-19, 20- C SW Bor*. **2** *of persons or their actions* smooth, cunning, sly; cajoling *18-19, 20- WC Bor*. **3** insecure, precarious *e18*. **4** changeable, uncertain *e16*. [related to SLIDE¹·²]
slidden *see* SLIDE¹·²
slidder¹·¹, sclidder, †sclither /'slɪdər, 'sklɪdər/ *n* **1** a sliding, slithering movement; a slip, a skid *19-*. **2** ice; an icy surface *20- NE T Bor*. **3** a stony area on a hillside, a scree; loose stones *19, 20- Bor*. **4** a slow-moving or dilatory person *la19, 20- WC*. **5** slipperiness *e16*. [see the adj]
slidder¹·², sclidder, sclither /'slɪdər, 'sklɪdər, 'sklɪðər/ *v* **1** to (cause to) slip or slide *19-*. **2** to walk or move in a casual or lazy way; to slip (away), take oneself off *la19, 20- T WC*. [ME *slideren, slitheren*, OE *slidrian*]
†slidder¹·³, slyddir *adj* slippery; inconstant, unreliable *la15-17*. [OE *slidor*]
slidderie, sliddry, †slydry, †slyddry /'slɪdəre, 'slɪdre/ *adj* **1** slippery, causing slipping or sliding *la15-*. **2** insecure, unstable, shaky; changeable, uncertain *la16-*. **3** sly, deceitful, unreliable, untrustworthy *17-*. **4** having a slippery surface, not easy to hold on to *16-19, 20- NE T EC*. **5** *of food* soft, sloppy *19, 20- Sh NE T*. [SLIDDER¹·² + -IE²]
slide¹·¹ /slʌɪd/ *n* **1** the action of sliding; a surreptitious or deceitful action *la16-*. **2** a mechanism, bolt or window that slides *la18-*. **3** a slippery track on which to slide *la19-*. [see the verb]
slide¹·², †slyde, †slyd /slʌɪd/ *v pt* **slid, slade, sled, †slaid**, *ptp* **slidden 1** to slip or glide over a surface *la14-*. **2** to slip, lose one's foothold *la14-*. **3** to pass, disappear (from memory) in the course of time; *of an occasion or season* to pass by *la15-*. **4** to deviate from the strict truth, tell a mild lie, exaggerate *19, 20- NE*. **5** to fall from good fortune or grace, lapse, err *la15-17*. **6** *of farm animals* to lose weight or condition *e19*. **†slide on sleip** to fall asleep *la15-e16*. [OE *slīdan*]
slide *see* SLID
slider /'slʌɪdər/ *n* **1** ice-cream sandwiched between two wafers *20-*. **2** the movable metal loop sliding on a rod on a cart-shaft, to which the back-chain is hooked *20- Ork N NE T EC*. [SLIDE¹·² + -*er* agent suffix]
slidey, slidy /'slʌɪde/ *adj of surfaces* slippery, very smooth *17-*. [SLIDE¹·² + -IE²]
slie *see* SLEE¹·²
slieck *see* SLEEK¹·¹
†slig, skleg *v* to lie, practise deceit *19 Bor*. [unknown]
slight *see* SLICHT²·², SLICHT³
slighten *see* SLICHTEN
slik, slike *see* SLEEK²
slim¹·¹, *N* **slime** /slɪm; *N* slʌɪm/ *v* to treat (work) with insufficient care, neglect (a job) *19- N NE SW Bor*. **slemmer** a careless or neglectful worker; a lazy, idle person *20- N H&I*. **slim awa** to waste, fritter away (time) *19, 20- N*. **slim ower** = SLIM¹·¹. [see the adj]
slim¹·² /slɪm/ *adj* **1** thin, slender; narrow *19-*. **2** *of clothing and footwear* flimsy, insubstantial *19, 20- Sh NE T*. **3** wily, sly, crafty; specious, dishonest *17-19, 20- NE SW*. **slim-jim** a kind of confectionery, long strips of coconut or liquorice *la19- WC*. [Du, LG *slim* mean, dishonest, crafty]
slime *see* SLIM¹·¹
sling¹·¹ /slɪŋ/ *n* **1** a device for securing or carrying objects; the swivels, hooks and chains of the draught-harness of a cart *15-*. **2** a swinging vigorous gait, a long striding step *19, 20- Bor*. [MLG *slinge*]
sling¹·², †slyng /slɪŋ/ *v pt* **slang 1** to throw, hurl, fling *la14-*. **2** to walk with a long vigorous stride, swing along *19, 20- Bor*. [see the noun; and compare ON *slyngva* to knock down by means of a sling]
sling *see* SLUNG
slinger¹·¹ /'slɪŋər/ *n* a twisting, a twining; a heave or swell in the sea *20- Sh*. [see the verb]
slinger¹·² /'slɪŋər/ *v* to swing, sway, roll, reel *la18, 20- Sh*. [Du *slingeren*]
slingers /'slɪŋərz/ *npl* **1** bread sops boiled in milk *20- NE*. **2** sausages *20- N NE T C*. [*Services slang*, derived from SLING¹·²]
slink¹·¹ /slɪŋk/ *n* a smooth, crafty person; a despicable character *19, 20- T C SW Bor*. [see the verb]
slink¹·² /slɪŋk/ *v pt* **slunk 1** to move or go quietly, stealthily or sneakily *la18-*. **2** to cheat, deceive, act dishonestly *19*. [OE *slincan* to creep, crawl]
slink¹·³ /slɪŋk/ *adj* thin, scraggy, lank *19-*. [see the verb; and compare SLINK²]
slink² /slɪŋk/ *n* **1** an aborted, premature, or newly-born, unfed calf or other animal *18-19, 20- T C SW*. **2** an emaciated or spent fish, especially a cod or salmon *19, 20- NE WC*. [Eng *slink* an aborted calf, (of a cow) to abort, perhaps variant of SLING¹·²].

slip¹·¹ /slɪp/ *n* **1** a (moral) fault, error *la16-*. **2** a loose (protective) garment for slipping over one's clothes, a pinafore *la16-*. **3** an abortion, a miscarriage *20- N NE T C*. **4** a metal ring attaching the swingle-trees of a plough to the trace-chains from the harness *19, 20- N H&I*. **5** a device for drawing ships out of the water for repair *19*. [see the verb]

slip¹·², †**slyp**, †**sleip** /slɪp/ *v* **1** to (cause to) move with an easy, gliding motion; to go quietly or secretly; to escape, evade (justice) *16-*. **2** to slide, move involuntarily *16-*. **3** *of a cow* to have the pelvic ligaments relaxed before calving *20- NE T WC SW*. **4** to fail or neglect (to do something), miss (an opportunity) *16-19, 20- Ork T*. **5** to allow to escape, let go, dismiss, release *la16-17, 20- Sh*. **6** to overlook, refrain from noticing, fail to mention *16, 20- Sh*. **7** to remove a garment; *of a snake* to slough (its skin) *e16*. **slippie** an undervest *20- Sh Ork*. **slip-band** a straw binding for a sheaf which, because of a defective knot, slips open *la19- Ork NE*. **slip-body** an under-bodice, a camisole *la19-*. **slip-bolt** a door- or sash-bolt made to slip into a cylindrical socket, a barrel-bolt *20-*. **slip-by** a carelessly-performed task, shoddy work *la19- Sh Ork N NE T C*. **slip-ma-labor** a lazy, untrustworthy person *19, 20- Sh*. **slip-me-laav** badly done work; a negligent person *la19- Ork*. †**slippon, slipon, slippond** a metal ring or buckle used as a part of harness or in the construction of a window *16-e19*. **slip-raip** = *slip-band 20- NE T WC*. **slip-shod 1** badly shod; shabby *la17-*. **2** wearing shoes but no stockings *19- T C SW Bor*. **3** having one's shoelaces hanging loose *20- WC SW Bor*. **slip aff o yer feet** to take your shoes off *la19- Sh*. **slip awa** to die quietly *la18-*. **slip on, slyp on** to dress quickly *la19- Sh*. **slip the tether** to throw off a restraint *19, 20- Sh*. **slip the timmers** to die *20- NE*. **slip yer ways** to depart, take yourself off *19, 20- Ork*. [ME *slippen*, MLG *slippen*]

slip² /slɪp/ *n* **1** a narrow strip or piece of something; a small piece of paper; a betting slip *la18-*. **2** a young person; one of small or slender build *19-*. **3** a twig or shoot from a plant; a tree-branch; a cutting *la19-*. **4** a measure of yarn, usually a hank weighing two pounds *la16-19, 20- Bor*. **5** a saddle flap *la16-e18*. [MDu, MLG *slippe* a strip]

slipe¹·¹, **slype**, †**slip**, †**slyp** /slʌɪp/ *n* **1** a wooden wheelless platform for moving heavy loads, a sledge *la15-19, 20- NE T C SW Bor Uls*. **2** a rail or wooden runner by which barrels etc are unloaded from a lorry *20- WC Bor*. **3** *mining* a curved wooden box on iron runners for taking coal away from the cutting-face *19*. [LG *slipe* a sledge]

slipe¹·² /slʌɪp/ *v* to transport by means of a drag or sledge *18-*. [see the verb]

slipe², †**slype** /slʌɪp/ *v* to move in a slanting direction, fall over sideways *la18-*. [compare MLG *slipen* to slip, slide]

slipper¹·¹ /'slɪpər/ *n* a slippery state or condition; that which causes slipperiness *la19- NE*. [see the adj]

†**slipper**¹·² *adj* slippery, smooth *la16-18*. [OE *slipor*]

slippy /'slɪpe/ *adj* slippery *la18-*. [SLIP¹·² + -y (-IE²)]

slit¹·¹ /slɪt/ *n* **1** a narrow cut, tear, or opening *17-*. **2** a sheep-mark, a cut in the ear *la18-19, 20- SW*. **3** a narrow aperture in a wall; a window *la16-18*. [see the verb]

slit¹·², *WC SW Bor* **slite** /slɪt; *WC SW Bor* slʌɪt/ *v pt also* **slate**, *ptp* **slitten 1** to cut, rip up, split *16-*. **2** to make sharp, whet *la18-e19*. **3** to score or incise meat *la16*; compare SLOT²·². †**slit mill** a slitting mill, for splitting iron bars or plates *18*. [ME *slitten*, OE *slītan*]

slitter¹·¹, **sluitter** /'slɪtər, 'slutər/ *n* **1** (messy) semi-liquid matter, an unpalatable mixture of food; a state of untidiness or dirtiness *20- T C SW Bor Uls*. **2** a slovenly, untidy, or messy person *20- T C SW Bor Uls*. **3** a tricky, complicated job or situation *la20- C*. **slittery** wet and messy, sloppy *19- T C SW Bor*. [variant of SLUTTER¹·¹]

slitter¹·² /'slɪtər/ *v* **1** to work or walk messily in water, splash about untidily; to eat or drink messily *la19- T C SW Bor*. **2** to smear with something wet or messy, make messy or stained *la19- T C SW Bor*. **3** to work at something tricky with little effect; to work in a slovenly way *la20- EC SW Uls*. [see the noun]

slitter² /'slɪtər/ *n* a tattered, ragged state *20- Ork*. [compare Icel *slitur* rags]

slive¹·¹ /slaev/ *n* a thin slice, a sliver *20- Bor*. [see the verb]

slive¹·² /slaev/ *v* to slice *20- Bor*. **sliver** the tailboard of a cart *19- EC Bor*. [Eng *slive*, OE *tōslīfan* to split]

sliver see SLAVER¹·¹, SLAVER¹·²

slo, sloo /*Sh* slo; *Ork* slu/ *n* the core of an animal's horn *la19- Sh Ork*. [Norw dial *slo*]

slo see SLAE¹

sloam see SLOOM¹·²

sloan /slon/ *n* a sharp retort, a snub, a rebuke *19, 20- Bor*. [Eng *slon* a sneer]

sloap see SLAP³

sloch¹·¹, **slough, sluch,** †**slowch,** †**slouch** /slɔx, slʌx/ *n* **1** an outer covering, a skin, a shell; a snake skin; the husk or skin of fruit or vegetables *16-*. **2** the pelt of a dead sheep *18- T H&I SW*. **3** the membrane covering the intestines in fish *20- Ork*. **4** a suit of clothes; clothing *la16-e19*. **5** a cataract (on the eye) *16-17*. **6** a lumpish or soft person *19*. [ME *slough*; compare MHG *slūch*]

sloch¹·², **slough, sluch** /slɔx, slʌx/ *v* to remove the wool from a dead sheep by skinning rather than shearing *19- SW*. [see the noun]

sloch²·¹, **slauch** /slɔx, slox/ *n* **1** a noisy intake of food or drink; a hearty drink, a good swig *la19-*. **2** a slatternly person *20- NE T*. **slochy** slimy, dirty and disgusting *20- NE T SW*. [see the verb]

sloch²·² /slɔx/ *v* to swallow (food or drink) in a noisy, slobbering way *19- N NE T C*. [onomatopoeic]

sloch see SLOCK²

slochen see SLOCKEN

slock¹·¹ /slɔk/ *n* a draught of liquid, a drink *19-*. [from the verb or Du *slok*]

slock¹·², **sloke,** *NE* **slyock** /slɔk, slok; *NE* sljɔk/ *v* **1** to quench (thirst) *15-*. **2** to slake (lime) *17-*. **3** to satisfy the thirst of (a person, animal); to satisfy wishes or desires *19-*. **4** to extinguish, quench (a fire or light) *la14-19, 20- Sh Ork N WC SW*. **5** *of fire* to go out *la15, la19- Sh Ork N*. **6** to moisten, soak, drench *la19- NE T*. **7** to thicken (water or soup) with meal *20- Sh*. **8** to suppress, eliminate, bring to an end *la14-15*. **slockin** enough (drink) to slake one's thirst, a drink *19- Sh Ork NE*. **slockit** drunk *20- Ork NE*. †**slock yer drouth** to quench your thirst *la18-19*. [ON *slokinn*, ptp of *sløkkva* to be extinguished]

slock², **sloch,** *NE* **slug** /slɔk, slɔx; *NE T* slʌg/ *n* **1** a hollow between hills, a narrow pass, frequently in place-names *la18- N NE T SW*. **2** a creek or gully in the sea, a long deep inlet between rocks, often revealed at low tide *19- NE T SW*. **the Sloch** a nickname for the village of Portessie *la19- NE*. **the Slug Road** the road through the pass between Banchory and Stonehaven *19- NE*. [Gael *sloc, slochd* a hollow, a dell, a pool]

slocken, *EC* **slochen,** *NE* **slyocken,** †**slokkin,** †**slokyn** /'slɔkən; *EC* 'slɔxən; *NE* 'sljɔkən/ *v ptp* †**sloknyt 1** to quench (thirst), satisfy (the desire to drink) *15-*. **2** to abate, subdue, alleviate; to extinguish, suppress *15-*. **4** to moisten, drench, soak *18-*. **5** to inaugurate or celebrate with a drink *19-*. **6** to make a paste of (meal) *19-*. **7** to extinguish (fire or a light) *la14-19, 20- N SW Uls*. **8** to slake (lime) *16-19, 20- SW Uls*. **9** *of thirst* to become slaked; *of a person* to have their thirst or another desire satisfied *19, 20- NE*. **10** *of fire or love* to go out, be extinguished *la15-e17*. **11** to sate, satisfy (a desire) *16-17*. **slockener** a thirst-quenching drink *19-*. **slockenin** a thirst-quenching; a satisfying drink *19, 20- Sh NE*. [ON *slokna* (of a fire) to go out]

sloe *see* SLAE¹

slogan, †sloggorn, †slughorn /'slogən/ *n* **1** a call to arms or of identification, a battle-cry or rallying-cry, mainly consisting of a family name or location; a password *16-*. **2** a distinctive catchword or motto adopted by a person, group or institution *la16-*. [Gael *sluagh-ghairm* the rallying cry of an army]

slogg /slog/ *n* a marsh, bog *19- NE Bor*. [compare SLAG², SLOCK², Gael *sloc* a hollow, a pool]

slogger¹·¹ /'slogər/ *n* a slovenly, dirty, or untidy person *19- WC SW Bor*. [see the verb]

slogger¹·² /'slogər/ *v* to loiter, hang back *20- WC*. [perhaps imitative; or altered form of LAGGER¹·²]

sloggerin /'slogərɪn/ *adj* slovenly in appearance, dirtily or untidily dressed *19- WC SW Bor*. [participial adj from SLOGGER¹·²]

sloggorn *see* SLOGAN

slogie-riddle /'slogeˈrɪdəl/ *n* a wide-meshed riddle *19- Bor*. [unknown first element + RIDDLE¹·¹]

sloindie /'sloɪndi/ *n* a rabble, a mob *la19- Sh*. [unknown]

†sloit¹·¹ *n* a lazy, slovenly person *19*. [see the verb]

sloit¹·², **slowt** /slɔɪt, slʌut/ *v* to walk in a slow, slouching way; to stroll idly or carelessly about *19, 20- EC*. **sloiterin** = SLOIT¹·² *la19- C Uls*. [probably onomatopoeic]

sloit *see* SLOT¹·¹

sloith *see* SLEUTH¹

sloke *see* SLAKE¹, SLOCK¹·²

slokkin, sloknyt, slokyn *see* SLOCKEN

slomer *see* SLUMBER¹·²

slong *see* SLUNG

slonk *see* SLUNK¹

sloo¹·¹ /slu/ *n* **1** an evenly spread layer (of dung, peat or compost) *19- Sh*. **2** a lanky or sluggish person or animal *la19- Sh*. [Norw dial *sloe* a drag made of branches, a lanky or sluggish person]

sloo¹·² /slu/ *v* to spread a layer of earth, seaweed or dung *19- Sh*. [Norw dial *sloe* to trail, drag]

sloo *see* SLO

slooan *see* SLUAN

sloob *see* SLUIB

slooch¹·¹, **slouch** /slutʃ, slʌutʃ/ *n* **1** (a person having) a stooping, ungainly posture or walk *la18-*. **2** an idle, work-shy person *la19, 20- Sh T*. **†slouchy** drooping *la17*. [EModE *slouch*]

slooch¹·², **slouch** /slutʃ, slʌutʃ/ *v* to crouch, cower, skulk furtively; to slouch *18-*. [see the noun]

slooch *see* SLUCH

sloom¹·¹ /slum/ *n* a dreamy or sleepy state; a daydream; a light or unsettled sleep *19-*. [OE *slūma* a slumber]

sloom¹·², *Uls* **sloam** /slum; *Uls* slom/ *v* **1** to move easily and quietly; to slink, sneak *la19, 20- Sh T*. **2** *of plants* to show luxuriant, soft or unnatural growth *la19- Uls*. **3** *of plants* to (cause to) become soft or flaccid; to (cause to) wilt and decay *la18-19*. **4** to sleep lightly or fitfully, doze *la18-19*. **†sloomy, sloumy, slomie 1** *of corn* not well filled out, stunted *18-e19*. **2** *of plants or animals* exhibiting soft, weak growth *la17-e19*. [ME *slumen* to doze; and compare Norw dial *sluma* to slouch]

sloom², **sloon** /slum, slun/ *n* a rumour, a piece of hearsay or gossip *la19- NE*. **sloomin, sleumin** a rumour, gossip *la19 NE*. [unknown]

sloomit /'slumit/ *adj* sly, underhand *19- Sh Ork*. [participial adj from SLOOM¹·²]

sloopsy /'slupsi/ *adj* having an odd appearance, uncouth *20- Ork*. [unknown]

sloor *see* SLOUR

sloosh¹·¹, **sluice**, *Sh* **slus, †slouse** /sluʃ, slus/ *n* **1** a structure by which the (level or quantity of) water in a canal or river can be controlled; a sluice *la16-*. **2** a dash of water, a splashing *la19-*. [ME *scluse*, OFr *escluse*, Lat *slūsa*]

sloosh¹·² /sluʃ/ *v* to splash with water, throw water about in large splashes, flush *20-*. [see the noun]

sloosht /sluʃt/ *n* a disreputable character, a reprobate *20 NE*. [unknown]

sloot /slut/ *v* to slant, slope, incline *la19- Sh*. [Norw dial *sluta* to hang down]

sloother *see* SLOUTER

slop, slope /slop, slop/ *npl* **sloppis 1** an outer garment, a loose-fitting seaman's or field worker's jacket or tunic *16- NE T EC*. **2** baggy trousers *16-e19*. **3** *literary* trailing clouds *16*. [ME *slop*, OE *oferslop*]

slop *see* SLAP¹·¹, SLAP²·¹, SLAP²·²

slope /slop/ *v* **1** to avoid paying, defraud *la19-*. **2** to shirk, idle *20- NE WC SW*. **sloper** a shirker *20- NE EC Uls*. [US *slope* to run away, decamp]

slope *see* SLOP

slopra *see* SLUPPER

slorach¹·¹, *NE* **schlorach** /'slorəx, 'slorəx; *NE* 'sklorəx/ *n* **1** a noisy gulping down of food *la19- NE*. **2** a wet, disgusting mess *la19- NE*. [onomatopoeic; perhaps SLOUR with intensifying suffix -OCH]

slorach¹·², *NE* **schlorach** /'slorəx, 'slorəx; *NE* 'sklorəx/ *v* **1** to eat or drink messily and noisily, slobber, slaver *la19- NE T*. **2** to clear the throat loudly, breathe or speak through catarrh *la19- NE T*. [see the noun]

slork¹·¹ /slork/ *n* **1** a noisy sucking up of food or drink *20- WC SW Bor*. **2** a reinhalation of nasal mucus *20- SW*. [onomatopoeic; compare Norw *slurk* a noisy gulp]

slork¹·² /slork/ *v* **1** to make a slobbering noise, when eating or drinking; to suck up (food or drink) noisily *19- WC SW Bor*. **2** to reinhale nasal mucus, sniff or snort *20- WC SW*. **3** *of shoes or persons* to make a squelching noise in walking *19- Bor*. [see the noun; compare Norw *slurke* to swallow with a gurgle]

slorp¹·¹ /slorp/ *n* a noisy mouthful, a slobber, a swig *19- EC SW Bor*. [see the verb]

slorp¹·² /slorp/ *v* **1** to eat or drink noisily and slobberingly *19-*. **2** *of shoes* to make a squelching sound *19- Bor*. **slorp an greet** to weep noisily and with gulps of indrawn breath, sob convulsively *19- Bor*. [Du, MLG *slorpen*]

slot¹·¹, **†slote, †sloit, †slott** /slɔt/ *n* **1** a bar or bolt for a door or window *16-*. **2** (metal) bar or rod used for support or to secure something; a cross-piece in a harrow or cart *la15-19, 20- N SW*. [MDu, MLG *slot*]

slot¹·² /slɔt/ *v* to bolt, lock (a door, window), secure with a bolt or bar *16-*. [see the noun]

slot²·¹ /slɔt/ *n* **1** the hollow running down the middle of the chest *16-*. **2** a narrow aperture, a slit *20-*. **3** the hem of a garment etc in which a drawstring runs *19, 20- N T*. **4** a pit, a hole in the ground *19- SW*. **Gallows Slot** a pit or hole on the shores of Carlingwark Loch at Castle Douglas *19- SW*. **the slot of yer breist** = SLOT²·¹ (sense 1). [ME *slot*, OFr *esclot*]

†**slot**[2.2] *v* to make one or more slits or scores on (the carcass of a slaughtered animal) *17-e18*. Compare SLIT[1.2] (sense 3). [see the noun]

slot[3] /slɔt/ *n* a dish of fish livers and roe mixed with flour and oatmeal, then boiled and fried *19- Sh*. [unknown]

slotch[1.1] /slɔtʃ/ *n* a lazy, slouching person, a layabout *19, 20- EC Bor*. [see the verb]

slotch[1.2] /slɔtʃ/ *v* to move or walk in a slouching, hangdog way; to drag the feet in walking *19-*. [probably onomatopoeic]

slote, slott *see* SLOT[1.1]

†**slotter** *v* to act in a slovenly way, work messily in a liquid; to act slothfully *16-e19*. [probably onomatopoeic; compare Du *slodderen* to hang about]

slottery, slottry /'slɔtəre, 'slɔtre/ *adj* sluggish, slothful *e16, 19-*. [SLOTTER + *-y* (-IE²)]

slouch *see* SLOCH[1.1], SLOOCH[1.1], SLOOCH[1.2]

slough *see* SLOCH[1.1], SLOCH[1.2]

sloughan *see* SLUAN

slough hound *see* SLEUTH HOUND

sloumy *see* SLOOM[1.2]

slounge[1.1], **slunge** /slundʒ, slʌndʒ/ *n* **1** a lazy person *19-*. **2** a person or animal always on the lookout for food, a scrounger, a glutton *19- EC SW Bor*. **3** a skulking, sneaking, sly, trouble-making person *19, 20- SW*. [see the verb]

slounge[1.2], †**slunge** /slundʒ/ *v* **1** to idle or loaf about; to walk in a slouching, lethargic way *la18-*. **2** to behave furtively and stealthily *la17-*. **3** to hang about in the hope of getting food *20- Sh NE SW Bor*. **slounger** an idler, loafer *19, 20- N Uls*. [altered form of LOONGE]

slounge *see* SLUNGE[1.1], SLUNGE[1.2]

slour, sloor /slur/ *n* a noisy gulp (of food or drink), a mouthful of soft, sloppy food *19- NE*. [onomatopoeic]

slouse *see* SLOOSH[1.1]

slouster[1.1], **sluister** /'slʌustər, 'slustər/ *n* **1** a careless, messy person *19- C SW Bor Uls*. **2** a wet, sloppy kiss *19- Uls*. **3** something wet or messy *19*. [see the verb]

slouster[1.2], **sluister** /'slʌustər, 'slustər/ *v* **1** to dabble in water or mud, work untidily or messily *19- T EC SW Uls*. **2** to swallow noisily and ungracefully, gulp, slobber *20- T C*. **3** to kiss in a sloppy way *19- Uls*. [onomatopoeic; compare SLAISTER[1.2]]

slout *see* SLUTE[1.1]

slouter, *Uls* **sloother** /'slutər; *Uls* also 'sluðər/ *n* a coarse, slovenly, idle person *la19, 20- N NE T Uls*. [perhaps derivative of SLUTE[1.1]]

†**slouth**[1.1], **sleuth, slewth** *n* laziness, idleness; sloth; slowness, negligence *15-17*. Compare SLEETH. **slouthful** negligent, careless; lazy; slow, lethargic; characterized by negligence, laziness or sluggishness *la15-19*. [OE *slæwð*]

slouth[1.2], †**sleuth**, †**slewth** /sluθ, slʌuθ/ *v* **1** to carry out (a task) in a lazy, idle, careless way, treat with indifference or neglect; to delay *16-19, 20- NE T*. **2** to waste (time) *la16*. [see the noun]

slow *see* SLAW[1.1], SLAW[1.2]

slowan *see* SLEUTH HOUND

slowch *see* SLOCH[1.1]

slow hound *see* SLEUTH HOUND

slownk *see* SLUNK[3.1]

slowt *see* SLOIT[1.2]

sloy *see* SCLY[1.1]

sluan, sloughan, slooan /'sluən/ *n* **1** a slow-moving, lazy, soft person *18-19, 20- Ork N NE Bor*. **2** a covetous or greedy person *19- Bor*. [reduced form with extended meaning of SLEUTH HOUND]

slub *see* SLUIB

slubber[1.1] /'slʌbər/ *n* **1** a noisy, slobbering way of eating *19, 20- Ork N NE*; compare SLABBER[1.1]. **2** any sloppy, jelly-like matter; pus; slush; a jelly-fish *19, 20- N NE T*; compare SLUIB. [see the verb]

slubber[1.2] /'slʌbər/ *v* to swallow sloppy food; to eat or drink in a noisy, gulping way *20-*. Compare SLABBER[1.2]. [EModE *slubber*, LG *slubbern*]

slubber[2] /'slʌbər/ *n* tangled yarn *19- Bor*. [Eng *slub* a yarn containing thickened parts]

sluch, slooch, †**sleugh,** †**slughe** /slʌx, slux/ *n* a marsh, quagmire; boggy ground *la16-19, 20- Sh NE*. [OE *slōh*]

sluch *see* SLOCH[1.1], SLOCH[1.2]

slud /slʌd/ *n* **1** an interval (between showers), lull; an occasion, opportunity *19- Sh*. **2** a girlfriend or boyfriend, a date *la19- Sh*. [Norw dial *slot*]

sludder, sluther /'slʌdər, 'slʌðər/ *n* something wet and slimy, mud, filth *19, 20- Bor*. [onomatopoeic; compare LG *sleuder* lather, Ger *Schluder* slush, mud]

sluff /slʌf/ *v* to drink in noisy gulps *20- Sh*. [probably onomatopoeic]

slug[1] /slʌg/ *n* **1** a sluggard *la16-*. **2** a sleep, a nap, a state of inactivity *20- WC SW*. [ME *slugge*; compare Norw dial *slugg* a heavy person]

slug[2] /slʌg/ *n* a loose upper garment worn to protect the clothing; an overall *la18-19, 20- Sh SW*. [compare Swed *sloka* to hang down loosely]

slug *see* SLOCK[2]

sluggard, *Bor* **sluigger,** †**sluggart,** †**sluggird,** †**slugird** /'slʌgərd; *Bor* 'slugər/ *n* a sluggish or lazy person *15-*. [ME *slogard, slugger*; SLUG[1], with *-ard* suffix]

†**sluggardry** *n* slothfulness *e16*. [SLUGGARD, with *-ry* suffix]

†**sluggardy** = SLUGGARDRY *la15-16*. [SLUGGARD + *-y* (-IE³)]

sluggart /'slʌgərt/ *adj* sluggish, slothful, negligent *16, 20- literary*. [from the noun SLUGGARD]

sluggie /'slʌgi/ *n* the opening at the foot of a corn-kiln which creates the draught for the fire *20- Sh*. [probably Norw *slok* the channel which brings water to a mill, conflated in form and sense with LOGIE]

sluggird *see* SLUGGARD

slughe *see* SLUCH

slughorn *see* SLOGAN

slugird *see* SLUGGARD

sluib, sloob, †**slub** /slub/ *n* a messy, viscous substance, slime *la19- Sh*. [perhaps MDu *slubbe* mud]

sluice *see* SLOOSH[1.1]

sluigger *see* SLUGGARD

sluister *see* SLOUSTER[1.1], SLOUSTER[1.2]

sluit *see* SLUTE[1.1]

sluitter *see* SLITTER[1.1]

slumber[1.1], †**slummer,** †**slummyr** /'slʌmbər/ *n pl* †**slumrys** (a period of) sleep or rest *la15-*. [see the verb]

slumber[1.2], †**slummer,** †**slummyr,** †**slomer** /'slʌmbər/ *v* to sleep, doze *la15-*. [ME *slomberen*, MDu *slumeren*, MLG *slummeren*]

slump[1.1], *N* **slamp** /slʌmp; *N* slamp/ *n* **1** *building* a rough estimate *la19-*. **2** a large quantity, a great number; a lump sum (in payment), an approximate total *la17-*. [LG (*im*) *slump* (*köpen*) (to buy in) the lump = a heap, a mass]

slump[1.2] /slʌmp/ *v* to treat (several things) as one, lump together, deal with as a whole *la17-19, 20- Sh NE T WC*. [see the noun]

slump[2] /slʌmp/ *n* a marsh, a boggy place, a morass *19- SW Bor Uls*. **slumpy** marshy, muddy; *of ice* soft, unsafe *19, 20- Bor*. [perhaps conflation of Eng *sump* with SLUNK[1]; and compare SLUMP[3]]

slump³ /slʌmp/ *v* to sink into mud or slush *19- SW Bor Uls*. [onomatopoeic; compare Norw dial *slumpa*]

slumrys *see* SLUMBER¹·¹

slung, sling, †slong /slʌŋ, slɪŋ/ *n* **1** an implement or weapon used for hurling stones *la14-*. **2** a tall, lanky, stupid person; a disreputable person, a rascal *19- NE*. **like a slung stane** like a bolt from the blue *la18- NE*. [variant of SLING¹·¹; and compare Norw dial *slyngja* a long thin person]

slung *see* SLANG²

slunge¹·¹, slounge /slʌnʒ, slundʒ/ *n* **1** a plunging motion, a headlong fall, a splash made by a heavy object *la18-*. **2** a quick rinse or wash *la20- C*. [see the verb]

slunge¹·², slounge /slʌnʒ, slundʒ/ *v* **1** to make a plunging movement or noise *19-*. **2** to drench with water *20-*. **3** to wade, splash, blunder through water or mud *la18, 19- Bor*. [onomatopoeic]

slunge *see* SLOUNGE¹·¹, SLOUNGE¹·²

slunk¹, †slonk /slʌŋk/ *n* a (wet and muddy) hollow; a soft, deep, wet rut in a road; a ditch *la15-19, 20- SW Uls*. **slunky** *of roads* muddy, rutted, full of wet holes *la19- Uls*. [compare Dan *slånk, slunk* a hollow in the ground]

slunk² /sluŋk/ *n* a long, lean, lanky person or animal *20- Sh*. **sloonky** lean, emaciated *20- Ork*. [Norw dial *slunk*; and compare SLUNKEN]

slunk³·¹, N slownk /slʌŋk/; *N* slʌuŋk/ *n derogatory* a lazy, sneaking person, a shirker *20- N WC*. [see the verb and compare Norw dial *slunk* a sluggard]

slunk³·² /slʌŋk/ *v* to go unobtrusively; to creep, sneak about *la19- Sh N*. Compare SLINK¹·² (sense 1). [compare Swed *slunka* to sneak]

slunk *see* SLINK¹·²

slunken /ˈslʌŋkən/ *adj* lank, emaciated, sunken *19- Sh WC SW Bor*. [perhaps participial adj from *slink*, the verb corresponding to SLINK²; and compare Norw *slunken* lean]

slunkit, slunket /ˈslʌŋkət/ *adj* = SLUNKEN *20- Sh*. [perhaps participial adj from *slink*, the verb corresponding to SLINK²]

slupper, slopra /ˈslʌpər, ˈslɔprə/ *n* a soft, wet substance; slush *la19- Sh*. [Faer *slupur* a slimy mess]

slus *see* SLOOSH¹·¹, SLUSH¹·¹

slush¹·¹, †slus /slʌʃ/ *n* **1** wet, half-melted snow or ice *la18-*. **2** a speech peculiarity in which *sh* or some similar sound is used in place of the usual *s la20- C*. **3** a wet marshy place, a puddle, a quagmire *la15-19, 20- Bor*. **4** a slovenly, untidy person; a menial worker, drudge *19, 20- Sh*. **slushy 1** *of drink* weak, insipid *19, 20- Sh Ork N*. **2** dirty, slovenly, slatternly *20- Sh Ork N*. [probably onomatopoeic; and compare Dan *slus* sleet, mud]

slush¹·² /slʌʃ/ *v* **1** to wade messily through wet mud; to walk with shuffling or dragging steps; to make a splashing noise *18-19, 20- WC Bor*. **2** to work in a messy, untidy or careless way *20- Sh Ork N*. **slushit** slovenly *20- Sh*. [see the noun]

slut *see* SLUTE¹·¹, SLUTE¹·²

†slutch *v* to walk or move heavy-footedly and messily through mud *e19*. [compare ME *sluchched* muddied; probably onomatopoeic]

slute¹·¹, slout, †slut, †sluit /slut/ *n* a slovenly, sluggish person *la15-19, 20- Ork N SW*. [ME *slutte*]

†slute¹·², slut, slutt *adj* sluttish, untidy, disreputable *16*. [see the noun]

sluther *see* SLUDDER

slutt *see* SLUTE¹·²

slutter¹·¹, sclutter /ˈslʌtər, ˈsklʌtər/ *n* **1** a mess, a mass of dirty (semi-)liquid matter *la19-*. **2** a state of confusion, a muddle *20- T C*. **3** a splash or slop *19, 20- Bor*. **sluttery 1** slovenly, sluttish *19- T C*. **2** messy, soft and wet, sloppy and sticky *la19, 20- C Bor*. Compare SLITTER¹·¹. [perhaps imitative or a derivative of SLUTE¹·¹]

slutter¹·², sclutter, T skleuter, T sleuther /ˈslʌtər, ˈsklʌtər; *T* ˈsklutər, ˈsluðər/ *v* **1** to work in a slovenly, dirty way or in something messy *la19-*. **2** to walk in a slouching, slovenly way *la19- Ork N NE T*. **3** to make a splashing sound; to plunge or flounder in mud *la19- NE T*. Compare SLITTER¹·². [see the noun]

sly /slae/ *n* green algae *19- Sh Ork N*. [Norw dial *sli*]

sly *see* SCLY¹·¹, SCLY¹·², SLEE¹·²

slycht *see* SLICHT¹·¹, SLICHT¹·²

slychten *see* SLICHTEN

slyd *see* SLIDE¹·²

slyddir *see* SLIDDER¹·³

slyddry *see* SLIDDERIE

slyde *see* SLID, SLIDE¹·²

slydry *see* SLIDDERIE

slygoose /ˈslaegøs/ *n* the shelduck *Tadorna tadorna la18- Ork*. [probably SLY, on which it feeds + *goose* (GUSE¹·¹)]

slyke *see* SLEEK²

slyng *see* SLING¹·²

slyocken *see* SLOCKEN

slyp *see* SLIP¹·², SLIPE¹·¹

slype¹·¹, sclype /slʌip, sklʌip/ *n* **1** (the noise of) a hard slap or smack, a thud caused by falling heavily *la19- NE*. **2** *derogatory* a lazy, coarse, dissolute, worthless person, usually a man *18-19, 20- NE*. [perhaps onomatopoeic]

slype¹·², sclype /slʌip, sklʌip/ *v* **1** to throw or fall down forcibly with a hard smack *la19- NE*. **2** to walk with a heavy, flat-footed step *la19- NE*. [see the noun]

slype *see* SLIPE²

†slyre *n* a fine linen or lawn *17*. **slyris lane** = SLYRE. [LG *sleier*]

slyster *see* SLAISTER¹·²

sma¹·¹, small /smɔ, sma, smɔl/ *n* **1** the narrow part of the back or leg *la15-*. **2** mainly *pl* small sums (of money); small coins, small change *e18, 20- NE T*. **3** *pl* small wares, small (drapery) goods; small quantities of *la15-19, 20- Ork T*. **4** a period of calm at sea, a lull *la19- NE EC*. **5** *pl* small quantities; a little, not much *la19, 20- Sh*. **by smas** = in smas *17-19, 20- Sh Ork N NE T EC*. **in smas** in small amounts; piecemeal, little by little; retail *15-19, 20- Sh Ork N NE T EC*. [see the adj]

sma¹·², small, *Sh Ork* **smaa, †smale, †smaill, †smaw** /smɔ, sma, smɔl; *Sh Ork* sma/ *adj* **1** little in size or dimension; not large in comparison with others of its type *la12-*. **2** *of children* young, not fully grown *la14-*. **3** *of persons or animals* slim, slender, slightly-built; *of things* narrow, thin, of small width or diameter *15-*. **4** little in amount or quantity *15-*. **5** *of cloth or mesh* fine in texture *la15-*. **6** fine, composed of small particles or droplets *16-*. **7** *of money, coins* of low value *16-*. **8** *of the sea or a lake* smooth, calm, undisturbed *la18-*. **9** *of a river* low, not in spate *la18-*. **10** *of alcoholic drink* not strong, light, weak *15-19*. **11** short, brief *15-e19*. **12** *of measures* constituting a lower standard, lesser size or valuation than another or the same designation *la16-17*. **13** *of people* of no authority or rank, ordinary, originally describing foot-soldiers *la14-e19*. **14** of little or minor consequence or importance *la14-e19*. **smally** *of persons* undersized, small and slight; *of things* small, slight, meagre *la18-19, 20- T C SW Bor*. **sma-boukit** of little bulk, small, compact *la19-*. **sma breid 1** bakery wares including scones, rolls, buns and biscuits *19-*. **2** a cheaper or inferior type of bread *17*. **†small corn** = *small oats 17-19*. **†small custom** a tax levied on goods entering a burgh for sale in its market *15-18*. **smaa evens** insufficient means *la19- Sh*.

sma faimily a family of young children *18-*. **small fish** fish such as haddock or herring caught inshore with *small lines la18- Sh NE T SW*. **sma hunner** one hundred; approximately one hundred *la16, 20- Ork NE*. **sma laird** a small landowner *la19, 20- Ork*; compare *bonnet laird* (BONNET). **sma lines** the lines used by inshore fishermen to catch *small fish la16-*. **small maa** the common gull *Larus canus la19- Sh*. **sma murr** a mass of small objects; people of no importance, small fry *la19- Sh Ork*. **small music** piping light music such as reels or strathspeys *la20-*. **small oats** a variety of oat sown on the poorest soil, the bristle oat *Avena strigosa la16-19, 20- historical*. **sma oors** the very early hours of the morning, just after midnight *18-*; compare *wee sma oors* (WEE[1,2]). **small pipe** a bagpipe of smaller dimensions and softer sound *19-*. **sma-raip** the sole-rope in a herring drift-net *20- T EC*. **sma saut**, †**small salt** fine salt, table salt *16-*. **sma-shot** a strengthening thread inserted in Paisley shawls at intervals of 6 or 8 threads *la19- WC*. †**sma stell** a small still with a lower boiler which distils the wash more quickly, supposed to produce mellower whisky *19*. †**small teinds** tithes from produce other than grain, originally paid to the vicar installed by a PARSON *la16-e19*. **sma thing** a small sum of money *20- Ork N NE T EC SW*. **sma write** small text, ordinary cursive handwriting *19, 20- N NE WC SW*. **Scallowa sma drink** an inhabitant of Scalloway *la19- Sh*. **small debt court** a court set up under a Justice of the Peace in 1801 for dealing with debts under £5, and under a sheriff in 1837 for debts up to £20 *19-*. **sma-shot Saturday** *in Paisley* a holiday on the first Saturday of July, originally a weavers' union holiday *la19- WC*. **sma steens and stew** the dust kicked up by sudden flight or hurry *20- NE*. **think yersel nae sma drink** to consider yourself to be a person of some importance *la18-*. [OE *smæl*]

sma[1,3], **small** /smɔ, sma, smɔl/ *adv* **1** in a small voice, quietly *la19, 20- T WC*. **2** to a small extent or degree, little, not much *la14-16*. **sma-spoken** having a thin, soft voice *20- Bor*. [see the adj]

smaa *see* SMA[1,2]

smacher /ˈsmaxər/ *v* to eat in a secretive way, nibble at unobtrusively *19, 20- NE*. [perhaps back-formation from SMACHRIE]

smachrie, smacherie, smackery, †**smaggrie** /ˈsmaxrə, ˈsmaxərə, ˈsmakərə/ *n* **1** a hotchpotch or mixture of food, especially sweets *la18- NE T EC*. **2** a large number of small objects or people, especially children, usually in disorder or confusion *19- NE*. [perhaps a frequentative form of SMACK[2]]

smack[1,1] /smak/ *n* **1** a (loud or hearty) kiss *17-*. **2** a blow *la19-*. [EModE *smack*; MDu *smack*, LG *smacke*]

smack[1,2] /smak/ *v* **1** to make a smacking sound; strike *19-*. **2** to kiss, especially in a loud hearty way *la19-*. **3** to move along with speed *19, 20- T*. †**smack-smooth** completely smooth and even; level, flush with the surface; evenly; uninterruptedly *la18-e19*. [EModE *smack*; MDu, MLG *smacken*]

smack[2], **smak** /smak/ *n* (a) flavour, taste *la15-*. [OE *smæc*]

smackery *see* SMACHRIE

smad[1,1], **smud**, *Sh T* **smodd** /smad, smʌd; *Sh T* smɔd/ *n* a small stain, a smut, a dirty mark; a very small quantity of anything *19- Sh Ork NE T*. **smaddy, smuddy** stained, spotted, messy *20- Sh T*. [from the verb, perhaps influenced by Gael *smad* a spot, a stain]

smad[1,2] /smad/ *v* **1** to stain, soil, blemish with dirt *la15-19, 20- Sh NE T*. **2** *of a fire* to smoulder and emit clouds of sooty smoke; to cause smuts *19- SW Uls*. [compare LG *smadderen* to befoul]

smag /smag/ *n* a sweet, a tasty morsel *la19- NE*. [probably back-formation from *smaggrie* (SMACHRIE)]

smagan /ˈsmagən/ *n* a toad *20- N*. [Gael *smàigean*]

smaggrie *see* SMACHRIE

smaik[1], †**smake** /smek/ *n* a rogue, a rascal, a ruffian *la15-*. †**smaikrie** mean or contemptible behaviour; roguery, trickery *la16*. [compare Norw dial *smeik* a fawner, a flatterer]

†**smaik**[2], **smak** *n* an imported commodity used for making a black dye *la16-e17*. [unknown]

smaill *see* SMA[1,2]

smairg /smerɡ/ *v* to smear with something oily or messy; to apply tar to sheep to protect them from damp and parasites *19- WC SW Bor*. [conflation of SMEAR[1,2] with SLAIRG[1,2]]

smairt *see* SMERT[1,1], SMERT[1,2], SMERT[1,3]

smait *see* SMITE[2]

smak *see* SMACK[2], SMAIK[2]

smake *see* SMAIK[1]

smale *see* SMA[1,2]

small *see* SMA[1,1], SMA[1,2], SMA[1,3]

†**smaragdine, smaragdane** *n* the emerald *15-e16*. [Lat *smaragdinus*]

smaroo *see* SMORA

smarrach /ˈsmarəx/ *n* a confused crowd or collection, especially of children *la19- NE*. [unknown; compare SWARRACH[1,1]]

smart *see* SMERT[1,1], SMERT[1,2], SMERT[1,3], SMERT[1,4]

smash[1,1] /smaʃ/ *n* **1** an act of or the sound of breaking; a heavy blow *19-*. **2** a shattered, smashed or pulpy state *la18-*. [see the verb]

smash[1,2] /smaʃ/ *v* to break in pieces *la18-*. †**smashery** destruction, utter ruin, annihilation *e19*. **smashie** a game of marbles in which a heavy marble is thrown with force at smaller marbles; the heavy marble used in this game *20-*. †**smashing** *of persons* well-built, strapping, vigorous *19*. [probably onomatopoeic]

smat *see* SMITE[2]

smatchet, smatchert, *Sh* **smatshard,** †**smatscheit** /ˈsmatʃət, ˈsmatʃərt; *Sh* ˈsmatʃərd/ *n* a mischievous or nasty child, a little rogue; a small insignificant person (or animal); a contemptible person *la16-*. [unknown]

smate *see* SMITE[2]

smatter[1,1], **smather** /ˈsmatər, ˈsmaðər/ *n* **1** a small jumbled collection of people or things, especially children *la18-*. **2** *pl* bits and pieces, smithereens; odds and ends, small amounts *la18-19, 20- T Bor*. **smatterie** a group of rowdy children *19, 20- C*. **smytrie** = SMATTER[1,1] (sense 1) *la18-19, 20- NE*. [see the verb]

smatter[1,2], **smather** /ˈsmatər, ˈsmaðər/ *v* **1** to smash, shatter *la19- SW Bor*. **2** to work untidily or unmethodically, (appear to) be busy with trivial jobs *19, 20- NE*. **smatter awa** to consume or dissipate bit by bit, fritter away (money); to nibble at (food) *19, 20- T*. [ME *smateren* to dirty, to talk idly]

smattering /ˈsmatərɪŋ/ *n* a small amount of skill, knowledge, fun *la17-*. [verbal noun from SMATTER[1,2]]

smaw *see* SMA[1,2]

smear[1,1] /smir/ *n* **1** a mark, a smudge; a patch of something smeared *la19-*. **2** a preparation for smearing sheep *e19*. **smeerich** a thin layer or spread (of butter) *20- N NE*. [see the verb]

smear[1,2], *NE* **smeer** †**smeir** /smir; *EC* smer/ *v* **1** to spread, daub with a greasy or sticky substance; to anoint *la15-*. **2** to treat (a sheep's fleece) with a tar-and-grease compound to protect it from damp and parasites *la16-*. **smeerich** to smear; to make a mess of *20- NE*. **smearing house** the shed in which sheep were treated *19-*. †**smear-docken, smeirdoken** mercury goosefoot *Blitum bonus-henricus*, the plant used in herbal medicine *16-19*. [OE *smierwan*]

smeddum /ˈsmɛdəm/ *n* **1** a finely ground meal or malt; the finest particles lost in the grinding process *la17-19*,

smedy *see* SMIDDY

20- historical. **2** the pith, strength or essence of a substance *la18-*. **3** spirit, energy, drive, vigorous common sense and resourcefulness *la18-*. [OE *smedma* fine flour]

smedy *see* SMIDDY

smeech *see* SMIACH[1.1], SMIACH[1.2]

smeeg[1.1] /smig/ *n* a smirk *20- Sh.* [see the verb]

smeeg[1.2] /smig/ *v* to smirk, leer, smile *20- Sh.* [Dan *smige* to ingratiate oneself]

smeek[1.1], †**smeke**, †**smeik** /smik/ *n* **1** the fumes from something burning, smoke *15-*; compare SMUIK[1.1]. **2** a contrivance for smoking out bees *20- WC SW Bor.* **3** a whiff or stifling puff of fumes; the act of smelling, a sniff *20- N WC SW.* **4** an unpleasant smell, a stuffy fetid atmosphere *18-19, 20- EC SW.* **smeeky** smoky *la16-*. [OE *smīc*]

smeek[1.2], †**smeke**, †**smeik** /smik/ *v* **1** to emit smoke or fumes *la18-*. **2** to affect or suffocate with smoke or soot, make smoky *la14-19, 20- T C SW Bor.* **3** to drive out (bees) with smoke or fumes; to smoke out (persons) as a joke *la17-19, 20- T C SW Bor.* **4** to preserve, cure (fish or meat) by smoking *19, 20- Bor.* **5** to fumigate with smoke *la19, 20- Bor.* **smeeker** a contrivance for smoking out bees (or playing practical jokes) *la19- T C SW Bor.* **smeekit 1** smoke-stained; stifled or blinded by smoke *19, 20- NE C.* **2** drunk *la19, 20- H&I WC SW.* **smeek oot** to smoke out (persons) as a joke *20-*. [OE *smīcan* to smoke, fumigate]

smeeo *see* SMOO[1.1]

smeer *see* SMEAR[1.2]

smeerich *see* SMEAR[1.1], SMEAR[1.2]

smeerless *see* SMERGHLESS

smeeth *see* SMUITH[2]

smeik *see* SMEEK[1.1], SMEEK[1.2]

smeir *see* SMEAR[1.2]

smeith *see* SMUITH[2]

smeke *see* SMEEK[1.1], SMEEK[1.2]

smell[1.1], †**smel** /smɛl/ *n* **1** odour, perfume, aroma; stench *la14-*. **2** a small quantity, a taste (especially of alcohol); a trace, a suggestion *la15-*. [OE *smelle*]

smell[1.2] /smɛl/ *v* **1** to perceive a smell *la15-*. **2** to give off an odour *16-*. **3** to detect, suspect; to perceive as if by smell *la16-*. **4** to seem, indicate, give an impression *16-17*. [OE **smellan*]

smelt, **smilt** /smɛlt, smɪlt/ *n* a calm patch on the sea *20- Ork N NE.* Compare SMOLT. **smelty** *of water* calm, oily *20- WC*. [compare OIcel *smeltr* lustrous]

smergh, *N* **smeuch** /smɛrx; *N* smjux/ *n* **1** bone-marrow, pith *la18-e19*. **2** energy, vitality *la18-19, 20- N*. [conflation of *mergh* (MARRA) with SMEAR[1.1]]

smerghless, *NE* **smeerless** /'smɛrxləs, 'smɪrləs/ *adj of persons* lacking in spirit or energy, sluggish, feckless, stupid; *of things* insipid, uninteresting *18- N NE T.* [SMERGH, with adj-forming suffix]

smert[1.1], **smart**, †**smairt** /smɛrt, smart/ *n* **1** (a sharp) physical pain; mental anguish, sorrow *la15-*. **2** a penalty *la19*. [probably OE **smiertu*]

smert[1.2], **smart**, †**smairt** /smɛrt, smart/ *v* to cause or feel pain or suffering *15-*. [OE *smeortan*]

smert[1.3], **smairt**, **smart** /smɛrt, smert, smart/ *adj* **1** *of a blow* painful, sharp, severe *la14-*. **2** *of pain, a wound, sorrow* sharp, keen *la15-*. **3** *of a person* quick, vigorous; skilled, clever *la14-*. **4** neat and trim; stylish, elegant, fashionable *la18-*. **smerter** = *smartie 20- N T C SW.* **smartie** a lively and efficient person, one who is quick to understand and act *20-*. **smertly 1** swiftly, vigorously *la14-*. **2** sharply, keenly *15-*. **3** neatly; cleverly *20-*. [OE *smeart*]

smert[1.4], **smart** /smɛrt, smart/ *adv* powerfully, vigorously; swiftly *18-*. [see the adj]

†**smervie** *adj in the North-East and Angus* full of substance or flavour *la18-19*. [variant of SMERGH, with -IE[2] suffix]

smeth *see* SMITH

smethy *see* SMIDDY

smeuch *see* SMERGH

smeuk *see* SMUIK[1.1], SMUIK[1.2]

smiach[1.1], **smeech** /'smiəx, smix/ *n in negative constructions* not a sound, whisper or murmur; not a trace, not a sign of life *20- N NE T.* [Gael *smiach* a syllable, a sound]

smiach[1.2], **smeech** /'smiəx, smix/ *v in negative constructions* not to utter a sound, keep quiet *20- N.* [see the noun]

†**smick** *n in the North and North-East* a spot, trace or small amount *19*. [probably a variant or altered form of SMACK[2] a taste, a small quantity]

smicker, †**smikker** /'smɪkər/ *v* to smile, laugh; to snigger *19- Sh Ork EC Bor.* [EModE *smicker* to look amorously]

smiddle /'smɪdəl/ *v* to behave furtively; to conceal *19, 20- SW.* [unknown]

smiddy, **smithy**, †**smydy**, †**smedy**, †**smethy** /'smɪde, 'smɪðe/ *n* a blacksmith's workshop, a forge *la14-*. **smiddy-coal** a small smokeless type of coal suitable for burning in a forge *la15-*. **smiddy coom** = *smiddy-coal la19, 20- SW Uls.* †**smiddy craft** the work of a blacksmith *16-e17*. **smethow cramps** slag from a forge or a fierce fire *20- Ork.* †**smithy-dander** a cinder from a forge *19*. †**smiddy-land** land on which a forge is situated; lands attached or pertaining to a forge *la15-e17*. **smiddy-sparks** the sparks which fly off a blacksmith's anvil *19, 20- NE T.* [ON *smiðja*]

smikker *see* SMICKER

smile, †**smyle**, †**smyll** /smʌɪl/ *v* to indicate pleasure with the mouth; to show emotion by smiling *la14-*. **smiler** a wide-toothed rake for use on stubble *20- N NE.* [ME *smilen*]

smilt *see* SMELT

smird /smɪrd/ *n* a smut, smudge, a spot of dirt or rain *20- Sh NE.* [perhaps conflation of SMIT[1.1] with SMIRR[1.1]]

smirk[1.1] /smɪrk/ *n* a smile, a friendly expression *la15-*. **smirkie** having a good-natured, amiable, friendly expression *18-19, 20- NE.* [see the verb]

smirk[1.2], †**smyrk** /smɪrk/ *v* **1** to smile pleasantly, amiably or flirtatiously *la15-*. **2** to smile mockingly or affectedly; to leer *16-*. †**smirkle** = SMIRK[1.2] (sense 1) *la16-e19*. [ME *smirken* to smile, OE *smearcian*]

smirk[2] /smɪrk/ *n* a kiss *la19- NE T.* [unknown; compare SMACK[1.1]]

smirk[3] /smɪrk/ *v* mainly *literary* to smirch, stain *la19- NE EC.* [altered form of Eng *smirch* by analogy with BIRK[1], KIRK[1.1]]

smirkle *see* SMIRK[1.2]

†**smirl** *n* a sneer, mocking smile; a snigger, sneering laugh *la19*. [perhaps onomatopoeic or reduced form of SMIRTLE[1.1]]

smirlin *see* SMISSLEN

smirr[1.1], *SW* **smurr** /smɪr; *SW* smʌr/ *n* fine rain, drizzle; sometimes fine sleet or snow *19-*. **smirr o rain** fine rain, drizzle *19-*. [perhaps onomatopoeic]

smirr[1.2], **smur** /smɪr, smʌr/ *v of rain or snow* to fall gently and softly, drizzle *19-*. [see the noun]

smirr[2] /smɪr/ *n* butter *la19- Sh.* [Norw *smør*]

smirsit /'smɪrsət/ *adj of a dark sheep* marked with white round the mouth *la19- Sh.* [derivative of SMIRR[2] or Norw dial *smyrsl* a smearing + -IT[2]]

smirtle[1.1] /'smɪrtəl/ *n* a sarcastic smile, a smirk of satisfaction; a cynical laugh *la18-*. [see the verb]

smirtle[1.2], †**smurtle**, †**smyrtle** /'smɪrtəl/ *v* to smile knowingly, smirk; to laugh coyly, giggle, snigger *la16-*. [variant of *smirkle* (SMIRK[1.2])]

smisslen, **smirlin** /'smɪzlɪn, 'smɪrlɪn/ *n* the sand-gaper shell-fish *Mya arenaria 18- Sh Ork.* [Icel, Faer *smyrsling(u)r*]

smit[1.1], †**smyt** /smɪt/ *n* **1** a smut, smudge; a taint, blemish *la14-*. **2** infection, contagion *la19-*. **get the smit** to become infected (by a disease); to fall in love *20-*. [OE *smitte* a spot, stain]

smit[1.2], †**smyt** /smɪt/ *v pt* **smit, smittit**, *ptp* **smit, smittit, smitten 1** to contaminate, affect (with) *la14-*. **2** to affect by contagion, infect; to taint *la14-*. **3** stain *la14-16*. **smittin**, †**smitand** contagious, infectious; liable to taint *15-*. **smit-some** = *smittin la19, 20- Ork SW*. [OE *smittian* to befoul, pollute]

smitch /smɪtʃ/ *n* **1** a stain, blemish, taint, smudge *19- WC SW Bor Uls.* **2** a very small amount, speck, trace *19- WC SW Bor Uls.* [variant of Eng *smutch*]

smite[1] /smʌɪt/ *n* a small insignificant person, a weak or puny creature *la19- NE T.* [unknown; compare SMOUT]

smite[2], †**smyte**, †**smyt** /smʌɪt/ *v pt* **smat** †**smate**, †**smait**, *ptp* **smitten** †**smyttyn**, †**smyte**, †**smyt 1** to strike *la14- literary*. **2** *of a cause or event* to have a (violent or disruptive) effect; to affect, impress *15-16*. [ME *smiten* to strike, OE *smītan* to pollute, blemish]

smith, †**smyth**, †**smeth** /smɪθ/ *n* **1** a worker in metal *12-*. **2** *pl* the incorporation of metal workers *15-e18*; compare **hammerman** (HAIMMER[1.1]). [OE *smið*]

smithy *see* SMIDDY

smitin /ˈsmʌɪtɪn/ *n* a hole in a sail for a reef-point *la19- Sh.* [derivative of SMYT]

smittal, smittell *see* SMITTLE

smitten *see* SMIT[1.2], SMITE[2]

smittit *see* SMIT[1.2]

smittle, smittal, †**smittell** /ˈsmɪtəl/ *adj* infectious; contagious *la16-*. [SMIT[1.2], with adj-forming suffix]

smizzle /ˈsmɪzəl/ *v* to rain lightly, drizzle *20- SW Bor.* [conflation of SMIRR[1.2] with Eng *drizzle*]

smoak *see* SMOKE

smoar *see* SMORE[1.2]

smoch[1] /smox/ *n* thick choking smoke; thick fog *20- T EC Bor.* **smochy** smoky; *of the air* close, sultry, stifling *19-*. [altered form of SMOKE, perhaps with influence from MOCH[2.1]]

†**smoch**[2], **smush** *adj* perhaps rotten, fusty *16-e17*. [perhaps altered form of MOCH[2.3]]

smochle /ˈsmoxəl/ *v* to grope, fumble *la19, 20- T.* [perhaps onomatopoeic]

smock *see* SMUCK, SMOKE

smodd *see* SMAD[1.1]

smoik *see* SMOKE

smoir *see* SMORE[1.2]

smoith *see* SMUITH[2]

smoke, *Sh* **smokk**, *Ork H&I* **smock**, †**smoik**, †**smoak** /smok; *Sh Ork H&I* also smɔk/ *n* **1** fumes from something burning *16-*. **2** an inhabited house *la18- N H&I*; compare SMUIK[1.1], SMEEK[1.1]. **smoke-board** a wooden flap or canopy over a fireplace to regulate the draught and prevent the chimney from smoking *la19-*. **smoke o tobacco** as much tobacco as will fill a pipe *19-*. [OE *smoca*]

smokie /ˈsmoke/ *n* a haddock smoked whole in Arbroath *la19-.* Compare ARBROATH SMOKIE. [SMOKE +-IE[3]]

smokk *see* SMOKE

†**smolet, smollat** *n* the penis *e16.* [unknown]

†**smolt, smowt** *adj* **1** *of weather* fine, fair, calm *la15-e16.* **2** bright, serene *e19.* [OE *smolt*]

smolt *see* SMOUT

smoly[1.1] /ˈsmoli/ *n* scorn, disdain, contempt *la19- Ork.* [unknown]

smoly[1.2] /ˈsmoli/ *v* to disdain, scorn, hold in contempt *la19- Ork.* [unknown]

smoo[1.1], *Ork* **smeeo** /smu; *Ork* ˈsmio/ *n* a narrow gap or passage *20- Sh Ork.* [Dan *smuga*]

smoo[1.2] /smu/ *v* to move about furtively, slink, sneak, prowl; to slip away or through a narrow opening or into (or out of) clothes *19- Sh Ork.* [Norw dial *smjuga*]

smoochter *see* SMUCHTER[1.1]

smoogle *see* SMUGGLE[1.2]

smook, *Sh* **smjug** /smuk; *Sh* also smok, smjug/ *v* **1** to slink or sneak about, go about furtively looking for something to pilfer, prowl *19, 20- Sh C.* **2** to hide, keep (something) to oneself *la19, 20- Sh.* **3** to take oneself off unobtrusively, steal away quietly *20- Sh.* **4** to pull (clothes) on or off *la19- Sh.* **smookit** sly, cunning *la19, 20- Sh.* [ON *smjúga*]

smook *see* SMUIK[1.1], SMUIK[1.2]

smooky /ˈsmuki, ˈsmoki/ *n* a fisherman's oilskin smock; a pullover, undershirt *20- Sh.* [SMOOK (sense 4) + -y (-IE[3])]

smool[1.1] /smul/ *n* **1** *frequently of a child* a wheedler *20- T.* **2** a small or insignificant person *20- NE.* [see the verb]

smool[1.2] /smul/ *v* **1** to slink, sneak, go about furtively *19-*. **2** to ingratiate oneself, fawn, wheedle *19-*. **3** to remove stealthily, steal *19, 20- literary.* **smool in wi, smoolie in wi** to cajole, ingratiate oneself with *19, 20- T EC Bor.* **smoolachin** sly *20- NE.* [perhaps onomatopoeic]

smool[2.1] /smul/ *n* a scowl; a snarl by a horse when threatening to bite *20- SW.* [see the verb]

smool[2.2] /smul/ *v* to look petulant or discontented, scowl, frown; to look scornful and unfriendly; *of a horse* to threaten to bite *la19- SW.* [perhaps onomatopoeic]

smoor *see* SMUIR[1.2]

smoorich[1.1], **smoorach, smourock** /ˈsmurəx, ˈsmurək/ *n* a kiss, caress, cuddle *la19, 20- Sh Ork NE T.* **smooriken** a kiss, a cuddle *19, 20- Sh.* [see the verb]

smoorich[1.2], *Sh* **smoorik** /ˈsmurəx; *Sh* ˈsmurik/ *v* to exchange kisses, cuddle, pet *19, 20- Sh NE T.* [intensive form of SMUIR[1.2]]

smoosk /smusk/ *v* to smile slyly *20- Ork.* [Norw dial *smuska*]

smoost *see* SMUIST[1.2]

smoot /smut, smɔt/ *v* **1** to hide furtively, put out of sight *la19- Sh.* **2** to sneak about, take oneself off unobtrusively; to move quietly, slip *la19- Sh.* [Norw *smutte* to glide]

smooth *see* SMUITH[2]

smoother *see* SMUDDER

smor *see* SMORE[1.2]

smora, *Ork* **smaroo** /ˈsmorə; *Ork* ˈsmaro/ *n* **1** clover *Trifolium repens 19- Sh Ork.* **2** bird's-foot trefoil *Lotus corniculatus 20- Ork.* [Icel *smári*, Norw *smære*]

smord *see* SMORE[1.2]

smore[1.1] /smor/ *n* a thick, close, stifling atmosphere full of smoke, snow, fine rain, or dust *la19- NE T.* **smorie** *of weather* close and drizzling *19- EC.* [see the verb]

smore[1.2], †**smoir**, †**smor**, †**smoar** /smor/ *v ptp* also †**smord 1** *of snow or smoke* to fall or come out in a dense stifling cloud; *of the atmosphere* to be thick with snow or smoke *19-*. **2** to smother, suffocate, crush to death, stifle with smoke; to drown *la14-19, 20- Sh NE T EC.* **3** to be smothered, suffocate; to drown *15-19, 20- Sh NE T.* **4** to suppress, extinguish, overwhelm *la14-19, 20- NE T.* **5** to confine or cover thickly with snow *la18-19, 20- NE T.* **6** to conceal, obscure *16-e17.* **smorin** *of a head-cold* thick, choking, heavy *20- NE.* **be smorin wi the cauld** to have a very bad cold *20- NE.* **smore up** to hush up (a rumour) *20- T.* [OE *smorian* to strangle, choke, suffocate; compare SMUIR[1.2]]

smot[1.1], **smote**, †**smott** /smɔt, smot/ *n* **1** a stain, blemish *la16.* **2** an identification or other mark put on sheep *la17-19, 20- SW Bor.* [see the verb]

smot[1,2] /smɔt, smot/ *v* 1 to stain, blemish *16*. 2 to mark (sheep) with ruddle as an indication of covering *19, 20- Bor*. [ME *smotten* to defile; compare MDu *besmodden*]

smot *see* SMIT[1.1], SMIT[1.2]

smote *see* SMOT[1.1]

smoth *see* SMUITH[2]

smother *see* SMUDDER

smott *see* SMOT[1.1]

†**smotter** *v ptp* **smottryt** to bespatter; to soil or stain *16-19*. [frequentative form of SMOT [1.2]]

smottyt *see* SMIT[1.2]

smouder[1.1], **smouther**, **smoulder** /'smudər, 'smuðər, 'smoldər/ *n* a slow burning; material so burned *19-*. [ME *smolder*]

smouder[1.2], **smouther**, **smoulder** /'smudər, 'smuðər, 'smoldər/ *v* to burn slowly without flame, smoulder; to continue in a suppressed state *la16-*. [see the noun]

smourock *see* SMOORICH[1.1]

smout, smowt, smolt /smʌut, smolt; *SW Bor* also smut/ *n* 1 a young salmon (or sea trout) between the parr and grilse stages *15-*. 2 a small insignificant person, a small child, animal or thing *la18-*. **smouty** small, insignificant *20- C*. [unknown]

smouther *see* SMOUDER[1.1], SMOUDER[1.2]

smowk *see* SMUIK[1.1], SMUIK[1.2]

smowt /smʌut/ *n* a term used in the game of marbles *20-*. **up for smowt** used in a marbles game like MOSH when a player is about to play the final sequence *20- WC SW*. [perhaps a reduced form of Eng *that's me out*]

smowt *see* SMOLT, SMOUT

smucht /smʌxt/ *n* thick smoke *20- NE*. **smuchty** smoky, fuggy; misty, close *20- NE*. [perhaps altered form of SMOKE, with influence from MOCH[2.1]; compare SMOCH[1]]

smuchter[1.1], **smoochter** /'smʌxtər, 'smuxtər/ *n* 1 thick smoke, frequently from damp fuel or a faulty chimney; slight smoke from a fire not properly lit; a thick stuffy atmosphere *la19- NE*. 2 a thin light mist or rain *la19- NE*. 3 a thick choking cold, a heavy catarrh *20- NE*. **smoochtery weather** misty, steamy, close *20- NE*. [see the verb]

smuchter[1.2] /'smʌxtər, 'smuxtər/ *v* 1 to smoulder, emit thick black smoke, burn slowly *la19- NE*. 2 *of rain or snow* to fall in a fine mist, drizzle persistently *la19- NE*. 3 *of persons* to be short of breath, breathe with difficulty; *of the voice* to be muffled or thick *19- NE*. [SMUCHT with frequentative suffix]

smuck, smock /smʌk, smɔk/ *n* 1 a carpet slipper; originally a thick, woollen shoe or slipper made of several layers sewn or stuck together *19- Sh*. 2 a ragged, fibrous peat *la19- Sh*. 3 a native of Aithsting *la19- Sh*. **smukket** *of a hen's feet* wrapped in rags (to prevent scratching) *la19- Sh*. [compare Norw *smokk* a sheath]

smucks /smoks/ *v* to make the sound of a slipper striking the ground; to shuffle *la19- Sh*. [derivative of SMUCK]

smud *see* SMAD[1.1]

smudder, smother, †**smoother** /'smʌdər, 'smʌðər/ *v* to suffocate, stifle; to suppress; to conceal *la16-*. [ME *smorther* suffocating smoke]

smuddy *see* SMAD[1.1]

smudge[1.1] /smʌdʒ, smudʒ/ *n* a quiet half-suppressed laugh, a smirk, simper *19, 20- Sh Ork WC SW Bor*. [see the verb]

smudge[1.2] /smʌdʒ, smudʒ/ *v* to laugh in a suppressed way, laugh quietly to oneself, smirk *18-19, 20- Sh Ork WC SW Bor*. [perhaps onomatopoeic]

smue /smu; *Ork* smju/ *v* to smile placidly, blandly or ingratiatingly, smirk; to laugh in a suppressed or furtive way *19, 20- Ork SW*. [perhaps a variant of extended sense of SMOO[1.2]]

smug /smʌg/ *v* to go about in a stealthy, furtive way *20 Sh*. [compare slang *smug* to steal, to run away with]

smugga, smoga /'smʌgə, 'smɔgə/ *n* a passageway, opening *20- Sh*. [Norw *smuge*]

smugger /'smʌgər/ *n* fisherman's taboo an eel *la19- Sh*. [SMUG + agent suffix]

smuggle[1.1] /'smʌgəl/ *n in rugby and handball* a struggle for the ball in which one side tries to pass the ball out of sight of their opponents towards the goal *20- Ork Bor*. [see the verb]

smuggle[1.2], *N* **smoogle** /'smʌgəl; *N* 'smugəl/ *v* 1 to convey clandestinely *19-*. 2 *in rugby and handball* to get the ball unobtrusively out of a scrummage *20-*. 3 to distil whisky illegally *la19, 20- historical*. **smuggler** a distiller of illegal whisky *la19, 20- historical*. **smuggle-the-gig, smugglety-geg** a game the aim of which is to convey an object to a safe area or to prevent this *la19-*. [Eng *smuggle*]

smuik[1.1], **smook,** †**smuke,** †**smowk,** †**smeuk** /smuk/ *n* 1 smoke, fumes *16-19, 20- T EC SW Bor*. 2 fine thick snow or rain *19- Ork NE*. [OFlem *smuick*]

smuik[1.2], **smook, smeuk,** †**smowk** /smuk/ *v* 1 to smoke, smoulder giving off thick smoke *16-19, 20- T Bor*. 2 to expose to smoke; to fumigate; to cure (meat) by smoking; to smoke out (bees); to discolour by smoke; to suffocate *17-19, 20- SW Bor*. [OFlem *smuycken*]

smuir[1.1] /smur/ *n* a thick atmosphere, a dense enveloping cloud of smoke, snow, rain, mist *la19-*. **smuirach** a covering (of snow) *20- T*. [see the verb]

smuir[1.2], **smoor,** †**smure,** †**smuyr** /smur/ *v* 1 to suffocate, smother, crush to death *16-*. 2 to suppress, deaden, quench *la15-*. 3 to damp down (a fire) so that it smoulders quietly *18-*. 4 to be choked, suffocate, undergo smothering, especially by being buried in a snowdrift *la18-*. 5 *of snow, darkness, mist or vegetation* to bury, cover over thickly, envelop *19-*. 6 to cover with a thin coating, smear a sheep with tar *la19, 20 N SW*. 7 to drown in a river or bog *19, 20- Sh*. 8 *of honour* to be extinguished or forgotten *la15-16*. **smooring** a ritual damping down of the domestic fire at night, once common in districts of the Highlands *20-*. **smooring the fire** = *smooring*. [MLG *smören*]

smuirach *see* SMURACH

smuist[1.1] /smust/ *n* (a smell of) thick, choking, sulphurous smoke *19, 20- SW Bor*. [perhaps onomatopoeic; and compare SMUIK[1.1]]

smuist[1.2], **smoost** /smust/ *v* to emit smoke without much fire, smoulder *19, 20- EC Bor*. †**smuister** to emit thick smoke or vapour; be smoky *19*. [see the noun]

smuith[1] /smuð/ *n* the sandy bottom of the sea *20- N NE*. [probably extended sense of SMUITH[2]]

smuith[2], **smooth**, *N NE* **smeeth,** †**smoith,** †**smeith,** †**smoth** /smuð; *N NE* smiθ, smið/ *adj* 1 having a surface free from projections; even, regular, level; not abrasive or harsh *la15-*. 2 persuasive, plausible, practised *17-*. [OE *smōð, smēðe*]

smuke *see* SMUIK[1.1]

smur *see* SMIRR[1.2]

smurach, smuirach /'smurəx; *NE* also 'smjurəx/ *n* (anything crushed to) fine dust or powder; crumbled peat *19, 20- N NE*. [Gael *smùrach* dust, ashes]

smure *see* SMUIR[1.2]

smurl /smʌrl/ *v* to eat little and slowly without appetite; to nibble half-heartedly or furtively *la19- NE T*. [altered form of MURL[1.2]]

smurr *see* SMIRR[1.1]

smurtle *see* SMIRTLE[1.2]

smush[1.1] /smʌʃ/ *n* 1 a mass of tiny crushed fragments, something reduced to pulp or powder, over-boiled potatoes, coal-dross *19-*. **2** fine drizzle *19, 20- Sh*. **smushie** drizzly *20- Sh*. **smushlach** = SMUSH[1.1] (sense 1) *la19-*. [altered form of MUSH[1]]

smush[1.2] /smʌʃ/ *v* **1** to break into very small fragments, crush, smash *19-*. **2** to drizzle *20- Sh*. [see the noun]

smush[2] /smʌʃ; *Ork* smuʃ/ *n* a thick cloud of smoke or soot particles, grime, a sulphurous smell *19, 20- Ork NE*. **smushy** foul, fumy, suffocating *20- Sh Ork*. [perhaps altered form of SMUIST[1.1], influenced by SMUSH[1.1]]

smush *see* SMOCH[2]

smutherin /ˈsmʌðərɪn/ *n* a little piece, a small amount *20- Ork*. [perhaps altered form of SMATTERING, with influence from smother (SMUDDER)]

smuyr *see* SMUIR[1.2]

†**smy** *n* a knave, rascal, scoundrel *16*. [unknown]

smyagger[1.1] /ˈsmjagər/ *n* a smear; a mess, bespattered state *20- N*. [see the verb]

smyagger[1.2] /ˈsmjagər/ *v* to smear, daub, bespatter *20- N*. [probably a variant of SMACHER]

smydy *see* SMIDDY

smyl *see* SMILE[1.1]

smyle *see* SMILE[1.1], SMILE[1.2]

smyll *see* SMILE[1.2]

smyrk *see* SMIRK[1.2]

smyrtle *see* SMIRTLE[1.2]

†**smyt** *n* the rope for making fast a sail *la15-e17*. [MDu *smiete*, MLG *smite*]

smyt *see* SMIT[1.1], SMIT[1.2], SMITE[2]

smyte *see* SMITE[2]

smyth *see* SMITH

smytrie *see* SMATTER[1.1]

smyttyn *see* SMITE[2]

snaa *see* SNAW[1.1], SNAW[1.2]

snaar /snɑr/ *n* **1** a loop of cord forming the fulcrum of a weighing-machine, by movement of which the point of equilibrium is reached *la18- Sh Ork*. **2** the turn of the tide *19- Sh Ork*. **3** a critical or opportune moment *20- Sh*. [Norw dial *snar* a turn, a kink in a thread]

snab[1] /snab/ *n* a cobbler; a cobbler's assistant or apprentice *19- T C Bor*. **snabbin**, *NE* **snobbin** shoemaking, cobbling *la19- NE EC*. [*snob* a cobbler, a vulgar person, a pretentious person]

snab[2] /snab/ *n* a steep short slope, a projection of rock *la18- C Bor*. [compare Flem *snabbe* a point of land]

snack[1.1], †**snak** /snak/ *n* **1** a bite, snap, especially of a dog *16-*. **2** a small amount or taste of food in advance of or instead of a meal *la19-*. **3** a short time, a snatch of time *e16*. [MDu *snack*]

snack[1.2], †**snak** /snak/ *v* **1** to snap with the teeth, bite *la16- C SW Bor*. **2** to break off sharply, snap *la15-19*. [compare MDu *snacken* to snap, Norw dial *snaka* (of an animal) to snatch]

snack[2.1], †**snak** /snak/ *adj* **1** nimble, active, quick; acute, clever, sharp-witted *17-19, 20- Ork N NE*. **2** *of speech* easy, smooth, voluble *18*. **3** sharp, severe, exacting *la19*. **snackie** = SNACK[2.1] (sense 1) *20- NE SW*. **snackit** a small, active, alert, brisk person *la19- NE*. [perhaps onomatopoeic]

†**snack**[2.2] *adv* quickly, sharply *18-19*. [see the adj]

snae *see* SNEE[1.1], SNEE[1.2]

snaffle[1.1] /ˈsnafəl/ *n* derogatory a wicked or ineffective person *19- WC SW Uls*. Compare *snaffler* (SNAFFLE[1.2]). [see the verb]

snaffle[1.2] /ˈsnafəl/ *v* to snuffle, speak through the nose *la16-19, 20- Bor*. †**snaffler** a weak-spirited sycophant, a rogue *e17*. **snafflin** mean, paltry; cringing *20- Bor*. [onomatopoeic]

snag[1.1] /snag/ *n* a titbit, a piece of confectionery *la19- Sh N NE T*. [variant of SNACK[1.1]]

snag[1.2] /snag/ *v* to snarl (at); to nag, grumble, taunt *19, 20- Sh NE T*. **snagger** to snarl, growl; to snore harshly *la19- NE*. [variant of SNACK[1.2]]

†**snaggy** *adj* sarcastic, snappish *19*. [SNAG[1.2] + -y (-IE[2])]

snaik, †**snake** /snek/ *v* to skulk, do something in a mean, furtive or underhand way; to prowl *la17-19, 20- T*. [ON *snaka* to go snuffing or searching about]

snaik *see* SNAKE

snail, †**snaill** /snel/ *n* **1** a gastropod of the genus *Helix*, having a shell *15-*. **2** a slug *17-*. **3** a sluggard, a slow or lazy person *e16*. [OE *snægl*]

snaith *see* SNED[2]

snak *see* SNACK[1.1], SNACK[1.2], SNACK[2.1]

snake[1] /snek/ *n* a slug, especially the large grey or black garden slug *20- N Bor*. [perhaps altered form of Eng †*snag* a snail, influenced by SNAKE[2]]

snake[2], †**snaik** /snek/ *n* a limbless scaly reptile *15-*. [OE *snaca*]

snake *see* SNAIK

†**snaker, sneaker** *n* a small bowl of punch or glass of brandy *18-e19*. [Eng †*sneaker*]

snap[1.1] /snap/ *n* **1** a hard ginger biscuit, a ginger snap *la18-*. **2** a sharp blow *la19- Sh N NE*. **3** a small piece, scrap, especially of food *la18-19, 20- Sh N T*. **4** (the firing mechanism of) a gun; the release mechanism of the MAIDEN (sense 5) *la16-e17*. **snappous, snappus** hasty in temper, irascible *19, 20- NE*. **snappy** hard-bargaining *19- T*. †**snapsy** short-tempered *la18-e19*. †**snap gun** a gun using a snaphaunce or flint-lock firing mechanism *e17*. †**snaphaunce, snaphans** (a gun with) a flint-lock firing mechanism *la16-e18*. †**snapmaker** a maker of guns with snaphaunce firing mechanisms *la16-e17*. †**snapwark, snapwork** = the firing mechanism of a (snaphaunce) gun *la16-17*. **in a snap, upon snap** like a shot, with no delay *la18- Sh N NE*. [from the verb or Du, LG *snap*]

snap[1.2] /snap/ *v* **1** to make a snapping noise; originally to release the firing mechanism of a gun; *of a gun* to go off *la17-*. **2** to snatch, catch or seize quickly or suddenly *la16-*. **3** to gobble; to eat hastily or with relish *19-*. †**snapper** *adj* snappish, tart, curt *la17-e19*. **snapper** *n* something large, heavy or excellent of its kind *19- T WC Uls*. **snappert** snappish, curt *19- NE T*. **snappie 1** a small cod *Gadus morhua callarias 20- N*. **2** a small haddock *Melanogrammus aeglefinus 20- Ork*. **snappit** *adj* snappish *20- Ork T*. **snap and rattle** toasted oatcakes crumbled in milk *20- NE*. [MDu, MLG *snappen* to make a sudden bite]

snap[1.3] /snap/ *adj* **1** quick, eager, smart *18-*. **2** short-tempered, surly *19, 20- Sh*. [see the verb]

†**snap**[2] *n* a top layer or coping of stones set on their edges so as to taper upwards *la18-19*; compare *Galloway dyke* (GALLOWAY). **snap-dyke** a wall with a coping of stones set on their edges *18- SW*. **snap-topped dyke** = *snap-dyke 19- SW*. [perhaps Eng *snape* to taper]

snapper[1.1] /ˈsnapər/ *n* **1** a stumble, false step, jolting motion *la16-19, 20- N NE*. **2** a slip in conduct, blunder; an unfortunate accident *17-19*. [see the verb]

snapper[1.2] /ˈsnapər/ *v* **1** to stumble, trip, fall *la15-19, 20- Sh Ork N NE WC*. **2** to fall into error, blunder, trip up *la15-17*. [ME *snaperen*]

snar *see* SNARRE

snarl[1.1] /snɑrl/ *n* **1** a snare *20-*. **2** a loop of cord forming the fulcrum of a weighing-machine, by movement of which the point of equilibrium is reached *20 Sh Ork*; compare SNAAR. [ME *snarle*, probably *snāre* a snare + *-le* suffix]

snarl[1,2] /snarl/ *v* **1** to tangle *17-*. **2** to snare *20-*. [see the noun]
snarre, †**snar** /snar/ *adj* **1** severe, strict, sharp-tongued *19, 20- EC*. **2** astute, shrewd, efficient *e19*. [ON *snarr* hard-twisted, keen, sharp]
snash[1,1] /snaʃ/ *n* abuse, impudence, cheek, insolence *la18-*. **snash-gab** petulant, insolent talk *19- T EC Bor*. [probably onomatopoeic]
snash[1,2] /snaʃ/ *v* **1** to insult, speak impertinently to, sneer at *19-*. **2** to snap, bite *la19, 20- Ork*. [see the noun]
snashters /'snaʃtərz/ *npl derogatory* sweets, cakes, pastries; junk food *19- T H&I C*. [perhaps derivative of SNASH[1,2]; and compare MLG *snascherie* eating of dainties]
snatchack /'snatʃək/ *n* a small quantity of alcohol, a dram *20- N NE*. [Gael *snathteag*]
snauchle /'snɔxəl/ *n* an insignificant, puny or feeble person; a dwarf *19- WC SW*. [altered form of *nauchle* (NOCHT[1,2])]
snaw[1,1], **snaa**, **snow** /snɔ, sna, sno/ *n* snow, a fall of snow, a covering of snow, snowy weather *la14-*. **snaw-bree**, **snowbree** melted snow or ice, frequently that carried down in rivers, slush *la19, 20- NE WC SW Bor*. **snaw-broo** = *snawbree la18-19, 20- NE T C SW Bor*. **snow fleck, snow flake** the snow bunting *Plectrophenax nivalis la17-19, 20- NE WC*. **snaw-fool** = *snow flake la19- Sh N*. †**snaw-mail**, **snow-mail** grazing-rent for hill sheep on lowland farms *e19*. **snow-wreath, snaw-wreath** a snowdrift *19-*. **cast snaw-bas** to jeer, make insulting remarks *la16-*. **like snaw aff a dyke** (to disappear, happen) very quickly *19-*. **thraw snaw-bas** = *cast snaw-bas la18-*. [OE *snāw*]
snaw[1,2], **snaa**, **snow** /snɔ, sna, sno/ *v pt also Sh* **snew 1** *of snow* to fall; to fall as snow *20-*. **2** to be snowed up *20- Sh*. [see the noun]
Snawdoun *see* SNOWDON
snawil *see* SNEEVIL[1,2]
snead *see* SNED[2]
sneak, †**sneik** /snik/ *n* a person who behaves in an underhand manner *la16-*. [perhaps related to OE *snīcan* to creep]
sneaker *see* SNAKER
sneck[1,1], †**snick**, †**snek** /snɛk/ *n* **1** a latch, the catch of a door; the lever or bolt which activates the latch *la15-*. **2** *building pl* small stones packed in between the larger ones in a rubble wall *la18- NE*. **3** *building* a section of a dry-stone wall built of stones extending through the whole width of the wall *19- EC SW Bor*. **4** *mining* points on a HUTCH[1,1] railway *la18-20, la20- historical*. **sneck-drawer** a crafty, deceitful person *19-*. **sneck-drawing, snick-drawing** *n* guile *la19-*. †**sneck-drawing, snick-drawing** *adj* full of guile, crafty *la18-19*. **sneck-shifter** *mining* a pointsman *20-*. **draw a sneck** to open a latch; to insinuate oneself into something surreptitiously; to act craftily or stealthily *la15-*. **aff the sneck** *of a door* unlatched, with the catch left off *la19-*. **lift a sneck** = *draw a sneck la18-*. **on the sneck** latched but not locked *19-*. [probably Lat *snecka* a latch, from OE **sneccan* to snap]
sneck[1,2], *H&I* **snick** /snɛk; *H&I* snɪk/ *v* **1** to latch, fasten with a latch; to make (a catch) fast *la16-*. **2** *of a door* to close on a latch, shut *la19-*. **3** to catch or squeeze (something) between two objects *20- WC SW Bor*. **4** to shut (one's mouth), keep quiet *20- NE T*. **5** *building* to close or fill (a crevice in a rubble wall) by packing smaller stones tightly between the large ones, or by filling the small spaces with lime *la18-19, 20- NE*. **sneck aff** to switch off (an electrical appliance) *20- Sh NE T EC*. [see the noun]
sneck[2,1] /snɛk/ *n* **1** a notch, a slight cut or incision; an indentation in an animal's horn as a sign of age *la18- Sh Ork N NE T*. **2** a dip in the ground, a saddle between hills *la19- NE T*. **3** the power or act of cutting; a cutting remark, a snub *19, 20- N T*. [see the verb]
sneck[2,2], *Bor* **sneg**, *SW Uls* **snig**, †**snek** /snɛk; *Bor* snɛg; *SW Uls* snɪg/ *v* **1** to cut, sever with a sharp instrument, cut into, prune, notch *la16-*. **2** to surpass, beat *la19- NE T*. †**sneck aff** to remove by cutting; to prune *18-19*. [probably onomatopoeic]
sneck[3,1] /snɛk/ *n* a greedy grasping person; a nickname for an Aberdonian *19- Ork N NE T EC*. [see the verb]
sneck[3,2], **snick** /snɛk, snɪk/ *v* to snatch, seize, steal *19-*. [EModE *sneck*; compare SNACK[1,2]]
sneckler /'snɛklər/ *n* a short circle of rope attached to the stern of a COBLE[2] for taking a rolling hitch on standing gear *la20- N NE*. [perhaps a variant of Eng *snickle* to catch with a noose with agent suffix]
sned[1,1] /snɛd/ *n* a cut, a cutting; a slash, a slight wound; a lopping or pruning *19-*. [see the verb]
sned[1,2] /snɛd/ *v* **1** to chop, lop off (a branch); to prune, trim (a tree) *16-*. **2** to cut (off); to sever *la16-*. **3** to trim (turnips); to cut the tops off (thistles) *la18-*. **snedder** a pruner *la16-*. †**snedding** pruning; *pl* prunings, branches removed *la16-e19*. †**snedding knife** a pruning knife *17-19*. [OE *snǣdan* to cut, slice, lop off, hew]
sned[2], **snead**, *NE* **snaith** /snɛd; *NE* sneð/ *n* the shaft of a scythe *la17-*. [OE *snǣd*]
snee[1,1], **snae** /sni, sne/ *n* **1** a cut, an incision; a slice *20- Sh Ork*. **2** inclination, liking; *of fish* readiness to take the bait *20 Sh*. [see the verb]
snee[1,2], **snae** /sni, sne/ *v* to cut, cut up *19- Sh Ork*. [Norw dial *sni* to cut, *sne* a cut]
snee[2] /sni/ *v* to twist, distort *20- Ork*. [compare Norw *snida* to go to the side]
sneed *see* SNOOD[1,1]
sneeg *see* SNIG[1,1]
sneekit /'snikət/ *adj* two-faced, underhand *20- N NE*. [conflation of SNEAK with SLEEKIT]
sneel *see* SNEEVIL[1,2], SNOOL[1,1]
sneer[1,1], †**sneir** /snir/ *n* **1** an expression of derision or scorn *la18-*. **2** *especially of a horse* a snort, noisy breathing (in or out) through the nose *la15-e19*. [see the verb]
sneer[1,2] /snir/ *v presp also* †**sneryng 1** to deride, scorn *la16-*. **2** to snort, snuffle, inhale or exhale heavily or noisily *16-19, 20- Ork*. [perhaps onomatopoeic]
sneerim-snaarim /'snirəm'snɑrəm/ *n* a violent quarrel, an uproar *20- Sh*. [a reduplicative formation based on SNAAR]
sneerko /'snirko/ *n* a twist, tangle, confusion *20- Ork*. [unknown]
sneesh[1,1], †**snish** /sniʃ/ *n* (a pinch of) snuff *la18-*. [back-formation from SNEESHIN]
sneesh[1,2] /sniʃ/ *v* **1** to take, inhale snuff *19-*. **2** to sneeze *20- C Bor*. [see the noun]
sneeshan *see* SNYSIN
sneeshin, †**snishing**, †**sneising**, †**snizing** /'sniʃən/ *n especially in Highland contexts* (a pinch of) snuff *17- literary*. †**sneeshin box** a snuffbox *17-19*. **sneeshin draps** drops of snuff-laden nasal mucus *19- NE T*. **sneeshin horn** a snuffbox made from a horn *la18-19, 20- T*. **sneeshin-mull**, **sneeshin mill** a snuffbox, originally one which ground the snuff *la17-*. **sneeshin pen** a small quill or spoon for taking snuff *19- NE T*. [Gael *snaoisean* snuff]
sneesl /'snisəl/ *v* to (begin to) rain or snow slightly *20- Sh*. [perhaps onomatopoeic; compare SMIZZLE]
sneest *see* SNEIST[1,2]
sneet *see* SNIT, SNITE[3]

sneeter /ˈsnitər/ v **1** to giggle, snigger *20- Ork N NE T WC*. **2** to weep, blubber *20- N NE*. [probably onomatopoeic; compare SNITTER¹]

sneevil¹·¹, **snivel** /ˈsnivəl, ˈsnɪvəl/ n **1** pl a severe cold in the nose *19-*. **2** a nasal intonation, a twang *19-*. **the sneevils** a cold *19- Ork N C* [see the verb]

sneevil¹·², **snivel**, †**snevil**, †**snawil**, †**sneel** /ˈsnivəl, ˈsnɪvəl/ v **1** to speak through the nose, speak with a nasal snuffling tone, whine *la14-*. **2** to cringe, act sycophantically or insincerely *la18-*. [OE *snyflan*]

sneg *see* SNECK²·²

snegg *see* SNIG²·²

sneik *see* SNEAK

sneir *see* SNEER¹·¹

sneising *see* SNEESHIN

sneist¹·¹ /snist/ n a taunt, a jibe; an air of disdain or impertinence *19, 20- EC Bor*. **sneisty, snisty** cheeky, sneering, uncivil, tart *19, 20- NE T EC Bor*. [see the verb]

sneist¹·², **sneest** /snist/ v to behave in a contemptuous and arrogant way, be scornful or supercilious *18-19, 20- WC*. **sneister 1** to laugh in a suppressed way, snigger *19, 20- Sh*. **2** to sniff, snuffle *19, 20- Sh*. [perhaps onomatopoeic]

†**sneith**, **sneth** adj smooth, polished *16-e19*. [perhaps altered form of *smeith* (SMUITH²)]

snek *see* SNECK¹·¹, SNECK²·²

snell¹·¹ /snɛl/ adj **1** *of weather* biting, bitter, severe *la14-*. **2** severe in manner or speech, tart, sarcastic *la16-19, 20- Sh NE T EC*. **3** sharp to the taste or smell, pungent, acrid *la18- NE C SW*. **4** hard, severe, harsh *15-19, 20- NE WC*. **5** *of sound* sharp, clear, shrill *19, 20- Sh*. **6** sharp, smart, clever; quick, nimble, active; powerful *la16-e19*. **7** *of a weapon* sharp, keen *15-e17*. [OE *snell*]

snell¹·² /snɛl/ adv **1** keenly, eagerly, quickly *la15-*. **2** harshly, unfeelingly, vigorously *la14-*. **3** *of wind* keenly, piercingly *18-*. **snell-white** pure white *la19- Sh*. [see the adj]

snell² /snɛl/ n a blaze or stripe (of white) on the face of an animal *20- Sh Ork*. **snellie** the coot *Fulica atra 20- Ork*. [perhaps reduced form of *snell white* (SNELL¹·²)]

snepp, †**snyp** /snɛp/ v to tie, bind, tether *17- Sh*. **sneppick** a tether, a halter *20- Sh*. [perhaps altered form of Norn *nepp* to tie together, ON *hneppa* to squeeze]

sneryng *see* SNEER¹·²

sneth *see* SNEITH

sneug /snjug/ n a hump-like projection, the shoulder or slope of a hill, a crag, a round hill top, frequently in place-names *19- Sh* [altered form of Norw dial *nuk* a hill crag]

sneuk /snjuk; *Ork also* snøk/ n a whim, a peculiarity of temper *20- Sh Ork*. **sneukit** insidious, crafty *19- Sh NE*. [probably back-formation from *ill-sneukit* (ILL¹·³)]

sneuter /ˈsnjutər/ n a slow, unskilful, stupid person *20- NE*. [unknown]

snevil *see* SNEEVIL¹·²

snew *see* SNAW¹·²

†**sneyster**¹·¹ n a piece of grilled meat, a roasted joint; a pork sausage for grilling *19*. [unknown]

sneyster¹·² /ˈsnʌɪstər/ v to burn, scorch, roast; to cauterize *19- WC*. [unknown]

snib¹·¹ /snɪb/ n **1** a catch, a small bolt for a door *19-*. **2** a check, a rebuke, a rebuff, a calamity, a reverse *15-19, 20- T WC Uls*. **3** a short steep hill or ascent *20- T C*. **4** a sixpence *20- N NE*. **snibble** *mining* a bar of wood or iron used as a brake or drag on a wagon *la18-19, 20- C historical*. [see the verb]

snib¹·², †**snyb** /snɪb/ v **1** to check, suppress, restrain; to reprove, punish *15-19*. **2** to cut (short or off), slice, cut into *la18-19, 20- Sh NE WC Uls*. **3** to fasten (a door) with a catch *19-*. **4** to shut in; to catch in a trap *la18-19*. **snibbit** cut short, curtailed, trimmed; *of hair* cropped very close *la19, 20- Sh NE C*. [compare OIcel *snubba*, Dan *snibbe* to rebuke]

snicher¹·¹ /ˈsnɪxər/ n a snigger, a titter *la19-*. [onomatopoeic]

snicher¹·² /ˈsnɪxər/ v to snigger, laugh in a suppressed way *19-*. [see the noun]

snick *see* SNECK¹·¹, SNECK¹·², SNECK³·²

sniffell *see* SNIFFLE²

sniffle¹·¹ /ˈsnɪfəl/ n a runny nose; the act of sniffling *19-*. **the sniffles** a head cold, causing difficulty in breathing *19- Sh N T EC Uls* [see the verb]

sniffle¹·² /ˈsnɪfəl/ v **1** to sniff or snuffle *19-*. **2** to be slow in motion or action, loiter *19, 20- NE*. **snifflin** slow, sluggish, lazy, weak, procrastinating, frivolous *la16-19, 20- NE*. †**sniffler** a strong gusty wind; a difficult business *la18-19*. [onomatopoeic; compare SNEEVIL¹·²]

†**sniffle**², **sniffell** n a snaffle *la17-18*. **sniffle bit** a snaffle bit *la17-18*. [variant of EModE *snaffle*]

snift /snɪft/ v to puff, snort, blow *la19-*. [perhaps back-formation from SNIFTER¹·¹]

snifter¹·¹ /ˈsnɪftər/ n **1** a (noisy) sniff, from a cold, grief, or disdain; a snivel, whimper or snigger *19-*. **2** a strong blast, gust or flurry (of wind or sleet) *18-19, 20- Sh Ork NE T C Uls*. **3** a shock, reverse, rebuff or quarrel *19, 20- NE Bor*. **snifter-dichter** a handkerchief *20-*. **the snifters** a (severe) head cold, catarrh, a stuffed nose *19-*. [see the verb]

snifter¹·² /ˈsnɪftər/ v **1** to sniff; to snivel, snuffle (with a cold); to snort, snore *18-*. **2** *of wind* to blow in strong gusts; *of vapour* to escape in clouds *la19- Sh NE*. [ME *sniftern*]

snifty /ˈsnɪfte/ adj haughty, disdainful *20- T EC SW Bor*. [probably back-formation from SNIFTER¹·¹ + *-y* (-IE²)]

snig¹·¹, **sneeg** /snɪg, snig/ n a sharp jerk, a sudden pull *20- N*. [onomatopoeic]

snig¹·² /snɪg/ v to pull sharply, jerk *20- N Uls*. [see the noun]

snig²·¹ /snɪg/ n a neigh, a whinny *la19- Sh*. [see the verb]

snig²·², **snegg** /snɪg; snɛg/ v *of a horse* to neigh, whinny *19- Sh*. **snigger, snegger** = SNIG²·² *la19- Sh*. [altered form of Norn *negg*; compare Icel *hneggja*]

snig *see* SNECK²·²

snigger¹·¹ /ˈsnɪgər/ n a grappling implement used in catching salmon *20- N NE*. [altered form of Eng *sniggle* a device for catching eels]

snigger¹·² /ˈsnɪgər/ v to catch (salmon) illegally by dragging a cluster of weighted hooks along the river bed; to fish (a pool) by this method *la19-*. [altered form of Eng *sniggle* to catch eels in their holes with a sniggle]

snip¹·¹ /snɪp/ n **1** a small piece (cut off something) *18-*. **2** a small white patch on a horse's face *la17-*. **snippy** adj quick in speech, curt *20- EC*. **snippy** n a sharp-tongued person *la19- Sh T*. **go snips** to share, divide equally *la17-*. **rin snips** = *go snips 19, 20- Sh*. [from the verb and LG *snip*]

snip¹·² /snɪp/ v to cut *16-*. **snippen** surly, abrupt *20- Sh*. †**snippin, snypand** nipping, bitingly cold *16-19*. **snippit 1** niggardly, giving short measure *la19, 20- Sh N NE Bor*. **2** quick in speech, curt *20- Ork EC*. **3** *of a horse* with a small white patch on the face *17-19, 20- NE*. †**snip-white** bright, dazzling *e19*. [Du, LG *snippen*]

snipe¹, †**snip** /snʌɪp/ n **1** a wading bird *Gallinago gallinago*, characterized by a very long slender bill *16-*. **2** *derogatory* a contemptible, insignificant person *la19-*. **snipie 1** a kettle or teapot *la19- NE T*. **2** *games* a particular game of marbles *20- EC*. **snippy** = *snipie* 1. [ME *snipe, snippe*; compare OIcel *mȳri-snīpa*, MDu, MLG *snippe*]

snipe²·¹ /snʌɪp/ n **1** a smart blow *18- NE Bor*. **2** a setback, a loss by being cheated, a let-down, a fraud, a cheat *la19- NE*. [altered form of SNIP¹·¹]

snipe[2,2] /snʌɪp/ *v* **1** to strike smartly *19- NE Bor.* **2** to cheat, defraud, bring loss on *la19- NE.* [see the noun]

snipper[1,1] /'snɪpər/ *n* **1** something wrinkled, shrivelled or tangled *20- Sh.* **2** a peevish mood, a surly temper *20- Sh.* **snipperie** shrivelled, shrunken *20- Sh.* **sniprek 1** a tangle, a wrinkled condition *la19- Sh.* **2** a boorish, unpleasant person *20- Sh.* [see the verb]

snipper[1,2] /'snɪpər/ *v of the face* to pucker, wrinkle up *la19- Sh.* **snippert** wrinkled, wizened, sharp *la19- Sh.* **sniprin** tart, snappish, cross *20- Sh.* **snirpet** bad-tempered, peevish, surly *20- Sh Ork.* [metathesis of Norw dial *snyrpa* to wrinkle]

snippik, snippack /'snɪpək/ *n* **1** a wading bird *Gallinago gallinago*, characterized by a very long slender bill *19- Sh.* **2** a sharp-tongued woman *20- Sh.* [SNIPE[1], with diminutive suffix -OCK]

snirk[1,1], **snyirk** /snɪrk, snjɪrk/ *n* a creaking, grating sound *20- Sh.* [see the verb]

snirk[1,2], **snyirk** /snɪrk, snjɪrk/ *v* to creak, cause a grating sound *la19- Sh.* [onomatopoeic]

snirk[2,1] /snɪrk/ *n* a snort, a snigger *20- Sh SW Bor.* [see the verb]

snirk[2,2] /snɪrk/ *v* to snort, wrinkle the nose, snigger *19- SW Bor.* **snirket** *of a face* pinched, wizened, puckered *20- Sh Bor.* **snirkim, snyirkim** strong drink, spirits *la19- Sh.* [ON *snerkja* to wrinkle, screw up one's face]

snirl[1,1] /snɪrl/ *n* a snarl, a contemptuous wrinkling of the nose *20- Ork Bor.* **snirly** a gusty biting wind *20- Sh SW.* [altered form of Eng *snarl*]

snirl[1,2] /snɪrl/ *v* **1** to snigger, laugh in a suppressed way *19- Bor.* **2** *of wind* to blow in gusts *20- NE.* [see the noun]

snirl *see* SNORL[1,1], SNORL[1,2]

snirt[1,1] /snɪrt/ *n* **1** a snigger, a suppressed laugh *19- T C SW Bor.* **2** a small insignificant person *19- C Bor.* **3** a snort *la18-19, 20- Bor.* [onomatopoeic]

snirt[1,2] /snɪrt/ *v* **1** to snigger, make a noise through the nose when trying to stifle laughter; to sneer *18-.* **2** to snort, breathe sharply through the nose *19-.* **snirtle 1** to snigger *la18-.* **2** to snort, breathe sharply through the nose *20- T.* [see the noun]

snish *see* SNEESH[1,1]

snishing *see* SNEESHIN

snisty *see* SNEIST[1,1]

snit, sneet /snɪt, snit/ *n* a small unpleasant person *la19- Sh Ork.* [unknown; compare SNOT[1,1], SNITE[2]]

snitchers /'snɪtʃərz/ *npl* handcuffs *la19-.* [Eng *snitch* to catch with a noose or loop, with agent suffix]

snite[1,1], **snyte** /snʌɪt/ *n* **1** a sharp blow, especially on the nose *19- NE C Bor.* **2** a blowing or wiping of the nose *19, 20- Sh NE.* **3** a reproof, a gibe *20- SW Bor.* [see the verb]

snite[1,2], **snyte** /snʌɪt/ *v* **1** to blow (one's nose) *la16- Sh Ork NE.* **2** to snuff (a candle) *19- NE.* **3** to strike, deliver a blow at *19- Bor.* **to snite someone's niz** to tweak someone's nose; to take someone down a peg *19- SW.* [OE *snȳtan*]

snite[2] /snʌɪt/ *n derogatory* a person perceived to be worthless; a small insignificant person or thing *la17- Sh NE T SW.* Compare SNIT. [perhaps extended sense of SNITE[1,1]]

snite[3], **sneet** /snʌɪt, snit/ *v* to move about or work in a lazy, careless or stupefied way, laze about, be listless, be at a loose end *19, 20- NE.* [unknown]

snitter[1] /'snɪtər/ *v* to giggle, snigger *19, 20- C SW Bor.* [probably onomatopoeic; compare SNIRT[1,2]]

snitter[2] /'snɪtər/ *n* a twitch for a horse *20- Sh Ork.* [unknown]

snitter[3] /'snɪtər/ *n* a bitingly cold wind *la19- Sh Ork.* **snitteret** bitterly cold *20- Sh.* [perhaps onomatopoeic]

snivel *see* SNEEVIL[1,1], SNEEVIL[1,2]

sniverrie /'snɪvəri/ *n* a home-made wooden button, a fastener *20- Sh.* **sniverrie-pin** a wooden pin, (part of) a fish-hook *la19- Sh.* [unknown; compare Norw dial *knuvr* a pin in a bar, a ring in a pig's nose]

snizing *see* SNEESHIN

snjug *see* SNUG[2]

snjuker *see* SNUKER

snjulted *see* SNOILTET

snocher[1,1], †**snocker** /'snɔxər/ *n* a snort or snore, the act of breathing heavily through the nose *19, 20- NE T EC.* **the snochers** a severe nose cold, causing nasal blockage *19, 20- NE T EC.* [see the verb]

snocher[1,2], †**snocker** /'snɔxər/ *v* to snort, breathe heavily and noisily through the nose, snuffle; to snuff up *18-19, 20- NE T EC Bor.* [onomatopoeic]

snochter[1,1], *SW* **snoichter** /'snɔxtər; *SW* 'snɔɪxtər/ *n* nasal mucus *20- NE WC SW.* **snochter-dichter** a handkerchief *20-.* [probably conflation of SNOCHER[1,1] with SNOTTER[1,1]]

snochter[1,2] /'snɔxtər/ *v* to sniffle, dribble or blow mucus from the nose *20.* [see the noun]

snock *see* SNOKE[1,2]

snocker *see* SNOCHER[1,1], SNOCHER[1,2]

snod[1,1] /snɔd/ *n* a trimming *20- T EC.* [see the adj]

snod[1,2] /snɔd/ *v* **1** to make trim or neat, tidy, put in order *la18-.* **2** to prune, cut, trim, smooth, make level *la18-19, 20- NE T SW Bor.* **3** to put to rights morally, put (someone) in his place, punish, defeat *la19.* [see the adj]

snod[1,3] /snɔd/ *adj* **1** smooth, level, evenly cut *la15-.* **2** neat, trim, smart; tidy; compact, well laid out, in good order *18-.* **3** comfortable, snug, at ease *la18-.* **snod up** a tidying, a smartening *la19- NE SW.* **snoddie up** = *snod up 20- NE SW.* [probably participial adj from SNED[1,2]]

snöd *see* SNUD[1,1], SNUD[1,2]

snoddie /'snɔde/ *n* a stupid person *19- Bor.* [altered form of Eng *noddy*]

snoddy /'snɔdi/ *n* a thick oatcake or barley-cake *19- Sh Ork.* [Norw dial *knoda* a lump of dough]

snodge /snɔdʒ/ *v* to walk deliberately or steadily *19- Bor.* [perhaps onomatopoeic]

snog *see* SNUG[1]

snoichter *see* SNOCHTER[1,1]

snoif *see* SNOOVE

snoilk, snølk /snɔɪlk, snølk/ *n* a frown, a fit of anger or sulks *la19- Sh.* **snoilket** angry, offended, sulky *la19- Sh.* [perhaps onomatopoeic]

snoiltet, snjulted /'snɔɪltət, 'snjultət/ *adj* shortened, closely cut, stumpy; polled *19- Sh.* [Norw dial *snollete*]

snoiter /'snɔɪtər/ *v* to breathe loudly through the nose, snore; to snooze *19, 20- NE T.* [probably onomatopoeic]

snok *see* SNOKE[1,2]

snoke[1,1], **snowk** /snok, snʌuk/ *n* **1** an act of smelling, a sniff *la18-19, 20- NE C SW.* **2** a prowler, a sneak; an inquisitive person *20- NE Uls.* [see the verb]

snoke[1,2], **snook, snowk, †snock, †snok** /snok, snuk, snʌuk/ *v* **1** to snuff, smell, poke with the nose; *of a dog* to scent out *la15-.* **2** to hunt, prowl, go about or search out furtively *la18-.* **3** to snort, snigger *la19, 20- Bor.* [compare Norw dial *snoka* to snuff, smell]

snoke *see* SNUKE

snöl *see* SNOOL[1,1]

snood[1,1], **snude**, *Sh* **snüd**, *NE* **sneed**, †**snud** /snud; Sh snød; *NE* snid/ *n* **1** a ribbon; the band or ribbon bound round the brow and fastened at the back under the hair, traditionally worn by young unmarried women; a symbol of virginity *16-.* **2** the hemp part of a sea-line to which the hook is attached; the twisted loop of horsehair by which the hook

snood is sometimes attached to this *la16-*. Compare *tippin* (TIP¹·²).

snooding 1 the short hair line to which a fishing-hook is attached *20- Uls.* **2** (the material used for making) ribbon *la16-e17*. [OE *snōd*]

snood¹·² /snud/ *v* **1** to bind (the hair) with a band *18-19, 20- historical*. **2** *fishing* to tie (the short hair line) to the hook *la19, 20- EC Uls*. [see the noun]

snooie¹·¹ /ˈsnui/ *n* a jerk or toss of the head *20- Ork N*. [Norw dial *snu* a turn, twist + -IE¹]

snooie¹·² /ˈsnui/ *v of cattle* to toss the head *20- N*. [see the noun]

snook *see* SNOKE¹·², SNUKE

snool¹·¹, *Sh* **snöl**, *NE* **sneel** /snul; *Sh* snøl; *NE* snil/ *n* **1** a spiritless, cringing, abject or cowardly person; a lazy, inactive person; a simple-minded person *18-19, 20- Sh T SW Bor Uls*. **2** an insult *20- Ork T*. [unknown]

snool¹·², *EC* **snule** /snul/ *v* **1** to submit tamely, cringe; to act meanly, deceitfully or spiritlessly *la18-*. **2** to subdue, keep in subjection; to humiliate, reprove, snub *18-19, 20- Ork*. **3** to show lack of energy, loaf about shiftlessly, move slowly and lethargically *19, 20- EC*. [unknown]

snoot, snout, †snowt /snut, snʌut/ *n* **1** the projecting part of an animal's face, the nose and jaws, the muzzle *la15-*. **2** *derogatory* the nose or face of a person *la15-*. **3** the peak (of a cap) *la18-*. **4** a detective, a policeman *20- NE T WC SW*. **5** a projecting point of land; a projecting part of a building or structure *16-19, 20- NE*. **6** the prow of a ship or armoured beak of a warship *16*. **snootit** *of a cap* peaked *la18-*. [ME *snout*, MDu, MLG *snūte*]

snoove, snuve, †snoif /snuv/ *v* **1** to twist, twirl, spin (yarn) *16-*. **2** to move smoothly or easily, at a steady, even pace; to glide *18-19, 20- NE C Bor*. **3** to move carelessly, lazily or abjectly; to slink or sneak *la18-19, 20- WC SW Bor*. **snoovle** = SNOOVE (sense 3). **snuivie** a layabout; an abject or cringing person; a dull-witted person *19- Bor*. [altered form of ON *snúa* to turn, twist]

snoozle /ˈsnuzəl/ *v* **1** to snooze, doze *la19, 20- NE T EC*. **2** to nuzzle, poke with the nose; to snuggle *la19, 20- WC SW*. [frequentative form of Eng *snooze*, in sense 2 conflated with *nuzzle*]

snore¹·¹, **†snor** /snor/ *n* **1** a snort, roar, loud roaring or droning noise *16-19, 20- Sh N Bor*. **2** *pl* an animal disease causing snuffling, the snivels *la16-e19*. [ME *snore* snorting, OE *fnora* sneezing]

snore¹·² /snor/ *v* **1** to make a (loud) noise in breathing while asleep *16-*. **2** *of wind, fire, or something vibrating* to make a rushing, whirring, droning sound *19-*. **3** to move at speed with a rushing, roaring sound *19, 20- Sh Ork T EC SW*. **4** *of animals* to snort *la18-19, 20- SW*. **snorer** a toy made from a piece of wood and cord which, when the cord is twisted and untwisted, produces a buzzing sound *20- SW Uls*. **snorik**, *N* **snorag** = *snorer la19- Sh N*. **snorie-ben, snorie-bane** = *snorer la19- Sh Ork*. [ME *snoren*]

snork¹·¹ /snork/ *n* a snort *19- SW*. [see the verb]

snork¹·² /snork/ *v* **1** to snort, snore, snuffle *19- WC SW Bor*. **2** *of things* to make a roaring or explosive sound *19- Bor*. [EModE *snork*, MDu, MLG *snorken*]

snorl¹·¹, **snurl, snirl**, *NE* **snorrel** /snɔrl, snʌrl, snɪrl; *NE* ˈsnɔrəl/ *n* **1** a knot, tangle, kink or twist (in a thread or rope) *19-*. **2** a predicament, a scrape; a muddle or confusion *19, 20- Sh N NE*. **snorly** twisted, tangled, knotted *19-*. [variant of SNARL¹·¹]

snorl¹·², **snurl, snirl** /snɔrl, snʌrl, snɪrl/ *v* to ruffle, wrinkle, twist, tangle; to become confused *18-*. [see the noun]

snorrel *see* SNORL¹·¹

snort /snort/ *n* a tangle *19- NE*. [perhaps conflation of SNORL¹·¹ with KNOT¹·¹]

snort *see* SNURT

†snosh *adj* chubby and contented *19*. [perhaps conflation of SNOD¹·³ with COSH]

snot¹·¹ /snɔt/ *n* **1** nasal mucus *la18-*. **2** a contemptible, worthless or stupid person *19, 20- T C SW Bor*. **3** the burnt wick of a candle *19- NE Bor Uls*. [OE *gesnot*]

snot¹·² /snɔt/ *v* **1** to blow or clear the nose *la17-*. **2** to snub, reprimand *la19-*. [see the noun]

snotter¹·¹ /ˈsnɔtər/ *n* **1** nasal mucus *la17-*. **2** the burnt wick of a candle *18-19, 20- NE SW*. **3** the red membranous part of a turkey-cock's beak *19, 20- N T EC*. **4** a contemptible, worthless or stupid person *la18- N EC SW Uls*. **snotter-box 1** the nose *la18-*. **2** a soft, stupid, untidy person *la19- N EC Bor*. **snotter-dichter** a handkerchief *20-*. [derivative of SNOT¹·¹, or from MDu *snoter*, MLG *snotter*]

snotter¹·² /ˈsnɔtər/ *v* **1** to snivel, weep noisily *19-*. **2** to snuffle, snort, breathe heavily through the nose *18-19, 20- N T EC*. **3** to snooze, doze *18-19, 20- NE*. [see the noun]

snottery /ˈsnɔtəre/ *adj* **1** slimy, running at the nose *19-*. **2** surly, brusque, snooty *20- T C SW*. **3** tearful, lugubrious *20- WC SW*. [SNOTTER¹·¹ + -y (-IE²)]

snottum /ˈsnɔtəm/ *n Travellers' language* a metal hook or crook used to hang a pot or kettle over a fire *20-*. [unknown]

snotty /ˈsnɔte/ *adj* **1** having mucus running from the nose *17-*. **2** short-tempered, curt, huffy *la19-*. [SNOT¹·¹ + -y (-IE²)]

snoury /ˈsnɔri/ *adj* irascible, easily offended *20- Ork*. [compare Norw dial *snorren* offended, annoyed]

snout *see* SNOOT

snow *see* SNAW¹·¹, SNAW¹·²

†Snowdon, Snawdoun *n* one of the Scottish heralds *15-19*. **Snowdon herald** = SNOWDON. [from the name of part of the hill on which Stirling Castle is built]

snowk *see* SNOKE¹·²

snowt *see* SNOOT

snubbert /ˈsnʌbərt/ *n* **1** *humorous* or *derogatory* the nose *19- NE*. **2** the red membranous part of a turkey-cock's beak *20- NE*. [derivative of Eng *snub* a short, turned-up nose]

snud¹·¹, *Sh* **snüd** /snøɖ/ *n* **1** a twist, coil or loop, especially one of the twists in a strand of rope *20- Sh Ork*. **2** (a sign of) irritation, peevishness, sulkiness; a toss of the head *la19- Sh Ork*. [Swed dial *snod*, with influence from *snüd* (SNOOD¹·¹)]

snud¹·², *Sh* **snüd** /snøɖ/ *v* **1** to twist, coil, wind; to put a twist in rope *la19- Sh Ork*. **2** to toss the head threateningly *20- Sh*. [see the noun]

snüd, snud *see* SNOOD¹·¹

snude *see* SNOOD¹·¹

snuff¹·¹ /snʌf/ *n* **1** a sniff, a snuffle, the act of snuffling *19-*. **2** a persistent snuffling; a disease in sheep *la16*. [see the verb]

snuff¹·² /snʌf/ *v* to sniff, inhale, clear (the nose) *la16-*. [MDu *snuffen* to snuffle]

snuff²·¹ /snʌf/ *n* **1** (a pinch or inhalation of) powdered tobacco *17-*. **2** a very small amount; something of little significance or value *18-*. **snuffy hanky** a handkerchief for use after taking snuff *20- T EC SW*. **snuff-horn** a snuffbox made from the tip of an animal's horn *19- Sh T WC*. **snuff-mill, snuff-mull** a snuffbox *17-*. **†snuff napkin** = *snuffy hanky la17-e18*. **†snuff-pen** a small spoon or quill for taking snuff *19*. [Du, Flem *snuf*]

snuff²·² /snʌf/ *v* to take snuff *18-*. **snuffing** the taking of snuff, especially as part of the Common Riding ceremony in Hawick *la17-*. [see the noun]

†snuff³ *n* a rage, a huff *la17-19*. [extended sense of EModE *snuff* the remains of a burnt candle wick]

snuff

†**snuff**⁴ *interj* expressing annoyance or impatience nonsense *18-19*. [compare SNUFF²·¹ sense 2]

snuffy /'snʌfe/ *adj* sulky, touchy, huffily displeased *19-*. [SNUFF³ + -y (-IE²)]

snug¹, **snog** /snʌg, snɔg/ *adj* **1** comfortable, warm, cosy, secure *18-*. **2** close, tight together *19-*. **3** neat, trim, tidy *17, 18- Ork N H&I EC*. **4** smooth, sleek, close-cropped *16-19, 20- Sh Ork*. [uncertain; compare LG *snügger, snögger* slender, smooth, dainty; and ON *snǫggr* smooth, short-haired]

snug², **snjug** /snʌg, snjʌg/ *v of cattle* to strike, push, try to prod with the horns *19, 20- Sh*. [Norw dial *snugga* to push, shove]

snuivie *see* SNOOVE

†**snuke, snoke, snook** *n* a projecting piece of land, a promontory *la14-15*. [unknown; compare SNEUG]

snuker, snjuker /'snjuker/ *n* a bad smell, an ill-smelling smoke or vapour, a fug *la19- Sh*. [Faer *snykur* a rancid smell]

snule *see* SNOOL¹·²

snurkle /'snʌrkəl/ *v of hard-twisted thread* to tangle, knot *19- Bor*. [uncertain; compare Norw *snirkel* a twist and SNORL¹·¹]

snurl *see* SNORL¹·¹, SNORL¹·²

snurt, snort /snʌrt, snɔrt/ *n* **1** nasal mucus *la19- Sh*. **2** the burnt end of the wick of a candle *20- Sh*. **3** *derogatory* a feckless person *e19*. **snorty** *of a person* useless, feckless *20- N*. [probably altered form of SNOT¹·¹ with influence from Eng *snort*]

snush¹·¹ /snøʃ/ *n* a sniff, a snort, a noisy breathing through the nose *la19- Sh*. [see the verb]

snush¹·² /snøʃ/ *v* to sniff audibly, snort, speak nasally *la19- Sh Ork*. [Norw dial *snøsa*]

snuve *see* SNOOVE

sny /snae/ *n especially of a horse* a white marking on the face, a blaze *la19- Sh Ork*. **snied** *of an animal* having a white mark on the nose, blazed *la19- Sh*. [perhaps back-formation from Norw dial *snøydd* bare, bald]

snyb *see* SNIB¹·²

snyirk *see* SNIRK¹·¹, SNIRK¹·²

snyp *see* SNEPP

snyse /snʌis/ *n* a wooden muzzle to prevent a calf from suckling *20- Ork*. **snyst** *of an animal* having a white mark on the nose of an animal *20- Ork*; compare *snied* (SNY). [Norw dial *sneis*]

snysin, sneeshan /'snʌisin, 'sniʃən/ *n* the coot *Fulica atra 20- Ork*. [derivative of SNYSE, because of the white stripe on its forehead]

snysters /'snʌistərz/ *npl* sweets, cakes, pastries *19- WC*. [altered form of SNASHTERS]

snyte *see* SNITE¹

†**snyth** *n in Orkney* the coot *Fulica atra la18-19*. Compare SNYSIN. [related to SNY or SNYSE]

so *see* SAE²·¹, SAE²·²

soach *see* SOUCH¹·²

soad, soadie *see* SOD¹

soak *see* SOCK³

soam, †**soyme,** †**soum,** †**some** /som/ *n* **1** a trace, the chain or rope attaching a draught animal to a plough *la14-*. **2** a rope, strap or chain for dragging or tying up a large, heavy object *16-e18*. [probably OFr *some* a pack saddle, a burden]

soap *see* SAIP

soart *see* SORT¹·¹, SORT¹·²

sob *see* SAB¹·¹, SAB¹·²

sober¹·¹, †**sobir** /'sobər/ *v* **1** to become sober; to become calm; to settle *15-*. **2** to pacify, calm, quieten *la14-19*. [see the adj]

sod

sober¹·², †**sobir,** †**sobyr** /'sobər/ *adj* **1** modest, not grand; decent, respectable; plain, unadorned *la15-*. **2** moderate, not excessive or given to excess; serious, prudent *la14-*. **3** small in size or amount; slight; slightly-built *la15-19, 20- NE T*. **4** in poor or only moderate health, sickly, weak *19, 20- NE T*. **5** poor, mean, paltry, miserable *la15-19, 20- NE*. **6** few in number; small in value; trifling; trivial *16-e17*. **7** of low rank or status; humble *la15-16*. **soberly** **1** gravely, seriously; quietly, calmly; in a measured fashion *la14-*. **2** moderately, temperately, without excess; respectably; sparingly, frugally *la15-*. **3** poorly, badly *la15-17*. **4** severely *la17*. [OFr *sobre*, Lat *sōbrius*]

soch *see* SOUCH¹·¹, SOUCH¹·²

socher /'sɔxər/ *v* to pamper oneself, be fussy about one's health *19, 20- WC*. †**socherin, saughrin** lacking in energy, sluggish, soft and flaccid in character or action *la18-19*. [conflation of Gael *socair* calm, ease, quiet with Gael *sochar* weakness, ficklness]

socht *see* SEEK¹

social /'soʃəl/ *adj* **1** friendly, well-disposed; co-operative; sociable *16-*. **2** taking place in a group (usually of friends or people connected in some way) meeting for a usually pleasurable purpose; *of an action or event* intended for such a purpose *la18-*. **3** of or relating to society *19-*. [MFr *social*, Lat *sociālis*]

society, †**societie,** †**societe** /sə'saeəte/ *n* **1** association, contact, communication; fellowship, social intercourse *la15-*. **2** (a) political or other association; a community, a group united by a common aim or government *16-*. **3** an association, a group of persons with a common interest, purpose or trade *17-*. **4** *pl* certain groups of Presbyterians who refused to recognize the 1679 Indulgence and 1688 Revolution Settlement *18-19, 20- historical*. **5** (a contract of) partnership in business or commerce *la16-17*. **Society Men** = SOCIETY (sense 4) *19, 20- historical*. †**The Society** the property of the Society of Brewers of the Burgh of Edinburgh, the part of Edinburgh bounded by Candlemaker Row and the Cowgate and incorporating 'Sciennes Acres', the land near Greyfriars Port formerly belonging to the Convent of St Catherine of Siena *la16-17*. [MFr *société*]

sock¹, †**sok** /sɔk, sok/ *n* a ploughshare *la15-*. **sock-spade** a spade for removing stones obstructing the plough *20- C*. †**sok and culter** a furrow ploughed on the boundary line of a piece of land indicating extent and confirming possession *la16-19*. †**sok and scythe** (fit for) ploughing and mowing; *of land* arable *la16-e19*. [ME *soc*, OFr *soc*, Lat *soccus*]

sock², †**sok** /sɔk, sok/ *n* **1** a (short) stocking *la15-*. **2** a piece of knitting *20- Sh*. †**sok-heid** perhaps the top of a sock or stocking or perhaps a footless sock *la16-17*. [OE *socc*]

sock³, **soak,** †**sok,** †**soke** /sɔk, sok/ *v* to steep; to saturate *la15-*. [OE *socian*]

socket¹·¹, †**sokkat** /'sɔkət/ *n* **1** a hollow part forming a holder into which something is fitted *16-*. **2** the part of a golf club into which the shaft is fitted; a stroke played off the socket *la19-*. **3** the head of a spear or lance *e16*. [ME *soket*, AN *soket*]

socket¹·² /'sɔkət/ *v in the game of golf* to hit the ball in the angle between the head and the shaft of the club *20-*. [see the noun]

sod¹, **soad** /sɔd, sod/ *n* **1** a cut piece or slice of grass with the earth in which it is growing, a turf *la18-*. **2** the surface of the earth *la18-*. **3** a piece of surface turf used as fuel *19, 20- Ork N NE T H&I Bor*. **4** a kind of bread, a roll made of coarse flour *la18- NE WC*. **5** a heavy, fat person; a dead weight *19- Bor Uls*. **soddie** a seat made of turf *la19- Sh N*. **sodick** = SOADIE *20- Sh*. **soadie** **1** a large heavy person; a slovenly person *la19, 20- C*. **2** a boring, spiritless, unimaginative person *la20- WC*. [EModE *sod*, MDu, MLG *sode*]

sod² /sɔd/ *n* the rock-dove *Columba livia la19- T*. [unknown]

sod *see* SAD¹·³

soda *see* SODIE

sodden, †**soddin**, †**sottyne** /'sɔdən/ *adj* **1** soaked, saturated; ruined by wetness *la16-*. **2** boiled, cooked by boiling *la14-19*. [OE *soden*, ptp of *sēoðan* to seethe]

†**soddin** *n* (a piece of) boiled meat *la15-17*. [from the adj SODDEN]

soddin *see* SODDEN

soddis *see* SODS

sodger¹·¹, **sojer**, **soldier**, †**souldiour**, †**sojour** /'sodʒər, 'sʌdʒər, 'soldʒər/ *n* **1** a man engaged in military service, a member of an army or militia, especially an unpromoted soldier *la14-*. **2** the ladybird *19-*. **3** the stem and flower-head of the ribwort plantain *Plantago lanceolata*; a children's game played with them *la19-*. **4** *pl* smuts of burning soot *la19- N NE T EC SW*. **5** an injured child or animal *20- NE T SW*. **6** the red-breasted minnow *Phoxinus phoxinus 20- NE C*. **7** *joinery* a packing piece or plug, used to make a bolt fit tightly *20- C*. **8** a nickname for a native of Ceres in Fife *20- EC*. **sodger-clad but major-minded** having a strong sense of pride and self-respect in spite of a humble position *20- NE T C SW*. [OFr *soudier*, *soldier*]

sodger¹·², **soldier** /'sodʒər, 'soldʒər/ *v* **1** to serve as a soldier *19-*. **2** to march in a stolid, dogged way, trudge *20- NE C SW*. [see the noun]

sodie, **soda** /'sode, 'sodə/ *n* soda *17-*. [Lat *soda*]

sodie-heid /'sodehid/ *n* an empty-headed, irresponsible person *20-*. [SODIE + HEID¹·¹]

†**sods**, **soddis** *npl* a saddle made of cloth bags stuffed with straw *la16-e19*. [extended sense of SOD¹]

soe¹·¹ /so/ *n* **1** half-boiled limpets or other shellfish chewed and used as bait in fishing *19- Sh*. **2** fragments, small pieces *19- Sh*. [Norw dial *så* seed, sowing]

soe¹·² /so/ *v fishing* to throw or spit out bait; to spit out *19- Sh*. [see the noun]

soft *see* SAFT¹·¹, SAFT¹·², SAFT¹·³

sog, *Sh Ork* **sugg** /sɔg; *Sh Ork* sʌg/ *n* a state of wetness, a bog, a mire *20- Sh Ork N*. **sogy** a mixture of oatmeal and buttermilk, eaten uncooked *20- Ork*. **suggo** a thick, sodden mess *20- Ork*. [EModE *sogge* a wet place; compare SOGGIT]

soggit /'sɔgət/ *adj* soaked *20- NE*. [participial adj from EModE *sog* to become soaked; compare Norw dial *soggjast*]

sohod /sɔ'hɔd/ *interj* a call to encourage a dog to drive sheep *20- Ork N*. [unknown]

soil *see* SILE⁶

soill *see* SOLE¹·¹

soill fluk *see* SOLE²

soind /'soind/ *n* a sight, view *20- Sh*. **soindick** the eye *19- Sh*. [Norw dial *synd*]

†**soir**, **soyr** *adj* **1** *of a horse* light chestnut, sorrel in colour *la15-17*. **2** *of a bird of prey* red *e16*. **soirit**, **soird 1** = SOIR (sense 1) *la16-e19*. **2** = SOIR (sense 2) *la15*. [OFr *sor* (of a hawk) red, unmoulted]

soir *see* SAIR¹·³

soireé *see* SUREE

soirt *see* SORT¹·¹

soit *see* SUIT¹·¹

soiurne *see* SOJOURN¹·²

sojer, **sojour** *see* SODGER¹·¹

sojourn¹·¹, †**sudiorne**, †**sugeorne** /'sodʒərn/ *n* **1** a stay (at a place); a halt *la14-*. **2** a period of rest, inactivity or leisure *15-e16*. †**but sojourne** without delay *15-e16*. [AN *sojorn*]

sojourn¹·², †**soiurne**, †**sudiorne** /'sodʒərn/ *v* to stay (briefly), tarry; to reside, dwell *la14-*. [OFr *sojorner*]

sok *see* SOCK¹, SOCK², SOCK³

soke *see* SOCK³

sokkat *see* SOCKET¹·¹

sokken /'sɔkən/ *n* slack water at the turn of the tide *la19- Sh*. [verbal noun from Norw dial *søkka* (of water) to subside]

sol *see* SILE⁶

solace¹·¹, †**soles** /'sɔləs/ *n* comfort, consolation; joy, happiness, celebration; pleasure, entertainment *la14-*. †**solacious**, **solacius** giving comfort, pleasure; cheerful, joyful *la14-e19*. [OFr *solas*, Lat *sōlācium*]

solace¹·² /'sɔləs/ *v* to comfort, console; to supply, take pleasure, entertain oneself *la14-*. [OFr *solacier*]

solan, †**soland** /'solən/ *n* the gannet *Morus bassanus la15-*. **solan-guse** = SOLAN *16-*. [ON *súla* + perhaps ON *ǫnd* a duck]

sold *see* SOWD¹, SOWD²

soldane *see* SOWDAN

solder, †**sowder** /'soldər/ *n* a fusible metal alloy used for joining one metal item to another *16-*. Compare SOWTHER. [ME *soudur*, OFr *soldure*, *soudure*]

soldier *see* SODGER¹·¹, SODGER¹·²

sole¹·¹, †**soill**, †**soll** /sol/ *n pl* **solis solys 1** the under surface of the foot *15-*. **2** the under side of a shoe or stocking *16-*. **3** the stone or wooden beam forming the sill of a window or the threshold of a door *16-*. **4** the foundation of a structure; the base of an oven or plough *16-*. **5** the flat bottom of a golf club or the under surface of a curling stone *19-*. **6** the base of a bagpipe chanter *20-*. **7** the sward or surface vegetation of a pasture *20- N NE T H&I C SW*. **8** the lower crust of a loaf of bread *17-19, 20- N T C*. **9** the bottom rope of a fishing net *la19, 20- Sh WC SW*. **10** a flat plate under a gravy boat or cheese-dish *18, 20- NE*. **11** the subsoil; the under surface of land *la17-18, 20- Sh*. **sole-clout** the iron shoe covering the sole of a plough *19, 20- SW*. **sole-plate 1** = *sole-clout 19, 20- EC*. **2** = SOLE¹·¹ (sense 5) *17*. **sole-raip** = SOLE¹·¹ (sense 9) *la19, 20- Sh N C*. **sole-shaif** the end slice of a loaf *20- N T C*. **sole-tree 1** a horizontal beam of wood which provides the base of the vertical posts of a structure; the beam forming the manger on the floor of a byre *la17-19, 20- Sh T Bor*. **2** the beam on which the axle of the wheel of a horizontal water-mill rests *20- Sh Ork*. [ME *sole*, OFr *sole*]

sole¹·² /sol/ *v* **1** to provide with a sole *17-*. **2** to throw a curling stone so that it lands smoothly on the ice *20-*. **sole grund** to tread the ground, be alive *20- Sh Ork*. [see the noun]

sole² /sol/ *n* a common British and European flat-fish *Solea solea*, used as food *16-*. †**sole fleuk**, **soill fluk** a species of sole; the lemon sole *Microstomus kitt 16-19*. [ME *sole*, OFr *sole*]

soleit *see* SOLID

solemn, †**solempne**, †**solempt** /'sɔləm/ *adj* **1** serious; performed with due ceremony; duly convened; sacred *15-*. **2** of a formal and serious or deliberate character; of force or import; weighty *la15-*. **3** extremely bad *20- Sh*. **4** of great significance, impressive; famous, renowned *15-16*. **solemnity**, †**solempnyte 1** (the observance of) ceremony, special formality on important occasions *la14-*. **2** a ceremonial occasion, a celebration *la14-*. **3** *law* a formality, procedure or ceremony required to make an act or document valid *la15-17*. †**solemnit**, **solempnit** = SOLEMN *la14-e17*. [OFr *solemne*, *solempne*, Lat *sollemnis*, *sollempnis*]

soles *see* SOLACE¹·¹

†**solicit¹**, **solist** *adj* characterized by solicitude or concern; solicitous, concerned; anxious *16-e17*. [Lat *sollicitus*]

solicit², †**solist**, †**solyst**, †**sollist** /səˈlɪsɪt/ v 1 to entreat; to importune; to request; to petition, seek (a favour) la15-. 2 to attempt to seduce, seek sexual favours 16-. 3 to conduct (a lawsuit) as a legal agent or solicitor la17-. 4 to persuade; to incite; to urge 16-. 5 to expedite, carry out (a transaction); to promote (an aim) 16-e17. [OFr *solliciter*, Lat *sollicitāre*]

solicitation, †**solistation** /səlɪsɪˈteʃən/ n 1 the action of pleading, seeking (to obtain a favour); an urgent request la15-. 2 (management of) a transaction la15-e16. [OFr *sollicitation*, Lat *sollicitātiōn*-]

solicitor, †**solistar** /səˈlɪsɪtər/ n 1 *law* an accredited legal representative or law agent la16-. 2 a person who entreats or petitions, frequently acting as an agent for another la15-17. 3 an official representing the monarch's interests, a royal agent 16-17. **Solicitor General (for Scotland)** a Law Officer of the Crown, and the deputy of the Lord Advocate, whose duty is to advise the Crown and the Scottish Government on Scots Law 19-. **The King's Solicitor** an official representing the monarch's interests la17-e18. **Solicitor in the Supreme Courts of Scotland** a member of an incorporated society of solicitors practising in Edinburgh la18-. [OFr *solliciteur*]

solid, *WC Bor* **solit**, †**soleit** /ˈsɔlɪd; *WC Bor* ˈsɔlɪt/ *adj* 1 dense, compact; strong, firm, steady, substantial 16-. 2 sane; in full possession of one's mental faculties, of sound mind 17-19, 20- *T EC*. [OFr *solide*, Lat *solidus*]

solis see SOLE¹·¹

solist see SALIST, SOLICIT¹, SOLICIT²

solistar see SOLICITOR

solistation see SOLICITATION

solit see SOLID

†**solitare**, **solitair**, **solitar** *adj* solitary la15-e17. [OFr *solitaire*, Lat *sōlitārius*]

†**soll** v to make foul, defile; to be soiled or defiled la14. [OE *solian* to become foul]

soll see SOLE¹·¹

sollist see SOLICIT²

†**solomonical**, **salamonicall** *adj* wise like Solomon 16-e17. [from the name of the biblical king]

solp see SOWP²

solpit see SOWP¹·²

solum /ˈsolǝm/ *n originally law* soil or ground; the ground on which a building stands 18-. [Lat *solum* ground]

solution, †**solutioun** /səˈluʃən/ n 1 the action or process of solving (a problem); an answer, an explanation la14-. 2 a liquid in which a solid has dissolved 19-. 3 the action of paying; payment la15-e18. [OFr *solucion*, Lat *solūtiōn*-]

solvendie, **salvendo**, †**solvendo** /sǝlˈvɛndi, sɔlˈvɛndo/ *adj* 1 firm, safe, adequate, sure 19, 20- *Ork NE*. 2 *of persons* strong, in good health, fit 19, 20- *NE*. 3 financially sound, solvent 17-e19. [Lat *solvendō* (*esse*) (to be) solvent]

solyst see SOLICIT²

some¹·¹, **sum**, †**sume**, †**sowm** /sʌm/ *adj* 1 *qualifying a singular noun* one or other of a number of instances; an unspecified amount, degree or extent la14-. 2 *qualifying a plural noun* certain la14-. 3 *qualifying a singular noun* a certain 16-. 4 *qualifying a singular noun* large, considerable: ◇ *a some hack on my thoomb* 20- *T*. **somebit** somewhere 20- *C SW Bor*. **sumdy** somebody la20-. **somepairt** 1 somewhat la15-e17. 2 somewhere 20- *C*. **someplace** somewhere la18-. **sometime** 1 at one time or another, from time to time, occasionally la14-. 2 at a certain time, on a particular occasion; in the past; formerly 15-. 3 at some (indefinite) future time la15-. 4 for a period, for some time 16-. 5 former, deceased la14-e18. **sometimes** 1 = *sometime* (sense 1) la15-. 2 formerly 15-17. **somewey** 1 somehow; in some fashion la16-. 2 somewhere 19, 20- *Sh NE*. †**sum ... othir sum** some ... others la14-17. **somean idder** someone else la19- *Sh Ork*. **some idder een** someone else 20- *Sh Ork NE*. **some ither wey** somewhere else la19- *NE T*. [OE *sum*]

some¹·², †**sum** /sʌm/ *adv* 1 *modifying adjectives* somewhat, a little; very, a great deal la16-. 2 *modifying verbs* to some extent, rather, a little la18-19, 20- *Sh NE T*. [see the adj]

some¹·³, †**sum** /sʌm/ *pron* a small unspecified number (of persons or things), a few, several la14-. [see the adj]

some see SOAM

-some, †**-sum** /səm/ *suffix* 1 forming adjectives, *eg* **eeriesome** (EERIE), **waesome** (WAE¹) la14-. 2 *used in country-dancing and golf* after cardinal numbers, denoting a group or team of that number; originally, also indicating an approximation or estimate la14-. Compare **twasome** (TWA). [OE *-sum*]

†**somedeal¹·¹**, †**sumdeill** *n* a part; a good deal la14-19. [SOME¹·¹ + DALE¹·¹]

somedeal¹·², †**sumdele**, †**sumdeill** /ˈsʌmdil/ *adv* somewhat, to some extent, a good deal la14-19, 20- *SW*. [see the noun]

somegate, †**sum gait** /ˈsʌmget/ *adv* 1 somewhere; in some places la16-. 2 somehow, in some way 19-. **somegates** = SOMEGATE (sense 1) 19-. [SOME¹·¹ + GATE]

somer see SIMMER¹·¹, SIMMER¹·³

something¹·¹, **sumhin**, *Sh Ork* **suntin**, †**sumthing** /ˈsʌmθɪŋ, ˈsʌmhɪn; *Sh Ork* ˈsʌntɪn/ *n* some unspecified or indeterminate thing la14-. [OE *sum ðing*, SOME¹·¹ + THING¹]

something¹·², †**sumthing** /ˈsʌmθɪŋ/ *adv* somewhat, to some extent, a little la14-19, 20- *WC SW*. [see the noun]

somir see SIMMER¹·¹

somler see SUMMELEIR

sommair see SUMMARY

sommer see SIMMER¹·², SIMMER²

sommon see SUMMON

somond see SUMMON

somp see SUMP

son see SIN¹, SUN¹·¹

†**sonach** *n* one of several varieties of seaside grass la17. [compare Gael *sonnag* a chair made of twisted straw or sea-bent]

sonce see SONSE

sond see SOUND²

Sonday see SUNDAY

sone see SIN¹, SUN¹·¹, SUNE¹·²

sonet see SONNET

song see SANG¹, SING¹·²

songer see SONKER

songie /ˈsɔŋi/ *n* 1 *of a sheep or pig* a hermaphrodite 19- *Sh*. 2 *derogatory* a person 20- *Sh*. [unknown]

sonk see SUNK¹

sonken see SUNKEN

sonker, **songer** /ˈsɔŋkər, ˈsɔŋɡər/ *v* to boil gently, simmer la19- *Sh*. [Norw dial *sångra* to murmur]

sonkin see SUNKEN

sonkyn see SINK¹·²

sonne see SIN¹

sonnet, †**sonet** /ˈsɔnət/ *n* 1 a (short lyric or love) poem, a sonnet in the French or English pattern la16-. 2 a song, ditty la18-19, 20- *NE T*. 3 a tale, a yarn, a (tall) story, nonsense la19- *NE T*. 4 a fuss, a to-do la19- *T*. [MFr *sonnet*, Ital *sonetto*]

sonse, **sonce**, †**sons** /sɔns/ *n* abundance, plenty; prosperity, good fortune 15-19, 20- *N EC Uls*. †**sonse fa ye** *sonse on ye* 18-e19. **sonse on ye** may you have good fortune, bless you 19, 20- *N*. [Gael *sonas* good luck, prosperity]

sonsie, **sonsy** /ˈsɔnse/ 1 *especially of women* comely, attractive; *of the figure* buxom, plump; *of young children* chubby, sturdy *18-*. **2** friendly, hearty, jolly; good, honest *18-*. **3** big, roomy, substantial *18-19, 20- Sh NE T EC Uls*. **4** fine, handsome, impressive; pleasant, cheery *la18-19, 20- C SW*. **5** bringing good fortune; lucky *16-19, 20- Uls*. **6** *of animals* manageable *la18-19*. **7** sensible, shrewd *16-e18*. [SONSE + -IE²]

†**sonȝe**¹·¹ *n* an excuse, a plea *15-17*. [OFr *soigne* or aphetic form of ESSONȝE¹·¹]

†**sonȝe**¹·², **swnye** *v* to hesitate *15-16*. [see the noun]

soo¹, **sow**, †**sou** /su, sʌu/ *n* **1** a mature female pig *la14-*. **2** a large oblong stack of hay or straw *la17-*. **3** *derogatory* a person *16-*. **4** a piece of oatcake dough *20-*. **5** a pig of either gender *la16-19, 20- T EC Bor*. **6** the ballan wrasse *Labrus bergylta 20- Sh NE*. **7** a siege-machine with a protective roof for military personnel *la14-17, 19 historical*. **8** the small ball or puck used in shinty *19*. **sooie** a piece of oatcake dough *20- NE*. †**sowie** a siege-machine with a protective roof for military personnel *e19*. **soo's bands** *in boat-building* strips of wood used to keep the boat boards in place temporarily *20- Sh*. **soo-boat** a small, square-sterned rowing boat used as a tender *la19- Ork*. **soo-crue** = *soo-cruive la19-*. **soo-cruive**, **soo's cruive** a pigsty *la19-*. †**sow-kiln** a type of mound-shaped limekiln *la18-19*. †**sow-libber** a person who castrates pigs; also used as a term of abuse *la16-e18*. **soo's lug 1** one of the mould-boards of a drill- or double-breasted plough *20- NE T EC*. **2** *in soldering* an overlap of lead to strengthen the joint at a corner *20- N EC*. **3** *in packing a parcel* an overlapped triangle of paper *20- N EC*. **soo-luggit** *of animals* having long, floppy ears *18-19, 20- T Bor*. **soo-moo'd** *of animals* having a projecting upper jaw *20- NE C*. **soo-stack** a haystack *20- N C SW*. **soo's tail**, **soo-tail**, **sow-tail** a wrongly-tied knot *la19- Ork T*. **soo's troch** a pig's trough *20- Sh N NE T*. **a soo wi a anither snoot** another story, a different situation *20-*. **soo's tail tae ye** an expression of defiance or derision *e18, 20- EC*. [OE *sugu*]

soo², †**sow** /su/ *v* **1** to ache; to throb, tingle *15-19, 20- WC SW Bor*. **2** to inflict pain on, hurt *la14-16*. [perhaps OE **sugian* to cause pain]

soo³ /su/ *v of wind* to breathe, murmur, sigh *la19- Sh WC*. [reduced form of SOUCH¹·²]

sooans *see* SOWANS

soo back, **soo's back** /ˈsu bak, ˈsuz bak/ *n* **1** a ridge or natural hump *19-*. **2** *mining* a ridge in the roof or pavement of a coalworking *la18-19, 20- C SW*. **3** a woman's cap with a ridge from back to front *19, 20- T*. **soo-back mutch**, **soo-backit mutch** = SOO BACK (sense 3). [SOO¹ + BACK¹·¹]

sooch *see* SOUCH¹·¹, SOUCH¹·²

soogan, **sugan** /ˈsugən/ *n* a type of coarse, thick blanket *19- SW Uls*. [HibEng *soogan*, *suggan* a straw pad used on a horse's back when carrying loads, IrGael *súgán* a straw rope, a straw mat]

sook¹·¹, **souk**, **suck**, †**sowk** /suk, sʌk/ *n* **1** the action or an act of sucking *16-*. **2** a sycophant, a flatterer *20-*. **3** the drying action of the wind *la19- Sh Ork N*. **4** a stupid person *19, 20- Bor*. **5** a cheat, a deception, a swindle *20- NE*. **6** liquid; moisture; sap *la16-e17*. [see the verb]

sook¹·², **souk**, **suck**, †**sowk**, †**sowik**, †**suk** /suk, sʌk/ *v* **1** to draw (liquid) into the mouth by suction; to perform the action of sucking *la14-*. **2** to suckle, give suck to *20-*. **3** *of the wind or clothes* to (cause to) become dry *19- Sh Ork N*. **4** to flow in a certain direction, as if drawn by suction, seep *la19, 20- Ork T*. **5** *of the sun* to extract, draw up (moisture) *la15-16*. **6** *of the sea*, a whirlpool to draw in, pull, drag *e16*. **sooker**, †**soukar 1** something that works by or causes suction *18-*. **2** a hard, boiled sweet *20-*. **3** one who sucks (nourishment, blood); a parasite, a scrounger *16-e18*. **sooking**,

†**soukand 1** *of a baby or young animal* unweaned *la14-*. **2** *of a female animal* suckling *16-e17*. **3** *of a whirlpool* that draws in (ships) *e16*. **sookit**, **sookid 1** *of fish* half-dried *19- Sh Ork N*. **2** *of animals* exhausted *19- N Uls*. **3** *of clothes* hung out to dry but not sufficiently dried, partly dry *20- Ork N*. †**sookin bairn** a child at the breast, a suckling; a helpless creature *19*. **sook-the-bluid** a red beetle *Rhagonycha fulva 20- EC Bor*. **sookit gimmer** a ewe that has lambed *20- SW*. **sook-the-pappie** *derogatory* a fairly old but babyish child, a child lacking toughness; an effeminate person *20- N T WC SW*. †**soukand sand** quicksand *e16*. **sookin teuchit** = *sookin turkey 19- NE*. **sookin turkey** a feeble or foolish person *19, 20- Sh Ork N NE T SW*. **sook in wi** to curry favour, ingratiate oneself *la19-*. **sook oot 1** to remove (poison) by sucking *la14-*. **2** to obtain (something) from a source (as if) by sucking *la16-*. **sook up tae** = *sook in wi 20-*. [OE *sūcan*]

sook¹·³, **souk**, **suck** /suk, sʌk/ *interj* a call to a calf, lamb or pig *la19-*. **sookie** = SOOK¹·³ *20- WC Uls*. **sucko** = SOOK¹·³ *20- Ork*. **sook sook**, **souk souk** = SOOK¹·³. [see the verb]

sook² /suk/ *v* to (cause to) sink, subside *la19- Sh Ork*. [Norw dial *søkka*]

sookan, **sugan** /ˈsukən, ˈsugən/ *n* a one-ply rope of straw, grass or hay used for tying bundles of straw or thatching ricks *la19- Ork WC*. [Gael *sùgan* a hay- or straw-rope]

sookie, **sookey**, †**sucky** /ˈsuke/ *n* **1** *derogatory* a petted or over-indulged child; a spoilt person *20-*. **2** clover *18-19, 20- NE T EC*. **3** a suckling *20- T Bor*. **4** the red clover *Trifolium pratense 19, 20- Sh*. **sooky leather** a child's toy; a small piece of leather on a string *20- T C SW Bor*. **sookie-mae** a clover flowerhead *20- EC*. **sookie-mammy** = *sookie-mae 20- C*. **sookie-soo** = *sookie-mae 19, 20- EC*. **sookie-sourocks** wood sorrel *Oxalis acetosella 20- N NE T C*. [SOOK¹·¹ + -IE¹]

sool *see* SWEEL³·¹

soolp¹·¹ /sulp/ *n* a soft wet mass, a soaked state; wet or muddy ground *la19- Sh*. [altered form of Norw dial *surp* mire]

soolp¹·² /sulp/ *v* to be wet, soaked or boggy *20- Sh*. [see the noun]

soom /sum/ *n* the swim-bladder or air-bladder of a fish *la18-19, 20- Sh NE WC Uls*. [altered form of SOUND², with influence from soom (SWEEM¹·²)]

soom *see* SOUM¹·¹, SWEEM¹·¹, SWEEM¹·²

soomans *see* SUMMONS¹·¹

soon *see* SOOND²·¹, SUNE¹·²

soond¹·¹, **soun**, **sound**, †**sown**, †**sownd** /sund, sun, sʌund/ *n* **1** something heard, (an) auditory sensation, (a) noise or sound *la14-*. **2** (a) melodious or harmonious noise, music; a poetical or liturgical composition *15-*. **3** a rumour, a report; widespread talk or gossip *la19, 20- Ork NE T SW*. **sounstick** the sound-post of a violin *19, 20- Sh WC SW*. [ME *soun*, AN *soun*]

soond¹·², **soun**, **sound**, †**sownd** /sund, sun, sʌund/ *v* **1** to make a noise; to reverberate; to utter (a sound); to proclaim *15-*. **2** to cause (a musical instrument or bell) to emit sound; to play (an instrument) *la15-*. **3** to convey an impression (by sound) *la15-*. **4** to test (a building) for its acoustics *la19*. **5** to tend towards, lead to be associated with *la15-16*. **sounding**, †**soundand**, †**soundyng** emitting sound; sonorous, resonant; resounding *16-*. **soundin box** a canopy over a pulpit to amplify the speaker's voice *la19, 20- Sh T*. [ME *sounen*, AN *suner*]

soond²·¹, **soon**, **sound**, †**soun**, †**sownd** /sund, sun, sʌund/ *adj* **1** fit, healthy; uninjured; sane *la14-*. **2** reliable, trustworthy *16-*. **3** solid, in good condition *16-*. **4** *of sleep* deep, profound *la16-*. **5** *of a blow or beating* severe *18-*. **6** smooth,

soond *see* SOUND¹·², SOUND²

soond²·², **soun, sound, †sownd** /sund, sun, sʌund/ *adv of sleeping* profoundly, deeply *la15*-. [see the adj]

sound *see* SOUND¹·², SOUND²

soop¹·¹, **sweep, †sweip** /sup, swip/ *n* **1** (everything encompassed in) a sweeping movement *la17*-. **2** an apparatus or implement which makes sweeping movements (such as a pump, the sail of a windmill or an implement for gathering hay) *la16*-. **3** sweepings, refuse; originally, scraps of silver swept up in the mint *la17, 20- Sh Ork*. **4** only **sweep** a cord or piece of rope by which the stone-sinkers of a herring net were attached *la19*. [see the verb]

soop¹·², **swoop, sweep,** *Sh* **swüp,** *NE* **swype, †soup, †sweip, †swop** /sup, swup, swip; *Sh* swøp; *NE* swʌɪp/ *v* **1** to clean (a surface) with a broom; to brush (the ground) with the hem of a garment; to remove (something) by sweeping *la15*-. **2** *curling* to sweep (the ice) in the path of a curling stone to assist its progress *19*-. **3** *originally mainly of ships* to move with a rapid, flowing movement *16*-. **sooper** a brush *19*-. **sweep-the-fluir** a move in the game of CHUCK² (sense 2) *20- T C*. **soop up** = SOOP¹·² (sense 2) *19*-. [ME *swepen*, OE *swēop* ptp of *swāpan*]

soople¹·¹, **souple, supple** /ˈsupəl, ˈsʌpəl/ *v* **1** to make flexible; to soften (by soaking); to soak; to wash *16*-. **2** to be or make compliant or submissive; to mollify; to weaken *la15-19*. **3** to make agile *el7*. [see the adj; compare MFr *soupler*]

soople¹·², **souple, supple, †soupill, †sowpill** /ˈsupəl, ˈsʌpəl/ *adj* **1** soft; flexible *15*-. **2** agile, nimble, athletic *17*-. **3** ingenious, cunning, astute, devious *18*-. **4** limp, helpless (with laughter or drink); drunk *19*-. **5** *of speech* fluent, prattling, loquacious *la18-19, 20- Sh T WC*. **6** compliant, open to persuasion or manipulation *17*. **suppleness, †souplenes 1** flexibility *19*-. **2** compliance, deviousness, cunning *la17-e18*. **†souple scones** thin, pliable scones, usually of barley meal *la18-19*. **†souple Tam** a jointed wooden toy figure, a puppet *19*. **soople-tongued** ready of speech *la19, 20- Sh T*. [ME *souple*, AN *souple*]

soople¹·³, **souple, supple** /ˈsupəl, ˈsʌpəl/ *adv* nimbly, agilely *18-19, 20- Ork NE T Uls*. [see the adj]

soople², **supple, souple, †soupell** /ˈsupəl, ˈsʌpəl/ *n* **1** the part of a flail which beats the grain *la16-19, 20- Sh Ork N NE Uls*. **2** a cudgel, a stout stick *el9*. [ME *swepyl*, from sweep (SOOP¹·²) with instrumental suffix]

soor¹·¹, **sour** /sur, sʌur/ *v* **1** to cause to become sour *16*-. **2** *of the action of water on lime* to macerate, soften, slake *18*-. [see the adj]

soor¹·², **sour, †sowr, †sowre** /sur, sʌur/ *adj* **1** tart, having an acid taste; fermented; spoiled or decayed, sour *la15*-. **2** *of events, people, or language* disagreeable, unpleasant *la15*-. **3** *of weather* unpleasant, cold and wet *la15-19, 20- NE T WC Bor*. **†sour breid** a kind of sour dough bread baked with wheat or rye flour *16-19*. **†sour-cake** a kind of oatcake baked for festivals, *eg* in Rutherglen for St Luke's Fair; originally also barley cakes *la16-19*. **soor-cloot** someone of a harsh, gloomy or fault-finding disposition *20*-. **†sour cogue** a dish, probably curds, made from sour-cream *la17-e19*. **sour dock** = *sour docken*. **sour docken** common sorrel *Rumex acetosa la19- SW Bor*; compare SOOROCK. **sour drap 1** an acid drop *la19- Sh NE*. **2** melancholy *20- NE*. **soor-face, sour-face** a bad-tempered, disagreeable person *20- C*. **soor-faced, sour-faced** = *sour-moued la20*-. **sour fish** fish kept until it has a gamey flavour *19- Sh*. **†sour-kit** = *sour cogue e16*. **soor-leek** = *sour docken la19- SW Bor Uls*. **†soure like** of a sullen, discontented disposition *la17*. **soor-milk, sour-milk 1** sour milk *16*-. **2** buttermilk *18-19, 20- Sh C SW*. **sour-moued** sulky-looking *la18, 19- NE T*. **sour-mood-like, sour-like-mood** = *sour-moued la19- NE*. **sour poos** a coarse, sour-flavoured oat bread or scone baked at Christmas-time *la19- NE*. **sour scone, sour skon** = *sour poos 19*-. [OE *sūr*]

soorce, source, †sowrs, †sours, †surs /surs, sors/ *n* **1** an origin, originally the spring from which a river derives *16*-. **2** the upward flight of a bird of prey, an act of soaring *e16*. **3** a well or fountain *el7*. [ME *sours*, AN *surse*, OFr *sors*]

soor dook, sour dook /ˈsur duk, ˈsʌur duk/ *n* **1** buttermilk, sour milk *la18*-. **2** yoghurt *20*-. **3** a sour, mean person *la19, 20- N T C SW*. **sour-dook sodger** nickname a member of the Lothian militia *19, 20- historical*. [SOOR¹·² + DOOK¹·¹]

soorik *see* SOOROCK

soorldab /surlˈdab/ *n* the finishing action or event, the knockout blow *20- T C*. **gie something its soorldab** to put paid to, finish off, spoil *20- T C*. [unknown]

soorn /surn/ *v* to turn sour, rot *la19- Sh*. [Norw dial *surna*]

soorock, sourock, *Sh* **soorik,** *N* **sourag, †sourok, †souroch,†sowrok** /ˈsurək; *N* ˈsurəg/ *n* **1** any of various varieties of sorrel, *eg* common sorrel *Rumex acetosa*, sheep's sorrel *Rumex acetosella*, wood sorrel *Oxalis acetosella la15*-. **2** a sulky, perverse, sour-tempered person *18-19, 20- NE T C*. [SOOR¹·² + -OCK; compare MDu *zuric*, MLG *sureke* sorrel]

soor ploom, sour ploom /sur ˈplum/ *n* **1** a tart-flavoured, round, green boiled sweet, originally associated with Galashiels *20*-. **2** a native of Galashiels *18-19, 20- WC Bor*. **3** *pl* an attitude of disparagement, sour grapes *19, 20- C SW*. **4** a fault-finding gloomy person *20- C*. [SOOR¹·² + PLOOM]

soos *see* SOUSE¹·²

soose *see* SOOZE, SOUSE¹·³

soosh /suʃ/ *v* **1** to beat, punish severely; to deal rigorously with *19, 20- NE*. **2** to swill, splash, wash over *la19- NE*. **3** to taunt, upbraid *e19*. [onomatopoeic, perhaps with infl from *swish* and *souse*]

soosler, sooshler /ˈsuslər, ˈsuʃlər/ *n* a thin fish; a cod in poor condition *20- N*. [unknown]

soost *see* SOUSE²

sooster *see* SOUSTER

soot *see* SUIT²

sooth¹·¹, **south** /suθ, sʌuθ/ *n* **1** the part of a place or point of the compass opposite the north; the part of Scotland south of the Aberdeen/Moray Firth area *la14*-. **2** (the people or society of) (the south of) England *17*-. [see the adv]

sooth¹·², **south, †suth, †sowth** /suθ, sʌuθ/ *adj* **1** situated in or belonging to the south, southern, southerly *la12*-. **2** *of the wind* blowing from the south *16*-. **soothie** left-handed *20- WC*. **southlan, †southland** (from or belonging to) the southern part of a place, originally and mainly of Scotland, usually from south of the Forth to the Border *la15*-. **sooth moother** an incomer to Shetland *20- Sh Ork*. **†south-part** = *south-side 15-16*. **†south-partis** the southern region of Scotland, England or Britain *16-e17*. **south-side** the southern side of a building or street, the southern part of a place or area; the area to the south of a river *13*-. **†the South Isles** the Hebrides south of Ardnamurchan, and also Kintyre *16-e17*; compare *the West Isles* (WAST¹·³). **†on south half, on southalf** on or to the south (of) *la14-e16*. [see the adv]

sooth¹·³, **south, sowth, †sowtht** /suθ, sʌuθ/ *adv* towards the south (in a direction opposite to north) *la14*-. **soothawa** in the south *20*-. **south by** = *sooth-awa la18*-. **sooth ower, †southour** southwards *la15-19, 20- Sh Ork*. **sooth troo** = *sooth ower la19- Sh*. **sooth trow** southern *20- Sh*. [OE *sūð*]

sooth²·¹, **south** /suθ, sʌuθ/ *n* singing or whistling in a low voice, a low murmur (of music) *18- SW*. [altered form of SOWFF¹·¹]

sooth²·², **south** /suθ, sʌuθ/ *v* to hum, sing or whistle softly *la18-19, 20- NE T*. [see the noun]

sooth *see* SUITH¹·¹, SUITH¹·²

soother /'suðər/ *v* 1 to soothe, calm *la19-*. 2 to coax, cajole, flatter *la19-* mainly *H&I WC Uls*. [HibEng *soother*, frequentative form of Eng *soothe*]

soothfast *see* SUITHFAST

soothward, southward, *Sh Ork* **suddert,** *NE* **sothert,** †**southert,** †**southwart** /'suθwərd, 'sʌuθwərd; *Sh Ork* 'sudərt; *NE* 'sʌðərt/ *adv* towards the south *la14-*. [OE sūðeweard]

sooze, soose /suz, sus/ *v* to smoulder with a hissing sound *20- NE*. [onomatopoeic]

†**sop** *n* 1 a troop (of soldiers) *la14-e16*. 2 a cloud or densely-packed mass (of mist or smoke) *e16*. [perhaps ON *soppr* a ball]

sop *see* SAP¹, SAP²·¹

sope *see* SUP¹·¹

†**sophistic** *adj of arguments or doctrines* imbued with sophistry; specious, fallacious *la15-e17*. [Fr *sophistique*, Lat *sophistic*-]

†**sopit, sowpit** *adj* 1 rendered dull or sluggish; sunk, exhausted, overwhelmed with (effort, sleep or sorrow) *16*. 2 *of a dream* characterized by tiredness or dejection *la15-e16*. [Lat sōpīt-, ptp of sōpīre to render unconscious, put to sleep]

†**sopite, sopit** *v ptp* **sopite, sopit** *law* to quash, settle, put an end to (a dispute, or claim) *la15-19*. [Lat sōpīt-, ptp stem of sōpīre to put to sleep]

soppy *see* SAPPIE

Sorby *see* ROB SORBY

sorcery, †**sorsery,** †**sossery,** †**sossary** /'sɔrsəre/ *n* witchcraft; a magical rite or practice *la14-*. [OFr *sorcerie*]

sore *see* SAIR¹·¹, SAIR¹·³, SAIR¹·⁴

sorefull *see* SORROWFU

sorely *see* SAIRLY

sorn /sɔrn/ *v* 1 to scrounge, sponge; to abuse hospitality, act as a parasite *18-*. 2 to exact free food and lodging, usually by aggressive or threatening behaviour; to beg importunately *la16-19, 20- historical*. 3 to scrounge (food); to forage, graze *19, 20- N T WC*. 4 to harass, despoil, live off (a population) by demands for free food and lodging *la16-e18*. 5 to idle, waste time *e19*; compare SORTHYN. **sorner, †sornar, †soirner,** †**soroner** a person who lives by exacting free food and lodging by threats or force; a scrounger *15-*. [IrGael *sorthan* free quarterage]

sornie /'sɔrni/ *n* the flue from the fireplace to the underside of the drying platform of a kiln; the fireplace itself *19- N*. [Gael sòrn + -IE¹]

soroful *see* SORROWFU

sorp /sɔrp/ *v* to be soaked or drenched *19- Bor*. [emphatic variant of *sop* (SAP²·²)]

sorple /'sɔrpəl/ *v* to make a sucking noise when drinking *20- Bor*. perhaps onomatopoeic; compare SLORP¹·²]

sorra¹·¹, **sorrow, sorry** /'sɔrə, 'sɔro, 'sɔre/ *n* 1 distress, deep sadness, grief *la14-*. 2 a cause of distress; *pl* troubles, sufferings *la16-*. 3 a rascal, a troublesome child, a pest of a person *19-*. 4 *as emphatic negative* not a: ◊*sorra a la16-19, 20- Sh Ork N NE SW*. 5 *in questions expressing impatience:* ◊*whit the sorra?* ◊*where in sorra? 17-19, 20- Sh Ork N NE T*. 6 the Devil *la18-19, 20- Sh NE SW Uls*. 7 the expression of grief or suffering *la14-e17*. **no hae yer sorrow tae seek, no hae yer sorrows tae seek** to have many troubles or difficulties *la19-*. †**send siluer sorrow** = *sorra fa ye e16*.

sorra care too bad, bad luck *la18- N NE T*. **sorra fa ye,** †**sorrow fall yow** may misfortune befall you *la16-19, 20- Sh N NE T*. **sorra tak ye** = *sorra fa ye la18-19, 20- Sh N NE T H&I*. [OE *sorg*]

sorra¹·², **sorrow** /'sɔrə, 'sɔro/ *adj* sad, sorry *19- N T WC*. [from the noun, with influence from Eng *sorry*]

sorrowfu, sorrowful, †**sorrowfull,** †**soroful,** †**sorefull** /'sɔrəfu, 'sɔroful/ *adj* 1 grieving, sad, unhappy; contrite, repentant; lamentable, distressing *la14-*. 2 indicative of, expressing sorrow or grief *15-*. 3 causing vexation, troublesome *19, 20- Sh N T*. [OE *sorgful*]

sorry *see* SAIRIE, SORRA¹·¹

sorryn *see* SORTHYN

sorsery *see* SORCERY

sort¹·¹, **soart,** †**soirt** /sɔrt, sort/ *n* 1 a kind, class, type, variety; a species (of something) *16-*. 2 a setting to rights, a repair, a tidying up *19-*. 3 a considerable number, a fair amount *19- Bor*. 4 a troop, band or company *la15-16*. **sort up** = SORT¹·¹ (sense 2). [ME *sorte*, OFr *sorte* a kind, category; but with some senses developed from the verb]

sort¹·², **soart** /sɔrt, sort/ *v* 1 to put in order, arrange, classify *la15-*. 2 to deal with by rebuke or punishment, put (a person) in his place, scold *la17-*. 3 to provide for, furnish or supply *la18-*. 4 to tidy or change one's clothes *19-*. 5 to restore to proper or working order, repair, mend, fix; to heal *19-*. 6 to attend to the needs of (livestock) *19, 20- N NE T C Bor*. 7 to castrate *20- Sh NE EC*. 8 to attend a child or sick person *la19, 20- NE*. 9 to bring together, pair, match *e19*. 10 to come together, keep company, live in harmony *la18-19*. 11 to come to an agreement *17-e19*. 12 *of matters, events* to work out *la16-17*. 13 to allot *e16*. **sort by** to put away (dishes or clothes) *20- Sh*. **sort up** to mend *la19*. **sort wi** 1 to provide with *19*. 2 to live in harmony with, be agreeable to *19*. 3 to gather up, collect together *e16*. [Lat *sortīri*, OFr *sortir* to divide or obtain by lot, but in many senses aphetic form of OFr *assorter* to arrange into groups, classify; or from the noun]

†**sort**² *n* 1 a lot (cast or drawn); a division by lot *15-16*. 2 *with poss pron* a person's lot or fate *la15-e16*. [ME *sort*, OFr *sort*, Lat *sort-*]

†**sort**³ *v* 1 to leave, come or go out *16-e17*. 2 *of armed men* to sally out; to make a sortie *la16-17*. [MFr *sortir*]

†**sorthyn, sorryn** *n* a service required of vassals to provide hospitality to the superior; a levy made in lieu of this *la12-14*. Compare SORN. [IrGael *sorthan* free quarterage]

sory *see* SAIRIE

†**sosh**¹ *adj* sociable, frank, open *la18-19*. [shortened form of Eng *sociable*]

sosh² /sɔʃ/ *n* a Co-operative Society shop *la19- T EC*. **soshie** 1 a manager of a Co-op store *la19*. 2 = SOSH² *la19-*. [shortened form of SOCIETY]

soss¹·¹ /sɔs/ *n* 1 a mixture of food or drink, a wet, soggy mess of food *18-19, 20- Sh N NE T EC*. 2 a wet state, a sopping condition, a dirty wet mess *19, 20- Sh N NE T EC Bor*. 3 a state of dirt and disorder, a muddle or confusion *la19- Sh N NE T EC*. 4 a slattern, a slut *20- NE T*. [compare ME *sos* a call to food to dogs and pigs]

soss¹·² /sɔs/ *v* 1 to make wet and dirty, make a mess of *20- Sh NE T Bor*. 2 to make a mess, work dirtily or in dirty conditions *la19- N NE EC Bor*. 3 to mix (especially liquids) in a messy way *19, 20- Sh T*. 4 to nurse over-tenderly, fuss over; to pester *la19- NE*. 5 to cuddle, fondle, pet *20- NE*. 6 to take one's ease, lie or remain idle *la19, 20- NE*. 7 to eat sloppy or messy food; to eat in an uncouth, slovenly way *la18-e19*. [see the noun]

soss²·¹ /sɔs/ *n* a thud, a heavy awkward fall, a heavy blow *18-19, 20- EC Uls*. [perhaps onomatopoeic]

soss²·² /sɔs/ *v* to fall or sit down with a thud *la18-19, 20- H&I EC SW Uls*. [see the noun]

sossary, sossery *see* SORCERY

sot¹ /sɔt/ *n a* fool, simpleton, a stupid person *la14-*. [OFr *sot*]

sot², **sut** /sɔt, sʌt/ *adv used to contradict a negative* on the contrary, far from it: ◊*It is not. – It is sot. la19-*. [altered form of *so* (SAE²·¹) by analogy with *not*; compare YO]

sotheroun *see* SOUTHRON¹·²

sothert *see* SOOTHWARD

sothroun *see* SOUTHRON¹·¹

sotter¹·¹ /'sɔtər/ *n* **1** a mess, a muddle, a confused mass, chaos *la19, 20- Sh NE T EC*. **2** the noise made by something boiling, frying or bubbling up *19, 20- T EC SW*. **3** a state of wetness *la19- NE*. **4** a considerable number, especially of small creatures; a swarm *19- Bor*. **in a sotteril** affected by a skin disease *20- NE*. [see the verb]

sotter¹·² /'sɔtər/ *v* **1** to boil, simmer; bubble or sputter in cooking *la18-*. **2** to work in a dirty unskilful way; to handle in a disgusting way *la19- Sh N NE T*. **3** to sputter, crackle; to come bubbling *19-*. **4** to saturate, soak, wallow *19- SW Bor*. **5** to idle, loaf, potter *la19- NE T*. **6** to abound, swarm *20- Bor*. **sotter aboot** = SOTTER¹·² (sense 5). **sotter oot** = SOTTER¹·² (sense 2). [compare Ger *dial sottern*]

sottle /'sɔtəl/ *v* to simmer, bubble in cooking *19- H&I WC*. [perhaps altered form of SOTTER¹·²]

sottyne *see* SODDEN

sou *see* SOO¹

souce *see* SOUSE¹·¹

souch¹·¹, **sooch, sough,** *Sh* **soch,** *Uls* **sugh,** *NE H&I* **seuch,** †**sowch,** †**swouch,** †**swoch** /sux; *Sh* sɔx; *Uls* sʌx; *NE H&I* ʃux/ *n* **1** a rushing, rustling, whistling or murmuring sound (of the wind, water or fire) *16-*. **2** a deep sigh or gasp; heavy breathing, panting *la18-*. **3** the sound or timbre of a voice, an accent, a way of speaking *la18-*. **4** *in preaching* a high-pitched, nasal way of speaking, a whine *18-*. **5** gossip, rumour, scandal *19-*. **6** the whizzing noise of a weapon or heavy blow *la18- Sh NE T C Uls*. **7** an uproar, a fuss *la19- NE T SW Bor Uls*. **8** a song, a tune, a melody *19, 20- NE T*. **9** heavy breathing in sleep; a state of sleep or trance, a snooze *16-19, 20- SW*. **10** general feeling or opinion, attitude, style *18-19, 20- WC*. **haud a sober souch** = *keep a calm souch 20-*. **keep a calm souch** to keep quiet, hold one's tongue; to keep calm or still *19-*. **keep a quaeit souch** = *keep a calm souch la19-*. [see the verb]

souch¹·², **sooch, sough,** *Sh* **soch,** *Uls* **sugh,** *N* **soach,** †**sowch,** †**swouch,** †**swowch** /sux; *Sh* sɔx; *Uls* sʌx; *N* ʃox/ *v* **1** *of the wind or a moving object* to make a rustling, whispering, murmuring or whizzing sound *la15-*. **2** to sing softly, hum, whistle *18-*. **3** to breathe heavily, sigh, wheeze, or blow *17-19, 20- Sh N NE SW Uls*. **4** *of music* to sound, waft *19, 20- NE T C SW*. **sough awa** to breathe one's last, die *la18-*. [OE *swōgan*]

souch *see* SHEUCH¹·¹, SHEUCH¹·²

soucht *see* SEEK¹

soucie *see* SUSSIE¹·²

soucy *see* SUSSIE¹·¹

soud *see* SOWD²

soudan *see* SOWDAN

soude *see* SOWD¹

souder *see* SOWTHER

souflet /'sʌflət/ *n* a stroke, a blow with the hand, a smack *19- Sh NE*. [Fr *soufflet*]

sough *see* SOUCH¹·¹, SOUCH¹·²

souk *see* SOOK¹·¹, SOOK¹·², SOOK¹·³

soul *see* SOWL¹·¹, SOWL¹·²

sould *see* SUD

souldiour *see* SODGER¹·¹

soull *see* SWEEL³·¹

soum¹·¹, *EC* **soom, sum,** †**soume,** †**sowm** /sum, sʌm/ *n* **1** a quantity or amount (of money) *la14-*. **2** the total amount, entirety (of anything) *15-*. **3** the number of livestock which can be supported by a certain area of pasture *15-19, 20- Sh T H&I Uls*. **4** the unit of pasturage which will support a certain number of livestock *16-19, 20- H&I Uls*. **5** a summary, digest or summing-up *15-e17*. †**soums grass, soumis girse** = SOUM¹·¹ (sense 4) *15-18*. †**in a sowme** *of money* in one instalment, in a lump sum *15-17*. [ME *somme*, OFr *somme*, Lat *summa*]

soum¹·², **sum,** †**soume,** †**sowm** /sum, sʌm/ *v* **1** to count, calculate *15-*. **2** to determine the number of grazing animals a pasture can support; to allocate pasture to specified numbers of livestock *la15-19, 20- Sh H&I Uls*. †**souming and rouming** *law* a legal action to determine each tenant's share of pasture *17-19*. [ME *sommen*,OFr *somer*, Lat *summāre*]

†**soum**², **sowm** *n* a (horse-)load, a pack; a burden *la14-e17*. [OFr *some*]

soum³ /sum/ *v* to surmise, assume *19- NE T*. [aphetic form of ASSUME]

soum *see* SOAM

soume *see* SOUM¹·¹, SOUM¹·²

soun *see* SOOND¹·¹, SOOND¹·², SOOND²·¹, SOOND²·², SOUND¹·¹, SUN¹·¹, SUNE¹·²

sound¹·¹, †**swound,** †**swoun,** †**soun** /sund/ *n* fainting, a fainting-fit, (a period of) unconsciousness *15-*. [see the verb]

sound¹·², *Sh* **soond,** *H&I* **swound,** †**swoune,** †**swone,** †**swown** /sund; *H&I* swund/ *v* to swoon or faint; to lose consciousness *la14-*. [ME *swounen, sounen*]

sound², *Sh* **soond,** †**sownd,** †**sond** /sʌund; *Sh* sund/ *n* **1** a narrow channel, a strait; an inlet of the sea *16-*. **2** the swimbladder of a fish *la16-19, 20- Sh Ork NE T EC*. †**sound- is bere** a cargo, probably originally barley, from a ship which has passed through the Sound, between Sweden and Denmark and paid sound-dues *la16-e17*. †**soundis last** = *soundis bere e15*. [OE *sund* sea, ocean, water, ON *sund* a strait, a narrow passage, a channel]

sound *see* SOOND¹·¹, SOOND¹·², SOOND²·¹, SOOND²·²

Sounday *see* SUNDAY

sounder *see* SINDER¹·²

soune *see* SIN¹

soup, *NE* **shoop** /sup; *NE* ʃup/ *n* a liquid food, usually made by boiling vegetables and meat or fish; a broth *la16-*. **soup-tatties** potato soup *20- NE EC*. [Fr *soupe*]

soup *see* SOOP¹·², SUP¹·¹, SUP¹·², SUP²

soupe *see* SOWP²

soupell *see* SOOPLE²

soupere *see* SUPPER¹·¹

soupill *see* SOOPLE¹·²

souple *see* SOOPLE¹·¹, SOOPLE¹·², SOOPLE¹·³, SOOPLE²

sour *see* SOOR¹·¹, SOOR¹·²

sourag *see* SOOROCK

source *see* SOORCE

sourd *see* SWURD

sour dook *see* SOOR DOOK

souroch, sourock, sourok *see* SOOROCK

sour ploom *see* SOOR PLOOM

sours *see* SOORCE

souse¹·¹, **sowse,** †**souce** /sʌus/ *n* **1** a heavy blow, a thump *la17-19, 20- N WC SW Uls*. **2** (the sound of) a heavy fall *la18-19, 20- EC Uls*. [EModE *souse*; perhaps onomatopoeic]

souse¹·², *N* **soos,** †**souss** /sʌus; *N* sus/ *v* to strike, thump *la16-19, 20- N WC SW Uls*. **souse doon** to let (something, oneself) fall; to sit down heavily *19, 20- N Uls*. [see the noun]

souse[1.3], *Sh* **soose** /saus; *Sh* sus/ *adv* violently, heavily, with a thud *19, 20- Sh WC SW Uls*. [see the noun]

souse[2] /sus/ *v pt* **soost** to reprove, put (a person) in his place, silence *la18-19, 20- NE T*. [perhaps extended sense of SOUSE[1.2] or SOUSE[3]]

souse[3] /sʌuz, saus/ *v ptp* †**soust** †**sowsit**, †**sust** 1 to plunge, immerse (in water); to soak, drench; to steep *16-*. 2 to pickle *la16-*. [ME *sousen*, from OFr *souse* pickled pork]

souse[4], †**sowce** /saus/ *n* a (messy) mixture of food; a dish made from oatmeal, *eg* porridge *la18-19, 20- N*. [altered form of SOSS[1.1]]

souss *see* SOUSE[1.2]

soust *see* SOUSE[3]

souster, sooster /'sustər/ *n* something very large; a large amount *20- N T EC*. [SOUSE[1.1], with agent suffix]

sout[1.1] /sʌut/ *n* a sudden leap, bounce, jolt or bump *19- SW*. [Fr *saut*]

†**sout**[1.2] *v* to shake or heave convulsively with sobs *19*. [probably from the noun]

souter[1.1], **soutar, sutor**, †**sowtar** /'sutər/ *n* 1 a shoemaker, a cobbler *13-*. 2 an opening in the game of draughts *la19-*. 3 a nickname for a native of Selkirk *la18- WC Bor*. 4 a nickname for a native of Forfar *la19- T*. †**souter's clod** a small coarse loaf *la18-e19*. **souter's ends** the waxed thread used by cobblers *19, 20- NE T SW*. **sutter's lingles** = *souter's ends la18, 20- NE T*; compare *lingle en* (LINGLE[1]). **the Souters** the two hills at the entrance to the Cromarty Firth *19-*. [OE *sūtere*]

souter[1.2], **sutor** /'sutər/ *v* 1 to cobble, make or mend shoes *20-*. 2 to get the better of; *in games* to cause a defeat in which an opponent fails to score *la18-19, 20- SW*. [see the noun]

south *see* SOOTH[1.1], SOOTH[1.2], SOOTH[1.3], SOOTH[2.1], SOOTH[2.2], SUITH[1.1]

†**southen, sowthin** *adj* southerly; southern; to, in or from the south *16-19 literary*. [OE *sūðan*]

southern *see* SOUTHRON[1.1], SOUTHRON[1.2]

southert *see* SOOTHWARD

southron[1.1], **southern**, †**sothroun**, †**sudron**, †**sutheroun** /'sʌðrən, 'sʌðərn/ *n* 1 the English; an English person *la15-*. 2 the English language *16-e19*. [see the adj]

southron[1.2], **southern, sudron**, †**sotheroun** /'sʌðrən, 'sʌðərn, 'sʌdrən/ *adj* 1 *of people* belonging to or living in England, English *la14-*. 2 *of things* of or characteristic of England or the English *la16-*. 3 situated in or belonging to the south of a place *16-*. **sudderin wid**, †**suthernewod** southernwood *Artemisia abrotanum la16, 20- N NE SW Bor*. [OE *sūðerne* southern]

southward, southwart *see* SOOTHWARD

souverane *see* SOVEREIGN[1.1]

sove[1.1] /sov/ *n* a stunning blow; a shove *20- Ork*. [see the verb]

sove[1.2] /sov/ *v* 1 to stun, be stunned (by a blow) *19- Sh*. 2 to sink into a stupor *20- Sh*. **söven** a doze *20- Sh*. [Norw dial *søva* to stun, Norw *sove* to sleep]

†**sover**[1.1] *v* 1 to trust in (something) *la15-e16*. 2 to make safe, especially by a safe-conduct *la15-16*. [see the adj]

†**sover**[1.2], **sovir, sovyr** *adj* 1 sure, secure, safe; reliable *la14-16*. 2 stoutly constructed, strong *16-e17*. 3 certain, assured, guaranteed *15-e17*. 4 accurate, true *16*. 5 efficacious *16*. **soverty** 1 making safe, safeguarding *15-16*. 2 a binding assurance, a guarantee *15-e17*. 3 a pledge *16-e17*. 4 a person who becomes surety *la15-17*. [altered form of OFr *soür* sure; compare MOVIR]

†**sover**[1.3] *adv* surely, securely *la15-16*. [see the adj]

†**soverance, surance** *n* a guarantee of safety, a safe-conduct, a truce *15-e18*. [OFr *surance*; compare SOVER[1.2]]

sovereign[1.1], †**soverane**, †**souverane** /'sʌvrən, 'sɔvrən, 'sovrən/ *n* 1 a superior, a person in authority; a monarch, a ruler *15-*. 2 a gold coin *la16-*. [ME *soverain*, OFr *soverain*]

sovereign[1.2], †**soverane** /'sʌvrən, 'sɔvrən, 'sovrən/ *adj* 1 having supreme authority; royal *la14-*. 2 peerless, incomparable, excelling all others; highly efficacious *la14-*. 3 *of a council or court* possessing the highest authority, supreme *16-17*. [see the noun]

sovir, sovyr *see* SOVER[1.2]

†**sow** *n* 1 a bride's outfit of clothes, a trousseau *la17-19*. 2 a shroud, a winding-sheet *la18-19*. [unknown]

sow *see* SAW[1], SOO[1], SOO[2]

sowans, sowens, sooans, †**swins** /'sʌuənz, 'suənz/ *n* 1 *pl* a dish made from the solid residue of fermented oat husks and fine meal *la16-*; compare SWATS. 2 *sing, weaving* a flour-and-water size applied to warp threads *18-19, 20- T*. †**sowan boat** a wooden barrel or tub used for steeping and fermenting sowans *la18-e19*. **sowan bowie** = *sowan boat la18-19, 20- NE*. **sowany daigh** solidified sowans *20- Ork*. †**sowan kit** = *sowan boat 18-e19*. **Sowans Nicht** Christmas Eve (Old Style), the fourth of January *20- NE*. †**sowan pot, sowans pot** the pot in which SOWANS was cooked *la18-19*. **sowan scone, sooan scone** a pancake made with sowan swats instead of milk *20- Ork N*. **sowan seeds** the husks of oats used in making sowans *la17-19, 20- N NE Uls*. **sowan-sieve** a strainer for SOWANS (after the initial steeping) *18-19, 20- NE*. **sowan swats** the liquid poured off sowans *la19, 20- Sh Ork N*. [Gael *sùghan*]

sowce *see* SOUSE[4]

sowch *see* SOUCH[1.1], SOUCH[1.2]

sowd[1], †**sold**, †**soude** /sʌud/ *n* 1 a large, ungainly person *20- NE T*. 2 a (large) quantity or amount of money or possessions *la15-19, 20- NE*. 3 a large amount or number; a lot *19, 20- NE*. 4 wages; remuneration received by a cottar *15-16*. **sowdie** *usually of a woman* large and ungainly *19, 20- Sh NE T Uls*. [OFr *soulde, soude* wages]

sowd[2], †**sold**, †**soud** /sʌud/ *v* 1 to agree (to), sympathize with (so as to curry favour); to come to an agreement *la19- NE Uls*. 2 to solder *la15-e17*. [ME *souder* to join, to solder, OFr *souder* to unite, combine]

sowdan, *Sh* **sowdian**, †**soudan**, †**soldane** /'sʌudən; *Sh* also 'sʌudɪən/ *n* 1 *derogatory* a tyrannical, cantankerous person *20- Ork NE*. 2 *derogatory* a big, clumsy, corpulent person *la19- Sh*. 3 a sultan; the ruler of an Islamic country *15-e17*. 4 a powerful and frightening figure *la15-e16*. [ME *soudan* a sultan, OFr *soudan*, Lat *soldanus*]

sowden *see* SUDIN

sowder *see* SOLDER

sowdian *see* SOWDAN

†**sowdie** *n* a hotchpotch, a heterogeneous mixture *18-19*. [unknown]

sowens *see* SOWANS

sowf, sowff /sʌuf/ *n* a foolish person; a stupid, silly person *19- NE*. [onomatopoeic; compare SUMPH]

sowff[1.1] /sʌuf/ *n* 1 wheezing, heavy breathing; a snooze, a sleep *19-*. 2 a low whistling, singing or humming *la18- NE T*. 3 a stroke, a blow, a smack *18- NE T*. 4 a person's (normal) line of thought or action *19, 20- NE*. 5 a copious drink, a draught *la18-19*. [see the verb]

sowff[1.2] /sʌuf/ *v* 1 to pant, sob, snore, doze *19-*. 2 to drink, quaff *19-*. 3 *of wind or water* to murmur softly; *of a breeze or smoke* to puff gently *la19-*. 4 to sing, hum or whistle softly or under one's breath *18-19, 20- NE*. [probably onomatopoeic]

sowff *see* SOWF

sowik *see* SOOK[1.2]

sowk *see* SOOK[1.1], SOOK[1.2]

sowklar see SUCKLER

sowl[1.1], **saul**, **soul**, †**saull**, †**sawl**, †**sall** /sʌul, sol/ *n* **1** the spiritual part of a person; a person's spirit as distinct from the body *la14-*. **2** a being endowed with a soul, a person *la14-*. **3** spirit, courage *la18-*. **4** a person who endows another with life or action or who animates, controls or manipulates another *la14-16*. †**saulie** a hired mourner at a funeral *17-18*, *19- historical*. **saulless**, †**saules** ignoble, mean-spirited, lacking in courage *la16-19, 20- NE*. †**saulmes**, **soul-mass** a mass for the soul of a dead person *la15-e19*. †**Saul mes day** All Souls' Day *16*. **for sowl and body** with great vigour, as if one's life depended on it *20- Sh Ork Uls*. **say yer saul is yer ain** in negative constructions to be independent of others *16-*. **the sowl, the wee sowl, my sowl** a term of familiarity, pity or mild disparagement *la19-*. [OE *sāwol*]

sowl[1.2], **soul** /sʌul, sol/ *interj* upon my word *la18-*. [see the noun]

sowm see SOME[1.1], SOUM[1.1], SOUM[1.2], SOUM[2], SWEEM[1.2]

sown see SOOND[1.1]

sownack see SHANNACK

sownd see SOOND[1.1], SOOND[1.2], SOOND[2.1], SOOND[2.2], SOUND[2]

sowp[1.1] /sʌup/ *n* **1** rain, wet weather *18- NE Bor*. **2** water for washing (clothes), soapsuds *19- WC SW*. [see the verb]

sowp[1.2] /sʌup/ *v ptp* †**sowpyt** †**ysowpit**, †**solpit** to soak, drench, saturate, steep *la15-19, 20- NE T C SW*. [OE *soppian*]

†**sowp**[2], **solp**, **soupe** *v* to tire, weary, become exhausted; to become dejected *la15-e17*. **sowpit**, **sopit** *adj* **1** rendered dull or sluggish; exhausted or overwhelmed with (effort, sleep or sorrow) *16*. **2** *of a dream* characterized by tiredness or dejection *la15-e16*. [perhaps back-formation from SOPIT, Lat *sōpīre* to render unconscious, put to sleep]

sowp see SUP[1.1], SUP[1.2], SUP[2]

sowpill see SOOPLE[1.2]

sowpyt see SOWP[1.2]

sowr, **sowre** see SOOR[1.2]

sowrchargis see SURCHARGE

sowrok see SOOROCK

sowrs see SOORCE

sowse see SOUSE[1.1]

sowsit see SOUSE[3]

sowtar see SOUTER[1.1]

sowth see SOOTH[1.2], SOOTH[1.3]

sowther, **solder**, **souder** /'sʌuðər, 'soldər, 'sʌudər/ *v* **1** to join items of metal with a fusible metal alloy, to solder *la16-*. **2** to settle, patch up (a quarrel, disagreement) *17-*. **3** to confirm, strengthen (a friendship); to seal, cement (a bargain) *la16-19, 20- NE T*. **4** to agree, get on well together *18-19, 20- T EC*. **5** to unite in matrimony; to make (a marriage) *19, 20- NE T*. **6** to mend, repair; to mitigate, alleviate (strong emotion) *la16-19, 20- T*. [from the noun SOLDER]

sowthin see SOUTHEN

sowtht see SOOTH[1.3]

soye, †**soy** /sɔi/ *n* silk *la18-19, 20- T*. [Fr *soie*]

soyl see SULƷE

soyme see SOAM

soyr see SOIR

soyt see SUIT[1.1]

spa see SPAE[1.2]

spaarl see SPARREL

space[1.1], †**spaice**, †**spais** /spes/ *n* **1** *with the definite article* an extent, a period of time *la14-*. **2** linear distance; a particular distance or extent *la14-*. **3** a lapse, extent or interval of time *la14-*. **4** room on paper available for writing; a gap between letters or words (on a page) *la14-*. **5** an (empty) area, an expanse *15-*. **6** a pace, a stride, used as a unit of measurement, approximately 3 feet (1 metre) *17- Sh N NE*. **7** time or opportunity (to do something) *la14-16*. [AN *space*]

space[1.2] /spes/ *v* **1** to measure (by pacing) *16-*. **2** to walk, stroll, pace *la15-17*. [see the noun; and compare MFr *spacier* to take a walk]

space see SPESHIE

spaceis, **spaces** see SPECIES

spacious see SPASHIOUS

spack see SPEAK[1.2]

spad /spad/ *v* to walk energetically *20 NE*. **spad on** = SPAD. [PAD[2.2], by wrong division of words in phrases such as *he's paddin on*]

spade, *NE* **spadd**, *NE* **spaud**, †**spaid**, †**spead** /sped; *NE* spad, spɔd/ *n* **1** a tool for digging or cutting *la14-*. **2** the female pubes *e18*. **spadin**, **spading** a spade's depth (or breadth) of earth, the amount of earth that can be taken on a spade; a trench of one spade-depth *la17-*. **spade-bearer** in Langholm Common Riding the person who carries the spade used to cut sods at various places indicating the boundaries of the communal land *20- Bor*. **spade's casting** a quantity of peats *la18-*. †**spadarrack** the number of peats that can be cut with a spade by one man in one day, a spade DARG[1.1] *18*. **spade peat** a surface peat cut with an ordinary spade, not the specialized peat-spade *18- Sh Ork N*. †**spaid-silver** payment for work with a spade *la16-17*. **the spade** = *spade-bearer*. [OE *spadu*]

spae[1.1], †**spay**, †**spe** /spe/ *n* **1** enchantment, sorcery *la19-*. **2** a prediction; an omen *la14-17*. †**spay craft** the art of predicting the future *16-19*. [ON *spá*]

spae[1.2], **spey**, †**spay**, †**spa** /spe/ *v* **1** to prophesy, foretell, predict, tell (fortunes); to utter a prophecy *la15-*. **2** to read (someone's hand) *la19, 20- NE*. [ON *spá*]

spaegie /'spegi/ *n* muscular pain or stiffness caused by overexertion *la19- Sh*. **spaegied** stiff, sore *20- Sh*. [compare Norw dial *speika* to walk stiffly]

spaek see SPEAK[1.2]

spaekalation see SPECULATION

spaeman /'speman/ *n* a fortuneteller; a diviner, prophet *15-19, 20- Uls*. [SPAE[1.2] + MAN]

spaewife, **spey wife** /'spe wʌif/ *n* a female fortune-teller *18-*. [SPAE[1.2] + WIFE]

spag, *N* **spaig** /spag; *N* speg/ *n* a paw, hand or foot; a big clumsy hand or foot *20- N NE Uls*; compare SPYOG[1.1]. **spagach** *adj* flat-footed, with clumsy or misshapen feet *la19- N H&I*. **spagach** *n* a clumsy, flat-footed person *20- H&I*. **spaggy-fitted** splay-footed *20- H&I SW*. [Gael *spàg* a claw, a paw, an (animal's) foot]

spahshous see SPASHIOUS

spaice see SPACE[1.1]

spaid see SPADE

spaig see SPAG

spaik, **spake**, **spoke**, *Ork* **spoag**, *NE* **spyauck** /spek, spok; *Ork* spog; *NE* spjɔk/ *n* **1** one of the bars or rods radiating from the hub of a wheel, a spoke *la14-*. **2** a supportive person *19-*. **3** the perch of a bird's cage, a roosting bar *19- WC SW Bor*. **4** one of the rungs of a ladder *la19, 20- T WC SW Bor*. **5** a wooden bar, rod or batten; a stake, slat or pale in a wooden fence *la15-19, 20- N WC Bor*. **6** one of the poles on which a coffin is carried to the graveside *17-19, 20- T SW Bor*. **spaikit** made of spokes or bars of wood *17, 20- T WC Bor*. **drap aff the spaik** to collapse with weariness, sleep or astonishment *20- Bor*. **fa aff the spaik** = *drap aff the spaik*. [OE *spāca*]

spail see SPALE[1.1]

spain see SPEAN

spaingie, *Sh* **spenyi**, *NE* **spengyie**, †**spanʒie** /'spɛɲi; *Sh* 'spɛnji; *NE* 'spɛnjе/ *n* **1** Spain *la14-e17*. **2 (a)** cane *la17- Sh NE T*. [AN *Espaigne*]

spair *see* SPARE[2.1]

spairge[1.1], **sperge, sparge** /spɛrdʒ, spardʒ/ *n* **1** a splash, sprinkling or splodge of water or mud *19-*. **2** *in brewing and distilling* the water sprinkled over the malt; the liquor produced by this process *19-*. **3** a drink, a mouthful, a drop of spirits *19- T SW*. **spergie** = SPAIRGE[1.1] (sense 2) *20- T*. [see the verb]

spairge[1.2], **sperge, sparge** /spɛrdʒ, spardʒ/ *v* **1** *in brewing and distilling* to sprinkle water over the malt *19-*. **2** to scatter, sprinkle, dash (water or mud) *la18-19, 20- NE WC*. **3** to bespatter, besprinkle *la18-19, 20- NE*. **4** to plaster, roughcast or perhaps whitewash (the interior or exterior walls of a building) *16-17*; compare SPARGEN. **spairge aboot** to flounder as if walking through mud, water or snow *19-*. [OFr *espargier*, Lat *spargere* to sprinkle, with influence from PARGEN]

spais *see* SPACE[1.1]

spaiver, spaver /'spevər/ *n* the opening in the front of trousers *19-*. [altered form of SPARE[1]]

spak *see* SPEAK[1.2]

spake *see* SPAIK, SPEAK[1.2]

spald, *N* **spowl** /spɔld; *N* spʌul/ *v* **1** to sprawl, lie stretched out; to knock (a person) flat *e16*. **2** to split, lay open or flat for cooking *19*. **3** to take long strides *20- N*. Compare SPELD[1.2]. [MLG *spalden* to split]

spald *see* SPAUL

spalder /'spɔldər/ *v* **1** to split (a fish) *la19, 20- Bor*. **2** to sprawl, stretch out, extend; to clamber *19- N Bor*. Compare SPELDER. [SPALD, with frequentative suffix]

spale[1.1], **spail, speal**, *Sh* **spil**, *Sh NE* **spell**, *Ork* **speill** /spel, spil; *Sh* spɪl; *Sh NE* spɛl; *Ork* speal/ *n* **1** a splinter, chip or sliver of wood (broken off, frequently by an axe or plane); a wood-shaving; a thin strip or lath of wood *15-*. **2** a splinter in the skin *16-*. **3** a wooden spill or taper used for lighting *18-*. **4** a small piece, a fragment; something of little or no value *la18-*. **5** a shroud-like shape of candlegrease on a guttered candle, thought to foretell the death of the person in whose direction it forms *la18-19, 20- NE T Bor*. **6** a wooden skewer for stretching a split fish apart to dry *20- Sh*. **spailing 1** a wood-shaving *la19, 20- T SW*. **2** the action of cutting a shaving from a barrel (as a means of identification) *la17*. **spale-basket** a two-handled (potato-)basket made of thin strips of wood *20-*. **spale-box** a (small) box made of thin strips of wood, for storing money or pills *18-19, 20- Ork NE WC*. **speill seive** a sieve set in a plywood frame *18- Ork*. [compare ON *spal-* a bar of wood, Norw dial *spila, spel* a splinter]

spale[1.2], *Sh* **spil** /spel; *Sh* spɪl/ *v* **1** *of a candle* to form spales *20- Sh*. **2** to skewer a split fish to keep it open while drying *20- Sh*. [see the noun; and compare Norw *spila* to skewer a split fish]

spale *see* SPEEL[1.1], SPELL[2.1]

spale bane, spale-bone *see* SPAUL

spalter /'spaltər/ *v* to walk awkwardly, stumble; to splash through water, flounder *20- SW Uls*. [perhaps Eng *spalter* to split off; related to SPALD]

span /span/ *n* *in Shetland, Orkney and Caithness* a measure of weight or capacity of butter (mainly used to assess the skatt to be paid) *16-19, 20- historical*. [ON *spann*]

span *see* SPANG[1.1], SPANG[1.2], SPIN[1.2]

spane *see* SPEAN

spang[1.1], **span** /spaŋ, span/ *n* **1** the distance from the tip of the thumb to the tip of the pinkie or index finger, about 9 inches; the grasp; the full stretch of anything *15-*. **2** a small extent of time; the duration of a human life *la18-*. **spangie** a game played with marbles or buttons *19, 20- C*. **a spang nievefu** as much of something as can be grasped in the hand *la19- EC Bor*. [OE *spann*; perhaps with influence from SPANG[2.1]]

spang[1.2], **span** /spaŋ, span/ *v* to encircle (with the hand), grasp *la14-*. **span the nose** to thumb one's nose *20- C SW*. [see the noun]

spang[2.1] /spaŋ/ *n* **1** a pace, a long vigorous step or bound *18-*. **2** (the sound of) a sharp, powerful or jerky movement; a smack, a sharp blow *16-e18*. [perhaps onomatopoeic]

spang[2.2] /spaŋ/ *v* **1** to walk or run with long vigorous steps, leap, bound *18-*. **2** to cross with a stride or bound, leap over; to make your way by leaping or in haste; to pace out, measure by pacing *la16-*. **3** to cause to leap up, throw, jerk, flick (up)*16-*. **4** *of an arrow* to spring from the bowstring *e16*. **spanghew** to jerk or catapult (something) violently into the air *19, 20- NE C SW Bor*. [see the noun]

spang[3] /spaŋ/ *n* **1** a buckle, a clasp, a metal plate *20- Sh*. **2** a spangle, an ornament or decoration *15-17*. [MDu *spange* a glittering ornament, Du *spang* a buckle]

†**spangit** *adj of cattle* speckled, variegated *la16-e18*. [SPANG[3] + -IT[2]]

spang-new /spaŋ'nju/ *adj* absolutely new, brand-new *19, 20- N WC SW*. Compare SPLIT NEW. [altered form of Eng †*span-new*, ON *spán nýr*]

spank /spaŋk/ *v* to move nimbly and briskly on foot, horseback or in a vehicle *19-*. **spanker 1** a spirited, fast horse *19, 20- N NE T WC SW*. **2** a person who walks quickly with a brisk, regular stride *19, 20- N NE T WC*. **spankie** frisky, nimble, spirited *la18-19, 20- EC Uls*. [Eng *spank*, perhaps onomatopoeic]

spanker-new /spaŋkər'nju/ *adj* = SPANG-NEW *19, 20- Bor*. [conflation of SPANG-NEW with *spanker* (SPANK)]

spankie-new /spaŋke'nju/ *adj* absolutely new, brand-new *la19, 20- Bor*. [conflation of SPANG-NEW with *spankie* (SPANK)]

†**spanys** *v of a flower* to open *e15*. **spanyst, spynist** *of a flower* opened *la14-e16*. [OFr *espaniss-*, stem of *espanir* to expand, spread out]

spanʒie *see* SPAINGIE

spar[1.1], *Bor* **spare**, *Sh* **sper** /spar; *Bor* spɛr; *Sh* spɛr/ *n* **1** a piece of timber, a beam, rafter, pole or rail *la14-*. **2** a wooden bolt for securing a door, a linchpin *19-*. **3** a rung of a chair or ladder *la19- NE T C Bor*. **4** a crossbar or wooden slat in a kitchen dresser *la19, 20- NE T WC*. **5** a bar or rail of a wooden fence or gate *la19, 20- NE*. **spardie** a perch for a bird *20- N T*. **spardan** = spardie *20- N*. **sparred,** †**sparit** slatted, made of spars *la16-*. †**sparret** a small spar or bar *e17*. [ON *sparri, sperra*; MDu, MLG *sparre*]

†**spar**[1.2], **sper** *v* **1** to fasten (a door or gate) with a bolt *la14-e19*. **2** to shut (a person) out *e15*. **Spardur** used as nickname or surname perhaps a jailer or gate-keeper *15*. [OE *gesparrian*, MDu *sperren*; or from the noun]

spar[2], †**sparr** /spar/ *n* one of a number of crystalline, nonmetallic minerals, for example, calcite or feldspar *17-*. **spar coal** a kind of coal containing spar *19- EC*. **sparry coal** = *spar coal*. [MLG *spar*]

spard *see* SPARE[2.1]

spare[1] /spɛr/ *n* **1** the opening or slit in a woman's skirt or petticoat *la16-19, 20- Sh Ork N C Bor Uls*. **2** the opening in the front of trousers *la18-19, 20- N NE T C SW*; compare SPAIVER. [ME *spair*]

spare[2.1], †**spair,** †**spayr** /spɛr/ *v pt* †**spard 1** to allow to remain unharmed or undamaged; to forbear; to hesitate; to fail to do something *la14-*. **2** to dispense with, do without; to reserve; to expend, spend; to set aside *la14-*. **3** to forgive *la14-e17.* **4** to save, hoard; to avoid incurring (expense); to keep clear of (obstacles) *15-17.* [OE *sparian*]

spare[2.2] /sper/ *adj* **1** held in reserve, not in use; surplus, superfluous *16-.* **2** meagre, scanty; thin *la16-.* [probably from the verb]

†**spare**[2.3] *adv* sparely, in a frugal manner *19.* [see the verb]

spare *see* SPAR[1.1]

spare rib, †**spar rib**, †**spere ribb**, †**sparreb** /sper 'rɪb/ *n* a cut of meat taken from the ribs *16-.* Compare FORESYE. [probably an altered form of MLG *ribbesper* a dish made of a stuffed ribcage]

†**spargen**, **spargeon** *v* to plaster, roughcast *16-e17.* **spargener** a plasterer *la16-e17.* [altered form of PARGEN; perhaps with influence from SPAIRGE[1.2]]

†**sparhalk** *n* a sparrowhawk *15-17.* [OE *spearhafoc*]

spark[1.1], *NE* **spirk**, *Bor* **sperk**, †**sprak** /spark; *NE* spɪrk; *Bor* sperk/ *n* **1** a tiny particle (of fire or light) *la14-.* **2** a trace, a fragment *16-.* **3** a person, a fellow, a character *la16-.* **4** a very small amount of a liquid or semi-liquid *16-19, 20- Sh NE T EC Bor Uls.* **5** a drop of water, a raindrop *19, 20- NE T Uls.* **6** a splash or spot of mud *16-19, 20- NE.* **7** a small diamond; a ruby *16-e19.* **8** a nip of spirits *19.* **sparkie** emitting sparks; bright, sharp, quick-witted; lively *19, 20- NE T.* †**a spark in yer throat** an unquenchable thirst *la18-19.* [OE *spearca*]

spark[1.2] /spark/ *v* **1** to emit sparks; to emit or reflect light *16-.* **2** to set alight; to light (a match or fire) *la19- T C SW.* **3** to spatter with liquid or mud; to spot with mud *16-19, 20- Sh Ork NE Bor Uls.* **4** to throw out a fine spray; to sputter, spit forth; to issue as or like sparks *16-.* **5** to rain slightly; to spit with rain *19, 20- Sh Ork NE Uls.* **sparkin** a sprinkling *la19- Ork NE.* **spark in** to mix in (a small quantity), sprinkle, scatter thinly (seed or dung) *19- NE.* [ME *sparken*, and from the noun]

sparl *see* SPARREL

sparling *see* SPIRLING

sparpal, **sparple** *see* SPERFLE

sparr *see* SPAR[2]

sparra, **sparrow**, **sparry**, *Sh Ork* **sporrow** /'spara, 'sparo, 'spare; *Sh Ork* 'spɔro/ *n* a small brownish-grey bird of the family *Passeridae*, especially the house sparrow *Passer domesticus la15-.* **sparrabaldy** having thin legs *20- NE.* **sparrow-drift** = *sparrow-hail 20- NE C Bor.* **sparrow-hail** shot for shooting small birds *la19- NE C Bor.* **sparrow-shot** = *sparrow-hail 20- NE C Bor.* [OE *spearwa*]

sparreb *see* SPARE RIB

sparrel, **sparl**, **spaarl** /'sparəl, sparl/ *n* **1** the long intestine between the stomach and the anus; the rectum *19- Sh.* **2** a sausage *19- Sh.* **3** a nickname for a native of Delting parish *la19- Sh.* **sparl pudding** = SPARREL (sense 2). [Faer *sperðill*]

spar rib *see* SPARE RIB

sparrow *see* SPARRA

sparse /spars/ *adj* **1** *of writing* spread out, widely spaced *la17-.* **2** thinly dispersed or scattered; thin, scanty *la19-.* [Lat *sparsus*, ptp of *spargere* to scatter]

sparsle *see* SPERFLE

spart /spart/ *v* to scatter (dung); to bespatter *20- Sh N.* [perhaps an altered form of SPARK[1.2]; and compare Gael *spairt* to plaster, spatter]

†**sparth** *n* perhaps a mistake for *pard*, a leopard *la15.* [erroneous]

spartickles *see* SPENTACLES

spartle *see* SPURTLE[2]

spashious, **spacious**, *H&I* **spahshous**, †**spatious**, †**spawcious** /'speʃəs; *H&I* 'spaʃəs/ *adj* **1** large; extensive; roomy *17-.* **2** conceited, pretentious *20- H&I.* [ME *spacious*, MFr *spacieux*, Lat *spatiōsus*]

spat *see* SPIT, SPOAT

spatch[1.1] /spatʃ/ *n* a patch, as on a garment *19- Bor.* [altered form of Eng *patch*]

spatch[1.2] /spatʃ/ *v* to patch, mend (clothes) *19- Bor.* [see the noun]

spatchell /'spatʃəl/ *adj* well-dressed, neat *20- N NE.* [Gael *spaideil*]

spate[1.1], *Sh* **speet**, †**speat**, †**spait**, †**speyt** /spet; *Sh* spit/ *n* **1** a flood, a sudden rise of water level; flooding, inundation, a swollen condition of water *15-.* **2** a torrential fall or heavy downpour (of rain) *16-.* **3** a torrent (of words); an outburst of emotion or activity; an overwhelming rush of incidents or events *16-.* **4** a flood of tears *17-.* **5** a bout (of drinking) *19.* **6** a powerful public outcry *17-e18.* **in spate** in flood *la16-.* †**on spait** = *in spate 15-e16.* [unknown]

spate[1.2] /spet/ *v* **1** to rain heavily *la19- Sh Ork NE EC Bor.* **2** *of a river* to flood, swell with flood-water *19.* [unknown]

spatious *see* SPASHIOUS

spatril *see* SPOAT

spattill *see* SPITTLE

spaud *see* SPADE

spaul, **spauld**, †**spald**, †**spule** /spɔl, spɔld/ *n* **1** *in a person or animal* the shoulder; the shoulder-bone *14-.* **2** one of the four quarters of an animal; a limb, a human or animal's leg *16-.* **3** *food* a joint of meat, a shoulder or leg of mutton or beef; the wing or leg of a fowl; a shoulder cut of beef, shoulder steak *16-19, 20- NE T WC.* **spule-bane**, **spale-bone 1** a shoulderblade; a shoulder joint of meat *la18-.* **2** a cut of beef from the shoulder, blade-bone steak *20-.* [OFr *espalle*, *espalde* a shoulder]

spave /spev/ *v* to spay, neuter (a female animal) *la18, 19- SW.* [altered form of Eng *spay*]

spaver *see* SPAIVER

spavie, †**speavie** /'spevi, 'speve/ *n* **1** spavin, a disease of horses *la17-.* **2** also *humorous* a human rheumatic disease, or injury causing lameness *19.* **spavied** affected with spavin *18-.* [shortened form of Older Scots, Eng *spavin*, OFr *espavain*]

spawcious *see* SPASHIOUS

spawny /'spɔne/ *adj* very lucky, fortunate *la20-.* [unknown]

spay *see* SPAE[1.1], SPAE[1.2]

spayr *see* SPARE[2.1]

spead *see* SPADE

speak[1.1], †**spek**, †**speke**, †**speik** /spik/ *n* **1** a chat, a conversation *la14-.* **2** gossip, scandalmongering *la19-.* **3** words, discourse *15-.* **4** a subject of conversation, especially of current gossip or rumour, the talk (of a place) *la18-19, 20- Sh NE T C SW.* **5** a speech, a statement, a comment; a popular saying *la14-19, 20- NE T EC.* **6** talking for the sake of talking, talk; make-believe *20- Sh NE.* **7** the action of speaking; a manner of speaking *la14-e15.* **8** (the power of) speech *la14.* Compare SPEECH. [ME *speke*, OE *spǣc*]

speak[1.2], **speik**, *Sh* **spaek**, *NE* **spike**, *NE* **spikk**, *Ork Uls* **spake**, †**speke** /spik; *Sh* spɛk; *NE* spʌɪk; *NE* spɪk; *Ork Uls* spek/ *v pt* **spak** †**spack**, *ptp* **spoken** †**spokkyn 1** to exercise or possess the faculty of speech; to communicate, converse, talk; to express one's views verbally, preach, make a speech, give testimony, make a revelation, tell a story *la14-.* **2** to (have the ability to) communicate or express oneself in a foreign language *la14-.* **3** *of an action or object* to express, signify, indicate (something) *la14-.* **4** *of a bird* to imitate the sounds of speech *16-.* **5** frequently *imperative* to listen (to), attend (to) *la18-.* **6** to order (goods), bespeak *20- Sh NE T C.* **speaker**, †**speikar 1** a person who speaks *16-.* **2** a person who delivers a (prepared) speech *la16-.* **3** a person who speaks on behalf of another, a spokesman *15-18.* **spoken**

after names of places or areas having the speech characteristic of the place mentioned: ◊*Sooth-spoken* ◊*Glesca spoken 20-*. †**for to speke** so to speak *e16*. **speak a wird tae** to rebuke, admonish, advise *la19- Sh N T*. **speak back 1** to reply (in argument) *la18-*. **2** to reply impertinently and defiantly, talk back *la19-*. **speak for 1** to petition, speak on a person's behalf *la14-*. **2** to order (goods); originally also to redeem (a pledge), hire (a workman) *15-17, 20- Sh*. **speak in** to pay a fleeting visit, drop in *19, 20- Ork T SW*. **speak tae, speak till 1** to ask in marriage *20-*. **2** *of a farmer* to engage (a worker) for a further term *19-*. **3** to talk to, converse with; to petition; to discuss, address, deal with (an issue) *la14-*. **speak like a prent buik** to speak with an air of knowledge or affectedly *18-*. **speak pink** to speak affectedly *la20- NE T EC*. [OE *specan*]

speaking, †**speking**, †**speiking** /ˈspikɪŋ/ *n* **1** the action of speaking *la14-*. **2** (a) speech, talk, discourse or conversation *la14-*. **3** a person's) way of talking *la14-16*. **4** *pl* statements, remarks *15-16*. **5** the faculty or power of speech *la14*. **speakan sweetie** a piece of confectionery with a motto printed on it, a conversation lozenge *20- Sh Ork N*. **speaking-time** the time of year at which employers, especially farmers, renew or terminate workers' contracts *la19-*. [verbal noun from SPEAK[1,2]]

†**speaking drink, speakyng drynk** *n* a payment paid for entry to a trade incorporation *17-e19*. [SPEAKING + DRINK[1,1]]

†**speaking pint** *n* = SPEAKING DRINK *la17-18*. [SPEAKING + PINT[1]]

speal *see* SPALE[1,1], SPEEL[1,1]

spean, spane, spen, *Sh* **spend,** *NE* **speen,** †**spain** /spɛn, spɛn; *Sh* spɛnd; *NE* spin/ *v* **1** to wean (an infant or suckling animal) *16-*. **2** to put (a person or animal) off food through disgust, fear etc *la18-19, 20- NE T SW*. **3** to draw (a person) away from (a habit or idea); to separate, part from *17-19, 20- NE T C*. **4** to be (in the process of being) weaned *la18-19, 20- T SW*. **5** to stop (a person) from doing something (as a punishment) *16*. **6** to be deprived of membership of a craft incorporation *16*. **speaning brash** an illness affecting children or young animals on being weaned *19, 20- SW Uls*. **speaning time** weaning time *la16-19, 20- N NE Uls*. [ME *spanen*, OFr *espanir*, MDu, MLG *spanen, spenen*]

spear, †**spere,** †**sper,** †**speir** /spir/ *n* **1** a weapon, a long wooden staff with a sharp, usually metal, head, for thrusting or throwing *la14-*. **2** a soldier armed with a spear *15-e19*. **3** *pl* the thorns or prickles of a plant *la15-e16*. †**speir rinning** jousting with spears *la16, e19*. †**spere-silver** a tax levied for military purposes *la15-16*. [OE *spere*]

spearimint /ˈspirimɪnt/ *n* spearmint, a common, cultivated species of mint *Mentha spicata la19- T C Bor*. [altered form of Eng *spearmint*]

speat *see* SPATE[1,1]

speavie *see* SPAVIE

speccy *see* SPECKY

spece *see* SPESHIE

spech *see* SPEECH

†**specht, speicht** *n* the green woodpecker *Picus viridis la15-e16*. [MDu, MLG *specht*]

special[1,1] /ˈspɛʃəl/ *n* **1** a carbonated *heavy* beer (HEAVY[1,2]) *la20-*. **2** a particular point, statement or detail *la15-e17*. **3** a close friend or supporter; an intimate *la16-17*. **4** a distinguished or important public figure, a member of the nobility *la16-e17*. [see the adj]

special[1,2], *Sh NE* **speeshal,** †**specyall,** †**spyciall** /ˈspɛʃəl; *Sh NE* ˈspiʃəl/ *adj* **1** exceptional; esteemed; trustworthy, reliable *la14-*. **2** exclusive, distinguished; set apart, distinctive *15-*. **3** having a particular or limited application or purpose *la14-*. **4** *of a second or sometimes third year class at St Andrews University, originally describing higher courses in all Scottish universities* advanced *18-20, 21- historical*. **5** important; main, principal *16-e17*. **specially 1** exceptionally; especially; principally; particularly *la14-*. **2** expressly, for a particular purpose *15-*. **3** explicitly, in detail *15-19*. †**special charge** *law* a particular procedure with regard to the service of heirs to particular lands *la17*. **special service** *see* SERVICE. [AN *special*, Lat *speciālis*]

†**special**[1,3], **speciall** /ˈspɛʃəl/ *adv* **1** expressly *15-17*. **2** exceptionally *16-17*. **3** especially *16-17*. †**in special 1** particularly, especially, above all *la15-17*. **2** specifically, in detail *la15-e17*. **3** individually, separately, personally *la15-16*. **4** relating to a procedure in the inheritance of particular lands *la15-17*; compare *special charge* (SPECIAL[1,2]). **5** exclusively, only *la15-16*. †**in to special** = *in special 5 la15*. [see the adj]

speciality /spɛʃeˈalətɛ/ *n* **1** a product, skill or quality for which a person or place is particularly known *20-*. **2** special favour or affection, friendship *la15*. **3** a particular point or detail *la16-17*. †**in specialitee** in detail *15*. †**but specialitie** without partiality or favour *la15*. [OFr *spécialité*]

specie *see* SPESHIE

species, †**spaces,** †**spaceis** /ˈspiʃiz/ *n* **1** a class, sort or kind *la16-*. **2** money in the form of coins; a denomination of coinage *la16-17*. **3** a visible, actual or apparent form (of something); *Christian Church* the physical form of the elements of the Eucharist *17*. Compare SPESHIE. [Lat *speciēs*]

specification, †**specificatioun** /spɛsəfəˈkeʃən/ *n* **1** specific mention; a specific character or nature *la16-*. **2** *law* the formation of a new property from materials belonging to another by conversion into a different form *la17-*. [OFr *specification*, Lat *specificātiō-*, noun from *specificāre* to specify]

specky, speccy /ˈspɛki, ˈspɛke/ *adj derogatory* wearing spectacles *20-*. [shortened form of Eng *spectacles* with -IE[2] suffix]

spectacles *see* SPENTACLES

speculation, *Sh* **spaekalation,** †**speculatione** /spɛkjuˈlɛʃən; *Sh* spɪkəˈlɛʃən/ *n* **1** *in commerce* the attempt to make a profit by predicting what will sell or what will rise in value *19-*. **2** thought based on slight evidence and guesswork *20-*. **3** a spectacle, a subject for remark or gossip, an object of contempt *la19, 20- Sh*. **4** contemplation, profound thought, assiduous study *la15-16*. [Lat *speculātiō-* observation]

specyall *see* SPECIAL[1,2]

sped *see* SPEED[1,2]

spede *see* SPEED[1,1], SPEED[1,2]

speeach /ˈspiək/ *n* an oak stake; an oak branch without the bark; a small stick *20-*. [Gael *spitheag* a small piece of wood]

speech, †**speche,** †**spech,** †**speiche** /spitʃ/ *n* talk, conversation, an utterance; the act of speaking, the faculty of speech *la14-*. **tak speech in hand** to (take the opportunity to) speak, make a speech, hold forth *la14-19, 20- WC*. Compare SPEAK[1,1]. [OE *spǣc*]

speed[1,1], †**spede,** †**speid** /spid/ *n* **1** quickness, swiftness, promptness *la14-*. **2** the capacity to move quickly *15-*. **3** success, prosperity, good fortune *15-19, 20- Uls*. †**spedefull** profitable, advantageous, expedient *la14-e19*. **speedy 1** swift *la14-*. **2** prompt *16-*. **come speed** to be successful *16-19, 20- Ork NE EC Uls*. **come nae speed** to be unsuccessful *16-19, 20- Ork NE EC Uls*. **come better speed** = *come speed la16-19, 20- NE*. †**come good spede** = *come speed la17-e19*. **come little speed** = *come nae speed 16-19, 20- H&I*. **speed of foot** fleetness of movement *16-*. [OE *spēd*]

speed[1,2], †**spede,** †**speid** /spid/ *v pt* **sped 1** to go quickly, hurry *la14-*. **2** to cause to move quickly *la15-*. **3** to promote, expedite, accomplish, deal with *la14-*. **4** *in greetings* good luck: ◇*speed ye* ◇*we wiss him speed* ◇*weel may ye speed 18-19, 20- NE.* **5** to meet with success, prosper, attain a purpose *la14-e19.* **6** to help (a person), cause (a person) to prosper *la14-16.* †**speid hand, speid your hand** to make haste *e16.* **speed the ploo, Speed the Plough 1** (the tune of) a country dance *19-.* **2** a well-wishing phrase at a *pleuch feast* (PLOO[1.1]) *la19*. [OE *spēdan* to succeed, prosper]

speeder, spider, *SW* **speedart** /ˈspidər, ˈspaedər; *SW* ˈspidərt/ *n* **1** an arachnid of the insectivorous order *Araneidae*, a spider *la16-.* **2** a penny-farthing bicycle *20 Ork NE.* **3** *fishing* a trout-fly dressed without wings *20-.* **speeder jenny** the cranefly or daddy-long-legs, an insect of the family *Tipulidae 20- SW Bor.* **speederlegs** = *speeder jenny 20- Sh Ork Bor.* **spider webster** = SPEEDER *20- T WC.* **the Spiders** a nickname for Queen's Park Football Club, from their black-and-white hooped jerseys *20-.* [OE *spiðra*]

speekit *see* SPICKET

speel[1.1]**, spell,** *Ork* **spale,** †**speal** /spil, spɛl; *Ork* spel/ *n* **1** a period of time *19-.* **2** a time of rest or relaxation, a break in work *la18-19, 20- Sh Ork WC SW.* **3** a task, a job *la19- Sh Ork N.* [from the verb]

speel[1.2]**, spell** /spil, spɛl/ *v* **1** to take a turn at work for (someone), relieve (someone) at work, substitute for (someone) *20- Sh N C SW.* **2** to work or walk with great energy *la19- NE SW Uls* [OE *spelian*]

speel[2.1]**, speil** /spil/ *n* the act of climbing; a climb *19- NE T C SW.* [see the verb]

speel[2.2]**, spiel,** †**spele,** †**speil,** †**speill** /spil/ *v* **1** to climb, clamber *16-.* **2** to rise (up) (in the world) *la16-.* **speeler 1** a climber *20- NE Bor Uls.* **2** a spiked crampon attached to the foot for climbing trees or poles *18-19, 20- Bor.* **spiel-the-wa** (a nip of) (inferior) whisky (from its supposed effects on the drinker) *la19- WC SW Bor.* [back-formation from SPELAR]

speel *see* SPIEL

speen *see* SPEAN, SPUIN

speen-drift *see* SPINDRIFT

speengie rose /ˈspiŋə roz/ *n* the peony *Paeonia officinalis la19- NE T EC.* [altered form of Eng *peony rose*]

speer /spir/ *v of liquid* to squirt *la19- Sh.* [Norw dial *spira*]

speer *see* SPEIR[1.1], SPEIR[1.2]

speerack /ˈspirak/ *n* a lively, alert person *20- N.* [perhaps Gael *speireag* a slender-limbed girl, literally a sparrow-hawk]

speerin *see* SPEIRIN[1.1], SPEIRIN[1.2]

speerit[1.1]**, spirit, spreit, spret,** *N* **spreet,** †**sperit,** †**sprit,** †**sprete** /ˈspirət, ˈspɪrət, sprʌɪt, sprɛt; *N* sprit/ *n* **1** the principle of life; the soul *la14-.* **2** a supernatural being, a spirit *la14-.* **3** the essential power of God *la14-.* **4** the emotional part of a person; the essence, the mind; the character, nature or disposition of a person *la14-.* **5** a person of a particular (specified) character or disposition; a body, a being *la15-.* **6** *pl* distilled liquid, especially alcohol; strong alcoholic drink *17-.* **spiritless,** †**spiritles 1** lacking boldness, courage or strength of character *la15-.* **2** drained of emotion; sorrowful; exhausted *16-e17.* **speerity** spirited, vivacious, full of energy *16-.* †**spreit of lyfe 1** = SPEERIT[1.1] (sense 1) *e16.* **2** blood *e16.* **the Spirit** = the essential power of God *la14-*; compare *Haly spreit* (HALY). [AN *spirit*, Lat *spīritus*]

speerit[1.2]**, spirit,** †**sprete** /ˈspirət, ˈspɪrət/ *v* **1** to move by unseen means; to kidnap, abduct *19-.* **2** to inspire, encourage *16-e18.* [see the noun]

speeritual, spiritual, †**spirituall,** †**sperituall** /ˈspirətʃəl, ˈspɪrətjuəl/ *adj* **1** of or affecting the spirit or soul of a person *la14-.* **2** describing a relationship to the church; ecclesiastical *15-.* **3** with reference to a relationship through the spirit *15-16.* **4** holy *15-e17.* **spirituality,** †**spiritualite 1** the quality or state of being spiritual; the aspect of life concerned with spiritual matters *la15-.* **2** *law* the part of a bishopric or benefice considered to belong to it by divine right rather than being endowed *la15-17.* **3** the clergy *la15-16.* [OFr *spirituel*, Lat *spīrituālis*]

speeshal *see* SPECIAL[1.2]

speet[1.1]**, spit,** †**speit,** †**spet,** †**spete** /spit, spɪt/ *n* **1** a pointed rod of metal or wood used to skewer meat for roasting *la15-.* **2** a pointed stick or skewer on which fish are hung to dry *19- Sh Ork N NE EC Bor.* **3** *of a fishing line* an iron rod (stuck horizontally through the sinker) from which hooked cords hang down *20- Sh.* **4** a rod for suspending the wicks in the making of tallow candles *20- SW.* **5** (a spit used as) a sharp-pointed weapon *15-17.* **6** *derogatory* a sword *19.* †**speit staff** a sharp-pointed staff *17.* [OE *spitu*]

speet[1.2]**, spit,** †**spet,** †**spete** /spit, spɪt/ *v* **1** to hang fish on a spit to dry *la19- Sh Ork N NE EC Bor.* **2** to put on a spit, pierce or impale (as with a spit) *16-e19.* **speet up** to put on a spit *la19- Sh N.* [see the noun]

speet *see* SPATE[1.1]

speiche *see* SPEECH

speicht *see* SPECHT

speid *see* SPEED[1.1], SPEED[1.2]

speik *see* SPEAK[1.1], SPEAK[1.2]

speiking *see* SPEAKING

speil *see* SPEEL[2.1], SPEEL[2.2]

speill *see* SPALE[1.1]

speir[1.1]**, speer** /spir/ *n* **1** a question; questioning, inquiry, investigation *la17-19, 20- NE T SW Bor Uls.* **2** a person who is continually asking questions; a prying inquisitive person *la19- NE C Bor Uls.* [see the verb]

speir[1.2]**, speer,** †**spere,** †**sper** /spir/ *v* **1** to ask (a question), inquire, make inquiries *la14-.* **2** to seek out (an opinion), request (something) *16-.* **3** to invite *19-.* **4** to ask (a person) a question, put a question to (a person) *15-19, 20- Ork N T WC SW.* **5** to inquire about or trace stolen property *la16-17.* **6** to search out, find (a particular sort of person) *la14-16.* **7** to inquire one's way; to make one's way to a place *la15-e17.* **speir at** to put a question to, inquire of (a person) *la14-.* **speir efter** to inquire about (a person or thing) *la14-.* **speir for 1** to inquire about, ask after (a person or their health); to seek information about (a person or thing); to seek out (a person) *la14-.* **2** to request, ask for (something) *la17-.* **3** to ask in marriage, make a proposal of marriage to, ask for the hand of *la18-19, 20- NE T C SW.* **speir guesses** to ask riddles *la19- C SW Uls.* †**speir of** to ask, make inquiries about *la14-16.* **speir oot** to seek out, search for, track down, trace; to find by inquiry *la16-.* **speir a person's price** *humorous* to make a proposal of marriage *la18-19, 20- NE C.* **speir questions** to catechize *la19-.* †**speir the votes** to ask the members of an official body to vote *17.* [OE *spyrian*]

speir *see* SPEAR

speirin[1.1]**, speerin,** †**spering** /ˈspirən/ *n* **1** the action of asking or inquiring; questioning, (an) inquiry; prying, (an) interrogation or investigation *la14-.* **2** a proposal of marriage *la19-.* **3** frequently *pl* information (obtained by inquiry); news *la14-19, 20- C SW Bor.* [verbal noun from SPEIR[1.2]]

speirin[1.2]**, speerin** /ˈspirən/ *adj* inquisitive, searching *la19-.* [participial adj from SPEIR[1.2]]

speit *see* SPEET[1.1]

†**spek** *n* lavender or spikenard *14-17.* [OFr *spic*]

spek *see* SPEAK[1.1]

speke *see* SPEAK[1.1], SPEAK[1.2]

speking *see* SPEAKING

spel *see* SPELD[1.2], SPELL[2.1]

†**spelar, spelair** *n* an acrobat, a performer *la15-e16.* [MDu *speler* a player, an actor]

spelch see SPELK¹·¹

†**speld**¹·¹, **spell** *n in Shetland and Orkney* a piece or measure of land *17-18*. [Norw dial *spjell* a strip of ground]

speld¹·², *NE* **spel** /spɛld; *NE* spɛl/ *v* **1** to split, slice open; to lay (a fish or chicken) open or flat (for drying or cooking) *la15-19, 20- Sh Ork N*. **2** to stretch out, splay; to knock (a person) flat; *of a person* to lie stretched out *la15-19, 20- Sh NE*. **3** to crack, crumble *17*. **spelding** a split and dried or smoked fish *la15-19, 20- Sh N NE T EC*. [variant of SPALD]

spelder /ˈspɛldər/ *v* **1** to split, spread or pull open or apart (a fish) *la17-19, 20- Ork T EC Bor Uls*. **2** to stretch out, sprawl; to thrash about awkwardly *18-19, 20- Ork C Bor*. **3** to wrench oneself or pull one's muscles by falling with the legs apart *19, 20- Ork Bor*. **speldrin** a split and dried or smoked fish *19, 20-* mainly *C Bor*. [SPELD¹·², with frequentative suffix]

spele see SPEEL²·²

spelk¹·¹, *Sh* **spyolk**, †**spelch** /spɛlk; *Sh* spjɔlk, spjʌlk/ *n* **1** a sharp splinter (of wood, glass or iron); a small strip of wood *la16-*. **2** a surgical splint *19, 20- Sh Ork N Bor*. **3** a skewer for hanging fish on to dry *la19- Sh N*. [OE *spelc*, Norw dial *spjålk* a splint]

spelk¹·², *Sh* **spyolk** /spɛlk; *Sh* spjɔlk, spjʌlk/ *v* **1** to bind (a broken limb) with a splint, repair (something broken) with splints *17-19, 20- Sh Ork N Bor*. **2** to splinter; to fly about like splinters *la19-*. **3** to skewer (a split fish) to keep it open for drying *20- Sh*. †**spelkit** splintered, damaged *16*. [OE *spelcan*]

spell¹·¹ /spɛl/ *n* **1** spelling, a spelling lesson *la19- NE Bor*. **2** a spelling book *19*. †**spell book** a spelling book *19*. [see the verb]

spell¹·² /spɛl/ *v* **1** to arrange (letters) to form a word; *of letters* to form (a word) *16-*. **2** to (have the ability to) understand the arrangement of letters forming a word *17-*. **3** to complete (literary writing) with difficulty *e19*. **4** to consider, scan *e19*. **5** to read *15-e19*. [OFr *espeller*]

spell²·¹, †**spel**, †**spale** /spɛl/ *n* **1** *witchcraft, folklore* an incantation, a charm *la17-*. **2** discourse, talk; a tale, a story *la14-18*. **3** a device, a trick *e18*. [OE *spel* discourse, speech, fable]

spell²·² /spɛl/ *v* **1** to talk; to tell (someone) (something) *la15-16*. **2** to state falsely; to exaggerate *la18-19, 20- SW*. **3** to swear, blaspheme *la19- NE T C Bor*. [OE *spellian*]

spell see SPALE¹·¹, SPEEL¹·¹, SPEEL¹·², SPELD¹·¹

spen see SPEAN

spence, **spense**, †**spens** /spɛns/ *n* a storeroom, a pantry; an inner apartment of a house, used as a sitting room or small bedroom *la13-19, 20- NE C SW*. †**spensar**, **spenser** the person in charge of the provisions in a household; a steward *15*. [aphetic form of OFr *despense*]

spencie /ˈspɛnsi/ *n* the storm petrel *Hydrobates pelagicus 19- Sh*. [perhaps from its appearance of wearing a short regency *spencer* jacket, with -IE¹ suffix]

spend¹ /spɛnd/ *v pt* **spent** †**spendit 1** to pay out, disburse, expend (money or, originally, also goods or property); to incur expenditure *la14-*. **2** to pass, occupy, use (time, one's life) *la14-*. **3** *of time* to elapse, pass *la19- Sh*. **4** to use, employ (one's faculties or body); to expend (effort) *15-16*. **5** to use up, consume (a commodity); to make use of (raw materials) *15-17*. **6** to suffer the loss of, lose (one's life) *la15-16*. **spending 1** the paying out (of money) *la15-*. **2** what may be spent, money, means of support *la14-17*. **3** use; consumption (of something); provisions *16-17*. **spent** *of a fish, especially herring* having spawned, in poor condition after spawning *la18-*. **spendrife** (a) spendthrift *19- NE T*. [OE **spendan*]

spend²·¹ /spɛnd/ *n* a spring, a bound, a leap *19- EC*. [see the verb]

†**spend**²·² /spɛnd/ *v* **1** *of a liquid* to spatter, splash *e16*. **2** *of a person or horse* to spring, leap, dash *e19*. [perhaps a conflation of STEND¹·² with SPANG²·²]

spend see SPEAN

spengyie see SPAINGIE

spens, **spense** see SPENCE

spent /spɛnt/ *n* a fish in poor condition after spawning *la19-*; compare *spent* (SPEND¹). **spyntie**, **speinty** = SPENT *la19- NE*. [from the ptp of SPEND¹]

spent see SPEND¹

spentacles, **spectacles**, †**spartickles**, †**spectaklis** /ˈspɛntəkəlz, ˈspɛktəkəlz/ *n* a device for assisting vision, spectacles *16-*. [altered form of Eng *spectacles*]

spenyi see SPAINGIE

sper, *NE* **sperr** /spɛr/ *v* **1** to brace (the limbs) in order to resist a strain *la19- Sh NE*. **2** to kick out with the legs *20- Sh*. **3** to stride out so as to stretch the legs *la19- Sh*. [Norw dial *sperra*]

sper see SPAR¹·¹, SPAR¹·², SPEAR, SPEIR¹·²

spere see SPEAR, SPEIR¹·²

spere ribb see SPARE RIB

sperfle, †**sparple**, †**sparpal**, †**sparsle** /ˈspɛrfəl/ *v* **1** to scatter, spread about, disperse; to squander *la15-*. **2** to distribute, divide (among persons); to disseminate *16-e17*. [ME *sparplen*, OFr *esparpeillier*]

sperge see SPAIRGE¹·¹, SPAIRGE¹·²

spering see SPEIRIN¹·¹

sperit see SPEERIT¹·¹

sperituall see SPEERITUAL

sperk see SPARK¹·¹

sperling see SPIRLING

†**sperthe** *n* a battle-axe *19 literary*. [ME *sparthe*, ON *sparða*]

speshie, †**specie**, †**spece**, †**space** /ˈspiʃi/ *n* **1** a class, sort or kind *17- N NE T C*. **2** money in the form of coins; a denomination of coinage *la16-e18*. **3** a visible, actual or apparent form (of something); *Christian Church* the physical form of the elements of the Eucharist *la16-e17*. [from the Lat phrase *in specie* specifically, perhaps mistaken as a singular of SPECIES, thought of as plural]

spet, **spete** see SPEET¹·¹, SPEET¹·²

speuchan see SPLEUCHAN

speug, **spug** /spjʌg, spʌg/ *n* **1** a sparrow *Passer domesticus 19-*. **2** a child; a small, plucky person; an insignificant, helpless person *20- T EC SW*. **spuggie**, **speugie** a sparrow *20-*. [altered form of SPURG]

speun see SPUIN

spew see SPUE¹·¹, SPUE¹·²

spey see SPAE¹·²

speyt see SPATE¹·¹

spey wife see SPAEWIFE

spiae /ˈspje/ *n* derision, scorn, mockery *la19- Sh*. [Norw dial *spe*]

spial see SPYALE

spiall /ˈspjal/ *n* a tall, slender person *19- Sh*. [Norw dial *spjole*]

spice¹·¹, †**spyce** /spʌɪs/ *n* **1** an aromatic seasoning for food *15-*. **2** pepper *la18-19, 20- Sh Ork N NE*. †**spicery**, **spiceri** 1 spices *la14-17*. **2** a flavour *e19*. **spicy 1** having the flavour or scent of spices *la18-*. **2** peppered, peppery; proud, testy *la18-*. †**spice house**, **spyshous** (part of) a building used for storing spices *la15-e17*. [ME *spice*, OFr *espice*]

spice¹·², †**spyce** /spʌɪs/ *v* **1** to season with spices; to affect *la15-*. **2** to embalm; to preserve with spices *la15-*. [OFr *espicer*, or from the noun]

†**spicing**, **spyceing** *n* the splicing of ropes *17*. [verbal noun from OFr *espisser* to splice]

spick, spikk /spɪk/ *n* fat, grease, lard; blubber (of a whale or seal) *17- Sh Ork N*. **spikket** excessively fat *20- Sh*. [OE *spic*, ON *spik*]

spicket, spigot, *Bor* **spriggit,** *T* **speekit,** †**spickot** /ˈspɪkət, ˈspɪɡət; *Bor* ˈsprɪɡət; *T* ˈspɪkət/ *n* **1** a vent-peg or tap used to regulate a flow of liquid (on a barrel or cask) *la17-*. **2** an outdoor tap; a stand-pipe supplying water for a locality; a drinking fountain *20-*. [ME *spigot*]

spider *see* SPEEDER

spieker /ˈspɪkər/ *n* a large nail, a spike nail *la19- Sh*. [Norw dial *spikar*, MDu, MLG *spiker*]

spiel, †**speel** /spil/ *n* **1** a curling match *la18-*. **2** any kind of game or play *19*. [shortened form of BONSPIEL, and compare Ger *Spiel* a game]

spiel, speill *see* SPEEL[2.2]

spigot *see* SPICKET

spike *see* SPEAK[1.2]

spikk *see* SPEAK[1.2], SPICK

spil *see* SPALE[1.1], SPALE[1.2], SPILL

spile[1.1] /spʌɪl/ *n* **1** a wooden plug for stopping the vent of a cask, a spigot *20-*. **2** a pointed stake or post used as a support for a wall or the foundation of a building *16-e17*. [MDu, MLG *spile*]

spile[1.2] /spʌɪl/ *v* to hang up (fishing lines) on a pole to be cleaned *20- NE*. **spile tree, spil tree** a pole on which fishing lines are hung to be cleaned or baited *la19- NE*. **spilin tree** = *spile tree 20- N NE EC*. [see the noun]

spile[2], **spoil** /spʌɪl, spɔɪl/ *v* to ruin, wreck, spoil *18-*. Compare SPULYIE[1.2]. [ME *spoilen*, OFr *espoillier*]

spilk /spɪlk/ *v* to shell (peas) *19- NE*. **spilkard** split peas *20- NE*. †**spilkins** = *spilkard la18-19*. [ME *spelked* (of beans) bruised, crushed, pounded; compare Eng *spelk* to bruise (beans)]

spill, †**spyll,** †**spil** /spɪl/ *v pt* **spilt 1** to cause (blood) to be shed *15-*. **2** to cause (liquid) to run out of its container; *of liquid* to run out of its container *15-*. **3** to spoil, damage, mar, ruin *la14-e19, 20- literary*. **4** to kill, put to death; to commit suicide *la14-16*. **5** to violate; to degrade, tarnish morally *la14-e17*. **6** *of food* to rot, spoil; *of weather* to deteriorate *la14-19*. **7** to die, perish; to fail; to come to ruin; to be lost or destroyed; to bring to misery or ruin *la14-e17*. **spilt 1** *of blood* shed *16-*. **2** *of a liquid* that has run out of a container *la16-*. **3** *of a person* leprous *20- Sh*. **4** *of a thing* damaged, rendered unfit for use, ruined *16-17*. [OE *spillan* to kill]

spil tree *see* SPILE[1.2]

spin[1.1] /spɪn/ *n* **1** an action of turning *19-*. **2** a journey, a trip *19-*. **3** a (made-up) story; gossip, rumour *la19- NE*. **aff at a spinner** off at great speed *la18- NE*. **on the spin** on a drinking spree *la19- T WC SW*. [see the verb]

spin[1.2], †**spyn** /spɪn/ *v pt* **spun,** *Ork NE* **span,** *ptp* **spun 1** to make a thread by drawing out and twisting fibres; to twist (fibres) into a thread *la14-*. **2** *of an object* to revolve; to move at speed *19-*. **3** to progress favourably, go well *20- NE T*. **4** *of a cat* to purr *20- Sh Ork*. **5** to weave (a garment, cloth) *16-18*. **6** to roll (tobacco leaf) into a continuous rope or coil, twist (tobacco) *18-19*. **7** to write or tell a story or poetry *la18-19*. **spinner 1** the cranefly or daddy-long-legs *Tipula oleracea 19- N NE T C Bor*. **2** a spider of the order *Araneidae 19, 20- NE*. **spinni** a device for twisting horsehair for fishing lines *20- Sh*. **spinnie** a spinning-wheel *la19- Sh*. **spinnin jenny 1** = *spinner* 1 *20-*. **2** a home-made spinning toy *20- WC Bor*. **spinnin meggie** = *spinner* 1 *la19- NE T C Bor*. **spinwillie** = *spinner* 1 *20- Sh*. **spin aff** to depart at speed *la19- Ork*. **spin the knife** a party game *20- T C SW*. [OE *spinnan*]

spindill, spindle *see* SPINLE

spindrift, *NE* **speen-drift,** *Sh* **spündrift** /ˈspɪndrɪft; *NE* ˈspindrɪft; *Sh also* ˈspʌndrɪft/ *n* **1** spray whipped up by gusts of wind and driven across the tops of waves *la16-*. **2** snow blown up from the ground in swirls by gusts of wind, driving snow *19- NE EC Uls*. [unknown]

spink[1] /spɪŋk/ *n* **1** a flower, especially the common primrose *Primula vulgaris*, also the lady's smock *Cardamine pratensis* or maiden pink *Dianthus deltoides la18-19, 20- NE T EC*. **2** an attractive young person *19*. [altered form of PINK[1]]

spink[2.1] /spɪŋk/ *n* **1** the chaffinch *Fringilla coelebs la17-19, 20- Bor*; compare GOWDSPINK. **2** *derogatory* a person *e16*. [ME *spinke* a finch, probably onomatopoeic]

spink[2.2] /spɪŋk/ *v of a bird* to utter the note 'spink' *la19-*. [see the noun]

spinle, spinnel, spinnle, spindle, †**spindill,** †**spyndill,** †**spynnill** /ˈspɪnəl, ˈspɪndəl/ *n* **1** an instrument used in spinning to twist fibres into thread *15-*. **2** the quantity of yarn that can be spun on a spindle at one time, a (varying) measure in which yarn was sold *la16-19*. **3** a rod used as an axis on which or by means of which something revolves *la15-*. **4** a weather-vane *16-e19*. **5** a rod on which the core of a gun is moulded *16*. †**spinnelled** *mainly of diseased teats of animals* spindle-shaped *18-19*. **spindle-wids** splinters *la19- Sh*. **spindle-shanks, spindle-shank** *derogatory* a person with long legs; a long leg *la18-*. [OE *spinel*]

spinnel, spinnle *see* SPINLE

spinner /ˈspɪnər/ *v* to move with a spinning or spiral motion; to move swiftly *19, 20- literary*. [frequentative form of SPIN[1.2]]

spiog *see* SPYOG[1.1]

†**spire**[1] *n* a vertical timber structure reaching from floor to ceiling in a building, found at the end of a wooden seat in a church or by the fireside in a house *16-e19*. **spire wall** a wall or screen between the fireplace and the door of a cottage *18-e19*; compare HALLAN. [OE *spīr* a spike, a blade of grass]

spire[2], †**spyre** /spaer/ *v* **1** to dry out; to become parched *la18-19, 20- Bor*. **2** *of hot, dry weather or wind* to (cause to) wither, dry up *19- EC Bor*. **3** to exude, emit *e17*. **4** to breathe (life) in *la15*. [ME *spiren* to exhale, OFr *spirer*, Lat *spīrāre* to breathe]

spirie *adj* tall, slender, spindly *19*. [SPIRE[1] a spike, a blade + -IE[2]]

spirit *see* SPEERIT[1.1], SPEERIT[1.2]

spiritual, spirituall *see* SPEERITUAL

spirk *see* SPARK[1.1]

spirl[1] /spɪrl/ *n* **1** a small, slender shoot *20- EC Bor*. **2** a tall, thin person *20- NE Bor*. **spirlie, spurly** *adj* slender, thin, spindly *la18-19, 20- T EC Bor Uls*. **spirlie** *n* a slender person *19, 20- EC Bor*. [probably a derivative of SPIRE[1] in the sense of a young shoot, OE *spīr* a spike, a blade; compare Norw dial *spirl* a long, thin woman or tree]

†**spirl**[2] *v* to run about, whirl around *19*. [altered form of PIRL[1.2]]

spirling, sparling, †**sperling** /ˈspɪrlɪŋ, ˈsparlɪŋ/ *n* the smelt *Osmerus eperlanus*, or, perhaps, other small fish *16-19, 20- NE T WC*. [AN *esperlinge*]

spirtle *see* SPURTLE[1]

spit, †**spitt** /spɪt/ *v pt* **spat,** †**spittit,** *ptp* **spitten,** †**spittit** to eject (saliva) from the mouth *la14-*. **spittery** a spittoon *la17*. **spittin 1** frequently *pl* spittle *la14-*. **2** a small hot-tempered person or animal *19- NE*. **spitty** a nickname for someone who spits frequently *20- Sh Ork NE EC*. **spitten image** the exact likeness *20-*. **spit and gie ower** to give in, admit defeat *19, 20- NE T*. **spit and gie up** = *spit and gie ower 20- NE T*. **spit upon** to make the slightest impression, get close to *la19- Sh*. [OE *spittan*]

spit see SPEET[1.1], SPEET[1.2]

spital, spittal, †spittaill, †spytaile /'spɪtəl/ *n* **1** a shelter or rest-house for travellers *18-19, 20- historical*. **2** a house or place of refuge for the sick and destitute, a charity hospital; lands whose revenue supported a hospital *13-e19*. [aphetic form of HOSPITAL]

spite /spʌɪt/ *n* **1** malice, ill-will, hatred *la15-*. **2** a disappointment, a cause for annoyance or grief *la19, 20- NE WC*. **in spite of your teeth** despite (someone's) wishes or efforts, in defiance of (someone) *la16-*. [ME *spite*, aphetic form of DESPITE[1.1]]

spitle see SPITTLE

spitt see SPIT

spittaill, spittal see SPITAL

spitten see SPIT

spitter[1.1] /'spɪtər/ *n* **1** a slight shower of rain or snow *19, 20- N NE T C SW*. **2** *pl* small drops of wind-driven rain or snow *la18-19, 20- NE T SW*. [see the verb]

spitter[1.2] /'spɪtər/ *v of rain or snow* to fall in small drops or flakes, drizzle *la19-*. [frequentative form of SPIT]

spittit see SPIT

spittle, †spattill, †spitle /'spɪtəl/ *n* **1** saliva, spit *16-*. **2** a quantity of saliva ejected at one time *18-*. [OE *spātl* with influence from SPIT]

splairge[1.1] /splerdʒ/ *n* a splash, sprinkling or splodge of water or mud *19- C SW Bor*. [see the verb]

splairge[1.2] /splerdʒ/ *v* **1** to slander, besmirch *la18- C*. **2** to bespatter, splash (a person) *19- T C Bor*. **3** to sprinkle, splash (a liquid) *20-*. **4** to fly or splash in all directions, scatter *19, 20- SW Bor*. **5** to splash, move clumsily through water or mud *la19, 20- T Bor*. **6** to run wild, squander one's resources or talents heedlessly *la19, 20- NE T*. **splairge oot** to sprawl *20- EC*. [altered form of SPAIRGE[1.2]]

splash[1] /splaʃ/ *n* the plaice *Pleuronectes platessa 20- NE*. **splashack** = SPLASH[1] *20- N NE*; compare PLASHACK. [altered form of PLASH]

splash[2] /splaʃ/ *v* **1** *of liquid* to dash (up), fly about; *of a person* to cause liquid to splash; to make a splashing noise; to fall with a splash *19-*. **2** to fish with a *splash net la19, 20- H&I WC SW*. **splash net** a net suspended in the water, into which fish are driven by a splashing in the water *la19, 20- H&I SW*. **splash netting** a method of fishing using a *splash net 20- H&I SW*. [EModE *splash*, altered form of PLASH[1.2]]

splash-fitted /'splaʃ fɪtət/ *adj* having a splay foot *la19- NE*. [perhaps figurative from SPLASH[1]]

†splash foot *adj* = SPLASH-FITTED *19*. [perhaps figurative from SPLASH[1]]

splatch[1.1] /splatʃ/ *n* a splodge or blot, especially of something semi-liquid or sticky, a patch of colour or dirt *19-*. [see the verb]

splatch[1.2] /splatʃ/ *v* **1** to bedaub, splash *19, 20- Sh NE T EC Bor*. **2** to splash, flounder through water or mud *20- Sh*. [onomatopoeic]

splatter[1.1] /'splatər/ *n* **1** a splashing, clattering or rattling sound; a commotion *19- N NE T C SW*. **2** a splash of liquid or mud *19- Sh N NE*. **3** a thin sprinkling *20- Sh T*. [see the verb]

splatter[1.2] /'splatər/ *v* **1** to scatter, splash, sprinkle about, spatter *la19-*. **2** to blurt out, babble, spout (words) *la18-19, 20- WC*. **3** to bespatter, bedaub, splash with liquid or mud *19-*. **4** to splash noisily; to move about, walk or run with a clattering or rattling noise *19, 20- Sh N NE T SW Bor*. [onomatopoeic]

splay[1.1] /sple/ *n* a seam finished by hemming the upper projecting edge over the lower one *19, 20- NE WC*. [see the verb]

splay[1.2] /sple/ *v sewing* to finish a seam by hemming the upper projecting edge down over the lower one *19, 20- Sh Ork NE C SW*. [Eng *splay* to bevel]

splay[2] /sple/ *n* a stroke, a slap *19- Bor*. [perhaps extended use of Eng *splay*; compare SPLAY ON]

splay on /'sple ɔn/ *v* to work vigorously *20- EC Bor*. [perhaps extended use of Eng *splay*]

spleen, †splene /splin/ *n* **1** an organ in vertebrates that regulates red blood cells and the immune system; the spleen *la15-*. **2** a grudge; spite, ill-will, resentment; anger *17-*. **3** the spleen seen as the seat of the emotions *la15-e17*. **†from the splene, fra the splene** from the heart *la15-16*. **†to the splene** to the core, to the heart *la16*. [ME *splene*, OFr *esplen*, Lat *splēn*]

spleet[1.1] /split/ *n* **1** a splinter *la19- Sh*. **2** the armhole of a jersey *20- Sh*. Compare SPLIT[1.1]. [EModE *spleet* a small strip of split wood, perhaps MDu *spleet*]

spleet[1.2], **†spleit** /split/ *v pt, ptp* **spleet** to break, split, burst; originally to break up (a ship); *of a ship* to break up *la17- Sh Ork N NE T EC Bor*. Compare SPLIT[1.2]. **spleeter** a person who splits fish and removes the backbone *la19- Sh N NE*. [EModE *spleet* to split; compare SPLIT[1.2] and LG *spleeten*]

spleeter[1.1], **spleiter** /'splitər/ *n* **1** a splash, a patch of spilt liquid, a blot *20- NE T H&I*. **2** a wind-driven shower of rain or snow *20- NE*. [see the verb]

spleeter[1.2], **spleyter** /'splitər, 'splʌɪtər/ *v* to spill, spatter messily *20- NE T*. [onomatopoeic; compare SPLEUTER[1.2]]

spleet new /split 'nju/ *adj* = SPLIT NEW *la18-*. [variant of SPLIT NEW; compare SPLEET[1.2]]

spleit see SPLEET[1.2]

spleiter see SPLEETER[1.1]

splender see SPLINDER

splenner /'splɛnər/ *v* to stride; to stand with the feet apart *19- SW*. [unknown]

splenshen /'splɛnʃən/ *n* a large nail or spike *la19- Sh*. Compare PLENSHIN. [altered form of PLENSHIN]

splent see SPLINT

splente coall see SPLINTY

splerrie /'splere/ *v* to bespatter, splash with liquid or dirt *20- EC*. [altered form of SLAIRY[1.2]]

splet see SPLIT[1.2]

spleuchan, speuchan /'spluxən, 'spjuxən/ *n* **1** a tobacco pouch *la18-*. **2** a pouch for holding money *la18-19, 20- Ork NE T SW Uls*. **3** a woman's genitals *la18*. [Gael *spliùchan*]

spleut /splut/ *n* (the noise caused by) a sudden spluttering gush of liquid *la19- NE*. [onomatopoeic]

spleuter[1.1], **splooter** /'splutər/ *n* **1** a sudden gush, a wet mess; wet mud *la19- NE T Uls*. **2** weak watery drink *la19- NE*. **3** diarrhoea *20- T*. **4** a dirty, messy person *20- T*. [see the verb]

spleuter[1.2], **splooter** /'splutər/ *v* **1** to burst or gush out with a spluttering noise; to spill in a messy, splashing manner *la19- NE T*. **2** to flounder; to splash around *20- T*. [onomatopoeic]

spleuterie[1.1], **spyooterie** /'splutəre, 'spjutəre/ *n* weak watery food; a dirty mess *la19- NE*. [see the adj]

spleuterie[1.2], **splootery** /'splutəre/ *adj* **1** *of weather* wet, rainy *20- NE T EC*. **2** weak and watery *la19- NE*. [SPLEUTER[1.2] + -IE[2]]

splew /splu/ *v* to spit out, spew, vomit *19, 20- NE*. [altered form of SPUE[1.2]]

spleyter see SPLEETER[1.2]

splice /splʌɪs/ *n* a sliver of wood, a splinter *20- T EC Bor Uls*. [altered form of SCLICE[1.1]]

splicer /'splʌɪsər/ *n* an instrument for twisting straw ropes *la20- C Bor*. [Eng *splice* to join ropes, with agent suffix]

splinder, †**splender** /ˈsplɪndər/ *n* a splinter, a fragment *15-19, 20- Sh Ork*. [ME *splinter*, MDu *splinter*, *splenter*; compare Norw dial *splindre*]

splinder new, *SW* **splinner new** /splɪndər ˈnju; *SW* splɪnər ˈnju/ *adj* brand-new, absolutely new *19, 20- Sh SW*. [SPLINDER, by analogy with SPLIT NEW]

splint, †**splent** /splɪnt/ *n* **1** a piece of armour, for the arms and legs *15-e19*. **2** a splinter, chip or fragment *la19-*. **3** = SPLINT COAL *la18-19, 20- C*. [MDu, MLG *splinte*, MLG *splente* a metal plate or pin]

splint coal /ˈsplɪnt col/ *n* a hard coarse splintering coal which burns with great heat *la18-19, 20- C*. [SPLINT + COAL]

splint new, †**splent new** /splɪnt ˈnju/ *adj* = SPLIT NEW *la19- T C SW*. [SPLINT, by analogy with SPLIT NEW]

splinty /ˈsplɪnte/ *adj of coal* like SPLINT COAL *20- C*. †**splinty coall**, **splente coall** = SPLINT COAL *la17-e18*. [SPLINT + -*y* (-IE¹)]

split¹·¹ /splɪt/ *n* **1** a cut, a tear *20-*. **2** a quarrel, a rift *18-*. **3** *weaving* a small piece of thin metal, originally split reed or cane, forming one of the divisions through which a warp thread passes in a loom *la18-19, 20 T C Bor*. **4** a piece of wood formed by splitting, *eg* an unfinished barrel stave *la17*. [see the verb]

split¹·² /splɪt/ *v pt* **split**, *Ork N T EC Bor* **splet 1** to break (in pieces), rend (in two), cleave lengthwise or along the grain *17-*. **2** to divide, separate; *of a religious sect* to secede *la18-*. **3** *curling* to separate (two stones lying together) by striking them with a third *la19-*. **4** to part (the hair) *20- NE C SW Uls*. [MDu *splitten*]

split new /splɪt ˈnju/ *adj* brand-new, absolutely new *la17-*. [ptp of SPLIT¹·² + NEW¹·²]

splitter¹·¹ /ˈsplɪtər/ *n* (the noise of) a splashing or splattering of liquid; a hubbub *la19-*. [see the verb]

splitter¹·² /ˈsplɪtər/ *v* to make a spluttering noise; to make a mess by splashing liquid about *la19- Ork C SW Bor*. [onomatopoeic]

sploit /sploɪt/ *v* to spout, squirt; to splash *la18- Sh NE SW*. [altered form of PLOWT]

sploiter¹·¹ /ˈsploɪtər/ *n* a splash *20- Sh NE*. [see the verb]

sploiter¹·² /ˈsploɪtər/ *v* to splash, spill *20- Sh NE*. [frequentative form of SPLOIT]

splooter *see* SPLEUTER¹·¹, SPLEUTER¹·²

splootery *see* SPLEUTERIE¹·²

splore¹·¹ /splor/ *n* **1** a party, a period of noisy enjoyment, alcoholic revelry *la18-*. **2** an exploit, an escapade *19-*. **3** a controversy, a quarrel; a state of excitement or commotion, a fuss *la18-19, 20- NE WC Bor*. [unknown]

splore¹·² /splor/ *v* **1** to frolic, make merry *la18-19, 20- T C Bor*. **2** to show off, boast, brag *19- C*. [unknown]

†**sploy** *n* a frolic; a funny story *la18-19*. [altered form of PLOY¹, perhaps with influence from *exploit*]

splunge /splʌndʒ, splʌndʒ/ *v* to splash in water; to become soaked *la19- C Bor*. [altered form of PLUNGE¹·²]

splunt /splʌnt/ *v* to go wooing or courting *19- SW Bor*. [unknown]

splurt¹·¹ /splʌrt/ *n* a spurt, a splutter, a sharp movement; a minor fracas *19, 20- T*. [see the verb]

splurt¹·² /splʌrt/ *v* to squirt, eject liquid from the mouth in a splash *la18, 20- Sh N T*.

splush /splʌʃ/ *n* plush *20- NE C Bor*. [altered form of Eng *plush*]

spoach¹·¹, †**spotch** /spotʃ/ *n* a prying, inquisitive person *19- Bor*. [see the verb]

spoach¹·², **spotch** /spotʃ, spotʃ/ *v* **1** to poach *la16-19, 20- SW Bor*. **2** to sponge, scrounge *19, 20- Bor*. **3** to pry, rummage *20- Bor*. **spoacher 1** a poacher *19, 20- Bor*. **2** a sponger, a scrounger *19, 20- Bor*. [altered form of POACH]

spoag /spog/ *n* a joke, a jibe *20- Ork*. [Dan *spøg*]

spoag *see* SPAIK

spoat, **spat**, **spot** /spot, spat, spɔt/ *n* **1** a mark of a different colour; a stain, a blemish; originally a moral stain, stigma or disgrace *15-*. **2** a place; originally a small extent of land; a particular point or area *la12-*. **3** a small piece or amount; a drop *19-*. **spatril** a musical note, especially as written on a score *19-*. **spottie** *see like spottie* (LIKE¹·⁴). **spat o preens** a round pin-cushion with a supply of pins in it *19, 20- NE*. [OE *spot* a speck, ON *spottr* a small piece]

spoil *see* SPILE²

spoken, **spokkyn** *see* SPEAK¹·²

spoliate, **spolʒe** *see* SPULYIE¹·²

spon, **spön** *see* SPUIN

†**spone** *v* to spend *la15*. [aphetic form of DISPONE]

spone *see* SPUIN

sponge *see* SPOONGE¹·¹, SPOONGE¹·²

sponget /ˈspɔŋɡət/ *adj of cattle* black with white markings *la19- Sh*. [Norw dial *spongad* spangled]

sponk *see* SPUNK¹·¹

†**sponsible** *adj* responsible, reliable, respectable *16-19*. [aphetic form of RESPONSIBLE]

spool *see* SPULE¹

spoon *see* SPUIN

spoonge¹·¹, **sponge**, †**spounge**, †**spunge** /spʌndʒ, spʌndʒ/ *n* a sponge; originally also a brush *la15-*. [OE *sponge*]

spoonge¹·², **sponge**, †**spounge** /spʌndʒ, spʌndʒ/ *v* to clean with a sponge; to brush *la16-*. [see the noun]

spoot¹·¹, **spout**, †**spowt** /sput, spʌut/ *n* **1** a pipe or conduit for conveying water or waste *16-*. **2** a projection from which liquid issues; a lip to facilitate pouring *la16-*. **3** a forceful discharge of water; a swiftly-flowing stream; a spring, a well *la16-*. **4** the razor fish *16-*. **5** frequently in place-names, a narrow enclosed pathway; a gully in a cliff-face *19-*. **6** a horizontal roof gutter *18-19, 20- Sh Ork NE T EC Bor*. **7** frequently in place-names, a waterfall, a cataract *16-, 20- Sh T C SW Bor*. **8** an outside tap or standpipe *la19- NE C SW Bor*. **9** (a plant stem used as) a water-pistol *la19, 20- Sh C SW*. **10** a small quantity of liquid *20- C SW Bor*. **11** a rush, dart or sudden movement *la18-19, 20- Sh N EC*. **12** an implement used in dyeing *16*. **13** a cascade of excrement *e16*. **spoutie** *of soil or ground* full of springs, marshy, undrained *la17-19, 20- NE T EC*. **spoutiness** a soggy condition (of soil) *la18-e19*. †**spoutrach** weak, thin liquid *19*. **spoutie-drum** = *spout-girse 20- Sh*. **spout-fish** the razor fish *18-*. **spout-girse** angelica *Angelica archangelica 20- Ork*. **spoot-gun**, **spout-gun** a popgun *la19- EC SW*. †**spout-well**, **spoot-well** a spring of water; a well *la16-19*. †**spout-whale** *in Orkney and the North* a porpoise *Phocoena phocoena la17-19*. [see the verb]

spoot¹·², **spout**, †**spowt** /sput, spʌut/ *v* **1** to discharge liquid forcefully *15-*. **2** *of liquid* to issue forcefully or copiously *16-*. **3** to dart, spring, bound out suddenly *19- Sh N T C SW*. **spoot-ma-gruel** any unappetizing food *20- NE*. †**spout oot** = SPOOT¹·² (sense 3) *la19*. [ME *spouten*, MDu *spouten*, MLG *spūten*]

spör, **spuir** /spør/ *v* to ask, enquire about; to propose marriage *la19- Sh Ork*. **spuirin bottle** a bottle of whisky offered by the prospective bridegroom to the parents of his intended bride *la19- Sh*. **spuir up** to search for; to turn up *la19- Sh*. [Norw *spørre*]

spord *see* SPURD

sporran /'spɔrən/ *n* the pouch worn in front of a man's kilt, used to hold money and other small articles *la18-*. [Gael *sporan*]

sporrow *see* SPARRA

sport[1.1] /spɔrt/ *n* (a) game; (an) entertainment, recreation or amusement; a joke *la15-*. †**sportsum** entertaining *16*. [aphetic form of Older Scots *disport*, AN *disport*]

sport[1.2] /spɔrt/ *v* 1 to amuse or entertain oneself, especially by taking part in an activity or pastime, enjoy oneself *15-*. 2 to display (an attitude); to wear (a hat) *19-*. [from the noun or aphetic form of Older Scots *disport*, AN *desporter*]

†**sportour** *n* a person who amuses others, a jester *16*. [SPORT[1.2], with agent suffix]

spot *see* SPOAT

spotch *see* SPOACH[1.1], SPOACH[1.2]

spoucher, †**spoutcheor** /'sputʃər/ *n* a ladle or scoop for baling a boat or lifting fish from a net *16-*. [ME *spuchour*, OFr *espuchoir*, from *espuchier* to drain, empty of water]

spoug *see* SPYOG[1.1]

spounge *see* SPOONGE[1.1], SPOONGE[1.2]

spounk *see* SPUNK[1.1]

spouse[1.1], †**spous**, †**spows** /spʌus/ *n* a married person, a husband or wife *la14-*. †**spousage 1** marriage, wedlock *15-e17*. **2** the act or ceremony of marriage, a wedding *la15-e16*. **3** = SPOUSE[1.1] *e16*. †**spousal 1** = *spousage 1 la14-15*. **2** = *spousage 2 15-e16*. †**spous-brekare** an adulterer *16-e17*. [AN *spous(e)*]

†**spouse**[1.2] *v* **1** to give in marriage *15-e16*. **2** to take as a husband or wife, marry *la14-e16*. **spousit 1** married *la14-e17*. **2** born in wedlock, legitimate *15-e16*. **spouse one's fortune** to try one's luck, seek one's fortune *e19*. **spouse a quarrell** to take up a cause *la16*. [AN *espouser*]

†**spousing** *n* marriage; betrothal; a wedding ceremony *la15-18*. **spousing chalmyr** the bedchamber of a newly married couple *16*. **spousing goune** a wedding dress *la15-16*. **spousing ring** a wedding ring *16-e17*. [verbal noun from SPOUSE[1.2]]

spout *see* SPOOT[1.1], SPOOT[1.2]

spowl *see* SPALD

spows *see* SPOUSE[1.1]

spowt *see* SPOOT[1.1], SPOOT[1.2]

sprach *see* SPRAICH[1.1]

sprachle *see* SPRAUCHLE[1.1], SPRAUCHLE[1.2]

sprack[1] /sprak/ *adj* lively, animated, alert *19*, *20- N NE* mainly *literary*. [Eng *sprack*]

sprack[2] /sprak/ *n* a chip of wood, a splinter; waste scraps of wood or tree branches, wood or straw litter *20- Ork H&I*. [compare Norw dial *sprek* a dry twig]

sprackle *see* SPRAUCHLE[1.1], SPRAUCHLE[1.2], SPRECKLE[1.1], SPRECKLE[1.2]

spraff[1.1] /spraf/ *n* **1** idle chat, small talk *la20-*. **2** boastful talk *la20-*. **spraffer** a braggart, someone who bluffs or tells lies *la20-*. [see the verb]

spraff[1.2] /spraf/ *v* **1** to talk nonsense, chatter idly *la20-*. **2** to boast, brag, embellish *la20-*. [onomatopoeic]

sprag /sprag/ *n* a bradnail *20- NE T C Bor*. [altered form of Eng *sprig*]

spragled *see* SPRECKLE[1.2]

spraich[1.1], *Sh* **sprech**, †**sprauch**, †**sprach** /sprex; *Sh* sprɛx/ *n* a scream, a cry, a shriek; the sound of weeping or wailing; an outcry *16-18, 19- Sh NE EC*. [see the verb]

spraich[1.2], *NE* **sprauch**, *Sh* **sprech** /sprex; *NE* sprɔx; *Sh* sprɛx/ *v* to cry shrilly, scream, shriek; to squawk *19, 20- Sh NE*. [onomatopoeic]

spraich[2] /sprex/ *n* first light, the crack of dawn *la19- C Bor*. **spraich of day** break of day *la19- C Bor*. [SPRAICH[1.1] by analogy with SKREEK]

spraichrie *see* SPREATH

spraikle *see* SPRECKLE[1.1]

spraing[1.1], †**sprayng**, †**sprang** /spreŋ/ *n* a stripe or streak (of colour); a glittering or brightly-coloured ray or beam *16-19, 20- Sh*. [see the verb]

spraing[1.2], †**sprang** /spreŋ/ *v* to variegate, ornament with coloured stripes *16-19, 20- NE*. **spraingit** variegated, striped *la16-*. †**spraingled** = *spraingit 18-e19*. [unknown; compare ME *sprengen*, OE *sprengan* to sprinkle]

spraint *see* SPRENT[1.2]

sprak *see* SPARK[1.1]

sprang *see* SPRAING[1.1], SPRAING[1.2], SPRING[1.2]

sprat *see* SPROT[1]

sprattle[1.1] /'spratəl/ *n* a scramble, a struggle *19, 20- NE*. [see the verb]

sprattle[1.2] /'spratəl/ *v* to scramble, struggle *la18-19, 20- NE C Bor*. [imitative, or metathesis of *spartle* (SPURTLE[2])]

sprauch *see* SPRAICH[1.1], SPRAICH[1.2]

sprauchle[1.1], **sprachle**, **sprackle**, *SW* **sprockle** /'sprɔxəl, 'spraxəl, 'sprakəl; *SW* 'sprɔkəl/ *n* **1** a scramble, a struggle *la19-*. **2** a stunted feeble creature, *20- SW*. [see the verb]

sprauchle[1.2], **sprachle**, **sprackle** /'sprɔxəl, 'spraxəl, 'sprakəl/ *v* to move laboriously or in a hasty, clumsy way (especially upwards), clamber; to struggle (especially to get out of or through something), flounder about *la18-*. [probably onomatopoeic; but compare ON *sprökla*, Faer *sprakla* to sprawl, kick about with the feet]

sprawl[1.1], *N* **spravle** /sprɔl; *N* 'spravəl/ *n* **1** a straggling array (of persons or things) *19-*. **2** a rush, struggle or scramble *la18-19, 20- NE*. [see the verb]

sprawl[1.2], *N* **spravle**, †**sprewl** /sprɔl; *N* 'spravəl/ *v* **1** to lie in an ungainly, spread-out fashion; to (struggle uselessly to) move, crawl, be unable to stand *15-*. **2** to stretch, spread (something) out; *of a thing* to spread out, straggle *19-*. **sprawlach** *v* to sprawl, flail about with the limbs, flounder *19- NE*. **sprawlach** *n* a sprawling, flailing movement of the limbs *19- NE*. [OE *sprēawlian*]

sprayng *see* SPRAING[1.1]

spread *see* SPREID

spreath, **spreeth**, **spreith**, **spreagh**, **spreich**, †**spreth** /sprɛθ, spriθ, sprɛx, sprix/ *n* **1** cattle stolen in a raid, especially by Highlanders into the Lowlands; cattle taken as booty *16-19, 20- historical*. **2** driftwood, wreckage from ships *20- NE T*. **3** a great many, a crowd, a collection *18-19, 20- NE*. **4** booty, plunder; stolen property *15-19*. **5** a foray to steal cattle *la18-19*. †**spreagherie**, **spraichrie 1** household goods of little value, trash *la16-e19*. **2** booty, plunder, loot *la18-e19*. [Gael *sprèidh* cattle]

sprech *see* SPRAICH[1.1], SPRAICH[1.2]

spreckle[1.1], **sprackle**, †**spraikle** /'sprɛkəl, 'sprakəl/ *n* a speckle, a spot, a freckle *16-*. [MHG *spreckel*, Norw *sprekla*, Swed *spräckla*]

spreckle[1.2], **sprackle** /'sprɛkəl, 'sprakəl/ *v* to speckle, mottle *la19-*. **spreckled**, **spreckelt**, *Ork* **spragled**, †**spraikled** speckled, mottled, flecked, variegated *la18-*. [see the noun]

spred, **sprede** *see* SPREID

spree[1.1] /spri/ *n* **1** a spell of noisy, enthusiastic socializing usually involving the consumption of alcohol *la19-*. **2** a (boisterous) quarrel, a spirited argument; a disturbance, a fuss *19*. **on the spree** enjoying a spell of noisy, enthusiastic socializing *la19-*. [see the verb]

spree[1.2] /spri/ *v* to go courting *20- Ork*. [unknown; compare SPREE[2.2]]

spree[2.1], **spry** /spri, sprae/ v to spruce, smarten up la19, 20- T C Bor. [see the adj]

spree[2.2], **spry** /spri, sprae/ adj 1 active, nimble la18-. 2 spruce, neat, smartly dressed 19, 20- T WC. [variant of Eng spry]

spreet see SPEERIT[1.1]

spreeth, spreich see SPREATH

spreid, spread, †**spred**, †**sprede** /sprid, spred/ v 1 to stretch out, extend; to expand, grow, multiply; to open la14-. 2 to scatter; to disseminate; to distribute la14-. 3 to cover, overlay with 15-. 4 to put (a thin layer of) butter or jam on (a slice of bread) 19-. 5 to turn the top covers of (a bed) down or up la19-. **spread-field** the ground where cut peats are spread for drying la16-. [OE sprǣdan]

spreit see SPEERIT[1.1]

spreith see SPREATH

sprenkill see SPRINKLE

†**sprent**[1.1] n 1 a spring, a leap e16. 2 the spring or clasp of a lock la15-19. [see the verb]

†**sprent**[1.2], **spraint** v 1 to move quickly, spring, bound, run la14-19. 2 to split, burst apart (in splinters) 15. [ON *sprenta to make to spring]

sprent[2] /sprent/ n in baking a hollow made in a heap of flour to contain liquid before mixing 19-. [unknown]

spret[1.1], **sprit** /sprɛt, sprɪt/ n a sudden, quick movement, a dash, a leap or bound la19- Sh Ork N. [see the verb]

spret[1.2], **sprit** /sprɛt, sprɪt/ v 1 to scamper; to bound; to run very quickly 19- Sh Ork. 2 of plants to sprout, grow 20- Sh Ork. 3 to unravel, unwind, burst, tear, split 19, 20- Sh Ork. 4 to spread the feet apart when standing 20- Sh. **sprettow** a footless stocking 20- Ork. [Norw dial spretta]

spret see SPEERIT[1.1], SPROT[1]

sprete see SPEERIT[1.1], SPEERIT[1.2]

spreth see SPREATH

sprewl see SPRAWL[1.2]

sprickle[1.1], **sprikkle** /ˈsprɪkəl/ n a struggle, a fight; wriggling la19- Sh. [see the verb]

sprickle[1.2] /ˈsprɪkəl/ v especially of a fish taken out of water to struggle, wriggle, thrash about 19- Sh. [Norw dial sprikla to lay about one, Icel sprikla to throw one's limbs about]

sprig /sprɪg/ n a tune, a snatch of song, a dance tune la19- N NE T C SW. [altered form of SPRING[1.1]]

spriggit see SPICKET

sprikkle see SPRICKLE[1.1]

spriklybag /ˈsprɪkləbag/ n a stickleback Gasterosteus aculeatus 19- WC Uls. [altered form of prickly, the adj from PRICKLE + BAG[1.1]]

spring[1.1], †**spryng** /sprɪŋ/ n 1 the source of a water supply, a well; a stream issuing from such a source 15-. 2 a lively dance tune or dance la15-. 3 the first season of the year 17-. 4 the rise, slope or height (of an arch) 16-19, 20- WC SW. 5 the growth of vegetation, especially in spring la16-e19. 6 a source of virtue 16-17. 7 a tide occurring just after the new or full moon in which the high-water is at its maximum 15-16. 8 a bound, a leap; a pounce or attack la15-e16. †**springald** a young man, a youth 16-e19. **spring-bauk** the main top-rope of a herring-net la19- NE WC. **play yersel a spring** to go one's own way, do what one pleases la18-19, 20- Sh. **play yer ain spring** = play yersel a spring. **spring of the day** dawn e16. **spring o the year** the first season of the year 16-. **tak a spring o yer ain fiddle** = play yersel a spring. [OE spring]

spring[1.2], †**spryng** /sprɪŋ/ v pt **sprang**, ptp **sprung**, †**sprungen**, †**sprungyn**, †**spruning** 1 of liquid to arise, issue (from a source) la14-. 2 of a sentiment to arise from, have as its source 15-. 3 of plants, hair etc to (cause to) grow la14-. 4 to move; to leap, bound la15-. 5 of a person or family to descend, take one's lineage or origins from; to be born from (a mother) 16-. 6 to cause (something) to spring up, appear, or happen la16-. 7 to cause to break, split; to strain (something, oneself) to breaking point la18-19, 20- Sh Ork N. 8 to dance (a reel) e19, 20- Ork. 9 of milk in a churn to begin to form butter 20- Ork. 10 of the day to begin; of the sun or moon to rise 15-16. 11 of news or fame to spread la14-16. [OE springan]

springing /ˈsprɪŋɪŋ/ n grazing from the first grass of the year, spring pasture 20- SW. [verbal noun from SPRING[1.2], with noun-forming suffix]

†**sprinkill, sprynkill** v to wriggle, dart e16. [unknown; compare ME spranklen to emit sparks, from MDu sprankel a spark]

sprinkill see SPRINKLE

sprinkle, †**sprinkill**, †**sprenkill** /ˈsprɪŋkəl/ v to scatter (liquid) in droplets 16-. [ME sprenklen, MLG sprenkelen]

sprit see SPEERIT[1.1], SPRET[1.1], SPRET[1.2], SPROT[1]

sprit-new /sprɪtˈnju/ adj = SPLIT NEW 19, 20- C SW. [altered form of SPLIT NEW]

sprittled see SPURTLED

sproan[1.1] /sprɔn/ n bird excrement 19- Sh. [see the verb]

sproan[1.2] /sprɔn/ v 1 of liquid to spray; to splash, bespatter la19- Sh. 2 of a bird to void excrement 19- Sh. 3 to scatter, radiate, broadcast (signals) la20-. [Norw dial sprǣna to squirt; perhaps influenced by STRONE[1.2]]

sprockle see SPRAUCHLE[1.1]

sprool[1.1] /sprul; Sh sprøl; sprɔl/ n fishing a short length of wire or bone pushed through the sinker of a hand-line, with a hook attached at either end la19- Sh Ork N NE T EC. [unknown]

sprool[1.2] /sprul/ v to fish offshore with a SPROOL[1.1] 20- NE T EC. [unknown]

sproosh /spruʃ/ n lemonade 20- NE. [perhaps shortened form of spruce beer, compare SPRUSH[1.1]; or onomatopoeic, compare SKOOSH[1.1]]

sproot[1.1], **sprout**, †**sprowt** /sprut, sprʌut/ n 1 new growth, a shoot 16-. 2 a Brussels sprout la20-. 3 a child 19- N NE C Bor. [see the verb]

sproot[1.2], **sprout**, SW Bor **spruit** /sprut, sprʌut/ v 1 to (cause to) grow; to spring up 16-. 2 to rub or break off the growing buds of potatoes 20- Sh Ork N NE T. [OE *sprūtan to sprout forth]

sproot[2] /sprut/ v to eject, emit; to spout, spit la19- Sh. [Norw dial spruta]

†**sprose**[1.1] n bragging, boastful talk la18-e19. [see the verb]

sprose[1.2], †**sprowse** /sproz/ v 1 to boast, swagger la18- mainly WC. 2 to exaggerate, 19- C. 3 to brag la18-19. [perhaps altered form of PROSS or Eng prose]

sprot[1], EC Bor **sprat**, WC SW Bor **spret**, H&I **sprut**, SW Bor Uls **sprit** /sprɔt; EC Bor sprat; WC SW Bor sprɛt; H&I sprʌt; SW Bor Uls sprɪt/ n a rush, coarse reedy grass of the genus Juncus la16-. **sprotty** of or like rushes; abounding in rushes 18-19, 20- NE SW. [probably extended sense of SPROT[2]]

†**sprot**[2] n in the Borders a small stick or twig, especially as used for fuel e19 mainly literary. [ME sprote a twig, a chip of wood, OE sprota a shoot, a sprout, a twig]

sproug see SPRUG

sprout see SPROOT[1.1], SPROOT[1.2]

sprowse see SPROSE[1.2]

sprowt see SPROOT[1.1]

spruce see SPRUSH[1.1], SPRUSH[1.2], SPRUSH[1.3]

sprud /sprʌd/ *n* a knife for prising limpets from a rock *la19- NE*. [altered form of Eng *spud* applied to various (chisel-shaped) tools]

sprug, sproug /sprʌg, sprʌug/ *n* **1** a sparrow *Passer domesticus 19, 20- N C*. **2** a bright but undersized boy *20- N C*. [metathesis of SPURG]

spruice *see* SPRUSH[1.3]

spruit *see* SPROOT[1.2]

sprung, sprungen, sprungyn, spruning *see* SPRING[1.2]

sprunt[1] /sprʌnt/ *v* to sprint *la19- H&I Bor*. [altered form of Eng *sprint*]

sprunt[2] /sprʌnt/ *n* weaving yarn stolen by a weaver *20- EC*. [unknown]

sprush[1.1], **spruce, †sprusche** /spruʃ, sprus/ *n* **1** a coniferous, evergreen tree of the family *Pinaceae 17-*. **2** a smartening up, a tidying or setting in order *la19, 20- Sh T C*. **3** Prussia *16-17*. **†sprush stane** a unit of weight in use in Prussia, the Baltic region, equal to 28 lb troy (25 lb avoirdupois, 11 kg) *16-e18*. [see the adj]

sprush[1.2], **spruce** /spruʃ, sprus/ *v* to smarten up *la19-*. [see the adj]

sprush[1.3], **spruce, †spruice** /spruʃ, sprus/ *adj* **1** smart in appearance *17-*. **2** brisk, smart in one's movements, spry *la18-*. [altered form of Older Scots *pruce* Prussian, OFr *prusse* Prussia(n)]

sprushle /'sprʌʃəl, 'spruʃəl/ *v* to scuffle *19, 20- NE T*. [altered form of STRUISSLE[1.2]]

†sprush-new *adj* absolutely new *e18*. Compare SPLIT NEW. [SPRUSH[1.3] + NEW[1.2]]

sprut *see* SPROT[1]

†sprutlis, sprutillis *npl* spots, speckles *e16*. [MLG *sprutle* a freckle]

sprutlit, spruttit *see* SPURTLED

spry *see* SPREE[2.1], SPREE[2.2]

spryng *see* SPRING[1.1], SPRING[1.2]

sprynkill *see* SPRINKILL

spue[1.1], **spew** /spju/ *n* **1** a retch, a vomiting motion *19-*. **2** (a puff of) smoke *la19- Sh T WC*. **3** an ugly or disgusting sight *20- Sh*. [see the verb]

spue[1.2], **spew** /spju/ *v* **1** to vomit; to discharge (something noxious) from the mouth *la15-*. **2** to bring forth or out abusive language *la16-*. **3** *of liquid or smoke* to flow, pour (out) in a copious stream, billow out *la18-*. **4** *of a pudding or sausage* to burst, split open *la19- Sh NE*. **spewins** vomit *20- Sh C*. **spuin fou** replete, especially with drink, to the point of vomiting *e18, 20- NE T SW*. [OE *spīwan*]

spug *see* SPEUG

spuilzie *see* SPULYIE[1.1], SPULYIE[1.2]

spuin, spune, spoon, *Sh* **spön**, *Ork* **speun**, *NE* **speen**, **†spone, †spon** /spɪn, spun; *Sh Ork* spøn; *NE* spin/ *n* **1** a utensil, a handle with a bowl-shaped end, for stirring or conveying liquid or soft food *15-*. **2** *golf* a wooden club with a slightly hollowed head and backward-sloping face, corresponding to the number 3 wood *19-*. **3** a roofing shingle *16*. **spunefu**, *NE* **speenifu, †sponfull** enough to fill a spoon *la15-*. **spoon-creel** a small basket hung on a kitchen wall for holding spoons *19- NE T C SW*. **speun-cubbie** = *spoon-creel la19- Ork*. **spune-gabbit** having a thick, protruding lower lip *20- C*. **spoon-meat, spune-meat** soft or liquid food eaten with a spoon *la19- Ork NE T C SW*. **have mair in the heid than the spune pits in** to be more than usually clever *la19- NE T SW*. **have naithin in the heid but what the spune pits in** to be more than usually stupid *la19- NE T WC SW*. **mak a spune or spoil a horn** to either succeed or fail in a big way *19-*. **pit in yer spune** to interfere *20- NE C*. **the spön o the breest** the hollow at the bottom of the breast-bone *20- Sh*. [OE *spōn* a thin piece of wood]

spulder /'spʌldər/ *n* a convulsion, a violent, noisy disturbance *20- Sh*. [perhaps altered form of PULDER]

spule[1], **spool** /spul/ *n* **1** a bobbin *16-*. **2** the shuttle in which the bobbin is placed *19, 20- Sh T*. [MLG *spōle*, OFr *espole*]

†spule[2] *n* a roofing shingle *la15-e16*. [altered form of SPUIN]

spule *see* SPAUL

spulie *see* SPULYIE[1.2]

spulyie[1.1], **spulzie, spuilzie, †spulʒe, †spolʒe** /'spulji, 'spulje/ *n* **1** (an instance of) spoliation, plundering, depredation, devastation; *law* the wrongful taking or theft of movable goods; spoliation as alleged theft, a claim at law for spoliation *15-19, 20-*. **2** *law* seizure of goods, claiming them as one's own, as payment for a debt or with the intention of returning them after use *la15-19*. **3** booty, spoil, plunder *16-*. **4** jetsam, anything cast ashore; trash, junk *la19- Sh Ork NE*. **5** an uproar, a fracas, a commotion *la19- Sh Ork*. **6** confusion, a mix-up *20- Ork*. **7** a legal action for spoliation *la16-17*; compare *action of spuilzie* (ACTION). **†under spulʒe** *law, of land or its produce* subject to an action for spoliation *e17*. [OFr *espoille*, AN *espuille*]

spulyie[1.2], **spulzie, spuilzie, spulie, †spulʒe, †spolʒe** /'spulji, 'spulje, 'spuli/ *v ptp also* **†spoliate 1** to despoil, plunder; rob (a person or place) *la14-*. **2** to deprive (someone) of (something), usually by stealing, violence or illegality *15-*. **3** to damage, harm *15-*. **4** to take as spoil or plunder, steal; *law* to carry off (a person's movable possessions) without legal warrant or against his will *15-*. **5** to loot, plunder, thieve, maraud *la15-19, 20- NE T*. **6** to strip of clothes or office, unfrock; to strip of a quality or benefit *la14-17*. **7** to take a cut of meat from a carcass before it is sold in the public market *la16-e17*. **8** to deprive a person of his life *16*. Compare SPILE[2].

†spulyier, spulʒear a robber, a plunderer *15-e19*. [OFr *espoillier*, AN *espuiller*]

spun *see* SPIN[1.2]

spunder[1.1] /'spøndər/ *n* a gallop *la19- Sh Ork*. [see the verb]

spunder[1.2] /'spøndər/ *v* to race, rush, gallop *la19- Sh Ork N*. [altered form of SPINNER]

spündrift *see* SPINDRIFT

spune *see* SPUIN

spung[1.1] /spʌŋ/ *n* **1** a purse, a pouch for money, frequently with a spring clasp *18-*. **2** a fob, a watch-pocket in trousers *la18-*. [altered form of ME *pung*, OE *pung*]

†spung[1.2] *v* to rob, steal; to pick a person's pocket *18-19*. [see the noun]

spunge *see* SPOONGE[1.1]

spunk[1.1], *N* **spounk, †sponk** /spʌŋk; *N* spʌuŋk/ *n* **1** a match for producing fire, originally tinder, touchwood or a sliver of wood tipped with sulphur *la17-*. **2** a sliver of wood suitable for making a match, matchwood; a splinter, a chip of wood *19-*. **3** a spark (of fire), a quick flicker of light, a glimmer *16-19, 20- Sh Ork N NE T C*. **4** a trace, an indication; the least particle or vestige of some moral quality *la15-19, 20- Sh Ork N NE T*. **5** a tiny, poor, miserable fire; a domestic fire *la18-19, 20- NE T*. **6** the spark (of life); life *17-19*. **7** a hot-tempered, irascible person *19*. **spunkie 1** = SPUNK[1.1] (sense 3) *19-*. **2** = SPUNK[1.1] (sense 2) *19-*. **3** the will-o-the-wisp, *ignis fatuus 18-*. **4** a spirited, lively young person *19, 20- NE C*. **5** whisky, spirits *la18*. **6** wild-fire, sheet lightning *20- Ork*. **spunk-box** a match-box, originally a tinder-box, a source of fire *18-*. **spunk-wud** = SPUNK[1.1] (sense 6) *19- C*. **a spunk o fire** = SPUNK[1.1] (sense 5). [compare Gael *spong*, IrGael *sponc* tinder]

spunk[1.2] /spʌŋk/ *v* to emit sparks (in all directions) *la19- Sh Ork T*. **spunk oot** *of news or scandal* to leak out, become

spur[1.1] /spʌr/ *n* **1** a device attached to a horserider's heel, used to urge a horse forward *la14-*. **2** an incentive, a stimulus *16-*. **3** a token payment *16*. **spurrie** a quick-moving beetle *la20- Ork*. †**spur-band** a strut or diagonal stay in a roof *16-18*. †**spur haste** great haste *e17*. †**spur silver** money paid to choristers in certain chapels by anyone entering wearing spurs *e16*. †**spur-whang** the leather strap or thong attaching a spur to the heel; something of little value *la17-19*. †**a spur in the head** a drink of alcohol *e18*. [OE *spura*]

spur[1.2] /spʌr/ *v* **1** to use spurs to urge on a horse; to ride quickly *la15-*. **2** to hurry, run fast *20- Sh*. **3** to scrape or scratch around, like a fowl in search of food *19- Bor*. **4** to urge, incite *16-*. **5** to take action *16*. **6** to kick *la15-e19*. [see the noun]

spur[2] /spʌr/ *n* a house sparrow *Passer domesticus 19-*. Compare SPURG, SPRUG, SPUG. **spurdie 1** = SPUR[2] *la19-, Ork NE T EC*. **2** a hedge sparrow *Prunella modularis 20- EC Bor*. **3** a small lively person *la19- NE*. †**spur hawk** = *blue spur hawk* (BLUE[1.2]) *19*. [perhaps Norw dial *sporr*]

spurd, spord /spord/ *n* **1** one of the lobes or flukes of a fish's tail *la19- Sh*. **2** the loop of a fish-hook where it is tied to the line *20- Sh*. **3** *in place-names* a projecting ridge of a coastline partly submerged; a low rocky reef or point *20- Sh*. [Norw dial *spord* a fish's tail]

spurg /spʌrg/ *n* a sparrow *Passer domesticus 19- NE*. Compare SPRUG. **spurgie** = SPURG. [perhaps reduced form of *spurrock, from SPUR[2] + -OCK]

spurkle *see* SPURTLE[1]

spurl /spʌrl/ *v* to struggle, kick or throw the legs or arms about *19, 20- WC SW Bor*. [frequentative form of SPUR[1.2]]

spurly *see* SPIRL[1]

spurn, †spurne /spʌrn/ *v* **1** to resist, reject, repulse; to strike, push *15-*. **2** to meet with disaster *15-e16*. [OE *spurnan*]

spurtelt *see* SPURTLED

spurtle[1], **spirtle**, *Ork N NE T C SW* **spurkle**, †**spurtill** /'spʌrtəl, 'spɪrtəl; *Ork N NE T C SW* 'spʌrkəl/ *n* **1** a wooden utensil for stirring porridge or soup *16-*. **2** an implement for thatching *19- C SW Uls*. **3** *in baking* a long-handled, flat-bladed implement for turning oatcakes, scones etc *16-19, 20- Ork T EC*. **4** a sword *la17-e19*. **spurtle-blade** = SPURTLE (sense 3) *la18- literary*. **spurtle-grup** a sudden gripping pain, a stitch *la19- WC*. **spurtle-legs** stick-like legs *la19- NE C*. **spurtle-leggit** having stick-like legs *la19- NE C SW*. **spurtle shanks** = *spurtle-legs 19- NE C*. [perhaps altered form of ME *spatil*, Lat *spatula* a spatula]

spurtle[2], †**spartle** /'spʌrtəl/ *v* to move the body or limbs in a sprawling or struggling way; to kick about, wriggle *18-19, 20- SW*. Compare SPRATTLE[1.2]. [Du, LG *spartelen*]

spurtled, spurtelt, †sprutlit, †sprittled, †spruttit /'spʌrtəld, 'spʌrtəlt/ *adj* spotted, speckled *la15-19, 20- Bor*. [derivative of SPRUTLIS]

†**spyale, spial** *n* **1** spying; observation, watch *la14-e17*. **2** a spy or spies *la15-e19*. [aphetic form of ME *espiaille*, OFr *espiaille* the action of spying, spies]

spyauck *see* SPAIK
spyaug *see* SPYOG[1.1]
spyce *see* SPICE[1.1], SPICE[1.2]
spyceing *see* SPICING
spyll *see* SPILL
spyn *see* SPIN[1.2]
spyndill *see* SPINLE
spynist *see* SPANYS
spynnill *see* SPINLE
spyntie *see* SPENT

spyog[1.1], *NE WC* **spyaug**, †**spiog** /spjɔg; *NE WC* spjʌug/ *n* **1** a paw, hand, foot or leg *la18-19, 20- Ork N NE WC*; compare SPAG. **2** a bare, stumpy branch *20- N NE*. [Gael *spòg* a paw, a claw]

spyog[1.2] /spjɔg/ *v* to walk in a stilted, stiff-legged or sedate way *la19- Ork SW*. [see the noun]

spyolk *see* SPELK[1.1], SPELK[1.2]
spyooterie *see* SPLEUTERIE[1.1]
spyre *see* SPIRE[2]
spytaile *see* SPITAL
squaak *see* SQUAIK[1.2]

†**squabash** *v* to squash, crush (a person); to quell, demolish (an argument) *e19*. [conflation of SQUASH[1.2] with BASH[1.2]]

†**squabblement** *n* a wrangle, disturbance of the peace *18-19*. [Eng *squabble*, with noun-forming suffix]

squad, *Sh Ork* **swad** /skwɔd; *Sh Ork* swad/ *n* **1** a small number of soldiers *la17-*. **2** a group or bunch of (a particular sort of) people *la18-*. [EModE *squad*, Fr *escouade*]

Squadrone, †Squadronie /skwɔ'drone/ *n* the New Party, a group of politicians in the Scottish Parliament, which vacillated between the opposition and government parties, and finally decided the Union issue in 1707; the group continued until 1725 in the British Parliament *e18, 20- historical*. **Squadrone Volante** = SQUADRONE. [Ital *squadrone volante* literally a flying squadron of ships, applied to a 17th-century faction of cardinals]

squaik[1.1] /skwek/ *n especially of a trapped bird or animal* a loud scream or screech *19-*. [see the verb]

squaik[1.2], **squeck**, *NE* **squaak**, *Sh* **squeech** /skwek, skwɛk; *NE* skwak; *Sh* skwix/ *v especially of birds or trapped animals* to squeal, squeak, screech, squawk *19-*. [onomatopoeic]

squaint *see* SQUINT
squair *see* SQUARE[1.3]

squall /skwɔl/ *n* **1** a sudden, violent gust of wind *19-*. **2** a row, a disturbance, a quarrel *la18-e19*. [probably onomatopoeic]

squalloch[1.1] /'skwaləx, 'skwɔləx/ *n* a loud cry; the noise of children playing *la19- NE*. [see the verb]

squalloch[1.2] /'skwaləx, 'skwɔləx/ *v* to scream, squeal, cry out shrilly, make a noise and commotion *19- Sh NE*. [Eng *squall* to squeal, probably the same word as SQUALL, with -OCH suffix]

squar *see* SQUARE[1.3]

square[1.1], *WC* **squerr** /skwer; *WC* skwɛr/ *n* **1** a geometrical figure with four equal sides joined at right angles *la15-*. **2** *joinery* an instrument for measuring and determining right angles *16-*. **3** *in freemasonry* a mason's square, used as a central symbol *la17-*. **4** an open area in a town surrounded by buildings *18-*. **5** a standard size of (fire)brick *20-*. †**squareman** a workman who regularly uses a square, a carpenter or mason *la18*. **squaremen 1** the section of the incorporation of wrights specializing in work involving use of the carpenter's square *17-19*. **2** freemasons *20-*. **square-wright** a member of the *squaremen* 1; a carpenter *la17-*. **the square** farm buildings, a farm steading, when forming the sides of a square *20- Ork N NE Bor*. [OFr *esquare*]

square[1.2] /skwer/ *v* **1** to cut to a square shape; to make square *16-*. **2** to regulate, set to rights *la16-*. [OFr *esquarrer*]

square[1.3], *NE* **squar**, *WC* **squerr**, †**squair**, †**sqwair** /skwer; *NE* skwar; *WC* skwɛr/ *adj* **1** square-shaped *la15-*. **2** *of the body or limbs* solid, well-built, powerful *la14-*. **3** straightforward, honest, direct *la16-*. **4** *of an object or weapon* solid, strong, heavy, substantial *la14-16*. **square go** a violent encounter, a fight with no holds barred *la20-*. **square sausage** sausage-meat cut into flat slices and grilled or fried *la20-*; compare LORNE SAUSAGE, SLICED SAUSAGE. [OFr *esquarré*]

square see SQUIRE^{1.1}

†squash^{1.1} *n* (the sound of) splashing or a blow smashing on something soft *19*. [see the verb]

squash^{1.2} /skwɔʃ/ *v* **1** to crush *19-*. **2** to splash *19*. [EModE *squash*, OFr *esquasser*]

squat^{1.1}, *NE* **scot**, **†sqwat** /skwɔt; *NE* skɔt/ *n* **1** a heavy fall, a blow, a jolt *16-e19*. **2** the act of squatting or crouching *la17-*. [see the verb]

squat^{1.2}, *NE* **scot** /skwɔt; *NE* skɔt/ *v* **1** to crouch *la18-*. **2** to strike with the open hand, smack, slap *19, 20- NE*. **†squattle** to squat, lie low, nestle *la18-19*. [ME *squatten*, OFr *esquatir*]

squatter^{1.1} /'skwɔtər, 'skwatər/ *n* a large number of small creatures or objects, a disorderly, confused crowd *la19-*. [see the verb]

squatter^{1.2} /'skwɔtər, 'skwatər/ *v* **1** to flutter, flap about in mud or water, splash along *la18-19, 20- WC SW*. **2** to scatter, or squander *la17-19, 20- WC SW*. [onomatopoeic]

squattle see SWATTLE^{1.2}

squeak^{1.1} /skwik/ *n* **1** a high-pitched sound *la18-*. **2** a narrow escape *19-*. **3** *humorous* a local newspaper *20-*. [see the verb]

squeak^{1.2} /skwik/ *v* to make a high-pitched, squealing noise *19-*. **squeaker** a local newspaper *20- C SW*. [Eng *squeak*]

squeal see SQUEEL^{1.1}, SQUEEL^{1.2}

squeck see SQUAIK^{1.2}

squeeb, squib /skwib, skwɪb/ *n* **1** a firework; something explosive *la17-*. **2** a mean, scrounging, insignificant person *20- NE*. [EModE *squib*]

squeech see SQUAIK^{1.2}

squeef /skwif/ *n derogatory* a mean, disreputable, shabby or worthless person *19- T WC SW Bor*. [unknown; compare SQUEEB]

squeegee, squeejee /'skwi'dʒi/ *adj* askew, twisted *20-*. [conflation of SKEW^{2.3} with AJEE^{1.1}]

squeel^{1.1}, squeal, *NE* **squile**, **†skoil** /skwil; *NE* skwʌɪl/ *n* **1** a high-pitched noise, a yell, a screech *la18-*. **2** an outcry, uproar; a spree *la18-19*. [see the verb]

squeel^{1.2}, squeal, *NE* **squile**, **†squele**, **†squeill**, **†skoil** /skwil; *NE* skwʌɪl/ *v* to utter a loud, sharp cry; to make a high-pitched noise *la14-*. [onomatopoeic]

squeel see SCHULE

squeenge see SCUNGE^{1.1}, SCUNGE^{1.2}

squeerie see SCURRY

squeesh, squish, †squische /skwiʃ, skwɪʃ/ *v* to crush, squash *16-*. [onomatopoeic]

squeeter^{1.1} /'skwitər/ *n* a state of confusion, a mix-up, a botched job *la19- NE*. [see the verb]

squeeter^{1.2} /'skwitər/ *v* **1** to spatter, (cause to) fly in all directions *la19- NE*. **2** to work in a weak, unskilful manner *la19- NE*. [emphatic form with extended sense of SKITTER^{1.2}]

squeill see SQUEEL^{1.2}

squele see SQUEEL^{1.2}

squere see SQUIRE^{1.1}

squerr see SQUARE^{1.1}, SQUARE^{1.3}

squib see SQUEEB

squile see SQUEEL^{1.1}, SQUEEL^{1.2}

†squink *adj* squint, crooked *e17*. **squink-eyed** squint-eyed *e17*. [altered form of SQUINT]

squinny see SQUINTY^{1.1}

squint, squaint /skwɪnt, skwɛnt/ *adj* off the straight, set at a slant, oblique *17-*. [aphetic form of ME *asquint* obliquely]

†squinty^{1.1}, squinny *n* a woman's plain bonnet, tied under the chin *e19*. **squinty mutch** = SQUINTY^{1.1} *la19*. [see the adj]

squinty^{1.2} /'skwɪntɛ/ *adj* squint *la20-*. [SQUINT + -y (-IE²)]

squire^{1.1}, *WC* **square**, **†squere**, **†squyar**, **†squyer** /skwaer; *WC* skwɛr/ *n* **1** *in the feudal system of military service* a man ranking immediately below a knight; a young man of noble family before he becomes a knight, frequently attached to or in the household of a knight *la13-19, 20- historical*. **2** a person belonging to the social class immediately below a knight; a country gentleman or landed proprietor *la14-19, 20- historical*. **3** a lover *la15-16*. **†squyary** squires or attendants collectively; a group of squires *la14-15*. [OFr *esquier*]

squire^{1.2}, †squyar /skwaer/ *v* to escort, accompany, conduct *15-*. [see the noun]

squirk /skwɪrk/ *v* to squirt out (liquid) suddenly *20- C*. [probably altered form of Eng *squirt*]

squirl /skwɪrl/ *n* an ornamental flourish at the end of a letter; a piece of trimming, a flounce *19- N NE T EC*. [probably altered form of SWIRL^{1.1}]

squische see SQUEESH

squish see SQUEESH

squyar, squyer see SQUIRE^{1.1}

squyary see SQUIRE^{1.1}

squyer see SQUIRE^{1.1}

sqwair see SQUARE^{1.3}

sqwat see SQUAT^{1.1}

sqway see SKEW¹

St see SAINT^{1.3}

sta^{1.1}, stall, *NE* **staa**, **†staw** /stɔ, stɑl; *NE* sta/ *n* **1** accommodation for an animal in a byre or stable *15-*. **2** a stand for the display and sale of merchandise; a market stall *15-*. **3** a space, a cubicle, storage space *la16-19, 20- Ork NE*. **4** an (enclosed) seat in (the choir of) a church *la15-e17*. [OE *steall*]

sta^{1.2}, stall, †stail, †stale /stɔ, stɑl/ *v ptp also* **†stald 1** to put (an animal) in a stall *la15-*. **2** to come or bring to a halt, stop; to be or get into difficulties; to delay, equivocate *15-*. **3** to put in a place or position, install *15-17*. Compare STELL^{1.2}. [from the noun and AN *estaler* to stalemate]

sta see STAW^{1.1}, STEAL^{1.2}

staa see STA^{1.1}, STAW^{1.2}

staag /stɑg/ *v* to roam, saunter, stroll *la19- Sh*. [Norw dial *staga* to stagger]

stab^{1.1}, *NE* **stob** /stab; *NE* stɔb/ *n* (a wound caused by) a thrust with a pointed weapon or thorn; a poke, prod *la15-*. Compare STOB^{1.1}. **stab inn** a rough pub where there is a risk of violence *la20- C*. [see the verb]

stab^{1.2}, *NE* **stob** /stab; *NE* stɔb/ *v* **1** to thrust, pierce, prick, jab with a pointed weapon or sharp object; to wound or kill with a pointed object or stabbing movement *la14-*. **2** to make thrusting movements with a staff or club *e16*. [variant of STOB^{1.2}]

stab^{2.1} /stab, stɑb/ *n* a stout thickset man *la19, 20- Sh Uls*. **†stabby** in Ayrshire = STAB^{2.2} *19*. [variant of STOB^{1.1} used figuratively]

stab^{2.2} /stab/ *adj* stocky, stout; substantial *19- Bor*. [see the noun]

stab³ /stab/ *n* a stool, small, wooden seat *19- Sh*. [Norw *stabbe* a block, tree stump]

stab see STOB^{1.1}, STOB^{1.2}

stabb see STOB^{1.1}

stabell see STABLE^{1.1}

stabil see STABLE^{2.2}

stabill see STABLE^{1.1}, STABLE^{1.2}, STABLE^{2.1}, STABLE^{2.2}

stable^{1.1}, †stabill, †stabell /'stebəl/ *n* housing for horses *15-*. **†stable-meal** the meal bought by a farmer at an inn on market days in return for the stabling of his horse *la18*. [ME *stable*, OFr *estable*, Lat *stabulum*]

stable^{1.2}, †stabill /'stebəl/ *v* to house (a horse) in a stable *15-*. **stabler, †stabillar** a (public) stable-keeper *la15-19, 20- historical*. **stabling, †stabillyng** the action of accommodating a horse; accommodation for a horse in a stable *15-*. [from the noun or OFr *establer*]

†**stable**[2.1], **stabill** *v* **1** to establish, install *la14-e16*. **2** to found (a city); to put (laws) into effect; to appoint (an official) *15-16*. **3** to cause to become stable or peaceful; to secure, take into one's possession *la14-16*. **4** *of the sea, weather* to become calm, settle *16*. [aphetic form of ESTABILL]

stable[2.2], †**stabill**, †**stabil** /ˈstebəl/ *adj* **1** unmoving, immovable, still, calm; fixed; unchanging, securely established, permanent *la14-*. **2** *of a person* resolute; steadfast; loyal; constant, dependable *la14-17*. †**stabilnes** steadfastness *15-e17*. [OFr *stable, estable*, Lat *stabilis*]

†**stablish**, **stablis**, **stablisch** *v* **1** to establish, put in place *la14-17*. **2** to bring into being; to put into effect *15-17*. **3** to appoint (a person) *la14-e17*. **4** to bring to a settled state; to establish order *la14-16*. [aphetic form of *establish* (ESTAIBLISH)]

stacher[1.1] /ˈstaxər/ *n* a stumble, a false step *la19- NE T C SW*. **staucherie** unsteady in gait *20- NE T C SW*. [see the verb]

stacher[1.2], **staucher**, †**stakker**, †**stackar** /ˈstaxər, ˈstɔxər/ *v* to walk unsteadily, stumble, totter *la14-*. **stachering**, †**stakkerand 1** tottering, unsteady *la16-*. **2** unreliable, vacillating *la16-17*. [ON *stakra* to stagger]

stack /stak/ *n* **1** a rick (of sheaves of grain or hay) *15-*. **2** a man-made pile of peats *la15-19, 20- Sh N NE*. **3** a pile (of materials, timber or turf) *la15-*. **4** a tall column of rock rising out of the sea, separated from the cliffs by weathering *la18-*. **5** *pl* stacks of grain, indicative of wealth *16-17*. **stack-hill**, *Ork* **stack-ald** the ground or mound on which a peat-stack is built *la16-19, 20- Ork N NE*. **stack-mou** that end of a peat-stack from which the peats are taken for use *la19- NE*. **stackyaird**, **stackyard** a rick-yard *la16-*. [ME *stak*, ON *stakkr* a haystack]

stack *see* STICK[1.2]

stackar *see* STACHER[1.2]

†**stacket** *n* a palisade *e17, e19*. [Du *staket*]

stack rope *see* STALK[1]

stack yaird, **stackyard** *see* STACK

stad *see* STAND[1.2], STEID[1.2]

stadel *see* STATHEL[1.1]

staelt *see* STEAL[1.2]

staff, *SW* **stave**, †**stafe**, †**staif**, †**stalf** *n pl* **staves**, †**staffis**, †**stalffis** /staf; *SW* stev/ *n* **1** a long stick used as a walking aid; a pole as a prop or support *la14-*. **2** a body of persons employed in the work of an establishment or company *19-*. **3** the shaft of a weapon or implement *14-*. **4** a stick or pole used as a weapon, a quarterstaff; a cudgel; a lance *la14-19, 20- historical*. **5** *in ceremonial use* a rod or wand of office *la14-e18*. †**staff-hird** *n* a herdsman in charge of animals grazing on common land *16-17*. †**staff-hird** *v* to tend (grazing) animals *la16*. †**staffman** a town officer or constable; an official *17-e18*. †**stafsling**, **staf slung**, **staf slong** a sling attached to a shaft of wood from which stones were hurled; a catapult or balista *la14-16*. †**keep someone at the staff en** to keep someone at a distance, remain aloof *la18-19*. †**staff and bastoun**, **staff and baton** the symbols by which a vassal resigned his feu into the hands of his superior *la14-e19*. [OE *stæf*]

staff *see* STAVE[1.1]

†**staffage**, **stafische** *adj* stubborn, unmanageable; unmitigated *16-e19*. [STAFF, with adj-forming suffix]

staffed *see* STAVE[1.3]

staffis *see* STAFF

stafische *see* STAFFAGE

stag *see* STAIG

stage[1.1] /stedʒ/ *n* **1** a level, position, step *la14-*. **2** a period or point of time; *15-*. **3** a raised platform (for actors, speakers or dignitaries) *la15-*. **4** a measure of length, a stadium, 600 Greek or Roman feet *la14-16*. **5** scaffolding *la16-17*. **6** a storey of a building *e16*. †**bring to the stage** to bring to trial *la17*. †**put on the stage** = *bring to the stage*. [OFr *estage*]

stage[1.2] /stedʒ/ *v* **1** to bring to trial; accuse *la17-e18*. **2** to strut about in a stately way (as if on a stage) *e19*. [see the noun]

staggie, †**staiggie** /ˈstegə/ *n* = STAIG *la18-*. **staiggie-man** the groom of a stallion *20- Ork*. [STAIG + -IE[1]]

Staggies /ˈstegɪz/ *npl* nickname for Ross County Football Club *20-*. [so called because of a representation of a red deer stag on their club badge]

staif *see* STAFF

staiff *see* STAVE[1.2]

staig, †**stag** /steg/ *n* **1** a young, unbroken horse usually of one to three years old *la15-19, 20- Sh Ork N C SW*. **2** a stallion *16-19, 20- Ork N NE T H&I C SW*. **3** a young castrated, male horse, a gelding *19, 20- Sh Ork N C SW*. **4** a bullock *e19*. **staiger** a man who takes a stallion around different farms for breeding purposes *20- NE T EC*. [OE *stagga* a stag]

staiggie *see* STAGGIE

staik *see* STAKE[1], STAKE[2]

stail *see* STA[1.2], STEAL[1.2]

staill *see* STALE[1], STALE[2], STELL[4]

stain, †**stenȝie**, †**steinȝie**, †**stane** /sten/ *v ptp also* †**stenyt 1** to (cause to) lose colour; to obscure, eclipse *la16*. **2** to blemish, discolour; to mar *16-*. **3** to depict in colour *e16*. [ME *steinen* to impart colour, aphetic form of OFr *desteindre* to (cause to) lose colour, perhaps with influence from ON *steina* to paint]

stain *see* STANE[1.1], STANE[1.2]

stainch *see* STENCH[1.2], STENCH[2.1], STENCH[2.2]

stainchel[1.1], †**stanchel**, †**stenchel** /ˈstenʃəl/ *n* **1** an iron bar, usually as part of a grating for a window *la16-19, 20- N C SW Bor*. **2** a bar for securing a door or gate *19, 20- C SW*. [probably OFr *estanchele* some kind of wooden prop used in a game]

†**stainchel**[1.2], **stanchel**, **stenchel** *v* to fit (a window) with iron bars *la16-19*. [see the noun]

staincheon[1.1], †**stancheoun**, †**stenchion** /ˈstenʃən/ *n* an iron upright or bar, usually used to secure a window *la15-19, 20- Ork N NE*. [OFr *estanchon*]

†**staincheon**[1.2], **stainshon**, **stanchen** *v* to provide (a window) with bars *la16-17*. [see the noun]

staincher[1.1], †**stancher**, †**stancheour**, †**stencher** /ˈstenʃər/ *n* an iron upright or bar, used for support or security, usually forming part of a window-grating *la15-19, 20- C SW*. [altered form of STAINCHEON[1.1]]

†**staincher**[1.2], **stancheour** *v* to provide (a window) with bars *16-e17*. [see the noun]

stainshon *see* STAINCHEON[1.2]

stair, *WC* **sterr**, †**stare** /ster; *WC* ster/ *n pl also* †**staris 1** *sing* a staircase giving access to the upper storeys of a building, originally frequently on the outside of the building; a flight of steps *la15-*. **2** *pl* (a flight of) steps, a staircase *16-*. **3** *sing* the shared staircase giving access to individual flats in a tenement *19-*; compare *common stair* (COMMON[1.3]). **4** *sing* an (upper) flat in a tenement; the tenement building itself *20-*. **5** *mining* the stairway giving access to (a section of) a mine *16-19*. **6** the space under an outside stair, enclosed for use as storage *15-e16*. **stair-fit**, †**stair-fute 1** (the space at) the bottom of a staircase *la16-*. **2** a flat at the bottom of a common stair *19-*. **doon the stair** downstairs *19-*. **up the stair** upstairs *19-*. [OE *stæger*]

stair *see* STARE[1.1], STARE[1.2]

stairch, sterch, †stearch /stertʃ, stertʃ/ *n* starch, a substance used to stiffen cloth *la17-*. [ME *sterche*, from OE **stercan* to make rigid]

stairge /sterdʒ/ *v* to stalk, strut *19- Bor*. [emphatic or intensive variant of STAGE[1,2]]

stairheid, stairhead /ˈsterhid, ˈsterhɛd/ *n* (the landing at) the top of a flight of stairs or at the top of a common stair *la16-*. **stairheid rammy 1** a quarrel between neighbours in a common stair *20-*. **2** a localized dispute; an inconsequential quarrel (which has become exaggerated out of proportion) *la20-*. [STAIR + HEID[1.1]]

stairt *see* START[1.2]
stairve *see* STERVE
stait *see* STATE[1.1], STATE[1.2]
staive *see* STAVE[1.2]
staiver *see* STAVER
stak *see* STALK[1], STICK[1.2]

stake[1], †staik, †stak /stek/ *n* **1** a post; an upright in the construction of a fence (or wall) *la14-*. **2** a young ling *Molva molva la18- NE*. **3** *weaving* apparently a rod used in measuring the length of the warp (threads) *17-e18*. **stakie** = STAKE[1] (sense 2) *20- NE*. **stake-net** a salmon-fishing net fixed on stakes in tidal waters *19-*. **stake and rice** *n* = *stab and rice* (STOB[1.1]) *la15-*. **stake and rice** *adj* sketchy, in outline only *19-*. [OE *staca*]

†stake[2], staik *v* **1** to be sufficient for, supply the needs or wants of, provide for, satisfy *16-e17, e18 historical*. **2** *of a person* to perform (a task), supply (an enterprise) as a worker; *of a church* to be provided with a minister *la16-e17*. **3** to suffice *la16-e17*. [unknown, perhaps related to STAKE[1] or STOCK[1.2]]

stakey /ˈsteke/ *n games* a game of marbles in which stakes are laid *la19- C*. [Eng *stake* an amount placed at hazard + *-y* (-IE[3])]

stakker *see* STACHER[1.2]
stald *see* STA[1.2]

stale[1], †staill /stel/ *n* **1** the foundation, made of a layer of stones or brushwood on which a corn- or hay-stack is built *la16-19, 20- T C Bor*. **2** a stock, colony or hive of bees *16-e19*. [MDu *stael*, MLG *stale*]

†stale[2], staill, stall *n* **1** a fixed, military position *la14-e15*. **2** the main body of an army *la14-e17*. **3** a division or (small) group of fighting men intended for a particular purpose; a band of hunters *15-e16*. **4** battle array *15-e16*. **in stale** in reserve; in battle array *15-e16*. [OFr *estal*]

stale[3.1] /stel/ *n* urine, especially that collected for making bleach or manuring *19, 20- T*. [see the verb]

stale[3.2] /stel/ *v* to urinate *15-*. [OFr *estaler*]

stale *see* STA[1.2], STELL[1.1]
stalf *see* STAFF
stalffis *see* STAFF

stalk[1], †stak /stɔk/ *n* **1** a thin support or rod *la14-*. **2** the stem of a flower or plant *la15-*. **3** the stem of a pipe or candle *la19-*. **4** a chimney-stack *19, 20- NE T C SW Bor*. **5** apparently a rope or tether attached to a halter to tie or lead a horse *la15-16*. **†stalkit** stemmed; branched *la16-17*. **stalk-raip, stack rope** a rope passed through a ring on a stable manger, weighted at one end and tied to the horse's stall halter at the other *20- C SW*. **be ca'ed aff its stalk** *of the heart* to be stopped by a sudden fright *20- EC*. **gan aff the stalk** = *be ca'ed aff its stalk 20- EC*. **†loup aff the stalk** = *be ca'ed aff its stalk 19*. [ME *stalk*]

stalk[2], †stauk /stɔk/ *v* **1** to walk stealthily in hunting game; to prowl *16-*. **2** to walk without haste; to stroll *la15-19*. **3** to stride *la18-e19*. **stalker, †stalkar 1** a person who stalks and hunts game; a person employed to hunt game *15-*. **2** a person who prowls about for purposes of theft *e16*. [OE *bestealcian*]

stall *see* STA[1.1], STA[1.2], STALE[2], STEAL[1.2]

†stallage, stellage *n* **1** a fee paid for the freedom to erect a stall in a market; the levy imposed on a STALLANGER *15-17*. **2** in Galloway, a brewery, a *brewland* (BREW) *la16-e19*; compare STALLANGE (sense 2). [ME *stallage*, OFr *estalage*]

†stallange *n* **1** the fee paid by a *stallangar 15-17*. **2** in Galloway, a brewery *16-e17*. [altered form of STALLAGE, with influence from STALLENGER]

stallanger *see* STALLENGER

†stallar *n* the vicar of a canon or prebendary serving in a cathedral *16*. **stallarie** the office of a STALLAR *la16-e17*. [Lat *stallārius*]

†stallenger, stallanger *n* a tradesman or craftsman not a member of a trade incorporation who by payment of a fee was able to carry on his business within a burgh *15-18*. [altered form of OFr *estalagier* one who pays STALLAGE]

stalouartly *see* STALWARTLY
stalp *see* STAMP[2]
stalwardly *see* STALWARTLY

stalwart[1.1] /ˈstalwart, ˈstɔlwart/ *n* **1** a dependable supporter *la19-*. **2** a strong valiant fighting man *la15-e16*. **the stalwart** strong, dependable people *la19-*. [see the adj]

stalwart[1.2], †stalworth /ˈstalwart, ˈstɔlwart/ *adj* **1** *of people and animals* physically strong, powerful; valiant, brave, resolute; determined *la14-*. **2** *of things* strong, strongly built; capable of inflicting a severe blow or withstanding great force *la14-18*. **3** *of fighting* fierce, hard, violent *la14-16*. [OE *stælwierðe*]

†stalwartly, stalwardly, stalouartly *adv* strongly, bravely *la14-16*. [STALWART[1.2], with adv-forming suffix]

stalworth *see* STALWART[1.2]

†stam[1] *n* the stem or prow of a ship *16-e17*. [ME *stampne*, ON *stamn*]

stam[2] /stam/ *v* to walk with a quick heavy tread, stamp along; to stumble, stagger *19- Bor*. [perhaps onomatopoeic or a variant of STAMP[1.2]]

stamack[1.1], stomach, stamach, †stammok, †stomak, †stomok /ˈstamək, ˈstʌmək, ˈstaməx/ *n* **1** the hollow dilated part of the alimentary canal in which food is digested; the part of the body containing the stomach, the belly, abdomen *la14-*. **2** temper, disposition, mind, spirit *la16-*. **3** appetite *la18-*. **4** a stomacher, a woman's bodice or a man's waistcoat *la15-17*. **5** desire, inclination, wish *e16*. **6** the stomach viewed as the seat of the emotions *la16*. **find the bottom o yer stamack** to feel ravenously hungry *la19- NE T*. **find the grund o yer stamack** = *find the bottom o yer stamack la18-19, 20- T H&I EC*. [OFr *estomac*]

stamack[1.2], stomach, †stammach, †stomak /ˈstamək, ˈstʌmək/ *v* **1** to bear, put up with, tolerate *19-*. **2** to digest, retain in the stomach *19, 20- NE*. **3** to resent; to take offence *la16-e17*. **†stomakit** offended, resentful *la16-17*. [see the noun, and compare Lat *stomachārī*, Fr *s'estomaquer* to take offence]

stame *see* STEAM[1.1]

†staminger, stammager, stommager *n* = STAMACK[1.1] (sense 4) *17-e18*. [ME *stomacher*, OFr *estomachier*]

stammach *see* STAMACK[1.2]

stammagast[1.1] /ˈstaməˌgast/ *n* = STAMMYGASTER[1.1] *la18-*. [a fanciful formation]

stammagast[1.2] /ˈstaməgast/ *v* = STAMMYGASTER[1.2] *19-*. [see the noun]

stammager *see* STAMINGER

stammer[1.1] /ˈstamər/ *n* **1** a hesitation or stumble in speech; stuttering *la19-*. **2** a stumble, stagger; a staggering, shambling gait *17-19, 20- NE T EC SW*. [see the verb]

stammer[1.2], *Ork* **stummer** /ˈstamər; *Ork* ˈstʌmər/ *v pt* †**stummyrryt**, †**stumryt 1** to stutter *la19-*. **2** to stumble, stagger, falter, blunder about; to hesitate *la15-*. **stammering**, †**stummerand 1** stumbling, not surefooted, insecure *la15-*. **2** *of the tongue, speech* stuttering, hesitant; incoherent *17-*. **stammery** *of a horse* unsure of its footing, stumbling, tottery *20- NE T EC SW*. [OE *stamerian, stomrian*]

stammerin /ˈstamərɪn/ *n* the transom knee in the bow and stern of a boat which binds the sides and the stem together; in the stern, used as a seat by the helmsman *19- Sh N*. [Norw dial *stamn* prow or stern + Norw dial *rong* stern seat]

stammering /ˈstamərɪŋ, ˈstamərɪn/ *n* **1** stuttering; incoherent, stumbling speech *la17-*. **2** hesitation, doubt *la16*. **3** foolish or loquacious speech *la18*. [verbal noun from STAMMER[1.2]]

stammle *see* STUMMLE

stammok *see* STAMACK[1.1]

stammrel *see* STAUMREL[1.1], STAUMREL[1.2]

stammygaster[1.1] /ˈstameˈɡastər/ *n* a great and sudden disappointment, an unpleasant surprise, a shock *20- NE T*; compare FLAMAGASTER. [STAMMAGAST[1.2] with agent suffix]

stammygaster[1.2] /ˈstameɡastər/ *v* **1** to disappoint, astonish, bewilder *la19- NE T EC SW Bor*. **2** to sicken, nauseate *20- NE C*. [see the noun]

stamp[1.1] /stamp/ *n* **1** a tool used to impress a mark or seal guaranteeing authenticity *16-*. **2** a mark, seal, impression or official label applied to something as a guarantee of authenticity *la16-*. **3** a spit or spadeful of earth *19- NE*. [from the verb and OFr *estampe*]

stamp[1.2] /stamp/ *v ptp also* **stampt 1** to bring the feet or a foot down forcible, violently or noisily *la14-*. **2** to mark or impress (a coin or letter) with a stamp or die (as a seal of authentication) *la16-*. **3** to crush, pound (in or as in a mortar) *la16-e17*. [OE **stampian*]

stamp[2], †**stalp** /stamp/ *n* a trap for catching small animals, especially one that is released when trodden on *16-19, 20- T EC*. [unknown, perhaps influenced in form by STAMP[1.1]]

stamp-cole *see* STANKLE

stampt *see* STAMP[1.2]

stamyng *see* STEMMING

stan *see* STAND[1.2]

stance[1.1], **staunce**, †**stans** /stans, stɔns/ *n* **1** the place where or the position in which something or someone stands *la18-*. **2** the site of a building, especially the building-site where a house etc is to be built *la16-*. **3** a person's place in life; a moral or philosophical position, an attitude *17-*. **4** a site for an open-air market or fair, a space for a single stand, market stall or side-show, a street-trader's pitch *la16-*. **5** a standing place for buses or taxis (at a terminus); a designated berth or bay for public vehicles *la17-*. **6** *games* the position of a player's feet when about to strike the ball; a position or spot where action occurs *la18-*. **7** an overnight stopping-place for a drove of cattle *19, 20- historical*. **8** a site or foundation on which something is laid or set up *17-19, 20- Sh N T EC Bor*. **9** the place where an animal stands in a stable or is tethered to graze *20- N NE*. **10** a room, a cell *e17*. **11** a compartment in a shield *e17*. **at a stance** at a standstill *la17-*. **take a stance, take up yer stance** to take (up) a position; to adopt a point of view *20-*. [MFr *estance* a residence, situation]

stance[1.2] /stans/ *v* to place, site, assign a position (to); to exhibit (an animal) for sale at a market *la17-19, 20- N NE T Bor*. [see the noun]

stanch *see* STENCH[1.2], STENCH[2.1]

stanche *see* STENCH[1.1]

†**stanchel**, **stanchell**, **stainchel** *n* the kestrel *Falco tinnunculus 13-e19*. [altered form of OE *stāngella*]

stanchel *see* STAINCHEL[1.1], STAINCHEL[1.2]

stanchen *see* STAINCHEON[1.2]

stancheoun *see* STAINCHEON[1.1]

stancheour *see* STAINCHER[1.1], STAINCHER[1.2]

stancher *see* STAINCHER[1.1]

stand[1.1], **staun** /stand, stɔn/ *n* **1** a place for standing in, a position, station; a point of view *la15-*. **2** a stall or booth for the sale or display of goods and provision or information *16-*. **3** a complete set or outfit of various kinds of equipment eg ropes, knitting needles, measures *16-19, 20- Sh Ork N NE T EC SW Bor*. **4** a set or suit (of clothes, vestments, armour) *la15-19*. **stauner** an erect penis; an erection *la20-*. †**stand bed** = *standing bed* (STANDING[1.2]) *la15-18*. †**stand-maill** a fixed rent *17-e18*; compare STANDING[1.2] (sense 2). **stand of pipes** a complete set of Scottish bagpipes, bag, drones and chanter *19-*. **at a stand** at a halt, standstill *la17-19, 20- Sh*. [see the verb]

stand[1.2], **staun, stan**, †**stant** /stand, stɔn, stan/ *v pt, ptp also* **stude**, *NE* **steed**, *NE* **stan't**, †**stud**, †**stad** *ptp also C Bor* **stuiden**, †**standyn**, †**stand 1** to be, remain (in an upright position); to cease moving, remain motionless *la14-*. **2** *of a building or wall* to remain erect, intact, undamaged or as described *la14-*. **3** *of a tree or plant* to grow (upright) *la14-*. **4** *of property or a commodity* to cost *la17-*. **5** *of a clock or watch* to stop, be stopped *la18-*. **6** *in imperative, in calls to a horse* stop!, stand quiet! *16-19, 20- N NE T C Bor*. **7** *in negative constructions* to hesitate, be reluctant, refuse *la16-e19*. **8** *of an event, especially a wedding* to take place, be celebrated *la15-19*. **9** to abide by, obey (a decree) *la15-16*. **10** *in battle* to take up and maintain a position for fighting; to give a good account of oneself; to make a stand *la14-e17*. **11** to be present; to be established; to dwell, reside; to be kept *la14-e17*. **12** *of a place etc* to be located *la14-e17*. **13** *of a payment* to be at a particular level or price *15-17, 20-*. **14** to withstand, suffer (a blow etc) *la15-17*. **as it stands** *of property* in the state in which it is found *la15-*. †**stand about** to stand farther off, keep one's distance, get out of the way *la18-19*. †**stand at 1** to adhere to; to accept *la15-17*. **2** to balk at *17*. †**stand at the bar** to be in a courtroom as an advocate or witness *la15-18*. †**stand aw of** to be afraid of *la14-e17*. **stand-by 1** to remain beside or near at hand; to support, help *la14-*. **2** to be present as an unconcerned spectator *19-*. **3** to afford (a loss) *e19*. **stand for 1** to uphold, defend, support; to guarantee *la14-e17*. **2** to represent; to take the place of *15-*. **3** to refuse *e19*. †**I stand for it, I stand ford** *parenthetic* I guarantee it *la15-16*. **stand good for** to stand surety for, guarantee *la18, 20- Sh Ork N NE T C*. †**stand in 1** to remain, continue in a situation or in doing something *15-17*. **2** to stand in an instrument or place of punishment *16-17*. **3** to have its source in; to depend on *15-17*. **stand in for** = *stand good for la19, 20- Sh NE T*. †**stand in judgement** to appear in court to defend oneself *15-16*. †**stand in a person's service and retinew** to hold an appointment *e16*. †**stand in a studie** to muse, be thoughtful *e16*. †**it stands in** it is the concern or responsibility of *15-16*. †**it stands on** = *it stands in 15-e17*. **stand on** *of wind or adversity* to blow head on; to be very arduous *20- Sh*. †**stand on, stand upon 1** to hesitate, delay on account of something; to scruple; to be influenced or impeded *15-17*. **2** = *stand in* 3 *la15-16*. **stand on da winterband** *of cattle* to be tied up in a stall throughout the winter *20- Sh*. †**stand on stappin stanes** to be excessively fussy; to dither *la17-19*. **stand oot** to remain solvent *20- NE*. **stand ower**, †**stand our 1** *as a command to a horse* move to the other side of the stall 20-. **2** to prorogue (Parliament); to postpone (business) 16-17. **stand tae the wa** *of a door* to be wide open *20- Sh Ork NE T.* †**stand to** to adhere to, abide by *15-17.* †**stand Tom Callendar** to foot the bill *e19.* †**stand under** to owe obedience to; to be subject to *la15-16.* †**stand with** to accord, agree; to please *la14-e19.* **stand your hand** to pay the bill in a restaurant or pub *19-.* **stand yont**, †**stand yon** to stand back, keep your distance, get out of the way *la18-19, 20- NE T EC Bor.* [OE *standan*]

stand[2] /stand/ *n* a tub, barrel or cask set upright to contain water, meal or salted beef *la15-19, 20- T.* [MLG *stande*]

standand *see* STANDING[1,2]

standand stane *see* STANDING STONE

standart, staunart, standard, stannert, †**standert,** †**stander** /ˈstandərt, ˈstɔnərt, ˈstandərd, ˈstanərt/ *n* **1** a flag displaying the symbols of identification of a country, king etc, as a rallying point or a symbol of allegiance *la14-.* **2** an upright timber, pole, post; a support *16-.* **3** the prescribed size of a unit of measure, weight or capacity; the authorized exemplar (usually held by a public authority) *15-.* **4** a level of correctness, a criterion *17-.* **5** mainly **stander** *in Kirkintilloch* one of sixteen land-holders each holding sixteen acres; the land-holding itself *la17.* **6** an inkwell *17.* **7** a candlestick *17-19.* **standard-bearer** the chief male participant in the Selkirk Common Riding, who carries the burgh flag round the town's boundaries *la19- Bor.* **Standard Grade** until 2014, applied to a certificate, examination or course awarded to pupils in secondary schools at the end of the fourth year *la20-.* **Standard Habbie** the name applied by Ramsay to the stanza form aaabab, with the b's forming a bob-wheel, used in the mock elegy *The Piper of Kilbarchan*, later much used by Burns and others *18-.* †**standart ledder** perhaps a particularly long ladder *16-e17.* **standard security** the form of heritable security which is now the only way of creating a security over land *la20-.* [OFr *estandard, estandart*]

†**standfray, standfra** *adj* aloof, rebellious *la15-16.* [STAND[1,2] + FRA]

standing[1.1] /ˈstandɪŋ/ *n* reputation, (high) status *16-.* [verbal noun from STAND[1,2]]

standing[1.2], †**standand** /ˈstandɪŋ/ *adj* **1** in an upright position; erect; vertical *15-.* **2** constant, permanent; *of rent* fixed, set *la14-.* **3** on a base or foot, free-standing *la16-17.* **4** *of trees* growing *la16-17.* **5** *of buildings* built; in good repair *17.* **6** *of water* not flowing, stagnant; perhaps, not tidal *15-.* **standing band** the tether by which a cow is fastened in her stall *la19- Sh.* †**standand bed** a (fourposter) bedstead *la15-e18.* †**standing-drink** a drink taken standing, indicating haste, impermanence or lack of commitment *17-19.* †**standand graith 1** the fixed or stationary parts of a mill *la16-19.* **2** the erect penis *la18.* **standing kirn** a churn worked by pushing a plunger up and down *20- N C.* [participial adj from STAND[1,2]]

standing stone, †**standand stane** /ˈstandɪŋ ˈston/ *n* **1** a monolith, a menhir, used as a landmark or meeting-place *la12-.* **2** an upright stone forming part of a boundary *la12-e17.* [STANDING[1,2] + STANE[1.1]]

standyn *see* STAND[1,2]

stane[1.1], **stain, stone,** *Sh Ork N NE T* **steen,** *Sh* **sten,** †**stayn** /sten, ston; *Sh Ork N NE T* stin; *Sh* also stɛn/ *n* **1** (a) (piece of) rock, a pebble; (a) stone used in building or roofing; a building block; a missile; a gemstone *12-.* **2** a unit of weight for goods in bulk, 16 pounds (originally to some extent depending on the period and produce weighed) *15-.* **3** a stone or piece of metal used as a standard stone-weight *la15-e17.* **4** *curling* a curling stone *18-.* **5** a testicle *16-.* **6** a mass of rock, a rocky crag or hill *16.* **7** a particular stone; a landmark; a boundary stone; a memorial or monument *13-.* **8** = *Stone of Scone 15.* **9** a gravestone *la15-.* **10** a millstone *16-17.* **11** a kidney- or gall-stone *la14-17.* **stonack, stonach** a large, brown, glazed earthenware marble *la19- N H&I.* **stoneder, stonder** = *stonack 20- NE.* **stoner** = *stonack la19- NE EC.* **stondie** = *stonack 20- NE.* **stanit, stained 1** *of a male horse* uncastrated *16-18, 20- Sh Ork Bor.* **2** *of a fruit* having a stone or stone-like seeds *16-.* **stane-bing** a heap or pile of stones *la19- C SW.* **stenbiter,** *Ork* **stein-biter** the catfish *Anarhichas lupus la18- Sh Ork.* **stone-blind** completely blind *la14-.* **stone-bruise** a boil or abscess on the foot *20- Uls.* †**stane buik** perhaps a tablet of slate used to make notes or a book with a cover decorated with gemstones *17.* **stone-cast, stane-cast** a stone's throw *la14-19, 20- Sh NE T EC.* **stane-chacker, stane-chackart, stane-chack,** *Sh* **sten-shakker 1** the stonechat *Saxicola torquata 18- T C Bor.* **2** the wheatear *Oenanthe oenanthe 19, 20- Sh Ork N NE.* **stane-chipper** the wheatear *Oenanthe oenanthe 20- WC SW.* †**stane-crase, stane-graze** *in the South-West* apparently a boil or bruise on the foot *e19.* **stane-dumb** completely silent *19- Sh Bor.* **stone-dyke, stane-dyke** a wall built of stone *15-;* compare *dry stane dyke* (DRY). **stane-dyker, stone-dyker** a person who builds (dry stone) walls *20-.* †**stone-fish** the gunnel *Pholis gunnellus 16-e19.* **stone horse** an uncastrated horse *18, 20- Sh Ork Bor.* **stane-knapper, stane-napper** a person who breaks stones *la19- NE C Bor.* †**stane-knot** a very tight knot *la18-19.* **stane-loppen** bruised, crushed *la19- Sh.* **stane-mine, stone-mine** mining a road from underground workings which cuts across the strata *20- C.* †**stane naig** = *stone horse e19.* **stane-pecker, stane-pikker** the wheatear *Oenanthe oenanthe* or the turnstone *Arenaria interpres la19- Sh.* **stane-putter, steenie-pouter** the turnstone *Arenaria interpres la19- Ork.* **stone-raw** the lichen *Parmelia saxatilis* used in dyeing *la18-19, 20- SW.* †**stane-still** motionless, inactive; remaining, continuing *la14-17.* **stane-tired** very tired; lazy, bone idle *20- Bor.* †**stane tron** = *tron stane 19.* †**stane-wecht 1** = STANE[1.1] (sense 2) *la15-19.* **2** = STANE[1.1] (sense 3) *16-e17.* **stiennie-warrag** a boil *20- N;* compare WERROCK. †**stane wring** colic attributed to the presence of a stone in the kidneys *e16.* **stane and lime,** †**lyme and stane** masonry *la14-.* †**cast the stane, hurl the stane, putt the stane** to throw a heavy stone as a test of athletic prowess *16-e19.* †**fra the hiest stane of the hill to the lawest stane of the eb** *in Shetland and Orkney* a formula indicating the extent of a land-holding *la15-e16.* †**the stane** a kidney- or gall-stone *14-17.* **the Stone of Scone** the Stone of Destiny *16-.* [OE *stān*]

stane[1.2], **stone,** *NE* **steen,** †**stain** /sten, ston; *NE* stin/ *v* **1** to pelt with stones; to punish, put to death by stoning *la14-.* **2** to furnish or pave with stone *17-.* **3** to press (a cheese) by weighting the cheese vat with stones *19, 20- NE WC.* **4** to toast bread or cakes by placing them on the hearthstone of a fire *20- NE.* [from the noun]

stane *see* STAIN

Stane-hyve *see* STEENHIVE

stanelock *see* STENLOCK

stane pirrie /ˈsten ˈpɪre/ *adj* hare-brained, scatty *la20- Bor.* [*stane* as in *stone-blind* (STANE[1.1]) + probably PIRR[2.1], with a play on *Pirrie*, the name of a manufacturer of stone ginger in Hawick]

stanerie *see* STANNERY

stang[1.1] /staŋ/ *n* **1** the sting (of an insect); the fang (of a snake) *15-.* **2** the wound caused by a sting or sharp object *la15-.* **3** a sharp pain, such as that caused by a sting, a pang *16-*. **4** the capacity to injure in word or deed; a harsh or cutting remark *la15-19, 20- Sh NE WC Bor*. **5** the sting of death *la16-19*. [see the verb]

stang[1,2] /staŋ/ *v* **1** to sting, pierce with a fang or sting *la14-*. **2** to shoot with pain, throb, ache *19-*. [ON *stanga*]

stang[2,1] /staŋ/ *n* **1** a pole, wooden bar or rod *17-19, 20- NE T SW Bor*. **2** a shaft or draught pole of a cart *la19, 20- Bor*. **3** a spike, prong or rod of metal *17- NE*. **4** a punt-pole *20- NE*. **5** *fisherman's taboo* the mast of a boat *19- Sh*. **6** the beam or shaft of a plough *la16, 20- Ork EC*. **7** a rough pole or tree trunk astride which an offender was mounted and carried about in public; punishment by this means *18-e19*. †**stangril** *in Tayside* an implement for thatching *e19*. **the stang o the trump** the indispensable or most effective person in a group or activity *19- NE T EC*. [ME *stang, stong*; ON *stǫng, stöng* a pole, a stake; compare STING[2,1]]

†**stang**[2,2] *v* to carry (a person) astride a pole as a punishment; to humiliate (a person) thus *la17-e19*. [see the noun]

stang see STING[1]

stanie see STANY[1,2]

stank[1,1] /staŋk/ *n* **1** a pond, a pool; a small semi-stagnant sheet of water, especially one overgrown with vegetation, a swampy place *la14-*. **2** a ditch, an open water-course, frequently a natural stream which has been straightened to serve as a boundary or as part of a drainage system *16-*. **3** an obstacle, a difficulty *20- NE*. **4** a street gutter *20- T C*. **5** a grating in a gutter *20- WC*. **6** the ground around a pool or pools *la16-18*. **7** a moat *16*. **stank brae** the edge of a stank *la16-17*. **stank hen** = STANKIE *la18-19, 20- T*. **doon the stank** irretrievably lost; *of money* squandered *20- C*. [OFr *estanc* a pool]

stank[1,2] /staŋk/ *v* **1** to dam (a stream); *of a ditch or pond* to retain water, fail to drain *la15-*. **2** to dig ditches; to drain with ditches *19- Sh N*. **3** to surround (a building) with a moat; *of land* to be bounded by a ditch or ponds *16-17, e20*. **4** to bury (a dead animal) *20- Ork*. **stankit 1** dammed up, blocked; choked *la19, 20- NE T*. **2** sated with food, satisfied *19- NE T*. [see the noun]

stankie /ˈstaŋkə/ *n* the water hen *Gallinula chloropus 19- T C SW Bor*. **stankie hen** = *stankie*. [STANK[1,1] + -IE[3]]

stankle, *Bor* **stamp-cole** /ˈstaŋkəl; *Bor* ˈstampkol/ *n* a small, temporary hay-rick *19- Ork N SW*. [STAMP[1,2] + COLE[1,1]]

stanners, †**stanneris**, †**stannyris** /ˈstanərz/ *npl* pebbles, shingle *16-19, 20- NE T*. [OE *stæner* stony ground, or a derivative of STANE[1,1]]

stannert see STANDART

†**stannery**, **stanerie**, **stenory** *adj* gravelly, stony, rocky *16-18*. [STANNERS + -IE[2]]

stannyris see STANNERS

stans see STANCE[1,1]

stant, stan't see STAND[1,2]

stan-tae, *NE* **stan-tee** /stanˈte, stanˈti/ *n* a set-to, a tussle *20- Sh N NE T EC SW*. [STAND[1,2] + TAE[3,1]]

stany[1,1], **stonie**, *NE* **steenie** /ˈstene, ˈstone; *NE* ˈstini/ *n* **1** a small coloured marble *la19- NE T C SW*. **2** a variety of tig *19- NE EC SW*. **stonie-tig** a variety of tig *20- SW*. [STANE[1,1] + -IE[1]]

stany[1,2], **stonie**, †**stanie** /ˈstene, ˈstone/ *adj* containing many stones; characterized by stone or stones *la12-*. **stonie gravell** stones in the kidneys or gall-bladder *17*. [OE *stānig*]

stap[1,1], **step**, *Bor* **staup**, †**stop** /stap, stɛp; *Bor* stɔp/ *n* **1** a tread (of a ladder or stair) *la14-*. **2** (a move in) a direction or course of action; a stage (in a process) *15-*. **3** a pace, a stride; progress made by stepping *la15-*. **4** a (short) distance, the length of a pace or stride *la16-*. **5** only **step** a place or piece of a road (on which the foot lands) *18-19, 20- NE T SW*. **6** a stepping-stone in a river *18- T SW*. **7** only **step** *mining* a fault or slip in the strata of a mine *la18-19, 20- WC*. **tak a stap** to take a short walk, make a short journey *19-*. **tak a person doon a stap** to deflate someone's self-importance *20- Sh Bor*. **like staps and stairs** *of the children in a family* born in quick succession *19- Sh T*. [OE *stæpe, stepe*]

stap[1,2], **step**, *Bor* **staup** /stap, stɛp; *Bor* stɔp/ *v* to take a step; to progress by stepping *la14-*. †**step-aside** to commit a fault, go astray *la17-19*. [OE *steppan*, with influence from the noun, and compare Du *stappen*]

stap[2,1], **stoap, stop** /stap, stop, stɔp/ *n* **1** a veto, a prohibition; an order prohibiting something *15-*. **2** an impediment, hindrance, obstruction or obstacle; a delay *la15-*. **3** the act of cramming or stuffing, or of blocking up a hole; a surfeit *la19- Sh Ork NE SW*. [see the verb]

stap[2,2], **stoap, stop**, †**stope** /stap, stop, stɔp/ *v* **1** to block up, choke, plug (an aperture), make (a way or passage) impassable *la14-*. **2** to bring to a halt; to (cause to) cease *la15-*. **3** to push, thrust, cram or poke (something (or someone) into something) *la14-*. **4** to cram, pack (a receptacle with something) *17-*. **5** to thrust (a pointed implement) into something; to put (a plant) in the ground *la17-*. **6** to gorge oneself (with food) *20- Sh N NE T Bor*. **7** to tuck or pack bedclothes around (someone) *la19- NE T*. **stappin** *food* **1** stuffing *20- NE T*. **2** the stuffing used for filling fishes' heads *19- NE*. **stap-fu** crammed full *la15-*. †**stap of** to deprive (a person) of something *la15-16*. †**stap someone's breath** to suffocate, end a person's life *18-e19*. [OE **stoppian* or MDu, MLG *stoppen*]

stap[3] /stap/ *n* a dish consisting of cod's liver and the soft parts of fish heads, which are mixed, seasoned and cooked together *19- Sh N*. **in stap** in a mashed or broken-up state *la19- Sh*. [Norw dial *stappa* a mash of food]

stap[4], †**step**, †**staup** /stap/ *n* a stave of a barrel or pail *la16-19, 20- SW Bor*. †**fa aa staps** = *gae aa tae staps la18*. **gae aa tae staps** to fall to pieces, disintegrate; to go to ruin *19- Bor*. **tak a stap oot o somebody's bicker** to humble a person *18-19, 20- SW Bor*. **tak a stap oot o somebody's cog** = *tak a stap oot o somebody's bicker*. [compare LG *stop* a stave]

stap-, step- /stap, stɛp/ *prefix* related as the result of a second marriage *15-*. [OE *stēop-*, with influence from STAP[1,1]]

stapill see STEEPLE[1]

staple, †**stapill** /ˈstepəl/ *n* **1** a basic principle or element; a basic commodity or foodstuff *la18-*. **2** one of various towns in the Netherlands designated as the entry port and market for Scottish goods *la15-e18, 20- historical*. **3** (a royal burgh designated as) the market for the sale of staple goods *16-e17*. †**staple gudis** goods for export through the staple port *la15-e18*. †**stapillhand** = *staple gudis la14*. [AN *estaple* an emporium, a mart]

staple see STEEPLE[1]

stappit, stoppit, *Ork* **stappid** /ˈstapət; ˈstɔpit; *Ork* ˈstapəd/ *adj* **1** stuffed *16-*. **2** replete, gorged *la18-19, 20- Sh NE T*. **3** taciturn *20- Ork*. **4** hoarse *la15*. **stappit-haddie** a stuffed haddock *la19- N NE*. **stappit-heidies** stuffed fish heads *19, 20- N NE*. **stappit fu** *of a person* replete; *of a receptacle* crammed full *la19-*. [participial adj from STAP[2,2]]

stapple[1], †**stoppell** /ˈstapəl/ *n* a stopper, plug or bung *la15-19, 20- Ork*. [ME *stoppel*, OFr *estoupail*]

stapple[2] /ˈstapəl/ *n* a bundle of straw or rushes tied like a sheaf and used for thatching *19- C SW Uls*. [Du *stoppel* straw for thatching]

stapple[3], †**stople** /ˈstapəl/ *n* **1** the stem of a tobacco-pipe *la17-19, 20- Sh C SW Bor*. **2** *mining* a short shaft connecting one coal-seam vertically with another *19, 20- EC*. [MDu *stapel* a stem, a stalk]

stappy, steppie /ˈstape, ˈstɛpe/ *n* a stepfather *19, 20- EC*. [STAP- + -y (-IE¹)]

star¹, *Bor* **ster** /star; *Bor* ster/ *n* any of the celestial bodies visible as points of light in the night sky *la14-*. Compare STARN¹. **starred**, †**starrit**, †**sterrit**, †**sturrit 1** covered with stars *16-*. **2** *of cattle* marked with a star *la16*. **starrie** a kind of confectionery, the cross section showing a star-like shape *20- T*. †**starshot** *in Orkney* a shooting star *la18*. **the star o the ee** the pupil of the eye *20- Sh T SW Bor*. †**the sterris sevin** the Pleiades *e16*; compare *the seven starns* (SEEVEN). [OE *steorra*]

star² /star/ *n* (ground covered with) coarse grass or sedge *la15-19, 20- NE*. †**starry** *of ground* covered with *star-grass 18*. **star-grass** coarse grass or sedge growing mainly in moorland or boggy ground *la18-19, 20- NE*. [ME *star*, ON *stǫr* bent-grass, sedge]

star³ /star/ *n* a cataract affecting the eye *la19- Sh*. [Norw *stær*]

stardied /ˈstarded/ *adj* Travellers' language imprisoned *la19- NE T Bor*. [Romany STARDY, with adj-forming suffix]

stardy, stardie, †**staurdie** /ˈstarde/ *n* Travellers' language a prison *la19- NE T Bor*. [back-formation from STARDIED; compare Romany *staripen*]

stare¹·¹, †**stair**, †**stayr** /ster/ *n* a fixed gaze *19-*. †**in a stare, in to ane stair** in a state of astonishment, musing or wonder indicated by staring *la15-e16*. [see the verb]

stare¹·², †**stair** /ster/ *v* **1** to gaze fixedly *la15-*. **2** *of things* to obtrude, become conspicuous; *of the hair* to stand on end *18-*. **3** to concentrate the attention on *e16*. **stare someone in the face** to resemble someone closely *la19, 20- NE EC*. [OE *starian*]

stare, staris *see* STAIR¹

stark¹·¹, †**sterk** /stark/ *adj* **1** *of persons or animals* physically strong, sturdy, vigorous, healthy *la14-19, 20- Ork N T*. **2** *of material objects and structures* strongly built or made, durable, resistant *la14-19, 20- SW Uls*. **3** *of a reason or argument* convincing *la15-e17*. **4** *of a military action* vigorous; strong in numbers *la14-16*. **5** *of alcoholic drink* strong, potent *la15-19*. **6** *of a thief* arrant, unmitigated *la14-e19*. **7** *of a weapon, instrument of torture or punishment* strong, stout; capable of inflicting severe pain or a heavy blow *la14-18*. **8** *of wind, water, currents etc* strong, violent, rough *la16-18, 20- Ork*. **9** *of a person, army etc* displaying great strength of will, determined, courageous; powerful *la14-19*. **10** *of foodstuffs* hard to digest *la15-19*. **stark deid** quite dead, utterly dead *15-19, 20- Sh*. [OE *stearc*]

stark¹·², **sterk** /stark, sterk/ *adv* **1** strongly, powerfully, vigorously, energetically *la15-19, 20- WC*. **2** completely, utterly *17-*. **3** rigidly *la19*. [see the adj]

starkyn *see* STURKEN

starling *see* STERLING¹·²

starn¹, stern, †**sterne** /starn, stern/ *n* **1** a star *la14-*. **2** a star-shaped decoration or object *16-e19*. **3** a particle, a grain, a piece; a small amount *16-19, 20- NE SW*. **4** a spot or star-shaped patch of white hair on the forehead of an animal *20- Sh*. **5** a comet *15-17*. **6** a person (seen as a source of illumination, goodness or beauty) *la14-16*. **7** the Virgin Mary *15-16*. **8** Christ *16-e17*. **9** (the pupil of) the eye *la16-19*. **10** *heraldry* a representation of a star *15-16*. **11** apparently a fixture for holding a number of lights *16-e17*. **staarna** *Sh, Ork* **starnoo**, *N* **starnag** a name for an animal with a white patch on its forehead *la19-*. **starned**, †**sternit 1** *of an animal* having a white patch of hair on the forehead *la17- Ork N*. **2** starred, starry *la15-e16*. **3** decorated with star-like decoration; studded with precious stones *la16*. **starnlicht** starlight *19, 20- NE Bor*. †**starnschoit** a comet or shooting star *e16*. **the starn o the ee** the pupil of the eye *19- Bor*. [ON *stjarna*; compare STAR¹]

starn², stern, †**sterne** /starn, stern/ *n* **1** the back part of a boat *16-*. **2** the back part of an object; the hindquarters of an animal *la17-*. **starn-stuil** the short seat furthest aft in a small boat, on which the steersman sits *20- NE EC*. [ME *sterne*, ON *stjórn* steering]

starnie¹, sterny, †**starny** /ˈstarne, ˈsterne/ *adj* **1** starry, covered with stars *16-19, 20- Ork NE T Bor*. **2** (glittering) like stars *16-e17*. [STARN¹ + -IE²]

starnie² /ˈstarne/ *n* **1** a star *la18-19*. **2** a grain, a particle *18-19, 20- NE*. [STARN¹ + -IE¹]

starrach /ˈstarəx/ *adj of weather* cold, bleak, disagreeable *20- N*. [probably altered form of STARK¹·¹]

start¹·¹, stert /start, stert/ *n* **1** a short time, a moment *15-19, 20- Sh*. **2** a leap, a sudden movement *16-*. **3** a commencement; an action (beginning something) *17-*. †**start and owerlowp** *in the South-West and Borders* the trespassing of farm-animals due to their leaping boundaries (generally tolerated as unavoidable) *la17-e19*. [see the verb]

start¹·², stert, stairt /start, stert, stert/ *v pt, ptp* also **stert, start 1** to begin; to initiate, bring about *la15-*. **2** to startle, disturb suddenly *la15-*. **3** *of the hair* to stick up in an unkempt fashion, bristle; to stand on end *16-e17, 20- WC SW Bor*. **4** to bounce (a ball) *20- Sh N*. **5** *of a horse (and rider)* to move, leap into motion swiftly, in a spirited or startled fashion *15-e16*. **6** to jump in fright; to be startled or disturbed *15-17*. **7** to move (away); to rush; to act (swiftly, suddenly) *la14-17*. **8** *of a feeling, a thing, the heart* to rise up *la14-16*. **start fae steeshie** to begin from scratch *20- T*. †**start on** to leap on (a horse etc) *la14-16*. †**start on fute** to jump to one's feet *15-16*. **start oot 1** to wake or leap out of bed abruptly; to leave off an action abruptly *15-*. **2** *of a thing* to come (abruptly) out of a position *la15-e16*. †**start to** to make for, move (swiftly) towards *la15-e17*. **start up 1** to leap up, get to one's feet quickly *la14-e19*. **2** *of an enterprise* to begin, come into being *la16-*. [OE **stertan*]

start² /start/ *n* **1** part of a bucket on a water-wheel *16-e17*. **2** one of the uprights of a box-cart onto which the side-boards are fixed *19- NE T WC SW*. **start an ave, start-an-ave wheel, startin ave** an undershot water-wheel *la19- NE*. [OE *steort* a tail]

startle, stertle /ˈstartəl, ˈstertəl/ *v* **1** to cause to feel sudden shock or alarm; to react (involuntarily) in fright or surprise *16-*. **2** *especially of agitated cattle* to rush about wildly; to stampede *la14-19, 20- WC SW Bor*. **3** to move swiftly; to prance *16*. [OE *steartlian* to kick, struggle]

starty /ˈstarti/ *adj of an animal* nervous, excitable, fidgety *19, 20- Sh Ork N*. [START¹·¹ + -IE²]

starve *see* STERVE

stashie *see* STUSHIE

state¹·¹, †**stait**, †**stayt** /stet/ *n* **1** a set of circumstances or conditions, a situation; a mood or attitude *la14-*. **2** a body of people living under a sovereign government; the body politic or government of a country *15-*. **3** status; rank *la14-*. **4** a statement of facts or figures (in the pleas of a law-suit or in financial transactions) *18-*. **5** a right or title to possession of property *15-19*. **6** a rank or division of society or the realm *la14-e18*. **7** *pl* (the classes of people of) a country, especially applied to the Netherlands *15-17*. Compare ESTATE. †**state and sasine, state and sesing** *law* the formal phrase used in the transfer of HERITABLE property *15-19*. †**state and possession** = *state and sasine 15-16*. †**in state of** in possession of, having SASINE of (property) *la15-e16*. **of state** appropriate to one of high rank or authority *16-*. **oot o a state**

out of patience, in a disturbed mood *la19- Sh*. †**state of a question** the formulation of a question *17*. †**the States of Scotland** (the governing classes or parliament of) the country of Scotland *e15, e19*; compare *The Estates* (ESTATE). †**state of a vote** the formulation of a motion as it is to be put to a vote *18-e19*. [variant of ESTATE or from Lat *status*]

state[1,2], †**stait**, †**steat** /stet/ *v* **1** to express verbally; to declare; to explain *la16-*. **2** to set out, represent (a case); to formulate a question or a motion to be voted on *17-e18*. **3** to place, settle, install (a person in a position, situation) *la17-e18*. **4** to constitute, give (a person) the status of *la17*. **stated 1** set down, formulated; avowed *la17-*. **2** fixed, set; certain *17-*. [see the noun]

stathel[1.1], **stethle**, *N* **stadel**, †**stathill** /ˈstaθəl, ˈsteθəl, ˈstɛθəl/ *N* ˈstadəl/ *n* **1** the stone or timber foundation of a stack of grain *la18-19, 20- N NE T EC SW*. **2** the main part of a corn-stack; a stack in the process of building or dismantling *17- N NE T EC Bor*. [OE *staðol* a foundation, a base]

stathel[1.2], **stethell** /ˈstaθəl, ˈsteθəl, ˈstɛθəl/ *v* to make a foundation for a corn-stack *20- T*. **stethlin**, †**staddlin** (the materials used for) the foundation of a stack *la19, 20- T*. [OE *staðolian* to found, establish]

stathill *see* STATHEL[1.1]

station, †**statioun** /ˈsteʃən/ *n* **1** a place allocated, a guardpost; a place designated for stopping; a halt *16-*. **2** a position of office held; a person's position in society *17-*. **stationie** a station-master *20- NE T*. **station agent** a station-master (whose duties were originally mainly to bring traffic to the railway) *20-*. [ME *stacioun*, AN *statiun*, Lat *statiōn-*]

†**stationeir** *adj of a planet* apparently stationary *la15*. [Lat *statiōnārius*]

statioun *see* STATION

stature, †**statur** /ˈstatʃər/ *n* **1** height; bodily form or build *la14-*. **2** social status *la15-*. **3** a likeness, an effigy *15-e16*. [AN *stature*, Lat *statūra*]

statute[1.1] /ˈstatʃut/ *n* a law; a regulation *la14-*. **statute law** *law* **1** a law enacted and published as a statute *15-16*. **2** the body of laws compiled and published as statutes *16-*. [AN *statute*, Lat *statūtum*]

†**statute**[1.2] *v ptp* also **statute 1** to ordain, decree *la14-19*. **2** to enact (a law); to institute (a penalty) *15-17*. **3** to appoint (a time of meeting or a payment) *15-16*. **4** to bring (a kingdom) to order or under the rule of law *la15-e16*. [Lat *statūt-*, ptp stem of *statuere*]

stau *see* STAW[1.2]

staucher *see* STACHER[1.2]

stauk *see* STALK[2]

staul[1.1] /stɔl/ *n* a squint *la19- NE*. [see the verb]

staul[1.2] /stɔl/ *v* to squint *la19- NE*. [perhaps stall (STA[1.2] (sense 2))]

staumrel[1.1], **staumril**, †**stammrel** /ˈstɔmrəl/ *n* an awkward, clumsy, stupid person *la19-*. [STAMMER[1.2], with pejorative *-rel* suffix]

†**staumrel**[1.2], **stammrel** *adj* awkward, clumsy, stupid *la18-19*. [see the noun]

staumril *see* STAUMREL[1.1]

staun *see* STAND[1.1], STAND[1.2]

staunart *see* STANDART

staunce *see* STANCE[1.1]

staunch *see* STENCH[2.1]

staup *see* STAP[1.1], STAP[1.2], STAP[4]

staurdie *see* STARDY

stave[1.1], †**staff** /stev/ *n* **1** one of the vertical sections of a barrel *la16-*. **2** *in poetry* a stanza *19-*. **3** a set of lines for musical notation *19-*. **4** a forceful blow, a jab *19*. **5** a sprain or wrench of a joint *19-*. **ding in staves** to smash, break *la18-19,* *20- Sh Ork T*. **fa intae staves** to fall or go to pieces *18-19, 20- Sh Ork T*. †**a staff out o yer bicker** a reduction in one's income, a drain on one's resources *19*. [back-formation from *staves* (STAFF)]

stave[1.2], †**staive**, †**staiff** /stev/ *v pt* **stove**, *ptp* **stove**, †**staved**, †**staffed**. **1** to jab, thrust; to aim blows at; to hit, belabour *16-*. **2** to sprain or bruise (a joint) *19-*. **3** to thicken (iron) by heating and hammering *la18-19, 20- N WC SW*. **4** to break up casks into staves; to destroy goods by breaking the barrels in which they are being transported *la17-18*. [see the noun]

stave[2] /stev/ *v* to stagger, totter; to barge *19, 20- N NE T H&I C Bor Uls*. **stavin** staggering with drunkenness *20- N*. [perhaps back-formation from STAVER]

stave *see* STAFF

staved *see* STAVE[1.2]

stavel[1.1] /ˈstevəl/ *n* a stumble *19- Bor*. [see the verb]

stavel[1.2], †**stevel** /ˈstevəl/ *v* to walk in a halting uncertain way, stumble, blunder on *19, 20- EC SW Bor*. [altered form of STAVER]

staver, **staiver** /ˈstevər/ *v* to stagger, stumble *15-19, 20- NE T EC*. [unknown; compare Norw *stavre* to stagger, totter]

staves *see* STAFF

stavie /ˈstevi/ *v* to walk in a leisurely way, saunter, stroll *la19- NE*. [STAVE[2] + -IE[1]]

staw[1.1], **sta** /stɔ, stɑ/ *n* **1** a surfeit, a feeling of nausea, disgust or aversion caused by satiety *la18-19, 20- C SW Bor Uls*. **2** an annoyance, a nuisance; a pest, a bore *19- WC SW Bor*. **gie (someone) a staw** to give (someone) an aversion to *19-*. **hae a staw at** to bear a grudge against *la20- WC*. **take a staw at** to take an aversion to *20- WC*. [see the verb]

staw[1.2], *Bor* **staa**, †**stau** /stɔ; *Bor* stɑ/ *v* **1** to satiate, sicken or disgust *la18-* mainly *T C SW Bor*. **2** to become cloyed or sated with or nauseated by food; to become bored or fed up *18- T WC SW*. **3** to tire, weary, bore with monotony or repetition *la19-* mainly *T EC Bor*. **stawsome 1** *of food* nauseous, repugnant to the taste or appetite *19- C SW Bor*. **2** tiresome, boring *19- NE Bor*. [extended sense of STA[1.2]]

staw *see* STA[1.1], STEAL[1.2]

stawn *see* STEAL[1.2]

stay *see* STEY[1], STEY[2.1], STEY[2.2], STEY[3.1], STEY[3.2]

stayn *see* STANE[1.1]

stayr *see* STARE[1.1]

stayt *see* STATE[1.1]

stead *see* STEID[1.1], STEID[1.2]

steadin, **steading**, *Bor* **steeding**, †**steding**, †**steiding** /ˈstɛdɪn, ˈstɛdɪŋ; *Bor* ˈstidɪŋ/ *n* **1** the buildings on a farm, sometimes but not always including the farmhouse *16-*. **2** a building site; a piece of ground on which a house or row of houses is built; the site of the buildings on a farm *la17-19, 20- Uls*. **3** landed property held under a lease; a farm, comprising both land and buildings *la15-17*. †**in steding** by leasehold *la16-e17*. [*stead* (STEID[1.1]) with *-ing* suffix]

steady[1.1], *Sh SW* **studdy**, *Bor* **steedy** /ˈstɛdɪ; *Sh SW* ˈstʌdɪ; *Bor* ˈstɪdɪ/ *v* to keep or become stable or balanced *19-*. [see the adj]

steady[1.2], *Sh SW* **studdie**, *Bor* **steedy**, †**steddy** /ˈstɛdɪ; *Sh SW* ˈstʌdɪ; *Bor* ˈstɪdɪ/ *adj* unwavering, stable, balanced; continuous *la17-*. [EModE *steady*; STEID[1.1] + *-y* (-IE[2])]

steady[1.3], *Sh SW* **studdie**, *Bor* **steedy** /ˈstɛdɪ; *Sh SW* ˈstʌdɪ; *Bor* ˈstɪdɪ/ *adv* **1** steadily *la16-*. **2** continuously, all the time *la19-*. [see the adj]

steal[1.1] /stil/ *n golf* a long putt which reaches the hole contrary to expectation *19-*. [see the verb]

steal[1.2], **stail**, †**steil**, †**stele**, †**stell** /stil, stɛl/ *v pt* **staw**, **sta**, **stole**, *Sh* **stule**, *Ork T EC* **staelt**, *NE T C* **stealt**, *Ork*

stoll, †**stall**, †**stealed**, *ptp* **stown**, *NE EC* **stealt**, *T EC* **staelt**, †**stollin**, †**stowin**, †**stawn** **1** to take dishonestly; to commit or practise theft *la14-*. **2** to move quietly or surreptitiously *la14-*. **3** *of sleep or forgetfulness* to creep over (a person) *16-*. **4** to carry off, kidnap (a person) *15-e17*. **5** to achieve (a goal) by dishonest means *16-e17*. **stowlins** in a hidden or secretive way, furtively *la18-*. **stealer**, †**stelar**, †**steillar** a thief *15-*. †**steil someone doun** to murder in a surreptitious manner *la16*. †**steil fellowis**, **steill fallowis** *in the Borders* members of a cross-border raiding party; fellow thieves *la16*. †**steal a dint** to seize an opportunity, take advantage *la15-18*. †**steil to the horn** to cause (a person) to be outlawed falsely *la16-e17*. **who stole your scone?** why are you so dejected? *20- C*. [OE *stelan*]

steam[1.1], *NE* **stame** /stim; *NE* stem/ *n* water vapour, fumes, (used to drive machinery) *la18-*. **steam-mill** a (travelling) threshing-mill driven by a steam-engine *la19-20*, *21- historical*. **steamboats** very drunk *la20-*; compare STEAMIN. [OE *stēam*]

steam[1.2] /stim/ *v* to give off (water) vapour or fumes *la19-*. [OE *stēman*]

steamie /'stimi/ *n* a public wash-house *20 T C SW Bor*, *la20- historical*. Compare *the talk of the steamie* (TALK[1.1]). [STEAM[1.1] + -IE[3]]

steamin, **steaming** /'stimən, 'stimən/ *adj* very drunk *20-*. Compare *steamboats* (STEAM[1.1]). [when licensing laws forbade the sale of alcohol on Sunday except to bona-fide travellers, a trip on a steamer allowed travellers to buy drink]

steanch see STENCH[2.1]

stearch see STAIRCH

steat see STATE[1.2]

stech[1.1], *H&I* **stoich** /stɛx, stex; *H&I* stɔix/ *n* **1** a gasp, a grunt *19- EC SW Bor*. **2** the stuffy, fetid atmosphere produced by a dense crowd in a small place, a fug; a noxious stench *19*, *20- NE H&I*. **3** disorder or lack of cleanliness; smelly or dirty rubbish *19*, *20- T*. [see the verb]

stech[1.2], **steigh**, **stegh**, *NE* **steech** /stɛx, stex; *NE* stix/ *v* **1** to stuff or cram (oneself or one's stomach) with food *18-19*, *20- EC*. **2** to create a strong unpleasant stifling atmosphere (in a place), fill with bad air or fumes, stink *19*, *20- NE*. **3** to gasp, pant, puff from over-eating *19- T C SW Bor*. [probably onomatopoeic]

stechie /'stɛxe/ *adj of persons* stiff-jointed or slow-moving due to stiffness, corpulence or indolence; stodgy *19- T C*. [probably STECH[1.2] + -IE[2]]

stechle see STICHLE[1.1], STICHLE[1.2]

sted see STEED, STEID[1.1], STEID[1.2]

steddy see STEADY[1.2]

stede see STEED, STEID[1.1]

steding, **stedding** see STEADIN

stedit see STEID[1.2]

steech see STECH[1.2], STITCH[1]

steed, †**steid**, †**stede**, †**sted** /stid/ *n* a (riding) horse, originally a great horse or war-horse; a stallion *la14-*. †**stede hors** a stallion or stud-horse *e15*. †**steid-meir** a stud-mare *la16-e17*; compare *stud mere* (STUD[1]). [OE *stēda*]

steed see STAND[1.2]

steeding see STEADIN

steedy see STEADY[1.1], STEADY[1.2], STEADY[1.3]

steek[1.1], †**stek** /stik/ *n* **1** a clasp, a fastening *20- NE C*. **2** a stopping or closing (of a door) *e16*. [see the verb]

steek[1.2], *Sh* **stekk**, †**steke**, †**steik**, †**stik** /stik; *Sh also* stɛk/ *v pt* **steekit**, †**stickit 1** to close, fasten, lock (a door, gate or window) *la14-*. **2** *of a door* to shut *15-*. **3** to shut, lock up (a place or room) *la15-*. **4** to close (the eyes) *la15-*. **5** to shut up, lock away (a person or thing) *la17-*. **6** to stuff, cram *19- Sh SW*. **7** to shut (a book) *19*, *20- NE T*. **8** to stop up, block (an opening or passageway) *la14-18*. **9** to shut out, exclude (a person) *la14-18*. **steeker 1** a boot-lace *19- EC SW Bor*. **2** the back-board of a farm cart *20- T EC*. †**stekyne**, **stekyng** the (means of) fastening of a door *la14-e15*. **steekit mist** a dense mist *la19- Sh*. **steekit nieve** the clenched fist *la16-*. **steek-and-hide** *games* hide-and-seek *la18-19*, *20- NE T EC*. †**steke your eris** to fail to listen or pay attention; to refuse to hear *la15*. **steek yer gab** to keep silent, shut your mouth *la18-*. †**steke yer lips** = *steek yer gab e18*. **steek yer lugs** = *steke your eris 20-*. **steek yer hert** to harden (one's heart) *20-*. **steek yer mooth** = *steek yer gab 19-*. **steek yer nieve on** to keep quiet about *la19- NE*. **steek somebody in** to enclose, shut in (a place) *la14-*. **steek somebody oot** to shut out, exclude a person *la16-*. †**steke up 1** to close, block up (a door, window or passageway) *16-17*. **2** to close up (a shop) for a period *la16*. **3** to lock up a person or thing *la16-e19*. [OE **stecan* to stab]

steek[2.1], **stick** /stik, stɪk/ *n* **1** *sewing, knitting* a stitch *18-*. **2** the least article of clothing, a fragment of cloth *19-*. **3** a sharp pain, a stitch in the side *la19-*. **4** a quick rate or pace *la19- T*. **keep steeks wi** to keep pace with; to compete with *la18-19*, *20- SW Bor*. **let doon a steek** to make a mistake, commit a fault *19*, *20- Sh*. **tak up a steek** to amend a fault, retrieve a mistake *19*, *20- Sh*. **tak up a steek in yer stockin** = *tak up a steek e19*, *20- Sh*. [see the verb]

steek[2.2], **stick**, †**steik**, †**stik**, †**styk** /stik, stɪk/ *v* to stitch, sew; to embroider *16-*. **steekit**, †**stekit 1** stitched; embroidered *16-*. **2** *of books* constructed by stitching together the pages *e17*. [perhaps OE **stecan* to stab; compare STEEK[1.2]]

steel[1], †**steill**, †**stele** /stil/ *n* **1** steel, a harder, more elastic variety of iron *la14-*. **2** a steelyard or weighing bar *20- T SW*. **3** weapons and armour (made of steel) *la14-16*. †**steling** the application of an edge or overlay of steel to an iron implement *e16*. †**stelit**, **stelyt** made of steel or furnished with a covering, edge or point of steel *e16*. †**stele bonet** a metal helmet *16-e17*. **steelbow** a form of land-tenancy whereby a landlord provided the tenant with stock, grain or implements under contract that the equivalent should be returned at the end of the lease; the stock belonging to the landlord under this arrangement *15-19*, *20- historical*. †**stele sadill** apparently a war saddle fitted with protective steel plates *16*. **the Steelmen** a nickname for Motherwell Football Club *20-*. [OE *stǣli*]

steel[2], †**steil**, †**stele** /stil/ *n in place-names* a steep bank, especially a spur on a hill ridge *la12- Bor*. [OE *stigel*]

steel[3] /stil/ *n* **1** = *finger steel* (FINGER) *20- NE Bor*. **2** = *heid staill* (HEID[1.1]) *20- Bor*. [confusion of Eng *(finger-)stall* with *steel* (STUIL)]

steel see STIEL, STUIL

steelie /'stile, 'stili/ *n* a marble made of steel (usually a ball bearing) *20-*. [STEEL[1] + -IE[3]]

steen see STANE[1.1], STANE[1.2]

steenge[1.1] /stindʒ/ *n* a sharp pain *20- T EC SW Bor*. [OE *stincg* a sting, a stab]

steenge[1.2] /stindʒ/ *v* to attack with a sharp pain *20- EC SW Bor*. [see the noun]

steengie, **stingy**, †**stingie** /'stindʒi, 'stɪndʒi/ *adj* **1** mean, ungenerous, miserly *20-*. **2** having a poor appetite, fastidious about food *la19- Sh*. **3** haughty, supercilious; peevish, petulant *la18-e19*. **4** reluctant *la17*. [perhaps STEENGE[1.1] + -IE[2]]

Steenhive, **Steenhyve**, †**Stane-hyve** /stin'haev/ the original Scots name of Stonehaven, Aberdeenshire *16-*. [*steen* (STANE[1.1]) + ME *have* variant of HAVEN]

steenie see STANY[1.1]

steep¹·¹, †**steip** /stip/ *n* **1** the act or process of steeping, originally of barley in brewing *17-*. **2** a place or container in which things are put to soak *17-19, 20- historical*. **3** rennet or some substitute for curdling milk *la19- SW*. **4** a quantity of barley sufficient for one steeping *17*. **in steep** in the process of being soaked or macerated *17-19, 20- NE*. **set yer brains in steep** = *set yer brains tae steep* (STEEP¹·²) *la19-, 20- C*. [see the verb]

steep¹·², †**steip**, †**step** /stip/ *v* **1** to soak (to soften), macerate *15-*. **2** to soak, saturate *la16-*. **3** to curdle milk *20- SW Uls*. **4** to infuse (tea) *20- SW*. **steepies** bread sops (as food for children or pets) *la19- NE T EC*. **steepit** wet through, sodden *19-*. †**steipstane** a stone trough in which barley (for brewing) or wool was steeped *la15-18*. †**steip watter** liquid produced by or used for steeping *la16-17, e19*. **lat something steep** to allow something to mature *20- NE SW*. **set yer brains tae steep** to think hard about a problem *la19- T C SW Bor*. **set yer harns tae steep** = *set yer brains tae steep*. **steep in** to soak in, seep, percolate *20- Sh*. **steep yer brains** = *set yer brains tae steep*. **steep yer heid** don't be silly *20- N NE T C SW*. [probably OE **stēpan*]

steepend, stipend /ˈstipənd, ˈstæpənd/ *n* **1** *Presbyterian Church* the salary of a minister, originally also of a reader or other official *la16-*. **2** the salary of a teacher, judge or other employee of an authority or institution *la16-17* **preach according tae yer steepends** to act as one's circumstances will allow, use discretion *la19, 20- NE Uls*. [OFr *stipende*, Lat *stipendium*]

steepid *see* STUPIT

steeple¹, **staple**, †**stiple**, †**stepill**, †**stapill** /ˈstipəl, ˈstɛpəl/ *n* **1** the supporting, looped part of a fastening, into which a hasp, bolt or bar is hooked or slotted *la15-*. **2** *in place-names* a pillar, a post *13-17*. [OE *stapol*]

steeple², **stepill**, †**stiple** /ˈstipəl/ *n* **1** a tall tower (attached to a church, tolbooth or other public building) *la14-*. **2** a stack of fish laid crossways in a pile to dry *la18- Sh*. **3** a building (with a steeple) used as a prison *la16-19*. [OE *stēpel*]

steer¹·¹, **stur**, **stir**, †**steir**, †**stere**, †**sturre** /stir, stʌr, stɪr/ *n* **1** movement, bustle, commotion, muddle *la15-*. **2** affray, tumult, riot, insurrection *la14-17*. **on steer 1** in motion *la14-19, 20- SW*. **2** in a state of commotion, tumult or civil disorder *la14-16*. **3** in a state of physical or mental turmoil *15-16*; compare ASTEER. [from the verb, or perhaps ON *styrr*]

steer¹·², **stur**, **stir**, †**steir**, †**stere**, †**sture** /stir, stʌr, stɪr/ *v* **1** to start into motion; to begin to act; to change *15-*. **2** to (cause to) move, move (a part of the body), bestir oneself *la14-*. **3** *of things* to be in motion, show signs of life; *of body parts* to move involuntarily *la14-*. **4** to affect emotionally, inspire, excite *15-*. **5** to agitate with an implement; to mix *16-*. **6** *of persons* to move about vigorously; to be in a bustle; to be hard-pressed with work; to work or go about in a confused, harassed way *la19-*. **7** to disturb, tamper with, molest, pester, provoke *la14-19, 20- NE T EC SW*. **8** to start off on a journey, set out on one's way *la15-19, 20- NE T WC SW*. **9** to plough, usually to replough or cross-plough (land already ploughed once) *17-19, 20- T*. **10** to cause (an implement) to move or be in motion *la15-e16*. **11** to exhibit displeasure or resistance *la16*. **12** to raise (troops) *e16*. **13** *of work* to go forward *e16*. †**sterage** movement, commotion *16-18*. **steer yer fit** to bestir oneself *19-*. †**stere yer time** to make vigorous use of one's opportunity *la15-16*. **stir up 1** to arouse; to encourage, inspire; to incite *16-*. **2** to raise up, bring to prominence *la16-e17*. [OE *styrian*]

†**steer**²·¹, **stere**, †**steir** /stir/ *n* **1** a rudder, a helm *la14-16*. **2** the action of directing or governing; guidance, control, rule, government *15-16*. **3** a plough-team *19*. **4** a means or instrument of control *15-16*. [OE *stēor*]

steer²·², †**stere**, †**steir** /stir/ *v* **1** to navigate (a course), sail or row (a ship) in a particular direction *la14-*. **2** to govern, rule, lead (a country); to guide, control (an institution) *la14-*. **3** to guide (a plough) *la15-*. **4** to guide, control (a person); to wield (authority) *la14-16*. **5** *of a course or route* to take a direction *e16*. †**sterage 1** management or control (of goods) *la15-16*. **2** steering, guidance (of a ship) *18-e19*. **steerer** *fishermen's taboo* a rudder *e17, 19- Sh*. **stereburd** the right-hand side of a ship *16-17*. [OE *stēran*]

steerie¹·¹ /ˈstiri/ *n* a bustle, a commotion, a muddle *la18-19, 20- EC*. [STEER¹·¹ + -IE¹]

steerie¹·² /ˈstiri/ *adj* lively, bustling *19- N NE EC Bor*. **steeriefyke** confused bustle, agitation, excitement *19-*. [STEER¹·¹ + -IE²]

steerin¹·¹, **steering**, **stirring**, †**stering** /ˈstirɪn, ˈstirɪŋ, ˈstɪrɪŋ/ *n* **1** (the action of) moving, movement; disturbance *la14-*. **2** (a second) ploughing *la17-19*. **3** the movement of an army, (a) military action; trouble-making, civil disturbance *la14-17*. †**stering up** agitation *la16-e17*. [verbal noun from STEER¹·²]

steerin¹·², **steering**, **stirring**, †**sterand**, †**stowrand** /ˈstirɪn, ˈstirɪŋ, ˈstɪrɪŋ/ *adj* **1** *of persons, especially children* active, restless, lively *la17-*. **2** *of places* full of activity, in a tumult *la19-*. **3** stimulating *la15-e17*. †**sterand steid** a swift, energetic horse *la14-e16*. [participial adj from STEER¹·²]

steesh /stiʃ/ *n games* home or base *20- T*. **steeshie** = STEESH. [perhaps child's alteration of STATION]

steet *see* STUIT¹·¹, STUIT¹·²

steeth *see* STEID¹·¹, STEID¹·²

steeve *see* STIEVE¹·¹, STIEVE¹·², STIEVE¹·³, STIVE¹, STIVE²

steeven *see* STIVVEN, STEVEN³

steevil *see* STIEVE¹·²

steg¹·¹ /stɛg/ *n* a hold-up of work in a factory or mine *20- WC*. [unknown]

steg¹·² /stɛg/ *v* to cause a hold-up of work (in a factory or mine) *la19- WC*. [unknown]

steg² /stɛg/ *n* a gander, a male goose *19- SW Bor*. [Eng *steg*, ON *steggr* a male bird]

steg³ /stɛg, steg/ *v* to walk with long heavy steps, stride, stalk, prowl *19, 20- C SW*. [unknown]

stegh *see* STECH¹·²

steich *see* STEY¹

steiche *see* STITCH¹

steid¹·¹, **stead**, **sted**, *Sh Ork N* **steeth**, †**stede**, †**steyd**, †**steith** /stid, stɛd; *Sh Ork N also* stið/ *n* **1** the site or foundation of a building or wall *13-19, 20- Sh Ork N WC*. **2** the foundation or base of a corn-, hay-, or peat-stack *18- Sh Ork N*. **3** a farmhouse and its outbuildings *18-19, 20- SW*. **4** a mark, imprint or impression *16-19, 20- SW*. **5** service, favour; advantage, profit *la15-19, 20- Ork*. **6** *fishing* a sinker or anchor-weight; the place where the stone is dropped *19- Sh*. **7** a dense, stationary shoal of fish *la19- Sh*. **8** (a) lodging; a dwelling-place *15-16*. **9** an area of land; a landed property or estate *13-17*. **10** a place, a location; an inhabited place, a village, town or city *la14-17*. **11** a part of or place on the body *la14-16*. **12** circumstances *la14-e16*. **13** a position, an office *la14-16*. †**stedabill, stedable** serviceable, helpful, useful, profitable *la15-17*. **steidfast** constant, dependable, unvarying *la14-*. †**steidful** = *steidfast* *16*. †**stedhaldand** a substitute, a deputy *la14-e16*. †**stedhaldar** = *stedhaldand* *la15-e17*. **steeth-stone, steethe stane** a foundation stone *19- Ork N*. †**in the stede** in the place of, as a successor or substitute *la15-17*. †**the Steidis** the cities of the Hanseatic

League *la15-16*. **stead of** instead of *18-19, 20- C SW Bor.* [OE *stede*]

steid¹·², **stead**, *Sh Ork* **steeth** /stid, stɛd; *Sh Ork* also stið/ *v pt* **sted**, †**stad**, †**stedit 1** *passive* to be placed in a difficult or bad condition or position; to beset (with difficulties) *la14-19, 20- Bor.* **2** to lay a foundation for, make the base of (a building or stack) *la18- Sh Ork.* **3** *of fish* to shoal *la19- Sh.* **4** *passive* to be placed in a location, be settled in a place *la14-e16.* **5** to establish, settle (a person) in a situation; to install a tenant *15-e16.* **6** to supply the needs of *la15-e16.* **7** to serve, be useful *16.* [see the noun]

steid *see* STEED

steiding *see* STEADIN

steif *see* STIEVE¹·², STIEVE¹·³

steiffing *see* STIFFIN

steigh *see* STECH¹·²

†**steik, stek, stik** *n* **1** a piece or item of goods; a number or quantity of the same good; the quantity belonging to one merchant *15-17.* **2** a quantity, probably a cask, of wine *15-e17.* **3** a single skin or a small number of skins *la14-16.* **4** a piece or length of cloth *la15-17.* **5** a piece of money, a coin *la15-17.* **6** a piece (of work); a matter or concern *la16-17.* [MDu *stic* a piece]

steik *see* STEEK¹·², STEEK²·², STICK¹·²

steil *see* STEAL¹·², STEEL², STELL¹·²

steill *see* STEEL¹, STELL⁴

†**steillar** *n applied abusively to a tailor* apparently a person who inserted steel into stomachers, punning with a person who stole stomachers *e16.* [paronomasia of STEEL and STEAL¹·²]

steillar *see* STEAL¹·²

steilt *see* STILT¹·¹

†**steine** *n in Orkney* a court *16.* [ON *stefna* an appointed meeting, a summons]

steing *see* STING²·¹

steinȝie *see* STAIN

steip *see* STEEP¹·¹, STEEP¹·²

steir *see* STEER¹·¹, STEER¹·², STEER²·¹, STEER²·²

steith *see* STEID¹·¹

steive *see* STIEVE¹·¹

stek *see* STEEK¹·¹, STEIK

steke *see* STEEK¹·²

†**stekill** *n* the bar of a door *la15.* [probably STEEK¹·², with noun-forming suffix]

stekit *see* STICK¹·²

stekk, stekyne *see* STEEK¹·²

stel *see* STEAL¹·², STEEL¹, STEEL², STIEL

stell¹·¹, *H&I* **stale** /stɛl; *H&I* stel/ *n* **1** a (circular) stone-built enclosure or shelter for sheep *18-19, 20- WC SW Bor.* **2** *mining* a prop or wooden stay used for underpinning a roof *19, 20- C.* **3** a clump or plantation of trees used as a shelter for sheep *la18-19, 20- Bor.* **4** *curling* the iron footboard or notches in the ice to prevent players' feet from slipping when delivering the stone *19- SW*; compare CRAMPET (sense 2). [see the verb]

stell¹·², *N* **stile**, †**steil**, †**still** /stɛl; *N* stʌɪl/ *v* **1** *chess* to undergo stalemate; to checkmate (an opponent) *la16-.* **2** to brace or stay (oneself) by planting the feet against something *la18- NE WC SW Bor.* **3** to fix (the eyes) in a stare; *of the eyes* to become fixed, protrude *19, 20- C SW Bor.* **4** to place in position, set up; to prop *la15-19, 20- N WC SW.* **5** to corner, shut in; to put (sheep) in a STELL¹·¹ (sense 1) *19, 20- SW Bor.* **6** to halt, come or bring to a standstill, make immobile *la19- WC SW Bor.* **7** to load (a ship) evenly, trim the cargo in (a ship) *18.* **8** to put (a horse) in a stall *la16.* †**stelling place** a place of refuge or shelter *e16.* [OE *stellan* to place, put, set]

stell²·¹, **still** /stɛl, stɪl/ *n* a container or vessel; an apparatus for distilling (whisky) *16-.* [see the verb]

†**stell**²·², **still** *v* to distil; to discharge (liquid) in small drops *la15-19.* [aphetic form of DISTIL]

stell³ /stɛl/ *v* to go with a firm, purposeful step, stride *19- WC SW.* [unknown]

†**stell**⁴, †**steill**, †**staill** *n* a place in a river or estuary where nets were set up to catch salmon *13-e19.* †**stell fishing** a fishery with a STELL⁴ *la17-e19.* †**stell-net** a net stretched out into or across a river *la16-19.* [OE *stællo* catching of fish, a standing-place, a stable, a fishing ground; compare ON *stallr* a stall]

stell *see* STEAL¹·²

stellage *see* STALLAGE

†**stellat** *adj of the sky* studded with stars *la15-16.* [Lat *stellātus*]

stellionate /ˈstɛljənɛt/ *n law* **1** a crime, originally fraud, for which there is no specific name *la17-.* **2** a real injury against the person which has no specific name *la18-19, 20- historical.* [Lat *stelliōnātus* from *stellio* a kind of lizard with star-like spots, a fraudulent person]

stelt *see* STILT¹·¹

stem¹·¹ /stɛm/ *n* **1** a dam of stones in a stream, used as a fish-trap or to form a watering-place for cattle *18, 20- N T C Bor.* **2** resistance; a check *la16-19.* [see the verb]

stem¹·² /stɛm/ *v* **1** to stop, staunch (bleeding) *la15-.* **2** to stop, dam up (water) *la16-.* [ME *stemmen*, ON *stemma*]

stem² /stɛm/ *n* the peak of a cap *20- SW.* **stemmed bunnet**, **stemmed bonnet** a cap with a peak *la19- SW.* **stemmed cap** = *stemmed bunnet 20- SW.* [extended sense of Eng *stem* the prow of a boat]

†**stem**³ *v nautical* to keep a certain course *la14.* [OE *stemn* the prow of a boat]

†**stemmet, stemmat** *n* a (fine) woollen cloth *16.* [OFr *estamet*]

†**stemming, stamyng** *n* a woollen cloth *15-17.* Compare TEMMING. [MFr *stamine*, Lat *stāmen*]

sten *see* STANE¹·¹, STEND¹·²

stench¹·¹, †**stanche** /stɛnʃ/ *n* **1** a satisfying, especially of hunger *la18-19, 20- NE.* **2** a stopping (of talk) *la16.* [see the verb]

stench¹·², **stanch, stainch** /stɛnʃ, stanʃ, stɛnʃ/ *v* **1** to check the flow of (water or blood) *15-.* **2** to allay (hunger or thirst); to satisfy (a person) with food, satiate; to satisfy desire *15-19, 20- NE T.* **3** to put a stop to, cause to cease, suppress activity, quell *la14-e19.* **4** to extinguish, suppress (emotion); *of emotion* to cease *15-17.* **5** to restrain from violence, suppress (troublemakers) *15-16.* **6** to cease flowing *la15-16.* **7** *of persons* to cease doing something *la15-16.* **8** *of activity* to cease *16.* [OFr *estanchier*]

stench²·¹, **staunch**, *NE C* **stainch**, *NE T* **stinch**, †**steanch**, †**stanch** /stɛnʃ, stɔnʃ; *NE C* stɛnʃ; *NE T* stɪnʃ/ *adj* **1** strong, dependable, firm; principled; in good health *la17-19, 20- NE C.* **2** serious, severe-looking, reserved; inflexible, uncompromising; austere, rigid *la18-19, 20- NE.* [ME *staunche*, OFr *estanche* watertight]

stench²·², **stainch** /stɛnʃ, stɛnʃ/ *adv* strictly, closely, exactly *la19- NE.* [see the adj]

stenchel *see* STAINCHEL¹·¹, STAINCHEL¹·²

stencher *see* STAINCHER¹·¹

stenchion *see* STAINCHEON¹·¹

stend¹·¹ /stɛnd/ *n* **1** a leap, a spring, a bound *15-19, 20- Sh WC.* **2** a long, firm, bouncing step, a stride *18-19, 20- Sh.* **3** a sudden start, a thrill of excitement or fear *la18-19.* [see the verb]

stend[1,2], **sten** /stɛnd, stɛn/ v **1** to leap, bound, spring up; *of animals* to rear, start, be restive *16-*. **2** to stride, walk or march purposefully *18-19, 20- Sh*. **3** *of emotion* to soar; to throb, pulsate *18-19*. †**stendling** leaping or bounding repeatedly *e16*. [perhaps aphetic form of EXTEND]

stendie /ˈstɛndi/ *n* a stroke of the TAWSE[1] *e19, 20- EC*. [Lat *extende (manum)* hold out (your hand)]

steng *see* STING[2,1]

stengle /ˈstɛŋəl, ˈstɛŋɡəl/ *v* to close up (a door or gate); to shut in (an animal) *la19- Sh*. [Norw dial *stengla*]

stenlock, stanelock /ˈstɛnlək, ˈstɛnlək/ *n* a (fully grown) coalfish, a SAITHE *19, 20- H&I WC Uls*. [unknown]

†**stennis**[1,1] *n* a sprain *19*. [unknown]

†**stennis**[1,2], **stinnish** *v* to sprain, wrench (a joint or muscle) *19*. [unknown]

stenory *see* STANNERY

stent[1], **stint** /stɛnt, stɪnt/ *v* **1** to extend, stretch out (a sail or net) in its proper position; to pitch (a tent or pavilion); to make taut *la14-*. **2** to strive, exert oneself *la18-19, 20- EC*. **3** to stretch, distend (the stomach) with food *19, 20- Sh*. **4** to extend, stretch (a person) on an instrument of torture; to suspend (a person) as a punishment *la14-e18*. **5** to spread out, stretch, keep in place, shape, line, stiffen (cloth, a garment) *la15-18*. **6** to hang (a window) with curtains; to hang (curtains) *la15-e17*. **7** to set up, put in position (a tomb or ordinance) *16-17*. **8** to extend, raise (a weapon) *e16*. **9** *of branches* to spread over, fill (a place); to fill (a place) with branches *e16*. †**stentar** a person in charge of setting up a tent or pavilion *e16*. **stenter 1** a clothes prop *20- C SW*. **2** a framework on which cloth is stretched during manufacture to prevent shrinkage *18*. †**stenting** material used to stiffen or line a garment *la15-18*. **stentit** extended, stretched, taut; stiff *16-*. †**stentour** stiffening for a doublet *e16*. **stenting post** a strainer in a wire fence *la19- C SW Bor*. †**stent-net** a fishing net stretched on stakes across a river *la17-19*. †**stent tree** = *stenter* 2 *17-e18*. **stent at** = STENT[1] (sense 2) *20- Sh*. [probably aphetic form of EXTEND]

stent[2,1], **stint** /stɛnt, stɪnt/ *n* **1** (money paid in) tax, usually an *ad hoc* tax imposed by the burghs or trade incorporations on those liable; an exaction for burghal or parochial purposes *15-19, 20- NE EC*. **2** the proportion of pasture on a common land allocated to each tenant; the number of animals allowed on each pasturage *15-19, 20- Bor*. **3** an (annual) assessment of the value of land or property, used to determine taxation and record rights and obligations *16-19*. **4** *in Orkney* the proportion of butter SKATT[1,1] exacted in kind *la15-e16*. **5** an extent or quantity (of a thing) *la15*. Compare EXTENT[1,1]. †**stent butter** *in Orkney* butter paid as a proportion of SKATT[1,1] *la15-e17*. †**stentmaister 1** a person appointed to assess the taxes of a town or parish *17-19*. **2** *pl* a committee of final-year students at Glasgow University appointed to assess the graduation fee for their fellow-graduands *18-19*. †**stent oil** = *stent butter la16-17*. **stent-roll**, †**stent-row** a list of taxable persons and the rate at which they were taxed; an assessment roll *16-18, 19- historical*. †**stent for trade** a tax based on the trade done by each burgess of a town *e18*; compare *trade's stent* (TRADE[1,1]). [AN *extente*, Lat *extenta* valuation for tax]

stent[2,2], †**stint** /stɛnt/ *v* **1** to assess for taxation, impose a tax or levy on (property, a person or community) *la15-19, 20- historical*. **2** to be liable for tax, pay tax *16-e17*. **3** to levy (money, goods, taxation); to impose taxation *la16-17*. Compare EXTENT[1,2]. †**stenter, stentour** an official in charge of assessing and raising taxes *la15-e19*. [see the noun]

stent[3,1] /stɛnt/ *n* **1** limits, bounds, restraint; the limit to which one is prepared to go *18- C SW Bor*. **2** an allotted task, a portion of work to be covered in a given time *18-*. Compare STINT[1,1]. [see the verb]

stent[3,2] /stɛnt/ *v* **1** to leave off, desist, halt, discontinue *la14-e19*. **2** to restrict, limit, curb *la17-19, 20- Bor*. **3** to apportion (work); to allocate an amount of work to (a person); to make (a person) work hard *la18-19, 20- T*. **4** to cease moving, come or bring to a halt *18*. [variant of STINT[1,2]]

stenyt, stenʒie *see* STAIN

step *see* STAP[1,1], STAP[1,2], STAP[4], STEEP[1,2]

step- *see* STAP-

stepbairn /ˈstɛpbern/ *n* a stepchild *16-*. **mak a stepbairn o** to treat unkindly, neglect, spurn *19-*. [step- (STAP-) + BAIRN[1,1]]

stepill *see* STEEPLE[1], STEEPLE[2]

steppie *see* STAPPY

ster *see* STAR[1]

sterand *see* STEERIN[1,2]

sterap *see* STIRRUP

sterch *see* STAIRCH

sterde *see* STURDY[1,2]

stere /stɪr/ *adj* harsh, stern *15, la19- literary*. [ME *ster* strong, stout; perhaps related to STURE[1]]

stere *see* STEER[1,1], STEER[1,2], STEER[2,1], STEER[2,2]

sterf *see* STERVE

stering *see* STEERIN[1,1]

sterk *see* STARK[1,1], STARK[1,2], STIRK

sterling[1,1], †**stirlin** /ˈstɛrlɪŋ/ *n* **1** the currency of the United Kingdom *18-*. **2** the Norman silver penny minted in England and Scotland *13-15, 16- historical*. [unknown]

sterling[1,2], **sterlin**, †**starling**, †**stirling**, †**striviling** /ˈstɛrlɪŋ, ˈstɛrlɪn/ *adj* **1** *frequently postpositionally, eg pund sterlin, shilling sterlin* describing English money or coin, or the currency of the United Kingdom *la15-*. **2** with reference to the English or Scottish coinage of the reign of David II or as mentioned in the original infeftments of the burghs *la16-e17*. **3** genuine, dependable *19-*. †**sterling money** = STERLING *16-e19*. **sterling silver** silver of the quality of the Norman silver penny; of standard quality *17-*. [unknown]

stern, †**sterne** /stɛrn/ *adj* **1** bold, courageous, ferocious, resolute *15-*. **2** severe, austere *16-*. **3** *of a battle* fiercely fought *e16, la19*. **4** *of a weapon or blow* fiercely wielded, ferocious *16-e19*. **5** *of winter* harsh *e16*. **6** *of a beard* stiff, rigid *e16*. **7** *of a person's constitution* strong *la15*. [OE *styrne*]

stern *see* STARN[1], STARN[2]

sterne *see* STARN[1], STERN

sterny *see* STARNIE[1]

sterr *see* STAIR[1]

stert *see* START[1,1], START[1,2]

stertle *see* STARTLE

sterve, starve, stairve, †**sterf**, †**stervyn** /stɛrv, starv, stɛrv/ *v* **1** to die of cold or hunger; to suffer the effects of lack of food or warmth *16-*. **2** to cause to die by lack of food *17-*. **3** to affect with extreme cold *19-*. **4** to die, perish; to suffer extremely; to cause to die *15-e17*. **stervation** bitter cold *20-*. †**sterve for hunger** to die or come close to dying for lack of nourishment *la16-17, la20-*. **serve o cauld** to be much affected by cold, feel severely chilled *la18-*. **serve wi cauld** = *sterve o cauld*. [OE *steorfan* to die]

stethell *see* STATHEL[1,2]

stethle *see* STATHEL[1,1]

steuch *see* STEW[1,1], STEW[1,2]

steue *see* STIEVE[1,3]

steug *see* STUG[1,1]

steul *see* STUIL

steve *see* STIEVE[1,1]

stevel *see* STAVEL[1,2]

†**steven**¹, **stevin**, **stevyn** *n verse* **1** a voice *la14-19*. **2** a loud outcry, a din *la15-e19*. **3** the voice of a poet, poetry *e16*. **4** birdsong *la15-16*. **5** the noise made by musical instruments *la15-e16*. **with ane stevin**, **with a stevin** in unison *la14-15*. [OE *stefn*]

†**steven**², **stevin**, **stevyn** *n* the prow or stern of a boat *16-19*. [OE *stefn*, or Du, LG *steven*, cognate with OE *stefn* the prow or stern]

steven³, **steeven** /ˈstivən/ *n* a coalfish in its third year *19-Sh*. [unknown; compare Norw dial *styving* a half-grown halibut]

stevie *see* STIFFIE

†**stevin**, **stevyn** *v* to direct one's course; to sail (a ship) *e16*. [STEVEN²; for the sense development compare STEM³]

stevin *see* STEVEN¹, STEVEN²

steving *see* STIFFIN

stevyn *see* STEVEN¹, STEVEN², STEVIN

stew¹·¹, **stue**, *NE* **styew**, *Sh SW* **steuch** /ˈstju; *Sh SW* ˈstjux/ *n* **1** a stench *16-19, 20- Sh WC SW Uls*. **2** (a cloud of) dust, smoke or vapour *la14-19, 20- Sh NE T*. **3** a hubbub, uproar or commotion; trouble, turmoil *la16, la19- Sh NE*. **4** a coating or sprinkling of dust or powder *20- NE*. **5** sea-spray *la19- Sh*. **stewie** dusty; floury *20- NE*. [unknown]

stew¹·², *Sh SW* **steuch** /ˈstju; *Sh SW* ˈstjux/ *v* **1** to emit smoke or vapour, smoulder *20- SW*. **2** to stink, cause a stench *la16, la19- Sh C SW*. †**stewat** a stinker; one who stinks *e16*. †**stew out** to come forth in the manner of smoke or a stink *la16*. [unknown]

steward *see* STEWART

stewart, **steward**, †**stwart**, †**stuart** /ˈstjuərt, ˈstjuərd/ *n* **1** an official of the highest status under a ruler; a chief executive officer; an official holding a supervisory or managerial position *14-*. **2** the title of the SHERIFF in Orkney and Shetland or in Kirkcudbright *18-19, 20- SW*. **3** an executive officer of the Crown having jurisdiction over lands held directly by the monarch, especially a *stewartry 15-e18*. **stewartry 1** an area that was formerly a STEWARTRY (sense 2) and continues to be so called after the abolition of that administrative unit, mainly Kirkcudbright and Orkney and Shetland *la18-*. **2** the territory under the jurisdiction of a STEWART (sense 3) *la15-e18*. **3** the office of STEWART (sense 3) *la15-e18*. †**stewart court** the court of justice or administration having jurisdiction within a *stewartry la15-18*. †**stewart deput** the judge delegated by the STEWART (sense 3) to administer justice in a *stewartry la15-18*. **Stewart of Scotland 1** a title of the monarch's eldest son *15-*. **2** the officer of state next after the king in authority *la14-e15, 18- historical*. [OE *stīweard*]

stewat *see* STEW¹·²

stey¹, **stay**, *T* **steich** /stae, ste; *T* staɪx/ *adj* **1** *of a hill or road* (very) steep; difficult to climb *la14-*. **2** upright, unbending; reserved, haughty *la16-e17*. **stey-coal** a coal seam set at a very steep angle *20- EC*. **set a stoot hert tae a stey brae** *see* STOOT. [OE *stǣge*; compare OE *stīgan* to ascend, rise, ON *stigi* a step, ladder, steep ascent]

stey²·¹, **stay** /stae, ste/ *n* **1** the action of coming or bringing to a halt, cessation; a delay *la16-*. **2** the action or fact of remaining in or occupying a place; a period of residence *la16-*. **3** a means or cause of stopping, a brake or obstacle *la16-e17*. [see the verb]

stey²·², **stay** /staɪ, ste/ *v* **1** to stop, prevent (something), desist from (something), come or bring to a halt; to arrest, detain (a person) *16-*. **2** to dwell, reside; to make one's home (in a place) *la16-*. **3** to wait (for) *la16-17*. **4** to remain, tarry; to delay departure, fail to leave *la16-*. [ME *steien*, OFr *estai-* stem of *ester* to stand]

stey³·¹, **stay** /stae, ste/ *n* **1** also *pl* a supportive (element of a) garment *17-*. **2** (a) support *la16-e19*. **stey-band**, **stay-band**, †**steband 1** a bar to fasten the two leaves of a double door *la16-19, 20- NE T C*. **2** a supportive band attached to a (child's) bonnet or cap *la17-e19*. [from the verb and OFr *estaye*]

†**stey**³·², **stay** *v* to support, sustain; to comfort *la16-e19*. [OFr *estayer* to prop up]

steyd *see* STEID¹·¹

steyng *see* STING²·¹

stibbill *see* STIBBLE

†**stibblart** *n in Aberdeen* a young lad, a (half-grown) youth *18-e19*. [probably STIBBLE in the sense of beard stubble with derogatory suffix]

stibble, **stubble**, †**stibbill**, †**stubbill** /ˈstɪbəl, ˈstʌbəl/ *n* the stalks of corn or other crops left on a field after reaping; reaped land *la15-*. **stibbler 1** a harvest-worker who gathers up odd straws, a gleaner *18-e19*. **2** *Presbyterian Church* a probationer not yet in a settled charge, who preaches wherever required *la18-19, 20- C*. **stibbly** stubbly *20- T*. **stibble-butter** high-quality butter made from the milk of cows grazed on stubble fields *19-*. **stibble-land**, **stubble-land** the stubble of the first crop of corn grown after grass *19, 20- EC*. **stibble-rig 1** a stubble field *la18-*. **2** the leader in a team of reapers *la18-e19*. [OFr *stuble*]

stichle¹·¹, **stechle** /ˈstɪxəl, ˈstɛxəl/ *n* a rustle, bustling noise *19, 20- NE*. [see the verb]

stichle¹·², **stechle**, †**stychle** /ˈstɪxəl, ˈstɛxəl/ *v* to rustle, stir, bustle; to move energetically *la15-19, 20- NE*. [probably altered form of ME *stightelen* to govern, arrange]

†**sticht** *n* battle array *la14*. [OE *stihtan* to set in order, arrange]

stick¹·¹ /stɪk/ *n* a stoppage, breakdown or standstill; an obstacle *17-19, 20- Sh SW*. [see the verb]

stick¹·², †**steik**, †**stik**, †**stek** /stɪk/ *v pt* **stuck**, *NE* **stack** **stickit**, †**stak**, †**stikkit**, †**stekit**, †**stokit**, *ptp* **stuck**, **stickit**, *Sh NE C Bor* **stucken**, †**sticken**, †**stekit 1** to stab, pierce (with a pointed weapon), injure or kill by stabbing *la14-*. **2** *of a thing* to thrust, pierce in (into) *15-*. **3** *of a horned animal* to gore, stab or butt with its horns *la16-*. **4** to come to a premature halt in, break down in the middle of (a job); to botch *16-*. **5** to remain fixed in a position or place; to stay attached (to), remain loyal *15-*. **6** to proceed with, complete, persist with, resolve *20-*. **7** to be thwarted by something; to suffer delay or hindrance; to be unable to progress or proceed ◊*he'll no stick 20-*. **8** *in sorting fishing-lines* to turn each hook back into the horse-hair of the SNOOD¹·¹ (sense 2) to prevent its entangling the line *20- NE T EC*. **9** to slaughter (an animal) as part of a ritual sacrifice *e16*. **10** to place (a mark) *e16*. **sticker**, †**stikkar** a stabber, a slaughterer *la16-19, 20- Sh*. **stickers** = *sticky-willie* (STICKY) *20- EC SW Bor*. **stickin** stiff and unsocial in manner, unwilling to join in; obstinate *19- T C SW Uls*. **stickit 1** *of a task* left spoilt or incomplete *la18-19, 20- T*. **2** *of persons* halted in their trade or profession, failed, insufficiently qualified: ◊*a stickit minister la18-*. **3** *of plants* stunted, checked in growth *19, 20- N T*. **stuck** = *stickit la19-*. **stick bubbly** a coarse imprecation *la20-*. **stick in** to persist doggedly, work hard, persevere, go energetically (at) *19-*. **stick in tae** = *stick in la19-*. **stick in wi** = *stick in la19-*. **stick tee** to adhere, keep close to *20- Sh NE*. **stick up tae 1** usually *of a lover* to pay court to, ingratiate oneself with *la18- NE*. **2** to stand up to, oppose defiantly *19-*. †**stick with** to cause difficulty or annoyance, bother *la17-e19*. [OE *stician*]

stick²·¹, †**stik** /stɪk/ *n* **1** a thin piece of wood broken or cut from a tree *la14-*. **2** a piece of wood used as an implement or weapon; a staff *la16-*. **3** a stick-like implement, an aspergillum *15-16*. **4** a dried up, miserable or perverse person *la16-*. †**stickle** a small stick, especially one laid across the joists of a mill kiln to support the straw or cloth on which the grain was dried *la17-19*. **a tae sticks** all to pieces, to ruin; completely and utterly *19-*. **a tae sticks and staves** = *a tae sticks e19*. †**all in sticks** = *a tae sticks e17*. **nae great sticks at** not adept at, not very good at *19, 20- Sh NE T*. †**stick and stour** = *stick and stow 16-e19*. **stick and stow** completely, entirely *la18-19, 20- EC*. †**stick of wax**, **stick wax** a stick-shaped piece of sealing wax *la17-e18*. **tak up the sticks** to exert oneself, act in support of *la19- Sh NE*. [OE *sticca*]

stick[2.2] /stɪk/ *adj* wooden, made of timber *18-*. [see the noun]
stick *see* STEEK[2.1], STEEK[2.2]
sticken *see* STICK[1.2]
stickit *see* STEEK[1.2], STICK[1.2]
†**stickle**[1], **stighill** *n* the trigger of a gun *la17-e18*. [unknown; compare Du *stekel* a thorn, Dan *stikkel* a pointed piece of metal]
stickle[2] /'stɪkəl/ *v* **1** to hesitate, scruple *18-19, 20- Bor*. **2** to dispute, argue, raise objections *la16-e18*. [probably back-formation from EModE *stickler* a moderator, a meddler]
stickly /'stɪkle/ *adj* prickly, bristly, stubbly; *of peat* rough, fibrous *19, 20- NE*. [unknown; perhaps a conflation of *stibbly* (STIBBLE) and STICK[2.2]]
sticky /'stɪke/ *adj* adhesive; gummy, tacky *19-*. **sticky-fingered** having a tendency to steal *19-*. **sticky grass** = *sticky willie la19- SW Bor*. **sticky willie 1** goose grass *Galium aparine 20-*. **2** sundew *Drosera 20- Sh*. [STICK[1.2] + -y (-IE[2])]
sticky-out, **sticky oot** /'stɪke ˈʌut, 'stɪke 'ut/ *adj* sticking out, at right-angles to *la20-*. [STICK[1.2] + -y (-IE[2]) + OOT[1.4]]
stiddie *see* STUDDIE
stiel, **steel**, †**stele** /stil/ *n* the handle of a barrow or plough *16-19, 20- NE Bor*. [ME *stele* a handle, a shaft, OE *stela* a stalk, a support]
stieve[1.1], **steeve**, †**steive**, †**steve** /stiv/ *v* to make firm, stiff, taut or steadfast *16-19, 20- SW*. [see the adj]
stieve[1.2], **steeve**, †**stive**, †**steif** /stiv/ *adj* **1** firmly fixed, stable; rigid *la16-*. **2** *of (the limbs of) persons or animals* firm, strong, sturdy *la18-19, 20- T EC SW*. **3** steady, resolute, staunch; loyal, dependable *la18-19, 20- NE T H&I EC SW*. **4** hard-hearted, relentless, obstinate *la16-19, 20- T C*. **5** shrewd in business, prudent; mean *la18-19, 20- SW*. **6** *of a struggle* hard, grim; *of haste* pressing *19, 20- WC*. **7** *of a road* difficult, steep and rough *la19, 20- Sh NE*. **8** *of food or drink* strong, thick, full of body *la18-19, 20- Sh Ork N*. **9** *of wind* strong *e19*. **stievie** = STIEVE[1.2] (sense 8) *20- SW*. **steevil**, *Ork* **stivval 1** = STIEVE[1.2] (sense 8) *19-*. **2** *of cloth* thick, hard-wearing *20- Ork*. [uncertain; compare Du, LG *stevig*]
stieve[1.3], **steeve**, †**steue**, †**steif** /stiv/ *adv* firmly, stoutly, securely, staunchly, unyieldingly; tautly *16-, 20- Ork EC*. [see the adj]
stif *see* STIFF[1.2]
stife /staɪf/ *n* a suffocating atmosphere, smoke or vapour *19-*. **stifin** stifling *20- WC SW Bor*. [probably back-formation from STIFLE]
†**stiff**[1.1], **stuff** *v* to make stiff; to starch *16-e19*. [see the adj]
stiff[1.2], †**stif**, †**styf**, †**stiffe** /stɪf/ *adj* **1** rigid, hard, unpliable *la15-*. **2** firm, unyielding, obstinate *la15-*. **3** fierce, forceful, strong *la15-*. Compare STIEVE[1.2]. [ME *stif*, OE *stīf*]
stiffen /'stɪfən/ *v* to make or become stiff; to starch (clothes) *19-*. [EModE *stiffen*, STIFF[1.2] with verb-forming suffix]

stiffenin, †**stifining** /'stɪfnɪn/ *n* **1** starch *19, 20- C*. **2** material used for stiffening a garment *e17*. [verbal noun from STIFFEN]
stiffie, **stevie** /'stɪfi, 'stivi/ *n* a broad vertical bar of light across the moon or sun, a sign of bad weather *20- N NE*. [unknown]
stiffin, **stiffing**, †**steiffing**, †**stuffing**, †**steving** /'stɪfɪn, 'stɪfɪŋ/ *n* **1** starch *la16-19, 20- N Bor*. **2** material used for stiffening a garment *la16-e17*. [verbal noun from STIFF[1.1]]
stifin *see* STIFE
stifining *see* STIFFENIN
stifle /'staɪfəl/ *n mining* foul air from an underground fire; miners' asthma (from this or from coal-dust), pneumoconiosis *19, 20- EC*. [Eng *stifle* to suffocate]
stiflin /'staɪflɪn/ *n* bronchitis *20- EC*. [verbal noun from Eng *stifle* to suffocate]
stiggie /'stɪɡi/ *n* **1** a stile; a set of steps in a drystane dyke *19- Sh*. **2** a lane between walls *20- Sh*. [Norw *stige* a ladder, steps]
stiggle[1] /'stɪɡəl/ *n* a poor, thin straw or stalk of grain *20- Ork*. **stiggly** *of a crop of grain* thin, insubstantial *20- Ork*. [Norw dial *stikla* stubble, a straw]
stiggle[2] /'stɪɡəl/ *v* to walk unsteadily, stumble *20- Sh*. [Norw dial *stigla*]
stighill *see* STICKLE[1]
stik *see* STEEK[1.2], STEEK[2.2], STEIK, STICK[1.2]
stikkit *see* STICK[1.2]
stilch /stɪltʃ/ *n* a young, fat, clumsy man *19- SW Uls*. [altered form of STILT[1.2], from the way of walking]
stile, †**style**, †**styill**, †**styll** /staɪl/ *n* a means of access; steps over or a passageway through a wall; a doorway in a wall *15-*. [OE *stigel*]
stile *see* STELL[1.2], STYLE[1.1], STYLE[1.2]
stilk, **stylk** /staɪlk/ *n* a stalk or stem *20- Sh*. [Norw *stilk*]
still[1.1] /stɪl/ *n* **1** *of the tide* the pause between ebb and flow *19- Sh SW*. **2** stillness *e16*. [see the adj]
still[1.2], †**styll** /stɪl/ *v* **1** to be or become quiet *17-*. **2** to cause activity or sound to cease; to calm (wind); to lull, soothe (a child); to silence (the law) *16-19*. **stillin** *of the tide* the pause between ebb and flow *20- Sh*. [OE *stillan*]
still[1.3], **stull**, †**styl**, †**styll** /stɪl, stʌl/ *adj* **1** motionless, inactive; calm *la14-*. **2** reserved, taciturn, unforthcoming *19, 20- NE T WC*. **3** silent, quiet *la14-18*. **stilly 1** unmoving *15-*. **2** quietly, secretly *15-*. **still-minded** reserved, taciturn *20- Bor*. †**stilly or loud** clandestinely or openly, in any way, at all *la15*. [OE *stille*]
still[1.4], **stull**, †**styll** /stɪl, stʌl/ *adv* **1** motionlessly; without changing location, at rest *la14-*. **2** continuously, constantly; thereafter *la14-*. **3** nonetheless *la16-*. **4** noiselessly, calmly *16-*. **still an on 1** yet, nevertheless, for all that *la18-*. **2** always, continuously, without intermission *la18-19, 20- N*. [OE *stille*]
still[1.5] /stɪl/ *interj* a call to stop, *eg* in games or to a horse *la19- N NE T*. **still an yow** a ball game in which a ball is thrown against a wall *20- Bor*. [see the verb]
still *see* STELL[1.2], STELL[2.1], STELL[2.2], STYLE[1.1]
stillicide /'stɪləsaɪd/ *n law* the SERVITUDE permitting the shedding of rainwater from a roof onto the adjoining property *la17-*. Compare EAVESDROP. [Lat *stillicidium* a dripping from the eaves]
†**still-stand** *n* an armistice *17-e19*. [Du *stilstand*]
stilp /stɪlp/ *v* to walk with long stiff steps, stalk *la18- NE T*. [altered form of STILT[1.2]]
stilpert[1.1] /'stɪlpərt/ *n* **1** a stilt *la19- NE*. **2** a tall, lanky person; an animal with long legs *la19- NE*. [STILP, with derogatory suffix]

stilpert[1,2] /'stɪlpərt/ *v* to walk with long, stiff strides, lifting the feet high *la19- NE*. [see the noun]

stilt[1,1], †**stult**, †**steilt**, †**stelt** /stɪlt/ *n* **1** one of the handles of a plough *la16-*. **2** a crutch *la16-19, 20- C SW Bor*. **3** a prop, a support *e17*. **stiltie** a wading bird, the redshank *Tringa totanus* or the greenshank *Tringa nebularia 20- N*. [ME *stilt*]

stilt[1,2], †**stult** /stɪlt/ *v* **1** to go on stilts or crutches *19, 20- C Bor*. **2** to cross (a river) on stilts *la18-19, 20- WC SW Bor*. **3** to walk on high heels *20- Bor*. **4** to walk stiffly or haltingly; to lift the legs high in walking *la18-e19*. [see the noun]

stilter /'stɪltər/ *v* to walk unsteadily, totter *la19- Ork*. [frequentative form of STILT[1,2]]

stim /stɪm/ *n* a haze, a mist *20- Ork*. **stimmy** hazy, foggy *20- Sh Ork*. [unknown]

stime[1,1], **styme** /staɪm/ *n* **1** a faint trace, a glimpse; an awareness (of something) *la15-*. **2** a tiny amount, a vestige, a particle, a jot *la18-*. **3** a glimmer of light *la18- literary*. **see a stime** see SEE. [ME *stime*]

stime[1,2], **styme** /staɪm/ *v* **1** to peer, attempt to see distinctly *19, 20- Sh N*. **2** to fail to see *e17*. **stymel** a person who does not see or understand quickly *19, 20- Bor*. †**stymie** a person who does not see well *17-e19*. [see the noun]

stimie[1,1], **stymie** /'staɪmi/ *n golf* the ball of an opponent lying on the green in a line between the ball of the player and the hole he is playing for, the distance between the balls being more than six inches (if it is less the intervening ball may be lifted) *19-20, 21- historical*. [unknown]

stimie[1,2], **stymie** /'staɪmi/ *v* **1** *golf, of a ball or player* to lie or play as a STIMIE[1,1] *la19-20, 21- historical*. **2** to obstruct, thwart *la19-*. [unknown]

stimna /'stɪmnə/ *n* strength, vitality, substance *la19- Sh Ork*. [compare Faer *stimbur* strength, power]

stimpart /'stɪmpərt/ *n* **1** *in dry measure* the fourth part of a PECK[2] *la18- C SW*. **2** *in Ayrshire and Lanarkshire*, a measure of land, the fourth part of a RIG[1,1] (sense 3) *la19, 20- historical*. [reduced form of *sixteen* (SAX) + PART, one sixteenth of a FIRLOT]

stinch *see* STENCH[2,1]

stinckett *see* STINK[1,2]

sting[1] /stɪŋ/ *v pt* **stung**, *NE T C Bor* **stang**, †**stingit** to pierce with a fang; to wound with a sting *la16-*. **stinging ether** the dragonfly *20- C*. [OE *stingan*]

sting[2,1], †**steng**, †**steing**, †**steyng** /stɪŋ/ *n* **1** a pole, stake, staff, bar or beam *la14-19*. **2** a staff used as a weapon; the shaft of a pike *15-17*. **3** a pole used to manoeuvre a boat *la18-19, 20- NE*; compare STANG[2,1] (sense 4). **4** a stick with a forked iron tip used in thatching *e19*. **5** *fisherman's taboo* the mast of a boat *19- Sh*; compare STANG[2,1] (sense 5). †**stinging** the action of thatching or mending thatch *la16-e18*. †**stingis-dint** a fine for an assault with a stick *15*. †**stingman** a porter who with another carried loads suspended on a pole *la16-e17*. †**sting and ling 1** a means of transporting something using ropes suspended from a pole resting on the shoulders of two bearers *la16-19*. **2** lock, stock and barrel, without ceremony, forcibly *e19*. [OE *steng* a stake, a pole, a staff]

sting[2,2] /stɪŋ/ *v* **1** to propel a boat with a pole *19*. **2** to use a STING[2,1] (sense 3) *18-19, 20- Bor*. [see the noun]

stingie /'stɪŋi/ *n* the starling *20- T*. [reduced and altered form of *stirling* (STIRLIN) + -IE[1]]

stingie *see* STEENGIE

stingit *see* STING[1]

stingy *see* STEENGIE

stink[1,1], †**stynk** /stɪŋk/ *n* a foul smell, a stench; foul-smellingness, stench *14-*. **stinkers** = *stinky dails*. **stinky dails** a children's game in which two opposing sides try to capture one another, or some object, across a dividing line *la19- WC SW*. [see the verb]

stink[1,2], †**stynk** /stɪŋk/ *v ptp* **stunk**, †**stinckett**, †**stinked 1** to emit a foul smell, reek *la15-*. **2** to be offensive or abhorrent *15-*. **3** to fill (a place) or affect (a person) with an offensive smell or foul atmosphere *18- Sh Ork NE T EC*. **stink in someone's nese, stink into someone's nese** to be offensive to someone *la15-16*. [OE *stincan*]

stinkin, stinking, †**stinkand**, †**stynkand** /'stɪŋkɪn, 'stɪŋkɪŋ/ *adj* **1** foul-smelling *13-*. **2** offensively haughty, snobbish, superciliuous *la18-19, 20- Sh NE T*. **3** offensive to the feelings, morally foul or repugnant *la14-e17*. **stinkin Billy** sweet william *Dianthus barbatus 20-*. **stinking-coal** an impure kind of coal which burns with a strong sulphurous smell *la19- C*. **stinking Elshender** = *stinkin Willie 19, 20- T EC*. †**Stinkand Styll** *in Edinburgh* the means of access to St Giles Church, passing into the alley through the luckenbooths *16-17*. **stinkin Tam, stinkin Tammy** one of various strong-smelling plants, especially the rayless mayweed *Matricaria discoidea la19- Bor*. **stinkin Willie** ragwort *Jacobaea vulgaris 19-*. [participial adj from STINK[1,2]]

stinkle /'stɪŋkəl/ *n* a wheatear *Oenanthe oenanthe 19- Sh Ork*. **stinklin** = STINKLE *20- Sh*. [altered form of Norw dial *steindolp*, or one of its variants]

stinnan /'stɪnən/ *presp* **stinnan wi fill** groaning with repletion *20- Ork*. [compare Norw dial *stynja* to groan]

stinnish *see* STENNIS[1,2]

stint[1,1], †**stynt** /stɪnt/ *n* **1** a lack, a shortage of something; a restriction or limitation (in quantity) *la15-*. **2** an allotted period of work; a specific period of time *la19-*. **3** delay, hesitation; a cessation of action *la14-e16*. Compare STENT[3,1]. †**but stint** without delay, pause or hesitation *15-e16*. †**forowtyn stint** = *but stint la14*. [see the verb]

stint[1,2], †**stynt** /stɪnt/ *v* **1** to leave off, desist, halt, discontinue *la14-*. **2** to limit, restrict, keep short *16-*. **3** *of plants* to shrivel, droop *la18-19, 20- Ork*. **4** to stop (a blow) *la14-e17*. †**but stinting** without delay, pause or hesitation *e16*. [OE *styntan* to blunt, dull]

stint *see* STENT[1], STENT[2,1], STENT[2,2]

stipend *see* STEEPEND

stiple *see* STEEPLE[1], STEEPLE[2]

stippit *see* STUPIT

†**stir** *n* as a polite form of address, sir *la18-e19*. [probably shortened form of MAISTER[1,1], conflated with SIR]

stir *see* STEER[1,1], STEER[1,2]

stirk, *Sh* **strik**, *Ork* **strick**, †**sterk** /stɪrk; *Sh Ork* strɪk/ *n* **1** a young bullock or sometimes heifer between one and two years old *14-*. **2** a young, countrified man, especially one who is well-built or stupid or oafish *16-*. **stirkie** = STIRK *la18-*. **in the stirk's sta** *of a child* supplanted in its parents' attention by a new baby *19-*. [OE *stirc* a calf]

stirlin, †**stirling**, †**styrlyng** /'stɪrlɪn/ *n* **1** a starling *Sturnus vulgaris 15-*. **2** a nickname for an inhabitant of Kirkwall in Orkney *la19- Ork*. **stirlin snaa** a period of wintry weather in May *20- Ork*. [ME *sterling*, OE *stærlinc*]

stirlin *see* STERLING[1,1]

stirling *see* STERLING[1,2]

Stirling jug *see* JOUG[1,1]

stirn /stɪrn/ *v* to become stiff with cold, be chilled, freeze; to shiver *la19- Sh*. [compare Faer *stirðna*]

stirrah, †**stirra**, †**stirrow** /'stɪrə/ *n* a young lad, a boy; a fellow *la17-19, 20- Bor*. [altered form of EModE *sirrah*; compare STIR]

stirring *see* STEERIN[1,1], STEERIN[1,2]

stirrop *see* STIRRUP

stirrow *see* STIRRAH

stirrup, †**sterap**, †**stirrop** /'stɪrəp/ *n* **1** the support suspended from a saddle for a horserider's foot *la14-*. **2** a metal fixing or support for *eg* a lamp or barrow *16-e17*. †**sterap irn** a metal support for the foot, forming part of the STIRRUP *la15-17*. †**sterap leddir** the (leather) strap by which a stirrup iron hangs from the saddle *15-17*. †**sterapman** an attendant on a horserider; specifically, a member of the royal household with duties with regard to the monarch's horses and their equipment *e16*. [OE *stigrāp*]

stishie *see* STUSHIE

stitch[1], †**steiche**, †**steech** /stɪtʃ/ *n* **1** a single in-and-out movement of a needle in sewing; the thread left in the material by this movement, a stitch (of a particular sort, especially in embroidery) *17-*. **2** a sharp pain *la17-*. **stitchy** a kind of sunbonnet *la19- SW Bor*. [OE *stice*]

stitch[2] /stɪtʃ/ *n* a furrow or drill, of turnips or potatoes *19- SW*. [EModE *stitch*, probably extended sense of STITCH[1]]

†**stith**[1.1] *v* to set firmly, cause to remain immovable *la14*. [see the adj]

†**stith**[1.2], **styth** *adj* **1** unyielding, strong; powerful, firm, immovable *la14-19*. **2** *of a stream* strong-flowing *la14-16*. **3** *of weather* hard, severe *15-19*. **4** stiff, rigid as in death *la18-19*. †**stithly 1** purposefully, steadfastly; courageously, valiantly *la14-e16*. **2** stiffly, rigidly *e16*. [OE *stīð*]

†**stith**[1.3] *adv* powerfully, vigorously *15-e16*. [OE *stīðe*]

stithy *see* STUDDIE

stive[1], **steeve** /staev, stiv/ *v* to stuff, pack, cram; to gorge with food *17-19, 20- T EC Bor Uls*. **stiver** an ample meal *20- T*. [OFr *estiver*]

stive[2], **steeve** /staev, stiv/ *v* to walk stiffly, march, stalk *20- Ork N*. [perhaps an altered form of STAVE[2] or extended sense of STIVE[1]]

stive *see* STIEVE[1.2]

stivn *see* STIVVEN

stivval *see* STIEVE[1.2]

stivven, **stivn**, †**steeven** /'stɪvən/ *v* to become stiff or numb, especially with cold; to congeal *19, 20- Sh Ork*. [Norw *stivne*]

St Johnston, **St Johnstoun** /sənt 'dʒɔnstən/ *n* **1** a former name for the town of Perth, of which St John the Baptist is patron *13-e19, 20- historical*. **2** a football team that plays in Perth; compare *the Saints* (SAINT[1.3]). **St Johnston's ribbon** the hangman's noose or rope *la16-19, 20- historical*. [from the name of the saint + TOUN]

†**stö** *n fisherman's taboo* the wind *19 Sh*. [compare Norw dial *vederstoe* the state of the weather]

stoackin, **stockin**, **stocking**, †**stokin** /'stokɪn, 'stɔkɪn, 'stɔkɪŋ/ *n* **1** a close-fitting garment covering the leg, usually to the knee or thigh *la16-*. **2** a stocking used as a receptacle for savings; savings, a hoard *la19-*. **stockin-fit** = STOACKIN (sense 2) *la19-*. **stockin-needle** a darning needle *la19-*. †**cast the stockin** = *throw the stocking la18*. **throw the stocking** to throw the stocking of the bride or bridegroom among the guests at a wedding as a way of predicting who will marry next *19, 20- N*. [STOCK[1.2] a sock, a stocking, with *-ing* suffix]

stoap *see* STAP[2.1], STAP[2.2]

stoat *see* STOT[2.1], STOT[2.2]

stoater *see* STOTTER[2]

stoat weasel /'stot 'wizəl/ *n* a stoat *Mustela erminea la19-*. [Eng *stoat* + WEASEL]

stob[1.1], **stab**, †**stobe**, †**stabb** /stɔb, stab/ *n* **1** a sharpened stake or pole; a post or stake used in fencing, originally a boundary-marker in a burgh *la15-*. **2** a prickle, a thorn; a splinter, especially one driven into the skin *17-*. **3** a bradawl; an implement for piercing *la19, 20- Sh NE T SW*. **4** an incomplete rainbow showing only the lower ends of the bow (believed to forewarn of a storm at sea) *19, 20- NE T EC*. **5** a pin for securing thatching, a Y-shaped stick used like a staple *16-19, 20- NE*. **6** a two-pronged stick used to push thatching straw into position *19- NE*. **7** a short thick nail; a spike *la15-19, 20- Bor*. **8** the stump of a tree or shrub; the stump of a broken standing stone or cross; a broken off branch or twig *la12-19, 20- N*. **stobber** a thatcher *la17*. †**stobbit** *of a cow* apparently having horns present only as stumps *e17*. **stobby 1** rough and spiky, prickly, bristly *19- N NE T*. **2** *of a bird* = *stob-feathert 20- Ork*. **stob-feathert** *of a bird* having stumpy, undeveloped feathers; *of persons* provided for, well off *19- N NE*. **stob-fence** a wire fence fixed on wooden posts *20-*. †**stob hornit** = *stobbit la16*. **stob-nail** a short thick nail *18-19, 20- NE Bor*. **stob-thack** thatch with pins to secure the thatching *18-19, 20- NE*. **stob-thackit**, †**stob-theekit** with pins securing the thatching *la18- NE T*. †**haf stob and stake** to own property (usually in a burgh) *la15-16*. †**hald stob and stake** = *haf stob and stake 16*. †**stab and rice** a method of construction by which twigs were woven horizontally between vertical stakes; a fence constructed thus *18-*. [OE *stubb*, *stobb* a stump]

stob[1.2], **stab** /stɔb, stab/ *v* **1** to fence with stakes, mark or bound with posts *16-19, 20- Sh WC SW Bor*. **2** to prop up (plants) with stakes *la18-19, 20- WC SW Bor*. **3** to fix down (thatch) with pins *16- NE T*. **4** to dress or trim (a stack of grain) by poking in projecting sheaves with a hay-fork *la19- Ork N NE*. †**stob and stake** to fence with stakes *16-e17*. [see the noun]

stob *see* STAB[1.1], STAB[1.2]

stobbie /'stobi/ *n* a dependable or trustworthy person or thing; a standby *la19- Sh*. [unknown]

stobe *see* STOB[1.1]

stock[1.1], †**stok**, †**stuke** /stɔk, stok/ *n* **1** a store, provision or supply (of goods) *17-*. **2** the progenitor of a family or kindred; a kinship group, a lineage or line of descent; a breed or strain (of animals or people) *la15-*. **3** the rail of a bed, originally a box bed; the side of a bed away from the wall; a bedstead *17-*. **4** the socket of a bagpipe drone, to which the bag is tied *20-*. **5** that proportion of a crop remaining after the teind had been deducted *18-19, 20- historical*. **6** a chap, a fellow, a creature *19, 20- NE T EC Uls*. **7** the hard stalk or stem of a plant (especially cabbage or kail); the whole plant *16-19, 20- Sh N*. **8** a pack of playing cards *la16-18, 20- Sh T*. **9** a block of wood, a tree trunk, a stump, a (stripped) log; a stake, a pole, a boundary post *la13-19, 20- NE*. **10** the main (upright) part of a structure; a framework or main element *16-19, 20- NE*. **11** the trunk of a body, a headless corpse; a lifeless, unfeeling person or thing *la15-19, 20- Ork*. **12** the wooden support attached to the barrel of a handgun or musket *17-*. **13** the shaft of a tool or weapon; the hilt of a sword or dagger *la15-19*. **14** *in Aberdeen* a board, bench or stall at an open-air market on which wares were displayed *la17-e19*. **15** a saddle-tree *la15-e18*. **16** the block of wood from which a bell is hung *la16-e18*. **17** *pl* the framework supporting a ship during construction *16-17*. **18** the lower part of a pair of hose, a stocking *16-e17*. **19** a plant stem on which a graft is inserted *la15-17*. **20** a butcher's or fishmonger's cutting block or table *la15-17*. **21** a gun carriage *la15-e17*. **22** an alms-box *la15-e17*. **23** an executioner's block *la15-e17*. **24** a stick or cudgel *la14-e15*. **25** a sum of money, a fund, wealth; an invested sum, capital (as distinct from revenue); a financial legacy or grant *la15-*. **26** a fishing station, a place where fish were caught (and cured) *la12-19*. **27** a living tree, a tree trunk still attached to its roots *16*. **stock-annet** the shelduck *Tadorna tadorna 18-19, 20- T*

EC SW. **stock-boat** *fishing* a boat used to transport cured herring and equipment between outlying fishing stations and the depots *20- Sh N NE.* **stock-duck,** *Sh* **stock-dyook** the wild duck or mallard *Anas platyrhynchos 19- Sh Ork N.* †**stok-fisch** a cod or whitefish cured by splitting open and drying hard in the air without salt *la13-17.* **stock-hawk** the peregrine falcon *Falco peregrinus la19- Sh.* †**stockmaker, stokmakar** a maker of gun-carriages *la16-e19.* †**stukemart, stoc mart** perhaps an ox or cow fattened for the table *la15-e16.* †**stock-owl, stock-oule** mainly in Orkney the eagle owl *Bubo bubo la17-e19.* †**stock-purse** a fund kept for the common purposes of a group *17.* †**stok sadill** perhaps a saddle with a wooden tree *e16.* †**stok shears** perhaps shears for cutting metal *e17.* **stock-whaup, stock-whaap** the curlew *Numenius arquata la18- Sh.* **stock and brock** one's whole property, every bit *17-.* †**stock and teind, teind and stock** *law* the gross produce of a farm or fishery, without deduction of the TEIND *la16-17.* †**stok or stane, stok and stane 1** *of religious (pagan) images* wood or (and) stone, in reference to worship of false gods *la14-e19.* **2** what is most basic, anything *la15.* **stock-still** as still as a lump of wood, completely motionless *la15-.* [OE *stocc* a stump, a stake, a log]

stock[1,2], †**stok** /stɔk, stok/ *v* **1** to furnish, supply, provide *la16-.* **2** *of the body or limbs* to become stiff, cramped, wobbly or swollen *19, 20- Uls.* **3** *of a plant* to send out shoots, sprout, develop side-shoots, spread *la18-19, 20- N NE T.* **4** to invest (money); to entrust (funds) to another for saving or investment *la16-19.* **5** to furnish a piece of artillery with a gun-carriage *16-17.* †**stoker** a workman who makes or fits gunstocks *la16-e17.* †**stoking 1** the action of fitting (a gun or a bell) to a stock *la15-e17.* **2** the livestock and implements of a farm *la17-.* **stockit 1** obstinate, stubborn *la16-19, 20- NE.* **2** *of hose* having the stocking part of a particular sort *16.* **3** *of a gun* fitted with a stock *la16-17.* †**stock in with** to join with others in an enterprise *17.* [see the noun]

†**stock and horn, stock-in-horn, stock horne** *n* a wind instrument *la15-19.* [Gael, IrGael *stoc*, OE *stocc* a horn, a trumpet, probably the same as STOCK[1,1] + HORN]

stockin, stocking *see* STOACKIN

stod *see* STUD[1]

stoddert, studdert /'stɔdərt, 'stʌdərt/ *n* an area of green grass on a hill or heath surrounding a spring of water *20- NE.* [probably an altered form of STROTHER]

stodge, *Sh* **studge** /stɔdʒ, stodʒ; *Sh* stʌdʒ/ *v* to walk with a long slow step; to step uncertainly or unsteadily; to travel heavily or laboriously (carrying a burden) *20- Sh NE SW Bor.* **stodgel** a slow, lumbering, rather stupid person *la19, 20- NE.* **stodger** = *stodgel 20- NE.* [compare EModE *stodge* to stuff full, probably onomatopoeic]

stöels /støls/ *n* the cut end of a sheaf of corn *20- Sh.* [compare Norw dial *stjøl*]

stog *see* STUG[1,1], STUG[1,2], STUG[2,1], STUG[2,2]

stoich *see* STECH[1,1]

stoif *see* STOVE[1,1], STOVE[2]

stoir *see* STORE[1,1], STORE[1,2]

stoit[1,1], *NE* **styte** /stɔit; *NE* stʌit/ *n* **1** a lurch, a stagger, a tottering step *19, 20- Sh Ork NE T.* **2** foolish talk, stupid rubbish, nonsense *19- Ork N NE.* **3** a buffet, a blow *20- SW Bor.* **4** a stupid, ungainly, blundering person *19, 20- NE.* **5** a stroll *20- NE.* [perhaps Du *stuit* a bounce of a ball; compare STOIT, STOT[2,1]]

stoit[1,2], *NE* **styte,** †**stoyte** /stɔit; *NE* stʌit/ *v* **1** to stagger, stumble (from drink), walk in a dazed uncertain way *18-.* **2** to stroll, saunter *la19- NE T.* **3** to (cause to) bounce, rebound *19- N.* [perhaps Du *stuiten* to rebound, bump, bounce; compare STOT[2,2]]

stoit[1,3] /stɔit/ *adv* with a bump or bounce *la19- NE T SW.* [see the noun]

stoit[2] /stɔit/ *n* a fit of obstinacy or sulking *20- Sh.* [compare Norw *bli støtt* to be offended]

stoit *see* STOT[1]

stoitek /'stɔitək/ *n* **1** a small sack of grain *la19- Sh.* **2** a short, stocky person *20- Sh.* [perhaps a derivative of Norw dial *stytt* stumpy + -OCK]

stoiter[1,1], *NE* **styter** /'stɔitər; *NE* 'stʌitər/ *n* **1** a staggering motion, a stumble, reeling about *19-.* **2** a stroll, a saunter *20- NE.* [see the verb]

stoiter[1,2], *NE* **styter** /'stɔitər; *NE* 'stʌitər/ *v* **1** to walk unsteadily, reel, totter *18-.* **2** to stumble or falter in speech, stammer *19, 20- SW.* [frequentative form of STOIT[1,2]]

stok *see* STOCK[1,1], STOCK[1,2], STUG[1,1], STUG[1,2]

stokin *see* STOACKIN

stokit *see* STICK[1,2]

stole[1,1] /stol/ *n forestry* a tree-stump; a new shoot from a cut stump *la18-19, 20- SW.* [Eng *stole* the sucker of a stolon, and STUIL]

†**stole**[1,2] /stol/ *v of a tree-stump* to throw up new shoots *la18-e19.* [see the noun]

stole *see* STEAL[1,2], STUIL

stoll /stɔl, stʌl/ *v* to walk with difficulty *20- Sh Ork.* [Norw dial *stulla* to go slowly, *stolla* to stump about]

stollin *see* STEAL[1,2]

stolum /'stoləm/ *n* **1** a pen-nibful of ink *la18-19, 20- N NE EC.* **2** a large piece broken or cut off something *19-, 20- EC.* **stollie** = STOLUM (sense 1) *20- T.* [compare ME *stulle* a chunk of food, MDu *stolle*; perhaps with mock-Latin suffix]

stomach *see* STAMACK[1,1], STAMACK[1,2]

†**stomachat, stomakat** *adj* indignant, angry *16-e17.* [Lat *stomachāt-*, ptp stem of *stomachārī* to be resentful]

stomak *see* STAMACK[1,1], STAMACK[1,2]

stomakat *see* STOMACHAT

stommager *see* STAMINGER

stomok *see* STAMACK[1,1]

stomp *see* STUMP[1,1]

stonach, stonack *see* STANE[1,1]

stond /stɔnd/ *n* the direction of a sea current or the tide *la19, 20- Ork.* [Norw *stand* (of wind) to come from a position]

stond *see* STOUND[1,1]

stonder, stondie *see* STANE[1,1]

†**stone** *v of plants and trees* to make new growth after pruning *la18-e19.* [perhaps ME *stoven*, OE *stofn* a tree trunk, a stem, a branch, a shoot; compare STOO[1,2], STOLE[1,2]]

stone *see* STANE[1,1], STANE[1,2]

stoneder, stoner *see* STANE[1,1]

stonie *see* STANY[1,1], STANY[1,2]

†**stonis, stoneis, stwnys** *v* **1** to shock, dismay, fill with fear *15-16.* **2** to astonish, amaze *la15-16.* **3** to be shocked, exhibit surprise *16.* [aphetic form of Older Scots *astonis*; compare ASTONIST]

stoo[1,1] /stu/ *n* **1** a slice, a chunk, a piece cut *18-e19.* **2** a cut on the ear (*eg* of a sheep) as a mark of ownership *18- Sh Ork SW.* [see the verb]

stoo[1,2], **stow** /stu, sto/ *v* **1** to cut, trim (hair) *20- Sh Ork NE SW.* **2** to cut off (the stem or shoots of a plant or tree) *la18-19, 20- Sh NE.* **3** to cut off an animal's tail or part of its ear (especially as a mark of ownership), originally also a person's ears or nose *16-19, 20- Sh.* **stowans** *food* the young leaves of the colewort, used as food *18-.* [ME **stuven*, from ON *stúfr* a stump]

stood *see* STUTH

stoog /stug/ *n* the core of a boil, the pus in an abscess *20- N.* [Gael *stùc* a little, conical hill]

stook[1.1], †**stouk** /stuk/ *n* **1** a number of sheaves set up in pairs to dry in the field *la15-*. **2** the (quantity of) straw or fodder contained in a stook *la16-e18*. **stookie Sunday** the Sunday in the harvest period when all the corn has been cut and stands in stooks *la19-*. **stook o duds** a person dressed in rags *19, 20- NE.* [ME *stouk*, MLG *stūke*]

stook[1.2], †**stowk** /stuk/ *v* **1** to set up (sheaves) in groups of self-supporting pairs to dry *la16-*. **2** *of sheaves* to go into stooks *19, 20- Sh NE T.* [see the noun]

stookie[1.1] /'stuki, 'stuke/ *n* **1** plaster of Paris, stucco; a plaster cast encasing a broken limb *la18-*. **2** pipeclay *20- WC SW*. **3** a stucco figure *la19-*. **4** a slow-witted, dull or shy person *la19-*. **5** *pl* a children's game in which the players are required to remain motionless *20- T C SW*. **stookie eemage 1** a plaster statue(tte) *la19- NE*. **2** an effigy; a scarecrow *la19- EC* **stand like a stookie** to stand motionless, as if helpless *la19-*. [Ital *stucco* a type of fine plaster]

stookie[1.2] /'stuki, 'stuke/ *v* to hit a person very hard *la20-*. [see the noun]

stool *see* STUIL

stoon *see* STOUND[2.2]

stoond *see* STOUND[1.1]

stoop[1], †**stoup**, †**stowp** /stup/ *v* **1** to bend over, bow *la14-*. **2** to humble oneself *la16-*. [OE *stūpian*]

stoop[2] /stup/ *interj* be quiet, shut up *20- Ork*. [probably an instinctive utterance]

stoor[1.1], **stour**, †**stower**, †**store**, †**stowr** /stur/ *n* **1** (a cloud or layer of) dust; any fine powdery substance *15-*. **2** commotion, fuss, disturbance *la18-*. **3** strife, conflict, battle *la14-19, 20- NE WC SW Bor literary*. **4** a storm, wild weather; a blizzard *la15-19, 20- Sh Ork*. **5** the violent movement of water; water moving violently; a cloud of fine spray *15-19, 20- Sh*. **6** a pouring out of liquid, a steady outflow, a gush *19- NE*. **7** a moral or emotional conflict; a struggle *la14-17*. †**bide the stour** to suffer adversity or hardship *la18-19*. †**escape the stour** to avoid adversity or hardship *la18-19*. **knock the stour oot o** to beat, thrash (someone) *la19-*. **like stour** like a whirl of dust, with a rush, very quickly *20-*. †**stand the stour** to put up with adversity or hardship *la18-19*. [OFr *estour* tumult, conflict]

stoor[1.2], **stour** /stur/ *v* **1** to go quickly, rush, bustle about *16-*. **2** *of dust or spray* to swirl, rise in a cloud *16-19, 20- Sh Ork WC Bor*. **3** to cover with powder or dust *17-19, 20-* mainly *N NE*. **4** to (cause to) gush out in a strong stream *19, 20- Sh NE*. [see the noun]

stoor[2] /stur/ *v* to stare dejectedly or vacantly *la19- Sh*. [Norw dial *stura*]

stoor *see* STURE[1]

stoorie[1.1], **stourie** /'sturi/ *n* oatmeal gruel *18-19, 20- Ork*. **stoorack** = STOORIE[1.1] *20- N NE*. **stoorin** = STOORIE[1.1] *19- NE T*. **stoorie-drink, stourie-drink**, *Sh* **stoor-a-drink** = STOORIE[1.1] *20 Sh T*. [see the adj]

stoorie[1.2], **stoory** /'sturi, 'sture/ *adj* **1** dusty, full of or covered with dust *la18-*. **2** *especially of a young child* active, restless *19, 20- T C*. **3** wild, stormy *20- H&I*. **stourie fit** *in Falkland and Peebles* a resident who is not a native of the town, an incomer; originally, a traveller or gipsy, a stranger who has arrived on foot *20- EC Bor*. **stourie lungs** pneumoconiosis; silicosis *20- EC*. [STOOR[1.1] + -IE[2]]

stooshie *see* STUSHIE

stoot[1.1], **stout**, †**stowt** /stut/ *adj* **1** strong *la15-*. **2** bold, valiant *la14-*. **3** corpulent, fat *19-*. **4** in good health, robust *la18-*. **5** *of wind* strong, violent *15-19*. **6** *of a mountain* imposing, formidable *e16*. **stoutfullie** stoutly *la16*. **stootly 1** very, greatly *20- Ork*. **2** boldly; fiercely *la14-17*. **3** resolutely *15-16*. **stoutness**, †**stoutnes 1** corpulence *20-*. **2** courage, pride *la14-16*. **3** firmness, determination *15-e17*. **set a stoot hert tae a stey brae** to face difficulties with resolution *18-*. **stootrife** strongly built, powerful *20 SW Bor*. [OFr *estout* brave, fierce, proud]

†**stoot**[1.2], **stout** /stut/ *adv* **1** powerfully, strenuously, strongly *la15-19*. **2** boldly, valiantly, proudly *la16-e17*. [see the adj]

stoot *see* STOT[3.2], STUIT[1.2], STUT

stooter *see* STOTTER[1.2]

stoothe /stuð/ *v* to make or cover (a wall) with lath and plaster *la18- SW Bor*. [ME *stuthe* a wooden post (especially one in a lath and plaster wall), OE *stuðu* a post]

stop *see* STAP[1.1], STAP[2.1], STAP[2.2], STOWP

stope *see* STAP[2.2]

stople *see* STAPPLE[3]

stoppell *see* STAPPLE[1]

stoppit *see* STAPPIT

stopple *see* STAPPLE[1]

store[1.1], †**stoir**, †**stor** /stor/ *n* **1** a stock, a supply; a large number, a flock, a host; wealth *la15-*. **2** a place where goods are stored; a shop *19-*. **3** livestock *14-18*. **the Store** the popular name for an area's Co-operative Society or its local retail branch *20-*. **store-ferm** a (usually upland) farm on which sheep are reared and grazed *la18-19, 20- SW Bor*. †**store-fermer** a person who runs a *store-ferm 19*. †**store-maister 1** = *store-fermer la16-e19*. **2** the person in charge of the stores in a royal palace or castle *la17-e18*. †**store-room** land used for grazing sheep *17-18*. [OFr *estor*]

store[1.2], †**stoir** /stor/ *v* **1** to keep in store, reserve; to preserve *la15-*. **2** to furnish, supply *la16-17*. **3** to breed, rear (cattle); *of cattle* to grow, fatten or perhaps breed *la16-e17*. †**storour**, **storer** a keeper of livestock *16-e17*. **store the kin** to keep the human race in existence; to survive *la19- NE T*. [OFr *estorer*]

store *see* STOOR[1.1]

storkyn *see* STURKEN

storm[1.1], †**storme** /stɔrm/ *n* **1** (a spell of) violent, disturbed weather, turbulence *la14-*. **2** fallen snow, especially when lying in quantity for a long time; a period of wintry weather with alternating frost and snow; originally, the result of heavy snowfall *la16-19, 20- N NE T EC Bor*. **3** a violent or furious outburst (of emotion, anger etc); trouble *la15-17*. **stormy**, †**stormie 1** characterized by storms; tempestuous *la15-*. **2** associated with or indicating storms *16*. **3** frosty, icy *16*. **4** violently perturbed, severely troubled *la15-16*. **5** exposed to wintry weather; snowy *la18-e19*. **storm-cock** the mistle thrush *Turdus viscivorus 20-*. **stormhead window** = *storm-window 19, 20- N SW*. **stormont window** = *storm-window la18, 20- N SW*. **storm-stayed, storm-stead**, †**storm-sted**, †**storm-staid** held up on a journey by bad weather *la15-*. **storm-window** a projecting window with a small roof and sides, a dormer window *la16-19, 20- NE T EC*. [OE *storm*]

storm[1.2] /stɔrm/ *v* **1** to assail violently, assault; to trouble, perturb; to complain violently, rage at *la16-*. **2** to block, cover (up) with snow or frost *la18-19*. [see the noun]

storour *see* STORE[1.2]

story *see* TORIE

stot[1], †**stoit** /stɔt/ *n* **1** a young castrated ox, a bullock, usually in its second year or more *la14-*. **2** a stupid, clumsy person *la19-*. **stot-stirk** a bullock in its second year *19-*. [OE *stot* a kind of horse, ON *stútr* an ox, a bull]

stot[2.1], **stoat** /stɔt, stot/ *n* **1** a bounce, a rebound, the act of rebounding; a spring or hop in a dance *la16-*. **2** a sharp (recoiling) blow *16-19, 20- T SW Bor*. **3** a sudden erratic movement, a fitful motion; a stumble or stagger *la19, 20- NE*. **4** *pl* a fit of the sulks, a whim *la19, 20- Sh NE*. **5** a beat, a rhythm *18-19, 20- NE T*. **6** the sequence of events in a story; the details or thread of a speech *la19- NE EC*. **7** a stroll, a saunter *20- NE*. **aff the stot** out of the rhythm or regular pace of something *la19- NE C Bor*. [see the verb]

stot^{2.2}, **stoat** /stɔt, stot/ *v* **1** *of a ball* to bounce, rebound *16-*. **2** to cause to bounce *19-*. **3** to walk with a springy, active step *la18-*. **4** *of an animal* to bound, go by leaps *la19-*. **5** to stumble, stagger, walk unsteadily *la16-*. **stottin** very drunk *la19-*. **stottin bits** scraps of meat used by butchers as makeweights *20- T EC*. **stottin fou** very drunk *la19-*. [compare STOIT^{1.2} and STOT^{3.2}]

stot^{2.3} /stɔt, stot/ *adv* with a rebound, with a bouncing thump *19-*. [see the verb]

stot^{3.1} /stɔt/ *n* a stutter, a stammer, a speech impediment *la17, 20- Ork*. [see the verb]

stot^{3.2}, †**stoot** /stɔt/ *v* **1** to stutter, stammer *la17-19, 20- Ork*. **2** to stop; to bring to a halt; to pause, hesitate *la14-e17*. [ME *stoten* to stop, stammer, MDu, MLG *stōten*]

stotter^{1.1} /ˈstɔtər/ *n* a stumble, a stagger, an unsteady gait *la18-*. [see the verb]

stotter^{1.2}, **stooter** /ˈstɔtər, ˈstutər/ *v* to stagger, totter, stumble *19-*. [frequentative form of STOT^{2.2}]

stotter², **stoater** /ˈstɔtər, ˈstotər/ *n term of admiration (mainly for women)* an excellent example *la20-*. [STOT^{2.2}, with agent suffix]

†**stouff, stuff** *n* dust, fine powder *e19*. [perhaps Du *stof*]

†**stouk, stowk** *n in Shetland and Orkney* a prebend, the benefice supporting a prebendary; the lands with which a prebend was endowed *16-17*. [ON *stúka* a wing of a building, especially of a church]

stouk *see* STOOK^{1.1}

stoun *see* STOUND^{1.1}, STOUND^{1.2}, STOUND^{2.1}, STOUND^{2.2}

stound^{1.1}, **stoun, stoond,** †**stond,** †**stund** /stund, stun/ *n* **1** a sharp throb of pain; an intermittent ache *la14-*. **2** a pang of mental pain or emotion: a throb of grief, a thrill of pleasure or excitement *15-*. **3** a period of time, a while; a moment *la14-19, 20- Sh T*. **4** a mood, a whim; a fit of depression, sullenness etc *20- Ork N NE T*. **5** a blow, an impact *la15-16*. **stoonie,** *Ork* **stoondie** moody, temperamental *20- Ork N*. [OE *stund* a short space of time, a moment]

stound^{1.2}, **stoun** /stund, stun/ *v* to (cause to) throb, ache, smart, thrill with pain or emotion *16-*. [see the noun]

stound^{2.1}, **stoun** /stund, stun/ *n* **1** a stunning blow *la18-19, 20- NE T EC*. **2** a stupefying din, a resounding noise *19-*. **3** a stunned condition, a state of insensibility *19-, 20- NE T EC SW*. [see the verb]

stound^{2.2}, **stoun, stoon** /stund, stun/ *v* **1** to stun, stupefy, make insensible with a blow *19-, 20- T C SW Bor*. **2** to stupefy with surprise or astonishment, bewilder *19, 20- WC*. **3** to resound, reverberate, ring with noise *18-19, 20- T*. [aphetic form of ME *astonen*, OFr *estoner*]

stoup /stup; *NE* stʌup/ *n* **1** a wooden post, a pillar, a prop *15-*. **2** *mining* a pillar of coal left to support the roof of the working *16-*. **3** a loyal supporter, adherent or ally (especially of a church) *la16-*. **4** a leg of a table or chair *la16-*. **5** the pillar of a gateway *20- Sh NE*. **6** the butt-end of the under-rail of a farm cart, on which it rests when tilted; the STILT^{1.1} or handle of a plough *la19- NE*. **7** one of the posts marking out a racetrack, especially the turning-post or winning-post *17-e19*. **8** a post where a wrongdoer was attached for punishment, the stake *la16-e17*. **9** a post of a four-poster bed *16-18*. **stouped** *of a bed* having posts *17-19, 20- NE*. **stoup-bed** a four-poster bed *19, 20- N EC*. †**stoup-net** a type of salmon fishing net stretched on poles *17-18*. **stoup and room** pillar-and-stall,

a method of working coal by leaving pillars of coal to support the roof *19-*. [ON *stulpe, stolpe* a post, a pillar, MLG, MDu *stupe* a whipping-post, a stake]

stoup *see* STOOP¹, STOWP

stour, *Ork* **stower,** †**stowr** /stʌur/ *n* **1** a stake, a post, a pole *la14-19, 20- SW*. **2** the reed *Phragmites australis la19- Ork*. [ON *staurr*]

stour *see* STOOR^{1.1}, STOOR^{1.2}, STURE¹

stourie *see* STOORIE^{1.1}

stoussie^{1.1} /ˈstuse/ *n* a plump, sturdy small child *19, 20- WC*. [unknown]

†**stoussie**^{1.2} *adj* stout and stocky, sturdy, chubby *la18-19*. [unknown]

stout *see* STOOT^{1.1}, STOOT^{1.2}

†**stouth, stowth** *n* **1** theft *15-e19*. **2** (something done by) stealth, an action carried out secretly *15-e19*. **stoutherie,** †**stowthry** goods and chattels, sometimes stolen *19*. [ON *stulðr*]

†**stouth and routh** *n* plenty *19*. [compare Older Scots *stout and rout* completely; of unknown origin]

stouthreif, stouthrief /ˈstuθrif/ *n* theft with violence *la15-19, 20- C*. [STOUTH + REIF]

stove^{1.1}, †**stoif,** †**stow** /stov/ *n* **1** an apparatus for producing heat or for use in cooking *la16-*. **2** a stew *18-*. **3** (heated) air or vapour *16-e19*. **4** a state of great heat *la17-e19*. **5** a hot-air bath; a steam-room *la15-17*. †**stofe pan** a pan for use on a cooking stove, perhaps a stew-pan *la17*. [MLG, MDu *stove*]

stove^{1.2} /stov/ *v* **1** to cook food by stewing (in very little liquid) *17-*. **2** to steam, emit vapour; *of smoke* to billow out in clouds; *of persons* to reek with alcoholic fumes *la18-19, 20- H&I C*. **3** to have a hot-air bath *la15*. †**stoving pan** a pan for stewing in a very little liquid *17*. **stoved tatties** = STOVIES *la19-*. [see the noun]

†**stove**², **stoif** *n in Shetland* apparently a room or house, perhaps originally one heated by a furnace *17 Sh*. [perhaps ON *stofa*, cognate with STOVE^{1.1}]

stove *see* STAVE^{1.2}

stovies, †**stoves** /ˈstoviz/ *n* **1** potatoes and onions, pieces of fat and sometimes small pieces of meat, cooked in a closed pot in very little liquid *la19-*. **2** a dish cooked by stewing *la17*. [STOVE^{1.2} and -IE³]

stow^{1.1} /stʌu/ *n coopering* a stack or stockpile of barrels stored away ready for use *20-*. [see the verb]

stow^{1.2} /stʌu/ *v* **1** to put (things or persons) in a place; to pack (cargo) in a ship *la14-*. **2** to fill (the stomach) with food, feed (oneself or another) *18-*. **3** to satisfy *20- Sh Ork*. **4** to silence *20- Sh Ork SW*. [ME *stouen*, from OE *stōw* a place]

stow² /stʌu/ *adv only as second element in phrases* **stick and stow** (STICK^{2.1}), **stab and stow** (STOB^{1.1}) completely, entirely *18-19, 20- EC*. [compare Du *stuk of stol*]

stow *see* STOO^{1.2}, STOVE^{1.1}

stower *see* STOOR^{1.1}, STOUR

stowff^{1.1} /stʌuf/ *n* (the sound of) a heavy-footed gait *la19- NE*. [probably onomatopoeic]

stowff^{1.2} /stʌuf/ *v* to plod along *la19- NE*. [see the noun]

stowfie *see* STUFFIE^{1.2}

stowin *see* STEAL^{1.2}

stowk *see* STOOK^{1.2}, STOUK

stowlins, stown *see* STEAL^{1.2}

stowp, stoup, *H&I WC* **stop** /stʌup; *Sh Ork* stup; *H&I WC* stop/ *n* **1** a vessel for holding liquids; a bucket, a cask, a pitcher *la14-*. **2** a vessel containing liquid for drinking, a drinking vessel; a flagon, decanter, tankard, cup or mug *la15-*. **3** a jug, especially for milk or cream *la18- NE T Bor*. **4** *Presbyterian Church* the flagon containing the communion wine prior to distribution *17*. **5** a vessel of a particular size,

stowp used as a measure *la15-17*; compare *pint stowp* (PINT[1]), *chopin stoup* (CHOPIN). **stowpfu**, **†stoupfull** the fill of a stowp *la16-*. [ON *staup* a drinking vessel, MDu *stoop* a jug, OE *stoppa* a bucket]
stowp *see* STOOP[1]
stowr *see* STOOR[1.1], STOUR
stowrand *see* STEERIN[1.2]
stowt *see* STOOT[1.1]
stowth *see* STOUTH
stoy[1] /stɔɪ/ *n* a float used to mark the position of sunken fishing-lines or crab-traps *la18-19, 20- NE*. [Gael *stuthaidh* a marker buoy]
stoy[2] /stɔɪ/ *v* to saunter, stroll *la19- NE*. [perhaps shortened form of STOIT[1.2]]
stoyte *see* STOIT[1.2]
stra *see* STRAE[1.1], STRATH
strab /strab/ *n* a stalk of corn that has been missed or merely broken by the scythe or reaper; any odd bit of straw or loose straw *19- NE*. [variant of STRAP[1.1]]
strabush *see* STRAMASH[1.1]
strachle, strauchle /'straxəl, 'strɔxəl/ *v* 1 to move or walk laboriously or with difficulty, struggle; to labour ineffectually *19- WC SW Bor Uls*. 2 to straggle, grow in a loose untidy way *20- C SW Bor*. [conflation of *straggle* (STRAIGGLE[1.2]) with TRAUCHLE[1.2]]
stracht *see* STRAUCHT[1.3]
strade *see* STRIDE[1.2]
strae[1.1], **stra, straw, †stray, †stro** /stre, stra, strɔ/ *n* 1 the dried stalks of cereal crops, straw *la14-*. 2 a single stalk of straw, a piece of straw, something of no significance *la14-*. **straen** made of straw *la18- Sh NE*. **strawzer** a strawberry *20- T*. **straw-back** a chair with a back of stitched straw, an Orkney chair *20- Ork*. **strae-bread, †stray breid** the breadth of a straw, a measure of smallness or insignificance *16-19, 20- Sh* **strae-buits** twisted straw bound round the feet and legs instead of or on top of the boots *19- Ork*. **straw crook** a rope twister, a *thrawcruik* (THRAW) *20- N NE T EC*. **strae-draw** a thin slice cut off the side of a sheep's ear as a mark of ownership *20- Sh*. **strae en** the end of a barn where the straw is put *la19- Ork N NE T EC*. **strae heuk** = *straw crook 20-*. **strae-hoose** a place for storing straw *la16-19, 20- Ork NE SW*. **strae-man** a mechanical elevator *20- C*. **strae-merr** a board along the edge of a box-bed to keep in the bedding *20- Ork historical*. **strae-moose** the shrew *Sorex araneus 19- NE EC SW*. **strae raip** a rope of twisted straw *la17-*. **†strae-sonk** a straw cushion used as a saddle *18-19*. **strae-thackit** thatched with straw *19- Ork NE T*. **†straw-wald** dyer's rocket or yellow-weed *Reseda luteola la16-e19*. **bind wi a strae** used to describe someone who is helpless with laughter: ◇*ye micht hae bund me wi a strae 19, 20- SW*. **in the strae** in childbed *19, 20- NE*. **†lay a strae** to stop, take a break *la15-16*. **†stra for** expressing contempt *e16*. **tie wi a strae** = bind wi a strae *19, 20- SW*. [ON *strá*; Eng *straw* is from OE *strēaw*]
strae[1.2], **straw** /stre, strɔ/ *v* to supply (animals) with straw for fodder or bedding *20-*. [see the noun]
straff /straf/ *n* a difficulty, predicament or state of anxiety *la19- Sh*. [compare Norw *straff* a punishment, Du *straf* a trial, an affliction]
strag /strag/ *n* 1 a thin, straggly crop; thin wispy hair *19- WC SW*. 2 a person of no fixed abode; a promiscuous woman *20- WC SW*. 3 a stray pigeon *20- C SW Bor*. [perhaps back-formation from *straggle* (STRAIGGLE[1.2])]
straggle, stragill *see* STRAIGGLE[1.1], STRAIGGLE[1.2]
straicht *see* STRAUCHT[1.1], STRAUCHT[1.3], STRAUCHT[1.4]
straict *see* STRICK[1]

straid *see* STRIDE[1.2]
straif *see* STRIVE[1.2]
straiggle[1.1], **straggle, †stragill** /'stregəl, 'stragəl/ *n* a scattering of objects or persons; a few *la19-*. **†at the stragill, at stragill, to the stragill** straggling, in disorder *la15-16*. [see the verb]
straiggle[1.2], **straggle, †stragill** /'stregəl, 'stragəl/ *v* to wander, roam (in an uncoordinated manner), singly or in small groups *16-*. [ME *stragelen, stragelen*]
straight *see* STRAUCHT[1.3]
straik[1.1], **strake, strak, stroke, †streak** /strek, strak, strok/ *n* 1 (the impact of) a blow; a stab, cut or thrust with a weapon *la14-*. 2 an action or event causing misfortune, distress, pain or death; an act of chastisement or vengeance *la15-*. 3 *golf* an act of striking the ball; a single (attempted) hit; the forward movement of the club with the intention of striking at and moving the ball *19-*. 4 coinage, imprint of coin *15-e17*. 5 (the sound of) the striking of a clock *15-17*. 6 a surgical incision *e16*. 7 a thrust (of the penis) *e16*. 8 the beating of a drum *la16-e17*. **stroke play** *golf* a competition scored on the gross score of each competitor *20-*. **†on the straik, upon the straik** in motion, in a state of activity, on the move *19*. [ME *strak*; Eng *stroke* is from ME form *strōk*; related to STRIK[1.2]]
straik[1.2], **strake, strak, stroke** /strek, strak, strok/ *v* to strike, beat, aim a blow at *16-19*. [see the noun]
straik[2.1], **stroke,** *Uls* **streek** /strek, strok; *Uls* strik/ *n* 1 a stroking, caressing movement of the hand; a sleeking, smoothing action *19-*. 2 the motion or marks of a harrow; the ground covered by one journey of a harrow *19-*. 3 a tool for sharpening a scythe *18-19, 20- NE EC SW Bor*. 4 a whetting or paring motion *20- Sh N WC*. 5 a stroke or mark of a pen *17, 20- Sh T*. [see the verb]
straik[2.2], **stroke,** *Uls* **streek, †streak** /strek, strok; *Uls* strik/ *v* 1 to rub gently, stroke, smooth *la15-*. 2 to level off (grain etc) in a measure *la18-*. 3 to rub, smear, spread (with something oily) *16-*. 4 to sharpen (a scythe) with a STRAIK[2.1] (sense 3) *20-*. 5 to harrow ground *20- N T*. 6 to fill up (a road) with snow *la19- N NE*. 7 to sprinkle (powder) on *20- NE*. **†straiking** the grain removed by a straik from a heaped measure *la16-17*. **†straik against the hair** to annoy, provoke *la16-19*. **†straik cream in someone's mouth** to flatter, mollify *17*. **straik tails** to exchange or barter *19, 20- N*. **†straik wi the hair** to soothe, humour *la18-19*. [OE *strācian*]
straik[3.1], **†strake, †stroack** /strek/ *n* 1 a stripe (of colour), a ray (of light) *16-*. 2 a small amount *la18-19, 20- Sh WC SW*. 3 a (long, narrow) tract of land or water; a sheep walk *la16-19, 20- NE T EC*. 4 a journey, a long walk *19- EC*. 5 a mark of a blow, a weal *16-e17*. [OE *strica*, with influence from STRAIK[2.1]]
straik[3.2] /strek/ *v* to streak, mark with streaks of a different colour *la19- Ork N NE T WC*. [see the noun]
straik[4], **†streak, †strake** /strek/ *n* 1 a cylindrical rod with one straight edge for levelling grain in a measure *15-*. 2 the quantity of heaped-up grain removed from the top of a container by a straik *16-e19*. 3 a level measure (of malt); (the measure of the strength of) the alcoholic liquid brewed or distilled from this *e19*. **straikit, straiked** *of grain etc* measured by use of a straik, having the surface level with the top of the container, not heaped *la14-*. **†strakmett, straik mesour** 1 measurement by use of a straik *la15-17*. 2 also **†straik firlot** a measure (firlot) enlarged to take account of the use of a straik in measuring the contents *16-e17*. [ME *stric*, OFr *estrique*, with influence from STRAIK[2.1]]
straik *see* STREEK[1.2], STRIK[1.2]

†straiken, straiking, strakin *n* a kind of coarse linen *la16-e19*. [perhaps related to STRAIK[2.1]; compare STREEK[2]]

strain[1.1], *Bor* **streen**, **†streinʒe** /stren; *Bor* strin/ *n* **1** pressure; the effect of pressure *la17-*. **2** constraint, bondage; compulsion *la15-e17*. **3** tone, style of expression, especially in music; a melody; a line of song or verse *17-19*. [see the verb]

strain[1.2], *Bor* **streen**, **†strenʒe**, **†strengʒe**, **†strene** /stren; *Bor* strin/ *v* **1** to press hard, squeeze tightly, grasp *la14-16*. **2** to extract by pressure, extort *la17*. **3** originally, to constrain, force, compel (a person) *la14-e17*. **4** to strike with a glancing blow *e16*. **5** to hurt, afflict, distress *16*. **6** to bind fast, fasten firmly *e16*. **7** to tighten (bonds, a line, a fence etc) *16-*. **8** to struggle, stretch oneself, make a great effort *la19-*. **9** to rid (solid matter) of liquid or clear (solids) from liquid by pressure in passing through a sieve *17-*. **10** to damage (a part of the body) by (undue) pressure *la18-* [OFr *estreign-*, stem of *estreindre* to bind tightly]

strainge see STRANGE[1.2]

strait[1.1] /stret/ *n* **1** a narrow, confined space; a mountain pass or defile; a narrow channel of water *la14-*. **2** a difficult situation, a dilemma; financial difficulties; penury *la16-*. **3** a narrow lane or passage; the narrow part of a street or thoroughfare *la16-18*. [see the adj]

strait[1.2] /stret/ *v* **1** to tighten, tauten, put tension on *la18-19, 20- NE*. **2** to restrict, constrain *la16-17*. **3** to afflict, oppress; to compel; to press (a person for payment); to subjugate *la16-17*. **†straitly 1** tightly *la14-e19*. **2** in close confinement, securely *la14-17*. **3** closely, intimately *la15-17*. **4** severely *la14-e17*. **5** *of swearing an oath* rigorously; without reservation or ambiguity *la14-17*. [see the adj]

strait[1.3], *Sh NE* **stret**, **†strate**, **†strat** /stret/ *adj* **1** *of clothing, footwear or fetters* tight, close-fitting *la16-*. **2** tense, taut, rigid; full to bursting *20- Sh NE WC*. **3** *of mountainous terrain* steep, originally also impassible, inaccessible *la15-19, 20- Sh NE T*. **4** poverty-stricken, lacking means, originally perhaps stingy *16-19, 20- NE*. **5** *of a legal instrument* stringently worded, unambiguous, perhaps peremptory *15-e17*. **6** strict, severe; stern, unbending *la14-16*. **7** harsh, repressive; *of imprisonment* strictly enforced, rigorous *la14-e19*. **8** *of a place or passage* narrow; cramped, confined *la14-19*. **9** *of friendship* close, intimate *la16-17*. [OFr *estreit*]

†strait[1.4] *adv* **1** tightly; with tight bonds *la14-16*. **2** securely *la16-17*. [see the adj]

straiten /ˈstretən/ *v* **1** to tighten (a knot etc) *la18-19, 20- Sh N NE T*. **2** to press hard, put in difficulty, inconvenience, impede; to exert oneself to the utmost *la17-18*. **3** to narrow, restrict *17*. [STRAIT[1.3], with verb-forming suffix]

straith see STRATH

straitie /ˈstrete/ *n* the shank of a sheep; a leg of mutton *la19- Sh*. [compare Norw dial *strate* a stake, *stratt* a stiff branch of a tree]

strak see STRAIK[1.1], STRAIK[1.2], STRIK[1.2]

strake see STRAIK[1.1], STRAIK[1.2], STRAIK[3.1], STRAIK[4], STRIK[1.2]

strakin see STRAIKEN

stram[1] /stram/ *n* excitement, anxiety *20- Ork*. [perhaps shortened form of STRAMASH[1.1]]

stram[2] /stram/ *n* a big, clumsy, blundering man *la18- NE*. [unknown; compare Eng *strammel* a lean, ungainly person and Du *stram* blunt, coarse, obtuse]

stramash[1.1], *EC* **strabush** /strəˈmaʃ, strəˈbuʃ/ *n* **1** an uproar, a commotion, a row *19-*. **2** a smash, a crash; an accident or disaster *la19, 20- Sh Ork T C*. **3** a state of ruin, wreckage; a smashed or shattered state *19, 20- Sh Ork T C*. **4** a state of great excitement or rage *20- Sh N NE*. [perhaps onomatopoeic]

stramash[1.2] /strəˈmaʃ/ *v* to create a disturbance, be rowdy *la19-*. [see the noun]

stramlach, stramlich /ˈstramləx/ *n* **1** anything long and trailing *19- NE*. **2** a tall, lanky, gangling person *20- NE*. [STRAMMEL + -OCH]

strammel /ˈstraməl/ *n* straw; a thin, straw-like object; a string *e19, 20- NE*. [EModE *strommell*, perhaps AN **estramaille* straw bedding]

stramp[1.1] /stramp/ *n* **1** a tread or stamp of the foot; a trampling on something *la16-19, 20- Sh Ork N Bor*. **2** a stride, a step *20- Sh Ork*. **3** a journey on foot *19- Sh*. [conflation of STAMP[1.2] with TRAMP[1.1]]

stramp[1.2] /stramp/ *v* **1** to bring the foot down heavily, stamp, tread; to trample *15-*. **2** to go about with a firm or heavy step; to march energetically or purposefully *la19-*. **†stramp doun, stramp under fute** to suppress *16-e17*. [see the noun]

strample /ˈstrampəl/ *v* = STRAMP[1.2] (sense 1) *la19, 20- Bor*.

†strampill doun = *stramp doun* (STRAMP[1.2]) *e17*. [frequentative form of STRAMP[1.2]]

strand[1] /strand/ *n* **1** a beach or shore of the sea; a sand-bank etc exposed at low water; the bank of a river *15-19, 20- N*. **2** *pl* regions, climes *e16 literary*. [OE *strand*]

strand[2], **straun** /strand, strɔn/ *n* **1** a stream, a rivulet *la15-19, 20- T WC SW*. **2** the sea *16*. **3** an artificial water channel, a (street-)gutter *16-19, 20- N NE T C*. **4** a stream or gushing forth (of blood or tears) *16-e17*. [perhaps STRIND[2.1] with influence from STRAND[1]]

strang[1.1] /straŋ/ *n* urine which has been allowed to stand for some time, used as a bleach or in making manure *17-19, 20- Sh Ork N NE T SW*. **strang bing** a hole in the ground in which urine is collected *20- Ork*. **strang hole** a seepage pit in a dung heap *20- Sh N NE T*. **strang pig** a large container for holding urine *19, 20- Ork NE*. [from the adj, with extension of meaning]

strang[1.2], **strong** /straŋ, strɔŋ/ *adj* **1** (physically) powerful; solidly constructed; assertive *la15-*. **2** able-bodied, robust *16-*. **3** bold, resolute *la14-16*. **4** *of emotion* fervid, intense *16-*. **5** *of odour or flavour* powerful, strong *la15-*. **strangly 1** fiercely, energetically, determinedly *16-*. **2** *of loving* intensely, passionately *e16*. **3** greatly, markedly, to an alarming degree *la16-17*. **†strang wesche** urine which has been allowed to stand for some time, used as a bleach or in making manure *la15-e16*. [OE *strang*]

strang[1.3], **strong** /straŋ, strɔŋ/ *adv* with force, powerfully, violently; intensely; securely *15-19, 20- WC*. [OE *strange*]

strang see STRING[1.2]

strange[1.1] /strenʒ/ *v* to marvel or wonder (at), find surprising *la17-19, 20- Sh Uls*. [see the adj]

strange[1.2], **strynge**, **†strainge** /strenʒ, strʌɪnʒ/ *adj* **1** foreign; belonging to another place *la14-*. **2** unknown, unfamiliar *15-*. **3** unusual, abnormal, peculiar *la15-*. **4** unfriendly, aloof *16-*. **5** *especially of children* shy, self-conscious *20-*. **stringie** aloof, shy, stiff, affected *19, 20- NE T*. **strangeness**, **†strangenes 1** the quality of being strange; peculiarity *la16-*. **2** unfriendliness, aloofness *la15-17*. [OFr *estrange*]

stranger, **†strangear**, **†straunger** /ˈstrenʒər/ *n* **1** a person belonging to another place (originally another parish or town), a visitor, an incomer; an unknown person, a person not previously encountered; one who is not a member of one's family *15-*. **2** anything thought to foretell the arrival of an unexpected visitor, *eg* a tea-leaf floating on the surface of a cup of tea *la19-*. **3** a foreigner *la14-17*. **be a stranger to**, **†be a stranger from** to be ignorant of or unacquainted with *16-*. [OFr *estrangier*]

strap[1.1], *Sh Bor* **strop** /strap; *Sh Bor* strɔp/ *n* **1** a strip of leather, a band, a thong *16-*. **2** *building* a strip of wood (or metal) serving as a base to which something else may be nailed or attaching one element to another *16-*. **3** black treacle, molasses *19, 20- NE T*. **4** *pl* trouser braces *la19- Sh N*. **5** the band of corn-stalks used to tie up a sheaf at harvest *la18- WC SW*. **6** a string or bunch of objects tied together *19- Bor*. **the strap** *in former times* corporal punishment inflicted on schoolchildren with a leather strap *la19-20, 21- historical*. [OE *strop*]

strap[1.2], *Sh Bor* **strop** /strap; *Sh SW Bor* strɔp/ *v* **1** *building* to fix strips of wood on (a wall) as a base for a lath, skirting etc *19-*. **2** to clamp, clinch or strengthen with strips of wood or metal *la19-*. **3** to string (beads) together, tie together in a bunch *20- C SW Bor*. **strapper** a groom; a person who straps and cares for horses *la19-*. [see the noun]

strate, strat *see* STRAIT[1.3]

strath, †**straith**, †**stra** /straθ/ *n* a broad, flat river valley; frequently in place-names *la12-*. **Strathclyde 1** a historic name for the ancient kingdom of the Britons in the area of South-West Scotland south of the kingdom of the Scots in Dalriada *19- historical*. **2** a Scottish region formed from the former counties of the City of Glasgow, Bute, Dunbarton, Lanark, Renfrew and Ayr and parts of the former counties of Argyll and Stirling *la20, 21- historical*. [Gael, IrGael *srath*]

strathspey, †**stravetspy** /straθˈspe/ *n* **1** a kind of dance, slower than a reel *17-*. **2** a Highland dance performed by four people *20-*. †**strathspey minuet** apparently a slow strathspey *la18*. †**strathspey reel** a kind of dance *18*. [from the Moray place-name]

strauchle *see* STRACHLE

straucht[1.1], **straicht** /strɔxt, strext, strɛxt; *Sh NE* straxt/ *n* **the straucht** a straight line; the straight part of a line or route; a direct route or straightforward attitude *la18-*. **off the straucht** out of one's way or sight *20- NE EC*. [see the adj]

straucht[1.2], **straught**, *SW Uls* **strecht** /strɔxt; *SW Uls* strext/ *v* **1** to stretch, extend *la14-*. **2** to make straight, straighten; to smooth, set to rights *la17-19, 20- Sh N NE T EC SW Uls*. **3** to lay out (a corpse) *18-19, 20- NE SW*. **4** to urge on (an animal) *15*. **strauchten** to straighten the limbs of, lay out (a corpse) *19-*. **strauchtin brod** the board on which a corpse is laid out *19, 20- NE SW*. [see the adj]

straucht[1.3], **straicht**, **straight**, **strecht**, *Sh NE* **stracht**, †**streight**, †**stricht**, †**strek** /strɔxt, strext, strext; *Sh NE* straxt/ *adj* not crooked, bent or curved; *of hair* not curly; *of a route* direct, undeviating *14-*. **straucht-forrit** straightforward; without deviation, circumlocution or duplicity *19-*. **a straight-line** a direct route *la15-*. [OE **strœht*, OE *streaht*, ptp of *streccan* to stretch]

straucht[1.4], **straicht**, **strecht**, †**strek** /strɔxt, strext, strɛxt; *Sh NE* straxt/ *adv* **1** by a direct route, without stopping or deviating; in a straight line *la14-*. **2** immediately, without delay *la14-*. **3** erect, upright *la15-*. **4** frankly, forthrightly *la19-*. **straucht-forrit** straight forward, straight ahead *19-*. **straucht-oot** frank, candid *la19 Ork NE T*. **straucht-oot-the-gate** = *straucht-oot*. [see the adj]

straucht *see* STREEK[1.2]

straught *see* STRAUCHT[1.2]

straun *see* STRAND[2]

straunger *see* STRANGER

stravaig[1.1] /strəˈveg/ *n* a roaming about, an aimless casual ramble, a stroll *19-*. [see the verb]

stravaig[1.2], **stravague** /strəˈveg/ *v* **1** to roam, wander about idly or aimlessly *la18-*. **2** to traverse, go up and down (a place) *la19-*. [aphetic form of EXTRAVAGE; compare VAIG[1.2]]

strave *see* STRIVE[1.2]

stravetspy *see* STRATHSPEY

straw, strew, strow /strɔ, stru, strʌu/ *v* **1** to scatter, sprinkle, spread *la14-19, 20- Sh Ork NE T EC Bor*. **2** to lay low, fell (a person) *e16*. [OE *streawian, streowian*]

straw *see* STRAE[1.1], STRAE[1.2]

strawcht *see* STREEK[1.2]

†**stray** *n* **on stray** wandering, at large, astray *la14-e16*. [aphetic form of ME *astray*]

stray *see* STRAE[1.1]

streach *see* STREETCH[1.1]

streak *see* STRAIK[1.1], STRAIK[2.2], STRAIK[4]

†**streaker, strekour** *n* **1** a kind of (hunting) dog *la14-e19*. **2** a term of abuse for a person *e16*. [AN *stracur*]

stream[1.1], *Sh* **strem**, †**streme**, †**streym** /strim/ *Sh* strɛm/ *n* **1** a brook, rivulet or river *la14-*. **2** the spring tide, originally any tide *17, 20- Sh*. **3** *pl* the waters of a river *16-e19 literary*. **4** water; the sea *16-e19*. **5** the middle of a river where the current is strongest *15-e19*. **6** a copious flow of blood *la14-16*. **7** a line, streak or stripe *la15-16*. **8** a flow or streak of fire *e16*. **stream tide** high tide *la17- NE EC*. †**upon the streme** *of a ship* lying offshore, at sea *la15-16*. [OE *strēam*]

stream[1.2], †**streme** /strim/ *v* to flow copiously *la14-*. [see the noun]

streamer[1.1], †**stremar**, †**stremer**, †**stremour** /ˈstrimər/ *n* **1** the male minnow near spawning time *20- WC SW Bor*. **2** *pl* the aurora borealis *la18-19, 20- T SW*. **3** a heavenly body emitting light *e16*. **4** a flag, a long narrow banner or pennant *16*. [STREAM[1.2], with agent suffix]

†**streamer**[1.2] *v* to deck out or furnish with flags *e19*. [see the noun]

streatch *see* STREETCH[1.2]

strecht *see* STRAUCHT[1.2], STRAUCHT[1.3], STRAUCHT[1.4]

streck *see* STRIK[1.2]

streek[1.1] /strik/ *n* **1** a stretch, a drawing out; the full extent, the maximum length to which a thing can be stretched *19, 20- T EC SW Bor*. **2** a continuous extent of time or space *la19, 20- EC Bor*. **3** *mining* the horizontal extent or direction of a seam of coal; a coal level *la17-19*. **4** the orientation of a harbour *la17*. [see the verb]

streek[1.2], **streik**, *Ork T* **straik**, †**streke**, †**strek**, †**strick** /strik; *Ork T* strek/ *v pt also* †**straucht** †**strawcht 1** to stretch, spread out, extend *la14-*. **2** to hurry, hasten; to go at full speed *la15-*. **3** to lay out (a corpse) *17-*. **4** to put (a plough etc) into action, plough; to start work, get going *la16-19, 20- NE*. **5** to question closely, cross-examine *20- Bor*. **6** to exert oneself *19, 20- NE*. **7** to hold out, extend (a spear, olive branch or wand or authority) *la14-e17*. **8** *of a heavenly body* to emit (light) *la14-e15*. **9** to stretch (a person) on the rack *la14*. **streeker** a very tall, thin person *la19- NE Uls*. **streekin** tall and agile *19- Bor*. **streekin buird** the board on which a corpse is laid out *la19- NE WC*. †**strekbed**, **strak bed** a folding bed *16*. †**streking time** ploughing time *la15-16*. †**streke a borch** to put forward a pledge or security *15-e17*. †**streke doun** to stretch out, lie down *la15-e19*. †**streke hands** to shake hands, in friendship or to confirm a bargain *la14-19*. **streek yer hochs**, **streek yer shanks** to take a walk; to hurry *19, 20- WC*. †**streek yoursell up beside** to compete, vie with *e19*. [OE *streccan*]

†**streek**[2] *n* a bundle of broken flax for scutching *18-19*. [ME *stric*, related to STRAIK[2.1]]

streek[3] /strik/ *n* **streek o day** daybreak, the first light of day *20- Sh NE T*. [altered form of SKREEK, with influence from STRAIK[2.1]]

streek *see* STRAIK[2.1], STRAIK[2.2]

streel *see* STRULE

streen *see* STRAIN[1.1], STRAIN[1.2]

street[1], †**strete**, †**streit**, †**streyt** /strit/ *n* **1** a (main, paved) road in a town or village *la14-*. **2** a route, path, way *la15-16*. †**street-raking** roaming the streets, vagrant *e19, 20- Sh*. **on the street 1** in the street, out of doors *la14-*. **2** roaming the streets; homeless *la16-*. [OE *strǣt*]

street[2] /strit/ *n* a jet or squirt of milk from a cow's teat *20- Ork*. [compare Swed dial *stritta*]

streetch[1.1], **stretch**, †**streach** /stritʃ, stretʃ/ *n* **1** an extent of distance or time *la17-*. **2** an unwarranted exercise of power or a straining of the meaning of the law or a person's authority beyond acceptability; an unfair or prejudiced argument *la17-e18*. [see the verb]

streetch[1.2], **stretch**, †**streich**, †**streatch** /stritʃ, stretʃ/ *v* **1** to extend, stretch *la16-*. **2** to stretch the legs, walk, take exercise by walking or dancing; to strut about haughtily *17-19, 20- SW*. **3** to lay out (a corpse) *19*. **4** to lay (a person) out like a corpse *la16*. **5** to put (a plough) into action *la16*. **6** to exert oneself *17*. **streetcher 1** a clothes-prop *la19-*. **2** a frame for stretching a shawl *la19- Sh*. **streetching board** the board on which a corpse is laid out *19, 20- SW*. [OE *streccan*]

streetle /'stritəl/ *v* to go askew or awry *20- Ork*. [perhaps related to Norw dial *stritla* to spray in all directions]

streeve *see* STRIVE[1.2]

streich *see* STREETCH[1.2]

†**streiche** *adj describing speech* perhaps stiff or affected *e16*. [perhaps OE *strǣc* rigid]

streight *see* STRAUCHT[1.3]

streik *see* STREEK[1.2], STRIK[1.2]

streinȝe *see* STRAIN[1.1]

streit *see* STREET[1]

strek *see* STRAUCHT[1.3], STRAUCHT[1.4], STREEK[1.2]

streke *see* STREEK[1.2], STRICK[1]

strekour *see* STREAKER

strem *see* STREAM[1.1]

stremar, stremer, stremour *see* STREAMER[1.1]

streme *see* STREAM[1.1], STREAM[1.2]

strene *see* STRAIN[1.2]

strenge *see* STRANGE[1.2]

strength *see* STRENTH[1.1], STRENTH[1.2]

strenkell *see* STRINKLE[1.2]

strenth[1.1], **strength**, *Sh Ork* **strent**, †**strinth** /strenθ, strenθ; *Sh Ork* strent/ *n* **1** power, force; energy *la14-*. **2** a fortress, a stronghold, a fortification; a defensible place; a place of greatest security *la14-*. **3** a fighting force, armed men *la14-16*. **4** *in the steelbow system* goods or money supplied at the beginning of a lease to be repaid at its end *la16-e18*. †**strenthily, strenthly 1** with force, powerfully *la14-15*. **2** in a durable manner, strongly *16*. †**strenthy 1** *of persons* strong, powerful *la14-16*. **2** *of a site or position* defensible; impregnable *la15-16*. **3** *of action or feelings* powerful in effect or influence, difficult to contend with *16*. **4** physically strong, robust, healthy *la15-e19*. **5** *of a plant* full of health-giving properties *e16*. **6** *of age* mature *e16*. †**strenth silver** = STRENTH[1.1] (sense 4) *e17*. [OE *strengð*]

strenth[1.2], **strength**, †**strinth** /strenθ, strenθ/ *v* **1** to strengthen, reinforce, make more secure *la14-*. **2** *law* to support a case with additional evidence; to justify, validate *15-16*. [see the noun]

†**strenuitie, strenewite** *n* vigour, energy *16*. [Lat *strēnuitas*]

†**strenȝe** *v* to seize (goods) to enforce payment *15-e17*. **strenȝeable, strenȝeabill** *of property* suitable for repossession; *of people* subject to distraint, liable to be distrained *la15-e17*. [aphetic form of DISTRENZIE]

strenȝe, strengȝe *see* STRAIN[1.2]

stress[1.1], †**stres** /strɛs/ *n* **1** shock, trauma; emotional pressure *la17-*. **2** hardship, adversity, affliction; bodily suffering or injury *la15-16*. **3** the overpowering pressure of some adverse force, especially bad weather; a storm, a gale *15-*. **4** the oppressive force of death *e16*. **5** *law* a distraint or seizure of property to pay debts etc; the property seized *15-e17*. [ME *stres*, probably aphetic form of DISTRESS[1.1]]

stress[1.2], †**stres** /strɛs/ *v* **1** to subject to pressure, hardship or harassment *la15-*. **2** to strain, overwork, fatigue *la17-19, 20- C Bor Uls*. **3** to subject (a person) to distraint *16-17*. [see the noun]

stret *see* STRAIT[1.3]

stretch *see* STREETCH[1.1], STREETCH[1.2]

strete *see* STREET[1]

streuk *see* STRIK[1.2]

strew *see* STRAW

streym *see* STREAM[1.1]

streyt *see* STREET[1]

strib *see* STRIP[3]

stribbly /'strɪble/ *adj of hair* straggly, loose and trailing *20- NE*. [perhaps conflation of Eng *straggly* with Eng *dribbly*]

stricht *see* STRAUCHT[1.3]

strick[1], **strict**, †**streke**, †**straict** /strɪk, strɪkt/ *adj* **1** severe, characterized by severity; punitive *la15-*. **2** *of an act, order or regulations* stringently worded; precise, unambiguous; requiring literal interpretation *16-17*. **3** rigorous, not lax; austere; scrupulous, unwavering *17-*. **4** *of friendship* close, intimate *la16*. [Lat *strictus* tight, severe]

strick[2], †**strict** /strɪk/ *adj of running water* rapid, swift-flowing *18-19, 20- SW*. [compare Norw dial *stryk* swift current]

strick *see* STIRK, STREEK[1.2], STRIK[1.2]

stricken *see* STRIK[1.2]

strict *see* STRICK[1], STRICK[2]

striddle[1.1], **stridle** /'strɪdəl/ *n* a standing or sitting with legs apart; the spreading apart of the legs in walking or dancing; a wide stride or pace *18-19, 20- EC Bor*. **striddlie-legs, striddle-legs, stridle-legs, straddle-leggit** especially *of riding a horse* with the legs apart, astride *20- SW Bor*. [see the verb]

striddle[1.2], **stridle** /'strɪdəl/ *v* **1** to stand or sit with the legs apart, straddle *17-19, 20- C SW Bor*. **2** to walk with long steps, stride, step out *la16-19, 20- SW Uls*. **striddler** a farm worker who stands on a corn-stack and passes sheaves from the cart to the stack-builder *20- Bor historical*. [back-formation from STRIDLINS]

stride[1.1] /straɪd/ *n* **1** a long step taken in walking or running; the line of a person's walking or running *18-*. **2** *pl* trousers *la19-*. **3** the stretch of the legs in striding *e17*. **stridelegs** astride *la18-*. [ME *stride*]

stride[1.2], †**stryde** /straɪd/ *v pt* **strade**, †**straid 1** to mount, sit astride (a horse) *15-16*. **2** to walk with long, energetic steps *la15-*. [OE *strīdan*]

stridle *see* STRIDDLE[1.1], STRIDDLE[1.2]

stridlins, †**strydlingis** /'strɪdlɪnz/ *adv* astride, with the legs apart *16-*. [ME *stridlinges*]

strife, †**stryfe**, †**strive** /straɪf/ *n* **1** discord; contention, dispute *la14-*. **2** combat *15*. **3** trouble, distress, pain *la14-16*. **4** a quarrel or fight; a struggle *la15-e19*. [OFr *estrif*]

striffe *see* STRIVE[1.2]

striffin, †**striffen** /'strɪfən/ *n* a thin membrane or film; a long thin strip *17-19, 20- Sh Ork N NE Uls*. [Gael *streafon*]

strik[1.1], **strike**, †**stryke** /strɪk, straɪk/ *n* **1** a blow *la16-*. **2** the infestation of sheep by maggots *20-*. [see the verb]

strik[1.2], **straik**, **strike**, *Sh T* **strick**, †**stryke**, †**streik**, †**streck** /strɪk, straɪk/ *v pt* also **strak, straik, strook**, *Sh Ork* **streuk**, †**strake** *ptp* also **strucken, strukken, stricken,** †**strikken,** †**strykkyn 1** to hit with force, strike *la14-.* **2** *curling* to hit away (an opponent's stone) *la18-.* **3** *of a clock or bell* to indicate (the time) by striking or pealing *16-.* **4** *of the time* to be indicated by the striking of a clock or bell *17-.* **5** to cause to be deprived of sight, speech etc *17-.* **6** to make one's way, go (in a direction) *la16-.* **7** *of fish* to become enmeshed in a net *la19-.* **8** *of maggots* to infest (a sheep's wool) *20- WC SW.* **9** *ptp* also **striked** to level (a measure) *la18-19, 20- WC SW.* **10** to fight (a battle) *la14-e19.* **11** to be afflicted with disease *la14-e17.* **12** *of a boundary or path* to take a direction *la14-e17.* **13** to beat (flax) before heckling; to tie (flax) in bundles for beating; to beat (threshed barley) to remove the awns *la18-19.* **14** to chop, slice (meat) *la15-16.* **15** *of a feeling, sense or impression* to affect as if by a blow *la15-.* **16** *of the law* to apply, take effect *la16-17.* **17** to beat (a drum) *la16-e19.* **18** *of a moving body* to collide, smash etc as a result of collision *la14-e17.* **19** *of a ship* to run aground *16-17.* **striking** *of a clock or watch* having a mechanism that indicates the hour etc by striking a bell etc *16-.* **strucken hour** a full hour by the striking of a clock, implying tedium *19-.* **striker**, †**strikar 1** a person who hits (another, an animal or thing) *15-.* **2** a person who coins money *15-17.* **3** *mining* a person who had some function in a coalmine *la17.* **strike away** to remove with a blow *la15.* **strike doon** to knock down with blows; to fell *la14-.* **strike fiars**, **strike the fiars** to fix the annual prices of (each variety of) grain *la17- see* FIAR[1]. †**strike furth** = *strike oot* **2** *la15-17.* †**strike hands** to shake hands as a token of striking a bargain *la14-19.* †**strikin in age** advanced in years, old *15-17.* **strike of**, **strike off 1** to remove; to cut off with a blow *la14-.* **2** *golf* to drive (a ball) *17-.* **strike oot 1** *of the head, face or body* to break out in sores or a rash; *of a boil* to erupt *la16-18.* **2** to make a hole, especially an opening in a wall (for a door or window) *16-19, 20- NE.* **strik tek** to cut heather for use in thatching *la19- Sh.* **strike throw** = *strike oot* **2** *17.* †**strike under** to yield, give in *18-e19.* **strike up 1** to open (a container); to remove (goods) from a container *la15-e17.* **2** to burst open or break down (a door or gate) *la15-e17.* **3** *of a leak* to open up *la16-17.* †**strike upon** *of a legal remedy* to apply to, take effect on (a person) *16-e17.* [OE *strīcan* to pass lightly over, go, stroke]

strik *see* STIRK

strike *see* STRIK[1.1], STRIK[1.2]

strikken *see* STRIK[1.2]

strin *see* STRIND[2.1]

strind[1], †**strynd** /strʌnd/ *n* descent, lineage; inherited characteristics *15-19, 20- Sh EC.* [OE *strȳnd* generation, stock]

strind[2.1], **strin** /strɪnd, strɪn/ *n* **1** a (very small) stream; a trickle of water; the run from spilt liquid *15-.* **2** the jet of milk from a cow's teat *la19- NE.* [OE **strynd*]

strind[2.2] /strɪnd/ *v* to spray; to trickle *la19- NE.* [see the noun]

string[1.1], †**stryng** /strɪŋ/ *n* **1** a slender line or cord (for tying or binding); a bow-string; objects strung together, a necklace; a rope *la15-.* **2** a section or proportional length of a fishing-line *la16- NE EC Bor.* **3** a road crossing a watershed or hill ridge; frequently in place-names *17- H&I WC.* **4** the mechanism of the eye *e16.* **stringle** a string of objects tied together, a long trailing piece or strip *la19- NE T EC.* **string-girse** couch grass *Elymus repens* 20- *NE T EC.* [OE *streng*]

string[1.2] /strɪŋ/ *v pt* also *Sh NE* **strang 1** to furnish with a string or strings; to thread on a string *16-.* **2** *originally of soldiers* to draw up, move in a line or row *17-19, 20- Bor.* **3** *of seedlings especially turnips* to sprout in a line along the drills *20 NE.* **stringing** ornamental lace or tape *la16-19, 20- NE T WC.* **stringin ingans** the game of leapfrog *20- NE.* [see the noun]

string[2] /strɪŋ/ *n* a strong tide or current in the sea *la19- Sh Ork.* [ON *strengr*]

stringie *see* STRANGE[1.2]

strinkill *see* STRINKLE[1.2]

strinkle[1.1] /ˈstrɪŋkəl/ *n* a quantity scattered or strewn; a small amount, especially of a liquid or powder *20- NE EC SW Bor.* [see the verb]

strinkle[1.2], †**strinkill**, †**strynkil**, †**strenkell** /ˈstrɪŋkəl/ *v* **1** to scatter, strew, sprinkle (something) *16-19, 20- Sh N NE T EC Bor.* **2** to sprinkle *la15-e19.* **strinkling** = STRINKLE[1.1] *18-19, 20- Sh NE.* [probably altered form of SPRINKLE]

strinth *see* STRENTH[1.1], STRENTH[1.2]

strintle[1.1] /ˈstrɪntəl/ *n* a small stream or trickle of liquid; a spurt, a squirt *20- N.* [see the verb]

strintle[1.2] /ˈstrɪntəl/ *v* to sprinkle, scatter, strew; to squirt, spurt; to trickle, straggle *20- N NE.* [altered form of STRINKLE[1.2]]

strip[1.1], †**stryp** /strɪp/ *n* **1** a stripe, a long, narrow line of colour or light *la16-.* **2** a narrow tract of land *15-.* **3** a narrow piece of cloth or metal *16-.* **4** a single journey or turn of harrows over a ploughed field *20- N NE T EC SW.* **5** a long narrow belt of trees *19-, 20- NE T C Bor.* **6** the indication of rank of a non-commissioned officer *19, 20- NE.* **7** a piece of armour *la15-e17.* **strip o a laddie** a young fellow, a youth *19, 20- Ork WC Uls.* [MLG *strippe*]

strip[1.2] /strɪp/ *v* **1** to mark or ornament with stripes *19.* **2** to pull up (a turnip crop) in strips, to pull up every alternate drill or set of drills *19.* [see the noun]

strip[2] /strɪp/ *v* **1** to divest (oneself, a person) of clothing or possessions *la15-.* **2** to remove (something) from an object *20-.* **3** to skin (an animal); to take (bark, foliage) off a tree or plant; to shear (a sheep) *16-.* **4** to pull up (a turnip crop) in strips; to pull up every alternate drill or set of drills *19.* **strip the willow** a Scottish country dance *20-.* [ME *stript* pt and ptp of *strēpen*, OE **strēpan*]

strip[3], **strib** /strɪp, strɪb/ *v* **1** to milk (a cow), especially to take the last drops of milk *19-.* **2** to remove (water) from a washed garment *20- Sh Ork.* **3** to draw an edged tool across a rough surface to trim or sharpen it *20- NE T SW.* **strippins** the last milk drawn off at a milking *19-.* **strippin block** a block or frame with a flat file, over which a saw is drawn to reduce the teeth to a uniform height before sharpening *20- NE T SW.* [compare Flem *strippen* to squeeze out between the fingers, LG *strippen* to milk out]

strip[4] /strɪp/ *v* to hurry, go quickly *la19- Sh.* [Norw †*strippe*]

strip *see* STRIPE[2]

stripe[1], †**strype** /strʌɪp/ *n* **1** a long, narrow piece of cloth *19- Bor.* **2** a line of colour *la16-.* **3** a narrow tract or strip of country *18-e19.* **4** a long narrow belt of trees *la18-e19.* **stripey** a red-and-yellow striped worm used as angling bait, a bramble-worm *20- T WC SW.* [ME *stripe*, MDu, MLG *stripe*]

stripe[2], †**strip**, †**strype**, †**stryp** /strʌɪp/ *n* **1** a small stream, a rivulet *13-19, 20- Sh Ork NE.* **2** a street gutter *la16-19, 20- EC.* [probably extended sense of STRIPE[1] or STRIP[1]]

stripe[3] /strʌɪp/ *v* **1** to thrust, pull or draw (an object) over or through something, or between the fingers, to wipe or sharpen it *la18-19, 20- Sh.* **2** to draw off the last of a cow's milk *20- Ork NE.* [variant of STRIP[3]]

strippit, **stripped**, *Ork* **strippid**, †**stripit**, †**stript** /ˈstrɪpɪt, strɪpt, Ork ˈstrɪpɪd/ *adj* marked or ornamented with stripes of different colours or materials, variegated, ribbed *la16-.* **strippit ba** a round, peppermint-flavoured sweet with usually black and white stripes *20-.* [participial adj from STRIP[1.2]]

strip-wind /ˈstrɪpwɪnd/ *adj of an egg* addled, going bad *20- Ork.* [Norw *stroppen* (of an egg) to develop + WYNT]

stristle see STRUISSLE[1.1]

strive[1.1] /straev/ *n* a scattering of coins, especially at a wedding *20- N WC Bor.* [see the verb]

strive[1.2], †**stryve**, †**stryfe**, †**striffe** /straev/ *v pt also Sh Bor* **strave**, *NE* **streeve**, †**straif** 1 to exert oneself, work hard; to endeavour *la14-*. 2 to be on hostile terms; to quarrel, argue with *la14-19, 20- Sh N NE*. 3 to scatter coins or sweets at a wedding for children to scramble for *20- Bor*. 4 to engage in conflict; to compete, vie *la14-17*. 5 to wrestle *e17*. 6 *of winds* to move against each other *e16*. **striven** having quarrelled, at loggerheads, out of friendship *19- NE*. †**strive aganis, strive agane** to resist, struggle against *la14-e17*. [OFr *estriver* to quarrel, contend]

strive see STRIFE

striviling see STERLING[1.2]

stro see STRAE[1.1]

stroack see STRAIK[3.1]

stroag /strog/ *v* to stroll; to trudge *20- Sh Ork*. [compare Norw dial *stroka*]

stroan see STRONE[1.1], STRONE[1.2]

strod, strodge /strɔd, strɔdʒ/ *v* to stride, strut *19- Bor*. [perhaps back-formation from EModE *stroddle* to walk with the legs wide apart]

strodie /ˈstrɔdi/ *n* a lane with a wall on both sides; a grassy strip between two cultivated pieces of ground *19- Sh*. [perhaps Norw *strodd* a funnel, with -IE[1] suffix]

stroint /strɔint/ *n* a pipe, a spout *20- Sh*. [Norw dial *strunt* a spout, funnel]

stroke see STRAIK[1.1], STRAIK[2.1], STRAIK[2.2]

stromalty /ˈstrɔmalti/ *n* a difficult situation; a mix-up or confusion *20- Ork*. [perhaps altered form of Eng *extremity*]

stron /strɔn/ *n* a beach or shore of the sea; a sand-bank etc exposed at low water *20- Ork*. Compare STRAND[1]. [ON *strǫnd*]

strone[1.1], **stroan** /stron/ *n* 1 the discharge of urine *19, 20- EC Bor*. 2 a gush or spurt of liquid; the stream of milk from a cow's teat *la19- NE C SW*. [unknown; compare ME *stronde*, a variant of STRAND[2]]

strone[1.2], **stroan** /stron/ *v* 1 *frequently of dogs* to urinate *18-19, 20- T EC SW Bor*. 2 *of water etc* to spout, spurt, gush *18-19, 20- WC Bor Uls*. [see the noun]

strong see STRANG[1.2], STRANG[1.3]

strontian /ˈstrɔnʃən/ *n* a carbonate containing the element strontium *la18-19, 20- historical*. [from the village of *Strontian*, where it was first found in the waste from lead mines]

strood /strud/ *n* 1 a suit (of clothes), an outfit *la19- Sh Ork N*. 2 *pl* the sails, the shrouds or ropes supporting the mast of a boat *la19- Sh Ork*. [perhaps altered form of SHROOD[1.1]]

strook see STRIK[1.2]

stroop, stroup /strup/ *n* 1 the spout or mouth of a kettle, jug or pump *16-*. 2 a pipe supplying water; the faucet, spout or outlet of a spring or well; a water-tap *la17-19, 20- N NE T*. **stroupach, stroupan** a drink of tea *20- N H&I*. **stroupie** a teapot *la19- Sh NE*. [ME *stroup* the throat, ON *strúpe*]

stroosh see STRUSH[1.1], STRUSH[1.2]

strop see STRAP[1.1], STRAP[1.2]

†**strother, struther, strudir** *n* a marsh *la12-16*. [related to OE *strōd* a marsh]

†**strouble, struble** *v* 1 to disturb, distress; to molest *la14-e16*. 2 to make turbid or cloudy *la14-15*. **stroublance, strublance** (the action of causing) civil disturbance or a breach of the peace; molestation; *15-16*. [aphetic form of DISTROUBLE]

stroud /straud/ *n* 1 a popular song, a street ballad; derogatory verse *19- NE*. 2 a piece of nonsense; rubbishy talk or writing *la19- NE*. [unknown]

strounge, strunge /strunʒ, strʌnʒ/ *adj* 1 harsh to the taste, rank, astringent, bitter *la19-*. 2 *of persons* gruff, surly, sullen, morose *la18-19, 20- N NE Bor*. [unknown]

stroup see STROOP

strouth /struθ/ *n* force, violence, might *19-*. [unknown]

strow[1] /strʌu/ *n* a contention, struggle or quarrel; a commotion or bustle *la18-19, 20- Bor*. [probably ME *strowen*, a variant of strew (STRAW)]

strow[2] /strʌu/ *n* the shrew *Sorex araneus la18- SW*. [altered form of *skrow* (SCREW[1])]

strow see STRAW

struan /ˈstruən/ *n* a cake made from the various cereals grown on a farm, usually oats, barley and rye, and baked with a special ritual on Michaelmas Eve (29th September) *20- H&I*. [Gael *strùthan*]

strubba /ˈstrʌba/ *n* (a dish of) sour, coagulated milk, curds *19- Sh*. **strubbet** curdled *20- Sh*. [compare Norw dial *stropa* slush]

struble see STROUBLE

strucken see STRIK[1.2]

strud /strʌd/ *v* to pull, tug *19- Sh*. [compare Dan *strutte* to struggle against]

strudir see STROTHER

strug /strʌg/ *n* toil, struggle; perplexity *20- Sh*. [compare Swed *strug* contention, strife]

struie /ˈstrui/ *v* to sweep threshed straw to the side with one movement of the flail *20- N*. [Norw dial *strøya* to sweep aside]

struissle[1.1], **strussel, stristle** /ˈstrusəl, ˈstrʌsəl, ˈstrɪsəl/ *n* a struggle; contention; toil; a hard or exacting task *19-*. [see the verb]

struissle[1.2] /ˈstrusəl/ *v* to struggle, wrestle with something bulky and unmanageable or with difficulties *19, 20- EC SW*. [perhaps onomatopoeic]

strukken see STRIK[1.2]

strule, streel /strul, stril/ *n* a stream or steady trickle of liquid *la19, 20- NE T*. [MDu *struylen* to urinate]

strum[1.1] /strʌm/ *n* a fit of ill-humour, a perverse mood *19, 20- NE T EC Bor*. †**tak the strum, tak the strums** to become ill-humoured, sulk *la18-19*. [perhaps onomatopoeic]

strum[1.2] /strʌm/ *v* to sulk, look surly *19- NE T EC*. [see the noun]

strum[2] /strʌm/ *n mining* the fuse of a shot or explosive charge, a narrow tube of paper filled with gunpowder and placed in a blasting borehole *la19- C SW*. [perhaps a shortened form of EModE *strommell* straw]

strummel /ˈstrʌməl/ *n* the half-smoked tobacco left at the bottom of a pipe *19- WC Bor*. Compare DOTTLE[1.1]. [compare STRAMMEL, STRUM[2]]

†**strummill**[1.1] *n* a term of abuse for a person *e16*. [unknown]

†**strummill**[1.2], **strummall, strwmill** *adj* ungainly, stumbling *e16*. [unknown]

strunge see STROUNGE

strunt[1.1] /strʌnt/ *n* 1 a huff, the sulks *la18-19, 20- C Bor Uls*. 2 strife, enmity, hostility *la18-19*. **tak the strunt, tak the strunts** to sulk *18-*. [perhaps an altered form of ME *strout* strife]

strunt[1.2] /strʌnt/ *v* 1 to offend, affront *19-*. 2 to sulk *la19-*. **struntit** offended, in a huff *19-*. [see the noun]

strunt[2] /strʌnt/ *v* to strut, walk about in a stately or affected way *la18-*. [altered form of Eng *strut*]

†**strunt**[3] /strʌnt/ *n* whisky *la18-19*. [unknown]

†**struntin, strunting** /ˈstrʌntɪn/ *n* a kind of coarse, narrow, worsted tape or braid *17-e19*. [unknown]

strunty /'strʌnte/ *adj* short, stumpy, stunted, shrunken, of poor growth *la18-19, 20- NE WC.* [perhaps derivative of Eng *stunt*, with -IE² suffix]

strush[1.1], **stroosh** /strʌʃ, struʃ/ *n* 1 a disturbance, tumult or squabble; a commotion *19-.* 2 a bustling, swaggering gait *20- N.* **strushie** = STRUSH[1.1] (sense 1). [probably onomatopoeic]

strush[1.2], **stroosh** /strʌʃ, struʃ/ *v* to bustle, strut, swagger *20- N.* **strushin** a disturbance, uproar or fuss *19- Bor.* [see the noun]

strushle[1.1] /'strʌʃəl/ *n* an untidy, slovenly person *20- NE.* **strushlach** = STRUSHLE[1.1] *20- N NE.* [see the adj]

strushle[1.2] /'strʌʃəl/ *adj* untidy, slovenly, disorderly *la19- NE.* [derivative of STRUSH[1.1]]

strussel *see* STRUISSLE[1.1]

†**strute** *adj* crammed full *18-e19.* [participial adj from ME *strouten* to bulge, swell, OE *strūtian* to stand out stiffly]

struther *see* STROTHER

stryde *see* STRIDE[1.2]

strydlingis *see* STRIDLINS

stryfe *see* STRIFE, STRIVE[1.2]

stryke *see* STRIK[1.1], STRIK[1.2]

strykkyn *see* STRIK[1.2]

strynd *see* STRIND[1]

stryng *see* STRING[1.1]

strynge *see* STRANGE[1.2]

strynkil *see* STRINKLE[1.2]

stryp *see* STRIP[1]

strypal /'strʌɪpəl/ *n* anything long and slender; a tall, slender person *la19- N NE.* [derivative of STRIPE[1]]

strype *see* STRIPE[1], STRIPE[2]

stryth /strʌɪθ/ *n* the work-animals on a farm, plough-horses and -oxen *19- N.* [Gael *sreath* an array, a flock]

stryve *see* STRIVE[1.2]

stuart *see* STEWART

stubbill, stubble *see* STIBBLE

stuck, stucken *see* STICK[1.2]

stuckie, stushie /'stʌke, 'stʌʃe/ *n* the starling *Sturnus vulgaris 20- T C.* [probably imitative, with influence from STIRLIN + -IE¹]

stuckin /'stʌkɪn/ *n* a stake *19- EC Bor.* [probably variant of STOCK[1.1], with *-ing* suffix]

stud[1], †**stude**, †**stod** /stʌd/ *n* 1 a group of horses kept for breeding *15-.* 2 a brood-mare *la15-17.* †**stodfald** an enclosure for brood-mares *13-17.* †**stude-mere** a brood-mare *la15-18.* [OE *stōd*]

stud[2], †**stood**, †**stuth** /stʌd/ *n* 1 a device (on a garment) for attaching or closing *20-.* 2 an ornamental knob or nail (on a garment, harness etc) *la15-.* **stuthit** having studs *16-.* [OE *studu* or ON *stoð* a post, a prop]

stud *see* STAND[1.2]

studdert *see* STODDERT

studdie, stithy, †**study**, †**stiddie**, †**stydde** /'stʌde, 'stɪθe/ *n* 1 an anvil *la14-.* 2 *in phonetics* the passive articulator *e17.* 3 *applied to (the community of) the Presbyterian Church* something able to withstand blows *17.* [ON *steði*]

studdie *see* STEADY[1.2], STEADY[1.3]

studdy *see* STEADY[1.1]

stude *see* STAND[1.2], STUD[1]

student, †**studyand** /'stjudənt/ *n* a person studying at a college or university; a pupil, a scholar *la15-.* **Students' Representative Council, S.R.C.** the statutory body elected in each of the Scottish universities by the matriculated students to discuss student affairs, and represented on the university court *20-.* [Lat *student-*]

studge *see* STODGE

study *see* STUDDIE

studyand *see* STUDENT

stue *see* STEW[1.1]

stuff[1.1], †**stuf**, †**stufe** /stʌf/ *n* 1 material, fabric *la15-.* 2 something unspecified *la15-.* 3 corn, grain, a crop *la15-.* 4 the substance of a person or situation *la16-.* 5 provisions, a store of food *la15-19, 20- Ork T.* 6 apparently padding or stiffening used in a garment; the quilted material worn under armour; clothing *la15-e16.* 7 military resources; plenishing; troops, a garrison, reinforcements; equipment, gear *la14-17.* 8 the materials of which bread is made: meal, flour, malt; the dough, the bread itself *la15-17.* 9 the materials of which something is made; building materials *14-17.* 10 merchandise, wares, finished goods presented for sale *16-17.* [OFr *estoffe* material, furniture]

stuff[1.2], †**stuf** /stʌf/ *v* 1 to fill completely, cram full *la15-.* 2 to furnish (troops) with support; to support, aid (a war) *la15-16.* 3 to fortify, garrison, supply (a castle, town or country) *la14-e17.* 4 to furnish (a person) with money *la14-16.* †**stuff a chace** to provide hostile pursuit *la15-e16.* [OFr *estoffer* to furnish, equip]

†**stuff**[2], **stuf** *v* to quilt, stiffen (a garment) *la15-16.* [perhaps an extended sense of STUFF[1.2], and compare STIFF[1.1]]

stuff *see* STIFF[1.1], STOUFF

†**stuffet** *n* perhaps a groom or a lackey, or an unspecific term of abuse *e16.* [MFr *estaffette* a mounted courier]

stuffie[1.1] /'stʌfe/ *n* **the stuffie** whisky *la19-* mainly *NE T.* [STUFF[1.1] + -IE¹]

stuffie[1.2], *NE* **stowfie** /'stʌfe; *NE* 'stʌufi/ *adj* 1 in good health, sturdy, full of vigour *19, 20- C SW Bor.* 2 spirited, plucky, game *19- T C SW Bor.* 3 sturdily built, stocky, stout, stolid *19-.* [STUFF[1.1] + -IE²]

stuffing *see* STIFFIN

stug[1.1], **stog**, †**steug**, †**stok** /stʌg, stɔg/ *n* 1 a prick, stab or thrust with a pointed object *la16-.* 2 a pointed object, a dart, a thorn *19-.* †**stok swerd** a thrusting sword *16.* [ME *stok*, Fr *estoc* a sword point, a thrust]

stug[1.2], **stog**, †**stok** /stʌg, stɔg/ *v* 1 to stab, prick, thrust with a weapon, jab, pierce *16-.* 2 to dress (stone) roughly with a pointed chisel *20- EC Bor.* [ME *stoken*; compare Fr *estoquer* to stab with a pointed weapon]

stug[2.1], **stog** /stʌg, stɔg/ *n* 1 a jagged or uneven cut, anything left rough by careless cutting; *pl* unevenly-cut stubble *18-19, 20- Bor.* 2 a stump of a tree or bush *19-.* 3 a stocky, coarsely-built person (or animal); one whose movements are stiff and awkward *la18-.* **stuggie** = STUG[2.1] (sense 3) *20- Ork.* **stuggal** = STUG[2.1] (sense 3) *20- Ork.* †**stug taillit** of a horse having a docked tail *la16-18.* [perhaps an altered form of STOCK[1.1] with influence from STUG[1.1]]

stug[2.2], **stog** /stʌg, stɔg/ *v* 1 to cut with a rough edge, especially in harvesting grain with a sickle; to cut (the stubble) unevenly *la17-e19.* 2 *of a clumsy, old or infirm person* to walk in a heavy-footed way, plod *19, 20- Sh Bor.* [see the noun]

stugg[1] /stʌg/ *v* to thicken *20- Ork.* [compare Norw dial *stokka*]

stugg[2] /stʌg/ *n* an aversion (to food) *la19- Sh.* **stuggit** replete, sick of food *20- Sh.* [Norw dial *stugg*]

stuiden *see* STAND[1.2]

stuil, stool, stule, *Ork* **steul**, *NE* **steel**, †**stole** /stul; *Ork* støl; *NE* stil/ *n* 1 a seat (without a back), originally also a chair *la14-.* 2 = *stool of repentance la16-20, 21- historical.* 3 a bench, counter or trestle *16-.* 4 the base and growing shoots of a plant; a dense bed of vegetation, especially grass roots *la17-19, 20- Sh Ork.* 5 a support, stand, base or foundation; the support for the upper millstone *15-19.* 6 an Orkney chair *20- Ork.* †**stuling** 1 timber used for supports or props *la16-18.* **2** (cargo used as) ballast *16-17.* **stool-bent, stuilbent** the heath rush *Juncus squarrosus la18-.* †**stule of es** a close stool or commode *16.* †**stool of repentance** = *repentance stool* (REPENTANCE). [OE *stōl*]

stuir, sture, stör /stør/ *n* a penny, originally a small Dutch coin; *pl* cash *la15-17, 19- Sh.* [Du *stuiver*]

stuir *see* STURE[1]

stuit[1.1], *N NE T* **steet**, †**stut** /stut; *N NE T* stit/ *n* a prop, a support *la16-19, 20- N NE T.* [MDu, MLG *stutte*]

stuit[1.2], *N NE* **steet**, *NE* **stoot**, †**stut** /stut; *N NE* stit/ *v* to prop, support, shore up *17-19, 20- NE T.* [MDu *stutten*]

stuke *see* STOCK[1.1]

stule *see* STEAL[1.2], STUIL

stull *see* STILL[1.3], STILL[1.4]

stult *see* STILT[1.1], STILT[1.2]

stumba /ˈstʌmba/ *n* a thick mist or fog; drizzle, a dense cloud of smoke *la19- Sh.* [compare Norw dial *stump-myrk* pitch dark]

stumble *see* STUMMLE

stumer, shtumer /ˈstjumər, ˈʃtjumər/ *n derogatory* a foolish or incompetent person *la20-.* [compare slang *stumer* a worthless cheque, a dud, a bankrupt person]

stummer *see* STAMMER[1.2]

stummle, stumble, *Bor* **stammle** /ˈstʌməl, ˈstʌmbəl; *Bor* ˈstaməl/ *v* **1** to miss one's footing, stagger, blunder, hobble *16-.* **2** to upset, disturb, puzzle, confuse (a person) *17.* **stumbling 1** that stumbles *19-.* **2** that causes stumbling *la16-e17.* [ME *stomblen*, ON **stumla*]

stummyrryt *see* STAMMER[1.2]

stump[1.1], †**stomp** /stʌmp/ *n* **1** the cut, broken off or left over end of something, originally a severed limb *15-.* **2** the core of an apple *20- C SW Bor.* **3** a short, stocky person or animal; a stiff, slow-moving or sluggish person; a toddler *la18-, 20- Sh N.* **4** a stupid person *19- Bor.* **stumparts** (sturdy) legs *20- NE.* **stumpie 1** a short, stocky or dumpy person; a plump, sturdy, young child *19-.* **2** the stump of a worn quill pen *la18-19.* **stump and rump** completely *la19- NE T C Uls*; compare *rump and stump* (RUMP[1.1]). [ME *stumpe*, MLG *stump*, MDu *stomp*]

stump[1.2] /stʌmp/ *v* to walk heavily, in a stumping way *19-.* **stumpart** = STUMP[1.2] *la19 NE.* **stumper** to walk with a clumsy, heavy or hobbling step *la19- NE.* **stumpit** short, stunted; *of a person* stocky, dumpy *la18-.* †**stumple** to walk with a stiff hobbling gait *e19.* [see the noun]

stumryt *see* STAMMER[1.2]

stumse[1.1] /stʌms/ *n* stupefaction *20- Sh.* [see the verb]

stumse[1.2] /stʌms/ *v* to bewilder; to be rendered speechless *19- Sh.* [compare Swed dial *stumsen* speechless with amazement]

stund *see* STOUND[1.1]

stunder[1] /ˈstʌndər/ *n* a whim, an impulse, a freakish notion; *of a horse* a spook *20- Ork.* [intensive form of STOUND[1.1]]

stunder[2] /ˈstʌndər/ *v* to astonish, perplex, flabbergast *20- Ork.* [intensive form of STOUND[2.2]]

stunk[1.1] /stʌŋk/ *n* a pant, gasp or grunt *la19- Sh.* [see the verb]

stunk[1.2] /stʌŋk/ *v* to pant or gasp with exertion; to groan or grunt with satisfaction *19- Sh.* [Norw dial *stanka*]

stunk[2] /stʌŋk/ *n* mainly *pl* (the stake in) a game of marbles *19- C SW Bor.* [unknown]

stunk[3] /stʌŋk/ *v* to sulk *la19, 20- NE.* **the stunkles** the sulks *19-, 20- NE.* [probably back-formation from STUNKARD]

stunk *see* STINK[1.2]

stunkard /ˈstʌŋkərd/ *adj* sulky, surly, perverse, obstinate *la17-19, 20- WC SW.* [unknown; perhaps imitative, with derogatory *-ard* suffix]

stunt /stʌnt/ *v* to bound, bounce, walk with a springy step *19, 20- WC SW Bor.* [probably onomatopoeic; compare STOT[2.2]]

stupe /stjup/ *n* a fool, a stupid person *19, 20- N NE T EC.* [back-formation from STUPIT]

stuperat *see* STUPRAT

†**stupifak, stupefact** *adj* stupefied *16-e17.* [Lat *stupefact-*, ptp stem of *stupefacere*]

stupit, *C Bor* **stippit,** *NE* **steepid** /ˈstjupɪt; *C Bor* ˈstɪpɪt; *NE* ˈstipɪd/ *adj* lacking sense or intelligence *la16-.* [Lat *stupidus* stunned, benumbed]

†**stuprat, stuperat** *v* to violate (a woman) *la16-e17.* **stupratioun** violation (of a woman) *la15-16.* [Lat *stuprāt-*, ptp stem of *stuprāre* to defile]

stur *see* STEER[1.1], STEER[1.2]

sturdy[1.1] /ˈstʌrde/ *n* **1** a brain disease of sheep, causing staggering and ultimately collapse *la16-.* **2** a sheep affected with STURDY[1.1] (sense 1) *19, 20- SW.* **sturdied** *of a sheep* affected with STURDY[1.1] (sense 1) *la18-.* **tak the sturdy, tak the sturdies** to sulk, be in a perverse or obstinate mood *la18-19, 20- T C SW Uls.* [see the adj]

sturdy[1.2], †**sturdie,** †**sterde** /ˈstʌrde/ *adj* **1** healthy, robust; strong; vigorous; originally, bold, fierce *la14-.* **2** giddyheaded; (as if) affected with STURDY[1.1] (sense 1) *18, 20- Sh N SW.* [OFr *estourdi* stunned, reckless, violent]

sture[1], **stour, stoor,** †**stuir,** †**stuyr** /stur/ *adj* **1** big, stout, burly, substantial; strong; valiant *la14-19, 20- Sh Ork EC SW.* **2** *of a sound, especially the voice* deep and hoarse, harsh, rough; powerful, commanding *la15-19, 20- WC SW Bor.* **3** rough in manner or appearance; grim, gruff, stern; hard, determined, unyielding; fierce *la14-19, 20- WC Bor.* [conflation of OE *stōr* great with MDu, MLG *sture* rough, fierce]

†**sture**[2] *n* a sturgeon *la15-16.* [compare Lat *sturio*; MDu, MLG *störe*]

sture *see* STUIR, STEER[1.2]

sturken, *Ork* **sturten,** †**storkyn,** †**starkyn** /ˈstʌrkən, ˈsturkən; *Ork* ˈstʌrtən/ *v* **1** to restore to robustness; to recover one's strength *19- SW Bor.* **2** to stiffen, coagulate, congeal, solidify *19- Sh Ork.* **3** *of the penis* to become stiff *e16.* **4** to become strong; to thrive *15.* [ON *storkna* to congeal, coagulate]

sturre *see* STEER[1.1]

sturt[1.1] /stʌrt/ *n* **1** trouble, vexation; contentious or violent behaviour *la14-.* **2** disquiet, sorrow, misery, melancholy *la15-.* †**sturtsum** quarrelsome, contentious, vexatious *la16.* **sturt and strife** = STURT[1.1] (sense 1) or STURT[1.1] (sense 2) *16-.* [metathesis of OE **strūt*]

sturt[1.2] /stʌrt/ *v* **1** to trouble, disturb, annoy; to attack, molest *16-19, 20- Sh.* **2** to rouse oneself, begin to do something *20- Ork.* †**sturtan** to take fright, be uneasy *la18-e19.* **sturtensome** easily roused or upset, not easy-going or lazy *20- Sh Ork.* [see the noun]

sturten *see* STURKEN

sturtin-stringin /ˈstʌrtɪn ˈstrɪŋɪn/ *n* a coarse worsted thread, with blue and red strands, like carpet-binding *19, 20- EC.* [metathesis of STRUNTIN + derivative of STRING[1.1]]

stushie, stooshie, stishie, stashie /ˈstuʃi, ˈstɪʃi, ˈstaʃi/ *n* an uproar, commotion, quarrel or row; a fuss or bother *19-.* [unknown]

stushie *see* STUCKIE

stut, †**stoot** /stʌt/ *v* to stutter, stammer *la15-19, 20- Bor.* [ME *stutten*; compare MLG *stöteren*]

stut *see* STUIT[1.1], STUIT[1.2]

†**stuth, stood** *n* **1** an ornamental stud or nail (on a garment, harness etc) *la15-e17.* **2** a device (on a garment) for attaching or closing *e18.* **stuthit** having studs *16-17.* [OE *studu, stuðu*]

stuyr *see* STURE¹
stwart *see* STEWART
stwnys *see* STONIS
styan, *N* **styal**, †**styen** /'staeən; *NE* stjal/ *n* an inflammation and swelling on the eyelid *18-19, 20- Ork N NE*. [OE *stīgend*]
stychle *see* STICHLE¹·²
stydde *see* STUDDIE
stye *see* BUFF³
styen *see* STYAN
styew *see* STEW¹·¹
styf *see* STIFF¹·²
styill *see* STILE
styk *see* STEEK²·²
styl *see* STILL¹·³
style¹·¹, †**stile**, †**still**, †**styll** /stʌɪl/ *n* 1 (a manner of) writing *15-*. 2 *law* the (approved) form or model for drawing up a legal document *la14-*. 3 one's condition, as revealed to others *la15-17*. 4 *law* the manner of functioning of (a process laid down by) a court *16-e17*. 5 *law* a regulation of a local court, especially the WHITSUNDAY court *e16*. 6 *pl* things written, writings *16*. 7 the manner in which a date is expressed *16-e17*. 8 a (legal or official) designation, an honorific title; a descriptive designation; a nickname *la15-*. **New Style** the manner of expressing the date adopted after the introduction of the Gregorian calendar in 1582 *19-*. **Old Style** the manner of expressing the date prior to the introduction of the Gregorian calendar in 1582 *20-*. **style-book** *law* a book containing examples of the correct wording of legal documents; originally also apparently drafts of legal transactions and parliamentary records *la16-*. [OFr *style*, Lat *stilus* a writing implement]
style¹·², †**stile** /stʌɪl/ *v ptp* also †**styld** 1 to give a name or designation, call by a name usually descriptive of a person's occupation, status or character *la15-*. 2 to name or address with an honorific title; to honour with a title *16-17*. [see the noun]
style *see* STILE
stylk *see* STILK
styll *see* STILE, STILL¹·², STILL¹·³, STILL¹·⁴, STYLE¹·¹
styme *see* STIME¹·¹, STIME¹·²
stymel *see* STIME¹·²
stymie *see* STIME¹·², STIMIE¹·¹, STIMIE¹·²
stynk *see* STINK¹·¹, STINK¹·²
stynkand *see* STINKIN
stynt *see* STINT¹·¹, STINT¹·²
styrlyng *see* STIRLIN
styte *see* STOIT¹·¹, STOIT¹·²
styter *see* STOITER¹·², STOITER¹·²
styth *see* STITH¹·²
sua *see* SAE²·¹
suadde *see* SWADE
suage *see* SWAGE
suaidge *see* SWEDGE¹·¹
suak *see* SWACK²·²
suallow *see* SWALLA
sualter *see* SWATTER¹·²
suap *see* SWAP¹·¹, SWAP¹·²
suave, †**swaif** /swav/ *adj* 1 pleasing, agreeable; smooth-mannered *la16-*. 2 gracious, kindly *16*. [OFr *suef*, MFr *suave*, Lat *suāvis*]
subaltern /'sʌbəltərn/ *adj* 1 *law, of a land-hold or the land* held of or granted by a SUPERIOR¹·¹ (sense 2) who is himself a VASSAL, subinfeudated *17-20, 21- historical*. 2 subordinate, inferior *la16-e19*. [Lat *subalternus* subordinate]
†**subbasmont** *n* a valance (of a bed) *e16*. [MFr *soubassement*]
subcharge, **subchettis** *see* SURCHARGE

†**subcommit** *v* to refer to a subcommittee *la17-e18*. [*sub-* prefix + Older Scots, Eng *commit*]
†**subdelegat**¹·¹ *n* a deputy or assistant of a person delegated to do something *16*. [see the verb]
†**subdelegat**¹·² *v* to appoint as a deputy or representative *e17*. [*sub-* prefix + Eng *delegate*; compare MFr *subdéléguer*, Lat *subdelegare*]
subdelegat *see* JUDGE
†**subdit**¹·¹ *n* a monarch's subject *la14-e17*. [Lat *subditus* a vassal]
†**subdit**¹·² *adj* subject to *15-e16*. [Lat *subditus* subject (to authority)]
†**subduce** *v* 1 to seduce, withdraw from allegiance *la16*. 2 to subtract *la16*. [Lat *subdūcere* to withdraw or take away]
†**suberbillis** *npl* suburbs *e16*. [ME *subarblis*, altered form of ME *suburbes* suburbs]
subfeu¹·¹ /'sʌbfju/ *n law* a FEU granted by a VASSAL to a SUBVASSAL *la17-20, 21- historical*. †**subfeudation** subinfeudation *la17*. [*sub-* prefix + FEU¹·¹]
subfeu¹·² /sʌb'fju, 'sʌbfju/ *v law* to make a grant of (lands) in SUBFEU¹·¹, subinfeudate *18-20, 21- historical*. [see the noun]
†**subitane** *adj* sudden, unpremeditated *15-17*. [Lat *subitāneus*]
subjeck¹·¹, **subject**, †**subiect** /'sʌbdʒɪk, 'sʌbdʒɪkt/ *n* 1 a topic of discourse *la16-*. 2 a person owing allegiance to a monarch; a feudal tenant or vassal *15-*. 3 *law* HERITABLE property, *eg* a piece of land, a house *18-*. 4 a person in subjection to another, a prisoner or slave *la15-16*. 5 mainly *pl* property, goods *17-19*. †**subject-superior** = SUPERIOR¹·¹ (sense 2), frequently when a SUPERIORITY (sense 3) is held *18-19, 20- historical*. [MFr *subject*, Lat *subiectus*]
subjeck¹·², **subject**, †**subiect** /sʌb'dʒɛk, sʌb'dʒɛkt/ *v* 1 to subjugate *la15-16*. 2 to subordinate, render submissive or obedient *la15-e17*. 3 to expose to an influence *16-*. [from the noun and MFr *subjecter*, Lat *subiectāre*]
subjeck¹·³, **subject**, †**subiect** /'sʌbdʒɪk, 'sʌbdʒɪkt/ *adj* 1 subservient to another, the law etc *la14-*. 2 dependent on, affected or enslaved by (a vice or virtue) *15-16*. 3 submissive, obedient *e16*. 4 likely to be affected by, exposed to *16-*. [MFr *subject*, Lat *subiectus*]
submission, †**submissioun**, †**summissiovn** /sʌb'mɪʃən/ *n* 1 the action of submitting, submissiveness *18-*. 2 *law* a contract, or the document embodying it, by which parties in a dispute agree to arbitration *15-*. [AN *submissioun*, *submission*, Lat *submissiōn-*]
†**submissour**, **summissour** *n* an arbiter or adjudicator (of a dispute) *15*. [Lat *submiss-*, *summiss-*, ptp stem of *submittere*, *summittere*]
submit /sʌb'mɪt/ *v* 1 to surrender, yield to the control of another *15-*. 2 to refer the parties in a dispute to an arbiter or assize *la14-17*. 3 to entrust to another's care *16-*. †**submitter**, **submittar** a person who makes a SUBMISSION (sense 2) *17-e19*. [AN *submittre*, Lat *submittere*]
subordinate /sʌ'bɔrdənət/ *adj* lesser, inferior *la15-*. [Lat *subordinātus*]
†**sub-principal**, **subprincipall** *n* the deputy of the PRINCIPAL¹·¹ (sense 3) of King's College, Aberdeen *la16-19*. [*sub-* prefix + PRINCIPAL¹·¹]
†**subreption** *n law* the act of obtaining gifts of ESCHEAT¹·¹ from the Crown by concealing certain facts *la17-e19*. [Lat *subreptiōn-* the act of taking secretly]
†**subscribent** *n* a signatory, a subscriber *17-e18*. [Lat *subscribent-* presp stem of *subscrībere* to underwrite, subscribe]
subscription, †**subscriptioun** /sʌb'skrɪpʃən/ *n* 1 a contribution, money collected or paid to support a cause, join an organization *19-*. 2 a signature; the action of signing (as

validation of a document or assent to its contents) *la15-e19*.
subscription manual signature, signed name *la15-17*. [Lat *subscriptiōn-*]
†**subscrive** *v* **1** to sign (a document); to signify assent to (a doctrine, course of action etc) by signing (a document) *la15-e19*. **2** to agree by one's signature to the purchase of a number of issues of a newspaper *e18*. **subscriver, subscrivar** a signatory *la16-e18*. [MFr *subscriv-*, pres stem of *subscrire*]
†**subset**[1.1] *n* a sub-lease *18-e19*. [see the verb]
†**subset**[1.2] *v* to sublet *la17-19*. [*sub-* prefix + SET[1.2]]
†**subsidiarie** *adv law* in a secondary or subsidiary manner, as a second resort *la18-e19*. [Lat *subsidāriē*]
subsist /sʌbˈsɪst/ *v* **1** to keep on, persevere in supporting or maintaining oneself *17-*. **2** to maintain, support (a person) *16-19*. **3** to cease, stop *17*. [MFr *subsister*, Lat *subsistere*]
†**substantious** *adj* **1** *of a structure* substantial, solid *16-19*. **2** wealthy, well-to-do *la15-17*. **3** *of a provision, course of action, remedy etc* ample, considerable; sufficient *16-e17*. **4** *of writing etc* full of useful content; sound, worthwhile *16-e17*. [MFr *substantieux*]
substitute[1.1] /ˈsʌbstɪtjut/ *n* **1** one who takes the place of another; a representative, proxy, delegate or deputy *la14-*. **2** *law* a beneficiary who will take a gift of property after the death of the first beneficiary *la17-*; compare INSTITUTE. [AN *substitut*, Lat *substitūtus*]
substitute[1.2] /ˈsʌbstɪtjut/ *v* **1** to replace *la18-*. **2** to appoint as a deputy or assistant *la15-17*. **3** to name a substitute heir *la17*. [Lat *substitūt-*, ptp stem of *substituere*]
substitute[1.3] /ˈsʌbstɪtjut/ *adj* usually *following a noun* **1** nominated to act in place of another, as a deputy *la16-*; compare *sheriff substitute* (SHERIFF). **2** nominated to replace a predeceasing person in an inheritance *la17-*. **substitute heir** an heir nominated to replace a predeceasing heir *la18-*; compare *heir substitute* (HEIR[1.1]). [Lat *substitūtus*]
substitution /sʌbstɪˈtjuʃən/ *n* **1** replacement *19-*. **2** the designation of a substitute heir in the event of the death of the first-named heir *la17-18*. **3** a writ or deed appointing a substitute or deputy *18*. [MFr *substitution*, Lat *substitūtiōn-*]
substract /sʌbˈstrakt/ *v* **1** to take away one number from another *la16-*. **2** to withdraw (oneself), retire; to remove (a person or thing) *16*. [Lat *substract-*, ptp stem of *substrahere*]
substraction, †**substractioune** /sʌbˈstrakʃən/ *n* an act of withdrawal or taking away; subtraction *15-*; compare SUBTRACK. [Lat *substractiōn-*, ptp stem of *substrahere*, variant of *subtrahere* to withdraw, with noun-forming suffix]
subsume /sʌbˈsjum/ *v* **1** to state; to add, subjoin (information, a proposition) (under a larger whole or category) *16-*. **2** *law* to state, allege *17-18*. **3** to assume, infer *la16-17*. [Lat *subsūmere* under + Lat *sūmere* to take]
†**subsumption** *n* a description of an alleged crime, setting out the known facts *17-19*. [Lat *subsumptiōn-*]
†**subsynod** *n* (a meeting of) a subcommittee of a SYNOD *17*. [*sub-* prefix + SYNOD]
subtack, †**subtak** /ˈsʌbtak/ *n* a lease granted by a tenant to a subtenant *la16-*. [*sub-* prefix + TACK[2]]
†**subtacksman, subtaksman** *n* a subtenant *17-e18*. [*sub-* prefix + *tacksman* (TACK[2])]
subtak *see* SUBTACK
subtenant /ˈsʌbtɛnənt/ *n* a tenant with a lease granted by a tenant *15-*. [*sub-* prefix + TENANT]
subtle, †**subtill**, †**suttel**, †**scitell** /ˈsʌtəl/ *adj* **1** skilful, ingenious, clever; skilfully made *15-*. **2** abstruse, obscure *15-*. **3** thin, fine, ethereal *la15-e17*. **4** wise, perspicacious; cunning, sly, deceitful *la14-17*. [AN *suttil, subtil*, Lat *subtīlis*]

subtrack, subtract, †**subtrak** /sʌbˈtrak, sʌbˈtrakt/ *v* to withdraw, remove, take away *16-*. [Lat *subtract-*, ptp stem of *subtrahere*]
†**subvassal** *n* a person who held his lands from a VASSAL *la15-e19*. [*sub-* prefix + VASSAL]
†**subvene** *v* to help, assist, rescue *la15-16*. [MFr *subvenir*]
subversion, †**subversioun** /sʌbˈvɛrʃən/ *n* **1** overthrow, ruin *16-*. **2** destruction, demolition *15-16*. [AN *subversioun*, Lat *subversiōn-*]
succar *see* SUGAR
succeed, †**succede**, †**succeid** /səkˈsid/ *v* **1** to take the place of, follow as heir or in an office; to descend in succession; to come down as an inheritance *la14-*. **2** to come next after, follow after *la15-*. **3** to follow as a consequence of, ensue, result *16-*. **4** to be successful, prosper *15-*. **5** to happen, transpire, turn out (to a person's advantage or disadvantage) *16-17*. †**succede in the vice and violence of a person** to take possession without permission of lands from which a tenant had been removed *la16-e17*. [OFr *succeder*, Lat *succēdere*]
success, †**succes** /səkˈsɛs/ *n* **1** an outcome, the result of a course of action etc *la16-17*. **2** a successful outcome, good fortune *la16-*. [Lat *successus*]
succession, †**successioun**, †**sucessioun** /səkˈsɛʃən/ *n* **1** the transmission (originally of royal or other inherited power) to succeeding generations; (the process or line of) inheritance; descendants, progeny *la14-*. **2** the course or passage (of time) *la15-16*. [OFr *succession*, Lat *successiōn-*]
†**succine** *n* amber *la16*. [Lat *succinum, sūcinum*]
succodrous *see* SUCCUDRUS
succour[1.1], †**succur**, †**succours**, †**secours** /ˈsʌkər/ *n* **1** help; a remedy; military reinforcements *la14-*. **2** a place of refuge *15-16*. [AN *sucurs*]
succour[1.2], †**succur** /ˈsʌkər/ *v* to help, assist; to rescue; to supply with military reinforcements *la14-*. [OFr *succurre*, Lat *succurrere*]
†**succudrus, succodrous** *adj* presumptuous, arrogant *la14-e16*. [SUCCUDRY, with adj-forming suffix]
†**succudry, sucquedry** *n* presumption, arrogance *la14-16*. [OFr *surcuiderie*]
succumb /səˈkʌm/ *v* **1** to give way, submit, yield *la16-*. **2** to bring low, overwhelm *e16*. **3** *law* to fail (in proving a case) *16-e18*. [OFr *succomber*, Lat *succumbere*]
succur *see* SUCCOUR[1.1], SUCCOUR[1.2]
such *see* SIC[1.1], SIC[1.2], SIC[1.3]
sucharge *see* SURCHARGE
suck /sʌk/ *n* **1** a mess; disorder, dirtiness *la19- Sh Ork*. **2** a slatternly person *20- Ork*. [Icel *sukk*]
suck *see* SOOK[1.1], SOOK[1.2], SOOK[1.3]
sucken[1.1], †**sukin** /ˈsʌkən/ *n* **1** an obligation on tenants requiring them to have their grain ground at a particular mill; the payment due in kind, service or money for the use of the mill *15-e19*. **2** tenants or lands restricted or bound to a particular mill; the grain belonging to those tenants *la15-19*. **3** *in Orkney and Shetland* the area of a bailiff's jurisdiction *la16-17*. **suckener**, *Ork* **sookaner** a tenant bound to a particular mill *la16-e19, 20- historical*. [OE *sōcn* resort (to a place), a seeking, a visit, ON *sókn* an assembling of people]
†**sucken**[1.2], **suckine** *v* to bind (tenants) to a particular mill for the grinding of grain *17-e18*. [see the noun]
†**sucken**[1.3] *adj* bound to a particular mill *la16-19*. Compare BUNSUCKEN. [see the noun]
sucken[2], †**sukkin** /ˈsʌkən/ *n* a small drag or grapnel, especially one used by fishermen in searching for lost lines *la19- Sh NE*. [Norw dial *sokn*]
sucker *see* SUGAR

suckine see SUCKEN¹·²
suckler, †**sowklar**, †**suklar** /'sʌklər/ *n* **1** an unweaned farm animal, a suckling *la15-19, 20- C Bor*. **2** a cow which suckles its calf; a herd of cows in which the calves remain with the mothers until naturally weaned *20- Bor*. **3** a flowerhead of clover *Trifolium pratense 18-19, 20- EC*. **4** a term of endearment or abuse *16-17*. [ME *sukelen* to suckle, with agent suffix]
sucky /'suke/ *adj of a wound or blow* painful, stinging *20- EC*. [unknown]
sucky see SOOKIE
sucquedry see SUCCUDRY
sud, **suld**, **sould**, **should**, **sid**, *Ork NE EC* **shid**, †**schuld**, †**shuld** /sud, ʃud, sɪd; *Ork NE EC* ʃɪd/ *v* **1** the past tense of SALL with temporal function, was to, were to; should, would; was or were about to *la14-*. **2** *in expressions of duty, obligation, propriety, the rightness or justice of something, entitlement etc* ought to *la14-*. **3** *in expressions of wishing or fearing* should, would, might (come about) *la14-e17*. **4** *as a modal verb* used in statements of presumed fact, mainly indicating uncertainty or the speaker's lack of commitment to the truth of the alleged fact *la14-17*. Compare SALL. [OE *sceolde*, pt of *sculan*]
sudcharge see SURCHARGE
suddan, **suddand** see SUDDENT¹·¹
suddane see SUDDENT¹·¹, SUDDENT¹·²
suddante, **suddanty** see SUDDENTY
†**suddart**, **suddert** *n* a mercenary soldier *16-e17*. Compare SODGER¹·¹. [MFr *souldart*]
suddent¹·¹, **sudden**, †**suddand**, †**suddane**, †**suddan** /'sʌdənt, 'sʌdən/ *adj* **1** happening without warning, unexpected, unforeseen; unpremeditated, spontaneous *la14-*. **2** prompt, immediate, instant *la15-*. **3** *of people* impetuous *la16-e19*. **4** *of a remedy* prompt in effect, efficacious *e17*. **5** brief *16*. **suddently 1** without warning, unexpectedly; without delay or premeditation, promptly, immediately *la14-*. **2** after a brief lapse of time, very soon *la16*. †**suddan cas** unforeseen or accidental circumstances; misfortune *15-e16*. †**upon a suddane**, **upon the suddane**, **upoun suddane** unexpectedly, promptly, without premeditation or delay *16-e19*. [AN *sudein*; with the form in *t* compare CERTAINT]
suddent¹·², **sudden**, †**suddane** /'sʌdənt, 'sʌdən/ *adv = suddently* (SUDDENT¹·¹) *la15-*. [see the adj]
suddenty, †**suddentie**, †**suddanty**, †**suddante** /'sʌdənte/ *n* **1** suddenness, unexpectedness *17-19, 20- N NE T*. **2** *law* a sudden outburst of rage, an act done in hot blood, without premeditation *la16-19*. **3** hastiness *17*. †**be ane suddante** *of actions* without premeditation *16-e17*. **in a suddenty**, †**in suddante** all of a sudden *la16-19, 20- NE*. **o a suddenty**, †**of suddante** = *in a suddenty 15-19, 20- NE*. **on a suddenty**, †**upon suddante** all of a sudden *la15-19, 20- NE*. **wi suddenty** = *in a suddenty la16-19, 20- N NE*. [MFr *sodeineté*]
suddert see SUDDART, SOOTHWARD
suddle¹·¹, †**suddill** /'sʌdəl/ *v* to soil, dirty *16-*. †**suddillit**, **suddled** = SUDDLE¹·² *la16-17*. [MHG *sudlen* to wallow in mire]
†**suddle**¹·², **suddill** /'sʌdəl/ *adj* filthy *la15*. **suddly** soiled, dirty *la15-16*. [see the verb]
sudiorne see SOJOURN¹·¹, SOJOURN¹·²
sudron see SOUTHRON¹·¹, SOUTHRON¹·²
sue, †**sew** /su/ *v* **1** *law* to institute legal proceedings, prosecute, make a claim *15-*. **2** to ask for (mercy) *16-*. **3** to pursue (a way of life etc) *16*. [ME *seuen* to follow, AN *suer*]

†**sueit**, **sweit** *n* suede, undressed kid-skin *17*. [Fr (*de*) *Suède* (from) Sweden]
sueit see SWEET¹·²
suelly see SWALLIE¹·²
suelt see SWELT¹
suer see SWEER¹·²
suerd see SWURD
suerthbak see SWART¹·²
suet see SHUET
suete see SWEET²
Suethin see SWADEN
suey see SWEY¹·²
suffer, *Sh* **siffer**, †**suffir** /'sʌfər/ *v* to undergo, endure, be adversely affected; to allow, tolerate, put up with *la14-*. †**suffer law**, **suffer ane assyise** to undergo trial, be tried *la14-16*. †**suffer to** to accept, consent to *la15-e19*. [AN *suffrir*]
suffice, †**suffys**, †**suffyis** /səˈfʌɪs/ *v* to be enough, satisfy; to be equal to *la14-*. [OFr *suffis-*, pres stem of *suffire*]
sufficiand see SUFFICIENT¹·¹, SUFFICIENT¹·²
sufficiency, †**sufficience**, †**suffisance** /səˈfɪʃənse/ *n* **1** sufficient provision, enough *la14-*. **2** the condition of being sufficient, suitable, satisfactory or adequate *la16-*. **3** sufficient capacity or skill *15-e18*. †**at sufficience** in sufficient quantity *la15-e16*. †**in sufficyans** in comfort *15-e16*. [OFr *sufficience*, Lat *sufficientia*]
sufficient¹·¹, †**sufficiand** /səˈfɪʃənt/ *adj* **1** adequate, satisfactory *la14-*. **2** *of things* substantial, solid, of adequate strength or quality *la14-*. **3** having adequate means, financially secure, prosperous *la14-17*. **4** *of livestock, produce, food or drink* of satisfactory quality *15-17*. **5** *law, of a pledge, testimony, witness etc* conforming to the requirements of the law *15-17*. **sufficiently 1** adequately, well enough *la14-*. **2** thoroughly, completely, in full compliance with a standard; well-made, sound, substantial *la14-*. **3** sufficient means or resources *la15*. [OFr *sufficient*, Lat *sufficient-*]
†**sufficient**¹·², †**sufficiand** *adv* of a satisfactory standard, quality or ability *la14-16*. [see the adj]
suffisance see SUFFICIENCY
suffrage /'sʌfrədʒ/ *n* **1** the action of voting; (a) vote or mandate *16-*. **2** (intercessory) prayers *la15-e17*. **3** help, assistance *la15-e16*. [Fr *suffrage*, Lat *suffrāgium*]
suffyis, **suffys** see SUFFICE
sugar, **shuggar**, **succar**, **sucker**, †**sugour** /'ʃugər, 'ʃʌgər, 'sʌkər/ *n* a sweet substance obtained from sugar-cane or sugar-beet *la15-*. **sugared**, †**sugarit**, †**sugarat**, †**sugarait 1** covered, coated or sprinkled with sugar *17-*. **2** *of sound, birdsong, speech, poetry etc* melodious, eloquent, pleasing *16-e17*. †**sugary**, **suggarie** a sugar factory *la17-e18*. †**sucker alacreische** liquorice *la16*. †**sucur lacrissye**, **sucker lacreische** = *sucker alacreische la15-16*. †**sugar biscuit** *food* a thin crisp biscuit, baked with sugar on top *la17-e19*. **sugar bool** a round boiled sweet, frequently striped *la19-*. **succar candy** sugar candy *la15-*; compare CANDY¹·¹. **sugardoddle** = *sugar bool 20- C*. **sugar piece** a slice of bread sprinkled with sugar *la19-*. **shuggar stane** quartz *20- Sh*. †**sugar work**, **suggar works** a sugar factory *la17-e18*. [OFr *sucre*]
sugarallie, **sugarellie** /ʃugəˈrale, ʃugəˈrɛle/ *n* (a piece of) liquorice *19-*. **sugarallie hat** a tall black silk hat, originally worn by policemen *la19- T C*. **sugarallie water** a (children's) drink made by dissolving a piece of liquorice in water *la19-*. [shortened form of *sugar alicreesh*; compare ALICREESH]
sugeorne see SOJOURN¹·¹

sugg /sʌg/ *n* a fat, easy-going person *19, 20- Ork NE T*. [Norw dial *sugg* a slovenly, lazy person, a big stout man]

sugg *see* SOG

†**suggeroun aitis, suggeorne** *npl* in Ross-shire a variety or quality of oats *16-17*. [compare Fr *soco(u)ran*, OFr *secourjon* a variety of barley + AIT]

suggie /'sʌge/ *interj* a call word to a sow *19, 20- Sh*. [Norw *sugge* a sow]

suggle /'sʌgəl/ *v* to drink in a sucking, slobbering way *20- Ork*. [probably onomatopoeic, but compare Eng *suckle*]

sugh *see* SOUCH¹·¹, SOUCH¹·²

sugour *see* SUGAR

suil /søl/ *v* to walk or move slowly or sluggishly *la19- Sh*. [compare Norw dial *søyla* to be slovenly and lazy]

suilkie /Sh 'sɔɪlkə; Ork 'sølkji/ *n* **1** a damp, dirty mass; a mess *20- Sh Ork*. **2** a person's or animal's usual haunts *20- Ork*. **suilkie drink** a mixture of water or whey, oatmeal and salt given as a drench to a sick animal *la19- Sh*. [perhaps metathesis of Norw dial *sukl* a clotted liquid mixture]

suilȝe *see* SILE⁶

suin *see* SUNE¹·²

suir *see* SHAIR²·¹, SURE

suit¹·¹, *NE T* **shoot**, *NE* **shuit**, †**sute**, †**soit**, †**soyt** /sut; *NE T* ʃut/ *n* **1** a legal action, litigation; a lawsuit *15-*. **2** wooing, solicitation of a woman's hand in marriage *la16-*. **3** a person's apparel; a set of garments designed to be worn together *15-*. **4** a set of items or entities; a number of the same item *16-*. **5** (the obligation of) a tenant to attend the court of his feudal lord, or by landowners to attend parliament; the right of the landholder to hold such a court *la14-e18, la18- historical*. **6** a representative of a person obliged to give suit in court *la15-16*. **7** seeking or pursuing (something); investigation by due process of law *la16*. **8** petitioning *la15-e19*. **9** a company, a retinue *15-16*. **10** a kind, a sort *15-16*. **suitable**, *N C* **sitable**, †**sutabil**, †**seuthable** appropriate; requisite *16-*. **suit-roll** a list of tenants bound to attend the court of their feudal lord or the sheriff court; a list of burgesses or craftsmen bound to attend at and vote in the burgh court *16-e18, la18- historical*. **suit-stock** *joinery, building* an adjustable square used for determining a right angle *la18-19, 20- N NE T*. †**call the suits** to call out the names of those bound to attend a court or parliament *la15-e18*. [AN *suite*]

suit¹·², †**sute** /sut/ *v* **1** to plead, petition; to request, solicit (a benefit) *16-17*. **2** *law* to sue for (a thing) in a court of law; to take legal action against, prosecute, sue (a person) *16-e18*. **3** to pursue with hostile intent, threaten *la16-e17*. **4** to pursue, aim at; to seek to obtain *la16-17*. **5** to seek in marriage, woo, pay court to (a woman); to cultivate (a person) *la16-17*. **6** to be agreeable or convenient to *la16-*. **7** mainly in *ptp* to please, give pleasure to ◊*she's no suitit 20-*. **8** *of a person* to look becoming in (a colour, dress): ◊*she suits blue 20-*. [see the noun]

suit², **soot, sit, shute**, *NE* **seet** /sut, sɪt, ʃut; *NE* sit/ *n* fine, black particles resulting from the burning of coal *la14-*. **suity, suitty**, †**suty**, †**suttie** like, composed of, covered with soot *la16-*. **suit-drap** a flake of soot *18-19, 20- Sh N NE T EC*. †**sootyman, sutiman** a chimney-sweep *17-e19*. [OE *sōt*]

suith¹·¹, **sooth**, †**suth**, †**suyth**, †**south** /suθ/ *n* (the) truth *la14-19, 20- NE T SW*. **my suith, by my suith** upon my word, to tell the truth *la18-19, 20- NE T SW*. [OE *sōð*]

suith¹·², **sooth**, †**suth**, †**suythe** /suθ/ *adj* **1** real, genuine; true, in accordance with the truth, not false *la14-*. **2** truthful *la16-19*. [OE *sōð*]

†**suith**¹·³, **sieth, sith** *adv* truly, really, indeed *15-19*. [OE *sōðe*]

suithfast, soothfast, †**suthfast**, †**suythfast** /'suθfast/ *adj* **1** *of people* truthful, reliable, trustworthy *la14-*. **2** true, accurate; reliable, certain, sure *la14-*. **3** *of people or things* genuine *la14-e16*. †**suthfastnes 1** truth, truthfulness *la14-16*. **2** *with a determiner* the true or actual state of affairs *la14-16*. [OE *sōðfæst*]

suize /swiz/ *v* **1** to snatch, seize *20- Ork*. **2** to pitch, throw *20- N*. [perhaps onomatopoeic]

suk *see* SOOK¹·²

sukin *see* SUCKEN¹·¹

sukkalegs /'sʌkəˌlɛgz/ *npl* footless stockings used as gaiters *19- Sh*. [probably Norw *sokk* sock + Norw *legg* the leg of a stocking; compare Faer *sokkalegald*]

sukkatoo /'sʌkəˌtu/ *n* coarse or loosely spun yarn *la19- Sh*. [probably Norw *sokk* sock + Norw *tó* yarn; compare Faer *sokkatógv*]

sukkin *see* SUCKEN²

suklar *see* SUCKLER

sul¹ /sul/ *n* **1** a glow of sunlight and heat, the influence of the sun *la19- Sh*. **2** the basking shark *Cetorhinus maximus la19- Sh*. [ON *sól* the sun]

sul² /sul/ *n* one of the boards of a clinker-built boat *la19- Sh*. [compare ON *sólborð* a gunwale]

sulch *see* SELCH

suld *see* SUD

sulfurious *see* SULPHUREOUS

†**sulliart, sulȝart, sulyeart** *adj of a horse* light, bright-coloured *16-18*. [probably Gael *soilleir* bright]

sulyeart, sulȝart *see* SULLIART

†**sulȝe, soyl** *v* to make foul, defile; to be soiled or defiled *16-17*. [OFr *suill(i)er, soill(i)er*]

sulȝe *see* SILE⁶

sum *see* SOME¹·¹, SOME¹·², SOME¹·³, SOUM¹·¹, SOUM¹·²

-sum *see* -SOME

sumdeill *see* SOMEDEAL¹·¹, SOMEDEAL¹·²

sumdele *see* SOMEDEAL¹·²

sume *see* SOME¹·¹

sum gait *see* SOMEGATE

sumhin *see* SOMETHING¹·¹

†**summa** *n* the whole amount payable, the sum total *16-18*. [Lat *summa*]

summary, †**summar**, †**sommair** /'sʌmərɪ/ *adj* **1** mainly *law, of proceedings (especially in minor cases)* expeditious, dispensing with written pleadings and formalities *16-*. **2** precipitate, hasty *la16-17*. **summarily**, †**summarly 1** *law* with a minimum of formality; expeditiously *16-*. **2** concisely *16-e17*. **summar-roll** *law* the list of cases to be heard in the Court of Session requiring to be dealt with quickly *19-*. [Lat *summārius*]

summeleir *see* SOMLER

†**summeleir, symleir, somler** *n* an officer of the royal household responsible for selecting and supplying wine *la16*. [OFr *sommelier*]

summer *see* SIMMER¹·¹, SIMMER¹·², SIMMER¹·³, SIMMER²

†**Summereve's Fair, Summaruff's Fair, Sanct Maruifis fair** *n in the North-East* the market or holiday on St Maolrubha's day, at the end of August or in September *17-18*. [run together SAINT¹·¹ and *Maolrubha* + FAIR²]

†**summock, summok** *n in Perthshire* a saddle-cloth or -pad *16-e19 H&I*. [Gael *sumag*]

summon, †**summond**, †**somond**, †**sommon** /'sʌmən/ *v* **1** to require the presence of a person; to arraign (a person) before a court *la14-*. **2** to assemble, call together; to cause a legal or other assembly to come into being *la14*. **3** to cause (something) to be brought *la16-*. †**summoner**,

summondar an official charged with executing summonses *15-e17*. [AN *sumun-*, pres stem of *somondre*]

summons[1.1], *Ork* **soomans**, †**summonds**, †**summondis**, †**summoun** /'sʌmənz; *Ork* 'sumənz/ *n* **1** an order by an authority requiring a person's presence, especially an official document, from the *Court of Session* (COORT[1.1]) or a SHERIFF, informing a person that civil proceedings are being taken against them, detailing the circumstances of the action and the redress sought, and granting warrant to cite him to appear in court *la14-*. **2** a (peremptory) command, direction or instruction *la15-*. **3** *informal* a citation to appear in a criminal court *20-*. **4** an order requiring an accused person to answer charges in a criminal case *18-19*; compare *criminal letters* (CRIMINAL). [AN *sumunse*]

summons[1.2] /'sʌmənz/ *v* to initiate legal action by taking out a SUMMONS[1.1] (sense 1) against *17-*. [see the noun]

sump, †**somp** /sʌmp/ *n* **1** *mining* a pit or well to collect water *17-*. **2** *in Galloway and the Borders* a sudden heavy fall of rain, a deluge *e19*. †**sumpting** the digging of a pit or well *la17*. †**somp holl** = SUMP (sense 1) *17*. †**sumpting coall** perhaps coal obtained in digging a sump *la17*. [MDu, MLG *sump*, *somp*]

sumph[1.1] /sʌmf/ *n* **1** a slow-witted person, a boorish person, someone with learning difficulties *la17-*. **2** a surly, sullen person *18-*. **sumphish** stupid *18-*. **sumphy** stupid *la19, 20- NE*. [perhaps onomatopoeic]

sumph[1.2] /sʌmf/ *v* to act stupidly; to laze or lie about in a dull, stupid way; to sulk, be sullen *la17-*. [see the noun]

sumphion *see* SYMPHIOUN

sumptuous, †**sumptuus** /'sʌmtʃəs, 'sʌmtjuəs/ *adj* **1** splendid, luxurious; originally costly *la15-*. **2** *of expenses* substantial, exorbitant *la14-16*. **3** incurring expense; wasteful *16-e17*. [OFr *sumpteux*, Lat *sumptuōsus*]

sumthing *see* SOMETHING[1.1], SOMETHING[1.2]

sun[1.1], **sin**, †**sone**, †**son**, †**soun** /sʌn, sɪn/ *n* **1** the brightest body of the solar system, around which the earth and other planets revolve; sunlight, sunshine *la14-*. **2** sunrise or sunset *la15-e17*. **3** a particular day as measured from sunrise to sunset or perhaps sunset to sunrise *15-17*. **sunny 1** exposed to, warmed or illuminated by (the rays of) the sun *16-*. **2** full of or characterized by sunshine *la18-*. †**sunny half** = *sun side 16-e18*. **sun-blink** a gleam or spell of sunshine *16-*. **sun-broch** a halo round the sun *la19- Sh Ork NE T EC Bor*. **sin-cassen** *of an egg* tainted by exposure to the sun *20- Sh*. †**sone-cavill** *in Fife* the drawn lot indicating that the division of land should begin at the sun side (the east); also perhaps the land thus allotted *16*. **sindoon** sunset *19-*. **sungates**, *Sh* **sungaets** following the sun, from east to west *16-19, 20- Sh*. †**sone half** = *sun-side la16-17*. †**sun-rising 1** sunrise *la14-17*. **2** the quarter in which the sun rises, the east *e16*. **sun-side** the side or aspect of a place facing the morning sun, the east side *18-19, 20- N NE T C*. **sun-sitten 1** = *sin-cassen 19- Sh*. **2** *of a potato* having a greenish colour due to exposure to light *20- Sh*. **sunny sodger** the red wild bee *20- C*. **sunways** = *sungates la17-*. †**between sone and sky** between dawn and sunrise *la17-19*. [OE *sunna, sunne*]

sun[1.2] /sʌn/ *v* **1** to expose oneself to sunshine *la16-*. **2** to spear a salmon dazzled by reflected sunlight *e19*. [see the noun]

sunckat *see* SUNKET

Sunday, †**Sonday**, †**Sounday** /'sʌnde/ *n* the day before Monday, the first day of the week; *Christian Church* the Sabbath and church worship *la14-*. **Sunday blacks** the black suit formerly always worn by men for attending church on Sunday *20-*. **Sundaybraws** clothes worn to church, one's best clothes **Sunday claes** clothes worn to church, one's best clothes *la18-*. **Sunday face** a solemn, sanctimonious look *la18-*. **Sunday-Monday** the name of a ball game *20- NE T*. **Sunday name** one's formal baptismal name, as opposed to a familiar form of it *la19- C*. **Sunday-salt** salt made at the weekend, large-grained from having been left longer to crystallize *la18-19, 20- historical*. **Sunday sark** one's best shirt; a clean shirt *la18-*. **Sunday strae** an extra amount of straw threshed to tide the animals over the weekend and so avoid threshing on Sunday *19- Sh Ork N NE T*. **gie Sunday kirk mense** to wear garments to church on Sunday *19- WC SW Bor*. [OE *Sunnandæg*]

sundry *see* SINDRY[1.1], SINDRY[1.2], SINDRY[1.3]

sune[1.1] /sun, sɪn; *Sh Ork* søn; *N* ʃin/ *adj* quick; direct *la15-19, 20- Sh N T SW*. [see the adv]

sune[1.2], **soon**, **suin**, **sin**, **shune**, *N* **sheen**, *NE* **seen**, *C* **shin**, †**sone**, †**soin**, †**soun** /sun, sɪn, ʃun; *Sh Ork* søn; *N* ʃin/ *NE* sin; *C* ʃɪn/ *adv* **1** within a short time; straight away *la14-*. **2** early, before it is late *la14-19, 20- Sh SW*. **sune as syne** sooner rather than later, soon for preference *19- C Bor Uls*. **sune or syne** sooner or later *la16-19, 20- Sh EC*. **sune or late** sooner or later, in the end, inevitably *la19, 20- Sh*. [OE *sōna*]

sung *see* SING[1.2], SING[2.2]

sunk[1], †**sonk** /sʌŋk/ *n* **1** a turf seat, a kind of sofa made of layers of sods, frequently at a fireside or against a sunny gable *16-*. **2** a bank or wall, especially of earth or turf *19 NE*. **3** a straw pad or cushion, especially one used as a substitute for a saddle, frequently in a pair slung on either side of the horse *16-19*. **4** a fat, shapeless person *19- NE T*. **sunkie** a little bench or stool, *eg* a milking-stool *19- Bor*. [unknown]

†**sunk**[2] *v* to sulk, be sullen or gloomy *e18*. **sunkan** sullen, surly *e18*. [unknown]

sunken, †**sonken**, †**sonkin** /'sʌŋken/ *adj* **1** immersed, absorbed in *la15-*. **2** *of the eyes* deep set, hollow *la15-*. [ptp of SINK[1.2]]

sunket, †**sunkot**, †**sunckat** /'sʌŋkət/ *n* **1** also *pl* something *la17-19*. **2** *pl* eatables, provisions, especially titbits or delicacies *18-*. [altered form of *sumquhat* somewhat]

sunna *see* SINNA

sunner *see* SINDER[1.1]

sunnin /'sʌnən/ *n* something *la19- Sh Ork*. [reduced form of SOMETHING[1.1]]

suntin *see* SOMETHING[1.1]

suoufe *see* SWOOF[1.2]

sup[1.1], *T C SW Bor* **soup**, *T C Bor Uls* **sowp**, †**sope** /sʌp; *T C SW Bor* sup; *T C Bor Uls* sʌup/ *n* **1** *frequently with omission of 'of'* a small amount (to drink or of semi-liquid food), a mouthful; a draught, a swig, a drink (of alcohol); something to drink: ◇*a sup tea 16-*. **2** a quantity or amount (of fluid or rain) *la16-19, 20- NE T C*. **3** a small quantity of foodstuffs or dry goods *20- NE*. **suppie** = SUP[1.1] *la19- NE T*. [see the verb]

sup[1.2], *Sh* **soup**, †**sowp** /sʌp; *Sh* sup/ *v* **1** to take (liquid or soft food) into the mouth in small quantities; to consume in mouthfuls; to eat with a spoon *16-*. **2** *of a boat* to take in water *e16*. **3** *literary* to consume, swallow *e16*. **suppable** fit to be eaten, palatable *19, 20- NE EC SW Bor*. †**suppins** soft, semi-liquid food *la18*. **suppin sowans** SOWANS thick enough to eat with a spoon *20- Ork NE*. [OE *sūpan*]

sup[2], †**soup**, †**sowp** /sʌp/ *v* to have supper, eat an evening meal *la15-*. [AN *supper, souper*]

superannuate /supər'anjuet/ *adj* mentally deranged, senile; stupefied, dazed *18-19, 20- EC Bor*. [Lat *superannuātus*]

superb /su'pɛrb/ *adj* originally *of buildings* magnificent, splendid *16-*. [MFr *superbe* proud]

supercloth *see* SURPCLAITH

†**superexcrescence** *n* increase in profit or value, surplus, *la15-16*. [Lat *superexcrescent-*, presp stem of *superexcrescere* to increase exceedingly, from *super-* above + *excrescere* to grow out]

†**superexpend** *v* to spend (time) wastefully *e16*. **superexpendit, super expendit, superexpended 1** overspent, ruined financially *la13-e18*; compare SUPERSPENDIT. **2** *of time* spent wastefully *e16*. [Lat *superexpendere*, Lat *super-* above + Lat *expendere* to spend]

†**superexpense, superexpens** *n* overspending, expenditure above receipts or income; out-of-pocket expenses *la15-e17*. [Lat *superexpensa*, *super-* above + Lat *expēnsa* payments]

†**superflue, superflew** *adj* **1** superfluous, excessively abundant *16*. **2** excessive, immoderate *la15-16*. **3** unnecessary *15-16*. **superflue chairgit** charged in excess, excessively *16-e17*. [Lat *superfluus*]

†**superinduction** *n law* the substitution or insertion of a word or letter in a document in place of another *la17-e18*. [Lat *superinduction-* the bringing in of superfluous matter or people, *super-* above + Lat *inductio*]

superintendence /supərɪnˈtɛndəns/ *n* **1** a body of superintendents of a church *la16*. **2** the action, function or duty of superintending or supervising *17-*. [MFr *superintendence*, Lat *superintendentia*]

superintendent *n* **1** a person in charge of something, a supervisor or overseer *la19-*. **2** *Presbyterian Church* a MINISTER appointed to supervise the administration of the newly-reformed church in a particular district *la16-17, la18- historical*. †**superintendentrie** the district supervised by or the duties of a SUPERINTENDENT (sense 2) *la16*. [Lat *superintendent-*]

†**superintromission** *n law* an additional INTROMISSION *la17-18*. [Lat *super-* above + INTROMISSION]

superior[1.1], †**superiour** /suˈpɪrɪər/ *n* **1** a person of higher rank or authority *16-*. **2** *law* a feudal overlord, a person who has made a grant of heritable property to another who thereby becomes a VASSAL in return for payment of *feu duty* (FEU[1.1]), or originally for the performance of services *la15-20, 21- historical*. [MFr *superior*, Lat *superior*]

superior[1.2], †**superiour** /suˈpɪrɪər/ *adj* higher (in rank or authority) *la16-*. [ME *superior*, AN *superior*, Lat *superior*]

superiority, †**superiorite** /supɪrɪˈɔrɪte/ *n* **1** superior rank, authority or status *15-*. **2** the position or status of feudal SUPERIOR[1.1] (sense 2), the rights which an overlord enjoys in land held by his vassals, *ie* the feu duties and services stipulated *la14-20, 21- historical*. **3** before the 1832 Reform Act, the feudal title which conferred the county franchise on its holder *e19, la19- historical*. [MFr *superiorite*]

†**supernal** *adj* existing in, located in, or pertaining to heaven *la15-16*. [MFr *supernal*, Lat *supernalis*]

†**superne** *adj* = SUPERNAL *la15-16*. [MFr *superne*, Lat *supernus*]

†**supernumerale lordis** *adj* = EXTRAORDINAR LORD OF SESSION *la16-e17*. [Lat *super-* above + Lat *numerālis* relating to or expressing a number + LORD]

†**superplus**[1.1] *n* **1** a surplus, excess *16-19*. **2** what remains to be paid, a sum still owed; over-budget expenses *la16-17*. [Lat *superplus*]

†**superplus**[1.2] *adj* extra, additional; surplus *la16-17*. [see the noun]

superscription, †**superscriptioun** /ˈsupərskrɪpʃən/ *n* **1** an inscription on or above something *15-*. **2** *humorous* or *informal* a subscription, especially a collection of money *19-*. [MFr *superscription*, Lat *superscriptiōn-*, ptp stem of *superscrībere*]

†**superscrive** *v* to add a signature; to sign (a document) at the head or top *17-19*. [ME *superscribe* with influence from SCRIEVE[2.2]; compare SUBSCRIVE]

supersede /supərˈsid/ *v* **1** frequently *in legal contexts* to postpone, defer, delay *la15-*. **2** to delay dealing with, reprieve (a person) (from debt or imprisonment) *16-17*. **3** to desist, refrain from *15-17*. †**supersedement** postponement, adjournment *la15-16*. [MFr *superseder*, Lat *supersedēre*]

supersedere /supərˈsidəre/ *n law* a judicial order or agreement among creditors granting a debtor (originally also other lawbreakers) immunity from or a delay in prosecution *16-*. [Lat *supersedēre* to sit on top of, forbear, refrain (from)]

†**superspendit** *adj* overspent *la16-17*. Compare SUPEREXPENDIT. [Lat *super-* above + ptp of SPEND[1]]

superstition, supersteetion, †**superstitioun** /supərˈstɪʃən, supərˈstɪʃən/ *n* **1** credulity, irrational belief *16-*. **2** religious observance *e16*. [MFr *supersticion*, Lat *superstitiōn-*]

†**superveniency** *n law* the fact of coming after or being subsequent *la17-e18*. [SUPERVENIENT, with noun-forming suffix]

supervenient /supərˈvɛnjənt/ *adj* frequently *in legal terminology* following; subsequent; consequent on what has happened previously *la16-e18*. [Lat *supervenient-*, presp stem of *supervenīre* to come on top (of another event)]

suple, suplie *see* SUPPLY[1.1]

suport *see* SUPPORT[1.2]

supper[1.1], †**sipper,** †**suppar,** †**soupere** /ˈsʌpər/ *n* **1** the last meal of the day *15-*. **2** the last meal of the day given to an animal *19-*. †**the Supper** = *the Supper of the Lord*. †**the Supper of the Lord** *Presbyterian Church* the service of Communion *la16-e17*. [AN *super*, *souper*]

supper[1.2] /ˈsʌpər/ *v* **1** to give an animal its last meal of the day *la17-*. **2** *of fodder* to serve or suffice for the supper of (an animal) *la18-19, 20- N NE EC*. **supper up** = SUPPER[1.2] (sense 1). [see the noun]

supple *see* SUPPLY[1.1], SUPPLY[1.2]

supplee *see* SUPPLY[1.1]

supplement /ˈsʌpləmənt/ *n* an addition making good a deficiency *la16-*. †**in supplement** *law, of an oath or additional evidence* delivered in order to confirm imperfect evidence *la16-17*. **letters of supplement** see LETTER. [OFr *suppleement*, Lat *supplēmentum*]

supplementary /sʌpləˈmɛntəre/ *adj education* applied to a course between the end of primary schooling and the school-leaving age, for children not continuing with academic education *e20, la20- historical*. [SUPPLEMENT, with adj-forming suffix]

supplie *see* SUPPLY[1.2]

suppline *see* SIPLING

supply[1.1], *NE* **supplee,** †**supple,** †**suplie,** †**suple** /səˈplae; *NE* səˈpli/ *n* **1** (a) provision of funds, food or necessities *16-*. **2** charitable assistance, (the giving of) money, food or money to one in need; originally, financial assistance for any particular purpose (*eg* completion of building work) or the making good of a deficit *16-*. **3** the amount of a commodity available for purchase *la18-*. **4** an additional body of troops, reinforcements *la15-18*. **5** a tax on land, for defraying the sovereign's expenses, levied from shires and burghs over and above other sources of revenue *la17-e19*. **6** assistance, (a) support, relief *15-e18*. **7** *pl* supporters, fighting men *e16*. **8** *Presbyterian Church* the filling of a vacant ministerial charge *17*. **supplier,** †**supplear 1** a purveyor, a provider *20-*. **2** a helper, supporter or accomplice *la14-e17*. [see the verb]

supply[1.2], †**supple,** †**supplie** /səˈplae/ *v* **1** to satisfy (a need); to furnish (supplies) *la14-*. **2** to help, aid; to reinforce (an army) *la14-17*. **3** to make up (a number); to fill (a vacancy); to compensate (a fault or lack) *la14-17*. **4** to provide (a school) with a teacher or (a parish) with a minister *17-e18*. [MFr *supploier*]

suppois *see* SUPPOSE

†**suppone** *v* to believe something to be the case; to anticipate, expect; to presume, suppose, take for granted *la15-17*. [Lat *suppōnere*]

support[1.1] /sə'port/ *n* **1** financial, spiritual or other maintenance; care, welfare *16-*. **2** *law* the requirement for a SERVIENT tenement in a building to support the weight of the DOMINANT TENEMENT above *la17-*. **3** payment (of expenses) *16*. **4** (money raised by) a tax or levy *la16-e17*. **5** the action of holding (something or someone) up *la16-*. [see the verb]

support[1.2], †**suport** /sə'port/ *v* **1** to strengthen, make more secure by lending assistance or backing; to uphold (a person's) rights; to assist, provide for (spiritually or financially) *la15-*. **2** to supply, satisfy (a person etc or a need); to make good (a deficiency) *16-e17*. [ME *supporten*, AN *supporter*]

†**supportation**, **supportatioun** /sʌpor'teʃən/ *n* **1** support *la15-16*. **2** maintenance, preservation in being *la15-e16*. **3** mainly *law* the action of physically supporting a person to prevent his collapse *16-18*. [AN *supportacion*, Lat *supportatiōn-*]

suppose, †**suppois** /sə'poz/ *v* **1** to believe, expect something to be the case *la14-*. **2** to presume *16-*. **3** *in passive* to be expected, required to: ◊*ye're supposed tae be here at nine o'clock 20-*. **4** *in negative passive* not to be permitted to: ◊*ye're no supposed to dae that 20-*. **5** *in imperative, used as conj* if, even if, although: ◊*I widnae tell ye suppose I kent la14-*. [ME *supposen*, AN *supposer*]

suppost, †**supposit** /sə'post/ *n* **1** an adherent, supporter, servant or representative; specifically, a person in the service of Satan *la16-e17*. **2** a member of St Andrews or Glasgow University *16-19, 20- historical*. **3** *grammar* the subject (of a verb) *e17*. [OFr *suppost*, Lat *suppositus* a subordinate, supporter, ptp of *suppōnere*]

†**suppowel**[1.1], **suppovel**, **suppovell** *n* support, help *la14-e16*. [AN *suppowelle*]

†**suppowel**[1.2], **suppowell** *v* to support, help *la14-e16*. [AN *suppoweler*]

supprise *see* SURPRISE[1.1], SURPRISE[1.2]

suppryis, **supprys** *see* SURPRISE[1.1]

supreme /sə'prim, su'prim/ *adj* **1** *of an institution, court or person* highest *la15-*. **2** *of God* highest, most exalted *16-*. **3** *of a class of students* most advanced *e17*. [MFr *supreme*, Lat *suprēmus*]

sur *see* SHAIR[2.2]

†**surage gray**, **surriche gray** *n* some kind of grey fabric *e16*. [perhaps OFr **souriche* a female mouse + GRAY[1.1]]

surance *see* SOVERANCE

surcharge, †**subcharge**, †**sucharge**, †**sudcharge** /sər'tʃardʒ/ *n pl also* †**sowrchargis**, †**subchettis** **1** a second or additional dish or course of food *la15-e16*. **2** an additional amount, load or burden *la15-*. [Lat *sub-* under + *charge* (CHAIRGE[1.1]), with influence from prefix *sur-*]

surcoat /'sʌrkət/ *n* an undershirt or waistcoat; a fisherman's jersey *la18-19, 20- N*. [Eng *surcoat*, with influence from *sarket* (SARK[1.1])]

sure, †**suir**, †**sever** /ʃur/ *v* **1** to make safe, secure; to bind (by allegiance) *16*. **2** *usually in first person* to assure, tell (a person) for certain *la16-19, 20- NE*. [aphetic form of *assure* (ASHAIR)]

sure *see* SHAIR[2.1], SHAIR[2.2]

surety, †**surete**, †**surte**, †**suretye** /'ʃurte, 'ʃurəte/ *n* **1** safety; assurance of safety *la15-e17*. **2** a binding assurance, a pledge *la15-*. **3** imprisonment, safe custody *15-17*. **4** certainty, assurance, reassurance *16-e19*. **5** a person standing pledge for another, guaranteeing their behaviour *16-e18*. †**for a surety**, **for surety**, **of surety** for certain *16-19*. [AN *surete*]

†**surfeit**[1.1] /'sʌrfət/ *n* **1** (the effects of) gluttony, intemperance *15-e19*. **2** excess, extravagance *16-*. [AN *surfeit*]

†**surfeit**[1.2], **surfet**, **surfit** *v* to indulge to excess *la16-17*. [see the noun]

surfeit[1.3], †**surfet**, †**surfat**, †**surfait** /'sʌrfət/ *adj* excessive, immoderate, intemperate *16-19, 20- SW*. [see the noun]

surfle /'sʌrfəl/ *v* to gather, ruck a hem; to overcast an edge of cloth; to trim with lace edging *la19, 20- T SW Bor*. [ME *surfilen*, AN **surfiler*]

surmount, †**surmont**, †**surmunt**, †**surmint** /sər'mʌunt/ *v* to excel, surpass; to exceed *15-*. [ME *surmounten*, AN *surmunter*]

surname, †**sirname** /'sʌrnem/ *n* **1** a heritable family name *la14-*. **2** a family or clan *la15-17*. **3** an (alternative) name or descriptive epithet given to a person, group, place etc *la14-e17*. [OFr *sur-* + *name* (NEM[1.1]); compare OFr *surnom*]

†**surpclaith**, **supercloth** *n* a surplice *la16-17*. [altered form of Eng *surplice*, with influence from claithes (CLAES)]

surprise[1.1], *SW* **surpreese**, †**supprise**, †**supprys**, †**suppryis** /sər'praez; *SW* sər'priz/ *n* **1** (a feeling of astonishment etc caused by) something unexpected *18-*. **2** injury, outrage, oppression *15-16*. **3** an unexpected attack *16-e18*. **4** a military defeat *15-e16*. [OFr *surprise*, compare the verb]

surprise[1.2], *SW* **surpreese**, †**supprise** /sər'praez; *SW* sər'priz/ *v* **1** to cause or strike with astonishment, wonder etc, astonish; to take unawares *la14-*. **2** to attack without warning; to take or capture by surprise *la14-*. **3** to dishonour, injure or rape (a woman) *la14-e16*. **4** to oppress, persecute; to suppress, put down *15-e17*. **5** to overpower, defeat *15-16*. [OFr *surprise*, ptp of *surprendre*]

surree *see* SWARREE

surrender[1.1], †**surrander** /sə'rɛndər/ *n* **1** capitulation *17-*. **2** *law* the handing over to the Crown of the right to receive tithes *17-e18, 19- historical*. **at an awfu surrender** at a great rate, at breakneck speed *la19- NE*. [ME *surrender*, AN *surrender*]

surrender[1.2], †**surrander** /sə'rɛndər/ *v* **1** to hand over (property) in the process of capitulating to an enemy *17-*. **2** to hand over (property) to a feudal superior *16-17*. [EModE *surrender*, AN *surrender*]

surriche gray *see* SURAGE GRAY

†**surrigeane**, **surrigian**, **surrugyne** *n* a surgeon *16-*; compare CHIRURGIAN. **surriginare** = SURRIGEANE *16-e17*. **surregenrie** surgery *16-17*. [AN *surrigien*]

†**surrogate**, **surrogat** *v presp* **surrogand** **1** to appoint as a substitute *16-17*. **2** to exchange (one person or thing for another) *16-17*. [Lat *surrogāt-*, ptp stem of *surrogāre*]

†**surrogatioun** *n* **1** the substitution by appointment or election of a person for another *16*. **2** *law* the appointment of interested parties as executors of an intestate estate in place of a procurator-fiscal already appointed *17*. [Lat *surrogātio*]

surrogatum /sʌrə'getəm/ *n law* something which stands in the place of another, a substitute or equivalent, *eg* the monetary value of a thing instead of the thing itself *la18-*. [neuter singular of Lat *surrogātus*, ptp of *surrogāre*]

surrugyne *see* SURRIGEANE

surt /sʌrt/ *v* to boil gently, simmer *20- Ork*. [probably onomatopoeic; compare Norw dial *søyda* to boil]

†**suscitat** *v* mainly *ptp* **suscitat**, **suscitate** **1** to incite rebellion *la16*. **2** *law* to raise, set in motion (an action) *la16*. [Lat *suscitāt-*, ptp stem of *suscitāre*]

†suspeck¹·¹, suspect, suspek *n* suspicion *la14-e17*. [Lat *suspectus*]

suspeck¹·², suspect /sə'spɛk, sə'spɛkt/ *v* **1** to believe guilty of a crime without evidence or proof; to view with suspicion as dishonest, untrustworthy or false *la14-*. **2** to believe possible or likely without proof; to conceive of, envisage, surmise *16-*. **3** to expect, anticipate *la15-16*. [Lat *suspect-*, ptp stem of *suspicere*]

suspeck¹·³, suspect, †suspek /'sʌspɛk, 'sʌspɛkt/ *adj* **1** arousing suspicion; thought to possess some (mainly negative) characteristic, *eg* being harmful, dangerous or dishonest *15-*. **2** *of a judge* suspected of bias or partiality *15-e17*. [see the verb]

suspeecion, suspicion, †suspicioun, †suspitioun /sə'spiʃən, sə'spɪʃən/ *n* the action of suspecting; (a) feeling, apprehension or conjecture *15-*. [ME *suspecion*, AN *suspecioun*]

suspend /sə'spɛnd/ *v* **1** to discontinue temporarily; to delay *15-*. **2** *of a court of law* to defer or stay (execution of a warrant, writ etc or any legal process) usually temporarily or until a condition has been met *la15-*. **3** *law, of a litigant or convicted person* to ask for SUSPENSION as a form of appeal *17-*. **4** to abrogate or annul a law or clause in a legal deed; to cancel, lift (a sentence) *la15-16*. **suspender, †suspendar** *law* a person who raises a bill of SUPENSION, suspending execution of a judgement, decree or sentence *17-*. [ME *suspenden*, OFr *suspendre*, Lat *suspendere*]

suspension, †suspensioun /sə'spɛnʃən/ *n* **1** the debarring, *eg* of a pupil from school, originally of a cleric or minister from office *la15-*. **2** *law* (a warrant for) a stay of execution of a sentence until the matter can be reviewed, used when ordinary appeal is incompetent *la16-*. [Lat *suspensio*]

suspensive /sə'spɛnsəv/ *adj* **1** *law* capable of causing or liable to cause a postponement of a legal process *la17-*. **2** liable to be suspended or kept undetermined, subject to doubt; disallowed *16*. **suspensive condition** *law* a condition which suspends the coming into force of a contract until the condition is fulfilled *la17-*. [Lat *suspensivus*]

suspicion, suspicioun see SUSPEECION

sussie¹·¹, sizzie, †sussy, †soucy /'sʌse, 'sɪzi/ *n* care, trouble, bother, *eg* in dealing with a drunk person *16-19, 20- Sh EC SW*. [OFr *soussy*]

sussie¹·², †soucie /'sʌse/ *v in negative constructions* **1** to shrink, hesitate *19, 20- Sh NE*. **2** to care, be anxious or concerned *la16-19, 20- Sh*. **3** not to refuse (to do something) *la16*. [OFr *soussier*]

sussy see SUSSIE¹·¹

sust see SOUSE³

sustain, susteen, †sustene, †sustein, †susteyn /sə'sten, sə'stin/ *v* **1** to support; to maintain, preserve; to provide for *la14-*. **2** *of a church court* to give formal approval to (a call from a congregation to a new MINISTER) *18-*. **3** to endure, withstand; to undergo (hardship); to incur (expenses) *la14-*. **4** *of a court of law* to support the validity of (a claim), uphold authoritatively, approve *la15-19*. [AN *susteiner*]

†sustent, sustentt *v* to lift or hold up *e16*. [Lat *sustent-*, ptp stem of *sustinēre*]

sustentation, *Sh* **sistentation, †sustentatioun** /sʌstən'teʃən/ *n* **1** provision, maintenance *la14-*. **2** Roman Catholic Church financial upkeep of church services *la15-e16*. **3** the smallest quantity of food to maintain life *19- Sh*. **Sustentation Fund** a fund for the support of the Free Church of Scotland ministry *19-*. [AN *sustentacion*, Lat *sustentātiōn-*]

susteyn see SUSTAIN

susy see SHUSY

sut see SIT¹·², SOT²
sute see SUIT¹·¹, SUIT¹·²
suth see SOOTH¹·², SUITH¹·¹, SUITH¹·²
Sutherland /'sʌðərlənd/ *n* a former county in northern Scotland *la13-*. **†Sutherland Highlander** a soldier in the *Sutherland Highlanders 18-19*. **Sutherland Highlanders** a regiment raised in 1799 as the 93rd Highland regiment; in 1861 it became the 93rd Sutherland Highlanders *la18-20, 21- historical*; compare *Argyll and Sutherland Highlanders* (ARGYLL). **Sutherland Clearances** *the Clearances* (CLEARANCE) in the county of Sutherland *la19- historical*. [from the place-name]

sutheroun see SOUTHRON¹·¹
suthfast see SUITHFAST
sutor see SOUTER¹·¹, SOUTER¹·²
sutshkin, sutchkin /'søtʃkɪn, 'sʌtʃkɪn/ *n* a brother and sister of the same parents *la19- Sh*. [Norw dial *systkin*]
suttel see SUBTLE
sutten see SIT¹·², SITTEN
suyr see SHAIR²·¹
suyth see SUITH¹·¹
suythe see SUITH¹·²
suythfast see SUITHFAST
swa see SAE²·¹, SWAAR²

swaabie, swabie /'swɑbi/ *n* the great black-backed gull *Larus marinus 19- Sh*. [perhaps reduced form of *swartback* (SWART¹·²) + -IE¹]

swaam¹·¹, †swalm, swame /swɑm/ *n* **1** (a) swelling *16*. **2** a fainting fit, giddiness *la19- Sh*. [ME *swalm*, related to SWALL]

swaam¹·², †swalm *v* to faint, swoon *la16*. [see the noun]

swaander see SWANDER¹·¹, SWANDER¹·²

swaar¹ /swɑr/ *n* the darkest part of the night *19- Sh*. **da swaar o da dim** = SWAAR¹. [compare Norw dial *sval* dark, dusky, and Norw *svart* dark, black]

swaar², †swa /swɑr/ *n* the noise of the sea at a distance *la19- Ork*. [uncertain; compare SWAW¹·²]

swaar³ /swɑr/ *n* a swath, the amount of grass or corn cut at one stroke of a scythe *20- Sh N*. [reduced form of SWARTH]

swaar⁴ /swɑr/ *n* **1** a covering of grass, a sward *20- Ork*; compare SWAIRD¹·¹. **2** the surface of the ground or a sheet of water *20- Ork N*. [reduced form of Eng *swarth* sward, or Norw dial *svord*]

swaarlick, swarlek /'swɑrlək/ *n* boggy ground, a marsh; a miry hole *20- Sh*. [unknown]

swabble¹·¹ /'swabəl/ *n* **1** a thrashing *e19*. **2** a long pliant stick *20- Bor*. **3** an unsteady motion *20- Bor*. **4** a tall thin person *e19*. [probably from the verb]

swabble¹·² /'swabəl/ *v* to beat, thrash *19- EC Bor*. [perhaps LG *swabbeln* to be agitated, sway about]

swabie see SWAABIE
swache see SWACK²·²

swack¹·¹, †swak /swak/ *n* **1** (the sound made by) a heavy blow or fall; a sudden or powerful movement *la14-*. **2** a big mouthful, a deep draught of drink *la18- NE EC Bor*. [onomatopoeic]

†swack¹·² *v* to throw forcibly, dash down; to deal violent blows; to brandish (a weapon) *la14-19*. [see the noun]

swack²·¹, †swak /swak/ *v* to make pliant, supple or weak *la19, 20- NE*. [see the adj]

swack²·², †suak, †swache /swak/ *adj* **1** *of people or animals* active, lithe, supple; *of the mind* quick, sharp *la18-19, 20- Sh Ork N NE T EC*. **2** soft, moist and easily moulded; *of cheese* not crumbly *18, 19- N NE*. **3** pliant, easily bent or stretched *la15-18, 19- N NE*. **4** unsteady, jerky and loose in movement *la19- Sh Ork*. **5** *of a person* hungry *20- Ork*. **6** thin, slender *16-19*. [Flem *zwak* lithe, MDu *swac* pliant]

swacken /'swakən/ *v* to make or become soft and pliant, loosen *19- Sh Ork N NE*. [SWACK[2.2], with verb-forming suffix]

swad *see* SQUAD

Swade, *NE* **Swad**, †**suadde** /swed; *NE* swad/ *n* **1** a native of Sweden *17-19, 20- NE*. **2** a swede, a variety of turnip *17-*. [compare SWADEN]

†**Swaden, Suethin** *n* Sweden *16-e17*. [MLG, MDu *Sweden*]

swadge *see* SWAGE

swag[1.1] /swag; *Sh* swag/ *n* **1** (the act of) swinging or swaying *19-*. **2** an extra-large sail on a boat to increase speed *20- Sh*. **3** a bag or wallet, especially one carried by a beggar or thief *18-19*. [see the verb]

swag[1.2] /swag/ *v* to sway from side to side, wag to and fro; to hang down heavily and lopsidedly *18-19, 20- Sh N SW*. [unknown; compare Norw dial *svagga* to sway]

swag[2] /swag, swag/ *n* a quantity of drink, a long draught *19, 20- Sh Ork*. [perhaps altered form of SWACK[1.1]]

swag[3] /swag/ *v* to assume, surmise *la19- T*. **I'll swag** I'll bet, I'll be bound *la19- T*. [altered form by wrong division of *I'se wad*, WAD 1.2]

swagate *see* SAE[2.1]

swage, *N NE* **swadge**, †**suage** /swedʒ; *N NE* swadʒ/ *v* **1** to consume, digest (food or drink) *20- Sh Ork N NE*. **2** *of flooding or swelling* to subside, go or settle down, shrink from a swollen state *15-19, 20- Sh Ork N NE*. **3** to satisfy (appetite, curiosity); to slake (thirst) *16-18*. **4** to assuage, moderate, alleviate (anger or sorrow); *of a person or emotion* to calm down *15-e17*. **5** to waver, vacillate *16*. [aphetic form of Eng *assuage*]

swagger /'swagər/ *v* **1** to behave as if superior; to seem superior; to strut *19-*. **2** to stagger, sway *18-19*. **3** to quarrel, behave boorishly *17*. [SWAG[1.2], with *-er* suffix]

swaible /'swebəl/ *v* to splash, wash, scour energetically *la19- Ork Bor*. [uncertain; compare LG *swabbeln* to make the sound of splashing water, Flem *swabbelen* to draw backwards and forwards in water]

swaif *see* SUAVE

swail[1], *NE* **swyle**, †**swell**, †**swaill** /swel; *NE* swʌɪl/ *n* a wet hollow, a boggy place *16-19, 20- NE*. [unknown, compare SWALLIE[1.1]]

†**swail**[2], **swale** *adj* sleek, fat *e16*. [unknown]

swaill *see* SWAIL[1]

swain, †**swane**, †**swayne** /swen/ *n* **1** a lovesick youth, a lover *la18- literary*. **2** *in military contexts* a young attendant, a follower *la14-e16*. **3** a servant *la15-e16*. **4** a man, a lad; a farm worker *15-e19*. **5** a man of disreputable character *e16*. [ON *sveinn*]

swaip[1.1] /swep/ *n* a slanting direction, a slope *20- Bor*. [see the verb]

swaip[1.2] /swep/ *v of a road or slope* to rise or descend obliquely *20- Bor*. [ON *sveipa* to sweep, wrap, be twisted]

swaip[1.3] /swep/ *adj* slanting or sloping, oblique *19- Bor*. [see the verb]

swair *see* SWEER[1.2], SWIRE

swaird[1.1], **sward** /swerd, sward/ *n* **1** the (grassy) surface of the ground; (the layer of) plant growth, turf; meadowland *la15-*; compare SWAAR[4]. **2** the scalp *la14*. †**swaird-cutter, sward-cutter** a machine which cuts into and chops up the grassy surface of the ground *la18*. **swear dyke** a turf wall *20- NE*. †**sward erd** grassland *16-17*. [OE *sweard* skin, hide]

†**swaird**[1.2], **sward** *v of ground* to develop a dense surface of grass or turf *la17-19*. **swardit, swarded** covered with grass or turf *16-19*. [see the noun]

swairm[1.1], **swarm** /swerm, swarm/ *n* a swarm of bees; a mass or crowd (of insects, people) *15-*. [OE *swearm*]

swairm[1.2], **swarm**, †**swerm** /swerm, swarm/ *v* **1** *of people* to mill around in large numbers; to crowd; to throng *16-*. **2** *of bees* to come together in a mass *19-*. **3** *of fire* to billow out in flames *e16*. [see the noun]

swairten *see* SWIRTEN

swait *see* SWEET[1.1]

swaittis *see* SWATS

swak *see* SWACK[1.1] SWACK[2.1]

swale *see* SWAIL[2]

swall, swell, *WC* **sweel**, †**swoll** /swal, swɛl; *WC* swil/ *v pt* **swelt**, *ptp* **swallen, swelt 1** to swell, increase in size, puff up *la14-*. **2** *of water* to rise *la16-*. [OE *swellan*]

swalla, swallow, †**suallow** /'swalə, 'swɔlə, 'swɔlo/ *n* **1** the swallow *Hirundo rustica*, a passerine bird with a long, forked tail and curved, pointed wings *la15-*. **2** the martin, another member of the *Hirundinidae la19-*. **swallow-hawk** the swift *Apus apus 20- Ork WC*. [OE *swealwe*]

swalla *see* SWALLIE[1.1]

swallen *see* SWALL

swallie[1.1], *NE* **swalla**, †**swellie** /'swɔle, 'swale; *NE* 'swalə/ *n* **1** an alcoholic drink *la20-*. **2** the throat, the gullet; an act of swallowing *19, 20- Sh Ork NE*. **3** an abyss in the sea; a whirlpool; a sink (of vice) *la16*, compare SWELCHIE. [OE *geswelg* a gulf, an abyss]

swallie[1.2], **swallow**, †**swelly**, †**swelle**, †**suelly** /'swɔle, 'swale, 'swɔlo/ *v pt also* **swellit**, *ptp also* **swolit 1** to cause (food) to pass from the mouth to the stomach through the gullet, eat, devour *la14-*. **2** to take in (a sensation) eagerly *16-*. **3** to consume, destroy; *of the sea* to engulf *la14-*. [OE *swelgan*]

swallow *see* SWALLA, SWALLIE[1.2]

swalm *see* SWAAM[1.1], SWAAM[1.2]

swalt *see* SWELT[1], SWELT[2]

swame *see* SWAAM[1.1]

swamp /swamp/ *adj* thin, lean, skinny; lithe *la14-19, 20- Sh*. [unknown]

swander[1.1], *Sh* **swaander** /'swɔndər; *Sh* 'swandər/ *n* a fit of giddiness; a reeling movement, a stagger *20- Sh Ork*. [see the verb]

swander[1.2], *Sh* **swaander** /'swɔndər; *Sh* 'swandər/ *v* to become giddy or faint; to reel about, stagger; to hesitate, dither *19- Sh Ork EC*. [perhaps altered form of *wander* (WANNER[1])]

†**Swane, Swen** *n* Sweden *16-e17*. [reduced form of SWADEN]

swane *see* SWAIN

swang *see* SWING[1.2]

swank /swaŋk/ *adj* lithe, agile, strong; *especially of a young man* smart, well set-up *la18-*. **swankin** active, agile, athletic *19-*. [MDu *swanc* supple, pliant, slender]

swankie[1.1], **swanky** /'swaŋke/ *n* a smart, active, strapping young man; originally a servant lad *la15-19, 20- C SW*. [see the adj]

swankie[1.2], **swanky** /'swaŋke, 'swaŋki/ *adj* **1** lithe, agile, active *19-*. **2** smart, fashionable; well set-up, self-assured, pretentious *19-*. [SWANK + -IE[2]]

Swankie's doo /swaŋkiz 'du/ *n humorous* a seagull *la20- T*. [from a surname common in Arbroath + DOO]

Swankie's hen /swaŋkiz 'hɛn/ *n humorous* a seagull *la20- T*. [from a surname common in Arbroath + HEN[1.1]]

swanky *see* SWANKIE[1.1], SWANKIE[1.2], SWINKY

swap[1.1], †**suap** /swap, swɔp/ *n* **1** an exchange *la16-*. **2** a sudden gust of wind *20- Sh Ork N*. **3** a blow, a stroke, a slap *16-19, 20- Sh N*. **4** *in mowing* a downward sweep of the scythe *20- Sh Ork*. [see the verb]

swap[1.2], †**suap** /swap, swɔp/ *v* **1** to exchange, barter; to strike a bargain *la17-*. **2** to strike, hit; to fling, swipe, swing, brandish (a weapon); to fight, deal blows *la14-19, 20- Sh*. **3** to fold or wind (a rope or strip of cloth) over itself, criss-cross *la19- Sh NE*. **4** to throw (a rope) over a hay- or cornstack to hold down the thatch; to rope (a stack) thus *la19- NE*. **5** *of wind* to blow in gusts, bluster, sweep down *20- Sh Ork N*. **6** to pounce upon, seize, catch (a bird in a net) *20- Ork*. **7** to drink in long, quick gulps *16-19*. **8** to fall abruptly in a faint or stupor; to swoon *la15-16*. †**swappit** perhaps dozy, sluggish or drunken *e16*. [ME *swap*, perhaps onomatopoeic]

swap[1.3] /swap/ *adv* with a sudden violent movement, forcibly *19, 20- Sh*. [see the verb]

swap[2.1], *NE T* **swype** /swap, swɔp; *NE T* swʌɪp/ *n* the cast of someone's features, a resemblance, a facial trait or characteristic in a family *19, 20- Sh NE T*. [Norw dial *svipe*]

swap[2.2] /swap, swɔp/ *v* **1** to resemble, show a family likeness to *19- Ork SW*. **2** to match (patterns or colours) *20- Ork*. [see the noun]

swap[3], **swaup**, *SW Bor* **swab** /swap, swʌup; *SW Bor* swab/ *n* (the shell or pod of) peas or beans *19- EC SW Bor*. [unknown]

swarales, **swaralos** /ˈswarələs/ *n* a deep mire or hole in a bog *la19- Sh*. [ON *svarðlauss* without turf]

†**swarbit**, **sarbit**, **swarbett** *n* a prohibition or curse *la16-18*. **Deil swarbit on** the Devil's curse on *18*. **God swarbett** God forbid *la16*. [EModE *swarbout* a corruption of *(God')s forbote* God's forbidding]

sward see swaird[1.1], swaird[1.2]

sware see sweer[1.2], swire

swarf[1.1], †**swerf** /swarf/ *n* a swoon, a faint; a stupor *la15-19, 20- Sh NE*. [see the verb]

swarf[1.2], †**swerf**, †**swarth** /swarf/ *v* **1** to faint, swoon; to lose consciousness *16-19, 20- Sh NE SW*. **2** to cause to faint; to stupefy *19- WC SW Bor*. †**swarffand** *of receding waves* drained of power, spent *e16*. [unknown; compare ON *svarfa* to agitate, be upset]

swarf[2] /swarf/ *n* (part of) a shallow bay or inlet, uncovered at low tide *20- Sh*. [Norw dial *svarv* a bay]

swarfish /ˈswarfɪʃ/ *n* the spotted blenny, a type of spiny fish *Pholis gunnellus 19- Sh Ork*. [Norw *sverd* a sword + fish[1.1]]

swarlek see swaarlick

swarm /swarm/ *v* to turn, move (a pot or kettle) over the heat; to stir around *la19- Sh*. [variant of Norw dial *svarva* to turn round, perhaps with influence from Norw dial *svarma* to be dizzy]

swarm see swairm[1.1], swairm[1.2]

swarra /*Sh* ˈswarə; *NE* ˈswarə/ *n* (a jersey, underclothing or other garment knitted with) a thick, heavy, woollen yarn *la19- Sh NE*. [unknown]

swarrach[1.1] /ˈswarəx/ *n* a crowd, a swarm (especially of young children in a family) *19- NE*. [perhaps *swarm* (swairm[1.1]) + -och]

swarrach[1.2] /ˈswarəx/ *v of a place* to swarm with living creatures *20- NE*. [see the noun]

swarree, **swarry**, **swuree**, **surree**, **siree** /swɔˈri, ˈswɔre, swʌˈri, səˈri/ *n* a soirée, a social gathering, especially organized by a church or Sunday school *19-*. [Fr *soirée*]

†**swart**[1.1] *n* black dyestuff *la16*. [see the adj]

swart[1.2] /swɔrt; *Sh* swart/ *adj* **1** black *la19- Sh*. **2** swarthy *20- T C*. **swartback**, †**swerthbak**, †**suerthbak** the greater black-backed gull *Larus marinus la15-19, 20- Sh*. [OE *sweart*, ON *svartr*]

†**swarth** *n* the cut made by one sweep of a scythe *la18-19*. Compare sway and swaar[3]. [EModE *swarth*, variant of Eng *swath*, from OE *swæþ* a track, a trace]

swarth see swarf[1.2]

swarve /swarv/ *v* to turn over (hay) *20- Sh*. [Norw dial *svarva* to turn round]

swarve see swerve

swasche see swesch

swash[1.1] /swɔʃ, swaʃ/ *n* **1** the splash of water; the dash or wash of waves *la18-19, 20- Sh Ork N*. **2** a large amount, especially of drink or food *19, 20- Sh Ork NE*. **3** (the noise of) a blow, a clashing *18-19*. **4** affected ostentatious behaviour; a swagger; a strutting, haughty gait *19*. **5** a swaggerer, a vain, ostentatious person *19*. **swashie** ostentatious, dashing; strapping *la19, 20- NE*. [EModE *swash*, onomatopoeic]

swash[1.2] /swɔʃ, swaʃ/ *v* **1** to throw down; to slash; to beat; to swish *17-*. **2** to swagger, cut a dash; to rush, go about excitedly, energetically or arrogantly *17-19, 20- NE T*. **3** to dash or splash (liquid) about or over *19-, 20- Sh Ork*. [see the noun]

†**swash**[2] *adj* **1** fuddled with drink *18-19*. **2** perhaps broad, squat *18-e19*. [unknown; perhaps related to swash[1.1]]

swat see sweet[1.2]

swatch[1.1] /swatʃ/ *n* **1** a glimpse, a partial view, a half-look *la19-*. **2** a pattern or sample (of cloth or wallpaper) *la16-*. **3** a typical piece, example or selection *la17-*. **4** a point or amount of similarity, a feature in common *18, 20- Sh T*. **5** a short spell, a turn *20- C*. **tak a swatch o**, **tak swatch o** to take an appraising, critical look at, scrutinize; to check on, glance at *la19- N T C*. **tak the swatch o** to take the measure of, be a match for *la19- NE*. [unknown]

swatch[1.2] /swatʃ/ *v* **1** to match, select; to make, copy, or supply according to a pattern *la19*. **2** to look appraisingly at, size up; to glimpse, glance at *la19- T C*. [unknown]

swats, *Ork* **swets**, †**swaittis** /swɔts; *Ork* swɛts/ *npl* **1** newly-brewed weak beer; a substitute for this, made of molasses, water and yeast *16-*. **2** the liquor resulting from the steeping of oatmeal husks in the making of sowans *19- Sh Ork N NE T*. [OE *swatan* (*n pl*) beer]

swatter[1.1] /ˈswatər, ˈswɔtər/ *n* **1** a splashing or floundering about in water *19*. **2** a large collection or crowd, especially of small creatures, a swarm *19, 20- NE Bor*. [see the verb]

swatter[1.2], †**sualter**, †**swelter** /ˈswatər, ˈswɔtər/ *v* to dabble, flounder or wallow in water *la15-19, 20- SW Uls*. [onomatopoeic; compare Du *zwadderen*]

swattit see sweet[1.2]

swattle[1.1] /ˈswatəl/ *n* liquid food, soup or drink *la19- Sh*. [see the verb]

swattle[1.2], †**squattle** /ˈswatəl/ *v* **1** to splash about in something wet, wallow *19, 20- Sh*. **2** to drink greedily or noisily *la18-19*. [onomatopoeic; compare swatter[1.2] and Ger dial *schwatteln*]

swaup see swap[3]

swaver[1.1] /ˈswevər/ *n* an inclination to one side, a lurch, a stagger *la19- NE*. [see the verb]

swaver[1.2] /ˈswevər/ *v* to totter, sway, move unsteadily or wearily *la18-19, 20- Sh Ork NE*. [ME *swafren*; compare Norw dial *sveiva* to swing]

swaw[1.1], †**swow** /swɔ/ *n* a wave, a ripple *19-*. [perhaps altered form of *waw* (waff[1.1])]

†**swaw**[1.2] *v* to form waves, ripple; to undulate *e19*. [see the noun]

sway /swe, swae/ *n* a swath, the width of grass cut by the sweep of a scythe or the cut of a reaper *19- T C Bor*. [reduced form of Eng *swath*]

sway see swey[1.1], swey[1.2]

swayne see swain

sweamish /ˈswimɪʃ/ *adj* inclined to be nauseated *20- Sh Ork N EC*. [Eng *squeamish*]

swear see sweer[1.1], sweer[1.2]

swear dyke see swaird[1.1]

sweat see sweet[1.1], sweet[1.2]

swecht /swɛxt/ *n* a rush, impetus, force *la15-e19, 20- T*. [ME *sweight*]

sweddell see SWEEL².²
swedge¹·¹, †**suaidge** /swɛdʒ/ *n* a tool for making the grooves and nail-holes in a horseshoe *la17-*. [ME *swage* a decorated strip of border on a piece of metal work, OFr *souage*]
swedge¹·² /swɛdʒ/ *v* to make a groove or hole in (metal, *eg* a horseshoe) *19, 20- NE.* [see the noun]
swedge²·¹ /swɛdʒ/ *n* a fight; a gang fight *la20- C.* [unknown]
swedge²·² /swɛdʒ/ *v* to fight *la20- C.* [unknown]
swee¹·¹ /swi/ *n* stinging or tingling pain; the pain of a burn *17- Sh Ork.* [see the verb]
swee¹·² /swi/ *v* **1** to burn; to singe, scorch; to roast; to sizzle; to bore with a hot iron *19- Sh Ork.* **2** to toast oneself before a fire *20- Ork.* **3** to sting, smart with excessive heat or cold *19- Sh Ork.* **4** (the pain caused by) a burn or scald *19- Sh Ork.* **sweein irn** a metal bar heated for boring wood *20- Sh.* **sweeoo-iron** = *sweein irn 20- Ork.* [Norw *svi* to burn, scorch, smart]
swee see SWEEG², SWEY¹·¹, SWEY¹·²
sweeg¹ /swig/ *v of a boat* to move to leeward, go off course, drift *19- Sh.* [Norw dial *sviga* to give way]
sweeg², **swee** /swig, swi/ *v* to ooze, leak *la19- Sh Ork.* [Norw dial *svikja* to leak]
sweek see SWICK¹·¹
sweel¹·¹, **swill** /swil, swɪl/ *n* **1** a rinsing, washing or swilling; a hasty wash *la18-.* **2** a circular motion, a swirl, spin or twist *19-.* **3** pig swill, left over food given to pigs *20-.* **4** *of water* a swirling motion; the breaking of waves on the shore *la19- Sh NE.* **5** hearty drinking *la18-19, 20- NE.* [see the verb]
sweel¹·², **swill** /swil, swɪl/ *v* **1** to wash (the throat) down with liquor; to wash (food) down with a drink; to swallow in copious draughts; to drink to excess *la16-.* **2** to wash, rinse (a floor); to wash away; to dash or throw (water) about; to cause (a liquid) to swirl round *18-.* **3** to swirl, spin or revolve (quickly) *19-.* **4** *of water, waves* to roll, flow with a swirling motion *la19-.* **5** *of dancers* to whirl, spin round *19- T C SW.* [OE *swillan, swilian*]
sweel²·¹ /swil/ *n* the act of swathing or swaddling *la19- WC.* [see the verb]
sweel²·², *NE* **swyle**, †**swele**, †**sweddell** /swil; *NE* swʌil/ *v* **1** to wrap (a person, especially an infant) in cloth or clothing, to swaddle *15-.* **2** to wrap, wind, tie or bind round *19, 20- Uls.* **sweeler** a cloth body-belt, a binder, especially for an infant *19-.* †**swele belt** = *sweilling clais 16-17.* †**sweilling clais** swaddling clothes *la16.* †**swealing clouts**, **swedling clouts** = *sweilling clais la16-17.* [ME *swethelen*]
sweel³·¹, **swill**, **swivel**, *NE WC* **sweevil**, *N T* **sool**, †**sweill**, †**swoul**, †**soull** /swil, swɪl, 'swɪvəl; *NE WC* 'swɪvəl; *N T* sul/ *n* a coupling or fastening which allows the attached object (frequently a tethered animal) to move about the point of attachment, a swivel *16-.* **swiveltree** the swingletree of a plough *20- Ork NE T.* [ME *swivel*]
sweel³·² /swil/ *v* **1** to tether (animals) together with a swivel on the rope to allow them limited freedom of movement *la19- Sh Uls.* **2** to swing round *20- Sh.* [see the noun]
sweel see SWALL, SWILL
sweem¹·¹, **soom**, **swim**, †**swoum** /swim, sum, swɪm/ *n* **1** an extremely wet state, a flood, *la17-19, 20- Sh NE.* **2** a period of swimming; the act of swimming *20-.* [see the verb]
sweem¹·², **soom**, **swim**, †**swome**, †**swym**, †**sowm** /swim, sum, swɪm/ *v pt* **swam**, *NE* **sweemed** *ptp* **swum**, *Sh T* **swummed 1** to travel in water by the action of limbs or fins *la14-.* **2** *of fish* to be present, be found (in a particular stretch of water); *of water* to abound in fish *la15-.* **3** to float (on water); *of a ship* to move over water; to glide, float (as if over water) *16-17.* [OE *swimman*]
sweeng see SWING¹·²

sweep see SOOP¹·¹, SOOP¹·²
sweepit /'swipɪt/ *n mainly in negative constructions* a particle, the least little bit *20- Ork Uls.* [shortened form of *deil sweep it*; compare DEIL]
sweer¹·¹, **swear** /swir, swer/ *n* **1** a bout of swearing *la19-.* **2** a swear word *20-.* **3** a solemn oath or promise *la17.* **sweery word** a swear word *la20-.* [see the verb]
sweer¹·², **swear**, †**sweir**, †**suer**, †**swair** /swir, swer/ *v pt* **swore**, **swure**, **sware**, *WC SW Bor* **sweered**, †**swour**, †**swoir**, †**swoor 1** to take an oath, confirm or assent to by oath or solemn assertion, promise *la14-.* **2** to utter an oath frivolously, as an expression of strong feelings; to use bad language *la14-.* **3** *passive* to be bound by an oath, be put on oath as a witness; to be inducted into an office or function, especially a court, by the administration of an oath *15-.* **4** to value (goods) on oath *la15-e17.* **sweer to** to promise something on oath *la15-.* [OE *swerian*]
sweer see SWEIR
sweerie /'swire/ *n* a box or basket for holding bobbins of yarn, constructed so as to make easier the spinning of two- or three-ply thread *18- Sh Ork.* [perhaps SWEIR, from the idea of saving work + -IE³]
sweerta, **sweerty** see SWEIRTIE
sweesh /swiʃ/ *v* to swish *la19-.* [variant of Eng *swish*]
sweesh see SWESCH
sweet¹·¹, **sweat**, †**swete**, †**swait** /swit, swɛt/ *n* **1** perspiration *la14-.* **2** a state or episode of being sweaty; a fit of sweating *la14-.* **3** hard labour, toil, exertion *15-.* **4** stress; a state of anxiety or excitement *18-.* **sweeting** the action of producing sweat, a state or episode of sweating *la15-.* †**lose the swete, tyne the sweit** to lose one's life-blood, die *la14-16.* [see the verb]
sweet¹·², **sweit**, **sweat**, **swat**, *Sh NE T* **swite**, †**swete**, †**sueit** /swit, swɛt, swat; *Sh NE T* swʌit/ *v pt* **swat**, **swattit**, *N* **sweitit**, †**swet** *ptp* also *NE SW* **swutten**, *NE* **sweitit**, *Bor* **sweeten**, †**swat 1** to perspire *la14-.* **2** to exude (moisture) *la15-.* **3** to exert oneself; to work hard *la15-.* [OE *swǣtan*]
sweet², †**sweit**, †**suete** /swit/ *adj* **1** tasting of sugar; pleasant, agreeable *la14-.* **2** *of salmon* fresh, not spoiled *la15-16.* **3** *of fermented grain* sweet-tasting *la16-17.* **4** *of water* fresh, not salt, also not bitter or stagnant *la15-16.* **5** *of discourse, rhetoric, poetry, a poet* pleasant, agreeable; persuasive *15-e17.* **6** *of rain or sleep* having an agreeable or beneficial effect *15-e16.* **sweetly 1** pleasantly *la14-.* **2** emphatically, with force or feeling *la19- Ork.* **sweet-bread** fancy cakes, pastries *la18, 20- Sh Ork.* **sweet butter** unsalted butter *la18- Ork NE T EC Bor.* **sweet-meat**, †**sweit-meit 1** sweet food, especially confectionery *16-.* **2** tasty food *la15.* **sweet-milk** fresh, untreated milk that is not skimmed or sour *15-.* **sweet-milk cheese** cheese made from unskimmed milk; DUNLOP cheese *la18-e19, 20- N NE T.* †**Swete Singers** *Presbyterian Church* a sect known for ostentatious praying and psalm-singing *la17.* **sweet-willie** the red campion *Lychnis dioica 20- Sh Ork.* [OE *swēte*]
sweeten /'switən/ *v* **1** to make sweet *17-.* **2** to bribe *la18-.* **sweetnin** a sweetmeat, a titbit *20- Ork NE.* [SWEET², with verb-forming suffix]
sweeten see SWEET¹·²
sweetie, †**sweitie** /'switi, 'swite/ *n* **1** a sweet(meat), a piece of confectionery *la17-.* **2** as a term of endearment, darling *la19-.* **3** a considerable sum of money, a stiff price *20- NE.* **sweetie-bool**, **sweetie-boolie** a round boiled sweet *20- NE.* **sweetie-bottle** a glass jar for holding sweets *la19, 20- NE.* **sweetie-bun** a bun baked with sweetmeats or raisins *19, 20- Sh.* **sweetie-fole** a PARKIN sprinkled with sugar-coated caraway seeds *20- Ork.* **sweetie-loaf** = *sweetie-bun*

la18-19, 20- NE. **sweetie-man** a confectioner, a sweet-seller *19-.* **sweetie-merchant** = *sweetie-man la19-.* **sweetie-poke** a bag of sweets *la18-.* **sweetie-scone** = *sweetie-bun 19, 20- NE.* **sweetie-shop** a sweet-shop *la19-.* **sweetie-stand** a sweet-stall at a fair *la19-.* **sweetie-wife 1** a female sweet-seller *la18-.* **2** a garrulous person, a gossip *20-.* **he couldnae run a sweetie shop** he is incompetent *20-.* **work for sweeties** to work for a pittance; to be badly paid *20-.* [SWEET² + -IE³]

sweetie-trump /ˈswititrʌmp/ *n* a water-pistol *20- Sh.* [Norw dial *skvetta* a squirter made from a plant stem + -IE¹ + TRUMP¹·¹]

sweevil /ˈswivəl/ *n* a gust of wind, a short, sharp gale *la19, 20- Sh Ork.* [Norw dial *svivla* a swirl of wind]

sweevil *see* SWEEL³·¹

sweeze /swiz/ *v* to squeeze *20- Sh Ork.* [variant of Eng *squeeze*]

sweill *see* SWEEL³·¹

sweip *see* SOOP¹·¹, SOOP¹·²

sweir, sweer, †swere, †swer /swir/ *adj* **1** lazy, slothful, unwilling to be active or to work *la14-.* **2** unwilling, reluctant, loath *la14-.* **3** mean *19, 20- T.* **4** oppressed in mind, dull, depressed *la14-15.* **sweir-draw** a children's game in which each of two players, sitting on the ground with the soles of their feet pressed together and holding a stick between them, tries to pull the other up *la19-.* **sweir-drawn** reluctant, hesitating *19- Bor.* **sweir-erse** = *sweir-draw.* **sweir-pin** = *sweir-draw 20- N.* **sweero stick** = *sweir-draw 20- Ork.* **sweir-tree, sweer-tree** = *sweir-draw 19, 20- NE T C SW.* [OE *swǣr*]

sweir *see* SWEER¹·²

sweird *see* SWEIRT

sweirie /ˈswiri/ *adj* rather lazy; somewhat reluctant (to do anything) *19- Sh Ork.* **sweirie geng** *knitting* the first or most difficult row *20- Sh.* **sweirie well** a well which is dependable only after rain *19, 20- N.* [SWEIR + -IE²]

sweirt, sweert, sweird /swirt, swird/ *adj* sluggish, loath, reluctant *19-.* [SWEIR + -IT²]

sweirtie, sweerty, *Sh* **sweerta** /ˈswirti; *Sh* ˈswirtə/ *n* laziness *19- Sh NE.* [SWEIRT + -IE³]

sweit *see* SUEIT, SWEET¹·², SWEET²

sweitit *see* SWEET¹·²

swelchie, swelth /ˈswɛlki, swɛlθ/ *n* **1** a whirlpool in the sea *la14-16, la17- Ork N.* **2** a sink (of vice) *la14-16.* [ON *svelgr*]

swele *see* SWEEL²·²

swell *see* SWAIL¹, SWALL

swelle *see* SWALLIE¹·²

swellie *see* SWALLIE¹·¹

swellit, swelly *see* SWALLIE¹·²

swelt *see* SWALLIE¹·²

†swelt¹, suelt *v pt* **sweltit, swelt, swalt 1** to die *la14-e17.* **2** to become faint with weakness or emotion, be physically overcome, swoon *la15-19.* **3** to suffer from excessive heat or sweating; to swelter *la16-e17.* [OE *sweltan* to die]

swelt², swalt /swɛlt/ *v* **1** to be famished, to starve *20- Ork.* **2** to become faint with weakness or emotion, be physically overcome, swoon *20- Ork.* **sweltin** *of a cod* emaciated; *of a child* hungry *19- Sh NE.* [Norw dial *svelta* to die, especially of hunger]

swelt *see* SWALL

swelter *see* SWATTER¹·²

swelth *see* SWELCHIE

sweltit *see* SWELT¹

sweltry /ˈswɛltrɪ/ *adj* oppressively hot, sultry *19-.* [frequentative form of SWELT + -IE²]

Swen *see* SWANE

swengeour, swenʒour *see* SWINGER¹

swepyr *see* SWIPPER¹·²

swer *see* SWEIR

swerd *see* SWURD

swere *see* SWEIR

swerf *see* SWARF¹·¹, SWARF¹·², SWERVE

swerm *see* SWAIRM¹·²

swerthbak *see* SWART¹·²

swerve, †swarve, †swerf /swɛrv/ *v* to turn (away); to (allow oneself to) be deflected *16-.* [ME *swerven*, OE *sweorfan* to rub, scour, with influence from LG *swarven* to swerve]

†swesch, sweesh, swasche, swische *n* **1** a small drum, beaten to attract public attention *16-19.* **2** perhaps a trumpet *16-19.* **swescher** a drummer *16-17.* **sweschman** in Aberdeen, a drummer *la16-e17.* **swesch taburn** a drum *16-e17.* [perhaps a variant of SWASH¹·¹, or from the adj *Swesche* Swiss (tabor)]

swet *see* SWEET¹·²

swets *see* SWATS

†swevyn, sweving *n* a dream *la15-e16.* **swevynyng, suevenyng, sweyning** dreaming, sleeping *15-16.* [OE *swefn*]

swey¹·¹, swy, swee, sway /swʌɪ, swi, swe/ *n* **1** controlling influence, prevailing power *la15-.* **2** a swinging semicircular motion; a sudden move to one side, a swerve or lurch; a swinging blow; a veering of the wind *16-.* **3** an iron bar which can be swung over a fire, on which pots or kettles can be hung *la18-.* **4** a swing for children *19-.* **5** a lever, a crowbar *16-19, 20- Sh.* **6** a derrick or crane; a steelyard *la17-e19.* **7** an inclination or bias, a trend, tendency *18-e19.* **8** an iron bracket, a street-lamp bracket *17-18.* **swey-boat, sway-boat** a funfair swing-boat *20-.* **swee chain** the chain hanging from the SWEY¹·¹ (sense 3) on which pots or kettles are hooked *20- N T H&I WC SW.* [see the verb]

swey¹·², swy, swee, sway, †sweye, †suey /swʌɪ, swi, swe/ *v* **1** *of a balance* to move in a particular direction; to cause (a balance) to swing to one side; to divert (one's thoughts) in a particular direction *16-.* **2** to vacillate *16-.* **3** to cause to swing, move (an object) to one side or the other; *of an object* to swing backwards and forwards *la18-.* **4** to press down, bend to one side; to lean, favour (one side) *la15-19.* **5** to wield (a sword or sceptre) as an emblem of authority; to command, control, direct, rule *la16-17.* **†swey doun** to collapse, fall *la15-16.* [ME *sweien* to go, move, probably ON *sveigja* to bend, give way]

sweyrd *see* SWURD

swick¹·¹, sweek, †swik /swɪk, swik/ *n* **1** (a piece of) deceit, a trick, a swindle *la14-.* **2** a cheat, a swindler, a deceiver *la19- Sh Ork N NE T C.* **swickery** cheating, swindling *la19-.* **†swikful** deceitful, treacherous *e15.* **the swick o 1** the responsibility for (something bad or unfortunate) *19- NE.* **2** the knack or ability to do (something) *19-.* [OE *swic* deceit, OE *swica* a deceiver]

swick¹·², †swyk /swɪk/ *v* to cheat, swindle, deceive *16-.* [OE *swican* to wander, deceive]

swidder *see* SWITHER¹·²

swiff¹·¹, swuff /swɪf, swʌf/ *n* the whizzing or whirring (sound) of an object flying through the air, a rush of air *19, 20- Sh NE.* [onomatopoeic]

swiff¹·² /swɪf/ *v* to rush through the air with a hissing noise *19.* [see the noun]

swift /swɪft/ *v* to reef (a sail) *19- Sh.* [Norw dial *svifta*]

swig /swɪg/ *v* to go with a swinging motion, rock, jog *19, 20- NE.* [compare Norw dial *sviga* to swing, work quickly, beat, *sveiga* to walk with a swing]

swik *see* SWICK¹·¹

swilk see SIC[1.1]

swill, swull, sweel /swɪl, swʌl, swil/ *n* a large shallow basket for carrying potatoes, clothes etc *19- EC Bor*. [uncertain; compare Flem *swyle* a bucket]

swill see SWEEL[1.1], SWEEL[1.2], SWEEL[3.1]

swilter /'swɪltər/ *v* to splash *20- Sh Ork*. [perhaps frequentative form of SWEEL[1.2], with influence from SWITTLE[1.2]]

swim see SWEEM[1.1], SWEEM[1.2]

swimp /swɪmp/ *n* a quick, bustling movement, a flounce *la19- Sh*. [compare Norw dial *svip, svim* a gesture, mannerism]

swine, †swyne /swʌɪn/ *n* **1** a pig, pigs *la14-*. **2** pork *15-17*. **3** a wild boar *e16*. **swine's arnit, swine arnit** the tall oatgrass *Arrhenatherum elatius 18-* mainly *NE*. **swine-beads** = *swine's arnit 20- Ork*. **swine-crue swine-cruive** a pigsty *16-19, 20- EC SW*. **swine-meat** pigswill *20-*. **swine's murricks** = *swine's arnit 19- Sh*. **swine-pot** a pot in which pigs' food is boiled *20- Ork NE SW*. **swine-thrissel** the sowthistle *Sonchus oleraceus 19- SW Bor*. **the swine has run through it** the plan, affair etc has been completely ruined *18-19, 20- Ork NE EC SW*. [OE *swīn*]

swing[1.1] /swɪŋ/ *n* **1** the action of swinging a golf club so as to hit the ball *la17-*. **2** a boat's mooring rope *la16-19, 20- Sh N NE T EC*. **3** *in herring-fishing* the line of nets to the stern of the boat *19, 20- Sh N NE T EC*. **4** a swinging blow with a weapon *la14*. **swing-rope, swing-tow** a boat's mooring rope or herring fishing nets *17- Sh N NE T EC*. **swing-tree** the swingletree of a plough etc *19, 20- Ork NE*. [see the verb]

swing[1.2], *NE T* **sweeng** /swɪŋ, swiŋ/ *v pt* **swang, swung 1** to move freely backwards and forwards from a fixed point *la15-*. **2** to strike a blow; to wield a sword; to throw, hurl *la15-16*. **sweengin lum** *in a cottage* a wooden chimney or smoke vent suspended over the fire *20- Ork NE*. **swing the tattie** to be in charge *20- SW*. [OE *swingan* to move violently]

†swing[2] *v* to labour, toil *la15*. [SWING[1.2] with influence from SWINK]

swinge[1.1] /swɪnʒ/ *n* a heavy blow, a dash or clash, a forcible impetus *la18- C SW Bor*. [see the verb]

swinge[1.2] /swɪnʒ/ *v* to beat, flog, drive with blows *la18-19, 20- Sh*. [OE *swengan*]

†swinger[1], **swengeour, swenʒour** *n* a rogue, a scoundrel *16-e19*. [compare MDu, MLG *swentzen* to roam about idly, Ger *Schwänzer* a vagabond]

swinger[2] /'swɪnʒər/ *n* a big, stalwart fellow *20- Sh N*. [SWINGE[1.2], with agent suffix]

swingle[1], **†swyngill** /'swɪŋəl, 'swɪŋgəl/ *v* to beat or scrape flax *la15-*. [MDu *swinghelen*]

swingle[2] /'swɪŋəl, 'swɪŋgəl/ *v* **1** to swing from side to side, be hung or suspended, oscillate *19- Bor*. **2** *of sheep* to walk with a swinging, jerky motion due to disease of the spine *la19- N*. [frequentative form of SWING[1.2]]

swingletree, †swingill-tre /'swɪŋəltri, 'swɪŋgəltri/ *n* **1** the cross-bar (of a plough) to which the traces are fastened *la16-*. **2** the free arm or beater of a flail *la18-*. **3** = *sweir tree* (SWEIR) *la19- NE C*. **4** a bar forming part of various mechanisms *17*. [SWINGLE[1] + TREE[1.1]]

swink /swɪŋk/ *v* to work hard, toil; to struggle hard or intensely *la14-*. [OE *swincan*]

swinkle /'swɪŋkəl/ *v of liquid* to splash about in a container *20- Sh*. **swinklan** drunk *la19- Sh*. [Norw dial *skvinkla* to ripple]

swinky, swanky /'swɪŋki, 'swaŋki/ *n* the earthworm *Lumbricus terrestris 20- Ork*. [compare Dan *skvinke* to wriggle]

swins see SOWANS

swint /swɪnt/ *v* to rush, dash *la19- Sh*. [Norw dial *svinte*]

swipe[1.1] /swʌɪp/ *n* **1** a blow with a full swing of the arm, a sweeping stroke *18-*. **2** a swinging stroke made with a golf club or cricket bat *19*. [probably variant of *sweep* (SOOP[1.1])]

swipe[1.2] /swʌɪp/ *v* to deliver a long swinging blow or stroke *19-*. [see the noun]

swipe[2] /swʌɪp/ *n mining* a crossing-switch or curved plate in a mine railway *la19- C*. [unknown; compare Eng *swape* a lever, related to SWAIP[1.2]]

swipper[1.1] /'swɪpər/ *n* a lithe, agile person *20-, NE*. [see the adj]

swipper[1.2], *NE T* **swippert, †swippir, †swypir, †swepyr** /'swɪpər; *NE T* 'swɪpərt/ *adj* quick, nimble, active *la14-19, 20- NE T*. [OE *swipor* crafty, cunning]

swipper[1.3] /'swɪpər/ *adv* agilely, nimbly, quickly, abruptly *la19- NE*. [see the adj]

swippir see SWIPPER[1.2]

swird see SWURD

swire, swyre, †sware, †swair /swaer/ *n* **1** the neck *la15-e16*. **2** a hollow or declivity between hills; a hollow or level place near the top of a hill *13-19, 20- WC Bor*. [OE *swīra* a neck]

†swirk *v* to spring (forth, up) *e16*. [unknown]

swirl[1.1], **swurl, sworl, †swyrl, †sworll** /swɪrl, swʌrl, sworl/ *n* **1** a whirling movement of water, smoke etc, an eddy, a whirlpool *15-*. **2** a twist, twirl or coil; a twisted or tangled state *la18-*. **3** a twist or knot in the grain of wood *19-*. **4** a tuft or curl of hair, a forelock *19-, 20-* [see the verb]

swirl[1.2], **swurl, †sworl** /swɪrl, swʌrl/ *v* **1** to (cause to) move round and round, whirl, eddy *16-*. **2** to have a twist, give a twist or curl to, coil, spin *e19*. [compare Norw dial *svirla*, Du *zwirrelen* to whirl]

swirlie, †swurly /'swɪrle, 'swʌrle/ *adj* **1** *of wood* with twists in the grain, knotty, gnarly; *of rock* knobby, with an uneven grain *la18-19, 20- Sh N NE*. **2** tangled, twisted *19-, 20- SW*. **3** especially *of the hair* curly, frizzy *19-, 20- Sh SW*. [SWIRL[1.1] + -IE[2]]

swirten, †swairten /'swɪrtən/ *v* to waste away; to flatten *la19- Sh*. [perhaps altered form of *sweltin* (SWELT[2])]

swische see SWESCH

switch /swɪtʃ/ *v* **1** to beat (eggs) *20-*. **2** to trim (a tree or hedge) *19-*. **3** to strike with a switch *la17-*. **4** to thresh (grain); to beat, scutch (flax) *19*. [Eng *switch* a slender stick or whip]

switchbell /'swɪtʃbel/ *n* an earwig *la19- WC Bor*. Compare COACHBELL. [altered form of Eng *twitch-ballock, twitch-bell*]

swite /swʌɪt/ *v* originally *fisherman's taboo* to bale out (water) *20- Sh*. [compare Norw dial *skvetta* to squirt]

swite see SWEET[1.1]

†swith[1.1] *v* to go (away) quickly *la18-19*. [see the adv]

swith[1.2] /swɪθ/ *adj* quick, speedy *19-*. [see the adv]

swith[1.3], **†swyth, †swyith, †switht** /swɪθ/ *adv* **1** quickly, rapidly; at once *la14-*. **2** suddenly, without warning *e16*. [OE *swīþe* strongly, forcibly]

swith[1.4] /swɪθ/ *interj* quick! *18-19, 20- WC*. **†swith awa** frequently *as a command to a dog* quick!, away! *18-19*. [see the adv]

swither[1.1] /'swɪðər/ *n* **1** a state of indecision or doubt, hesitation, uncertainty *la17-*. **2** a state of nervousness or agitation, a panic or fluster *la17-*. **3** a state of confusion, a tangled or muddled condition *la19-*. **4** a dithering, undecided person *20-*. [see the verb]

swither[1.2], **swuther**, *NE* **swudder, †swidder** /'swɪðər, 'swʌðər; *NE* 'swʌdər/ *v* **1** to doubt, falter, hesitate, dither *16-*. **2** *of things* to be indeterminate or uncertain, have a doubtful appearance, fluctuate, move fitfully *19-* mainly *literary*. **3** to feel faint or sick *e19*. [uncertain; perhaps extended sense of SWITHER[2.2]]

swither[2.1] /ˈswɪðər/ *n* a rushing movement, swirl, flurry *20- Sh NE*. [see the verb]
swither[2.2] /ˈswɪðər/ *v* to rush, swirl, move with haste and flurry *19- Sh NE T Bor*. [probably onomatopoeic; compare Norw dial *svidra* to rush to and fro, Icel *sviðra* to swirl]
†**swither**[3] *v* to beat, thrash, *la18-e19*. [unknown]
swither[4.1] /ˈswɪðər/ *n* a swelter, great heat *20- Sh NE*. [see the verb]
swither[4.2] /ˈswɪðər/ *v of weather* to be very hot, swelter *la19- Sh NE SW*. [ON *sviðra* to burn, singe]
switherel, switherum, *EC* **swithers** /ˈswɪðərəl, ˈswɪðərəm; *EC* ˈswɪðərz,/ *n* a jellyfish, in its adult or medusa stage (from its stinging properties) *20- T EC*. [SWITHER[4.2] with agent suffix -*el*]
swith see SWITH[1.3]
swittek /ˈswɪtək/ *n* a water-pistol *20- Sh*. [Norw dial *skvetta* a squirter made from a plant stem with -OCK suffix]
switter[1] /ˈswɪtər/ *v* to splash; to flounder (in water); *of water* to ripple, splash *la17-19, 20- H&I*. [onomatopoeic]
switter[2] /ˈswɪtər/ *v* to swirl, to spill carelessly *20- Sh Ork*. [onomatopoeic; compare Norw dial *skvitra*]
swittle[1.1] /ˈswɪtəl/ *n* **1** the gentle splash of water *20- Sh*. **2** watery, wishy-washy food or drink *19- Sh*. [see the verb]
swittle[1.2] /ˈswɪtəl/ *v* to splash gently in water, dabble; *of water* to splash, lap *la19- Sh*. [Norw dial *skvitla*]
swivel see SWEEL[3.1]
swiz /swɪz/ *n* a whizzing noise *la19- Sh*. [onomatopoeic]
swnye see SONƷE[1.2]
swo /swo/ *n* the smarting pain of a burn or scald *20- Ork*. [compare Norw dial *svode* an abrasion]
swoch see SOUCH[1.1]
swoir see SWEER[1.2]
swolit see SWALLIE[1.2]
swoll see SWALL
swome see SWEEM[1.2]
swone see SOUND[1.2]
swoof[1.1] /swuf/ *n* a swishing, blowing sound *20- Sh*. [onomatopoeic]
swoof[1.2], †**suoufe** /swuf/ *v* **1** *of the wind* to make a rustling, swishing sound *19, 20- Sh*. **2** to breathe or sigh *la16*. [see the noun]
swoop see SOOP[1.2]
swoor see SWEER[1.2]
swop see SOOP[1.2]
sword see SWURD
swore see SWEER[1.2]
sworl see SWIRL[1.1], SWIRL[1.2]
sworll see SWIRL[1.1]
swouch see SOUCH[1.1], SOUCH[1.2]
swoul see SWEEL[3.1]
swoum see SWEEM[1.1]
swoun see SOUND[1.1]
swound see SOUND[1.1], SOUND[1.2]
swoune see SOUND[1.2]
swour see SWEER[1.2]
swourd see SWURD
swow see SWAW[1.1]
swown see SOUND[1.2]
swudder see SWITHER[1.2]
swuff see SWIFF[1.1]
swull see SWILL
swum see SWEEM[1.2]
swung see SWING[1.2]
swüp see SOOP[1.2]
swurd, sword, swourd, swird, sourd, swerd, †**sweyrd,** †**suerd** /sɔrd, swʌrd, surd/ *n* **1** a long-bladed weapon, a sword *la14-*. **2** a cross-piece; the crossbar in a barred gate or between chair- or table-legs *19- Sh N SW*. **3** a slat of wood or tang of metal on the end of a ladder, used to prevent it from slipping *20- T EC*. **sword-belt** a belt from which a sword in its scabbard is suspended *la15-*. **sword-dance** a Highland dance (HIELAND[1.2]), usually danced solo, consisting of a series of steps between two swords laid cross-wise on the ground *la16-*. †**sword-hand** the handle of a sword *16*. †**sword-slipper, swerd-slippar** a sword-sharpener *la14-19*. [OE *sweord*]
swure see SWEER[1.2]
swuree see SWARREE
swurl see SWIRL[1.1], SWIRL[1.2]
swurly see SWIRLIE
swuther see SWITHER[1.2]
swutten see SWEET[1.2]
swy see SWEY[1.1], SWEY[1.2]
†**swyfe, swiff, swyve** *v* to copulate *16*. **swyvear** a person who copulates *e16*. [ME *swiven*, specialized sense of OE *swīfan* to sweep]
swyith see SWITH[1.3]
swyk see SWICK[1.2]
swyle see SWAIL[1], SWEEL[2.2]
swym see SWEEM[1.2]
swyne see SWINE
swyngill see SWINGLE[1]
swype see SWAP[2.1], SOOP[1.2]
swypir see SWIPPER[1.2]
swyre see SWIRE
swyrl see SWIRL[1.1]
swyth see SWITH[1.3]
swyve see SWYFE

sybow, syboe, †**sebow,** †**sybae** /ˈsʌɪbo/ *n* a spring onion; a scallion or Welsh onion *la16-*. †**sybow-tail** the green shoots of the young onion *la18-19*. [Fr *ciboule*]
sych see SICH[1.1]
sycht see SICHT[1.1], SICHT[1.2]
sychtis see SICHTIS
syd see SIDE[1]
syde see SIDE[1], SIDE[2.1]
sydelingis see SIDELINS[1.4]
sydrapis see SIDE[1]
sye[1.1] /sae/ *n* a strainer or sieve for liquids, especially milk *la19-*. **sey clout** a piece of gauze stretched across a frame, used for straining liquid *20-*. **sye-dish** a milk-strainer *18- NE EC*. **sye-milk** = *sye-dish 18- NE*. **sye-sowans** a strainer for SOWANS *la19-*. [see the verb; compare MDu *sye* a strainer]
sye[1.2]**, sey, sie** /sae/ *v* to pass (liquid) through a sieve, drain, filter *18-*. **syer** = SYE[1.1] *la19-*. [OE *sīon*]
syes[2] /saez/ *n* mainly *pl* chives *19- N NE T*. [Fr *cives*, pl]
syid see SIDE[1]
syith see SITH[1]
syk see SIC[1.1]
syke, sike /sʌɪk/ *n* **1** a small stream or water course; a ditch or the channel of a stream, especially in a hollow or on flat, boggy ground, and often dry in summer *13-19, 20- C Bor*. **2** a marshy hollow, especially one with a stream, a cleft in the ground *18-19, 20- EC SW Bor*. †**siket** a small watercourse *13-e14*. †**sykie** *of ground* full of sluggish rivulets, soft, boggy, though dry in summer *la18-e19*. [OE *sīc*]
sykkyn see SICCAN[1.1]
syklyke see SICLIKE[1.1], SICLIKE[1.2]
syk wys see SIC WISE
syl see SILE[4]

syle, †**cile**, †**syll** /sʌil/ *v* **1** to line the interior roof or walls of a building; to provide with a ceiling *la15-e18, 20- NE*. **2** to cover or enclose a bed with a tester *16*. Compare CIEL. [ME *ceelyn*, related to Fr *ciel* canopy]

syle *see* CIEL, SILE¹, SILE⁵

syling, **ceiling**, †**siling**, †**seling** /'sʌilɪŋ, 'silɪŋ/ *n* **1** the lining of the roof of a room; originally (boards for) the lining or panelling of walls or roof *16-*. **2** the action of lining the walls or roof of a room *la14-17*. [verbal noun from SYLE]

syll *see* SYLE

syllab¹·¹, †**sillab** /'sɪləb/ *n* **1** a syllable *16-*. **2** a small portion or detail (of something written), the slightest part (of a letter) *la15-17*. [OFr *sillabe*, Lat *syllaba*]

†**syllab**¹·² *v* to divide words into syllables, especially in teaching reading *18-e19*. [see the noun]

syllowr *see* SYLOUR¹·²

syllyn *see* SHILLING

†**sylour**¹·¹, **silour** *n* **1** a canopy *la15-e17*. **2** a ceiling *16*. [ME *celure*, OFr *celure*, Lat *celura*]

†**sylour**¹·², **syllowr** *v* to provide with a ceiling; to line with wainscotting *la16-e17*. **sylouring**, **sylring**, **seyloring 1** a ceiling; wainscotting *la15-e18*. **2** the action of providing with a ceiling or wainscotting *la16-17*. **3** a canopy *16*. **sylourit** provided with a ceiling, wainscotting, a top or a canopy *16-e17*. [see the noun]

syluyr *see* SILLER¹·¹

sylver *see* SILLER¹·³

symbol /'sɪmbəl/ *n* **1** a thing or action which stands for or represents something else, especially an object representing an abstract principle, *eg* legal possession *17-*. **2** a letter of the alphabet (as representing a speech sound) *e17*. †**symbolical**, **symbolick** *law* pertaining to the giving of symbols, *eg* earth and stone, as a token that heritable property has been transferred from one person to another *la17-e19*. †**symbolize** to represent by means of a SYMBOL (sense 2) *e17*. [Lat *symbolum*, Fr *symbole*]

Symie, †**Simmie** /'sʌimi/ *n humorous* the devil *la18-*. [from the personal name *Simon, Simeon*]

symleir *see* SUMMELEIR

symmer *see* SIMMER¹·¹

symmyr *see* SIMMER¹·³

†**symphioun**, **sumphion** *n* a musical instrument *la15-16*. [altered form of ME *symphan*, OFr *simphoine*]

†**symphony** *n* a musical instrument; (a harmonious sound played on) various musical instruments *la15-e16*. [OFr *simphonie*]

syn *see* SIN²·¹, SIN²·²

synd *see* SYNE¹·¹, SYNE¹·²

syndry *see* SINDRY¹·²

syne¹·¹, **sine**, **synd** /sʌin, sʌind/ *n* a washing or rinsing out, a swill, a hasty wash *la18-*. [see the verb]

syne¹·², **sine**, **synd**, †**seynd** /sʌin, sʌind/ *v* **1** to wash, rinse (dishes or clothes) *la15-*. **2** to wash (food) down with drink *la18- C SW Bor*. †**syndins** rinsings, slops, swill *19*. **syne oot** to rinse out (dishes or clothes) *la18-*. [ME *sinden*, compare ON *synda* to swim]

syne²·¹, **sin**, *NE* **seen**, †**sen**, †**sene** /sʌin, sɪn/ *NE* sin/ *adv* **1** *in sequential or subsequential use* thereupon, directly after, next, afterwards; subsequently *la14-*. **2** *in retrospective use* ago, since, before now *15-*. **3** *in prospective or consequential use* from then, since, thereafter; as a result, consequently *15-*. **4** *in inferential use* in that case, so, then: ◊*and syne, ye're no gaun la19- NE T EC*. †**aforesyne** at that time, then *la19*. **fae syne** since that time *20- Sh*. [OE *siþþan* since then]

syne²·², **sin**, †**sen**, †**sene** /sʌin, sɪn/ *prep* after *la14-*. [see the adv]

syne²·³, **sin**, †**sen**, †**sene** /sʌin, sɪn/ *conj* **1** since, from the time that *la14-*. **2** since, because, seeing that *la14-19, 20- Sh NE EC*. [see the adv]

syne *see* SIGN¹·¹, SIN²·¹

syng *see* SIGN¹·¹, SING¹·²

syngill *see* SINGLE¹·³

synk *see* SINK¹·²

synny *see* SINNIE¹

synod /'sɪnəd/ *n* **1** *Presbyterian Churches* the court immediately superior to the PRESBYTERY *17-*. **2** *in the Christian Church* a general council of clergy *la15-*. †**synodal 1** = SYNOD *la16-e17*. **2** a payment made by the inferior clergy to a bishop or archdeacon on a visitation *la16*. †**synodal assembly** = SYNOD *la16-e17*. [ME *sinod*, Lat *synodus*]

†**synoper**, **synopar** *n* (the colour or pigment) red or reddish-brown *la15-e16*. [OFr *synopre*]

synsyne *see* SINSYNE

syon *see* SCION

syour *see* SYVER

sype¹·¹, **sipe**, **seep** /sʌip, sip/ *n* **1** a leakage, dripping; an oozing *la15-*. **2** a small quantity of liquid; dregs *19, 20- Sh Ork*. [see the verb]

sype¹·², **seyp**, **seip**, **seep** /sʌip, sip/ *v* **1** to drip, ooze, trickle, leak *16-*. **2** to cause to drip or ooze, drain, drip-dry *la19- Sh Ork NE SW*. **3** to soak up, absorb *la19, 20- N T Bor*. **seipage** leakage *19-*. **sypin** *of rain* soaking; *of a person* soaked, wet through *la19, 20- Sh NE*. **sypins** oozings, leakage; dregs, the last drops from a container *19, 20- Ork NE EC SW*. **sypit** soaked, wet through *19-*. [MDu *sīpan*]

†**syper**, **sypir**, **cipir** *n* cypress wood *15-16*. [shortened form of ME *cipres*, OFr *cipres*]

sypher *see* SEVER

syphir *see* CEEPHER

syre *see* SYVER

syrop, **syrup** *see* SEERUP

sys *see* SICE

Systeus *see* CISTEUS

syt *see* SIT¹·²

syte¹·¹, †**site**, †**syt** /sʌit/ *n* **1** care, solicitude *20- SW*. **2** sorrow, grief, suffering *la14-18*. [ON **sýt*, variant of *sút*]

syte¹·² /sʌit/ *v* to care for, tend *19- SW*. [see the noun]

†**syth**¹·¹ *n* satisfaction, compensation *la16-17*. †**get your heart's syth, get your hart syth** to be revenged *17-e18*. [aphetic form of ASSYTH¹·¹]

†**syth**¹·² *v* to satisfy, compensate; to be satisfied *15-17*. [see the noun]

syth *see* SCYTHE

sythe¹·¹, **syth** /sʌið/ *n* a (milk-)strainer, a filter *la16-19, 20- T*. [probably variant of Eng *sieve*]

sythe¹·², †**syth** /sʌið/ *v* to strain (milk) through a sieve, filter *la16-19, 20- T*. [see the noun]

†**sythment**, **sithement** *n* satisfaction, compensation, redress *16-18*. [aphetic form of ASSYTHMENT]

syttyn *see* SIT¹·²

syver, **syre**, †**syour** /'saevər/ *n* **1** a ditch, a drain, a water channel, a field drain; a street gutter *16-*. **2** the opening and, frequently, grating of the drain-trap in a street gutter *19-*. [probably OFr *essevour* a drainage channel]

T

't *see* IT
ta *see* TAE[1], TAE[2], TAE[3.2], TAK[1.2]
taak *see* TALK[1.1], TALK[1.2]
taam *see* TAUM
taat *see* TAUT[1.2]
taave[1.1] /tɑv/ *n* rags; tattered pieces of cloth *20- Sh.* [Norw dial *tave* a cloth, rag]
taave[1.2] /tɑv/ *v* **1** to caulk, to plug timbers with oakum *la19- Sh.* **2** to tear or rend *20- N.* [see the noun]
taavers *see* TAIVERS[2]
tab /tab/ *n* **1** a short broad strap or flat loop; a small flap or projecting tag *20-.* **2** a cigarette stub *20- NE C Uls.* **tabbie** a cigarette stub *20-.* [Eng *tab*]
tabackie, tabacca, tobacco, *Sh* **tabacha,** †**tabacco** /təˈbaki, təˈbakə, təˈbako; *Sh* təˈbaxə/ *n* a plant of the genus *Nicotiana* used for smoking or chewing *17-.* **tobacco fleuk** a lemon sole *20- NE.* **tobacco lord** a wealthy Glasgow tobacco merchant *19- historical.* **tabacha-speel** the fibre with which tobacco twist is tied in coils *20- Sh.* [EModE *tabaco, tobacco,* Spanish *tabaco*]
tabor *see* TABOUR[1.1]
†**tabet, tebbit, tibit** *n* physical sensation; energy, strength *19.* **tibbits** = TABET. [unknown]
tabetless, tapetless /ˈtebətləs, ˈtepətləs/ *adj* **1** without feeling, numb *la18-19, 20- NE T C.* **2** dull, lethargic, spiritless *la18-19, 20- NE EC Bor.* **3** heedless, foolish *la18-19, 20- literary.* [TABET + *-less* suffix]
tabill *see* TABLE[1.1]
tabillar *see* TABLE[1.2]
table[1.1], *Ork* **teeble,** *T* **tebill,** †**tabill** /ˈtebəl; *Ork* ˈtibəl; *T* ˈtɛbəl/ *n* **1** a piece of furniture with a flat surface *15-.* **2** the company assembled round a table *15-.* **3** a list or index; an arrangement of information in columns *la15-.* **4** *Presbyterian Church* the Communion table *la16-.* **5** *Christian Church* Communion; the communicants taking part in Communion *la16-20, 21- historical.* **6** *mining* a platform or plate on which coals are screened and picked *la19, 20- C.* **7** a tablet or surface for writing or painting *la14-17.* **8** a game of backgammon *la15-17.* **9** a backgammon board *16-17.* **10** *building* a flat piece of stone used as a coping or base *16-e17.* **tabling** *building* the stone coping of a wall or gable *la16-.* **table claith** a cloth for covering a table *17-.* **table cloot** a cloth for covering a table *la19-.* **table heid 1** the surface of a table, a table-top *la19-.* **2** the seat at the head of a table *20- NE C.* **table stane, table stone 1** a horizontal gravestone *la18-.* **2** a flat stone; a coping stone *la16-17.* **table tombstone** a flat tombstone *la19-.* **serve the tables** *Presbyterian Church of a minister* to administer the Sacrament; *of the elders* to distribute the elements to the tables *la16-19, 20- historical.* **the Tables, the tables 1** *Presbyterian Church* Communion; the Communion table *la16-.* **2** the committee formed in 1637 from representative commissioners appointed by presbyteries to defend the Presbyterian system against Charles I and which framed the National Covenant *17, 18- historical.* [ME *table,* AN, OFr *table*]
table[1.2] /ˈtebəl/ *v ptp* **tabled,** †**tabulit,** †**tabulat 1** *law* to lodge a summons before a court as a preliminary to its being called *16-.* **2** to submit for discussion *la17-.* **3** to tabulate, list *la15-17.* **4** to sit at a table to drink *17.* †**tabillar, tabular** *law* the officer of the court responsible for tabling cases *16-e17.* [see the noun]
tablet, taiblet /ˈtablət, ˈteblət/ *n* **1** a medicinal pill *la16-.* **2** a kind of sweet made from butter, sugar and milk (of the consistency of a stiff crumbly fudge) *la17-.* **3** an ornament or piece of jewellery *16-17.* [ME *tablet,* OFr *tablet* a writing tablet]
†**tabour**[1.1]**, tabor, taburne, tabroun, tawberne, talberone** *n* **1** a small drum, sometimes used to attract public attention *15-17.* **2** a drummer *16-e17.* **tabourer** a drummer *14-e17.* [ME *tabour, taborne,* OFr *tabour, taborne*]
tabour[1.2]**, toober, tober** /ˈtabər, ˈtubər/ *v* to beat, thrash *19- C Bor.* [see the noun]
tabular, tabulat, tabulit *see* TABLE[1.2]
taburne *see* TABOUR[1.1]
tac /tak/ *n* tact, good sense *la19, 20- Sh NE.* [variant of Eng *tact*]
†**tach** *v* **1** to seize or arrest *la15-e17.* **2** to attach *e16.* [aphetic form of ATTACH]
tach *see* TASH[1], TYACH
tacht, †**taught,** †**taght** /taxt/ *adj* tightly drawn, under tension *19, 20- Sh Ork N.* **tachten** to tighten *20- Sh.* [ME *tought*]
tacit[1.1] /ˈtasɪt/ *adj* not openly expressed, implicit *17-.* **tacit relocation** *law* the assumed continuation of a lease or contract of employment on unchanged terms if no action is taken at the date of expiry *la17-.* [Lat *tacitus,* ptp of *tacēre* be silent]
†**tacit**[1.2] /ˈtasɪt/ *adv* tacitly, by implication *la16-e17.* [see the adj]
taciturnity /tasɪˈtʌrnɪti/ *n* **1** silence, disinclination to speak *16-.* **2** *law* the silence of a creditor in regard to a debt or obligation, which can be pleaded in extinction of it, as implying that the claim has been satisfied or abandoned *16-.* [MFr *taciturnité,* Lat *taciturnitās*]
tack[1.1] /tak/ *n* **1** a small nail *16-.* **2** a thread, a stitch *17-.* **3** a small amount of clothing *20- Uls.* [ME *tak,* OFr *taque* a clasp]
tack[1.2] /tak/ *v* **1** to fasten, nail; to stitch loosely *16-.* **2** to join or unite *19- T WC.* [ME *takken,* from the noun]
tack[2], †**tak,** †**take** /tak/ *n* **1** *law* a lease granting tenancy of land or property; the period of tenure of a lease *la14-.* **2** land that has been leased; a farm or farmland *15-.* **3** the leasehold tenure of mining or fishing rights, or of tax or toll collecting rights *la15-.* **4** an agreement, a bargain *la18-.* **5** a specific period of time *18- Ork NE T EC Uls.* **tackie** a farm or piece of land held on lease *la19- N.* †**takar** a person who grants a tack *15-e17.* **tack duty** rent paid for property leased or for the right to collect taxes *17-19, 20- Ork NE SW.* †**tak fisch** rent paid in fish *la16-17.* **tacksman,** †**takkisman,** †**taxman 1** a person who holds a tack, a tenant or lessee; the holder of a coastal salmon-fishing lease *la15-19, 20- NE T.* **2** a chief tenant, frequently a relative of the landowner, who leased land directly from him and sublet it to lesser tenants *la16-19, 20- historical.* †**tackswoman, takiswoman** a female tenant or lessee *la16-18.* †**in tack, in tak** on lease *la15-18.* †**in tack and assedation** on leasehold terms *la15-18.* †**letter of tak** the document setting out the

tack *see* TAK[1.2]

tacket, tackit, †takkat /'takət/ *n* a small nail; a hobnail used to stud the soles of shoes or boots *la15-.* **tacketed** studded with tackets *la19-.* **tackety, tackity** studded with tackets *19-.* **tackety boots, tacketty buits** hobnailed boots *la19-.* **tackety jock** a shoemaker's last *la19- C.* [TACK[1.1] + *-et* diminutive suffix]

tackle[1.1], taickle, teckle, †takill, †taikill /'takəl, 'tekəl, 'tɛkəl/ *n* **1** a ship's rigging *la14-.* **2** rope; a rope used as part of a pulley system *16-.* **3** equipment, gear *18-.* **4** an arrow *la14-18.* [MLG *takel*]

tackle[1.2] /'takəl/ *v* **1** to adjust the rigging of a ship *16-.* **2** to take in hand, to resolve *19-.* **†tackling, †taikling** a ship's rigging *la15-17.* **tackle to** to set to work vigorously on *la19-.* [see the noun]

taddie /'tade, 'tadi/ *n* a tadpole *20- C.* [shortened form of Eng *tadpole* + -IE[1]]

taddy /'tade, 'tadi/ *n* a kind of snuff *la19-e20, la20- historical*. [from the manufacturer's name *Taddy and Co.*]

tadge *see* TARGE[1.2]

tadger, tadge /'tadʒər, tadʒ/ *n* a slang word for the penis *20-.* [Eng and slang]

tadgewangle /'tadʒwaŋgəl/ *n* a mix-up, confusion; a commotion *20- NE.* [unknown]

tae[1], toe, †ta, †tay /te, to/ *n* **1** a digit on a foot, a toe *la14-.* **2** the prong of a fork, rake or salmon spear *la18-.* **3** *golf* the point or fore-part of a club *la19-.* **4** one of the thongs at the end of a tawse *19, 20- Sh Ork N EC.* **5** the claw of a crab or lobster *16-17.* **tae bit** the iron toe-plate on the front of the sole of a boot *la19-.* **tae breadth** the shortest possible distance *la19, 20- Sh.* **tae length, tae's length** a very short distance *la19-.* [OE *tā*]

tae[2], †ta /te/ *adj* one (of two) *la14-.* **†her tae fit** one of her feet *16-18.* **†on the ta part** *law* **1** of one of two parties to an agreement *la14-e17.* **2** one of the boundaries of a property *15-e16.* [variant of TANE; compare AE]

tae[3.1], to, *NE* **tee, †too** /te, tu; *NE* ti/ *adv* **1** towards, as far as *14-.* **2** also, besides, as well: ◇*Ah kent his brither tae la14-.* **be tee** to be up to schedule *20- NE.* **tae and fra** back and forth *la14-.* **weel tee** up to time, well in hand *20- NE.* [see the prep]

tae[3.2], to, tu, te, ti, *NE* **tee, †ta** /te, tu, tə, tɪ; *NE* ti/ *prep* **1** in the direction of: ◇*drivin fae Ayr tae Kilmarnock la14-.* **2** as far as: ◇*the yaird wis paved tae the west wa o the hoose la14-.* **3** with regard to, about: ◇*hae ye heard ony word tae yer sister la14-.* **4** onto: ◇*he held tae the ladder wi baith hauns la14-.* **5** over to, into the possession of: ◇*Ah gied it tae the meenister la14-.* **6** until: ◇*gie me tae the morn la14-.* **7** for: ◇*coal tae the fire la14-.* **8** on behalf of: ◇*Ah'm buyin tabacca tae ma faither la14-.* **9** with, on: ◇*dae ye want ony saut tae yer tatties? la14-.* **10** as: ◇*he had a meenister tae his faither la14-.* **11** in relation to, compared with: ◇*ma hoose is toty tae yours la14-.* **12** by: ◇*she had a bairn tae him 16-.* **13** within: ◇*it wisnae his daein, tae ma knowledge 17-.* **14** at, towards: ◇*look tae that sunset 16-19, 20- Sh N SW.* **15** against, to the detriment of: ◇*there were rumours tae his character 17-19.* Compare TILL[2.2]. **†to-hungin** *of a seal* attached or appended to a document *la15-16.* **†to put** = *to-hungin la14-e15.* **†to name** for or as a name; named: ◇*he hath to name Thomas* ◇*the king to name Alexander la14-17.* **tae trade, to trade** by trade: ◇*he's a jyner tae trade 18-.* [OE *tō*]

tae[3.3] /te/ *conj* till, until: ◇*the shop will be closed tae the Spring comes* ◇*the dyke rins doon tae it meets the sea la14-.* **†to that** while *la14-15.* [see the prep]

tae *see* DEY[2], TEA

tae- *see* TO-[3]

tae bread /'te brɛd/ *n* an extra loaf given free by a baker as a discount after the purchase of a certain amount *la19, 20- Sh NE C Bor.* [TAE[3.1] + *bread* (BREID)]

tae come, †tocum /'te kʌm/ *n* **1** an increment; a profit on resale *20- EC.* **2** an extra loaf given by a baker as a discount *20- EC.* **3** an approach, an entrance *e16.* [TAE[3.1], TO-[3] + COME[1.1]]

taed *see* TAID

tae fa, tu-fa, to fall /'te fa, 'tufa, 'tu fɔl/ *n* **1** a lean-to porch or outhouse *15-.* **2** an addition, accretion; an extra charge or burden *19, 20- NE.* **†tae fa o the day** evening, dusk *18-e19.* **†tae fa o the night** = *tae fa o the day.* [TAE[3.1], TO-[3] + FA[1.1]]

taegither *see* THEGITHER

taen *see* TAK[1.2]

taet *see* TAIT[1.1]

†taffell *n* a table *la16.* [Du *tafel*]

taffie, toaffee, toffee /'tafi, 'tofi, 'tɔfi/ *n* a sweet made with boiled sugar, toffee *19-.* **toffee aipple** an apple coated in toffee and mounted on a stick *la19-.* **taffie join** a social gathering of young people who club together to buy treacle to make toffee *la19, 20- Bor.* [unknown; Eng *toffee* is a later variant]

taffle, taiffle, tuffle /'tafəl, 'tefəl, 'tʌfəl/ *v* to handle roughly; to ruffle or rumple, disarrange *19, 20- T SW Bor.* [probably onomatopoeic]

taft, †toft /taft/ *n* **1** a homestead (and the attached land); the site of a house and buildings *13-.* **2** an enclosed vegetable plot *la18- N.* **†tafting, tofting** (the tenancy of) a homestead with attached land *16-19.* **†toftstead, toftsteid** a homestead *16-19.* **toft and croft** an entire holding of buildings and land *15-19, 20- historical.* [late OE *toft* from ON *topt*]

taft *see* THAFT

tag[1.1], †taig /tag/ *n* **1** a small attached piece; a flap or loop; a pendant or tassel *16-.* **2** a long thin strip or slice of flesh or tissue *18-19, 20- Sh EC.* **3** the strap used for corporal punishment in schools, the tawse *19-20, 21- historical.* **4** a thin, worn-out horse *20- NE.* **5** a weaving fault in cloth, producing a hole where there should be pattern *la20- C.* **6** a strip of parchment to which a seal is appended *la16-19.* **7** a leather buckle-strap *16-18.* **8** a torn piece of a garment *15-e16.* **†taggie, tagie** *of a cow* having a white-tipped tail *16-19.* **taggin, tagging 1** the fitting of a leather strap *16-.* **2** the material used to make a tag *17.* **†taggit** *of a cow* having a white-tipped tail *16-17.* **tagsy** untidy, unkempt *la20- Ork.* **tag hole** a weaving fault in cloth *la20- C.* **be in the tag** to be oppressed with work *20- NE.* [unknown; compare MLG *tagge* a twig, spike and Norw *tagg* a point, prong]

tag[1.2] /tag/ *v* to beat with a leather strap *la19-20, 21- historical.* [see the noun]

tagedder, tagidder *see* THEGITHER

taghairm /'tagərəm/ *n* folklore a form of (magical) divination said to have been practised in the Highlands *la18-19, 20- historical.* [Gael *toghairm* a summons, invocation]

taght *see* TACHT

taiblet *see* TABLET

taich *see* TAUCH

taickle *see* TACKLE[1.1]

taid, taed, toad, †tead /ted, tod/ *n* **1** a froglike amphibian, a toad *15-.* **2** term of endearment for a child or young woman *la18- NE T Bor.* **3** a sheep-tick *19- WC SW Bor.* [OE *tāde*]

taiffle *see* TAFFLE

taig /teg/ *n derogatory* a nickname for a Roman Catholic *20- C Uls*. [EModE nickname for an Irishman, IrGael personal name *Tadhg, Teague*]

taig *see* TAG[1.1]

taigle[1.1] /ˈtegəl/ *n* a tangle, a muddle *20- NE EC SW Bor*. [see the verb]

taigle[1.2], **†teagle** /ˈtegəl/ *v* **1** to tangle or entangle; to confuse or muddle *17-*. **2** to impede or hinder; to harass *17-19, 20- C*. **3** to confound, bamboozle, perplex *la19, 20- EC SW Bor*. **4** to linger or delay; to dawdle or loiter *la18-19, 20- C SW Bor*. **5** to drag the feet; to walk slowly and heavily *la19, 20- EC*. **taigled, taiglit 1** tangled, confused *la19-*. **2** tired, weary, harassed *19- C SW Bor*. **†taiglement** a delay; a cause of delay *e19*. **taiglesome 1** time-consuming, causing delay *19, 20- C SW*. **2** tiring, tedious *20- EC Bor*. **taigle the cleek 1** *mining* to hinder the working of a pit *la19, 20- EC*. **2** to impede progress, cause a delay *la20- C*. **†taigle wi** to have a dalliance with *19*. **†taigle after** to follow a woman around *19*. [compare Swed *taggla* to disorder and AN *entagler* to entangle]

taik[1.1] /tek/ *n* **1** a rope, wire, or chain used to secure a ship's sails *18-19, 20- Sh N EC*. **2** a stroll, a saunter *20- Sh N NE*. **3** mood, humour, disposition *20- Sh NE*. [shortened form of *taickle* (TACKLE[1.1])]

taik[1.2] /tek/ *v* **1** to sail obliquely against the wind *18-19, 20- N NE T EC*. **2** to stroll, saunter; to move unobtrusively *20- N NE T*. [see the noun]

taik *see* TAK[1.2]

taiken[1.1], **token**, **†takin** /ˈtekən, ˈtokən/ *n pl also* **†taknis 1** a sign or symbol; a vestige; a small gift or keepsake *la14-*. **2** *Presbyterian Church* a small piece of stamped metal used to gain entry to the Communion service (now replaced by a printed card) *la16-20, 21- historical*. **3** a metal badge worn by beggars giving permission to beg in a burgh or parish *15-e18*. **4** *law* a piece of written evidence or proof *la15-e17*. **5** a symbol or badge of identification of a craft *15-17*. **6** a shop sign *15-16*. **†takynar** a portent *e16*. **†in takin of** *law* as a sign or witness of *la14-17*. **†in takin that** = *in takin of*. **†to the taikin** in proof *la15-e17*. [OE *tācen*]

taiken[1.2], **token** /ˈtekən, ˈtokən/ *v* **1** to indicate, signify *la15-19, 20- NE*. **2** to mark with a sign *la14-e16*. [OE *tācnian*]

taikill *see* TACKLE[1.1]

tail[1.1], **†tale**, **†teill** /tel/ *n* **1** the hinder part of anything *13-*. **2** the tail of an animal or bird *la14-*. **3** an additional piece of land attached to a larger piece; the further or lower end of a holding of land *15-*. **4** the loose lower part of a garment *la15-*. **5** a person's buttocks *la15-*. **6** a retinue or following; the entourage of a Highland chief *la16-19, 20- literary*. **7** the end of a sandbank *18-19, 20- WC*. **8** the end or edge of water in a mine *la19, 20- C*. **9** a fish *20- Sh N*. **10** a promiscuous woman; a prostitute *20- C*. **11** a man's back trouser-pocket *la20- C*. **12** the horizontal section of the cords in the harness of a draw-loom *e19*. **13** the female sexual organs *la15-18*. **14** a strip of parchment to which a seal is appended *15-16*. **tailer, tailert** a hand turnip-cutter *20- Ork N*. **tails onion** leaves *la19, 20- EC Bor*. **tail dam** the tail-race of a mill *17-19, 20- EC*. **†tail-ill** one of several diseases of the tail in cattle *19*. **tail lead** the tail-race of a mill *la18-*. **tail-net** the herring-net first to be shot and therefore the farthest from the boat *la19, 20- Sh N*. **†tail rig** (a narrow) strip of land lying at the furthest extremity of a piece of land *16-18*. **tailsman** the sawmill worker who takes and sorts the timber from the saw *20-*. **tail toddle 1** sexual intercourse *18-*. **2** the name of a Scottish country dance tune *la19-*. **the tail of level** *mining* the lower or discharging end of a drainage shaft *la19, 20- C*. **Tail o the Bank** a stretch of the River Clyde just below Greenock, at the end of a long sandbank *19-*. [OE *tægel*]

tail[1.2] /tel/ *v* to trail, straggle after; to follow on behind *19-*. **†tailing rig, tailling rigg** (a narrow) strip of land lying at the furthest extremity of a piece of land *17-e19*. [see the noun]

tail *see* TALE

Tailie Day /ˈtele de/ *n* the second day of April, when children fixed paper tails with various messages to the backs of unsuspecting victims *20, 21- historical*. [TAIL[1.1] + -IE[1] + DAY]

taillie *see* TAILYIE[1.1]

tailor, teylor, tylor, *Sh* **teelyir,†taylour**, **†tailyour**, **†telʒour** /ˈtelər, ˈtʌɪlər; *Sh* ˈtiljər/ *n* a person who makes or alters clothes *13-*. **tailor's gartens** ribbon-grass *la19-*. [AN *taillour*]

tailyie[1.1], **tailzie, taillie**, **†tailʒe**, **†tailye**, **†talʒe** /ˈtelji, ˈteli/ *n* **1** a cut or slice of meat, especially pork, for boiling or roasting *la15-19, 20- Bor*. **2** *law* an entail, the settlement of heritable property on a specified line of heirs *la14-18*. **3** an account or reckoning *la15-e17*. **4** a length of cloth *17*. **5** a tax *la14-16*. **6** an arrangement or agreement *e15*. [OFr *tailliee* a cut, *taille* a cutting, division]

†tailyie[1.2], **tailzie, tailʒe** *v* **1** *law* to determine or prescribe the succession to an estate by means of an entail *la14-e19*. **2** to cut, shape or fashion *15-e17*. **3** to keep an account or tally of materials *la15-16*. **4** to decide, settle *la14-e15*. **tailʒeit** *of coins* specified as being a particular kind *16-17*. [OFr *taillier* to cut]

tailyour *see* TAILOR

tailʒe *see* TAILYIE[1.1], TAILYIE[1.2]

†tailʒeve[1.1] *n* a rocking motion; a lurch *la16*. **tak a tailʒeve** *of a boat* to make a lurch *la16*. [unknown]

†tailʒeve[1.2] *v of a boat* to rock, lurch *e16*. [unknown]

tailzie *see* TAILYIE[1.1], TAILYIE[1.2]

taim *see* TUIM[1.2]

taimet *see* TAMET

†tainge *n* a pair of tongs *la16-17*. [OE *tang*]

†tainghle *v* to harass; to weary with hard work *e19*. [unknown; perhaps a conflation of TINCHEL and TAIGLE[1.2]]

taings *see* TANGS[1.1]

taint[1.1], **†tint** /tent/ *n* **1** a stain or blemish; a slur, a stigma *la16-*. **2** a sign or vestige; a report or trace *la18-19, 20- literary*. **3** *law* proof leading to a conviction *la14-19*. **4** a verdict of perjury by a jury of 24 men; the jury itself *15-17*. [OFr *taint* a colour, tinge, fallen together with an aphetic form of OFr *atteinte* a conviction for misconduct]

taint[1.2], **†taynt**, **†tent** /tent/ *v* **1** to sully or corrupt; to spoil or tarnish *17-*. **2** *law* to convict a person *la14-16*. **3** *law* to catch a criminal *15-16*. **4** *law* to prove a charge *15-e16*. [AN *teinter* to colour, tinge, fallen together with an aphetic form of Older Scots *attaint* to accuse, convict, from OFr *ataint* convicted]

taip *see* TAPE[1.1]

tair *see* TEAR[2.2]

taird *see* TURD

tairge *see* TARGE[1.2]

tairget *see* TARGET[1], TARGET[2]

tairgin *see* TARGE[1.2]

tairie *see* TARRIE[2], TARY[1.1]

tairm *see* TERM

†tairrie[1.1], **tary** *n* **1** delay, procrastination *la14-16*. **2** a stay, a sojourn *la14-16*. **3** a hindrance *la15-e16*. [unknown]

tairrie[1.2], **tarry** /ˈtere, ˈtari/ *v* **1** to linger, stay *la14-*. **2** to delay, hinder *la14-e17*. **†tarisum** slow, lingering; wearisome *e16*. **†tary upon** to wait for *16-e17*. [unknown]

tairt, tert /tert, tɛrt/ *n* **1** a sweet or savoury dish made with baked pastry, a tart *la16-*. **2** a (promiscuous) girl or woman *la19-*. **3** a girlfriend *la19- NE EC*. [MFr *tarte*]

tairtan *see* TARTAN[1.1]

taisch, taish /teʃ, tʌɪʃ/ *n* a vision seen in second sight, especially an apparition of a person about to die *la18- literary*. [Gael *taibhse* an apparition, ghost]

taisel *see* TOSSEL

taisle[1.1] /'tezəl/ *n* an instance of vexing or teasing; an instance of bamboozling with questions *19, 20- SW*. [see the verb]

taisle[1.2], **teasle** /'tezəl, 'tizəl/ *v* **1** to entangle, mix up; to put or get into disorder *la19, 20- C SW Bor Uls*. **2** to tease, irritate, vex *la17-19, 20- SW*. [frequentative form of *taise* (TEASE), with influence from TAISLE [2.2]]

taisle[2.1], **†tassel, †tassil, teazle** /'tezəl, 'tizəl/ *n* **1** a plant of the genus *Dipsacus*; a head of the fuller's teasel *Dipsacus fullonum 15-17*. **2** an instance of buffeting or knocking about; a tussle *18-19, 20- SW*. [OE *tǣsel*, with some senses from the verb]

taisle[2.2], **†tassel, teazle** /'tezəl, 'tizəl/ *v* **1** to raise the nap on cloth with teasels *18* **2** to toss or throw about; to stir up, turn over (hay) *19, 20- NE T EC SW*. [from the noun, perhaps with influence from TAISLE [1.2]]

taist *see* TASTE[1.1], TASTE[1.2], TEST[1.1]

taistrel /'testrəl/ *n* a vagabond; a scruffy person *la17-19, 20- Bor*. [unknown; compare Gael *taistealach* a traveller, a wanderer]

tait[1.1], **tate, taet, tet**, *NE* **tit, †teat** /tet, tɛt; *NE* tɪt/ *n* **1** a tuft, lock or strand of hair or wool (or other fibrous material) *la15-*. **2** a small amount, a bit, a little *18-*. **3** a tuft of grass, a bundle of hay or straw *la18-* **a tait** somewhat *18-*. **a wee tait** a bit, a little: ◊*a wee tate tipsy 18-*. [unknown; compare Icel *tæta* a shred]

tait[1.2] /tet/ *v* to pull or pluck; to tease out (fibres) *la19, 20- Sh*. **taettet** fine-spun *20- Sh*. [unknown; compare Icel *tæta* to tear to shreds and TIT[1.2]]

†tait[2.1] *v* to cavort with; to make love to *la15-16*. **tait and tig** to cavort *la15-16*. [see the adj]

†tait[2.2], **tate** *adj* active, lively *14-e16*. [ON *teitr* glad, cheerful]

taitht *see* TATHE[1.1]

taiver, †taver /'tevər/ *v* **1** to annoy, irritate; to bewilder with talk or questioning *la19, 20- T EC Uls*. **2** to wander, stray; to dally, waste time *la16-19, 20- T C*. **3** to wander in mind or speech, to rave *19, 20- T Uls*. **taivert** exhausted; bewildered, confused *16-*. [frequentative form of ME *taven* to throw oneself about; compare Norw *tava* to toil vainly]

taivers[1], *Ork* **taavers** /'tevərz; *Ork* 'tɑvərz/ *npl* idle, foolish talk *la19- C*. [from the verb TAIVER]

taivers[2], *Ork* **taavers** /'tevərz; *Ork* 'tɑvərz/ *npl* rags, tatters, shreds *la18- Sh Ork EC*. **boiled to taivers** *of food* overcooked *19-*. [compare Swed dial *tavra* fibres]

tak[1.1] /tak/ *n* **1** a catch or haul of fish *la16-*. **2** goods or money taken or received, a haul *la16-*. **3** a state of excitement, agitation or rage: ◊*she wis in an affae tak 19-*. **4** a state of growth; the sprouting of a crop *la20-*. [see the verb]

tak[1.2], **take, ta, †taik, †tack** /tak, tek, ta/ *v pt* **tuik, teuk, tuke, taen**, *NE* **tyeuk** *ptp* **tane, taen, taken, tooken**, *Sh N NE* **teen, †tein, †tone** **1** to acquire, seize; to catch or grasp *la14-*. **2** to choose: ◊*neivie, neivie nick nack; which han will ye tak? la14-*. **3** to accept as husband or wife, to marry *la14-*. **4** to receive, accept: ◊*will ye tak a drink? la14-*. **5** to experience, undergo: ◊*she's tane a bad fa la14-*. **6** to understand *la14-*. **7** to undertake, carry out a task *la14-*. **8** to follow a route; to embark on a journey: ◊*you'll tak the high road la14-*. **9** *law* to acquire ownership or jurisdiction; to collect payment, duty or tax *la14-*. **10** *law* to lease property *la14-*. **11** to purchase goods *la15-*. **12** to cost; to use up resources or time: ◊*it tuik fower yairds o claith tae mak thae curtains la15-*. **13** to make for; to resort to something: ◊*the fiddle wad gar us tak the flair 16-*. **14** *of water or a bog* to have a certain depth (in relation to the height of a person) ◊*that bog wad tak a man tae the oxters or abune the heid la18-*. **15** to catch fire: ◊*the wid wis weit it widnae tak 20-*. **16** to be caught on or tripped by; to catch one's foot on something: ◊*Ah tuik ma fit oan the cairpet 18- NE T C*. **17** to check or restrain oneself: ◊*I was juist on the pynt o sayin't, fan I min't fa he wis, and I tuik mysel la18-19, 20- NE EC*. **18** to appropriate a crop for the grazing of livestock *la19- NE T*. **19** to require the utmost strength and effort from: ◊*it'll tak ye to jump thon burn 19, 20- EC*. **20** to consume food or drink: ◊*sit ye doon an tak la19- N*. **21** to shine brightly: ◊*'e stars are aa takin 20- N*. **22** to administer an oath; to require or accept a promise in a formal matter *17-e19*. **23** *law* to follow the appropriate steps in a legal action ◊*tak instruments la15-18*. **24** to agree to do something: ◊*he tuke to preive it la15-16*. **25** to select as a guide or mediator *15-16*.

taen, taken, takken 1 surprised, embarrassed, disconcerted *19, 20- C*. **2** *folklore* bewitched *19, 20- N*. **taker, †takar, †takkar 1** a person who takes or seizes; a thief *14-*. **2** a person who takes a prisoner for ransom *15-e17*. **takin** a way of thinking *la19- NE SW*. **takkie** the game of tig; the pursuer in the game *la19- NE T*. **†taen-awa** *folklore* a fairy changeling *e19*. **taen-like** surprised, embarrassed, disconcerted *19- literary*. **Tak' a'** a school attendance officer *20- NE*. **†taker-up 1** a person who collected rents *16-e17*. **2** a precentor *la16-e17*. **†I tak on hand** I swear, I dare say *la14-16*. **no a tak-it** nothing at all: ◊*What's du been doin da day? No a tak-it 20- Sh*. **on the tak** *of fish* rising readily to the bait *20-*. **tak a hairst** to engage oneself as a harvest labourer *la19- NE T SW*. **tak an ug at** to take a dislike to *la19- NE T*. **tak a tig, tak the tig** to take a sudden whim or notion; to get a fit of the sulks *19- NE T*. **tak a tune tae yersel** to play a tune by yourself *19-*. **†tak aboot, tak about 1** to take care of, manage *la18- Sh Ork NE*. **2** to prepare a body for burial *20- Ork N NE*. **3** to secure a crop or harvest successfully *la18- Sh NE*. **4** to wrap oneself up warmly *la19- Sh*. **tak aff 1** to remove *la14-*. **2** to drink up *la18-*. **3** to take after, resemble *la19-*. **4** to lease land *la19- Sh NE*. **5** to turn off or shut down *la19- Sh*. **6** to annoy *20- Sh Ork*. **7** *of bad weather* to cease, abate *20- Sh*. **8** to take measurements for new clothes *18-e19*. **9** *law* to remove a penalty *16-17*. **†tak again** to take back; to withdraw (a promise) *18*. **tak at** to proceed; to exert oneself *la18-19, 20- Sh*. **tak awa 1** to remove; to seize; to kill *15-*. **2** *folklore* to spirit away a human child and substitute a fairy child *la16-19, 20- Uls*. **3** to consume food or drink; to eat heartily or gulp down liquor *19, 20- Sh Ork*. **tak back** to go back, return *19, 20- Sh EC*. **tak bound** to require someone to make an oath; to promise or undertake in a formal matter *18-e19*. **tak doon, tak doun 1** to demolish, dismantle *16-*. **2** to impair in health or strength, to weaken; to cause to lose weight *19-*. **3** to reduce the potency of spirits, to dilute *la20-*. **4** to unpick a garment to make another *la18- Sh EC SW*. **5** to reduce in circumstances, impoverish or bankrupt *la19- Ork N*. **6** to launch a boat *la19, 20- Sh*. **tak end** to come to an end; to be settled *la14-19, 20- Sh*. **†tak handis fra the recognition** *law* to withdraw from the legal process *la15-e16*. **tak ill** to become ill *19-*. **tak in 1** *of a boat* to let in water, to leak *la16-*. **2** to house livestock, bring animals under cover *la19-*. **3** to dismantle a cornstack for threshing *la19-*. **4** to arrest, take into custody *20-*. **5** to bring in, welcome a new day or year *20- N NE H&I*. **6** to cover a distance: ◊*ye can fairly tak in the road nooadays wi a car* *la18- NE.* **7** to catch up with; to overtake *19- NE.* **tak in aboot** to take in hand, discipline a person: ◊*I'll hae tae tak you in about 19, 20- Sh NE.* **tak in fur** to stand up for *la19- Sh.* **tak in hand** to undertake a task *16-.* †**tak land** to strike or reach land *la14-e16.* **tak nae weel** to become ill *19-.* **tak o** to take after, resemble *19-, 20- Ork N.* **tak o it** to take the consequences *la19- NE.* **tak on 1** to take responsibility for; to undertake *15-.* **2** to buy on credit *la18-.* **3** to get excited or emotional, be worked up; to mope or sulk *19-.* **4** to affect physically: ◊*the heat wis fair takkin on me la19-.* **5** to joke with or tease a person *la19-.* **6** to start, begin *19, 20- N.* **7** to take the consequences, make the best of it *la19, 20- Sh.* **8** to embrace a religion *la16-17.* **9** to enlist as a soldier *17.* **10** to put on clothes *16.* **taen on wi** favourably impressed with, attracted by *20-.*†**tak one to one's fute** to go on foot, flee *16-17.* **tak on hand, take upon hand** to undertake a task, do something *la14-.* **tak oot, tak out 1** to produce something; to remove something; to take something outside *la18-.* **2** to enrol in a university class: ◊*this year I'm taking out Latin 20-.* **3** to drink up, drain a glass *la18-19, 20- Sh NE.* **tak tae, tak till 1** to acknowledge to oneself the truth of an accusation; to feel guilt or remorse, be sensitive about: ◊*he took tae him that he had never lookit near his folk 19-.* **2** to exert oneself *la19- Sh.* **3** to criticize adversely, speak ill of; to mock *la20- Sh.* **tak the turn oot o** to trick, fool *20- Sh Ork T.* **tak up 1** to raise; to lift; to pick or gather up *la14-.* **2** to begin a song or dance *16-.* **3** *Presbyterian Church* to lead the singing of psalms in church, to act as precentor *la16-.* **4** to understand, get the meaning of *la16-.* **5** *of a school or college* to reopen after a holiday *18-.* **6** to take a collection at a meeting *20-.* **7** to run into debt; to live on credit *la19, 20- Ork NE EC.* **8** to raise one's foot to kick *la18- NE T.* **9** to improve oneself in conduct or character; to pull oneself together *la19- T Bor.* **10** to strike against: ◊*her heid teuk up on a steen la19- Sh Ork.* **11** *of wind* to rise, begin to blow *20- Sh SW.* **12** to draw up an inventory or list *17.* **13** to teach a class; to establish a school *17.* **14** to collect payment or rent *15-17.* **15** to remove a restriction *la15-17.* **16** to take possession of property *15-e17.* **taen up aboot** charmed by, favourably impressed by; concerned about *la19-.* †**tak up dittay** *law* to pursue a legal process to obtain information and proof with a view to prosecution *la15-19.* **tak up house** to set up house; to become a householder *17-.* **tak up wi 1** to form an association with *19-.* **2** to be charmed by *19-.* **tak wi 1** to take to; to be pleased by *la14-.* **2** to put up with; to accept or acquiesce *la14-.* **3** to acknowledge; *Presbyterian Church* to admit to a fault (such as paternity outside marriage) *la16-19, 20- NE T.* **4** to welcome *20- Sh.* **5** to give or pay attention to *la15-e19.*†**tak to witnes** *law* to cite as a witness or evidence *15-e17.* †**tak witnes of 1** to cite as a witness or evidence *15-e17.* **2** to take note of *la15-16.* †**tak yer bed** to take to your bed *16-19.* **tak yer breath** to affect strongly, cause someone to gasp: ◊*her sheer effrontery fair tuik ma breath la19-.* **take yer death** to die *20- NE T.* **tak yer hand aff someone's face** to slap someone's face *20-.* **tak yer heid** to go to your head, make you giddy *la19, 20- T.* **tak yer tap in yer lap** to pack up and go; to leave in a hurry (from the practice of taking flax to spin in a neighbour's house and wrapping it in one's apron on departure) *19-.* **tak yer wind** = *tak yer breath.* [OE *tacan* from ON *taka*]

tak *see* TACK[2]
take *see* TACK[2], TAK[1.2]
taken *see* TAK[1.2]
takill *see* TACKLE[1.1]
takin *see* TAIKEN[1.1]
takkat *see* TACKET

takkie *see* TAK[1.2]
talberone *see* TABOUR[1.1]
talch *see* TAUCH
tald *see* TELL[1.2]
tale, †**tail**, †**teal** /tel/ *n* **1** an account, a (true or fictional) story *la14-.* **2** a lie; a rumour, gossip *la14-.* **tale pyet 1** a telltale *19- T EC SW Bor.* **2** a fisherman's taboo word for a compass *la19- Sh.* **by my tale** according to me, as I would have others believe *19- Sh Ork SW.* **true tale** an expression of disbelief *20- Sh.* **with my tale** = *by my tale.* [OE *talu*]
tale *see* TAIL[1.1]
talesman /'telzmən/ *n* **1** a storyteller; the source for a story or statement *la15-19, 20- Sh.* **2** a spokesman *la15.* **gie baith tale and talesman** to tell the complete truth *20- Sh.* [pl of TALE + MAN]
talian iron *see* TALLIE
talk[1.1], tauk, taak /tɔk, tak/ *n* **1** a verbal exchange, conversation *la15-.* **2** speech, an utterance *16-.* **3** an informal lecture *la19-.* **4** gossip *20-.* **the talk of the steamie** the subject of gossip *la20-.* [see the verb]
talk[1.2], tauk, taak, †**tawk** /tɔk, tak/ *v* to speak, converse *15-.* [ME *talken*]
Tallie, Tally /'tali, 'tale/ *n* **1** an Italian *19-.* **2** an Italian-run shop selling ice cream or fish and chips *20-.* **Tallie's blood** *humorous* raspberry-flavoured syrup poured over ice cream *20-.* **tally iron, talian iron** an Italian or goffering iron *20-.* [reduced form of Eng *Italian* + -IE[1]]
†**talloun, tallon** *v* to smear with tallow or grease *la15-e16.* [from the noun *talloun* (TAUCH)]
talloun, tallow, tally *see* TAUCH
Tally *see* TALLIE
tally lamp /'tale lamp/ *n* an oil or tallow lamp, especially a miner's lamp *20- C.* [*tally* (TAUCH) + LAMP[1]]
talʒe *see* TAILYIE[1.1]
tam /tam/ *n* **1** a short form of the name Thomas, sometimes used as a general term of address to a man *la18-.* **2** a bite, a morsel of food *20-.* **3** a small freshwater fish *20- SW.* **tam o' tae end 1** a kind of large haggis *19- SW.* **2** the skin in which a haggis is stuffed *20- SW.* **Tam the bam** nickname for a stupid or foolhardy person *la20-.* **tam trot** a kind of toffee *19- Bor.* [shortened form of TAMMAS]
tamar-spinnle /'tamər spɪnəl/ *n* an instrument for twisting ropes *20- Ork.* [Norw dial *taumarne* of the ropes + SPINLE]
tamatie /tə'mate, tə'mati/ *n* a tomato *20- T EC.* [variant of Eng *tomato*]
tamet, taimet /'tamət, 'temət/ *n* the line on a fishing rod; a handline with one or two hooks *20- NE T.* [unknown; perhaps altered form of TOME]
†**Tammas** *n* Thomas *la18-20.* [the personal name *Thomas*]
Tammasmass /'taməsmas/ *n* St Thomas's Day, the 21st December, traditionally regarded as a day of rest *la19- Sh.* [TAMMAS + MASS[2]]
tammie, tammy /'tami, 'tame/ *n* **1** a Tam o Shanter bonnet *19-.* **2** a loaf of coarse brown bread; food, provisions *19, 20- EC Bor.* **3** the puffin *Fratercula arctica la18-e19.* **tammie a'thing** a small general store; the owner of a shop of this kind *la19- EC Bor*; compare *Johnnie a'thing* (JOHNNY). **tammy book** a shop account-book recording goods supplied on credit *la19-20, 21-* historical. **tammy cheekie** the puffin *Fratercula arctica 19- NE T.* **tammy-nid-nod** the chrysalis of the butterfly *20- WC Bor.* **tammie norrie** the puffin *Fratercula arctica 18-.* **tammy reekie** a kind of smoke gun made from a cabbage stem, used to blow smoke through keyholes to annoy those inside *la19- Ork EC Bor.* [shortened form of TAMMAS + -IE[1]]
tammock *see* TUMMOCK

Tam o Shanter /tam o ˈʃantər/ *n* a round, flat-crowned woollen cap, frequently with a pompom *19-*. [from the eponymous hero of Burns' poem, described as wearing such a cap; compare TAMMIE]

Tamson's mear /ˈtamsənz ˈmir/ *n* the act of travelling on foot; walking *la19-*. [from the surname *Thomson* used in the sense of everyman, or any ordinary man + MEAR[1]]

tan /tan/ *v* **1** to beat up, inflict damage on *19- C Bor*. **2** to eat or drink with enthusiasm: ◇*we tanned aw the beer an pies. la20- C*. **3** to steal; to burgle *la20- C*. [Eng *tan* to thrash (orginally, to cure hide)]

tand /tɑnd/ *n* **1** a spark of fire; a piece of burning coal or peat *la19- Sh Ork*. **2** a hereditary trait; an inherited bad habit *20- Ork*. **tander** a hereditary trait *20- Ork*. [related to Norw dial *tandre* a spark]

tandle *see* TANNEL

tane, *NE* **teen** /ten; *NE* tin/ *pron* one *la14-*. **the tane** one (of two) *la14-*. [by wrong division of ME *þat an*, *þet ān* the one; compare TITHER[1,2]]

tane *see* TAK[1.2]

tang[1] /taŋ/ *n* a general name for large, coarse seaweed growing above low-water mark, especially sea-wrack *Fucus 18- Sh Ork N NE T*. **tang bow** a knob or vesicle on seaweed *la19- Sh*. **tangy-buckie** the flat periwinkle *Littorina obtusata 20- Ork*. **tang-cow** a branch of wrack *la19- Sh Ork*. †**tang kelp** kelp made by burning wrack *la19*. **tang maw**, **tangie maw** the common gull *Larus canus la19- Sh*. **tang sparrow** the shore- or rock-pipit *Anthus petrosus la19- Sh Ork*. **tang-whaup** the whimbrel *Numenius phaeopus 19- Sh Ork*. [Norw *tang*]

tang[2], *Sh Ork* **teeng**, *NE* **tyang** /taŋ; *Sh Ork* tiŋ; *NE* tjaŋ/ *n* **1** the prong of a digging-fork or pitchfork *18- Sh N NE Bor*. **2** the tongue of a Jews' harp *la19- Sh Ork N C Bor*. **3** a tongue of land projecting into the sea; frequently in place-names *la17- Sh Ork N*. **the tang o the trump** the most important person in a group *la19- Sh Ork N WC Bor*. [ME *tang*, ON *tangi* a spit of land, the tang of a knife]

Tangerines /tandʒəˈrinz/ *npl* a nickname for Dundee United Football Club *20-*. [from the team's colours]

tangie /ˈtaŋi/ *n* **1** *folklore* a sea-spirit, a type of kelpie *19- Sh Ork*. **2** the common inshore or brown seal *20- Ork N*. **tangie fish** the common inshore seal *19- Sh Ork*. [TANG[1] + -IE[3]]

tangle[1.1], *T* **tankle** /ˈtaŋəl, ˈtaŋgəl; *T* ˈtaŋkəl/ *n* **1** seaweed; the long stalk and fronds of seaweed *la17-*. **2** a tall, lanky person *la18-*. **3** an icicle *17-19, 20- NE T EC*. **sea tangle** seaweed *16-*. [Norw *tångel* the stalk of TANG[1]]

†**tangle**[1.2] *adj* long and limp, lank and loose-jointed *e19*. [see the noun]

tangs, **taings**, **tings**, **tongs**, *Sh Ork* **teengs**, *NE* **tyangs** /taŋz, teŋz, tɪŋz, tɔŋz; *Sh Ork* tiŋz; *NE* tjaŋz/ *npl* large pincers for grasping and lifting, tongs *la15-*. **a tangs**, **a taings**, †**a tangis** a pair of tongs: ◇*gie me a tangs and shovel 15-*. **find it where the Hielandman fand the tings** to take something from its rightful place and appropriate it, to steal *18-19, 20- T EC*. **taings o fire** as much burning peat or coal as can be lifted with a pair of tongs *la19- Sh*. [OE *tang* a pair of tongs]

tanist /ˈtanɪst/ *n law* the successor to a Celtic king or chief elected during his predecessor's lifetime from within certain degrees of kinship *la18- historical*. **tanistic** relating to a tanist *19- historical*. **tanistry** the system of succession through a tanist; the office of a tanist *la17- historical*. [Gael *tànaiste* the next heir]

tank *see* TUNK

tanker, †**tankert** /ˈtaŋkər/ *n* a tankard *la14-19, 20- EC Bor*. **tanker backit** round-shouldered and hollow-backed *20- C Bor*. [MDu *tanckaert*; Fr *tanquart*, pl *tanquars*]

tankle *see* TANGLE[1.1]

†**tannage** *n* **1** a tannery, a leatherworks *18-19*. **2** the process of tanning *e17*. [Fr *tannage*]

tannel, **tawnle**, †**tandle**, †**tendal** /ˈtanəl, ˈtɔnəl/ *n* a beacon; a bonfire (kindled at festivals such as Midsummer Eve or Halloween); frequently in place-names *la15- WC*. [MIrGael *teannáil*]

tanner *see* TENOR[2.1], TENOR[2.2]

tanner ba, **tanner baw** /ˈtanər ˈba, ˈtanər ˈbɔ/ *n* a cheap football *20-*. **tanner baw player** a football player whose skills have been learned on the streets *20-*. [Eng *tanner* sixpence + BA[1]]

tanners /ˈtanərz/ *npl* the small or fibrous roots of a tree or other plant *19, 20- Bor*. [perhaps altered form of Eng *tendron* a young shoot]

†**tanny**[1.1] *n* tawny-coloured cloth *la15-17*. **tannicannellie** a kind of tawny-coloured cloth *la16-e17*. [see the adj]

tanny[1.2] /ˈtane, ˈtani/ *adj* **1** tawny *la15-19, 20- literary*. **2** sombre, gloomy *la19* [MFr *tanné*]

tanshik /ˈtanʃɪk/ *n* a tooth *la19- Sh*. [diminutive form from Norw dial *tann-* a tooth]

tansy /ˈtanzi/ *n* **1** the yellow flowering plant *Tanacetum vulgare 16-*. **2** the yellow weed ragwort *Jacobaea vulgaris 18-*. [ME *tanseie*, OFr *tanesie*]

tant[1.1], **taunt** /tant, tɔnt/ *n* a jibe, an insult *16-*. [MFr *tant pour tant* tit for tat]

tant[1.2], **taunt** /tant, tɔnt/ *v* **1** to mock or scorn *16-*. **2** to upset the digestion or appetite *la19- Sh Ork*. **3** to argue, shout; *of the wind* to blow a gale *la19*. [see the noun]

tanter /ˈtantər/ *n* a rage, a fury *20- Sh*. [perhaps Norw dial *tantra* to scold, pick a quarrel]

tantersome /ˈtantərsəm/ *adj* exasperating, annoying *20- NE*. [TANTER + adj-forming suffix]

tantie *see* TWENTY[1.1]

tantrum /ˈtantrəm/ *n* an affected air, a whim *19, 20- Sh Ork T*. [Eng *tantrum* a fit of bad temper]

tanty /ˈtanti/ *adj* unstable, giddy; touchy, moody *la19- Ork*. [unknown]

tap[1.1], **top**, **toap** /tap, tɔp, top/ *n* **1** the highest, uppermost or most important place or position *la14-*. **2** a tuft of hair, wool or feathers; a forelock; a bird's crest *15-*. **3** the surface of water *18-*. **4** *of milk* the part that rises to the top, the cream *19-*. **5** the head *19, 20- Sh NE T*. **6** the tip, the end *19, 20- Sh Ork N T*. **7** a fir cone *la19, 20- NE EC Bor*. **8** *spinning* the tuft of flax or tow put on a distaff at one time *la17-19*. **9** a platform near the head of the lower mast on a ship *15-17*. **tappie** pet name for a hen with a tufted crest *la19- Sh Ork NE C*. **tap-pit**, **toppit** crested, tufted *19-*. **tappock** = *tappie*. **tops 1** the best sheep or lamb in a flock *19-*. **2** a framework fitted round a cart to facilitate the transport of large loads of hay or other goods *19, 20- T EC*. **3** the uppermost division of a seam of coal or mineral *la19, 20- C*. **tapster** a leader, the person in authority *la19- Sh*. †**top annual** *law* annual rent payable on a building as distinct from the land on which it stood *la16-17*; compare *grund annual* (GRUND[1.1]). **top coal** the uppermost division of a seam of coal *la19- C*. **tap flude**, †**top-flood** *of water* in full flood, at its highest point *18-19, 20- Sh NE Bor*. **tap pickle** the highest ear on a stalk of oats, usually considered to be of the best quality *la18-19, 20- Sh*. †**toppe-royall** a top gallant, a platform at the head of the topmast *e16*. **tapsman** the man in charge of a drove of cattle, the head drover *la18-*. **tap square** on one's dignity; *of a boat* top-heavy *la19- Sh Ork*. †**tap swarm** the first swarm of bees from a hive *la17-19*. **tap thrawn** headstrong, perverse, obstinate *19-*. **†in top with** in conflict with *17*. **never off yer tap** always criticizing, continually quarrelling *19-*. **on yer tap** attacking, severely reproving someone *la17-*. **tap o lint** *spinning* the tuft of flax or tow put on a distaff at one time *la17-e19*. **the tap o the road** the middle of the road (in reference to setting out on a journey) *20- Sh N NE*. **†tap ower tail** upside down, head-over-heels, topsy-turvy *la14-e19*. **nae mak tap, tail or main o** not to make sense of: ◊*I cannae mak tap, tail or main o whit yer sayin 18-19, 20- NE SW*. **tap o tow 1** a fiery-tempered, irritable person *19- C Uls*. **2** a head of flaxen hair *la18-19, 20- C*. **3** *spinning* the tuft of flax or tow put on a distaff at one time *la18-e19*. **the tap o the water** high water, full tide *20-* [OE *top*]

tap[1.2], **top** /tap, tɔp/ *v* **1** *golf* to hit the ball on its upper part, making it spin rather than fly forward *la19-*. **2** *farming* to cut the tip of the ear of an animal as a mark of ownership *18-19, 20- Sh SW*. **3** to oppose; to argue with *17*. [see the noun]

tap[1.3] /tap/ *adj* **1** first-rate, excellent *19-*. **2** *of sheep* of the best grade *19-*. [see the noun]

tap[2] /tap/ *n* **1** a spinning toy, especially a whipping top *la15-*. **2** *in rope-making* a conical, grooved piece of wood used to keep the strands apart and under tension *20- Sh N Bor*. [OE *top*]

tap[3.1] /tap/ *n* a spigot, a water-tap *18-*. **†taptree** *in brewing* a bung inserted in the outlet hole of a mash-tub or cask *la16-e18*. [OE *tæppa*]

tap[3.2], **†top** /tap/ *v* **1** to draw off and sell alcoholic drinks in small quantities *la15-*. **2** to retail any commodity *15-e18*. **†tapper, topper, toper 1** a seller of ale; an innkeeper *16-17*. **2** a retailer *la15-17*. **†tapstar** a (female) tapper *16-17*. [OE *tæppian* to broach (a cask)]

†tap[4], **top** *n* **1** a basket (of figs or raisins) of a precise weight or quantity *la15-e17*. **2** *in Aberdeen* a minor custom duty of six apples or onions from each barrel imported *17*. [MLG *toppe* a basket (as a measure for goods)]

tape[1.1], **†taip** /tep/ *n* a narrow strip of material for binding or measuring *17-*. [OE *tæppe*]

tape[1.2] /tep/ *v* to measure exactly (with a tape-measure); to dole out or use sparingly *18-19, 20- NE T C*. [see the noun]

taper /'tepər/ *v* to use (food) sparingly, eke out *la19- Sh T EC Bor*. [Eng *taper*, with influence from TAPE[1.2]]

tapetless *see* TABETLESS

tapie *see* TAUPIE[1.1], TAUPIE[1.2]

tapner, tapon *see* TAUPIN

tappent *see* TAPPIN

tappietoorie /tapi'turi/ *n* **1** a pile or heap; a cairn on a hilltop *19-*. **2** a turret, a structure embellished with towers; a pinnacle *19-*. **3** hair piled up on top of the head, a bun *la19-*. **4** a knot of ribbons or wool on the top of a cap, a tassel, pompom; a bonnet with these decorations *la19- NE T C Bor*. **5** something which rises to a peak; an ornament on top of something *19- Ork C*. **6** a pastry decoration around the centre hole in a pie *19- C*. [TAP[1.1] + -IE[1] + TOUR[1] + -IE[1]]

tappin /'tapɪn/ *n* **1** the top *19-*. **2** a hairstyle where the hair is combed into a crest or bun *19-*. **3** a tuft or crest of feathers on a bird's head *19, 20- C SW Uls*. **4** the peaked top of a hill; a cairn on a hilltop *20- SW Bor*. **5** a woollen toorie on the top of a bonnet *e19*. **†tappint, tappined, tappent** tufted, crested *19- SW Uls*. **tappin lift** *nautical* a halyard that is used to set the peak of a mainsail *19- Sh SW*. [verbal noun from TAP[1.2]]

tappit hen /'tapɪt 'hɛn/ *n* **1** a hen with a tuft of feathers on its head *18-*. **2** a kind of (pewter) decanter containing a standard measure, its lid knob resembling a fowl's tuft *18-*. [participial adj from TAP[1.2] + HEN[1.1]]

tapsalteerie[1.1] /tapsəl'tiri/ *n* disorder, chaos *19-*. [see the adj]

tapsalteerie[1.2], **tapsie-teerie, †tapsie-turvie** /tapsəl'tiri, tapsi'tiri/ *adj* upside down, topsy-turvy; in utter confusion or disorder *17-*. [variant of EModE *topsy-turvy*]

taptaes /'taptez/ *npl* tiptoes *19- Sh C SW*. [altered form of TIPTAES, with influence from TAP[1.1]]

tar[1.1], **taur, ter** /tar, tɔr, tɛr/ *n* a dark, thick inflammable liquid *la14-*. **tar buist** a box containing tar for smearing and marking sheep *19- N C SW Bor*. [OE *teoru, taru*]

tar[1.2] /tar/ *v* to smear or coat with tar *16-*. **tarrit** covered in or impregnated with tar *la16-*. **a tarrit wi the same stick** all sharing the same defects *19-*. [see the noun]

†tar[2] *v* to toy or meddle with *la15-16*. **tar and tig** to interfere with *la15-16*. Compare *tig and tar* (TIG[1.2]). [ME *terren* to provoke, OE **terwan, tergan*]

†tarage *n* character *la15*. [ME *tarage*]

tarbet, tarbert /'tarbət, 'tarbərt/ *n* an isthmus or neck of land between two navigable stretches of water (over which boats were pulled) *19-*. [Gael *tairbeart*]

†tardation *n* delay, tardiness *e16*. [Lat *tardātiōn-*, OFr *tardation*]

tards, tawrds, targe /tardz, tɔrdz, tardʒ/ *n* a leather strap formerly used in schools for hitting a pupil's palm, as a form of corporal punishment *16-20, 21- historical*. [unknown]

tare *see* TEAR[2.2], TEER[1]

tarf /tarf/ *adj* **1** harsh, bad-tempered *la18- Ork*. **2** bitter-tasting *20- Ork*. **3** *of weather* severe *20- Ork*. [variant of DERF]

targe[1.1] /tardʒ/ *n* a violent, scolding or domineering woman *la19-*. [unknown]

targe[1.2], **tairge,** *EC* **tadge** /tardʒ, terdʒ; *EC* tadʒ/ *v* **1** to scold severely *19- C SW Bor Uls*. **2** to bustle about, do something actively or vigorously *19- SW Bor Uls*. **3** to discipline; to beat *19*. **4** to question closely, cross-examine rigorously *la18-19*. **targer 1** a violent, quarrelsome, domineering person, especially a woman *la19-*; compare TARGE[1.1]. **2** a big, active, bustling person *19- EC SW Uls*. **tairgin** a scolding *19- EC SW Bor Uls*. [unknown]

targe *see* TARDS

target[1], **tairget** /'targət, 'tergət/ *n* **1** a shield *16-19, 20- historical*. **2** something to aim at *19-*. **3** a (circular) ornament, worn on headgear *16*. [ME *target*, MFr *targette*]

target[2], *Bor* **tairget** /'targət; *Bor* 'tergət/ *n* **1** a thin strip of flesh (from a lacerated wound) *la18-*. **2** a long narrow shred of cloth, a tatter *la18-19, 20- Sh Bor*. **3** a long thin strip of dried skate *19, 20- Sh*. **4** an oddly- or untidily-dressed person *20- NE*. [unknown; compare Swed *targa* to tear]

tarisum *see* TAIRRIE[1.2]

tarlach *see* TARLOCH

tarleddir, †tarleather /tar'lɛdər/ *n* hide taken from the belly of an animal, used as a thong or strap *la15-19, 20- Sh*. **†tarledderit** *of a hide* having had strips of skin cut from the belly *la16-18*. [Gael *tarr-leathar* belly leather, with influence from LEATHER[1.1]]

tarloch, tarlach /'tarlax/ *n* a small, weak or useless person, animal or thing *17-19, 20- NE*. [perhaps Gael *tàrlaid* a serf, a contemptible creature]

tarmachan *see* TARMIGAN

tarmegant *see* TERMIGANT

tarmigan, †tarmachan, †termigant /'tarməgən/ *n* the ptarmigan *Lagopus mutus 16-*. [Gael *tàrmachan*]

tarragat /'tarəgət/ *v* to question closely and persistently; to pester *19, 20- Sh T EC*. [aphetic form of Eng *interrogate*]

tarraneese, tarranize *see* TIRRAN

tarrie[1] /'tare, 'tari/ *n* a terrier *la18- C*. **tarry-dog** a terrier *19- C*. [shortened form of Eng *terrier*, †*tarrier* + -IE[1]]

tarrie², **tarry**, **taurie**, †**tairie** /'tare, 'tari, 'tɔre/ *adj* **1** covered in or impregnated with tar *la16-*. **2** given to stealing *19-*. **tarrie bogie** a dried whalegut sack for oil or tar *la19- Sh Ork*. **tarry breeks** a nickname for a sailor *18-*. **tarry fingered** given to stealing *19-*. †**tarry oo** wool from a sheep which has been smeared with tar *18-19*. [TAR¹·¹ + -IE²]

tarrock /'tarək/ *n* the kittiwake *Rissa tridactyla*, especially the young bird *20- EC*. [extended sense of *tarrock* (TIRRICK)]

†**tarrock** *see* TIRRICK

tarrow /'taro/ *v* **1** to delay, linger, hesitate *la14-18, 20- Sh Ork*. **2** to complain; to be perverse *19, 20- Sh*. †**tarrowing** *of a child* peevish *16-e17*. **tarrow at 1** to be fractious or fastidious about; to be overly fastidious about food *17-19, 20- Sh Ork*. **2** to be reluctant or disdainful; to spurn *17-19*. †**tarrow on** to be disdainful or hesitant *18*. [variant of *tarry* (TAIRRIE¹·²)]

tarry *see* TAIRRIE¹·², TARRIE²

tarrykrook /'tarikruk/ *n* a fork for gathering seaweed *19- Sh*. [Norw *tare* Laminaria + CRUIK¹·¹]

tartan¹·¹, **tairtan**, **tertan** /'tartən, 'tertən, 'tɛrtən/ *n* **1** woollen cloth with a pattern of stripes of different colours crossing at right angles; since the late 18th-century particular patterns have become associated with particular clans, and although this is unhistorical, it is thought that in former times particular colours became associated with specific areas because of the natural vegetable dyes available *16-*. **2** a tartan garment, especially a Highland plaid *18-e19*. †**tartaned** dressed in tartan *19*. **tartanry** sentimental Scottishness *la20-*. **Tartan Army** the supporters of the Scottish national football team *la20-*. **tartan purry** a dish of boiled oatmeal mixed with chopped red cabbage or boiled with cabbage water *18-*. [probably MFr *tiretaine*, *tertaine* a cloth of wool and other mixed fibres]

tartan¹·², **tairtan**, **tertan** /'tartən, 'tertən, 'tɛrtən/ *adj* **1** made of tartan; having a pattern like tartan *16-*. **2** Scottish *la20-*. [see the noun]

tartar¹·¹ /'tartər/ *n* a disturbance, a noise, a row *20- N*. [see the verb]

tartar¹·² /'tartər/ *v* to move about restlessly and noisily *20- N*. [derivative of Eng *Tartar*]

†**Tartar²** *n* Hell *e16*. **Tartareane** hellish *e16*. [Fr *Tartare*, Lat *Tartarus*]

tartle¹ /'tartəl/ *n* a tuft of hair or wool on an animal matted with excrement or dirt *20- H&I C SW Uls*. **tartles** tatters, torn or trailing edges of (dirty) cloth *la19- H&I C SW Uls*. [metathesis of EModE *tratle*, perhaps from OE *tyrdelu* pl, droppings]

tartle² /'tartəl/ *v* **1** to discern, recognize (after some uncertainty) *la17- C Bor*. **2** to hesitate, be uncertain *18-19*. [compare OE *tealtrian* to waver, be uncertain]

tary¹·¹, **tairie**, **terra** /'tari, 'teri, 'tɛrə/ *n* **1** a name for the Devil *18- NE*. **2** vexation, trouble *16-e19*. [see the verb]

†**tary¹·²** *v* to provoke, harass *e15*. [ME *tarien*, OFr *tarier*]

tary *see* TAIRRIE¹·¹

tas *see* TASS

†**tascal¹·¹**, **taskell** *n* a demand for a reward for the recovery of stolen property; the reward itself *la13-17*. **tascal money** *in the Highlands* (the demand for) a reward for the recovery of stolen property *17-19*. [Gael *taisgeal* a reward for returning something lost]

†**tascal¹·²** *v* to return stolen property (especially cattle) after payment of a reward *17-e18*. [see the noun]

tase *see* TEE¹·²

tash¹, †**tach** /taʃ/ *n* a strap or rope for fastening; a clasp *la15-19, 20- T*. [probably extended sense of OFr *tache* a clasp]

tash²·¹ /taʃ/ *n* **1** a stain, a blemish; damage *la16-19, 20- NE T WC*. **2** a blot on one's character, a slur, stigma *la15-19, 20- Sh*. **tashy** scruffy, unkempt, shabby *19-*. [MFr *tache*]

tash²·² /taʃ/ *v* **1** to besmirch a person's reputation, to stigmatize *la15-*. **2** to damage or deface; to spoil, ruin *la17-*. **3** to fatigue, tire out with hard work *la19-*. **4** to scold *19, 20- T*. **5** *of a football team* to defeat an opponent heavily *la20-*. [MFr *tacher* to stain]

task /task/ *n* **1** a job; a piece of work *16-*. **2** a set lesson to be prepared, a piece of school homework *la18-*. †**taskman** a journeyman *16-17*. [ME *task*; OFr *tasque* a tax, Lat *tasca*]

taskell *see* TASCAL¹·¹

tasker /'taskər/ *n* a worker paid for specified tasks; a pieceworker; a thresher of corn *la14-20, 21- historical*. [TASK with agent suffix]

taskit /'taskɪt/ *adj* **1** fatigued by hard work, exhausted *19-*. **2** stressed, harassed *19-*. [participial adj from TASK]

†**taslet**, **teslot** *n* **1** plate-armour for the thighs *16-e17*. **2** a decorative plate or tassel *e16*. [MFr *tasselet* a decorative plaque, and compare MFr *tassete* plate-armour for the thighs]

tass, †**tas**, †**tays** /tas/ *n* **1** a drinking cup *16-19, 20- literary*. **2** *Presbyterian Church* (a cup for) the collection *e17*. [MFr *tasse*]

tassel *see* TAISLE¹·², TOSSEL

tassie /'tasi, 'tase/ *n* **1** a drinking cup *la18- literary*. **2** a trophy, an ornamental cup offered as a prize *la20-*. [TASS + -IE¹]

taste¹·¹, †**taist** /test/ *n* **1** the tasting or consuming of food or drink *la15-*. **2** flavour; the sense by which flavour is detected *16-*. **3** a sample or small quantity; a hint or inkling *16-*. **4** a partiality or relish, a liking for something *16-*. **5** a small drink, a dram *la19-*. **6** the act of touching; hostile contact *la15-e16*. **lose taste o** to lose interest in or liking for *la20- Ork N NE T*. [ME *taste* the act of tasting, OFr *tast* touching, touch]

taste¹·², †**taist**, †**test** /test/ *v* **1** to perceive the flavour; to experience by tasting *la14-*. **2** to sample a small amount of food or drink *16-*. **3** to drink liquor in small amounts, to tipple *la18-*. **4** to touch *la14*. †**tastar 1** a person appointed to test the quality of ale and fix its price *15-17*. **2** a cup used for tasting *17*. **tastin 1** the act of consuming; a small portion taken to assess the taste *16-*. **2** the drinking of a dram *19-*. **3** the sense of taste *la14-16*. **taste yer gab** to cause a pleasant taste in your mouth, stimulate the appetite *19-*. **taste yer hert** = *taste yer gab 20-*. **taste yer mou** = *taste yer gab la18-*. [OFr *taster* to touch, feel, taste]

tat *see* TAUT¹·¹, THAT¹·¹, THAT¹·²

tatbore *see* TEET¹·¹

tate *see* TAIT¹·¹, TAIT²·²

tathe¹·¹, *NE* **toth**, †**taitht** /teθ; *NE* toθ/ *n* **1** the grass which grows on ground manured by grazing animals *la17-19, 20- NE C Bor*. **2** the dung of grazing animals left on the pasture as manure *la15-e19*. **3** ground manured by grazing animals *la15-17*. †**tathe fold**, **toth fold** a piece of enclosed ground on which cattle and sheep were confined to manure it with their dung *la16-e19*. †**breke tathe** to contravene the local regulations regarding the manuring of land *e16*. †**kepe tathe** to observe the local regulations regarding the manuring of land *17*. [ON *tað* dung, ON *taða* the manured homefield, hay from this field]

tathe¹·², *NE* **toath**, †**ted** /teð; *NE* toð/ *v* **1** to manure land by pasturing cattle or sheep on it *la16-19, 20- NE*. **2** *of grazing animals* to drop dung onto land and manure it *18-e19*. **toathin-fauld** a fold in which cattle were enclosed in order to manure it *20- historical*. [ON *teðja* to dung, manure]

tatie *see* TATTIE

tatter[1] /'tatər/ *n* a rag; a piece of torn cloth *16-*. **tattery 1** ragged, hanging loose *19, 20- T.* **2** very windy *la20- WC Bor*. **tatter-wallop 1** a rag, a piece of torn, flapping clothing *19, 20- Sh NE T EC*. **2** a ragged person, a ragamuffin *19, 20- Ork NE*. [ME *tater*, ON **taturr*]

tatter[2] /'tatər/ *v* **1** to talk idly, prattle *la19, 20- SW Bor*. **2** to scold *20- SW Bor*. [ME *tateren*; MDu, MLG *tateren* to babble]

tattie, tatty, tatie, tawtie, tottie /'tati, 'tate, 'tɔti, 'tɔte/ *n* **1** a potato *18-*. **2** a foolish or stupid person *la19-*. **3** a humorous term for the head *la19, 20- Sh NE EC*. **tattie ait, tattie oat** a kind of oat, the potato-oat *20-*. **tattie bannock** a scone made of flour, milk and mashed potato *20- Sh Ork N*. **tattie beetle, tatie beetle** a potato-masher or pestle *18-*. **tattie bing** a potato clamp, for winter storage *19-*. **tattie bloom, tattie bleem** the flower or flower and foliage of the potato plant *20- N Bor*. **tattie blots** water in which potatoes have been boiled *19- Sh*. **tattie bluitter** water in which potatoes have been boiled *20- EC*. **tattie bockie** a home-made toy consisting of a potato stuck with feathers *20- Sh*. **tattie bogie** a scarecrow *20- NE*. **tattie bogle, tawtie bogle 1** a scarecrow *19-*. **2** a ragged, unkempt or oddly-dressed person *la19-*. **3** a large raw potato with matchsticks stuck in it as a toy *la20- EC Bor*. **tattie boodie, tattie bootie 1** a ghost, a hobgoblin *19- NE*. **2** a foolish or cowardly person *20- NE*. **3** a scarecrow *20- NE*. **tattie bree** water in which potatoes have been boiled *la19- NE EC*. **tattie broo** = *tattie bree 20- Ork*. **tattie broth** potato soup *20-*. **tattie brunie, tautie brunie** a pancake made with mashed potatoes, milk and flour *20- Sh*. **tattie champer, tattie chapper** a potato-masher or pestle *19-*. **tattie claw, tatie claw** potato soup *20- EC Bor*. **tattie creel** a basket for gathering potatoes *19-*. **tattie cruse** a potato stuffed with fish liver and oatmeal and roasted *20- Sh*. **tattie deevil** a machine for digging potatoes *20- NE T*. **tattie doolie** a scarecrow; a ragamuffin *19- NE T*. **tattie graip** a fork for digging potatoes *19-*. **tattie grubber** a kind of harrow for digging up potatoes *la19- NE T*. **tattie grund** ground used for growing potatoes *la19-*. **tattie heid** a stupid person *20-*. **tattie hol** a pit for storing potatoes *20- Sh*. **tattie holidays** an autumn holiday to allow school children to help with the potato harvest *20, 21- historical*. **tattie holin** the potato harvest *20- NE T*. **tattie house** a potato-clamp built of sods like a corn stack *20- Sh N*. **tattie howker** a person who works at the potato harvest *la19-*. **tattie howkin** the potato harvest *19-*. **tattie kro** a kind of bunker in a house in which potatoes are stored *19- Sh*. **tattie liftin** the potato harvest *19-*. **tattie man** an itinerant potato-seller or greengrocer *la19- NE T*. **tattie müld** ground used for growing potatoes *la19- Sh*. **tattie parer 1** a person who peels potatoes *la19-*. **2** an instrument for peeling potatoes *20-*. **tattie parins** potato peelings *20-*. **tattie park** a field of potatoes *20- N NE T*. **tattie peel** potato peelings *la19-*. **tattie peelin** *of speech* affected, prim *la20- EC Bor*. **tattie pie** shepherd's pie *la19-*. **tattie pit** a pit for winter storage of potatoes *19-*. **tattie ploom** the fruit of the potato plant *20- NE T SW Bor*. **tattie poke** a sack or bag for holding potatoes *20- NE T EC*. **tattie pourins** the discarded water in which potatoes have been boiled *la19-*. **tattie rig** a rig used for growing potatoes *19- Sh*. **tattie scone** a dough of flour, milk and mashed potato, rolled out thinly and baked on a girdle *la18-*. **tattie shaw** the stalk and leaves of the potato plant *la19-*. **tattie sheevik** a slice of potato *19 Sh*. **tattie swinger** a foreman; an overseer of farm-workers at the potato harvest *20- WC SW*. **tattie trap** the mouth *la19- T C*. **tattie washins** water in which potatoes have been washed *20- Sh*. **tattie weather, tatie weather** weather favourable for the potato harvest *20- Sh NE T*. **tattie yard** a yard for growing potatoes *19, 20- Sh*. **the tattie** the right person, one who can be trusted or relied on *la19-*; compare *the clean tattie* (CLEAN[1,3]). **no the full tattie** having learning difficulties; in a state of emotional distress *20- NE C*. **tatties and dab** potatoes boiled in their skins and dipped in melted fat or gravy *la19-*. **tatties and dip** = *tatties and dab*. **tatties and point** a frugal meal of potatoes (the non-existent meat being symbolically pointed at) *la19-*. **a tattie short** = *no the full tattie 20- NE C*. **the vera tattie** the very thing *20-*. [shortened form of *potato* (PITAWTIE)]

tattle /'tatəl/ *v* to handle carelessly or messily *la20- Sh Ork*. [unknown; compare TAUT[1,2]]

tatty see TATTIE, TAUTIE

tauch, tallow, tally, †talloun, †talch, †taich /tɔx, 'talo, 'tale/ *n* animal fat (used to make candles) *15-*. **tauchie, tauchy, †tachy 1** greasy; sticky; smeared with tallow *la18-19, 20- EC SW*. **2** sweaty, damp *la19, 20- Ork*. [ME *talgh, talou*, OE **talg*]

taucht see TEACH

taught see TACHT

tauk see TALK[1,1], TALK[1,2]

taul, tauld see TELL[1,2]

taum, tawm, taam /tɔm, tam/ *n* a fit of rage, a bad temper; a sullen, sulky mood *19, 20- H&I*. [ME *talme* a state of being incapacitated, probably from ON *tálma* to obstruct, hinder]

taunt see TANT[1,1], TANT[1,2]

taupie[1,1], **tawpie, †tapie** /'tɔpi, 'tapi/ *n* a thoughtless, untidy or careless person *18-*. [compare Norw *tåpe* a foolish or weak-minded person]

†taupie[1,2], **tawpie, tapie** *adj* foolish, awkward; thoughtless, careless *18-19*. [see the noun]

taupin, †tawpon, †tapon /'tɔpən/ *n* **1** a subsidiary root of a tree or plant; the tap-root of a turnip *17-19, 20- NE T*. **2** a peg or pin *16-17*. **3** a bung *16-e17*. **4** a wooden wad for a cannon *16*. **taupiner, tapner** a curved knife with a hooked tip with which turnips are pulled from the ground and then topped and tailed *20- NE T*. [MFr *tapon* a plug]

†taupit foolish *19*. [TAUPIE[1,1] + -IT[2]]

taur see TAR[1,1]

taurie see TARRIE[2]

taut[1,1], **tat** /tɔt, tat/ *n* a tangled, matted tuft of wool or lock of hair *18-*. [perhaps back-formation from TAUTIE]

taut[1,2], **taat** /tɔt, tat/ *v* **1** to tangle; to make matted or tangled *la19-*. **2** to make rugs with thick, rough worsted yarn *la19- Sh*. **tautit, tattit 1** matted, tangled; shaggy, unkempt *18-*. **2** *of a rug* made of thick, rough worsted yarn *la19- Sh*. [see the noun]

tautie, tatty /'tɔti, 'tati/ *adj of hair or wool* matted, tangled; shaggy, unkempt *la15-*. [perhaps OE *tætteca* a rag, tatter; compare also TAIT[1,1]]

tauve see TYAUVE[1,1], TYAUVE[1,2]

taver see TAIVER

taw[1,1] /tɔ/ *n* **1** a leather thong, the thong of a whip; dressed leather *17-19, 20- SW*; compare TAWSE[1,1]. **2** the penis *la20- C*. [see the verb]

taw[1,2] /tɔ/ *v* **1** to dress leather *17-*. **2** to pull and tug at *la17-19, 20- NE*. **3** to work laboriously, struggle *la18- NE T*; compare TEW[1,2], TYAUVE[1,2]. **4** to draw out or twist something adhesive or pliable *19- T Bor*. [EModE *taw*, OE *tāwian*]

taw[2], *NE* **tyave** /tɔ; *NE* tjav/ *n* **1** a fibre or filament of a plant or tree; a fibrous root (preserved in peat) *16- Sh Ork N NE*. **2** a narrow streak of light *la19- Sh*. **3** fibrous tissue in the liver of a fish *20- Sh*. [ON *tág* root, fibre, thread]

tawberne see TABOUR[1,1]

tawis see TAWSE[1,1]

tawk see TALK[1,2]
tawm see TAUM
tawnle see TANNEL
tawpie see TAUPIE[1.1], TAUPIE[1.2]
tawpon see TAUPIN
tawrds see TARDS
tawse[1.1], †**taws**, †**tawis** /tɔz/ *n pl* **tawses 1** a leather strap divided at one end into two or more strips, used as a punishment in schools; abolished by legislation enacted in 1980 and 1993 *16-20, 21- historical*. **2** the whip for spinning a top *16-20, 21- historical*. [plural of TAW[1.1]]
tawse[1.2] /tɔz/ *v* to beat or whip with a tawse *la18-20, 21- historical*. [see the noun]
tawtie see TATTIE
tax, †**taxt** /taks/ *n* a contribution to state revenue levied on individuals or businesses *15-*. †**taxter**, **taxtar**, **taxatour** the person who assessed, imposed and levied a tax *15-e18*. †**taxt marriage** a marriage on which the feudal casualty of avail was payable *la17*. †**taxt master** the person appointed to set the rate of taxation *la16-17*. †**taxt roll** a list of its members drawn up by the Convention of Royal Burghs with the proportionate liability of each in the total tax payable by the burghs *16-e18*. †**taxt ward** a form of feudal land tenure in which a fixed annual sum was paid to the superior in lieu of the full income from the lands *17-e18*. [ME *taxe*; OFr *taxer* to tax, Lat *taxāre*]
†**taxative** *adj law* limited in power or scope; not definitive or absolute *la17*. [Lat *taxātīvus*]
taxt see TAX
tay see TAE[1], TEA
tayle see TILE[1.2]
taylour see TAILOR
taynt see TAINT[1.2]
tays see TASS, TEE[1.2]
Taysiders /ˈtesʌɪdərz/ *npl* a nickname for Dundee Football Club *20-*. [from the name of the River Tay]
tazie, **teesie** /ˈtezi, ˈtizi/ *n* a struggle, a tussle; strenuous effort *19, 20- N T Bor*. [derivative of *taise* (TEASE)]
†**tchick**[1.1] *v* to make a clicking sound to urge on a horse *e19*. [see the interj]
tchick[1.2], **tchuck** /tʃɪk, tʃʌk/ *interj* a sound expressing annoyance; a tut *la19-*. [a natural utterance]
tchop, **tchoppie** see SHOP
tchuck see TCHICK[1.2]
te see TAE[3.2], TIE[1.1], TIE[1.2]
tea, **tae**, **tay**, †**tee** /ti, te/ *n* **1** a hot drink made from an infusion of leaves *la17-*. **2** a meal eaten in the early evening; high tea *la19-*. **tea blade** a tea leaf *la19- EC*. **tea bread** a bun or scone; a fruit loaf *19-*. **tae flour** the plant sneezewort *20- Sh*. **tea hand** a person who drinks a lot of tea *la19-*. **tea jenny** a person of either sex who drinks a lot of tea *20-*. †**tea kitchen** a tea urn *la18*. **tea piece** a mid-afternoon snack *la19- NE EC*. **tae plate** a saucer *20- Sh*. **tea skiddle**, **tea skittle** *derogatory* a tea party *20- NE C*. **tae well** a well supplying good tea-making water *20- Sh*. **tea shine** a tea party *19-*. **tea and till't** tea served with a cooked meal *20- C SW*. **yer tea's oot 1** a call to children, to say that the evening meal is ready *20- C*. **2** an indication that someone is in serious trouble; a threat *la20- C*. [EModE *tea*, Fr *thé*]
teach, †**teche**, †**teich** /titʃ/ *v pt, ptp* **taucht**, **teachit**, *Sh NE H&I Bor* **teached 1** to instruct, train *la14-*. **2** to teach a school or class *la16-*. **3** to inform *15-16*. **4** to hand over, give or entrust to *la14-e16*. †**techement** teaching, instruction *la15-16*. **teaching elder** *Presbyterian Church* a minister *la19-*. [OE *tǣcan*]
tead see TAID

teagle see TAIGLE[1.2]
teal /til/ *v* to entice; to coax or wheedle *la19, 20- NE WC*. [probably ME *telen* to betray, deceive, OE *tǣlan* to blame, insult, despise]
teal see TALE
tear[1.1], †**tere**, †**teir** /tir/ *n* **1** lachrymal fluid, a teardrop *la14-*. **2** dew; blood *16-e17*. **3** *heraldry* a representation of a tear *la16-17*. **wi the tear in yer ee** in an emotional or tearful state; in mourning or grief *la18-*. [OE *tēar*; compare TICHER[1.1]]
tear[1.2] /tir/ *v* to weep *la16-19, 20- SW*. [see the noun]
tear[2.1], **teir**, **teer**, *C* **terr** /ter, tir; *C* tɛr/ *n* **1** a rent or rip *19-*. **2** merrymaking, a drinking binge *20-* **3** a joke, a piece of fun *20-*. **4** a lively entertaining person, a comic *20-*. **5** a substantial amount, a large quantity: ◇*Whit a tear o wark she did the day. 20- Sh NE T EC Uls*. **6** the angle of adjustment of a plough between the coulter and the point of the ploughshare, which regulates the cut in the furrow *20- N Bor*. [see the verb]
tear[2.2], **tair**, **teir**, **teer**, *C* **terr**, †**toir** /ter, tir; *C* tɛr/ *v pt* **tore**, *EC* **tare**, †**tuir** *ptp* **torn**, **tore**, †**teared 1** to rend, lacerate, rip *16-*. **2** to work strenuously with speed and vigour *19-*. **3** *of wind* to blow hard, gust violently *la19-*. **4** to rage or express fury *19*. **tearer** a person who is quick to anger *la19- Sh N WC*. **torn bellie** a herring split or broken by careless handling *la19- Sh N NE EC*. **torn-hattie** *derogatory* a name for a native of Brechin (used by the people of Montrose) *20- T*. **tear him up** *of weather* to improve *20- Sh*. **tear in** to cultivate waste or rough ground *19, 20- N*. **torn-doun** disreputable, dissipated, broken-down *19, 20- Sh*. **be torn out** to be asked out a lot, be popular *la20- NE*. **tear the tartan** to speak Gaelic *20-*. **tear up** to tackle vigorously *la19-*. [OE *teran*]
tearin[1.1] /ˈtɛrɪn/ *n* **1** rowdy behaviour *la19-*. **2** an angry reproof, a thorough dressing-down *20- NE T C*. [verbal noun from TEAR[2.2]]
tearin[1.2] /ˈtɛrɪn/ *adj* rowdy, boisterous *la19- Sh NE C*. [participial adj from TEAR[2.2]]
tearm see TERM
teary-weary /ˈtiriˈwiri/ *adj* boring *20- NE EC*. [rhyming formation from TEAR[1.1] + WEARY[1.3]]
tease, **taise** /tiz, tez/ *v* to vex in a jocular or mischievous way *18-* [OE *tǣsan* to card (wool)]
tease see TEE[1.2]
teat see TAIT[1.1]
teaze see TEE[1.1]
teazle see TAISLE[1.2]
tebbit see TABET
tebill see TABLE[1.1]
teche see TEACH
teckle see TACKLE[1.1]
ted[1] /tɛd/ *v* **1** *in farming* to spread out grass or another crop to dry *la17-*. **2** to spread out or arrange in an orderly way; to make tidy *la19-*. **3** to scatter, strew, dissipate *la16-19*. [ME *tedden*, OE **teddan*]
Ted[2] /tɛd/ *n* a player for, or supporter of, Rangers Football Club *la20-*. [shortened form of TEDDY BERRS]
ted see TATHE[1.2]
tedder see TETHER[1.1], TETHER[1.2]
Teddy Berrs, **Teddy Bears** /ˈtɛdi ˈbɛrz, ˈtɛdi ˈbɛrz/ *npl* a nickname for Rangers Football Club *la20-*. [rhyming slang for GERS]
tedious, †**tidious** /ˈtidɪʌs/ *adj* **1** wearisome, boring *15-*. **2** weary, bored, depressed *e16*. [Lat *tediōsus*]
tedisome, **teedisome** /ˈtidɪsəm/ *adj* **1** tedious, tiresome, boring *19-*. **2** peevish and sluggish; obstinate, reluctant *la19- EC*. [TEDIOUS + with altered suffix -SOME]

tee[1.1], †**teaze** /ti/ *n* **1** *golf* the small heap of sand or peg from which the ball is driven at the start of each hole *la17-*. **2** *curling* the target, a mark on the ice at the centre of several concentric circles *la18-*. **3** *golf* the area from which the first stroke of a hole must be played *20-*. **4** *bowling* the target or goal *19, 20- SW*. **tee shot** *golf* the first stroke at a hole, played from the tee *la19-*. [see the verb; the later form *tee* is by reinterpretation of *teaze* as a plural]

tee[1.2], †**tease**, †**tase**, †**tays** /ti/ *v* **1** to place a golf ball on a tee *la17-*. **2** to aim or prepare a projectile for shooting or throwing *la14-17*. **tee'd ball, teed ba 1** a golf ball which has been placed on a tee *18-*. **2** a person or state of affairs bound to succeed *18-19*. **tee'd shot** a golf stroke played from a tee *20-*. **teeing ground** the area from which the first stroke of a hole must be played *la19-*. **tee off, tee aff** to strike the ball from the tee to begin play *20-*. **tee up** to place a ball on a tee *20-*. [OFr *teser* to stretch, bend; the form *tee* is from the noun]

tee *see* TAE[3.1], TAE[3.2], TAE[3.1], TEA, THEE[1], TIE[1.1]

teeble *see* TABLE[1.1]

teebro /ˈtibro/ *n* an atmospheric shimmering or mirage *20- Ork*. [compare Icel *tíðbrá* a mirage]

teed /tid/ *adj of a cow* giving milk *Sh*. Compare TIDY. [Norw dial *tid* of a cow, about to calve]

teedisome *see* TEDISOME

teedle *see* DIDDLE[2.2]

teedy, teethy /ˈtidi, ˈtiði/ *adj* ill-tempered; sharp; *of children* fractious *19- SW Bor*. [variant of Eng *teety, teethy*, ME *tēthī*]

teef *see* THIEF[1.1]

teeger, tiger, †**tygir**, †**tigir**, †**tegir** /ˈtigər, ˈtaegər/ *n* **1** a large carnivorous cat, a tiger *la14-*. **2** a person with a fierce, quarrelsome nature *la15-*. [OFr *tigre*, Lat *tigris*]

teek /tik/ *v* to coax *20- Ork*. **teeked** (of an animal) petted, spoilt *20- Ork*. [unknown]

teek *see* TICK[4]

teel[1.1] /til/ *n* cultivation *la19, 20- Sh*. **oot o teel** uncultivated, desolate *la19, 20- Sh*. [see the verb]

teel[1.2], **till**, †**tele**, †**teil** /til, tɪl/ *v* to cultivate land, plough *la14-*. †**teelar, telare** a person who cultivates the soil, a ploughman or farmer *16-17*. †**teilman, teleman** = *teelar la14-15*. †**telisman** = *teelar 16*. †**teilland, teleland** cultivated or arable land *15-e16*. †**teill ryge** = *teilland 16-e17*. †**teillit land** = *teilland la14-17*. [OE *tilian*]

teel *see* TUIL

teelyir *see* TAILOR

teem *see* TUIM[1.1], TUIM[1.2]

†**teemse** *n* a fine sieve, especially for sifting flour *18-e19 Bor*. [ME *temse*, OE **temes*]

teen[1.1], **tene, teyn** /tin/ *n* **1** harm, hurt; sorrow, grief *la14-*. **2** wrath, anger, rage *la14-19*. †**teenfu, teinfull, teneful** angry; malicious; sorrowful *16-18*. [OE *tēona*]

teen[1.2] /tin/ *v ptp* **teened, teended, teendit** to trouble, annoy, provoke *16-19, 20- T*. [OE *tēonian*]

†**teen**[1.3] *adj* angry, enraged; fierce *la14-16*. [see the noun]

†**teen**[2] *adv* in the evening *la18-e19*. [shortened form of *at een* (EVEN[1])]

teen *see* TAK[1.2], TANE, TUNE[1.1]

tee name *see* TO NAME

teend *see* TEIND[1.2]

teended, teendit *see* TEEN[1.2]

teeng *see* TANG[2]

teenge, tinge /tindʒ, tɪndʒ/ *n* **1** a touch or admixture (of some colour or quality) *18-*. **2** colic in horses *19, 20- T*. [EModE *tinge* to tint, Lat *tingere*]

teengs *see* TANGS

teenie, teeny /ˈtini, ˈtine/ *n* **1** a girl or woman of any age *la19-*. **2** *derogatory* an effeminate man *20-*. **3** a junior maidservant *20, 21- historical*. **teenie bash** a term of address to a girl *20-*. **Teenie fae Troon** *derogatory* an oddly dressed or fussily dressed woman or girl *20-*. **Teenie fae the neeps** = *Teenie fae Troon la20- T EC*. [petform of the female forename *Christine*]

teenty /ˈtɪnti/ *numeral in children's rhymes* two *la19-*. [nonsense word derived from a system of counting sheep]

teeny *see* TEENIE

teeock, teeoo /ˈtiɔk, ˈtiu/ *n* the lapwing *Vanellus vanellus la19- Ork*. **teeack snaa** wintry weather in March when lapwings nest *la20- Ork*. [imitative of the bird's call]

teep[1.1], **type** /tip, tʌɪp/ *n* **1** a representation *la15-*. **2** a stamp; type or letters in printing *la17-*. [MFr *type*, Lat *typus*]

teep[1.2], **type** /tip, tʌɪp/ *v* **1** to prefigure, foreshadow *19-*. **2** to typify, symbolize, exemplify *19-*. **3** to create text using a keyboard *la19-*. **4** to classify *20-*. **5** to stamp a letter or figure on wood or metal with a die *la20- C*. **6** *weaving* to print a pattern on a piece of cloth *19*. [see the noun]

teep *see* TUP[1.1]

teepical /ˈtipəkəl/ *adj* typical *20-*. [EModE *typical*, Lat *typicālis*]

teer[1], †**tare** /tir/ *n* wild vetch *Vicia 16-19, 20- NE T Bor*. [ME *tare*]

teer[2] /tir/ *adv* barely, by the skin of one's teeth; ◊*it wis aw by teer Ah caught the bus 20- WC SW*. **aw the teer** only just *19, 20- WC SW*. [reduced form of *aw that e'er* reinterpreted as *(aw the) teer*]

teer *see* TEAR[2.1], TEAR[2.2]

teerant *see* TIRRAN

teerd *see* TURD

Teerie *see* TERI

teerie-orrie /ˈtiri ˈɔri/ *n* the game of throwing a ball against a wall, and then catching and bouncing it in various ways *20- EC*. [reduplicated nonsense words recited while playing the game]

teeset /ˈtisɛt/ *n* **1** *fishing* the first of a fleet of lines to be shot from a boat *20- NE*. **2** *fishing* the man whose turn it is to shoot the first line and to whom its catch is assigned *20- NE*. [**tee** (TAE[3.1]) + SET[1.2]]

teesick, †**tisicke**, †**phtisik** /ˈtizɪk, ˈtɪsɪk/ *n* **1** a spell of illness, frequently of an indefinite nature *20-*. **2** pulmonary consumption *la16-e17*. [ME *tisike*, AN *tisike*, influenced in spelling by Lat *phthisicus*]

teesie *see* TAZIE

teet[1.1] /tit/ *n* a shy peep; a sly glance *19- Sh N NE T EC*. **teetbo** the game of peep-bo; an exclamation used in the game *la18-*. **teetiebo** = *teetbo la19-*. †**titbore tatbore** = *teetbo 17*. [see the verb]

teet[1.2], †**tete**, †**tute** /tit/ *v* to peep or peer; to glance slyly or surreptitiously *16-19, 20- Sh N NE T EC*. [OE *tōtian*]

teet[2] /tit/ *n* the smallest sound or word; a squeak *la19- Sh N NE EC*. [onomatopoeic]

teeter /ˈtitər/ *v* **1** to totter or walk with short, tripping or uncertain steps *20-*. **2** to hesitate; to hover indecisively *20-*. [Eng *teeter*]

teeth *see* TUITH

teethe /tið/ *v* **1** to develop or cut teeth *la17-*. **2** to set teeth in; to furnish with teeth or spikes *la18-*. **3** to face; to stand up to *la19- NE*. **4** to point with mortar *la18-e19*. [ME *tethen*, from the plural of TUITH]

teethy *see* TEEDY

teetick /ˈtitɪk/ *n* a pipit, especially the meadow pipit *Anthus pratensis la19- Sh*. [probably Norw *tit* a small bird + *-ick* (-OCK) diminutive suffix]

teetin /ˈtitɪn/ *n* the meadow pipit *Anthus pratensis* 19- Ork N. [Norw dial *titing* a small bird]

teetle[1.1], **title**, †**titill**, †**tittle** /ˈtitəl, ˈtʌɪtəl/ *n* **1** a name, a title *la14-*. **2** *law* legal right, entitlement *la14-*. **3** *law* the evidence of a right to land or property, a title-deed *la15-*. [OE *tītul*; and later in the form *teetle* from OFr *title*]

teetle[1.2] /ˈtitəl, ˈtʌɪtəl/ *v* **1** to entitle, provide with a name or title *15-*. **2** to enrol or put oneself forward as burgess or citizen *15-e17*. [see the noun]

teetle *see* TITTLE[1]

teet-meet *see* TOOT-MOOT[1.1]

teetotum /tiˈtotəm/ *n* a small, insignificant person *19-*. Compare TOTUM[2] (sense 2). [Eng *teetotum* a TOTUM[1]]

teewheet, teewhip *see* TEUCHIT

tefter /ˈtɛftər/ *v* to idle, lounge *20- Ork*. [unknown]

tegir *see* TEEGER

teh /tɛ/ *interj* an expression of impatience or derision *la19- C Bor*. [a natural utterance]

†**tehe, tohie, teshee** *interj* a representation of derisive laughter *la15-18*. [ME *tē he*, onomatopoeic]

te-hent /təˈhɛnt/ *prep* behind *la19- NE T EC*. [reduced from *tae the hent* (HINT[1.1])]

teich *see* TEACH

teicher *see* TICHER, TICHWR

teicht *see* TICHT[1.3]

teikin *see* TICKING

teil *see* TEEL[1.2]

teill *see* TAIL[1.1]

tein *see* TAK[1.2], TEIND[1.1]

teind[1.1], †**teint**, †**tend**, †**tein** /tind/ *n* **1** the tenth in a sequence *la14-*. **2** a tenth part *la14-19, 20- literary*. **3** *Presbyterian Church* the tithe granted by the Crown to the owner of ecclesiastical property, subject to provision for the clergy *la16-20, 21- historical*. **4** *Christian Church* a tenth of the produce of land or other profits collected annually and given over to the upkeep of the religious establishment *la14-16*. †**Teind Clerk** the clerk of the Court of Teinds, the person in charge of the Teind Office *19-20, 21- historical*, compare *Clerk of Teinds* (CLARK[1.1]). †**Teind Court** the Commissioners of Teinds, functioning as part of the Court of Session *18-20, 21- historical*, compare *Court of Teinds* (COORT). **teind duty** money paid as tithe in lieu of goods *17-19, 20- historical*. †**teind free** exempt from payment of tithes *17-e18*. †**teindmaister** a person who had the right to tithes *17-e19*. **Teind Office** the administrative arm of the Teind Court *20, 21- historical*. †**teind penny, tent pennie 1** the tithe payable to ecclesiastics on legal transactions *15-17*. **2** a tax of one tenth of the value of land *16-17*. **3** a commission or rebate of a tenth of a value or sum *17*. **4** *in Orkney* the tenth part of the land or property which under udal law could be transferred or sold without consultation with the heirs *16*. **teind sheaf** every tenth sheaf, paid as tithe *15-19, 20- historical*. **teind silver** money paid as tithe in lieu of goods *16-19, 20- historical*. **teind to hell** a tribute or price required of his minions by the Devil *la18- literary*. **teind and stock** the gross produce of a farm or fishery, without deduction of the tithe *la16-17*; compare *stock and teind* (STOCK[1.1]). [see the adj TENT[4], and compare ON *tiunde* a tenth]

teind[1.2], †**teynt**, †**teend** /tind/ *v* to assess or take the tithe of crops *16-20, 21- historical*. [see the noun]

teir *see* TEAR[1.1], TEAR[2.1], TEAR[2.2]

teirce *see* TERCE[1.1]

teiroung *see* TIRUNG

Teisday *see* TYSDAY

teistie, †**toist** /ˈtʌɪsti/ *n* the black guillemot *Cepphus grylle la17- Sh Ork N NE*. [Norw dial *teiste*]

teith *see* TUITH
tele *see* TEEL[1.2]
telfer *see* TILFER
telisman *see* TEEL[1.2]
tell[1.1] /tɛl/ *n* a word, a report *la19-*. [see the verb]
tell[1.2], *Ork* **toll** /tɛl; *Ork* tol/ *v pt, ptp* **telt, tald, tauld, tellit**, *NE* **taul 1** to relate, inform, reveal *la14-*. **2** to enumerate, list, mention *la14-*. **3** to foretell *la14-e17*. **tell aff** to match, pair off *la19- Sh Bor*. **tell awa** *folklore* to remove by means of a spell or incantation, to exorcize *la19- Sh*. Compare TELL OOT. **tell doon** to count out money in payment *16-19, 20- Sh*. **telling** countable, of value *17-*. **tellie-speirie** a tell-tale *20- T*. **tell pie, tell piet** a tell-tale *20- Ork N SW Bor*. **be tellin** to be to the interest or advantage of (a person) *17-*. **d'ye tell me?** an expression of surprise or disbelief *20-*. **tell oot** *folklore* to remove by means of a spell or incantation, to exorcize *18- Sh Ork*. **tell upon** to inform on *la18-*. [OE *tellan*]
tell[2] /tɛl/ *v* to ail *19- Sh Ork*. [perhaps by wrong division of Eng *what ails*]
tellin, telling /ˈtɛlɪn, ˈtɛlɪŋ/ *n* a lesson, a warning *19-*. **let that be a tellin tae ye** let that be a lesson or warning *20-*. **tak a tellin** to accept an admonition or warning *19-*. [verbal noun from TELL[1.2]]
tellit *see* TELL[1.2]
telt *see* TELL[1.2]
telʒour *see* TAILOR
†**tem**[1.1] *n* a state of distention or strain *la19 Ork*. [shortened form of TEMBA]
tem[1.2] /tɛm/ *v* to stretch a skin to dry *20- Ork*. [see the noun and compare Norw dial *tenja* to stretch]
temba /ˈtɛmbə/ *n* a state of tension, alertness or watchfulness *la19- Sh*. **be upo temba** to be on the alert; to be on tenterhooks or on one's guard *la19- Sh*. [compare Norw dial *temba* distention (of the stomach)]
teme *see* THEME[1], TUIM[1.1]
†**temerare** *adj* reckless, rash *16-17*. [MFr *temeraire*, Lat *temerārius*]
†**temeraritie** *n law* culpable or wilful recklessness or heedlessness *la15-e17*. [Lat *temerārius* rash + *-ity* noun-forming suffix]
†**temming** *n* fine woollen cloth *15-e19*. [aphetic form of STEMMING]
temp, tempt, †**tent** /tɛmp, tɛmpt/ *v* to entice, tempt *la15-*. [ME *tempten*, OFr *tenter, tempter*, Lat *temptāre*]
temper[1.1], †**tempyr** /ˈtɛmpər/ *n* **1** the quality of hardness or resilience of a blade *la15-*. **2** composure under provocation *18-*. **3** uncontrolled anger *18-*. **temper pin 1** the wooden screw which controls the tension of the band of a spinning-wheel *18-19, 20- Uls*. **2** a tuning peg on a violin *la18*. †**in temper** *of a clock* well regulated *la16-e17*. [see the verb]
temper[1.2], †**tempir**, †**tempre**, †**tempor** /ˈtɛmpər/ *v* **1** to moderate, restrain *15-*. **2** to regulate a mechanism *16-*. [OE *temprian*]
temperate, †**temperat**, †**temperit** /ˈtɛmpərət/ *adj* **1** *of the weather* moderate, mild *la14-*. **2** *of a person* measured, conciliatory *la15-*. [Lat *temperātus*, ptp of *temperāre*]
temperit, tempered /ˈtɛmpərɪt, ˈtɛmpərd/ *adj* **1** having or developing a moderate temperament; moderated, balanced *15-*. **2** *of steel* hardened and made resilient *16-*. **3** *weather* moderate, mild *e16*. [participial adj from TEMPER[1.2]]
tempill *see* TEMPLE[1]
tempir *see* TEMPER[1.2]
temple[1], †**tempill** /ˈtɛmpəl/ *n* **1** (something belonging or relating to) the religious order of Knights Templar; frequently in place-names *la12-*. **2** a building used for worship *la14-*. **templar** a tenant or owner of land belonging to or formerly

belonging to the Knights Templar *15-17, 18- historical*. **temple land** property belonging or having belonged to the Knights Templar and as such not subject to tithes *15-e19, la19- historical*. [OE *tempel*]

†**temple**² *n* a (hazel) rod used to hold down thatch *14-18*. [OFr *temple*]

tempor, tempre *see* TEMPER¹·²

tempt *see* TEMP

tempyr *see* TEMPER¹·¹

ten, †**tene** /tɛn/ *numeral* the cardinal number after nine *la14-*. **tenfauld**, †**tenfald** tenfold *18-*. †**tensome** (a group of) ten *la16-19*. **ten hours** ten o'clock *15-*. †**ten hour bell** a curfew bell rung at 10 pm, especially in Edinburgh *la16-e19*. **ten waurs** ten times worse *la19, 20- NE SW*. [OE *tīen*]

tenaby /'tɛnəbi/ *numeral in children's rhymes* ten *la19- Sh Ork N*. [TEN + nonsense suffix]

tenant, *NE* **tenan**, †**tenand**, †**tennent**, †**tennend** /'tɛnənt; *NE* 'tɛnən/ *n* a person who rents land or a building, a lessee, one who pays rent *15-*. **tenandry, tenantry 1** land or other property let for rent; the parts of an estate let to tenants rather than retained in the hands of a feudal superior *la14-19, 20- historical*. **2** the tenants of an estate *la16-19, 20- NE T*. **3** the state of being a tenant *la14-e18*. †**tenant stead** *of land or property* occupied by a tenant, let out *la17-18*. [OFr *tenant*]

Tenants-Day /'tɛnənts de/ *n* a fair day and holiday held in August in the town of Beith in Ayrshire *19-20, 21- historical*. [altered form of *Saint Inan's Day*, from the 9th-century Celtic saint]

tend¹ /tɛnd/ *v* **1** to attend to, look after *la19-*. **2** to intend (to do something) *la15-17*. **3** to show, indicate; to reveal *la15-e17*. †**tendour 1** *freemasonry* a member chosen by a novice to instruct him in the mysteries of the craft *e17*. **2** a person who tutored or instructed *la15*. [aphetic form of INTEND and of Older Scots *attend* from MFr *atendre*]

tend² /tɛnd/ *v* **1** to be disposed or inclined (towards an outcome or goal); to head or move towards (a place) *la15-*. **2** *of land or a boundary* to extend in a particular direction *la15-e17*. [ME *tenden*, MFr *tendre*, Lat *tendere* to stretch (out)]

tend *see* TEIND¹·¹, TENT⁴

tendent *see* TENON

†**tender**¹·¹ *v* to care about; to have regard for *16-17*. [from the adj, and compare OFr *tendrir*]

tender¹·², **tener**, †**tendir** /'tɛndər, 'tɛnər/ *adj* **1** gentle, kind *la14-*. **2** easily harmed, delicate *la14-*. **3** weak, feeble; ailing, infirm *la14-*. **4** *of coal* soft, crumbly; easily broken or split off *la18-e19*. **5** careful *la17*. **6** closely related, kindred *la14-e17*. **7** dear, beloved *la15-16*. **tenderness**, †**tendirnes 1** compassion, kindness *la14-*. **2** ill-health *e18*. **3** closeness of kinship *15-16*. †**tendir of blude** closely related *la15-e17*. †**tendernes of blude** closeness of kinship *16*. [OFr *tendre*]

tender² /'tɛndər/ *n* **1** an offer; the act of offering *la17-*. **2** *law* an offer of a sum in settlement made during an action by the defender to the pursuer *la19-*. **3** the offer of union between England and Scotland made during the period of the Commonwealth *la17*. [EModE *tender* to offer, an offer, MFr *tendre* to offer]

tendir *see* TENDER¹·²

tendon *see* TENON

tene *see* TEEN¹·¹, TEN

tenement, †**tennement** /'tɛnəmənt/ *n* **1** a large building of several storeys, divided into flats occupied by separate householders; the section of such a building served by one stair *la16-*. **2** a holding of land; land held in tenure and built on; a house or other buildings erected upon a tenement of land *15-18, 19- historical*. **tenementer** the holder of a tenement of land, a person who has a feu of land in a village *la18-19, 20 historical*. **tenement of houses** rented flats within a large building *la16-19, 20- historical*. **tenement of land** (housing built on) land held in tenure *la15-18, 19- historical*. [OFr *tenement* tenure of property]

tenendas /tə'nɛndas, tə'nɛndəz/ *n law* the clause in a feudal charter expressing the manner in which lands are to be held of a feudal superior *la17-20, 21- historical*. [from the Lat legal phrase *tenendas (praedictas terras)* (the aforementioned lands) to be held]

tener *see* TENDER¹·²

tennement *see* TENEMENT

tennend, tennent *see* TENANT

tennon *see* TENON

tennour *see* TENOR¹, TENOR²·¹

tenon, tendon, †**tennon**, †**tendent** /'tɛnən, 'tɛndən/ *n* **1** body tissue, a tendon *la16-*. **2** a root *17*. [ME *tenoun*, EModE *tendon*; Lat *tenōn-, tendōn-*]

tenor¹, †**tenour**, †**tennour** /'tɛnər/ *n* **1** *law* the meaning or substance of a document *la14-*. **2** the tenor part in a musical composition *la16-*. **3** *law* the process or method by which a legal procedure was carried out *la15-e17*; compare *prove the tenor* (PRUIVE). [OFr *tenor, tenour*, Lat *tenor*]

tenor²·¹, **tanner**, †**tennour** /'tɛnər, 'tanər/ *n* **1** a tenon or projection on a piece of wood cut to fit into a mortise or cavity on another to join the pieces *19-*. **2** the crossbar between the legs of a chair *la19- Sh*. **3** a crosspiece *la16*. **tenor saw, tanner saw** a small saw used to make tenons *17-*. [altered form of ME *tenoun*, OFr *tenon*]

tenor²·², **tanner** /'tɛnər, 'tanər/ *v* to cut a tenon (on a piece of wood) *la19-*. [see the noun]

tenour *see* TENOR¹

tensket /'tɛnskət/ *adj* peevish *20- Sh*. [perhaps Norw dial *tynsket* pointed, sharpened]

tent¹ /tɛnt/ *n* **1** a portable (weatherproof) shelter; a pavilion *la14-*. **2** *Presbyterian Church* a movable pulpit (with steps and canopy) erected in the open air, especially at half-yearly Communion services when the congregation was too large for the church *la17-19*. [OFr *tente*, Lat *tenta*]

tent²·¹ /tɛnt/ *n* attention, heed, care *la14-*. **tak tent 1** to pay attention; to notice or observe *la14-*. **2** to take care, beware *la14-*. [aphetic form of ATTENT¹·¹]

tent²·² /tɛnt/ *v* **1** to pay attention to; to listen to, heed *15-*. **2** to watch over, care for; to look after (animals or children) *la16-19, 20- T SW*. **3** to beware, be careful of: ◊*tent wha ye tak by the hand 18-19, 20- EC*. **4** to observe, take notice of *18-e19*. [see the noun]

†**tent**²·³ *adj* watchful, attentive, intent *la18-19*. [see the noun]

†**tent**³ *v* **1** to treat a wound *15-16*. **2** to probe or investigate *la16-17*. [ME *tent* a probe, a roll of lint, OFr *tente*]

tent⁴, **tenth**, †**tend**, †**teynd** /tɛnt, tɛnθ/ *adj* tenth *la14-*. Compare TEIND¹·¹. [TEN + -*t*, -*th*, -*d* ordinal suffix]

tent *see* TAINT¹·², TEIND¹·¹, TEMP

tenter¹ /'tɛntər/ *n* **1** a frame for stretching cloth *16-*. **2** a bar of wood fitted with hooks on which fish are hung to dry *20- NE T EC*. †**tenter hooks** the hooks by which cloth was attached to the tenter *17-18*. [ME *tentour*, Lat *tentor*]

tenter² /'tɛntər/ *n* **1** a loom-tuner *20- T C*. **2** a weaver's assistant who attended a loom *19*. [TENT²·² with agent suffix]

tenth *see* TENT⁴

tentie /'tɛnti/ *adj* attentive, careful; circumspect *la16-19, 20- NE*. [TENT²·¹ + -IE²]

†**tentive, tentife** *adj* attentive, careful *15-18*. [OFr *tentif*]

tentless /'tɛntləs/ *adj* inattentive, heedless, careless *la16-*. [TENT²·¹ + adj-forming suffix]

tep /tɛp/ *v* to stop or dam water *20- Ork*. [Norw dial *teppa* to stop, close, block up]

tepat *see* TIPPET

ter *see* TAR[1.1]

teran *see* TIRRAN

terbutche, terbuts, †trebuck /tərˈbʌtʃi, tərˈbʌts/ *interj* a call indicating a person's awareness of an error committed, especially when a player has made a false move in a game and wants to make a second attempt *la19, 20- WC*. [Fr *trébucher* to stumble]

†terbynthyn, terebynthine *n* (the wood or oil of) the turpentine tree *e16*. [ME *terebint*, Lat *terebinthus*, + *-ine*]

terce[1.1]**, †ters, †teirce** /tɛrs/ *n* **1** *law* a widow's legal inheritance, the liferent of one third of her husband's heritable estate, provided that she had agreed to no other arrangement and the marriage had lasted for a year and a day and had produced a living child *la15-20, 21- historical*. **2** a third part or share of something *la15-e18*. **3** a measure of capacity equating to one third of a pipe cask; a cask of this capacity *16-17*. **4** tierce, the third canonical hour *la14-e16*. **†tersell** a measure of capacity *16*. **tercer, †tercear** a widow possessing a terce *la16-*. **†terce landis** lands whose income was assigned to a widow's terce *la15-17*. [OFr *terce, tierce* a third]

†terce[1.2] *adj of fever* tertian, recurring every third day *la16-e17*. [shortened form of Older Scots *tercian*, Lat *tertiānus*]

†tere *adj* irksome, tedious; distressing *la15-e16*. [ME *tere*, perhaps related to TIRE[1.2]]

tere *see* TEAR[1.1]

terebynthine *see* TERBYNTHYN

†terepoile, tere pyle *n* a particular length of nap of velvet *la15-e16*. Compare *thre pile* (THREE). [MFr *a treis poils*]

Teri, Teerie /ˈtɛri, ˈtiri/ *n* a native or inhabitant of Hawick, Roxburghshire *la19- Bor*. [shortened form of TERIBUS]

teribus, tiribus /ˈtɛrɪbəs, ˈtɪrɪbəs/ *n* **1** the slogan of the town of Hawick *19- Bor*. **2** a popular song with this slogan in its chorus, sung especially at the Hawick Common Riding *19- Bor*. **teribus and teriodin** = TERIBUS. [unknown]

terlass *see* TIRLIS, TIRLISS

terlys *see* TIRLIS

term, tairm, †tearm /tɛrm, term/ *n* **1** a (limited) period of time *la14-*. **2** *law* one of the four days of the year on which payments become due, or leases begin and end, traditionally Candlemas, Whitsunday, Lammas, Martinmas *la14-*. **3** a word or expression *la15-*. **4** a subdivision of a school or university year *19-*. **5** the days on which contracts of employment (on farms) began and ended: *la14-20, 21- historical*. **6** *law* the time fixed by a court for establishing the evidence in a case *la15-e18*. **terms** conditions, circumstances *la15-*. **termly 1** occurring or falling due every term or at the end of a term *la15-*. **2** in each term, once every term *la15-e19*. **term day 1** the days on which contracts of employment begin and end *la18-*. **2** a limit date *la14-17*. **term time 1** the days on which contracts of employment begin and end *la19-*. **2** the part of a year when a school or university is in session *20-*. **†term of law** the period prescribed for an action to take place *la15-e18*. **term and life** for all time *19, 20- Sh*. [OFr *terme* limit (of time or place)]

termigant, termagant, †tarmegant, †termagaunt /ˈtɛrməgənt/ *n* **1** a quarrelsome, violent woman *la16-*. **2** a deity supposedly worshipped by the Saracens *la15-e19*. **3** a braggart *16*. **4** the devil *la15*. [ME *Termagaunt*, OFr *Tervagant* a fictitious deity]

termigant *see* TARMIGAN

terminate /ˈtɛrmɪnet/ *v* **1** to bring to an end, conclude *la16-*. **2** *law* to bring a legal process to a conclusion *la16-*. [Lat *termināt-*, ptp stem of *termināre* to limit, end]

†tern *n* gloom *la16*. [probably from the adj TERNE]

†ternar *n* a student at St Andrews University of the third or lowest social rank *la17-e19*. Compare PRIMAR, *Seconder* (SECOND[1.2]). [Lat *ternārius* in third place]

†terne, terned *adj* gloomy, fierce *16-e17*. **tarnedness** sorrow, gloom *la16*. [MFr *terne* dull, tarnished]

terr *see* TEAR[2.1], TEAR[2.2]

terra *see* TARY[1.1]

terran *see* TIRN

terrible[1.1]**,** *EC SW* **terrel, †terribill** /ˈtɛrəbəl; *EC SW* ˈtɛrəl/ *adj* dreadful, awful *la15-*. [OFr *terrible*, Lat *terribilis*]

terrible[1.2] /ˈtɛrəbəl/ *adv* **1** in a terrible manner *la16-*. **2** extremely, awfully: ◊*she wis terrible ill 19-*. [see the adj]

terrie /ˈtɛri/ *n* a storage area made of boards or netting on the crossbeams of the kitchen or an outbuilding *la19- Sh*. [Norw dial *terre* the cross-spars of a corn or malt kiln]

terrifee, †terrife /ˈtɛrɪfi/ *v* to terrify *la16-*. **terrification** the action of terrifying; a cause or state of terror *17-*. [MFr *terrifier*]

territory, †territoure, †territor /ˈtɛrɪtəre, ˈtɛrɪtre/ *n* **1** a particular region or district (originally under the jurisdiction of a burgh) *la15-*. **2** *law* the area over which a judge holds jurisdiction *17-*. **territorial 1** relating to a particular locality *la18-*. **2** *of the jurisdiction of a sheriff* limited to a defined area or district *la18-*. **3** *of a church in a large town* serving an area not co-terminous with the parish *19*. [ME *territorie*, Lat *territōrium*; MFr *territoire*]

terror, †terrour /ˈtɛrər/ *n* **1** intense fear *la14-*. **2** a cause of terror *la16-*. **3** a deterrent *la16-17*. [MFr *terreur*, Lat *terror*]

†ters *n* a penis *16*. [OE *teors*]

ters *see* TERCE[1.1]

tersell *see* TERCE[1.1]

tersie versie[1.1] /ˈtɛrsi ˈvɛrsi/ *adj* topsy-turvy; random or disordered *19- Bor*. [euphemistic form of Eng *arsy-versy*, perhaps with influence from *topsy-turvy*]

tersie versie[1.2] /ˈtɛrsi ˈvɛrsi/ *adv* in a random or disorderly way *19- Bor*. [see the adj]

tert *see* TAIRT

tertan *see* TARTAN[1.1]

tertian[1.1] /ˈtɛrʃən/ *n* a third-year student (at St Andrews or Aberdeen University) *la17-*. [see the adj]

tertian[1.2] /ˈtɛrʃən/ *adj* in the third year (at St Andrews or Aberdeen University) *la17-* [Lat *tertiānus* of or belonging to the third]

terty *see* THIRTY[1.2]

terung *see* TIRUNG

teshee *see* TEHE

teslot *see* TASLET

tesment *see* TESTAMENT[1.1]

test[1.1]**, †taist** /tɛst/ *n* **1** a means of determining something, an assessment; an exam *18-*. **2** the cupel for melting metal or refining precious metals *16-19, 20- historical*. **3** *Episcopal Church* the oath or declaration prescribed by the Test Act of 1681, aimed at imposing on the extreme Covenanters compliance with Episcopacy in the Church of Scotland *la17-19, 20- historical*. **the Test** *Episcopal Church* the oath prescribed by the Test Act *la17-19, 20- historical*. [OFr *test* a pot, Lat *testa*; and, in some senses, from the verb]

test[1.2] /tɛst/ *v* **1** to assess, examine *18-*. **2** *Episcopal Church* to swear the oath required by the Test Act of 1681 *la17*. [see the noun]

†test[2] *n* a statement of evidence presented before a court *la15-17*. [aphetic form of EModE *attest* evidence]

test³ /tɛst/ *v* **1** *law* to make a will *la17-*. **2** *law* to include in a will or testament *la17-e18*. †**testable, testabil** *of possessions* that may be bequeathed *16-17*. [MFr *tester* to bequeath]

test *see* TASTE¹·²

testament¹·¹, †**tesment** /'tɛstəmənt/ *n* **1** *law* a will; the part of a will in which an executor is appointed *la14-*. **2** each of the two main divisions of the Bible *la15-*. **3** a work concerned with the wishes of the author or protagonist after his death *16*. **testament dative** *law* a will drawn up by the court when a person dies intestate in order to appoint and confirm an executor on their behalf *16-*. **testament testamentar** *law* a testament in which the nomination of executors and disposal of goods is specified by the person whose testament it is *16-*. **testament testamentary** = *testament testamentar la18-*. †**mak testament** to record in a document one's intentions as to the disposal of one's possessions after death *la15-16*. [OFr *testament*, Lat *testāmentum*]

†**testament**¹·² *v* to bequeath *la19*. [see the noun]

testamentar /tɛstə'mɛntər/ *adj* **1** *law* pertaining to a will *la15-*. **2** *of a person* nominated executor or executrix testamentar in a will *17*. [MFr *testamentaire*, Lat *testāmentārius*]

†**testamentrix** *n* a woman appointed as a trustee by a will *17-e18*. [altered form of TESTAMENTAR by analogy with EXECUTRIX]

†**testan, testoun** *n* **1** a Scottish silver coin of the reign of Mary *la16-e17*. **2** an Italian, French or English silver coin bearing a portrait head *la15-16*. **make a mark of your testan** to make a profit; to invest one's capital or efforts to advantage *e18*. [MFr *teston*]

testat, testate *see* TESTIT

testifee, †**testife,** †**testifie** /'tɛstəfi/ *v* to testify *15-*. [ME *testifien*, AN *testifier*]

†**testificate, testificat** *n* **1** a solemn declaration of fact or belief put in writing; a certificate; a testimonial *17-18*. **2** a character reference (written by a minister) *17-e19*. **testificatioun** a document containing testimony; a character reference *16-17*. [Lat *testificātum* that which is testified, verbal noun from *testificārī*]

testifie *see* TESTIFEE

testimonial, †**testimoniall** /tɛstə'mɔnɪəl/ *n* **1** documentary proof *la15-*. **2** a character reference *16-*. **3** a letter or recommendation issued by a minister or kirk session to a person joining the congregation of another church *la16-e18*. †**the testimoniale of the grete sele** a Chancery seal (consisting of a replica of the upper half of the great seal, obverse and reverse), compare *quarter seal* (QUARTER¹·¹) *la15-e18*. [MFr *testimonial*, Lat *testimōniālis*]

testimonie, testimony /'tɛstəməni/ *n* **1** attestation of the truth or validity of something; *law* evidence in court *16-*. **2** a character reference *la16-17*. [ME *testimonie*, MFr *testimonie*, Lat *testimōnium*]

testing clause /'tɛstɪŋ klɔz/ *n law* the attestation clause authenticating a deed, giving the names of the witnesses and the date and place where it was signed *la18-*. [participial adj from TEST² + CLAUSE]

testit, testate, †**testat** /'tɛstɪt, 'tɛstet/ *adj* **1** *of a deceased person* having left a valid will *la16-*. **2** *of possessions* recorded as a bequest in a will *la15-16*. [participial adj from TEST³]

testoun *see* TESTAN

tet *see* TAIT¹·¹

tete *see* TEET¹·²

†**teth** *interj* a mild oath *19*. Compare HAITH. [probably euphemistic form of FETH¹·¹]

teth *see* TUITH

tether¹·¹, *Sh Ork N* **tedder** /'tɛðər; *Sh Ork N* 'tɛdər/ *n* **1** a rope for securing an animal *la14-*. **2** resources; options; scope *19, 20- Sh Ork N*. **3** a hangman's noose *16-e19*. **put a tether to his tongue** to silence a person, restrain someone from speaking *19, 20- Sh N*. [ON *tjóðr*]

tether¹·², *Sh Ork N* **tedder** /'tɛðər; *Sh Ork N* 'tɛdər/ *v* **1** to confine with a tether *16-*. **2** to restrict; to limit freedom *la15-19, 20- Ork NE*. **3** to marry, unite in marriage *19, 20- N NE*. **4** to moor a boat *18-19, 20- NE*. **5** *of a ship* to stick fast *e17*. **tethering,** *Sh Ork N* **teddering** the tying of animals to restrict their grazing; the grazing itself *la16-*. [see the noun]

tethery /'tɛðəre/ *numeral in children's rhymes* three *19- T C* [nonsense word derived from a system of counting sheep]

tetht *see* TUITH

teuch¹·¹, **tyeuch, cheuch, tough,** *Sh Ork N* **tyoch,** †**tewch,** †**tuch,** †**teugh** /tjux, tʃux, tʌf; *Sh Ork N* tjɔx/ *adj* **1** strong and pliable, not easily broken or torn; hard; unyielding *la14-*. **2** *of people or animals* physically or mentally strong; difficult to contend with *la15-*. **3** *of food* hard to chew *16-*. **4** *of people* rough, coarse *la19-*. **5** *of weather* wet and windy *20- Sh N NE*. **6** sticky, viscous *la16-18*. **teuchen** cause to become tough *19-*. **teuchie 1** *of people* tough or coarse *20- NE EC*. **2** *of weather* wet and windy *20- NE*. **teuchly** toughly; strongly; persistently *la16-*. **teuch Jean, cheuch Jean** a sticky, chewy boiled sweet *20-*. [OE *tōh*]

†**teuch**¹·² *adv* vigorously, stoutly; persistently, pertinaciously *la15-19*. [see the adj]

teuch *see* DEUCH

teuchit, teewheet, *Ork N* **teewhip,** †**tuchet,** †**tuquheit** /'tjuxət, 'tʃuxət, 'tiwit; *Ork N* ti'wɪp/ *n* the lapwing *Vanellus vanellus 14-*. **teuchats storm** a period of bleak wintry weather in early spring (when the birds arrive and begin to nest) *19- NE T*. [imitative of the bird's call; compare PEESWEEP]

teuchter, teuchtar, cheuchter, choochter /'tjuxtər, 'tʃuxtər/ *n* **1** a (Gaelic-speaking) Highlander; a native of the North of Scotland *20-*. **2** *derogatory* an uncouth, countrified person *20-*. [unknown; perhaps imitative of Gaelic occupational nouns ending in *-(a)dair*]

teug *see* TUG¹·¹

teugh *see* TEUCH¹·¹

teuk *see* TAK¹·²

teulie *see* TULYIE¹·¹

teven /'tɛvən/ *numeral in children's rhymes* seven *la19- N*. [probably altered form of Eng *seven*]

†**tew**¹·¹ *n* a piece of hard work or exertion *19*. Compare TYAUVE¹·¹. [see the verb]

tew¹·² /tju/ *v* **1** to exhaust *19-*. **2** to toil, struggle *19-*; compare TYAUVE¹·². **tewed 1** *of food* tough, shrivelled *19, 20- Bor*. **2** exhausted *19, 20- SW Bor*. [variant of TAW¹·²]

tew² /tju/ *interj* an expression of disgust, contempt or impatience *la19- WC*. [a natural utterance]

tew *see* TYAUVE¹·²

tewch *see* TEUCH¹·¹

tewel *see* TUIL

tewk *see* TUCK

†**textour** *n* a weaver *la16*. [AN *textour*, Lat *textōr-*]

teylor *see* TAILOR

teyn *see* TEEN¹·¹

teynd *see* TENT⁴

teynt *see* TEIND¹·²

tha *see* THAE¹·¹, THAE¹·², THAY

thack¹·¹, **theek,** *N NE* **theck,** *N* **thaik,** †**thak** /θak; *Ork* tɛk; *N* θɛk/ *n* **1** straw used for roofing; originally also roofing material in general, including slate; the roof itself *la14-*. **2** a thick covering of hair or foliage *la19-*. **thack-gate** the ledge at the top of a gable-wall on which the thatch was extended and supported *la17-19, 20- Sh.* †**thack-hathir** heather used for thatching *la14-15.* **thack-house** a thatched house *la15-.* †**thack-nail** = *thack-pin la15-19.* **thack-pin** a wooden peg used to fasten down thatch *17-.* **thack-raip** a straw-rope used to secure thatch on a house or stack *la19-.* **thack-scythe** a scythe for cutting heather or thatching material *18- Sh.* †**thack-sheaf** a bundle of thatching material *17-e18.* †**thak skew** a stone forming part of the coping of a gable where it meets the thatch *e16.* †**thack-stane** stone used as roofing *16-17.* **thack-wyse, thack-weyse** a bundle of straw for thatching *20- NE.* **thack and raip 1** the thatch of a house or stack and the ropes tying it down; used with reference to giving possession of a building by handing over symbols of it *la16-.* **2** describing something tidy, comfortable, well-secured *la18- literary.* [OE *ðæc*, ON *þak*]

thack[1,2], †**thaick** *v* to thatch, cover a roof *17-;* compare THEEK. **thacker** a thatcher *18-.* [OE *ðacian*]

thack *see* THEEK

thackin /'θakın/ *n* a beating; a severe scolding *la19-.* [verbal noun from *thack*, variant of Eng *thwack*, OE *ðaccian* to pat, clap]

thae[1.1], **they**, *N NE* **ey**, †**thai**, †**tha** /ðe/ *pron pl* those *la14-.* [OE *ðā*]

thae[1.2], **they, thai,** †**tha** /ðe/ *dem adj* those *la14-.* [see the pron]

thaft, *Sh* **taft**, †**thoft** /θaft; *Sh* taft/ *n* a rower's bench, a thwart *16-.* [OE *ðoft*]

thai *see* THAE[1.1], THAE[1.2], THAY, THY

thaick *see* THACK[1.2]

thaik *see* THACK[1.1]

thaim[1.1], **them, thame,** *Sh* **dem** /ðem, ðɛm; *unstressed* ðəm; *Sh* dɛm/ *pron* **1** third person plural, objective of THAY *la14-.* **2** as the third person plural indirect object, sometimes with *to* omitted: ◊*He said thaim thae things la14-.* **3** occasionally used in subject position, only in collocation with other personal pronouns they: ◊*Them and us is no speakin 19-.* **4** as the antecedent of a relative pronoun those: ◊*Them that haes siller aye gets mair 19-.* **5** = THEIRSELS *la14-16.* **them-lane** alone *19-.* [ON *þeim*]

thaim[1.2], **them,** *Sh* **dem,** †**tham** /ðem, ðɛm; *Sh* dɛm/ *dem adj* those: ◊*ye'll pey for the mess them beasts made 15-.* [see the pron]

thaim self *see* THEIRSEL
thaim selfis *see* THEIRSELS
thaim selwyn *see* THAME SELVIN
thain *see* THANE[2]
thair *see* THAUR, THERE, THIR[1.3]

†**thaircuming** *n* arrival *la16-e17.* [*thair* (THERE) + verbal noun from COME[1.2]]

thairm, therm, †**tharm** /θerm/ *n* **1** intestine, gut *16-.* **2** the cord driving the mechanism of a clock or watch *la17-.* **3** a fiddle-string *la18-.* **4** gut used as the skin of a sausage *la18-.* **5** gut dried and twisted into a string or cord, catgut *19, 20- Sh T.* **6** the cord driving a spinning-wheel *la19- Sh NE.* [OE *ðearm*]

thairsel *see* THEIRSEL
thairsels *see* THEIRSELS
thais *see* THIS[1.3]
thak *see* THACK[1.1]
tham *see* THAIM[1.2]
thame *see* THAIM[1.1], THEME[1]
thame selff *see* THEIRSEL
thameselffis *see* THEIRSELS

†**thame selvin, thaim selwyn, thame selfin** *pron* themselves *la14-15.* [variant of *thaim selfis* (THEIRSELS)]

than[1.1], †**thyne** /ðan/ *n* that time, a particular time: ◊*by than we'll aa be deid la14-.* [see the adv]

than[1.2], **then, an** /ðan; *NE unstressed* an/ *adv* **1** at a particular time *la14-.* **2** subsequently *la14-.* **3** consequently, in that case *la14-.* **or than, or thance** or else; or even; otherwise *la14-.* **than-a-days** in those days *la18-19, 20- Ork NE.* [OE *ðanne*]

than[1.3], †**then** /ðan/ *conj* **1** introducing the second element in a comparison *la14-.* **2** except, but *la14-e15.* [see the adv]

thanage *see* THANE[1]
thance *see* THAN[1.2]

thane[1], †**thayn** /θen/ *n* **1** the pre-feudal equivalent of an earl or baron; the governor, mainly of royal lands, responsible for the collection of revenues and the administration of justice; under the feudal system, incorporated into the ranks of earl or baron *12-15, 16- historical.* **2** a nobleman, an earl *18-e19 literary.* **thanage** lands originally under the jurisdiction of a THANE[1] (sense 1), a barony *13-17, 19- historical.* **thanedom** = *thanage 15-18, 19- historical.* [OE *ðegn* a retainer]

†**thane**[2], **thain, thean** *n* a vane, a metal plate in the form of a flag or banner often bearing a coat of arms; a pennant; a weathercock *la15-18.* [variant of FANE[1]]

thang, thong, *Sh Ork* **twang,** *EC Bor* **thwang,** †**twhang** /θaŋ, θɔŋ; *Sh Ork* twaŋ; *EC Bor* θwaŋ/ *n* a thong or lace *15-.* Compare WHANG[1.1] (sense 1). [OE *ðwang, ðwong*]

thank[1.1], **thenk** /θaŋk, θɛŋk/ *n* gratitude, the expression of gratitude *la14-19, 20- Ork NE SW.* **thankful,** †**thankfull 1** feeling or expressing gratitude, grateful *la14-.* **2** worthy of gratitude; acceptable *la14-17.* **3** *of a payment* satisfactory, adequate, complete *la15-17.* **thankfully 1** in a manner expressing gratitude *la14-.* **2** graciously, willingly *la14-16.* **3** so as to please, acceptably, satisfactorily *la14-16.* **4** *referring to a payment or transaction* (paid or achieved) satisfactorily, fully *15-17.* **thankrife** full of thanks, grateful *la20- T C SW.* **thanks 1** = THANK[1.1] (sense 1). **2** services rendered, favours *la15-e16.* **thanksgiving,** †**thanksgeving 1** the giving of thanks to God, especially in a public manner *la16-.* **2** a religious service expressing thanks for some event or state of affairs *17.* **thanks be** exclamation expressing relief *20-.* **thanksgiving service** the service after Communion, in which special thanks are given to God *18-.* **give thanks** to say grace before or after a meal *19-.* **my thank** *expressing reproach or displeasure* inadequate thanks for or recognition of a service: ◊*Is this a my thank for my hard work? 19-.* **the thank** = *my thank.* [OE *ðanc*]

thank[1.2], **thenk** /θaŋk, θɛŋk/ *v* to express gratitude *la14-.* **be thankit 1** *interj* God be thanked, exclamation expressing relief *la18-.* **2** *n* a grace said after a meal *la18-.* **for thank ye** for no more than an expression of gratitude, for nothing: ◊*That's nae been pit there for thank ye. There maun be a guid reason. 20-.* †**thankit be God** thank God *la15-e17.* [OE *ðancian*]

thar *see* THAUR, THERE

†**tharf, thraffe** *adj* **1** *of bread* unleavened *la15-17.* **2** cold, stiff in manner *18-19.* **tharfly** in a surly manner *la16.* **tharf caik** a cake of unleavened bread *la15.* [OE *ðearf* unleavened]

tharm *see* THAIRM
tharth *see* THAUR

that[1.1], *Sh Ork* **dat,** †**tat** /ðat; *Sh Ork* dat/ *dem pron* **1** a more distant or less immediate person, thing or circumstance indicated, previously named or understood *la14-.* **2** this: ◊*I'll say that for you, you write a good letter. 19-.* **3** used to emphasize or confirm a previous phrase: ◊*It's very cold. It is that. 19-;* compare AT[2]. **aa that** = THAT[1] (sense 3) *20- N C.* **and that** and so on, et cetera *20-.* **like aa that** with the utmost energy or speed *la20*-. **or that** or the like, or something similar *20*-. [OE *ðæt*, neuter of *se* dem pron and adj]

that[1,2], **thit**, *Sh Ork* **dat**, †**tat** /ðat, ðɪt; *Sh Ork* dat/ *pron* **1** who, which, whom *la14*-; *often omitted*: ◇*the wifie bides doon the road feeds ma cat.* **2** *the possessive can also be expressed by 'that' plus possessive inflection or pron* **that's** whose *la14*-: ◇*the faimly that thair hoose wis broken intae*; ◇*the man that's sister mairrit the postie.* **3** *not used of persons* (of) which: ◇*the hoose that the end o't fell doon la19*-. [see the dem pron]

that[1,3], *Sh Ork* **dat** /ðat; *Sh Ork* dat/ *dem adj* **1** preceding a person or thing indicated and denoting distance, contrasting with this and YON[1,3] *la14*-. **2** *used as a pl* those: ◇*whit's wrang wi that coos? 15-18, 19- Sh Ork N NE T.* **3** without its following noun (which is understood from the previous clause): ◇*she's the clever one that 19-.* **4** such, so much: ◇*a man o that mense maun dae weel la18-.* **thattan** = THAT[1,3] (sense 4) *20*-. [see the dem pron]

that[1,4], **thit**, *Sh Ork* **dat** /ðat, ðɪt; *Sh Ork* dat/ *dem adv* so; to such a degree; to that extent; very *la16*-. [see the dem pron]

that[2], **thit**, *Sh Ork* **dat** /ðat, ðɪt; *Sh Ork* dat/ *conj* introducing a subordinate clause, indicating a statement or purpose *la14*-. [OE *ðæt* conj]

thattan see THAT[1,3]

thaur, thar, †**thair,** †**tharth** /θɔr/ *v pt* †**thurt,** †**thurft** to need, be obliged to *la14-19, 20- N.* [OE *ðurfan* to need]

thaveless see THIEVELESS

thaw see THOW[1,1], THOW[1,2]

thay, thai, they, †**tha,** †**thei** /ðe/ *pron* third person plural subject, the people, animals or things already mentioned or under discussion *la14*-; compare THAIM, THAIR **they're, thur** they are *20*- [ON *þeir*]

thayn see THANE[1]

the[1,1] /ðə/ *adv* preceding a comparative adjective or adverb to form an adverbial phrase by so much: ◇*a problem tackled is the sooner solved. la14*-. **the ... the ...** in correlative constructions: ◇*let's do it, the sooner the better la14*-. [OE *ðē*, instrumental case of *se* dem pron and adj]

the[1,2], **ra**, *Sh* **da**, *NE* **de**, *N NE T* **ee** /ðə; *Sh* da; *NE* də; *N NE T* i, ə/ *def art* **1** as a determiner, denoting one or more persons, animals or things already under discussion or whose identity is understood *la14*-. **2** used instead of the possessive adjective with the names of parts of the body: ◇*dinna haud him by the thrapple or he'll loss the heid wi ye la14*-. **3** with nouns denoting activities, pastimes or branches of learning: ◇*you've been at the maths*; ◇*they're at the fishing la14*-. **4** before titles: ◇*The Lord Neill Campbell la14*-. **5** before nouns denoting a period of time: ◇*in the night time*; ◇*about the Martinmass la14*-. **6** before some place-names: ◇*the Bas*; ◇*the Langholm*; ◇*the Crail*; ◇*the Dam la14*-. **7** with names of diseases: ◇*she's got the measles 15*-. **8** with the names of languages: ◇*the Gaelic 15*-. **9** with measures, quantities or periods, indicating the rate for one unit, per: ◇*five shillings the ton*; ◇*ten barrels the day 15*-. **10** with non-count nouns denoting mainly abstract concepts: ◇*the peace is better nor the war 15*-. **11** with a noun used generically or as a type of its class: ◇*guid wine warms the hert and loosens the tongue 15*-. **12** with a noun phrase differentiated, usually by an adjective, as particular in some way: ◇*the maist noble prince*; ◇*is it not the strange thing? 16*-. **13** used with nouns denoting aspects of domestic life: ◇*up the stair*; ◇*sit at the table*; ◇*say the grace*; ◇*we'll hae fish for the tea 18*-. **14** used with nouns denoting a fit of annoyance or sulks: ◇*tak the huff 18*-. **15** with items of clothing: ◇*he wears the kilt 18*-. **16** with adjectives, adverbs or determiners, often comparatives, used substantively: ◇*the baith o them*; ◇*the maist folks 18*-.

17 used with nouns denoting public institutions with no restriction as to a particular location: ◇*she's at the school now*; ◇*he's in the jail la18*-. **18** used with commodities: ◇*price of the milk la18*-. **19** used instead of possessive adjective with names of relatives, especially ◇*the wife 19*-. **20** denoting the chief of a Highland clan: ◇*the Mackintosh 19*-. **21** before the names of schools or colleges: ◇*at the Waid Academy 19*-. **22** implying approval: ◇*Eat up your kail! That's the boy! 20*-. **23** before the surname of the chief member of a family: ◇*Robert the Bruce*; ◇*the Chisholm la14-16, 19- historical.* **24** *used before a relative pronoun* = THE[1,2] (sense 1) *la14-19, 20- in legal phraseology.* **25** with numerals denoting a year: ◇*in the 1667*; ◇*he wis oot in the '45 17-e19, 19 literary, 20- historical.* **26** sometimes omitted with river-names and place-names: ◇*drowned in Doun* ◇*Bridge of Don 18-19, 20- historical.* **27** in the; on the; of the ◇*a skelp ee jaw 19- NE T.* **28** with an adverb expressing location, especially THE BEN[1], THE BUT, THE FURTH: ◇*the snaw is cauld an deep the oot 18- NE.* **the self, the sell** itself *la14*-. **the morra** tomorrow *la20- C.* **the-noo** at the present time; a moment ago *la15*-. **the year** this year *17*- [late OE *ðe*, variant of *se* dem pron and adj]

the see THEE[1], THEE[2], THEE[3], THERE

theame see THEME[2]

thean see THANE[2]

theat, theet, †**thete** /θit; *EC* θet/ *n* **1** a trace attaching a draught animal to a vehicle or plough *19, 20- N NE T C.* **2** a tow, pulled by a trace-horse *20- T.* **3** the restraint imposed upon conduct *18-19, 20- NE.* **theater** a trace-horse of a cart or plough *20- C.* **theats,** †**thetis** traces, the ropes by which a draught animal is attached to a swingle-tree in order to pull a plough, harrow or vehicle *la15-19, 20- N NE T C.* †**hae nae theat o** to dislike, have no inclination for *la19.* **oot o theat 1** disordered; out of control; going beyond normal bounds *18-19, 20- NE T.* **2** in addition to what is expected or needed, extra *la20- NE.* [unknown]

theck see THACK[1,1]

thee[1], **thei**, *Sh* **tee,** †**the,** †**thie** /θi; *Bor* θae; *Sh* ti/ *n* **1** the part of the leg between the hip and the knee *la14*-. **2** the thigh of an animal as meat; a leg of smoked dried meat, especially mutton *17- Sh.* **3** the part of a garment covering the thigh *16.* [OE *ðēh*]

†**thee**[2], **the** *v literary* to thrive, prosper *la14-19.* [OE *ðēon*]

thee[3], *Sh Ork* **dee,** †**the,** †**thie** /ði; *Sh Ork* di/ *pron* **1** second person singular personal pronoun, the accusative and dative of THOU *la14-e19, 20- Sh Ork N SW.* **2** *used reflexively* thyself *la14-e19, 20- Ork.* **3** *used as a nominative and vocative* = THOU *la14-17.* Compare THOU, THY, YE. **dee sell** thyself *20- Sh.* [OE *ðē*]

thee see THY

theedle see THEEVIL

theek, thack, thick, †**thik,** †**theik** /θik, θak, θɪk/ *v* **1** to roof, cover (a building, hay-, corn-, or peat-stack) with straw, bracken, heather, rushes or sod *16*-. **2** to cover, protect with a thick covering of hair or clothes *17*-. **3** to roof (a building) with stone, slate, lead or tile *la14-18*; compare THACK[1,2]. **theeking spurtle** a flat-bladed implement, sometimes forked, for pushing thatching straw into position on a roof *19- SW Uls.* [ME *ðeccan*, ON *þekja*]

theek see THACK[1,1]

theel see THEEVIL

theer see THERE

theet see THEAT

theevil, *N NE T EC* **theedle**, *EC* **theel,** †**thivel** /'θivəl; *EC* 'θidəl, θil/ *n* a stick used to stir food during cooking, a SPURTLE[1] (sense 1) *18*-. [ME *thivel*]

thefe see THIEF¹·¹

theft, †thift, †theift /θɛft/ *n* **1** stealing; *law* the appropriation of moveable things belonging to another, without consent, with the intent of depriving the owner permanently, indefinitely or temporarily *la14-*. **2** *law* stolen goods *15-17*. **3** stealth, treachery, wickedness *la15-17*. **†theftdom** theft; thievery *la16-e19*. **†theftuous** thievish; furtive, stealthy *16-19*. **†thiftwis** = *theftuous 15-16*. **theft-bute, theft-boot** a bribe given by a thief to secure his release *15-17, 19- historical*. [OE ðēoft]

thegither, thegether, thegidder, taegither, *Sh* **tagidder,** *Sh* **tagedder,** *N NE* **egither, †togidder** /ðə'gɪðər, ðə'gɪdər; *Sh* tə'gɪðər; *N NE* i'gɪðər/ *adv* **1** expressing joining or intermingling; association or proximity; simultaneity; unity of being or purpose *la14-*. **2** with verbs expressing mutual or reciprocal action *la14-*. **3** *of a period of time* continuously; altogether *15-*. **thegither wi, thegither with** along with, in addition to; in company with, at the same time as *la15-*. [OE tōgædere, with influence from THE¹·²]

thei see THAY, THEE¹
theift see THEFT
theik see THEEK
theilk see THILK

theirsel, thairsel, themsel, †thaim self, †thame selff /ðər'sɛl, ðəm'sɛl/ *pron* emphatic or reflexive form of them (latterly in a collective sense) *la14-*. [THAIM + SEL¹·²; *their-* forms are by analogy with first and second person reflexive pronouns]

theirsels, thairsels, themsels, †thaim selfis, †thameselffis /ðər'sɛlz, ðəm'sɛlz/ *pron* emphatic or reflexive form of them *15-*. **theirsels twa** just the two of them *18-*. **†within theirsels** within their own property *la17*. [plural form of THEIRSEL]

theis see THIS¹·²
them see THAIM¹·¹, THAIM¹·²

†theme¹, thame, teme *n law* the right of jurisdiction in a suit for the recovery of goods alleged to have been stolen *12-e17*. **toll and theme** see TOLL. [OE tēam]

theme², †theame /θim/ *n* **1** a topic for composition or discussion *la15-*. **2** *in schools and universities* a topic for an exercise or essay, or translation into or out of Latin or Greek *16-17*. [OFr *theme*, Lat *thema*]

themsel see THEIRSEL
themsels see THEIRSELS
then see THAN¹·², THAN¹·³
thenk see THANK¹·¹, THANK¹·²

†theolog, theologue *n* **1** a theologian; a teacher of theology in a university *15-17*. **2** a university student of theology *17-e18*. **3** in pre-Christian contexts, a religious or moral authority and scholar *la15-e16*. [Lat *theologus*]

there, thair, thur, the, they, *Bor* **theer,** *Sh Ork* **der, †thar** /ðer; *unstressed* ðər, ðə, ðe; *Bor* ðir; *Sh Ork* der/ *adv* **1** in that place, at that time; to that place; at which place, where *la14-*. **2** *with the verb 'to be'* to indicate the existence of something: ◊*there is a muckle coo in the gairden la14-*. **3** *elliptical for* there is, there are: ◊*there naebody aboot 16-*. **†thereanent, thereanentis** about or relating to what has been said above *la16-e17*. **thereat 1** at the place, thing, occasion mentioned *la14-*. **2** at that, because of that *la14-*. **3** as regards that matter, about that *15-16*. **†thereatoure** furthermore, in addition; concerning what has been said above *la14-e16*. **thereawa, thereaway** in that direction; thereabouts *la14-*. **†thereben** in the inner part of a house or building *16-19*. **†therebut** in the outer part of a house or building *la16-19*. **thereby 1** by that place *la14-*. **2** by that, because of or by means of that *15-*. **3** around that time, amount, thereabouts *la15-*. **†theredown, thar doun** down there, down below *la14-18*. **therefore, †therefoir** for that, on that account; consequently; for that reason *la14-*. **†therefra, therefrae** from that place, time or action, thence *la14-19*. **†therefurth** outside; in the open *15-e16*. **therein** inside; within, indoors, at home; in; into *la14-*. **†thereintil, thereintill** in (a place, thing, matter); into *la15-e19*. **thereof** of, belonging to or with respect to that place, thing or matter *la14-*. **thereon** on a thing, place or matter *la14-*. **thereoot, †thereout 1** outside (place, circumstance); arising from (a source) *la14-*. **2** out of doors, in the open *15-*. **3** outside that place *la14-19*. **4** abroad, in existence *la15-e18*. **therethrough, †therethrow** by reason or means of that *la14-*. **theretill** = *thereto la14-*. **thereto 1** for that purpose; about that matter; to that thing, place or person *la14-*. **2** in addition, besides *la14-15*. **thereupon, thereapon 1** upon, on top of, on the outside or surface of *la14-*. **2** upon that subject or matter *la14-*. **3** in consequence of or directly after that *15-*. **therewith 1** with, by means of that thing or action; in consequence or on account of that *la14-*. **2** with that thing in one's possession, with a person in one's company; along with or as well as that *15-*. **3** that being said or done, at that *la14-*. **4** in addition to that, moreover *la14-*. **5** with or concerning that affair, action or person *15-17*. **†tharewithall, thairwithal** = *therewith*. [OE ðǣr]

thereckly /ðə'rɛkle/ *adv* directly, straight away, at once *la19- SW Bor*. [Eng *thereckly*, altered form of *directly*]

therm see THAIRM
therteen see THIRTEEN¹·²
therty see THIRTY¹·²
thes see THIS¹·²
thesaurar see THESAURER
thesaure see TREISURE

thesaurer, treasurer, †tresaurar, †thesaurar, †thresaurar /'θɛzərər, 'trɛʒərər/ *n* a treasurer, a person who administers a treasury, collects revenues, makes payments *15-*. **thesaurery 1** the post of treasurer; the office or department of treasurer of an organization *la15-*. **2** the office or department of the LORD HIGH TREASURER of Scotland *la15-e18, 18- historical*. **thesaurer hous** a treasury or repository for valuables *la15-17*. [Lat *thēsaurārius*, OFr *tresorer*]

thesis, †these /'θisɪs/ *n pl* **theses 1** a proposition or topic which was argued and the conclusions defended in debate *la16-*. **2** a written essay or spoken address or sermon on a THESIS (sense 1) *17-*. [Greek θέσις, Lat *thesis*, MFr *thèse*]

the streen¹·¹, *Sh Ork* **da streen** /ðə 'strin; *Sh Ork* də 'strɪn/ *n* yesterday evening *la18-*. [altered form of YESTREEN¹·¹, with influence from THE¹·²]

the streen¹·², *Sh Ork* da streen, †the strene /ðə 'strin; *Sh Ork* də 'strɪn/ *adv* last night; yesterday *la15-*. Compare YESTREEN¹·². [see the noun]

thete see THEAT
thevis nek see THIEF¹·¹
thewes, thewis see THOWS
thewles, thewless see THOWLESS
they see THAE¹·¹, THAE¹·², THAY, THERE
theyn furth see THYNE
thi see THY

thibet /'θɪbət/ *n* (cloth made from) a kind of fine Tibetan wool *19-*. [from the obsolete spelling *Thibet* of the place-name *Tibet*]

thick¹·¹, thik /θɪk/ *n* the midst of something; the densest part of a crowd *la16-*. [see the adj]

†thick¹·², thik *v* **1** to thicken the texture (of cloth) by fulling *17*. **2** to flock, crowd *16*. [OE ðiccian]

thick[1,3], *Sh Ork* **tick**, †**thik** /θɪk; *Sh Ork* tɪk/ *adj* **1** having relatively great extension, not thin; wide, broad *la14-*. **2** dense, difficult to penetrate, closely packed; solid, coagulated *la14-*. **3** broad, muscular, burly *18-*. **4** very friendly, intimate *19-*. †**thikkest** the most densely occupied part (of a crowd) *la14-15*. †**thikfald** thickly together; in crowds *16-e17*. **thickness**, †**thiknes 1** width, density *15-*. **2** a dense fog or sea-mist *la19-*. **3** familiarity, intimacy *la19*. **thick black** a brand of strong tobacco *20-*. **thick and threefauld 1** very friendly, intimate *la19, 20- Sh T Uls*. **2** in large numbers, in a crowd *19, 20- N*. **thick as mince** very stupid *la20-*. [OE *đicce*]

thick[1,4], †**thik** /θɪk/ *adv* **1** in large numbers, in close proximity, in a densely crowded manner *la14-*. **2** to considerable depth or width *15-*. **3** in rapid succession, quickly *la16-*. [OE *đicce*]

thick *see* THEEK

thicken, †**thikkyn**, †**thikkin** /ˈθɪkən/ *v* to (cause to) become thicker or denser in consistency *16-*. **thickenin, thickening, thicknen 1** an agent which curdles milk, rennet *la18-*. **2** the action of making thicker *19-*. [THICK[1,3] + verb-forming suffix]

thidder *see* THITHER

thie *see* THEE[1], THEE[3]

thief[1,1], *Sh Ork* **teef**, †**thefe** /θif; *Sh Ork* tif/ *n pl* **thieves**, †**thevis**, †**thewis**, †**thefis 1** a person who steals, a robber *la14-*. **2** a rascal, a scoundrel *la14-*. **3** the Devil *la17-*. **thiefie**, *Sh* **teefi** disreputable, given to stealing *la19-*. **thievish**, †**theyfage** given to stealing, dishonest *16-*. **thief-like** thievish; disreputable; stealthy, furtive *la18-19, 20- Sh*. †**theiflie** by stealth *la16*. **thief's hole, thieves' hole** a cell or dungeon (in a tollbooth), in which thieves and other criminals were imprisoned *16-18, 19- historical*. **thief lookin 1** disreputable *19-*. **2** *of the sky* ominous, foretelling bad weather *20- N*. †**thieves geit** the lapwing *Vanellus vanellus 19*. **tieves nacket, thievnick** the lapwing *Vanellus vanellus 20- Sh Ork*. †**thevis nek 1** the call of the lapwing *la15-16* **2** *derogatory* one fit for the gallows *la15-16*. **thief taker** a person who detects and captures thieves *16-*. [OE *đēof*]

thief[1,2] /θif/ *v* to steal *la19-*. [see the noun]

thieveless, thaveless /ˈθivləs, ˈθevləs/ *adj* **1** ineffective; feeble, listless *18-*. **2** cold, frigid, forbidding (in manner) *la18-e19*. [variant of *thewless* (THOWLESS)]

thift *see* THEFT

thig, *Sh* **tig** /θɪg; *Sh* tɪg/ *v* **1** to beg, ask for charity; to solicit (food) by begging *la14-19, 20- Sh Ork NE SW*. **2** to take for one's own use with or without permission *18, 20- NE*. **3** to crave, beseech, invoke (a favour or a curse) *la14-e19*. **thigger**, †**thiggar** a person who begs, especially a beggar who lives by begging food and lodging from particular houses *15-*. **thigging 1** the practice of begging *16-19, 20-*. **2** a gift or contribution obtained by begging *18-19, 20- historical*. [ON *þiggja* to receive]

thight *see* TICHT[1,3]

thik *see* THEEK, THICK[1,1], THICK[1,2], THICK[1,3], THICK[1,4]

thikkin, thikkyn *see* THICKEN

†**thilk, theilk** *adj* the same (as has already been mentioned) *15-e16*. Compare ILK[1]. [THE[1,2] + ILK[1,2]]

thimble, thimmle *see* THUMMLE

thin[1,1], *Sh* **tin** /θɪn/ *Sh* tɪn/ *n* something lacking thickness *18-*. **the thin** = *the thins*. **the thins** diarrhoea *20- NE T*. **da tin o da side** the flank *la19- Sh*. **da tin o da rib** = *da tin o da side*. [see the adj]

thin[1,2], *Sh* **tin**, †**thyne** /θɪn; *Sh* tɪn/ *v* **1** to make or become thin *la16-*. **2** to pick the bones out of cooked fish *la19- Sh N*. [OE *đynnian*]

thin[1,3], *Sh* **tin**, †**thyn**, †**thyne** /θɪn; *Sh* tɪn/ *adj* **1** having relatively little extent; not thick; narrow, slender *la14-*. **2** not dense; loose, runny, watery; insubstantial, weak *la14-*. **3** lacking flesh, spare, bony *la15-*. **4** *of a group or class* few, sparse, scanty, scarce *16-*. **5** *of wind or weather* cold, bitter *20-*. **6** *of a shot in bowls or curling* narrow, not having enough bias *20-*. **7** annoyed; unfriendly *la19- NE WC*. [OE *đynne*]

thin[1,4], †**thyn** /θɪn/ *adv* thinly, sparsely, sparingly *la14-*. [see the adj]

thin *see* THYNE

thine, *Sh* **dine**, †**thyne** /ðaɪn; *Sh* dʌɪn/ *pron* yours; belonging to you *la14-*. Compare THY, THOO. [OE *đīn*, genitive of *đū*]

thing[1], **hing**, *Sh Ork* **ting**, †**thyng** /θɪŋ, hɪŋ; *Sh Ork* tɪŋ/ *n* **1** a material object *la14-*. **2** an action or event, a matter or item for consideration *la14-*. **3** an entity, a phenomenon: ◊*the horse wis a canny auld thing*. *la14-*. **4** something said, written or thought, a fact, opinion or story *la14-*. **5** the male or female sexual organ *16-*. **6** an amount or number, an extent or cost: ◊*she ate an awfu thing o tatties*. *la18-*. **7** a reason, a cause *e19*. **things** goods, possessions, property; food or drink *la14-*. **ting o bairn** a child *la19- Sh Ork N*. **Thing-at's-awa** a dead person *20- Sh*. [OE *đing*]

thing[2], *Sh Ork* **ting** /θɪŋ/; *Sh Ork* tɪŋ/ *n in areas of Scandinavian settlement* a public assembly with legislative and judicial powers *18- historical*. Compare LAWTHING. [Norw *ting*, ON *þing*]

thingie, thingy /ˈθɪŋe, ˈθɪŋi/ *n* **1** a (small) thing, frequently something the name of which has been forgotten *la18-*. **2** a (small) person; a person of a specified sort: ◊*he wis jist a puir sharger thingie*. *la18-*. [THING[1] + -IE[1]]

thingmy, thingwi, hingmy /ˈθɪŋmi, ˈθɪŋwi, ˈhɪŋmi/ *n* a term used to indicate a person or thing, the name of which one cannot remember or cannot be bothered to give precisely *20-*. **thingum** = *thingmy 20-*. **thingumdairie** = *thingmy la19- NE*. [variants of Eng *thingummy*, extended sense of THING[1]]

thingy *see* THINGIE

think[1,1] /θɪŋk/ *n* a thought, an idea, an opinion; a spell of thinking *19-*. [see the verb]

think[1,2], **hink**, *Sh Ork* **tink**, †**thynk** /θɪŋk, hɪŋk; *Sh Ork* tɪŋk/ *v pt, ptp* **thocht, thoucht, thoat, thunk**, *Sh Ork* **toucht 1** to form in the mind, conceive mentally; to meditate on, ponder; to engage in mental activity *la14-*. **2** to have in mind, intend *la14-*. **3** to believe, judge, consider, regard; to suspect, expect *la14-*. **4** to call to mind, reflect on, remember, bear in mind *la15-*. **5** to appear, seem (to someone): ◊*him thinks* ◊*methinks la14-16*. **Ah'm thinkin** I presume, it's my opinion *la18-*. **think at** to be offended, take amiss *20- Sh*. **think black burnin shame** to be very ashamed *la15-*. **think ill to do** to be unwilling to do, have scruples about doing *la19, 20- Sh N*. †**think lak** to be ashamed *la16-e19*. **think lang** to long for, miss *la15-19, 20- Sh T SW*. **thinkna** do not think *la18-*. **think on 1** to reflect on, think of or about *15-*. **2** to devise, invent, hit upon *la18-19, 20- NE EC SW*. **think shame** to be ashamed *la15-*. **think tae, think till** to think of *20- NE EC*. [OE *đencan* to form in the mind, conflated with OE *đyncan* to seem]

thir[1,1], **thur** /ðɪr, ðʌr/ *dem pron* these *la14-*. Compare THIS[1,2]. [unknown]

thir[1,2], **thur** /ðɪr, ðʌr/ *dem adj* these *la14-*. Compare THIS[1,3]. [unknown]

thir[1.3], **thur, thair, their,** *Sh* **der,** †**thar** /ðɪr, ðʌr, ðer; *Sh* der/ *pron* of or belonging to them; their *14-*; compare THAIM. **their lane** by themselves, without a companion *la16-*. [ON *þeira*]

third[1.1]**, thurd,** *Sh* **trid,** †**thrid** /θɪrd, θʌrd; *Sh* trɪd/ *n* **1** a third part *la14-*. **2** the third part of the personal property and effects of a deceased husband which was allowed to the widow *la14-e17*. **3** the third part of a person's moveable estate which could be disposed of before death *la16-e17*. **thirdie** a loaf of coarse or inferior flour, with a large amount of bran *la19- NE T.* **thirds 1** the residue of grain left after milling or brewing, third-quality flour *la19-*. **2** *Presbyterian Church* a third of the ecclesiastical revenues collected by the Crown and used to ensure adequate provision for the clergy of the post-Reformation church *la16*. †**third and teind** a lease whereby the tenant paid one third of his crop as rent as well as a tenth in tithe *la18-19*. **trids of kin,** †**thirds of kin** related in the third degree of consanguinity *16-19, 20- Sh*. †**thirds of benefices** a third of the ecclesiastical revenues used to provide for the clergy *la16*. [see the adj]

third[1.2]**, thurd,** *Sh* **trid,** †**thrid** /θɪrd, θʌrd; *Sh* trɪd/ *v* to divide into thirds *la15-*. [see the adj]

third[1.3]**, thurd,** *Sh* **trid,** †**thrid,** †**thred** /θɪrd, θʌrd; *Sh* trɪd/ *adj* the ordinal number corresponding to the cardinal number three; of the third in a sequence *la14-*. **thirdsman** a third person, especially one acting as arbiter between two disputants *la18-*. [OE *ðridda*]

thirl[1.1]**,** †**thyrl** /θɪrl/ *n* **1** a hole, an aperture *16-19, 20- N*; compare NOSETHIRL. **2** the sensation caused by the intense excitation of the emotions or nerves *la19-*. [OE *ðyrel*]

thirl[1.2]**, thrill,** *Sh Ork* **tirl,** †**thirll** /θɪrl, θrɪl; *Sh Ork* tɪrl/ *v* **1** to pierce, bore through, penetrate, perforate *la14-*. **2** to pierce or affect with emotion *la15-*. **3** to vibrate, quiver, (cause to) experience a tingling sensation *18-*. **4** *mining* to cut through a wall of coal *la18-*. †**thirling** *n mining* a hole connecting one working with another *la18-19*. †**thirling** *adj of weather* piercingly cold, bitter *19*. [OE *ðyrlian*]

thirl[2.1]**,** †**thrill,** †**thrall,** †**threll** /θɪrl/ *n* **1** a person bound in servitude, a slave *la14-19, 20- literary*. **2** *law* the obligation of being bound in thirlage to a particular mill *la15-19, 20- historical*. **3** the lands subject to thirlage, the sucken of a mill *la16-e19*. **4** the body of tenants bound to a particular mill *la17-18*. †**thirl multure** *law* the multure paid by tenants bound by thirlage; the right to exact it *la14-e18*. [OE *ðræl* from ON *þræll* a thrall; but most senses develop from the verb]

thirl[2.2]**, thrill,** †**thrall,** †**threll** /θɪrl, θrɪl/ *v* **1** to bind with ties of affection, duty, loyalty or habit *15-*. **2** *law* to restrict or bind (lands or tenants) to have grain ground at a particular mill *15-19, 20- historical*. **3** to bind or oblige (a person) to give his services or custom to a particular person *19, 20- NE*. **4** to engage as a servant *20- Bor*. **5** to enthral, overwhelm, hold in subjection; to embroil in debt *16-17*. **6** to mortgage (land or property) *la15-e17*. **7** to enslave, reduce to or hold in bondage or servitude *la15-16*. **thirled, thirlit 1** bound in thirlage *16-*. **2** bound by ties of affection or duty *la16-*. **3** hidebound by an idea or belief *la19-*. †**thirlit multure** the multure paid by tenants bound by thirlage; the right to exact it *16-17*. [see the noun]

†**thirl**[2.3]**, thryl, thrall** *adj of tenants* bound to a particular mill *15-19*. [see the verb]

†**thirl**[3] *v* to furl *16-e17*. [variant of EModE *furl*]

thirlage, †**thrillage** /ˈθɪrlədʒ/ *n* **1** *law* the obligation on the tenants of an estate to have their grain ground at a particular mill *la16-e20, la20- historical*. **2** the multure or payment made to a mill for grinding grain *18-e19*. **3** the land or body of tenants bound to a mill *la17-18*. **4** *law* service due to a superior *la15-17*. **5** thraldom, bondage *la14-16*. [THIRL[2.1] + -*age* suffix]

thirldom, thraldom, †**thrildom** /ˈθɪrldəm, ˈθrɔldəm/ *n* slavery, servitude to a superior or tyrant; bondage *la14-*. [THIRL[2.1] + -*dom* suffix]

thirll *see* THIRL[1.2]

thirlman, †**thrillman** /ˈθɪrlman/ *n* a (farm) servant, a bondsman, a slave *la14-19, 20- literary*. [THIRL[2.1] + MAN]

thirsill *see* THRISSEL

thirst[1.1]**, thrist,** *Sh Ork* **trist** /θɪrst, θrɪst; *Sh Ork* trɪst/ *n* **1** the need to drink *la14-*. **2** an overwhelming desire or longing for (something) *la15-*. **thirsty, thristy** afflicted by thirst *15-*. [OE *ðurst*, with vowel influenced by the verb]

thirst[1.2]**, thrist,** *Sh Ork* **trist** /θɪrst, θrɪst; *Sh Ork* trɪst/ *v* **1** to crave, long for (something)*la14-*. **2** to experience a need to drink, be thirsty *la15-*. †**thristing** the need to drink *la15-e18*. [OE *ðyrstan*]

thirstle *see* THRISSEL

thirteen[1.1]**,** †**thretten, threttein,** †**thrattene** /θɪrˈtin/ *adj* thirteenth *la14-*. [see the numeral]

thirteen[1.2]**, therteen,** *Sh* **tretten,** †**thretten,** †**threttein,** †**thrattene** /θɪrˈtin, θerˈtin; *Sh* ˈtretən/ *numeral* the cardinal number between twelve and fourteen *la14-*. **thirteent** thirteenth *la16-19, 20- NE*. [OE *ðrēotīne*]

†**thirty**[1.1]**, threty, thrittie** *adj* thirtieth *16-17*. [see the numeral]

thirty[1.2]**, thurty, therty, thretty,** *Sh Ork* **tretty,** *Ork* **terty,** †**thritty** /ˈθɪrti, ˈθʌrte, ˈθerte, ˈθrete; *Sh Ork* ˈtreti; *Ork* ˈterti/ *numeral* the cardinal number between twenty-nine and thirty-one *la14-*. **thirtytwosome** a reel danced in sets of thirty-two dancers *20-*. [OE *ðrītig*]

this[1.1]**,** *Sh* **dis** /ðɪs; *Sh* dɪs/ *adv* **1** so, to such a degree or extent *la16-*. **2** thus *la14-16*. [OE *ðys*, instrumental of *ðes* dem pron and adj]

this[1.2]**,** *Sh* **dis,** *N NE* **is,** †**thes,** †**theis** /ðɪs; *Sh* dɪs; *N NE* ɪs/ *dem pron* **1** the one nearer in place, the one closer to mind *la14-*. **2** this time, this place, now, here: ◇*he gaed fae this tae Ayr 14-*. **3** these: ◇*this is them la18- Sh NE*. Compare THIR[1.1]. **this o't** this state of affairs, this point or pitch *19, 20- literary*. [OE *ðis*, neuter nominative sg of *ðes* dem pron and adj]

this[1.3]**,** *Sh* **dis,** *N NE* **is,** †**thais** /ðɪs; *Sh* dɪs; *N NE* ɪs/ *dem adj* **1** the nearer in place, the closer to mind *la14-*. **2** these *18-*. **3** *with expressions of time* this: ◇*this nicht la15-*. [see the dem pron]

thissell cok *see* THROSTLE

Thistle /ˈθɪsəl/ *n* a nickname for any Scottish football club with the word 'thistle' in its name *20-*. [shortened from the team name]

thistle *see* THRISSEL

thit *see* THAT[1.2], THAT[1.4], THAT[2]

thither, †**thidder** /ˈθɪðər/ *adv* to that place, there *la14-*. †**thitherward, thidderwart** = THITHER *la14-e19*. [OE *ðider*]

thivel *see* THEEVIL

†**tho**[1] *adv* then, at that time; subsequently; thereupon *la15-16 literary*. [southern ME *tho*, ON *ðā*]

tho[2]**, though,** †**thof,** †**thoch,** †**thoucht,** *Sh Ork* **to** /ðo; *Sh Ork* to/ *conj* **1** despite the fact that, although *la14-*. **2** even if, even supposing *la14-*. **3** if, in the event that *15-16*. **4** irrespective of (whether) *la15-e16*. [ON **þóh*]

thoat *see* THINK[1.2]

thoch *see* THO[2]

thocht, thoucht, thought, thoat, *Sh Ork* **toght,** *Sh Ork* **tought,** †**thowcht** /θɔxt, θɔt, θot; *Sh Ork* tɔxt; *Sh Ork* tʌut/ *n* **1** an idea, a thought *la14-*. **2** intention, purpose, opinion *la14-*. **3** anxiety, care, sorrow; a cause for anxiety, a burden, worry *la15*-. **4** consideration, care, regard *la16*-. **5** a small amount (of) *19*-. **6** memory, recollection *la14-15*. **thochtful 1** mindful, considerate, careful *la14*-. **2** engaged in thinking, pensive *19*-. **3** anxious, melancholy *la15-19, 20- Sh*. **thouchtish** serious, pensive *20- Bor*. **thochtit** worried, anxious, troubled *la19, 20- EC*. **thocht bane** the wishbone of a fowl *19- NE*. **a thocht, a thochtie** a little, somewhat *19*-. **it's my thocht** it's my belief *la19, 20- Sh NE*. **to a thocht** precisely, exactly *la19*-. [OE *ðōht*]

thocht see THINK[1,2]

thochtie[1], **thochty**, †**thoughty** /ˈθɔxti/ *n* **1** a very small amount, a little *la18*-. **2** a thought *20- NE* [THOCHT + -IE[1]]

thochtie[2], **thochty**, †**thoughty** /ˈθɔxti/ *adj* heedful, attentive; serious-minded; anxious *la14*-. †**thochtiness** anxiety; melancholy *la17-e18*. [THOCHT + -IE[2]]

thock /θɔk/ *v* to pant, breathe heavily with exertion *19- Bor*. [perhaps onomatopoeic]

thof see THO[2]

thoft see THAFT, THORT[1,1]

thoill see THOLE[1,2]

thole[1,1] /θol/ *n* patience, endurance *e17, 20- SW Uls*. [see the verb]

thole[1,2], †**thoill**, †**tholl** /θol/ *v* **1** to endure with patience or fortitude, put up with, tolerate *la14*-. **2** to be patient, wait patiently *la14*-. **3** to have to bear pain or grief; to be afflicted with (some evil) *la14*-. **4** *of people or things* to be able to endure; to have capacity for, withstand *15*-. **5** to allow, permit *la14-19*. **tholeable** bearable, tolerable *19*-. †**tholance** sufferance, toleration; permission *15*. **tholer** a person who endures or perseveres *la20*-. †**tholing** sufferance, permission, leave *la14-e16*. †**tholmod**, †**tholmude** patient, meek, long-suffering *la14-e18*. **thole amends** *of health* to be capable of improvement *la18-19, 20- WC SW Bor*. †**thoill arriest** to be arrested, get caught *la15*. **thole an assize** *law* to stand trial *15*-. †**thole fire and water** *of grain* to undergo a process of steeping in water and kiln-drying in preparation for grinding at a mill *17-e19*. †**thole the law** = thole an assize *15-17*. **thole through** to recover from an illness *la19- T EC*. **thole wi** to put up with, tolerate *19*-. [OE *ðolian*]

tholl see THOLE[1,2], TOLL

tholmont see TOWMOND

thon[1,1] /ðɔn/ *dem pron* that, those, the thing or person more remote from the speaker than another or others *19*-. [altered form of YON[1,3] with influence from THAT]

thon[1,2] /ðɔn/ *dem adj* that; those *19*-. [see the dem pron]

thonder, thonner /ˈðɔndər ˈðɔnər/ *adv* over there, at some distance, yonder *la19*-. [altered form of YONNER[1,1] with influence from THERE]

thong see THANG

thonner see THONDER

thoo see THOU

thoom[1,1], **thoum, thoomb, thumb**, *Sh Ork* **toom** /θum, θʌm; *Sh Ork* tum/ *n* **1** the inner digit of the human hand, opposable to the fingers *la14*-. **2** the part of a glove designed to cover the thumb *17*-. **3** the thumb used as a measure of length, the width of the thumb taken as an inch *15-17, la19- historical*. **4** a thumb-shaped part of the liver of a ruminant *20- Sh*. **thoomack** a violin peg *la19- NE T*. **thoumie** the wren *20- NE*. **thoumkins, thumbikins** thumbscrews *la17, 18- historical*. **thoum hand** the nearest free available hand; the right hand *la19- NE T*. **thumb note** piping high A, the top note of the bagpipe scale *20*-. **thumb piece**, *Ork* **toom piece** a slice of bread with butter spread on with the thumb *20- Ork NE C Bor*. **thoom raip** a hay or straw rope made by twisting the strands under the tip of the thumb *19- NE H&I C SW*. **thoum stall** a sheath for protecting an injured thumb *la18*-. **toomy snuid** = *thoom raip 20- Sh*. **thumb variation** piping a doubling of the ground in which the *thumb note* is usually substituted for the highest note in each phrase *20*-. †**aboon yer thumb** beyond your reach, power or abilities *18-19*. **aside yer thoom** in an uncertain manner *20- NE*. **he cannae bite his thoum** he is drunk *la18, 19- NE T*. †**under thoume** covertly *la16-17*. **there's my thumb** an offer to strike a bargain by joining of thumbs *18*-. [OE *ðūma*]

thoom[1,2], **thoum, thumb**, *Sh Ork* **toom** /θum, θʌm; *Sh Ork* tum/ *v* to touch, rub, spread or manipulate with the thumb(s) *18*-. [see the noun]

thoomack see THOOM[1,1]

thoomb see THOOM[1,1]

thoosand, thoosant, thoosan, thousand, *Sh Ork* **toosan**, †**thowsand** /ˈθuzənd, ˈθuzənt, ˈθuzən, ˈθʌuzənd; *Sh Ork* ˈtuzən/ *numeral* **1** the cardinal number equal to ten times one hundred *la14*-. **2** an indefinitely large number *15*-. **thousandfauld 1** a thousand times as much *19*-. **2** a thousand times (in succession) *e16*. [OE *ðūsend*]

thorl see WHURL[2]

thorn, *Sh* **torn**, †**thorne** /θɔrn; *Sh* tɔrn/ *n* **1** a prickle or spine; a thorn tree or bush *12*-. **2** a spine or prickle on an animal or fish *la15*-. **thorny, thornie 1** filled with or composed of thorn trees or bushes; frequently in place-names *la13*-. **2** painful, contentious, difficult to handle *17*-. **thorn-back** the ray *Raja clavata la16*-. †**thorne rone** thorny undergrowth *15-16*. **thorny-back** = *thorn-back la18*-. **toarny-ware** barbed wire *20- Sh*. [OE *ðorn*]

thorough[1,1] /ˈθʌrə/ *n* a thorough cleaning or tidying *20*-. [see the adj]

thorough[1,2], †**thorow** /ˈθʌrə/ *v* to clean thoroughly *20*-. [see the adj]

thorough[1,3], †**thorow**, †**throw**, †**throuche** /ˈθʌrə/ *adj* **1** complete, full; without omissions; *of a person* painstaking, methodical *17*-. **2** mentally alert, intelligent; sane *17-19, 20- SW Bor*. [OE *ðurh* through, throughout; compare THROU[1,2]]

thoroughfare, †**throuchfare** /ˈθʌrəfər/ *n* **1** a street leading into another street *16*-. **2** a town or village on a highway (which is not a burgh), through which traffic passes regularly *15-17*. †**throuchfair toun** a non-burghal town on a highway *16*. [ME *thurgh-fare*, OE *ðurh*, THROU[1,2] + OE *faru* a way]

thorow see THOROUGH[1,2], THOROUGH[1,3], THROU[1,2], THROU[1,3]

thort[1,1], **thwart**, †**thoft** /θɔrt, θwɔrt/ *n* **1** a crosswise board in a boat, a rower's bench *16*-; compare THAFT. **2** the transverse member of a window *la16*. [see the adv]

thort[1,2], **thwart** /θɔrt, θwɔrt/ *v* **1** to foil, obstruct, frustrate *la16*-. **2** to cross-plough or harrow *20- NE*. **3** to clash, conflict (with) *la17*. [see the adv]

thort[1,3], **thwart**, *Sh Ork* **twart** /θɔrt, θwɔrt; *Sh Ork* twɑrt/ *adj* **1** lying transversely, crosswise *19- Sh Ork*. **2** *of a person* perverse, awkward *la19*. **twart-bauk, twart-back** a joist or crossbeam *19- Sh Ork*. [see the adv]

thort[1,4], **thwart**, *Sh Ork* **twart**, †**thuart** /θɔrt, θwɔrt; *Sh Ork* twɑrt/ *adv* transversely *la17- Sh Ork SW*. [ME *thwart*, ON *þvert*]

thort[1,5], *Sh Ork* **twart**, †**thwart** /θɔrt; *Sh Ork* twɑrt/ *prep* across, from side to side of *la17*-. [see the adv]

†**thorter**[1,1], **thortour, thworter** *n* **1** a difficulty or dilemma, a setback, contention *la16-17*. **2** the transverse member of a window *16*. [see the adv]

thorter[1,2], †**thourtour** /ˈθɔrtər/ *v* **1** to cross the path of; to oppose, contradict, clash with *la16*-. **2** to do something in a direction at right angles to what has been done before (such as in ploughing and harrowing, or in spreading butter) *la17-19, 20- NE*. [see the adv]

thorter[1.3], *Sh* **twarter**, †**thortour**, †**thwortour** /'θɔrtər; *Sh* 'twɑrtər/ *adj* **1** *of wood* cross-grained *19, 20 Sh NE*. **2** crossing, lying across, transverse; contrary *la15-e18*. **thorter ill** paralysis in sheep causing distortion of the neck; a palsy *la18-19, 20- literary*. †**thorter knot** a knot in wood where a branch has grown out of the tree *e19*. [see the adv]

thorter[1.4], †**thortour**, †**thwortour** /'θɔrtər/ *adv* transversely, across, from side to side *la15-*. Compare OVERTHORT[1.1]. [ME *thwert-over*, THORT[1.4] + OWER[1.3]]

thorter[1.5], †**thortour** /'θɔrtər/ *prep* on or to the other side of, across, over *16-19, 20- Sh*. [see the adv]

thortour *see* THORTER[1.1], THORTER[1.3], THORTER[1.4], THORTER[1.5]

thou, *Sh Ork* **du**, *Ork N* **thoo**, *Ork N* **thu**, †**tou**, †**thow** /ðʌu; *Sh Ork* du; *Ork N* ðu/ *pron* you *la14-19, 20- Sh Ork N SW*. Compare THY, THEE, YE. [OE *ðū*]

thoucht *see* THINK[1.2], THO[2], THOCHT

though *see* THO[1], THO[2]

thought *see* THOCHT

thoughty *see* THOCHTIE[1.1], THOCHTIE[1.2]

thoum *see* THOOM[1.1], THOOM[1.2]

thoumart *see* FOUMART

thourtour *see* THORTER[1.2]

†**thousand** *adj* thousandth *la16-17*. [extended sense of *thousand* (THOOSAND)]

thousand *see* THOOSAND

thow[1.1], **thowe**, **thaw**, *Sh Ork* **tow** /θʌu, θɔ; *Sh Ork* tʌu/ *n* (weather causing) the process of melting snow or ice *16-*. **thow wind** a wind bringing a thaw *20-*. [see the verb]

thow[1.2], **thowe**, **thaw**, *Sh Ork* **tow** /θʌu, θɔ; *Sh Ork* tʌu/ *v of ice or snow* to (cause to) melt *la16-*. [OE **ðōwan*]

thow *see* THOU

thowe *see* THOW[1.1], THOW[1.2]

thowl, **thowal**, *N EC* **thow** /θʌul, 'θʌuəl; *N EC* θʌu/ *n* one of the pins which hold the oar in a boat *19-*. **thow pin**, **thowal pin** = THOWL *la19-*. [OE *ðol*]

thowless, *C Bor* **thewless**, †**thewles** /θʌuləs; *C Bor* 'θjuləs/ *adj* **1** lacking energy or spirit, listless, inactive; lacking initiative, ineffectual *18-*. **2** immoral, dissolute *la14-e16*. [OE *ðēawlēas* ill-mannered; compare THOWS]

thows, †**thewes**, †**thewis** /θʌuz/ *npl* **1** muscles, tendons *19-*. **2** personal characteristics, customs, habits; behaviour *la14-e16*. [plural of OE *ðēaw* a habit; in pl virtues]

thowsand *see* THOOSAND

thra *see* THRAE

†**thra**[1.1] *n* eagerness, haste, fury of battle *15-e16*. [ON *þrá* obstinacy, hard struggle]

†**thra**[1.2] *adv* boldly; persistently; violently *la15-e16*. [from the adj *thra* (THRAE)]

thra *see* THRAE

thraa *see* THRAW[1.1], THRAW[1.2]

thrab *see* THROB[1.1], THROB[1.2]

thrae, *Sh Ork SW* **tray**, †**thra** /θre; *Sh Ork SW* tre/ *adj* **1** obstinate, persistent, perverse *la14-19, 20- Sh Ork*. **2** reluctant, unwilling; reserved, aloof *la14-19, 20- SW*. **3** keen, zealous, earnest *la14-e16*. [ON *þrár* obstinate, zealous, keen]

thrae *see* FAE[2.1], FAE[2.2]

thraetin *see* THREATEN

thrafe *see* THREAVE[1.1]

thraffe *see* THARF

thraif *see* THREAVE[1.1], THRIVE[1.2]

thrain[1.1], †**thren** /θren/ *n* a sad refrain; a dirge or lamentation *la19, 20- literary*. [EModE *threne*, Greek θρῆνος a funeral lament]

thrain[1.2] /θren/ *v* to beg persistently; to nag *la19- EC*. [see the noun]

thraip *see* THREAP[1.2]

thraist *see* THRUST[1.2]

thraiten *see* THREATEN

thraldom *see* THIRLDOM

thrall *see* THIRL[2.1], THIRL[2.2], THIRL[2.3]

thram /θram/ *v* to thrive *la18- NE*. [unknown; compare Eng †*frame* to prosper]

thrammel /'θraməl/ *n* **1** the rope or chain by which cattle are tied in their stalls, specifically the part linking the post to the SELL[2] *19- N NE*. **2** the leather hinge connecting the hand-staff and swipple of a flail *20- Ork NE*. [altered form of Eng *trammel*]

thrammel *see* THRUMMLE

thrang[1.1], **throng**, *Sh Ork* **trang** /θraŋ, θrɔŋ; *Sh Ork* traŋ/ *n* **1** a multitude of people; a milling crowd *la14-*. **2** intense pressure; hectic activity, a busy time *la17-*. **3** a large quantity or number *la19, 20- NE*. **4** close friendship, intimacy *la18-e19*. **5** affliction, distress; difficulties *la14-16*. [OE *geðrang*]

thrang[1.2], **throng**, **thring**, †**thryng** /θraŋ, θrɔŋ, θrɪŋ/ *v pt* †**thrang** *ptp* **thronged**, †**thrung**, †**thrungin 1** to assemble in a crowd; to press or push forward or past *la14-*. **2** to thrust, force, impale *la14-17*. †**thring doun** to press or force down; to subdue *la14-16*; compare *doun thring* (DOON[1.3]). [from the noun and OE *ðringan*]

thrang[1.3], **throng**, *Sh Ork* **trang** /θraŋ, θrɔŋ; *Sh Ork* traŋ/ *adj* **1** pressed together; densely packed *la15-*. **2** pressing, urgent; busily occupied *la15-*. **3** crowded with people *la16-*. **4** intimately associated, on very friendly terms *la18-*. **thrangity 1** intense pressure; hectic activity *19-*. **2** a bustling crowd, a press of people *20- T C*. †**thronged** busily occupied with a difficult task *18*. **thrang o** full of, crowded with *18-19, 20- literary*. [see the noun]

thrang[1.4], *Sh Ork* **trang**, †**throng** /θraŋ; *Sh Ork* traŋ/ *adv* **1** busily, assiduously *la18-19, 20- Sh*. **2** in large numbers; densely packed *17-19*. [see the noun]

thrapple[1.1], **thropple**, *Sh Ork* **trapple**, †**throppill**, †**thropill** /'θrapəl, 'θrɔpəl; *Sh Ork* 'trapəl/ *n* the windpipe; the throat, the gullet *la14-*. **thrapple bow** the Adam's apple *20- N NE*. [compare OE *ðrot-bolla* the Adam's apple]

thrapple[1.2], **thropple**, *Sh Ork* **trapple** /'θrapəl, 'θrɔpəl; *Sh Ork* 'trapəl/ *v* to grip by the throat; to throttle *la18-*. [see the noun]

thrapple[2], **thropple** /'θrapəl, 'θrɔpəl/ *v* **1** to draw the edges of a hole in cloth roughly together instead of darning *20- SW Bor*. **2** *of wool* to tangle *20- Bor*. [altered form of RAPPLE]

thrapple plough /'θrapəl plʌu/ *n* a single-stilted wooden plough formerly used in the Highlands *la18- historical*. [unknown]

thrash *see* RASH[1], THRESH

thrashel *see* THRESHOLD

thrashen *see* THRESH

thrast *see* THRUST[1.2]

thratch[1.1] /θratʃ/ *n* a jerk, a twist of the body; a convulsion *la15-19, 20- N NE T*. Compare THRAW[1.1]. [unknown]

thratch[1.2] /θratʃ/ *v* to twist the body about; to writhe or convulse *18- N NE T*. Compare THRAW[1.2]. [unknown]

thrattene *see* THIRTEEN[1.1], THIRTEEN[1.2]

thrave *see* THREAVE[1.1], THREAVE[1.2], THRIVE[1.2]

thraveless *see* THRIEVELESS

thraw[1.1], **throw**, **throe**, *Sh Ork* **traa**, *NE* **thraa** /θrɔ, θro; *Sh Ork* trɑ; *NE* θrɑ/ *n* **1** a convulsion, a spasm, a writhing of the body in pain *15-*. **2** a turn or twist; an act of twisting *16-*. **3** a distortion, a tilt, a warp *la16-*. **4** a fit of obstinacy or ill-humour *la18-*. **5** the action of throwing; the distance a missile is thrown *19-*. **6** an argument, a quarrel *19-*. **7** a check, a reverse, a setback *19-*. **8** *piping* a series of grace notes preceding a melody note of higher pitch *20-*. **9** a wrench of a muscle, a sprain *la18-19, 20- Sh NE T EC*. **10** a contortion of the face, a wry expression *la19, 20- Sh Ork NE*. **11** *mining* a fault or dislocation in a vein or stratum *la19, 20- C*. **a thraw in the raip** a drawback, an unforeseen difficulty *20- EC*. **oot o thraw** *of a stone or brick* into alignment; straightened, squared *19, 20- NE SW*. [see the verb]

thraw[1,2], **throw**, *Sh Ork* **traa**, *NE* **thraa** /θrɔ, θro; *Sh Ork* trɑ; *NE* θrɑ/ *v pt* **thrawit, thrawed, threw**, *ptp* **thrawn, thrown**, *Sh Ork* **traan**, †**thrawin 1** to project with force; to fling, hurl *la14-*. **2** to twist or turn; to wring or screw *la14-*. **3** to turn a key, a knob or a wheel *la14-*. **4** to writhe or convulse *la14-*. **5** to wrench or sprain a joint or muscle *la15-*. **6** to distort or pervert the meaning or interpretation of something *la15-*. **7** to twist straw or withies together to make rope *la15-*. **8** to thwart, oppose; to quarrel or contend with *la16-*. **9** to curl, shrivel; to become warped or twisted *la18-*. **10** to discolour, fade or cause to fade *19-*. **11** to throw up, vomit *la19-*. **12** to snatch or wrench something *15-e17*. **13** to attack, strike *15*. †**thrawand** struggling painfully; suffering the agony of death *la14-e16*. **thraw-cruik**, †**thrawcruk 1** an implement for twisting straw into rope *la16-*. **2** a twisted straw rope *20-*. **thraw-huik**, *NE* **thraa-heuk** an implement for twisting straw into rope *20- NE H&I Uls*. †**thraw-mow** a name for a cannon *la16*. **thraw-moose, thraa moose** the common shrew *19- NE*. **thraw rape** an implement for twisting straw into rope *20-*. **be thrown back** to suffer a relapse in an illness *20-*. **throw down** to demolish; to destroy *la15-*. **throw off 1** to produce with ease *la18-*. **2** to print *19-*. **thraw the neck** to wring the neck (of a fowl or a person) *17-*. †**thraw your neb** to tweak a person's nose *17*. †**thraw your nose** = *thraw your neb 17*. **throw out** to emit, discharge, expel *16-*. **throw together** to bring into casual contact *19-*. **thraw yer face** to screw up or contort the face *18-*. [OE *ðrāwan*]

thraw *see* THRAWN

thrawart, *Sh Ork* **traaward**, †**thraward**, †**throwart** /'θrɔwərt; *Sh Ork* 'trɑwərd/ *adj* **1** perverse, contrary, obstinate *la15-*. **2** adverse, unfavourable *la16-*. **3** twisted, crooked *19*. [variant of FRAWART, with influence from THRAWN]

thrawin *see* THRAW[1,2], THRAWN

thrawn, *Sh Ork Uls* **trawn**, †**thrawin**, †**thraw**, †**threw** /θrɔn; *Sh Ork Uls* trɔn/ *adj* **1** perverse, obstinate; intractable; sullen, surly *la15-*. **2** *of the facial features* contorted with pain or rage *la15-*. **3** twisted, crooked; distorted, misshapen *16-*. **4** *of weather* disagreeable, inclement *la19, 20- NE*. **5** *of string or thread* fashioned from strands twisted together *la16-e17*. **6** *of jewellery or metalware* made by turning or patterned with a twisting pattern *16-17*. **thrawness, thrawnness** obstinacy, stubbornness *la19-*. **thrawn faced** having a twisted or scowling face *17-*. **thrawn gabbit** having a twisted or scowling mouth *18-*. **thrawn heidit** perverse, contrary *la18-19, 20- T Bor*. †**thrawn mou'd** having a twisted or scowling mouth *16-18*. [participial adj from THRAW[1,2]]

thrawn *see* THRAW[1,2]

thre *see* THREE

thread *see* THREID[1.1], THREID[1.2]

threap[1.1], **threep**, *Sh Ork* **traep**, *Sh Ork* **trep**, †**threpe**, †**threip** /θrip; *Sh Ork* trep/ *n* **1** an argument, a conflict; a dispute, a quarrel *la14-*. **2** a vehemently-held opinion or attitude *la17-*. **3** superstition; a traditional belief or saying *19- C Bor*. **4** the swingletree of a plough *19- SW*. **5** the angle between the point of the coulter and the point of the share of a plough *20- T*. **threapland**, †**threipland** land whose ownership is disputed (especially the Debatable Land of the Scottish/English border) *13-*. [see the verb]

threap[1.2], **threip**, **thraip**, *Sh Ork* **traep**, *Sh Ork* **trep**, †**threpe** /θrip, θrep; *Sh Ork* trep/ *v* **1** to argue; to quarrel *la15-*. **2** to assert something positively, vehemently or persistently *la15-*. **3** to nag, be insistent *19-*. **threep doon yer throat** to force an opinion on a person *19-*. **threap on, threap upon** to force an opinion on *15-*. †**threap kindness on** to beg kindness or mercy (from God) *la16-e18*. [OE *ðrēapian* to rebuke]

threat[1.1], **threit**, †**threte**, †**threyt** /θrɛt, θrit/ *n* **1** a declaration of intent to harm; an indication of trouble *la14-*. **2** compulsion, pressure *la14-16*. †**in threyt, in thretis** in close proximity *e16*. [OE *ðrēat*]

threat[1.2], **threit**, †**threte** /θrɛt, θrit/ *v* **1** to threaten *la14-*. **2** to compel or induce by threats *15-e17*. [OE *ðrēatian*]

threaten, threiten, *Sh* **traeten**, †**thretten**, †**thraiten**, †**thraetin** /'θrɛtən, 'θritən; *Sh* 'tretən/ *v* **1** to utter a threat, to menace *la16-*. **2** *of an event* to appear likely *18-*. **3** to command, order sternly *16-19, 20- Sh*. **4** to predict *la16-e17*. [OE *ðrēatnian*]

threave[1.1], **thrave**, *Sh Ork* **trave**, †**thrafe**, †**thraif** /θriv, θrev; *Sh Ork* trev/ *n* **1** a quantity of cut unthreshed grain or straw, consisting of two stooks *14-*. **2** a measure of straw or reeds for thatching *15-*. **3** a large number or quantity; a crowd *la15-19, 20- Sh NE*. [ON *þrefi, *þrafe*]

threave[1.2], **thrave** /θriv, θrev/ *v* to harvest; to reap stalks of grain and bind them into sheaves *19, 20- historical*. **threaver, thraver** a reaper paid by the measure of a grain that was cut *19, 20- historical*. [see the noun]

thred *see* THIRD[1.3]

threde *see* THREID[1.1]

three, *Sh Ork* **tree**, *EC* **chree**, *WC* **hree**, *Bor* **threy**, †**thre**, †**thrie** /θri; *Sh Ork* tri; *EC* tʃri; *WC* hri; *Bor* θre/ *numeral* the cardinal number between two and four *la14-*. **threesie 1** a move in the game of chuckstones *20- C*. **2** the third square or box in the game of peever *20- C*. **threesome**, †**thresum 1** a group or company of three *la14-*. **2** *of a dance* performed by groups of three people *17-*. **threeie** the third square or box in the game of peever *20- C*. **three bawbee** costing three halfpence; cheap, worthless *19-*. **threefauld, threefold**, †**trefald** *adj* **1** consisting of three parts *la14-*. **2** enacted three times *la16-*. **threefauld** *n* the marsh trefoil, the bog-bean *Menyanthes trifoliata 19- Sh SW Bor*. **three fower** three or four; a few *la19-*; compare TWA-THREE. **threepenny, thrippeny** costing three pence *19-20, 21- historical*. †**thre pile, thrie pild** a particular length of nap of velvet *la16-17*. †**be sic thre** three times as much *la15-16*. **three threeds and a thrum** a cat's purr *19- Ork SW Uls*. **The Three Estates** the three classes of the community of Scotland (prelates, nobility and burgesses) which, with the king, made up the Scottish Parliament *17, 18- historical*. [OE *ðrīe*]

threed *see* THREID[1.1], THREID[1.2]

threep *see* THREAP[1.1]

threeple[1.1] /'θripəl/ *v* to increase threefold, treble *20- NE T*. [see the adj]

threeple[1.2] /'θripəl/ *adj* triple, threefold *19- NE T EC Bor*. [altered form of Eng *triple*, with influence from THREE]

threeplet /'θriplət/ *n* a triplet *20-*. [altered form of Eng *triplet*, with influence from THREE]

threesh *see* THRESH

threid[1.1], **threed, thread**, *Sh Ork* **treed**, †**threde**, †**freid** /θrid, θrɛd; *Sh Ork* trid/ *n* **1** a fine cord or yarn *15-*. **2** the course of a person's life *la15-* **3** the main narrative course of a story or events *la17-*. **threadbare**, †**threidbair** *of cloth* worn, shabby *la15-*. **threid dry** completely dry *la19- Sh*

SW. †**thrums and threids** scraps and waste fragments *la16-e19* [OE *ðræd*]

threid[1,2], **threed**, **thread**, *Sh Ork* **treed** /θrid, θrɛd; *Sh Ork* trid/ *v* **1** to pass the end of a thread through the eye of a needle *18-*. **2** to run throughout, pervade; to negotiate a narrow or difficult course *la18-*. **3** to string beads or other objects together *19-*. **4** to pay out a rope or line gradually *la19- Sh*. [see the noun]

threip *see* THREAP[1.1], THREAP[1.2]
threit *see* THREAT[1.1], THREAT[1.2]
threiten *see* THREATEN
threll *see* THIRL[2.1], THIRL[2.2]
thren *see* THRAIN[1.1]
threpe *see* THREAP[1.1], THREAP[1.2]
thresaurar *see* THESAURER
threschald *see* THRESHOLD
thresh, **thrash**, *Sh Ork* **tresh** /θrɛʃ, θraʃ; *Sh Ork* trɛʃ/ *v pt* **thrasht**, **thrashed**, **thruish**, **throosh**, *Sh Ork* **treush**, *NE* **threesh** *ptp* **thrashed**, *NE WC* **thrashen**, *T EC* **thruishen**, *Sh Ork* **treshen**, †**thrushen**, †**throoshen 1** to separate grain from husks and straw by beating or mechanical means *la14-*. **2** to beat a person or animal soundly; to defeat thoroughly *16-*. **thrashing machine** a power-driven machine for separating grain from straw *la18-*. **thrashing mill** = *thrashing machine*. †**thresch out** *law* to thresh and confiscate a crop *la15-e17*. [OE *ðerscan*]

thresh *see* RASH[1]
threshold, **thrashel**, **threshwart**, †**threschald**, †**threswald** /'θrɛʃhold, 'θraʃəl, 'θrɛʃwərt/ *n* **1** a door sill, an entrance *la14-*. **2** a starting point, an outset; a border or limit *19-*. [OE *ðerscold*, *ðerscwald*]

thresour *see* TREISURE
threte *see* THREAT[1.1], THREAT[1.2]
threttein *see* THIRTEEN[1.1], THIRTEEN[1.2]
thretten *see* THIRTEEN[1.1], THIRTEEN[1.2], THREATEN
thretty *see* THIRTY[1.2]
threty *see* THIRTY[1.1]
threw *see* THRAW[1.2], THRAWN
threy *see* THREE
threyt *see* THREAT[1.1]
thrid *see* THIRD[1.1], THIRD[1.2], THIRD[1.3]
thrie *see* THREE
thrieveless, **thraveless** /'θrivləs, 'θrɛvləs/ *adj* thriftless, careless, negligent *19- WC Uls*. [altered form of THIEVELESS, with influence from THRIFT, THRIVE[1.1]]
thrif *see* THRIVE[1.2]
thrife *see* THRIVE[1.1]
thrift, *Sh Ork* **trift** /θrɪft; *Sh Ork* trɪft/ *n* **1** success, prosperity; good fortune, good luck *15-*. **2** prudence, economy; savings or accumulated wealth *16-*. **3** work, industry; profitable occupation *18-19, 20- Sh T EC*. **4** willingness to work; energy or enthusiasm *19, 20- Ork*. **thrifty**, †**thriftie** *adj* **1** thriving, prosperous *la15-*. **2** careful, prudent *la15-*. **3** worthy, estimable; profitable, useful *16*. **thriftie** *n* a child's moneybox *20- EC Bor*. **thriftless** worthless, useless *la15-*. [ME *thrift*, ON *þrift*; compare THRIVE]
thrildom *see* THIRLDOM
thrill *see* THIRL[1.2], THIRL[2.1], THIRL[2.2]
thrimbill, **thrimlar**, **thrimmle** *see* THRUMMLE
†**thrin** *adj* triple *e15*. [ON *þrinnr*]
†**thrinfald**[1.1], **thrynfald** *adj* threefold, tripartite *la14-16*. [THRIN + *-fald* suffix, compare FAULD[1.2]]
†**thrinfald**[1.2], **thrynfald** *adv* triple *e16*. [see the adj]
thring *see* THRANG[1.2]
thringle *see* TRINKLE[1.2]

†**thripplin kame** *n* an instrument for removing the seeds from flax *18-19*. [altered form of *rippling comb* (RIPPLE)]
thrissel, **thistle**, **thustle**, *Sh Ork* **tistle**, *N* **thirstle**, *C* **thrustle**, †**thrissill**, †**thirsill** /'θrɪsəl, 'θɪsəl, 'θʌsəl; *Sh Ork* 'tɪsəl; *N* 'θɪrsəl; *C* 'θrʌsəl/ *n* **1** a prickly herbaceous plant *Onopordum acanthium* with a globular flower-head and purple flower *la15-*. **2** the thistle or a representation of a thistle as the emblem of Scotland *la15-*. **thistle cock** the corn bunting *Emberiza calandra la19- Ork N*. **tistle sporrow** = *thistle cock 20- Sh*. †**thrissell noble** a Scottish gold half MERK of James VI, with a thistle on the reverse *la16*. **the Thistle** the Order of the Thistle *la18-*. [OE *ðistel*]
thrist *see* THIRST[1.1], THIRST[1.2], THRUST[1.1], THRUST[1.2]
thristill *see* THROSTLE
thristle *see* THROSTLE
thristle-cock *see* THROSTLE
thrittie *see* THIRTY[1.1]
thritty *see* THIRTY[1.2]
thrive[1.1], †**thrife** /θraev/ *n* prosperity; a thriving state *17-19, 20- SW*. [see the verb]
thrive[1.2], *Sh Ork* **trive**, †**thrif**, †**thryff**, †**thryve** /θraev; *Sh Ork* traev/ *v pt* **thrave**, †**thraif** *ptp* **thriven**, *Sh Ork* **triven**, †**thryvin 1** to prosper, enjoy good fortune *la14-*. **2** to grow vigorously; to flourish *la14-*. †**sa mot I thrive** may I prosper *la15-16*. **sae hae me trivan, sae micht I trive** upon my word *la19- Ork*. [ON *þrífask* (reflexive) to thrive]
throat, *Sh Ork* **trot**, †**throt**, †**throte**, †**thrott** /θrot; *Sh Ork* trot/ *n* **1** the front part of the neck; the windpipe, the gullet *la14-*. **2** the vocal organs, the voice *16-*. **3** a narrow passage; a narrow stretch of a river, a ravine or gully; frequently in place-names *16-*. †**throtcutter** a cut-throat, an assassin *16-17*. [OE *ðrote*]
throb[1.1], **thrab** /θrɔb, θrab/ *n* a strong pulsing or vibrating *19-*. [see the verb]
throb[1.2], **thrab** /θrɔb, θrab/ *v* to pulse or vibrate strongly *19-*. †**throbbing** croup *la18*. [ME *throbben*, onomatopoeic]
throch *see* THROU[1.3], THROUCH, THRUCH[1]
throcht *see* TROCH
throck, †**frock** /θrɔk/ *n* the third, fourth, or fifth pair of oxen in a twelve-oxen plough team *19, 20- NE*. [compare Eng *throck*, OE *ðroc* the sharebeam of a plough]
throe *see* THRAW[1.1]
throm /θrɔm/ *prep* from *20- N NE Bor*. [variant of Eng *from*; compare *thrae* (FRAE)]
throne, †**trone**, †**trowne**, †**troyn** /θron/ *n* the seat of a monarch or bishop; the position of supreme authority or power *la4-*. †**Tronis** one of the nine orders of angels *la15-16*. [AN *throne*, Lat *thronus*; OFr *trone*]
throng *see* THRANG[1.1], THRANG[1.2], THRANG[1.3], THRANG[1.4]
throosh /θruʃ/ *v* to play truant from school *la19- SW*. [unknown]
throosh *see* THRESH
throppill, **throppill** *see* THRAPPLE[1.1]
thropple *see* THRAPPLE[1.1], THRAPPLE[1.2], THRAPPLE[2]
throstle, †**thristle**, †**thristill** /'θrɔsəl/ *n* the song thrush *la14-19, 20- literary*. †**throstle cock**, **thissell cok** the male song thrush or mistle thrush *la16-19*. [OE *ðrostle*]
throt, **throte** *see* THROAT
throttle[1.1] /'θrɔtəl/ *n* **1** the throat, the gullet, the windpipe *19-*. **2** a valve for controlling the flow of steam or petrol to an engine *19-*. [see the verb]
throttle[1.2] /'θrɔtəl/ *v* to seize by the throat; to choke, strangle *19-*. [Eng *throttle*]
throu[1.1], **through** /θru/ *adj* **1** finished, complete *17-*. **2** at the end; close to death *20-*. [see the prep]

throu[1,2], **through**, **throw**, *Sh Ork* **trou**, †**throucht**, †**throwght**, †**thorow** /θru, θrʌu; *Sh Ork* trʌu/ *adv* **1** so as to penetrate or pierce *la15-*. **2** across country, from start to destination: ◊*they came throu frae Fife la15-*. **3** to a favourable conclusion: ◊*we won throu la15-*. **4** from beginning to end, throughout *16-*. **5** towards the inner part of a house *la19-*. **6** across; over a surface *18-19, 20- NE C Bor*. **thrower**, †**throuar** *mining* a passage made by the removal of coal from a seam worked in the stoup-and-room manner; an access point between two levels for ventilation *17-19, 20- C*. †**throughly** thoroughly, completely *la16-19*. **through band** a stone which goes through the whole thickness of a wall *la18-*. **through bearing** support, livelihood, maintenance; a way out of difficulty or hardship *la17-19, 20- Sh*. **through-ca** energy, drive *20- NE T*. **throucome** an ordeal; hardship *20- Sh NE*. **through flat** a tenement flat with rooms facing both the front and the back of the building *la20-*. **throu gate, throughgate,** †**throwgait** a passageway; an alley, a lane *la15-*. †**throu gyrd, throw gird** to pierce, run through *e16*. **through house** a house whose rooms lead off one another *20- C SW*. †**throughlet** a narrow passage or sea channel *la18-e19*. **throu-pit, through-pit 1** energy, activity *19-*. **2** production, output *20-*. **through-pittin** rough handling; a severe cross-examination *19- C SW Uls*. **throu an throu** thoroughly, completely *16-*. [see the prep]

throu[1,3], **through**, **throw**, **throch**, *Sh Ork* **trou**, †**throuch**, †**thorow** /θru, θrʌu, θrɔx; *Sh Ork* trʌu/ *prep* **1** from side to side or end to end of *la14-*. **2** over the whole extent of; throughout *la14-*. **3** by means of; on account of *la14-*. **4** across or over the surface of *15-*. **5** during, in the course of *15-*. **6** further into, in the interior of; in another part or end of *18-*. **through-hochie** a throw in a game of marbles in which the marble is thrown through the legs from behind *20- NE*. **speak through the cauld** to talk in a choked, difficult manner due to a cold *la19, 20- NE T EC*. **throu the wa** on the other side of a wall; next door *la19-*. **throw-the-wud-laddie** a severe scolding *19- SW*. **throu the bile up** and beyond boiling point *20-*. **throu-the-muir** *n* a severe scolding; a violent row *la19- NE T EC*. **throu-the-muir** *adj* untidy, heedless *20- NE*. **through the week** during the week; on a weekday *20-*. **through time** in time, eventually *18-*. [OE *ðurh*]

†**throuch, throch, thrugh** *n* a sheet of paper *16-17*. [unknown]

throuche *see* THOROUGH[1,3]
throuchfare *see* THOROUGHFARE
throuch out *see* THROUGHOOT
throucht *see* THROU[1,2]
throuch uther *see* THROUITHER[1,3]
througal *see* FRUGAL
through *see* THROU[1,1], THROU[1,2], THROU[1,3], THRUCH[1], THRUCH[2]
through-gang /ˈθrugaŋ/ *n* a way through; a passageway, a corridor; a thoroughfare, a lane *la15-*. [THROU[1,2] + GANG[1,2]]
through-gaun[1,1], **through-gaen, through-going** /ˈθrugɔn, ˈθrugeən, ˈθrugɔɪŋ/ *n* **1** a critical examination of conduct; a severe reproof *19-*. **2** a passageway; an alley *la19-*. [see the adj]
through-gaun[1,2], **through-gaen, throw-gaen, through-going** /ˈθrugɔn, ˈθrugeən, ˈθrugɔɪŋ/ *adj* **1** providing access from one street or house to another *la19-*. **2** passing through, traversing *20-*. **3** energetic, active *19, 20- C SW Bor Uls*. [THROU[1,2] + *gaun* presp of GAE]
through-ither *see* THROUITHER[1,3]

throughoot, throughout, †**throuch out,** †**throw out** /θruˈut, θruˈʌut/ *prep* through the full extent of, during the entire course of *la14-*. [OE *ðurhūt*]
through other *see* THROUITHER[1,2], THROUITHER[1,3]
throuither[1,1], †**throwther** /θruˈɪðər/ *n* **1** an unmethodical, muddled person *20-* **2** confusion, a row; a muddle or mess *la18-19, 20- NE*. [see the adj]
throuither[1,2], **through other,** *NE* **throwder,** †**throuther** /θruˈɪðər, θru ˈʌðər; *NE* ˈθrʌudər/ *adj* **1** *of things* confused; untidy or badly arranged *18-*. **2** *of people* untidy, disorganized, slovenly *19-*. **3** *of children* unruly, difficult *19, 20- NE Bor*. **throughitherness** muddle-headedness; lack of method *la19, 20- NE*. [THROU[1,3] + ITHER[1,2]]
throuither[1,3], **through-ither, through other,** †**throuther,** †**throuch uther,** †**throu other** /θruˈɪðər, θru ˈʌðər/ *adv* in an intermingled or mixed up manner; in a state of confusion *la15-*. [see the adj]
throu other *see* THROUITHER[1,3]
throw *see* THOROUGH[1,3], THRAW[1,1], THRAW[1,2], THROU[1,2], THROU[1,3]
throwart *see* THRAWART
throw-gaen *see* THROUGH-GAUN[1,2]
throwght *see* THROU[1,2]
thrown *see* THRAW[1,2]
throw out *see* THROUGHOOT
throwth *see* TRUITH
thruch[1], **throch, through, thruff, thruck** /θrʌx, θrɔx, θru, θrʌf, θrʌk/ *n* a flat gravestone or funerary monument (placed across a grave or over a tomb inside a church) *la15-19, 20- SW Bor*. **thruch stane, throch stane,** †**throuch stone** a flat gravestone *la15-19, 20- C SW Bor*. [OE *ðrūh* a tomb, coffin]
thruch[2], †**through,** †**thorow,** †**thro** /θrʌx/ *v* **1** to succeed, win or pull through *17-19, 20- SW*. **2** to put into effect, complete or resolve *la15-e18*. [from the prep THROU[1,3]]
thruck *see* THRUCH[1]
thruff *see* THRUCH[1]
thrugh *see* THROUCH
thruish *see* THRESH
thrum[1,1] /ˈθrʌm/ *n* **1** the end of a warp-thread *15-*. **2** a short piece of waste thread or yarn; a scrap, a shred *19-*. **3** a perverse streak in a person's character; a fit of ill-humour *la19, 20- Sh NE T*. **4** a horse hair *20- Sh*. **thrummie 1** covered with or made of ends of thread *la19- NE T*. **2** threadbare, frayed *la19- NE T*. †**thrummit** *of a hat* fringed or decorated with ends of thread *16*. **thrummy 1** a nickname for the Devil *la19- NE*. **2** a weaver *20- NE*. **thrums** the ends of warp-threads; scraps of waste thread *15-*. **thrummy caip** a nickname for the Devil *la19- NE*. †**thrum bonnet** a hat made of waste yarn *16-19, 20- H&I*. †**thrum keel 1** the ruddle mark indicating the end of a piece of cloth *19*. **2** the tail-end or conclusion of something *19*. [OE (*tunge*)*ðrum* ligament (of the tongue)]
†**thrum**[1,2] *v* to twist or coil loosely or carelessly; to tie up in a makeshift manner *19*. [see the noun]
thrum[2,1] /θrʌm/ *n* **1** a cat's purr *19-*. **2** a monotonous humming noise *la20-*. **3** a monotonous conversation *19*. [see the verb]
thrum[2,2] /θrʌm/ *v* **1** to strum (a musical instrument) *la18-*. **2** *of a cat* to purr *19, 20- NE*. **3** to make a monotonous humming noise *la20-*. **4** to speak monotonously *e19*. [Eng *thrum*, onomatopoeic]
thrummle, thrimmle, †**thrumble,** †**thrimbill,** †**thrammel** /ˈθrʌməl, ˈθrɪməl/ *v* **1** to press, squeeze, crush *16-*. **2** to push or jostle *la15-19, 20- literary*. **3** to grasp; to press or rub with the hands *18- NE SW Bor*. **4** to fumble or grope with the fingers; to handle awkwardly *la18-19, 20- NE*. †**thrimlar** a

jostler; a hustler *e16*. [probably a frequentative form of ME *thrumen* to compress; compare THRUMP]

†**thrump, thrymp** *v* to push, jostle *16-e19*. [a variant of ME *thrumen* to compress; compare THRUMMLE]

thrumple[1.1] /'θrʌmpəl/ *n* the state or condition of being creased, crumpled or crushed *20- NE T*. [see the verb]

thrumple[1.2] /'θrʌmpəl/ *v* to crumple up, crush *19- NE Bor*. [a variant of FRUMPLE; with influence from THRUMMLE]

†**thrunter** *n* a three-year-old (female) sheep *19 Bor*. [EModE *thrinter*; OE *ðriwintre* of three winters; compare TWINTER]

thrushen *see* THRESH

thrust[1.1], *Sh Ork* **trist**, †**thrist** /θrʌst; *Sh Ork* trɪst/ *n* **1** an act of thrusting; a push or shove *la15-*. **2** a bite *19- Ork Bor*. **3** a hug, an embrace *19*. **4** oppression, hardship *16*. [see the verb]

thrust[1.2], *Sh Ork* **trist**, †**thrist**, †**thraist**, †**thrast** /θrʌst; *Sh Ork* trɪst/ *v pt* **thrust**, †**thrist**, †**thristit** *ptp* **thrust**, †**thrusted**, †**thristit**, †**threst** **1** to push with force; to penetrate *la14-*. **2** to push against, jostle *la14-*. **3** to compress, squeeze or wring *la14-19*. **thrust out** to expel or eject *la16-*. †**thrist togidder** to copulate *e16*. [ON *þrýsta*]

thrustle *see* THRISSEL

thryff *see* THRIVE[1.2]

thryl *see* THIRL[2,3]

thrymp *see* THRUMP

thrynfald *see* THRINFALD[1.1], THRINFALD[1.2]

thryng *see* THRANG[1.2]

thryve, thryvin *see* THRIVE[1.2]

thu *see* THOU

thuart *see* THORT[1.4]

thud[1.1], *Sh Ork* **tud**, †**thuid** /θʌd; *Sh Ork* tʌd/ *n* **1** the dull sound of a heavy impact; a loud report *15-*. **2** a thump, a blow *la15-19, 20- Ork N WC*. **3** a noisy blast of wind; a sudden squall or gust *16-19, 20- Sh Ork*. **4** a misfortune; an affliction *18-19* †**thuddert** a violent storm *la16*. [perhaps onomatopoeic, but compare OE *ðoden* a violent wind]

thud[1.2], *Sh Ork* **tud** /θʌd; *Sh Ork* tʌd/ *v* **1** to make a dull sound on impact *la18-*. **2** of wind to come in noisy blasts; to bluster *16-19, 20- Sh*. **3** to beat, strike or thump *19*. **thudder** *of wind* to come in noisy blasts; *of thunder* to resound *la19, 20- literary*. **thuddin** a beating; a severe scolding *la19, 20- NE C SW Bor*. [see the noun and compare OE *ðyddan* to stab, thrust]

thumb *see* THOOM[1.1], THOOM[1.2]

thumbikins *see* THOOM[1.1]

thumble *see* THUMMLE

thummart *see* FOUMART

thummle, thimmle, thimble, †**thumble,** †**thymmil,** †**thymbill** /'θʌməl, 'θɪməl, 'θɪmbəl/ *n* **1** a bell-shaped sheath to protect the finger pushing a needle *la15-*. **2** the foxglove *Digitalis purpurea 20- T Bor*. **3** *mining* an iron ring round a heart-joint in a pumping apparatus *la19, 20- EC*. **thummles** raspberries *20- NE*. [OE *ðȳmel*]

thump[1.1] /θʌmp/ *n* **1** a heavy blow; a pounding *la18-*. **2** a large piece, a lump *19-*. **3** a sturdy child *la19- T WC*. **4** a vigorous dance *20- EC*. [see the verb]

thump[1.2], *Sh* **tump** /θʌmp; *Sh* tʌmp/ *v* **1** to beat, batter; to defeat *la17-*. **2** to walk with a heavy or noisy tread *la18-19*. **3** to dance *la18-19*. [EModE *thump*, onomatopoeic]

thunk *see* THINK[1.2]

thunner[1.1], **thunder**, *Sh* **tunnir**, †**thundir**, †**thwndir** /'θʌnər, 'θʌndər; *Sh* 'tʌnər/ *n* the loud noise accompanying a flash of lightning; a thunder-bolt *la14-*. **thunnered milk, thundered milk** milk which has become tainted or soured by thundery weather *19, 20- NE EC Bor*. **thunner plump, thunder plump** a sudden heavy thunder-shower *19-*. **thunner spale** a thin piece of wood whirled round on a string to make a thunder-like noise *19, 20- historical*. **thunner-anlichtenin** the lungwort *Pulmonaria officinalis* or a similar plant with white-spotted leaves *la19-*. [OE *ðunor*]

thunner[1.2], **thunder**, *Sh* **tunnir** /'θʌnər, 'θʌndər; *Sh* 'tʌnər/ *v* **1** to make a loud noise *16-*. **2** *of thunder* to resound, reverberate *la16-*. [OE *ðunrian*]

thur *see* THAY, THERE, THIR[1.1], THIR[1.2], THIR[1.3]

thurd *see* THIRD[1.1], THIRD[1.2], THIRD[1.3]

Thursday, Fuirsday, Forsday, *NE* **Fiersday,** †**Thurisday,** †**Furisday** /'θʌrzde, 'fʌrzde, 'fɔrzde; *NE* 'fɪrzde/ *n* the day of the week before Friday *la14-*. [OE *ðunresdæg* influenced by ON *þórsdagr*]

thurt *see* THAUR

thurty *see* THIRTY[1.2]

thus /ðʌs/ *adv* **1** in the present or following manner *la14-*. **2** to this extent *15-*. **3** consequently *la15-*. †**thusgate, thusgatis** in this way, thus *la14-e19*. †**thuswis, thuswys, thuswayes** in this manner *15-e17*. [OE *ðus*]

thustle *see* THRISSEL

thwang *see* THANG

thwart *see* THORT[1.1], THORT[1.2], THORT[1.3], THORT[1.4], THORT[1.5]

thworter *see* THORTER[1.1]

thwortour *see* THORTER[1.4]

thy, *Sh* **dee,** *Sh* **dy,** *Ork N* **thee,** †**thi,** †**thai** /ðaɪ; *Sh* di; *Sh dae; Ork N* ði/ *pron* your; of or belonging to you *la14-19, 20- Sh Ork N SW*. Compare THOU. [variant of THINE]

thycht *see* TICHT[1.3]

thyn *see* THIN[1.3], THIN[1.4]

†**thyne, thin, theyn** *adv* thence; from that time or place *la14-e17*. **thynefurth, thin furth** thenceforth *la14-16*. [reduced form of ON *þeðan*]

thyne *see* THAN[1.1], THIN[1.2], THIN[1.3], THINE

thyng *see* THING[1]

thynk *see* THINK[1.2]

thyrl *see* THIRL[1.1]

ti *see* TAE[3,2]

tial /'taeəl/ *n* something used for tying, *eg* a cord, ribbon *19- Sh Ork N NE H&I*. [OE *tygel* a tow-rope, rein]

tibbie thiefie, tibbie fithie /'tɪbi 'θifi, 'tɪbi 'fɪθi/ *n* a sandpiper *20- NE T*. [onomatopoeic of the bird's cry, assimilated to the personal name *Tibbie*; compare *thevis nek* (THIEF[1.1])]

tibit *see* TABET

†**tibrick** *n* the young of the coalfish *Pollachius virens la18 Ork*. [possibly an altered form with extended sense of DOOBRACK]

Tic /tɪk/ *n* a nickname for Celtic Football Club *la20-*. [shortened form of *Celtic*]

tice, tyse, †**tyst** /taɪs, taɪz/ *v* **1** to entice, seduce, persuade; to coax, wheedle *14-18, 19- Sh Ork NE*. **2** to provoke, harass *16-17*. [AN *ticer*]

†**ticher**[1.1], **tichwr, tychir, teicher** *n* **1** a tear *e16*. **2** a drop of water, sweat or blood *16-e17*. [OE *tehher*; compare TEAR[1.1]]

ticher[1.2], †**teicher** /'tɪxər, 'tɪxər/ *v* **1** *of a wound or sore* to weep, exude moisture *19- SW Bor*. **2** to weep *20- SW*. [see the noun]

tichle *see* TUCKLE

ticht[1.1] /tɪxt/ *n* a tightening ◊ *gie that screw yin mair ticht 20-*. [see the adj]

ticht[1.2] /tɪxt/ *v* **1** to tighten, make secure *19-*. **2** *of barrels* to make watertight *16-*. [from the adj, fallen together with ME *tighten*, OE *tyhtan* to stretch, draw, pull]

ticht[1.3], **tight,** *Ork* **thight,** †**thycht,** †**teicht** /tɪxt, təɪxt, təɪt; *Ork* θəɪt/ *adj* **1** impervious, close-textured; without holes or damage, in good repair *la15-*; compare *waterticht* (WATER[1.1]). **2** *of clothes or covers* fitting very closely, firmly fixed, closely fastened, not loose *16-*. **3** neat in build, well-made, shapely *la16-*. **4** competent, capable, alert, vigorous *17-*. **5** *of persons* neat, smart, tidily or carefully dressed *18-*. **6** *of things* neatly kept or arranged, snug *la18-*. **7** *of persons* parsimonious, close-fisted; short of money *la19-*. **8** *of things* in short supply *la19-*. **9** strict, severely critical *la18-19, 20- N*. **10** *of ale* strong *la18*. [ON **þéhtr* dense, thick, with influence from the verb]

ticht¹·⁴ /tɪxt/ *adv* strictly, closely, neatly *19-*. **ticht-hauden** hard-pressed, harassed *20- SW Bor*. [see the adj]

tichten¹·¹ /ˈtɪxtən/ *n* = TICHT¹·¹ *20- Ork N NE T EC*. [see the verb]

tichten¹·² /ˈtɪxtən/ *v* to make tight, secure *la19-*. [TICHT¹·³, with verb-forming suffix]

tichtly /ˈtɪxtlɪ/ *adv* **1** neatly, tidily *la19-*. **2** strictly, rigorously; severely *la16-19, 20- N EC Uls*. [TICHT¹·³, with adv-forming suffix]

tick¹ /tɪk/ *n* a small quantity, a grain, drop *la19-*. **tickie** = TICK¹ *NE T*. [probably Du *tikje* a small amount]

tick²·¹ /tɪk/ *n* the game of TIG¹·¹ (sense 2) *19, 20- Sh*. **ticky tack**, **tick an tack** = TICK²·¹ *20- NE T*. [ME *tik* a light touch; compare Du *tik* a touch]

tick²·² /tɪk/ *v* to tap lightly, especially in the game of TIG²·¹ *19- Sh NE T C*. [ME *tiken*; compare Du *tikken* to pat]

tick³ /tɪk/ *n* **play the tick** to play truant *20- EC*. [unknown]

tick⁴, **teek** /tɪk, tik/ *interj* a call to chickens to come for food *19- Ork N NE T*. **tickie** = TICK⁴. **tick-tick** = TICK⁴. [onomatopoeic of a hen's cluck; compare TUCK]

tick *see* THICK¹·³

tickerie, *Sh* **tukkeri** /ˈtɪkəre, ˈtɪkərɪ; *Sh* ˈtʌkərɪ/ *numeral* a number used in counting rhymes, used to determine who will start a game *19-*. [nonsense word derived from a system for counting sheep]

ticket¹·¹, †**tikkat** /ˈtɪkət/ *n* **1** a piece of paper or card indicating an entitlement, penalty or price *la18-*. **2** a person dressed in a slovenly or unconventional way *20-*. **3** contemptuous a person *20- C Uls*. **4** *Presbyterian Church* a Communion *token* (TAIKEN) permitting participation in the rite of communion *la16-18 NE T C, 19- WC historical*. **5** *law* a notice posted in a public place or delivered to a person, especially a summons *16-17*. **6** a note containing an instruction, request, evidence or other information *16-17*. **7** *law* a summary of a legal document *e17*. **8** a list, inventory *16-17*. **9** a piece of writing by which a gift or bequest was made *16-e17*. **10** an account or bill listing expenses *16-17*. **11** *mining* the piece of paper for recording a collier's expenses, or the lead token representing them *17*. **12** a receipt for payment made *16-17*. **13** a promissory note *la16-18*. **14** a licence or permit to travel; a safe-conduct *16-e17*. **15** *Presbyterian Church* a permit to have a child baptized *17*. **16** = *burgess ticket* (BURGESS¹·¹) *16-e18*. **17** a severe beating or punishment *19*. †**in ticket in** writing *16-e17*. **that's the ticket for tattie soup** *humorous* that's the very thing, that's just what was wanted *la19- NE T EC*. [aphetic form of MFr *etiquet*]

ticket¹·² /ˈtɪkət/ *v* **1** to attach a TICKET¹·¹ (sense 1); to label, designate, license with a ticket *19-*. **2** *of Glasgow Town Council* to put an official notice on the door of (a dwelling) to certify its cubic capacity and the number of people allowed to spend the night in it *la19-e20 historical*. **3** to post a public notice *e16*. [see the noun]

tickie /ˈtɪki/ *n* children's name for a hen or chicken *20- NE T*. **tickie taed** pigeon-toed *20- T EC*. [see *tickie* (TICK⁴)]

tickie *see* TICK¹

ticking, **tykin**, **teikin** /ˈtɪkɪŋ, ˈtɪkɪn, ˈtʌɪkɪn/ *n* **1** a strong fabric used mainly for making mattress covers *la16-*. **2** = TIKE² *19-*. **3** a mattress *19, 20- EC Bor*. [TIKE² + -*ing* suffix]

tickle¹·¹ /ˈtɪkəl/ *v* **1** to lightly touch a person to cause a sensation that makes them laugh or itch *17-*. **2** to puzzle, perplex *19-*. Compare KITTLE¹·² [OE *tinclian*]

†**tickle**¹·² /ˈtɪkəl/ *adj* tricky, difficult *17-18*. Compare KITTLE¹·³ [see the verb]

tickle² /ˈtɪkəl/ *v* to catch, tangle, become entangled (in) *la19- T EC*. [perhaps TAIGLE¹·² with influence from TICKLE¹·¹]

tickler /ˈtɪklər/ *n* a problem, puzzle *19-*. [TICKLE¹·¹, with instrumental suffix]

tickly /ˈtɪklɪ/ *adj* puzzling, difficult *19- N NE*. [TICKLE¹·¹ + -IE²]

ticky wife /ˈtɪke wʌɪf/ *n* a truant officer *20- EC*. [TICK³ + WIFE]

†**tic-tac-toe** /ˈtɪkˈtakˈtoː/ *n* a game in which numbers are written down on a slate, the player shuts his eyes and taps on the slate with a piece of slate-pencil to the rhythm of a rhyme and at the conclusion of the rhyme is awarded the score of the number on which his pencil came to rest *la19*. [TICK²·² with echoic alliterative extension]

tid¹·¹ /tɪd/ *n* **1** a mood, humour *la18- C SW Bor Uls*. **2** a favourable time or season; an occasion or opportunity *18, 19- T C*. **3** the proper or favourable season or suitable condition of the soil for cultivation *la18-19, 20- C Uls*. **in tid**, **in the tid 1** *of a river* in the proper condition for angling. **2** *of a fish* ready to take the bait *la19- WC*. [variant of TIDE¹·¹]

†**tid**¹·² *v* to cultivate at the right season *la18-19 C Bor*. [see the noun]

tidder *see* TITHER¹·¹, TITHER¹·²

tiddo /ˈtɪdo/ *interj* a call to a lamb *20- Ork*. [perhaps altered form with extended sense of CADDIE²]

tide¹·¹ /tʌɪd/ *n* **1** (a moment or period of) time *la14-*. **2** the ebbing or flowing of the sea *la15-*. **3** a period of ebbing and flowing, the time between one tide and the next *la15-*. **4** the sea, ocean *19-*. **5** *fishing* a good catch *20- Sh Ork N*. **6** the foreshore, the land between high and low water marks *la19- NE EC*. **7** an occasion; an opportunity *la14-19, 20- Sh*. **8** the time of a tide, as a period of work *16-17*. **9** the period of a tide, with reference to the (quantity of) fish caught *14-17*. **10** a flow of excrement *e16*. †**tide gate** *in Shetland and Orkney* the channel where the tide was strongest *la17-e18*. **tide line** the last section of a fishing line to be shot *20- NE T*. [OE *tīd*]

tide¹·² /tʌɪd/ *v* **1** to leave (fishing lines) for sufficient time to let fish take the bait *19, 20- Sh WC*. **2** to (cause something to) happen *la14-19*. **tidin 1** the period during which fishing lines are left down *20- NE WC*. **2** *in Shetland and Orkney*, the expert use of the tide *e18*. [OE *tīdan* to happen, with some senses from the noun]

tidin *see* TIDE¹·²

tidy, †**tyddie** /ˈtʌɪde, ˈtʌɪdɪ/ *adj* **1** *of a cow* giving milk; in calf, pregnant *la15-*. **2** *of people* attractive; shapely; plump *19-*. **3** orderly *19-*. **4** *of animals, mainly cattle* in good condition, fat *16-19, 20- Ork*. **5** timely, seasonable, propitious *e18*. [ME *tīdi* timely, healthy; compare TIDE¹·¹]

tie¹·¹, **te**, †**tee** /tae/ *n* **1** a tie or fastening *la15-*. **2** an obligation, a restricting force, constraint *17-*. **3** *fishing* a section of line (with a specific number of hooks attached) *la16-19, 20- EC*. **4** a strap, part of a horse's tack, especially the strap attaching the crupper to the saddle *la15-17*. **5** an element of a ship's cordage *14-e17*. **tie-back** a short rope tied between two horses of a plough team to prevent their heads moving to the side *20-*. [OE *tēag*]

tie¹·², †**ty**, †**te** /tae/ *v* **1** to fasten, tether, bind, attach (with a rope) *la14-*. **2** to bind by obligation *16-*. **3** usually *passive* to bind by marriage; to be married *la18-*. **4** to fasten (with nails) *e16*. **5** *law* to bind by a legally binding agreement *la16-17*. **tied** *of persons or circumstances* bound, certain *la19-*. [OE *tīgan, tēgan*]

tie² /tae/ *n* a small strip of land, probably a part of a runrig system *20- Ork.* [Norw dial *teig* a strip of hay meadow]

tiff see TIFT¹·¹, TIFT²

tift¹·¹, **†tiff** /tɪft/ *n* order, condition; fettle *18-19, 20- SW Bor.* **†in tift** in good or proper condition *18-19.* [see the verb]

†tift¹·² *v* to adjust, put in good order or spirits *la18-e19 N NE T.* [variant of Eng †*tiff* to dress, deck out, OFr *tiffer* to adorn]

†tift¹·³ *adj* ready *la14.* [participial adj from OFr *tiffer*; see the verb]

tift², **tiff** /tɪft, tɪf/ *n* **1** a quarrel, dispute; the act of quarrelling *la17-.* **2** a sudden breeze, gust of wind *la18-.* **3** a fit of ill-humour, the sulks *la18-19, 20- C.* **tifter 1** = TIFT² (sense 1) *19-.* **2** = TIFT² (sense 2) *19-.* **tifty** quarrelsome, touchy *20- WC Bor.* [probably onomatopoeic, from the sound of a puff of wind]

tift³ /tɪft/ *v* **1** to thicken or full cloth by beating it, WAULK cloth *la19- Sh.* **2** to beat; to throb *la19- Sh Ork.* [unknown]

†tift⁴ *v* to drink, gulp down liquor *18-e19.* [variant of Eng slang †*tiff* to drink, sip]

tig¹·¹ /tɪg/ *n* **1** a light (playful) touch, tap, slap *18-.* **2** the tap given in the children's chasing game, usually accompanied by the call 'tig!' *18-.* **3** a children's chasing game, varieties include: *aeroplane tig, chain(y) tig, high tig, lame tig, low tig, plainy tig, tigtow, tunnel tig 19-.* **4** a sudden whim, mood or humour; a fit of sullenness *la18, 19- NE T EC.* **in tig tire** in suspense *19- Ork NE.* [see the verb]

tig¹·² /tɪg/ *v* **1** to touch lightly, pat *la15-.* **2** to meddle, interfere, have to do (with) *la15-.* **3** to tap or touch lightly with the hand while playing tig *19-.* **4** *of cattle* to run in panic or when tormented by flies *19, 20- T EC.* **5** to take a sudden whim, go off in a huff *la19- NE T.* **tig tow** to play at tig; to romp, flirt *19, 20- SW.* **†tig and tar, tar and tig** to toy, meddle (with) *la15-16*; compare *tar and tig* (TAR²). [perhaps an altered form of ME *tiken*; see TICK²·²]

tig¹·³ /tɪg/ *interj* called out in the game of tig when the pursuer touches someone *19-.* [see the verb]

tig see THIG

tiger see TEEGER

tiggie /ˈtɪgi/ *adj* fractious, cross *19- NE T.* [TIG¹·¹ + -IE²]

tight see TICHT¹·³

tigir see TEEGER

tigsam /ˈtɪgsəm/ *adj* vexatious, tedious *la19- Ork.* [TIG¹·¹ + -SOME]

tig-tag¹·¹ /ˈtɪgtag/ *n* a state of suspense *la19- Sh Ork.* [see the verb]

tig-tag¹·² /ˈtɪgtag/ *v* **1** to dally amorously, tease *20- Sh WC.* **2** to (suffer) delay; to haggle *17-e19.* [reduplication of TIG¹·²]

tikabed, **tyke-o-bed**, **ticky bed** /ˈtɪkəbed, ˈtaɪkobed, ˈtɪke bɛd/ *n* a mattress *19, 20- WC SW Bor.* [TIKE² + *o* (OF) + BED¹·¹]

tike¹, **tyke** /tʌɪk/ *n* **1** a dog, sometimes ill-tempered, rough or unkempt *la15-.* **2** *contemptuous* a rough, disreputable person *16-.* **3** a mischievous child *19-.* **4** a fellow, chap *19-.* **5** an otter *18- Sh.* **tyke-auld** very old *19, 20- NE.* **tike-tired, tyke-tired**, *Ork* **tig-tired** dog-tired, worn out *la18-.* [ON *tík* a bitch]

tike², **†tyk** /tʌɪk/ *n* **1** a mattress *19- EC Bor.* **2** a mattress cover; ticking *la15-e19.* [MDu *tīke*]

til see TILL²·²

tile¹·¹, **†tild**, **†till** /tʌɪl/ *n* **1** a thin slab of burnt clay, shaped according to the purpose for which it is required; tiles or bricks collectively *15-.* **2** a top hat *20-.* **tile-hat** a top hat. **†tile stane** a brick or tile *16-e17.* [OE *tigel*]

tile¹·², **†tyle**, **†tyld**, **†tayle** /tʌɪl/ *v* **1** to cover, usually a roof, with tiles *la14-.* **2** to cover over with cloth or curtains *16, 19- T.* **†tiled** *of white fish* dried in the sun in Prestonpans, East Lothian *la18-e19.* [see the noun]

tile see TOIL¹·²

tilfer, telfer, †tulfar /ˈtɪlfər, ˈtɛlfər/ *n* a loose floor-plank or moveable board on the bottom of a boat *19- Sh Ork.* [Norw *tilfar*]

till¹ /tɪl/ *n* **1** a stiff, usually impervious, clay, found in glacial deposits and forming a poor subsoil, now adopted in English as a geological term *la17-.* **2** *mining* a hard laminated shale formed from TILL¹ (sense 1), a kind of fireclay or BLAES *la17-19.* **†tillie** composed of TILL¹ (sense 1) *la18-19.* **†tillie clay** cold, stiff, unproductive soil *la18-e19.* **tillie airn** a crowbar *la19- WC SW.* [compare *northern* ME *thil* fireclay, OE *ðille* a floor, flooring]

till²·¹ /tɪl/ *adv* used idiomatically with verbs towards, in contact *la14-.* [see the prep]

till²·², **tull, til** /tɪl, tʌl/ *prep* **1** in expressing family relationships: ◊*John wis sib till yer Auntie Betty. la14-.* **2** *of distance* as far as: ◊*he vaiged till Aiberdeen. la14-.* **3** indicating the person or thing to which words or actions are directed: ◊*wae be till her. la14-.* **4** expressing proximity or contact: ◊*she took him till her bosom. la14-.* **5** indicating a limit of time until: ◊*I winnae ken till Tuesday. la14-.* **6** before vowel and h in C and Bor to, towards: ◊*she ran till him wi a face like thunder. la14-.* **7** expressing the outcome of an action: ◊*the accused beat him till his nose was broken. la14-.* **8** as far as a person or thing is concerned; with regard to: ◊*they wir indifferent til the lave. 15-.* **9** *of direction frequently with verbs of looking or listening* at: ◊*luik till the bairns. 18-.* **10** *with a verb of motion understood* to (an activity or place), frequently implying beginning something: ◊*A'm till the gairden. 18-.* **11** *of paternity* by: ◊*she had a bairn till the milkman. la18-.* **12** *of food* as a constituent of, accompaniment to, or flavouring for a meal: ◊*wull ye hae ony pepper till't? la19-.* **13** indicating the person or thing for whose use or benefit something is done for, on behalf of: ◊*I wis pechin aboot wi messages till ma faither. la14-, 20- Sh N NE T.* **14** indicating a limit of size up to *la15-16.* **15** in the formal greeting in the preamble of a letter to *la14-16.* **16** indicating purpose for, as *la14-16.* **17** in comparisons, to, with *la14-e19.* Compare TAE³·². **tea and till't** = HIGH TEA *20- C.* **†till trade** by trade *19.* [ON *til*]

till²·³ /tɪl/ *conj* **1** *of time* until *la14-.* **2** *of distance* as far as *15-.* **3** while: ◊*Ah'll bide here till Ah feenish ma denner. la14-.* **4** with a negative main clause before, when *la15-.* **5** in order that: ◊*gie us a match till Ah licht the caunle. la19-.* Compare TAE³·³. [see the prep]

till²·⁴ /tɪl/ *adv* to: ◊*if ye're keen till ken. la14-.* Compare *for till* (FOR¹·¹). [see the prep]

till see TEEL¹·², TILE¹·¹

tiller /ˈtɪlər/ *v of corn or other crops* to produce side-shoots from the root or base of the stem *18-.* [OE *telgor* a branch, twig]

tillie /ˈtɪle, ˈtɪli/ *n* a tiller (of a boat) *20- N NE EC.* [shortened form of Eng *tiller* + -IE¹]

†tillieloot *n* a cry of reproach, a taunt of Galashiels boys to those of the neighbouring parish of Bowden *19- Bor.* [unknown]

tillie-pan /ˈtɪleˈpan/ *n* a flat, iron cooking pan; a saucepan with a folding handle *18- NE EC.* [unknown first element + PAN¹·¹]

†tilliesoul *n* a small private inn erected by a landowner for the servants and horses of his guests and any others whom he did not want to entertain himself, frequently in place-names *la17-19.* [unknown]

tilt /tɪlt/ *n* euphoria; self-satisfaction, over-confidence *la19-Sh*. [unknown]

tilt *see* TILTH

tilter /ˈtɪltər/ *v* to sway, totter *20- Ork WC*. [Eng *tilter*, frequentative form of *tilt*]

tilth, *Ork* **tilt** /tɪlθ; *Ork* tɪlt/ *n* **1** cultivation; cultivated land *la14-*. **2** condition of cultivated soil: ◊ *a fine tilth for seedlings, a coorser tilth for tatties 17-*. **3** a hard struggle *20- Ork*. [OE *tilð*]

tim *see* TUIM[1.1], TUIM[1.2]

timber *see* TIMMER[1.1]

time, †**tyme** /tʌim; *unstressed* tɪm/ *n* time, measurement of duration *la14-*. **at aa time** at any time, at all times *20-*. **at a time** at times, now and again *la19-*. †**for the time** at that time; at the moment *la15-e18*. **in time coming, in all time coming** for all time to come, for the indefinite future *la16-*. **time aboot** alternately, in turn(s) *16-*. **time o day 1** the appropriate time *18-*. **2** a clock *20- Sh N NE EC Bor*. **3** *ironic* a severe manhandling or reproof *la19- Ork WC*. **the time that** while, during the time that *18-*. **a time or twa** once or twice *20- Sh N T SW Uls*. [OE *tīma*]

timeous, timous, †**tymous** /ˈtɪmiəs, ˈtʌɪməs/ *adj* frequently; *law* (sufficiently) early, prompt, in good time; timely; opportune *la15-*. [TIME + *-ous* adj-forming suffix]

timid /ˈtɪmɪd/ *adj* lacking in boldness *16-*. **timidity,** †**timidite** shyness, fearfulness *la15-*. **timidness** timidity *19-*. [MFr *timide*, Lat *timidus*]

timmer[1.1], **timber**, †**tymmer** /ˈtɪmər, ˈtɪmbər/ *n* **1** wood, especially as used in construction *la14-*. **2** wood as the material from which objects are made *15-*. **3** a wooden dish, cup or utensil *18-19*. †**timmer bush** the timber yard at Leith; also used for the storage of other goods *17-19*. **Timber Bush** the area of Leith where the timber yard was located *19-*. †**timmer houf, timmer holf** = HOWF (sense 3), an alternative name for *timmer bush la16-19*. †**timberman** a wood-cutter; a carpenter; a wood merchant *la15-17*. **timmer mercat 1** a fair held in Aberdeen during August (originally mainly for the sale of wood or wooden objects) *la18-*. **2** a timber market *la15-e17*. [OE *timber*]

timmer[1.2] /ˈtɪmər/ *v* **1** to beat, thrash *19- NE WC Uls*. **2** to act or move briskly or vigorously, go at (something) with verve and energy *19- NE*. **3** to build or furnish with wood *16-17*. **timmer up** = TIMMER[1.2] (sense 2). [OE *timbran* to build]

timmer[1.3] /ˈtɪmər/ *adj* **1** wooden, made of wood *16-*. **2** wooden, dull, stupid, unresponsive *19-*. **3** unmelodious, unmusical, tuneless *19-*. **timmer tongue** the disease actinomycosis, which causes swelling and hardening of the tongue in cattle *20- N NE T WC*. **timmer tuned** having a harsh unmusical voice, unable to sing in tune *19-*. †**timmer wark 1** the wooden part of a structure *la15-17*. **2** wooden furnishings or furniture *la16-e17*. [see the noun]

timmer[2] /ˈtɪmər/ *adj* shy, fearful *20- WC Bor*. [back-formation from TIMORSOME or Eng *timorous*]

timorsome /ˈtɪmərsəm/ *adj* nervous, timid, fearful *18-*. [EModE *timorsome*, altered form of *timorous* with change of suffix]

timothy /ˈtɪməθɪ, ˈtɪməθi/ *n* **1** a downpour of rain *20- Ork*. **2** an alcoholic drink; a drinking glass *la19*. [from the biblical character, who was advised to take a little wine for the sake of his health]

†**timous, tymous** *adv* early in the day *la16-19*. [see the adj TIMEOUS]

timous *see* TIMEOUS

timously /ˈtʌiməsli/ *adv* promptly, expeditiously, in due time *la15-*. [*timous* (TIMEOUS), with adv-forming suffix]

timpan *see* TYMPAN

timple /ˈtɪmpəl/ *v* to finger, handle so as to spoil *20- Ork*. [unknown]

tin[1.1], †**tyn,** †**tun** /tɪn/ *n* a silver-coloured, highly malleable metal used in manufacture and in making alloys such as bronze or pewter *15-*. [OE *tin*]

tin[1.2], †**tyn** /tɪn/ *v* to coat with tin *la15-*. [see the noun]

tin *see* THIN[1.1], THIN[1.2], TUNE[1.1]

tinchel, †**tynchell,** †**tinckell** /ˈtɪŋxəl/ *n* a ring of beaters used to drive a quarry, especially deer, towards the hunters *16-19, 20- historical*. [Gael *timcheall* an act of surrounding, a circuit]

tincklarian *see* TINKLER

tinclar *see* TINKLER

tindle box /ˈtɪndəl bɔks/ *n* a box containing tinder and a flint or steel, producing a spark for lighting (a pipe) *la18-19 WC Bor, 20- historical*. [altered form of Eng *tinderbox*; perhaps with influence from *tendal* (TANNEL)]

tine[1], †**tyne,** †**tynd** /tʌin/ *n* **1** a prong, spike; originally (a branch of) a deer's antler *la14-*. **2** a tooth (of a harrow or clock wheel) *16-*. [OE *tind*]

tine[2], **tyne,** †**tyine** /tʌin/ *v pt, ptp* **tint,** †**tynt,** †**tyned 1** to lose, suffer the loss, destruction or disappearance of, cease to have or enjoy, fail to retain, forfeit *la14-*. **2** to lose (a contest, legal action or battle) *la14-*. **3** to spend unprofitably or in vain, waste (time or labour) *la14-*. **4** to mislay *la15-*. **5** to cause the loss of, confiscate *la15-*. **6** to get rid of, free oneself from, abandon *la18-*. **7** to lose or miss (one's way), get lost, lose sight of (land); to go astray *la14-19, 20- Sh N NE T WC*. **8** *of things* to decline, lose value or prestige, fade away; *of persons or animals* to perish, die *la14-19, 20- Sh NE T*. **9** to fail to obtain, miss, come short of, be deprived of *la14-19,20- NE T*. **10** to forget, be oblivious of *16-19, 20- NE T*. **11** to lose (one's footing), miss (a step) *18- NE*. **12** to lose by letting fall; *knitting* to drop a stitch *la19- NE*. **13** to draw away from, leave behind *la19- NE*. **14** to ruin, destroy *la15-e17*. **15** to incur (a penalty) *15-e17*. †**between (the) tyning and (the) winning** in a critical or doubtful state, hovering between success and failure *la18-e19*. [ON *týna* to destroy, lose, perish]

ting *see* THING[1], THING[2]

tinge *see* TEENGE

tinged, tingt, †**tingde** /tɪŋd, tɪŋt/ *adj of cattle* swollen, acutely distended because of overeating *17- WC Uls*. [unknown]

tingle[1.1] /ˈtɪŋl/ *n* **1** a prickling, stinging sensation; a thrill *la18-*. **2** a ringing, jingling noise *la17, 20- NE T*. [see the verb]

tingle[1.2] /ˈtɪŋl, ˈtɪŋgəl/ *v* **1** to affect with a prickling, stinging sensation; to thrill, excite *18-*. **2** to (cause to) tinkle, ring or chime *19- NE C Bor*. [variant of TINKLE]

tingle[2] /ˈtɪŋl/ *v* to patch a leak in the clinkers of a boat *20- NE EC*. [Eng *tingle* a small nail, a sheet of metal for repairing a boat]

†**tingle naill** *n* a small nail *la17*. [Eng *tingle*, see TINGLE[2], + NAIL]

tings *see* TANGS

tingt *see* TINGED

tink /tɪŋk/ *n* **1** an itinerant pedlar *la19-*. **2** *contemptuous* a dishonest or contemptible person; a vagrant; a foul-mouthed, abusive person *20-*. **3** *affectionately, of a child la20-*. Compare TINKER (sense 1). **tinkie** an itinerant pedlar *20- NE T EC*. **tinking** an abusive scolding, a slanging *la20- NE*. [shortened form of TINKER]

tink *see* THINK[1.2]

tinker /ˈtɪŋkər/ *n* **1** an itinerant pedlar or trader, some being descendants of dispossessed Highland peasantry and others of mixed gipsy descent *la17-*. **2** a dishonest or contemptible person *17-*; compare TINK (sense 2). **3** a worker in metal; a tinsmith *la17-*; compare TINKLER (sense 2). **tinker's tartan** mottled skin on the legs caused by sitting too close to a fire *20- N H&I C*; compare *fireside tartan* (FIRE), *grannie's tartan* (GRANNIE[1.1]). **tinker's tea** tea brewed in a pan rather than a teapot *20-*. [ME *tinker*; perhaps from TIN[1.1] or from the later attested *tink* to mend, solder]

tinkle /'tɪŋkəl/ *v* to (cause to) ring, jingle *16-*. †**tinkle on**, **tinkle upon** to talk idly about *17-19*. [ME *tinklen*]

tinkler, †**tynklar**, †**tinclar** /'tɪŋklər/ *n* **1** = TINKER (sense 1) *la16-*. **2** in personal names, a worker in metal; a tinsmith *12-*; compare TINKER (sense 3). †**tincklarian** of the tinker sort, a term devised to describe himself by the early 18th-century Edinburgh pamphleteer William Mitchell, a tinsmith by trade *18-e19*. [variant of TINKER]

tinnel *see* TUMMELL

tinnie[1], **tinny** /'tɪne/ *n* a tin mug *19-*. [TIN[1.1] + -IE[1]]

tinnie[2], **tinny** /'tɪne/ *n* name for a tinsmith *la18-*. [TIN[1.1] + -IE[3]]

tino[1.1] /'tʌɪno/ *n* a spit or skewer for drying fish *la19- Ork*. [Norw dial *tein* + -O[2]]

tino[1.2] /'tʌɪno/ *v fishing* to skewer (fish) for drying *la19- Ork*. [see the noun]

tinsel[1.1], **tinsal**, †**tynsall**, †**tynsell** /'tɪnsəl/ *n* **1** loss, destruction, harm, detriment *la14-*. **2** spiritual loss, perdition, damnation *la14-16*. **3** *law* forfeiture (of a thing or right) by failure to perform some stipulated condition; deprivation or confiscation as a penalty or punishment *la14-e19*. **4** loss incurred by the effects of damage, mistreatment or neglect, damage, ruination *16-17*. **5** waste (of time) *la15-e17*. **6** failure to gain (something) or win (a contest) *la14-17*. †**tinsel of the feu** forfeiture of a FEU by failure to pay the *feu duty 19*. [ON *týnsla*]

†**tinsel**[1.2], †**tynsall** *v* **1** to lose, damage (goods); to cause loss or harm to (a person) *15-16*. **2** to penalize, punish by a fine *la16-e17*. [see the noun]

tint /tɪnt/ *n* a taste, touch, drop, especially of alcohol *la19- Sh*. [extended sense of Eng *tint* a colouring]

tint *see* TAINT[1.1], TINE[2]

tinter /'tɪntər/ *n* a trace *la19- Sh Ork*. [altered form of Eng *tincture* a colouring]

tintle *see* TRINNLE[1.2]

tip[1.1] /tɪp/ *n* **1** an end or point, an apex; an end-piece *la16-*. **2** an over-dressed person, a dandy *la19- Sh*. **have a guid tip o yersel** to have a good opinion of yourself *la20- C Bor*. [ME *tip*, ON *typpi*, MDu *tip*]

tip[1.2] /tɪp/ *v* **1** to furnish with a tip or end-piece *15-*. **2** to walk or dance on tiptoe; to tread lightly *19-*. **3** to kick a football lightly with the point of the toe *19-*. **4** to touch lightly *19-*. **5** to remove the tip of something *la19, 20- T SW*. **tipper** to walk on tiptoe or with little pressure on the foot *la18-*. **tippin** *fishing* the cord used to attach the hook to the snood *la19- N NE T EC*; compare TIPPET. **tippit** having a tip (of a particular sort) *la15-*. **tip up** to dress up, smarten oneself *la19- NE T EC*. [ON *typpa* to tip or top; and compare Du, LG *tippen* to touch lightly]

tip *see* TUP[1.1]

tippence, †**twa penyis**, †**tuppens** /'tɪpəns/ *n* **1** a coin worth two pennies; money to the value of two pennies *15-*. **2** something worth very little *17-*. **want tippence o the shillin** *derogatory* to be considered to be mentally disadvantaged *19-*. [reduced form of TWA + *pence* (PENNY)]

tippeny[1.1], **tuppeny** /'tɪpəne/ *n* **1** weak ale or beer sold at twopence a (Scots) pint *18, 19- historical*. **2** a child's elementary reading book, succeeding the *penny book* (PENNY) *la19-e20, la20- historical*. [reduced form of TWA + PENNY]

tippeny[1.2], **tuppeny**, †**twa penny** /'tɪpəne, 'tʌpəne/ *adj* costing or worth two pence *16-*. **tippeny reel** a lively dance *20- Sh*. **tuppeny struggle** *humorous* a Scotch pie *20- C*. **tuppeny tightener** *humorous* a twopenny portion of fish and chips *la19-e20, la20- historical*. †**The Twa-penny Faith** a popular name for Archbishop Hamilton's tract *Ane Godlie Exhortatioun* published in 1559, also misapplied to his *Catechism* of 1552 *la16*. [see the noun]

tippeny-nippeny /'tɪpəne 'nɪpəne/ *n* a kind of leapfrog *20- EC Bor*. [perhaps reduplicative form of TIP[1.2], and assimilated to TIPPENY[1.1], TIPPENY[1.2]]

tippertin /'tɪpərtɪn/ *n games* a cardboard spinning-top *19, 20- NE*. [derivative of *tipper* (TIP[1.2])]

tippet, †**tepat** /'tɪpət/ *n* **1** a (fur) garment worn around the neck and shoulders; a scarf-like part of a garment *la15-*. **2** *fishing* a length of twisted horsehair to which the hook is attached on a line *19, 20- N NE T*; compare *tippin* (TIP[1.2]). **3** a handful of stalks of straw, used in thatching *19, 20- NE*. **4** a tuft or handful of hair or wool *19, 20- NE*. [unknown; compare TIP[1.1]]

tiptaes, †**tip-tais**, †**typtays** /'tɪptez/ *npl* the tips of the toes *16-*. Compare TAPTAES. [TIP[1.1] + TAE[1]]

tird[1] /tɪrd/ *n* a state of excitement or rage; a commotion *20- Sh*. [variant of TIRR[2.1]; perhaps influenced by TIRD[2]]

tird[2] /tɪrd/ *v* **1** to tear off a covering; to strip off clothes *la19- Sh*. **2** to work with speed and vigour *la19- Sh*. [variant of TIRR[1.2]]

tire[1.1] /taer/ *n* a state of being or becoming tired, fatigue, weariness *19- Sh N NE T EC*. [see the verb]

tire[1.2], †**tyre** /taer/ *v* **1** to (cause to) tire, become exhausted *15-*. **2** to cause a person to lose interest *15-*. **3** to become or be weary or sick of something, lose patience or interest *la15-*. **4** to grow weary of waiting *la18-e19*. †**tyre ʒour thowmes** to be bothered, trouble yourself *e16*; compare *fash yer thumb* (FASH[1.2]). [OE *tēorian*]

†**tire**[2], **tyre** *n* **1** a row or course of stones (or turf) on a wall *17-18*. **2** a tier or rank (of guns on a ship) *la16-17*. **3** a stack of timber *e16*. **tyring**, **tiring** *of timber* stacking *e16*. [MFr *tire* a rank, sequence]

tiresome, †**tyrsum** /'taersəm/ *adj* tedious, wearisome, irksome *16-*. [TIRE[1.2], with adj-forming suffix]

tirf *see* TURF[1.1]

tiribus *see* TERIBUS

tirl[1.1] /tɪrl/ *n* **1** a turning or twisting movement, a twirl *la16-19, 20- Sh Ork N WC*. **2** an overturning, a twisting or whirling motion leading to a fall; a fall; a disease characterized by falling *la16-19, 20- Sh Ork N*. **3** a knock, rattle or tap (on a door) *19, 20- NE T EC*. **4** a breeze; a flurry of snow *18-19, 20- NE*. **5** a slight pat or touch; a pecking kiss *19*. **6** a short spell of some activity, a bout, round or turn of doing something (such as dancing or drinking) *la17-18*. [see the verb]

tirl[1.2] /tɪrl/ *v pt also* **tird 1** to spin, swirl, whirl *17-*. **2** to turn or bowl over; to upset; to trip *20-*. **3** to turn, twist; *of a door fitting* to open the door or produce a noise; to tap, knock, rattle on a door *la15-19, 20- Sh NE T*. **tirlin pin 1** a door-latch *la19, 20- historical*. **2** a door-knocker *la20- T EC*. [metathesis of ME *trillen* to rotate, roll; compare Norw *trille*, TRILL]

tirl[2] /tɪrl/ *n* a device serving the purpose of a wheel in a horizontal water-mill *la18- Sh Ork*. [compare Faer *tyril* a milk whisk, Swed dial *tyril* the plunger of a churn]

tirl[3] /tɪrl/ *v* **1** to pull off clothes or bedclothes; to strip thatch from a roof *17-*. **2** to take the surface off a piece of ground for quarrying or peat-cutting *19-*. **3** to take the covering off (a person or thing) *18-19, 20- Bor*. **tirler** the person who strips the surface layer off the ground, especially from a quarry or coal mine *17*. [perhaps a frequentative form of TIRR¹·²]

tirl⁴ /tɪrl/ *v* **1** to cause the string of a musical instrument to vibrate or tremble *la16*-. **2** to quiver, vibrate, thrill *19*-. †**tirl at** to pluck at (a beard) *la15*. **tirl on** to pluck on the strings of a musical instrument *la16*-. [perhaps an extended sense of TIRL¹·²; and compare THIRL¹·²]

tirl *see* THIRL¹·²

tirlie¹ /ˈtɪrli, ˈtɪrle/ *n* **1** a curlicue, a decorative scroll used in carving, a flourish *la19*-. **2** a latch for a door *20*- *Ork*. **3** a spinning top *20*- *Ork*. **4** a mechanism which twirls or spins round to help vent smoke from a chimney *e17*. †**tirlie mirlie 1** a term of endearment or familiar name *16-19*. **2** an ornament *e17*. **tirlie-tod** the greater plantain *Plantago major 20*- *NE*. **tirlie-whirlie 1** an ornament, knick-knack *la18*-. **2** *in singing* a trill, a grace note *la19*- *T C*. **3** an intricate device or mechanism, a gadget *la18-e19*. **4** the female pudendum *la18-e19*. [TIRL¹·² + -IE³]

†**tirlie**² *n* a barred wicket gate or turnstile *18*. **tirlie door** a barred wicket gate *e18*. [back-formation from TIRLISS reinterpreted as a plural]

tirlis, **terlass**, †**tyrleis**, †**terlys** /ˈtɪrlɪs, ˈtɛrləs/ *v* to fit a door or window with a lattice or grating *16-19*, *20*- *historical*. [from the noun TIRLISS]

tirliss, †**tirleis**, †**tyrlis**, †**terlass** /ˈtɪrlɪs/ *n* **1** a grill, grating or screen for a door or window *la15*-. **2** a trellis for supporting plants *16*-. **3** a barred wicket gate or turnstile *18*-. **4** a grid or rack for drying goods indoors *20*- *NE*. **5** a grating over a drain *16-e17*. †**tirles yett** a barred wicket gate *16-17*. †**tirlie door** a barred wicket gate *17-18*. [metathesis of OFr *treliz*]

tirn, **terran** /tɪrn, ˈtɛrən/ *adj* **1** *of weather* threatening, gloomy *20*- *Sh Ork*. **2** *of a person* irritable, bad-tempered, angry *19*- *Sh*. **3** *of a sight* fearful *la19*- *Ork*. [Norw *tirren, terren* cross, surly]

tirn *see* TURN¹·²

tirr¹·¹ /tɪr/ *n* the layer of turf or soil removed from the rock of a quarry *la18-19*, *20*- *N EC Bor*. [see the verb]

tirr¹·², **turr**, **tirve** /tɪr, tʌr, tɪrv/ *v* **1** to take the top layer off a piece of ground; to remove surface turf or soil from ground to allow digging for peat or quarrying for stone *la16*-. **2** to strip or tear off roofing *16-19*, *20*- *Sh Ork N NE C*. **3** to undress a person or oneself *la15-19*, *20*- *NE T*. **4** to strip a room or bed; to dismantle *20*- *NE EC Bor*. **5** to rob a fruit tree *la20*- *NE*. **tirrin 1** the action of stripping a roof from a building *16-19*, *20*- *Ork N*. **2** the layer removed before digging or quarrying *18-19*, *20*- *Ork N*. **3** the material removed from a roof being stripped *e17*. †**tirr the kirk to theek the quire** to pay off one debt by incurring another *la16-e19*. [ME *tirven*, probably related to TURF¹·¹. Compare TIRL³]

tirr²·¹ /tɪr/ *n* a fit of bad temper or rage; a quarrel *20*- *Sh Ork EC SW Bor*. [see the verb]

tirr²·² /tɪr/ *v* to snarl; to grumble or reproach *19*, *20*- *Bor*. [perhaps onomatopoeic]

tirr²·³ /tɪr/ *adj* bad-tempered, quarrelsome *19*- *SW*. **tirrie** angry *19*- *Sh Ork*. [see the verb]

tirr³ /tɪr/ *v of a heart* to beat, thump *20*- *T*. [perhaps onomatopoeic]

tirran, **teerant**, **tyran**, †**tyrand**, †**tirrant**, †**teran** /ˈtɪrən, ˈtɪrənt, ˈtaerən/ *n* **1** a despot, a tyrant *la14*-. **2** a cantankerous, awkward or exasperating person *19*, *20*- *N NE*. **3** a violent person, a villain *la14-16*. **tirraneese**, **tarraneese**, **taraneze**, **tarranize**, **tyrannize** 1 to behave like a despot *la16*-. **2** to harass or vex; to tease or irritate *20*- *NE T*. **3** to treat roughly, assault *la19*- *NE*. †**tyranfull** tyrannical *16*. †**tirannitie** tyranny *e16*. †**tyranlie** tyrannically, harshly *la15-16*.

†**tyrandry** tyranny *15-16*. **tirrany**, †**tiranie 1** despotism *la14*-. **2** violent, lawless behaviour; fierce fighting *la15-16*. [OFr *tyrant, tiran*]

tirrick, †**tarrock** /ˈtɪrɪk/ *n* the Arctic tern *Sterna paradisaea*, or common tern *Sterna hirundo la18-19*, *20*- *Sh*. [probably related to Eng *tern*, with -ick (-OCK) suffix]

tirrievirrie *see* TIRRY-MIRRY

tirrivee /ˌtɪrɪˈvi, ˈtɪrɪvi/ *n* **1** a fit of rage or temper, a tantrum *19*-. **2** a whim, an odd notion *19*-. **3** a state of excitement or bustle; a disturbance or fight *19*-. [perhaps derivative of TIRR²·¹ or altered form of TAIL3EVE¹·¹]

tirr-wirr¹·¹, **tur-wur** /ˈtɪrˈwɪr, ˈtʌrˈwʌr/ *n* a commotion, a disturbance; a noisy quarrel *la19*- *NE T EC*. [TIRR²·¹ + WIRR¹·¹]

tirr-wirr¹·² /ˈtɪrwɪr/ *v* to quarrel or fight noisily; to complain or reproach *la19*- *NE T EC*. [see the noun]

†**tirryfyke** *n* bustle, stress, excitement *la18*. [perhaps a conflation of TIRRIVEE with FYKE¹·¹]

tirry-merry /ˈtɪrɪˈmɛri/ *adj* in a state of excitement or uproar *20*- *Sh*. [variant of TIRRY-MIRRY]

tirry-mirry, †**turry-wurry**, †**tirrievirrie** /ˈtɪrɪˈmɪri/ *n* **1** a fit of ill-temper *20*- *Sh T*. **2** a commotion, a disturbance; a noisy quarrel *20*- *Sh N*. [altered form of TIRR-WIRR¹·¹ with -y (-IE¹) suffix]

tirse¹·¹ /tɪrs/ *n* **1** a jerk or tug; a sudden movement *19*- *Sh Ork*. **2** a sudden wind or storm *la19*- *Sh*. **3** a state of excitement, impatience or rage *20*- *Sh*. [see the verb]

tirse¹·² /tɪrs/ *v* to tug or jerk impatiently; to tear, rend *19*- *Sh Ork*. [compare Norw dial *tersa* to drive, force]

tirsipel, †**tirsibald** /ˈtɪrsɪpəl/ *n* a shred, a rag or tatter of cloth *la19*- *Sh*. Compare TRUSSIE BELT. [perhaps TIRSE¹·² + PEEL⁴ or PELT²]

tirsoo, **tirso** /ˈtɪrso/ *n* **1** the marsh ragwort *Jacobaea aquatica la19*- *Ork*. **2** the common dock *Rumex obtusifolius 20*- *Ork*. [perhaps a derivative of TIRSE¹·²]

tirung, †**terung**, †**teiroung** /ˈtɪrʌŋ/ *n in the Western Isles* land with a rental value of one ounce of silver *la15-17*, *18*- *historical*. [Gael *tìr-unga*]

tirve *see* TIRR¹·²

tirvis *see* TURF¹·¹

tische *see* TISHIE

Tiseday *see* TYSDAY

tishie, †**tische**, †**tusche**, †**tisshew** /ˈtɪʃi/ *n* **1** flesh, sinews *19*-. **2** soft, gauzy paper; a paper hankerchief *la19*-. **3** a fine fabric woven with gold or silver thread; a band or belt made of rich cloth *la15-e17*. [OFr *tissu*]

tisicke *see* TEESICK

†**tisshew**, **tissue** *v ptp* **tissu** to weave with gold or silver thread *16-17*. [from the noun *tisshew* (TISHIE)]

tisshew *see* TISHIE

tissle *see* TOUSLE¹·²

tissue *see* TISSHEW

tistle *see* THRISSEL

tit¹·¹ /tɪt/ *n* a pull, a tug, a jerk; a snatching movement *15-19*, *20*- *Sh NE T*. [see the verb]

tit¹·² /tɪt/ *v pt, ptp* **tittit**, †**tit**, †**tytt** 1 to pull, tug, jerk *la14-19*, *20*- *Sh NE T*. **2** to snatch, seize *la14-e15*. **3** to grab or pull a person *15*. †**tit up** to string up, hang *la14-e16*. [perhaps onomatopoeic]

†**tit**²·¹, **tid** *n* a touch or stroke; a light tap *18-19*. [EModE *tit*, onomatopoeic]

tit²·² /tɪt/ *v* to strike lightly, tap *20*- *C*. [see the noun]

tit³ /tɪt/ *n* a nipple or teat; an artificial teat *la19*-. [OE *titt*]

tit⁴ /tɪt/ *n* a fit of temper or rage *la19*- *NE T C*. **tittie** short-tempered, irritable *19*- *C*. [variant of TID¹·¹]

†**tit**⁵ *n* a type of button *e17*. [perhaps an extended sense of TIT³]

tit *see* TAIT¹·¹

tita, tyta, tyty /ˈtɪta, ˈtaeta, ˈtaete/ *n* an affectionate term for a father or grandfather *la18-19, 20- Ork.* [compare Gael *taididh*]

†**Titan** *n* the sun *la15-16.* [Lat *Titan* applied in poetry to the sun god Helios]

titbore tatbore *see* TEET[1.1]

titbow dance /ˈtɪtbo dans/ *n* a heat haze, the shimmering of light in hot weather *20- Sh.* [unknown first element + DANCE[1.1]]

titbow reel /ˈtɪtbo ril/ *n* = TITBOW DANCE *20- Sh.* [unknown first element + REEL[1.1]]

titch *see* TOUCH[1.2]

†**tite**[1.1] *adj* quick, swift; ready, prepared *la15-16.* [see the adv]

tite[1.2], †**tyte** /tʌɪt/ *adv* **1** immediately, directly; quickly *la14-19, 20- Sh Ork.* **2** readily, willingly; easily *la14-e19.* †**titter, tittar, tytar** sooner *la14-18.* †**tittest** soonest *16.* [ON *títt* frequently]

titersome /ˈtʌɪtərsʌm/ *adj of a job* tricky, tediously difficult *20- NE.* [*toiter* (TOIT[1.2]) + -SOME]

tither[1.1], *Sh NE* **tidder**, †**tother** /ˈtɪðər; *Sh NE* ˈtɪdər/ *adj* **1** the other; the second of two (or more) *la14-.* **2** additional, extra *la14-.* **3** previous, recent *la15-.* [see the pron]

tither[1.2], *Sh NE* **tidder**, †**tothir**, †**tuther**, †**tuder** /ˈtɪðər; *Sh NE* ˈtɪdər/ *pron* the other (of two) *la14-.* **tane or tither**, †**tane or tother** one or the other *16-19, 20- literary.* [by wrong division of ME *þat oþer, þet oþer* the other; compare TANE]

titill, title *see* TEETLE[1.1]

title *see* TITTLE[1]

titlin, titling /ˈtɪtlɪn, ˈtɪtlɪŋ/ *n* **1** the meadow pipit *Anthus pratensis 16-19, 20- Ork N NE Uls.* **2** the smallest and weakest in a brood; the runt in a litter of pigs *la20- NE T Uls.* [compare Norw dial *titlingur* any small fish or bird]

tits *see* TOOT[2.2]

tit-tat /ˈtɪtˈtat/ *n* an argument, an altercation *20- N.* [reduced form of Eng *tit for tat*]

titter /ˈtɪtər/ *v* **1** to shiver, tremble *la19- Sh Ork.* **2** *of the teeth* to chatter *20- Ork.* [Norw dial *titra*]

titter *see* TITE[1.2]

tittie[1], **titty** /ˈtɪti, ˈtɪte/ *n* a familiar term for a sister *17-19, 20- literary.* [perhaps an infantile pronunciation of SISTER[1]]

tittie[2] /ˈtɪti/ *n* a girl or young woman *20- Sh.* [Norw dial *titta*]

tittit *see* TIT[1.2]

tittle[1], **teetle**, †**title**, †**tutle** /ˈtɪtəl, ˈtitəl/ *v* to whisper; to chatter or gossip *la15-.* †**tittillar, titlar, tutlar** a gossip *la15-16.* [probably onomatopoeic]

tittle[2] /ˈtɪtəl/ *v* to vex, irritate *la19- Ork.* [perhaps conflation of KITTLE[1.2] with TICKLE[1.1]]

tittle *see* TEETLE[1.1]

titty *see* TITTIE[1]

titular, †**titulair**, †**tittular** /ˈtɪtjələr/ *n* **1** *law* a lay owner of formerly ecclesiastical property *16-.* **2** a possessor of a title to ecclesiastical property *16-18.* **3** a possessor of a title to property or office *la16-e17.* **titular of the teinds** *law* a layman owning the tithes of formerly ecclesiastical property *16-e19, la19- historical.* [MFr *titulaire*]

†**titup** *n* **1** a type of bit for a horse *e16.* **2** the trigger of a crossbow *e16.* [TIT[1.2] + UP]

to *see* TAE[3.1], TAE[3.2], TAE[3.4], THO[2], TOO[3]

†**to-**[1] *prefix* expressing violent or forceful separation or movement apart. **tobet** beaten to pieces *15-e16.* **to-brokin, to-brok** broken into pieces, smashed *15-e16.* **to-brist** burst apart *la14-e16.* **to-claif** split apart *15-e16.* **to-ga** to go away, to flee *la14-16.* **toganging** the setting (of the sun) *15-16.* **to-hew** cut to pieces *14-e15.* **to-rent** to tear to pieces *15-16.* **to-schake** to shake or tremble violently, to shake to pieces *e16.* **to-schulder** to fly asunder *e16.* **to-schyde** to split asunder *e16.* **to-tor, to-torn** torn to pieces, lacerated *e16.* **to-trynsch** to cut to pieces, to slaughter *e16.* [OE *tō-*]

†**to-**[2] *prefix intensifier* utterly, completely. **to-baith** wet copiously *e16.* **tobasyt** dismayed, fearful *e16.* **tochange** to change completely *e16.* **to-grane** to groan deeply *e16.* **to-holkyt** dug up, eroded *e16.* **to-hungyn** left undecided *e16.* **to-irkyt** deeply troubled *e16.* **to-lame** badly maimed *e16.* **to-quake** to show extreme fear *15-e16.* **to-schent** gravely wounded *la15-e16.* **to-smyte** utterly stricken *e16.* **to-sparpill** to scatter everywhere *e16.* [OE *tō-*]

to-[3], **tae-**, †**too-** /tu, tə, te/ *prefix* **1** with verbs and nouns expressing movement or direction towards *la14-*; compare to LUIK. **2** expressing something additional *la17-.* **3** with verbs (especially past participles) expressing attachment or adherence, mainly with reference to the attachment of a seal on a document *15-16.* †**to-hungyn** (of a seal) hung on, appended *15-16.* [see the prep *to* (TAE[3.2])]

toad *see* TAID

toaffee *see* TAFFIE

toal *see* TOUL

toaly, toly, toley, tollie /ˈtole/ *n* a lump of excrement, also a term of abuse *18-.* [altered form of DOLL[1] + -IE[1]]

toap *see* TAP[1.1]

toarny-ware *see* THORN

†**toast**[1.1], **tost** /tost, tɔst/ *n* a piece of toasted bread *la16-17.* [see the verb]

toast[1.2], **tost** /tost, tɔst/ *v* to brown (bread) by exposure to heat *17-.* **toaster 1** a device for toasting bread *20-.* **2** a metal rack or a stone for drying and toasting oatcakes in front of an open fire after baking *la19, 20- NE T WC.* [ME *tosten*, OFr *toster*]

toath *see* TATHE[1.2]

toatie *see* TOTTIE

tobacco *see* TABACKIE

tobackie /təˈbake/ *n* one of the actions in a children's ball-game *20- C.* [TO-[3] + BACK[1.1] + -IE[1]]

tobasyt *see* TO-[2]

tobe /tob/ *v* **1** to be talkative, babble inconsequentially *la19- Sh.* **2** to grumble, complain *la19- Sh.* [probably related to Norw *tåpe* a fool; compare TAUPIE]

tober *see* TABOUR[1.2]

tobet *see* TO-[1]

tobooth *see* TOLBOOTH

toby /ˈtobe/ *n* **1** a stopcock or valve in a water or gas main, usually in a roadway, at which the supply may be cut off *la19-.* **2** *humorous* the penis *la20- NE T EC.* [unknown; compare Gael *tobar* a well or fountain and Eng slang *toby* the buttocks, the female pudendum, from the personal name *Toby*]

toch /tɔx/ *interj* call to a calf to come to food *20- N.* [unknown]

tochange *see* TO-[2]

tocher[1.1], †**tochir**, †**toucher**, †**toquhir** /ˈtɔxər/ *n* a marriage portion, usually a bride's dowry *la15-20, 21- historical.* **tocherless** having no dowry *la18-.* †**tocher-band** a marriage settlement *la18-e19.* †**tocher-gear** property given as a dowry *16-e19.* †**tocher-gude** = *tocher-gear 16-18.* [Gael †*tochar*]

†**tocher**[1.2] *v* to provide with a dowry *la16-19.* [see the noun]

tochir *see* TOCHER[1.1]

†**tocum** *v* to come to a person's attention, arrive *15-17.* [ME *tocomen*, TO-[3] + COME[1.2] +]

tocum *see* TAE COME

tod[1], †**todd**, †**tode** /tɔd/ *n* **1** a fox, frequently in place-names *la12-.* **2** a sly, cunning, untrustworthy person *la15-19, 20- T C SW.* †**toddis** fox fur *la15-e17.* **Toddie's grund** *WC,*

Ork **Toddo's grund** the den in children's games *la19-*. †**Toddie's birds** offspring of bad stock, an evil brood *la16-e18*. **tod-hole, tod's hole 1** a fox's hole or den, frequently in place-names *la12-*. **2** a refuge; the grave *la18-19*. **tod-hunt** a fox-hunt *19-*. †**tod-hunter** a person employed to exterminate foxes *la19*. **tod-lowrie** the fox *la15-* literary; compare LOWRIE. †**tod pultis** = *tod skins e16*. **tod skins,** †**tod skynnis** fox skins or furs *15-*. **tod-tail, tod tails, tod's tails 1** the stagshorn clubmoss *19, 20- N*. **2** the foxglove *20- Bor*. **hunt the tod** children's games hide-and-seek *la19- NE T*. **the tod and the lambs, tod and lambs** a draughts-like board game, fox and geese *19, 20- NE T*. †**tod-i-the-fauld** name of various games *19*. [unknown]

tod[2] /tɔd/ *interj euphemism* a mild oath, a form of 'God' *la19-*. [altered form of GOD]

todd see TOD[1]

toddie /'tɔde/ *n* a type of bread or scone *la18-19, 20- Bor*. [probably a variant of *dod* (DAD[1.1]) + -IE[1]]

toddle[1.1] /'tɔdəl/ *n* **1** a leisurely walk or stroll *la19-*. **2** a toddler, toddling child; a small neat person *19*. [see the verb]

toddle[1.2], †**todle** /'tɔdəl/ *v* **1** *especially of a young child or an old, infirm or drunk person* to walk with small, uncertain or unsteady steps *la16-*. **2** *humorous* to set (off), walk with short, unhurried steps *19-*. **3** *of running water* to babble, ripple *la18-19*. **4** to make small movements (as in play) *e16*. [unknown; perhaps imitative, with frequentative suffix]

tode see TOD[1]

toe see TAE[1]

to fall see TAE FA

toffee see TAFFIE

toft, toftsteid see TAFT

toga /'toga/ *n Scottish Universities* the scarlet gown worn by undergraduates, especially at Aberdeen *la19-*. Compare *red gown* (REID[1.2]). [Lat *toga*]

toght see THOCHT

togidder see THEGITHER

tohie see TEHE

toholkyt see TO-[2]

toil[1.1] /tɔɪl/ *n* (a period or time of) labour, (hard) work *15-*. [see the verb]

toil[1.2], **tile,** †**toyle** /tɔɪl, tʌɪl/ *v* **1** to labour, work hard *17-*. **2** to exhaust (oneself) with hard work *la19, 20- Sh*. [ME *toilen*; AN *toiller* to dispute; compare TULYIE]

toill see TOLL

toillie see TULYIE[1.1]

†**toilʒe, toyle** *n* a type of cloth, perhaps linen *15-16*. **toildor, toldoir** *of cloth* shot through with gold threads *e16*. [OFr *toille* linen cloth, canvas]

toir see TEAR[2.2]

toiseach, †**toscheoch** /'tɔʃəx, 'tɪʃəx/ *n* the head of a clan, a chieftain *16-17, 18- historical*. **toschederach,** †**toscheoderach,** †**toschachdor** an executive officer of the crown in Gaelic-speaking areas, whose duties evolved into those of the *mair of fee* (MAIR[2]); the office itself *16-e18, la18- historical*. **toscheochdoraship** the office of the *toschederach la14-17, 18- historical*. [Gael *toiseach*]

toist see TEISTIE

toit[1.1] /tɔɪt/ *n* **1** a fit of bad temper *19-*. **2** an attack of illness, a dizzy turn *19, 20- Ork SW Bor*. [see the verb]

toit[1.2] /tɔɪt/ *v* **1** to walk with short unsteady steps, totter, especially from weakness or old age *la18- NE C*. **2** to move about doing odd jobs, work steadily but not very strenuously *19, 20- NE*. **toiter** to totter *19, 20- NE T*. [perhaps a variant of TOT[3]]

toitle[1.1] /'tɔɪtəl/ *n* a short, quick or uncertain step *la19- NE*. [see the verb]

toitle[1.2] /'tɔɪtəl/ *v* to totter; to toddle; to idle aimlessly *la19, 20- NE*. [frequentative form of TOIT[1.2]]

token see TAIKEN[1.1], TAIKEN[1.2]

tolbooth, tobooth, *N* **towbeeth,** †**tolbuith,** †**tolbuth,** †**towbooth** /'tɔlbuθ, tə'buθ; *N* 'tʌubiθ/ *n* **1** a public or municipal building in a burgh, formerly the centre of civic and financial administration, originally used for the collection of tolls and customs, the town hall *15-18, 19- historical*. **2** a building housing the town jail *la15-19, 20-*. **3** a building used for the administration of justice *la15-17*. [TOLL + BUITH]

toldie see DOLL[1]

tole /tol/ *adj* imperturbable *20- Ork*. [compare Norw dial *tolen* patient, tolerant]

tolerance /'tɔlərəns/ *n law* permission or licence given, sometimes by tacit consent, to someone to do or enjoy something to which he has no formal right *la15-*. [OFr *tolerance*]

toley see TOALY

toll, †**tholl,** †**toill** /tol/ *n* **1** a tax or duty *la13-*. **2** a tollgate on a road requiring payment for its use; frequently in place-names *la18-*. **3** the right to tax, one of the rights of jurisdiction of major landowners *12-17*. **tollie, towlie** nickname a toll-collector *19-*. **toll-bar** a toll barrier, the collection point for toll; also the toll-collector's house; the toll road itself *19-*. †**toll beir** (the right to) barley paid as duty *16-e17*; compare BEAR[1]. †**toll-fre** exempt from paying duty *la15-e17*. †**toll mony** money paid as a tax *la17*. †**toll penny** = *toll mony la16*. †**toll silver** = *toll mony la16*. †**toll master** a collector of tolls *la16-e17*. **toll-road** a road on which tolls are charged *la18-19, 20- historical*. **toll and theme** in the list of rights in the TENENDAS clause of a charter, the right to exact a tax or duty from tenants, the two elements, toll and theme, apparently not being distinguished as different in meaning *12-17, 18- historical*. [OE *toll*]

toll see TELL[1.2], TOWL

†**tollet, tulat** *n* **1** a piece of cloth, perhaps made into a bag, for wrapping clothes for travelling *e16*. **2** = *tollet clayth e18*. **tollet clayth** a cloth, frequently embroidered or of rich fabric, perhaps for laying over a dressing-table *la16*. **tollar cloath** = *tollet clayth la17-e18*. [MFr *toilete*]

tollie see TOALY

tolmonth see TOWMOND

tolook see TO LUIK

tolter[1.1], **toolter** /'tɔltər, 'tultər/ *n* an insecure structure *20- Ork N*. [see the verb]

tolter[1.2], **toolter, totter** /'tɔltər, 'tultər, 'tɔtər/ *v* **1** to totter, waver; oscillate; to hobble *la15-19, 20- Ork N*. **2** to shake, rock to and fro *17*. **3** to walk unsteadily *17-*. [ME *toteren* to sway, waver, rock; compare OE *tealtrian* to totter, waver, Norw dial *totra* to tremble, MDu *touteren* to totter, waver]

tolter[1.3], **toolter,** †**towter,** †**totyre** /'tɔltər, 'tultər/ *adj* unstable; precarious *la14-19, la19- Ork N*. [see the verb]

†**to luik, tolook** *n* an outlook, prospect *la16-e19*. [TO-[3] + LEUK[1.1]]

toly see TOALY

†**Tolyig's day, Tulya's day, Tolyigisday** *n* the feast of Thorlak, Bishop of Skalholl in Iceland (died 1193), 4th January Old Style, 23rd December New Style. **Tolyig's e'en** the evening before Tolyig's day *la19- Sh*. [from the name of the saint + DAY]

†**toman** *n* a little hill, mound, frequently one formed by the moraine of a glacier; in *folklore* associated with a fairy dwelling *19*. [Gael *toman*]

toman see TOWMOND

tome, *N* **toum,** *Sh* **toam** /tom; *N* tʌum/ *n* **1** *fishing* a cord of twisted horsehair; a fishing line; the cord to which the hook is attached in floating lines; the SNOOD[1.1] (sense 2) joining the hook to the hemp in a handline *la17-19, 20- Sh Ork N T*. **2** any horsehair band or cord; as on a spinning-wheel *la19- Sh Ork*. **tōmekins** a three-strand rope-twister *20- Sh*. **tomeline** = TOME (sense 1) *18- Sh*. **tome spinner, toamin spindle** a spindle for twisting fishing lines *la19- Sh*. [ON *taum* a cord, fishing line]

tome *see* TUIM[1.1], TUIM[1.2], TUME

†**to-morn**[1.1], **to-morne** *n* tomorrow *la14-16*. Compare *the morn* (MORN). [see the adv]

†**to-morn**[1.2], **to-morne** *adv* tomorrow *la14-16*. Compare *the morn* (MORN). [OE *tō morgen*]

ton *see* TUN[1.1]

to name, *NE* **tee name**, †**too name** /'tu nem; *NE* 'ti nem/ *n* an additional name, a nickname or additional surname, especially one used in a community where many have the same surname *la16-*. [TO-[3] + NEM[1.1]]

tone[1], †**toone** /ton/ *n* a tone, a musical note or sound; vocal expression, intonation *la15-*; compare TUNE. **toner** a person who talks endlessly on the same subject *20- WC SW*. [OFr *ton*, Lat *tonus*]

†**tone**[2] *n* the buttocks; the anus *16-17*. [Gael *tòn*]

tone *see* TAK[1.2], TUNE[1.1]

tong *see* TONGUE[1.1]

tongs *see* TANGS

Tongs ya bass /'tɔŋz ja bas/ *n* a gang slogan *20- WC*. [from the Calton Tongs, a Glasgow gang from the 1930s]

tongue[1.1], **tong, tung,** †**toung** /tʌŋ/ *n* **1** the tongue; language; speech *la14-*. **2** a narrow strip of land *16-*; compare TANG[2] (sense 3). **3** impudence, abuse, violent language *la19- NE T C SW Uls*. **4** a narrow piece of metal, part of a weighing BAUK[1.1] *e15*. **tonguie** glib, loquacious, fluent *la18-19, 20- Sh N*. **tongue-betrusht** blunt, outspoken *20-* mainly *NE*. **tongue-deaving** tiresomely talkative *la19, 20- Sh NE*. †**tongue grant** *law* oral admission or confession *la15-16 NE*. **tongue-lowser** a stimulant to talk *20- Ork NE*. †**tongue-raik** volubility, flow of language *19*. **tongue-tackit** tongue-tied *17-*. **tongue thief** a slanderer *la19- Sh*. **aff your tongue** by word of mouth, orally *19-*. †**be tongue** by word of mouth, orally *16-17*. **on your tongue** ready to be expressed or recited *la19- Sh N NE T Uls*. **tongue of the trump** the vibrating fork in a Jew's harp; hence, figuratively, the chief person in an enterprise; the life and soul of a party *la17-19, 20- Sh Ork NE*; compare TANG[2]. [OE *tunge*]

tongue[1.2] /tʌŋ/ *v* to scold; to revile, abuse *la19-*. [see the noun]

tonie /'tone/ *n* a jellyfish *20- NE*. [shortened form of CLUNKERTONIE]

Tontine face /'tɔntin 'fes/ *n* a wry face, a grimace, from the grotesque faces on the facade of Glasgow Town Hall, which was acquired by the Tontine Society in 1781 *19- C*. [Fr *Tontine* from the surname of Lorenzo Tonti, a Neapolitan banker who invented the financial schemes known as Tontine Societies]

tonyied /'tɔnjed/ *adj of food* shrivelled, dried up, frizzled *20- Ork*. [compare Norw dial *tvinna* to shrink, shrivel]

too[1] /tu/ *n* a mound, hillock; frequently in place-names *la19- Sh Ork*. **toog, tuack,** †**towick** hillock, knoll; tussock, mole-hill *la18- Sh Ork N*. [compare Dan *tue*]

too[2.1] /tu/ *n* a toot on a horn; a whistle *20- Sh*. [see the verb]

too[2.2] /tu/ *v* to blow on or sound like a horn, toot *20- Sh Ork*. [onomatopoeic]

†**too**[3], †**to** *adv* modifying an adjective or adverb to a greater or lesser extent than is needed, excessively *la14-17*; compare OWER[1.3]. **too-too** very, utterly *17*. [from the preposition *to* (TAE[3.2]); in ModSc only as an introduction from Eng]

too *see* TAE[3.1]

too- *see* TO-[3]

toober *see* TABOUR[1.2]

tooch[1.1] /tuʃ/ *n* the sound of a shot, a bang, puff *20- Bor*. [onomatopoeic]

tooch[1.2] /tuʃ/ *interj* implying an immediate or instantaneous result, like a shot *la19- T SW*. [see the noun]

tood /tud/ *v of a young animal* to suckle *la19- Sh*. **toodick 1** an artificial teat for feeding a piglet or lamb *la19- Sh*. **2** *fisherman's taboo* a bilge-plug in a boat *e19 Sh*. [compare Dan *tud* a spout]

tooel *see* TOUL

too-hoo /tu'hu/ *n* **1** a fuss; hullabaloo *la19-*. **2** a spiritless, useless person *19, 20- T SW Bor*. [onomatopoeic]

tooken *see* TAK[1.2]

tool *see* TUIL

toolter *see* TOLTER[1.1], TOLTER[1.2], TOLTER[1.3]

toom /tum/ *n* a rubbish dump *19, 20- EC Bor*. [spelling pronunciation; see the adj *toom* (TUIM[1.2])]

toom *see* THOOM[1.1], THOOM[1.2], TUIM[1.1], TUIM[1.2]

toon *see* TOUN, TUNE[1.1]

too name *see* TO NAME

toone *see* TONE[1]

toontie *see* TWENTY[1.2]

toop *see* TUP[1.1]

toopick, toopichen, toopickin *see* TOUPACHAN

toorie /'turi, 'ture/ *n* **1** an ornamental top, tuft, topknot, pompom *19-*; compare *tourie, tourock* (TOUR[1]). **2** a hat or bonnet (often with a pompom), short for **toorie hat, toorie bunnet** *20-*. [TOUR[1] + -IE[1]]

toosan *see* THOOSAND

toose /tuz/ *n* withered tufts of grass roots *la18- Ork*. [probably an altered form of TOOSK]

toosh /tuʃ/ *numeral* a word used in games and counting rhymes, often indicating when an action takes place *20-*. [nonsense word]

toosht[1.1] /tuʃt/ *n* **1** a loose untidy bundle (of rags or straw); a bunch, tuft; a small quantity, a pinch *la19- NE*. **2** a dirty, untidy person *la19- NE*. **3** a nasty, unpleasant person *la19-* mainly *NE*. **tooshlich** = TOOSHT (sense 1). [unknown; compare Norw dial *tust* a tuft, and TOOSK]

toosht[1.2] /tuʃt/ *v* **1** to rumple, bundle up carelessly *la19, 20- T*. **2** to toss or be strewn about; to dash hither and thither *la19- NE*. [see the noun]

toosip /'tusəp/ *n* **1** withered grass roots *20- Ork*. **2** ravelled wool *20- Sh*. [perhaps TOOSE + Norw *hop* a heap, mass]

toosk[1.1] /tusk/ *n* a tuft of grass or hair; a tangled mass of hair *la19- Sh NE*. [unknown; compare Swed *tuskug* matted, and TOOSHT[1]]

toosk[1.2] /tusk/ *v* to tousle (hair) *la19- Sh*. **tooskie** matted, tangled *20- Sh*. [see the noun]

toot[1], †**tout,** †**tute** /tut/ *n* a projection, something jutting out *19, 20- Ork*. †**toot mou'd** having protruding lips *16-19*. **toot-net** a salmon net hung between the shore and a boat (in the Tay estuary), and hauled as soon as a watcher in the boat saw a fish strike the net *la18-19, 20- T EC historical*. [OE **tūtian* to protrude]

toot[2.1] /tut/ *v* to express disapproval or protest *19, 20- Ork NE T*. [see the interj]

toot[2.2], **toots, tits** /tut, tuts, tɪts/ *interj, frequently reduplicated* an expression of disapproval or protest *18-*. [a natural utterance; compare HOOT[1.2]]

toot[3.1], **tout** /tut/ *n* the characteristic sound of a horn or other wind instrument *16-*. **ae toot and yer oot, one toot and yer oot** keep quiet! *20-*. **a new toot in an auld horn, an auld toot in a new horn** an old idea or piece of news dressed up as new *la16-e19*. [see the verb]

toot[3.2], **tout** /tut/ *v* **1** to make a noise on a horn or other wind instrument *la17-*. **2** to make a noise like a horn; to speak loudly, shout *la17-*. **3** *especially of a child* to cry, sob *19-*. **4** to spread (a report), blab, broadcast *la18-19*. **tooting horn** a cow's horn sounded by a cowherd driving his animals *18-*. **toot your ain horn** to proclaim your own merits *la19-*. **toot on your ain trumpet** = toot your ain horn. [EModE *toot*, compare LG *tuten*]

toot[4.1], **tout** /tut/ *n* **1** a draught, swig, a large single drink *la18-*. **2** a small but repeated drink, a tipple *la18-*. **3** a drinker, tippler *20- WC SW*. **tootie 1** = TOUT[4.1] (sense 1) *19, 20- NE*. **2** = TOOT[4.1] (sense 2) *la18-e19*. **tootlie** = tootie **1**. [see the verb]

toot[4.2], **tout** /tut/ *v* **1** to drink alcohol constantly, tipple *la18-*. **2** to drink down, empty (a glass) to the last drop *la18-19, 20- Bor*. [probably TOOT[3.2] with reference to drinking horns]

tooter[1.1] /'tutər/ *n* **1** a botched job *la19- NE*. **2** a feckless worker, a botcher *20- NE*. **3** a tottery gait *20- NE*. [see the verb]

tooter[1.2] /'tutər/ *v* **1** to work ineffectually, potter ineptly *la19- N*. **2** to toddle, walk with short mincing steps *20- NE*. **tooterie** *of persons* fussy, pottering; *of things* fiddling, irritatingly trivial or intricate; *of weather* changeable, preventing steady outdoor work *la19- NE*. [perhaps a conflation of FOOTER[1.2] with TOTTER]

tooter[2], **touter** /'tutər/ *n* **1** a horn, trumpet, frequently a toy trumpet *la19- NE*. **2** trivial gossip, tittle-tattle *la19- NE*. **tooteroo** = TOOTER[1.2] (sense 1). [TOOT[3.2] with instrumental suffix]

tooth see TUITH

toot-moot[1.1], *NE* **teet-meet** /'tut'mut; *NE* 'tit'mit/ *n* a low muttered conversation, a whispering together *19, 20- NE SW*. [see the verb]

†**toot-moot**[1.2] *v* to converse in a low mutter, whisper *la19*. [reduplicative compound; TOOT[3.2] + MOOT[1.1]]

toots see TOOT[2.2]

toove see TOVE[2]

top see TAP[1.1], TAP[1.2], TAP[3.2], TAP[4]

†**to-put** *adj of a seal* attached, appended (to a document) *la14-15*. [TO-[3] + *put* (PIT[2])]

toquhir see TOCHER[1.1]

tore see TEAR[2.2], TORR

torfle /'torfəl/ *v* **1** to decline in health, pine away; to perish, be lost *19- Bor*. **2** to toss or tumble about *19- Bor*. [altered form of Eng *torfer* to die, fail, ON *torfœra* a difficult or dangerous passage]

torie, *Sh Ork N* **story** /'tore; *Sh Ork N* 'stori/ *n* the grub of the cranefly or daddy-long-legs *Tipula paludosa 18-*. **toriet** = torie eaten *la19- NE*. **torie eaten** *of land* infested with cranefly grubs *18-19, 20- NE*. **story worm** the grub of the cranefly or daddy-long-legs *Tipula paludosa 18- Sh*. [Gael *toran* literally, the borer, with -IE[1] suffix]

torment[1.1] /'tormənt, tər'mɛnt/ *n* **1** (a means of) torture, punishment, a state of suffering *la14-*. **2** a nagging physical pain *la19- Sh*. [OFr *torment* an instrument of torture, Lat *tormentum*]

torment[1.2] /tər'mɛnt/ *v* to afflict with pain *la14-*. [OFr *tormenter*, Lat *tormentāre*]

torn see TEAR[2.2], THORN, TURN[1.2]

†**tornach** *n* a heap (of rubbish), a midden *la17*. [compare Gael *torran*]

torn face /'torn fɛs/ *n* a bad-tempered or disgruntled person *la20-*. [*torn* (TEAR[2.2]) + FACE[1.1]]

torn faced /'torn 'fɛst/ *adj* bad-tempered, disgruntled *la20-*. [*torn* (TEAR[2.2]) + participial adj from FACE[1.2]]

torr, **tore**, **tour** /tɔr, tor, tur/ *n* **1** a projection, especially a knob on a cradle or chair *la15-*. **2** the pommel of a saddle *la16-19*. **3** a hill, mound *la15-e19*. **tore-bane** the prominence on the pelvic bone of a horse, cow or sheep *la19- WC SW*. †**schippis of tour** beaked warships *15-16*. [Gael *torr* a conical hill, mound]

†**torrall** *n* a small tower *16*. **torrall house** a tower used as a residence, a defensible dwelling house *16*; compare *tour house* (TOUR[1]). [ME *torel*, OFr *torelle*]

torret see TURRET[1]

torsk see TUSK[1]

†**tort**[1], **torte** *n* harm, injury; physical suffering *la16-e17*. **tort and na reson** *law* = *wrang and unlaw* (WRANG[1.1]), wrongdoing in a civil matter *15-e17*. [ME *tort*, OFr *tort*, Lat *tortum*]

†**tort**[2] *v* to harm, twist *16-e17*. [Lat *tort-*, ptp stem of *torquēre* to turn, twist]

torte see TORT[1]

tortie /'tɔrte/ *n* a tortoise *18-*. [ME *tortu*, Fr *tortue*]

tortieshell, †**tortois shell** /'tɔrtəʃɛl/ *adj* made of tortoiseshell; tortoise-shell coloured *la17-*. [TORTIE + SHELL[1.1]]

torture[1.1], *Sh N* **torter**, †**tortour** /'tɔrtʃər; *Sh N* 'tɔrtər/ *n* (means or instrument of) torture *la16-*. [OFr *torture*, Lat *tortūra*]

torture[1.2], *Sh N* **torter**, †**tortour** /'tɔrtʃər; *Sh N* 'tɔrtər/ *v* to torture, inflict extreme pain on *17-*. [MFr *torturer*]

toschachdor, **toschederach**, **toscheoch**, **toscheoderach** see TOISEACH

tosh[1.1] /tɔʃ/ *v* to make neat or tidy, smarten up *19-*. **tosh up** = TOSH[1.1]. [unknown]

tosh[1.2] /tɔʃ/ *adj* **1** neat, tidy, smart *18-*. **2** intimate, friendly *19-*. [unknown]

tosh[1.3] /tɔʃ/ *adv* neatly; in a comfortable, friendly way *la18-*. [unknown]

tosh up /'tɔʃ 'ʌp/ *n* a tidy-up *la19-*. [from the verb *tosh up* (TOSH[1.1])]

tosie /'tose, 'tosi/ *adj* **1** comfortable, cosy, snug *18-*. **2** slightly intoxicated, tipsy and merry *18-*. **3** *of the cheeks* red; flushed *19-*. [unknown]

tosk see TUSK[1]

†**to smyte** see TO-[2]

toss[1] /tɔs/ *n* a toast, a drink to someone's health; the subject of a toast *18-*. [reduced form of Eng *toast* perhaps influenced by TASS]

†**toss**[2.1] *n* a bout, an encounter *18*. [see the verb]

toss[2.2], †**tost** /tɔs, tos/ *v* **1** to pitch to and fro, throw around *16-*. **2** to toss a coin with (a person) *20- NE T*. [unknown; compare Norw *tossa* to spread, strew]

tossel, **taisel**, **tassel** /'tɔsəl, 'tɛsəl, 'tasəl/ *n* **1** a tassel *la17-*. **2** the penis *20- NE T EC SW*. **3** a tuft or fringe of hair *20- Sh NE T*. [ME *tassel*; OFr *tassel* a clasp, Lat *tassellus*]

tossing see TOSTIN

tosslin /'tɔslɪn/ *n weaving* the forming of the thread-ends of a web into tassels *20- T C*. [derivative of TOSSEL]

tost see TOAST[1.1], TOAST[1.2], TOSS[2.2]

tostin, †**tossing** /'tɔstɪn/ **1** a bout, encounter *20- Sh*. **2** consideration, discussion *17*. [derivative of TOSS[2.2]]

tot[1] /tɔt, tot/ *n* **1** a small child, toddler *18-*. **2** *child's word* the penis *20- N*. **totie**, **tottie** = TOT[1] (sense 1) *19-*. [unknown; compare the later attested TOT[3]]

tot[2] /tɔt, tot/ *n* the sum total, the whole lot *19- C SW*. [shortened form of Eng *total* or Lat *totum*]

tot[3] /tɔt, tot/ *v* to toddle; to totter *19, 20- WC*. [perhaps shortened form of TOTTER]

total /'totəl/ *adj* teetotal *19- NE T Bor*. [shortened form of Eng *teetotal*]

totey see TOTTIE

toth see TATHE[1.1]

tother see TITHER[1.1]

tothir *see* TITHER[1,2]
totie *see* TOT[1], TOTTIE
totter /'tɔtər/ *v* **1** to bob about in boiling water *20- T.* **2** *of running water* to ripple, babble *e19.* [perhaps a variant of TOTTLE or extended sense of *totter* (TOLTER); compare HOTTER[1,2]]
totter *see* TOLTER[1,2]
tottie, totie, toatie, totey /'tɔte, 'tote/ *adj* small, tiny *20-.* **totey-wee** extremely small *20-.* [TOT[1] + -IE[2]]
tottie *see* TATTIE
tottle /'tɔtəl/ *v* **1** *of food* to simmer, boil gently *19, 20- T EC Bor.* **2** to totter and fall, topple over *19, 20- Ork T.* **3** to walk unsteadily, toddle, totter *19, 20- T.* **4** to cause (food) to simmer *18.* **5** *of running water* to ripple, babble *19.* [probably onomatopoeic with frequentative suffix, or altered form of *totter* (TOLTER) and TOTTER]
tottum *see* TOTUM[2]
totum[1] /'totəm/ *n in games of chance* a four-sided disc with a letter on each side: T totum, A aufer, D depone, N nihil, spun like a top, the player's fortune being decided by the letter uppermost when the disc falls; the game itself *16-.* [Lat *tōtum* the whole lot]
totum[2], **tottum** /'totəm, 'tɔtəm/ *n* **1** any diminutive neat person, animal or thing *la18-.* **2** a small child, a TOT[1] *la19, 20- N T C.* [probably TOT[1] with mock-Latin suffix, but compare TEETOTUM]
totyre *see* TOLTER[1,3]
tou *see* THOU
toub *see* TUB
touch[1,1], †**twich**, †**tuiche**, †**toutch** /tʌtʃ, tɪtʃ/ *n* **1** an act of touching; contact *16-.* **2** a brief narration, a mention *la15-e18.* **3** a short space of time, a moment *la18-e19.* [AN *tuche,* OFr *touche*]
touch[1,2], **titch**, †**twech**, †**twich**, †**tuich** /tʌtʃ, tɪtʃ/ *v* **1** to touch, make physical contact with, come into contact *la14-.* **2** to affect, concern, have a bearing on *la14-.* **3** to touch an Act of the Scottish Parliament with the sceptre, indicating royal assent *17- historical.* **4** to touch so as to heal, lay hands on *la14-17.* **5** to touch a copy of the Gospels, as a symbolic gesture witnessing to the truth of something or expressing assent, while taking an oath *la14-e17.* **6** *of a person unable to write* to touch the pen of a notary, acknowledging one's name *16-17.* **7** to touch a document, rendering it legal *e16.* **8** to pluck the strings of a musical instrument *la15-e17.* [AN *tuchier, tochier,* MFr *toucher*]
toucher *see* TOCHER[1,1]
toucht *see* THINK[1,2]
tough *see* TEUCH[1,1]
tought *see* THOCHT
touk[1,1] /tuk/ *n* **1** a tuck, a fold in cloth *19-.* **2** an embankment or jetty built to prevent soil erosion *18-19, 20- SW.* **3** a hasty tug or pull *18-19, 20- Bor.* [see the verb]
touk[1,2], **tuck** /tuk, tʌk/ *v* to tuck, gather in folds *16-.* [OE *tūcian* to ill-treat, MDu, MLG *tucken* to draw, pull sharply]
touk[2] /tuk/ *n* a disagreeable flavour or aftertaste *19- C SW.* [unknown; perhaps extended sense of TOUK[1,1]]
†**touk**[3,1] /tuk/ *n* **1** a blow, a hit *15-e17.* **2** a stroke or tap on a drum *16-19.* **by touk of drum** *of a proclamation* (made) by a public crier with his drum *17-18.* [see the verb]
touk[3,2], †**tuck**, †**tuik** /tuk/ *v* **1** *of the wind* to blow in gusts *19-.* **2** to push or hit (a person) *la16-17.* **3** to beat (a drum) *17-19.* **4** *of a drum* to sound, beat *17-18.* [OFr *toker, toukier* to touch, strike; compare TOUCH[1,2]]
toukin /'tukɪn/ *n* bran and bran-dust fed to poultry *20- Sh.* [unknown]
toul, tooel, *SW* **toal,** †**towell,** †**towall** /tul, 'tuəl; *SW* tol, 'toəl/ *n* a towel *15-.* [ME *touail,* OFr *toaile*]

toul *see* TUIL
toum *see* TOME
toun, toon, town /tun, tʌun/ *n* **1** a settlement, a group of dwellings and farm buildings inhabited by the tenants of an estate; a farm or estate including dwellings, farm buildings and land, frequently in place-names *la14-.* **2** a settlement large enough to have its own administration, a town or burgh; a city *la14-.* **3** the community of a town, the townspeople *15-.* **4** the arable enclosed land of a farm *19- Sh.* **toundie** the person left in charge of a farm when the rest of the household are away *20- NE.* **tounie** an inhabitant of a town *20- Sh NE T EC.* **tounser** usually *disparaging* a town-dweller *20- NE T.* **township 1** the inhabitants or community of a town *la15-.* **2** a settlement of crofters in the Highlands *19-.* †**toun's bairn, toun bairn** a native of a particular town *17-19.* **toun's bodie** a town-dweller *la18-19, 20- Sh Ork NE.* **Toon Champion** the participant in the Riding of the Marches in Musselburgh whose duty it is to protect the *Turf Cutter* (TURF) *la17-.* **town-drummer, toun's drummer** a drummer employed to make burgh proclamations to the beating of his drum *la16-19, 20- historical.* **toundyke, town-dyke** the wall enclosing the arable ground on a farm *la18- Sh.* **town-end, toun-end 1** the end of or way out from a town *15-.* **2** a row of cottages, usually on a farm *20- NE Uls.* **toun fit** the lower end of a town, frequently in place-names *19-.* **toun's folk** townspeople *20-.* **toun-gate, toon-gate, town-gate** the main street of a town or village *la18- Bor.* **town-guard** an armed corps, mainly of ex-soldiers, enrolled for police duties, particularly in Edinburgh *la17-18, 19- historical.* **toun-heid** the higher or upper end of a town, frequently in place-names *16-.* †**town-herd** the public herdsman who looked after the cattle on the common pasture *la18-19.* **town-house, toun-house, toon-house, toun's house,** †**tounes hous** a municipal building housing the public offices of a municipality, a town hall *la17-.* **town-keeper, tound-keeper 1** the person left in charge of a farm when the rest of the household are away *20- NE.* **2** an official acting as a kind of constable *la18-e19.* **toun land 1** = TOUN (sense 2) *20- Sh.* **2** the land of a TOUN (sense 1) *16-19.* **3** a land-holding in a town or burgh *la16-17.* **toun-loan, toon-loan, town-loan** an open space round a farmstead or hamlet *18- Sh NE EC.* †**toun major** in Edinburgh, the major of the *town-guard la17.* **tounmal, towmal,** †**tumel** a piece of land attached to a farmstead or settlement *la15- Sh Ork.* **town-officer 1** an official attending on the provost or councillors in the Council Chamber and in public *la17-.* **2** an officer charged with keeping public order *la17-19.* †**toon-piper, town-piper** the official bagpiper of a municipality *la17-18.* **toun sergeant** in Aberdeen and Dundee, = *town-officer 18-.* **toun skerrie** *fisherman's taboo* a cockerel *20- Sh.* **toun's speak** the talk of the town, the local scandal *20-.* **a clean toun** a farm from which all the hired servants have left at one TERM (sense 3) *la19- NE.* **keep the toun** to act as *town-keeper 1* or *toundie la19- NE.* †**the Toun Rats** the Edinburgh Town Guard *e19.* †**toun and parochin** the whole of a parish including the main centre of population and the rural hinterland *16-17.* [OE *tūn*]
toun *see* TUN[1,1]
toung *see* TONGUE[1,1]
toupachan, toopichen, toopickin, toopick /'tupəxən, 'tupɪkən/ *n* a topknot or knob-shaped ornament on the top of a hayrick or hill, a bobble on a bonnet; the top of a boiled egg *la18- NE.* [derivative of TOUPIE]
toupie /'tupi/ *n* any high pointed object; a knob on the top of something *la19- Sh NE.* [perhaps Gael *topan* a topknot, tuft of wool on a distaff or extended sense of Eng *toupee*]

tour[1], **touer, tower, †towre** /tur, 'tuər, 'tʌuər/ *n* **1** a tall building, a tower *la14*-. **2** part of a castle; in the names of particular towers *la14*-. **3** = *tour-house la15*-. **tourie 1** a little tower *la19*-. **2** = TOORIE. **tourock** = *tourie*. **tour-house, towerhouse** a tower used as a residence, a defensible dwelling house mainly built in the 15th–17th centuries *la15*-. [AN *tur*, OFr *tour*]

tour[2], **tower** /tur, 'tʌuər/ *n* **1** only /tur/, one's turn or spell in a regular sequence *16*-. **2** a circular route *la18*-. **tour about** turn about, alternately *18- C SW Bor*. **tour and turn** = *tour about*. [ME *tour*, Lat *tour*; *tower* is a hypercorrect form]

tour *see* TORR

tourn *see* TURN[1,2]

tournepyke *see* TURNPIKE

touse /tuz/ *v* **1** to disorder, dishevel (hair or clothes) *17*-. **2** to pull or knock about, handle roughly *19*-. **3** to tease out *20- WC*. **4** to tease (a woman) roughly or boisterously *18-19, 20- Sh N*. [OE **tūsian*]

toush, toosh /tuʃ/ *n* a woman's jacket or short-skirted working-dress *19- EC*. [shortened form of CARTOUSH]

tousie, tousy, towsy /'tuzi, 'tuze, 'tʌuzi, 'tʌuze/ *adj* **1** (often of hair) dishevelled; tangled; untidy, in a disorderly state *16*-. **2** rough, boisterous, rowdy, violent *la19*-. **tousie tea** = HIGH TEA *19*-. [TOUSE + -IE[2]]

tousle[1,1] /'tuzəl/ *n* **1** a struggle, tussle, contest *19*-. **2** a rough physical encounter of a sexual nature *la18-19, 20- Sh NE*. [see the verb]

tousle[1,2], **toozle**, *Ork* **tissle**, **†tussill** /'tuzəl; *Ork* 'tɪsəl/ *v* **1** to pull about (roughly); to rumple *la15*-. **2** *of lovers* to pull one another about playfully, fondle one another *19*-. **3** to rummage about in, turn out the contents of; to unravel, disentangle *19, 20- N NE*. **touslie 1** *of the hair* dishevelled, ruffled *20- C*. **2** *of wind* blustery, boisterous *20- C*. [frequentative form of TOUSE]

†toust, towst *n law* a tax levied mainly on imports and exports *la16-17*. [AN *touste*]

toustie /'tusti, 'tuste/ *adj* testy, irascible *19*-. [unknown]

tousy *see* TOUSIE

tout *see* TOOT[1], TOOT[3,1], TOOT[3,2], TOOT[4,1], TOOT[4,2], TOWT[1,1], TOWT[1,2]

toutch *see* TOUCH[1,1]

touter *see* TOOTER[3]

touteroo *see* TOOTER[3]

touther[1,1] /'tuðər/ *n* a rough handling; a throwing into confusion; a state of disorder, a mess *19, 20- Sh NE EC*. **toutherie** dishevelled, untidy, slovenly *19*-. [unknown; compare THROUITHER[1,1]]

touther[1,2], **towder, tudder** /'tuðər, 'tʌuðər, 'tʌudər, 'tʌdər/ *v* to handle roughly, throw into disorder *19-, 20- Sh NE EC*. [see the noun]

toutlie *see* TOOT[4,1]

toutour *see* TUTOR

†tøva-kuddie *n* a place on the sea-shore where cloth was put to be fulled or thickened by action of the tide *la19 Sh*. [Norw dial *tøva* fulling + perhaps Norw dial *kudde* a nest]

tove[1,1] /tov/ *n* a chat, talk, gossip *la19, 20- WC SW Bor*. [see the verb]

tove[1,2] /tov/ *v* to talk at length, gossip, chat *19, 20- Bor*. [perhaps extended sense of TOVE[2]]

tove[2], **toove** /tov, tuv/ *v* **1** to smoke (tobacco) *19*-. **2** to cause to swell *19*-. **3** to puff up with praise, flatter *19, 20- SW Bor*. **4** *of a fire* to emit smoke or flames *19, 20- Bor*. **5** *of smoke* to billow out, rise in the air *19, 20- Bor*. **6** to rise into the air, soar; to hurry along *19, 20- Bor*. **7** to swarm or stream out *la19- Bor*. **tovie 1** boastful, especially in drink *19, 20- Uls*. **2** steaming; giving warmth and comfort *e19*. [perhaps an aphetic form of STOVE[1,2]]

tow[1] /tʌu/ *n* flax or hemp fibre *15*-. **tow band** a strap or band of woven tow; a skirt- or trouser-waistband *19, 20- NE*. **†tow card** a toothed instrument for carding flax *17-e19*. **tow grown** *of wood* reduced to a fibrous state *20- Sh*. **tow gun** a popgun with tow wadding *19- T C*. **†tow rock** a distaff used in spinning hemp *la18*. **hae ither tow on yer rock** to have other concerns or intentions *la17*-. **hae ither tow to tease** = *hae ither tow on yer rock 19-, 20- Bor Uls*. [compare OE *tow-* spinning, as in *towcræft* the product of spinning, and ON *tó* uncleansed wool or flax]

tow[2,1] /tʌu/ *n* **1** a rope, cord, length of strong twine or string *la15*-. **2** a skipping-rope *20- Sh NE T WC*. **3** a cord used to lower a coffin into the ground *la17, 20- NE*. **4** a whip, whiplash *20- NE EC*. **5** the main cord of a fishing line *19- Sh Ork*. **6** *mining* the winding-rope which hoists or lowers a cage, the cage itself *la19- C*. **7** *mining* the journey up or down in the cage *la20- EC*. **8** the bonds of marriage *20- Sh NE*. **9** a gallows rope, hangman's noose *la16, la18- literary*. **10** cords for suspending the weights of a clock *la16-e19*. **tows** the halyards of a sailing ship *la19- Sh*. **lat the tow gang wi the bucket** *proverb* to give up, get rid of something impatiently, cut one's losses *20- NE EC*. **ower the tow** out of control, beyond bounds *19*. [see the verb and compare MLG *touwe* a rope]

tow[2,2] /tʌu/ *v* **1** to pull along or drag using a rope *la14*-. **2** to raise or lower by means of a rope *la16-18*. [OE *togian*]

tow *see* THOW[1,1], THOW[1,2]

towall *see* TOUL

towbeeth, towbooth *see* TOLBOOTH

towder *see* TOUTHER[1,2]

†towdy *n* the buttocks or genitals *16-e19*. **towdy mowdy** term of endearment *e16*. [unknown]

towell *see* TOUL

tower *see* TOUR[1], TOUR[2]

towin, town /'tʌuɪn, tʌun/ *v* **1** to toss, rumple, disorder (clothes or straw) *19- SW*. **2** to toss and turn, bustle (about), rummage *la19- SW*. **3** to beat; to tame by beating *18-19*. [unknown]

towl, toll /tʌul, tol/ *v* **1** to toll (a bell) *la17*-. **2** *of a queen bee* to emit an intermittent series of single clear notes as a signal to swarm *18-e19*. [ME *tollen* to pull, OE **tollian* to attract]

towl *see* TUIL

towler /'tʌulər/ *n* a large marble *20- Bor*. [unknown]

towlie *see* TOLL

towmond, †tolmonth, †tholmont, †toman /'tʌumənd/ *n* **1** (the period of) a year *15*-. **2** *with a date or day* a year before the date mentioned *la15-16*. **3** *with a date or day* a year after the date mentioned *la16-e17*. **4** a sheep or wether in its second year *19-, Bor*; compare DINMONT *Compare* TWALMONTH. **†towmond auld** a yearling *16*. [ON *tólfmánuðr*]

town *see* TOUN, TOWIN

townty *see* TWENTY[1,2]

towrist, towerist /'tʌurɪst, 'tʌuərɪst/ *n frequently humorous* a tourist *20-* [*tower* (TOUR[2]) + agent suffix; hypercorrect form originally imitative of Highland speech]

towrow[1,1] /'tʌuˌrʌu/ *n* a noisy uproar, rumpus, disturbance *la19- Sh NE T*. [reduplicative form of Eng *row* a commotion]

towrow[1,2] /'tʌuˌrʌu/ *v* **1** to make a noisy disturbance *20- Sh EC*. **2** to be tossed or buffeted by the sea *la20- Sh*. [see the noun]

towsy *see* TOUSIE

towt[1,1], **tout** /tʌut/ *n* **1** a slight or temporary ailment, an indisposition *19*-. **2** a sudden (usually bad) mood, huff *la18*-. **3** a teasing remark, taunt *20- Bor*. **towtie 1** subject to frequent attacks of slight illness *19*-. **2** touchy, irritable *20*-. **3** *of things* uncertain, changeable *e19*. [unknown]

towt[1,2], **tout** /tʌut/ *v* **1** to tease, annoy, taunt *la18-19, 20- Bor.* **2** to throw into disorder, rumple; to upset *la16-19.* **3** argue with *e17.* [unknown]
towter *see* TOLTER[1,3]
toy[1,1] /tɔɪ/ *n* **1** a cap with a flat crown and a back-flap reaching to the shoulders, worn by married and elderly women, a style of MUTCH *17-18, 20- historical.* **2** a notion, idea; a trick, prank *16-17.* [probably MDu *tooy* attire, finery]
toy[1,2] /tɔɪ/ *v* **1** to treat (a person) in an offhand, frivolous or dismissive way *la19, 20- Bor.* **2** to behave frivolously *e17.* [see the noun]
toyik, **toyack**, **toyeg**, **toig** /'tɔjək/ *n* a small basket *la19- Sh.* [Norw dial *taaje* a creel made of root fibres + *-ack* (-OCK)]
toyle *see* TOIL[1,2], TOIL3E, TUIL, TULYIE[1,2]
†**tozee** *n* the mark at which a curler aims his stones, the TEE[1] *la18-19.* [perhaps a hypercorrect form of *tase* (TEE[1,2]) + -IE[1]]
traa *see* THRAW[1,1], THRAW[1,2]
traan *see* THRAW[1,2]
traath *see* TROWTH
traaward *see* THRAWART
traboond[1,1] /'trɑbund/ *n* a rebound, a blow moving the object struck out of position, a tumble *la19- Ork.* [altered form of REBOUND]
traboond[1,2] /trɑ'bund/ *interj* thud, crash *20- Ork.* [see the noun]
†**trabuschet**, **trebuschet** *n* an assay balance or (small) pair of scales *la16-17.* [Fr *trébuchet*]
trace[1], **tress** /tres, tres/ *n* a rope, chain, strap connecting a draught animal to a vehicle *e16-.* **tracer 1** a trace-horse, a horse which works in traces rather than shafts *19-.* **2** the man in charge of a trace-horse *la19-.* **traces** the pair of ropes connecting a draught animal to a cart *la14-.* [ME *trais* reinterpreted as sg, OFr *trais*, plural of *trait*]
trace[2,1], †**trays** /tres/ *n* **1** a track, the footprints or scent left by a person or animal *la14-.* **2** a way, course; course of action *la14-.* **3** a series of dance steps; a processional dance *la15-e16.* [OFr *trace*]
†**trace**[2,2], **trase** *v* **1** to step, go; also in dancing *e16.* **2** to track *16-e17.* **3** to describe (a plan) *e17.* †**traschor** shoemaking a tool used for marking out designs *16-e17.* [ME *tracen*, OFr *tracier* to proceed along a path; with some senses from the noun]
trace *see* TRESS [2]
trachelt *see* TRAUCHLED
trachle *see* TRAUCHLE[1,1], TRAUCHLE[1,2]
trachled, **trachlit** *see* TRAUCHLED
trachour *see* TRECHOUR
trachy /'tratʃi/ *adj* stiff, not moving easily *20- Sh.* [a variant of DRATCH + -y (-IE[2])]
track[1,1], **tract**, **trait**, †**treit**, †**treitt** /trak, trakt, tret/ *n* **1** a track, course or way *la16-.* **2** a trench *la20-.* **3** a line *la16-.* **4** *of the face* a lineament, feature, trait *16-19, 20- Sh.* **5** the course of a stream *la17.* **6** in Edinburgh, material taking passage along a course, effluent *16.* **7** a course (of conduct), manner (of behaving) *la17.* [ME *trak*, OFr *trac* a trail; fallen together with ME *tracte*, Lat *tractus* a dragging, a track, MFr *trait*]
track[1,2] /trak/ *v* **1** to train an animal *la19- NE.* **2** to train, discipline (a person) *20- NE.* [see the noun]
track[2] /trak/ *n* a tract, a (religious) pamphlet *la18-.* [Lat *tractus*, shortened form of *tractātus*; compare TRACTAT]
track[3], **tract** /trak, trakt/ *n* **1** a period or spell (of time or weather) *la16-.* **2** a tract or extent of land, a district *17-.* **3** a continuing state, a settled and protracted condition *17-19, 20- Sh.* [Lat *tractus* a dragging, a track, a tract of time or space]

track[4] /trak/ *n* a poorly- or untidily-dressed person *20- NE.* [variant of TRAG]
track[5], **trakk** /trak/ *v* to infuse (tea) *la19- Sh.* **trackie** = *track-pot la19- NE.* **track-pot**, **tract-pot** a teapot *18-19, 20- NE.* [Du *trekken* to draw, make (tea)]
†**track-boat**, **trakboat** *n* a boat intended to be towed (along a river or canal) *17-19.* [Du *trekken* to draw + BOAT[1,1]]
trackle *see* TRAUCHLE[1,1], TRAUCHLE[1,2]
†**tract** *v* to track, trace *la16-17.* [Lat *tract-* participial stem of *trahere* to draw]
tract *see* TRACK[1,1], TRACK[3]
†**tractat** *n* **1** a literary work; a treatise *la15-17.* **2** negotiation, discussion *16.* [Lat *tractātus*]
†**tractive** *n* = TRACTAT (sense 1) *la16.* [Lat *tractāre* to handle + -*ive* suffix]
tract-pot *see* TRACK[5]
trad *see* TRADE[1,1]
traddle *see* TREADLE, TRIDDLE
trade[1,1], **tred**, **tread**, †**trad** /tred, tred/ *n* **1** trading, commercial dealing, business *16-.* **2** an occupation, trade, craft *la16-.* **3** a corporation of master craftsmen in a particular trade in a BURGH, which formerly elected members to the town council *17-.* **4** coming and going; a fuss or carry-on *la19-.* **5** way of life, mode of behaviour, habitual practice, custom, procedure *la15-19, 20- NE T.* **6** a track or trail of foot- or hoofprints *la15-e19.* **7** a corporation of craftsmen in contradistinction to the merchants *la17-e18.* **8** a course, way *la14-16.* †**trades bailie** a BAILIE or member of a town council elected by *the Trades* **1** *18-e19.* †**trades councillor** = *trades bailie.* **trades hall** a meeting house of *the Trades* **1** in a burgh *la18-.* **Trades holiday**, **Trades holidays** the annual summer holiday, originally of the craftsmen of Edinburgh *la19-.* †**trades hospital** a home for pensioners of a burgh *18-19.* **trades house** a deliberative body or council consisting of representatives of the fourteen *Incorporated Trades* (INCORPORATE) of Glasgow, presided over by the *Deacon Convener* (DEACON[1]) *18- WC.* **tradesman** a person who practises a trade, an artisan, craftsman; a member of a trade *17-.* †**trade's stent** tax based on the trade done by each burgess of a town *la18-e19.* **mak a trade o** to make a habit of *la17- NE T Bor.* **the Trades 1** the incorporated trades collectively *la17-.* **2** = *Trades holiday 20-.* **to trade** by profession or occupation *19-.* [MDu *trade* a path, course, way of life, MLG *trade* a track]
trade[1,2] /tred, tred/ *v* **1** to deal (in goods) *la16-.* **2** to do business *la16-.* **3** to have dealings (in) *e19.* **trader**, †**treddar** a trader *16-.* **trading**, **tredding** commerce *17-.* [see the noun]
trade *see* TREAD[1,1], TREAD[1,2]
tradeetion *see* TRADITION
trade widdie *see* TRAGWIDDIE
tradition, **tradeetion**, †**traditioun** /trə'dɪʃən, trə'dɪʃən/ *n* **1** tradition, long-established custom *la19-.* **2** *Roman Catholic Church* belief or practice handed down from the past, not deriving directly from the Bible *16-.* **3** the process of handing down beliefs *la15-.* **4** *law* the transfer of ownership of property by customary means *16-17.* [OFr *tradicion*, Lat *trāditiōn-*]
traep *see* THREAP[1,1], THREAP[1,2]
traes ace *see* TRES-ACE
traeten *see* THREATEN
traff /traf/ *n* rope fibres, frayed material *19- Sh.* [Norw dial *trav* a rag, tatter]
traffeck[1,1], **trafficque**, **traffic**, *N* **trafike**, †**treffik**, †**traffect** /'trafek, 'trafɪk/ *n* **1** trading, the transportation of merchandise for the purpose of commerce, buying and selling; transportation more generally *16-.* **2** dealing,

communication; a transaction *la16-19, 20- NE T.* **3** work, progress with a job, activity *la19- Sh NE T.* **traffecks** odds and ends; spare parts; trash *20- Sh N.* [MFr *trafique*]

traffeck¹·² /'trafɛk, 'trafɪk/ *v* **1** to trade, buy and sell, latterly illicitly *la16-.* **2** to deal, have to do, negotiate, or have (frequently illicit, secret or improper) relations (with); to intrigue, conspire *16-19, 20- Sh NE T.* **3** to proselytize for (mainly Catholicism) *la16-17.* **traffecker 1** a trader, merchant or dealer *la16-.* **2** a go-between, negotiator; mainly a person who engages in clandestine dealings, an intriguer *la16-19.* **3** a proselytizer for Catholicism *la16-e18.* [MFr *trafiquer*]

traffic, trafficque, trafike *see* TRAFFECK¹·¹

trag /trag/ *n* **1** something of poor quality or little value, trash *19- Sh NE.* **2** riff-raff *19- NE.* [perhaps an altered form of *trog* (TROKE¹·²)]

tragwiddie, †**trade widdie,** †**trodwoddie** /'tragwɪdɛ/ *n farming* the draught chain, originally a rope of twisted withy, with hook and swivel connecting a plough or harrow to the swingle-trees *la17-18, 19- historical.* [TRADE¹·¹ + WIDDIE]

traheelsoo /trəˈhilsu/ *n* a somersault *20- Ork.* [nonce formation based on HEEL]

traichle *see* TRAUCHLE¹·²

traicle, treacle, tryacle, *NE Bor* **trykle, trekkle** /'trɛkəl, 'trikəl, 'traekəl; *NE Bor* 'trʌɪkəl/ *n* **1** molasses, syrup, a by-product of sugar-refining *la16-.* **2** a medicinal salve *la15-17.* **traicle ale** light ale brewed from treacle, water and yeast *19-.* **traicle-bendy, treacle-bendy** = *traicle ale la19-.* **traicle-bun** a bun with treacle as an ingredient *20-.* **traicle gundy** candy or toffee made from treacle *20- N C.* **treacle-peerie** = *traicle ale la19- T EC Bor.* **traicle pig** a treacle jar *20- N.* **traicle scone** a scone with treacle as an ingredient *la19-.* **traicle-wheech** = *traicle ale la19- Bor.* [ME *triacle,* OFr *triacle* a medicinal salve]

traik¹·¹ /trek/ *n* **1** plague, pestilence; destruction, ruin, harm *16-.* **2** an illness, especially of an epidemic type *la18-.* **3** the flesh of sheep which have died of natural causes *19-.* **4** fatigue *20- Ork N.* †**traikie** sickly, ailing, declining *la18-19.* [unknown]

traik¹·² /trek/ *v* to be ailing or ill, decline in health; to become weak; to pine and die *16-.* **traikit 1** wasted, worn out; fatigued, bedraggled *16-19, 20- WC SW.* **2** *of animals* dead of exhaustion or disease *16-19.* **3** *of skins* deriving from animals which have died (of natural causes) *la16-e17.* [unknown]

traik²·¹ /trek, trɛk/ *n* **1** a long tiring walk, a trudge, the act of roaming *la19-.* **2** a person or animal that is always roving or wandering *la19, 20- WC Bor.* [see the verb and compare Afrikaans *trek* a stage of a journey by ox-drawn wagon]

traik²·² /trek, trɛk/ *v* **1** to tramp, trudge, walk wearily or with difficulty *la19-.* **2** to roam, wander about idly or aimlessly, prowl *19-.* **3** frequently *of young poultry* to wander, stray, become lost *19-.* **traik efter (upon)** to follow, pursue in courtship *19-.* [Du *trekken*]

trail¹·¹ /trel/ *n* **1** a long wearisome walk, a tramp, trudge *la19-.* **2** a trailing piece of cloth, a rag *la19-.* **3** a careless, dirty, slovenly person *19, 20- NE T Bor.* **4** a large accumulation of articles, a haul *la19- NE T.* **5** something dragged, a sledge or hurdle *la15-e18.* **trailach** = TRAIL¹·¹ (sense 1) *19, 20- SW.* [see the verb]

trail¹·² †**trale,** †**trayl** /trel/ *v* **1** to drag, haul (a person or thing) behind one on the ground; *of clothes* to drag on the ground *la14-.* **2** to tramp, trudge (laboriously or dispiritedly); to wander about idly *19-.* **3** to search (a water channel) with grappling irons *la19, 20- Sh.* **4** to walk with trailing garments *la15-e16.* **trailach** to go (about) in an idle or slovenly manner *la19, 20- Uls.* **trail-en, trail-end** the first of a fleet of herring nets to be shot, the net furthest from the boat *20- Sh NE.* †**trail-fly** the last fly on a trout-fishing line *e19.* †**trail syde** *of a garment* so long that it trails *e16.* [OFr *trailler* to haul, tow (a boat)]

†**trailʒe, trailye, trelʒe** *n* cloth of various sorts *la15-16.* [MFr *treillis* net-work]

train¹, †**tryne** /tren/ *n* **1** a retinue; procession *la15-.* **2** the course or direction of thoughts or affairs *16-.* **3** a series of carriages, a locomotive with its carriages or trucks, anything pulled along behind *19-.* **4** a rope or trace for dragging a plough *la18 Ork.* **5** a line or trail (of gunpowder) *16-e17.* **6** importance, authority or honour (perhaps originally as implied by possession of a retinue) *16.* [ME *traine,* OFr *train, traine* something trailing]

†**train**², **trane, tryne** *n* **1** treachery, trickery, deceit *la14-e17.* **2** a snare or trap to catch prey *la15-17.* [AN *trayne*]

train³, †**trane,** †**trayne** /tren/ *v* **1** to discipline, teach, instruct; to manage *la15-.* **2** to drag, pull *e19.* **3** to entice, ensnare *la14-17.* **train up** = TRAIN³ (sense 1) *la16-.* [OFr *trainer* to drag]

traipse¹·¹ /treps/ *n* a long weary trudge, a tiring walk *20-.* [see the verb]

traipse¹·², **trapeez** /treps, trəˈpiz/ *v* to tramp, trudge wearily; to shuffle through mud and dirt; to go about, gad about *20-.* [EModE *traipse, trapess,* perhaps OFr *trapasser* to pass beyond]

trais *see* TRESS²

traison, treason, †**tresoun,** †**tressone,** †**tressoun** /'trɛzən, 'trizən/ *n* the action of being disloyal, (the crime of) treachery, betrayal *la14-.* **traisonable,** †**traisonabill** of or characteristic of treason; treacherous *la14.* [AN *tresun*]

traissle /'trɛsəl/ *v* to tread or trample down (growing crops or grass) *19, 20- Bor.* [altered form of TAISLE¹·², with influence from TRAMPLE]

traist¹·¹, **trust,** †**trest,** †**traste,** †**trast** /trest, trʌst/ *n* **1** confidence; assurance; firm expectation *la14-.* **2** the quality of being trustworthy or reliable; trustworthiness, reliability *la15-.* **3** *law* the requirement that a person be trustworthy in carrying out an obligation *la17.* **4** *law* a list of indictments *la16-e17.* **5** the confidence that someone will pay, credit *la15-e19.* **traisty** trustworthy, faithful, reliable *16-.* [see the verb]

traist¹·², **trust,** †**trest,** †**trast,** †**thrist** /trest, trʌst/ *v* **1** to have confidence (in), depend (on) *la14-.* **2** to commit (the safety of something to someone or something), entrust *la15-.* **3** to expect; to hope *la14-.* **4** to supply (goods) on credit *15-16.* **truster** *law* one who sets up a trust for the administration of property or funds *la17-.* [ON *treysta* to make safe]

†**traist**¹·³, **traste, trest** *adj* **1** faithful, trustworthy, reliable *la14-16.* **2** assured, confident *la14-e16.* **3** *of a place* secure *15-e16.* **4** firm, strong *la15-e16.* [ON *treystr,* ptp of *treysta;* see the verb]

†**traist**¹·⁴ *adv* **1** securely *la15-e16.* **2** truly *la15.* [see the adj]

traist *see* TRESS¹

trait *see* TRACK¹·¹, TREAT¹·¹, TREAT¹·²

†**traith, treth** *n* a herring-fishing ground *17-19.* [perhaps a variant of TRADE¹·¹]

traitor, †**tratour,** †**traytour** /'tretər/ *n* a person who betrays a trust, especially their allegiance to their sovereign or country; an untrustworthy person or thing *la14-.* †**tratourly** treacherously *15-16.* †**tratoury** treachery *la14-e17.* [AN *traitor,* accusative of *traitre*]

traivel[1.1], **trevel**, **travel**, †**travail**, †**trawaill** /'trevəl, 'travəl/ *n* **1** an act of travelling or journeying, a journey *la14*-. **2** a walk, a journey on foot *18*-. [see the verb]

traivel[1.2], **trevel**, **travel**, †**travaill** /'trevəl, 'travəl/ *v* **1** to (make a) journey, move about, go; to rove *la14*-. **2** to walk; to go about or make a journey on foot *16*-. **3** to go about (originally on foot) begging or selling small wares *la17*-. **4** to drive (cattle) from place to place *la19*-. **5** to walk back and forth, pace up and down *19- NE*. **travelled** *of soil or stones* deposited at a distance from their original site *19*- also *geological term*. **traveller, treveller, traiveller 1** a person engaged in journeying, going from place to place, one who is on a journey, a wayfarer, a passenger *la14*-. **2** a person engaged in transporting merchandise from place to place as a living *15*-. **3** an itinerant person who deals in small or tin goods *19*-; compare *Scottish Traveller* (SCOTS[1.2]). **4** an agent of a commercial firm engaged to travel around arranging the sale of commodities, a commercial traveller *20*-. **5** a hawker *20*-. **6** *humorous* a head-louse *20- Ork NE EC SW*. **7** a person walking, a pedestrian *la18-19, 20- Uls*. **traivel the countra** to go about, journey through the whole country *19*-. **traivel the road, traivel the roads** to journey on road(s) for some purpose; to infest the roads as thieves or beggars; to travel extensively *la17*-. [extended sense of TRAVAIL[1.2]]

trakboat *see* TRACK-BOAT

trakk *see* TRACK[5]

trale *see* TRAIL[1.2]

traleel /trə'lil/ *n* something long and trailing; something of poor quality *la19- NE EC*. [unknown; compare TRAIL[1.1]]

trallop *see* TROLLOP[1.1]

tram /tram/ *n* **1** a shaft of a barrow or cart *16*-. **2** a passenger car on rails; a car in a coalmine *20*-. **3** a very tall, thin, ungainly person (with long legs) *la19- NE*. **4** *pl* the two upright posts of a gallows *la17*. **trams** especially *humorous* or *contemptuous* the legs *19*-. **tram girth** a loose girth attached to the shafts of a cart to prevent a load from tipping back *19, 20- Ork*. **tram horse** a horse harnessed between the shafts of a cart *la18-19, 20- Ork*. **tram sach 1** a big, ungainly person or animal *la19- NE*. **2** a rough, untidy person *20- N*. [LG *traam*]

†**trammell net, tramalt net, tramble net** *n* a type of fishing net *16-17* [ME *tramaile*, OFr *tramail* + NET]

tramort /tra'mɔrt/ *n* a corpse *e16, e20*. [Lat *tra-* beyond + Lat *mort-* death]

tramp[1.1] /tramp/ *n* **1** a stamp of the foot; an injury to the foot by having it trodden on *19*-. **2** a vagrant *la19*-. **3** a horizontal strip of iron on the top of a spade-blade for the foot to press on *19*-. **4** *curling* a piece of spiked iron on a boot-sole to prevent slipping on the ice *19*-. **5** an iron plate on the sole of a boot or shoe used in digging *19- N WC Bor*. **trampers 1** the feet *19- N C*. **2** heavy boots *la18-19*. **trampie** = TRAMP[1.1] (sense 2) *20- NE T SW Bor*. **tramp cock, tramp cole** a heap of hay compressed by tramping *18*-. **tramp pick** a crowbar with an iron bracket for the foot to press on *19, 20- N NE C*. †**tramp ruck** = *tramp cock la16-19*. **tramp wife** a female vagrant *la19- NE T*. [see the verb]

tramp[1.2] /tramp/ *v* **1** to step, tread (on) *15*-. **2** to stamp, tread (heavily), trample (on); to hurt by treading (on) *la15*-. **3** to wash (clothes or bedclothes) by treading them in soapsuds *17*-. **4** to tread, press (down), crush, destroy by treading or stamping *16-19, 20- Sh Ork N NE T*. **5** to press down compactly by hand, compress or pack firmly *19- NE T Uls*. **tramp on somebody's taes** to encroach on a person's interests, take advantage of, offend a person *19*-. **tramp underfoot,** †**tramp vnder feit** = TRAMP[1.2] (sense 4) *la15*-. [ME *trampen*, MLG *trampen*]

†**tramp**[2] *v* to steep, soak *la15-16*. [MFr *tremper*]

trample, †**trampill** /'trampəl/ *v* to crush by treading underfoot *17*-. [frequentative form of TRAMP[1.2]]

trance[1], †**transe** /trans/ *n* **1** a narrow passage between buildings, an alley, a lane *la15*-. **2** a passage within a building, especially one connecting the two main rooms of a cottage, a lobby, a corridor *16-, 20- N NE T C*. **trance door** the door of a passage, especially an inner door leading from the outside door to the kitchen of a cottage *19- NE T C*. [OFr *transe* the passage from life to death, with the sense of Lat *transitus* a passage, way through]

trance[2], †**trans** /trans/ *n* **1** excitement, abstractedness, rapture, terror, a stunned or dazed state of mind *la15*-. **2** unconsciousness, a swoon or fainting fit, a fit associated with a disease or injury *16*-. **3** a semi-conscious state between sleeping and waking *e16*. [OFr *transe* the passage from life to death]

trane *see* TRAIN[2], TRAIN[3]

trang *see* THRANG[1.1], THRANG[1.3], THRANG[1.4]

†**tranont, tranount** *v in military use* to shift position, especially rapidly and stealthily; to make a forced march *la14-e16*. [unknown]

trans *see* TRANCE[2]

transack[1.1], **transact** /tran'zak, tran'zakt/ *n* a transaction, matter of business *la19*-. [from the verb or Lat *transactum*]

transack[1.2], **transact** /tran'zak, tran'zakt/ *v* to negotiate, conduct (business), settle, manage (affairs), come to an agreement *la16*-. [Lat *transact-*, ptp stem of *transigere* to drive through, accomplish]

transaction, †**transactioun** /tran'zakʃən/ *n* **1** an agreement, originally *law* the settlement of disputed claims *la16*-. **2** a record of the proceedings of a society *la17*-. [OFr *transaction*, Lat *transactiōn-*]

transcend /tran'sɛnd/ *v* **1** to surpass, excel *la15*-. **2** to go beyond (a boundary), exceed (a limit) *16*-. [OFr *transcender*, Lat *transcendere* to climb over]

transe *see* TRANCE[1]

transfer /trans'fɛr/ *v* **1** to convey, remove from one place or person to another *15*-. **2** *law* to move (a case or action) to another jurisdiction *15*-. **3** *law* to convey or make over (a right or title) to another *la15*-. **4** *law* to move a legal action in the process of being heard from a deceased person to their heir or representative *la16*-. **transference** *law* the procedure by which an action is transferred to an heir or representative from a person who dies during the process *la17*-. †**transferring** = *transference la16-17*. [OFr *transferrer*, Lat *transferre*]

†**transfigurat** *v pt, ptp* **transfigurat** to alter in appearance, transform *la15-16*. Compare TRANSFIGURE. [Lat *transfigūrāt-*, ptp stem of *transfigūrāre*]

transfiguration, †**transfiguratioun** /transfɪgə'reʃən/ *n* a change in appearance or form *la14*-. [OFr *transfiguration*, Lat *transfigūrātiōn-*]

transfigure, †**transfigur** /trans'fɪgər, tranz'fɪgər/ *v* to alter in appearance, transform *la15*-. [OFr *transfigurer*, Lat *transfigūrāre*]

transform /trans'fɔrm/ *v ptp* **transformit,** †**transformate 1** to change in appearance or form; metamorphose *16*-. **2** to change morally or spiritually *la15*-. [OFr *transformer*, Lat *transformāre*]

transgression, †**transgressioun** /trans'grɛʃən, tranz'grɛʃən/ *n* a sin, crime, misdemeanour *15*-. [OFr *transgression*, Lat *transgressiōn-*]

translacione *see* TRANSLATION

translate, †**translait** /trans'let, tranz'let/ *v* **1** to turn from one language into another *la14*-. **2** to remove (a person,

translation especially a body or bones, or thing) from one place to another; to convey to heaven; to deify *la14-*. **3** *Presbyterian Church* to transfer (a minister) from one charge to another *la16-*. **4** to change the nature or composition of (something), frequently to its opposite; to alter, transform; to remake (clothes) *15-17*. **5** to remove (something) from the possession of one group and pass it to another *15-16*. **translater**, †**translatour**, †**translatar** a person who translates from one language to another *la15-*. [OFr *translater* to relocate; Lat *translāt-*, ptp stem of *transferre*]

translation, †**translatioun**, †**translacione** /trans'leʃən, tranz'leʃən/ *n* **1** the action or process of translating from one language to another; the text translated *la15-*. **2** removal from one place to another *15-*. **3** *law* transference of property, mainly transference of an inheritance away from the direct heir *15-*. **4** the transference of a person (frequently a minister of religion) from one charge or post to another *la17-*. **5** alteration, change *la15-16*. [OFr *translation*, Lat *translātiōn-* a transporting]

†**transmeridiane** *n* the region beyond a meridian, either that in the Atlantic, beyond which is the New World, or the equator, hence, in the southern hemisphere; a remote place *e16*. [*trans-* prefix + Lat *merīdiānum* the position of the sun at midday]

transmogrify /tranz'mɔgrɪfae/ *v* **1** to alter or change in form or appearance, metamorphose *la18-*. **2** to astound, astonish *19-*. [EModE *transmogrify*]

transplant /trans'plant/ *v* **1** to remove (a plant) from one place to another; to remove (people) to another place *17-*. **2** *Presbyterian Church* to transfer (a minister or other ecclesiastic) from one charge to another *17*; compare TRANSLATE (sense 3). [Lat *transplantāre*]

†**transplantation**, **transplantatioun** *n* the action of transplanting; originally *Presbyterian Church* the transfer of a minister to another charge *17*. [TRANSPLANT + noun-forming suffix]

transport[1.1] /'transport/ *n* **1** the conveyance of people or things *la16-*. **2** a means of conveyance *20-*. **3** transference or conveyance (of property) *la15-17*. [see the verb]

transport[1.2] /trans'port/ *v* **1** to (cause to) move, remove (to another place); to transfer, carry (people or things) (to another place) *la16-*. **2** to move, carry (goods) for the purpose of trade *la16-*. **3** to go into exile, migrate *16-*. **4** *Presbyterian Church* to cause or permit (a minister) to move from one charge or post to another *la16-*; compare TRANSLATE (sense 3). **5** *Presbyterian Church* to remove (the site of a church) to a different place *17-*. **6** to carry away with emotion, enrapture *la16-e17*. **transportable**, †**transportabill 1** able or allowed to be transported *la16-*. **2** *Presbyterian Church of a minister* permitted to transfer to another charge *la16-*. †**act of transportability** *Presbyterian Church* formal permission granted by a presbytery to one of its ministers to move to another charge *17-e18*. [OFr *transporter*, Lat *transportāre*]

transportation, †**transportatioun** /transpor'teʃən/ *n* **1** the act of conveying (people or things) *16-*. **2** deportation used as a punishment *la17-*. **3** *Presbyterian Church* a minister's transferring from one charge to another *la16-18*. [TRANSPORT[1.2] + noun-forming suffix]

†**transume** *v pt, ptp* **transumit, transsumpt** *law* to make an official copy of (a legal document) *15-18*. [OFr *transumer*, Lat *transsumere, transsumptāre* to transcribe, make a copy of]

†**transumpt, transump** *n* **1** *law* a transcript or copy of a document or record authenticated so as to give it equivalence in law with the original *la15-19*. **2** the action or process of copying a legal document *la16-17*. **3** a copy *17-19*. [Lat *transsumpt-*, ptp stem of *transsumptāre* to transcribe, make a copy of]

trantle, †**trantill**, †**trental**, †**trigental** /'trantəl/ *n* **1** in plural, trifles; miscellaneous bits of equipment *17-*. **2** a set of thirty requiem masses *16-19*. **trantlement, trintlement** = TRANTLE (sense 1) *20 NE*. **trantles** odds and ends *17-*. **trantlum**, *SW* **tranklum** = TRANTLE (sense 1) *la18-*. †**trentalis of mysdedis** sets of thirty sins, a very large number of sins *e16*. [OFr *trentel* a set of thirty requiem masses, Lat *trentāle*, perceived as vain after the Reformation; with influences from Lat *trīgintā* thirty and Eng *trinket*]

trantlum *see* TRANTLE

trap[1] /trap/ *n* **1** a ladder, a (movable) flight of steps *la16-*. **2** the trapdoor giving access to a loft, a small door at the top of a flight of steps, a small door set into a larger door *la15-17*. **trap ladder** = TRAP[1] (sense 1) *19, 20- Ork Bor*. **trap stair, trap stairs** = TRAP[1] (sense 1) *N T C Bor*. [Du *trap* a stair]

trap[2] /trap/ *v* **1** to ensnare, catch (out) *la15-*. **2** to correct another pupil's mistake and thus take his place in order of merit in a school class *19-*. [OE **træppan*]

trap[3] /trap/ *n* a slut *20- N*. [Gael *dràb*, itself from Eng *drab*]

†**trap**[4] *n* a fastening or clasp; an embellishment *16*. [perhaps OE *trappe* a snare, or compare TRAPPIT]

trapach /'trapəx/ *adj* slovenly, slatternly *20- N*. [Gael *dràbach*; compare TRAP[3]]

trapeez *see* TRAIPSE[1.2]

trappin, trapping /'trapɪn, 'trapɪŋ/ *n* **1** material used to trim or tie garments, lace, tape, ribbon, thread; originally used for decorating a horse's caparison or harness *16-19, 20- Ork NE T*. **2** small wares, a hawker's stock-in-trade *la19- Bor*. [ME *trappinge*; compare TRAPPIT]

†**trappit** *adj of a horse* protected (with armour) or decorated (with rich cloth) *la14-16*. [derivative of AN *trappe* cloth, covering]

trapple *see* THRAPPLE[1.1], THRAPPLE[1.2]

†**trappour, trapper, trapour** *n* trapping or housing for a horse *la15-e16*. [ME *trappour*, OFr *drapure, *trapeure*]

trasche *see* TRASH[1]

traschor *see* TRACE[2.2]

trase *see* TRACE[2.2], TRESS[2]

trash[1], †**trasche** /traʃ/ *n* **1** objects of little value, rubbish *17-*. **2** waste materials, especially timber *la17-*. †**trashrie, trashery, trusterie** = TRASH[1.1] (sense 1) *la15-19*. **trashtrie 1** = TRASH[1] (sense 1) *19-*. **2** *of food* lacking in substance or value *la18-*. **trashy** *of weather* wet, unpleasant *19- H&I Bor*. [unknown; compare Norw dial *trask* lumber, trash]

trash[2] /traʃ/ *v* to wear out, exhaust, abuse with overwork and exertion *19- SW Bor*. **trashy** fatiguing *20- Bor*. [EModE *trash*; compare Norw *traske* to walk heavily]

trast *see* TRAIST[1.1], TRAIST[1.2]

traste *see* TRAIST[1.1], TRAIST[1.3]

†**trat, trattes** *n* an old woman, an old hag *la14-e16*. [compare AN *trote*]

trate /tret/ *n* a piece of cloth dipped in a mixture of beeswax and lard, used as a dressing for sores or boils *la18- N NE EC*. [OFr *trait* an adhesive plaster]

trath *see* TRUITH

tratle *see* TRATTLE

tratlys *see* TRATTLES

tratour *see* TRAITOR

trattes *see* TRAT

trattillis *see* TRATTLES

trattle, †**trattill**, †**tratle** /'tratəl/ *v* to talk idly; to chatter, prattle, gossip *15-19, 20- EC*. †**trattlar** a gossip *la15-16*. [probably onomatopoeic]

†**trattles, trattillis, tratlys** *npl* idle talk or tales; gossip; chatter *la15-17*. [from the verb TRATTLE]

trauchle[1.1], **trachle, trackle** /ˈtrɔxəl, ˈtraxəl, ˈtrakəl/ *n* **1** a struggle, a hard time *la17-*. **2** a long, tiring trudge or walk *19-*. **3** tiring labour, drudgery, fatiguing or dispiriting work *la19-*. **4** a source of trouble or anxiety, a burden, encumbrance *la19-*. **5** a careless incompetent person, an inefficient slovenly worker *la19-*. **6** a state of chronic muddle caused by having too much to do *20-*. **trauchlesome** exhausting, laborious *20- NE T.* [see the verb]

trauchle[1.2], **trachle, traichle, trackle** /ˈtrɔxəl, ˈtraxəl, ˈtrɛxəl, ˈtrakəl/ *v* **1** to walk slowly and wearily, drag oneself along *19-*. **2** to bedraggle, injure, spoil (by dragging, trampling, knocking about) *19-*. **3** to exhaust with overwork or travelling, overburden, harass *19-*. **4** to hamper, trouble, worry *19-*. **5** to drudge, labour on in a harassed way *19-*. **6** to draw, trail, drag through mud *la19-*. **trackle soam** *farming* the draught-rope and pin on the beam of an Orkney single-stilted plough *20-*. [perhaps back-formation from TRAUCHLED; or from Flem *tragelen, trakelen* to trudge, drag]

trauchled, trachled, †**trachelt,** †**trachlit** /ˈtrɔxəld, ˈtraxəld/ *adj* **1** bedraggled, dishevelled *16-*. **2** exhausted, tired out; overworked, harassed with cares *la16-*. [perhaps Gael *treachailte*, IrGael *trocailte* tired out; or participial adj from the verb TRAUCHLE[1.2]]

travaig /traˈveg/ *v* to wander idly or aimlessly *20- Sh Ork.* [aphetic form of STRAVAIG[1.2]]

travail[1.1], †**travel** /traˈvel/ *n* **1** hardship, suffering; exertion, toil; a particular struggle *la14-*. **2** the labour of childbirth *la16-*. **3** (distress associated with) sickness *la14-e17*. **4** *Presbyterian Church* the deliberations of the commissioners of the Church of Scotland on particular matters *17*. [OFr *travail*]

travail[1.2], †**travel** /traˈvel/ *v* **1** to harass, torment, bother; tire *la14-*. **2** to exert oneself, toil, labour, perform (a task) *la14-*. **3** to suffer the labour of childbirth *la14-*. [OFr *travailler*]

travail *see* TRAIVEL[1.1]

travaill *see* TRAIVEL[1.2]

travally *see* TREVALLIE

trave *see* THREAVE[1.1]

travel *see* TRAIVEL[1.1], TRAIVEL[1.2], TRAVAIL[1.1], TRAVAIL[1.2]

travellye *see* TREVALLIE

†**travers** *n law* a formal denial; a change in circumstances, a reversal of fortune *15-17*. [ME *travers*, OFr *travers* something that crosses, an obstacle]

traverse, †**travers,** †**trevis,** †**travis** /traˈvɛrs/ *v* **1** to move (to and fro) across, cross *la14-*. **2** to go through, pierce *e16*. **3** to be contrary, run counter to *la15*. [OFr *traverser*]

travise, trevis, †**trevice,** †**trivice,** †**travers** /ˈtrɛvɪs, ˈtrɛvɪs/ *n* **1** the wooden partition between two stalls in a stable or cowshed *16-*. **2** a stall or loose-box in a stable *18-19*. **3** a screen, partition *15-e17*. **4** a partitioned-off space *la16*. †**travise pece** a crosspiece or transom *e16*. [variant of ME *travers*, OFr *travers* something that crosses, an obstacle, and OFr *traverse* a cross-piece, enclosure]

traw *see* TRAWL[1.1]

trawaill *see* TRAIVEL[1.1]

†**trawe, trye** *n* a trick *16*. [ME *traie* from AN *traier* to betray]

trawl[1.1], †**traw** /trɔl/ *n* a bag-shaped net dragged along the bottom of fishing grounds or a seine-net, a net used to surround a shoal of fish *la17-*. **trawl-net** = TRAWL[1.1]. [see the verb]

trawl[1.2] /trɔl/ *v* to fish with a trawl-net or seine-net, by encircling shoals of fish *la19-*. [EModE *trawl*, compare MDu *traghelen* to drag]

trawn *see* THRAWN

†**tray**[1] *n* pain, trouble, vexation *la14-16*. **tray and tene** trouble and pain *la14-16*. [OE *trega*]

†**tray**[2] *n* a three in dice *15*. [ME *trei*, AN *trei*; compare TRES-ACE]

tray *see* THRAE

trayl *see* TRAIL[1.2]

trayne *see* TRAIN[3]

trays *see* TRACE[2.1]

trayst *see* TRYST[1.1]

traytour *see* TRAITOR

tre *see* TREE[1.1], TREE[1.2]

treacle *see* TRAICLE

tread[1.1], †**trade** /trɛd/ *n* **1** a footprint, a trail of footprints, a track, way (of life) *la15-*; compare TRADE[1.1] (sense 5), (sense 6), (sense 8). **2** the felloe of a wooden wheel *la17, 19- C.* [see the verb]

tread[1.2], †**tred,** †**trade** /trɛd/ *v pt* **treadit, trod,** *NE T WC* **tread,** †**trode,** †**tred,** *ptp* **treadit,** *WC* **treddin,** †**tred 1** to step on, crush, trample *16-*. **2** to follow (a path, track, animal or example) *la16-*. [OE *tredan*]

tread *see* TRADE[1.1]

treadle, treddle, †**traddle,** †**tredle** /ˈtrɛdəl/ *n* a foot-operated lever, as on a loom or sewing machine *la16-*. †**treidling** woven goods *la16-e17*. **treadle-hole, treddle-hole** *weaving* an open space under the loom for the treadle shafts *19- C.* [TREAD[1.2] + *-le* suffix]

treason *see* TRAISON

treasure *see* TREISURE

treasurer *see* THESAURER

treat[1.1], **trait,** †**treit** /trɛt, trit/ *n* an entertainment, special occasion offered (as a celebration), originally usually of food and drink *la14-*. [see the verb]

treat[1.2], *NE* **trait,** †**trete,** †**treit** /trit, trɛt/ *v pt* **treatit, tret,** *ptp* **treatit, tret, treat 1** to discuss, negotiate; to deal with; to concern oneself with *la14-*. **2** to behave, act towards (people) *la14-*. **3** to feast, regale (someone with something) *16-*. **4** to beseech, beg, request *la14-19*. **5** to deal kindly with, show respect to; to honour; to flatter *la15-16*. **treatable,** †**tretabill 1** *of a disease or condition* able to be treated *20-*. **2** *of a person* tractable, willing, agreeable *la15-e17*. †**treater, treatar** a negotiator *la14-e18*. **treatise,** †**tretis 1** a book or writing, a literary work, a dissertation *15-*. **2** negotiation *la14-17*. **3** a negotiated settlement *la14-16*. **4** earnest solicitation, entreaty; an offer of truce *14-16*. **treaty,** †**trete,** †**trety,** †**traitie 1** a negotiated settlement, binding agreement; arrangement *15-*. **2** negotiation *15-17*. **3** earnest solicitation, entreaty; an offer of truce *15-e17*. **4** a book or writing, a literary work, a dissertation *la15-e17*. [OFr *tretier, traitier*]

Treaty of Union /ˈtritɛ əv ˈjunjən/ *n* the Acts of the Scottish and English Parliaments uniting Scotland and England *18-*. Compare *Act of Union* (ACK[1.1]). [*treaty* (TREAT) + *of* (O[2]) + UNION]

treb, †**treve** /trɛb/ *n archaeology* an earth-mound or dyke found in Orkney, thought to be Pictish, perhaps a boundary wall or settlement enclosure; also in place-names *18-*. **treb-dyke** = TREB *20-*. [Norw *trev* a shelf, Norw *trip* a step]

treble, †**tribill** /ˈtrɛbəl/ *n* the highest part in a three-part vocal or instrumental composition; high-pitched, youthful *16-*. [OFr *treble* threefold]

treble *see* TRIPLE[1.3]

trebling /ˈtrɛblɪŋ/ *n piping* in PIBROCH, the form in which the *doubling* (DOOBLE[1.2]) of a variation is sometimes repeated with further development *20-*. [OFr *treble* threefold + *-ing* suffix]

trebuck *see* TERBUTCHE

trebuschet *see* TRABUSCHET

†**trechour, trichour, trachour, treitcheoure** *n* a deceiver, liar, cheat *15-16.* **trechour tung** the tongue of a liar, hence, a treacherous, lying tongue *e16.* [ME *trechour, trichour,* AN *trecheor, tricheur*]
tred *see* TRADE[1.1], TREAD[1.2]
treddin *see* TREAD[1.2]
treddle, tredle *see* TREADLE
tree[1.1], †**tre,** †**trie** /triː/ *n* **1** a woody plant, a tree *la14-.* **2** wood, timber *la14-19, 20- literary.* **3** *mining* a pit-prop *20- C.* **4** a pole or staff, a walking-stick; a club, a cudgel *la14-19.* **5** a balk or beam, a rafter, a post, a mast *15-19.* **6** a wooden barrel, a keg *la15-19.* **7** a gallows or gallows-cross *la14-e17.* **8** the wooden part of a plough or saddle *la14-17.* †**trey buits** wooden boots *la16.* †**tre crop** a treetop *la16.* **tree-ladle** a wooden ladle *18-19, 20- Ork.* **tree-speeler** the treecreeper *Certhia familiaris la19, 20- C SW.* †**tree-leg** a wooden leg *la17-19.* [OE *trēow*]
†**tree**[1.2], **tre** *v* **1** to provide the roof of a coal-working with supporting timbers or props *la19.* **2** to shape a boot on a block of wood *la16* [see the noun]
tree *see* THREE
treece *see* TREESH[1.2]
treed *see* THREID[1.1], THREID[1.2]
treel *see* TRILL
treelip *see* TROLLOP[1.1]
treen[1.1], †**treyne,** †**trene** /triːn/ *n* wooden objects or wares *17-.* [see the adj]
†**treen**[1.2], **treyn, trene** *adj* wooden, made of wood *la14-19.* **treen-mare** a wooden horse used as an instrument of punishment *la17-19.* [OE *trēowen*]
treeple *see* TRIPLE[1.2]
treesh[1.1] /triːʃ/ *v* **1** to entreat, cajole, entice *19- NE.* **2** to run after, court *19- NE.* **3** to call an animal *la19- NE.* [unknown]
treesh[1.2], **treece** /triːʃ, triːs/ *interj* a call to cattle, especially calves, to come *la19- NE T.* [unknown]
treeska /ˈtriːskə/ *n* the sulks, resentment *20- Ork.* **treeskie** sulky, bad-tempered *20- Ork.* **play treeska** to play truant *20- Ork.* [Faer *treiski*]
treetle, *NE* **trytle,** *SW* **trittle** /ˈtriːtəl; *NE* ˈtrʌɪtəl; *SW* ˈtrɪtəl/ *v* **1** to trickle or fall in drops or in a slender stream *la19- Sh Ork NE.* **2** to walk with short steps, trot, move reluctantly *20- NE SW.* [probably an altered form of dreetle (DRIDDLE[1.2])]
trefell *see* TRIFFLE[1]
treffik *see* TRAFFECK[1.1]
treffle *see* TRIFFLE[2]
tregallion /trəˈɡaljən/ *n* a rabble, an untidy collection; a rambling story *19, 20- Ork N.* [extended sense of TREVALLIE]
treget *see* TRIGIT
treh *see* TRY
treist *see* TRYST[1.2]
treisure, treasure, †**tresour,** †**thesaure,** †**thresour** /ˈtriːʒər, ˈtrɛʒər/ *n* **1** (a hoard of) money, precious metals or jewels; wealth *la14-.* **2** a thing or person of great value, a rich source of something, an asset or resource *la15-.* **3** treasure-trove *16-17.* †**thesaury 1** a treasure-house, a repository for valuables *la15-17.* **2** the office of treasurer *la15-17.* †**thesaurhous** a repository for valuables *la15-16.* [OFr *tresor,* Lat *thēsaurus*]
treit *see* TRACK[1.1], TREAT[1.1], TREAT[1.2]
treitcheoure *see* TRECHOUR
treitt *see* TRACK[1.1]
trekkle *see* TRAICLE
†**trelapse, trilapse** *n Presbyterian Church* **1** a third offence against church discipline, especially fornication *la16-19.* **2** = *trelapser la16-17.* **trelapser** a person guilty of a third offence against church discipline *17-19.* [Lat *tri-* three- + Lat *lapsus* a fall]
trelȝe *see* TRAIL3E
tremble *see* TREMMLE
tremendous[1.1]**, tremendious,** †**tremenduous** /trəˈmɛndəs, trəˈmɛndɪəs/ *adj* **1** great, strong; extraordinary *19-.* **2** awful, terrible *17.* [Lat *tremendus* that is to be trembled at]
tremendous[1.2] /trəˈmɛndəs/ *adv* very much, extremely *la19-.* [see the adj]
tremmle, tremble, trimmle, trummle, †**trimble,** †**trimbill,** †**trymmill** /ˈtrɛməl, ˈtrɛmbəl, ˈtrɪməl, ˈtrʌməl/ *v* **1** *of a person* to shake involuntarily; *of a thing* to quake, quiver *la14-.* **2** to experience apprehension or dread *la16-.* **tremmlin, trembling** a virus disease of sheep, causing paralysis, tremor and spasms *19-.* †**trembling aixies** an acute fever, ague *la17-19.* †**tremmlin fever** = *trembling aixies la16-e19.* **tremmlin tree** the aspen *Populus tremula 20-.* **trimmlin strae, tremmlin strae** unthreshed straw *20- NE.* **trimmlin tam 1** potted head *la19- T C.* **2** a fruit jelly *20- C SW.* **trimmlin tammie** a fruit jelly *20- C.* [OFr *trembler,* Lat *tremulāre*]
tremskit /ˈtrɛmskɪt/ *adj* badly arranged, disorderly, scruffy *20- Sh.* [Norn *tremsek* a rag, tatter + *-IT*[2]]
trench[1.1]**,** †**trinsch,** †**trensch** /trɛnʃ/ *n* **1** a channel cut in the ground, a (defensive) ditch *la15-.* **2** the earthwork created by excavating a ditch *16-17.* [ME *trench,* AN *trench*]
trench[1.2]**,** †**trynch,** †**trynsch** /trɛnʃ/ *v* **1** to excavate a cutting, furrow or hollow in the earth, dig a trench; to fortify with a trench *la16-.* **2** to cut or slice meat, cut in pieces *la15-e16.* †**trynschand** cutting, sharp *la15-e16.* †**trench upon** to encroach upon, infringe *17.* [Fr *trenchier* to cut, slice; with some senses from the noun]
trenchman *see* TRUNCHEMAN
trene *see* TREEN[1.1], TREEN[1.2]
trensch *see* TRENCH[1.1]
trental *see* TRANTLE
trentlet /ˈtrɛntlət/ *adj of clothes and shoes* long and narrow, tight-fitting; *of persons* lanky *20- Sh Ork.* [unknown]
trep *see* THREAP[1.1], THREAP[1.2]
†**tres-ace, traes ace, tre trace** *n* **1** a game similar to musical chairs *la18-e19.* **2** a throw of three and one in a game of dice *la16-17.* [ME *treis,* AN, OFr *treis* a three in dice; + ACE; compare TRAY[2]]
tresaurar *see* THESAURER
tresh *see* THRESH
tresoun *see* TRAISON
tresour *see* TREISURE
trespass[1.1]**,** †**trespas** /ˈtrɛspas/ *n* **1** an offence, sin, wrongdoing *la14-.* **2** *law* a crime or misdemeanour, criminal activity *la14-.* [OFr *trespas*]
trespass[1.2]**,** †**trespas** /ˈtrɛspas/ *v* **1** to sin against; to commit an offence *la14-.* **2** *law* to enter another's land without permission *15-.* [see the noun]
tress[1]**,** †**trest,** †**traist** /trɛs/ *n* **1** a trestle supporting a board or boards; a bench or table formed with a trestle *la15-.* **2** a small wooden jetty *la19- Sh.* **3** a wooden framework used to support scaffolding; a section of a bridge *16-19.* **4** a rest for a firearm *16.* **5** a tripod *e16.* [OFr *trest, trast*]
tress[2]**,** †**trace,** †**trais, trase** /trɛs/ *n* **1** a plait or braid of hair; a lock of hair *16-.* **2** a ribbon or braid of gold or silver thread for trimming a garment or cloth *16.* **3** *heraldry* a narrow band *la15-17.* †**tressit** *of hair* plaited, braided *16-17.* †**tressing** braid, ribbon, trimming *16-17.* [ME *tresse, trāce,* OFr *tresse*]
tress *see* TRACE[1]
tressone, tressoun *see* TRAISON

tressure, †**tressour** /ˈtrɛʃər/ n *heraldry* a narrow band *la15-*. [ME *tressour*, AN *tressour*]
trest see TRAIST[1.1], TRAIST[1.2], TRAIST[1.3], TRESS[1]
tret, **trete** see TREAT[1.2]
treth see TRAITH
tre trace see TRES-ACE
tretten see THIRTEEN[1.2]
trettind-day /ˈtrɛtəndˈde/ n Epiphany, Twelfth Night, the thirteenth day of Christmas *20- Sh*. [Norw *trettende dag*]
tretty see THIRTY[1.2]
Treuel see TREWALL
treush see THRESH
treuth see TRUITH
trevallie, **travally**, *Ork* **travellye** /trəˈvali; *Ork* trəˈvɛlje/ n **1** a disturbance, brawl *19, 20- Ork Uls*. **2** a startling noise, a crash, a prolonged clatter *20- N Uls*. **3** a miscellaneous collection; a retinue of followers, a swarm, rabble *19, 20- Uls*. **4** a reveille beaten on a drum *e18*. [EModE *trevally*, altered form of *reveille*]
treve see TREB
trevel see TRAIVEL[1.1], TRAIVEL[1.2]
treveller see TRAIVEL[1.2]
trevis see TRAVERSE, TRAVISE
trevmphe see TRIUMPH[1.1]
trew, **troo**, *T* **trow**, †**true** /truː/ v pt, ptp **trowed 1** to believe; to have confidence in, trust *la14-*. **2** to expect *la14-17*. [OE *trēowan*; with *troo* etc forms from OE *trūwian* reinforced by ON *trúa*]
trew see TRUCE, TRUE
†**Trewall**, **Treuel** n abbreviated form of St Rule *la16-17*. **Treuelday** St Rule's day, the second Tuesday in October *la16-17*. **Truel fair** a fair held on St Rule's day *la16-17*. [from the name of the saint]
trewis see TRUCE
trewker see TROOKER
trews, †**trowse**, †**trewis**, †**trues** /truːz/ n **1** close-fitting (tartan) trousers worn by Highlanders and certain Scottish regiments; originally a garment which covered the legs and feet *16-*. **2** trousers *19-*. [Gael, IrGael *triubhas*]
trewth see TROWTH
treyn see TREEN[1.2]
treyne see TREEN[1.1]
trial, †**tryall**, †**tryell** /ˈtraɛəl/ n **1** *law* the formal judging of a person in a court of law *la16-*. **2** a test of quality, performance or suitability *la16-*. **3** *Presbyterian Church* the examination of ministers or probationers by a Presbytery before they are licensed to preach *la16-*. **4** *law* the testing of a candidate for the legal profession or of a new judge before he was admitted to the bench *la16-e20, la20- historical*. **5** evidence, proof *la16-17*. †**tak trial** to investigate, examine *la16-e18*. [ME *trial*, AN *trial*]
tribble see TROUBLE[1.1]
tribe /traɪb/ n **1** a community claiming descent from a common ancestor *15-*. **2** a (highland) clan or subdivision of a clan *16-17*. [ME *tribe*, OFr *tribu*, Lat *tribus*]
tribill see TRIPLE[1.3]
†**tribulance** n **1** harassment, interference; *law* (the crime of) disorderly or violent behaviour, breach of the peace *16*. **2** distress, suffering *16*. [OFr *tribulance*]
tribule see TROUBLE[1.1]
tribunal, †**tribunall** /traeˈbjunəl/ n **1** a judicial assembly *17-*. **2** a judge's seat, a seat of judgement *la15-16*. †**tribunall sait** a judge's seat *16*. [ME *tribunal*, OFr *tribunal*, Lat *tribūnāl*]
trichour see TRECHOUR
trick[1.1], †**trik** /trɪk/ n **1** an underhand or fraudulent stratagem designed to cheat or mislead; a prank; a dodge *la16-*. **2** a feat of dexterity, a skill, a knack *17-*. **by trick of thoum** as a matter of routine, automatically *20- Ork*. [MFr *trique*]
trick[1.2], †**trik** /trɪk/ v to cheat or deceive *17-*. [see the noun]
tricker[1] /ˈtrɪkər/ n the trigger of a gun *18-19, 20- N NE C*. [Du *trekker*]
tricker[2], **trigger** /ˈtrɪkər/ n *curling* the iron plate on which a player places his foot to prevent it from slipping on the ice *19, 20- historical*. [perhaps TRIG[1.1] with instrumental suffix, altered by analogy with TRICKER[1]]
trickit, **triket** /ˈtrɪkət/ adj **1** mischievous *20-*. **2** pleased, happy, delighted *20- NE*. [TRICK[1.1] + -IT[2]; compare *ill-trickit* (ILL[1.3])]
trid see THIRD[1.1], THIRD[1.2], THIRD[1.3]
†**triddle**, **traddle** v to tramp, trudge, go frequently *la18-e19*. [frequentative form of TREAD[1.2]]
triddle see TRIPLE[1.3]
trie see TREE[1.1]
triffle[1], **trifle**, †**triffill**, †**trefell** /ˈtrɪfəl, ˈtrʌɪfəl/ n **1** something of little importance *16-*. **2** a small amount *la16-19, 20- NE C*. [ME *triffle*, AN *triffle*]
†**triffle**[2], **treffle**, **trifoly** n the name of various plants with three-lobed leaves *la15-19*. [AN *trefle*, Lat *trifolium*]
trift see THRIFT
trifoly see TRIFFLE[2]
trig[1.1] /trɪg/ v to neaten, set in order *la17-19, 20- Sh NE*. **trig up** to smarten up *19, 20- Sh NE*. [see the adj]
trig[1.2], †**tryg** /trɪg/ adj **1** active, nimble, brisk, alert *la15-*. **2** *of people* smart, well turned out; *of places or things* neat, tidy *16-*. **trigly** neatly, smartly *la18-*. [ON *tryggr* trusty, faithful]
trigental see TRANTLE
trigger see TRICKER[2]
†**trigit**, **trygget**, **treget** n enchantment, trickery, deceit *la14-e17*. [OFr *treget*]
trigle see TRINKLE[1.2]
trik see TRICK[1.1], TRICK[1.2]
triket see TRICKIT
trilapse see TRELAPSE
trilka /ˈtrɪlkə/ n the sulks *20- Ork*. **tak the trilka** to take the sulks, become huffy *20- Ork*. [compare Norw dial *tryllskjin* sour, cross]
trill, **treel** /trɪl, trɪl/ v to run (slowly) *20- Ork*. [Norw *trille* to spin, roll, trundle; compare TIRL[1.2]]
trim[1.1] /trɪm/ v to adjust, adapt; to modify by cutting *la16-*. [OE *trymman*, *trymian* to make firm]
trim[1.2], **trum** /trɪm, trʌm/ adj **1** neat, well-ordered; smart or attractive *16-*. **2** able, proficient *16-17*. **trimmie** a pert, impudent girl *19, 20- SW*. **trimly**, †**trimlie 1** neatly, handsomely *16-*. **2** ably, well *16*. [see the verb]
trimbill, **trimble**, **trimmle** see TREMMLE
trimse /trɪms/ v to move about restlessly or painfully; to move impatiently *20- Ork*. [perhaps Norw dial *dremba* (seg) to press or exert (oneself)]
trincher see TRUNCHER
trinchman see TRUNCHEMAN
trindle see TRINNLE[1.2]
trinity, †**trinite**, †**trinitie** /ˈtrɪnɪti/ n the state of being three; *Christian Church* the threefold nature of God, the Father, Son and Holy Spirit *la14-*. **Trinity College** the Church of the Holy Trinity in Edinburgh *la15-e19, la19- historical*. **Trinity Fair** a fair or market taking place around *Trinity Sunday 16-*. **Trinity friars**, †**Trinitie freiris** the Trinitarian Friars, the Order of the Holy Trinity *la16-18, 19- historical*. **Trinity Monday** the day after *Trinity Sunday 17-*. **Trinity Sunday** the Sunday after Whitsunday *15-*. [OFr *trinite*]
trink /trɪŋk/ n **1** a trench or channel; a ditch, a gutter, an open drain *la16-*. **2** a narrow inlet of the sea, a creek; a

watercourse *la17-*. **3** a rut in a road *la19- NE T*. **trinkit 1** rutted, filled with ruts *la19- NE*. **2** long and narrow, contracted *20- Sh*. **trinky** narrow, slender, thin *20- Sh Ork*. [MFr *trenque*; compare TRENCH¹·¹]

†**trinket** *v* to intrigue, scheme *17-e19*. [unknown; compare TRICK¹·², Eng *trinket* and TRIGIT]

trinkle¹·¹ /ˈtrɪŋkəl/ *n* a trickle, a tiny stream, a drop *la19-*. [unknown]

trinkle¹·², †**tryngle**, †**thringle**, †**trigle** /ˈtrɪŋkəl/ *v* **1** *of liquid* to trickle, flow, drip *la14-*. **2** to besprinkle or scatter (something) over *la19- NE*. [unknown]

†**trinkum** *n* a trinket, a knick-knack *la18-19*. **trinkums** odds and ends *la18-19*. [altered form of Eng *trinket*, with mock-Latin suffix]

trinnell *see* TRINNLE¹·²

trinnle¹·¹, **trunnel**, **trintle**, †**tryndill**, †**trundill** /ˈtrɪnəl, ˈtrʌnəl, ˈtrɪntəl/ *n* **1** a circular revolving object; a wooden roller or the wheel of a wheelbarrow *16-19, 20- C Bor*. **2** a lantern- or cog-wheel (in the gearing machinery of a mill) *la15-19*. **3** a rolling or flowing motion *19*. **trinnly** roundish, suitable for rolling *20- Bor*. **trintlet** a small ball or pellet (of sheep's dung) *20-*. **trundle bed**, †**trinnell bed** a low bed on wheels or castors to allow storage under another bed, a truckle-bed *17-*. †**trinnle broad**, **trinell brod** one of the two parallel plates on a cog-wheel *la16-e18*. [OE *trendel* a circle, ring]

trinnle¹·², **trintle**, *Sh* **tintle**, †**trindle**, †**trinnell**, †**truntle** /ˈtrɪnəl, ˈtrɪntəl; *Sh* ˈtɪntəl/ *v* **1** to (cause to) roll or trundle along *17-*. **2** to walk steadily; to saunter or amble along *19, 20- Sh Ork NE Bor*. **3** to trail or trudge behind, totter unsteadily; to waddle or straggle, dawdle *19, 20- Sh Ork NE Bor*. **4** to (cause to) flow or trickle *la18- NE C*. [see the noun]

trinsch *see* TRENCH¹·¹

trintle *see* TRINNLE¹·¹, TRINNLE¹·²

trip¹·¹, †**tripp** /trɪp/ *n* **1** an act of tripping up; a fault, a misdemeanour *la17-*. **2** a turn at dancing *18-e19*. [see the verb]

trip¹·² /trɪp/ *v* **1** to move nimbly or lightly, skip, flit; to dance, prance *la15-*. **2** to trip up, catch out *la16-*. **tripping 1** moving lightly, dancing *la15-*. **2** the action of tripping up or falling over; an error, fault *la17-*. [ME *trippen*, OFr *tripper*]

trip² /trɪp/ *n* a pile of stones set up as a division on a beach *20- Ork N*. [Norw *trip* an obstruction to be crossed on a path]

trip *see* TROOP

tripe¹, †**trype** /trʌɪp/ *n* entrails, bowels, the stomach (of a ruminant) *la15-*. **trypal** a tall, thin, ungainly person *18- NE* [ME *tripe*, OFr *tripe*]

†**tripe²**, **trype**, **tryp** *n* an imitation velvet *la16-e17*. [MFr *tripe*; supposedly from its resemblance to TRIPE¹]

tripill *see* TRIPLE¹·¹, TRIPLE¹·³

triping /ˈtrʌɪpɪŋ/ *n* coal from which the larger lumps have been separated; unscreened coal; a kind of dross *la19, 20- C*. [unknown]

triple¹·¹, †**tripill** /ˈtrɪpəl/ *n* (a quantity) three times as much or as many *la16-*. [see the adj]

triple¹·², **treeple** /ˈtrɪpəl, ˈtripəl/ *v* **1** to multiply by three *la14-*. **2** to play or dance to a tune in triple time, to waltz; to beat time with the foot to a dance tune *19-*. [Lat *triplāre*; in sense 2 perhaps with some influence from TRIP¹·²]

triple¹·³, **treble**, †**triddle**, †**tripill**, †**tribill** /ˈtrɪpəl, ˈtrɛbəl/ *adj* **1** three times as much or many *la14-*. **2** having three components; occurring three times; threefold *17-*. †**triplar** *of music* having an interval of a third *la15*. †**triplat** = *triplar e16*. [OFr *triple*, Lat *triplus*]

tripling /ˈtrɪplɪŋ/ *n* *in a pibroch or strathspey* a melody note divided into three by the insertion of two short cutting grace notes *la19-*. [verbal noun from TRIPLE¹·²]

triply¹·¹ /trɪˈplae/ *n law* a third answer made by the pursuer in reply to the DUPLY¹·¹ of the defender; sometimes a second rejoinder by the defender *16-19, 20- historical*. [Lat *tri-* three- + *-ply* as in DUPLY¹·¹, and compare OFr *triplique*]

triply¹·² /trɪˈplae/ *v law* to make a third answer *16-19, 20- historical*. [see the noun and compare OFr *tripliquer*, Lat *triplicare*]

tripp *see* TRIP¹·¹

trip-trap-truiscae /ˈtrɪpˈtrapˈtrøskɛ/ *n* the game of noughts and crosses *20- Ork N*. [Norw *tripp-trapp-tresko*]

†**trist**, **tryst** *adj* sad, sorrowful, melancholy *la15-16*. [MFr *triste*]

trist *see* THIRST¹·¹, THIRST¹·², TRYST¹·¹, TRYST¹·²

trith *see* TRUITH

tritle-trantles *see* TRITTLE-TRATTLES

†**trittill-trattill** *interj* an expression of contempt or dismissal *e16*. [reduplicative form of TRATTLE]

trittle *see* TREETLE

†**trittle-trattles**, **trittil trattilis**, **tritle-trantles** *npl* **1** cheap articles, knick-knacks *la17-19*. **2** foolish or idle talk *la16*. [reduplicative form of TRATTLE; perhaps with influence from TRINKUM, TRANTLE]

triumph¹·¹, †**triumphe**, †**tryumphe**, †**trevmphe** /ˈtraeəmf/ *n* **1** a victory; joy relating to a victory or success *la15-*. **2** pomp, magnificence *16-e17*. **3** a public festivity or celebration; a spectacle or pageant *16*. **triumphal**, †**triumphall 1** relating to a victory or the victor; betokening or celebrating victory *la15-*. **2** triumphant, victorious *16*. **triumphant**, †**triumphand 1** victorious; relating to a victory *16-*. **2** splendid, magnificent *la15-16*. †**triumphous** betokening or celebrating victory *e16*. [ME *triumphe*, OFr *triumphe*, Lat *triumphus*]

triumph¹·², †**trivmph**, †**tryumph** /ˈtraeəmf/ *v* **1** to be victorious, prevail *la15-*. **2** to rejoice, exult (over a victory) *la15*. **3** to excel, be pre-eminent *16*. [OFr *triumpher*, Lat *triumphāre*]

trive, **triven** *see* THRIVE¹·²

trivice *see* TRAVISE

trivmph *see* TRIUMPH¹·²

trivvle, **trivvel** /ˈtrɪvəl/ *v* to grope, fumble in the dark *19- Sh Ork*. [Norw dial *trivla*]

troak, **truck** /trok, trʌk/ *v* to tramp or trudge, walk aimlessly *la19- Sh N*. [perhaps extended sense of TROKE¹·² or TRUCK²]

troce *see* TROYES

troch, **trough**, **trow**, **trouch**, †**trowch**, †**throcht** /trɔx, trʌu, trʌux/ *n* **1** a container or vessel for holding liquid; a vat for some specified purpose *la14-*. **2** a channel or conduit for water; the channel conducting water to a mill-wheel *la15-*. **3** the channel or (rocky or stony) bed of a river; a channel among sea rocks *16-*. **4** a narrow passage between houses *19-*. **5** *derogatory* a person who eats or drinks to excess *19-*. **6** a communal dish used by a family at meals *la19- Sh*. **7** a river valley or basin *la17-e19*. **trochie** a narrow passage between houses *19- NE*. **trows** a flat-bottomed river barge built in two sections with a space through which salmon can be speared *19- Bor*. **trowmill** a watermill, frequently in place-names *19- Bor*. **troch stane** a trough hollowed out from a single piece of stone *la16-19, 20- C Bor*. [OE *trog*]

troch *see* TROKE¹·²

trock *see* TROKE¹·¹, TROKE¹·²

trocker *see* TROKER

trod *see* TREAD¹·²

troddle /ˈtrɔdəl/ *v* to walk with short, quick steps, toddle, trot *19, 20- NE*. [conflation of TODDLE¹·² with TROT¹·²]

troddle *see* TROTTLE

trode *see* TREAD¹·²

trodge /trɔdʒ/ v to walk laboriously or wearily; to travel on foot *18-*. [variant of Eng *trudge*]
trodwoddie see TRAGWIDDIE
trog see TROKE[1,2]
trogger see TROKER
trogs, trugs /trɔgz, trʌgz/ *interj* a mild oath or expletive *la18-*. †**by my troggs** by my faith, by my word *la18-e19*. **guid trogs** goodness, good gracious *20-*. [altered form of *troth* (TROWTH)]
†**Troilus verse** *n* rhyme-royal, the stanza form of seven decasyllabic lines *la16*. [as used by Chaucer in his poem *Troilus and Criseyde*]
troint[1.1] /trɔɪnt/ *n* a (pig's) snout; a snout-shaped peak or projection *20- Sh.* **trointie** a pointed, snout-shaped object, a spout *la19- Sh.* [compare Norw dial *trunt* a snout]
troint[1.2] /trɔɪnt/ *v of a pig* to grunt *la19- Sh.* [see the noun]
trois see TROYES
troitska /ˈtrɔɪtska/ *n* a bad mood, a huff *la19- Sh.* [compare ON *þrjózka* obstinacy]
troke[1.1], **truck, trock** /trok, trɔk/ *n* **1** barter, exchange; a bargain or business deal *la16-*. **2** dealings, association; intimacy (sometimes implying improper familiarity) *la18-*. **3** worthless or rubbishy goods; insubstantial trash *19-*. **4** *pl* small articles of merchandise, odds and ends, trinkets *18-19, 20- N NE T EC*. **5** a small piece of work or business, a task, errand *19- Sh NE T EC*. **6** nonsensical talk, rubbish *20- Sh N*. **7** *of persons or animals* worthless specimens, riff-raff *19*. **trockerie, trock'ry** miscellaneous merchandise, odds and ends *la19, 20- Sh NE T*. [MFr *troc*]
troke[1.2], **truck, trock, troch**, *SW Uls* **trog**, †**truk** /trok, trʌk, trɔk, trɔx; *SW Uls* trog/ *v* **1** to bargain or barter; to trade, deal in a small way (with) *16-*. **2** to associate with; to have nefarious or illicit dealings with; to be on friendly or intimate terms with *18-*. **3** to potter or bustle about, occupy oneself with trivial matters *la18-19, 20- NE T H&I C*. **4** to spread or carry about news or gossip *la19, 20- NE*. **troggin** miscellaneous merchandise, odds and ends *la18-*. [MFr *troquer*]
troker, trocker, trogger /ˈtrokər, ˈtrogər/ *n* a bargainer, dealer, petty trader, pedlar *18-*. [TROKE[1.2] with agent suffix]
troll /trol/ *n* an untidy, slovenly person *la19- NE Bor*. [Eng *troll* a trull, prostitute, from OFr *troller* to quest for game]
troll see TROW[1]
trollie-bags /ˈtrolibagz/ *n* **1** the intestines or entrails *19-*. **2** *derogatory* a fat, unshapely person *20-*. [altered form of Eng *trillibubs*]
trollop[1.1], **trallop**, *NE* **treelip** /ˈtrɔləp, ˈtraləp; *NE* ˈtrilɪp/ *n* **1** a disorganized, untidy or slovenly woman *la18-*. **2** a long, trailing piece of cloth, a tatter; a large, ugly, a straggling mass or bundle *19-*. **3** a long, gangling, ungainly person or animal *la19-* **trollopie, trollopy** untidy, hanging loose *20-*. [EModE *trollop*, perhaps related to TROLL]
trollop[1.2] /ˈtrɔləp/ *v* to hang or trail loosely or untidily *la19-*. [see the noun]
trompet see TRUMPET
tron[1.1], †**trone** /tron/ *n* **1** a steelyard, a weighing machine (for public use) in or near a burgh marketplace *15-e19, la19- historical*. **2** the place or building where the weighing machine stood and the area round it; the marketplace, the town centre *16-*. **3** the post of the weighing machine used as a pillory or as a place of public exposure and punishment *15-e19*. †**tronar, troner** the official in charge of the public weighing machine, the keeper of the tron *15-17*. †**stane tron** = *tron stane 19*. **Tron Church** the name of a church standing near the site of the weighing machine *18-*. **Trongate** a street name in Glasgow where the weighing machine formerly stood *16-*. **Tron Kirk** = TRON CHURCH *la17-*. †**Tron lord, Trone lord 1** an Edinburgh chimney sweep *18-e19*. **2** *in Edinburgh* a porter, labourer or odd-job man (who probably stood for hire at the Tron) *17-e19*. †**tron man 1** an Edinburgh chimney sweep *17-e19, la19- historical*. **2** a porter or odd-job man *18*. **3** the keeper or operator of the weighing machine *16*. **tron pound** one pound measured by *tron weight*, varying from 21 to 28 ounces avoirdupois *la17-19, 20- historical*. **tron stane, tron stone** one stone measured by *tron weight*, a weight for weighing one stone *la16-19, 20- historical*. **tron weight**, †**tron wecht** the standard weight for home-produced commodities *15-e19, la19- historical*; compare TROYES. [OFr *trone*]
†**tron**[1.2], †**trone** *v* to weigh on a (public) weighing machine *la15-e19*. **trone on the treis** to hang on the gallows *16*. [see the noun]
trone see THRONE, TROON[1.1], TROON[1.2], TRUAN
tronie /ˈtrone/ *n* a long story; rambling conversation *19- T*. [perhaps altered form of *rone* (RANE[1])]
Tronis see THRONE
troo /tru/ *interj* a call to cows or calves *la19-*. [compare PROO]
troo see TREW, TROON[1.1]
trooker, †**trucker**, †**truiker**, †**trewker** /*Sh* ˈtrukər/ *n* **1** a disreputable person; a cheat; a rogue *la15-*. **2** a mischievous child or animal *20- Sh*. [ME *truken, troken* to deceive, OE *trucian* to fail + agent suffix]
troon[1.1], **trone, truan, truant**, *NE* **troo**, †**trowan** /trun, tron, ˈtruən, ˈtruənt; *NE* tru/ *n* a truant (from school) *16-*. **play the troon** = TROON[1.2] *19-*. [OFr *truant, truan*]
troon[1.2], **trone** /trun, tron/ *v* to play truant *20-*. **troon the schule** *19-* = TROON[1.2]. [see the noun]
troon[1.3], †**trowan** /ˈtruən/ *adj* **1** perverse, stubborn, lazy *20- Sh Ork*. **2** trivial *16*. **3** feigned *17*. [see the noun]
troop, †**trowp**, †**troup**, †**trip** /trup/ *n* **1** a company (of fighting men); soldiers *la16-*. **2** a band or company (of people) *la16-*. **3** a herd or flock *la15-16*. **trooper** a soldier in a troop of cavalry *17-*; compare *moss trooper* (MOSS[1.1]). †**trooping horse** cavalry mounts *17*. **in triphirsill** the separate pasturing of the animals belonging to an individual *17*. [MFr *troupe*]
troosers /ˈtruzərz/ *npl* trousers *la19-*. [conflation of TREWS with Eng *trousers*]
troosh[1.1] /truʃ/ *v* to drive, cause to move *20- WC*. [see the interj]
troosh[1.2] /truʃ/ *interj* a command to an animal, especially a dog, to move away *la19- H&I*. [Gael *truis*]
trooshlach[1.1] /ˈtruʃləx/ *n* trash, worthless things; a contemptuous term for a person *19- NE T H&I SW*. [probably an altered form of Gael *trusdaireachd* filthiness; compare TROOSHTER]
trooshlach[1.2] /ˈtruʃləx/ *adj of persons* dirty, slovenly *20- NE*. [see the noun]
trooshter /ˈtruʃtər/ *n* **1** useless rubbish *la19- NE*. **2** troublesome children *20- N NE*. [variant of TRUSDAR or shortened form of Gael *trusdaireachd* filthiness; compare TROOSHLACH[1.1]]
troot, trout, †**trowt** /trut, trʌut/ *n* a trout, usually the brown trout *Salmo trutta la14-*. **trootie** a term of endearment to a child *la19- NE T SW*. **trooter** a trout-fisher *18-*. **trooting** trout-fishing *17-*. **there's a troot in the well, there's a trootie in the well** said of a woman expecting a child, especially if illegitimate *la19, 20- NE*. [OFr *troute*]
trophy, †**trophe**, †**trophee** /ˈtrofe/ *n* **1** a memorial, originally to victory in battle *16-*. **2** anything won in battle or taken in hunting *16-*. **3** a token or symbol of victory *16-*. †**tropheall** pertaining to a victory memorial *e16*. [MFr *trophee*, Lat *trophaeum*]

trosk /trɔsk/ *n* a stupid or silly person or animal *20- N.* [Gael *trosg* a cod fish; a silly person]

tross *see* TURSE[1.1]

trot[1] /trɔt/ *n* trot, the gait between walking and running *la15-.* [MFr *trot*]

trot[2] /trɔt/ *v of a quadruped* to move at the pace between a walk and canter, jog, move briskly *16-.* **trottin** *of a stream* babbling *18-19.* **trottle 1** = TODDLE (sense 2) *19-.* **2** dawdle, idle *20- SW.* †**trottand horse** = *trotting naig la15.* †**trotting naig** a horse with an aptitude for trotting *la16-18.* [MFr *troter*]

trot *see* THROAT

†**trotcosy** *n* a hood, usually as part of a cloak or other warm outer garment *la18-19.* [probably THROAT + COSIE]

troth *see* TROWTH, TRUITH

trøttin /ˈtrɒtɪn/ *adj* sulky *20- Sh.* [participial adj from Norw *tryta* to pout, sulk]

trottle, troddle /ˈtrɔtəl, ˈtrɔdəl/ *n pl* small round pellets of excrement *la19-.* **trottlick** = TROTTLE. [EModE *trottle*, perhaps from OE *tyrdelu* pl, droppings]

tröttle, trütel /ˈtrøtəl/ *v* to grumble, mutter; gossip *la19- Sh.* [frequentative form of Norw *tryta* to pout, sulk, mutter]

trou *see* THROU[1.2], THROU[1.3]

troublance *see* TRUBLANCE

trouble[1.1]**, tribble,** †**trubill** /ˈtrʌbəl, ˈtrɪbəl/ *n* **1** public disorder *15-.* **2** care, labour, effort, pains; inconvenience *15-.* **3** adversity, hardship; affliction, distress; difficulties *la15-.* **4** a conflict *16-.* **5** sickness, disease; an ailment *18-.* **6** *mining* a break or intrusion in strata; a fault *la17- C.* **7** harm, injury *la15-16.* **8** *of natural phenomena* turbulence, commotion *la15-e16.* **9** *law* an oppressive legal action *16-e17.* **10** controversy, dissension *16-e17.* †**trubly** *weather* stormy *e16.* **the troubles, the Troubles** political and military strife, civil unrest *17-.* [ME *trouble*, AN *truble*, OFr *trouble*]

trouble[1.2]**,** †**trubill,** †**truble,** †**tribule** /ˈtrʌbəl/ *v* **1** to disturb, hinder, interrupt, harass, pester *15-.* **2** to agitate, make (air or water) turbid or cloudy *15-16.* **3** to harm; to injure; to oppress *la14-e18.* **troublit** afflicted *la15-.* [ME *troublen*, AN *trubler*, OFr *troubler*]

trouch *see* TROCH

trough *see* TROCH

trounce[1] /trʌuns/ *v* **1** to defeat heavily *18-.* **2** to beat down, smash *la19- SW.* [EModE *trounce* to thrash, defeat]

†**trounce**[2] *v* to rush off or along briskly *e19.* [perhaps a variant of ME *trauncen* to move about, prance]

trounsour *see* TRUNCHER

troup *see* TROOP

troush /truʃ/ *interj* a call to cattle *19- NE T.* [compare PROOCHIE, TROO]

trouss *see* TURSE[1.1], TURSE[1.2]

trout *see* TROOT

trow[1]**,** †**troll** /trʌu/ *n* **1** a mythical being usually associated with Orkney and Shetland *17-.* **2** *disparaging* an unlucky, feeble or stupid person or animal *la19- Sh Ork.* **3** the Devil *19- Sh Ork.* **trowie** = TROW[1] *la19- Sh Ork.* †**trowing** a baby *e19 Sh.* **trulshket, trullyet** untidy, slovenly *la19- Sh.* **trowie buckie** a snail-shell *la19 Sh.* †**trowbund** bewitched by trows TROW[1] (sense 1) *la19 Ork.* **trowie cairds** fern fronds *20- Sh.* **trowie flaachts** summer lightning, wildfire *20- Sh.* **trowie girse** the foxglove *Digitalis purpurea 20- Ork.* **trowie glove** = *trowie girse 20- Sh Ork.* †**trowis glove** a sea-sponge *17-18 Sh Ork.* **trows kairds** = *trowie cairds 20- Sh.* **trowie tune** fiddle music *la20-.* **trow tak me, trow tak ye** *imprecation* may the Devil take me, you TROW[1] (sense 3) *19- Sh Ork.* [ON *troll* a giant, fiend]

trow[2]**, trowl** /trʌu, trʌul/ *v* **1** to roll, descend by rolling, spin round *la18-.* **2** to cause to roll, spin, turn round *19-.* **3** to walk with a rolling or waddling gait *19- Bor.* [ME *trollen*, Ger *trollen*]

trow *see* TREW, TROCH, TRUE

trowan *see* TROON[1.1], TROON[1.3]

trowch *see* TROCH

trowen *see* TRUAN

trowie /ˈtrʌui/ *adj* **1** sickly, ailing, unhealthy; supernaturally afflicted *19- Sh Ork N.* **2** of or pertaining to mythical beings; supernatural *19- Sh.* **3** superstitious *20- Sh.* [TROW[1] + -IE[2]]

trowl *see* TROW[2]

trowne *see* THRONE

trowp *see* TROOP

trowse *see* TREWS

trowt *see* TROOT

trowth, troth, truth, *Sh* **traath,** †**trewth** /trʌuθ, troθ, truθ; *Sh* traθ/ *interj* indeed, upon my word *18-.* **God's truth** = TROWTH *19-.* **guid trowth** = TROWTH *la18-19.* **in trowth, of trowth, on trowth** in fact, to be sure *la15-.* [from the noun TRUITH]

trowth *see* TRUITH

troyes, trois, †**troce** /trɔɪz/ *n* of or pertaining to a standard system of bullion or merchant weights *15-18, 19- historical.* [probably from the French town of Troyes]

troyn *see* THRONE

truaghan /ˈtruəxən/ *n* a poor, destitute person, a down-and-out; also *humorous* a small child *20- N.* [Gael *truaghan* a wretched creature]

truan, trone, †**trowen** /ˈtruən/ *n* a trowel *19-.* [altered form of TRUEL]

truan, truant *see* TROON[1.1]

trubill *see* TROUBLE[1.1], TROUBLE[1.2]

†**trublance, troublance, trubulance** *n* **1** harassment, interference; *law* (the crime of) disorderly or violent behaviour, breach of the peace *la15-e16.* **2** distress, suffering *16-19.* [OFr *trublance*]

truble *see* TROUBLE[1.2]

trubulance *see* TRUBLANCE

truce, †**trewis,** †**trew** /trus/ *n* a (period of) suspension of hostilities *la14-.* [OE *trēow* fidelity to a promise;, plural reinterpreted as singular]

truck[1] /trʌk/ *n* turf from hill ground used to improve arable land *19- Sh.* [unknown; perhaps an extended sense of truck (TROKE[1.1])]

truck[2]**, trukk** /trʌk/ *v* to trample, tread down *la19- Sh.* [Norw dial *trokka*]

truck *see* TROKE[1.1], TROKE[1.2], TROAK

trucker *see* TROOKER

trudder /ˈtrʌdər/ *n* rubbish, trash *19- NE.* [variant of *tudder* (TOUTHER[1.1]), perhaps with influence from TRASH[1]]

true, †**trew,** †**trow** /tru/ *adj* **1** faithful, loyal; real, genuine *la14-.* **2** honest; factually correct; accurate, precise *15-.* **3** conforming to a standard *17-.* **truelins** truly, indeed *la18-.* **true blue** (of) a 17th-century COVENANTER (from their chosen colour, the blue of the St Andrew's flag); (of) any staunch or devoted Presbyterian; (of) a supporter of the Whigs of the 17th and 18th centuries *18, 19- historical.* [OE *trēowe*]

true *see* TREW

truel /ˈtruəl/ *n* a trowel *19- Ork N T.* [OFr *truele*]

truen /ˈtruən/ *n* a wooden bait box *20- Sh.* [Norw dial *tron* a hollowed out block of wood]

trues *see* TREWS

†**truff**[1.1] *n* a trick *e16.* [MFr *truffe*]

†**truff**[1.2] *v* to steal, pilfer *18*. **truffer, truffur** a cheat, thief *16-18*. **trufinge** trickery, deceit *la14*. [MFr *truffer* to trick, deceive]
truff *see* TURF[1.1]
trufinge *see* TRUFF[1.2]
truggel /ˈtrʌɡəl/ *n farming, fishing* a small wooden trough *la19- Sh*. [diminutive form of Norw dial *trog* a trough]
trugs *see* TROGS
truiker *see* TROOKER
truith, truth, trowth, troth, throwth, trith, treuth, *Sh Ork* **trath** /truθ, trʌuθ, troθ, θrʌuθ, trɪθ; *Sh Ork* traθ/ *n* **1** one's pledged word, an oath of allegiance *la14-*. **2** *in abstract or spiritual senses* what is true as distinct from illusory or false; faith, belief; specifically a religious faith *la14-*. **3** that which is true or which actually occurred; (a) fact *la15-*. **4** loyalty, faithfulness *la14-17*. **5** honesty, integrity *15-e17*. Compare TROWTH. †**treuthles 1** lying *16*. **2** faithless *16*. [OE *trēowð*]
truk *see* TROKE[1.2]
trukk *see* TRUCK[2]
†**trulis** *npl* a game, perhaps played with balls or bowls *e16*. [unknown; perhaps ME *trollen, trullen* to roll; compare TROW[2]]
trulls /trʌlz/ *npl* testicles *20- Ork*. [compare Norw *droll* a little knob]
trullyet, trulshket *see* TROW[1]
†**trum** *n* a drum *16*. [MDu *tromme*, LG *trumme*]
trum *see* TRIM[1.2]
trump[1.1] /trʌmp/ *n* **1** a trumpet *la14-*. **2** a Jew's harp *16-*. [AN *trumpe*]
†**trump**[1.2] *v* **1** to assemble or raise an army by blowing a trumpet *la14-e16*. **2** to proclaim with a trumpet *la15-e16*. **3** to play on a Jew's harp *la19*. [AN *trumper*]
†**trump**[2], *EC* **trumph** *n* a thing of small value, a trifle; rubbish *16-19*. [perhaps back-formation from *trumperie* (TRUMPHERY)]
†**trump**[3] *v* to deceive, trick *la14-16*. **trumpour** a deceiver, cheat *la15-e17*. [OFr *tromper*]
trump[4] /trʌmp/ *v of a horse* to stamp, kick restively *19- Sh*. [Dan *trumpe* to stamp the foot]
trumperie *see* TRUMPHERY
trumpet, †**trumpat,** †**trompet** /ˈtrʌmpət/ *n* **1** a trumpet, originally used to herald an event or proclamation *la14-*. **2** a person who or thing that proclaims (something) *16-*. **3** a trumpeter *la15-17*, also as a surname *15*. Compare *draucht trumpet* (DRAUCHT[1.1]). **trumpetour, trumpeter** a trumpeter *la15-*. [MFr *trompette*]
trumph /trʌmf/ *n* trump, the chief suit in a card game; a splendid person or thing *19-*. **what's trumph?** what's doing?, how are things?; what's to be done next? *la20- Sh NE T*. [variant of Eng *trump*, itself an altered form of *triumph*]
trumph *see* TRUMP[2]
trumphery, trumperie, †**trumpry** /ˈtrʌmfəre, ˈtrʌmpəre/ **1** nonsense, rubbish *la15-*. **2** trash, rubbish *la18-19, 20- Sh Ork NE T*. **3** deceit, trickery *la15-16*. [MFr *tromperie*]
trums[1.1] /trʌms/ *n* sulkiness *20- Sh*. **trumset, trumsket, trumpset, trumpsket, troinsket, troinshket, trønsket** sulky *la19- Sh*. [see the verb]
trums[1.2] /trøms/ *v* to sulk *la19- Sh*. [Faer *trumsa* to be in a bad humour]
†**truncheman, trenchman, trinchman** *n* an interpreter or translator *la16-17*. [altered form of MFr *trucheman*, Lat *turchemannus*, Arabic *turjamān*]
truncher, trincher, †**trunscheour,** †**trynschour,** †**trounsour** /ˈtrʌnʃər, ˈtrɪnʃər/ *n* **1** a large flat dish, a (wooden or metal) platter *16-19, 20- Sh NE WC*. **2** a flat cake of bread used as a platter *e16*. **3** a spearhead *la16*. [ME *trenchour*, AN *trenchour*, OFr *trencheor*]
trunch-gilt /ˈtrʌnʃɡɪlt/ *n* a group of guests at a table who share the same dish *20- Ork*. [shortened form of TRUNCHER + GUILD]
trundill *see* TRINNLE[1.1]
trunie /ˈtrøni/ *n* **1** a pig's snout *19- Sh*. **2** *of a person* a pouting grimace *la19- Sh*. **swap a trunie** to exchange a kiss *la19- Sh*. [Norw dial *tryne* a snout]
trunnel *see* TRINNLE[1.1]
trunscheour *see* TRUNCHER
truntle *see* TRINNLE[1.2]
trusdar /ˈtrusdər, ˈtrusṭər/ *n* an untrustworthy person, a rogue *19- N H&I*. [Gael *trusdar* a lecher]
trushel[1.1] /ˈtrʌʃəl/ *n* a muddle, confusion; a slovenly or ungainly person *20- N*. [unknown]
trushel[1.2] /ˈtrʌʃəl/ *v* to walk in a shuffling, ungainly manner *20- N*. [unknown]
truss[1.1] /trʌs/ *n* rubbish, trash; scraps *la19- Sh*. [Norw dial *tros* woody refuse, Icel *tros* rubbish]
truss[1.2] /trʌs/ *v* to work in a slapdash way *la19- Sh*. **trusset** untidy, slovenly *20- Sh*. [Norw dial *trosa* to break in bits]
trussie belt /ˈtrʌsɪ bɛlt/ *n* seaweed, probably a variety of *Laminaria 20- Sh*. [altered form of TIRSIPEL]
trussie-laverick /ˈtrʌsɪˈlavərək/ *n* the corn bunting *Emberiza calandra 20- Sh*. [unknown first element + LAVEROCK]
trust *see* TRAIST[1.1], TRAIST[1.2]
trütel *see* TRÖTTLE
truth *see* TROWTH, TRUITH
trwoo /trwu/ *interj* a call to cows or calves *19- NE EC*. [variant of TROO]
try, *T* **treh** /trae, trɛ/ *v* **1** to attempt *16-*. **2** *law* to examine judicially; to submit to a legal process *16-*. **3** to discover, investigate *la16-17*. **4** to test (truth, quality) *la16-17*. **5** to interrogate *la16-17*. **6** to prove *la16-e17*. †**tryit 1** having been tested as satisfactory; excellent; trustworthy *la15-e17*. **2** proven to be bad, infamous *16-e17*. [ME *trien*; OFr *trier* to separate out]
tryacle *see* TRAICLE
tryall *see* TRIAL
trye *see* TRAWE
tryell *see* TRIAL
tryg *see* TRIG[1.2]
trygget *see* TRIGIT
tryist *see* TRYST[1.1]
trykle *see* TRAICLE
trymmill *see* TREMMLE
trynch *see* TRENCH[1.2]
tryne *see* TRAIN[1], TRAIN[2]
tryngle *see* TRINKLE[1.2]
trynsch *see* TRENCH[1.2]
trynschour *see* TRUNCHER
tryp *see* TRIPE[2]
trype *see* TRIPE[1], TRIPE[2]
tryst[1.1], †**trist,** †**tryist,** †**trayst** /trʌɪst/ *n* **1** an agreement, covenant, mutual pledge *la14-*. **2** an appointment to meet at a specified time and place; an assignation *la14-*. **3** an appointed meeting or assembly, a rendezvous *16-*. **4** an appointed meeting-place *la14-19, 20- NE T EC*. **5** a conspicuous object chosen as a rendezvous; frequently in place-names *19-*. **6** a market, established by agreement between buyers and sellers rather than public authority or the crown, for the sale of livestock *la16-19, 20- historical*. **7** a fair, originally a TRYST[1.1] (sense 6) *18-19, 20- N NE T*. **8** trouble, bother, difficulty *la19- Sh Ork*. **bide (yer) tryst** to wait for someone

at a pre-arranged meeting-place *19, 20- Uls.* [OFr *triste* an appointed place of ambush in hunting, Lat *trista*]

tryst[1.2], †**trist**, †**treist** /trʌɪst/ *v* **1** to make an appointment or assignation, fix a time and place of meeting *15-*. **2** to order (goods); to arrange for the hire of (services); to have (clothes) made to measure *la16-*. **3** to meet (with) by pre-arrangement *la17-, 20- NE T EC*. **4** to betroth, form an engagement to be married *19, 20- NE C Uls*. **5** to invite, encourage, entice, make a fuss of, coax, wheedle *19, 20- N NE Bor*. **6** to fix (a time or place) for a meeting to perform a service *16-19, 20- NE T*. **7** to ordain, arrange for (something); to afflict or favour (with bad or good fortune) *17-19*. **8** to coincide (in time) (with); to arrange for (things) to coincide (in time) *17*. **9** to negotiate, have dealings (with) *16-17*. †**trystar** a mediator, go-between, matchmaker *17*. [see the noun]

tryst *see* TRIST

trysting /'trʌɪstɪŋ/ *n* **1** an assignation *la16-*. **2** (a meeting arranged for the purpose of) negotiation, arbitration *la16-17*. **3** the action of arranging (something) *la16-17*. **trysting place** a meeting-place *17-*. **trysting tree** a tree used as a meeting-place *la18-*. [verbal noun from TRYST[1.2]]

trytle *see* TREETLE
tryumph *see* TRIUMPH[1.2]
tryumphe *see* TRIUMPH[1.1]
tsill *see* CHILD
tu *see* TAE[3.2]
tua *see* TWA

tub, †**toub** /tʌb/ *n* **1** an open, flat-bottomed container *la15-*. **2** a TUB used as a measure *16-18 Ork NE*. **3** *mining* a HUTCH[1.1] for carrying cut coal; a measure of coal (varying in weight) *19- C Uls*. [ME *tubbe*, MDu, MLG *tubbe*]

tuch *see* TEUCH[1.1]
tuchet *see* TEUCHIT

tuchin /'tjuxən, 'tuxən/ *n* a husky cough, hoarseness *20- N NE*. [Gael *tùchan*]

tuck, tewk /tʌk, tjuk/ *interj* a call to hens to come for food *19-*. **tuckie** *child's word* a hen or chicken *19-*. **tuckie hen** = *tuckie 20- T*. [onomatopoeic of a hen's cluck; compare TICK[4]]

tuck *see* TOUK[1.2], TOUK[3.2]

tuckie /'tʌke/ *adj* **1** awkward, clumsy *20- NE*. **2** *of a limb* disabled, deformed *20- NE*. [perhaps *tuck* (TOUK[1.2]) + -IE[2]]

tuckle, †**tichle** /'tʌkəl/ *n* frequently *contemptuous* a line or file (of people or animals) *19- Bor*. [unknown]

tuckshon /'tʌkʃən/ *n* a rough handling, a knocking about *20- Ork*. [unknown]

tud *see* THUD[1.1], THUD[1.2]
tüd *see* TUID

tuddick /'tʌdək/ *n humorous* a child or small person *la19- Sh*. [unknown]

tuder *see* TITHER[1.2]

tudset /'tʌdsət/ *v* to drive an animal into a location from which it cannot escape; to corner *la19- Sh*. [unknown]

tuedlit *see* TWEEDLE[1.2]
tueidill *see* TWEEDLE[1.1]
tueill *see* TWEEL[1.1]
tuelf *see* TWAL
tuelft *see* TWALT
tuentie *see* TWENTY[1.1]
tuentieth *see* TWENTIETH
tuenty *see* TWENTY[1.2]
tu-fa *see* TAE FA

†**tuffing** *n* caulking material; oakum *e16*. [derivative of OFr *tuffe* a bunch, tuft]

tuffle *see* TAFFLE

tug[1.1], **chug, teug** /tʌg, tʃug, tjʌg/ *n* **1** a jerk, a pull *16-*. **2** a tug-boat, a towing vessel *19-*. **3** a tangle in the hair *20-*. **4** a pull or draught of liquor *la19- Ork*. **5** a strip of skin pulled off the hide of a slaughtered animal and, frequently, used as harness straps or traces *la17-19*. **6** a strap or rope used in pulling a load; part of a draught animal's harness *16-18*.

teugie a moment, instant *20- N*. **tuggy** *of the hair* full of tangles *20-*. [see the noun]

tug[1.2], **chug** /tʌg, tʃug/ *v* **1** to jerk, pull *15-*. **2** to pull a strip off (the hide of a slaughtered animal) *17-18*. †**tug-net** *fishing* a net pulled behind a boat at the mouth of a river *15-e19*. [ME *tuggen*, probably from OE *tugon*, preterite plural of *tēon*]

tuggill *see* TUGGLE[1.2]

tuggimø /'tʌgɪmø/ *n* a mist, a thick haze *20- Sh*. [Norw dial *toka* fog + Norw dial *mo* a haze]

tuggle[1.1], *NE* **tyuggle,** *SW* **chugle** /'tʌgəl; *NE* 'tjʌgəl; *SW* 'tʃʌgəl/ *n* a struggle *20- Sh N NE SW*. [see the verb]

tuggle[1.2], **tyuggle,** *SW* **chuggle,** †**tuggill** /'tʌgəl, 'tjʌgəl, 'tʃʌgəl/ *v* to wrestle, pull (about) roughly and jerkily *la15-19, 20- Sh N SW*. [ME *tuggelen*, frequentative form of TUG[1.2]]

tugs /tʌgz/ *npl* clothes *19*. **tuggery** *Travellers' language* clothes; fine clothes *20-*. [variant of Eng *togs*]

tuich *see* TOUCH[1.2]
tuiche *see* TOUCH[1.1]

tuid, tüd /tød/ *v* to rant, carp *la19- Sh*. [Norw dial *tjota, tyta* to howl, roar]

tuik *see* TAK[1.2], TOUK[3.2]

tuil, tool, *NE* **teel,** *Sh Ork SW* **tewel,** †**towl,** †**toul,** †**toyle** /tul; *NE* til; *Sh Ork* 'tjuəl; *SW* also tjul/ *n* **1** an implement, piece of equipment *la16-*. **2** the blade of a knife *la17*. **3** a weapon *e19-*. **4** *contemptuous* a person *19-*. **5** a penis *20-*. **6** *fisherman's taboo* a boat *e19 Sh*. [ME *tol, toile*, OE *tōl*]

tuill *see* TULYIE[1.1]

tuiltry /'tøltri/ *adj* in tatters *20- Ork*. [Norw *tultre* a rag + -IE[2]]

tuilyie *see* TULYIE[1.1]
tuilʒe *see* TULYIE[1.2]

tuim[1.1], **toom, teem, tim,** †**teme,** †**tume,** †**tome** /tum, tim, tɪm; *Sh Ork* tøm/ *v* **1** to empty a container *la14-*. **2** to pour, empty out (the contents) from a container *la15-*. **3** to discharge (a gun or shot) *16-17, 18- NE T EC*. **4** to drain water from (potatoes) *20- T EC Bor Uls*. **5** to empty, be or become empty *la18-19, 20- Sh N NE T*. **6** *of water* to flow or gush copiously; *of rain* to pour, come down in torrents *19-*. [ON *tœma* giving *teme* etc; with *tuim* etc from the adj]

tuim[1.2], **toom, tume,** *N NE* **teem,** *T EC* **taim,** *C Bor* **tim,** †**tome** /tum; *N NE* tim; *T EC* tem; *C Bor* tɪm; *Sh Ork* tøm/ *adj* **1** empty; void of contents; vacant *15-*. **2** empty of food, fasting, hungry *la15-*. **3** *of a place* unoccupied *la15-*. **4** *of people* thin, lean, lank *19, 20- Sh NE EC*. **5** vain, insubstantial, futile *15-19, 20- Sh*. **6** empty-headed, foolish *la16-19, 20- Sh*. **7** *of a machine* idling, not processing material *20- NE T EC Bor*. **8** hollow-sounding, echoing *20- NE C*. **tume-brained** empty-headed, foolish *la18-19, 20- Sh EC*. **tume-handit, toom-handit** empty-handed, bearing no gifts *18-19, 20- Sh NE C*. **tume-heid** an empty-headed, foolish person *la19, 20- Sh C*. **tume-heidit** = *tume-brained 17-*. **gang on like a tume mill** to chatter on without pause *20- T*. [OE *tōm*, ON *tómr*]

tuink /tøŋk/ *n* a thump, crack, blow *20- Ork*. [Norw dial *dunk*]

tuip *see* TUP[1.2]
tuir *see* TEAR[2.2]
tuird *see* TURD
tuist *see* TWIST[1.2]

tuith, tooth, *N NE T Bor* **teeth,** †**tutht** /tuθ; *N NE T Bor* tiθ/ *n pl* **teeth** †**teth,** †**tetht,** †**teith 1** an enamel-coated structure in the jaw of a person or animal *la14-*. **2** the tooth of an implement or mechanism *la16-*. **3** a fragment of rainbow seen near the horizon, regarded as a sign of bad weather

20- *NE*. **4** *figurative* the mouth, face or person *15-17*. **tuithfu** a mouthful, especially of liquor *la18*-. **tuithy 1** sharp-toothed; ravenous, hungry *19*. **2** sharp in manner; critical, acrimonious *la18*-. **teethache, tuith aik** toothache *la16*-. **tuith tuil** *masonry* a serrated chisel or punch used for dressing stones *la20*- *EC Bor*. [OE *tōð*]

tuix *see* TWIXT
tuke *see* TAK[1.2]
tukkeri *see* TICKERIE
tulat *see* TOLLET

tulbert scatt, tillberdskatt /'tʌlbərt 'skat, 'tɪlbərdskat/ *n* grazing rent *la18*- *Sh Ork*. [unknown first element; perhaps an altered form of Icel *tilbót* extra + SKATT[1.1]]

tulchan /'tʌlxən/ *n* **1** a substitute, a person appointed nominally to an office, the power and emoluments being diverted to another; originally one of the bishops created by Regent Morton in 1572 to enable him and his supporters to appropriate Church revenues *la16-19, 20- historical*. **2** a large or fat person *19*- *NE T*. **3** a calfskin, usually that of a cow's own dead calf, stuffed with straw and put beside the cow to induce her to give milk freely or wrapped round another calf to encourage the cow to foster it *la16-19*. **4** used as a term of endearment *e16*. [Gael *tulchan* a dummy calfskin]

tulfar *see* TILFER
tull *see* TILL[2.2]

tullie /'tʌli/ *n* a large knife; a clasp-knife; a sheath-knife *19*- *Sh*. [reduced form of Norw dial *tolekniv*]

tulliment /'tʌlɪmənt/ *v of stars* to sparkle, dance *20*- *Ork*. [unknown]

tullitan /'tʌlətən/ *n* = TULLIE *20 Ork*. [nonce variant of TULLIE]

tulloch, †tulloiche /'tʌləx/ *n* a mound, hillock; frequently a fairy mound; frequently in place-names *13-19, 20- N T*. [Gael *tulach* a small hill]

tully *see* TULYIE[1.1]

tulshoch /'tʌlʃəx/ *n* **1** a small bundle or heap *19*- *NE*. **2** *contemptuous* a person *19*- *NE*. [altered form of *dulshoch* (DULSHET)]

Tulya's day *see* TOLYIG'S DAY

tulyie[1.1], **tulzie, tully, toillie,** *Ork* **teulie, †tulʒe, †tuilyie, †tuill** /'tule; *Sh Ork* 'tøle, 'tølje/ *n* **1** a quarrel, brawl, fight; fighting, disturbance of the peace *la14*-. **2** a verbal quarrel, wrangle, argument *18*-. **3** trouble, turmoil; toil, exertion *15-19, 20- Sh*. **tuilyiement** = TULYIE[1] (sense 3) *la19*-. **†tulyiemulie** a quarrel, brawl, turmoil *19*. [AN *toylle* a battle, a quarrel]

tulyie[1.2], *SW* **tweelzie, †tulʒe, †tuilʒe, †toyle** /'tule; *Sh Ork* 'tøle, 'tølje; *SW* 'twile, 'twilje/ *v* **1** to quarrel verbally, argue, squabble *la16-19, 20- Sh Ork NE SW*. **2** to quarrel, fight *15-19, 20- Sh Ork NE*. **3** mainly **toyle** to work hard, labour, toil *17-19, 20- Sh*. **4** to assault, attack, harass, fight (an opponent) *la14-16*. **†tulyieour** a quarrelsome person, a brawler *15-e17*. [AN *toiller* to dispute, quarrel]

tulʒe *see* TULYIE[1.1], TULYIE[1.2]
tulzie *see* TULYIE[1.1]

tümald /'tumald/ *n* a downpour of rain, a cloudburst *la19*- *Sh*. [derivative of TUIM[1.1]; possibly influenced by Eng *tumult*]

tumbil, tumble *see* TUMMLE

tumbler, †tumlar /'tʌmblər, 'tʌmlər/ *n* **1** *mining* an apparatus for tipping coal hutches or waggons *la19- EC*. **2** a cart with fixed wheels, a tumbrel *16-e19*. [TUMMLE + *-er* instrumental suffix]

†tume, tome *n* unoccupied time, sufficient time or leisure (to do something) *la14-16*. [ON *tóm*; compare TUIM[1.2]]

tume *see* TUIM[1.1], TUIM[1.2]

tumfie, tumphie /'tʌmfi/ *n* a silly or foolish person *la18*-. [unknown; compare TUMSHIE (sense 2)]

tumlar *see* TUMBLER

†tummell, tinnel *n* a funnel used for pouring the wort of ale into casks *la16-e18*. [unknown; compare ME *tinel*, OFr *tinel* a tub, and TUN[2]]

tummle, tumble, †tummyll, †tumbil /'tʌməl, 'tʌmbəl/ *v* **1** to fall suddenly and violently *la14*-. **2** to knock down, demolish; to throw, cast down *la14*-. **3** to roll in water or on the ground *la15*-. **†tumbling cart** a cart with fixed wheels *la16-19*. **tummlin Tam 1** a horse-drawn hay-gatherer which turned right over when depositing its load *20, 21- historical*. **2** a set of scales for weighing heavy copper George III coins *la18-e19*. **†tumbling verse** a kind of irregular anapaestic verse *la16*. **tummle the cat** to somersault *20- Sh NE*. **tummle the wilkie** to somersault *la19*-. [ME *tumblen*, AN *tumbler*, MLG *tummeln*]

tummock, †tammock /'tʌmək/ *n* a small hillock; a tuft or tussock of grass; a molehill *la18- NE C SW Uls*. [Gael *tom* a knoll; a bush, thicket; a tuft + *-ock* diminutive suffix]

tummyll *see* TUMMLE
tump *see* THUMP[1.2]
tumphie *see* TUMFIE

tumphy /'tʌmfi/ *n mining* coaly fireclay *la19- EC*. [unknown]

tumshie /'tʌmʃi, 'tʌmʃe/ *n* **1** a swede *20*-. **2** *derogatory* a silly or foolish person *20*-. **tumshie heid** a foolish person *la20*-; compare *neep heid* (NEEP[1.1]). [perhaps a children's variant of *turmit* (TURNEEP)]

tun[1.1], **ton, †toun** /tʌn/ *n* **1** a barrel or cask, mainly for wine; a tub or vat *la14*-. **2** *measures* (a barrel of a standard size used as) a measure of capacity or weight *15*-. **3** the capacity of a ship *16*-. **4** a casket for human remains *16-e17*. **5** a buoy *la16-17*. **tunnage** a duty on casks of merchandise *15-19, 20- historical*. [OE *tunne*]

†tun[1.2] *v* to put (ale) into barrels *15-17*. [see the noun]
tun *see* TIN[1.1]

†tunag *n* a woollen shawl or plaid worn by Highland women *la18-e19*. [Gael *tonnag*]

tunder, †tundir /'tʌndər/ *n* tinder *la14*-. **tunder-dry** of washing too dry to iron *20- T*. [OE *tynder, tunder*, ON *tundr*]

tune[1.1], **toon,** *NE* **teen,** *C* **tin, †tone** /tjun, tun; *NE* tin; *C* tɪn/ *n* **1** music, a melody *16*-. **2** intonation of speech (associated with a particular dialect) *16*-. **3** vocal expression, attitude expressed in language *la16*-; compare TONE[1]. **4** state, mood, humour, temper *la16*-. **5** birdsong *16-e17*. **in guid tune** in good humour *la16*-. **in ill tune** in bad humour *la16*-. **hae a tune till yersel** to play a tune by oneself *19, 20- Ork NE T*. **tak a tune tae yersel** = *hae a tune till yersel*. [OFr *ton*, Lat *tonus*]

tune[1.2] /tjun/ *v* **1** to tune an instrument *la15*-. **2** to put in proper working order, adjust or repair *19*-. **3** to chastise, discipline; to develop or improve by correction *la16-e17*. **4** to modulate the tone or feeling of a poem *16*. **†tune yer pipes** to start to cry, wail *la17-19*. [see the noun]

tung *see* TONGUE[1.1]

tunie /'tʃuni/ *adj* moody, changeable in temperament *19- Bor*. [TUNE[1.1] + *-IE*[2]]

tunk, tank /tʌŋk, taŋk/ *n games* a sum of money played for *20- C*. [aphetic form of STUNK[2]]

tunkit /'tʌŋkɪt/ *adj* bankrupt, penniless; *in the game of marbles* beaten *20- T*. [TUNK + -IT[3]]

tunnir *see* THUNNER[1.1]

†tunykill *n* **1** *Roman Catholic Church* an ecclesiastical vestment *15-16*. **2** *heraldry* a coat or tabard bearing a coat of arms *la15-16*. [ME *tunicle*, Lat *tunicula*, OFr *tunicle*]

tuo *see* TWA

tup[1.1], **tip,** *N* **toop,** *NE* **teep** /tʌp, tɪp; *N* tup; *NE* tip/ *n* **1** a ram *15*-. **2** *derogatory* a man *19, 20- N*. **tup headed** stupid *19*-.

tup hog a young ram; a male sheep till its first shearing *la17-*. **tup-lamb**, †**toop-lamb** a male lamb *la18-*. †**toop horn spoon** a spoon made from a ram's horn *18*. **tup-yeld** *of a ewe* barren, infertile *19, 20- N C Bor*. [unknown]

tup[1,2], **tuip** /tʌp, tup/ *v of a ram* to copulate *18-*. [unknown]

tuppens see TIPPENCE

tuppeny see TIPPENY[1.1], TIPPENY[1.2]

tuquheit see TEUCHIT

turbot, turbit, †**turbat** /ˈtʌrbət/ *n* a fish, either the turbot *Scophthalmus maximus*, or halibut *Hippoglossus hippoglossus la14-*. †**turbat fluik** a flat fish, the turbot *16-e18*. [ME *turbot*, AN *turbut*, MDu *turbot*]

†**turcas, turkas, turkose** *n* a turquoise, the precious stone *15-17*. [AN *turkeise*, OFr *turquoise* literally, Turkish (stone)]

Turcas see TURK[1.1]

turd, tuird, *NE* **teerd,** *NE* **tyoord,** *C* **taird** /tʌrd, turd; *NE* tird; *NE* tjurd; *C* terd/ *n* **1** a lump of excrement *la16-*. **2** a term of abuse for a person *17-*. [OE *tord*]

turf[1.1], **turr,** *N NE* **truff,** †**tirf** /tʌrf, tʌr; *N NE* trʌf/ *n pl* **turves turfs, truffs,** †**turris,** †**tirvis 1** a piece of peat used as fuel *12-*. **2** a sod used as a building material *12-19, 20- historical*. **3** sods over a grave; the grave itself *la17-19*. **Turf Cutter** the participant in the Riding of the Marches ceremony at Musselburgh, whose duty it is to verify the boundaries of the burgh, marking twelve points by cutting a turf *la17-*. [OE *turf*]

turf[1.2], **turve** /tʌrf, tʌrv/ *v* **1** to remove surface turf *la19- Sh N NE*; compare TIRR[1] (sense 1). **2** to cover with turf *la16-17*. **3** *of the sky* to become covered with small, fleecy clouds *la19- Sh*. **turvin, turfing** the cutting of turf; the right to cut turf; a quantity of turf cut *la15-19, 20- Sh*. **turfy** *of the sky* covered with small, fleecy clouds *la19- Sh*. [see the noun]

Turk[1.1] /tʌrk/ *n* **1** a Turkish person *la14-*. **2** a fierce or aggressive person or animal *16-19*. **3** a kind of cloth *la17*. **Turkish,** †**Turkas,** †**Turcas** pertaining to Turkey *15-*. †**Turk upon Turk** upholstery fabric (of wool and canvas with a thick pile) *18-19*. [MFr *Turc*, Lat *turcus*]

turk[1.2] /tʌrk/ *v* to become enraged *20- NE*. [see the noun]

turk[1.3] /tʌrk/ *adj* fierce, truculent, sullen *la19- NE T WC*. [see the noun]

turkas, turkis /ˈtʌrkəs/ *n* pincers or pliers used by a blacksmith, cobbler or carpenter *la15-17, la19- NE*. [OFr *turcaise* literally, Turkish (nippers)]

turkas see TURCAS

†**Turkey work** *n* Turkish fabric, tapestry or carpeting *16-17*. [from the name of the country + work (WARK[1.1])]

turkis see TURKAS

turkose see TURCAS

turmit see TURNEEP

turn[1.1], †**turne** /tʌrn/ *n* **1** an action, deed or exploit *la14-*. **2** the rotation of a wheel *16-*. **3** a change in direction or circumstances *16-*. **4** a period of action *16-*. **5** a spell or piece of work, a task, chore or duty *16-*. **6** inclination; aptitude *19-*. **7** the action of pulling oneself together: ◊*he took a turn tae hissel*. *20-*. **8** a trick, prank *la18-19, 20- Sh Ork T*. **9** a rebuff, a setback *19, 20- N*. **10** a section or passage of a tune; a refrain *19, 20- Sh*. **11** something done as a favour *20- C*. **12** a stroke of good luck *20- C*. **13** a dispute *la16-17*. **14** a purpose *la16-e17*. **15** an estimation of a crop as a multiple of the seed sown *la16-e17*. †**turngrese, turngree** a spiral stair, a stair revolving round a central axis *la15-e17*; compare TURNPIKE. **aff the turn** *of a door* at rest, still *la19-*. **on the turn 1** *of the day or the year* changing in length of daylight or temperature, especially between winter and spring *19-*. **2** *of food or drink* about to go off *20-*. †**your awin turnis** one's personal affairs or circumstances *la16-e17*. **the turn o the nicht** midnight, the dead of night *la19-*. **the turn o the year** the time of year when the days begin to lengthen *la19-*. [from the verb, also AN *turn* a rotation]

turn[1.2], **tirn,** †**torn,** †**tourn** /tʌrn, tɪrn/ *v* **1** to revolve; to change direction *la14-*. **2** to become, grow: ◊*ye're turnin a big boy la18-*. **3** to turn (cut hay or peats) to dry; to dismantle and rebuild (a small stack of peats or turf) for drying *19-*. **4** to twist or spin a rope from straw *20-*. **5** to change one's religion, especially to become a Roman Catholic *20-*. **6** *of property* to return to the former owner *15-16*. **turner,** †**turnour** a person who turns wood on a lathe, a wood-worker *la14-*. **turn-fittin** stacking piles of peats *19- SW Bor Uls*. †**turn agane** to retreat, flee *la14*. **turn yer hand** to relieve you from financial straits: ◊*it juist turned oor hand la19-*. **turn someone's head** to make someone feel giddy, intoxicate someone *la19-*. **turn ower tae years** to grow old, age *la19- NE T EC*. †**turning of the riddle, turning the riddle** *witchcraft* a method of divination (used for finding lost or stolen objects) *la16-e19*. †**turn one's style** to change to another subject *15-e17*. †**turning the siefe and the sheare** *witchcraft* a method of divination *17-e18*. **turn tae the door** to put out of one's house, eject, expel *20- Sh N NE*. **turn up the wee finger** to tipple, drink alcohol *19-*. **turn the cat** to do a somersault, go head over heels *20- Sh N T*. **turn yer taes** to change direction *20- Sh*. **turn yer thoum** to make an effort *20- NE T SW*. [OE *turnian, tyrnan*]

turne see TURN[1.1]

turneep, turnip, *C Bor Uls* **turmit,** †**turnepe** /ˈtʌrnip, ˈtʌrnɪp; *C Bor Uls* ˈtʌrmɪt/ *n* a turnip, a swede *la17-*. **turnipy** *of milk or butter* tasting as if the cow has been fed on turnips *20- Ork Bor*. **turneep purry** a puree of boiled turnip, butter, salt, pepper and ginger *20-*. [EModE *turnepe*, OE *nǣp* with unknown first element]

turnepyk see TURNPIKE

turner, †**turnour,** †**turnor** /ˈtʌrnər/ *n* a copper coin, originally valued at two Scots pennies, a BODLE *la16-e18, la18- historical*. [altered form of OFr (*denier*) *tournois* a coin struck in Tours]

turning /ˈtʌrnɪŋ/ *n* **1** the action of rotating or changing *la14-*. **2** carving wood on a lathe *la15-*. **3** a section or passage of a tune; a refrain *19- literary*. **turning-loom** a turning lathe *la16-19, 20- Sh*. **turning tree** a wooden stick for stirring *19- Sh NE*. [verbal noun from TURN[1.2]]

turnor, turnour see TURNER

turnpike, †**turnepyk,** †**tournepyke** /ˈtʌrnpʌɪk/ *n* a spiral stair, a stair revolving round a central axis *15-*. †**turnpike foot** the foot of a turnpike staircase *la16-e18*. †**turnepyk heid** the head of a turnpike *16-e17*. **turnpike-stair** a spiral staircase *18-19, 20- historical*. †**turnepyk yet** a gate or door at the foot or top of a turnpike staircase *16-e17*. [TURN[1.2] + PIKE[1.1]]

turr see TIRR[1.2], TURF[1.1]

Turra coo /ˈtʌrə ku/ *n* a cow which was distrained for debt in 1913 because of the refusal of her owner, a farmer near Turriff, to pay his employees' National Insurance contributions (she was later bought by sympathizers and returned to her farm) *20- NE*. [variant of *Turriff* + COO]

Turra neep /ˈtʌrə nip/ *n* a nickname for a native or inhabitant of Turriff *20- NE*. [of *Turriff* + NEEP[1.1]]

Turra tattie /ˈtʌrə ˈtati/ *n* a nickname for a native or inhabitant of Turriff *20- NE*. [variant of *Turriff* + TATTIE]

turret[1], †**turrett,** †**torret** /ˈtʌrət/ *n* **1** a small tower *15-*. **2** an ornamental representation of a turret *16*. **3** a high, turret-shaped head-dress worn by a woman *la15-16*. [AN *turret*, OFr *torete*]

†turret², turet, turat *n* a ring on a dog's collar to which a leash can be attached *12-e18*. [OFr *toret* a ring]

turris *see* TURF¹·¹

turry-wurry *see* TIRRY-MIRRY

turse¹·¹, *SW,* **trouss, †turs, †tross** /tʌrs; *SW* trus/ *n* **1** a bundle or bale (of hay, straw, thatch or sticks) *la15-19, 20- Ork N NE T H&I.* **2** a tuck, fold, or hem in a garment *19- Sh SW Uls.* **3** a big, ungainly woman *20- Sh N.* **4** *on a ship* a rope that hauled back the yard to the mast *16.* **5** a rope for securing a bundle or pack *e16.* [AN *trusse*, OFr *torse, trouse*]

turse¹·², *NE* **trouss, †turs** /tʌrs; *NE* trus/ *v* **1** to pack up, make into a bundle or bale *la14-.* **2** to fasten, adjust or tuck up clothes; to get dressed *la17- N NE T.* **3** to carry a heavy burden laboriously *20- Ork.* **4** to carry away, transport, bring, convey *15-19.* **5** to start off, set to work; to take oneself off *18-19.* **6** to convey a person or animal *la15-e17.* **7** to send packing, drive off *16.* **8** to bind, tie, fasten *16-e17.* **9** *on a ship* to fasten ropes *e16.* **†tursabill** portable *16-17.* [AN *trusser,* OFr *torser, trousser*]

†tursel *n* **1** a bundle *15-16.* **2** a stamp used to imprint the obverse side of a coin or a trademark on cloth *la16-e17.* [OFr *torsel, toursel*]

turve *see* TURF¹·²

turves *see* TURF¹·¹

turvin *see* TURF¹·²

tusche *see* TISHIE

tush, †tusche /tʌʃ/ *interj* an expression of impatience or contempt *la16-19, 20- literary.* [a natural utterance]

tushery /'tʌʃəre/ *n* a conventional style of historical fiction, using many archaisms *la19-.* [coined by R L Stevenson from TUSH]

tushilago¹, dishilago /tʌʃɪ'lego, dɪʃɪ'lago/ *n* coltsfoot *Tussilago farfara 18-.* [Lat *tussilāgo*]

tushilago² /tʌʃɪ'lego/ *n* the butterbur *Petasites japonicus 20-.* [extended sense of TUSHILAGO¹]

tushkar, tuskar, tusker /'tuʃkər, 'tʌʃkar, 'tʌskər/ *n* a peat-cutting spade *la16- Sh Ork N.* [ON *torfskeri*]

tusk¹, *Sh* **tosk,** *Sh* **torsk** /tʌsk; *Sh* tɔsk; *Sh* tɔrsk/ *n* a ling-like fish of the cod family *Brosme brosme la16-19, 20- Sh Ork N.* **tusk fish** = TUSK¹ *17-19, 20- Sh Ork N NE.* [Norw *tosk, torsk,* ON *þoskr, þorskr*]

tusk²·¹ /tʌsk/ *n* **1** *of an animal* a long or canine tooth *la15-.* **2** *pl building* projecting end-stones for bonding with an adjoining wall, toothing *20- NE T EC.* **3** the projecting wing on the blade of a peat-cutting spade *20- NE.* **†tuskit** having prominent canine teeth *e16.* **†tusk stones** *building* projecting end-stones for bonding with an adjoining wall *la18.* [OE *tūsc, tusc-*]

tusk²·² /tʌsk/ *v* **1** to cut peat from above the bank *la19- N NE.* **2** to join two walls by means of projecting stones *la15-16.* **tuskin, tusking** *in building* projecting end-stones for bonding with an adjoining wall, toothing *20- NE T EC.* **†tusking stones** = *tuskin la18.* [see the noun]

tusk³ /tʌsk/ *v* to empty out the contents of a bag; to empty one container into another *20-.* [Gael *taosg* to pour out, empty]

tuskar, tusker *see* TUSHKAR

tusket /'tʌskət/ *adj of the weather* stormy, violent *20- Sh.* [probably Norw *tuska* to crash, clatter, make a noise + -IT¹]

tussi /'tʌsi/ *n* a tassel; a tuft of grass or hair *20- Sh.* **tussi-girse** a species of coarse meadow grass *20- Sh.* [perhaps a shortened form of Eng *tussock,* but compare TOOSK and TOOSHT¹·¹]

tute *see* TEET¹·², TOOT¹

tuther *see* TITHER¹·²

tutht *see* TUITH

†tutivillar *n* a rogue, a wicked person *e16.* [altered form of TUTIVILLUS]

†tutivillus *n abusive* a rogue, a wicked person *e16.* Compare TUTIVILLAR. [Lat *Tutivillus* a devil or demon in the mystery plays]

tutle *see* TITTLE¹

tutor, †tutour, †toutour /'tjutər/ *n law* the guardian and administrator of the estate of a minor *15-.* **tutorial** relating to a guardian or his office *18-.* **tutory 1** *law* guardianship, protection of a minor or their estate, the office of a guardian *15-.* **2** tuition, instruction *17-e18.* **tutor dative** a guardian appointed by a court in the absence of a *tutor testamentar* or *tutor at law la15-.* **†tutor legitim** = *tutor at law 16-e19.* **tutor nominate** = *tutor testamentar la17-.* **tutor testamentar** a guardian appointed by the parent of a minor to act in the event of his or her death *15-.* **tutor at law** *law* the nearest male relative on the father's side, who becomes guardian of a minor in default of one appointed by the parents *16-.* [OFr *tutour,* Lat *tūtor;* compare CURATOR with which it is sometimes confused]

tutrix, †tutrice /'tjutrɪks/ *n law* a female guardian or tutor *la15-.* **tutrix dative** a female *tutor dative* (TUTOR) *la16-.* **†tutrix testamentar** a female *tutor testamentar* (TUTOR) *16-17.* [Lat *tutrix,* OFr *tutrice*]

tutti-taitie, †tutti-taiti /'tuti 'teti/ *interj* **1** an exclamation representing the sound of a trumpet *la18-e19, 20- historical.* **2** an exclamation expressing impatience, disbelief or derision *la18-e19.* [onomatopeoic]

tuyse *see* TWICE

twa, twaa, twae, two, *T EC* **qua, †tway, †tua, †tuo** /twa, twe, tu; *T EC* kwɔ/ *numeral* **1** the cardinal number after one *la14-.* **2** a few, several *la19- Sh.* **twaerie** *in children's rhymes* two *19, 20- Sh EC.* **twaeock, tweck** *in the game of buttony* a larger button counting as two in scoring *20- T EC.* **twosie** the second move in various games *20- C Bor.* **twasome, †twasum 1** a group or company of two, a couple, a pair *la14-.* **2** a Scottish country dance *la18-19, 20- NE T C.* **twa-bedded** twin-bedded *20- Sh T EC.* **twabiggin** two farms built end to end *20- Ork.* **two-built hoose** = *twabiggin.* **twa cord** *of rope* having two strands, two-ply *la19- Sh Ork.* **twa-eyed steak** a humorous term for a herring or kipper *la19- N NE T EC Uls.* **twa-fanglet** indecisive *20- NE.* **twa-hand crack** a conversation between two people *19, 20- C SW.* **twa-handit crack** = *twa-hand crack.* **twa-handit sword** a sword wielded using both hands *16-.* **twa-handit wark** work so badly done that it has to be done again *19, 20- Sh Ork NE T EC.* **twa-horse** *of a farm* (only) needing two horses to work it *la19- Ork NE T.* **twa-beast tree** the swingle-tree of a two-horse plough *la18-19, 20- Ork.* **twa-horse tree** = *twa-beast tree.* **†twa-lofted** *of a house* three-storeyed *e19.* **twa-pair** *of a farm* worked by two pairs of horses *20- Ork N NE.* **twa-skippet** *of a cap* having a peak back and front *la19- C.* **twa-snooted** = *twa-skippet la19- NE T EC Bor.* **†tua of ten** the level of interest of ten percent reduced by two percent which was paid as an extraordinary tax to the Crown *e17.* **twa words** a discussion, argument or dispute *19, 20- T Uls.* **twa year auld, twa year'l** (an animal of) two years of age *la15-.* **in twa** in two parts, pieces or directions *la14-.* [OE *twā*]

twad *see* WID²

twae *see* TWA

twaet *see* WHITE²

twafauld /'twafɔld/ *adj* **1** *of persons* bent double, doubled up (from injury, pain or infirmity) *15-.* **2** double, folded over *la16-.* **3** deceitful, two-faced *la18-19, 20- NE.* [TWA + *-fauld* suffix; compare FAULD¹·²]

twain, †**twane** /twen/ *numeral* two *la14-19, 20- literary*. **in twain** in two pieces, apart *la14-19, 20- literary*. [OE *twēgen*]

twal, twel, twol, twull, qual, quel, twelve, †**twelf,** †**tuelf** /twal, twɛl, twol, twʌl, kwɔl, kwɛl, twɛlv/ *numeral* **1** the cardinal number after eleven *la14-*. **2** a set or group of twelve persons or things *la16-*. **3** twelve o'clock *la16-*. **4** a midday snack or drink *20- Sh*. **twelvesie** the last move in the game of chucks *20- C*. **twalsome** a group of twelve *la19-*. **twal cup** tea or a drink taken at midday *la19- Sh*. **twall oors, twal hoors 1** twelve noon (or sometimes midnight) *16-*. **2** a midday snack or drink; a midday meal *19-*. **twal hundred** medium-fine linen woven on a reed of twelve hundred splits *la18-19, 20- Ork*. **twalpenny** twelve pennies, a shilling *la16-20, 21- historical*. **twalpiece** a midday snack *20- Ork*. **twal-time** = *twall oors 20- Sh*. [OE *twelf, twælf*; OE *tuoelf, tuoel*]

twalmonth, †**twelf month** /ˈtwalmʌnθ/ *n* **1** (the period of) a year *la14-*. **2** *with a date or day* a year after the date mentioned *la15-17*. †**twalmonth auld** a yearling, an animal a year old *la15-e19*. [TWAL + MONTH¹]

twalt, twelt, †**twelft,** †**tuelft** /twalt, twɛlt/ *adj* the ordinal number after eleventh *la14-*. [OE *twelfta*, with influence from TWAL]

twane *see* TWAIN

twang /twaŋ/ *n* a sudden sharp pain, a pang; a sudden sharp feeling *18-*. [EModE *twang* a vocal imitation of a plucked string]

twang *see* THANG

twantie *see* TWENTY¹·²

twa part /ˈtwa part/ *n* two thirds *la14-*. [TWA + PAIRT¹·¹]

twa penny *see* TIPPENY¹·²

twa penyis *see* TIPPENCE

'twar *see* BE

twarrow /ˈtwaro/ *n* the head rig in a ploughed field *20- Ork N*. [Norw dial *tverre* the short side of a rectangle, a strip of land lying beyond another]

twart *see* THORT¹·³, THORT¹·⁴, THORT¹·⁵

twarter *see* THORTER¹·³

twartle /ˈtwartəl/ *v* to annoy *20- Sh*. **twartled** easily irritated *20- Sh*. [frequentative form of *thwart* (THORT)]

twartree *see* TWA-THREE

twa-three, *Sh Ork* **twartree** /ˈtwa ˈθri; *Sh Ork* ˈtwartri/ *adj* two or three, a few, several *la14-*. [TWA + THREE]

tway *see* TWA

twayt *see* WHITE²

twech *see* TOUCH¹·²

tweck *see* TWA

twee /twi/ *interj* a call to calves at feeding time *20- NE*. [compare PREE and TROO]

tweed /twid/ *n* a twilled, rough-textured woollen cloth made of yarn of two or more colours *19-*. [supposedly a misreading of TWEEL¹·¹ but more probably a reduced form of *tweeled* (TWEEL¹·²) or TWEEDLE¹·¹, with confusion with the name of the River Tweed]

tweedle¹·¹, †**tueidill,** †**twidle** /ˈtwidəl/ *n* a twilled cloth *la16-*. [perhaps metathesis of *tweeled* (TWEEL¹·²)]

†**tweedle**¹·² *v ptp* **tuedlit** to weave so as to produce diagonal ridges on the surface of the cloth *la16-19*. **tweedling, twidling, tueidling** twilled cloth, especially linen *la16-18*. [see the noun]

tweedle², **twiddle** /ˈtwidəl, ˈtwɪdəl/ *v* **1** to twist, agitate (the fingers) *19-*. **2** to cheat, deceive *19, 20- NE*. [EModE *twiddle*]

tweel¹·¹, **twill,** †**tweill,** †**tweyll,** †**tueill** /twil, twɪl/ *n* **1** a diagonally-ribbed cloth produced by passing the weft threads over one and under two or more warp threads *la15-*. **2** *ploughing* the angle at which the coulter is set in the beam, which determines the lie of the furrow *20- T EC*. [OE *twilic* woven of double thread]

†**tweel**¹·² *v ptp* **tueillit, tweillit, tweeled** to weave diagonally-ribbed cloth produced by passing the weft threads over one and under two or more warp threads *la16-19*. **tweeling, tweilling** a diagonally-ribbed cloth *la16-19*. [see the noun]

tweel² /twil/ *adv* truly, indeed *la18-19, 20- C*. Compare ATWEEL [shortened form of *I wat weel* literally, I know well]

tweel-brook-dee-new /ˈtwilbrukdiˈnju/ *n* an expression of good luck *20- Sh*. [reduced form of *mat weel etc*; compare MAT, BROOK², dee (THEE³)]

tweelzie *see* TULYIE¹·²

tween /twin/ *prep* between *la16-*. **tween hands** between times, meantime *20-*. **tween heid** *ploughing* the part of the reins joining the heads of two horses in a team *20- C SW*. [aphetic form of BETWEEN¹·², ATWEEN¹·²]

tweest *see* TWIST¹·¹, TWIST¹·²

tweet *see* WHITE²

tweetanshae, tweeteeshee *see* TWEETISHEE

tweeter *see* TWITTER¹·²

tweetie-twattie /ˈtwitiˈtwati/ *n* a humorous term for a gun *20- Sh*. [nonce formation]

tweetishee, tweeteeshee, tweetanshae /twitiˈʃi, twitənˈʃe/ *interj* an expression of anger or contempt, used as a malediction *20- Sh*. [probably ON *tví fie* + ON *svei fie*]

†**tweetle**¹·¹ *n* a dance, an occasion for dancing *19 NE*. [see the verb]

tweetle¹·² /ˈtwitəl/ *v* **1** to whistle, warble, sing *20-*. **2** to walk nimbly and quickly *20- Sh*. [onomatopoeic]

tweezlick /ˈtwizlɪk/ *n* an iron hook used in twisting straw or rush rope *20- NE*. [perhaps TWISTLE¹·² + a reduced form of HEUK or TWISTLE¹·¹ + *-ick* (-OCK)]

tweill *see* TWEEL¹·¹

tweise *see* TWYS

twel, twelf *see* TWAL

twelf month *see* TWALMONTH

twelft, twelt *see* TWALT

†**twelter-aith** *n* an oath of twelve compurgators or witnesses as to the innocence of the accused *e17*. Compare SAXTER-AITHE and LAWRICHT-AITH. [ON *tylftar-eiðr*]

twelve, twelvesie *see* TWAL

twentieth, †**tuentieth,** †**twentyd,** †**twentiand** /ˈtwɛntɪəθ/ *adj* the ordinal number after nineteenth *14-*. [OE *twēntigoða*; for the *-and* suffix, compare ON *tuttugandi*]

†**twenty**¹·¹, **tuentie, tantie** *adj* the ordinal number after nineteenth *17-18*. [extended use of TWENTY¹·²]

twenty¹·², **twinty, twunty,** *Bor* **twonty,** *Bor* **toontie,** †**twantie,** †**townty,** †**tuenty** /ˈtwɛnti, ˈtwɪnti, ˈtwʌnti; *Bor* ˈtwɔnti; *Bor* ˈtunti/ *numeral* **1** the cardinal number after nineteen *la14-*. **2** in large numbers, plentiful, numerous *la15-17, la19 Sh*. †**twenty days** the period of warning or notice (before the date of a term day or summons) *17-18*. [OE *twēntig*, OE Northumb *tuoentig*]

twentyd *see* TWENTIETH

twet /twɛt/ *n* **1** a tiring spell of work *la19- Sh*. **2** a quarrel *20- Sh*. [perhaps Norw dial *tveta* to wrangle, dispute]

tweyll *see* TWEEL¹·¹

twhang *see* THANG

twice, *Sh* **twyse,** *Sh Ork* **twise,** *T H&I WC* **twicet,** †**twyis,** †**twys,** †**tuyse** /twʌis; *Sh Ork* twʌɪz; *T H&I WC* twʌɪst/ *adv* **1** two times, on two occasions *la14-*. **2** double, two times as much *15-*. **twiser** *in the game of buttons* a button valued at two shots *la19- T*. **at twice** on two occasions *la15-*. **the twice** for a second time *20-*. **twice or thrice,** †**twyse**

or thryse two or three times, more than once *la15-*. [OE *twiges*]
twich *see* TOUCH[1.1], TOUCH[1.2]
twiddle *see* TWEEDLE[2]
twidle *see* TWEEDLE[1.1]
twig[1.1] /twɪg/ *n* a jerk, tug, twitch *19, 20- Sh Ork*. [see the verb]
twig[1.2] /twɪg/ *v* to jerk, tug or twitch *la18-19, 20- Sh Ork N*. [onomatopoeic; compare Eng *tweak, twitch*]
twig[2] /twɪg/ *n* a quick or sidelong glance; a glimpse *19- NE*. [Eng *twig* to watch]
twill *see* TWEEL[1.1]
twilt[1.1], **quilt** /twɪlt, kwɪlt/ *n* a padded bedcover *la17-*. [ME *quilte, twilte*, AN *quilte*]
twilt[1.2], **quilt** /twɪlt, kwɪlt/ *v* to pad; to sew in padding *19-*. **twilted** padded *la17-*. [see the noun]
twin[1.1] /twɪn/ *v* to take a lamb from a weak ewe and give it to a strong one to suckle with her own *20- C SW Bor*. [see the adj]
twin[1.2], †**twynn** /twɪn/ *adj* **1** born as one of two at one birth *la14-*. **2** double *la14-*. [OE *twinn*]
twin *see* TWINE[2]
twine[1.1], †**twyne**, †**quyn** /twʌɪn/ *n* **1** string, thread *16-*. **2** a short attack (of an ailment) *19*. [OE *twīn*]
twine[1.2], †**twyne** /twʌɪn/ *v pt* **twinit, twined,** †**twane 1** to twist strands together to make thread; to make ropes by twisting fibres *la15-*. **2** to join, unite in marriage *19-*. **3** to twist part of the body, wriggle, writhe *19, 20- N SW*. **4** to work with effort and perseverance, push oneself to the limit *la19- N*. **twiner** a person or machine employed to twist spun yarn into a thicker thread *la19- Bor*. †**twiners** a pair of pincers *e16*. †**twynrys** = *twiners*. †**twine off** to compose a story, spin a yarn *e19*. [ME *twinen*]
twine[2], **twin,** †**twyn** /twʌɪn, twɪn/ *v* **1** to put asunder, divide, separate, cause to part *la14-*. **2** *of two people* to part company, separate *la14-*. **3** to deprive *18-*. **4** to depart *la14-e17*. **twine with** to relinquish *16-19, 20- Sh Ork N*. [from the adj TWIN[1.2]]
†**twingle-twangle**[1.1] *n* a twanging sound *la18*. [reduplicative, onomatopoeic]
twingle-twangle[1.2] /ˈtwɪŋəlˈtwaŋəl/ *v* to twang *20- SW*. [see the noun]
twinkle, †**twinkill,** †**twynkle** /ˈtwɪŋkəl/ *v* **1** *of light* to shine intermittently, sparkle, glitter *15-*. **2** *of an eye* to blink, wink *la14-e19*. [OE *twinclian*]
twinter, quinter, †**twyntir** /ˈtwɪntər, ˈkwɪntər/ *n* a two-year-old farm animal *16-19, 20- SW Bor*. Compare THRUNTER. [ME *twinter*; OE *twīwintre* of two winters; compare THRUNTER]
twinty *see* TWENTY[1.2]
twise *see* TWICE
twist[1.1], *Ork NE* **tweest** /twɪst; *Ork NE* twist/ *n* **1** thread *la16-*. **2** a turn or shot (at doing something) *20- Sh NE*. **3** a small amount (of food or drink); a small, undersized person *20- NE*. **4** homespun cloth formed by weaving black and white threads together *20- Ork*. **5** a surly, perverse mood *20- Sh*. **6** curling a shot in which the curling stone is made to spin *19*. **7** a twig, branch *la14-16*. [OE (*candel-*)*twist* a pair of (snuffers), ON *kvistr* a twig, branch, MDu *twist* thread]
twist[1.2], *Ork NE* **tweest,** †**tuist** /twɪst; *Ork NE* twist/ *v* to make (thread or rope) by turning two or more strands over another or others; to turn, wind (anything) *17-*. **twister** a tool used in twisting or spinning yarn or rope *20-*. **twisting** *curling* the action of making a curling stone spin *19- SW*. [ME *twisten*, MDu *twisten*]
twistle[1.1] /ˈtwɪsəl/ *n* **1** the action of twisting *19-*. **2** rough treatment, a shaking or pulling about *la18-19*. [see the verb]

twistle[1.2], †**twussle** /ˈtwɪsəl/ *v* **1** *weaving* to join threads by twisting together without a knot *20-*. **2** to twist, screw, wring *la18-19*. [frequentative form of TWIST[1.2]]
twit /twɪt/ *v* to chirp, twitter *la19- Ork T Bor*. [onomatopoeic]
twitter[1.1] /ˈtwɪtər/ *n* a state of nervous excitement or apprehension *19-*. [see the verb]
twitter[1.2], **tweeter** /ˈtwɪtər, ˈtwɪtər/ *v* to (cause to) quiver or tremble *19-*. [ME *twiteren* to chirp, onomatopoeic]
twitter[2] /ˈtwɪtər/ *n* **1** a thin part of unevenly spun yarn *18-*. **2** a very slender, small or feeble person or thing *19-*. [onomatopoeic]
twixt, †**tuix** /twɪkst/ *prep* between *la16-19, 20- literary*. †**twixt and** between now and (a date), before (a date) *la17-e18*. [aphetic form of BETWIXT]
two *see* TWA
twol *see* TWAL
twonty *see* TWENTY[1.2]
twull *see* TWAL
twunty *see* TWENTY[1.1]
twussle *see* TWISTLE[1.2]
twyis *see* TWICE
twyn *see* TWINE[2]
twyne *see* TWINE[1.1], TWINE[1.2]
twynkle *see* TWINKLE
twynn *see* TWIN[1.2]
twynrys *see* TWINE[1.2]
twyntir *see* TWINTER
†**twys, tweise** *n* a case for keeping instruments or valuables *la15-17*. [aphetic form of MFr *etuis* pl of *etui*]
twys *see* TWICE
twyte *see* WHITE[2]
ty *see* TIE[1.2]
tyach, tach /tjax, tax/ *interj* an expression of impatience, contempt or petulance *la19-*. [a natural utterance]
tyang *see* TANG[2]
tyangs *see* TANGS
tyarr /tjar/ *v* to fight or be prone to quarrelling *20- N*. [voiceless variant, due to Gaelic influence, of Eng *jar*]
tyauve[1.1], **chauve,** †**tauve** /tjav, tʃav/ *n* an act of labouring, exertion, a hard struggle; a laborious walk *la19- NE*. [see the verb]
tyauve[1.2], **chauve,** †**tauve** /tjav, tʃav/ *v pt* **tyauved, tew,** †**tyeuve** *ptp* **tyauved 1** to knead, work dough *19- N NE*. **2** to struggle physically, tumble or toss about *19- NE*. **3** to walk heavily or with difficulty through snow or mud *19- NE*. **4** to pull or knock about, treat roughly *la19- NE*. **5** to strive, struggle (with little result), live or work hard, exert oneself *la19- NE*. **6** to become fatigued, exhaust oneself *20- NE*. [variant of TAW[1.2]]
tyave *see* TAW[2]
tyce /tʌɪs/ *v* to move about slowly and easily, walk cautiously *la18- NE*. [unknown]
tychir *see* TICHWR
tyddie *see* TIDY
tye /tae/ *interj* an expression of affirmation or approval *la19- NE*. [shortened form of *hoot aye* (HOOT[1.2])]
tyeuch *see* TEUCH[1.1]
tyeuk *see* TAK[1.2]
tyeuve *see* TYAUVE[1.2]
tygir *see* TEEGER
tyine *see* TINE[2]
tyistar *see* TYSTIR
tyk *see* TIKE[2]
tyke *see* TIKE[1]
tyke-o-bed *see* TIKABED
tykin *see* TICKING

tyld, tyle *see* TILE[1,2]
tylor *see* TAILOR
tymber *see* TYMMER[2]
†**tymbrell, timberall** *n* a musical instrument, a tambourine *16-17*. [diminutive form of TYMMER[1]]
tyme *see* TIME
†**tymmer**[1] *n* a musical instrument, a drum or tambourine *la16*. Compare TYMBRELL. [ME *timber*, OFr *timbre*]
†**tymmer**[2], **tymber** *n* the crest of a helmet *la14-e16*. **tymbret** *n* the crest of a helmet *e16*. **tymbret** *adj of a helmet* having a crest *e16*. **tymeral, tymbrell** the crest of a helmet *e15*. [MFr *timbre*]
tymmer *see* TIMMER[1.1]
tymous *see* TIMEOUS, TIMOUS
tympany[1], †**tympan** /ˈtɪmpəni/ *n* the gable-shaped raised middle part of the front of a house *18-19, 20- NE*. [Lat *tympanum*]
†**tympany**[2] *n* a swelling of the stomach *la17*. [Lat *tympanias*]
†**tympathy** *n* a morbid swelling or tumour *e19*. [conflation of TYMPANY[2] with Eng *sympathy*]
tyn *see* TIN[1.1], TIN[1.2]
tynchell *see* TINCHEL
tynd *see* TINE[1]
tyne *see* TINE[1], TINE[2]
tyned *see* TINE[2]
tynklar *see* TINKLER
tynsall *see* TINSEL[1.1], TINSEL[1.2]
tynt *see* TINE[2]

tyoch *see* TEUCH[1.1]
tyoll /tjɔl/ *n* a heavy burden *20- Ork*. [perhaps Norw dial *talla* to work slowly]
type[1] /tʌɪp/ *n* a low conical hill; frequently in place-names *20- SW*. [EModE *tipe* a cupola]
type[2] /tʌɪp/ *v* to become weary with hard work, to toil; to walk wearily or feebly *la19- NE*. [unknown]
type *see* TEEP[1.1], TEEP[1.2]
typtays *see* TIPTAES
tyran, tyrand *see* TIRRAN
†**tyre** *v* to inter *e15*. **tyrement, terment, tyrment** interment, burial *la15-e16*. [aphetic form of *entyre* (INTER)]
tyre *see* TIRE[1.2]
tyrleis *see* TIRLIS
tyrlis *see* TIRLISS
†**Tyrrhene, Tyrrhean** *adj* Tyrrhenian, Etruscan *e16*. [Lat *Tyrrhēnus*]
tyrsum *see* TIRESOME
Tysday, Teisday, Tiseday /ˈtʌɪzde/ *n* Tuesday *la14-19, 20- Sh Ork NE T EC*. [ON *Týsdagr* the day of the god Týr]
tyse, tyst *see* TICE
†**tystir, tyster, tyistar** *n* (a cover for) the Gospels as kept on the high altar or carried in procession *15-17*. [AN *tistre*]
tyta *see* TITA
tyte *see* TITE[1.2]
tyty *see* TITA
tyuggle *see* TUGGLE[1.1], TUGGLE[1.2]

U

uag see WAG[2]

†**uberior, vberior** *adj law* fuller, fullest *16*. **in uberior form** in a fuller or the fullest possible form *16*. [Lat *ūberior* fuller]

†**ubiquiter** *n Christian Church* a Lutheran, a ubiquitarian *la16*. [from the stem of Lat *ubiquitarius* someone or something ubiquitous, with *-er* suffix]

†**uche, vche, ouch** *n* a clasp, a buckle, a brooch; a gold or silver setting for a precious stone *la14-17*. [by wrong division of ME *a nouche, a nuche*, AN *nouche*, OFr *nuche*]

udal, odal, †**uthall,** †**owthall** /ˈjudəl, ˈudəl, ˈodəl/ *n* freehold tenure by which land is held in absolute ownership, without feudal superior or obligations *la15- Sh Ork*. **udaller,** †**udelar** a person holding land by udal tenure *17- Sh Ork*. †**udal-man** = *udaller 16*. [ON *óðal* property held by inheritance, patrimony]

udder, *Ork N NE T EC* **ether,** *NE* **edder,** *EC Bor* **uther** /ˈʌdər; *Ork N NE T EC* ˈɛðər; *NE* ˈɛdər; *EC Bor* ˈʌðər; *Ork N* also ˈɪðər/ *n in animals* the mammary gland, an udder *la16-*. **udder-locking** the plucking of the wool from a ewe's udder to facilitate suckling *la18-*. **udder-locks** the wool growing on a ewe's udder *la18-*. [OE *ūder*]

uddie /ˈʌdi/ *adj* small, insignificant *20- Ork*. [variant of ODD[1.2] + -IE[2]]

uder see ITHER[1.1], ITHER[1.3]

ue /ø/ *v* to hum (a tune) *20- Ork*. [by wrong division of for example *sittan nuean*; see NUE]

U.F. /ˈju ˈɛf/ *n* a member of the UNITED FREE CHURCH *20-*. [abbreviation]

ug[1.1] /ʌg/ *n* **1** a dislike; a sensation of nausea *la19- NE T*. **2** an object of disgust; a person with disgusting manners *la19- NE*. [see the verb and compare ME *ugge* fear, dread, ON *uggr*]

ug[1.2], †**vgg,** †**wg** /ʌg/ *v* **1** to find offensive or repellent; dread, dislike, loathe, feel disgust or horror at *15-*. **2** to disgust, nauseate; to annoy, upset, exasperate *19- Sh NE T EC Bor*. **uggin** disgusting, loathsome; objectionable; annoying, vexatious *19- NE*. **uggit** upset, annoyed; disgusted; fed up *20- Sh NE Bor*. †**ugrines** horror, dread *la14*. [ME *uggen* to fear, dread, ON *ugga*]

ug[2], **ugg** /ʌg/ *n* the pectoral fin and adjacent parts of a fish *20- N*. **ugg-bone** the bone behind the gills of a fish *20- Ork*. [Norw *ugge* gills, ON *uggi* the pectoral fin]

uggle see AGGLE[1.2]

ugly[1.1] /ˈʌgle/ *n* a protective shade attached to the front of a woman's bonnet; a bonnet on a high cane frame worn by women field-workers *20- EC Bor*. [see the adj]

ugly[1.2], **oogly,** *H&I* **oagly,** †**hugly,** †**vgly** /ˈʌgle, ˈugli; *H&I* ˈogli/ *adj* **1** unsightly, unattractive, repulsive *la14-*. **2** inspiring dread or horror, terrifying *15-17*. [ON *uggligr* to be feared or dreaded]

†**ugly**[1.3], **vgly, wgly** *adv* in an unpleasant manner; unpleasantly, horribly *la14-e15*. [see the adj]

ugsome, *Bor* **augsome,** *T* **ogsome,** †**ugsum,** †**vgsum,** †**wgsum** /ˈʌgsəm; *T Bor* ˈɔgsəm/ *adj* disgusting, repulsive, horrible, loathsome, dreadful *15-*. †**ugsumnes, wgsumnes** the quality of being loathsome or dreadful *16-e19*. [UG[1.2] + -SOME adj-forming suffix]

uhuh, uhha /ˈʌhʌ, ˈʌhə/ *interj* indicating attentiveness or agreement *19-*. [a natural utterance]

uik /øk/ *v* to retch, vomit *20- Ork N*. [Norw dial *øga* to feel sick]

uilie see ILE[1.1]

uise see USE[1.1], USE[1.2]

uiter-kap see ETTERCAP

uivigar, †**ivigar** /ˈøvɪgər/ *n* a sea urchin; something clumsy *la17- Ork*. [compare Icel *igulkera* sea urchin]

uiz see AES[1.1]

uizer see AES[1.2]

ule /øl/ *n* sultry heat, warm vapour, mist *la19- Sh*. [Norw *yl*]

ule see ILE[1.1]

†**ulipy, ully py,** †**vlypy** *n* probably an oilskin material used for making a coat or jacket *la15-16*. [probably Du *olie* oil + *pije* a coat]

ull see ILL[1.1], ILL[1.3], ILL[1.4]

Ullans /ˈʌlənz/ *n* a name for the dialect of Scots spoken in Ireland *la20-*. Compare *Ulster Scots* (ULSTER). [a blend of ULSTER + LALLANS]

ulless see ILL-LESS

ullier see OLLER

ull-wullie see ILL-WILLIE

ullya-pluck see OO[1]

ully py see ULIPY

†**ulne, wln** *n* **1** a measure of length *la15-16*. **2** a measure for cloth *la14-e17*. [Lat *ulna*]

Ulster, †**Vllister** /ˈʌlstər/ *n* one of the four provinces of Ireland *la14-*. **Ulster Scots** the dialect of Scots spoken in Ireland *la20-*. Compare ULLANS. [AN *Ulvestre*]

ultimus haeres, †**ultimus heres** /ˈʌltɪməs ˈhɛrəz/ *n law* the last or ultimate heir, a title applied to the Crown when succeeding to the property of someone who has died intestate without any known heir *17-*. [Lat *ultimus haerēs*]

ultroneous /ʌlˈtronɪəs/ *adj* **1** voluntary *17-*. **2** *law of a witness* one who gives evidence spontaneously without being formally cited; *of evidence* given voluntarily *la17-*. †**ultroneousness** voluntary action *17-19*. [Lat *ultrōneus*]

ulyie see ILE[1.1]

um see HIM

†**um-, umb-, umbe-** *prefix* round, around, but there is some confusion with UN-. [ON *umb-, um-*]

-um *suffix* added to nouns or verbs to form diminutives or terms of endearment, *eg breekums* (BREEK[1.1]). [mock-Lat suffix]

umast see UMEST[1.2]

umb- see UM-

†**umbdraw, undraw** *v pt* **umbedrew, onbydrew** to withdraw, retreat *la15-16*. [UM- or UN- + DRAW[1.2]]

umbe- see UM-

†**umbecast** *v pt* **umbekest 1** to make the circuit of, travel round *la15*. **2** to consider, ponder *la14-e15*. [*umbe-* (UM-) + CAST[1.2]]

umbedrew see UMBDRAW

umbelie see HUMMLE[1.2]

†**umberaucht, omberaucht** *v pt, ptp* encompassed, surrounded *e16*. [*umbe-* (UM-) + *raucht* (REAK[1.2])]

umberella, umbrella, †**umbrell** /ʌmbəˈrɛlə, ʌmˈbrɛlə/ *n* an umbrella, an implement for protection against rain or sun;

anything shaped like or offering protection like an umbrella *la18-*. **Hielandman's Umbrella** see HIELANDMAN. [Ital *ombrella*]

umbersorrow /'ʌmbərsɔro/ *adj* fit, robust; resisting disease or the effects of severe weather *19- Bor*. [unknown]

†**umbeschew, wmchew, ombyschew** *v* to avoid, shun *la15-16*. [*umb-* (UM-) + ESCHEW]

†**umbesege, ombesege** *v* to besiege *e16*. [UM- + Older Scots *besege*; compare SIEGE[1,1]]

†**umbeset**[1,1] *n in Orkney* a piece of wasteland enclosed and taken into cultivation *e16*. [see the verb]

†**umbeset**[1,2], **ombeset, unbesett** *v* to surround, beset; to attack, besiege; to obstruct *la14-17*. [UM- + Older Scots *beset*, OE *besettan*]

†**umbethink, unbethink, ombethynk** *v* to think, consider; to call to mind, remember *la14-17*. [UM- + Older Scots *bethink*, and compare OE *ymbðencan*]

†**umbeweround** *adj* surrounded *la14*. [participial adj from *umbe-* (UM-) + ENVERON]

umboth /'ʌmbəθ, 'ʌmbəd/ *n* **1** *in Shetland and Orkney* a tithe payable from lands originally belonging to the bishops of Orkney, then the Crown, and finally the earldom of Zetland *la16-19, 20- historical*. **2** *in Orkney* agency, procuratory *la15-e16*. †**umbothisman** *in Orkney* an agent or representative *la15-16*. †**umbothman** = *umbothisman 16*. [ON *umboð* a charge delegated for collection, a commission]

umbrage see UMMERAGE

†**umbrakle, vmbrakill** *n* shade, shadow *e16*. [Lat *umbrāculum* a shady place]

†**umbrate** *adj* shady *e16*. [Lat *umbrāt-*, ptp stem of *umbrāre* to shade]

umbrell, umbrella see UMBERELLA

umel see HUMMEL[1,3]

†**umest**[1,1], **vmaste** *n* that which is highest, uppermost or of the highest importance; a salient point, the gist *15-e16*. [see the adj]

umest[1,2], *NE* **eemost**, †**umast**, †**humast**, †**immost** /*Sh Ork* 'ɔmɪst *NE* 'ɪməst/ *adj* **1** uppermost, highest *15-*. **2** *of clothes* outermost *15-16*. †**umast clathe** the coverlet of a bed, claimed as a perquisite by the parish priest on the death of a parishioner *la15-16*. [OE *ufemast*, superlative of *uferra* higher]

†**umest**[1,3], **vmast** *adv* highest; foremost *15-e16*. [see the adj]

umff see HUMPH[2,3]

†**umgang** *n* circuit, circumference *15-e16*. [ON *umgangr*]

umik see OOMIK

umman see WOMAN

ummerage, umrage, umbrage, †**vmbrage** /'ʌmredʒ, 'ʌmredʒ, 'ʌmbrɪdʒ/ *n* **1** shadow, shade *16-19*. **2** displeasure *18-*. **3** a hint, an inkling, a suspicion *17*. [OFr *umbrage*]

umnae see BE

umph see HUMPH[2,3]

umplist see ONPLAST

umquhile[1,1], †**umquhill,** †**wmquhyll** /'ʌmʍʌɪl/ *adj* mainly *of persons* former, late; especially *law frequently without determiner* deceased *15-*. [altered form of OE *ymb hwīle* with substitution of UM- for *ymb*]

†**umquhile**[1,2], **umquhill, wmquhile** *adv* **1** at times, sometimes *la14-16*. **2** formerly *la14-19*. **3** at some future time *la14-e16*. [see the adj]

umrage see UMMERAGE

un-, on-, *Sh NE* **oon-,** †**one-** /ʌn, ɔn, on; *Sh NE* un/ *prefix* **1** expressing both negation and deprivation or reversal; mainly with adjectives or adverbs, but also with participles, nouns and verbs: ◊*unsonsie, unawaurs, onbekent, unattempting, oonhonesty, unfankle la14-*. **2** with active past participles or present participles not having done or without doing or being (something): ◊*he mist sum of the Strathbogie men oncum thair la15-*. **3** with passive past participles or past participle phrases not (having been done) or without (something being done), not or without (doing): ◊*gif thar be ony of thar gudis in place ondisponit apoun la15-19*. **4** used with first item only of a series of negated items: ◊*onhurt or slaine 16-19*. [OE *un-*]

†**unabasit, onabasit** *adj* undaunted *la15-e17*. **unabasitly, onabasitly** boldly *la14-16*. [UN- + *abaisit* (ABAIS)]

unable, †**unabill,** †**onabill,** †**onhabill** /ʌn'ebəl/ *adj* **1** not able, unsuitable; incapable, incompetent; ineligible, prohibited *la15-*. **2** physically weak, incapacitated *16-19*. **unable for 1** unfit for, incapable of (doing something) *19-*. **2** having no appetite for (food) *20-*. [UN- + ABLE[1,1]]

unacquaint, unacquent /ʌnə'kwɛnt, ʌnə'kwɛnt/ *adj* unacquainted, unfamiliar, ignorant *la16-*. [UN- + ACQUANT[1,2]]

†**unaffectionat** *adj* unbiased, impartial *16*. [UN- + Older Scots *affectionat* prejudiced, Lat *affectionātus* inclined, well disposed]

†**unagaist, unagast, vnagast** *adj* unafraid, fearless *la15-16*. [UN- + Older Scots *agast* aghast]

unalike /ʌnə'lʌɪk/ *adj* different, dissimilar, unlike *20- Sh NE T*. [UN- + ALIKE[1,1]]

†**unamiable, vnamyabill** *adj* unfriendly *la15*. [UN- + Older Scots *amiable*, OFr *amiable*]

†**unaspyit, unespyit** *adj* unnoticed, unobserved *16-17*. [participial adj from UN- + ESPY[1,2]]

unawaurs, unawares, *Sh* **unawaars,** †**vnawars** /ʌnə'wɔrz, ʌnə'wɑrz; *Sh* onə'wɑrz/ *adv* without warning *la16-*. [UN- + AWAUR with *-s* adv-forming suffix]

†**unbawndonit** *adj of animals* loose, not fastened or under control *la14*. [participial adj from UN- + BANDOUNE[1,2]]

†**unbegrave, onbegrave** *adj* unburied *e16*. [participial adj from UN- + ME *bigraven* to inter]

unbeist see ONBEAST

unbekent, unbekenned, †**ombekend** /ʌnbɪ'kɛnt, ʌnbɪ'kɛnd/ *adj* **1** unknown, strange, unfamiliar *16-*. **2** unobserved, unnoticed *20- T WC*. [participial adj from UN- + BEKEN]

unbeknowins /ʌnbɪ'nowɪnz, ʌnbɪ'nonz/ *adv* unperceived, unnoticed, secretly, unobtrusively *20- NE T H&I*. [Eng *unbeknown* + *-s* adv-forming suffix]

unbesett see UMBESET[1,2]

†**unbet, onbet** *adj* not beaten down, not destroyed *e16*. [participial adj from UN- + BATE[1,2]]

unbethink see UMBETHINK

unbiddable /ʌn'bɪdəbəl/ *adj* perverse, obstinate; undisciplined *19-*. [UN- + *biddable* (BID[1])]

unbiggit, †**unbigged** /ʌn'bɪɡət/ *adj* **1** *of land* not built on, not occupied *15-*. **2** *of a building* not built, derelict *la15-*. [UN- + *biggit* (BIG[1]) ditto

†**unblist** *adj* unblessed, evil *e16*. [participial adj from UN- + BLISS]

†**unblomit, vnblomit** *adj* without flowers *e16*. [UN- + *blomit*, participial adj from *blome* (BLUME[1,2])]

†**unbodyit, onbodeit** *adj* incorporeal *e16*. [UN- + Older Scots *bodyit* bodied, compare BODY]

unbonnie, unbonny /ʌn'bɔne/ *adj* ugly, unsightly: ◊*that's no unbonny 19-*. [UN- + BONNY[1,1]]

unbowsome /ʌn'bʌusəm/ *adj* stiff; unable to bend or stoop; obstinate *19- Bor*. †**vnbowsumly** ungraciously, reluctantly *15*. [UN- + BOWSOME]

†**unbranslable** *adj* unshakable, firm *e17*. [UN- + EModE *bransle* a kind of dance + *-able* adj-forming suffix]

unbraw, †**onbraw** /ʌn'brɔ/ *adj* plain, unattractive *19- WC SW*. [UN- + BRAW[1,1]]

unca *see* UNCO¹·²
unca'd, †**uncald**, †**uncallit**, †**oncallyt** /ʌnˈkɔd/ *adj* not summoned or invited; unwelcome, intrusive *15-*. [participial adj from UN- + CA¹·²]
uncal *see* UNCO¹·¹
uncan¹·¹ /ˈʌŋkən/ *n* **1** mainly *pl* strange or unusual things, rarities, novelties, curiosities *20- Sh*. **2** *pl* news, gossip *20- Sh*. [see the adj]
uncan¹·², **unkin** /ˈʌŋkən/ *adj* **1** unknown, unfamiliar, strange *20- Sh Ork*. **2** unusual; odd, strange, peculiar; unnatural, weird; remarkable *20- Sh Ork*. **3** reserved, shy, unfriendly *20- Sh*. **4** foreign, belonging to another nation or culture *19- Sh*. [altered form of UNCO¹·² with influence from Norw dial *ukjend* strange]
uncannie, **uncanny**, *NE* **oncanny** /ʌnˈkane; *NE* ɔnˈkane/ *adj* **1** dangerous, unreliable, insecure, treacherous, threatening *17-*. **2** weird, mysterious, ominous, *19-*. **3** awkward, not easy to manage *la19- Sh NE T EC*. **4** unlucky, inauspicious *19, 20- Sh N NE*. **5** *of a blow or fall* hard, violent, severe *la18-19, 20- NE T*. **6** unskilful, clumsy, careless *17-e19*. **7** mischievous, malicious *la16*. [UN- + CANNY¹·¹]
uncassen, †**uncassin**, †**uncastin**, †**oncasin** /ʌnˈkasən/ *adj* **1** *of clothes* not faded or worn *20- NE T*. **2** not dug up; *of peats* not cut or extracted by digging *la15-19, 20- Sh NE*. **3** not damaged or broken, whole *16-e17*. **4** not cast or thrown *la14-16*. [UN- + cassen (CAST¹·²)]
unce *see* OUNCE
†**uncert** *adj* uncertain *e16*. [Lat *incertus* with change of prefix]
†**unchance** *n* misfortune, calamity *16-e19*; compare WANCHANCE. [UN- + CHANCE¹·¹]
unchancy, *NE* **oonchancy** /ʌnˈtʃanse; *NE* unˈtʃanse/ *adj* **1** inauspicious, unlucky, ill-fated, unfortunate *16-*. **2** dangerous, threatening, treacherous, not to be meddled with *la18-*. Compare WANCHANCY. [UN- + CHANCY]
†**unchargit** *adj* **1** not called upon, not summoned *la15-e17*. **2** not burdened *la15-16*. [participial adj from UN- + charge (CHAIRGE¹·²)]
†**unciate** *n* in Highland Scotland and Skye a piece of land the annual rent of which is one ounce of silver *16-17*. Compare *ounce-land* (OUNCE). [extended sense of Lat *uncia* the twelfth part (of a pound), a measure of land; compare unce (OUNCE)]
uncioun *see* UNCTION¹
uncle, †**vnkill**, †**oncle**, †**onkill** /ˈʌŋkəl/ *n* the brother of a person's father or mother; an aunt's husband *la15-*. [ME *uncle*, AN *uncle*, OFr *oncle*]
unco¹·¹, †**uncal** /ˈʌŋkə/ *n* **1** mainly *pl* strange or unusual things, rarities, novelties, curiosities *19-*. **2** *pl* news, gossip *la18-*. **3** mainly *pl* strangers, foreigners *la17-19*. [see the adj]
unco¹·², **unca**, †**uncow** /ˈʌŋkə/ *adj* **1** unknown, unfamiliar, strange *16-*. **2** unusual; odd, strange, peculiar; unnatural, weird; remarkable; *as an intensifier* extraordinary, great, awful ◊*ye mak an unco sang about your taxes 17-*. **3** reserved, shy, unfriendly *17-*. **4** foreign, belonging to another nation or culture *19-*. **5** so much altered as to be scarcely recognizable *19, 20- NE*. **6** rude, unseemly *18-e19*. **uncoly**, **uncaly** very much, to a great or remarkable degree *la17-19, 20- literary*. **unconess 1** strangeness, peculiarity, eccentricity *19, 20- Sh EC*. **2** coldness of manner, unresponsiveness; hostility *17*. †**unco body** a stranger, outsider, newcomer *19*. **unco folk** strangers *la18-*. **unco men** strangers, outsiders, newcomers *la18-19, 20- Sh*. **unco-leukin** having a strange, wild, rough or unpleasant appearance; looking out of sorts, woebegone *20-*. [variant of UNCOUTH¹·²]
unco¹·³ /ˈʌŋkə/ *adv* very, exceedingly, extremely *18-*. [see the adj]

†**uncoactit**, **uncoakit** *adj* not compelled or constrained *16-17*. [UN- + Older Scots *coactit* compelled, Lat *coact*-, ptp stem of *coagere*]
unco guid /ˈʌŋkə ˈɡɪd/ *n* the self-righteously moral or pious *la18-*. [UNCO¹·² + GUID¹·¹]
unco-like¹·¹, †**unkie-like** /ˈʌŋkəlʌɪk/ *adj* **1** unusual, unfamiliar, uncanny, weird *17-*. **2** having a strange, wild, rough or unpleasant appearance; looking out of sorts *la17-*. [UNCO¹·² + -LIKE]
†**unco-like**¹·² *adv* in a strange or distant manner *e17*. [see the adj]
†**unconform** *adj* non-conforming *17*. **unconformist** non-conformist *17*. [UN- + CONFORM]
†**uncorn**, **oncorn** *n* poor quality oats; wild oats *16-e19*. [UN-, with pejorative force + CORN¹·¹]
uncost *see* ONCOST
†**uncouth**¹·¹, **onkouth**, **vncoutht**, **uncowth** *n* **1** a stranger *e16*. **2** an unusual or remarkable event *e16*. **3** an uncultivated person *la16*. [see the adj]
uncouth¹·², †**wncouth** /ʌnˈkuθ/ *adj* **1** strange unusual; remarkable, marvellous; unnatural, weird; *as an intensifier* extraordinary *15-*. **2** uncultured, unsophisticated, lacking manners, rude; ignorant, unknowing *16-*. **3** unknown, unfamiliar; not belonging to local jurisdiction, especially of a burgh *la14-e19*. **4** unpleasant; unattractive; vile *la15-19*. **5** foreign *la14-e17*. Compare UNCO¹·². [OE *uncūð*]
uncouthie /ʌnˈkuθi/ *adj* unfriendly, hostile, fear-inspiring *la18-*. [UN- + COUTHIE]
†**uncouthlike** *adj* = UNCO-LIKE¹·¹ (sense 2) *la16-17*. [UN-COUTH¹·² + -LIKE]
uncow *see* UNCO¹·²
uncowth *see* UNCOUTH¹·¹
†**unct**, **unt** *v* to anoint *15-16*. Compare OINT. **unctment** ointment, salve *la15-16*. [Lat *unct-*, ptp stem of *unguere*]
unction¹, †**unctioun**, †**uncioun** /ˈʌŋʃən, ˈʌŋkʃən/ *n* **1** (sacramental) anointing (of a dying person or monarch) *15-*. **2** *ironic* punishment; an unpleasant or dangerous experience *20- NE*. [Lat *unctiōn-*]
unction²·¹, †**aunction** /ˈʌŋʃən, ˈʌŋkʃən/ *n* an auction *19-*. [Eng *auction* confused in form with UNCTION¹ perhaps with ironic reference to the smooth talk of an auctioneer]
unction²·² /ˈʌŋʃən, ˈʌŋkʃən/ *v* to auction *19-*. [see the noun]
unctioun *see* UNCTION¹
†**uncum**, **oncum** *adj* not yet arrived *16-17*. [participial adj from UN- + COME¹·²]
†**uncustom**, **uncustum** *n* an improper or illegal tax *la16*. [UN-, with pejorative force + CUSTOM¹·¹]
†**uncustomit**, **uncustumate** *adj of goods* not having paid duty *la14-17*. [participial adj from UN- + CUSTOM¹·²]
undaemin *see* UNDEEMAN
undali *see* ONDALI
undauntit, †**undantit**, †**ondantit**, †**undantonit** /ʌnˈdɔntɪt/ *adj* **1** not daunted, intrepid, bold *16-*. **2** disorderly, wild; unbridled, unrestrained; *of horses* not broken in, untamed *16-17*. [UN- + *dauntit*, participial adj from DAUNT]
undecent, *Uls* **ondacent** /ʌnˈdisənt; *Uls* ɔnˈdesənt/ *adj* **1** unbecoming, unseemly; improper, indecent *la16-*. **2** unattractive *17*. [UN- + DACENT]
undeeman, **undaemin** /ʌnˈdimən, ʌnˈdemən/ *adj* = UNDEEMOUS *la19- Ork*. [altered form of UNDEEMOUS with presp ending substituted for *-ous*]
undeemous, *Sh* **undömious**, *NE* **ondeemous**, †**undemous** /ʌnˈdiməs; *Sh* ʌnˈdømɪəs; *NE* ɔnˈdiməs/ *adj* huge, immense, unparalleled in size or scope; incalculable; extraordinary *15-*. [ME *undemes*, ON *údǿmis* genitive of *údǿmi* a

monstrous, inconceivable thing or deed, with substitution of adj suffix *-ous* for *-is*]

†**undegest**, **ondegest** *adj* **1** *of food* undigested *la15*. **2** *of an event* untimely, premature; *of a person* rash *e16*. [UN- + *degest* (DIGEST[1,2])]

†**undeid** *adj* alive *la15-16*. [UN- + DEID[1,2]]

†**undeip**, **ondepe** *n* a shallow, a shoal *e16*. [OE *undēop* shallow adj]

†**undemandit**, **ondemandit** *adj* **1** not demanded or required (by another) *e15*. **2** arising from a natural impulse, spontaneous *e16*. [participial adj from UN- + Older Scots *demand*, OFr *demander*]

undemous *see* UNDEEMOUS

under[1.1], **unner**, **onder**, *Sh NE* **oonder**, †**undir** /ˈʌndər, ˈʌnər, ˈɔndər/; *Sh NE* ˈundər/ *adv* **1** below, underneath *la14-*. **2** in subjection; suppressed *la14-*. †**at under** in an inferior place or position; in subjection *la14-17*. [see the prep]

under[1.2], **unner**, **onder**, *Sh NE* **oonder**, *NE* **ooner**, †**undir**, †**wndyr** /ˈʌndər, ˈʌnər, ˈɔndər/; *Sh NE* ˈundər/; *NE* ˈunər/ *prep* **1** below, beneath, lower than; at or close to the bottom of (a hill) *la14-*. **2** subject to, restrained within (authority, domination, guidance, protection or other specified terms or circumstances) *la14-*. **3** concealed, hidden, disguised by *15-*. **4** lower in rank than, inferior to *la15-*. **5** *of land* planted, sown or stocked with; used for growing or rearing *la16-*. **6** behind *la15*. **under nicht** during the night, by night; under the cover of night *15-*. **under thoum** secretly, in an underhand manner *la16-17, 19- Sh SW Bor*. [OE *under*]

under-, **unner-**, †**wunder-** /ˈʌndər, ˈʌnər/ *prefix* beneath, lower than, inferior to *15-*. [OE *under-*]

underboard /ʌndərˈbɔrd, ˈʌndərbɔrd/ *adj of a corpse* laid out awaiting burial *18- SW Uls*. [UNDER- + *board* (BOORD[1.1])]

underbod /ˈʌndərbɔd/ *n* the swelling of the sea under a boat or floating object *20- Sh*. [UNDER- + BOD[2]]

undercoat *see* UNDERCOT

†**under-coit** *n* an undergarment *17*. **undercoatie** a petticoat *la18-e19*. [UNDER- + *coit* (COAT)]

undercot, **undercoat** *v* to fester *la16-e18*. [UNDER- + unknown second element]

underfold *see* UNDERFOWDE

underfoot, †**underfit**, †**vnderfeit** /ʌndərˈfut/ *adv* **1** beneath the feet *15-*. **2** down below; underneath; underground *19*. [UNDER- + FIT[1.1]]

†**underfowde**, **underfold** *n in Orkney and Shetland* a parish official with responsibilities similar to those of a bailiff or sheriff *16-e17*. [UNDER- + FOUD]

undergo, †**underga** /ʌndərˈgo/ *v* **1** to submit to; to suffer, endure *la14-*. **2** to undertake, assume, take on (a duty or responsibility) *la15-17*. [OE *undergān*]

undergro /ˈʌndərgro/ *n* a swelling or disturbance of the sea *20- Sh*. [UNDER- + GRO[1.1]]

underhand /ʌndərˈhand/ *adv* **1** sneakily, secretly, covertly *la16-*. **2** in reserve *20- Ork*. [UNDER- + *hand* (HAN[1.1])]

underhoos, **underhus**, †**unner-hous** /ˈʌndərhus/ *n* **1** the basement of a horizontal water-mill *20- Sh*. **2** the lower part of a house, a basement; perhaps sometimes the inner part of a house *16*. [UNDER- + HOOSE[1.1]]

†**underlie**, **vndirly**, **onderly** *v* **1** to be subject or subjected to, submit to, undergo (a penalty, something unpleasant or arduous; a charge or payment) *la14-19*. **2** to be liable to (the process of law, legal procedures and penalties), have imposed upon one, or accept (the judgement of a court) *15-18*. **underlie the law** = UNDERLIE (sense 2) *la15-19*. [OE *underlicgan*]

†**underlout**[1.1], **underlowt** *n* **1** a subject or servant, an inferior *la14-e16*. **2** one who is forced to submit, a loser *e16*. [see the adj]

†**underlout**[1.2], **onderlowt** *adj* subservient, subject (to); submissive *la14-e16*. [participial adj from OE *underlūtan* to stoop beneath; compare LOUT[1.2]]

underlowt *see* UNDERLOUT[1.1]

undermoor /ˈʌndərmʊr/ *n* the second or under layer of peat in a peat-bank *20- Sh*. [UNDER- + *moor* (MUIR)]

undermost, †**vnermaste** /ˈʌndərmost/ *adj* **1** having the lowest position *17-*. **2** *of the planets* innermost *e16*. [UNDER[1.2] + *-most* superlative suffix]

underply /ˈʌndərplae/ *n mining* a band or division of the upper portion of a thick seam of coal *la19-*. [UNDER- + PLY[1.1]]

†**underscriber**, **underscriver** *n* = UNDERSUBSCRIBER *17-18*. [agent noun from UNDER- + SCRIBE[1.2], SCRIEVE[2.2]; compare ODu *onderschrijver*]

†**underset** *n* = UNDERSETTILL *e16*. [shortened form of UNDERSETTILL]

†**undersettill**, **undirsedill** *n* a subtenant; a person who occupies part of another's house *la15-e16*. **undersettillar** = UNDERSETTILL *la15*. [ME *undersetle*, UNDER- + OE *-setla* occupant]

undersook /ˈʌndərsuk/ *n* an undercurrent flowing against the direction of the surface water *20- Sh NE EC*. [UNDER- + SOOK[1.1]]

†**underspecifeit**, **onderspecifeit** *adj* specified below *16-17*. [participial adj from UNDER- + Older Scots *specifie*, OFr *specifier*]

underspey /ˈʌndərspe/ *adj of land* boggy, fed by underground springs *20- Ork*. [UNDER- + Norn *späi* a spring of water]

†**understand**[1.1] *n* **1** understanding, knowledge *15-16*. **2** support, basis *la16*. [see the verb]

understand[1.2], **unnerstaun**, **unnerstan**, **oonerstan**, **onerstan**, *NE* **winnerstan**, †**onderstand** /ʌndərˈstand, ʌnərˈstɔn, ʌnərˈstan, unərˈstan, ɔnərˈstan; *NE* wɪnərˈstan/ *v pt also NE* **unersteed**, **oonersteed** to comprehend, realize; to learn, become aware or informed of; interpret *la14-*. [OE *understandan*]

understane /ˈʌndərsten/ *n* the nether or lower millstone; the bed-stone *20-*. [UNDER- + STANE[1.1]]

†**undersubscriber**, **undersubscriver** *n* a signatory to a document, the undersigned *la16-18*. [UNDER- + *subscriver*, agent noun from SUBSCRIVE; with influence from SCRIBE[1.2]]

†**undersubscrivand**, **undersubscriband**, **undersubscriving** *v presp* signing (a document) below, (I, we) the undersigned *la16-e18*. [UNDER- + *subscrivand*, presp of SUBSCRIVE; with influence from SCRIBE[1.2]]

undertak, **unnertak**, **undertake**, †**underta**, †**ondertak** /ʌndərˈtak, ʌnərˈtak, ʌndərˈtek/ *v* **1** to take on (a task, assignment or responsibility); to begin (an action) *la14-*. **2** to give a pledge or promise; to enter into a compact or contract *la14-*. **undertaker 1** a person who arranges funerals *la19-*. **2** a supporter *la16-17*. **3** one who undertakes a task or accepts a responsibility; one who carries out work or business on behalf of another, a contractor; a tax-collector *la15-e19*. **4** a colonist in Ireland *17*. **undertaking**, †**ondyrtakyn** *n* an action or work undertaken; an enterprise *15-*. **undertaking** *n* readiness to undertake a task; enterprise, zeal *la14-15*. †**I undertak** *parenthetic* I guarantee, I assure you *la14-e16*. [UNDER- + TAK[1.2]]

under-watter *see* UNNER-WATTIR

undir *see* UNDER[1.1], UNDER[1.2]

undirsedill *see* UNDERSETTILL

undo, †**omdo** /ʌnˈdu/ v **1** to destroy, ruin *la14-*. **2** to unfasten, unbind, unlock *15-*. **3** to remove, take away; to cut off *la15-16*. **4** to uncover, reveal *e16*. **5** to explain, interpret, answer *la14-15*. [OE *undōn*]
undocht, undought, ondocht /ˈʌndoxt, ˈɔndoxt/ n a feeble, weak or ineffective person *16-19, 20- Ork N*. Compare WANDOCHT[1.1]. [participial adj from UN- + *docht*, ptp of DOW[1]]
undömious *see* UNDEEMOUS
undraw *see* UMBDRAW
undrawn /ʌnˈdrɔn/ adj of straw not arranged in uniform length for thatching *la19, 20- Sh Ork NE*. [participial adj from UN- + DRAW[1.2]]
†**unduchtie** adj lacking in good qualities; worthless, vile *la16*. [UN- + *duchtie* (DOCHTY)]
†**undynd** adj unfed *e16*. [participial adj from UN- + DINE[1.2]]
†**une** v pt **unit, vnyte, unitt** to join, bind together; to combine; to reconcile *la15-17*. [OFr *unir*, Lat *ūnīre*; compare UNITE[1.1], UNITE[1.2]]
une *see* OAVEN
uneardly, uneirdlie *see* UNYIRDLY
†**uneis, unneis, oneth** adv not easily, (only) with difficulty, scarcely *la14-16*. [OE *unēaðe* difficult with *-s* adv-forming suffix]
unersteed *see* UNDERSTAND[1.2]
unespyit *see* UNASPYIT
unet *see* UNITE[1.1], UNITE[1.2]
uneven[1.1], †**unevin,** †**onevyn** /ʌnˈivən/ adj **1** unequal; irregular; not smooth or level *15-*. **2** upset, out of sorts *la19- Sh*. [OE *unefn*]
†**uneven**[1.2], **unevin** adv inequitably, unjustly *e16*. [OE *unefne*]
†**unevenly, onevynly** adj **1** ill-matched *e16*. **2** uneven, not level *la17*. [un- + EVENLY[1.1]]
unexhausted teinds /ˌʌnɛgˈzɔstəd ˈtinds/ npl that part of the tithe of a parish not yet allocated to a minister's stipend *la19-20, 21- historical*. [Eng *unexhausted* + TEIND[1.1]]
unfaensindry /ʌnfɑnˈsɪndri/ adj not quite fallen apart, still in one piece *20- Sh Ork*. [UN- + *faen* ptp of FA[1.2] + SINDRY[1.3]]
†**unfain, unfane** adj sorry; unhappy; displeased; not fond *15-e19*. [UN- + FAIN[1.2]]
unfair[1.1] /ʌnˈfer/ adj **1** unjust, inequitable *18-*. **2** unattractive; foul, unclean *la14-e15*. **3** bad, wicked *la14*. [OE *unfæger*]
†**unfair**[1.2] adv without entitlement; unattractively *la15*. [OE *unfægre*]
unfald *see* UNFAULD
unfane *see* UNFAIN
unfarrant, †**onfarrand** /ʌnˈfarənt/ adj unattractive, unpleasant; unrefined, unsophisticated, rude *16-19, 20- Sh*. [UN- + FARRANT]
unfauld, unfold, unfald, †**onfald** /ʌnˈfɔld, ʌnˈfold, ʌnˈfald/ v to open, spread out, unwrap; to reveal *16-*. [OE *unfealdan*]
†**unfeary, unfery, onfery** adj weak, infirm *la15-e19*. [UN- + *fearie* (FERE[3])]
unfeel, †**onfeel** /ʌnˈfil/ adj unpleasant, dirty; rough; uncomfortable *19- Bor*. [OE *unfǣle*; compare FEEL[2]]
unfierdy, †**unferdie** /ʌnˈfirdi/ adj **1** clumsy, awkward *la16-*. **2** overgrown, unwieldy, not in proper trim *19, 20- Sh Ork*. [UN- + FERDY]
unfiskalee /ʌnˈfɪskəli/ adj not fisherman-like, not suited to fishing *19- Sh*. [UN- + FISKALIE]
unfold *see* UNFAULD
unforbidden /ʌnfɔrˈbɪdən/ adj unruly, disobedient, spoilt *20- Sh*. [UN- + FORBIDDEN]
unfordersome, unfurthersome /ʌnˈfordərsʌm, ʌnˈfʌrðərsʌm/ adj slow, causing delay or hindrance *19- Bor Uls*. [UN- + *fordersome* (FORDER[1.1])]

unforgiven, †**unforgevin,** †**unforgiffyn** /ʌnfɔrˈɡɪvən/ adj **1** unpardoned *la16-*. **2** of a penalty without any remission *15-17*. [OE *unforgifen*]
†**unforlatit** adj not drawn off from one container into another *e16*. [participial adj from UN- + MDu *verlaeten* to draw off, rack (wine)]
†**unforleyt, onforleit** adj not abandoned or forsaken *e16*. [OE *unforlǣten*; compare FORLEET]
†**unformal, unformall** adj not in proper form, not properly drawn up *la16-18*. [UN- + Older Scots *formale*, Lat *formālis*]
unfree, †**unfre,** †**unfrie** /ʌnˈfri/ adj **1** restricted, not enjoying freedom *20-*. **2** not having the rights of a freeman or burgess in a burgh, not being a member of a guild or incorporation *15-18*. **3** of a town not having the privileges of a free burgh; subject to trading restrictions *16-17*. **4** not official, not authorized *la17*. †**unfreeman** a man who is not a freeman or burgess in a burgh *15-19*. [UN- + FREE[1.3]]
unfreely, †**unfrely** /ʌnˈfrili/ adj **1** heavy, weighty, unwieldy *19, 20- NE*. **2** unattractive, unsightly *la15-16*. [UN- + FREELY[1.1]]
unfriend, unfreen, †**unfreind,** †**unfrend,** †**onfrend** /ʌnˈfrend, ʌnˈfrin/ n one who is not a friend, an enemy, opponent, antagonist *15-*. †**unfreindfull** hostile *la15-16*. †**unfreindfully** in an unfriendly or hostile manner *e16*.
unfriendship enmity, ill-will *19, 20- Sh*. [UN- + FREEND[1.1]]
†**unfulʒeit** adj not exhausted *e16*. [UN- + *fulʒeit* (FULZIE[1.2])]
unfurthersome *see* UNFORDERSOME
†**unfylet, unfylit, onfylit** adj undefiled, pure *la14-19*. [participial adj from UN- + FYLE]
†**unganand, vnganand, wnganand** adj inappropriate, unbecoming, unsuitable *15-16*. [UN- + *ganand* (GAIN)]
†**ungane, ungone** adj not having gone or departed *la15-17*. [participial adj from UN- + GAE]
ungasto /ˈʌŋɡəstɔ/ n a strong headwind, a contrary wind *la19- Sh*. [unknown]
†**ungear** v to strip naked; to disarm; to castrate *18*. [UN- + GEAR[1.2]]
ungone *see* UNGANE
†**ungrate** adj **1** unpleasant, obnoxious *17*. **2** ungrateful *16-e19*. [altered form, with change of prefix, of Older Scots *ingrate*, Lat *ingrātus*, OFr *ingrate*]
†**ungument, unʒement, vnguent** n ointment *la14-e17*. [AN *unguent*, Lat *unguentum*, with influence from OINTMENT]
unhaandy, †**unhanty** /ʌnˈhɑndi/ adj **1** inconvenient *19, 20- Sh*. **2** clumsy, obese, unwieldy *la18-19*. [UN- + HANDY[1.1], HANTY]
unhairtsome *see* UNHEARTSOME
unhalesome, unhailsome, unwholesome, †**vnhailsum,** †**vnhelsum** /ʌnˈhelsʌm, ʌnˈholsʌm/ adj **1** unhealthy, unsalubrious *15-*. **2** ugly, repulsive *la15*. [UN- + HAILSOME]
unhanty *see* UNHAANDY
†**unhap**[1.1] n bad luck; a misfortune *15-17*. [ME *unhap*; compare HAPPEN]
†**unhap**[1.2] v to bring misfortune *la16*. [see the noun]
†**unhappin** adj miserable, wretched *e16*. [UN- + Older Scots *happin* fortunate, ON *heppinn*]
unheartsome, unhairtsome /ʌnˈhartsʌm, ʌnˈhertsʌm/ adj disagreeable, cheerless, melancholy, dismal *17-*. [UN- + *heartsome* (HERTSOME)]
unhearty *see* OONHERTY
†**unhed, vnheid** v to behead *la14*. [UN- + HEID[1.1]]
†**unhine** adj excessive *19*. [ME *unhende*; compare HENDE]
unhonest /ʌnˈɔnəst/ adj dishonest, disreputable; dishonourable, shameful *15-*. [UN- + HONEST]
unhool /ʌnˈhul/ v to disembody, frighten *18-*. †**unhool someone's saul** to frighten the life out of someone *18-e19*. [UN- + HOOL[1.2]]

unhorsed, †**unhorsit** /ʌnˈhɔrst/ *adj* **1** thrown or dragged from a horse *15-*. **2** dismounted, not provided with a horse *la15-16*. [participial adj from UN- + HORSE¹,²]

†**unhovin** *adj* unbaptized *la14-e17*. [participial adj from UN- + HEAVE¹,²]

unicorn, †**vnicorne** /ˈjunɪkɔrn/ *n* **1** a mythical horse-like animal, with a horn *15-*. **2** *heraldry* one of the supporters of the royal arms of Scotland until 1603, now incorporated in the present royal arms of Great Britain as displayed in Scotland *15-*. **3** a Scottish PURSUIVANT, originally also a herald *15-*. **4** a gold coin worth 18 shillings Scots *la15-16, 19- historical*. **5** a unit of weight, one eighth of a troy ounce *e16*. †**unicorn wecht** = UNICORN (sense 5) *16*. [ME *unicorn*, AN, OFr *unicorne*, Lat *ūnicornis*]

union, †**unioun** /ˈjunjən/ *n* **1** the uniting of two or more persons, peoples or things to form a new entity; the state of being united *15-*. **2** *of Scotland and England* the action of uniting the two realms in friendship or a formal political relationship *16-*. **3** a student union; the building in which a student union is housed *la19-*. **4** a group of people joined together for a common purpose or action; a trade union *20-*. **5** *law* (the combining or annexing of non-contiguous properties into) a single united holding of lands or tenements *la15-e19*. **6** agreement, unanimity *15-16*. **the Union** the joining of the Scottish and English crowns in 1603, or more commonly, the Parliaments in 1707 *17-*; compare *Act of Union* (ACK¹,¹), TREATY OF UNION. [MFr *union*, Lat *union-*]

†**unirkit**, **onyrkyt** *adj* unwearied, not tired; without tiring *e16*. [UN- + IRKIT]

unit *see* UNE

†**unite**¹,¹, **unet**, **unitie** *n* a gold coin marking the Union of the Crowns of Scotland and England in 1603 *17*. [from the ptp of the verb or ptp of UNE; with influence from UNITY]

unite¹,², †**unet** /juˈnʌɪt/ *v ptp* also †**unite** to join, make as one *15-*. [Lat *ūnīt-*, ptp stem of *ūnīre*; compare UNE]

unite *see* UNITY

united, †**unitit** /juˈnʌɪtəd, jəˈnʌɪtəd/ *adj* **1** joined together, merged, combined; characterized by unity *la16-*. **2** in titles of Presbyterian churches which united or reunited after schisms and separations *18-*. †**United Associate Synod** name taken by the NEW LICHTS parties in the BURGHER and ANTIBURGHER branches of the *Original Seceder* (ORIGINAL¹,²) faction on their reunion in 1820 *e19*; compare UNITED PRESBYTERIAN CHURCH. †**United Associate Synod of the Secession Church** = *United Associate Synod*. †**United Secession Church** = *United Associate Synod 19*. **United Provinces** the seven northern provinces of the Netherlands comprising the Dutch Republic *17-18, 19- historical*. [participial adj from UNITE¹,²]

United Free Church, **United Free Kirk** /juˈnʌɪtəd ˈfri ˈtʃʌrtʃ, juˈnʌɪtəd ˈfri ˈkʌrk/ *n* **1** the church formed by the union in 1900 of the majority of the members of the FREE CHURCH OF SCOTLAND with the UNITED PRESBYTERIAN CHURCH, the majority of whose members rejoined the CHURCH OF SCOTLAND in 1929 *e20, la20- historical*. **2** also CONTINUING UNITED FREE CHURCH the minority group of members of the UNITED FREE CHURCH who did not rejoin the CHURCH OF SCOTLAND in 1929 *20-*. [UNITED + FREE¹,³ + KIRK¹,¹]

United Presbyterian Church /juˈnʌɪtəd prɛzbəˈtɪriən ˈtʃʌrtʃ/ *n* the church formed in 1847 by the union of the *United Associate Synod* (UNITED) and *the Relief Church* (RELIEF) *19-*. [UNITED + PRESBYTERIAN¹,² + CHURCH]

unitie *see* UNITE¹,¹, UNITY
unitit *see* UNITED
unitt *see* UNE

unity, †**unitie**, †**unite** /ˈjunəti/ *n* **1** agreement, unanimity, harmony *15-*. **2** the fact or state of being one and undivided, oneness *la15-16*. [AN *unitee*, OFr *unité*]

universal /junəˈvɛrsəl/ *adj* **1** all-encompassing, comprehensive; global; prevalent over all *la15-*. **2** *law of an heir* taking over the total rights and obligations of his or her predecessor *la16-*. **3** *law of an executor or intromitter* taking custody or control of all the effects of a deceased person *la16-19*. †**universal legator** sole legatee *17-e18*. **universal successor** an heir taking over the total rights and obligations of his or her predecessor *17-*. [ME *universal*, OFr *universal*, Lat *ūniversālis*]

universitas /junəˈvɛrsɪtas/ *n law* the whole property of a deceased person *la18-*. [Lat *ūniversitās* the totality]

unjust /ʌnˈdʒʌst/ *adj* **1** *of a person* that does not act justly or fairly; *of an action* not in accordance with justice or fairness *16-*. **2** *of weights or measures* false, inaccurate *la16-17*. [ME *unjust*; compare JIST¹,¹]

unjustice /ʌnˈdʒʌstɪs/ *n* injustice *la17-19, 20- Sh*. [UN- + JUSTICE]

unken, *NE* **oonken** /ʌnˈkɛn; *NE* unˈkɛn/ *v* not to know, to fail to recognize, be ignorant of *19, 20- NE*. [UN- + KEN¹,² or back-formation from UNKENT]

unkend, **unkenned** *see* UNKENT

unkennin, **unkenning**, †**unkennand** /ʌnˈkɛnɪn, ʌnˈkɛnɪŋ/ *adj* unknowing, ignorant *la14-19, 20- Sh NE EC*. [participial adj from UN- + KEN¹,²]

unkent, **onkent**, **unkenned**, *NE* **oonkent**, †**unkend**, †**onkend**, †**wnkennit** /ʌnˈkɛnt, ɔnˈkɛnt, ʌnˈkɛnd; *NE* unˈkɛnt/ *adj* unknown, unfamiliar, strange; unseen, unnoticed *la14-*. **unkent by** unknown to, without someone's knowing *19-*. **unkent tae**, **unkent to** not known to a person; without a person's knowing, being aware of or affected by *15-*. [UN- + KENT¹]

unkie-like *see* UNCO-LIKE¹,¹
unkin *see* UNCAN¹,²
unla *see* UNLAW¹,¹
unlaid *see* UNLAW¹,²

†**unland** *n* non-arable land *16-e17*. [OE *unland* desert, waste land]

†**unlandit** *adj* not possessed of land *15-e17*. [UN- + *landit* (LAND¹,¹)]

†**unlaw**¹,¹, **unla**, **vnlay** *n* a fine, penalty; the revenues raised from fines *la14-e18*. **not worth the king's unlaw** *of a pauper* unable to pay a fine, hence, unsuitable as a witness *17-18*. **wrang and unlaw** *see* WRANG¹,¹. [OE *unlagu* an illegal action]

†**unlaw**¹,², **vnlay** *v ptp* also †**unlaid** **1** to impose a financial penalty, fine *la15-e18*. **2** to pay a fine *16-17*. [see the noun]

unleeze /ʌnˈliz/ *v* to disentangle *la19- C SW*. [UN- + LEASE¹,²]

†**unlegitimat** *v ptp* **unlegitimate** not to make legitimate, not legalize *16-17*. [UN- + Lat *legitimāt-*, ptp stem of *legitimāre* to legalize]

†**unleif**, **onleif** *adj* unacceptable, disagreeable *15-e16*. [OE *unlēof* hated; compare LEIF¹,¹]

†**unleifit** *adj* without leaves *e16*. [UN- + LEAF + -IT²]

unleifsum *see* UNLEISUM
unleil *see* UNLELE

unleisum, **unlessum**, †**unlesum**, †**onlesum**, †**unleifsum** /ʌnˈlisʌm, ʌnˈlɛsʌm/ *adj* unlawful, illegal; forbidden, prohibited *la14-19, 20- WC SW*. [UN- + LEESOME²]

†**unlele**, **unleil**, **onleill** *adj* **1** faithless; disloyal; untrustworthy *la14-16*. **2** unjust, unfair *e16*. [UN- + LEAL¹,¹]

unless¹,¹, **onless**, *NE* **oonless**, *Sh* **aless**, †**onles**, †**unles** /ʌnˈlɛs, ɔnˈlɛs; *NE* unˈlɛs; *Sh* əˈlɛs, aˈlɛs/ *conj* unless, if not, except *la16-*. [see the prep]

unless[1,2], †**onles**, †**unles**, †**ales** /ʌnˈlɛs/ *prep* except, but for *la19-*. **unless that** except that *la16-17*. **ales than** = *unless that la15*. [ME *unlesse*, ON[1,2] + LESS[1,2]]

unlessum, unlesum *see* UNLEISUM

unlikely, †**unliklie**, †**onlykly** /ʌnˈlʌɪkli/ *adj* **1** having little chance of coming about, improbable; not likely to succeed, unpromising *la14-*. **2** unattractive, repellent, unacceptable, disagreeable, poor in quality or condition *la15-e18*. [UN- + LIKELY[1,2]]

unlucky, †**unlukie** /ʌnˈlʌki/ *adj* **1** unfortunate; inauspicious; having or bringing bad luck *la16-*. **2** slatternly, slovenly: ◇*she's a foul unlucky trollop* 20- *NE*. [UN- + LUCKY[1,2]]

†**unmaculat** *adj* immaculate *16-e17*. [UN- + MACULAT]

unmainnerfu /ʌnˈmenərfu/ *adj* rude, discourteous, unmannerly 20- *Sh NE*. [UN- + MAINNER, + -FU adj-forming suffix]

†**unmoderly** *adv* unkindly *15*. [UN- + Older Scots *moderly*, OE *mōdorlīc* motherly]

unmoved, †**unmovit** /ʌnˈmuvd/ *adj* **1** unaffected by emotion or conflict; steadfast; undisturbed, tranquil; not moved in position *la14-*. **2** unmoving, fixed *e16*. [participial adj from UN- + MOVE]

unnatural, *NE* **oonnaitral** /ʌnˈnatʃərəl/ *NE* unˈnetrəl/ *adj* **1** contrary to natural feelings, attitudes or behaviour *16-*. **2** abnormal, monstrous; simple-minded; peculiar *16-*. [UN- + NATURAL[1,2]]

unneis *see* UNEIS

unner *see* UNDER[1,1], UNDER[1,2]

unner- *see* UNDER-

unner-hous *see* UNDERHOOS

unnerstan, unnerstaun *see* UNDERSTAND[1,2]

unnertak *see* UNDERTAK

unner-wattir, **under-watter** /ˈʌnərwatɪr, ˈʌndərwɔtər, ʌndərˈwatər/ *n* water that has accumulated in the foundations of a house *la15-19*, 20- *Sh Ork NE*. [UNDER- + WATTER[1,1]]

unoorament /ʌnˈurəmənt/ *adj* uncomfortable, unpleasant *19*, 20- *N*. [unknown]

†**unpait, unpayit, unpeyit** *adj* not paid *15-17*. [participial adj from UN- + *pay* (PEY[1,2])]

†**unpay** *v* to leave unpaid; to fail to pay *16-17*. [UN- + *pay* (PEY[1,2]) or back-formation from *unpait*]

unpayit, unpeyit *see* UNPAIT

†**unplane, onplayn, onplane** *adj* devious, dishonest; of terrain difficult *e16*. [UN- + PLAIN[1,2]]

unpossibill, unpossible *see* ONPOSSIBLE

unprisit *see* ONPRISIT

unprofitable, †**unproffitabill**, †**onprofitabil** /ʌnˈprɔfɪtəbəl/ *adj* **1** yielding no profit or advantage, useless *la15-*. **2** *of a person* of no consequence, worthless; unsatisfactory as a worker *la15-17*. [UN- + *profitable* (PROFIT[1,1])]

unproven, †**unprovyn** /ʌnˈprovən/ *adj* **1** *of (the outcome of) a case brought before a court* not proved *la16-*. **2** *law* attracting a verdict of *not proven* (PROVEN) *la19-*. [UN- + PROVEN]

†**unprovidedly** *adv* unexpectedly, without warning *la16-17*. [UN- + Older Scots *provyditlie* prudently; compare PROVIDE]

†**unprovisit** *adj* unexpected, unforeseen, unconsidered *la15-16*. **unprovisitly, onprovisitly 1** unexpectedly, without warning *la15-16*. **2** perhaps without consideration or imprudently *e16*. [participial adj from UN- + Older Scots *provise* to provide, pre-arrange, Lat *prōvīs-*, ptp stem of *prōvidēre* to foresee]

unprovyn *see* UNPROVEN

†**unquarrelable** *adj law* indisputable, unchallenged, incontrovertible *la17-e18*. [UN- + *quarrellable* (QUARREL[2,2])]

†**unquietatioun** *n* a disturbance *e17*. [UN- + QUIETACIOUN]

unreason, †**unresoun**, †**unressoun** /ʌnˈrizən/ *n* **1** absence of reason; that which is contrary to or devoid of reason *la15-*. **2** unreasonable action or intention; injustice, impropriety *la15-e17*. **Abbot of Unreason** *see* ABBOT. [UN- + REASON[1,1]]

unreasonable, *NE* **oonrizzonable**, *Bor* **unrizzonable**, †**onressonabill**, †**oneresonabile** /ʌnˈriznəbəl; *NE* unˈrɪzənəbəl; *Bor* ʌnˈrɪzənəbəl/ *adj* **1** beyond the bounds of reason or acceptability; irrational, nonsensical *la14-*. **2** *of animals* lacking in the faculty of reason *la15-17*. [UN- + RIZZONABLE]

†**unreducit** *adj* not revoked, annulled or repealed *la16-e17*. [participial adj from UN- + REDUCE]

unremovable /ʌnrəˈmuvəbəl/ *adj* **1** *of things* incapable of being moved, immovable; fixed, steady *la15-*. **2** *of tenants* that cannot be legally moved or ejected *la16*. [UN- + REMOVABILL]

unresoun *see* UNREASON

†**unresponsall** *adj* unresponsible, lacking substance or standing; insolvent *la16-e17*. [UN- + RESPONSALL[1,2]]

unressoun *see* UNREASON

unrest, †**onrest** /ʌnˈrɛst/ *n* trouble, turmoil; disturbance *la14-*. †**unrestles** restless *e16*. **unresty** unrestful, ill at ease, troubled *la15*, *19- N Bor*. [UN- + REST[1,1]]

†**unricht**[1,1], **onrycht** *n* wrongdoing, injustice *la14-16*. [OE *unriht* noun]

unricht[1,2], †**onrycht** /ʌnˈrɪxt/ *adj* **1** not right, unjust; dishonest, improper *15-19*, 20- *N T EC SW*. **2** incorrect, inaccurate *16-e17*. [OE *unriht* adj]

†**unricht**[1,3], **onrycht** *adv* wrongly, incorrectly, improperly, unjustly *15-16*. [OE *unrihte*]

unrizzonable *see* UNREASONABLE

†**unrockit, vnrokkit** *adj* in a state of excitement, lacking control *la15-16*. [participial adj from UN- + ROCK[2]]

unrove *see* UNRUFE

†**unrude, onrude, vnryde** *adj* violent, rough; dreadful, outrageous *la15-e19*. [OE *ungerȳde*, with form influenced by RUDE[1]]

†**unrufe, unrove** *n* unrest, disquiet *la15-16*. [UN- + *ruve* (RO[2,1])]

†**unruleful, vnrewlful** *adj* unruly, rebellious *15-17*. [UN- + REULFUL]

unsaired *see* UNSERVED

unscathed, unscathit *see* UNSKAITHED

unscaumit /ʌnˈskɑmɪt/ *adj* not burned or scorched, unscathed *la19- Sh NE*. [participial adj from UN- + *scaum* (SCAM[1,2])]

†**unscrapit tongue** *n* a foul mouth; abusive or uncivil speech *18-19*. [participial adj from UN- + SCRAPE[1,2] + TONGUE[1,1]]

†**unseely, unseli, onsilly** *adj* **1** unfortunate, unhappy *la15-e16*. **2** causing or involving misfortune, unhappiness or danger *16-19*. [OE *unsǣlig*; compare SEELY]

†**unsell**[1,1] *n* **1** misfortune *la14-16*. **2** a wicked, disreputable or troublesome person *la16-e19*. [OE *unsǣl*]

†**unsell**[1,2], **unsel, vnsall** *adj* unlucky, wretched; wicked *la14-e17*. [OE *unsǣle*]

unsensible /ʌnˈsɛnsəbəl/ *adj* **1** lacking sense, or reasoning power *17-19*, 20- *N*. **2** unappreciative; callous *la17*. [UN- + Older Scots *sensible*, OFr *sensible*, Lat *sensibilis*]

unserved, unsaired, †**unservit** /ʌnˈsɛrvd; ʌnˈsɛrd/ *adj* **1** not attended to; not furnished with *la16-*. **2** *law* not returned as heir *la15-e17*. [participial adj from UN- + SAIRVE]

†**unset** *adj* **1** *of time or place* not previously appointed or arranged *la16*. **2** *of land or property* unlet, not rented out; not allocated to someone *15-18*. **3** not seated at a table *la15*. [UN- + SET[1,3]]

†**unsichtfull** *adj* invisible *la14*. [UN- + Older Scots *sichtfull* visible; compare SICHT[1.1]]
unskaithed, unscathed, †**unscathit** /ʌnˈskeθd, ʌnˈskeðd/ *adj* unhurt, unharmed *la14*-. [participial adj from UN- + SKAITH[1.2]]
†**unsmart** *adj of a bow* slack, dull, feeble *la15*. [UN- + *smart* (SMERT[1.3])]
unsolt *see* ONSLAUCHT
unsonsie, unsonsy /ʌnˈsɔnsi/ *adj* **1** capable of causing harm or injury; malign, nasty; unpleasant, treacherous; troublesome, mischievous *la16*-. **2** bringing bad luck, ill-omened; unfortunate, luckless, hapless *18-19*. **3** plain, unattractive; slovenly, untidy *19*. [UN- + SONSIE]
unspoken, onspoken, †**unspokin** /ʌnˈspokən, ɔnˈspokən/ *adj* **1** not uttered *la16*-. **2** *folk-medicine of a curative substance or procedure* not spoken over, gathered, handled or carried out in silence *la16-19*. **3** without speaking or having spoken, in silence *la16*. **4** not spoken of; not mentioned *la14*. [participial adj from UN- + SPEAK[1.2]]
unspuilȝeit *see* ONSPULȝEIT
†**unstraight** *adj* devious, untrue *la17*. [UN- + *straight* (STRAUCHT[1.3])]
†**unsufficient, unsuffyciande** *adj* **1** insufficient; *of a person* unsatisfactory; deficient in skill or ability; inadequate, incompetent *la15-17*. **2** *of workmanship or construction* inadequate, unsatisfactory; unsound, insecure *16-18*. [UN- + SUFFICIENT[1.1]]
unsure, †**onsure** /ʌnˈʃur/ *adj* **1** not known or understood *la16*-. **2** dangerous *16*. **3** insecure, vulnerable; precarious *16-e18*. **4** unreliable *la16-19*. [UN- + *sure* (SHAIR[2.1])]
†**unsynnand** *adj* unsinful *la14*. [participial adj from UN- + SIN[2.2]]
unt *see* UNCT
untellin, †**untelland** /ʌnˈtɛlən/ *adj* past reckoning, impossible to tell, beyond words *e16, 19- C Bor*. [ME *untelland* innumerable; compare TELL[1.2]]
†**untender** *adj* lacking religious feeling *la17-e19*. **untenderness** lack of proper religious feeling *la17-e18*. [UN- + TENDER[1.2]]
unthochtful /ʌnˈθɔxtfəl/ *adj* **1** not taking thought, unheeding (of) *la15*. **2** thoughtless *20*-. [UN- + *thochtful* (THOCHT)]
†**unthrift, onthrift** *n* **1** a worthless wretch, a waster; a spendthrift *la14-e19*. **2** lack of thrift, extravagance; lack of success; vain or wasted labour *16-e19*. **unthriftines** foolish or misguided behaviour *e16*. **unthrifty** wasteful, extravagant; foolish *la15-e19*. [UN- + THRIFT]
†**unthrive** *v* to fail to thrive *e17*. **unthriven** = *unthriving 19*. **unthriving** *of living things* sickly, unhealthy *17-19*. [ME *unthriven*; compare THRIVE[1.2]]
until[1.1], ontil /ʌnˈtɪl, ɔnˈtɪl/ *prep in OSc usually before vowels and h* **1** up to a point in time *la15*-. **2** in, into *16-19, 20- NE*. **3** to, unto, as far as, towards (a place) *15-e19*. **4** indicating the person or thing towards or against which an attitude, request or action is directed *15-e19*. **5** to *15-16*. **6** for *la15-e17*. [ME *until*, ON **und* as far as + TILL[2.2]]
until[1.2] /ʌnˈtɪl/ *conj* **1** up to the point when *16*-. **2** *with a negative in the main clause* before *la16*-. [see the prep]
unto *see* ONTO[1.1]
untowtherly, untodderly /ʌnˈtʌuðərli, ʌnˈtɔdərli/ *adj* **1** big, clumsy and unwieldy; badly put together *20- NE*. **2** slovenly, unkempt, dishevelled *20- NE*. [perhaps an altered form of Eng *untowardly*, with influence from TOUTHER[1.1]]
unused, †**unusit,** †**onvsyt,** †**vnwsit** /ʌnˈjuzd/ *adj* **1** unaccustomed, not used to; inexperienced *la15*-. **2** not made use of *la15*-. **3** unusual, uncommon *16-17*. [participial adj from UN- + USE[1.2]]

†**unvincible, vnvynsable, wnvinsabell** *adj* invincible *la15-e17*. [altered form, with change of prefix, of Older Scots *invincible*, Lat *invincibilis*]
unwaft /ʌnˈwaft/ *v* to disentangle *20*-. †**unwafted** left unwoven *la17*. [UN- + WAFT[1.2]]
unwaiting *see* ONWAIT[1.2]
†**unwarnist, onwarnyst, onawarnyst** *adj* unforewarned, unprepared; unannounced *15-16*. **unwarnistly** unexpectedly, without warning *e16*. [participial adj from UN- + WARNIS, with influence from WARN[1]]
unwashen, †**unweschin,** †**onwaschin** /ʌnˈwaʃən/ *adj* unwashed *16-19, 20- Sh NE*. [OE *unwæscen*; compare WASH[1.2]]
†**unwaukit** /ʌnˈwɑkɪt/ *adj of cloth* not shrunk or fulled *la19- Sh NE Bor*. [UN- + *waukit* (WAULK)]
unweel, unwell, *Sh NE* **oonweel;** *N NE T* **onweel,** †**unweill** /ʌnˈwil, ʌnˈwel; *Sh NE* unˈwil; *N NE T* ɔnˈwil/ *adj* in poor health, sickly, ailing; suffering from an illness *17*-. **unweelness,** †**unweelnes** bad health; illness *17-19, 20- N NE*. [UN- + WEEL[1.1]]
†**unweildable** *adj* unwieldy *e16*. [UN- + WIELD, with adj-forming suffix]
unweill *see* UNWEEL
†**unweirdit** *adj* ill-fated *la16*. [UN- + WEIRD[1.1] + -IT[2]]
unwell *see* UNWEEL
†**unwenandly** *adv* unexpectedly *la14*. [UN- + *wenand*, presp of WEEN[1.2], with adv-forming suffix]
unweschin *see* UNWASHEN
unwholesome *see* UNHALESOME
unwinnable, †**unwinnabil,** †**wnwynnabill** /ʌnˈwɪnəbəl/ *adj* not winnable; *of a stronghold* impregnable *la15*-. [UN- + WIN[1.2], with adj-forming suffix]
unwiselike /ʌnˈwaezlʌɪk/ *adj* indiscreet, imprudent, foolish *la17-19, 20- N*. [UN- + *wise-like* (WISE[2])]
unwittens /ʌnˈwɪtənz/ *adv* unwittingly, inadvertently *19, 20- literary*. [UNWITTING, with *-s* adv-forming suffix]
unwitting, †**unwittand** /ʌnˈwɪtɪŋ/ *adj* unknown to; not or without knowing, unaware *la14*-. [OE *unwitende*]
†**unwollit** *adj* lacking wool, shorn *e16*. [UN- + *woll* (OO[1]) + -IT[2]]
†**unworth[1]** *n* a very low price *e18*. [UN- + WORTH[1.1]]
†**unworth[2]** *adj* unworthy, undeserving; worthless *17-18*. [OE *unweorð*, or new formation UN- + WORTH[1.2]]
†**unwrokin, onwrokyn** *adj* unavenged *e16*. [participial adj from UN- + WREKE]
unyirdly, †**uneirdlie,** †**uneardly** /ʌnˈjɪrdli/ *adj* supernatural; mysterious; weird *17*-. Compare WANEARTHLIE. [UN- + Older Scots ȝerdly, erdly, OE *eorðlic*]
unyiverish /ʌnˈjɪvərɪʃ/ *adj* sluggish *20- Ork*. [UN- + YIVVER, + *-ish* suffix]
unȝement *see* UNGUMENT
unȝeon *see* INGAN
up[1.1], †**uppe** /ʌp/ *adj* **1** *of a river* in flood *18*-. **2** *of a child* grown up, adult *la19*-. **3** *of a chimney* on fire *20- Ork N T EC*. **4** *of people* in a state of excitement or irritation *19, 20- NE T*. **5** open, ajar; extending outwards *la14-19*. **neither up nor doon 1** nowhere *20- Sh Ork NE*. **2** *especially of feelings* unaffected by events, equable *19*-. **up in life** *of a person* advanced in years, elderly *19*-. **up in years** = *up in life la19*-. **up to high doh** in a state of extreme anxiety or excitement *la20*-. **up wi 1** equal, as good as; fit for, capable of *la18*-. **2** even with, quits with *19, 20- Sh T*. [see the adv]
up[1.2], oop, †**upe,** †**uppe,** †**oup** /ʌp, up/ *adv* **1** to or towards a higher level or place, or vertical position *la14*-. **2** to completion or (en)closure, entirely *la14*-. **3** *of activity* to a greater degree, more intensely *la14*-. **4** to or towards a higher valuation *la16*-. **uplins** upwards *19, 20- Sh NE*. **up aboot**

somewhere in or near *20-*. **up again** all over again *20- Sh*. **up an doon, up and doun 1** to and fro, throughout (a place); in both directions; everywhere, anywhere *la14-*. **2** from top to bottom; from every angle, in every aspect, thoroughly *la14-17, la19- Ork N NE T*. †**up of land** = UPONLAND *la15*. **up or doon** *in negative constructions* neither one way nor the other, neither here nor there *19, 20- NE*. **up wi't** *in songs* hurrah!, bravo! *la18-19, 20- historical*. [OE *upp, ūp*]

up[1,3], **oop**, †**upe** /ʌp, up/ *prep* **1** from a lower to a higher level, upwards, uphill; in the direction of the source of a river or stream *la14-*. **2** at or near the top of (a slope) *la16-*. **up hill and doon dale** *especially of someone pursuing another with abuse* relentlessly, without restraint *la19- Sh Ork N NE T EC*. **up street** up the street; going to or associated with the upper end of a town or village *la19- Ork*. **up the country** in or from the upland or interior part of a district *19, 20- NE T SW*. **up the gates** *in Kirkwall, Orkney* a person born in the inland part of the town, south of the Bishop's and Earl's palaces, and playing as an UPPIE in the annual HAND-BA game *la19-*. **up the hoose** into the interior of a house, from the door inwards *18-19, 20- Sh Ork T*. **up the kyte** *see* KYTE. [OE *uppan* assimilated to the adv]

U.P. /'ju 'pi/ *n* a member of the UNITED PRESBYTERIAN CHURCH *la19-*. [abbreviation]

upaland *see* UPELAND, UPONLAND.

upald *see* UPPLE[1,2]

†**upbeild** *v* to build, construct *16*. [UP[1,2] + *beild* (BUILD)]

†**upber** *v pt* **vpbair** *ptp* **vpborne, vpbore** to hold up, support, carry; to raise up *15-e17*. **upberar** a supporter *16-e17*. [UP[1,2] + BEAR[2]]

upbiggit /ʌp'bɪgɪt/ *adj* **1** built up, repaired *15-19, 20- NE*. **2** elated *20- NE*. [UP[1,2] + *biggit* (BIG[1])]

†**upblawand** *adj of wind* rising, blowing more strongly *e16*. [participial adj from UP[1,2] + BLAW[1,2]]

†**upblese** *v of fire* to blaze up, erupt in flames *16*. [UP[1,2] + *blese* (BLEEZE[1,2])]

†**upboltyt** *adj* arisen, sprung up *e16*. [participial adj from UP[1,2] + bolt (BOWT[1,2])]

up-brae /'ʌpbre/ *adj* uphill *la19- Ork SW*. [UP[1,3] + BRAE]

upbraid /ʌp'bred/ *v* **1** to abuse verbally, scold *16-*. **2** to spring up *e16*. [OE *upbregdan*]

upbrak /'ʌpbrak/ *n* **1** the dispersal (of a gathering) *20- Sh NE*. **2** the beginning (of a thaw) *20- N*. **3** a shipwreck *20- Ork*. [UP[1,2] + BRAK[1,1]]

†**upbraking, upbreking, upbreaking** *n* (the action of) breaking into, forcing open; raping *la15-17*. [verbal noun from UP[1,2] + BRAK[1,2]]

upbring[1,1] /'ʌpbrɪŋ/ *n* training, education, maintenance during childhood *la19- Sh NE T C*. [see the verb]

upbring[1,2] /ʌp'brɪŋ/ *v* **1** to bring up, rear *la14-*. **2** to raise up, exalt *e16*. **upbringing 1** rearing, nurture, early training *16-*. **2** fetching, transporting *la15-e17*. [UP[1,2] + BRING]

upby /ʌp'bae/ *adv* up there, up the way, up at or to a place, especially somewhere thought of as being more exalted than where the speaker is, for example the *big hoose* (BIG[2]) or heaven; upstairs *la18-*. [UP[1,2] + BY[1,1]]

upcast[1,1] /'ʌpkast/ *n* **1** a taunt, reproach, ground or occasion for criticism *17-*. **2** *mining* a fault in a seam of coal which forces it upwards *la18-*. **3** *mining* the shaft by which the ventilating current returns to the surface *19-*. **4** an upset, a state of being overturned *19, 20- Sh*. **5** an upward glance *15*. **upcast shaft** = UPCAST[1,1] (sense 3) *20-*. [see the verb]

upcast[1,2] /ʌp'kast/ *v* **1** to taunt, reproach, allege as a fault *19-*. **2** to throw or force open (a gate) *15-e16*. **3** to throw oneself (onto a horse's back) *e16*. **4** to cause to stand on end *e16*. **upcastin 1** a gathering of clouds, a cloud formation *19, 20- Sh NE*. **2** digging up, removing by digging *la16-e17*. [UP[1,2] + CAST[1,2]]

upcome /'ʌpkʌm/ *n* **1** a comment, saying, turn of phrase *la19- N NE T*. **2** the final or decisive point, the result, outcome *19, 20- Sh T*. **3** an ascent, way up, slope *la14, la19*. **4** outward appearance, especially as being an indication for the future; promising aspect: ◊*if all be good that is upcome e17, e19*. **upcomin**, †**upcumming 1** rise, development, growth; the upbringing and development of a child *16-19, 20- Sh*. **2** the action of ascending or rising; journeying to or arrival at (a place) *la14-19*. **3** an ascent, a way up, a slope *la14-16*. [UP[1,2] + COME[1,1]]

†**updaw** *v* to dawn, become light *e16*. [UP[1,2] + DAW[1,2]]

updraw /ʌp'drɔ/ *v* **1** to catch up with, overtake *la19- Sh*. **2** to lift, raise up; to (cause to) rise *la15-e16*. [UP[1,2] + DRAW[1,2]]

†**updrive** *v ptp* **vpdryve** to drive, force upwards or into a higher place *la15-e16*. [UP[1,2] + DRIVE[1,2]]

upe *see* UP[1,2], UP[1,3]

upeat /ʌp'et/ *v* to annoy, vex *20- Sh*. [UP[1,2] + EAT[1,2]]

†**upeland, upaland, uplande** *adj* living or situated in the countryside (as opposed to the town), rustic, rural *la13-e17*. [see the adv *upeland* (UPONLAND)]

upeland *see* UPONLAND

uper *see* UPPER

upfeshin, up-fessen /'ʌpfɛʃɪn, 'ʌpfɛsɪn/ *n* upbringing, the rearing (of a family) *la19- NE EC*. [verbal noun from UP[1,2] + FESH]

†**up-flureis** *v* to grow, flourish *e16*. [UP[1,2] + *flureis* (FLOURISH[1,2])]

upga *see* UPGAE[1,2]

upgae[1,1] /'ʌpge/ *n mining* a rise in the stratum of a coal-seam *la17, 20- EC*. [see the verb]

upgae[1,2], †**upga** /ʌp'ge/ *v* to go, rise up *la15-*. [UP[1,2] + GAE]

upgaen[1,1], **upgaun** /'ʌpgen, 'ʌpgɔən/ *n* an ascent *la19, 20- Sh Ork T*. [verbal noun from UPGAE[1,2]]

upgaen[1,2] /'ʌpgeən/ *adj* reckless *20- Sh*. [participial adj from UPGAE[1,2]]

upgaister *see* OPGESTER

upgaistrie *see* OPGESTRIE

upgang, *Sh* **uppgeng** /'ʌpgaŋ, 'ʌpgɛŋ/ *n* **1** a sudden rising of the wind; a storm *la19- Sh Ork*. **2** an act of ascending; an ascent, a slope *la14-e19*. [OE *upgang*; compare GANG[1,1]]

upgaster *see* OPGESTER

upgaun *see* UPGAEN[1,1]

†**upget** *v* to get up, rise; to put together *la19*. **upgeter** one who instigates something *e17*. [UP[1,2] + GET[1,2]]

upgie, upgive, †**upgif** /ʌp'gi, ʌp'gɪv/ *v* **1** *law* to give up, deliver up, resign (possession) *la14-*. **2** to abandon, relinquish (an allegiance); to hand over (information) *e16*. †**upgiver, upgiffar** an informant or informer *la16-17*. †**upgiving 1** *law* surrender, relinquishment (of property or rights) *15-e17*. **2** *law* a declaration, presentation (of accounts or information); a statement on oath *la15-e18*. **3** abandonment (of friendship) *la16-17*. [UP[1,2] + GIE]

uphald *see* UPHAUD[1,1], UPHAUD[1,2]

uphaldin *see* UPHAUD[1,2]

uphalieday, *Ork* **Uphelli Day**, †**uphalyday**, †**huphallowday** /'ʌphelɪde; *Ork* 'ʌphɛli 'de/ *n* the festival of the Epiphany as the end of the Christmas holidays, the 6th January *la15-18, 20- historical*. [UP[1,2] with the sense of completion + HALY + DAY; compare UP-HELLY-AA]

†**uphaly-evin, vphelly-ewin, huphally-evin** *n* (the evening of) the eve of Epiphany, 5th January *16-e17*. [formed on UPHALIEDAY with substitution of evin (EVEN[1]) for *day*]

†**uphalymes, vphellymes** = UPHALIEDAY *16*. [formed on UPHALIEDAY with substitution of mess (MASS[2]) for *day*]

uphaud[1.1], **uphud**, †**uphald**, †**uphold** /'ʌphɔd, 'ʌphʌd; *NE* 'ʌpəl/ *n* **1** a person or institution that upholds another; a support, mainstay *15-*. **2** the support or maintenance of a person or estate; the upkeep of property *la14-19, 20- Sh Ork N*. **3** a means of support for a physical structure, a prop *16*. [see the verb]

uphaud[1.2], **uphud**, **uphald**, **uphold** /ʌp'hɔd, ʌp'hʌd, ʌp'hald, ʌp'hold/ *v pt, ptp* **upheld**, *NE* **upheeld**, †**vpheild**, †**vpheildit**, †**vphald** *ptp* also **uphauden** †**uphaldin 1** to support, preserve, sustain *la14-*. **2** to raise, lift up, originally especially of the hand raised to take an oath *la14-*. **3** to maintain in argument, warrant, guarantee *15-*. **4** to keep in a state of good repair, maintain, look after *la14-19, 20- Sh T C*. **5** to provide for, support financially *15-16*. [UP[1.2] + HAUD[1.2]]

†**uphaving** *n* transport, carrying (up) *e16*. [verbal noun from *uphaue* (UPHEVE)]

upheeld *see* UPHAUD[1.2]

upheeze, †**upheis**, †**uphes** /ʌp'hiz/ *v* to lift up, raise; to exalt, elate *16-19, 20- C*. [UP[1.2] + HEEZE[1.2]]

upheld *see* UPHAUD[1.2]

Uphelli Day *see* UPHALIEDAY

†**uphellie-nicht** *n* = UPHALY-EVIN *la19*. [formed on UP-HELLY-AA with substitution of NICHT[1.1] for *aa*]

Up-Helly-Aa /ʌp'hɛli'ɑ, 'ʌphɛle'a/ *n in Shetland* the fire festival held in Lerwick on the last Tuesday of January *la19-*. [altered form of UPHALIEDAY with assimilation to HELLY and the final syllable understood as *aa* (AW[1.1])]

uphe *see* UPHIE

uphes *see* UPHEEZE

†**upheve**, **uphaue** *v* to raise, lift up *la14-e16*. [UP[1.2] + HEAVE[1.2]]

upheyt *see* UPHIE

†**uphie**, **uphe**, **vphei** *v ptp* also **upheyt** to exalt; to raise up *la15-16*. [UP[1.2] + *he* (HEICH[1.2])]

uphold *see* UPHAUD[1.1], UPHAUD[1.2]

uphud *see* UPHAUD[1.1], UPHAUD[1.2]

uphug[1.1], **uphoug** /'ʌphʌg/ *n* ruin, bankruptcy *19- Sh*. [see the adj]

†**uphug**[1.2], **uphoug** *adj* **1** worn out *e20 Sh*. **2** fatted and ready for slaughter *e20 Sh*. [UP[1.2]; for the second element compare Norw *hugge* to hack, cut up]

†**uphynt**, **wphint** *adj* raised, lifted up *e16*. [participial adj from UP[1.2] + *hint* (HENT[2])]

upkummel /ʌp'kʌməl/ *v* to overturn, capsize *20-*. [UP[1.2] + CUMMEL]

uplande *see* UPELAND

†**uplandis** *adj* = UPELAND *15-17*. [OE *uplendisc*]

uplayer /'ʌpleər/ *n* a person who prepares the loads for a beast of burden, especially in the transport of peats *la19- Sh*. [UP[1.2] + LAY[1.2], with agent suffix]

uplift[1.1] /'ʌplɪft/ *n* **1** a refuse collection *la20-*. **2** a contribution or payment to a common fund; the collection of accounts (by a shopkeeper) *la19- C*. **3** an exaction or levy *la17*. [see the verb]

uplift[1.2], †**vplyft** /ʌp'lɪft/ *v* **1** to lift up, raise to a higher level or position; elevate *15-*. **2** to collect, draw, take possession of (money, rents or taxes) *la15-*. **3** to collect, fetch (tickets or parcels), pick up, take on (passengers) *la16-*. **4** to dig up, harvest (potatoes and other root crops) *la19-*. **5** to gladden, make proud *19-*. **6** to conscript (soldiers) *la16-e18*. †**upliftable** *of taxes* due, leviable *la17-18*. **uplifted**, *Sh* **upliftet** elated, in high spirits, proud *19-*. †**uplifter** a collector (of rents or taxes) *la16-17*. †**uplift the psalm** *Presbyterian Church* to lead the singing of the psalm *e19*. [UP[1.2] + LIFT[2.2]]

uplook /'ʌpluk/ *n* a respite, let-up *la19- T*. [UP[1.2] + *look* (LEUK[1.1])]

uplös /ʌp'løs/ *v* to reveal, disclose *la19- Sh*. [Norw *oplyse*]

uplowsin /'ʌplʌuzən/ *n* a thaw; a deluge of rain *20- Sh*. [verbal noun from UP[1.2] + LOWSE[1.2]]

upluppen /'ʌplʌpən/ *adj* impulsive, excitable *la19- Sh*. [participial adj from UP[1.2] + LEAP]

upmade /'ʌpmed/ *adj* pleased, elated *20- Bor*. [participial adj from UP[1.2] + MAK[1.2]]

upmaist, **upmost** /'ʌpmest, 'ʌpmost/ *adj* **1** uppermost, highest *17-*. **2** outermost *la16-e17*. Compare UMEST[1.2]. **upmaist clathe** = *umest clathe* (UMEST[1.2]) *la16*. [UP[1.1] + *-maist* suffix; compare MAIST[1.1]]

upmak[1.1] /'ʌpmak/ *n* **1** invention, composition, a made-up story, song or plan *19- Sh NE*. **2** compensation, reparation *la19- Sh Ork NE*. **3** *in dressmaking* the creation of a garment *la19- Sh NE*. **4** a lie *20- Sh*. **5** a person's disposition *20- Sh*. [see the verb]

†**upmak**[1.2] *v* **1** to make good, compensate for (a defect, damage, harm done) *la15-e17*. **2** to construct, build; to repair *la15-e17*. [UP[1.2] + MAK[1.2]]

upmaker, **upmakker** /'ʌpmekər, 'ʌpmakər/ *n* a storyteller, composer *20- Sh NE*. [UP[1.2] + MAK[1.2], with agent suffix]

upmaking[1.1] /'ʌpmekɪŋ, 'ʌpmakɪŋ/ *n* **1** the preparation of (land for planting), the making up of (garments) *18-*. **2** = UPMAK[1.1] (sense 1) *la19- Sh NE T*. **3** the assembly of lines of type into pages for printing *la19-20, 21- historical*. **4** compensation *la17-e18*. **5** building, construction; reconstruction, repair *la15-17*. **6** the satisfying or satisfaction (of a spiritual need) *la17*. [verbal noun from UPMAK[1.2]]

†**upmaking**[1.2] *adj* compensating, satisfying; ingratiating *la17-19*. [participial adj from UPMAK[1.2]]

upmakker *see* UPMAKER

upmost *see* UPMAIST

upoland *see* UPONLAND

upon, **upo**, **upoan**, *Sh NE* **apon**, *Sh Ork* **apo**, *Sh* **ipo**, *Ork N NE* **'po**, *Ork* **apae**, †**upoun**, †**upone**, †**avpone** /ʌ'pɔn, ʌ'po; *Sh NE* ə'pɔn; *Sh Ork* ə'po; *Sh* ɪ'po; *Ork N NE* po; *Ork* ə'pa/ *prep* **1** positioned above and supported by or in contact with *la14-*. **2** *especially with verbs of remembering or thinking* about, concerning: ◇*Ah mind upon being sent la14-*. **3** in, on, at, beside: ◇*meet ye upon the street* ◇*we waur upon nae hurry la14-*. **4** at (a price or cost) *la15-*. **5** (be married) to, with *la15-*. **6** belonging to, having membership of *16-*. **7** during, in the course of, on the occasion of: ◇*sleep upon the day la14-19, 20- Sh Ork NE*. **8** on, onto, at, towards; against, from *la14-19, 20- Sh*. **9** for: ◇*expensis maid upon the artilʒery 15-17*. **10** on the basis of, because of *la14-17*. **upon the heid o** at the head of *la18, 20- Sh NE*. [OE *upp on*, UP[1.2] + ON[1.2], with influence from ON *upp á*]

†**uponland**, **upoland**, **upaland**, **upeland**, **aponlande** *adv* in the country (as opposed to the town) *15-19*. [OE *uppe on londe, uppe lande*; compare UPELAND]

†**uponlandis** *adj* = UPELAND *la15*. [conflation of UPLANDIS with UPONLAND]

upoun *see* UPON

†**uppa** *n in Shetland and Orkney* the first RIG[1.1] (sense 3) in a *sheed* (SHED[1.1] (sense 4)), especially at the edge of a township *17*. [ON *uppi up*]

uppabrak /'ʌpəbrak/ *n* anxiety *la19- Sh*. [compare Norw *oppbrakt* upset, distressed]

uppaled *see* UPPLE[1.2]

uppe *see* UP[1.1], UP[1.2]

uppelt *see* UPPLE[1.2]

upper, †**uper** /'ʌpər/ *adj* **1** of higher rank or level, senior *la15-*. **2** (situated) higher; lying above *16-*. **3** *in place-names* the highest of two or more places with the same name; *in farm names* the section of a divided estate situated on the highest ground *la17-*. **upper mor** the upper layer of peat in a moss *20- Sh*. [comparative of UP¹·¹]

†**uppermair, uppermore** *adv* higher up, further up *la14-18*. [UPPER + *-mair* suffix; compare MAIR¹·²]

uppgeng *see* UPGANG

uppgester *see* OPGESTER

uppie /'ʌpe, 'ʌpi/ *n* in the game of HAND-BA, a member of the team playing towards the upward goal, an UPPIE usually coming from the upper part of the town *20- Ork Bor*. Compare DOONIE. [UP¹·¹ + -IE³]

uppie-killie-donkey /'ʌpi 'kɪli 'dɔŋki/ *n* the game of seesaw *20- Ork*. [altered form of HEDDERKINDUNK]

†**uppit, upput** *v* to construct, erect (buildings) *16-17*. **upputter** a construction worker *17-e18*. **uppiting, upputting** raising, putting, setting up; constructing, building *16-e18*. [UP¹·² + PIT²]

uppittin, upputtin, †**upputting** /'ʌp'pɪtɪn, 'ʌp'pʊtɪn/ *n* lodging, accommodation *19, 20- EC SW Bor*. [verbal noun from UP¹·² + PIT²]

upple¹·¹ /'ʌpəl/ *n* a break in wet weather *19- NE*. [uphald (UPHAUD¹·¹) with shift of stress to the first syllable; compare Norw *opphald* an interval of fine weather]

upple¹·² /'ʌpəl/ *v pt* **uppaled, uppelt,** †**upald** *of rain or snow* to stop falling, let up, clear *17-19, 20- NE*. [see the noun]

upput, upputing, upputter *see* UPPIT

upputtin, upputting *see* UPPITTIN

upputting *see* UPPIT

upredd¹·¹ /'ʌpred/ *n* the act of clearing away, a cleaning, tidying *20- Sh NE T EC Bor*. [see the verb]

upredd¹·² /ʌp'red/ *v* to tidy, put in order *19, 20- Sh*. [UP¹·² + REDD¹·²]

upreddin /'ʌpredɪŋ/ *n* a scolding *la19- Sh EC SW*. [verbal noun from UPREDD¹·²]

upricht¹·¹, upright /'ʌprɪxt, 'ʌprʌɪt/ *n* 1 a vertical bar or support, a perpendicular stone or post *16-*. 2 *pl* a pious, upstanding group of people *20-*. 3 a goalpost *20-*. [see the adj]

†**upricht¹·²** *v in Aberdeen* to make reparation, compensate *la15*. [see the adj]

upricht¹·³, upright /'ʌprɪxt, 'ʌprʌɪt/ *adj* 1 erect; directed upwards *la14-*. 2 honest, honourable *la14-*. 3 genuine, authentic; rightful, legitimate *la15-17*. [OE *upriht*; compare RICHT¹·³]

upride /ʌp'rʌɪd/ *v* to dandle (a baby) *la19- Sh*. [UP¹·² + RIDE¹·²]

upright *see* UPRICHT¹·¹, UPRICHT¹·³

uprin /ʌp'rɪn/ *v* to catch up with by running *la19- Sh*. [UP¹·² + RIN¹·¹]

uprise, †**vpryse** /ʌp'raez/ *v* 1 to stand up; to get out of bed *15-*. 2 to ascend (into view), appear; to arise, become erect *la15-18*. 3 to advance in power or consequence *16*. 4 to grow up, mature; to spring up *16*. **uprisin,** †**oprisin** removal from a house *la19- Sh* [UP¹·² + RISE¹·²]

†**uproll** *v* 1 to drive, propel upwards *e16*. 2 to roll, wind, tuck up *16-e19*. [UP¹·² + *roll* (ROW¹·¹)]

†**upseed-time** *n* harvest *la17-e18*. [UP¹·² with the sense of completion + Older Scots *seed-time*; compare SEED¹·¹, TIME]

upset¹·¹ /'ʌpset/ *n* 1 *mining* a working place driven upwards following the course of the coal seam *18- EC*. 2 = *upset price* (UPSET¹·³) *19-*. 3 the fee paid to an INCORPORATION on becoming a freeman and commencing trading *la15-e19*. 4 setting up in business, the action or occasion of setting up one's booth to begin trading or of becoming a freeman in a trade *16-e18*. 5 insurrection, revolt *e15*. †**upsetter, upsettar** 1 a person who sets up as a master workman or starts in business *16-e18*. 2 a person who erects a sign or monument *la16-e17*. 3 a person who founds or establishes something *la16*. 4 an instrument for cleaning the bore of a cannon *e17*. [see the verb]

upset¹·² /ʌp'sɛt/ *v* 1 to put into a prominent or raised position; to place upright; to erect, build *15-*. 2 to overturn, spill, capsize *19-*. 3 to distress, disturb *la19-*. 4 to make good, make up for, compensate; to get over, recover from *16-e19*. 5 to (cause to) catch fire, burn *e16*. [UP¹·² + SET¹·²]

upset¹·³ /'ʌpsɛt/ *adj* 1 set up, raised, erected *16-*. 2 of good proportions *la15*. **upset price** the lowest acceptable selling price (of a property, or goods to be sold by auction) *la18-*. [see the verb]

upsettin¹·¹, upsetting /'ʌpsɛtɪn, 'ʌpsɛtɪŋ/ *n* 1 the action of placing or fixing in an elevated position; erecting, constructing *16-*. 2 setting up in business; setting up a stall or booth *la15-e18*. 3 raising to, or establishing in, position or power *la16-e18*. 4 arrogance, an unwarranted assumption of superiority *e19*. [verbal noun from UPSET¹·²]

upsettin¹·², upsetting /'ʌpsɛtɪn, ʌp'sɛtɪŋ/ *adj* haughty, presumptuously ambitious, giving oneself airs *19-*. [participial adj from UPSET¹·²]

upsides /ʌp'sʌɪdz, 'ʌpsʌɪdz/ *adv* alongside, on a level (with) *la17-*. **upsides doon wi** = *upsides wi* 1 *la19- N NE*. **upsides wi** 1 even, quits or equal with; revenged on *la18-*. 2 alongside *la17*. [UP¹·² + SIDE¹, with *-s* adv-forming suffix]

†**upsitten** *adj* indifferent, inactive *la17-e18*. [participial adj from UP¹·² + SIT¹·²; compare UPSITTING]

upsitting /'ʌpsɪtɪŋ/ *n* 1 indifference, lethargy *la17-*. 2 staying up late, deferring going to bed until a late hour *16-17*. 3 the celebration of a woman's first sitting up in bed after giving birth *16*. [verbal noun from UP¹·² + SIT¹·²; compare *sit up* (SIT¹·²)]

upslaag, *NE* **upslay** /'ʌpslɑg/; *NE* 'ʌpsle/ *n* a thaw *la19- Sh NE*. [Norw dial *uppslag*]

upsook /'ʌpsuk/ *n* a swell in the sea near land indicating worsening weather *20- Sh*. [UP¹·² + SOOK¹·¹]

upspraet /'ʌpsprɛt/ *n* (unravelled) thread or yarn *20- Sh*. [UP¹·² + ptp of SPRET¹·²]

upstand, upstan, upstaun /ʌp'stand, ʌp'stan, ʌp'stɔn/ *v* 1 to stand up, rise to one's feet *15-*. 2 to stand erect or upright *la14-16*. [UP¹·² + STAND¹·²]

upstandand *see* UPSTANNIN¹·²

upstander, *Sh* **opstander,** †**upstandar,** †**ouipstander** /ʌp'standər; *Sh* ɔp'standər/ *n* 1 one who stands up (in the pulpit), replacing the fisherman's taboo terms clergyman or minister *la19- Sh Ork*. 2 *in a jacquard lace loom* an upright needle *20- WC*. 3 an upright timber, a support *la16-e17*. [UPSTAND with agent suffix]

upstannin¹·¹, upstanding, †**oupe-standeng** /ʌp'stanɪn, ʌp'standɪŋ/ *n* 1 *usually of foodstuffs* substance, nutrition *la19- NE T*. 2 apparently a support, an upright *la16*. [verbal noun from UPSTAND]

upstannin¹·², upstaunin, upstanding, †**upstandand** /ʌp'stanɪn, ʌp'stɔnɪn, ʌp'standɪŋ/ *adj* 1 standing erect, upright; intact *16-*. 2 *of wages* regular, fixed, basic *la19- WC SW Bor*. **be upstanding** to stand up, as a sign of respect or ceremonially, to drink a toast or for a prayer ◊ *be upstanding for the bride and groom la19-*. [participial adj from UPSTAND]

upstart¹·¹ /'ʌpstart/ *n* 1 an upward start or spring *e17*. 2 *building* an upright or vertically set jamb- or reveal-stone in a door or window-case *la18-*. 3 a nouveau-riche person *la16-e19*. [see the verb]

†**upstart¹·²** *v* to start up, begin; to rise up, spring forward *15-19*. [UP¹·² + START¹·²]

upstaun *see* UPSTAND

upstaunin *see* UPSTANNIN¹·²

upsteer[1.1] /ˈʌpstir/ *n* a commotion, disturbance *20- Sh*. [see the verb]

upsteer[1.2], **upstir**, †**upsteir** /ʌpˈstir, ʌpˈstɪr/ *v* to stir up, throw into turmoil; to stimulate, encourage, arouse, incite *la16-*. [UP[1.2] + STEER[1.2]]

†**upstent** *v* to set up, erect; to make taut *16*. [UP[1.2] + STENT[1]]

†**upsticken** *adj* stuck up, priggish, snobbish *la19*. [participial adj from UP[1.2] + STICK[1.2]]

upstir *see* UPSTEER[1.2]

†**upstour** *v of dust* to fly up; *of the sea* to foam, froth *e16*. [UP[1.2] + STOOR[1.2]]

upstrake *see* UPSTREKE

upstraucht /ʌpˈstrɔxt/ *v* to stand up straight, straighten oneself up *la19- NE*. [UP[1.2] + STRAUCHT[1.2]]

†**upstreke**, **upstrik** *v pt* **upstrake**, *ptp* **upstraucht** to stretch, reach or rise up; to stand upright *e16*. [UP[1.2] + STREEK[1.2]]

†**upstriking**, **upstricking** *n* breaking down; breaking into; stealing (by forced entry) *la15-16*. [verbal noun from UP[1.2] + STRIK[1.2]]

†**up-sun** *n* **with up-sun** at sunrise; in daylight *17-e19*. [UP[1.2] + SUN[1.1]]

uptail /ʌpˈtel/ *v* to bolt, run away; to turn tail *20-*. **uptail and awa** having left in haste, fled at once *20- Ork NE T*. **uptail doon** = *uptail and awa 20- Ork*. [UP[1.2] + TAIL[1.1]]

uptak[1.1], **uptake** /ˈʌptak, ˈʌptek/ *n* **1** the capacity for understanding, power of comprehension, intelligence *19-*. **2** dealings, involvement, relationship *20- Sh T*. **3** lifting or gathering of a crop, especially a root-crop *20- Sh NE*. **4** *weather* an onset or recurrence of bad weather *la19- Sh*. **5** responsibility *la20- Sh*. [see the verb]

uptak[1.2], **uptake** /ʌpˈtak, ʌpˈtek/ *v* **1** to understand, comprehend *la17-19, 20- Sh*. **2** to lift, pick up *la15-19*. **3** to collect, levy payments, rents or taxes *la15-18*. **4** to take possession of, capture *15-e16*. **5** to cause (a person) to rise, get up *e16*. †**uptaker**, **uptakar 1** a collector of rents or taxes *la15-e17*. **2** *Presbyterian Church* a PRECENTOR *17-19*. [UP[1.2] + TAK[1.2]]

uptaking[1.1], **uptakin** /ʌpˈtekɪŋ, ʌpˈtakɪn/ *n* **1** comprehending, understanding *17-*. **2** raising, picking or lifting up *la15-19*. **3** the collection, levying (of rents or other payments) *la15-17*. **4** recruiting (of soldiers) *la16-e17*. **5** *Presbyterian Church* leading of psalm-singing *la16-e17*. **6** borrowing (of money) *e18*. †**to a person's uptaking** as far as someone can understand, in someone's opinion *la17-e18*. [verbal noun from UPTAK[1.2]]

†**uptaking**[1.2], **uptakin** *adj* **1** engrossing, absorbing, preoccupying *17-e18*. **2** intelligent *la18*. [participial adj from UPTAK[1.2]]

uptene *see* OBTAIN

upthraw *see* UPTHROW[1.2]

upthrou[1.1], **upthrough**, **upthrowe** /ʌpˈθru, ʌpˈθrʌu/ *adj* upland, inland *19, 20- NE*. **upthrowe heat** a warming of the lower body by sitting open-legged in front of a fire *la20- NE*. [see the adv]

upthrou[1.2], **upthrough**, **upthrowe**, †**upthrow** /ʌpˈθru, ʌpˈθrʌu/ *adv* **1** in the upper part of the country, in or from the uplands, in the Highlands inland from the sea *19, 20- Sh N NE*. **2** upwards through a place *la15*. †**upthrow and down-throw** upwards and downwards through a place *la15*. [UP[1.2] + THROU[1.2]]

†**upthrou**[1.3], **upthrow** *prep* upwards through a place *la16*. **upthrow and down-throw** up and down, through a place *la17*. [see the adv]

upthrough *see* UPTHROU[1.1], UPTHROU[1.2]

upthrow[1.1] /ˈʌpθro/ *n geology, mining* an upward dislocation of a stratum or seam *19- C*. [see the verb]

†**upthrow**[1.2], **upthraw** *v* to throw upwards, cause to rise; to vomit *16-19*. [UP[1.2] + THRAW[1.2]]

upthrow *see* UPTHROU[1.2], UPTHROU[1.3]

upthrowe *see* UPTHROU[1.1], UPTHROU[1.2]

upwalx *see* UPWAX

upward *see* UPWART

†**upwark** *n* the completion of a piece of work, cessation of work *15-16*. [UP[1.2] with the sense of completion + WARK[1]]

†**upwarp** *v* to throw up, throw open *la15-16*. [UP[1.2] + WARP[1.2]]

upwart, **upward** /ˈʌpwərt, ˈʌpwərd/ *adv* to or towards a higher point, in an ascending course, so as to rise *la14-*. [OE *upweard*]

†**upwax**, **upwalx** *v* to grow *e16*. [UP[1.2] + WAX[2]]

†**upwelt** *v* to fly upwards *e16*. [UP[1.2] + *welt* (WALT[2])]

†**upwelter** *v* to stir up, cause to be turbulent *e16*. [UP[1.2] + WELTER[2.2]]

†**upwith**[1.1], **up-with** *n* a crucial stage, (sexual) climax *16-17*. [see the adv]

†**upwith**[1.2] *adj* having an upward course, rising *la15-19*. [see the adv]

upwith[1.3], **upwuth** /ˈʌpwɪθ, ˈʌpwʌθ/ *adv* upwards *16-19, 20- NE*. [UP[1.2] + *with* (WI)]

†**upwith**[1.4] *prep* up along the course of *e16*. [see the adv]

†**upwrele** *v* to push or pull up or off with a twisting motion *e16*. [UP[1.2] + WRELE]

upwuth *see* UPWITH[2.2]

ur *see* BE

urban /ˈʌrbən/ *adj* **1** pertaining to a town or city *16-*. **2** *law of a lease* relating to a building, as opposed to land (whether in town or country) *la17-*; compare RURAL. **urban Scots 1** the language spoken in the cities of Scotland *la20-*. **2** city-dwelling Scots *la20-*. [Lat *urbānus*]

urdeen *see* ORDEEN

ure[1], **yower** /jur, ˈjʌuər/ *n* the udder, especially of a cow or ewe *la18- SW Bor*. [ON *júgr*]

ure[2] /ur/ *n* **1** a damp mist; fine rain, drizzle *19, 20- Ork*. **2** an atmospheric haze, especially when radiated by sunbeams *19, 20- EC Bor*. [ON *úr*]

ure[3], *NE* **eer** /ur; *NE* ir/ *n* **1** ore, the naturally occurring material from which metal is obtained *la15-e19*. **2** clay containing iron, barren ferruginous soil, red gravelly earth *18-19, 20- Sh*. **3** an iron stain on cloth *20- NE*; compare *iron eer* (AIRN[1.2]). **4** *law* apparently used metonymically of a metal weapon *15-17*. **5** apparently, precious metal *e16*. [OE *ōra*]

†**ure**[4] *n of the valuation of land in Shetland and Orkney* the monetary value of an ounce of silver *16-e19*. **uriscop** *in Orkney* = URISLAND *16-e17*. **uris thift** *in Shetland* stolen goods to the value of an ounce of silver *e17*. **uris of land**, **ure of land** = URISLAND *la16-e19*. [ON *øyrir* an ounce of silver]

urf *see* WURF

uriscop *see* URE[4]

urisland, *Ork* **eyrisland**, *Ork* **ursland** /ˈørɪslənd, ˈurɪslənd; *Ork* ˈerɪslənd; *Ork* ˈʌrslənd/ *n* **1** *in Shetland and Orkney* a measure of land, originally assessed at the monetary value of an ounce of silver *16-19, 20- historical*; compare *ounceland* (OUNCE). **2** *in Orkney* a part of a parish which functioned as a unit for burial and other ecclesiastical arrangements *19, 20- historical*. [possessive of URE[4] + LAND[1.1]; the form *eyrisland* is from ON *eyrisland*]

urison *see* ORISON

urlar /ˈurlər/ *n piping* in a PIBROCH, the basic theme of the tune *la19-*. [Gael *ùrlar* a floor]

urmal *see* ORMAL

urn *see* ERN

urnae *see* BE

†**urse** *n* **1** *pl astronomy* the Great and Little Bear constellations *16-e17*. **2** a bear *la16-e17*. [Lat *ursa*, *ursus* a bear]

ursland *see* URISLAND

us, uz, iz, hiz, huz, his, wis, wiz, ous /ʌs, ʌz, ɪz, hɪz, hʌz, hɪs, wɪs, wɪz, us/ *pron* **1** us *la14-*. **2** me: ◊ *I tell'd him a lee... he jist felled iz like a herrin la19-*. **us anes, us yins** we, those of our group *la19-*. Compare WE. [OE *ūs*]

usage, *NE* **eesage** /ˈjusədʒ; *NE* ˈisədʒ/ *n* **1** (usual, regular) behaviour, conduct; a means of proceeding; regular practice; custom, habit *la14-*. **2** use, employment (of something) *la15-*. [OFr *usage*]

†**usance**, **vsans** *n* custom, practice *la15-16*. [ME *usaunce*, OFr *usance*, Lat *ūsantia*]

usar *see* USE[1,2]

usche *see* ISH[1.1], ISH[1.2]

uscher *see* USHER

use[1.1], **yuise, uise, yiss**, *Sh* **ös**, *Ork* **euse**, *Ork* **yeuse**, *N NE* **yeese**, *N NE* **eese**, †**ois**, †**vs**, †**ws** /juz, jɪs; *Sh Ork* øs; *Ork* jøs; *N NE* jis; *N NE* is/ *n* **1** the (continuous or repeated) employment of something for a particular aim or purpose; an aim or purpose *la14-*. **2** habit, custom, practice; established procedure, tradition; conduct *15-*. **3** the right to make use of land, property or a resource *15-*. **4** need, occasion, reason (for something) *la18-19*, *20- Sh Ork N T*. **5** *Presbyterian Church* (the part of a sermon devoted to) the practical application or purpose of a doctrine; a specific precept drawn from a general theological principle *17-e19*. **6** the ability or opportunity to use (a faculty or skill) *la14-e17*. †**as use is** as is customary *la15-e18*. †**be in use to do, be in use of doing** to be in the habit of doing *16-e19*. †**use and consuetude** = *use and wont 16-e19*. †**use and custom** = *use and wont 15-17*. †**use and possessioun** = USE[1.1] (sense 3) *16*. **use and wont** the usual practice and procedure *la15-*. [OFr *use*, Lat *ūsus*]

use[1.2], **uise, yuise**, *N NE* **yeese**, *NE* **eese**, †**ois**, †**ows**, †**oys** /juz, jez; *N NE* jiz; *NE* iz/ *v* **1** to make use of, employ (something) *la14-*. **2** to be or become inured or accustomed to *la14-*. **3** to carry out an activity, (habitually), practise (a trade or profession) *la14-*. **4** to observe (a custom), comply with, enforce (a law) *15-*. **5** to utter, say (words), speak (a language), employ (a manner of speaking) *15-*. **6** to have the use of, occupy (land or property) *15-*. **7** to use for sexual pleasure *la15-*. **8** to consume (food or drink) *la15-*. **9** to go to, frequent (a place); to hold (a market) *la15-*. **10** to behave, act, conduct oneself, treat another (in a particular way) *la15-*. **11** to take a drug, especially an illegal one habitually and regularly *la20*. **12** to pass (time) in some fashion, follow or pursue (a lifestyle) *15-e19*. **user**, †**usar 1** one who uses or makes use of; one who practises an activity or behaviour *la16-*. **2** *law* a person who enforced or executed a legal document *la16-e17*. †**usit** customary *la15-17*. †**used and wont, usit and wont** customary, usual, according to use and custom *la15-e19*. †**usit in** = *used wi la14-e19*. **used wi**, *NE* **eest wi** made familiar with, habituated to, accustomed to *18-*. [OFr *user*]

useless[1.1], **yaisless**, *NE* **eesless**, *Ork* **euseless**, †**uselesse** /ˈjusləs, ˈjesləs; *NE* ˈisləs; *Ork* ˈøsləs/ *adj* **1** of no practical value or benefit *17-*. **2** indisposed in health; incapacitated by illness or exhaustion *20-*. [USE[1.1] with adj-forming suffix]

useless[1.2], *NE* **eeseless** /ˈjusləs; *NE* ˈisləs/ *adv* exceedingly, so much as to be ineffectual, far too: ◊ *the lassie's pit on useless mony coals la19-*. [see the adj]

uselesse *see* USELESS[1.1]

†**ush** *v* to usher, escort, guide *19*. [back-formation from USHER]

ush *see* ISH[1.1], ISH[1.2]

usher, †**uscher**, †**ischear** /ˈʌʃər/ *n* a doorkeeper, originally especially of the royal household; an official of the court or exchequer *14-*. †**Hereditary Usher** an officer of the crown who directed court ceremonial, including the opening of Parliament *e18*. †**Heritable Usher** = *Hereditary Usher la17-18*. **Usher of the Green Rod** the official master of ceremonies in the ORDER OF THE THISTLE *18-*. [AN *usser*]

usmal *see* OSMAL

†**usquae, usky** *n* whisky *e18*. [shortened form of USQUEBAE]

usquebae, usquebaugh, †**usquebay**, †**iskie bae** /ˈuskəbe, ˈuʃkəbe, ˈuskəbɔx/ *n* whisky *la16-*. [Gael, IrGael *uisge beatha* literally, water of life]

usual, uswal, *NE* **eeswal**, *Sh* **öswal**, *Ork* **euswal**, †**usuall** /ˈjuʒəl, ˈjuʒwəl; *NE* ˈizwəl; *Sh* ˈøʒwəl; *Ork* ˈøswəl/ *adj* **1** *of money, terms or payment* that is in ordinary use; having general currency *la14-*. **2** commonly used, practised or observed; normal, customary *15-*. **a person's usual** a person's usual state of health, frame of mind: ◊ *he's in his usual. la18-*. [OFr *usual*, Lat *ūsuālis*]

ut efter *see* OOT[1.4]

utensil, †**outainsell** /juˈtɛnsəl/ *n* frequently in singular as collective domestic equipment *la14-*. [OFr *utensile*, Lat *ūtēnsile*]

uter *see* OOTER, UTTER

uterance *see* UTTERANCE

uter fyne *see* UTTER-FINE[1.1]

uterli *see* OOTERLY

utgie *see* OUTGIE

uthall *see* UDAL

uther *see* UDDER, ITHER[1.1], ITHER[1.3]

utland *see* OUTLAND[1.2]

utlaw *see* OOTLAW[1.1]

utmaist, utmost, †**utmast** /ˈutmɛst, ˈʌtməst/ *adj* most extreme, far-reaching, important *la14-*. Compare OOTMAIST. [OE *ūtmest*]

utouth *see* OUTWITH[1.3]

Utrik *see* UTTRECHT

uts *see* HOOTS

utter, †**uter**, †**vtir**, †**outer** /ˈʌtər/ *adj* complete, total, ultimate; uttermost; last *la15-*. **utterly** without reserve, thoroughly, totally *la14-*. Compare OOTER. [OE *ūtera*]

utter *see* OOTER, OUTER

utterage *see* OOTRAGE

†**utterance, uterance, vtyrrans** *n* the most extreme action, the utmost extremity *la16*. **at the utterance** with the utmost energy, to the utmost (of one's power) *e16*. **at utterance** = *at the utterance la15-e17*. **put to utterance** to put to death *e16*. [OFr *outrance*, with influence from UTTER]

†**utter-fine**[1.1], **uter fyne** *n* cloth of the finest quality *16*. [see the adj]

†**utter-fine**[1.2] *adj of precious metals* highly refined, superfine *16-17*. [UTTER + FINE[1.2]]

Utter Hous *see* OUTER HOUSE

uttounes *see* OUT-TOUN[1.2]

†**Uttrecht, Utrik, Outrecht** *n* a gold coin minted in Utrecht *la15*. **Uttrecht guldyn** = UTTRECHT *la15*. [from the name of the Dutch city]

utward *see* OOTWARD[1.1]

uver *see* OWER[1.2]

uvirmest *see* OWERMAIST

uz *see* US

V

va /va/ *n* a wet piece of ground *20- Sh.* [reduced form of Norw dial *vad* a ford]

vaalen /ˈvɑlən, ˈvelən/ *adj* **1** numb with cold *la19- Sh.* **2** awkward, lacking in dexterity *20- Sh.* [Norw dial *valen*]

vaam[1.1] /vam/ *n* **1** a spell, a hypnotic influence *la19- Sh.* **2** a smell, a flavour *la19- Sh.* [Norw dial *vam* a mishap, a disappointment, bewilderment]

vaam[1.2] /vam/ *v* to bewitch, cast a spell on *20- Sh.* **vamd** decaying, having a (bad) smell *la19- Sh.* [see the noun]

vaan, vaun, van /vɑn/ *adj* **come vaan** to fail (to get), miss, lose, fall short (of) *19- Sh.* [Norw dial *van-* lacking]

†**vaana** *n* water, the sea *la19 Sh.* [Norw *vann*]

vaar[1.1] /var/ *n* heed, attention *la19- Sh.* [Norw (*ta*) *vare* (*på*) (to take) heed (of)]

vaar[1.2] /var/ *v* to pay attention (to), be wary of *la19- Sh.* **varin** a warning *20- Sh.* [Norw dial *vara*]

vaar[2] /var/ *n* the moment of stillness when the tide is about to turn *20- Sh.* [perhaps an extended use of VAAR[3]]

vaar[3] /var/ *v* to (cause to) drift to one side, (cause a boat) to veer *19- Sh.* [compare Norw dial *vara* to point or move in a given direction]

vaardie *see* VAIRDIE

vaarious *see* VARIOUS

vaarline *see* VARLINE

vaarnakle *see* VARNIGLE

vaav[1], **vav** /vav/ *n* a woollen thread for tying bait to the VARNIGLE or fish-hook *la19- Sh.* **vaaving** a VAAV[1]. [Norw dial *vav* a wrapping, strip of binding]

vaav[2] /vav/ *v* to tie fish-bait onto a hook *la19- Sh.* [see the noun]

vabrat *see* WARBOO

vabried leiff *see* WAAVERIN LAEF

vacabound *see* VAGABOND[1.1]

vacance, vacans, vagans, †**vacant** /ˈvekəns, ˈvegəns/ *n* **1** a vacation, holiday; *law* period of recess of the law courts, suspension of business *16-.* **2** a vacancy, an unfilled post or tenancy; the fact of becoming vacant, the vacation (of a post) *la15-18.* **3** a vacant period, an interregnum *e16.* [MFr *vacance*, Lat *vacantia*]

vacancy /ˈvekənsi/ *n* **1** a VACANCE (sense 1) *la16-19.* **2** a VACANCE (sense 2) *17-.* **3** a VACANCE (sense 3) *la17.* [Lat *vacantia* or VACANT + noun-forming suffix]

vacans *see* VACANCE

vacant, †**vacand,** †**vakand,** †**vaiking** /ˈvekənt/ *adj* **1** *of a position* unfilled *15-.* **2** *of lands or houses* unassigned, untenanted *17-.* **3** *law of a court* in recess *17-18.* **4** *of time* not occupied with work, given over to holidays *17.* **5** *of a bird* lacking a mate *e16.* †**vacanted** *law of a court* in recess *18.* [ME *vacant*, from OFr *vacant*, Lat *vacant-*, oblique stem of *vacans*; fallen together with the present participle of VAIK]

vacant *see* VACANCE

vacation /vəˈkeʃən/ *n* **1** a VACANCE (sense 2) *15-.* **2** a VACANCE (sense 1) *15-e17.* [OFr *vacation*, Lat *vacātiōn-*]

vaddle /ˈvadəl/ *n* a sea-pool that empties and fills as the tide ebbs and flows *19- Sh.* [compare ON *vaðill* shallow water and VA]

vaedik, vyaedick /ˈvedək, ˈvjedək/ *n* **1** a small stream, a ditch, drain or open sewer *19- Sh.* **2** a dirty mark (left by a cursory wash), a tidemark *20- Sh.* [Norw dial *veit* a ditch, trench + *-ick* (-OCK) diminutive suffix]

vaegle *see* VEEGIL

vaelensi, vailensi /ˈvalənsi/ *n* violence (of weather), turbulence *la19- Sh.* [altered form of Eng *violency*]

vaer *see* VAIR

vagabond[1.1], †**vacabound,** †**vagabound,** †**vagabund,** †**vagabon,** †**vaigabon** /ˈvegəbɔnd, ˈvagəbɔnd/ *n* a wanderer; vagrant; a rogue *16-.* [see the adj]

vagabond[1.2] /ˈvegəbɔnd, ˈvagəbɔnd/ *adj* **1** wandering, nomadic *15-.* **2** *of laws or sayings* not properly recorded; stray; inconsequential *la15-e16.* [OFr *vagabond*, Lat *vagābundus*]

vagabund *see* VAGABOND[1.1]

vagans *see* VACANCE

vage *see* VAIG[1.2], VAIGE

vaggel /ˈvagəl/ *n* a small spar between beams in a roof on which meat or fish is hung for smoke-curing *19- Sh.* [Norw dial *vagl* a hen roost]

vague *see* VAIG[1.2]

vaig[1.1], **vyaug** /veg, vag; *NE* vjag/ *n* **1** a vagrant, vagabond, tramp *19-.* **2** a rough-living disreputable person, a rascal, rogue *la19-.* **3** *of a woman* a coarse, disreputable, gossipy person *la19-.* [from the verb or a reduced form of *vaigabon* (VAGABOND[1.1])]

vaig[1.2], *NE* **vyaug,** †**vage,** †**vague** /veg, vag; *NE* vjag/ *v* to wander about idly, roam aimlessly, swan around *15-.* **vaiger** a footloose, idle wanderer, a gadabout; a rogue *17-.* **vaigin** idle rambling, wandering *la16-.* [MFr *vaguer*, Lat *vagāri* to roam]

vaigabon *see* VAGABOND[1.1]

vaige, veage, voyage, *N* **veege,** †**viage,** †**vayage,** †**veyage** /vedʒ, ˈveadʒ, ˈvɔɪədʒ; *N* vidʒ/ *n* **1** a commercial trip by sea (to a foreign port and back) *la14-.* **2** a journey; a trip, an outing, an expedition *la14- Sh NE EC.* **vaiger** traveller *20- Sh.* **ill vage to ye** bad luck to you *20- Sh NE.* [AN *vaiage*, OFr *veage, viage, voiage*]

†**vaik,** †**vake** *v* **1** *of an (especially ecclesiastical) office or position* to fall vacant; to remain unfilled *15-e18.* **2** *of property* of a TACK[2] or tenancy, to fall vacant; to remain unfilled *la15-17.* **3** to attend (upon), give one's attention or time to *la15-e17.* **4** to absent oneself (from an occupation or business) *la15-e17.* [MFr *vaquer*, Lat *vacāre*]

vaik *see* WAUK[1.2]

vaiking *see* VACANT

†**vail**[1.1], **vale** *n* **1** value, worth; account, estimation *la15-e17.* **2** advantage, benefit *la15.* [see the verb]

†**vail**[1.2], **vailʒe, valʒe** *v* to be of use, avail *la14-16.* †**of (na, nane) vail** *law* of (no) validity, without authority *15-e16.* **vail quod vail** = *vail que vail.* **vail que vail** no matter what, whatever the outcome *la14-16.* [OFr *vail-* participial stem of *valoir* to be of value]

vailable, †**valabill,** †**valiable,** †**vailʒeabill** /ˈveləbəl/ *adj* **1** valuable; (morally) profitable *la15-.* **2** *law* legally valid *la15-e17.* **3** of sufficient means, solvent *la16-e17.* [VAIL[1.2] + adj-forming suffix]

vailensi *see* VAELENSI

vailey, †**valé,** †**valay** /ˈvele/ *n* a low area between hills *la14-.* [OFr *valee*]

vaillie, vailye *see* VALUE[1.1], VALUE[1.2]

vailyeant *see* VALIANT
vailȝand *see* VALIANT, VALIENT
vailȝe *see* VAIL[1.2]
vailȝeabill *see* VAILABLE
vain *see* VEIN[1.1]
vainish, wainish, †**vanis,** †**vanisch,** †**wanis** /'venɪʃ, 'wenɪʃ/ *v* to disappear *la14-*. **wainisht** shrunken-looking, emaciated *19-*. [aphetic form of OFr *evaniss-* stem of *evanir*]
vainity, †**vanite,** †**vanitie** /'venəte/ *n* vanity *la14-*. [OFr *vanite*]
vaiper, †**vapoure** /'vepər/ *v* 1 to boast, swagger, act with bravado *17-e19*. 2 to saunter, stroll aimlessly *18-19, 19- Sh Ork*. [Lat *vapōrāre* to emit vapour]
vair, vaer, ver /ver/ *adj* having no appetite, fussy about food *19- Sh Ork*. [unknown]
vair *see* WARE[5]
vairdie, verdie, vaardie /'verdi, vɛrdi, 'vɑrdi/ *n* a charm supposed to bring luck; a superstition *la19- Sh*. [shortened form of ON *varðlokkur* a song used against enchantment + -IE[1]]
vairnish *see* VERNISH[1.1], VERNISH[1.2]
vaister *see* WASTER[2]
vaistie *see* WASTY
vakand *see* VACANT
vake *see* VAIK
vakster *see* WALKSTER
valabill *see* VAILABLE
valairie /və'lere/ *n* common valerian *Valeriana officinalis la19- H&I Uls*. [shortened form of Eng *valerian* or Lat *valeriana* + -IE[1]]
valay, valé *see* VAILEY
vale *see* VAIL[1.1], VEAL
valeat *see* VALID
†**valent** *n law* the value of an estate or piece of land *la18-19*. **valent clause** the clause in a RETOUR[1.1] or *special service* (SERVICE) in which the *auld extent* (AULD[1.2]) and *new extent* (NEW[1.2]) of the lands were specified *la18-19*. [Lat (*dictae terrae*) *valent* (the said lands) are worth]
Valentine, †**wallantyne** /'valəntʌɪn/ *n* 1 one of several saints of this name, especially Valentine of Rome *16-*. 2 a lot, a piece of paper containing a person's name to be drawn to determine an outcome *16-e17*. 3 a writ listing the names of suspected lawbreakers, requiring their apprehension *la16-17*. **dealing o the Valentines** a custom observed on St Valentine's eve of drawing by lot the name of one's sweetheart for the following year *la18-19*. **Valentine's deal** = *dealing o the Valentines*. [from the name of the saint]
valet, †**wally,** †**vallett,** †**wallett** /'vale/ *n* an attendant, a personal servant *la16-*. [MFr *valet*]
valeur *see* VALOUR[1.1]
valew *see* VALUE[1.1], VALUE[1.2]
valiable *see* VAILABLE
valiant, †**vailyeant,** †**vailȝand** /'valɪənt, 'veljənt/ *adj* 1 courageous, bold *15-*. 2 worth in respect of wealth or value *16-e17*. 3 *law* valid *la16-e17*. [AN *vailliant*; fallen together with the presp of vailȝe (VAIL[1.2])]
valid, †**valied,** †**valeat** /'valɪd/ *adj law* sufficient, legally binding *la16-e17*. **validitie** 1 *law* the state of being valid *la16-e17*. 2 value, worth *la16-*. [MFr *valide*, Lat *validus*]
†**valient, vailȝand** *n law* a person's worth; his goods or property *16-17*; compare VALENT. [from the adj VALIANT (sense 2)]
valiorm /valɪ'orm/ *v* to ornament, decorate *20- Sh*. [altered form of VARIORUM]
valisone *see* WALANSONE

valkie /'vɑlki/ *n* the Iceland gull *Larus glaucoides* or glaucous gull *Larus hyperboreus 20- Sh*. [unknown; compare Gael *faoileag* a gull]
vall *see* WA[1.1]
vallett *see* VALET
vallies *see* WALISE
valour[1.1]**,** †**valur,** †**valure,** †**valeur** /'valər/ *n* 1 honour, chivalry, bravery *la14-*. 2 moral or monetary value *15-17*. 3 *law* the validity of a document or process *15-e16*. [OFr *valour* worth, courage, Lat *valor*; and OFr *valure* strength, potency]
†**valour**[1.2] *v* to value *la16-17*. [see the noun]
valsket /'vɑlskət, 'vjɑlskət/ *adj* numb, fumbling, slow in one's movements *20- Sh*. [perhaps related to VAALEN]
value[1.1]**,** *T EC Bor* **vaillie,** *NE* **vailye,** †**walu,** †**valew,** †**wallow,** †**walow** /'valju; *T EC Bor* also 'veli; *NE* also 'velji/ *n* 1 worth *la14-*. 2 = VALOUR[1.1] (sense 2) *la14-e17*. [OFr *value*]
value[1.2]**,** *T EC Bor* **vaillie,** *NE* **vailye,** †**valew,** †**wallow,** †**walow** /'valju; *T EC Bor* also 'veli; *NE* also 'velji/ *v* to have a high opinion of, consider the worth of *la16-*. †**valued rent** a valuation of land made in 1667 for the purpose of computing the land-tax and the apportionment for public and parochial expenditure, superseding the *auld extent* (AULD[1.2]) and *new extent* (NEW[1.2]) *la17-19*. †**valued teinds** tithes on which a fixed monetary value has been set *la17-*. [from the noun and MFr *valuer* to be worth, to evaluate]
valur, valure *see* VALOUR[1.1]
valȝe *see* VAIL[1.2]
†**vambrace, wambras, vantbras** *n* defensive armour for the (fore-)arm *16-e19*. [ME *vauntbras, vaumbrāce*, AN *vantbras*]
vamd *see* VAAM[1.2]
vamit *see* VOMIT[1.1], VOMIT[1.2]
van *see* VAAN, VEIN[1.1]
vand *see* VYND[1.1], VYND[1.2]
vandgard *see* VANGAIRD
vandit /'vɑndɪt/ *adj* 1 *of a cow* having striped sides *20- Ork N*. 2 *of socks* dyed so as to be variegated in colour *20- Ork*. [Faer *vond* a woven pattern, ON *vǫndr* a stripe on cloth + -IT[2]]
vandlup, †**vandlob** /'vɑndləp/ *n* a heavy shower (of rain) *la19- Sh*. [compare ON *vatnahlaup* floods, rushing water]
vane /ven/ *interj* call to a horse in harness to turn to the left *19- C*; compare YAIN. [unknown]
vane *see* WAN[1]
vangaird, †**vandgard,** †**vantgarde** /'vangerd/ *n* the foremost division of an army *la14-*. [AN *vantgarde*; compare VAWARD]
†**vangel, vangyle, wangele** *n* the Gospel; a copy of the gospel(s), especially as used in oath-taking *la14-16*. **vangelist** one of the writers of the gospels *la14-16*. [aphetic form of EVANGEL]
vanis, vanisch *see* VAINISH
vanite, vanitie *see* VAINITY
vanquish[1.1] /'vaŋkwɪʃ/ *n* a disease in sheep caused by cobalt deficiency *19- SW*. [see the verb]
vanquish[1.2]**,** *SW* **vinkish,** †**vencus,** †**vinqueis** /'vaŋkwɪʃ; *SW* 'vɪŋkɪʃ/ *v ptp* also †**vencust** to conquer, defeat *la14-*.
†**vincust, vencust** *adj* 1 defeated *la15-16*. 2 exhausted, tired out *e20 T*. [OFr *vencus, venquis*, ptp and pt of *veintre*]
vant *see* VAUNT[1.1], VAUNT[1.2]
vantage /'vantɪdʒ/ *n* 1 advantage, profit, benefit *15-*. 2 tactical advantage, superiority in a battle situation *la14-16*. [AN *vantage*]
vantbras *see* VAMBRACE
vantgarde *see* VANGAIRD
vantplat *see* WAMPLATE
vapoure *see* VAIPER

vareez /ˈvariz/ *v* to notice, observe *19- Sh.* [derivative of VAAR[1.2]]

varefy *see* VERIFY

varg[1.1], †**verg** /varg/ *n* **1** a mess, dirt, rubbish *la19- Sh.* **2** messiness, dirty work or conditions *20- Sh.* [see the verb]

varg[1.2] /varg/ *v* **1** to dirty *la19- Sh.* **2** to work in dirty conditions, perform a messy task; to work in a laborious way, slave *20- Sh.* **vargit** covered with dirt *20- Sh.* [Icel *verga* to dirty]

variable, †**variabill** /ˈverɪəbəl/ *adj* **1** inconstant, fickle *la15-*. **2** *of weather or seasons* changeable *la15-*. [ME *variable*, OFr *variable*, Lat *variābilis*]

varie, variit *see* VARY

varin *see* VAAR[1.2]

variorum /varɪˈorəm/ *n* **1** a decoration, a flourish, an ornament, a trinket *la19-*. **2** a change, novelty; a constant variation *la18-19*. [Lat *variōrum* in the phr *editio cum notis variorum* an edition with notes by various hands]

various, *NE EC* **vaarious**, †**vawrious** /ˈverɪəs; *NE EC* ˈvarɪəs/ *adj* diverse, different *16-*. [Lat *varius*]

varitie *see* VERITY

varless /ˈvarləs/ *adj* inattentive, careless; clumsy *la19- Sh.* [VAAR[1.1] + *-less* adj-forming suffix]

varline, vaarline /ˈvarlɪn, ˈvarlʌɪn/ *n fishing* a secondary or auxiliary line connecting a fishing boat with the buoy of a fleet of lines *la19- Sh.* [compare *var-* in VARNIGLE + LINE[1.1]]

varnes *see* VERNISH[1.1], VERNISH[1.2]

varnigle, vaarnakle, vernyaggle /ˈvarnəgəl/ *n* a pin, usually wooden, used especially for fastening the two pieces of a CLIBBER or used as a fish-hook *la19- Sh.* [Norw dial *varnagle* a linch-pin]

varr /var/ *v mainly in negative expressions* to have an appetite for, stomach *20- Ork.* [unknown]

varra, varraye *see* VERRA[1.1], VERRA[1.2]

vary, †**varie** /ˈvere/ *v ptp* also †**variit** **1** to change, differ *15-*. **2** to show the first symptoms of delirium *19- Bor.* **3** to wander in the mind, rave *la15-e16.* **variant, variand 1** changeable, differing *la15-e17*. **2** varied in colour, variegated *la15-17* [OFr *varier*, Lat *variāre*]

vase, *C* **vawse** /vaz, vez; *C* vaz/ *n* a container, usually decorative, used as an ornament or for displaying flowers *18-*. [Fr *vase*, Lat *vās*]

†**vaskene, waskyne, vasquine** *n* a petticoat *la16-e17*. [MFr *vasquine*]

†**vassal** *n* **1** one who owes allegiance to another, specifically, *law* a person who holds HERITABLE property in FEU[1.1] from a SUPERIOR[1.1] (sense 2) *la14-20*. **2** a man, a warrior *e15*. **3** applied to the relationship of man with God *la15-e17*. [OFr *vassal*]

†**vassalage, waslage** *n* **1** *law* the duties or servitude of one holding land as a VASSAL *la17-20*. **2** bravery, valour as befitting a vassal or knight; military prowess *la14-17*. **3** a brave or chivalrous act; a gallant exploit *la14-17*. **do vassalage** to act bravely, carry out a valorous exploit *15-17*. **win vassalage** to achieve honour in battle, gain the rewards of valour *la15-e17*. [OFr *vassalage*]

vast[1.1] /vast/ *n* a large number, quantity or amount, a great deal *la18-*. [see the adj]

vast[1.2] /vast/ *adj* enormous in amount *la17*. [Fr *vaste*, Lat *vastus*]

vat, *Sh* **fat**, †**fatt**, †**falt**, †**vautt** /vat; *Sh* fat/ *n* a vat, a container for either liquid or dry goods *la14-*. [OE *fæt*; the form *vat* is from *southern* ME]

vater *see* WATTER[1.1]

vatick, vatik /ˈvatɪk/ *n* a (water) bucket *la19- Sh.* [probably an altered form of FIDDICK assimilated to VAT]

vatsgairen, vatsgaarin /ˈvatsgerən, ˈvatsgarən/ *n* a halo round the sun, supposed to indicate rain, bad weather *la19- Sh.* [Norw dial *vats* genitive of *vatr* water + Norw dial *gard* an enclosure, ring around the moon with Norw *-in, -en* suffix article]

vattaband, vaytaband /ˈvatɑband, ˈvatəband/ *n* **1** a wristband to prevent water entering the sleeve *19- Sh.* **2** a string by which a pair of sea-mittens are suspended around the neck when not in use *la19- Sh.* [Norw dial *vette* gloves + BAND[1.1]]

vauch spear *see* WAWSPER

vaudie /ˈvɔde, ˈvade/ *adj* proud, vain, ostentatious, showing off; elated; frisky, merry *18-*. [perhaps an altered form of VAUNTIE, influenced by GAUDY]

vaun *see* VAAN

†**vaunt**[1.1], **vant** *n* a boast, boasting *la15-e19*. [from the verb or aphetic form of AVANT[1.1]]

†**vaunt**[1.2], **vant** *v* to boast *la15-e19*. [AN *vaunter*, OFr *vanter*, Lat *vantāre*; compare AVANT[1.2]]

vauntie /ˈvɔnte, ˈvante/ *adj* proud, boastful, vain; proud-looking, ostentatious, jaunty; pleased, elated *18-*. [VAUNT[1.2] + -IE[2]]

vaut[1.1], **vowt**, *Sh* **vult**, †**vout**, †**volt** /vʌut, vɔt; *Sh* vult/ *n* **1** a vault *la14-*. **2** a cavern or vaulted rock formation *15-e16*. **3** an attic or upper room; the space under a roof *16*. [AN *vaute*, OFr *voute, volte*]

vaut[1.2], **vowt**, *Sh* **vult**, †**vout**, †**volt** /vʌut, vɔt; *Sh* vult/ *v* to construct (a building) by means of vaulting *la14-*. [OFr *vouter, volter, vaulter*]

vautt *see* VAT

vav *see* VAAV[1]

†**vaward, wawart** *n* the foremost division of an army *la14-e16*. Compare VANGAIRD. [aphetic form of OFr *avantwarde*; compare VANGAIRD]

vawrious *see* VARIOUS

vawse *see* VASE

vax *see* WAX[1], WAX[2]

vayage *see* VAIGE

vayndis *see* WANDYS

vaytaband *see* VATTABAND

vberior *see* UBERIOR

vche *see* UCHE

ve *see* WE

veage *see* VAIGE

veal, vale, *Sh Ork* **veel**, †**vele**, †**veil** /vil, vel/ *n* **1** a calf, especially one killed for food or reared for this purpose *la15-18, 20- Ork*. **2** the flesh of a calf as food *16-*. **3** a fool, an idiot *20- Ork*. [AN *vele, veal*]

veallience /ˈveljɪns/ *n* an area of open land, an old flat pasture *20- Ork*. [extended sense of Norw dial *veller* fields]

vedmell *see* WADMAL

veeand /ˈviənd/ *adj* lacking common sense; in one's dotage *19- Bor*. [perhaps participial adj from *vee to be foolish, witless; compare VEED]

veeat, viad /ˈviat/ *n* a stretch of open ground *20- Ork*. [Norw dial *viåtta* a wide expanse]

veecious, veetious, vitious, vicious /ˈviʃəs, ˈviʃɪəs, ˈvɪʃəs/ *adj* **1** immoral, depraved; malicious *15-*; compare VITIOUS INTROMISSION. **2** *weather* severe, inclement *la19-*. **3** illegal, unlawful, offending against the law; null *la16-17*. **vitious intromissatrix** a female *vitious intromitter la16-*. **vitious intromitter**, †**vicious intromittor** a person who interferes with the property of another without authority *17-*. [ME *vicious*, AN *vicious*, Lat *vitiōsus*]

veed /vid/ *adj* lacking understanding; in one's dotage, senile *la19- Bor*. [perhaps participial adj from **vee* to be foolish, witless; compare VEEAND]

veegal, veetney, veekney /ˈvigəl, ˈvitni, ˈvikni/ *n* **oot o veegal** out of order, in confusion *20- Ork*. **veekalty** = VEEGAL. [compare Norw dial *vikl* disorder]

veege *see* VAIGE

veegil, vaegle, vegwal /ˈvigəl, ˈvɛgəl, ˈvɛgwəl/ *n* a tether, a wooden stake with a hole through it driven into the BYRE wall *19- Sh*. [Norw dial *vegg* a wall + Norw *vol* a stake]

veekalty, veekney *see* VEEGAL

veel *see* VEAL

veelage *see* VILLAGE

veeper, viper, †veper /ˈvipər, ˈvaepər/ *n* **1** an adder *la16-*. **2** a venomous or spiteful person *la16-*. **veeperate** venomous, malicious *20- NE*. [MFr *vipere*, Lat *vīpera*]

vees *see* VISE

veesion *see* VISION

veesit¹·¹, visit /ˈvizɪt, ˈvɪzɪt/ *n* **1** a charitable, social or official call *17-*. **2** an inspection *17*. [from the verb or Fr *visite*]

veesit¹·², visit, †vesit /ˈvizɪt, ˈvɪzɪt/ *v* **1** to visit, come to or call on, charitably, socially or officially *la15-*. **2** to afflict (with sickness) *17-*. **3** to go to (a place) for recreation or interest *17-*. **4** to observe, examine, scrutinize *17-*. Compare VIZZY¹·². **visitation 1** an act of visiting *la16-*. **2** a (time of) tribulation or affliction *16-*. **3** the action or duty of inspecting or examining churches (especially post-Reformation), schools and universities *16-17*. **buik of visitation 1** a record of inspection *la16*. **2** the record of (perhaps the mapping of) the boundaries of Orkney *la16*. [OFr *visiter*, Lat *visitāre*]

veesitor, visitor, *Ork* **viseetor, †vesitour** /ˈvizɪtər, ˈvɪzɪtər/ *n* **1** one who visits *la19-*. **2** a superintendent or inspector of the craft guilds *la15-17*. **3** an inspector, especially of churches or schools, in the post-Reformation period *16-17*. **4** a person who inspects the sick or investigates the incidence of disease as a matter of public health *la16-e17*. [AN *visitour*]

veet /vit/ *n* a veterinary surgeon *20- N NE*. [altered form of Eng *vet*]

veetious *see* VEECIOUS

veetney *see* VEEGAL

veeve *see* VIEVE

†veezable *n* the least thing: ◊*gin du tinks itt du kens veezable aboot grammar 19 Sh*. [Scots form of Eng *visible* a visible thing implying a barely visible thing]

veeze *see* VIZZY¹·¹, VIZZY¹·²

†vega *n fisherman's taboo* rain *e19 Sh*. [compare ON *vekka* moisture]

vegwal *see* VEEGIL

vehement¹·¹, †viement /ˈviimənt/ *adj* **1** forceful, intense, extreme *la15-*. **2** *of presumption or suspicion* very strong *la15-e17*. **3** *of natural phenomena such as sun or wind* strong, fierce *la15-e17*. **4** *of a sound* very loud *la16*. **5** *of troubles, difficulties* terrible, overwhelming *16*. **vehemencie 1** intensity, severity *la16*. **2** *of natural phenomena* great force or violence *la16*. **3** *applied to sound* loudness *la16-e17*. **vehementlie** forcefully, intensely *16-17*. [MFr *vehement*, Lat *vehement-*, oblique stem of *vehemēns*]

†vehement¹·² *adv* extremely *16-e17*. [see the adj]

veikes *see* VICCES

veil *see* VEAL

veillane *see* VILLAIN¹·¹

vein¹·¹, †van, †vain, †veyne /ven/ *n* **1** a blood vessel (for blood returning to the heart) *la14-*. **2** a sap-vessel in a plant; a vein of a leaf *e16-*. **3** a slender stripe of a different colour or material on a garment *16-*. **4** literary talent *16-e17*. **†vainorgane** the jugular vein *16-17* [OFr *veine, vaine*]

†vein¹·² *v* to ornament (a garment) with narrow stripes of a contrasting material *16-17*. [see the noun]

veir *see* VER

velane, velanous, velany *see* VILLAIN¹·¹

vele *see* VEAL

†vellous, velvous *n* velvet *15-e17*. [OFr *velous*]

vellye, velya /ˈvɛljə/ *n* a sudden jerk, a crash, a heavy fall or thud *la19- Ork*. [unknown, perhaps a variant of FAILZIE¹·¹]

velterin, veltrin /ˈvɛltərən, ˈvɛltrən/ *n* a young cod *la19- Sh*. [compare Norw dial *voltr* a cylinder + *-in* article suffix]

velvous *see* VELLOUS

velya *see* VELLYE

venace *see* VENDACE

venamous, venamuse *see* VENOM

vencus, vencust *see* VANQUISH¹·²

vend /vɛnd/ *v* to present for sale *la17-*. Compare VENT²·². [Fr *vendre*, Lat *vendere*, or back-formation from VENDAR]

vend *see* VENT²·¹

vendace, †vendiss, †venace /ˈvɛndes, ˈvɛndɪs/ *n* a species of char, a small trout-like fish, *Coregonus albula*, found in Britain only at Lochmaben, Dumfriesshire *la17-*. [MFr *vendese* the dace]

†vendar, vender, vyndour /ˈvɛndər/ *n* a seller *la15-*. Compare VENTAR. [AN *vendor, vendour*]

vender /ˈvɛndər/ *v* **1** to wander *la19- Sh*. **2** *of the tide* to turn *20- Sh*. [perhaps a conflation of Norw *vandre* to wander, with Norw dial *vende* to turn]

vender *see* VENDAR

vendicate *see* VINDICATE

†vendicatife, vindicative *adj* vengeful *la15-e17*. [MFr *vindicatif*, Lat *vindicātīvus*]

vendiss *see* VENDACE

venell *see* VENNEL

†venerable¹·¹ *n* a person worthy of respect, especially an ecclesiastic *la15-16*. [see the adj]

venerable¹·², †venerabill /ˈvɛnərəbəl/ *adj* revered, held in esteem *15-*. [MFr *venerable*, Lat *venerābilis*]

†venga, vengi *n fisherman's taboo* a cat *la19- Sh Ork*. [unknown]

†venge *v* to avenge *la14-16*. **†vengeable, vengeabill** *adj* **1** vengeful, vindictive, cruel, destructive *la15-e19*. **2** accursed *16*. [ME *vengen*, AN *venger*]

vengeance, †wengeans /ˈvɛndʒəns/ *n* retribution *la14-*. [AN *vengeance*]

vengi *see* VENGA

venim *see* VENOM

venison, †venysoun /ˈvɛnɪsən/ *n* **1** (the meat or carcass of) hunted game, later specifically deer *la14-*. **2** *law* the right to hunt and kill game; compare *vert and venysoun* (VERT¹) *la15-e17*. [AN *venison*]

vennel, †venell, †vennall, †vinell /ˈvɛnəl/ *n* **1** a narrow lane or thoroughfare in a town or city; frequently in street names *15-*. **2** a (covered) drain, sewer *19- Sh*. [OFr *venelle*, Lat *venella*]

venom, †vennome, †venim, †vinume /ˈvɛnəm/ *n* **1** poison *la14-*. **2** a spiteful or vicious person *16, la19- Sh*. **3** vicious thoughts or talk *la15-17*. **venomit** poisoned; malevolent; corrupt *la14-16*. **venomous, venomus, †vennemous, †venamuse** *adj* poisonous; malicious *14-*. **venamous** *adv intensifier* very, extremely *20- Sh*. [AN *venim*]

vent¹·¹ /vɛnt/ *n* **1** an opening or aperture of the body *15-*. **2** an opening in a building or container to allow light to enter, air to circulate or gases to escape *15-*. **3** specifically, the flue of a chimney; the duct used to convey smoke out of a room *17-*. **4** a chimney head or stack *18-*. **5** the opening of a fireplace *20- Sh NE EC*. **6** (an opportunity for) ventilation; emission, discharge *16-e17*. [aphetic form of MFr *esvent* the action of venting, possibly influenced by Lat *ventus* wind]

vent[1.2] /vɛnt/ *v* **1** *of a chimney or opening* to allow smoke to pass out *la16-*. **2** to give expression to (emotion, rumour, opinion) *la16-*. **3** *of smoke or foul air* to find a way out, (have room to) pass away *17-19*. **4** to put (counterfeit) coins into circulation or currency *17-e19*. **5** to open (a cask of wine) in preparation for use *la16-17*. **6** to disseminate, circulate (a book) illegally *la16-17*. **7** *of wine* to emit vapour *e17*. †**ventar** *n* **1** a person who circulates counterfeit coin *17*. **2** a person who disseminates forbidden literature *17*. †**venting** ventilation, the allowing of smoke to escape from a chimney *la16-e17*. †**take vent** *of coin* to pass into circulation *e17*. [from the noun or aphetic form of MFr *esventer*]

†**vent**[2.1], **vend** *n* sale, the action of selling *la16-17*. [MFr *vente*, Lat *venditus*]

†**vent**[2.2] *v* to sell (originally especially wine) *la15-17*. [see the noun and compare VEND]

ventar *n* a seller of wine; one who broaches a cask of wine for the purpose of selling it *la15-17*. Compare VENDAR. [VENT[1.2] fallen together with VENT[2.2] + agent suffix]

venture[1.1], †**ventour**, †**venter** /ˈvɛntʃər/ *n* **1** a commercial enterprise involving risk, originally mainly in overseas trading *17-*. **2** a chance *la16-e18*. †**ventour schip** a ship carrying a speculative cargo *17*. †**in ventour 1** *of a trading venture overseas* entailing or accepting some financial risk *la16-17*. **2** in case, by chance *la16-e18*. †**upon (one's awin) ventour** at (one's own) risk, perhaps, by way of a speculative venture (in trading overseas) *la16*. [aphetic form of AVENTURE[1.1]]

venture[1.2] /ˈvɛntʃər/ *v* **1** to risk (one's life or possessions) *16-*. **2** to dare to go, travel, proceed *la16-*. **3** to hazard (a commodity) in overseas trading *la16*. †**venturar**, **venturer** a military adventurer *la16-e17*. †**venturous** adventurous, bold *la15-e19*. †**gentilman venturar** a *venturar* engaged in the pacification of Lewis *la16-e17*. [from the noun or aphetic form of AVENTURE[1.2]]

Venus /ˈviːnəs/ *n* **1** Roman goddess of love and beauty; the planet Venus *15-*. **2** sexual intercourse; lust *16*. [Lat *Venus*]

venysoun *see* VENISON

veol *see* VIOL

veper *see* VEEPER

†**ver**, **veir** *n* spring, springtime *la14-e16*. [OFr *ver*, *vere*, Lat *vēr*]

ver *see* VAIR

vera *see* VERRA[1.1], VERRA[1.2]

†**verbo** *adv* verbally *la16-e17*. [Lat *verbō*, dative of *verbum* word]

verd *see* VERT[1]

verdick, †**verdyt** /ˈvɛrdɪk/ *n* decision, judgement *15-*. [AN *verdit*, Lat *verdictum*]

verdie *see* VAIRDIE

verdingale *see* FARTINGAILL

verdyt *see* VERDICK

†**verecund** *adj* modest; shamefaced *la15-16*. **verecundity** modesty *e17*. [Lat *verēcundus*]

verefeit *see* VERIFY

verely *see* VERILY

verg *see* VARG[1.1]

vergens ad inopiam /ˈvɛrdʒɛnz ad ɪnˈɔpiam, ˈvɛrdʒəns ad ɪnˈɔpiəm/ *adj law* in the state preceding bankruptcy, approaching insolvency *18-*. [Lat *vergens ad inopiam* close to being in need]

vergus, †**virgus** /ˈvɛrdʒus/ *n* sour fruit-juice *16-*. [ME *verjous*, OFr *verjus*]

verification, †**verificatioun** /vɛrɪfɪˈkeʃən/ *n* **1** *originally law* the formal attestation of the validity or authenticity of something *la15-*. **2** something that attests to the truth (of something), a proof *la16-*. **3** authentication (of a document) by a seal or signature *la15-17*. [OFr *verificacion*, Lat *vērificātiōn-*]

verify, †**varefy**, †**werify** /ˈvɛrɪfae/ *v ptp also* †**verefeit 1** to confirm as true *la14-*. **2** *law* to prove by testimony or evidence *la15-17*. **3** to authenticate (a document) with a seal or signature *16-e17*. **4** to confirm, ascertain or demonstrate (the truth) *la16-17*. †**verefying** = VERIFICATION (sense 1) *16-e17*. [OFr *verifier*]

verilies *see* VERILYS

verily, †**verralie**, †**verely**, †**verrelie** /ˈvɛrɪli/ *adv* truly *la14-*. [VERRA[1.1] + adv-forming suffix]

verilys, **verilies** /ˈvɛrɪlez/ *adv* truly, indeed *20-*, Ork NE. [VERILY + -*s* adv-forming suffix]

verity, †**verite**, †**varitie** /ˈvɛrɪti/ *n* **1** the truth *la14-*. **2** *law* the truth in law or of a case at law *15-e17*. †**aith of verite** *law* an oath volunteered by pursuer or defender the effect of which is to conclude the case *17*. †**of verite 1** true *la15-19*. **2** *adverbially with emphatic force* truly, indeed *la15-17*. †**the chayre of verite** the pulpit *la16-e17*. [OFr *verite*]

vermin, †**vermine**, †**verming** /ˈvɛrmɪn/ *n* **1** obnoxious creatures, *specif* applied to people *15-*. **2** dangerous or unpleasant people *15-*. **3** unwanted or unpleasant creatures such as mice or snakes *la15-*. **4** *pejorative* a large quantity, swarm, crowd *18- N NE T*. [ME *vermin*, OFr *vermin*, *vermine*]

vernish[1.1], **vairnish**, †**vernis**, †**varnes** /ˈvɛrnɪʃ, ˈvɛrnɪʃ/ *n* varnish *16-*. [OFr *vernis*]

vernish[1.2], **vairnish**, †**vernis**, †**varnes** /ˈvɛrnɪʃ, ˈvɛrnɪʃ/ *v* to coat with varnish *la16-*. [OFr *vernisser*]

vernyaggle *see* VARNIGLE

verra[1.1], **vera**, **very**, **varra**, **wery**, †**verray**, †**varraye**, †**werray** /ˈvɛrə, ˈvɛre, ˈvarə, ˈwɛrɪ/ *adj* **1** true, genuine *la14-*. **2** *law of a person* rightful, true, legally entitled *la14-e17*. **3** *law of a thing* properly established in law, legal *15-16*. [AN *verrai*]

verra[1.2], **vera**, **very**, **varra**, **wery**, †**verray**, †**varraye**, †**werray** /ˈvɛrə, ˈvɛre, ˈvarə, ˈwɛrɪ/ *adv* **1** to a considerable degree, extremely; completely *la15-*. **2** truly, genuinely *15-17*. [see the adj]

verralie, **verrelie** *see* VERILY

verray *see* VERRA[1.1], VERRA[1.2]

version /ˈvɛrʃən/ *n* **1** an account from one person's viewpoint, an edition or translation, a variant as performed or adapted *20-*. **2** the translation of a passage of English prose into Latin mainly as a school exercise; the passage so translated *18- NE T C*. **3** the translation of a passage of English prose into Latin associated with the bursary competition in Aberdeen University *18-19*. [EModE *version*, Fr *version*, Lat *versiōn-*]

versmoia /ˈvɛrsmɔɪa/ *n fisherman's taboo* a mother-in-law or sister-in-law *19- Sh*. [Norw *ver-* in-law + Norw dial *moi* mother]

†**vert**[1], **verd** *n* **1** green vegetation, trees *la15-17*. **2** *law* the right to cut green wood *la15-17*. **vert and venysoun** the right to cut green wood and take venison *la15-17*. [AN *verd*, OFr *vert*]

†**vert**[2] *v* **1** to turn up, root up (the ground) *la16*. **2** to redirect one's attention *la16*. [Lat *vertere* to turn, overturn]

verteis *see* VERTISE

verter *n* **verter spring, well, etc** a medicinal spring, well, etc *19 Bor*. [altered form of *vertew* (VIRTUE)]

vertew *see* VIRTUE

vertie, †**verty** /ˈvɛrte/ adj **1** energetic, active, up early and at work, early-rising *19, 20- NE*. **2** cautious, prudent *la14-18*. [aphetic form of AVERTY]

vertise, †**verteis** /ˈvɛrtɪz/ v to inform; to warn *16- Sh*. [aphetic form of ADVERTEESE]

vertu see VIRTUE

verty see VERTIE

very see VERRA[1.1], VERRA[1.2]

veseit see VIZZY[1.2]

veshel, vessel, *NE* **weshell**, †**veschell** /ˈvɛʃəl, ˈvɛsəl; *NE* ˈwɛʃəl/ n **1** a container, utensil, kitchenware, tableware *la14-*. **2** an animal's udder *20- N T WC SW*. **3** the amount contained in a vessel, paid as MULTURE[1.1] *la15-e17*. [OFr *vessel*]

vesiar see VIZZY[1.2]

vesit see VEESIT[1.2]

vesitour see VEESITOR

vessel see VESHEL

vest /vɛst/ v **1** *law* to establish (a person) in full or legal possession or occupation of property *15-*. **2** to clothe, robe *la15-16*. **vestit and sesit** established in full or legal possession or occupation of property *15-e17*. [OFr *vestir* to clothe, Lat *vestīre*]

vestige /ˈvɛstɪdʒ/ n a surviving trace (of something) *17-*. [Fr *vestige*, Lat *vestīgium* a footprint, trace]

vestin see WASTEN[1.2]

vestry /ˈvɛstri/ n the room in a church used for storing vestments and conducting local or parish business *15-*. [AN *vestrie]

vesy see VIZZY[1.1], VIZZY[1.2]

veto /ˈvito/ n a prohibition *17-*. **Veto Act** an act passed by the General Assembly in 1834, providing that no minister should be presented to a parish against the wish of the congregation; the precipitating cause of *the Disruption* (DISRUPTION) *19*. [Lat *veto* I forbid]

vevaris see VIVERS

vew see VIEW[1.1]

vex[1.1] /vɛks/ n a source of regret, sorrow or annoyance *19-*. **vexsome** sorrowful, full of vexation *19-, 20- WC*. [see the verb]

vex[1.2] /vɛks/ v ptp also **vext 1** to harass, threaten, trouble (a person) *15-*. **2** to cause (a person) mental agitation, make anxious or depressed, distress *15-*. **be vexed for** to be sorry for (a person) *la19-*. [OFr *vexer*, Lat *vexāre* to shake, disturb]

veyage see VAIGE

veynd see VYND[1.1]

veyne see VEIN[1.1]

vgg see UG[1.2]

vgly see UGLY[1.2], UGLY[1.3]

vgsum see UGSOME

viad see VEEAT

viage see VAIGE

vicar, †**vicare** /ˈvɪkər/ n **1** *RC and Episcopalian Church* the incumbent in a parish, originally substituting for the holder of the benefice *la14-*. **2** a layman who claimed the title of the *vicarage teinds* (VICARAGE) after the Reformation *la17-e18 Sh*. **3** the church precentor who was given the vicarage teinds as his salary *19 Bor*. **vicar-pensionar** a vicar receiving a fixed payment out of the revenues of a benefice *la15-16*. [AN *vicar*, OFr *vicaire*, Lat *vicārius* a substitute]

vicarage /ˈvɪkərɪdʒ/ n **1** the portion of the benefice of a PARSON assigned to his vicar; the vicar's share of the TEIND[1.1] of a parish, usually *vicarage teinds*; the living of a vicar *la15-*. **2** an ecclesiastical payment for the upkeep of a minister or reader based originally on the emolument of a vicar *la16*. **vicarage pensionar 1** the fixed payment received by a *vicar-pensionar* (VICAR) *16-e17*. **2** the benefice of a *vicar-pensionar* (VICAR) *la16-17*. **vicarage teinds** *small teinds* (SMA[1.2]), frequently used to pay the vicar or minister of a parish *la16-*. [VICAR + *-age* suffix]

†**vicces, veikes** npl public disputations held for bachelors at the University of St Andrews as they prepared for their examinations; a feast held in celebration of this *la16-e17*. [Lat (*per*) *vicēs* in turn]

vice[1] /vʌɪs/ n **1** the place, position, stead (of another) *16-*. **2** one's turn in a rota; one of the recurrent periods in a continuous series *la16-18*. **3** the right to present a minister to a parish where the patronage was shared by two or more heritors who exercised their right in turn *la18-e19*. **succeed in the vice (of a person)** *law* to take over a tenancy by collusion with the outgoing tenant and without the landlord's consent *16-19, 20- historical*. [Lat *vice* in place of]

vice[2], †**phise**, †**phese**, †**fize** /vʌɪs/ n **1** a mechanism for gripping and holding an object being worked on *16-*. **2** a screw or mechanism operated by a screw *15-17*. Compare FEEZE[1.1]. [OFr *vis* a spiral staircase, MDu *vize* a screw]

†**vice**[3] n ADVICE *la15-17*. [aphetic form of *avyse* (ADVICE)]

vice see VOICE[1.1], VOICE[1.2]

vice- /vʌɪs/ prefix in place of, in the absence of (the person specified in the noun with which it occurs) *la15-*. [Lat *vice* in place of]

vice-chancellor, †**vice-chancellar** /ˈvʌɪsˈtʃansələr/ n **1** the deputy of a chancellor in a diocese *la15-*. **2** the deputy of the chancellor of Scotland *la16-17*. [VICE- + CHANCELLOR]

†**vicennial** adj lasting for or occurring every 20 years *la17-*. **vicennial prescription** *law* a 20-year period of prescription applied to retours and to holograph bonds *la17-19, 20- historical*. [adj from Lat *vīcennium* a period of 20 years]

†**vice-president** n a person appointed to act in the place of the president of the Court of Session *16-17*. [VICE- + PRESIDENT]

viciat see VITIAT

vicious see VEECIOUS

†**vicissim** adv in turn *16-17*. [Lat *vicissim*]

victor, †**victour** /ˈvɪktər/ n **1** a winner of a contest or battle *15-*. **2** the DUX of a school *la17-e18*. †**victoriall** victorious *la15-17*. **victorious**, †**victorius** victorious *la15-*. †**victrice** a female victor *e16*. [AN *victor*, *victour*, Lat *victor*]

victory, victorie, †**victore**, †**victour** /ˈvɪktəri/ n victory *la14-*. [AN *victorie*, OFr *victoire*]

victual[1.1], **vittal**, †**vittail**, †**vittel**, †**vitale** /ˈvɪtəl/ n **1** *used collectively* provisions, foodstuffs *la14-*. **2** corn, grain; a crop before or after harvesting *la15-*. **victuals** provisions, foodstuffs *la14-*. **victual-farm** farm rent paid in grain *18*. **victual house** a granary, especially the grain-store of an estate *la16-e18*. **victual rent** rent paid in grain *la17-18*. **victual stipend** that part of a minister's stipend formerly paid in grain or the cash equivalent *19-*. [AN *vitelle*, OFr *vitaile*, Lat *victuālia*]

victual[1.2], †**vitale**, †**vittal** /ˈvɪtəl/ v to supply with provisions *la14-*. [from the noun and AN, OFr *vitailler*]

†**vidimus** n **1** an examination or inspection confirming authenticity; verification *la15-19*. **2** an authenticated copy of a document *16-e17*. [Lat *vīdimus* we have seen]

viduity see *widowity* (WEEDA).

viement see VEHEMENT[1.1]

vieu see VIEW[1.1]

vieve, vive, veeve /viv/ adj **1** *of a person* living, alive; lively, alert, brisk *16-*. **2** *of colours, impressions, sights, sounds* bright, clear, vivid, distinct *la16-*. **3** *of a visual or verbal representation* true to life, lifelike; accurate *la16-19, 20- Sh NE EC*. **4** *of a person as a representation or example* living, actual *la16-17*. **vively 1** clearly, distinctly, vividly *la16-*. **2**

in a lively way *la16-17*. **vive voice** a person's actual voice or speech *la16-e17*. **be vive voice** by word of mouth *la16-e17*. [OFr *vive*, Lat *vīvus*]

vievers *see* VIVERS

view[1.1], *NE* **vyow**, †**vew**, †**vieu** /vju; *NE* also vjʌu/ *n* prospect, sight *17-*. [ME *vewe*, *vieu*, AN *vewe*, *vieu*]

view[1.2], *NE* **vyow** /vju; *NE* also vjʌu/ *v* **1** to inspect, examine; look at *la16-*. **2** to consider *la19 Sh*. [see the noun]

vigour /ˈvɪɡər/ *n* **1** energy, force, strength *la14-*. **2** *law* legal force or validity of an instrument of law or government *la15-17*. **vigorouslie** with energy, force or strength *la14-*. **stand in vigour** *law* to be in force *16-17*. [OFr *vigour*]

†**vig vise** *n fisherman's taboo* a compass *e19 Sh*. [Norw dial *vegvisar* a guide, signpost]

vikkend /ˈvɪkənd/ *adj of a young man or boy* stout, sturdy, robust *20- Ork*. [probably participial adj from Norw dial *kvika* to thrive, grow]

vilan *see* VILLAIN[1.2]

†**vilderas** *n* a velvet fabric *e17*. [perhaps a variant of OFr *velour* + RAZE]

vildroo *see* VILLYAROO

vilipend, *NE* **wallipend** /ˈvɪləpɛnd; *NE* also ˈwaləpɛnd/ *v* to show contempt for authority or the law, despise, abuse *la15-*. **vilipendar** a person who treats authority with contempt *16-17*. [OFr *vilipender*, Lat *vīlipendere*]

†**vilipensioun** *n* contempt for others or the law, scornful or arrogant behaviour *la15-17*. [OFr *vilipension*, Lat *vīlipensiōn-*]

village, *Ork NE T* **veelage**, †**welage** /ˈvɪlədʒ; *Ork NE T* ˈvilədʒ/ *n* a large hamlet or very small rural township *la15-*. [OFr *village*]

villain[1.1], †**veillane**, †**velane**, †**villan** /ˈvɪlən/ *n* **1** a person at the bottom of the social hierarchy; a rascal, rogue, scoundrel *la15-*. **2** a feudal serf bound in agricultural service *la15-17*. **villainous**, **velanous** base, evil *la14-*. **villainy**, **velany**, **villanie** wickedness, cruelty, harm *la14-*. [AN *vilan*, OFr *vilein*, *villain*]

†**villain**[1.2], **villan**, **villayn**, **vilan**, **wellien** *adj* low-born, base, vile *la15-16*. [AN *vilein*, OFr *vilain*]

villyaroo, *Ork* **vildroo** /ˈvɪljəru, ˈvɪləru; *Ork* ˈvɪldru/ *n* **1** gossip, chatter *la19- Sh*. **2** confusion; destruction *20- Ork*. [compare Norw *villrede*, Dan *vilderede* confusion, perplexity]

vils /vɪls/ *npl* the small intestines of a ruminant *la19- Sh*. [Faer *vil*]

vimmer[1.1] /ˈvɪmər/ *n* a state of trembling, a flutter *la19- Sh*. [see the verb]

vimmer[1.2] /ˈvɪmər/ *v* to tremble, flutter *la19- Sh*. [frequentative form of Norw dial *vima* to tumble, be dazed or stupefied]

vincust *see* VANQUISH[1.2]

vindicate, †**vendicate** /ˈvɪndɪket/ *v ptp* also **vindicate 1** to justify *la16-*. **2** to avenge (a person), vent (anger) in revenge *e16*. **3** to rescue, deliver (from error or injury) *la16*. **4** to assert or establish possession *la16-17*. [Lat *vindicāt-*, ptp stem of *vindicāre*]

†**vindicatioun** *n* justification for a claim or defence against censure *17*. [Lat *vindicātiōn-* a laying claim to a thing, and compare OFr *vindication* vengeance]

vindicative *see* VENDICATIFE

vinell *see* VENNEL

vinkish, **vinqueis** *see* VANQUISH[1.2]

vinster /ˈvɪnstər/ *n* = BRAXY *la18-*. **vinster sickness** braxy *la18- Sh*. [Norw dial *vinster* the fourth stomach of a ruminant]

vinume *see* VENOM

viol, †**veol** /ˈvaeəl/ *n* a stringed musical instrument played with a bow *16-*. †**violer**, †**violar** a player of the viol; a fiddler *la16-e19*. [OFr *viole*]

viola, †**viole** /ˈvaeələ/ *n* a flower of the viola or pansy family; a violet *la15-*. [Lat *viola*]

†**violent**[1.1] *v* **1** to harm, damage (a public office) *la16-18*. **2** to treat with violence, coerce, ride roughshod over *17-18*. [MFr *violenter*, Lat *violentare*]

violent[1.2] /ˈvaeələnt/ *adj* **1** *of natural forces* possessed of or operating with great force or strength, moving strongly and impetuously *la14-*. **2** exhibiting violence, prepared to use physical force *la15-*. **3** *law of the possession or use of property while withholding rent* by force; without consent, illegal, also *of the occupier of property so seized la15-17*. **4** *law of suspicion or presumption* intense, strong *16-17*. **violentlie 1** violently *15-*. **2** *of seizure of property* forcibly, unlawfully *la15-17*. †**violent possessor** a person occupying (property) by force *la16*. **violent presumption 1** willingness to use violence *15-e17*. **2** *law* strong PRESUMPTION (sense 2) *15-17*. **violent profits** *law* revenues, including penal damages, from property held by force, exacted from the illegal occupier *la16-*. **lay violent hands on**, **put violent hands on** to attack, seize with violence *la14-*. [OFr *violent*, Lat *violentus*]

violet[1.1] /ˈvaeələt/ *n* **1** the flower of the genus *Viola* *15-*. **2** the purple colour associated with the flower; cloth or dress violet in colour *15-*. [OFr *violete*]

violet[1.2] /ˈvaeələt/ *adj* violet in colour *16-*. [OFr *violet*]

viper *see* VEEPER

vippick, **whippack** /ˈvɪpək, ˈmɪpək/ *n* a small fishing rod *19- Sh*. [perhaps WHIP + *-ack* (-OCK) diminutive suffix]

viral *see* VIRL

vire[1] /vaer/ *n* the best or most outstanding person, animal or thing *19- Sh Ork*. [unknown]

†**vire**[2] *n* a bolt for a crossbow *la14-e17*. [OFr *vire*]

vire[3], †**vyre** /vaer/ *v* **1** to move from one place to another *20- Sh Ork*. **2** *fisherman's taboo* to turn a pot over the fire; to move the contents of the pot from one side to another while cooking *20- Sh*. **3** to throw or move; to throw or move on a curving or circular path *la14-15*. **4** to wind (a rope or string); to adjust by pulling or winding *16-17*. **5** to (cause a ship) to alter course *la16-e17*. [OFr *virer* to turn]

Virgilian /vɪrˈdʒɪlɪən/ *adj* in the style of the poet Virgil *16-*. [Lat *Virgiliānus*]

Virginia, †**Virginie** /vɪrˈdʒɪnɪə, vɪrˈdʒɪnjə/ *n* Virginia, the place in North America, now a US state *17-*. **Virginia leaff tobacco** tobacco leaf from Virginia *la17*. **Virginia trade** the tobacco trade between Glasgow and Virginia *18*. [from the place-name]

virgule /ˈvɪrɡjul/ *n* a sloping or upright line used in manuscripts and musical notation *la16-*. [MFr *virgule*, Lat *virgula*]

†**virgultis** *npl* bushes, shrubs *e16*. [Lat *virgulta*]

virgus *see* VERGUS

virilitie /vɪˈrɪləti/ *n* manhood; masculine vigour, strength *la15-*. [MFr *virilité*, Lat *virīlitas*]

virl, **virrel**, †**viral**, †**virol** /vɪrl, ˈvɪrəl/ *n* **1** a ferrule, a band fitted round a rod, pipe or the like to prevent splitting *la15-*. **2** a ring or eddy in water, especially as caused by the stroke of an oar *20- Sh*. **virled** having a ferrule; clasped round as by a ferrule *19*, *20- Ork T*. [OFr *virol*, *virelle*, Lat *virola*]

virmish *see* FIMIS[1.2]

virp /vɪrp/ *v* to vomit *20 Sh*. [Norw dial *virpa* to throw]

virpa /ˈvɪrpa/ *n* thin SOWANS (sense 1) *la19- Sh*. [perhaps a jocular derivative of VIRP]

virr /vɪr/ *n* vigour, energy, force, impetuosity *la16-*. [probably onomatopoeic]

virrel *see* VIRL

virry *see* WIRRY[1.2]

virtue, †vertu, †vertew /ˈvɪrtju/ *n* **1** virtue, a moral quality, the courage or strength *of persons la14-*. **2** power or efficacy *of things la14-*. **3** cleverness, skill, ability *15*. **4** a bodily sense or ability; one of the five senses *e15*. **5** *education* (the principles of) morality as taught in a school or university *16*. **6** a useful practical skill or ability, associated with the virtues of work *16-17*. **7** the efficacious application (of money, skill or effort) to the general good; industry, diligence *la15-19*. **virtuous, †vertuous** *adj* possessing virtue *la14-*. **virtuously, †vertuously 1** with virtue, in a virtuous manner *la14-*. **2** with great skill or excellence *e15*. **†hous of vertew** a parish institution set up for teaching the practical skill of cloth-making *e17*. [OFr *virtu, vertu*]
vis *see* WISH[1.2]
vise, vees, †weyse /vʌɪs, vis/ *n* mining the line of fracture of a fault in a coal-seam, usually marked by a deposit of earth, clay or the like *la17-*. [unknown]
viseetor *see* VEESITOR
visek /ˈvisək/ *n* a ballad or song sung to accompany dancing *17-18, 19- Sh historical*. [ON *vísa* a verse, stanza + *-ick* (-OCK) diminutive suffix]
visie *see* VIZZY[1.1], VIZZY[1.2]
vision, veesion, *NE* **weezhan, †visioun** /ˈvɪʒən, ˈvɪʒən; *NE* ˈwiʒən/ *n* **1** sight *la14-*. **2** a person seen as a dream figure or apparition *16-*. **3** a person of unusual beauty *19-*. **4** a puny, emaciated person or animal, one who is wasting away; an insignificant characterless person *19, 20- Sh Ork C SW*. **5** a perverse child *la20- N*. [AN *visioun*, OFr *vision*, Lat *vīsiōn-*]
visit *see* VEESIT[1.1], VEESIT[1.2]
visitor *see* VEESITOR
vis major /ˈvɪs ˈmedʒər/ *n law* a circumstance, such as a natural disaster, which cannot be reasonably expected or prevented, an act of God, a DAMNUM FATALE, which excludes responsibility for loss, damage or the non-performance of a contract *la19-*. [Lat *vīs mājor* superior force]
†visnet *n law* trial by a jury made up of a person's neighbours *15-16*. [OFr *visnet*, Lat *visnetum*]
visnomy *see* PHYSIOGNOMY
vissie *see* VIZZY[1.1], VIZZY[1.2]
vissier *see* VIZZY[1.2]
vissil *see* WISSEL[1.2]
vissit *see* VIZZY[1.2]
vistie /ˈvɪsti/ *n* a visit, trip *19- Ork*. [perhaps a conflation of VIZZY[1.1] with *visit* (VEESIT[1.1])]
vitale *see* VICTUAL[1.1], VICTUAL[1.2]
vitch /vɪtʃ/ *v* to visit, drop in on, exchange gossip *19- Sh*. [Norw dial *vitja*]
†vitiat *v ptp* **vitiat, viciat 1** *law* to spoil, deface or tamper with fraudulently *15-18*. **2** to diminish, harm *la16-17*. [Lat *vitiāt-*, ptp stem of *vitiāre*]
vitious *see* VEECIOUS
vitious intromission /ˈvɪʃəs ɪntroˈmɪʃən/ *n* the unwarrantable interference with the moveable estate of a deceased without legal title, whereby liability for all the deceased's debts may be incurred *17-*. Compare VEECIOUS. [*vitious* (VEECIOUS) + INTROMISSION]
†Vitrie canves *n* canvas from Vitré in Brittany *la15-e17*. [from the place-name + *canves* (CANNAS)]
vitta /ˈvɪtə/ *n* a wooden bit for a horse's bridle *la19 Ork*. [perhaps a variant of WIDDIE]
vittail *see* VICTUAL[1.1]
vittal *see* VICTUAL[1.1], VICTUAL[1.2]
vittel *see* VICTUAL[1.1]
vivda /ˈvɪvdə/ *n* meat cured and dried in the open air without salt *17-19, 20- Sh Ork historical*. [perhaps Norw dial *vovde* muscle, the fleshy part of a limb]

†vive *adv* accurately, exactly *la16-e17*. [see the adj *vive* (VIEVE)]
vive *see* VIEVE
vivers, †vevaris, †vievers /ˈvivərz, ˈvaevərz/ *npl* provisions; food, victuals; necessities *16-*. **victuals and vivers** provisions, grain and other necessities *16-17*. [MFr *vivres*]
†vizicater *n* an application used to raise blisters on the skin *16-e18*. [Lat *vēsīcatōrius*]
vizzy[1.1]**, vizy,** *Ork* **veeze, †visie, †vesy, †vissie** /ˈvɪzi, ˈvizi; *Ork* viz/ *n* **1** a visit, a charitable or social act of visiting *17-*. **2** a look, glimpse, scrutiny, survey *18-*. **3** a view, prospect *18-*. **4** an aim (with a weapon) *18-*. **5** the sight on the barrel of a gun *19-*. **6** an inspection or official investigation *la16-17*. **7** a *vizzy-hole e17*. **vizzy-hole** a peephole, or spyhole *20- Ork*.
†vesymaster an inspector *16-17*. [MFr *visée* a view, aim, with some senses from the verb]
vizzy[1.2]**, vizy,** *Ork* **veeze, †visie, †vesy, †vissie** /ˈvɪzi, ˈvizi; *Ork* viz/ *v pt, ptp* **vizzied, †veseit, †vissit 1** to visit, come to or call on, charitably, socially or officially *la14-*. **2** to go to (a place) for recreation or interest *15-*. **3** to observe, examine, scrutinize *15-*. **4** to afflict (with sickness) *la15-*. **5** to squint at so as to see clearly *19-20, 20- Sh*. **6** to study, pore over *20- Sh Ork*. **7** to take aim (with a gun), aim (at something) *la16-19, 20- Sh*. **8** to make an official inspection or examination of a person, place, commodity or circumstances *la15-17*. **9** to make an official inspection or examination of evidence *15-17*. **10** *of books* to inspect for the purpose of censorship *la16-e17*. **11** to view, look at, pay attention to *16*. **†vesiar, vissier** an inspector *la15-16*. † **vizzying hole** peephole, spyhole *19*. [OFr *viseer* to visit, with some senses from the noun]
Vllister *see* ULSTER
vlypy *see* ULIPY
vmast *see* UMEST[1.3]
vmaste *see* UMEST[1.1]
vmbrage *see* UMMERAGE
vmbrakill *see* UMBRAKLE
vnagast *see* UNAGAIST
vnamyabill *see* UNAMIABLE
vnawars *see* UNAWAURS
vnblomit *see* UNBLOMIT
vnbowsumly *see* UNBOWSOME
vncoutht *see* UNCOUTH[1.1]
vnderfeit *see* UNDERFOOT
vndirly *see* UNDERLIE
vnermaste *see* UNDERMOST
vnganand *see* UNGANAND
vnguent *see* UNGUMENT
vnhailsum *see* UNHALESOME
vnheid *see* UNHED
vnhelsum *see* UNHALESOME
vnicorne *see* UNICORN
vnkill *see* UNCLE
vnlay *see* UNLAW[1.1], UNLAW[1.2]
vnrewlful *see* UNRULEFUL
vnrokkit *see* UNROCKIT
vnryde *see* UNRUDE
vnsall *see* UNSELL[1.2]
vnvynsable *see* UNVINCIBLE
vnwsit *see* UNUSED
vnyte *see* UNE
voaler /ˈvolər/ *n fisherman's taboo* a cat *19- Sh*. [agent noun from Norw dial *våla*, Icel *vola* to howl, wail]
voamd /vomd/ *adj of meat or fish* tainted, gone off, putrescent *19- Sh*. [participial adj from the stem of Norw dial *våmen* tainted, gone off]

voar see WARE⁵
vocable /ˈvokəbəl/ *n* a word *16-*. **vocables** a word list *18*. [MFr *vocable*, Lat *vocābulum*]
vocation, †**vocatioun** /voˈkeʃən/ *n* **1** a sense of calling (to an occupation or way of life) *16-*. **2** the summoning of an assembly or its members *la15*. [MFr *vocation*, Lat *vocātiōn-*]
voce see VOICE¹·¹
vocky see VOGIE
vodd, vode see VOID¹·², VOID¹·³
voe /vo/ *n* an inlet of the sea, creek, bay *17- Sh Ork*. [Norw *våg*, ON *vágr*]
voge see VOGUE
vogerous /ˈvogərəs/ *adj* keen, eager; brisk, strong *la19- Sh*. [perhaps a conflation of Eng *vigorous* with Norw dial *vak* wide awake, early up, brisk]
vogie, †**vougy**, †**voky**, †**vocky**, †*N NE* **vyokie** /ˈvogɪ, ˈvogi/ *adj* **1** *of persons* proud, elated, vain *17-*. **2** *of things* imposing, ostentatious *18-*. **3** merry, light-hearted, happy *18-*.
vokish proud, elated, vain *la19 Ork*. [unknown]
vogue, voge /vog/ *n* popularity, social approval *16-*. **in vogue 1** in fashion, in use *16-*. **2** *of people* known to be active, flourishing *17*. **the vogue** the principal or foremost place in the estimation of society *la16-*. [MFr *vogue* success (originally in a rowing contest)]
voice¹·¹, **vos, voss, vice, vyce**, †**voce** /vɔɪs, vos, vʌɪs/ *n* **1** a sound from the larynx emitted orally; an utterance *la14-*. **2** report or rumour; fame or renown *la15-17*. **3** (the right of) speaking or deciding in matters of communal decision-making or elections; a vote *la15-17*. **4** an opinion or point of view *16-17*. **in ane voice** unanimously *la15-e17*. †**the commoun voce** public opinion *la14-e17*. [AN *voice*, Lat *vōc-* oblique stem of *vōx*]
voice¹·², **vos, voss, vice, vyce** /vɔɪs, vos, vʌɪs/ *v* **1** to express verbally *17-*. **2** to vote *17*. **voicer** a person entitled to vote, a voter *17*. **voicing** voting (in an assembly or election) *17*. [see the noun]
void¹·¹, †**voyd**, †**voud** /vɔɪd/ *n* an empty space, a hole; a gap between buildings *16-*. [see the adj]
void¹·², *Sh* **vodd**, †**voyd**, †**vode**, †**vyde**, †**voud** /vɔɪd; *Sh* vəd/ *v* **1** to empty, quit, clear (a place) *la14-*. **2** to be free (of) a fault *la14-e16*. **voyded** heraldry of a figure empty, having a different colour from its border *la15-17*. **voidour 1** a receptacle into which leftovers are emptied *e16*. **2** the container, packing or wrapping from which goods are emptied or removed *la15-e17 EC*. **void and redd** *law of a property* vacated, cleared and ready for a new occupant *la15-*. [AN *voider*]
void¹·³, *Sh* **vodd**, †**voyd**, †**vode**, †**vyde**, †**voud** /vɔɪd; *Sh* vəd/ *adj* **1** empty, unoccupied *la14-*. **2** *law* null *15-*. **3** abandoned; derelict *la19-*. **4** *heraldry of a figure* empty, having a different colour from its border *la15-17*. **mak void** to clear, render free from obstructions *16-17*. [AN *voide*]
voite see VOTE¹·¹, VOTE¹·²
vokish, voky see VOGIE
volage, †**fallauge** /ˈvolədʒ, vəˈladʒ/ *adj* **1** lavish, profuse, prodigal with money *19- NE*. **2** fickle, foolish, rash *16-19*.
†**volageous** fickle, foolish, rash *la14-19*. [OFr *volage*]
†**voler** *n* a robber, pirate *17*. [MFr *voleur*]
†**volier** *n* a birdcage, aviary *la16-17*. [MFr *volière*]
volley, †**voly**, †**wollie**, †**woilley** /ˈvɔli/ *n* **1** the simultaneous discharge of a number of weapons *la16-*. **2** the discharge of artillery specifically as a salutation on a formal occasion *la16-*. **3** a torrent of invective *20-*. [MFr *volée*]
vollum see VOLUME
volt see VAUT¹·¹, VAUT¹·²

volume, †**vollum**, †**volum** /ˈvɔljum/ *n pl* also †**volummis** a book, tome *15-*. **the volum of creation** the created world as a source of knowledge *la17*. [OFr *volume*, Lat *volūmen* a scroll]
†**volunté** *n* will, desire *la15-e16*. [ME *volunte*, AN *voluntie*]
†**voluntair** *n* a person who undertakes a task or enters military service of their own free will *e17*. [from the adj VOLUNTAR]
voluntar /ˈvɔləntər/ *adj* **1** done of one's own free will *la15-19, 20- NE*. **2** *law of an act, judgement, or deed* undertaken of one's own free will, also *of the resultant right 17*. **3** *of wrongdoing* done deliberately *la15-16*. [OFr *voluntaire*, Lat *voluntārius*]
†**volve** *v* to turn over, roll *la15*. [MFr *volver*, Lat *volvere*]
voly see VOLLEY
†**vome** *v ptp* also †**vomeit** †**vomet** to vomit *16*. [MFr *vomir*, Lat *vomere*]
vomit¹·¹, **vamit** /ˈvɔmɪt, ˈvamɪt/ *n* **1** the act of regurgitating stomach contents; ejected stomach contents *la15-*. **2** an emetic *la15-e18*. [AN *vomit*, Lat *vomitus*]
vomit¹·², **vamit** /ˈvɔmɪt, ˈvamɪt/ *v* to regurgitate stomach contents *la16-*. **vomiter** an emetic *17-18*. [Lat *vomitāre*]
voo¹·¹, **vow, wow** /vu, vʌu, wʌu/ *n* a solemn promise *la14-*. [OFr *vou*]
voo¹·², **vow, wow** /vu, vʌu, wʌu/ *v* **1** to make a solemn promise *la15-*. **2** to curse, swear *la20- Ork NE*. [OFr *vouer*]
voracious /vɔˈreʃəs/ *adj* ravenous *la16-*. [MFr *vorace*, Lat *vorāci-* oblique stem of *vorax*, with *-ous* suffix]
vos, voss see VOICE¹·¹, VOICE¹·²
vost see VOUST¹·¹, VOUST¹·²
vote¹·¹, †**vot**, †**vott**, †**voite** /vot/ *n* **1** a ballot, the process of decision-making or election *16-*. **2** an opinion, decision or choice *la15-e17*. **3** a vow, a solemn promise *e16*. **have ane vote** to be entitled to vote *la15-*. **in ane vote** unanimously *16-17*. **put to a vote, put to the vote** to submit to the decision of the meeting *la16-*. [Lat *vōtum* a vow, wish]
vote¹·², †**vot**, †**vott**, †**voite** /vot/ *v* **1** to express (an opinion) usually by a recorded ballot or by a show of hands; to consider and decide (a matter) by submitting (it) to a vote *16-*. **2** to elect into office by a ballot or a show of hands *16-*. **3** to vow (to do something) *e16*. **voter** a person who has a right to vote, especially an elector *la16-*. [Lat *vōt-*, ptp stem of *vovēre* to vow, desire, or Lat *vōtāre*]
vou see WOW²
†**vouch**, †**woche** *v law* to affirm or assert ownership (of land) before a legal authority, lacking documentary evidence *la15-16*. [ME *vouchen*, OFr *voucher*, *vocher*]
voud see VOID¹·¹, VOID¹·², VOID¹·³
vougy see VOGIE
†**voust**¹·¹, **vost** *n* a boast *15-19*. [perhaps onomatopoeic or an altered form of BOAST¹·¹]
voust¹·², †**vost** /vust/ *v* to boast, brag *16-*. **vouster**, †**voustour** a braggart *16-*. [see the noun]
vout see VAUT¹·¹, VAUT¹·²
vow see VOO¹·¹, VOO¹·²
vow see WOW²
vowt see VAUT¹·¹, VAUT¹·²
voyage see VAIGE
voyd see VOID¹·¹, VOID¹·², VOID¹·³
vpbair, vpbore, vpborne see UPBER
vpdryve see UPDRIVE
vphald see UPHAUD¹·²
vphei see UPHIE
vpheild, vpheildit see UPHAUD¹·²
vphelly-ewin see UPHALY-EVIN
vphellymes see UPHALYMES

vplyft see UPLIFT[1.2]
vpryse see UPRISE
vrack see WRACK[1.1], WRACK[1.2]
vraith see WREATH[1.1]
vrang see WRANG[1.3]
vrapper see WRAPPER
vratch see WRATCH[1.1]
vreet see WRITE[1.1], WRITE[1.2]
vreeter see WRITER
vreetin see WRITING
vricht see WRICHT
vrigling see WRIGGLING
vring see WRING
vrow see WIRL[1]
vrutten see WRITE[1.2]
vs see USE[1.1]
vsans see USANCE
vtir see UTTER
vtlaw see OOTLAW[1.2]
vtouth see OUTWITH[1.2]
vtterlie see OOTERLY
vtyr see OOTER
vtyrrans see UTTERANCE
vulgar[1.1] /ˈvʌlgər/ *n* **1** the vernacular language *16-e17*. **2** the common, ordinary people *16-17*. [see the adj]
vulgar[1.2], †**wlgar**, †**vulgair** /ˈvʌlgər/ *adj* **1** *of people* not of noble birth *16-*. **2** *of knowledge* familiar to ordinary people, commonplace, ordinary *la15-e17*. **3** *of language* Scots (rather than Latin) *la16-17*. **4** written in or translated into the vernacular *16-e17*. **vulgar schole** elementary school, teaching reading and writing in the vernacular rather than Latin *la16-17*. [OFr *vulgaire*, Lat *vulgāris*]
†**vulgate**, †**wlgat** *adj* commonly known *e16*. [Lat *vulgāt-*, ptp stem of *vulgāre* to make public or common]
†**vult**, †**wlt**, †**wlte** *n* **1** the face, countenance; especially facial expression *la14-e17*. **2** mood, attitude *16*. [OFr *vult*, Lat *vultus* the face]
vult see VAUT[1.1], VAUT[1.2]
vyaedick see VAEDIK
vyaug see VAIG[1.1], VAIG[1.2]
†**vyce** *n* a section, division, boundary *la17*. [aphetic form of DIVISE[1.1]]
vyce see VOICE[1.1], VOICE[1.2]
vyde see VOID[1.2], VOID[1.3]
†**vyis**, **wyse** *v* to bethink (oneself), take careful thought *la14-16*. **vysment** careful consideration, advice *15-16*. [aphetic form of *avise* (ADVISE)]
vyll see WILE[1.1], WILE[2]
vynd[1.1], **vand**, †**veynd** /vʌɪnd, vɑnd, vjɑnd/ *n* **1** a skill, knack, aptitude *la19- Sh*. **2** attitude, manner of behaving *la19- Sh*. [Norw dial *vand* custom, habit]
vynd[1.2], **vand** /vʌɪnd, vɑnd, vjɑnd/ *v* to arrange, contrive, fit or adapt (one thing to another) *la20- Sh*. [Icel *vanda* to perform something with care]
vyndour see VENDAR
vyokie see VOGIE
vyow see VIEW[1.1], VIEW[1.2]
vyre see VIRE[3]
vysment see VYIS

W

wa[1.1], **waa**, **waw**, **wall**, †**wae**, †**wal**, †**vall** /wa, wɔ, wɔl/ *n* **1** a wall, a rampart or embankment constructed for defensive purposes; a construction composed of bricks, turf or stones, forming part of a building or enclosure *la14-*. **2** *pl* a roofless building, ruins *18-19, 20- SW*. **waa-back** a paraffin lamp with a flat back-plate for hanging against a wall *20- Sh*. †**wa-bag** a bag hung on a wall, for holding odds and ends *la17-19*. †**wall-rase**, **walreis** a wall-plate *16-17*. **wall-stade**, †**walsted** the foundation of a wall; a walled area or enclosure *la17-19, 20- Sh*. †**wall toun** a walled or fortified town *la15-16*. [OE *wall*]

wa[1.2], **wall** /wa, wɔ, wɔl/ *v* to build a wall; to provide a town with a (defensive) rampart; to surround with a wall *la14-*. [see the noun]

wa[2.1], **way** /wa, we/ *adv* away *la15-*; compare AWA. **wa-cast** something of little value *19- Sh Ork N NE T*. †**waycoming** departure *la16-17*. †**way passing** departure *la15-16*. **wa pittin** **1** putting away, storing; removal or sending away (of a person) *16-19, 20- Sh*. **2** a burial, a funeral *la19-, 20- Sh*. **wa-takin**, †**waytaking** removal, carrying off, especially by theft or violence *la15-19, 20- Sh NE WC* [aphetic form of AWA[1.1]]

wa[2.2], **way** /wa, we/ *interj* an exclamation of disbelief or dismissal *19-*; compare AWA. †**do way** go away *la15-16*. **gae wa** go away *la16-*. **gae wa wi ye** go away *20-*. [see the adv]

wa see WAE[1.1], WAE[1.2], WAE[1.3], WAE[2], WEY[1]
waadge see WAGE[1.1]
waager see WAGER[1.2]
waak see WALK[2.1], WAUK[1.2]
waal see WALE[1.1], WALE[1.2], WALL[1]
waald, †**wald** /wald/ *n* command, control *la14-19, 20- Ork*. [OE *gewald*; compare WIELD]
waalse /wals/ *v* to move (a person) lightly and quickly, sweep (along) *20- Sh*. [altered form of Eng *waltz*]
waan see WAN[2]
waand see WAND[1.1]
waant see WANT[1.2]
waar see WARE[1.1]
waard /ward/ *v* to award *20- Sh*. [EModE *ward*, aphetic form of *award*]
waarm see WARM[1.3]
waash see WASH[1.2]
waasp see WASP
waatch see WATCH[1.1], WATCH[1.2]
waater see WATTER[1.1]
waavel see WAVEL

waaverin laef, †**wayburn leaf**, †**wabroun leaf**, †**vabried leiff** /'wɑvərɪn lef/ *n* the greater plantain *Plantago major* *16-19, 20- Sh Ork*. Compare WARBOO. [OE *weʒbrǣden lēaf* compare WARBOO]

wab, **wob**, **web**, **wub** /wab, wɔb, wɛb, wʌb/ *n* **1** piece of woven material; a piece of cloth in process of being woven *15-*. **2** a spider's web, a cobweb *la15-*. **3** the fatty covering of the large intestine, the omentum *19- Sh N SW*. **4** *mining* the extent of a face of coal, especially in thickness *la18-19*. **wobby** covered with cobwebs *20- NE EC*. **wub-fat** the fatty covering of the large intestine *20- Sh N SW*. **wub gless** a magnifying glass for examining a web of cloth *la19- EC*. **wab o the wame** = *wub-fat 20- Ork*. **web tallon** = *wub-fat 20- Sh*. **gie in the wab** *weaving* to assist a weaver to thread his loom by handing him the threads *la19, 20- historical*. **have yer wab oot** *weaving* to have completed your piece of cloth and removed it from the loom *la20- T WC*. [OE *web*]

wabbit, **wubbit** /'wabɪt, 'wʌbɪt/ *adj* **1** exhausted, feeble, lacking in energy *la19-*. **2** *of things* worn out, dilapidated; no longer useful *la20-*. **wabbit out** tired out *20- T C*. [unknown; perhaps onomatopoeic]

wabble[1] /'wabəl/ *n* drink or liquid food that has no distinct flavour or is weak or tasteless *la19- NE*. [perhaps from WABBLE[2], and compare OFr *wape* weak, lacking in strength; insipid]

wabble[2], **wauble**, **waible** /'wabəl, 'wɔbəl, 'webəl/ *v* **1** to walk unsteadily, totter; to waddle *la18-*. **2** to wriggle *20- Sh T C*. [LG *wabbeln*]

wabblie /'wabli/ *adj* weak, wishy-washy, thin *20- NE C SW*. [WABBLE[1] + -IE[2]]

wabbly /'wabli/ *adj* unsteady, likely to wobble *20- C*. [WABBLE[2] + -y (-IE[2])]

wabred see WARBOO
wabroun leaff see WAAVERIN LAEF

wabster, **webster**, *NE* **wobster** /'wabstər, 'wɛbstər; *NE* 'wɔbstər/ *n* **1** a weaver *la14-*. **2** a spider *la18- C SW*. [OE *webbestre* a female weaver]

wach see WATCH[1.1], WATCH[1.2]
wachle see WAUCHLE[1.2]
wacht see WAUCHT[1.1], WAUCHT[1.2], WECHT[1.1]

†**wack**[1.1], **wak** *n* moisture, wetness *la15-e17*. [see the adj]
†**wack**[1.2], **wak** *adj* moist, damp, wet *16-19*. **waknes** moisture, humidity *16-e19*. [MDu *wak*, ON **wakw-*]
wack see WAULK

wad[1.1], †**wadd**, †**wed**, †**wod** /wad/ *n* **1** a stake, bet *la14-*. **2** a pledge, something deposited as security *la14-19, 20- Sh SW Uls*. **3** a forfeit; *pl* the name for various games in which forfeits are demanded *la18-19, 20- Sh*. †**wedfee**, **wedfe** a wager; a prize in a contest *16-e17*. †**wedwife**, **wedwyf** a (female) pawnbroker; a woman who deals in clothing and household linen *16-17*. **wad shooting** a shooting match for prizes *18-19, 20- historical*. **be in a wad 1** to be liable to a forfeit in a game *19- Sh SW*. **2** to be in error about something *20- Sh*. †**lay in wad** to pawn *la14-e19*. †**lie in wad** to be in pawn *15-e19*. **sell wads** to play at forfeits *20- Sh*. [OE *wedd* a pledge]

wad[1.2], **wed** /wad, wɛd/ *v* **1** to marry; to be married *la14-*. **2** to wager, bet *16-*. [OE *weddian* to pledge]

wad[2], **waud**, †**wade**, †**wodd** /wad, wɔd/ *n* **1** *mining* black lead, graphite; a mine of black lead *la18-19, 20- historical*. **2** a lead pencil *la19- WC SW Bor*. [Eng *wad*]

wad[3] /wɔd/ *n* wadding, cotton wool *20-*. [unknown; compare Swed *vadd*, Du *watte*]

wad see WADE[1.2], WID[2]
wadd see WAD[1.1]
wadder see WEATHER, WEDDER

waddin¹, wadding, weddin, wedding, *Ork N H&I* **wedeen**, †**wading** /ˈwadɪn, ˈwadɪŋ, ˈwɛdɪn, ˈwɛdɪŋ; *Ork N H&I* ˈwɛdin/ *n* **1** marriage, marriage festivities; a wedding *la14-*. **2** (the action of) wagering or betting *16-17*. **waddin braws** wedding clothes *19-*. **waddin coat** the coat worn by a bridegroom *20- Ork SW*. **wedding needs** a bride's trousseau *la19, 20- Ork*. †**weddin treat** *in Shetland* a continuation of the festivities celebrating a marriage *la19*. †**weddin kirk door** the church door or porch at which marriages were performed *16*. †**wedding door** = *weddin kirk door la17*. [verbal noun from WAD¹·²]

waddin², †**waldin**, †**walding**, †**waldyne** /ˈwadən/ *adj* **1** young, vigorous, active *19- Bor*. **2** physically or mentally supple, (excessively) compliant *15-e18*. [participial adj from *wald* (WIELD)]

waddy /ˈwadi/ *n* a wading place, a ford *20- Ork*. [ON *vaði* locative of *vaða* a ford]

wade¹·¹, *NE* **wyde** /wed; *NE* wʌɪd/ *n* **1** the act of wading; a distance covered by wading *la19-, N NE T EC*. **2** shallow water, a ford *19- Sh Ork*. †**wadeable** fordable, that can be crossed on foot *la17-19*. [from the verb]

wade¹·², **wad**, **wide**, **wyde**, †**waid** /wed, wad, wʌɪd/ *v pt* †**woyd**, *ptp NE* †**widden 1** to walk through water or boggy ground; to travel across a river on foot *la14-*. **2** *of the moon or sun* to move through cloud or mist *18-*. **3** *of fish* to appear on the surface of water; to leap out of water *19- Sh*. **wade the water** to endure a particular experience *la19- Ork EC*. [OE *wadan* to go, move, ON *vaða* to wade, Norw dial *vada* (of fish) to swim at the surface]

wade², **wed** /wed, wed/ *n* the after-part of a boat where the fish are drawn in [probably an extended use of WADE¹·² (sense 3)]

wade *see* WAD²

Wadensday *see* WEDNESDAY

wadge¹·¹, **wedge**, †**wege**, †**waige** /wadʒ, wɛdʒ/ *n* **1** a piece of wood or metal, thicker at one end than at the other (used as a tool) *16-*. **2** a thick slice of bread, cake or cheese, a chunk of butter; a large lump *16-*. **3** a gold ingot *17*. [OE *wecg*]

wadge¹·², **wedge** /wadʒ, wɛdʒ/ *v* **1** to wedge, fix firmly, fasten tightly (with a wedge) *16-*. **2** *in Shetland* to prod, nudge forcibly *la19*. [see the noun]

wadge *see* WAGE¹·²

wading *see* WADDIN¹

wadmal, †**vedmell** /ˈwɑdməl/ *n in Shetland and Orkney* a coarse woollen homespun cloth *16-19, 20- historical*. [ON *vaðmál*]

wadna, **wadnae** *see* WID²

Wadnesday *see* WEDNESDAY

wadset¹·¹, †**wedset**, †**wodset** /ˈwadsɛt/ *n* **1** *law* a mortgage of property, with a conditional right of redemption *15-18, 19- historical*. **2** a pledge; that which is pledged *la18-e19*. **wadsetter**, †**wedsettar** the creditor or holder of a conditional mortgage; a person who puts his land in pledge *la16-18, 19- historical*. [see the verb]

wadset¹·², †**wedset**, †**wodset** /ˈwadsɛt/ *v law* to pledge (land or other heritable property) in security; to pawn, mortgage *la14-18, 19- historical*. [WAD¹·¹ + SET¹·²]

wae¹·¹, **woe**, †**wa**, †**wo** /we, wo/ *n* a state or condition of misery, misfortune, distress, affliction or trouble *la14-*. **waefu**, †**waful**, †**wofull** sorrowful *la14-*. **waesome**, **waesum** sorrowful; causing sorrow *19-*. †**wae be to** a curse upon, may sorrow befall *16-19*. **wae's me** woe is me *la14-*. †**wae's the craws!** dear me! *e19*. †**wae to** = *wae be to 16-18*. **wae-worth** may ill or harm befall, a curse upon *la14-*. [OE *wā*]

wae¹·², **wey**, †**wa**, †**wo** /we/ *adj* filled with grief, wretched, sorrowful *la14-*. **wae's my heart** woe is me *la18-19, 20- N T*. [see the noun]

wae¹·³, †**wa**, †**way** /we/ *interj* an exclamation of sorrow or despair *la14-*. [OE *wā* interj]

wae², **wey**, †**wa** /we/ *interj* an exclamation used to introduce an assertion: ◇*wae, he wis here the day la18-*. [probably a natural utterance; compare ME *wē*]

wae *see* WA¹·¹, WI

waebegane, †**wo begone**, †**wobegon** /ˈwebəgen/ *adj* troubled by sorrow, distress, grief *la15-*. [WAE¹·¹ + *begane* beset, from the ptp of OE *begān*]

waeden, †**waiden** /ˈwedən/ *adj* soft, supple, flaccid *la19- Sh*. [Dan *vaeden*]

waek *see* WAIK¹·²

waer *see* WIRE¹·¹

wa'er *see* WATTER¹·¹, WATTER¹·²

waeren, **waring**, *Ork* **wiring** /ˈwerɪn, ˈwerɪŋ; *Ork* ˈwaerɪŋ/ *n* a strap of wood nailed to the ribs of a boat on the inside below the gunwale *la19- Sh Ork N*. [Du *wegering, wijgering*]

waesucks /ˈwesʌks/ *interj* an exclamation of sorrow or despair *la18-*. [WAE¹·¹ + pl of SAKE]

waett *see* WIT¹·²

wafer *see* WAFFER

waff¹·¹, **wave**, **wauf**, †**waif** /waf, wev, wɔf/ *n* **1** a flapping, oscillating, waving movement *16-*. **2** a signal (made by waving), a hand gesture *16-*. **3** a puff or blast of air, a flurry of snow *17-*. **4** a whiff, a faint sound, a glimpse, a touch; a mild illness; a brief or incidental experience *la17-*. **5** a flag *19, 20- Ork SW*. **6** an apparition, ghost *18-e19*. [see the verb]

waff¹·², **wave**, †**wauff**, †**waif**, †**waw** /waf, wev/ *v* **1** to move to and fro, flap *la14-*. **2** *of water or wind* to move in a rolling, surging fashion *15-*. **3** to signal by waving with the hand *17-*. **4** to set (air) in motion; to fan *19, 20- Sh NE C*. **5** to move, drive *19, 20- Sh*. **6** to move erratically, waver *e16*. **wave on** to attract the attention of (someone) with a wave of the hand *20- Sh N T*. [OE *wafian* to wave; *waw* is from OE *wagian* to move, shake, swing but the Older Scots spelling is ambiguous as 'w' and 'v' are interchangeable; compare WAW³]

waff²·¹, **waif** /waf, wef/ *n* **1** *law* a lost item or stray animal for which no claim of ownership is made (and whose ownership ultimately devolves to the crown) *14-*; compare WAITH¹·¹. **2** a helpless person, an abandoned or neglected child *19-*. **3** a person viewed as having little ability or strength of character, a feeble or disreputable person *la19-*. [AN *waif* something loose or wandering]

waff²·², **waif**, **wauf** /waf, wef, wɔf/ *adj* **1** *of animals* strayed, wandering; *of goods* abandoned, ownerless *la16-*; compare WAITH¹·². **2** *of people or places* solitary, lonely *18-*. **3** *of people* disreputable, viewed as lacking worth or merit; scruffy *la18-*. **4** *of people* feeble in body or mind *19-*. **5** *of things* lacking strength or substance, of poor quality, of little account *19-*. **6** *of people* vagrant, wandering, homeless *18-e19*. **waffish** *of people* disreputable, worthless *la19- NE T EC*. **wauf like 1** having a feeble or sickly appearance *19-*. **2** shabby *19*. **waff looking**, **wauf looking** scruffy, disreputable or feeble *19-*. [see the noun]

waffer, **wafer** /ˈwafər/ *n* a wastrel *20-*. Compare WIFFER-WAFFER. [WAFF²·¹ with agent suffix]

waffie¹·¹ /ˈwafi/ *n* a tramp, vagrant; an outcast; a person viewed as lacking worth or merit *19-*. [from the adj or WAFF²·¹ + -IE¹]

waffie¹·² /ˈwafi/ *adj* **1** *of objects or qualities* flimsy, shoddy, of little account *19-*. **2** *of persons* disreputable, viewed as lacking worth or merit; scruffy *la19-, N NE T EC*. [WAFF²·¹ + -IE²]

waffinger, †**wavengeour** /ˈwafɪndʒər/ *n* a tramp, vagrant *la15-19, 20- literary*. [probably an extended form of WAFF²·¹; compare *messenger, passenger* etc]

waffle¹·¹, *Sh* **weffle** /ˈwafəl; *Sh* ˈwɛfəl/ *n* **1** a weak or foolish person *la19- C Bor*. **2** an act of tossing something around *la19- Sh*. **3** *pl* flatulence *20- Sh*. **4** a tangle, a confusion; an untidy heap *la20- Sh*. **waffly, weefly 1** limp from weakness or exhaustion, feeble; tottery *la19- Sh Ork NE T EC*. **2** volatile, easily blown about, shaky *20- Ork NE*. [see the verb]

waffle¹·², **wuffle**; *Sh* **weffle** /ˈwafəl, ˈwʌfəl; *Sh* ˈwɛfəl/ *v* **1** to wave about, flap, flutter *19-*. **2** to rifle, shuffle (paper) *la19-*. **3** to crease, wrinkle; to tangle *19- Sh NE Bor*. **4** to stagger, totter *la20- Sh N SW*. **5** to waver, vacillate, hesitate *19- C Bor*. **6** *of wind* to blow in gusts (from different directions) *20- Sh SW*. **waffled** limp from weakness or exhaustion *la18-19, 20- EC Bor*. [frequentative form of WAFF¹·²]

waffle¹·³ /ˈwafəl/ *adj* **1** inert, limp, feeble, sluggish *19-*. **2** supple, pliant *19, 20- N NE*. [see the verb]

waft¹·¹, **weft**, *Bor* **woft** /waft, wɛft; *Bor* wɔft/ *n weaving* the woof or cross-threads of a piece of cloth *15-*. **weft clew, waft clew** a hank or ball of yarn *18-*. [OE *weft*]

waft¹·², *NE* **wuft** /waft; *NE* wʌft/ *v* **1** *weaving* to use as the woof thread; to weave *la17-*. **2** to trounce; to outmanoeuvre *20- N NE*. [see the noun]

wag¹·¹ /wag/ *n* **1** an act of moving something to and fro *la16-*. **2** a hand-signal, gesture *19- NE C*. **waggie** the pied wagtail *la19- C Bor*. **waggitie** = *waggie 20- T EC*. [see the verb]

wag¹·² /wag/ *v* **1** to move to and fro, sway, stagger *15-*. **2** to cause to move or shake; to brandish (a weapon) *16-*. **3** to beckon, signal to; to wave to (a person) *18-*. **4** to proceed, continue *19-*. **5** to interact, associate with *la15-e17*. **wag-at-the-wa, waggity-wa 1** a wall clock originally with an exposed pendulum *19-*. **2** *folklore* a household goblin with a supposed habit of swinging on domestic equipment *e19*. **wag yer heid in a pupit** to be a minister *20-*. †**wag yer pow in a pupit** = *wag yer heid in a pupit 19*. [OE *wagian*]

wag², †**uag** /wag/ *n archaeology* (the remains or site of) an iron-age building in Caithness *la18- N*. [Gael *uamhag* a little cave]

wa-gang, wa'gang, †**waygang** /ˈwagən/ *n* **1** the outflow of water from a millwheel, the tail-race *18-*. **2** departure, going away *17-19, 20- NE*. **3** a lingering taste or flavour; an aftertaste *la18-19, 20- Sh NE T*. [WA²·¹ + GANG¹·¹]

†**wa-ganging** *n* departure, going away *la15-19*. [WA²·¹ + verbal noun from GANG¹·²]

wag-at-the-wa *see* WAG¹·²

wa-gaun¹·¹, **waygoing,** †**waygaeing** /ˈwagɔn, ˈwegɔɪŋ/ *n* **1** departure, going away *la16-*. **2** the departure of a farmer from his tenancy *la18-*. †**wa-gaun crop** the last crop sown by a tenant farmer before the end of his tenancy *la18-19*. **way-going sale** the sale of the stock and effects of someone who is leaving a farm or giving up a business *20-*. [WA²·¹ + verbal noun from GAE]

wa-gaun¹·², **way-going** /ˈwagɔn, ˈwegɔɪŋ/ *adj* departing, going away *19-*. **way-going tenant** an outgoing tenant *19-*. [WA²·¹ + participial adj from GAE]

wage¹·¹, *NE* **waadge,** †**wauge,** †**wedge** /wedʒ; *NE* wadʒ/ *n* **1** payment or reward for work or service; recompense *la14-*. **2** *pl* school fees *17-19*. **3** pledge *la14-16*. **4** a bribe *la15-e17*. †**lay in wage** to give as security *la15-e16*. [AN *wage*]

wage¹·², **wadge,** *NE* **wodge,** †**wauge** /wedʒ, wadʒ; *NE* wɔdʒ/ *v* **1** to engage in combat *15-*. **2** to hire, employ for wages *la15-*. **3** to wield an implement, brandish or hurl a weapon *19- NE T EC*. **4** to wager, bet *19- N C*. **5** to pledge *la15-18*. †**wageour** a soldier hired for wages, a mercenary *la14-e17*. [OFr *wagier*]

wager¹·¹ /ˈwedʒər/ *n* **1** a stake, a bet *17-*. **2** a prize in a contest *16-e17*. [ME *wagour*, AN *wageure*]

wager¹·², **wauger,** *Sh* **waager,** *H&I SW* **wudger** /ˈwedʒər, ˈwɔdʒər; *Sh* ˈwadʒər; *H&I SW* ˈwʌdʒər/ *v* to stake (something) on the likelihood of a particular result, bet *18-*. [from the noun]

waggitie *see* WAG¹·¹

waggity-wa *see* WAG¹·²

waggle¹·¹ /ˈwagəl/ *n* **1** a shake, a wobble *la19-*. **2** a marsh, a bog, a pool *la18-e19*. [see the verb]

waggle¹·², **waigle** /ˈwagəl, ˈwegəl/ *v* to move to and fro, shake, wobble *18-*. [frequentative form of WAG¹·²]

waghorn, *NE* **waugram** /ˈwaghɔrn; *NE* ˈwɔgrəm/ *n* **1** *folklore* a character in fable, the greatest of all liars *18-*. **2** an alternative name for the Devil *19-*. **3** a liar, boaster *la16*. [perhaps WAG¹·² + HORN; compare HORNIE¹·¹]

waible *see* WABBLE²
waich *see* WATCH¹·¹
waicht *see* WECHT²
waichty *see* WECHTY
waid *see* WADE¹·²
waiden *see* WAEDEN
waif *see* WAFF¹·¹, WAFF¹·², WAFF²·¹, WAFF²·²
waige *see* WADGE¹·¹
waigle *see* WAGGLE¹·²

†**waik**¹·¹ *v* to (cause to) become weak; to weaken, diminish in strength or efficacy *la15-19*. [see the adj]

waik¹·², **wake,** *Sh* **waek,** *NE* **wyke** /wek; *Sh* ˈweək; *NE* wʌɪk/ *adj* lacking in strength, feeble, weak *la14-*. [OE *wāc*]

waik *see* WAUK¹·¹
waikin *see* WAUKEN
waikrife *see* WAUKRIFE
wail *see* WEEL¹·²
wail-a-day *see* WALLY-DYE
waill *see* WALE¹·¹
wailowit *see* WALLOW

wain¹·¹, †**wane** /wen/ *n* a large vehicle drawn by oxen or horses and used to transport heavy, bulky goods, a wagon *la14-19, 20- EC*. †**waingate, wayne get** a cart-track *16-17*. [OE *wægn*]

†**wain**¹·² *v* to transport in a carriage *e19*. [see the noun]

wain *see* WEAN
waine *see* WANE¹·¹
waingle *see* WINGLE¹·²
wainish *see* VAINISH
waint *see* WYNT

†**wair** *adj* causing exhaustion *la15*. [unknown; perhaps a back-formation from WEARY¹·³]

wair *see* WARE¹·¹, WARE³, WARE⁴, WARE⁵, WEAR, WEIR¹·¹
waircodling *see* WARE¹·¹
waird *see* WARD¹·¹, WARD¹·², WEIRD¹·²
wairdane *see* WARDEN
wairdroip *see* WARDROBE
wairm *see* WARM¹·³
wairn *see* WARN¹
wairp *see* WARP¹·²
wairsh *see* WERSH
waiscot *see* WESKIT

waist, weyst, †**west,** †**wast** /west, wʌɪst/ *n* **1** the narrow middle part (of the body) *la15-*. **2** the waist of a garment *la15-*. **waist of Scotland** the Central Belt of Scotland *la20-*. [ME *wast*, OE **wæst*]

waist *see* WASTE¹·¹, WASTE¹·², WASTE¹·³, WASTE¹·²
waister *see* WASTER¹
waistie *see* WASTY
waistour *see* WASTER¹

wait[1.1], †**wate** /wet/ *n* **1** the act of waiting or watching; a lying in wait *la15-*. **2** an ambush *16-18*. **3** *in Edinburgh* a musician who signalled the time early in the morning (during Winter) *la17-e18*. **4** an attendant *la16-e17*. †**at the wait** by secret observation, secretly *la15-e16*. †**at wait** = *at the wait*. [AN *waite*, with some senses from the verb]

wait[1.2], *NE* **wyte**, †**wate**, †**wayt** /wet/; *NE* wʌɪt/ *v* **1** to await, remain (in expectation of); to delay, postpone *la14-*. **2** to lodge, make one's (temporary) home *la20- C SW*. **3** to waylay, ambush *la14-e17*. **4** to watch, look intently, watch out for; to keep watch over, spy on *la15-16*. **waiter 1** an attendant, a person who serves (food and drink) *17-*. **2** a watchman at the gates of Edinburgh *la17-18, 19- historical*. **3** a customs officer *la16-e19*. **4** one who watches over or guards (a person) *la16*. †**wait of** to call on, pay one's respects to; to attend (the summons of) *18*. **wait on 1** to wait for, await *la14-*. **2** to attend to someone, see to someone's needs *la15-*. **3** to look after a sick or dying person *16-*. **4** to linger, remain in attendance, stay on *18- NE T H&I*. **5** to be on the point of death *19- N Bor Uls*. **wait or** wait until *19-*. **wait the table** to serve a meal *la19-*. **wait table** = *wait the table*. [AN *waiter*]

†**wait**[2] *v* to treat (a person) with unkindness *la14-16*. [ON *veita*]

wait *see* WEET[1.3], WIT[1.2]

waiter *see* WATTER[1.1]

†**waith**[1.1], **weth** *n* lost or shipwrecked property; strayed or ownerless livestock *15-19*. Compare WAFF[2.1]. [altered form of *waif* (WAFF[2.1])]

waith[1.2] /weθ/ *adj of an animal* strayed, roaming loose; not under the control of an owner *15-19, 20- historical*. [see the noun]

†**waith**[2] *n* cloth (made up into garments) *17-e19*. [ON *váð*]

†**waith**[3] *n* the taking of game; hunting or fishing (unlawfully); the game itself *15-16*. †**waithing** fishing; a catch of fish *la15-e17*. †**waithman** a hunter, especially a forest outlaw *15-16*. [ON *veiðr* hunting, fishing, OE *wāð* pursuit, hunting]

†**waith**[4], **wath**, **wouth** *n* danger, harm *la14-16*. [ON **wáðe*]

waiting *see* WEYTING

wak *see* WACK[1.1], WACK[1.2], WAUK[1.1], WAUK[1.2]

wake *see* WAIK[1.2], WAULK, WAUK[1.1], WAUK[1.2]

waken *see* WAUKEN

waker *see* WAULKER

wakerife *see* WAUKRIFE

wal *see* WA[1.1]

†**walansone**, **valisone** *n* a variety of eel *la15*. [unknown]

walawa[1.1], †**wallova**, †**wallaway** /ˈwaləwa/ *n* **1** the Devil *19- Sh Ork*. **2** a lamentation, a cause of lamentation *la15-19*. [see the interj]

walawa[1.2], †**wellaway**, †**willywa**, †**walloway** /ˈwaləwa/ *interj* an expression of sorrow or dismay *16-*. **willawins** an expression of sorrow *la18-*. **willawackits** = *willawins 19-*. [OE *wālāwā*]

welcome[1.1], **welcome**, *Sh* **wylcome** /ˈwalkəm, ˈwɛlkəm; *Sh* ˈwɪlkəm/ *n* a greeting; a means by which an arrival is celebrated *17-*. [see the verb]

welcome[1.2], **welcome**, †**welcum** /ˈwalkəm, ˈwɛlkəm/ *v* to receive (a visitor) gladly; to provide hospitality to a guest *la14-*. [OE *wilcumian*]

welcome[1.3], **welcome** /ˈwalkəm, ˈwɛlkəm/ *adj* **1** gladly received, acceptable, pleasing (as a guest, visitor or companion) *la14-*. **2** freely permitted (to do something) *15-*. [see the interj]

welcome[1.4], **welcome**, †**welcum** /ˈwalkəm, ˈwɛlkəm/ *interj* an expression of greeting (addressed to a visitor) *la14-*. [OE *wilcume*]

†**wald**[1], **wold**, **wauld** *n* a hill, a piece of open country *la14-e19*. [OE *wald*]

†**wald**[2] *n* dyer's rocket, the plant *Reseda luteola*; the yellow dye obtained from it *15-e18*. [OE **walde*]

wald *see* WAALD, WALL[2], WID[2], WIELD

waldin *see* WADDIN[2]

walding *see* WADDIN[2]

waldin-heat *see* WALL[2]

waldyne *see* WADDIN[2]

wale[1.1], *Ork* **waal**, *NE T* **wile**, *SW* **waul**, †**waill** /wel; *Ork* wɑl; *NE T* wʌɪl; *SW* wɔl/ *n* **1** choice, the act of choosing, scope for choice *la14-*. **2** the pick, choice, the thing chosen as the best *la15-*. †**to wale** freely available, abundant *la15-e16*. †**at wale** = *to wale 15*. [ON *val*]

wale[1.2], *Ork* **waal**, *NE T* **wyle**, *SW* **waul**, †**weil** /wel; *Ork* wɑl; *NE T* wʌɪl; *SW* wɔl/ *v* **1** to choose, select, pick out *15-*. **2** to arrange, separate into lots, sort *20-*. **waled**, †**walit** (carefully) chosen, choice *la15-*. **walin 1** the pick, the best *la16-19, 20- NE T SW Bor*. **2** the leavings, rubbish *20- C SW Uls*. **3** the act or process of choosing *la16-19, 20- NE T*. **wale amang** to choose between *la19- Sh NE T*. **wale for** to choose carefully, search for *la18-19, 20- NE T*. **wale out** to pick out, choose *18-*. **waled wight men** elite fighting men, the best and bravest men *la18- literary*. **wale yer feet** to pick your way, step forward cautiously *la19- Sh T C*. [see the noun]

walgin, **walgan** /ˈwalgən/ *n* **1** a leather wool-sack, a bag *19- NE T*. **2** a large clumsy overgrown person or thing *20-, NE*. [Gael *bhalgan*, lenited form of *balgan* a little bag, wallet]

walie, †**wally** /ˈwɔli, ˈweli/ *adj of the sea* tempestuous, wave-tossed, swelling *16- literary*. [wall variant spelling of WAW[3] + -IE[2]; the intrusive *ll* latterly leading to spelling pronunciations]

†**walise**, **vallies** *n* a travelling bag, a suitcase; a saddlebag *17-e19*. [Fr *valise*]

†**walk**[1] *n* a cloud, clouds *16*. [perhaps a shortened and altered form of WELKIN]

walk[2.1]; *Sh* **waak** /wɔk; *Sh* wɑk/ *n* **1** a path or avenue; a place set aside for walking *15-*. **2** a spell of walking, a stroll; travel, wandering (on foot) *la15-*. **3** a ceremonial procession *17-*. **4** a way of life, conduct *la17-*. **5** a passageway in a cowshed *20- Sh Ork N H&I*. **6** a pasture for cattle *19, 20- T WC*. **The Walk** Leith Walk, a street in Edinburgh leading to the port of Leith *la20-*. [see the verb]

walk[2.2], **wauk** /wɔk/ *v pt* †**woik**, †**wouk 1** to travel on foot, stroll; to journey, wander *15-*. **2** *of things* to move about, be in motion *19, 20- N NE H&I*. **3** *of persons* to live, exist; to behave *la15-17*. **4** *of information* to circulate, spread *la15-16*. [ME *walken* to travel on foot, OE *wealcan*, *wealcian* to roll; compare WAULK]

walk *see* WAUK[1.1], WAUK[1.1], WAULK

walkar, **walker** *see* WAULKER

walkin *see* WAUKEN

walkrife, **walkryfe** *see* WAUKRIFE

walkster, **waukster**, †**vakster** /ˈwɔkstər/ *n* a fuller of cloth *la16-*. [WAULK + -*ster* occupational suffix, or altered form of WAULKER with change of suffix]

wall[1], **waal**, **well**, **woll** /wɔl, wal, wɛl, wol/ *n* **1** a source of water, a spring, a pool or stream fed by a spring *la12-*. **2** a source of water for drinking or domestic purposes; a drawwell or drinking fountain *la14-*. **3** a mineral spring reputed to have medicinal qualities *la15-*. **4** a water stand-pump *19- N NE T C*. **5** a cold-water tap at a sink *20- NE T C*. **6** a strong current in the sea *18- Ork*. **wallie 1** a discharge of urine *20-*. **2** a small stream, pool, well *la19- NE T*. **wall ee**, **well eye 1** a place in a bog from which a spring rises *16-*.

2 a spring, a well *19-*. **well grass, wall girse,** †**walgrase** water-cress *17-*. **wall-heid, well head 1** the place where a spring breaks out of the ground; the source of a stream or river *16-19, 20- historical*. **2** a spring which feeds a boggy piece of ground *19, 20- historical*. **wallink** brooklime, the plant *19, 20- SW Uls*. †**wall kerse** = *wall grass la16-e19*. †**well strand** a streamlet from a spring *19*. **wall-wesher** a water-spider *20- SW Bor*. [OE *wælle, welle*]

wall[2], **well, weld,** *N NE* **wauld,** *EC* **wald,** †**weel,** †**weal,** †**weil** /wɔl, wal, wɛl, wɛld; *N NE* wɔld; *EC* wald/ *v* **1** to join metals by means of heat, weld *16-*. **2** to unite people *la16-*. **3** *of liquids* to rise, boil up *19-*. **wallin heat, waldin-heat 1** the degree of heat necessary for welding metals *19-*. **2** fever pitch, the heights of passion *19-*. [OE *wællan, wellan* to boil, melt]

wall *see* WA[1.1], WA[1.2], WAW[2], WAW[3]
wallack *see* WALLOCH[2.1]
wallan, wallant, †**wallowand** /'wɔlən, 'walən, 'wɔlənt/ *adj of flowers* withered, faded, drooping *la19- NE*. [participial adj from WALLOW]
wallantyne *see* VALENTINE
wallap *see* WALLOP[1.2]
wallat *see* WALLET
wallaway *see* WALAWA[1.1]
waller[1.1] /'walər/ *n* a confused crowd of living things, especially when in motion *19- Bor*. [see the verb]
†**waller**[1.2] *v* to toss or thrash about; to surge, heave *19*. [probably an altered form of WALLOW with *-er* frequentative ending substituted for the second syllable]
wallet, †**wallat** /'walət, 'wɔlət/ *n* **1** a fund of stories or poems *19-*. **2** a pocket-book for holding money and other items; a purse *20-*. **3** a bag for carrying or storing clothing and possessions, a merchant's or pedlar's pack *16-19*. [ME *walet*]
wallett *see* VALET
wallicoat *see* WYLIECOAT
wallidrag *see* WALLYDRAG
wallie[1.1], **wally** /'wali, 'wɔle/ *n* **1** *pl* a set of false teeth *20-*. **2** porcelain, china, glazed earthenware (tiles); a porcelain or china dish or ornament *la19- C Bor*. **3** *pl* broken pieces of china used as toys *20- C*. **4** *pl* fine clothes, finery *18-19*. **5** an ornament, trinket, toy *la17-e19*. **6** *pl* the (male) genitals *la17-e19*. **7** a daisy *la18-e19*. [see the adj]
wallie[1.2], **wally, waly** /'wali, 'wɔle/ *adj* **1** fine, beautiful, excellent *16-19, 20- Ork T EC*. **2** *of people and animals* big and strong, thriving, sturdy, plump *18-19, 20- Sh Ork T EC*. **3** *of a fist or grip* big, strong *la18-19, 20- literary*. **4** large, heavy, substantial, imposing *18-19, 20- Sh Ork NE EC*. **5** made of porcelain, china, glazed *20- C Bor*. **wally close** a tiled entrance hall or close, typical of 19th- and early 20th-century tenement buildings *20- C*. **wally dugs** ornamental porcelain dogs usually displayed in pairs *20-*. †**wally gowdy, wally gowdie** a lovely jewel *e16, la19*. **wally money** broken pieces of china used as toy money *20- T C*. †**wallie fall, wally fa** may things turn out well, may good fortune befall (you) *16-e19*. [perhaps related to WALE[1.1]]
†**wallie**[1.3] *interj* an expression of admiration or wonder *la18-19*. [see the adj]
wallied *see* WALLOW
wallin heat *see* WALL[2]
wallipend *see* VILIPEND
wallit *see* WALLOW
walloch[1.1] /'wɔləx, 'waləx/ *n* **1** the act of wallowing, or of walking with difficulty; a floundering movement *19- NE*. **2** the lapwing *Vanellus vanellus 19- NE*. Compare *heilan walloch* (HIELAND[1.2]). [see the verb]

walloch[1.2] /'wɔləx, 'waləx/ *v* **1** to make violent heavy movements, especially in water or mud; to move clumsily, flounder *la18-19, 20- N NE T*. **2** to dance, skip, romp noisily *19*. [altered form of WALLOP[1.2] with -OCH suffix substituted for the second syllable]
walloch[2.1], *NE* **wallack** /'wɔləx, 'waləx; *NE* 'walək/ *n* a scream, howl, wail *la19- NE T*. [see the verb]
walloch[2.2] /'wɔləx, 'waləx/ *v* to cry, shriek, howl *19, 20- NE*. [probably an onomatopoeic first element + -OCH suffix]
wallop[1.1], †**walope** /'wɔləp, 'waləp/ *n* **1** a heavy blow, thump, whack *19-*. **2** a violent jerky movement, a floundering *19, 20- Sh NE T*. **3** a strong beat of the heart or pulse, a throb *la18- Sh T SW*. **4** a fluttering rag, a piece of ragged clothing *18- NE T*. **5** a constant motion to and fro, a wagging (of the tongue) *la19- Sh NE*. **6** a leap, bound or movement in a lively dance *19- NE C*. **7** a gangling loose-limbed person or animal *la19- T Uls*. **8** a horse's gallop *la15*. **gae wallop** to land heavily with a thud; to move very suddenly *la19- Sh N NE T EC*. **play wallop** to thrash about, tumble over *19- T EC*. [see the verb]
wallop[1.2], **wallap,** †**walop** /'wɔləp, 'waləp/ *v* **1** *of a horse* to gallop; *of a person* to ride a horse at a gallop *la14-*. **2** to move to and fro, dangle, swing, flap *la16-*. **3** to make violent struggling or convulsive movements, thrash about, flounder *la18-*. **4** to beat, thrash *19-*. **5** to move at great speed *17-19, 20- NE T EC Uls*. **6** *of the heart* to throb, beat violently *la18- Sh Ork N NE T EC*. **wallop at** to put all one's energies into *la18-19, 20- Sh N*. [OFr *waloper to gallop]
wallop[2] /'waləp, 'wɔləp/ *n* the lapwing *Vanellus vanellus la19- Sh Ork N NE*. Compare WALLOCH[1.1]. **wallopie** = WALLOP[2]. **wallopieweet** = WALLOP[2]. [probably WALLOP[1.2], with reference to its movements when feigning injury to protect its nest]
walloper /'wɔləpər, 'waləpər/ *n* **1** the penis *la20-*. **2** a foolish person *la20-*. [WALLOP[1.2], with agent suffix]
wallova *see* WALAWA[1.1]
wallow /'walə, 'wɔlə/ *v pt* **wallit, wallied,** †**wallowit,** †**wailowit** to wither, fade, waste away *15-19, 20- N T WC SW*; compare WALLAN. [OE *wealwian*]
wallow *see* VALUE[1.1], VALUE[1.2]
wallowand *see* WALLAN
walloway *see* WALAWA[1.2]
wally *see* VALET, WALIE, WALLIE[1.1], WALLIE[1.2]
wallydrag, *NE* **warridrag,** †**wallidrag** /'walidrag; *NE* 'waridrag/ *n* **1** an aimless person, a person viewed as being of low worth; a slovenly, untidy person *16-19, 20- NE Bor*. **2** a thin, undeveloped or undersized person or animal *19, 20- NE*. **3** the smallest, weakest or youngest bird in a nest *la18-e19*. **wallydraigle,** *NE* **warydraggel,** †**wallydraggle** = WALLYDRAG *18-*. [unknown; compare WALY and DRAIGLE[1]]
wally-dye, weel-a-day, †**wail-a-day** /'walɛdʌɪ, 'wiladə/ *interj* an expression of sorrow *18-19, 20- literary*; compare WALAWA[1.2]. [altered forms of WALAWA[1.2]]
walop *see* WALLOP[1.2]
walope *see* WALLOP[1.1]
walow *see* VALUE[1.1], VALUE[1.2]
†**walsh, welsh, welch** *adj* insipid, lacking in flavour; nauseous *16-19*. [unknown; compare WERSH]
walt[1.1], **waut, welt,** †**wat,** †**watt** /walt, wɔlt, wɔt, wɛlt/ *n* **1** the strip of material joining the sole and upper of a shoe *16-*. **2** the (reinforcing or decorative) border of a garment *16-19, 20- EC Bor*. [unknown; compare OE *wælt* a sinew]
†**walt**[1.2] *v* **1** to hem; to add a border to a garment (to strengthen or decorate it) *la15-19*. **2** to furnish with a joining strip *18-19*. **walting** (the action of adding) an edging, hem or

selvedge *16-e19*. **waltened** edged, having a welt, hem or selvedge *la18-19*. [see the noun]

walt[2], **welt** /walt, wɔlt, wɛlt/ *v* **1** to be on the point of falling, totter; to roll or tumble over *20- SW Bor*. **2** to (cause to) move violently or forcibly; to throw; to lash; to surge *e16*. [ON *welta* to roll]

waltams, **wull-tams** /'wɔltamz, wɔl'tamz, 'wʌltamz/ *npl* a pair of buckled leather straps fastened over the trousers to prevent the material flapping around loosely during manual labour *20-*, *NE T*; compare NICKIE-TAMS. [WALT[1.1] + TOME assimilated to TAM]

waltened *see* WALT[1.2]

walter *see* WATTER[1.1], WELTER[2.2]

walth, **wealth**, †**welth** /walθ, wɛlθ/ *n* **1** riches, material wealth, possessions *la14-*. **2** abundance, plenty, profusion *la16-*. **3** prosperity, good fortune, advantage, success *15-e17*. **4** happiness, well-being *la14-e17*. **walthy**, **wealthy**, †**welthie 1** rich *la15-*. **2** happy; prosperous *la14-16*. [OE *wela*, *wala* riches, with *-th* suffix]

waltir *see* WATTER[1.1]

walu *see* VALUE[1.1].

walx *see* WAX[1], WAX[2]

walxyn *see* WAX[2]

†**waly** *interj* an expressing of sorrow or dismay *la16-19*. **waly fa** woe betide, bad fortune will befall *la18-e19*. [compare WAE[1.3] and WALAWA[1.1]]

waly *see* WALLIE[1.2]

wambe *see* WAME[1.1]

wamble *see* WAMMLE[1.1], WAMMLE[1.2]

wambras *see* VAMBRACE

†**wambrase**, **wamebrace** *n* a part of a horse's harness perhaps to protect the belly *e16*. Compare *belly brace* (BELLY[1]). [WAME[1.1] + BRACE]

wame[1.1], **wime**, **womb**, †**wambe**, †**waym**, †**weam** /wem, wʌɪm, wum/ *n* **1** the stomach, intestines *la14-*. **2** the uterus *la14-*. **3** the seat of the passions or thoughts, the heart, the mind *16-*. **4** the belly-piece of a fur, skin or hide *la14-e17*. **5** tripe or roe used as food *18-e19*. **wamefu** a bellyful *17-19, 20- NE T Uls*. **wamie** big-bellied *19, 20- T EC*. **wame girt**, **wame gird** a belly-band, saddle girth *la19- Sh*. †**wame-ill** an illness affecting the stomach *16-18*. [OE *wamb* the belly]

wame[1.2], †**womb** /wem/ *v* to fill oneself with food, eat heartily *17-*. [see the noun]

wame *see* WAUM

wamebrace *see* WAMBRASE

wamfle[1.1] /'wamfəl, 'wɔmfəl/ *v* to flap, flutter, wave about *19-T EC*. [perhaps onomatopoeic or an altered form of WAFFLE[1.2]]

wamfle[1.2] /'wamfəl, 'wɔmfəl/ *adj* limp, weak, flexible *la19- N NE T SW*. [see the verb]

†**wamfler**, **wanfler** *n* a dandy, gallant *la16-e19*. [unknown; compare the later attested WAMFLE[1.1]]

-wamit, **-wimed**, †**-wamyt** /'wɛmɪt, 'wʌɪmd/ *adj* having a belly of a specified kind *15-*. †**gret-wamit** pregnant *15-16*. [WAME[1.1] + -IT[2]]

wammill *see* WAMMLE[1.2]

wammle[1.1], **wamble**, **waumle** /'waməl, 'wambəl, 'wɔməl/ *n* **1** a churning of the stomach, a feeling of sickness *la19- NE T EC*. **2** a rolling or unsteady motion, a wriggle *19- Ork NE C*. **wammily**, **wambly** tottery, weak, feeble *la19- NE T C*. **womle brees** a dish of the same ingredients as HAGGIS but of a liquid consistency *19- NE*. [see the verb]

wammle[1.2], **wamble**, **waumle**, **wummle**, †**wammill** /'waməl, 'wambəl, 'wɔməl, 'wʌməl/ *v* **1** to stagger, move with a weak, unsteady gait *la15-*. **2** *of things* to roll, toss, twist and turn; to coil, tangle *la15-*. **3** *of persons and animals* to roll about, wriggle, writhe *18-*. **4** *of thoughts* to creep into someone's mind, go round in someone's head *18-*. **5** *of the stomach or its contents* to churn, stir uneasily or queasily *la18- NE T EC*. **6** to move unsteadily to and fro in the air, sway, flap, dangle *17-19, 20- T SW Bor*. **7** to feel nauseous or queasy *la15-17*. [ME *wamelen*; compare Dan *vamle* to feel nausea, and Norw *vamla* to stagger]

wammle[1.3] /'waməl/ *adv* with a writhing or undulating motion *la19- NE*. [see the verb]

wampish /'wampɪʃ, 'wɔmpɪʃ/ *v* **1** to move to and fro, wave, flap about *19, 20- Uls*. **2** to wave, flourish, brandish *e19*. [onomatopoeic; compare WAMFLE[1.1], with *-ish* as in BRANISH etc]

†**wamplate**, **vantplat** *n* plate armour attached to a spear, to protect the hand in combat *e16*. Compare VAMBRACE. [ME *vamplate*, AN *vant-* before + PLATE]

wample *see* WIMPLE[1.1]

-wamyt *see* -WAMIT

wan[1], †**wane**, †**vane**, †**wone** /wan/ *n* **1** a place, territory, area *la15-e16, la19- NE*. **2** a place of habitation or shelter, a room in a dwelling, a group of buildings *la14-e19*. [probably ON *ván* hope, expectation, the place where one expects to find something]

wan[2], **wane**, *Ork N* **waan** /wan, wen; *Ork N* wɑn/ *n* **1** hope, expectation; course of action, option *la14-16, 19- Sh Ork N*. **2** liking *19- Sh Ork N*. **3** quantity, abundance *la14-15*. **wanless** hopeless, forlorn; destitute *la19- Sh Ork*. **wanlie 1** hopeful, likely, promising **2** agreeable, comfortable *la19- Sh Ork N*. **wansome** likely, probable *20- Ork*. †**gud wane** plentifully, in great quantity *la14-15*. †**gret wane** = *gud wane la14*. [ON *ván* hope, expectation]

wan *see* ANE[1.1], ANE[1.2], WAND[1.1], WANE[1.1], WAUM, WIN[1.2], WIN[2], WIND[2.2]

wan- /wan/ *prefix* = UN- *la14-*. [OE *wan-*, and in Ork and Sh from ON *van-*]

-wan /wən/ *suffix* in the direction of; towards: ◊*eastwan* ◊*gaein to Aberdeenwan 19-*. [unknown; compare WAN[1]]

†**wanboona** *n* a curse *20- Ork*. [WAN- + ON *bón* a prayer]

wancanny /wan'kani/ *adj* unsafe, risky; dangerous, unlucky *19, 20- N*. [WAN- + CANNY[1.1]]

wance *see* AINCE[1.1], AINCE[1.2]

wanchance /wan'tʃans/ *n* misfortune *la16, 20- WC Bor*. [WAN- + CHANCE[1.1]]

wanchancy, **wanchancie** /wan'tʃansi/ *adj* unlucky, ill-fated; dangerous, unreliable *la18-*. [WAN- + CHANCY]

wand[1.1], **waun**, **wan**, **whaun**, *Sh* **waand** /wɔnd, wɔn, wan, mɔn; *Sh* wɑnd/ *n* **1** a pole, a walking stick, a staff *la14-*. **2** a rod or switch used for punishment *la14-*. **3** a thin pliable stick cut from a young tree; a growing shoot, branch or sapling *15-*. **4** a young shoot of willow used in wicker work *15-*. **5** a fishing rod *la16-*. **6** a staff used as a symbol in various legal transactions, as the insignia of an office or sign of authority *15-19, 20- historical*. **7** the penis *la15-19, 20- SW*. **8** an administerer of punishment; a beating, defeat or harm *15-e19*. †**the wand hand** that side of a racecourse on which the jockey held his whip; the advantage *17*. †**brak your wand** *see* BRAK. †**under a person's wand** under the control, authority or jurisdiction of a person *15-e17*. †**under the wand** in the country *la15-e16*. **wand of peace** *law* a baton carried by the king's messenger and used to touch an outlaw to show his restoration to the king's peace *15-e19, la19- historical*. [ON *vandu-r, vǫndr*]

†**wand**[1.2] *v* **1** to beat with a wand or switch; to wield an official rod or staff *la16-18*. **2** to interweave, plait willow *la15*. [see the noun]

†**wand**[1.3] *adj of a thing* made of or encased in wickerwork; made with a thin, pliable branch or branches *16-19*. [see the noun]

wand see WAYND, WIND[2.2]
wander see WANNER[1], WANDRETH
wandered, wandert see WANNERT
wandir see WANNER[1]
wando see WINNOW
†**wandocht**[1.1], **wandought** *n* **1** a feeble, silly, sluggish or worthless person *18-19*. **2** lack of strength, feebleness *18-e19*. [WAN- + DOCHT]
wandocht[1.2], †**wandought** /'wandoxt/ *adj* feeble, puny, inert; contemptible, worthless *la18- literary*. [see the noun]
wandought see WANDOCHT[1.1], WANDOCHT[1.1]
wandrecht see WANDRETH
†**wandreth, wandrecht, wander** *n* sorrow, distress, hardship, misfortune *la15-17*. [ON *vandræði*]
†**wandys, vayndis** *v* to retreat or give way *la14*. [OFr *wandiss*- stem of *wandir*]
wane[1.1], *Sh Ork* **wan,** †**waine** /wen; *Sh Ork* wɑn/ *n* the act of decreasing or diminishing *la17-*. [OE *wana* lack, shortage with influence from the verb]
wane[1.2], *Sh Ork* **wann** /wen; *Sh Ork* wɑn/ *v* **1** to diminish, decrease *la14-*. **2** *of the moon* to wane *15-*. [OE *wanian*]
wane see WAN[1], WAN[2], WAYND, WEAN
wanearthlie, wanyirthlie, *Sh Ork* **wanertly** /wan'ɛrθlɪ, wan'jɪrθlɪ; *Sh Ork* wan'ɛrtlɪ/ *adj* supernatural, ghostly; unearthly *19-*. Compare UNYIRDLY. [WAN- + Older Scots *earthlie*; compare earth (YIRD[1.1])]
†**wanease, waneis** *n* uneasiness, distress *16-18*. [WAN- + EASE[1.1]]
wanertly see WANEARTHLIE
wanfine /'wanfaɪn/ *n* a bad ending or outcome, a loss *20- Sh Ork*. [WAN- + FINE[2.1]]
wanfler see WAMFLER
†**wanfortune, wanfortoun** *n* misfortune *la15-e18*. [WAN- + FORTUNE[1.1]]
†**wanfukkit** *adj* misbegotten *16*. [participial adj from WAN- + FUCK]
wangele see VANGEL
wangle /'waŋɡəl/ *v* to dangle, wag to and fro *20- Sh N*. [unknown; compare Eng *waggle* and Norw *vangla* to roam about]
wangrace[1] /'waŋɡres/ *n* **1** a disreputable or dishonest person *20- N*. **2** lack of grace, bad behaviour *16-e18*. [WAN- + GRACE]
wangrace[2], **wangrease** /'waŋɡres, 'waŋɡrɪs/ *n* thin oatmeal gruel with butter and honey given to invalids *18-19, 20- Uls*. [WAN- + unknown second element, perhaps *grease*]
wanhap /'wanhap, wan'hap/ *n* misfortune *la15-16, 19- literary*. [WAN- + *hap* as in UNHAP[1.1]]
wanhelt /wan'hɛlt/ *n* ill health *20- Sh*. [WAN- + *health* (HALTH)]
†**wanhew** *v* to stain *e15*. [WAN- + ME *heuen* to colour; compare HUE]
wanhoup, †**wanhope** /'wanhop, wan'hop/ *n* despair, hopelessness *la14-16, 20- Sh NE EC*. [WAN- + HOWP[1.1]]
wanis see VAINISH
wanjoy[1.1] /'wandʒɔɪ/ *n* sorrow, misery *la19- Ork*. [WAN- + JOY[1.1]]
wanjoy[1.2] /'wandʒɔɪ/ *adj* miserable, wretched *20- Ork*. [see the noun]
†**wankish** *v* to twist, interlace or entwine *e19 Bor*. [unknown; compare WAMPISH]
wanlass, †**wanlas,** †**wanles** /'wanləs/ *n* **1** a surprise, a shock *19-, literary*. **2** an ambush, a place of interception (of game) *15-16*. [AN *wanelace*]
wanle, †**wannel,** †**wannle** /'wɔnəl, 'wanəl/ *adj* supple, agile; active *19- Bor*. [probably a derivative of WAND[1.1]]
wanluck, †**wanluk** /'wanlʌk/ *n* bad luck, misfortune; an accident *la16-19, 20- Sh*. [WAN- + LUCK[1.1]]

wann see WANE[1.2]
wannel see WANLE
wanner[1], **wander, wauner,** †**wandir** /'wanər, 'wɔndər, 'wɔnər/ *v* **1** to travel aimlessly; to roam; to stroll; to saunter *la14-*. **2** to stray, deviate from a route, lose one's way *16-*. **3** to confuse, perplex, bewilder *la19-*. **wanderin folk** beggars, gipsies, tramps; travelling people *la19- N T SW*. **wander the road** to be a vagrant, have no home *la19- N T*. [OE *wandrian*]
wanner[2.1], **oner** /'wanər, 'wʌnər/ *n* a single action: ◇*she drank a gless o ginger in a wanner 20-*. [*wan* (ANE[1.2]), with *-er* instrumental suffix]
wanner[2.2], **oner** /'wanər, 'wʌnər/ *v* **1** to complete as a single action; to consume in one go: ◇*she wannered the cider 20-*. **2** to beat, hit, kick *20-*. [see the noun]
wannert, waunert, wandert, wandered /'wanərt, 'wɔnərt, 'wɔndərt, 'wɔndərd/ *adj* **1** lost, uncertain of one's whereabouts *18-*. **2** confused, bewildered; mentally disordered *la19-*. [participial adj from WANNER[1]]
wannle see WANLE
wanpace /'wanpes/ *n* irritation; strife *20- Sh*. [WAN- + PEACE[1.1]]
wanrest /'wanrɛst/ *n* **1** lack of rest, restlessness; uneasiness, anxiety *la16-*. **2** the pendulum of a clock *la18-e19*. **wanrestfu** restless, unsettled *la18-*. **wanrestie** = *wanrestfu 20- Sh N Bor*. **wanrestit** having slept poorly *20- Sh*. †**wanrest quheill** the escape wheel of a verge escapement in a clock *e17*. [WAN- + REST[1.1]]
wanreullie see WANRULY
wanrufe /wan'ruf/ *n* disquiet *la15, 20- literary*. [WAN- + *rufe* (RO[2.1])]
†**wanrule** *n* misconduct, bad behaviour *la16-17*. [WAN- + RULE[1.1]]
wanruly, †**wanreullie** /wan'rulɪ/ *adj* unmanageable, violent *17-19, 20- Sh N NE*. [WANRULE + -IE[2]]
†**wanshapen, wanschapen** *adj* misshapen, deformed *la16-17*. [participial adj from WAN- + SHAPE[1.2]]
†**wansonsie** *adj* mischievous, unpleasant, treacherous *17-19*. [WAN- + SONSIE]
wanst see AINCE[1.1]
want[1.1], *NE* **wint** /wɔnt, want; *NE* wɪnt/ *n* **1** a lack, a shortage; an absence *la14-*. **2** *mining* an interruption in a coal seam *la19, 20- C*. **3** *fishing* a defective or damaged part of a net or line *la19- NE Bor*. **4** a need or requirement *16-17*. **a dish o wint** nothing to eat *20- NE*. **hae a want** to have learning difficulties *19-*. **nae want** a great deal, very much *20- Sh*. [ON *vant* lacking, neuter of *vanr*]
want[1.2], **waant,** *NE* **wint,** *NE* **wunt** /wɔnt, want; *NE* wɪnt; *NE* wʌnt/ *v* **1** to feel the need for, wish, require, desire *15-*. **2** to lack, be without; to lose; to miss; to be free from; to be lacking or deficient *la14-*. **3** to lack the basic necessities of life *la15-*. **4** *frequently with negative* to be unable to do or go without, be unable to spare *16-*. **5** *with omission of verb of motion* to wish to go or come (in, out or home): ◇*the dug wants oot 19-*. **6** to be absent, missing *la15*. **wanter 1** someone who seeks to acquire something they lack *16-19*. **2** an unmarried man or woman, a widow(er) *18-*. **wantin,** †**wantand 1** lacking, missing; not having, without *la15-*. **2** mentally retarded *20-*. **dae wantin** to do without *la19- NE T SW*. **want a feather in the wing** to be mentally retarded *19-*. **want a penny o the shillin** = *want a feather in the wing*. **want a sclate** = *want a feather in the wing*. **want a slice** = *want a feather in the wing*. [ON *vanta* to be lacking, lack]

wanthrift, *Sh* **wantrift** /ˈwanθrɪft; *Sh* ˈwantrɪft/ *n* extravagance, lack of thrift *16-19, 20- Sh C*. **wantrifty** not thrifty *20- Sh*. [WAN- + THRIFT]

wanthriven, *Sh* **wantrivven**, *Ork* **wantrivan** /wanˈθrɪvən; *Sh Ork* wanˈtrɪvən/ *adj* in poor physical condition, sickly, stunted, *16-19, 20- Sh Ork Bor*. [participial adj from WAN- + THRIVE[1.2]]

wantin[1.1], **wanting**, †**wantyng** /ˈwantɪn, ˈwɔntɪŋ/ *n* **1** need, needing, requiring *la14-*. **2** lack, scarcity, shortage *15-17*. **3** loss (of a right or possession) *la15-17*. **4** lack or absence (of a person) *16*. [verbal noun from WANT[1.2]]

wantin[1.2] /ˈwɔntɪn, ˈwantɪn/ *adj* not having, without *la19- NE*. [participial adj from WANT[1.2]]

†**wanton**[1.1], **wantoun** *v* to be reckless, careless or heedless; overindulge; flourish *16-19*. **wantount** unrestrained, unchecked; proud, insolent; lustful *la16*. [see the adj]

wanton[1.2], †**wantoun**, †**wantone** /ˈwɔntən/ *adj* **1** unrestrained, unruly, reckless; uncontrollable; rude; lustful, lewd *15-*. **2** haughty, insolent, proud *la15-e16*. **3** carefree, not serious *15-16*. **4** *of clothing* unrestrained in colour; extravagant or luxurious *la15-16*. **wantonly 1** recklessly; boldly; defiantly *la14-*. **2** in a carefree manner, sportively, jovially *16*. **wantonness**, †**wantones 1** undisciplined, unruly or unchaste behaviour *la14-*. **2** lightheartedness, frivolity, extravagance, excess *la14-*. **3** pride, haughtiness; insolence, arrogance *la15-16*. [ME *wantoune*, WAN- + OE *towen* ptp of *tēon* to bring up, educate]

†**wanton**[2], **wantoun** *n* a saddle girth for a horse, or a strap for securing a pack or pack saddle *16-e19*. [altered form of ME *wame-tow*, WAME[1.1] + TOW[2.1]]

wantone *see* WANTON[1.2]
wantoun *see* WANTON[1.1], WANTON[1.2], WANTON[2]
wantrift *see* WANTHRIFT
wantrivan *see* WANTHRIVEN
wantrivven *see* WANTHRIVEN
wantyng *see* WANTIN[1.1]

wanwardy, †**wanwordy**, †**wanwordie** /ˈwanwardi/ *adj* unworthy, worthless *la16-*. [WAN- + *wordy* (WORTH[1.1])]

†**wanweird**, **wanwerd** *n* misfortune, bad luck; an unhappy fate *16-19*. [WAN- + WEIRD[1.1]]

†**wanwit** *n* foolishness, lack of sense *15*. [WAN- + WIT[1.1]]

wanworth[1.1], *Sh* **wanwirt** /ˈwanwʌrθ; *Sh* ˈwanwɪrt/ *n* **1** a very low price for an article, a bargain *18-*. **2** a thing of little value, something worthless *20- Sh T*. **3** a contemptible or useless person *19, 20- Sh NE*. **at a wanworth** at a bargain price, excessively cheaply *18-19, 20- Sh NE Bor*. **for a wanworth** = *at a wanworth Sh NE*. [WAN- + WORTH[1.1]]

wanworth[1.2] /ˈwanwʌrθ/ *adj* unworthy, worthless *19, 20- NE EC*. [see the noun]

wanyirthlie *see* WANEARTHLIE

wap[1.1], **whap**, **wop**, **waup** /wap, ʍap, wɔp, wʌup/ *n* **1** a blow, thump *la16-*. **2** a sweeping or swinging movement; a flap, wave or shake *17-*. **3** a disturbance, a brawl, a din, a quarrel *19-*. **4** a puff or gust of wind *19, 20- Sh NE*. [see the verb]

wap[1.2], **whap**, **wop**, †**whop**, †**weipe** /wap, ʍap, wɔp/ *v* **1** to throw violently, thrust, fling *la14-*. **2** to strike, thrash, hit *la17-*. **3** to (cause to) flap, wave or shake; to move to and fro, move jerkily *19-*. **4** to cast a fishing line; to fish a river *la19- C SW Bor*. **5** to fight, riot, cause a disturbance *19- WC SW Bor*. [perhaps onomatopoeic; compare WARP]

wap[2.1], *Uls* **wop** /wap; *Uls* wɔp/ *n* **1** a tie or splice joining by means of a cord or twine tied round, a turn or loop of string round something *19, 20- literary*. **2** a bundle of hay or straw *19- SW Bor Uls*. **3** (a turn of) a handle *20- Ork*. **wap kirn** a kirn turned by a handle, a revolving churn *20- Ork*. **wap-organ** a barrel-organ *20- Ork*. **waptree** a cord or rod connecting the treadle and the axle of a spinning-wheel *20- Sh*. [see the verb]

wap[2.2], **wop**, †**wep**, †**weap** /wap, wɔp/ *v* **1** to wrap, enfold, envelop *la14-*. **2** to bind, tie or join (by splicing); to whip with cord *18-19, 20- Ork C Bor*. [unknown; compare WRAP and LAP[1.1]]

wap[3] /wap/ *n* a child's word for a wasp *20-*. [from *waps* (WASP), reinterpreted as a plural]

wapinschaw *see* WAPPENSHAW

wappen, **weapon**, *Sh Ork* **wapon**, †**wapyn** /ˈwapən, ˈwɛpən; *Sh Ork* ˈwapən/ *n* an instrument used in combat or warfare, a weapon; *pl* arms *la14-*. [ON *vápn*; *weapon* is from OE *wǣpen*]

wappenshaw, **wapinschaw**, **weaponshaw**, †**wapynschaw** /ˈwapənʃɔ, ˈwɛpənʃɔ/ *n* **1** a review of military capability and preparedness; a muster of the men *16-e18, la18-historical*. **2** a gathering or games (with military contests) *18-19, 20- historical*. **3** a rifle-shooting competition organized by volunteers and private rifle clubs *la19-*. [shortened form of WAPPENSHAWING]

wappenshawing, †**weaponshawing**, †**wapynschawing** /ˈwapənʃɔɪŋ/ *n* a muster or review of the men under arms in a particular lordship or district *15-e18, la18- historical*. [verbal noun from SHAW[1.2]; compare Du *wapenschouwinge*]

wapper /ˈwɔpər/ *n* something exceptionally large or fine of its kind *19, 20- N NE*. [WAP[1.2], with instrumental suffix]

wappin, **wapping**, †**whapping** /ˈwɔpɪn, ˈwɔpɪŋ/ *adj* strikingly large *18-*. [participial adj from WAP[1.2]]

wappy /ˈwapi/ *adj* showy; smart *20- NE*. [WAP[1.2] + -IE[2]]

waps *see* WASP
wapyn *see* WAPPEN
wapynschaw *see* WAPPENSHAW
wapynschawing *see* WAPPENSHAWING

†**war** *n* (a knot in) an olive tree *e16*. **warryn tre** a knotty, dense or hard tree; an oak tree *e16*. [OE *wearr* a piece of hard skin, callosity]

war *see* BE, WARE[1.1], WARE[4], WAUR[1.1], WAUR[1.2], WAUR[1.3], WAUR[1.4], WEIR[1.1], WEIR[1.2]

warand *see* WARRANT[1.1]
warandar *see* WARRANDER
warandy *see* WARRANTY
warba *see* WARBOO
warback *see* WARBLE[2]

warble[1.1], †**warbill**, †**wrable**, †**wrible** /ˈwɔrbəl/ *n* **1** melodious singing, birdsong *16-*. **2** *music* a group of grace notes *20-*. [OFr *werble* a melody]

warble[1.2] /ˈwɔrbəl/ *v* **1** to make melodious sounds, sing with trills *la16-*. **2** *music* to embellish a tune with a group of grace notes *19-*. **warbler** *piping* a group of (five or more) grace notes *19-*. [OFr *werbler* to play a stringed instrument]

warble[2], †**warbill** /ˈwɔrbəl/ *n* **1** an abscess or swelling on the backs of cattle or deer (caused by the larva of the gadfly or warble fly) *la16-*. **2** (the larva of) the gadfly, a fly of the genus *Hypoderma 19-*. **warback**, **warribowg** (the larva of the) gadfly *19- Sh Ork N T* [unknown; compare WAR]

warble *see* WURBLE

warboo, †**warba**, †**wabred**, †**vabrat** /ˈwarbu/ *n* the greater plantain *Plantago major 16-19, 20- N*. †**warba blade** the greater plantain *19*. [OE *wegbrǣde*; compare WAAVERIN LAEF]

ward[1.1], †**waird** /wɔrd/ *n* **1** an (administrative) division of a shire, region or area *15-*. **2** an (enclosed) piece of land, a field, paddock, a pasture for animals, frequently in place-names *15-*. **3** a division or room in a hospital *18-*. **4** a section of the defences of a castle; the position of particular guards; (a position held by) a division or part of an army drawn up or deployed for battle *la14-e16*. **5** (a place of) custody,

confinement or imprisonment *15-19*. **6** *law of a minor, heir to land held by military service, or the land itself* the guardianship or custody reverting to the feudal superior due to the minor's inability to supply the military service required by this tenure *15-19*. **7** *law* tenure by military service *la15-17*; compare *taxt ward* (TAX). **8** a division of the underworld *e16*. **ward dyke** a wall enclosing grazing land *16-17*. †**wardegard** a receptacle for clothes *16-e17*. †**wardholding** *law* the tenure of land by WARD[1.1] (sense 2) *la17-e18, e19 historical*. †**wardhous** a prison *la16-17*. †**ward land** land held in return for military service *13-e18, la19 historical*. †**wardvassal** *law* a vassal, having tenure by military service, who was a minor and in the guardianship of his superior *la17-19*. †**ward and warsel** in *Aberdeen* security, a pledge *la16-e19*. †**have in ward** to have custody of (a place) *la14-15*. [OE *weard* guard, observation; with legal senses from OFr *warde*]
ward[1.2], †**waird** /wɔrd/ *v* **1** to put or keep in custody or confinement, imprison, jail *la15-*. **2** to guard, protect *16-*. **3** to ward off or parry a blow; to avert danger *la17-*. **4** *of the lands of a minor* to be in the control of the feudal superior *la15-16*. †**wardar, wardour** *n* **1** the feudal superior or their assignee having the lands to which a minor was heir during the minority *16*. **2** a person in custody, a prisoner *16-17*. [OE *weardian*]
ward see WARE[3]
†**wardatar, wardatour** *n law* the feudal superior or their assignee having the lands to which a minor was heir during the minority *16-18*. [Latinized form of *wardar* (WARD[1.2]), perhaps on the model of DONATOR]
warden, †**wardan,** †**wardane,** †**wairdane** /ˈwɔrdən/ *n* **1** a guardian, custodian or official *15-*. **2** a regent appointed to govern during the absence or minority of a monarch; one of the Guardians appointed after the death of Alexander III and during the Wars of Independence *la14-e16, la19- historical*. **3** the governor and military commander of a province, region, district, town or castle *la14-16*. **4** one of the governors or military commanders of the Scottish/English border *la15-e17*. **5** an overseer or superintendent of a guild or incorporation, especially the incorporation of masons *15-e18*. **6** the chief officer of the Scottish Mint *la15-17*. **7** the superior of a community of friars, especially the Franciscans *la15-16*. †**wardanry** the office or jurisdiction of WARDEN (sense 3) *la15-16*. †**Wardane of the March, Wardane of the Marchis** = WARDEN (sense 4). [OFr *wardein*]
wardill see WARLD
warding /ˈwɔrdɪŋ/ *n* **1** imprisonment *la15-18, 19- historical*. **2** the action or fact of lands falling into the control of the feudal superior because of the minority of their heir *la15-e16*. †**warding place** a jail, a prison *la16-18*. †**act of warding** *law* a warrant for imprisonment for debt issued by magistrates in a royal burgh *la16-e19*. [verbal noun from WARD[1.2]]
wardle see WARLD
†**wardone, werdoune** *n* a reward, a recompense *la14*. [variant of Older Scots *guerdoun*, OFr *guerdon*]
wardrobe, †**wardrop,** †**wairdroip** /ˈwɔrdrob/ *n* **1** a person's stock of wearing apparel; a store or collection of clothing *16-*. **2** a piece of furniture for hanging or storing clothes *la19-*. **3** a room for storing clothes and household gear; a private apartment *16-19*. **4** the department of the royal or a noble household concerned with the care of wearing apparel and other household gear *13-17*. †**wardropar, wardraipair, wardraipper** a servant in the wardrobe of a royal or noble household *15-17*. [OFr *warderobe*]
ware[1.1], **wair, war, waar, waur** /wer, war, wɔr/ *n* **1** seaweed, especially for use as manure *la15-*. **2** *law* the right of gathering seaweed, one of the rights attaching to property *la15-17*.

waury, *Sh* **waari** pertaining to, covered with, living among seaweed *19- Sh NE*. †**ware barley** barley manured with seaweed *la18-e19*. **ware bear** = *ware barley la18- NE*. **wareblade** a frond of seaweed *la18- Sh Ork*. **waar brak,** †**ware break** the breaking off and washing ashore of quantities of seaweed *la19- Sh Ork*. **ware cod** an inshore cod *la18- Ork N*. †**waircodling** = *warry codlin 16*. **ware goose** the brent goose *Branta bernicla la19-*. **ware pick** a mattock for uprooting seaweed *la19- Ork*. **war sea** a heavy sea *la19- Ork EC*. **warry codlin** a young inshore cod *20- Sh NE*. [OE *wār*]
ware[1.2], †**wayr** /wer/ *v* to manure with seaweed *la16- Ork N NE*. [see the noun]
†**ware**[2.1] *v* **1** to look out for, take care of *15-17*. **2** to beware of *e16*. **wary, waurro** beware, be on one's guard; watch out *18-19*. [OE *warian* fallen together with OFr *warer*]
ware[2.2], **waur, waar,** †**war,** †**wair** /wer, wɔr, war/ *adj* **1** aware, conscious of; cautious, careful, wary *la14-19, 20- Sh Ork Uls*. **2** well informed, prepared; alert, vigilant, cunning *la15-17*. †**warlie, warrily** carefully, cautiously; conscientiously, thoroughly, vigilantly *la14-17*. †**ware and wis** skilled, competent, cunning *la14-16*. [OE *wær*]
ware[3], **wair, waur** /wer, wɔr/ *v pt* also **ward 1** to spend, lay out, dispose of money or goods *15-*. **2** to expend, use up, waste, squander, sacrifice (something) *la15-*. **3** to pass time in a particular way or for a purpose *la15-19*. **4** to make use of a person or resource *15-e17*. **5** to conduct oneself *la14-16*. **waarin,** †**waring** goods, merchandise *la15-17, 20- Ork*. †**bettir warit** better spent *16-18*. **ill wared** ill-spent, wasted, out of place *la16-*. **weel waired** well-spent or bestowed, well deserved, worthwhile *la16-*. **weel wared on him** it served him right *la19-*. †**ware out 1** to spend, lay out money *la16-e19*. **2** to expend words *e16*. [ON *variðr* ptp of *verja*]
ware[4], †**war,** †**wair** /wer/ *n* **1** *pl* goods; possessions; merchandise *la14-*. **2** money, cash *la18-19*. **3** a pillowcase *la15-e18*. **4** a thing or things *la15-e17*. †**wair almery** a store cupboard *la15-e17*. †**warestaw, warestall** a store cupboard *la15-e17*. [OE *waru*]
ware[5], *Sh Ork* **voar,** †**wair,** †**vair,** †**were** /wer; *Sh Ork* vor/ *n* **1** spring, springtime *la14-*. **2** sowing, planting or ploughing in spring *18- Sh Ork*. †**ware quarter** the season of spring, the months of February to April *17-19*. **ware day,** *Sh Ork* **voar day** the first day of spring *la19- SW Uls*. **ware time,** *Sh Ork* **voar time** springtime *17- Sh Ork SW Bor*. [ON *vár*; with Sh Ork *voar* compare Norw *vår*]
warfare, †**weirfair,** †**werefare** /ˈwɔrfer/ *n* the action or fact of engaging in war or fighting, a conflict *15-*. †**pas in werefare** to go to war; to be at war *la15-e16*. [WEIR[1.1] + FARE[1.1]]
wargeld see WERGELT
waring see WAEREN
†**warisoun, warysoun, warison** *n* **1** reward, payment, recompense *la14-17*. **2** one's deserts, due punishment *15-16*. [OFr *warison*]
wark[1], **werk, wurk, work,** †**wirk** /wark, wɛrk, wʌrk/ *n* **1** labour, employment; a task, job; workmanship *la14-*. **2** a fortification, an edifice; an imposing public building *la14-*. **3** the action of or activity concerned with building or repairing *la14-*. **4** an action, deed, achievement *la14-*. **5** a literary composition, an author's writings *la14-*. **6** something manufactured, the result of workmanship *la15-*. **7** *pl* an organized and shared activity, an industrial or commercial enterprise; a workshop or factory, a works *la15-*. **8** *pl* the mechanism of a clock or gun *la16-*. **9** behaviour, conduct; goings-on; trouble, outcry; a fuss *la16-*. **10** a religious revival; originally the evangelical campaign at Cambuslang in 1742 *18-19*. **11** sexual activity *la14-e16*. **warklike** industrious *la19- Sh NE T*.
†**wark hors, work-horse** a draught- or pack-horse *16-e19*.

†**wark house** a workshop or factory *la15-e18*. **wark-lume** 1 *pl* tools, implements, instruments *la15-*. 2 the penis; *pl* the male genitals *la16-18*. **warkman, workman** 1 a labourer or craftsman *la14-*. 2 a porter *la16-18*. **hae a wark aboot** to make a great fuss over *la19-*. **mak a wark aboot** = *hae a wark aboot la18-*. **haud a wark** = *hae a wark aboot 19-*. †**put in wark** *of materials* to be put to use *17*. [OE *weorc*; compare WIRK]
†**wark**² *v* to hurt, ache *16*. **wark and wound, wirkand wound, werkand wound** a painful, aching or severe wound *la15-16*. [OE *wærcan*]
wark *see* WIRK
warld, warlt, warl, wurld, world, wardle, wordle *Uls* **worl,** †**wardill** /warld, warlt, warl, ˈwʌrəld, ˈwardəl, ˈwʌrdəl; *Uls* wɔrl/ *n* 1 human life, the people on earth collectively; earth as opposed to heaven; secular as opposed to spiritual life; the material universe; a planet *la14-*. 2 an age or period of time in the history of mankind *la14-*. 3 (an area or region of) the physical world; the physical globe, the earth *15-*. 4 worldly wealth, riches *la19- Sh N NE*. 5 *pl* a state of affairs, one's circumstances *19- N NE*. **warld-like** normal in appearance, like everyone else *19-*. **warldlin,** †**warldling,** †**wardling** a materialist; a mean, grasping person *la16-19, 20- NE SW*. **warldly** 1 of, belonging to or with reference to the world and its inhabitants; earthly, mundane; temporal; human; secular *la14-*. 2 greedy *la18-19, 20- Uls*. **warld's end,** †**warldis end** 1 the farthest distance possible, the most distant point on the earth *16-*. 2 the end or destruction of life on earth *16*. **world's föl** a complete fool *20- Sh*. **warld's gear** possessions *la18-19, 20- Sh*. †**warldis gud** = *warld's gear la14-e16*. †**warldis win, warldlie win** prosperity *la14-e16*. **warld's wunner, warld's wonner** 1 a person whose conduct is notorious and surprising *18- Ork NE T EC*. 2 an object of scorn or wonder *la18- NE T*. †**warldis wrack, warldis wrak** 1 = *warld's gear la15-16*. 2 the troubles and hardships of life *la18*. †**a warld of** an enormous number or quantity of *15-17*. †**like the warld** like everyone else, normal *la18-19*. [OE *woruld*]
warlock¹·¹, †**warlo,** †**warlok,** †**warloch** /ˈwɔrlɔk/ *n* 1 a man (or woman) thought to possess occult powers, a sorcerer or wizard *16-*. 2 an old, ugly or misanthropic man; a mischievous or troublesome man; a scoundrel, reprobate *16-19, 20- NE*. 3 a devil or fiend *la14-16*. [OE *wǣrloga* a traitor, devil]
warlock¹·², †**warlo** /ˈwɔrlɔk/ *adj* malevolent, mischievous; bewitched, magical, supernatural *la16-19, 20- literary*. [see the noun]
warlt *see* WARLD
warm¹·¹ /warm/ *n* warmth; an act of warming *16-*. [see the adj]
warm¹·² /warm, wɔrm/ *v* 1 to heat, cause to become warm; to (cause to) feel uplifted or joyful *la14-*. 2 to beat, thrash, hit *19-*. **warmer** an outstanding or formidable character *20- WC SW Bor*. **warm-hearted,** †**warm hartit** generous, affectionate *16-*. [OE *wearmian* to become warm fallen together with OE *wyrman* to warm, make warm]
warm¹·³, **waarm, wairm, warum,** †**warme** /warm, wɔrm, werm, ˈwɔrəm/ *adj* 1 having or giving out a moderate heat *15-*. 2 filled with emotion; angry, heated *la15-*. [OE *wearm*]
warme *see* WARM¹·³
warn¹, **wairn** /warn, wern/ *v* 1 to give advance notice, inform (of danger); to supply with information or knowledge *la14-*. 2 *of a clock* to make a clicking or whirring noise prior to striking *la19, 20- Ork NE T*. 3 to give (official or legal) notice, summon (to fulfil an obligation), summons (before a court) *la14-19, 20- Ork N*. 4 to invite to a funeral *19*. **warning** 1 advance notice (of danger or difficulty) *la14-*. 2 a premonition, portent *la19-*. 3 legal or official notification, especially notice given to vacate premises or resign from a post; a summons *16-18*; compare *precept of warning* (PRECEPT). 4 *in a clock* an alarm *e16*. [OE *warnian*]
†**warn**² *v* to refuse, deny, prevent; to oppose, forbid *la14-17*. [OE *wiernian, wearnian*, ON *varna*]
warnice *see* WARNISH
†**warnis, warnys** *v* to supply, equip; to protect; to be endowed with *la14-15*. **warnysing, warnisicioun** provision(s) *la14-16*. [AN *warniss-*, stem of *warnir*]
warnish, †**warnice** /ˈwarnɪʃ/ *v* 1 to warn, caution, advise *19-*. 2 *of a clock* to make a clicking or whirring noise prior to striking *la19*. **warnisin** warning *19- NE T EC*. **warnishment** advice *19- NE T EC*. [extended sense of WARN¹ with *-ish* suffix]
†**warnour, wernour** *n* a wretch, miser *e16*. [WARN² + agent suffix]
warnys *see* WARNIS
warp¹·¹ /warp/ *n* 1 the lengthwise yarn of a piece of cloth *15-*. 2 a stroke in rowing *la19- Sh Ork*. [OE *wearp*]
warp¹·², **wairp,** †**werp,** †**wrap** /warp, werp/ *v* 1 *weaving* to prepare the warp threads for a piece of cloth; to weave *17-*. 2 *farming* to interlace ropes in thatching a cornstack *20- T EC*. 3 to plait; to knit, cast on (stitches) *19, 20- NE*. 4 to cast, throw, fling *la14-16*. 5 to utter, say (words); to talk *15-16*. 6 to fling open (a door); *of a door* to open *e16*. 7 *of the wind or sea* to toss, throw around, carry along *e16*. 8 to (cause to) move in an erratic or whirling trajectory; to swing round, whirl *16-19*. †**warpit** prepared for weaving; woven *la15-17*. [OE *weorpan* to throw, cast]
warp *see* WRAP
warpin, warping /ˈwɔrpɪn, ˈwarpɪŋ/ *n* 1 *weaving* the preparation of the warp threads *la16-*. 2 *joinery* a strut, brace or angle-piece *16-*. 3 *weaving* = *warpin staik 17-e18*. †**warping ale** a drink of ale given to the weaver after setting up a warp of homespun wool *la17-e18*. †**warping fatt** a tub or trough in which the clews of yarn are laid for warping *la16-e18*. **warpin staik** one of the set of wooden uprights round which the yarn is wound in warping *17-*. [verbal noun from WARP¹·²]
†**warpis** *v* to abandon, give up *la14-e15*. [OFr *werpiss-*, stem of *werpir*]
warple /ˈwarpəl/ *v* 1 to intertwine, twist, entangle; to confuse *la18-*. 2 to wrestle, tumble, wriggle *la18- N NE*. 3 to stagger, move erratically; to struggle through (a difficulty) *la19- SW Bor*. [frequentative form of WARP¹·²]
warran *see* WARRANT¹·²
warrand *see* WARRANT¹·¹, WARRANT¹·²
†**warrander, warandar** *n* a person in charge of a rabbit-warren *la15-17*. [altered form of OFr *warrennier*]
warrandice, †**warrandise,** †**warandice,** †**werrandis** /ˈwarandɪs/ *n* 1 a guarantee which secures another against risk or loss, especially given by the seller of goods as protection to the buyer; the legal obligation to indemnify another *la14-*. 2 *law* the undertaking by a granter or seller, especially of heritable property, to indemnify a grantee or buyer if possession is lost through defect of title *la14-*. 3 (a document conferring) authorization, authority *19*. [AN *warandise*]
warrandy *see* WARRANTY
warrant¹·¹, †**warrand,** †**warand,** †**werrand** /ˈwarənt/ *n* 1 (a document giving official or formal) authorization or permission *15-*. 2 a protector, defender *la14-e19*. 3 (a place of) security, safety or shelter; protection *la14-e17*. 4 a guarantor; a person who stands as surety *15-e17*. 5 justification, authority for an action or belief *15-e19*. **warrant sale** a sale carried out by a *sheriff officer* (SHERIFF) under warrant,

usually of a householder's goods *20, 21- historical*. [OFr *warant, warand*]

warrant[1,2], **warran**, †**warrand**, †**werrand** /ˈwarənt, ˈwarən/ *v* **1** to protect, keep safe, take care of; to guarantee the safety or security of *la14-*. **2** to vouch for, guarantee the truth of (an opinion): ◊*I ken a better place, I'se warrant ye for that la14-*. **3** to authorize, sanction *15-*. **4** to stand as guarantor, be surety for *la15-17*. [OFr *warantir, warandir*]

warranty, †**warrandy**, †**warandy** /ˈwarənti/ *n* **1** *with regard to a legally binding agreement, especially the sale of goods* a guarantee *19-*. **2** an assurance *19-*. **3** (the part of) a document expressing a legal obligation or guarantee *la14-e15*. [AN *warantie*]

†**warray**, **werray** *v* **1** to wage war *la14-15*. **2** to persecute *la14-e17*. **warraying**, **werraying** warfare *la14-e16*. [AN *warreier*, OFr *werier*]

warrayour *see* WARRIOR

warridrag *see* WALLYDRAG

warrior, †**weriour**, †**werrayour**, †**warrayour** /ˈwɔrɪər; *NE* ˈwʌrɪər/ *n* **1** one who practises warfare, a fighting man *la14-*. **2** *humorous* a lively, spirited child *20-*. **3** a rival or fellow-combatant *e16*. **the Warriors** nickname for various football clubs, specifically Stenhousemuir and occasionally Third Lanark and Dumbarton *la20-*. [OFr *werreieor*]

warroch /ˈwarəx/ *n* **1** a stunted, feeble, person or plant; a good-for-nothing *19- NE T*. **2** a knotty stick; a knot in wood *e19*. [WAR + -OCH]

warry codlin *see* WARE[1.1]

warryn tre *see* WAR

wars *see* WARSE[1.2]

warsch *see* WERSH

warse[1.1], †**wers** /wars/ *n* that which is worse *la15-*. Compare WAUR[1.1]. **the worse of drink** the worse for drink, having drunk too much alcohol *18-*; compare *the waur o* (WAUR[1.3]). [see the adj]

warse[1.2], **worse**, †**wers**, †**wars**, †**wors** /wars, wʌrs/ *adj* bad or ill in a greater or higher degree; inferior, in a less good condition, worse *16-*. Compare WAUR[1.3]. [OE *wærsa, wiersa*; *worse* is from *southern* ME *wurse*, OE *wyrsa*]

warse[1.3], **worse**, †**wers**, †**wors** /wars, wʌrs/ *adv* less well, more seriously or severely, worse *16-*. Compare WAUR[1.4]. [from the adj and OE *wiers*]

†**warset**, **wersslete**, **warseth** *n* a hunting dog *15-e17*. [altered form of ME *berselet*, AN *bercelet*]

warsill *see* WARSLE[1.2]

warsle[1.1], **warstle**, **wrestle**, **wrastle**, *Sh Ork* **wassle** /ˈwarsəl, ˈrɛsəl, ˈrasəl; *Sh Ork* ˈwɑsəl/ *n* **1** a wrestling match, a physical tussle; a struggle, an effort *19-*. **2** a mental or moral struggle, a fight against circumstances or hardship *la18-*. [see the verb]

warsle[1.2], **warstle**, **wrestle**, **wrastle**, *Sh Ork* **wassle**, †**worsill**, †**warsill**, †**worsle** /ˈwarsəl, ˈrɛsəl, ˈrasəl; *Sh Ork* ˈwɑsəl/ *v* **1** to wrestle (as a sport); to struggle with, fight (an opponent) *15-*. **2** to pray earnestly *19-*. **3** to labour, try hard, exert oneself *la15-*. **4** to fight, overcome (circumstances) *la18-*. **5** to writhe, wriggle, flounder, *la15-*. **6** to toil or struggle through life, scrape along; to travel with difficulty *la16-*. **7** to get by striving, achieve (an end) by great effort *la18- NE T WC*. **8** to drive or force (someone) out of (something) as by wrestling *17-19*. **warslin** struggling; energetic, hardworking *la19-*. **warstle through** to scrape through, get by *20-*. **warsle wi 1** to fight with an opponent *15-*. **2** to contend, struggle, strive with circumstances *16-*. [metathesis of OE **wræstlian*, and compare MDu *werstelen, worstelen*]

warst[1.1], **worst**, †**werst** /warst, wʌrst/ *n* **1** the most reprehensible behaviour *la14-*. **2** a most wicked, cruel or morally reprehensible person *15-*. **3** the most unpleasant period; the most unacceptable aspect; the most grievous outcome *la15-*. Compare WAUR[1.1]. [see the adj]

warst[1.2], **worst**, †**werst** /warst, wʌrst/ *adj* **1** *of a situation* most unpleasant or unfavourable *la14-*. **2** *of a person* most wicked, cruel or morally reprehensible *la15-*. **3** least desirable, most inferior, of poorest quality *15-*. Compare WAUR[1.3]. [OE *wierresta, wurresta*, ON *verstr*]

warst[1.3], **worst**, †**werst** /warst, wʌrst/ *adv* most unfavourably or ineffectively; most badly; least well; worst *la15-*. Compare WAUR[1.4]. [OE *wierrest* ON *verst*]

warstle *see* WARSLE[1.1], WARSLE[1.2]

wart, †**warth** /wart, wɑrt/ *n* **1** a lookout point on high ground; a mound, a cairn, a beacon; a watch-tower *17- Sh Ork N*. **2** a small, stone-built shelter *20- Ork*. **warto** = WART (sense 2).

†**warthill**, **wert hill** in Orkney, Shetland and the Northeast, (a hill surmounted by) a beacon *14-19*. [ON *varða*]

wart *see* WRAT

-wart /wərt/ *suffix* in the direction indicated, towards *la14-*. [OE *-weard*]

warth *see* WART, WORTH[1.1], WORTH[1.2], WRAITH[1]

warum *see* WARM[1.3]

†**warwoof**, **warwoolf**, **werwoif** *n* **1** a werewolf *la15-17*. **2** a puny child; an ill-grown person *e19*. [OE *werewulf*]

†**wary** *v* **1** to curse, lay a curse on, utter a curse; to pronounce a formal curse against; to blaspheme *la14-e17*. **2** to curse (one's fate), bemoan (one's lot); to regret (one's birth) *la14-16*. **weriour** a person who curses or maligns another *e16*. **waryit**, **warʒit**, **wareit** cursed, reviled, hated *la14-16*. [OE *wærgan*]

wary *see* WARE[2.1]

warydraggel *see* WALLYDRAG

warysoun *see* WARISOUN

was *see* WIS

wasche *see* WASH[1.2]

wascher *see* WASHER

wash[1.1], **wesh**, †**wesche** /waʃ, wɛʃ/ *n* **1** the action of washing; a bathe, swim *la17-*. **2** (stale) urine, used as a cleansing agent or fixing agent in dyeing *la15-*. **3** a bevelled edge or slope on a board or stone *20- NE EC*. **wash-board** skirting-board *19- NE C SW*. [see the verb]

wash[1.2], **waash**, **wesh**, *Sh* **wish**, †**wesche**, †**wysche**, †**wasche** /waʃ, wɛʃ; *Sh* wɪʃ, wʌɪʃ/ *v pt* **washt**, *Sh* **wysh**, *Sh EC* **woosh**, *NE* **weesh**, *T EC Bor* **wuish**, *ptp* **washt**, **weshed**, *Sh T C* **wishen**, *N NE* **washen**, *T EC Bor* **wuishen**, *EC* **wooshen**, *Bor* **weshen**, †**weschin**, †**weschyn 1** to cleanse, clean; to bathe *la14-*. **2** to cut to a slope or bevel, chamfer *19- WC*. **3** to flow over, inundate *16-*. **4** to carry away in a flow of water; to wash away *16-*. **wash-bine** a portable wash-tub *la19-*. **wash-hoose** a (public) wash-house *20, 21- historical*. **wash doon**, †**wash doun 1** = WASH[1.2] (sense 2) *20-*. **2** to wash away; to clean off *16-*. †**wash off** = WASH[1.2] (sense 2) *e19*. **wash its face** *of a commercial venture* to pay its way, break even *20-*. [OE *wascan*]

washen *see* WASH[1.2]

washer, †**wascher**, †**weschar** /ˈwaʃer/ *n* **1** one whose occupation is washing, especially clothes or linen *16-*. **2** a person who scrubs and cleans fish after gutting, in preparation for curing *19- Sh NE*. **washer wife 1** a washer-woman, laundress *17-*. **2** a water spider *Argyroneta aquatica 20- NE T WC*. [WASH[1.2], with agent suffix]

washin, **washing** /ˈwaʃɪn, ˈwaʃɪŋ/ *n* the act or action of washing *la14-*. †**washing-board** skirting-board *la18-19*. **washing-boyne**, **washing-bine** a (portable) wash-tub *19-*. **washin-hoose** a wash-house *17-*. †**washing an**

apron an initiation rite of apprentices *18-19*; compare *apron washing* (APRIN). [verbal noun from WASH[1,2]]

washt *see* WASH[1,2]

†**wasie** *adj* wise, clever, quick-witted *19 NE T*. [unknown]

waskyne *see* VASKENE

waslage *see* VASSALAGE

wasna, wasnae *see* WISNAE

wasp, waasp, waps, *SW* **wesp** /wɔsp, wasp, wɔps; *SW* wɛsp/ *n* **1** a wasp, an insect of the family *Vespidae la14-*. **2** *derogatory* a malicious person *15-e17*. **wasp bike** a wasps' nest *19-*. **the Wasps** nickname for Alloa Athletic Football Club (from the yellow and black hoops on their jerseys) *20-*. [OE *wæsp, wæps*]

wasper *see* WAWSPER

wassie, *Sh* **wizzie** /'wazi, 'wɪzi/ *n* **1** a straw horse-collar or pad *19-20 Sh Ork*. **2** bushy, unkempt hair or whiskers *20- Sh*. [Norw *vase* a straw bundle, pad, tangle; compare WEASE]

wassle *see* WARSLE[1.1], WARSLE[1.2]

wast[1.1]**, west** /wast, wɛst/ *n* **1** the westerly point of the compass or direction *la14-*. **2** the western part of a place; the western area of Scotland *15-*. [see the adv]

wast[1.2]**, west** /wast, wɛst/ *v of the wind* to veer or back to the west *la19- Ork NE EC*. [see the adv]

wast[1.3]**, west** /wast, wɛst/ *adj* situated in or belonging to the west *13-*. †**west country** the western part of Scotland *la15-17*. **west end** the western end of a place or building *la15-*. **west ender** an inhabitant of the *west end* of Hawick *20- Bor*. **wastland** *n* the west of Scotland, *of the wind* westerly, blowing from the west *la15-19, 20- C*. **wastland** *adj* coming from or situated in the west of Scotland, western; *of the wind* westerly, blowing from the west *la15-*. †**westlander** an inhabitant of the west of Scotland *la17-e19*. †**west part** the western section of an area or country *la14-e18*. †**west se, west seis** the sea on the western side of Scotland *la15-17*. **the West Isles** the Hebrides south of Ardnamurchan, and also Kintyre *17*; compare *the South Isles* (SOOTH[1.2]). [see the adv]

wast[1.4]**, west,** †**wost** /wast, wɛst/ *adv* **1** in a westerly direction, westwards *la15-*. **2** away from or to the left of the speaker or the person addressed *18-*; compare EAST[1.3] (sense 3). **wastle, wasla,** †**wassil,** †**westell, wostell** westward, to the west (of) *16-e17, 19- SW Bor*. **wastlin** western, from or in the west, westerly *18-*. **wastlins** westward, to or in the west *18-*. **westmaist, westmost** most westerly, furthest west *la15-*. **wastward,** *NE* **wastert,** †**wastwart** in a westerly direction, towards the west *la14-*. **wastru, waastroo** western, from the west *20- Sh*. **west-by** westward, in a westerly direction *la18- NE T EC*. †**westcuming** (making) a journey to the west or in a westerly direction *la16-17*. †**westgoing** = *westcuming 17*. †**go west** *of the sun* to set *la15*. †**wast about** = *wast awa la16-19*. **wast awa** in or to the west *19, 20- C*. **wast ower** westwards, to or in the west *e17, 19- Sh NE*. [OE *west*]

wast[1.5]**, west** /wast, wɛst/ *prep* above, along, across, over, to the west, on the west side of *la15-19, 20- NE T EC*. [see the adv]

wast *see* WAIST, WASTE[1.1], WASTE[1.2], WASTE[1.3]

wastair *see* WASTER[2]

wastall *see* WASTEL

wastcoat, wastcoit *see* WESKIT

waste[1.1]**, waist,** †**wast,** †**west** /west/ *n* **1** an area of wild or sparsely populated land *la14-*. **2** debris, refuse, rubbish *la17-*. **3** land (adjacent to buildings) left waste, land not maintained or used *la15-18*. **4** a cavity, hole *16-17*. **wastage 1** loss by use, decay or damage *la19-*. **2** a piece of waste ground; a ruin *la17-19*. †**in waste** in vain, to no effect *la14-16*. **waste o wind** a waste of breath *20-*. [OFr *waste*]

waste[1.2]**, waist,** †**wast,** †**west** /west/ *v* **1** to expend (effort, energy) to little effect; to use (resources) extravagantly, squander; to exhaust (a supply); to deteriorate, diminish, wear out through use; to spend (time) idly *la14-*. **2** to spoil, ruin by misuse or neglect *la14-*. **3** to spoil, pamper *20-*. **4** to beat up *la20-*. **5** to harry, lay waste, destroy *15-17*. **waistit, wasted 1** worn out, exhausted, impotent *16-*. **2** laid waste, damaged *e16*. **3** spent, squandered *la16-*. **wastry,** †**wastrie** reckless extravagance, wastefulness *la14-*. **waste yer wind** to waste one's breath, argue or plead in vain *19- N NE*. †**wast wind** = *waste yer wind la15-16*. [OFr *waster*]

waste[1.3]**, waist, wyste,** †**wast,** †**west** /west, wʌɪst/ *adj* **1** no longer useful or required, superfluous; discarded *la14-*. **2** *of land* uncultivated; uninhabited, not built on; wild, desolate; barren; laid waste *la14-*. **3** *of effort* unprofitable, useless *la15-e17, 20- Sh Ork*. **4** *of a building or room* ruined, derelict; unoccupied, empty, disused *la14-e19*. **5** *of an idea* abandoned *16*. **wastrife** wasteful, extravagant *19-*. †**wast fracht** a duty payable on any empty cargo space in a ship *la15-16*. †**wast of** devoid of *15-16*. [OFr *waste*]

†**waste**[1.4]**, waist** *adv* in vain, to no purpose *16*. [see the adj]

wastel, wastle, †**wastall** /'wasəl/ *n* a kind of bread, scone or cake baked with the finest flour; a large scone made of oatmeal and wholemeal flour *15-19, 20- NE*. [ME *wastel*, OFr *wastel*]

wasten[1.1]**, westin** /'wastən, 'wɛstən/ *n* the western part of a district *20- Sh*. [see the adj]

wasten[1.2]**, westin,** †**vestin** /'wastən, 'wɛstən/ *adj* western, from the west *e16, 20- Sh*. **Westin Sea** in Papa Stour, a heavy sea driven by a North-Westerly gale on to the North-West coast *20- Sh*. [OE *westan* adv from the west, Norw *vestan*]

waster[1]**, waister,** †**waistour,** †**westar** /'westər, 'wʌɪstər/ *n* **1** an extravagant squanderer, an idler, a good-for-nothing *15-*. **2** something on the wick of a candle causing it to gutter *la18-19, 20- T EC Bor*. **3** a person, animal or object of no further use, due to age or disease *la19-*. **4** a destroyer (of something) *la14*. **wasterfu** wasteful, extravagant *19-*. **wastry** wasteful, extravagant *la18-19, 20- N Bor*. [WASTE[1.2] with agent suffix]

waster[2]**,** †**wastair,** †**vaister** /'westər, 'wastər/ *n* a (salmon) fishing spear *16-19, 20- Bor*. †**wausterin, wastering** spearing (salmon) *la16-19*. [conflation of WAWSPER with LEISTER[1.1]]

waster[3]**, wester,** †**westir** /'wastər, 'wɛstər/ *adj* **1** western, lying towards the west, frequently in place-names *la12-*; compare EASTER[1.3]. **2** *of the wind* from a westerly direction *17*. **wasterly** in the direction of, towards or (coming) from the west *16-*. [OE *westra*]

wastern, western, †**wasterin** /'wastərn, 'wɛstərn/ *adj* situated in or coming from the west (of Scotland) *17-*. **western remonstrance** = REMONSTRANCE (sense 2). **the Western Isles 1** the (Outer) Hebrides, a chain of islands off the North-West mainland of Scotland *la16-*. **2** the administrative area of Lewis, Harris, North Uist, Benbecula, South Uist and Barra *la20-*. [OE *westerne*]

Wastie /'wasti/ *n* (the occupant of) a farm the name of which includes WAST or WASTER[3] *la19- NE*. Compare EASTIE. [WAST[1.3] + -IE[1]]

wastle *see* WASTEL

wastrife *see* WASTE[1.3]

wastry *see* WASTE[1.2]

†**wasty, waistie, vaistie** *adj* desolate, deserted, uninhabited *la14-16*. **wasty wanis** a stripped or emptied house *15-16*. [WASTE[1.1] + -IE[2]]

wasyll *see* WEASEL

wat *see* WALT[1.1], WEET[1.1], WEET[1.2] WEET[1.3], WIT[1.2]

watch[1.1], **waatch**, †**wach**, †**waich**, †**weche** /wɔtʃ, watʃ/ *n* **1** the action of watching, guarding, protecting; the duty of a guard *la14-*. **2** a guard, an outpost or scout, a look-out man; a body of military guards *la14-*. **3** a vigil *la16-*. **4** a timepiece small enough to be carried in the pocket or worn on the wrist *17-*. **5** a patrol of burgesses in a burgh, the town guard *15-17*. **6** the action of watching to do harm, (persons) lying in wait, an ambush; a place liable to ambush *15-e17*. **watchie 1** a watchmaker *la18-19, 20- NE T*. **2** a watchman *19-*. †**watchfell** = *watch-knowe e15*. **watch-knowe** a hill used as a look-out station or beacon; frequently in place-names *17- Bor*. **watchman 1** a sentinel, a military guard; a member of the town guard *15-17*. **2** *Presbyterian Church* a pastor *la16-e17*. †**watch and ward** a feudal obligation owed by burgesses in a burgh requiring participation in the town guard *16-17*. †**Wach of day** Venus, the morning star *e16*. [OE *wæcce*]

watch[1.2], **waatch**, †**wach** /wɔtʃ, watʃ/ *v* **1** to observe; to keep a watch; to keep under surveillance; to guard, protect; to fulfil the duty of a watchman, sentinel or guard *la14-*. **2** to be alert; to be vigilant, watch out; to pay attention *la16-*. †**watch youself with** to guard oneself against *la14*. **watch yersel** to look after oneself, be on one's guard, watch out *la19-*. †**watch and ward** to perform the civic duty of *watching and warding la15-17*. †**watching and warding** the civic duty of a burgess to patrol the streets of a burgh and maintain order *la16-e19*. [OE *wæccan*]

wate *see* WAIT[1.1], WAIT[1.2], WIT[1.2]

water *see* WATTER[1.1], WATTER[1.2]

waterin, watering /ˈwatərɪn, ˈwɔtərɪŋ/ *n* **1** the action of wetting or sprinkling with water; the action of supplying with water *la15-*. **2** *law* the right to take water from the land of a vassal for use on that of the superior *la17*; compare *watirgang 2* (WATTER[1.1]). **3** mainly *pl* a spring, trough or pool in a stream where farm animals go to drink *la18-19, 20- Ork NE*. **4** *in the game of handball* the continuation of the game in the river when the ball lands in the water *20- Bor*. †**watering bridill** a bridle with a snaffle bit, mainly used when taking a horse to drink *16-e17*. **watering chyne** a chain used on a bridle used when taking a horse to drink *20- N NE*. **waterin-stane** a stone horse-trough *la18-*. [verbal noun from WATTER[1.2]]

Waterloo /watərˈluː/ *n marbles* a soft, brittle, clay marble *20- T EC*. [from the place-name]

watery *see* WATTERY[1.2]

†**wath, wouth** *n* **1** (exposure to) harm or danger *la14-e15*. **2** *law* (an accusation of) harm having been done *la13-16*. [ON *wáðe*]

wath *see* WAITH[4]

wather *see* WEATHER, WEDDER

wathir *see* WEATHER

watir *see* WATTER[1.1]

watry *see* WATTERY[1.2]

watt *see* WALT[1.1]

wattell *see* WATTLE[1.2]

watter[1.1], **waaater, water, wa'er**, *Sh T* **wattir**, *EC Bor* **waiter**, †**watir**, †**walter**, †**vater** /ˈwatər, ˈwɔtər, ˈwaər, ˈwɔər; *Sh T* ˈwatɪr; *EC Bor* ˈwetər/ *n* **1** a large stream (between a burn and a river in size); a tributary of a river; a small river, frequently in place-names *13-*. **2** water *la14-*. **3** bodily fluids, especially urine or tears *la14-*. **4** mainly *pl* the seas and oceans belonging to a particular nation, territorial water(s) *la15-*. **5** mainly *pl* an area or stretch of a river or sea identified as belonging to an individual or town, *eg* coastal waters *la15-*. **6** a liquid similar to and containing water, a decoction or infusion for use as a medicine, flavouring or cosmetic; distilled water *16-*. **7** dropsy; a disease of sheep *la19-*. **8** a body of water, a loch, frequently in place-names *la14-19, 20- Sh*. **9** a river valley, the area and its inhabitants bordering a river *la15-19, 20- Bor*. **10** a measurement for goods *15-e17*. **11** waste water; sewage *17*. **12** mainly *pl* alcoholic drink *17*. **water arvo** chickweed *Stellaria media 20- Sh Ork*. **water-bailie 1** a water-bailiff employed to prevent poaching in rivers; originally to enforce fishing law more generally *la15-19, 20- N NE T*. **2** the magistrate with jurisdiction for shipping and maritime affairs *16-19, 20- historical*. **3** an aquatic insect or water-bug, especially the water-strider of the family *Gerridae*, or water boatman of the family *Corixidae 20- NE*. †**water bailliery** the jurisdiction of a *water-bailie 2 la16-e17*. †**wattirbairge** a stone or wooden ledge on the edge of a roof for protection from rain *la16-18*. †**wattir bank** a shore *la14-16*. **water-bird** a chick that has died in the egg *20- Ork*. **water blackbird** the dipper *Cinclus cinclus la19, 20- Bor Uls*. **water-bobbie** = *water blackbird la19- NE T*. †**watter boll** a BOLL of the *wattermett* series of measures *la15-17*. †**wattir brae** a riverbank or shore *16-17*. **water-brash** heartburn, a reflux of gastric fluid *19-*. †**wattir brek** a sudden rush of water, a flood *16*. **water-brod** a bench or board on which water buckets can be set *la19- Sh*. **water-broo** oatmeal mixed with boiling water *19, 20- EC*. **water-brose** = *water-broo la18-19, 20- N NE T*. **water-buggie** a person who drinks a lot of water *20- Sh*. **water-burn** phosphorescence on the sea *19, 20- NE*. **water-calf** the amnion of a cow, the membrane around the foetus *20- Sh*. †**wattir claith 1** a cloth or towel for wiping up water *la16-e18*. **2** a cloth (apparently an altar cloth) with a lustrous finish *la15*. **water-clearer** one of the small insects that skim over the surface of water and in doing so are said to clean it *20- T H&I C*. **water-cock** = *water blackbird 19- NE*. **water-cog**, †**wateir coig** a wooden water vessel, a bucket *la16-19, 20- Ork*. †**watter corne** the grain paid by tenant-farmers for the upkeep of the dams and waterways of the estate mill *17-e19*. †**wattir court** a court dealing with issues relating to waterways *la15-e17*. †**water cow** *Celtic folklore* a mythical amphibious beast supposed to live in lakes *la18-e19*. **water-craw** = *water blackbird la18-19, 20- NE T C*. **water-dog 1** a dog for hunting in wetlands and rivers *16-*. **2** a water vole *Arvicola amphibius la18- NE*. †**water-drap** = EAVESDROP *e19*. †**watterfaw** the line or inclination of descent of water (on a hill) *16-17*. †**waterfast** = *waterticht 16-19*. **watter firlot** a FIRLOT of the *watter-mett* series of measures *la16-17*. **waterfit** the mouth of a river, frequently in place-names *18-*. **water-fur** *n* a drainage furrow to carry off surface water *la18-*. †**water-fur** *v* to provide (land) with drainage furrows *18-19*. †**water-furrowed** ploughed with deep furrows for drainage *la17*. **watergang 1** a watercourse, especially a ditch or a channel for a mill *15-19*. **2** *law* a burden on property giving the right of conveying water from the property of a vassal for use on that of the superior *la17*. **water-gate 1** a grating suspended over a stream to prevent animals from straying or floating rubbish from passing *20-*. **2** a name for a street leading to or from water *la16-*. **3** a river valley, the area and its inhabitants bordering a river *la19- Bor*. **4** a road and its branches which serve a valley *18- Bor*. **5** a channel for water, a watercourse *la16-19*. **watergaw** an imperfect or fragmentary rainbow *la19-*. **water-glass** a glass container for water *17-*.

waterheid the source of a river, the upper end of a valley *la16-*. **water-hole 1** a hole or pit in which water collects or is collected, a well or pool *17-19, 20- Sh N NE T*. **2** a detention cell under the old Guard-house in the High Street of Edinburgh, so called because there was always water in it *la18-e19*. **water-horse** *Celtic folklore* a mythical spirit in the form of a horse which frequents lakes and rivers *19-*. †**water-kail, water-caill** BROTH¹ made without meat *la15-19*. **water-kelpie** *Celtic folklore* a water demon, usually in the form of a horse, said to haunt rivers and lochs and lure the unwary to their deaths *la18-*; compare *water-horse*. **water-kit** a large wooden bucket or barrel; a wooden tub *19-, 20- Sh N*. **watter lead** a channel for water, a mill lade *la15-e17*. **water-lip** the brink of a stream *19- WC*. **water-lump** a bank of dark, rainy cloud *20- Sh*. †**wattir-mail** rent for fishing a stretch of water *la14-e18*. †**wattirmaill** apparently the fur of a small animal *la15-e16*. †**watterman 1** the proprietor or owner of a stretch of water, especially with regard to fishing rights *la16-17*. **2** a man who removed water from a mine *17*. **3** a mariner or seaman *e17*. **water-mark 1** the line forming the limit to which the tide rises *la19-*. **2** a boundary mark indicating the line of separation between the waters of rivers owned by different proprietors *e17*. **water-meggie** = *water blackbird 20- C Bor*. †**watter-mett** a measurement used for (imported) goods transported by sea, mainly grain and salt *15-17*. **water money** *mining* extra payment for working in wet conditions *20-*. †**water mouse** a water vole *Arvicola amphibius la18-e19*. **water-mooth, water-mou** the mouth of a river *la16-19, 20- NE T EC*. †**water-neb** in Renfrewshire, the confluence of the rivers Cart and Clyde *19*. †**watter passage** = *watergang 1 la15-17*. **water-pig** a container for water, a pitcher *la16-19, 20- Sh T*. **water pleep** the common sandpiper *Actitis hypoleucos 20- Ork*. **water-purpie** brooklime *Veronica beccabunga 17-*. **water-pyet** = *water blackbird 19, 20- T WC*. †**water-run** a runnel of water, a surface drain or gutter for carrying off water, a streamlet *la18-19*. †**water-serjant** in Glasgow, an officer of the court of the *water-bailie* **2** *17-e18*. **water-side** the side or brink of water, the bank of a river; a district in the vicinity of a river *la14-*. †**watter sponge** a sponge for washing oneself *la15-e17*. **water-stank** a pond, a pool of water *la15-e18*. **water stowp**, †**watter stop** a wooden bucket; a drinking vessel, a pitcher *la15-*. **watter strype** a strip of water, a stream *la16-e17*. **waterticht** impervious to water *la14-*. **watter-traa** heartburn *19- Sh Ork N*. **water trip** the annual inspection of the waterworks, an occasion for a social outing for the local government Councillors *20-*. **water-waggie** the water wagtail *Motacilla alba la19-*. **water water** river water *19- Bor*. **watter-wik** as weak as water, frail, delicate *20- Sh N*. **watter-wark, water-work 1** structures concerned with the supply or control of water *17-*. **2** the part of a handball game played in the river *20, 21- historical*. **3** in Inverness, a structure or structures built in the river Ness to facilitate fishing *la16-e17*. **water-wrack, watter wrak** weeds, leaves, sticks and other flotsam carried down by a river *la17-*. †**water-wraith** *folklore* a water spirit haunting streams and lakes *la18-19*. **water-yett 1** = *water-gate 3 20- T C SW Bor*. **2** an entrance gate (of a town) close to or leading to a river, especially in Edinburgh and the Canongate *la16-17*. **tak yer water aff** to make a fool of, take a rise out of *la19, 20- T*. **Water of** a designation for a particular river or stream ◊*the Water of Leith*, frequently in river names *la14-*. **Water of Ayr stone** a kind of stone found on the banks of the river Ayr used for making whetstones and in polishing *19, 20- WC*. [OE *wæter*]

watter[1,2], **water, wa'er,** †'**wattir,** †'**waltir** /ˈwatər, ˈwɔtər, ˈwaər, ˈwɔər/ *v* **1** to sprinkle, dampen (with water) *la16-*. **2** to give water to animals or people (to drink); to supply (a garden, plant) with water *17-*. **3** *of the eyes* to shed tears, water *16-*. **4** to coat or plate (with (precious) metal); to cause to shine *17-e18*. **5** to supply with the means to grow or flourish *la16-e17*. **wattered, watterit 1** supplied with water or drink *la16-*. **2** *of textiles* having a lustrous finish *16-*. **3** soaked, wetted, steeped in water *17-*. **4** *of a coal mine* subject to flooding *la19-*. **5** *of metal* gilded by a process of water gilding *17*. [OE *wæterian*]

wattery[1,1] /ˈwatəri/ *n* **1** a water closet *20- Ork NE T EC*. **2** the pied wagtail *Motacilla alba la19- NE T*. [shortened form of various compounds of WATTER[1,1] + -IE¹]

wattery[1,2]**, watery, watry** /ˈwatəri/ *adj* **1** full of water, well watered or irrigated, frequently in place-names *13-*. **2** like water in some respect; of the colour or texture of water *16-*. **3** *of food* having too much water in it, thin, insipid *18-*. **4** pertaining to water or the sea; consisting of water *16-e18*. **watery-arvie** = *water arvo* (WATTER[1,1]) *20- Sh*. **wattery drums** groundsel *Senecio vulgaris 20- Sh*. **watery-nebbit** pale and sickly; starved-looking; having a drip at the end of one's nose *la19- NE T*. **watery-pleep** = *water pleep* (WATTER[1,1]). **watery-pox** chicken-pox *la19- T EC*. **watery swirl** a knot in timber thought to presage the wreck of the boat in which it is found *la19- Sh*. **watery wagtail** the pied wagtail *Motacilla alba* or the yellow wagtail *Motacilla flava la19-*. **watery winky** the pied wagtail *20- EC*. [WATTER[1,1] + -IE²]

wattill see WATTLE[1,1]

wattir see WATTER[1,1], WATTER[1,2]

wattle[1,1]**,** †**wattill** /ˈwɔtəl, ˈwatəl/ *n* **1** *pl thatching* the interwoven twigs on which the turf or thatch was laid; originally also *building* thin branches used to construct walls or partitions *16-19, 20- T*. **2** a tangle, mix-up, confused mess *20- N*. **3** a pliable rod, twig or wand used as a whip *la18-19*. [OE *watel*]

wattle[1,2]**,** †**wattell** /ˈwɔtəl, ˈwatəl/ *v* **1** to tie down the thatch of a stack with interlacing ropes (originally pliable branches) *20-*. **2** to furnish, use wattles (WATTLE[1,1] (sense 1)) in building work *la16-17*. †**wattlin,** †**wattelling** twigs or branches which have been or can be plaited to form wattle-work *14-19*. [see the noun]

wattle², †**wattill** /ˈwatəl/ *n* in Shetland and Orkney, a tax deriving originally from the obligation of a subject to provide hospitality for (the representative of) the monarch; the goods going to provide what was due *la15-19, 20- historical*. [ON *veizla* a grant, gift, revenue, Norw *veitsla*]

wauble see WABBLE²

wauch, *NE* **waugh,** *SW Bor* **wauf** /wɔx; *SW Bor* wɔf/ *adj* **1** good-for-nothing, worthless, feeble *19-*. **2** unwell, faint, weary *19- NE EC SW Bor*. **3** *of food* tasteless, unappetizing; not nourishing *19- NE T SW*. **4** *of a taste or smell* unpleasant, stale, unappetizing *la18-19, 20- NE T*. [ME *walh*, OE *wealg* nauseous; the form *wauf* is from *northern* Eng *dial*]

wauch see WAUCHT[1,1]

wauchie /ˈwɔxe/ *adj* swampy, boggy *19- C SW*. [probably WACK[1,2] + -IE²; perhaps with influence from WAUCH]

wauchle[1,1] /ˈwɔxəl/ *n* **1** a struggle, laborious effort *19, 20- Sh NE T SW*. **2** a staggering ungainly movement, a wobble *la19, 20- C*. [see the verb]

wauchle[1,2]**, wochle, wachle** /ˈwɔxəl, ˈwaxəl/ *v* **1** to walk or make one's way laboriously or with difficulty, walk in a clumsy, ungainly way, stumble with fatigue *19-*. **2** to plod on amid difficulties, struggle with a situation or task *19-*. **3** to last out (a period of time) in a weary, listless way *la18-*. **4** to confuse *19- WC*. **wauchled** perplexed, bewildered, muddle-headed *20- T EC*. [perhaps onomatopoeic; compare TRAUCHLE[1.2], SPRAUCHLE[1.2]]

waucht[1.1], **wacht**, †**waught**, †**wauch** /wɔxt, waxt/ *n* **1** a draught of liquid, a swig or gulp of a drink *18-*. **2** a deep breath of air, a full inhalation *19-*. [see the verb]

waucht[1.2], **wacht**, †**waught** /wɔxt, waxt/ *v* to drink (a great amount of) alcohol, drink deeply, drain *16-19, 20- EC*. **waucht oot** to empty, drain (a glass) of drink *la16-19, 20- EC*. [probably onomatopoeic]

waucht see WECHT[1.1]

waud see WAD[2]

wauer see WAVER

wauf see WAFF[2.2], WAUCH

wauff see WAFF[1.2]

wauge see WAGE[1.1], WAGE[1.2]

wauger see WAGER[1.2]

waugh see WAUCH

waught see WAUCHT[1.1], WAUCHT[1.2]

waugram see WAGHORN

wauk[1.1], **wake**, †**walk**, †**wak**, †**waik** /wɔk, wak, wek/ *n* **1** a vigil over a corpse *la14-*. **2** the action of watching; guard duty *la14*. **3** *pl* a small band of musicians, maintained by a town to play in the streets, usually at Christmas and New Year *la19*. **4** a serenade, a midnight concert *e19*. [OE *(niht)-wacu* (night)-watch]

wauk[1.2], **wake**, **waak**, †**walk**, †**wak**, †**vaik** /wɔk, wak, wek, wak/ *v pt* **woke**, †**woik**, †**wouk 1** to wake up, awaken from sleep *la14-*. **2** to be or remain awake (all night), be sleepless *la14-*. **3** to guard, watch over (property or livestock), tend, especially during the night; to stand guard; to be on the lookout *la14-*. **4** to stay up all night with, watch over (a sick person or corpse) *la14-*. **5** to be diligent, alert, wary; to be vigilant, watch out; to pay attention *la15-16*. †**waking and warding** = *watching and warding* (WATCH[1.2]) *la15-e16*. [OE **wacan, wacian*]

wauk see WALK[2.2], WAULK

wauken, **waken**, †**walkin**, †**waikin** /'wɔkən, 'wakən, 'wekən/ *v* **1** to arouse (oneself or another) from sleep, wake *la14-*. **2** to rouse, stir up *la15-*. **3** *law* to revive (a legal process) in which no action has been taken for a year *la16-*; compare SLEEP[1.2] (sense 3). **4** to watch (over), guard *la15-e16*.

waukened awake *20-*. †**walkiner**, **walknar 1** a person or thing that rouses or stirs up *16-17*. **2** an alarm attached to a clock *la16-e17*. **waukenin 1** the action of wakening or rousing *15-*. **2** the action of reviving a legal process; an instance of this *la16-*. **3** a severe reproof, a dressing-down *19-*. **wauken on** to lose one's temper with *19, 20- Ork N NE T*. [OE *wæcnan, wæcnian*]

wauker see WAULKER

waukrife, *Uls* **wakerife**, †**walkrife**, †**walkryfe**, †**waikrife** /'wɔkrɪf, 'wakrɪf, 'wɔkrʌɪf; *Uls* 'wekrɪf/ *adj* **1** disinclined or unable to sleep; able to do with little sleep *la15-*. **2** watchful, alert, vigilant *la15-*. **3** easily awakened, lightly sleeping *19, 20- Ork NE T*. **waukrifeness** sleeplessness, insomnia; vigilance *la16-19*. [WAUK[1.2] + -RIFE]

waukster see WALKSTER

waul[1], †**wawl** /wɔl/ *v* **1** *of the eyes* to roll wildly *e16, 19- Bor*. **2** to roll the eyes, look (at someone) with wide rolling eyes in a stupid, surprised or aggressive way *e16, 19- Bor*. **3** to move with a rolling motion *la15*. Compare WAVEL. [variant of WAVEL; for the sense compare WAVILL]

waul[2] /wɔl/ *adj* supple, nimble, agile *19- Bor*. [probably an altered form of YAULD, perhaps with influence from WALLIE[1.2]]

waul see WALE[1.1], WALE[1.2]

wauld see WALD[1], WALL[2]

waulk, **wauk**, †**walk**, †**wack**, †**wake** /wɔk/ *v* **1** to full (cloth), make (cloth) thick and felted by a process of soaking, beating and shrinking *la15-*. **2** *of cloth* to shrink as a result of being wetted *19-*. **waukit 1** *of cloth* fulled, thickened by fulling; shrunk *la15-*. **2** *of skin* hardened, roughened, calloused *la18-*. **waulking song** a Gaelic song sung to provide a suitable rhythm for the team of women engaged in fulling cloth, a song belonging to this tradition *la19-*. **wauk mill**, †**walkmyln** a mill for fulling cloth *15-*. [OE *wealcian* to roll, or back-formation from WAULKER; compare WALK[2.2]]

waulker, **wauker**, †**walker**, †**walkar**, †**waker** /'wɔkər/ *n* a fuller of cloth *la14-*. Compare WALKSTER. [OE *wealcere*]

waum, †**wame**, †**wem**, †**wan** /wɔm/ *n* a scar, a blemish, a bruise *la14-16, 19-*. [OE *wamm*]

waumish /'wɔmɪʃ/ *adj* faint, nauseous, dizzy, out of sorts *la19- T EC Uls*. [unknown; compare Eng †*walm* the bubbling and heaving of water]

waumle see WAMMLE[1.1], WAMMLE[1.2]

waun see WAND[1.1]

wauner see WANNER[1]

waunert see WANNERT

waup see WAP[1.1]

waur[1.1], **war**, †**wer** /wɔr, war, wʌr/ *n* the worse, that which is inferior, less desirable or more reprehensible *la14-*. **come by the waur** to come off worst, get the worst of something *19, 20- Sh N*. †**get the war** = *come by the waur 16*. †**hae the war** = *come by the waur la14-e15*. **win the waur** = *come by the waur la18-19, 20- Sh N*. [see the adj]

waur[1.2], **war**, †**wer** /wɔr, war, wʌr/ *v* **1** to defeat, get the better of, overcome; to outdo, surpass *15-*. **2** to damage, harm *15*. [see the adj]

waur[1.3], **war**, *Sh* **wer**, †**wor** /wɔr, war, wʌr; *Sh* wer/ *adj* **1** worse, inferior *la14-*. **2** in poorer condition or health *la15-*. **waurer** worse *18-*. **the waur o**, †**the waur of** the worse for, in a less favourable position than *16-*. [ON *verre*]

waur[1.4], **war**, †**wer** /wɔr, war, wʌr/ *adv* worse *la14-*. **waurfaured**, **waur-faurt**, †**waur-far'd** more ill-favoured, uglier *la18-19, 20- Ork NE T*. [ON *verr*]

waur see WARE[1.1], WARE[2.2], WARE[3]

waut see WALT[1.1]

wauther see WEATHER

wave /wev/ *n* a swivel-catch on the jamb of a door which opens outwards *20- Sh*. [compare Swed dial *veiv* a revolving wooden door-handle]

wave see WAFF[1.1], WAFF[1.2]

wavel, *Sh* **waavel** /'wevəl; *Sh* 'wavəl/ *v* **1** to rock unsteadily, sway to and fro, stagger *17-19, 20- Sh NE T*. **2** to flutter, waver, wag to and fro, move (with a rolling, waving motion) *16-17, 20- Sh NE*. Compare WAUL[1]. [frequentative form of *wave* (WAFF[1.2])]

wavengeour see WAFFINGER

waver, †**wauer** /'wevər/ *v* **1** to move indecisively; to vacillate *la14-*. **2** *of water or waves* to surge *e15*. **3** to move erratically, totter, stagger *16*. †**waverand**, **wawerand 1** wandering, moving erratically *la14-16*. **2** unreliable, unstable, inconstant; fleeting, changeable *la14-e17*. †**waver fra** to stray; to wander *la15-e17*. [ON *vafra* to move unsteadily, flicker]

†**wavill** *adj of the feet* twisted *16*. **wawill-eit** having mismatched eyes *la15*. [see the verb WAVEL]

waw[1.1] /wɔ/ *n* the sound made by a cat or child in distress *19, 20- NE*. [onomatopoeic]

waw[1.2] /wɔ/ *v* to mew, caterwaul, wail *la18-19, 20- Ork NE*. [see the noun]

†**waw[2]**, **wall** *n* a measure of weight, of twelve stones, used of merchandise and other materials *la14-e17*. [MLG, MDu *wage*]

†**waw**³, **wall** *n* a wave (of the sea) *la14-19*. [see the verb *waw* (WAFF¹·²); compare WALIE]
waw *see* WA¹·¹, WAFF¹·²
wawart *see* VAWARD
wawl *see* WAUL¹
†**wawsper, wasper, vauch spear** *n* a (salmon-)fishing spear *la15-e17*. [*waw* (WAFF¹·²) + SPEAR]
wax¹, †**walx**, †**vax** /waks/ *n* **1** wax, beeswax *la14-*. **2** a seal (made of wax) *15-16*. †**waxy** made of wax *16*. †**vax-cayme** a honeycomb *la14*. **wax cloth** canvas cloth coated with wax used especially for floor and table coverings; oilcloth; linoleum *19-*. †**waxt buittis** boots dressed with wax *la16-17*. [OE *weax*]
wax², †**walx**, †**vax** /waks/ *v pt* also †**woux, wox, wolx**, *ptp* also †**walxyn** to increase in size or number; to grow, become, turn into (something) *la14-*. **waxen kernel, waxing kernal** a swollen gland or boil *18-*. †**wax with child** to become pregnant *la15*. †**wax full** = *wax with child e16*. [OE *weaxan*]
way /we/ *interj* **1** a call to a sheepdog to make a detour or move away from the sheep *20-*. **2** a call to a horse to stop *la19- T WC Bor*; compare WO. [probably an aphetic form of *away* (AWA¹·¹)]
way *see* WA²·¹, WA²·², WAE¹·³, WEY¹
wayburn leaf *see* WAAVERIN LAEF
waygaeing *see* WA-GAUN¹·¹
waygang *see* WA-GANG
waygoing *see* WA-GAUN¹·¹
way-going *see* WA-GAUN¹·²
waym *see* WAME¹·¹
†**waymentyng, womenting** *n* lamentation *la15-*. [verbal noun from ME *waimenten*, OFr *waimenter*, with influence from WAE¹·¹]
†**waynd, wand, wane** *v* to hesitate; to refrain *la14-16*. [OE *wandian*]
wayr *see* WARE¹·²
†**wayre** *adj* varied or variegated in colour *e15*. [OFr *vair*, Lat *varius*]
Waysiders /ˈwesʌɪdərz/ *npl* a nickname for Airdrieonians Football Club *20, 21 historical*. [from the name *Wayside Club* given to the club by one of its players]
wayt *see* WAIT¹·²
waywart /ˈwewərt/ *adj* wayward, disobedient, perverse; perverted *e16, 19- C*. [aphetic form of Older Scots *awaywart away*, off adv, *away* (AWA¹·¹) + -*wart* suffix]
wazz *see* WEASE
wazzin *see* WIZZEN
we, *C SW Bor* **oo**, †**wee**, †**ve** /wi; *C SW Bor* also u/ *pron* **1** *used as subject* denoting the speaker and one or more others associated as the protagonist of whatever is said, we *la14-*. **2** *mainly in documents* denoting a single person, a ruler or person in high authority *la14-*. **3** *used as object* = US *la19- Ork T EC Bor*. **we's** we shall *la18-19, 20- NE*. [OE *we*, OE *woe*]
we *see* WEE¹·¹, WEE¹·², WI
weal *see* WALL², WEEL²
wealnesse *see* WEEL¹·¹
wealth *see* WALTH
weam *see* WAME¹·¹
wean, wain, wane, †**we'an**, †**wyne** /wen/ *n* a (young) child *la16-*. **weanish** childish *20- C SW*. **weanly** = *weanish 19- C SW*. [reduced form of WEE¹·² + ANE¹·¹]
weap *see* WAP²·²
weapon *see* WAPPEN
weaponshaw *see* WAPPENSHAW
weaponshawing *see* WAPPENSHAWING

wear, werr, weer, weir, †**wer**, †**were** /wer, wɛr, wir/ *v pt* **wore**, *Sh* **wure**, *H&I* **weered**, †**wour**, †**woir**, †**wair**, †**weer**, †**weir**, *ptp* **worn, wurn**, †**wore 1** to wear, be dressed in, carry on one's person *la14-*. **2** to (cause to) deteriorate, decay, erode; to (cause to) become weak or infirm *15-*. **3** to go or proceed (slowly and cautiously) *la15-19, 20- Sh Ork NE T EC*. **wearin cheena** everyday crockery *20- Ork SW*. **wearin claes**, †**wering clathis** clothing for everyday use *la16-*. **wear aff 1** to go away quietly, slip away; to crumble; to die *la18, 20- Sh*. **2** to pay off (a debt) gradually *la19, 20- T*. **wear awa 1** = *wear aff* **1** *19, 20- Ork NE T*. **2** to pass away, die *19-*. **3** = WEAR (sense 3). **wear doon** to grow old *19, 20- Ork NE*. **wear doon the brae** = *wear doon*. **wear in by** to approach *la18, 20- T EC*. **weer in o** to get the hang of *la19- NE*. **wear intae** to proceed (slowly or gradually); to approach *19, 20- NE Uls*. **wear on 1** to be advancing in age, grow older *20- Ork N NE T EC*. **2** = *wear intae la19, 20- Ork*. **wear oot** *of news* to leak out *19, 20- Sh*. †**wear out** to cause to fly or flutter *la15*. **wear oot o** to lose touch, become estranged *18, 20- NE*. **wear ower 1** *of time* to grow late *la19- NE T EC*. **2** *of persons* = *wear on* **2** *20- Sh NE*. **wear roun** to prevail on, get round, persuade *la19, 20- Sh Ork*. **wear throu 1** to get through a task by degrees *20- Ork N NE T*. **2** to waste, consume *la19- NE T*. **wear tae** *weather* to show signs of changing, turn to *20- NE WC*. †**wear yer wa, wear yer wa's** *in the North East* to make one's way, make off *la18-19*. **wear up** to grow, advance in time, age or amount *la18-19, 20- Sh NE*. **wear a petticoat** to be a woman *19-*. [OE *werian*]
weary¹·¹ /ˈwiri/ *n* a curse, an invocation *la18-*. **weary fa** *used to express exasperation* damn!, the devil take ... *la18-19, 20- Uls*. †**weary on** = *weary fa e19*. **weary tak** = *weary fa la19*. **da weary o'd** the devil of it, the annoying thing about it *la19- Sh Ork*. [see the adj]
weary¹·², †**wery** /ˈwiri/ *v* **1** to become tired *la15-*. **2** to become bored, discontented or listless *la15-*. **3** to make tired or exhaust; to trouble, vex *la16-e19*. **weary for** to long for, yearn for *19-*. [OE *wērgian* to weary, exhaust]
weary¹·³, †**wery**, †**werie** /ˈwiri/ *adj* **1** tired, exhausted, worn out *la14-*. **2** depressing, dispiriting *18-19, 20- Sh NE SW*. **3** sickly, puny, weak, feeble; paltry, insignificant *la14-19*. **4** *of persons* sad, miserable, dispirited, wretched *la15-18*. **5** annoying, troublesome *18-*. **6** causing tiredness *la16-e17*. **wearifu** troublesome, annoying, vexatious; sad, dismal *18-19, 20- NE*. **weariness**, †**werynes**, †**weirines** exhaustion, tiredness *la14-*. **weary warroch** a good-for-nothing *19- NE T EC*. [OE *wērig*]
wease, *N* **wazz**, *NE* **weyse**, *EC Bor* **weeze** /wis; *N* waz; *NE* wʌɪs; *EC Bor* wiz/ *n* **1** *mining* packing in the joints of metal water-pipes *la19-*. **2** a pad used to relieve pressure when carrying heavy weights on the head *19- NE EC Bor*. **3** a bundle of straw, especially for thatching *la18- NE T*. **4** a horse-collar; *humorous* a bulky necktie, collar or scarf *19- Ork N*. **5** (a bundle of twigs, brushwood or straw placed against a cottage door as) a windbreak or draught-excluder *e19*. †**weasie** a straw collar or pad used in the harness of oxen *17*. **wassock**, *NE* **wussock**, *WC* **wussuck 1** tuft, tussock, wisp; a tangle *20- NE*. **2** = WEASE (sense 5) *la19- WC SW Uls*. **3** the laths in a lath and plaster wall *20- WC*. **4** bushy, unkempt hair or whiskers *20- WC*. [ME *wase* a bundle of straw, MDu *wase* a bundle, straw pad; compare WASSIE]
weased *see* WEEST
weasel, *C Bor* **wheasel, wheesel, whaizle**, †**weazel**, †**wasyll**, †**quhasill** /ˈwizəl; *C Bor* ˈmizəl, ˈmezəl/ *n* **1** the weasel *Mustela nivalis la15-*. **2** a sharp, restless, prying, sneaky person *la19-*. †**weasel-blawn** *of an animal* affected

weason see WIZZEN

weather, wather, wedder, *Sh* **wadder,** *NE* **widder,** *NE EC* **wither,** *SW* **wauther,** †**weddir,** †**wethir,** †**wathir** /'wɛðər, 'waðər, 'wɛðər; *Sh* 'wɑðər; *NE* 'wɪðər; *NE EC* 'wɪðər; *SW* 'wɔðər/ *n* **1** atmospheric conditions *la14-.* **2** bad weather, wet stormy weather, rain or snow with blustery winds, rain *15-.* **3** favourable or seasonable weather (suitable for a particular purpose) *la14-17, 20- Sh Ork NE.* **4** circumstances, prevailing conditions *19- H&I WC Bor.* **weatherfu** stormy, wet and windy *19- Bor.* †**weather days** a period or occasion of a particular sort of weather *la15-e19.* **weathergaw 1** an atmospheric appearance regarded as a portent of bad weather *18-.* **2** a bright calm spell between two periods of bad weather thought to indicate snow *19- NE Bor.* **wedderglim, weather-gleam 1** (a band of clear sky above the horizon often visible at) twilight *19-.* **2** a place exposed to the elements *la19- NE.* **wadder-head** a bank or pillar of cloud *la19- Sh.* **wadder-mooth** a cloud formation in which long trails of cloud appear to converge making a mouth-like shape *la19- Ork N.* **this weather** just now, at the moment *20- NE H&I C Bor.* [OE *weder*]

weave, *NE T* **wyve,** †**weve,** †**weif** /wiv; *NE T* wʌɪv/ *v presp* also †**wefand,** *pt* **wove,** *NE* **weave,** *Bor* **wuive,** *NE* **weivt,** *ptp* **woven,** *NE* **wivven,** *Bor* **wuven,** *NE T* **weyvt,** †**wovyn,** †**wiffen,** †**woffen,** †**weif 1** to make (cloth) by interlacing yarns, weave *15-.* **2** to knit *la17-19, 20- NE T.* **3** to make the mesh work of (a herring net) *20- NE T.* **weavin** (a piece of) knitting *la18, 19- NE T.* †**in a weavin** in a moment, in a jiffy *18-e19.* [OE *wefan*]

weaver, *NE T* **wyver,** †**wevar** /'wivər; *NE T* 'wʌɪvər/ *n* **1** a person who makes cloth by weaving *la15-.* **2** a spider *19-;* compare WABSTER. **3** a knitter *19- NE.* **weaver-kneed 1** knock-kneed *20- C SW.* **2** having sensitive or ticklish knees *20- WC.* [WEAVE, with agent suffix]

weazel see WEASEL
web see WAB
webster see WABSTER
wech see WITCH¹·¹, WITCH¹·²
weche see WATCH¹·¹
wecht¹·¹, weicht, weight, *NE* **wacht,** *NE* **waucht,** †**weght,** †**wycht,** †**weiht** /wɛxt, wext, wet; *NE* waxt, wɔxt/ *n* **1** relative heaviness, weight, mass *la14-.* **2** physical force, impetus created by the movement of a heavy object, *eg* in propelling a curling-stone *la14-.* **3** a quantity (of something) determined by its weight *15-.* **4** an object having a standard heaviness used for weighing goods *15-.* **5** seriousness, gravity, importance *la15-.* **6** a heaviness or burden of oppressive feelings, suffering or pain *16-.* **7** *pl* a set of scales *19-.* **8** a large amount, a great number (of things) *la19-.* **9** coinage the correct or lawful weight for a particular coin *la15-17.* **10** a system for weighing (goods) *15-17;* compare *tron weight* (TRON¹·¹), TROIS. †**of wecht** *of coins* of correct or lawful weight *la15-17.* [OE *wiht*, with vowel influenced by ON *vétt*]

wecht¹·², weight, /wɛxt, wext/ *v* **1** to ascertain the weight of; to evaluate, judge (according to a standard); to have weight or heaviness *17-.* **2** to oppress (the mind) *17-e18.* **3** to add weight to, weigh down, increase the burden on, press down by weight *la19-.* [see the noun]

wecht², weicht, †**waicht** /wɛxt, wext/ *n* a wooden hoop with skin or canvas stretched over it, mainly used for carrying grain or potatoes, originally used for winnowing corn *la16-19, 20- Sh N NE T SW Uls.* †**wechtfu** the amount contained in a WECHT², used as a measure *19.* [perhaps a specif usage of WECHT¹·¹, originally denoting a container made to hold a certain weight of grain]

wechtie see WECHTY
wechty, wechtie, *NE* **waichty,** †**weghty,** †**wichty,** †**weichtie** /'wɛxte; *NE* 'wexte/ *adj* **1** heavy *16-.* **2** serious, important, solemn *la15-.* **3** onerous, burdensome *la16-.* **4** *of persons or animals* physically heavy and solidly corpulent *19, 20- NE.* [WECHT¹·¹ + -IE²]

wed see WAD¹·¹, WAD¹·², WADE², WEED¹·¹, WEED¹·², WEED²
wedder, wether, wather, †**weddir,** †**woddir,** †**wadder** /'wɛdər, 'wɛðər, 'waðər/ *n* an immature or castrated male sheep *13-.* †**wedder bouk** the carcass of a wether *16.* †**wether gammond** a leg of mutton *la18.* †**weddergang** a (range of) sheep pasture; also in place-names *la16-e17.* †**wether haggis** a haggis boiled in the stomach of a wedder *la18.* †**wether head** the head of a wedder; a stupid person *la18.* **wedder lamb** a (castrated or immature) male lamb *16-.* **wether-hogg** a young castrated male sheep *18-.* †**wadder silver** money in lieu of a wether paid as a customary rent or tax *la16.* [OE *weðer*]

wedder see WEATHER
weddin, wedding see WADDIN¹
Weddinisday see WEDNESDAY
weddir see WEATHER, WEDDER
†**wede, weid** *v* **1** to be or become insane *la14-16.* **2** to rage, behave in a frenzied manner, go wild with fury or ferocity *15-e16.* **wedand** raving, frenzied, furious *la14-e15.* [OE *wēdan*]

wede see WEED¹·¹, WEED¹·², WEED²
wedeen see WADDIN¹
wedge see WADGE¹·¹, WADGE¹·², WAGE¹·¹
Wednesday, Wensday, Widdinsday, Wadensday, Wadnesday, *Bor* **Wodensday,** †**Wednysday,** †**Weddinisday,** †**Wodnisday** /'wɛdənzde, 'wɛnzde, 'wɪdənzde, 'wadənzde; *Bor* 'wodənzde/ *n* the day after Tuesday, the fourth day of the week *la14-.* †**the Wednesdays** the five winter (cattle-)markets held on a Wednesday, *la18-19.* **Big Wednesday** see BIG². [OE *wōdnesdæg* literally, Woden's day]

Wednysday see WEDNESDAY
wedo see WEEDA
wedonynpha see WEIDINONFA
wedow see WEEDA
wedset see WADSET¹·¹, WADSET¹·²
wedy see WIDDIE

wee¹·¹, †**we,** †**wie,** †**wy** /wi/ *n* **1** a short time, a moment *la14-.* **2** a small amount, a bit; a short distance *la14-.* †**a little wee** see LITTLE¹·². [OE *wēge* a weight]

wee¹·², †**we,** †**wie,** †**wy** /wi/ *adj* **1** small, little *la15-.* **2** *as intensifier with nouns meaning 'a small amount'* (very) small, tiny *18-.* **3** *football* the reserve team: ◊ *wee Celtic 20-;* compare *the wee Rangers.* **little wee** see LITTLE¹·². **wee ane,** †**wie-one** a (young) child, a little one *la17-;* compare WEAN. **wee boukit** of small size, physically small *la19- C.* **wee boy, wee boay** term of address to a small boy or small man *la20- C.* **wee coal** a shallow seam coal *19- WC SW.* **wee hairy, wee herry** a woman from the slums, thought to be promiscuous; a prostitute *la20-.* Compare HAIRY¹·¹. **wee hauf, wee half 1** a nip (35 ml) of spirits *la20-.* **2** originally a nip of spirits, a small whisky, usually a fifth of an imperial gill, and less than half a gill *la19-20.* **3** a half-pint of beer *la20-;* compare *half and a half* (HALF¹·¹). **wee heavy** a type of strong beer, usually sold in small bottles of 1/3 pint (approx. 0.2 litre) *20-.* **wee hoose** an earth-closet, an outside toilet *20-.* **wee heidies** a game of *heidies* (HEIDIE¹·¹) played in a confined space such as a common stair *la20-.* **wee lassie** a young girl *la19-*. **wee man 1** the devil ◊*in the name o the wee man 20-*. **2** term of endearment or address used to a small person or child *la20-*. **3** the penis *la20-*. **4** a man of below average height *la19-*. **5** an odd-job man *20- WC SW*. †**wee pawn** an unlicensed pawnbroker, often one engaged in illicit dealings *19*. **the wee Rangers** nickname for Berwick Rangers Football Club *la20-*. **wee refreshment** a small alcoholic drink *la20-*. **wee schule 1** the infant or junior department in a school *la19-*. **2** a primary school (as opposed to a secondary school) *la20-*. **wee sma** very small *20-*. **wee team** a reserve football team *la20-*. **wee thing** a small child or person *18-*. **wee tottie**, **wee toattie** extremely small *20-*. **wee wee** very small, tiny *18-*. **wee wee man** a very small or tiny man, an elf *la18-*. **wee yin 1** a young child *20-*. **2** a dram, a drink of spirits *20-*. **a wee bit 1** a small amount; to a small extent, somewhat, rather *la18-*. **2** describing something on a small scale; not out of the ordinary: ◊*a wee bit land* ◊*a wee-bit pot, an a wee-bit pan* ◊*a wee bit collie dug 18-*. **a wee half and half** a nip of whisky with a half-pint of beer chaser *la20-*. **wee sma oors** the early hours of the morning, just after midnight *20-*; compare *sma oors* (SMA[1.2]). **a wee thing** a small amount, a bit; somewhat, rather, a little *la18-*. **a wee thingie** = *a wee thing*. **the wee boy** see the *boy* (BOY). [see the noun]

wee[2.1] /wi/ *n* a squeal or neigh *20- Ork*. [see the verb]
wee[2.2] /wi/ *v* to squeal; to neigh *20- Ork*. [onomatopoeic]
wee see WE, WEY[2.2]
weeack[1.1] /'wiək/ *n* a squeak, squeal, high-pitched utterance *19- NE*. [see the verb]
weeack[1.2], **weik** /'wiək, wik/ *v* to chirp, whine, speak or sing in a thin squeaky voice *18- NE*. [onomatopoeic]
weebie, **weebo**, **weepie** /'wibi, 'wibo, 'wipi/ *n pl* ragwort *Jacobaea vulgaris 19- T EC*. [unknown]
weed[1.1], †**weid**, †**wede**, †**wed** /wid/ *n* a noxious or unwanted plant *la15-*. **weedock**, †**weedick**, †**weidok**, †**weidheuk** a hooked implement for cutting weeds; a weapon *la16-19, 20- T EC*. [OE *wēod*]
weed[1.2], †**weid**, †**wede**, †**wed** /wid/ *v pt* also **wed**, **wede 1** to clear (land) of weeds; to thin or weed (woodland) *la15-*. **2** to remove (weeds) *la16-*. **wede awa** to remove, carry off, especially by death *la18- literary*. [OE *wēodian*]
weed[2], †**wede**, †**wed**, †**weid** /wid/ *n* **1** dress, apparel; distinctive clothing; a garment or cloak; *pl* clothes; armour; mourning clothes *la14-*. **2** foliage *15-e16*. **3** the language, style or vocabulary of a literary work *la15-e16*. **4** the attributes or behaviour of a person *16*. [OE *wǣd*]
weed[3] /wid/ *n* **1** a high fever, a sudden feverish attack; puerperal fever *la18-*. **2** a chill *19-*. **3** *in farm animals* a feverish ailment thought to have been caused by a chill; *in female animals* mastitis *19-*. [shortened form of WEIDINONFA]
weeda, **weedy**, **widow**, †**wedow**, †**wedo**, †**weido** /'wida, 'wide, 'wɪdo/ *n* a man or woman whose spouse is dead *la14-*. †**wedowhed**, **widowheid**, **widowhood** the state of being a widow *la14-19*. †**widowity**, **viduity** widowhood *la15-18*. **widow-man** = WIDOW *la16-*. **widow-wumman** = WIDOW *16-*. [OE *weoduwe, widuwe*]
weedgie, **weedjie** see WEEGIE
Wee Free *n* (a member of) the minority of the Free Church of Scotland, which refused to enter the Union with the United Presbyterian Church in 1900 and which continues under its original name *20-*. [WEE[1.2] + FREE[1.1]]
weeg /wig/ *n* the kittiwake *Rissa tridactyla 19- Sh*. [onomatopoeic of the bird's call]
weegaldie-waggaldie see WEEGLTIE-WAGGLTIE
weegie, **weedgie**, **weedjie** /'wɪdʒe/ *n* a Glaswegian *la20-*. [reduced form of *Glaswegian* + -IE[1]]

weegle[1.1], **wiggle** /'wigəl, 'wɪgəl/ *n* a wiggling movement *19-*. [see the verb]
weegle[1.2], **wiggle** /'wigəl, 'wɪgəl/ *v* to move to and fro; to jiggle, wriggle; to waddle *19-*. [MLG *wiggelen*]
weegltie-waggltie, **wigglety-wagglety**, *Ork* **weegaldie-waggaldie** /'wigəlti'wagəlti, 'wɪgəlte'wagəlte; *Ork* 'wigəldi'wagəldi/ *adj* very unstable, tottery; unsteady *19-*. [WEEGLE[1.2] + WAGGLE[1.2] with adj-forming suffixes]
weegly-waggly /'wɪglɪ'waglɪ/ *adj* waggling, unstable *19, 20- EC Bor*. [WEEGLE[1.2] + WAGGLE[1.2] with -IE[2] adj-forming suffixes]
week[1], **wick**, †**weik** /wik, wɪk/ *n* a candle or lamp wick *la15-*. [OE *wēoce*]
week[2], *NE* **ouk**, *Sh NE SW* **ook**, *NE EC* **wick**, †**wouk**, †**wolk**, †**oulk** /wik; *Sh NE SW* uk; *NE EC* wɪk/ *n* a period of seven consecutive days *la14-*. **weekday 1** a day other than Saturday or Sunday *la15-*. **2** a day of the week other than market-day *la15-17*. †**oukis penny** the weekly contribution to the funds of an incorporation made by its members *la15-16*. [OE *wice, wiece, uke*]
week see WICK[1]
weekly[1.1], *NE* **ookly**, *NE* **wikkly** /'wikle; *NE* 'ukli; *NE* 'wɪkle/ *n* a weekly paper or magazine *20-*. [see the adj]
weekly[1.2], †**ookly**, †**wolklie**, †**oukly** /'wikle/ *adj* that is done or occurs once a week *16-*. †**oukly penny** the weekly contribution to the funds of an incorporation made by its members *la15-17*. [WEEK[2] with adj-forming suffix]
weekly[1.3], †**wolklie**, †**ouklie** /'wikle/ *adv* per week, weekly *la15-*. [WEEK[2] with adv-forming suffix]
weel[1.1], **well**, †**wele**, †**wel**, †**weill** /wil, wɛl/ *adj* **1** *used predicatively* good; proper, fitting, suitable *la14-*. **2** healthy *la16-*. **3** *of food* cooked, ready to eat *19, 20- H&I Bor*. **4** fortunate, lucky; happy *15-17*. **weelness**, †**wealnesse** good health *la17-*. **weel foggit** well-off as the result of thrift *18- NE T*. †**it's very weel** = *it's weel and weel eneuch e19*. **it's weel and weel eneuch** it's all very well *20- N NE*. **weel at anesel** in good physical condition, plump, stout *la18-*. **weel I wat**, †**weel wat I** I know, indeed, I must say, I can tell you *18-*. **weel tae be seen** having a good appearance, very presentable *20- Sh NE SW*. **weel-saired** well satisfied with food or drink *la18-19, 20- NE*. †**weel to live** in comfortable circumstances, well-off; tipsy *19*. †**weel to pass** affluent, prosperous *19*. †**weel to pass in the warld** affluent, prosperous *19*. **weel upon't** = *weel to live la19- NE*. †**weel weel** may you be fortunate, good luck *15-19*. [see the adv]
weel[1.2], **well**, †**wele**, †**weill**, †**wail** /wil, wɛl/ *adv* **1** in accordance with a high standard, to a high degree, satisfactorily, properly, successfully; safely; certainly; completely *la14-*. **2** *as intensifier* fully, very, rather, quite, much *la14-*. **3** as might be expected, with good reason *la14-*. **4** fully, not less than *la14-e17*. **weel amis** well deserved, merited *20- Ork*. †**wele bakyn** *of bread* properly or thoroughly baked *15-e17*. †**wele bekend** well-known, familiar *e16*. **wele beknaw** = *wele bekend* †**wele besene** well dressed, well equipped; attractive in appearance *la15-16*. **weel boukit** well-sized *16-*. **weel come 1** arriving at an opportune moment, welcome *la19, 20- NE*. **2** *of persons* of good lineage, of honourable parentage *la18*. **weel-comed** = *weel come 2 20- NE SW*. **weel-daein** well-to-do, prosperous *19-*. †**weel-farrant** of pleasant appearance or behaviour *la14-15, la19*. **weel-faured**, †**weel-fard**, †**weel-favourit** *of persons* **1** good-looking *la15-*. **2** decent, respectable *19-*. †**weel faurdly** in a decent, proper or pleasant way *la18-19*. **weel fells...** lucky is... *la18-19 NE*. †**weel-hained 1** *of persons* well preserved, in good shape *18-19*. **2** used sparingly

or economically, assiduously saved *la18-19*. **weel-handit** dexterous; competent *19-*. **weel happit** well covered up, well-protected, wrapped up against the cold *19-*. **weel-hauden-in** saved to good purpose *la19- NE*. †**weel-hertit 1** courageous *la15-18*. **2** good-hearted, generous, liberal *la18-19*. †**weel lookit** good-looking, handsome *18-19*. **weel lookit tae** well-looked-after, blessed by fortune *la19, 20- NE*. †**weel-natured 1** good-natured, kindly and amiable *la18-19*. **2** well-disposed *la17*. **weel-peyd 1** very satisfactory, well remunerated *la17-*. **2** thoroughly beaten *18-19*. **weel pit on** smartly dressed *19-*. **weel pitten on** = *weel pit on*. **well-redd-up** clean and tidy *19-*. **weel seen 1** evident, plainly visible *18-*. **2** well-versed, proficient, very knowledgeable in *la17-19*. **weel set 1** well placed or firmly established *la19-*. **2** morally sound, of good intention, well disposed *la15-17*. **3** well matured *e18*. **weel-thriven** well-grown, plump *20- Sh SW Bor*. **weel-tochtid** thinking well of, having a good opinion of *20- Sh*. **weel usit** well practised or exercised *la15*. †**wele willit** = *weel-willie la15-19*. **weel-willie** eager, ready, well disposed *la14-*. †**wele willing, wele willand** *adj* eager, ready, well disposed *la14-e17*. †**wele willing, wele willand** *n* a well-disposed, compliant person, a well-wisher *15-16*. **weel and warl-like** *of a new-born baby* normal physically and mentally *20-*. **weel-gaithered** rich, well-to-do *la19- NE T Bor*. †**weel's me on** happy am I (because of), blessings on *18-e19*. †**weel is on** = *weel's me on 19*. **weel lo'es me o** blessings on, good luck to *la18*. †**weel to pass in the warld** affluent, prosperous *19*. **weel to pass** = *weel to pass in the warld*. **weel upon't** = *weel to live la19- NE*. **that's weel mindit** what a good thing that you remembered *18-*. **the weel warst** the very worst, the worst of the lot *la17-19, 20- NE* †**weel to live** comfortably off *19*. Z [OE *wel*, ON *val*]

weel[1.3], **well,** †**weill** /wil, wɛl/ *interj introducing a remark or qualifying something said previously, frequently little more than a resumptive word* well! *la15-*. **well a well** very well, all right *la18-*. **weel than, well then,** *SW* **wi than,** †**waethan 1** right, okay; all right then *la18-*. **2** *emphatic affirmative* very much so *20- NE*. **weel weel** reduplication of WEEL[1.3]. [see the adv]

weel[2], **weal,** †**wele,** †**weill** /wil/ *n* **1** wellbeing, happiness, welfare (of a group or community) *la14-*. **2** a benefit, favour or advantage *16-17*. **3** what is good, virtue *15-e17*. **4** prosperity, wealth *15*. **5** a commonwealth, state, community *16*. [OE *wela*]

weel[3], **wiel,** †**weill,** †**well** /wil/ *n pl also* **welis** a deep pool; an eddy, a whirlpool; frequently in place-names *la12-*. [OE *wǣl*]

weel *see* WALL[2], WIELD

weel-a-day *see* WALLY-DYE

weelfare, welfare, †**weilfair,** †**welefare** /'wilfər, 'welfər/ *n* **1** good fortune, success, prosperity; wellbeing, happiness *la14-*. **2** material abundance, good cheer *la14-15*. [WEEL[1.2] + FARE[1.1]]

weel-kent, weill-kent, weel-kenned /wil'kɛnt, wil'kɛnd/ *adj* well-known, familiar *la18-*. [WEEL[1.2] + KENT[1]]

weem /wim/ *n* **1** a cave, a natural cavity in the ground or in a rock, also in place-names *18-19*. **2** an Iron Age underground storehouse, mainly in the form of a curved slab-lined passageway *18- Sh NE T*. [Gael †*uaim*, MIrGael *uaim*]

weemen *see* WOMAN

†**ween**[1.1], †**wene** *n* doubt *la14-16*. [OE *wēn* opinion, supposition]

ween[1.2], †**wene,** †**weyn,** †**wein** /win/ *v pt* †**wend,** †**weind,** †**wount** *v* **1** to surmise, suppose, think *la14-19, 20- literary*. **2** to expect, anticipate, hope *la14-17*. [OE *wēnan*]

ween *see* WIND[1.1], WIND[1.2]

weeng *see* WING

weenkle *see* WINGLE[1.2]

weenth /winθ/ *n* width *20- WC SW*. [altered form of Eng *width* by analogy with breenth (BRENTH)]

weep *see* WIPE[1.2]

weeper /'wipər/ *n* a small cross-wall between the sleeper walls in the foundation of a house, constructed so as to direct the ventilation through the foundations and dry out condensation *la20- EC SW*. [Eng *weep* to exude moisture + instrumental suffix]

weepie *see* WEEBIE

weer, †**were,** †**weir,** †**wer** /wir/ *n* **1** danger, jeopardy *la14-16*. **2** (a) doubt, uncertainty, apprehension; dread *la14-17, 18- NE*. **3** a doubtful or difficult point of law *15-17*. **werefull** doubtful *la15*. **but were** without doubt *la14-e17*. **the weers o** in danger of, on the brink of, just about to *la19- NE*. [perhaps extended meaning of WEIR[1.1]]

weer *see* OOR[3], WEAR, WIRE[1.1]

weered *see* WEAR

wees *see* WEYS

weesh /wiʃ/ *interj* a call to a horse in harness to turn right *19- Sh Ork N NE T*. [a distinctive sound for a horse to contrast with the *hi* call to turn left]

weesh *see* WASH[1.2], WISH[1.2]

weeshie-washie *see* WISHY-WASHY[1.1], WISHY-WASHY[1.2]

weesht *see* WHEESHT[1.1], WHEESHT[1.2], WHEESHT[1.4]

weesk[1.1] /wisk/ *n* a squeak or squeal *20- Ork*. [see the verb]

weesk[1.2] /wisk/ *v* to squeak, squeal, creak *20- Ork*. [onomatopoeic]

weest, weased /wist, wizd/ *adj* depressed, doleful; anxious, fidgety *19- NE*. [unknown]

weet[1.1], **weit, wet,** *C Bor* **wat,** †**weyt** /wit, wɛt; *C Bor* wat/ *n* **1** wetness, damp, moisture *la14-*. **2** (a period of) wet weather, rain, drizzle *15-*. **3** dew *la18-*. **4** a drink *18-19*. [OE *wǣt*]

weet[1.2], **wet,** *C Bor* **wat,** †**weit** /wit, wɛt; *C Bor* wat/ *v pt* **wet, wat, weetit,** *ptp also NE* **wutten 1** to (cause to) become wet; to moisten, soak *la14-*. **2** to celebrate with a drink, drink to the success of (a bargain) *la19-*. **3** to wet (a weapon) with blood, kill *la15-e16*. **weetin** a quantity of liquor, a drinking party *19, 20- EC*. **weet the bairn's heid** to toast the health of a newborn baby *20-*. **wat a cup o tea** to make (a cup of) tea *20- WC*. **weet-my-fit** the landrail or corncrake *Crex crex* (from its cry) *19, 20- Uls*. **weet thoums** the practice of confirming a bargain by wetting and joining thumbs *19-*. **weet yer thrapple** to have something to drink, quench one's thirst *la18-*. †**weet yer throttle** = *weet yer thrapple 19*. [OE *wētan*]

weet[1.3], **weit, wet,** *C Bor* **wat,** †**weyt,** †**wait** /wit, wɛt; *C Bor* wat/ *adj* **1** exposed to rain, water or other liquid; wetted; soaked; spoiled by moisture; *of land* boggy, waterlogged *14-*. **2** *of weather* rainy *la15-*. **3** *redundantly of a liquid* wet *15-*. **4** *of foodstuffs, especially fruits, spices or fish* preserved in alcohol, syrup or brine *la15-17*. **weetie** wet, damp, rainy *17-19, 20- Sh NE EC*. †**weit ledder** a type of leather *la16-e17*. †**weitschod 1** having wet feet *la15-*. **2** *of the eyes* wet with tears *la18- WC SW*. **weet thow** a thaw unaccompanied by wind or rain *20- NE C*. **wet as muck** soaking wet *19, 20- Sh NE SW*. [OE *wēt*, ON *vátr*; *wet* is from the ptp of the verb]

weet *see* WIT[1.2]

weetit *see* WEET[1.2]

weeze, †**wheese** /wiz/ *v* to ooze, seep *17-19, 20- NE*. [OE *wēsan*]

weeze *see* WEASE

weezened *see* WIZENED

weezhan *see* VISION
wefand *see* WEAVE
weffle *see* WAFFLE[1.1], WAFFLE[1.2]
weft *see* WAFT[1.1]
wege *see* WADGE[1.1]
weght *see* WECHT[1.1]
weghty *see* WECHTY
weicht *see* WECHT[1.1], WECHT[2]
weichtie *see* WECHTY
weid *see* WEED[1.1], WEED[1.2], WEED[2]
†**weidinonfa, wedonynpha** *n* a high fever; puerperal fever *la15-e19*. [first element of OE *wēdensēoc*, *wēdenheort* mad + ONFA]
weido *see* WEEDA
weif *see* WEAVE
weigh *see* WEY[2.1], WEY[2.2]
weighs *see* WEYS
weight *see* WECHT[1.1], WECHT[1.2]
weiht *see* WECHT[1.1]
weik *see* WEEACK[1.2], WEEK[1]
weil *see* WALE[1.2], WALL[2]
weild *see* WIELD
weilfair *see* WEELFARE
weiliecoat *see* WYLIECOAT
weill *see* WEEL[1.1], WEEL[1.2], WEEL[1.3], WEEL[2], WEEL[3]
weill-kent *see* WEEL-KENT
wein *see* WEEN[1.2]
weind *see* WEEN[1.2]
weing *see* WING
weipe *see* WAP[1.2], WIPE[1.2]
weir[1.1]**, war,** †**were,** †**wer,** †**wair** /wir, wɔr/ *n* **1** warfare, hostilities, (an episode of) fighting *la14-*. **2** conflict, quarrelling, contention *15-*. †**warly** *adj* **1** = weirlike **1** *15-e17*. **2** = weirlike **2** *la15-16*. †**warly** *adv* in a warlike, martial manner; in a manner suitable for war *e16*. **weirlike,** †**weirlyk 1** *of persons* aggressive, given to fighting; martial *15-*. **2** *of actions or things* martial in character, aggressive, hostile *la15-e19*. **3** *of dress or behaviour* for or appropriate to warfare *15-*. †**weir cairt** a chariot or a cart for use in warfare *16*. †**were man 1** a fighting man, warrior, soldier *la15-e19*. **2** a man-of-war, warship *e16*. **were ship** a ship armed and manned for fighting or warfare *la15-*. †**were wall** a defensive wall or means of defence; a bulwark, rampart *la15-e17*. [OFr *werre*]
weir[1.2]**, war,** †**were,** †**wer** /wir, wɔr/ *v* **1** to make war; to fight *15-*. **2** to harass, annoy *15*. [see the noun]
weir[2.1], † **wer** /wir/ *n* **1** a river dam; a barrier or trap to prevent the movement of fish; an embankment at the side of a river (to prevent erosion) *la15-*. **2** a hedge, fence *la18-19*. **weir-buist** a partition between stalls in a byre *19- WC Bor*. [OE *wer*]
weir[2.2], †**were,** †**wer** /wir/ *v pt* also **wore,** *ptp* also **worn 1** to guard, defend, protect *la14-*. **2** to keep off, ward off; to stop *la15-*. **3** to drive, bring, cause (people or animals) to move gradually (in a desired direction), shepherd *18-*. **4** *of a sheepdog* to stand guard over (sheep) to prevent them breaking loose; originally to keep a watch on, hold, control (an entrance) *la15-19, 20- Bor*. **weir aff** to keep off, ward off, hold at bay *la18-*. **weirer** a dog which is skilful in herding animals *20- H&I SW Bor*. [OE *werian*]
weir *see* WEAR, WEER, WIRE[1.1], WIRE[1.2]
weird[1.1], †**werd** /wird/ *n* **1** fate, fortune, destiny; a person's fate *la14-19, 20- literary*; compare *dree yer weird* (DREE[1.2]). **2** someone with supernatural skill or knowledge *la17-*. **3** an omen, prophecy, prediction *15-19*. **4** *pl* the Fates, the three goddesses of destiny *15-e19*. **5** an event destined to happen; predetermined events *la15-e17*. **6** a decree (of a god) *e16*. **weirdfu** fateful, fraught with the supernatural *la19-*. **weirdless** unfortunate; inept, incapable; improvident *la18-19, 20- NE T EC*. †**weirdlessness** thriftlessness, mismanagement of one's life and affairs *19*. **weirdly 1** magical, eerie, dismal, sinister *19-*. **2** lucky, prosperous *19*. [OE *wyrd*]
weird[1.2], †**waird** /wird/ *v* **1** to ordain by fate, destine; to assign a specific fate or fortune to *la16-*. **2** to prophesy (someone's fate); to warn ominously *la18-19*. [see the noun]
weird[1.3], †**werd** /wird/ *adj* **1** strange, peculiar, uncanny *19-*. **2** having the power to control the destiny of men *15-17*. **3** troublesome, mischievous, harmful *19*. †**weird sisteris 1** the Fates *15-17*. **2** the three prophetesses or witches in the story of Macbeth *15-16*. **weird wife** a prophetess, fortuneteller *la18-*. [see the noun]
weirdie /'wirdi, 'werdi/ *n* the smallest or least thriving of a brood or litter *19- T EC*. [perhaps WEIRD[1.3] + -IE[3]]
weirfair *see* WARFARE
weirines *see* WEARY[1.3]
weise *see* WISE[2]
weist *see* WHEESHT[1.4]
weit *see* WEET[1.1], WEET[1.2], WEET[1.3]
weivt *see* WEAVE
wekit *see* WICKIT
wel *see* WEEL[1.1]
welage *see* VILLAGE
welch *see* WALSH
welcome *see* WALCOME[1.1], WALCOME[1.2], WALCOME[1.3], WALCOME[1.4]
welcum *see* WALCOME[1.2], WALCOME[1.4]
weld *see* WALL[2], WIELD
wele *see* WEEL[1.1], WEEL[1.2], WEEL[2]
welefare, welfare *see* WEELFARE
welis *see* WEEL[3]
welkin /'wɛlkɪn/ *n* the sky; the upper atmosphere *17-*. Compare WALK[1]. [OE *weolcen*]
well *see* WALL[1], WALL[2], WEEL[1.1], WEEL[1.2], WEEL[1.3], WEEL[3]
wellaway *see* WALAWA[1.2]
wellien *see* VILLAIN[1.2]
welsh *see* WALSH
welt *see* WALT[1.1], WALT[2]
welter[2.1], †**walter** /'wɛltər/ *n* **1** a confused mass *19-*. **2** an upset, upheaval; a state of turmoil *la16-19*. [see the verb]
welter[2.2], *Sh Uls* **walter,** †**weltir,** †**wolter** /'wɛltər; *Sh Uls* 'wɔltər/ *v* **1** *of a person or object* to roll to and fro, writhe, wallow, flounder, toss on the sea *15-19, 20- Sh Uls*. **2** to walk unsteadily, totter, stagger *19, 20- Sh N NE*. **3** *of water or waves* to surge, roll *la14-19*. **4** to damage, overturn, overthrow *la14-e17*. **5** to cause (the sea) to toss or (water) to rise in waves; to roll (a stone) *e16*. †**weltir doun** to (cause to) fall *la15-e16*. [MDu *welteren*, MLG *weltern* or frequentative form of WALT[2]]
welth *see* WALTH
weltir *see* WELTER[2.2]
wem *see* WAUM
wench *see* WINCH[2.1]
wend /wɛnd/ *v pt*, **went,** †**wynt 1** to go, travel; to make one's way; to depart *la14-*. **2** to die; to pass away, disappear, perish; *of time* to elapse *la14-16*. **3** to direct one's attention or effort; to aim to achieve (a goal) *la14-16*. **4** *of an event* to happen *e16*. Compare GAE. [OE *wendan*]
wend *see* WEEN[1.2], WIND[2.2]
wene *see* WEEN[1.1], WEEN[1.2]
wengeans *see* VENGEANCE
wengle *see* WINGLE[1.2]
Wensday *see* WEDNESDAY

went[1], *NE* **wint** /wɛnt; *NE* wɪnt/ *n* **1** a glimpse *19- N NE*. **2** a moment *la19- Sh Ork N*. [unknown]

†**went**[2.1] *n* **1** a route, course, path, way *16*. **2** an occasion, event; state of affairs *e16*. [related to WEND]

†**went**[2.2] *adj* gone, departed, past *16*. [participial adj from WEND]

went *see* WEND, WYNT
wep *see* WAP[2.2]
wepe *see* WIPE[1.2]
wer *see* OOR[3], WAUR[1.1], WAUR[1.2], WAUR[1.3], WEAR, WEER, WEIR[1.1], WEIR[1.2], WEIR[2.1], WEIR[2.2]
werch *see* WRATCH[1.1]
werd *see* WEIRD[1.1]
were *see* WARE[5], WEAR, WEIR[1.1], WEIR[1.2], WEIR[2.2], WEER, WIR
werefare *see* WARFARE
weregeheld *see* WERGELT

†**wergelt**, **weregeheld**, **wargeld** *n* **1** *law* the sum paid by way of compensation or fine to the victim or his family mainly in cases of homicide, to free the offender from further obligation or punishment *15-e17*. **2** a requital, a recompense *la14*. [OE *wergild*]

werie *see* WEARY[1.3]
werify *see* VERIFY
weriour *see* WARRIOR
werk *see* WARK[1], WIRK
wernour *see* WARNOUR
werp *see* WARP[1.2]
werr *see* WEAR
werrand *see* WARRANT[1.1], WARRANT[1.2]
werrandis *see* WARRANDICE
werray *see* WARRAY, VERRA[1.1], VERRA[1.2]
werrayour *see* WARRIOR

werrock, **werruck**, †**wirrok** /ˈwɛrək/ *n* a corn, bunion or lump on the foot *16-*. [OE *wearr* or MDu *weer* a callus, with -OCK diminutive suffix]

werruck *see* WERROCK
wers *see* WARSE[1.1], WARSE[1.2], WARSE[1.3]

wersh, **wairsh**, †**warsch** /wɛrʃ, wɛrʃ/ *adj* **1** *of food or drink* tasteless, insipid, unpalatable; cooked without salt; *of beer* flat *la17-*. **2** *of food or drink* bitter, harsh in taste, sour *20-*. **3** *of weather* raw, cold and damp *19-*. **4** *of people* sickly, feeble in appearance; spiritless, depressed *la15-*. **5** *of discourse or writing* dull, uninspiring *la16-*. **6** *of land* of poor quality, exhausted, lacking fertility *18-*. **7** *of life, feelings, activity* dull, humdrum, lacking zest *17-*. **8** *of the stomach or appetite* disinclined towards food; faint from hunger, squeamish *la18-19, 20- NE Uls*. **wershly** insipidly, without cordiality *17-*. **wershie** *of discourse or writing* dull, uninspiring *19- Sh Ork N*. †**wersh crap** *farming* the third and last crop taken from the OUTFIELD[1.1] before the fallow period *18-19*. [ME *werish*]

wersill *see* WARSLE[1.2]
wersslete *see* WARSET
werst *see* WARST[1.1], WARST[1.2], WARST[1.3]
werwoif *see* WARWOOF
wery *see* VERRA[1.1], VERRA[1.2], WEARY[1.2], WEARY[1.3]
werynes *see* WEARY[1.3]
wes *see* WIS
wesand *see* WIZZEN
weschar *see* WASHER
wesche *see* WASH[1.1], WASH[1.2]
weschin, **weschyn** *see* WASH[1.2]
wescot *see* WESKIT
wesh *see* WASH[1.1], WASH[1.2]
weshed *see* WASH[1.2]
weshell *see* VESHEL

weshen *see* WASH[1.2]

weskit, **wastcoat**, *NE* **wystcoat**, †**wastcoit**, †**wescot**, †**waiscot** /ˈwɛskɪt, ˈwastkot; *NE* ˈwʌɪstkot/ *n* a waistcoat *la16-*. [WAIST + COAT]

wesp *see* WASP

west *see* WAIST, WAST[1.1], WAST[1.2], WAST[1.3], WAST[1.4], WAST[1.5], WASTE[1.1], WASTE[1.2], WASTE[1.3]
wester *see* WASTER[3]
western *see* WASTERN

West Highland /ˈwɛst ˈhʌɪlənd/ *n* **1** a hardy breed of beef cattle *la18-*. **2** a small, white, rough-haired breed of terrier *20-*. **West Highlander** one of the West Highland breed of cattle *19-*. [*west* (WAST[1.3]) + *Highland* (HIELAND[1.2])]

West Highland Way /ˈwɛst ˈhʌɪlənd ˈwe/ *n* a path (154 km 96 miles) used by hillwalkers from Milngavie to Fort William *la20-*. [*west* (WAST[1.3]) + *Highland* (HIELAND[1.2]) + *way* (WEY[1])]

Westie /ˈwɛsti/ *n* a West Highland Terrier *20-*. [shortened form of WEST HIGHLAND + -IE[1]]

westin *see* WASTEN[1.1], WASTEN[1.2]
westir *see* WASTER[3]
wet *see* WEET[1.1], WEET[1.2], WEET[1.3]
weth *see* WAITH[1.1]
wether *see* WEDDER
wethir *see* WEATHER
wethy *see* WIDDIE

†**weuch**, **wewche**, **wouch** *n* wrong, injury, harm *la15-e17*. [OE *wōh*]

wevar *see* WEAVER
weve *see* WEAVE
wewche *see* WEUCH

wey[1], **wye**, **way**, †**wa** /wʌɪ, we/ *n* **1** a (particular) road, track, path, street, passageway; a spiritual or moral path, a course of action, a manner of doing something; a distance *la14-*. **2** a person's circumstances, way of life, business *la19-*. **weydaein** = *wey o daein* 2. †**wayfare**, **wafair** a passage or roadway *la16-*. **way-flude**, **wa'-fleed** the outflow of water from a mill wheel, the tail-race; a water channel *la18-19, 20- NE*. **waygate 1** a passageway, a thoroughfare; room, space; an outlet *19- Bor*. **2** speed, progress; push, drive, energy *19- C SW Bor*. †**walaid**, **wayleid** = *way-flude 16*. **be in the wey o** to have a habit of *18-*. **by his wey o't** according to him by his account *la19-*. **by way of** by the action of a person or a method specified *15-*. **that wey** in that manner, so; in that respect *la19-*. **the wey 1** because of the way or manner in which, from the way (that) *la19-*. **2** because, the reason why *la19-*. **the wey at** the reason why *la20- Sh T*. **the wey o** in the direction of *la19- Sh Ork N NE T EC*. **wey o daein 1** a means of livelihood, a job *19-*. **2** a fuss; a disturbance, uproar; a celebration *la19- T EC*. **3** method of working, habits *20- C*. [OE *weg*]

wey[2.1], **weigh** /wʌɪ, we/ *n* a measure of weight varying according to district and commodity *17-19, 20- historical*. [OE *wǣge*]

wey[2.2], **wye**, **weigh**, *EC Bor* **wee** /wʌɪ, we; *EC Bor* wi/ *v* **1** to ascertain the weight of; to evaluate, judge (according to a standard); to have weight or heaviness *15-*. **2** to weigh anchor *la15-*. **3** to apply (the law), administer (justice) impartially *16*. **4** to value, estimate at a particular valuation *16-e17*. **5** to pay heed or deference to *15*. †**weyage** a tax on weighing goods on the public scales *16-17*. **weigh-bauk** (the beam of) a pair of scales *16-*. **weigh-brods** the boards used on scales for weighing heavy objects *la16-17, 20- N*. **weigh-house**, †**weyhous** the building containing the public scales *la16-*. **wey-wechts** (the weights used with) scales *la19- NE T C*. **wey butter**, **wey cheese** a game in which two people stand back to back with arms linked and lift each other alternately *19-*. **weigh down** (to cause) to weigh more heavily; to have a greater effect on *la16-*. †**wey up** *of a scale* to rise up *la14*. [OE *wegan*]

wey *see* WAE[1.2], WAE[2]

weycht *see* WICHT[1]

†**weygilt** *n* a payment for weighing *la15-16*. Compare *wey-age* (WEY[2.2]). [WEY[2.2] + Older Scots *gilt* money; compare Du *waaggeld*]

weyis *see* WEYS

weyn *see* WEEN[1.2]

weynd *see* WYND[1], WYND[2.1]

weys, weighs, *N C* **wees,** †**weyis** /wʌɪz, wez; *N C also* wiz/ *npl* a (public) weighing-machine; the weights used with scales *15-*. [pl of WEY[2.1]]

-weys /wʌɪz, wez/ *suffix* -wise, in the manner specified: ◇ *says he, affhand-weys 19-*. [pl of WEY[1]]

weyse *see* VISE, WEASE

weyst *see* WAIST

weyt *see* WEET[1.1], WEET[1.3]

†**weyting, waiting** *n in the North East and Angus* entertainment, hospitality owed by a vassal *la12-e14*. Compare CONVETH. [ON *veiting*]

weyvt *see* WEAVE

wg *see* UG[1.2]

wglie *see* UGLY[1.2]

wgly *see* UGLY[1.3]

wgsum *see* UGSOME

wgsumnes *see* UGSOME

wha, who, *N NE* **fa,** *C SW Bor* **whae,** *Bor* **whee,** †**quha,** †**quhay,** †**quho** /ʍa, hu; *N NE* fa; *C SW Bor* ʍe; *Bor* ʍi/ *pron* **1** *in direct and indirect questions* which person *la14-*. **2** *in indefinite or generalized use* any person who, any person that, whoever *la14-*. **3** *as a relative pronoun* who, that *la14-17, 18-* mainly *literary*; compare THAT. **4** *in definite use* the person (or persons) who, the one that *15-16*. **5** *as the subject of a clause with conditionality* (even) if anyone, when anyone *la14-e17*. **whaever, whaiver 1** whichever person or persons; no matter who *15-*. **2** *in a rhetorical question used to express astonishment* who? *16-e17*. **wha sae,** †**quhasa,** †**quha so** whoever, anyone who *la14-*. **whaasay, whaarsay** *conj* as much as to say, as if to say *la19- Sh*. **whaasay, whaarsay** *n* a rumour, hearsay; a pretence *19- Sh Ork*. †**quha-sum-ever** *pron* any person who, whoever *la14-e17*. †**quha-sum-ever** *adj* whichever, whatever (person or persons) *15-16*. **wha but he, wha but him** *of a self-assured person* the one and only, the cock of the walk *17-19, 20- NE T EC*. †**wha but him** = *wha but he la18-e19*. **wha daur meddle wi me** free translation of the national motto *nemo me impune lacessit*; also applied to the thistle *la19-*. **wha deil** who the devil? *18, 20- Sh Ork*. **wha like** whoever (it may be), no matter who *la18, 20- Sh Ork*. **wha's aucht** = who is the owner or parent of? *19- NE T C*. **wha's got the thummle** games hunt the thimble *la19, 20- T WC*. **wha tae be mairrit first** a card game *19, 20- Ork*. [OE *hwā*]

whaak *see* QUACK[1.1], QUACK[1.2], QUAK

whaal, whale, *NE* **whaul,** *NE* **faal,** *NE* **fawl,** †**quhale,** †**quhaill,** †**quhail** /ʍal, ʍel; *NE* ʍɔl; *NE* fal; *NE* fɔl/ *n* **1** a marine mammal of the order *Cetacea*, a whale; originally apparently any particularly large sea-creature *15-*. **2** *pl* long, undulating, unbroken waves *la19- Sh N*. **whaal-bubble** the jellyfish *20- Sh NE EC*. †**quhaill horne** whalebone *la16*. †**quhale-schot** spermaceti, a fatty substance found in the head of a sperm whale *la16-17*. [OE *hwæl*]

whaap *see* WHAUP[1.1]

whaar *see* WHAUR[1.1]

whaarl *see* WHURL[2]

whaarm, †**quarm** /ʍarm/ *n* the rim of the eyelid on which the eyelash grows *19- Sh*. [Norw dial (*augne-*)*kvarm* (eye) lash]

whaasel WHEEZLE[1.1], WHEEZLE[1.2]

whack[1.1] /ʍak/ *n* **1** a sharp, heavy stroke or blow, a thump, smack *18-*. **2** a cut, incision; a large slice *la18-19*, *20- N NE T*. **3** a great number, a large quantity *la19-*. **get yer whacks** to be punished, get one's just deserts *18-*. [see the verb]

whack[1.2]**, whauk,** †**whake** /ʍak, ʍɔk/ *v* **1** to beat, thrash, wallop *16-*. **2** to slash, cut severely with a sharp instrument *la18-19*. **whackin, whauken** great, big, thumping *la18-19, 20- Ork NE T WC*. [onomatopoeic]

whack *see* QUAK

whae *see* WHA

whaen /ʍen, ˈʍeən/ *n* a ram incapable of procreation, a hermaphrodite sheep *la19- Sh*. [variant with extended sense of QUEAN; compare Du *kween* literally a woman, a hermaphrodite bull]

wha-hup /ʍaˈhʌp/ *interj* a call to a horse to move (off or to the right) *20- C Bor*. [extended sense of HUP[1.2]]

whaig *see* QUEY

whair *see* WHAUR[1.1], WHAUR[1.2]

whaisk /ʍesk/ *v* to wheeze, breathe with difficulty, as with a heavy cold, gasp for breath *19- Bor*. [perhaps a conflation of *whaizle* (WHEEZLE[1.2]) with HASK[1.1]]

whaiver *see* WHA

whaizle *see* WEASEL, WHEEZLE[1.1], WHEEZLE[1.2]

whake *see* WHACK[1.2]

whale *see* WHAAL

whality *see* QUALITY[1.1]

whalm *see* FOLM[1.2]

whalp[1.1]**, whulp, whelp,** *N NE* **folp,** *N NE* **fulp,** †**quhelp,** †**quhalp,** †**quholp** /ʍalp, ʍɔlp, ʍʌlp, ʍɛlp; *N NE* fɔlp, fʌlp/ *n* **1** the young of a dog or of other wild animals, a puppy or cub *13-*. **2** term of abuse for a person *la18-*. [OE *hwelp, hwealp*]

whalp[1.2]**, whulp, whelp,** *N NE* **folp,** *N NE* **fulp** /ʍalp, ʍɔlp, ʍʌlp, ʍɛlp; *N NE* fɔlp, fʌlp/ *v of a dog* to produce puppies *19-*. [see the noun]

wham[1]**,** †**quhawme,** †**quhame** /ʍam; *Sh* ʍɑm/ *n* **1** a dale or valley, a broad hollow among hills through which a stream runs; frequently in place-names *la16-19, 20- Sh SW Bor*. **2** a hollow or (boggy) depression in a field *19- Sh C Bor*. **3** the hollow of a person's hand or foot *20- Sh*. [ON *hvammr*]

wham[2] /ʍam/ *n* **1** a blow *18-*. **2** a thud, a dull sound *20-*. †**whample** = WHAM[2] *e19*. [onomatopoeic]

wham[3] /ʍam, ʍɑm/ *n* a trick, a dodge; a whim *20- Ork*. Compare WHEEM. [shortened form of Eng *whim-wham*]

wham[4]**, whom,** †**quham,** †**quhom,** †**quam** /ʍam, hum/ *pron* **1** what or which person?; him or her, those; whatever person, anyone; that particular person *la14-*. **2** *with a preposition immediately following* from, of, to whom: ◇ *it specifyit nocht quham fra the gudis wes takin. la14-16*. **whomever** anyone whom, that person whom *la14-*. †**quham-so** anyone whom *la15-e19*. †**quham of** from, of, concerning whom *la14-e17*. †**quham-till** to what person or persons, to whom *15-e16*. †**quham-to** = *quham-till la14-16*. †**quham-with** with whom *la14-e17*. [OE *hwām* dative sg of *hwā* WHA]

whammle *see* WHUMMLE[1.1], WHUMMLE[1.2]

whamsy /ˈʍamsi, ˈʍɑmsi/ *adj* out of sorts, slightly unwell *20- Ork*. [probably a variant of Eng *qualm* + *-sie* adj-forming suffix]

whan[1.1]**, when, whaun, whin, whun,** *N NE* **fan,** *NE* **fin,** †**quhen,** †**quhan,** †**quhone** /ʍan, ʍɛn, ʍɔn, ʍɪn, ʍʌn; *N NE* fan; *NE* fɪn/ *adv in direct and indirect questions* inquiring about or stating the time or occasion of an event or circumstance, when *la14-*. **whenas**, †**quhen-as** at a time in which, in a case in which *15-*. [OE *hwanne,hwenne, hwonne*]

whan[1,2], **when**, **whaun**, **whin**, **whun**, *N NE* **fan**, *NE* **fin**, †**quhen**, †**quhan**, †**quhone** /ʍan, ʍɛn, ʍɔn, ʍin, ʍʌn/; *N NE* fan; *NE* fɪn/ *conj* **1** at or during the time that; at which time or on which occasion; as soon as, after; while *la14-*. **2** considering that; since; even though; if *15-*. **whanever 1** on any or every occasion or time; if on some occasion; on the occasion that, when in due course *la14-*. **2** as soon as, at the very moment when *18-*. †**quhen-swa** when, whenever *la14-16*. [see the adv]

whan awhan *see* OCHONE

whang[1,1], *NE* **fang**, *EC Bor* **whank**, *Bor* **whing**, †**quhang**, †**quhayng** /ʍaŋ/; *NE* faŋ; *EC Bor* ʍaŋk; *Bor* ʍiŋ/ *n* **1** a strip of leather, a thong, a band, a strap *16-*. **2** a (leather) lace for boots or shoes *18-*. **3** a large thick slice of food, especially cheese *18-*. **4** a large amount or number, a chunk, large slice of anything *19-*. **5** a stroke, blow; a cut with a whip *19-*. **6** the penis *20- C Bor*. **7** a strip of dried (eel- or sheep-)skin or whale's sinew, used as a hinge for a flail *la18-19, 20- Sh*. **8** the lash of a whip *18-19, 20- EC*. **9** a length of twist tobacco *20- Sh*. **10** a rascal, disagreeable person *la19- NE*. [OE *ðwang*]

whang[1,2], *NE* **fang**, *EC Bor* **whank**, *Bor* **whing** /ʍaŋ/; *NE* faŋ; *EC Bor* ʍaŋk; *Bor* ʍiŋ/ *v* **1** to cut in chunks or sizeable portions, slice *18-*. **2** to beat, lash (as) with a whip; to best, defeat *la18-*. **3** to cut with a slicing movement, slash, chop, snip *19, 20- SW Bor*. **4** to move with sudden force; to push or pull with a jerk *la19, 20- SW Bor*. **whanker** a large or impressive specimen of its kind *19- C SW Bor*. **whankie** a sickle-blade mounted on a long handle, for cutting thistles *19- EC Bor*. **whing-hole** an eyelet for a lace in a boot or shoe *20- C Bor*. **the Whangie** a split rock through which a path runs in the Kilpatrick Hills, Dunbartonshire *la19-*. [see the noun]

whank *see* WHANG[1,1], WHANG[1,2]
whap *see* WAP[1,1], WAP[1,2], WHAUP[3], WHAUP[4]
whapping *see* WAPPIN
whar *see* WHAUR[1,1], WHAUR[1,2]
whark *see* KWARK[1,2]
wharl *see* QUARREL[2,1], QUARREL[2,2]
wharry *see* QUARRY
wharter *see* QUARTER[1,1], QUARTER[1,2]
wharve /ʍarv, ʍarv/ *v* to turn over mown hay with a rake *la19- Sh*. [Norw dial *kverva* to turn]
whase, **whause**, **whose**, †**quhais**, †**quhase**, †**quhois** /ʍez, ʍɔz, huz/ *pron* **1** *of a person* of whom; he whose; whosever, whosesoever *la14-*. **2** *of a thing* of which (the) *la15-*. [OE *hwæs* genitive of *hwā* WHA, with vowel assimilated to *hwā*]
whassaco[1,1] /'ʍasəko/ *n* a pretence, insincere behaviour *20- Ork*. [unknown]
whassaco[1,2] /'ʍasəko/ *adv* ostensibly, on a pretext, as a pretence *la19- Ork*. [unknown]
what, **whet**, †**quhet** /ʍat, ʍɔt, ʍɛt/ *v* to sharpen *la15-*. **whatstick** *shoemaking* a hone or emery-board *20- NE WC SW Bor*. [OE *hwettan*]
what *see* WHIT[1,1], WHIT[1,2], WHIT[1,3], WHIT[1,4]
whatten, *N NE* **fatten**, †**quhattin** /'ʍatən, 'ʍɔtən; *N NE* 'fatən/ *adj* **1** *in questions, indirect questions or exclamations* what sort of, what kind of; what *16-*. **2** which, of two or more *la18-*. **whitna**, **whatna**, *N NE* **fitna**, *N NE* **fatna** = WHATTEN *19-*. [reduced form of *quhatkin* (WHIT[1,1])]
whatty *see* WHEETIE[1,1]

whauk *see* WHACK[1,2]
†**whauky** *n* whisky *la18-e19*. [conflation of AQUA with WHISKY]
whaul *see* WHAAL
whaun *see* WHAN[1,1], WHAN[1,2], WAND[1,1]
whaup[1,1], *Sh* **whaap**, *N NE* **faap**, *N NE* **faup**, †**quhaip**, †**quhape**, †**quhawpe** /ʍɔp; *Sh* ʍap; *N NE* fap, fəp/ *n* **1** the curlew *Numenius arquata 16-*. **2** a nickname or term of abuse for a person *la16-*. **whaup nebbit** having a long beaky nose *18-*. †**whaup in the nest** something annoying or unpleasant, likely to arise or come to light *la18-e19*. [perhaps related to OE *hwilpe* a kind of sea bird or onomatopoeic of the bird's call]
whaup[1,2] /ʍɔp/ *v* to whistle shrilly like a curlew *19, 20- WC SW Bor*. [see the noun]
whaup[2], **faup** /ʍɔp; *NE* fɔp/ *n* **1** an (empty) pea or bean pod *19- NE EC*. **2** a scoundrel, a scamp *19- NE T*; compare WHAUP[1,1]. [unknown]
whaup[3], †**whap**, †**quhap** /ʍɔp/ *n* a hitch, a snag; a drawback, an unforeseen difficulty *17-19, 20- NE Bor*. **a whaup in the raip** = WHAUP[3]. [perhaps an altered form of WAP[2,1] a turn of a string wrapped round something]
whaup[4], **whap** /ʍɔp, ʍap/ *n* a shrill noise, yelp, screech, outcry *la19- N SW*. [onomatopoeic; perhaps with influence from WHAUP[1,2]]
whaur[1,1], **whar**, **whair**, **where**, *Sh* **whaar**, *N NE* **far**, **faar**, †**quhare**, †**quhair**, †**quhere** /ʍɔr, ʍar, ʍer; *Sh* ʍar; *N NE* far/ *adv* **1** *in questions, indirect questions or statements* in or to which place, the place in or to which, in or to any place; whereas *la14-*. **2** *with a person as the object of feelings* in whom *la15-e16*. †**whereanent** *law* concerning which, on account of this *la16-e18*. **whereawa** away in or to what place, whereabouts, where on earth, whither *16-*. **whauriver**, †**quhair evir 1** in, at, to any or every place; no matter where *la14-*. **2** *with a person as the object of feelings* whomever *la15*. †**wharfor** why; for, on account of; on that account; therefore, so *la14-19*. **whaurfrae 1** *in direct and indirect questions* from what place, whence? *16-e19*. **2** *introducing statements* from which (place or course of action) *la14-*. †**quherintill** wherein *16-17*. †**quherinto 1** (in)to which *la16-17*. **2** in which *16-e17*. **whar-pairt** where, whereabouts, where on earth *20- Sh*. **whar-piece** = *wharpairt 20- Ork*. †**quharsa** wherever *la14-e16*. **whereto 1** to what place or thing *15-*. **2** for what purpose, why *15-19, 20- Sh Ork*. **wherewitha**, †**wharewitha**, †**whairwithall** (a means) whereby *17-*. [OE *hwār*, *hwǣr*]
whaur[1,2], **whar**, **whair**, **where**, *N NE* **far**, †**quhare**, †**quhar**, †**quhair** /ʍɔr, ʍar, ʍer; *N NE* far/ *conj* **1** at whatever place or circumstance described in the dependent clause *la14-*. **2** that *la14-16*. [see the adv]
whause *see* WHASE
whauze *see* WHEEZE[1,1], WHEEZE[1,2]
wheasel *see* WEASEL
wheat, *NE T* **white**, †**quhete**, †**quheit**, †**quhite** /ʍit; *NE T* ʍʌit/ *n* wheat, a cereal (plant and grain) of the genus *Triticum* most commonly used in bread-making *la14-*. [OE *hwǣte*]
whee *see* WHA
wheeber[1,1] /'ʍibər/ *n* **1** a whistle *20- NE T*. **2** a person with disagreeable manners; a lean, tall, ungainly person *la19- NE*. **wheebert** = WHEEBER[1,1] (sense 2). [see the verb]
wheeber[1,2] /'ʍibər/ *v* **1** to whistle *20- NE T*. **2** to walk with hurried, ungainly steps, scurry *la19- NE*. [frequentative form of WHEEP[1,2]]
wheech[1,1], **wheek** /ʍix, ʍik/ *n* **1** a sudden sweeping motion, a whisk, a breath of wind *20-*. **2** a whizzing sound *19- NE*

EC. **3** a blow delivered with a whizzing sound *la19-* NE T C. **4** *pl* strokes with the TAWSE, a belting at school *20-* C. **wheeky-whacky day** a day at school in which the TAWSE is much in use *20-* C. [see the verb]

wheech[1,2], **wheek** /ʍix, ʍik/ *v* **1** to move quickly rush, dash (with a whizzing sound) *19-*. **2** to remove (something) with a speedy, sweeping, forcible movement; to snatch or whisk away *la19-*. **3** to beat, whack, hit *la19-* T WC SW. **wheecher 1** something big or outstanding of its kind, something of top quality or excellence *20-* C SW Bor. **2** = *coal wheecher* (COAL). [onomatopoeic]

wheech[2] /ʍix/ *n* a stench *20-* N EC. [a natural utterance; compare FEECH[2]]

wheeda /ˈʍidɑ/ *n fishing taboo* the ling *Molva molva la19-* Sh. [Norw *hvide* the white one]

wheedle, †**whidle** /ˈʍidəl/ *v* to cajole, persuade with flattery *la17-*. [unknown; compare OE *wǣdlian* to beg]

wheef see WHEICH, WHIFF[1,1], WHIFF[1,2]

wheefle[1,1], **whiffle**, †**whifle** /ˈʍifəl, ˈʍɪfəl/ *n* a puff, spurt, whiff, hint or whisper; a slight insignificant thing *17-*. [see the verb]

wheefle[1,2], **whiffle** /ˈʍifəl, ˈʍɪfəl/ *v* **1** to puff, blow *19-*. **2** to vacillate, dither *19, 20-* Sh. [frequentative form of WHIFF[1,2]]

†**wheegee** *n* a whim; a humming and hawing, prevarication *19*. [reduplicative formation, perhaps onomatopoeic]

wheegle /ˈʍigəl/ *v* to cajole *la18-19, 20-* C Bor. [altered form of WHEEDLE]

wheek[1,1], †**quaik**, †**quake** /ʍik/ *n* a squeak, squeal *la15-19, 20-* NE T. [see the verb]

wheek[1,2] /ʍik/ *v* to squeak, squeal, whine, cheep; to complain peevishly *19, 20-* NE T. [onomatopoeic]

wheek see WHEECH[1,1], WHEECH[1,2]

wheel[1,1], †**quhele**, †**quheil**, †**wheill** /ʍil/ *n* **1** a circular object used as a means of locomotion on a vehicle or as part of a mechanism, a wheel *la14-*. **2** a spinning wheel or yarn winder *19-*. **3** an instrument of torture *la14-*. **4** *in poetry* the wheel of fortune *la14-e17*. **wheelit** having (a (specified) number of) wheels *16-*. **wheel band** *spinning* the driving belt of a spinning wheel, usually made from the dried intestines of a sheep *la16-19, 20-* Sh Ork N. **wheel brae** *mining* a mechanism whereby the descent of full hutches causes the ascent of empty ones, a COWSY *la19-* C. **wheel guts** = *wheel band 20-* Ork. **wheel mitten** *fishing* the steersman's glove (in a boat without a wheelhouse) *20-* Sh. **wheelsman** *mining* = *wheeler* (WHEEL[1,2]) *la19-* EC. **wheel term** = *wheel band 20-* Sh. **wheel tree** *mining* the wooden post or pivot on which the wheel of a *wheel brae* turns *la19-* C. **wheelwright**, †**quhele-wricht** a maker of wheels and wheeled vehicles *la14-*. †**quheill makar** = *wheelwright la16*. [OE *hwēol*]

wheel[1,2], †**quhele**, †**quheil** /ʍil/ *v* **1** to turn in a circle, (as) on a wheel or with circular motion, rotate, wheel *la15-*. **2** *dancing* to whirl round, swing (one's partner) round, pirouette, reel *19, 20-* Sh NE T. **3** to make a bid at an auction for the purpose of raising the price *la19-* NE. **4** to travel in a wheeled vehicle *e18*. **wheeler 1** a person who wheels or conveys something in a wheelbarrow *la17-* C. **2** *mining* the person who operates the *wheel brae* (WHEEL[1,1]) *20-* EC. **wheelin** *spinning* a coarse, thick type of worsted yarn, originally from uncombed wool spun on the *muckle wheel* (MUCKLE) *17-*. **wheel a brae** to operate the haulage system on a *wheel brae* (WHEEL[1,1]) *20-* EC. [see the noun]

wheel[2] /ʍil/ *v* to sit down, rest *la19-* Ork. [Norw *hvile* to rest]

wheelie-oe /ˈʍilio/ *n* the willow-warbler *Phylloscopus trochilus 20-* WC SW. [onomatopoeic of the last notes of the bird's call; compare WHEETIE[1,1]]

wheem, **whim** /ʍim, ʍɪm/ *n* a fancy or notion *18-*. †**whimwham**, **quhum-quhame** a trinket, trifling ornament; a fantastic notion *16-e19*. Compare WHAM[3] [onomatopoeic]

wheen[1,1], †**quhene**, †**quheyne**, †**quhoyn** /ʍin/ *n* **1** quite a large number, a lot *la17-*. **2** a small number, a few *la14-*. **3** mainly *pl* a separate or distinct number (of persons), a group, some as opposed to others *la18-*. **a wheen** *in adverbial use* a bit, somewhat *la19-*. [see the adj]

wheen[1,2], †**quhene**, †**quhoyn**, †**whine** /ʍin/ *adj* **1** few, not many, some *la14-*. **2** many, lots *la17-*. [OE *hwēne* somewhat, instrumental case of *hwōn* few]

wheen see QUEEN

wheen ann /ˈʍinɑn/ *n* quinine *20-* Sh. [altered form of Eng *quinine*, punning on the Sh pronunciation of *Queen Anne*]

wheenge see WHINGE[1,1], WHINGE[1,2]

wheenk see WHENK[1,1], WHENK[1,2]

wheep[1,1] /ʍip/ *n* a sharp cry or whistle *la19-*. [see the verb]

wheep[1,2] /ʍip/ *v* **1** to whistle, especially to call a dog or attract attention; to pipe shrilly like a bird, especially the lapwing *19-*. **2** to make a shrill noise, squeak, emit a high-pitched buzz or hiss *19, 20-* NE. [onomatopoeic]

wheep see WHUP[1,1], WHUP[1,2], WHUP[1,3]

wheeple[1,1] /ˈʍipəl/ *n* **1** the shrill call or whistle of a bird, especially the curlew *la18-*. **2** a tuneless, unmusical whistling or playing on a whistle *19-*. [see the verb]

wheeple[1,2] /ˈʍipəl/ *v* **1** *of a bird* to whistle shrilly or with a long drawn-out note *19-*. **2** *of the wind* to whistle *19-*. **3** *of persons* to whistle, especially tunelessly or ineffectually *19-*. **4** to whistle (a tune) *20-*. **5** to whine, whimper *19-* T Bor. [frequentative form of WHEEP[1,2]]

wheer see QUEER[1,1]

wheeriorum /ʍɪrɪˈorəm/ *n* a trifle, toy; a thingumajig *la19-* N NE T. [conflation of WHEERUM with VARIORUM]

wheerum /ˈʍirəm/ *n* a trifle, something insignificant; a toy *19-*. [perhaps an altered form of QUEER, with mock-Latin suffix]

wheery see WHERRY

wheese see WEEZE, WHEEZE[2]

wheesel see WEASEL

wheesh see WHEESHT[1,1], WHEESHT[1,2], WHUSH[1,2]

wheesher /ˈʍiʃər/ *n* anything large of its kind *20-* C SW Bor. [*wheesh* (WHUSH[1,2]), with instrumental suffix]

wheesht[1,1], **weesht**, **wheesh**, **whush** /ʍɪʃt, wɪʃt, ʍɪʃ, ʍʌʃ/ *n* the slightest sound, the least whisper; the faintest rumour or report *la18-19, 20-* Sh N C. **whishie** = WHEESHT[1,1]. **haud yer wheesht** see HAUD[1,2]. [see the interj]

wheesht[1,2], **weesht**, **wheesh**, **whush** /ʍɪʃt, wɪʃt, ʍɪʃ, ʍʌʃ/ *v* **1** to silence, cause to be quiet, quieten *19-*. **2** to be quiet, remain silent *la18-*. **3** to say *wheesht!*, call for silence *20-* Sh N NE C. [see the interj]

wheesht[1,3], **whush'd**, †**whist**, †**whush** /ʍɪʃt, ʍʌʃd/ *adj* quiet, silent, hushed *18-*. [see the interj]

wheesht[1,4], **weesht**, **whisht**, **whush**, **wisht**, †**whist**, †**fusht**, †**weist** /ʍɪʃt, wɪʃt, ʍɪʃt, ʍʌʃ, wɪʃt/ *interj* be quiet!, shut up!; hush! *la16-*. [a natural utterance]

wheesk /ʍisk/ *n* a creaking sound; the noise made by a mouse *19-* Ork Bor. [onomatopoeic]

wheesp /ʍisp/ *n* a whisper, rumour, the slightest sound *20-* Ork. [back-formation from *whisper* (WHUSPER[1,2])]

wheet, **whit**, †**quheit**, †**quhit** /ʍit, ʍɪt/ *n* a very small amount, the least part, a jot *16-*. [OE *wiht* a thing, something, anything]

wheetie[1,1], NE **quytie**, Bor **whatty** /ˈʍiti; NE ˈkʍʌɪti; Bor ˈʍate/ *n* **1** a young bird, especially a duckling or chicken *19*. **2** the whitethroat *Sylvia communis 19-*. **wheetie whitebeard**, **wheaty whybeard 1** = WHEETIE[1,1] (sense 2) *19-* H&I

WC SW Bor. **2** the willow-warbler *Phylloscopus trochilus 19- WC*. †**wheetle** = WHEETIE¹·¹. [onomatopoeic of a bird's chirp]

wheetie¹·² /ˈʍiti/ *interj* call to ducks *19-*. **wheetle** = WHEETIE¹·². [see the noun]

wheetie² /ˈʍiti/ *adj* mean, stingy, shabby; underhand, shifty, evasive *19- NE*. [unknown]

wheetle /ˈʍitəl/ *v* **1** *of persons* to whistle, warble, usually tunelessly *la19-*. **2** *of birds* to twitter, chirp *19, 20- EC Bor*. [onomatopoeic]

wheety-whattie¹·¹, **whittie-whattie**, †**whytie-whatie** /ˈʍɪtɪˌʍatɪ, ˈʍɪtɪˌʍatɪ/ *n* frivolous excuses, circumlocutions intended to conceal the truth; indecision *la17-*. **wheety-whattieing** shilly-shallying, indecision *19, 20- Sh*. [reduplicative formation perhaps based on WHEET or WHEETIE²]

wheety-whattie¹·², **whittie-whattie** /ˈʍɪtɪˌʍatɪ, ˈʍɪtɪˌʍatɪ/ *adj* indecisive, shilly-shallying, vague *20- Sh T*. [see the noun]

wheeze¹·¹, *NE* **foze**, *NE* **whauze** /ʍiz/; *NE* foz, mɔz/ *n* **1** noisy or asthmatic breathing; difficulty of breathing *la19-*. **2** a joke; a clever action *la19-*. [see the verb]

wheeze¹·², *NE* **foze**, *NE* **whauze** /ʍiz/; *NE* foz, mɔz/ *v* to breathe noisily or with difficulty; to cough *19-*. [probably ON *hvæsa* to hiss]

wheeze², †**wheese** /ʍiz/ *v* to flatter, coax, cajole *la18-e19, 20- NE*. [unknown]

wheezle¹·¹, *Sh* **whaasel**, *NE* **fozle**, †**whaizle** /ˈʍizəl; *Sh* ˈʍazəl; *NE* ˈfozəl/ *n* a wheeze, hard rough breathing *19-*. †**wheezloch** *in horses* broken-windedness *e18*. **the wheezles** asthma; bronchitis *la19-*. [see the verb]

wheezle¹·², *Sh* **whaasel**, *NE* **fozle**, *Bor* **huizle**, †**whaizle**, †**whosle** /ˈʍizəl; *Sh* ˈʍazəl; *NE* ˈfozəl; *Bor* ˈhuzəl/ *v* to wheeze, pant *la18-*. [frequentative form of WHEEZE¹·²]

wheich, **wheuch**, **wheef** /ʍix, ʍjux, ʍif/ *n* alcohol; whisky *la19- NE T EC Bor*. [perhaps an extended sense of WHEECH¹·¹, WHEECH²; compare Eng *whiff* a draught of liquor, WHIFF¹·¹]

wheill *see* WHEEL¹·¹
whelm *see* FOLM¹·¹
whelp *see* WHALP¹·¹, WHALP¹·²
when *see* WHAN¹·¹, WHAN¹·²

whence¹·¹, †**quhence**, †**quhens** /ʍɛns/ *adv* from where *15-*. [ME *whennes*]

whence¹·², †**quhence**, †**quhens** /ʍɛns/ *conj* from where *la15-*. [see the adv]

whenk¹·¹, **wheenk**, **whink** /ʍɛŋk, ʍiŋk, ʍɪŋk/ *n* a sudden, jerky movement, an odd gesture *20- Sh Ork*. [see the verb]

whenk¹·², **wheenk**, **whink** /ʍɛŋk, ʍiŋk, ʍɪŋk/ *v* to make an odd or jerky movement or gesture; to flounce *20- Sh Ork*. [onomatopoeic; compare Norw dial *vinka* to push, to swing to and fro]

where *see* WHAUR¹·¹, WHAUR¹·²

wherry, **whurry**, †**wheery**, †**whiry** /ˈʍɛri, ˈʍʌri/ *n* **1** a rowing boat or barge *17-*. **2** a kind of sailing barge with one sail, and a mast stepped forward *la18- C*. [unknown]

whess /ʍɛs/ *v* to pant, wheeze *la19- Ork*. [Norw dial *kvæsa*]
whestin *see* QUESTION
whet, †**quhet** /ʍɛt/ *v* **1** to sharpen *la15-*. **2** to incite, entice *la15-*. **whetstone**, †**quhit-stane**, **quhetstane** a stone used for sharpening cutting tools *16-*. [OE *hwettan*]
whet *see* QUIT¹·¹, WHAT
whether *see* WHITHER¹·²
wheuch *see* WHEICH

†**wheugh**, **whieu**, **quhew** *interj* whew! *15-19*. [a natural utterance]

†**whew**, **quhew** *n* a whistling sound *16-19*. [onomatopoeic]

whey, *N NE T* **fye**, **fy**, †**quhay**, †**quhey** /ʍe, ʍʌɪ; *N NE T* fʌɪ/ *n* the watery part of milk remaining after the separation of the curd in cheese making *la15-*. **whey brose** BROSE made with whey instead of water *19- Ork NE EC Bor*. **whey parritch** porridge made with whey instead of water *la19- WC SW Bor*. [OE *hwæg*]

which *see* WHILK³·¹, WHILK³·²

whicker /ˈʍɪkər/ *v* to whimper, titter, giggle *19-*. [onomatopoeic]

whid¹·¹, †**quhyd** /ʍɪd/ *n* **1** *frequently of a hare* a rapid, noiseless movement, a gambol, spurt *la18-*. **2** a squall, (sudden) gust of wind *la16, 20- Sh Ork*. **3** a sudden notion, fad, whim *20- Sh Ork*. **4** a slight movement, gesture *20- Sh*. †**in a whid** *in literature* in a moment *18-e19*. †**wi a whid** = *in a whid la18-e19*. [perhaps ON *hvíða* a squall]

whid¹·², **whud** /ʍɪd, ʍʌd/ *v* **1** *frequently of a hare* to move quickly and noiselessly, especially in a jerky or zigzag way; to whisk, scamper, run *18-*. **2** *of or like wind* to sweep in gusts *19, 20- Sh Ork*. **3** to turn (the head or body) quickly in different directions *20- Sh*. [see the noun]

whid²·¹, **whud** /ʍɪd, ʍɪd, ʍʌd/ *n* a lie, an exaggeration, a fib *la18- C SW Bor*. [unknown; compare Eng thieves' cant *whid* a word]

whid²·², **whud** /ʍɪd, ʍɪd, ʍʌd/ *v* to lie, tell fibs *19- C SW*. [see the noun]

whidder¹·¹, **whudder**, **fudder**, †**quhidder** /ˈʍɪdər, ˈʍʌdər, ˈfʌdər/ *n* **1** a sudden or loud gust of wind; a whirlwind *la15-19, 20- Sh NE*. **2** an impetuous rush, a flurry; a scurry *16-19, 20- NE*. **3** a blow, smart stroke *la18-e19*. **4** the spouting of a whale *e16*. **whitherspale** a small whizzing toy *19- Bor*. [see the verb]

whidder¹·², **whither**, **whudder**, *NE* **fudder**, *T* **futher**, *Bor* **whuther**, †**quhidder**, †**quhedir**, †**quhether** /ˈʍɪdər, ˈʍɪdər, ˈʍʌdər; *NE* ˈfʌdər; *T* ˈfʌðər; *Bor* ˈʍʌdər/ *v* **1** to move with force or impetus, rush about; to hum or whizz through the air, bluster or rage like the wind *la14-19, 20- NE T Bor*. **2** *of the wind* to bluster, blow fiercely in gusts *19- Sh NE SW Bor*. **3** to beat, hit; to deal a blow to, floor *19- N Bor*. **4** to potter, trifle in a bustling way *la19- NE T*. **5** to run nimbly; *of a bird* to dart, flutter *19*. [probably ON **hviðra*; related to WHID¹·¹]

whidder *see* WHITHER²
whidle *see* WHEEDLE
whiet *see* QUAIT¹·³
whieu *see* WHEUGH

whiff¹·¹, **whuff**, *Sh Ork* **wheef**, *Ork* **quiff**, †**whiffe** /ʍɪf, ʍʌf; *Sh Ork* ʍif; *Ork* kwɪf/ *n* **1** a small amount, a sip; a slight attack (of illness), a touch *la17-*. **2** a puff (of smoke) *19-*. **3** a smell *la20-*. **whiff of grapeshot** a discharge, a small amount of shot *19-*. **in a whiff** in an instant, a jiffy *la19-*. [EModE *whiff*, onomatopoeic]

whiff¹·², **whuff**, *Sh Ork* **wheef** /ʍɪf, ʍʌf; *Sh Ork* ʍif/ *v* **1** to puff, blow; to drive or carry by blowing; to blow out (a candle) *17-*. **2** to move easily or lightly *la19, 20- Sh*. [see the noun]

whiffe *see* WHIFF¹·¹
whiffle *see* WHEEFLE¹·¹, WHEEFLE¹·²
whifle *see* WHEEFLE¹·¹

whig¹, †**wig** /ʍɪg/ *n* whey, buttermilk *la18-*. [ME *whig*, perhaps a northern variant of WHEY]

†**whig**² *v* **1** to spur, urge on (a horse) *la17*. **2** to go quickly, move at an easy, steady pace, jog *la17-19*. [probably onomatopoeic; compare WHEECH¹·²]

whig³, †**quhigg** /ʍɪg/ *n* **1** an adherent of the National Covenant, one of the Covenanters of South-West Scotland who rose in arms in the reigns of Charles II and James VII and II, an extreme Presbyterian *la17-19*. **2** *in the politics of Great Britain* a member or supporter of the anti-Jacobite parliamentary party which became the Liberal Party *18-*. †**whiging, whigging** behaving like a WHIG³, adhering to Presbyterian and anti-Jacobite principles *la17-e19*. [probably a shortened form of WHIGAMORE]

whig *see* WIG³

whigamore, †**whiggamaire,** †**whigamyre,** †**whiggimuir** /ˈʍɪgəmor/ *n* a Covenanter, originally one who participated in the Whiggamore Raid of 1648, an extreme Presbyterian of the latter part of the 17th century *la17-19, 20- historical*. [perhaps WHIG² + MEAR, literally, spur on a mare, with the final element variously reinterpreted]

whigamyre *see* WHIGAMORE

whigga /ˈʍɪgə/ *n* couch grass *Elymus repens 19- Sh*. [Norw dial *kvika*]

whiggamaire *see* WHIGAMORE

whigget, whugget /ˈʍɪgət, ˈʍʌgət/ *n* a lump, chunk (of bread or cheese etc) *20- Ork*. [unknown]

whiggimuir *see* WHIGAMORE

whigmaleerie, *NE C* **figmaleerie,** *T* **feelimageery,** †**figmalirie** /ʍɪgməˈliri; *NE C* fɪgməˈliri; *T* filɪməˈgiri/ *n* **1** a decorative object, a piece of ornamentation in dress or stonework; *derogatory* a fantastic contrivance or contraption; a bauble, an overly-ornate object *la18-*. **2** a whim, fanciful notion, fad *18-*. [fanciful formation, perhaps based on FYKE¹]

while¹·¹**, whill,** *NE* **file,** †**quhile,** †**quhill** /ʍʌɪl, ʍɪl; *NE* fʌɪl/ *n* **1** a period of time; a (fairly) short time *14-*. **2** a point of time, an occasion *la14-e17*. **a while back** some time ago, in the past *20-*. **a while's time** some time, a period of time *19, 20- Ork NE T*. **a while syne** a certain time ago, for some time past *19-*. **this while** for some time past, for the past few days or weeks *la15-*. **this while back** = *this while la19-*. **this while past** = *this while back e17*. [OE *hwīl*]

while¹·²**, whill,** *Sh Ork N* **fill,** *NE* **file,** †**quhile,** †**quhill,** †**quhell** /ʍʌɪl, ʍɪl; *Sh Ork N* fɪl; *NE* fʌɪl/ *conj* **1** until, up to the time that, up to the point where *la14-*. **2** during, as long as; within the time when *la14-*. **3** when, at the same time as *la15-*. **4** *in co-ordinating use* and then; but then *la14-16*. **5** with the result that *la14-17*. **6** before *15-e17*. **7** provided that, if only *la14-16*. **while that** = WHILE¹·³ *la14-16, 20- NE*. [shortened form of OE *þā hwīle þe*]

†**while**¹·³**, whill, quhill** *prep* till, until *la14-e18*. [see the conj]

whileock, *NE* **fileock** /ˈʍʌɪlək; *NE* ˈfʌɪlək/ *n* a short time, a while *19-*. [WHILE¹·¹, with -OCK diminutive suffix]

whiles¹·¹**,** *NE* **files, fyles,** †**quhilis,** †**quhylis** /ʍʌɪlz; *NE* fʌɪlz/ *adv* **1** sometimes, at times, occasionally *la14-*. **2** formerly, once *la14-16*. [WHILE¹·² with adv-forming suffix]

†**whiles**¹·²**,** †**quhilis** /ʍʌɪlz/ *conj* **1** while, whilst *15-19*. **2** until *la14-e15*. **3** when *la16-e17*. **whiles that** = WHILES¹·² (sense 2) *la14-e15*. [see the adv]

whilie, *NE* **filie** /ˈʍʌɪli; *NE* ˈfʌɪle/ *n* a short time, a while *19-*. [WHILE¹·¹ + -IE¹]

whilin /ˈʍɪlɪn/ *n* a ram with undescended testicles *20- Sh*. [perhaps Norw dial *tvilling* a twin, twin animals being sometimes sexually imperfect or sterile]

whilk¹·¹**, quilk** /ʍɪlk, kwɪlk/ *n* a gulp, a large mouthful, a draught *20- Sh*. [see the verb]

whilk¹·² /ʍɪlk/ *v* to gulp, swallow noisily, suck *la19- Sh*. [probably onomatopoeic]

whilk² /ʍɪlk/ *v* to grasp, pull, pluck, whisk *20- Sh*. †**whilkin** lively, playful as a kitten *19*. [perhaps onomatopoeic]

whilk³·¹**, whulk, which,** †**quhilk,** †**quhich,** †**wich** /ʍɪlk, ʍʌlk, ʍɪtʃ/ *adj pl* †**quhilkis,** †**whilkis 1** *relative* which (person, thing etc) *la14-*. **2** *in direct and indirect questions seeking to know a specification, or requiring a choice to be made,* which, what (person, thing etc) *la14-*. †**the quhilk, the whilk** = **1** *la14-19*. [see the pron]

whilk³·²**, whulk, which,** *N NE T* **filk,** †**quhilk,** †**quhich,** †**wich** /ʍɪlk, ʍʌlk, ʍɪtʃ; *N NE T* fɪlk/ *pron pl* †**quhilkis,** †**whilkis 1** *introducing any kind of relative clause* which, who, whom; that which, those whom, what *la14-*. **2** whichever *la14-e16*. **3** *in direct and indirect questions seeking to know a specification, or requiring a choice to be made,* which person or thing *la14-*. †**the quhilk, the whilk** = **1** *la14-19*. †**the quhilk that, quhilk that** = **1** *la14-e16*. [OE *hwilc*]

whilkis *see* WHILK³·¹, WHILK³·²

whill *see* WHILE¹·¹, WHILE¹·², WHILE¹·³

whillie, *Ork* **whullo** /ˈʍɪli; *Ork* ˈʍʌlo/ *n* a small boat, a skiff *19- Sh Ork*. [perhaps a variant of WHERRY]

whillilu /ˈʍɪlɪlu/ *n* an uproar, a commotion *la18- WC SW Bor Uls*. [onomatopoeic]

whilliwha *see* WHILLYWHA¹·¹

whilly /ˈʍɪli/ *v* to cheat, trick; to wheedle, cajole *18-19, 20- WC*. [shortened form of WHILLYWHA¹·²]

whillywha¹·¹**,** †**whilliwha** /ˈʍɪlɪʍa/ *n* **1** a flatterer, a person who deceives by wheedling; a cheat, trickster; a highwayman *la17-*. **2** flattery, cajolery *19-*. [see the verb]

whillywha¹·² /ˈʍɪlɪʍa/ *v* **1** to wheedle, coax, cajole *19-*. **2** to talk intimately *e19*. [reduplicative formation, perhaps onomatopoeic]

†**whillywha**¹·³ *adj* flattering, deceitful, unreliable *19*. [see the verb]

†**whilom**¹·¹**, quhilum, quhilom** *adj* deceased, late *la14-e19*. [see the adv]

whilom¹·²**,** †**quhilum,** †**qwhylum,** †**quhilom** /ˈʍʌɪləm/ *adv* **1** sometimes, occasionally *la14-16, 20- T*. **2** formerly, once, at some past time *la14-e19*. **3** during a person's lifetime, before the decease of the person named *la14-15*. **whiloms,** †**quhilumis** sometimes, at times *la15-16, la18- literary*. [OE *hwīlum*, dative pl of *hwīl* WHILE¹·¹]

whilom¹·³**,** †**quhylum** /ˈʍʌɪləm/ *conj* while, at the time or period when *e15, la19- literary*. [see the adv]

†**whilter** *n* *in draughts* a game characterized by a particular opening exchange of moves *la19*. [unknown]

†**whiltie-whaltie** *n of the heart* a palpitation, a rapid beating *la18-e19*. [reduplicative formation, perhaps onomatopoeic]

whim *see* WHEEM

whime /ʍʌɪm/ *v* to sneak, insinuate oneself *la19- Ork*. [compare Norw dial *kvima* to flit about, to trifle]

whimmel *see* WHUMMLE¹·²

whimper¹·¹**,** *N NE* **fumper** /ˈʍɪmpər; *N NE* ˈfʌmpər/ *n* **1** a feeble cry, a complaint *19-*. **2** a rumour, a whisper *la19-*. [see the verb]

whimper¹·²**,** *N NE* **fumper,** †**quhimper,** †**quhymper** /ˈʍɪmpər; *N NE* ˈfʌmpər/ *v* to utter a feeble cry, whine, complain *16-*. [onomatopoeic]

whin¹**, whun,** *NE* **fun,** †**quhin,** †**quhyn** /ʍɪn, ʍʌn; *NE* fʌn/ *n* **1** a hard, crystalline, igneous rock, *eg* basalt, flint or diorite; any hard stone used as road stone *16-*. **2** a piece of whin rock, a boulder, slab or stone *16-19, 20- C Bor*. **whin boul** a hard nodule of whin rock embedded in sandstone *la18- T*. **whin dust** whinstone dust or small rubble *20- T C SW*. **whin float** an intrusion or surface overflow of igneous rock *la19, 20- WC*. †**whin rock** = WHIN¹ (sense 1) *la17-e19*. [unknown]

whin²**, whun,** *NE* **fun,** †**quhin,** †**whine** /ʍɪn, ʍʌn; *NE* fʌn/ *n* **1** common furze or gorse *Ulex europaeus*; *pl* a clump or area of furze *16-*. **2** broom *Cytisus scoparius 20- Ork N NE T Bor*. **whinnie** composed of or overgrown with gorse *la17-*. **whin buss** a gorse bush *17-*. **whin chackart** the whinchat

Saxicola rubetra la19-. **whin cow** a tuft or branch of gorse *18-19, 20- T.* **whin dyke** a fence consisting of gorse bushes *19, 20- N EC Bor.* **whun howe** a mattock for uprooting gorse bushes *19- EC SW.* **whin lintie 1** = *whin chackart 19- NE T Bor.* **2** the linnet *Linaria cannabina 19- SW Bor.* **whin mill** a mill for crushing gorse as fodder *la18-19, 20- historical.* **whin-sparrow** the dunnock or hedge sparrow *Prunella modularis 19-.* **through the whins** an unpleasant or painful experience; a dressing-down *19, 20- C Bor.* [ME *whin*; compare Norw *hvine* applied to certain grasses]

whin[3.1] /mɪn/ *n* a (dried up) bannock *20- Ork.* [see the verb]

whin[3.2] /mɪn/ *v* to dry up, harden, scorch (bread) *la19- Sh Ork.* **whinner** plough hard ground *20- Ork.* **whinney** a dried up, hardened piece of bread or cheese *20- Ork.* **whinnery** dried up, shrivelled *20- Ork.* [unknown; perhaps an extended usage of WHIN[1]]

†**whin**[4], **quhyn** *v* to whine, complain *la16-e20.* [OE *hwīnan* to whizz]

whin *see* WHAN[1.1], WHAN[1.2]
whinder *see* WHINNER[1.1]
whine *see* WHEEN[1.2], WHIN[2]
whing *see* WHANG[1.1], WHANG[1.2]

whinge[1.1], **wheenge**, †**quhinge** /mɪndʒ, mɪndʒ/ *n* a whine, whimper, a querulous complaint *16-.* [see the verb]

whinge[1.2], **wheenge**, †**quhinge**, †**quhynge** /mɪndʒ, mɪndʒ/ *v* **1** *of a dog* to whine, whimper, fret *16-.* **2** *of a person* to whine, complain peevishly *17-.* **whinger** a person who whines or complains, a malcontent *la18-.* [OE *hwinsian*]

whinger, †**quhinʒar**, †**quhingar**, †**quhingear** /ˈmɪndʒər, ˈmɪnər/ *n* a short stabbing sword, a long knife or dagger *la15-19, 20- historical.* [unknown]

whink[1.1] /mɪŋk/ *n* a sharp bark or yelp, a whimper *19- Bor.* [see the verb]

whink[1.2] /mɪŋk/ *v of dogs* to bark sharply, yelp *19- Bor.* [probably onomatopoeic; but compare Norw dial *kvinka* to yelp]

whink *see* WHENK[1.1], WHENK[1.2]

whinner[1.1], **whunner**; *Sh* **whinder** /ˈmɪnər, ˈmʌnər; *Sh* ˈmɪndər/ *n* **1** a whizzing sound, the noise made by rapid flight or motion *e19.* **2** a crash, clatter; (the sound of) a heavy fall *19, 20- Sh Ork SW.* **3** a resounding blow, a whack, wallop *19, 20- Sh Ork.* [see the verb]

whinner[1.2], **whunner** /ˈmɪnər, ˈmʌnər/ *v* **1** to whizz, whistle through the air; to move quickly *19-.* **2** to go at, attack with all one's strength, hammer at *19, 20- Sh.* **3** to strike (a person) *e17.* [frequentative form of WHIN[4]]

whinstane[1.1], *NE* **funstane**, †**quhin stane** /ˈmɪnsten; *NE* ˈfʌnsten/ *n* **1** a hard, dark type of rock *16-.* **2** a slab or boulder of whin rock *16-.* [WHIN[1] + STANE[1.1]]

whinstane[1.2] /ˈmɪnsten/ *adj* hard-hearted, inflexible; solid, durable *la18-.* [see the noun]

whint *see* QUAINT
whip *see* WHUP[1.1], WHUP[1.2]
whippack *see* VIPPICK
Whippitie Stourie *see* WHUPPITY STOURIE
whire *see* QUEIR
whirk *see* KWARK[1.2]
whirken *see* WHURKEN
whirl *see* WHURL[1.1], WHURL[1.2]
whirlie *see* WHURLY

whirligig, *NE* **furligig** /ˈmʌrləgɪg; *NE* ˈfʌrləgɪg/ *n* **1** a rotating contrivance or piece of machinery; a child's rotating toy *la19-.* **2** a spiral or fancy ornament; a piece of unnecessary finery; an intricate symbol, design or diagram *la18-.* **3** a revolving chimney cowl *la19- C Bor.* **whirligigum** = WHIRLIGIG. [ME *whirlegig*, compare *whirl* (WHURL[1.2])]

whirliwha[1], *NE* **furlie-fa** /ˈmʌrləʍa; *NE* ˈfʌrləfa/ *n* **1** a piece of fanciful ornamentation *19-.* **2** a revolving piece of machinery *20- NE.* [fanciful formation based on *whirl* (WHURL[1.2])]

†**whirliwha**[2] *v* to flatter, deceive by flattery, trick *19.* [altered form of WHILLYWHA[1], with influence from WHIRLIWHA[1]]

whirm /mɪrm/ *v* to (cause to) disappear, vanish (suddenly); to spirit away *19- Sh Ork.* [unknown]

whirr[1.1], †**quhir**, †**quhirr** /mɪr/ *n* **1** (the sound of) a rapid, rushing movement *16-.* **2** commotion, rush, hurrying about *la19- NE.* **3** a burr in speech, the use of the uvular *r 20- WC SW.* [see the verb]

whirr[1.2], †**whurr**, †**quhir**, †**quhyr**, †**quhuir** /mɪr/ *v* **1** to rush (through the air) with a whirring sound *la15-.* **2** to use a strongly burred or uvular *r* in one's speech *la19- WC SW.* **3** *of a cat* to purr *la19, 20- Ork.* [perhaps onomatopoeic; but compare Dan *hvirre*, Norw *kvirra*]

†**whirry** *v* **1** to carry off, drive away *18-e19.* **2** to move rapidly, rush, fly *e19.* [EModE *whirry*, WHIRR[1.2] with influence from HURRY[1.2]]

whiry *see* WHERRY
whishie *see* WHUSHIE
whisht *see* WHEESHT[1.4]

whisk[1.1], †**wisk**, †**quhisk** /mɪsk/ *n* **1** a rapid, sweeping movement; a blow, swipe; a sweep (of a brush) *la14-.* **2** mainly *pl* a pair of small reels used to facilitate the winding of yarn onto a bobbin *19.* [from the verb and compare LG *wisk* a quick movement]

whisk[1.2], †**wisk**, †**whusk**, †**quhisk**, **wysk** /mɪsk/ *v* **1** to move quickly with a sweeping motion, whirl, rush; to move briskly *la15-.* **2** to rub down (a horse) *la16-.* **3** to beat, whip *la18-e19.* **4** to chase *e16.* †**whiskins** palpitations (of the heart) *e19.* **whisk awa** to move or take away quickly *16-.* [compare Dan *viske* to whisk (off), to sponge, LG *wisken* to wipe off]

whisker *see* WUSKER

whisky, **whusky**, *NE* **fuskie** /ˈmɪski, ˈwʌski; *NE* ˈfʌski/ *n* a spirit distilled from malted barley in a pot still, or with the addition of unmalted grain spirit made in a patent still *17-*; compare *malt whisky* (MAUT) and *blended whisky* (BLAND[1]). **whiskied** affected by whisky, tipsy *19-.* †**whiskified** = *whiskied 19.* †**whisky-house** a tavern where whisky could be obtained *la18-e19.* **whisky pig** an earthenware jar for holding whisky *19, 20- Sh Ork.* **whisky-plook** a pimple on the face ascribed to too much whisky-drinking *la18, 20- T.* **whisky-tacket** = *whisky-plook 19, 20- NE C.* [variant of USQUAE]

whisper *see* WHUSPER[1.1], WHUSPER[1.2]

whiss[1], †**qwis** /mɪs/ *v* **1** to whisper *20- Sh Ork.* **2** to hiss *la15.* [probably onomatopoeic, but compare Norw dial, ON *kvisa*]

whiss[2.1] /mɪs/ *n* a morsel, scrap of food *20- Sh.* [see the verb]

whiss[2.2] /mɪs/ *v* **1** to trim, dress (stone) *la19- Sh.* **2** to scold severely *20- Sh.* **3** to strip the kernel from grains of oats; to eat corn in this way *la19- Sh.* **4** to pick (the bones of), eat (an animal) *19- Sh.* [Norw dial *kvista* to trim (wood)]

whiss *see* QUIZ
whissall *see* WHUSTLE[1.1]
whissle *see* WISSEL[1.2]
whist *see* WHEESHT[1.3], WHEESHT[1.4]
whistle *see* WHUSTLE[1.1], WHUSTLE[1.2]
whistler *see* WHUSTLER

whit[1.1], **whut**, **what**, *N NE* **fit**, *N NE* **fat**, †**quhat** /mɪt, mʌt, mɒt; *N NE* fɪt; *N NE* fat/ *adj* **1** *in direct and indirect questions of the nature or identity of things* what kind, what sort of; which *la14-.* **2** *of the amount of a thing or things* how much, how great, how many : ◇*whit wecht is it? la14-.* **3** *introducing a statement* the, that, those; any, whichever, whatever *15-*. **4** *with indef art + pl noun* how many, what a lot of : ◊*whit a hooses la19-*. **5** *of (the identity of) a person* which, what sort of *la14-17*. **6** *as an exclamation or after verbs of thinking or perceiving* how much, how great what a *15-e17*. **whatever** any (person or thing) that, no matter what, notwithstanding any *15-*. †**quhatkin 1** *in questions, indirect questions or exclamations* what (sort of) *la14-16*; compare WHATTEN. **2** no matter what or which (thing) *la14-15*. †**quhatkynd** = *quhatkin* 1 *e16*. **whatsomever**, †**whatsumever** whatever, any (person or thing) at all, no matter what or which (person or thing) *la14-19, 20- Sh N NE EC Bor*. †**quhatsumevery** = *whatsomever* 16. **what time** when, whenever, as soon as *la14-16, la19- NE T*. **what wey**, †**quhat way 1** how?, in what manner? *15-*. **2** why?, for what reason? *18-*. †**quhat wys** = *what wey* 1 *e16*. **what o'clock is it?** the dandelion *Taraxacum officinale*, from the children's practice of using the seeded head of the flower as a clock *la19-*. **what reck**, †**quhattrak** what does it matter?, no matter, it does not matter *16-*. [see the pron]

whit[1,2], **what**, *N NE* **fit**, *N NE* **fat**, *H&I* **whoot**, *H&I* **hoot**, †**quhat** /ʍɪt, ʍɔt; *N NE* fɪt; *N NE* fat; *H&I* ʍut; *H&I* hut/ *adv* **1** *in exclamatory statements* how greatly, how much *la14-15*. **2** *as exclamation* with an adjective, how, how very: ◊*what pretty it is!* 19-. **3** *in questions* why?, in what way?, to what extent?, how? *la15-19, 20- Sh NE*. **4** *introducing a statement* after than or as, in resumptive use, recalling the subject referred to in the object clause: ◊*I think I laughed heartier then than what I do now 19, 20- Sh Ork N NE T EC*. **whatever** in any case, however, nevertheless, under any circumstances *la19-*; compare Gaelic *co-dhui*. [see the pron]

whit[1,3], **whut**, **what**, *Sh* **quit**, *Sh* **quat**, *N NE* **fit**, *N NE* **fat**, *H&I* **whoot**, *H&I* **hoot**, †**quhat** /ʍɪt, ʍʌt, ʍɔt; *Sh* kwɪt; *Sh* kwat; *N NE* fɪt; *N NE* fat; *H&I* ʍut; *H&I* hut/ *pron* **1** *in direct and indirect questions* seeking information about a thing or things, what *la14-*. **2** *after verbs indicating disbelief or disparagement* indeed: ◊*I worked it aa oot in ten minutes. Did ye whit?* 20-. **3** *introducing a statement* that or those which; anything that, whatever *la14-*. **4** *introducing a statement* that amount which, that number which *la15-19*. **5** *in questions or statements of a person or persons* asking for or expressing the need for information about name, identity or character *la14-e17*. **6** *introducing a statement* that *la16-e18*. **whateverwhitever**, †**quhat evir 1** anything that, all that; no matter what *la14-*. **2** whoever, whatever (sort of) person, no matter who *la14-e17*. †**whatsomever**, **whatsumever** whatever, whoever, no matter what (thing or person) *la14-e17*. **what ... at** why?: ◊*whit's she greetin at? la19-*. **what be** what about ...?, how about ...? *20- Sh Ork Bor*. **whatwhit for 1** why?, for what reason? *la18-*. **2** what kind of (a) *17-19, 20- Ork*. **what for no** why not? *la18-*. **what itherwhatither** what else?, of course *19- Ork N NE T*. **what like** what sort of?, resembling what in appearance or nature?, how? *18-*. **fit like**, **fat like** how are you? *20- NE*. **what recks**, †**what raiks**, †**whatrax 1** what does it matter?, it doesn't matter *la16-19, 20- NE C*. **2** why not? *16-e17*. [OE *hwæt*, neuter sg of *hwā* WHA]

whit[1,4], **what**, †**quhat** /ʍɪt, ʍɔt/ *conj* **1** *after negative verbs of saying, thinking, doubting etc* that: ◊*I dinna think but what it'll be rain la18-*. **2** to the utmost that; as much, as far or as hard etc as: ◊*she cried what she could cry 19-*. **3** *introducing two or more co-ordinating expressions* indicating alternative or cumulative states or causes, both ... and, partly ... partly, whether ... or: ◊*a ... forton what in land, what in money la14-17*. †**quhat for** as a result of *e16*. [see the pron]

whit *see* WHEET

white[1,1], *NE* **fite**, †**quhite**, †**quhit**, †**quhyte** /ʍʌɪt/ *NE* fʌɪt/ *n* **1** the colour white, whiteness; white cloth or a white garment *15-*. **2** the white of the eye or an egg *la15-*. **3** white paint *16-*. **4** the white part of an archery target, the bull's eye, the mark *la15-e19*. **5** *in Shetland fisherman's taboo* the ling *Molva molva la19*. **whitie 1** *fisherman's taboo* the ling *Molva molva 20- Sh*. **2** the whiting *Merlangius merlangus la19- H&I WC*. **whited-broon**, **whitit-broon** unbleached linen thread *la18- NE*. **whitie-broon** = *whited-broon* 19- *Ork T EC Uls*. [OE *hwīt* noun]

white[1,2], *NE* **fite**, †**quhite**, †**quhit**, †**quhyt** /ʍʌɪt; *NE* fʌɪt/ *adj* **1** white or light in colour; lustrous; colourless, pale *12-*. **2** *of hair* white or grey; fair, blonde *la14-*. **3** *of the skin or complexion* pale, fair; not sunburned *15-*. **4** *of coins* silver *la15-19, 20- Sh Ork NE C*. **5** *of land* fallow, unploughed *la14-19, 20- N SW*. **6** *of hill-land* covered with coarse bent or natural grass instead of heather, bracken or scrub *19- T C SW Bor*. **7** flattering, fair-seeming, plausible, usually implying an intention to deceive *la15-e19*. **8** *of metal* silver, a silver-coloured alloy or steel; *of commodities* white in colour; of high quality, not spoiled *15-17*. **fiteichtie** rather white, whitish *20- NE*. **whitely**, †**quhitlie** pale, whitish, delicate-looking *la15-19, 20- T*. **white bonnet** a person at an auction sale engaged by the seller to raise the bidding *la18-*. **white cockade** a white rosette, originally worn by Jacobites to represent the *white rose* as an emblem of the Stewart cause *18-*. **white cow** remains of heather, whin and broom bleached by sun and rain after the annual burning *la19- T*. **White Craw** nickname for a native of Carnwath, Lanarkshire *20- WC*. **white drap** a snowfall *la19- Sh*. **white-faced** *of a sheep* applied to a breed with a white face *la18- Sh N NE Bor*. **white hare** the Alpine, Scottish, mountain or blue hare *Lepus timidus*, especially in its white winter coat *19, 20- N NE T H&I*. †**white hause** an oatmeal pudding cooked in a sheep's gullet *e16, e19*. **white head** a large, white cloud on the horizon *20- Sh*. †**white herring** herring cured by salting or pickling *17-e19*. **white hoolet** the barn owl *Tyto alba la19- C*. **white house** a house built with stone and lime as opposed to a *black house* (BLACK) *la19- N H&I*. **white ice** curling the ice up the middle of the rink, whitened and roughened by the friction of the stones *19- T WC SW*. **white iron** tin-plate, tinned iron *la15-19, 20- NE T*. **white lily** a pheasant's eye narcissus *Narcissus poeticus la19-*. **white meal** apparently mainly oatmeal as distinct from barley meal *la16-19, 20- N C*. **white meat** the flesh of poultry or game *18-*. **white moss** sphagnum moss *20- Sh*. **white owl** the snowy owl *Bubo scandiacus la19- Sh*. **white peat** a layer of mosses, mainly sphagnum, under the surface layer of vegetation in a peat bog *la18- NE T*. **white puddin** a pudding or sausage stuffed mainly with oatmeal, suet, salt, pepper and onions *17-*. **white rizzar** white currant *18- EC Bor*. **white room** a room in a textile factory where finished cloth is inspected and prepared for despatch *20- WC*. **white rose**, †**quhit rois 1** the emblem of royalism and legitimacy, adopted in Scotland as the symbol of adherence to Jacobitism and the Stewart cause *19, 20- historical*; compare *white cockade*. **2** Perkin Warbeck, the Yorkist Pretender to the English Throne *e16*. †**white seam** plain needlework *18-19*. **white settler** an incomer into a rural area, someone resented by the local population *la20-*. **white shower** a shower of snow *19- Sh NE*. **white siller**, †**quhite silver 1** silver money as opposed to coppers, cash in silver *15-19, 20- Sh Ork N NE T C*. **2** (ungilt or unalloyed) silver *15-e17*. **white sookie** white clover *Trifolium repens la19, 20- T C*. †**quhite staff** a white rod used as a sign of authority (or, sometimes, infection) *la16-17*. **white throat** *fisherman's taboo* a minister *20- Sh Ork*. **white victual** a cereal or grain crops as opposed to green crops *la18- T C*. †**quhite**

wand 1 = *quhite staff* 1 *15-16*. **2** a stripped twig carried by a bridegroom *e19*. †**quhite wax** natural, uncoloured beeswax, used for making seals *16-e17*. †**quhite-werk 1** tinned iron or tin-plate *16-e17*. **2** silver-work or silver-ware *16-17*. **3** embroidery executed with silver or white thread *la16-e17*. **white wood**, †**quhyt wod 1** light-coloured wood *la16-*. **2** the outer circles of new wood on a tree trunk *19*. †**under the quhite wax** *of a document* authenticated by the use of the *quarter-seal* (QUARTER) *15-e16*. †**quhite and red** = *reid and quhyt* (REID[1,2]) *la15*. [OE *hwīt* adj]

white², *Sh* **twaet**, *Sh* **tweet**, *N* **twayt**, *NE* **fite**, †**quhite**, †**twyte** /ʍʌɪt/ *Sh* twɑət; *Sh* twit; *N* twet; *NE* fʌɪt/ *v* to cut with a knife, pare, whittle *16-*. **fite the idle pin** to fritter away time *la19- NE*. [OE ðwītan]

white see WHEAT

white breid, **white bread**, †**quhyte breid**, †**quhete brede**, †**quhitt breid** /'ʍʌɪt brid, 'ʍʌɪt brɛd/ *n* white bread, bread made from refined wheat flour and so white in appearance *15-*. [WHITE[1,2] + BREID]

whiteret see FUTRET

whither¹, *Sh* **whidder**, †**quhether**, †**quhidder** /'ʍɪðər; *Sh* 'ʍɪdər/ *adv* to what place, where *la14-*. [OE *hwider*]

†**whither**[2,1], **quhethir**, **quhithir** *pron* which (of alternatives); whichever *la15-17*. [OE *hweðer*]

whither[2,2], **whether**, *NE T* **fither**, *NE* **fudder**, *Bor* **whuther**, †**quhethir** /'ʍɪðər, 'ʍɛðər; *NE T* 'fɪðər; *NE* 'fʌdər; *Bor* 'ʍʌðər/ *conj* **1** indicating choice, doubt or indecision between alternatives, whether, if *14-*. **2** if *la14-16*. **3** *introducing a direct question* indicating a question *la14-16*. †**quhethir gif** = WHITHER[1,2] *la15-16*. **whether-or-no** uncertain, indecisive, dithering *la19- C SW*. †**whither sa, quhidder so** = WHITHER[1,2] (sense 1) *la14-e16*. [see the pron]

whither see WHIDDER[1,2]

whitherspale see WHIDDER[1,1]

whitin, *NE* **fitin**, †**quhiting**, †**whitting** /'ʍʌɪtɪn; *NE* 'fʌɪtən/ *n* **1** the whiting *Merlangius merlangus 15-*. **2** an immature sea trout *Salmo trutta la18-e19* [probably WHITE[1,2] + -*ing* suffix, but compare MDu *witinc*, MLG *witink* the whiting and WHITLING]

whitling /'ʍɪtlɪŋ/ *n* an immature sea trout *Salmo trutta* at the stage of development equivalent to the GRILSE of the salmon *la18- T C Bor*. [WHITE[1,2] + -*ling* suffix; compare OE *hwītling* an unidentified fish]

whitret, whitrick, whitrit see FUTRET

Whitsun, †**Witson** /'ʍɪtsən/ *n* = Whitsun, pertaining to (the period around) WHITSUNDAY *la14-*. **Whitsun Term** *in the Universities of St Andrews and Glasgow* the third or summer term *20-*. [shortened form of WHITSUNDAY, reanalysed as *Whitsun Day*]

Whitsunday, **Whussenday**, †**Witsonday**, †**Quhissonday**, †**Witsounday** /'ʍɪtsəndɛ, 'ʍʌsəndɛ/ *n* **1** Whit Sunday, the seventh Sunday after Easter, the feast of Pentecost *la14-*. **2** a quarter day, one of the *term days* (TERM), originally the normal term for changes in tenancy, fixed at 15 May in 1690, though the date for removals and for the employment of servants was changed in 1886 to 28 May *la14-*. **Whitsunday term** = WHITSUNDAY (sense 2); the period from an earlier term-day to the Whitsun term-day *15-*. [OE *Hwīta Sunnandæg*, WHITE[1,2] + SUNDAY]

whittell see WHITTLE²

whitter¹ /'ʍɪtər/ *n* a small or insignificant object; a trifle *la18-19, 20- EC*. [perhaps an extended form of *whit* (WHEET)]

whitter² /'ʍɪtər/ *v* to diminish by taking away small portions; to whittle *19- Ork T WC Bor*. [altered form of WHITTLE[1,2]]

whitter³ /'ʍɪtər/ *n* an alcoholic drink, alcohol *la18-19, 20- H&I C*. [compare EModE *whittle* to ply with alcohol]

whitter[4,1] /'ʍɪtər/ *n* chatter, prattle; a talkative person *19- Bor*. [see the verb]

whitter[4,2], †**quitter**, †**quytter**, †**quhitter** /'ʍɪtər/ *v* **1** *of birds* to twitter, warble, chirp *16-*. **2** to flutter, flicker, quiver; to scamper, scurry, patter *16-*. **3** *of persons* to mutter, prattle, gossip *19-*. [onomatopoeic of a bird's chirp, with frequentative suffix]

whitterick /'ʍɪtərɪk/ *n* the curlew *Numenius arquata la19- C Bor*. [perhaps onomatopoeic of its cry, with the form influenced by *whitterick* (FUTRET)]

whitterick see FUTRET

whittie-whattie see WHEETY-WHATTIE[1,1], WHEETY-WHATTIE[1,2]

whitting see WHITIN

whittle[1,1], **whuttle**, *N NE* **futtle**, †**quhittil** /'ʍɪtəl, 'ʍʌtəl; *N NE* 'fʌtəl/ *n* **1** a knife *la15-*. **2** an implement or bill-hook for pruning; a sickle or scythe *18-19, 20- WC*. **3** a whetstone for sharpening scythes *19, 20- Sh WC*. **4** a blunt knife; a useless tool *20- N*. [ME *thwitel* a type of knife, WHITE², with *-le* suffix]

whittle[1,2], **whuttle**, *N NE* **futtle** /'ʍɪtəl, 'ʍʌtəl; *N NE* 'fʌtəl/ *v* to cut, carve, pare (with a knife) *19-*. [see the noun]

whittle², †**whittell** /'ʍɪtəl/ *n* an abscess-like inflammation in a finger or thumb, a whitlow *17-19, 20- H&I C SW Bor Uls*. **whittle-beal** = WHITTLE² *la19, 20- Sh Ork N T C*. **whittle bealin** = *whittle-beal*. **whitly-beal**, *NE* **futley bealin** = *whittle-beal la19- NE T*. [reduced form of EModE *whitlow*]

whittrock see FUTRET

whizz see QUIZ

who see WHA

whoast see HOAST[1,1]

whole see HAIL[1,1], HAIL[1,2], HAIL[1,3]

wholme see FOLM[1,2]

whom see WHAM⁴

whommle see WHUMMLE[1,2]

whoogh see HOOCH[1,3]

whoom /ʍum/ *n* a blaze; a roaring sound *20-, NE*. [onomatopoeic]

whooper /'ʍupər/ *n* nickname for a native of Ayton, Berwickshire *la19, 20- historical*. [perhaps a variant of Eng *hooper*, i.e. a cooper in the local barrel factory]

whoor see HOOR

whoot see WHIT[1,2]

whop see WAP[1,2], WHUP[1,1]

whope see HOPE¹

whose see WHASE

whosle see WHEEZLE[1,2]

whost see HOAST[1,2]

whow /ʍʌu/ *interj* expressing astonishment or surprise, usually with regret or weariness *19, 20- EC Bor*. [a natural utterance; compare WOW²]

whow see HOO¹

whud see WHID¹·², WHID²·¹, WHID²·²

whudder see WHIDDER[1,1], WHIDDER[1,2]

whuff see WHIFF[1,1], WHIFF[1,2]

whulk see WHILK[3,1], WHILK[3,2]

whullo see WHILLIE

whulp see WHALP[1,1], WHALP[1,2]

whult /ʍʌlt/ *n* anything large of its kind *19- WC SW*. **whulter** = WHULT *19- C SW*. [perhaps Scots †*quhult* to 'quilt', beat, thrash or onomatopoeic]

whum, home /ʍʌm, hom/ *v* to finish off the top on a stack (of corn) *20- Ork*. [compare Norw dial *kvelm* a truss of hay which fills a space in a drying frame, Swed *valm* a small haycock]

whumble see WHUMMLE[1,2]

whummle[1.1], *T H&I SW Uls* **whammle** /ˈʍʌməl; *T H&I SW Uls* ˈʍaməl/ *n* **1** a capsizing, an overturning, an upset *19-*. **2** a turning, a whirling round; a rocking, tossing or rolling from side to side *19*. **3** a tumble, a fall, an avalanche; a downfall, a reversal of good fortune *19, 20- T H&I WC SW*. **dish o whammle, plate o whammle** no food, nothing to eat or drink *20-*. **whammle net** *fishing* a drift-net *la19- SW*. [see the verb]

whummle[1.2], **whommle**, *Ork* **whimmel**, *NE* **fummle**, *NE* **fommle**, *T SW Uls* **whammle**, †**whumble**, †**quhomle** /ˈʍʌməl, ˈʍɔməl; *Sh* ˈkʌməl; *Ork* ˈʍɪməl; *NE* ˈfʌməl, ˈfɔməl; *T SW Uls* ˈʍaməl/ *v* **1** to capsize, overturn, turn upside down *17-*. **2** to empty (a container) by tilting it, pour out (the contents of a container) *17-*. **3** to overthrow, throw into ruin or confusion *la17-*. **4** to go head over heels, fall or tumble suddenly; to stumble *la18-*. **5** to (cause to) turn or revolve, rock or toss about *la18-*. **6** to knock down, push over *19-*. **7** to cover or conceal (something) by inverting a hollow container over it *19- Sh Ork SW Uls*. **8** to overpower, defeat; to astonish *la19- NE EC Bor*. **9** to overwhelm, drown *la16-19*. **whummlin, whammlum** *humorous* what is left when a pot has been emptied; nothing *20- WC SW Bor*. **whamlins** = *whummlin 20- WC SW*. [metathesis of *wholme* (FOLM[1.2])]

whump /ʍʌmp/ *n* a toss of the head, a gesture of impatience *20- Ork*. [compare Dan *hvimpe* (of a horse) to toss the head]

whun *see* WHAN[1.1], WHAN[1.2], WHIN[1], WHIN[2]

whunner *see* WHINNER[1.1], WHINNER[1.2]

whup[1.1], **whip**, *Ork NE T EC* **wheep**, *N NE* **fup**, *T* **whop**, †**quhip**, †**quhyp** /ʍʌp, ʍɪp; *Ork NE T EC* ʍip; *N NE* fʌp; *T* ʍɔp/ *n* **1** a rod with a lash attached, a whip *la14-*. **2** a blow with a whip *15-*. **3** a sudden quick movement, a start, a jerk, a swirl; a gust or blast of wind *la16-*. **4** a crack, a shot, a go at *la19-*. **5** *mainly pl* plenty, lots *la19- N H&I SW*. **6** *weaving* a thread separate from the basic warp and weft which is introduced into the weave to form a pattern *19*. **whuppie** *n* **1** a derogatory term for a mischievous or pert girl *19*. **2** a rope of twisted straw *20- EC Bor*. **whuppie** *adj* quick or brisk in movement, nimble, agile *19- C SW*. **whiplicker** a carter; *in St Andrews* a member of the Incorporated Society of Whiplickers or Carters *19, 20- historical*. **whipman** a carter, a driver of horses; a member of one of a number of benevolent societies of carters and ploughmen *la16-19, 20- historical*. **at ae whup** at one stroke or swoop, suddenly *19-*. **in a whup** = *at ae whup*. **whip o dearth** an unexpected hardship, an emergency *la19- T C*. [from the verb and MDu, MLG *wippe* a quick movement]

whup[1.2], **whip**, *N NE* **fup**, *NE* **wheep**, †**quhip**, †**quheip** /ʍʌp, ʍɪp; *N NE* fʌp; *NE* ʍip/ *v* **1** to beat, flog *la16-*. **2** to drink, gulp down *la17-19*. **3** to strike rapidly, cut swiftly *e16*. **whipper-in** a school attendance-officer *19-*. **whippert** hasty and sharp in manner or behaviour *19-, 20- SW*. **fup a haud o** to seize in one's grip *20- NE*. **whip the cat** *mainly of a tailor* to go from house to house practising one's trade *19, 20- historical*. [MDu, MLG *wippen* to swing, oscillate]

whup[1.3], †**wheep** /ʍʌp/ *adv* with a quick or sudden movement, like a shot, in a jiffy *19- Sh NE T EC*. [see the verb]

whup *see* HOPE[1]

whupper /ˈʍʌpər/ *n* something very large or outstanding of its kind, a whopper *la19, 20- Ork N SW Bor*. [altered form of Eng *whopper*]

Whuppity Scoorie /ˈʍʌpɪti ˈskuri/ *n in Lanark* a traditional custom among young people celebrated on 1 March *20- WC*. [unknown; compare WHUP[1.1] and SCOUR[2.1]]

Whuppity Stourie, Whippitie Stourie /ˈʍʌpɪti ˈsturi, ˈʍɪpɪti ˈsturi/ *n* **1** a household fairy or BROONIE *19-*. **2** a light-footed nimble person *20- C*. [unknown; compare WHUP[1.1] and STOORIE[1.2]]

whure *see* HOOR

whurken, whirken /ˈʍʌrkən, ˈʍɪrkən/ *v* to choke, suffocate *19- Bor*. [ME *querkenen*]

whurl[1.1], **whirl**, *NE T* **furl**, †**quhirl** /ʍʌrl, ʍɪrl; *NE T* fʌrl/ *n* a (rapid) turn or circular movement; the swift or violent whirling motion of water or wind *la15-*. **whirlock** anything twisted into a knot or tangle *la19- Sh*. **whirl-dodie** a spinning top *20- Sh*. **furlin yett** a turnstile *la19- NE*. **furl o birse, furly birse** the ace of spades, so called because of the intricate, flowery ornamentation usually found on this card *20- NE*. [see the verb]

whurl[1.2], **whirl**, *NE T* **furl**, †**quhirl** /ʍʌrl, ʍɪrl; *NE T* fʌrl/ *v* **1** to (cause to) rotate, spin; fly, hurtle, move rapidly *16-*. **2** to propel on wheels, trundle, cart; to drive on *16-*. [probably ON *hvirfla*]

whurl[2], *Sh* **whaarl**, *N NE* **forl**, *C* **horl**, †**thorl**, †**quhorle**, †**quorill** /ʍʌrl; *Sh* ʍarl; *N NE* fɔrl; *C* hɔrl/ *n* **1** *spinning* the small perforated disc placed on a spindle as a counter balance *16-e19, 20- N NE*. **2** a (small) wheel, caster or pulley *la18-19, 20- NE EC*. **3** *folklore* a naturally perforated stone, supposed to be used by the fairies *la19- N NE*. †**quhorlebane** the hip-bone or joint; a vertebra *la17-19*. [ME *whirl, wharle, whoril*, ON *hvirfill* a circle, ring, MDu *wirvel, warvel, worvel* a spindle, vertebra]

whurly, whirlie /ˈʍʌrli, ˈʍɪrli/ *n* **1** a chimney-cowl *20-*. **2** a bed on castors which can be rolled under another bed when not in use *20- H&I*. **3** *mining* a box-like container on wheels, for taking coal to the surface *19- WC*. **whurly bed** = WHURLY (sense 2) *20- WC*. **whurly-gate** a turnstile *20- C Bor*. **whurlie-wheeter** a whelk-type seashell *20- Sh*. [WHURL[1.2] + -IE[3]]

whurn *see* HORN

whurr *see* WHIRR[1.2]

whurry *see* WHERRY

whush[1.1] /ʍʌʃ/ *n* a rushing noise; a stir, a commotion *19-*. [onomatopoeic]

whush[1.2], **wheesh** /ʍʌʃ, ʍɪʃ/ *v* to make a rushing sound *19, 20- NE*. [see the noun]

whush *see* WHEESHT[1.1], WHEESHT[1.2], WHEESHT[1.3], WHEESHT[1.4]

whush'd *see* WHEESHT[1.3]

†**whushie, whishie** *n* the whitethroat *Sylvia communis la19*. **whushie-whey-beard** = WHUSHIE; *see also* WHUSKY TAM. [onomatopoeic of the bird's song; compare WHEETIE[1.1]]

whusk *see* WHISK[1.2]

whusky *see* WHISKY

whusky Tam /ˈʍʌski tam/ *n* = WHUSHIE *20- WC*. [WHUSHIE with influence from WHISKY + TAM]

whusper[1.1], **whisper**, †**quhisper** /ˈʍʌspər, ˈʍɪspər/ *n* **1** a soft, sibilant sound *16-*. **2** a whispered word or remark; a hint, a rumour *la16-*. [see the verb]

whusper[1.2], **whisper**, †**quhisper** /ˈʍʌspər, ˈʍɪspər/ *v* to speak softly; say (something) in a whisper; to talk confidentially or secretly; to gossip *16-*. [OE *hwisprian*]

Whussenday *see* WHITSUNDAY

whust *see* HOAST[1.1]

whustle[1.1], **whistle**, *NE* **fussle**, †**whissall**, †**quhissill**, †**quyschile** /ˈʍʌsəl, ˈʍɪsəl; *NE* ˈfʌsəl/ *n* **1** a whistle, a flute or pipe *la14-*. **2** a wallop, a swipe, a swingeing blow *19, 20- N NE*. **3** a factory hooter *20- T*. †**whistle kirk** a church with an organ; an Episcopalian Church *19*. **whustle-wud** tree with a slippery bark so that twigs can be used to make a whistle *19, 20- SW*. **kist o whistles** *see* KIST[1.1]. **no gie a whistle (for)** not to give a damn, have nothing but contempt for *la19- Sh Ork N T EC SW*. [OE *hwistle*]

whustle[1,2], **whistle**, *NE* **fussle**, †**quhissill**, †**quhisle** /ˈʍʌsəl, ˈmɪsəl; *NE* ˈfʌsəl/ *v* **1** to utter or produce a shrill whistling sound or cry; to play a whistle *15-*. **2** to beat sharply, strike *la19- NE*. **3** *of snakes* to hiss *15-e17*. **whistlin Sunday, fusslin Sunday** *Presbyterian Church* the fast day (usually a Thursday) of the pre-Communion service when, unlike Sundays, whistling was permitted *la19- NE*. **fusslebare, whistlebare** *of land* poor, hilly, exposed; frequently in place-names *la19- Ork NE SW Uls*. **whistlebinkie** a person who attends a *penny wedding* (PENNY) without paying and had no right to share in the entertainment; a mere spectator (who might whistle for his own amusement) *e19-*. **whistle on yer thoum** to act in an idle or ineffectual manner, especially after a rebuff or failure; to twiddle one's thumbs *18-19, 20- Sh NE T*. [OE *hwistlian*]

whustler, whistler, *NE* **fussler**, †**quhisilar** /ˈʍʌslər, ˈmɪslər; *NE* ˈfʌslər/ *n* **1** a person or bird that whistles; a piper or flute-player *16-*. **2** a big specimen of anything *20- N T EC*. **3** nickname for an inhabitant of Fife *la19- T EC*. **4** a heavy blow, a wallop *20- N T*. [from the verb WHUSTLE[1,2] with agent suffix]

whut *see* WHIT[1.1], WHIT[1.3]
whuther *see* WHITHER[1,2], WHIDDER[1,2]
whuttle *see* WHITTLE[1.1], WHITTLE[1.2]
why[1.1], †**quhy** /ʍae/ *n* (the) reason, cause *15-*. [see the adv]
why[1.2], †**quhy**, †**quhi** /ʍae/ *adv* **1** *in direct and indirect questions* for what reason, why *la14-*; compare FORQUHY. **2** *as a relative* because of which; for which *la14-*. **why fur?** why? *19-*. **why fur no?** why not? *19-*. [OE *hwȳ*, instrumental of *hwæt* WHIT[1.3]]
why[1.3], †**quhy** /ʍae/ *interj* an exclamation of surprise *la15-*. [see the adv]
why *see* QUEY, QUOY
whytie-whatie *see* WHEETY-WHATTIE[1.1]

wi, wae, with, †**we,** †**wyth** /wi, wɪ, we, wɪθ/ *prep* **1** in the company of, accompanied by *la14-*. **2** mainly *with passive verb* by means of, by the action of: ◊*eaten wi the mice la14-*. **3** *with verbal noun* because of, by means of: ◊*wi being ill he couldna come la14-*. **4** having, bringing, in ownership or possession of: ◊*she left hir keys wi me la14-*. **5** against, in opposition to, in resistance to: ◊*the laddies were aye fechtin wi yin anither la14-*. **6** in the culture, estimation, or opinion of: ◊*wi us a windae bar is cried an astragal la14-*. **7** referring to procreation by (either parent): ◊*he had fower weans wi Jeannie 15-*. **8** *with negative* to indicate inability: in consequence of; on account of: ◊*they coudna fecht wi cauld 19-*. **9** expressing a means of travel, by the conveyance of: ◊*he came wi the bus 20-*. †**with the mare** and more, and something over *la15-e17*. **with their tale** according to their account *19, 20- Bor*. **wi me** (cannot be done) by me: ◊*that buik winna read wi me 19, 20- Sh N NE*. [OE *wið*]

wice *see* WISE[2]
wich *see* WHILK[3.1], WHILK[3.2], WITCH[1.1], WITCH[1.2]
wicht[1], **wight,** †**weycht** /wɪxt/ *n* **1** a supernatural being; a being with supernatural powers *16-*. **2** a human being, a person *la14-19, 20- NE Bor*. [OE *wiht*]
wicht[2], **wight,** †**wycht** /wɪxt/ *adj literary* **1** *of a person* physically strong, powerful, valiant, courageous *la14-*. **2** *of an animal or bird* strong, powerful *la14-19*. **3** *of a thing or building* strongly constructed, stout *15-19*. **4** swift; energetic *la14-19*. [ON *vígt* neuter of *vígr* battle ready]
wichty *see* WECHTY
wick[1], **week** /wɪk, wik/ *n* **1** a corner of the mouth *18-*. **2** the corner of the eye *19, 20- Sh Bor*. †**hing by the wicks of the mouth** to hang on for as long as possible, refuse to give up easily *17-19*. [ON -*vik*, as in *munnvik* the corner of the mouth]
wick[2], †**wik** /wɪk/ *n* **1** a wicked person *la14*. **2** a naughty child *20- NE C*. [OE *wicca* a wizard]
wick[3] /wɪk/ *n* an inlet of the sea, a small bay; frequently in place-names *17, la18- Sh Ork N*. [ON *vík*]
wick[4.1] /wɪk/ *n curling, bowls* a cannon of one stone or ball off another towards the TEE[1] *19-*. [unknown]
wick[4.2] /wɪk/ *v curling, bowls* to cannon one stone or ball off another *la18-*. [unknown]
wick *see* WEEK[1], WEEK[2]
wicked *see* WICKIT
wicker[1], †**wickir,** †**wicir,** †**wekirr** /ˈwɪkər/ *n* **1** wickerwork *16-*. **2** a hut or tent made of wickerwork *20- SW*. **3** a withy, osier or thin pliable branch *14-18*. [ME *wiker*, compare MSwed *viker*, Dan *vigger* willow, osier]
wicker[2.1] /ˈwɪkər/ *n* **1** a short, sharp shower *19- WC*. **2** a flicker *la19*. [see the verb]
wicker[2.2] /ˈwɪkər/ *v* to flicker, twitch involuntarily *19- SW*. [perhaps an altered form of Eng *flicker*, with influence from WICK[1]]
wicket, †**wykket** /ˈwɪkət/ *n* **1** a small door or gate, usually in or beside a larger one *la15-*. **2** a small opening or unglazed window in a wall *17-19*. [AN *wiket*]
wickit, wicked, wicket, †**wikkit,** †**wykkit,** †**wekit** /ˈwɪkɪt, ˈwɪkɪd, ˈwɪkət/ *adj* **1** bad, evil, cruel, malicious, criminal *la14-*. **2** bad-tempered, ill-natured, (viciously) angry *la15-*. **3** *of weather* severe, destructive *la14-e16*. **4** *of a place, route or terrain* dangerous, difficult *e16*. [WICK[2] + -IT[2]]
†**Wiclefit** *n* a Wycliffite, a follower of the theologian John Wycliffe *la16*. [from the surname]
wid[1.1], **wuid, wud, wood,** †**wode,** †**wod,** †**woud** /wɪd, wʌd, wud/ *n* **1** an area of trees, smaller than a forest; trees, wooded land *12-*. **2** (a piece of) wood, as a material or commodity, timber, originally especially as fuel *la14-*. **3** an inferior type of small coal *la17-e19*. **wudy 1** wooded, abounding in trees *la14-*. **2** consisting of, of the texture of wood *19-*. †**wood-forester** a forester, a person in charge of the woods on an estate *la18-19*. †**wood-ill** a disease of cattle *la18-e19*. **wood laid** floored with wood *20- N NE EC*. **woodlark** the tree pipit *Anthus trivialis la18-*. †**wood leave,** †**wodeleve** permission to cut growing timber *la13-18*. **wood-pecker** the treecreeper *Certhia familiaris la19-*. [OE *wudu*]
wid[1.2], **wud, wood** /wɪd, wʌd, wud/ *v ptp also* †**woddit 1** to construct or furnish with wood *la16-*. **2** to plant with trees *19-*. **wooding** (a planting of) trees; a copse or wood *la18-*. [see the noun]
wid[2], **wad, wud,** †**wald** /wɪd, wad, wʌd/ *v* **1** was able to, could; was accustomed to; was bound to *la14-*. **2** would or should like, desire to, wish to, seek to *la14-*. **3** chooses to; be willing to, intend to *la14-*. **widna, widnae, wadna, wadnae, wudna, wudnae** would not *18-*. **twad** it would *la18-19, 20- NE T*. [OE *wolde*, pt of *willan* WILL[1.2]]
wid *see* WILL[1.2]
widden, wudden, wooden, †**wodin** /ˈwɪdən, ˈwʌdən, ˈwudən/ *adj* (made) of wood, timber *17-*. **wooden breeks** a coffin *19- T C Bor*. **wudden jeckit** a coffin *20- T C*. [WID[1.1], with adj-forming suffix]
widden *see* WADE[1.2]
widder *see* WEATHER, WITHER
widdergaets /ˈwɪdərgets/ *adv* anticlockwise *la19- Sh*. [*widder-* as in WIDDERSHINS or WIDDERWISE[1.2] + GAIT[3], with adv-forming suffix]
widderlok *see* WITHERLOCK
widdershins, withershins, †**withersones,** †**wodershins** /ˈwɪdərʃɪnz, ˈwɪðərʃɪnz/ *adv* **1** anticlockwise; in a

direction contrary to the apparent course of the sun, with the implication of bad luck or disaster, *16-.* **2** in a direction opposite to the usual, the wrong way round *16-19, 20- Ork.* Compare DEASIL¹·¹. **widdershins about** anticlockwise *18-.* [MDu *wedersins*, MLG *weddersinnes*, with influence from *widder-* as in WIDDERWISE¹·²]

widderwise¹·¹ /ˈwɪdərwʌɪz/ *adj* contrary, stubborn *20- Sh.* [see the adv]

†**widderwise**¹·², **witherwys** *adv* anticlockwise *17-19.* [OE *wiðer-* counter-, + WISE¹]

widdie, woodie, wuddie, †**wedy,** †**wethy** /ˈwɪdi, ˈwudi, ˈwʌde/ *n* **1** a rope, originally made of twisted or intertwined withies or flexible branches *la15-.* **2** a halter or harness *16-.* **3** a container made of withies for carrying things over the shoulder *19-.* **4** the gallows rope *la15-.* **5** a willow tree, especially the dwarf willow *Salix repens 20- Sh.* **6** a quantity of iron, originally a bundle tied with rope *15-e17.* **7** a door fastening *16-.* **widdiefu,** †**widdefow** *n* a person who deserves hanging, a scoundrel; a rogue *16-19, 20- NE.* **widdiefu** *adj* deserving hanging; rascally; ill-natured; troublesome *16-.* †**widdieneck, widdienek** a person who deserves hanging *la15-16.* **widdie-wand** a withy or branch of willow *la19-.* **in the widdienecks** at loggerheads, in a quarrel or dispute *20- NE.* [OE *wīðig*]

Widdinsday *see* WEDNESDAY

widdle¹·¹ /ˈwɪdəl/ *n* **1** a struggle *la18-.* **2** a bustle, a tumult *e19.* [unknown]

†**widdle**¹·², **widdill** *v* to curse *16-e17.* [unknown]

widdle² /ˈwɪdəl/ *v* **1** to move slowly and unsteadily, stagger, totter *la18-.* **2** to progress slowly and laboriously, struggle *la18- NE C Bor.* [altered form of Eng *waddle*]

wide¹·¹, †**wyde,** †**wyd** /wʌɪd/ *adj* **1** of great extent, vast, spacious; not narrow *la14-.* **2** *of clothes* capacious, generously cut *15-16.* **3** *of speech* unrestrained *la16.* **wide-gab** the anglerfish *Lophius piscatorius 19-.* **wide tae the wa** *of a door* wide open *19-.* [OE *wīd*]

wide¹·², †**wyde,** †**wyd** /wʌɪd/ *adv* widely, over a wide area, extensively; having a wide opening; opening widely or extensively *la14-.* †**wydequhar** far and wide *la14-e16.* **gae wide** *of a sheepdog* to go ahead but well away from the sheep *la19-.* **keep wide** *of a sheepdog* to go ahead but well away from the sheep *19-.* **haud wide o** *see* HAUD¹·². **wide waukin** wide-awake *19, 20- Ork.* [OE *wīde*]

wide *see* WADE¹·²

wideo, wido /ˈwʌɪdo/ *n* a hooligan, a gangster *20- C.* [shortened form of Eng *wide-boy* + *-o* intensive suffix]

widge /wɪdʒ/ *v* to shift the body uneasily *20- Sh.* [compare FIDGE¹·²]

widna, widnae *see* WID²

widow *see* WEEDA

wie *see* WEE¹·¹, WEE¹·²

wiel *see* WEEL³

wield, *Ork* **wald,** *NE* **weel,** †**weld,** †**weild** /wild; *Ork* wald; *NE* wil/ *v* **1** to use (a weapon or ability); to exercise (an attribute) *la14-.* **2** to direct, control (one's body) *la14-e19.* **3** to govern, control, command *la14-17.* **4** to possess; to obtain *15-18.* **5** to gain mastery; to achieve (success) *15-16;* compare WAALD. **hae the weelins o** to have control or full use of (one's body) *20- NE.* [OE **weldan, waldan*]

wife, †**wif,** †**wyfe,** †**wyff** /wʌɪf/ *n* **1** a woman *la14-.* **2** a married woman *14-.* **3** a disparaging term for a woman *18-.* **4** the mistress or wife of a churchman *15-e17.* **5** the mate of a male fowl *e16.* **wifie 1** a woman *19-.* **2** an old-fashioned little girl *19-.* **wifikie, wifeikie,** *NE* **wifockie** = *wifie la18- NE Bor.* **wifeock** = WIFE (sense 1) *la19-.* **wife-carl** a man who occupies himself with women's affairs or work traditionally carried out by women *16-e19.* [OE *wīf*]

wiffen *see* WEAVE

wiffer-waffer /ˈwɪfərˈwafər/ *n* an ineffectual person *20- NE.*

wifferty-wafferty ineffectual, doddering *20- NE T.* [reduplicative form of WAFFER]

wifie, wifockie *see* WIFE

wig¹ /wɪg/ *v* to shake, wag; to move, go, walk *la19- Sh.* [shortened form of *wiggle* (WEEGLE¹·²), and compare Norw dial *vigga* to rock, move]

wig² /wɪg/ *n* **frae wig to wa,** †**from wigge to wall** back and forward, from pillar to post *17-e19, 20- NE.* [ON *veggr* a wall]

wig³, **whig** /wɪg, ʌɪg/ *n* a small oblong currant bun *la18-.* [ME *wig* a small loaf, cake, bun, MDu *wigge* a wedge, wedge-shaped cake]

wig *see* WHIG¹

wiggle *see* WEEGLE¹·¹, WEEGLE¹·²

wigglety-waggglety *see* WEEGLTIE-WAGGLTIE

wight *see* WICHT¹, WICHT², WYTE¹·¹

wi'in *see* WITHIN¹·¹, WITHIN¹·²

wik *see* WICK (sense 2)

wikkit *see* WICKIT

wikkly *see* WEEKLY¹·¹

wil *see* WILL¹·²

wild¹·¹, **wile, wull,** *Ork* **will,** †**wyld,** †**wyll** /wʌɪld, wʌɪl, wʌl; *Ork* wɪl/ *adj* **1** untamed, undomesticated; not bred or kept in captivity; not cultivated; barren, desolate *la14-.* **2** unrestrained, out of control, unstable *14-.* **3** strong-tasting, rank, strong-smelling *16, 19- Sh Ork NE EC.* **4** *of people* fierce, warlike; savage, uncivilized *15-.* **5** *of natural phenomena, weather* violent *15-.* **6** nickname for the extreme Evangelical party in the CHURCH OF SCOTLAND *la18-19.* **wildrife** extremely wild *la19-.* **wild coal** poor-quality coal *19-.* **wild hyacinth** the English bluebell *Hyacinthoides non-scripta la19-.* **wild-kail** the wild radish *Raphanus raphanistrum* or charlock (wild mustard) *Sinapis arvensis la18- WC SW.* **wild parrot** an inferior kind of soft coal *20- C.* **wild rhubarb** butterbur *Petasites hybridus la19- T C SW Bor.* **wild willie** ragged-robin *Lychnis flos-cuculi 20- Sh.* †**the wild aventouris** customs duty levied on goods imported, apparently outwith the control of the authorities, by foreigners or unfreemen *la15-16; see unfreeman* (UNFREE). [OE *wilde*]

wild¹·² /wʌɪld/ *adv* extremely, very; originally, to a mad or crazy extent *16-.* **wild and ...** = WILD¹·²: ◊ *the weather's wild an cold 20- H&I EC.* [see the adj]

wildcat, wullcat, will cat /ˈwʌɪldkat, ˈwʌlkat, ˈwɪlkat/ *n* the wild cat *Felis silvestris grampia la15-.* [WILD¹·¹ + CAT¹]

wildfire, wulfire, †**wilfire** /ˈwʌɪldfaər, ˈwʌlfaər/ *n* **1** a furious, destructive fire, wildfire *18-.* **2** lightning, especially without thunder *15-19, 20- Ork N NE T.* **3** *mining* fire-damp; originally ignis fatuus, phosphorescence seen over marshland *la17-19, 20- EC.* [ME *wilde fire*, WILD¹·¹ + FIRE¹·¹]

wile¹·¹, †**wyle,** †**vyll** /wʌɪl/ *n* **1** guile; cleverness *14-.* **2** a trick, a stratagem involving deception or cunning *la14-.* **3** an idea, means (not necessarily involving cunning) *15-e17.* **wylie, wily,** †**wyly 1** cunning *la15-.* **2** clever, sagacious, wise *15-19, 20- Sh NE T.* [ME *wile*]

wile¹·², †**wyle** /wʌɪl/ *v* **1** to beguile, deceive *la14-.* **2** to entice, persuade, achieve or obtain by cunning or persuasion *la15-.* [see the noun]

wile², †**wyle,** †**vyll** /wʌɪl/ *adj* **1** despicable, loathsome, disgusting, depraved *la14-.* **2** physically repulsive, filthy; diseased; producing or seeking out corruption *la14-e17.* **3** lowly, mean *16-e17.* [AN *vile*]

wile *see* WALE¹·¹, WILD¹·¹

wilfire see WILDFIRE

wilk see WULK

wilkie, †**willick** /ˈwɪlki/ n the razorbill *Alca torda*, originally also applied to the common guillemot *Uria aalge* and the puffin *Fratercula arctica* la18-19, 20- *Sh*. [EModE *willock*, *Will* + diminutive suffix -OCK, with second diminutive suffix -IE¹]

will[1.1], **wull**, †**wyll** /wɪl, wʌl/ n 1 a person's disposition, inclination or drive towards the achievement of their ends la14-. 2 wish, intent, purpose la14-. 3 what a person in authority determines, a command la14-. 4 a fine consequent on a person's submission to the authority of the monarch for a crime or misdemeanour 16; compare *come in (someone's) will*. 5 *pl* the Fates e16. †**willed** headstrong, wilful, 19. †**willy** = *willed* la19. †**at (someone's) will** under the control, according to (someone's) judgement or wishes la14-16. **at yer ain wull** under one's own authority or control, as one wishes la14-19, 20- *N T C*. **at a wull** as much as one could wish for; in all conscience 19, 20- *Sh NE T*. †**come in (someone's) will** to submit (to someone's authority or wishes) la14-e19. **get yer will o, hae yer will o, tak yer wills o** to get one's way, do what one likes with la16-. **hae (nae) will o** *frequently in negative construction* to take (no) pleasure in, have (no) liking for; hope not la16-19, 20- *NE*. †**gif your willis be** if you will, wish, please la14-15. †**in will** determined, fully intending (to do something) la14-e16. †**of (a person's) will** by the authority or command of (someone) la14-e17. †**o will, of will** willingly, spontaneously la14-19. †**the will of the summons, the will** *law* the clause in a summons expressing a royal command la17-. **what's your will?** what do you want? la15-. **wi a will** = *at a wull* 20- *NE T* †**with a will** of a single determined purpose la14-e16 **wi yer will** with one's consent or approval 15-. †**will and wale** free choice la15, 18-e19. [OE *willa*]

will[1.2], **wull**, †**wil** /wɪl, wʌl/ v pt **wid** 1 to desire, want; to wish, seek to do (something) la14-. 2 expressing authoritative intention, to ordain, decree la14-. 3 expressing intention with future reference, or simple futurity, will la14-; compare SALL. 4 expressing consent, acquiescence, or necessity, to be willing, have to la14-. 5 without temporal force, describing a possible course of action or state of affairs la14-. 6 expressing capacity, can, be able to 15-. 7 expressing determination or insistence; used to give force to a statement 16-. 8 with omission of a verb of motion: to want, intend, seek to go, act la14-16. **willna, willnae, winna, wunna** will not 17-. **wilta**, †**wiltu, wultu**, †**wilter** will you 13-. **it will be ..., there will be ...** *in estimates or conjectures* I think or expect it is ..., it is approximately ... 16-. [OE *willan*]

will[2] /wɪl/ v 1 to bequeath la15-. 2 to wish, desire, intend 16-e17. 3 to ask, enjoin; to command la16-17. [OE *willian*]

will[3.1] /wɪl/ v to go astray, lose one's way 14-15, 19- *Sh Ork*. [ON *villask*]

will[3.2], **wull**, †**wyll** /wɪl, wʌl/ adj 1 misguided, erring, wayward la14-. 2 going or gone astray, wandering la14-19, 20- *Ork NE T*. 3 bewildered, perplexed, at a loss 15-19, 20- *NE*. 4 *of a place* out of the way, desolate e16, 19- *NE*. **will-like** perplexed; *of appearance* having a dazed look la19- *NE*. **willness** dizziness la19- *Ork*. **wilsom, wullsome**, †**wilsum** 1 *of a path, place or journey* treacherous, remote, desolate, wild la15-19, 20- *Sh Ork NE*. 2 *of people* lost, wandering; bewildered; forlorn 15-e19. **gae wull** to lose one's way, go astray; to err, go wrong la14-19, 20- *Ork N NE T EC*. †**will of rede** at a loss, not knowing what to do next la14-16. †**will of wane** = *will of rede* la14-e17. [ON *villr* bewildered, astray]

will see WILD[1.1]

willand see WILLIN

willawins see WALAWA[1.2]

will cat see WILDCAT

William and Mary /ˈwɪljəm ən ˈmɛre/ n lungwort *Pulmonaria officinalis* 20- *NE T*. [male-and-female name representing the change in the developing flowers from pink to blue]

willick see WILKIE

willie[1], **willow**, †**willing** /ˈwɪlɪ, ˈwɪlo/ n a plant of the genus *Salix*, willow; a willow tree or branch la15-. **willie-muff, willie-muftie** the willow-warbler *Phylloscopus trochilus* 19- *NE EC Bor*. †**willow wand** a thin, pliable branch of willow; a weak person 16-19. [OE *welig, wilig*]

Willie[2], **Wullie** /ˈwɪle, ˈwʌle/ n short form of William 16-. **Wullie A'thing** = *Johnnie a'thing* (JOHNNY) la19- *Bor*. **Willie beeb** the common sandpiper *Actitis hypoleucos* or purple sandpiper *Calidris maritima* 20- *N*. **Willie Cossar, Wull o Cossar** a long thick pin, originally used for fastening shawls or the like 19, 20- *WC SW Bor* [from the name of the maker]. **willie goo 1** the herring gull *Larus argentatus* la19-. **2** a lost- or stupid-looking person la19- *NE T*. **willie wagtail** the pied wagtail *Motacilla alba* 19-. **Willie Wassle** a children's game in which a den or territory is defended 19- *C*. **Willie Winkie** a character in a nursery rhyme whose job it was to send children to sleep 19- [1844 Songs for the Nursery by William Miller]. †**Sir Willie's picture, Sir Willie** a bank-note of the Edinburgh banking house Messrs Coutts (later Forbes, Hunter and Co.), bearing the portrait of its chairman, Sir William Forbes of Pitsligo (1739–1806) e19. †**Willie and the Wisp, Willie with a Wisp, Willie's wisp** ignis fatuus, will-o'-the-wisp 18-19. **Willie Gunn's cannles** birch-bark washed up by the sea and saturated with salt which crackles and sparkles when burned 20- *Sh*. **willie lang-legs** the cranefly, daddy-long-legs 20- *Sh Ork*. **willie-run-hedge** goosegrass, sticky willy *Galium aparine* la19- *NE C*. **Willie-whip-the-wind** the kestrel *Falco tinnunculus* 19- *T*. **if Willie be wi im** if he really wishes 20- *Sh*. **tak Willie wi ye** to put willingness and determination into a task 20- *NE*. [familiar form of the personal name *William*]

willie-waught /ˈwɪlɪˈwɔxt/ n a hearty swig of ale or other alcohol 19-. [from wrong division of the words in Burns' *Auld Lang Syne*; see *guidwillie* (GUIDWILL) and WAUCHT[1.1]]

willin, wullin, *T Bor* **willint**, †**willand** /ˈwɪlɪn, ˈwʌlən; *T Bor* ˈwɪlɪnt/ adj 1 eager, desirous; deliberately intending 15-. 2 compliant, ready, prepared, willing la16-. **willintly 1** voluntarily, without compulsion; gladly, eagerly, willingly la15-. 2 intentionally, deliberately la16-19, 20- *T*. [participial adj from WILL[1.2]]

willing see WILLIE[1]

willint see WILLIN

willow see WILLIE[1]

willsome /ˈwɪlsʌm/ adj wilful e19, 20- *N*. [WILL[1.1] + -SOME adj-forming suffix]

willyart, †**wilȝart** /ˈwɪljərt/ adj 1 bewildered; undisciplined, wayward 19-. 2 *of people* awkward, shy la18- *NE WC SW*. 3 wilful, obstinate; unmanageable 17-19, 20- *H&I SW*. 4 *of animals* wild, untamed or astray la16-19. [derivative of WILL[3.2] fallen together with derivative of WILL[1.1]]

willywa see WALAWA[1.2]

willywaying, willy-wha-ing, †**willywawin** /wɪlɪˈweɪŋ, wɪlɪˈmɔɪŋ/ n bemoaning, lamenting; screeching, yelling 19- *T SW*. [WALAWA[1.1], with -*ing* suffix]

wilroun see WOLRON

wilter, wiltu see WILL[1.2]

wily see WILE[1.1]

wily coyt see WYLIECOAT

wilȝart see WILLYART

wimble see WUMMLE

wime *see* WAME¹·¹

-wimed *see* -WAMIT

wimple¹·¹, *NE* **wumple**, *SW* **wample**, †**wympil**, †**womple**, †**wempill** /ˈwɪmpəl; *NE* ˈwʌmpəl; *SW* ˈwampəl/ *n* **1** a type of headdress worn by women, latterly only by nuns *la14-*. **2** a twist, a turn, a coil, a winding or meandering; a twisting movement, a ripple *16-*. **3** a tangle, a complication *19-*. **4** a wile, a piece of trickery *17-e19*. [OE *wimpel*]

wimple¹·², *Sh NE* **wumple**, *SW* **wample**, †**wymple**, †**womple** /ˈwɪmpəl; *Sh NE* ˈwʌmpəl; *SW* ˈwampəl/ *v* **1** to wriggle, writhe; to whirl; to curl (up) *la15-19, 20- Sh N*. **2** to enfold, enwrap, entangle; to wind up *la15-19, 20- NE*. **3** *of a river or a road* to meander, twist, turn; to ripple *18-*. **4** *of a boat* to wobble *la19- Sh Ork*. **5** to complicate; to bewilder, perplex; to tell a story in an involved deceitful way *la17-19*. [see the noun]

win¹·¹ /wɪn/ *n* **1** (a) victory in a game *20-*. **2** the quantity of standing corn cut by a team of reapers; the team itself *19, 20- N*. **3** wealth, possessions *la14-15*. **4** profit, earnings; livelihood *la15-19*. **winnie** *marbles* a game in which the winner keeps the gains *la19-*; compare FUNNY. [OE *winn* labour, profit, with some senses from the verb]

win¹·², **won**, **wun**, †**wyn** /wɪn, wʌn/ *v pt* **wan**, **won**, *ptp* **wun**, **won**, †**win**, †**wonnin 1** to seize, take possession of; to get, acquire, obtain *la14-*. **2** to beat, defeat, overpower *la14-*. **3** to earn (a living), gain by labour *la14-*. **4** to gather in (crops), harvest *la14-*. **5** to extract from the ground by mining, quarrying or digging; to sink a pit or shaft to (a coal seam) *la14-*. **6** to reach (a destination or state); to achieve (a goal) *la14-*. **7** to make one's way, travel; to manage to make a journey; to be permitted to go *la14-*. **8** to be victorious, succeed *la14-*. **9** to bring to a way of thinking, convert *la14-*. **10** to deliver, drive home (a stroke, a blow) *19- Bor*. **11** to cultivate or manage (land) *la15-e17*. **12** to save, bring to safety, rescue *la14-16*. **winner 1** a victor *la15-*. **2** *curling* the stone played nearest the TEE¹ *la18-19*. **3** a harvester (of crops) *la14-17*. **4** a miner, a quarrier *16-e17*. **winning 1** victory *15-*. **2** profit, gain, earnings; advantage *la14-19, 20- Sh*. **3** a pit and its fittings and machinery; a seam; a coal working *la18-19, 20- EC*. **4** booty, plunder, gain from conquest, seizure (of a town or stronghold) *la14-e17*. **5** *mining* the extraction (of coal, stone or peat) from the ground *la15-19*. **6** *farming* the harvesting and safe storage of a crop *15-17*. **7** the cultivation of land *la15-e17*. **win abune** to get over, overcome, recover from (illness or misfortune) *la18-19, 20- Sh NE T*. **win aff 1** to depart; to get away, escape; to be acquitted, get off *18-19, 20- Sh Ork NE T*. **2** to finish work *la19- Sh*. **win afore** to get ahead of, outrun, anticipate *19, 20- NE T*. **win after** to pursue *la19, 20- Sh*. **win asleep** to get to sleep *20- Sh Ork NE T*. **win at** to reach, get at or to *17-*. **win awa 1** to leave; to escape, be permitted or find it possible to go *la14-*. **2** to die, especially after great suffering *17-*. **win by** to get past; to avoid *17-*. **win farrer ben**, †**win fardest benn** to be admitted to greater grace or favour *la17, 20- Sh Ork T*. **win frae** to escape from; to be allowed to leave *la14-19, 20- Sh Ork*. **win free** to become free, escape, be released *19-*. **win hame** to arrive, reach your destination *la19-*. **win in** to obtain entry, get in *16-*. **win in aboot** to get near or close to *20- NE*. **win in ahin** to get the better of, outsmart *20- NE*. **win in wi** to find favour with *20-*. **win the kirn** to gain the honour of cutting the last sheaf; to be the first to finish reaping *la18-*. **win on** to achieve (something); to get on; to mount (a horse) *la14-19, 20- Sh NE T*. †**win on fute** to get to one's feet *la15*. **win oot 1** to go, make one's way out, escape *15-*. **2** *mining* to widen out a working *la17-19, 20- EC*. **win ower 1** to (be allowed to) cross, pass or climb over *la14-*. **2** to recover from, overcome *18-*. **win redd o** to escape from, get rid of *la19- NE T*. **win tae 1** to arrive at, reach *la14-19, 20- Sh Ork NE EC*. **2** to succeed in, manage or contrive to *17-19, 20- Sh Ork NE* **3** to begin eating *e19*. **win tae fit**, **win tae the fit** to get to one's feet *la16-19, 20- Sh Ork*. **win tae the road** to get an opportunity; to make a start (on an activity or journey) *la19- Sh NE*. **win tae wi** to overtake, make up on; to be even with *la19- NE*. **win till** to arrive, reach *15-19, 20- Sh N NE T*. †**win throu** to get through, succeed in doing something, accomplish *16-19*. †**win or tyne 1** to (be liable to) win or lose (in an affair), be a participant, be partial *la14-17*. **2** *law* to bring (an action) to a conclusion *la15-16*. **3** to have the means to risk loss while aiming at profit *la16-17*. **win up 1** to rise to one's feet, stand up *la16-*. **2** to travel, climb up (a river, on a wall, to a place) *la14-17*. **win up tae** to get to or as far as, catch up on, overtake *la15-19, 20- NE*. **win up wi** = *win up tae 19, 20- NE*. **win a watch** to have a piece of good luck *la20- C SW*. [OE *winnan*]

win², **wun**, **won** /wɪn, wʌn/ *v pt* **wan**, *ptp* **won**, **win 1** *of cut crops, hay or peats* to dry outdoors, ready for storage *la17-*. **2** to dry out, season, mature (wood, cheese or the like) *e17-*. [extended sense of WIN¹·²]

win³ /wɪn/ *n* pleasure, joy *la14-e16, 20- Ork*. [OE *wynn*]

win *see* WIND¹·¹

wincey /ˈwɪnsi/ *n* a cloth with a woollen weft and a linen or cotton warp *la18-*. [shortened form of LINSEY-WINSEY]

winch¹ /wɪnʃ/ *v* **1** to wince, start back, flinch *la15-e19*. **2** to kick, prance *19-*. [AN *wenchir* to turn aside, avoid]

winch²·¹, **wench** /wɪnʃ, wenʃ/ *n* a girl, a young woman, frequently a little girl; a sweetheart *la14-*. [shortened form of OE *wenchel* a child]

winch²·² /wɪnʃ/ *v* to court, keep company with someone of the opposite sex, originally of a man with a girl: ◊*are ye winchin? la18-*. [see the noun]

wind¹·¹, **win**, **wund**, **wun**, *NE* **ween**, †**wynd**, †**wound** /wɪnd, wɪn, wʌnd, wʌn; *NE* win/ *n* **1** air in motion, wind *la14-*. **2** breath as used for speaking; talk, speech, what one has to say *la14-*. **3** breath, the air breathed *la18-*. **4** intestinal or stomach gas *15-*. **5** boasting; a braggart *18-19, 20- SW Bor*. †**wind-bill** a bill of exchange drawn as a means to raise credit, a bill which negotiates a loan of money *la18-19*. **wind-blawn** *of a horse* broken-winded *20- N EC SW*. **wincasten** blown down by the wind; cast down by circumstance *20- Sh NE WC*. **oon-egg** a wind-egg, an egg laid without a shell *19-*. **wind-feed**, **wind-feeder** a shower of rain followed by an increase of wind *la19- Sh Ork N*. †**wind-flaucht** with the force or speed of wind *e16, 19*. **wind-mill**, *NE* **win-mull**, †**wyndmyln 1** a windmill *15-*. **2** a notion, a fancy *20- NE*. **windrawing**, †**uindrawing** the act of making a row or line of mown hay in which small piles of cut peats may be set, to aid drying *la17-*. **windskew 1** a smoke deflector in a chimney, a chimney cowl *la18-19, 20- Ork NE*. **2** the stone coping of a gable *la16-17*; compare SKEW¹ (sense 1). **windspel** a whirligig *20- Sh*. **keep yer wind tae cool yer kail** to hold one's tongue, be quiet *la19- Sh N NE T*. **let the win intil't** to squander money or resources *20- NE*. **wind and watertight**, †**windticht and watterticht** *of a building* secure against wind and rain *la16-*. †**where wind and weather shears**, **as wind and watter scheris** on a watershed or high ridge *la15-19*. [OE *wind*]

wind¹·², **ween** /wɪnd, win/ *v* to exaggerate, boast *19, 20- NE T*. [see the noun]

†**wind**²·¹, **wynd** /wʌɪnd/ *n* **1** a twist or turn in movement; a turning point *16-*. **2** a reel or instrument for winding yarn; as much yarn as a reel will hold; a twist (of tobacco) *la15-e18*.

windie an apparatus for winding straw ropes *20- Sh.* [OE *wind* a spiral, *gearn-winde* a reel]

wind[2.2], **wund**, *NE* **wun**, †**wynd**, †**wend** /wɪnd, wɪn, wʌɪnd, wʌnd; *NE* wʌn/ *v pt also N NE* **wan**, †**wand**, *ptp also* **wundit**, †**wynd**, †**woon 1** to turn round and round or back and forth; to twist, weave *15-*. **2** to wrap (a corpse in a shroud, baby in a shawl) *la14-e19*. **3** to draw (coal) to the pithead by means of a winding-engine; originally, to pull up (a sail, clock weights) by winding a rope or chain round a roller *la15-*. †**windar** (a person who operates) a windlass *15-19*. **windband** an iron hoop or band put round a wooden bar to strengthen it and prevent splintering; the nave-band of a wheel *la15-19, 20- SW.* **wind the clue** *folklore* to wind a ball of worsted in a kiln at Halloween to divine the name of one's future spouse *18- NE*; compare *blue clue* (BLUE[1.2]). **wind a (bonnie, ill) pirn** to create difficulties for oneself or another *16-*. †**wynd our** to extend over; encroach upon *e16*. †**wynd upoun** = *wynd our la16-17*. [OE *windan*]

wind[3], †**wynd** /wɪnd/ *v* to winnow *16-19, 20- Ork Uls.* [shortened form of *window* (WINNOW)]

wind *see* WOUND[1.1], WYND[2.1], WYNT

windae, window, wundae, wunda, wundow, *NE WC* **winda**, *C* **windy**, *EC* **wundy**, †**wondow**, †**wyndo** /ˈwɪnde, ˈwɪndo, ˈwʌnde, ˈwʌndə, ˈwʌndo; *NE WC* ˈwɪndə; *C* ˈwɪndi; *EC* ˈwʌndi/ *n* **1** a glazed opening in a wall to admit light; a window *la14-*. **2** a shop window used to display goods *15-*. **3** an opening or breach in a barrier *16-*. **4** the window of a public building used to display the names of those summoned to appear in court *16-e17*. **window band** a hinge for a window *16-17*. **window bole** an unglazed window opening, usually with a wooden shutter *19, 20- NE T.* **window-brod, window-bred, window-board** a window shutter *16-19, 20- NE T WC.* **windae hing** the act of leaning out of a tenement window to watch events in the street *20- T C SW.* **windae-sole** a window sill *18-*. **window-stane** a stone window sill *20- Ork.* **wunda-swalla** the house martin *Delichon urbica 20- EC Bor.* [ON *vindauga* literally, wind eye]

windass, †**wyndas**, †**wyndois**, †**windes** /ˈwɪndəs/ *n* **1** a windlass; specifically, the winching mechanism for taking up water from the shaft of a coal mine *15-19, 20- EC.* **2** a fan for winnowing grain *18-19, 20- Bor.* **3** the winch mechanism used to draw a cross-bow *e16.* **windass cord** the bowstring of a cross-bow *e16.* [AN *windas*]

winder *see* WUNNER[1.1]
windes *see* WINDASS
windil stra *see* WINDLESTRAE[1.1]
windir *see* WONDER[1.1]

windle[1.1], †**wyndill** /ˈwɪndəl/ *n* **1** *weaving* a device for winding yarn or thread onto bobbins *la16-19, 20- WC.* **2** a bundle of straw or hay *19.* **windlin** a (small) bundle of straw *16-19, 20- Sh Ork N NE.* [WIND[2.2] + instrumental suffix]

windle[1.2], **winle**, **wunnle** /ˈwɪndəl, ˈwɪnəl, ˈwʌnəl/ *v* **1** to make (straw or hay) into bundles *la17-19, 20- Bor.* **2** to wind (thread and the like) *15-17.* **3** to move with circular motion, whirl, stagger *la14.* **windlin** a bundle of straw *la16-19, 20-.* [frequentative form of WIND[2.2]]

windlestrae[1.1], **wunnelstrae**, †**wyndill stray**, †**windil stra** /ˈwɪndlstre, ˈwʌnəlstre/ *n* **1** a tall, thin, withered stalk of grass; also applied to various grasses with long thin stalks, such as the crested dog's-tail grass *Cynosurus cristatus*, Yorkshire fog *Holcus lanatus*, tufted hair-grass *Deschampsia cespitosa 16-*. **2** something of little or no value, a jot, a scrap *16-*. **3** *derogatory* a thin or lanky person; a person who is weak in health or character *19-*. **4** *derogatory* a dagger or a sword *19.* [OE *windelstrēaw*, with substitution of STRAE[1.1] for *straw*]

windlestrae[1.2] /ˈwɪndəlstre/ *adj* easily blown about; weak, thin, delicate *19-*. [see the noun]

windo *see* WINNOW
windock *see* WINNOCK
window *see* WINDAE, WINNOW

windrift /ˈwɪndrɪft/ *n* ruin, destruction *20- Ork.* [altered form of WANTHRIFT]

windy, †**wyndy** /ˈwɪndɪ, ˈwɪndi/ *adj* **1** characterized by or exposed to wind *13-*. **2** verbose, garrulous *16-*. **3** conceited; boastful *19, 20- T.* **4** changeable, fickle *16-e17.* **windy-ask** a haze presaging wind *la19- Sh.* **windy rogs** lines of cloud portending rain *20- Sh.* **windy-wallets** a person who talks in a boastful, exaggerated way *19- Bor.* [OE *windig*]

windy *see* WINDAE

wine, †**wyne**, †**wyn**, †**wyine** /wʌɪn/ *n* **1** fermented grape juice *la14-*. **2** *in urban areas* cheap fortified red wine or sherry *la20- WC.* **wine grape** *derogatory, rhyming slang* pape, a Roman Catholic *la20- C.* **wine shop** a public house which serves cheap wine *la20- WC.* **wine slide** a coaster for a wine bottle or decanter which can be slid along a table *20-.* [OE *wīn*]

wing, *NE T* **weeng**, †**wyng**, †**weing** /wɪŋ; *NE T* wiŋ/ *n* **1** the wing of a bird or insect *la14-*. **2** a lateral projection similar to a wing; a division on one side of the main body of an army in battle formation *15-*. **3** a detachable board which can be added to the side of a cart to increase its capacity *20- N EC Uls.* **4** the part of a fish next to the gill and side fin, often used as bait *la19- Sh.* [ON *væng*r]

wingle[1.1] /ˈwɪŋgəl/ *n* something winding or twisty *la18, 20- NE.* **wingle-wankle** a coiling, a convolution *20- SW.* [see the verb]

wingle[1.2], *Sh* **wengle**, *Ork* **weenkle**, *SW* **winkle**, †**waingle** /ˈwɪŋəl; *Sh* ˈwɛŋgəl; *Ork* ˈwɪŋkəl; *SW* ˈwɪŋkəl/ *v* **1** to walk unsteadily, reel, stagger *19, 20- Sh Uls.* **2** to twist, bend, wriggle; *of a stream* to meander *19- Sh N SW.* **3** to hang loosely, dangle; to flap, wag *19, 20- Sh Ork.* **wingle-wankle** in a wobbly fashion, unsteadily *20- Sh Ork.* [for *Sh* and *Ork*, compare Norw dial *vingla*; elsewhere, compare WANGLE and wiggle (WEEGLE[1.2])]

wink[1.1], †**wynk** /wɪŋk/ *n* the closing of an eye or the eyes; the time taken to close and open the eyes; a moment *la14-*. **winkie 1** a (flickering or unsteady) lamp or light *19- Bor.* **2** the lighted buoy marking the end of a line of herring nets *20-.* [see the verb]

wink[1.2], †**wynk** /wɪŋk/ *v* **1** to close, then open an eye, blink *la15-*. **2** to close the eyes, sleep, doze *la14-19.* **3** to shut one's eyes to, overlook, tolerate (an offence or fault) *la16-e18.* **winkers** the eyelids or eyelashes *19, 20- T.* [OE *wincian*]

winkie /ˈwɪŋki/ *n* a child's word for the little finger *20- Sh Ork.* [shortened form of *pinkie-winkie* reduplicative form of PINKIE[1]]

winkle *see* WINGLE[1.2]
winle *see* WINDLE[1.2]
winna *see* WILL[1.2]

winnel-skewed /ˈwɪnəlˈskjud/ *adj* suffering from an optical illusion; squint-eyed; askew *19- SW.* [probably WINDLE[1.1] + participial adj from SKEW[2.2]]

winner *see* WUNNER[1.1], WUNNER[1.2]
winnerstan *see* UNDERSTAND[1.2]
winnie *see* WIN[1.1]
winning *see* WIN[1.2]

winnish, †**dwinnish** /ˈwɪnɪʃ/ *v* to pine away, diminish *la19- Sh.* [perhaps a conflation of DWINE[1.2] with Eng *diminish*]

winnock, **windock**, **wunnock**, †**wondok**, †**wyndok** /ˈwɪnək, ˈwɪndək, ˈwʌnək/ *n* a window *la15-*. †**winnock bole** an unglazed window opening, usually with a wood shutter *19*. †**wyndok brod** a window shutter *16-e19*. †**winnock bunker** a window-seat *la18-e19*. †**winnock neuk** a window-corner *la18-19*. **winnock sole** a window sill *la18-*. [altered form of WINDOW; compare ELBUCK]

winnow, *Sh Ork* **windo**, †**wando**, †**window**, †**woundow** /ˈwɪno; *Sh Ork* ˈwɪndo/ *v* to separate chaff from grain *16-*. †**winder** a winnower *la16*. †**winnowster**, †**windostar**, †**windister** a woman engaged in winnowing *16-e17*. **winnister** a machine for winnowing; the fanning apparatus on a threshing machine *19- NE*. †**winnow-claith** a winnowing sheet *la14-e19*. **windo-cubbie** a basket for the grain about to be winnowed *20- Ork*. [OE *windwian*]

winsome, †**winsom** /ˈwɪnsəm/ *adj* attractive, charming *la17-*. [OE *wynsum* pleasant, gracious]

wint *see* WANT¹·¹, WANT¹·², WENT¹, WONT¹·², WONT¹·³

winter¹·¹, †**wynter**, †**wintare**, †**wyntir** /ˈwɪntər/ *n* **1** the season of the year, winter *14-*. **2** the last person to turn up for work on HOGMANAY *la20- WC*. **3** the last load of grain to be brought to the stackyard in harvest *la18-19, 20- NE*. **4** the feast held to celebrate the end of harvest *19*. **5** the person who moved the last of the grain from the field to the stackyard *la19*. **winter-dykes** a clothes-horse *18- C SW*. **winter-fish** fish pickled for winter *la19- Sh*. **winter green** a clothes-horse *20- WC*. **winter toon** the arable part of a farm as opposed to the summer pasture *la18-*. **get winter, hae winter, mak winter, tak winter** to reach the end of the harvest, complete the bringing in of the crops *19- NE*. **ye never died o winter yet** *of a person* you survived all difficulties or hardships *la19-*. [OE *winter*]

winter¹·² /ˈwɪntər/ *v* to keep (animals) over the winter *16-*. **winterer** a farm animal kept over winter for fattening in the following spring and summer *la18-*. **winterin 1** a winter pasture, winter keep for animals *16-*. **2** an animal kept over the winter *18-19, 20- N NE*. **wintering money** money paid for the winter keep of animals *18-, 20- T*. †**winter and simmer** *see simmer and winter* (SIMMER¹·²). [see the noun]

winter² /ˈwɪntər/ *n* an iron or rack which hangs on the bars of a fire-grate to support a kettle or pot; a trivet *la17-19, 20- T*. [perhaps in jocular antithesis to SIMMER² a beam, punning on SIMMER¹·¹]

wintle, **wuntle** /ˈwɪntəl, ˈwʌntəl/ *v* to stagger, reel; to tumble, rock from side to side, *la18-*. †**wintle in a widdie** to be hanged *la18-e19*. **wintle ower** to tumble, capsize *19-*. [MDu *wintelen* to roll]

winya /ˈwɪnja/ *n* ruin, destruction *20- Ork*. [unknown]

winyaless /ˈwɪnjaləs/ *adj* frail, infirm; unwell *20- Ork*. [perhaps Norw dial *vinn* energy, with *-less* suffix]

†**winze** *n* a curse *la18-e19*. [MDu *wens* an imprecation]

wi'oot *see* WITHOUT¹·²

wip *see* WUP¹·¹, WUP¹·²

wipe¹·¹ /wʌɪp/ *n* **1** an act of wiping *18-*. **2** a cutting remark, a sneer *la16-19*. [see the verb]

wipe¹·², †**weep**, †**wepe**, †**weipe** /wʌɪp/ *v* **1** to clean by wiping, clear away, erase *la14-*. **2** to strike, beat, attack *la17-19, 20- WC*. [OE *wīpian*]

wipple *see* WUPPLE¹·¹, WUPPLE¹·²

wir, **wur**, **were** /wɪr, wʌr, wer/ *v* had been, were *la14-*. [OE *wǣron* pt pl of *wesan* to be; compare WIS]

wir *see* OOR³

wird *see* WORD¹·¹, WORD¹·²

wirdy *see* WORTH¹·¹

wire¹·¹, *Sh* **waer**, *NE* **weer**, *NE* **weir**, †**wyre** /waer; *Sh* wer; *NE* wir/ *n* **1** (a length of) metal in a fine rod or strand, a thin metal bar or strap *15-*. **2** a knitting needle *la18-*. **3** a metal grille for a window *17-e18*. **4** wirework *16-17*. †**wyre window** a glazed or unglazed window with a metal grille *17-e19*. †**wyrin** (made) of wire *e16*. [OE *wīr*]

wire¹·², †**weir** /wʌɪr/ *v* **1** to secure with wire *16-*. **2** to furnish (a window) with a wire grille *16-e18*. **wire in, wire intae** to eat heartily, do something with energy and enthusiasm *la20-*. [see the noun]

wiring *see* WAEREN

wirk, **wark**, **work**, **wurk**, †**wyrk**, †**werk** /wark, wɪrk, wʌrk/ *v pt also* **wrocht**, **wroucht**, **wrought**, **wraucht 1** to carry out, perform (one's job or profession); to do a job of work *la14-*. **2** to operate on, influence, affect; to have an effect, bring about *la14-*. **3** to act in a specified way, behave, function; *of a machine or mechanism* to operate effectively *la14-*. **4** to invent, create; to build, repair; to make (an artifact or product) *la14-*. **5** to till land; to work a mine or quarry *16-*. **6** to affect physically or mentally; to trouble, annoy *la18-*. **7** to purge, act as a laxative *20- Sh Ork NE T*. **8** to look after, herd animals *20- T EC Bor*. **9** to sprain *19- NE SW*. **10** *of ale* to ferment *la16-e19*. **11** to inflict a wound; to harm *15-e17*. **12** to write something *15-16*. **warker**, **worker**, **wirker**, †**wirkar 1** someone who does a job of work, a labourer, craftsman; a working animal *la15-*. **2** an author or creator *la15-e17*. **work for** to deserve or earn punishment or retribution *la19, 20- Sh N NE T*. **wirk yer wark** to do one's work, perform what one is employed to do *16-19, 20- Sh Ork NE*. **wirk wi** to employ, use *la19- Sh N NE T*. [OE *wyrcan*; compare WARK¹]

wirk *see* WARK¹

wirl¹, **wirral**, **wurl**, *NE EC* **vrow**, †**wirle** /wɪrl, ˈwɪrəl, wʌrl; *NE EC* vrʌu/ *n* **1** a puny, malformed person, animal or plant, a stunted or deformed creature *18-19, 20- NE T EC*. **2** a mischievous child *20-*. **wirlie** puny, stunted, undersized; wrinkled, wizened *19-*. [unknown; perhaps a back-formation from WIRLING; compare YRLE]

wirl² /wʌrl/ *v* to fret, whine, be peevish *19- Sh*. [perhaps onomatopoeic]

†**wirlar** *n* a puny or stunted person *e17*. [perhaps an altered form of WIRLING with change of suffix]

wirle *see* WIRL¹

wirlie /ˈwʌrli/ *n* an opening at the bottom of a wall or fence for passage of a stream *la19- Sh*. [unknown]

†**wirling**, **wurlyon**, **worling** *n* a puny or stunted person or animal; a wretch *16-19*. [ME *wyrling*]

wirm *see* WORM

wirned /wʌrnd/ *v ptp* become, happened (to) *la19- Sh*. [Norw dial *voren*]

wirnie, **wurnae** /ˈwɪrne, ˈwʌrne/ *v negative* were not *20-*. [WIR + -NA]

wirr¹·¹, **wurr** /wɪr, wʌr/ *n* **1** the growl of a dog *la18- NE T*. **2** a fit of bad temper *la19*. [see the verb]

wirr¹·², **wurr** /wɪr, wʌr/ *v* to growl, snarl *la18- NE T*. [onomatopoeic]

wirral *see* WIRL¹

wirricow, †**worricow** /ˈwʌrɪkʌu, ˈwɪrɪkʌu, ˈwɪrekʌu/ *n* **1** *folklore* a frightening monster, a supernatural creature *18-19, 20- EC*. **2** a frightening- or repulsive-looking person *19, 20- WC SW Bor*. **3** the Devil *18-19*. [perhaps WIRRY¹·² + COW³]

wirrok *see* WERROCK

wirry¹·¹, **worry** /ˈwɪri, ˈwʌri/ *n* **1** (a source of) anxiety *20-*. **2** a dispute, wrangle, argument *la19- NE T*. [see the verb]

wirry¹·², **worry**, †**virry** /ˈwɪri, ˈwʌri/ *v* **1** *of an animal* to savage, attack ((the throat of) a victim) *la14-*. **2** to (cause to) die, kill by strangulation, strangle *la14-19, 20- Sh Ork WC*. **3** to (cause to) choke (on a mouthful of food), suffocate *15-*.

wirschep | 831 | **witch**

4 *of smoke* to stifle, suffocate *18-19, 20- Ork.* 5 to devour, swallow greedily, gobble up *18-19, 20- NE T.* 6 to gather up greedily *e17*. **wirriar** 1 a dog that attacks sheep *16-*. 2 a guzzler or swiller (of wine) *la16*. **wirry carl** 1 a snarling, ill-natured person *19- Bor.* 2 in Roxburghshire, a large coarse winter pear *e19*. **no wirry upo kliers** to speak one's mind freely *la19- Sh.* †**worry in the band like MacEwin's caff** to be hanged *e18*. [OE *wyrgan* to strangle]

wirschep, wirschip *see* WORSHIP[1.1], WORSHIP[1.2]

wirsel, wirsels *see* OOR[3]

wirsit *see* WORSET

wirsom *see* WURSOM

wirsum *see* WURSOM

wirt, wort /wɪrt, wart, wɔrt/ *n brewing* the infusion of malt fermented to make beer *la15-*. **wort-stane** a stone used in making wort, for keeping the barrel steady *16-19, 20- Ork.* †**play wirt** to work the mash in the brewing vessel *17*. [OE *wyrt*]

wirt *see* WORT[1,2], WORTH[1.1]

wirth *see* WORTH[1.1]

wis, was, wes, wus, wur /wɪz, wɔz, wɛz, wʌz, wʌr/ *v* was, had been *la14-*. [OE *wǣs* pt 1st and 3rd sg of *wesan* to be]

wis *see* US, WISE[1], WISE[2], WISE[3], WISH[1.1]

wisch *see* WISH[1.2]

wise[1], †**wis**, †**wyse**, †**wyis** /waez/ *n* manner, way, means *la14-*. [OE *wīse*]

wise[2], **wice, wyss, weise**, †**wis**, †**wys**, †**wyice** /waez, wʌɪs/ *adj* 1 of sound judgement, sensible, prudent; skilled *la14-*. 2 clever, knowledgeable, well-informed, erudite *la14-19, 20- Ork N T EC.* 3 in one's right mind, sane, rational *18-19, 20- Ork N NE T Bor Uls.* **wise-like, wice-like** 1 prudent, sensible, reasonable *19-*. 2 respectable, proper, decent *19-*. 3 of good appearance, handsome, pretty *19-*. 4 suitable, fitting, appropriate *19, 20- WC.* **wise-lookin** handsome, good-looking *19, 20- Sh Ork N T SW.* **wise saying** a proverb *20- Sh EC.* **wice-spoken** wise, sensible in speech *la19- Sh Ork NE T WC.* **wise wife** a woman skilled in magic, possessing powers of witchcraft *la14-19, 20- Ork EC.* **wise woman** a woman skilled in the art of medicine; a sorceress *la16-19, 20- historical.* †**wise behind the hand** wise after the event *la16-e19*. **wise and warl-like** *of a new-born baby* normal physically and mentally *19-*. **no wise,** †**not wise** not sane *18-*. **no wise eneuch** insane *la18- NE.* [OE *wīs*]

wise[3], *Sh* **wiss,** †**wis** /waez; *Sh* wɪs/ *v* 1 to instruct, inform; to advise; to persuade *15-*. 2 to guide, direct (a person) (to a place) *la14-*. 3 to move, go *18-*. 4 *of a shepherd or his dog* to direct, lead sheep *19-*. 5 to aim, propel, shoot (a missile) *18-19, 20- SW.* 6 to manoeuvre, cause to move *18-19, 20- Bor.* 7 to contrive, obtain by guile *19.* 8 to expend, use up (time, money) *19.* 9 to lead, conduct (water) in a channel *19.* [OE *wīsian*]

wisgan /ˈwɪzɡən/ *n derogatory* a stunted, useless, feckless person or creature *la19- NE T.* [perhaps Gael *ùruisgean*, diminutive of *ùruisg* a brownie, hobgoblin]

wish[1.1], †**wuss**, †**wis**, †**wys** /wɪʃ/ *n* a desire *15-*. **to a wish, to a very wish** just as one would wish, to one's complete satisfaction *la18-*. [see the verb]

wish[1.2], **wush, wiss**, *NE* **wuss**, *T Uls* **weesh**, †**wys**, †**vis**, †**twisch** /wɪʃ, wʌʃ; *NE* wʌs; *T Uls* wiʃ/ *v* 1 *with direct object or infinitive, or both* to want, desire, wish for: ◇*do you wish any more? la15-*. 2 *with clause object* to desire, want, hope, trust: ◇*I wish I binna fou la16-*. [OE *wȳscan*]

wish *see* WASH[1.2]

wishen *see* WASH[1.2]

wisht *see* WHEESHT[1.4]

wishy-washy[1.1], **weeshie-washie** /ˈwɪʃɪˈwaʃɪ, ˈwɪʃɪˈwaʃɪ/ *n* 1 a thin, watery drink, *eg* weak tea *19- Ork T WC SW.* 2 circumlocutions, procrastination, humming and hawing *la18- NE T.* [see the adj]

wishy-washy[1.2], **weeshie-washie** /ˈwɪʃɪˈwaʃɪ, ˈwɪʃɪˈwaʃɪ/ *adj* feeble; insipid *la17-*. [reduplicative compound based on EModE *washy* weak, watery]

wisk /wɪsk/ *n* a bunch, a tangled mass (of threads) *20- Sh Ork N NE.* [Norw *visk* a wisp]

wisk *see* WHISK[1.1], WHISK[1.2]

wisker *see* WUSKER

wisnae, wisna, wasnae, wasna, wusnae, wusna, *NE* **wiznan** /ˈwɪzne, ˈwɪznə, ˈwɔzne, ˈwɔznə, ˈwʌzne, ˈwʌznə; *NE* ˈwɪznən/ *v negative* was not *la19-*. [WIS + -NA]

wisnit *see* WIZENED

wisp[1.1], **wusp,** †**wosp** /wɪsp, wʌsp/ *n* 1 a handful or twist (of hay) *15-*. 2 a bundle or parcel (of a definite quantity) of a commodity, *eg* steel *16-e17, 20- NE.* 3 a small bundle of hay or straw *la17*. [perhaps OE **wisp*]

wisp[1.2] /wɪsp/ *v* 1 to rub down a horse with a handful of hay *la16-*. 2 to put straw into (footwear) as an insole *19- EC SW Bor.* [see the noun]

wiss *see* WISE[3], WISH[1.2], WUSS

†**wissel**[1.1] /ˈwɪsəl/ *n* 1 the changing of coin, change given *17-e19*. 2 a building where merchants transacted business *la15*. **wiselhous** = WISSEL[1.1] (sense 2) *la16*. **get the wissel of one's groat** to be paid in one's own coin, get one's just deserts *18-e19*. [MDu *wissel*, MLG *wissele*]

wissel[1.2], †**whissle,** †**wissyll,** †**vissil** /ˈwɪsəl/ *v* 1 to exchange, barter *la14-16, 20- N.* 2 to exchange, bandy (words) with *la16-e19*. 3 to change (money), give out (change); to spend (money) *la15-e19*. †**wislar** a money-changer employed by the Crown *la15-16*. †**in wisselling** in exchange *la14-e17*. [MDu, MLG *wisselen*]

wissen *see* WIZEN

wissyll *see* WISSEL[1.2]

wist *see* WIT[1.2]

wista /ˈwɪstə/ *n* an open, exposed situation *la19- Sh.* [unknown; compare Eng *vista*]

wit[1.1], **wut,** †**wyt** /wɪt, wʌt/ *n* 1 the mind, consciousness *la14-*. 2 intelligence, wisdom, common sense *la14-*. 3 knowledge, information *la14-*. 4 a person of great mental ability or knowledge; an important person, a dignitary *15-*. 5 sanity, reason, one's senses *la14-19, 20- Sh Ork N NE T.* **witty** 1 clever, intelligent *la14-*. 2 wise, sagacious; knowledgeable *la14-17, 20- Ork.* 3 sane, rational, sensible *la19- Ork.* **get wit o** to learn, find out, become aware of *la14-19, 20- NE T EC.* †**have wit of** to know *15-e19*. **oot o yer wits** out of one's senses *la14-*. **tak wit o** = *get wit o*. [OE *witt*]

wit[1.2], **wat,** *NE T* **wite**, *SW Bor* **weet,** †**wate,** †**wait,** †**waett** /wɪt, wat; *NE T* wʌɪt; *SW Bor* wit/ *v pt* †**twist,** †**wyttyt** *ptp* †**wittin, witting** 1 to know, be or become aware (of); to learn, discover, realize; to understand *la14-*. 2 to expect, feel certain, be sure of *la15*. †**wittandlie** 1 knowingly, deliberately *15-16*. 2 cleverly, skilfully *la14-e15*. †**witting, witin** known to one, of which one is aware; notorious *16-17*. **I wat,** †**I wot** I know, indeed, I must say, I can tell you *la15-16, 19-*. **let wit** 1 to let (a person) know something, inform of *18-*. 2 *law in imperative* let it be known that, take notice that *18*. †**wit ye, ye sall wit, ȝe wait** *in injunctions* understand, be assured, know *la14-17*. [OE *witan*]

wit *see* WYTE[1.1], WYTE[1.2]

witch[1.1], **wutch,** †**wich,** †**wech** /wɪtʃ, wʌtʃ/ *n* 1 a (mainly female) sorcerer *la14-*. 2 a moth *la19, 20- NE T.* 3 a tortoiseshell butterfly probably *Aglais urticae la19- Bor.* 4 the pole flounder *Glyptocephalus cynoglossus* or dab *Limanda*

limanda la19-. **5** a (red clay) marble *la19- NE.* †**witch-carline** a witch *16-e19.* **witches' paps** the foxglove *Digitalis purpurea 20- H&I WC.* **witches'-thummles** (the flowers of) the foxglove *Digitalis purpurea 19-.* **witchiebody** a witch *20- Sh Ork.* **witchie-clock** a burrowing beetle of the family *Carabidae la19- Sh.* **witchiflooer** the scentless mayweed *Tripleurospermum inodorum 20- Sh.* **witch wife** a witch *la16-.* [OE *wicce*]
witch[1,2], †**wich**, †**wech** /wɪtʃ/ *v* to bewitch, affect (as if by) by witchcraft *la14-.* [OE *wiccian*]
wite *see* WIT[1,2], WYTE[1,1], WYTE[1,2]
with *see* WI
witha, †**withal**, †**withaw** /wɪθ'a/ *adv* **1** as well, besides *la14-.* **2** with that, by that means *16-17.* **3** concerning, with respect to that *15-17.* [*with* (WI) + AW[1,1]]
wi than *see* WEEL[1,3]
withaw *see* WITHA
withdraw /wɪθ'dra/ *v* **1** to remove, take away; to absent oneself; to retreat, retract *la14-.* **2** to leave, depart *15-e19.* †**withdrawer** *Presbyterian Church* a person who did not conform to the established church *17.* **withdrawing 1** the action of removing, retracting or departing *la14-.* **2** *Presbyterian Church* failing to attend church services *la17.* [*with* (WI) + DRAW[1,2]]
wither, *NE* **widder**, †**wydder** /'wɪðər; *NE* 'wɪdər/ *v* **1** to dry up, become dried up *la14-.* **2** to wash the starch out of (summer garments) and put them away for winter unironed *20- C SW.* **witherit 1** dried up; dead; shrivelled, wasted *la15-.* **2** worn out *la15.* **3** *of timber* dried out, seasoned *la15-16.* [extended sense of *wither* (WEATHER)]
wither *see* WEATHER
witherlins /'wɪðərlɪnz/ *adv* anticlockwise *19, 20- NE.* Compare WIDDERGAETS, WIDDERSHINS, WITHERSHINS. [OE *wiðer* against, with adv-forming suffix]
witherlock, †**widderlok** /'wɪðərlok/ *n* the tuft of a horse's mane above the withers *la15-19, 20- N.* [EModE *wither* + LOCK[2]]
withershins, **withersones** *see* WIDDERSHINS
wither-wecht, †**wodderweght** /'wɪðərwɛxt/ *n* a counterweight *17-19, 20- N NE T.* [OE *wiðer-* counter- + WECHT[1,1]]
witherwirt, †**witherwardis**, †**woderwardis** /'wɪðərwɪrt/ *adv* **1** *in witchcraft* anticlockwise *e17.* **2** wavering, lurching *20- Ork.* [OE *wiðer* against, with -WART suffix]
witherwys *see* WIDDERWISE[1,2]
†**withgang**[1] *n* profit, success, prosperity *la15-e16.* [ON *viðgangr* increase]
†**withgang**[2] *n* free access, licence *la15-16.* [ON *viðganga* access, admission]
†**withgate** *n* freedom, licence, permission *la16-e18.* [altered form of WITHGANG[2], substituting GAIT[3]]
with-haud, **withhold**, †**withhald** /wɪθ'had, wɪθ'hold/ *v* **1** to keep, retain; to keep in one's possession something belonging to another *15-.* **2** to hold back *e16.* **3** to hold *e16.* [ME *withholden; with* (WI) + *hold* (HAUD[1,2])]
within[1,1], **wi'in** /wɪ'θɪn, wɪ'ɪn/ *adv* **1** inside; on the inner surface *la14-.* **2** less than (a number etc) *la14-.* †**within-namit**, **within-nominat** named in this document *la17.* †**within-written** mentioned in this document, herein *16-17.* [OE *wiðinnan* adv]
within[1,2], **wi'in**, †**wythin** /wɪ'θɪn, wɪ'ɪn/ *prep* **1** inside, in (a place, thing, limit) *la14-.* **2** less than a specified period of time, before a period of time has elapsed *la14-.* **3** less than (a specified distance) *la15-.* **within itsell** *of a house* not shared in its accommodation, self-contained *la18-19, 20- NE.* †**within themsell** within the confines of their own property *la17.* [OE *wiðinnan* prep]

withoot[1,1], **without** /wɪ'θut/ *adv* outside; on the outside *la14-.* [OE *wiðūtan* adv]
withoot[1,2], **wi'oot**, *literary* **withooten**, †**withowt**, †**withoutin**, †**withowttin** /wɪ'θut, wɪ'ut, wɪ'θutən/ *prep* **1** in the absence of, lacking (an impediment, participant etc) *la14-.* **2** with no use of, without resort to (a means, the law etc) *la14-.* **3** outside (a boundary or limit) *la14-.* [OE *wiðūtan* prep]
withoot[1,3], **without** /wɪ'θut/ *conj* unless, except (that) *la15-19, 20- T C SW Uls.* [see the prep]
witless, †**witles**, †**wytles** /'wɪtlɪs/ *adj* **1** stupid; mentally deficient *16-19, 20- Sh Ork N NE.* **2** mad, raving, furious *la14-16.* [OE *witlēas*]
†**witnesbirtht** *n* evidence *la16-e17 Sh Ork.* [ON *vitnisburðr*]
witness[1,1], †**witnes** /'wɪtnɪs/ *n* testimony, evidence; a person able to attest to something; one called to give evidence in court *la14-.* [OE *witnes*]
witness[1,2], †**witnes** /'wɪtnɪs/ *v* **1** to supply testimony, attest to *15-.* **2** to record, chronicle *la15-e17.* **3** to take note, observe (as evidence of something) *la15-.* **4** to spectate at *la19-.* [see the noun]
†**witnessmen**, **witnesmen** *npl* witnesses *la14-e17.* [ON *vitnismenn* pl of *vitnismaðr*]
Witsounday, **Witsonday** *see* WHITSUNDAY
witter[1,1], †**wittir**, †**wyttir** /'wɪtər/ *n* **1** *curling* the tee *la18- WC SW.* **2** the marker-buoy at the tail of a fleet of herring nets *20- Sh.* **3** a sign or identifying mark; an indication *16-e19.* †**witter-hole** in Aberdeen, a mark or depression made in a *witter stane e17, e19 historical.* †**witter stane** a boundary stone *17.* [see the verb and compare Norw *vitr* a warning sign]
witter[1,2], †**wytter** /'wɪtər/ *v* to inform, tell *la14-e15, la19- Sh.* [ON *vitra* to reveal, make to know]
witter[2], **wutter** /'wɪtər, 'wʌtər/ *n* **1** the barb of a fish-hook or gaff *la18-.* **2** *pl* the teeth *la19-.* **witterd 1** barbed, jagged *19, 20- Sh NE.* **2** stuck, entangled *la18- Sh NE.* †**be in witters** in the North-East, to start a quarrel with *la18-19.* **flee in witters** = *be in witters* [unknown; compare ME *witherhōked* barbed]
witter[3,1], **wutter** /'wɪtər, 'wʌtər/ *n* a sharp, active, restless, impatient, frequently disagreeable person *20- NE T Bor.* **witterous** bad-tempered, stubborn *la19- NE.* [see the verb]
witter[3,2] /'wɪtər/ *v* **1** to be restless, impatient, fretful; to grumble; to mutter *20- NE T Bor.* **2** to struggle, earn one's living precariously *19- NE* [unknown; compare WHITTER[4,2]]
witterin, **wutterin**, †**wittering** /'wɪtərɪn, 'wʌtərɪn/ *n* information, knowledge, news; a hint, sign *la14-19, 20- WC Bor.* [verbal noun from WITTER[1,2]]
wittin, **witting** /'wɪtɪn, 'wɪtɪŋ/ *n* **1** the fact of knowing or being aware of something, knowledge, understanding *la14-.* **2** *pl* knowledge imparted, information, intelligence, news *la14-.* **get wittings** to obtain information, find out *la14-19, 20- Sh Ork N NE T.* †**by one's witting**, †**eftir one's witting** *law in bearing witness* according to one's knowledge or information *15-16.* †**have witting** to know *la14-16.* **withoot wittings**, †**for-owtyne witting** without one's knowledge *la14-.* [verbal noun from WIT[1,2] and compare ON *vitand* consciousness, knowledge]
wittin *see* WIT[1,2]
witting *see* WIT[1,2], WITTIN
wittir *see* WITTER[1,1]
wivven *see* WEAVE
wiz *see* US
wizen, **wissen** /'wɪzən, 'wɪsən/ *v presp* **wisnand** to (cause to) shrivel, shrink, wither, dry *16-.* [OE *wisnian* to dry up, wither]

wizened, weezened, wuzzened, †wisnit, †wysnit /ˈwɪzənd, ˈwizənd, ˈwʌzənd/ *adj* dried up, shrivelled, shrunken; withered, parched *16-*. [participial adj from WIZEN]
wiznan *see* WISNAE
wizzen, *Sh Ork N* **wazzin, †wyson, †weason, †wesand** /ˈwɪzən; *Sh Ork N* ˈwazən/ *n* **1** the gullet, oesophagus *la14-.* **2** the windpipe, trachea; the throat *17-.* **3** the throat as the source of the voice *la18-.* **4** the breath, life itself *e18.* †**weet yer wizzen** to have a drink *18-e19.* [OE *wāsend, wesend*]
wizzie *see* WASSIE
wizzy /ˈwɪzi/ *n child's word* an act of urination *20- EC.* **dae a wizzy** to urinate *20- EC.* [Eng *whizz* + -IE¹]
wlgar *see* VULGAR¹·²
wlgat *see* VULGATE
wln *see* ULNE
†**wlonk** *n* a beautiful woman *e16.* [OE *wlonc* proud, magnificent]
wlt, wlte *see* VULT
wmchew *see* UMBESCHEW
wmquhile *see* UMQUHILE¹·²
wmquhyll *see* UMQUHILE¹·¹
wncouth *see* UNCOUTH¹·²
wndyr *see* UNDER¹·²
wnganand *see* UNGANAND
wnkennit *see* UNKENT
wnvinsabell *see* UNVINCIBLE
wnwynnabill *see* UNWINNABLE
wo /wo/ *interj* a call to a horse to stop *la19-.* **wo back 1** a call to a horse to stop or go backwards *la19, 20- Ork N NE T WC.* **2** a call to a horse to turn right *20- T EC.* **wo hie** a call to a horse to turn left *20- N T Bor.* **wo hup** a call to a horse to turn right *20- N T Bor.* [variant of HO²·³]
wo *see* WAE¹·¹, WAE¹·²
wob *see* WAB
wobart, wobat *see* OOBIT
wobegon *see* WAEBEGANE
wo begone *see* WAEBEGANE
wobster *see* WABSTER
woche *see* VOUCH
wochle *see* WAUCHLE¹·²
wod *see* WAD¹·¹, WID¹·¹, WUD¹·²
wodd *see* WAD²
wodderweght *see* WITHER-WEICHT
woddir *see* WEDDER
woddit *see* WID¹·²
woddy *see* WID¹·¹
wode *see* WID¹·¹, WUD¹·¹
wodeleve *see* WID¹·¹
Wodensday *see* WEDNESDAY
wodershins *see* WIDDERSHINS
woderwardis *see* WITHERWIRT
wodge *see* WAGE¹·²
wodin *see* WIDDEN
Wodnisday *see* WEDNESDAY
wodset *see* WADSET¹·¹, WADSET¹·²
†**wodwys** *n* a wild man, a savage; an outsider or foreigner; apparently also construed as some sort of animal; a heraldic figure *la15.* [OE *wuduwāsa* a faun, satyr, perhaps with influence from WY]
woe *see* WAE¹·¹
woffen *see* WEAVE
woft *see* WAFT¹·¹
woggie catte mattie /ˈwɔgɪ ˈkat ˈmati/ *n* noughts and crosses *20- Ork.* [unknown]
woid *see* WUD¹·¹

†**woidre** *n* probably cunning *la14.* [perhaps OFr *voidie* cunning]
woik *see* WALK²·², WAUK¹·²
woilley *see* VOLLEY
woir *see* WEAR
woke *see* WAUK¹·²
wold *see* WALD¹
wolf *see* OOF¹·¹, OOF¹·²
wolk *see* WEEK¹
wolklie *see* WEEKLY¹·², WEEKLY¹·³
woll *see* OO¹, WALL¹
wollbutter *see* OO¹
wollie *see* VOLLEY
†**wolron, wilroun, wolroun** *n a term of abuse* a savage creature *16-e19.* [WILD¹·¹ or WILL³·¹, with abusive suffix *-roun*; compare laidron (LAITHERIN)]
wolter *see* WELTER²·²
wolx *see* WAX²
woman, wumman, wummin, *NE* **umman** /ˈwumən, ˈwʌmən; *NE* ˈʌmən/ *n pl* **weemen, †wemen 1** an adult, female human being *la14-.* **2** as a familiar form of address, sometimes applied to a little girl *la18-.* **3** a wife or lover *17-.* †**woman bairn** a female child, a girl *la16-19.* **woman body** a woman *19-.* **weemen-folk** women *la19-.* **woman-grown** grown to womanhood, adult *la18-19, 20- Sh T.* †**woman hoose 1** accommodation for female servants or workers *la16-18.* **2** the laundry of a mansion house *la16-e19.* **woman length** grown to womanhood, adult *20- Sh T C.* **woman-muckle** grown to womanhood, adult *19-.* [OE *wīfmann*]
womb *see* WAME¹·¹, WAME¹·²
womenting *see* WAYMENTYNG
womill *see* WUMMLE
womle brees *see* WAMMLE¹·¹
wommill *see* WUMMLE
womple *see* WIMPLE¹·¹, WIMPLE¹·²
won, wone, †win /wɔn/ *v pt* **wonned, †wond, †wonnit, †wynnit** *ptp* †**woun 1** to dwell, reside, stay *la14-.* **2** to live, remain in a certain state *la14-16.* †**wonnyng, winning, wynnyng** (place of) habitation; dwelling place *la14-17.* [OE *wunian*]
won *see* OON, WIN¹·², WIN²
wond *see* WON, WOUND¹·¹, WOUND¹·²
†**wonder¹·¹, wondir, windir** *adj* marvellous, extraordinary *la14-16.* [OE *wundor-* in compounds]
†**wonder¹·², wondir, woundir** *adv* wondrously, surprisingly; very, exceedingly *la14-19.* [OE *wundor-* in compounds and OE *wundrum*, dative pl of *wundor* WUNNER¹·¹]
wonder *see* WUNNER¹·¹, WUNNER¹·²
wondir *see* WUNNER¹·¹, WUNNER¹·², WONDER¹·¹, WONDER¹·²
wondok *see* WINNOCK
wondow *see* WINDAE
wone *see* WAN¹, WON
wonned *see* WON
wonner *see* WUNNER¹·¹, WUNNER¹·²
wonnin *see* WIN¹·²
wonnit *see* WON
wont¹·¹ /wʌnt; *Sh Ork T* wɪnt/ *n* habit, custom *15-.* †**have wont** to be accustomed to, be in the habit of *16-e17.* †**wont and use** customary procedure; as is customary *la15.* [see the adj]
wont¹·², *Sh Ork T* **wint** /wʌnt; *Sh Ork T* wɪnt/ *v* to be in the habit of, be accustomed or used to *16-19, 20- Ork N.* [see the adj]
wont¹·³, *Sh Ork T* **wint, †wount, †wontit** /wʌnt; *Sh Ork T* wɪnt/ *adj* **1** accustomed to *14-.* **2** customary, usual;

established; ordinary *15-e19*. **wont wi** accustomed or used to, familiar with *e16, la19- Sh Ork*. †**wont and usit** customary procedure; as is customary *la15*. [OE *gewunod* ptp of *wunian* WON]
woo *see* OO[1]
wood *see* WID[1.1], WUD[1.1], WUD[1.2]
wooden *see* WIDDEN
woodie *see* WIDDIE
wooee *see* OO[2]
†**wooer-bab** *n* a garter, a scarf tied with lover's knots *la18-19*. [Eng *wooer* + *bab* (BOB[1])]
woof *see* OOF[1.2]
wool *see* OO[1]
woolster *see* OO[1]
woon *see* OO[1]
woop *see* WUP[1.1]
woord *see* WORD[1.1]
woosh, wooshen *see* WASH[1.2]
wooster /ˈwustər/ *n* a wooer *19 literary*. [Eng *woo*, with occupational suffix]
wop *see* WAP[1.1], WAP[1.2], WAP[2.1], WAP[2.2]
wor *see* WAUR[1.3], WORTH[1.2]
worble *see* WURBLE
word[1.1]**, wird, †wourd, †wowrd, †woord** /wʌrd, wɪrd/ *n* **1** a written or spoken unit of language *la14-*. **2** news, information; rumour, report *la14-*. **3** reputation, character *la14-*. **4** the faculty of speech; the sound of one's voice by which one is recognized *18-*. **5** a secret word (implying some sort of supernatural power); the secret watchword of those initiated into a craft or similar group *17-*. **6** *pl* prayers *la18-19*. **wirdie** a prayer *20- NE*. **get word o, get a word o** to converse with, talk to *18-19, 20- Sh*. **put up a word** to say a prayer *la19-*. **pit words on, pit words tae** to describe, express adequately *la19- Sh Ork*. **tak the word frae** to interrupt *20- Sh*. **word of mouth** an oral communication, a word *la18-*. [OE *word*]
word[1.2]**, wird** /wʌrd, wɪrd/ *v* to express (oneself) *20- Sh*. [see the noun]
wordle *see* WARLD
wordy *see* WORTH[1.1]
wore *see* WEAR, WEIR[2.2]
work *see* WARK[1], WIRK
worl, world *see* WARLD
worling *see* WIRLING
worm, *Sh* **wirm, †worme** /wʌrm; *Sh* wɪrm/ *n* **1** an earthworm, a member of the genus *Lumbricus*, or other creeping animal *la15-*. **2** a maggot *la14-*. **3** a larva or grub; a woodworm; the worm originally supposed to be the source of the barnacle goose or the phoenix *16-*. **4** *pl* parasitic worms *16-*. **5** a vile, unpleasant or venomous person *16-*. **6** an endless screw or worm-gear; the screw used to remove the charge or wad from a muzzle-loading gun *la16-*. **7** applied to a person, expressing tenderness, playfulness or commiseration *la19- Sh T*. **8** a snake or other reptile or reptilian monster *la15-19*. **wirmit** wretched, miserable *20- Sh*. **wirming** a gnawing pain *la19- Sh*. **worm-eaten 1** (as if) eaten by worms *16-*. **2** discontented; decrepit *17, 20- Ork NE*. **worm month** July, or late July and early August, when caterpillars etc are most numerous *19- T Uls*. †**worm web** a spider's web, a cobweb; flimsy clothing *18-e19*. **worm in the cheek** = *the worm* 1 *la16, e20*. **the worm 1** toothache *la16-19, 20- Ork NE*. **2** colic; a gnawing pain in the stomach *16-19*. [OE *wyrm, wurm*]
wormit, wormwood, †wormot, †wormed /ˈwʌrmət, ˈwʌrmwəd/ *n* wormwood *Artemisia absinthium la15-*. [ME *wermode*, also *worm-wōde* altered as if WORM + wood (WID[1.1]), OE *wermōd*]

worn *see* WEAR, WEIR[2.2]
worricow *see* WIRRICOW
worry *see* WIRRY[1.1], WIRRY[1.2]
wors *see* WARSE[1.2], WARSE[1.3]
worschip *see* WORSHIP[1.1], WORSHIP[1.2]
worse *see* WARSE[1.2], WARSE[1.3]
worset, wirsit /ˈwʌrsət, ˈwɪrsət/ *n* worsted, a woollen fabric or yarn *la14-*. [altered form of the place-name *Worstead*]
worship[1.1]**, †worschip, †wirschip, †wirschep** /ˈwʌrʃɪp/ *n* **1** *with possessive adjective* a title of respect *la16-*. **2** *Christian Church* (an act or rite of) veneration; family prayers *la15-*. **3** honour, worth; renown; wellbeing *la14-16*. **4** valour *la14-15*. **5** a source of honour *la15-16*. **6** respect; veneration *la14-e17*. [OE *weorðscipe* worth, honour, dignity]
worship[1.2]**, †worschip, †wirschip, †wirschep** /ˈwʌrʃɪp/ *v* **1** to honour, revere, venerate *la14-*. **2** to engage in an act of worship *16-*. [see the noun]
†**worsing** *n* deterioration *la16*. [verbal noun from EModE *worse* to become worse]
worsle *see* WARSLE[1.2]
worst *see* WARST[1.1], WARST[1.2], WARST[1.3]
worsum *see* WURSOM
†**wort**[1.1] *n* a pig's snout *e16*. [metathesis of OE *wrōt*]
†**wort**[1.2]**, wirt** *v of pigs* to root or dig up (ground) *16*. [metathesis of OE *wrōtan*]
wort *see* WIRT, WORTH[1.2]
wortchat *see* ORCHARD
worth[1.1]**, wirth, warth,** *Sh Ork* **wirt** /wʌrθ, wɪrθ, warθ; *Sh Ork* wɪrt/ *n* **1** financial or monetary value *la14-*. **2** the esteem in which something or someone is held, merit, highstanding *15-*. **worthy, wordy, †wirdy 1** of high or sufficient merit or value; fitting, suitable, competent, reliable; deserving *la14-*. **2** worth (so much), of the value of *18-e19*. **little worth** worthless, of small value *la15-19, 20- Sh Ork*. **na worth 1** (something) of no use or value *la14-19, 20- Ork N T*. **2** hardly, scarcely; not even *19, 20- Sh Ork*. [OE *weorð, worð, wurð* noun]
worth[1.2]**, wirth, warth, †wourth, †wor, †wort** /wʌrθ, wɪrθ, warθ/ *adj* **1** of a value which can be specified according to some standard *la14-*. **2** of sufficient merit, suitable: ◊*somethin wirth the fryin la15-*. **3** of use, suitability, competence or service (for some purpose) *la14-19, 20- Sh Ork N NE T*. **no worth a bean, †nocht wirth a bene** useless *16-*. †**nocht worth ane mite** of no value *la14-16*. [OE *weorð, worð, wurð* adj]
†**worth**[1.3] *adv* in a meritorious manner; correctly, as might be expected *la15-16*. [see the adj]
worth[2]**, wuth, wirth** /wʌrθ, wʌθ, wɪrθ/ *adv* **gae wuth** to become spoilt or useless, go to ruin *18- NE T*. [probably a variant of *awalt* (AVAL[1]), reinterpreted as *aa worth*]
†**worth**[3]**, wourd, wirth** *v* **1** to come to be, become, befall *la14-e19*. **2** to need, be necessary *la14-16*. [OE *weorðan, wurðan*]
†**wortis** *npl* plants, vegetation *15-e16*. [ME *wurt, wort,* OE *wyrt*]
wosp *see* WISP[1.1]
wost *see* WAST[1.4]
wouch *see* WEUCH
woud *see* WID[1.1], WUD[1.1]
wouk *see* WALK[2.2], WAUK[1.2], WEEK[2]
woun *see* WON
wound[1.1]**, woun,** *Bor* **oon, †wounde, †wond, †wind** /wund, wun; *Bor* un/ *n* a break in the skin, an injury, a wound *la14-*. [OE *wund*]
wound[1.2]**, woun,** *Bor* **oon, †wond** /wund, wun; *Bor* un/ *v* to injure, harm, wound; to inflict pain *la14-*. [OE *wundian*]

wound see WIND¹·¹
woundir see WONDER¹·², WUNNER¹·¹, WUNNER¹·²
woundow see WINNOW
wount see WEEN¹·², WONT¹·³
woup see WUP¹·²
wour see WEAR
wourd see WORD¹·¹, WORTH³
wourth see WORTH¹·²
wouth see WAITH⁴, WATH
woux see WAX²
wove, woven, wovyn see WEAVE
wow¹·¹ /wʌu/ *n* a howl, deep-throated call or cry, bark *la18-Sh Ork NE T EC*. [onomatopoeic]
wow¹·² /wʌu/ *v* to howl, bark, bay *19- Sh NE*. [see the noun]
wow², **†vow**, **†vou** /wʌu/ *interj* 1 expressing admiration, astonishment or surprise *la15-*. 2 expressing regret *la18-19*; compare WAE¹·¹. [a natural utterance]
wow see OO¹, OO², VOO¹·¹, VOO¹·²
wowf /wʌuf/ *adj* touched, mad, violently agitated or excited *19, 20- WC*. [unknown]
wowf see OOF¹·¹
wowff¹·¹ /wʌuf/ *n* a dog's bark *la18-*. [onomatopoeic]
wowff¹·² /wʌuf/ *v of a dog* to bark *19-*. [see the noun]
wowff¹·³ /wʌuf/ *adv* with a dull thudding noise, thump! *20- NE T*. [see the noun]
wowff see OOF¹·²
wowrd see WORD¹·¹
wox see WAX²
woyd see WADE¹·²
†wpbrynt *v pt* burned *e16*. [UP¹·² + *brint* (BURN²·²)]
wphint see UPHYNT
†wra, wrey, wray *n* 1 a nook, corner; a sheltered spot *13-e16*. 2 perhaps a place of refuge *la16*. 3 in Shetland and Orkney, perhaps a bay or inlet *la16*. [ON *wrá, rá*]
wrable see WARBLE¹·¹
wrach see WRATCH¹·¹
wrachit see WRETCHED
wrack¹·¹, **rack**, *NE* **vrack**, **†wrak**, **†wraik**, **†wrek** /rak, rɛk; *NE* vrak/ *n* 1 ruin, destruction, disaster; the downfall of a person; (a) shipwreck *16-*. 2 material washed up by the sea *16-*. 3 field weeds, vegetable rubbish *la17-*. 4 fresh- or salt-water weed, river or marine algae *18-19, 20- NE EC*. 5 vengeance; persecution; retribution, punishment *la14-e17*. 6 (the wreckage of) a wrecked ship; a ship unfit for use *14-e18*. 7 (the roots of) couch grass *Elymus repens la18-*. 8 goods, gear *16*. **†wrakment** harm, disaster *la16-e17*. **†wrak and wair** material washed up by the sea *la15-17*. **†wreck and waith** flotsam and jetsam *la15-19*. [OE *wracu*, *wræc* misery, vengeance, fallen together with MDu, MLG *wrak* wreckage, refuse, AN *wrec* wreckage]
wrack¹·², **wreck**, *NE* **vrack**, **†wrak**, **†wraik** /rak, rɛk; *NE* vrak/ *v* 1 to harm, hurt, ruin, cause the destruction of *la15-*. 2 to undergo shipwreck *la16-19, 20- Sh Ork N NE T*. 3 to suffer harm, destruction or ruin *la16-19, 20- NE EC*. 4 to punish, exact retribution *la14-16*. 5 to give vent to (feelings of rage) *18-19*. [from the noun and in some senses conflated with WREKE]
wrack¹·³, **†wrak**, **†wraik** /rak/ *adj* 1 damaged *la16-*. 2 doomed, bound to suffer ruin *la16*. **†wrakful** 1 vengeful *la15-16*. 2 disastrous; destructive *15-e17*. **†wrack goods**, **wrak gudis** *law* goods washed ashore from a wreck *la16-e19*. **wrack ship** a wrecked or unseaworthy ship *17, 20- Sh*. **wrack wid** driftwood *19- Sh Ork Bor*. [see the noun]
†wrack², **wraik** *v* to examine (fish) for damage *la16-e17*. **wracker** an inspector of fish *la16-e18*. [MLG *wracken* to reject, refuse]

wraethe see WREATH¹·¹
†wraiglane, wraggilland *adj* wriggling *e16*. [compare ME *wragelinge* noun, LG *dial wraggeln* to wriggle]
wraik see WRACK¹·¹, WRACK¹·², WRACK¹·³, WRACK², WREKE
wraikful see WRACK¹·³
wraist see WREST¹·²
wrait see WRITE¹·²
wraith¹, **†wrath**, **†warth**, **†wreath** /reθ/ *n* 1 an apparition of a living person, usually taken as an omen of their death; any warning sign of danger or misfortune *16-*. 2 a ghost, an apparition of a dead person *16-*. 3 any kind of fantastic image or apparition *19-*. [unknown]
wraith², **wrath**, **†wreth**, **†wreith**, **†wroth** /reθ, raθ/ *adj* 1 angry, furious, enraged *la14-18, 20- NE*. 2 grieved, sorrowful *15-16*. [OE *wrāð*]
wraith see WRATH¹·¹, WRATH¹·², WREATH¹·²
wrak see WRACK¹·¹, WRACK¹·², WRACK¹·³
†wrakling *n* a type of nail *la15*. [MLG *wrakelinge*]
†wramp¹·¹ *n* a wrench, twist, sprain; a twisted view or understanding *la17-18*. [compare Dan *vrampet* warped, twisted]
†wramp¹·² *v* to wrench, twist, sprain *la18-19*. [see the noun]
wran, wren /ran, rɛn/ *n* 1 the wren *Troglodytes troglodytes la15-*. 2 term of endearment especially to a child *19-*. 3 a cowrie shell *20- Sh*. **wrannie** the wren *la18-*. [OE *wrenna*]
wranch¹·¹, **wrench**, *N WC SW* **runch**, **†wrinche** /ranʃ, rɛnʃ; *N WC SW* rʌnʃ/ *n* 1 a twist *la19-*. 2 a spanner *17-*. [see the verb]
wranch¹·², **wrench**, *N WC SW* **runch** /ranʃ, rɛnʃ; *N WC SW* rʌnʃ/ *v* to twist *la16-*. [OE *wrencan*]
wrang¹·¹, **wrong** /raŋ, rɔŋ/ *n* 1 wickedness, injustice, harm *la14-*. 2 wrong behaviour, evil or unjust action, harm, injury done; an act of wrongdoing; a mistake *15-*. 3 *law* a crime or misdemeanour *15-*. 4 physical or material harm, damage *la18-19*. **say (a person) wrang** to speak ill of (a person) *la19- Sh Ork T*. **†wrang and unlaw** (the right to prosecute) wrongdoing of a relatively minor sort, not involving a capital penalty *la13-16*. [OE *wrang*, from ON **wrangr* adj]
wrang¹·², **wrong** /raŋ, rɔŋ/ *v* 1 to do (undeserved) harm, injustice or injury; to treat badly or unfairly *la14-*. 2 to cause physical harm or injury to, damage, hurt; to spoil *la16-*. 3 to commit a crime or misdemeanour *16*. **wrang your stamack** to make oneself sick by eating or drinking too much *19- WC Bor*. [see the adj]
wrang¹·³, **wrong**, *NE* **vrang** /raŋ, rɔŋ; *NE* vraŋ/ *adj* 1 not right, immoral, illegal; erroneous, false; incorrect *la15-*. 2 disordered, not functioning properly *la16-*. 3 *of a person or limb* crooked, deformed; *of a joint* dislocated *19- NE T*. 4 deranged, insane *19, 20- NE*. 5 on the left side *la15-e16*. 6 *of succession or inheritance* illegitimate *la15*. **wrangweys** incorrectly, the wrong way round *19-*. **†wrang handit** left-handed *e17*. **fa wrang till** *of a woman* to lose her virginity, be seduced (by) *la19- SW*. **get the wrong end of the tether** to misunderstand, be confused *la19- Ork*. **not come wrang (tae)** not to come amiss (to), not to be unwelcome (for), not to disconcert *la19-*. **not say a wrang word** not to use harsh, unjust or improper language *20-*. **on the wrang side o the blanket** out of wedlock *la18-*. **rise aff your wrang side** to get up in a bad temper *la19*. **wrang in the heid** insane *18-*. [OE **wrang*, from ON **wrangr*]
wrang¹·⁴, **wrong** /raŋ, rɔŋ/ *adv* in a wrong or mistaken fashion or direction, erroneously, incorrectly *la14-*. **gae wrang** 1 to take a wrong direction *16-*. 2 to fail to function properly *16-*. 3 *of food etc* to go bad, decompose *la19- Sh Ork NE*. [see the adj]
wrang see WRING

†**wrangis**, **wrayngis** *npl* the timbers or ribs of a ship *e16*. [plural form of OE *wrang* from ON **wrǫng*]
wranglesome /ˈraŋəlsʌm/ *adj* quarrelsome, contentious *la19, 20- Sh Ork NE*. [Eng *wrangle*, with -SOME adj-forming suffix]
wrangous, †**wrangwis**, †**wrangwys**, †**wrangus** /ˈraŋəs/ *adj* 1 unjust, immoral, unfair; fostering harm *15-*. 2 *law* illegal, wrongful *15-*. 3 *of goods* ill-gotten; *of actions* injurious *15-*. 4 *of the processes of the law, documents* inaccurate, incorrect, mistaken *la15-17*. **wrangously** 1 improperly, illegally *la14-*. 2 unjustly, immorally, unfairly, falsely *la14-e18*. 3 incorrectly, mistakenly; in a manner not in keeping with the processes of the law *la15-e17*. 4 undeservedly, without justification *15-17*. **wrongous imprisonment** *law* false imprisonment, imprisonment without the due form of law *la17-*. [ME *wrangwise*, WRANG[1.3] + WISE[1], with change of suffix in some forms]
wrap, *NE EC* **warp** /rap; *NE EC* warp/ *v* 1 to wind around (part of the body) with something; to wrap something about the body; to envelop or enfold (in something, originally especially an emotion) *la15-*. 2 to permeate, envelop, enclose *e16*. [unknown; compare WAP[2.2]]
wrap *see* WARP[1.2]
wrapper, *NE* **vrapper** /ˈrapər; *NE* ˈvrapər/ *n* 1 a woman's household overall, a smock *19-*. 2 a loose robe or gown worn as a dressing-gown or bed-jacket *19, 20- NE*. 3 a boot of thin leather, fastened by wrapping the upper part around the leg *la18-e19*. [WRAP, with instrumental suffix]
wrastle *see* WARSLE[1.1], WARSLE[1.2]
wrat, **wart** /rat, wɔrt/ *n* a small, rough growth, a wart *la15-*. **warty girse** sun spurge *Euphorbia helioscopia*, the fluid in the stems was used as a treatment for warts *20- Ork*. [OE *weart*]
†**wrat** *see* WRITE[1.2]
wratch[1.1], **wretch**, *NE* **vratch**, †**wrach**, †**wreche**, †**werch** /ratʃ, retʃ; *NE* vratʃ/ *n* 1 an unfortunate person, a poor, miserable creature *la14-*. 2 a miser, a mean person *la15-19*. 3 a person without riches or resources *la15-16*. 4 a despicable person, capable of vile, wicked behaviour *la14-e17*. [OE *wræcca, wrecca* an exile]
wratch[1.2], †**wreche** /ratʃ/ *v* to become mean or stingy; to cheat, stint *la16-19, 20- Uls*. [see the noun]
wratchit *see* WRETCHED
wrath[1.1], *Sh* **wreth**, †**wraith**, †**wroth**, †**wroith** /raθ, raθ; *Sh* vreθ/ *n* anger; rage, (violent) fury *la14-*. [OE *wrǣððu*]
†**wrath**[1.2], **wraith**, **wreth** *v* to make (a person) angry, enrage; to become angry or enraged *la14-15*. [see the noun]
wrath *see* WRAITH[1], WRAITH[2]
wrattle, **wruttle**, **writtle**, *EC* **wortril**, †**wratwel**, †**wartweil** /ˈratəl, ˈrʌtəl, ˈritəl; *EC* ˈwɔrtrəl/ *n* a hang-nail *19, 20- C*. [OE *wyrtwala, wurtwala* a root]
wraucht *see* WARK[1.2]
wrax *see* RAX[1.1], RAX[1.2]
wray *see* WRA, WRY[1.2]
wreat *see* WRITE[1.2]
wreath[1.1], **wride**, *NE* **vraith**, †**wreth**, †**wryth**, †**wraethe** /riθ, rid; *NE* vrʌiθ/ *n* 1 a wreath, originally a laurel wreath *17-*. 2 a bank or drift of snow, probably originally an accumulation of swirls of snow *18-*. 3 a necklace *la14-e16*. [OE *wriða* a band, thong, collar]
wreath[1.2], †**wreith**, †**wraith** /rið/ *v* 1 to turn, roll up (a sleeve) *la16*. 2 figuratively, to fasten (a yoke) around a person's neck; to subjugate *la17-e19*. [see the noun]
wreath *see* WRAITH[1]
†**wreche** *see* WRATCH[1.1], WRATCH[1.2]
wreck *see* WRACK[1.1], WRACK[1.1]

wregling *see* RIGLEN
wreicht *see* WRICHT
wreik *see* WREKE
wreist *see* WREST[1.1], WREST[1.2]
wreit *see* WRITE[1.1], WRITE[1.2]
wreith *see* WRAITH[2], WREATH[1.2]
wreittar *see* WRITER
wreitten *see* WRITE[1.2]
†**wreke**, **wreik**, **wrek**, **wraik** *v ptp* **wrokkin**, **wrokin** 1 to avenge (oneself, another, an injury etc) *la14-16*. 2 to give vent to (feelings of rage) *la14-17*. **wrekar** an avenger *e16*. [OE *wrecan* to drive, punish]
wrek *see* WRACK[1.1]
wrekis *see* WRIKIS
†**wrele**, **wreil** *v* apparently, to turn (around); to struggle *e16*. [perhaps onomatopoeic]
wren *see* WRAN
wrench *see* WRANCH[1.1], WRANCH[1.2]
wrest[1.1], **wrist**, †**wreist** /rest, rɪst/ *n* 1 a sprain *17-19, 20- Sh*. 2 a tuning key for tightening the strings of a musical instrument *la15-e17*. 3 a twist of a tuning key *16*. [see the verb]
wrest[1.2], **wrist**, **reist**, †**wreist**, †**wraist** /rest, rɪst, rist/ *v* 1 to tear, seize *la16-*. 2 to sprain, wrench (a muscle or joint) *16-*. 3 to turn over (thoughts), change, influence (one's own or another's mind) *15-e17*. 4 to misinterpret *la16-17*. **wrestin threed** *in folk medicine* a string, cord or length of wool used to treat sprains *17- Sh Ork*. [OE *wrǣstan* to bend, twist, ON **wreista*]
wrest *see* REEST[3.1], WRIST
wrestle *see* WARSLE[1.1], WARSLE[1.2]
wret *see* WRIT, WRITE[1.2]
wretch *see* WRATCH[1.1]
wretched, †**wretchit**, †**wratchit**, †**wrachit** /ˈretʃɪd/ *adj* 1 miserable; causing misery; vile *la14-*. 2 small, of little account; base; poverty-stricken *la14-e16*. 3 miserly, mean *la15-17*. [WRATCH[1.1] + -IT[2]]
wreth *see* WRAITH[2], WRATH[1.1], WRATH[1.2], WREATH[1.1]
wrett *see* WRITE[1.2]
wrettin *see* WRITE[1.2]
wrey *see* WRA, WRY[1.2], WRY[1.3]
wrible *see* WARBLE[1.1]
wricht, **wright**, *NE* **vricht**, †**wrycht**, †**wreicht** /rɪxt, rʌit; *NE* vrɪxt/ *n* 1 a craftsman; a carpenter or joiner *la13-*. 2 *pl* the incorporation or craft guild of wrights *la15-e19, la19- historical*. **wrichtin** the job of a carpenter or joiner; carpentry, joinery *la19- NE T*. †**wricht work** carpentry, joinery *la16-18*. [OE *wyrhta*]
wride *see* WREATH[1.1]
wriggling, †**vrigling** /ˈrɪɡlɪn, ˈrɪɡlɪŋ/ *adj* twisting and turning, wriggling *la16-*. [participial adj from EModE *wriggle*, MLG *wriggeln*]
wright *see* WRICHT
†**wrikis**, **wrekis** *npl* acts of reaching or stretching movements *e16*. [perhaps a variant of RAX[1.1]]
wrinche *see* WRANCH[1.1]
wring, *NE* **vring** /rɪŋ; *NE* vrɪŋ/ *v presp also* †**wrinkand**, *pt also* †**wrang** to twist, writhe; to squeeze, crush; to wring the hands (in sorrow) *la14-*. [OE *wringan*]
†**wrink**, **wring** *n* a cunning action, a trick *la15-e17*. [ME *wrinke*, OE *wrenc*]
wrinkand *see* WRING
wrinkle *see* WRUNKLE[1.1], WRUNKLE[1.2]
wrist, †**wrest** /rɪst/ *n* the wrist *17-*. **wristie** a woollen muff or knitted cuff for the wrist *20- Sh*. †**wristikin** = *wristie 19*. **wristy** a throw in the game of *knifie* (KNIFE) in which

the wrist has to be touched before the throw is made *20- T EC.* [OE *wrist*]

wrist *see* WREST¹·¹, WREST¹·²

writ, †**wryt**, †**wret**, †**wyrt** /rɪt/ *n* **1** something written; a chronicle or story *la14-.* **2** handwriting *16-19, 20- Sh Ork WC.* **3** *law* a document, usually witnessed and signed or sealed, a deed, a writing having legal force *la14-.* **4** scripture *la14-.* Compare WRITE¹·¹. †**in writ** in writing *la14-17.* [OE *writ*]

writ *see* WRITE¹·²

writar *see* WRITER

write¹·¹, *NE* **vreet**, †**wreit** /rʌɪt; *NE* vrit/ *n* **1** writing, as opposed to speech *la19-;* compare *in write.* **2** handwriting, especially in ink; the art or style of writing, penmanship *la16-19, 20- NE.* **3** = WRIT (sense 4) *la14-16.* **4** = WRIT (sense 1) *15-17.* **in write** a written record or document of any transaction, especially of a legal or formal nature *15-19, 20- NE.* †**in wreit** in writing *la15-e19.* Compare WRIT. [from the verb and in some senses from WRIT]

write¹·², **wreat**, *NE* **vreet**, †**writ**, †**wreit**, †**wret** /rʌɪt, rɪt; *NE* vrit/ *v pt* **wrait**, **wrat**, **writ**, †**wreit**, †**wrett**, †**wreat**, *ptp* **written**, *NE* **vrutten**, †**wrettin**, †**wreitten** to form (letters), transcribe; to draw up (a document); to put into writing, set down in words; to chronicle, compose; to communicate by letter *la14-.* **write-book** a (school) writing- or exercise-book *18-19, 20- Ork.* †**wrett on** to continue to write *la15.* **write up 1** to record in writing; to list *15-.* **2** to communicate (something) in writing to an authority or someone of higher status *17.* [OE *wrītan*]

writer, *NE* **vreeter**, †**writar**, †**writtar**, †**wreittar** /ˈrʌɪtər; *NE* ˈvritər/ *n* **1** an author; a person who writes *15-.* **2** a lawyer, notary, solicitor, attorney *16-19, 20- NE T EC.* **3** a person employed to make an official account of proceedings and prepare documents; a legal secretary *la15-18.* †**writer-chiel** an author or lawyer *la18-e19.* **Writer to the Signet (W.S.)** a member of a society of solicitors in Edinburgh, originally the clerks by whom signet writs (see SIGNET¹·¹ (sense 4) and WRIT) were prepared, *latterly* having the exclusive privilege of signing all SIGNET WRITS and drawing up crown writs and charters *la15-.* [OE *wrītere*]

writhe, †**wryth**, †**wryith** /rʌɪð/ *v ptp* also †**writhen 1** to twist, turn, squirm; to wring, wrench *15-.* **2** to turn, direct (a feeling); to change (one's mind); to turn away from *la14-16.* **3** to screw up, avert (the face) in anger *la15-e16.* **4** to throw into confusion *e16.* [OE *wrīðan*]

writing, **writin**, *NE* **vreetin** /ˈrʌɪtɪŋ, ˈrʌɪtɪn; *NE* ˈvritɪn/ *n* **1** the action of writing; something written *la15-.* **2** a literary composition *la15-.* **3** handwriting *la15-.* **4** the skill or ability to form letters *la16-.* **5** the action or profession of drawing up and copying documents and letters *la15-17.* **6** a legal document, documentary evidence, a written agreement *la15-16.* **7** a message or instruction in writing, a letter *15-17.* **8** (a piece of) paper etc with writing on it *16.* †**writing buith** a place for the preparation of legal documents *la16-e17.* †**writing chamber** = *writing buith;* a lawyer's office *la16-e19.* [verbal noun from WRITE¹·²]

writtar *see* WRITER

written *see* WRITE¹·²

wrocht *see* WARK¹·²

wroith *see* WRATH¹·¹

wrokin, **wrokkin** *see* WREKE

wrong *see* WRANG¹·¹, WRANG¹·², WRANG¹·³, WRANG¹·⁴

wroth *see* WRAITH², WRATH¹·¹

wroucht *see* WARK¹·²

wrought *see* WARK¹·²

wrunkle¹·¹, †**wrinkle**, †**wrynkle** /ˈrʌŋkəl/ *n* **1** a crease, fold, wrinkle *la19-;* compare RUNKLE¹·¹. **2** a sinuous, sweeping movement *e16.* **wrunklie** crumpled *la20-.* [see the verb]

wrunkle¹·², **wrinkle**, †**wrynkle**, †**wrynkkill** /ˈrʌŋkəl, ˈrɪŋkəl/ *v* to crease, fold, wrinkle *16-.* †**wrinklit** winding, tortuous *e16.* [compare OE *gewrinclod* winding, serrated]

†**wry**¹·¹ *n* a grimace *e19.* **on wry**, **upon wry**, **a wrie** distortedly, crookedly, awry *la14-16.* [see the verb]

†**wry**¹·², **wray**, **wrey** *v* **1** to move with a turning or twisting motion; to (cause to) change (beliefs) *la14-17.* **2** to twist, distort or avert (the face); to make a wry face, grimace *16-e19.* **3** to wrest meaning from; to understand *e16.* **4** to twist, misinterpret *la16.* [OE *wrīgian* to go, turn, twist]

wry¹·³, †**wrey** /rae/ *adj* twisted *la16-.* [see the verb]

wrycht *see* WRICHT

wryith *see* WRITHE

wrynkkill *see* WRUNKLE¹·²

wrynkle *see* WRUNKLE¹·¹, WRUNKLE¹·²

wryt *see* WRIT

wryth *see* WREATH¹·¹, WRITHE

ws *see* USE¹·¹

W.S. *see* WRITER

wtelau, **wtlaw** *see* OOTLAW¹·¹

wub *see* WAB

wubbit *see* OOBIT, WABBIT

wud¹·¹, **wuid**, **wude**, **wood**, **wid**, *Ork* **wod**, †**wode**, †**woid**, †**woud** /wʌd, wud, wɪd; *Ork* wɔd/ *adj* **1** *of people* mad, insane, demented *la14-.* **2** *of animals, especially dogs* rabid, mad *16-.* **3** *of animals* fierce, violent, wild; not tame *la14-.* **4** furiously angry, enraged *la14-.* **5** *of weather or the elements* fierce, furious, wild *la14-e19.* **6** *of people* reckless, wild or savage in behaviour *la15-e19.* **7** lacking sense, stupid *la14-16.* **8** *of a state, emotion or event* fierce, furious, crazy; maddening *la15-e17.* **wudness**, †**wodnes** mad rage, a paroxysm affecting the brain; recklessness, extreme folly *la14-19, 20- literary.* **wudden dream** a dazed, frantic or frenzied state, mental confusion; a brainstorm; a fantasy *la18-.* **wuddrum**, †**widdrim**, †**wodrome** = *wudden dream 17-19, 20- literary.* †**wodeman 1** a madman *la14-e17.* **2** a wild, savage, fierce man *16.* **aince wud and aye waur** getting madder and madder *18-.* **wud for** eager keen for, *la17-.* [OE *wōd*]

†**wud**¹·², **wood**, **wod** *adv* crazily, madly, ferociously; utterly *la15-19.* [see the adj]

wud *see* WID¹·¹, WID¹·², WID²

wudden *see* WIDDEN

wuddie *see* WIDDIE

wude *see* WUD¹·¹

wudger *see* WAGER¹·²

wudna *see* WID²

wuffle *see* WAFFLE¹·²

wuft *see* WAFT¹·¹

wuid *see* WID¹·¹, WUD¹·¹

wuish, **wuishen** *see* WASH¹·²

wuive *see* WEAVE

wulfire *see* WILDFIRE

wulk, **wilk**, *Sh* **wylk** /wʌlk, wɪlk; *Sh* wʌɪlk/ *n* **1** a whelk or periwinkle *Buccinum* or similar mollusc *16-.* **2** a nickname for an inhabitant of the island of Veira *19- Ork.* **wylk-ebb** the seashore where whelks are accessible at low-tide *20- Sh.* **gang i da wylk ebb** to be reduced to penury *20- Sh.* **pick yer wulk** to pick your nose *20- T C.* [OE *wioloc*]

wull *see* WILD¹·¹, WILL¹·¹, WILL¹·², WILL³·²

wullcat *see* WILDCAT

Wullie *see* WILLIE²

wullin *see* WILLIN

wullsome see WILL[3.2]
wull-tams see WALTAMS
wumble see WUMMLE
wumman, wummin see WOMAN
wummle, wimble, womill, †wumble, †wommill /ˈwʌməl, ˈwɪmbəl, ˈwoməl/ *n* **1** a drill or auger, a tool for boring *la15-*. **2** *mining* a drill for boring through soil and rock for coal or water *18-19*. **wummle bore 1** an auger-hole *18-*. **2** a cleft palate *19, 20- EC Bor.* [AN *wimble*]
wummle see WAMMLE[1.2]
wumple see WIMPLE[1.1], WIMPLE[1.2]
wumplefeyst see AMPLEFEYST
wun see WIN[1.2], WIN[2], WIND[1.1], WIND[2.2]
wund see WIND[1.1], WIND[2.2]
wunda see WINDAE
wundae, wunda-swalla see WINDAE
wunder- see UNDER-
wundy see WINDAE
wunna see WILL[1.2]
wunnelstrae see WINDLESTRAE[1.1]
wunner[1.1]**, wonder, wonner,** *Sh N* **winder,** *NE* **winner, †wondir, †woundir** /ˈwʌnər, ˈwʌndər, ˈwɒnər; *Sh N* ˈwɪndər; *NE* ˈwɪnər/ *n* **1** surprise, astonishment, amazement; something amazing; a miracle, portent, omen *la14-*. **2** *derogatory* a nasty, unpleasant or insignificant person *la18-19, 20- N NE T*. **wunnerfu, †wondirfull** *adj* amazing; extraordinary; very great *la14-*. **wunnerfu, †wondirfull** *adv* to an amazing extent, extremely, remarkably *la15-*. **†wondirlie** amazingly, exceedingly *la14-16*. **wondersome** exceedingly, remarkably *20- WC SW*. [OE *wundor*]
wunner[1.2]**, wonder, winner,** *Uls* **wonner, †wondir, †woundir** /ˈwʌnər, ˈwʌndər, ˈwɪnər; *Uls* ˈwɒnər/ *v* **1** to feel wonder, admiration, astonishment; to look upon in amazement *la14-*. **2** to be eager to know, be curious (about) *16-*. **3** *reflexive* to be surprised: ◊*A wonder me that ee wad dae a thing lek at 20- N*. **4** to be amazed, marvel at (something) *la14-16*. **wunnerin, †wondryng, †woundring 1** surprise, amazement *la14-*. **2** an object of wonder, a marvel *e16*. **I widna wunner but what** I wouldn't be surprised if *20-*. [OE *wundrian*]
wunnle see WINDLE[1.2]
wunnock see WINNOCK
wunt see WANT[1.2]
wuntle see WINTLE
wup[1.1]**, wip, woop** /wʌp, wɪp, wup/ *n* **1** a ring; a finger ring without stones; an earring *16-*. **2** a splice, a tying or binding with cord twined round; a coil or loop of string or rope *19, 20- Sh Ork N NE*; compare WAP[2.1]. **3** a strake or side-plank of a boat *20- Sh*. **4** a journey up, round and down, a circuit, a turning movement *20- Ork*. **5** a bandage *e16*. **6** a garland or head-dress of entwined foliage *e16*. **7** a hoop or band (for the shaft of a cart) *16*. [see the verb]
wup[1.2]**, woup, wip, †wyp** /wʌp, wup, wɪp/ *v* **1** to coil, become entangled or involved *20-*. **2** to bind (together), splice; to secure, fasten, tie *la15-19, 20- Sh Ork N NE T EC*. **3** to wind (a cord) tightly and regularly round an object, overlay with cord *16-19, 20- Sh Ork N NE T*. Compare WAP[2.2]. [unknown; compare WAP[2.2], WHUP[1.1]]
wup[2] /wʌp/ *n* someone who drives horses, a ploughman or horseman *20- NE*. [altered form of WHUP[1.1]]
wuppen see OPEN[1.2]
wupple[1.1]**,** *N* **wipple** /ˈwʌpəl; *N* ˈwɪpəl/ *n* **1** a tangle *20- Sh*. **2** a predicament *20- Sh N*. [see the verb]
wupple[1.2]**,** *N* **wipple** /ˈwʌpəl; *N* ˈwɪpəl/ *v* **1** to wrap, bundle up, roll tightly *la19- Sh Ork N*. **2** to become entangled *20- Sh N*. **3** to buckle under one *20- Sh*. [frequentative form of WUP[1.2]]
wur see OOR[3], WIR, WIS
wurble, †worble, †warble /ˈwʌrbəl/ *v* **1** to move in a twisting, sinuous way, wriggle, crawl; to struggle *la16-19, 20- Bor*. **2** to entwine, twist *19*. [unknown; compare Du *wervelen*]
wure see WEAR
wurf, †urf /wʌrf/ *n* a puny, ill-grown person, especially a child *19, 20- Bor*. [unknown; perhaps a reduced form of WARWOOF]
wurk see WARK[1], WIRK
wurl see WIRL[1]
wurld see WARLD
wurlyon see WIRLING
wurn /wʌrn/ *v* to be querulous, complain *19- literary*. [perhaps onomatopoeic]
wurn see WEAR
wurnae see WIRNAE
wurp see ORP
wurpie see ORPIE
wurr see WIRR[1.1], WIRR[1.2]
wursom, *Sh* **wirsom, †worsum, †wirsum** /ˈwʌrsʌm; *Sh* ˈwɪrsʌm/ *n* pus, the discharge from a festering sore *16-19, 20- Sh Ork N NE*. **wursom-eed** having rheumy eyes, suffering from conjunctivitis *20- Ork WC*. **wursom-midder** the core of a boil *20- Sh Ork*. [OE *worsm*]
wus see WIS
wush see WISH[1.2]
wusker, wisker, whisker /ˈwʌskər, ˈwɪskər, ˈʍɪskər/ *n* **1** a bunch of feathers or short straws tied at one end to form a brush *19- NE*. **2** a belt for supporting a knitting needle, originally a bunch of straw used for that purpose; a leather belt *19- NE*. [WHISK[1.2] + instrumental suffix]
wusna, wusnae see WISNAE
wusp see WISP[1.1]
wuss, wiss /wʌs, wɪs/ *n* juice, the liquid obtained from vegetable substances *19, 20- Sh*. [OE *wōs* moisture, exuded liquid]
wuss see WISH[1.1], WISH[1.2]
wut see WIT[1.1]
wutch see WITCH[1.1]
wuth[1.1] /wʌθ/ *n* wrath, anger *la19- literary*. [see the adj]
†wuth[1.2] *adj* mad, deranged *20 Bor*. [ME *oth*, ON *óðr*]
wuth see WORTH[2]
wutten see WEET[1.2]
wutter see WITTER[2], WITTER[3.1]
wutterin see WITTERIN
wuven see WEAVE
wuzzened see WIZENED
†wy *n* **1** a fighting man, warrior, soldier *la15-e16*. **2** a man, a person *15-16*. [OE *wiga*]
wy see WEE[1.1]
wycht see WECHT[1.1], WICHT[2]
wyd see WIDE[1.1], WIDE[1.2]
wydder see WITHER
wyde see WADE[1.1], WADE[1.2], WIDE[1.1], WIDE[1.2]
wye see WEY[1], WEY[2.2]
wyfe, wyff see WIFE
wyght see WYTE[1]
wyice see WISE[2]
wyine see WINE
wyis see WISE[1]
wyke see WAIK[1.2]
wykket see WICKET
wykkit see WICKIT

wylcome see WALCOME[1.1]
wyld see WILD[1.1]
wyle see WALE[1.2], WILE[1.1], WILE[1.2], WILE[2]
wylie /ˈwʌɪli/ *n* an instrument for twisting straw into ropes *19- C SW Bor.* [probably an altered form of WYLOCK with the second element reinterpreted as -OCK, and -IE[1] substituted]
wylock, †**wavelock** /ˈwʌɪlək/ *n* = WYLIE *19- WC Bor.* [probably a reduced form of WAVEL, from the twisting motion of the instrument, + HEUK]
wylie see WILE[1.1]
wyliecoat, †**wily coyt**, †**weiliecoat**, †**wallicoat** /ˈwʌɪlɪkot/ *n* **1** a man's undergarment, frequently in warm material, sometimes with long sleeves, originally sometimes decorated or of rich material to be seen under the outer garments *la15-*. **2** a woman's undergarment or petticoat, sometimes intended to be seen *16-19, 20- literary*. **3** a child's outer garment or undergarment *16-*. **4** a woman's nightdress *17-18*. [unknown first element + COAT]
wylk see WULK
wyll see WILD[1.1], WILL[1.1], WILL[3.2]
wyly see WILE[1.1]
wympil see WIMPLE[1.1]
wymple see WIMPLE[1.2]
wyn see WIN[1.2], WINE
wynd[1], †**wyne**, †**weynd** /wʌɪnd/ *n* mainly in street names a narrow, frequently winding street or alley, mainly in towns or cities *la13-*. **wynie** = WYND[1] *la19- NE.* †**wyndheid** the top end of a WYND[1] *la15-18*. [OE *gewind* a winding ascent]
wynd[2.1], **wyne**, †**wind**, †**weynd** /wʌɪnd, wʌɪn/ *v* **1** *in ploughing or other agricultural field-work* to (command draught-animals to) turn to the left *19, 20- EC SW Uls*. **2** to turn a plough (at the end of a rig); to plough *la15-e18*. †**wyner** *in a ploughing team* the leading animal on the right-hand side, which took the first steps to the left on the command to WYND *la18-19*. **wyndin** an awkwardly shaped piece of land which can only be ploughed in one direction; a field divided into sections for the convenience of ploughing; the rigs at each end of a field on which the plough team or tractor turns *18- NE EC Uls*. [variant of WIND[2.2]]
wynd[2.2] /wʌɪnd/ *interj* a call to a yoked animal to turn to the left *19, 20- SW Uls*. [see the verb]
wynd see WIND[1.1], WIND[2.1], WIND[2.2], WIND[3]
wyndas see WINDASS
wyndill see WINDLE[1.1]
wyndill stray see WINDLESTRAE[1.1]
wyndo see WINDAE
wyndois see WINDASS
wyndok see WINNOCK
wyndy see WINDY

wyne see WEAN, WINE, WYND[1], WYND[2.1]
wyne seck see SECK WYNE
wyng see WING
wynk see WINK[1.1], WINK[1.2]
wynnit see WON
wynt, **wint**, **went**, **waint**, †**wind** /wʌɪnt, wɪnt, wɛnt, went/ *v* of food or drink to (allow to) spoil (originally by exposure to the air) *la18-*. **wyntit**, **wynted** spoiled, soured, tainted *la16-*. [variant of WIND[1.1]]
wynt see WEND
wynter, **wyntir** see WINTER[1.1]
wyp see WUP[1.2]
wyre, **wyrin** see WIRE[1.1]
wyrk see WIRK
wyrt see WRIT
wys see WISE[2], WISH[1.1], WISH[1.2]
wysche see WASH[1.2]
wyse see VYIS
wysh see WASH[1.2]
wysk see WHISK[1.2]
wysnit see WIZENED
wyson see WIZZEN
wyss see WISE[2]
wystcoat see WESKIT
wyste see WASTE[1.3]
wyt see WIT[1.1], WYTE[1.1], WYTE[1.2]
wyte[1.1], **wite**, **wight**, †**wit**, †**wyt** /wʌɪt/ *n* **1** blame, reproach; blameworthiness, responsibility (for some error or mischief) *la14-*. **2** the person or thing to blame, the source of blame *16-e19*. **3** *law* fault, responsibility (for a crime) *16-17*. **wyteless**, †**wyteles** blameless, innocent *16-e18, 20- literary*. †**wytleyir** *law* an accuser or prosecutor, apparently in a personal name *e14*. [OE *wīte* punishment]
wyte[1.2], **wite**, †**wyght**, †**wit**, †**wyt** /wʌɪt/ *v* to blame, impute blame or guilt to (a person or thing), accuse a (person) of responsibility for something *la14-*. **tae wyte** to blame, at fault *15-19, 20- Sh NE*. **wyte me** used as an expletive *20- Sh*. [OE *wītan*]
wyte see WAIT[1.2]
wyth see WI
wythin see WITHIN[1.2]
wytles see WITLESS
wytter see WITTER[1.2]
wyttir see WITTER[1.1]
wyttyt see WIT[1.2]
wyve see WEAVE
wyver see WEAVER

Y

†y- *prefix mainly attached to (past) participles* in imitation of English poetic models *la15-e16.* [OE *ge-* perfective prefix]

-y *see* -IE[1], -IE[2], -IE[3]

ya *see* AE, YEA[1.1], YEA[1.2]

yaa /jɑ/ *n* an eel *Anguilla anguilla la19- N NE.* [compare ON *áll*]

yaa *see* YEA[1.1]

yaag[1] /jɑg/ *v* **1** to nag, demand persistently, annoy with persistent demands *19- Sh Ork.* **2** *fishing* to keep the line constantly in motion, jerk the hook up and down *la19- Sh Ork.* [Norw *jaga* to hunt, move to and fro; 'harp on one string']

yaa[2.1] /jɑg/ *n* gossip, chatter *la19- NE.* [see the verb]

yaag[2.2] /jɑg/ *v* to gossip, chatter *la19- NE.* [aphetic form of *lyaag* (LAIG[1.2])]

yaager /'jɑgər/ *v of dogs* to tear, bite at, worry *20- Ork.* [altered form of YAGGLE with change of frequentative suffix]

yaager *see* YAGGER

yaakie *see* YACK

yaarm *see* YARM

yaave /jɑv/ *n farming* a spoke or paddle on the fanner of a winnowing machine or on the vane of a corn-reaper or -binder *20- NE.* [variant of AVE[3]]

yaavel *see* AVAL[2.2]

yaavin *see* YAWIN

ya bass /jɑ ˈbas/ *n* a term of abuse *la20- WC.* [probably a shortened form of Eng *you bastard*]

yabb /jɑb/ *v* to harp on a subject, talk incessantly; gabble *19- Sh NE T.* [probably onomatopoeic, and compare Norw *jabba*]

yabble[1.1] /'jɑbəl/ *n* **1** a noisy clamour of voices *19- NE C.* **2** a garrulous person, a chatterbox *19- NE T.* [see the verb]

yabble[1.2] /'jɑbəl/ *v* **1** to talk volubly or excitedly, chatter, gossip *19-.* **2** to scold, be querulous *19- EC.* **3** *of animals or birds* to chatter or bark excitedly *la19- Ork NE T.* [frequentative form of YABB]

yable *see* ABLE[1.1]

yachis *see* HAICHES

yacht *see* YATT

yack /jɑk/ *n* an Inuit *la19- Sh Ork NE T.* **yackie, yaakie** an Inuit *la19- Sh Ork NE T.* **yackie yaw** an Inuit *la19- T EC.* [originally a whalers' word, perhaps imitative of Inuit speech]

yackie-thunder /'jɑkiˈθʌndər/ *n* a sudden, loud noise which proves to be nothing serious *20- Ork.* [perhaps reduced form of *yark o thunder*, YERK[1.1]]

yackle[1.1], *N* **aickle** /'jɑkəl; *N* 'ekəl/ *n* **1** a molar tooth *19- Sh Ork N.* **2** a small, white, tooth-shaped cloud *20- Sh.* [Norw dial *jakle*]

yackle[1.2] /'jɑkəl/ *v* to gnaw, chew *la19- Sh Ork.* [see the noun]

yad, yade *see* YAUD

yae *see* AE

yaes *see* YE

yaff[1.1], **yauff** /jɑf, jɔf/ *n* **1** a chatterbox, a pert person; *derogatory* a peevish, insignificant person *la19- C Bor.* **2** a bark, a yelp; a sharp bird-call *la19- C.* [see the verb]

yaff[1.2], **yauff** /jɑf, jɔf/ *v* **1** to bark, yelp *19- C Bor.* **2** to chatter, talk pertly *19- C Bor.* **3** to chide, scold, criticize *19- EC Bor.* [onomatopoeic]

yafu *see* AWFY[1.1]

yag /jɑg/ *n* poorly developed grains of corn or small, worthless fish; originally the fine dust of flour or meal *la19- Sh.* [unknown]

yagger, yaager, †jagger /'jɑgər/ *n* **1** a tender, originally a vessel which attended to the needs of the Dutch herring-fishing fleet *18-19*, *20- Sh.* **2** a pedlar, hawker, originally a small trader who bought fish clandestinely *19- Sh Ork.* [Du (*haring*)*jager*]

yaggle /'jɑgəl/ *v* **1** to chew with difficulty; to work laboriously *20- Sh Ork.* **2** to argue *la20- Ork.* [Norw dial *jagla*]

yagiment /'jɑgɪmənt/ *n* a state of excitement, a flurry, agitation *19- NE.* [altered form of *argument* (AIRGUMENT)]

yain /jen/ *interj* a call to a horse in harness to turn left *20- C.* [perhaps an altered form of VANE]

yair, †ȝair, †ȝare, †yhar /jer/ *n* a fish-trap in a river or bay in the form of an enclosure or barrier *la12-19, 20- WC SW.* [OE (*mylen*)*gear* an enclosure (on a millstream)]

†yairaman, yarromang, yarromanna *n in Shetland and Orkney* a portion or division of land *la16-17.* [ON *jarðarmeginn, jarðmunr*]

yaird[1.1], **yard, yerd, yird, †yeard, †ȝaird, †ȝard** /jerd, jard, jerd, jɪrd/ *n* **1** an area of enclosed ground planted with grass or trees, or crops or vegetables; an orchard or (kitchen) garden *14-.* **2** an enclosed and uncultivated area adjacent to or enclosed by a building; a courtyard *la14-.* **3** an (enclosed) area used for storage; a stackyard *la15-.* **4** a churchyard *18-*; compare YIRD[1.1] (sense 4). **5** also *pl* a school playground, *eg* High School Yards in Edinburgh *la18-.* **6** a boat or ship manufacturers' yard; an oil or gas fabrication yard *la19-.* **7** the garden of Gethsemane *16.* **yaird dyke** a garden wall *la15- Sh Ork N C.* **†yaird end** the *yaird fit 16.* **yaird fit** the bottom end of a YAIRD (sense 1) *17- C SW.* **Yaird heads**, **†yaird hedis 1** the name of an area in Leith *la17-.* **2** *in Dumfriesshire, Selkirk and Elgin* (the name of) the top part of a YAIRD (sense 1) *16-e17.* [OE *geard* a yard, enclosure]

yaird[1.2], **yard** /jerd, jard/ *v* to store (goods, especially crops) in a yard *la15-19, 20- Ork.* [see the noun]

yaird[2], **yeard, yard, †yerd, †ȝerd** /jerd, jerd, jard/ *n* **1** a unit of lineal measure, now 36 inches (0.9144 m), formerly 37 inches (0.940 m) *la15-.* **2** a spar attached to a ship's mast to extend the sail *14-.* **3** a staff, rod or stick; the penis *16.* [OE *gerd*]

yairn, yarn, †yearn, †ȝairn, †ȝarn /jern, jarn/ *n* spun fibre suitable for weaving or knitting; yarn *15-.* **yairn clew** a ball of knitting wool or yarn *16-19, 20- Sh.* **yarnell, yarlin** = *yairn winds la18- NE.* **†yairn winders** = *yairn winds la17.* **yairn winds, yairn wins** a machine for winding yarn *18- Sh Ork N.* **†yairn winnle, †yairn windle, †yairn wyndill** = *yairn winds la16-19.* [OE *gearn*]

yaise *see* USE[1.2]

yaisless *see* USELESS[1.1]

yak /jɑk/ *n* the eye *20- NE SW Bor.* [Travellers' language, Romany *yack*]

yak *see* YAWK

yake /jek/ *n* a marble used as a stake in a contest *19*, *20- NE WC.* [altered form of LAIK[1.1]]

yalder[1.1] /'jɑldər/ *n* loud, continuous barking *la19- Sh.* [see the verb]

yalder[1,2], *Ork* **yolder**, *N* **yaller** /'jɑldər; *Ork* 'joldər; *N* 'jɑlər/ *v of a dog* to bark continuously *20- Sh Ork*. [frequentative form of YALL[1,2], perhaps with influence from GALDER[1,2]]

yaldie /'jɑldi/ *n* the yellowhammer *Emberiza citrinella la19- NE*. [shortened form of *yaldrin* (YOLDRIN) + -IE[1]]

yaldrin *see* YOLDRIN

yale *see* ALE[1,1]

yalk[1,1] /jɑlk/ *n* a dog's bark, a yelp *la19- Sh*. [see the verb]

yalk[1,2] /jɑlk/ *v of a dog* to bark, yelp *la19- Sh*. [onomatopoeic]

yall[1,1], †**yawl** /jɑl/ *n* a shout, cry, howl *19, 20- Sh N NE T*. [see the verb; and compare Norw dial *hjal* a yell]

yall[1,2], †**yawl** /jɑl/ *v* to yell, scream, howl *17-19, 20- Sh N NE T*. [variant of YOWL[1,2]; and compare Norw dial *hjala*]

yall *see* YEA[1,2], YOAL

yalla *see* YELLA[1,2]

yaller *see* YALDER[1,2]

yallicrack /'jɑlikrɑk/ *n* a commotion, hubbub, outcry *la19- Sh*. [probably YALL[1,2] + CRACK[1,1]]

yallochie, **yallock**, **yallow** *see* YELLA[1,2]

yalmer *see* YAMMER[1,2]

yalp *see* YELP[1,1], YELP[1,2]

†**yam** *n* a (large, coarse) variety of potato usually fed to animals *la18-19*. [extended sense of Eng *yam*]

yamal, **yammald**, **yamalt** /'jɑməl, 'jɑməld, 'jɑməlt/ *n* **1** a contemporary, one born in the same year as another *19- Sh Ork*. **2** a twin *la19- Sh*. Compare GEMMELL. [Norw dial *jamaldre*]

yammer[1,1], **yaumer**, †**ȝammyr**, †**ȝawmer** /'jɑmər/ *n* **1** lamentation, wailing, whining; a cry, a whimper *16-*. **2** a great outcry, clamour, incessant talk *la18-*. [MDu, MLG *jammer*]

yammer[1,2], **yaumer**, †**ȝammer**, †**yamour**, †**yalmer** /'jɑmər/ *v* **1** to howl, wail; lament, cry out in distress; whine, whimper; grumble, complain *la15-*. **2** to clamour, make a loud noise or din; talk volubly, incoherently or insistently, harp on *la18-*. **3** *of a bird or animal* to utter repeated cries, chatter *la19-*. [MDu, MLG *jammeren*]

yamp, **yamph** /jɑmp, jɑmf/ *adj* hungry *20- NE*. [altered form of YAUP[1,2]]

yamph[1,1] /jɑmf/ *n* a dog's bark *19-*. [see the verb]

yamph[1,2] /jɑmf/ *v* to bark, yap, yelp *18-19, 20- Bor*. [altered form of YAFF[1,2]]

yamph *see* YAMP

yamse /jɑms/ *adj* greedy, covetous *20- Sh*. [unknown; perhaps a reduced form of *yampish*, YAMP]

yane *see* ANE[1,1]

yank[1,1] /jɑŋk/ *n* **1** a sudden jerk or pull *20-*. **2** a sudden blow, a thump (with the fist) *la18-19*. **yankie** *n* an agile person *la18-e19*. **yankie** *adj* nimble, agile *la19*. [see the verb]

yank[1,2] /jɑŋk/ *v* **1** to pull vigorously with a sharp sudden movement, jerk, twitch *la18-*. **2** (cause) to move quickly and vigorously *19- C SW*. **yanker** a smart, agile person *19-*. [perhaps onomatopoeic]

yanks /jɑŋks/ *npl farming* straps tied around trouser legs below the knee *la19- NE T*. Compare BOOYANGS, NICKIE-TAMS. [unknown; compare YANK[1,2]]

yap[1,1], **yaup** /jɑp/ *n* **1** incessant talking; nagging *19-*. **2** the call of a bird in distress; the squawking of chickens *19- SW Uls*. **3** a bark, yelp *20-*. **4** a yelping dog *20-*. **5** a chatterbox; a windbag *20-*. [see the verb]

yap[1,2], **yaup** /jɑp/ *v* **1** to yelp, bark *20-*. **2** to chatter, nag, speak querulously, harp on *19-*. **3** to speak affectedly or with an English accent *la19-*. **4** to cry shrilly, scream; whimper; chirp plaintively *la18- Sh N C SW Bor*. [onomatopoeic]

yap[2], **yapp** /jɑp/ *n child's word* an apple *la19- Edinburgh*. [reduced form of *yapple*, variant of apple (AIPPLE)]

yap *see* YAUP[1,1], YAUP[1,2]

yape *see* APE, YAUP[1,2]

yapp *see* YAP[2]

yard *see* YAIRD[1,1], YAIRD[1,2], YAIRD[2]

yardfast, **yarfast** /'jɑrdfɑst, 'jɑrfɑst/ *v* to secure (to the ground); fasten *la19- Sh*. [see the adj YIRDFEST[1,2]]

yare[1,1], †**ȝare**, †**ȝor** /jer/ *adj* **1** ready, prepared *la14-e16, 19- literary*. **2** eager, agile *19- literary*. [OE *gearo*]

†**yare**[1,2], **ȝare**, **ȝar**, †**ȝor** *adv* **1** quickly, promptly *la14-16, 19*. **2** well, thoroughly; doubtless *15-e16*. [OE *gearwe*]

yarf /jɑrf/ *n* a peat-bog *la19- Sh*. [shortened form of YARPHA]

yarfast *see* YARDFAST

yarg[1,1] /jɑrg/ *n* incessant complaining; nagging *20- Sh*. [see the verb]

yarg[1,2] /jɑrg/ *v* to complain incessantly, carp *19- Sh Ork NE*. [perhaps an aphetic form of *nyarg* (NARG[1,2]), and compare Icel *jarga* to repeat tediously]

yark /jɑrk/ *n* the instep *20- Sh Ork*. **yarken** the instep *19- Sh*. [Norw dial *jark* the outer edge of the foot]

yark *see* YERK[1,1], YERK[1,2]

yarlin *see* YAIRN, YORLIN

yarm, **yaarm** /jɑrm/ *v* **1** *of a sheep* to bleat *19- Sh Ork*. **2** *of a cat* to mew *19- Sh Ork*. **3** *of a person* to yell, scream *la19- Sh Ork*. **4** to grumble *20- Ork*. **yarmer**, **jarmer** *fisherman's taboo* **1** a cat or a sheep *20- Sh*. **2** a church precentor *la19- Sh Ork*. [Icel *jarma* to bleat]

yarms /jɑrmz/ *npl* caterwauling, mewing of a cat *la19- Sh Ork*. [see the verb YARM]

yarn *see* YAIRN

yarnell *see* YAIRN

yarp /jɑrp/ *v* to grumble, carp, whine; harp on *19, 20- NE*; compare ORP, YIRP. [onomatopoeic, and compare Norw dial *jarpa* to chatter]

yarpha /'jɑrfə/ *n* peat moss, fibrous peat which burns poorly; a peaty soil combined with clay or sand *la18- Sh Ork N*. [compare ON *jorfi* sand, gravel, a sandbank]

yarpoan /'jɑrpon/ *v* to thatch a roof with turf *la19- Sh*. [Norw *jord* earth + POAN[1,1]]

yarr[1] /jɑr/ *n* corn-spurry *Spergula arvensis la18-*.

†**yarr**[2] *v* to snarl, growl *la17-18*. [onomatopoeic]

yarrib *see* YERB

yarromang, **yarromanna** *see* YAIRAMAN

yarrow[1], †**ȝarrow** /'jaro/ *n* yarrow *Achillea millefolium 16-*. [OE *gearwe*]

†**yarrow**[2] *v* to prepare (grain) for use, make meal *19 Sh*. [compare ON *gjǫrva*, OE *gearwian* to prepare]

yarta /'jɑrtə/ *n* a term of endearment, my dear, darling *19- Sh*. [Norw dial *hjarta* heart]

yask *see* ASK[2,1]

yasp /jɑsp/ *adj* lively, energetic *la19- Sh*. [unknown]

yat, **yatt**, †**yet**, †**ȝet** /jɑt/ *v pt also* †**ȝet**, †**yet**, *ptp also* †**ȝet**, †**yet** **1** to cast (an object) in metal; to melt (metal) for casting *15-e17, 20- Sh*. **2** to pour forth (in a large quantity), flow copiously; gush *16, la19- Sh*. **3** to pour *la14-e17*. **4** to fasten or attach (*eg* iron in stone) with molten lead *16-e19*. †**yat furth** to pour out, emit, shed; to cause to flow *la15-e16* = *yat furth*. [OE *gēotan*]

yate *see* YETT

yatlen *see* YETLIN[1,1], YETLIN[1,2]

yatt, **yacht**, †**yaucht**, †**yaught**, †**ȝeaught** /jɑt, jɔt/ *n* a small light sailing vessel, a yacht *17-*. [EModDu *jaght*]

yatt *see* YAT

yatter[1,1] /'jɑtər/ *n* **1** continuous chatter, rambling and persistent talk *19-*. **2** an incessant talker; a gossip *19-*. **3** the confused noise of many people talking loudly all together, clamour, unintelligible speech *19, 20- Sh Ork NE T H&I*. **4**

yatter (continual) scolding, grumbling *19, 20- Ork NE T.* **yattery** fretful, querulous, scolding *19-*. [see the verb]

yatter[1,2] /ˈjatər/ *v* **1** to nag, harp on querulously, scold *19-*. **2** to chatter; prattle, talk interminably *19-*. **3** to gabble incomprehensibly or in a foreign language *19-*. **4** *of an animal* to yelp *19-*. **5** *of nerves* to jar, fire *20-*. **6** *of teeth* to rattle, chatter (from fear or cold) *20- T Bor.* **yatterin** fretful, querulous, scolding *19-*. [onomatopoeic]

yaucht *see* AUCHT[2], YATT

yaud, yad, †**yade,** †**ȝad, ȝawd, ȝaid,** †**ȝald** /jɑd, jad/ *n* **1** an old mare or horse in poor condition *16-19, 20- NE EC Bor.* **2** a derogatory term for a woman *16-19*. **3** badly wound yarn *e19*. [ON *jalda* a mare]

yauff *see* YAFF[1,1], YAFF[1,2]

yaught *see* YATT

yaul *see* YEA[1,2]

yauld, yaul /jɑld, jɔld, jɑl, jɔl/ *adj* active, alert, vigorous, healthy, strong *17-19, 20- C SW Bor.* [unknown]

yaumer *see* YAMMER[1,1], YAMMER[1,2]

yaup[1,1]**, yawp,** †**yap** /jɑp/ *v* to be ravenously hungry; *of baby birds* to gape with hunger *18-*. **yaupit** pinched or starved-looking *20- WC.* [see the adj]

yaup[1,2]**, yawp, yap,** †**yape,** †**ȝape,** †**ȝaip** /jɑp, jap/ *adj* **1** having a keen appetite, hungry *18-*. **2** clever, cunning; shrewd, astute *la14-16*. **3** fit, active; alert, keen; eager, ready *la15-19*. **yaupish** having a keen appetite, hungry *la18-19, 20- WC.* [OE *gēap* shrewd]

yaup *see* YAP[1,1], YAP[1,2]

yaval *see* AVAL[1,2], AVAL[2,2]

yavil *see* AVAL[2,1]

†**yaw** *v* to mew, caterwaul; squeal *19*. [onomatopoeic]

yaw *see* AWE

yawin, *N NE* **yaavin,** *N NE* **yewn,** *Sh Ork Uls* **ann,** *T* **aan,** †**awne** /ˈjɑwɪn; *N NE* ˈjɑvɪn; *N* jun; *Sh Ork Uls* ɑn; *T* ɑn/ *n* the awn or beard of barley or oats *la14-19, 20- Sh Ork N NE T Uls.* **awny,** †**awnie** *of grain* having awns, bearded *la18-*. [ON *ǫgn-* pl stem of *ögn*]

yawk, yak, †**ȝak,** †**ȝaik,** †**aik** /jɑk, jak/ *v* to ache, suffer (severe or prolonged) pain *16-*. [OE *acan*]

yawl *see* YALL[1,1], YALL[1,2]

yawn /jɑn/ *n in place-names on the coast of Kincardineshire* a long sea-inlet or gully *la19- NE.* [extended sense of Eng *yawn* a chasm]

yawp /jɑp/ *n* a fool, oaf *la19- NE T EC Bor.* [perhaps onomatopoeic or related to YAP[1,1]]

yawp *see* YAUP[1,1], YAUP[1,2]

yax *see* AIX

yaxtra *see* AIXTRA[1,2]

ybaik *see* BAKE[1,2]

ybe *see* BE

ybent *see* BEND[2,2]

Ybernian *see* HIBERNIAN[1,2]

yberyit *see* BEERIE

ybet *see* BEET[2,2]

ybocht *see* BUY

ybond, ybondyn *see* BIND[1,2]

yborn *see* BEAR[2]

ybrokkyn *see* BRAK[1,2]

ybrynt *see* BURN[2,2]

yburnyst *see* BIRNIS

yce *see* ICE

†**ych** *adj* each *e16*; compare ILK[2,2]. [ME *ich*, OE *ælc*]

yclepit *see* CLEPE[1,2]

yclos *see* CLOSE[1]

ydant *see* EIDENT

ydeotry *see* IDIOTRY

ydil, ydilteth *see* IDLE

ydoll *see* EEDOL

ydraw *see* DRAW[1,2]

ydrunkin *see* DRINK[1,2]

ydy *see* ITHY

ye, you, *WC Bor* **yow,** †**ȝe,** †**ȝow** /ji, ju; *WC Bor* jʌu/ *pron pl* also **yez,** *EC* **yaes,** *C* **yeez,** *C* **yous, youse,** *C Uls* **yiz** **1** you *la14-*. **2** yourself: ◊*haid ȝe wmbethocht ȝow la14-16*. Compare THOU. **yiv** you have *20- C Uls.* [OE *gē* subject, *ēow* object]

yea[1,1]**,** *Sh* **ya,** *Ork* **yaa,** †**ȝha,** †**ȝe** /je; *Sh Ork* jɑ/ *n* an utterance of the word 'yea'; the affirmative; affirmation *la15-19, 20- Sh Ork.* [see the adv]

yea[1,2]**,** *Sh Ork NE* **ya,** †**ȝa,** †**ȝe,** †**ȝee** /je; *Sh Ork NE* jɑ/ *adv* **1** *expressing surprise, disbelief, vague assent or opposition* really, indeed: ◊*yea, d'ye think sae, Tammas? la15-*. **2** *in answering a question or expressing agreement* yes, indeed *la14-19, 20- Sh Ork NE T.* **3** *used before a repeated verb* again, over and over: ◊*he tried and yea tried la19- NE.* †**yall, yaul** = *yeltow la18-e19.* **yeltow,** †**yeltie** you would, would you; be careful; that's enough, now *la18-19, 20- WC.* **yea yea** used derisively expressing contempt *20- NE T.* [OE *gēa*, Norw, Du *ja*]

yeables *see* ABLES

yeal *see* ALE[1,1]

yealie *see* ELY

yealins, yealings *see* EILD[1,1]

†**yean** *v of a ewe* to give birth to (a lamb) *la18-19*. Compare INGY. [ME *enen*, OE *ēanian*]

year, 'ear, †**ȝeir,** †**ȝhere,** †**ȝer** /jir, ir/ *n* **1** a period of twelve months; a particular year *la14-*. **2** uninflected pl with reference to an age or duration of time a year: ◊*twa year auld la14-*. **year auld** *n* a one-year-old farm animal, a yearling *16-*. **year auld** *adj* year-old *16-*. †**year tak** a year's lease *la15-17.* **a year and a day,** †**year and day** a period of twelve months with the addition of a day to ensure that a full year has elapsed *15-*. **monie a year and day** for a very long time *la19- NE T EC.* **the year** this year *17-*. **up in years** elderly *19-*. †**year of God** a particular year of the Christian era (denoted by a number following) *la15-e18*. [OE *gēar*]

yeard *see* YAIRD[1,1], YAIRD[2], YIRD[1,1]

yearn *see* EARN, YAIRN, YIRN[1], YIRN[2,2]

yearnin *see* YIRNIN

yearth *see* YIRD[1,1]

yech /jɛx/ *interj* expressing impatience *20-*. [a natural utterance]

†**yed** *n* strife, wrangling; struggle *18-19*. [ME *yed* keening, OE *giedd* a song, poem]

yee *see* AE

yeel *see* YELD[1,2], YULE

yeese *see* USE[1,1], USE[1,2]

yeesp /jisp/ *n* a cheep, the slightest sound *20- Ork.* [onomatopoeic]

yeez *see* YE

yeild *see* EILD[1,1]

yeit *see* YIT[1,1]

yeld[1,1] /jɛld/ *n* a barren cow or ewe *la19- Ork NE T.* [see the adj]

yeld[1,2]**, eild, eel,** *Sh* **yield,** *SW Uls* **yell,** †**yeel,** †**ȝeld,** †**ȝeild** /jɛld, ild, il; *Sh* jild; *SW Uls* jɛl/ *adj* **1** *of land or objects* sterile, unproductive, unprofitable *15-*. **2** *of female farm animals* barren; not bearing young; not giving milk *la15-*. **3** *of birds* without a mate; not having nested or produced young *16-19*. **4** *of a man* impotent *e16*. [OE *gelde*]

yeldrick, yeldrin *see* YOLDRIN

yell[1.1], †**ȝell** /jɛl/ *n* **1** a shout, a loud cry *la14-*. **2** loud, incomprehensible noise; a groan *e16*. [see the verb]

yell[1.2], †**ȝell** /jɛl/ *v pt* also †**ȝeld** **1** to shout, make a loud noise; utter as a shout *la14-*. **2** (cause (a thing)) to make a loud, cracking noise *19-*. **3** to be invoked or celebrated by yelling *e16*. †**yellyhoo** shouting and screaming, yelling *19*. [OE *gellan*]

yell *see* YELD[1.2]

yella[1.1], **yelly**, **yellow**, †**ȝallow** /ˈjɛlə, ˈjɛle, ˈjɛlo/ *n* **1** the colour yellow *la15-*. **2** a gold coin *e19*. **3** yellow fabric *16*. [see the adj]

yella[1.2], **yelly**, **yalla**, **yellow**, **yallow**, †**ȝallow**, †**ȝallo**, †**yhalow** /ˈjɛlə, ˈjɛle, ˈjalə, ˈjɛlo, ˈjalo/ *adj* yellow-coloured; golden; blonde; fair; tawny *14-*. **yallochie** yellowish *la19- N NE T*. **yallock** the yellowhammer *Emberiza citrinella la19- NE*. †**yella beak** a first-year student at Aberdeen University, a BEJAN *la19*. **yella cod** smoked cod *20- Ork NE*. **yella fin** the young of the sea-trout *19-*. **yella fish** smoked (or dyed) fish, especially haddock *la19-*. **yella Geordie** a guinea coin *la18-20, 21- historical*. **yella gowan 1** the marsh marigold *Caltha palustris 20- Ork*. **2** the common buttercup *Ranunculus acris e19*. **yella gum** jaundice, especially in the newborn *20-*. **yella haddie, yella haddock** smoked haddock *20- NE T EC*. **yella lily** the yellow iris *Iris pseudacorus la18- NE T*. **yella lintie** the yellowhammer *Emberiza citrinella 20- NE T WC*. †**yella neb** a *yella beak 18*. **yella neb lintie** the twite *Linaria flavirostris la19- N H&I SW*. **yella plover** the golden plover *Pluvialis apricaria la19- NE T EC*. †**yella tang** the knotted tang *Ascophyllum nodosum* or perhaps *Fucus serratus*, a kind of bladderwrack *la18-19*. **yella wagtail** the grey wagtail *Motacilla cinerea la19- T EC Bor*. **yella yite** the yellowhammer *Emberiza citrinella 19-*. **yella yitie** the yellowhammer *20-*. **yella yoldrin** the yellowhammer. †**Protestants of the yellow stick** adherents of *the religion of the yellow stick la18-e19, 20- historical*. **the religion of the yellow stick** (with reference to) the conversion to Presbyterianism of the inhabitants of the island of Rhum (by a blow administered by their Protestant laird, and a demand that they go to the Kirk) *la18-e19, 20- historical*. [OE *geolu*]

yellings *see* EILD[1.1]

yelloch[1.1], †**ȝelloch** /ˈjɛləx/ *n* a yell, shriek, scream *16-*. [YELL[1.1] + -OCH intensive suffix]

yelloch[1.2], *NE* **ellach** /ˈjɛləx; *NE* ˈɛləx/ *v* **1** *of a cooking pot* to make the sound of boiling, hiss, whistle *20- NE*. **2** to yell, scream, shriek *la18-19*. [see the noun]

yellow, yelly *see* YELLA[1.1], YELLA[1.2]

yellyhoo *see* YELL[1.2]

yelp[1.1], *Ork T* **yalp**, †**ȝelp** /jɛlp; *Ork T* jɑlp/ *n* **1** a sharp, shrill bark; a high-pitched cry *16-*. **2** *derogatory* a yapping dog; a peevish person *20- NE T EC*. [see the verb and compare OE *gelp* vainglory]

yelp[1.2], *Ork T* **yalp**, †**ȝelp** /jɛlp; *Ork T* jɑlp/ *v* to make a high-pitched sound, yelp *16-*. **yelpin stane 1** a loose stone underfoot *20- Ork*. **2** an echoing rock *19, 20- WC*. [OE *gelpan* to boast]

†**Yelt** *n* an inhabitant of Shetland *17-e18*. [Norw dial *hjelte*; compare Yetland (ZETLAND)]

yeltie, yeltow *see* YEA[1.2]

yemit *see* ȝEME

†**yeoman, ȝeman, ȝoman** *n* **1** a free man ranking below a gentleman or burgess; a small landowner; a commoner *la14-19*. **2** a (foot) soldier *la14, e19*. **3** a retainer or servant in a royal or noble household *15-16, e19*. **yeoman man** a man of the YEOMAN (sense 1) class, especially a small landowner *la14-17*. [ME *yoman, yēman*]

yeomanry, †**ȝemanry**, †**ȝhumanry** /ˈjomənri/ *n* **1** the name of various Scottish regiments in the Territorial Army, which had their origin in volunteer cavalry regiments *la18-*. **2** the class of small landowners, farmers and commoners; such persons as fighting men *la14-17*. [YEOMAN + -*ry* suffix]

yer, yur, yir, your, yere, *NE Bor* **eer**, †**ȝowr**, †**ȝour**, †**yhoure** /jer, jʌr, jɪr, jur, jir; *NE Bor* ir/ *determiner* **1** of, belonging or connected to you *la14-*. **2** as part of a title of respect: ◊*yhoure noble lordship 15-*. **yours** belonging to you ◊*thon's yours la14-*. [possessive form of YE; OE *eower*]

yerb, herb, *Bor* **yirb**, *Uls* **yerrib, yarrib**, †**hairb**, †**erbe** /jɛrb, hɛrb; *Bor* jɪrb; *Uls* ˈjɛrɪb, ˈjarɪb/ *n* a (medicinal) plant; a herb *la14-*. [OFr *erbe*]

yercke *see* YERK[1.1]

yerd *see* YAIRD[1.1], YAIRD[2], YIRD[1.1]

yere *see* YER

yerk[1.1], *Sh Ork N NE* **yark**, †**yercke** /jɛrk; *Sh Ork N NE* jɑrk/ *n* **1** a blow, a hard knock, a slap *17-*. **2** a jerk, tug, twitch, grab *19-*. **3** a crack, crash; the sound of a blow *la19- NE T*. **4** a large gulp of food or drink *la19- Sh*. **5** a throb of pain; an ache *20- NE T*. **6** an oversized person or house *20- Sh N*. **come yerk against** to come against, collide with *20- Sh NE*. **hae a yerk at** to make a vigorous attempt, have a go at *20- Sh NE*. [see the verb]

yerk[1.2], **yirk**, *Sh Ork N NE T* **yark**, *Sh Ork* **yirg** /jɛrk, jɪrk; *Sh Ork N NE T* jɑrk; *Sh Ork* jɪrg/ *v* **1** to perform in a vigorous, lively way *18-*. **2** to drive hard, put pressure on, stir to activity; to set to, exert oneself, press on *18-*. **3** to beat, whip, strike; to break by striking; to hammer *18-*. **4** to strike on or against, make a sharp sound by striking *la18- NE SW*. **5** to bind, tie, fasten tightly, pull tight *19-*. **6** to snatch, tug, wrench, pull, grab forcibly *19- 7* to throw vigorously, toss, pitch; *19-*. **8** to throb, ache, tingle *19- NE T EC SW*. **9** to nag, find fault, carp *19- Sh NE Bor*. **10** to take a quick drink or bite, gulp *la19- Sh*. **11** to move jerkily *la19, 20- Sh Ork*. **yerker** anything very large of its kind *19-*. **yerkin 1** the side seam in a boot or shoe *19, 20- Sh*. **2** a beating, a blow *19- Bor*. †**yarking fat** a vat or tub *e16*. **yerk aff** to do (something) in a vigorous, practised way *la18-*. **yerk oot** to rattle off (a speech) *18-*. **yerk up** to strike up (a tune) *19-*. [ME *yerken* (of a shoemaker) to draw (stitches) tight]

yerker *see* JERKER

yerl *see* EARL, HERLE

Yerlston fever /ˈjɛrlstən ˈfivər/ *n* a fit of laziness, a lazy mood *20- Bor*. [from the place-name Earlston, in Berwickshire, the inhabitants being thought lazy by their neighbours]

yerp *see* YIRP

yerrib *see* YERB

yersel, yersell, yirsel, yursel, yoursel, yourself, *EC Bor* **ersel**, †**ȝour self**, †**ȝour sell** /jərˈsɛl, jɪrˈsɛl, jʌrˈsɛl, jurˈsɛl, jurˈsɛlf; *EC Bor* ərˈsɛl/ *pron* **1** yourself *15-*. **2** *referring to more than one person* yourselves *16-18*. **3** *in Highland speech, in emphatic use* you: ◊*och, it's yersel la14-*. [YER + SEL[1.1]]

yes, *Sh* **yis**, †**ȝes**, †**ȝis**, †**ȝhis** /jɛs; *Sh* jɪs/ *adv* **1** the affirmative, yes *la14-*. **2** as an expression of opposition or contradiction *la14-e16*. [OE *gēse*]

yesk[1.1], *NE* **esk** /jɛsk; *NE* ɛsk/ *n* hiccups, a belch *17-*. [OE *gesca*]

yesk[1.2], *N* **isk**, *N NE* **esk**, *EC* **yex**, †**yisk**, †**ȝesk**, †**ȝisk** /jɛsk; *N* ɪsk; *N NE* ɛsk; *EC* jɛks/ *v* **1** to hiccup, belch, vomit *16-19, 20- NE*. **2** to sob *la16, 20- N*. [OE *giscian* to sob]

yestreen[1.1], †**ȝistrene** /jɛˈstrin/ *n* yesterday evening *16-*. Compare THE STREEN[1.1]. [see the adv]

yestreen[1.2], *NE* **estreen**, †**ȝestrene**, †**ȝistreyn**, †**ȝisterevin** /jɛˈstrin; *NE* ɛˈstrin/ *adv* on yesterday evening; last night;

yesterday *la14-*. Compare THE STREEN¹·². [shortened form of *yester-*, OE *gestor-*, + EVEN¹]

yet *see* YAT, YIT¹·¹, YIT¹·¹

yether¹·¹ /ˈjɛðər/ *n* **1** a blow *19- WC SW Bor*. **2** the mark left by a blow or by tight binding with cord, a weal, bruise *19- SW Bor*. **3** a long rod or withy *e19 Bor*. [see the verb]

yether¹·² /ˈjɛðər/ *v* **1** to tie very firmly; to leave a pressure mark by tight binding *19- SW Bor*. **2** to beat severely, bruise with a cane *19 SW Bor*. [variant with extended sense of *ether* (EDDER¹·²)]

yetin *see* ETIN

yetland *see* YETLIN¹·²

Yetland *see* ZETLAND

yetlin¹·¹, **yetling**, *Sh* **yatlen**, *Ork* **yettleen**, †**ʒetling** /ˈjɛtlɪn, ˈjɛtlɪŋ; *Sh* ˈjatlɪn; *Ork* ˈjɛtlɪn/ *n* **1** a cast-iron artifact, especially a pot, pan or kettle *la14-19, 20- WC Bor*. **2** a griddle or girdle for baking scones or oatcakes *la19- Sh Ork*. **3** cast iron *la18-19, 20- Sh*. **4** a small, cast-iron cannon *la16-e17*. **yetlins** a game played with an iron ball *la19, 20- EC historical*. [*yet* (YAT) + *-ling* noun-forming suffix]

yetlin¹·², *Sh* **yatlen**, *SW* **yetland**, †**yetling**, †**ʒetling** /ˈjɛtlɪn; *Sh* ˈjatlɪn; *SW* ˈjɛtlənd/ *adj* made of cast metal, mainly cast-iron *16-19, 20- Sh SW*. [see the noun]

yett, **yate**, †**ʒet**, †**ʒett**, †**ʒat** /jɛt, jet/ *n* **1** a gate; a gateway or entrance *la14-*. **2** *archaeology* a door made of interlacing iron bars *la19-*. **3** *mainly in place-names* a pass between hills: ◇*Yetts o' Muckhart 19-*. †**yett cheik** the side-post of a gate *16-17*. **as daft as a yett in a windy day** scatter-brained, flighty, crazy *la19- C SW*. [OE *geat*]

yettleen *see* YETLIN¹·¹

yeuk¹·¹, **yuke**, **youk**, *Sh* **yuck**, *Ork* **yuk**, *N NE* **heuk**, †**yook**, †**ʒuik** /juk, jok, jɔk; *Sh Ork* jʌk; *N NE* hjuk/ *n* **1** itching, an itch or itchiness *la16-*. **2** something disgusting, something of very poor quality *20- C SW*. [see the verb]

yeuk¹·², **yuke**, **youk**, **yuck**, *NE* **yock**, *NE* **heuk**, †**ʒuik** /juk, jok, jʌk; *NE* jɔk; *NE* hjuk/ *v* **1** *mainly of a part of the body* to itch, feel ticklish or itchy *15-*. **2** to crave; to have a strong urge (to do something); to long to hear, be curious about *16-*. **3** to scratch *20- Sh Ork NE*. **a person's neck is yeukin** the person is heading for the gallows *la17-*. †**gar you scart where you youk not** to make you regret what you have done *e18*. †**yeukand earis** ears straining to hear or itching with curiosity *15-16*. [MDu *jeuken*, MLG *jucken*]

yeukie, **youkie**, **yokie**, **yuckie**, *N* **heuchy**, **heukie** /ˈjuke, ˈjoke, ˈjɔke, ˈjʌke; *N* ˈhjuxe, ˈhjuke/ *adj* **1** *of a part of the body* itching, itchy *18-*. **2** prickly *20-*. **3** excitedly eager, impatiently waiting to do something *18-19, 20- Sh NE T EC*. **4** sexually excited *20- NE T WC*. **5** *derogatory* mean, shabby, rough, filthy *20- C SW Bor*. **6** *of work* rough and careless, badly finished; perfunctory *20- C*. **gar somebody claw where it's no yeukie** *frequently in threats* to make someone smart or regret what they have done *19-*. [YEUK¹·² + -IE²]

yeuse *see* USE¹·¹

yewn *see* YAWIN

yex *see* YESK¹·²

yez *see* YE

†**yfere**, **yfeir**, **efeir** *adv* together, in company *16*. [ME *ifere*, IN¹·⁴ + FERE¹]

yfetterit *see* FETTER¹·²

ygrant *see* GRANT

ygraven *see* GRAVE¹·²

yhalow *see* YELLA¹·²

yhar *see* YAIR

yhoure *see* YER

yibble *see* ABLE¹·¹

yibbles *see* ABLES

yiblins *see* AIBLINS

yicker /ˈjɪkər/ *v* to quarrel; to complain *la19- Sh*. [onomatopoeic]

yickie-yawkie /ˈjɪkiˈjaki/ *n shoemaking* a tool used to polish the soles of shoes *19- SW*. [onomatopoeic from the sound made by the tool scraping across the leather]

yield¹·¹, †**ʒeild**, †**ʒelde** /jild/ *n* **1** the product of a crop, or plant *19-*. **2** money raised by taxation; compensatory payment; tribute, debt *la14-16*. [from the verb and OE *gield* money, payment]

yield¹·², †**ʒeild**, †**ʒelde**, †**ʒald** /jild/ *v pt* †**yieldit**, †**ʒald**, †**ʒeild**, *ptp* also **yowden**, †**ʒoldin**, †**yoldyn** **1** to render (something owed), give in return, repay; to hand over, relinquish; to surrender *la14-*. **2** to produce, bear *16-*. **3** *of things* to bend, give way *la16-*. †**yield the breth** to die *e16*. †**yield the gast** to die *la14-e16*. †**yield the spreit** to die *la14-16*. [OE *gieldan*, *geldan*]

yield *see* YELD¹·²

yieldit *see* YIELD¹·²

yiff-yaff /ˈjɪf ˈjaf/ *n* **1** a small, insignificant, chattery person *19- C Bor*. **2** chatter *20- EC Bor*. [onomatopoeic]

yik *see* AIK

yill *see* ALE¹·¹, ALE¹·²

yillee *see* ELY

yim¹ /jɪm/ *n* a (very) small particle, a bit, a fragment *19- T SW Bor*. [probably an aphetic form of *nyim* (NIMP)]

yim²·¹ /jɪm/ *n* a thin film or coating on a surface, a scum, a layer of dust or condensed vapour *la19- NE*. [variant of EEM²]

yim²·² /jɪm/ *v* to cover or become covered with a layer of dust or dirt *la19- NE*. [see the noun]

yin *see* ANE¹·¹, ANE¹·², YON¹·¹, YON¹·³

yince *see* AINCE¹·¹, AINCE¹·²

yince erran *see* AINCE ERRAND¹·²

yind, †**aynd**, †**aind**, †**ein** /jɪnd/ *v* **1** to breathe *la14-19*. **2** to knock the breath out of (by chasing) *20- SW Bor*. Compare END. [ON *anda*]

ying *see* YOUNG

yink *see* ENK¹·¹, ENK¹·²

yinst *see* AINCE¹·¹

yins yirrint *see* AINCE ERRAND¹·²

yip /jɪp/ *n* a cheeky child *20- EC Bor*. [perhaps a variant of *yape* (APE), or onomatopoeic]

yir *see* YER

yirb *see* YERB

yird¹·¹, **yirth**, **earth**, **eird**, **eard**, **yerd**, **erd**, *Sh* **eart**, *Sh* **aert**, *EC* **yearth**, †**yeard**, †**ʒerd**, †**erth** /jɪrd, jɪrθ, ɛrθ, ird, ɛrd, jɛrd, ɛrd; *Sh* ert; *Sh* ert; *EC* jɪrθ/ *n* **1** (a piece of) ground; soil; (the surface of) the world *la14-*. **2** ploughing (the angle of the plough-sock for any particular) depth of furrow *18-*. **3** a heap of large boulders forming a den or small cave; a fox's earth *19- SW*. **4** the grave *19*. **yirden** earthen; of the world *19-*. †**yirdlins** earthwards; along or towards the ground *18-e19*. **eart bark** the roots of tormentil *Potentilla erecta*, used medicinally and in tanning leather *19- Sh*. **aert bile** a quagmire *la19- Sh*. **yird-din**, †**erddyn**, †**erdine 1** thunder *19- NE*. **2** an earthquake *la14-16*. †**yird dike** a wall made of earth *16-e17*. **yird-drift 1** drifting snow *19- NE Bor*. **2** a sandstorm *20- NE*. **earth-house**, †**erdhous** a building with earthen walls; an Iron-Age underground, walled dwelling *la15-*. **erd hun** an animal which is said to burrow in graveyards, feeding on corpses *la19- NE*. †**yird-hunger** a strong desire to possess land *18-19*. **yird kent** universally known, of worldwide reputation *la19- Sh*. **yerd-meel** grave-mould, the dust of the churchyard *18- NE*. **yird pig** an *yird hun 20- NE*. **yird silver** payment for burial ground *la15-16*. †**yird swine** a *yird hun la19- NE*. **yird taid** the common toad *Bufo bufo 19*. **earth-worm** a money-grubber *19, 20- NE*. †**at the yird** *of buildings* completely demolished *16-e17*. **by a the yird** for all the world, exactly *la19- NE T EC*. **let the yird bear the dyke** let the cost of something come out of subsequent profits *19, 20- Sh*. †**let the yird big the dike** = *let the yird bear the dyke e18*. **yird and stane** the symbols of ownership used in the formalized transfer of landed property *15-19, 20- historical*. [OE *eorðe* ground, soil, fallen together with OE *eard* native land]

yird[1.2], **eard**, †**ȝerd**, †**erd**, †**erth** /jɪrd, ird/ *v* **1** to bury; to inter; to conceal objects in the ground; to cover (over) with earth *la14-19, 20- Sh NE T C*. **2** to sink into the ground *19, 20- Sh Ork*. **3** to bring violently to the ground; to strike with force *19, 20- NE*. **4** to drive (a hunted animal) to earth *e19*. **yirdit 1** buried *16-*. **2** bogged down *20- Sh NE*. **yird the cogie** *children's game* a rhythmic chant and quick stamping (to warm the feet) *20- NE*. [see the noun]

yird *see* YAIRD[1.1]

yirdfast *see* YIRDFEST[1.2]

yirdfest[1.1] /ˈjɪrdfɛst/ *n* a stone firmly embedded in the earth *19- NE SW Bor*. [see the adj]

yirdfest[1.2], **yirdfast**, **earthfast**, *Sh* **aertfast**, *Sh* **ertfast**, *Bor* **eardfast**, †**ȝerdfast**, †**erdfast** /ˈjɪrdfɛst, ˈjɪrdfast, ˈɛrθfast; *Sh* ˈɛrtfast; *Bor* ˈɛrdfast/ *adj* fixed in the ground *la15- Sh NE T WC Bor*. [YIRD[1.1] + *fast* (FEST[1.1])]

yirdie, **yirdy** /ˈjɪrdi/ *adj* earthen, earthly *19-*. **yirdie bee** a miner bee, of the family *Andrenidae 19- C Bor*. **yirdie tam** a mound of earth and weeds, a compost heap *20- NE*. [YIRD[1.1] + -IE[2]]

yirg, **yirk** *see* YERK[1.2]

yirl *see* EARL

yirm /jɪrm/ *v* **1** to whine, wail; to complain incessantly, nag *19- C Bor*. **2** *of a bird or insect* to chirp, cry, sing *19- C*. [OE *gyrman* to lament]

yirn[1], **earn**, **yearn**, †**ȝyrne** /jɪrn, jʌrn, ɛrn, jɛrn/ *v* (to cause milk) to coagulate or curdle and form curds *16-*. **yirned milk 1** curds; junket *19-*. **2** milk curdled in preparation for cheese-making *e17*. [OE *gerinnan*, *iernan*, variants of *rinnan* to run, run together]

yirn[2.1] /jɪrn, jʌrn/ *n* a complaint, a whine *la19- C SW*. [see the verb]

yirn[2.2], **yearn** /jɪrn, jʌrn, jɛrn/ *v* to whine; to whimper; to wail, complain *19, 20- SW Bor Uls*. [probably a conflation of YIRM and GIRN[1.2]]

†**yirn**[3], **ȝarne**, **ȝerne** *v* **1** to desire, yearn for *la14-19*. **2** to have compassion *e16*. [OE *geornan*, *girnan*]

yirn *see* EARN

yirnin, **yirning**, **yearnin**, †**ȝirning** /ˈjɪrnɪn, ˈjʌrnɪn, ˈjɪrnɪŋ, ˈjʌrnɪŋ, ˈjɛrnɪn/ *n* **1** rennet *la16-*. **2** the act of curdling milk to produce cheese *19-*. **3** the stomach of an unweaned calf used in making rennet *19, 20- Sh Ork N NE*. **4** the human stomach *la19- NE*. **5** curdled milk *20- Sh*. **6** a native of Orphir parish *20- Ork*. **yearnin-bag** the stomach of an unweaned calf used in making rennet *la18-*. **yirnin puddin** the stomach of an unweaned calf used in making rennet *20- Ork*. [verbal noun from YIRN[1]]

yirp, **yerp** /jɪrp, jɛrp/ *v* **1** *of a baby bird* to chirp *19-*. **2** *of persons* to make a fuss, argue, complain incessantly *la19-*; compare YARP. [onomatopoeic]

yirr *see* HIRR[1.1], HIRR[1.2], HIRR[1.3]

yirran *see* EERAN

yirsel *see* YERSEL

yirth *see* YIRD[1.1]

yis *see* YES

yisk *see* YESK[1.2]

yiss *see* ACE, USE[1.1]

yit[1.1], **yet**, †**yeit**, †**ȝit**, †**ȝet** /jɪt, jɛt/ *adv* **1** in addition, moreover, besides; even *la14-*. **2** *in temporal expressions* at, during or up to the present time, or some time in the past, or stretching into the future; still: ◊*best that I've heard yit* ◊*in-to Carrik ȝeit wes the king* ◊*a debt yit tae pey la14-*. **3** *as a cheer or rallying cry* hurrah for ...!, ... for ever!: ◊*Haddington yet! la18-19*. †**yet as of before** again *la15-16*. †**yet as than** again *e15*. †**ȝit than** nevertheless *la14-16*. [OE *ġiet*, *ġīt*]

yit[1.2], **yet**, †**ȝit**, †**ȝeit**, †**ȝett** /jɪt, jɛt/ *conj* in spite of that; nevertheless *la14-*. [see the adv]

yit *see* AIT

yite[1], **yowt**, **yoit** /jʌɪt, jʌut, jɔɪt/ *n* **1** the yellowhammer *Emberiza citrinella 19-*. **2** a small person; *derogatory* a person *la19- C SW*. **yella yite** *see* YELLA[1.2]. [onomatopoeic of the bird's call]

yite[2] /jʌɪt/ *v* to play truant *20- T EC*. [perhaps an extended use of YITE[1], with reference to the harrying of the birds by boys]

yittel /ˈjɪtəl/ *n* **1** a (swollen) gland (in the neck) *20- Sh*. **2** a nodule in a stone, *eg*, quartz in sandstone *20- Sh*. [Norw dial *eitel*]

yitter /ˈjɪtər/ *v* to chatter *20- NE C SW Bor*. [onomatopoeic]

yitter *see* ETTER[1.2]

yiv *see* YE

yivver, †**aiver** /ˈjɪvər/ *adj* eager, ardent *19- Ork NE Bor*. **yivvery**, **yivverie**, †**ȝevery** eager for food, hungry; greedy *16-19, 20- Ork NE EC*. **yivverin** keen, eager *la19- NE*. [OE *gīfre* greedy, voracious]

yix *see* AIX

yiz *see* YE

yl *see* ILL[1.3]

yland *see* ISLAND

yll *see* AISLE

ylyke *see* ALIKE[1.1], ALIKE[1.2]

ymage *see* EEMAGE

ymagin, **ymagyn** *see* IMAIGINE

†**ymangis** *prep* amongst *la15*. [altered form of *amangis* (AMANGST)]

ymn, **ympne** *see* HIME

ymyddis *see* AMIDS[1.2]

Ynd *see* INDIE

yneuch *see* ENEUCH[1.1], ENEUCH[1.3]

Yngland *see* INGLAND

ynk *see* INK

ynnys *see* INNS

ynsche *see* INCH[2]

ynsted *see* INSTEID

yo /jo/ *adv* a strong affirmative contradicting another's negative *20- Sh Ork N NE T*. [altered form of YEA[1.2] by analogy with *no*; compare SOT[2]; and compare Norw, Dan *jo*]

yoag /jog/ *n* the large horse-mussel *Modiolus modiolus 19- Sh Ork*. [unknown]

yoal, **yole**, †**yoll**, †**yall**, †**ȝoll** /jol/ *n* a six-oared boat, originally a fishing- or ferry-boat *la16-19, 20- Sh Ork N NE T EC*. **yollie**, **yowlie** a six-oared boat *18-19, 20- N NE*. [MLG *jolle*]

yoam[1.1], **oam**, †**ome** /jom, om; *Sh Ork* øm/ *n* **1** steam, vapour; condensation *la16-19, 20- Sh Ork NE T*. **2** a warm aroma, *eg* from cooking *la19- Sh Ork NE*. **3** a warm stuffy atmosphere; a gust of hot air; a heat haze *la19- Sh Ork NE*. **4** a jet of thick billowing smoke *la19- Sh NE*. Compare EEM[2]. [Norw dial *ome* smoke; the smell of burning; a warm breeze]

yoam[1.2], **oam** /jom, om; *Sh Ork* øm/ *v* **1** *of smoke* to pour out thickly *20- Sh NE*. **2** *of a smoker* to puff *la19- NE*. [from the verb or Norw dial *oma* to be hot and hazy, to smell]

yochel /ˈjɔxəl, ˈjoxəl/ *n* **1** a countryman, rustic, ploughman *la19- T*. **2** a lout *la19, 20- T*. [altered form of Eng *yokel*]

yock see YEUK[1.2], YOKE[1.1]

yod /jɔd/ *interj as an oath* God! *19- NE*. [euphemistic form]

yoger /'jogər/ *n* pain and swelling of the wrist *la19- Sh*. [Norw dial *gjøgr*]

yogle /'jogəl/ *n* the short-eared owl *Asio flammeus la19- Sh*. [Norw *ugla*]

yoit see YITE[1]

yoke[1.1], *Sh Ork T Uls* **yock**, †**ʒok**, †**ʒock**, †**ʒoik** /jok; *Sh Ork T Uls* jɔk/ *n* **1** subjection, oppression; an oppressive or onerous state; the submission required by religious faith *la14-*. **2** a shaped wooden bar by which two draught animals are coupled to pull a plough; a pair of animals coupled by a yoke *la14-*. **3** something constricting or controlling or requiring co-operation *16-*. **4** the time a yoked plough team works at a time; a shift or stretch of work *la18-*. **5** a spell of activity, a task or job *19-*. **6** a wooden bar fitted to the neck and shoulders for carrying two buckets *la19-*. **7** the harness of a plough or cart, the swingle-tree of a plough *la18-19, 20- Ork N NE*. **8** a snatch, grab or grasp *la19- Sh*. **9** a horse and cart or carriage, attached in full harness *20- T EC Bor*. **10** marriage *16-17*. **11** = YOKIN (sense 7) *16-17*. **12** a yoke placed over the neck of an enemy, symbolizing defeat *e16*. †**in the yoke** wearing a yoke, yoked up, harnessed *16-19*. †**under the yoke, under yoke** = *in the yoke 15-19*. [OE *geoc*]

yoke[1.2], †**ʒok**, †**ʒock**, †**ʒolk** /jok/ *v* **1** to join, unite, associate with; to marry *16-*. **2** to start on some activity, set to, go about something (vigorously); to start up (an activity) *la16-*. **3** to set (a person) to do something, start (a person) to work *17-19, 20- NE T EC*. **4** to attack; to start a dispute or quarrel; to engage in battle with *16-19, 20- Sh H&I*. **5** to start work *19-*. **6** to grasp, grip, seize hold of *la19- Sh*. **7** to burden, oppress; to subjugate *16-19*. **8** to attach (draught animals) to a plough, attach (a plough or cart) to draught animals *la14-e18*. **yokit tuillie** a string of squatting skaters, each pulled along by clinging to the one in front *19- Bor*. **yoke a had o** = YOKE[1.2] (sense 6) *20- Sh Ork*. †**yoke by the lugs** to get the attention of *19*. **yoke horns** to clash head-on, fight, come to grips with *20- Sh*. **yoke on** to set upon, attack (a person) *la19-*. **yoke tae 1** = YOKE[1.2] (sense 3) *la18-*. **2** = *yoke on 19-*. †**yoke upon** to set (dogs) on *la17*. **yoke wi 1** = YOKE[1.2] (sense 2) *17-*. **2** to have to do, associate with (a person); to contend, argue, join battle with (an adversary) *16-*. [OE *geocian*]

yoke see YOLK

yokie see YEUKIE

yokin, yoking, †**ʒoking** /'jokɪn, 'jokɪŋ/ *n* **1** the period during which a team of horses or oxen is in harness at one stretch *16-*. **2** the act of yoking a plough *17-*. **3** a spell of work, a stint, shift *19-*. **4** a spell, bout of some (leisure) activity, a stretch *18-*. **5** a fight, contest, scuffle *la16-*. **6** a verbal attack or dispute; a severe reprimand; an argument *17-19, 20- NE*. **7** a measure of land, probably originally the amount ploughed in one YOKIN (sense 1) *16-e18*. **yokin time** the time to start work *la19-*. [verbal noun from YOKE[1.2]]

yolder see YALDER[1.2]

yoldrin, †**yaldrin**, †**yeldrin** /'joldrɪn/ *n* the yellowhammer *Emberiza citrinella la18-*. †**yeldrick** the yellowhammer *Emberiza citrinella 19*. [altered form of EModE *yowlring* literally, yellow ring]

yoldyn see YIELD[1.2]

yole see YOAL

yolk, yowk, †**yoke**, †**ʒok**, †**ʒoik** /jok, jʌuk/ *n* **1** the yellow centre of an egg *la16-*. **2** a kind of soft, free, good-burning coal *la18-*. **3** an opaque part in window glass *19-*. **4** a hard nodule in a softer rock or piece of metal *18-e19*. **5** the best part; the core or substance *la16-19*. [OE *geolca*]

yoll see YOAL

yöll see YULE

yoller /'jɔlər/ *v* to speak loudly, excitedly, angrily or incoherently, shout, bawl *19- SW Bor*. [frequentative form of ME *yollen*, a variant of YELL[1.2]]

yomf see YOWFF[1.1], YOWFF[1.2]

yon[1.1], *Sh* **yun**, *Ork N* **yin**, †**ʒon**, †**ʒone** /jɔn; *Sh* jʌn; *Ork N* jɪn/ *dem adj* **1** that (one), those over there, at some distance; previously mentioned or known; *derogatory* other, especially indicating (something involving) a stranger or enemy; qualifying a noun that is antecedent to a relative clause *la14-*. **2** that (person or) thing (with no sense of being at a distance) *20- Sh*. **ʒongat** in that way *la14-15*. **yon kin** describing an unspecifiable emotion or state of an unmentionable or embarrassing sort *20- Sh N NE*. **yon time** some unspecifiable time in the distant future or past *20-*. [OE *geon*; compare THON]

yon[1.2], *Sh* **yun**, *Ork N* **yin**, †**ʒon**, †**ʒone** /jɔn; *Sh* jʌn; *Ork N* jɪn/ *dem pron* **1** that person or thing, those people (at a distance); other, strange; already mentioned or known) *la14-*. **2** that thing, those things (as opposed to another or others) *20- Sh*. [see the dem adj]

yon[2] /jɔn/ *adv* **1** over there, yonder, at or in that place *19, 20- Sh N NE T*. **2** to that place over there *20- NE C* [shortened form of *yond* (YONT[1.2])]

yond see YONT[1.1], YONT[1.2], YONT[1.3]

yonner[1.1], **yonder**, †**ʒondir** /'jɔnər, 'jɔndər/ *adj* **1** (that) over there, at some distance, originally, within sight *16-*. **2** *in place-names* part of the name of the farther of two farms with the same name *16-*. **3** farther, more distant, other; originally frequently describing the other side or bank of a stretch of water *la15-17*. [see the adv]

yonner[1.2], **yonder**, *Sh* **yunder**, †**ʒonder**, †**ʒondir** /'jɔnər, 'jɔndər; *Sh* 'jʌndər/ *adv* in that place, over there, indicating a person or thing at some distance (within sight) *la14-*. **yonneraboots** in that district, thereabouts *19- Sh T Bor*. †**yonnerawa** = *yundroo 19*. **yonnermaist** farthest, most distant *16-19, 20- NE*. **yundroo** over there, in that place *20- Sh Ork*. †**ʒonder mar** at a farther place, farther over *e16*. †**ʒonderwart** in a direction away from or farther off from the speaker *e16*. [ME *yonder*, derivative of *yond* (YONT); compare THONDER]

yonsi /'jɔnsi/ *n fisherman's taboo* a hen *20- Sh*. [diminutive form from Norw dial *høns* hens]

†**yont**[1.1], **yond, ʒond** *adj* **1** farther, more distant, other *la14-e19*. **2** = YON[1.1] (sense 1) *la15-e17*. **3** that, yonder *18*. **4** distant, remote *la19*. [see the adv]

yont[1.2], †**yond**, †**ʒond** /jɔnt/ *adv* **1** farther away or along, onwards, beyond, aside, apart *16-*. **2** yonder, over there, at or to a (far) distance *15-19, 20- C*. †**yontby** in Angus, over yonder, across *19*. **yontmaist**, †**ʒondmost** farthest, most distant; last; uttermost *17-*. [OE *geond* adv]

yont[1.3], †**yond** /jɔnt/ *prep* **1** beyond, on or to the other side of *17-*. **2** along, further along, onwards through or over *la18-*. [OE *geond* prep]

yoof see YOWF[1.2]

yoofer /'jufər/ *n* **1** a log of wood nine feet long by nine inches in diameter; a fir-pole *la18- Sh*. **2** a large, clumsy oar *la19- Sh*. [Du *juffer* a long squared beam of wood used in shipbuilding]

yook see YEUK[1.1]

yoot see YOWT[1.1], YOWT[1.2]

†**yopindaill, yowpindail, ʒopindale** *n* a silver coin *16*. [LG *jochimdailer*]

yorks /jɔrks/ *npl farming* NICKIE-TAMS, straps fastening the trousers below the knee *20- C SW*. Compare YANKS. [perhaps a variant of YERK[1.1]]

yorlin, *N NE Uls* **yarlin**, †**youlring** /'jɔrlɪn, 'jɔrlɪn; *N NE Uls* 'jarlɪn/ *n* the yellowhammer *Emberiza citrinella la17-*. [reduced form of YOLDRIN]

you *see* YE

youch /jʌux/ *v of a dog* to bark *la19- SW Uls*. Compare YOWF[1.2]. [onomatopoeic]

youdith /'judɪθ/ *n* youth, the state or time of being young; young people *18- literary*. [metathesis of *youthheid* (YOUTH)]

youk *see* YEUK[1.1], YEUK[1.2]

youkie *see* YEUKIE

youlring *see* YORLIN

young, †**ying**, †**ȝung**, †**ȝong** /jʌŋ/ *adj* **1** in the earlier part of life; not fully grown, immature *la14-*. **2** *in titles* prefixed to the name of a Highland chieftain or his estate to indicate his eldest son and heir: ◇*young Lochiel 18-*. **3** *of the sun* early in the morning *e16*. **younger**, †**youngar** **1** less old than another, frequently a sibling *la14-*. **2** used after a person's name to distinguish him from an older person of the same name, frequently son from father *la14-*. **3** in the title for the heir of a person with a territorial designation as part of his surname or with the style of a Highland chieftain: ◇*Malcolm MacGregor, younger of MacGregor*, or (and now officially preferred) ◇*Malcolm MacGregor of MacGregor, younger la16-*. **young anes**, **young yins** young people; children *la16-*. **young communicant** Presbyterian Church a person intending (and receiving instruction) to become a communicant member of a church *18-*. **young folk** a newly-married couple, irrespective of age *19, 20- Ork T C*. **young laird** the heir of a landowner below peerage rank *la15-*. **young man 1** a young man, one in early manhood *la14-*. **2** a boyfriend, fiancé, lover *la14-*. **3** the best man at a wedding *19- Ork NE*. **4** an unmarried man *18, 20- Ork EC*. **5** the eldest son and heir *17-18*. **6** a soldier or warrior *16*. **young yule** the beginning of the Christmas period; the early stages of a celebration or period of time *20- Sh*. [OE *geong*]

youngling *see* YOUNKLIN

younk /jʌŋk/ *n* a young bird, a nestling *20-*. [shortened form of YOUNKER]

younker, †**ȝounker**, †**ȝonker**, †**ȝonkeir** /'jʌŋkər/ *n* **1** a youngster, a young lad or girl, a youth *16-*. **2** a young bird, a nestling *20-*. **3** a young man of rank, a young knight; a young man of the burgess class *16-17*. [MDu *jonckher*]

younklin, †**youngling**, †**ȝoungling**, †**ȝynglyng** /'jʌŋklɪn/ *n* a youngster *16-19, 20- NE*. [OE *geongling*]

youp /jʌup/ *n* howling, wailing like a dog; a scream; complaining *la18- Ork NE*. [onomatopoeic]

youph *see* YOWF[1.2]

your, yours *see* YER

yoursel, yourself *see* YERSEL

yous, youse *see* YE

youth, †**ȝouth**, †**ȝowth**, †**ȝewth** /juθ/ *n* **1** the fact or state of being young *la15-*. **2** the time of a person's being young, the early part of a person's life *la14-*. **3** young persons, the young *la15-*. **youthheid 1** youth, the state or time of youth *la14-18, 19- literary*. **2** young people *la16-e19*. **youthie** young, youthful (looking) *la18-19, 20- Ork*. †**youth age 1** = YOUTH (sense 1) *e16*. **2** = YOUTH (sense 2) *la15-16*. [OE *geoguð*]

yow *see* YE, YOWE

yowden, †**ȝoldin** /'jʌudən/ *adj* **1** soft; submissive; exhausted *16-*. **2** having surrendered *16*. [participial adj from YIELD[1.2]]

yowden *see* YIELD[1.2]

yowdendrift, †**ewindrift** /'jʌudəndrɪft/ *n* snow driven by the wind *17-18, 19- literary*. [unknown first element + DRIFT[1.1]]

yowder, **yowther**, †**ewder**, †**euther** /'jʌudər, 'jʌuðər/ *n* **1** a stink; fumes *18-19 20- NE*. **2** the fluff or dust of flax *19, 20- Uls*. **3** steam, smoke, vapour *e19*. [perhaps a variant of Older Scots *odour*, AN *odour*]

yowe, **ewe**, †**ȝow**, †**yow**, †**ȝew** /jʌu, ju/ *n* **1** a female sheep *la15-*. **2** a stupid, weak-willed person *la19- NE T*. **yowie** a fir cone *20- NE T*. **yowe bucht** a pen for ewes at milking- or weaning-time; the time of day or period of the year when this happens *18-19, 20- NE T Bor*. †**ewe gowan** the common daisy *Bellis perennis 19*. **ewe-hog** a young female sheep *la16-*. **ewe-lamb**, †**ewe-lam** a female lamb *16-*. **yow-lammie** a little ewe lamb *la19-*. **ewe-milk**, **yowe-milk** ewe's milk *16-*. **yow-trummle** a cold spell in early summer, about the time of sheep-shearing *20- NE EC Bor*. [OE *ēowu*]

yower *see* URE[1]

yowf[1.1] /jʌuf/ *n* a bark, barking sound *19-*. [see the verb]

yowf[1.2], †**youph**, †**yoof** /jʌuf/ *v of a dog* to bark *la17-*. [onomatopoeic]

yowff[1.1], *SW* **yomf** /jʌuf; *SW* jɔmf/ *n* **1** a sharp blow, a swipe, thump; a smack *18-19, 20- Sh NE Bor*. **2** a thrashing *la19- Sh*. [onomatopoeic]

yowff[1.2], †**yomf** /jʌuf/ *v* to knock, strike, swipe *18- NE SW Bor*. [see the noun]

yowk *see* YOLK

yowl[1.1], †**ȝoule**, †**ȝowle** /jʌul/ *n* **1** a howl, whine, mournful cry of a dog or other animal; a yell, a wail, a shriek *16-*. **2** the cry of a bird *la15-e16*. [see the verb]

yowl[1.2], †**ȝoule**, †**ȝowl** /jʌul/ *v* **1** *of dogs or wild animals* to bark, howl, yell; *of persons* to bawl, wail; to complain, whine *la14-*. **2** *of a bird* to hoot, coo *la15-e16*. [ME *youlen*, conflation of GOWL[1.2] with YELL[1.2]]

yowlie *see* YOAL

yowpindail *see* YOPINDAILL

yowris *see* YER

yowt[1.1], **yoot**, †**ȝowt** /jʌut, jut/ *n* a shout, roar, yell, cry *la16-19, 20- T EC Bor Uls*. [see the verb]

yowt[1.2], **yoot**, †**ȝowt** /jʌut, jut/ *v* to cry, roar, shout, howl, hoot *la15-19, 20- T EC Bor*. [perhaps onomatopoeic; compare Flem *juyten*]

yowt *see* YITE[1]

yowther *see* YOWDER

†**Yper, Ypir, Ipar** *n* cloth from Ypres *la15-e17*. **Yper blak** a type of cloth *la15-e16*. [from the place-name]

yplet *see* PLET[1.3]

†**Ypocras, hypocras, ipocras** *n* Hippocras, spiced wine *16*. [OFr *ipocras* from the name of the Greek physician *Hippocrates*]

ypocreit, ypocrit *see* HYPOCREET

†**ypodorica** *n* the Hypodorian mode of music, the lowest of the classical keys *la15*. [Lat *hypodōricus*]

†**ypolerica** *n* the Hypolydian mode of music, an interval below the highest of the classical keys *la15*. [perhaps a nonce formation in contrast to YPODORICA]

ypothec *see* HYPOTHEC

ypothecary *see* APOTHECARIE

ypothegar *see* APOTHICAR

ypothingar, ypotingair *see* IPOTINGAR

Yrland *see* IRELAND[1.1], IRELAND[1.2]

†**yrle** *n* a dwarf; a stunted person *e16*. [unknown; compare WIRL]

yrn *see* AIRN[1.2]

Yrysch *see* IRISH[1.1]

yschappit see SHAPE[1.2]
yschrowdyt see SHROOD[1.2]
yset see SIT[1.2]
ysowpit see SOWP[1.2]
yssen see EISEN
ysundir see SINDER[1.2]
ythand see EIDENT
†**ytwyn** adv apart *la14-e16*. [A[3] + *twain*]
yuchle /ˈjʌxəl/ *n* a gob of sputum *la20- C*. [onomatopoeic]
yuck /jʌk/ *n* a stone, pebble *20- C Bor*. [originally schoolboy slang, perhaps a reduced form of *dyuck* (DEUK) as in the game of *ducks and drakes*]
yuck see YEUK[1.1], YEUK[1.2]
yuckie see YEUKIE
yuffie /ˈjʌfi/ *n* **1** a water-closet, especially one on a tenement stair *20- EC SW Bor*. **2** a dry closet *20- EC*. [unknown; compare DUFFIE]
yuise see USE[1.1]
yuk see YEUK[1.1]
yuke see YEUK[1.1], YEUK[1.2]
Yule, *Sh* **yöll**, *N NE* **eel**, *NE* **yeel**, †**ʒule**, †**ʒuill**, †**ʒoull** /jul; *Sh* jøl; *N NE* il; *NE* jil/ *n* **1** Christmas, the date or time of the year, frequently beginning before Christmas Day and continuing until after New Year, originally for about twenty days; the festive season associated with it; the day itself *la14-*. **2** the celebrations associated with Christmas and the entertainment provided; Christmas cheer *15-19, 20- Sh NE*. **3** the word, as an exclamation of joyful greeting *la15-e18*. **Yule bannock 1** frequently *pl*, oatcakes specially baked on Christmas Eve both for one's own family and for children going from door to door *19, 20- historical*. **2** a gratuity of oatmeal paid at Christmas by tenants of a barony to the baron court officer *18*. **Yule breid** a richly seasoned oatbread baked for Christmas *19, 20- historical*. **Yule brunie** = *Yule bannock* **1** *20- Sh Ork*. **Yule candle** a Christmas candle *19, 20- Sh Ork*. †**Yule clais** wearing apparel given to an employee at Christmas *e16*. **Yule day 1** Christmas Day *la14-19*. **2** Christmas Day, Old Style, 6th January *20- Ork historical*; compare *auld yule* (AULD[1.2]). **Yule e'en**, **Yule even**, †**Yule evin** Christmas Eve *la14-19, 20- N NE*. **Yule feast** a Christmas dinner *la16-19, 20- Sh*. **Yule fire** the fire kindled on the hearth on Christmas morning *la19- Sh*. † **Yule girth** a time of immunity from criminal prosecution proclaimed at Christmas *16*. **Yule guse** a goose given or eaten at Christmas time *17-19, 20- SW*. **Yule mairt** an ox or cow slaughtered and salted for Christmas and the winter *19, 20- NE*. **Yule mornin** Christmas morning *la19, 20- Sh NE*. **Yule nicht** Christmas night *la15-19, 20- Sh*. † **Yule oulk**, **Yule wolk** Christmas week *15-e16*. **Yule pins** pins used as stakes in a Christmas game *19, 20- Sh*. **Yule play** the Christmas school-holidays *la19- Sh NE*. **Yule preens** = *Yule pins 19- NE*. **Yule rant** Christmas merrymaking *20- Sh*. **Yule shard**, **eelshard** = *Yule's yaud la19- NE*. **Yule sheep** a sheep killed and eaten at Christmas *la18- Sh Ork*. **Yule sowans** SOWANS specially made for Christmas into which were stirred a ring, a coin or button for predicting who would marry in the coming year *la18-19, 20- NE*. **Yule stack** a stack of peats sufficient to last over the whole Christmas period *la19- Sh*. **Yule steek** a badly or hurriedly made stitch, referring to the bustle of Christmas *19- Sh*. † **Yule stok** a Yule log *la15*. **Yule strae** the supply of straw needed on a farm over Christmas and the New Year *la19- NE*. **Yule tide** Christmas time *la15-*. **Yule time** = *Yule tide 17-19, 20- Sh*. † **Yule vacance** the Christmas holidays *17-19*. **Yule yagger** a person who has nothing new to wear at Christmas *20- Sh*. † **Yule's yaud** derogatory **1** a person ill-prepared for YULE, one who leaves work unfinished before Christmas or the New Year or who has nothing new to wear at Christmas *la18-19*. **2** an old horse left to fend for itself over the Christmas period *e16*. **Yule yow** = *Yule sheep la19- Sh*. [OE *gēol*]
yule-girse /ˈjølgɪrs/ *n* meadowsweet *Filipendula ulmaria 20- Sh Ork*. [Norw *jul-gras* applied to various plants, assimilated to YULE + GIRSE[1.1]]
yulger /ˈjølgər/ *n* surf, foam, commotion from breaking waves *la19- Sh*. [frequentative form of Norw dial *gjelg* a stir in the sea]
yulter /ˈjʌltər/ *n* a sea-urchin of the genus *Echinus 20- Sh*. [Norw dial *julkjer*]
yumer see HUMOUR
yun see YON[1.1], YON[1.2]
yunder, **yundroo** see YONNER[1.2]
yungie /ˈjʌɲi/ *n fisherman's taboo* a foal or horse *la19- Sh*. [probably YOUNG + -IE[3]]
yunk[1] /jʌŋk/ *n marbles* a marble staked in a game *20- C*. [unknown]
yunk[2] /jʌŋk/ *v of a horse* to rear and plunge, buck *20- EC*. [unknown]
yunk-the-cuddie /ˈjʌŋkəˈkʌdi/ *n* the game of leapfrog *20- EC*. [YUNK[2] + CUDDY]
yur see YER
yursel see YERSEL
yvor see EVOR

ȝ

ȝ /j/ *letter* this letter-form was commonly used in Middle Scots manuscripts and prints to represent the sound /j/. In Early Scots it varied with *y*, *ȝh* and (then the most common form) *yh*. In Middle Scots it predominated over its chief alternative *y*. It was indistinguishable in form from the (much less commonly used) letter-form *z*, used to represent the sound /z/. In manuscripts and black-letter prints (predominant in *e16*), a 'tailed' form of *ȝ/z* was used, but this gave way to the modern tail-less *z* in *la16* prints in roman and italic types. From the eighteenth century the regular use of *ȝ/z* for the sound /j/ was given up in favour of *y*, except for fossilized occurrences in a limited number of words such as *capercailzie* (CAPERCAILLIE), GABERLUNZIE, *tailzie* (TAILYIE), and in place-names and personal names such as ZETLAND and *Menzies*. In many cases the fossilized spellings gave rise to new spelling pronunciations with /z/ where the etymological pronunciation was with /j/, some of these spelling pronunciations, such as that of *Mackenzie*, being now the only surviving pronunciation.

ȝa *see* YEA[1.2],
ȝad *see* YAUD
ȝaid *see* YAUD
ȝaik *see* YAWK
ȝaip *see* YAUP[1.2]
ȝair *see* YAIR
ȝaird *see* YAIRD[1.1]
ȝairn *see* YAIRN
ȝak *see* YAWK
ȝald *see* YAUD, YIELD[1.2]
ȝallo *see* YELLA[1.2]
ȝallow *see* YELLA[1.1], YELLA[1.2]
ȝammer *see* YAMMER[1.2]
ȝammyr *see* YAMMER[1.1]
ȝane *see* ANE[1.2]
ȝape *see* YAUP[1.2]
ȝar *see* YARE[1.2]
ȝard *see* YAIRD[1.1]
ȝare *see* YAIR, YARE[1.1], YARE[1.2]
†ȝarn, **ȝarne** *adv* eagerly; energetically; firmly, fast *la14-e16*. [ON *gjarna*, OE *georne*]
ȝarn *see* YAIRN
ȝarne *see* YIRN[3], ȝARN
ȝarrow *see* YARROW[1]
ȝat *see* GAIT[3], YETT
ȝawd *see* YAUD
ȝawmer *see* YAMMER[1.1]
ȝe *see* YE, YEA[1.1], YEA[1.2]
ȝeaught *see* YATT
ȝee *see* YEA[1.2]
ȝeid *see* GAE
ȝeild *see* YELD[1.2], YIELD[1.1], YIELD[1.2]
ȝeir *see* YEAR
ȝeit *see* YIT[1.2]
ȝeld *see* YELD[1.2]
ȝelde *see* YIELD[1.1], YIELD[1.2]
ȝell *see* YELL[1.1], YELL[1.2]
ȝelloch *see* YELLOCH[1.1]
ȝelp *see* YELP[1.1], YELP[1.2]
ȝeman *see* YEOMAN
ȝemanry *see* YEOMANRY
†ȝeme, **ȝym** *v pt also* **yemit** 1 to take care of, guard, protect *la14-16*. 2 to keep in custody, confine *la14-e16*. 3 to keep, adhere to (conditions, laws) *la14-e15*. [OE *gīeman* to care for, guard, entertain (guests)]
†ȝemsel *n* 1 care, protection, keeping *la14-e15*. 2 rule, governance *la14-16*. [ON *geymsla*]
ȝer *see* YEAR
ȝerd *see* YAIRD[2], YIRD[1.1], YIRD[1.2]
ȝerdfast *see* YIRDFEST[1.2]
ȝerl *see* EARL
ȝerne *see* YIRN[3]
ȝes *see* YES
ȝesk *see* YESK[1.2]
ȝestrene *see* YESTREEN[1.2]
ȝet *see* YAT, YETT, YIT[1.1]
ȝetland *see* ZETLAND
ȝetling *see* YETLIN[1.1], YETLIN[1.2]
ȝett *see* YETT, YIT[1.2]
ȝevery *see* YIVVER
ȝew *see* YOWE
ȝewth *see* YOUTH
ȝha *see* YEA[1.1]
ȝhere *see* YEAR
ȝhis *see* YES
ȝhumanry *see* YEOMANRY
ȝirning *see* YIRNIN
ȝis *see* YES
ȝisk *see* YESK[1.2]
ȝisterevin *see* YESTREEN[1.2]
ȝistrene *see* YESTREEN[1.1]
ȝistreyn *see* YESTREEN[1.2]
ȝit *see* YIT[1.1], YIT[1.2]
ȝock *see* YOKE[1.1], YOKE[1.2]
ȝoik *see* YOKE[1.1], YOLK
ȝok *see* YOKE[1.1], YOKE[1.2], YOLK
ȝoking *see* YOKIN
ȝoldin *see* YIELD[1.2], YOWDEN
ȝolk *see* YOKE[1.2]
ȝoll *see* YOAL
ȝoman *see* YEOMAN
ȝon, **ȝone** *see* YON[1.1], YON[1.3]
ȝond *see* YONT[1.1], YONT[1.2]
ȝonder *see* YONNER[1.2]
ȝondir *see* YONNER[1.1], YONNER[1.2]
ȝong *see* YOUNG
ȝongat *see* YON[1.1]
ȝonker, **ȝonkeir** *see* YOUNKER
ȝopindale *see* YOPINDAILL
ȝor *see* YARE[1.1], YARE[1.2]
ȝoule *see* YOWL[1.1], YOWL[1.2]
ȝoull *see* YULE
†ȝoungfrow *n* a dead-eye, a wooden disc with holes to receive lanyards *la15-e17*. [EModDu *jongvrouw* a young lady, a beam in shipbuilding]
ȝoungling *see* YOUNKLIN
ȝounker *see* YOUNKER
ȝour *see* YER
ȝour self, **ȝour sell** *see* YERSEL

ȝouth *see* YOUTH
ȝow *see* YE, YOWE
ȝowl *see* YOWL[1.2]
ȝowle *see* YOWL[1.1]
ȝowr, **ȝowris** *see* YER
ȝowt *see* YOWT[1.1], YOWT[1.2]
ȝowth *see* YOUTH
ȝude *see* GAE

ȝuik *see* YEUK[1.1], YEUK[1.1]
ȝuill, **ȝule** *see* YULE
ȝung *see* YOUNG
ȝym *see* ȜEME
ȝynglyng *see* YOUNKLIN
ȝyrne *see* YIRN[1]

Z

zeal, †**zeill**, †**zele** /zil/ *n* **1** fervent devotion or intense ardour (in pursuit of some end) *16-*. **2** great affection or devotion (for a person) *la15-16*. **3** something ardently desired *e15*. †**gude zeill** good intent, kindly disposition *16*. [Lat *zēlus*]

zeenty, **zeendi**, **zeentee**, **zinty** /ˈzinti, ˈzindi, ˈzinti, ˈzɪnti/ *numeral in sheep-counting and children's rhymes* one *la19- Ork N NE C SW*. [from a system of counting sheep in Northern England and Southern Scotland; compare TEENTY, TETHERY, METHERY]

zeill, **zele** *see* ZEAL

†**Zephyrus**, **Zepherus** *n* the west wind, a westerly breeze *la15-e16*. [Lat *zephyrus*]

Zetland, †**Ʒetland**, †**Yetland** /ˈzɛtlənd/ *n* Shetland, used as the official name of the county until 1975, and as a peerage title *16-*. [ON *Hjaltland*; a spelling pronunciation following the replacement of yogh with z had developed by the early 19th century]

†**zickety** *numeral in Edinburgh* the first word in a children's counting-out rhyme, one *19*. [probably a children's variant derived from a system of counting sheep in Northern England and Southern Scotland; compare ZEENTY]

zinty *see* ZEENTY

zulu, **Zulu** /ˈzulu/ *n* a type of fishing boat common especially in the Moray and Clyde Firths *la19- NE H&I*. [eponymous from the Zulu War]